# ARCHITECTURAL
# Graphic
# STANDARDS

ELLIOTT CARROLL, FAIA
Chairman, Architectural Graphic Standards Task Force

ROBERT T. PACKARD, AIA
Editor Emeritus

## The American Institute of Architects

MARC A. GIACCARDO, AIA
Senior Editor

STANLEY N. HALL
Managing Editor

DAVID W. JOHNSON
Senior Draftsman

JANET H. RUMBARGER
Manuscript Editor

MAHBOOB ALI
Assistant Editor

ANDREA ROUDA
Art Director

ANTHONY DYSON
Illustration Coordinator

TERRI L. SISLEY
Production Assistant

LEISA CHESTER WEIR
Editorial Assistant

## John Wiley & Sons

CAROL L. BEASLEY
Publisher

ROBERT J. FLETCHER IV
Production Director

ISHAYA MONOKOFF
Illustration Reproduction Director

JEAN MORLEY
Design Coordinator

JOHN SOLLAMI
Copyeditor

JENIFER A. McKENNA
Production Assistant

 **JOHN WILEY & SONS**

*New York / Chichester / Brisbane / Toronto / Singapore*

*Ramsey / Sleeper*

# ARCHITECTURAL
# *Graphic*
# STANDARDS

*Eighth Edition*

JOHN RAY HOKE JR., AIA
Editor in Chief

# THE AMERICAN INSTITUTE OF ARCHITECTS

## SUBSCRIPTION NOTICE

*Architectural Graphic Standards* is updated on a periodic basis (e.g., annual supplements) to reflect important changes in the subject matter. If you purchased this product directly from John Wiley & Sons, we have already recorded your subscription for this update service.

If, however, you purchased this product from a bookstore and wish to receive any current update at no additional charge, and future updates, revised, or related volumes billed separately with a 30-day examination review, please send your name, company name (if applicable), address, and the title of this product to:

Supplement Department
**John Wiley & Sons, Inc.**
One Wiley Drive
Somerset, NJ 08875
1-(800)-225-5945

**Library of Congress Cataloging-in-Publication Data**

Ramsey, Charles George, 1884–1963.
   Ramsey/Sleeper architectural graphic standards.

   "The American Institute of Architects."
   Includes index.
   1. Building—Details—Drawing.  I. Sleeper, Harold
Reeve, 1893–1960.  II. Hoke, John Ray, 1950–
III. American Institute of Architects.  IV. Title.
V. Title: Architectural graphic standards.
TH2031.A84   1988      721'.022'2      87–31746
ISBN 0-471-81148-3

Printed in the United States of America

10  9  8  7  6  5  4  3

# Contents

# Publisher's Note

In the fall of 1932, the lowest point of the Great Depression, I joined the House of Wiley and soon learned that there had been published in May a promising new book. Martin Matheson, then Manager of Marketing, had persuaded Charles George Ramsey, AIA, author of an earlier Wiley textbook, and his younger colleague, Harold Reeve Sleeper, FAIA, to develop their ideas and prepare the plates for what became *Architectural Graphic Standards*. Subsequently, Matheson directed the design and layout of the book and personally oversaw its production and manufacture.

The immediate acceptance and success of *Architectural Graphic Standards* extended far beyond its anticipated audience of architects, builders, draftsmen, engineers, and students. Interior designers, real estate agents and brokers, homeowners, insurance underwriters, and lovers of fine books all came to be among its known users and admirers.

Soon after the publication of *Architectural Graphic Standards* suggestions and requests came from many enthusiastic readers. These called for changes and additions and inevitably the decision was made to publish a second edition, which was almost 25 percent larger. It appeared in 1936, not long after the first. Recovery from the Great Depression had begun when the second edition came out, and with rising construction activity the demand for *Architectural Graphic Standards* increased. To serve its users' growing needs work soon began on a third edition which, when published in 1941, was almost twice as large as the original edition.

World War II lengthened the interval between editions; the fourth edition, prepared by Sleeper, appeared in 1951; the book had grown to 614 pages. The fifth edition (with 758 pages), Sleeper's last revision, was issued in 1956. The co-authors' achievements in the initial decade, followed by the efforts of Sleeper, provided untold thousands of users with an invaluable resource for almost 30 years.

Harold Sleeper's foresight led to his suggestion, heartily supported by John Wiley & Sons, that the American Institute of Architects be asked to assume the editorial responsibility for the sixth and subsequent editions. This was proposed at the June 1964 annual convention of the American Institute of Architects, and within a month a contract between John Wiley & Sons and the Institute led to the fulfillment of Harold Sleeper's wish.

I commend to all users of *Architectural Graphic Standards* a careful reading of the Foreword by Elliott Carroll, FAIA, chairman of the AIA task force for the eighth edition, and the Preface by John Ray Hoke Jr., AIA, editor in chief.

Now, nearly sixty years after publication of the first edition, we look back on a remarkable record. Each edition has surpassed its predecessors. The book has grown fourfold in size and immeasurably in depth. The collected editions are a chronicle of twentieth century architectural practice and reflect as well those times when progress has meant preserving (and hence respecting) our architectural heritage. This edition, for the first time, presents substantial material on historic preservation, leading to the satisfying notion that buildings created with the aid of the first edition may now benefit from material presented in the eighth.

Since change in this work has always been guided by its users, we expect them to lead us to new formats in the future, especially as electronic design and drafting tools become commonplace in the architectural office.

John Wiley & Sons takes pride in the part its officers and staff have played in the enduring success of *Architectural Graphic Standards* and in the association with the American Institute of Architects. Over two generations of readers have benefited from this work, and we look forward to meeting the needs of generations to come.

W. BRADFORD WILEY
Chairman
John Wiley & Sons, Inc.

# Foreword

In June 1964 at the American Institute of Architects' annual convention in St. Louis a meeting took place that laid the foundation for the book you now see. On that occasion I vividly recall working with Robert F. Hastings, FAIA, treasurer and later president of AIA; William H. Scheick, FAIA, the Institute's executive director; and Walker G. Stone, editor in chief of professional publications and later vice president of John Wiley & Sons, to negotiate a contract that would realize Harold Reeve Sleeper's wish that the Institute assume his editorial responsibilities for *Architectural Graphic Standards*.

After bringing several editions to completion, Sleeper realized that the work had grown to such an extent that no individual working alone or with a group of colleagues could do justice to the material. The AIA accepted sponsorship, recognizing its responsibility to provide practice and educational aids for AIA members. A drafting table reference was viewed as one of the most important practice aids the Institute could support and it seemed a natural progression for the AIA to carry on the work maintained through five editions by Sleeper and his colleague Charles George Ramsey. The AIA leaders also recognized that the Institute was uniquely able, through its members, to bring together the expertise to maintain and expand the book's value to the profession.

In return for the AIA's agreement to assure that up-to-date editions of *Architectural Graphic Standards* would continue to be available to the profession, the Institute received a royalty interest in the book. Royalties to the Institute over the years have supported major projects of value to the members that would otherwise not have been possible.

Over the course of the book's 56-year history *AGS* has maintained its place as the leading architectural reference work. As envisioned by Sleeper in 1964, this enduring legacy is due in large part to the continued participation of AIA members in the book's research, writing, and production.

AIA membership involvement, for example, led to publication of the sixth *AGS* in 1970. The sixth edition, edited by Joseph W. Boaz, AIA, was a completely new book, not simply a revision. Harold D. Hauf, FAIA, chaired the editorial advisory board and acted as final arbiter of page approvals. Assisted by coordinating editor Douglas S. Stenhouse, AIA, I was honored to serve as project director for the AIA, enlisting the assistance and expertise of some 100 architects, landscape architects, engineers, and their firms.

The sixth edition established both the form and precedent for member participation that has endured through three revisions. The task force members make a tremendously generous contribution of professional effort; their tangible reward is small in comparison. However, as a task force leader and member for over two decades I can attest to the satisfaction that accompanies the issue of each new edition.

The groundwork for production of the seventh edition was laid in 1975 and again relied on Institute and member participation.

Robert T. Packard, AIA, assumed the editorship, with John Ray Hoke Jr., AIA, as assistant editor and William G. Miner, AIA, technical editor.

By then, I had left the AIA to become assistant to the Architect of the U.S. Capitol, but was recalled to serve as chairman of the 11-member AIA Committee on *Architectural Graphic Standards*, which oversaw the editing of the seventh edition. Joseph A. Wilkes, FAIA, succeeded Harold Hauf as chairman of the editorial review board. William Dudley Hunt, Jr., FAIA, former senior editor of *Architectural Record*, publisher of the *AIA Journal*, and a close friend from my days on the AIA staff, was appointed Wiley's editor for the project. The high quality of that edition, published in 1981, can in large measure be credited to his guidance, encouragement, and encyclopedic knowledge of architecture.

Despite the extensive revisions of the seventh edition, continual change in the professional practice of architecture led to the decision, three years later, to start on the current edition. Bob Packard, John Hoke, and I were once again signed up, along with 16 task groups that were responsible for editorial content, review, and page approval. Eighty-four AIA members and other experts shared these responsibilities; they deserve our highest commendation for their selfless contributions. With the eighth edition, the number of editorial board members and task force participants exceeds 200; many have lent their support to more than one edition. Victor C. Gilbertson, FAIA, deserves special mention for his long history of service on the AIA Board of Directors and the editorial review boards of all three AIA editions of *AGS*.

Bob Packard retired in 1986. We are deeply indebted to him for his exemplary role as editor for two editions. As the new editor, John Hoke has infused the eighth edition with his own brand of energy, efficiency, and professional excellence.

Thanks to AIA member commitment, *Architectural Graphic Standards* continues to grow and evolve. The eighth edition adds three new chapters—on sports facilities, energy conservation, and historic preservation. I am especially pleased to see that historic preservation has been given well-deserved emphasis, in view of my own participation in the field and, according to a recent survey, that of some 80 percent of the Institute's members.

So, to the hundreds of AIA members and other professional colleagues who over the past 56 years have served as editors, review board members, page contributors, editorial staff, and providers of technical and professional documentation, my heartfelt thanks. Your contributions of time and talent are recognized on every page; they substantiate Sleeper's vision of a profession continually growing, nurturing, and challenging itself. You deserve our admiration for making his idea of *Architectural Graphic Standards* an enduring reality.

ELLIOTT CARROLL, FAIA
Chairman, AIA Task Force
*Architectural Graphic Standards*

# Acknowledgments

**TASK FORCE CHAIRMAN**

**Elliott Carroll, FAIA**

**Consulting Editors**
Harrison D. Goodman, P.E.
Harry T. Gordon, AIA
Richard F. Humenn, P.E.
Joseph R. Loring, P.E.
William G. Miner, AIA
Lee H. Nelson, FAIA

**Light Frame Construction**
Frederick R. Bentel, FAIA
C. William Brubaker, FAIA
Albert O. Bumgardner, FAIA
Harvie P. Jones, FAIA
James A. Smith, Jr., AIA

**Energy Design**
David J. Bennett, FAIA
Benjamin H. Evans, FAIA
Edward Mazria, AIA
P. Richard Rittelmann, AIA
Donald Watson, FAIA
Steven Winter, AIA

**Sports Facilities Design**
David Body, AIA
Ernest R. Lord, AIA
David Sheffield, AIA
Henry Teague, AIA

**Historic Preservation**
Richard C. Frank, FAIA
Raymond Girvigian, FAIA
Harvie P. Jones, FAIA
Lee H. Nelson, FAIA
Baird Smith, AIA

**Interior Design and Space Planning**
Norm DeHaan, AIA
James T. Fitzgerald, AIA
Tom L. Heideman, AIA
Yee Leung, AIA
Gini L. Pettus, AIA
William L. Pulgram, AIA

**Life Safety Design**
John L. Fisher, FAIA
Hollye Fisk, AIA, Esq.
Tom Jaeger, P.E.
Gerald L. Johnson, AIA
Kirby W. Perry, AIA
Robert L. Robinett, AIA
Ralph Rowland, FAIA
Raymond Ziegler, FAIA

**Land, Urban, and Site Development**
Stephen M. Ervin
Francis Ferguson, AIA
Richard C. Frank, FAIA
Jay Graham, ASLA
David Lewis, FAIA, AICP
Carl Maston, FAIA
Kathrin Moore, AICP
Kurt N. Pronske, P.E.
Clarence Roy, FASLA
Barry R. Thalden, AIA

**Public Assembly**
Victor C. Gilbertson, FAIA
Larry D. Hurlbert, AIA, CSI
Theodore Maffitt, FAIA
William W. Rupe, AIA

**Building Envelope Detailing**
Michael D. Flynn, R.A.
Jack Heitmann
Charles A. Hubbard, AIA
Thomas F. O'Connor, AIA
Norma Sklarek, FAIA
Mark Williams, AIA

**Acoustical and Lighting Design**
Benjamin H. Evans, FAIA
Paul Marantz
David P. Walsh, AIA
Maurice W. Wasserman, AIA

**Accessibility and Handicapped Design**
Edward Matthei, FAIA
Hunt McKinnon, AIA
Alfonso W. Nardi, AIA
Theresa Rosenberg, AIA

**Waterproofing, Flashing, and Roof Design**
Charles B. Goldsmith, AIA
Charles H. Kerner, AIA
Terrence M. Lallak, AIA
Ron Marrs, AIA

**Mechanical, Electrical, and Conveying Systems**
G. Z. Brown, AIA
Benjamin H. Evans, FAIA
Don Felts, AIA, P.E.
John L. Fisher, FAIA
Joseph R. Loring, P.E.
Paul Marantz
Henn Rebane, P.E.
LeRoy S. Troyer, AIA

**Structural Detailing**
Christopher Arnold, AIA
Edward A. De Vilbiss, AIA
Michael D. Flynn, R.A.
David Geiger, Ph.D., P.E.
Victor C. Gilbertson, FAIA
Robert A. Halvorson, P.E.

**Specialties and Equipment**
Michael Chambers, AIA, CSI
Ray E. Cumrine, AIA, FCSI
Victor C. Gilbertson, FAIA
Anne M. Lewis, AIA
William W. Rupe, AIA
Michael Steiner, AIA

**New Technology**
Thomas A. Amsler, AIA
John L. Fisher, FAIA
Edward L. Jenkins, Jr., AIA
Steve Parshall, AIA
Lev Zetlin, Ph.D., P.E.

# Preface

*This graphic and diagrammatic assembly of data, standards, and information is for the use of those concerned with architecture, building, and their allied fields.*

Charles George Ramsey, AIA
Harold Reeve Sleeper, FAIA
Preface, first edition, 1932

Once again, we are proud to present a new edition of *Architectural Graphic Standards*, published for the first time 56 years ago. This eighth edition is the third prepared by the American Institute of Architects. Every effort has been made to continue the important work of Charles George Ramsey, AIA, and Harold Reeve Sleeper, FAIA, who first conceived and produced *AGS* in 1932.

Our mission for the eighth edition was twofold: to expand the book to include new areas of building construction technology and design not covered in previous editions, and to improve and update existing material that has been used by over a generation of architects. We began by reorganizing the book around issues rather than chapters. In other words, by examining the book horizontally rather than vertically we hoped to establish better connections among the pages and to show how the many common elements throughout the book relate to one another. In addition, every effort was made to remove redundant and inconsistent information.

The eighth edition resembles the seventh in scope and organization, yet much has been changed. In all, 129 pages were omitted, 303 were revised, 282 remain unchanged, and 226 were added, increasing the eighth edition to 811 technical pages—nearly quadrupling the first edition size of 213 pages and making this the largest yet published.

The book is organized, generally, according to the principles of *Masterformat*, published by the Construction Specifications Institute. Increased emphasis has been placed on light frame construction, roofing and waterproofing, curtain wall construction, energy conservation, seismic design, sports design data, building security, aircraft, space planning, special purpose rooms, floor wiring systems, interior finishes, furnishings including classical furniture, and historic preservation.

There are three new chapters: Sports, Energy Design, and Historic Preservation. While materials on sports and energy design were published in the seventh edition, these are extensively revised and expanded in the eighth. To do justice to this coverage, separate chapters have been formed.

Our special thanks are due to the Department of Energy for sponsoring the research on which 25 new pages on energy design were based. Despite relatively stable energy costs in recent years, the AIA task group and I believe that current, in-depth coverage of energy aspects of design will serve the profession well in coming years.

The chapter on historic preservation appears for the first time, and reflects the enormous upsurge of involvement by architects in restoration and preservation work. A recent industry survey indicates that the involvement of firms offering services in this aspect of architecture approaches 80 percent. Special credit goes to consulting editor Lee H. Nelson, FAIA, and H. Ward Jandl of the Preservation Assistance Division of the National Park Service and their staff, and to Eric J. Gastier of Darrel Downing Rippeteau Architects, P.C., who created this magnificent chapter.

A work of this magnitude can only be completed with the commitment of hundreds of individuals, most making time for the project despite a full load of other professional responsibilities. Even the in-house AIA staff was drawn largely from the community of professional architects and draftspeople. We believe the project is better for this breadth of involvement, and commend to the reader the credit lines on individual pages and the Data Sources at the end of the book, for an overview of the participants.

The first phase of this revision was accomplished with the aid and guidance of the *AGS* task force comprising 84 members and chaired by Elliott Carroll, FAIA. All of the participants were identified by the AIA as experts in their respective fields. The eighth edition is Carroll's third in the role of task force chairman, and we are grateful for his commitment to this project over the past 24 years.

The editorial work for the eighth edition began in January 1984. Bob Packard was named editor, and I was named managing editor. Both of us had fulfilled these roles previously on the seventh edition. The team's first efforts were devoted to capturing the task force's suggestions and assembling the research materials that would become the basis for new and revised pages. As a result of meetings held between March 1984 and April 1986, the task force recommended a 55 percent revision of the seventh edition and proposed adding 250 new pages.

By the summer of 1985, the task force had nearly completed its page-by-page review of the seventh edition. Following their recommendations, AIA members were invited to develop new pages or to revise and update existing pages for the eighth edition. Since that time more than 200 professionals have been involved in shaping the book.

One of the highest priorities during this period was to produce high-quality pencil drawings for ink illustrators, and AIA members and consultants worked under tight schedules toward that end. Our special thanks are extended to them; their talents have made this the finest edition yet published.

Some staff changes over the course of the project should also be noted. Carol Beasley, publisher for the Scientific and Technical Division at Wiley, assumed responsibility for the project in July 1985, after the retirement of Bob Polhemus, vice president. After

Bob Packard's retirement in October 1986, I became editor in chief and was charged with completing the project.

In November 1986 we appraised the entire book and devised a plan to complete each page's required editorial work by July 1987. In order to accomplish this, an expanded team was formed to devote full attention to the editorial content. This team, which made the final result possible, included: Marc A. Giaccardo, AIA, senior editor; Stanley N. Hall, managing editor; David W. Johnson, senior draftsman; Janet H. Rumbarger, manuscript editor; Mahboob Ali, assistant editor; Andrea Rouda, art director; Anthony Dyson, illustration coordinator; Terri L. Sisley, production assistant; and Leisa Chester Weir, editorial assistant.

Final copyediting, inking, proofing, and page makeup were completed with the cooperation of the Wiley production staff under the direction of Robert J. Fletcher, also a seventh edition veteran. The team included Ishaya Monokoff, illustration reproduction director; Jean Morley, design coordinator; John Sollami, copyeditor; Jenifer A. McKenna, production assistant; and Mary Lohmann, proofreader.

Other key people who made tremendous contributions are Gordy Becker of Automated Composition Services, Inc., who set type and did page makeup, and June E. Morse of Editorial Experts, Inc., who compiled the index.

We thank the following people who worked either as AIA staff or independent consultants. Without them this project would not have come into being: Allan G. Assarsson, Compton Boodhoo, Karin Buchanan, Ron L. Chase, Donald Freehof, AIA, Kevin W. Green, Mark A. Jarvinen, Lynne H. Jennrich, George M. John, Kevin Kennedy, Kelvin Matthews, Timothy B. McDonald, Judy Pittman, Narcisa Sanchez, Georgina Seldon, Scott Siegel, and M. Stephanie Stubbs.

Special thanks are due to the consulting editors for their contribution in assuring the integrity of every page. They are: Harrison D. Goodman, P.E.; Harry T. Gordon, AIA; Richard F. Humenn, P.E.; Joseph R. Loring, P.E.; William G. Miner, AIA; and Lee H. Nelson, FAIA.

Now for a personal note. I wish to acknowledge three important people for whose support I am grateful: Carol Beasley; Steve Etkin, corporate vice president of the AIA; and my good friend Bob Fletcher, manager of production at Wiley.

In his foreword to the fifth edition, Eero Saarinen eloquently described the place of *AGS* in contemporary architecture: "Just as Vitruvius gives us understanding of the vocabulary of Renaissance architects, so *Architectural Graphic Standards* will show the future the dizzying speed and expanding horizons of architectural developments and practice in our time." I am grateful for all of the creative energy that was gathered over the past four years to pursue anew this worthy goal. This edition is dedicated to the members of the American Institute of Architects.

JOHN RAY HOKE Jr., AIA
Editor in Chief

# CHAPTER 1

# General Planning and Design Data

## INTRODUCTION TO ANTHROPOMETRIC DATA

The following anthropometric drawings show three values for each measurement: the top figure is for the large person or 97.5 percentile; the middle figure, the average person or 50 percentile; and the lower figure, the small person or 2.5 percentile. The chosen extreme percentiles thus include 95%. The remaining 5% include some who learn to adapt and others, not adequately represented, who are excluded to keep designs for the majority from becoming too complex and expensive. Space and access charts are designed to accept the 97.5 percentile large man and will cover all adults except a few giants. Therefore, use the 97.5 percentile to determine space envelopes, the 2.5 percentile to determine the maximum "kinetospheres" or reach areas by hand or foot, and the 50 percentile to establish control and display heights. To accommodate both men and women, it is useful at times to add a dimension of the large man to the corresponding dimension of the small woman and divide by 2 to obtain data for the average adult. This is the way height standards evolve. Youth data are for combined sex. Although girls and boys do not grow at the same rate, differences are small when compared with size variations.

Pivot point and link systems make it easy to construct articulating templates and manikins. Links are simplified bones. The spine is shown as a single link; since it can flex, pivot points may be added. All human joints are not simple pivots, though it is convenient to assume so. Some move in complicated patterns like the roving shoulder. Reaches shown are easy and comfortable; additional reach is possible by bending and rotating the trunk and by extending the shoulder. Stooping to reach low is better than stretching to reach high. The dynamic body may need 10% more space than the static posture allows. Shoes have been included in all measurements; allowance may need to be made for heavy clothing. Sight lines and angles of vision given in one place or another apply to all persons.

The metric system of measurement has been included, since it is used in scientific work everywhere and is the most practical system of measurement ever devised. Millimeters have been chosen to avoid use of decimals. Rounding to 5 mm aids mental retention while being within the tolerance of most human measurements.

Disabilities are to be reckoned as follows: 3.5% of men and 0.2% of women are color blind; 4.5% of adults are hard of hearing; over 30% wear glasses; 15 to 20% are handicapped, and 1% are illiterate. Left-handed people have increased in number to more than 10%.

## SAFETY INFORMATION

Maximum safe temperature of metal handles is 50°C (122°F) and of nonmetallic handles, 62°C (144°F); maximum air temperature for warm air hand dryers is 60°C (140°F); water temperatures over 46.1°C (115°F) are destructive to human tissue. Environmental temperature range is 17.2 to 23.9°C (63 to 75°F). Weights lifted without discomfort or excessive strain are 22.7 kg (50 lb) for 90% of men and 15.9 kg (35 lb) for women; limit weight to 9.07 kg (20 lb) if carried by one hand for long distances. Push and pull forces, like moving carts, are 258 N (58 lbf) and 236 N (53 lbf) initially, but 129 N (29.1 lbf) and 142 N (32 lbf) if sustained. Noise above the following values can cause permanent deafness: 90 dB for 8 hr, 95 dB for 4 hr, 100 dB for 2 hr, 105 dB for 1 hr, and 110 dB for 0.5 hr.

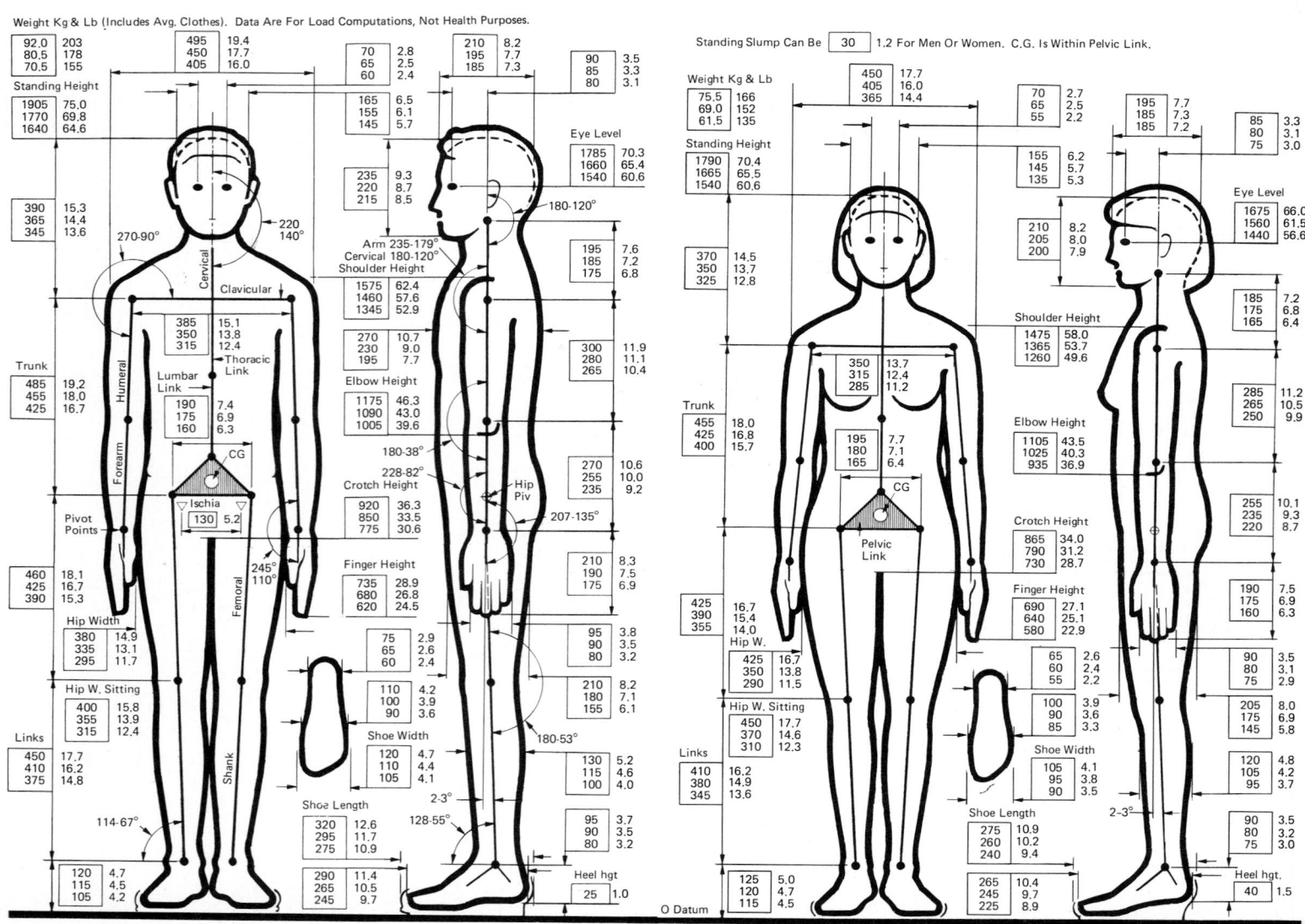

Weight Kg & Lb (Includes Avg. Clothes). Data Are For Load Computations, Not Health Purposes.

Standing Slump Can Be [ 30 ] 1.2 For Men Or Women. C.G. Is Within Pelvic Link.

Male and female standing heights (including shoes):

| 1905 | 75.0 | 1790 | 70.4 | large = 97.5 percentile | includes |
| 1775 | 69.8 | 1665 | 65.5 | average = 50 percentile | 95% U.S. |
| 1640 | 64.6 | 1540 | 60.6 | small = 2.5 percentile | adults. |

Dimensional notation system:

| 1000 | 39.3 | Numbers appearing in boxes are measurements |
| 100 | 3.9 | in millimeters. Numbers outside boxes are |
| 25.4 | 1.0 | measurements in inches. |

Niels Diffrient, Alvin R. Tilley; Henry Dreyfuss Associates; New York, New York

# 1 ANTHROPOMETRIC

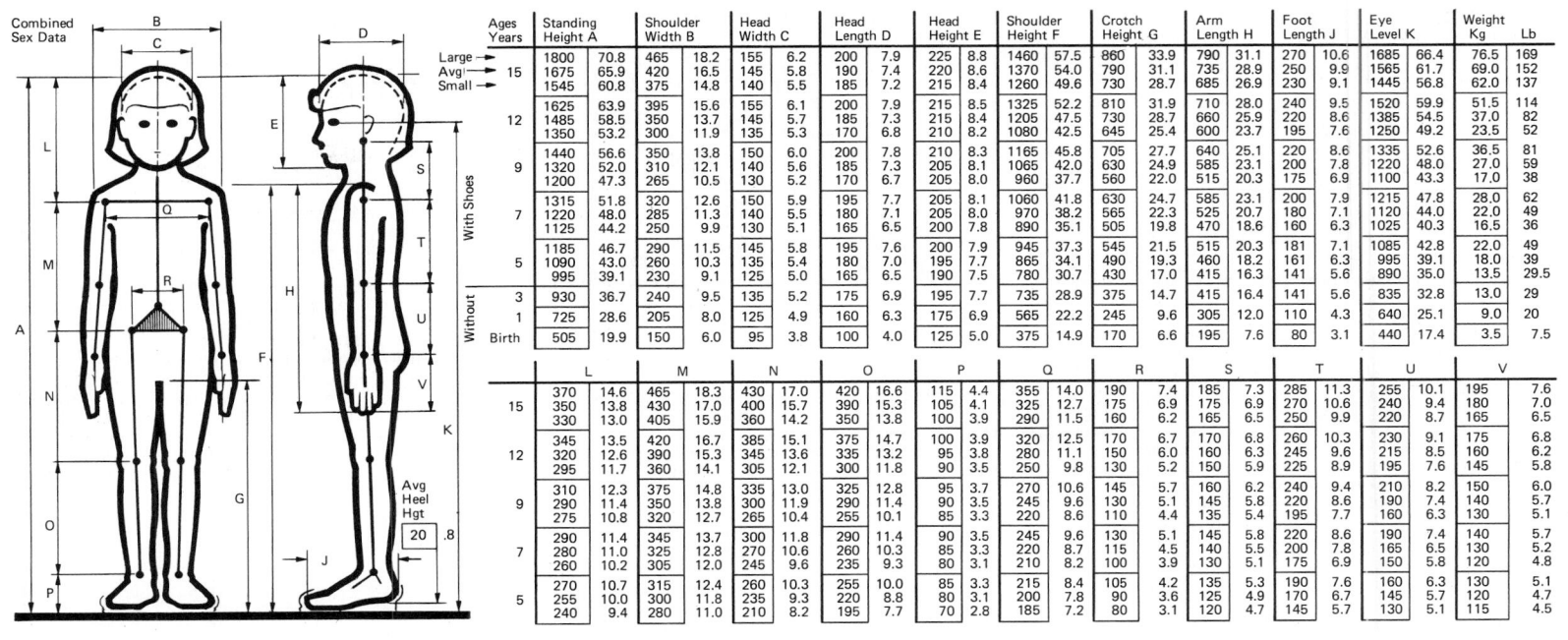

Combined Sex Data

| Ages Years | Standing Height A | | Shoulder Width B | | Head Width C | | Head Length D | | Head Height E | | Shoulder Height F | | Crotch Height G | | Arm Length H | | Foot Length J | | Eye Level K | | Weight Kg | Lb |
|---|---|---|---|---|---|---|---|---|---|---|---|---|---|---|---|---|---|---|---|---|---|---|
| 15 Large | 1800 | 70.8 | 465 | 18.2 | 155 | 6.2 | 200 | 7.9 | 225 | 8.8 | 1460 | 57.5 | 860 | 33.9 | 790 | 31.1 | 270 | 10.6 | 1685 | 66.4 | 76.5 | 169 |
| Avg | 1675 | 65.9 | 420 | 16.5 | 145 | 5.8 | 190 | 7.4 | 220 | 8.6 | 1370 | 54.0 | 790 | 31.1 | 735 | 28.9 | 250 | 9.9 | 1565 | 61.7 | 69.0 | 152 |
| Small | 1545 | 60.8 | 375 | 14.8 | 140 | 5.5 | 185 | 7.2 | 215 | 8.4 | 1260 | 49.6 | 730 | 28.7 | 685 | 26.9 | 230 | 9.1 | 1445 | 56.8 | 62.0 | 137 |
| 12 | 1625 | 63.9 | 395 | 15.6 | 155 | 6.1 | 200 | 7.9 | 215 | 8.5 | 1325 | 52.2 | 810 | 31.9 | 710 | 28.0 | 240 | 9.5 | 1520 | 59.9 | 51.5 | 114 |
|  | 1485 | 58.5 | 350 | 13.7 | 145 | 5.7 | 185 | 7.3 | 215 | 8.4 | 1205 | 47.5 | 730 | 28.7 | 660 | 25.9 | 220 | 8.6 | 1385 | 54.5 | 37.0 | 82 |
|  | 1350 | 53.2 | 300 | 11.9 | 135 | 5.3 | 170 | 6.8 | 210 | 8.2 | 1080 | 42.5 | 645 | 25.4 | 600 | 23.7 | 195 | 7.6 | 1250 | 49.2 | 23.5 | 52 |
| 9 | 1440 | 56.6 | 350 | 13.8 | 150 | 6.0 | 200 | 7.8 | 210 | 8.3 | 1165 | 45.8 | 705 | 27.7 | 640 | 25.1 | 220 | 8.6 | 1335 | 52.6 | 36.5 | 81 |
|  | 1320 | 52.0 | 310 | 12.1 | 140 | 5.6 | 185 | 7.3 | 205 | 8.1 | 1065 | 42.0 | 630 | 24.9 | 585 | 23.1 | 200 | 7.8 | 1220 | 48.0 | 27.0 | 59 |
|  | 1200 | 47.3 | 265 | 10.5 | 130 | 5.2 | 170 | 6.7 | 205 | 8.0 | 960 | 37.7 | 560 | 22.0 | 515 | 20.3 | 175 | 6.9 | 1100 | 43.3 | 17.0 | 38 |
| 7 | 1315 | 51.8 | 320 | 12.6 | 150 | 5.9 | 195 | 7.7 | 205 | 8.1 | 1060 | 41.8 | 630 | 24.7 | 585 | 23.1 | 200 | 7.9 | 1215 | 47.8 | 28.0 | 62 |
|  | 1220 | 48.0 | 285 | 11.3 | 140 | 5.5 | 180 | 7.1 | 205 | 8.0 | 970 | 38.2 | 565 | 22.3 | 525 | 20.7 | 180 | 7.1 | 1120 | 44.0 | 22.0 | 49 |
|  | 1125 | 44.2 | 250 | 9.9 | 130 | 5.1 | 165 | 6.5 | 200 | 7.8 | 890 | 35.1 | 505 | 19.8 | 470 | 18.6 | 160 | 6.3 | 1025 | 40.3 | 16.5 | 36 |
| 5 | 1185 | 46.7 | 290 | 11.5 | 145 | 5.8 | 195 | 7.6 | 200 | 7.9 | 945 | 37.3 | 545 | 21.5 | 515 | 20.3 | 181 | 7.1 | 1085 | 42.8 | 22.0 | 49 |
|  | 1090 | 43.0 | 260 | 10.3 | 135 | 5.4 | 180 | 7.0 | 195 | 7.7 | 865 | 34.1 | 490 | 19.3 | 460 | 18.2 | 161 | 6.3 | 995 | 39.1 | 18.0 | 39 |
|  | 995 | 39.1 | 230 | 9.1 | 125 | 5.0 | 165 | 6.5 | 190 | 7.5 | 780 | 30.7 | 430 | 17.0 | 415 | 16.3 | 141 | 5.6 | 890 | 35.0 | 13.5 | 29.5 |
| 3 | 930 | 36.7 | 240 | 9.5 | 135 | 5.2 | 175 | 6.9 | 195 | 7.7 | 735 | 28.9 | 375 | 14.7 | 415 | 16.4 | 141 | 5.6 | 835 | 32.8 | 13.0 | 29 |
| 1 | 725 | 28.6 | 205 | 8.0 | 125 | 4.9 | 160 | 6.3 | 175 | 6.9 | 565 | 22.2 | 245 | 9.6 | 305 | 12.0 | 110 | 4.3 | 640 | 25.1 | 9.0 | 20 |
| Birth | 505 | 19.9 | 150 | 6.0 | 95 | 3.8 | 100 | 4.0 | 125 | 5.0 | 375 | 14.9 | 170 | 6.6 | 195 | 7.6 | 80 | 3.1 | 440 | 17.4 | 3.5 | 7.5 |

(With Shoes: ages 15–5; Without: ages 3, 1, Birth)

| Ages | L | | M | | N | | O | | P | | Q | | R | | S | | T | | U | | V | |
|---|---|---|---|---|---|---|---|---|---|---|---|---|---|---|---|---|---|---|---|---|---|---|---|
| 15 | 370 | 14.6 | 465 | 18.3 | 430 | 17.0 | 420 | 16.6 | 115 | 4.4 | 355 | 14.0 | 190 | 7.4 | 185 | 7.3 | 285 | 11.3 | 255 | 10.1 | 195 | 7.6 |
|  | 350 | 13.8 | 430 | 17.0 | 400 | 15.7 | 390 | 15.3 | 105 | 4.1 | 325 | 12.7 | 175 | 6.9 | 175 | 6.9 | 270 | 10.6 | 240 | 9.4 | 180 | 7.0 |
|  | 330 | 13.0 | 405 | 15.9 | 360 | 14.2 | 350 | 13.8 | 100 | 3.9 | 290 | 11.5 | 160 | 6.2 | 165 | 6.5 | 250 | 9.9 | 220 | 8.7 | 165 | 6.5 |
| 12 | 345 | 13.5 | 420 | 16.7 | 385 | 15.1 | 375 | 14.7 | 100 | 3.9 | 320 | 12.5 | 170 | 6.7 | 170 | 6.8 | 260 | 10.3 | 230 | 9.1 | 175 | 6.8 |
|  | 320 | 12.6 | 390 | 15.3 | 345 | 13.6 | 335 | 13.2 | 90 | 3.8 | 280 | 11.1 | 160 | 6.3 | 160 | 6.3 | 245 | 9.6 | 215 | 8.5 | 160 | 6.2 |
|  | 295 | 11.7 | 360 | 14.1 | 305 | 12.1 | 300 | 11.8 | 90 | 3.5 | 250 | 9.8 | 130 | 5.2 | 150 | 5.9 | 225 | 8.9 | 195 | 7.6 | 145 | 5.8 |
| 9 | 310 | 12.3 | 375 | 14.8 | 335 | 13.0 | 325 | 12.8 | 95 | 3.7 | 270 | 10.6 | 145 | 5.7 | 160 | 6.2 | 240 | 9.4 | 210 | 8.2 | 150 | 6.0 |
|  | 290 | 11.4 | 350 | 13.8 | 300 | 11.9 | 290 | 11.4 | 90 | 3.5 | 245 | 9.6 | 130 | 5.1 | 145 | 5.8 | 220 | 8.6 | 190 | 7.4 | 140 | 5.7 |
|  | 275 | 10.8 | 320 | 12.7 | 265 | 10.4 | 255 | 10.1 | 85 | 3.3 | 220 | 8.6 | 110 | 4.4 | 135 | 5.4 | 195 | 7.7 | 160 | 6.3 | 130 | 5.1 |
| 7 | 290 | 11.4 | 345 | 13.7 | 300 | 11.8 | 290 | 11.4 | 90 | 3.5 | 245 | 9.6 | 130 | 5.1 | 145 | 5.8 | 220 | 8.6 | 190 | 7.4 | 140 | 5.7 |
|  | 280 | 11.0 | 325 | 12.8 | 270 | 10.6 | 260 | 10.3 | 85 | 3.3 | 220 | 8.7 | 115 | 4.5 | 140 | 5.5 | 200 | 7.8 | 165 | 6.5 | 130 | 5.2 |
|  | 260 | 10.2 | 305 | 12.0 | 245 | 9.6 | 235 | 9.3 | 80 | 3.1 | 210 | 8.2 | 100 | 3.9 | 130 | 5.1 | 175 | 6.9 | 150 | 5.8 | 120 | 4.8 |
| 5 | 270 | 10.7 | 315 | 12.4 | 260 | 10.3 | 255 | 10.0 | 85 | 3.3 | 215 | 8.4 | 105 | 4.2 | 135 | 5.3 | 190 | 7.6 | 160 | 6.3 | 130 | 5.1 |
|  | 255 | 10.0 | 300 | 11.8 | 235 | 9.3 | 220 | 8.8 | 80 | 3.1 | 200 | 7.8 | 90 | 3.6 | 125 | 4.9 | 170 | 6.7 | 145 | 5.7 | 120 | 4.7 |
|  | 240 | 9.4 | 280 | 11.0 | 210 | 8.2 | 195 | 7.7 | 70 | 2.8 | 185 | 7.2 | 80 | 3.1 | 120 | 4.7 | 145 | 5.7 | 130 | 5.1 | 115 | 4.5 |

|  | Ages | High Reach A | | Low Reach B | | Reach Distance C | | High Reach D | | Reach Radius E | | Eye Level F | |
|---|---|---|---|---|---|---|---|---|---|---|---|---|---|
| HS | 15 | 2085 | 82.0 | 815 | 32.0 | 735 | 29.0 | 1440 | 56.7 | 660 | 25.9 | 1215 | 47.8 |
|  |  | 1915 | 75.3 | 730 | 28.7 | 685 | 27.0 | 1375 | 54.1 | 610 | 24.1 | 1100 | 43.3 |
|  |  | 1765 | 69.4 | 665 | 26.2 | 635 | 25.1 | 1315 | 51.7 | 570 | 22.4 | 1100 | 43.3 |
| Jr. HS | 12 | 1860 | 73.2 | 705 | 27.6 | 665 | 26.2 | 1320 | 52.0 | 600 | 23.6 | 1100 | 43.3 |
|  |  | 1705 | 67.1 | 630 | 24.7 | 620 | 24.3 | 1250 | 49.2 | 555 | 21.9 | 1040 | 41.0 |
|  |  | 1545 | 60.9 | 560 | 22.1 | 565 | 22.3 | 1185 | 46.6 | 510 | 20.1 | 990 | 38.9 |
| 4th. | 9 | 1645 | 64.8 | 605 | 23.8 | 600 | 23.6 | 1175 | 46.3 | 540 | 21.2 | 975 | 38.4 |
|  |  | 1510 | 59.4 | 555 | 21.8 | 550 | 21.7 | 1120 | 44.0 | 495 | 19.5 | 925 | 36.5 |
|  |  | 1345 | 53.0 | 510 | 20.0 | 485 | 19.1 | 1040 | 40.9 | 435 | 17.1 | 880 | 34.6 |
| 2nd. | 7 | 1505 | 59.3 | 545 | 21.5 | 550 | 21.7 | 1080 | 42.6 | 500 | 19.6 | 890 | 35.0 |
|  |  | 1370 | 53.9 | 510 | 20.1 | 495 | 19.5 | 1015 | 40.0 | 445 | 17.5 | 850 | 33.5 |
|  |  | 1245 | 49.0 | 485 | 19.0 | 445 | 17.5 | 960 | 37.7 | 395 | 15.6 | 815 | 32.0 |
| KDG | 5 | 1330 | 52.3 | 500 | 19.7 | 480 | 19.0 | 970 | 38.1 | 430 | 16.9 | 815 | 32.1 |
|  |  | 1210 | 47.7 | 465 | 18.3 | 435 | 17.1 | 915 | 36.1 | 385 | 15.2 | 770 | 30.4 |
|  |  | 1085 | 42.7 | 425 | 16.7 | 390 | 15.3 | 865 | 34.1 | 345 | 13.6 | 720 | 28.4 |

Starting School Grades

| Up To Ages | Hat Shelf Height G | | Lavatory Height H | | Work Top J | | Work Depth K | | Table Height L | | Seat Length M | |
|---|---|---|---|---|---|---|---|---|---|---|---|---|
| 15 | 1675 | 66.0 | 760 | 30.0 | 915 | 36.0 | 460 | 18.0 | 650 | 25.5 | 370 | 14.6 |
| 12 | 1485 | 58.5 | 685 | 27.0 | 795 | 31.3 | 420 | 16.5 | 590 | 23.3 | 340 | 13.3 |
| 9 | 1320 | 52.0 | 635 | 25.0 | 695 | 27.3 | 380 | 15.0 | 525 | 20.7 | 300 | 11.8 |
| 7 | 1220 | 48.0 | 585 | 23.0 | 635 | 25.0 | 355 | 14.0 | 480 | 18.9 | 275 | 10.8 |
| 5 | 1090 | 43.0 | 485 | 19.0 | 570 | 22.5 | 330 | 13.0 | 445 | 17.5 | 250 | 9.9 |

| Ages | Seat Height N | | Seat To Backrest O | | Min Backrest Height P | | Armrest Spacing Q | | Seat Width R | | Basic Table Width S | |
|---|---|---|---|---|---|---|---|---|---|---|---|---|
| 15 | 405 | 15.9 | 150 | 6.0 | 175 | 6.8 | 445 | 17.5 | 380 | 15.0 | 760 | 30.0 |
| 12 | 370 | 14.6 | 145 | 5.7 | 160 | 6.2 | 420 | 16.5 | 370 | 14.5 | 710 | 28.0 |
| 9 | 325 | 12.8 | 135 | 5.4 | 140 | 5.6 | 355 | 14.0 | 330 | 13.0 | 610 | 24.0 |
| 7 | 290 | 11.4 | 130 | 5.1 | 130 | 5.1 | 330 | 13.0 | 305 | 12.0 | 610 | 24.0 |
| 5 | 265 | 10.4 | 120 | 4.8 | 125 | 5.0 | 305 | 12.0 | 280 | 11.0 | 535 | 21.0 |

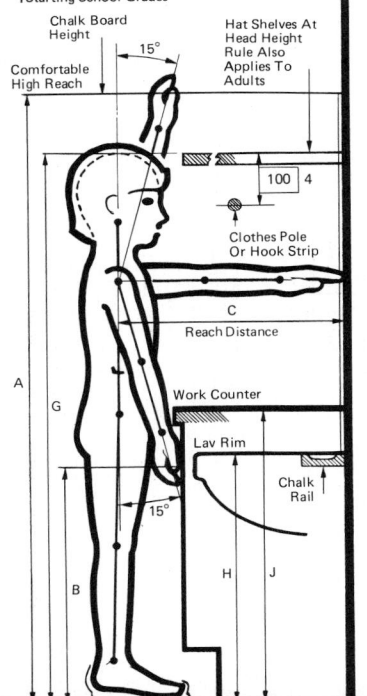

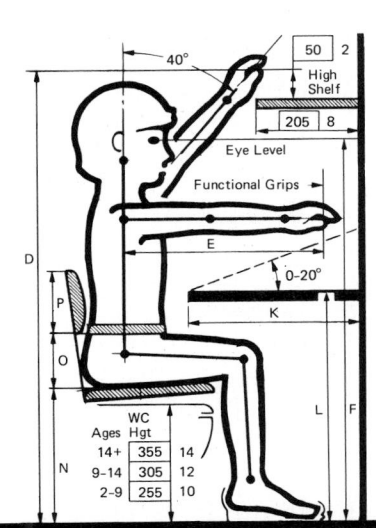

| Ages | WC Hgt | |
|---|---|---|
| 14+ | 355 | 14 |
| 9–14 | 305 | 12 |
| 2–9 | 255 | 10 |

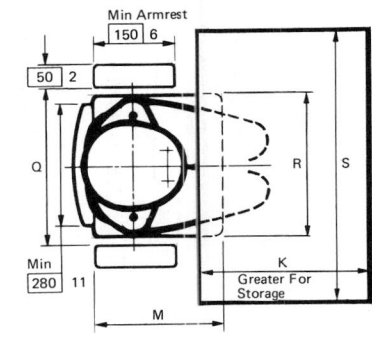

Standing heights (including shoes)—typical example:
| 1800 | 70.8 | large 15 year youth = 97.5 percentile |
| 1675 | 65.9 | average 15 year youth = 50 percentile |
| 1545 | 60.8 | small 15 year youth = 2.5 percentile |

} combined sex data U.S. youths

Dimensional notation system:
| 1000 | 39.3 | Numbers appearing in boxes are measurements |
| 100 | 3.9 | in millimeters. Numbers outside boxes are |
| 25.4 | 1.0 | measurements in inches. |

Niels Diffrient, Alvin R. Tilley; Henry Dreyfuss Associates; New York, New York

**ANTHROPOMETRIC**   1

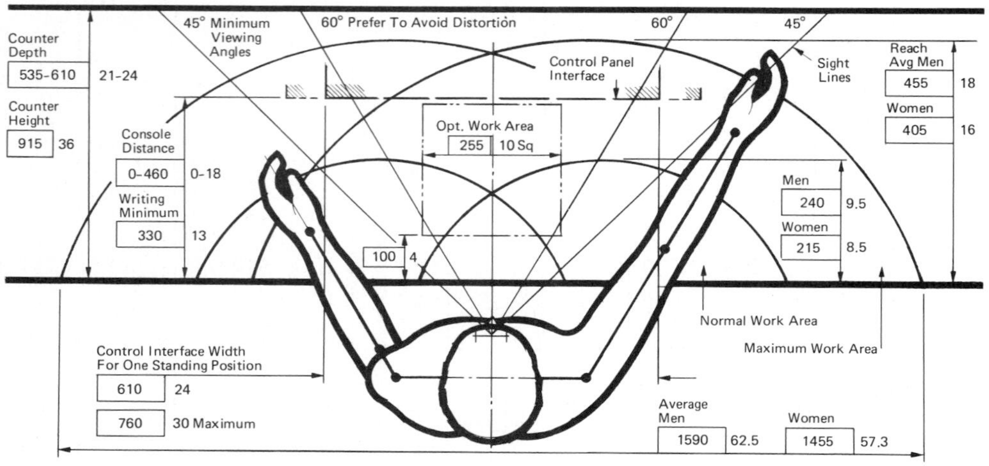

## Top left diagram (viewing angles / work area)

- 45° Minimum Viewing Angles
- 60° Prefer To Avoid Distortion
- 60°
- 45°
- Control Panel Interface
- Sight Lines

| Counter Depth | 535-610 | 21-24 |
| Counter Height | 915 | 36 |
| Console Distance | 0-460 | 0-18 |
| Writing Minimum | 330 | 13 |

- Opt. Work Area | 255 | 10 Sq
- 100 | 4

| Reach Avg Men | 455 | 18 |
| Women | 405 | 16 |
| Men | 240 | 9.5 |
| Women | 215 | 8.5 |

- Normal Work Area
- Maximum Work Area

Control Interface Width For One Standing Position
| 610 | 24 |
| 760 | 30 Maximum |

| Average Men | 1590 | 62.5 |
| Women | 1455 | 57.3 |

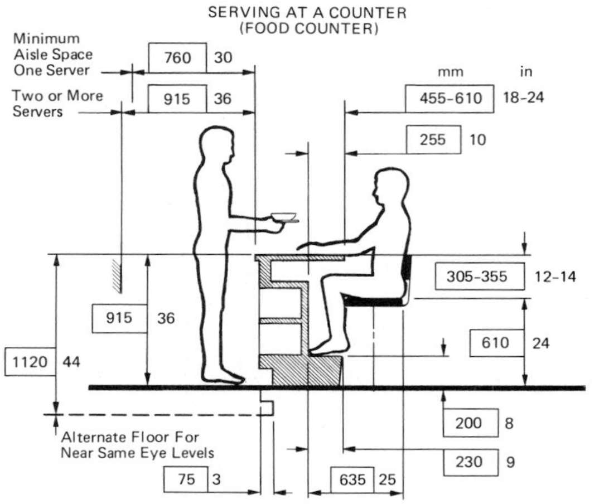

## Top right diagram — SERVING AT A COUNTER (FOOD COUNTER)

| Minimum Aisle Space One Server | 760 | 30 |
| Two or More Servers | 915 | 36 |

| | mm | in |
| | 455-610 | 18-24 |
| | 255 | 10 |
| | 915 | 36 |
| | 1120 | 44 |
| | 305-355 | 12-14 |
| | 610 | 24 |

- Alternate Floor For Near Same Eye Levels
| 75 | 3 |
| 635 | 25 |
| 200 | 8 |
| 230 | 9 |

## Left elevation diagram

| 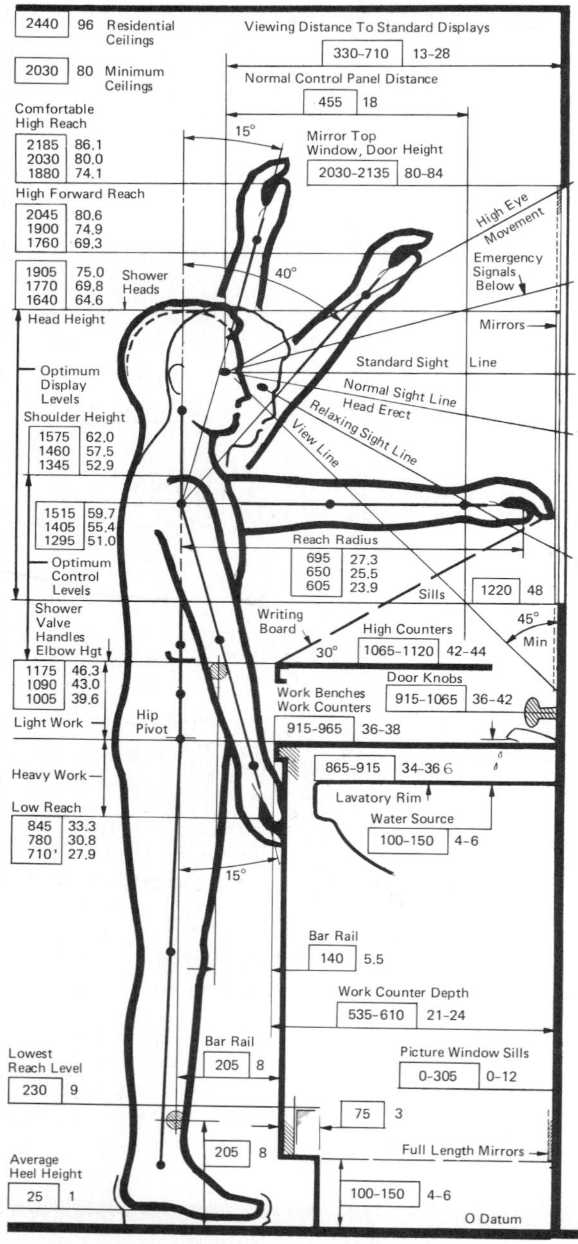 2440 | 96 | Residential Ceilings |
| 2030 | 80 | Minimum Ceilings |

Viewing Distance To Standard Displays
| 330-710 | 13-28 |

Normal Control Panel Distance
| 455 | 18 |

15°

Mirror Top Window, Door Height
| 2030-2135 | 80-84 |

Comfortable High Reach
| 2185 | 86.1 |
| 2030 | 80.0 |
| 1880 | 74.1 |

High Forward Reach
| 2045 | 80.6 |
| 1900 | 74.9 |
| 1760 | 69.3 |

High Eye Movement +30°
Emergency Signals Below +15°
Mirrors

Shower Heads
| 1905 | 75.0 |
| 1770 | 69.8 |
| 1640 | 64.6 |

40°

Head Height

Optimum Display Levels

Standard Sight Line 0°
Normal Sight Line
Head Erect
Relaxing Sight Line −10°
View Line

Shoulder Height
| 1575 | 62.0 |
| 1460 | 57.5 |
| 1345 | 52.9 |

| 1515 | 59.7 |
| 1405 | 55.4 |
| 1295 | 51.0 |

Optimum Control Levels

−30°

Reach Radius
| 695 | 27.3 |
| 650 | 25.5 |
| 605 | 23.9 |

Sills | 1220 | 48 |

Writing Board
High Counters 45° Min
| 1065-1120 | 42-44 |
30°

Door Knobs
| 915-1065 | 36-42 |

Work Benches Work Counters
| 915-965 | 36-38 |

Shower Valve Handles Elbow Hgt
| 1175 | 46.3 |
| 1090 | 43.0 |
| 1005 | 39.6 |

Light Work
Hip Pivot

| 865-915 | 34-36 | 6 |

Lavatory Rim
Water Source
| 100-150 | 4-6 |

Heavy Work

Low Reach
| 845 | 33.3 |
| 780 | 30.8 |
| 710' | 27.9 |

15°

Bar Rail
| 140 | 5.5 |

Work Counter Depth
| 535-610 | 21-24 |

Bar Rail
| 205 | 8 |

Picture Window Sills
| 0-305 | 0-12 |

| 75 | 3 |
| 205 | 8 |

Full Length Mirrors
| 100-150 | 4-6 |

Lowest Reach Level
| 230 | 9 |

Average Heel Height
| 25 | 1 |

## Center column — STANDING HEIGHT STDS. COMBINED ADULT SEX

| mm | in | Item |
|---|---|---|
| 2440 | 96 | Residential Ceiling |
| 2135 | 84 | Office Doors |
| 2030 | 80 | Residential Doors Min Ceiling, Chandeliers |
| 1980 | 78 | Min Door Hgt. Shower Head (Max) |
| 1905 | 75 | Highest Head Top |
| 1880 | 74 | Clothes Line (Max) |
| 1830 | 72 | No See Over Hat Hooks (Max) |
| 1830 | 72 | Highest Shelf (Men) Shower Head Clear (Min) |
| 1780 | 70 | Rail For Evening Dresses Top Of Mirror |
| 1730 | 68 | Highest Shelf (Women) |
| 1600 | 63 | Catwalk Head Clear (Min) |
| 1575 | 62 | Avg Adult Eye Level |
| 1475 | 58 | Thermostats |
| 1395 | 55 | See Over |
| 1370 | 54 | Grab Bars Phone Dial Hgt |
| 1320 | 52 | Highest File |
| 1270 | 50 | Door Push Plates Shower Valves |
| 1220 | 48 | Wall Switch Plate Deal Plate |
| 1145 | 45 | Push Bar On Doors |
| 1120 | 44 | Bar (Hi) |
| 1065 | 42 | Counters, Doorknob (Max) Safety Handrails, Bars |
| 1015 | 40 | Entrance Lock (Max) Ironing Board (Hi) |
| 915 | 36 | Handrails, Ironing Board (Hi) Counters, Doorknob (Min) |
| 840 | 33 | Panic Bars |
| 790 | 31 | Lavatory Rim |
| 760 | 30 | Letter Slot, Rails On Steps |
| 760 | 30 | Ironing Board (Lo) |
| 455 | 18 | Wall Outlets |
| 405 | 16 | Highest Step |
| 305 | 12 | Rung Spacing |
| 205 | 8 | Bar Rails |
| 190 | 7.5 | Stair Riser (Opt) |
| 150 | 6 | Toe Space (Max) |
| 75 | 3 | Toe Clear (Min) |
| 25 | 1 | Threshold (Max) |

2M
M
O Datum

## Right box — ADJUSTMENTS FOR THE ELDERLY

| High Reach, High Shelves | Lower | 75 | 3 |
| Low Reach, Low Shelves | Raise | 75 | 3 |
| Work Surfaces | Lower | 40 | 1.5 |

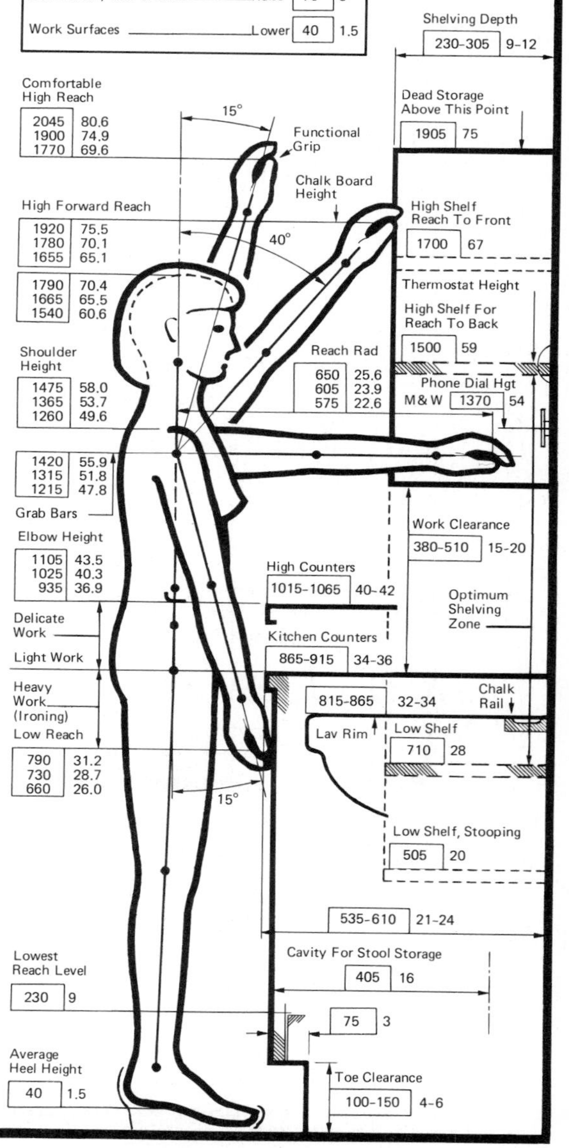

## Right elevation diagram

Comfortable High Reach
| 2045 | 80.6 |
| 1900 | 74.9 |
| 1770 | 69.6 |

15°
Functional Grip
Chalk Board Height

High Forward Reach
| 1920 | 75.5 |
| 1780 | 70.1 |
| 1655 | 65.1 |

| 1790 | 70.4 |
| 1665 | 65.5 |
| 1540 | 60.6 |

40°

Shoulder Height
| 1475 | 58.0 |
| 1365 | 53.7 |
| 1260 | 49.6 |

Reach Rad
| 650 | 25.6 |
| 605 | 23.9 |
| 575 | 22.6 |

| 1420 | 55.9 |
| 1315 | 51.8 |
| 1215 | 47.8 |

Grab Bars
Elbow Height
| 1105 | 43.5 |
| 1025 | 40.3 |
| 935 | 36.9 |

Delicate Work
Light Work
Heavy Work (Ironing)
Low Reach
| 790 | 31.2 |
| 730 | 28.7 |
| 660 | 26.0 |

15°

High Counters
| 1015-1065 | 40-42 |

Kitchen Counters
| 865-915 | 34-36 |

| 815-865 | 32-34 |

Lav Rim
Low Shelf
| 710 | 28 |

Lowest Reach Level
| 230 | 9 |

Average Heel Height
| 40 | 1.5 |

## Far right column

Shelving Depth
| 230-305 | 9-12 |

Dead Storage Above This Point
| 1905 | 75 |

High Shelf Reach To Front
| 1700 | 67 |

Thermostat Height
High Shelf For Reach To Back
| 1500 | 59 |

Phone Dial Hgt M&W
| 1370 | 54 |

Work Clearance
| 380-510 | 15-20 |

Optimum Shelving Zone

Chalk Rail

Low Shelf, Stooping
| 505 | 20 |

Cavity For Stool Storage
| 405 | 16 |

| 75 | 3 |

Toe Clearance
| 100-150 | 4-6 |

## Bottom

Male and female standing heights (including shoes):

| Male | | Female | | |
|---|---|---|---|---|
| 1905 | 75.0 | 1790 | 70.4 | large = 97.5 percentile |
| 1775 | 69.8 | 1665 | 65.5 | average = 50 percentile | includes 95% U.S. adults |
| 1640 | 64.6 | 1540 | 60.6 | small = 2.5 percentile |

Dimensional notation system:
| 1000 | 39.3 |
| 100 | 3.9 |
| 25.4 | 1.0 |

Numbers appearing in boxes are measurements in millimeters. Numbers outside boxes are measurements in inches.

Niels Diffrient, Alvin R. Tilley; Henry Dreyfuss Associates; New York, New York

**ANTHROPOMETRIC**

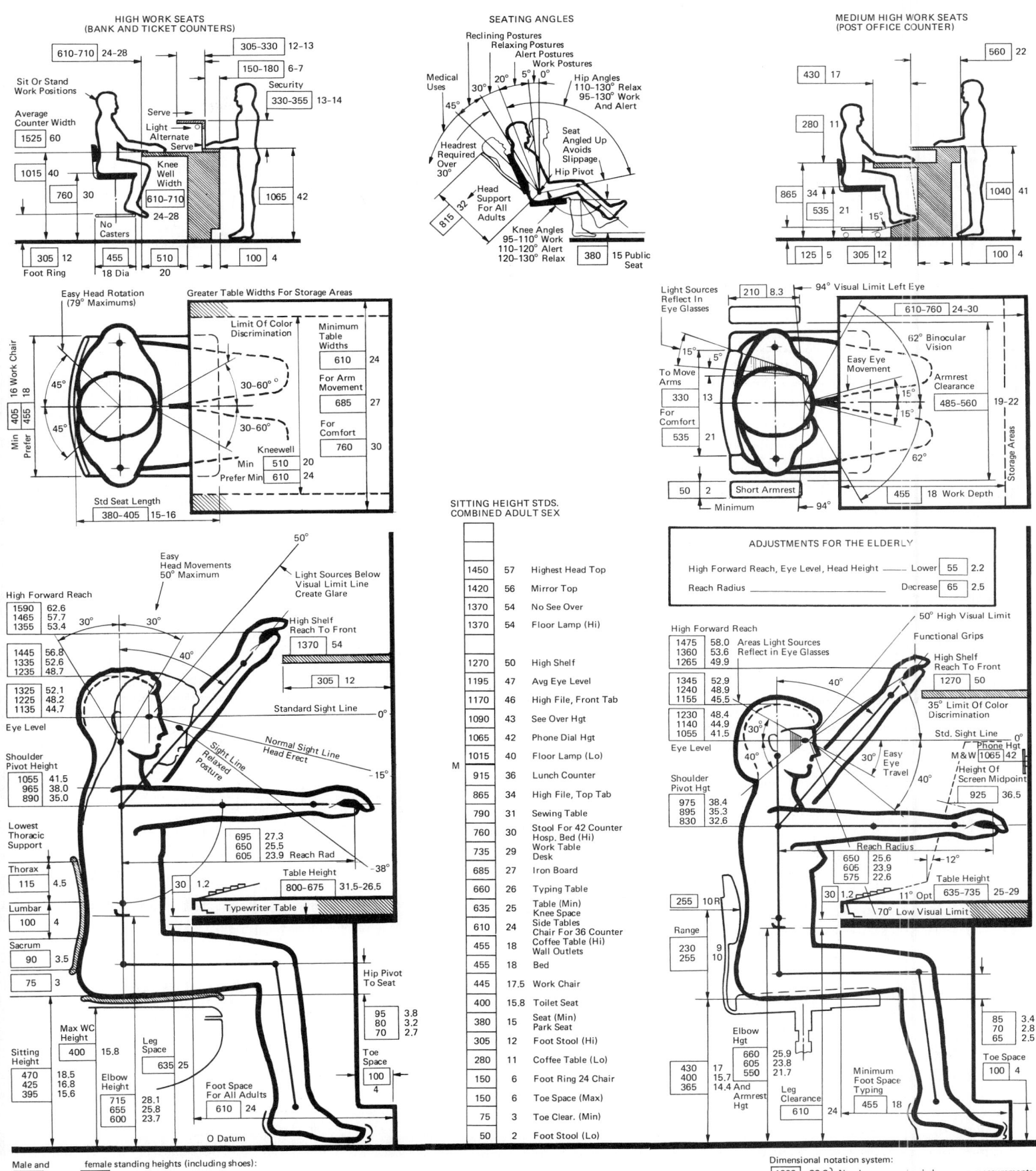

HIGH WORK SEATS
(BANK AND TICKET COUNTERS)

SEATING ANGLES

MEDIUM HIGH WORK SEATS
(POST OFFICE COUNTER)

SITTING HEIGHT STDS.
COMBINED ADULT SEX

| | | |
|---|---|---|
| 1450 | 57 | Highest Head Top |
| 1420 | 56 | Mirror Top |
| 1370 | 54 | No See Over |
| 1370 | 54 | Floor Lamp (Hi) |
| 1270 | 50 | High Shelf |
| 1195 | 47 | Avg Eye Level |
| 1170 | 46 | High File, Front Tab |
| 1090 | 43 | See Over Hgt |
| 1065 | 42 | Phone Dial Hgt |
| 1015 | 40 | Floor Lamp (Lo) |
| 915 | 36 | Lunch Counter |
| 865 | 34 | High File, Top Tab |
| 790 | 31 | Sewing Table |
| 760 | 30 | Stool For 42 Counter / Hosp. Bed (Hi) |
| 735 | 29 | Work Table / Desk |
| 685 | 27 | Iron Board |
| 660 | 26 | Typing Table |
| 635 | 25 | Table (Min) / Knee Space |
| 610 | 24 | Side Tables / Chair For 36 Counter |
| 455 | 18 | Coffee Table (Hi) / Wall Outlets |
| 455 | 18 | Bed |
| 445 | 17.5 | Work Chair |
| 400 | 15.8 | Toilet Seat |
| 380 | 15 | Seat (Min) / Park Seat |
| 305 | 12 | Foot Stool (Hi) |
| 280 | 11 | Coffee Table (Lo) |
| 150 | 6 | Foot Ring 24 Chair |
| 150 | 6 | Toe Space (Max) |
| 75 | 3 | Toe Clear. (Min) |
| 50 | 2 | Foot Stool (Lo) |

ADJUSTMENTS FOR THE ELDERLY

High Forward Reach, Eye Level, Head Height — Lower 55 | 2.2

Reach Radius — Decrease 65 | 2.5

**Male and female standing heights (including shoes):**

| | | | | | |
|---|---|---|---|---|---|
| 1905 | 75.0 | 1790 | 70.4 | large = 97.5 percentile | includes |
| 1775 | 69.8 | 1665 | 65.5 | average = 50 percentile | 95% U.S. |
| 1640 | 64.6 | 1540 | 60.6 | small = 2.5 percentile | adults |

**Dimensional notation system:**

| | | |
|---|---|---|
| 1000 | 39.3 | Numbers appearing in boxes are measurements |
| 100 | 3.9 | in millimeters. Numbers outside boxes are |
| 25.4 | 1.0 | measurements in inches. |

Niels Diffrient, Alvin R. Tilley; Henry Dreyfuss Associates; New York, New York

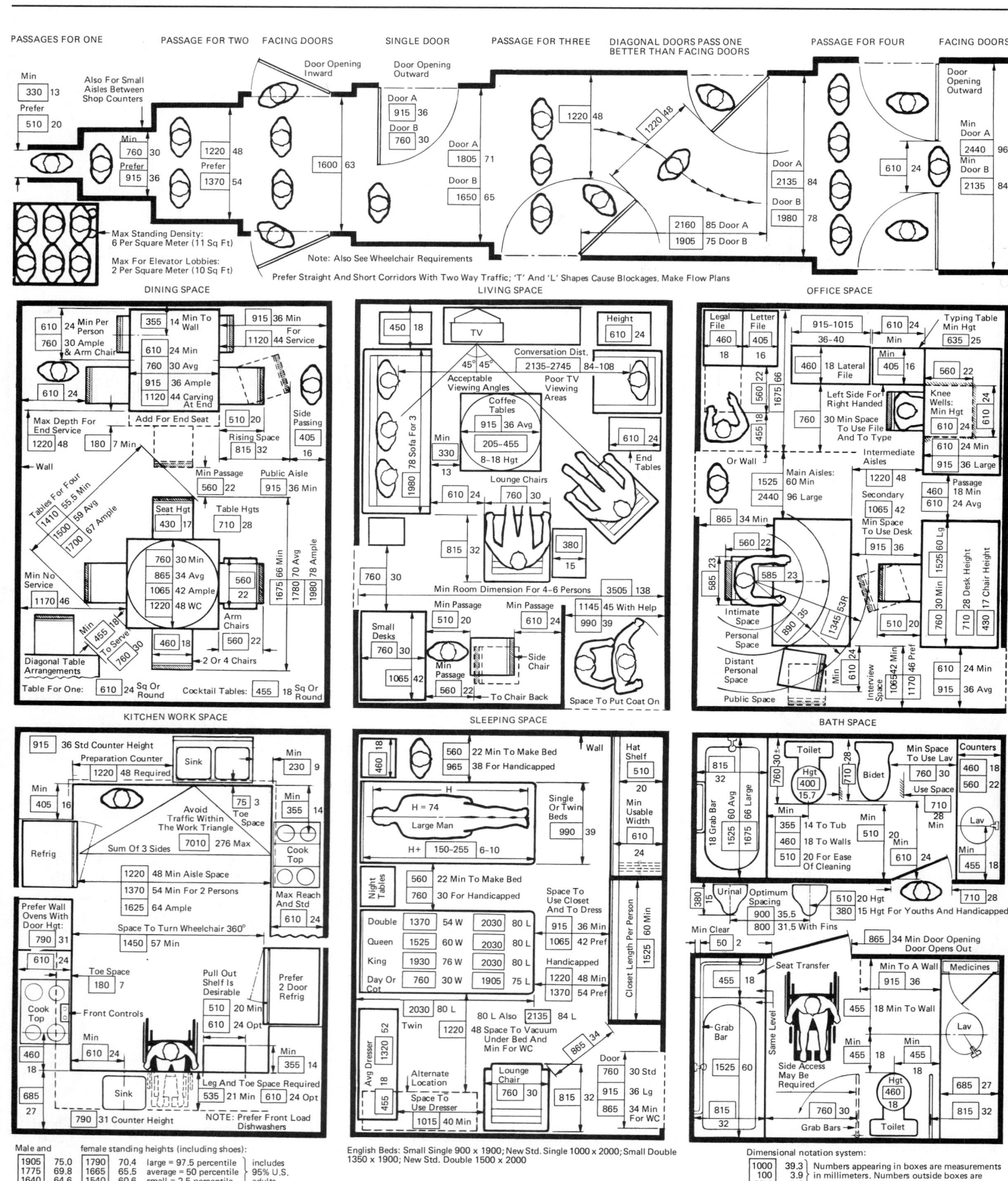

Niels Diffrient, Alvin R. Tilley; Henry Dreyfuss Associates; New York, New York

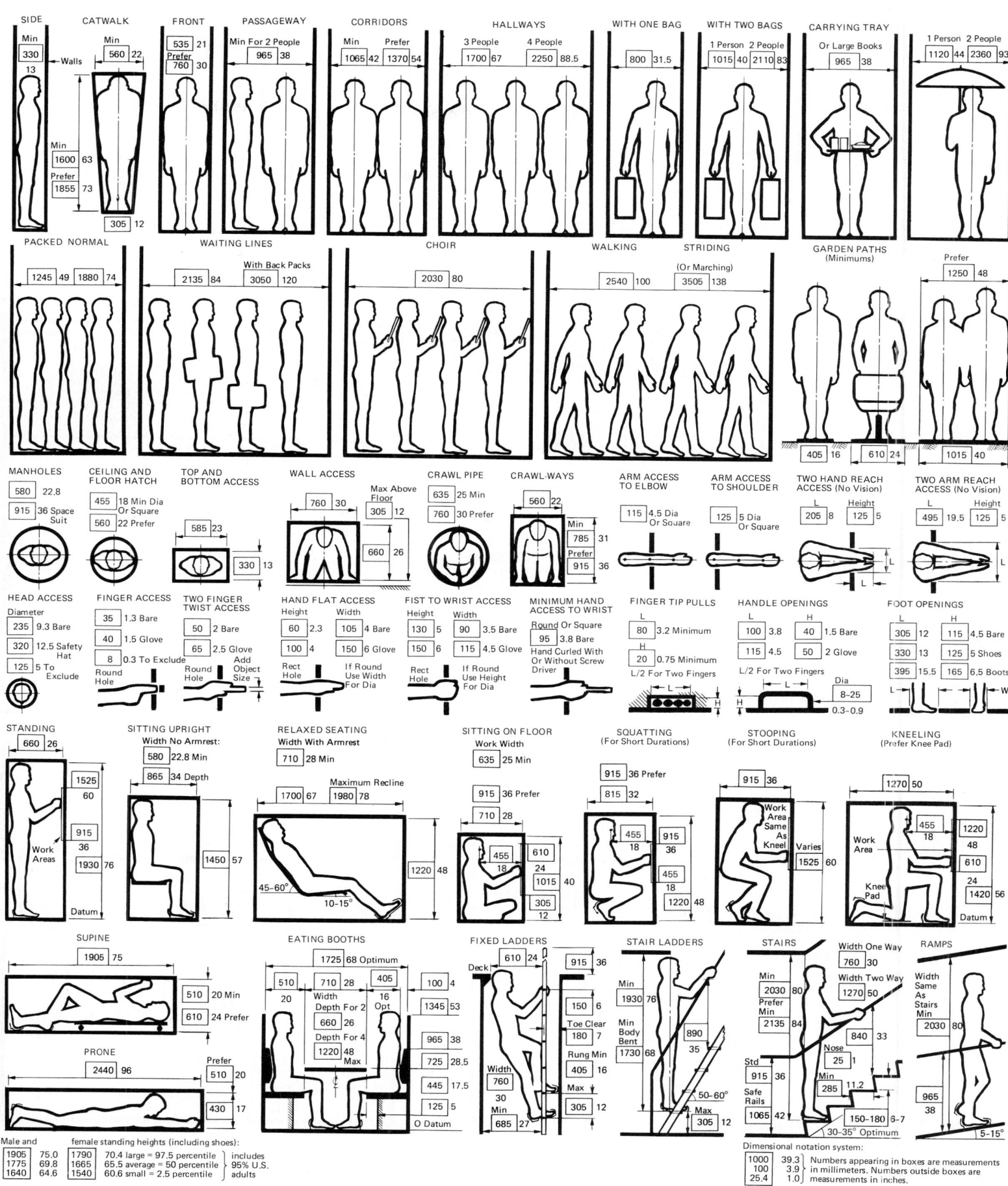

Niels Diffrient, Alvin R. Tilley; Henry Dreyfuss Associates; New York, New York

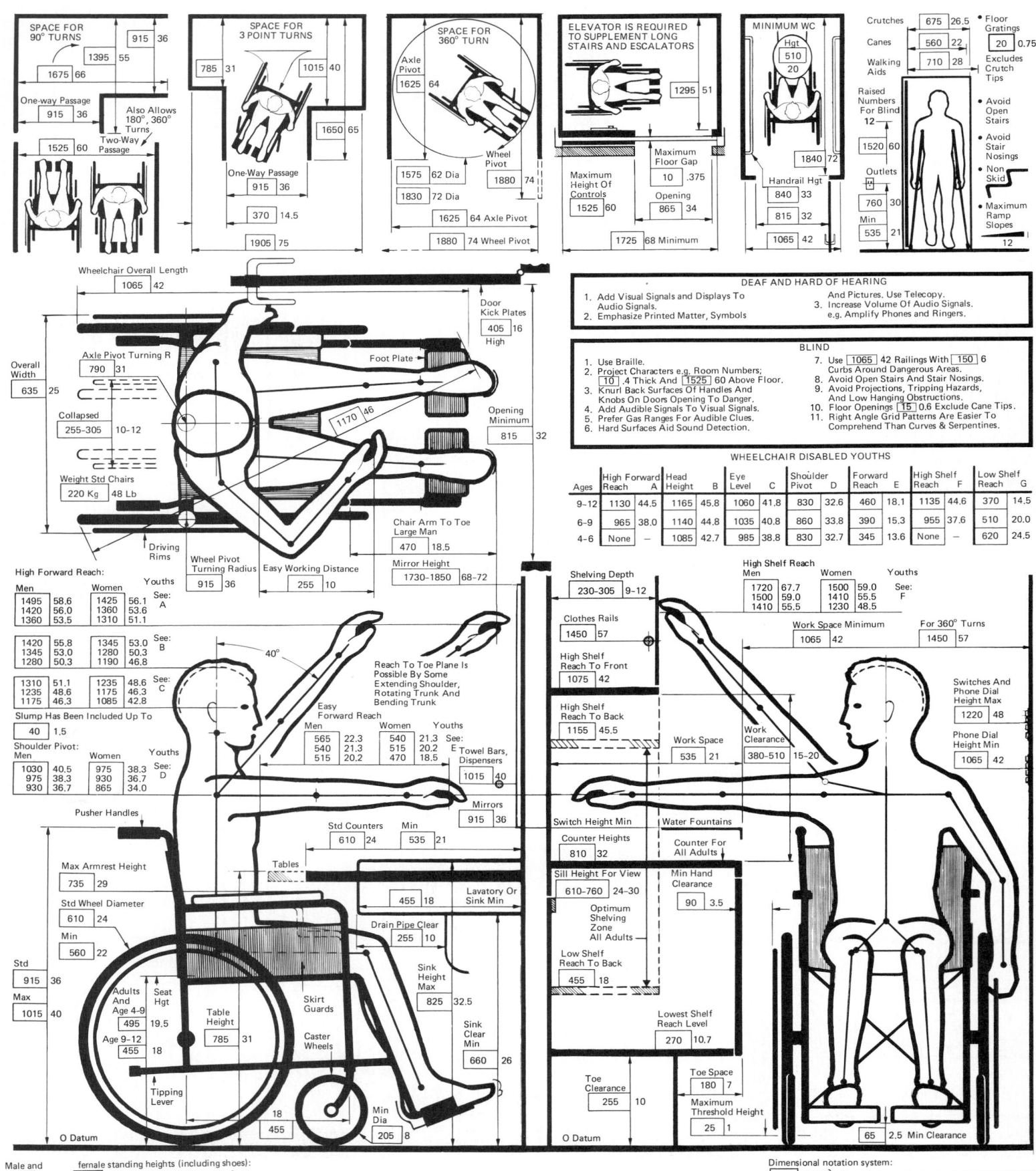

Niels Diffrient, Alvin R. Tilley; Henry Dreyfuss Associates; New York, New York

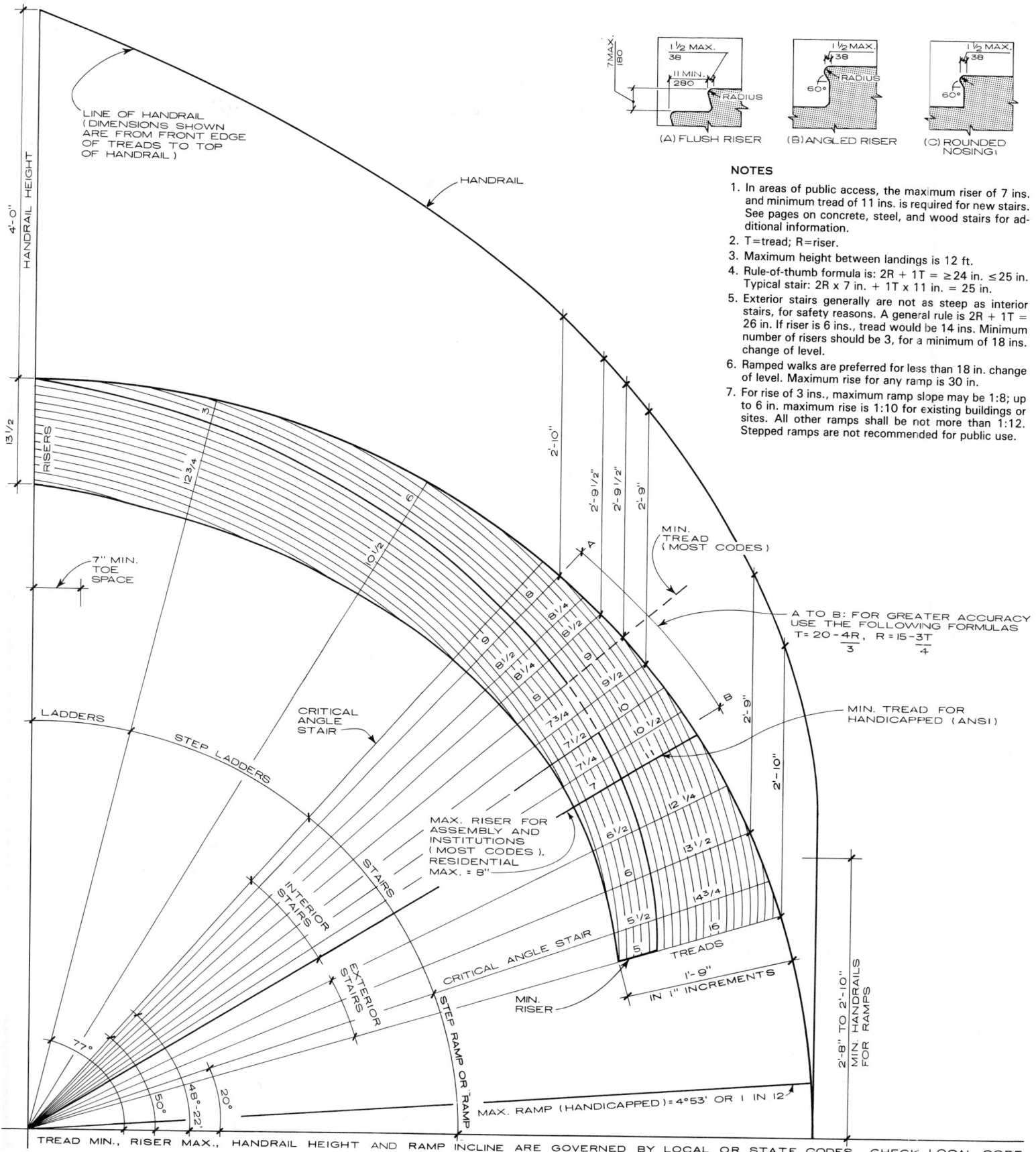

**NOTES**

1. In areas of public access, the maximum riser of 7 ins. and minimum tread of 11 ins. is required for new stairs. See pages on concrete, steel, and wood stairs for additional information.
2. T=tread; R=riser.
3. Maximum height between landings is 12 ft.
4. Rule-of-thumb formula is: 2R + 1T = ≥24 in. ≤25 in. Typical stair: 2R x 7 in. + 1T x 11 in. = 25 in.
5. Exterior stairs generally are not as steep as interior stairs, for safety reasons. A general rule is 2R + 1T = 26 in. If riser is 6 ins., tread would be 14 ins. Minimum number of risers should be 3, for a minimum of 18 ins. change of level.
6. Ramped walks are preferred for less than 18 in. change of level. Maximum rise for any ramp is 30 in.
7. For rise of 3 ins., maximum ramp slope may be 1:8; up to 6 in. maximum rise is 1:10 for existing buildings or sites. All other ramps shall be not more than 1:12. Stepped ramps are not recommended for public use.

A TO B: FOR GREATER ACCURACY USE THE FOLLOWING FORMULAS
$T = 20 - \frac{4R}{3}$, $R = 15 - \frac{3T}{4}$

**TREADS AND RISERS**

Paul Vaughan, AIA; Charleston, West Virginia

**ANTHROPOMETRIC** 1

## BED SIZES

| TYPES | W | L |
|---|---|---|
| KING | 72'' | 84'' |
| QUEEN | 60'' | 82'' |
| DOUBLE | 54'' | 82'' |
| SINGLE | 39'' | 82'' |
| DAYBED | 30'' | 75'' |
| CRIB | 30'' | 53'' |

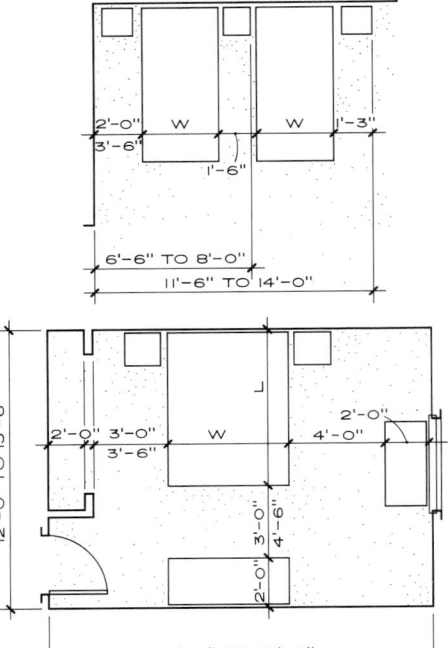

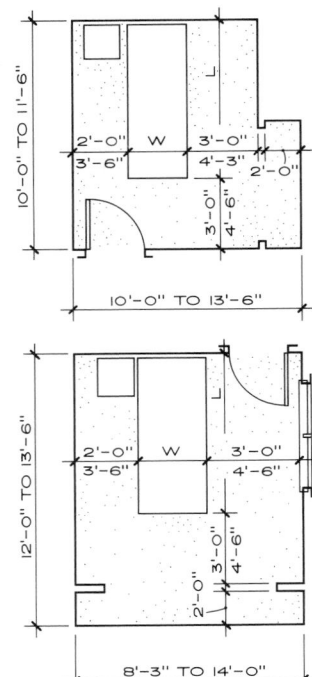

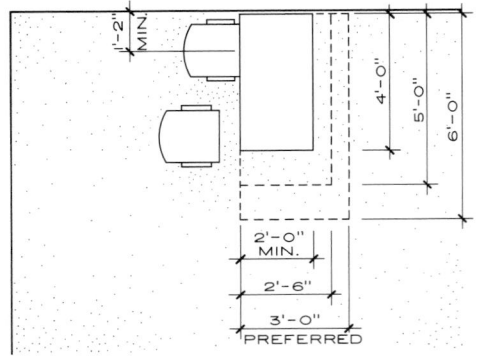

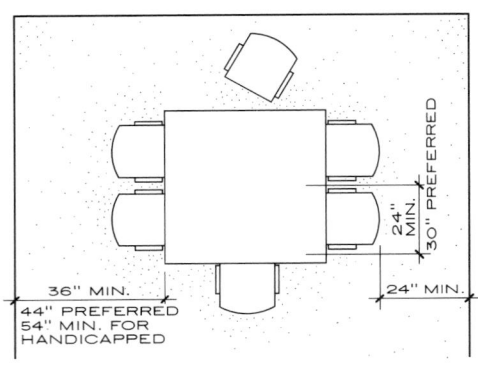

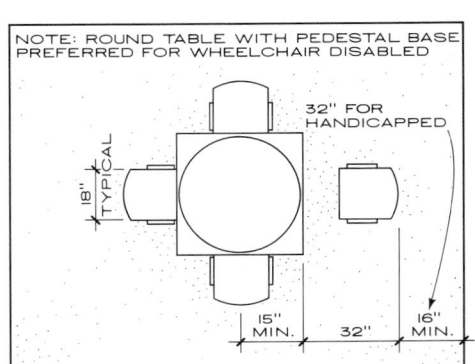

**BED CLEARANCES**

**BEDROOM FURNITURE**

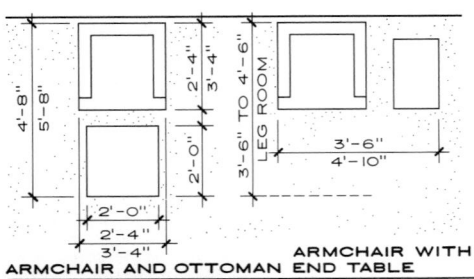

### RECTANGULAR TABLES (IN.)

| SIZE | SEAT | WHEELCHAIR |
|---|---|---|
| 24 x 48 | 4 | |
| 30 x 48 | 4 | 2 |
| 30 x 60 | 4-6 | 2-4 |
| 36 x 72 | 4-6 | 4-6 |
| 36 x 84 | 6-8 | 6 |

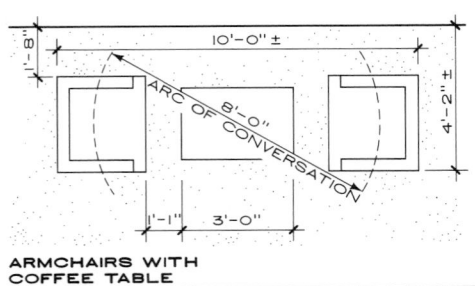

### SQUARE TABLES (IN.)

| SIZE | SEAT | WHEELCHAIR |
|---|---|---|
| 30 x 30 | 2 | |
| 36 x 36 | 2-4 | |
| 42 x 42 | 4 | 2 (TIGHT) |
| 48 x 48 | 4-8 | 2 |
| 54 x 54 | 4-8 | 4 |

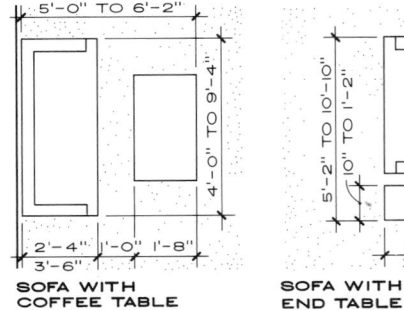

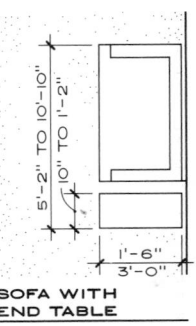

NOTE: ROUND TABLE WITH PEDESTAL BASE PREFERRED FOR WHEELCHAIR DISABLED

### ROUND TABLES (IN.)

| SIZE | SEAT | WHEELCHAIR |
|---|---|---|
| 30 | 2 | |
| 36 | 2-4 | |
| 42 | 4-5 | |
| 48 | 5-6 | 2 |
| 54 | 5-6 | 4 |

**DINING ROOM FURNITURE**

**ARMCHAIR AND OTTOMAN**

**ARMCHAIR WITH END TABLE**

**ARMCHAIRS WITH COFFEE TABLE**

**SOFA WITH COFFEE TABLE**

**SOFA WITH END TABLE**

**LIVING ROOM FURNITURE**

Robin Andrew Roberts, AIA; Washington, D.C.
Arthur J. Pettorino, AIA; Hicksville, New York

**RESIDENTIAL DESIGN**

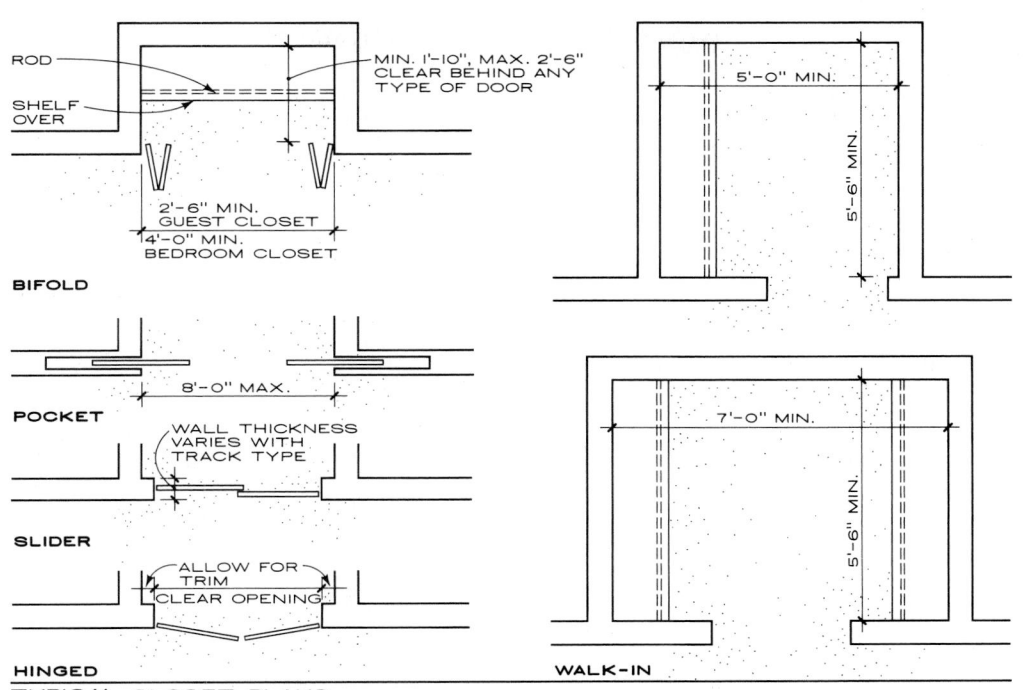

**TYPICAL CLOSET PLANS**

### NOTES

1. No closet bifold door should exceed a 2 ft panel. Largest door stock in pocket and sliding door is 4 ft.
2. All closet doors should allow easy access to top shelves.
3. Doors for children's closets can be used as tackboards, chalkboards, or mirrors.
4. Consider use of hinged doors for storage fittings and mirrors.
5. Walk-in closets should be properly ventilated and lit.
6. Provide clear floor space at least 30 by 48 in. for wheelchair approach. Pole and shelf height is 54" maximum for handicapped.
7. Percentage of accessibility of closets varies with door types used: Bifold at 66⅔% min.; pocket at 100%; sliding at 50% or more; and hinged at 90% depending on hardware and door thickness.

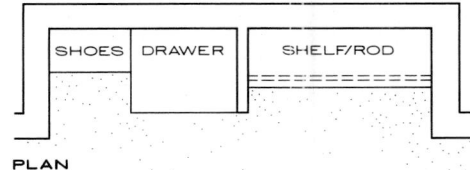

**PLAN**

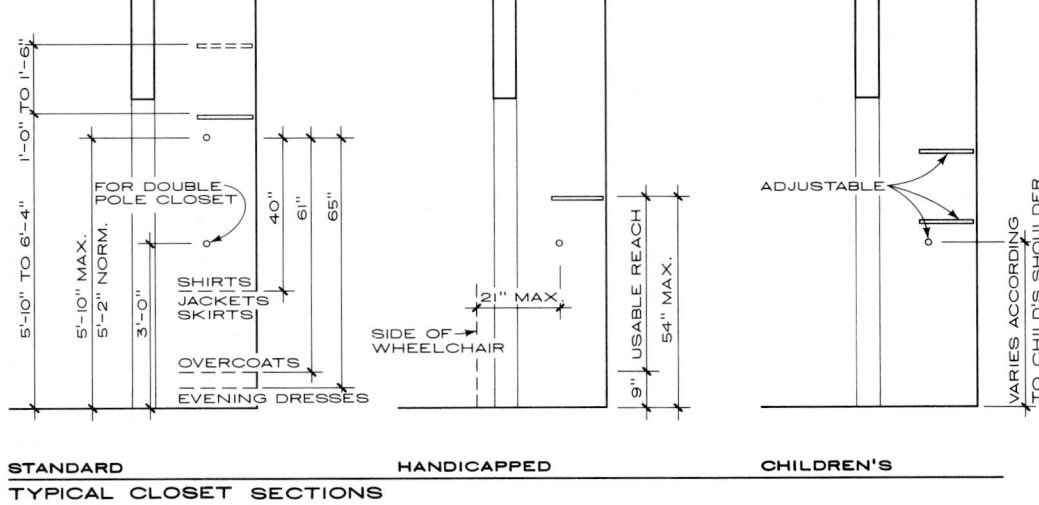

**STANDARD**    **HANDICAPPED**    **CHILDREN'S**

**TYPICAL CLOSET SECTIONS**

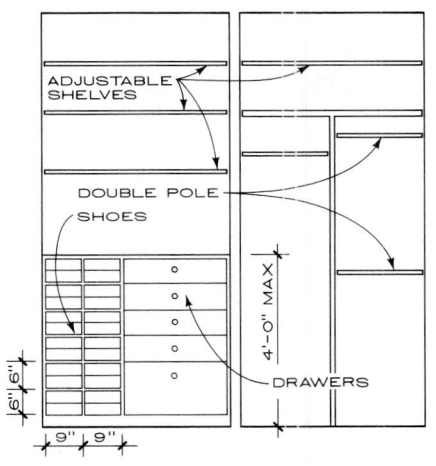

**ELEVATION**
**DIVIDED CLOSET**

## RESIDENTIAL STORAGE

SHELVING. Standard shelving sizes are 6, 8, 10, and 12 in., although shelving up to 18 in. deep is desirable for closet shelving. Shelving may be either fixed or adjustable.

DRAWERS. Typical drawers are from 16 to 24 in. deep, 12 to 36 in. wide, and 2 to 8 in. deep or deeper. Often built into casework, drawers may be of wood, metal, or molded plastic.

CLOSETS. Standard closet depth is 24 to 30 in. for clothing and 16 to 20 in. for linens.

BOXES. Closet storage fittings such as boxes and garment bags can be used for supplemental or seasonal storage.

Robin Andrew Roberts, AIA; Washington, D.C.
R. L. Speas, Jr.; Hugh N. Jacobsen, FAIA; Washington, D.C.

## STORAGE REQUIREMENTS

BEDROOM. Allow 4 to 6 ft of hanging space per person. Allow 8 linear ft of hanging space for closets shared by 2 people. Allow 12 in. of hanging space for 6 suits, 12 shirts, 8 dresses, or 6 pairs of pants.

LINEN STORAGE. Place near bedrooms and bathrooms in a closet with 12 to 18 in. deep shelves. Supplemental storage in bins or baskets may be needed. Provide minimum 9 sq ft for 1–2 bedroom house; 12 sq ft for 3–4 bedroom house.

BATHROOMS. A mirrored wall cabinet 4 to 6 in. deep is typical bathroom storage, supplemented by space for supplies of soap, toothpaste, and other toiletries.

COATS. A closet near an entry door for coats and rainwear is desirable in most areas of the country. Provide extra 2 to 3 in. in depth for air circulation and added bulkiness of overcoats.

CLEANING EQUIPMENT. A closet at least 24 in. wide for storage of vacuum cleaners and household cleaning supplies is helpful. Locate closet near center of house and provide electrical outlet so vacuum can be left connected.

KITCHEN/DINING. See pages on kitchen planning for recommendations.

OTHER STORAGE. Most families have additional storage needs. For custom design work, these needs must be analyzed and storage planned. Storage rooms and attic and basement areas are possible supplemental storage locations.

## KITCHEN SPACE PLANNING

The layouts shown here, together with their general area requirements, are based on studies of furniture, appliances, storage, and clearances for the average residential kitchen. They have been developed to accommodate work, storage, and floor areas required for various food preparation functions. The location and order of both appliances and associated work surfaces should be de- termined by physical limitations, traffic flow, individual preferences, and appliance type in determining kitchen size during the early planning stages. To simplify com- parison of the various room types, basic sizes of furni- ture, appliances, and clearances have been standardized.

Storage: Minimum 18 sq ft of space for basic storage with an additional 6 sq ft/person served.

Work Flow: Work flow should move from refrigerator work center (A) to sink work center (B) to cooking work center (C), then to the serving spot. The total length of the work triangle (ABC) should average less than 23 lin- eal feet and never exceed 26 lineal feet.

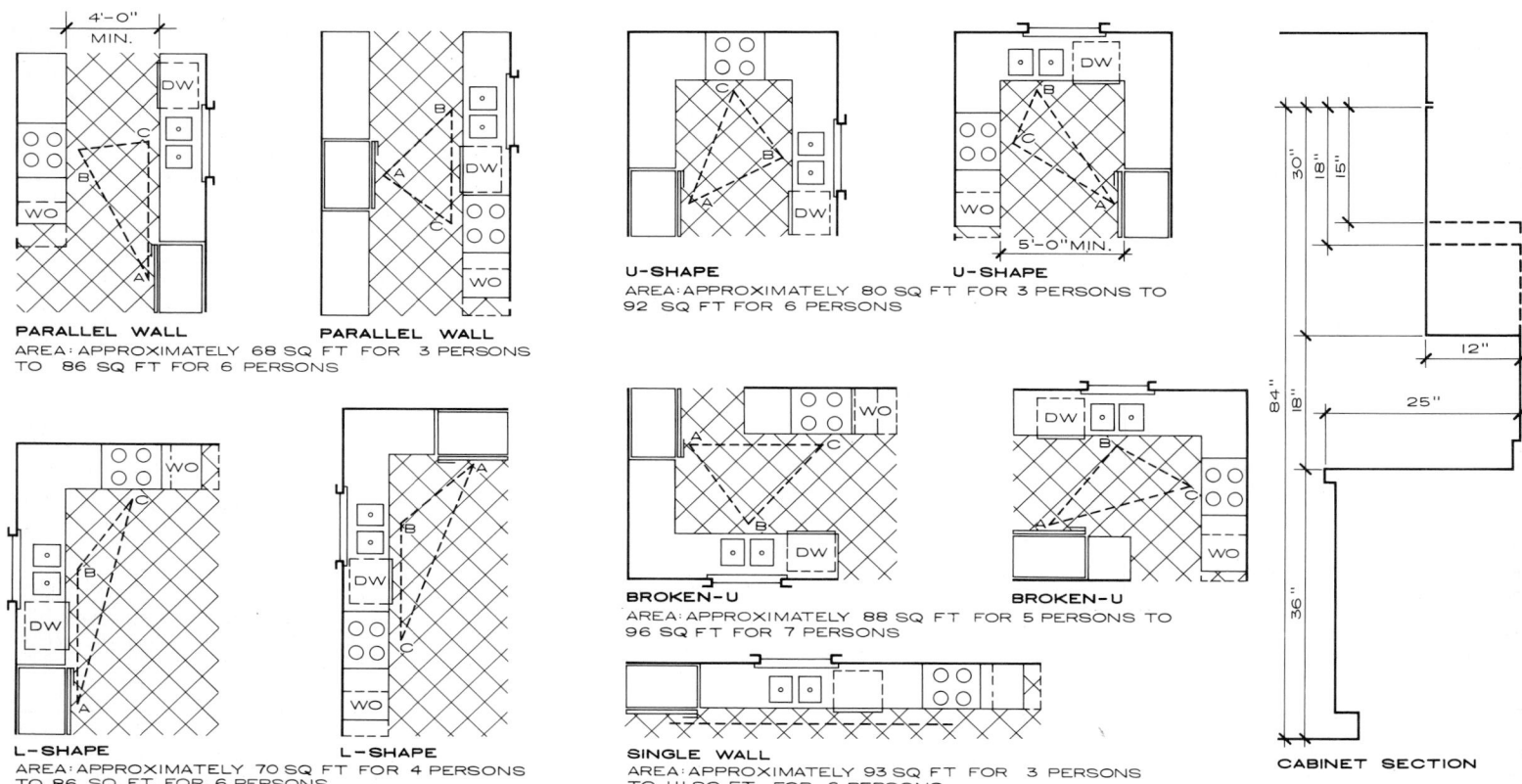

**PARALLEL WALL**
AREA: APPROXIMATELY 68 SQ FT FOR 3 PERSONS TO 86 SQ FT FOR 6 PERSONS

**PARALLEL WALL**

**U-SHAPE**
AREA: APPROXIMATELY 80 SQ FT FOR 3 PERSONS TO 92 SQ FT FOR 6 PERSONS

**U-SHAPE**

**L-SHAPE**
AREA: APPROXIMATELY 70 SQ FT FOR 4 PERSONS TO 86 SQ FT FOR 6 PERSONS

**L-SHAPE**

**BROKEN-U**
AREA: APPROXIMATELY 88 SQ FT FOR 5 PERSONS TO 96 SQ FT FOR 7 PERSONS

**BROKEN-U**

**SINGLE WALL**
AREA: APPROXIMATELY 93 SQ FT FOR 3 PERSONS TO 111 SQ FT FOR 6 PERSONS

**CABINET SECTION**

**RESIDENTIAL KITCHEN ARRANGEMENTS**

NOTE: SMALL KITCHENS USUALLY HAVE UP TO 10 RUNNING FEET OF COUNTER AND EQUIPMENT. AVERAGE KITCHENS HAVE UP TO 20 RUNNING FEET OF THE SAME. USUAL EQUIPMENT INCLUDES UNDERCOUNTER REFRIGERATOR

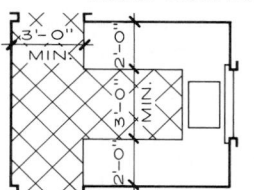
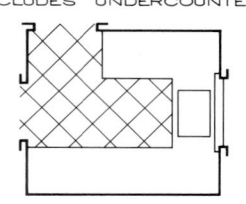
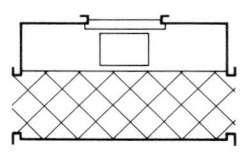
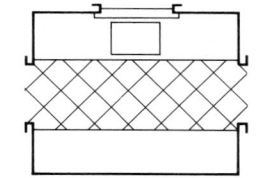
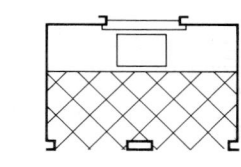

**PANTRY TYPES**

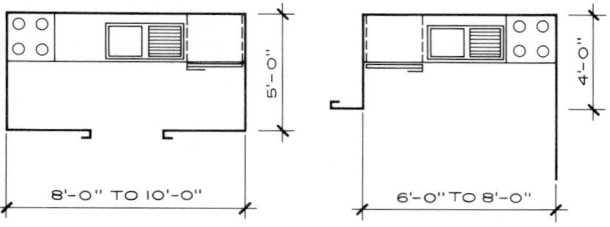
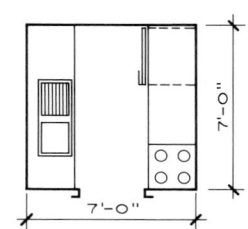

ABBREVIATIONS
DW = DISHWASHER
WO = WALL OVEN

**KITCHENETTES**

Robin Andrew Roberts, AIA; Washington, D.C.
R. E. Powe, Jr., AIA; Hugh N. Jacobsen, FAIA; Washington, D.C.

 **RESIDENTIAL DESIGN**

## KITCHEN WORK CENTERS

A residential kitchen may be considered in terms of three interconnected work centers: A, B, and C, as shown below. Each encompasses a distinct phase of kitchen activity, and storage should be provided for the items that are most used in connection with each center.

The functions of the sink center are most common to the other two centers. It is recommended, therefore, that the sink center's location be convenient to each of the others (usually between them). The refrigerator center is best located near the entry and the range center near the dining area.

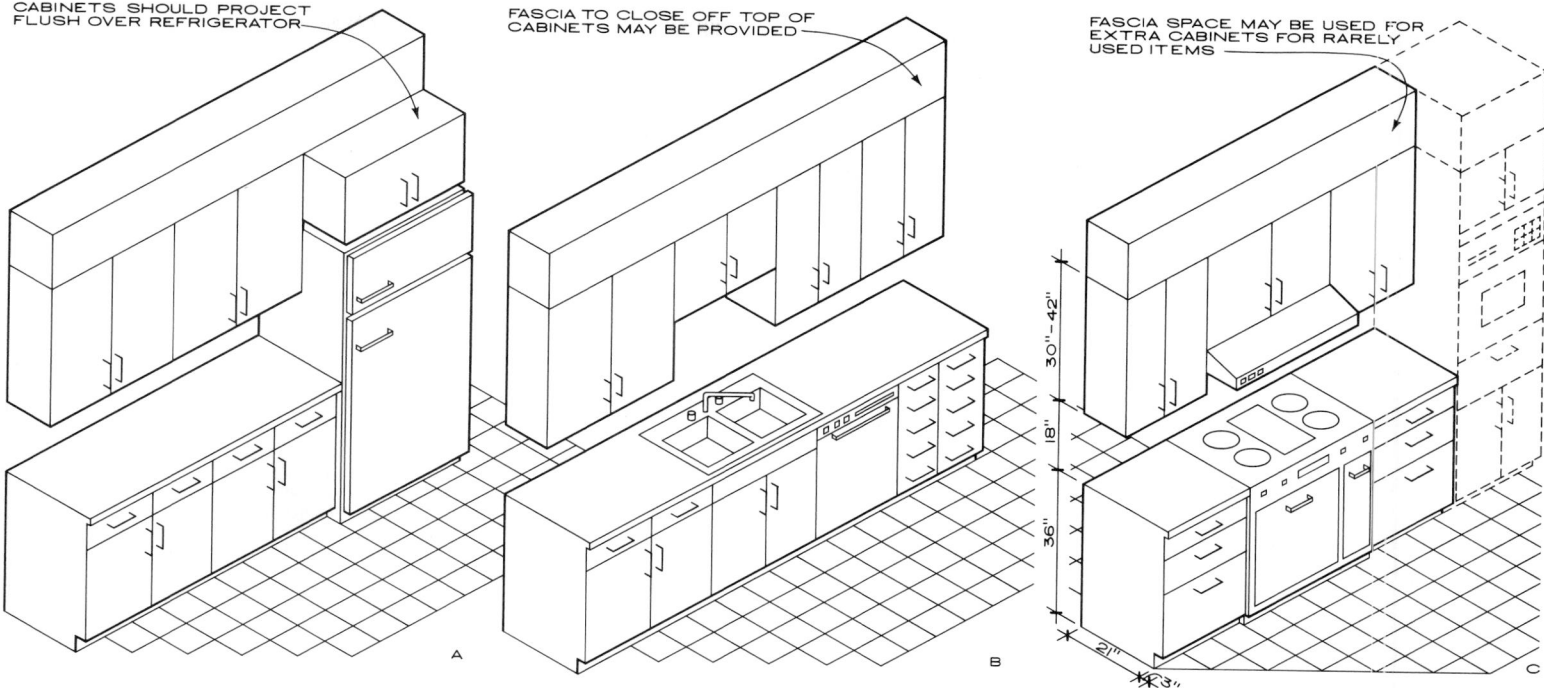

### REFRIGERATOR CENTER
(Receiving and Food Preparation)

Provide storage for mixer and mixing bowls; other utensils: sifter, grater, salad molds, cake and pie tins, occasional dishes, condiments, staples, canned goods, brooms, and miscellaneous items.

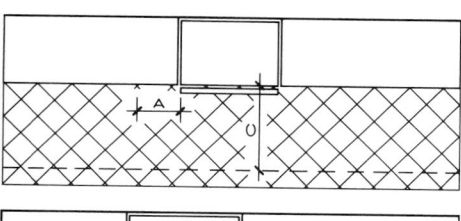

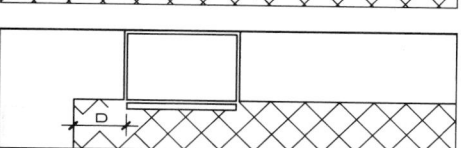

A = 15 in. minimum counter space at latch side of refrigerator for loading and unloading.

B = 18 in. minimum clearance between latch side of refrigerator and turn of counter.

C = 40 to 42 in. clearance from face of refrigerator to wall or facing counter.

### SINK CENTER
(Food Preparation, Cleaning, and Cleanup)

Provide storage for everyday dishes, glassware, pots and pans, cutlery, silver, pitchers and shakers, vegetable bins, linen, towel rack, wastebasket, cleaning materials and utensils, garbage can or disposal, and dishdrain. Some codes require louvers or other venting provisions in the doors under enclosed sinks.

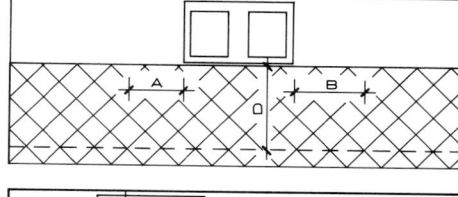

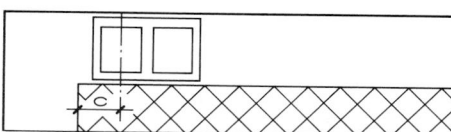

A = 18 to 36 in. counter space on side of sink.

B = 24 to 36 in. counter space on side of sink.
Provide 24 in. counter space at either right or left if dishwasher is used.

C = 14 in. minimum clearance between center of bowl and the turn of counter.

D = 40 to 42 in. minimum clearance from face of sink to wall or facing counter.

### RANGE CENTER
(Cooking and Serving)

Provide storage for pots, potholders, frying pans, roaster, cooking utensils, grease container, seasoning, canned goods, breadbin, breadboard, toaster, plate warmer, platters, serving dishes, and trays.

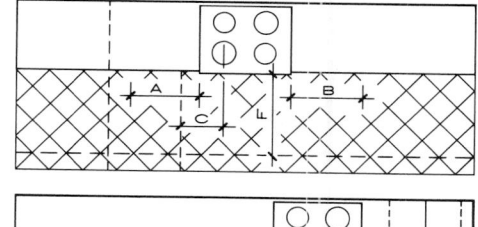

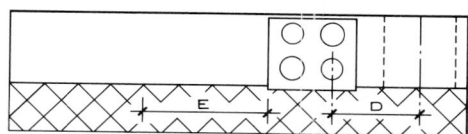

A, B = 18 to 24 in. counter space on either side of cooking facility.

C = 14 in. minimum clearance between center of front unit and the turn of counter.

D = 16 in. minimum clearance between center of front unit and nearest piece of high equipment or wall, or between center of wall oven and adjoining wall.

E = 36 to 42 in. counter space between range and nearest piece of equipment.

F = 40 to 42 in. clearance from face of range or oven to face of wall or facing counter.

## CLEARANCES

### KITCHENS FOR THE HANDICAPPED

The preferred cooktop and counter height is 30 to 33 in., but may be standard 36 in. Open floor space is necessary for wheelchair maneuverability; observe a 5 ft minimum turning radius. Smooth, nonskid flooring is required. Indoor–outdoor carpet is preferred, but difficult to maintain in a kitchen. Linoleum or vinyl tile is acceptable. Knee space is necessary under sink counter. Insulate pipes to avoid scalding. Provide cooktop controls at

front to avoid reaching across hot surfaces. Wall ovens should preferably be set so that top of open oven door is 2 ft 7 in. above floor. Side-by-side refrigerator-freezer is preferred, although units with freezer on bottom are acceptable. Dishwashers should be front-loading.

Round tables with pedestal bases are preferred. A 4 ft diameter will accommodate two wheelchair users; a 4 ft 5 in. diameter will accommodate four wheelchair users.

Storage considerations for the wheelchair disabled include use of pegboard for pots, pans, and utensils. Vertical drawers in base cabinets allow for storage of food that would otherwise be out of reach of wheelchair users. Narrow shelving mounted to the backs of doors in cabinets or closets provides accessible storage for food and utensils.

Robin Andrew Roberts, AIA; Washington, D.C.
Arthur J. Pettorino, AIA; Hicksville, New York
R. E. Powe, Jr., AIA; Hugh N. Jacobsen, FAIA; Washington, D.C.

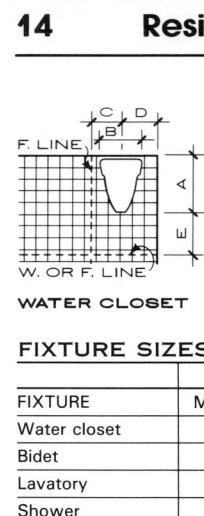
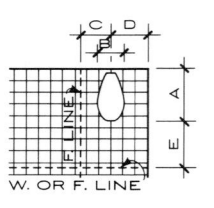
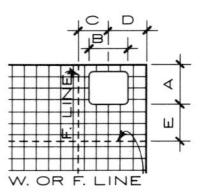
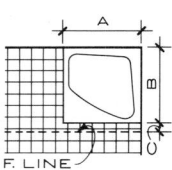

| WATER CLOSET | BIDET | LAVATORY | SHOWER | TUB (RECTANGULAR) | TUB (SQUARE) |

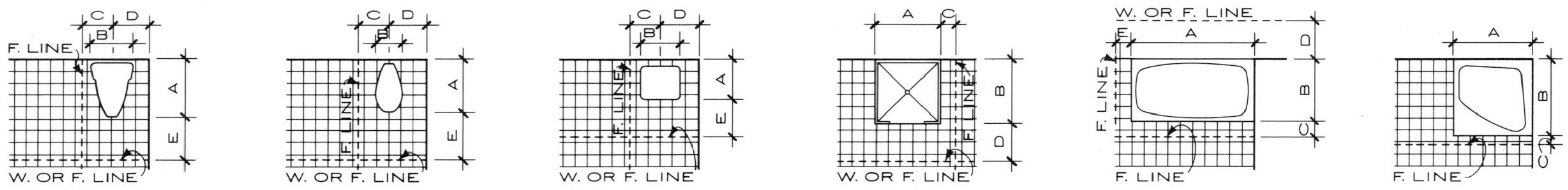

## FIXTURE SIZES AND CLEARANCES (IN.) W = WALL F = FIXTURE

| FIXTURE | A MINIMUM | A LIBERAL | B MINIMUM | B LIBERAL | C MINIMUM | C LIBERAL | D MINIMUM | D LIBERAL | E MINIMUM | E LIBERAL |
|---|---|---|---|---|---|---|---|---|---|---|
| Water closet | 27 | 31 | 19 | 21 | 12 | 18 | 15 | 22 | W = 18 F = 18 | W = 36 F = 34 |
| Bidet | 25 | 27 | 14 | 14 | 12 | 18 | 15 | 22 | W = 18 F = 18 | W = 36 F = 34 |
| Lavatory | 16 | 21 | 18 | 30 | 2 | 6 | 14 | 22 | 18 | 30 |
| Shower | 32 | 36 | 34 | 36 | 2 | 8 | 18 | 34 | | |
| Tub (rectangular) | 60 STD. | 72 | 30 STD. | 42 | 2 | 8 | W = 20 F = 18 | W = 34 F = 30 | 2 | 8 |
| Tub (square) | 38 | | 39 | | 2 | 4 | | | | |

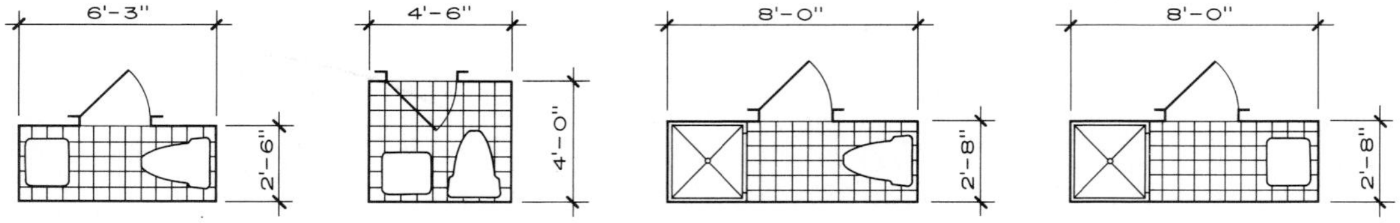

### NOTES
1. Typical bathroom accessories include medicine cabinet, mirror, soap dish, towel rack, and toilet paper holder.
2. Convenience outlets for electric toothbrushes, razors, and hair dryers should be provided. They should be electrically grounded for user safety.
3. Bathroom ventilations may be achieved by natural means (window or operable skylight) or with mechanical exhaust fan.

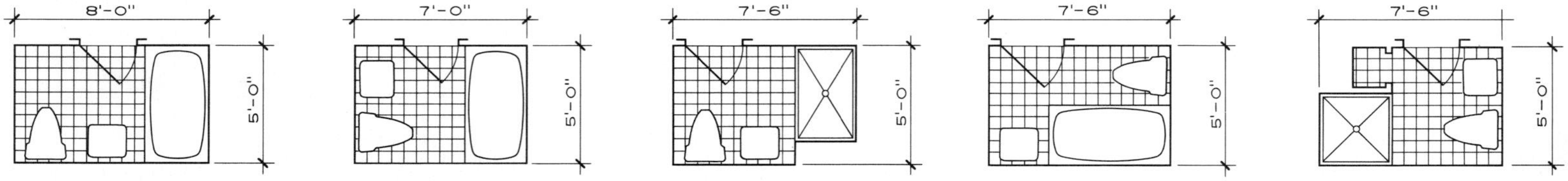

**TWO-FIXTURE**

**THREE-FIXTURE**

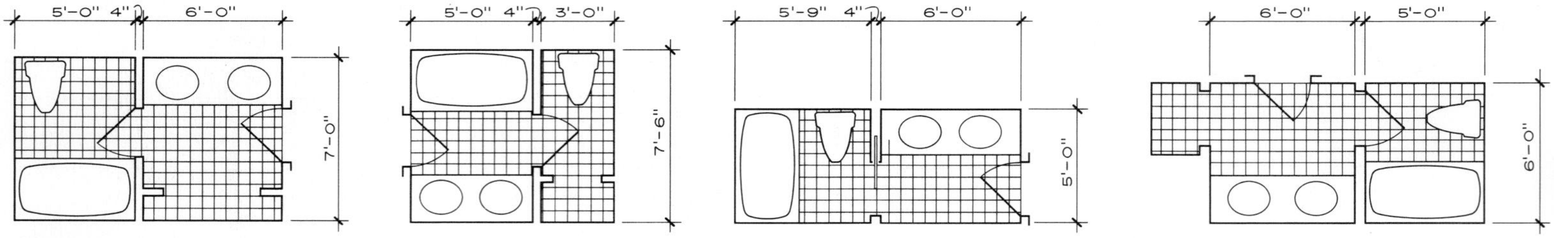

**FOUR-FIXTURE**

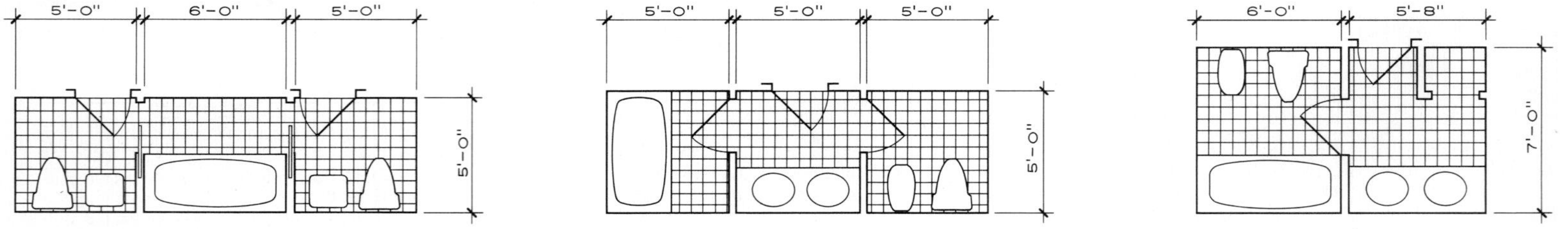

**FIVE-FIXTURE**

## TYPICAL ARRANGEMENTS

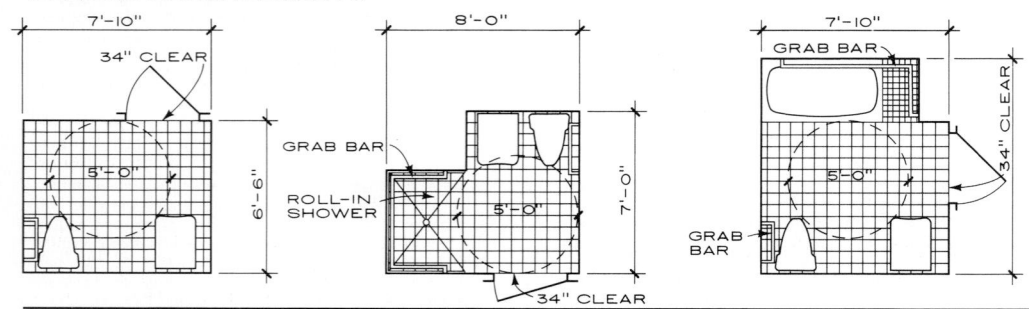

### NOTES
1. Provide space for wheelchair maneuverability; observe 5 ft minimum radius.
2. Additional space next to water closet will allow for side transfer from wheelchair.
3. Provide knee space under sink. Insulate pipes to avoid scalding.
4. Use grab bars around water closet and tub.
5. Roll-in shower may replace tub and is more convenient for many wheelchair disabled.
6. Bathroom door to be minimum 32 in. clear opening and to swing outward. Use lever hardware on both sides.

## ARRANGEMENTS FOR THE WHEELCHAIR DISABLED

Robin Andrew Roberts, AIA; Washington, D.C.
Arthur J. Pettorino, AIA; Hicksville, New York

# 1  RESIDENTIAL DESIGN

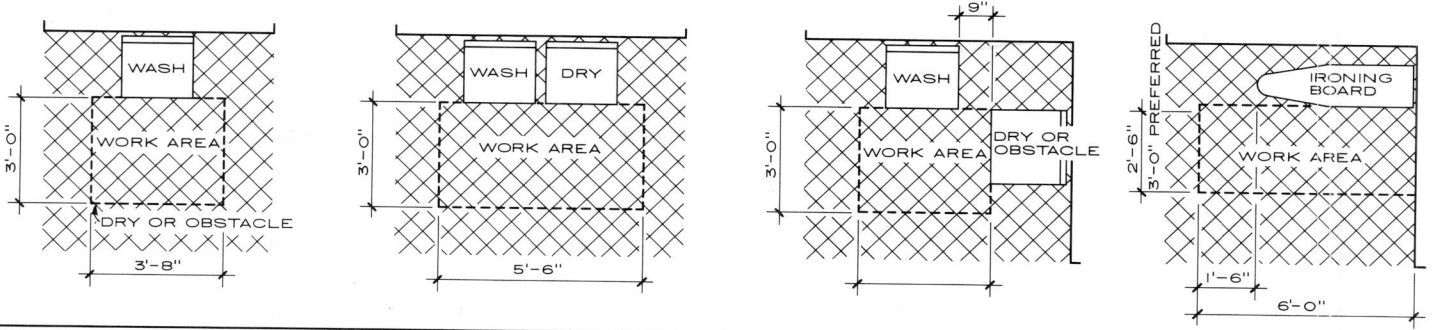

WASH
WORK AREA
DRY OR OBSTACLE
3'-0"
3'-8"
WASH
DRY
WORK AREA
3'-0"
5'-6"
9"
WASH
WORK AREA
DRY OR OBSTACLE
3'-0"
IRONING BOARD
WORK AREA
2'-6"
3'-0" PREFERRED
1'-6"
6'-0"


LAUNDRY EQUIPMENT CLEARANCES

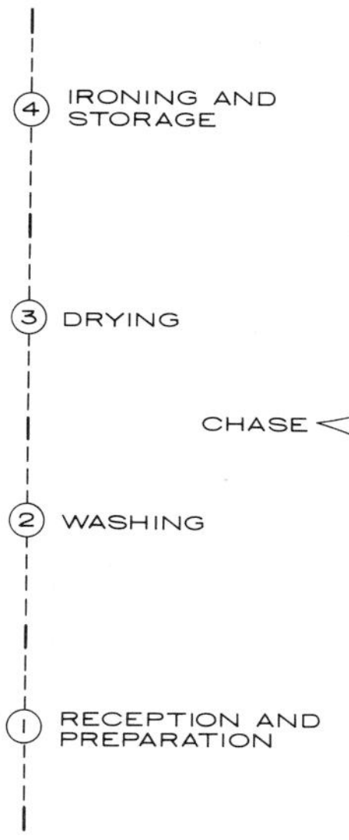

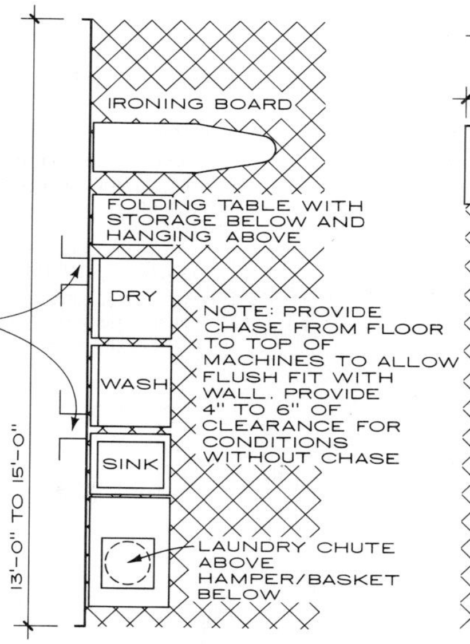

4 IRONING AND STORAGE
3 DRYING
2 WASHING
1 RECEPTION AND PREPARATION


SEQUENCE

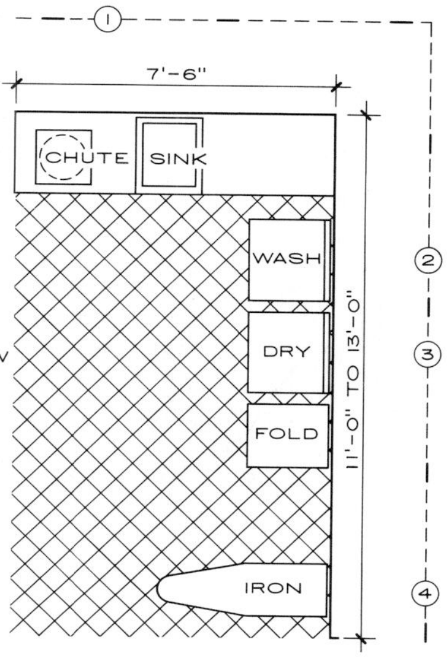

IRONING BOARD
FOLDING TABLE WITH STORAGE BELOW AND HANGING ABOVE
CHASE
DRY
WASH
SINK
NOTE: PROVIDE CHASE FROM FLOOR TO TOP OF MACHINES TO ALLOW FLUSH FIT WITH WALL. PROVIDE 4" TO 6" OF CLEARANCE FOR CONDITIONS WITHOUT CHASE
LAUNDRY CHUTE ABOVE HAMPER/BASKET BELOW
13'-0" TO 15'-0"


ONE-WALL LAUNDRY

7'-6"
CHUTE
SINK
WASH
DRY
FOLD
IRON
11'-0" TO 13'-0"


"L" LAUNDRY

8'-0"
WASH
DRY
SINK
FOLD
IRON
CHUTE
2'-6" MIN.
7'-6" TO 9'-0"


PARALLEL LAUNDRIES

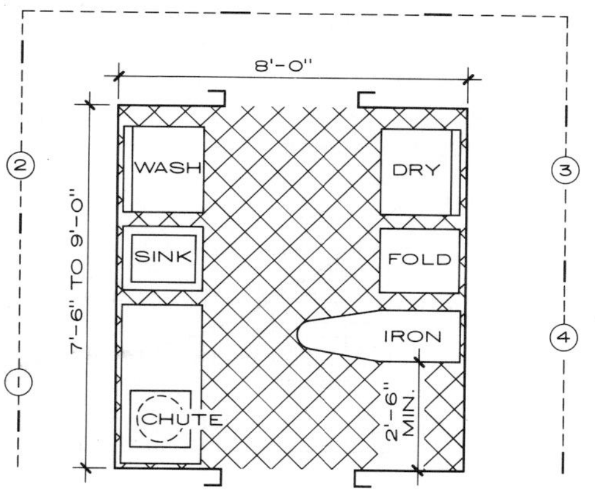

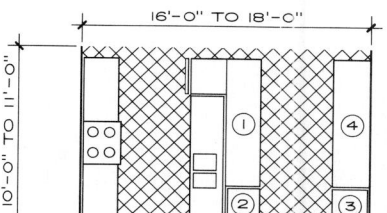

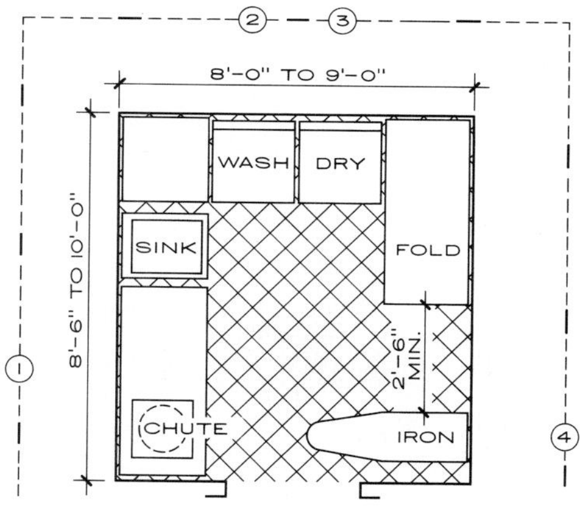

8'-0" TO 9'-0"
WASH
DRY
SINK
FOLD
2'-6" MIN.
CHUTE
IRON
8'-6" TO 10'-0"


"U" LAUNDRY

TYPICAL LAUNDRIES

16'-0" TO 18'-0"
8'-0" TO 9'-0"
16'-0" TO 18'-0"
10'-0" TO 11'-0"
16'-0" TO 18'-0"
8'-0" TO 9'-0"
17'-0" TO 22'-0"
9'-0" TO 11'-0"


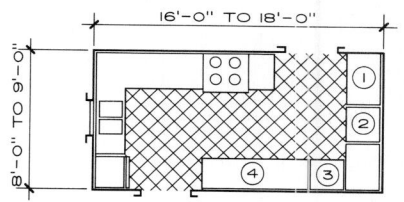

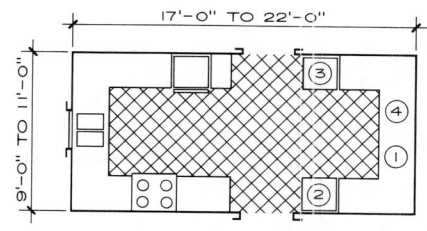

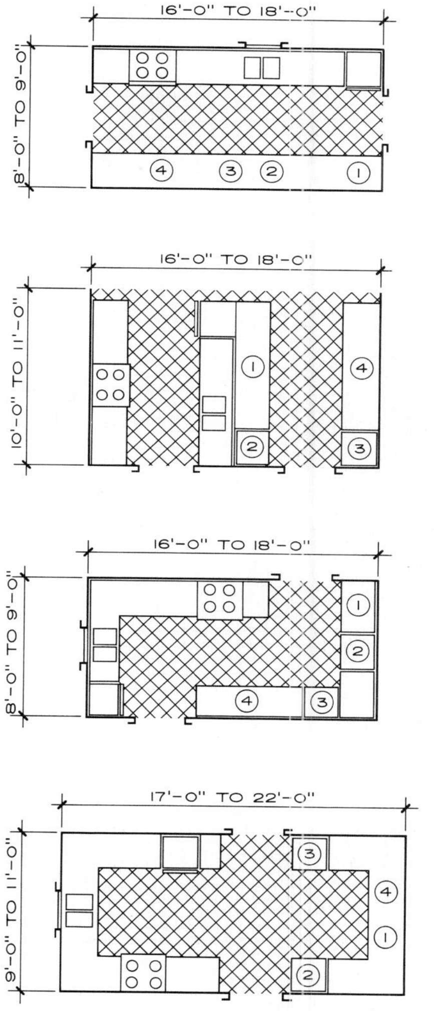

LAUNDRIES WITH KITCHEN

## LAUNDRIES FOR THE HANDICAPPED

For the wheelchair disabled, having laundry facilities close to the kitchen combines several time-consuming activities with a minimum of movement from place to place.

The basic necessities for an accessible laundry facility are the following: front-loading automatic washer, dryer, storage shelving for supplies, lightweight steam iron, ironing board, and a surface for folding.

Laundry equipment controls are to be within high forward or side reach ranges. Controls shall be operable with one hand and not require tight grasping, pinching, or twisting of the wrist.

For an accessible laundry area, provide storage for supplies within high forward or side reach ranges and all working surfaces at a comfortable seated work height of 29 in. with knee clearance below.

## APARTMENT HOUSE LAUNDRIES

In apartment houses, locate laundry rooms in the basement or on the ground floor of the building near necessary mechanical equipment, piping, and ventilation.

Locate laundry rooms on grade, to provide surfaces to absorb vibrations from operation and to not disturb the apartment dwellers.

Provide convenient access from dwelling units to laundry room. Incorporate into the laundry room design folding tables and vending machines for soap, bleach, and other laundry powders.

Provide the ability for visual inspection of the laundry room for the security of the users. Also, laundry rooms in large apartment buildings are public areas where apartment dwellers socialize and meet each other, so provide area to accommodate this necessary function.

Robin Andrew Roberts, AIA; Washington, D.C.
Arthur J. Pettorino, AIA; Hicksville, New York
R. E. Powe, Jr., AIA; Hugh N. Jacobsen, FAIA; Washington, D.C.

**NOTES**

Commercial kitchens usually are defined as those providing food to be consumed away from home. Typical of these are kitchens within restaurants, hotels and motels, cafeterias, snack bars and coffee shops, schools and colleges, office buildings, hospitals, and other institutions. The size, type, quantity, and layout of equipment in the kitchen and the related service areas are a direct function of the menu, amount of patronage, and the time in which the items are to be served.

The schematic drawings shown here do not attempt to present kitchen design solutions, but rather to familiarize the reader with typical characteristics of commercial kitchen design.

**FUNCTIONAL FLOW DIAGRAM**

**NOTES**

Workers and materials should travel minimum distances. They should proceed in a logical sequence with minimum crisscrossing and backtracking. Delay in processing and serving should be reduced to a minimum. Garbage and trash disposal facilities are required for all functions.

## GENERAL INFORMATION

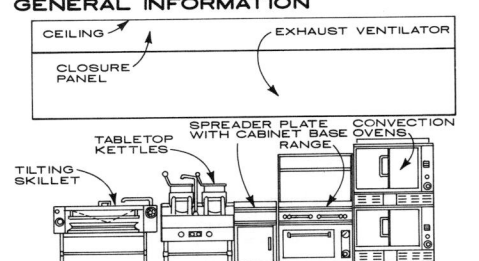

**HOT FOOD PREPARATION AREA-ELEVATION**

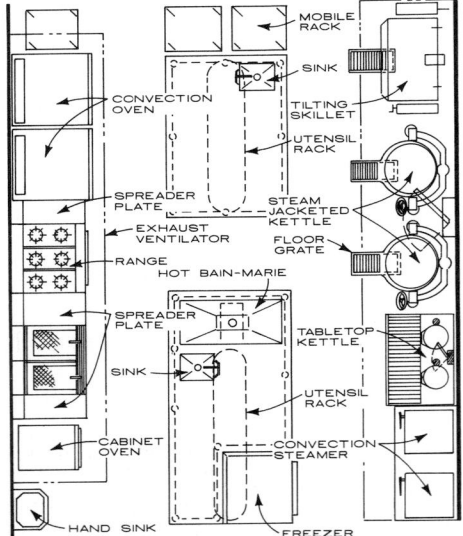

**HOT FOOD PREPARATION AREA-CAFETERIA/ BANQUET**

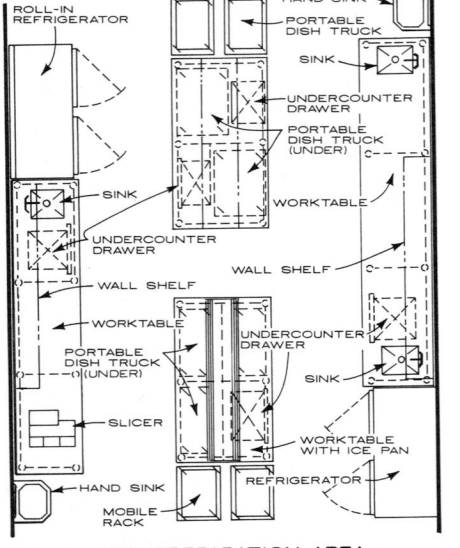

**COLD FOOD PREPARATION AREA- CAFETERIA/BANQUET**

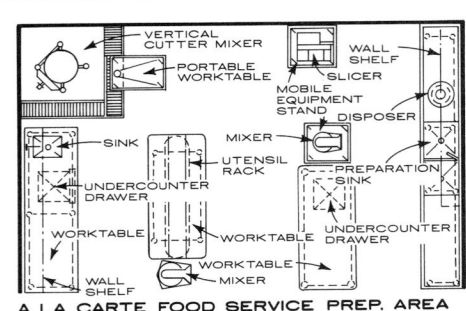

**A LA CARTE FOOD SERVICE PREP. AREA**

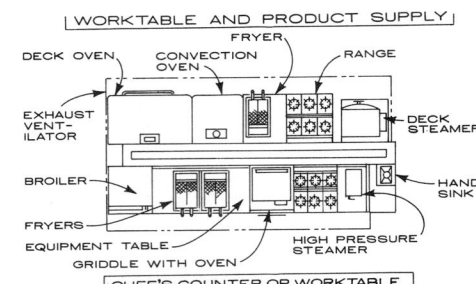

**HOT FOOD PREP. AREA—ISLAND TYPE**

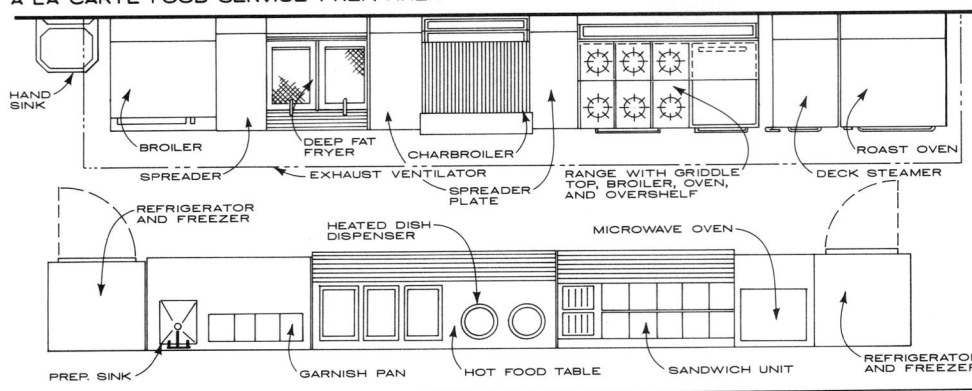

**A LA CARTE FOOD SERVICE AREA**

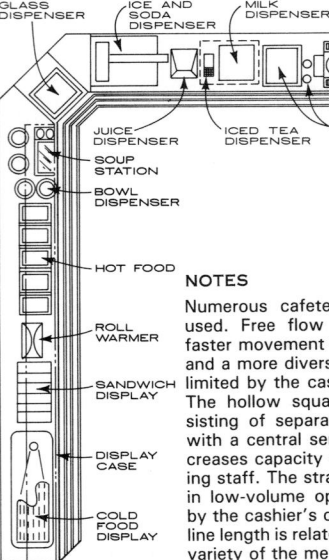

**CAFETERIA**

**NOTES**

Numerous cafeteria layouts are used. Free flow design permits faster movement through the line and a more diversified menu; it is limited by the cashier's capacity. The hollow square design, consisting of separate feeding lines with a central service facility, increases capacity without increasing staff. The straight line is used in low-volume operations limited by the cashier's capacity. Service line length is related directly to the variety of the menu.

**RECOMMENDED STORAGE TEMPERATURES**

1. DRY FOOD STORAGE: 65°F (15°C). Stored 4 in. off floor, 2 in. from wall.
2. COMMON STORAGE: 50°F to 60°F (10°C to 15°C).
3. FREEZER STORAGE: −10°F (−23°C).
4. REFRIGERATED STORAGE: 31°F to 40°F (−0.5°C to 4°C).

**RECOMMENDED WARE WASHING TEMPERATURES**

1. PRERINSE: 120°F to 140°F (49°C–60°C).
2. WASH: 140°F (60°C).
3. RINSE: 180°F (82°C) for 10 seconds. 170°F (77°C) for 30 seconds or longer.

(If sanitizing agent is used, 140°F (60°C) is acceptable for all ware washing functions.)

NOTE: Check local health codes for requirements.

**VENTILATORS**

Ventilators generally are required over all types of major cooking equipment. The exhaust system should be either a canopy type or high-speed backshelf exhaust. Grease should be removed through filters or internal centrifugal extraction. Fire extinguishing equipment must be installed in compliance with standard codes established by the National Fire Protection Association and local codes. The most commonly used systems are carbon dioxide and dry chemical extinguishing systems in conjunction with portable fire extinguishers. Water fog systems are being introduced and accepted in many areas.

Ventilator installations should cover completely the equipment being ventilated, with minimum overhangs on all sides regulated by national and local codes. Maximum floor to canopy height should be approximately 7 ft and the canopy from bottom to top should be 2 ft or more.

Cini-Grissom Associates, Inc.; Food Service Consultants; Washington, D.C.

# 1 SPACE PLANNING

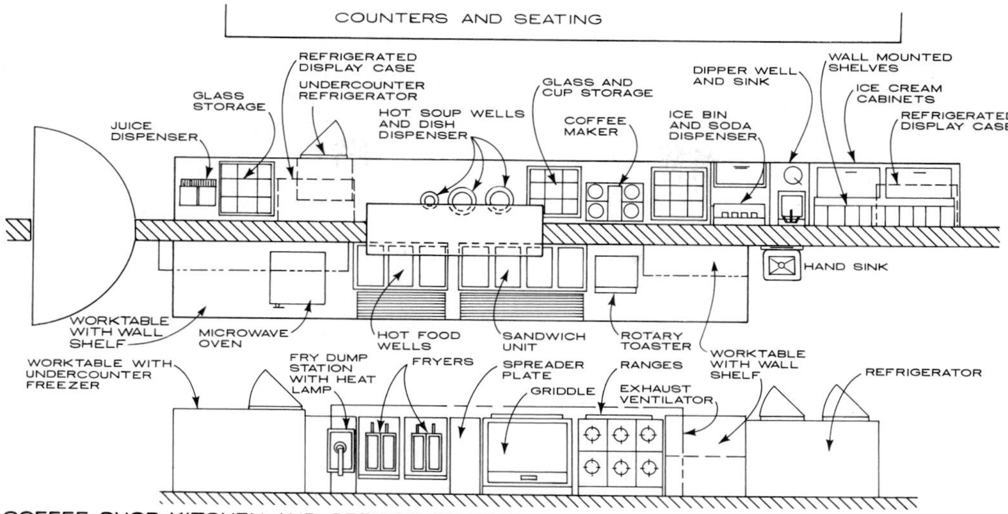

COUNTERS AND SEATING

JUICE DISPENSER

GLASS STORAGE

REFRIGERATED DISPLAY CASE
UNDERCOUNTER REFRIGERATOR

HOT SOUP WELLS AND DISH DISPENSER

GLASS AND CUP STORAGE

COFFEE MAKER

DIPPER WELL AND SINK

ICE BIN AND SODA DISPENSER

WALL MOUNTED SHELVES

ICE CREAM CABINETS

REFRIGERATED DISPLAY CASE

HAND SINK

WORKTABLE WITH WALL SHELF

WORKTABLE WITH UNDERCOUNTER FREEZER

MICROWAVE OVEN

FRY DUMP STATION WITH HEAT LAMP

FRYERS

HOT FOOD WELLS

SANDWICH UNIT

SPREADER PLATE

GRIDDLE

ROTARY TOASTER

RANGES

EXHAUST VENTILATOR

WORKTABLE WITH WALL SHELF

REFRIGERATOR

## COFFEE SHOP KITCHEN AND SERVICE PANTRY

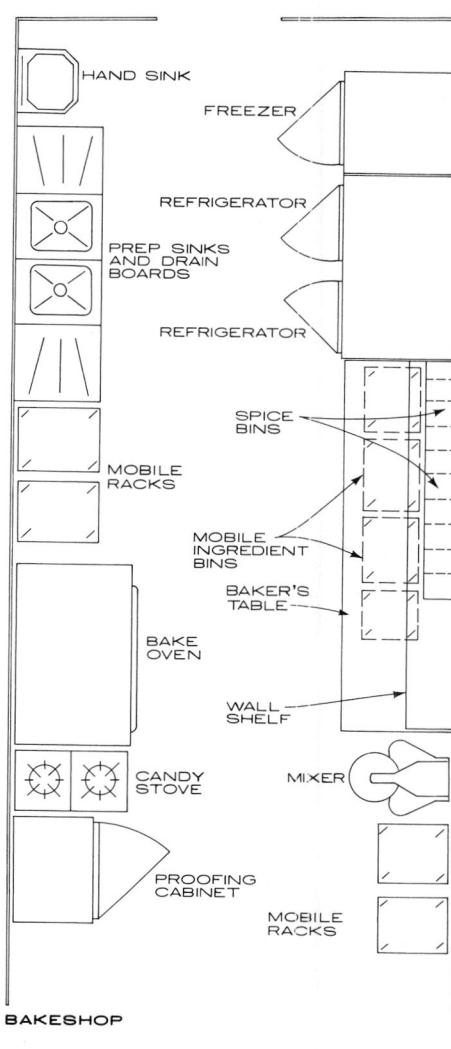

HAND SINK

FREEZER

REFRIGERATOR

PREP SINKS AND DRAIN BOARDS

REFRIGERATOR

MOBILE RACKS

SPICE BINS

MOBILE INGREDIENT BINS

BAKER'S TABLE

BAKE OVEN

WALL SHELF

CANDY STOVE

MIXER

PROOFING CABINET

MOBILE RACKS

### BAKESHOP

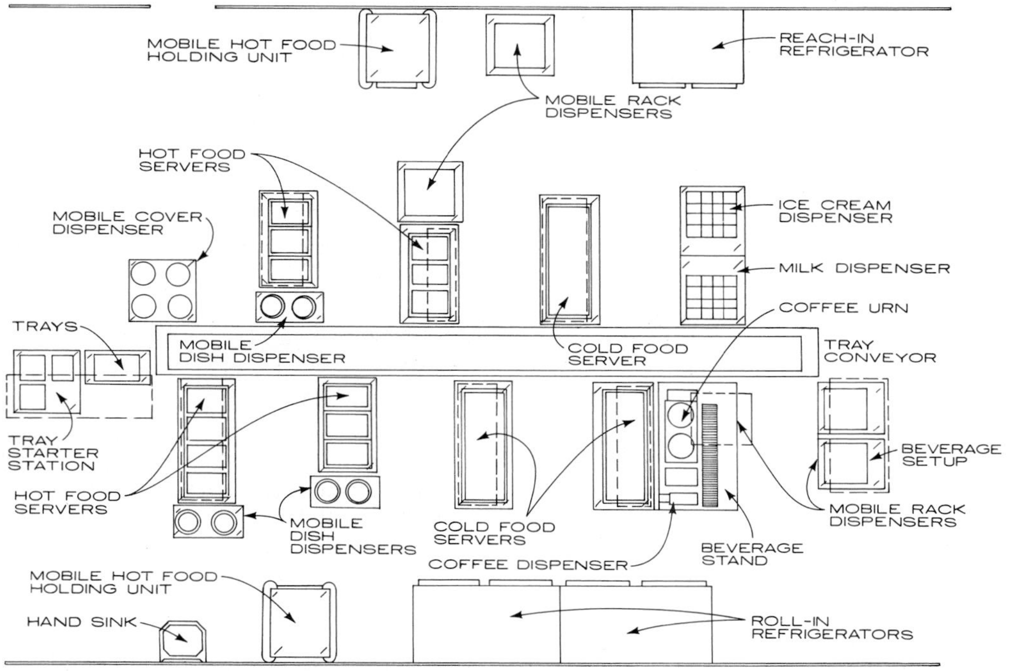

MOBILE HOT FOOD HOLDING UNIT

MOBILE RACK DISPENSERS

REACH-IN REFRIGERATOR

HOT FOOD SERVERS

MOBILE COVER DISPENSER

ICE CREAM DISPENSER

MILK DISPENSER

COFFEE URN

TRAYS

MOBILE DISH DISPENSER

COLD FOOD SERVER

TRAY CONVEYOR

TRAY STARTER STATION

HOT FOOD SERVERS

MOBILE DISH DISPENSERS

COLD FOOD SERVERS

BEVERAGE STAND

BEVERAGE SETUP

MOBILE RACK DISPENSERS

MOBILE HOT FOOD HOLDING UNIT

HAND SINK

COFFEE DISPENSER

ROLL-IN REFRIGERATORS

## HOSPITAL PATIENT TRAY ASSEMBLY SYSTEM
## INSTITUTIONAL

**NOTE**

This tray assembly system is designed for trays made up in advance of service. It is used most commonly in hospitals, extended care facilities, and hospices. In some cafeteria situations, this design may be modified for reduced customer food handling. Because of the modular design, the system may accommodate a wide variety of menu items.

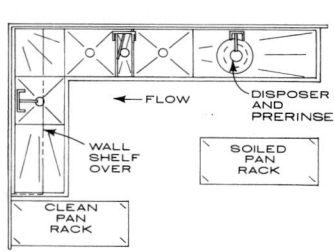

FLOW

DISPOSER AND PRERINSE

WALL SHELF OVER

SOILED PAN RACK

CLEAN PAN RACK

### POT WASHING

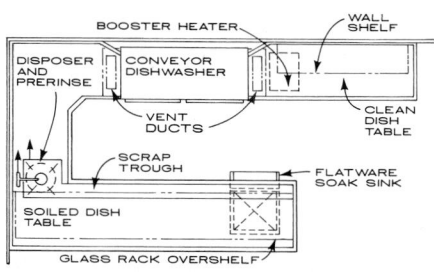

BOOSTER HEATER

WALL SHELF

DISPOSER AND PRERINSE

CONVEYOR DISHWASHER

VENT DUCTS

CLEAN DISH TABLE

SCRAP TROUGH

FLATWARE SOAK SINK

SOILED DISH TABLE

GLASS RACK OVERSHELF

### U-SHAPED CONVEYOR TYPE
**NOTE**

The conveyor type dish machine is less costly than a circular system and has a larger volume capacity than a single compartment machine. Many table configurations are available.

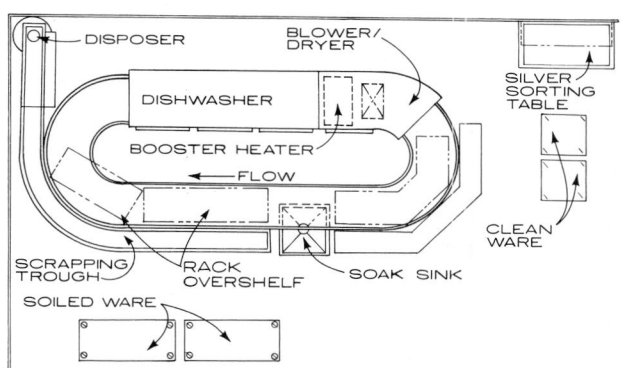

DISPOSER

BLOWER/ DRYER

DISHWASHER

BOOSTER HEATER

FLOW

SILVER SORTING TABLE

CLEAN WARE

SCRAPPING TROUGH

RACK OVERSHELF

SOAK SINK

SOILED WARE

### CIRCULAR TYPE
**NOTE**

The circular system is overall less labor intensive than other designs. It is most useful in a large volume operation.

## WARE WASHING SYSTEMS

Cini-Grissom Associates, Inc.; Food Service Consultants; Washington, D.C.

**SPACE PLANNING**   1

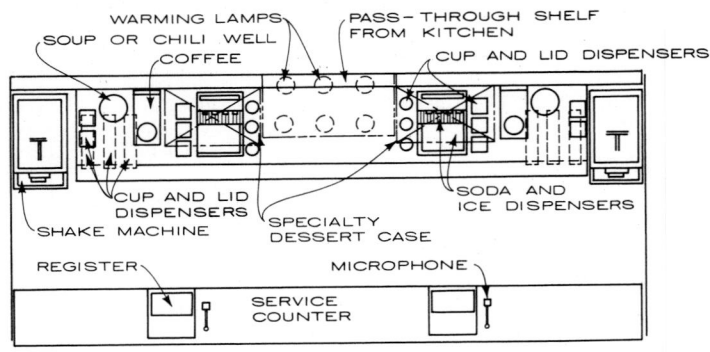

## BEVERAGE AND SERVICE COUNTER

**NOTE**

Design of the service counter depends on the number of stations required for efficient service and the amount of space available.

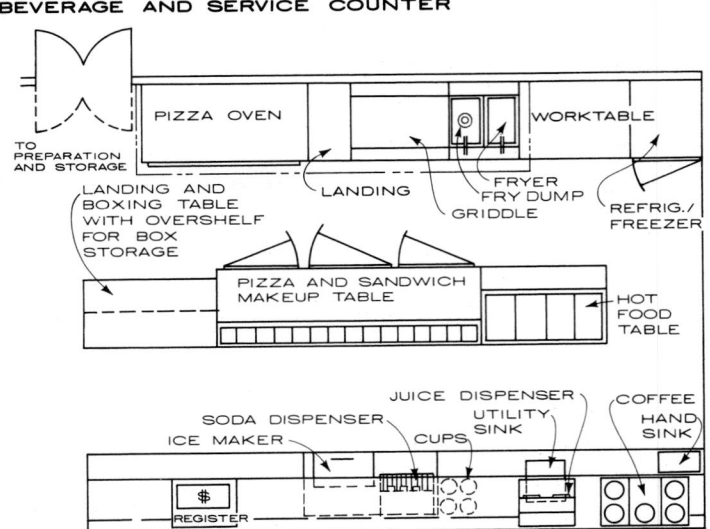

## PIZZA AND SANDWICH SHOP

**NOTE**

This type of operation has many variables. Sandwiches and hot entrees may or may not be offered. The equipment requirements are related directly to the menu, volume, and style of service.

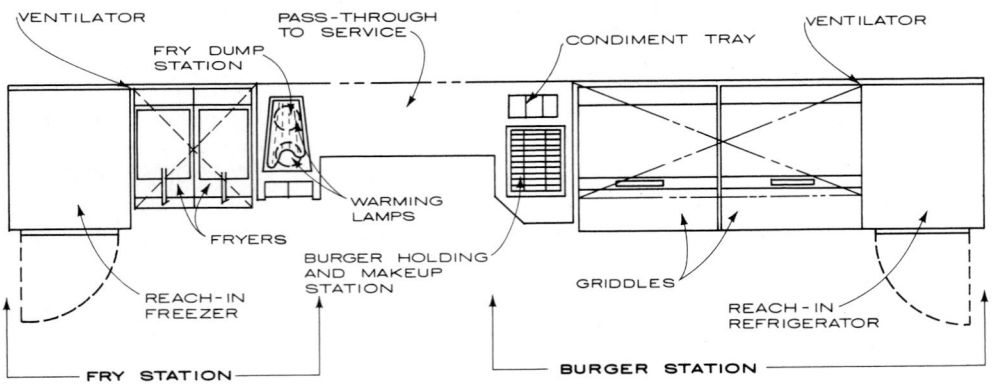

## FRY STATION BURGER STATION

**NOTE**

The area will vary depending on the menu and method of preparation. Alternate equipment would include a charbroiler, conveyor charbroiler, and more fry space for expanded fried menu items.

## HAMBURGER AND FRENCH FRY PREPARATION AREA

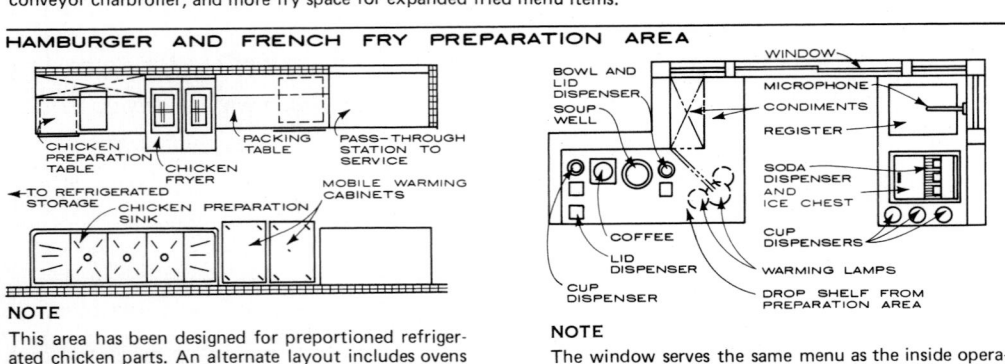

**NOTE**

This area has been designed for preportioned refrigerated chicken parts. An alternate layout includes ovens for prebreaded, frozen portions.

## CHICKEN PREPARATION

**NOTE**

The window serves the same menu as the inside operation. Service may be pass-window or bank-drawer type.

## DRIVE-UP WINDOW

Cini-Grissom Associates, Inc.; Food Service Consultants; Washington, D.C.

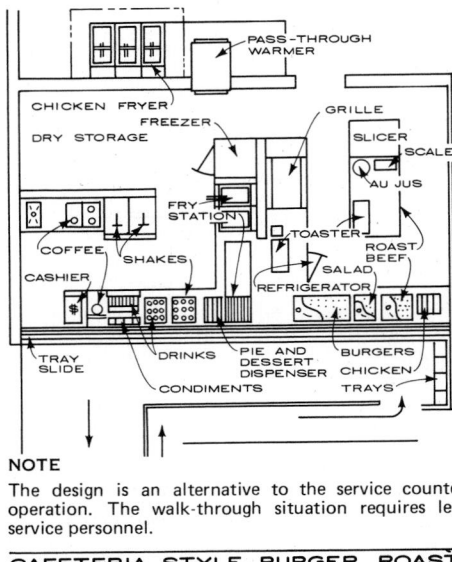

**NOTE**

The design is an alternative to the service counter operation. The walk-through situation requires less service personnel.

## CAFETERIA STYLE BURGER, ROAST BEEF, AND CHICKEN

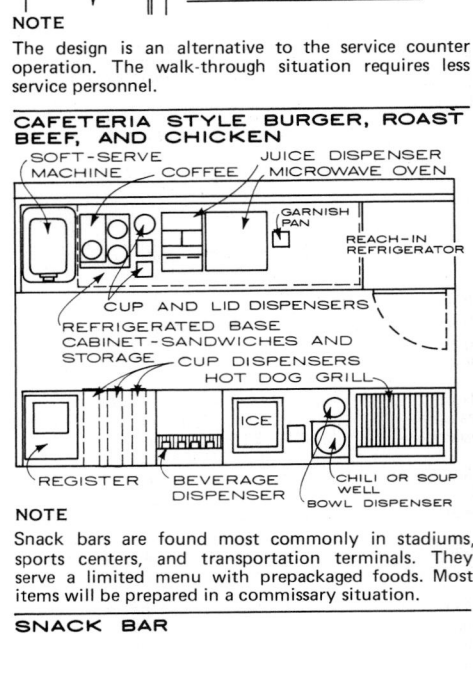

**NOTE**

Snack bars are found most commonly in stadiums, sports centers, and transportation terminals. They serve a limited menu with prepackaged foods. Most items will be prepared in a commissary situation.

## SNACK BAR

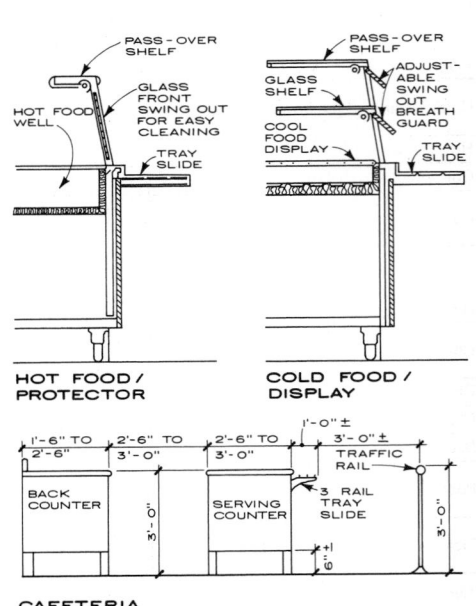

### HOT FOOD / PROTECTOR

### COLD FOOD / DISPLAY

## CAFETERIA COUNTERS

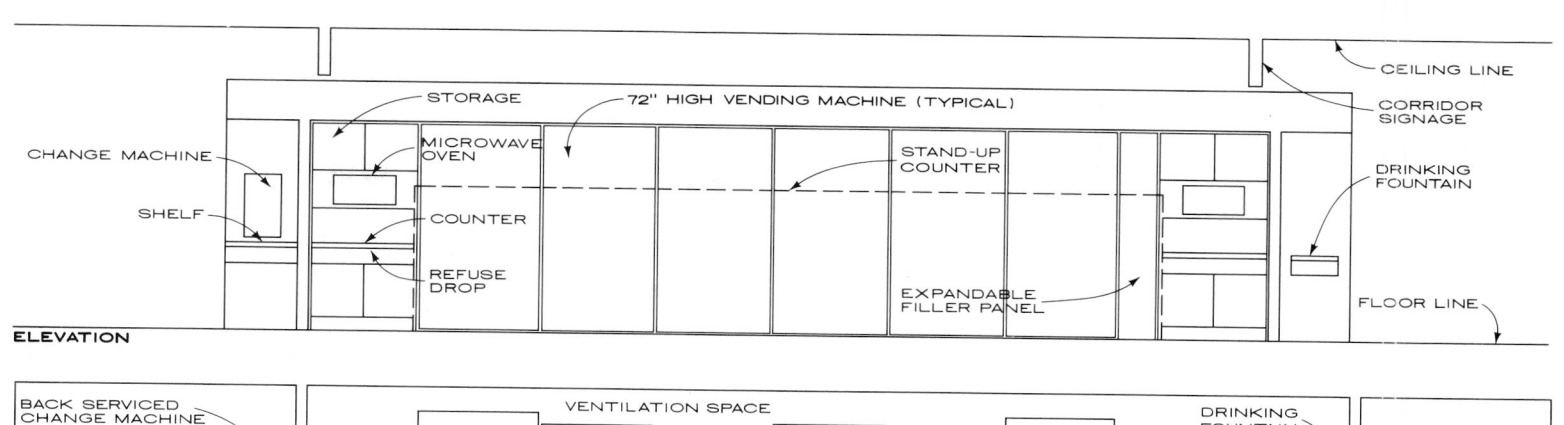

ELEVATION

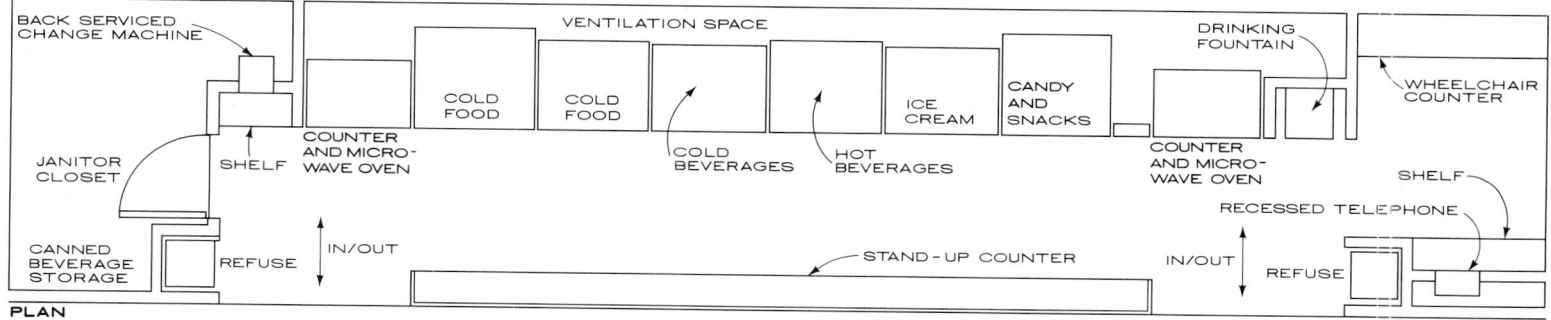

PLAN

## TYPICAL CORPORATE OR INSTITUTIONAL VENDING AREA

**NOTE**

Refrigerated vending machines and microwave ovens require a rear wall clearance of up to 8 in. to permit cooling.

No hot water required. Some beverage dispensing units require a cold water line with a shut-off valve. Overflow waste disposes into internal bucket or tray.

A separate, 115 volt electrical circuit for each machine is suggested. Delivery amperages range from approximately 2 to 20 amps per machine.

Service access generally is from the front; some cigarette units require top access.

Some machines require patron to use both hands, make extended arm reach, or use more than minimal force to access some items or controls, all of which can make use by handicapped persons difficult. Consult local codes.

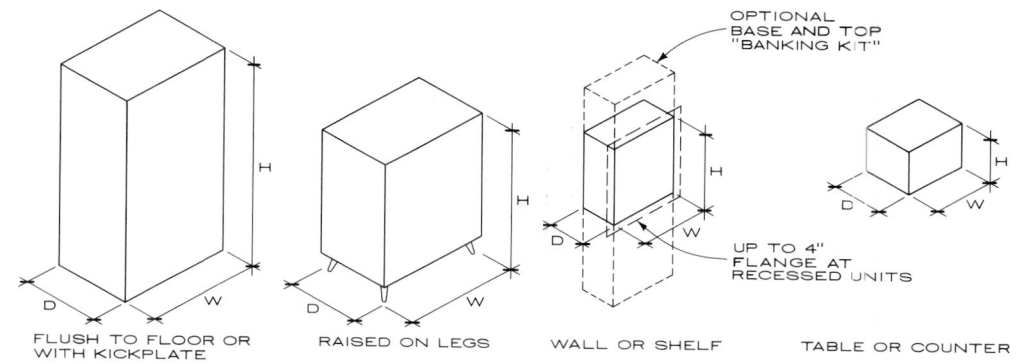

F-FLOOR TYPE
FLUSH TO FLOOR OR WITH KICKPLATE
RAISED ON LEGS

OPTIONAL BASE AND TOP "BANKING KIT"
UP TO 4" FLANGE AT RECESSED UNITS
WALL OR SHELF
TABLE OR COUNTER

W-WALL, SHELF, TABLE OR COUNTER TYPE

**VENDING MACHINE TYPES**

## VENDING MACHINE DATA

| FOOD VENDING UNITS | TYPE | TYPICAL | | | | APPROXIMATE RANGE | | | | | | | |
|---|---|---|---|---|---|---|---|---|---|---|---|---|---|
| | | | | | | MINIMUM | | | | MAXIMUM | | | |
| | | H (IN.) | W (IN.) | D (IN.) | LB.* | H (IN.) | W (IN.) | D (IN.) | LB.* | H (IN.) | W (IN.) | D (IN.) | LB.* |
| Cold Beverages | F | 72 | 38½ | 24½ | 510 | 55⅜ | 28¾ | 22⅝ | 460 | 79½ | 45¾ | 29⅝ | 790 |
| | W | 35 | 28¾ | 10¾ | 125 | 35 | 28¾ | 10¾ | 125 | | | | |
| Hot Beverages | F | 72 | 38 | 31 | 560 | 72 | 24 | 27½ | 340 | 72 | 38 | 33 | 585 |
| Cold Foods | F | 72 | 35½ | 31½ | 720 | 72 | 35¼ | 30¼ | 647 | 72 | 41 | 35⅝ | 950 |
| Candy, Pastry, and Snacks | F | 72 | 33 | 35 | 640 | 72 | 28 | 31 | 406 | 72 | 39 | 35½ | 760 |
| | W | 25 | 24⁷⁄₁₆ | 24⅝ | 100 | 25 | 24⁷⁄₁₆ | 24⅝ | 100 | | | | |

| OTHER UNITS | TYPE | TYPICAL | | | | APPROXIMATE RANGE | | | | | | | |
|---|---|---|---|---|---|---|---|---|---|---|---|---|---|
| | | | | | | MINIMUM | | | | MAXIMUM | | | |
| | | H (IN.) | W (IN.) | D (IN.) | LB.* | H (IN.) | W (IN.) | D (IN.) | LB.* | H (IN.) | W (IN.) | D (IN.) | LB.* |
| Change | F | 51⁹⁄₁₆ | 27⅞ | 19¼ | 275 | 56 | 22½ | 11 | 145 | 78 | 40 | | |
| | W | 31⅝ | 12¹⁄₁₆ | 15⅛ | 140 | 23¾ | 14¾ | 18½ | 175 | 38⅝ | 12¹⁄₁₆ | 18½ | 200 |
| Cigarettes | F | 51 | 38 | 21¼ | 410 | 50½ | 32½ | 21¼ | 300 | 72 | 36 | 25¼ | 485 |
| Microwave oven | W | 12¾ | 20½ | 14½ | 43 | | | | | 14⅞ | 20½ | 21 | 78 |
| Microwave Oven with "banking kit" | F | 72 | 25 | 31 | 204 | | | | | | | | |
| Postage Stamps | F | 71 | 37⅝ | | | | | | | | | | |
| | W | 21½ | 31½ | | | | | | | | | | |
| Tickets | F | 78 | 40 | | | | | | | | | | |
| | W | | | | | | | | | | | | |

*Net weight in pounds

William Xavier Fabis, Architect; San Francisco, California

**SPACE PLANNING    1**

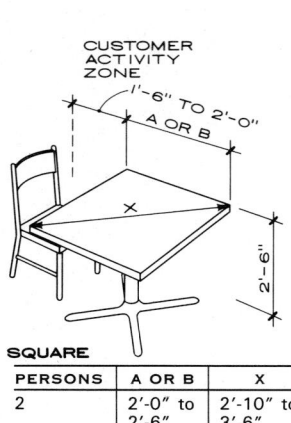

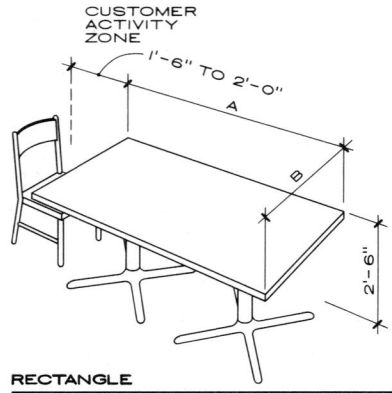

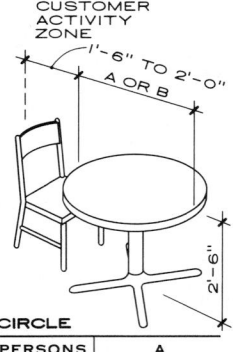

### NOTES

Round tables are usually recommended only for seating 5 persons or more.

Dimension "A" depends on the perimeter (1'-10" to 2'-0" per person) necessary to seat required number. For cocktails, 1'-6" is sufficient.

Tables wider than 2 ft-6 in. will seat one at each end.

Minimum sizes are satisfactory for drink service; larger sizes for food. Tables with widespread bases are more practical than four-legged tables.

Tables and arrangements are affected by the type of operations and the style of service. The use of flaming trays, busing carts, high chairs for children, and handicapped access must be considered.

### SQUARE

| PERSONS | A OR B | X |
|---|---|---|
| 2 | 2'-0" to 2'-6" | 2'-10" to 3'-6" |
| 4 | 2'-6" to 3'-0" | 3'-6" to 4'-3" |

### RECTANGLE

| PERSONS | A | B |
|---|---|---|
| 2 | 2'-6" to 3'-0" | 2'-0" to 2'-6" |
| 2 (on one side) | 3'-4" to 4'-0" | |
| 6 | 5'-10" to 6'-0" | 2'-6" to 3'-0" |
| 8 | 6'-10" to 7'-0" | |

### CIRCLE

| PERSONS | A |
|---|---|
| 4–5 | 3'-6" to 4'-0" |
| 6–7 | 4'-6" to 5'-0" |
| 7–8 | 5'-6" to 6'-4" |
| 8–10 | 6'-0" to 7'-2" |

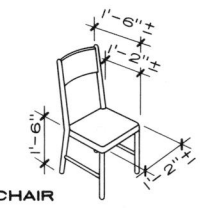

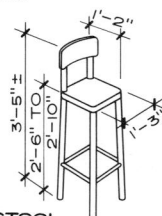

**CHAIR**          **STOOL**

### AVERAGE CAPACITIES PER PERSON

| TYPE OF ROOM | SQUARE FEET |
|---|---|
| Banquet | 10–12 |
| Cafeteria | 12–15 |
| Tearoom | 10–14 |
| Lunchroom/coffee shop | 12–16 |
| Dining room/restaurant | 13–16 |
| Specialty/formal dining | 17–22 |

**NOTE**

Figures are general and represent minimum average dimensions. No maximum exists. Seating allowances and requirements may vary to suit individual operations.

### GENERAL DESIGN CRITERIA

Service aisles: 30–42 in.
1. Square seating, 66 in. minimum between tables, 30 in. aisle plus two chairs back to back.
2. Diagonal seating, 36 in. minimum between corners of tables.
3. Wall seating, 30 in. minimum between wall and seat back.
4. Minimum of 30 in. for bus carts and flaming service carts.

Customer aisles:
1. Refer to local codes for restrictions on requirements.
2. Wheelchair requirements, 35–44 in. aisle.
3. Wall seating, 30 in. minimum between walls and table.

Tables:
1. Average 29 in. high.
2. Allow space around doors and food service areas.

### TABLE

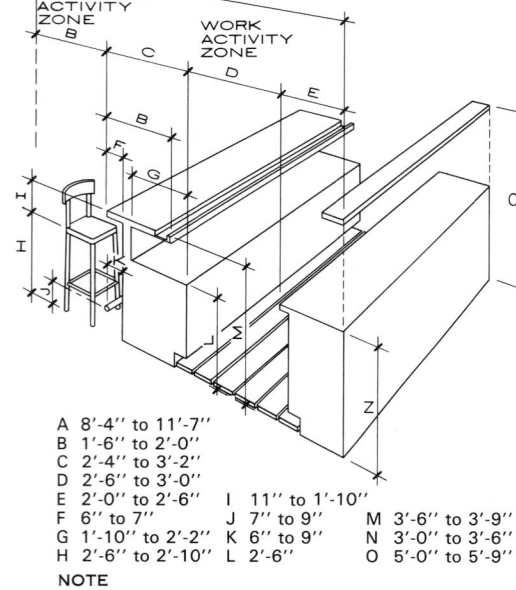

A Seat back to seat back: 5'-0" to 6'-2"
B One person per side: 2'-0" to 2'-6"
  Two persons per side: 3'-6" to 4'-6"
  Recommended maximum for serving and cleaning: 4'-0"
C 3'-0" to 4'-0"        F 0 to 4"
D 2'-6"                 G ± 1'-6"
E 1'-6"                 H 2'-0" to 2'-6"

**NOTE**

Local regulations determine actual booth sizes. Tables are often 2 in. shorter than seats and may have rounded ends. Circular booths have overall diameter of 6'-4"+.

A 8'-4" to 11'-7"
B 1'-6" to 2'-0"
C 2'-4" to 3'-2"
D 2'-6" to 3'-0"
E 2'-0" to 2'-6"        I 11" to 1'-10"
F 6" to 7"              J 7" to 9"        M 3'-6" to 3'-9"
G 1'-10" to 2'-2"       K 6" to 9"        N 3'-0" to 3'-6"
H 2'-6" to 2'-10"       L 2'-6"           O 5'-0" to 5'-9"

**NOTE**

Ratio of counter stools to servers is 10:1.

### BOOTHS

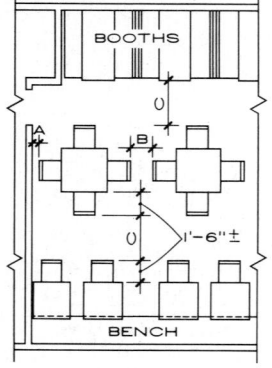

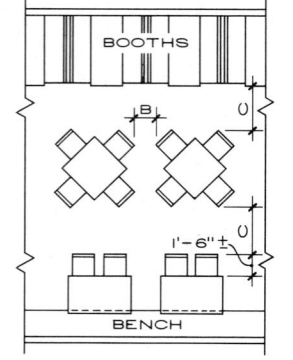

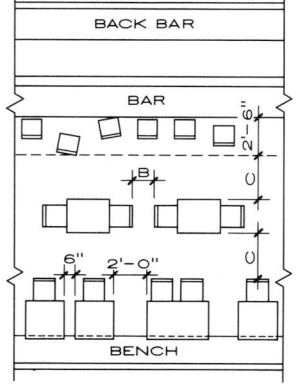

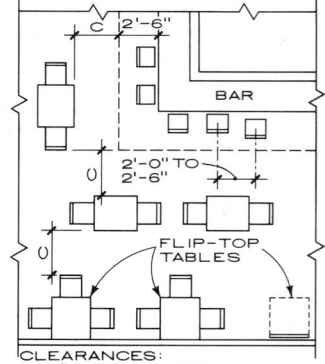

CLEARANCES:
A = 6" MIN. (NO PASSAGE)
B = 1'-6" LIMITED PASSAGE
C = 2'-6" TO 3'-0" SERVICE AISLE

**NOTE**

All dimensions are minimum clearances. Seating layouts show general configurations and are not intended to depict any specific type of operation. Tables may be converted from square to round to enlarge seating capacity. Booth seating makes effective use of corner space.

### TYPICAL SEATING ARRANGEMENTS

Richard J. Vitullo; Washington Grove, Maryland
Cini-Grissom Associates, Inc.; Food Service Consultants; Washington, D.C.

# 1  SPACE PLANNING

## GENERAL

Conference rooms should be located for proximity to user groups within a building and for accessibility to outside guests. Since a conference room typically serves to communicate a firm's "image" to others, finishes are usually selected from higher quality materials to suggest a prominent and visible location. When a conference room functions as a multiuser or multigroup space, the position of access doors is altered and acoustical folding partitions or movable walls may be used. The designer should note the additional requirements imposed by building codes for assembly occupancy for larger rooms.

## FINISHES

Carpeted floors, acoustical wall panels, or fabric wall coverings and acoustic ceilings should be used. Avoid using "attention-getting" patterns and colors on walls which may decrease focal emphasis of tables, seating,

and speaker or projection area. All finishes should be carefully examined for flame spread and smoke-generated ratings.

## LIGHTING

Parabolic lens fluorescent fixtures provide good general lighting with less glare. Directional fixtures such as track lighting may be used for presentation areas. Use dimming switches.

## MECHANICAL

Provide a minimum of eight air changes per hour plus a minimum of 10 cu ft/min of outside air per person for odor-free air and good ventilation. Provide an exhaust system to be manually controlled from the room. Careful attention should be given to sound attenuation of diffusers.

## TELECONFERENCING

The space and furniture requirements for teleconferencing are different from the typical conference room. All aspects are geared toward video camera requirements. Typically, the conference is held between groups in separate locations linked by video satellite. The standard layout includes two ceiling-mounted video cameras to cover the participants and an optional direct downward-aimed document camera, a projection television monitor (front or rear projecting) for the remote participants, and a control console which interfaces the video cameras, telephone, and satellite linkage. The room arrangement is such that all participants may view and be viewed simultaneously. Mixing presentation media (projection, boards, flip charts, etc.) becomes more difficult in teleconferencing, while the requirements for acoustics and ventilation remain unchanged from the typical conference room. Lighting must be in accordance with the requirements of the video system used.

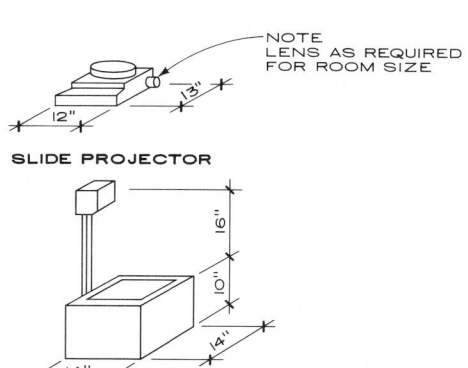

SLIDE PROJECTOR

OVERHEAD PROJECTOR

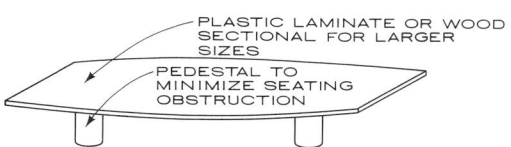

CONFERENCE TABLE
REFER TO FURNITURE SECTION FOR SIZE BASED ON SEATING

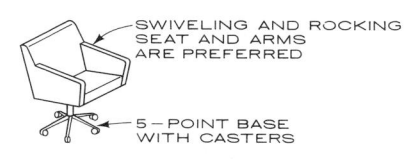

CHAIR

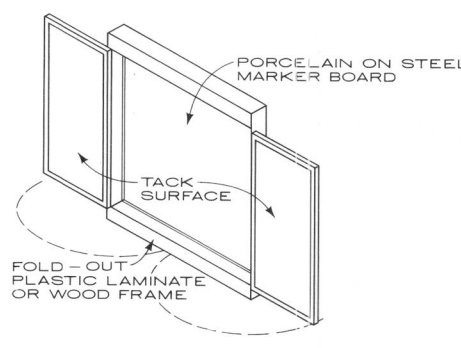

WALL-MOUNTED VISUAL CENTER

**CONFERENCE ROOM FURNITURE AND EQUIPMENT**

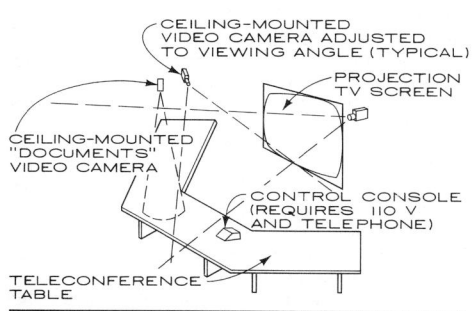

**COMPONENTS OF A TYPICAL TELECONFERENCE ROOM**

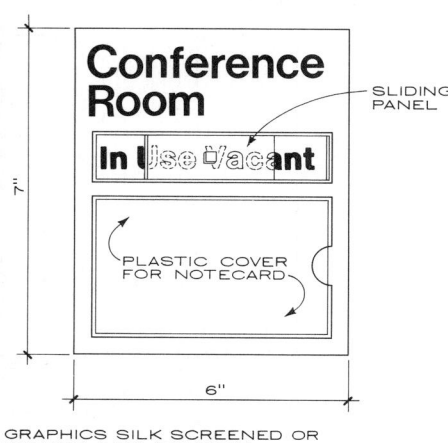

**CONFERENCE ROOM SIGN**

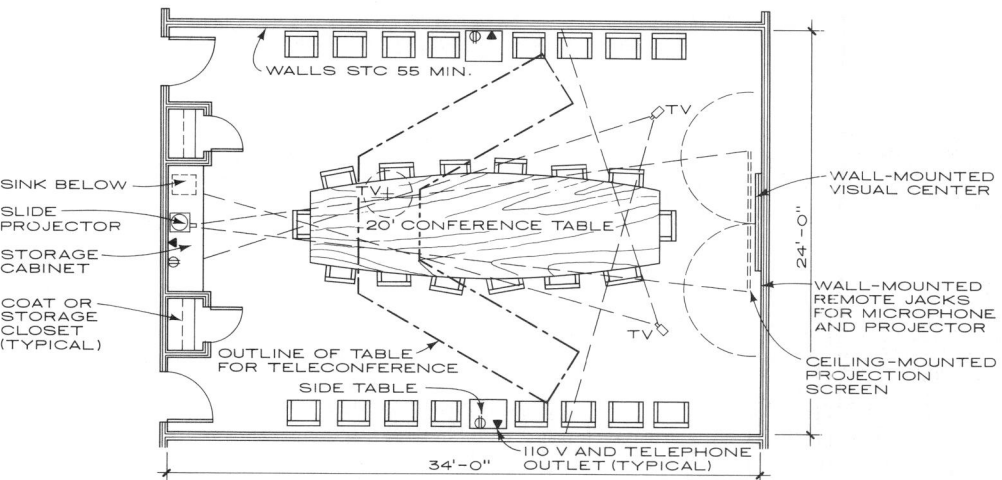

PLAN

NOTE

Components of both traditional and teleconferencing conference rooms are shown. The "board room" layout rendered here is not recommended for teleconferencing. See dashed layout, components at left, and general notes above.

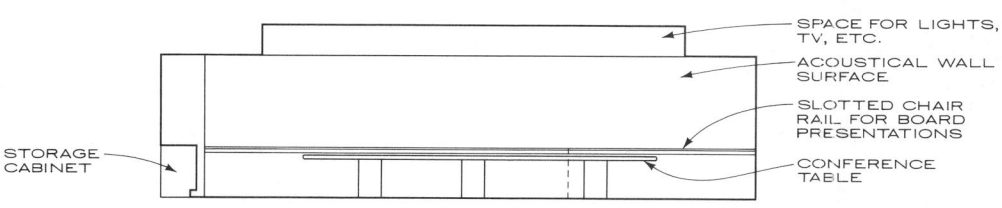

SECTION

**TYPICAL CONFERENCE ROOM (25 – 30 PERSONS)**

J. Kevin Lloyd, AIA; Barge, Waggoner, Sumner & Cannon; Nashville, Tennessee

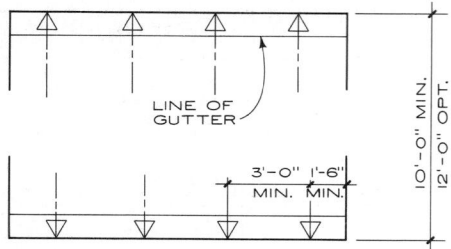

PLAN

## GROUP SHOWERS

There must be a sufficient number of shower heads. Educational facilities with time constraints should have 10 shower heads for the first 30 persons and 1 shower head for every 4 additional persons. In recreational facilities 1 shower head for each 10 dressing lockers is a minimum. Temperature controls are necessary to keep water from exceeding 110°F. Both individual and master controls are needed for group showers.

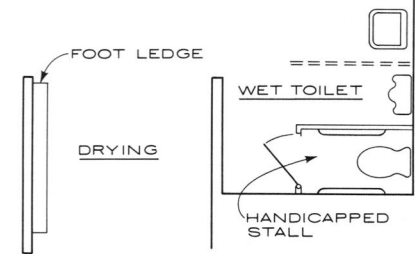

PLAN

## DRYING ROOM AND WET TOILET

The drying room should have about the same area as the shower room. Provision for drainage should be made. Heavy duty towel rails, approximately 4 ft from the floor, are recommended. A foot drying ledge, 18 in. high and 8 in. wide as shown in the drawing, is desirable. An adjacent wet toilet is suggested. Avoid curbs between drying room and adjacent space. Towel service is desirable in a school. Size of area varies with material to be stored (can be used for distributing uniforms), with 200 sq ft usually being sufficient.

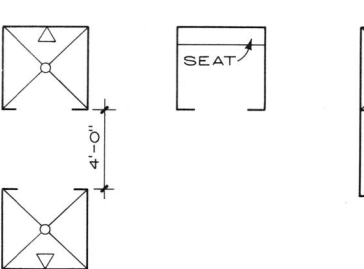

PLAN

## INDIVIDUAL SHOWERS AND DRESSING ROOMS

| INDIVIDUAL ROOMS | MINIMUM | OPTIMUM |
|---|---|---|
| Showers | 3'-0'' x 3'-6'' | 3'-6'' x 3'-6'' |
| Dressing Rooms | 3'-0'' x 3'-6'' | 3'-6'' x 4'-0'' |

Individual dressing rooms and showers can be combined in a variety of configurations to obtain 1:1, 2:1, 3:1, and 4:1 ratios, respectively.

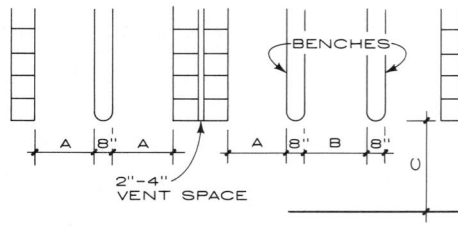

PLAN

## AISLE SPACE FOR DRESSING ROOM
## AISLE SPACE

|  | A | B | C |
|---|---|---|---|
| Recreation | 2'-2'' | 1'-8'' | 3'-6'' |
| School | 2'-6'' | 2'-2'' | 4'-0'' |

Bench should be minimum 8 in. in width and 16 in. from the floor. Traffic breaks 3 ft minimum wide should occur at maximum intervals of 12 ft. Main traffic aisle to be wider for large number of locker bays. Avoid lockers that meet at 90° corner.

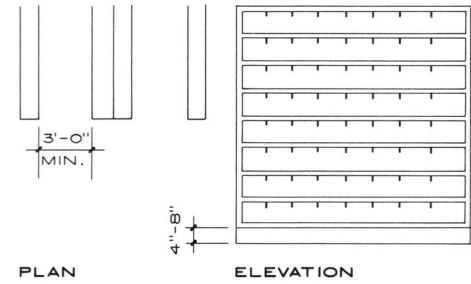

PLAN          ELEVATION

## BASKET ROOM AND BASKET RACK

Basket racks vary from 7 to 10 tiers in height. Wide baskets require 1 ft shelf space, small baskets 10 in. shelf space, both fit 1 to 1½ ft deep shelf. Back-to-back shelving is 2 ft 3 in. wide. Height shelf-to-shelf is 9¼ in.

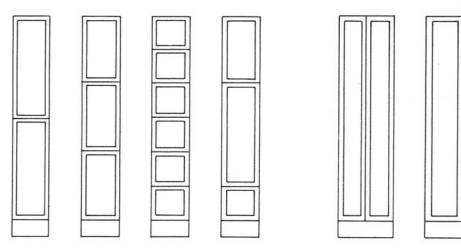

STORAGE          DRESSING

## LOCKERS
## STANDARD SIZES

|  |  |
|---|---|
| Width | 9'', 12'', 15'', 18'' |
| Depth | 12'', 15'', 18'' |
| Height | 60'', 72'' (overall) |

For schools, standard storage locker is 9 in. or 12 in. x 12 in. x 12 in. to 24 in. One storage locker per student enrolled plus 10% for expansion. Standard dressing lockers are 12 in. x 12 in. x 60 in. or 72 in. Number of dressing lockers should be equal to the peak period load plus 10 to 15% for variation.

## LOCKER ROOM FACILITIES
### ITEMS TO BE PROVIDED

1. Fixed benches 16 in. high.
2. Lockers on raised base.
3. Locker numbering system.
4. Hair dryers—one per 20 lockers.
5. Mirrors at lavatory.
6. Makeup mirror and shelf.
7. Drinking fountain (height as required).
8. Bulletin board.
9. Dressing booths if required.
10. Full length mirror.
11. Clock.
12. Door signs.
13. Sound system speaker if required.
14. Lighting at mirrors for grooming.
15. Lighting located over aisles and passages.
16. Adequate ventilation for storage lockers.
17. Windows located with regard to height and arrangement of lockers.
18. Visual supervision from adjacent office.

YMCA Building and Furnishings Service; New York, New York

## RECOMMENDED MOUNTING HEIGHTS

| Shower valve |  | 4'-0'' |
|---|---|---|
| Shower head |  |  |
| Men |  | 6'-6'' |
| Women |  | 6'-0'' |
| Children |  | 5'-0'' |
| Hand dryer outlet |  |  |
| Men |  | 3'-8'' |
| Women |  | 3'-6'' |
| Teenagers |  | 3'-1'' |
| Preteens |  | 2'-8'' |
| Hair dryer outlet |  |  |
| Men |  | 6'-0'' |
| Women |  | 5'-5'' |
| Teenagers |  | 5'-0'' |
| Preteens |  | 5'-0'' |
| Clock |  | 6'-6'' min. |
| Robe hook |  | 6'-3'' |
| Towel bar |  | 4'-0'' |

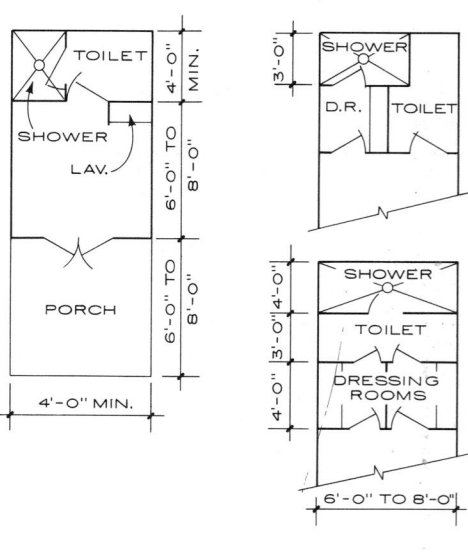

## CABANAS

# 1    SPACE PLANNING

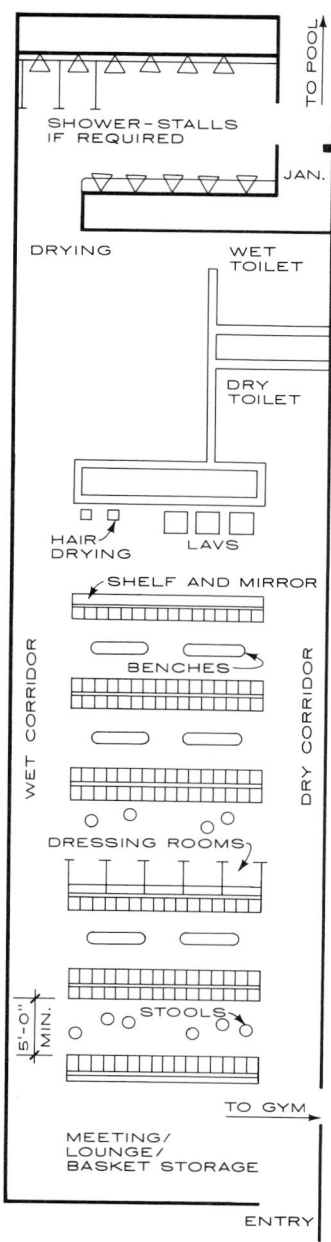

**LOCKER/SHOWER UNIT**

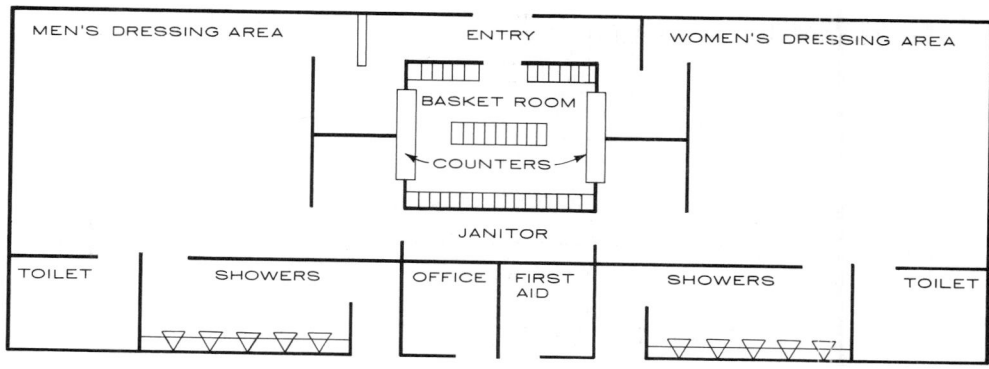

**DRESSING UNIT FOR POOL**

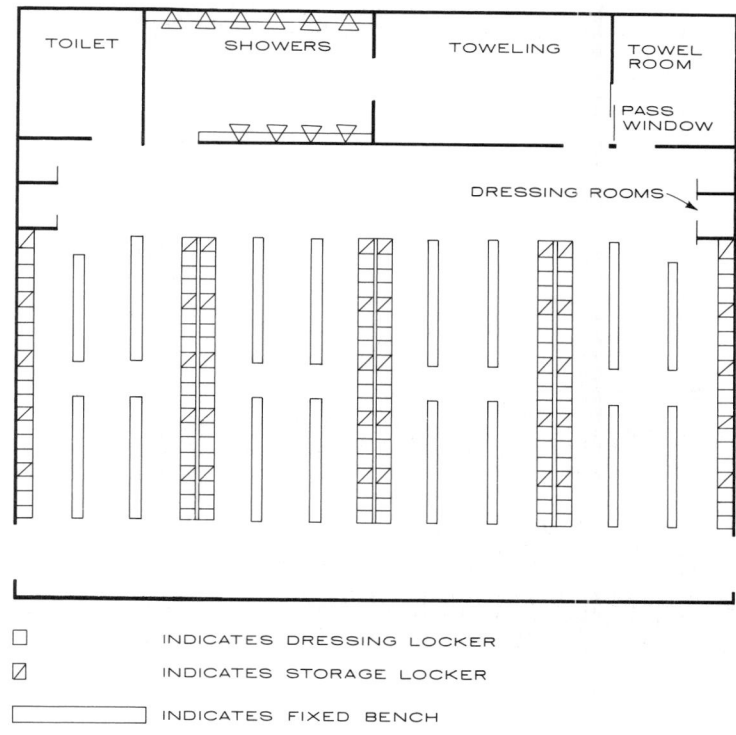

☐     INDICATES DRESSING LOCKER

▨     INDICATES STORAGE LOCKER

▭     INDICATES FIXED BENCH

## TO SERVE GYMNASIUM AND POOL

### NOTES

The best arrangement of lockers is the bay system, with a minimum 4 ft circulation aisle at each end of the bays. Ordinarily, the maximum number of lockers in a bay is 16. Locate dry (shoe) traffic at one end of the bays and wet (barefoot) traffic at the other end. For long bays with a single bench, make 3 ft breaks at 15 ft intervals.

Supervision of school lockers is the easiest if they are located in single banks along the two long walls, providing one or more bays that run the length of the room.

The number of lockers in a locker room depends on the anticipated number of members and/or size of classes. Separate locker areas should be encouraged. In small buildings interconnecting doors provide flexibility and allow for the handling of peak loads.

Individual dressing and shower compartments may be required for women's and girls' locker and shower rooms and for men's clubs. A shower stall for the handicapped may also be required.

YMCA Building and Furnishings Service; New York, New York

### GYMNASIUM LOCKER ROOM

Basket storage, if included, is self-service. Maximum height is 8 tiers. A dehumidifying system should be provided to dry out basket contents overnight. Separate auxiliary locker rooms may be required. These may serve teams, part time instructors, the faculty, or volunteer leaders. A small room for the coach's use may be desirable.

The shower rooms should be directly accessible to the toweling room and the locker room that it serves. When a shower room is designed to serve a swimming pool, the room should be located so that all must pass through the showers prior to reaching the pool deck.

Separate wet and dry toilet areas are recommended. Wet toilets should be easily accessible from the shower room. When designed for use with a swimming pool, wet toilets should be located so that users must pass through the shower room after use of toilets.

Locker room entrance and exit doors should have vision barriers.

All facilities should be barrier free.

Floors should be of impervious material such as ceramic or quarry tile, with a Carborundum impregnated surface, and should slope toward the drains. Concrete floors (nonslip surface), if used, should be treated with a hardener to avoid the penetration of odors and moisture.

Walls should be of materials resistant to moisture and should have surfaces that are easily cleaned. All exterior corners in the locker rooms should be rounded.

Heavy duty, moisture resistant doors at locker room entrances and exits should be of sufficient size to handle the traffic flow and form natural vision barriers. Entrance/exit doors for the lockers should be equipped with corrosion resistant hardware.

Ceilings in shower areas should be of ceramic tile or other material impervious to moisture. Locker room ceilings should be acoustically treated with a material impervious to moisture and breakage. Floor drains should be kept out of the line of traffic where possible.

## LOCATION WITHIN THE BUILDING

The courtroom is often the major space in the building and should be centrally located, with primary access to its support spaces (e.g., judge's office, jury rooms, witness rooms, court officer's spaces), the public lobby, and toilet facilities.

## REQUIRED SPACES

Courtrooms require 3 main areas or zones

1. The public space
2. The courtroom, including the jury box
3. The judge's bench and witness stand for observation of the trial proceedings. This space is also used by defendants and attorneys as a waiting area prior to the trial.

The public space should have access to the public corridor and good access to the public toilet facilities. The public space is usually divided from the courtroom space by a low divider rail with swinging gates.

The courtroom space is a restricted access space. Access to this space should be from private corridors, jury rooms, court officer offices, or the gates to the public space. This space contains the majority of courtroom activity. The jury, attorney, defendants, and sometimes the press occupy this space. The jury box, part of the courtroom space, usually has a raised floor to provide better visibility of the trial proceedings. The jury box should have direct access to the jury room(s) or to a private corridor leading to the jury room(s). The courtroom space should not be accessible from any public corridor.

The judge's bench and witness stand have the most restricted access. They are usually divided from the courtroom space by a divider rail. The floor of the judge's bench is usually raised above the raised floor level of the jury box and witness stand to provide the judge(s) the most prominent position in the courtroom space. The judge's bench has direct access to the judge's chamber or to a private corridor leading to the judge's chamber. The witness stand is located adjacent to the judge's bench and is accessible only from the courtroom space. The witness stand has a raised floor, usually at the same level as the jury box.

## SPACE RELATIONSHIPS

The jury should have direct access to the jury room without crossing the courtroom or any public space. A separate entrance to the jury room should be provided from the building corridor. Private toilet facilities should be provided, with direct access to the jury room. The judge should have direct access to the courtroom from his office. The size of the courtroom and its support spaces vary considerably depending on the volume of court proceedings. For example, in a small municipal or magistrate's courtroom, 50 seats in the public space and 6 seats for jury members are adequate, whereas in a federal district court or state circuit court, 80–100 seats should be provided for the public, 12–14 for jury members (includes 2 alternates), 3 for judges, 1 for clerk of court, and 1 for court reporter. Seating for the press reporters should be provided in or near the courtroom space.

## CONSTRUCTION

The courtroom does not require natural lighting. A lighting level of 50 fc at the attorneys' table and judge's bench and a lighting level of approximately 30 fc in the public space should be adequate. All perimeter walls should be insulated to reduce sound transmission (STC 47 minimum). Resilient floor covering should be used in the public space and carpet may be used in the courtroom itself.

## AREA REQUIREMENTS FOR SUPPORT SPACES

The jury room should be approximately 200 sq ft for municipal court and 350 sq ft for federal district court. Multiple jury rooms are often required for busy court facilities. A judge's office should be 150–350 sq ft. If pretrial hearings are held in the judge's office, area should be increased to approximately 750 sq ft. A clerk of court's office should be 150–350 sq ft.

## TYPES OF COURTS

Municipal or magistrate's courtrooms are usually small courtrooms located in City Hall or other municipal buildings. Municipal courts handle traffic and minor criminal cases. Magistrate's courts handle small civil and minor criminal cases.

State circuit courtrooms are usually large courtrooms located in the county courthouse of each county. State circuit courts handle all state trial proceedings, both civil and criminal.

Federal district courtrooms are usually large courtrooms located in federal governmental buildings serving each federal judicial district. Federal district courts handle all federal trial proceedings, both civil and criminal.

**RAIL DIVIDER**

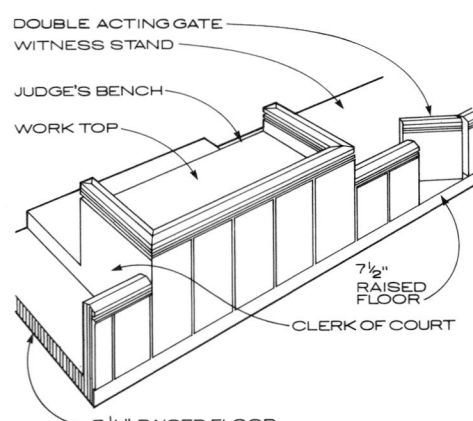

**VIEW OF JUDGE'S BENCH**

**JUDGE'S BENCH**

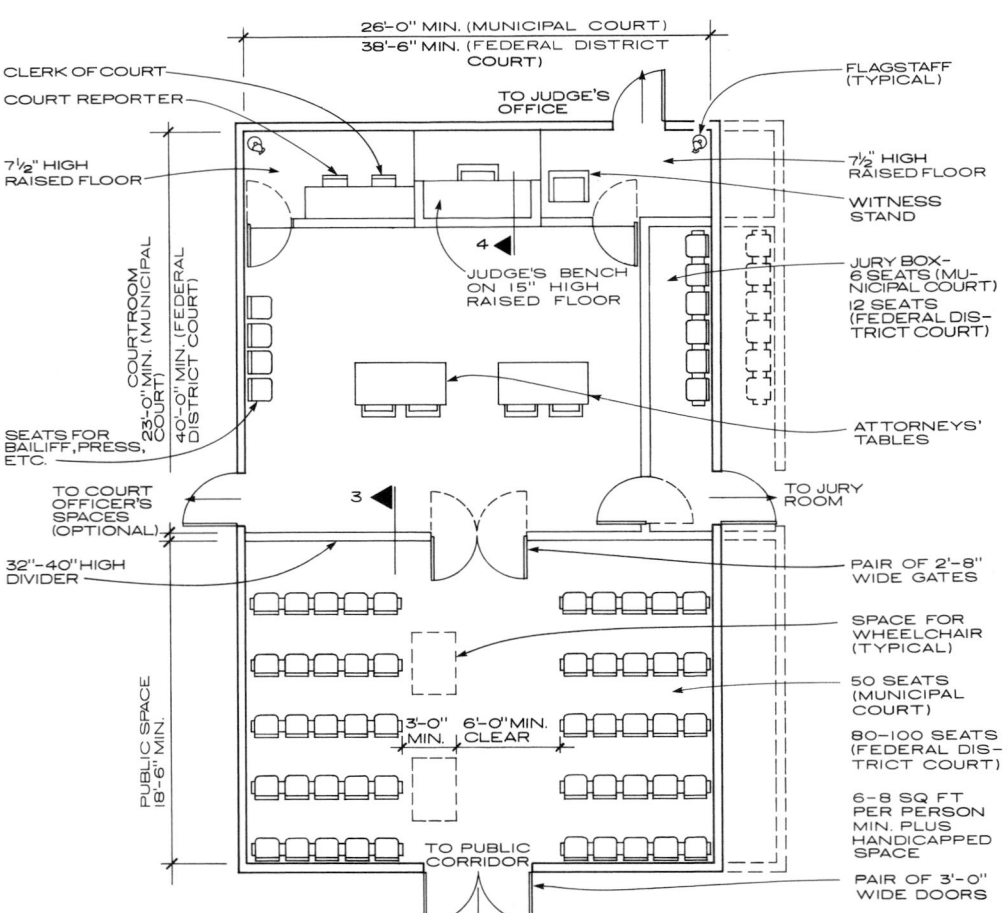

**FLOOR PLAN—MUNICIPAL COURTROOM**

T. John Gilmore, AIA; O'Cain & Gilmore Architects; Spartanburg, South Carolina

# 1     SPACE PLANNING

## PLANNING NOTES

Correctional facility design has experienced a dramatic shift away from the classic cellblock system to a centralized living unit concept. This system provides for greater control of a given number of inmates and economizes on staffing requirements by allowing control of several living units from a centralized location. Living units are sized to provide manageable groups of inmates, maximum flexibility in segregating different groups, and a high degree of fire protection without sacrificing security.

The living unit concept typically groups between 8 and 16 single cells around a communal dayroom, which provides areas for television, reading, conversation, and light activities. Each unit contains its own shower facility, with approximately one shower for every 6 inmates. Units are usually two tiers high, with a two-story dayroom. The inclusion of natural light in both cells and dayrooms is strongly encouraged.

There is a growing trend away from indirect inmate supervision (in which guards are placed in a secure control booth) to direct supervision where guards are in direct contact with inmates, encouraging an environment of greater interaction.

CELL
CELL
CENTRAL CONTROL STATION
DAYROOM

TYPICAL UNIT SECTION

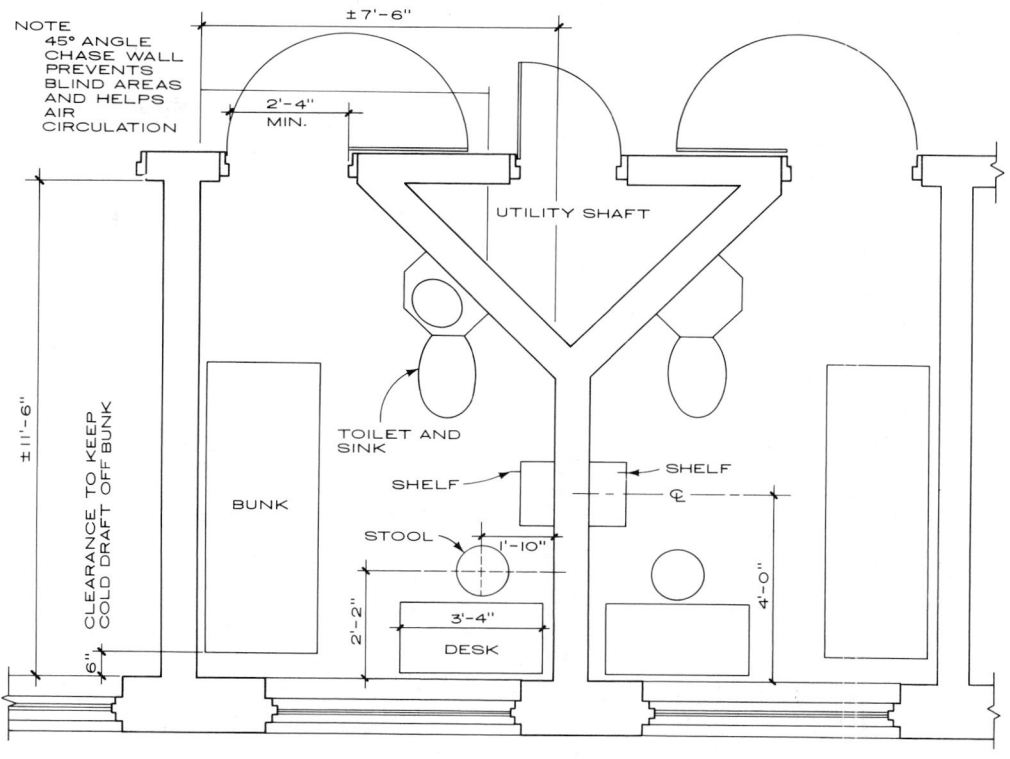

NOTE
45° ANGLE CHASE WALL PREVENTS BLIND AREAS AND HELPS AIR CIRCULATION
±7'-6"
2'-4" MIN.
UTILITY SHAFT
±11'-6"
CLEARANCE TO KEEP COLD DRAFT OFF BUNK
BUNK
TOILET AND SINK
SHELF
SHELF
℄
STOOL
1'-10"
2'-2"
3'-4"
DESK
4'-0"
6"

TYPICAL CELL LAYOUT

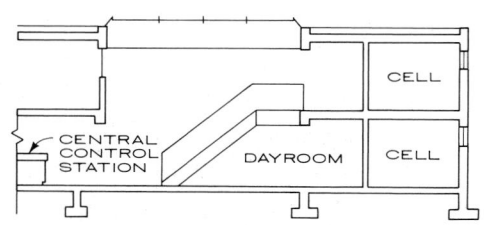

TO DINING, EXERCISE YARD, ETC.
CENTRAL CONTROL STATION
LINE OF MEZZANINE ABOVE
ACTIVE DAYROOM
UP
UP
UP
UP
PASSIVE DAYROOM
EMERGENCY DOOR
SHOWER
TYPICAL CELL

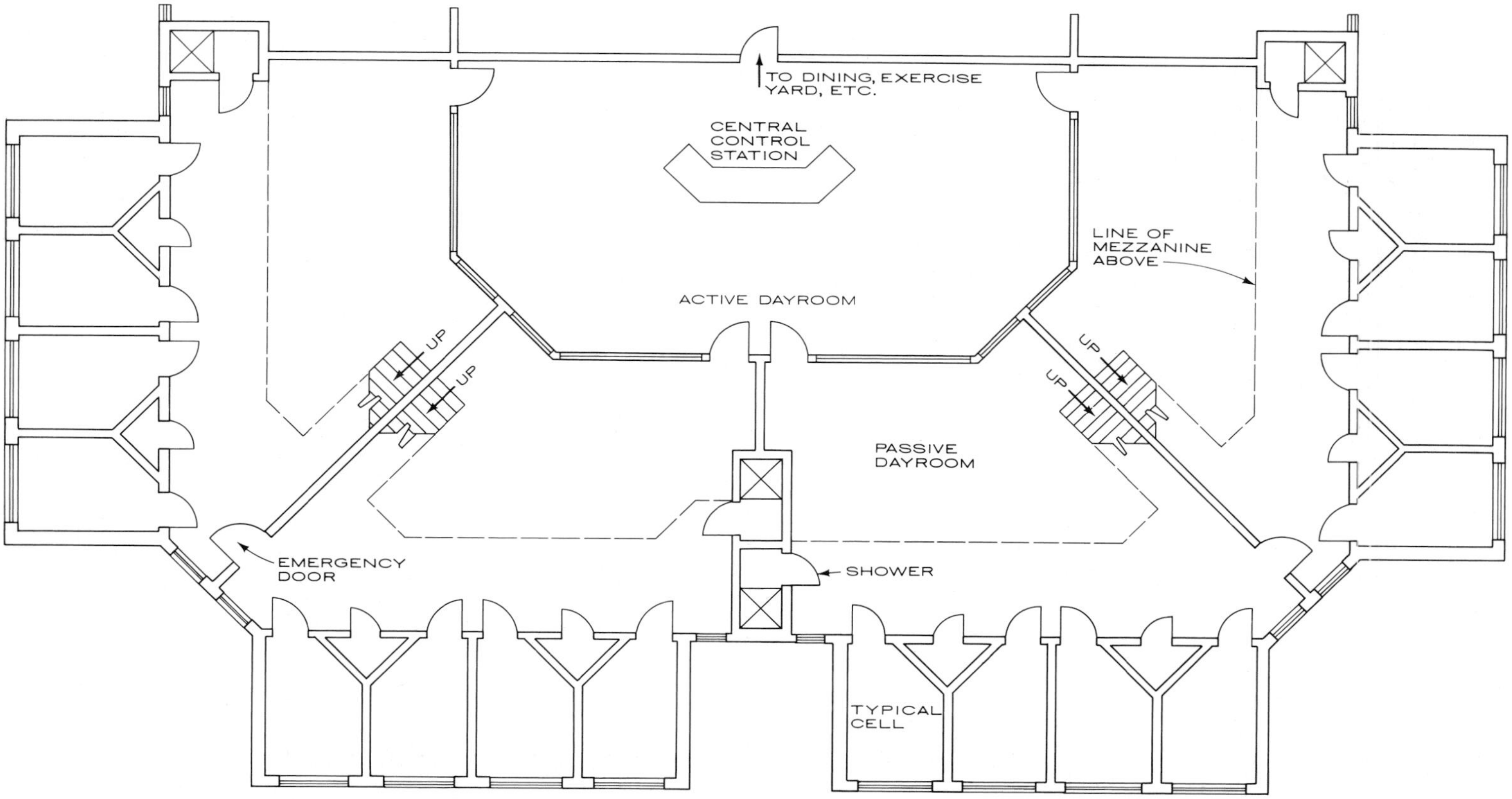

TYPICAL HOUSING UNIT PLAN

Gene L. Holtz; Hansen Lind Meyer; Orlando, Florida
Blythe + Nazdin Architects, Ltd.; Bethesda, Maryland

## PLANNING

### GENERAL

Patient rooms must be easily accessible to gurneys. Entry doors should be a minimum of 4 ft 0 in. wide. A clear area of 4 ft 0 in. should be maintained between foots of beds and partitions. With the exception of intensive care unit rooms, patient rooms should be equipped with several basic amenities: chairs for visitors, a television set, a wardrobe and bedside table for each bed, and a flower shelf. Patient rooms should be equipped with toilet facilities; however, centralized bathing areas may be provided in lieu of individual showers. Doors to toilet rooms should be a minimum of 2 ft 10 in. wide and should have a bolt release which permits the door to swing out. Lavatories should be located outside of toilet rooms to facilitate use by more than one patient, as well as hospital staff. Semiprivate patient rooms should contain cubicle curtains for examinations and general privacy.

### INTENSIVE CARE

Patients in an intensive care unit are under continuous observation, and each room must be visible from the nurse's station by means of the window wall. A patient's vital signs are typically monitored both within the room and remotely from the nurse's station. A small sink base and wall cabinet may be provided for minor procedures, or items may be supplied as required via rolling carts. Separate toilet rooms are not provided in these units.

Pediatric patient rooms should have a sleep sofa to accommodate parents who stay overnight with their child. Additional storage and a rocking chair can be provided. Because pediatric patients require closer supervision than older patients, a vision panel should be provided.

Finishes in patient rooms should be durable and easy to maintain: vinyl flooring, vinyl wall covering or painted gypsum board partitions, and plaster or gypsum board ceilings. Some hospitals contain several "V.I.P." patient rooms with carpeted floors and generally upgraded finishes throughout. Consult local codes for any restrictions on finishes in such rooms. All patient rooms should contain a built-in service module at the headwall of each bed. Depending on the room type, this unit contains a combination of nurse call button, reading light, controls for room lights, electrical outlets, monitor jacks, suction and vacuum lines, and medical gas outlets. Headwalls typically require framing with 6 in. studs.

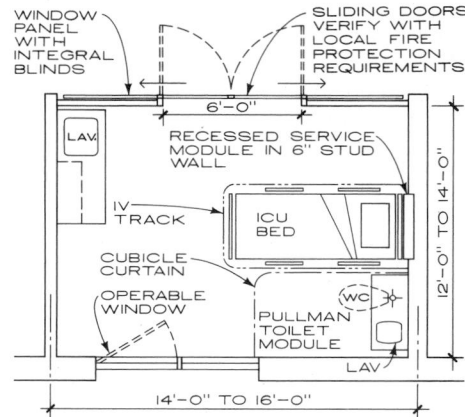

INTENSIVE CARE UNIT
PATIENT ROOM 170 SQ FT MIN.

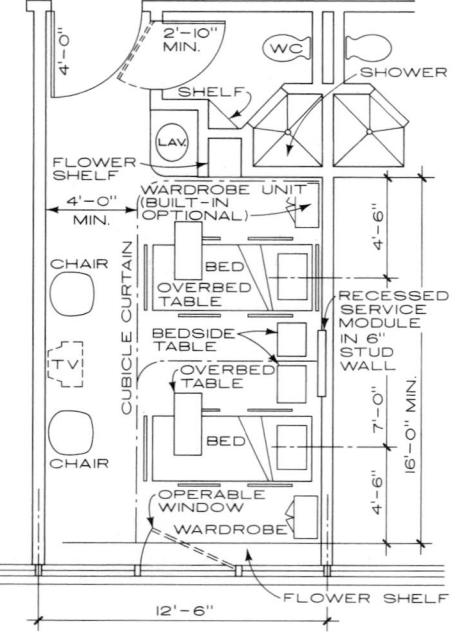

SEMIPRIVATE PATIENT ROOM
200 SQ FT (NET INCLUDING TOILET)

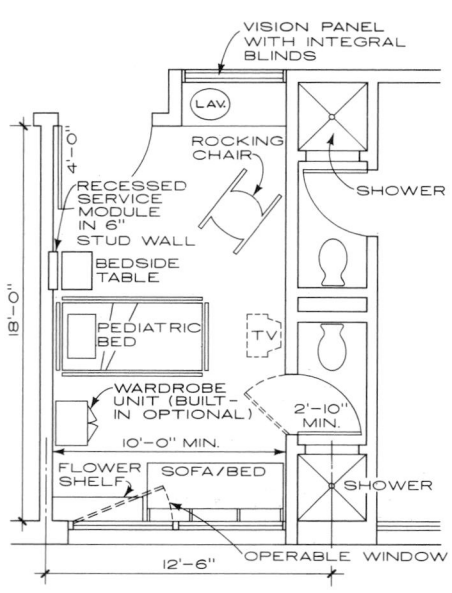

PEDIATRIC PATIENT ROOM
180 SQ FT

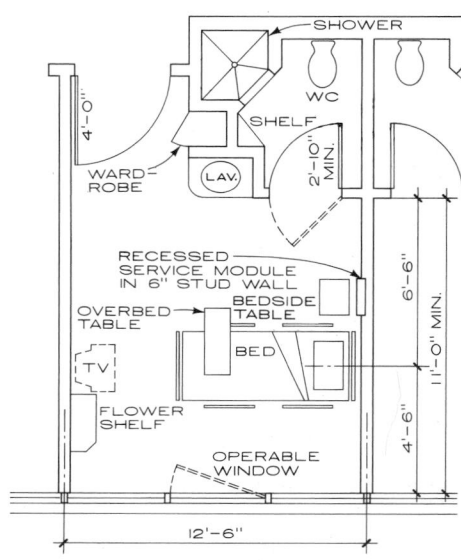

PRIVATE PATIENT ROOM
140 SQ FT (NET INCLUDING TOILET)

TYPICAL ROOM PLANS

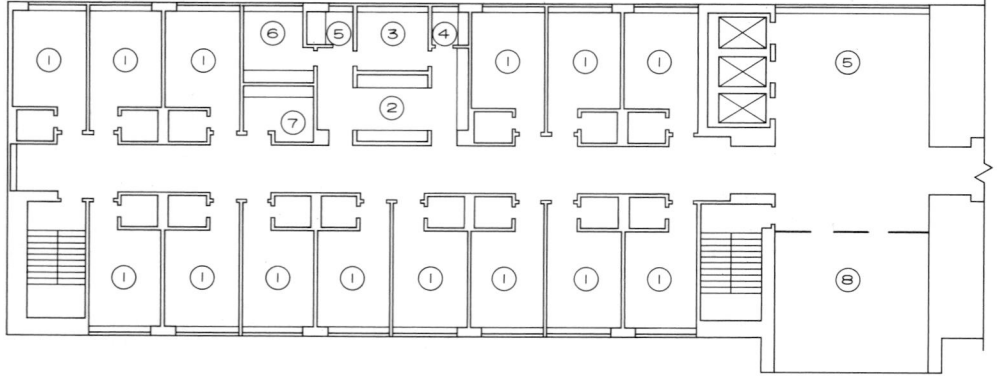

TYPICAL UNIT CONFIGURATION

### NOTES

1. A typical hospital floor consists of groups of units arranged around a common elevator lobby and lounge area.
2. Each unit contains a centrally located nurse's station and support areas.

### KEY

1. Patient room with bath
2. Nurse's station
3. Conference room
4. Head nurse's office
5. Nourishment station
6. Clean supply room
7. Soiled holding room
8. Lounge
9. Elevator lobby

Harwood K. Smith & Partner, Inc.; Dallas, Texas

# 1    SPACE PLANNING

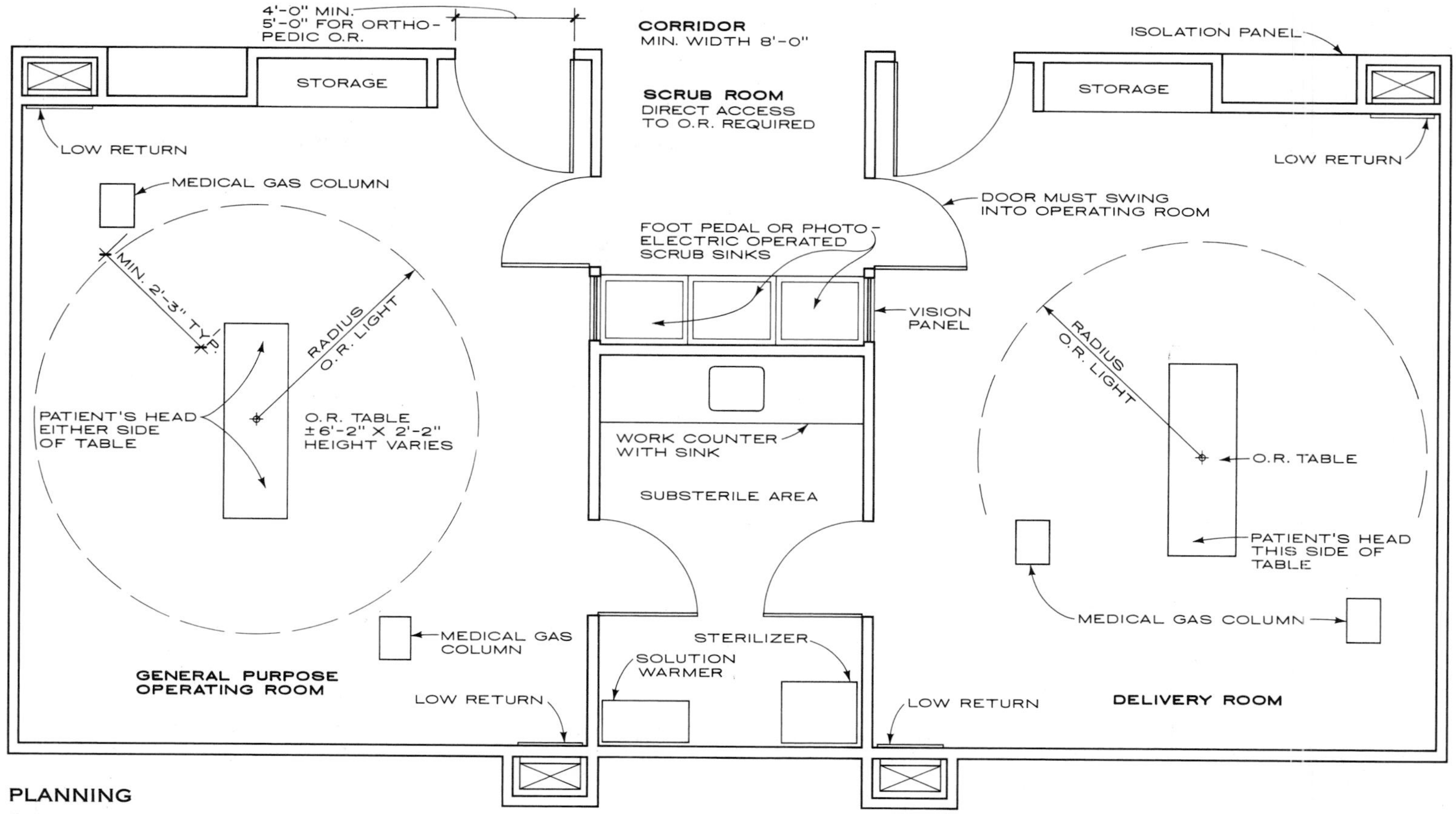

4'-0" MIN.
5'-0" FOR ORTHO-
PEDIC O.R.

STORAGE

LOW RETURN

MEDICAL GAS COLUMN

MIN. 2'-3" TYP.

PATIENT'S HEAD
EITHER SIDE
OF TABLE

RADIUS
O.R. LIGHT

O.R. TABLE
±6'-2" X 2'-2"
HEIGHT VARIES

GENERAL PURPOSE
OPERATING ROOM

MEDICAL GAS
COLUMN

LOW RETURN

CORRIDOR
MIN. WIDTH 8'-0"

SCRUB ROOM
DIRECT ACCESS
TO O.R. REQUIRED

FOOT PEDAL OR PHOTO-
ELECTRIC OPERATED
SCRUB SINKS

VISION
PANEL

WORK COUNTER
WITH SINK

SUBSTERILE AREA

STERILIZER

SOLUTION
WARMER

ISOLATION PANEL

STORAGE

LOW RETURN

DOOR MUST SWING
INTO OPERATING ROOM

RADIUS
O.R. LIGHT

O.R. TABLE

PATIENT'S HEAD
THIS SIDE OF
TABLE

MEDICAL GAS COLUMN

LOW RETURN

DELIVERY ROOM

## PLANNING

### ENCLOSURE

General purpose operating rooms must be extremely flexible due to widely varying spatial requirements of surgical procedures and personal preferences of the surgical staff. Public health codes limit the minimum size of these operating rooms to 360 sq ft, exclusive of casework. Certain procedures can require significantly more space. Operating rooms should be roughly square in plan and free of columns, with the operating room table located in the approximate center of the room to allow for maximum flexibility in positioning of equipment and personnel. Delivery rooms may be a minimum of 300 sq ft, exclusive of casework, for noncesarian births and 360 sq ft for cesarian. In delivery rooms, the operating room table is typically shifted from the center of the room to provide more space at the foot end. Endoscopy operatories may be as small as 250 sq ft, while orthopedic rooms should be at least 450 sq ft. Operating room finished ceiling height should be no lower than 9 ft 0 in., with an ample ceiling cavity for service space above.

### FINISHES

The primary concern in surgical room finishes is cleanliness. Flooring materials should be seamless and have an integral base for ease of maintenance. Walls should be finished with a scrubbable epoxy base paint or with vitreous ceramic tile and bacteria-resistant grout. Ceiling finishes should be either plaster or gypsum board. Built-in casework, countertops, sinks, and similar items should be stainless steel.

In operating rooms where flammable gases will be used an antistatic flooring surface must be specified to avoid sparks that could cause an explosion. Finishes throughout the operating room should be of light, neutral colors to avoid any distortion in skin color.

### ENVIRONMENTAL CONTROLS

Temperature and humidity in operating rooms must be strictly regulated to maintain a suitable environment for surgery. Positive air pressure must be maintained with respect to other areas to avoid infiltration of contaminants from outside the operating room. Air should be supplied at low velocities, with diffusers positioned to avoid formation of air eddies. Return registers should be at floor level, adjacent to medical gas columns, and at furthest points from each other for evacuation of

heavier-than-air gases, dust, and microbes. In areas where flammable gases will be used, electrical outlets must be explosion-proof, and high-hazard fire protection systems should be installed.

### EQUIPMENT

Medical gas columns typically contain a variety of gases, vacuum lines, and power used by the anesthesiologist during surgical procedures. They should be located adjacent to the anesthesiologist, who is positioned near the head of the patient. These columns are ceiling mounted and typically extend down to approximately 5 ft 6 in. above the floor. Retractable columns are also available. Depending on the anticipated use of the facility, a great variety of additional, highly specialized equipment will also be required.

Because of the extreme complexity of these areas, extensive participation by doctors, technicians, equipment manufacturers, and engineers is required throughout the design process.

---

**TYPICAL SURGICAL SUITE**

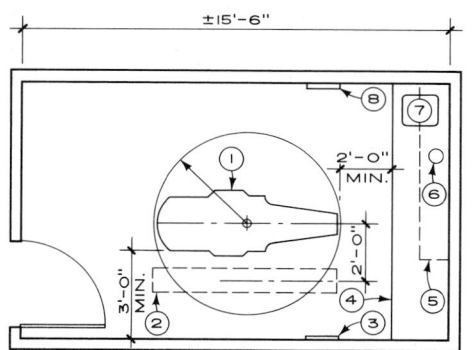

±15'-6"

2'-0" MIN.

2'-0"

3'-0" MIN.

## DENTAL EQUIPMENT KEY

1. Dental chair
2. Dual operating room light track
3. Medical gas console
4. Counter (cabinets below)
5. Overhead storage
6. Cutout in counter for waste
7. Stainless steel sink with foot control
8. Film illuminators (2)

## PLANNING

The dental chair base is equipped with hot and cold water, wet suction, compressed air, drainage if required for cuspidor, and power. In addition, a chair-mounted operating light may be used in lieu of a ceiling-mounted fixture.

The wall-mounted medical gas console typically includes nitrogen, oxygen, and nitrous oxide. If nitrous oxide gas is included, a scavenging system should be provided. Medical gases can be supplied by tanks on movable carts.

While room finishes are not as critical in dental operatories as in operating rooms, all surfaces should be washable.

---

**DENTAL OPERATORIES**

Deborah Hershowitz and Frank Giese; Rogers, Burgun, Shahine and Deschler Architects; New York, New York
Blythe + Nazdin Architects, Ltd.; Bethesda, Maryland

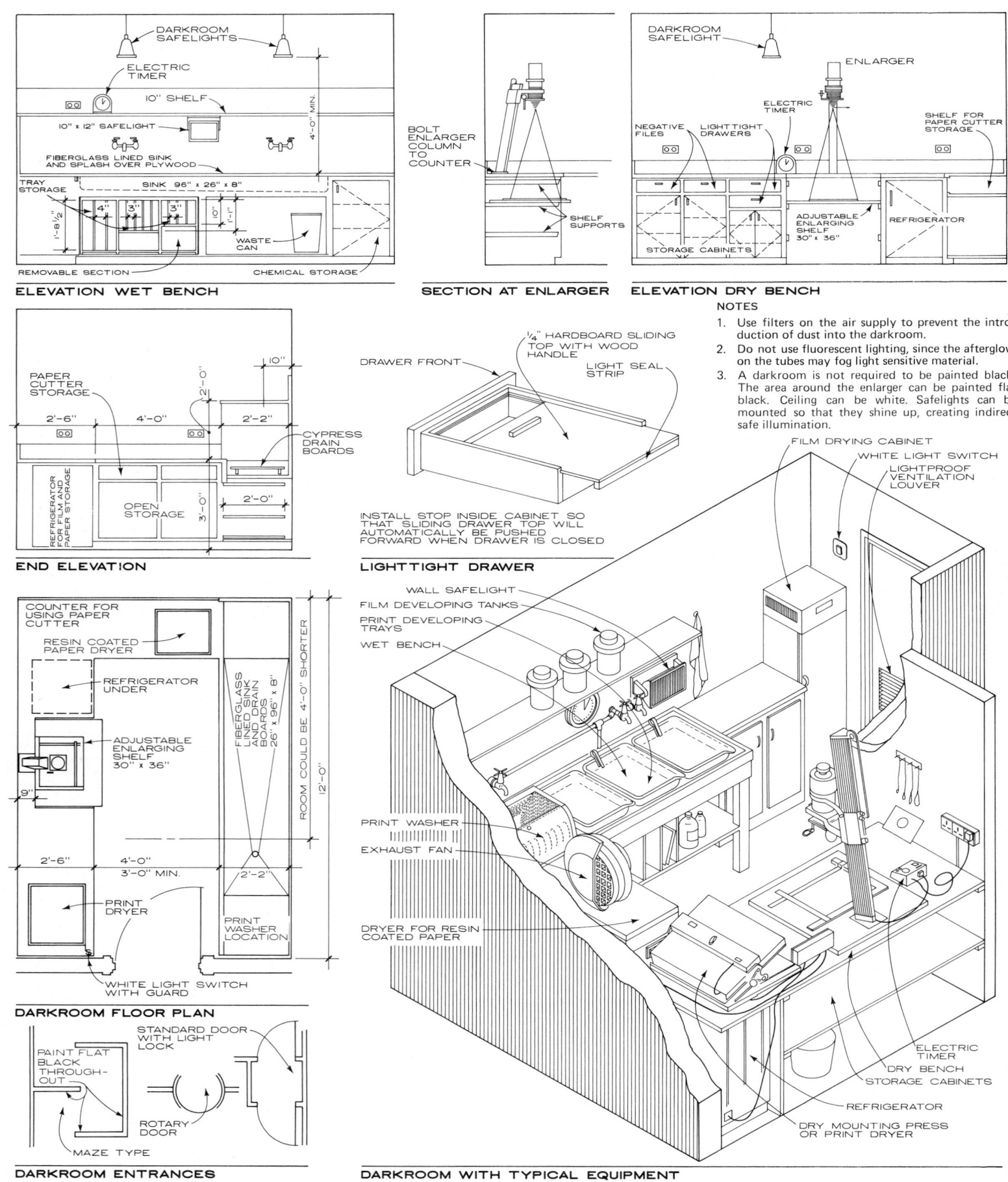

## ELEVATION WET BENCH

DARKROOM SAFELIGHTS
ELECTRIC TIMER
10" SHELF
10" x 12" SAFELIGHT
FIBERGLASS LINED SINK AND SPLASH OVER PLYWOOD
4'-0" MIN.
TRAY STORAGE
SINK 96" X 26" X 8"
1'-8½"
4" 3" 3"
10"
1'-1"
WASTE CAN
REMOVABLE SECTION
CHEMICAL STORAGE

## SECTION AT ENLARGER

BOLT ENLARGER COLUMN TO COUNTER
SHELF SUPPORTS

## ELEVATION DRY BENCH

DARKROOM SAFELIGHT
ENLARGER
ELECTRIC TIMER
NEGATIVE FILES
LIGHTTIGHT DRAWERS
SHELF FOR PAPER CUTTER STORAGE
STORAGE CABINETS
ADJUSTABLE ENLARGING SHELF 30" X 36"
REFRIGERATOR

### NOTES

1. Use filters on the air supply to prevent the introduction of dust into the darkroom.
2. Do not use fluorescent lighting, since the afterglow on the tubes may fog light sensitive material.
3. A darkroom is not required to be painted black. The area around the enlarger can be painted flat black. Ceiling can be white. Safelights can be mounted so that they shine up, creating indirect safe illumination.

## END ELEVATION

PAPER CUTTER STORAGE
10"
2'-0"
2'-6" 4'-0" 2'-2"
CYPRESS DRAIN BOARDS
REFRIGERATOR FOR FILM AND PAPER STORAGE
OPEN STORAGE
3'-0"
2'-0"

## LIGHTTIGHT DRAWER

¼" HARDBOARD SLIDING TOP WITH WOOD HANDLE
DRAWER FRONT
LIGHT SEAL STRIP

INSTALL STOP INSIDE CABINET SO THAT SLIDING DRAWER TOP WILL AUTOMATICALLY BE PUSHED FORWARD WHEN DRAWER IS CLOSED

## DARKROOM FLOOR PLAN

COUNTER FOR USING PAPER CUTTER
RESIN COATED PAPER DRYER
REFRIGERATOR UNDER
ADJUSTABLE ENLARGING SHELF 30" X 36"
9"
FIBERGLASS LINED SINK AND DRAIN BOARDS 26" X 96" X 8"
ROOM COULD BE 4'-0" SHORTER
12'-0"
2'-6" 4'-0" 2'-2"
3'-0" MIN.
PRINT DRYER
PRINT WASHER LOCATION
WHITE LIGHT SWITCH WITH GUARD

## DARKROOM WITH TYPICAL EQUIPMENT

FILM DRYING CABINET
WHITE LIGHT SWITCH
LIGHTPROOF VENTILATION LOUVER
WALL SAFELIGHT
FILM DEVELOPING TANKS
PRINT DEVELOPING TRAYS
WET BENCH
PRINT WASHER
EXHAUST FAN
DRYER FOR RESIN COATED PAPER
ELECTRIC TIMER
DRY BENCH STORAGE CABINETS
REFRIGERATOR
DRY MOUNTING PRESS OR PRINT DRYER

## DARKROOM ENTRANCES

PAINT FLAT BLACK THROUGHOUT
STANDARD DOOR WITH LIGHT LOCK
ROTARY DOOR
MAZE TYPE

Robert E. Fehlberg, FAIA; CTA Architects Engineers; Billings, Montana

# 1 SPACE PLANNING

## GENERAL NOTES

### HOME DARKROOM

The adjustable enlarging shelf is handy, but not necessary. The door should be made lighttight with weather-stripping and a bottom sweep. The floor covering should be dense and nonabsorbent. A homemade fiberglass or purchased tray developing sink could replace the plastic laminate cabinet top and sink. A rudimentary darkroom could function without a sink if a sink was available nearby. For consistency in developing, the water supply might require aeration, softening, temperature control, and possibly a vacuum breaker on the supply line. If waste disposal is through the plumbing, local code requirements should be checked as silver concentrations are regulated by sewer codes. To prevent electrical shock, ground fault interrupters should be used, particularly on outlet circuits. The safelights should be on separate circuits from the equipment and outlets. Color reproduction requires a voltage stabilizer.

### NEWSPAPER DARKROOM

Several darkrooms might be required as dictated by volume and variety of cameras used. Darkroom would include individual film darkrooms and a print darkroom with multiple stations. Film processing could be manual or automatic. Color and custom processing could require additional darkrooms. An adjacent small studio and copy camera room could serve for public relations and advertising photos.

### POLICE DARKROOM

Several darkrooms might be required, including a film darkroom and a printing darkroom. A large facility might include color processing and a crime lab. A finishing area and a fingerprint and mug shot room should be provided adjacent to the darkrooms.

### X-RAY LABS

The size of the X-ray darkroom is determined by the volume of film and may have several work stations. X-ray development requires different safelighting and can be manually or automatically processed. There are several different kinds of X-ray labs:

Dental    Darkrooms are usually for small facilities. Special sizes of film are involved and they are usually manually processed.

Hospital    Darkrooms are usually large, with multiple stations. Film is automatically processed and there is usually an adjacent viewing area.

Industrial    Darkroom size and quantities vary. Different kinds of film and processing might be used.

### SILVER RECOVERY

Economic feasibility and sewage codes might necessitate the recovery of silver from film processing affluent. Cartridge systems for automatic processors and remote systems are available.

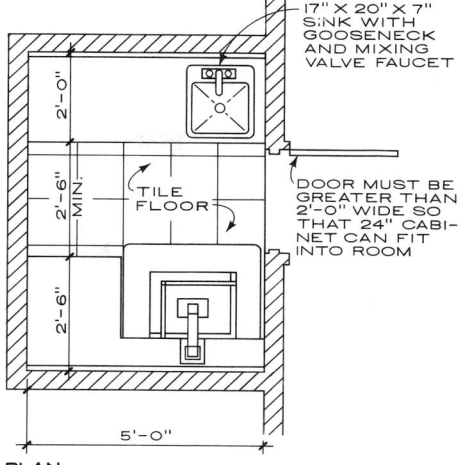

PLAN

SECTION

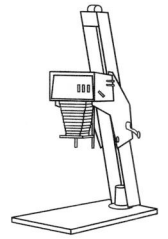

WET BENCH ELEVATION

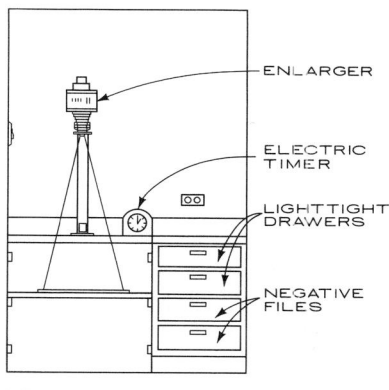

DRY BENCH ELEVATION

**HOME DARKROOM LAYOUT**

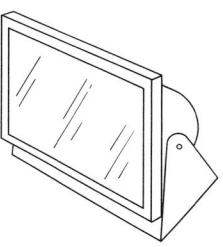

Color or black and white use different head assembly. Removable base is convenient to mount enlarger to counter. Power source is controlled by a remote timer.

**ENLARGER**

Wall, ceiling, or table mountable, with interchangeable filters for different kinds of film.

**SAFELIGHT**

Remote system to remove silver from discarded fixer. Various sizes available. Silver recovery is not usually cost-effective for home hobbyists.

**SILVER RECOVERY SYSTEM**

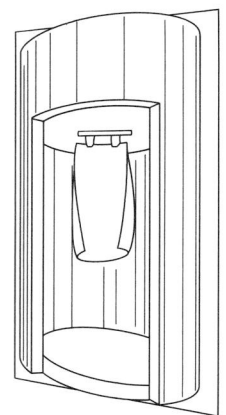

Allows film passage from room to room while remaining lighttight. Heating can be attached to modify to print dryer.

**FILM PASS-THROUGH**

Used for consistent high-volume processing. Different kinds of processors are available for various types of print development. Through-wall installation, silver recovery, and roll feed and take-up are options. Water supply line, drainage, and a power source are required. Maintain adequate space for maintenance and chemical changing.

**AUTOMATIC PROCESSOR**

CTA Architects Engineers; Billings, Montana

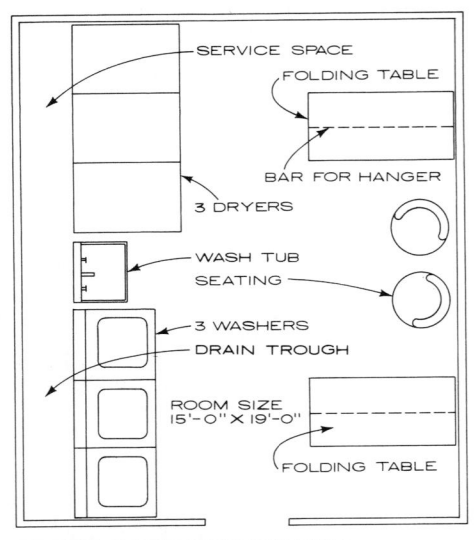

**20 UNIT APARTMENT BUILDING**

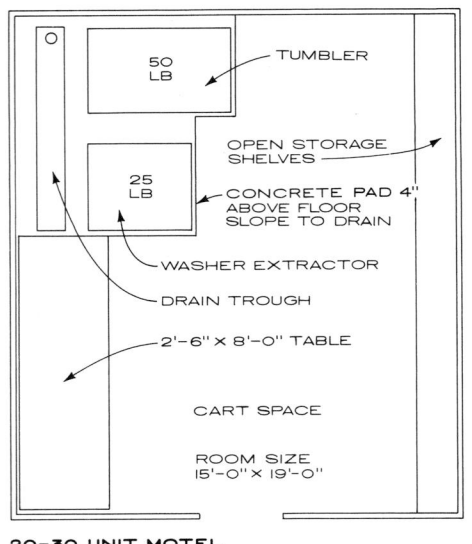

**20-30 UNIT MOTEL**

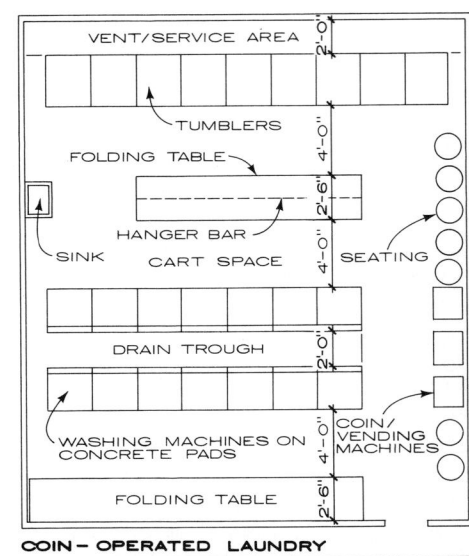

**COIN - OPERATED LAUNDRY**

**TYPICAL PLANS FOR LAUNDRY ROOMS**

## DRYER SIZES

| CAPACITY (LB) | WIDTH | DEPTH |
|---|---|---|
| 30 | 31'' | 44'' |
| 50 | 38'' | 44'' |
| 75 | 38'' | 49'' |
| 100 | 46'' | 62'' |
| 200 | 72'' | 54'' |

### NOTES

1. Drain trench underneath or behind washers is for washing machine overflow and is sized to contain one complete dump from all machines.
2. Variables that determine size of on-premise laundry machines for hotels include number of rooms and hotel occupancy (at 10 lb of laundry per room).
3. Variables that determine the mix of single, double, and triple load washing machines and size of tumblers in launderettes include the neighborhood and clientele expected.
4. Heavy-duty machines have fewer parts prone to breakage than coin-operated residential machines.
5. Tumbler capacity is twice washer capacity for permanent press fabrics.
6. Venting, electrical, and gas lines should run overhead and drop down to machines.
7. Washing machines in apartment buildings are generally coin-operated residential sizes.
8. Stackable dryers can provide a maximum utilization of space.

## WASHER/EXTRACTOR SIZES

| CAPACITY (LB) | WIDTH | DEPTH |
|---|---|---|
| 20 | 28'' | 30'' |
| 20–30 | 30'' | 32'' |
| 30–40 | 34'' | 36'' |
| 40–50 | 36'' | 44'' |
| 50–60 | 46'' | 40'' |

Above 60 lb, sizes may vary with manufacturer. Minimum clearances: 18 in. sides, 24 in. behind, and 48 in. front.

## TUMBLER SIZES

| CAPACITY (LB) | WIDTH | DEPTH |
|---|---|---|
| 30 | 32'' | 45'' |
| 50 | 39'' | 47'' |
| 65 | 39'' | 53'' |
| 100 | 47'' | 64'' |

Minimum clearances: 24 in. behind, none sides, 48 in. front.

Duane Fisher; Richard Newlon Associates; Washington, D.C.

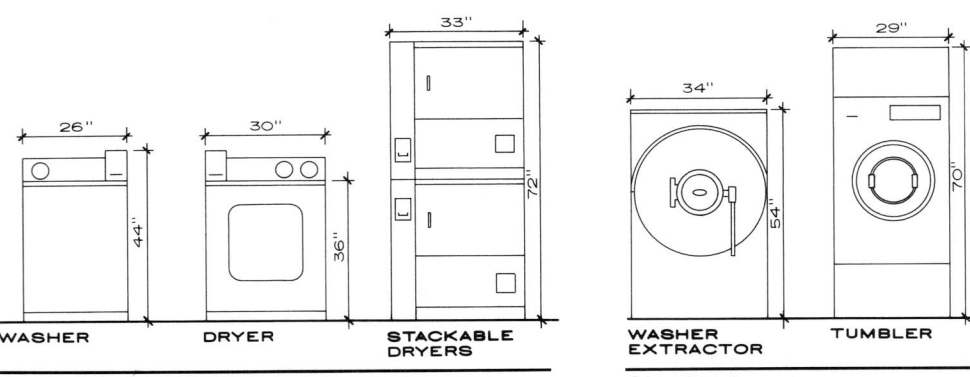

**COIN - OPERATED LAUNDRY**          **ON-SITE LAUNDRY**

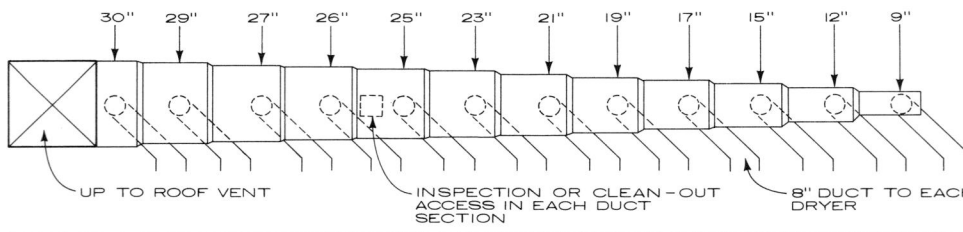

**EXHAUST DUCT**

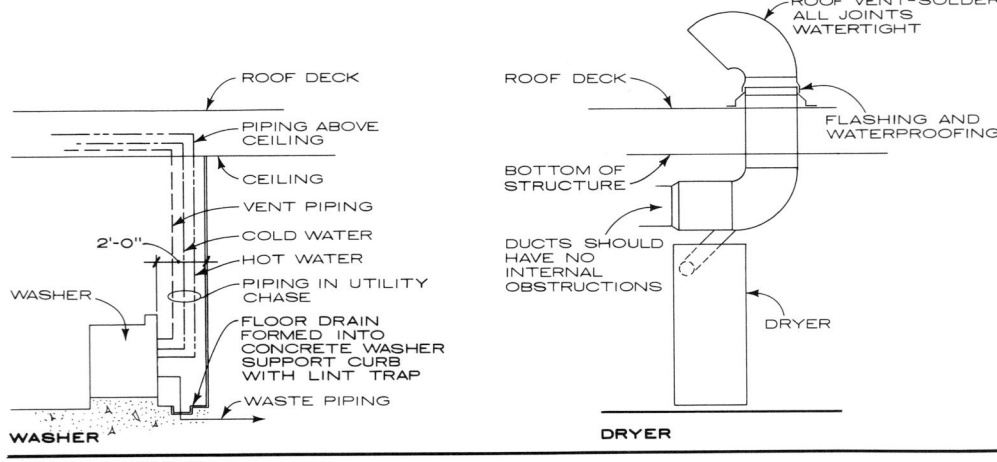

**UTILITY HOOKUP**

**1**     **SPACE PLANNING**

## STANDARD LINEN SIZES (IN.)

| | SIZE | SUGGESTED FOLDED SIZE | MIN. DEPTH OF SHELF |
|---|---|---|---|
| **Flat sheet** | | | |
| Twin | 66 x 104 | 8 1/4 x 13 | |
| Double | 81 x 104 | 10 1/8 x 13 | |
| Queen size | 90 x 110 | 11 1/4 x 13 3/4 | |
| King size | 108 x 110 | 13 1/2 x 13 3/4 | |
| **Fitted sheet** | | | 18" |
| Twin | 39 x 80 | 7 1/4 x 9 3/8 | |
| Double | 54 x 75 | 13 1/3 x 9 3/8 | |
| Queen size | 60 x 80 | 15 x 10 | |
| King size | 72 x 84 | 18 x 10 1/2 | |
| **Pillowcase** | | | |
| Standard | 21 x 33 | 7 x 11 | 12" |
| King | 21 x 33 | 7 x 15 | |
| **Pillows** | | | |
| Standard | 20 x 26 | Not | |
| Queen | 20 x 30 | Applicable | |
| King | 20 x 36 | | |
| **Blanket** | | | 24" |
| Twin | 66 x 90 | 16 1/2 x 22 1/2 | |
| | 72 x 90 | 18 x 22 1/2 | |
| Double | 80 x 90 | 20 x 22 1/2 | |
| Queen/king | 108 x 90 | 27 x 22 1/2 | |
| **Hand towel** | 11 x 18 | 5 1/2 x 9 | |
| | 12 x 20 | 6 x 10 | 12" |
| **Face towel** | 15 x 26 | 7 1/2 x 13 | |
| | 16 x 32 | 8 x 16 | |
| | 18 x 36 | 9 x 18 | |
| **Bath towel** | 22 x 44 | 11 x 11 | |
| | 24 x 48 | 12 x 12 | 18" |
| | 26 x 50 | 13 x 12 1/2 | |
| | 28 x 52 | 14 x 13 | |
| **Bath sheet** | 36 x 68 | 12 x 17 | |
| | 44 x 72 | 14 3/4 x 18 | |
| **Wash cloth** | 9 x 9 | 4 1/2 x 9 | |
| | 12 x 12 | 6 x 12 | |
| | 14 x 14 | 7 x 14 | |
| **Bath mat** | 20 x 30 | 10 x 7 1/2 | 12" |
| | 20 x 34 | 10 x 8 1/2 | |
| | 22 x 36 | 10 x 9 | |
| **Tablecloth** | | | |
| Rectangular | 52 x 52 | | |
| | 52 x 70 | | |
| | 62 x 85 | | |
| | 62 x 104 | | 18" |
| | 70 x 90 | | |
| | 70 x 126 | | to |
| Round | 72" diam. | | |
| | 90" diam. | | 24" |
| Oval | 52 x 70 | | |
| | 64 x 84 | | |
| | 72 x 90 | | |
| **Napkin** | 14 x 14 | 4 3/4 x 7 | |
| | 18 x 18 | 6 x 9 | 12" |
| | 22 x 22 | 7 1/2 x 11 | |
| **Dish towel** | 16 x 30 | 8 x 15 | |
| | 18 x 36 | 9 x 18 | |
| | 20 x 32 | 10 x 16 | 18" |
| **Sleeping bag** | Varies | 8 x 18 | |
| | | 11 x 22 | |

Kent Wong; Hewlett, Jamison, Atkinson & Luey; Portland, Oregon

### MAIN LINEN STORAGE ROOM IN HOTELS AND MOTELS

Requires a room with minimum 20-24 in. wide shelving. Shelving less than 20 in. may not accommodate linen processed by professional linen service. Provisions for storage of dining linen and uniforms and a sewing/mending room are recommended in hotels. A clear space in the room for loading of carts (24"W x 60"L x 60"H) is required.

### SECONDARY LINEN STORAGE ROOM IN HOTELS AND MOTELS

Requires a room with minimum 20-24 in. wide shelving. A clear space in the room for loading of two cleaning carts (24"W x 52"L) at one time is recommended. In most cases, the linen room is also used for storing some room service/nonlinen items.

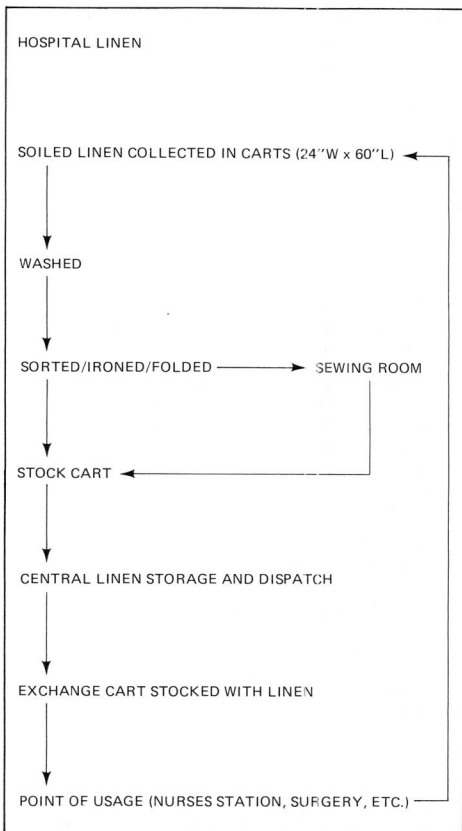

### GENERAL NOTES

1. Rolled-up size (diam. x length). Manufacturer recommends storing bag(s) by hanging up unrolled.
2. Requires a room large enough to accommodate 24 in. wide shelving and circulation space for parking and storing of stock carts (24"W x 60"L) and loading of exchange carts (28"W x 52"L x 72"H).
3. Exchange cart may be stored in a closet near point of usage. An overhead shelf in closet for extra blankets and pillows is recommended.
4. Consult with Joint Commission on Accreditation of Hospitals and American Hospital Association for guidelines and standards.

**SPACE PLANNING** 1

## GENERAL PLANNING NOTES

During the early stages of planning, consult with regional Postmaster General for regulations concerning postal facilities in office buildings.

### PLATFORM

A dock area that provides off-the-street loading and unloading of mail.

### MAILROOM

A security type room located at platform level, which has its own access door to the platform for off-hour service. Platform door should be 48 in. wide, security type. If window or lockbox service is provided, the mailroom should be located at the principal building entrance level. Standard interior treatment should apply in this space. Provide heavy-duty wall and corner guards.

### SERVICES

The size of mailroom and services provided by the post office vary with size and occupancy of the building. The U.S. Postal Service recognizes for its staffing and servicing two types of mailrooms for small, medium, and large office buildings.

1. LOCKBOX SERVICE: Buildings up to 200,000 sq ft of leasable space or with a maximum of 75 tenants. Provide one receptacle for each tenant and rear loading for 11 or more tenants. A building directory must be maintained.

   The vertical distance from floor to tenant locks on top tier of receptacles is 66 in. maximum; to bottom lowest tier 10 in. minimum, preferably 30 in. Install only at one entrance. Allow a minimum of 3 ft of clear working space behind units. Provide

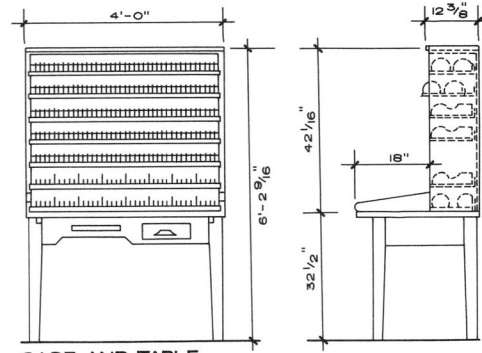

**CASE AND TABLE**

80 sq ft of working space for each additional carrier. Allow 1 sq ft of working space for every 1000 sq ft of leasable office space. Specifications for construction of mail receptacles shall be identical to those for Type II, horizontal apartment house receptacles as prescribed in USPS Publication 17, except that the minimum inside dimensions shall be 5¾ in. high, 10½ in. wide, and 16 in. deep.

2. CALL WINDOW SERVICE: Buildings with 75 or more tenants, one carrier for each 100,000 sq ft of leasable office space up to 500,000 sq ft, plus one carrier for each additional 200,000 sq ft of office building. Allow 1.5 sq ft for every 1000 sq ft of leasable space; the minimum call window service space is 100 sq ft.

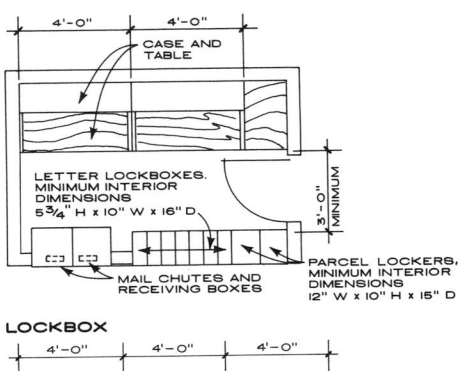

**LOCKBOX**

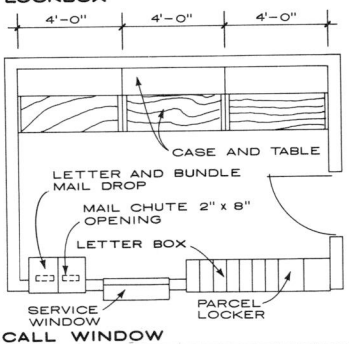

**CALL WINDOW**

## POSTAL SERVICES

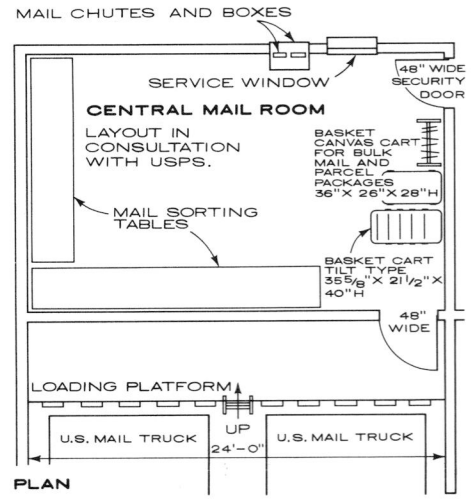

**PLAN**

### CENTRAL MAILROOM

Buildings larger than 200,000 sq ft and up to 2,000,000 sq ft of leasable space can be served on each floor from a central mailroom using a containerized mechanical system. Allow a minimum of 400 sq ft for first 50 tenants plus 135 sq ft for each additional 50 tenants, or 2 sq ft for each 1000 sq ft of leasable space.

Service mailrooms shall be provided on each multitenant floor, unless containers are conveyed mechanically to tenant offices. Allow 5 x 7 ft minimum floor area for service mailroom. Mechanical systems accommodating 8 to 19 containers may require a minimum area of 7 x 8 ft. Minimum inside container dimensions are 12 x 16 x 6 in.

Existing mechanical systems often are disbanded. U.S. Postal Service recommends a central mailroom with rear-loading lock boxes and parcel lockers. For high mail and parcel volumes, nutting trucks and BMC containers as shown may be used for transport to mailroom floor (48 in. wide security doors required).

### NOTES

1. Centralized mail delivery: Neighborhood Delivery & Collection Box Units (NDCBU) are popular in home and office complex developments. USPS can help plan centralized mail delivery (Pub. 265, August 1983).

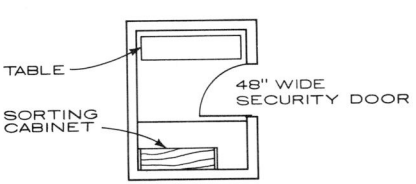

**SERVICE MAILROOM PLAN**

2. USPS lobby layouts in postal buildings designate specific vending machine areas, customer service lobby, and box lobby with parcel lockers having a lock system similar to public lockers, and customer leased box lockers. See USPS guidelines, "New Directions in Lobby Design Practices." Some equipment and features are applicable to office buildings.

3. Rehabilitating existing buildings: the form of mail handling should not change, i.e., an original central mailroom installation may not be changed to mail delivery on each floor. Same applies to mail chute installations. Relocation may be necessary, but discontinuation or introduction of a new installation needs approval. In all cases, early consultation with the local Postmaster should be initiated.

## CENTRAL MAILROOM

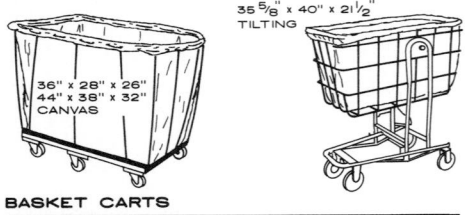

**BASKET CARTS**

**EQUIPMENT**

### MAIL CHUTES AND RECEIVING BOXES

1. Chutes: Used in buildings of at least four stories for first class mail only. The chute cross section must be approximately 2 x 8 in. and extend in a continuously vertical line from beginning point to receiving box or mailroom. Chute interior must be accessible its entire length. Chutes in pairs have a divider and dual receiving boxes.

**MAIL CHUTES AND RECEIVING BOXES**

2. Receiving boxes: Must be placed near the building's main entrance or near the loading, unloading area for USPS mail collection. Using the shortest line, receiving boxes may not be placed more than 100 ft from the entrance used by the collection person. Locations require local Postmaster approval. Receiving boxes must be placed on the same floor the collection person uses to enter the building. Doors must operate freely. Door openings must be at least 12 x 20 in. and not more than 18 x 30 in.

3. Auxiliary boxes: Located near receiving box when receiving box is too small to accommodate first class mail volume. Openings must be large enough to receive tied bundles of first class mail.

4. Bundle drops: Receiving boxes must have bundle drops with an opening for a bundle at least 6½ in. wide by 11½ in. long and 4 in. high. To prevent removal of mail through it, the deposit opening must be fully protected by inside baffle plates. Inlet doors must be inscribed "Letters" and "Letter Mail Tied in Bundles." Bottom of the opening must be at least 61 in. above floor level.

Reference: USPS Publication 16, September 1985

### NOTE

1. All installations must comply with USPS requirements and are subject to inspection.

2. Floor penetrations may need firestopping methods.

3. USPS provides listing of approved manufacturers.

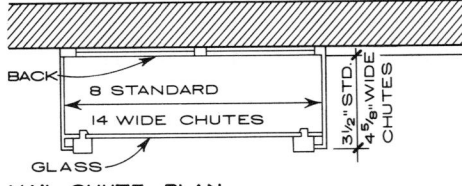

**MAIL CHUTE—PLAN**

### NOTES

1. May be recessed.

2. Use wide chutes for 8 x 10 in. envelopes.

3. Tempered glass at least ³⁄₁₆ in. thick, or heavy, shatterproof plate glass at least ¾ in. thick, or transparent, fire-resistant plastic material of equal or greater strength than ³⁄₁₆ in. tempered glass.

Walter Hart Associates, AIA; White Plains, New York

1 SPACE PLANNING

## THEATER DESIGN CRITERIA

The planning of seating areas in places of assembly should involve the following considerations:

1. EFFICIENCY: The floor area efficiency in square feet per seat is a function of the row spacing, the average chair width, and the space allocation per seat for aisles. See following pages for further discussion of these factors.

$$\text{Efficiency (F)} = \text{seat factor} + \text{aisle factor}$$

$$F \text{ (sq ft/seat)} = \frac{W_s T}{144} + \frac{IT}{144} \times \frac{1}{S_{avg}}$$

where $W_s$ = average seat width (in.)
  $T$ = row to row spacing (tread) (in.)
  $I$ = average aisle width (in.) (42 in. width is typical)
  $S_{avg}$ = average number of seats in a row per single aisle: 8 or fewer—inefficient layout; 14 to 16—maximum efficiency (multiple aisle seating); 18 to 50 and more—continental seating.

2. CAPACITY AND AUDIENCE AREA: Audience area = capacity x efficiency.

| | |
|---|---|
| 35-75 | Classroom |
| 75-150 | Lecture room, experimental theater |
| 150-300 | Large lecture room, small theater |
| 300-750 | Average drama theater in educational setting |
| 750-1500 | Small commercial theater, repertory theater, recital hall |
| 1500-2000 | Medium large theater, large commercial theater |
| 2000-3000 | Average civic theater, concert hall, multiple use hall |
| 3000-6000 | Very large auditorium |
| Over 6000 | Special assembly facilities |

3. PERFORMING AREA (not including adjacent support area) (sq ft):

| | MINIMUM | AVERAGE | MAXIMUM |
|---|---|---|---|
| Lectures (single speaker) | 150 | 240 | 500 |
| Revue, nightclub | 350 | 450 | 700 |
| Legitimate drama | 250 | 550 | 1000 |
| Dance | 700 | 950 | 1200 |
| Musicals, folk opera | 800 | 1200 | 1800 |
| Symphonic concerts | 1500 | 2000 | 2500 |
| Opera | 1000 | 2500 | 4000 |
| Pageant | 2000 | 3500 | 5000 |

4. ORIENTATION OF SEATED SPECTATOR: Head strain is minimized by orienting chairs or rows of chairs so that spectators face the center of action of the performing area.

5. ANGLE OF VISION OF SPECTATOR: The human eye has a peripheral spread of vision of about 130°. This angle of view from chairs in the front rows will define the outer limits of the maximum sized performing area.

6. ANGLE OF ENCOUNTER: The angle of encounter is defined by the 130° peripheral spread of vision of a single performer standing at the "point of command." Patrons seated outside the spread of this angle will not have simultaneous eye contact with performer. Natural sound communication will also deteriorate for these patrons.

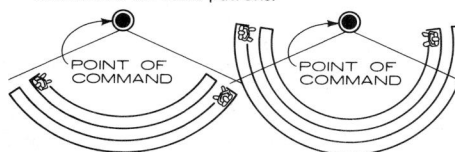

POINT OF COMMAND    POINT OF COMMAND

7. DISTANCE BETWEEN PERFORMANCE AND LAST ROW OF SPECTATORS: Achievement of visual and sound communication is enhanced by minimizing this distance while satisfying the preceding parameters.

Peter H. Frink; Frink and Beuchat: Architects; Philadelphia, Pennsylvania

## SCREEN PROJECTION
- The minimum distance between the first row and the screen ($D_F$) is determined by the maximum allowable angle between the sightline from the first row to the top of the screen and the perpendicular to the screen at that point. A maximum angle of 30 to 35° is recommended.
- The maximum distance between the screen and the most distant viewer (MDV) should not exceed eight times the height of the screen image. An MDV two to three times the screen width is preferred.
- Screen width (W) is determined by the use of the appropriate aspect ratio between the screen image width and height.
- Curvature of screens may reduce the amount of apparent distortion for a larger audience area. Curvature of larger screens may help to keep the whole of the image in focus and may provide a more uniform distribution of luminance.

## ZERO ENCIRCLEMENT (PROSCENIUM STAGE, PICTURE FRAME STAGE, END STAGE)
- The angle of audience spread in front of a masking frame is determined by the maximum size of the corner cutoff from a rectangularly shaped performing area that can be tolerated by seats at the side.
- Audience may not fill angle of encounter from point of command.
- Audience farthest from performing area.
- Large range in choice of size of performing area.
- Provisions for a large amount of scenic wall surfaces without masking sightlines.
- Horizontal movement of scenery typically made in both perpendicularly and parallel to centerline.
- Possibility of short differences in arrival time between direct and reflected sound at the spectator. This may be beneficial to music performances.

## 90° TO 130° ENCIRCLEMENT (PICTORIAL OPEN STAGE, WIDE FAN, HYBRID, THRUST STAGE)
- Audience spread defined and limited by angle of encounter from point of command.
- Performing area shape trapezoidal, rhombic, or circular.
- Audience closer to performing area than with zero encirclement.
- Picture frame less dominant.
- Range in choice of size of performing area.
- Provision for an amount of scenic wall surfaces possible without obscuring the performing area.
- Horizontal movement of scenery is possible in directions at 45° to and parallel to centerline.
- Shape of seating area places maximum number of seats within the directional limits of the sound of the unaided voice, beneficial for speech performance.

## 180° TO 270° ENCIRCLEMENT (GREEK THEATER, PENINSULAR, THREE-SIDED, THRUST STAGE, 3/4 ARENA STAGE, ELIZABETHAN STAGE)
- Audience spread well beyond angle of encounter from point of command in order to bring audience closer to performing area.
- Simultaneous eye contact between performer and all spectators not possible.
- Minimum range of choice in size of performing area.
- Provision of a small amount of scenic wall surfaces possible without masking sightlines.
- Horizontal movement of scenery is possible only parallel to centerline.
- Large encirclement by audience usually demands actor vomitory entrance through or under audience.

## 360° ENCIRCLEMENT (ARENA STAGE, THEATER IN THE ROUND, ISLAND STAGE, CENTER STAGE)
- Performer always seen from rear by some spectators.
- Simultaneous eye contact between performer and all spectators not possible.
- Audience closest to performance.
- No range of choice in size of performing area.
- No scenic wall surfaces possible without obscuring the view of the performing area.
- Horizontal movement of scenery not readily possible.
- Encirclement by audience demands actor vomitory entrance through audience area.

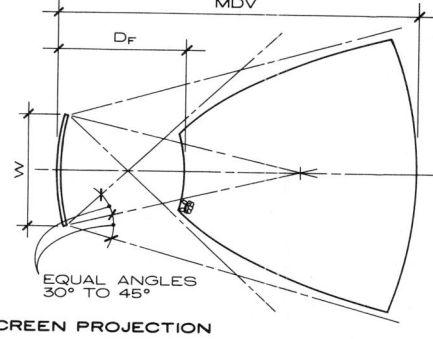

SCREEN PROJECTION

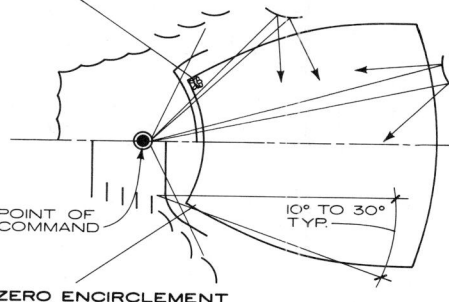

ZERO ENCIRCLEMENT

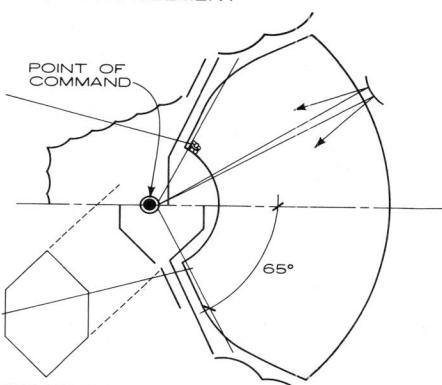

90° TO 130° ENCIRCLEMENT

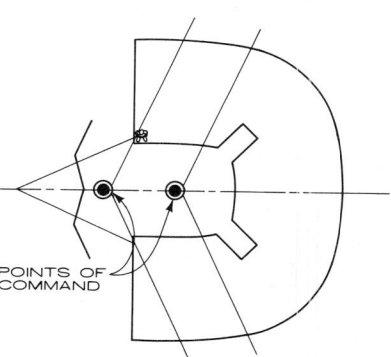

180° TO 270° ENCIRCLEMENT

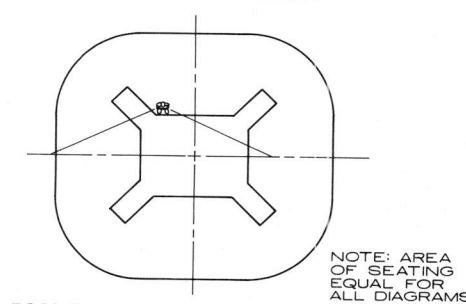

360° ENCIRCLEMENT

NOTE: AREA OF SEATING EQUAL FOR ALL DIAGRAMS

## THEATER DESIGN 1

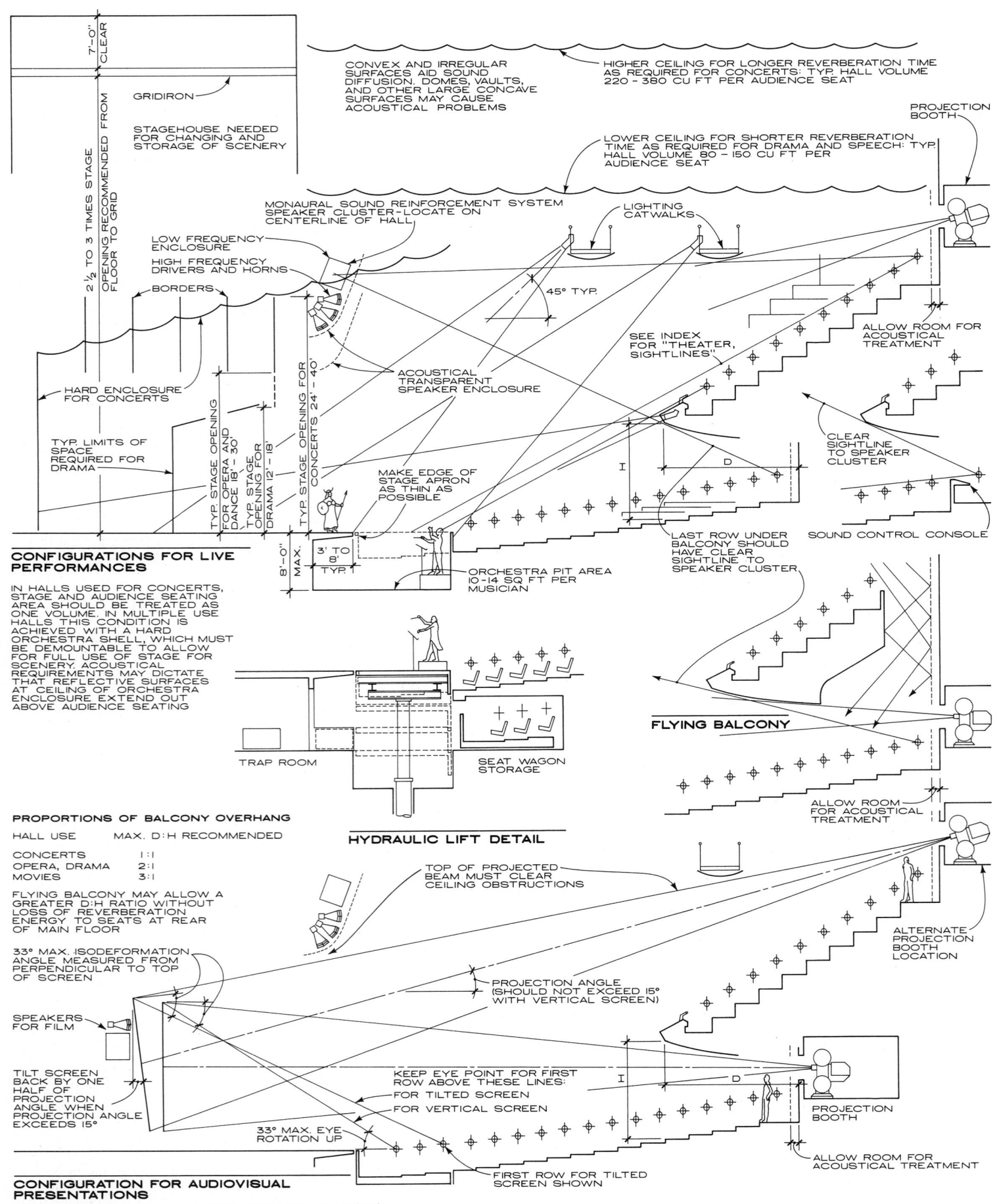

### CONFIGURATIONS FOR LIVE PERFORMANCES

7'-0" CLEAR

GRIDIRON

STAGEHOUSE NEEDED FOR CHANGING AND STORAGE OF SCENERY

2½ TO 3 TIMES STAGE OPENING RECOMMENDED FROM FLOOR TO GRID

CONVEX AND IRREGULAR SURFACES AID SOUND DIFFUSION. DOMES, VAULTS, AND OTHER LARGE CONCAVE SURFACES MAY CAUSE ACOUSTICAL PROBLEMS

HIGHER CEILING FOR LONGER REVERBERATION TIME AS REQUIRED FOR CONCERTS: TYP. HALL VOLUME 220 - 380 CU FT PER AUDIENCE SEAT

PROJECTION BOOTH

LOWER CEILING FOR SHORTER REVERBERATION TIME AS REQUIRED FOR DRAMA AND SPEECH: TYP. HALL VOLUME 80 - 150 CU FT PER AUDIENCE SEAT

MONAURAL SOUND REINFORCEMENT SYSTEM SPEAKER CLUSTER-LOCATE ON CENTERLINE OF HALL

LIGHTING CATWALKS

LOW FREQUENCY ENCLOSURE

HIGH FREQUENCY DRIVERS AND HORNS

45° TYP.

ALLOW ROOM FOR ACOUSTICAL TREATMENT

BORDERS

SEE INDEX FOR "THEATER, SIGHTLINES"

HARD ENCLOSURE FOR CONCERTS

ACOUSTICAL TRANSPARENT SPEAKER ENCLOSURE

CLEAR SIGHTLINE TO SPEAKER CLUSTER

TYP. LIMITS OF SPACE REQUIRED FOR DRAMA

TYP. STAGE OPENING FOR OPERA AND DANCE 18' - 30'

TYP. STAGE OPENING FOR DRAMA 12'-18'

TYP. STAGE OPENING FOR CONCERTS 24 - 40'

MAKE EDGE OF STAGE APRON AS THIN AS POSSIBLE

I    D

LAST ROW UNDER BALCONY SHOULD HAVE CLEAR SIGHTLINE TO SPEAKER CLUSTER

SOUND CONTROL CONSOLE

8'-0" MAX.

3' TO 8' TYP.

ORCHESTRA PIT AREA 10-14 SQ FT PER MUSICIAN

IN HALLS USED FOR CONCERTS, STAGE AND AUDIENCE SEATING AREA SHOULD BE TREATED AS ONE VOLUME. IN MULTIPLE USE HALLS THIS CONDITION IS ACHIEVED WITH A HARD ORCHESTRA SHELL, WHICH MUST BE DEMOUNTABLE TO ALLOW FOR FULL USE OF STAGE FOR SCENERY. ACOUSTICAL REQUIREMENTS MAY DICTATE THAT REFLECTIVE SURFACES AT CEILING OF ORCHESTRA ENCLOSURE EXTEND OUT ABOVE AUDIENCE SEATING

### FLYING BALCONY

ALLOW ROOM FOR ACOUSTICAL TREATMENT

### PROPORTIONS OF BALCONY OVERHANG

| HALL USE | MAX. D:H RECOMMENDED |
|---|---|
| CONCERTS | 1:1 |
| OPERA, DRAMA | 2:1 |
| MOVIES | 3:1 |

TRAP ROOM

SEAT WAGON STORAGE

### HYDRAULIC LIFT DETAIL

FLYING BALCONY MAY ALLOW A GREATER D:H RATIO WITHOUT LOSS OF REVERBERATION ENERGY TO SEATS AT REAR OF MAIN FLOOR

33° MAX. ISODEFORMATION ANGLE MEASURED FROM PERPENDICULAR TO TOP OF SCREEN

TOP OF PROJECTED BEAM MUST CLEAR CEILING OBSTRUCTIONS

ALTERNATE PROJECTION BOOTH LOCATION

PROJECTION ANGLE (SHOULD NOT EXCEED 15° WITH VERTICAL SCREEN)

SPEAKERS FOR FILM

TILT SCREEN BACK BY ONE HALF OF PROJECTION ANGLE WHEN PROJECTION ANGLE EXCEEDS 15°

KEEP EYE POINT FOR FIRST ROW ABOVE THESE LINES: - FOR TILTED SCREEN - FOR VERTICAL SCREEN

I    D

PROJECTION BOOTH

33° MAX. EYE ROTATION UP

ALLOW ROOM FOR ACOUSTICAL TREATMENT

FIRST ROW FOR TILTED SCREEN SHOWN

### CONFIGURATION FOR AUDIOVISUAL PRESENTATIONS

Peter H. Frink; Frink and Beuchat: Architects; Philadelphia, Pennsylvania

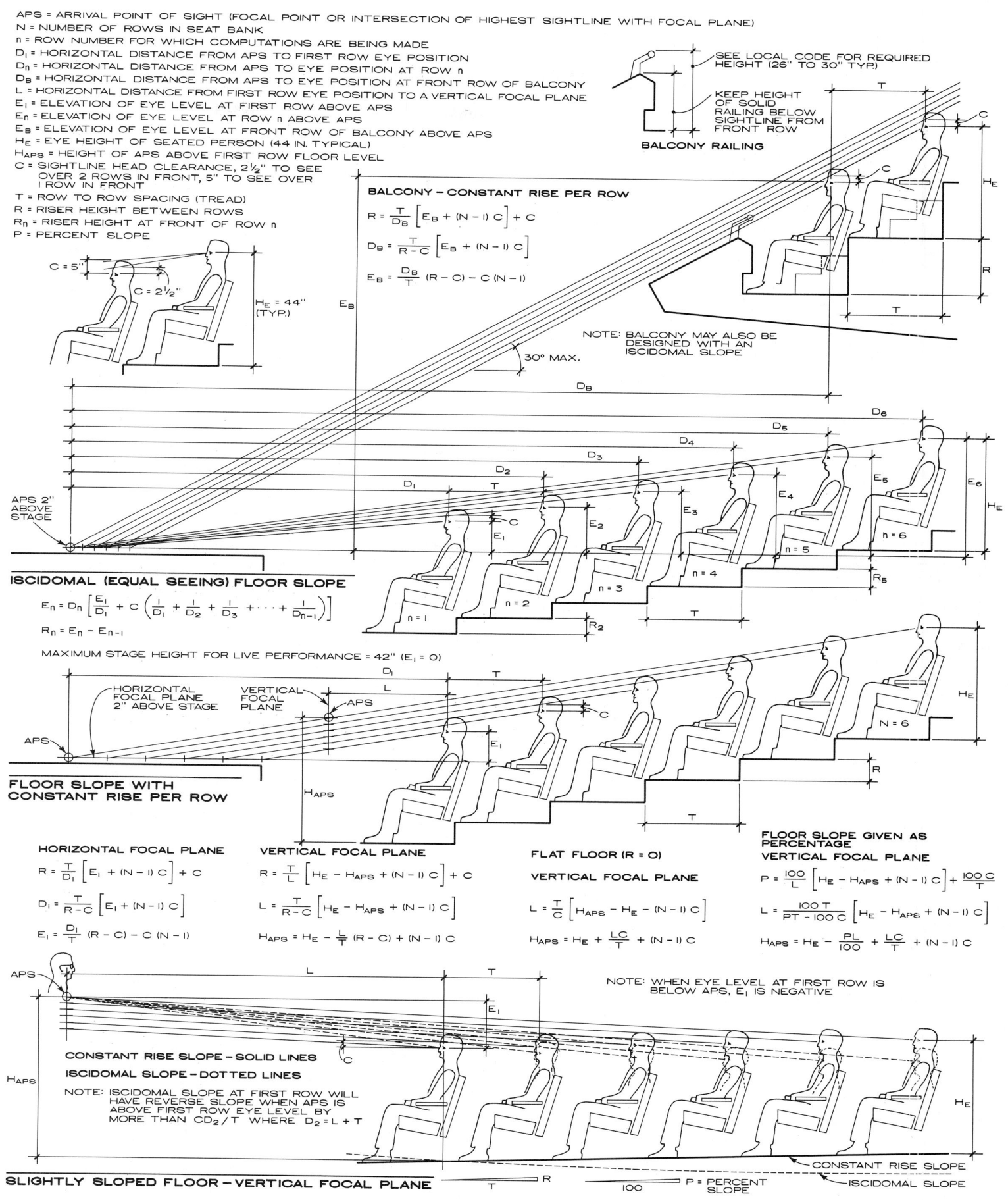

APS = ARRIVAL POINT OF SIGHT (FOCAL POINT OR INTERSECTION OF HIGHEST SIGHTLINE WITH FOCAL PLANE)
N = NUMBER OF ROWS IN SEAT BANK
n = ROW NUMBER FOR WHICH COMPUTATIONS ARE BEING MADE
$D_1$ = HORIZONTAL DISTANCE FROM APS TO FIRST ROW EYE POSITION
$D_n$ = HORIZONTAL DISTANCE FROM APS TO EYE POSITION AT ROW n
$D_B$ = HORIZONTAL DISTANCE FROM APS TO EYE POSITION AT FRONT ROW OF BALCONY
L = HORIZONTAL DISTANCE FROM FIRST ROW EYE POSITION TO A VERTICAL FOCAL PLANE
$E_1$ = ELEVATION OF EYE LEVEL AT FIRST ROW ABOVE APS
$E_n$ = ELEVATION OF EYE LEVEL AT ROW n ABOVE APS
$E_B$ = ELEVATION OF EYE LEVEL AT FRONT ROW OF BALCONY ABOVE APS
$H_E$ = EYE HEIGHT OF SEATED PERSON (44 IN. TYPICAL)
$H_{APS}$ = HEIGHT OF APS ABOVE FIRST ROW FLOOR LEVEL
C = SIGHTLINE HEAD CLEARANCE, 2½" TO SEE OVER 2 ROWS IN FRONT, 5" TO SEE OVER 1 ROW IN FRONT
T = ROW TO ROW SPACING (TREAD)
R = RISER HEIGHT BETWEEN ROWS
$R_n$ = RISER HEIGHT AT FRONT OF ROW n
P = PERCENT SLOPE

SEE LOCAL CODE FOR REQUIRED HEIGHT (26" TO 30" TYP.)
KEEP HEIGHT OF SOLID RAILING BELOW SIGHTLINE FROM FRONT ROW
**BALCONY RAILING**

C = 5"
C = 2½"
$H_E$ = 44" (TYP.)

### BALCONY – CONSTANT RISE PER ROW

$$R = \frac{T}{D_B}\left[E_B + (N-1)\,C\right] + C$$

$$D_B = \frac{T}{R-C}\left[E_B + (N-1)\,C\right]$$

$$E_B = \frac{D_B}{T}(R-C) - C(N-1)$$

NOTE: BALCONY MAY ALSO BE DESIGNED WITH AN ISCIDOMAL SLOPE

30° MAX.

APS 2" ABOVE STAGE

### ISCIDOMAL (EQUAL SEEING) FLOOR SLOPE

$$E_n = D_n\left[\frac{E_1}{D_1} + C\left(\frac{1}{D_1} + \frac{1}{D_2} + \frac{1}{D_3} + \cdots + \frac{1}{D_{n-1}}\right)\right]$$

$$R_n = E_n - E_{n-1}$$

MAXIMUM STAGE HEIGHT FOR LIVE PERFORMANCE = 42" ($E_1$ = O)

HORIZONTAL FOCAL PLANE 2" ABOVE STAGE
VERTICAL FOCAL PLANE
APS

### FLOOR SLOPE WITH CONSTANT RISE PER ROW

**HORIZONTAL FOCAL PLANE**

$$R = \frac{T}{D_1}\left[E_1 + (N-1)\,C\right] + C$$

$$D_1 = \frac{T}{R-C}\left[E_1 + (N-1)\,C\right]$$

$$E_1 = \frac{D_1}{T}(R-C) - C(N-1)$$

**VERTICAL FOCAL PLANE**

$$R = \frac{T}{L}\left[H_E - H_{APS} + (N-1)\,C\right] + C$$

$$L = \frac{T}{R-C}\left[H_E - H_{APS} + (N-1)\,C\right]$$

$$H_{APS} = H_E - \frac{L}{T}(R-C) + (N-1)\,C$$

**FLAT FLOOR (R = O)**
**VERTICAL FOCAL PLANE**

$$L = \frac{T}{C}\left[H_{APS} - H_E - (N-1)\,C\right]$$

$$H_{APS} = H_E + \frac{LC}{T} + (N-1)\,C$$

**FLOOR SLOPE GIVEN AS PERCENTAGE**
**VERTICAL FOCAL PLANE**

$$P = \frac{100}{L}\left[H_E - H_{APS} + (N-1)\,C\right] + \frac{100\,C}{T}$$

$$L = \frac{100\,T}{PT - 100\,C}\left[H_E - H_{APS} + (N-1)\,C\right]$$

$$H_{APS} = H_E - \frac{PL}{100} + \frac{LC}{T} + (N-1)\,C$$

APS
$H_{APS}$
$H_E$

**CONSTANT RISE SLOPE – SOLID LINES**
**ISCIDOMAL SLOPE – DOTTED LINES**

NOTE: ISCIDOMAL SLOPE AT FIRST ROW WILL HAVE REVERSE SLOPE WHEN APS IS ABOVE FIRST ROW EYE LEVEL BY MORE THAN $CD_2/T$ WHERE $D_2 = L + T$

NOTE: WHEN EYE LEVEL AT FIRST ROW IS BELOW APS, $E_1$ IS NEGATIVE

CONSTANT RISE SLOPE
ISCIDOMAL SLOPE
P = PERCENT SLOPE

### SLIGHTLY SLOPED FLOOR – VERTICAL FOCAL PLANE

Peter H. Frink; Frink and Beuchat: Architects; Philadelphia, Pennsylvania

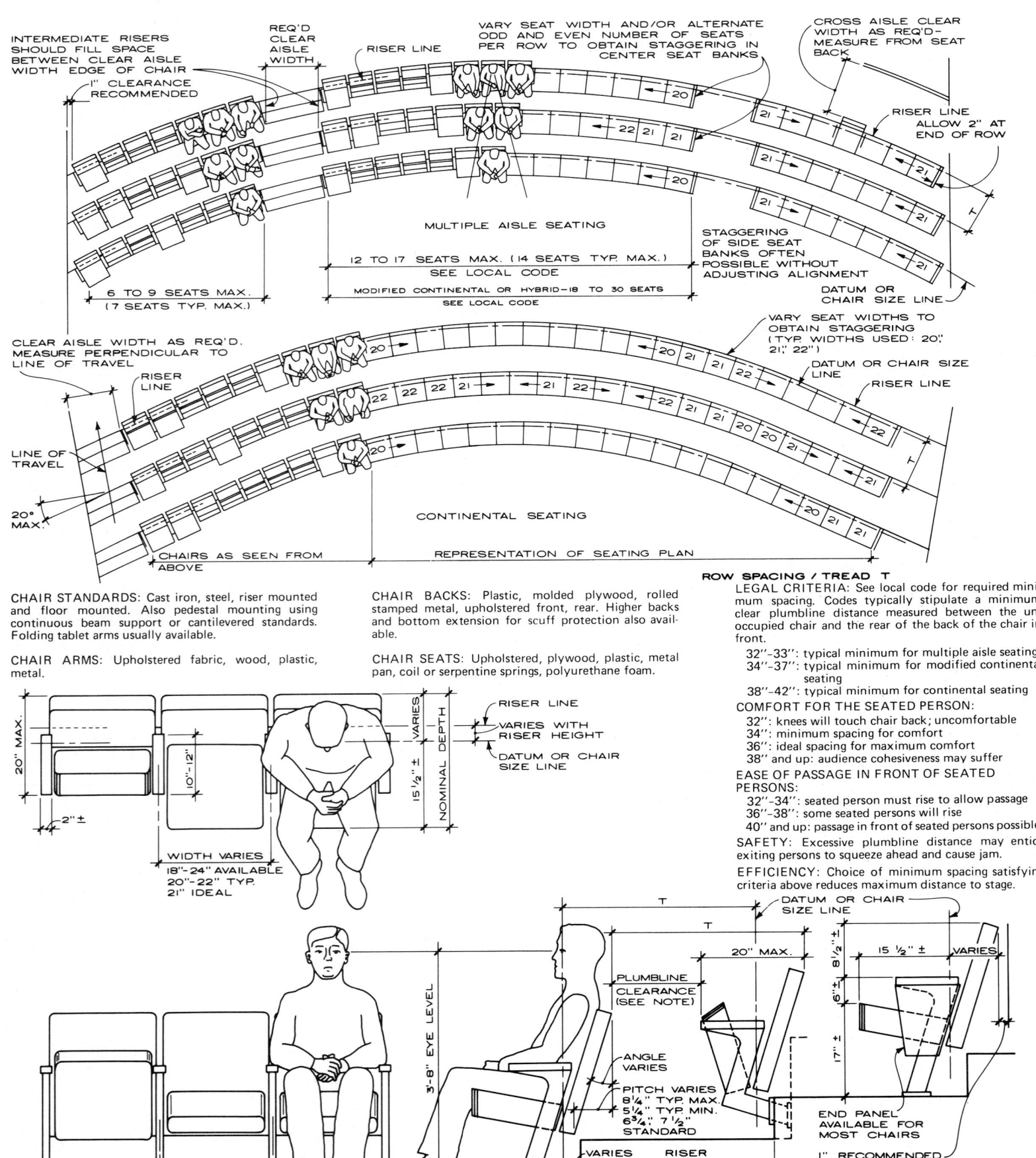

INTERMEDIATE RISERS SHOULD FILL SPACE BETWEEN CLEAR AISLE WIDTH EDGE OF CHAIR 1" CLEARANCE RECOMMENDED

REQ'D CLEAR AISLE WIDTH

RISER LINE

VARY SEAT WIDTH AND/OR ALTERNATE ODD AND EVEN NUMBER OF SEATS PER ROW TO OBTAIN STAGGERING IN CENTER SEAT BANKS

CROSS AISLE CLEAR WIDTH AS REQ'D—MEASURE FROM SEAT BACK

RISER LINE ALLOW 2" AT END OF ROW

MULTIPLE AISLE SEATING

12 TO 17 SEATS MAX. (14 SEATS TYP. MAX.) SEE LOCAL CODE

MODIFIED CONTINENTAL OR HYBRID—18 TO 30 SEATS SEE LOCAL CODE

6 TO 9 SEATS MAX. (7 SEATS TYP. MAX.)

STAGGERING OF SIDE SEAT BANKS OFTEN POSSIBLE WITHOUT ADJUSTING ALIGNMENT

DATUM OR CHAIR SIZE LINE

CLEAR AISLE WIDTH AS REQ'D. MEASURE PERPENDICULAR TO LINE OF TRAVEL

RISER LINE

VARY SEAT WIDTHS TO OBTAIN STAGGERING (TYP. WIDTHS USED: 20", 21," 22")

DATUM OR CHAIR SIZE LINE

RISER LINE

LINE OF TRAVEL

20° MAX.

CONTINENTAL SEATING

CHAIRS AS SEEN FROM ABOVE

REPRESENTATION OF SEATING PLAN

RISER LINE
VARIES WITH RISER HEIGHT
DATUM OR CHAIR SIZE LINE

20" MAX.
10"-12"
2"±
WIDTH VARIES
18"-24" AVAILABLE
20"-22" TYP.
21" IDEAL

VARIES
NOMINAL DEPTH
15 ½" ±

**CHAIR STANDARDS:** Cast iron, steel, riser mounted and floor mounted. Also pedestal mounting using continuous beam support or cantilevered standards. Folding tablet arms usually available.

**CHAIR ARMS:** Upholstered fabric, wood, plastic, metal.

**CHAIR BACKS:** Plastic, molded plywood, rolled stamped metal, upholstered front, rear. Higher backs and bottom extension for scuff protection also available.

**CHAIR SEATS:** Upholstered, plywood, plastic, metal pan, coil or serpentine springs, polyurethane foam.

### ROW SPACING / TREAD T

**LEGAL CRITERIA:** See local code for required minimum spacing. Codes typically stipulate a minimum clear plumbline distance measured between the unoccupied chair and the rear of the back of the chair in front.

32"-33": typical minimum for multiple aisle seating
34"-37": typical minimum for modified continental seating
38"-42": typical minimum for continental seating

**COMFORT FOR THE SEATED PERSON:**
32": knees will touch chair back; uncomfortable
34": minimum spacing for comfort
36": ideal spacing for maximum comfort
38" and up: audience cohesiveness may suffer

**EASE OF PASSAGE IN FRONT OF SEATED PERSONS:**
32"-34": seated person must rise to allow passage
36"-38": some seated persons will rise
40" and up: passage in front of seated persons possible

**SAFETY:** Excessive plumbline distance may entice exiting persons to squeeze ahead and cause jam.

**EFFICIENCY:** Choice of minimum spacing satisfying criteria above reduces maximum distance to stage.

3'-8" EYE LEVEL

CHAIR WIDTH

FLOOR MOUNTED CHAIR

DATUM OR CHAIR SIZE LINE

T
T
20" MAX.

PLUMBLINE CLEARANCE (SEE NOTE)

ANGLE VARIES

PITCH VARIES
8¼" TYP. MAX.
5¼" TYP. MIN.
6¾", 7½" STANDARD

VARIES   RISER MOUNTED CHAIR

8½" ±
6" ±
17" ±
15 ½" ±
VARIES

END PANEL AVAILABLE FOR MOST CHAIRS

1" RECOMMENDED FROM BACK WALL OR RAIL FOR STANDEE

T

Peter H. Frink; Frink and Beuchat: Architects; Philadelphia, Pennsylvania

1    **THEATER DESIGN**

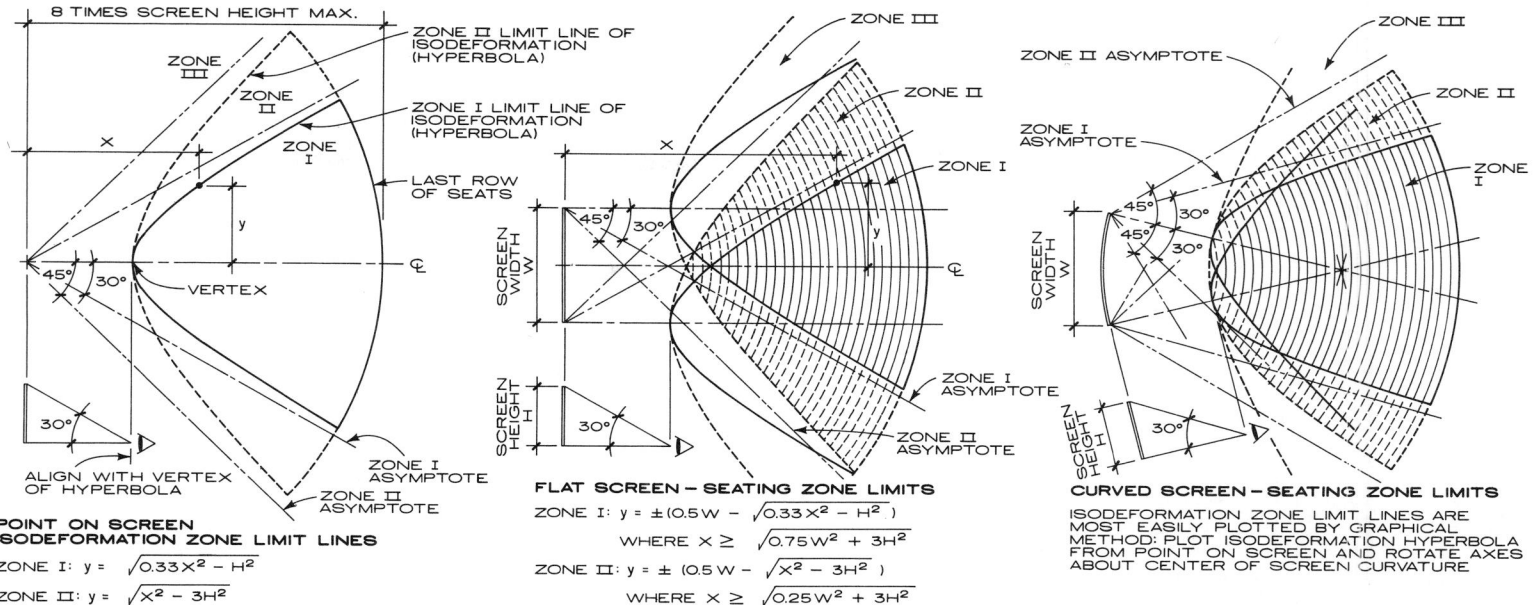

**POINT ON SCREEN ISODEFORMATION ZONE LIMIT LINES**

ZONE I: $y = \sqrt{0.33X^2 - H^2}$

ZONE II: $y = \sqrt{X^2 - 3H^2}$

WHERE H = SCREEN HEIGHT

**FLAT SCREEN – SEATING ZONE LIMITS**

ZONE I: $y = \pm(0.5W - \sqrt{0.33X^2 - H^2})$

WHERE $X \geq \sqrt{0.75W^2 + 3H^2}$

ZONE II: $y = \pm(0.5W - \sqrt{X^2 - 3H^2})$

WHERE $X \geq \sqrt{0.25W^2 + 3H^2}$

**CURVED SCREEN – SEATING ZONE LIMITS**

ISODEFORMATION ZONE LIMIT LINES ARE MOST EASILY PLOTTED BY GRAPHICAL METHOD: PLOT ISODEFORMATION HYPERBOLA FROM POINT ON SCREEN AND ROTATE AXES ABOUT CENTER OF SCREEN CURVATURE

## VIEWING OF A POINT ON A SCREEN

A projected image on a screen will have an apparent distortion when viewed from an angle beyond the perpendicular to a point on the screen in plan and section. The boundary of the seating area for which spectators will see the same apparent distortion is called the line of isodeformation. This shape in plan is a hyperbola, which is defined in plan by asymptotes from the point on the screen.

1. SEATING ZONE I: Distortion of a projected image exists but will not be noticed from seats falling within the hyperbola which is bounded by the asymptotes drawn from a point on the screen at an angle of no greater than 30° from the perpendicular at that point on the screen. The minimum horizontal distance from the vertex of the hyperbola to the screen is determined by the limitation of the vertical angle from the eye of the first row to the top of the screen to a maximum of 30 to 35°.

2. SEATING ZONE II: Distortions of the projected image will be noticed but tolerated from the seats falling outside of Zone I but within the hyperbola bounded by the asymptotes drawn from a point on the screen at an angle no greater than 45° from the perpendicular at that point.

3. SEATING ZONE III (seating placed beyond the limits of Zone II): Distortions of the projected image will not be tolerated and the viewer will refuse to use the seats placed here.

## VIEWING OF A FLAT SCREEN

A projected image occupies a space on a screen rather than a point. The seating area, defined by the isodeformation lines, for which the entire width of the projected image is considered, is represented by the area common to the space within the two hyperbolas which are drawn within asymptotes from both sides of the projected image. The area in Zone I for a wide, projected image is less than the Zone I seating area for a point on the screen. The seating area in Zone II for a wide image on a flat screen may approximately correspond to the Zone I area for a point on the screen.

## VIEWING OF A CURVED SCREEN

Zone I seating area for a given screen width can be increased by curving the screen. An appropriate screen curve will cause an overlap of the hyperbolas drawn from the sides of the projected image in such a way that they define a greater common seating area.

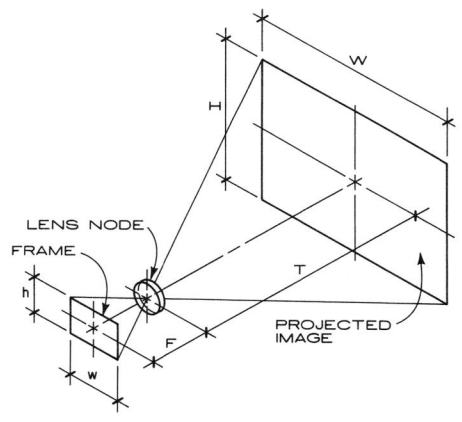

**BASIC PROJECTION GEOMETRY**

## PROJECTION FORMULAS

$T = F(W/w) = F(H/h)$
$F = T(w/W) = T(h/H)$
$W = w(T/F)$
$H = h(T/F)$

where

W = picture width
H = picture height
w = frame width
h = frame height
T = throw distance
F = focal length

## ASPECT RATIOS AND FRAME DIMENSIONS FOR PROJECTED MEDIA

| PROJECTION MEDIUM | FRAME (mm) h x w | ASPECT RATIO | FRAME (IN.) h | w |
|---|---|---|---|---|
| 8 mm motion picture | (3.28 x 4.37) | 1 : 1.33 | 0.129 | 0.172 |
| Super 8 motion picture | (4.01 x 5.36) | 1.33 | 0.158 | 0.211 |
| 16 mm motion picture | (7.21 x 9.65) | 1.34 | 0.284 | 0.380 |
| 16 mm CinemaScope | (7.21 x 9.65) | 2.68 | 0.284 | 2 x 0.380 |
| 35 mm motion picture | (15.2 x 20.9) | 1.375 | 0.600 | 0.825 |
| 35 mm CinemaScope | (18.2 x 42.6) | 2.34 | 0.715 | 2 x 0.839 |
| 70 mm motion picture | (22.1 x 49.0) | 2.21 | 0.868 | 1.913 |
| 70 mm IMAX | (51.0 x 71.0) | 1.39 | 2.00 | 2.80 |
| 35 mm filmstrip | (17.0 x 22.5) | 1.32 | 0.668 | 0.885 |
| 2 x 2 35 mm double frame slides | (22.9 x 34.2) | 1.493 | 0.902 | 1.346 |
| 2 x 2 35 mm half frame slides | (15.9 x 22.9) | 1.44 | 0.626 | 0.902 |
| 2 x 2 35 mm square slides | (22.9 x 22.9) | 1.00 | 0.902 | 0.902 |
| 126 Insta-Load slides | (12.7 x 17.0) | 1.34 | 0.500 | 0.669 |
| 2 x 2 Instamatic slides | (26.5 x 26.5) | 1.00 | 1.043 | 1.043 |
| 2 x 2 superslides | (38.0 x 38.0) | 1.00 | 1.496 | 1.496 |
| 2¼ x 2¼ slides | (51.6 x 51.6) | 1.00 | 2.030 | 2.030 |
| 2¾ x 2¾ slides | (55.5 x 55.5) | 1.00 | 2.187 | 2.187 |
| 3½ x 4 lantern slides | (69.9 x 76.2) | 1.09 | 2.75 | 3.00 |
| 3½ x 4 Polaroid slides | (61.0 x 82.8) | 1.36 | 2.40 | 3.26 |
| 4 x 5 lantern slides | (88.9 x 114.3) | 1.28 | 3.50 | 4.50 |
| Overhead projector | — | 1.26 | 7.50 | 9.50 |
| Overhead projector | — | 1.00 | 10.00 | 10.00 |
| Television projector | — | 1.33 | — | — |

Peter H. Frink; Frink and Beuchat: Architects; Philadelphia, Pennsylvania

## PROJECTION ROOM DETAILS

1. DIMENSIONS: 14 ft deep by 21 ft wide minimum for two projectors. Add 5 ft width for each additional piece of projection apparatus. Ceiling height should never be less than 8 ft; 9 ft is preferred.
2. WALL CONSTRUCTION: Wall separating projection room and auditorium should be made of brick, concrete, or concrete block to minimize sound transmission.
3. FLOOR CONSTRUCTION: Provide for a live load of 200 psf minimum. Recommend 4 in. reinforced concrete slab, 4 in. tamped cinder fill (to accommodate concealed conduit), and 2 in. topping slab.
4. FLOOR FINISH: Recommend heavy battleship linoleum. A good grade of vinyl tile is also acceptable.
5. PORTS: Projection ports should be glazed with ¼ in. optical quality or select water white glass. Observation ports may be glazed with ¼ in. select plate glass that is free from distortion.

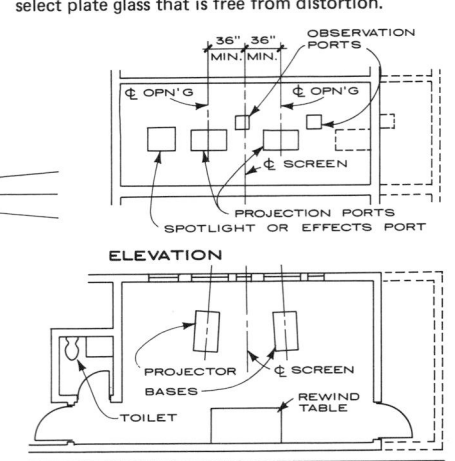

REAR VIEW     SIDE VIEW
**TYPICAL 35 MM MOVIE PROJECTOR**

ELEVATION

**TYPICAL PROJECTION ROOM PLAN**

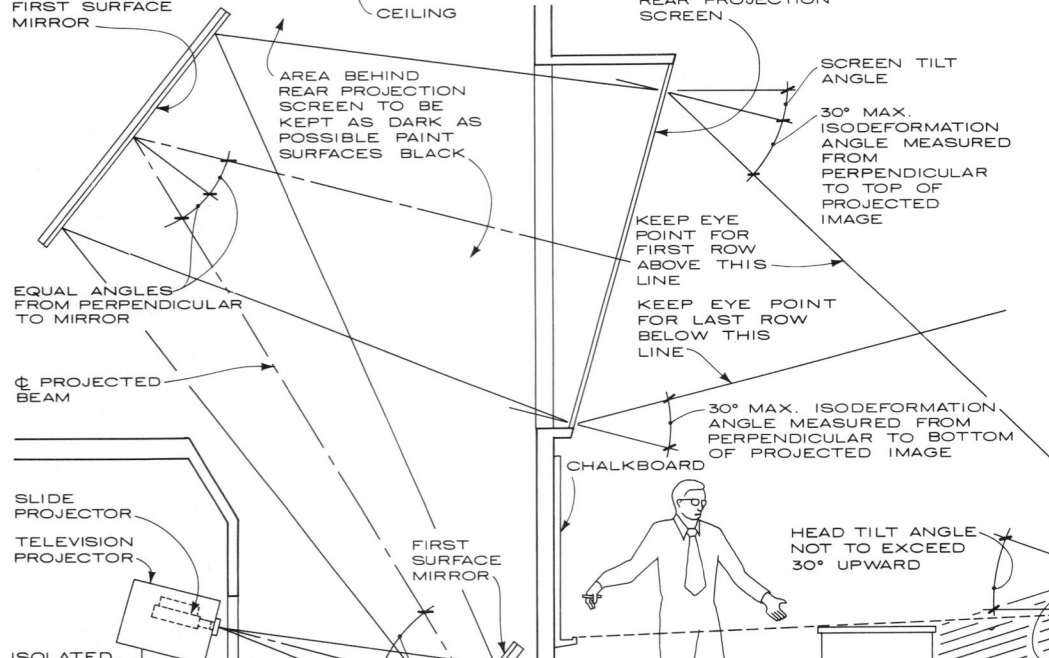

**REAR PROJECTION**

## SCREEN TYPES

An ideal screen would be one that would diffuse all the light from the projector into the audience spaces with uniform brightness for every viewer and simultaneously reject any stray light falling on the screen, reflecting it away from the audience. Most common screen materials possess characteristics that fall short of the ideal.

MATTE SCREEN     GAIN SCREEN

### MATTE WHITE SCREEN

Uniform brightness from all viewing angles. Good resolution and color fidelity. Because much of the light reflected from a matte white screen falls outside of the viewing area, the picture will be less bright than a picture from the same source on a gain screen. Rejects less stray light than gain screens.

### GAIN SCREENS

Mechanical or chemical treatment of screen surface increases the amount of light reflected in the direction of the audience and decreases the amount reflected in other directions. Because brightness from all viewing angles is not uniform, gain screens dictate a narrower viewing area. For high gain screens, viewing area should be restricted to zone I as described on other pages. While the picture on a gain screen will be brighter than on a matte screen, resolution and color fidelity may suffer somewhat depending on the type of gain screen used. Gain screen types include: beaded, silver, pearl, and lenticular.

### AVAILABLE SCREEN SIZES

1. Tripod screens: 30 x 40 to 72 x 86 in., bottom of screen usually 3 to 4 ft above floor (adjustable).
2. Table or wall hung screens: 18 x 24 to 36 x 36 in.
3. Wall or ceiling mounted, manually operated spring loaded roll-up: 50 x 50 in. to 12 x 12 ft.
4. Wall or ceiling mounted, electrically operated roll-up: 50 x 50 in. to 20 x 20 or 12 x 24 ft. Custom sizes: up to 40 ft wide.
5. Bottom roller, rope controlled: 5 ft 6 in. x 14 to 30 x 30 ft. Winch controlled: up to 40 ft wide.
6. Framed screen (lace and grommet): custom made to any size. Economical for larger sizes. Frames made of 2 x 6 in. lumber or steel tubing or angle. Wood frames usually 2 ft wider than screen size. Metal frames usually 1 ft wider than screen size.
7. Rear projection screens: 3 x 4 to 7 x 14 ft. Custom sizes, acrylic: up to 10 x 12 or 8 x 14 ft. Custom sizes, glass: up to 10 x 25 ft.

### NOTES

1. The average rear projection screen is usually smaller than a possible front projection screen because of physical and/or economic reasons. Front projection, therefore, is usually preferable for larger audiences. The size of a rear projection screen may be restricted by its greater cost and by limitations of projection geometry for lack of space.
2. Projection equipment and projection formulas are the same for both front and rear projection. Front projection usually permits an adequate throw distance over the heads of an audience in order to fill a larger screen. An equivalent depth is not typically available for rear projection. Larger images for rear projection can be achieved through the use of shorter focal length lenses which allow a shorter throw distance. Mirrors can also be used to bend or fold a projected beam into a shallower space behind the screen.
3. Front projection usually results in better resolution, better color fidelity, and better contrast ratios.
4. The principal advantage of rear projection over front projection is the ability of the rear projection screen to reject stray ambient light in the auditorium. This ability may allow a higher light level within a learning space for, for example, taking notes while viewing a projected image.
5. Rear projection will also allow a speaker or a spectator to stand in front of a screen without casting a shadow.

Peter H. Frink, AIA; Assembly Places International; Philadelphia, Pennsylvania

**1** **THEATER DESIGN**

## PLANNING AUDIOVISUAL FACILITIES

Audiovisual facilities, designed for easy operation, are electronically complex. Innovative products are developed continuously. Information here is for planning guidance. A qualified audiovisual specialist should be consulted.

## SIZING IMAGES

Because image widths vary, image height (H) is used as a determinate, assuming a horizontal format common to most projected images. V (or the maximum viewing distance) is equivalent to H x 8. The minimum comfortable viewing distance is about H x 2.5. These values, determined experimentally, assume graphics are prepared to standards recommended by Eastman Kodak Company and other audiovisual sources. Incorrectly prepared graphics may not be legible. For example, a comfortable viewing distance for a 5 ft. high image is figured: V = 5 ft. x 8 ft. = 40 ft. maximum.

Screen size for 35mm slides would be figured as follows: 5 ft. high x (aspect ratio* height) = 5 ft. x (1.49* x 5 ft.) or 5 ft. x 7.45 ft.

*NOTE: For aspect ratios for diverse projected media see slide, movie, and overhead projection page.

For vertical format intermixed with horizontal, the screen would be 7.4 ft. square. A standard 8 ft. x 8 ft. screen is ideal for slides, but an 8 ft. x 10 ft. screen provides flexibility for wide-screen film projection. Room ceiling height critically affects viewing area adequacy.

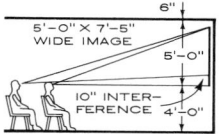
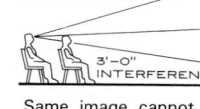

Bottom of image should be 4 ft. above floor to avoid excessive interference.

Same image cannot be used vertically without interference.

**ROOM CEILING HEIGHT FOR SCREEN**

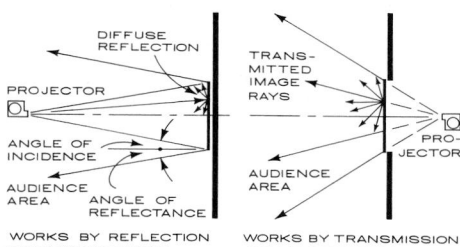

WORKS BY REFLECTION
**FRONT SCREEN**

WORKS BY TRANSMISSION
**REAR SCREEN**

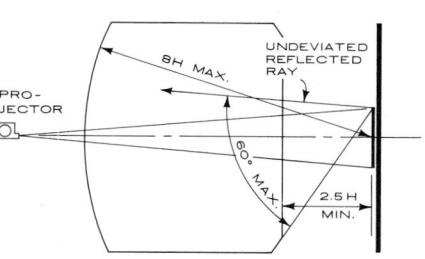

**FRONT SCREEN SEATING AREA**

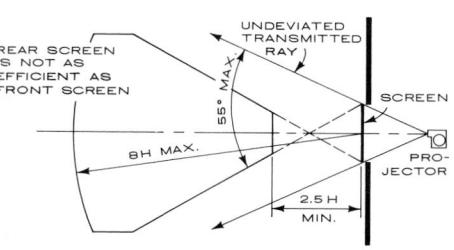

**REAR SCREEN SEATING AREA**

H. Thomas Wilson, AIA; Pasadena, California
Wadsworth, see data sources

## DUAL IMAGES

Seating area is reduced for dual images. Curved screens improve edge brightness and widen the effective viewing area. Triple images are undesirable except in multimedia presentations where screen brilliance and legibility for all seats is secondary to the impact of multiple images. The depth required for rear screen can be reduced with optical mirrors, either glass or stretched mylar.

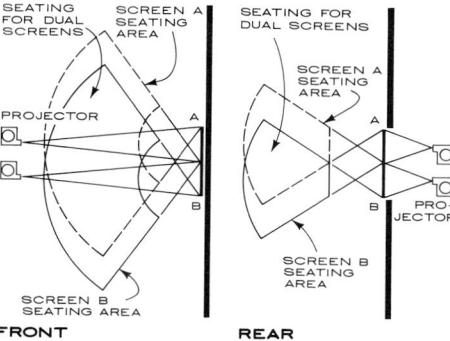

**FRONT DUAL SCREENS**

**REAR DUAL SCREENS**

| FRONT SCREEN | VS. | REAR SCREEN |
|---|---|---|
| Larger seating area | | Smaller seating area |
| Darkened room | | Partially lighted |
| Can use curved or flat screen | | Flat screen. Acrylic screens with fresnel lens pattern can brighten image at side of viewing area |
| Screen can be roll-up, portable, or flat wall | | Fixed screen with projection space behind |
| Durable screen materials | | Fragile material such as glass or plastic subject to scratching |
| Audience may interface with and block image | | Audience has less effect on image |
| Long focal length or zoom lenses, less distortion | | Short focal length lenses potentially have more distortion |

## PROJECTION EQUIPMENT

Common audiovisual optical projection equipment includes programmable 35mm slide projectors, 16mm motion picture projectors with sound track, overhead projectors for transparencies, and opaque projectors. Special light sources such as xenon can augment normal projector lighting to increase viewing distances. Special situations may require other equipment such as commercial motion picture projectors.

## TELEVISION

Video cassette players and television monitors or receivers gradually are replacing 16mm projectors. Television equipment costs more and film image quality is better; however, users have become accustomed to the convenience of recorded cassettes in VCRs.

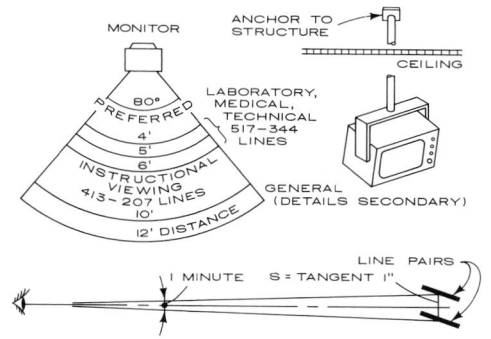

**TELEVISION/VIDEO VIEWING**

Television screen viewing distances are based on the human eye's ability to distinguish line pairs (not to be confused with television image lines). One minute of arc has been established experimentally as the minimum angle discriminated by viewers with normal vision.

| SCREEN DIAGONAL | 80° VIEWING AREA | | NUMBER OF CHAIRS AT EACH SET |
|---|---|---|---|
| 12 in. | 52 sf | 4.8 sq.M | 7 |
| 19 in. | 93 sf | 12.2 sq.M | 16 |
| 21 in. | 160 sf | 14.9 sq.M | 20 |
| 25 in. | 226 sf | 21.0 sq.M | 28 |

Projection television is feasible. Large screen projection requires special, expensive equipment. Small screen, liquid-cooled cathode ray systems, now available, allow up to a 6 ft. high screen. Larger screens theoretically can be used, but image brightness falls off rapidly. Keystone distortion can be corrected electronically.

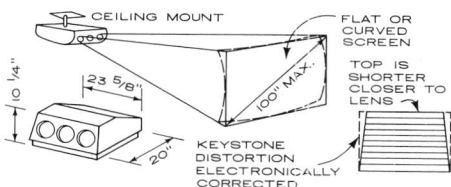

**LIQUID-COOLED VIDEO PROJECTOR**

## TELECONFERENCING AND VIDEOCONFERENCING

Teleconferencing is voice or data communication from and to remote locations with an origination site.

Videoconferencing is teleconferencing with visual contact and pictorial images added to voice and data communications.

1. Audioconferencing through three-way telephone calls or bridging services is least expensive.
2. Installing computer equipment and additional communication channels can add graphic capability via telephone lines, electronic blackboard, and computer-generated displays.
3. To add freeze-frame video slow scan requires one line for voice, one line for data, and more specialized electronic equipment.
4. Computer conferencing using personal computers and telephone modems is simple when confined to PC display screen. Larger images require reformatting for video.
5. Full-motion videoconferencing requires satellite dish antennae, receivers, or cable and an expensive investment in equipment such as uplinks, downlinks, and ground station equipment. It provides a good sense of participation, but it is the most expensive method of communication. Encryption is required if security must be maintained.

## VIDEOCONFERENCE FACILITY

Combination television studio with camera and audiovisual conference room. A minimum of two screens is necessary, one to display graphics and the other to focus on participants.

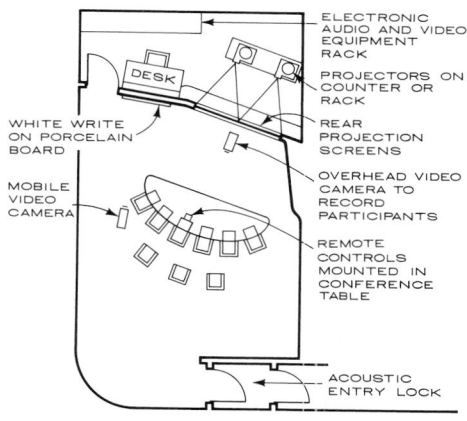

**VIDEO CONFERENCE FACILITY**

**THEATER DESIGN** 1

## STAGE LIGHTING SYSTEM DESIGN GENERAL COMMENTS

The purpose of a stage lighting system is to provide a flexible arrangement of dimmers, lighting positions, and outlet devices such that stage lighting fixtures may be placed where needed and controlled individually or in groups according to the differing requirements of each production. While it is impossible to develop rules of thumb which will be adequate or appropriate in all cases, several guidelines have been listed below as an aid to determining the proper scope of system required. Several generic cases have been listed. Common terms and equipment components are defined.

## CONSIDERATIONS

The planning of a stage lighting system should involve the following considerations:

1. Type of use
2. Size of performing area
3. Size of theater, location of stage lighting positions
4. Budget

Determinations will have to be made about the following subjects:

1. Dimmer-per-circuit or patched circuit system
2. Quantity of dimmers
3. Quantity and distribution of stage lighting circuits
4. Electrical feed size
5. Type of stage lighting outlet devices
6. Type of control console
7. Type and quantity of stage lighting fixtures and accessories

## STAGE LIGHTING SYSTEM TERMS AND COMPONENTS DEFINED

### DIMMER

A device which controls the intensity of stage lighting fixtures; a remotely controlled electronic device in current practice. Standard sizes are 1.2 kW, 2.4 kW, 6.0 kW, 12.0 kW, at 120 V. Dimmers may be purchased in rack cabinets in large quantities (96 or more) or in small portable packages which can be wall mounted (6, 12, or 18 dimmers).

### CIRCUIT

A grounded stage lighting circuit; usually no common neutrals are permitted. Load sizes depend in part on local codes—20 A is average, 15 A is maximum in some areas; some 50 A are often also provided. Circuits are distributed throughout the theater for fixture plug-in and terminate either at a dimmer rack, patch panel, or transfer panel.

### DIMMER-PER-CIRCUIT

A configuration whereby every stage lighting circuit home runs to an independent dimmer. This is more economical than a patch panel scheme in most cases.

### PATCH PANEL

A custom-made device for interconnecting a large number of stage lighting circuits to a small number of dimmers. This is more expensive than a dimmer-per-circuit configuration in most cases.

### TRANSFER PANEL

A custom-made device enabling permanent circuits to be disconnected from the theater's dimming system and connected to a show's touring dimming system. Front-of-house circuits are generally made "transferable" in this way in large multipurpose theaters that must accommodate tours.

### FRONT-OF-HOUSE

In a proscenium theater, the audience side of the proscenium. Abbreviated "FOH."

### FOLLOWSPOT

A very bright manually operated spotlight used to "follow" a performer around the stage. Light source can be incandescent, carbon arc, xenon, or HMI.

### LEKO, FRESNEL, ELLIPSOIDAL, PARCAN, SCOOP, FLOODLIGHT

Theatrical lighting fixtures.

### STRIPLIGHT

A continuous fixture containing a number of lamps, used for downlight, backlight, footlight, and cyclorama lighting—usually 6 or 8 ft long with 12 lamps in three or four circuits.

### CONTROL CONSOLE

Often called the "light board." A computerized, manual, or hybrid control device for stage lighting dimmers. Generic types include 2, 5, or 10 scene "preset consoles" (manual) and "memory consoles" (computerized). Older installations may have mechanically operated resistance or autotransformer dimmers in which the control console and the dimmer rack are essentially one device.

### CONNECTOR STRIP

A type of outlet device for stage lighting circuits; essentially a continuous wireway with outlets or pigtails.

### OUTLET BOX

An outlet device for stage lighting circuits. Box size and circuit quantities vary. Surface-mounted or recessed styles available. Circuit numbers must appear on the faceplate (with adhesive labels or engraved).

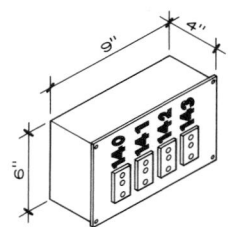

**OUTLET BOX**

### BOX BOOM

An important front-of-house side wall lighting position in a proscenium theater. See diagram below.

### COVE, BEAM, SLOT, TRUSS

A front-of-house lighting position located at the auditorium ceiling. See diagram below.

### FOLLOWSPOT BOOTH

Houses the followspots. Enclosed, if possible, and ventilated as per code. Usually at or near the rear of the house, and quite high; 30°–45° to the edge of the stage preferred. Four spots require a booth nominally 24 ft wide x 10 ft deep; two spots require one 12 ft wide x 10 ft deep.

### CONTROL BOOTH

Primary location for control console. Good view of stage preferred. Often located on the main level at the rear of the house. Houselighting controls should be duplicated here as well as backstage.

### DIMMER ROOM

Location for dimmer racks. Can be remote from the stage. Locate for efficiency of load and feed wire conduit runs. Ventilate to accommodate heat load (approximately 5% connected load). Control humidity to protect equipment.

### BOOMS, LADDERS, TORMS, TORMENTORS

On-stage side lighting positions. Nonarchitectural; located temporarily for each production as required.

### PIPES, BATTENS, ELECTRICS

On-stage overhead lighting positions. Usually rigging pipes or pipe grid members. In a proscenium theater often one or more rigging pipes will be permanently designated as "electrics" and served with connector strips attached directly to the pipe.

### CYCLORAMA, CYC

A large seamless white or pale blue backdrop, used scenically to represent the sky or provide a surface on which abstract colors and patterns can be projected with stage lighting fixtures. Usually cloth; some plaster cycs exist, but are difficult (some say impossible) to repair adequately once cracked or marred. Plaster is not recommended.

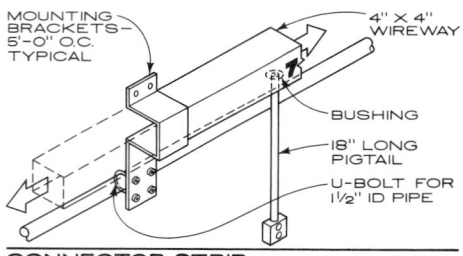

**CONNECTOR STRIP**

MOUNTING BRACKETS— 5'-0" O.C. TYPICAL

4" X 4" WIREWAY

BUSHING

18" LONG PIGTAIL

U-BOLT FOR 1½" ID PIPE

## RECOMMENDED PARAMETERS FOR STAGE LIGHTING SYSTEMS

| THEATER TYPE | NUMBER OF SEATS | FEED SIZE* | CIRCUIT QUANTITY | DIMMER QUANTITY |
|---|---|---|---|---|
| Elementary school | Varies | 100 | 24–36 | 18–36† |
| Junior high, or middle school | Varies | 300 | 75–100 | 75–100 |
| High school | Varies | 400 | 100–150 | 100–150 |
| Studio theater | 75–300 | 400 | 150–200 | 36–200† |
| Educational drama theater | 300–750 | 800 | 200–400 | 200–400 |
| Small professional theater | 750–1500 | 1200 | 300–500 | 300–500 |
| Medium size theater | 1500–2000 | 1600 | 400–600 | 400–600 |
| Large multipurpose theater, civic theater, road house | Over 2000 | 2400 | 600–800 | 600–800 |

*Feed size shown in amps, 3 phase, 120/208 V Y.
†A simple patch system where the circuits terminate in male pigtails which can be plugged directly into a small quantity of portable dimmer packs is generally more economical for small installations with limited budgets than a dimmer-per-circuit scheme.

Joshua Dachs; Jules Fisher Associates Inc., Theatre Consultants; New York, New York

1  THEATER DESIGN

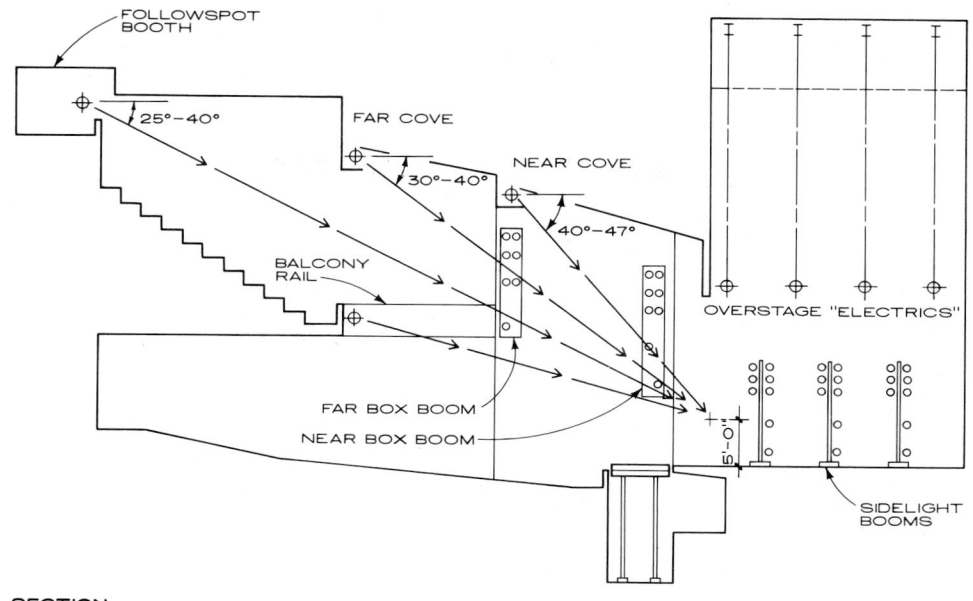

SECTION

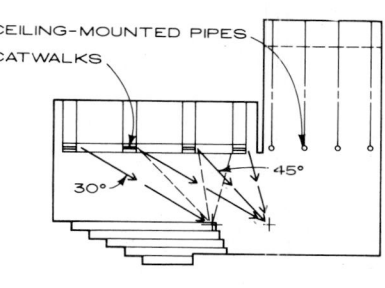

SECTION

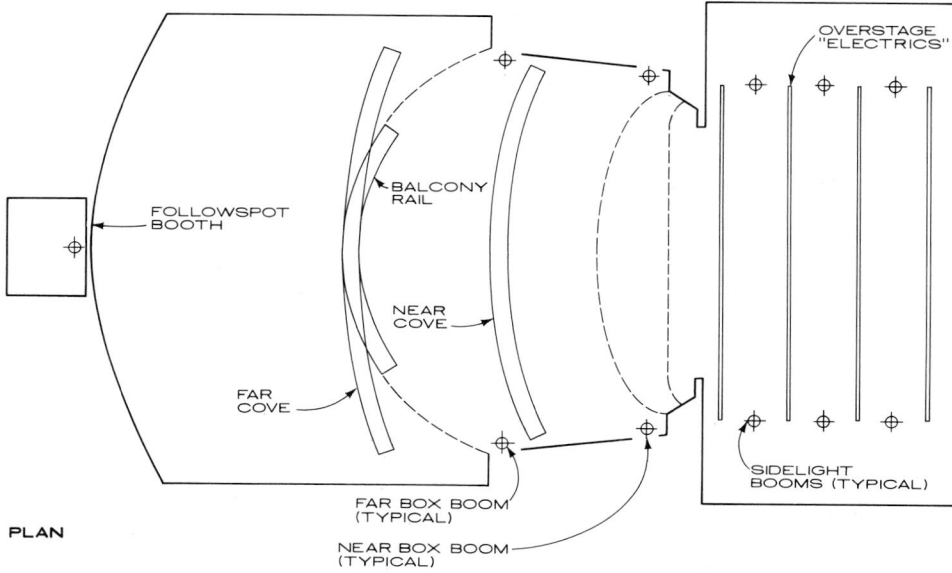

PLAN

PROSCENIUM THEATER

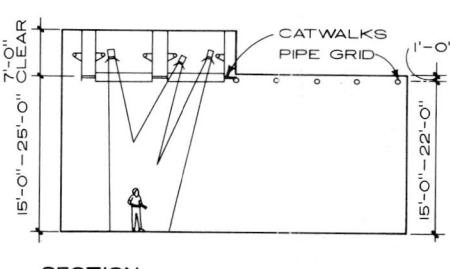

PLAN

THRUST THEATER

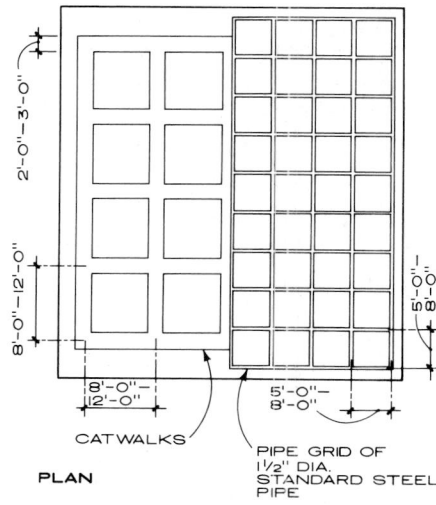

SECTION

## STAGE LIGHTING POSITIONS

It is crucial that a theater be provided with adequate, easily accessible stage lighting positions, served with an adequate quantity of circuits. Accessibility is a key issue. Lighting positions in an active theater need to be accessed daily to maintain, focus, and color the fixtures. Safety and ease must be kept in mind, as well as crew size, which is crucial to theater economics. Using a ladder is both time-consuming and dangerous and requires more than one stagehand. A catwalk is much safer, less time-consuming, and only requires one stagehand.

In a proscenium theater lighting is done from a variety of positions and angles. Frontlighting is provided by side wall positions called box booms, the balcony railing, and ceiling positions which can be recessed within the ceiling or exposed as catwalks. Followspots are generally located in a booth at the top rear of the theater (see definitions). On stage, rigging sets with dedicated stage lighting outlet devices (connector strips or drop boxes) and portable vertical floor-mounted pipes called booms provide positions for downlighting, sidelighting, and backlighting. These positions are *all* important, and every attempt should be made to provide them.

In flexible studio or black-box theaters a pipe grid or a system of catwalks should be provided over the entire floor area of the theater to which lighting equipment (and scenery) can be attached. This grid should be well served by stage lighting circuits in boxes or connector strips. A two-way grid of 1½ in. diameter pipe, nominally 4–6 ft o.c. should be adequate in most cases, accessed by ladder from the floor. The catwalk system is preferable, but requires a taller room.

In a thrust or arena theater, a grid or a series of catwalks should be provided over the main stage area to accommodate downlighting, sidelighting, and backlighting. Catwalks, ceiling slots, or ceiling-mounted pipes should be provided for frontlight and low washes, similar to the balcony rail or second cove in a proscenium theater. If there is a conventional stagehouse behind the thrust, it should be served in the same way as a proscenium theater's stagehouse, with overhead pipes and side booms.

## RECOMMENDED REFERENCE MATERIAL

*Stage Lighting—A guide to the planning of theatres and public building auditoriums*. Illuminating Engineering Society Report #CP-45, 1983.

In most cases it is recommended that the services of a qualified theater consultant be retained.

Joshua Dachs; Jules Fisher Associates Inc., Theatre Consultants; New York, New York

STUDIO THEATER ("BLACK BOX")

**THEATER DESIGN**    1

## NOTES

Sound is produced by a vibrating object or surface. In order for sound to be transmitted or propagated, it requires an elastic medium. The most common medium for transmission is the air. Such sound is called "air-borne sound." However, sound can also be easily transmitted through common building materials and components such as steel, concrete, wood and metal framing, piping, and gypsum wallboard. This type of sound is called "structure-borne sound."

A-weighted decibel [dB(A)] is a standard single-number rating representing the overall sound energy of a given source. The A-weighting network in a sound level meter filters sound in a manner similar to the human ear by downgrading low frequencies.

## DECIBEL SCALE

The decibel (dB) scale is a logarithmic scale based on 10 times the logarithm of a ratio of sound pressures. The decibel levels of two noise sources can not be added directly; instead use this simplified method:

| difference between two sound levels, in dB | 0–1 | 2–3 | 4–9 | >10 |
|---|---|---|---|---|
| add to the higher level | 3 | 2 | 1 | 0 |

For example:  90 dB + 20 dB = 90 dB
60 dB + 60 dB = 63 dB

## OCTAVE BAND

An octave band covers the range from one frequency (Hz) to twice that frequency, f to 2f.

## SUBJECTIVE FACTORS: EFFECT OF CHANGE IN SOUND PRESSURE LEVEL

| CHANGE IN SOUND PRESSURE LEVEL (+ OR −) (dB) | CHANGE IN APPARENT LOUDNESS |
|---|---|
| 3 | Barely perceptible |
| 5 | Clearly noticeable |
| 10 | Dramatic: Twice as loud (OR ½) |
| 15 | Dramatic: Three times as loud (OR ⅓) |
| 20 | Dramatic: Four times as loud (OR ¼) |

## FREQUENCY OF COMMON SOUNDS

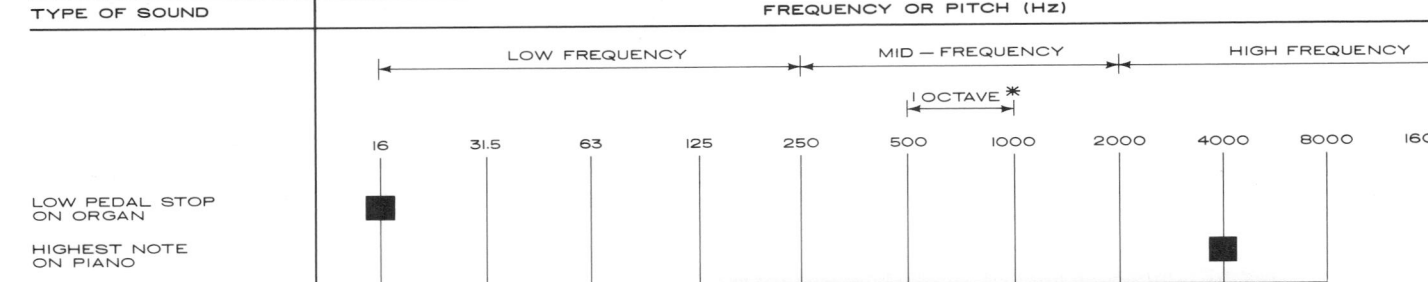
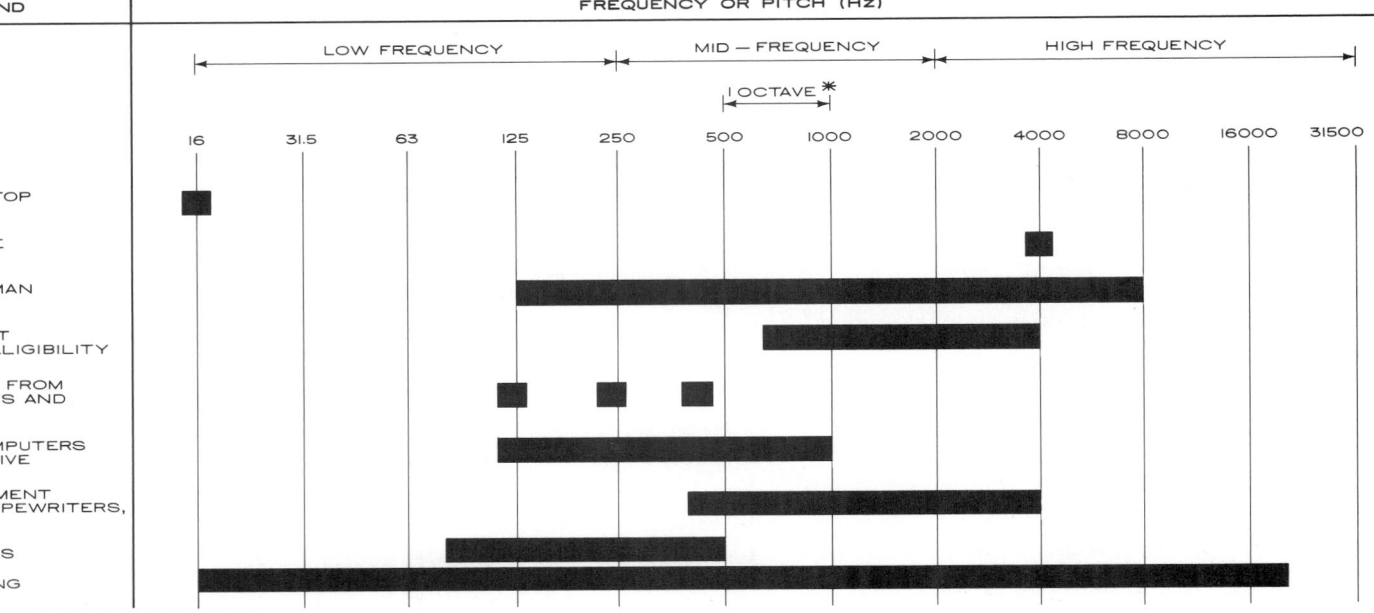

*OCTAVE — A FREQUENCY RATIO OF 2:1

## RELATIONSHIP OF SOUND LEVEL AND SUBJECTIVE LOUDNESS

| SOUND LEVEL (dBA) | SUBJECTIVE EVALUATIONS | ENVIRONMENT OUTDOOR | ENVIRONMENT INDOOR | COMMENTS |
|---|---|---|---|---|
| 140 | Deafening | Near jet aircraft and artillery fire | | |
| 130 | Threshold of pain | | | |
| 120 | Threshold of feeling | Elevated train | Hard rock band | |
| 110 | | Jet flyover at 1000 ft | Inside propeller plane | Continuous exposure above here is likely to degrade the hearing of most people |
| 100 | Very loud | Power mower, motorcycle at 25 ft, auto horn at 10 ft | | |
| 90 | | Propeller plane flyover at 1000 ft, noisy urban street | Full symphony or band, food blender, noisy factory | |
| 80 | Moderately loud | Diesel truck at 40 mph at 50 ft | Inside auto at high speed, garbage disposal, dishwasher | |
| 70 | Loud | | Face-to-face conversation, vacuum cleaner, electric typewriter | |
| 60 | Moderate | Air conditioning condenser at 15 ft, near freeway auto traffic | General office | |
| 50 | Quiet | Large transformer at 100 ft | | Range of Speech |
| 40 | | Birdcalls | Private office, soft radio music in apartment | |
| 30 | Very quiet | Quiet residential neighborhood | Bedroom, average residence without stereo | |
| 20 | | Rustling leaves | Quiet theater, whisper | |
| 10 | Just audible | | | |
| 0 | Threshold of hearing | | | |

Carl J. Rosenberg, AIA; BBN Laboratories, Inc.; Cambridge, Massachusetts

1 **ACOUSTIC DESIGN**

**NOTE**

The material below outlines a design procedure, in abbreviated form, for the architect to use in analyzing a noise control problem and developing a solution or solutions. The three major elements of an acoustical circuit—source, path, and receiver—can each be quantified as shown here; hence there is no need for guesswork.

1. SELECT RECOMMENDED BACKGROUND NOISE DESIGN CRITERIA FOR TYPICAL OCCUPANCIES

| TYPE OF SPACE | RECOMMENDED MAXIMUM BACKGROUND NOISE CRITERION CURVE* |
|---|---|
| Broadcast studios, concert halls | NC 15–25 |
| Legitimate theaters, churches (no amplification) | NC 20–30 |
| Large conference rooms, small auditoriums, orchestra rehearsal rooms, movie theaters, courtrooms, teleconferencing | NC 25–30 |
| Bedrooms (residences, apartments, hotels, hospitals) | NC 25–35 |
| Small conference rooms, classrooms | NC 30–35 |
| Small private offices, libraries | NC 30–35 |
| Hospitals, clinics | NC 30–45 |
| Restaurants, stores, general offices | NC 35–40 |
| Coliseums for sports only (with amplification) | NC 40 |
| Computer rooms | NC 40–50 |

*Noise Criteria (NC) Curves—The noise criteria curves provide a convenient way of defining the ambient noise level in terms of octave band sound pressure levels. The NC curves consist of a family of curves relating the spectrum of a noise to the environment being specified. Higher noise levels are permitted at the lower frequencies, since the ear is less sensitive to noise in this frequency region. By using one NC number, the complete octave band frequency of an acceptable ambient noise can be specified.

2. IDENTIFY ALL NOISE SOURCES—INTERIOR AND EXTERIOR: Note proximity of noise sensitive areas to all exterior and interior sources of intrusive background noise—whether speech (in corridors, outdoor play areas, etc.), music (auditorium, rehearsal and practice rooms, etc.), impact noise (pedestrian traffic, etc.), activity noise (recreation areas, workrooms, traffic, etc.), or mechanical equipment noise (rooftop, perimeter, basement, etc.). Measured sound pressure level data for all these sources are generally available or can be calculated.

3. CALCULATE REQUIRED NOISE REDUCTION (NR) = SOURCE LEVEL—NC: To minimize NR requirements, locate noisy spaces next to spaces having a relatively high NC; when this is not possible, a heavier and more expensive construction assembly is required. See Figs. 1 and 2.

4. SELECT PARTITION TYPES (AND FLOOR/CEILING ASSEMBLIES) WHOSE TRANSMISSION LOSS (TL) CURVES EXCEED REQUIRED NR CURVES.

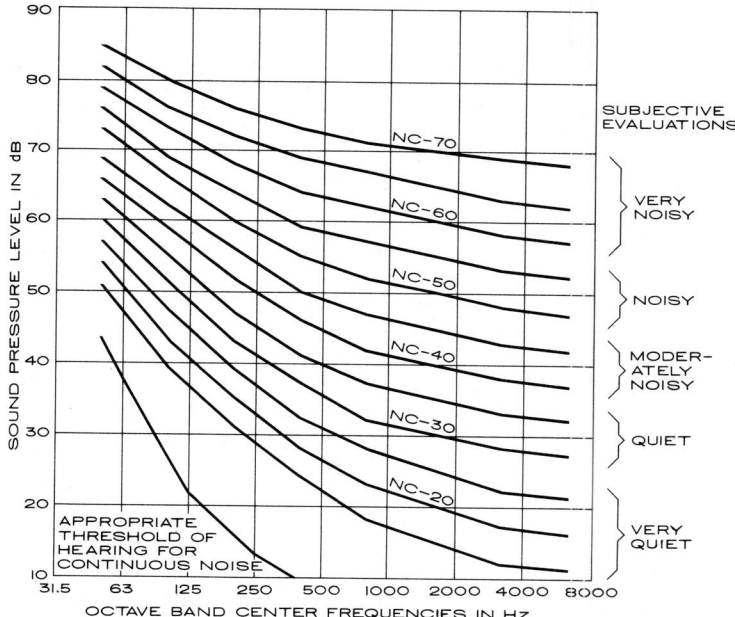

## NOISE CRITERIA SOUND PRESSURE LEVEL TABLE*

| NC CURVE | 63 Hz | 125 Hz | 250 Hz | 500 Hz | 1000 Hz | 2000 Hz | 4000 Hz | 8000 Hz |
|---|---|---|---|---|---|---|---|---|
| NC-70 | 83 | 79 | 75 | 72 | 71 | 70 | 69 | 68 |
| NC-65 | 80 | 75 | 71 | 68 | 66 | 64 | 63 | 62 |
| NC-60 | 77 | 71 | 67 | 63 | 61 | 59 | 58 | 57 |
| NC-55 | 74 | 67 | 62 | 58 | 56 | 54 | 53 | 52 |
| NC-50 | 71 | 64 | 58 | 54 | 51 | 49 | 48 | 47 |
| NC-45 | 67 | 60 | 54 | 49 | 46 | 44 | 43 | 42 |
| NC-40 | 64 | 57 | 50 | 45 | 41 | 39 | 38 | 37 |
| NC-35 | 60 | 52 | 45 | 40 | 36 | 34 | 33 | 32 |
| NC-30 | 57 | 48 | 41 | 36 | 31 | 29 | 28 | 27 |
| NC-25 | 54 | 44 | 37 | 31 | 27 | 24 | 22 | 21 |
| NC-20 | 50 | 41 | 33 | 26 | 22 | 19 | 17 | 16 |
| NC-15 | 47 | 36 | 29 | 22 | 17 | 14 | 12 | 11 |

*For convenience in using noise criteria data, the table lists the sound pressure levels (SFLs) in decibels for the NC curves from the above chart.

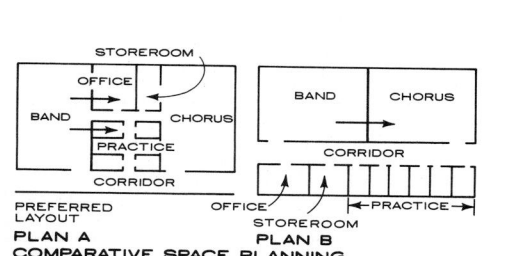

PREFERRED LAYOUT
PLAN A

PLAN B

COMPARATIVE SPACE PLANNING
FIGURE 1

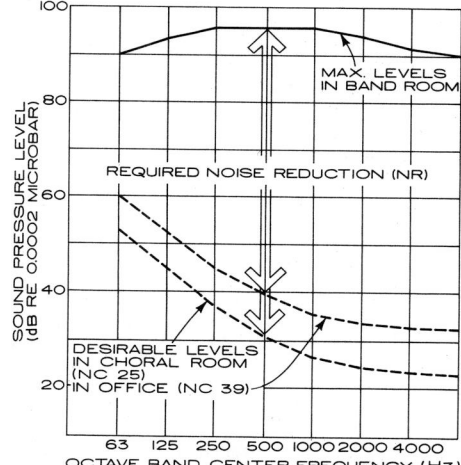

FIGURE 2

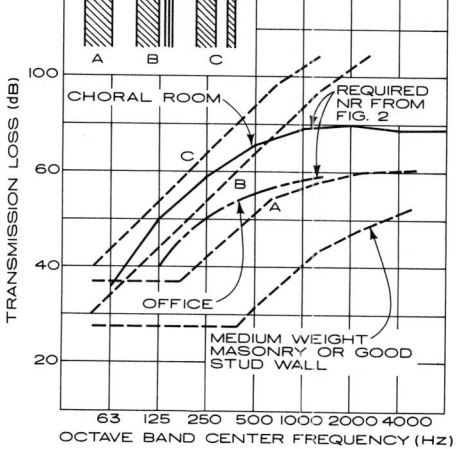

FIGURE 3

## ACOUSTICAL DESIGN CHECKLIST

1. Build in good acoustical design—sound isolation and reverberation control—from the beginning. It is much cheaper to avoid noise problems in the initial design than to correct them later. Good acoustics is not cosmetics; it must be an integral part of the building design and is not a superficially applied treatment either before or after the fact.

2. Select materials with adequate mass and sound isolation design; choose the simplest construction that meets the NR criteria. Detail well and build well; minimize penetrations of walls, floors, and ceilings and make all holes and openings airtight to maintain acoustical integrity. Use materials wisely: Do not confuse lightweight, porous, sound-absorbing materials (for echo and reverberation control) with heavy, impervious, sound-isolating materials (for sound transmission control). Both may be needed, but both cannot be achieved with the same material.

3. Consider the mechanical and electrical equipment as an integral part of the acoustical design. Choose quiet-rated fixtures and equipment and beware of the sound "leaks" that the ductwork, piping, and conduit provide. Use as needed vibration isolators and sound-absorbing duct lining together with flexible connections and low flow velocities in ducts and pipes.

4. Seek out qualified professional advice for all spaces with critical acoustical requirements. Do not rely solely on rules of thumb.

Carl J. Rosenberg, AIA; BBN Laboratories, Inc.; Cambridge, Massachusetts

## INSTRUCTIONS FOR THE PROPER USE OF SOUND TRANSMISSION CLASS (STC) DATA

### DESIGN CRITERIA FOR PARTITIONS

STC ratings are a measure of the effectiveness of a given partition construction in reducing airborne sound transmission, not the transmission of impact noise, low frequency noise sources (e.g., HVAC equipment and vehicular traffic), or amplified music. Because of the limited frequency range covered (125–4000 Hz), STC ratings are limited to evaluating the speech privacy potential of the various partitions and therefore are best used in the design of partitions separating adjacent offices, hospital patient rooms, classrooms (with little or no amplified speech or playback of recordings), dormitories, apartments, courtrooms, small conference rooms, etc. The single number STC ratings should not be relied on, solely, for the selection of partitions separating, say, movie theaters, large conference rooms, auditoriums, music practice rooms, computer and business machine rooms, and mechanical equipment rooms, from, say, private offices and apartments. Typically, a more extensive acoustical analysis is required for such adjacent locations; consult an acoustical consultant for additional information.

Note also that the STC ratings are based on test data measured in a laboratory installation of the given partitions, that is, under ideal construction conditions. Drywall manufacturers admit to a 5–15 point reduction in the lab ratings for the actual field performance, depending on the quality of detailing and workmanship. The importance of communication between the design team and the construction team cannot be overemphasized. The presence of flanking paths—interconnecting ductwork, nonairtight edge joints, inadequate door and window construction, untreated piping and conduit penetrations, and so on—in a completed building can result from improper design, improper construction, or both. The stated criteria assume no flanking paths.

Partitions with STC ratings within 1–2 points (1–2 dB) of the listed criteria would still be acceptable given the anticipated tolerances in test results. (Subjectively, the human ear would consider a 1–2 dB change as ''just barely audible'' at best, which is insignificant.)

The stated performance criteria assume acceptable background noise levels in the source and receiver rooms, that is, some masking of intrusive sounds without loss of speech intelligibility or other interference in listening conditions. The stated criteria are for buildings that fall into an average construction cost range and thus are not weighted toward any one type of construction or geographic region. The primary concern on which these criteria are based is the desire to provide adequate acoustical privacy for the building user. It is clear, however, that these acoustical criteria must be tempered by the designer's consideration of other design parameters—fire ratings, structural loads, energy conservation, and so on—which may downgrade (or even upgrade) the quality of the acoustical design.

For this reason the acoustical criteria listed here tend to be reasonably conservative, rather than lenient, given the many possible compromises.

### DESIGN CRITERIA FOR FLOOR/CEILING ASSEMBLIES

1. AIRBORNE SOUND: STC ratings for floor/ceiling assemblies should be equal to or greater than those for the partitions.
2. STRUCTUREBORNE (IMPACT) SOUND: Impact Isolation Class (IIC) ratings should be equal to or greater than the STC ratings.

Both criteria must be met to ensure adequate acoustical privacy.

STC values for constructions built in the field range from 10 (practically no isolation; an open doorway) to 65 or 70 (such performance requires special constructions). Average constructions might provide noise reduction in the range of STC 30 to STC 60.

It is extremely difficult to measure the STC performance of a single wall or door in the field because of the many flanking paths and nonstandard conditions. Field performance is measured as Noise Isolation Class (NIC), which includes the contribution of all sound transfer between rooms.

## SOUND ISOLATION CRITERIA

| SOURCE ROOM OCCUPANCY | RECEIVER ROOM ADJACENT | SOUND ISOLATION REQUIREMENT (MINIMUM) FOR ALL PATHS BETWEEN SOURCE AND RECEIVER |
|---|---|---|
| Executive areas, doctors' suites, personnel offices, large conference rooms; confidential privacy requirements | Adjacent offices and related spaces | STC 50–55 |
| Normal offices, regular conference rooms for group meetings; normal privacy requirements | Adjacent offices and similar activities | STC 45–50 |
| Large general business offices, drafting areas, banking floors | Corridors, lobbies, data processing; similar activities | STC 40–45 |
| Shop and laboratory offices in manufacturing laboratory or test areas; normal privacy | Adjacent offices; test areas, corridors | STC 40–45 |
| Mechanical equipment rooms | Any spaces | STC 50–60+[1] |
| Multifamily dwellings | Neighbors (separate occupancy) | |
| (a) Bedrooms | Bedrooms | STC 48–55[2] |
| | Bathrooms | STC 52–58[2] |
| | Kitchens | STC 52–58[2] |
| | Living rooms | STC 50–57[2] |
| | Corridors | STC 52–58[2] |
| (b) Living rooms | Living rooms | STC 48–55[2] |
| | Bathrooms | STC 50–57[2] |
| | Kitchens | STC 48–50[2] |
| School buildings | | |
| (a) Classrooms | Adjacent classrooms | STC 50 |
| | Laboratories | STC 50 |
| | Corridors | STC 45 |
| (b) Large music or drama area | Adjacent music or drama area | STC 60[3] |
| (c) Music practice rooms | Music practice rooms | STC 55[3] |
| Interior occupied spaces | Exterior of building | STC 35–60[4] |
| Theaters, concert halls, lecture halls, radio and TV studios | Any and all adjacent | Use qualified acoustical consultants to assist in the design of construction details for these critical occupancies |

### NOTES

1. Use acoustical consultants for mechanical equipment rooms housing other than air handling equipment—e.g., chillers, pumps, compressors—and for heavy manufacturing areas employing equipment generating noise levels at or above OSHA allowable levels or generating high vibration levels.
2. Depends on nighttime, exterior background levels, and other factors that affect actual location of building. Grades I, II, and III are discussed in ''Guide to Airborne, Impact and Structureborne Noise Control in Multifamily Dwellings,'' HUD TS-24, 1974.
3. The STC ratings shown are guidelines only. These situations require, typically, double layer construction with resilient connections between layers or, preferably, structurally independent ''room-within-a-room'' construction. The level of continuous background noise, such as that provided by the HVAC system or an electronic masking system, has a significant impact on the quality of construction selected and must be coordinated with the other design parameters.
4. Depends on the nature of the exterior background noise—its level, spectrum shape, and constancy—as well as the client's budget and on thermal considerations. Use qualified acoustical consultants for analysis of high noise outdoor environments such as airport areas, highways (with heavy truck traffic especially), and industrial facilities.

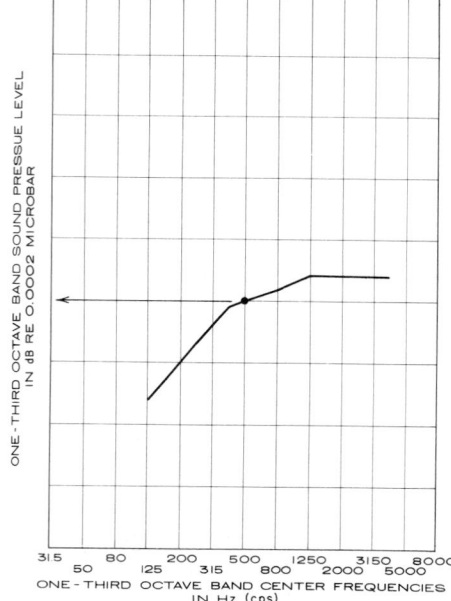

STC RATING CURVE

### DERIVATION AND USE OF THE STC CURVE

To determine the STC rating for a given construction, the STC curve shown in the adjacent figure is applied over the transmission loss (TL) curve for a laboratory test of that construction. Typical TL curves are shown on the next page, Fig. 2. The STC curve is then manipulated in accordance with prescribed rules to obtain the highest possible rating. The procedure states that the TL curve can not be less than the STC curve by more than 8 dB in any one-third octave band; nor can the TL curve be less than the STC curve by more than a total of 32 dB (average of 2 dB for each of 16 one-third octave band frequencies). Any values from the TL curve that are above the STC curve are of no benefit in the rating. The object is to move the STC curve up as high as possible, and to read the STC rating number from the point where the STC curve at 500 Hz crosses the TL curve.

The STC curve has three segments: the first segment, from 125 to 400 Hz, rises at the rate of 9 dB per octave (3 dB per one-third octave); the second segment, from 400 to 1250 Hz, rises at the rate of 3 dB per octave (1 dB per one-third octave); the third segment, from 1250 to 4000 Hz, is flat.

Carl J. Rosenberg, AIA; BBN Laboratories, Inc.; Cambridge, Massachusetts

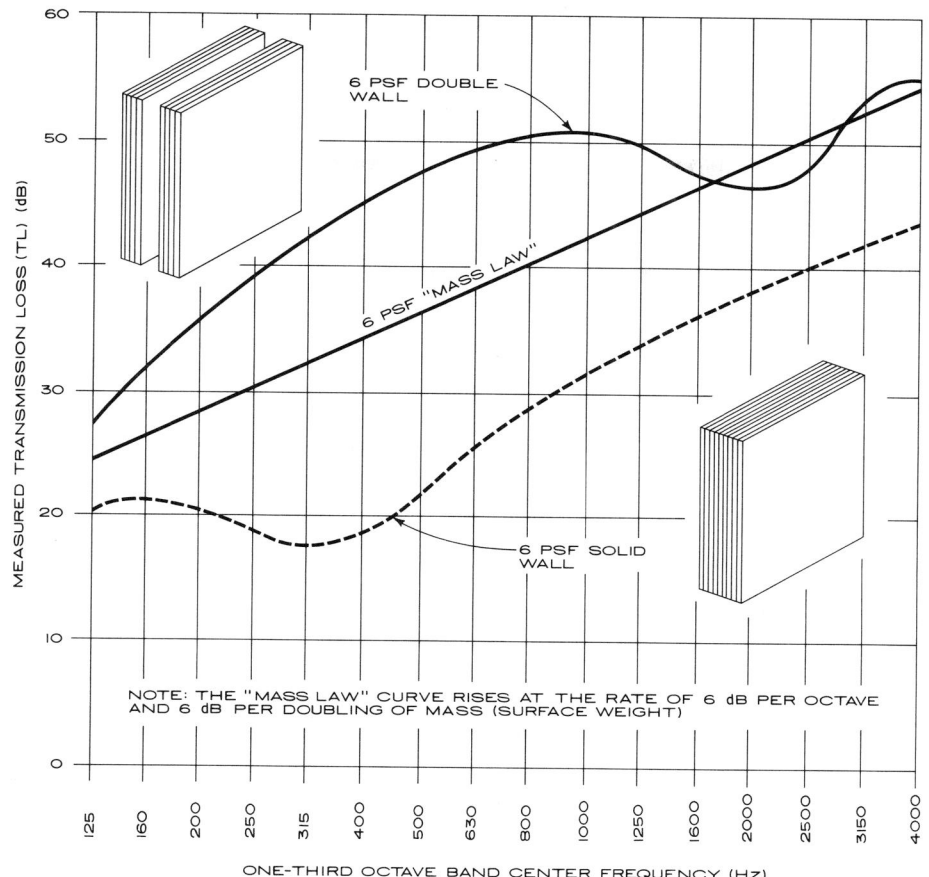

NOTE: THE "MASS LAW" CURVE RISES AT THE RATE OF 6 dB PER OCTAVE AND 6 dB PER DOUBLING OF MASS (SURFACE WEIGHT)

**FIGURE 1**

A. PARTITION WITH 31 dB AVERAGE, STC 22   B. PARTITION WITH 31 dB AVERAGE, STC 32

**FIGURE 2**

Carl J. Rosenberg, AIA; BBN Laboratories, Inc.; Cambridge, Massachusetts

## NOTES AND DEFINITIONS

1. TRANSMISSION LOSS (TL): The measure of the properties of a material to block sound; specifically, the attenuation of air-borne sound transmitted through construction when tested in a laboratory according to ASTM E90. The measured test data, as opposed to calculations, provide the most accurate information on which to base the single-number sound transmission class descriptor. (See note 2 below.)

Design of construction and materials for high transmission loss builds on three principles:

   a. MASS: Lightweight materials do not block sound. Sound transmission through walls, floors, and ceilings varies with the frequency of sound, the weight (or mass), the stiffness of the construction, and the cavity absorption. Theoretically, the transmission loss varies at the rate of 6 dB per doubling (or halving) of the surface weight of the construction.

   A single solid panel behaves less well than the mass law would predict, since the mass law assumes a homogeneous, infinitely resilient material/wall.

   b. SEPARATION: Improved TL performance without undue increase of mass can be achieved by separating materials. A true double wall of the same weight with separate unconnected wythes performed better than the mass law predicts. Note in Figure 1 the significant improvement in transmission loss with increased resiliency—approximately 15 dB ±, depending on the octave band.

   The transmission loss tends to increase about 5 dB for each doubling of the airspace between wythes (minimum effective space approximately 2 in.).

   Resilient attachment of surface skins to studs or structural surfaces provides similar benefit, as do separate wythes.

   c. ABSORPTION: Soft, resilient absorptive materials in the cavity between wythes, particularly for lightweight staggered stud construction, increase transmission loss significantly. Viscoelastic (somewhat resilient but not fully elastic) materials, such as certain insulation boards, dampen or restrict the vibration of rigid panels such as gypsum board and plywood and thus increase transmission loss appreciably. Installation details recommended by manufacturers should be followed.

2. SOUND TRANSMISSION CLASS (STC): A single-number rating system that compares the laboratory TL test curve for a particular material or assembly with a standard contour as described in ASTM E413. The contour is fitted to the test curve of the constructions, allowing for a certain maximum amount of deviation. See Figure 2 for an example that compares two constructions with identical average TL values but widely differing effectiveness (10 points).

   The sound transmission loss at all frequencies, from 125 to 4000 Hz, is important (in varying degrees), so a single TL number or an average is meaningless. The shape of the entire TL test curve as related to the standard contour is important. Deep dips (as in curve A) are harmful, and yet the numerical average misses this dip; the sound transmission class contour properly evaluates its effect by downgrading the overall performance accordingly.

3. NOISE REDUCTION (NR): This depends on the properties of the rooms and is the actual difference in sound pressure level between two spaces being considered. It is what the ear hears and what is actually of interest to us and consists of the noise reduction of the walls, floors, and ceilings as well as the sound absorption present in the receiver room being considered.

   Noise reduction also depends on the relative size of the room in question. If the noise source is in a small room next to a large receiving room, like an office next to a gymnasium, then the noise reduction will be greater than the transmission loss performance alone of the wall, because the sound radiating from the common wall between office and gym has such a large space to be dissipated into. On the contrary, if the noise source is in a large room next to a small one, like the gym next to the office, then the noise reduction will be far less than the transmission loss, because the common wall, which is radiating sound, is such a large part of the surface of the smaller room. This adjustment, plus the contribution of the absorptive finishes in the receiving room, enter into our calculation of actual noise reduction.

## IMPACT NOISE DESIGN CRITERIA

Floors are subject to impact or structure-borne sound transmission—noises such as footfalls, dropped objects, and scraping furniture. Parallel to development of laboratory Sound Transmission Class (STC) ratings for partition constructions is Impact Insulation Class (IIC), a single-number rating system to evaluate the effectiveness of floor construction to prevent impact sound transmission to spaces underneath the floor. The current IIC rating method replaces the previously used Impact Noise Rating (INR) method. To compare the ratings, note that IIC = INR + 51 ±. [The amount of deviation is relatively small ($\pm 2$), but should still be noted.] For example, INR = +4 would be equivalent basically to IIC = 55.

### IMPACT SOUND PRESSURE LEVELS MEASUREMENT (ASTM E492.77)

$$L_n = L_p - 10 \log (A_0/A_2)$$

where $L_n$ = normal impact sound pressure
  $L_p$ = sound pressure level in the receiving room
  $A_2$ = sound absorption of the receiving room
  $A_0$ = reference absorption (108 sabins)

### SUMMARY OF METHOD (ASTM E492.77)

A standard tapping machine is used on a test floor specimen, which forms a horizontal separation between two rooms, one directly above the other. The transmitted impact sound is characterized by the one-third octave band spectrum of the average sound pressure level produced by the tapping machine in the receiving room located directly beneath the test floor specimen.

Since the noise levels depend on the absorption of the receiving room, it is desirable to normalize the impact sound pressure levels to a reference absorption for purposes of comparing results obtained in different receiving rooms that differ in absorption.

To achieve adequate acoustical privacy in multifamily dwellings and other structures where both air-borne and structure-borne sound transmission are concerns, controlling impact sound transmission is as important as the control of air-borne sound transmission, or, expressed in its simplest terms: IIc ≥ STC for a given construction. Again, as with STC ratings, the higher the IIC number, the greater the sound control.

This method is based on the use of a standard tapping machine, which produces a series of continuous uniform impacts at a uniform rate on a test floor. It generates broadband sound pressure levels in the receiving room below which are sufficiently high to accurately reproduce them. The tapping machine, however, is not designed to simulate any one type of impact, for example, male or female footsteps.

Because it is portable, the tapping machine cannot simulate the weight of a human walker. Therefore, the creak or boom of a limber floor caused by such footsteps cannot be reflected in the single-figure impact rating. The correlation between tapping machine tests in the laboratory and field performance of floors under typical conditions may vary, depending on floor construction and the nature of the impact.

Often the greatest annoyance caused by footfall noise is generated by low-frequency sound energy beyond standardized test frequency range. Sometimes it is near or at the resonant frequency of the building structure.

To summarize, think resiliency. Wherever possible, use carpet with padding on floors of residential buildings. Use resilient, suspended ceilings with cavity insulation. For especially critical situations such as those involving pedestrian bridges or tunnels, use an acoustics consultant.

Other sources of impact noise are slamming of doors or drawers of cabinets. If possible, bureaus should not be placed directly against a wall. Door closers or stops can be added to cushion the impact of the energy so that it is not imparted directly into the structure. Common sense arrangements can help minimize problems in multifamily dwellings. Kitchen cabinets should not be placed on a common wall to a neighbor's bedroom, for example.

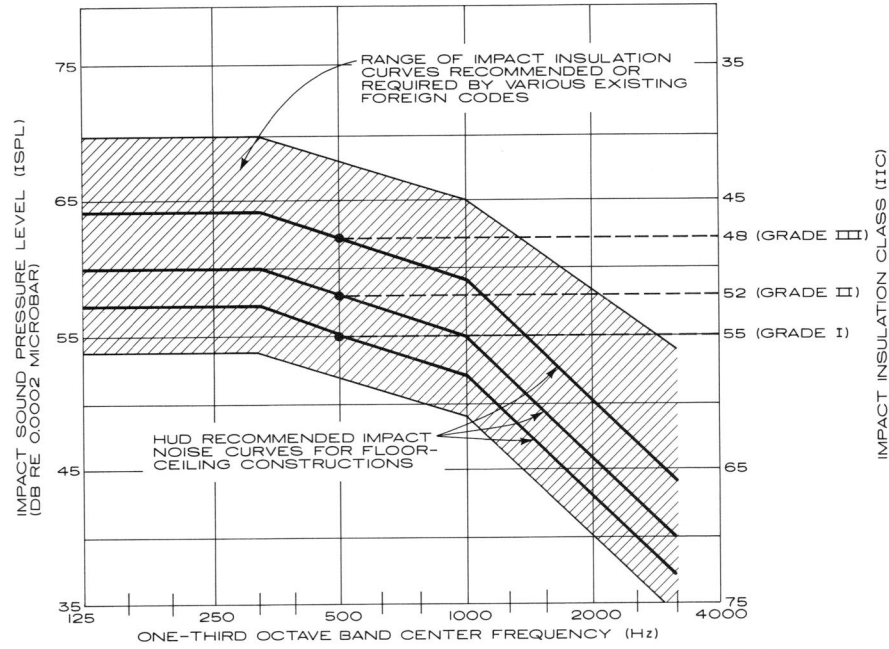

**IMPACT NOISE INSULATION CRITERIA**

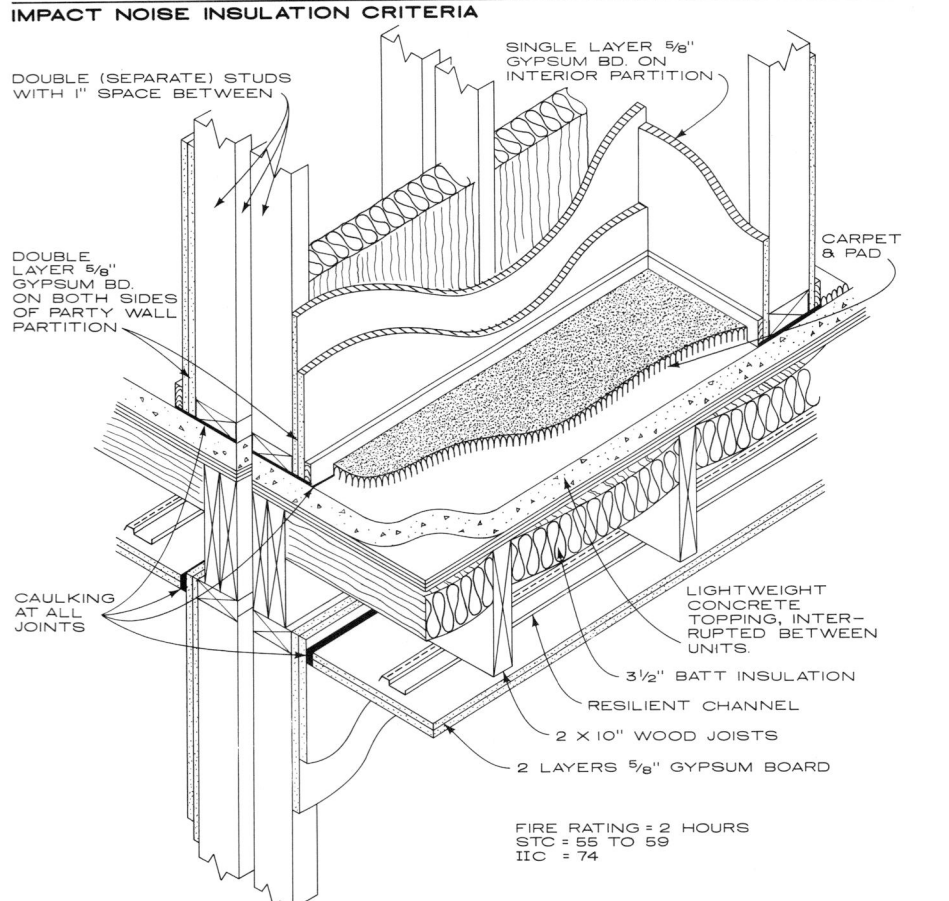

**GOOD SOUND ISOLATION CONSTRUCTION**

### NOTE

Edge attachment and junctions of walls, partitions, floors, and ceilings can cause large differences in TL performance. The transverse waves set up in continuous, stiff, lightweight walls or floors can carry sound a long distance from the source to other parts of the structure with little attenuation. Curtain walls, thin concrete floors on bar joists, and wood framed structures are particularly subject to this weakness.

Properly designed discontinuities such as interrupted floor slab/toppings are helpful in reducing structural flanking.
A resilient (airtight) joint between exterior wall and partition or partition and floor can appreciably improve TL.
Continuous pipes, conduits, or ducts can act as transmission paths from room to room. Care must be taken to isolate such services from the structure.

Carl J. Rosenberg, AIA; BBN Laboratories, Inc.; Cambridge, Massachusetts

1  **ACOUSTIC DESIGN**

## USE OF ABSORPTION IN COMMON OCCUPANCIES

| ROOM OCCUPANCY | CEILING TREATMENT | WALL TREATMENT | SPECIAL |
|---|:---:|:---:|:---:|
| Auditoriums, churches, theaters, concert halls, lecture halls, radio, recording and T.V. studios, speech and music rooms | | | ● |
| Classrooms, elementary | ● | ○ | |
| Classrooms, college | ○ | ○ | |
| Commercial kitchens | ● | | |
| Computer and business machine rooms | ● | ● | |
| Corridors and lobbies | ○ | | |
| Gymnasiums, arenas, and recreational spaces | ● | ● | |
| Health care patient rooms | ● | | |
| Laboratories | ● | | |
| Libraries | ● | | |
| Mechanical equipment rooms | | | ● |
| Meeting and conference rooms | ● | ○ | |
| Open office plan | ● | ● | |
| Private offices | ● | | |
| Restaurants | ● | ○ | |
| Schools and industrial shops, factories | ● | ● | |
| Stores and commercial shops | ● | | |

● Strongly recommend
○ Advisable

NOTES
1. This table lists conservative rule-of-thumb recommendations for use of absorption.
2. Wall treatment is advisable in addition to ceiling treatment for the reduction of reflections, flutter, or echo. This treatment will further reduce noise and control reverberation.
3. Complex applications require an acoustical consultant.

DEFINITIONS

The percentage of sound energy absorbed by a material is the coefficient of absorption (x), which ranges from 0 to .99; the coefficient varies with frequency.

The total sound-absorbing units (sabins) provided by a given material is a function of its absorptive properties and surface area, as defined by this formula:

$$a = Sx$$

where $a$ = sabins, units of sound absorption
$S$ = surface area, in square feet
$x$ = coefficient of absorption

The total sound absorption for a space is the sum of sabins for all surfaces in the room.

Reverberation time is directly proportional to the volume of a space and inversely proportional to the units of absorption:

$$R_t = \frac{.049V}{a}$$

where $R_t$ = reverberation time, in seconds
$V$ = volume, in cubic feet
$a$ = total sabins

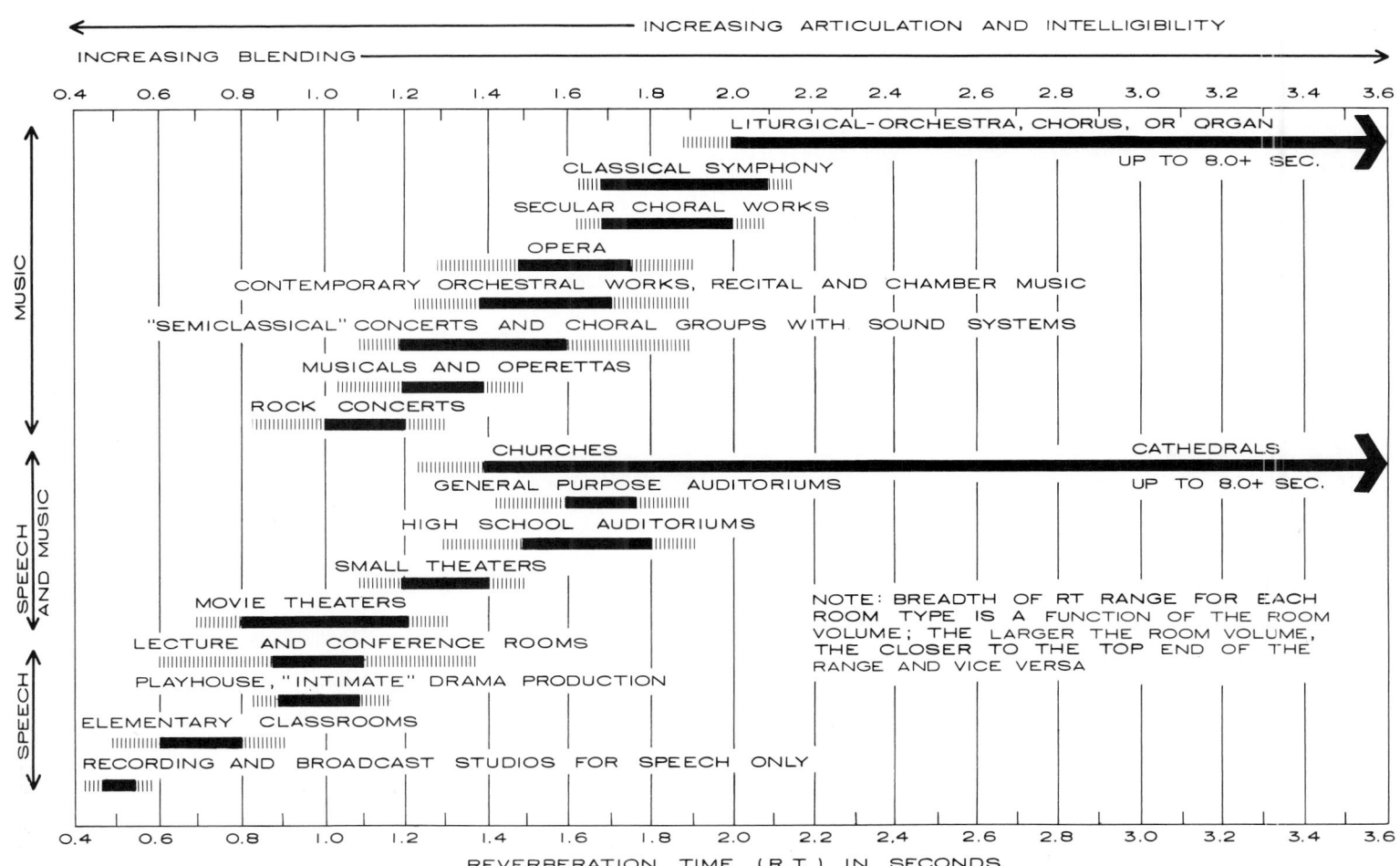

OPTIMUM REVERBERATION TIMES AT MID-FREQUENCIES (500/1000 Hz) FOR AUDITORIUMS AND SIMILAR FACILITIES

Carl J. Rosenberg, AIA; BBN Laboratories, Inc.; Cambridge, Massachusetts

ACOUSTIC DESIGN   1

## OPEN PLAN OFFICES

An open plan office uses partial height screens to separate work stations. With no full-height partitions or doors to block sound transmission, intruding conversations and noise from typewriters and other office machines often are sources of annoyance and distraction. Achieving a satisfactory acoustical environment requires careful acoustical design and treatment of all elements. Important background information is provided directly below, and guidelines for acoustical treatment are listed below. Open plan offices acoustically are marginal at best, and every one of the guidelines must be followed to achieve a satisfactory result.

## CHARACTERISTICS OF SPEECH

A person talking may use various voice levels, ranging from a lowered voice level to a shout. Open plan offices can be designed to accommodate normal conversational voice levels; raised voice levels cause serious privacy problems.

The human voice is loudest directly in front of a talker, less loud to the sides, and quietest to the rear. These directional characteristics should be considered when offices are laid out.

The frequency region that contributes most to speech intelligibility is the 2000 Hz octave band. This needs to be taken into account when selecting sound-absorbing materials for open plan offices.

## SPEECH PRIVACY

The most common complaints in open plan offices are lack of speech privacy and distraction due to intruding conversations. Freedom from the distraction of intruding speech, and the provision of speech privacy, depend on how loud the intruding speech is and how much it is covered up, or masked, by the steady background sound at the listener's location.

The degree of speech privacy can be defined by the articulation index (AI), which can range between 0 and 1.

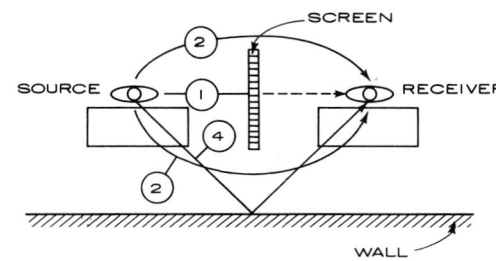

PLAN   SECTION

### SOUND TRANSMISSION IN OPEN PLAN OFFICES

Sound is transmitted between work stations in open plan offices by a number of different paths, as shown in the illustration: (1) by direct line of sight or through screens; (2) by diffraction over and around screens; (3) by reflection from ceilings, luminaires, walls, windows, and other surfaces.

In a well-treated open plan office the sound level drops off with distance from a source, much as it does out of doors. For example, at a distance of 10 ft from a sound source, the sound level will be judged by most people to be about half as loud as it is at 3 ft from the same source.

**SOUND TRANSMISSION PATHS BETWEEN TWO WORKSTATIONS**

Zero represents no intelligibility and complete privacy; 1 represents perfect intelligibility and no privacy. AI can be predicted for open plan layouts by means of computer programs that take into account all of the important acoustical variables.

NORMAL PRIVACY, or freedom from distraction, is the degree of privacy required by most office workers. It is achieved when the office occupant is not disturbed or distracted by intruding conversations, even though they may be audible and partially understandable. Normal privacy requires careful design.

CONFIDENTIAL PRIVACY is required if a person must carry on conversations without being overheard or understood by others. It requires an AI of 0.05 or less and is difficult to achieve in open plan offices. Fully enclosed offices are recommended for personnel who need confidential privacy. If confidential privacy is required in an open plan office, an acoustical consultant should be retained.

## ACOUSTICAL GUIDELINES FOR OPEN PLAN OFFICES

| | | |
|---|---|---|
| **ABSORB UNWANTED NOISE** | Ceilings should have a noise reduction coefficient (NRC) of at least 0.75 and a sound absorption coefficient at 2000 Hz of at least 0.90. | |
| | Ceiling-mounted luminaires with flat lenses wider than 12 in. are good sound reflectors and should be avoided. Eliminate ceiling-mounted fixtures or use 6 in. wide units or units with large parabolic louvers. | |
| | Use acoustical screens and sound-absorbing wall panels with an NRC of at least 0.75. | |
| | Carpet floors to reduce the noise of heel clicks, chair scraping, and other annoying noises originating at the floor. The NRC is not critical. | |
| **BLOCK UNWANTED NOISE** | Screens between work stations should break the line of sight in all directions by 1 ft or more. They should be at least 5 ft high and have an STC rating of at least STC22. Higher screens should be used around copy machines and other noisy equipment. | |
| **COVER UP UNWANTED NOISE** | Provide an electronic sound masking system to cover up intruding conversations and improve speech privacy and freedom from distraction. Most systems have loudspeakers located above the acoustical ceilings and produce a sound similar to a well-designed ventilating system. The sound level, tonal characteristics, and spatial uniformity of the sound masking system are critical; an acoustical consultant should be retained for its design and adjustment. | |
| **DISTANCE AND DIRECTION** | Because sound levels drop off with distance, personnel should be located as far apart as possible, commensurate with efficient use of space. If possible, locate adjacent workers at least 8 ft apart. | |
| | Whenever possible, orient adjacent workers back to back to take advantage of the directional characteristics of the human voice. | |

Carl J. Rosenberg, AIA; BBN Laboratories, Inc.; Cambridge, Massachusetts

1   ACOUSTIC DESIGN

# FUNCTIONS OF LIGHTING

Light is one of many tools available to help us design space. It is wise at the beginning of any project to recall the functions of lighting and to be certain that each function has been examined.

1. PERFORMANCE OF TASKS: Lighting to perform work, whether it be reading, assembling parts, or seeing a blackboard, is referred to as task lighting. Visual work is a primary reason for providing lighting.
2. ENHANCEMENT OF SPACE AND STRUCTURE: It is only through the presence of light that spatial volume, planes, ornament, and color are revealed. For centuries, structural systems evolved partly in response to aesthetic as well as functional desires for light of a certain quality. The progress from bearing wall to curtain wall was driven by the push of newly discovered technologies (both in materials and in technique), by evolving cultural desires for certain spatial characteristics, and by a desire to admit light of a particular quality—as with the Gothic church window, the Baroque oculus, or the Bauhaus wall of glass. With the advent of electric lighting systems, this connection of structure to light was no longer entirely necessary, but most architects continue to pay homage to this historic tie.
3. FOCUSING ATTENTION: The quality of light in a space profoundly affects one's perception of that space. The timing and the direction of one's gaze—which are the vanguards of understanding of the space—are often a function of the varying quality and distribution of light throughout the space. Lighting draws attention to points of interest and helps to guide the user of a space about.
4. PROVISION OF SECURITY: Lighting can enhance visibility and thereby engender a sense of security. Lighting can also be used to illuminate hazards, such as a changing floor plane or moving objects.

# ISSUES TO CONSIDER IN GOOD LIGHTING DESIGN

Good lighting design promotes (1) seeing—in the sense of performing such visual tasks as reading or operating equipment—and (2) perceiving the space and its various qualities (volume, color, texture, etc.).

To do visual work, a sufficient amount of light is required for the task. Most lighting standards discuss the quantity of light in terms of incident light or light that falls onto a surface. This light, called illuminance, is measured in footcandles or lux (S.I.). Although convenient to calculate, illuminance is not, of course, what actually enters our eyes.

When performing a visual task, the light that reaches our eyes and is therefore laden with whatever raw information our mind takes in is usually reflected light—that is, light reflected off the details of the task (typed letters), the immediate background (paper), and the surround (desk top and room). Important exceptions are electronic visual displays using CRTs and LEDs, which emit their own light. In these visual tasks, light reflected off their surfaces generally reduces their legibility, and much attention needs to be given to the lighting of the surround.

It should be recognized that exitance or luminance or even brightness is only one factor in a list of criteria for seeing, including contrast, task size, time (duration of gaze), and environmental distractions (noise, odors, etc.). While these items are by and large not part of the lighting design, contrast must be taken into account quite specifically. Tasks have their own inherent contrast, but under different lighting systems can produce differing perceived contrasts. This is primarily a matter of the position of the source of light relative to the task and the observer's eye.

Another factor in lighting design is the choice of the light source. Two issues are involved: color and size.

COLOR: Each lamp family has its own inherent color characteristics. The chart below describes in general terms the various perceived color effects.

SIZE: It is useful to think of sources and source/fixture combinations classified into point, line, or area sources. Point sources [for instance, bare incandescent lamps and recessed incandescent or high-intensity discharge (HID) fixtures with small apertures and specular reflectors] can be precisely controlled in terms of where light is and is not and can provide sparkle in a space by means of reflections off of polished room surfaces. Line sources

(bare fluorescent tubes and linear fluorescent fixtures) can be controlled in their transverse axis of output, but not longitudinally. This makes them useful for lighting large open areas where repetitive rows of fixtures are suitable. The most common area source is a window, but also included in this category are arrays of line sources covered by a diffusing element. These sources usually provide medium to high levels of light with little directional control.

The human eye/brain combination is a complex and sensitive perceptual apparatus and does not simply function as a camera, projecting pictures onto the mind. The many nerves and tissues necessary for translating the information carried as radiant energy by light into an image in the brain results in some anomalies that are significant to consider in lighting design.

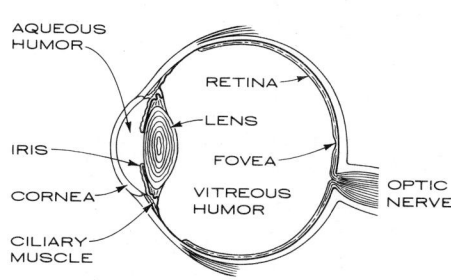

Light passes into the eye through a flexible lens, which passes the image through the vitreous humor and focuses it on the retina. The retina is actually a layer of light-sensitive receptors of two types: rods and cones. Millions of these receptors are spread over the retinal area, but they are not distributed evenly. The rods predominate in the peripheral zone, away from the center or fovea. Rods do not discriminate between colors, but are very sensitive to low light levels and movement. They are the primary transmitters of information at night when light levels are said to be in the scotopic range ("night vision"). Toward the center of the retina, and especially at the fovea, cones predominate. Cones are active at higher light levels (photopic range) and are divided into types that are sensitive to red, blue, and green light, which makes these hues the primary colors of light. The rods and cones are not equally sensitive to all wavelengths (colors) of light. Sensitivity peaks at about 550 nm for cones (a yellow-green color) and at about 500 nm for the rods, which do not "see" this wavelength as a color.

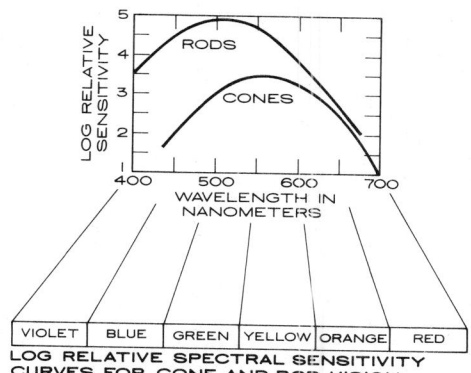

LOG RELATIVE SPECTRAL SENSITIVITY CURVES FOR CONE AND ROD VISION

Two important features of the human visual system for lighting design are adaptation to different light levels and color adaptation.

1. Adaptation to light levels: The visual system does not see a patch of a given luminance as a constant brightness across differing ambient light levels. Rather, it sees the patch as a brightness relative to another adjacent patch, or relative to the general surround. The visual system can be very discriminating in side-by-side, simultaneous comparisons of brightness. But judging the absolute brightness of a scene is near impossible, since the system adapts to the ambient light level. Also, because two different kinds of receptors (rods and cones) are used for night and daytime light levels, a transition from one extreme to the other—such as entering a movie theater at midday—requires time for the system to shift from photopic to scotopic sensitivity.
2. Adaptation of color: Analogously to brightness adaptation, the visual system does not have an absolute color sensitivity. When in an environment illuminated with light that primarily triggers the red sensitive cones, for instance, the blue and green receptors become acutely sensitive, and the red receptors become saturated or dulled to the dominant color. Because the visual system works in this way, two phenomena occur: (1) After a period of time (the adaptation), we see the red-light-dominated scene as more or less normal, since the sensing of red is attenuated and the sensing of blue and green is enhanced; (2) When we leave the red-light-dominated space and pass into one with less redness in the light, the blues and greens will, for a time (the adaptation period), be more apparent than their absolute value suggests. Color sensitivity is very much dependent on one's state of adaptation.

## PERCEIVED COLOR EFFECTS FROM LAMPS

| LAMP NAME | COLOR APPEARANCE | OBJECT COLORS ENHANCED | OBJECT COLORS DULLED |
|---|---|---|---|
| Incandescent, including tungsten halogen | Yellowish white | Warm colors | Cool colors |
| Fluorescent | | | |
| Cool white | White | Orange, yellow, blue | Red |
| Warm white | Yellowish white | Orange, yellow, blue | Red, blue |
| Cool white deluxe | White | All nearly equal | None appreciable |
| Warm white deluxe | Yellowish white | Red, orange, yellow | Blue |
| High-intensity discharge (HID) | | | |
| Clear mercury | Blue/green | Yellow, green, purple | Red, orange |
| Deluxe mercury | Purplish white | Orange, yellow, purple | Deep reds |
| Deluxe warm mercury | Yellowish white | Orange, yellow, purple | Deep reds |
| Metal halide | White | Orange, yellow, blue | Deep reds |
| High-pressure sodium | Yellow/orange | Yellow, orange | Green, blue |
| Low-pressure sodium | Yellow | Yellow | All except yellow |

Robert T. Prouse; Jules Fisher & Paul Marantz, Inc.; New York, New York

## TERMS COMMONLY USED IN LIGHTING DESIGN

| ENGLISH | SI | MEASURE OF |
|---|---|---|
| Footcandle (FC)<br>Lumens/sq ft<br>CP/D² (ft) | Lux (LX)<br>Lumens/sq m<br>CP/D² (meters) | Illuminance; incident light |
| Candlepower (CP) | Candela (CD) | Intensity of a "ray" of light in a given direction (used for point-by-point calculations) |
| Lumen (LM) | Lumen (LM) | Flux; total amount of light emitted by a source (used for lumen method calculations) |
| Candela/sq ft (CD/sq ft) | Candela/sq m (CD/sq m) | Luminance or luminous exitance, or simply exitance; flux leaving a surface at a point (formerly measured in footlamberts) |
| Reflectance (R) | Reflectance | $R(\%) = \dfrac{\text{Luminance of sample material}}{\text{Luminance of reflectance standard}}$<br>or<br>$\dfrac{\text{Flux reflected}}{\text{Flux incident}}$ |
| Transmission (T) | Transmission | $T(\%) = \dfrac{\text{Flux emerging}}{\text{Flux incident}}$ |

## ILLUMINANCE VALUES FOR VARIOUS TYPES OF ACTIVITIES IN INTERIORS

| TYPES OF ACTIVITY | FOOTCANDLES | REFERENCE WORK PLANE |
|---|---|---|
| Public spaces with dark surroundings | 2–3–5 | Hospital corridors (night) |
| Simple orientation for short temporary visits | 5–7.5–10 | CRT areas (veiling reflections need special consideration), transportation terminal concourses |
| Working spaces where visual tasks are only occasionally performed | 10–15–20 | Auditoriums, banks (general), hotel corridors and lobbies, hospital corridors (days) |
| Performance of visual tasks of high contrast or large size | 20–30–50 | Conference rooms, offices (high contrast), factory (simple assembly) |
| Performance of visual tasks of medium contrast or small size | 50–75–100 | Drafting rooms (high-contrast tasks), classrooms, offices, factory (low contrast), factory (moderately difficult assembly) |
| Performance of visual tasks of low contrast or small size | 100–150–200 | Drafting rooms (low-contrast tasks), laboratories, factory (difficult assembly) |
| Performance of visual tasks of low contrast and very small size over a prolonged period | 200–300–500 | Factory (very difficult assembly) |
| Performance of very prolonged and exacting visual tasks | 500–750–1000 | Factory (exacting assembly) |
| Performance of very special visual tasks of extremely low contrast and small size | 1000–1500–2000 | Cloth inspection areas |

## ENERGY MANAGEMENT

Many state governments have or are in the process of formulating laws, codes, and guidelines to control the use of energy. While the major impact is on building HVAC systems, lighting systems are also considered. The federal government is in the process of developing a model code for use by states and municipalities.

Most of these energy management guidelines are based on a procedure to limit the total connected load in units of overall watts per square foot. Most also recognize that time is a factor since power is measured in units of kilowatt hours (KWHRS).

The procedures being developed require that some assumptions be made about space use, but should not be confused with actual design of lighting systems. While the process will set an overall limit of connected load for a building, individual spaces within the building may vary widely from the watts-per-square-foot average. The procedure must often be invoked at a point in design when not enough is known about all the activities in the building; however, enough latitude is generally given to allow the law of averages to take its course.

Many special areas are typically excluded, although one must always check with the current local code. These typically include:

1. Performance spaces
2. Outdoor activities
3. Special lighting for medical or dental uses
4. Display lighting for art
5. Special lighting for research
6. Lighting for plant growth used only in off-peak hours
7. Normally off emergency lighting
8. Lighting for high-risk security areas
9. Classrooms for the visually handicapped
10. Store display windows
11. Lighting for dwelling units

To determine a building's power limit, each space type must be analyzed to determine a "base unit power density" (UPD). The UPD is stated in units of watts per square foot. The formula for UPD is:

$$\text{UPD} = \frac{(FC_t \times \text{task area \%}) + (FC_g \times \text{general area \%})}{GCU \times LSF \times LLF} \times AF$$

where:

$FC_t$ = recommended task area illuminance (in footcandles)

Task area % = percent that the task area is of the total

$FC_g$ = recommended illuminance for the general area around the task area (usually ⅓ × $FC_t$)

General area % = percent that the general area is of the total (100% − task area %)

GCU = generalized coefficient of utilization for a broad space or task type (the range is 0.50–0.75)

LSF = light source factor based on lamp efficacy (lumens/watt) appropriate for the space or task (the range is 20–90)

LLF = light loss factor taking into account the accumulation of dirt on fixture and room surfaces (the range is 0.70–0.75)

AF = adjustment factor to account for special conditions (rarely used).

Robert T. Prouse; Jules Fisher & Paul Marantz, Inc.; New York, New York

## LIGHTING THE HORIZONTAL PLANE

The most commonly used measure of a lighting system's performance is the resulting illuminance (the amount of footcandles delivered to the work surface). This is not because illuminance is an effective measure of all aspects of quality, but because the illuminance characteristics of lighting systems are well understood and easily predicted.

The work surface is usually a horizontal plane such as a desk top, a drafting board, or the floor. Hence, the most commonly used calculation technique (the lumen method described on the following page) permits the selection of fixtures and layouts to achieve approximate uniformity of illuminance (footcandles) at any desired horizontal plane in a room.

## UNIFORMITY

Uniformity is of interest to the lighting designer for two reasons. One is that it is thought that excessive variations in brightness in the observer's field of view in a work environment can be unpleasant and lead to feelings of fatigue and subsequently reduced performance. The most common example is looking up from one's desk at a bright, sunlit window, which causes the visual system to begin to adapt to that high brightness, and then looking back down at one's work surface, which has a lower brightness, causing the visual system to begin to readapt. A day full of such attempted adaptation to such extreme contrasts can be a tiring one. The second interest in uniformity has to do with the relatively common need to provide a fixed lighting system for a flexible (or unknown at the time of design) furniture plan. This situation requires uniformity of illuminance so that the required amount of footcandles is present wherever a work surface might be positioned.

Therefore, in addition to achieving a particular illuminance level, understanding of the uniformity of a lighting plan is necessary. In a typical room it is possible to achieve virtually any illuminance level with only one very powerful fixture. However, that one fixture would create unacceptably high brightness gradients.

To understand the uniformity aspect of any lighting system, it is necessary to look at the distribution of light from one fixture and consider how it relates to an adjacent one. As an example, here is a diagram of the output from a downlight:

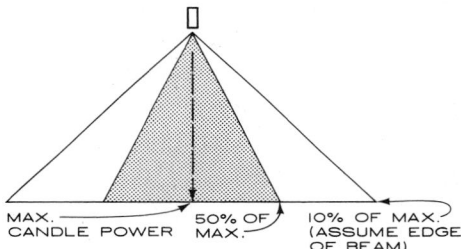

MAX. CANDLE POWER     50% OF MAX.     10% OF MAX. (ASSUME EDGE OF BEAM)

Manufacturers provide the angles off center of the points at which the intensity of light has dropped to 50% of the maximum value and 10% of the maximum value.

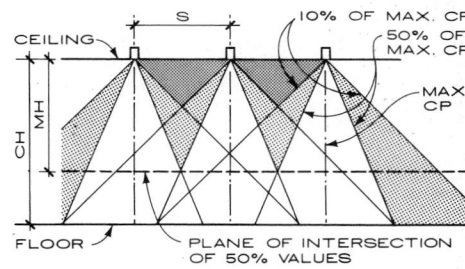

The maximum spacing (S) at a given mounting height (MH) above the work plane is chosen such that the illuminance halfway between fixtures due to two adjacent fixtures is equal to the illuminance under one fixture due to that one fixture. The MH and the ceiling height (CH) may or may not be the same, depending on the selection of the work plane height (i.e., floor vs. desk). The ratio of a suitable spacing to the mounting height (S/MH) is known as the spacing criterion (SC).

## 1    LIGHTING DESIGN

## TERMS COMMONLY USED IN LIGHTING DESIGN

| ENGLISH | SI | MEASURE OF |
|---|---|---|
| Candlepower | Candlepower | Intensity |
| Lumen | Lumen | Light flux |
| Footcandle (ft-c) | Lux | Density- lumen/ft² (lux/m²) |
| Reflectance (R) | Reflectance | ft-c $R = \dfrac{\text{ft-c (reflected)}}{\text{ft-c (incident)}}$ |
| Transmission (T) | | $T = \dfrac{\text{ft-c (transmitted)}}{\text{ft-c (incident)}}$ |
| Footlambert (ft-L) | Candlepower/m² | Luminance ft-L = ft-c × R |

## SUBJECTIVE IMPRESSION APPEARS TO BE AFFECTED BY:

| | |
|---|---|
| Visual clarity | Peripheral wall brightness Luminance in the center of the room Cool color light source and continuous spectrum output |
| Spaciousness | Peripheral lighting (not affected by color) |
| Relaxation | Nonuniform, peripheral (wall) lighting |
| Attention | Intensity of light and contrast Recommended contrast ratios: 2/1: subliminal differences 10/1: minimum for significant focal contrast 100/1: dominating contrast |
| Privacy, intimacy | Lighting of background and/or inanimate objects (centerpieces) |
| Gaiety, playfulness | Visual noise and "clutter" such as sparkle, random patterns |
| Somberness | Dimness and diffusion of light |

## SEEING

Although many of the characteristics of quality seeing conditions are known, it is a difficult area to define precisely. Research continues in an effort to uncover knowledge of how people see and what kind of lighting conditions are most desirable for every situation.

### RECOGNITION OF TASKS

The human ability to recognize detail generally varies with respect to (1) contrast between the details of a task and its immediate surround, (2) luminance (or brightness) of the task, (3) size of the task, and (4) time of viewing.

Maximum visibility is attained when the luminance contrast of details against their background is greatest (e.g., black ink on white paper). Significant savings of electric energy can occur when the task contrast is maximized because the level of illumination needed is reduced. The same opportunity occurs with task size (e.g., large size type on a typewriter saves on the need for illumination). The luminance of the task depends on the amount of incident illumination and the reflectivity of the task. A small amount of light on white paper may be as effective for seeing as a large amount of illumination on dark cloth. With increased time available for viewing, illumination levels can be reduced (e.g., when speed is not critical).

### VEILING REFLECTIONS

Substantial losses in contrast, hence in visibility and visual performance, can result when light is reflected from specular visual tasks (the task is "veiled"). This is perhaps the most significant factor in poor seeing conditions. Three factors govern these veiling reflections: (1) the nature of the task, (2) the observer's

Benjamin Evans, FAIA; Blacksburg, Virginia

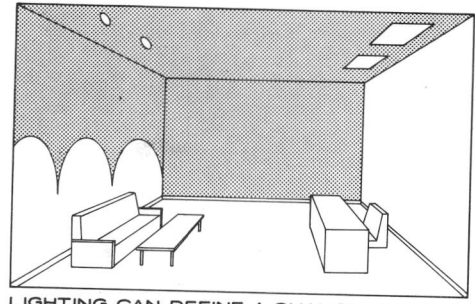

LIGHTING CAN DEFINE A CHANGE OF MOOD BETWEEN DESK AND MORE RELAXED SEATING AREA

LUMINAIRE PATTERNS THAT CONFLICT WITH STRUCTURE CAN DESTROY HARMONY OF SPACE

## ILLUMINATION

Proper illumination depends on the establishment of design goals that define the desired environment, rather than on the equipment needed. Lighting is the most expressive tool available for setting the tone for perception of the environment. It should be thought of as a design tool and not as an "add on" to provide light, and its consideration should be fundamental to any design effort.

Light should be considered to be what we "see by" and not that which we actually see. We do not see footcandles (the measure of quantity). We see luminance as a result of reflected or direct light. (When perceived rather than measured, it is called brightness.) The footlambert is the unit of measurement of brightness.

Of course, there must be enough light. (The unit of measure is the footcandle.) The quantities of illumination necessary for various visual tasks have been

orientation and viewing angle, and (3) the lighting system.

### THE TASK

The luminance of the task (e.g., writing or printing on paper) depends on both the amount of light being reflected from it and the bright object or surface (e.g., luminaire) that may be reflected in it. Diffusing or matte papers and inks tend to reduce veiling reflections.

### THE OBSERVER

If the eye is in such a position that the rays of light from the "offending zone" are reflected toward it, veiling reflections will occur. This situation can usually be observed in a space by placing a sheet of clear acetate or some other glossy surface over the task

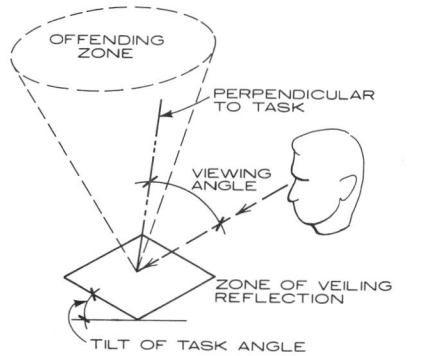

TASK LIGHTING

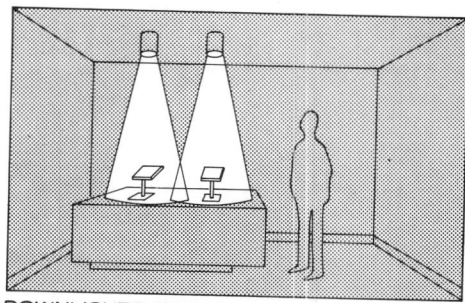

DOWNLIGHTS FOCUS ATTENTION ON OBJECT

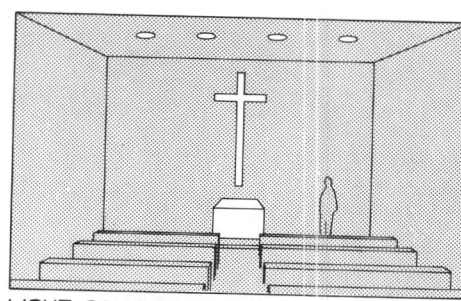

LIGHT CAN DIRECT ATTENTION TO A SPECIFIC FOCAL POINT BY A SHARP CONTRAST OF LIGHT AND DARK SURFACES

recommended by the Illuminating Engineering Society (IES) based on research. But the quantity of illumination needed on walls, floors, ceilings, and so on, for the creation of a beautiful and functional environment is very much left to the designer's logic, experience, and intuition. The proper lighting of all tasks, whether functional or esthetic, is vital to a total design, and recommended footcandle levels should be considered only as targets.

### PURPOSE

Lighting can define the intended use of a space by focusing on points of attention and subduing less important areas. It can be used to express structural concepts by silhouetting beams, arches, and columns or to emphasize unusual contours. Mechanical equipment can be made to visually recede with dark paint and the absence of light. Light can help to define space use changes through brightened ceiling areas or changes of light patterns on walls.

(such as a book or paper with writing or printing) and observing the reflections (if any). Sources of light in this offending zone should be minimized for best seeing conditions.

### LIGHTING SYSTEMS

The worst condition is a highly concentrated, bright source, above and forward, directed at the task. Paradoxically, it is also the condition under which the worker can most easily escape veiling reflections by tilting or reorienting the task so that the reflected rays do not reach the eye (e.g., as in turning the back so the light comes over the shoulder). Placement of lighting equipment and fenestrations in the general area above and forward of the task (or desk) should be avoided. When the nature of the tasks and their location are known, luminaires can be located to avoid the offending zone. When task locations are not known and flexibility is necessary, as for speculative office space, general low level ambient lighting, which tends to negate the effects of veiling reflections, and task lighting can be provided by plug-in units at the discretion of the tenant.

### EQUIVALENT SPHERE ILLUMINATION (ESI)

ESI is a unit adopted by the IES for measuring the visibility potential of a particular task at a particular location and with a specific lighting system. It is a unit of measurement just as is the meterstick. It is not a standard of quality, but a way of taking into consideration those elements by which quality is judged. ESI cannot be measured over the area of a room as simply as raw footcandles, because ESI depends on a task, a location, an orientation, and a lighting system. A task has 50 ESI when it is as visible as it would be when illuminated by 50 ft-c of illuminance produced by a photometric sphere.

## AVOIDING VEILING REFLECTIONS

The area above and directly in front of the task is called the offending zone, since it is the most likely to cause veiling reflections (reflected glare).

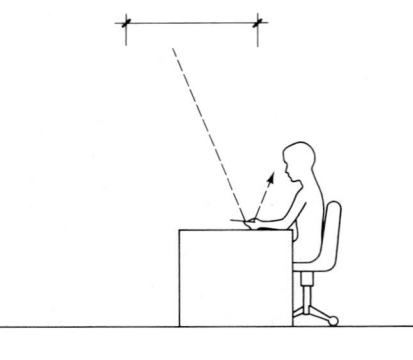

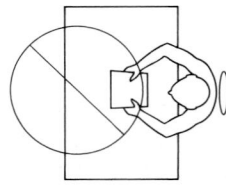

Fixtures located off to each side in an area 25°–45° off the task surface will tend not to produce veiling reflections:

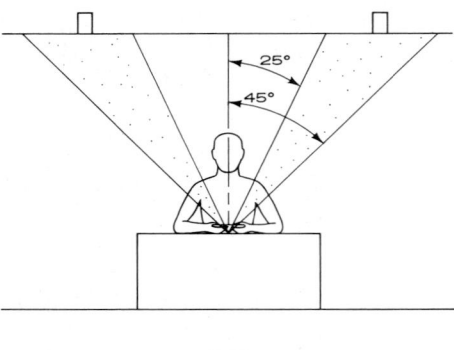

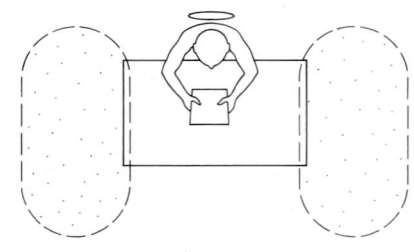

## LUMEN METHOD

The lumen method, also known as the zonal cavity system, is a way to calculate either horizontal illuminance from a proposed lighting fixture section and layout or quantity of fixtures from proposed fixture selection and horizontal illuminance value.

The lumen method is based on the definition of average footcandles over an area which is lumens per square foot. The method modifies this fundamental equation (FC = lumens/sq ft) to account for room size and proportion; reflectance of walls, ceiling, and floors; fixture efficiency; and the effects of time in reducing output due to dirt accumulation, deterioration of reflecting surfaces, and reduction of lumen output.

Robert T. Prouse; Jules Fisher & Paul Marantz, Inc.; New York, New York

The lumen method requires the following information:

1. Room dimensions (adequate to compute wall area and floor area)
2. Height of fixtures above work plane
3. Reflectances of major surfaces (ceiling, walls, and floor)
4. An estimate of the light loss factor (LLF)
5. Initial lamp lumens
6. A target illuminance level

The coefficient of utilization (CU) is the percentage of total lamp lumens that reaches the work plane. As such, it has nothing to do with the intensity of the fixture, but rather with the efficiency of the fixtures (lumens emitted from the fixture divided by lamp lumens) and the direction of the light output. (This direction of output is graphically represented by the candlepower distribution curve.) Since for purposes of this procedure, the plane of interest is invariably a horizontal plane (typically either the floor or desk level), a fixture that throws the greatest percentage of its lumens downward will necessarily have a higher CU [room cavity ratio (RCR) and reflectance values being equal] than one that distributes light in any other direction. A higher CU is not necessarily a virtue; it only ranks fixtures according to their ability to provide horizontal illuminance.

The lumen method/zonal cavity system is limited by the following:

1. It is based on a single number, average value, from which follows:
2. It assumes a uniform array of lighting fixtures.
3. It assumes that all room surfaces are a matte (lambertian) finish.
4. It assumes that the room is devoid of obstruction, at least down to the level of the work plane.

The LLF is used in calculating illuminance at a specific point in time in the life of a lighting system under given conditions. It incorporates variations from test conditions in temperature and voltage, dirt accumulation on lighting fixtures and room surfaces, lamp lumen output depreciation, maintenance procedures (mainly frequency of cleaning), and atmospheric conditions. The LLF is also known as the maintenance factor.

In order to use a CU table, one must first make assumptions about the reflectances of the major room surfaces: ceiling, walls, and floor. Then the RCR must be determined according to one of the following formulas:

RCR = (5 x H(L + W))/(L x W), for rectangular rooms

where H is the cavity height (see diagram)

RCR = 2.5 wall area/floor area, for odd-shaped rooms

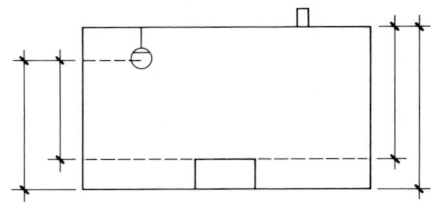

Any one of these dimensions may be the cavity height, depending on the location of the work plane of interest and the fixture mounting.

## BATWING DISTRIBUTION

Fixture manufacturers have developed luminaires (mostly fluorescent) that produce a light distribution that tends to reduce direct glare and veiling reflections if used in large, uniform arrays and typical open office geometries. This distribution pattern is called batwing and has the following characteristics:

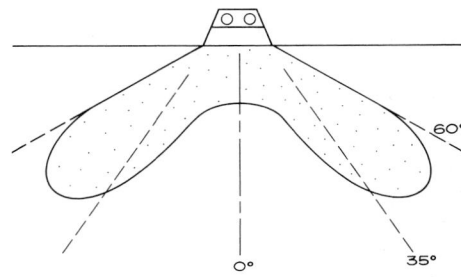

The intensity of light straight below the fixture (0°) is minimized so that even a fixture placed in the "offending zone" will not be as objectionable as it otherwise might. The intensity at angles between 35° and 60° is maximized so that at typical spacings, peak intensities overlap at the work surface:

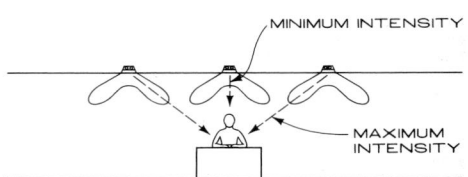

## SOME USEFUL FORMULAS FOR AVERAGE LIGHTING CALCULATIONS

$$\text{NUMBER OF LUMINAIRES} = \frac{\text{footcandles desired x room area}}{\text{CU x LLF x lamps/luminaire x lumens/lamp}}$$

$$\text{AVERAGE FOOTCANDLES} = \frac{\text{lumens/lamp x lamps/luminaire x CU x LLF}}{\text{area of room (sq ft)}}$$

$$\text{POWER DENSITY (W/sq ft)} = \frac{\text{footcandles desired}}{\text{source efficacy (lumens/watt) x CU x LLF}}$$

where   CU = Coefficient of Utilization (percentage of light that actually reaches task)
LLF = Light loss factor (time-dependent depreciation factors)

### NOTE

See manufacturer's photometric tables or the Lighting Handbook of the Illuminating Engineering Society for tables giving values of CU, LLF, lumens/lamp, and so on.

### TYPICAL EXAMPLES

Room size 25 x 40 ft; ceiling height 9 ft; office area 70 ft-c; 2 x 4 ft recessed troffers with 4–40 W T12 lamps (3100 lm) each. From IES tables, Room Index = E and CU = 0.67 (plastic lens):

$$\text{NUMBER OF FIXTURES} = \frac{70 \times 25 \times 40}{0.67 \times 0.7 \times 4 \times 3100} = 12.03 \text{ (use 12 luminaires)}$$

$$\text{POWER DENSITY (W/sq ft)} = \frac{70 \text{ FC}}{78 \text{ lumens/W} \times 0.67 \times 0.70} = 1.9 \text{ W/sq ft}$$

# 1   LIGHTING DESIGN

## LUMINAIRE SELECTION PARAMETERS

In selecting luminaires that will contribute to the making of an appropriate environment in a space, several factors are usually considered:

1. DISTRIBUTION is the shape of the light output from a luminaire. It is illustrated by the candlepower distribution curve, a polar plot of intensities at specific angles. Luminaires are classified by the percentage of their luminous output sent in various directions.

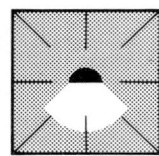

$$\frac{0-10\%}{90-100\%}$$

DIRECT

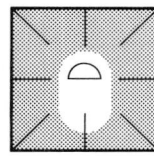

$$\frac{10-40\%}{60-90\%}$$

SEMIDIRECT

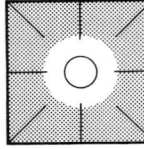

$$\frac{40-60\%}{40-60\%}$$

GENERAL DIFFUSE

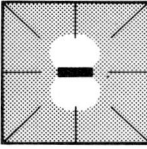

$$\frac{40-60\%}{40-60\%}$$

DIRECT-INDIRECT

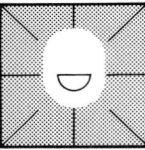

$$\frac{60-90\%}{10-40\%}$$

SEMIINDIRECT

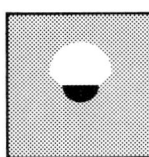

$$\frac{90-100\%}{0-10\%}$$

INDIRECT

2. WHERE IS THE FIXTURE relative to the space? Is it outside (i.e., recessed), inside on a surface (ceiling or wall), or within: portable (table or floor)?

Recessed fixtures primarily light major planes: downlights for floors and horizontal work surfaces (desks, drafting tables, lab tables, etc.) and wall washers for walls. Recessed adjustable accent lights can be used to highlight selected areas. Since their distributions are entirely "direct," the lighting quality tends to the dramatic: full of contrasts and shadows. Fixtures located in the space (surface, pendant, or portable) can illuminate the ceiling as well as the floor, work surfaces, and walls. These types of fixtures (except for those whose distribution is totally direct) tend to soften shadows and contrasts.

Robert T. Prouse; Jules Fisher & Paul Marantz, Inc.; New York, New York

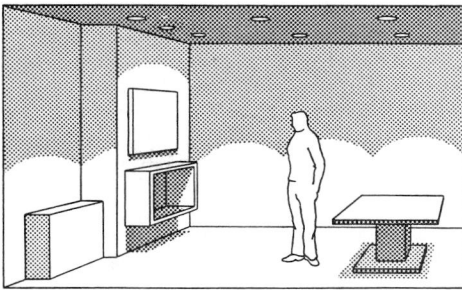

**DIRECT**

All recessed lighting is an example of a direct lighting system, but a pendant fixture could be direct if it emits virtually no light above the horizontal. Unless extensive wall-washing is used, the overall impression of a direct lighting system is one of low general brightness with the possibility of higher intensity accents.

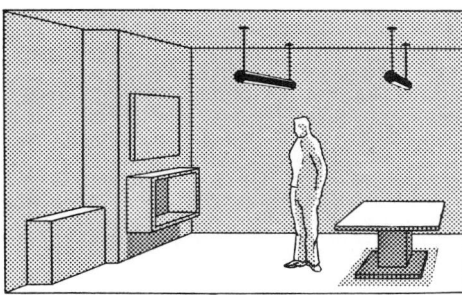

**SEMIDIRECT**

All systems other than direct ones necessarily imply that the lighting fixtures are in the space, whether pendant mounted, surface mounted, or portable. A semidirect system will provide good illuminance on horizontal surfaces, with moderate general brightness.

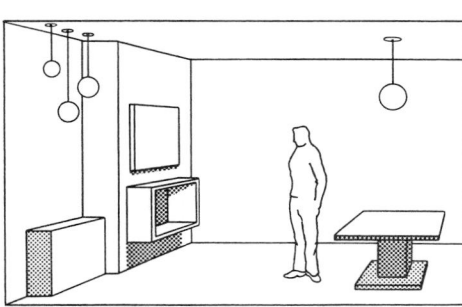

**GENERAL DIFFUSE**

A general diffuse system most typically consists of suspended fixtures, with predominantly translucent surfaces on all sides.

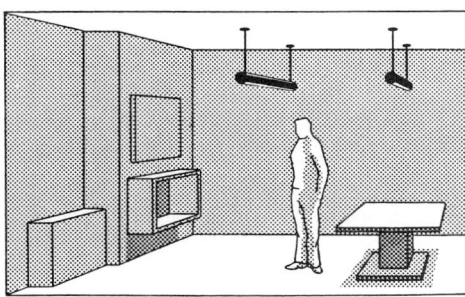

**DIRECT-INDIRECT**

A direct-indirect lighting system will tend to equally emphasize the upper and lower horizontal planes in a space (i.e., the ceiling and the floor).

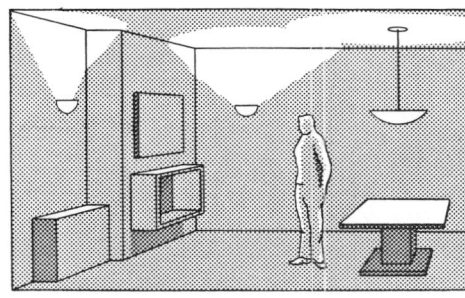

**SEMIINDIRECT**

A semiindirect system will place the emphasis on the ceiling, with some downward or outward-directed light.

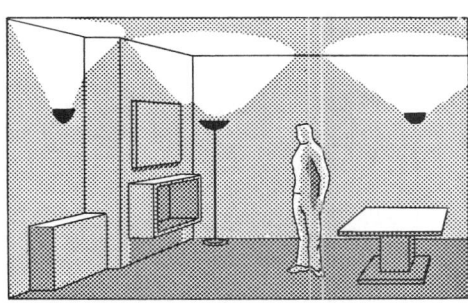

**INDIRECT**

A fully indirect system will bounce all the light off the ceiling, resulting in a low-contrast environment with little shadow.

3. DIRECT GLARE is produced by excessive luminance in the visual field which affects the visual systems as the individual looks around the environment. It is usually associated with the luminaire zone from 45° to 90°. To minimize direct glare, the luminous intensity should be kept out of the 45°–90° zone.

The design of a good lighting fixture is—in photometric terms—often a balance between a fixture that is efficient at delivering illuminance to a work surface (high CU) and one that is comfortable to live with (low glare). Excessive brightness at high angles (above 45°) will tend to cause fixtures to be perceived as glaring. Some manufacturers publish charts of luminous exitance values at critical angles, and some sense of this can be obtained from inspection of the candlepower distribution curve.

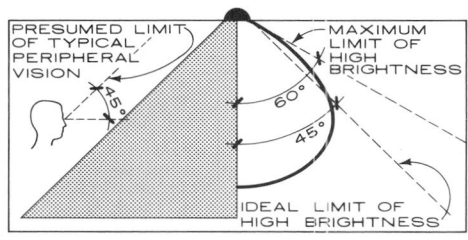

PRESUMED LIMIT OF TYPICAL PERIPHERAL VISION

MAXIMUM LIMIT OF HIGH BRIGHTNESS

45°

60°

45°

IDEAL LIMIT OF HIGH BRIGHTNESS

4. SOURCE TYPE AND MAGNITUDE: The lumen output of a fixture must be proportionate to the desired illuminance level and the size of the space. The color of the source must also be appropriate to the area/space and activity being lighted.

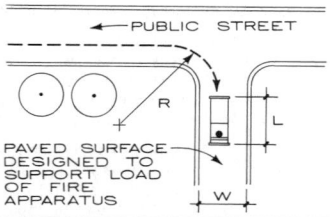

## FIRE APPARATUS ACCESS

Fire apparatus (i.e., pumpers, ladder trucks, tankers) should have unobstructed access to buildings. Check with local fire department for apparatus turning radius (R), length (L), and other operating characteristics.

### RESTRICTED ACCESS
Buildings constructed near cliffs or steep slopes should not restrict access by fire apparatus to only one side of the building. Grades greater than 10 percent make operation of fire apparatus difficult and dangerous.

### FIRE DEPARTMENT RESPONSE TIME FACTOR
Site planning factors that determine response time are street accessibility (curbs, radii, bollards, T-turns, culs-de-sac, street and site slopes, street furniture and architectural obstructions, driveway widths), accessibility for firefighting (fire hydrant and standpipe connection layouts, outdoor lighting, identifying signs), and location (city, town, village, farm). Check with local codes, fire codes, and fire department for area regulations.

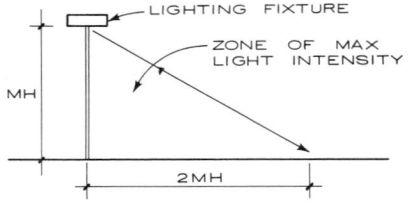

## OUTDOOR LIGHTING

Streets that are properly lighted enable fire fighters to locate hydrants quickly and to position apparatus at night. Avoid layouts that place hydrants and standpipe connections in shadows. In some situations, lighting fixtures can be integrated into exterior of buildings. All buildings should have a street address number on or near the main entrance.

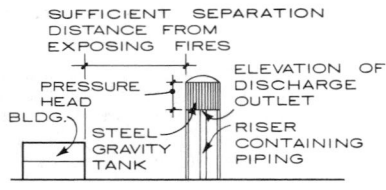

## GRAVITY TANK

Gravity tanks can provide reliable source of pressure to building standpipe or sprinkler systems. Available pressure head increases by 0.434 psi/ft increase of water above tank discharge outlet. Tank capacity in gallons depends on fire hazard, water supply, and other factors. Tanks require periodic maintenance and protection against freezing during cold weather. Locations subject to seismic forces or high winds require special consideration. Gravity tanks also can be integrated within building design.

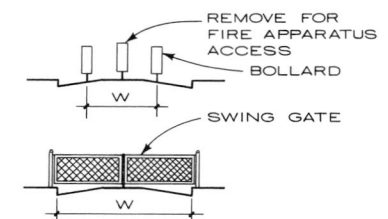

## ACCESS OBSTRUCTIONS

Bollards used for traffic control and fences for security should allow sufficient open road width (W) for access by fire apparatus. Bollards and gates can be secured by standard fire department keyed locks (check with department having jurisdiction).

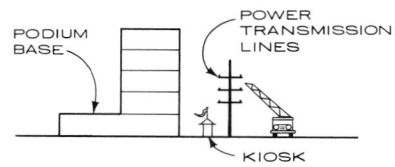

## STREET FURNITURE AND ARCHITECTURAL OBSTRUCTIONS

Utility poles can obstruct use of aerial ladders for rescue and fire suppression operations. Kiosks, outdoor sculpture, fountains, newspaper boxes, and the like can also seriously impede fire fighting operations. Wide podium bases can prevent ladder access to the upper stories of buildings. Canopies and other non-structural building components can also prevent fire apparatus operations close to buildings.

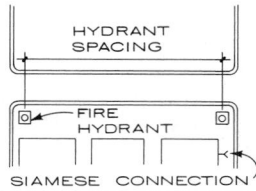

## FIRE HYDRANT AND STANDPIPE CONNECTION LAYOUT

Locate fire hydrants at street intersections and at intermediate points along roads so that spacing between hydrants does not exceed about 300 ft. (Check with local authority having fire jurisdiction for specific requirements.) Hydrants should be placed 2 to 10 ft from curb lines. Siamese connections to standpipes should be visible, marked conspicuously, and be within 200 ft of hydrant to allow rapid connection by fire fighters.

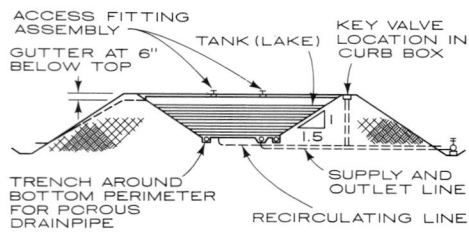

## ON-SITE LAKES

Man-made and natural on-site lakes are used for private firefighting in suburbs, on farms, and at resorts. Piped supply system (suction facilities) is preferred for its quantity flexibility, better maintenance, and accessibility. Man-made lakes such as reservoir liner are berm-supported or sunk in the ground. Lakes and ponds are natural water supplies dependent on the environment. See local codes, fire codes, and fire departments for on-site lake regulations.

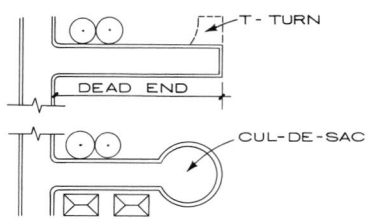

## DRIVEWAY LAYOUTS

Long dead ends (greater than 150 ft) can cause time consuming, hazardous backup maneuvers. Use t-turns, culs-de-sac, and curved driveway layouts to allow unimpeded access to buildings.

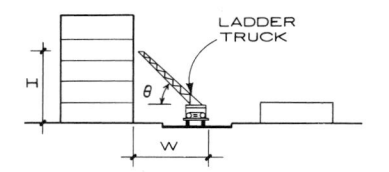

## DRIVEWAY WIDTHS

For full extension of aerial ladders at a safe climbing angle ($\theta$), sufficient driveway width (W) is required. Estimate the required width in feet by: $W = (H - 6) \cot \theta + 4$, where preferred climbing angles are 60 to 80°. Check with local fire department for aerial apparatus operating requirements.

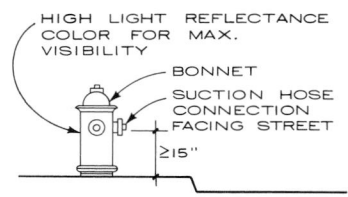

## FIRE HYDRANT PLACEMENT

Fire hose connections should be at least 15" above grade. Do not bury hydrants or locate them behind shrubs or other visual barriers. Avoid locations where runoff water and snow can accumulate. Bollards and fences used to protect hydrants from vehicular traffic must not obstruct fire fighters' access to hose connections. Suction hose connection should usually face the side of arriving fire apparatus.

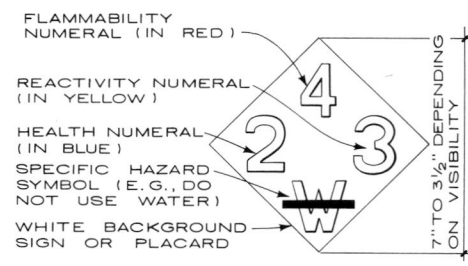

## NFPA 704 DIAMOND SYMBOLS

Standard diamond symbols provide information fire fighters need to avoid injury from hazardous building contents. 0 numeral is the lowest degree of hazard, 4 is highest. Locate symbols near building entrances. Correct spatial arrangement for two kinds of diamond symbols are shown. Consider integrating symbols with overall graphics design of building. (Refer to "Identification of the Fire Hazards of Materials," NFPA No. 704, available from the National Fire Protection Association.)

M. David Egan, P.E.; College of Architecture, Clemson University; Clemson, South Carolina
Nicholas A. Phillips, AIA; Lockwood Greene; New York, New York
National Fire Protection Association, see data sources

# 1   FIRE PROTECTION

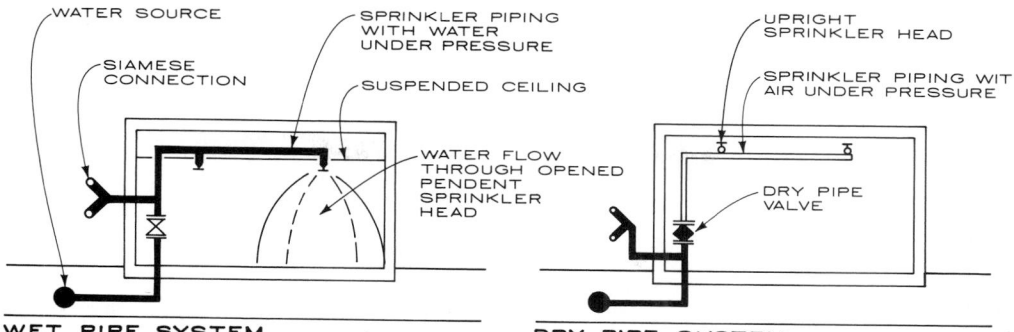

**WET PIPE SYSTEM**

**DRY PIPE SYSTEM**

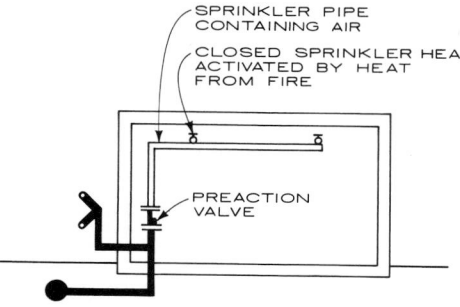

**PREACTION SYSTEM**

**DELUGE SYSTEM**

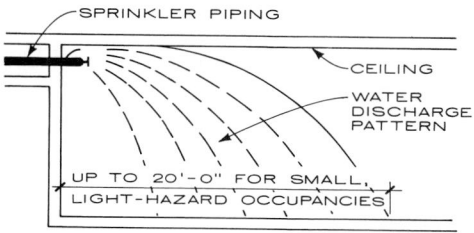

**SIDEWALL SPRINKLER HEAD**
(HORIZONTAL SIDEWALL SHOWN)

Piping can be unobtrusively installed along sides of exposed ceiling beams or joists. In small rooms, sidewall heads provide water discharge coverage without overhead piping.

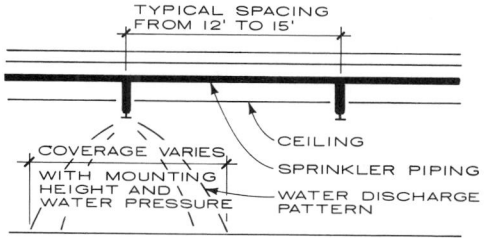

**PENDENT SPRINKLER HEAD**

Can be recessed in ceiling (e.g., coffered, modeled) or hidden above flat metal cover plate. (Flush sprinkler heads are also available.)

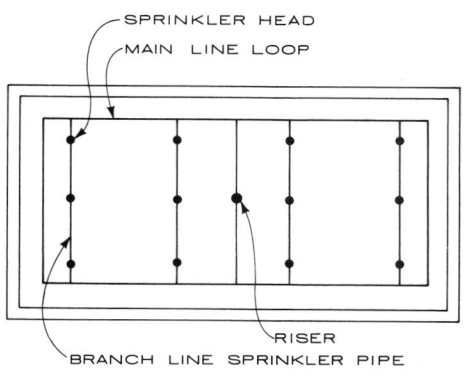

**HYDRAULICALLY DESIGNED SPRINKLER SYSTEM LAYOUT**

Loop provides water flow from two directions to operating sprinkler heads so pipe sizes will be small. Hydraulic calculations can assure delivery of adequate water flow and pressure throughout piping network to meet design requirements.

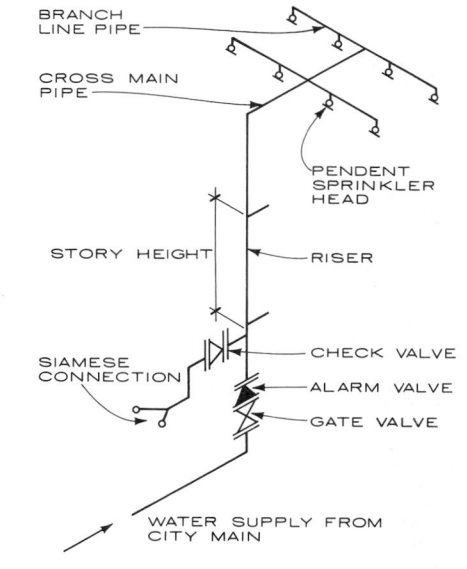

**SPRINKLER SYSTEM RISER**

## TYPES OF SYSTEMS

**WET PIPE:** Piping network contains water under pressure at all times for immediate release through sprinkler heads as they are activated by heat from fire. Wet pipe system is the most widely used system, since water delivery here is faster than with a dry pipe system.

**DRY PIPE:** Piping network contains air (or nitrogen) under pressure. Following loss of air pressure through opened sprinkler head, dry pipe valve opens allowing water to enter piping network and to flow through opened sprinkler head (or heads). Used where piping is subject to freezing.

**PREACTION:** Closed head, dry system containing air in piping network. Preaction valve is activated by independent fire detection system more sensitive than sprinkler heads. The opened preaction valve allows water to fill piping network and to flow through sprinkler heads, as they are activated by heat from fire. Used where leakage or accidental discharge would cause serious damage.

**DELUGE:** Sprinkler heads (or spray nozzles) are open at all times and normally there is no water in piping network. Mechanical or hydraulic valves, operated by heat, smoke, or flame sensitive devices, are used to control water flow to heads by opening water control clapper. Deluge systems are special use systems, as water discharges from all heads (or nozzles) at the same time.

**STANDPIPE AND HOSE:** Dry standpipes are empty water pipes used by fire fighters to connect hoses in buildings to water sources such as ground level fire hydrants. Wet standpipes are water filled pipes permanently connected to public or private water mains for use by building occupants on small fires or by fire fighters.

**FOAM:** Used to suppress flammable liquid fires. Foam can be distributed by piping network to nozzles or other discharge outlets (e.g., tubes, troughs, chutes) depending on the hazard.

**HALON** (halogenated hydrocarbon): Can be used where water damage to building contents would be unacceptable. Piping network connects fixed supply of halon to nozzles that discharge uniform, low concentration throughout room. To avoid piping network, discharge cylinders may be installed throughout room or area. Though generally nontoxic, delayed discharge can cause problems by allowing decomposition of halon. Rapid detection is necessary.

**$CO_2$** (carbon dioxide): Does not conduct electricity and leaves no residue after its use. Piping network connects fixed supply of $CO_2$ to nozzles that discharge $CO_2$ directly on burning materials where location of fire hazard is known (called "local application") or discharge $CO_2$ uniformly throughout room (called "total flooding"). In total flooding systems, safety requirements dictate advance alarm to allow occupants to evacuate area prior to discharge.

**DRY CHEMICAL:** Can be especially useful on electrical and flammable liquid fires. Powdered extinguishing agent, under pressure of dry air or nitrogen, commonly discharged over cooking surfaces (e.g., frying).

## PREPARATION FOR SPRINKLER SYSTEMS

1. Begin planning sprinkler system at the very earliest design stages of project.
2. Determine hazard classification of building and type of system best suited for suppression needs.
3. Refer to national standards (NFPA), state and local codes.
4. Check with authority having jurisdiction:
   a. State and local fire marshals.
   b. Insurance Services Office (ISO).
   c. Insurance underwriting groups such as IRI, OIA, or FM (if they have jurisdiction).
5. Use qualified engineers to design system. Be sure water supply is adequate (e.g., by water flow tests). Integrate system with structural, mechanical, and other building services.
6. Check space requirements for sprinkler equipment. Sprinkler control room must be heated to prevent freezing of equipment.
7. Consider possible future alterations to building.

M. David Egan, P.E.; College of Architecture, Clemson University; Clemson, South Carolina

**FIRE PROTECTION** 1

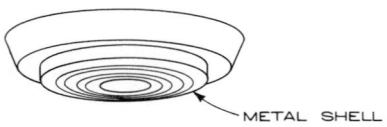

HEAT DETECTOR

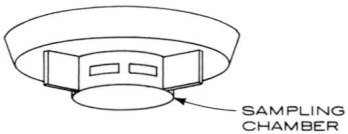

IONIZATION SMOKE DETECTOR

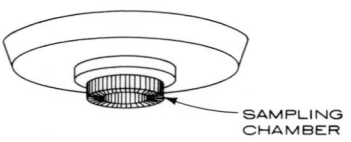

PHOTOELECTRIC SMOKE DETECTOR

**FIRE AND SMOKE DETECTORS**

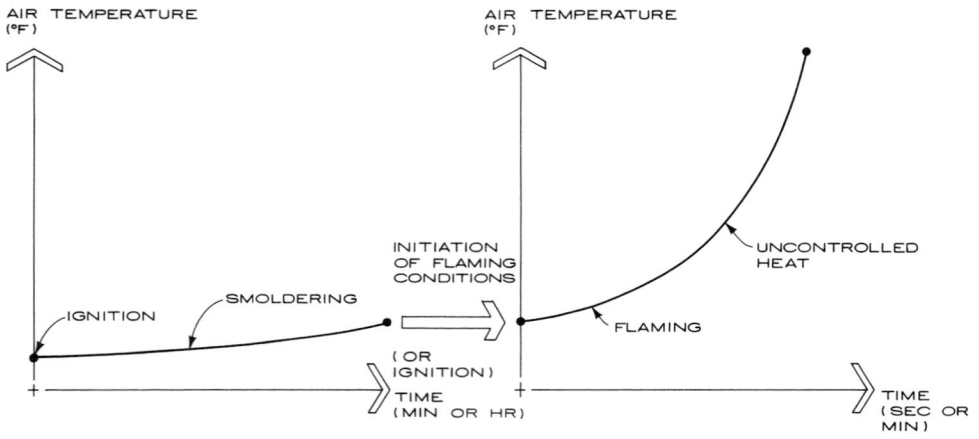

INFRARED FLAME DETECTOR

## HEAT DETECTOR

Fixed temperature heat detectors (e.g., those rated at 135 to 197°F) use low melting point solder or metals that expand when exposed to heat to detect fire. Rate-of-rise heat detectors alarm when rate of temperature change exceeds about 15°F/min. Expansion of air in chamber with calibrated vent is used to detect rapidly developing fires. Devices are available with both rate-of-rise and fixed temperature detection features.

## IONIZATION SMOKE DETECTOR

Ionization detectors use the interruption of small current flow between electrodes by smoke in ionized sampling chamber to detect fire. Dual chamber (with reference chamber exposed only to air temperature, pressure, and humidity) and single chamber detectors are available. Ionization detectors can be used in rooms and in air ducts to detect smoke in air distribution systems.

## PHOTOELECTRIC SMOKE DETECTOR

Photoelectric smoke detectors use the scattering of light by smoke into view of photocell. Sources of light may be either incandescent lamp or light emitting diode (LED). Photoelectric detectors can be used in rooms and in air ducts to detect smoke in air distribution systems.

## INFRARED FLAME DETECTOR

Infrared flame detectors respond to the high-frequency (IR) radiant energy from flames. Alarm is only triggered when IR energy flickers at rate which is characteristic of flames. Infrared detectors can be used in large open areas where rapid development of flaming conditions could occur (e.g., flammable liquids fire hazards).

**STAGES OF FIRE**

## STAGES OF FIRE

Carefully match fire detectors to anticipated fire hazard (e.g., photoelectric smoke detectors for smoldering fires, ionization smoke detectors for flaming fires, infrared flame detectors for flash fires). The time-temperature curves show growth to hazardous conditions for smoldering, flaming, and uncontrolled heat stages of fire.

**RESIDENTIAL OCCUPANCY** (WITH SINGLE SLEEPING AREA)

**RESIDENTIAL OCCUPANCY** (WITH SPLIT SLEEPING AREAS)

## CHECKLIST FOR RESIDENTIAL FIRE DETECTION

1. Use smoke detectors to protect the following (in decreasing order of importance):
   a. Every occupied floor and basement.
   b. Sleeping areas and basement near stairs.
   c. Sleeping areas only.
2. Use heat detectors to protect remote areas (e.g., basement shops, attics) where serious fires could develop before smoke would reach smoke detector or in areas such as garages or kitchens where smoke detectors would be exposed to high smoke levels during normal conditions.
3. Locate smoke detectors on ceilings near center of rooms (or on the upper walls 6 to 12 in. from ceiling) where smoke can collect. In long corridors, consider using two or more detectors.
4. Use closer spacing between detectors where ceiling beams, joists, and the like will interrupt flow of smoke to detector.
5. Do not place smoke detectors near supply air registers or diffusers, or near return air grilles where return air could remove smoke from the area before it reaches detector.
6. For guidelines on fire detection for residences, refer to "Household Fire Warning Equipment," NFPA No. 74, available from the National Fire Protection Association.

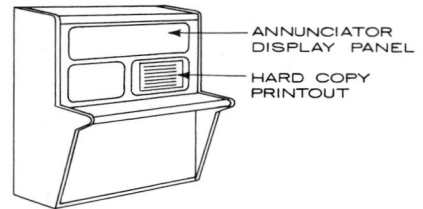

**AUTOMATED CONTROL CONSOLE**

NOTE

When fire is detected (e.g., by smoke, heat, infrared detectors, or water flow indicators in sprinkler system piping), automated control systems immediately summon the fire department. Floor plans of fire area can be projected on annunciator display panel to pinpoint trouble spots. Controls can be designed to automatically shut down fan systems or activate fans and dampers for smoke removal and control. In addition, remote firefighter control panel, with telephone communication to control console and to each floor in building, can be used to control and monitor status of elevators, pumps and emergency generators, fans, dampers, and the like.

M. David Egan, P.E.; College of Architecture, Clemson University; Clemson, South Carolina

**1**    **FIRE PROTECTION**

## NOTES

The simplest fire alarm system is the self-contained, UL approved, residential smoke detector. It senses products of combustion, sounds an alarm, and signals when the battery needs replacement. Local fire departments campaign for their use in homes and apartments. They are required in motel and hotel rooms by local and/or state codes.

Where public safety is involved in schools, hospitals, office buildings, and other commercial establishments or institutions, more complex systems evolve. Although there are still applications for small hardwired and relay-operated alarm signaling systems, the trend is toward microprocessor-based digital multiplex systems that not only signal events, but initiate events. These may include conditioning fans and dampers for smoke control, closing fire doors and shutters, releasing locked doors, capturing elevators, and transmitting voice messages. Voice communication is required in "high-rise buildings" of specific group occupancies as defined by the BOCA Code. It is also recommended for large low-rise buildings to enhance life safety.

Fire alarm systems can be "stand alone" or a subsystem, integrated with security and building management functions. Processors and their peripheral equipment are generally located in a fully manned central command center accessible to arriving firemen. Depending on the degree of reliability desired, redundancy can be provided in wiring and processors, along with battery backup.

Transponder cabinets can be 36 in. wide x 8 in. deep. They must have battery backup, be UL approved, conform to NFPA No. 72, and may also require local approval. In small systems where only one cabinet may be required, all the functions required at the command center can be incorporated in the same cabinet and located in the main entrance lobby. In larger systems, remote cabinets are generally located in wiring closets throughout the building and can be provided with programmed intelligence to function independent of the central processor, should it fail.

Basic signaling systems can be:

NONCODED: Continuous sounding evacuation signal.
MASTER CODED: Four rounds of a repeating signal.
SELECTIVE CODED: Same as above except individual devices generate an assigned number code of up to three groups per round.
PRESIGNAL: Same as above except signals sound only at selected areas to prompt investigation. If hazard is determined, evacuation signal is initiated by key.
VOICE: Direct (by microphone) or automatic prerecorded messages are transmitted over speakers, following an "alert" signal.

Range in size from 4 to 12 in. diameter. Can be recessed behind a grille. Operation can be single stroke or continuous.

**FIREMAN TELEPHONE JACK PLATE**

Approximately 10 in. high x 7 in. wide with visual signal. Visual signal can be flashing light or stroke. Can be provided with directional sound projector.

**SMOKE DETECTOR**

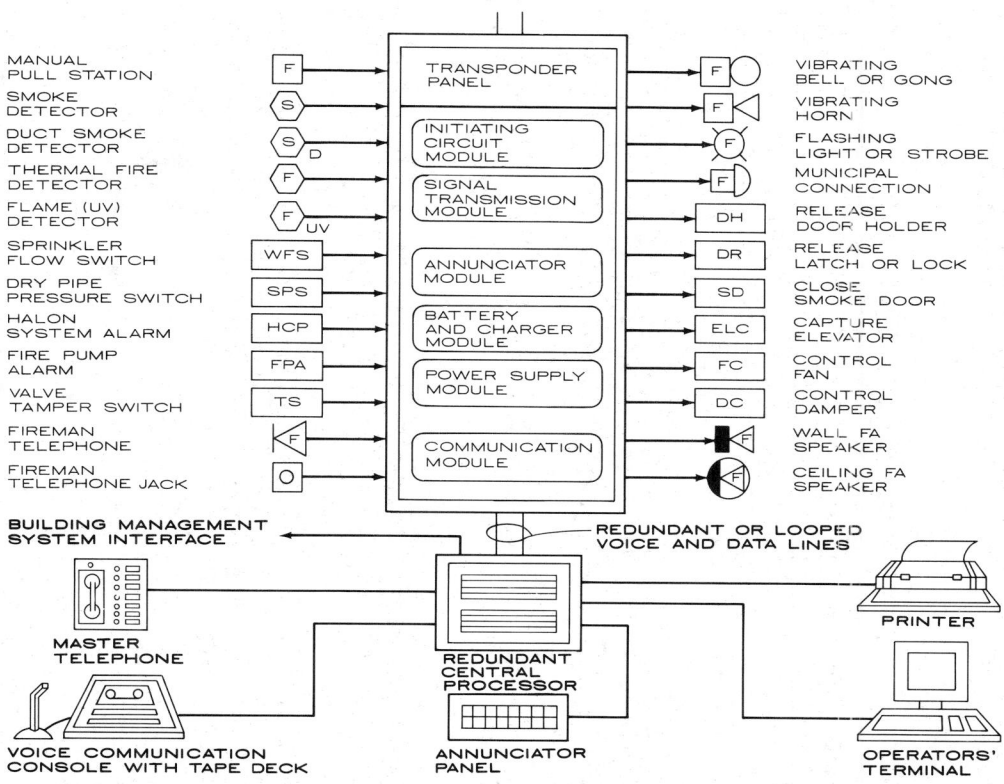

| MANUAL PULL STATION | F | | TRANSPONDER PANEL | | F | VIBRATING BELL OR GONG |
| SMOKE DETECTOR | S | | | | F | VIBRATING HORN |
| DUCT SMOKE DETECTOR | S D | | INITIATING CIRCUIT MODULE | | F | FLASHING LIGHT OR STROBE |
| THERMAL FIRE DETECTOR | F | | SIGNAL TRANSMISSION MODULE | | F | MUNICIPAL CONNECTION |
| FLAME (UV) DETECTOR | F UV | | | | DH | RELEASE DOOR HOLDER |
| SPRINKLER FLOW SWITCH | WFS | | ANNUNCIATOR MODULE | | DR | RELEASE LATCH OR LOCK |
| DRY PIPE PRESSURE SWITCH | SPS | | | | SD | CLOSE SMOKE DOOR |
| HALON SYSTEM ALARM | HCP | | BATTERY AND CHARGER MODULE | | ELC | CAPTURE ELEVATOR |
| FIRE PUMP ALARM | FPA | | POWER SUPPLY MODULE | | FC | CONTROL FAN |
| VALVE TAMPER SWITCH | TS | | | | DC | CONTROL DAMPER |
| FIREMAN TELEPHONE | F | | COMMUNICATION MODULE | | | WALL FA SPEAKER |
| FIREMAN TELEPHONE JACK | O | | | | F | CEILING FA SPEAKER |

BUILDING MANAGEMENT SYSTEM INTERFACE

REDUNDANT OR LOOPED VOICE AND DATA LINES

MASTER TELEPHONE

PRINTER

REDUNDANT CENTRAL PROCESSOR

VOICE COMMUNICATION CONSOLE WITH TAPE DECK

ANNUNCIATOR PANEL

OPERATORS' TERMINAL

**ELECTRONIC FIRE ALARM / COMMUNICATION SYSTEM FUNCTION DIAGRAM**

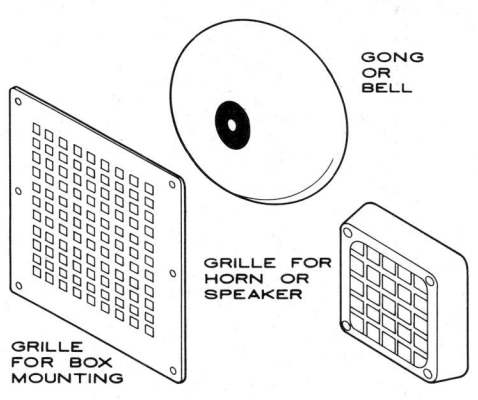

GONG OR BELL

GRILLE FOR HORN OR SPEAKER

GRILLE FOR BOX MOUNTING

Approximately 7 in. high x 5 in. wide surface or semi-flush mounted. Can be provided with break-glass (rod) feature. Operation can be coded or noncoded.

**BELL AND COVERS**

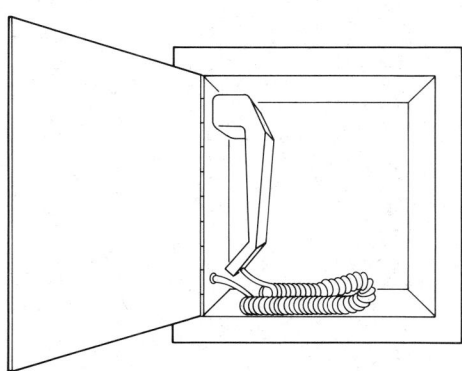

Standard single gang device plate size. Located at exit stair doors and elevator lobbies. Jack matches plug on phone carried by firemen.

**FIREMAN TELEPHONE CABINET**

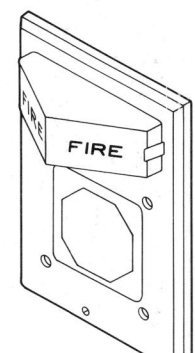

Approximately 6 in. diameter, 5 in. high (maximum). Can be hardwired or electronically addressable. Operation can be ionization or photoelectric.

**HORN / SPEAKER / VISUAL SIGNAL**

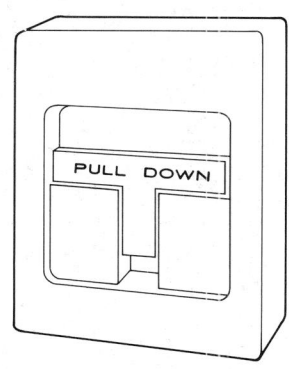

Approximately 12 in. high x 10 in. wide x 3 in. deep, surface or flush. Provided in lieu of jack plates for a total system. Door can be glass or plastic pane.

**MANUAL PULL STATION**

Richard F. Humenn, P.E.; Joseph R. Loring & Associates, Inc., Consulting Engineers; New York, New York

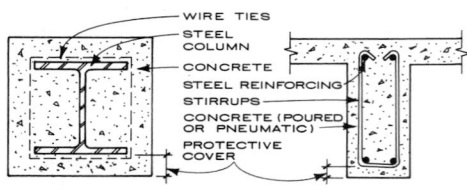

**CONCRETE ENCASEMENT**

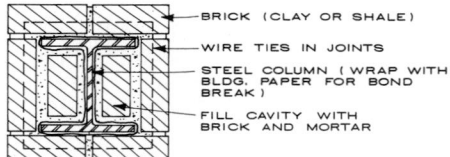

**MASONRY ENCLOSURE**

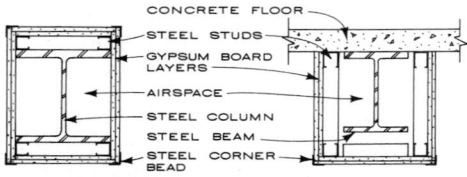

**GYPSUM MEMBRANE ENCLOSURE**

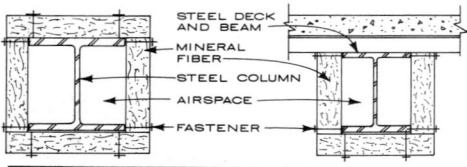

**MINERAL FIBER MEMBRANE ENCLOSURE**

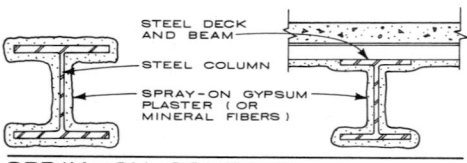

**SPRAY—ON CONTOUR**

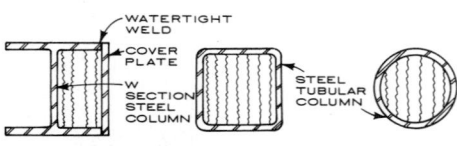

**LIQUID FILLED COLUMN**

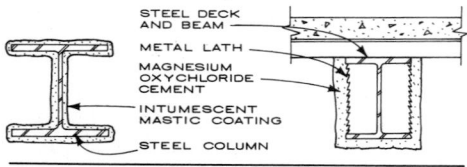

**COATINGS**

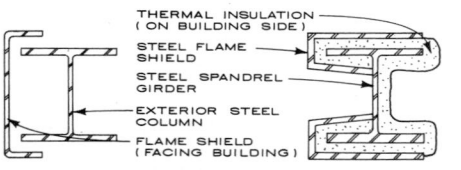

**FLAME SHIELDS**

## UNPROTECTED STEEL

At temperatures greater than 1000°F, mild steel loses about one half of its ultimate room temperature strength. Consequently, fire tests on steel beams and columns are terminated when the steel's surface temperatures reach a predetermined limit or when the applied design loading can no longer be sustained (specific alternate test procedures are given by ASTM Standard Methods E 119). Fire resistance ratings are expressed in terms of duration in hours of fire exposure to standard temperature conditions in a test furnace (e.g., 3/4 hr, 1 hr, 2 hr, 3 hr). For further information on fire resistance tests and fire protection of steel, see American Iron and Steel Institute's handbook, "Fire-Resistant Steel-Frame Construction."

## CONCRETE ENCASEMENT

Achieved fire resistance for steel members encased in concrete depends on thickness of protective concrete cover, concrete mixture, and structural restraint (i.e., method of support and method of confining thermal expansion). Lightweight aggregate concrete has better fire resistance than normal weight concrete because of its higher moisture content and higher thermal resistance to heat flow. Heavier members require less cover for equivalent fire resistance, since they have greater mass. For data on columns encased in concrete, see National Fire Protection Association's "Fire Protection Handbook." Gunite, a mixture of cement, sand, and water, can be spray-applied by air pressure, but requires steel reinforcing. For exterior applications, reinforcing steel with less than 2 in. of concrete cover usually requires corrosion resistant primers.

## MASONRY ENCLOSURE

Masonry materials (brick, concrete block, gypsum block, hollow clay tile) can be used to encase steel columns. The cores (or cells), which provide openings for reinforcing, also can be filled with mortar or insulating materials such as vermiculite to increase thermal resistance to heat flow. For data on fire resistance of masonry constructions, see National Concrete Masonry Association's "Fire Safety with Concrete Masonry."

## GYPSUM MEMBRANE ENCLOSURE

Gypsum board or troweled plaster (e.g., vermiculite-gypsum, perlite-gypsum) or lath can be used to protect steel at building locations not exposed to moisture. Gypsum retards heat flow to steel by releasing chemically combined water (called "calcination") at temperatures above 180°F. To protect steel columns, gypsum board layers can be attached to steel studs by means of self-tapping screws or installed behind a galvanized or stainless sheet steel cover. For data on fire resistance of gypsum constructions, see Gypsum Association's "Fire Resistance Design Data Manual."

## MINERAL FIBER MEMBRANE ENCLOSURE

When exposed to fire, mineral fiber (made from molten rock or slag) retards heat flow to steel because of its low thermal conductivity (it can withstand temperatures above 2000°F without melting). Mineral fiber requires a protective covering when exposed to outdoor conditions or the possibility of damage from accidental impact or abrasion.

## SPRAY-ON CONTOUR

Spray-on applied cementitious mixtures (lightweight aggregate plasters with insulating fibers or vermiculite) or mineral fibers mixed with inorganic binders provide thermal barrier to heat from fire. The steel surface must be clean and free of loose paint, rust, oil, and grease before spraying, and a protective primer may be required. In addition, spraying should not be scheduled during cold conditions. Lightweight spray-on contours can be easily damaged during installation of nearby gas and water pipes, air ducts, and the like, and they are subject to flaking during normal use. Pins, studs, and other mechanical fasteners can be used to secure moisture or abrasion resistant protective finish coatings. Applications more than 2 in. thick generally require wire mesh or lath reinforcement.

## LIQUID FILLED COLUMNS

During a fire the liquid, circulating by convection from fire floor columns, removes heat. Storage tanks or city water mains can be used to replace water converted to steam (vented by pressure relief valves or rupture discs). Pumps also may be used to avoid stagnant areas within an interconnected water circulation system of columns and piping. To prevent corrosion, use a rust inhibitor such as potassium nitrate. To prevent freezing in cold climates, use an antifreeze such as potassium carbonate. During construction, strict quality control is essential to achieve a watertight system.

## COATINGS

Intumescent mastic coatings can be spray-applied like paint. When exposed to fire, the coating absorbs heat above about 300°F by expanding into a thick, lightweight thermal barrier more than about 150 times its initial thickness. This gas filled multicellular layer retards heat flow by releasing cooling gases and blocks off oxygen supply. Coatings should only be applied to steel surfaces that are free of dirt, scale, and oil. A multilayer system, consisting of intumescent mastic layers with glass fiber reinforcing between, is needed to achieve fire resistance ratings greater than 1 hr.

When exposed to heat, magnesium oxychloride cement retards heat flow to steel by releasing water of hydration at temperatures above about 570°F. Corrosion resistant priming may be required to assure proper adhesion of magnesium oxychloride to steel surfaces. In high intensity fires (e.g., flammable liquid or gas fires), magnesium oxychloride does not spall and the magnesium oxide residue acts as an efficient heat reflector.

## FLAME SHIELDS

Steel flame shields can deflect heat and flames from burning building away from exterior structural steel members. For example, girder top and bottom flanges avoid direct flame impingement during fire by having flame shield protection with thermal insulation behind girder.

### NOTES

1. Check prevailing building code for required fire resistance ratings of building constructions. Begin planning steel fire protection during the early stages of a project so that it can be integrated into building design. Consult early with authority having jurisdiction and insurance underwriting groups such as Industrial Risk Insurers, American Insurance Association, or Factory Mutual System.

2. Refer to fire resistance data based on ASTM E 119 test procedures from Underwriters' Laboratories, Factory Mutual, and other nationally recognized testing laboratories.

3. In general, fire resistance of constructions with cavity airspace (e.g., walls, floor-ceilings) will be greater than similar identical weight constructions without airspace.

4. If possible, locate cavity airspace on side of construction opposite potential fire exposure.

5. For most situations, fire resistance of constructions with thermal insulating materials such as mineral fiber and glass fiber in cavity airspace (e.g., doors, walls) will be greater than identical constructions without cavity insulation. Be careful, however, since adding thermal insulation to suspended floor-ceiling assemblies may lower fire resistance by causing metal suspension grid system to buckle or warp from elevated surface temperatures.

6. When plenum spaces above suspended ceilings are used for mechanical system return airflow, fire resistance of floor-ceiling assemblies will be diminished. Conversely, plenums under positive pressure from supply airflow can achieve greater fire resistances than under neutral pressure conditions (e.g., no air circulation in plenum).

7. For beams and columns, the higher the ratio of weight (e.g., pounds per unit length) to heated perimeter (i.e., surface area exposed to fire) the greater the fire resistance.

8. Beams and columns with membrane enclosure protection will have less surface area exposed to fire than identical members with spray-on applied contour protection. In addition, membrane enclosures (e.g., gypsum board, mineral fiber, magnesium oxychloride, or metal lath) form airspaces on both sides of W and S section webs.

M. David Egan, P.E.; College of Architecture, Clemson University; Clemson, South Carolina

1 **FIRE PROTECTION**

## GENERAL

Life safety in long span buildings is of equal concern as appropriate form and cost in selection of a long span roof structure. Exit flow must be carefully evaluated by simulating exiting under a number of adverse conditions rather than by just complying with building codes. Fire safety begins by limiting fire load, as codes rarely require fire protection or sprinkler systems. Auxiliary uses having any fire risk (e.g., food handling) should be carefully fire separated from the rest of the structure.

Various examples of long span structures in the table are rated for sensitivity to the structural factors noted below.

## NATURAL CONDITIONS

a. Uneven or excessive snow and ice loads: Geometry, equipment, or exterior structure can contribute no multiple spaces to snow drifting or ice buildup.

b. Ponding: Provide positive drainage to dump water from the structure when roof drains clog.

c. Wind: Evaluate potential of wind to induce destructive vibration in members or connections.

d. Thermal: Diurnal and seasonal temperature cycles can cause significant changes in structural shape and member stresses and can lead to fatigue failure.

e. Freeze/thaw cycles: Corrosive atmosphere with long-term effect on structural performance, particularly exposed or concrete structures, should be evaluated.

## PRIMARY STRESSES

f. Two or more load paths for all loads should be provided wherever possible. The more area a single member supports, the greater should be its safety factor.

g. Compression failure: Resistance to lateral buckling of long members is crucial. Use members that assure initial and verifiable alignment.

h. Tension failure: Dynamic instability under wind or other vibration loading should be carefully verified.

## SECONDARY STRESSES

i. Deflection: Changed orientation of members at joints under load can increase stresses destructively.

j. Member interaction: Load flows through structures in a way to minimize structural work. Check all possible load paths of complex geometric structures.

k. Nonstructural connections: Assemblies attached to a structure will influence structural load flow and even become part of the load flow if the attachment changes the deflected shape.

l. Scale: Most systems have a span beyond which self-weight becomes a severe limit.

m. Stress concentration: Check stresses at changes of cross section, holes, and connections. High-strength materials are particularly sensitive.

## TOLERANCES

n. Erection alignment: True member length and spatial position are crucial for proper alignment and load flow.

o. Creep: Length change over time will influence both primary and secondary stresses for erection alignment.

p. Supports and foundations: Supports must accept movements due to deflections from primary and secondary stresses and differential foundation settlement.

## QUALITY CONTROL

q. Engineering design must not be compromised by time, scheduling, design changes, or building codes. Computerized design must be carefully verified as resolving all primary and secondary stresses.

r. Construction methods should be selected carefully to safely locate the structural components accurately in space.

s. Site observation: Only when the structure is properly established in space should it be accepted. Changes in construction should be carefully checked.

t. Structural building maintenance: Conditions and alignment of various members, especially crucial nonredundant members, should be verified on a regular schedule. Consider equipment to detect excessive deflections.

u. Nonstructural building maintenance: Condition of building components should not adversely affect the structure (e.g., keep roof drains open, prevent excessive equipment vibration, maintain expansion joints).

William Bauman Jr.; University of Oklahoma; Norman, Oklahoma

## LONG SPAN SYSTEMS

| SYSTEM | MATERIAL (OR SHAPE) | ONE WAY | TWO WAY | FLAT SURFACE | PITCHED PLANE | CURVED PLANE | CURVE SURFACE | SPAN RANGE (FT) | SPAN/DEPTH RATIO (FT) | STRONG FACTORS | SENSITIVITY FACTORS |
|---|---|---|---|---|---|---|---|---|---|---|---|
| Joist | Steel | • | | • | – | | | | 20–24 | p,q,s | a,b,f,g |
| Truss | Steel | • | | • | • | – | | | 16–22 | | a,b,f,g,m |
| | | | • | • | | – | | | 16–20 | a,b,f | m |
| | Wood | • | | • | • | – | | | 9–12 | | a,b,f,g |
| | | | • | • | | – | | | 9–12 | b,f | |
| Space frame | Steel | | • | • | | | | | 16–20 | f | a,i,j,n,p, q,s,u |
| Stress skin | Steel | • | | • | | – | | | 14–18 | f | a,i,j,n,p, q,s,u |
| Beam | Steel | • | – | • | | | | | 18–22 | a,q | b,f |
| | Wood | • | | • | | | | | 16–20 | | b,f |
| | Prestressed concrete | • | | • | | | | | 22–26 | | b,f |
| Rigid frame | Steel | • | – | • | – | | | | 20–24 | a | f |
| | Wood | • | | • | – | | | | 18–22 | | f |
| | Prestressed concrete | • | – | • | – | | | | 24–28 | | f |
| Cable stayed | | | | | | | | | | i,p | c,h,q |
| Folded plate | Steel | • | | | • | | | | 18–22 | a,b | f,m |
| | Concrete | • | | | • | | | | 10–14 | b | a,f,m |
| | Wood | • | | | • | | | | 12–16 | b | a,f,m |
| Cylindric shell | Concrete | • | | | | • | | | 10–14 | b | a,m,o |
| Vault | Concrete | • | • | | | • | | | 6–10 | b | c,o |
| Arch | Concrete | • | • | | | • | | | 3–7 | b | a,d,f |
| | Steel | • | • | | | • | | | 4–8 | b | a,d,f |
| | Wood | • | • | | | • | | | 3–7 | b | a,d,f |
| Dome | Concrete | | • | | | | • | | 5–8 | c,f,g,b | a,d,o |
| | Radial steel | | • | | | | • | | 4–8 | b,c | a,d,f,g |
| | Geodesic steel | | • | | | | • | | 2–5 | a,b,c,f,g | d,i,j,n |
| | Radial wood | | • | | | | • | | 3–6 | b,c | a,d,f,g |
| | Lamella wood | | • | | | | • | | 3–6 | a,b,c,f,g | d,n |
| Pneumatic | Steel | | • | | | | • | | 4–7 | d | a,b,c |
| Cable | Parallel | • | | | | • | | | 8–16 | d | a,b,c,f |
| | Radial | | • | | | | • | | 6–12 | d | a,c,f |
| | Hyperbolic | | • | | | | • | | 4–8 | b,d,f | a,c |
| | Tent | | • | | | | • | | 3–6 | b,f | a,c |
| Hyperbolic | Concrete | | • | | | | • | | 3–6 | f | a,d,o |

### NOTES

1. Steel is A-36; wood is laminated, heavy timber; concrete is reinforced with steel; prestressed concrete is prestressed with steel.

2. Cable stayed system can give auxiliary support to trusses, beams, or frames, greatly reducing span and member sizes, but adds a tension structure.

3. Lamella arches make two-way arch structures, improve redundancy.

4. Domes can also be structured with aluminum.

5. Pneumatics are fabric roofs, pressurized, stabilized with steel cables.

| FLOOR STRUCTURE ASSEMBLIES FOR ADDITIONAL INFORMATION CONSULT MANUFACTURERS' LITERATURE AND TRADE ASSOCIATIONS | | DEPTH OF SYSTEM (IN.) | STANDARD MEMBER SIZES (IN.) | DEAD LOAD OF STRUCTURE (PSF) | SUITABLE LIVE LOAD RANGE (PSF) | SPAN RANGE (FT) | DIMENSIONAL STABILITY AFFECTED BY |
|---|---|---|---|---|---|---|---|
| WOOD JOIST | PLYWOOD SUBFLOOR / WOOD JOIST / CEILING | 7-13 | Nominal joist 2 x 6, 8, 10, and 12 | 5-8 | 30-40 | Up to 18 | Deflection |
| WOOD TRUSS OR PLYWOOD JOIST | PLYWOOD SUBFLOOR / PLYWOOD JOIST (OR WOOD TRUSS) / CEILING | 13-21 | Plywood joists 12, 14, 16, 18, and 20 | 6-12 | 30-40 | 12-30 | Deflection |
| WOOD BEAM AND PLANK | WOOD PLANK / WOOD BEAM | 10-22 | Nominal plank 2, 3, and 4 | 6-16 | 30-40 | 10-22 | — |
| LAMINATED WOOD BEAM AND PLANK | WOOD PLANK / GLUE LAMINATED WOOD BEAM | 8-22 | Nominal plank 2, 3, and 4 | 6-20 | 30-40 | 8-34 | — |
| STEEL JOIST | PLYWOOD SUBFLOOR / WOOD NAILER / STEEL JOIST / CEILING | 9-31 | Steel joists 8-30 | 8-20 | 30-40 | 16-40 | Deflection |
| STEEL JOIST | CONCRETE SLAB / STEEL CENTERING / STEEL JOIST / CEILING | 11-75 | Steel joists 8-72 | 30-110 | 30-100 | 16-60 (up to 130) | Deflection |
| LIGHT-WEIGHT STEEL FRAME | PLYWOOD SUBFLOOR / LIGHTWEIGHT STEEL FRAME / CEILING | 7-12 | Consult manufacturers' literature | 6-20 | 30-60 | 10-22 | — |
| STEEL FRAME | CONCRETE SLAB / STEEL CENTERING / STEEL BEAM / CEILING | 9-15 | — | 35-60 | 30-100 | 16-35 | Deflection |
| STEEL FRAME | CONCRETE TOPPING / PRECAST CONCRETE PLANK / STEEL BEAM / CEILING | 8-16 | Concrete plank 16-48 W 4-12 D | 40-75 | 60-150 | Up to 50 Generally below 35 | Deflection and creep |
| PRECAST CONCRETE | CONCRETE TOPPING / PRECAST CONCRETE PLANK / CONCRETE BEAM | 6-12 | Concrete plank 16-48 W 4-12 D | 40-75 | 60-150 | Up to 60 Generally below 35 | Deflection and creep |
| ONE-WAY CONCRETE SLAB | CONCRETE SLAB / CONCRETE BEAM | 4-10 | — | 50-120 | 40-150 | 10-20 More with prestressing | — |
| TWO-WAY CONCRETE SLAB | CONCRETE SLAB / CONCRETE BEAM | 4-10 | — | 50-120 | 40-250 | 10-30 More with prestressing | — |
| ONE-WAY RIBBED CONCRETE SLAB | CONCRETE SLAB / RIB (JOIST) | 8-22 | Standard pan forms 20 and 30 W 6-20 D | 40-90 | 40-150 | 15-50 More with prestressing | Creep |
| TWO-WAY RIBBED CONCRETE SLAB | CONCRETE SLAB / RIB (JOIST) | 8-22 | Standard dome forms 19 x 19, 30 x 30 6-20 D | 75-105 | 60-200 | 25-60 More with prestressing | Creep |
| CONCRETE FLAT SLAB | CONCRETE SLAB / DROP PANEL / CAPITAL / COLUMN | 6-16 | Min. slab thickness 5 without } Drop 4 with } panel | 75-170 | 60-250 | 20-40 Up to 70 with prestressing | Creep |
| PRECAST DOUBLE TEE | CONCRETE TOPPING / PRECAST DOUBLE TEE | 8-18 | 4', 5', 6', 8', and 10' W 6-16 D | 50-80 | 40-150 | 20-50 | Creep |
| PRECAST TEE | CONCRETE TOPPING / PRECAST SINGLE TEE | 18-38 | 16-36 D | 50-90 | 40-150 | 25-65 | Creep |
| COMPOSITE | CONCRETE SLAB / WELDED STUD (SHEAR CONNECTOR) / STEEL BEAM | 4-6 | — | 35-70 | 60-200 | Up to 35 | Deflection |
| CONCRETE FLAT PLATE | COLUMN / CONCRETE FLAT PLATE | 5-14 | — | 60-175 | 60-200 | 18-35 More with prestressing | Creep |

Roger K. Lewis, FAIA, and Mehmet T. Ergene, Architect; Roger K. Lewis, FAIA, & Associates; Washington, D.C.

| BAY SIZE CHARAC-TERISTICS | REQUIRES FINISHED FLOOR SURFACE | REQUIRES FINISHED CEILING SURFACE | SERVICE PLENUM | COMPARATIVE RESISTANCE TO SOUND TRANSMISSION | | FIRE RESISTIVE RATING PER CODE AND UNDERWRITERS | | CONSTRUC-TION TYPE CLASSIFI-CATION | REMARKS |
|---|---|---|---|---|---|---|---|---|---|
| | | | | IMPACT | AIRBORNE | UNPRO-TECTED HOURS | MAXIMUM PROTECTED HOURS | | |
| — | Yes | Visual or fire protection purposes | Between joists —one way | Poor | Fair | — | 2 (combustible) | 4B (A) 3C (B) | Economical, light, easy to construct. Limited to lowrise construction |
| — | Yes | Visual or fire protection purposes | Between trusses and joists —two ways | Poor | Fair | — | 2 (combustible) | 4B (A) 3C (B) | Close dimensional toler-ances; cutting holes through web permissible |
| Maximum beam spacing 8'-0" | Optional | No | Under structure —one way | Poor | Fair | — | 2 | 3A 6" x 10" frame min. 4" planks min. | Most efficient with planks continuous over more than one span |
| — | Optional | No | Under structure —one way | Poor | Fair | — | 2 | 3A 6" x 10" frame min. 4" planks min. | — |
| Light joists 16" to 30" o.c. Heavy joists 4'–12' o.c. | Yes | Visual or fire protection purposes | Between joists —two ways | Poor | Poor | — | 1 | 3C (B) | — |
| Light joists 16" to 30" o.c. Heavy joists 4'–12' o.c. | No | Visual or fire protection purposes | Between joists —two ways | Poor | Fair | — | 1–3 | 1, 2 and 3 | Economical system, selective partition place-ment required. Canti-levers difficult |
| — | Yes | Visual or fire protection purposes | Under structure | Poor | Poor | — | 1 | 3C (B) | — |
| — | No | Visual or fire protection purposes | Under structure | Poor | Fair | 1–3 | 1–4 | 1, 2, and 3 | — |
| — | Optional | Visual or fire protection purposes | Under structure | Fair | Fair | — | 1–4 | 1, 2, and 3 | — |
| — | Optional | No | Under structure | Fair | Fair | 2–4 | 3–4 | 1 and 2 | — |
| — | No | No | Under structure | Good | Good | 1–4 | 3–4 | 1 and 2 | Restricted to short spans because of exces-sive dead load |
| L ≤ 1.33 W | No | No | Under structure | Good | Good | 1–4 | 3–4 | 1 and 2 | Suitable for concen-trated loads, easy parti-tion placement |
| — | No | No | Between ribs —one way | Good | Good | 1–4 | 3–4 | 1 and 2 | Economy through re-use of forms, shear at supports controlling factor |
| L ≤ 1.33 W | No | No | Under structure | Good | Good | 1–4 | 3–4 | 1 and 2 | For heavy loads, columns should be equidistant. Not good for cantilevers |
| L ≤ 1.33 W | No | No | Under structure | Good | Good | 1–4 | 3–4 | 1 and 2 | Drop panels against shear required for spans above 12 ft |
| — | Optional | Visual purposes; differential camber | Between ribs —one way | Fair | Good | 2–3 | 3–4 | 1 and 2 | Most widely used pre-stressed concrete product in the medium span range |
| — | Optional | Visual purposes; differential camber | Between ribs —one way | Fair | Good | 2–3 | 3–4 | 1 and 2 | Easy construction, lack continuity, poor earth-quake resistance |
| — | No | Visual or fire protection purposes | Under structure | Good | Good | — | 1–4 | 1, 2, and 3 | — |
| L ≤ 1.33 W | No | No | Under structure | Good | Good | 1–4 | 3–4 | 1 and 2 | Uniform slab thickness, economical to form, easy to cantilever |

Roger K. Lewis, FAIA, and Mehmet T. Ergene, Architect; Roger K. Lewis, FAIA, & Associates; Washington, D.C.

| ROOF STRUCTURE ASSEMBLIES<br>FOR ADDITIONAL INFORMATION CONSULT MANUFACTURER'S LITERATURE AND TRADE ASSOCIATIONS | | DEPTH OF SYSTEM (IN.) | STANDARD MEMBER SIZES (IN.) | DEAD LOAD OF STRUCTURE (PSF) | SUITABLE LIVE LOAD RANGE (PSF) | SPAN RANGE (FT) | BAY SIZE CHARAC-TERISTICS | DIMENSIONAL STABILITY AFFECTED BY |
|---|---|---|---|---|---|---|---|---|
| WOOD RAFTER | 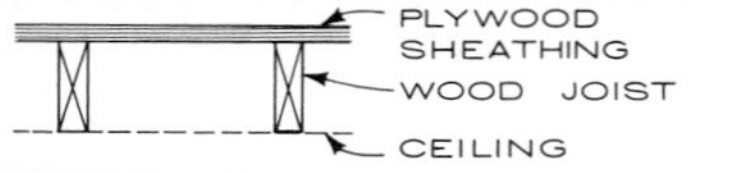 — PLYWOOD SHEATHING — WOOD JOIST — CEILING | 5–13 | Nominal rafters 2 x 4, 6, 8, 10, and 12 | 4–8 | 10–50 | Up to 22 | — | Deflection |
| WOOD BEAM AND PLANK |  — WOOD PLANK — WOOD BEAM (OR LAMINATED BEAM) | 8–22 | Nominal planks 2, 3, and 4 | 5–12 | 10–50 | 8–34 | Maximum beam spacing 8'-0" | — |
| PLYWOOD PANEL |  — PLYWOOD (STRESSED SKIN) PANELS | 3¼ and 8¼ | — | 3–6 | 10–50 | 8–32 | 4'-0" modules | — |
| WOOD TRUSS | 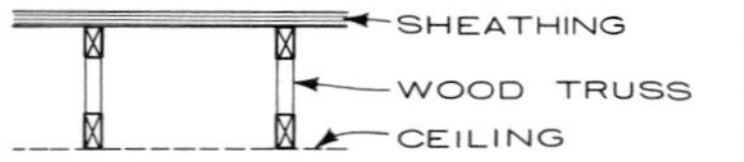 — SHEATHING — WOOD TRUSS — CEILING | Varies (1'–12') | — | 5–15 | 10–50 | 30–50 | 2'–8' between trusses | Deflection |
| STEEL TRUSS | 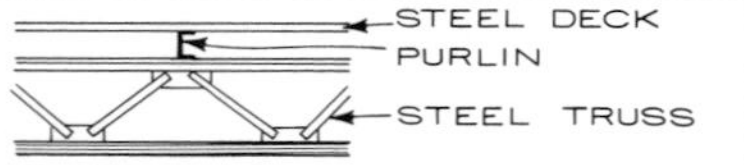 — STEEL DECK — PURLIN — STEEL TRUSS | Varies | — | 15–25 | 10–60 | 100–200 | — | Deflection |
| STEEL JOIST | 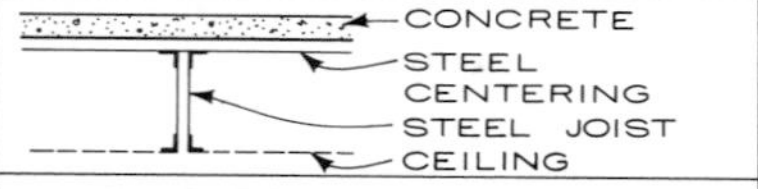 — CONCRETE — STEEL CENTERING — STEEL JOIST — CEILING | 11–75 | Steel joists 8–72 | 10–28 | 10–50 | Up to 96 | Light joists 16"–30" o.c. Heavy joists 4'–12' o.c. | Deflection |
| STEEL JOIST | 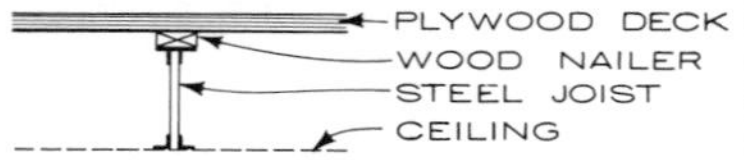 — PLYWOOD DECK — WOOD NAILER — STEEL JOIST — CEILING | 10–32 | Steel joists 8–30 | 8–20 | 10–50 | Up to 96 | Light joists 16"–30" o.c. Heavy joists 4'–12' o.c. | Deflection |
| STEEL JOIST | 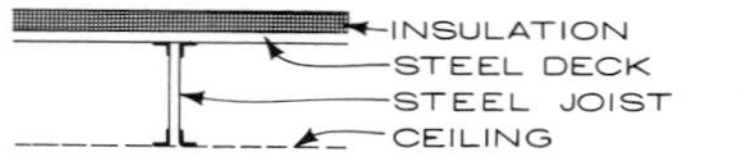 — INSULATION — STEEL DECK — STEEL JOIST — CEILING | 11–75 | Steel joists 8–72 | 6–24 | 10–50 | Up to 96 | — | Deflection |
| STEEL FRAME | 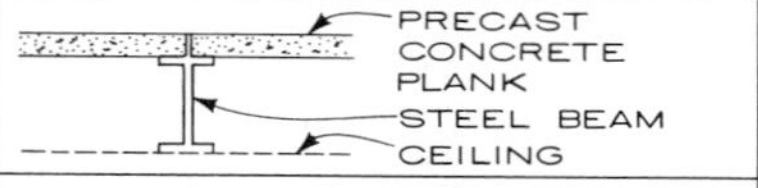 — PRECAST CONCRETE PLANK — STEEL BEAM — CEILING | 4–12 plus beam depth | Concrete plank 16–48 W 4–12 D | 40–75 | 30–70 | 20–60 Generally below 35 | — | Deflection and creep |
| PRECAST CONCRETE | 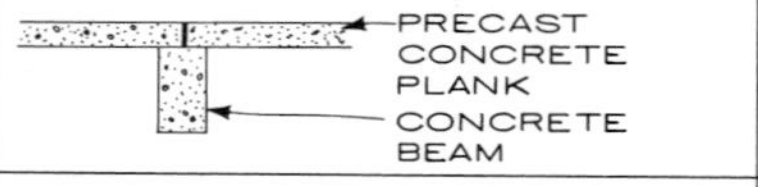 — PRECAST CONCRETE PLANK — CONCRETE BEAM | 4–12 plus beam depth | Concrete plank 16–48 W 4–12 D | 40–75 | 30–70 | 20–60 Generally below 35 | — | Deflection and creep |
| ONE - WAY CONCRETE SLAB | 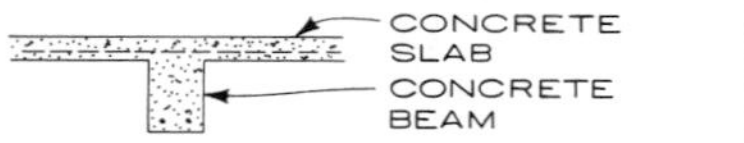 — CONCRETE SLAB — CONCRETE BEAM | 4–10 slab plus beam depth | | 50–120 | Up to 100 | 10–25 More with prestressing | — | — |
| TWO - WAY CONCRETE SLAB | 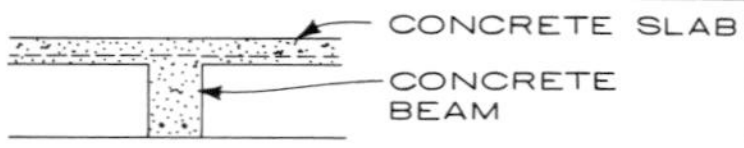 — CONCRETE SLAB — CONCRETE BEAM | 4–10 slab plus beam depth | | 50–120 | Up to 100 | 10–30 More with prestressing | L ≤ 1.33 W | — |
| ONE - WAY RIBBED CONCRETE SLAB |  — CONCRETE SLAB — RIB (JOIST) | 8–22 | Standard pan forms 20 and 30 W 6–20 D | 40–90 | Up to 100 | 15–50 More with prestressing | | Creep |
| TWO - WAY RIBBED CONCRETE SLAB |  — CONCRETE SLAB — RIB (JOIST) | 8–24 | Standard dome forms 19 x 19, 30 x 30 6–20 D | 75–105 | Up to 100 | 25–60 More with prestressing | L ≤ 1.33 W | Creep |
| PRECAST TEE | 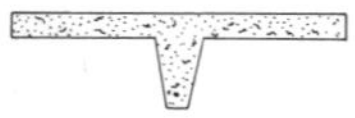 | 16–36 | 16–36 deep | 65–85 | 20–80 | 30–100 | — | Creep |
| PRECAST DOUBLE TEE | 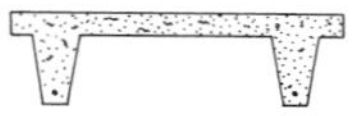 | 6–16 | 4', 5', 6', 8', and 10' wide 6"–16" deep | 35–55 | 25–60 | 20–75 | — | Creep |
| CONCRETE FLAT PLATE | 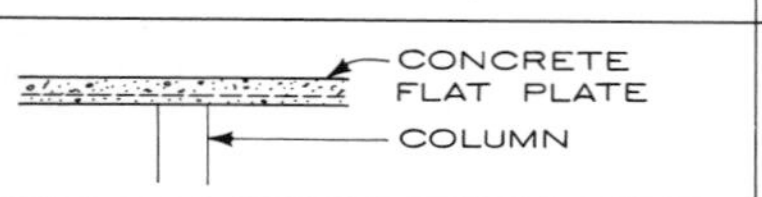 — CONCRETE FLAT PLATE — COLUMN | 4–14 | — | 50–160 | Up to 100 | Up to 35 More with prestressing | L ≤ 1.33 W | Creep |
| CONCRETE FLAT SLAB | 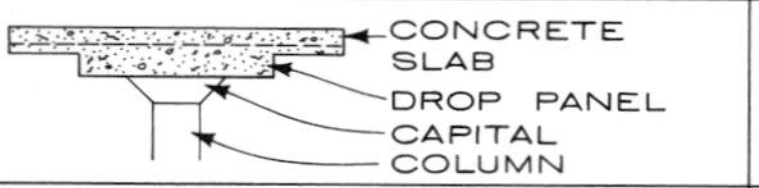 — CONCRETE SLAB — DROP PANEL — CAPITAL — COLUMN | 5–16 | Min. slab thickness 5 w/o Drop 4 w/ panel | 50–200 | Up to 100 | Up to 40 More with prestressing | L ≤ 1.33 W Equal column spacing required | Creep |
| GYPSUM DECK | 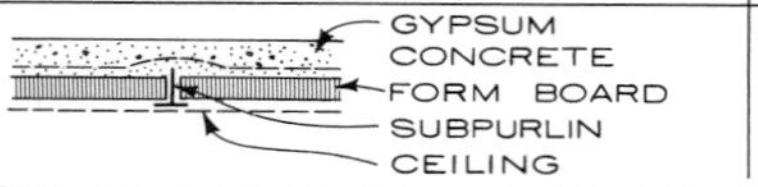 — GYPSUM CONCRETE — FORM BOARD — SUBPURLIN — CEILING | 3–6 | — | 5–20 | Up to 50 | Up to 10 | Up to 8' between subpurlins | Deflection and creep |

Roger K. Lewis, FAIA, and Mehmet T. Ergene, Architect; Roger K. Lewis, FAIA, & Associates; Washington, D.C.

1

**BUILDING SYSTEMS**

| SUITABLE FOR INCLINED ROOFS | REQUIRES FINISHED CEILING SURFACE | SERVICE PLENUM | RELATIVE THERMAL CAPACITY | COMPARATIVE RESISTANCE TO SOUND TRANSMISSION | | FIRE RESISTIVE RATING PER CODE AND UNDERWRITERS | | CONSTRUCTION TYPE CLASSIFICATION | REMARKS |
|---|---|---|---|---|---|---|---|---|---|
| | | | | IMPACT | AIRBORNE | UNPROTECTED HOURS | MAXIMUM PROTECTED HOURS | | |
| Yes | For visual or fire protection purposes | Between rafters —one way | Low | Poor | Fair | — | 2 (combustible) | 4B (A) 3C (B) | |
| Yes | For fire protection purposes | Under structure —one way | Medium | Poor | Fair | — | 2 | 3A 6″ x 10″ frame min. 4″ plank min. | |
| Yes | No | Under structure only | Low | Poor | Fair | — | 2 | 4B (A) 3C (B) | |
| Yes | For visual or fire protection purposes | Between trusses | Low | Poor | Fair | — | 2 (combustible) | 4B (A) 3C (B) | Truss depth to span ratio 1:5 to 1:10 |
| Yes Pitched trusses usually used for short spans | For visual or fire protection purposes | Between trusses | Low | Fair | Fair | — | 1–4 | 1, 2, and 3 | Truss depth to span ratio 1:5 to 1:15 |
| No | For visual or fire protection purposes | Between joists | Medium | Fair | Fair | — | 1–4 | 1, 2, and 3 | |
| Yes | For visual or fire protection purposes | Between joists | Low | Poor | Fair | — | 1 | 1, 2, and 3 | |
| Yes | For visual or fire protection purposes | Between joists | High | Excellent | Good | — | 2 | 1, 2, and 3 | |
| Yes | For visual or fire protection purposes | Under structure | High | Fair | Fair | — | 1–4 | 1, 2, and 3 | Easy to design; quick erection |
| Yes | No | Under structure | High | Fair | Fair | 2–4 | 3–4 | 1 and 2 | Provides finished flush ceiling. May be used with any framing system |
| No | No | Under structure | High | Good | Good | 1–4 | 3–4 | 1 and 2 | |
| No | No | Under structure | High | Good | Good | 1–4 | 3–4 | 1 and 2 | |
| No | For visual purposes | Between ribs —one way | High | Good | Good | 1–4 | 3–4 | 1 and 2 | |
| No | No | Under structure | High | Good | Good | 1–4 | 3–4 | 1 and 2 | Economy in forming; suitable for two-way cantilevering |
| Yes | For visual or fire protection purposes | Between ribs —one way | High | Fair | Good | 2–3 | 3–4 | 1 and 2 | Generally used for long spans |
| Yes | For visual or fire protection purposes | Between ribs —one way | High | Fair | Good | 2–3 | 3–4 | 1 and 2 | Most widely used prestressed concrete element. |
| No | No | Under structure | High | Good | Good | 1–4 | 3–4 | 1 and 2 | Uniform slab thickness; easy to form; suitable for vertical expansion of building |
| No | No | Under structure | High | Good | Good | 1–4 | 3–4 | 1 and 2 | Suitable for heavy roof loads |
| No | For visual or fire protection purposes | Under structure | High | Good | Good | — | 2 | 1, 2, and 3 | Provides resistance to wind and seismic loads |

Roger K. Lewis, FAIA, and Mehmet T. Ergene, Architect; Roger K. Lewis, FAIA, & Associates; Washington, D.C.
DeChiara and Koppelman, see data sources

BUILDING SYSTEMS    1

| EXTERIOR WALL ASSEMBLIES<br>FOR ADDITIONAL INFORMATION CONSULT MANUFACTURERS LITERATURE AND TRADE ASSOCIATIONS | | WALL THICKNESS (NOMINAL) (IN.) | WEIGHT (PSF) | VERTICAL SPAN RANGE (UNSUPPORTED HEIGHT) (FT) | WIND RESIST. | RACKING RESISTANCE | SERVICE PLENUM SPACE | HEAT TRANS-MISSION COEFFICIENT (U-FACTOR) (BTU/HR·SQ FT·°F) |
|---|---|---|---|---|---|---|---|---|
| C.M.U. | C.M.U. (GRAVEL AGGREGATE) | 8<br>12 | 55<br>85 | Up to 13<br>Up to 20 | | Good | None | 0.56<br>0.49 |
| C.M.U. (INSULATED) | C.M.U.<br>INSULATION<br>INT. WALL FIN. | 8 +<br>12 + | 60<br>90 | Up to 13<br>Up to 20 | | Good | Through insulation | 0.21<br>0.20 |
| C.M.U. AND BRICK VENEER (INSULATED) | BRICK VENEER<br>C.M.U.<br>INSULATION<br>INT. WALL FIN. | 4 + 4 +<br>4 + 8 + | 75<br>100 | Up to 13 (w/filled cavity)<br>Up to 20 (w/filled cavity) | | Good | Through insulation | 0.19<br>0.18 |
| CAVITY | BRICK VENEER<br>CAVITY (MIN. 2")<br>INSULATION (WATER REPELLENT)<br>C.M.U.<br>INT. WALL FIN. | 4 + 2 + 4<br>4 + 2 + 8 | 75<br>100 | Up to 9<br>Up to 13 | | Fair | None | 0.12<br>0.11 |
| C.M.U. AND STUCCO (INSULATED) | STUCCO<br>C.M.U.<br>INSULATION<br>INT. WALL FIN. | 8 + | 67 | Up to 13 | | Good | Through interior insulation | 0.16 |
| WOOD STUD | EXT. WALL FIN.<br>SHEATHING WITH MOISTURE BARRIER<br>WOOD STUD<br>INSULATION WITH VAPOR BARRIER<br>INT. WALL FIN | 4<br>6 | 12<br>16 | Up to 14<br>Up to 20<br>(L/d ≤ 50) | | Poor to fair | Between studs | 0.06<br>0.04 |
| BRICK VENEER | BRICK VENEER<br>SHEATHING WITH MOISTURE BARRIER<br>WOOD STUD<br>INSULATION WITH VAPOR BARRIER<br>INT. WALL FIN. | 4 + 4 | 52 | Up to 14 | | Poor to fair | Between studs | 0.07 |
| METAL STUD | EXT. WALL FIN.<br>METAL STUD AT 16" O.C.<br>INSULATION WITH VAPOR BARRIER<br>INT. WALL FIN. | 4<br>5 | 14<br>18 | Up to 13<br>Up to 17 | | Poor | Between studs | 0.06<br>0.04 |
| BRICK VENEER | BRICK VENEER<br>SHEATHING WITH MOISTURE BARRIER<br>METAL STUD AT 16" O.C.<br>INSULATION WITH VAPOR BARRIER<br>INT. WALL FIN. | 4 + 4 | 54 | Up to 15 | | Good | Between studs | 0.07 |
| INSULATED SANDWICH PANEL | METAL SKIN<br>AIRSPACE<br>INSULATING CORE<br>METAL SKIN | 5 | 6 | See manufacturers' literature | | Fair to good | None | 0.05<br>See manufacturers' literature |
| CONCRETE | CONCRETE | 8<br>12 | 92<br>138 | Up to 13 (w/reinf. 17)<br>Up to 20 (w/reinf. 25) | | Excellent | None | 0.68<br>0.55 |
| CONCRETE (INSULATED) | CONCRETE<br>INSULATION<br>INT. WALL FIN. | 8 + | 97 | Up to 13 (w/reinf. 17) | | Excellent | Through insulation | 0.13 |
| CONCRETE AND BRICK VENEER (INSULATED) | BRICK VENEER<br>CONCRETE<br>INSULATION<br>INT. WALL FIN. | 4 + 8 + | 112 | Up to 13 (w/reinf. 17) | | Excellent | Through insulation | 0.13 |
| PRECAST CONCRETE | CONCRETE (REINFORCED)<br>INSULATION<br>INT. WALL FINISH | 2 +<br>4 + | 23<br>46 | Up to 6<br>Up to 12 | | Fair to good | Through insulation | 0.99<br>0.85 |
| PRECAST CONCRETE SANDWICH | CONCRETE<br>INSULATION | 5 | 45 | Up to 14 | | Fair to good | None | 0.14 |

*Wind resistance depends on geographical location and height of building; wind velocity; wall material thickness; strength; workmanship; axial loads; and horizontal span. Design walls for both inward and outward pressures*

| GLASS | SEE INDEX UNDER "GLASS" | | | SIZE RANGE | | SHADING COEFFICIENT S.C. | |
|---|---|---|---|---|---|---|---|
| | | | | MAXIMUM ALLOWABLE GLASS AREA | WIND LOAD | | |
| SINGLE GLAZING | 1/4" GLASS | 1/4 | 3.2 | Four side supported 110 SF @ 10 PSF<br>20 SF @ 60 PSF<br>Two side supported 40 SF @ 10 PSF<br>17 SF @ 60 PSF | | Clear 0.94<br>Tinted 0.70 | Clear/tinted 1.1<br>Reflective 0.8–1.1 |
| DOUBLE GLAZING | 1/4" GLASS<br>1/4" CAVITY | 3/4 | 6.4 | Four side supported 55 SF @ 30 PSF<br>28 SF @ 60 PSF<br>Heat strengthened 70 SF @ 80 PSF<br>30 SF @ 200 PSF | | Reflective 0.44 | Clear/tinted 0.5–0.6<br>Reflective 0.3–0.6 |
| TRIPLE GLAZING | 1/4" GLASS<br>1/4" CAVITY | 1 1/4 | 9.6 | — | | | Clear/tinted 0.3–0.4<br>Reflective 0.2–0.4 |

Roger K. Lewis, FAIA, and Mehmet T. Ergene, Architect; Roger K. Lewis, FAIA, & Associates; Washington, D.C.

**1**    **BUILDING SYSTEMS**

**HAZARD CLASSIFICATION (FIRE)**

Classification provides data in regard to (1) flame spread, (2) fuel contributed, and (3) smoke developed during fire exposure of materials in comparison to asbestos-cement boards as zero and untreated red oak lumber as 100 when exposed to fire under similar conditions

| | FLAME SPREAD | FUEL CONTRIBUTED | SMOKE DEVELOPED |
|---|---|---|---|
| Paint on CMU | 5–25 | 0–5 | 0–10 |
| Gypsum board surfaced on both sides with paper | 15 | 15 | 0 |
| Gypsum board surfaced on both sides with paper, vinyl faced | 25–35 | 0–10 | 15–45 |
| Untreated wood particle board | 180 | 75 | 190 |
| Treated wood particle board with untreated wood face veneer | 25–180 | 10–160 | 10–250 |
| Vermiculite acoustical plaster | 10–20 | 10–20 | 0 |
| Glass fiber batts and blankets (basic) | 20 | 15 | 20 |
| (foil kraft faced) | 25 | 0 | 0 |
| Treated lumber (Douglas fir) | 15 | 10 | 0–5 |
| (Hemlock) | 10–15 | 5–15 | 0 |
| Laminated plastic (fr) | 20–30 | 0–15 | 5–30 |

**NFPA CLASSIFICATION:**

| CLASS | FLAME SPREAD | SMOKE DEVELOPED |
|---|---|---|
| A | 0–25 | 0–450 |
| B | 26–75 | 0–450 |
| C | 76–200 | 0–450 |

For lesser classifications, permitted in residential construction only, refer to regulating agency guidelines

| RESISTANCE TO EXTERIOR AIRBORNE SOUND TRANSMISSION | FIRE RESISTIVE RATING PER CODE AND UNDERWRITERS (HRS) | CONSTRUCTION TYPE CLASSIFICATION | SUBCONTRACTORS REQUIRED FOR ERECTION (PLUS FINISHES) | EXTERIOR MAINTENANCE REQUIREMENTS | REMARKS |
|---|---|---|---|---|---|
| Fair to good | 2–4 / 4 | 1, 2, and 3 | Masonry | Washing, re-pointing joints, painting, sand blasting | Properties of non-engineered masonry are drastically reduced |
| Fair to good | 2–4 / 4 | 1, 2, and 3 | Masonry Carpentry Drywall | Washing, re-pointing joints, painting, sand blasting | |
| Excellent | 3–4 / 4 | 1, 2, and 3 | Masonry Carpentry Drywall | Washing, re-pointing joints, sand blasting | |
| Excellent | 4 | 1, 2, and 3 | Masonry Drywall (Carpentry) | Washing, re-pointing joints, sand blasting | Cavity increases heat storage capacity and resistance to rain penetration |
| Good | 2–4 | 1, 2, and 3 | Masonry Drywall Lath and plaster (Carpentry) | Washing, painting, and re-stuccoing | The assembly is reversed for optimum energy conservation |
| Poor to fair | 1 (combustible) | 4 | Carpentry Drywall (Lath and plaster) | Washing, painting, and replacing exterior finish | Exterior wall finishes:<br>• wood, plywood,<br>• aluminum siding<br>• stucco |
| Good to excellent | 1–2 (combustible) | 3B, C | Masonry Carpentry Drywall | Washing, re-pointing joints, sand blasting | |
| Poor to fair | 1–2 | 1 (nonbearing) 2 and 3 | Carpentry Drywall (Lath and plaster) | Washing, painting, and replacing exterior finish | Exterior wall finishes:<br>• wood, plywood,<br>• aluminum siding<br>• stucco |
| Good to excellent | 1–2 | 1 (nonbearing) 2 and 3 | Masonry Carpentry Drywall | Washing, re-pointing joints, sand blasting | |
| Poor to good; see manufacturers' literature | See manufacturers' literature | See manufacturers' literature | Curtain walls —erection | Washing, steam cleaning, painting, replacing joint sealers | Temperature change critical<br>Minimize metal through connections |
| Good | 4 / 4 | 1, 2, and 3 | Concrete work | Washing, sand blasting | Concrete walls have very high heat storage capacity |
| Good | 4 / 4 | 1, 2, and 3 | Concrete work Drywall (Carpentry) | Washing, sand blasting | |
| Excellent | 4 | 1, 2, and 3 | Concrete work Masonry Drywall (Carpentry) | Washing, re-pointing joints, sand blasting | |
| Poor to fair | 1–3 | 1A (nonbearing) 1B, 2, and 3 | Curtain walls —erection Drywall (Carpentry) | Washing, sand blasting, re-placing joint sealers | Large size economical (fewer joints) units available with various finishes |
| Fair | 1–3 | 1A (nonbearing) 1B, 2, and 3 | Curtain walls —erection | Washing, sand blasting, re-placing joint sealers | 8' x 20' max. size for concrete sandwich panels<br>Plant quality control is very essential |
| Poor | — | — | Curtain walls —erection (Glazing) | Washing, re-placing joint sealers, gaskets | Anchorage to building is critical<br>Anchors must isolate wall to limit building movement transmitted to glass |
| Fair | — | — | Curtain walls —erection (Glazing) | Washing, re-placing joint sealers, gaskets | Wall design must limit wall movement transmitted to glass<br>Mullions should accommodate movement through gaskets, sliding connections, etc. |
| Good | — | — | Curtain walls —erection (Glazing) | Washing, re-placing joint sealers, gaskets | |

Roger K. Lewis, FAIA, and Mehmet T. Ergene, Architect; Roger K. Lewis, FAIA, & Associates; Washington, D.C.

BUILDING SYSTEMS    1

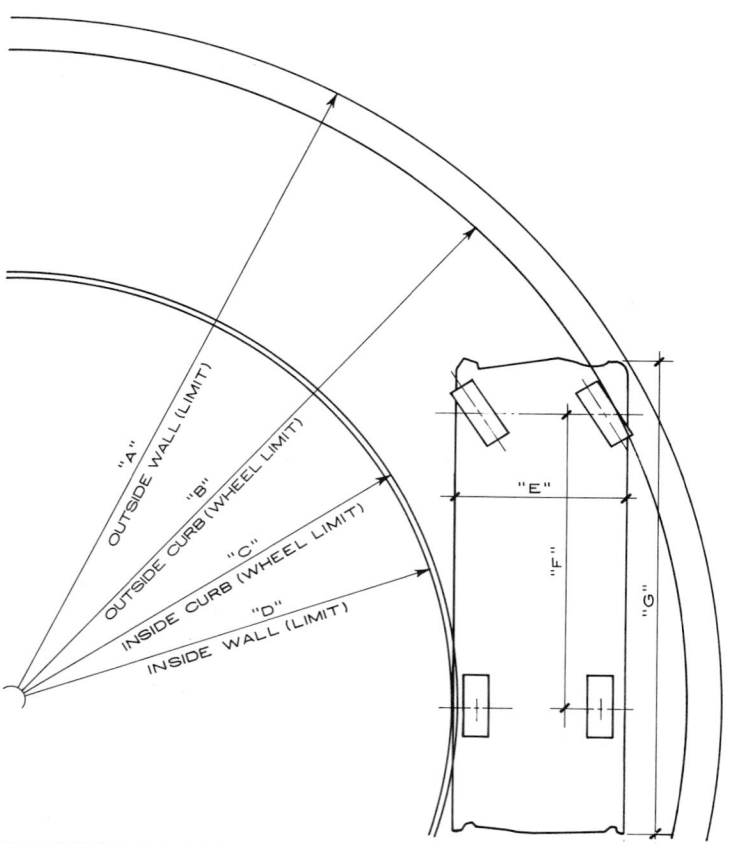

## AMBULANCES AND HEARSES
DIMENSIONS AND TURNING RADII

| MAKE OF CAR | A | B | C | D | E | F | G |
|---|---|---|---|---|---|---|---|
| BUICK | 28'-9'' | 27'-3'' | 18'-4'' | 17'-10'' | 6'-0'' | 11'-7'' | 19'-2'' |
| LINCOLN | 30'-2'' | 28'-5'' | 18'-6'' | 18'-4'' | 6'-6'' | 11'-5'' | 19'-8'' |

Dimensions vary—verify with individual coach builder.

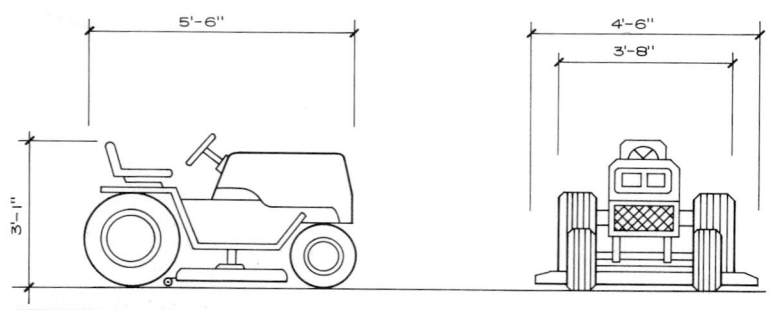

**GARDEN TRACTOR**

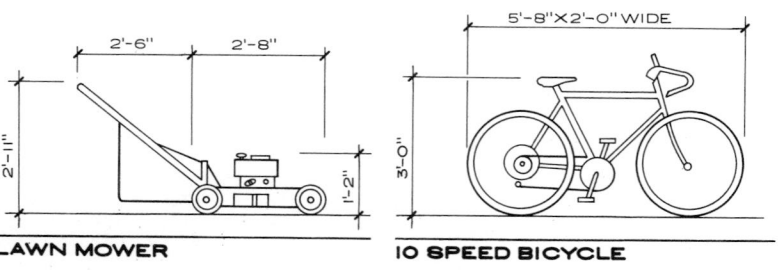

**LAWN MOWER**        **10 SPEED BICYCLE**

## GOLF CARTS GASOLINE OR ELECTRIC POWER

| 3 WHEELS | | 4 WHEELS |
|---|---|---|
| 46 3/4'' | Overall Height | 47 1/8'' |
| 10 3/4'' | Floorboard Height | 11 1/4'' |
| 27 3/4'' | Seat Height | 28 1/4'' |
| 102'' | Length | 102'' |
| 47'' | Width | 47'' |
| 68'' | Wheel Base | 68 3/4'' |
| — | Front Wheel Tread | 34'' |
| 34 5/8'' | Rear Wheel Tread | 34 5/8'' |
| 4 5/8'' | Ground Clearance | 4 5/8'' |
| 19'-6'' | Clearance Circle | 24'-0'' |

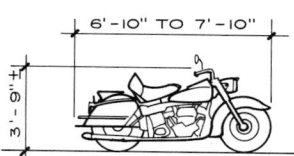 

WIDTH AT HANDLEBAR 2'-7'' TO 3'-6''

When parked on stand motorcycle leans about 10° to 12°. Large vehicle requires about 3'-8'' of space.

**HEAVYWEIGHTS WEIGH FROM ABOUT 400 LB TO 661 LB**

**HEAVYWEIGHT MOTORCYCLES**

Consult manufacturers' information for width of motorcycle and sidecar.

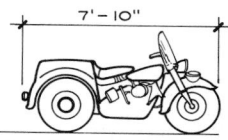

**POLICE TRICYCLE WIDTH AT BOX 4''-0''±**

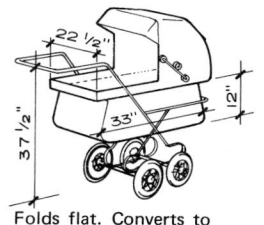 

Folds flat. Converts to stroller. Body makes car bed.
**BABY CARRIAGE**

Handlebar width 23'' and up.
Weight about 230 lb to about 300 lb

**LIGHTWEIGHT MOTORCYCLE**

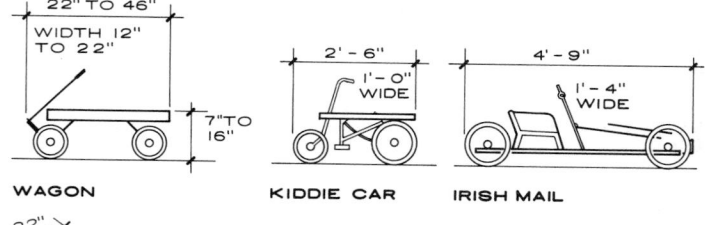

**WAGON**        **KIDDIE CAR**        **IRISH MAIL**

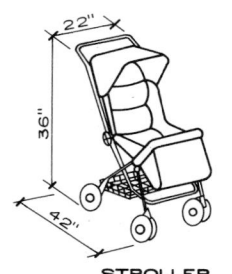 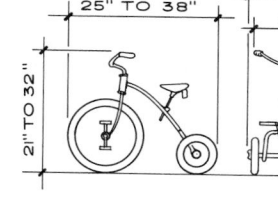

**STROLLER**      **TRICYCLE**        **SCOOTER**

Harold C. Munger, FAIA; Munger Munger + Associates Architects, Inc.; Toledo, Ohio
Foster C. Parriott; James M. Hunter & Associates; Boulder, Colorado

# 1    TRANSPORTATION

NOTE

Each design vehicle in Groups I, II, and III represents a composite of the critical dimensions of the real vehicles within each group below. Parking lot dimensions on the parking lot development page are based on these groups and dimensions. For parking purposes, both compact and standard size vehicles are in Group II. Turning dimensions R, R1, and C are shown on the private roads page.

## DESIGN VEHICLE

| GROUP I | | SUBCOMPACTS |
|---|---|---|
| L | Length | 13'–10'' |
| W | Width | 5'–5'' |
| H | Height | 4'–5'' |
| WB | Wheelbase | 8'–1'' |
| OF | Overhang front | 2'–6'' |
| OR | Overhang rear | 3'–9'' |
| OS | Overhang sides | 0'–7'' |
| GW | Gross Weight | 2100# to 2500# |

| GROUP II | | COMPACTS |
|---|---|---|
| L | Length | 14'–9'' |
| W | Width | 5'–8'' |
| H | Height | 4'–5'' |
| WB | Wheelbase | 8'–7'' |
| OF | Overhang front | 2'–8'' |
| OR | Overhang rear | 4'–3'' |
| OS | Overhang sides | 0'–8'' |
| GW | Gross Weight | 2300# to 2500# |

| GROUP III | | INTERMEDIATE |
|---|---|---|
| L | Length | 16'–8'' |
| W | Width | 6'–0'' |
| H | Height | 4'–6'' |
| WB | Wheelbase | 9'–0'' |
| OF | Overhang front | 2'–10'' |
| OR | Overhang rear | 4'–4'' |
| OS | Overhang sides | 0'–9'' |
| GW | Gross Weight | 2700# to 3200# |

| GROUP IV | | LARGE CARS |
|---|---|---|
| L | Length | 18'–5'' |
| W | Width | 6'–6'' |
| H | Height | 4'–9'' |
| WB | Wheelbase | 10'–2'' |
| OF | Overhang front | 2'–11'' |
| OR | Overhang rear | 4'–5'' |
| OS | Overhang sides | 0'–9'' |
| GW | Gross Weight | 3100# to 4030# |

| GROUP V | | LARGE PICK-UP |
|---|---|---|
| L | Length | 16'–4'' |
| W | Width | 6'–0'' |
| H | Height | 5'–8'' |
| WB | Wheelbase | 10'–5'' |
| OF | Overhang front | 2'–10'' |
| OR | Overhang rear | 4'–4'' |
| OS | Overhang sides | 0'–9'' |
| GW | Gross Weight | 3430# |

## LARGE VEHICLE DIMENSIONS*

| VEHICLE | (L) LENGTH | (W) WIDTH | (H) HEIGHT | (OR) OVERHANG REAR |
|---|---|---|---|---|
| Intercity bus | 45'–0'' | 9'–0'' | 9'–0'' | 10'–1'' |
| City bus | 40'–0'' | 8'–6'' | 8'–6'' | 8'–0'' |
| School bus | 39'–6'' | 8'–0'' | 8'–6'' | 12'–8'' |
| Ambulance | 20'–10¼'' | 6'–11'' | 10'–0'' | 5'–4'' |
| Paramedic van | 21'–6'' | 8'–0'' | 6'–6'' | 4'–0'' |
| Hearse | 22'–1'' | 6'–8'' | 9'–3'' | 5'–4'' |
| Airport limousine | 22'–5¾'' | 6'–4'' | 5'–0'' | 3'–11'' |
| Trash truck | 28'–2'' | 8'–0'' | 11'–0'' | 6'–0'' |
| U.P.S. truck | 26'–3'' | 7'–11'' | 10'–8'' | 8'–5'' |
| Fire truck | 32'–0'' | 8'–0'' | 9'–8'' | 10'–0'' |

*Exact sizes of large vehicles may vary
For truck and trailer information, see pages on truck and trailer sizes.

Harold C. Munger, FAIA; Munger Munger + Associates Architects, Inc.; Toledo, Ohio
William T. Mahan, AIA; Santa Barbara, California

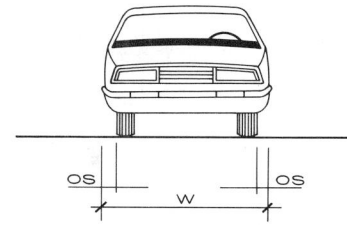

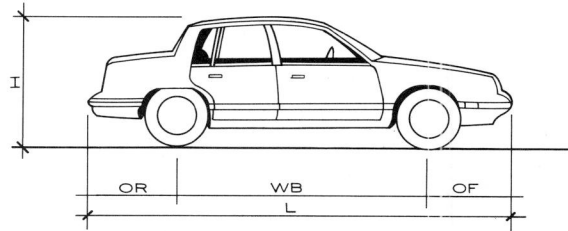

NOTE
Angles shown below may vary depending on speed, load, tire pressure, and condition of shock absorbers.

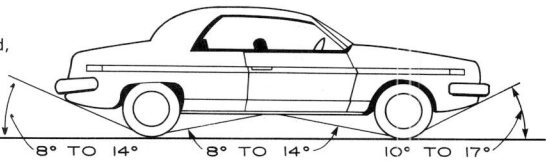

8° TO 14°   8° TO 14°   10° TO 17°

NOTE
Composite vehicle is shown with maximum wheelbase, front overhang, and rear overhang.

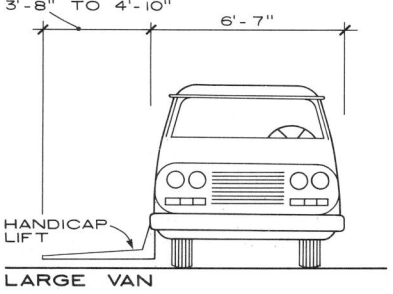

HANDICAP LIFT

LARGE VAN

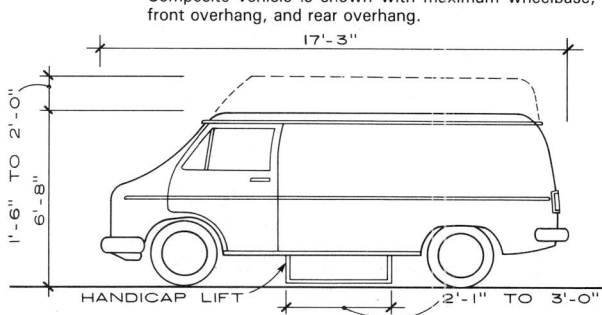

HANDICAP LIFT   2'–1'' TO 3'–0''

LARGE PICK-UP

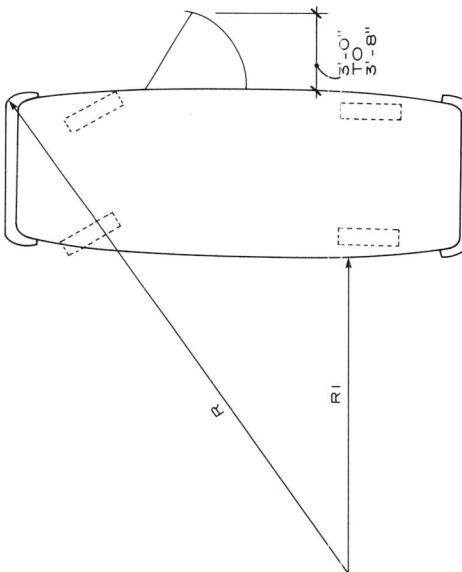

NOTE
For dimensions R and R1 see page on private roads. Typically parking for handicapped area requires 20 ft. × 12 ft.

For further parking information, see pages on parking lot development and parking garages.

See local codes and standards for parking requirements, size, and quantity of parking spaces and number of spaces required for the handicapped.

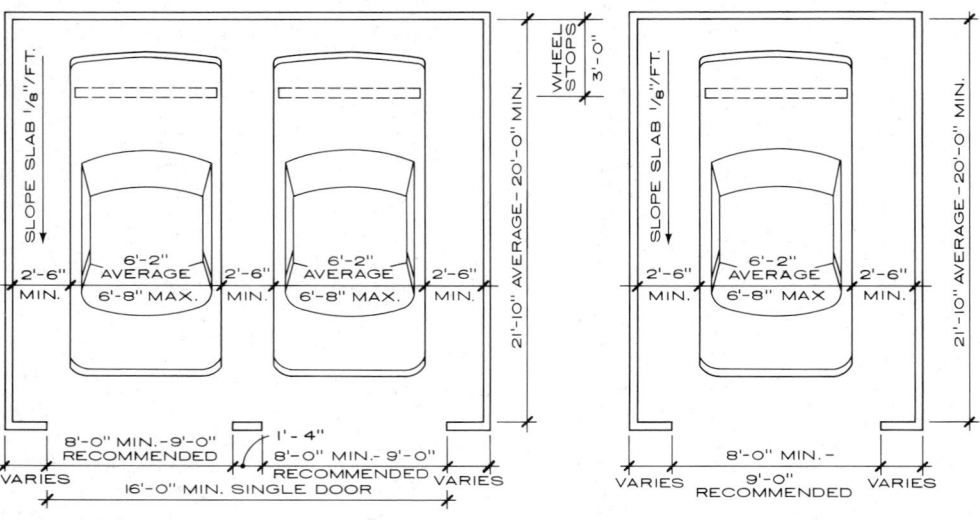

NOTES
1. Site location varies because of site constraints and design concept. Design considerations include circulation, visual safety for backing out, and visual consideration if garage is exposed to public view.
2. Garages may be enlarged to provide circulation ease by allowing spaces of 2 ft 6 in. minimum between all walls and other vehicles, and to provide space for work areas, photography laboratories, laundry room, and storage.
3. Garages may be attached directly to the house or be connected by a covered passage. Connection is preferable at or near the kitchen or utility area off the kitchen. If attached, refer to local code requirements.

**TWO-CAR GARAGE**    **ONE-CAR GARAGE**

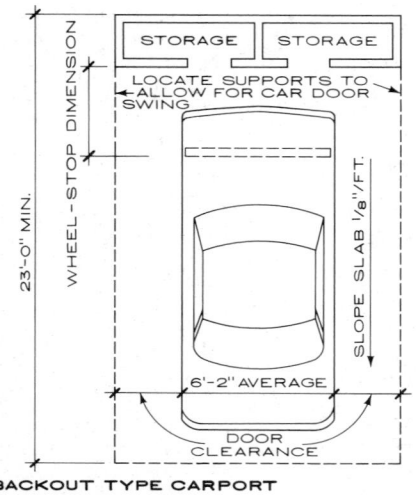
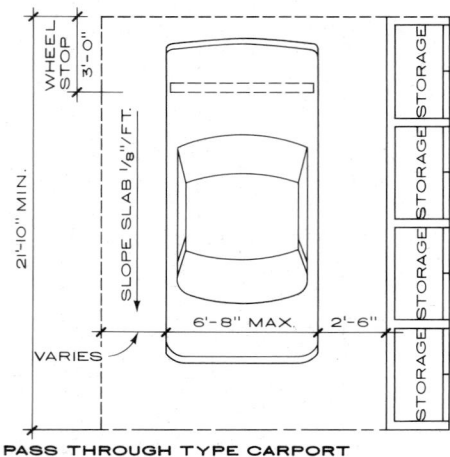

**BACKOUT TYPE CARPORT**    **PASS THROUGH TYPE CARPORT**

**CARPORTS**

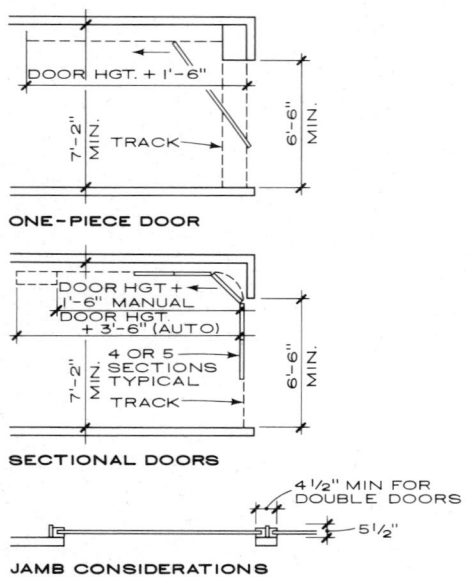
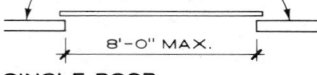

**ONE-PIECE DOOR**

**SECTIONAL DOORS**

**JAMB CONSIDERATIONS**

**LIFT DOORS – MOST WIDELY USED – AUTOMATIC OPTIONAL**
**NOTE:** HEIGHTS 6'-6", 6'-10", 7'-0", 7'-6" AND 8'-0"

**HINGED SECTION**
**MULTIPLE DOORS – TWO OR MORE CARS**
**SINGLE DOOR**

NOTE
6½ to 9 in. necessary from top of opening to ceiling (all sliding doors).

**SLIDING DOORS**

### SECTIONAL DOOR SIZES

| DOOR WIDTH | NUMBER OF PANELS ACROSS |
|---|---|
| To 8'-11" | 2 |
| 9'-0"–11'-11" | 3 |
| 12'-0"–14'-11" | 4 |
| 15'-0"–17'-11" | 5 |

NOTE: Doors up to 8'-6" high require 4 sections.

### HINGED GARAGE DOOR WIDTHS

| OPENING | TWO-DOOR | THREE-DOOR | FOUR-DOOR |
|---|---|---|---|
| 8'-0" | 4'-0" | 2'-8" | 2'-0" |
| 8'-6" | 4'-3" | 2'-10" | 2'-1½" |
| 9'-0" | 4'-6" | 3'-0" | 2'-3" |

**OFFSET HINGE – MULTI-LEAVE**

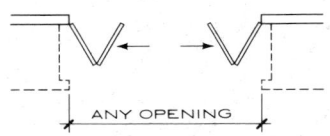

**MULTIPLE HINGED DOOR TWO OR MORE CARS**

**DOUBLE OR TRIPLE HINGED**

NOTE
For multiple and offset hinged doors, swinging to one or both sides, hinged in or out, and used for two or more cars: 6½ to 11 in. necessary from top of opening to ceiling.

**HINGED DOORS**

William T. Cannady, FAIA; Houston, Texas
DeChiara and Koppelman, see data sources

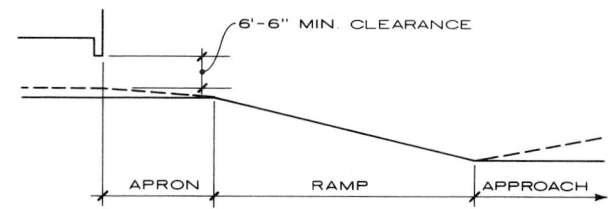

WIDEN FOR ALL TURNS

## CONCRETE RUNWAYS TO GARAGE

| RAMP | APPROACH | APRON |
|------|----------|-------|
| 4% | 0% to 4% | 0% to 2% |
| 5% | 0% to 3% | 0% to 2% |
| 6% | 0% to 2% | 0% to 2% |
| 7% | 0% to 1% | 0% to 1% |
| 8% | 0% | 0% |

## ROAD TO GARAGE RAMPS

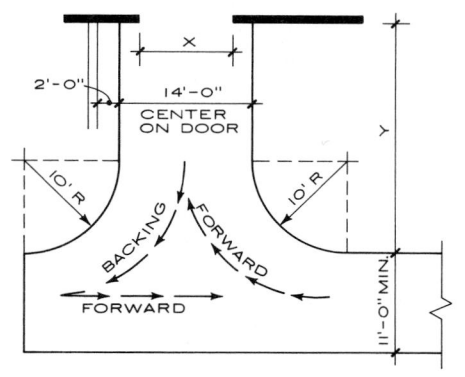

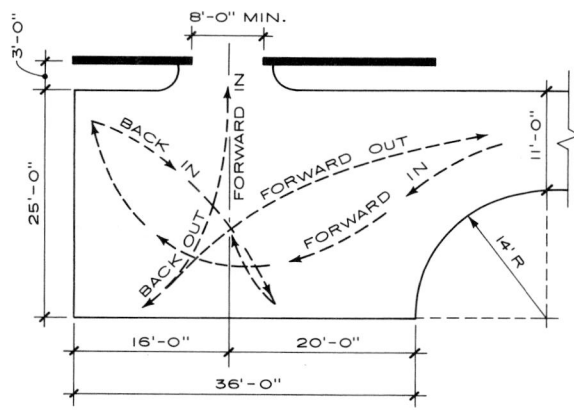

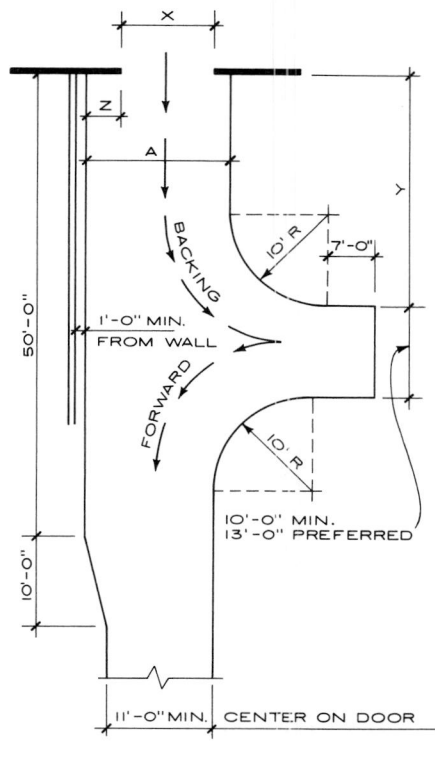

**NOTE**

Three maneuver entrance for single car garage. Employ only when space limitations demand use. Dimensioned for large car.

#### 90° IN—BACK OUT (1 CAR)

| X | 8'-9" | 9'-0" | 10'-0" | 11'-0" | 12'-0" |
|---|-------|-------|--------|--------|--------|
| Y | 25'-0" | 24'-6" | 23'-8" | 23'-0" | 22'-0" |

#### STRAIGHT IN—BACK OUT

| X | 9'-0" | 10'-0" | 12'-0" | 16'-0" |
|---|-------|--------|--------|--------|
| Y | 26'-0" | 25'-0" | 23'-6" | 24'-0" |
| Z | 3'-4" | 3'-1" | 2'-0" | 3'-0" |
| A | 14'-4" | 14'-5" | 14'-8" | 20'-0" |

## PRIVATE DRIVEWAYS TO GARAGES

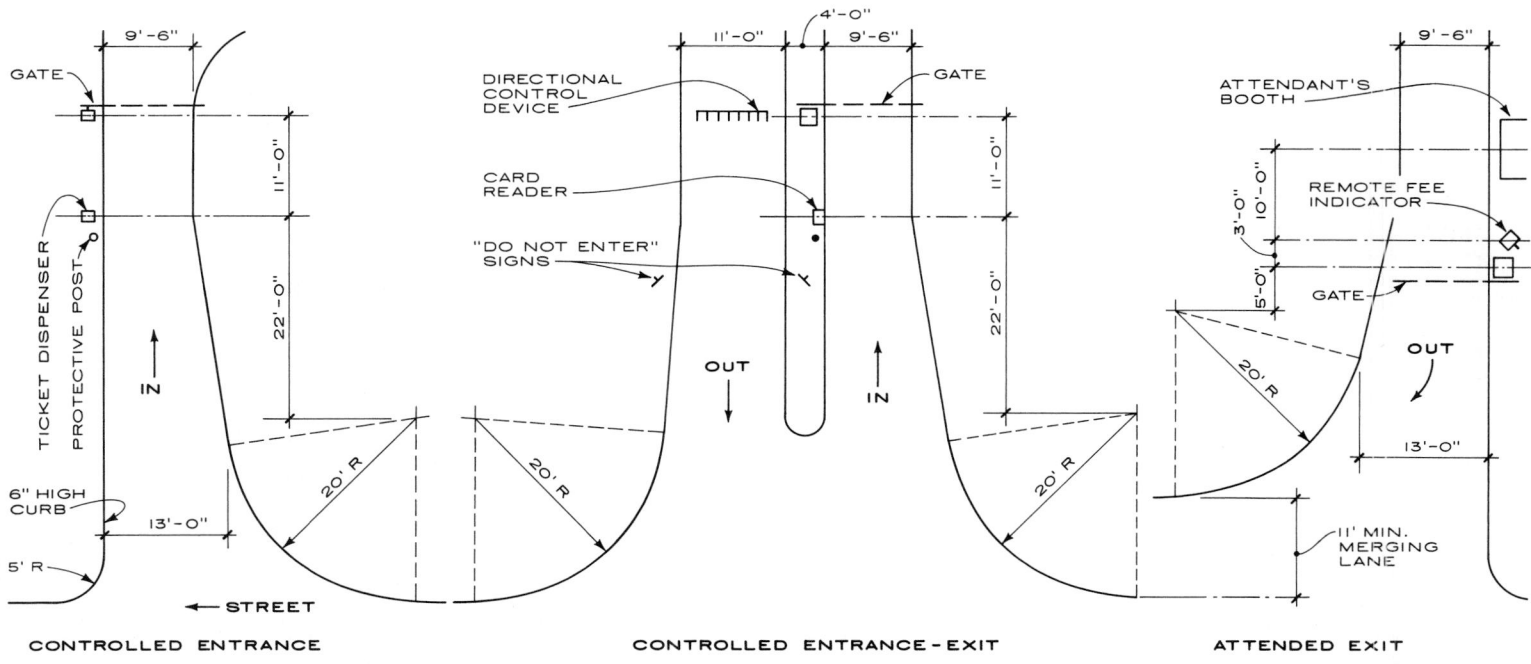

CONTROLLED ENTRANCE

CONTROLLED ENTRANCE - EXIT

ATTENDED EXIT

## DRIVEWAYS FOR PARKING FACILITIES

William T. Mahan, AIA; Santa Barbara, California

## GENERAL NOTES

Examples shown are for easy driving at moderate speed. See the preceding page for vehicle dimensions (L, W, and OR). The "U" drive shown below illustrates a procedure for designating any drive configuration, given the vehicle's dimensions and turning radii. The T (tangent) dimensions given here are approximate minimums only and may vary with the driver's ability and speed.

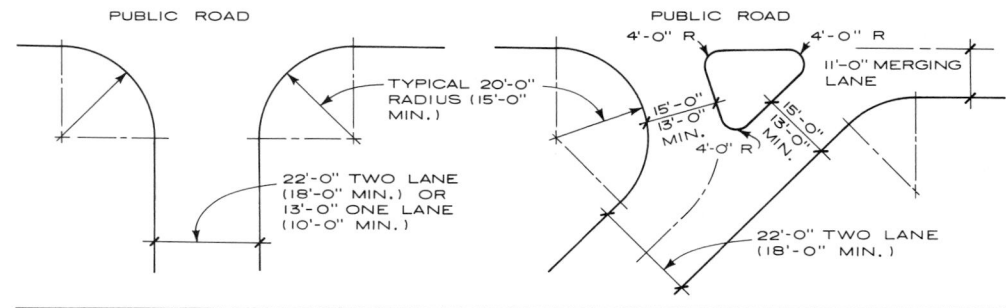

PRIVATE ROADS INTERSECTING PUBLIC ROADS

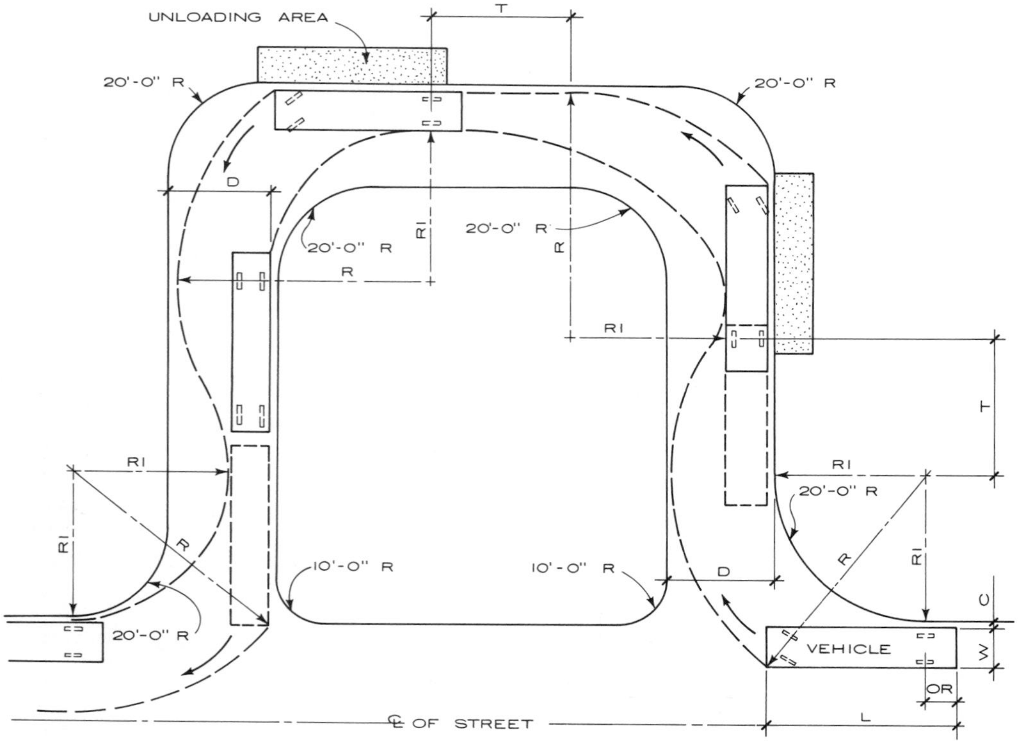

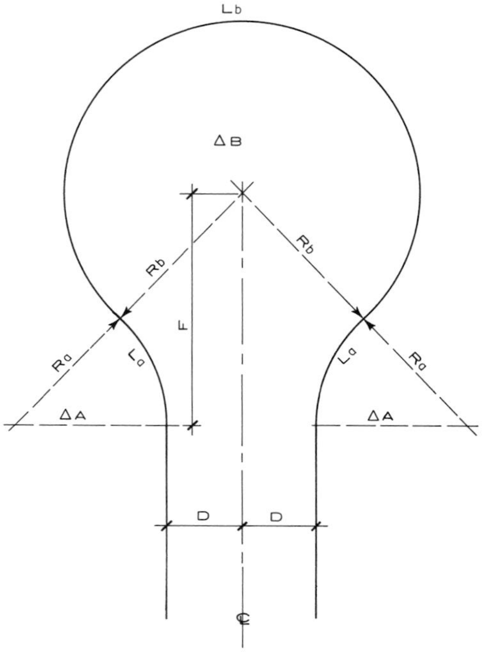

## "U" DRIVE AND VEHICLE TURNING DIMENSIONS

| VEHICLE | R | RI | T | D | C |
|---|---|---|---|---|---|
| Small car | 19'-10'' | 10'-9'' | 12'-0'' | 10'-0' | 6'' |
| Compact car | 21'-6'' | 11'-10'' | 15'-0'' | 10'-10'' | 7'' |
| Standard car | 22'-5'' | 12'-7'' | 15'-0'' | 11'-2'' | 8'' |
| Large car | 23'-0'' | 12'-7'' | 15'-0'' | 12'-0'' | 9'' |
| Intercity bus* | 55'-0'' | 33'-0'' | 30'-0'' | 22'-6'' | 1'-0'' |
| City bus | 53'-6'' | 33'-0'' | 30'-0'' | 22'-6'' | 1'-0'' |
| School bus | 43'-6'' | 26'-0'' | 30'-0'' | 19'-5'' | 1'-0'' |
| Ambulance | 30'-0'' | 18'-9'' | 25'-0'' | 13'-3'' | 1'-0'' |
| Paramedic van | 25'-0'' | 14'-0'' | 25'-0'' | 13'-0'' | 1'-0'' |
| Hearse | 30'-0'' | 18'-9'' | 20'-0'' | 13'-3'' | 1'-0'' |
| Airport limousine | 28'-3'' | 15'-1½'' | 20'-0'' | 15'-1½'' | 1'-0'' |
| Trash truck† | 32'-0'' | 18'-0'' | 20'-0'' | 16'-0'' | 1'-0'' |
| U.P.S. truck | 28'-0'' | 16'-0'' | 20'-0'' | 14'-0'' | 1'-0'' |
| Fire truck | 48'-0'' | 34'-4' | 30'-0'' | 15'-8'' | 1'-0'' |

*Headroom = 14'.
†Headroom = 15'.

William T. Mahan, AIA; Santa Barbara, California

### CUL-DE-SAC

| | SMALL | LARGE |
|---|---|---|
| O | 16'-0'' | 22'-0'' |
| F | 50'-11'' | 87'-3'' |
| A | 46.71° | 35.58° |
| B | 273.42° | 251.15° |
| Ra | 32'-0'' | 100'-0'' |
| Rb | 38'-0'' | 50'-0'' |
| La | 26'-1'' | 61'-8'' |
| Lb | 181'-4'' | 219'-2'' |

**NOTE:** R values for vehicles intended to use these culs-de-sac should not exceed Rb.

NOTE: Small car dimensions should be used only in lots designated for small cars or with entrance controls that admit only small cars. Placing small car stalls into a standard car layout is not recommended. Standard car parking dimensions will accommodate all normal passenger vehicles. Large car parking dimensions make parking easier and faster and are recommended for luxury, a high turnover, and use by the elderly. When the parking angle is 60° or less, it may be necessary to add 3 to 6 ft to the bay width to provide aisle space for pedestrians walking to and from their parked cars. Local zoning laws should be reviewed before proceeding.

**RECOMMENDED RANGE OF STALL WIDTHS (SW)**

WIDTH (ft) — 8 — 9 — 10 — 11 — 12

- Small car use
- All day parker use
- Standard car use
- Luxury and elderly use
- Supermarket and camper use
- Handicapped use*

*Minimum requirements = 1 or 2 per 100 stalls or as specified by local, state, or federal law; place convenient to destination.

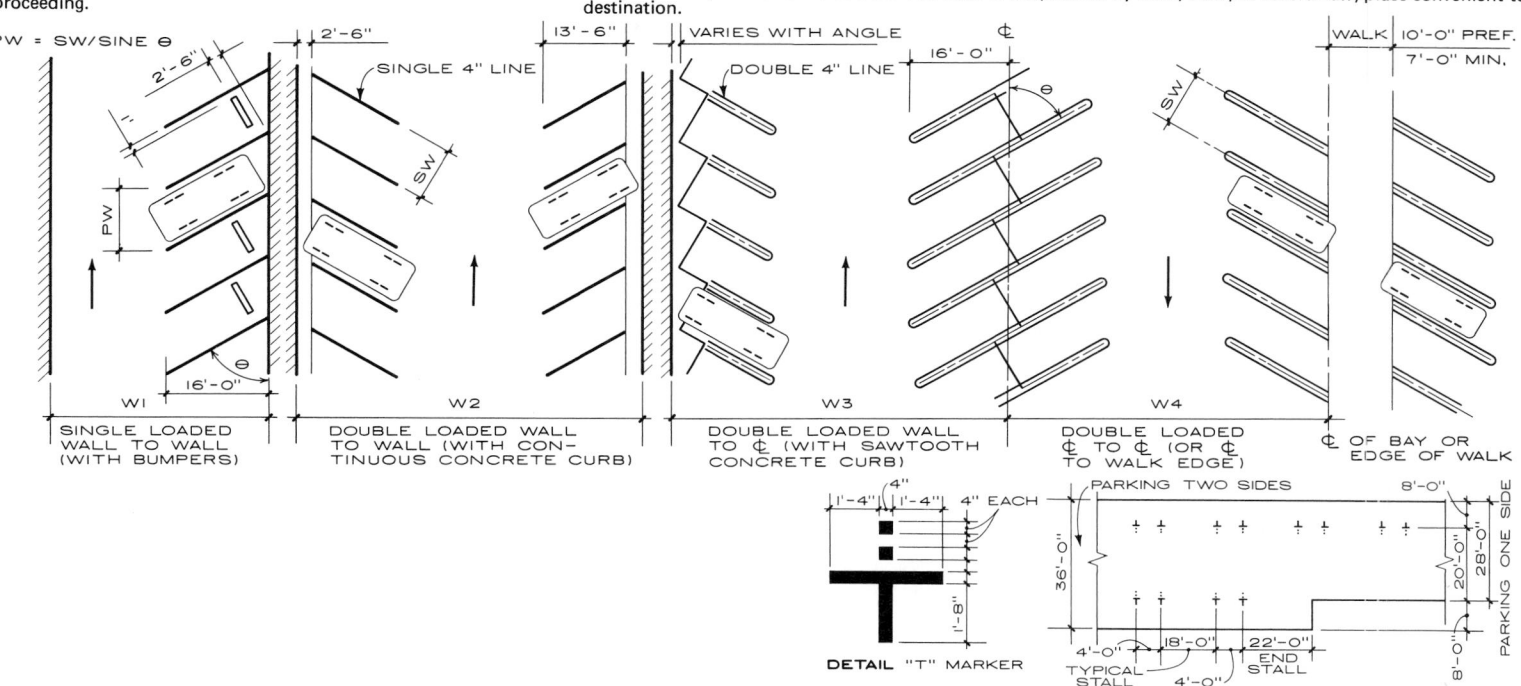

## PARKING DIMENSIONS IN FEET AND INCHES

### PARALLEL PARKING STALLS AND "T" MARKER DETAIL

| | SW | W | 45° | 50° | 55° | 60° | 65° | 70° | 75° | 80° | 85° | 90° |
|---|---|---|---|---|---|---|---|---|---|---|---|---|
| Group I: small cars | 8'-0" | 1 | 25'-9" | 26'-6" | 27'-2" | 29'-4" | 31'-9" | 34'-0" | 36'-2" | 38'-2" | 40'-0" | 41'-9" |
| | | 2 | 40'-10" | 42'-0" | 43'-1" | 45'-8" | 48'-2" | 50'-6" | 52'-7" | 54'-4" | 55'-11" | 57'-2" |
| | | 3 | 38'-9" | 40'-2" | 41'-5" | 44'-2" | 47'-0" | 49'-6" | 51'-10" | 53'-10" | 55'-8" | 57'-2" |
| | | 4 | 36'-8" | 38'-3" | 39'-9" | 42'-9" | 45'-9" | 48'-6" | 51'-1" | 53'-4" | 55'-5" | 57'-2" |
| Group II: standard cars | 8'-6" | 1 | 32'-0" | 32'-11" | 34'-2" | 36'-2" | 38'-5" | 41'-0" | 43'-6" | 45'-6" | 46'-11" | 48'-0" |
| | | 2 | 49'-10" | 51'-9" | 53'-10" | 56'-0" | 58'-4" | 60'-2" | 62'-0" | 63'-6" | 64'-9" | 66'-0" |
| | | 3 | 47'-8" | 49'-4" | 51'-6" | 54'-0" | 56'-6" | 59'-0" | 61'-2" | 63'-0" | 64'-6" | 66'-0" |
| | | 4 | 45'-2" | 46'-10" | 49'-0" | 51'-8" | 54'-6" | 57'-10" | 60'-0" | 62'-6" | 64'-3" | 66'-0" |
| | 9'-0" | 1 | 32'-0" | 32'-9" | 34'-0" | 35'-4" | 37'-6" | 39'-8" | 42'-0" | 44'-4" | 46'-2" | 48'-0" |
| | | 2 | 49'-4" | 51'-0" | 53'-2" | 55'-6" | 57'-10" | 60'-0" | 61'-10" | 63'-4" | 64'-9" | 66'-0" |
| | | 3 | 46'-4" | 48'-10" | 51'-4" | 53'-10" | 56'-0" | 58'-8" | 61'-0" | 63'-0" | 64'-6" | 66'-0" |
| | | 4 | 44'-8" | 46'-6" | 49'-0" | 51'-6" | 54'-0" | 57'-0" | 59'-8" | 62'-0" | 64'-2" | 66'-0" |
| | 9'-6" | 1 | 32'-0" | 32'-8" | 34'-0" | 35'-0" | 36'-10" | 38'-10" | 41'-6" | 43'-8" | 46'-0" | 48'-0" |
| | | 2 | 49'-2" | 50'-6" | 51'-10" | 53'-6" | 55'-4" | 58'-0" | 60'-6" | 62'-8" | 64'-6" | 65'-11" |
| | | 3 | 47'-0" | 48'-2" | 49'-10" | 51'-6" | 53'-11" | 57'-0" | 59'-8" | 62'-0" | 64'-3" | 65'-11" |
| | | 4 | 44'-8" | 45'-10" | 47'-6" | 49'-10" | 52'-6" | 55'-9" | 58'-9" | 61'-6" | 63'-10" | 65'-11" |
| Group III: large cars | 9'-0" | 1 | 32'-7" | 33'-0" | 34'-0" | 35'-11" | 38'-3" | 40'-11" | 43'-6" | 45'-5" | 46'-9" | 48'-0" |
| | | 2 | 50'-2" | 51'-2" | 53'-3" | 55'-4" | 58'-0" | 60'-4" | 62'-9" | 64'-3" | 65'-5" | 66'-0" |
| | | 3 | 47'-9" | 49'-1" | 52'-3" | 53'-8" | 56'-2" | 59'-2" | 61'-11" | 63'-9" | 65'-2" | 66'-0" |
| | | 4 | 45'-5" | 46'-11" | 49'-0" | 51'-8" | 54'-9" | 58'-0" | 61'-0" | 63'-2" | 64'-10" | 66'-0" |
| | 9'-6" | 1 | 32'-4" | 32'-8" | 33'-10" | 34'-11" | 37'-2" | 39'-11" | 42'-5" | 45'-0" | 46'-6" | 48'-0" |
| | | 2 | 49'-11" | 50'-11" | 52'-2" | 54'-0" | 56'-6" | 59'-3" | 61'-9" | 63'-4" | 64'-8" | 66'-0" |
| | | 3 | 47'-7" | 48'-9" | 50'-2" | 52'-4" | 55'-1" | 58'-4" | 60'-11" | 62'-10" | 64'-6" | 66'-0" |
| | | 4 | 45'-3" | 46'-8" | 48'-5" | 50'-8" | 53'-8" | 57'-0" | 59'-10" | 62'-2" | 64'-1" | 66'-0" |
| | 10'-0" | 1 | 32'-4" | 32'-8" | 33'-10" | 34'-11" | 37'-2" | 39'-11" | 42'-5" | 45'-0" | 46'-6" | 48'-0" |
| | | 2 | 49'-11" | 50'-11" | 52'-2" | 54'-0" | 56'-6" | 59'-3" | 61'-9" | 63'-4" | 64'-8" | 66'-0" |
| | | 3 | 47'-7" | 48'-9" | 50'-2" | 52'-4" | 55'-1" | 58'-4" | 60'-11" | 62'-10" | 64'-6" | 66'-0" |
| | | 4 | 45'-3" | 46'-8" | 48'-5" | 50'-8" | 53'-8" | 57'-0" | 59'-10" | 62'-2" | 64'-1" | 66'-0" |

*θ ANGLE OF PARK*

NOTE: θ angles greater than 70° have aisle widths wide enough for two-way travel.

William T. Mahan, AIA; Santa Barbara, California

Frederick J. Gaylord, AIA; McClellan/Cruz/Gaylord & Associates; Pasadena, California

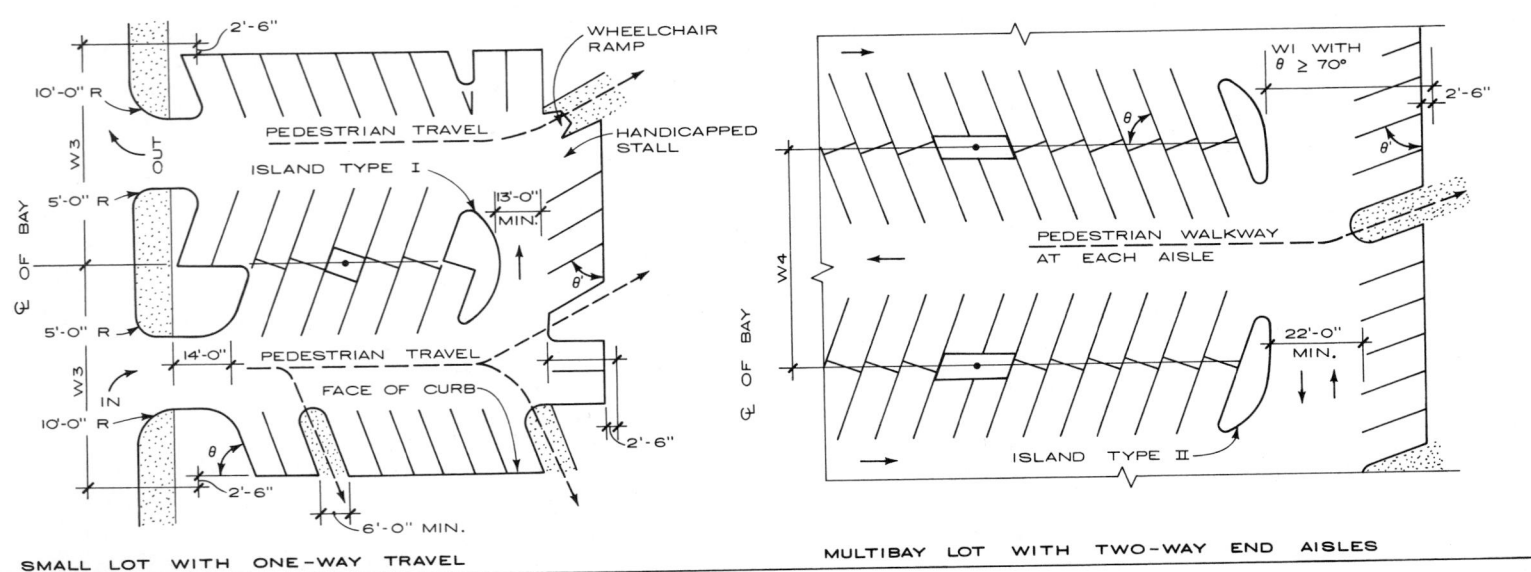

SMALL LOT WITH ONE-WAY TRAVEL

MULTIBAY LOT WITH TWO-WAY END AISLES

**TYPICAL PARKING LAYOUTS**

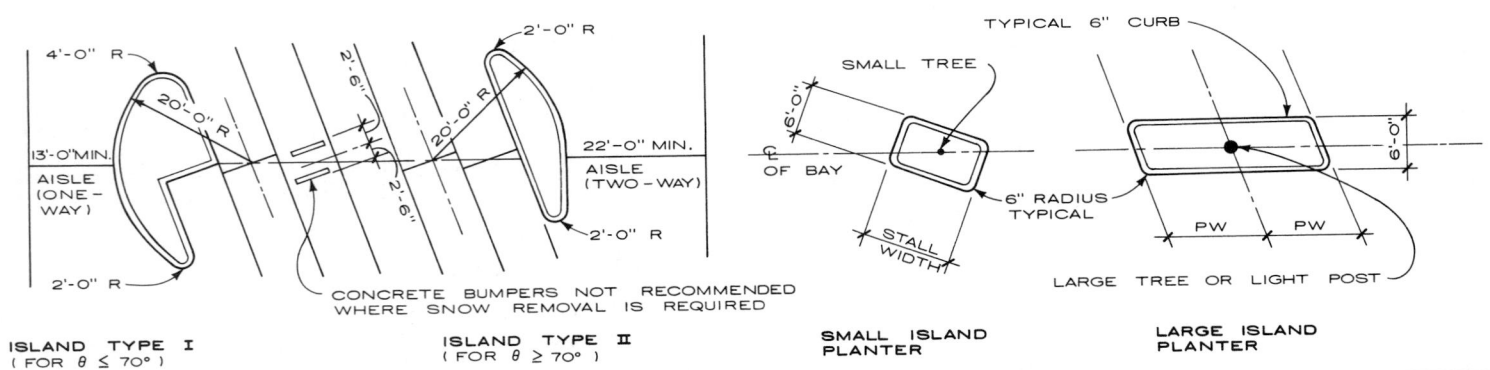

ISLAND TYPE I
( FOR θ ≤ 70° )

ISLAND TYPE II
( FOR θ ≥ 70° )

SMALL ISLAND
PLANTER

LARGE ISLAND
PLANTER

**TYPICAL PLANTER ISLANDS**

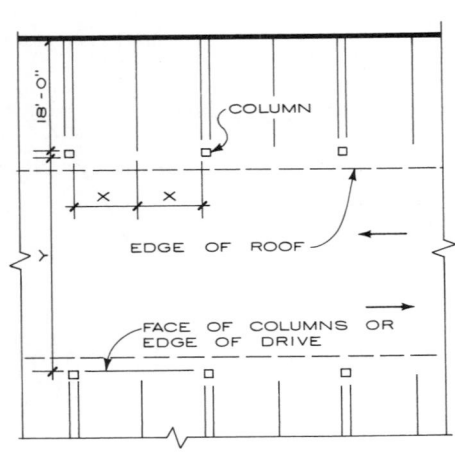

**TWO STALL 90° APARTMENT CARPORTS**

| X | 9'-0" | 10'-0" | 11'-0" | 12'-0" |
|---|-------|--------|--------|--------|
| Y | 35'-0" | 34'-0" | 33'-0" | 32'-0" |

**PARKING LAYOUTS WITH COLUMNS**

NOTE: STALL PRECEDING COLUMN IS ALWAYS WIDER

**ANGLE PARKING WITH 3 STALLS PER COLUMN**

| θ | PW | PW' | W2 | E | A | B | AREA/STALL |
|---|-----|------|------|------|------|------|------------|
| 60° | 10'-5" | 13'-0" | 55'-0" | 18'-0" | 19'-0" | 33'-10" | 310 sq ft |
| 70° | 9'-7" | 11'-1" | 59'-10" | 18'-0" | 23'-10" | 30'-3" | 302 sq ft |
| 80° | 9'-1" | 10'-2" | 63'-4" | 18'-0" | 27'-4" | 28'-4" | 300 sq ft |

William T. Mahan, AIA; Santa Barbara, California
Frederick J. Gaylord, AIA; McClellan/Cruz/Gaylord & Associates; Pasadena, California

**1**    **TRANSPORTATION**

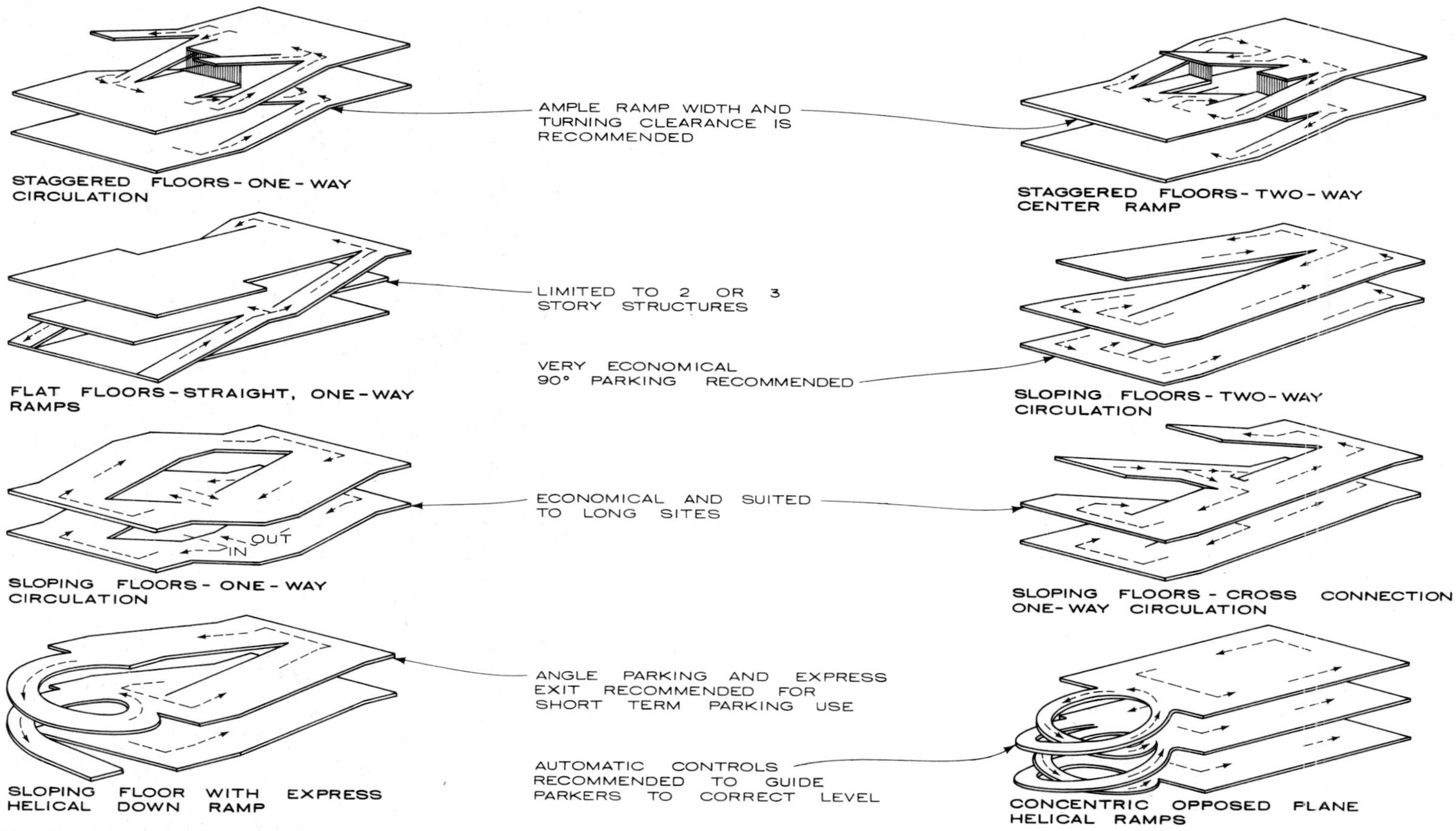

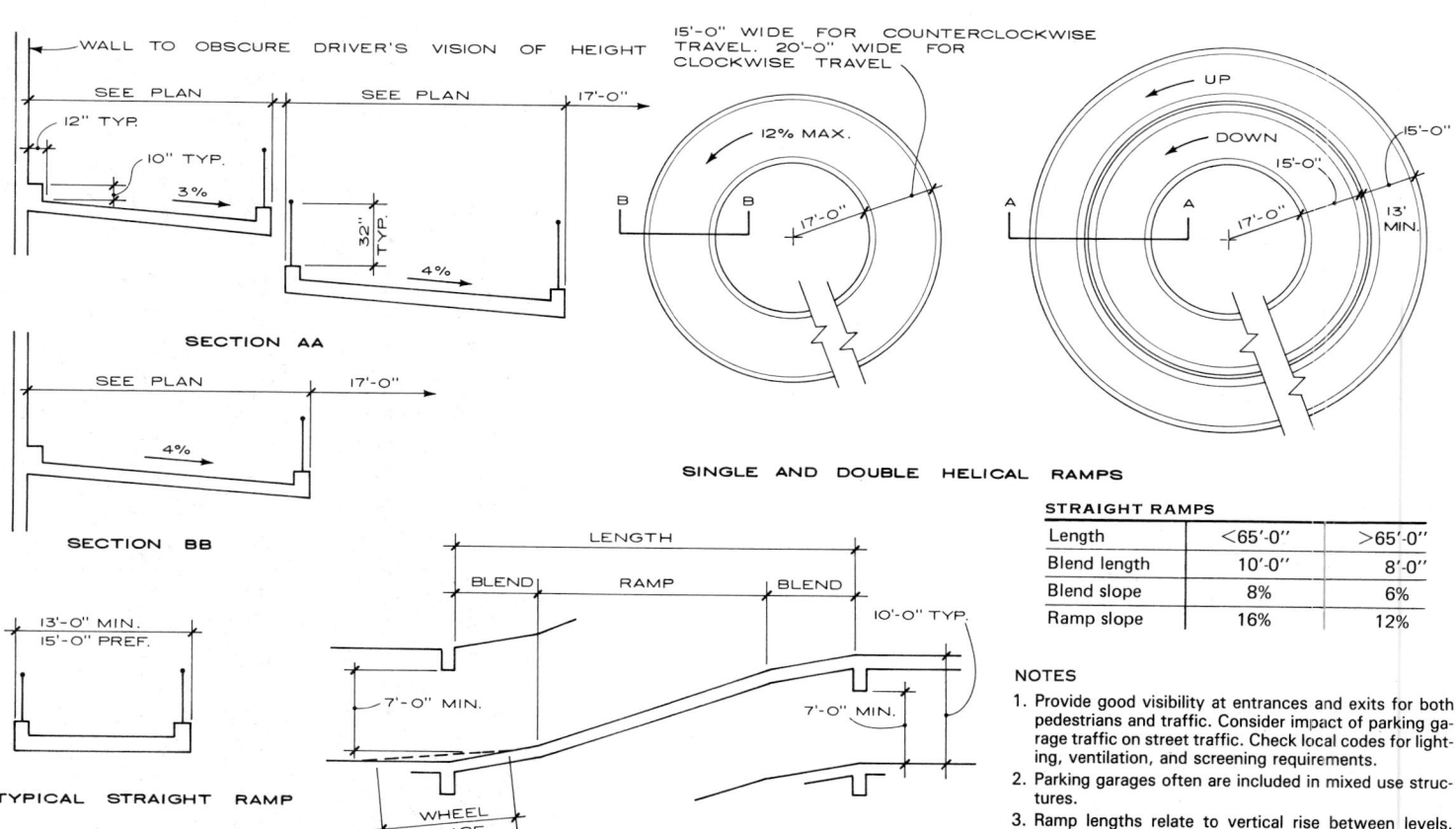

**STAGGERED FLOORS – ONE – WAY CIRCULATION**

**STAGGERED FLOORS – TWO – WAY CENTER RAMP**

AMPLE RAMP WIDTH AND TURNING CLEARANCE IS RECOMMENDED

**FLAT FLOORS – STRAIGHT, ONE – WAY RAMPS**

**SLOPING FLOORS – TWO – WAY CIRCULATION**

LIMITED TO 2 OR 3 STORY STRUCTURES

VERY ECONOMICAL 90° PARKING RECOMMENDED

**SLOPING FLOORS – ONE – WAY CIRCULATION**

OUT
IN

**SLOPING FLOORS – CROSS CONNECTION ONE – WAY CIRCULATION**

ECONOMICAL AND SUITED TO LONG SITES

**SLOPING FLOOR WITH EXPRESS HELICAL DOWN RAMP**

ANGLE PARKING AND EXPRESS EXIT RECOMMENDED FOR SHORT TERM PARKING USE

AUTOMATIC CONTROLS RECOMMENDED TO GUIDE PARKERS TO CORRECT LEVEL

**CONCENTRIC OPPOSED PLANE HELICAL RAMPS**

## TYPICAL RAMP SYSTEMS

WALL TO OBSCURE DRIVER'S VISION OF HEIGHT

SEE PLAN          SEE PLAN          17'-0"

12" TYP.
10" TYP.
3%
32" TYP.
4%

**SECTION AA**

SEE PLAN          17'-0"

4%

**SECTION BB**

13'-0" MIN.
15'-0" PREF.

**TYPICAL STRAIGHT RAMP**

15'-0" WIDE FOR COUNTERCLOCKWISE TRAVEL. 20'-0" WIDE FOR CLOCKWISE TRAVEL

12% MAX.
B     B
17'-0"

UP
DOWN
15'-0"
15'-0"
A     A
17'-0"
13' MIN.

## SINGLE AND DOUBLE HELICAL RAMPS

LENGTH
BLEND     RAMP     BLEND
10'-0" TYP.
7'-0" MIN.
7'-0" MIN.
WHEEL BASE

| STRAIGHT RAMPS | | |
|---|---|---|
| Length | <65'-0" | >65'-0" |
| Blend length | 10'-0" | 8'-0" |
| Blend slope | 8% | 6% |
| Ramp slope | 16% | 12% |

## NOTES

1. Provide good visibility at entrances and exits for both pedestrians and traffic. Consider impact of parking garage traffic on street traffic. Check local codes for lighting, ventilation, and screening requirements.
2. Parking garages often are included in mixed use structures.
3. Ramp lengths relate to vertical rise between levels. Maintain 7 ft. 0 in. minimum clearance for cars.

## TYPICAL RAMP DETAILS

William T. Mahan, AIA; Santa Barbara, California

## TRIPLE SEMITRAILER AND TRACTOR

**MAXIMUM ALLOWABLE LENGTH**
NOT PERMITTED, EXCEPT IN THOSE STATES LISTED BELOW

| UNIT | STATE |
|------|-------|
| 90'-0" | AK |
| (each trailer 27'-0") | AZ |
| 105'-0" | CO |
| 105'-0" | ID |
| 105'-0" | NV |
| 105'-0" | OR |
| 105'-0" | UT |
| 65'-0" | IN |
| 110'-0" | ND |

## DOUBLE SEMITRAILER AND TRACTOR

**MAXIMUM ALLOWABLE LENGTH**

| UNIT | EACH TRAILER | STATE |
|------|--------------|-------|
| 60'-0" | 28'-0" | GA, SC, VT, VA |
| 61'-0" | — | UT |
| 65'-0" | 30'-0" | LA |
| 65'-0" | 28'-6" | MA, MN, NY, TX |
| 65'-0" | 28'-0" | DE, HI, MD, MO, NM, PA |
| 65'-0" | — | ME, NB |
| 70'-0" | 28'-0" | CO, OK |
| 75'-0" | 28'-6" | CA, MT |
| 75'-0" | 28'-0" | ND |
| 75'-0" | — | AK, OR |
| 80'-0" | 28'-6" | SD |
| 85'-0" | — | WY |
| 105'-0" | — | ID |
| — | 30'-0" | MS |
| — | 28'-6" | AL, AZ, IN, IA, KS, MI, TN, WI |
| — | 28'-0" | AK, CT, DC, FL, KY, NH, NJ, NC, WV |
| — | 27'-6" | RI |
| — | — | IL, NV, OH, WA |

## SEMITRAILER AND TRACTOR

**MAXIMUM ALLOWABLE LENGTH**
**EACH**

| UNIT | TRAILER | STATE |
|------|---------|-------|
| 55'-0" | 53'-0" | DC |
| 55'-0" | 48'-0" | MD |
| 60'-0" | 53'-0" | DE, WI |
| 60'-0" | 48'-0" | GA, NC, SC, VA, WV |
| 60'-0" | 45'-0" | MA, NY |
| 60'-0" | — | MO, OR, VT |
| 65'-0" | 57'-0" | TX |
| 65'-0" | 53'-0" | OK |
| 65'-0" | 50'-0" | LA |
| 65'-0" | 48'-0" | HI, ME |
| 65'-0" | — | CA, MN, NM, PA |
| 70'-0" | 48'-0" | AK |
| 70'-0" | — | CO, NV |
| 75'-0" | 48'-0" | ID, MT |
| 75'-0" | — | ND |
| 80'-0" | 53'-0" | SD |
| 85'-0" | 60'-0" | WY |
| — | 53'-0" | NB, OH, IL, IN, IA, KS, KY |
| — | 51'-0" | AZ |
| — | 50'-0" | AL, MI, MS |
| — | 48'-0" | AR, CT, FL, NH, NJ, RI, UT, WA |
| — | — | TN |

## STRAIGHT BODY TRUCKS

**MAXIMUM ALLOWABLE LENGTH**

| UNIT | STATE |
|------|-------|
| 40'-0" | In all states, except those listed below |
| 35'-0" | FL, KY, MA, NH, NJ, NY, NC, SC, WV |
| 36'-0" | IN |
| 42'-0" | IL |
| 42'-6" | KS |
| 45'-0" | LA, ME, SD, TX, UT |
| 50'-0" | ND |
| 60'-0" | CT, GA, VT, WY |

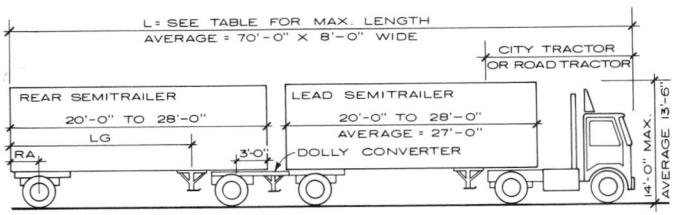

L = SEE TABLE FOR MAX. LENGTH
AVERAGE = 70'-0" X 8'-0" WIDE

**DOUBLE SEMITRAILER AND CITY TRACTOR**

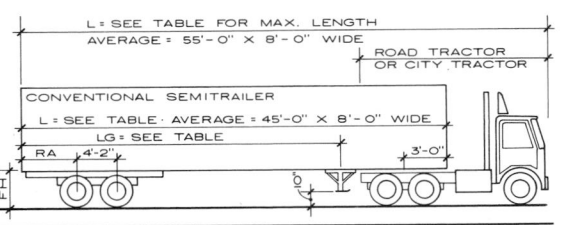

L = SEE TABLE FOR MAX. LENGTH
AVERAGE = 55'-0" X 8'-0" WIDE

**SEMITRAILER AND ROAD TRACTOR**
TIRE SIZE APPROX. 41" ± DIA. X 10" ± WIDE

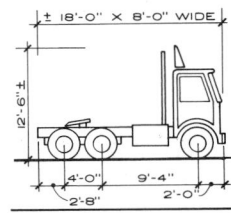

**CITY TRACTOR**

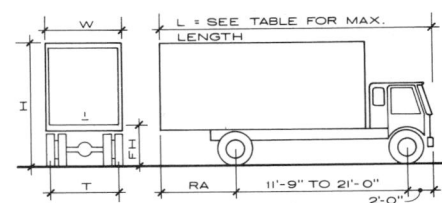

**ROAD TRACTOR**

## VEHICLE HEIGHT

**MAXIMUM ALLOWABLE**

| TOTAL HEIGHT | STATE |
|--------------|-------|
| 13'-6" | In all states, except those listed below |
| 13'-0" | FL |
| 14'-0" | CA, ID, ME, NV, ND, OR, UT, WA, WY |
| 14'-6" | CO, NB |

## VEHICLE WIDTH

**MAXIMUM ALLOWABLE**

| TOTAL WIDTH | STATE |
|-------------|-------|
| 8'-6" | In all states, except those listed below |
| 8'-0" | DE, DC, FL, IL, IA, KY, LA, MI, MO, NY, NC, PA, SC, TN, WV |

NOTE: Width is 8'-0" or 8'-6" according to state. Length and area restrictions vary with each state and locale. Verify exact dimensions and restrictions.

**STRAIGHT BODY TRUCK**

## AVERAGE SEMITRAILER DIMENSIONS

| | LENGTH (L) | | | |
|---|---|---|---|---|
| | 27'-0" | 40'-0" | 45'-0" | REFRIG. 40'-0" |
| Floor height (FH) | 4'-2" | 4'-2" | 4'-2" | 4'-9" |
| Rear axle (RA) | 3'-0" | 5'-2" | 5'-10" | 4'-5" |
| Landing gear (LG) | 19'-0" | 30'-0" | 34'-6" | 29'-5" |
| Cubic feet (CU) | 1564 ± | 2327 ± | 2620 ± | 2113 ± |

## AVERAGE DIMENSIONS OF VEHICLES

| | TYPE OF VEHICLES | | |
|---|---|---|---|
| | DOUBLE SEMITRAILER | CONVENTIONAL SEMITRAILER | STRAIGHT BODY TRUCK |
| Length (L) | 70'-0" | 55'-0" | 17'-0" to 40'-0" |
| Width (W) | 8'-0" | 8'-0" | 8'-0" |
| Height (H) | 13'-6" | 13'-6" | 13'-6" |
| Floor Height (FH) | 4'-0" to 4'-6" | 4'-0" to 4'-4" | 3'-0" to 4'-0" |
| Track (T) | 6'-6" | 6'-6" | 5'-10" |
| Rear Axle (RA) | 3'-0" to 4'-0" | 4'-0" to 12'-0" | 2'-3" to 12'-0" |

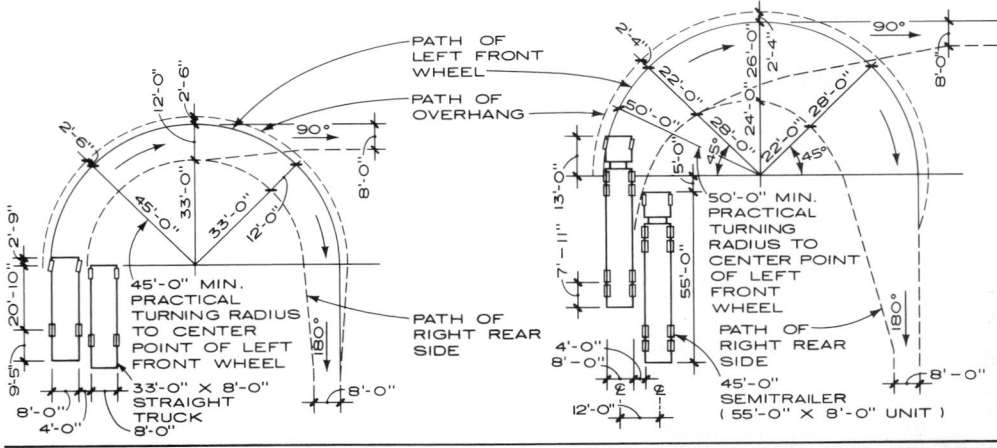

**33'-0" STRAIGHT BODY TRUCK MINIMUM PRACTICAL TURNING RADIUS OF 45'-0"**

**55'-0" SEMITRAILER AND TRACTOR COMBINATION MINIMUM PRACTICAL TURNING RADIUS OF 50'-0"**

Robert H. Lorenz, AIA; Preston Trucking Company, Inc.; Preston, Maryland
The Operations Council, American Trucking Association; Washington, D.C.

# 1 TRANSPORTATION

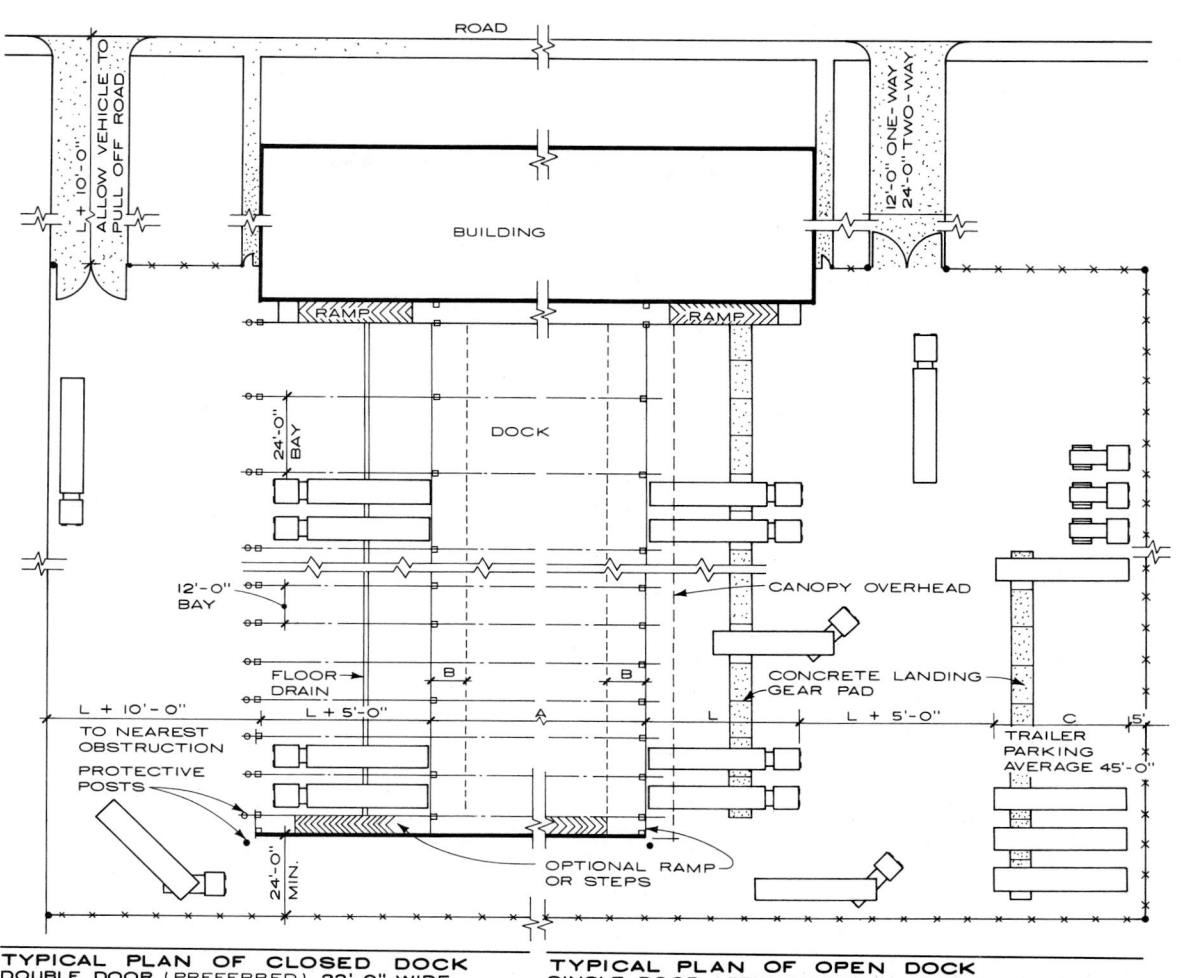

**TYPICAL PLAN OF CLOSED DOCK**
DOUBLE DOOR (PREFERRED) 22'-0" WIDE X 14'-6" HIGH. SINGLE DOOR (OPTIONAL) 11'-0" WIDE X 14'-6" HIGH

**TYPICAL PLAN OF OPEN DOCK**
SINGLE DOOR (PREFERRED) 9'-0" WIDE X 10'-0" HIGH. DOUBLE DOOR (OPTIONAL) 20'-0" WIDE X 10'-0" HIGH

### NOTES

1. Allow for off-street employee and driver parking.
2. Entrances and exits should be of reinforced concrete when excessive twisting and turning of vehicles are expected.
3. Average gate (swing or slide) 30 ft 0 in. wide for two-way traffic. People gate 5 ft 0 in. wide with concrete walkway 4 ft 0 in. to 6 ft 0 in. wide.
4. For yard security use a 6 ft 0 in. high chain link fence with barbed wire on top.
5. On-site fueling facilities are desirable for road units.
6. Provide general yard lighting from fixtures mounted on building or on 24 ft 0 in. high minimum poles at fence line. Mercury vapor or high pressure sodium preferred.
7. Tractor parking requires 12 ft 0 in. wide × 20 ft 0 in. long slot minimum. Provide motor heater outlets for diesel engines in cold climates.
8. Trailer parking requires 10 ft 0 in. wide slot minimum. Provide 10 ft 0 in. wide concrete pad for landing gear. Score concrete at 12 ft 0 in. o.c. to aid in correct spotting of trailer.
9. 4 ft 0 in. wide minimum concrete ramp from dock to grade. Slopes of 3 to 15% (10% average), score surface for traction.
10. Vehicles should circulate in a counterclockwise direction, making left hand turns, permitting driver to see rear of unit when backing into dock.
11. Double trailers are backed into dock separately.

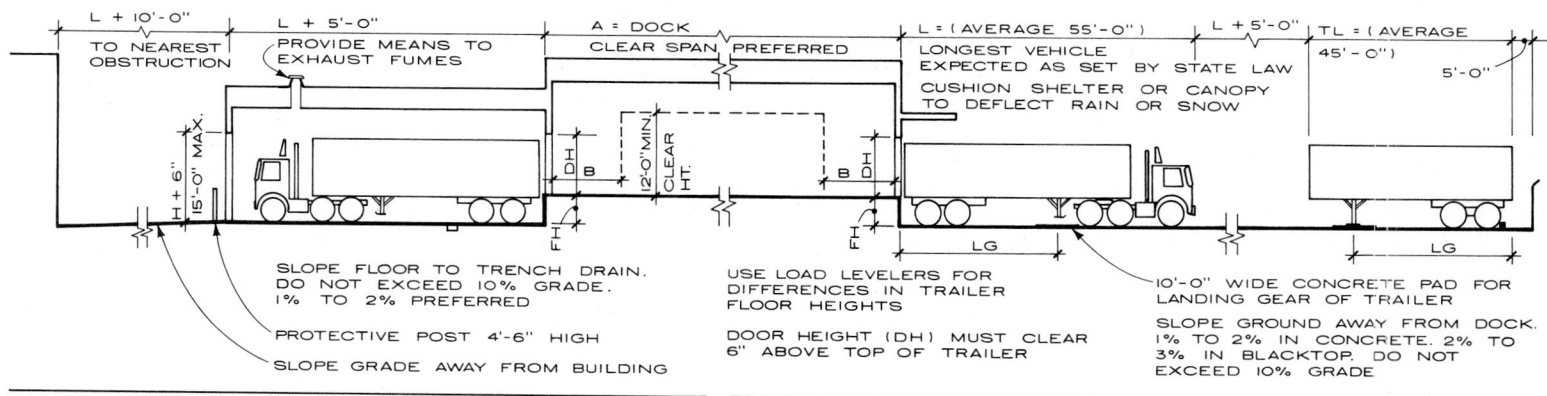

**TYPICAL SECTION OF CLOSED DOCK**

**TYPICAL SECTION OF OPEN DOCK**

### AVERAGE VEHICLE DIMENSIONS

| LENGTH OF VEHICLE (L) | FLOOR HEIGHT (FH) | VEHICLE HEIGHT (H) |
|---|---|---|
| 60 ft tractor trailer | 4'-0" to 4'-6" | 14'-0" |
| 45 ft trailer | 4'-0" to 4'-2" | 13'-6" |
| 40 ft straight body | 3'-8" to 4'-2" | 13'-6" |
| 18 ft van | 2'-0" to 2'-8" | 7'-0" |

NOTE: Refer to other pages for truck and trailer sizes.

### AVERAGE WIDTHS OF DOCKS

| TYPE OF OPERATION | TWO-WHEEL HAND TRUCK | FOUR-WHEEL HAND TRUCK | FORKLIFT TRUCK | DRAGLINE | AUTO SPUR DRAGLINE |
|---|---|---|---|---|---|
| Dock width (A) | 50'-0" | 60'-0" | 60'-0" to 70'-0" | 80'-0" | 120'-0" to 140'-0" |
| Work aisle (B) | 6'-0" | 10'-0" | 15'-0" | 10'-0" to 15'-0" | 10'-0" to 15'-0" |

Robert H. Lorenz, AIA; Preston Trucking Company, Inc.; Preston, Maryland
The Operations Council, American Trucking Association; Washington, D.C.

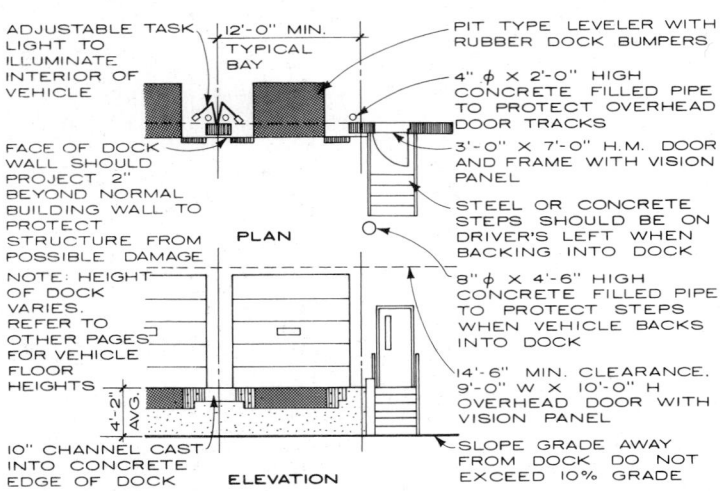

ADJUSTABLE TASK LIGHT TO ILLUMINATE INTERIOR OF VEHICLE

12'-0" MIN. TYPICAL BAY

PIT TYPE LEVELER WITH RUBBER DOCK BUMPERS

4" φ × 2'-0" HIGH CONCRETE FILLED PIPE TO PROTECT OVERHEAD DOOR TRACKS

3'-0" × 7'-0" H.M. DOOR AND FRAME WITH VISION PANEL

FACE OF DOCK WALL SHOULD PROJECT 2" BEYOND NORMAL BUILDING WALL TO PROTECT STRUCTURE FROM POSSIBLE DAMAGE

STEEL OR CONCRETE STEPS SHOULD BE ON DRIVER'S LEFT WHEN BACKING INTO DOCK

PLAN

NOTE: HEIGHT OF DOCK VARIES. REFER TO OTHER PAGES FOR VEHICLE FLOOR HEIGHTS

8" φ × 4'-6" HIGH CONCRETE FILLED PIPE TO PROTECT STEPS WHEN VEHICLE BACKS INTO DOCK

14'-6" MIN. CLEARANCE. 9'-0" W × 10'-0" H OVERHEAD DOOR WITH VISION PANEL

4'-2" AVG.

10" CHANNEL CAST INTO CONCRETE EDGE OF DOCK

ELEVATION

SLOPE GRADE AWAY FROM DOCK DO NOT EXCEED 10% GRADE

**TYPICAL LOADING DOCK BAY**

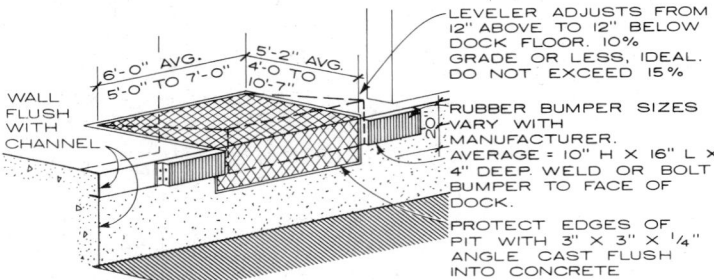

6'-0" AVG. 5'-0" TO 7'-0"

5'-2" AVG. 4'-0 TO 10'-7"

LEVELER ADJUSTS FROM 12" ABOVE TO 12" BELOW DOCK FLOOR. 10% GRADE OR LESS, IDEAL. DO NOT EXCEED 15%

WALL FLUSH WITH CHANNEL

RUBBER BUMPER SIZES VARY WITH MANUFACTURER. AVERAGE = 10" H × 16" L × 4" DEEP. WELD OR BOLT BUMPER TO FACE OF DOCK.

PROTECT EDGES OF PIT WITH 3" × 3" × ¼" ANGLE CAST FLUSH INTO CONCRETE

Automatic or manual operation for high volume docks where incoming vehicle heights vary widely; must be installed in a preformed concrete pit. Exact dimensions provided by manufacturer.

**PIT TYPE DOCK LEVELER**

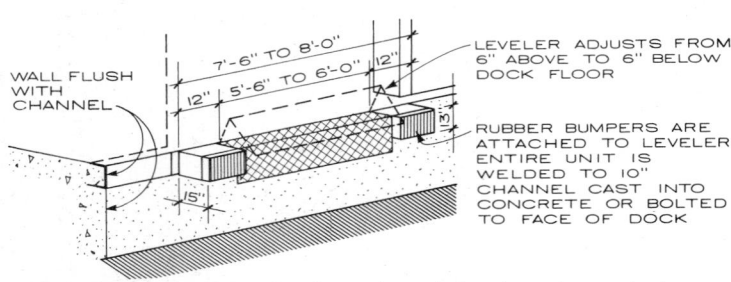

7'-6" TO 8'-0"

12"   5'-6" TO 6'-0"   12"

WALL FLUSH WITH CHANNEL

15"

LEVELER ADJUSTS FROM 6" ABOVE TO 6" BELOW DOCK FLOOR

RUBBER BUMPERS ARE ATTACHED TO LEVELER. ENTIRE UNIT IS WELDED TO 10" CHANNEL CAST INTO CONCRETE OR BOLTED TO FACE OF DOCK

Manual operation for high or medium volume docks where pit type levelers are impractical or leased facilities are being used.

**EDGE OF DOCK LEVELER**

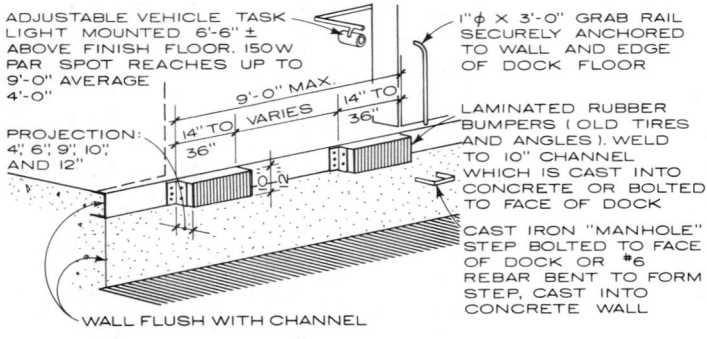

ADJUSTABLE VEHICLE TASK LIGHT MOUNTED 6'-6" ± ABOVE FINISH FLOOR. 150W PAR SPOT REACHES UP TO 9'-0" AVERAGE 4'-0"

1" φ × 3'-0" GRAB RAIL SECURELY ANCHORED TO WALL AND EDGE OF DOCK FLOOR

9'-0" MAX.   14" TO 36"

14" VARIES 36"

PROJECTION: 4", 6", 10", AND 12"

LAMINATED RUBBER BUMPERS (OLD TIRES AND ANGLES). WELD TO 10" CHANNEL WHICH IS CAST INTO CONCRETE OR BOLTED TO FACE OF DOCK

CAST IRON "MANHOLE" STEP BOLTED TO FACE OF DOCK OR #6 REBAR BENT TO FORM STEP, CAST INTO CONCRETE WALL

WALL FLUSH WITH CHANNEL

Used for low volume docks where incoming vehicle heights do not vary. Use portable type leveler such as a throw plate.

**LOADING DOCK WITHOUT LEVELER**

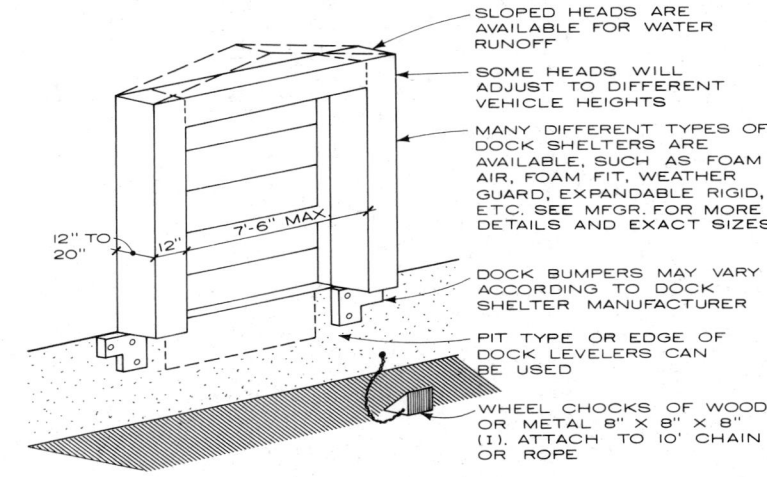

SLOPED HEADS ARE AVAILABLE FOR WATER RUNOFF

SOME HEADS WILL ADJUST TO DIFFERENT VEHICLE HEIGHTS

MANY DIFFERENT TYPES OF DOCK SHELTERS ARE AVAILABLE, SUCH AS FOAM AIR, FOAM FIT, WEATHER GUARD, EXPANDABLE RIGID, ETC. SEE MFGR. FOR MORE DETAILS AND EXACT SIZES

12" TO 20"   12"   7'-6" MAX

DOCK BUMPERS MAY VARY ACCORDING TO DOCK SHELTER MANUFACTURER

PIT TYPE OR EDGE OF DOCK LEVELERS CAN BE USED

WHEEL CHOCKS OF WOOD OR METAL 8" × 8" × 8" (I). ATTACH TO 10' CHAIN OR ROPE

Provides positive weather seal; protects dock from wind, rain, snow, and dirt. Retains constant temperature between dock and vehicle.

**CUSHIONED DOCK SHELTER**

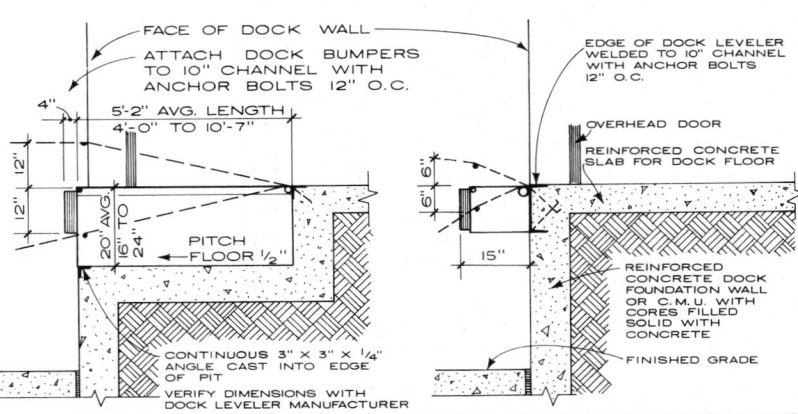

FACE OF DOCK WALL

ATTACH DOCK BUMPERS TO 10" CHANNEL WITH ANCHOR BOLTS 12" O.C.

EDGE OF DOCK LEVELER WELDED TO 10" CHANNEL WITH ANCHOR BOLTS 12" O.C.

4"   5'-2" AVG. LENGTH 4'-0" TO 10'-7"

OVERHEAD DOOR

12"

12"   20" AVG. 16" TO 24"

PITCH FLOOR ½"

6"   6"

REINFORCED CONCRETE SLAB FOR DOCK FLOOR

15"

REINFORCED CONCRETE DOCK FOUNDATION WALL OR C.M.U. WITH CORES FILLED SOLID WITH CONCRETE

FINISHED GRADE

CONTINUOUS 3" × 3" × ¼" ANGLE CAST INTO EDGE OF PIT

VERIFY DIMENSIONS WITH DOCK LEVELER MANUFACTURER

**SILL FOR PIT LEVELER**     **SILL FOR EDGE OF DOCK LEVELER**

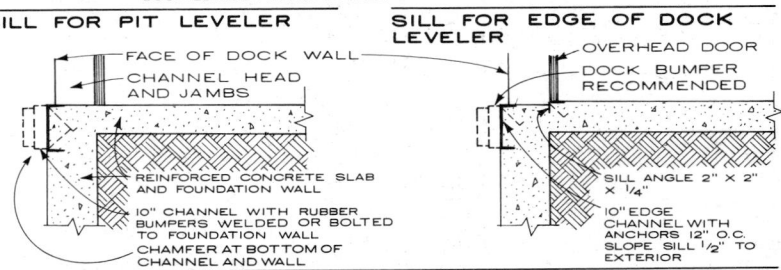

FACE OF DOCK WALL

CHANNEL HEAD AND JAMBS

OVERHEAD DOOR

DOCK BUMPER RECOMMENDED

REINFORCED CONCRETE SLAB AND FOUNDATION WALL

10" CHANNEL WITH RUBBER BUMPERS WELDED OR BOLTED TO FOUNDATION WALL CHAMFER AT BOTTOM OF CHANNEL AND WALL

SILL ANGLE 2" × 2" × ¼"

10" EDGE CHANNEL WITH ANCHORS 12" O.C. SLOPE SILL ½" TO EXTERIOR

**DOCK SILL WITHOUT LEVELERS**

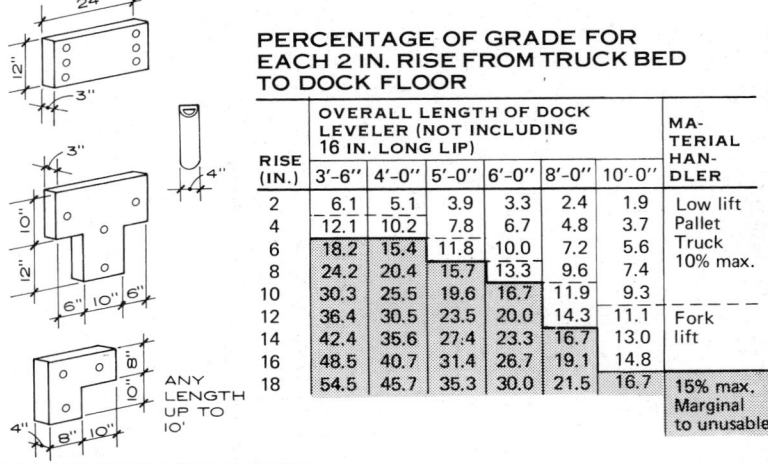

24"

12"   3"

3"

10"   4"

12"

6" 10" 6"

8"

ANY LENGTH UP TO 10'

4" 8" 10"

MOLDED HARD RUBBER DOCK BUMPERS

**PERCENTAGE OF GRADE FOR EACH 2 IN. RISE FROM TRUCK BED TO DOCK FLOOR**

| RISE (IN.) | OVERALL LENGTH OF DOCK LEVELER (NOT INCLUDING 16 IN. LONG LIP) | | | | | | MATERIAL HANDLER |
|---|---|---|---|---|---|---|---|
| | 3'-6" | 4'-0" | 5'-0" | 6'-0" | 8'-0" | 10'-0" | |
| 2 | 6.1 | 5.1 | 3.9 | 3.3 | 2.4 | 1.9 | Low lift Pallet Truck 10% max. |
| 4 | 12.1 | 10.2 | 7.8 | 6.7 | 4.8 | 3.7 | |
| 6 | 18.2 | 15.4 | 11.8 | 10.0 | 7.2 | 5.6 | |
| 8 | 24.2 | 20.4 | 15.7 | 13.3 | 9.6 | 7.4 | |
| 10 | 30.3 | 25.5 | 19.6 | 16.7 | 11.9 | 9.3 | |
| 12 | 36.4 | 30.5 | 23.5 | 20.0 | 14.3 | 11.1 | Fork lift |
| 14 | 42.4 | 35.6 | 27.4 | 23.3 | 16.7 | 13.0 | |
| 16 | 48.5 | 40.7 | 31.4 | 26.7 | 19.1 | 14.8 | |
| 18 | 54.5 | 45.7 | 35.3 | 30.0 | 21.5 | 16.7 | 15% max. Marginal to unusable |

Robert H. Lorenz, AIA; Preston Trucking Company, Inc.; Preston, Maryland

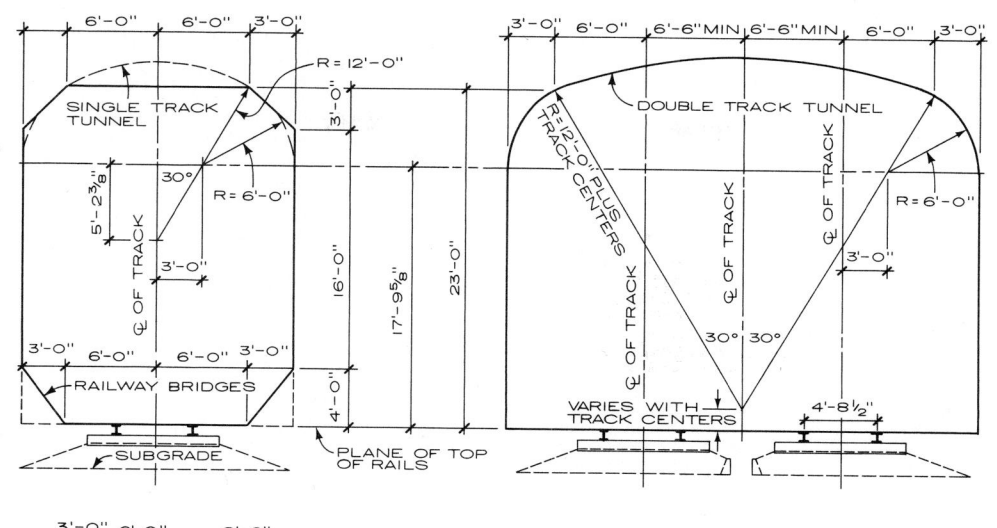

**NOTES**

1. Given clearances are the recommended minimums of the American Railway Engineering Association. Actual requirements vary from state to state.
2. Clearances shown are for the tangent track and new construction. Clearances for reconstruction work or for alteration are dependent on existing physical conditions and, where reasonably possible, should be improved to meet the requirements for new construction.
3. On curved track, the lateral clearances each side of track center line shall be increased 1½ in. per degree of curvature.
4. Common state requirement for lateral clearance of poles is 8 ft 6 in. (varies from 8 to 12 ft).
5. Standard American railroad gauge of 4 ft 8½ in. is measured between the inner faces of the rails.

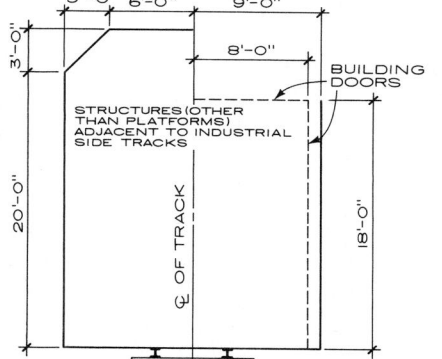

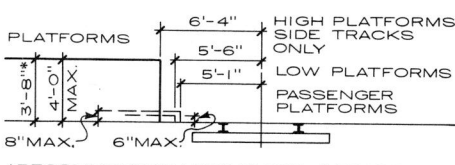

**NOTE**

The 6 ft 4 in. dimension will accommodate cars with either flush sliding doors or plug doors. Cars with hinged double doors require full clearance of 8 ft. Where 6 ft 4 in. platform is used, full clearance should be provided on opposite side, except inside buildings. (Several states allow a platform height of 4 ft 6 in. for refrigerator cars only, if the full lateral clearance of 8 ft is provided.)

**RAILWAY CLEARANCES**

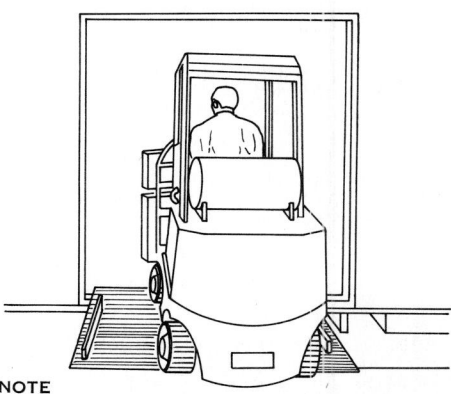

**NOTE**

Ramp travels laterally on rail mounted to edge of dock for positioning to rail car opening. It adjusts above and below dock level and locks to the rail when in the lowered position. Self-stores in vertical position when not in use. Available in varying lengths and widths.

**RAIL DOCK RAMPS**

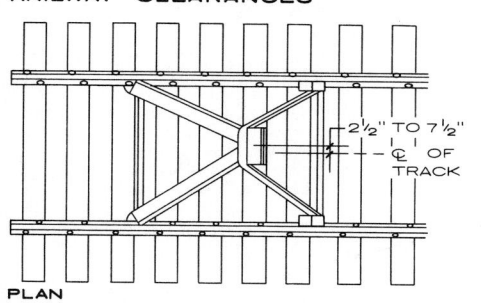

**PLAN**

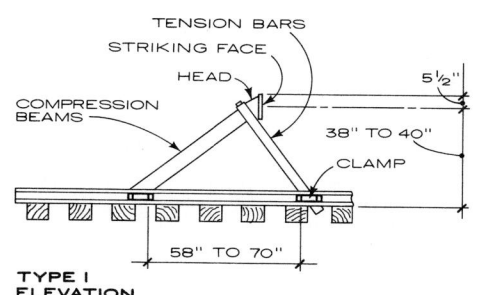

**TYPE 1 ELEVATION**

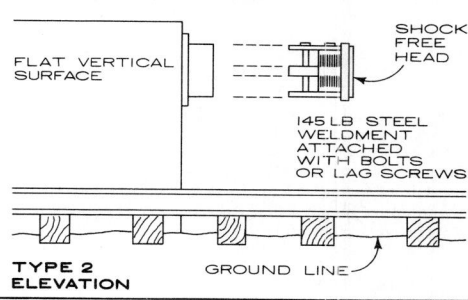

**TYPE 2 ELEVATION**

**TYPICAL BUMPING POSTS**

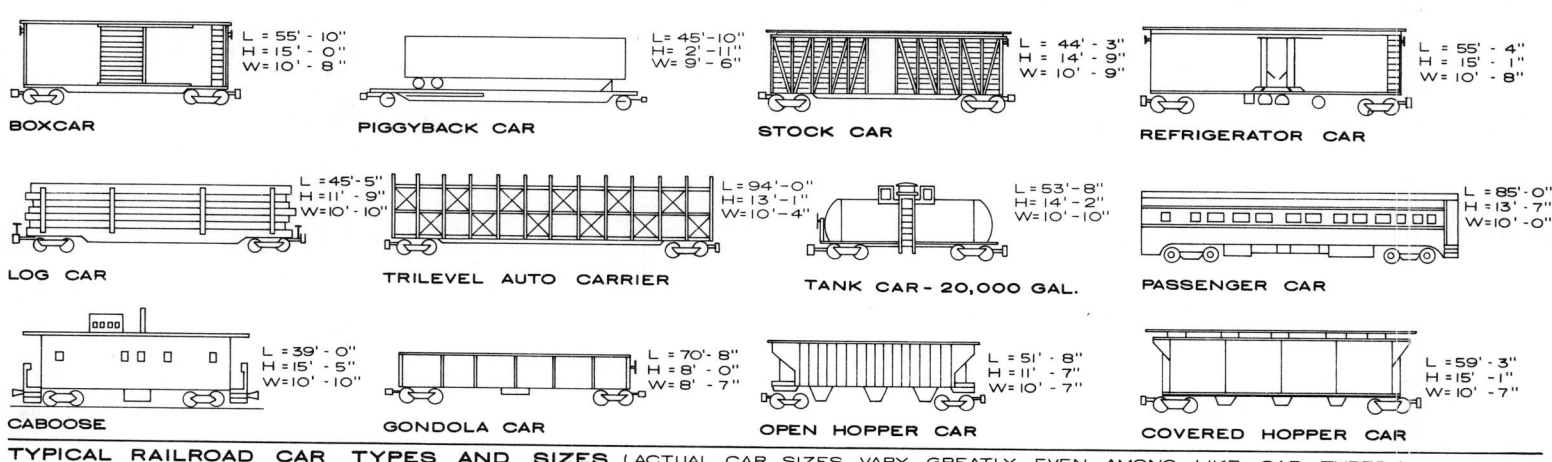

**TYPICAL RAILROAD CAR TYPES AND SIZES** (ACTUAL CAR SIZES VARY GREATLY EVEN AMONG LIKE CAR TYPES)

Ed Hesner; Rasmussen & Hobbs Architects; Tacoma, Washington
N. Claiborne Porter Jr., AIA; Anchorage, Alaska

# MANUFACTURED HOMES

## INTRODUCTION

The manufactured housing industry, formerly called mobile homes, has progressed in the past forty years: manufactured home unit widths have increased steadily from 6 to 8 ft (1950), 10 ft (1954), 12 ft (1962), 14 ft (1969), to 16 to 18 ft (1980).

The manufactured home usually has a wheeled chassis, an integral structural part of the housing unit. Manufactured home units are factory finished, interior and exterior.

## ACTS AND REGULATIONS

The U.S. Congress enacted the National (then Mobile Home) Manufactured Home Construction and Safety Act of 1974, directing the Department of Housing and Urban Development (HUD) to set national construction and safety standards preempting state laws. These standards are in the Code of Federal Regulations (CFR) as follows:

24 CFR 3280 (Standards)
24 CFR 3282 (Procedural Rules)
24 CFR 3283 (Consumer Installation Manual)

Manufactured home site installation requirements usually are adopted by local and state authorities from a model code such as the one developed by the National Conference of States on Building Codes and Standards, Inc. (NCSBCS), containing ANSI 225.1 and NFPA 501 specifications.

In 1980 Congress changed the designation ''Mobile Home'' to ''Manufactured Home.''

The HUD code, which became mandatory on June 15, 1976, as Manufactured Homes Procedural and Enforcement Regulations, established three agencies: State Administrative Agency (SAA); Design Approval Primary Inspection Agency (DAPIA); In-Plant Primary Inspection Agency (IPIA).

This inspection and approval system provides for a single inspection of a home's design and plant approval. The approved home can be shipped to any state for sale without further inspections other than local set-up and foundation requirements. The HUD code includes a provision that the manufacturer remains liable for repairing certain major design or structural defects.

Restrictive zoning requirements gradually are changing. One major difference is the classification of manufactured homes on a homeowner's lot as ''chattel'' (personal property) instead of as ''real estate.'' The Federal Housing Administration, FHA Title I of 1982, insured only chattel loans, which qualify for short-term, high interest bearing loans.

In 1983, HUD included manufactured housing in the FHA Title II, long-term mortgage financing programs, qualifying this form of housing for lower interest rates. Homes must comply with federal manufactured home construction and safety standards, and they must be attached to permanent site-built foundations meeting local building code requirements.

Legislation passed in 1984 allows the Veteran's Administration to guarantee mortgage financing for manufactured homes on the same basis as for site-built housing.

## POST–1986 INSTALLATION INSTRUCTION MANUALS

Manufacturers are required to provide HUD-approved consumer manuals, which must include: an installation manual with instructions for setting and anchoring, and for hookup and connecting utilities, and a homeowner's manual describing maintenance procedures.

The modular home manufacturers also provide installation and homeowner manuals; however, modular homes are built in sections, or pods, and must comply with state and local standards. Foundations, anchoring, and utilities must comply with local building codes. Certification procedures for modular homes differ in each state.

HUD-code and modular homes may be constructed in the same plant and on the same assembly line.

## DESIGN

Homes can be manufactured in multiple sections, in 24 to 28 ft widths, 50 to 60 ft long (up to 84 ft), with the option of adding on to. Cathedral ceilings are not uncommon, and even built-in whirlpool baths may be incorporated in the design.

## FOUNDATION

The foundation system design must meet installation requirements of the manufacturer's DAPIA-approved installation manual. Soil bearing properties must be known, or analysis is required by a professional engineer. The trend is to use foundations designed by registered architects and engineers, to be approved by regulatory authorities. See NFPA 501A, Chapter 3, Manufactured Home Foundation Systems, and Appendix C, Typical Designs of Piers or Load-Bearing Supports for Manufactured Homes.

## ANCHORING AND TIE-DOWN SYSTEMS

Anchors and tie-downs are used to secure the home from overturning due to wind. Systems for HUD-code homes are described in HUD-approved manuals.

Tie-downs must be weather resistant and have a minimum capacity of 3150 lb (plus a 50% overload factor) resistance to withdrawal in the direction of the tie. The same capacity applies when concrete slabs or continuous footings are used. See table below for the number of ties required for hurricane and nonhurricane resistive regions.

Over-the-roof ties are factory installed. Frame ties are furnished by the manufacturer/installer. The number of over-the-roof ties and frame ties varies by wind zone, pier height, and size of home.

The angle of the tie-down strap or cable with the horizontal or vertical plane is critical. Anchors and tie-down straps/cables should not extend outside the fascia or skirting.

## BOTTOM BOARD (SKIRT), GROUND VAPOR BARRIER, CLEARANCES, RECOMMENDATIONS

The entire area under the home shall be covered with an approved ground vapor barrier, such as polyethylene film 6-mil thick, 6 in. overlap at joints. The bottom board must be equipped with nonclosing vents. The free air opening of the vents must be equal to not less than $1/300$ of the crawl space plus two times the crawl space perimeter times $1/100$.

Additional vents must be installed adjacent to air intakes, oil burners, or sealed combustion water heaters. At least 75% of the covered area underfloor should have 18 in. clearance between bottom main chassis members and ground level, and not more than 25% of the covered area may have a minimum of 12 in. clearance.

## UTILITY CONNECTION, HOOK-UP TO ON-SITE SERVICES TESTING

Multiple section units require specific cross-over connections. Utility hookups must comply with local codes and ordinances. Utility systems and installations that have been equipped and factory tested must be tested on-site by qualified personnel in accordance with the manufacturer's manual and must have 12 in. minimum clearance underneath.

## ACCESSORY STRUCTURES

Carports, decks, porches, utility buildings, and fences, unless designed and constructed by the manufacturer or licensed installer, must have a separate structural system and must comply with local codes and ordinances.

## SITE LAYOUT

Layout of manufactured home developments does not differ from those for site-built housing developments.

Service buildings no longer are required.

The layout of manufactured home communities must take into consideration setbacks, access to community streets, community streets, walk systems, and maneuvering for the off-loading and installation of 12 to 18 ft wide units, which may be up to 84 ft in length.

See NFPA 501A, Section 2-4, Multiple Manufactured Home Site Development.

## NUMBER OF TIES REQUIRED PER SIDE OF SINGLE SECTION[1] MANUFACTURED HOMES[2]
BASED ON A MINIMUM WORKING LOAD PER ANCHOR OF 3150 LB (1429 KG) WITH A 50% OVERLOAD [4725 LB TOTAL]

| | HURRICANE RESISTIVE | | | | NONHURRICANE RESISTIVE | | | |
| | | | ALTERNATE METHOD[4] | | | | ALTERNATE METHOD | |
| LENGTH[3] (FT) | NO. OF VERTICAL TIES | NO. OF DIAGONAL TIES[5] | NO. OF BALING STRAPS | NO. OF DIAGONAL TIES[6] | NO. OF VERTICAL TIES | NO. OF DIAGONAL TIES[5] | NO. OF BALING STRAPS | NO. OF DIAGONAL TIES[6] |
|---|---|---|---|---|---|---|---|---|
| up to 40 | 2 | 4 | 2 | 5 | 2 | 3 | 2 | 3 |
| 40 to < 46 | 2 | 4 | 2 | 6 | 2 | 3 | 2 | 3 |
| 46 to < 49 | 2 | 5 | 2 | 6 | 2 | 3 | 2 | 3 |
| 49 to < 54 | 3 | 5 | 3 | 7 | 2 | 3 | 2 | 3 |
| 54 to < 58 | 3 | 5 | 3 | 7 | 2 | 4 | 2 | 4 |
| 58 to < 64 | 3 | 6 | 3 | 8 | 2 | 4 | 2 | 4 |
| 64 to < 70 | 3 | 6 | 3 | 9 | 2 | 4 | 2 | 5 |
| 70 to < 73 | 3 | 7 | 3 | 9 | 2 | 4 | 2 | 5 |
| 73 to < 84 | 4 | 7 | 4 | 10 | 2 | 5 | 2 | 5 |

[1] Double section manufactured homes require only the diagonal ties specified in column 3 or 7.
[2] Except when the anchoring system is designed and approved by a registered professional engineer or architect.
[3] Length of manufactured home (as used in this table) means length excluding draw bar.
[4] Alternate method. When this method is used, an approved wall reinforcement means shall be provided.
[5] Diagonal ties in this method shall deviate at least 45° from a vertical direction.
[6] Diagonal ties in this method shall be 45° ± 5° from vertical and shall be attached to the nearest main frame member.

Walter Hart Associates, AIA; White Plains, New York
Charles W. Graham, AIA; Texas A & M University; College Station, Texas

1 **TRANSPORTATION**

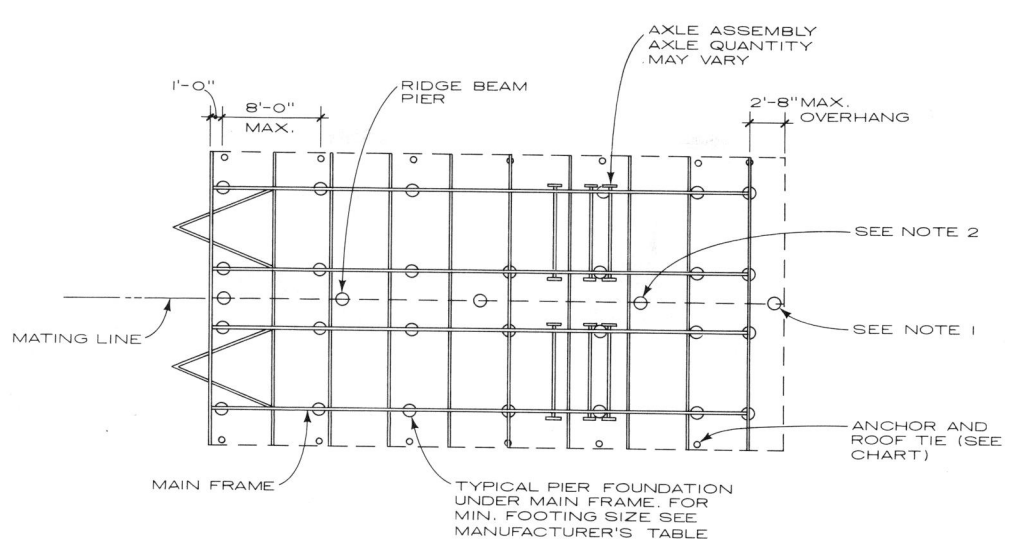

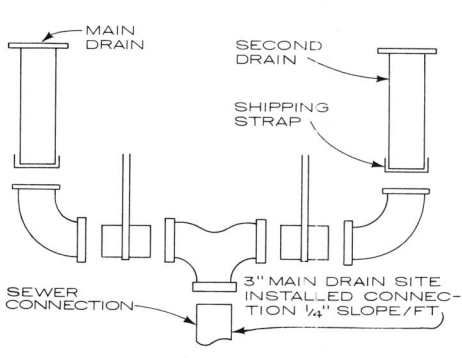

## NOTES

1. Required pier capacity at each end of home equals the total distance in feet to the next ridge beam post multiplied by 165 lb/lin. ft.

2. Required pier capacity at interior ridge beam posts equals the distance between each post on each side, in feet, multiplied by 165 lb/lin. ft.

## NOTE

Gutters, overflows not hooked up with the drain system shall discharge outside the home perimeter.

## EXAMPLES OF FOOTING MAIN FRAME TIE-DOWN

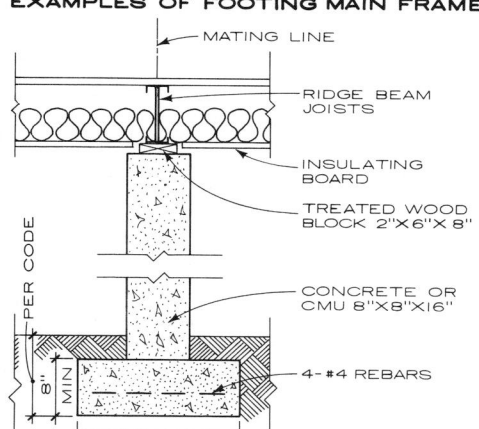

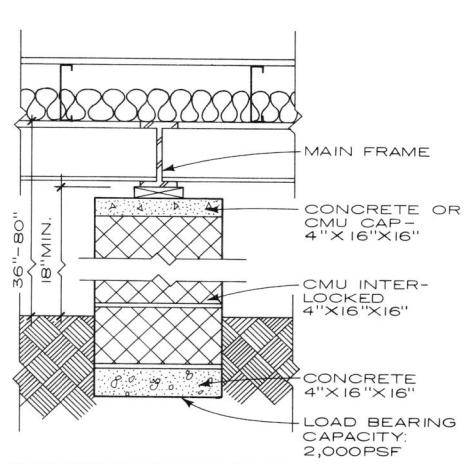

## DRAIN SYSTEM HOOKUP

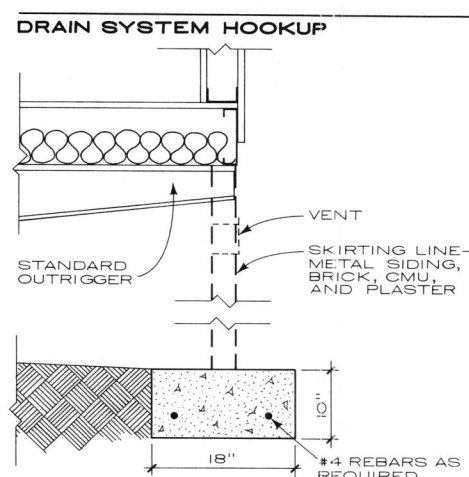

### RIDGE BEAM PIER

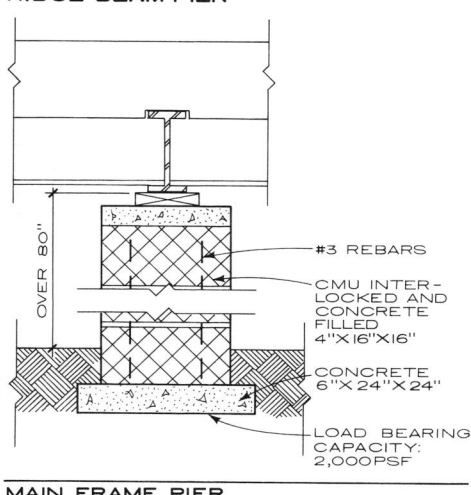

### MAIN FRAME PIER

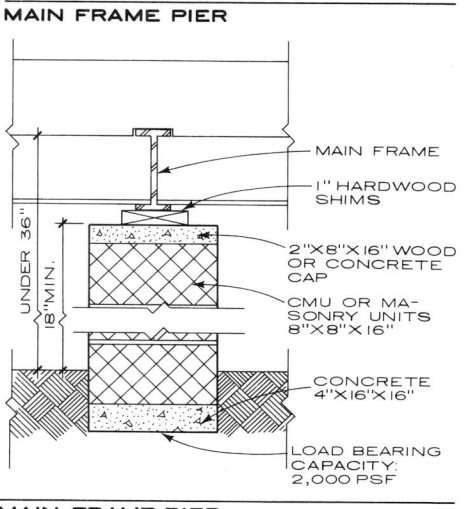

### MAIN FRAME PIER

### MAIN FRAME PIER

## TYPICAL SIDEWALL

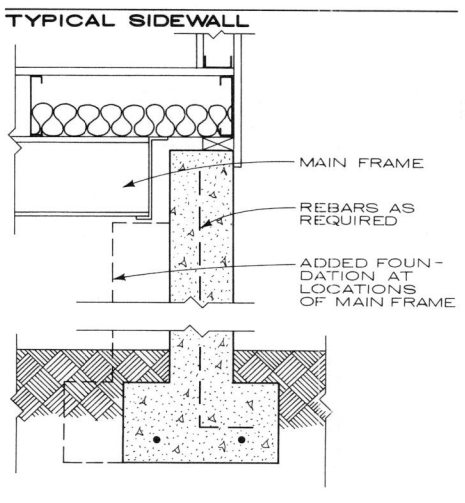

## TYPICAL ENDWALL

Walter Hart Associates, AIA; White Plains, New York
Charles W. Graham, AIA; Texas A & M University; College Station, Texas

## TRANSPORTATION    1

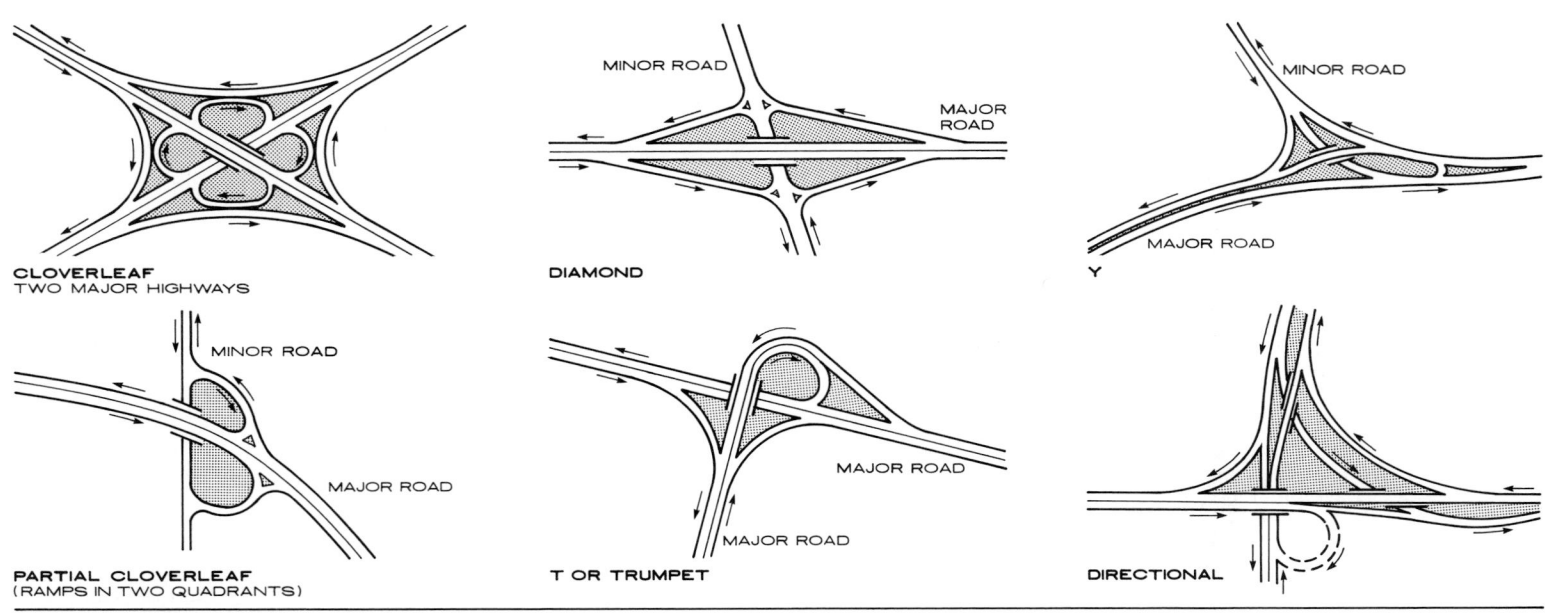

CLOVERLEAF
TWO MAJOR HIGHWAYS

MINOR ROAD
MAJOR ROAD

DIAMOND

MINOR ROAD
MAJOR ROAD

Y

MINOR ROAD
MAJOR ROAD

PARTIAL CLOVERLEAF
(RAMPS IN TWO QUADRANTS)

MAJOR ROAD
MAJOR ROAD

T OR TRUMPET

DIRECTIONAL

FREEWAY GRADE SEPARATED INTERSECTIONS

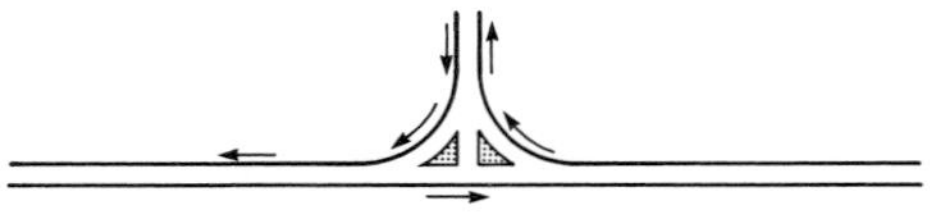

"T"

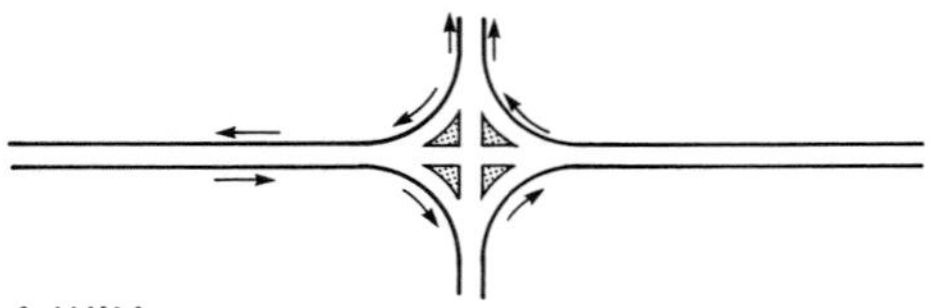

4-WAY

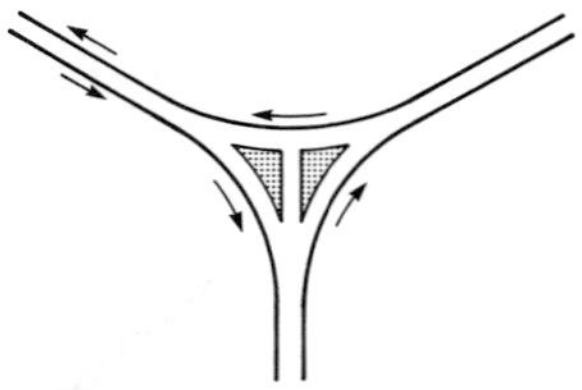

"Y"

EXPRESSWAY / RURAL HIGHWAY
AT GRADE CHANNELIZED INTERSECTIONS

| TYPE OF HIGHWAY | VEHICLE CAPABILITIES | WIDTHS: ROW | WIDTHS: PAVEMENT | FEATURES |
|---|---|---|---|---|
| Freeway: A high-speed, controlled access highway. Connects regional or metropolitan areas. | Design Flow rate: 1500 VPH/lane<br>Capacity: 200 VPH/lane | 200 ft.–300 ft.<br><br>300 ft.–400 ft. | Without access roads:<br>Driving lanes: 11 ft.–12 ft. per lane<br>Shoulders: 8 ft.–10 ft. (both sides each roadway)<br>Median: 16 ft.–60 ft.<br><br>With access roads | Divided traffic<br>Grade-separated crossings<br>Continuous traffic; no stops<br>DMG: 3%<br>Extensive landscape planting<br>Building setbacks: with service road: 50 ft. without service road: 75 ft. |
| Expressway/Rural Highway: Limited-access highway providing connections between metropolitan areas and cities | Design Flow rate: 900 VPH/lane<br>Capacity: 1500 VPH/lane | 150 ft.–250 ft. | driving lanes: 11 ft.–12 ft. per lane<br>Shoulders: 8 ft.–10 ft. | Two-way or divided traffic<br>Channelized at grade crossings<br>Traffic signals at major intersections<br>DMG: 4%<br>Landscape planting<br>Parking prohibited<br>Building setback: 75 ft. |

VPH: Vehicles per hour DMG: Desired maximum grade ROW: Right-of-way

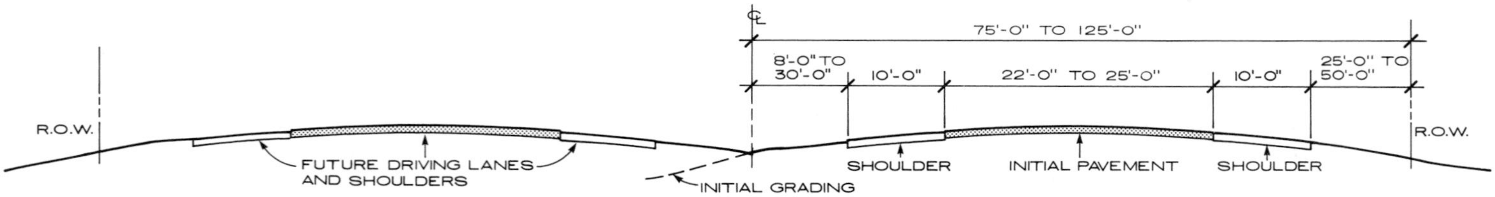

℄
75'-0" TO 125'-0"
8'-0" TO 30'-0"
10'-0"
22'-0" TO 25'-0"
10'-0"
25'-0" TO 50'-0"
R.O.W.
R.O.W.
FUTURE DRIVING LANES AND SHOULDERS
SHOULDER
INITIAL PAVEMENT
SHOULDER
INITIAL GRADING

EXPRESSWAY / RURAL HIGHWAY

℄
60'-0" TO 104'-0"
40'-0" TO 64'-0"
20'-0" TO 40'-0"
WITHOUT ACCESS ROAD
WITH ACCESS ROAD
R.O.W.
R.O.W.
R.O.W.
R.O.W.
FUTURE EXPANSION
8'-0" TO 30'-0"
150'-0" TO 200'-0"
24'-0"
10'-0"
55'-0" TO 83'-0"
28'-0"
26'-0"
MEDIAN
DRIVING LANES (12'-0" PER LANE)
SHOULDER
AREA FOR ON/OFF RAMPS AND EXPANSION
ACCESS ROAD URBAN ONE-WAY RURAL TWO-WAY

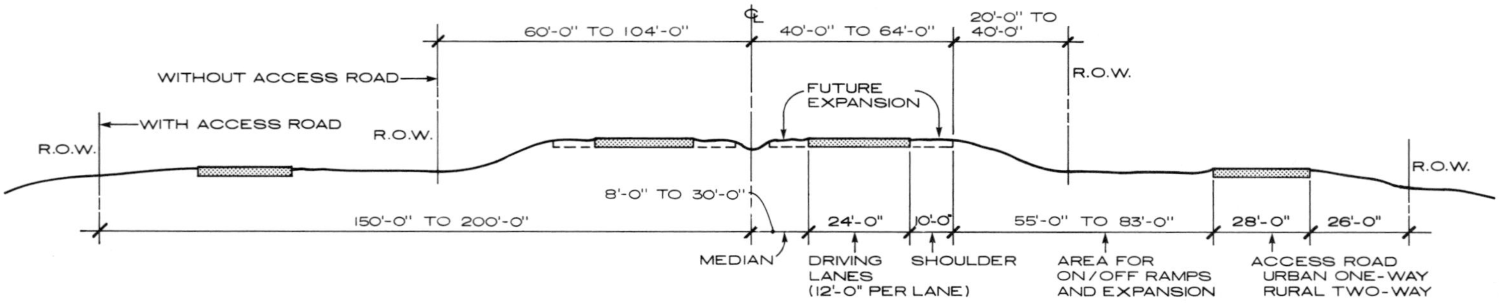

FREEWAY

SECTIONS

Connecticut Coastal Management Program, see data sources
William H. Evans, AIA; San Antonio, Texas

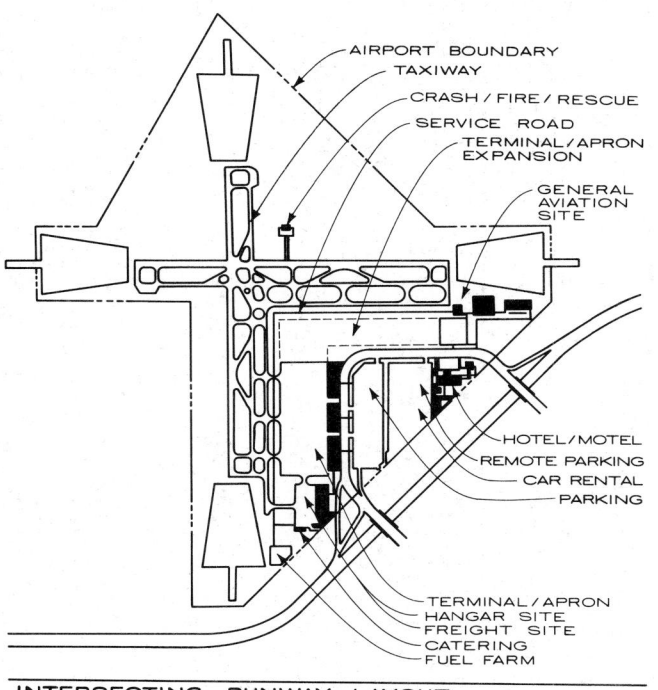

- AIRPORT BOUNDARY
- TAXIWAY
- CRASH / FIRE / RESCUE
- SERVICE ROAD
- TERMINAL / APRON EXPANSION
- GENERAL AVIATION SITE
- HOTEL / MOTEL
- REMOTE PARKING
- CAR RENTAL
- PARKING
- TERMINAL / APRON
- HANGAR SITE
- FREIGHT SITE
- CATERING
- FUEL FARM

**INTERSECTING RUNWAY LAYOUT**

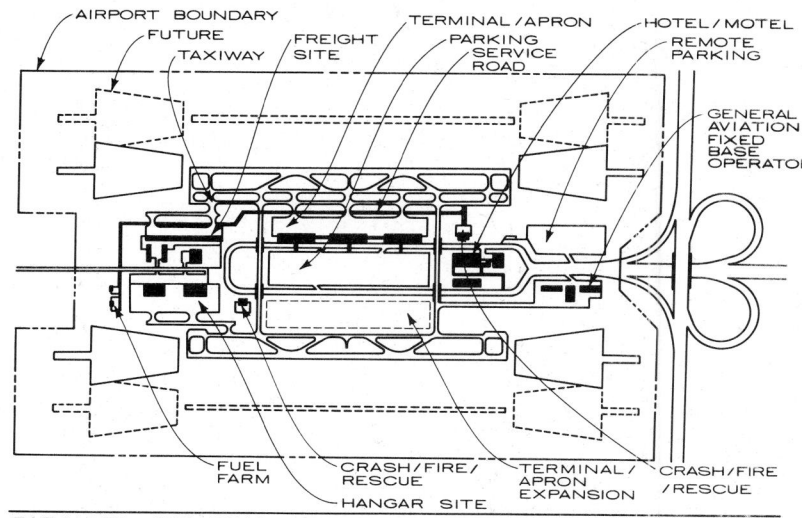

- AIRPORT BOUNDARY
- FUTURE TAXIWAY
- FREIGHT SITE
- TERMINAL / APRON PARKING SERVICE ROAD
- HOTEL / MOTEL REMOTE PARKING
- GENERAL AVIATION FIXED BASE OPERATOR
- FUEL FARM
- CRASH / FIRE / RESCUE
- HANGAR SITE
- TERMINAL / APRON EXPANSION
- CRASH / FIRE / RESCUE

**PARALLEL RUNWAY LAYOUT**

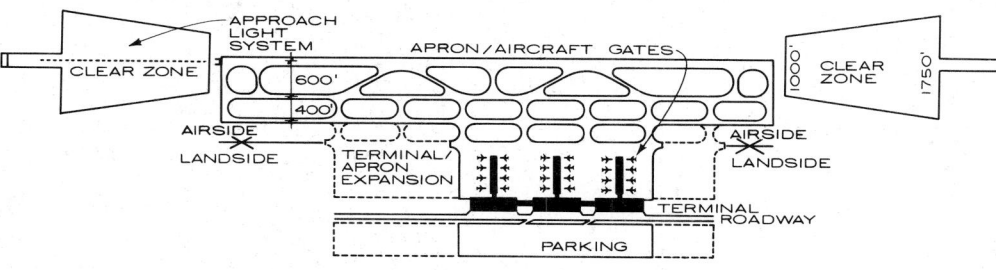

**AIRPORT AIRSIDE-LANDSIDE**

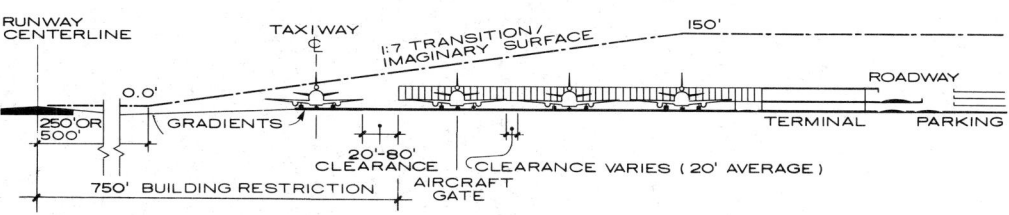

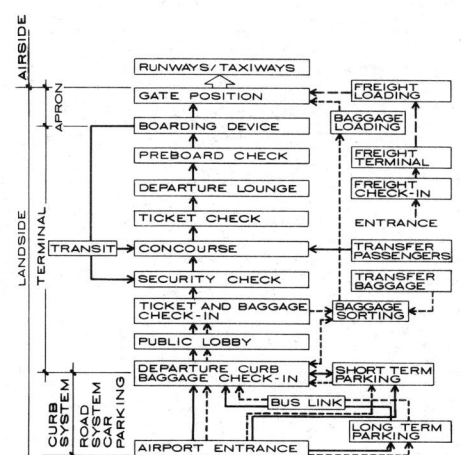

**OUTBOUND—U.S. DOMESTIC AND U.S. INTERNATIONAL PASSENGER BAGGAGE AND FREIGHT FLOW FEDERAL INSPECTION SERVICES (F.I.S.) NOT REQUIRED**

**INBOUND—U.S. DOMESTIC AND U.S. INTERNATIONAL PASSENGER BAGGAGE AND FREIGHT FLOW FEDERAL INSPECTION SERVICES (F.I.S.) REQUIRED**

Walter Hart Associates, AIA; White Plains, New York

Runway-taxiway configurations and apron terminal concepts appear in many variations, generally caused by climatic conditions, traffic characteristics, operational requirements, traffic volumes, and historical growth patterns.

Two airport plans are shown: (1) an intersecting runway configuration, total land area small to medium, the landside facilities are arranged within one quadrant, expansion capability is limited; (2) a parallel runway configuration, total land area medium to large, the landside facilities are arranged within the area between the runways, expansion capability is significant.

The airport airside consists of the runway-taxiway system, areas for clearances, and areas for navigational aides.

The airport landside consists of the passenger terminal with aircraft apron; airport ground transportation systems, roads, vehicular parking; support facilities, hangars, freight terminals, U.S. mail, catering, car rental, hotels, motels. The airside influences the location, plan development, and expansion capabilities of the landside facilities.

Requirements, recommendations, criteria, and guidelines are documented in the United States by the Department of Transportation/Federal Aviation Administration (DOT/FAA) and by the Air Transport Association of America (ATA), outside the United States by the International Civil Aviation Organization (ICAO) and the International Air Transport Association (IATA).

The following publications contain basic information on airport planning and design:

1. A Model Zoning Ordinance to Limit Height of Objects Around Airports, AC 150/5190-4, FAA, Dec. 5, 1983, Washington, D.C.
2. Utility Airports—Air Access to National Transportation, AC 150/5300-4B, FAA, June 24, 1975, incorporates Changes 1–6, Change 7, Sept. 23, 1983, Washington, D.C.
3. Airport Design Standards—Transport Airports, DOT/FAA, AC 150/5300-12, Feb. 28, 1983, Washington, D.C.
4. Planning and Design Guidelines for Airport Terminal Facilities, FAA AC 150/5360-7A, DOT/FAA, Washington, D.C.
5. Runway Capacity Criteria for Airport Planning Purposes, 5th edition, ATA, Washington, D.C.
6. Airline Aircraft Gates and Passenger Terminal Space Approximations, AD/CS Report No. 4, July 1977, ATA, Washington, D.C.
7. Aircraft Ground Support Air System Planning Guide Book, prepared for ATA, Nov. 1981, by Burns & McDonnell, Engineers, Architects, & Consultants, Kansas City, Mo.
8. Guidelines for Airport Signing and Graphics, ATA, Sept. 1984, Washington, D.C.

Small Airports:

9. Planning and Design of Airport Terminal Facilities at Non Hub Locations, AC 150/5360-9, FAA, Mar. 4, 1980.

Heliports:

10. Heliport Design Guide, AC 150/5390-1B, FAA, Aug. 1977.

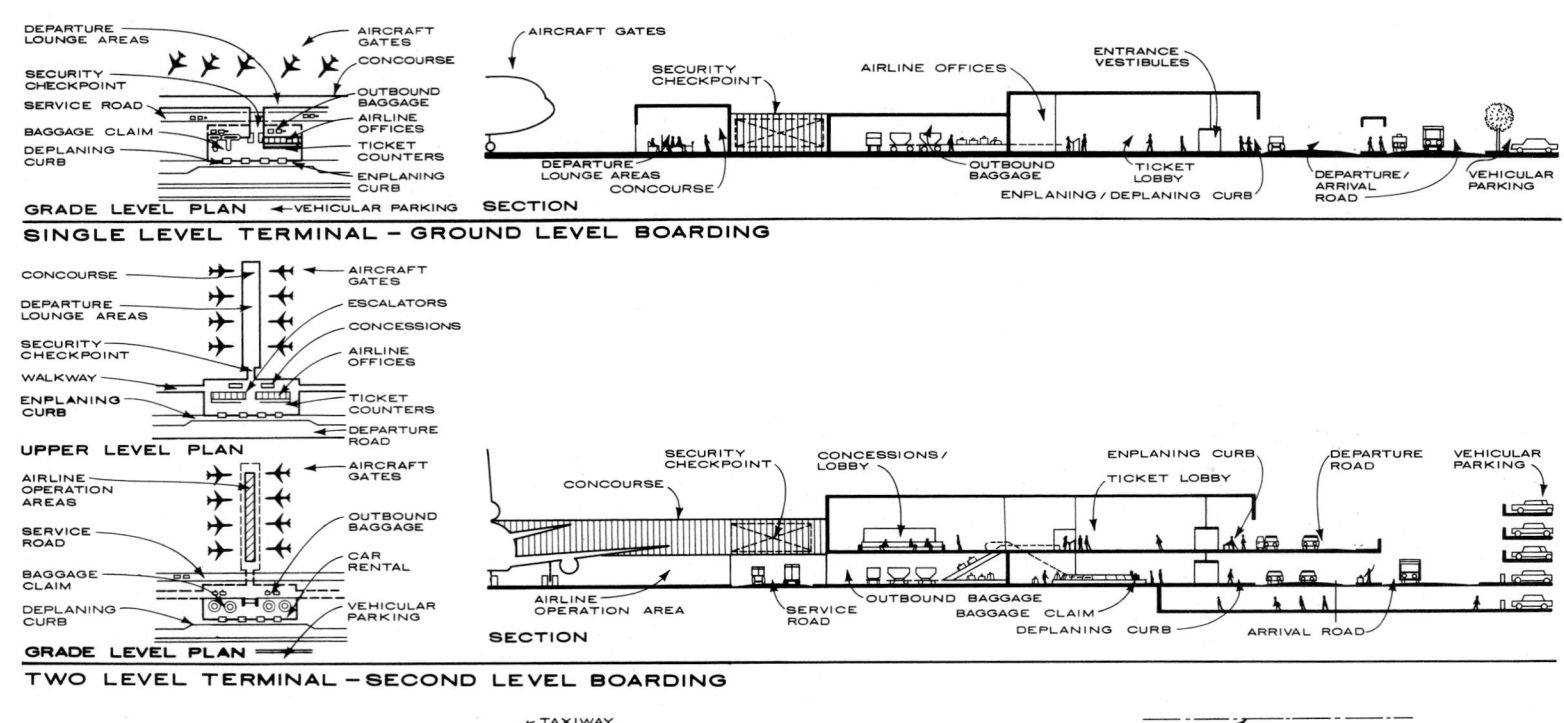

**SINGLE LEVEL TERMINAL – GROUND LEVEL BOARDING**

**TWO LEVEL TERMINAL – SECOND LEVEL BOARDING**

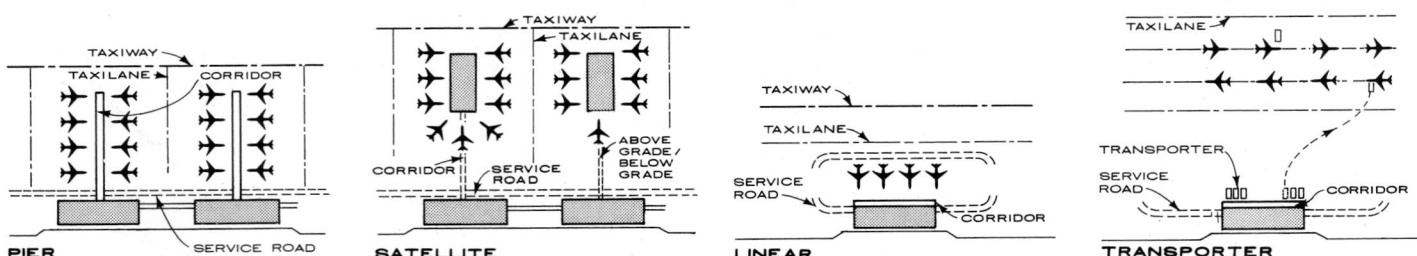

**TERMINAL CONCEPTS**

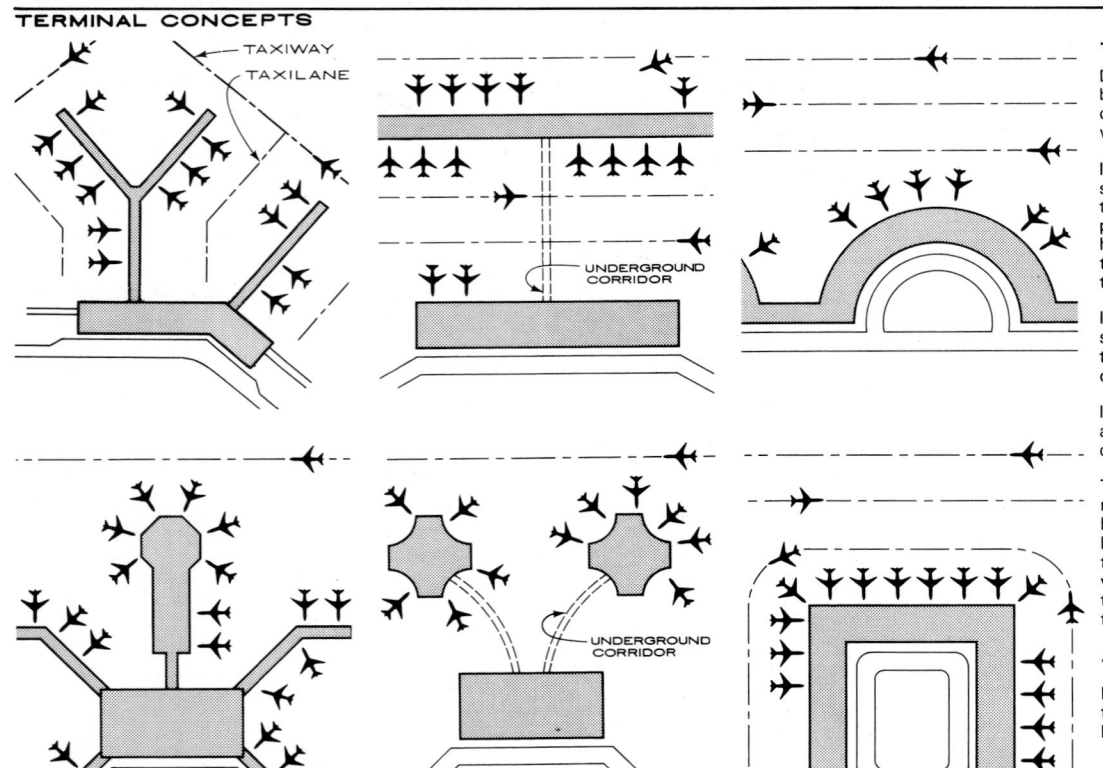

**CONCEPT VARIATIONS**

## TERMINAL CONCEPTS

During the past 10 years, a general understanding has been reached that the link that connects an aircraft gate configuration with a terminal is the dominant feature by which each terminal concept can be identified.

In the pier concept, aircraft are parked in a line at either side of a connecting corridor or concourse attached to the main terminal. In both the satellite and pier concepts, passenger ticketing and inbound and outbound baggage handling functions are centralized, mostly in the main terminal. However, there are variations and exceptions to this.

In the satellite concept, aircraft are parked in a cluster surrounding a structure that is connected to the main terminal by a corridor or concourse positioned below, on, or above grade.

In the linear concept, aircraft are parked in a single line at a corridor or concourse on the apron. All functions are centralized.

The transporter concept involves a return to earlier modes of operation when passengers were transported between aircraft and the terminal in buses or other vehicles. This concept involves separating aircraft positions from the main terminal and using a connecting vehicle to transport passengers to and from aircraft. In this concept, passenger and baggage handling is centralized in the main terminal.

## VARIATIONS

Existing solutions are shown schematically. Each needs thorough analysis before adoption in any form or combination.

Walter Hart Associates, AIA; White Plains, New York
Benito Lao, RA; Fort Worth, Texas

**1     TRANSPORTATION**

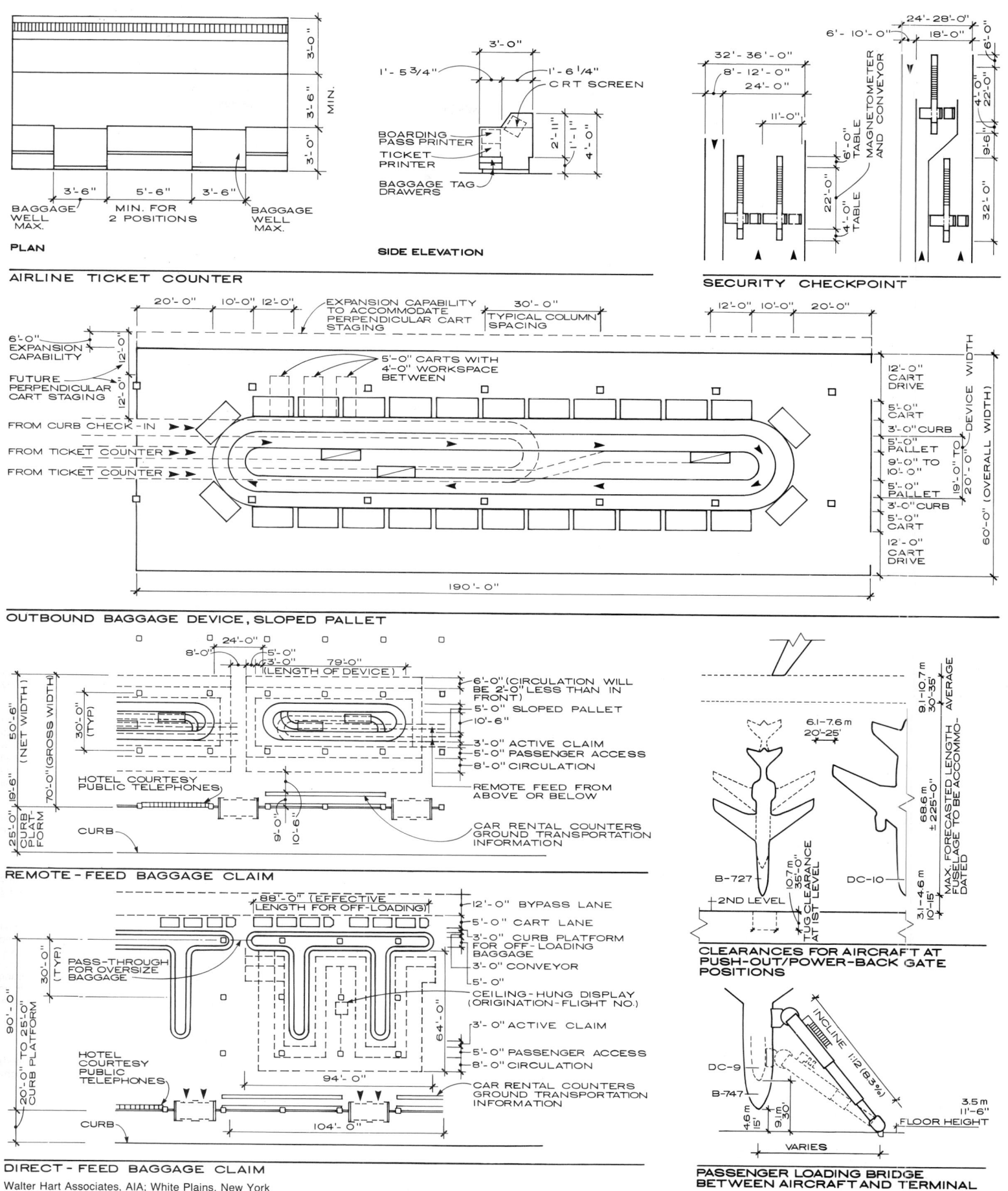

**PLAN**        **SIDE ELEVATION**

**AIRLINE TICKET COUNTER**

**SECURITY CHECKPOINT**

**OUTBOUND BAGGAGE DEVICE, SLOPED PALLET**

**REMOTE-FEED BAGGAGE CLAIM**

**DIRECT-FEED BAGGAGE CLAIM**

Walter Hart Associates, AIA; White Plains, New York

**CLEARANCES FOR AIRCRAFT AT PUSH-OUT/POWER-BACK GATE POSITIONS**

**PASSENGER LOADING BRIDGE BETWEEN AIRCRAFT AND TERMINAL**

DATA KEY: L-Length overall    W-Wingspan    H-Height overall    SEATS-Normal passenger accomodations

L 255'-2"
W 207'-8"
H 63'-5"

452 SEATS

**BOEING 747**

L 177'-5"
W 147'-1"
H 54'-7"

267 SEATS

**AIRBUS A-300**

L 182'-1"
W 165'-4"
H 58'-1"

255 SEATS

**McDONNELL-DOUGLAS DC-10**

L 177'-9"
W 155'-4"
H 55'-4"

256 SEATS

**LOCKHEED L-1011**

L 187'-5"
W 148'-5"
H 42'-5"

240 SEATS

**McDONNELL-DOUGLAS DC-8-70**

L 176'-1"
W 156'-1"
H 52'-0"

216 SEATS

**BOEING 767**

L 155'-3"
W 124'-10"
H 44'-6"

205 SEATS

**BOEING 757**

L 147'-10"
W 107'-10"
H 29'-8"

172 SEATS

**McDONNELL-DOUGLAS MD-80 (DC-9)**

L 153'-2"
W 108'-0"
H 34'-0"

145 SEATS

**BOEING 727**

L 203'-9"
W 83'-10"
H 37'-5"

128 SEATS

**CONCORDE**

L 100'-2"
W 93'-0"
H 37'-0"

115 SEATS

**BOEING 737**

L 97'-2"
W 82'-3"
H 27'-10"

85 SEATS

**FOKKER F-28**

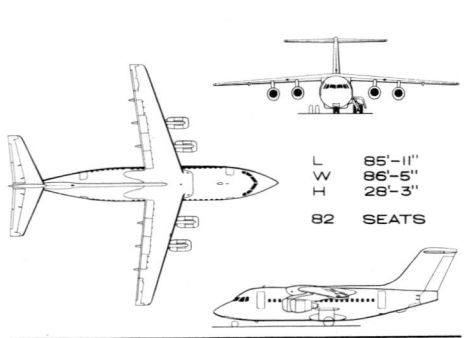

L 85'-11"
W 86'-5"
H 28'-3"

82 SEATS

**BAE-146**

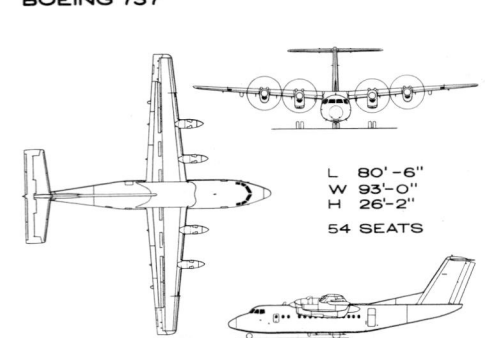

L 80'-6"
W 93'-0"
H 26'-2"

54 SEATS

**DeHAVILLAND DHC-7**

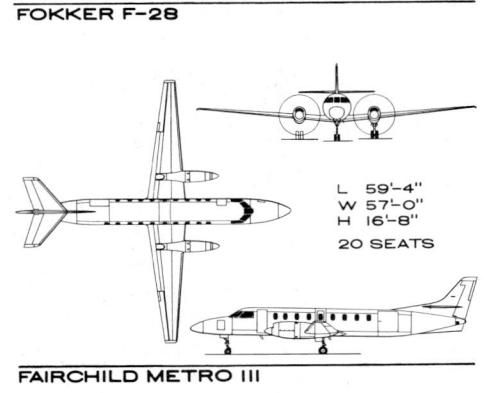

L 59'-4"
W 57'-0"
H 16'-8"

20 SEATS

**FAIRCHILD METRO III**

Stanley N. Hall; Washington, D.C.

# 1 TRANSPORTATION

DATA KEY

L-Length Overall   H-Height Overall
W-Wingspan   SEATS-Normal Passenger Accommodations

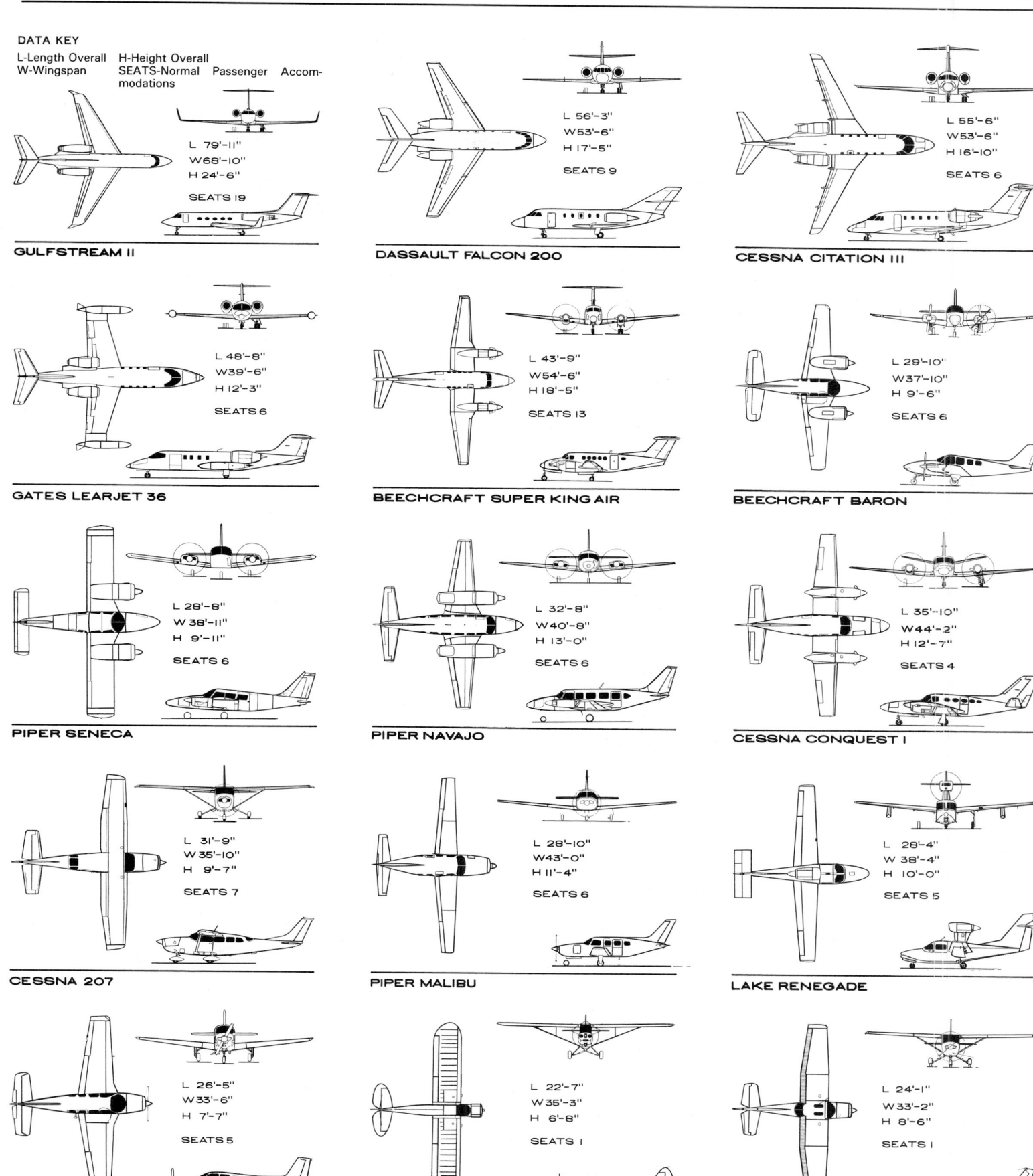

L 79'-11"
W 68'-10"
H 24'-6"

SEATS 19

**GULFSTREAM II**

L 56'-3"
W 53'-6"
H 17'-5"

SEATS 9

**DASSAULT FALCON 200**

L 55'-6"
W 53'-6"
H 16'-10"

SEATS 6

**CESSNA CITATION III**

L 48'-8"
W 39'-6"
H 12'-3"

SEATS 6

**GATES LEARJET 36**

L 43'-9"
W 54'-6"
H 18'-5"

SEATS 13

**BEECHCRAFT SUPER KING AIR**

L 29'-10"
W 37'-10"
H 9'-6"

SEATS 6

**BEECHCRAFT BARON**

L 28'-8"
W 38'-11"
H 9'-11"

SEATS 6

**PIPER SENECA**

L 32'-8"
W 40'-8"
H 13'-0"

SEATS 6

**PIPER NAVAJO**

L 35'-10"
W 44'-2"
H 12'-7"

SEATS 4

**CESSNA CONQUEST I**

L 31'-9"
W 35'-10"
H 9'-7"

SEATS 7

**CESSNA 207**

L 28'-10"
W 43'-0"
H 11'-4"

SEATS 6

**PIPER MALIBU**

L 28'-4"
W 38'-4"
H 10'-0"

SEATS 5

**LAKE RENEGADE**

L 26'-5"
W 33'-6"
H 7'-7"

SEATS 5

**BEECHCRAFT BONANZA**

L 22'-7"
W 35'-3"
H 6'-8"

SEATS 1

**PIPER SUPER CUB**

L 24'-1"
W 33'-2"
H 8'-6"

SEATS 1

**CESSNA 152**

Stanley N. Hall; Tulsa, Oklahoma

## GENERAL

A heliport is composed of both real and imaginary surfaces. Real surfaces are the takeoff–landing areas, which include the touchdown pad, peripheral area, taxiways, passenger service building (terminal), and maintenance and hanger facilities. Imaginary surfaces are the approach–departure paths and primary and transitional surfaces. The imaginary surfaces define the lines of flight to and from the real surfaces. Approach–departure paths are selected based on considerations of prevailing winds, the locations and heights of buildings or other objects in the area, and environmental factors. It is desirable for a heliport to have two approach–departure paths separated by an angle of at least 90°. Curved approach–departure paths are permitted and may be necessary in some cases to provide a suitable obstruction-free path.

## ENVIRONMENTAL FACTORS

Establishment of a heliport should include an assessment of the following in regard to the impact on the community:
1. Public safety
2. Noise
3. Exhaust emissions
4. Land-use zoning
5. Ground traffic

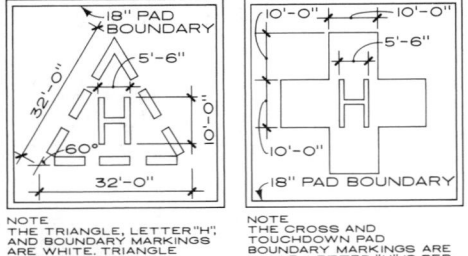

**RECOMMENDED HELIPORT MARKINGS**

## CLASSIFICATIONS OF HELIPORTS

### PERSONAL USE

A heliport used exclusively by the owner. Personal-use heliports are owned by individuals and corporations.

### PRIVATE USE

Any heliport that restricts usage to the owner or to persons authorized by the owner. It may be owned by a public body such as a hospital or police department.

### PUBLIC USE

A heliport that is open to the public and does not require permission of the owner for use. The extent of the heliport facilities may limit operations to helicopters of a specific size and weight.

### FEDERAL

Heliport facilities operated by a department or nonmilitary agency of the United States government.

### MILITARY

A heliport operated by one of the United States uniformed services; public use is generally prohibited.

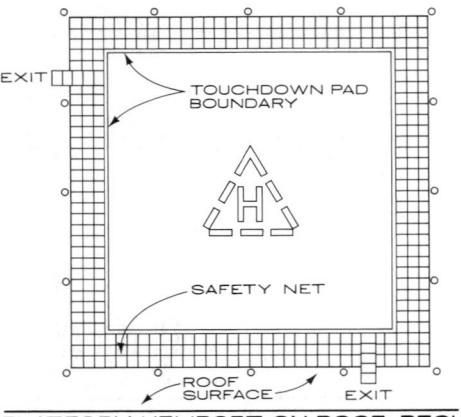

**PLATFORM HELIPORT ON ROOF-DECK**

Stanley N. Hall; Washington, D.C.

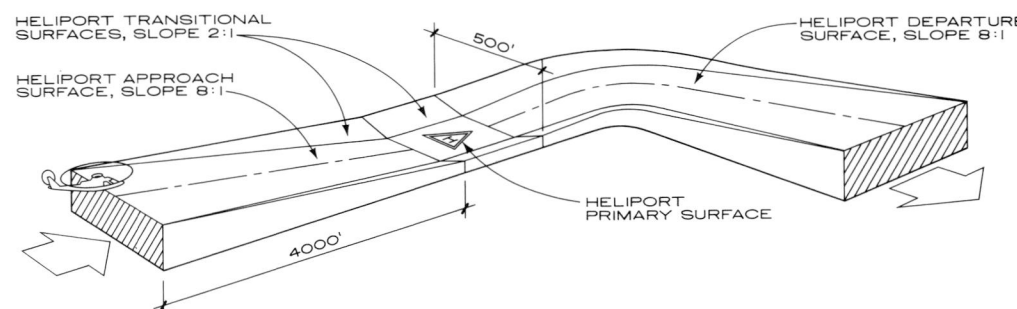

**HELIPORT APPROACH/DEPARTURE PATH**

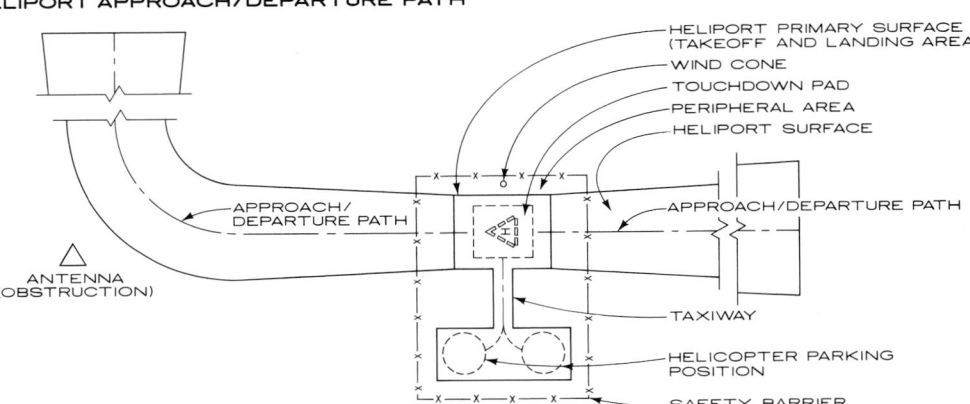

**HELIPORT SURFACE RELATIONSHIPS**

## RECOMMENDED DESIGN CRITERIA

| DESIGN FEATURE | HELIPORT CLASSIFICATION | |
| --- | --- | --- |
| | PUBLIC | PRIVATE |
| Helicopter Approach Surface | | |
|   Number of surfaces | 2 | |
|   Angular separation | 90° minimum, 180° preferred | |
|   Length | 4000 ft | |
|   Inner width | 1.5x helicopter overall length | |
|   Outer width | 500 ft | |
|   Slope | 8:1 | |
| Helicopter Transitional Surface | | |
|   Length | Full length of approaches and primary surface | |
|   Width | 250 ft measured from approach and primary surface centerlines | |
|   Slope | 2:1 | |
| Helicopter Primary Surface | | |
|   Length, width, and diameter | 1.5x helicopter overall length | |
|   Elevation | Elevation highest point of takeoff and landing area | |
| Takeoff and Landing Area | | |
|   Length, width, and diameter | 1.5x helicopter overall length | |
| Touchdown Pad | | |
|   Ground level, minimum | | |
|     Length and diameter | 2.0x wheelbase | 1.5x wheelbase |
|     Width | 2.0x tread | 1.5x tread |
|   Elevated, minimum | | |
|     Length and diameter | 1.0x rotor diameter | 1.5x wheelbase |
|     Width | 1.0x rotor diameter | 1.5x tread |
| Peripheral Area | | |
|   Recommended width | .25x helicopter overall length | |
| Taxiway | | |
|   Paved width | Variable, 20 ft minimum | |
| Parking Position | | |
|   Length, width, and diameter | 1.0x helicopter overall length | |
| Clearances—Rotor tip to object taxiways and parking positions | 10 ft minimum | |
| Pavement Grades | | |
|   Touchdown pad, taxiways, and parking positions | 2.0% maximum | |
| Other Grades | | |
|   Turf shoulders, infield area, etc. | Variable, 1.5 to 3% | |

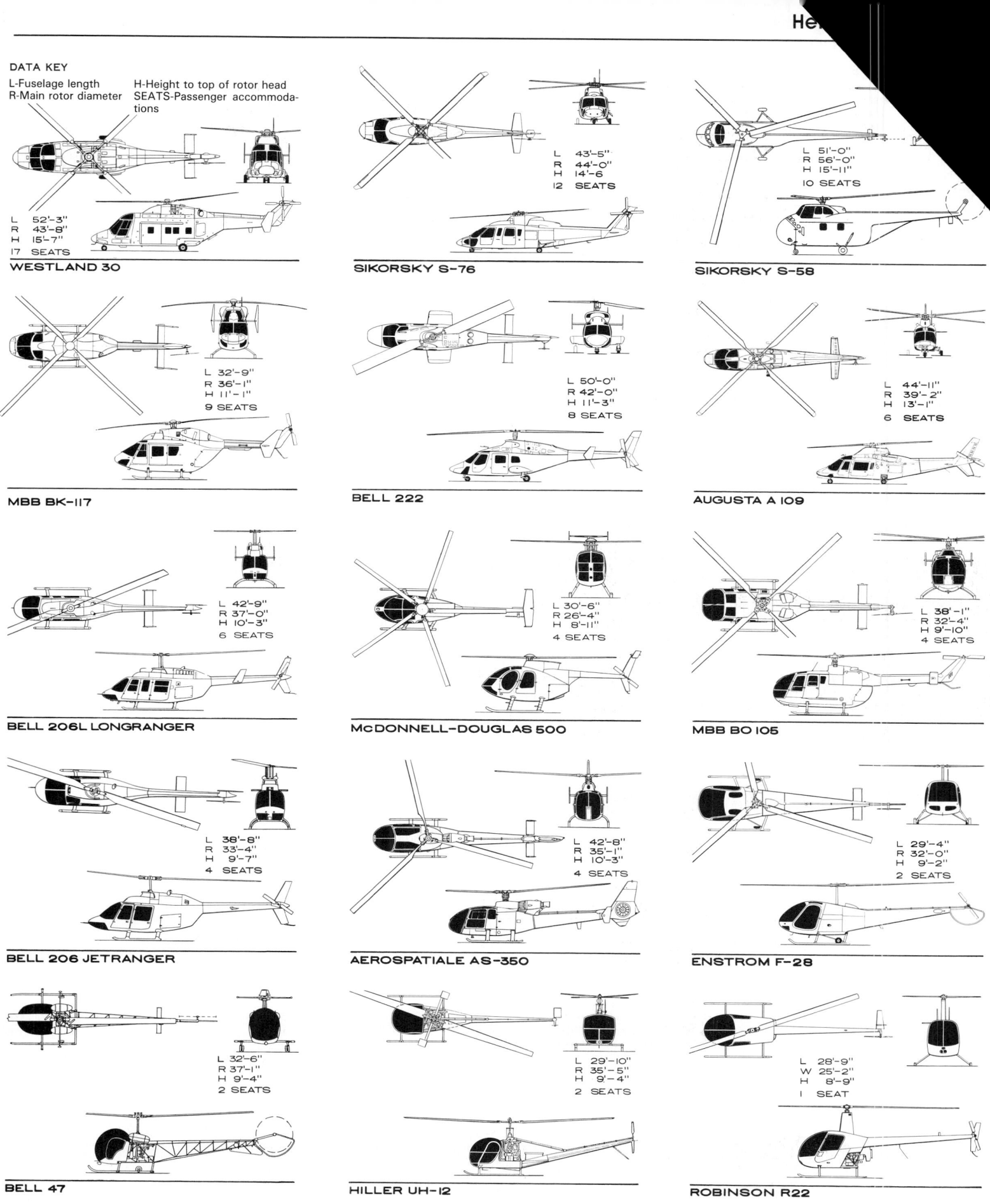

Stanley N. Hall; Washington, D.C.

...licopters  87

### ...TRIBUTED

| | LIVE LOAD (PSF) |
|---|---|
| | 150 |
| ...nbly | 60 |
| | 100 |
| | 100 |
| | 25 |
| | 80* |
| | 150 |
| Balconies | |
| Exterior | 100 |
| Interior (fixed seats) | 60 |
| Interior (movable seats) | 100 |
| Bowling alleys, poolrooms, and similar recreational areas | 75 |
| Broadcasting studios | 100 |
| Catwalks | 25 |
| Cold storage rooms | |
| Floor | 150 |
| Roof | 250 |
| Corridors | |
| First floor | 100 |
| Other floors, same as occupancy served except as indicated | |
| Dance halls and ballrooms | 100 |
| Dining rooms and restaurants | 100 |
| Dormitories | |
| Nonpartitioned | 80 |
| Partitioned | 40 |
| File rooms | |
| Card | 125* |
| Letter | 80* |
| Fire escapes on multifamily or single family residential buildings only | 100 |
| Foundries | 600† |
| Fuel rooms, framed | 400† |
| Garages (passenger cars only). For trucks and buses use AASHO† lane load | 50 |
| Grandstands | 100 |
| Greenhouses | 150 |
| Gymnasiums, main floors and balconies | 100 |
| Hospitals | |
| Operating rooms, laboratories | 60 |
| Private rooms | 40 |
| Wards | 40 |
| Corridors, above first floor | 80 |
| Hotels (see Residential) | — |
| Kitchens, other than domestic | 150† |
| Laboratories, scientific | 100 |
| Laundries | 150† |
| Libraries | |
| Reading rooms | 60 |
| Stack rooms (books and shelving at 65 pcf) but not less than | 150 |
| Corridors, above first floor | 80 |
| Manufacturing | |
| Light | 125 |
| Heavy | 250 |
| Ice | 300 |
| Marquees | 75 |
| Morgues | 125 |
| Office buildings | |
| Office | 50 |
| Business machine equipment | 100† |
| Lobbies | 100 |
| Corridors, above the first floor | 80 |
| File and computer rooms require heavier loads based on anticipated occupancy | |
| Penal institutions | |
| Cell blocks | 40 |
| Corridors | 100 |
| Printing plants | |
| Composing rooms | 100 |
| Linotype rooms | 100 |

| | |
|---|---|
| Paper storage rooms | § |
| Pressrooms | 150† |
| Public rooms | 100 |
| Residential | |
| Multifamily houses | |
| Private apartments | 40 |
| Public rooms | 100 |
| Corridors | 80 |
| Dwellings | |
| First floor | 40 |
| Second floor and habitable attics | 30 |
| Uninhabitable attics | 20 |
| Hotels | |
| Guest rooms | 40 |
| Public rooms | 100 |
| Corridors serving public rooms | 100 |
| Rest rooms and toilet rooms | 60 |
| Schools | |
| Classrooms | 40 |
| Corridors | 80 |
| Sidewalks, vehicular driveways, and yards subject to trucking | 250 |
| Skating rinks | 100 |
| Stairs and exitways | 100 |
| Storage warehouses | |
| Light | 125 |
| Heavy | 250 |
| Hay or grain | 300 |
| Stores | |
| Retail | |
| First floor, rooms | 100 |
| Upper floors | 75 |
| Wholesale | 125 |
| Telephone exchange rooms | 150† |
| Theaters | |
| Aisles, corridors, and lobbies | 100 |
| Orchestra floors | 60 |
| Balconies | 60 |
| Stage floors | 100 |
| Dressing rooms | 40 |
| Grid iron floor or fly gallery grating | 60 |
| Projection room | 100 |
| Transformer rooms | 200† |
| Vaults, in offices | 250* |
| Yards and terraces, pedestrians | 100 |

*Increase when occupancy exceeds this amount.
†Use weight of actual equipment when greater.
‡American Association of State Highway Officials.
§Paper storage 50 lb/ft of clear story height.

## LIVE LOAD

Live load is the weight superimposed by the use and occupancy of the building or other structure, not including the wind load, snow load, earthquake load, or dead load.

The live loads to be assumed in the design of buildings and other structures shall be the greatest loads that probably will be produced by the intended use or occupancy, but in no case less than the minimum uniformly distributed unit load.

## THRUSTS AND HANDRAILS

Stairway and balcony railings, both exterior and interior, shall be designed to resist a vertical and a horizontal thrust of 50 lb/linear ft applied at the top of the railing. For one- and two-family dwellings, a thrust of 20 lb/ft may be used instead of 50 lb/ft.

## CONCENTRATED LOADS

Floors shall be designed to support safely the uniformly distributed live load or the concentrated load in pounds given, whichever produces the greater stresses. Unless otherwise specified, the indicated concentration shall be assumed to occupy an area of 2½ feet square (6.25 ft$^2$) and shall be located so as to produce the maximum stress conditions in the structural members.

## PARTIAL LOADING

The full intensity of the appropriately reduced live loads applied only to a portion of the length of a structure or member shall be considered if it produces a more unfavorable effect than the same intensity applied over the full length of the structure or member.

## IMPACT LOADS

The live loads shall be assumed to include adequate allowance for ordinary impact conditions. Provision shall be made in structural design for uses and loads that involve unusual vibration and impact forces.

1. ELEVATORS: All elevator loads shall be increased 100% for impact, and the structural supports shall be designed within limits of deflection prescribed by American National Standard Safety Code for Elevators and Escalators, A17.1-1981, and American National Standard Practice for the Inspection of Elevators, Escalators, and Moving Walks (Inspector's Manual) A17.2-1979.

2. MACHINERY: For the purpose of design, the weight of machinery and moving loads shall be increased as follows to allow for impact: (a) elevator machinery, 100%; (b) light machinery, shaft or motor driven, 20%; (c) reciprocating machinery or power driven units, 50%; (d) hangers for floors or balconies, 33%. All percentages to be increased if so recommended by the manufacturer.

3. CRANEWAYS: All craneways, except those using only manually powered cranes, shall have their design loads increased for impact as follows: (a) a vertical force equal to 25% of the maximum wheel load; (b) a lateral force equal to 20% of the weight of trolley and lifted load only, applied one-half at the top of each rail; and (c) a longitudinal force of 10% of the maximum wheel loads of the crane applied at top of rail.

## MINIMUM ROOF LOADS

1. FLAT, PITCHED, OR CURVED ROOFS: Ordinary roofs—flat, pitched, or curved—shall be designed for the live loads or the snow load, whichever produces the greater stresses.

2. PONDING: For roofs, care shall be taken to provide drainage or the load shall be increased to represent all likely accumulations of water. Deflection of roof members will permit ponding of water accompanied by increased deflection and additional ponding.

3. SPECIAL PURPOSE ROOFS: When used for promenade purposes, roofs shall be designed for a minimum live load of 60 psf; 100 psf when designed for roof garden or assembly uses. Roofs used for other special purposes shall be designed for appropriate loads, as directed or approved by the building official.

## LIVE LOAD REDUCTION

In general, design live loads not in excess of 100 psf on any member supporting an area of 150 sq ft or more, except for places of public assembly, repair garages, parking structures, and roofs. The reduction shall not exceed the value of R from the following formulas:

$$R = .08(A-150)$$

$$R = 23(1 + D/L)$$

where R = reduction (%)
D = dead load per square foot of area supported by the member
L = live load per square foot of area supported by the member
A = area supported by the member.

In no case should the reduction exceed 60% for vertical members, nor 40 to 60% for horizontal members.

For live loads in excess of 100 psf, some codes allow a live load reduction of 20% for columns only.

## CODES AND STANDARDS

The applicable building code should be referred to for specific uniformly distributed live load, movable partition load, special, and concentrated load requirements.

In addition to the specific code requirements, the designer must consider the effects of special loading conditions, such as moving loads, construction loads, roof top planting loads, and concentrated loads from supported or hanging equipment (radiology, computer, heavy filing, or mechanical equipment).

The live loads given in this table are obtained by reference to ANSI A58.1-1982.

David H. Holbert; Hansen Lind Meyer, P.C.; Iowa City, Iowa

# ARCHITECTURAL AREA OF BUILDINGS

The architectural area of a building is the sum of the areas of the floors, measured horizontally in plan to the exterior faces of perimeter walls or to the center-line of walls separating buildings. Included are areas occupied by partitions, columns, stairwells, elevator shafts, duct shafts, elevator rooms, pipe spaces, mechanical penthouses, and similar spaces having a headroom of 6 ft and over. Areas of sloping surfaces, such as staircases, bleachers, and tiered terraces, should be measured horizontally in plan. Auditoriums, swimming pools, gymnasiums, foyers, and similar spaces extending through two or more floors should be measured once only, taking the largest area in plan at any level.

Mechanical penthouse rooms, pipe spaces, bulkheads, and similar spaces having a headroom less than 6 ft and balconies projecting beyond exterior walls, covered terraces and walkways, porches, and similar spaces shall have the architectural area multiplied by 0.50 in calculating the building gross area.

Exterior staircases and fire escapes, exterior steps, patios, terraces, open courtyards and lightwells, roof overhangs, cornices and chimneys, unfinished roof and attic areas, pipe trenches, and similar spaces are excluded from the architectural area calculations. Interstitial space in health care facilities is also excluded.

# ARCHITECTURAL VOLUME OF BUILDINGS

The architectural volume of a building is the sum of the products of the areas defined in the architectural area times the height from the underside of the lowest floor construction to the average height of the surface of the finished roof above, for the various parts of the building. Included in the architectural volume is the actual space enclosed within the outer surfaces of the exterior or outer walls and contained between the outside of the roof and the bottom of the lowest floor, taken in full: bays, oriels, dormers; penthouses, chimneys; walk tunnels; enclosed porches and balconies, including screened areas.

The following volumes are multiplied by 0.50 in calculating the architectural volume of a building; nonenclosed porches, if recessed into the building and without enclosing sash or screens; nonenclosed porches built as an extension to the building and without sash or screen; areaways and pipe tunnels; and patio areas that have building walls extended on two sides, roof over, and paved surfacing.

Excluded from the architectural volume are outside steps, terraces, courts, garden walls; light shafts, parapets, cornices, roof overhangs; footings, deep foundations, piling cassions, special foundations, and similar features.

# NET ASSIGNABLE AREA

The net assignable area is that portion of the area which is available for assignment to an occupant, including every type of space usable by the occupant.

The net assignable area should be measured from the predominant inside finish of enclosing walls in the categories defined below. Areas occupied by exterior walls, partitions, internal structural, or party walls are to be excluded from the groups and are to be included under "construction area."

1. "NET ASSIGNABLE AREA": Total area of all enclosed spaces fulfilling the main functional requirements of the building for occupant use, including custodial and service areas such as guard rooms, workshops, locker rooms, janitors' closets, storerooms, and the total area of all toilet and washroom facilities.

2. "CIRCULATION AREA": Total area of all enclosed spaces which is required for physical access to subdivisions of space such as corridors, elevator shafts, escalators, fire towers or stairs, stairwells, elevator entrances, public lobbies, and public vestibules.

3. "MECHANICAL AREA": Total area of all enclosed spaces designed to house mechanical and electrical equipment and utility services such as mechanical and electrical equipment rooms, duct shafts, boiler rooms, fuel rooms, and mechanical service shafts.

4. "CONSTRUCTION AREA": The area occupied by exterior walls, partitions, structure, and so on.

5. "GROSS FLOOR OR ARCHITECTURAL AREA": The sum of areas 1, 2, 3, and 4 plus the area of all factored non- and semienclosed areas equal the gross floor area or architectural area of a building.

In commercial buildings constructed for leasing, net areas are to be measured in accordance with the "Standard Method of Floor Measurement," as set by the Building Owners and Managers Association (BOMA).

The net rentable area for offices is to be measured from the inside finish of permanent outer building walls, to the office or occupancy side of corridors and/or other permanent partitions, and to the center of partitions that separate the premises from adjoining rentable areas. No deductions are to be made for columns and projections necessary to the building.

The net rentable area for stores is to be measured from the building line in case of street frontages and from the inside finish of other outer building walls, corridor, and permanent partitions and to the center of partitions that separate the premises from adjoining rentable areas. No deductions are to be made for vestibules inside the building line or for columns and projections necessary to the building. No addition is to be made for projecting bay windows.

If a single occupant is to occupy the total floor in either the office or store categories, the net rentable area would include the accessory area for that floor of corridors, elevator lobbies, toilets, janitors' closets, electrical and telephone closets, air-conditioning rooms and fan rooms, and similar spaces.

The net rentable area for apartments is to be measured from the inside face of exterior walls, and all enclosing walls of the unit.

## NOTE

Various governmental agencies have their own methods of calculating the net assignable area of buildings. They should be investigated if federal authority or funding apply to a project. Also, various building codes provide their own definitions of net and gross areas of building for use in quantifying requirements.

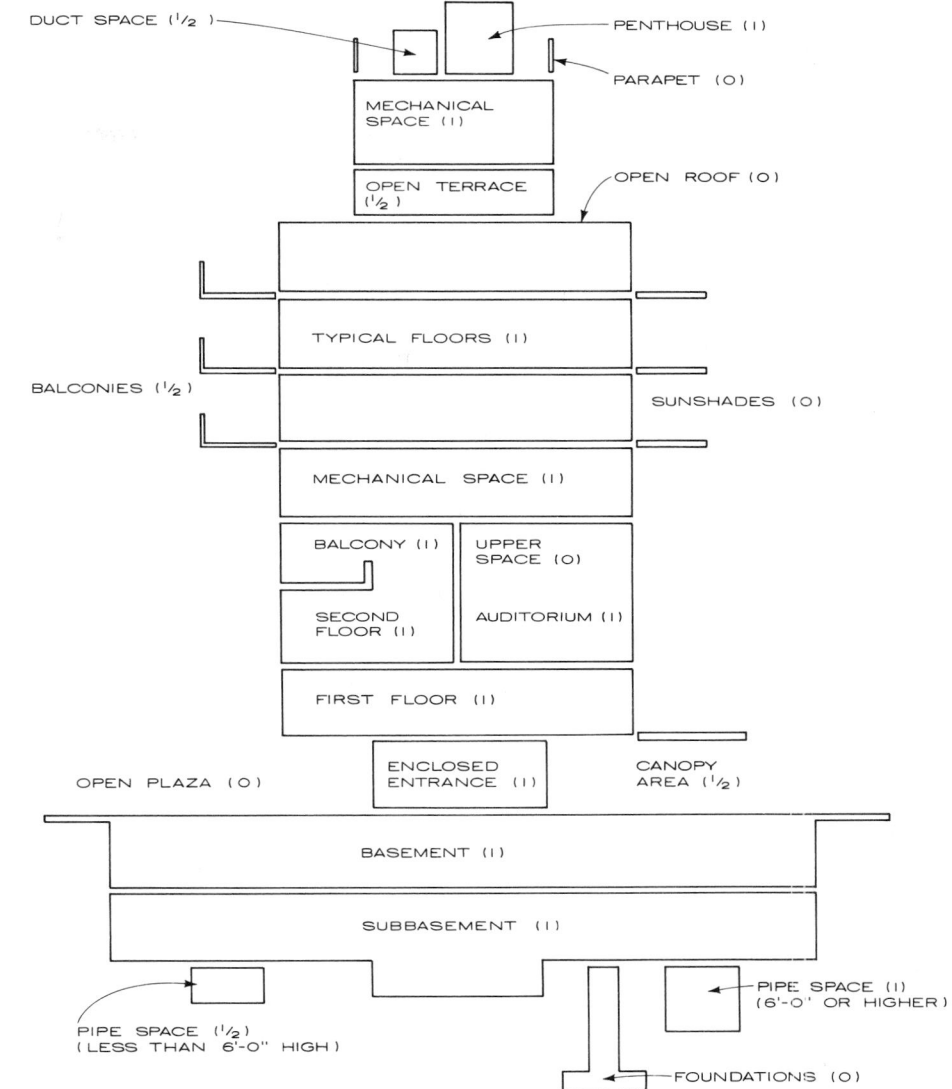

ARCHITECTURAL AREA DIAGRAM

T. Edward Thomas; Hansen Lind Meyer, P.C.; Iowa City, Iowa

BUILDING LOADS AND CALCULATIONS     1

## GENERAL

Information to determine occupant load is from three model building codes in use in the United States:

1. Uniform Building Code (UBC), 1985 edition, copyright 1985, with permission of the International Conference of Building Officials, publisher.
2. BOCA National Building Code (BOCA), 1986 edition, copyright 1986, with permission of the Building Officials and Code Administrators International, Inc., publisher.
3. Standard Building Code (SBC), 1985 edition, copyright 1985, with permission of the Southern Building Code Congress International, Inc., publisher, with all rights reserved.

Occupant load generally is defined as the maximum capacity of a building or room given as the total number of people present at any one time. For occupant loads, generally it is assumed that all areas of a building will be occupied at the same time, with some exceptions noted in specific codes. For example, the UBC states: "Accessory use areas, which ordinarily are used only by persons who occupy the main areas of an occupancy, shall be

provided with exits as though they are completely occupied, but their occupant load need not be included in computing the total occupant load of the building" [UBC-Sec. 3302.(a)].

Most codes require that to determine multiple use building or area occupancies, the occupant load (O.L.) be based on the use that produces the most occupants. For example, the occupant load for a school multiple use room, which also will be used for classroom activities (O.L. factor = 20), as well as for assembly space (O.L. factor = 15), is calculated using the 15 sq. ft. per occupant factor.

If buildings or areas contain two or more separate occupancies, the overall occupant load is determined by computing occupant loads for various areas and adding them together for an aggregate occupant load.

When calculating occupant load for areas with fixed seating in benches or pews, the number of occupants is based on one seat for each 18 in. of bench or pew. In dining areas with booth seating, the number of seats is based on 24 in. for each seat.

## EXITS

All three major codes use occupant loads to determine the size and number of required exits. Based on occupant loads and area usages, it is possible to determine the required exits, arrangement, and sizes of exit components. All three codes (BOCA, SBC, and UBC) consider an exit to be more than merely a door. Although specific definitions vary with each code, exits usually are considered to be continuous and unobstructed means of egress to a public way and may include such building elements as doors, corridors, stairs, balconies, lobbies, exit courts, etc. Elevators are not considered exits. Requirements for arrangements, size, and operation of exits vary; consult appropriate code for specific information.

## OCCUPANT LOADS

| USE | MAXIMUM FLOOR AREA PER OCCUPANT (SQ. FT. PER OCCUPANT) | | |
|---|---|---|---|
| | BOCA | SBC | UBC[1] |
| Assembly areas[2]—concentrated use (without fixed seats): auditoriums, bowling alleys[3], churches, dance floors, lodge rooms, reviewing stands, stadiums | 7 net | 7 net | 7 |
| Assembly areas—less concentrated use: conference rooms, dining/drinking areas, exhibit rooms, gymnasiums, lounges, stages[4] | 15 net | 15 net | 15 |
| Assembly areas—standing space | 3 net | 3 net | — |
| Business areas[7] | 100 gross | 100 gross | 100 |
| Courtrooms—(without fixed seats) | 40 net | 40 net | — |
| Daycare facilities | — | — | 35 |
| Dormitories | — | — | 50 |
| Educational | | | |
| classroom areas | 20 net | 20 net | 20 |
| shops and vocational rooms | 50 net | 50 net | 50 |
| Industrial areas[5] | 100 gross | 100 gross | 200 |
| Institutional[6] | | | |
| children's homes, homes for aged, nursing homes, sanitariums, hospitals | — | — | 80 |
| inpatient treatment areas | 240 gross | 240 gross | — |
| outpatient areas | 100 gross | 100 gross | — |
| sleeping areas | 120 gross | 120 gross | — |
| Kitchens (commercial) | — | — | 300 |
| Library | | | |
| reading rooms | 50 net | 50 net | 50 |
| stack areas | 100 gross | 100 gross | — |
| Lobbies (accessory to assembly area) | — | — | 7 |
| Locker rooms | — | — | 50 |
| Mechanical equipment areas | 300 gross | 300 gross | 300 |
| Mercantile[8] | | | |
| basements | 30 gross | 30 gross | 20 |
| ground floors | 30 gross | 30 gross | 30 |
| upper floors | 60 gross | 60 gross | 50 |
| storage, stockrooms, shipping areas | 100 gross | 100 gross | 300[9] |
| Parking garages | 200 gross | 200 gross | 200 |
| Residential[10] | 200 gross | 200 gross | — |
| hotels and apartments | — | — | 200 |
| dwellings | — | — | 300 |
| Skating rinks[11] | — | 15 net | — |
| rink area | — | — | 50 |
| deck | — | — | 15 |
| Storage areas | 300 gross | 300 gross | 300 |
| Swimming pools | | | |
| pool | — | — | 50 |
| deck | — | — | 15 |
| All other areas | — | — | 100 |

## MINIMUM EXITS BASED ON USAGE

| USAGE | MINIMUM TWO EXITS REQUIRED WHERE O.L. IS AT LEAST: |
|---|---|
| Aircraft hangars | 10 |
| Auction rooms | 20 |
| Assembly areas | 50 |
| Children's homes and homes for the aged | 6 |
| Classrooms | 50 |
| Dormitories | 10 |
| Dwellings | 10 |
| Hospitals, sanitariums, and nursing homes | 6 |
| Hotels and apartments | 10 |
| Kitchens (commercial) | 30 |
| Library reading rooms | 50 |
| Locker rooms | 30 |
| Manufacturing areas | 30 |
| Mechanical equipment rooms | 30 |
| Nurseries for children (daycare) | 7 |
| Offices | 30 |
| Parking garages | 30 |
| School shops and vocational rooms | 50 |
| Skating rinks | 50 |
| Storage and stockrooms | 30 |
| Stores (retail sales rooms) | |
| basements | 2 exits minimum |
| ground floors | 50 |
| upper floors | 10 |
| Swimming pools | 50 |
| Warehouses | 30 |
| All other | 50 |

### TABLE NOTES

1. Both BOCA and SBC use net and gross floor areas to determine occupant load. UBC does not differentiate between gross and net areas.
2. Occupant loads for assembly areas with fixed seats are determined by the actual number of installed seats.
3. Occupant load calculations for bowling alleys under BOCA and SBC use 5 persons per alley in addition to tabular values indicated.
4. Stages are considered assembly areas—less concentrated use (15 sq. ft. per occupant) in UBC; not separately classified in BOCA or SBC.
5. UBC classifies industrial areas as manufacturing areas.
6. BOCA and SBC classify areas within institutional occupancies, UBC classifies by occupancy description only.
7. UBC classifies business areas as office occupancy.
8. UBC classifies mercantile areas as store-retail sales rooms.
9. UBC considers storage and stockroom areas as storage occupancy (300 sq. ft. per occupant).
10. BOCA and SBC do not separate hotel/apartment and dwelling occupancies.
11. BOCA does not classify separately skating rinks from other assembly areas—less concentrated use (15 sq. ft. per occupant). SBC does not separate areas within skating rinks.

International Conference of Building Officials; Southern Building Code Congress International; Building Officials and Code Administrators International, Inc.; see data sources

James O. Rose, AIA; University of Wyoming; Laramie, Wyoming

# 1  BUILDING LOADS AND CALCULATIONS

## GENERAL

Life cycle costing (LCC) is a method for evaluating all relevant costs over time of alternative building designs, systems, components, materials, or practices. The LCC method takes into account first costs, including the costs of planning, design, purchase, and installation; future costs, including costs of fuel, operation, maintenance, repair, and replacement; and any salvage value recovered during or at the end of the time period examined. These costs are displayed in the adjacent charts.

## TIME ADJUSTMENTS

Adjustments to place all dollar values on a comparable time basis are necessary for valid assessment of a project's life cycle costs. The time adjustment is necessary because receiving or expending a dollar in the future is not the same as receiving or expending a dollar today. One reason for this "time value of money" is that the purchasing power of money may fall over time because of inflation. To ensure that all of a building's costs are expressed in dollars of equal purchasing power, they should be stated in "constant dollars," that is, with purely inflationary effects not included. Another reason for the "time value of money" is that money in hand may be invested productively to earn a return over time. Both inflation and the productive earning potential of resources in hand cause an investor usually to prefer to delay payments of costs or debts and to hasten receipts. The adjustment for time related earning potential can be accomplished by converting all costs to "present values," as though they were all to be incurred today, or to "annual values," as though they were all spread out over a given time in even, annual installments including the cost of money. This time adjustment, often called "discounting cash flows," is accomplished by using "discount formulas" or by multiplying dollar amounts by special "discount factors" calculated from the formulas. The most frequently used discount formulas for evaluating building projects are described below, where the following notation is used:

P = present value
F = future value
A = annual value
D = discount rate
N = number of periods
E = price escalation rate

## SINGLE PRESENT WORTH

The single present worth (SPW) formula is used to find the present value of a future amount, such as the value today of a future replacement cost.

SPW (single present worth)     $P = F(1 + D)^{-N}$

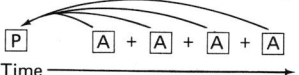

## UNIFORM PRESENT WORTH

The uniform present worth (UPW) formula is used to find the present value of a series of uniform annual amounts, such as the value today of the costs of future yearly routine maintenance.

UPW (uniform present worth)     $P = A\left[\dfrac{(1 + D)^N - 1}{D(1 + D)^N}\right]$

## UNIFORM PRESENT WORTH—MODIFIED

A modified version of the uniform present worth formula (here designated UPW*) is used to find the present value of an initial amount escalating at a constant annual rate, such as the value today of future yearly energy costs, when energy prices are expected to escalate at a given rate.

UPW* (uniform present worth—modified)

$$P = A\left[\left[\frac{1 + E}{D - E}\right]\left[1 - \left[\frac{1 + E}{1 + D}\right]^N\right]\right]$$

## UNIFORM SINKING FUND

The uniform sinking fund (USF) formula is used to find the annual amount that must be accumulated to yield a given future amount, such as how much money must be set aside each year at interest in order to cover expected future replacement costs.

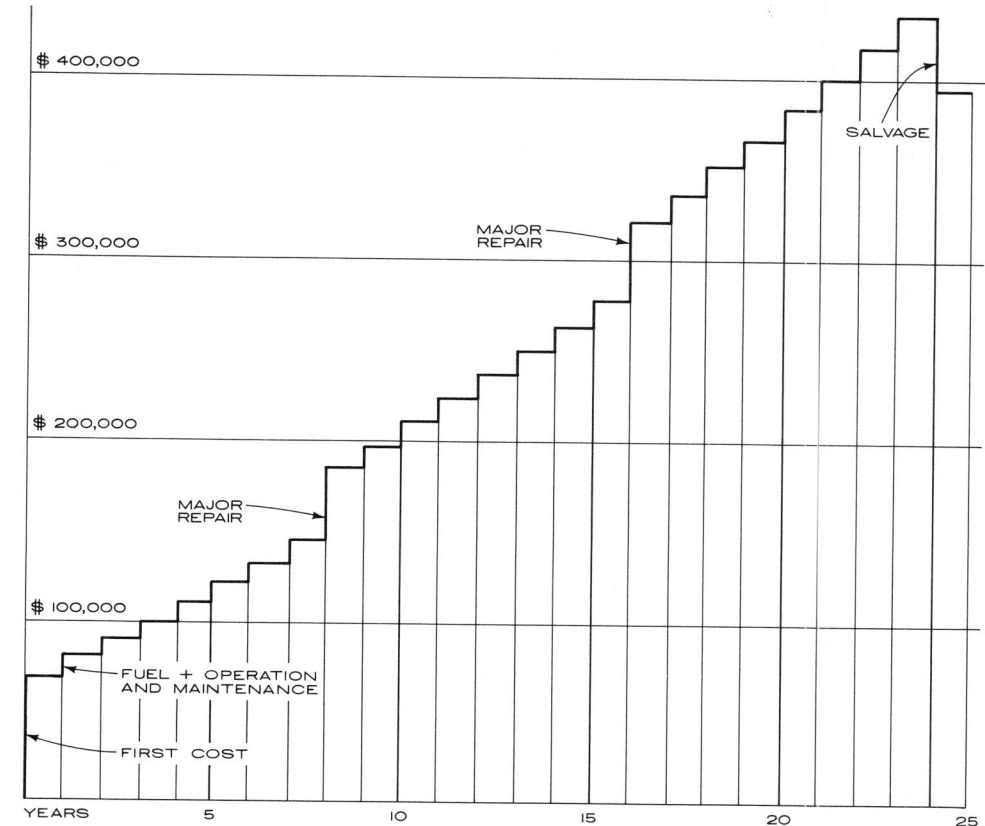

**CUMULATIVE COSTS**

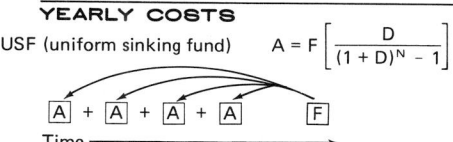

FUEL — $ 5000/YEAR INITIALLY, INCREASING 4%/YEAR
OPERATION AND MAINTENANCE — $ 5000/YEAR

**YEARLY COSTS**

USF (uniform sinking fund)     $A = F\left[\dfrac{D}{(1 + D)^N - 1}\right]$

## UNIFORM CAPITAL RECOVERY

The uniform capital recovery (UCR) formula is used to find the annual value of a present value amount, such as how much it would be necessary to pay each year in order to pay off a loan made today at a given rate of interest for a given period of time.

UCR (uniform capital recovery)     $A = P\left[\dfrac{D(1 + D)^N}{(1 + D)^N - 1}\right]$

### NOTE

The discount factors for each of these discounting formulas have been precalculated for a range of discount rates and time periods and put into tables to facilitate their use. These tables can be found in most engineering economics textbooks. A table of discount factors for a 10% discount rate is shown opposite.

## LIFE CYCLE COST FORMULA

To find the total life cycle cost of a project, sum the present values (or, alternatively, the annual values) of each kind of cost and subtract the present values (or annual values) of any positive cash flows such as salvage values. Thus, where all dollar amounts are adjusted by discounting either present values or annual values, the following formula applies:

LCC (life cycle cost formula)

Life cycle cost = first costs + maintenance and repair
                 + energy + replacement − salvage value

## APPLICATIONS

Alternative projects may be compared by computing the life cycle costs for each project using the formula above and seeing which is lower.

The LCC method can be applied to many different kinds of building problems. For example, it can be used to compare the long run costs of one building design to another; to determine the expected dollar savings of retrofitting a building for energy conservation or the least expensive way of reaching a targeted energy budget for a building; to select the most economical floor coverings and furnishings; and to determine the optimal size of a solar energy system.

In addition to the life cycle formula shown above, there are other closely related ways of combining present or annual values to measure a project's economic performance over time, such as the net savings technique, savings-to-investment ratio technique, internal rate of return technique, and discounted time to payback technique.

Harold E. Marshall and Rosalie Ruegg, Economists; Porter Driscoll, AIA, Architect; Center for Building Technology, National Bureau of Standards; United States of America

## SAMPLE LCC PROBLEM

Determine present value of costs occurring during the life of a component so that they can be compared with the costs of an alternative component to serve the same purpose. Cumulative and yearly costs are indicated on the charts of the preceding page.

### ASSUMPTIONS

| | |
|---|---|
| Time horizon | 25 years |
| Discount rate | 10% |
| Fuel price increases in excess of inflation | 4% |
| First cost of component | $70,000 |
| Repairs to component at 8th and 16th years | $30,000/repair |
| Operations and maintenance (constant dollars) | $ 5,000/year |
| Annual cost of fuel at onset | $ 5,000 |

NOTE: When financing costs and tax effects are relevant they should be incorporated into LCC analysis.

### SOLUTION

1. Establish present value of equipment. Convert all equipment costs (first cost, two major repair costs, and salvage value) to present value. Since the first cost occurs in the present, no change is made to the $70,000 sum.

   The first major repair, estimated to occur 8 years in the future, is discounted at the rate of 10% back to the present using the SPW factor (see Discount Factor Chart, column 2) for 8 years at 10%, 0.4665. Therefore, PV = $30,000 x 0.4665 = $13,995. This present value is added to the $70,000 first cost as shown in the Present Value of Equipment Chart.

   The second major repair is discounted 16 years back to the present in a similar manner. The SPW factor for 16 years at 10% = 0.2176. Therefore, PV = $30,000 x 0.2176 = $6528. This amount is also added to the present value in the chart.

   The $40,000 to be realized from salvage at the end of the 25 year period is discounted back to the present in the same manner. The SPW factor for 25 years, at 10% = 0.0923. Therefore, PV = $40,000 x 0.0923 = $3692. Since this sum is income, not expense, it must be subtracted from the sum of the other present values as indicated.

   Thus the present value of equipment is determined to be $86,832.

2. Establish present value of operation and maintenance costs and fuel costs. Operation and maintenance costs are estimated to be equal amounts that occur yearly during the period and are converted to present value using the UPW factor (column 3) for 25 years at 10%, 9.0770. Therefore, PV = $5000 x 9.0770 = $45,385. This amount is added to the present value of equipment as shown in the Total Present Value Chart.

   Annual fuel costs are estimated to be $5000 based on the initial price of fuel which is projected to increase at the rate of 4% per year. These costs are converted to present value using the modified UPW* factor (column 4) for 25 years at 10%, 13.0686. Therefore, PV = $5000 x 13.0686 = $65,343.

   This amount is also added to the present values of equipment and operation and maintenance costs as shown in the Total Present Value Chart.

3. Total life cycle cost in present value is the sum of the present value of equipment, operation, and maintenance and fuel costs which equals $197,559. The equipment, operation, and maintenance and fuel costs of other components to serve the same purpose can be compared to these figures to determine the best economic value.

### REFERENCES

1. Gerald W. Smith, Engineering Economy: Analysis of Capital Expenditures, Iowa State University Press, Ames, Iowa, 1973.
2. Donald Watson, ed., Energy Conservation through Building Design, "Life-cycle Costing Guide for Energy Conservation in Buildings" chapter by Harold E. Marshall and Rosalie T. Ruegg, McGraw-Hill, New York, 1979.
3. Simplified Energy Design Economics, NBS special publication 544, Center for Building Technology, National Bureau of Standards, Washington, D.C., 1980.

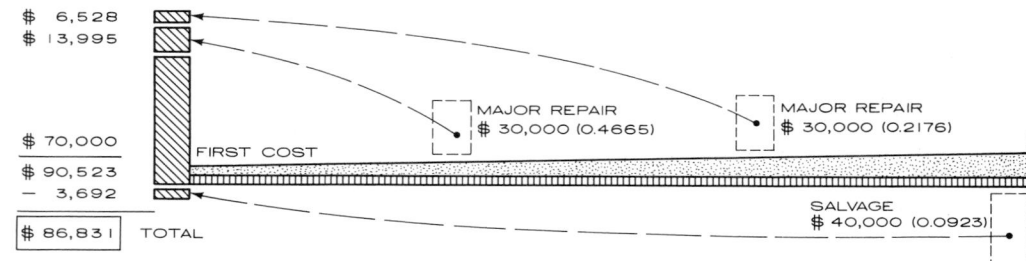

| | |
|---|---|
| $ 6,528 | |
| $ 13,995 | |
| $ 70,000 | FIRST COST |
| $ 90,523 | |
| − 3,692 | |
| $ 86,831 | TOTAL |

MAJOR REPAIR $ 30,000 (0.4665)
MAJOR REPAIR $ 30,000 (0.2176)
SALVAGE $ 40,000 (0.0923)

**PRESENT VALUE OF EQUIPMENT**

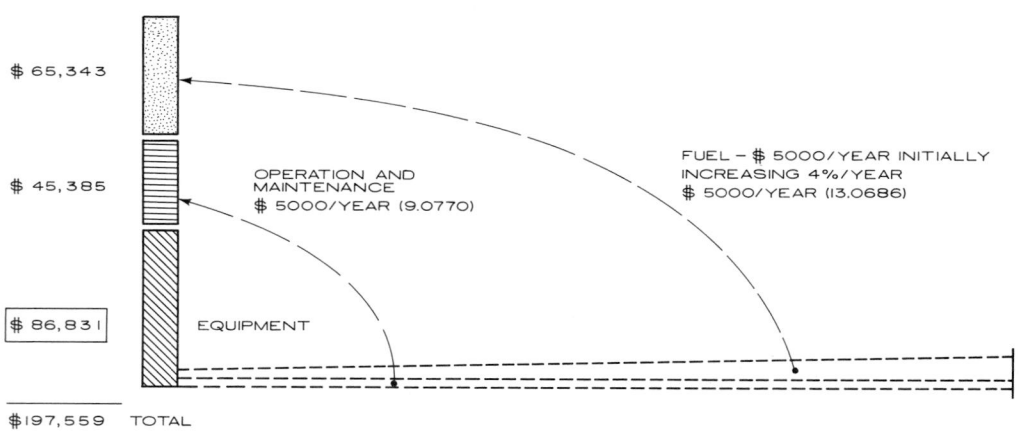

| | |
|---|---|
| $ 65,343 | |
| $ 45,385 | OPERATION AND MAINTENANCE $ 5000/YEAR (9.0770) |
| $ 86,831 | EQUIPMENT |
| $197,559 | TOTAL |

FUEL − $ 5000/YEAR INITIALLY INCREASING 4%/YEAR $ 5000/YEAR (13.0686)

**TOTAL PRESENT VALUE**

### DISCOUNT FACTORS

**BASED ON 10% DISCOUNT RATE**

| 1. YEARS | 2. SPW | 3. UPW | 4. UPW* (4% PRICE ESCALATION) | 5. USF | 6. UCR |
|---|---|---|---|---|---|
| 1 | 0.9091 | 0.909 | 0.9455 | 1.000 00 | 1.100 00 |
| 2 | 0.8264 | 1.736 | 1.8393 | 0.476 19 | 0.576 19 |
| 3 | 0.7513 | 2.487 | 2.6844 | 0.302 11 | 0.402 11 |
| 4 | 0.6830 | 3.170 | 3.4834 | 0.215 47 | 0.315 47 |
| 5 | 0.6209 | 3.791 | 4.2388 | 0.163 80 | 0.263 80 |
| 6 | 0.5645 | 4.355 | 4.9531 | 0.129 61 | 0.229 61 |
| 7 | 0.5132 | 4.868 | 5.6284 | 0.105 41 | 0.205 41 |
| 8 | 0.4665 | 5.335 | 6.2669 | 0.087 44 | 0.187 44 |
| 9 | 0.4241 | 5.759 | 6.8705 | 0.073 64 | 0.173 64 |
| 10 | 0.3855 | 6.144 | 7.4411 | 0.062 75 | 0.162 75 |
| 11 | 0.3505 | 6.495 | 7.9807 | 0.053 96 | 0.153 96 |
| 12 | 0.3186 | 6.814 | 8.4909 | 0.046 76 | 0.146 76 |
| 13 | 0.2897 | 7.103 | 8.9733 | 0.040 78 | 0.140 78 |
| 14 | 0.2633 | 7.367 | 9.4293 | 0.035 75 | 0.135 75 |
| 15 | 0.2394 | 7.606 | 9.8604 | 0.031 47 | 0.131 47 |
| 16 | 0.2176 | 7.824 | 10.2680 | 0.027 82 | 0.127 82 |
| 17 | 0.1978 | 8.022 | 10.6535 | 0.024 66 | 0.124 66 |
| 18 | 0.1799 | 8.201 | 11.0177 | 0.021 93 | 0.121 93 |
| 19 | 0.1635 | 8.365 | 11.3622 | 0.019 55 | 0.119 55 |
| 20 | 0.1486 | 8.514 | 11.6878 | 0.017 46 | 0.117 46 |
| 21 | 0.1351 | 8.649 | 11.9957 | 0.015 62 | 0.115 62 |
| 22 | 0.1228 | 8.772 | 12.2870 | 0.014 01 | 0.144 01 |
| 23 | 0.1117 | 8.883 | 12.5623 | 0.012 57 | 0.112 57 |
| 24 | 0.1015 | 8.985 | 12.8225 | 0.011 30 | 0.111 30 |
| 25 | 0.0923 | 9.077 | 13.0686 | 0.010 17 | 0.110 17 |

Harold E. Marshall and Rosalie Ruegg, Economists; Porter Driscoll, AIA, Architect; Center for Building Technology, National Bureau of Standards; United States of America

# CHAPTER 2

# Sitework

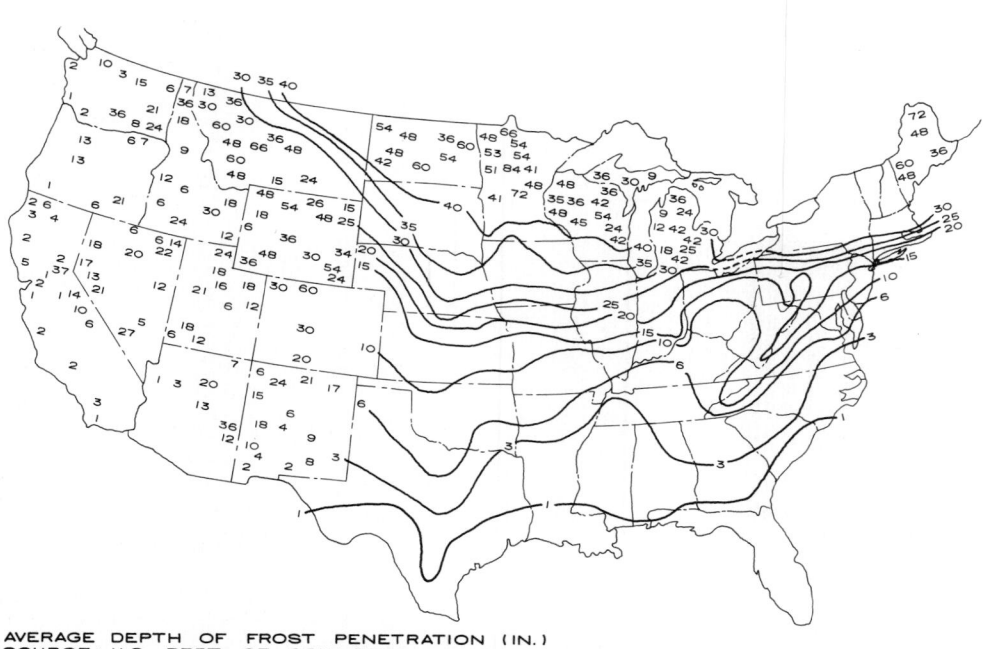

AVERAGE DEPTH OF FROST PENETRATION (IN.)
SOURCE: U.S. DEPT. OF COMMERCE WEATHER BUREAU

## PRELIMINARY SUBSURFACE INFORMATION

A. Collect available information for soil, rock and water conditions, including the following:
   1. Topographic and aerial mapping.
   2. Geological survey maps and publications.
   3. Local knowledge (history of site development, experience of nearby structures, flooding, subsidence, etc.).
   4. Existing subsurface data (boreholes, well records, water soundings).
   5. Reconnaissance site survey.
   6. Previous studies.
B. Evaluate available information for site acceptability. If available data are insufficient, consult a geotechnical engineer to perform a limited subsurface investigation to gather basic information.
C. Consult geotechnical engineer for potential foundation performance at each site as part of the selection process.

## DETAILED SUBSURFACE INFORMATION

After selection of a potential site a subsurface and laboratory test investigation should be carried out by a qualified geotechnical engineer before design is undertaken.

The investigation should provide an adequate understanding of the subsurface conditions and the information should be assessed to determine potential foundation behavior.

The engineer should evaluate alternative foundation methods and techniques in conjunction with the architect.

The engineer or architect should provide inspection during construction to ensure that material and construction procedures are as specified and to evaluate unexpected soil, rock, or groundwater conditions that may be exposed by excavations.

## SOIL TYPES AND THEIR PROPERTIES

| DIVISION | SYMBOLS LETTER | SYMBOLS HATCHING | SYMBOLS COLOR | SOIL DESCRIPTION | VALUE AS A FOUNDATION MATERIAL | FROST ACTION | DRAINAGE |
|---|---|---|---|---|---|---|---|
| Gravel and gravelly soils | GW | | Red | Well graded gravel, or gravel-sand mixture, little or no fines | Excellent | None | Excellent |
| | GP | | Red | Poorly graded gravel, or gravel-sand mixtures, little or no fines | Good | None | Excellent |
| | GM | | Yellow | Silty gravels, gravel-sand-silt mixtures | Good | Slight | Poor |
| | GC | | Yellow | Clayey-gravels, gravel-clay-sand mixtures | Good | Slight | Poor |
| Sand and sandy soils | SW | | Red | Well-graded sands, or gravelly sands, little or no fines | Good | None | Excellent |
| | SP | | Red | Poorly graded sands, or gravelly sands, little or no fines | Fair | None | Excellent |
| | SM | | Yellow | Silty sands, sand-silt mixtures | Fair | Slight | Fair |
| | SC | | Yellow | Clayey sands, sand-clay mixtures | Fair | Medium | Poor |
| Silts and clays LL < 50 | ML | | Green | Inorganic silts, rock flour, silty or clayey fine sands, or clayey silts with slight plasticity | Fair | Very high | Poor |
| | CL | | Green | Inorganic clays of low to medium plasticity, gravelly clays, silty clays, lean clays | Fair | Medium | Impervious |
| | OL | | Green | Organic silt-clays of low plasticity | Poor | High | Impervious |
| Silts and clays LL > 50 | MH | | Blue | Inorganic silts, micaceous or diatomaceous fine sandy or silty soils, elastic silts | Poor | Very high | Poor |
| | CH | | Blue | Inorganic clays of high plasticity, fat clays | Very poor | Medium | Impervious |
| | OH | | Blue | Organic clays of medium to high plasticity, organic silts | Very poor | Medium | Impervious |
| Highly organic soils | Pt | | Orange | Peat and other highly organic soils | Not suitable | Slight | Poor |

NOTES
1. Consult soil engineers and local building codes for allowable soil bearing capacities.
2. LL indicates liquid limit.

Mueser, Rutledge, Johnston & DeSimone; New York, New York

2   SUBSURFACE INVESTIGATION

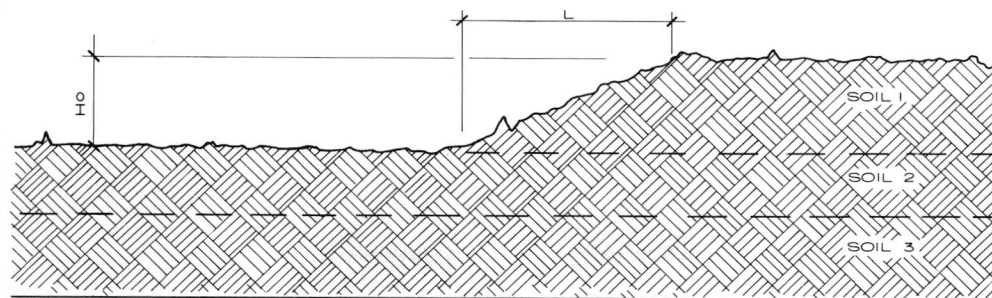

**OPEN EXCAVATION**

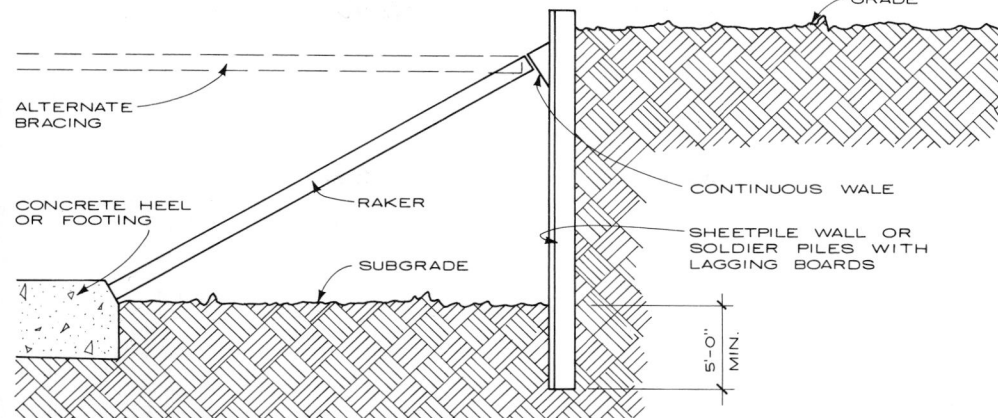

**BRACED EXCAVATION USING RAKERS**

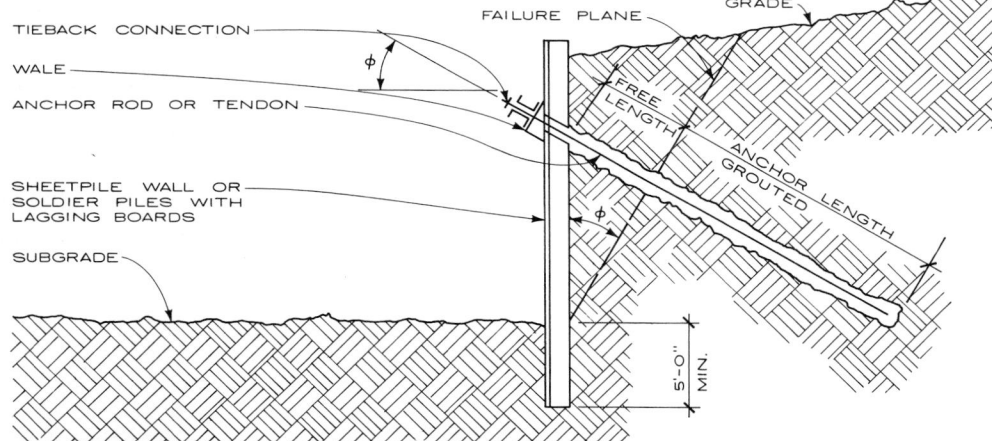

**BRACED EXCAVATION USING EARTH ANCHORS**

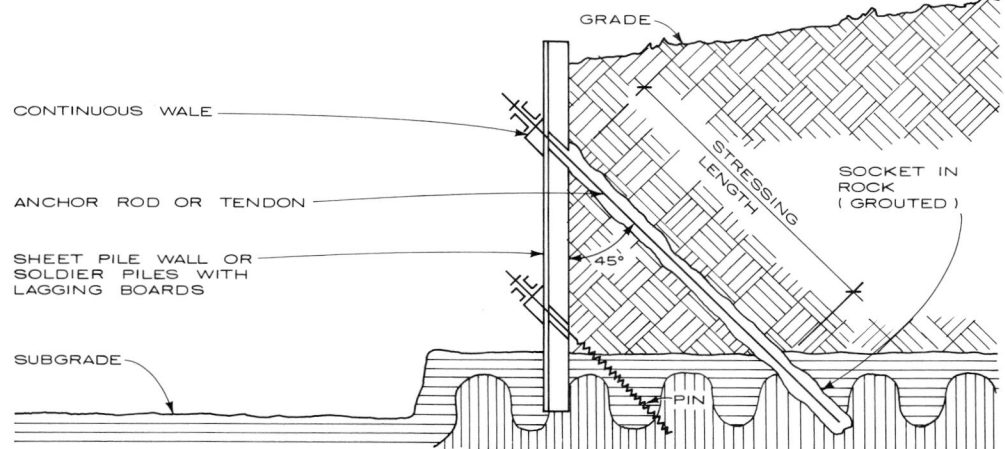

**BRACED EXCAVATION USING ROCK ANCHORS**

Mueser, Rutledge, Johnston & DeSimone; New York, New York

## EMBANKMENT STABILITY
### CONSULT FOUNDATION ENGINEER

| SOIL TYPES | | | $L/H_O$ | REMARKS |
|---|---|---|---|---|
| S1 | S2 | S3 | | |
| Fill | Rock | | >1.5 | Check sliding of S1 |
| Soft clay | Hard clay | Rock | >1.0 | Check sliding of S1 |
| Sand | Soft clay | Hard clay | >1.5 | Check lateral displacement of S2 |
| Sand | Sand | Hard clay | >1.5 | |
| Hard clay | Soft clay | Sand | <1.0 | Check lateral displacement of S2 |

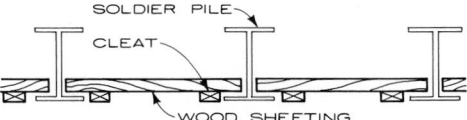

**TIMBER LAGGING**

**TIMBER SHEETING**

**STEEL SHEETING**

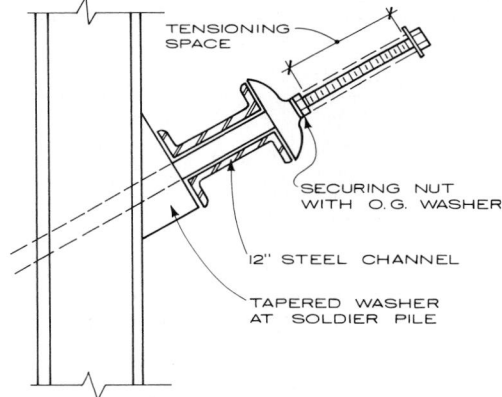

**CHANNEL WALER DETAIL**

### NOTES

1. For shallow depths of excavation cantilever sheeting may be used, if driven to sufficient depth.
2. For deep excavations, several tiers of bracing may be necessary.
3. If subgrade of excavation is used for installation of spreadfootings or mats, proper dewatering procedures may be required to avoid disturbance of bearing level.
4. At times it may be possible to improve the bearing stratum by excavation of compressible materials and their replacement with compacted granular backfill.
5. For evaluation of problems encountered with sheeting and shoring, a foundation engineer should be consulted.
6. Local codes and OSHA regulations must be considered.
7. Proximity of utilities and other structures must be considered in design.

## EXCAVATION SUPPORT SYSTEMS    2

Embankment stabilization is required where extremely steep slopes exist that are subject to heavy storm water runoff. The need for mechanical stabilization can be reduced by intercepting the runoff, or slowing the velocity of the runoff down the slope. Diversions are desirable at the tops of slopes to intercept the runoff. Slopes can be shelved or terraced to reduce the velocity of runoff to the point where a major erosion hazard is avoided. Use an armored channel or slope drain if concentrated runoff down a slope must be controlled.

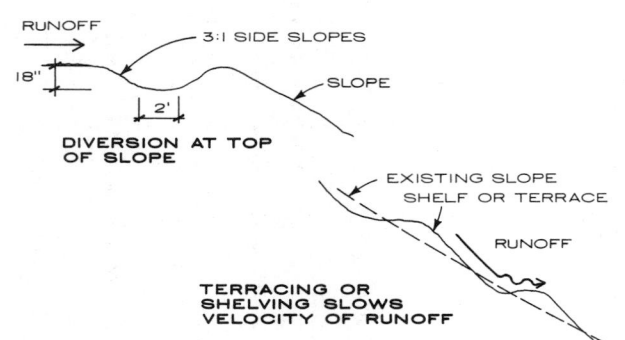

**DIVERSION AT TOP OF SLOPE**

**TERRACING OR SHELVING SLOWS VELOCITY OF RUNOFF**

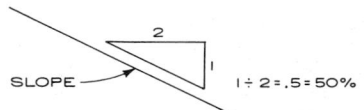

| SOIL | GRADIENT | RATIO |
|---|---|---|
| Dry sand | 33% | 3:1 |
| Loam | 40% | 2.5:1 |
| Compacted clay | 80% | 1.25:1 |
| Saturated clay | 20% | 5:1 |

**MAX. GRADIENTS FOR BARE SOILS**

---

## SLOPE STABILIZATION WITH RIPRAP

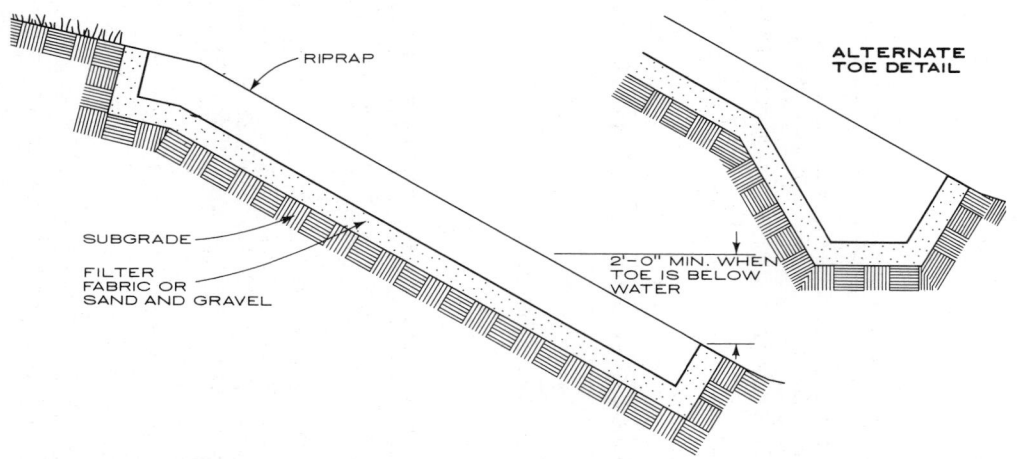

**ALTERNATE TOE DETAIL**

**2'-0" MIN. WHEN TOE IS BELOW WATER**

**NOTE**

A number of mechanical embankment stabilization materials are illustrated. Two important features all methods have in common are

1. Embedment of the toe and lateral limits to prevent undercutting and outflanking, and
2. Use of a granular or fabric filter to protect the soil beneath the protective layer from the effects of flowing water or existing groundwater.

---

### RIPRAP EMBANKMENT WITH ALTERNATE TOE

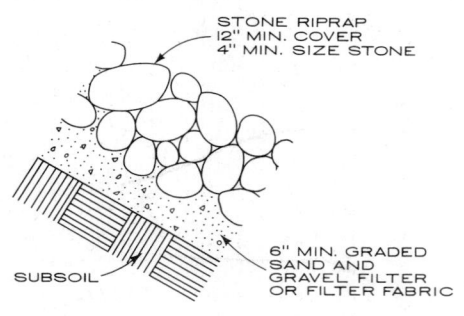

**STONE**

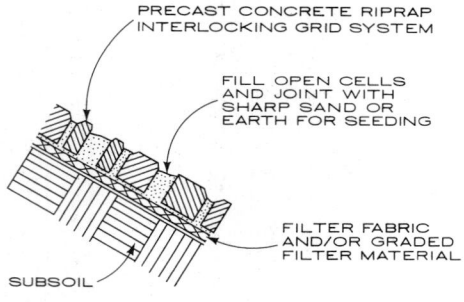

**PRECAST CONCRETE**

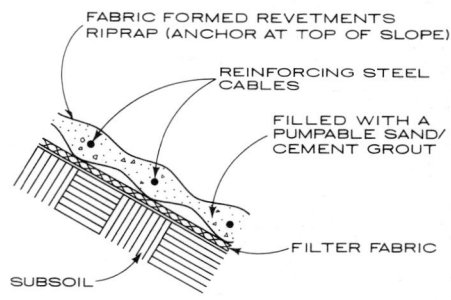

**FABRIC FORMED REVETMENTS**

---

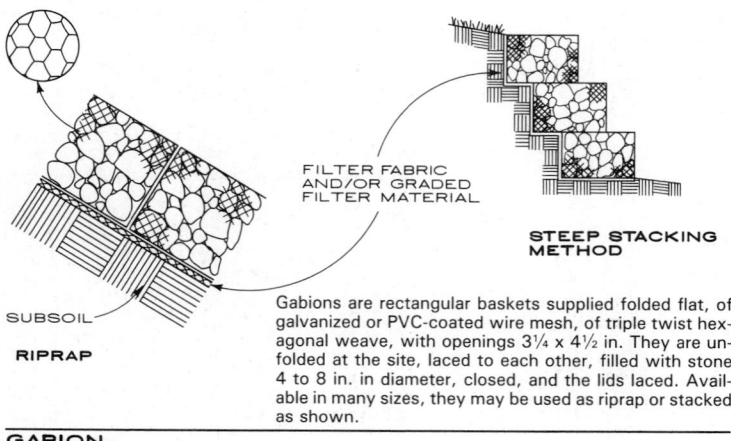

**STEEP STACKING METHOD**

Gabions are rectangular baskets supplied folded flat, of galvanized or PVC-coated wire mesh, of triple twist hexagonal weave, with openings 3¼ x 4½ in. They are unfolded at the site, laced to each other, filled with stone 4 to 8 in. in diameter, closed, and the lids laced. Available in many sizes, they may be used as riprap or stacked as shown.

**GABION**

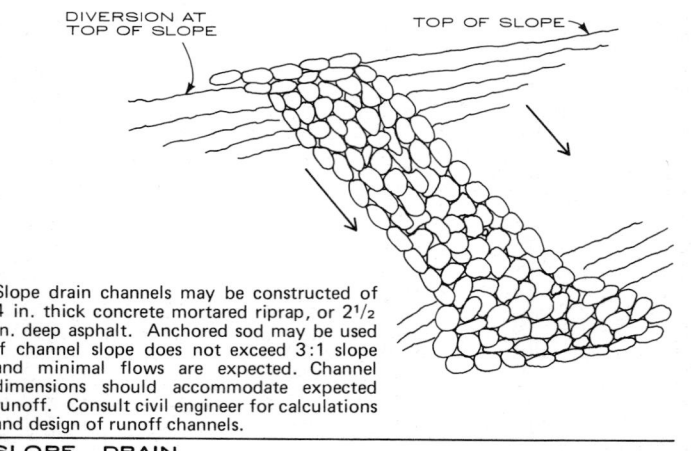

Slope drain channels may be constructed of 4 in. thick concrete mortared riprap, or 2½ in. deep asphalt. Anchored sod may be used if channel slope does not exceed 3:1 slope and minimal flows are expected. Channel dimensions should accommodate expected runoff. Consult civil engineer for calculations and design of runoff channels.

**SLOPE DRAIN**

Derek Martin, FAIA; Pittsburgh, Pennsylvania
John M. Beckett; Beckett, Raeder, Rankin, Inc.; Ann Arbor, Michigan
James E. Sekela, PE; United States Army Corps of Engineers, Pittsburgh, Pennsylvania

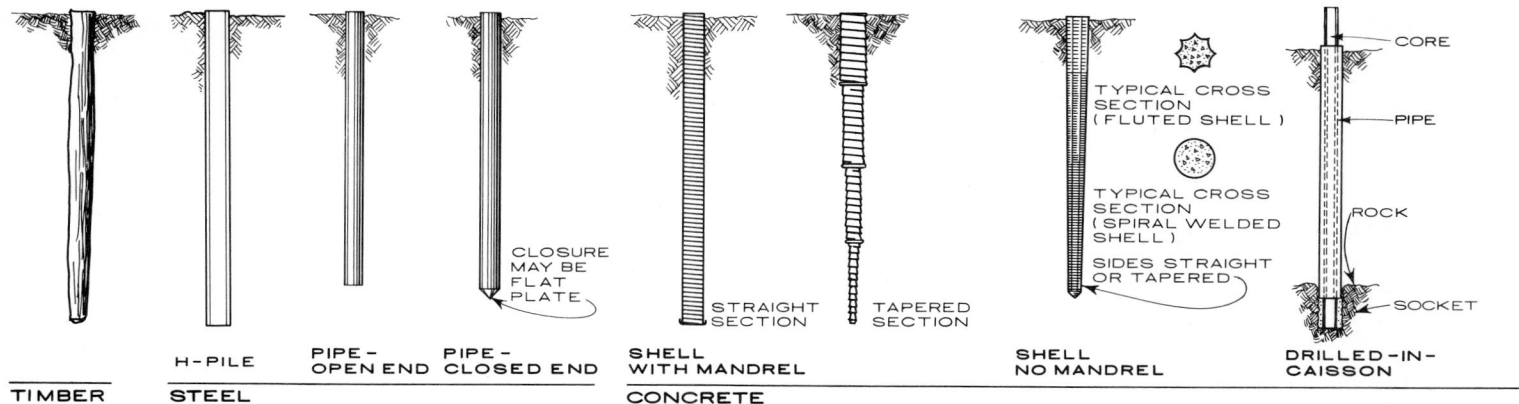

TIMBER | STEEL | CONCRETE | DRILLED-IN-CAISSON

**NOTE:** A mandrel is a member inserted into a hollow pile to reinforce the pile shell while it is driven into the ground.

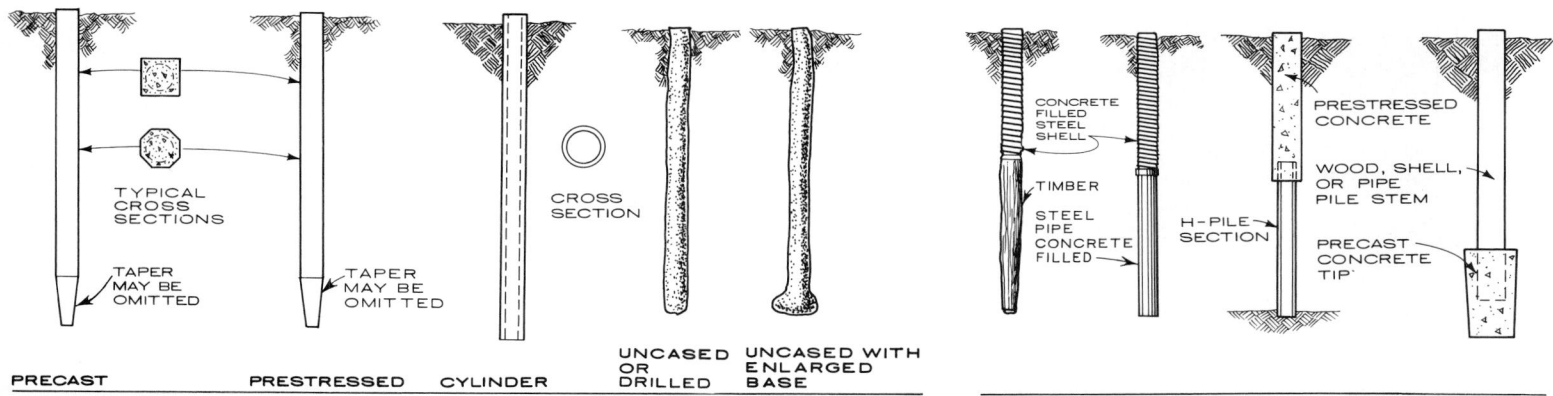

CONCRETE | COMPOSITE

## GENERAL PILE DATA

| PILE TYPE | MAXIMUM LENGTH (FT) | OPTIMUM LENGTH (FT) | SIZE (IN.) | MAXIMUM CAPACITY (TONS) | OPTIMUM LOAD RANGE (TONS) | USUAL SPACING |
|---|---|---|---|---|---|---|
| TIMBER | 110 | 45-65 | 5-10 tip 12-20 butt | 40 | 15-25 | 2'6" to 3'0" |
| **STEEL** | | | | | | |
| H-pile | 250 | 40-150 | 8-14 | 200 | 50-200 | 2'6" to 3'6" |
| Pipe—open end concrete filled | 200 | 40-120 | 10-24 | 250 | 100-200 | 3'0" to 4'0" |
| Pipe—closed end concrete filled | 150 | 30-80 | 10-18 | 100 | 50-70 | 3'0" to 4'0" |
| Shell—mandrel concrete filled straight or taper | 100 | 40-80 | 8-18 | 75 | 40-60 | 3'0" to 3'6" |
| Shell—no mandrel concrete filled | 150 | 30-80 | 8-18 | 80 | 30-60 | 3'0" to 3'6" |
| Drilled-in caisson concrete filled | 250 | 60-120 | 24-48 | 3500 | 1000-2000 | 6'0" to 8'0" |
| **CONCRETE** | | | | | | |
| Precast | 80 | 40-50 | 10-24 | 100 | 40-60 | 3'0" |
| Prestressed | 200 | 60-80 | 10-24 | 200 | 100-150 | 3'0" to 3'6" |
| Cylinder pile | 150 | 60-80 | 36-54 | 500 | 250-400 | 6'0" to 9'0" |
| Uncased or drilled | 60 | 25-40 | 14-20 | 75 | 30-60 | 3'0" to 3'6" |
| Uncased with enlarged base | 60 | 25-40 | 14-20 | 150 | 40-100 | 6'0" |
| **COMPOSITE** | | | | | | |
| Concrete—timber | 150 | 60-100 | 5-10 tip 12-20 butt | 40 | 15-25 | 3'0" to 3'6" |
| Concrete—pipe | 180 | 60-120 | 10-23 | 150 | 40-80 | 3'0" to 4'0" |
| Prestressed concrete H-pile | 200 | 100-150 | 20-24 | 200 | 120-150 | 3'6" to 4'0" |
| Precast concrete tip | 80 | 40 | 13-35 | 180 | 150 | 4'6" |

**NOTES**

Timber piles must be treated with wood preservative when any portion is above permanent groundwater table.

Applicable material Specifications Concrete—ACL 318; Timber—ASTM D25: Structural Sections ASTM A36, A572 and A696.

For selection of type of pile consult foundation engineer.

Mueser, Rutledge, Johnston & DeSimone; New York, New York

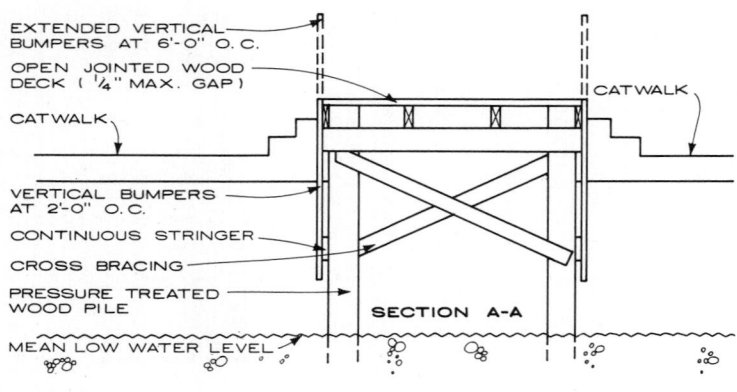

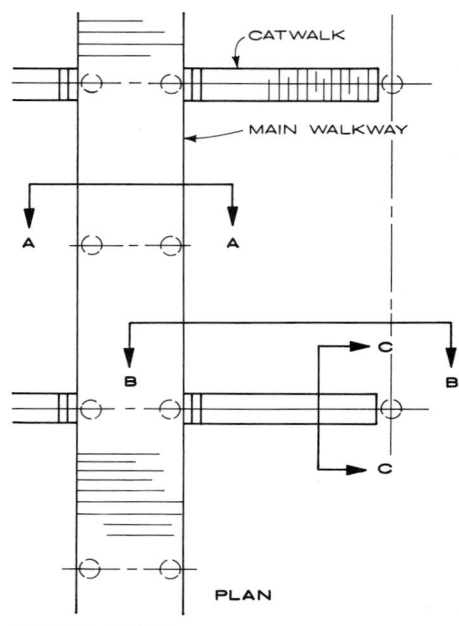

EXTENDED VERTICAL BUMPERS AT 6'-0" O.C.
OPEN JOINTED WOOD DECK ( 1/4" MAX. GAP )
CATWALK
CATWALK
VERTICAL BUMPERS AT 2'-0" O.C.
CONTINUOUS STRINGER
CROSS BRACING
PRESSURE TREATED WOOD PILE
MEAN LOW WATER LEVEL
**SECTION A-A**

CATWALK
MAIN WALKWAY
**PLAN**

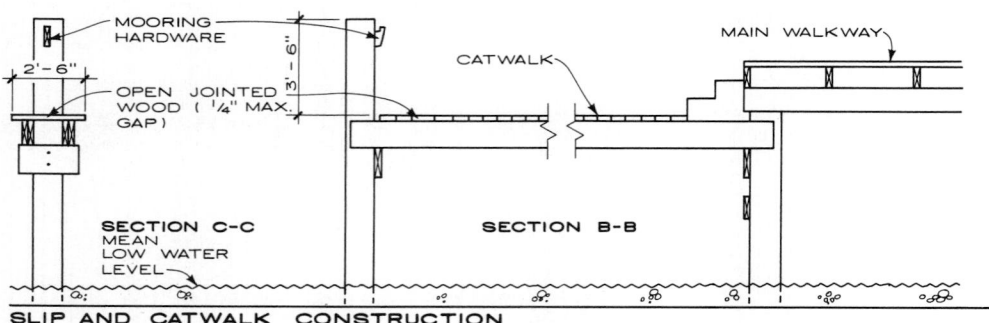

MOORING HARDWARE
2'-6"
3'-6"
OPEN JOINTED WOOD ( 1/4" MAX. GAP )
CATWALK
MAIN WALKWAY
**SECTION C-C**
MEAN LOW WATER LEVEL
**SECTION B-B**
**SLIP AND CATWALK CONSTRUCTION**

### GENERAL NOTES

1. Wood marine construction must be pressure treated with a preservative. Wood preservatives for use in marine applications fall into two general categories, creosote and waterborne. To select a specific preservative from within these categories, the decaying agents must be identified. A preservative may then be chosen based on the recommendations of the American Wood Preservers Institute.
2. Waterborne preservatives are recommended for decks because creosote stains shoes and bare feet.
3. The preservatives selected should be approved by the Environmental Protection Agency.
4. Dock height above water is determined by average deck levels and probable water level. Maintain a 12 in. minimum dimension between water and deck. Floating docks may be required in tidal waters. Consult manufacturer for construction information.
5. Cross bracing should be minimized to avoid entanglement of swimmers.

### LAUNCHING RAMPS

1. Launching ramps are for sheltered waters only.
2. A catwalk may be provided alongside the ramp.
3. Floating ramps may be required in tidal waters.

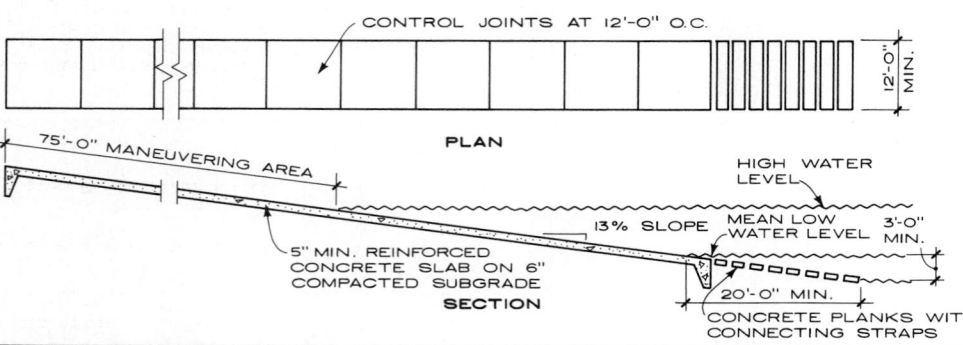

CONTROL JOINTS AT 12'-0" O.C.
12'-0" MIN.
**PLAN**
75'-0" MANEUVERING AREA
HIGH WATER LEVEL
13% SLOPE
MEAN LOW WATER LEVEL
3'-0" MIN.
5" MIN. REINFORCED CONCRETE SLAB ON 6" COMPACTED SUBGRADE
20'-0" MIN.
**SECTION**
CONCRETE PLANKS WITH CONNECTING STRAPS
**BOAT LAUNCHING RAMP**

## TABLE OF DIMENSIONS FOR SLIPS AND CATWALKS TO BE USED WITH PLAN DIAGRAM

| LENGTH GROUP FOR BOAT | BEAM TO BE PROVIDED FOR | MIN. CLEAR WIDTH OF SLIP | GROSS SLIP WIDTH TYPE A | GROSS SLIP WIDTH TYPE B | GROSS SLIP WIDTH TYPE C | 1ST CATWALK SPAN LENGTH D | 2ND CATWALK SPAN LENGTH E | 3RD CATWALK SPAN LENGTH F | DISTANCE G TO ANCHOR PILE |
|---|---|---|---|---|---|---|---|---|---|
| Up to 14' | 6'-7" | 8'-10" | 10'-9" | 10'-6" | 11'-2" | 12'-0" | | | 17'-0" |
| Over 14' to 16' | 7'-4" | 9'-8" | 11'-7" | 11'-4" | 12'-0" | 12'-0" | | | 19'-0" |
| Over 16' to 18' | 8'-0" | 10'-5" | 12'-4" | 12'-1" | 12'-9" | 14'-0" | | | 21'-0" |
| Over 18' to 20' | 8'-7" | 11'-1" | 13'-0" | 12'-9" | 13'-5" | 8'-0" | 8'-0" | | 23'-0" |
| Over 20' to 22' | 9'-3" | 11'-9" | 13'-8" | 13'-5" | 14'-1" | 10'-0" | 8'-0" | | 25'-0" |
| Over 22' to 25' | 10'-3" | 13'-1" | 15'-0" | 14'-9" | 15'-5" | 10'-0" | 8'-0" | | 28'-0" |
| Over 25' to 30' | 11'-3" | 14'-3" | 16'-2" | 15'-11" | 16'-7" | 10'-0" | 10'-0" | | 33'-0" |
| Over 30' to 35' | 12'-3" | 15'-8" | 17'-7" | 17'-4" | 18'-0" | 12'-0" | 10'-0" | | 38'-0" |
| Over 35' to 40' | 13'-3" | 16'-11" | 18'-10" | 18'-7" | 19'-3" | 12'-0" | 12'-0" | | 43'-0" |
| Over 40' to 45' | 14'-1" | 17'-11" | 19'-10" | 19'-7" | 20'-3" | 14'-0" | 12'-0" | | 48'-0" |
| Over 45' to 50' | 14'-11" | 19'-0" | 20'-11" | 20'-8" | 21'-4" | 9'-0" | 9'-0" | 10'-0" | 53'-0" |
| Over 50' to 60' | 16'-6" | 21'-0" | 22'-11" | 22'-8" | 23'-4" | 11'-0" | 11'-0" | 12'-0" | 63'-0" |
| Over 60' to 70' | 18'-1" | 23'-0" | 26'-8" | 24'-8" | 25'-4" | 11'-0" | 11'-0" | 12'-0" | 73'-0" |
| Over 70' to 80' | 19'-9" | 24'-11" | 28'-7" | 26'-7" | 26'-3" | 11'-0" | 11'-0" | 12'-0" | 83'-0" |

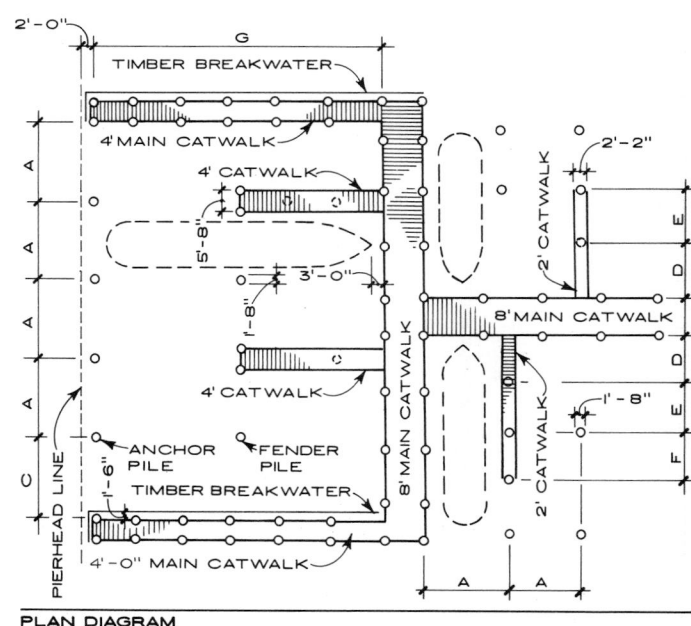

2'-0"
G
TIMBER BREAKWATER
4' MAIN CATWALK
4' CATWALK
2'-2"
2' CATWALK
5'-8"
3'-0"
8' MAIN CATWALK
4' CATWALK
1'-8"
1'-8"
2' CATWALK
ANCHOR PILE
FENDER PILE
TIMBER BREAKWATER
8' MAIN CATWALK
1'-6"
PIERHEAD LINE
4'-0" MAIN CATWALK
**PLAN DIAGRAM**

David E. Rose; Rossen/Neumann Associates; Southfield, Michigan

2    **MARINE WORK**

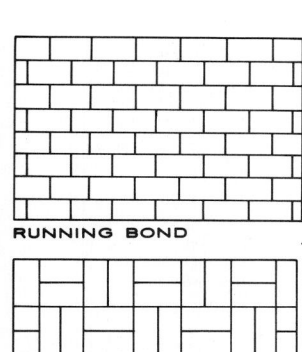

RUNNING BOND

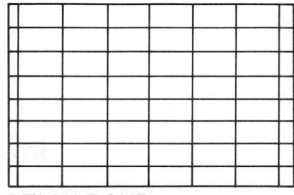

STACK BOND

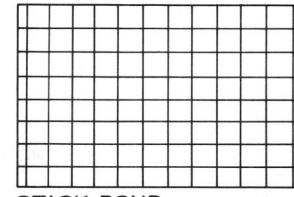

STACK BOND

## TYPICAL UNIT PAVER TYPES AND NOMINAL SIZES

BRICK PAVERS: 4 in. x 4 in., 4 in. x 8 in., 4 in. x 12 in.; ½ in. to 2¼ in. thick.

PRESSED CONCRETE BRICKS: 4 in. x 8 in., 2½ in. to 3 in. thick.

PRESSED CONCRETE PAVERS: 12 in. x 12 in., 12 in. x 24 in., 18 in. x 18 in., 18 in. x 24 in., 24 in. x 24 in., 24 in. x 30 in., 24 in. x 36 in., 30 in. x 30 in., 36 in. x 36 in.; 1½ in. to 3 in. thick.

ASPHALT PAVERS: 5 in. x 12 in., 6 in. x 6 in., 6 in. x 12 in., 8 in. x 8 in., 8 in. hexagonal, 1¼ in. to 3 in. thick.

### NOTES

1. Face brick, marble, and granite sometimes are used for paving.
2. See index for tile paver sizes and shapes.
3. Paving patterns shown often are rotated 45° for diagonal patterns.
4. Maximum 3 percent absorption for brick applications subject to vehicular traffic.
5. For pressed concrete and asphalt pavers subject to vehicular traffic, use 3 in. thickness.
6. Use modular size for brick paver patterns other than running and stack bond set with mortar joints. Use full size when set without mortar joints.

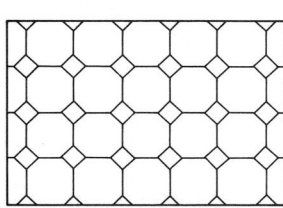

BASKET WEAVE OR PARQUET

HERRINGBONE

DIAGONAL RUNNING BOND

OCTAGON AND DOT

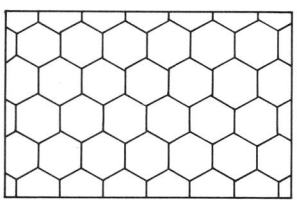

ROMAN COBBLE

HEXAGON

## UNIT PAVERS

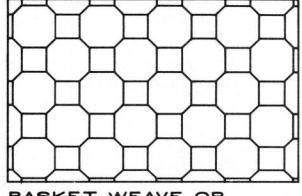

BASKET WEAVE OR PARQUET

DIAGONAL RUNNING BOND

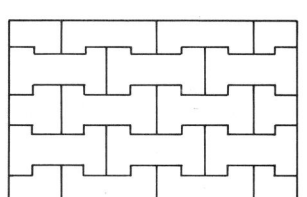

RUNNING BOND

### NOTES

1. Interlocking pavers are available in concrete, hydraulically pressed concrete, asphalt, and brick, and in different weight classifications, compressive strengths, surface textures, finishes, and colors. Consult local suppliers for availability.
2. Subject to manufacturer's recommendations and local code requirements, interlocking concrete pavers may be used in areas subject to heavy vehicle loads at 30 to 40 mph speeds.
3. Continuous curb or other edge restraint is required to anchor pavers in applications subject to vehicular traffic.
4. Concrete interlocking paver sizes are based on metric dimensions. Dimensions indicated are to nearest ⅛ in.
5. Where paver shape permits, herringbone pattern is recommended for paving subject to vehicular traffic.
6. Portions have been adapted, with permission, from ASTM C 939.

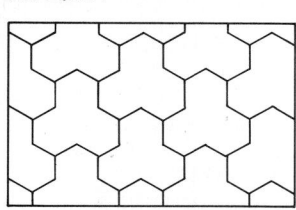

COMBINED HEXAGON

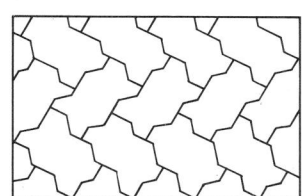

HERRINGBONE

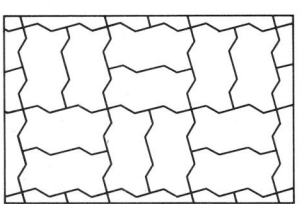

BASKET WEAVE

## INTERLOCKING PAVERS

DIAGONAL SQUARES

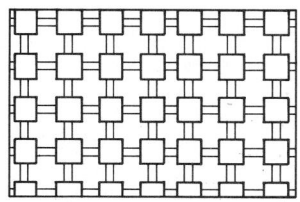

RUNNING SQUARES

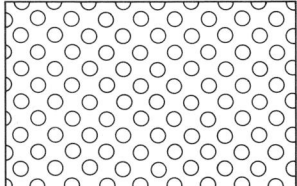

RINGS

### NOTES

1. Appearance of grass pavers when voids are filled are shown by stipple to the right of the cut line. Voids may be filled with grass, a variety of ground cover, or gravel.
2. Grass pavers may be used to control erosion.
3. Herringbone pattern is recommended for concrete grass pavers subject to vehicular traffic.
4. Grass rings are available with close ring spacing for pedestrian use or wide ring spacing for vehicular use.

## GRASS PAVERS

STACK BOND

RANDOM

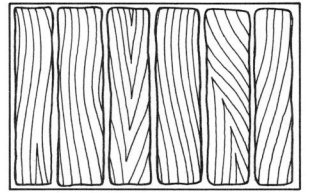

STACK BOND

BASKET WEAVE OR PARQUET

## WOOD PAVERS

Jeffrey R. Vandevoort; Talbott Wilson Associates, Inc.; Houston, Texas
John R. Hoke, Jr., AIA, Architect; Washington, D.C.

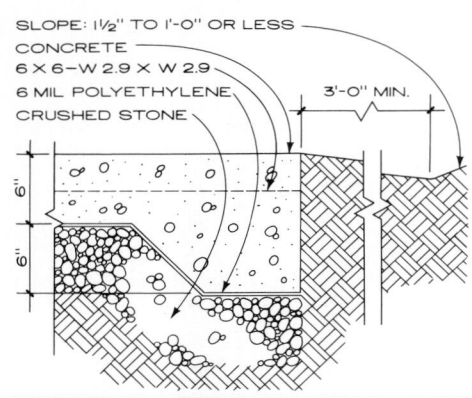

SLOPE: 1½" TO 1'-0" OR LESS
CONCRETE
6 × 6–W 2.9 × W 2.9
6 MIL POLYETHYLENE
CRUSHED STONE
3'-0" MIN.

**CONCRETE PAVING WITHOUT CURB**

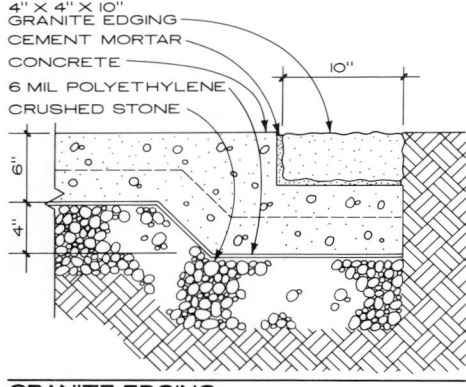

4" × 4" × 10"
GRANITE EDGING
CEMENT MORTAR
CONCRETE
6 MIL POLYETHYLENE
CRUSHED STONE
10"

**GRANITE EDGING**

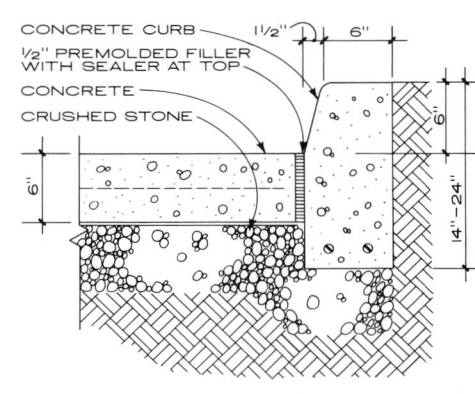

CONCRETE CURB
1½"    6"
½" PREMOLDED FILLER
WITH SEALER AT TOP
CONCRETE
CRUSHED STONE
14"–24"

**SEPARATE CONCRETE CURB**

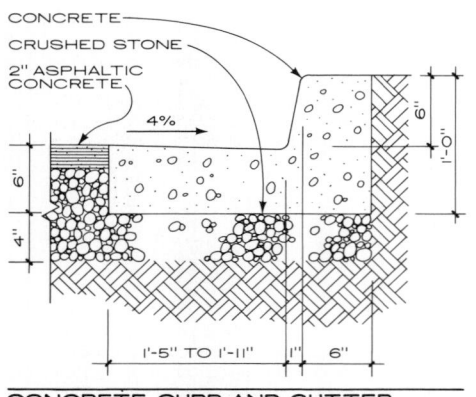

CONCRETE
CRUSHED STONE
2" ASPHALTIC
CONCRETE
4%
6"
4"
1'-0"
6"
1'-5" TO 1'-11"    1"    6"

**CONCRETE CURB AND GUTTER**

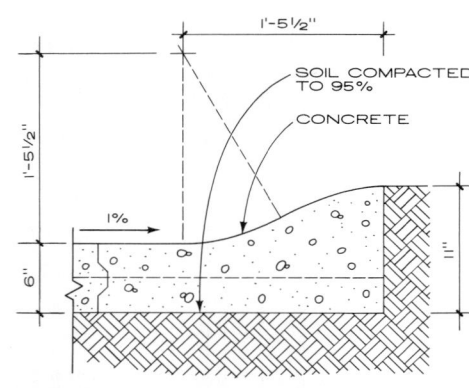

1'-5½"
SOIL COMPACTED
TO 95%
CONCRETE
1'-5½"
1%
6"    11"

**MOUNTABLE CONCRETE CURB**

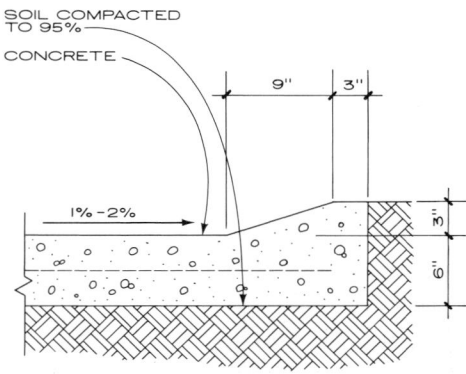

SOIL COMPACTED
TO 95%
CONCRETE
9"    3"
1%–2%
3"
6"

**IOWA CONCRETE CURB**

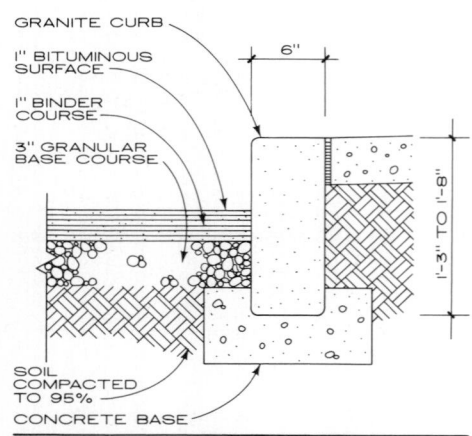

GRANITE CURB
1" BITUMINOUS
SURFACE
1" BINDER
COURSE
3" GRANULAR
BASE COURSE
6"
1'-3" TO 1'-8"
SOIL
COMPACTED
TO 95%
CONCRETE BASE

**ASPHALT PAVING WITH STONE CURB**

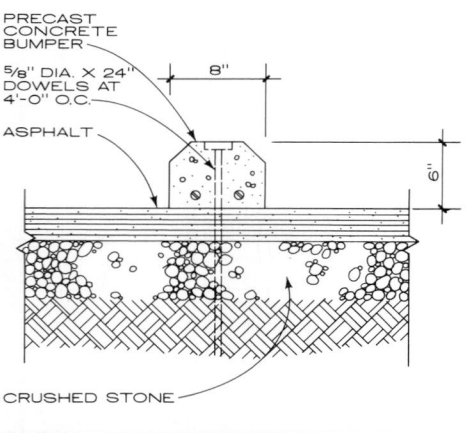

PRECAST
CONCRETE
BUMPER
⅝" DIA. × 24"
DOWELS AT
4'-0" O.C.
ASPHALT
8"
6"
CRUSHED STONE

**ASPHALT PAVING WITH PRECAST
CONCRETE BUMPER**

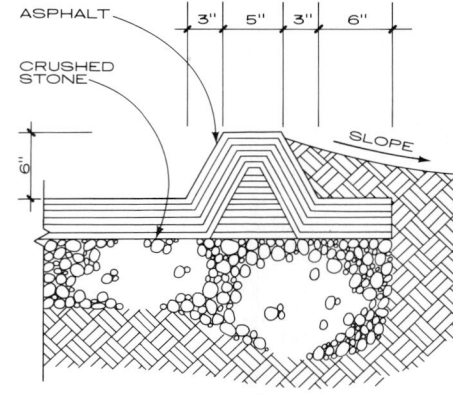

ASPHALT
CRUSHED
STONE
3"    5"    3"    6"
SLOPE
6"

**NOT RECOMMENDED AS WHEEL STOP**

**ASPHALT CURB AND PAVING**

GALVANIZED STEEL
EDGING AND STAKES
AT 3'-0" O.C.
2" CRUSHED STONE
¾" BITUMINOUS BINDER
2¾"
2"
¾"
6"
6" COARSE AGGREGATE

**CRUSHED STONE PAVING WITH
METAL EDGE**

REDWOOD OR
PRESSURE-TREATED
WOOD CURB WITH
2" × 4" × 24" STAKES
AT 3'-0" O.C.
4" CRUSHED STONE
6"
4"
8"
6"
6" COARSE AGGREGATE

**CRUSHED STONE PAVING WITH
TIMBER CURB**

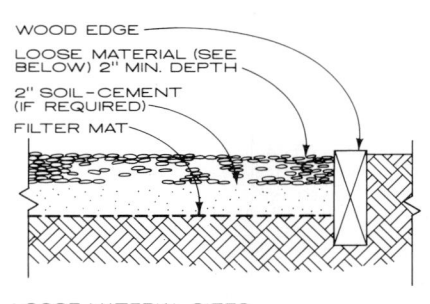

WOOD EDGE
LOOSE MATERIAL (SEE
BELOW) 2" MIN. DEPTH
2" SOIL-CEMENT
(IF REQUIRED)
FILTER MAT

LOOSE MATERIAL SIZES
WOOD CHIPS–1" NOMINAL        ½" DECOMPOSED
SHREDDED BARK MULCH         GRANITE
¼" STONE CHIPS                    ¾" CRUSHED
¾" PEA GRAVEL                     STONE
                                            1"–2" WASHED
                                            STONE

NOTE: ORGANIC MATERIALS WILL DECOMPOSE

**LOOSE MATERIAL PAVING WITH
WOOD EDGE**

Francisco J. Menendez; Washington, D.C.
Richard J. Vitullo; Washington Grove, Maryland

# 2   PAVING AND SURFACING

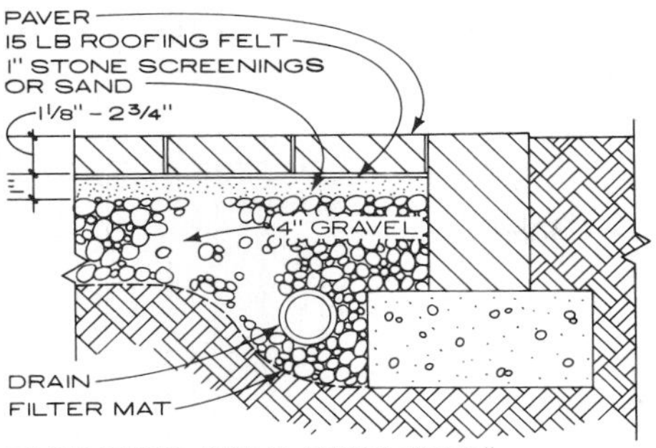
PAVER
15 LB ROOFING FELT
1" STONE SCREENINGS OR SAND
1 1/8"-2 3/4"
4" GRAVEL
DRAIN
FILTER MAT

PAVER SIZES: 4" × 4", 4" × 8", 4" × 12", 6" × 6", 8" × 8", 12" × 12", 5 3/4", 8", AND 12" HEXAGON

PAVER THICKNESS: 1 1/8"-2 3/4"

**BRICK, CLAY TILE, OR ASPHALT BLOCK PAVERS**

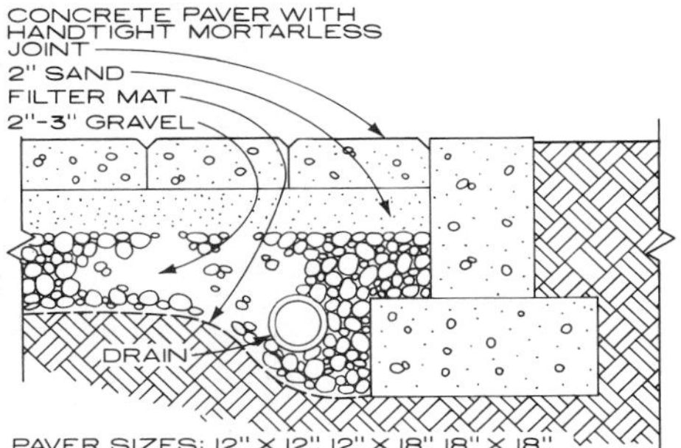
CONCRETE PAVER WITH HANDTIGHT MORTARLESS JOINT
2" SAND
FILTER MAT
2"-3" GRAVEL
DRAIN

PAVER SIZES: 12" × 12", 12" × 18", 18" × 18", 18" × 24", 24" × 36"

PAVER THICKNESS: 1 1/2"-2 1/2" PRECAST CONCRETE

TEXTURE: TROWEL FINISH, FLOAT FINISH, EXPOSED AGGREGATE FINISH

**CONCRETE PAVERS AND LONDON WALKS**

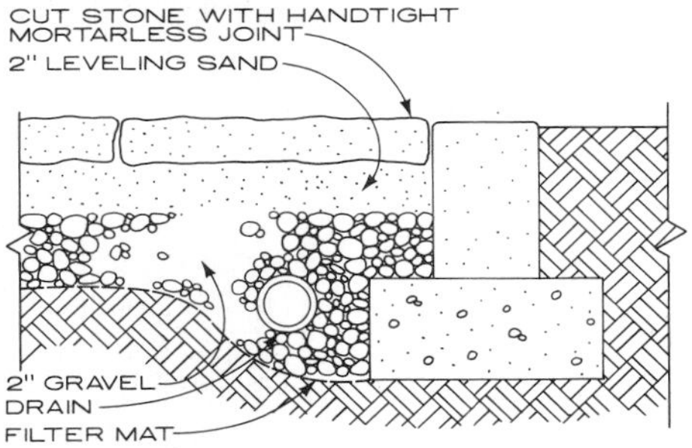
CUT STONE WITH HANDTIGHT MORTARLESS JOINT
2" LEVELING SAND
2" GRAVEL
DRAIN
FILTER MAT

STONE SIZES: 12" × 12", 12" × 18", 18" × 18", 18" × 24", 24" × 36", OR RANDOM SHAPES

STONE THICKNESS: 1"-2" CUT STONE

TEXTURE: HONED, NATURAL CLEFT, OR FLAME TREATED FOR NONSLIP FINISH

**CUT STONE PAVERS**

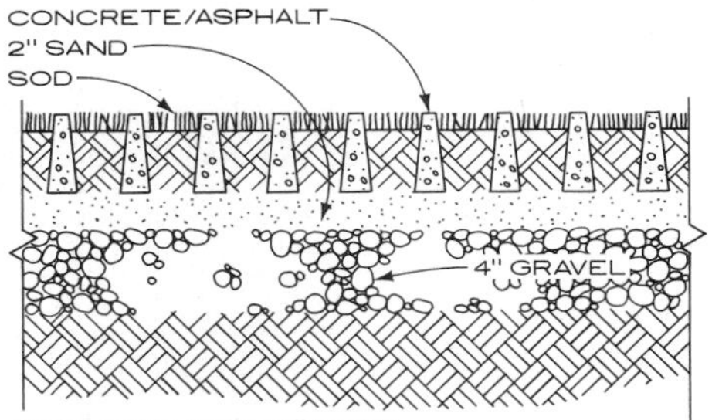
CONCRETE/ASPHALT
2" SAND
SOD
4" GRAVEL

SIZE: 24" × 24" × 4" DEEP

SURFACE TEXTURE: MODERATELY ABRASIVE

COLOR: STANDARD GRAY OR TAN INSTALLED WITHOUT SLAB, MORTAR, OR GROUT. A PREFORMED LATTICE UNIT USED FOR STORM RUNOFF CONTROL, PATHWAYS, PARKING AREAS, AND SOIL CONSERVATION

**GRID PAVING BLOCKS**

## UNIT PAVERS ON FLEXIBLE BASE

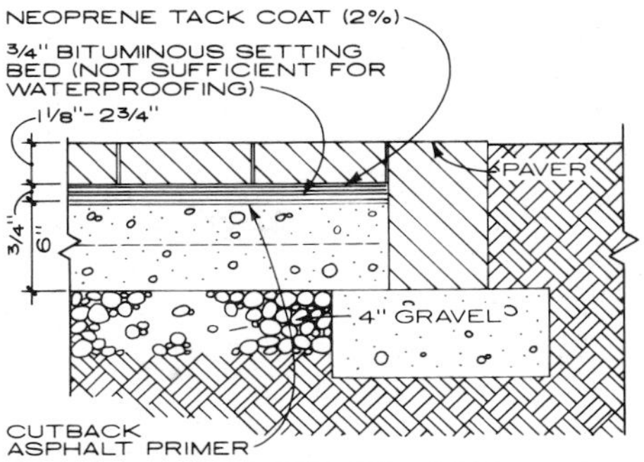
NEOPRENE TACK COAT (2%)
3/4" BITUMINOUS SETTING BED (NOT SUFFICIENT FOR WATERPROOFING)
1 1/8"-2 3/4"
PAVER
3/4"
6"
4" GRAVEL
CUTBACK ASPHALT PRIMER

WHERE WEATHER PERMITS, LATEX-MODIFIED MORTAR MAY BE USED FOR JOINTS AND SETTING BED

**BRICK, CLAY TILE, OR ASPHALT BLOCK PAVERS**

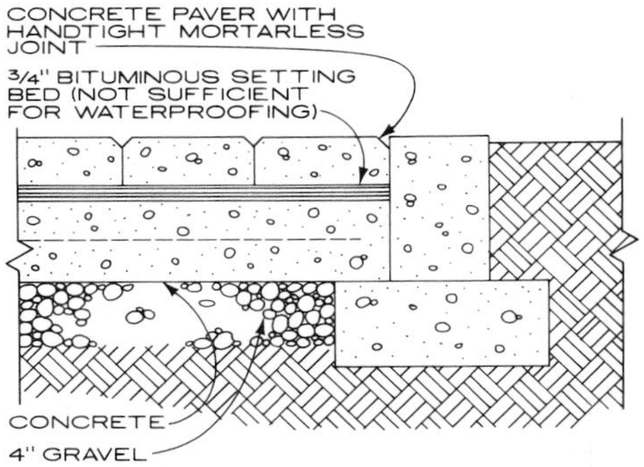
CONCRETE PAVER WITH HANDTIGHT MORTARLESS JOINT
3/4" BITUMINOUS SETTING BED (NOT SUFFICIENT FOR WATERPROOFING)
CONCRETE
4" GRAVEL

WHERE WEATHER PERMITS, LATEX-MODIFIED MORTAR MAY BE USED FOR JOINTS AND SETTING BED

**CONCRETE PAVERS AND LONDON WALKS**

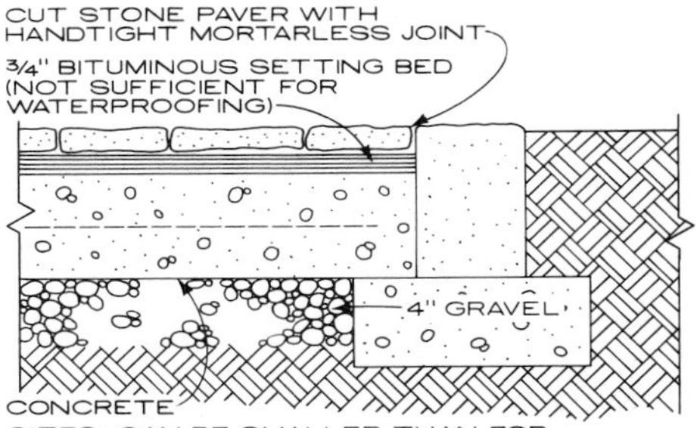
CUT STONE PAVER WITH HANDTIGHT MORTARLESS JOINT
3/4" BITUMINOUS SETTING BED (NOT SUFFICIENT FOR WATERPROOFING)
4" GRAVEL
CONCRETE

SIZES: CAN BE SMALLER THAN FOR FLEXIBLE BASE WHERE WEATHER PERMITS LATEX-MODIFIED MORTAR MAY BE USED FOR JOINT AND SETTING BEDS. JOINTS MAY BE STAGGERED OR RANDOM

STONE THICKNESS: 1/2" SLATE OR 1"-2" CUT STONE

**CUT STONE PAVERS**

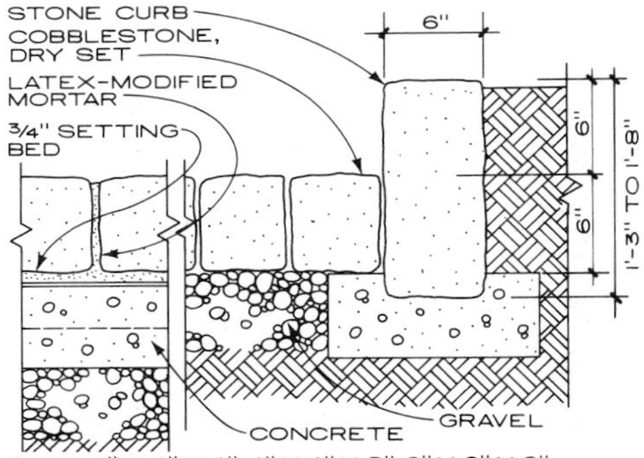
STONE CURB
COBBLESTONE, DRY SET
LATEX-MODIFIED MORTAR
3/4" SETTING BED
6"
6"
6"
1'-3" TO 1'-8"
GRAVEL
CONCRETE

SIZE: 4" × 4" × 4", 4" × 4" × 8", 6" × 6" × 6", 6" × 6" × 10", ETC.

STONE: GRANITE, BASALT, ETC.

**COBBLESTONE PAVERS**

## UNIT PAVERS ON RIGID BASE

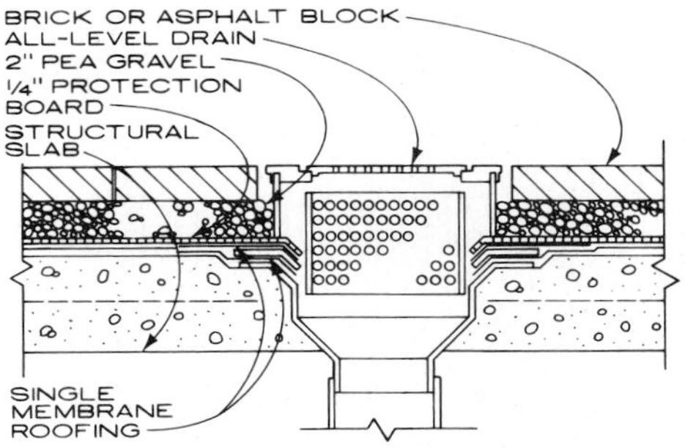
BRICK OR ASPHALT BLOCK
ALL-LEVEL DRAIN
2" PEA GRAVEL
1/4" PROTECTION BOARD
STRUCTURAL SLAB
SINGLE MEMBRANE ROOFING

FOR HEATED SPACES UNDER STRUCTURAL SLAB, USE CLOSED CELL INSULATION UNDER PAVERS

**BRICK, CLAY TILE, ASPHALT BLOCK, CONCRETE, OR STONE PAVERS OVER UNINSULATED BASE**

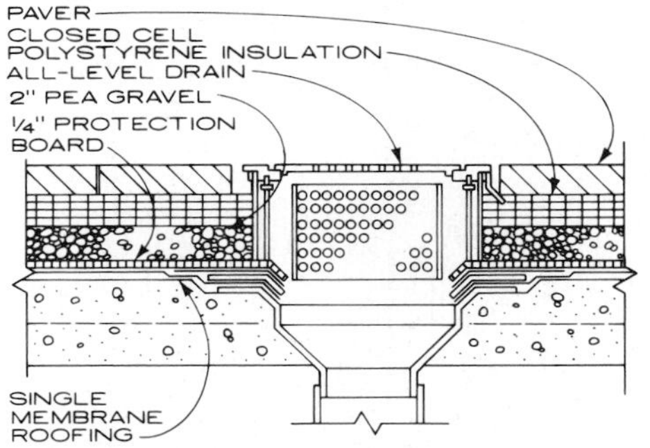
PAVER
CLOSED CELL POLYSTYRENE INSULATION
ALL-LEVEL DRAIN
2" PEA GRAVEL
1/4" PROTECTION BOARD
SINGLE MEMBRANE ROOFING

THIS SYSTEM SUITABLE FOR PEDESTRIAN TRAFFIC ONLY

**BRICK, CLAY TILE, ASPHALT BLOCK, CONCRETE, OR STONE PAVERS OVER INSULATED BASE**

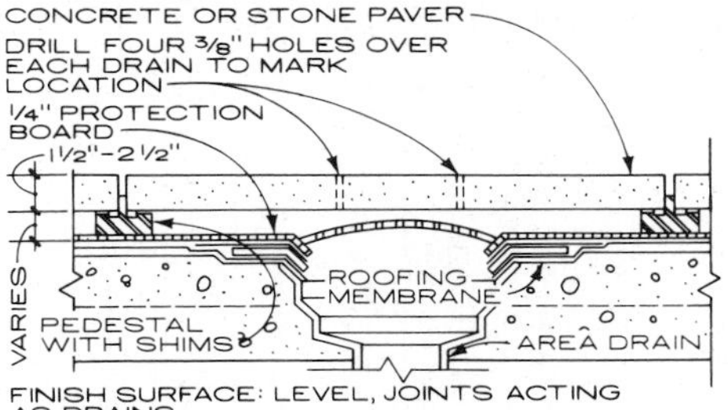
CONCRETE OR STONE PAVER
DRILL FOUR 3/8" HOLES OVER EACH DRAIN TO MARK LOCATION
1/4" PROTECTION BOARD
1 1/2"-2 1/2"
VARIES
ROOFING MEMBRANE
PEDESTAL WITH SHIMS
AREA DRAIN

FINISH SURFACE: LEVEL, JOINTS ACTING AS DRAINS

DRAINAGE SURFACE: SLOPE TO DRAIN 1/8"-1/4" PER FT

HEIGHT OF PEDESTALS: 1/2"-1 1/2"

PEDESTAL MATERIAL: NEOPRENE, METAL, VINYL, MORTAR

SHIMS: MULTIPLE OF 1/8"

**CONCRETE OR CUT STONE PAVER ON PEDESTALS OVER UNINSULATED BASE**

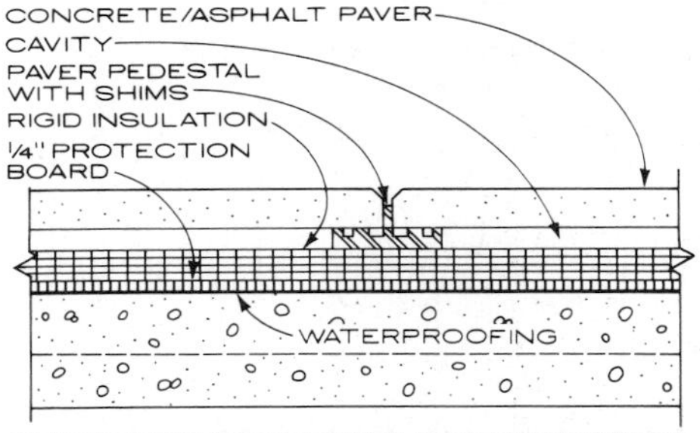
CONCRETE/ASPHALT PAVER
CAVITY
PAVER PEDESTAL WITH SHIMS
RIGID INSULATION
1/4" PROTECTION BOARD
WATERPROOFING

THIS SYSTEM IS SUITABLE FOR PEDESTRIAN TRAFFIC ONLY. RIGID INSULATION SHALL BE SUITABLE TO CARRY PEDESTRIAN LOADS

PEDESTAL MATERIAL: NEOPRENE, METAL, VINYL, MORTAR

SHIMS: SAME AS PEDESTAL MATERIAL

**CONCRETE OR STONE PAVERS ON PEDESTALS OVER INSULATED BASE**

## UNIT PAVERS ON SUSPENDED BASE

GENERAL NOTES

1. Drainpipes may be omitted at well-drained areas.
2. Provide positive outflow for drainpipes.
3. Do not use unsatisfactory soil (expanding organic).
4. Satisfactory soil shall be compacted to 95%.
5. Flexible and suspended bases shown are for light duty only.
6. Edging width: 2, 4, 8, 12 in.; depth: 8, 12, 16, 24 in.
7. Footing of edging width: 8, 12, 16, 20 in.; depth: 6, 8 in.
8. If freezing, depth is deeper than bottom of footing; provide gravel at footing.

Charles A. Szoradi; Washington, D.C.
Richard J. Vitullo; Washington Grove, Maryland

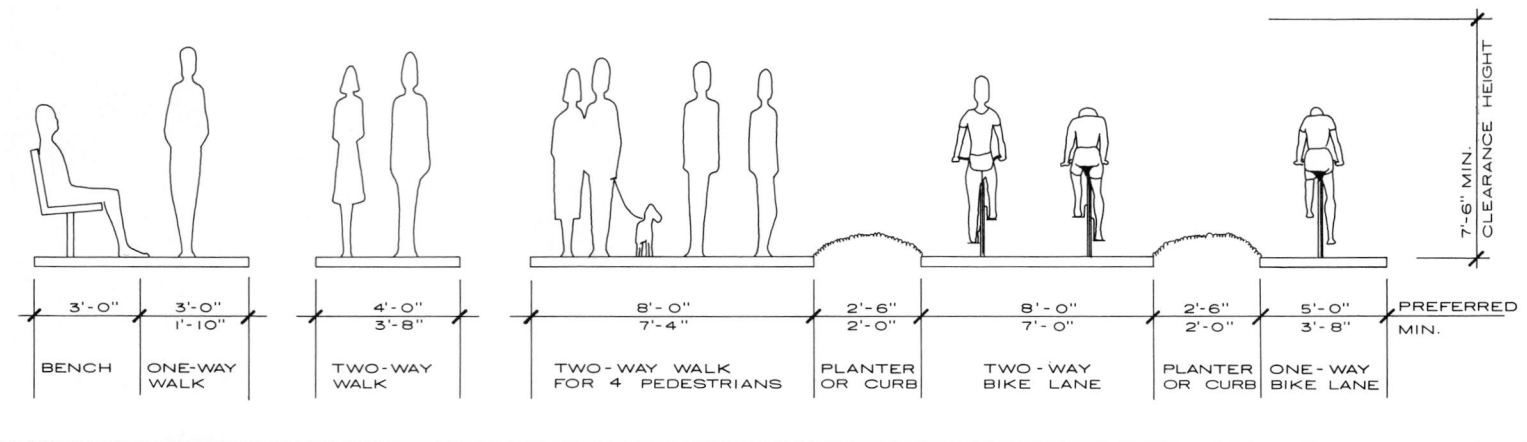

**WALK AND BIKE LANE WIDTHS**

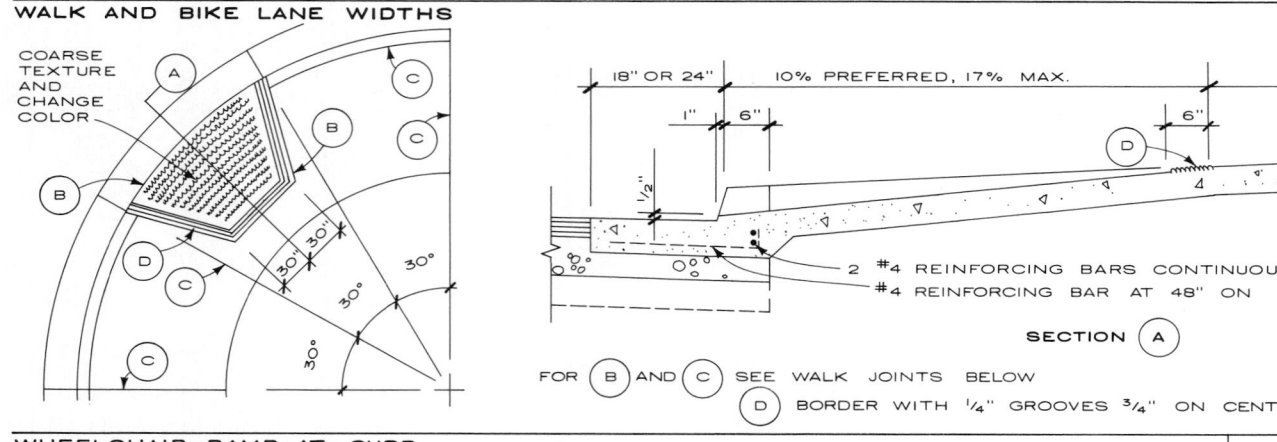

FOR Ⓑ AND Ⓒ SEE WALK JOINTS BELOW

Ⓓ BORDER WITH ¼" GROOVES ¾" ON CENTER

**WHEELCHAIR RAMP AT CURB**
( ROUND CURB SHOWN IN PLAN.
SECTION TYPICAL FOR ANY CURB )

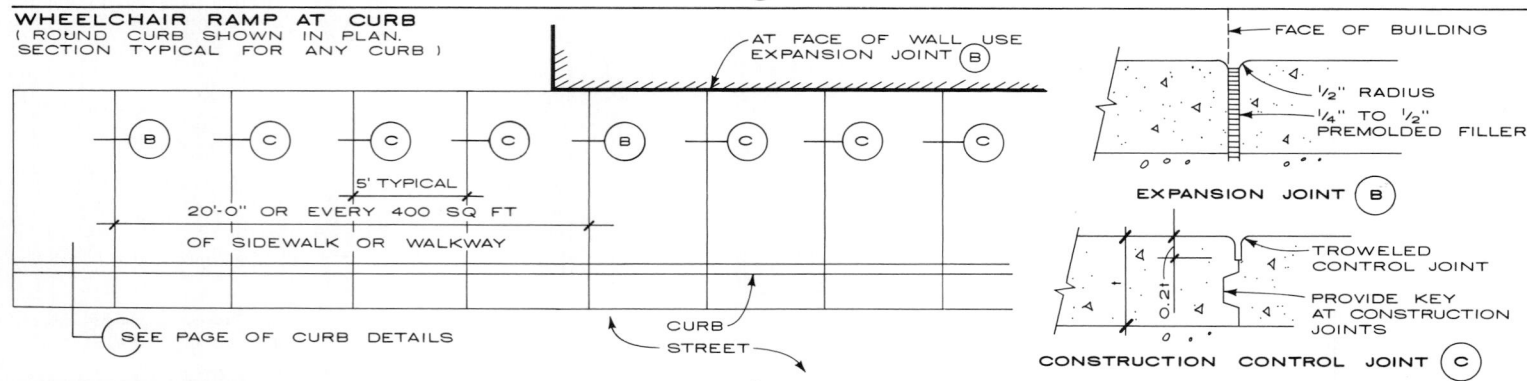

**WALK AND CURB JOINTS**

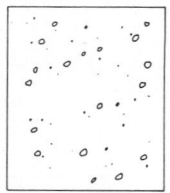

**ROCK SALT**

Spread on troweled surface and press in. Wash salt away after concrete hardens. Protect planting.

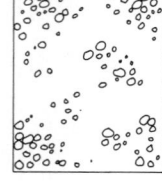

**EXPOSED AGGREGATE**

Seed aggregate uniformly onto surface. Embed by tamping. After setup, brush lightly and clean with spray. If using aggregate mix, trowel and expose by washing fines or use a retarder.

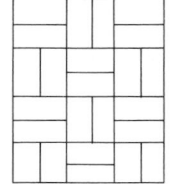

**PRESSED OR STAMPED**

Stock patterns are available. Use integral or dry shake colors. Joints may be filled with mortar.

**BROOM SURFACE**

Use stiff bristle for coarse texture. Use soft bristle on steel troweled surface for fine texture.

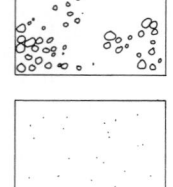

**TROWELED**

Use wood float for coarse texture. Use steel float for fine texture.

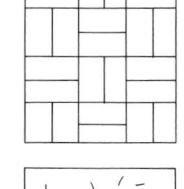

**NONSLIP**

Apply silicon carbide (sparkling) or aluminum oxide at ¼ to ½ psf; trowel lightly.

**WALK SURFACES AND TEXTURES**

William T. Mahan, AIA; Santa Barbara, California

**PAVING AND SURFACING**

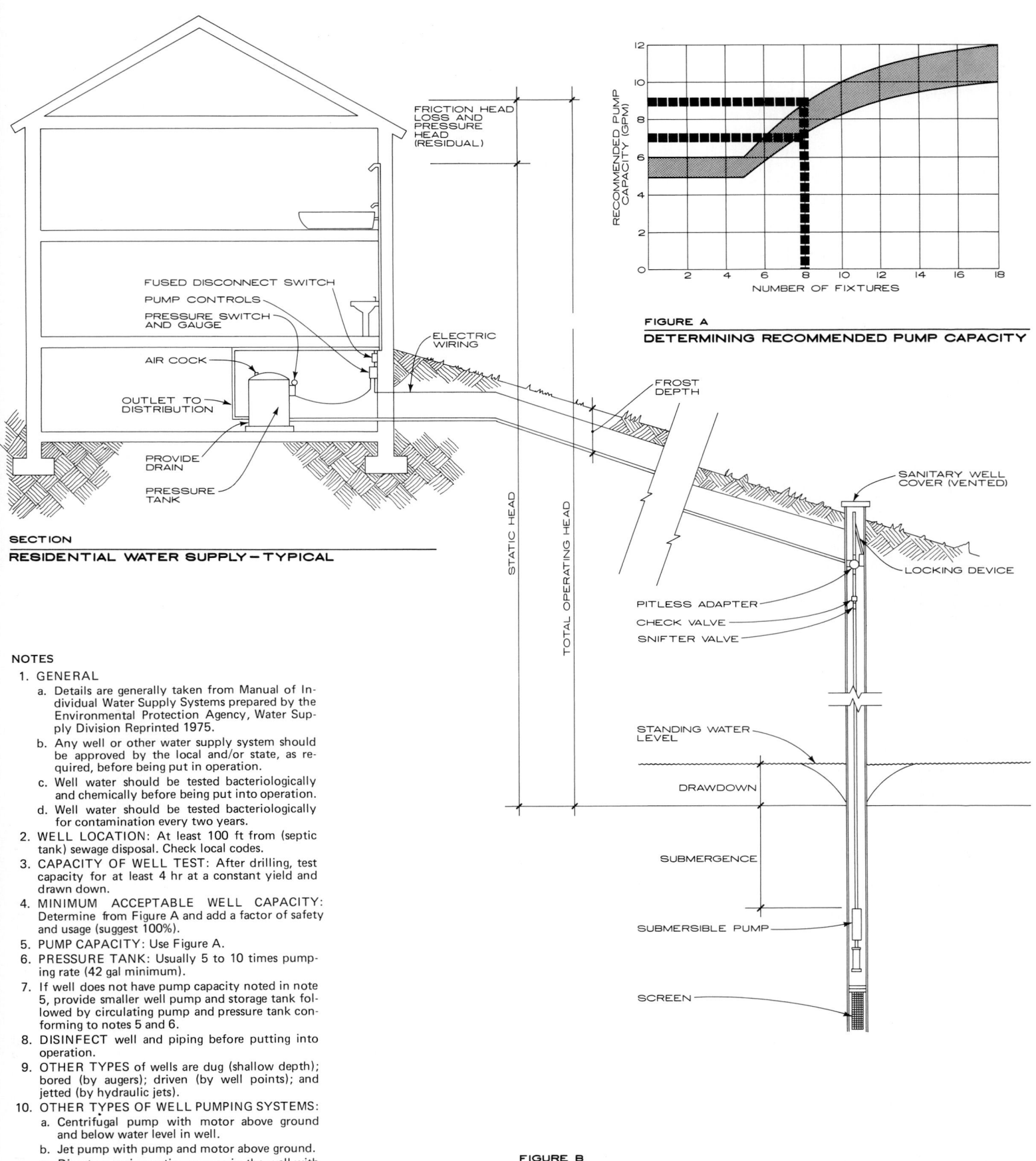

**SECTION**

## RESIDENTIAL WATER SUPPLY — TYPICAL

**FIGURE A**

## DETERMINING RECOMMENDED PUMP CAPACITY

**FIGURE B**

## DRILLED WELL — SECTION

### NOTES

1. **GENERAL**
   a. Details are generally taken from Manual of Individual Water Supply Systems prepared by the Environmental Protection Agency, Water Supply Division Reprinted 1975.
   b. Any well or other water supply system should be approved by the local and/or state, as required, before being put in operation.
   c. Well water should be tested bacteriologically and chemically before being put into operation.
   d. Well water should be tested bacteriologically for contamination every two years.
2. **WELL LOCATION:** At least 100 ft from (septic tank) sewage disposal. Check local codes.
3. **CAPACITY OF WELL TEST:** After drilling, test capacity for at least 4 hr at a constant yield and drawn down.
4. **MINIMUM ACCEPTABLE WELL CAPACITY:** Determine from Figure A and add a factor of safety and usage (suggest 100%).
5. **PUMP CAPACITY:** Use Figure A.
6. **PRESSURE TANK:** Usually 5 to 10 times pumping rate (42 gal minimum).
7. If well does not have pump capacity noted in note 5, provide smaller well pump and storage tank followed by circulating pump and pressure tank conforming to notes 5 and 6.
8. **DISINFECT** well and piping before putting into operation.
9. **OTHER TYPES** of wells are dug (shallow depth); bored (by augers); driven (by well points); and jetted (by hydraulic jets).
10. **OTHER TYPES OF WELL PUMPING SYSTEMS:**
    a. Centrifugal pump with motor above ground and below water level in well.
    b. Jet pump with pump and motor above ground.
    c. Direct or reciprocating pumps in the well with motor above ground.

Jack L. Staunton, P.E.; Staunton and Freeman, Consulting Engineers; New York, New York

## GENERAL NOTES

Seepage and runoff each require special engineering designs to protect against potential water damage. Drainage systems intercept and dispose of the water flow to prevent inordinate damage to an area or facility from seepage and direct runoff.

Subsurface drainage systems are designed to lower the natural water table, to intercept underground flow, and to dispose of infiltration percolating down through soils from surface sources. These systems typically are used under floors, around foundations, in planters, and under athletic fields and courts. Each system must be provided with a positive outfall either by pumped discharge or gravity drain above expected high water levels.

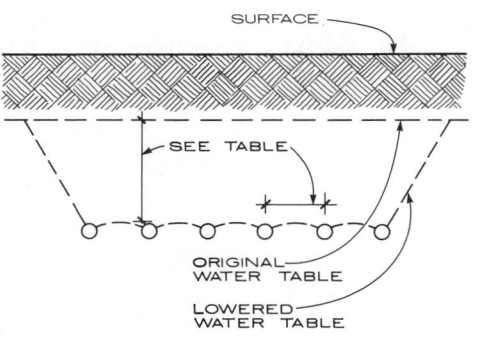

**SECTION**

Drain layout varies to meet need. May be grid, parallel, herringbone, or random pattern to fit topography.

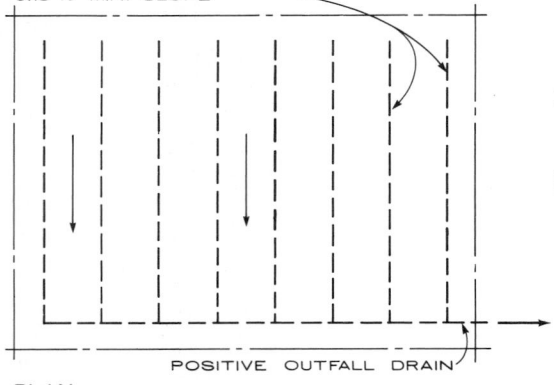

**PLAN**

Depths indicated in table below are minimum range. Greater depths may be required to prevent frost heave in colder climates or where soils have a high capillarity.

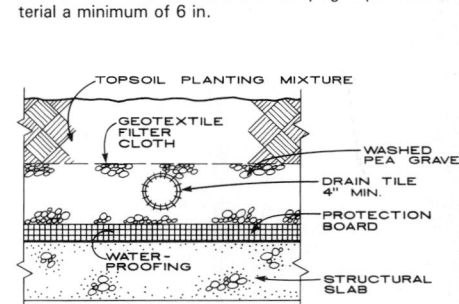

**FOOTING DRAIN**

**TYPICAL SECTION**

If perforated drain is used, it should be installed with the holes facing down.

When used to intercept sidehill seepage, the bottom of the trench should be cut into underlying impervious material a minimum of 6 in.

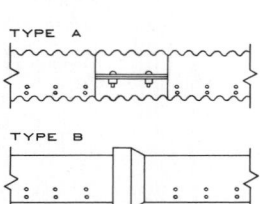

**SUBSURFACE DRAIN PIPES IN GENERAL USE**

## DRAIN PIPES

| DRAIN TYPE | MATERIAL | JOINT |
|---|---|---|
| A | Corrugated metal Flexible plastic | Collars |
| B | Concrete Clay tile | Bell and spigot |
| C | Rigid plastic | Sleeve socket |
| D | Porous concrete | Tongue and groove |

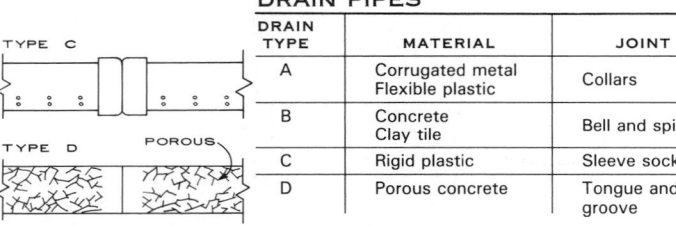

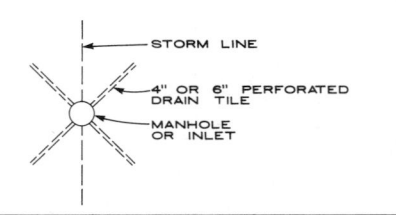

**PLANTER DRAIN**

**DRYWELLS**

Drywells provide an underground disposal system for surface runoff. Their effectiveness is in direct proportion to the porosity of surrounding soils, and they are efficient only for draining small areas. High rainfall runoff rates cannot be absorbed at the considerably lower percolation rates of most soils; the difference is stored temporarily in the drywell. Efficiency is reduced during extended periods of wet weather when receiving soils are saturated and the well is refilled prior to draining completely.

## DEPTH AND SPACING OF SUBDRAINS RECOMMENDED FOR VARIOUS SOIL CLASSES

| SOIL CLASSES | PERCENTAGE OF SOIL SEPARATES | | | DEPTH OF BOTTOM OF DRAIN (FT.) | DISTANCE BETWEEN SUBDRAINS (FT.) |
|---|---|---|---|---|---|
| | SAND | SILT | CLAY | | |
| Sand | 80–100 | 0–20 | 0–20 | 3–4<br>2–3 | 150–300<br>100–150 |
| Sandy loam | 50–80 | 0–50 | 0–20 | 3–4<br>2–3 | 100–150<br>85–100 |
| Loam | 30–50 | 30–50 | 0–20 | 3–4<br>2–3 | 85–100<br>75–85 |
| Silt loam | 0–50 | 50–100 | 0–20 | 3–4<br>2–3 | 75–85<br>65–75 |
| Sandy clay loam | 50–80 | 0–30 | 20–30 | 3–4<br>2–3 | 65–75<br>55–65 |
| Clay loam | 20–50 | 20–50 | 20–30 | 3–4<br>2–3 | 55–65<br>45–55 |
| Silty clay loam | 0–30 | 50–80 | 20–30 | 3–4<br>2–3 | 45–55<br>40–45 |
| Sandy clay | 50–70 | 0–20 | 30–50 | 3–4<br>2–3 | 40–45<br>35–40 |
| Silty clay | 0–20 | 50–70 | 30–50 | 3–4<br>2–3 | 35–40<br>30–35 |
| Clay | 0–50 | 0–50 | 30–100 | 3–4<br>2–3 | 30–35<br>25–30 |

Harold C. Munger, FAIA; Munger Munger + Associates Architects, Inc.; Toledo, Ohio
Kurt N. Pronske, P.E.; Reston, Virginia

**SEWERAGE AND DRAINAGE**

**SURFACE DRAINAGE SYSTEMS:** Designed to collect and dispose of rainfall runoff. There are two basic types. One, a ditch/swale and culvert, or open system, is generally used in less densely populated and more open areas where natural surfaces predominate. In urbanized areas where much of the land is overbuilt, the second type is used—the pipe, inlet/catchbasin and manhole, or closed system. Combinations of the two are quite common where terrain and density dictate.

## GENERAL NOTES

1. Lay out grades to allow safe flow away from building if drains becomes blocked.
2. It is generally more economical to keep water on surface as long as possible.
3. Consider the possibility of ice forming on surface when determining slopes for vehicles and pedestrians.
4. Determine which design criteria are set by code or governmental agency, such as intensity and duration of rain storm and allowable runoff.
5. Formulas given are for approx. only. A qualified engineer should be consulted to design the system.

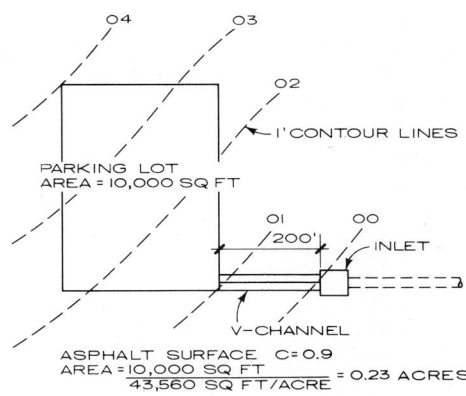

ASPHALT SURFACE C=0.9
AREA = 10,000 SQ FT
$\frac{10,000 \text{ SQ FT}}{43,560 \text{ SQ FT/ACRE}} = 0.23$ ACRES

## SITE PLAN—EXAMPLE

### RATIONAL FORMULA

Q = CIA
Q = Flow (cu ft/sec)
C = From table (Approximate Values for C)
I = Intensity (in./hr) Obtain from local code requirements
A = Area of site (acres)

EXAMPLE: Assume local code requires I = 5 in./hr

Q = CIA
Q = 0.9(5)0.23
= 1.04 cu ft/sec
= Approximate volume of water entering the V-channel per second from the parking lot

Note: Simplified method of calculation for areas of less than 100 acres.

## APPROXIMATE METHOD FOR CALCULATING RUNOFF

### APPROXIMATE VALUES FOR C

| | |
|---|---|
| Roofs | 0.95–1.00 |
| Pavement | 0.90–1.00 |
| Roads | 0.30–0.90 |
| Bare soil | |
| Sand | 0.20–0.40 |
| Clay | 0.30–0.75 |
| Grass | 0.15–0.60 |
| Developed land | |
| Commercial | 0.60–0.75 |
| High-density residential | 0.50–0.65 |
| Low-density residential | 0.30–0.55 |

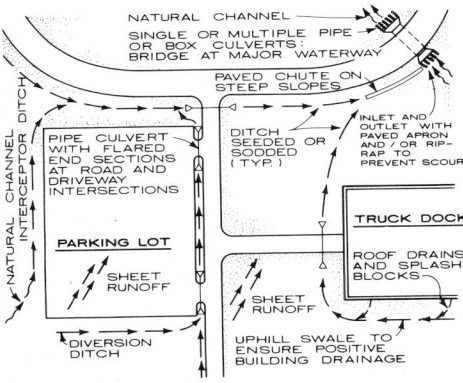

**OPEN SYSTEM**

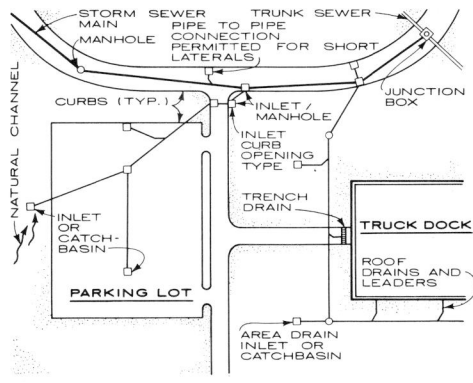

**CLOSED SYSTEM**

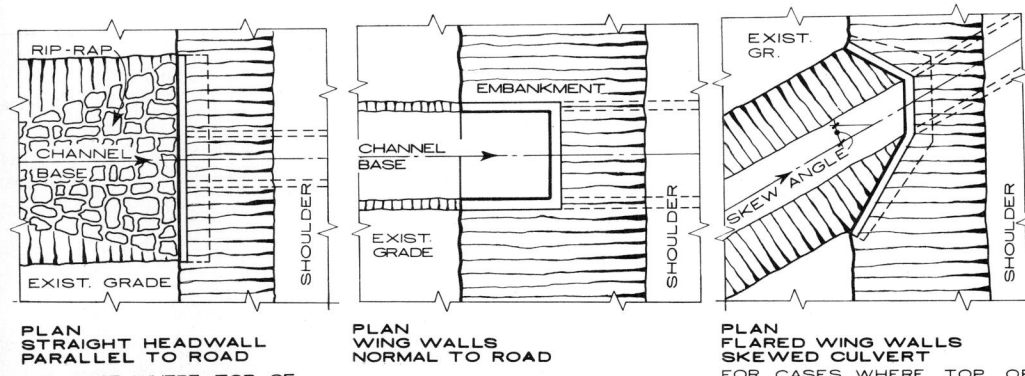

**PLAN STRAIGHT HEADWALL PARALLEL TO ROAD**
FOR CASE WHERE TOP OF DITCH SIDE IS ABOVE TOP OF CULVERT OR PIPE

**PLAN WING WALLS NORMAL TO ROAD**
SHALLOW DITCHES OR UNDERPASS

**PLAN FLARED WING WALLS SKEWED CULVERT**
FOR CASES WHERE TOP OF PIPE IS ABOVE TOP OF DITCH SIDES

## HEADWALL DESIGN AS CONTROLLED BY TOPOGRAPHY

## n VALUES FOR MANNING FORMULA

| CHANNEL SURFACE | n |
|---|---|
| Cast iron | 0.012 |
| Corrugated steel | 0.032 |
| Clay tile | 0.014 |
| Cement grout | 0.013 |
| Concrete | 0.015 |
| Earth ditch | 0.023 |
| Cut rock channel | 0.033 |
| Winding channel | 0.025 |

## NOTES

1. Determine velocity with Manning formula.
2. Check flow with formula Q = Va
   a = Cross-sectional area of water in sq ft.
3. For a given Q, adjust channel shape, size, and/or slope to obtain desired velocity (noneroding for earth and grass ditches, etc.)

## MANNING FORMULA

$$V = \left(\frac{1.486}{n}\right) r^{0.67} S^{0.5}$$

= Velocity (ft/sec)
n = From table (n Values for Manning Formula)
r = Hydraulic radius
See Channel Properties for derivation of r
S = Slope $\left(\frac{\text{drop in ft}}{\text{length in ft}}\right)$

EXAMPLE: Assume concrete V-channel

W = 2 ft
h = 0.5 ft
S = 0.005  (see site plan—example)
r = 0.37 (calculated using V-channel properties)
$$V = \left(\frac{1.486}{0.015}\right)(0.37)^{0.67}(0.005)^{0.5}$$
= 2.6 ft/sec (see runoff velocity table)

### CHECK FLOW

Q = Va (a from Channel Properties)
= 2.6 (0.5) = 1.3 cu ft/sec
1.04 cu ft/sec required from example above using the Rational Formula; therefore, flow is OK.

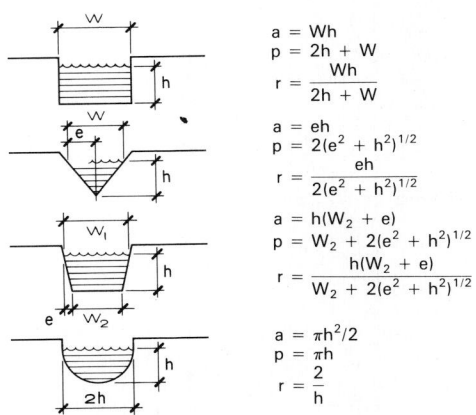

a = Wh
p = 2h + W
$r = \frac{Wh}{2h + W}$

a = eh
$p = 2(e^2 + h^2)^{1/2}$
$r = \frac{eh}{2(e^2 + h^2)^{1/2}}$

$a = h(W_2 + e)$
$p = W_2 + 2(e^2 + h^2)^{1/2}$
$r = \frac{h(W_2 + e)}{W_2 + 2(e^2 + h^2)^{1/2}}$

$a = \pi h^2/2$
$p = \pi h$
$r = \frac{2}{h}$

a = AREA OF WATER SECTION
p = WETTED PERIMETER
r = a/p = HYDRAULIC RADIUS

**CHANNEL PROPERTIES**

## APPROXIMATE METHOD FOR SIZING CHANNELS

Fred W. Hegel, AIA; Denver, Colorado
Seelye, see data sources

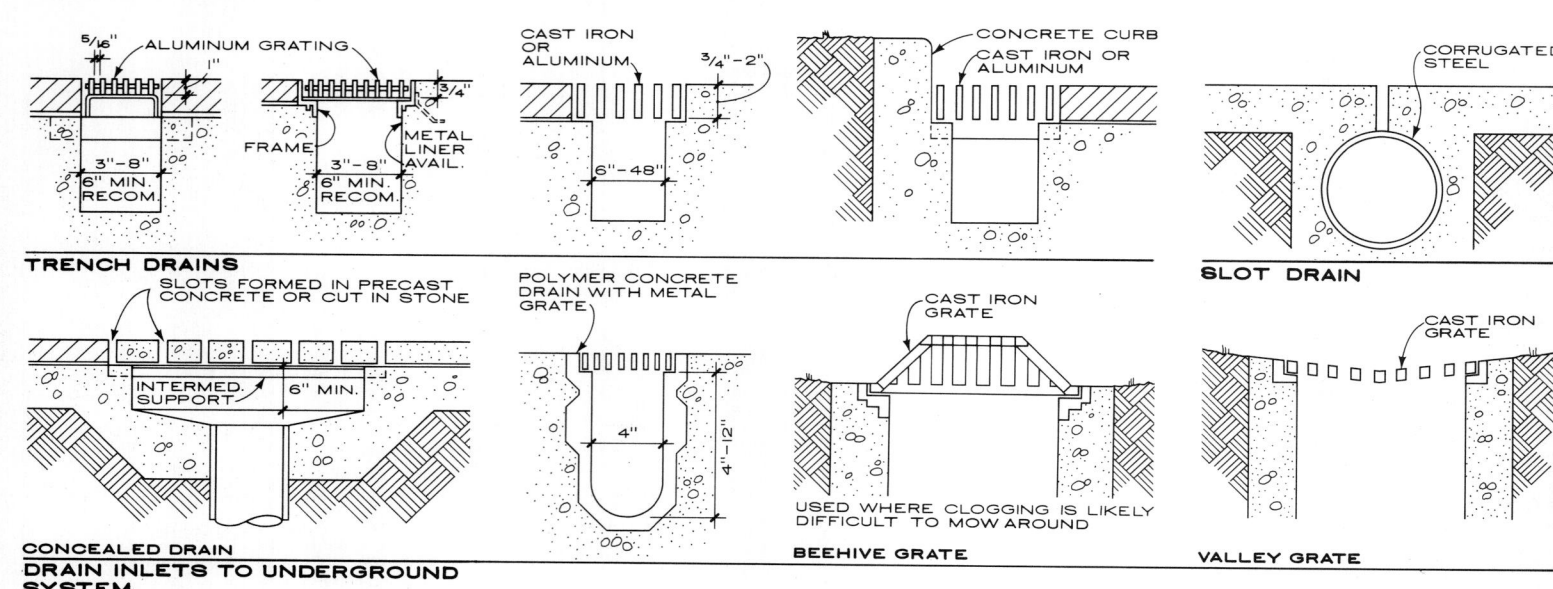

**TRENCH DRAINS**

**SLOT DRAIN**

**CONCEALED DRAIN**

USED WHERE CLOGGING IS LIKELY DIFFICULT TO MOW AROUND

**BEEHIVE GRATE**

**VALLEY GRATE**

**DRAIN INLETS TO UNDERGROUND SYSTEM**

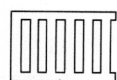 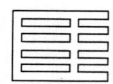 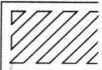     

USE GRATING DESIGNED FOR EXTERIOR USE AND CORRECT WHEEL LOAD

**GRATING DESIGNS–STANDARD**

## GRATE SIZING

Most gratings are oversized to prevent a buildup of water. See manufacturers' catalogs for free area.

Formula shown for sizing gratings is based on a given allowable depth of water (d) over the grating.

$Q = .66\ CA\ (64.4\ d)^{.5}$

A = Free area (square feet)
d = Allowable depth of water above grate (feet)
C = Orifice coefficient
    .6 for square edges
    .8 for round edges
.66 = Clogging factor

CHECK DAMS USED WHERE CHANNEL SLOPE AND VELOCITY WILL CAUSE EROSION

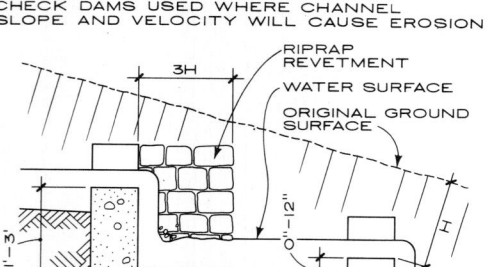

RIPRAP REVETMENT
WATER SURFACE
ORIGINAL GROUND SURFACE
SLOPE 0.002 MAX.

**CHECK DAMS**

## DETENTION

Check with local code requirements for control of storm water. Many require runoff to be maintained at predevelopment rates. This is accomplished with a detention facility upstream of a controlled outlet structure. The detention basin may be a structure or a paved or grass basin. If soil types permit, seepage may be used to dispose of runoff accumulated in a grass basin. The volume of detention required can be approximated by the following formula:

AMOUNT OF DETENTION:

$Vol. = (C_{dev.} - C_{hist.})AD$

D = Design storm depth (inches)
A = Area site (acres)
$C_{dev.}$ = C from table for developed land
$C_{hist.}$ = C from table for land prior to development

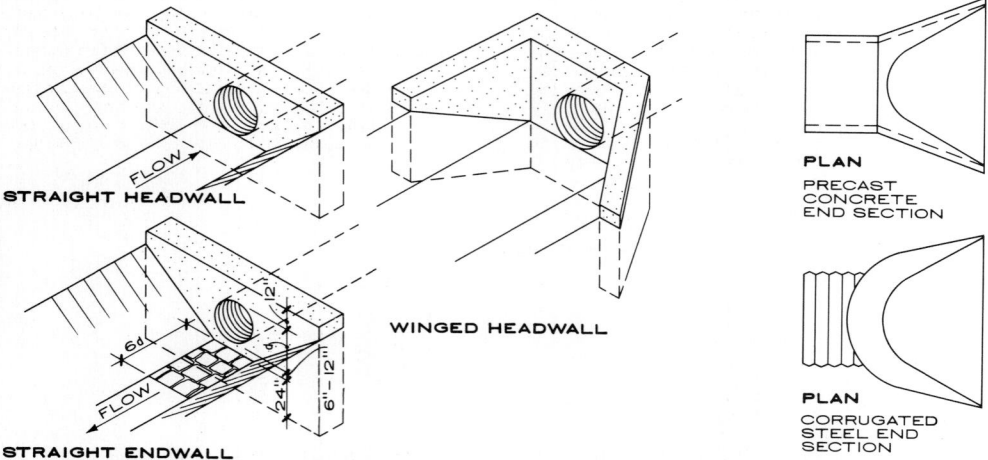

**STRAIGHT HEADWALL**

**WINGED HEADWALL**

**STRAIGHT ENDWALL**

**PLAN** PRECAST CONCRETE END SECTION

**PLAN** CORRUGATED STEEL END SECTION

**HEADWALLS AND ENDWALLS**

## SLOPES

| DESCRIPTION | MIN. % | MAX. % | REC. % |
|---|---|---|---|
| Grass (mowed) | 1 | 25 | 1.5–10 |
|   (athletic field) | .5 | 2 | 1 |
| Walks (Long.) | .5 | 12* | 1.5 |
|   (Transv.) | 1 | 4 | 1–2 |
| Streets (Long.) | .5 | 20 | 1–10 |
| Parking | 1 | 5 | 2–3 |
| Channels | | | |
|   Grass swale | 1 | 8 | 1.5–2 |
|   Paved swale | .5 | 12 | 4–6 |

*8.3% max. for handicapped

## RUN-OFF VELOCITY

| VELOCITIES | MIN. | MAX. |
|---|---|---|
| CHANNEL | FT/SEC | FT/SEC |
| Grass | 2 | 4 |
| Concrete | 2 | 10 |
| Gravel | 2 | 3 |
| Asphalt | 2 | 7.5 |
| Sand | .5 | 1.5 |

Fred W. Hegel, AIA; Denver, Colorado
Seelye; Landphair and Klatt; see data sources

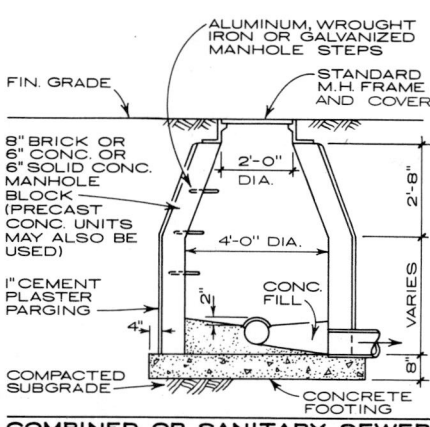

**COMBINED OR SANITARY SEWER MANHOLE**

**NOTES**

1. Parging may be omitted in construction of storm sewer manholes.
2. Brick and block walls to be as shown for manholes up to 12 ft deep. For that part of manhole deeper than 12 ft, brick and block walls shall be 12 in. thick. Manholes over 12 ft deep shall have a 12 in. thick base.

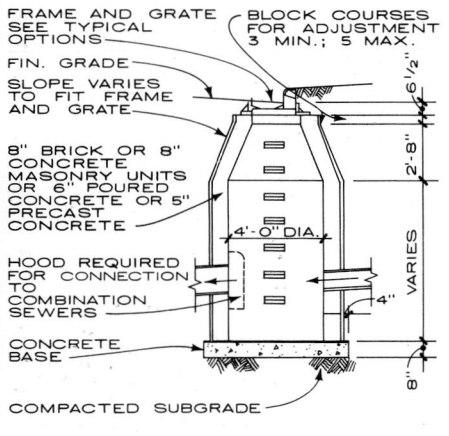

**CATCH BASIN**

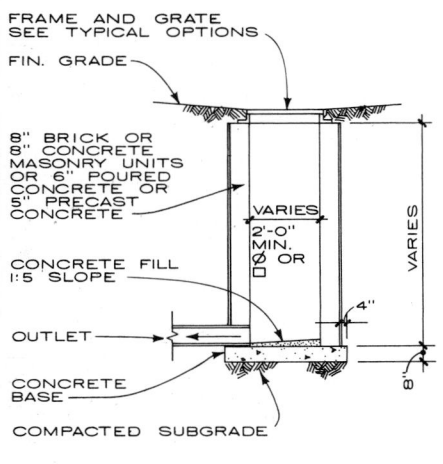

**INLET**

Kurt N. Pronske, P.E.; Reston, Virginia

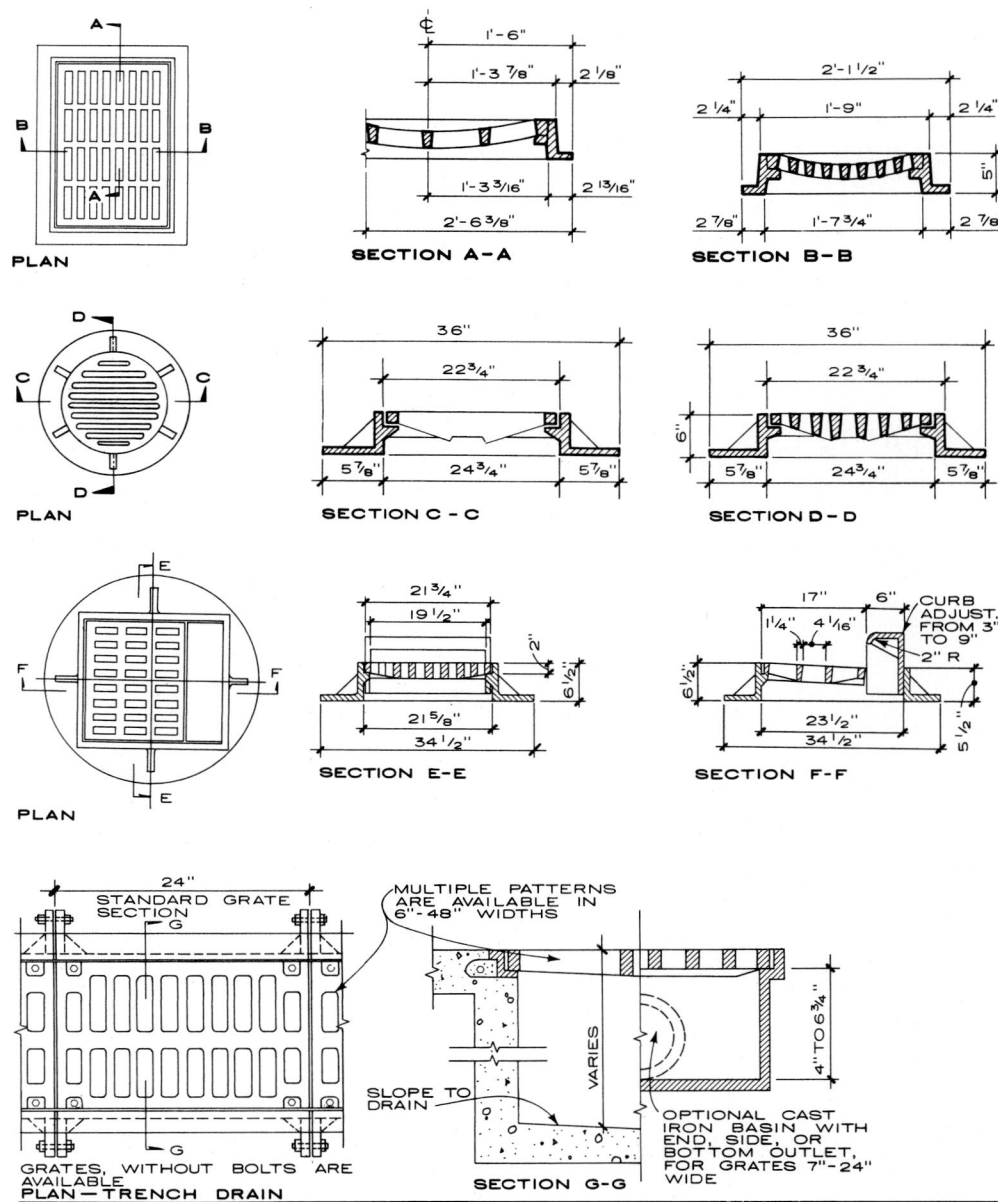

**TYPICAL FRAMES AND GRATES**

**NOTES**

1. A great number of standard shapes and sizes of frames and grates are available. They are constructed of cast or ductile iron for light or heavy duty loading conditions. The available shapes are shown above: round, rectangular or square, and linear. In addition, grates may be flat, concave, or convex. Manufacturers' catalogs and local foundries should be consulted for the full range of castings.

2. Drainage structures with grated openings should be located on the periphery of traveled ways or beyond to minimize their contact with pedestrian or vehicular traffic. Grates that will be susceptible to foot or narrow wheel contact must be so constructed as to prevent penetration by heels, crutch and cane tips, and slim tires, but still serve to provide sufficient drainage. This can be done by reducing the size of each unit opening and increasing the overall size or number of grates. Where only narrow wheel use is expected, slotted gratings can be used if the slots are oriented transversely to the direction of traffic.

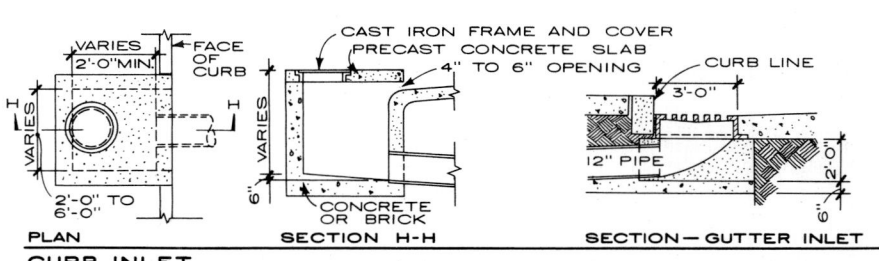

**CURB INLET**

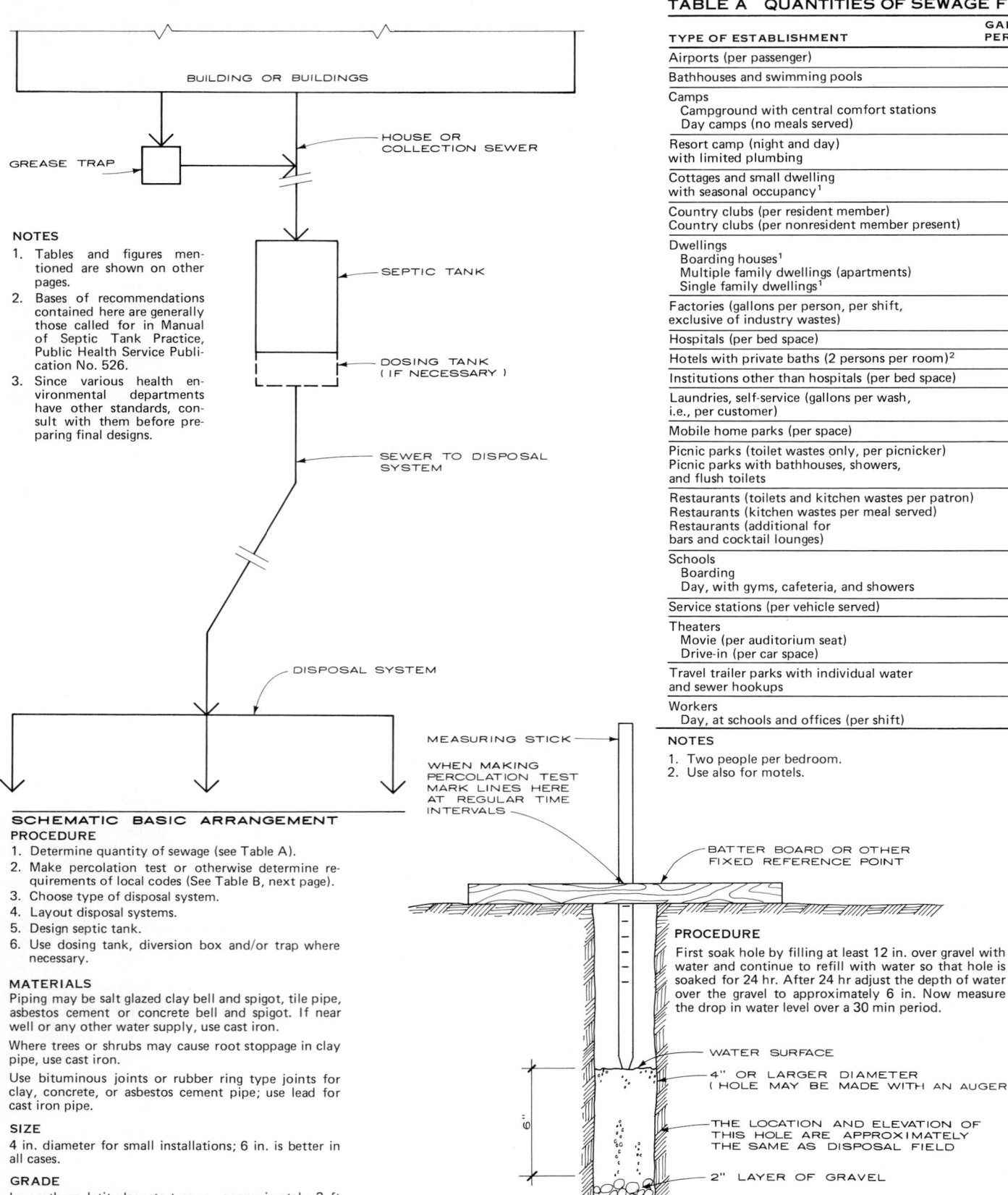

### NOTES

1. Tables and figures mentioned are shown on other pages.
2. Bases of recommendations contained here are generally those called for in Manual of Septic Tank Practice, Public Health Service Publication No. 526.
3. Since various health environmental departments have other standards, consult with them before preparing final designs.

## SCHEMATIC BASIC ARRANGEMENT

### PROCEDURE

1. Determine quantity of sewage (see Table A).
2. Make percolation test or otherwise determine requirements of local codes (See Table B, next page).
3. Choose type of disposal system.
4. Layout disposal systems.
5. Design septic tank.
6. Use dosing tank, diversion box and/or trap where necessary.

### MATERIALS

Piping may be salt glazed clay bell and spigot, tile pipe, asbestos cement or concrete bell and spigot. If near well or any other water supply, use cast iron.

Where trees or shrubs may cause root stoppage in clay pipe, use cast iron.

Use bituminous joints or rubber ring type joints for clay, concrete, or asbestos cement pipe; use lead for cast iron pipe.

### SIZE

4 in. diameter for small installations; 6 in. is better in all cases.

### GRADE

In northern latitudes, start sewer approximately 3 ft below grade. In southern latitudes, sewer may start just below grade.

### PITCH

Pitch 4 in. sewer $1/4$ in./ft minimum. Pitch 6 in. sewer $1/8$ in./ft minimum.

## TABLE A QUANTITIES OF SEWAGE FLOWS

| TYPE OF ESTABLISHMENT | GALLONS PER PERSON PER DAY |
|---|---|
| Airports (per passenger) | 5 |
| Bathhouses and swimming pools | 10 |
| Camps | |
|    Campground with central comfort stations | 35 |
|    Day camps (no meals served) | 15 |
| Resort camp (night and day) with limited plumbing | 50 |
| Cottages and small dwelling with seasonal occupancy[1] | 50 |
| Country clubs (per resident member) | 100 |
| Country clubs (per nonresident member present) | 25 |
| Dwellings | |
|    Boarding houses[1] | 50 |
|    Multiple family dwellings (apartments) | 60 |
|    Single family dwellings[1] | 75 |
| Factories (gallons per person, per shift, exclusive of industry wastes) | 35 |
| Hospitals (per bed space) | 250+ |
| Hotels with private baths (2 persons per room)[2] | 60 |
| Institutions other than hospitals (per bed space) | 125 |
| Laundries, self-service (gallons per wash, i.e., per customer) | 50 |
| Mobile home parks (per space) | 250 |
| Picnic parks (toilet wastes only, per picnicker) | 5 |
| Picnic parks with bathhouses, showers, and flush toilets | 10 |
| Restaurants (toilets and kitchen wastes per patron) | 10 |
| Restaurants (kitchen wastes per meal served) | 3 |
| Restaurants (additional for bars and cocktail lounges) | 2 |
| Schools | |
|    Boarding | 100 |
|    Day, with gyms, cafeteria, and showers | 25 |
| Service stations (per vehicle served) | 10 |
| Theaters | |
|    Movie (per auditorium seat) | 5 |
|    Drive-in (per car space) | 5 |
| Travel trailer parks with individual water and sewer hookups | 100 |
| Workers | |
|    Day, at schools and offices (per shift) | 15 |

### NOTES

1. Two people per bedroom.
2. Use also for motels.

### PROCEDURE

First soak hole by filling at least 12 in. over gravel with water and continue to refill with water so that hole is soaked for 24 hr. After 24 hr adjust the depth of water over the gravel to approximately 6 in. Now measure the drop in water level over a 30 min period.

NOTE: THIS TEST IS RECOMMENDED BY THE ENVIRONMENTAL PROTECTION AGENCY. CHECK LOCAL REQUIREMENTS FOR OTHER TEST CONDITIONS

## METHOD OF MAKING PERCOLATION TEST

Jack L. Staunton, P.E.; Staunton and Freeman, Consulting Engineers; New York, New York

**TABLE B. ALLOWABLE RATE OF SEWAGE APPLICATION TO A SOIL ABSORPTION SYSTEM**

| PERCOLATION RATE [TIME (MIN) FOR WATER TO FALL 1 IN.] | MAXIMUM RATE OF SEWAGE APPLICATION (GAL/SQ FT/DAY)[1] FOR ABSORPTION TRENCHES,[2] SEEPAGE BEDS, AND SEEPAGE PITS[3] | PERCOLATION RATE [TIME (MIN) FOR WATER TO FALL 1 IN.] | MAXIMUM RATE OF SEWAGE APPLICATION (GAL/SQ FT/DAY)[1] FOR ABSORPTION TRENCHES,[2] SEEPAGE BEDS, AND SEEPAGE PITS[3] |
|---|---|---|---|
| 1 or less | 5.0 | 10 | 1.6 |
| 2 | 3.5 | 15 | 1.3 |
| 3 | 2.9 | 30[4] | 0.9 |
| 4 | 2.5 | 45[4] | 0.8 |
| 5 | 2.2 | 60[4,5] | 0.6 |

**NOTES**

1. Not including effluents from septic tanks that receive wastes from garbage grinders and automatic washing machines.
2. Absorption area is figured as trench bottom area and includes a statistical allowance for vertical sidewall area.
3. Absorption area for seepage pits is effective sidewall area.
4. Over 30 is unsuitable for seepage pits.
5. Over 60 is unsuitable for absorption systems.

If permissible, use sand filtration system. For subsurface sand filters use 1.15 gal/sq ft/day.

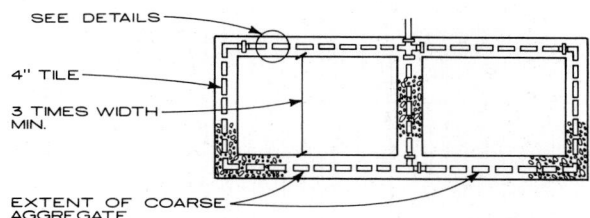

**ABSORPTION TRENCH ARRANGEMENT FOR LEVEL GROUND FOR HOUSEHOLD DISPOSAL**

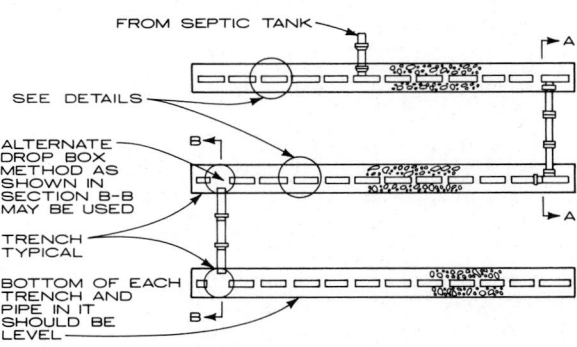

NOTE
INVERT OF THE OVERFLOW PIPE MUST BE AT LEAST 4" LOWER THAN INVERT OF THE SEPTIC TANK OUTLET

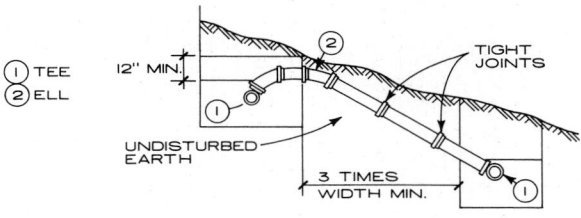

SECTION A-A

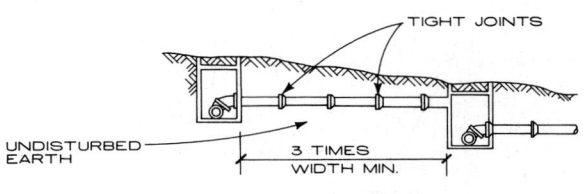

SECTION B-B

**ABSORPTION TRENCH ARRANGEMENT FOR HILLY SITE FOR HOUSEHOLD DISPOSAL**

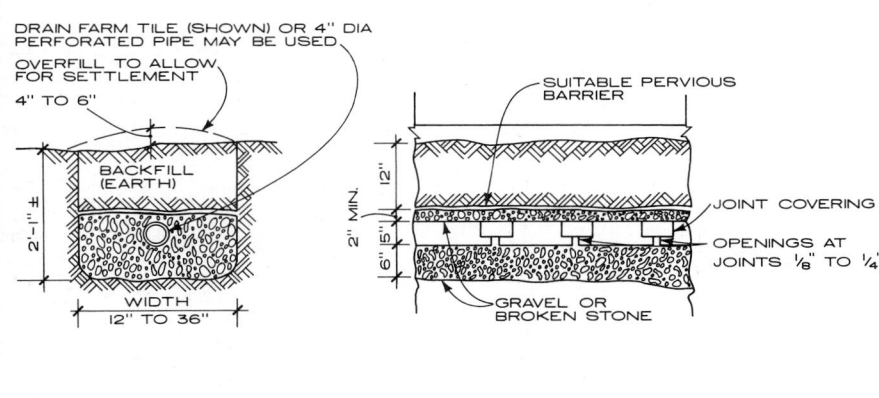

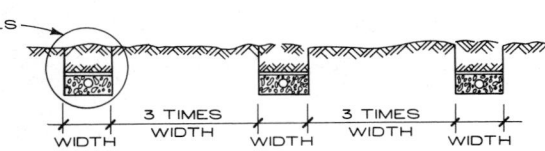

**ABSORPTION TRENCH SYSTEM DETAILS**

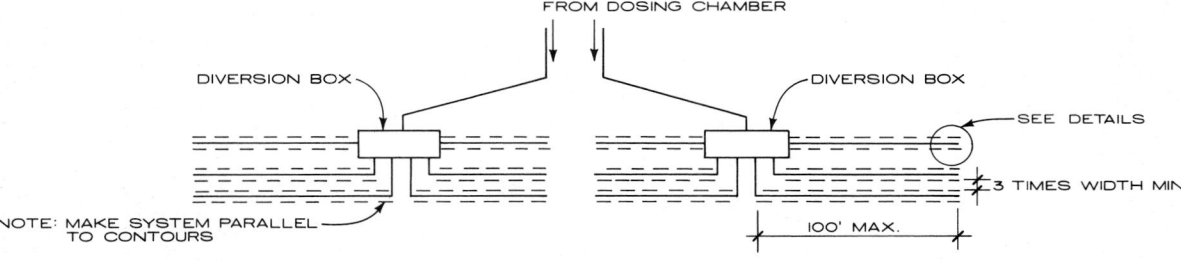

**ABSORPTION TRENCH ARRANGEMENT FOR INSTITUTIONAL AND LIGHT COMMERCIAL DISPOSAL**

Jack L. Staunton, P.E.; Staunton and Freeman, Consulting Engineers; New York, New York

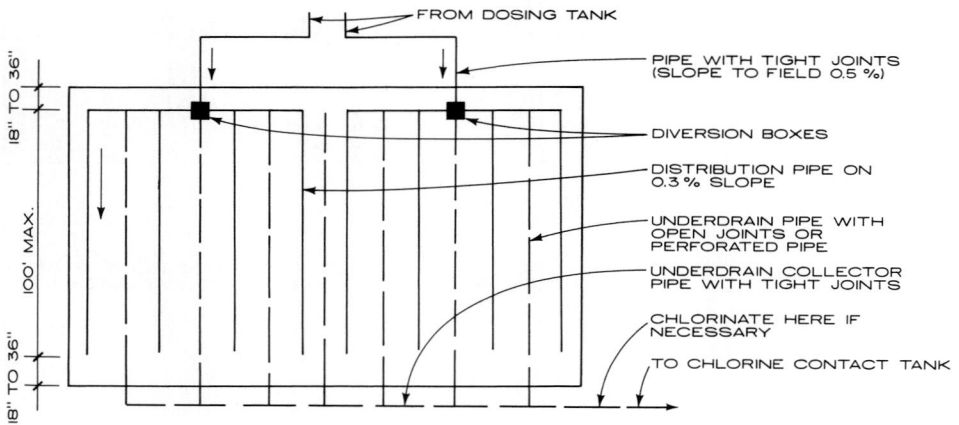

FROM DOSING TANK

18" TO 36"

100' MAX.

18" TO 36"

PIPE WITH TIGHT JOINTS (SLOPE TO FIELD 0.5 %)

DIVERSION BOXES

DISTRIBUTION PIPE ON 0.3 % SLOPE

UNDERDRAIN PIPE WITH OPEN JOINTS OR PERFORATED PIPE

UNDERDRAIN COLLECTOR PIPE WITH TIGHT JOINTS

CHLORINATE HERE IF NECESSARY

TO CHLORINE CONTACT TANK

**PLAN**

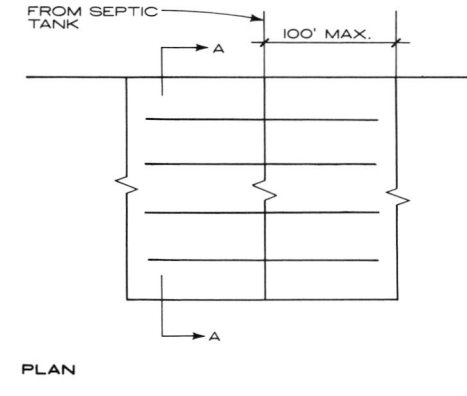

FROM SEPTIC TANK

100' MAX.

A

A

**PLAN**

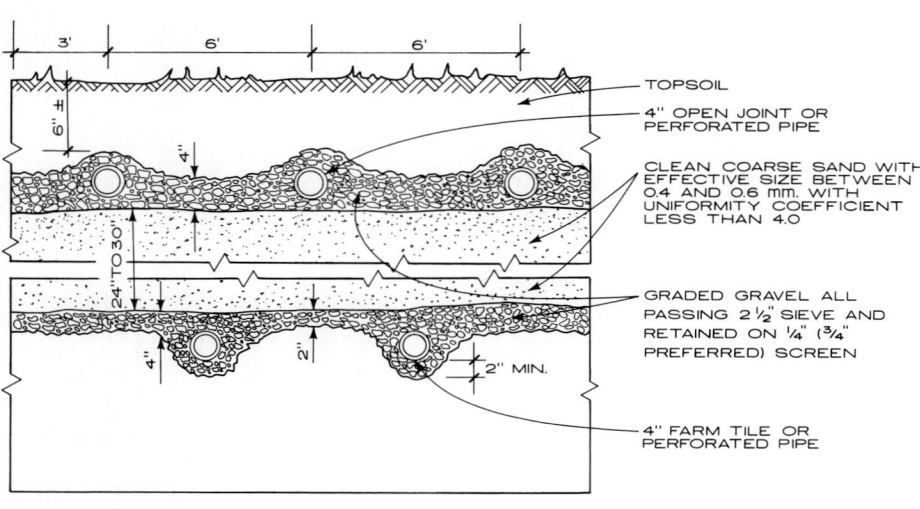

3'    6'    6'

TOPSOIL

4" OPEN JOINT OR PERFORATED PIPE

CLEAN COARSE SAND WITH EFFECTIVE SIZE BETWEEN 0.4 AND 0.6 mm. WITH UNIFORMITY COEFFICIENT LESS THAN 4.0

GRADED GRAVEL ALL PASSING 2½" SIEVE AND RETAINED ON ¼" (¾" PREFERRED) SCREEN

24" TO 30"

4"    2"    2" MIN.

4" FARM TILE OR PERFORATED PIPE

**SECTIONAL ELEVATION**

**SUBSURFACE SAND FILTER**

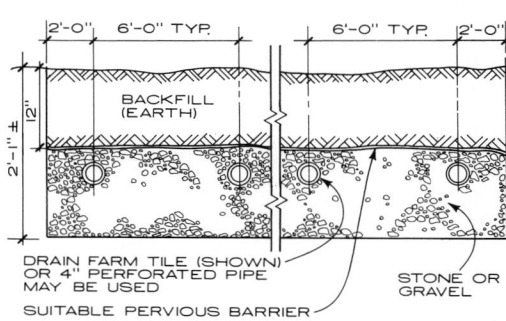

2'-0"    6'-0" TYP.    6'-0" TYP.    2'-0"

BACKFILL (EARTH)

2'-1" ±    12"

DRAIN FARM TILE (SHOWN) OR 4" PERFORATED PIPE MAY BE USED

SUITABLE PERVIOUS BARRIER

STONE OR GRAVEL

**SECTION A-A**

**SEEPAGE BED**

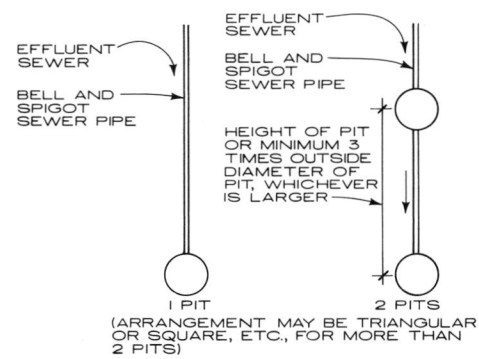

EFFLUENT SEWER

EFFLUENT SEWER

BELL AND SPIGOT SEWER PIPE

BELL AND SPIGOT SEWER PIPE

HEIGHT OF PIT OR MINIMUM 3 TIMES OUTSIDE DIAMETER OF PIT, WHICHEVER IS LARGER

1 PIT    2 PITS

(ARRANGEMENT MAY BE TRIANGULAR OR SQUARE, ETC., FOR MORE THAN 2 PITS)

**ARRANGEMENT**

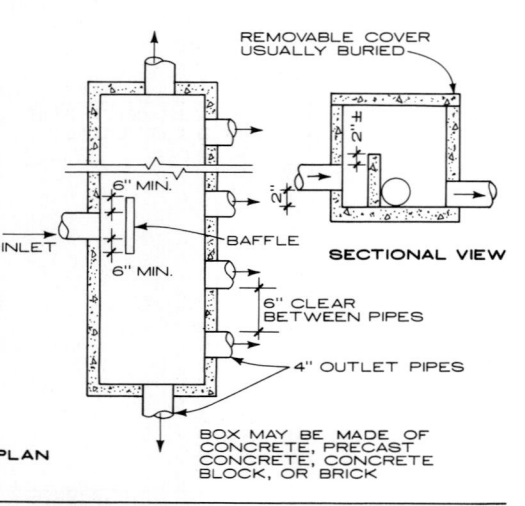

REMOVABLE COVER USUALLY BURIED

6" MIN.

2"

6" MIN.

INLET    BAFFLE

6" CLEAR BETWEEN PIPES

4" OUTLET PIPES

**SECTIONAL VIEW**

**PLAN**

BOX MAY BE MADE OF CONCRETE, PRECAST CONCRETE, CONCRETE BLOCK, OR BRICK

**DIVERSION BOX**

REINFORCED CONCRETE COVER WITH LIFTING RING

GRADE

PRECAST REINF. CONCRETE

INLET

2'-0"

OUTLET

SLOTS FOR LEACHING

STONE OR GRAVEL

4"  7'-6" DIA.  12"
USUALLY    4"

**SECTION**

CORBELED BRICK OR BLOCK IN MORTAR OR LAY BLOCK SO THAT HOLES ARE HORIZONTAL OR USE SPECIAL CONCRETE BLOCK

GRADE

STRAW

INLET

8"

**SECTION**

4" BLOCK WITH HOLES

INLET

STONE OR GRAVEL

12"

**PLAN OF 8" CONCRETE BLOCK PIT**

**SEEPAGE PITS**

Jack L. Staunton, P.E.; Staunton and Freeman, Consulting Engineers; New York, New York

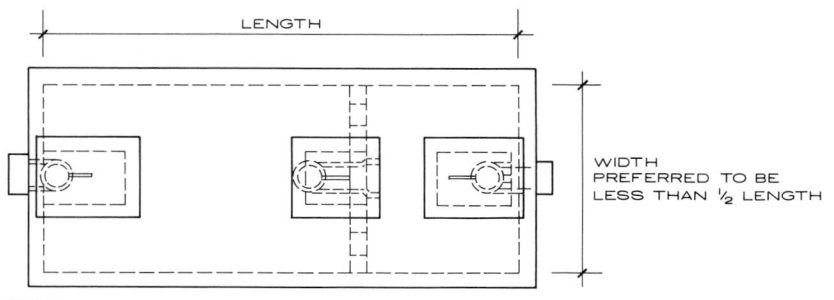

PLAN

LENGTH

WIDTH PREFERRED TO BE LESS THAN ½ LENGTH

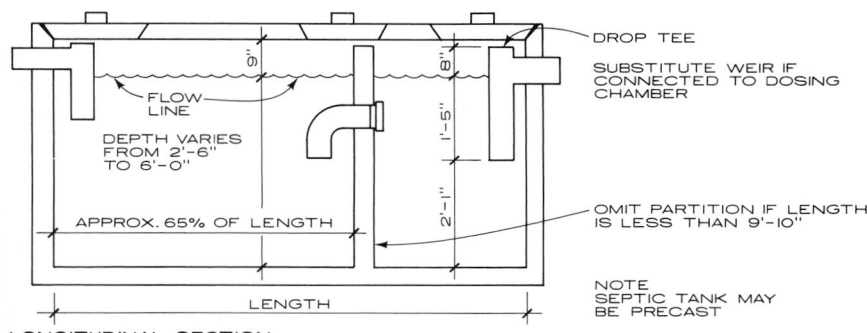

LONGITUDINAL SECTION

6"
8"
1'-5"
2'-1"

FLOW LINE

DEPTH VARIES FROM 2'-6" TO 6'-0"

APPROX. 65% OF LENGTH

LENGTH

DROP TEE

SUBSTITUTE WEIR IF CONNECTED TO DOSING CHAMBER

OMIT PARTITION IF LENGTH IS LESS THAN 9'-10"

NOTE
SEPTIC TANK MAY BE PRECAST

## SEPTIC TANK

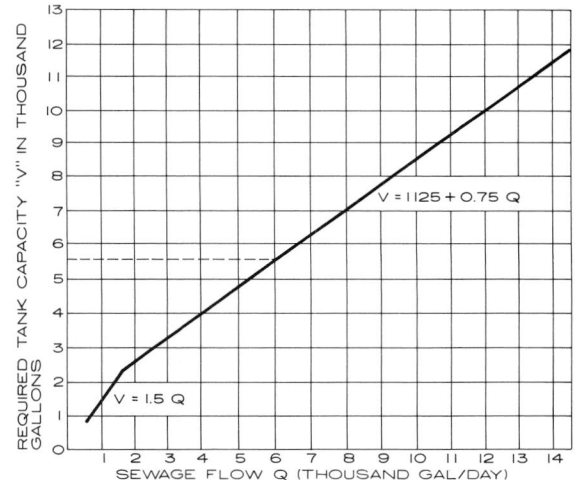

$V = 1125 + 0.75 Q$

$V = 1.5 Q$

REQUIRED TANK CAPACITY "V" IN THOUSAND GALLONS

SEWAGE FLOW Q (THOUSAND GAL/DAY)

## DETERMINATION OF SEPTIC TANK VOLUME

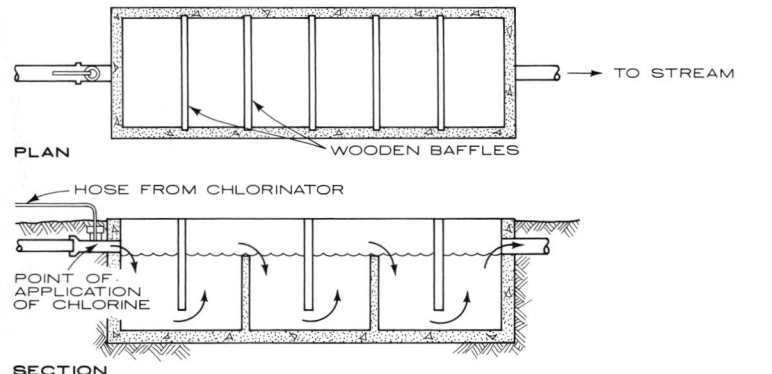

PLAN

WOODEN BAFFLES

TO STREAM

HOSE FROM CHLORINATOR

POINT OF APPLICATION OF CHLORINE

SECTION

## CHLORINE CONTACT CHAMBER

Jack L. Staunton, P.E.; Staunton and Freeman, Consulting Engineers; New York, New York

NOTES
• DOSE FROM CHAMBER TO EQUAL ¾ OF FARM TILE OR PERFORATED PIPE IN ONE FIELD
• PIPES MAY BE SUBSTITUTED FOR SIPHONS IF CONDITION DICTATES

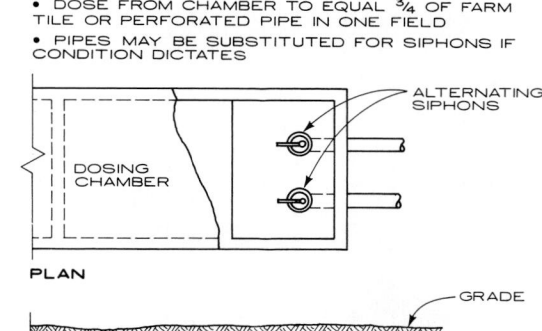

PLAN

DOSING CHAMBER

ALTERNATING SIPHONS

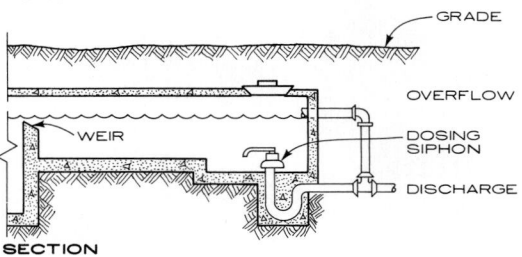

SECTION

GRADE

OVERFLOW

DOSING SIPHON

DISCHARGE

WEIR

## DOSING CHAMBER WITH ALTERNATING SIPHONS

NOTE
GREASE TRAPS TO BE USED ONLY IF THEY ARE CLEANED DAILY

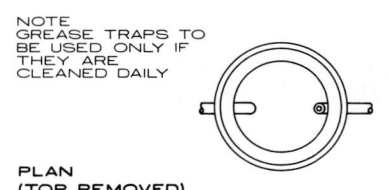

PLAN (TOP REMOVED)

INLET

OUTLET

3" TO 6"

12"

±3'-0"

6"

6"

CLAY TILE PIPE SEALED IN CONCRETE

SECTION

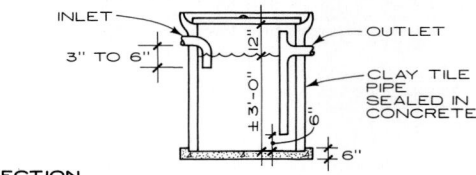

PLAN (TOP REMOVED)

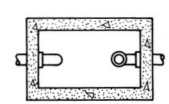

INLET

3" TO 6"

12"

±3'-0"

COVER OF REINFORCED CONCRETE, ALUMINUM, OR CAST IRON

OUTLET

SECTION
CONCRETE BOX

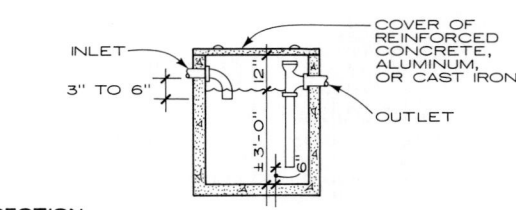

±3'-0"

2" INLET FROM KITCHEN SINK

2'-0"

±3'-0"

ALUMINUM OR CAST IRON COVER

CLEANOUT

4" OUTLET TO MAIN SEWER

3" TO 6"

## TYPICAL GREASE TRAPS

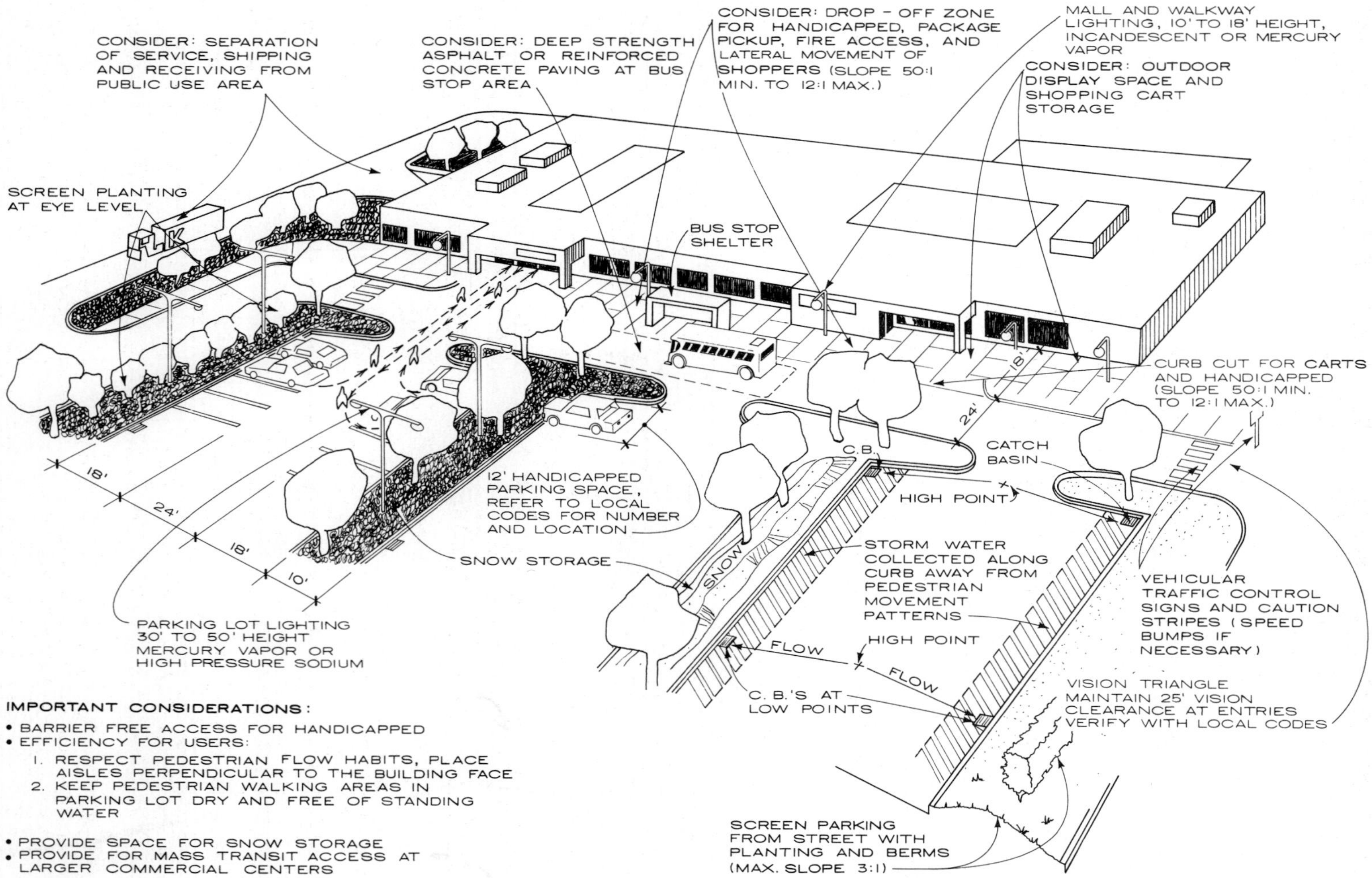

CONSIDER: SEPARATION OF SERVICE, SHIPPING AND RECEIVING FROM PUBLIC USE AREA

CONSIDER: DEEP STRENGTH ASPHALT OR REINFORCED CONCRETE PAVING AT BUS STOP AREA

CONSIDER: DROP - OFF ZONE FOR HANDICAPPED, PACKAGE PICKUP, FIRE ACCESS, AND LATERAL MOVEMENT OF SHOPPERS (SLOPE 50:1 MIN. TO 12:1 MAX.)

MALL AND WALKWAY LIGHTING, 10' TO 18' HEIGHT, INCANDESCENT OR MERCURY VAPOR

CONSIDER: OUTDOOR DISPLAY SPACE AND SHOPPING CART STORAGE

SCREEN PLANTING AT EYE LEVEL

BUS STOP SHELTER

12' HANDICAPPED PARKING SPACE, REFER TO LOCAL CODES FOR NUMBER AND LOCATION

SNOW STORAGE

CURB CUT FOR CARTS AND HANDICAPPED (SLOPE 50:1 MIN. TO 12:1 MAX.)

C.B.

CATCH BASIN

HIGH POINT

STORM WATER COLLECTED ALONG CURB AWAY FROM PEDESTRIAN MOVEMENT PATTERNS

HIGH POINT

FLOW

FLOW

VEHICULAR TRAFFIC CONTROL SIGNS AND CAUTION STRIPES (SPEED BUMPS IF NECESSARY)

C.B.'S AT LOW POINTS

VISION TRIANGLE MAINTAIN 25' VISION CLEARANCE AT ENTRIES VERIFY WITH LOCAL CODES

PARKING LOT LIGHTING 30' TO 50' HEIGHT MERCURY VAPOR OR HIGH PRESSURE SODIUM

SCREEN PARKING FROM STREET WITH PLANTING AND BERMS (MAX. SLOPE 3:1)

18'   24'   18'   10'

**IMPORTANT CONSIDERATIONS:**

- BARRIER FREE ACCESS FOR HANDICAPPED
- EFFICIENCY FOR USERS:
  1. RESPECT PEDESTRIAN FLOW HABITS, PLACE AISLES PERPENDICULAR TO THE BUILDING FACE
  2. KEEP PEDESTRIAN WALKING AREAS IN PARKING LOT DRY AND FREE OF STANDING WATER
- PROVIDE SPACE FOR SNOW STORAGE
- PROVIDE FOR MASS TRANSIT ACCESS AT LARGER COMMERCIAL CENTERS

## PLANTING CONSIDERATIONS

The distribution and placement of plants in parking areas can help to relieve the visually overwhelming scale of large parking lots. To maximize the impact of landscape materials, the screening capabilities of the plants must be considered. High branching canopy trees do not create a visual screen at eye level. When the landscaped area is concentrated in islands large enough to accommodate a diversified mixture of canopy and flowering trees, evergreen trees, and shrubs, visual screening via plants is much more effective. Planting low branching, densely foliated trees and shrubs can soften the visual impact of large parking areas. Consider the use of evergreens and avoid plants that drop fruit or sap.

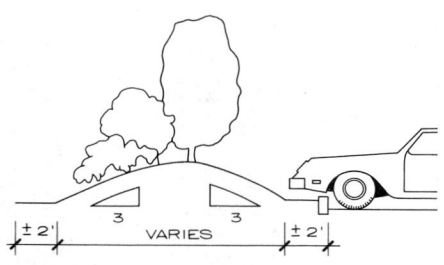

**BERM SECTION**

±2'   VARIES   ±2'   3   3

## DESIGN CONSIDERATIONS

While efficiency (number of spaces per gross acres) is the major practical consideration in the development of parking areas, several other important design questions exist. Barrier free design is mandatory in most communities. Parking spaces for the handicapped should be designated near building entrances. Curb cuts for wheelchairs should be provided at entrances. The lots should not only be efficient in terms of parking spaces provided, but should also allow maximum efficiency for pedestrians once they leave their vehicles.

Pedestrians habitually walk in the aisles behind parked vehicles. This should be recognized in the orientation of the aisles to building entrances. When aisles are perpendicular to the building face, pedestrians can walk to and from the building without squeezing between parked cars with carts and packages. Pedestrian movement areas should be graded to avoid creating standing water in the paths of pedestrians. Space should be provided for snow storage within parking areas, if required.

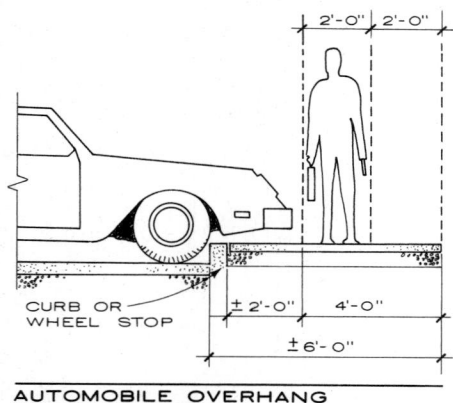

**AUTOMOBILE OVERHANG REQUIREMENT**

2'-0"   2'-0"   ±2'-0"   4'-0"   ±6'-0"

CURB OR WHEEL STOP

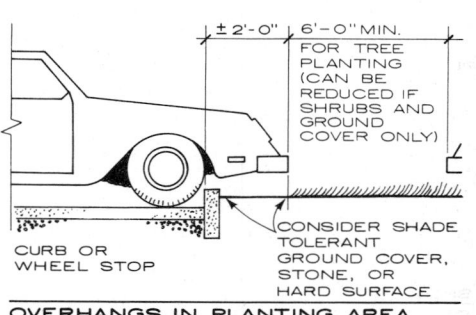

**OVERHANGS IN PLANTING AREA**

±2'-0"   6'-0" MIN. FOR TREE PLANTING (CAN BE REDUCED IF SHRUBS AND GROUND COVER ONLY)

CURB OR WHEEL STOP

CONSIDER SHADE TOLERANT GROUND COVER, STONE, OR HARD SURFACE

William H. Evans, AIA; San Antonio, Texas
Johnson, Johnson & Roy, Inc.; Ann Arbor, Michigan

**SITE IMPROVEMENTS**

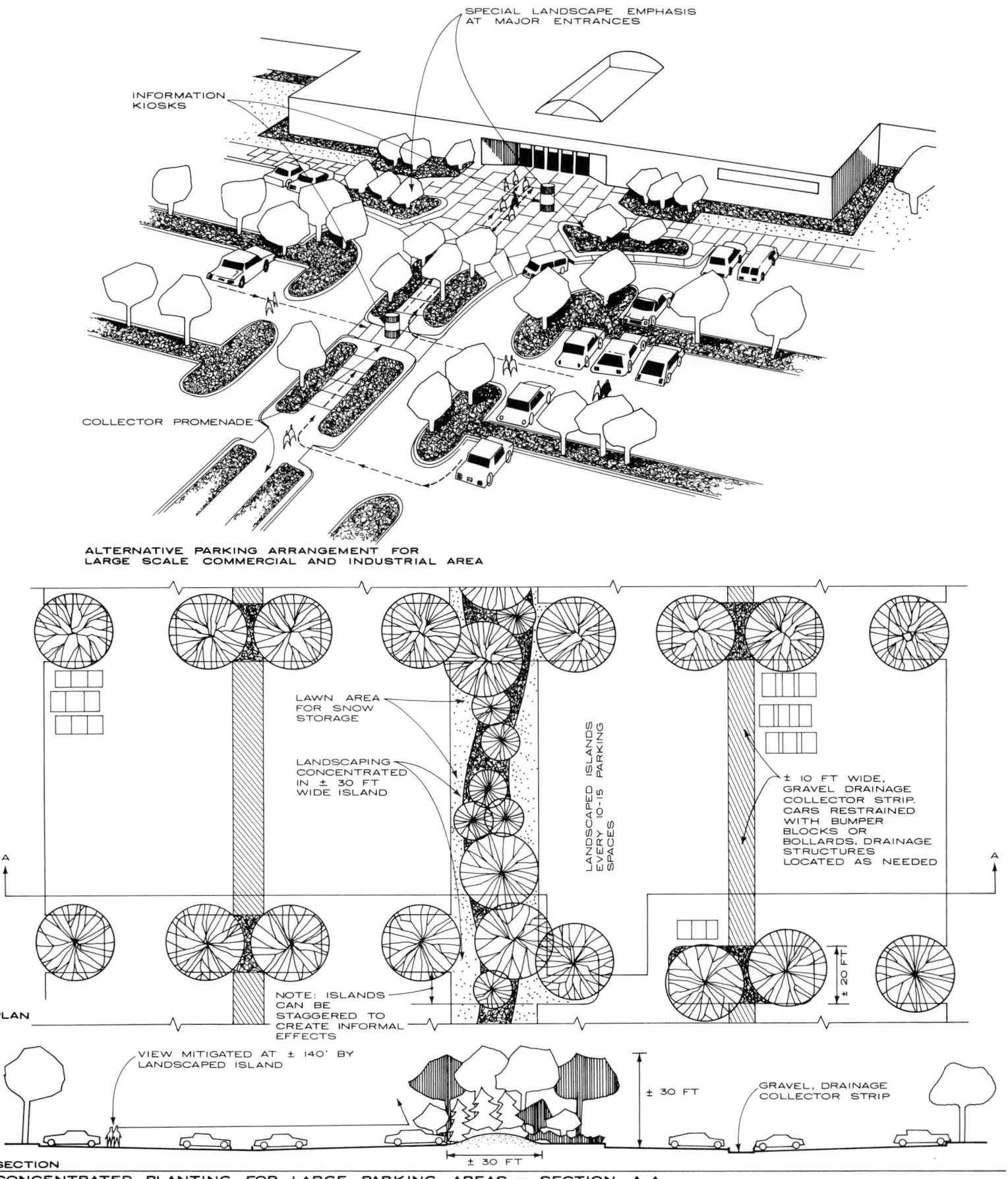

SPECIAL LANDSCAPE EMPHASIS AT MAJOR ENTRANCES

INFORMATION KIOSKS

COLLECTOR PROMENADE

ALTERNATIVE PARKING ARRANGEMENT FOR LARGE SCALE COMMERCIAL AND INDUSTRIAL AREA

LAWN AREA FOR SNOW STORAGE

LANDSCAPING CONCENTRATED IN ± 30 FT WIDE ISLAND

LANDSCAPED ISLANDS EVERY 10-15 PARKING SPACES

± 10 FT WIDE, GRAVEL DRAINAGE COLLECTOR STRIP. CARS RESTRAINED WITH BUMPER BLOCKS OR BOLLARDS. DRAINAGE STRUCTURES LOCATED AS NEEDED

± 20 FT

A

A

PLAN

NOTE: ISLANDS CAN BE STAGGERED TO CREATE INFORMAL EFFECTS

VIEW MITIGATED AT ± 140' BY LANDSCAPED ISLAND

± 30 FT

GRAVEL, DRAINAGE COLLECTOR STRIP

SECTION

± 30 FT

CONCENTRATED PLANTING FOR LARGE PARKING AREAS — SECTION A-A

Johnson, Johnson & Roy, Inc.; Ann Arbor, Michigan

**SITE IMPROVEMENTS** 2

## VEHICULAR CONSIDERATIONS

There are strong differences between the perceptual performance of the driver and that of the pedestrian. Increasing speed imposes five limitations on man:

1. MAN'S CONCENTRATION INCREASES: While stationary or walking, a person's attention may be widely dispersed. When moving in an automobile, however, he or she concentrates on those factors that are relevant to the driving experience.

2. THE POINT OF CONCENTRATION RECEDES: As speed or motion increases, a person's concentration is directed at a focal point increasingly farther away.

3. PERIPHERAL VISION DIMINISHES: As the eye concentrates on detail at a point of focus a great distance ahead, the angular field of vision shrinks. This shrinking process is a function of focusing distance, angle of vision, and distance of foreground detail.

4. FOREGROUND DETAIL FADES INCREASINGLY: While concentrating on more significant distant objects, a person perceives foreground objects to be moving and increasingly blurred.

5. SPACE PERCEPTION BECOMES IMPAIRED: As the time available for perceiving objects decreases, specific details become less noticeable, making spatial perception more difficult.

With an increasing rate of motion, it becomes more and more important that copy, including illustrations and symbols, be created specifically for out-of-doors use and not merely rescaled from other media of communication. The safety of the motorist and passengers can depend on the clarity of messages conveyed by signs.

### VEHICLE SPEEDS VERSUS LETTER HEIGHT ON TRAFFIC SIGNS

| INITIAL SPEED | DISTANCE TRAVELED WHILE READING | DISTANCE TRAVELED WHILE SLOWING | TOTAL DISTANCE | SIZE OF COPY AT 65 FT/IN. |
|---|---|---|---|---|
| 30 mph | 110 ft | 200 ft | 310 ft | 4.8 in. |
| 40 mph | 147 ft | 307 ft | 454 ft | 7.0 in. |
| 50 mph | 183 ft | 360 ft | 543 ft | 8.4 in. |
| 60 mph | 220 ft | 390 ft | 610 ft | 9.4 in. |

NOTE: It is recommended that street name signs have 4 in. letters in area where vehicle speeds are 30–35 mph. For speeds of 40 mph and over, a 5 in. letter size is recommended.

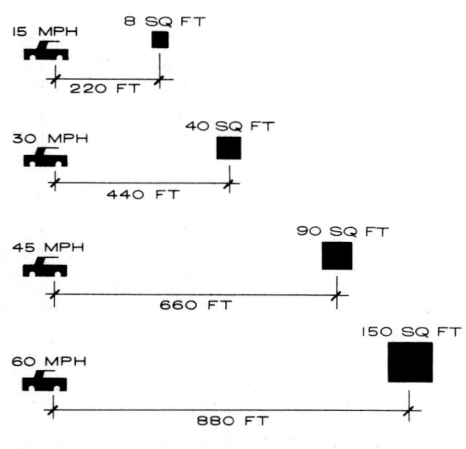

**SPEED, SIGHT DISTANCE AND GRAPHIC SIZE RELATIONSHIPS**
NOTE: LETTERS SHOULD CONSTITUTE APPROXIMATELY 40% OF GRAPHIC'S AREA

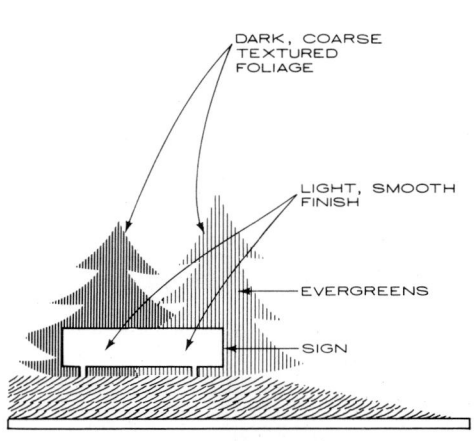

**CONSIDER BACKGROUND WHEN CHOOSING COLOR AND MATERIALS**

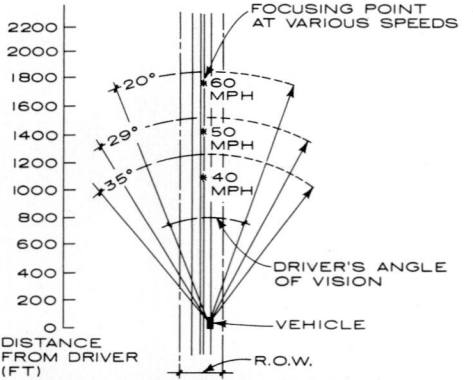

**RELATIONSHIP BETWEEN DRIVER'S FOCUSING POINT AND ANGLE OF VISION** DOES NOT CONSIDER EFFECT OF PRECEDING TRAFFIC

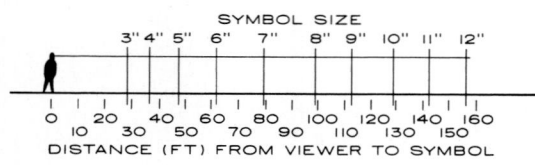

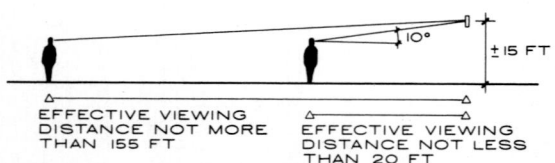

**PEDESTRIAN CONSIDERATIONS**

Johnson, Johnson & Roy, Inc.; Ann Arbor, Michigan

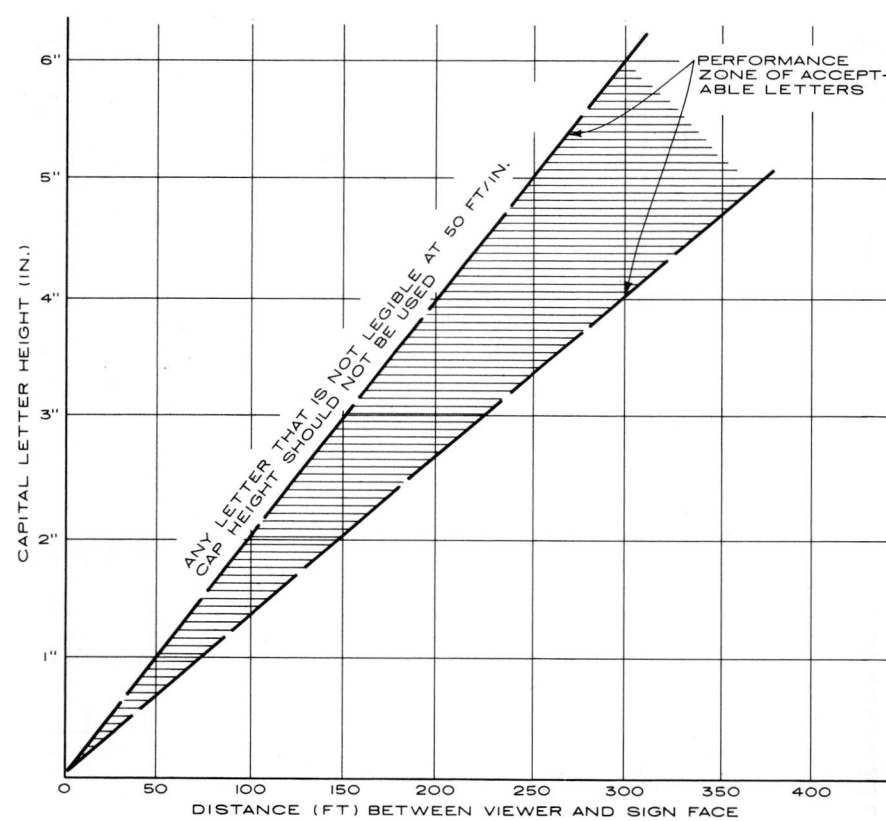

### NOTE

Under normal daylight conditions, with normal vision, and an angular distortion of 0° approximately 50 ft/in. of capital height can be taken as a guideline for minimal legibility, as seen from the chart.

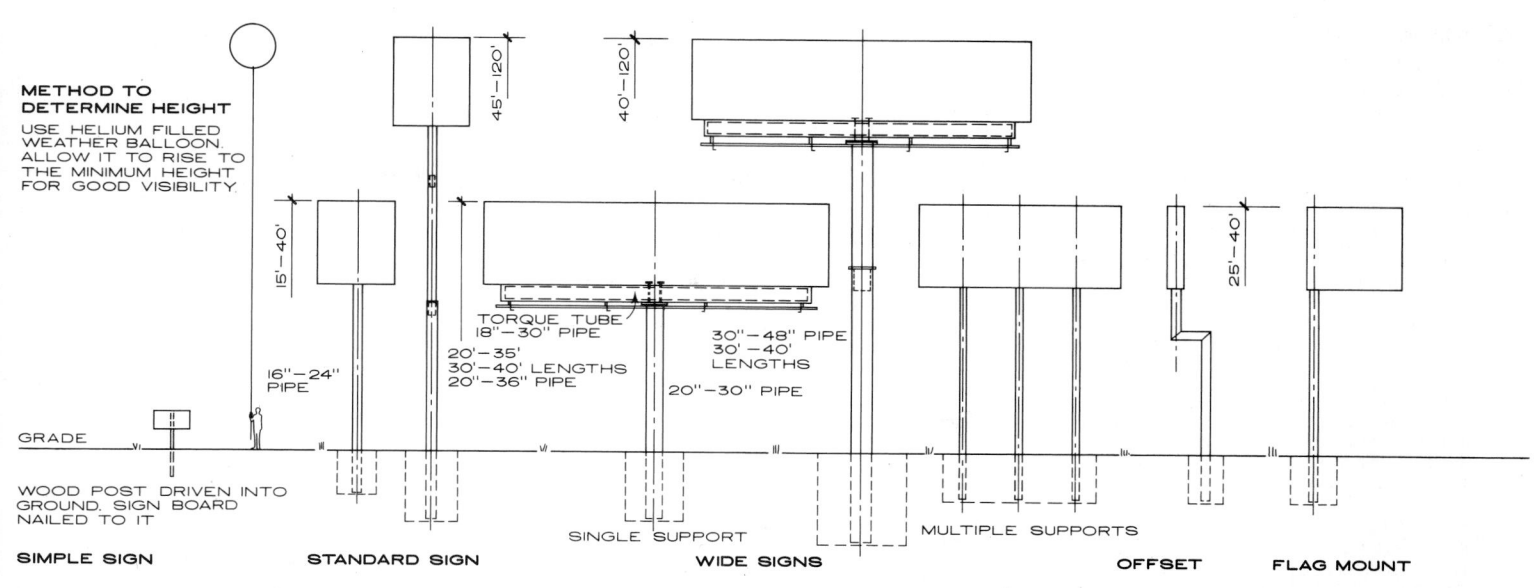

**METHOD TO DETERMINE HEIGHT**
USE HELIUM FILLED WEATHER BALLOON. ALLOW IT TO RISE TO THE MINIMUM HEIGHT FOR GOOD VISIBILITY.

WOOD POST DRIVEN INTO GROUND. SIGN BOARD NAILED TO IT

GRADE

16"–24" PIPE

TORQUE TUBE 18"–30" PIPE

20'–35' 30'–40' LENGTHS 20"–36" PIPE

30"–48" PIPE 30'–40' LENGTHS

20"–30" PIPE

SINGLE SUPPORT

MULTIPLE SUPPORTS

SIMPLE SIGN     STANDARD SIGN     WIDE SIGNS     OFFSET     FLAG MOUNT

## TYPES OF SIGNS

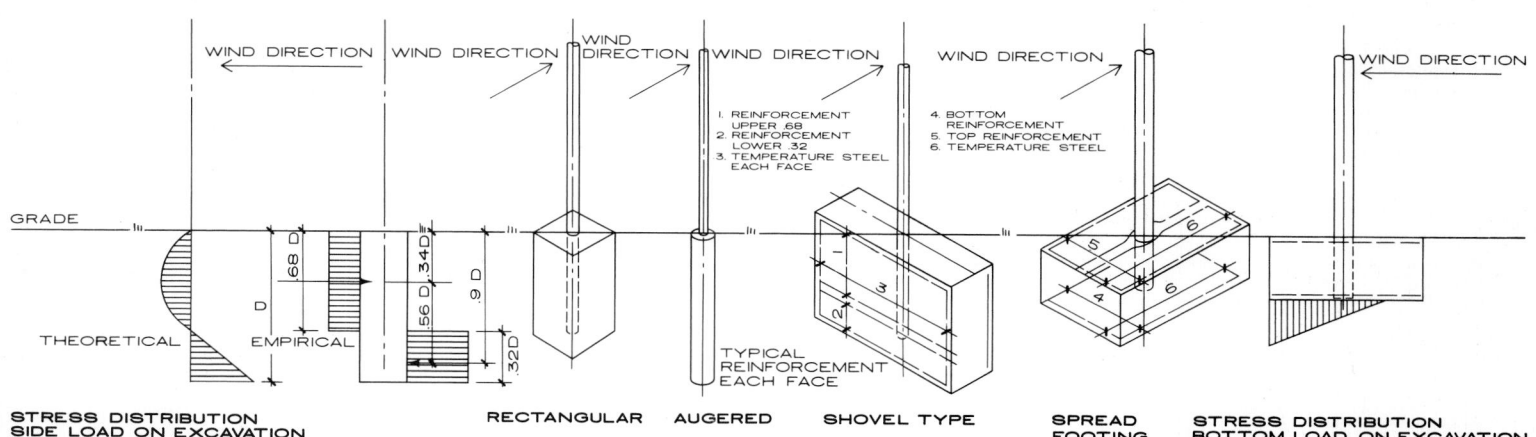

WIND DIRECTION

1. REINFORCEMENT UPPER .68
2. REINFORCEMENT LOWER .32
3. TEMPERATURE STEEL EACH FACE

4. BOTTOM REINFORCEMENT
5. TOP REINFORCEMENT
6. TEMPERATURE STEEL

GRADE

.68 D     .34 D     .9 D     .56 D     .32 D

THEORETICAL     EMPIRICAL

TYPICAL REINFORCEMENT EACH FACE

STRESS DISTRIBUTION SIDE LOAD ON EXCAVATION     RECTANGULAR     AUGERED     SHOVEL TYPE     SPREAD FOOTING     STRESS DISTRIBUTION BOTTOM LOAD ON EXCAVATION

## FOOTING TYPES

## STRUCTURAL DESIGN OF SIGNS

Signs are structurally designed primarily by wind forces and secondarily by gravitational forces. Wind forces are determined by wind speed, height, location, time interval for maximum wind (100 year, 50 year, etc.), gust factor, distribution on the surface, and codes. Although the basic wind load p is computed by the formula $p = 0.00258\,V$ where $V$ = velocity of the wind in miles per hour, the factors that modify it vary in different regions by the codes that apply. Therefore wind loads are computed differently in different parts of the country. A state code may also be modified by a local ordinance, so a designer has to make sure that code requirements are met. By following the applicable code requirements utilizing wind maps, tables, and directions, the designer is able to determine the wind load per square foot acting on the sign surface in the locality in which the sign is being erected.

½"–1½" PLATE GUSSETS WHERE NEEDED

¾"–1½" ANCHOR BOLTS

**ALTERNATE CONNECTION COLUMN TO FOOTING**

TORQUE TUBE 18"–30" PIPE

WELD PLUG

FULLY WELDED CONNECTION

ALIGNMENT COLLAR WELDED TO LOWER PIPE

**COLUMN SPLICE EQUAL DIAMETER PIPE**

8"–14" BEAMS

UPRIGHTS

½" PLATES BOLTED AS REQUIRED

10"–14" BEAMS

WALKWAY GRATING

5" CHANNEL MIN.

½"     PLUG WELD

**COLUMN SPLICE REDUCED PIPE SIZE**

**TORQUE TUBE CONNECTION TO COLUMN**

### NOTES

1. Use 24"–36" beams
2. Plates ¾"–1½"
3. Gussets may be required on pipe column to plate connection
4. Torque tube plate connected to column cap plate use ¾" to 1½" dia. bolts
5. Size and number determined by design conditions

**UPRIGHT CONNECTION TO TORQUE TUBE**

Leon Seligson, AIA; Columbus, Ohio

## CONSIDERATIONS

The following factors must be considered when installing or renovating outdoor lighting systems:

1. In general, overhead lighting is more efficient and economical than low level lighting.
2. Fixtures should provide an overlapping pattern of light at a height of about 7 ft.
3. Lighting levels should respond to site hazards such as steps, ramps, and steep embankments.
4. Posts and standards should be placed so that they do not create hazards for pedestrians or vehicles.

## NOTES

1. Because of their effect on light distribution, trees and shrubs at present height and growth potential should be considered in a lighting layout.
2. It is recommended to use manufacturer-provided lighting templates sized for fixture type, wattage, pole height, and layout scale.
3. Color rendition should be considered when selecting light source. When possible, colors should be selected under proposed light source.
4. Light pollution to areas other than those to be illuminated should be avoided.

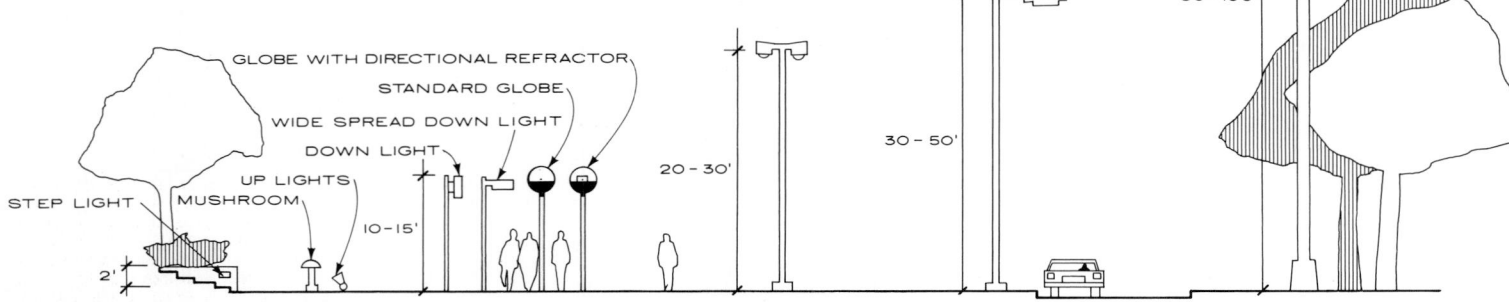

### LOW LEVEL LIGHTING

1. Heights below eye level.
2. Very finite patterns with low wattage capabilities.
3. Incandescent, fluorescent, and high-pressure sodium, 5 to 150 watt lamps.
4. Lowest maintenance requirements, but highly susceptible to vandals.

### MALL AND WALKWAY LIGHTING

1. 10 ft. to 15 ft. heights average for multiuse areas. Wide variety of fixtures and light patterns.
2. Mercury, metal halide, or high-pressure sodium, 70 to 250 watt lamps.
3. Susceptible to vandals.

### SPECIAL PURPOSE LIGHTING

1. 20 ft. to 30 ft. heights average.
2. Recreational, commercial, residential, industrial.
3. Mercury, metal halide, or high-pressure sodium, 200 to 400 watt lamps.
4. Fixtures maintained by gantry.

### PARKING AND ROADWAY LIGHTING

1. 30 ft. to 50 ft. heights average.
2. Large recreational, commercial, industrial areas, highways.
3. Mercury, metal halide, or high-pressure sodium, 400 to 1000 watt lamps.
4. Fixtures maintained by gantry.

### HIGH MASTLIGHTING

1. 60 ft. to 100 ft. heights average.
2. Large areas—parking, recreational, highway interchanges.
3. Metal halide or high-pressure sodium, 1000 watt lamps.
4. Fixtures must lower for maintenance.

## DEFINITIONS

A lumen is a unit used for measuring the amount of light energy given off by a light source. A footcandle is a unit used for measuring the amount of illumination on a surface. The amount of usable light from any given source is partially determined by the source's angle of incidence and the distance to the illuminated surface. See Chapter 1 on illumination.

**NOTE**

All exterior installations must be provided with ground fault interruption circuit.

## RECOMMENDED LIGHTING LEVELS IN FOOTCANDLES

| | COMMER-CIAL | INTERME-DIATE | RESIDEN-TIAL |
|---|---|---|---|
| **PEDESTRIAN AREAS** | | | |
| Sidewalks | 0.9 | 0.6 | 0.2 |
| Pedestrian ways | 2.0 | 1.0 | 0.5 |
| **VEHICULAR ROADS** | | | |
| Freeway* | 0.6 | 0.6 | 0.6 |
| Major road and expressway* | 2.0 | 1.4 | 1.0 |
| Collector road | 1.2 | 0.9 | 0.6 |
| Local road | 0.9 | 0.6 | 0.4 |
| Alleys | 0.6 | 0.4 | 0.2 |
| **PARKING AREAS** | | | |
| Self-parking | 1.0 | — | — |
| Attendant parking | 2.0 | — | — |
| Security problem area | — | — | 5.0 |
| Minimum for television viewing of important interdiction areas | 10.0 | 10.0 | 10.0 |
| **BUILDING AREAS** | | | |
| Entrances | 5.0 | — | — |
| General grounds | 1.0 | — | — |

*Both mainline and ramps.

Johnson, Johnson & Roy, Inc.; Ann Arbor, Michigan
Dewey Hou; Tomblinson Harburn Associates; Flint, Michigan

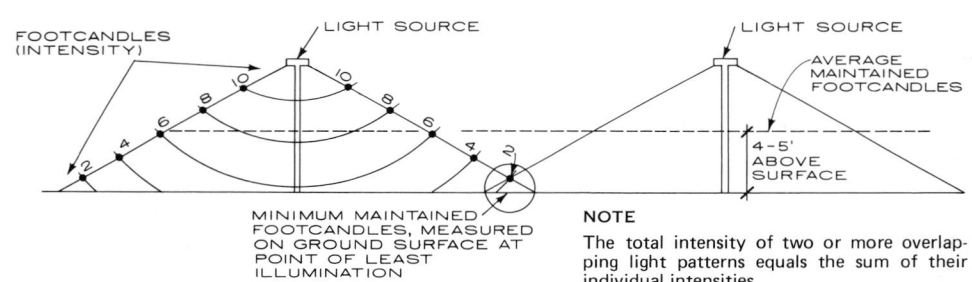

**MEASURING LIGHT INTENSITY IN FOOTCANDLES**

The total intensity of two or more overlapping light patterns equals the sum of their individual intensities.

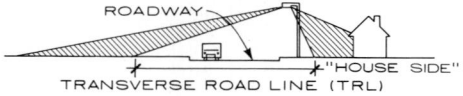

1. CUTOFF means that maximum of 10 percent of light source lumens fall outside of TRL area.
2. SEMICUTOFF means that maximum of 30 percent of light source lumens fall outside of the TRL area.
3. NONCUTOFF means that no control limitations exist.

**CUTOFF TERMINOLOGY**
(NOTE: "CUTOFF" IS MEASURED ALONG TRL.)

**NOTE**

Degree of cutoff is determined by one of the following:

(a) design of fixture housing
(b) incorporation of prismatic lens over light source
(c) addition of shield to fixture on "house side"

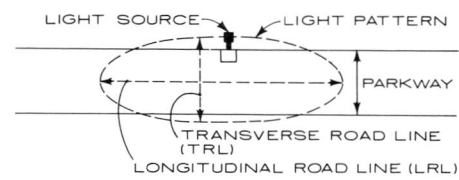

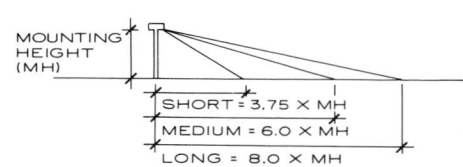

**TYPES OF DISTRIBUTION**
(NOTE: DISTRIBUTION IS MEASURED ALONG LRL)

## 2 SITE IMPROVEMENTS

## BIKE PATH CLASSIFICATIONS

### BIKE PATH (CLASS I BIKEWAY)

A bikeway physically separated from motorized vehicular traffic by an open space. It is located either within the roadway right-of-way or within an independent right-of-way (greenbelt).

### BIKE LANE (CLASS II BIKEWAY)

A portion of a roadway that has been designated by lane stripes or traffic buttons, signs, or other pavement markings for the preferential or exclusive use of bicyclists.

### BIKE ROUTE (CLASS III BIKEWAY)

A bikeway that shares the traffic right-of-way with motor vehicles and is designated only by signs. Bicycles are considered legal road vehicles, and bicyclists must obey all traffic laws. One-way bike travel only is permitted on a bike route.

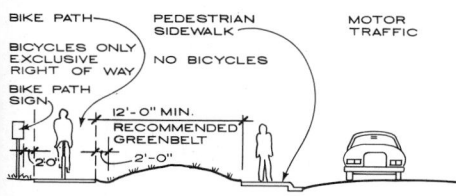

**CLASS I BIKEWAY**

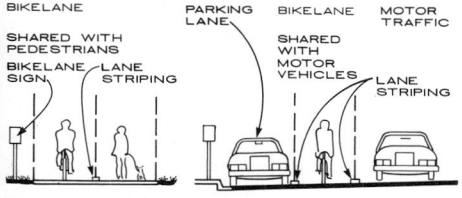

**CLASS II BIKEWAY**

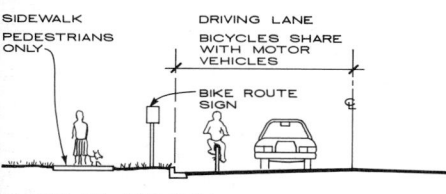

**CLASS III BIKEWAY**

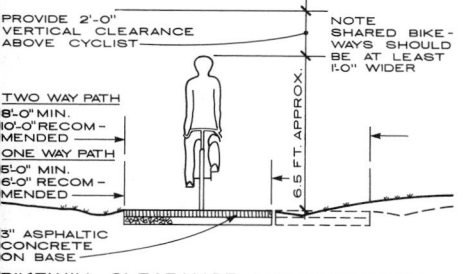

**BIKEWAY CLEARANCE AND DIMENSIONS**

## HORIZONTAL, VERTICAL LAYOUT

Except in terrain where unavoidable, such as in mountains with numerous curves, long steep inclines should be avoided. Slopes of one percent to one-half percent have no significant effect on the use of bicycle paths by cyclists. Three percent slopes to 500 ft. are acceptable. Grades of six percent and more that are longer than 250 ft. will discourage bicycle path use except by expert cyclists using lightweight bicycles. Cyclists prefer straight or gently curving paths to circuitous, meandering paths.

## PAVING SURFACE

Pavement must be smooth and durable, as 3 in. asphaltic concrete on a prepared subgrade or a minimum of 4 in. of crushed aggregate base (variable with climate and soil conditions). Concrete is satisfactory if it is well aligned. Tree root or frost heave displacement or differential settlement can create uneven paths in concrete unless doweling is provided.

## TRAFFIC SAFETY

Class I Bikeways, with bicycles separated from motorized traffic, provide the most safety for cyclists. Class III Bikeways, dependent on signs, provide the least safety. They do not encourage bicycle use, but often are the only option in urban areas. On Class II and Class III Bikeways hazards can arise from suddenly opened doors of parked cars and from cross-traffic turning into driveways. Bikeways beside pedestrian walks may get interference as walkers stray onto the designated bikeway.

## INTERSECTIONS

The major safety problem with bikeways is at grade intersections where motor vehicles, pedestrians, and cyclists converge or cross each other. The best solution is to provide a grade-separated intersection with an underpass or overpass planned as a part of a Class I Bikeway. Other possibilities include:

1. Provide a clearly defined mid-block crossing.
2. Merge bicycles and pedestrians a minimum of 100 ft. from four-way intersections using warning signs for both.
3. Provide warning signs for motorists approaching intersections where bikeways cross.
4. Provide and maintain adequate lighting.
5. Control planting and trimming of trees and plants to provide adequate intersection visibility.
6. Provide electronically activated signals for high traffic volume intersections.
7. At busy intersections or during peak traffic periods, restrict bicycle left turns.

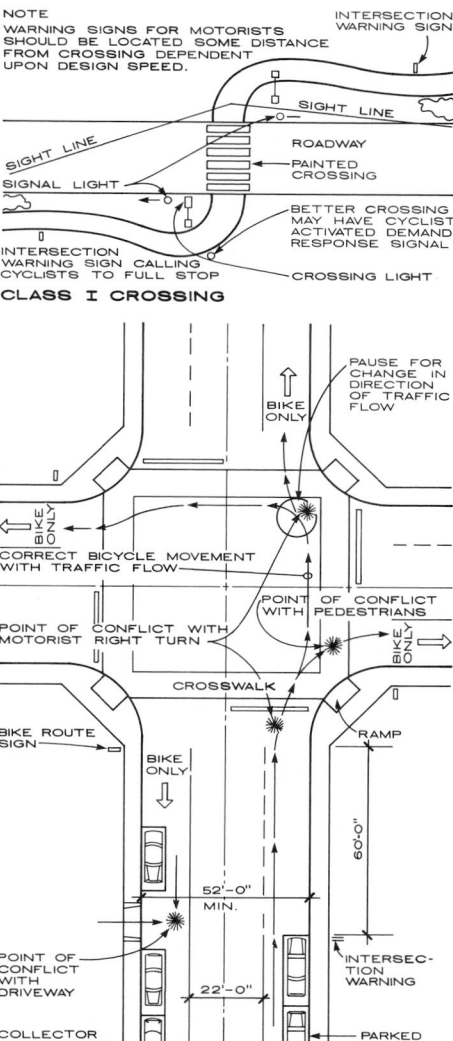

**CLASS I CROSSING**

**CLASS II INTERSECTION**

## BICYCLE PARKING

Bicycle parking should be close to, but not obstructing, the main entrances to buildings. Where feasible, parking should be visible from the interior of a building or CCTV monitored. Good exterior lighting is important.

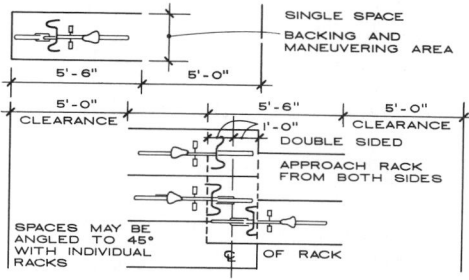

**BICYCLE PARKING SPACES**

Theft of bicycles, bicycle wheels, and accessories has become a significant problem. All bicycle parking devices must have provisions for locking mechanisms. Cyclists usually provide the locks. Coin-operated locks also are available on some devices. Case-hardened chains or high strength cable with heavy duty padlocks, or bar locks must be accommodated at the parking device. Parking devices shown are classified by the amount of theft protection offered.

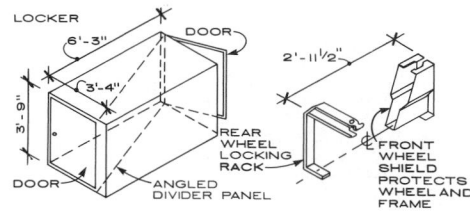

**TYPE A—HIGH PROTECTION**

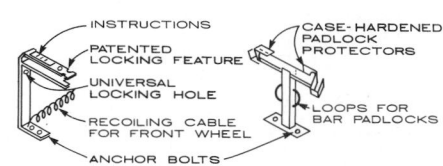

**TYPE B—MEDIUM PROTECTION**

All parking devices mentioned above must be constructed of hardened steel resistant to hacksaws and hammers. All must be anchored securely in concrete foundations or set with nonremovable bolts.

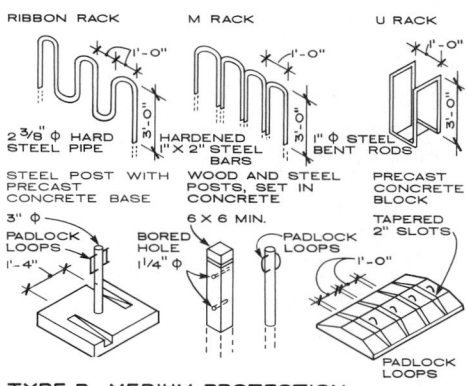

**SHELTERS FOR BICYCLES**

H. Thomas Wilson, AIA; Pasadena, California

Bicycle facilities designs courtesy of Rally Racks, Canterbury Designs, Brandir International, Sunshine U-Lok Corp.

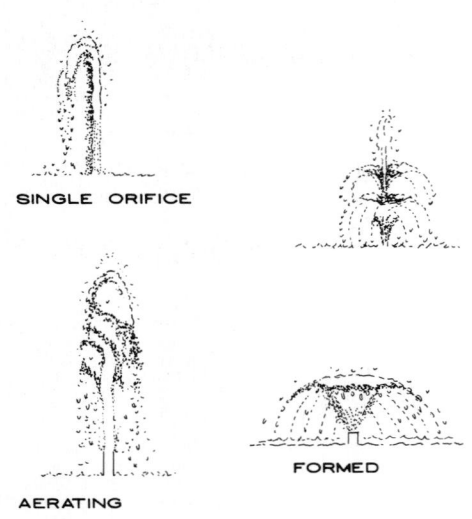

SINGLE ORIFICE

AERATING

FORMED

GENERAL JET TYPES

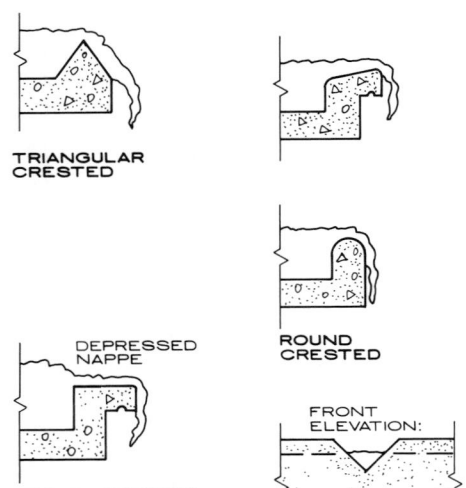

TRIANGULAR CRESTED

DEPRESSED NAPPE

BROAD CRESTED

ROUND CRESTED

FRONT ELEVATION:

'V' NOTCHED

WEIR SECTIONS

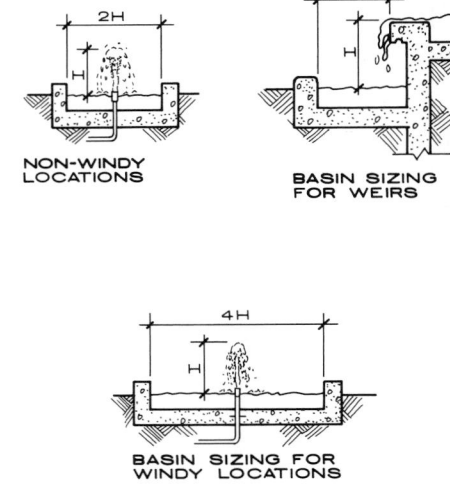

NON-WINDY LOCATIONS

BASIN SIZING FOR WEIRS

BASIN SIZING FOR WINDY LOCATIONS

BASIN SIZING FOR FOUNTAINS

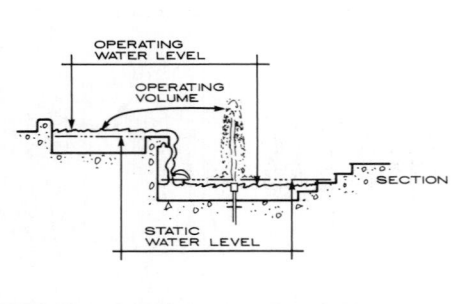

OPERATING WATER LEVEL

OPERATING VOLUME

SECTION

STATIC WATER LEVEL

$$\frac{\text{CIRCULATING VOLUME (CU FT)}}{\text{BASIN AREA (SQ FT)}} = \begin{array}{l}\text{DIFFERENCE BETWEEN}\\\text{STATIC AND}\\\text{OPERATING LEVELS}\\\text{(INCHES)}\end{array}$$

**STATIC AND OPERATING LEVELS OF FOUNTAINS**

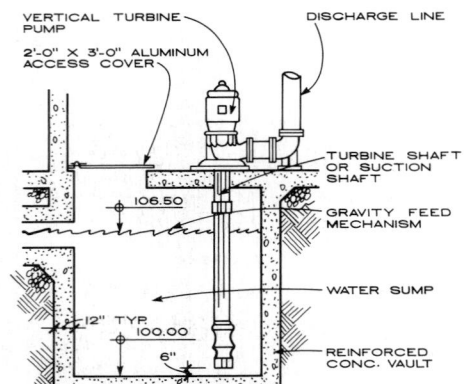

VERTICAL TURBINE PUMP

2'-0" X 3'-0" ALUMINUM ACCESS COVER

DISCHARGE LINE

TURBINE SHAFT OR SUCTION SHAFT

106.50

GRAVITY FEED MECHANISM

WATER SUMP

12" TYP. 100.00

6"

REINFORCED CONC. VAULT

6" GRAVEL ON COMP SUBGRADE

11'-0"

**VERTICAL TURBINE PUMP**

NOZZLE #1   NOZZLE #2

NOZZLE #3

NOZZLE #4

SECTION:

DISCHARGE

DISCHARGE

SUCTION

PUMP IN DRY VAULT

**PIPE SCHEMATIC — DRY CENTRIFUGAL PUMP**

## PURPOSE

Fountains can provide the following site considerations or program elements:

1. Recreation
2. An altered environment to increase comfort
3. Image
4. Visual focal point
5. An activities focal point
6. To frame views
7. Acoustical control

## FORMS

1. Held water in pools and ponds. Form and reflectivity are design considerations.
2. Falling water. The effect depends on water velocity, water volume, container surface, or the edge over or through which the water is moving.
3. Flowing water. The visual effect of the same volume of flowing water can be changed by narrowing or widening a channel, by placing objects in its path, by changing the direction of the flow, and by changing the slope and roughness of the bottom and sides.
4. Jets. An effect derived by forcing water into the air to create a pattern. Jet types include single orifice nozzles, aerated nozzles, and formed jets.
5. Surge. An effect created by a contrast between relatively quiet water and a surge (a wave or a splash), made by quickly adding water, by raising or lowering

an object in the water, by moving an object back and forth through the water, or by introducing strong air currents.

## OVERALL DESIGN CONSIDERATIONS

1. Scale. Size of the water feature in context to the surroundings.
2. Basin sizing: Width—consider fountain height and prevailing winds. Depth—consider weight (1 cu. ft. water = 62.366 lbs.). Safety—consider children playing near or in the pool. Cover—allow space for lights, nozzles, and pumps. Local codes may classify basins of a certain depth as swimming pools. Nozzle spray may be cushioned to prevent excessive surge.
3. Bottom appearance is important when clear water is maintained. It can be enhanced by patterns, colors, materials, three-dimensional objects, or textures. Dark bottoms increase reflectivity.
4. Edges or copings. In designing the water's edge, consider the difference between the operating water level and the static water level. Loosely defined edges (as in a pond) make movement into the water possible both visually and physically. Clearly defined edges (as in a basin) use copings to delineate the water's edge.
5. Lips and weirs—A lip is an edge over which flowing water falls. A weir is a dam in the water to divert the water flow or to raise the water level. If volume and velocity are insufficient to break the surface tension, a reglet on the underside of the edge may overcome this problem.

## MATERIAL SELECTION CRITERIA

1. Waterproof
2. Crack resistant
3. Weather resistant, durable
4. Stain resistant
5. Workable material appropriate for intended effect

## GENERATION OF WATER PRESSURE

1. Elevated dam structures, used in early fountains, are not feasible today.
2. Submersible pumps, used for low volume fountains only, are easy to install and require short pipe runs. The pump must be covered with water to operate correctly; it may be damaged if the water level drops. Vandalism can be a problem. Motors range from $1/20$ to 1 horsepower.
3. Dry centrifugal pumps are used most commonly for larger water features. Motors range from $1/4$ to 100 horsepower. The assembly consists of a pump, electric motor, suction line, and discharge line. The pump and motor are located in an isolated dry vault.
4. Vertical turbine pumps usually are more energy efficient than pumps with suction lines because the pump uses no energy to move the water to the pump. Water flows to the pump by gravity and thus reduces the amount of work exerted by the pump. The assembly consists of a pump and motor, a water sump in the equipment vault, a gravity feed mechanism to the pump, and a discharge line.

Barry R. Thalden, AIA; Thalden Corporation; St. Louis, Missouri

## SPRINKLER SYSTEMS

Spray: For residential or commercial planting beds, shrub areas, ground covers, and trees. Available in various arc and strip patterns. 2 in. to 12 in. pop-up shrub heads common. Recommended operating pressure: 20-50 psi.

Stream rotor: For residential or commercial small to large turf areas, slopes, ground covers, and planting beds. Available in various arc patterns. 3 in. to 12 in. pop-up shrub heads common. Recommended operating pressure: 35-60 psi.

Rotary (gear driven): For residential or commercial large turf areas, sports fields, parks, and cemeteries. Available in various arc patterns. 2 in. to 4 in. pop-up and shrub heads common. Recommended operating pressure: 25-90 psi.

Agricultural: For dust control, ground cover, nurseries, and frost protection. Available in different trajectory angles and nozzle volumes. Recommended operating pressure: 20-100 psi.

Drip: For special residential, commercial, and agricultural problems such as hillsides or individual plantings, or where excessive runoff, overspray, and wasted water are problems. Recommended operating pressure: 10-40 psi.

## DESIGN FACTORS

Supply line size, meter, available water pressure, code restrictions, type and scale of growing material, and soil conditions govern the type of system, spray heads, and pipe size used.

## TYPES OF CONTROL SYSTEMS

Quick coupler: This system normally is under pressure. A key is inserted into a spray head where water is needed.

Manual: This system is turned on with a valve, all heads in place.

Automatic: The two basic types are hydraulic, in which the signal between the controller and the valves is transmitted through fluid pressure in control tubing, and electric, in which the signal is transmitted to the valves directly through buried wire. Electric is the more common system. It is operated from a central control unit.

## PIPE

Polyvinyl chloride or polyethylene piping, easily cut and connected, commonly is used. Steel and copper pipe also are used. Pipe sleeves should be preset under walks and through walls for ease of installation and future extension of the system.

## PRECIPITATION RATES

The amount of water applied to turf areas must be adjusted according to the species of grass, the traffic it receives, subsoil conditions, and surface gradient.

## BACKFLOW PREVENTERS

A cross-connection device protects the potable water supply from contaminants caused by backsiphonage or backpressure. Many state and local plumbing codes require the use of such a device on an irrigation system. Types of cross-connections include atmospheric vacuum breakers, pressure vacuum breakers, double check valves, and reduced pressure valves.

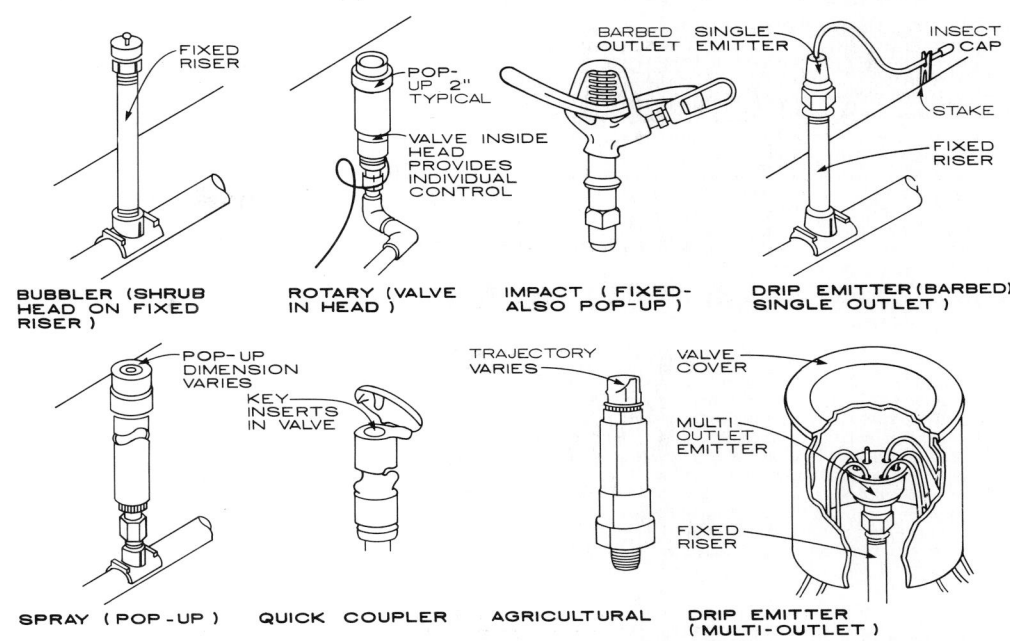

**SPRAY HEADS**

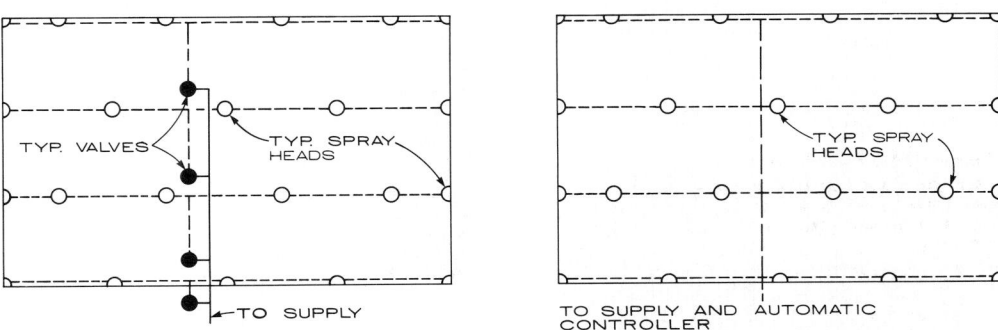

VALVE IN HEAD PROVIDES INDIVIDUAL HEAD CONTROL FOR MAXIMUM FLEXIBILITY TO FIT TURF USE, TOPOGRAPHY, AND SOIL.

BLOCK SYSTEM · VALVE IN HEAD

**TYPICAL LAYOUTS**

**TYPICAL TRAJECTORIES**

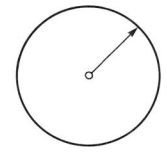

360° CIRCLE

OTHER TYPICAL PATTERNS AVAILABLE ARE 90°, 120°, 180°, 240°, AND 270°. SPECIAL ARCS ARE ALSO AVAILABLE

RADIUS DIMENSIONS VARY FROM 6' WITH SPRAY HEADS TO 100' WITH ROTARY HEADS.

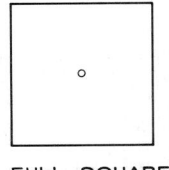

FULL SQUARE (SPECIAL)

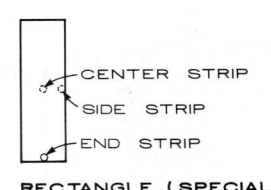

RECTANGLE (SPECIAL)

**NOZZLE PATTERNS**

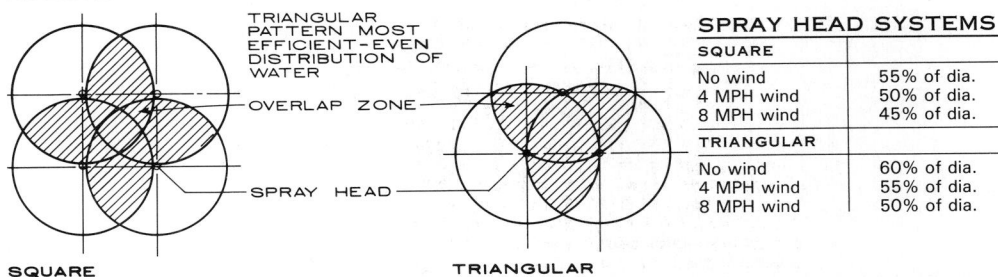

SQUARE · TRIANGULAR

**SPRAY HEAD SPACING**

| SPRAY HEAD SYSTEMS | |
| --- | --- |
| **SQUARE** | |
| No wind | 55% of dia. |
| 4 MPH wind | 50% of dia. |
| 8 MPH wind | 45% of dia. |
| **TRIANGULAR** | |
| No wind | 60% of dia. |
| 4 MPH wind | 55% of dia. |
| 8 MPH wind | 50% of dia. |

Robert K. Sherrill; Wilkes, Faulkner, Jenkins & Bass; Washington, D.C.

## GROWTH AND DEVELOPMENT

As children grow their physical abilities change, as does the scale of equipment that will challenge them. Physical growth is accommodated by social development resulting in different levels and types of interaction and activity. A child's play experience must be successful as well as challenging. Therefore play equipment should be designed and selected to meet the physical and intellectual requirements of groups that will use it. The height, distance between levels, and the ability and strength required to use the equipment should be scaled to the size and level of social and intellectual development of the child.

## SINGLE UNIT VS. INTEGRATED PLAY EQUIPMENT

Many types of play equipment are designed to stand alone as units. While they may often be linked to other equipment, they are generally single activity items. Where space or other conditions limit the scope of development such equipment is useful. However, since activity proceeds in a continuous flow, integrated play areas have proved to be more successful than arrangements of individual items. Linking of equipment and equipment that combines several activities on one structure increase the options available to the user and tend to increase the interest and challenge.

## PLAY COMPONENTS

Several basic elements are used to create play equipment. The most commonly employed include slides (standard, spiral, tube, rail, roller, and pole), swings (standard and tire), ladders (vertical, horizontal, chain net, cables, and arch), climbers (stepped wood posts, stacks, arch, chain, rungs, tire, and rope), and miscellaneous components (decks, panels, log rollers, spring pads, balance beams, parallel bars, rings, and clatter bridges).

## INTEGRATED PLAY STRUCTURES

Manufacturers offer predesigned arrangements, using a variety of play components to provide a multitude of ways to serve groups of 5 to 75 children. These systems are available in timber and powder-coated steel. Both offer modular construction, ease of installation, durability, and a variety of accessories, most of which are common to each. Plan space requirements on the number of children expected to use such a structure at one time. Allot each child about 65 to 70 sq. ft., which includes a 4 ft. safety zone around the structure.

## SAFETY CONCERNS

No playground or play activity is completely safe from all potential accidents because the element of risk is inherent in most play. To design an absolutely safe playground would remove all risk and thus would be counterproductive. Children would seek challenge elsewhere, usually where risk is unmanaged. As a goal, playground equipment should provide challenging activities in the safest way possible. Structures should be solidly built. Components should have rounded edges and corners. Metal fasteners should be covered or placed in recessed holes. Above all, playground equipment always should be installed on a bed of absorbing ground cover such as granulated pine bark (12 in. deep), pea gravel (10 in. deep), or sand (10 in. deep). Asphalt, packed dirt, or exposed concrete should never be an acceptable play surface. Manufacturers recommend a minimum of 4 ft. safety zone around the play area. Adequate seating space in clear view of all play equipment should be allotted for adults supervising children.

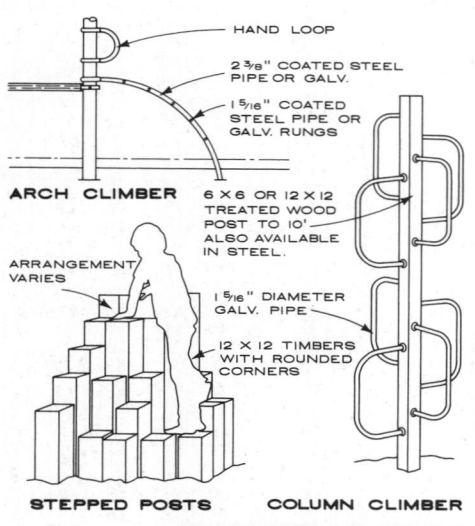

**SLIDES**

ALSO AVAILABLE ARE STANDARD STAINLESS STEEL AND PLASTIC SLIDES. HEIGHTS AND LENGTHS VARY. CONSULT MANUFACTURERS' DATA FOR SPECIFIC AVAILABILITY AND INFORMATION.

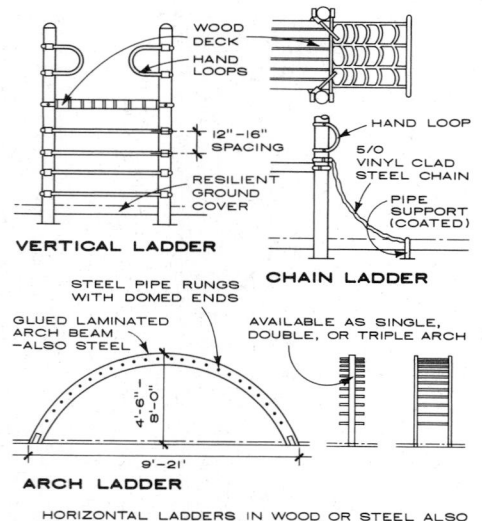

**LADDERS**

HORIZONTAL LADDERS IN WOOD OR STEEL ALSO ARE AVAILABLE IN VARIOUS DESIGNS.

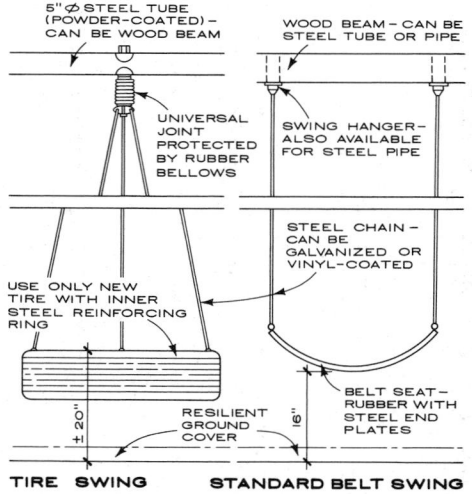

**SWINGS**

OPTIONAL SEATS FOR STANDARD SWING INCLUDE FULL OR PARTIAL BUCKET SEATS, FLAT MOLDED RUBBER SEATS, AND MOLDED CONTOUR CHAIRS.

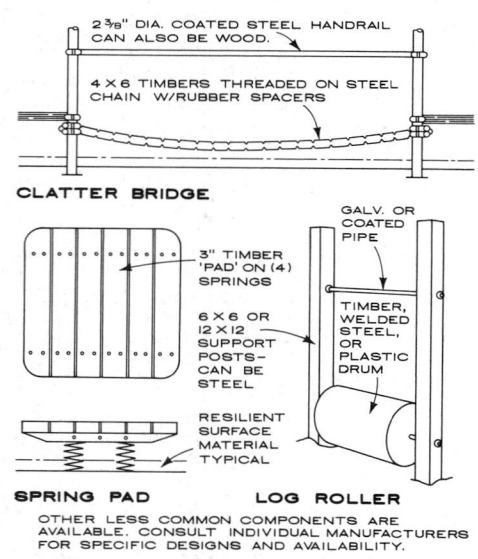

**CLIMBERS**

ARCH CLIMBERS ALSO AVAILABLE IN TIMBER DESIGNS.

**MISCELLANEOUS**

OTHER LESS COMMON COMPONENTS ARE AVAILABLE. CONSULT INDIVIDUAL MANUFACTURERS FOR SPECIFIC DESIGNS AND AVAILABILITY.

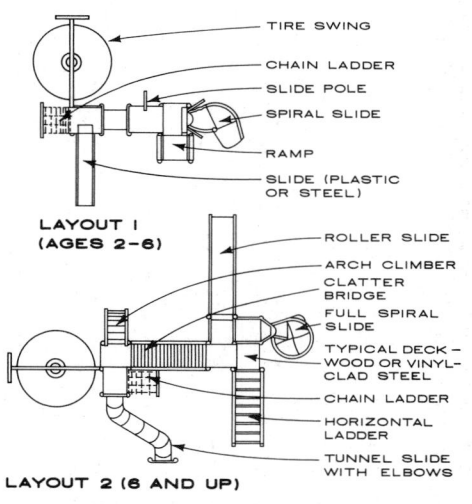

**INTEGRATED PLAYSYSTEMS**

LAYOUTS SHOWN SERVE AS EXAMPLES ONLY. OPTIONAL LAYOUTS ARE PRACTICALLY INFINITE. CONSULT MANUFACTURERS' DATA FOR SPECIFIC ARRANGEMENTS.

Robert K. Sherrill; Wilkes, Faulkner, Jenkins & Bass; Washington, D.C.

2 SITE IMPROVEMENTS

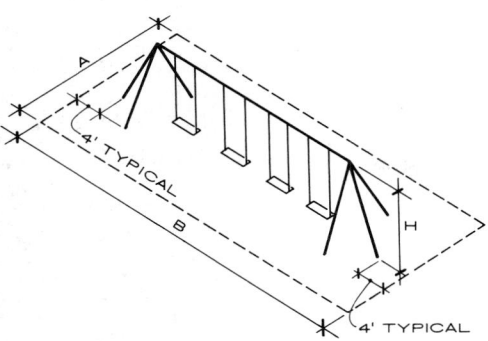

4' TYPICAL

4' TYPICAL

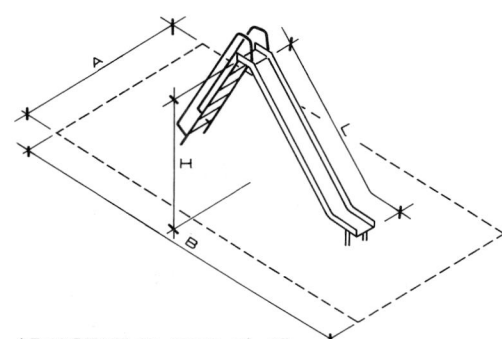

ADJACENT SLIDES: 7'-6"
(CHUTES C. TO C.) OTHERS 10' O.C.

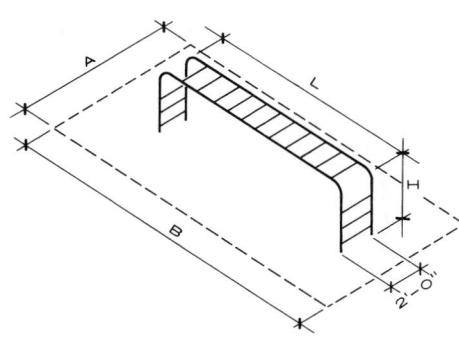

## SWINGS

| SWINGS | H (FT) | SAFETY ZONE | |
|---|---|---|---|
| | | A (FT) | B (FT) |
| 2 | 8 | 24 | 27 |
| | 10 | 28 | 27 |
| | 12 | 32 | 27 |
| 3 | 8 | 24 | 30 |
| | 10 | 28 | 30 |
| | 12 | 32 | 30 |
| 4 | 8 | 24 | 40 |
| | 10 | 28 | 40 |
| | 12 | 32 | 40 |
| 6 | 8 | 24 | 46 |
| | 10 | 28 | 46 |
| | 12 | 32 | 46 |
| 8 | 8 | 24 | 57 |
| | 10 | 28 | 57 |
| | 12 | 32 | 57 |
| 9 | 8 | 24 | 61 |
| | 10 | 28 | 61 |
| | 12 | 32 | 61 |

## SLIDES

| H | L | SAFETY ZONE | |
|---|---|---|---|
| | | A | B |
| 4 | 8 | 26 | 24 |
| 5 | 10 | 26 | 28 |
| 6 | 12 | 26 | 32 |
| 8 | 16 | 26 | 36 |

## HORIZONTAL LADDER

| H (FT-IN.) | L (FT-IN.) | SAFETY ZONE | |
|---|---|---|---|
| | | A (FT) | B (FT) |
| 6-6 | 12-6 | 14 | 25 |
| 7-6 | 16-0 | 14 | 30 |

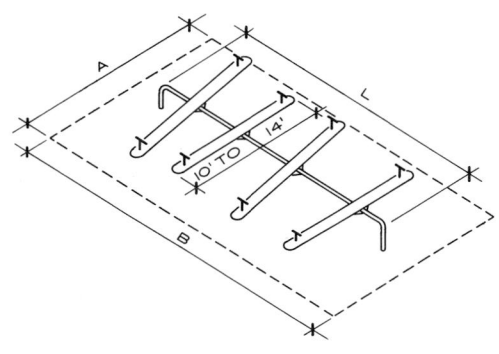

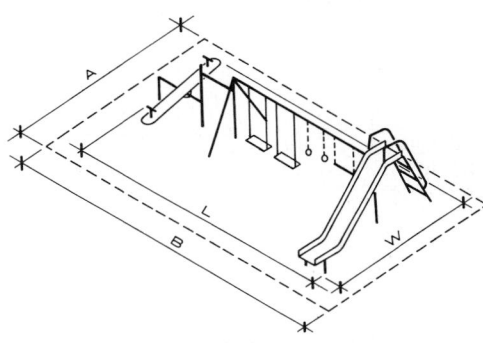

## GENERAL PLANNING INFORMATION

| EQUIPMENT | AREA (SQ FT) | CAPACITY (NUMBER OF CHILDREN) |
|---|---|---|
| Slide | 450 | 4–6 |
| Low swing | 150 | 1 |
| High swing | 250 | 1 |
| Horizontal ladder | 375 | 6–8 |
| Seesaw | 100 | 2 |
| Junior climbing gym | 180 | 8–10 |
| General climbing gym | 500 | 15–20 |

## SEESAWS

| BOARDS | 1 | 2 | 3 | 4 | 6 |
|---|---|---|---|---|---|
| L | 3 | 6 | 9 | 12 | 18 |
| A | 20 | 20 | 20 | 20 | 20 |
| B | 5 | 10 | 15 | 20 | 25 |

## COMBINATION UNITS*

| ENCLOSURE LIMITS |
|---|
| A = W + 12'-0'' |
| B = L + 6'-0'' |

*Types and no. of units are variable.

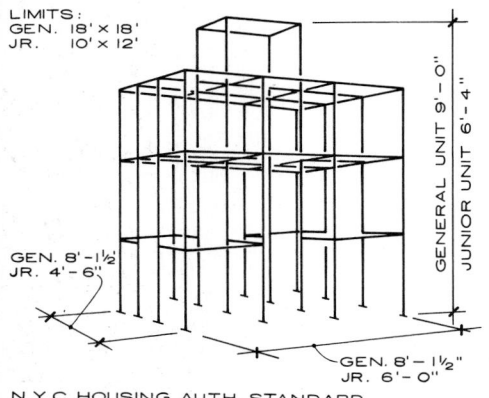

LIMITS:
GEN. 18' × 18'
JR. 10' × 12'

GENERAL UNIT 9'-0''
JUNIOR UNIT 6'-4''

GEN. 8'-1½'
JR. 4'-6'

GEN. 8'-1½''
JR. 6'-0''

N.Y.C. HOUSING AUTH. STANDARD
**CLIMBING GYM**

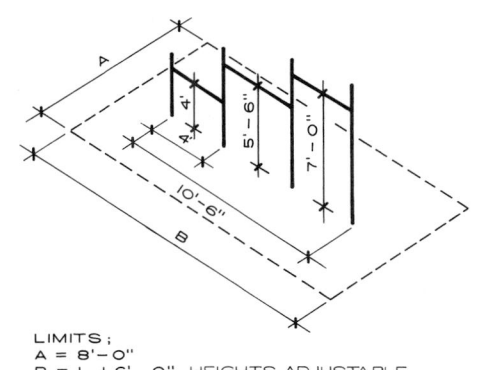

LIMITS;
A = 8'-0''
B = L + 6'-0'' HEIGHTS ADJUSTABLE
**HORIZONTAL BARS**

18'-22'

10'-0''

10 FT DIA. IS CONSIDERED STANDARD
OTHER DIA. = 6' AND 8'

**SPIN AROUND**

Robert K. Sherrill; Wilkes, Faulkner, Jenkins & Bass; Washington, D.C.
Vincent F. Nauseda; Sasaki, Dawson Associates, Inc.; Watertown, Massachusetts

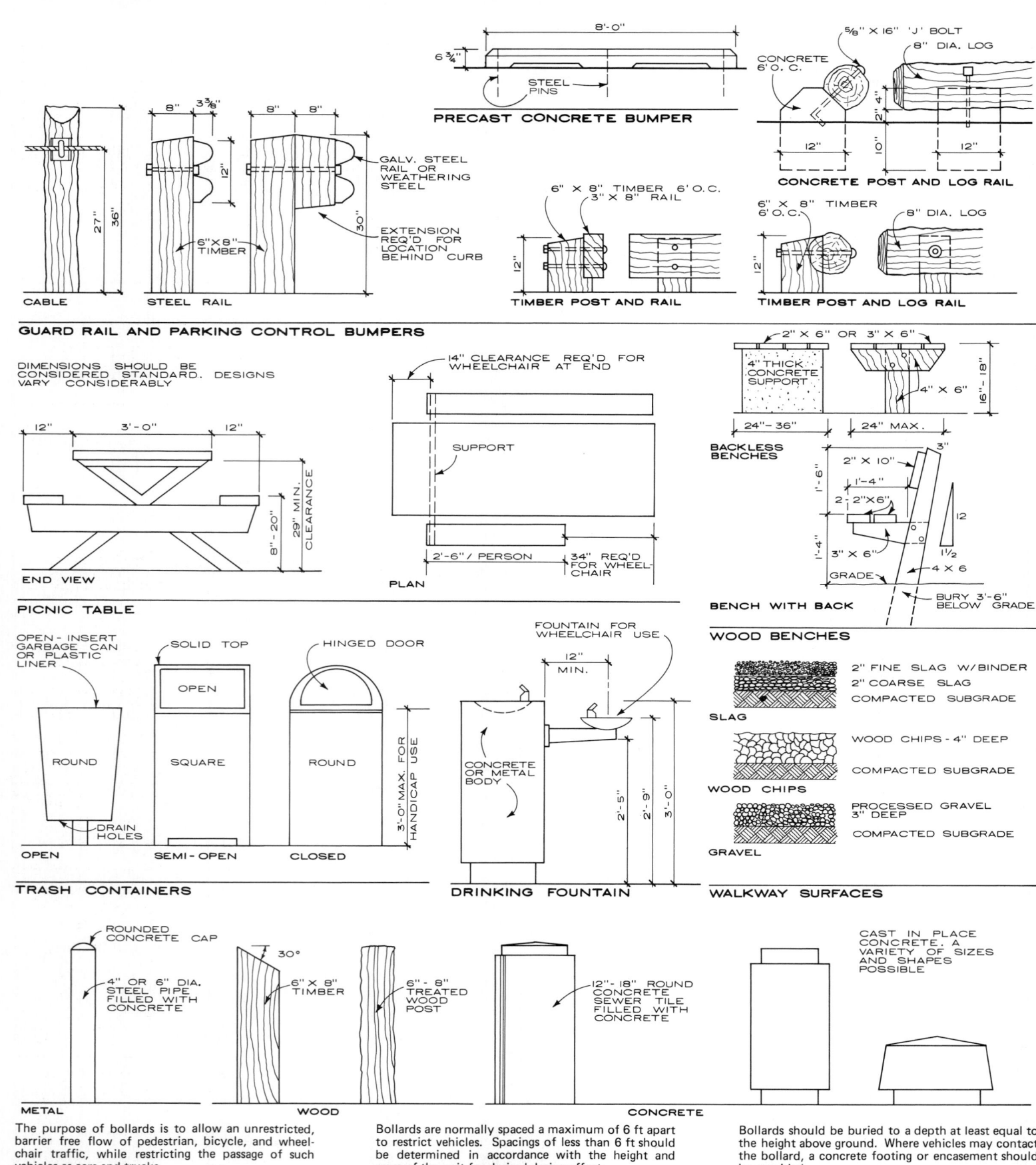

**PRECAST CONCRETE BUMPER**

**CONCRETE POST AND LOG RAIL**

**TIMBER POST AND RAIL**

**TIMBER POST AND LOG RAIL**

CABLE

STEEL RAIL

**GUARD RAIL AND PARKING CONTROL BUMPERS**

DIMENSIONS SHOULD BE CONSIDERED STANDARD. DESIGNS VARY CONSIDERABLY

END VIEW

PLAN

**PICNIC TABLE**

BACKLESS BENCHES

BENCH WITH BACK

**WOOD BENCHES**

OPEN

SEMI-OPEN

CLOSED

**TRASH CONTAINERS**

**DRINKING FOUNTAIN**

SLAG

2" FINE SLAG W/BINDER
2" COARSE SLAG
COMPACTED SUBGRADE

WOOD CHIPS

WOOD CHIPS - 4" DEEP
COMPACTED SUBGRADE

GRAVEL

PROCESSED GRAVEL 3" DEEP
COMPACTED SUBGRADE

**WALKWAY SURFACES**

METAL

WOOD

CONCRETE

The purpose of bollards is to allow an unrestricted, barrier free flow of pedestrian, bicycle, and wheelchair traffic, while restricting the passage of such vehicles as cars and trucks.

Bollards are normally spaced a maximum of 6 ft apart to restrict vehicles. Spacings of less than 6 ft should be determined in accordance with the height and mass of the unit for desired design effect.

Bollards should be buried to a depth at least equal to the height above ground. Where vehicles may contact the bollard, a concrete footing or encasement should be provided.

**BOLLARDS**

John M. Beckett; Beckett, Raeder, Rankin, Inc.; Ann Arbor, Michigan

2    **SITE IMPROVEMENTS**

## NOTES

Several factors should be considered when designing with plants:

1. The physical environment of the site:
   - Soil conditions (acidity, porosity).
   - Available sunlight.
   - Available precipitation.
   - Seasonal temperature range.
   - Exposure of the site (wind).

2. The design needs of the project:
   - Directing movement.
   - Framing vistas.
   - Moderating the environment of the site.
   - Creating space by using plants to develop the base, vertical, and overhead planes.

3. The design character of the plants chosen:
   - Height.
   - Mass.
   - Silhouette (rounded, pyramidal, spreading).
   - Texture (fine, medium, coarse).
   - Color.
   - Seasonal interest (flowers, fruit, fall color).
   - Growth habits (fast or slow growing).

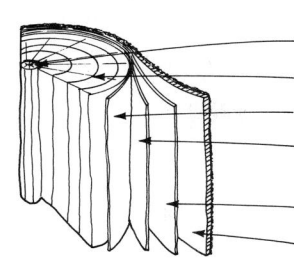

CROWN: THE HEAD OF FOLIAGE OF THE TREE LEAVES — THE FOLIAGE UNIT OF THE TREE THAT FUNCTIONS PRIMARILY IN FOOD MANUFACTURE BY PHOTOSYNTHESIS

HEARTWOOD: THE NONLIVING CENTRAL PART OF THE TREE GIVING STRENGTH AND STABILITY

ANNUAL RINGS: REVEAL AGE OF THE TREE BY SHOWING THE YEARLY GROWTH

SAPWOOD (XYLEM): CARRIES NUTRIENTS AND WATER TO THE LEAVES FROM THE ROOTS

CAMBIUM: LAYER BETWEEN THE XYLEM AND PHLOEM WHERE CELL GROWTH OCCURS, ADDING NEW SAPWOOD TO THE INSIDE AND NEW INNER BARK TO THE OUTSIDE

INNER BARK (PHLOEM): CARRIES FOOD FROM THE LEAVES TO THE BRANCHES, TRUNK, AND ROOTS

OUTER BARK: THE AGED INNER BARK THAT PROTECTS THE TREE FROM DESSICATION AND INJURY

ROOTS: THE ROOTS ANCHOR THE TREE AND HELP HOLD THE SOIL AGAINST EROSION

ROOT HAIRS: THE TINY ROOT HAIRS ABSORB THE MINERALS FROM THE SOIL MOISTURE AND SEND THEM AS NUTRIENT SALTS IN THE SAPWOOD TO THE LEAVES

### PHYSICAL CHARACTERISTICS

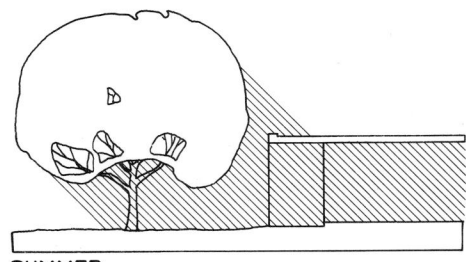

SUMMER

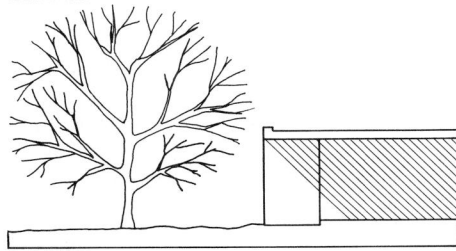

WINTER

### RADIATION PROTECTION

In summer deciduous plants obstruct or filter the sun's strong radiation, thus cooling the area beneath them. In winter the sun penetrates through.

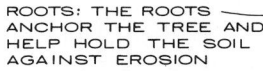

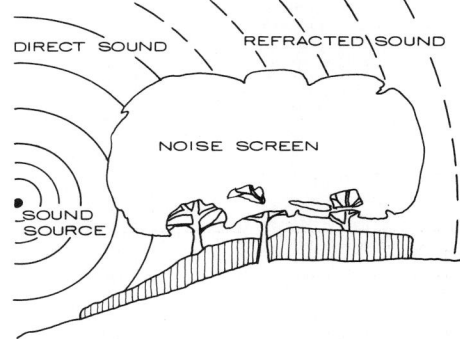

### SOUND ATTENUATION

Plantings of deciduous and evergreen materials reduce sound more effectively than deciduous plants alone. Planting on earth mounds increases the attenuating effects of the buffer.

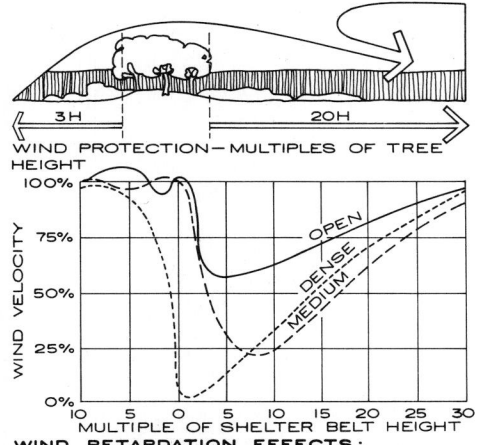

WIND PROTECTION — MULTIPLES OF TREE HEIGHT

### WIND RETARDATION EFFECTS:
1. REDUCE EVAPORATION
2. LOWER TEMPERATURE IN SUMMER
3. REDUCE HEAT LOSSES IN WINTER
4. INCREASE RELATIVE HUMIDITY
5. REDUCE DUST AND SNOW BLOWING

### DENSITY

The density of a planted wind buffer determines the area that is protected. Height and composition are also factors in wind protection.

PARTICULATE MATTER TRAPPED ON THE LEAVES IS WASHED TO THE GROUND DURING A RAINFALL. GASEOUS AND OTHER POLLUTANTS ARE ASSIMILATED IN THE LEAVES

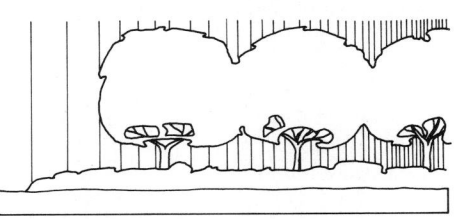

FUMES AND ODORS CAN BE MECHANICALLY MASKED BY FRAGRANT PLANTS AND CHEMICALLY METABOLIZED IN THE PHOTOSYNTHETIC PROCESS

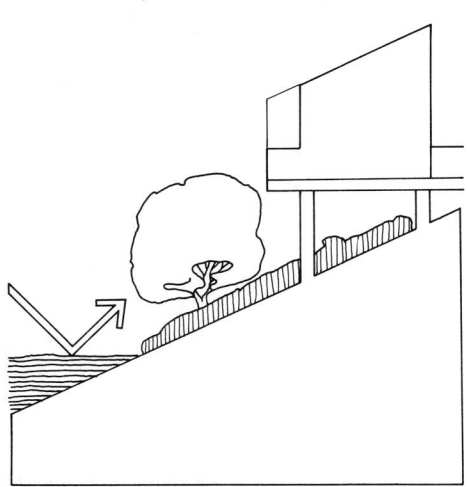

### GLARE PROTECTION

The sun's vertical angle changes seasonally; therefore, the area subject to the glare of reflected sunlight varies. Plants of various heights screen glare from adjacent reflective surfaces (water, paving, glass, and building surfaces).

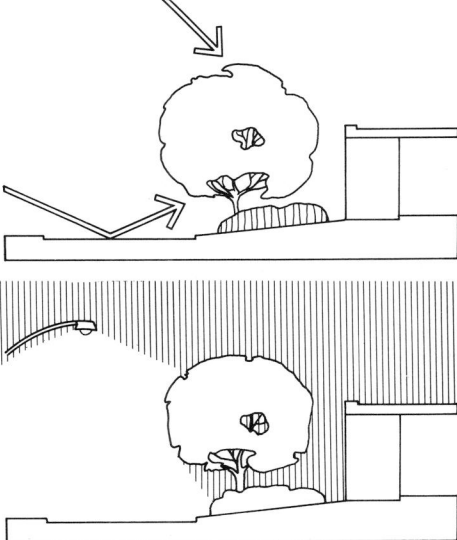

### GLARE PROTECTION

Glare and reflection from sunlight and/or artificial sources can be screened or blocked by plants of various height and placement.

### AIR FILTRATION

Large masses of plants physically and chemically filter and deodorize the air to reduce air pollution.

A. E. Bye and Associates, Landscape Architects; Old Greenwich, Connecticut
Robin Roberts; Washington, D.C.

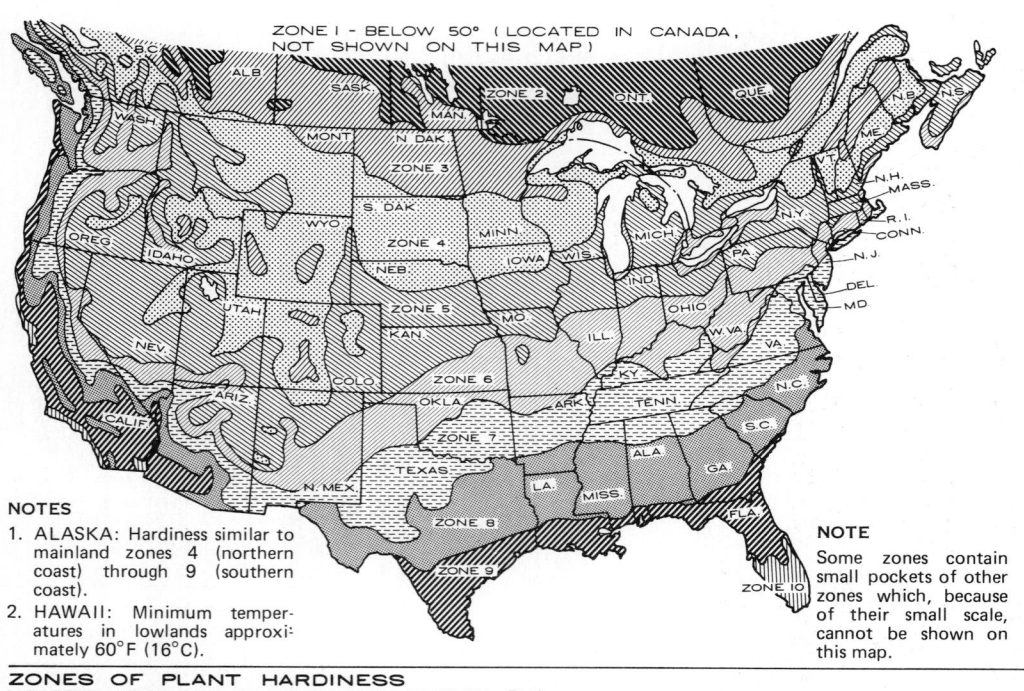

ZONE I - BELOW 50° (LOCATED IN CANADA, NOT SHOWN ON THIS MAP)

**NOTE**

The zone map shows in moderate detail the expected minimum temperature of most of the horticulturally important areas of the United States. Plants are listed in the coldest zone where they will grow normally, but they can be expected to grow in warmer areas.

**APPROXIMATE RANGE OF AVERAGE ANNUAL MINIMUM TEMPERATURES FOR EACH ZONE**

| Zone | Range |
|---|---|
| 2. | −50° TO −40° |
| 3. | −40° TO −30° |
| 4. | −30° TO −20° |
| 5. | −20° TO −10° |
| 6. | −10° TO 0° |
| 7. | 0° TO 10° |
| 8. | 10° TO 20° |
| 9. | 20° TO 30° |
| 10. | 30° TO 40° |

**NOTES**

1. ALASKA: Hardiness similar to mainland zones 4 (northern coast) through 9 (southern coast).
2. HAWAII: Minimum temperatures in lowlands approximately 60°F (16°C).

**NOTE**

Some zones contain small pockets of other zones which, because of their small scale, cannot be shown on this map.

**ZONES OF PLANT HARDINESS**
(ADAPTED FROM MAP IN U.S.D.A. PUBLICATION 814)

## NEEDLE EVERGREENS—30 FT AND OVER

| BOTANICAL NAME | COMMON NAME | Columnar | Conical | Spreading | Slow | Medium | Fast | Urban | Seashore | Ornamental | Windbreak | Green | Light Green | Dark Green | Silver Green | Blue Green | Full Sun | Dry Soil | Moist Soil | Acid | Alkaline | Well Drained | Average | 1 | 2 | 3 | 4 | 5 | 6 | 7 | 8 | 9 | 10 |
|---|---|---|---|---|---|---|---|---|---|---|---|---|---|---|---|---|---|---|---|---|---|---|---|---|---|---|---|---|---|---|---|---|---|
| Abies concolor | White fir | | ● | | | ● | ● | ● | | ● | ● | | | | | ● | ● | | | ● | | | | | | | ● | | | | | | |
| Araucaria excelsa | Norfolk Island pine | | ● | ● | | | | | ● | ● | | | | | ● | | ● | | | ● | | | | | | | | | | | | | ● |
| Cedrus atlantica glauca | Blue atlas cedar | | ● | ● | ● | | | | | ● | ● | | | | ● | ● | ● | | | | | | ● | | | | | | ● | | | | |
| Cedrus deodara | Deodar cedar | | ● | | | ● | | | | ● | ● | | ● | | | | ● | | | | | | ● | | | | | | | ● | | | |
| Cedrus libani stenocoma | Cedar of Lebanon | | ● | ● | | ● | | | | ● | | | | ● | | | ● | | | | | | ● | | | | | | ● | | | | |
| Chamaecyparis lawsoniana | Lawson false cypress | ● | | ● | | | | | | ● | ● | | | ● | | | ● | | ● | | | | | | | | | ● | | | | | |
| Chamaecyparis obtusa | Hinoki false cypress | | ● | ● | ● | | | | | ● | | | | ● | | | ● | | ● | | | | | | | | ● | | | | | | |
| Chamaecyparis pisifera | Sawara false cypress | ● | ● | | | | | | | ● | ● | ● | | | | | ● | | ● | | | | | | | ● | | | | | | | |
| Cryptomeria japonica | Cryptomeria | ● | ● | | | | | | ● | ● | | | | | | | ● | | ● | ● | | | | | | | | ● | ● | | | |
| Cunninghamia lanceolata | Common China fir | | | ● | ● | | | | | ● | ● | ● | | | | | ● | | ● | | | | | | | | | | | ● | | | |
| Cupressus sempervirens 'stricta' | Italian pyramidal cypress | ● | | ● | | | | | | ● | ● | | | | | | ● | ● | | | | | | | | | | | | ● | | | |
| Juniperus chinensis | Chinese juniper | | ● | | ● | ● | ● | | | ● | ● | | | | | | ● | | | ● | ● | | | | | | ● | | | | | | |
| Juniperus scopulorum | Western red cedar | ● | | ● | | | | | | ● | ● | | | | ● | ● | ● | | | ● | ● | | | | | | ● | | | | | | |
| Juniperus virginiana | Eastern red cedar | ● | ● | ● | | | | | | ● | ● | | | | | | ● | | | ● | ● | | | | ● | | | | | | | | |
| Larix leptolepis | Japanese larch | | ● | ● | | ● | ● | | | | | ● | | | | | ● | | ● | | | ● | | | | | ● | | | | | | |
| Libocedrus decurrens | California incense cedar | ● | ● | | | ● | | | | ● | | | | ● | | | ● | | ● | | | | | | | | | ● | | | | | |
| Metasequoia glyptostroboides | Dawn redwood | | ● | | | | ● | | | ● | ● | ● | | | | | ● | | ● | | | | | | | | | ● | | | | | |
| Picea* | Spruce | | | | | | | | | | | ● | | | | | | | | | | | | | | | | | | | | | |
| Pinus* | Pine | | | | | | | | | | | ● | | | | | | | | | | | | | | | | | | | | | |
| Podocarpus macrophyllus | Yew podocarpus | ● | | | | ● | | | | ● | ● | | | ● | | | ● | | | | | | | | | | | | | | ● | | |
| Pseudolarix amabilis | Golden larch | | ● | ● | | ● | | | | ● | ● | ● | | | | | ● | | | ● | | | | | | | ● | | | | | | |
| Pseudotsuga menziesii | Douglas fir | | ● | ● | | ● | | | | ● | ● | ● | | | | | ● | | | | | | | | | | ● | | | | | | |
| Sciadopitys verticulata | Umbrella pine | ● | ● | | ● | | | | | ● | | | | ● | | | ● | | | | | | | | | | | ● | | | | | |
| Sequoiadendron giganteum | Giant sequoia | ● | | ● | | | | | | ● | | | | | ● | ● | ● | | | | | | | | | | | | ● | | | | |
| Taxodium distichum | Bald cypress | ● | | ● | | | | | ● | ● | ● | ● | | | | | ● | ● | ● | | | | | | | | ● | | | | | | |
| Taxus Baccata | English yew | | ● | ● | | | | | | ● | ● | | | ● | | | ● | | ● | ● | | | | | | | | | ● | | | | |
| Taxus Baccata stricta | Irish yew | ● | | ● | | | | | | ● | ● | | | ● | | | ● | | ● | ● | | | | | | | | ● | | | | | |
| Thuja occidentalis | American arborvitae | ● | ● | ● | | | | ● | | ● | ● | | | | | | | | | ● | | | | | | ● | | | | | | | |
| Thuja plicata | Giant arborvitae | ● | ● | ● | | | | ● | | ● | ● | ● | | | | | | | | ● | | | | | | | ● | | | | | | |
| Tsuga canadensis | Canada hemlock | | ● | ● | | ● | | | ● | ● | | | | ● | | | ● | | ● | ● | | | | | | | ● | | | | | | |
| Tsuga caroliniana | Carolina hemlock | | ● | ● | | ● | | | | ● | | | | ● | | | ● | | ● | ● | | | | | | | | ● | | | | | |

*See other references for local species and varieties.

A. E. Bye & Associates, Landscape Architects; Old Greenwich, Connecticut

# BROAD LEAVED EVERGREENS

| Botanical Name | Common Name | Under 1 ft | 1 to 3 ft | 3 to 6 ft | 6 to 10 ft | 10 ft and over | White | Yellow-orange | Pink-red | Purple-blue | Spring | Summer | Fall | Winter | Partial sun | Full sun | Full shade | Moist soil | Dry soil | Acid soil | Alkaline soil | City | Seashore | Ornamental | Hedge | 1 | 2 | 3 | 4 | 5 | 6 | 7 | 8 | 9 | 10 |
|---|---|---|---|---|---|---|---|---|---|---|---|---|---|---|---|---|---|---|---|---|---|---|---|---|---|---|---|---|---|---|---|---|---|---|---|
| Abelia x grandiflora | Glossy abelia | | | • | | | | | • | | | • | | | • | • | | • | | | | • | | • | • | | | | | • | | | | | |
| Azalea varieties* | Azalea varieties | | | • | • | | • | • | • | | • | | | | • | • | | • | | • | | • | | • | | | | | | | | | | | |
| Buxus sempervirens | Common box | | | • | | | | | | | | | | | • | • | | • | • | | | | | | • | | | | | • | | | | | |
| Calliandra inaequilatera | Pink powder puff | | | • | | | | | • | | • | | | | | • | | | | • | | | | • | | | | | | | | | | | • |
| Callistemon citrinus | Lemon bottle brush | | | | • | • | | | • | | • | • | | • | | • | | | • | | | | | • | | | | | | | | | | • | |
| Calluna vulgaris | Heather | | • | | | | • | | • | • | | • | • | | | • | | • | | • | | | | • | | | | | • | | | | | | |
| Citrus sinensis | Sweet orange | | | | • | • | • | | | | • | • | • | • | • | • | | • | | | | | | • | | | | | | | | | | • | • |
| Codiaeum variegatum | Croton | | | • | | | | | | | | | | | • | • | | • | | | | | | • | • | | | | | | | | | | • |
| Cotoneaster species* | Cotoneaster species | | • | • | • | | • | | | | • | • | | | | • | | | | | | | | • | | | | | | • | • | • | • | | |
| Daphne cneorum | Rose daphne | • | | | | | | | • | | • | | | | • | • | | | | • | • | | | • | | | | | | • | | | | | |
| Elaeagnus pungens | Thorny elaeagnus | | | | • | • | • | • | • | | | | • | | | • | • | • | • | | • | | | • | | | | | | | | • | | | |
| Enkianthus campanulatus | Redvein enkianthus | | | | • | | • | | • | | • | | | | • | • | | • | | • | | | | • | | | | | | • | | | | | |
| Erica carnea | Spring heather | | • | | | | • | | • | • | • | | | | | • | | | | • | | | | • | | | | | | | • | | | | |
| Eriobotrya japonica | Loquat | | | | • | • | • | | | | | | • | • | | • | | | | • | | | | • | | | | | | | | • | | | |
| Euonymus japonica | Evergreen euonymus | | | | • | | | | | | | | | | • | • | | • | • | | | | | | • | | | | | | | | • | | |
| Euphorbia pulcherrima | Poinsetta | | | • | • | | | | • | | | | | • | • | • | | • | | | | | | • | | | | | | | | | | | • |
| Fatsia japonica | Japanese fatsia | | | | • | • | • | | | | | | • | | | | • | | | | | • | • | | | | | | | | | | • | | |
| Ficus benjamina | Weeping fig | | | | • | | | | | | | | | | • | | | | | | | | | • | | | | | | | | | | | • |
| Gardenia jasminoides | Gardenia | | | • | | | • | | | | • | • | • | | • | • | | • | | • | | | | • | | | | | | | | | • | | |
| Gaultheria shallon | Salal | | | • | | | • | | | | | • | | | • | • | • | • | • | | | | | • | | | | | | | • | | | | |
| Hebe traversii | Traverse hebe | | | • | | | • | | | | | • | | | | | • | | • | • | | | | • | • | | | | | | | • | | | |
| Hibiscus rosa-sinensis | Chinese hibiscus | | | | • | | | • | • | | | • | | | | • | | • | | | | | | • | • | | | | | | | | | • | |
| Hypericum species* | Saint-John's-wort species | | • | | | | | • | | | | • | • | | | • | | • | | | | | | • | | | | | | | • | | | | |
| Ilex (evergreen species)** | Holly (evergreen species) | | • | • | • | • | | | | | | | | | • | • | | • | | • | • | | | • | | | | • | • | • | • | • | • | | |
| Ixora coccinea | Ixora | | | | • | • | | • | • | | • | • | • | • | • | • | • | • | | | | | | • | | | | | | | | | | | • |
| Jasminum mesnyi | Primrose jasmine | | | | • | | | • | | | • | • | | | | • | | • | • | | | | | • | | | | | | | | | • | | |
| Kalmia latifolia | Mountain laurel | | | • | • | | • | | • | | • | | | | • | • | • | • | | • | | • | | • | | | | | • | | | | | | |
| Laurus nobilis | Laurel | | | | • | • | | | | | • | | | | | • | | • | • | | • | | | • | | | | | | | • | | | | |
| Ligustrum japonicum | Japanese privet | | | • | • | • | • | | | | | • | | | | • | | | • | | | | | • | • | | | | | | | • | | | |
| Mahonia aquifolia | Oregon holly-grape | | • | | | | | • | | | • | | | | • | | | | | | | | | • | | | | | • | • | | | | | |
| Myrtus communis 'compacta' | Compact Myrtle | | | • | • | | • | | | | | • | | | | • | | | • | | | | • | | • | | | | | | | | • | | |
| Nandina domestica | Nandina | | | • | | | • | | | | | • | | | | • | • | | | | | | | • | | | | | | | | • | | | |
| Nerium Oleander | Oleander | | | | • | • | • | • | • | • | • | • | | | | • | | • | • | • | | | | • | • | | | | | | | • | | |
| Olea europarea | Common olive | | | | • | • | • | | | | • | | | | | • | | • | | | | | | • | | | | | | | | | | • | |
| Osmanthus heterophyllus | Holly osmanthus | | | | • | • | • | | | | | | • | | | • | | • | | | | | | • | • | | | | | | | • | | | |
| Photinia serrulata | Chinese photinia | | | | • | • | • | | | | • | | | | • | | | | | | | | | • | | | | | | | | • | | | |
| Pieris floribunda | Mountain andromeda | | | • | | | • | | | | • | | | | • | • | | • | | • | | • | | • | | | | | • | | | | | | |
| Pieris japonica | Japanese andromeda | | | • | | | • | | | | • | | | | | • | | • | | • | | • | | • | | | | | | • | | | | | |
| Pittosporum tobira | Japanese pittosporum | | | • | | | • | | | | • | | | | | • | | • | | | | | | • | • | | | | | | | | • | | |
| Plumbago capensis | Cape plumbago | | • | | | | | | | • | • | • | • | • | • | • | | | | | | | | • | • | | | | | | | | | • | |
| Prunus laurocerasus 'schipkaenis' | Schipka cherry-laurel | | | • | • | | • | | | | • | | | | | • | | | | | | | | • | • | | | | | | • | • | | | |
| Pyracantha coccinea | Firethorn | | | | • | | • | | | | • | | | | | • | | | • | • | | | | • | | | | | | | • | | | | |
| Rhododendron species* | Rhododendron species | | • | • | • | • | • | | • | | • | • | | | • | • | | • | | • | | | | • | | | | | • | • | • | | | | |
| Schinus molle | California pepper tree | | | | • | • | | | | | | • | | | | • | | • | • | • | | | | • | | | | | | | | | | • | |
| Skimmia japonica | Japanese skimmia | | | • | | | • | | | | • | | | | • | | • | | | | | | | • | | | | | | | | | • | | |
| Ulmus parvifolia pendens | Evergreen elm | | | | | • | | | | | | | | | | • | | • | • | • | • | | | • | | | | | | | | | | | • |
| Viburnum rhytidophyllum | Leatherleaf viburnum | | | | • | • | • | | | | • | | | • | | | | • | | | | | | • | | | | | | | • | | | | |
| Xylosma senticosa | Xylosma | | • | | • | | | | | | | | | | • | | | • | | • | | | | • | | | | | | | | | • | | |

* See other references for local species and varieties.
** Also deciduous ilex available.

A. E. Bye & Associates, Landscape Architects; Old Greenwich, Connecticut

## DECIDUOUS TREES—20 TO 50 FT

| BOTANICAL NAME | COMMON NAME | Rounded | Weeping | Spreading | Conical | Columnar | Oval | Slow | Medium | Fast | Shade Tree | Ornamental | Street Tree | Urban Tree | Seashore Tree | Flowers | Fruit | Leaf Color | Bark | Light Shade | Full Sun | Dry Soil | Moist Soil | Well Drained Soil | Acid Soil | Alkali Soil | 1 | 2 | 3 | 4 | 5 | 6 | 7 | 8 | 9 | 10 |
|---|---|---|---|---|---|---|---|---|---|---|---|---|---|---|---|---|---|---|---|---|---|---|---|---|---|---|---|---|---|---|---|---|---|---|---|---|
| | | | | | | SHAPE | | | RATE OF GROWTH | | | | USES | | | | NOTABLE TRAITS | | | | | CULTURAL CONDITIONS | | | | | | | | | HARDINESS ZONES | | | | | |
| Acer campestre | Hedge maple | ● | | | | | | ● | | | | ● | ● | ● | | | | | | ● | ● | | | | | | | | | | | | ● | | | |
| Acer ginnala | Amur maple | ● | | | | | | | | ● | | ● | ● | ● | | ● | ● | ● | | | ● | ● | | | | | | | ● | | | | | | | |
| Acer palmatum | Japanese maple | ● | | | | | | ● | | | | ● | | ● | | | | ● | | | ● | ● | | ● | ● | | | | | | | | ● | | | |
| Ailanthus altissima | Tree of heaven | ● | | | | | | | | ● | | | ● | ● | ● | | ● | ● | | | ● | ● | ● | | ● | | | | | | | ● | | | | |
| Albizia julibrissin | Hardy silk tree | | | ● | | | | | ● | ● | ● | | ● | ● | | | | | | ● | ● | | | | | | | | | | | | ● | | |
| Amelanchier laevis | Allegany serviceberry | ● | | | | | | | ● | | | ● | | ● | ● | ● | ● | ● | ● | ● | ● | ● | ● | | | | | | | ● | | | | | |
| Arbutus unedo | Strawberry tree | | | ● | | | | ● | | | ● | | | ● | | | ● | ● | | ● | | | ● | | | ● | | | | | | | | | ● | |
| Bauhinia variegata | Buddhist bauhinia | ● | | | | | | | ● | ● | ● | ● | | | ● | | | | ● | ● | ● | | | | | | | | | | | | | ● |
| Betula populifolia | Gray birch | | | ● | | ● | | | ● | | | ● | | | | ● | ● | | | ● | ● | ● | ● | | | | | | ● | ● | | | | | |
| Broussonetia papyrifera | Common paper mulberry | ● | | ● | | | | | ● | | ● | ● | ● | | ● | ● | ● | | ● | ● | ● | ● | | | | | | | | | ● | | | |
| Camellia japonica | Common camellia | ● | | | | | | ● | | | ● | | | ● | | | ● | | ● | | ● | | | | ● | | | | | | | | ● | | |
| Carpinus caroliniana | American hornbeam | ● | | | | | | ● | | | | ● | ● | ● | | | | ● | ● | ● | ● | | | | | | | ● | | | | | | | | |
| Cassia fistula | Golden shower senna | ● | | | | | | | ● | | ● | ● | ● | | ● | ● | | | ● | ● | | | ● | | | | | | | | | | | | ● |
| Castanea mollissima | Chinese chestnut | | | ● | | | | | ● | ● | | | ● | | ● | ● | ● | | | ● | ● | | ● | | | | | ● | ● | | | | | |
| Cercis canadensis | Eastern redbud | ● | | ● | | | ● | | ● | | | ● | | ● | | ● | ● | | ● | ● | | | | | | | | ● | | | | | | |
| Chionanthus virginicus | Fringetree | ● | | ● | | | | ● | | | ● | | ● | | ● | ● | | ● | ● | | | | | | | | ● | | | | | | |
| Cladastris lutea | American yellowwood | ● | | | | | | ● | | ● | ● | ● | ● | | ● | ● | ● | ● | ● | ● | ● | | ● | | | ● | | | | | | | |
| Clethera barbinervis | Japanese clethera | | | ● | | | | ● | | | ● | | | ● | ● | ● | ● | ● | | | | | | ● | | | | | |
| Cornus florida | Flowering dogwood | ● | ● | ● | | | | ● | | | ● | | ● | | ● | ● | ● | ● | ● | ● | ● | ● | | ● | | | | | ● | | | | |
| Cornus kousa | Japanese dogwood | | | ● | | | | ● | | | ● | | ● | | ● | ● | ● | ● | ● | ● | ● | | ● | | | | | ● | | | | |
| Cornus mas | Cornelian cherry | ● | | ● | | | | ● | | | ● | | ● | | ● | ● | ● | ● | ● | ● | ● | | | | | | ● | | | | |
| Crataegus species* | Hawthorne species | ● | | ● | | | | ● | ● | ● | | ● | ● | ● | ● | ● | ● | ● | ● | ● | | ● | ● | | | | ● | | | | |
| Delonix regia | Royal poinciana | | | ● | | | | | ● | ● | ● | ● | ● | | ● | ● | | | ● | ● | | | | | | | | | | | ● |
| Elaeagnus angustifolia | Russian olive | ● | | ● | | | | | ● | | ● | ● | ● | | ● | ● | | ● | ● | ● | ● | | | | ● | | | | | | |
| Firmiana simplex | Chinese parasol tree | | | | ● | | | | ● | | | ● | ● | | ● | ● | | ● | | | | | | | | | | ● | |
| Fraxinus holotricha | Moraine ash | ● | | | | | | | ● | | ● | ● | | | ● | | | | | | | ● | | | | | | |
| Fraxinus velutina glabra | Modesto ash | ● | | | | | | | ● | ● | ● | | | | ● | | ● | | ● | ● | | ● | | | | ● | | | | |
| Halesia carolina | Carolina silverbell | ● | | | ● | | | | ● | | ● | | ● | | ● | | ● | | ● | ● | ● | | | | | ● | | | | |
| Koelreuteria paniculata | Goldenrain tree | | | ● | | | | | ● | ● | ● | ● | ● | ● | | ● | ● | | | ● | | | | | | ● | | | | |
| Laburnum watereri | Waterer laburnum | | | | | ● | | | ● | | ● | | | ● | | | ● | | ● | | ● | | | | | ● | | | | |
| Magnolia species* | Magnolia | ● | | | | | | | ● | | ● | | ● | ● | ● | ● | ● | ● | | ● | ● | | | | | ● | ● | ● | ● | ● |
| Malus species* | Crab apple species | ● | | ● | | | ● | | ● | | | ● | ● | | ● | ● | ● | | ● | ● | | | | | | ● | ● | ● | | | |
| Melia azedarach | Chinaberry | ● | | ● | | | | | ● | ● | | ● | ● | | ● | ● | | ● | ● | | ● | ● | | ● | | | | | ● | |
| Phellodendron amurense | Amur cork tree | | | ● | | | | | ● | | ● | ● | | ● | ● | | ● | | ● | | ● | ● | ● | ● | | | ● | | | | |
| Prunus species* | Cherries, apricots, plums, peaches | ● | | | | | | | ● | | ● | | ● | | ● | ● | ● | ● | | ● | | | | | ● | ● | ● | ● | ● | ● | |
| Pterocarya fraxinifolia | Caucasian wing nut | | | ● | | | | | ● | | ● | | | ● | | | ● | | | ● | | | | | | ● | | | |
| Pyrus calleryana "Bradford" | Bradford pear | | | ● | | | | ● | | | ● | ● | ● | | ● | ● | ● | | ● | | | | | | | ● | | | | |
| Salix babylonica | Babylon weeping willow | | ● | | | | | | ● | | ● | | | | ● | | | ● | ● | | ● | | | | | ● | | |
| Salix elegantissima | Thurlow weeping willow | | ● | | | | | | ● | | ● | | | | ● | | | ● | ● | | ● | | | | ● | | | |
| Sapium sebiferum | Chinese tallow tree | | | ● | | | | | ● | ● | | | ● | ● | | | ● | ● | ● | | | | | | | | | ● |
| Sorbus alnifolia | Korean mountain ash | ● | | ● | | | | | ● | ● | | ● | ● | ● | | ● | ● | ● | | | | | | | ● | | | | |
| Sorbus aucuparia | Rowan tree | ● | | ● | | | | | ● | ● | | ● | ● | | ● | ● | ● | | | | | | | ● | | | | |
| Stewartia koreana | Korean stewartia | | | ● | | | | | ● | | | ● | | ● | ● | ● | ● | ● | | | | | | ● | | | | |
| Styrax japonica | Japanese snowbell | ● | | ● | | | ● | | ● | | | ● | | ● | ● | ● | ● | ● | | ● | ● | | ● | | | ● | | | | |
| Syringa amurensis japonica | Japanese tree lilac | | | ● | ● | | | ● | ● | | ● | ● | ● | | ● | | | ● | | ● | ● | | | | ● | | | | |
| Ulmus parvifolia | Chinese elm | | ● | | | | | | ● | | | ● | | ● | ● | ● | ● | ● | ● | ● | ● | | ● | | | ● | | | |
| Viburnum sieboldii | Siebold viburnum | ● | | ● | | | | ● | | | ● | | ● | ● | ● | ● | ● | ● | | ● | ● | | | | ● | | | | |

*See other references for local species and varieties.

A. E. Bye & Associates, Landscape Architects; Old Greenwich, Connecticut

## LANDSCAPING

# LARGE DECIDUOUS TREES—50 FT AND OVER

| Botanical Name | Common Name | Rounded | Weeping | Spreading | Conical | Columnar | Oval | Slow | Medium | Fast | Shade Tree | Ornamental | Street Tree | Urban Tree | Seashore Tree | Flowers | Fruit | Leaf Color | Bark | Light Shade | Full Sun | Dry Soil | Moist Soil | Acid Soil | Alkaline Soil | Well Drained Soil | 1 | 2 | 3 | 4 | 5 | 6 | 7 | 8 | 9 | 10 |
|---|---|---|---|---|---|---|---|---|---|---|---|---|---|---|---|---|---|---|---|---|---|---|---|---|---|---|---|---|---|---|---|---|---|---|---|---|
| Acacia decurrens dealbata | Silver wattle | | | • | | | | | | • | | • | | | | • | | | | | • | | • | | | • | | | | | | | | | • | |
| Acer platinoides and varieties | Norway maple and varieties | • | | | • | • | | | • | • | • | • | • | • | | • | | | | | • | | | | | • | | | • | | | | | | | |
| Acer rubrum | Red or swamp maple | • | | | | | • | | • | • | • | | • | | | • | • | • | • | | | | • | | | | | | • | | | | | | | |
| Acer saccharum | Sugar maple | | | | • | | • | • | | | • | | • | | | | | • | | • | • | | • | | • | | | | • | | | | | | | |
| Aesculus hippocastanum | Horse chestnut | • | | | | | • | | • | | • | | • | | | • | | | | • | • | | • | | | | | | • | | | | | | | |
| Betula nigra | River birch | | | | • | | | | • | | • | | • | • | | | | • | • | • | • | • | • | • | | | | | | • | | | | | | |
| Betula papyrifera | Canoe or paper birch | | | | • | | • | | • | | • | | • | | | | | | • | • | • | • | | | | | | | • | | | | | | | |
| Betula pendula | European birch | | • | | • | • | | | | | | | | | | | | | • | • | • | • | • | | | | | | • | | | | | | | |
| Carpinus betulus | European hornbeam | • | | | | • | | • | | | | • | | • | • | | | | • | • | | | | | | | | | | | | • | | | | |
| Cercidiphyllum japonicum | Katsura tree | • | | | | | | | • | • | • | | • | • | | | | | • | • | • | • | | • | | | | | | | | • | | | | |
| Cornus controversa | Giant dogwood | | | • | | | | | • | | | • | | | | • | • | | • | | | | • | | | | | | | | • | | | | |
| Eucalyptus species* | Eucalyptus species | • | | | | | | | • | • | • | • | • | | | | | • | • | • | | | | | | | | | | | | | | | • | • |
| Fagus grandifolia | American beech | • | | | | | • | • | | | • | • | | | • | | | | • | • | • | | • | | | | | | • | | | | | | | |
| Fagus sylvatica and varieties* | European beech and varieties | • | • | • | | | • | • | | | • | • | | | • | | | | • | • | • | | | | | | | | | • | | | | | | |
| Fraxinus americana | White ash | • | | | | | | | • | • | • | | • | | | | | | • | | • | | | | | | | | • | | | | | | | |
| Fraxinus oregona | Oregon ash | | | | • | | | | • | | • | | • | | | | | | | | • | | | | | | | | | | | | | • | | |
| Fraxinus pennsylvanica lanceolata | Green ash | • | | | • | | | | • | | • | | • | | | | | | • | | • | | | | | | | • | | | | | | | | |
| Ginkgo biloba | Ginkgo | | | • | • | • | | | • | | | | • | • | | | | | • | | • | • | • | | | | | | | • | | | | | | |
| Gleditsia triacanthos and varieties* | Honey locust and varieties | | | • | | | | | • | • | • | | • | • | • | | | | • | • | | | | | | | | | | • | | | | | | |
| Gordonia lasianthus | Loblolly bay gordonia | | | | • | | | • | | | | • | | • | | | • | | | | • | • | • | • | | | | | | | | | | • | | |
| Liquidambar styraciflua | Sweet gum | | | | • | | | | • | | • | | • | | | | • | • | • | • | • | • | | • | | | | | | | • | | | | |
| Liriodendron tulipifera | Tulip tree | | | | | | • | | • | | • | | • | | | • | • | • | | • | • | • | | • | | | | | | | • | | | | |
| Magnolia grandiflora | Southern magnolia | | | | • | | | | • | | | • | | • | | | • | • | | | | | | | • | | | | | | | | • | | |
| Nyssa sylvatica | Black tupelo | | | | • | | | | • | | • | | • | | | | | | • | | • | • | • | • | • | | | | | | • | | | | |
| Pittosporum rhombifolium | Diamond leaf pittosporum | • | | | | | | | • | | | • | | • | | | • | | | | • | | | | | | | | | | | | | | | • |
| Platanus acerifolium | London plane tree | • | | • | | | | | • | | • | | • | • | | | | | • | • | • | | | • | | | | | | • | | | | | |
| Populus alba | White poplar | | | • | | • | | | • | • | | • | | | | | | | • | | • | | • | | | | | | | • | | | | | | |
| Populus tremuloides | Quaking aspen | | | • | | | | | | • | | • | | | | | | • | • | • | | • | • | • | • | • | | | • | | | | | | | |
| Prunus serotina | Black cherry | | | • | | | | | • | | • | • | | | • | | • | • | | • | | | | | | | | | | • | | | | | | |
| Quercus alba | White oak | • | | • | | | • | | | | • | • | | | • | | | | • | • | • | | • | | | | | | • | | | | | | | |
| Quercus borealis | Red oak | • | | • | | | • | | | • | • | • | • | | | | | | • | | • | | • | | | | | | • | | | | | | | |
| Quercus coccinea | Scarlet oak | • | | • | | | | | • | | • | | | | | | | | • | | • | | • | | | | | | • | | | | | | | |
| Quercus falcata | Southern red oak | • | | • | | | • | | | • | | | | | | | | | • | | • | | • | | | | | | | | • | | | | | |
| Quercus imbricaria | Shingle oak | • | | | • | | | • | | | • | | • | | | | | | • | | • | | • | | | | | | | | • | | | | | |
| Quercus kelloggii | California black oak | • | | • | | | • | | | • | | | | | | | | | • | | • | • | • | | | | | | | | | | | • | | |
| Quercus laurifolia | Laurel oak | | | | | | • | | | • | | | • | | | | | | | | • | | • | | | | | | | | | | | • | | |
| Quercus palustris | Pin oak | | | | • | | | | • | | • | | • | | | | | | • | | • | | • | | | | | | | • | | | | | | |
| Quercus phellos | Willow oak | • | | | • | | | | • | | • | • | • | • | | | | | • | | • | | • | • | | | | | | | | | | • | • | |
| Quercus robur and varieties* | English oak and varieties | • | | | • | • | • | | | | • | | • | | | | | | • | | • | | • | | | | | | | | • | | | | | |
| Quercus shumardii | Shumard oak | | | • | | | | | • | | • | • | | • | | | | | • | | • | | • | | | | | | • | | | | | | | |
| Quercus virginiana | Live oak | • | | • | | | • | | | • | | • | | • | • | | • | | • | | • | • | | | | | | | | | | | | • | | |
| Salix alba tristis | Golden weeping willow | | • | | | | | | • | | • | | • | | | • | | | • | | • | | • | | | | | | • | | | | | | | |
| Sassafras albidum | Sassafras | | | | • | | | | • | | • | | | | | • | • | • | • | • | • | | | | • | | | | | | • | | | | | |
| Sophora japonica | Japanese pagoda tree | • | | • | | | | | • | • | • | • | | • | • | | • | | • | | • | | | | | | | | | | • | | | | | |
| Tilia cordata | Little leaf linden | | | | • | | • | | | | • | • | • | • | | | • | | • | | • | • | • | | | | | | | | | • | | | | |
| Tilia euchlora | Crimean linden | | | | • | | | | | | • | • | • | • | | | • | | • | | • | • | • | | | | | | | | • | | | | | |
| Tilia tomentosa | Silver linden | | | | • | | • | | • | | • | • | • | • | | | • | | • | | • | • | • | | | | | | | | • | | | | | |
| Zelkova serrata and varieties* | Japanese zelkova and varieties | • | | | | | | | • | • | | • | | • | • | | • | | • | | • | • | • | | | • | | | | | | • | | | | |

*See other references for local species and varieties.

A. E. Bye & Associates, Landscape Architects; Old Greenwich, Connecticut

## DECIDUOUS SHRUBS

| Botanical Name | Common Name | 0 to 3 ft | 3 to 6 ft | 6 to 10 ft | 10 ft and over | Flowers | Fruit | Foliage Color | Good Winter Appearance | Rapid Growth | Easy Maintenance | White | Yellow-orange | Pink-red | Blue-purple | Spring | Summer | Fall | Winter | Urban | Seashore | Hedges | Sun | Shade | Light Shade | Acid Soil | Alkaline Soil | Moist Soil | Dry Soil | Well drained Soil | 1 | 2 | 3 | 4 | 5 | 6 | 7 | 8 | 9 | 10 |
|---|---|---|---|---|---|---|---|---|---|---|---|---|---|---|---|---|---|---|---|---|---|---|---|---|---|---|---|---|---|---|---|---|---|---|---|---|---|---|---|---|
| Amelanchier stolonifera | Running serviceberry |  | • |  |  | • | • | • |  |  | • | • |  |  |  | • |  |  |  |  | • |  | • |  | • |  |  | • | • |  |  |  |  | • |  |  |  |  |  |  |
| Aronia species* | Chokeberry species | • | • | • | • | • | • | • | • |  |  | • | • |  |  | • |  |  |  | • | • | • | • |  | • |  |  | • | • | • |  |  |  | • |  |  |  |  |  |  |
| Berberis species* | Barberry species | • | • | • |  | • | • | • | • |  |  |  | • | • |  | • |  |  |  | • | • | • | • |  | • |  |  | • | • | • |  |  |  | • |  |  |  |  |  |  |
| Calycanthus floridus | Sweet shrub |  | • | • |  | • |  | • |  |  | • |  |  | • | • |  | • |  |  |  |  |  | • |  | • | • |  |  | • |  |  |  |  | • |  |  |  |  |  |  |
| Caragana arborescens | Siberian pea tree |  |  | • | • | • | • |  |  |  |  |  | • |  |  | • |  |  | • |  | • | • |  |  |  |  |  | • | • | • |  | • |  |  |  |  |  |  |  |  |
| Cercis chinensis | Chinese redbud |  | • | • |  | • |  |  |  | • | • | • |  |  | • | • | • |  |  |  |  |  | • | • |  |  |  |  | • |  |  |  |  |  |  |  |  | • |  |  |
| Chaenomeles species* | Quince species | • | • |  |  | • | • |  |  |  |  | • | • | • |  | • |  |  |  | • | • | • | • |  | • |  |  | • | • |  |  |  | • |  |  |  |  |  |  |  |
| Clethra alnifolia | Summer sweet |  | • |  |  | • |  | • |  |  | • |  |  | • |  |  | • | • |  | • |  |  | • | • | • |  | • |  | • |  |  |  |  |  |  | • |  |  |  |  |
| Cornus species* | Dogwood species | • | • | • | • | • | • | • | • | • | • | • |  | • |  | • |  |  |  | • |  | • | • |  | • | • |  | • | • |  |  |  | • |  |  |  |  |  |  |  |
| Corylopsis species* | Winter hazel species | • | • | • | • | • |  | • |  |  |  | • |  | • |  | • |  |  |  |  | • | • | • | • |  | • |  |  | • | • |  |  |  |  |  |  |  | • |  |  |
| Cotinus species* | Smoke tree species |  | • | • |  | • |  | • |  |  |  | • |  | • | • |  | • |  |  |  |  |  | • |  |  |  | • | • | • |  |  |  |  |  |  |  |  | • |  |  |
| Cotoneaster species* | Cotoneaster species | • | • | • | • | • | • | • |  |  |  | • | • |  |  | • |  |  |  | • | • | • | • |  | • |  |  | • | • |  |  |  |  | • |  |  |  |  |  |  |
| Cytisus species* | Scotch broom species | • | • | • |  | • |  | • | • | • |  |  | • |  |  | • |  |  |  | • |  | • |  |  | • |  |  | • | • |  |  |  |  |  | • |  |  |  |  |  |
| Deutzia species* | Deutzia species |  | • | • |  | • |  |  | • |  |  | • |  | • |  | • |  |  |  | • |  |  | • |  | • |  |  | • | • |  |  |  |  |  | • |  |  |  |  |  |
| Euonymus species* | Euonymus species |  | • | • | • | • |  |  | • |  |  |  |  | • |  | • |  |  |  | • | • | • | • | • |  | • | • |  |  | • | • |  |  | • |  |  |  |  |  |  |
| Exochorda species* | Pearlbush species |  | • | • |  | • |  |  |  |  |  | • |  |  |  | • |  |  |  |  |  | • | • |  |  |  |  | • |  |  |  |  |  |  |  |  |  | • |  |  |
| Forsythia species* | Forsythia species | • | • | • |  | • |  |  |  | • | • |  | • |  |  | • |  |  |  | • |  | • | • |  | • |  |  | • | • |  |  |  |  |  | • |  |  |  |  |  |
| Fothergilla species* | Fothergilla species | • | • | • |  | • |  | • |  |  |  | • |  |  |  | • |  |  |  |  | • | • | • | • |  | • |  |  | • | • |  |  |  |  |  |  |  | • |  |  |
| Hamamelis species* | Witch hazel species |  | • | • | • |  | • | • |  |  |  | • |  | • |  | • | • | • | • | • |  | • | • |  | • |  | • | • | • |  |  |  |  |  | • |  |  |  |  |  |
| Hibiscus species* | Rose of Sharon species |  | • | • | • | • |  |  |  | • |  | • |  | • | • | • |  | • | • | • | • | • | • | • |  | • | • |  |  |  | • |  |  |  |  |  | • |  |  |  |
| Ilex verticillata | Winterberry |  | • |  |  |  | • | • | • | • |  | • |  |  |  | • |  |  |  |  | • | • | • |  | • | • |  | • | • |  |  |  |  | • |  |  |  |  |  |  |
| Jasminum nudiflorum | Winter jasmine | • | • | • |  |  |  | • |  |  |  |  | • |  |  | • |  |  | • | • |  | • |  |  | • |  |  | • |  |  |  |  |  |  |  |  |  | • |  |  |
| Kerria japonica | Kerria |  | • | • |  | • |  |  | • |  |  |  | • |  |  | • |  |  |  | • |  |  | • |  | • |  |  | • | • |  |  |  |  |  | • |  |  |  |  |  |
| Kolkwitzia amabilis | Beauty bush |  | • |  |  | • | • | • | • |  | • |  |  | • |  |  | • |  |  | • |  |  | • |  | • |  |  | • | • |  |  |  |  |  | • |  |  |  |  |  |
| Lagerstroemia indica | Crape myrtle |  | • | • |  | • | • |  | • | • |  |  | • | • | • |  | • | • |  |  | • |  |  | • |  | • |  |  | • | • |  |  |  |  |  |  |  |  | • |  |  |
| Lespedeza species* | Bush clover species |  | • | • |  | • |  |  |  |  |  |  | • |  | • |  |  | • | • | • |  |  |  |  |  | • |  |  | • | • |  |  |  |  | • |  |  |  |  |  |
| Ligustrum species* | Privet species |  | • | • |  | • | • | • |  | • |  | • |  | • |  | • |  |  |  | • | • | • | • | • | • | • |  |  | • | • |  |  |  | • |  |  |  |  |  |  |
| Lindera benzoin | Spicebush |  | • | • |  |  | • | • |  |  |  | • |  |  |  | • |  |  |  | • |  |  | • | • | • |  |  | • | • |  |  |  |  | • |  |  |  |  |  |  |
| Myrica pensylvanica | Bayberry |  | • | • |  |  | • | • | • |  | • |  |  |  |  |  | • | • |  | • | • |  | • |  |  | • | • |  | • | • |  | • |  |  |  |  |  |  |  |  |
| Photinia villosa | Oriental photinia |  |  | • | • | • | • | • |  |  | • |  |  |  | • |  |  |  |  | • |  |  | • |  | • |  |  | • | • |  |  |  |  | • |  |  |  |  |  |  |
| Plumeria rubra | Frangipani |  |  | • | • | • |  |  | • |  |  | • | • | • | • |  | • | • |  |  |  |  | • |  |  |  |  | • | • |  |  |  |  |  |  |  |  |  |  | • |
| Potentilla species* | Bush cinquefoil species | • |  |  |  | • |  |  |  |  |  | • | • | • |  | • | • | • | • |  |  |  | • |  |  |  |  | • | • |  |  |  |  | • |  |  |  |  |  |  |
| Rhamnus species* | Buckthorn species |  | • | • |  | • | • |  |  |  |  |  |  |  |  | • |  |  |  | • | • | • | • |  | • |  |  | • | • |  |  |  |  | • |  |  |  |  |  |  |
| Rhododendron | Azalea | • | • | • | • | • |  | • |  |  |  | • | • | • | • | • |  |  |  |  |  | • | • |  | • | • |  | • | • |  |  |  |  | • |  |  |  |  |  |  |
| Rosa species* | 'Shrub' rose species | • | • | • | • | • | • | • |  | • | • | • | • | • |  | • | • |  |  | • | • | • | • |  |  |  |  | • | • | • |  |  |  | • |  |  |  |  |  |  |
| Spiraea species* | Spiraea species | • | • | • |  | • |  | • |  |  |  | • | • | • |  | • | • |  |  | • |  | • | • |  | • |  |  | • | • |  |  |  |  |  | • |  |  |  |  |  |
| Stephanandra species* | Stephanandra species | • | • |  |  | • |  | • |  |  |  | • |  |  |  | • |  |  |  |  |  |  | • | • | • |  |  | • |  |  |  |  |  |  |  |  |  | • |  |  |
| Stewartia species* | Stewartia species |  |  | • | • | • |  | • | • |  |  | • | • |  |  |  | • |  |  |  |  |  | • |  | • |  | • |  | • |  |  |  |  |  |  |  |  | • |  |  |
| Symphoricarpos species* | Snowberry species | • | • |  |  |  | • |  | • |  |  | • |  |  |  |  |  |  | • |  | • | • | • | • |  | • |  |  | • | • |  |  |  | • |  |  |  |  |  |  |
| Symplocos paniculata | Sapphireberry |  |  | • | • | • | • |  |  |  |  | • |  |  |  | • |  |  |  |  |  | • |  | • | • | • |  |  |  | • |  |  |  |  |  |  |  | • |  |  |
| Syringa species* | Lilac species | • | • | • | • | • |  |  |  | • |  | • | • | • | • | • |  |  |  | • | • | • | • |  | • | • |  | • |  | • |  |  | • |  |  |  |  |  |  |  |
| Vaccinium corymbosum | Highbush blueberry |  | • | • |  | • | • | • | • |  |  | • |  |  |  | • |  |  | • | • |  | • | • |  | • | • |  | • | • |  |  |  |  |  |  | • |  |  |  |  |
| Viburnum species* | Viburnum species | • | • | • | • | • | • | • | • |  |  | • | • | • |  | • | • |  |  | • | • | • | • | • | • | • |  | • | • | • |  |  |  | • |  |  |  |  |  |  |

## NOTES

*See other references for local species and varieties. Listings in this chart represent large genera of many species and varieties. Other sources need to be consulted to obtain detailed information. The hardiness zone notations indicate that most of the species within the family are hardy to that zone but there are a few that are not.

A. E. Bye & Associates, Landscape Architects; Old Greenwich, Connecticut

LANDSCAPING

# GROUND COVERS

| BOTANICAL NAME | COMMON NAME | HEIGHT | | | | LIGHT RE-QUIRE-MENTS | | | SOIL TYPES | | SPECIAL AREAS | | MOISTURE NEEDS | | | FOLIAGE COLOR | | | | | FEATURES | | | | | | HARDINESS ZONES | | | | | | | | | |
|---|---|---|---|---|---|---|---|---|---|---|---|---|---|---|---|---|---|---|---|---|---|---|---|---|---|---|---|---|---|---|---|---|---|---|---|---|
| | | Less than 6 in. | 6 to 12 in. | 12 to 18 in. | 18 in. and over | Sun | Shade | Light Shade | Acid | Alkaline | Seashore | City | Moist Soil | Dry Soil | Well-drained Soil | Green | Dark Green | Blue Green | Gray Green | Purple Green | Flowers | Fruit | Mowable | Slopes | Rapid Growth | Easy Maintenance | 1 | 2 | 3 | 4 | 5 | 6 | 7 | 8 | 9 | 10 |
| **DECIDUOUS** | | | | | | | | | | | | | | | | | | | | | | | | | | | | | | | | | | | | |
| Asperula odorata | Sweet woodruff | | • | | | | | • | • | | | | • | | • | | | | | | • | | | • | • | | | | | • | | | | | | |
| Coronilla varia | Crown vetch | | | • | • | • | | • | • | • | | | • | • | • | | | | | | • | | | • | • | • | | | • | | | | | | | |
| Cotoneaster (spreading varieties) | Cotoneaster | | • | | | • | | | • | • | • | | | | • | | • | | | | • | • | | • | | • | | | | | | • | | | | |
| Gazania uniflora | Trailing gazania | • | | | | • | | | • | • | | | | • | | | • | | | • | | • | | | • | • | • | | | | | | | | | • | |
| Phlox subulata | Ground pink | • | | | | • | | | | | | | • | • | | | • | | | | | • | | | | • | | • | | | | | | | | | |
| Rosa wichuraiana | Memorial rose | | • | | | • | | | | | • | | | • | | • | | • | | | | • | | | • | • | • | | | | | • | | | | | |
| Trifolium repens | White clover | • | | | | • | | | | | | | • | | • | | | | | | • | | • | | • | | • | | | | | | | | | |
| Vaccinium angustifolium laevifolium | Low bush blueberry | | • | | | • | • | • | • | | | | • | | • | | | • | • | | | • | • | | • | • | • | | | | | | | | | |
| Veronica repens | Creeping speedwell | • | | | | • | • | • | | | | | • | | • | | | | | | • | | | • | | • | | | | | | | | | | |
| Xanthorhiza simplicissima | Yellowroot | | | • | • | • | | | | | | | • | | • | | | | | | • | | | • | • | | | | • | | | | | | | |
| **BROAD LEAVED EVERGREENS** | | | | | | | | | | | | | | | | | | | | | | | | | | | | | | | | | | | | |
| Ajuga reptans | Bugleweed | • | | | | • | • | • | | | | | • | | | • | • | | | • | • | | | • | | | | • | | | | | | | | |
| Anthemis nobilis | Chamomile | • | • | | | • | | | | | | | | | • | | | | | | • | | • | | • | | | • | | | | | | | | |
| Arabis albida | Wall rockcress | • | | | | • | | | | | | | | | • | • | | | • | | • | | | | • | | | • | | | | | | | | |
| Arctostaphylos uva-ursi | Bearberry | | • | | | • | | • | • | | | | | | • | | • | • | | | • | • | | • | | | • | | | | | | | | | |
| Baccharis pilularis | Coyote bush | | • | • | • | • | | | • | | • | • | | | | • | | • | | | • | | | • | • | • | | | | | | | | • | | |
| Carissa macrocarpa 'green carpet' | Green carpet natal plum | | • | | | • | | | • | | | | | | | • | | • | • | | | • | | | • | | | | | | | | | | • | |
| Carpobrotus edulis | Hottentot fig | • | | | | • | | | • | | | | | • | | | | • | • | | | • | • | | • | • | • | | | | | | | | | • |
| Ceanothus griseus horizontalis | Carmel creeper | | | • | • | • | | | • | | | | | • | | • | | • | | | • | | | • | • | | | | | | | | • | | | |
| Ceratostigma plumbaginoides | Leadwort | | • | | | • | | • | | | | | • | • | • | | • | | | | • | | | • | • | | | | | | | • | | | | |
| Cornus canadensis | Bunchberry | | • | | | | • | • | • | | | | • | | • | | • | • | | | • | • | | • | • | | • | | | | | | | | | |
| Cotoneaster dammeri | Bearberry cotoneaster | | • | | | • | | | • | • | • | • | • | • | | • | | • | • | | | • | • | | • | • | | | | • | | | | | | |
| Dichondra repens | Dichondra | • | | | | • | • | • | | | | | • | • | | • | | | | | | | • | • | | • | | | | | | | | | | • |
| Drosanthemum hispidum | Rosea ice plant | | • | | | • | | | | | • | | | | • | | | • | | • | | • | | | • | • | | | | | | | | | | • |
| Euonymus fortunei coloratus | Purple-leaf wintercreeper | • | | | | • | | • | • | | | | • | | • | | | | | • | • | | | • | • | | | | | • | | | | | | |
| Fragaria chiloensis | Wild strawberry | | • | | | • | | • | | | • | | | • | | • | | • | • | | | • | | | • | • | | | • | | | | | | | |
| Galax aphylla | Galax | • | • | | | | • | • | • | | | | • | | • | | • | | | | • | | | • | | | | • | | | | | | | | |
| Hedera helix | English ivy | | • | | | • | • | • | | | • | • | | • | | • | | | | | | | • | • | | | | • | | | | | | | | |
| Hypericum calycinum | Aaronsbeard Saint-John's-wort | | | • | | • | | • | | | | | • | • | • | | | | | • | | | • | • | | | | | • | | | | | | | |
| Iberis sempervirens | Evergreen candytuft | | • | | | • | | | • | • | • | | • | | • | | • | | | | • | | | • | | | • | | | | | | | | | |
| Leucothoe catesbaei | Drooping leucothoe | | • | • | • | • | • | • | • | | | | • | | • | | • | | | | • | | • | | • | | • | | | | | | | | | |
| Lotus bertholettii | Parrot's beak, coral gem | • | • | | | • | | | | | | • | • | • | | | • | | | | • | | | • | • | | | | | | | | | | • |
| Micromeria chamissonis | Yerba buena | • | | | | • | | | • | • | | | • | | • | | | | | | • | | | • | • | | | | | | | | | • | |
| Pachistima canbyi | Canby pachistima | | • | • | | • | • | • | • | | | | • | | • | | • | | | | • | | | • | | | • | | | | | | | | |
| Pachysandra terminalis | Japanese spurge | | • | | | | • | • | • | | | | • | | • | | • | | | | • | • | | • | | | • | | | | | | | | |
| Rosmarinus officinalis prostratus | Creeping rosemary | | | • | • | • | | | • | | | | • | • | • | | • | | | | • | | | • | • | | | | | | | | | • | |
| Saxifraga stolonifera | Strawberry geranium | • | | | | | | • | | | | | • | | • | | | | • | • | • | | | • | | | | | | | | | | • | |
| Trachelospermum jasminoides | Star jasmine | | • | • | | • | • | • | | | | | • | | • | | • | | | | • | | | • | • | | | | | | | | | • | |
| Vinca minor | Myrtle, periwinkle | • | | | | | • | • | | | | | • | | • | | | | | | • | | • | • | • | | | | • | | | | | | |
| **NEEDLE EVERGREENS** | | | | | | | | | | | | | | | | | | | | | | | | | | | | | | | | | | | | |
| Calluna vulgaris | Scotch heather | • | • | • | • | • | | • | • | | • | | • | | | • | | | | | • | | | • | | | | • | | | | | | | | |
| Erica carnea | Spring heath | | • | | | • | | • | • | • | | | | • | | | • | | • | | • | | | • | • | | | | • | | | | | | | |
| Juniperus chinensis varieties | Varieties of Chinese juniper | | • | • | • | • | | | • | | • | • | • | • | • | • | | • | • | | | | | • | | | | • | | | | | | | | |
| Juniperus conferta | Shore juniper | | • | | | • | | | • | | • | | | • | | | • | | | | | | | • | | | | | • | | | | | | | |
| Juniperus horizontalis douglasii | Waukegan juniper | • | • | | | • | | | • | | | | | • | | | • | | • | | | | | • | • | | • | | | | | | | | | |
| Juniperus horizontalis 'Bar Harbor' | Bar Harbor juniper | | • | | | • | | | • | | • | | • | • | | | • | • | • | | | | | • | • | | • | | | | | | | | | |
| Juniperus horizontalis 'wiltonii' | Wilton carpet juniper | • | | | | • | | | • | | | | • | • | | | • | | | | | | | • | • | | • | | | | | | | | | |
| Juniperus horizontalis 'plumosa' | Andorra juniper | | | • | | • | | | • | | | | • | • | | | | • | • | | | | | • | • | | | | • | | | | | | | |
| Juniperus procumbens 'nana' | Japanese garden juniper | • | • | | | • | | | • | | | | • | | • | | | • | | | | | | • | • | | | | • | | | | | | | |
| Juniperus sabina tamariscifolia | Tamarix juniper | | | • | | • | | | • | | • | • | • | • | | | • | | | | | | • | • | • | | • | | | | | | | | | |
| Taxus baccata repandens | Spreading English yew | | | • | • | • | • | | • | | | | • | | • | | • | | | | | | | • | | | • | | | | | | | | | |

A. E. Bye & Associates, Landscape Architects; Old Greenwich, Connecticut

## PLANT CHARTS

The intent of the plant chart is to indicate the wide variety of plants available to the designer. There are many unusual trees, shrubs, and ground covers for every environmental and design situation. In using the charts, the designer will obtain a general perception of the plants listed. It is strongly recommended that more specific information be sought in botanic journals. The charts note the northernmost reaches of the plant listed, but some plants will not grow where winters are too warm. The southern reach of those particular plants has not been included in the charts because of conflicting and inadequate information. There are many regional variations in climate that should be considered when selecting plants. The designer is urged to consult a landscape architect to ensure the best selection for the design.

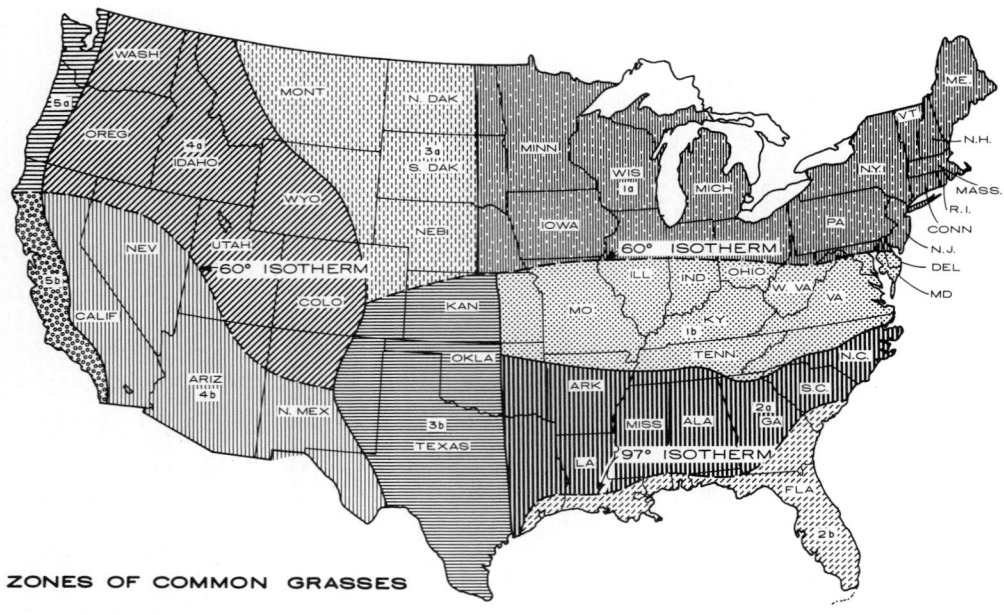

ZONES OF COMMON GRASSES

## GRASSES

In selecting a type of grass for lawn development the designer must consider both environmental and use factors. The amount of available sunlight, the temperature range, rainfall, soil type, and drainage will determine the type of grass that will survive in a given location while additional consideration of tolerance to traffic and recuperative rates will ensure the best possible lawn. For example, different grasses are used for athletic fields depending on environmental factors: bluegrasses and fescues in the northern zones; Bermuda grasses and zoysias in the southern zones, and St. Augustine grass in the extreme south. All are rugged, but require different environments to grow well. Another example is bent grass. Although it requires high maintenance, it is desirable for golf courses because of its fine texture and thick growth.

Lawns can be installed by seed, sprigging, or sod at varying costs. Careful installation at the proper time of the year will ensure the health and beauty of the lawn. Proper soil preparation including aerating the soil, adding topsoil, fertilizer, lime, if necessary, good drainage, and the use of high quality certified weedfree seed is important for success. Frequently, mixtures of seeds are used, since growing conditions are rarely uniform throughout the lawn area. This practice can also mitigate the effects of lawn disease. More specific information is available from local agricultural agents.

## GRASSES

| BOTANICAL NAME | COMMON NAME | LIGHT RE-QUIRE-MENTS | | | MOISTURE RE-QUIRE-MENTS | | | SOIL TYPE | | TEMP. PREFER-ENCE | | VISUAL CHARAC-TERISTICS | | | | MAIN-TEN-ANCE RE-QUIRE-MENTS | | | COLOR | | | | | | | ZONE | | | | | | | | | |
|---|---|---|---|---|---|---|---|---|---|---|---|---|---|---|---|---|---|---|---|---|---|---|---|---|---|---|---|---|---|---|---|---|---|---|---|
| | | Sun | Shade | Light Shade | Well-drained Soil | Moist | Dry | Acid | Alkaline | Cool | Warm | Coarse | Fine | Thick | Hairy | High | Moderate | Minimal | Green | Dark Green | Light Green | Blue Green | Gray Green | Brown (hot weather) | Brown (cold weather) | 1a | 1b | 2a | 2b | 3a | 3b | 4a | 4b | 5a | 5b |
| Agropyron | Wheat | • | | | | | • | • | • | | | | | • | | | • | | | | • | | | | • | • | • | • | | | | | | | |
| Agrostis | Bent | • | • | | • | | • | | • | | | • | • | | • | | • | | • | | • | • | | | | | • | • | | | * | | * | | • | * |
| Ammophila | Beach | • | | • | | | • | • | | • | | | • | | • | | • | | | • | | | | | | | • | • | • | | | | | | • | * |
| Axonopus | Carpet | • | • | | • | | • | | | • | • | | | | | | • | | | | • | | | • | | | | | • | • | | | | | | |
| Bouteloua | Blue gamma | • | | | | | • | • | • | | | | • | | | | • | | | | | | • | • | | | | | | | * | • | * | • | | * |
| Buchloë | Buffalo | • | | | | | • | • | • | | | • | | • | | | • | | | | | | • | • | | | | | | • | • | * | * | | | |
| Cynodon | Bermuda | • | | * | • | | • | | | • | • | • | | • | | • | | • | | | | | | | • | | | • | • | | * | | * | | • |
| Eremochloa | Centipede | • | | • | | • | * | • | | | • | • | | • | | • | | • | | | | | | • | | | | • | • | | * | | * | | • |
| Festuca | Fescue | • | • | • | • | • | • | • | | • | | | • | | | | • | | • | | | | | | | • | • | * | | * | | • | • | * | • |
| Lolium | Rye | • | | • | | • | | • | | • | | | • | | | | • | | • | | | | | | | • | • | * | * | | * | | • | * | • |
| Paspalum notatum | Bahia | • | | • | | • | * | • | | | • | • | | • | | | • | | • | | | | | • | | | | • | • | | | | | | |
| Poa | Bluegrass | • | | * | • | | • | • | | • | | | • | • | | | • | | • | | | | | • | | • | • | | | * | | * | | • | |
| Stenotaphrum | St. Augustine | • | • | • | | • | | • | | | • | • | | • | | • | | | | • | | | | • | | | | * | • | | * | | * | | • |
| Zoysia | Zoysia | • | • | • | | | • | | | • | | • | | • | | • | | | | | | | • | | | • | • | • | • | | * | | * | * | • |

*Will grow under special conditions: high altitude, proximity to water, or irrigation.

## NOTES

1. Consult local agricultural agent, horticulturist, or nurseryman in your area for best grasses for slopes, maintenance concerns, and general planting instructions.
2. Planting slopes: (a) 3 to 1 is maximum for mowed banks. (b) 2 to 1 is maximum for unmowed banks.

A. E. Bye & Associates, Landscape Architects; Old Greenwich, Connecticut

## LANDSCAPING

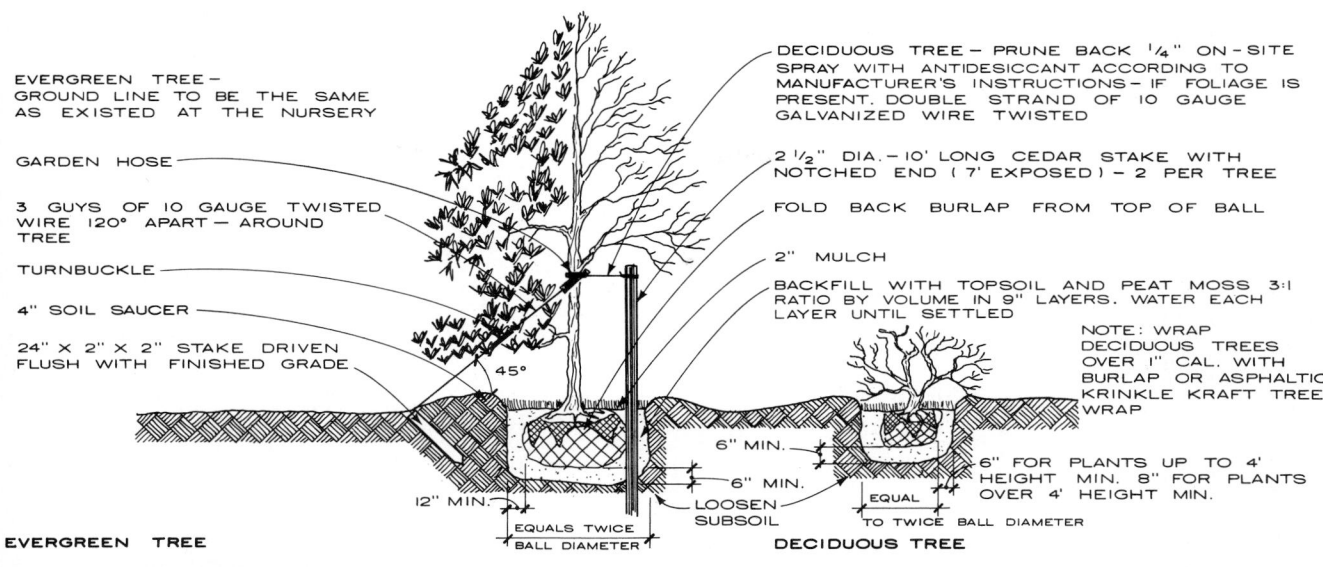

EVERGREEN TREE – GROUND LINE TO BE THE SAME AS EXISTED AT THE NURSERY

GARDEN HOSE

3 GUYS OF 10 GAUGE TWISTED WIRE 120° APART – AROUND TREE

TURNBUCKLE

4" SOIL SAUCER

24" X 2" X 2" STAKE DRIVEN FLUSH WITH FINISHED GRADE

DECIDUOUS TREE – PRUNE BACK 1/4" ON-SITE SPRAY WITH ANTIDESICCANT ACCORDING TO MANUFACTURER'S INSTRUCTIONS – IF FOLIAGE IS PRESENT. DOUBLE STRAND OF 10 GAUGE GALVANIZED WIRE TWISTED

2 1/2" DIA.–10' LONG CEDAR STAKE WITH NOTCHED END ( 7' EXPOSED ) – 2 PER TREE

FOLD BACK BURLAP FROM TOP OF BALL

2" MULCH

BACKFILL WITH TOPSOIL AND PEAT MOSS 3:1 RATIO BY VOLUME IN 9" LAYERS. WATER EACH LAYER UNTIL SETTLED

NOTE: WRAP DECIDUOUS TREES OVER 1" CAL. WITH BURLAP OR ASPHALTIC KRINKLE KRAFT TREE WRAP

45°

6" MIN.

6" MIN.

12" MIN.

LOOSEN SUBSOIL

EQUAL

EQUALS TWICE BALL DIAMETER

6" FOR PLANTS UP TO 4' HEIGHT MIN. 8" FOR PLANTS OVER 4' HEIGHT MIN.

TO TWICE BALL DIAMETER

**EVERGREEN TREE**

**DECIDUOUS TREE**

**PLANTING DETAILS – TREES AND SHRUBS**

## SHRUBS AND MINOR TREES BALLED AND BURLAPPED

| HEIGHT RANGE (FT) | MINIMUM BALL DIAMETER (IN.) | MINIMUM BALL DEPTH (IN.) |
|---|---|---|
| 1 1/2 – 2 | 10 | 8 |
| 2 – 3 | 12 | 9 |
| 3 – 4 | 13 | 10 |
| 4 – 5 | 15 | 11 |
| 5 – 6 | 16 | 12 |
| 6 – 7 | 18 | 13 |
| 7 – 8 | 20 | 14 |
| 8 – 9 | 22 | 15 |
| 9 – 10 | 24 | 16 |
| 10 – 12 | 26 | 17 |

NOTE: Ball sizes should always be of a diameter to encompass the fibrous and feeding root system necessary for the full recovery of the plant.

## STANDARD SHADE TREES—BALLED AND BURLAPPED

| CALIPER* (IN.) | HEIGHT RANGE (FT) | MAXIMUM HEIGHTS (FT) | MINIMUM BALL DIAMETER (IN.) | MINIMUM BALL DEPTH (IN.) |
|---|---|---|---|---|
| 1/2 – 3/4 | 5–6 | 8 | 12 | 9 |
| 3/4 – 1 | 6–8 | 10 | 14 | 10 |
| 1 – 1 1/4 | 7–9 | 11 | 16 | 12 |
| 1 1/4 – 1 1/2 | 8–10 | 12 | 18 | 13 |
| 1 1/2 – 1 3/4 | 10–12 | 14 | 20 | 14 |
| 1 3/4 – 2 | 10–12 | 14 | 22 | 15 |
| 2 – 2 1/2 | 12–14 | 16 | 24 | 16 |
| 2 1/2 – 3 | 12–14 | 16 | 28 | 19 |
| 3 – 3 1/2 | 14–16 | 18 | 32 | 20 |
| 3 1/2 – 4 | 14–16 | 18 | 36 | 22 |
| 4 – 5 | 16–18 | 22 | 44 | 26 |
| 5 – 6 | 18 and up | 26 | 48 | 29 |

*Caliper indicates the diameter of the trunk taken 6 in. above the ground level up to and including 4 in. caliper size and 12 in. above the ground level for larger sizes.

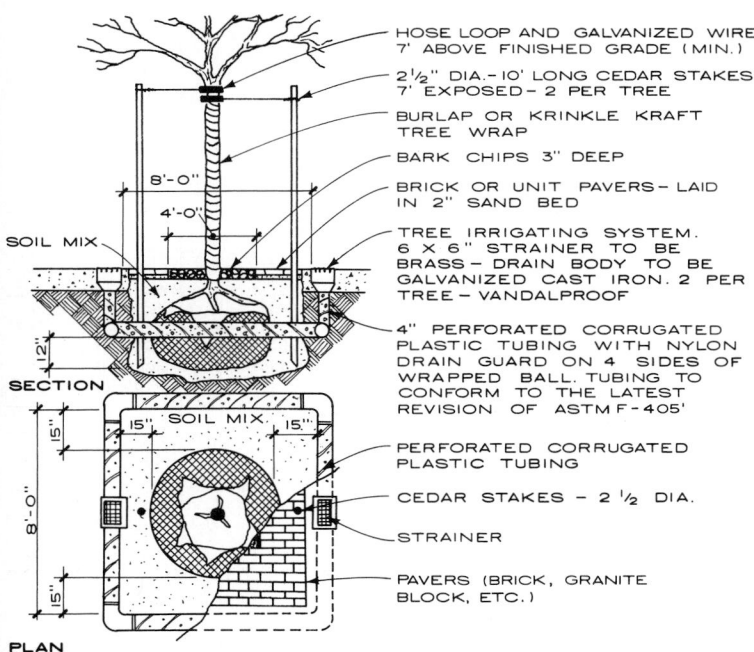

HOSE LOOP AND GALVANIZED WIRE 7' ABOVE FINISHED GRADE ( MIN. )

2 1/2" DIA.– 10' LONG CEDAR STAKES 7' EXPOSED – 2 PER TREE

BURLAP OR KRINKLE KRAFT TREE WRAP

BARK CHIPS 3" DEEP

BRICK OR UNIT PAVERS – LAID IN 2" SAND BED

TREE IRRIGATING SYSTEM. 6 X 6" STRAINER TO BE BRASS – DRAIN BODY TO BE GALVANIZED CAST IRON. 2 PER TREE – VANDALPROOF

4" PERFORATED CORRUGATED PLASTIC TUBING WITH NYLON DRAIN GUARD ON 4 SIDES OF WRAPPED BALL. TUBING TO CONFORM TO THE LATEST REVISION OF ASTM F-405'

PERFORATED CORRUGATED PLASTIC TUBING

CEDAR STAKES – 2 1/2 DIA.

STRAINER

PAVERS (BRICK, GRANITE BLOCK, ETC.)

8'-0"

4'-0"

SOIL MIX

12"

**SECTION**

15"    15"    SOIL MIX    15"

8'-0"

15"

**PLAN**

**PLANTING DETAIL – TREE IN PAVING**

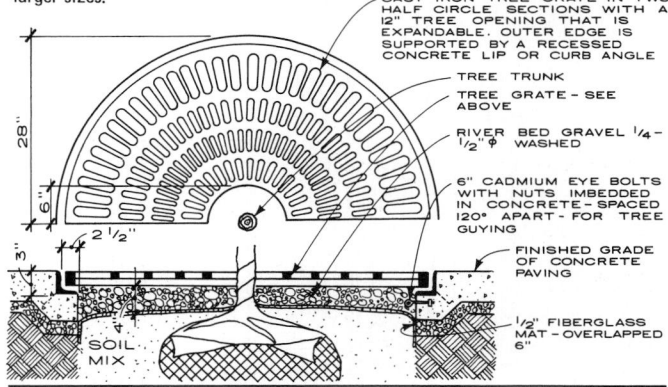

CAST IRON TREE GRATE IN TWO HALF CIRCLE SECTIONS WITH A 12" TREE OPENING THAT IS EXPANDABLE. OUTER EDGE IS SUPPORTED BY A RECESSED CONCRETE LIP OR CURB ANGLE

TREE TRUNK

TREE GRATE – SEE ABOVE

RIVER BED GRAVEL 1/4 – 1/2" Ø WASHED

6" CADMIUM EYE BOLTS WITH NUTS IMBEDDED IN CONCRETE – SPACED 120° APART – FOR TREE GUYING

FINISHED GRADE OF CONCRETE PAVING

1/2" FIBERGLASS MAT – OVERLAPPED 6"

28"

6"

3"

2 1/2"

SOIL MIX

**TREE GRATE DETAIL**

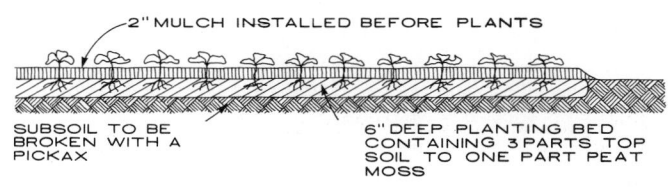

2" MULCH INSTALLED BEFORE PLANTS

SUBSOIL TO BE BROKEN WITH A PICKAX

6" DEEP PLANTING BED CONTAINING 3 PARTS TOP SOIL TO ONE PART PEAT MOSS

**GROUND COVER PLANTING DETAIL**
NOTE: GROUND COVERS SHOULD BE POT OR CONTAINER GROWN

A. E. Bye & Associates, Landscape Architects; Old Greenwich, Connecticut

**LANDSCAPING    2**

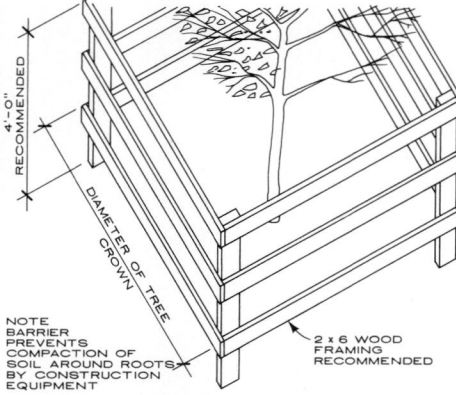

**TREE PROTECTION BARRIER**

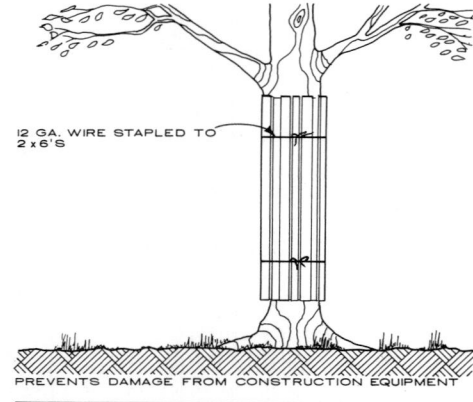

**TREE TRUNK PROTECTION**

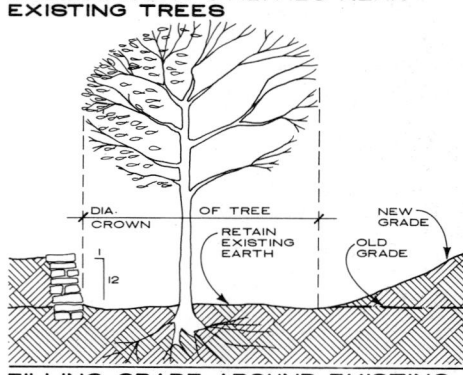

**UNDERGROUND UTILITIES NEAR EXISTING TREES**

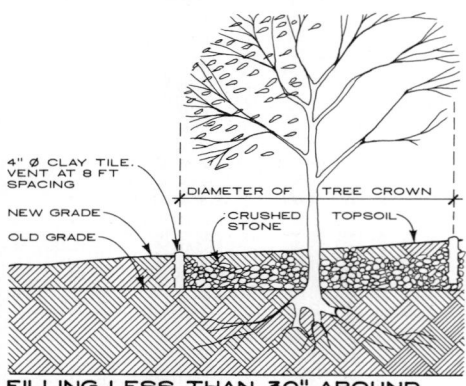

**FILLING LESS THAN 30" AROUND EXISTING TREE**

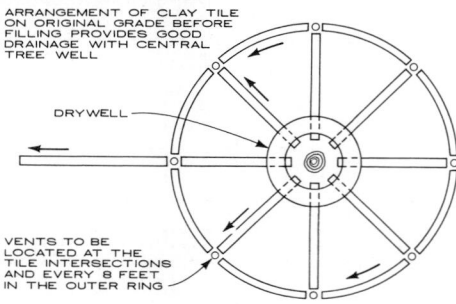

**PLAN**

**FILLING OVER 30" AROUND EXISTING TREE**

## CUTTING AROUND EXISTING TREES

Extreme care should be taken not to compact the earth within the crown of the tree. Compaction can cause severe root damage and reduce the air and water holding capacity of the soil.

If no surrounding barrier is provided, care should be taken not to operate equipment or store materials within the crown spread of the tree. If this area should be compacted, it would be necessary to aerate the soil thoroughly in the root zone immediately following construction. Certain tree species are severely affected by manipulation of the water table, and great care should be exercised to minimize this condition.

## SPECIAL USE OF TREES

Trees for special uses should be branched or pruned naturally according to type. Where a form of growth is desired that is not in accordance with a natural growth habit, this form should be specified. For example:

1. BUSH FORM: Trees that start to branch close to the ground in the manner of a shrub.
2. CLUMPS: Trees with three or more main stems starting from the ground.
3. CUT BACK OR SHEARED: Trees that have been pruned back so as to multiply the branching structure and to develop a more formal effect.
4. ESPALIER: Trees pruned and trained to grow flat against a building or trellis, usually in a predetermined pattern or design.
5. PLEACHING: A technique of severe pruning, usually applied to a row or bosque of trees to produce a geometrically formal or clipped hedgelike effect.
6. POLLARDING: The technique in which annual severe pruning of certain species of trees serves to produce abundant vigorous growth the following year.
7. TOPIARY: Trees sheared or trimmed closely in a formal geometric pattern, or sculptural shapes frequently resembling animals or flowers.

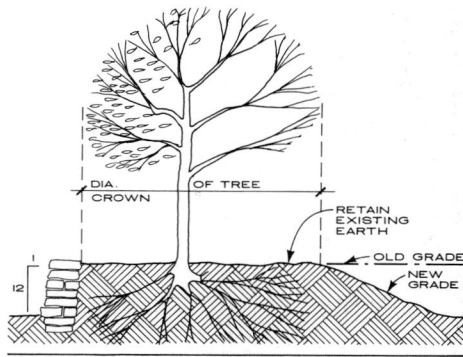

**FILLING GRADE AROUND EXISTING TREE**

**CUTTING GRADE AROUND EXISTING TREE**

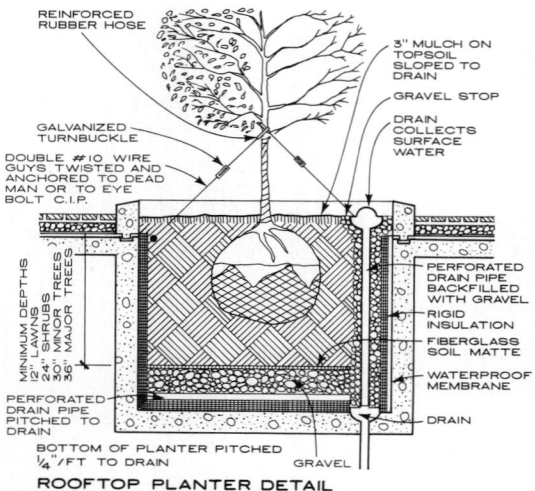

**ROOFTOP PLANTER DETAIL**

**PLANTING ON STRUCTURES**

## SELECTING PLANTS FOR ROOFTOPS

### WIND TOLERANCE

Higher elevations and exposure to wind can cause defoliation and increased transpiration rate. High parapet walls with louvers screen wind velocity and provide shelter for plants.

### HIGH EVAPORATION RATE

Drying effects of wind and sun on soil around planter reduce available soil moisture rapidly. Irrigation, mulches, moisture holding soil additives (perlite, vermiculite and peat moss), and insulation assist in reducing this moisture loss.

### RAPID SOIL TEMPERATURE FLUCTUATION

The conduction capacity of planter materials tends to produce a broad range of soil temperatures. Certain plant species suffer severe root damage because of cold or heat. Use of rigid insulation lining planter alleviates this condition.

### TOPSOIL

Topsoil in planters should be improved to provide the optimum growing condition. A general formula would add fertilizer (as per soil testing) plus 1 part peat moss or vermiculite (high water holding capacity) to 3 parts topsoil. More specific requirements for certain varieties of plants or grasses should be considered.

### ROOT CAPACITY

Plant species should be carefully selected to adapt to the size of the plant bed. If species with shallow fibrous roots are used instead of species with a tap root system consult with nurseryman. Consider the ultimate maturity of the plant species in sizing planter.

Jim E. Miller and David W. Wheeler; Saratoga Associates; Saratoga Springs, New York
Erik Johnson; Lawrence Cook and Associates; Falls Church, Virginia
Connecticut Coastal Management Program, see data sources

**LANDSCAPING**

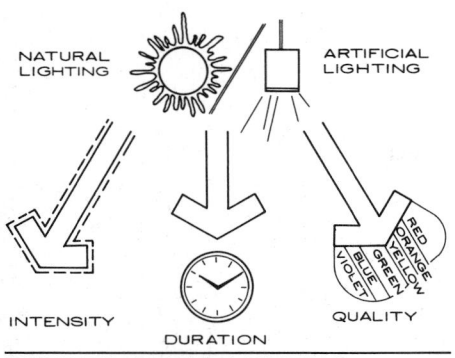

**INTERIOR PLANT LIGHTING FACTORS**

## LIGHTING DURATION NEEDS

1. Adequate lighting is the product of intensity times duration to yield "footcandle-hours"; therefore, compensation between the two exists (e.g., 300 ft-c x 12 hr = 360 ft-c x 10 hr).
2. Recommended rule of thumb: 10-12 hr of continuous lighting on a regular basis, 7 days a week.
3. Generally, it is believed that continuous 24 hr lighting period might be detrimental to plants, but no research bears this out and many projects are under this regime with no apparent bad effects.

## LIGHTING INTENSITY NEEDS

1. All plants desire good lighting, but many are tolerant and adaptable to lower light conditions.
2. Because most interior plants are native to areas with intensities of 10-14,000 ft-c, these plants must be "trained" through an acclimatization process of lowered light (2000-4000 ft-c), water and fertilizer levels for survival, and maintained appearance in the interior environment.
3. All plants have varying degrees of interior lighting intensity requirements, best understood as footcandle (lumens/square foot) requirements.
4. Lighting intensity for plants must be planned and is not simply a footcandle measurement after the building is complete (i.e., footcandle meters are "after the fact" instruments).
5. Intensity must always be above the individual light compensation point for each plant variety, for survival. (LCP is the intensity point at which the plant utilizes as much food as it produces; hence no food storage. Eventually, the plant could die with no food backup.)
6. Recommended rule of thumb: design for a MINIMUM of 50 ft-c on the ground plane for fixed floor type of planters and 75 ft-c at desk height for movable decorative floor planters.
7. Flowering plants and flowers require extremely high intensities (above 2000 ft-c) or direct sunlight to bud, flower, or fruit, as well as lighting high in red and far-red energy.

## RECOMMENDED LIGHTING SOURCES FOR PLANTS

Lighting sources are listed in order of priority, based on plant growth efficiency, color rendition preference, and energy efficiency.

| CEILING HEIGHT | RECOMMENDED LIGHT SOURCE |
|---|---|
| 10 ft and less | Daylight—sidewall glazing<br>Cool white fluorescent<br>Natural light fluorescent<br>Incandescent<br>Plant growth fluorescent |
| 10-15 ft | Daylight<br>  Sidewall glazing<br>  Major glazing<br>  Skylights<br>Metal halide lamp, phosphor coated<br>Mercury lamp, deluxe white<br>Mercury lamp, warm deluxe white<br>High pressure sodium (if color rendition not a design factor)<br>Quartz halogen lamp<br>Incandescent |
| 15 ft and greater | Daylight<br>  Sidewall glazing<br>  Major glazing<br>  Skylights<br>Metal halide lamp, clear<br>Metal halide lamp, phosphor coated<br>Mercury lamp, deluxe white<br>Mercury lamp, warm deluxe white<br>High pressure sodium (if color rendition not a design factor)<br>Quartz halogen lamp<br>Incandescent |

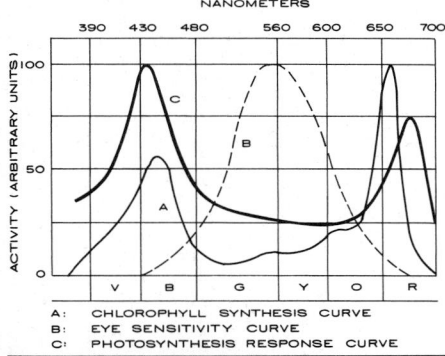

A: CHLOROPHYLL SYNTHESIS CURVE
B: EYE SENSITIVITY CURVE
C: PHOTOSYNTHESIS RESPONSE CURVE

**SPECTRAL ENERGY DISTRIBUTION CURVE SHOWING OPPOSING PLANT AND HUMAN EYE RESPONSES**

## LIGHT QUALITY NEEDS

1. Natural lighting is about twice as efficient as cool white fluorescent lighting for plant growth, because of sunlight's broad range spectrum (i.e., 200 ft-c of CWF = 95 ft-c of natural light).
2. Chlorophyll is most responsive to blue and red wavelength energy in the production of food. The human eye is least responsive to blue and red energy and most responsive to the green-yellow region of the spectrum.
3. High blue energy emitting sources are best for overall plant maintenance (stockier growth, dark green color, little elongation).
4. High red energy emitting sources produce lighter colored foliage, elongated growth, stragglier growth.
5. Designer must be cognizant of color rendition of source, as well as light quality, if lighting is to be used for both plant lighting and illumination. (See Lamp Responses table.)
6. Ultraviolet energy is believed to be somewhat helpful to the photosynthesis process, but is not considered necessary as an integral segment of plant lighting.

Richard L. Gaines, AIA; Plantscape House; Apopka, Florida

## LAMP RESPONSES ON INTERIOR PLANTS

| BULB | ROOM APPEARANCE | COLORS STRENGTHENED | COLORS GREYED | PLANT RESPONSES |
|---|---|---|---|---|
| CW | Neutral to cool | Blue, yellow, orange | Red | Green foliage, stem elongates slowly, multiple side shoots, flower life long |
| WW | Yellow to warm | Yellow, orange | Blue, green, red | |
| GRO-PL | Purple to pink | Blue, red | Green, yellow | Deep green foliage, stem elongates very slowly, thick stems, multiple side shoots, late flowers on short stems |
| GRO-WS | Warm | Blue, yellow, red | Green | Light green foliage, stem elongates rapidly, suppressed side shoots, early flowering on long stems, plant matures and dies rapidly |
| AGRO | Neutral to warm | Blue, yellow, red | Green | |
| VITA | Neutral to warm | Blue, yellow, red | Green | |
| HG | Cool | Blue, green, yellow | Red | Green foliage expands, stem elongates slowly, multiple side shoots, flower life long |
| MH | Cool green | Blue, green, yellow | Red | |
| HPS | Warm | Green, yellow, orange | Blue, red | Deep green, large foliage, stem elongates very slowly, late flowers, short stems |
| LPS | Warm | Yellow | All except yellow | Extra deep green foliage, slow, thick stem elongation, multiple side shoots, some flowering, short stems. Some plants require supplemental sun |
| INC | Warm | Yellow, orange, red | Blue | Pale, thin, long foliage, stems spindly, suppressed side shoots early, short-lived flowers |
| INC-HG | Warm | Yellow, orange, red | Blue | |

KEY

CW: cool white fluorescent.
WW: warm white fluorescent.
GRO-PL: Gro-Lux plant light.
GRO-WS: Gro-Lux wide spectrum.
AGRO: Agro-Lite.
VITA: Vita-Lite.

HG: mercury (all types).
MH: metal halide.
HPS: high pressure sodium.
LPS: low pressure sodium.
INC-HG: incandescent mercury.
INC-PL: incandescent plant light.

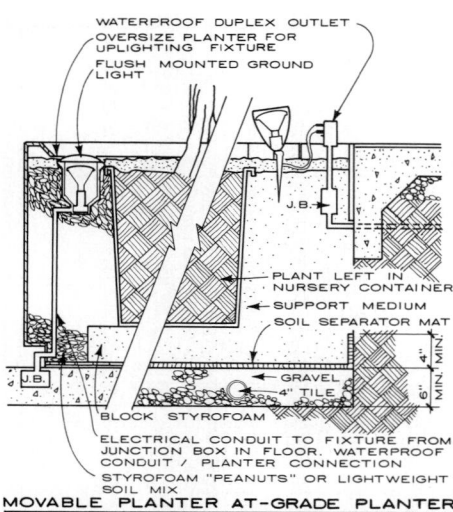

**MOVABLE PLANTER AT-GRADE PLANTER**
**UPLIGHTING / PLANTING DETAILS**

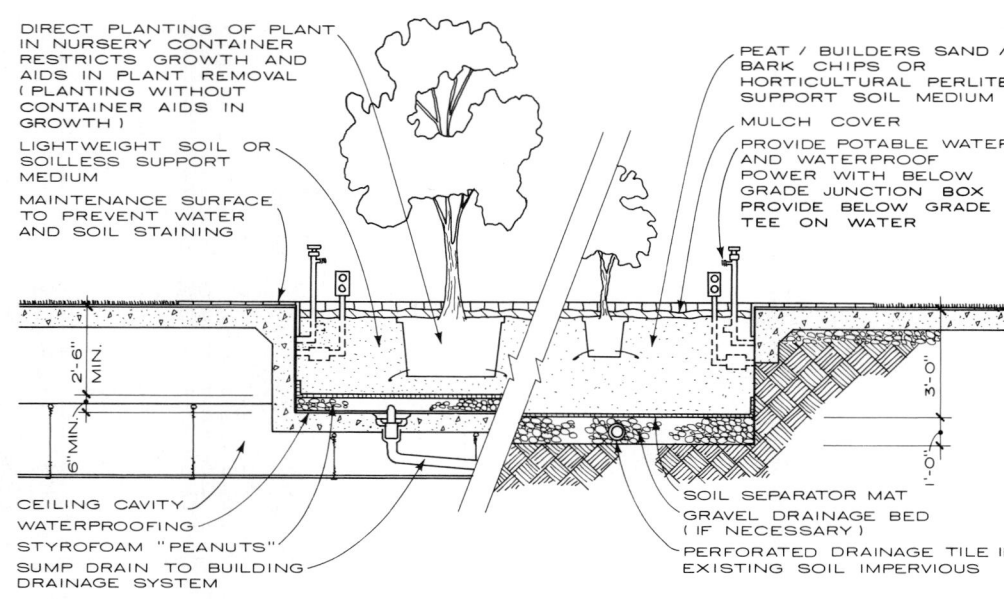

**ABOVE-GRADE PLANTER**          **AT-GRADE PLANTER**
**FLOOR PLANTER DETAILS**

## UPLIGHTING AND ELECTRICAL NEEDS

1. May be of some benefit to plants, but inefficient for plant photosynthesis because of plant physiological structure. Chlorophyll is usually in upper part of leaf.

2. Uplighting should never be utilized as sole lighting source for plants.

3. Waterproof duplex outlets above soil line with a waterproof junction box below soil line are usually adequate for "atmosphere" uplighting and water fountain pumps.

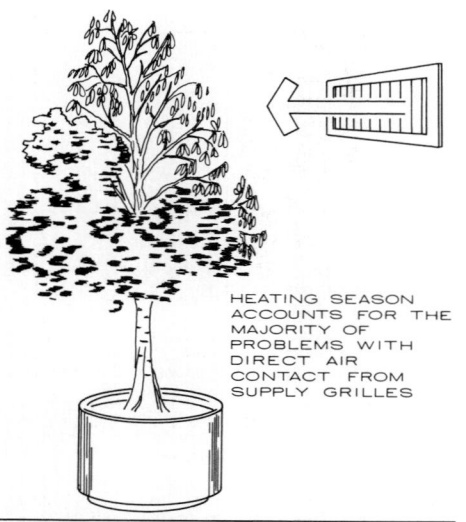

**FOLIAGE BURN FROM DIRECT HEAT CONTACT**

## HVAC EFFECT ON PLANTS

1. Air-conditioning (cooled air) is rarely detrimental to plants, even if it is "directed" at plants. The ventilation here is what counts! Good ventilation is a must with plants; otherwise oxygen and temperatures build up. Heat supply, on the other hand, when "directed" at plants, can truly be disastrous. Plan for supplies directed away from plants, but maintain adequate ventilation.

2. Extended heat or power failures of sufficient duration can damage plant health. The lower limit of temperature as a steady state is 65°F for plant survival. Brief drops to 55°F (less than 1 hr) are the lower limit before damage. Temperatures up to 85°F for only 2 days a week can usually be tolerated.

3. The relative humidity should not be allowed to fall below 30%, as plants prefer a relative humidity of 50-60%.

Richard L. Gaines, AIA; Plantscape House; Apopka, Florida

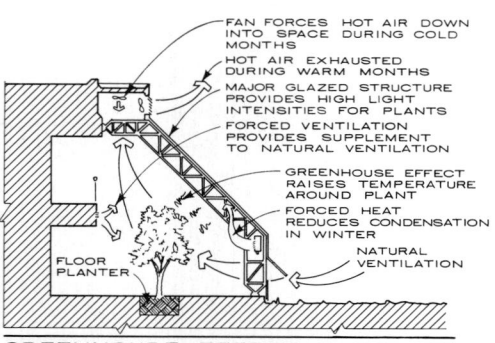

**GREENHOUSE EFFECT RAISES NEED FOR ADEQUATE VENTILATION**

## TEMPERATURE REQUIREMENTS

1. Most plants prefer human comfort range: 70-75°F daytime temperatures and 60-65°F nighttime temperatures.

2. An absolute minimum temperature of 50°F must be observed. Plant damage will result below this figure. Rapid temperature fluctuations of 30-40°F can also be detrimental to plants.

3. "Q-10" phenomenon of respiration: for every 10°C rise in temperature, plants' respiration rate and food consumption doubles.

4. Both photosynthesis and respiration decline and stop with time, as temperatures go beyond 80°F. Beware of the greenhouse effect!

## WATER SUPPLY REQUIREMENTS

1. Movable and railing planters are often watered by watering can. Provide convenient access to hot and cold potable water by hose bibbs and/or service sinks (preferably in janitor's closet) during normal working hours, with long (min. 24 in.) faucet-to-sink or floor distances. Provide for maximum of 200 ft travel on all floors.

2. At-grade floor planters are usually watered by hose and extension wand. Provide hose bibbs above soil line (for maximum travel of 50 ft) with capped "tee" stub-outs beneath soil line. If soil temperature is apt to get abnormally low in winter, provide hot and cold water by mixer-faucet type hose bibbs.

3. High concentrations of fluoride and chlorine in water supply can cause damage to plants. Provide water with low concentrations of these elements and with a pH value of 5.0-6.0. Higher or lower pH levels can result in higher plant maintenance costs.

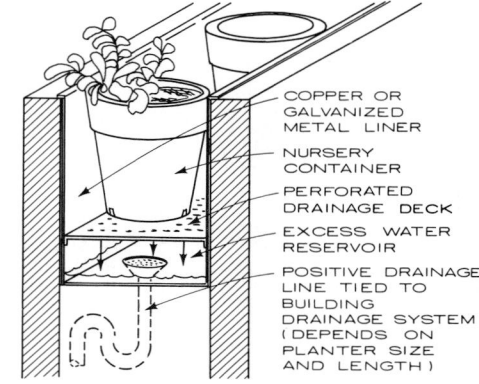

**RAILING PLANTER DETAIL**

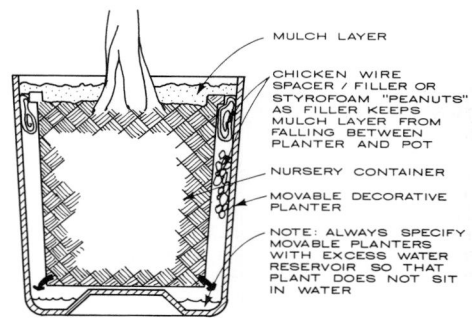

**MOVABLE DECORATIVE PLANTER DETAIL**

## STORAGE REQUIREMENTS

Provide a secured storage space of approximately 30 sq ft for watering equipment and other maintenance materials. It may be desirable to combine water supply and janitor needs in the same storage area.

## AIR POLLUTION EFFECTS ON PLANTS

Problems result from inadequate ventilation. Excessive chlorine gas from swimming pool areas can be a damaging problem, as well as excessive fumes from toxic cleaning substances for floor finishes, etc. Ventilation a must here!

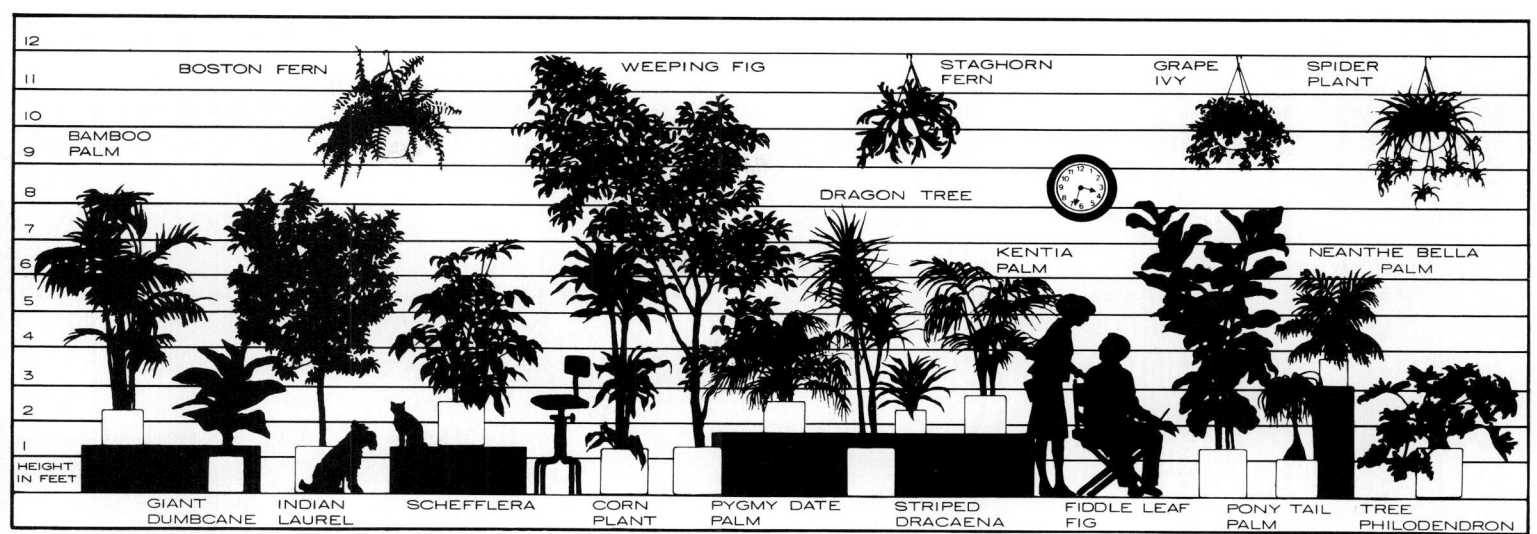

**FORM, TEXTURE, AND SIZES OF SOME TYPICALLY USED INTERIOR PLANTS**

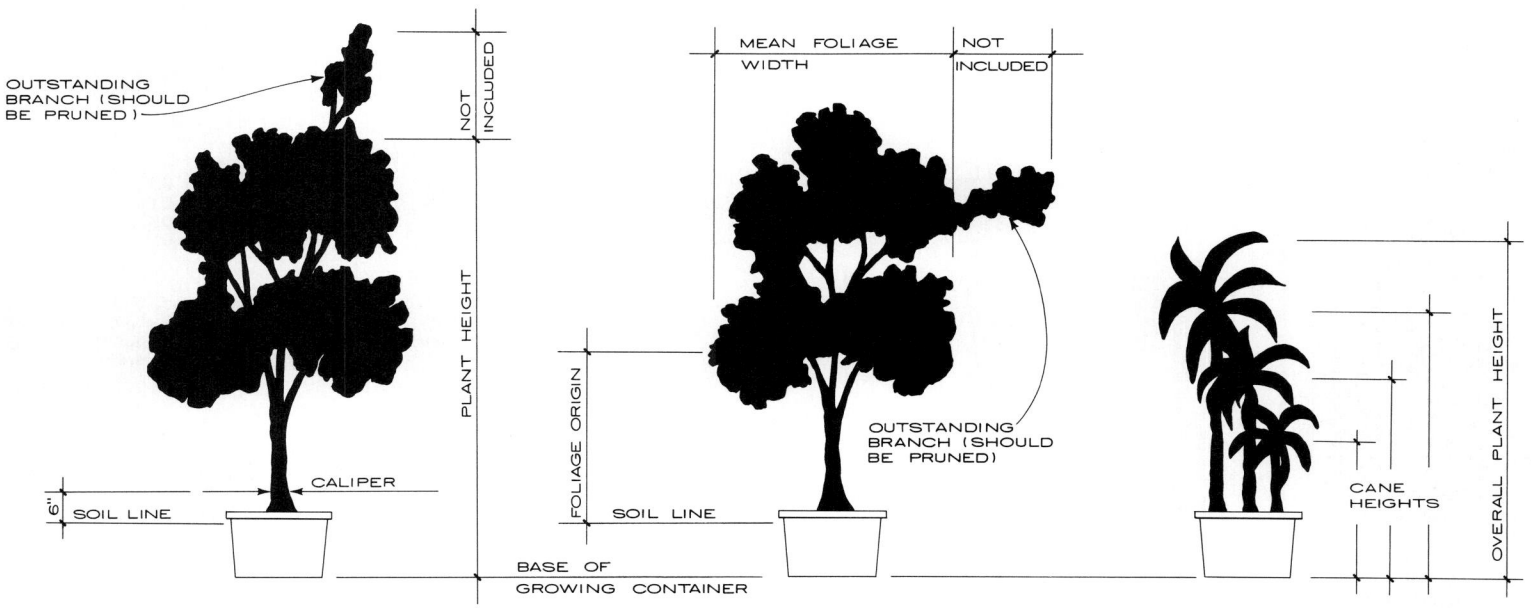

PLANT HEIGHT AND CALIPER    FOLIAGE WIDTH AND ORIGIN    CANE HEIGHTS

## INTERIOR PLANT SPECIFICATIONS

**NOTE**

Plant height should be measured as overall height from the base of the growing container to mean foliage top. Isolated outstanding branches should not be included in height. (Since most plants are installed in movable planters, this overall height measurement should be utilized.)

**NOTE**

Foliage width should be measured across the nominal mean width dimension. Isolated outstanding branches should not be included in foliage width. Origin or start of foliage should be measured from the soil line.

**NOTE**

Many plant varieties are grown from rooted canes, with the plant being made up of one or more canes. The number of canes must be specified, if plant form is to be identified. Cane heights should always be measured from the base of the growing container.

## OTHER PLANT SPECIFICATION FACTORS

1. Accurately describe plant form (e.g., multistem vs. standard tree form, clump form) and foliage spread desired. Indicate "clear trunk" measurements on trees, if desired. These measurements are from soil line to foliage origin point. Specify caliper, if significant.

2. Indicate lighting intensities designed or calculated for interior space where plants will be installed.

3. Indicate how plants will be used (i.e., in at-grade planter or in movable decorative planter). If movable decorative planters are used, indicate interior diameter and height of planter for each plant specified, since growing container sizes vary considerably.

4. Specify both botanical and common plant names.

5. Indicate any special shipping instructions or limitations.

6. Specify in-plant height column, whether plant height is measured as overall height or above-the-soil line height. Recommended height measurements:

   Interior plants: overall plant height (i.e., from bottom of growing container to mean foliage top).
   Exterior plants: above-the-soil line height.

7. Indicate whether plants are to be container grown or balled and burlapped (B & B) material.

8. Indicate location of all convenient water supply sources on all interior landscaping layouts.

Richard L. Gaines, AIA; Plantscape House; Apopka, Florida

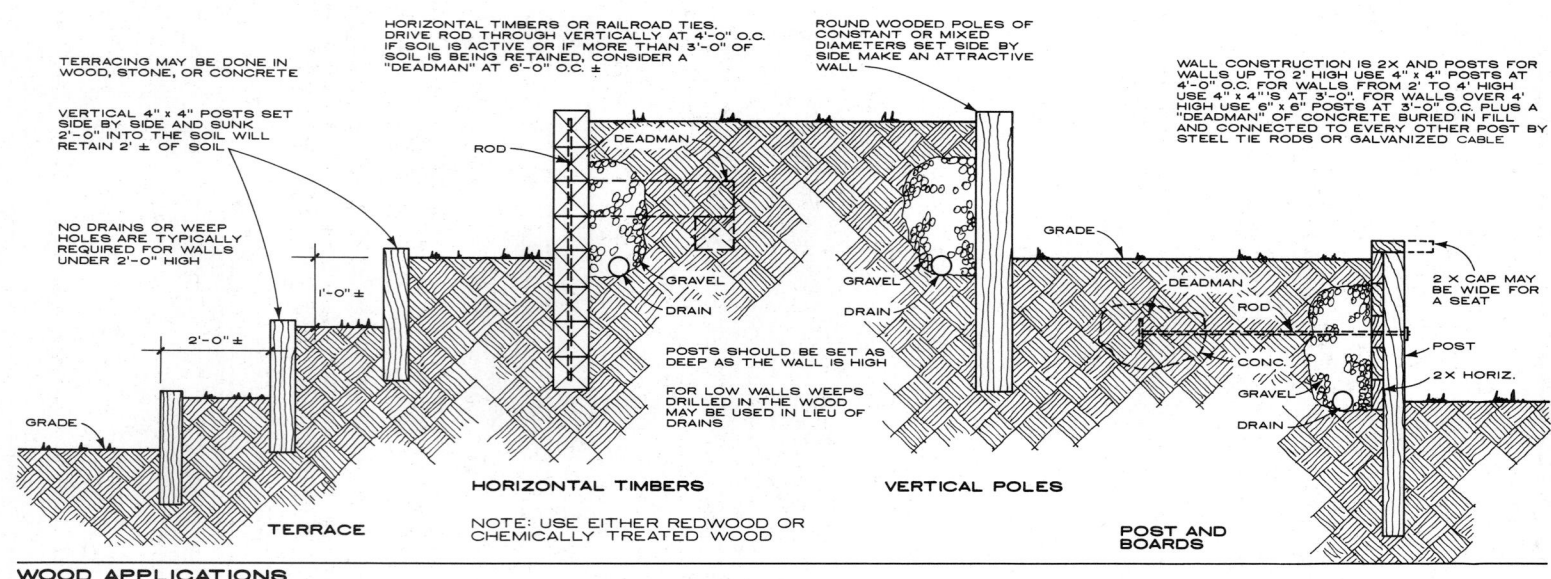

TERRACING MAY BE DONE IN WOOD, STONE, OR CONCRETE

VERTICAL 4" x 4" POSTS SET SIDE BY SIDE AND SUNK 2'-0" INTO THE SOIL WILL RETAIN 2' ± OF SOIL

NO DRAINS OR WEEP HOLES ARE TYPICALLY REQUIRED FOR WALLS UNDER 2'-0" HIGH

HORIZONTAL TIMBERS OR RAILROAD TIES. DRIVE ROD THROUGH VERTICALLY AT 4'-0" O.C. IF SOIL IS ACTIVE OR IF MORE THAN 3'-0" OF SOIL IS BEING RETAINED, CONSIDER A "DEADMAN" AT 6'-0" O.C. ±

ROUND WOODED POLES OF CONSTANT OR MIXED DIAMETERS SET SIDE BY SIDE MAKE AN ATTRACTIVE WALL

WALL CONSTRUCTION IS 2X AND POSTS FOR WALLS UP TO 2' HIGH USE 4" x 4" POSTS AT 4'-0" O.C. FOR WALLS FROM 2' TO 4' HIGH USE 4" x 4"'S AT 3'-0". FOR WALLS OVER 4' HIGH USE 6" x 6" POSTS AT 3'-0" O.C. PLUS A "DEADMAN" OF CONCRETE BURIED IN FILL AND CONNECTED TO EVERY OTHER POST BY STEEL TIE RODS OR GALVANIZED CABLE

ROD    DEADMAN    GRADE    DEADMAN    ROD    2 X CAP MAY BE WIDE FOR A SEAT

GRAVEL    GRAVEL    CONC.    POST    2 X HORIZ.    GRAVEL

GRADE    DRAIN    DRAIN    DRAIN

POSTS SHOULD BE SET AS DEEP AS THE WALL IS HIGH

FOR LOW WALLS WEEPS DRILLED IN THE WOOD MAY BE USED IN LIEU OF DRAINS

**TERRACE**         **HORIZONTAL TIMBERS**         **VERTICAL POLES**         **POST AND BOARDS**

NOTE: USE EITHER REDWOOD OR CHEMICALLY TREATED WOOD

## WOOD APPLICATIONS

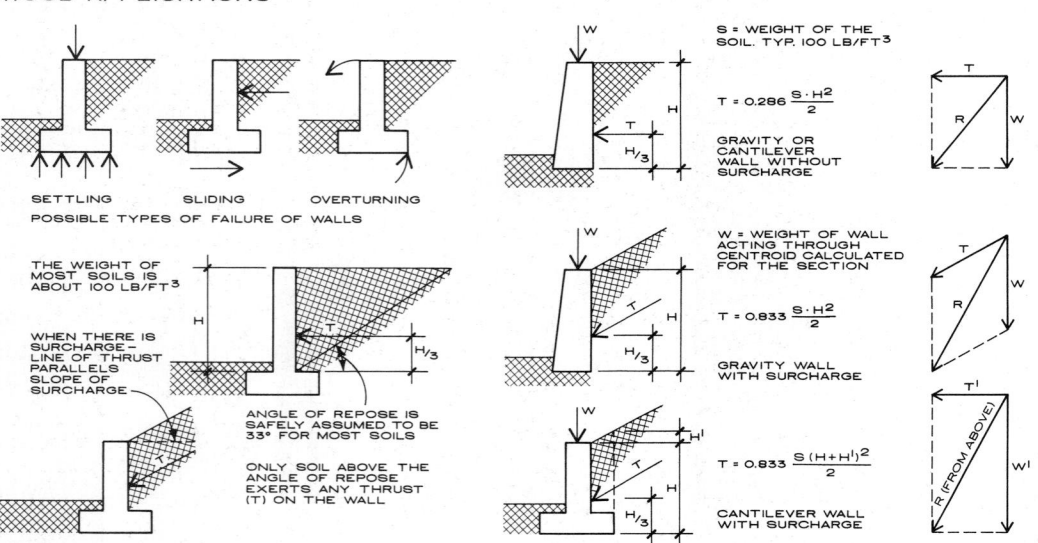

SETTLING     SLIDING     OVERTURNING

POSSIBLE TYPES OF FAILURE OF WALLS

THE WEIGHT OF MOST SOILS IS ABOUT 100 LB/FT³

WHEN THERE IS SURCHARGE — LINE OF THRUST PARALLELS SLOPE OF SURCHARGE

ANGLE OF REPOSE IS SAFELY ASSUMED TO BE 33° FOR MOST SOILS

ONLY SOIL ABOVE THE ANGLE OF REPOSE EXERTS ANY THRUST (T) ON THE WALL

**GENERAL RELATIONSHIPS**

S = WEIGHT OF THE SOIL. TYP. 100 LB/FT³

$$T = 0.286 \frac{S \cdot H^2}{2}$$

GRAVITY OR CANTILEVER WALL WITHOUT SURCHARGE

W = WEIGHT OF WALL ACTING THROUGH CENTROID CALCULATED FOR THE SECTION

$$T = 0.833 \frac{S \cdot H^2}{2}$$

GRAVITY WALL WITH SURCHARGE

$$T = 0.833 \frac{S (H + H')^2}{2}$$

CANTILEVER WALL WITH SURCHARGE

**FORMULAS**

**FORCE DIAGRAMS**

### SLIDING

The thrust on the wall must be resisted. The resisting force is the weight of the wall times the coefficient of soil friction. Use a safety factor of 1.5. Therefore:

$$W(C.F.) \geq 1.5T$$

Average coefficients:

| | |
|---|---|
| Gravel | 0.6 |
| Silt/dry clay | 0.5 |
| Sand | 0.4 |
| Wet clay | 0.3 |

### OVERTURNING

The overturning moment equals $T(H/3)$. This is resisted by the resisting moment. For symmetrical sections, resisting moment equals W times (width of base/2). Use a safety factor of 2.0. Therefore:

$$M_R \geq 2(M_o)$$

### SETTLING

Soil bearing value must resist vertical force. For symmetrical sections that force is W (or W')/bearing area. Use a safety factor of 1.5. Therefore:

$$S.B. \geq 1.5(W/A)$$

## STRUCTURAL DESIGN CONSIDERATIONS

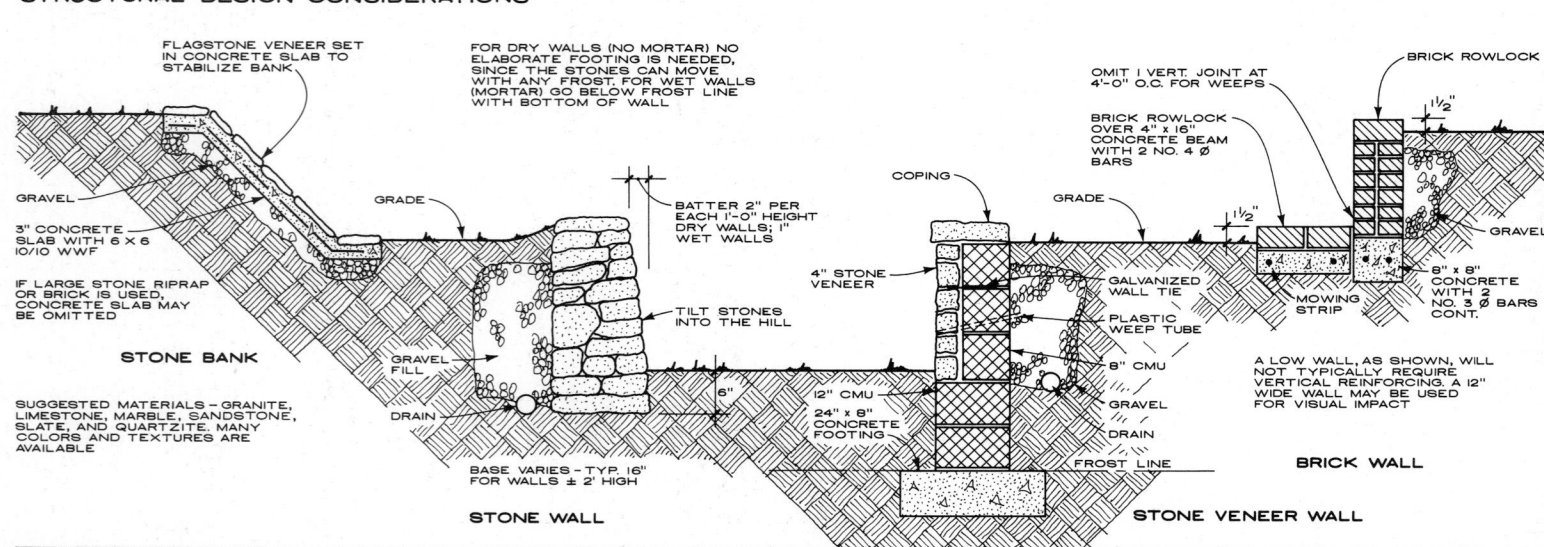

FLAGSTONE VENEER SET IN CONCRETE SLAB TO STABILIZE BANK

GRAVEL

3" CONCRETE SLAB WITH 6 x 6 10/10 WWF

IF LARGE STONE RIPRAP OR BRICK IS USED, CONCRETE SLAB MAY BE OMITTED

**STONE BANK**

SUGGESTED MATERIALS – GRANITE, LIMESTONE, MARBLE, SANDSTONE, SLATE, AND QUARTZITE. MANY COLORS AND TEXTURES ARE AVAILABLE

FOR DRY WALLS (NO MORTAR) NO ELABORATE FOOTING IS NEEDED, SINCE THE STONES CAN MOVE WITH ANY FROST. FOR WET WALLS (MORTAR) GO BELOW FROST LINE WITH BOTTOM OF WALL

GRADE

BATTER 2" PER EACH 1'-0" HEIGHT DRY WALLS; 1" WET WALLS

TILT STONES INTO THE HILL

GRAVEL FILL

DRAIN

BASE VARIES – TYP. 16" FOR WALLS ± 2' HIGH

**STONE WALL**

COPING

4" STONE VENEER

6"

12" CMU

24" x 8" CONCRETE FOOTING

FROST LINE

GALVANIZED WALL TIE

PLASTIC WEEP TUBE

8" CMU

GRAVEL

DRAIN

**STONE VENEER WALL**

OMIT 1 VERT. JOINT AT 4'-0" O.C. FOR WEEPS

BRICK ROWLOCK OVER 4" x 16" CONCRETE BEAM WITH 2 NO. 4 Ø BARS

GRADE

MOWING STRIP

BRICK ROWLOCK

1½"    1½"    1½"

GRAVEL

8" x 8" CONCRETE WITH 2 NO. 3 Ø BARS CONT.

A LOW WALL, AS SHOWN, WILL NOT TYPICALLY REQUIRE VERTICAL REINFORCING. A 12" WIDE WALL MAY BE USED FOR VISUAL IMPACT

**BRICK WALL**

## STONE AND MASONRY APPLICATIONS

Charles R. Heuer, AIA; Washington, D.C.

2    WALLS AND FENCES

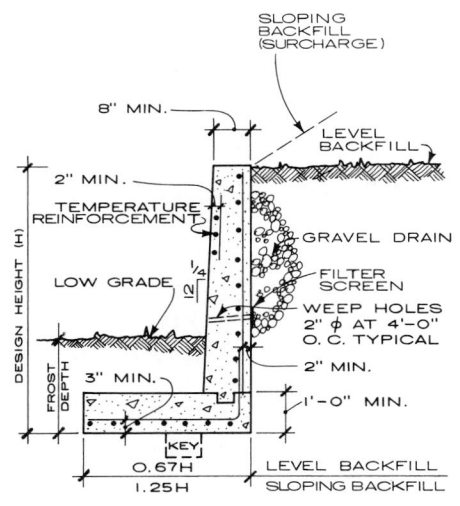

Place base below frost line. Dimensions are approximate.

**L TYPE RETAINING WALLS**

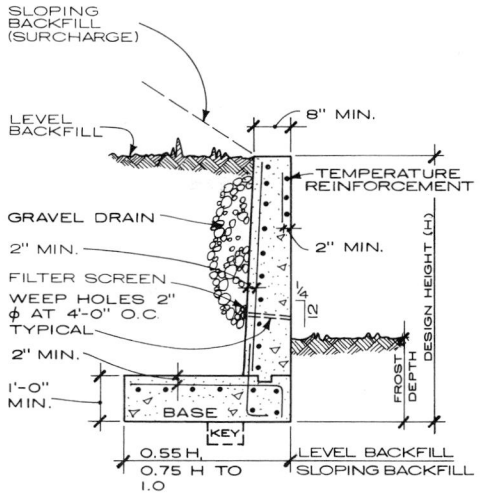

Soil pressure at toe equals 0.2 times the height in kips per square foot. Dimensions are preliminary.

**GRAVITY RETAINING WALL**

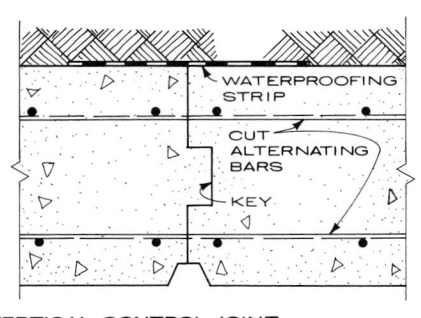

**VERTICAL CONTROL JOINT**

**VERTICAL EXPANSION JOINT**

**RETAINING WALL JOINTS**

**NOTES**

Provide control and/or construction joints in concrete retaining walls about every 25 ft and expansion joints about every fourth control and/or construction joint. Coated dowels should be used if average wall height on either side of a joint is different.

Consult with a structural engineer for final design of concrete retaining walls. An engineer's seal may be required for final design approval by local code officials.

Use temperature bars if wall is more than 10 in. thick.

Keys shown dashed may be required to prevent sliding in high walls and those on moist clay.

## PRELIMINARY DIMENSIONS

| BACKFILL SLOPING $\phi = 29°\ 45'\ (1\frac{3}{4}:1)$ | | | | |
|---|---|---|---|---|
| APPROXIMATE CONCRETE DIMENSIONS | | | | |
| HEIGHT OF WALL H (FT) | WIDTH OF BASE B (FT) | WIDTH OF WALL a (FT) | HEEL b (FT) | TOE c (FT) |
| 3 | 2'-8'' | 0'-9'' | 1'-5'' | 0'-6'' |
| 4 | 3'-5'' | 0'-9'' | 2'-0'' | 0'-8'' |
| 5 | 4'-6'' | 0'-10'' | 2'-6'' | 1'-2'' |
| 6 | 5'-4'' | 0'-10'' | 2'-11'' | 1'-7'' |
| 7 | 6'-3'' | 0'-10'' | 3'-5'' | 2'-0'' |
| 8 | 7'-0'' | 1'-0'' | 3'-8'' | 2'-4'' |
| 9 | 7'-6'' | 1'-0'' | 4'-2'' | 2'-4'' |
| 10 | 8'-6'' | 1'-0'' | 4'-9'' | 2'-9'' |
| 11 | 11'-0'' | 1'-1'' | 7'-2'' | 2'-9'' |
| 12 | 12'-0'' | 1'-2'' | 7'-10'' | 3'-0'' |
| 13 | 13'-0'' | 1'-4'' | 8'-5'' | 3'-3'' |
| 14 | 14'-0'' | 1'-5'' | 9'-1'' | 3'-6'' |
| 15 | 15'-0'' | 1'-6'' | 9'-9'' | 3'-9'' |
| 16 | 16'-0'' | 1'-7'' | 10'-5'' | 4'-0'' |
| 17 | 17'-0'' | 1'-8'' | 11'-1'' | 4'-3'' |
| 18 | 18'-0'' | 1'-10'' | 11'-8'' | 4'-6'' |
| 19 | 19'-0'' | 1'-11'' | 12'-4'' | 4'-9'' |
| 20 | 20'-0'' | 2'-0'' | 13'-0'' | 5'-0'' |
| 21 | 21'-0'' | 2'-2'' | 13'-7'' | 5'-3'' |
| 22 | 22'-0'' | 2'-4'' | 14'-4'' | 5'-4'' |

| BACKFILL LEVEL—NO SURCHARGE | | | | |
|---|---|---|---|---|
| APPROXIMATE CONCRETE DIMENSIONS | | | | |
| HEIGHT OF WALL H (FT) | WIDTH OF BASE B (FT) | WIDTH OF WALL a (FT) | HEEL b (FT) | TOE c (FT) |
| 3 | 2'-1'' | 0'-8'' | 1'-0'' | 0'-5'' |
| 4 | 2'-8'' | 0'-8'' | 1'-7'' | 0'-5'' |
| 5 | 3'-3'' | 0'-8'' | 2'-2'' | 0'-5'' |
| 6 | 3'-9'' | 0'-8'' | 2'-5'' | 0'-8'' |
| 7 | 4'-2'' | 0'-8'' | 2'-6'' | 1'-0'' |
| 8 | 4'-8'' | 1'-0'' | 2'-8'' | 1'-0'' |
| 9 | 5'-2'' | 1'-0'' | 3'-2'' | 1'-0'' |
| 10 | 5'-9'' | 1'-0'' | 3'-7'' | 1'-2'' |
| 11 | 6'-7'' | 1'-1'' | 4'-1'' | 1'-5'' |
| 12 | 7'-3'' | 1'-2'' | 4'-7'' | 1'-6'' |
| 13 | 7'-10'' | 1'-2'' | 5'-0'' | 1'-8'' |
| 14 | 8'-5'' | 1'-3'' | 5'-5'' | 1'-9'' |
| 15 | 9'-0'' | 1'-4'' | 5'-9'' | 1'-11'' |
| 16 | 9'-7'' | 1'-5'' | 6'-2'' | 2'-0'' |
| 17 | 10'-3'' | 1'-6'' | 6'-7'' | 2'-2'' |
| 18 | 10'-10'' | 1'-6'' | 7'-1'' | 2'-3'' |
| 19 | 11'-5'' | 1'-7'' | 7'-5'' | 2'-5'' |
| 20 | 12'-0'' | 1'-8'' | 7'-10'' | 2'-6'' |
| 21 | 12'-7'' | 1'-9'' | 8'-2'' | 2'-8'' |
| 22 | 13'-3'' | 1'-11'' | 8'-7'' | 2'-9'' |

**T TYPE RETAINING WALLS**

Kenneth D. Franch, AIA, PE; Phillips Swager Associates, Inc.; Dallas, Texas
Neubaur · Sohn, Engineers; Washington, D.C.

## DIMENSIONS AND REINFORCEMENT

| WALL | H | B | T | A | "V" BARS | "F" BARS |
|------|------|------|------|------|----------|----------|
| 8" | 3' 4" | 2' 4" | 9" | 8" | #3 @ 32" | #3 @ 27" |
|  | 4' 0" | 2' 9" | 9" | 10" | #4 @ 32" | #3 @ 27" |
|  | 4' 8" | 3' 4" | 10" | 12" | #5 @ 32" | #3 @ 27" |
|  | 5' 4" | 3' 8" | 10" | 14" | #4 @ 16" | #4 @ 30" |
|  | 6' 0" | 4' 2" | 12" | 16" | #6 @ 24" | #4 @ 25" |
| 12" | 5' 4" | 3' 8" | 10" | 14" | #4 @ 24" | #3 @ 25" |
|  | 6' 0" | 4' 2" | 12" | 15" | #4 @ 16" | #4 @ 30" |
|  | 6' 8" | 4' 6" | 12" | 16" | #6 @ 24" | #4 @ 22" |
|  | 7' 4" | 4' 10" | 12" | 18" | #5 @ 16" | #5 @ 26" |
|  | 8' 0" | 5' 4" | 12" | 20" | #7 @ 24" | #5 @ 21" |
|  | 8' 8" | 5' 10" | 14" | 22" | #6 @ 8" | #6 @ 26" |
|  | 9' 4" | 6' 2" | 14" | 24" | #8 @ 8" | #6 @ 21" |

NOTE: See General Notes for design parameters.

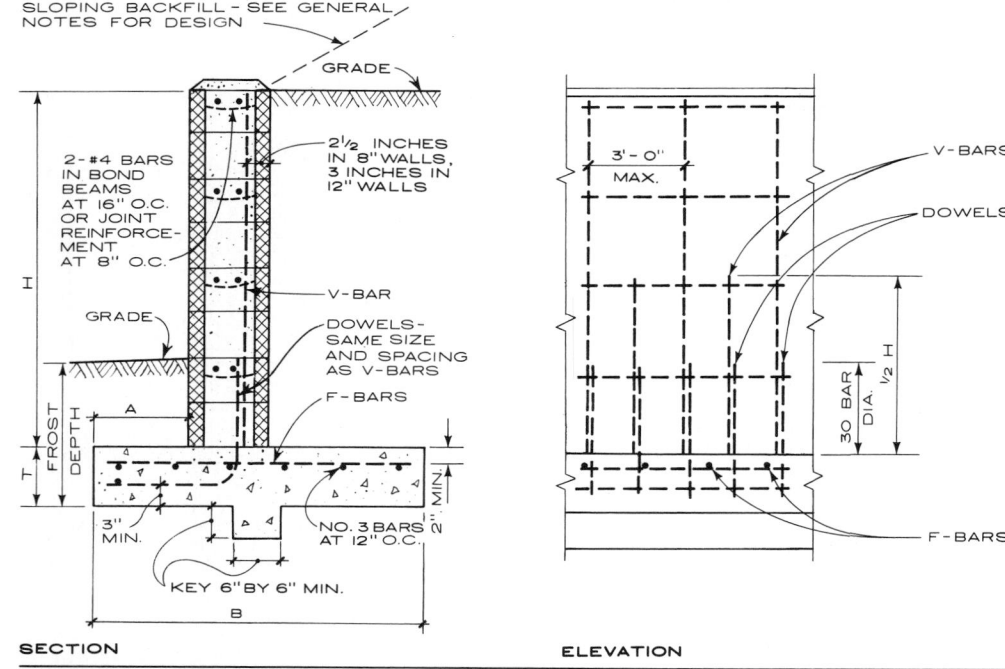

**SECTION**      **ELEVATION**

**TYPICAL CANTILEVER RETAINING WALL**

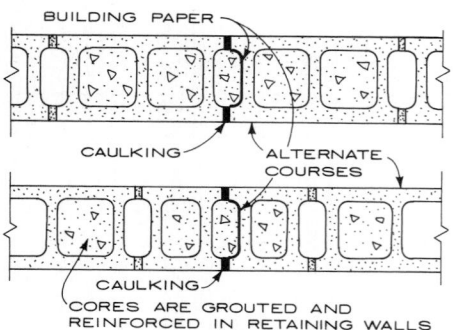

**SHEAR-RESISTING CONTROL JOINT**

**NOTE**

Long retaining walls should be broken into panels 20 ft. to 30 ft. long by vertical control joints designed to resist shear and other lateral forces while permitting longitudinal movement.

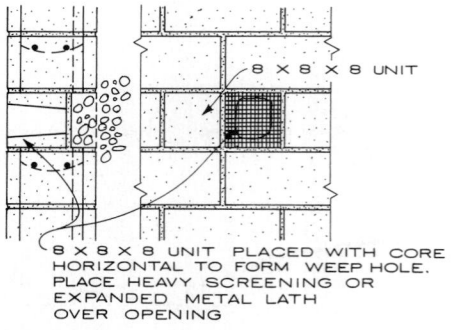

**ALTERNATE WEEP HOLE DETAIL**

**NOTE**

Four inch diameter weepholes located at 5 to 10 ft spacing along the base of the wall should be sufficient. Place about 1 cu ft of gravel or crushed stone around the intake of each weephole.

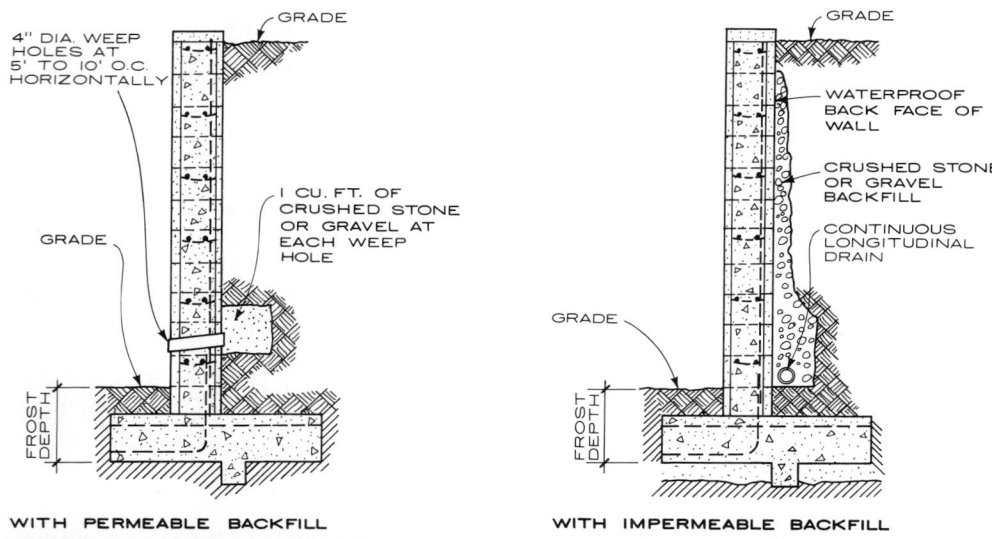

**WITH PERMEABLE BACKFILL**      **WITH IMPERMEABLE BACKFILL**

**DRAINAGE DETAILS FOR VARYING SOIL CONDITIONS**

## GENERAL NOTES

1. Materials and construction practices for concrete masonry retaining walls should comply with "Building Code Requirements for Concrete Masonry Structures (ACI 531)."

2. Use fine grout where grout space is less than 3 in. in least dimension. Use coarse grout where the least dimension of the grout space is 3 in. or more.

3. Steel reinforcement should be clean, free from harmful rust, and in compliance with applicable ASTM standards for deformed bars and steel wire.

4. Alternate vertical bars may be stopped at wall midheight. Vertical reinforcement usually is secured in place after the masonry work has been completed and before grouting.

5. Designs herein are based on an assumed soil weight (vertical pressure) of 100 pcf. Horizontal pressure is based on an equivalent fluid weight for the soil of 45 pcf.

6. Walls shown are designed with a safety factor against overturning of not less than 2 and a safety factor against horizontal sliding of not less than 1.5. Computations in the table for wall heights are based on level backfill. One method of providing for additional loads due to sloping backfill or surface loads is to consider them as an additional depth of soil, that is, an extra load of 300 psf can be treated as 3 ft. of extra soil weighing 100 psf.

7. Top of masonry retaining walls should be capped or otherwise protected to prevent entry of water into unfilled hollow cells and spaces. If bond beams are used, steel is placed in the beams as the wall is constructed. Horizontal joint reinforcement may be placed in each joint (8 in. o.c.) and the bond beams omitted.

8. Allow 24 hours for masonry to set before grouting. Pour grout in 4 ft. layers, 1 hour between each pour. Break long walls into panels of 20 ft. to 30 ft. in length with vertical control joints. Allow 7 days for finished wall to set before backfilling. Prevent water from accumulating behind wall by means of 4 in. diameter weepholes at 5 ft. to 10 ft. spacing (with screen and graded stone) or by a continuous drain with felt-covered open joints combined with waterproofing.

9. Where backfill height exceeds 6 ft., provide a key under the footing base to resist the wall's tendency to slide horizontally.

10. Heavy equipment used in backfilling should not approach closer to the top of the wall than a distance equal to the height of the wall.

11. A structural engineer should be consulted for final design.

Kenneth D. Franch, AIA, PE; Phillips Swager Associates, Inc.; Dallas, Texas
Stephen J. Zipp, AIA; Wilkes and Faulkner Associates; Washington, D.C.

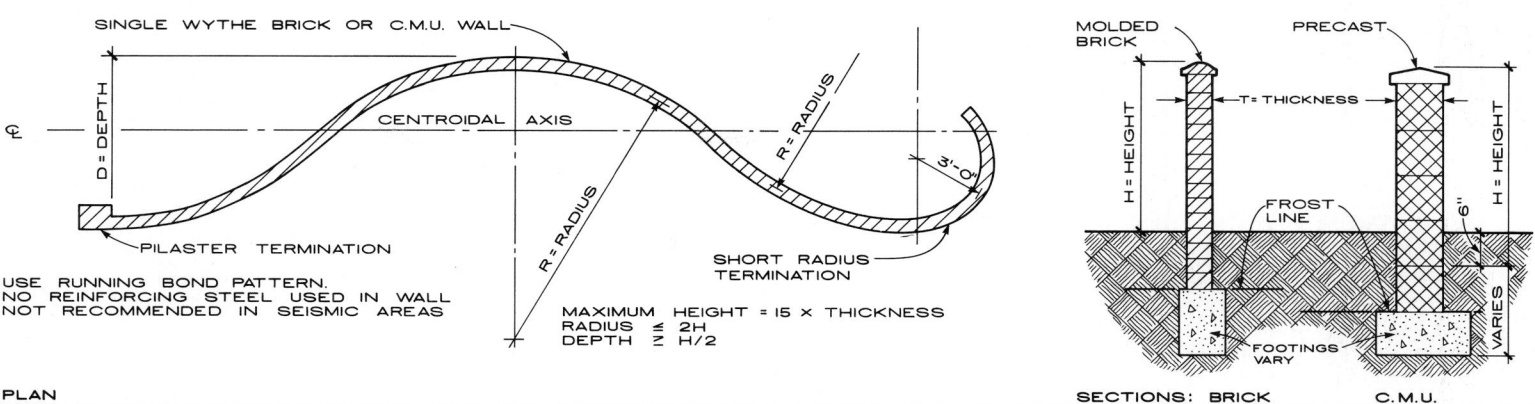

SINGLE WYTHE BRICK OR C.M.U. WALL

℄

D = DEPTH

CENTROIDAL AXIS

R = RADIUS

R = RADIUS

R = RADIUS

3'-0

PILASTER TERMINATION

SHORT RADIUS TERMINATION

USE RUNNING BOND PATTERN.
NO REINFORCING STEEL USED IN WALL
NOT RECOMMENDED IN SEISMIC AREAS

MAXIMUM HEIGHT = 15 × THICKNESS
RADIUS ≤ 2H
DEPTH ≥ H/2

MOLDED BRICK
PRECAST
T = THICKNESS
H = HEIGHT
H = HEIGHT
FROST LINE
6"
FOOTINGS VARY
VARIES

**PLAN**
**SERPENTINE GARDEN WALLS**

SECTIONS: BRICK    C.M.U.

12"× 12" OR 12"× 16" GROUTED, REINFORCED PIERS CENTERED OR OFFSET

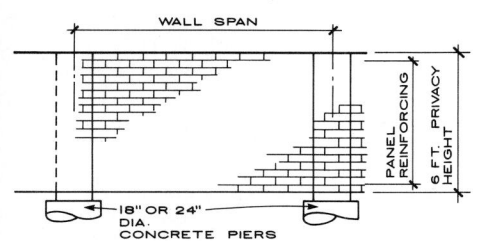

WALL SPAN

PANEL REINFORCING

6 FT. PRIVACY HEIGHT

18" OR 24" DIA. CONCRETE PIERS

**REINFORCED WALLS**
**PIER AND PANEL GARDEN WALLS**

## PANEL WALL REINFORCING STEEL

| WALL SPAN (FT.) | VERTICAL SPACING* (IN.) | | | | | | | | |
|---|---|---|---|---|---|---|---|---|---|
| | WIND LOAD 10 PSF | | | WIND LOAD 15 PSF | | | WIND LOAD 20 PSF | | |
| | A | B | C | A | B | C | A | B | C |
| 8 | 45 | 30 | 19 | 30 | 20 | 12 | 23 | 15 | 9.5 |
| 10 | 29 | 19 | 12 | 19 | 13 | 8.0 | 14 | 10 | 6.0 |
| 12 | 20 | 13 | 8.5 | 13 | 9.0 | 5.5 | 10 | 7.0 | 4.0 |
| 14 | 15 | 10 | 6.5 | 10 | 6.5 | 4.0 | 7.5 | 5.0 | 3.0 |
| 16 | 11 | 7.5 | 5.0 | 7.5 | 5.0 | 3.0 | 6.0 | 4.0 | 2.5 |

*A, two #2 bars; B, two 3/16 in. diameter wires; C, two 9-gauge wires.
NOTE: Wall spans between piers, no footing.

T = THICKNESS

L = LENGTH

## NON-REINFORCED WALLS L/T RATIO

| WIND PRESSURE (P.S.F.) | MAXIMUM LENGTH/THICKNESS RATIO |
|---|---|
| 5 | 35 |
| 10 | 25 |
| 15 | 20 |
| 20 | 18 |
| 25 | 16 |
| 30 | 14 |
| 35 | 13 |
| 40 | 12 |

**NON-REINFORCED WALLS WITH CONTINUOUS FOOTINGS**

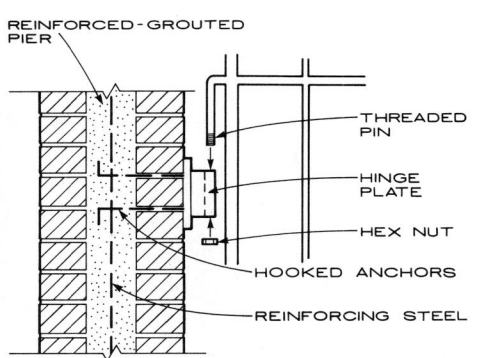

REINFORCED-GROUTED PIER

THREADED PIN

HINGE PLATE

HEX NUT

HOOKED ANCHORS

REINFORCING STEEL

**HINGE DETAIL**
**IRON GARDEN GATE**

ANALYSIS OF SECTIONS

$M_o$ = OVERTURNING MOMENT

$M_r$ = RESISTING MOMENT

W = WEIGHT OF WALL AND FOOTING (LB.)

P = WIND LOAD (LB./FT.$^2$) (FROM CODE)

$M_o = PL_1$    $M_r = WL_2$

FOR STABILITY $M_r \geq M_o$;

IF NOT, REDESIGN

CANTILEVER FOOTINGS ARE OFTEN USED AT PROPERTY LINES OR TO INCREASE RESISTANCE TO OVERTURNING. BE SURE TO CHECK FOR WIND FROM EITHER DIRECTION

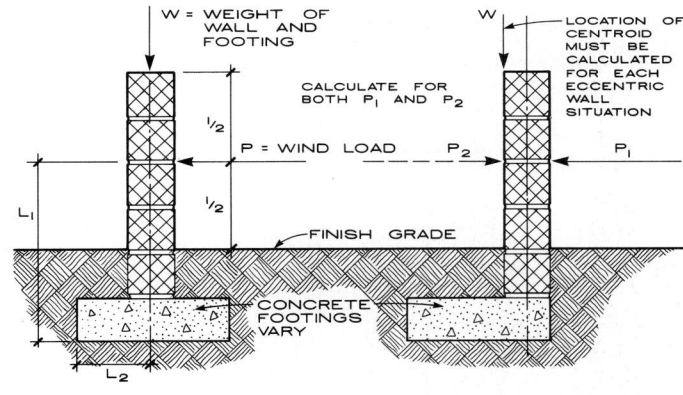

W = WEIGHT OF WALL AND FOOTING

W

LOCATION OF CENTROID MUST BE CALCULATED FOR EACH ECCENTRIC WALL SITUATION

CALCULATE FOR BOTH $P_1$ AND $P_2$

P = WIND LOAD    $P_2$    $P_1$

$L_1$

l/2

l/2

FINISH GRADE

CONCRETE FOOTINGS VARY

$L_2$

**SYMMETRICAL**    **CANTILEVER/ECCENTRIC**
**HORIZONTAL LOADING - FREESTANDING WALLS**

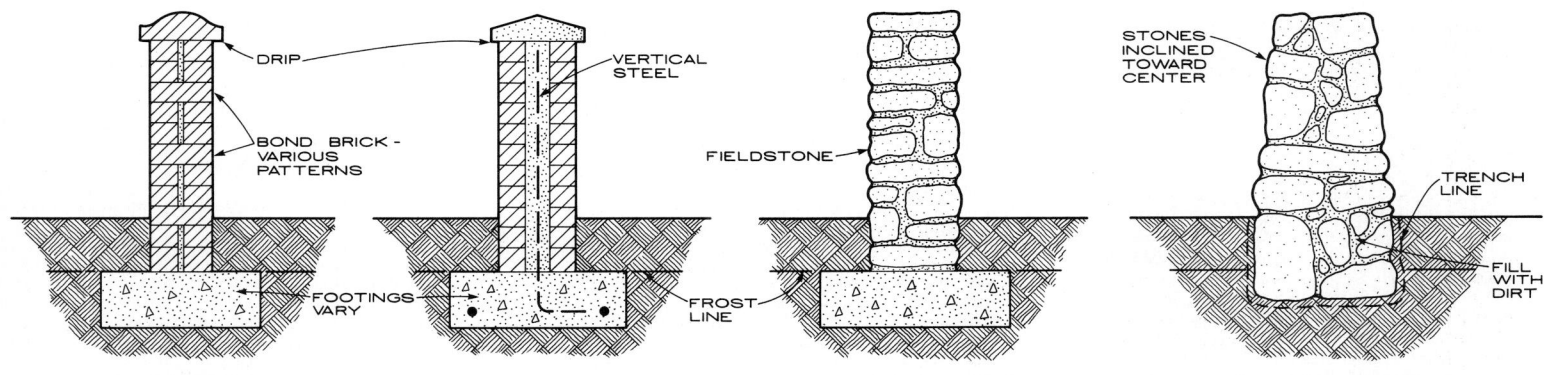

DRIP

BOND BRICK - VARIOUS PATTERNS

FOOTINGS VARY

VERTICAL STEEL

FROST LINE

FIELDSTONE

STONES INCLINED TOWARD CENTER

TRENCH LINE

FILL WITH DIRT

**SOLID MASONRY**    **GROUTED-REINFORCED**    **MORTARED STONE**    **DRY STACK STONE**
**FREESTANDING WALL TYPES**

Christine Beall, AIA, CCS; Austin, Texas
Charles R. Heuer, AIA; Washington, D.C.

**WALLS AND FENCES**    2

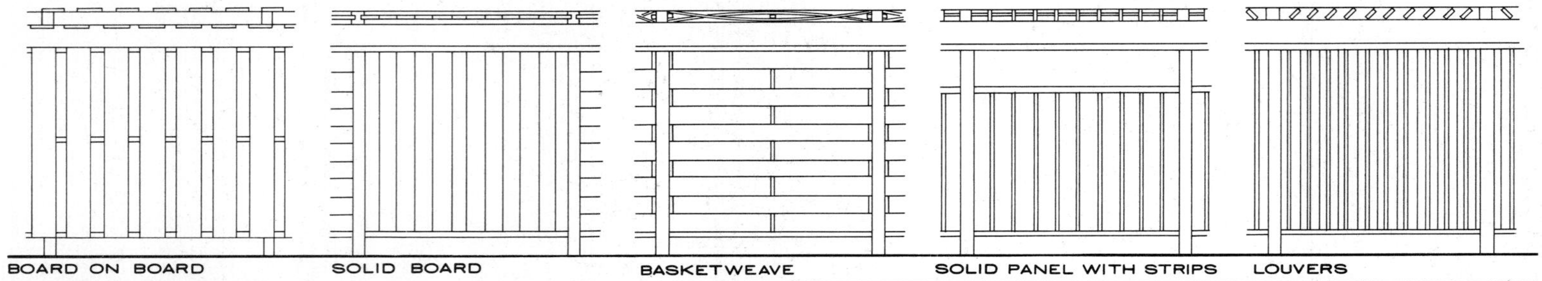

**BOARD ON BOARD**    **SOLID BOARD**    **BASKETWEAVE**    **SOLID PANEL WITH STRIPS**    **LOUVERS**

**SOLID FENCE TYPES**

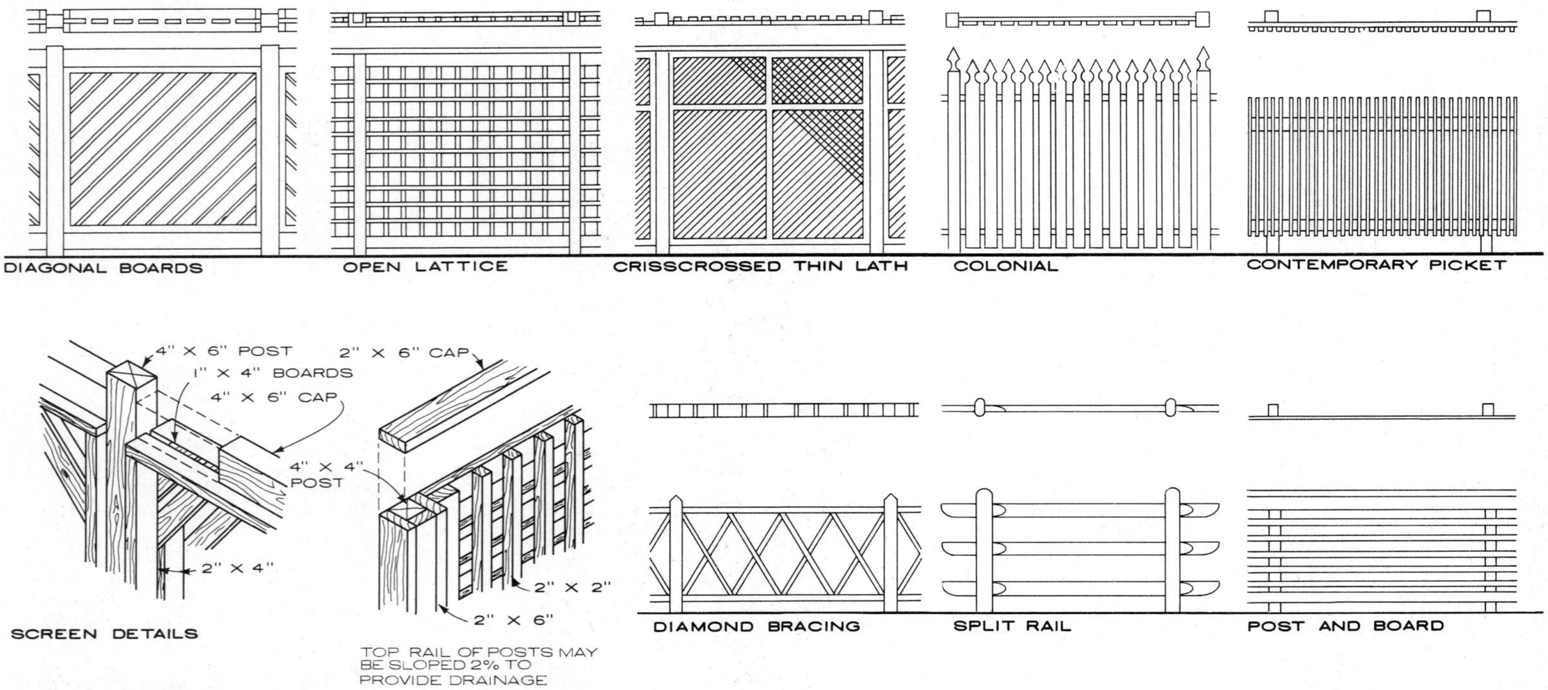

**DIAGONAL BOARDS**    **OPEN LATTICE**    **CRISSCROSSED THIN LATH**    **COLONIAL**    **CONTEMPORARY PICKET**

4" × 6" POST
1" × 4" BOARDS
4" × 6" CAP
2" × 6" CAP
4" × 4" POST
2" × 4"
2" × 2"
2" × 6"

**SCREEN DETAILS**

TOP RAIL OF POSTS MAY BE SLOPED 2% TO PROVIDE DRAINAGE

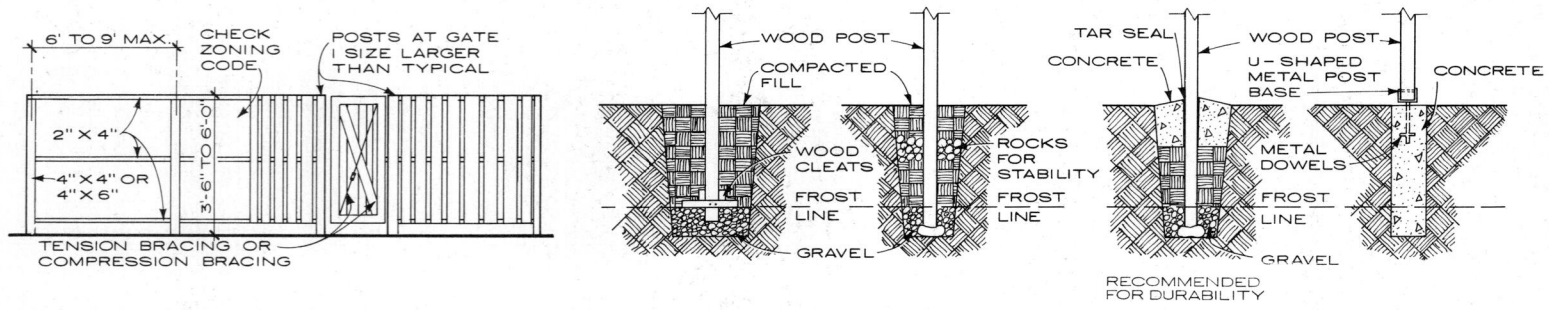

**DIAMOND BRACING**    **SPLIT RAIL**    **POST AND BOARD**

**TRANSPARENT FENCES AND SCREENS**

6' TO 9' MAX.    CHECK ZONING CODE    POSTS AT GATE 1 SIZE LARGER THAN TYPICAL

2" × 4"
4" × 4" OR 4" × 6"
3'-6" TO 6'-0"

TENSION BRACING OR COMPRESSION BRACING

**TYPICAL FENCE DIMENSIONS**

WOOD POST
COMPACTED FILL
WOOD CLEATS
FROST LINE
GRAVEL
ROCKS FOR STABILITY
FROST LINE

TAR SEAL
CONCRETE
WOOD POST
U-SHAPED METAL POST BASE
CONCRETE
METAL DOWELS
FROST LINE
GRAVEL

RECOMMENDED FOR DURABILITY

**FOOTING DETAILS**

## NOTES

When selecting a wood fence pattern, consider:

1. Site topography and prevailing wind conditions;
2. Architectural style of surrounding buildings and adjacent land use;
3. Required fence height and size of the property to be enclosed.

## PURPOSE

Wood fences are used for security, privacy, and screening of outdoor spaces. Picket fences 3 ft. or 4 ft. high keep small children or small dogs in the yard. Board-on-board fences, by standards built taller, provide greater wind and view barriers. Acoustical fences are built to keep out sound and wind, and to provide privacy. Open lattice or louvered fences, usually a minimum of 4 ft. high with self-closing gates and latches, are used for swimming pool enclosures. A semitransparent wood screen often is used to enclose an outdoor room to avoid totally obstructing the view or restricting natural ventilation. Long, open fence patterns are used best at the property line to define boundaries or limit access to a site.

## FASTENERS

Fasteners should be of noncorrosive aluminum alloy or stainless steel. Top quality, hot dipped galvanized steel is acceptable. Metal flanges, cleats, bolts, and screws are better than common nails.

Pressure-treated wood commonly is used for fencing. Certain species of nontreated woods, such as cedar and redwood heart, also are suitable. Refer to pages on wood uses in Chapter 6 for further information. Natural, stain, and paint finishes may be used.

Charles R. Heuer, AIA; Washington, D.C.

**WALLS AND FENCES**

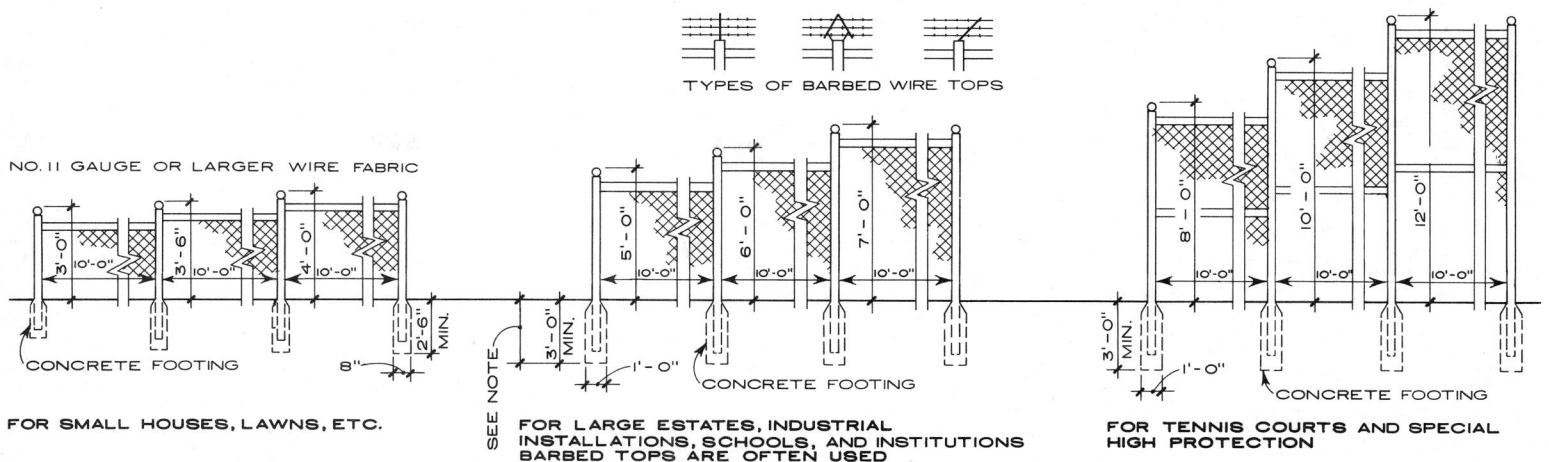

TYPES OF BARBED WIRE TOPS

NO. 11 GAUGE OR LARGER WIRE FABRIC

CONCRETE FOOTING    8"    2'-6" MIN.

**FOR SMALL HOUSES, LAWNS, ETC.**

SEE NOTE    3'-0" MIN.    1'-0"    CONCRETE FOOTING

**FOR LARGE ESTATES, INDUSTRIAL INSTALLATIONS, SCHOOLS, AND INSTITUTIONS BARBED TOPS ARE OFTEN USED**

3'-0" MIN.    1'-0"    CONCRETE FOOTING

**FOR TENNIS COURTS AND SPECIAL HIGH PROTECTION**

## HEIGHTS OF FENCES FOR VARIOUS USES

See note at middle right for depth of concrete footings.

## MATERIALS

### SIZES GIVEN ARE NOT STANDARD BUT REPRESENT THE AVERAGE SIZES USED

| | |
|---|---|
| Wire gauge | Usually No. 11 or No. 9 W & M. For specially rugged use use No. 6. For tennis courts usually No. 11 |
| Wire mesh | Usually 2″. For tennis courts usually $1^5/_8$″ or $1^3/_4$″ of chain link steel hot dip galvanized after weaving. Top and bottom salvage may be barbed or knuckled |
| Corner and end posts | For lawn fences usually 2″ O.D.<br>For estate fences 2″ for low and $2^1/_2$″ for medium and 3″ O.D. for heavy or high<br>For tennis courts 3″ O.D. |
| Line or intermediate posts | For lawn $1^3/_8$″ or 2″ O.D. round<br>For estate etc. 2″, $2^1/_4$″, $2^1/_2$″ H or I sections<br>For tennis courts $2^1/_2$″ round O.D. or $2^1/_4$″ H or I sections |
| Gate posts | The same or next size larger than the corner posts. Footings for gate posts 3′-6″ deep |
| Top rails | $1^5/_8$″ O.D. except some lawn fence may be $1^3/_8$″ O.D. |
| Middle rails | On 12′-0″ fence same as top rail |
| Gates | Single or double any width desired |
| Post spacing | Line posts 10′-0″ O.C., 8′-0″ O.C. may be used on heavy construction |

O.D. = outside diameter.

## POST SIZES FOR HEAVY DUTY GATES

| A.S.A. SCHEDULE 40 PIPE SIZES | SWING GATE OPENINGS | |
|---|---|---|
| | SINGLE GATE | DOUBLE GATE |
| $2^1/_2$″ | To 6′-0″ | Up to 12′-0″ |
| $3^1/_2$″ | Over 6′ to 18′ | Over 12′ to 26′ |
| 6″ | Over 13′ to 18′ | Over 26′ to 36′ |
| 8″ | Over 18′ to 32′ | Over 36′ to 64′ |

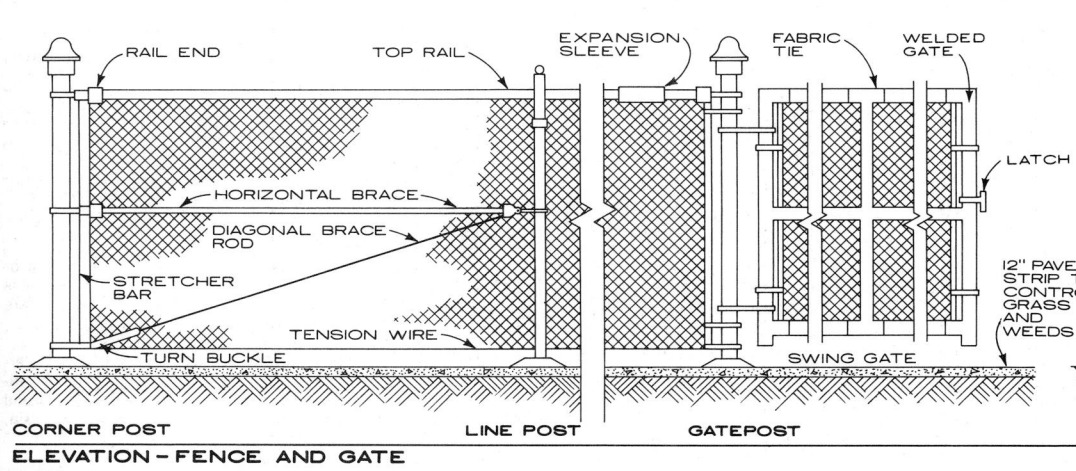

RAIL END    TOP RAIL    EXPANSION SLEEVE    FABRIC TIE    WELDED GATE

HORIZONTAL BRACE

DIAGONAL BRACE ROD

STRETCHER BAR

TENSION WIRE

TURN BUCKLE

LATCH

12″ PAVED STRIP TO CONTROL GRASS AND WEEDS

SWING GATE

CORNER POST    LINE POST    GATEPOST

## ELEVATION – FENCE AND GATE

NOTE

For fences 5′-0″ and taller a horizontal or diagonal brace, or both, is used for greater stability. Post spacing should be equidistant and should not exceed 10′-0″ O.C.

Charles Driesen; Ewing Cole Erdman & Eubank; Philadelphia, Pennsylvania

## CONCRETE FOOTING

Bottom of concrete footing to be set below frost line (see local code). Concrete footing sizes shown are the recommended minimum; they should be redesigned for conditions where soil is poor.

## TYPES OF WIRE FABRIC MESH

VINYL-COATED: Suitable for residential, commercial or industrial applications.
Mesh sizes: 1, $1^1/_4$, $1^1/_2$, $1^3/_4$, and 2 in.
Gauge sizes: 11, 9, 6, and 3.

## REDWOOD SLATS

Used for visual privacy and appearance. Suitable for homes, swimming pools, and gardens.
Mesh size: $3^1/_2$ x 5 in.
Gauge size: 9.

1. PREGALVANIZED: Should be restricted to such residential applications as residential perimeter fencing, swimming pool enclosures, private tennis courts, dog kennels, and interior industrial storage.
Mesh sizes: $1^1/_2$, $1^3/_4$, and 2 in. Gauge sizes: 13, 11, and 9.

2. HOT DIPPED GALVANIZED: Suitable for highway enclosures, institutional security fencing, highway bridge enclosures, exterior industrial security fences, parking lot enclosures, recreational applications, and any other environment where resistance to abuse and severe climatic conditions exist.
Mesh sizes: $1^1/_2$, $2^3/_4$, and 2 in. Gauge sizes: 9 and 6.

## COATINGS

Protective coatings used on fencing, such as zinc and aluminum. Various decorative coatings can be applied including vinyl bonded and organic coatings available from most manufacturers.

## SPECIAL FENCING

1. ORNAMENTAL: Vertical struts only—no chain link fabric required. Ideal for landscape or as barrier fence.

2. ELEPHANT FENCE: This fence can actually stop an elephant, hold back a rock slide, or bring a small truck to a halt. Size: 3 gauges x 2-in. mesh.

3. SECURITY FENCE: This fabric is nonclimbable and cannot be penetrated by gun muzzles, knives, or other weapons. Suitable as security barrier for police stations, prisons, reformatories, hospitals, and mental institutions. Mesh size: $3/_8$ in. for maximum security, $1/_2$ in. for high security, $5/_8$ in. for supersecurity, and 1 in. for standard security.

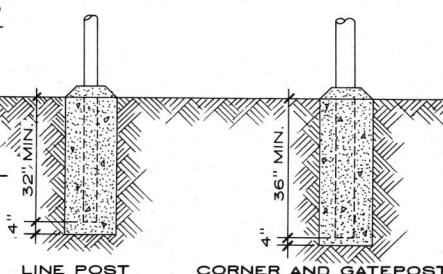

32″ MIN.    4″

LINE POST

36″ MIN.    4″

CORNER AND GATEPOST

## FLOOD DAMAGE MANAGEMENT

Flood damage results from a combination of floods and non-flood-resistant construction in flood-prone areas. Floods cannot be prevented, merely diverted from one area to another. Structural flood diversion facilities such as dams and levees encourage development of high-hazard areas with consequent increases in flood damage. For example, levee overtopping or failure is involved in about one-third of all flood disasters. Floodplain management, which regulates the use of floodplains and requires flood-resistant construction, can provide more reliable protection than structural flood diversion.

The designer bears the primary responsibility for flood damage management. The designer should evaluate building sites for their intrinsic suitability for the intended use. The designer also should select suitable architectural flood-resisting measures to compensate for deficiencies in the site and in public flood damage management programs.

Successful flood damage management requires the co-operation of the designer and public bodies. Public responsibility for flood damage management is shared by local and state governments and federal agencies, such as the Federal Emergency Management Agency (FEMA), the Office of Wetlands Protection, and the Army Corps of Engineers. Local governments often regulate floodplain use and drainage design. They also may require flood-resistant construction of buildings and infrastructures. Regional, state, and federal governments may provide regional floodplain management, protect ecosystems essential for flood damage control, such as wetlands, coastal dunes, and mangrove stands, and build regional flood diversion facilities.

The National Flood Insurance Program (NFIP) is a program to reduce federal expenditures for flood disaster relief. FEMA provides subsidized flood damage insurance to induce communities to adopt floodplain management programs. NFIP minimum standards require a low level of flood damage management based on historic condition. Many communities establish higher standards. They may regulate runoff, have freeboard requirements, or may base regulatory flood elevations on projections of effects of future development. Local standards more strict than NFIP supersede NFIP standards.

## FLOOD TERMS

Floodplain: The relatively flat area within which a river moves and upon which it regularly overflows.

Regulatory floodplain: That portion of the floodplain subject to floodplain regulations, usually that inundated by the base flood. Some communities regulate the 0.2% per year floodplain (500-year flood, NFIP Zone B).

Riverine flood: A great overflow of water from a river channel onto a floodplain. Riverine floods are caused by precipitation over large areas or by the melting of a winter's accumulation of snow, or both.

Flash flood: A local flood of great volume and short duration. Flash floods differ from riverine floods in their extent and duration. Flash floods generally result from a torrential rain or "cloudburst" on a relatively small drainage area. Flash floods also result from the failure of a dam or from the sudden breakup of an ice jamb.

Tidal flood: An overflow onto coastal lands bordering an ocean, an estuary, or a lake. These coastal lands, such as barrier islands, shores, and wetlands, occupy the same protective position relative to the sea that floodplains do to rivers.

Base flood (1% flood, 100-year flood): Under NFIP, the minimum size flood to be used by a community as a basis for its floodplain management regulations. It is presently required to be that flood which has a 1% chance of being equaled or exceeded in any given year.

The base flood is the still water height for riverine floods. The base flood for the Atlantic Coast and the Gulf of Mexico includes storm surge plus wave crest height because of "northeasters" and hurricanes. The base flood for the Pacific Coast includes astronomical tides plus wave runup because of tropical cyclones and tsunamis (seismic sea waves). For major lakes, the base flood includes seiche, "sloshing" because of wind, seismic activity, and storm surge.

Standard project flood: A flood that may be expected from the most severe combination of meteorological and hydrological conditions that are considered reasonably characteristic of the geographic area in which the drainage basin is located, but excluding extremely rare combinations. The peak flow for a standard project flood is generally 40–60% of the probable maximum flood for the same location. It is used in designing dams and other facilities with high damage potential.

Probable maximum flood: The most severe flood that may be expected from a combination of the most critical meteorological and hydrological conditions that are reasonably possible in a drainage basin. It is used in designing high-risk flood protection works and siting of structures and facilities that must be subject to almost no risk of flooding.

Base flood elevation (BFE): The height of the base flood in reference to mean sea level as defined by the National Geodetic Vertical Datum of 1929 (NGVD 1929).

Regulatory flood datum (RFD): The base flood plus a freeboard factor of safety established for each particular area, which tends to compensate for uncertainties that could contribute to greater flood height than that computed for a base flood.

Freeboard: A factor of safety for flood damage prevention expressed in feet above a design flood level.

Freeboard allows for hazards excluded from consideration and the uncertainties in analysis, design, and construction which cannot be fully or readily considered in an analytical fashion. Severe structural subsidence increases in floods because of obstructions in the floodplain or because of the urban runoff effect, and long-term increases in sea level and storms because of global temperature changes are often excluded from consideration. Urban conditions, low-accuracy map bases, and unplanned development are common sources of uncertainty which justify freeboard.

## USE ZONES

Floodway: The channel of a watercourse and those portions of the adjoining floodplain required to provide for the passage of a specified flood with an insignificant increase in the flood levels above that of natural conditions. As used by the NFIP, floodways must be large enough to pass the 100-year flood without causing an increase in elevation of more than a specified amount (1 ft in most areas).

Uses permitted in a floodway are those having a low flood damage potential and which do not obstruct flood flows, provided they do not require structures, fill, or storage of materials or equipment. Fill is prohibited. Most structures are prohibited or strongly discouraged. The following are generally permitted uses:

Agricultural uses such as general farming, pasture, grazing, outdoor plant nurseries, horticulture, viticulture, truck farming, forestry, sod farming, and wild crop harvesting.

Incidental industrial-commercial uses such as loading areas, parking areas, and airport landing strips (except in flash flood areas).

Recreational uses such as golf courses, tennis courts, driving ranges, archery ranges, picnic grounds, boat launching ramps, swimming areas, parks, wildlife and nature preserves, game farms, fish hatcheries, shooting preserves, target ranges, trap and skeet ranges, hunting and fishing areas, and hiking and horseback riding trails.

Incidental residential uses such as lawns, gardens, parking areas, and play areas.

Floodway fringe (flood fringe): The portion of the regulatory floodplain outside of the floodway, but still subject to flooding. The flood fringe is primarily a storage area for flood waters. Where permitted, property owners on each side of the floodplain may obstruct the flood flows to an equivalent degree.

Uses permitted in the floodway fringe include those permitted in floodways and elevated or otherwise floodproofed structures. Prohibited or strongly discouraged uses include storage of materials that are flammable or explosive in water, or toxic, and vital facilities such as hospitals and civil defense or rescue facilities, and difficult to evacuate facilities such as nursing homes and prisons.

## SOURCES

Coastal Construction Manual, FEMA-55, Dames & Moore, and Bliss & Nyitray, Inc. 1986.

Elevated Residential Structures, FEMA-54, American Institute of Architects, 1984.

Elevating to the Wave Crest Level: A Benefit:Cost Analysis, FIA-6, Sheaffer & Roland, Inc., 1980.

Facing Geologic and Hydrologic Hazards: Earth-Science Considerations, W. W. Hays, ed., U.S. Geological Survey, 1981.

Floodplain Management Handbook, Flood Loss Reduction Associates, U.S. Water Resources Council, 1981.

Floodproofing Nonresidential Structures, FEMA-102, Booker Associates, Inc., 1986.

The Floodway: A Guide for Community Permit Officials, Community Assistance Series No. 4, FEMA.

The Granite Garden: Urban Nature and Human Design, Anne Whiston Spirn, Basic Books, Inc., New York, 1984.

Guidelines for Determining Flood Flow Frequency, Bulletin #17B of the Hydrology Committee, U.S. Water Resources Council, 1981.

A Levee Policy for the National Flood Insurance Program, National Research Council, National Academy Press, 1982.

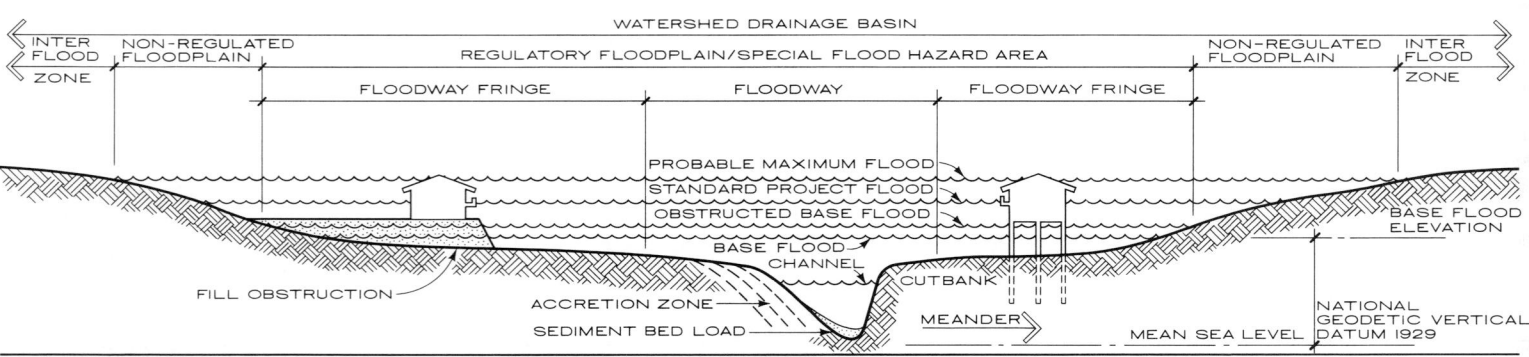

**IDEALIZED RIVERINE PROFILE**

Mattie Ann Fincher; Baton Rouge, Louisiana
National Research Council; Spirn; see data sources

# LAND PLANNING AND SITE DEVELOPMENT

## FLOOD RISK AND FLOOD RISK FACTORS

Flood risk is the hazard or exposure to the chance of injury or loss due to floods.

Freeboard can be used to compensate for uncertainties in estimating risk. For example, some communities require up to 3 ft freeboard to compensate for low-accuracy floodplain base maps. The margin of error of base maps may be estimated as plus or minus one-half of the contour interval. Maps developed from aerial photos usually have a contour interval of 5 ft. Thus, the margin of error is $\pm 2\frac{1}{2}$ ft. Field survey maps with a contour interval of 2 ft or less are used in some communities. This reduces the uncertainty of the risk and the need for freeboard.

Flood risk factors indicate the probability that one or more floods will exceed a given magnitude within a specified period of years. The risk factor (probability of exceedance, $P$) is the reciprocal of the recurrence interval ($T$): $P = 1/T$. Thus, there is a 1% chance or risk factor that the 100-year flood will be exceeded in a given year ($1\% = 1/100$). Actual risk may exceed the risk factor.

The risk factor chart can be used to determine the risk factor during a specified time period, and vice versa. Example: Estimate the flood risk factor for a house built at the base flood elevation (BFE) during the life of a 30-year mortgage. On the risk factor chart, (1) locate the recurrence interval, 30 years, at the bottom, (2) move up to the annual exceedance frequency curve for the base flood, 1%, and then (3) move left to interpolate the risk factor, 26%.

## FLOOD RISK ZONES

Structures in flood zones must protect their interiors and contents from inundation and must resist flotation, collapse, and lateral movement. Also, they should not increase flooding in other areas. There are five major risk zones, each with special flood resistance requirements.

Interflood zone: Low-risk upland areas of a watershed above the natural floodplain.

Nonregulated floodplain: Moderate-risk floodplain between the interflood zone and the regulatory floodplain.

In the interflood zone and the nonregulated floodplain, risks are usually caused by improper design of grading and drains or moderate- to low-frequency floods. In these zones, local agencies often regulate minimum building elevations above street or sewer levels. Local regulations may also control runoff, soil erosion, and sedimentation to prevent worsening floods.

Special flood hazard areas (zone A): High-risk areas, defined by the National Flood Insurance Program (NFIP) as riverine flood-prone areas identified as susceptible to inundation by the still water base flood.

Nonvelocity coastal flood areas (zone A): High-risk areas, defined by the NFIP as coastal flood-prone areas susceptible to inundation by the base flood, including storm surges with velocity waves of less than 3 ft and a still water depth of less than 4 ft. The water may be moving at high velocities in zone A because of the residual momentum of breaking waves.

In zone A, residences must have their lowest floor, usually including basements, elevated to the BFE. Flood-resistant residential basements are permitted only in communities that meet special NFIP flood criteria and adopt special local standards for their design and construction. Commercial structures must be elevated or otherwise floodproofed to the BFE.

Coastal high hazard areas (velocity zone, zone V): Very high-risk areas, defined by the NFIP as coastal flood-prone areas identified as susceptible to inundation by the base flood, including tidal surges with velocity waves greater than 3 ft. Generally, zone V indicates the inland extent of a 3-ft breaking wave, where the still water depth during the 100-year flood decreases to less than 4 ft.

In zone V the lowest horizontal structural member of the lowest habitable floor must be elevated above the BFE. Structural requirements are most stringent in zone V. Rigid frames and semirigid frames with grade beams are used in zone V. Semirigid frames without grade beams should be used only in areas not subject to potential scour. Free-standing pole structures are unsafe for use in zone V. They develop large rotations at moment connections which induce excessive deflection of pilings under sustained lateral loads.

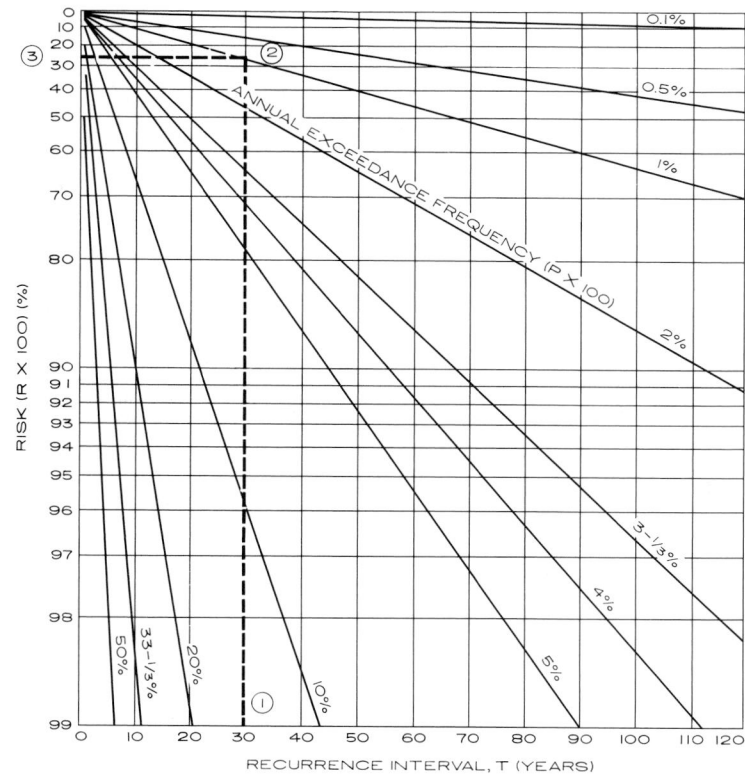

**RISK FACTOR CHART**

## GENERAL LIMITS OF FLOODPROOFING

| METHOD | DEPTH | VELOCITY | WARNING REQUIREMENTS |
|---|---|---|---|
| Levees | 4-7' | <10'/sec | Advance warning required for installation of floodgates in openings |
| Floodwalls | 4-7' | <12'/sec | |
| Closures (24 hr max) | 4-8' | <8'/sec | 5-8 hr advance warning required for installation of closures |
| Fill | 10'+ | <10'/sec | Evacuation time required unless fill connects to higher ground |
| Piles, piers, and columns | 10-12' | <8'/sec | Adequate evacuation time required |

Note: Information presented is general and warrants caution. Time available for warning may be severely limited by a flood's rate of rise.

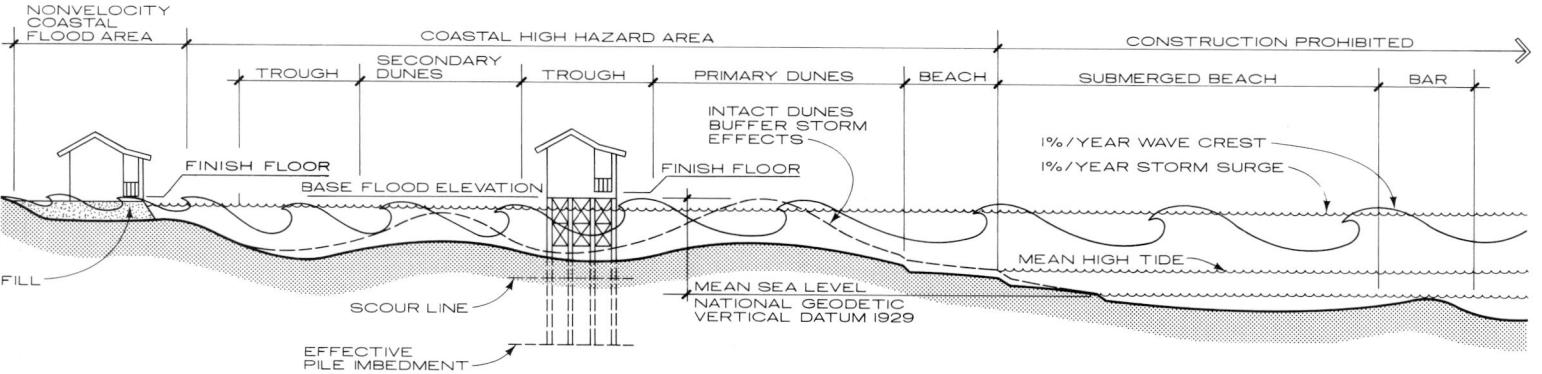

**IDEALIZED COASTAL PROFILE**

Mattie Ann Fincher; Baton Rouge, Louisiana

## SOCIAL IMPACTS

Social impacts are simply the effects on people— the way they live, work, play, and relate to one another—caused by the decision to develop a specific site. Although social impacts can be either beneficial or harmful, it is the latter that are of most concern. Historically there has been little equity in the distribution of adverse impacts. People who have had to bear the bulk of adverse social impact are members of minority groups, the poor, the elderly and the young, all of whom for one reason or another cannot exert sufficient influence on projects to defend adequately against the negative aspects of development. Planners and all other design professionals must be sensitive to the potential social impact their work may generate along with the economic and environmental aspects.

Social impacts can occur at any time during the life of a project. There are anticipatory effects such as land speculation, which occur when a project is still in the planning stage. Later, during construction, the physical intrusion of heavy machinery accompanied by noise, dust, and fumes may assume great importance. Finally, there may be social and other environmental consequences that occur after the completion of a project, sometimes many years later. Some negative impacts are short-lived and, at worst, annoying. Others may impair seriously an individual's ability to learn or to cope effectively in society; still others may precipitate grief, depression, and occasionally, in the case of the elderly, early death.

The social impact as well as economic and environmental impacts should be addressed in all impact studies. Some key questions must be answered in assessing the social impacts of a project:

1. What problems might the project create for the people in the community?
2. How many people will be affected (who gains and who loses)?
3. For how long and how severely will people be affected?
4. What alternatives exist? What happens if another location is selected or if development does not take place?
5. What can be done to lessen the severity of an adverse impact?
6. Is it possible to compensate people adequately for any adverse consequences of the project?
7. Will it significantly alter the pattern of urban development in the area?
8. Will it alter community or neighborhood infrastructure and transportation patterns?
9. Will it generate traffic hazards to pedestrians, motor vehicles, bicyclists or equestrians?
10. Will it create or alter the need for public services in the area, including fire and police protection, and hospital services?
11. Will it have an impact on, or result in the need for new or altered utilities in the area, including water, storm drainage, waste disposal, fuel supplies, and communication systems?
12. Will it adversely affect visibility, scenic resources or viewsheds?
13. Will it change the direction or flow rate of groundwaters?
14. Will it change the quantity or quality of groundwaters, through either direct additions, withdrawals, or through interception of an aquifer by cuts or excavations?
15. Will it substantially reduce the amount of water otherwise available for public water supplies?
16. Will it increase significantly the exposure of people or property to water-related hazards such as flooding or tidal waves?
17. Will it alter the quality of air by creating objectionable odors, altered wind patterns or changes in climate?
18. Will it release air pollutants or noise pollutants?
19. Will it change the patterns of light and solar exposure for adjacent properties?
20. Will it reduce the acreage of any agricultural crop or non-renewable natural resource such as agricultural soils or open space?
21. Will it cause the destruction or impairment of a significant archeological site?
22. Will it require the destruction, removal, or alteration of a significant historical site, structure, or other important cultural resource?

All identifiable potential impacts should be addressed and considered. Potentially adverse consequences should be dealt with thoroughly by the developer or avoided if possible. A relatively straightforward method of classifying potential consequences and responses is to:

1. Identify if a significant impact potential exists for a particular facet of the project;
2. Identify measures to be taken to mitigate and minimize negative impacts; and
3. For items of significant impact, qualify each relative to the long-term productivity versus short-term gain.

Some specific environmental and social concerns may be grouped as follows:

### LAND USE AND ZONING

1. Conflict with zoning or general plan designations for the property.
2. Conflict with adjacent, existing or planned land uses.
3. Induce urban growth or alter the location, distribution, density or growth rate of the human population of an area.
4. Affect existing housing or create a demand for additional housing.
5. Preclude opportunities for provision of lower income housing.

### TRANSPORTATION, ACCESS AND CIRCULATION

1. Alter present patterns of circulation or movement of people and goods.
2. Alter water, rail or air traffic.
3. Generation of additional vehicular movement.
4. Effects on existing parking facilities or demand for new parking.
5. Traffic hazards to equestrians, motor vehicles, bicyclists or pedestrians.

### PUBLIC SERVICES

Effect upon or result in a need for new or altered services in: education, open space and recreation, police, fire protection, hospital and ambulance.

### GEOLOGY AND SOILS

1. The destruction, covering or modification of any unique geologic or physical features.
2. Exposure of people or property to earthquake hazards like surface rupture or severe ground shaking.
3. Exposure of people or property to hazards of liquefaction, ground failure or similar hazards.
4. Unstable earth conditions or changes in geologic substructures.
5. Disruptions, displacements, compaction or overcovering of the soil.
6. Destruction, covering or modification of any soils of agricultural, mineral or construction value.
7. Any increase in wind or water erosion of soils, either on or off the site.
8. Changes in deposition or erosion of beach sands, or changes in siltation, deposition or erosion which may modify the channel of a river or stream or the bed of the ocean or any bay, inlet or lake.

### UTILITIES

Have an impact on, or result in need for, new or altered utilities in: water, sewer or septic tank, storm water drainage, solid waste and disposal, energy resources, or communications systems.

### TOPOGRAPHY

Change in topography or ground surface relief features, which affect: slopes, visibility, scenic resources, aesthetics, or viewsheds.

### HYDROLOGY

1. Changes in the currents, or the course or direction of water movements, in either marine or fresh waters.
2. Changes in absorption rates, drainage patterns, or the rate and amount of surface water runoff.
3. Alterations to the course or flow of flood waters.
4. Change in the amount of surface water in any body.
5. Discharge into surface waters, or in any alteration of surface water quality, including but not limited to temperature, dissolved oxygen or turbidity.
6. Alteration of the direction or rate or flow of groundwaters.

7. Change in the quantity or quality of groundwaters, either through direct additions or withdrawals, or through interception of an aquifer by cuts or excavations.
8. Substantial reduction in the amount of water otherwise available for public water supplies.
9. Exposure of people or property to water related hazards such as flooding or tidal waves.

### AIR QUALITY

1. Increased air emissions or deterioration of ambient air quality.
2. Creation of objectionable odors.
3. Alteration of air movement, moisture or temperature, or any change in climate, either locally or regionally.
4. Exposure of persons to locally elevated levels of air pollution.

### NOISE

Increase in existing noise levels.

### CLIMATE

Pattern changes in winds, precipitation, temperature, or sun angles.

### PLANT AND ANIMAL LIFE

1. Change in the diversity of species, or number of any species of plants or animals.
2. Reduction of the numbers of any unique, aesthetically significant, rare or endangered species of plants or animals.
3. Introduction of a new species of plants or animals into an area, or as a barrier to the normal replenishment or migration of existing species.

### PALEONTOLOGIC, ARCHAEOLOGICAL, AND HISTORIC

1. Destruction, removal or alteration of a significant paleontological site.
2. Destruction, removal or alteration of a significant historical site, structure, object or building or other important cultural or scientific resource.

### RANKING OF CONSTRUCTION RELATED SOCIAL IMPACTS USING A HIGHWAY CONSTRUCTION PROJECT EXAMPLE

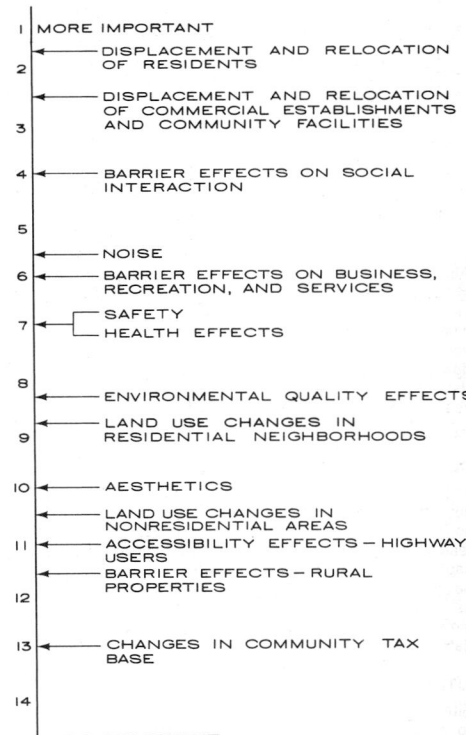

```
1  MORE IMPORTANT
          DISPLACEMENT AND RELOCATION
2             OF RESIDENTS

          DISPLACEMENT AND RELOCATION
            OF COMMERCIAL ESTABLISHMENTS
3           AND COMMUNITY FACILITIES

          BARRIER EFFECTS ON SOCIAL
4           INTERACTION

5
          NOISE
6         BARRIER EFFECTS ON BUSINESS,
            RECREATION, AND SERVICES
          SAFETY
7         HEALTH EFFECTS

8
          ENVIRONMENTAL QUALITY EFFECTS
          LAND USE CHANGES IN
9           RESIDENTIAL NEIGHBORHOODS

10        AESTHETICS
          LAND USE CHANGES IN
            NONRESIDENTIAL AREAS
11        ACCESSIBILITY EFFECTS – HIGHWAY
            USERS
          BARRIER EFFECTS – RURAL
            PROPERTIES
12

13        CHANGES IN COMMUNITY TAX
            BASE

14

15  LESS IMPORTANT
```

William H. Evans, AIA; San Antonio, Texas
Lynn G. Llewellyn, Ph.D., Social Psychologist; Rockville, Maryland
Connecticut Coastal Management Program, see data sources

# THE SITE PLANNING PROCESS

## INTRODUCTION

Site planning for any significant development project should be a sequential process, beginning with broad information-gathering and ending with specific, detailed design drawings. The process involves three basic stages: analysis, design, and implementation. The following chart indicates a planning process; however, it should be noted that the site planning process will be specific to the particular project. The following is a checklist approach to structure a project. Specifics of the site, such as physical site characteristics, urban or suburban location, and community criteria, will modify the process. The site planning process is interdisciplinary, and includes both architect and landscape architect. An integrated approach to site development and architecture helps create a quality environment.

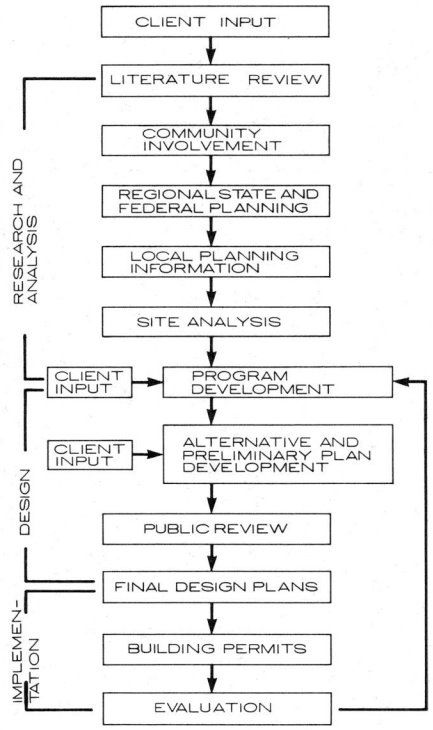

Also important, particularly in urban infill situations, is the involvement of the community in providing input to the design process. Although most site planning processes involve some form of public hearing, a less structured involvement early in the design process will be useful in designing a project that responds to existing community desires and aspirations. Certain steps in the following process may be taken simultaneously, rather than on a precise step-by-step basis.

## CLIENT CONTACT AND INPUT

The first step is the contact between client and site planner. Although the site planner should be involved as early as possible in the decision-making process, the client already may have some broad objectives based on financial capabilities and market feasibility. In many cases, it may be advisable for the client to retain the site planner for assistance in selecting a site that meets the client's basic aims. It is important that the site planner obtain all client data relative to the planning of the site.

## LITERATURE REVIEW

Site planning problems vary from rural and suburban sites to intensive urban sites. It often is beneficial to review literature relevant to the nature of the particular site planning problem. Current literature is available on responsibilities of designers working within an existing urban framework.

Gary Greenan, AICP; Miami, Florida
Rafael Diaz, Graphics Coordinator; Miami, Florida

## COMMUNITY INVOLVEMENT

Early in the design process it is important to contact community groups that have an interest in the proposed project. Involvement of such groups may provide valuable information about their concept of the existing community and their view of possible changes. It is particularly important for infill projects when edges of the proposed project are adjacent to existing development. The compatibility of the edges—building intensity, scale, lot size and design—are typical issues that should be resolved with community participation. Also, an early cooperative effort can defray problems later at public hearing stages. Citizen contact should be maintained throughout the design process.

## REGIONAL, STATE, AND FEDERAL PLANNING

In some areas of the country, regional planning agencies have been established for research and planning of intercommunity regional issues such as water management, transportation, population studies, pollution control, and other regional environmental concerns. Many communities have adopted plans that establish regional planning guidelines on land use planning. The site planner should pinpoint regional issues pertinent to the site design.

Some projects also may be affected by state and/or national criteria, although this is not a common occurrence. Adopted state plans may address broad issues applicable to large sites or impose constraints on sites involving issues of statewide concern. Also, some states require environmental impact statements for large-scale projects. At the national level, the Environmental Protection Agency, a non-permitting agency, has delegated its authority to various permitting agencies involved in the protection of air and water quality. Under the U.S. Clean Water Act, the U.S. Corps of Engineers is responsible for environmental review of proposed dredge and fill operations in navigable waters as well as wetlands. Another federal regulation that will affect many coastline projects is the Federal Flood Insurance Program, which establishes minimum elevations for potential flood areas.

## LOCAL PLANNING INFORMATION

At this stage the site planner becomes involved in collecting local planning information that will influence decisions made in the site planning process. Personal contact with local planning and zoning agencies is important in order to comprehend clearly local criteria. Following is a list of information to review.

## PLANNING DOCUMENTS

Many communities have adopted comprehensive plans that indicate in general terms, and in some instances in specific terms, the particular land use and intensity of the site. Also, valuable information on the availability and/or phasing of public services and utilities, environmental criteria, traffic planning information, and population trends can be found in most comprehensive plans. Some communities may require that rezoning meet the criteria provided in their comprehensive plans.

In addition to the comprehensive plan, some communities adopt neighborhood or area studies that refine the comprehensive plan as it relates to subareas. Many of these studies stipulate specific zoning categories for individual parcels of land.

## URBAN DESIGN STUDIES

Many communities have adopted urban design plans that provide guidance for the coherent development of their urban areas. These documents may range from a general conceptual nature to documents that incorporate specific zoning requirements. Some documents may include compliance with specific urban design requirements. Some provide bonuses in greater land use intensities for incorporating urban amenities such as plazas and squares. These plans usually are developed with major input from the design professions.

## ZONING

The intensity and type of land use that can occur is determined by the zoning on a tract of land. A zoning change is required if the planned project differs.

## PUBLIC SERVICES AND UTILITIES

Although some information on public services and utilities may be provided in the comprehensive plan or neighborhood study, the critical nature of the availability of these public facilities may require additional research, especially:

1. Availability of public sewer service, access to trunk lines, capacity of the trunk lines, and available in-

creases in the flow. (If sewage lines are not immediately available, the projected phasing of these services must be determined, as well as other possible alternatives to sewage collection and treatment.)
2. Availability of potable water, with the same basic research approach as indicated for sewer service determination.
3. Local and state regulations on freshwater wells and septic tanks.
4. Access to public roads, existing and projected carrying capacity, and levels of service of the roads. (State and local road departments can provide this information.)
5. Availability and capacity of schools and other public facilities such as parks and libraries.

## SITE ANALYSIS (SITE INVENTORY)

Site analysis is one of the site planner's major responsibilities. All of the on- and off-site environmental design determinants must be evaluated and synthesized during the site analysis process. The site analysis processes follow later in this section.

## PROGRAM DEVELOPMENT

At the program development stage, the background research, citizen input, and the site analysis are combined with client input and synthesized into a set of site development concepts and strategies. Elements that form the basis for program development include market and financial criteria, federal, state, regional, and local planning information, development costs, and the client's basic objectives, combined with site opportunities and constraints as developed in the synthesis of environmental site determinants. Trade-offs and a balancing of the various determinants would be needed to develop an appropriate approach to site development. Consideration of dwelling unit type, density, marketing, time phasing, and other similar criteria, as well as graphic studies of the site, constitute the program. Graphic representations depicting design concepts should be developed clearly for presentation to the client and others who may have input to the process. If the program cannot be accomplished under the existing zoning, the decision to request a zoning change becomes a part of the program.

## ALTERNATIVE AND PRELIMINARY PLAN PREPARATION

Once the program is established and accepted by the client, alternative design solutions that meet the program objectives, including basic zoning criteria, are developed. The accepted alternative is further developed into the preliminary plan. This plan should be relatively detailed, showing all spatial relationships, landscaping, and similar information.

## PUBLIC REVIEW

If a zoning change is required to implement the plan, review by the public will be required. Some communities will require substantial data, such as impact statements and other narrative and graphic exhibits, while others may require only an application for the zoning change. Local requirements for changes can be complex, and it is imperative for the site planner or the client's attorney to be familiar with local criteria.

## FINAL DESIGN PLANS

At this stage, the preliminary plan is further refined to include any modifications that may have been agreed upon at a public hearing. Final design plans, including landscape plans and all required dimensioning, must be provided in the final design.

At this stage, the preliminary plans are further refined into the final site development plans. The final site development plans include fully dimensioned drawings and all landscape plans and site details. Final development plans also include drawings such as legal plats, utilities, and street and drainage plans, prepared by the engineer or surveyor. Upon approval, final design plans are recorded in the public records in the form of plats. In addition, homeowner association agreements, deed restrictions, and other similar legal documents must be recorded, and they become binding on all owners and successive owners unless changed by legal processes. Bonding may be required for public facilities.

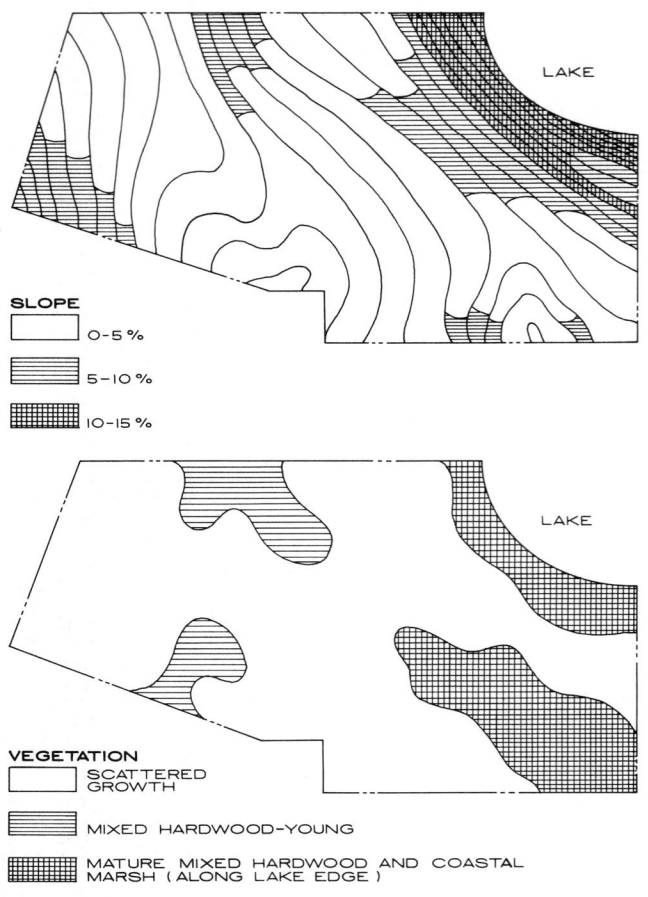

**SLOPE**

|       |         |
|-------|---------|
|       | 0-5 %   |
|       | 5-10 %  |
|       | 10-15 % |

**VEGETATION**

|       |         |
|-------|---------|
|       | SCATTERED GROWTH |
|       | MIXED HARDWOOD-YOUNG |
|       | MATURE MIXED HARDWOOD AND COASTAL MARSH (ALONG LAKE EDGE) |

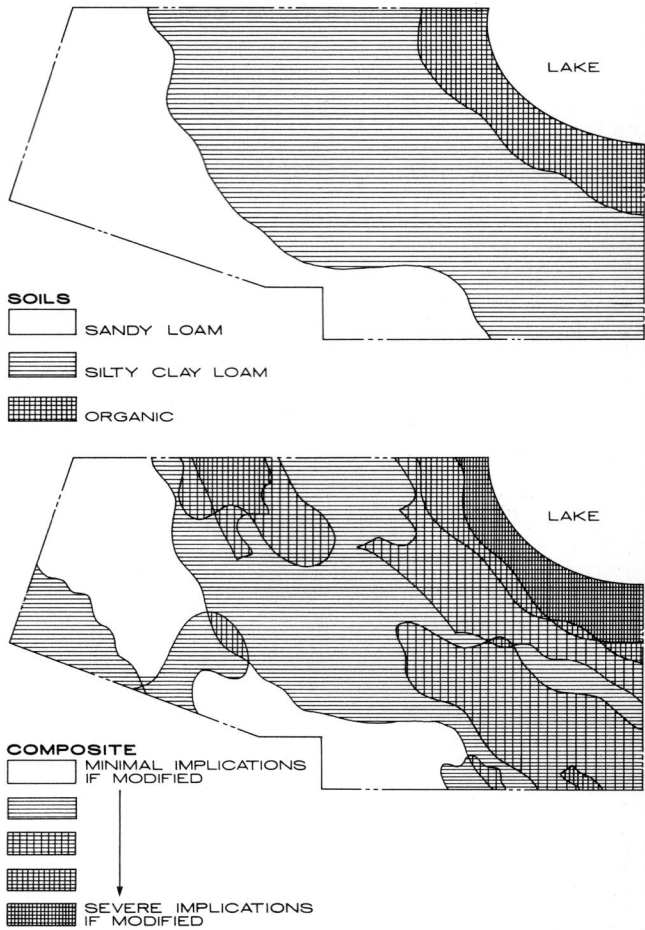

**SOILS**

|       |         |
|-------|---------|
|       | SANDY LOAM |
|       | SILTY CLAY LOAM |
|       | ORGANIC |

**COMPOSITE**

|       |         |
|-------|---------|
|       | MINIMAL IMPLICATIONS IF MODIFIED |
|       |         |
|       |         |
|       |         |
|       | SEVERE IMPLICATIONS IF MODIFIED |

## ENVIRONMENTAL SITE ANALYSIS PROCESS

If a site has numerous environmental design determinants, the site planner may analyze each environmental system individually in order to comprehend the environmental character of the site more clearly. This can be a complex process, and a site planner/landscape architect with expertise in environmental analysis should be retained to coordinate such an effort.

By preparing each analysis on transparencies, the site planner can use the overlay approach to site analysis. Values are assigned to each sheet based on impact, ranging from area of the site where change would have minimal effect to areas where change would result in severe disruption of the site. In essence, the separate sheets become abstractions with values assigned by the site planner and associated professionals. As each sheet is superimposed, a composite develops, which, when completed, constitutes the synthesis of the environmental design determinants. Lighter tones indicate areas where modification would have minimal influence, darker tones indicate areas more sensitive to change. The sketches shown simulate the overlay process. The site planner may give greater or lesser weight to certain parameters depending on the particular situation. In assigning values, the site planner should consider such factors as the value of maintaining the functioning of the individual site systems, the uniqueness of the specific site features, and the cost of modifying the site plan as an input in the site design process.

Following is a list of the environmental design determinants that, depending on the particular site, may be considered and included in an overlay format:

1. SLOPE: The slope analysis is developed on the contour map; consideration should include the percentage of slope and orientation of slope relative to the infrastructure and land uses.
2. SOIL PATTERNS: Consideration may include the analysis of soils by erosion potential, compressibility and plasticity, capability of supporting plant growth, drainage capabilities, possible sources of pollution or toxic wastes, septic tank location (if relevant), and the proposed land uses and their infrastructure.
3. VEGETATION: Consideration of indigenous species, (values of each in terms of the environmental system), size and condition, the succession of growth toward climax conditions, uniqueness, the ability of certain species to tolerate construction activities, aesthetic values, and density of undergrowth.
4. WILDLIFE: Consideration of indigenous species, their movement patterns, the degree of change that each species can tolerate, and feeding and breeding areas.
5. GEOLOGY: Consideration of underlying rock masses, the depth of different rock layers, and the suitability of different geological formations in terms of potential infrastructure and building.
6. SURFACE AND SUBSURFACE WATER: Consideration of natural drainage patterns, aquifer recharge areas, erosion potential, and flood plains.
7. CLIMATE: Consideration of microclimatic conditions including prevailing breezes (at different times of the year), wind shadows, frost pockets, and air drainage patterns.

### COMPUTER APPLICATION

The above process is labor intensive when developed by hand on individual sheets of mylar; however, this partic-

ular method of environmental analysis is easily adaptable to the CAD (Computer Aided Drafting) System. Commercial drafting programs suitable for the overlay approach are readily available. Simplified, the method is as follows:

1. A map, such as a soil map, is positioned on the digitizer and the information is transferred to the processor through the use of the stylus. One major advantage to the use of a computer is that the scale of the map being recorded will be transferred to the selected scale by the processor. A hatched pattern is selected, with a less dense pattern for soil types that would have minimal influence and with more dense patterns for soil types that are more sensitive to change. Once this information is programmed into the computer, it is stored.
2. The same process is repeated for development of the next overlay; for example, vegetation. Once again any scale map may be used. This process is repeated until all overlays have been stored. At any time one or all overlays can be produced on the screen.
3. Then the individual overlays or any combination of overlays can be drawn on mylar with a plotter. If appropriate for the particular analysis, the plotter will draw in color. The resulting overlay sheets would have taken considerably longer by hand and may have been less accurate. The site also can be studied directly on the computer monitor screen. Another advantage to the use of the computer is that any part of the overlay can be enlarged for greater detail.
4. The overlay process can be recorded by video tape or by slides from the screen for use in presentations.

Gary Greenan, AICP; Miami, Florida
Rafael Diaz, Graphics Coordinator; Miami, Florida

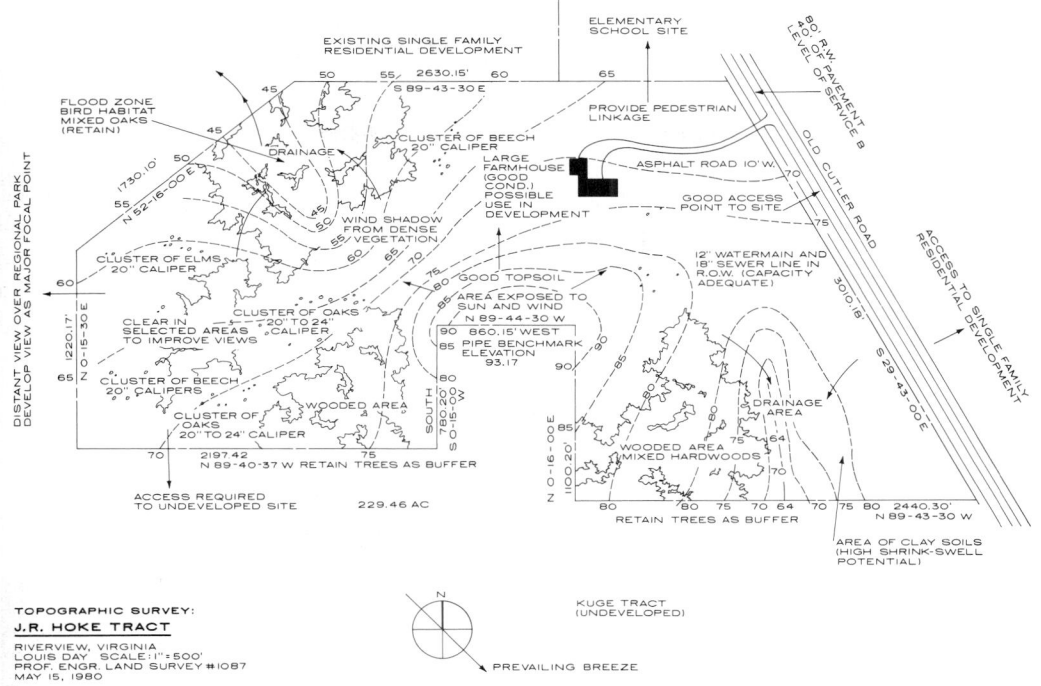

## ENVIRONMENTAL CONSIDERATIONS

1. Air movement: prevailing breezes characteristic of a region may be greatly modified by urban high rise structures. Predominant air movement patterns in a city may be along roadways and between buildings. In addition, the placement, shape, and height of existing buildings can create air turbulence caused by micro air movement patterns. These patterns may influence the location of building elements such as outdoor areas and balconies. Also, a building's design and placement can mitigate or increase local wind turbulence.

2. Sun and shadow patterns: existing structure sun and shadow patterns should be studied to determine impact on the proposed building. This is particularly important for outdoor terraces and balconies where sunlight may be desirable. Sun and shadow patterns also should be considered as sources of internal heat gain or loss. Building orientation, window sizes, and shading devices can modify internal heat gain or loss. Studies also should include daily and seasonal patterns, and the impact on existing buildings and open spaces of shadows cast by the proposed building.

3. Reflections: reflections from adjacent structures such as glass-clad buildings may be a problem. The new building should be designed to compensate for such glare, or if possible, oriented away from such glare.

## URBAN CONTEXTUAL ANALYSIS

1. Building typology and hierarchy: An analysis of the particular building type (residential, commercial, public) relative to the hierarchy of the various building types in the city is useful in deciding the general design approach of a new building. For example, public buildings may be dominant in placement and design, while residential buildings are subdominant. It is important to maintain any existing hierarchy that reinforces visual order in the city. Any predominant architectural solutions and details characteristic of a building type may be useful in the new building's design to maintain a recognizable building type.

2. Regional character: An analysis of the city's regional architectural characteristics is appropriate in developing a design solution that responds to unique regional characteristics. Regional characteristics may be revealed through unique architectural types, vernacular building resulting from local climatic and cultural characteristics, and from historically significant architecture. Historical structures should be saved by modifying them for the proposed new use or by incorporating parts of the existing structure(s) into the proposed design.

3. City form: The delineation of city form created by road layout, location of major open spaces, and architecture-created forms should be analyzed. Elements that delineate city form should be reinforced by architectural development solutions for a particular place within the city. For example, a building proposed for a corner site should be designed to reinforce the corner through building form, entrance, and design details. A building proposed for mid-block may be a visually unifying element providing connection and continuity with adjacent buildings. Sites at the end of important vistas or adjacent to major city squares probably should be reserved for important public buildings.

4. Building scale and fenestrations: It is important to analyze building scale and fenestration of nearby buildings. Such detailing may be reflected, although not necessarily reproduced, in the proposed building. This can provide visual unity and continuity in the architectural character of the city. One example is the use and placement of cornice lines to define the building's lower floors in relation to adjacent buildings. Cornice lines also can define the building's relationship to pedestrians in terms of scale and use.

5. Building transition: Sometimes it may be appropriate to use arcades and porches to provide transition between the building's private interior and the public sidewalk. It may be especially worthy to include them if adjacent buildings have these elements.

6. Views: Important city views of plazas, squares, monuments, and natural features such as waterfronts and parks should be considered. They are important as views from the proposed building. It is also important to design the proposed structure to enhance and preserve such views for the public and for inhabitants of nearby buildings.

## SURVEY DATA

The first step in any site analysis is the gathering of physical site data. An aerial photograph and an accurate survey showing the following information are basic to any site analysis process:

1. Scale, north arrow, benchmark and date of survey.
2. Tract boundary lines.
3. Easements: location, width, and purpose.
4. Names and locations of existing road rights-of-way on or adjacent to the tract including bridges, curbs, gutters, and culverts.
5. Position of buildings and other structures such as foundations, walls, fences, steps, and paved areas.
6. Utilities on or adjacent to the tract, including: location of gas lines, fire hydrants, electric and telephone poles, and street lights; and direction, distance to, and size of nearest water mains and sewers and invert elevation of sewers.
7. Location of swamps, springs, streams, bodies of water, drainage ditches, water shed areas, flood plains, and other physical features.
8. Outline of wooded areas with names and condition of plant material.
9. Contour intervals of 2 ft. to 5 ft. depending on the slope gradients, and spot elevations at breaks in grade, along all drainage channels or swales, and selected points as needed.

### ADDITIONAL INFORMATION

Considerable additional information may be needed, depending on design considerations and site complexities such as soil information and studies of the geological structure of the site.

## SUBURBAN SITE ANALYSIS

As indicated in the previous site planning process, the site analysis is a major responsibility of the site planner. The physical analysis of the site is developed primarily from field inspections. Using the survey, the aerial photograph and, where warranted, infrared aerial photographs, the site designer, working in the field and in the office, verifies the survey and notes site design determinants. Site design determinants should include but not be limited to the following:

1. Areas of steep and moderate slopes.
2. Macro- and microclimatic conditions, including: sun angles during different seasons; prevailing breezes; wind shadows; frost pockets; and sectors where high or low points give protection from sun and wind.
3. Solar energy considerations: if solar energy appears feasible, a detailed climatic analysis must be undertaken considering such factors as: detailed sun charts; daily averages of sunlight and cloud cover; daily rain averages; areas exposed to the sun at different seasons; solar radiation patterns; and temperature patterns.
4. Areas of potential flood zones and routes of surface water runoff.
5. Possible road access to the site, including potential conflicts with existing road systems and carrying capacities of adjacent roadways. (This information usually can be obtained from local or state road departments.)
6. Natural areas that from an ecological and aesthetic standpoint should be saved; all tree masses with name and condition of tree species and understory planting.
7. Significant wildlife habitats that would be affected by site modification.
8. Soil conditions relative to supporting plant material, areas suitable for construction, erosion potential, and septic tanks, if relevant.
9. Geological considerations relative to supporting structures.
10. Exceptional views; objectionable views (use on-site photographs).
11. Adjacent existing and proposed land uses with notations on compatibility and incompatibility.
12. Potential noise sources, particularly noise generated from traffic that can be mitigated by the use of plants, berming, walls, and by extending the distance between the source and the receiver.

## URBAN SITE ANALYSIS

Although much of the information presented for suburban sites may apply equally to urban sites, additional site design criteria may be necessary. The urban environment has numerous design determinants in the form of existing structures, city patterns, and microclimatic conditions.

Gary Greenan, AICP; Miami, Florida
Rafael Diaz, Graphics Coordinator; Miami, Florida

## INTENSITY STANDARDS FOR RESIDENTIAL DEVELOPMENT

| DWELLING UNIT TYPE | DWELLING UNITS PER ACRE | COMMON OPEN SPACE AS PERCENTAGE OF TOTAL SITE | PARKING PER UNIT (1) | TREES PER ACRE OF TOTAL SITE AREA (2) | PRIVATE OPEN SPACE (3) |
|---|---|---|---|---|---|
| Single family | 3 to 5 depending on lot size | Usually not provided | 2.5 +/− | 15+ | Depends on lot size |
| Duplex | 5 to 10 depending on lot size | Usually not provided | 2+(4+ for each structure) | 15+ | Depends on lot size (at least 50% of lot) |
| Zero-lot-line (9) | 4 to 8 units per acre | Usually not provided | 2.25+ | 15+ | At least 40% of lot |
| Single family cluster (4) | 4 to 7 | 25% to 50% | 2.25+ | 15 to 20 +/− for first 3 acres, 10+ for remaining acreage | Depends on lot size (at least 40% of lot) |
| Atrium (5) | 4 to 9 units per acre | Usually not provided | 2.25+ | 15+ | 25% of unit square footage |
| Suburban townhouse (6) | 6 to 9 | 25% to 40% | 2.25+ | 15 to 20 +/− for first 3 acres, 10 for remaining acreage | 500 to 700 square feet per unit |
| Urban townhouse (7) | 8 to 16 | 15% to 25% if provided | 2.0 +/− (Some parking may be on street) | 15 to 20 +/− for first 3 acres, 10 +/− for remaining acreage | 400 to 600 square feet per unit |
| Walk-up apartment | 10 to 25 (may be regulated by F.A.R.) | 25% to 50% | 2.0 +/− depending on number of bedrooms | 15 to 20 +/− for first 3 acres, 10 +/− for remaining acreage | Usually not provided except on ground floor units |
| Midrise apartment up to 6 stories | 15 to 35 (may be regulated by F.A.R.) | 25% to 50% | 2.0 +/− depending on number of bedrooms | 15 to 20 +/− for first 3 acres, 10 +/− for remaining acreage | Usually not provided except on ground floor units |
| Highrise apartments | 30 to 75 (may be 100+ in dense urban areas) | 20% to 60% (may include roof terraces) | 2.0 +/− depending on number of bedrooms | 15 to 20 +/− for first 3 acres, 10 +/− for remaining acreage | Usually not provided |
| Planned unit development (8) | 10 to 25 depending on type of PUD | 25% to 60% | 2.0 +/− depending on unit type(s) | 15 to 20 +/− for first 3 acres, 10 +/− for remaining acreage | Depends on individual unit type(s) |

## INTRODUCTION

The standards above should be used only as a basic reference to determine spatial site functions. The final determination of intensity and dwelling type of a particular site should evolve as the end of a thorough planning process. The designer also must refer to local zoning codes and ordinances for specific criteria.

## NOTES

1. PARKING PER UNIT: In determining parking requirements per unit, the site planner should consider available public transportation and the relationship of the development's location to employment centers and supporting facilities. Overestimating parking spaces to accommodate infrequent special activities can result in excess pavement. Depending on prevailing conditions, sometimes it is better to accommodate infrequent overflow parking on grassed areas, on commercial parking areas, or at community center parking lots.

2. TREES: A major unifying design element, trees also can act as climate modifiers. Extensive tree planting should be part of most site planning programs in appropriate climate areas unless the site already bears a substantial number of trees. The number of trees per acre is based more on the particular locale than on a uniform standard. Trees planted along streets at 30 ft. to 50 ft. on center provide roadway shading as well as visual unity for the development.

3. PRIVATE OPEN SPACE: Both visual and aural privacy is important in development design. Private open space for each unit may be provided by courtyards, entrance courts, porches, and rear, side, and front yards.

4. SINGLE FAMILY CLUSTER: Clusters of single-family units provide maximum open space. Units may or may not be attached.

5. ATRIUM: A single-family unit similar to early Greek and Roman structures that incorporated interior living spaces fronting on an internal court.

6. SUBURBAN TOWNHOUSE: A single-family unit attached to other single family units with a party wall. Open space usually is a major element in suburban townhouse development.

7. URBAN TOWNHOUSE: Early prototypes appear in many older cities. They are similar to suburban townhouses, although densities usually are higher and common open space usually is provided in public open space.

8. PLANNED UNIT DEVELOPMENT (PUD): All housing types included in the chart, plus associated retail support facilities and community amenities, may be found in a PUD. Emphasis is on total community design.

9. ZERO-LOT-LINE: Provides increased density over typical single-family developments by reducing individual lot sizes, and thereby reducing single-family housing costs. Zero-lot-line developments provide in-fill solutions in lower density urban areas where higher density is justified because of available urban services and higher land cost. Sketches indicate basic design considerations for zero-lot-line development.

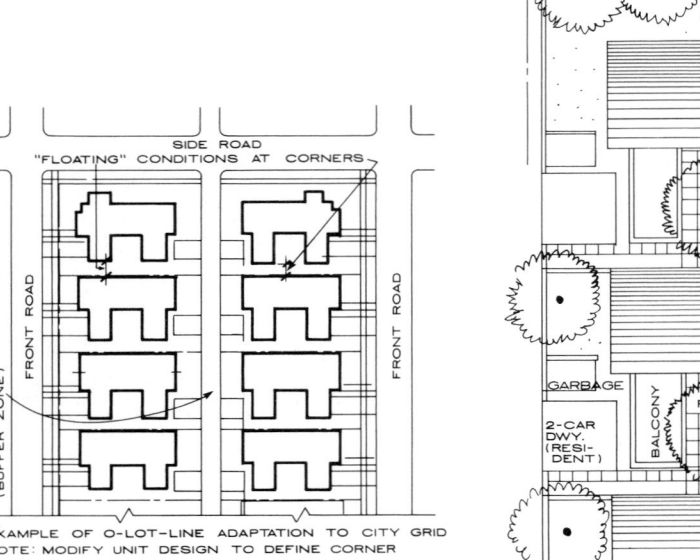

EXAMPLE OF O-LOT-LINE ADAPTATION TO CITY GRID
NOTE: MODIFY UNIT DESIGN TO DEFINE CORNER

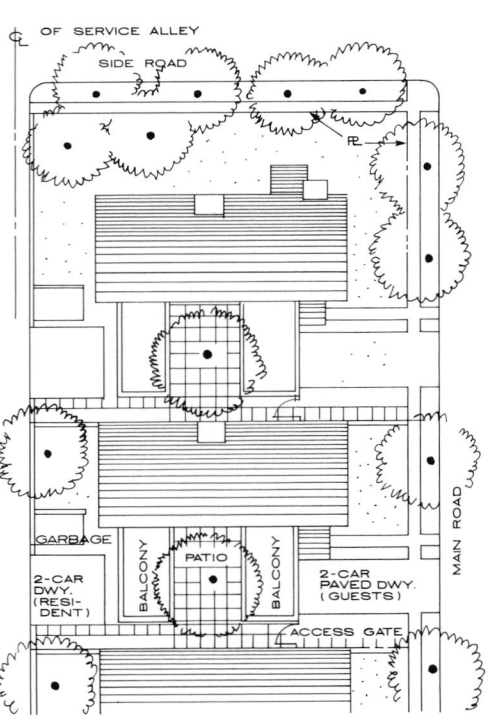

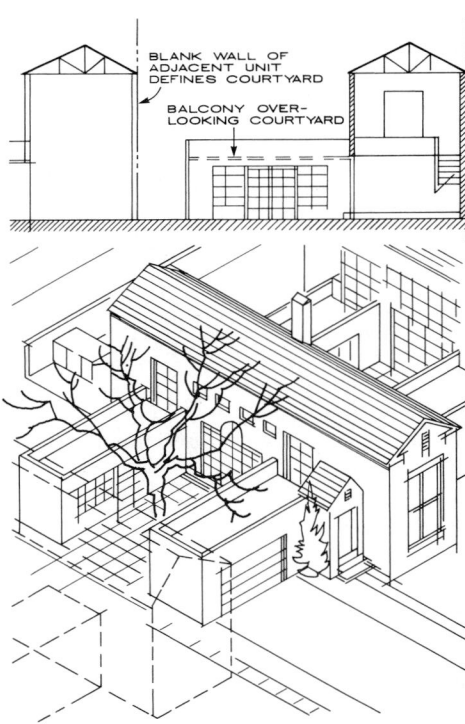

Gary Greenan, AICP; Miami, Florida
Rafael Diaz, Graphics Coordinator; Miami, Florida

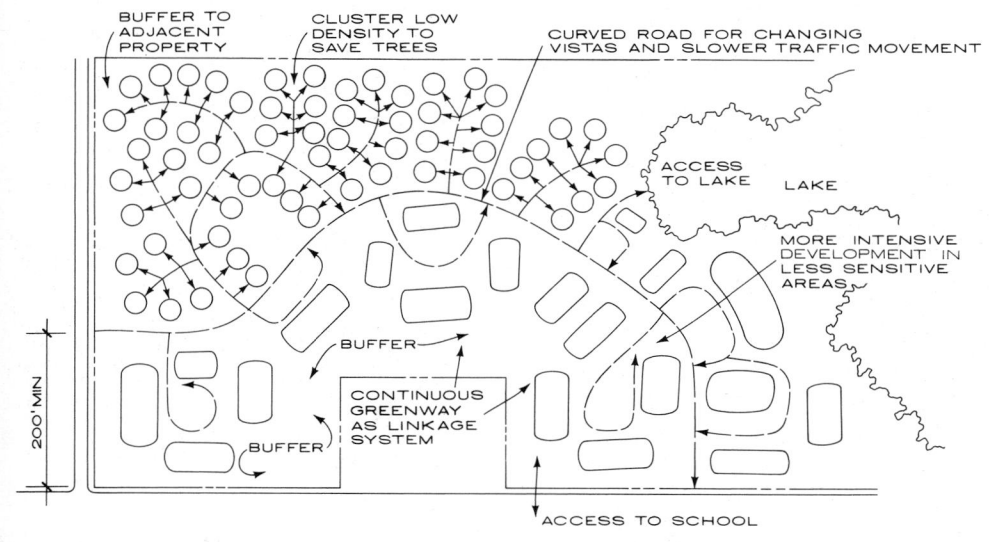

**SITE ANALYSIS**

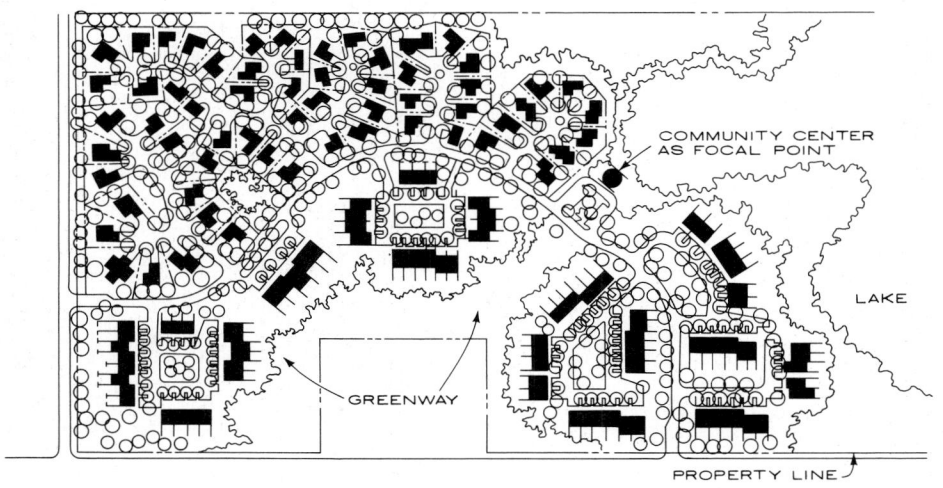

**CONCEPT PLANNING**

## INTRODUCTION

The following steps illustrate a design process:

1. SITE ANALYSIS: A synthesis of the physical environmental design determinants and offsite influences.
2. CONCEPT PLAN: A synthesis of the site analysis, research, citizen input, and client input into design concepts. Several concept plans may be prepared.
3. PRELIMINARY PLAN: A further sophistication and detailing of the concept plan.

## DESIGN SCALE

The site planner should be aware of four interdependent levels of design:

### COMMUNITY

At the community, or neighborhood, scale, the site planner should be aware of elements that create design unity and give identity to the development as a whole. Major natural features, circulation systems, greenway systems, and public use spaces such as schools, shopping, and parks act as focal points or linkages in the total design of the project.

### SUBCOMMUNITY

The first level down from the community scale is the subcommunity space. These spaces are created by the grouping or clustering of housing units and associated parking, paths, and landscape into a form that responds to the environmental characteristics of the site and gives identity to individual clusters.

### TRANSITION

Transition spaces in the form of porches, entrance courts, patios, and yards provide a transition from the private interior spaces of a housing unit to public spaces. Consideration should be given to privacy for the individual unit and to environmental site characteristics such as breezes, sun angles, and landscape.

### INTERIOR

This is the smallest scale with which the site planner is involved. Emphasis should be placed on the unit's interior design for its relationship to the exterior environment and for privacy. A close working relationship between architect and landscape architect is essential.

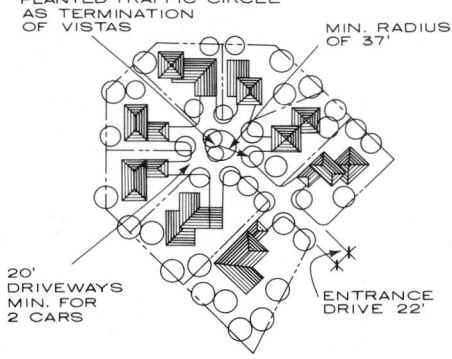

**SINGLE FAMILY CLUSTER**

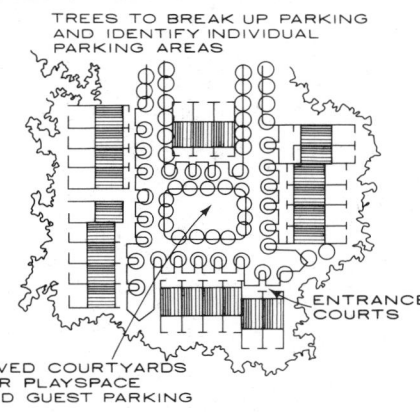

**TOWN HOUSE LAYOUT**

**PRELIMINARY PLAN**

Gary Greenan, AICP; Miami, Florida
Rafael Diaz, Graphics Coordinator; Miami, Florida

**LAND PLANNING AND SITE DEVELOPMENT**   2

# SUBDIVISION LAYOUT PROCEDURES

Residential subdivision of a tract of land requires considerable attention to design options and principles. Some of these are illustrated and described below.

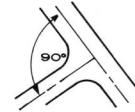

REDUCE TRAFFIC HAZARD POTENTIAL BY USE OF RIGHT ANGLE INTERSECTIONS

**ANGLE OF INTERSECTION**

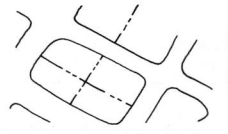

AVOID SMALL IRREGULAR BLOCKS THAT MAY BE DIFFICULT TO SERVICE AND NOT COST EFFECTIVE

**BLOCK SHAPE AND SIZE**

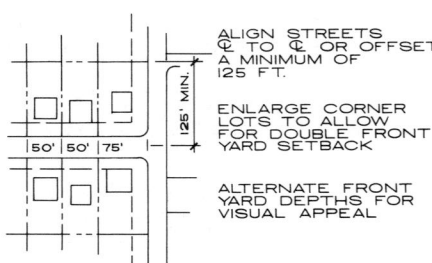

ALIGN STREETS ℄ TO ℄ OR OFFSET A MINIMUM OF 125 FT.

ENLARGE CORNER LOTS TO ALLOW FOR DOUBLE FRONT YARD SETBACK

ALTERNATE FRONT YARD DEPTHS FOR VISUAL APPEAL

**INTERSECTION OFFSET, FRONT YARD SETBACK, AND CORNER LOTS**

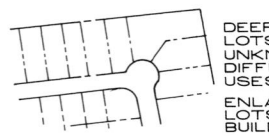

DEEPEN PERIMETER LOTS THAT ABUT UNKNOWN OR DIFFERENT LAND USES

ENLARGE CUL-DE-SAC LOTS FOR BUILDABLE AREA

**ADJACENT LAND USE CONDITION/ CUL-DE-SACS**

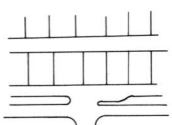

AVOID DOUBLE FRONTAGE OF RESIDENTIAL LOTS

**DOUBLE FRONTED LOTS**

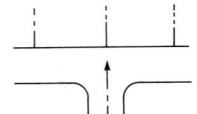

ALIGN LOT LINE WITH CENTERLINE OF STREET TO MINIMIZE NIGHTTIME GLARE OF AUTO LAMPS INTO HOUSE

**LOT LINE STREET OFFSET**

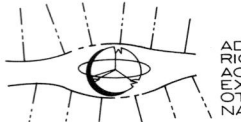

ADJUST STREET RIGHT OF WAY TO ACCOMMODATE EXISTING TREES OR OTHER SIGNIFICANT NATURAL FEATURES

**AMENITY CONSIDERATIONS**

## GENERAL INFORMATION

Much of the same equipment and procedures used in building layouts are used in subdivision layouts and staking. For further information, see building layout procedures page.

Usually a transit is used as the primary tool for locating and placing subdivision components. These components include, but are not limited to, streets, lots and respective lot lines, and utility systems. Horizontal and vertical control (distances and elevations) for the layout of these components usually is related to a bench mark or other monument, the location and elevation of which is more or less permanent and is recorded.

## STREETS

Streets are laid out in either an open or closed traverse by a series of station points and lines established along the street's centerline. These station points typically are staked at points of grade change, intersection, horizontal and vertical curvature, and at selected intervals of 25 ft., 50 ft., or 100 ft. A point of beginning (POB) typically is established where the proposed street's centerline intersects the existing road to which it is linked. The POB is "Station 0," and it is expressed numerically as 0 + 00. Station 1 is 100 ft. along the centerline from Station 0 and is expressed numerically as 1 + 00.

Intermediate stations are expressed in the same manner. For example, Station 5.20 is 520 ft. along the centerline from Station 0 and is read on engineering plans as 5 + 20 (see diagram.) Proposed elevations along the street's centerline are established by setting a marked stake into the ground with its top set at the desired elevation. A road-grading machine then cuts or fills soil to the stake's marked elevation.

## LOTS

Residential lots are laid out as closed traverses that have a POB, usually established at one of the lot's front corners on the street right-of-way. From the POB, lot lines are established with a series of horizontal angles (bearing/azimuths) and distance. Curved lot lines, if applicable, are laid out as circular curves with a known interior angle, tangent length, and length of curvature. They are most typically the front lot line on a curved street.

## UTILITIES

Sanitary sewers also are laid out by stationing along the centerline where pipes will be installed. Manholes and sewer intersections are plotted with station points and elevations much the same as a street. Utility easements typically are recorded with horizontal bearings and distances.

## CONVENTIONAL SUBDIVISION DEVELOPMENT

ELEMENTS—Lots, blocks, streets.

OBJECTIVES—Private lot ownership with public street frontage.

BENEFITS—Public street and utilities ownership or private fee, single-ownership of lots.

DENSITY—30 acres, 54 lots: density = 1.8 lots per acre (example shown).

## CLUSTER DEVELOPMENT

ELEMENTS—Lots, streets, common open space, usually requires zoning or special zoning such as PUD.

OBJECTIVES—Private lot ownership combined with community ownership of common open space (requires homeowners' association to maintain open space).

BENEFITS—Opportunity to separate vehicular and pedestrian traffic. Efficient road and utility system, reduced construction and maintenance costs to community, developer, and consumer. Opportunity for controlled entry with private roads. Environmentally sensitive areas may be held for open space.

DENSITY—30 acres, 54 lots: density = 1.8 lots per acre (example shown).

## ATTACHED SINGLE-FAMILY

ELEMENTS—Lots or units, private or public streets or easements, common open space (recreation facilities shown), usually requires zoning or special zoning such as PUD.

OBJECTIVES—Private ownership of lots or units, combined with community ownership of common open space (homeowners' association to maintain open space).

BENEFITS—Allows for larger, more continuous open spaces. Appeals to families or individuals who want home ownership without yard maintenance responsibilities. Cost savings mentioned in cluster development. Security, controlled access opportunities.

DENSITY—30 acres, 112 townhouses: density = 3.7 units per acre (example shown).

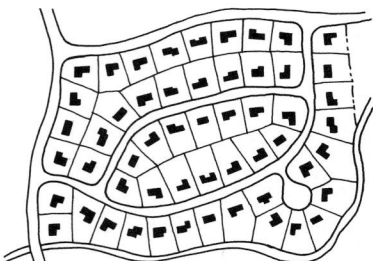

**CONVENTIONAL SUBDIVISION**

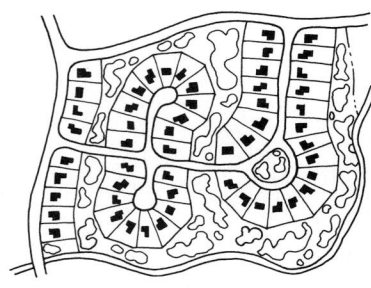

**CLUSTER DEVELOPMENT**

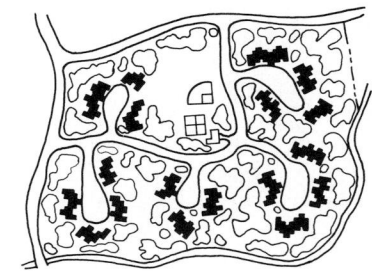

**CLUSTER DEVELOPMENT - TOWNHOMES**

**ROAD PLAN AND PROFILE**

William H. Evans, AIA; San Antonio, Texas
Connecticut Coastal Management Program, see data sources
Munson, see data sources

# 2    LAND PLANNING AND SITE DEVELOPMENT

## INTRODUCTION

A site designer needs a basic understanding of roadway layout to design circulation systems that function on the site and are compatible with systems off the site. Specific minimum standards that must be met are in effect for most municipalities.

## HIERARCHY OF ROAD SYSTEMS

A site designer needs to know the hierarchy of road systems and the purposes of each system. At the upper end is the limited access freeway, which carries up to 1,000 or 1,300 vehicles per lane per hour at 60 mph and up to 2,000 per hour at slower speeds. Site selection is affected by accessibility to freeway systems.

Major or principal arterials and minor arterials are intercommunity connectors that can carry, respectively, 600 to 800 cars per lane per hour and 400 to 500 cars per lane per hour, depending on traffic signals, on-street parking, intersections, and other physical impediments restricting traffic flow. Site selection is affected by these streets because they usually provide the direct access to a proposed development.

Collector streets are laid out by the site planner in the development to collect traffic from neighborhoods and local streets and direct it onto the arterials. They can carry efficiently 100 to 250 vehicles per lane per hour.

## TRAFFIC GENERATION

In projects where traffic generation is a major factor in the road system design, it may be advisable to retain the services of a transportation engineer. Technical information on traffic generation can be found in publications produced by the Institute of Transportation Engineers. This Institute projects the following trip generation factors for residential development:

## SUMMARY RATE TABLES OF DIFFERENT DWELLING UNITS

| TYPE OF DWELLING UNIT | AVERAGE WEEKDAY VEHICLE TRIP ENDS PER UNIT | | |
|---|---|---|---|
| | AVG. | MAX. | MIN. |
| Single-Family Detached Unit | 10.0 | 21.9 | 4.3 |
| Apartment, General | 6.1 | 12.3 | 0.5 |
| Low-Rise Apartment | 6.6 | 9.2 | 5.1 |
| High-Rise Apartment | 4.0 | 6.4 | 1.2 |
| Condominium | 5.2 | 11.8 | 0.6 |
| Mobile Home Park | 4.8 | 7.6 | 2.3 |
| Retirement Community | 3.3 | 4.9 | 2.8 |
| Planned Unit Develop. | 7.8 | 14.4 | 5.8 |

## ENVIRONMENTAL CONSIDERATIONS

A site's environmental characteristics affect the location and development of a road system. It is the responsibility of the site designer to develop systems that recognize the ecological constraints of a particular site. Following is a checklist of environmental considerations for road alignment:

1. Cause minimal disruption of existing topography by reducing cut and fill requirements, thus reducing erosion and sedimentation problems.
2. Cause minimal disruption of natural overland and subsurface water flows.
3. Cause minimal disruption to existing vegetation and animal life.
4. Avoid positive drainage along roadways into storm sewer systems where such systems directly outfall into water bodies and cause pollution. Systems of swales along the roadway help to filter nutrients from the roadway surface before entering natural water bodies, thus reducing water pollution.

## NOTES

1. Bike path grades should not exceed 5 to 6 percent for short distances (200 ft. to 400 ft.) or 2 percent for long distances. Separate bike path from roadway with swales and plantings. Where possible, bike paths can be integrated into greenway systems rather than along roadway.
2. Tree species that tolerate smog and dust and with root systems that do not damage underground utilities or pavements should be selected. Where snow removal

or icy conditions occur, trees should be placed far enough from the roadway edge to prevent damage from automobiles or chemicals applied to the roadway. Tree spacing should take into consideration species and design effect; as a general rule shade trees should be 35 ft. to 50 ft. apart.

3. Street lighting. Design considerations for spacing between lights should relate to amount of illumination needed based on street type, pedestrian use, crime prevention, and similar criteria. Approximate spacing for vehicular street use is 100 ft. to 150 ft. between standards.

Gary Greenan, AICP; Miami, Florida
Rafael Diaz, Graphics Coordinator; Miami, Florida
Institute of Transportation Engineers, see data sources

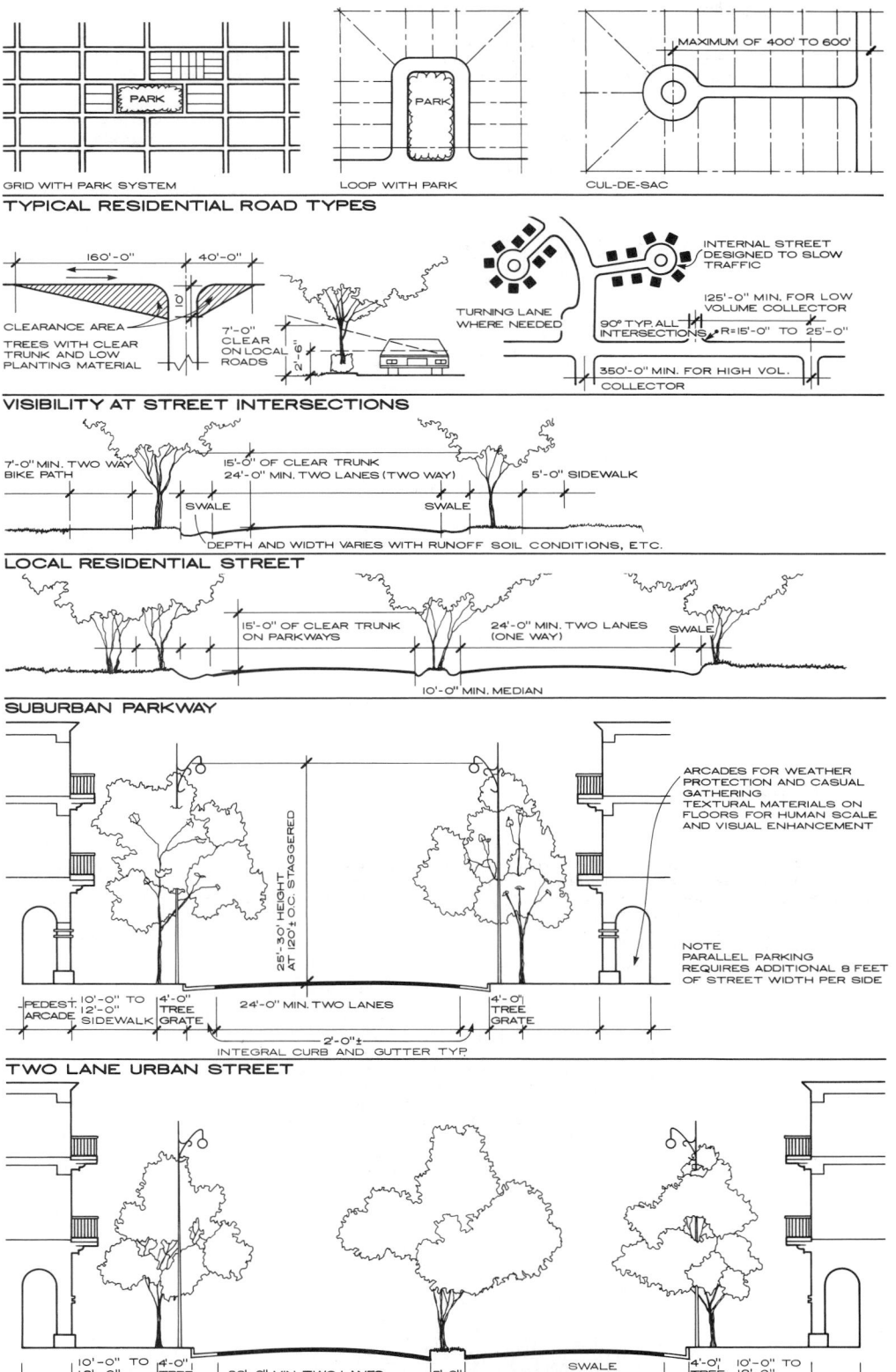

TYPICAL RESIDENTIAL ROAD TYPES

VISIBILITY AT STREET INTERSECTIONS

LOCAL RESIDENTIAL STREET

SUBURBAN PARKWAY

TWO LANE URBAN STREET

FOUR LANE URBAN STREET WITH LANDSCAPED MEDIAN

## FINAL DEVELOPMENT PLANS

After all necessary approvals under the zoning process have been granted, final site development plans are initiated. The final presentation drawing, as indicated below, is prepared by the site planner as part of the presentation for the zoning and public review process or as part of the final site development plans. The technical site development plans, as listed below, usually are prepared by a registered surveyor and/or engineer. The professional preparing these plans should obtain a copy of the local subdivision code and, if available, a copy of the public works manual for specific local requirements. All drawings should show the name and location of the development, the date of preparation and any revisions, the scale, north point, datum, and approvals of local authorities. The following list of exhibits are typical requirements for most communities.

## TENTATIVE OR PRELIMINARY PLAT

Platting is the process in which a piece of land, referred to as the parent tract, is subdivided into two or more parcels. A plat specifically and legally describes the layout of the development. A tentative plat is the first step in the preparation of the final drawings. It indicates the layout of the development in terms of lot layout and sizes of lots, lot frontages, road rights-of-way, setbacks, sidewalks, street offsets, and other graphic information relative to the project design. After approval of the tentative plat, the engineer can begin the utility, street paving, and drainage plans. Even if the local regulations do not require a tentative plat, it is advised that the designer prepare a sketch of the plat and meet with local authorities to avoid problems later in the final site development plan process.

## STREET PAVING AND DRAINAGE PLANS

Street paving and drainage plans are final construction drawings prepared by an engineer indicating:

1. Streets and parking area plans with starting points and radii.
2. Typical cross section (some communities also may require road profiles).
3. Details and specifications of pavement base, surfacing, and curbs.
4. Indication of methods to confine storm water runoff within the right-of-way (soil tests for percolation may be required). Also, details and specifications for inlets, manholes, catch basins, and surface drainage channels.
5. Indication that roads will meet local, state, and federal flood criteria.

## UTILITY PLANS

Utility plans are final drawings prepared by an engineer that indicate the location of water supply lines, sewage disposal lines, fire hydrants, and other utility functions usually located in the road right-of-way. In addition to approval by local public works departments, some communities require review of utility plans by the public health board, fire department, and departments involved in pollution control.

## FINAL PLAT

The final plat is usually the last stage of the final site development process prior to the issuance of building permits. A subdivision plat, when accepted and recorded in the public land records, establishes a legal description of the streets, residential lots, and other sites in the development. If roads and other improvements are not constructed at the time of final platting, a bond, usually in excess of the estimated cost of the improvements, will be required. Following is a typical list of information that should be shown on the final plat.

1. Right-of-way lines of streets, easements, and other sites with accurate dimensions, bearings, and curve data.
2. Name and right-of-way width of each street or other right-of-way.
3. Location, dimensions, and purpose of any easements.
4. Identifying number for each lot or site.
5. Purpose for which sites, other than residential lots, are dedicated or reserved.
6. Minimum building setback line on all lots and other sites.
7. Location and description of monuments.
8. Reference to recorded subdivision plats of adjoining platted land by record, name, date, and number.
9. Certification by surveyor or engineer.
10. Statement by owner(s) dedicating streets, rights-of-way, and any sites for public use.
11. Approval by local authorities.
12. Title, scale, north arrow, and date.

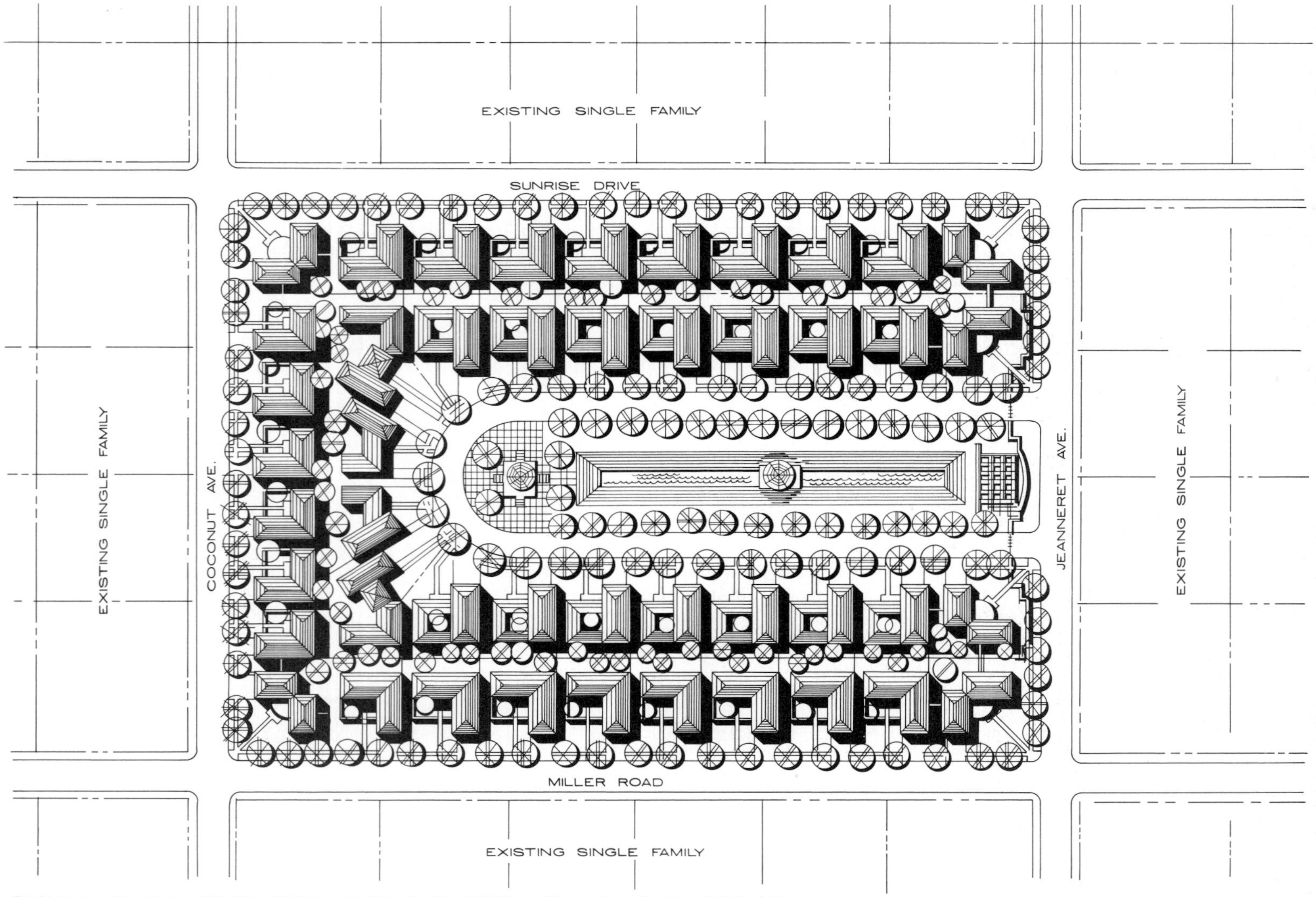

EXISTING SINGLE FAMILY

SUNRISE DRIVE

EXISTING SINGLE FAMILY

EXISTING SINGLE FAMILY

COCONUT AVE.

JEANNERET AVE.

MILLER ROAD

EXISTING SINGLE FAMILY

EXAMPLE OF FINAL PRESENTATION DRAWING OF ZERO-LOT-LINE AS AN URBAN INFILL
NOTE: MODIFY UNIT DESIGN TO DEFINE CORNER

Gary Greenan, AICP; Miami, Florida
Rafael Diaz, Graphics Coordinator; Miami, Florida

LAND PLANNING AND SITE DEVELOPMENT

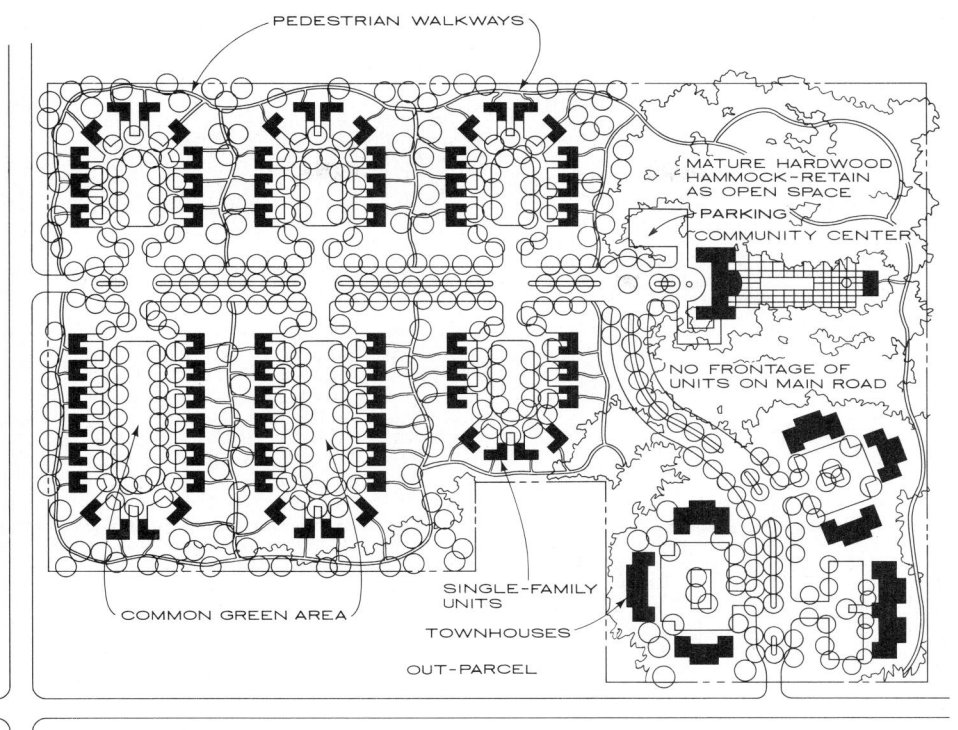

PEDESTRIAN WALKWAYS

MATURE HARDWOOD HAMMOCK—RETAIN AS OPEN SPACE

PARKING

COMMUNITY CENTER

NO FRONTAGE OF UNITS ON MAIN ROAD

COMMON GREEN AREA

SINGLE-FAMILY UNITS

TOWNHOUSES

OUT-PARCEL

**PLANNED UNIT DEVELOPMENT (TWO-STORY UNITS)**

The planned unit development ordinance usually incorporates standards for dwelling unit density, open space, and other spatial requirements. PUD ordinances usually place emphasis on total community design, with review of plans by local agencies and public hearing bodies as a primary requirement.

## ADVANTAGES OF PLANNED UNIT DEVELOPMENT AND CLUSTER ZONING CONCEPTS

Although the lot-by-lot type of subdivision is still the prevalent development type in many suburban areas, the amenities that can be realized by the planned unit development and cluster zoning concepts are such that these approaches should be seriously considered.

In some communities the terms planned unit development (PUD) and cluster may be synonymous. Usually, however, the PUD is a more comprehensive approach than the cluster, with provisions for both single family and multifamily development and, in some instances, commercial and industrial activities. The combination of commercial and recreational development in the town or community center can be found in some PUDs. Fee simple ownership and condominium ownership usually are permitted. Often PUDs are divided into tracts and developed over a long-term period such as 10 to 20 years. The term cluster refers to the grouping of single family residences in clusters on lots smaller than permitted by the single family zoning district and compensating for the smaller lots with common open space areas of substantial and usable configurations.

Both methods offer the designer not only the flexibility of locating structures in a manner that responds to site features, but also the opportunity for developing imaginative architectural forms. A key element of these approaches is the common green space that gives design cohesiveness to the total project.

The responsibility for the maintenance of common space and associated common facilities is a major concern that must be resolved in PUD and cluster developments. The homeowners' association is the most commonly accepted approach. The association should be established by recorded agreement before the sale of the first unit by the developer. Each homeowner is automatically a member and is assessed a proportionate share of the cost in maintaining the common facilities. The developer or his attorney should evaluate the best methods of developing a homeowners' association before the initiation of site development. Many jurisdictions require a legal instrument for the association prior to final approval of the project.

The use of common open space usually allows more flexibility in effectively fitting the development to the land than does the more typical lot-by-lot approach. Following are some of the obvious advantages gained by the proper use of the planned unit development concept:

1. With smaller individual lots, excess land can be massed together to provide larger and more useful community recreational space.
2. With the use of connecting community open spaces and fewer through traffic streets, children are better protected from vehicular traffic.
3. With larger amounts of open space, the natural character of the site can be preserved.
4. With the shorter networks of streets and utilities, construction costs can be reduced.

It should be emphasized that the standard subdivision approach still retains a major part of the housing market. Where the program suggests a more typical subdivision layout, the site planner has a responsibility to respond to the same environmental design determinants of the site as for a project being developed under more flexible zoning criteria. Creative planning can be accomplished using either approach.

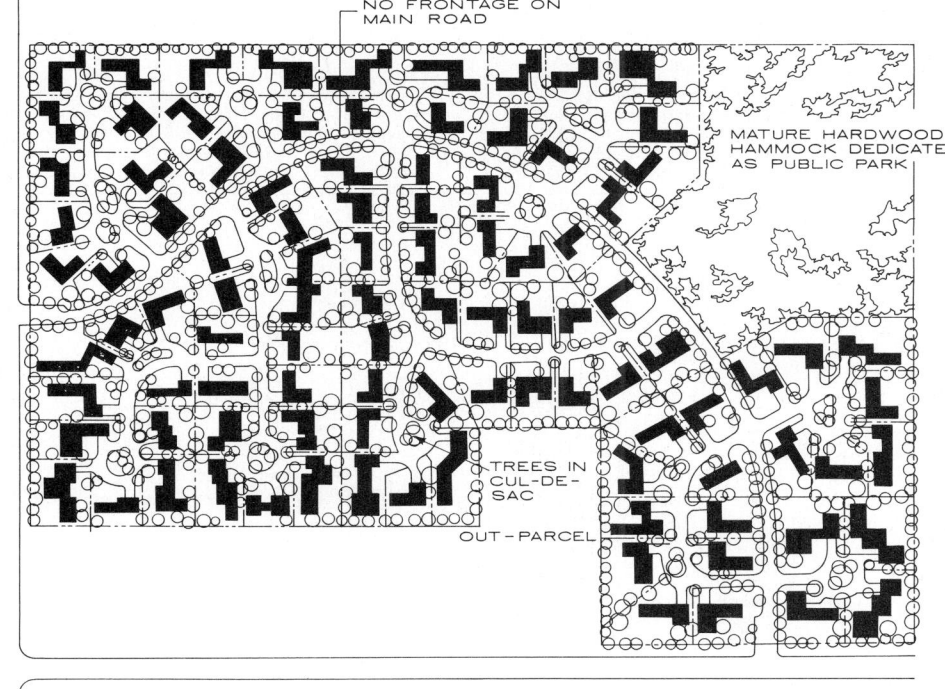

NO FRONTAGE ON MAIN ROAD

MATURE HARDWOOD HAMMOCK DEDICATE AS PUBLIC PARK

TREES IN CUL-DE-SAC

OUT-PARCEL

**CONVENTIONAL SINGLE FAMILY (ONE-STORY UNITS)**

Gary Greenan, AICP; Miami, Florida
Rafael Diaz, Graphics Coordinator; Miami, Florida

## CONVENTIONAL SINGLE FAMILY RESIDENTIAL ZONED DEVELOPMENT

The density determination for conventional single family residential zoning is based on minimum lot size requirements as provided by local ordinances. For planning purposes, the site planner can translate lot size to a net density figure which represents the total number of dwellings per acre within the site, after deducting for roads, parks, school sites, and other public facilities.

## GENERAL INFORMATION AND TERMINOLOGY

Building layout requires a site plan that has been accurately drawn to a specific scale (e.g., 1 in. = 20 ft), showing all relevant information regarding: building outline (footprint) dimensioned location from the property lines, existing and new streets and curbs, above and below ground utilities, easements, all site improvements (other than the building footprint) such as driveways, retaining walls, and patios, and other features unique to the site. Existing and new contour lines, spot grade elevations, and bench marks should be shown on a site plan if there is not a separate grading plan. All information, especially building location, should be verified to conform to local codes and zoning ordinance requirements prior to layout.

1. Angles: The difference in direction of two intersecting lines.
2. Azimuths: Angles measured clockwise from any meridian, usually north; however, the National Geodetic Survey uses south.
3. Bearings: The acute angle between the meridian and a line, measured from north or south, toward east or west to give a reading of less than 90° (e.g., S 31° 13′ E).
4. Transit: A precise general-purpose surveying instrument primarily used for measuring horizontal (azimuth and bearing) angles, vertical (altitude) angles, and to run level lines. It can also be used to measure distances directly by subtense and stadia measurement.
5. Taping: Tape lengths are not guaranteed accurate. Certified tapes are those having their lengths verified at the National Bureau of Standards, checked at a temperature of 68°F at both 10 lb pull (fully supported) and 12 lb pull (ends supported). To obtain accurate measurements, the measured distance must be corrected for temperature differences. The coefficient of thermal expansion for steel tapes is 0.0000065/unit of length/°F. Invar tapes, made of special nickel steel alloy, do not need temperature corrections. A spring balance is used to measure standard pull. The tape must be horizontal and in true alignment.
6. Stadia measurement: A rapid, efficient method of measuring distances accurately enough for locating topographic details. The transit has two horizontal cross hairs, spaced equidistant from the center cross hair. The interval between hairs gives a vertical intercept of 1 ft on the rod for every 100 ft of distance to the rod; thus the distance to a point can be read directly by counting the number of hundredths of a foot between stadia hairs.
7. Subtense bar: The angle between targets is determined by using a transit reading to an accuracy of 1 sec of an arc or less. The horizontal distance from the transit to the bar is computed mathematically or read from a table.
8. Bench mark (BM): An established elevation point, used as a reference for survey purposes. Mean sea level is the national reference elevation. Local datum may exist in many areas.
9. Leveling: The process of finding the difference in elevations between points. The transit is set up approximately one-half the distance between the BM and the point to be determined. A back sight (BS) is taken on the BM and the height of instrument (HI) determined by reading the rod at the center cross hair (rod reading + BM + HI). The rod is then placed on the new point. A foresight is taken and the rod reading subtracted from HI to determine the elevation of the point (HI − rod reading = elevation in ft).
10. Leveling rods: Tall rods, usually wood, graduated in feet, tenths, and hundredths of a foot; or in metric using meters, centimeters, and millimeters.
11. Cadastral surveys: Surveys that are made to establish property boundary lines. Deed descriptions are essential parts of any document denoting ownership or conveyance of land. The basic rule of property lines and corners is that they shall remain in their original positions as established on the ground. This basic rule is important because most land surveys are resurveys. The original description may be followed, but this description is merely an aid to the discovery of the originally established lines and corners. Substantial discrepancies are frequently found. In some states, surveys are conducted on the metes and bounds principle, and in others, the basic subdivisions are rectangular. If boundaries to be described border an irregular line (a winding stream), the line can be located by a series of closely spaced perpendicular offsets from an auxiliary straight line.

John J. Hare, AIA; Haddonfield, New Jersey
Walter H. Sobel, FAIA, and Associates; Chicago, Illinois

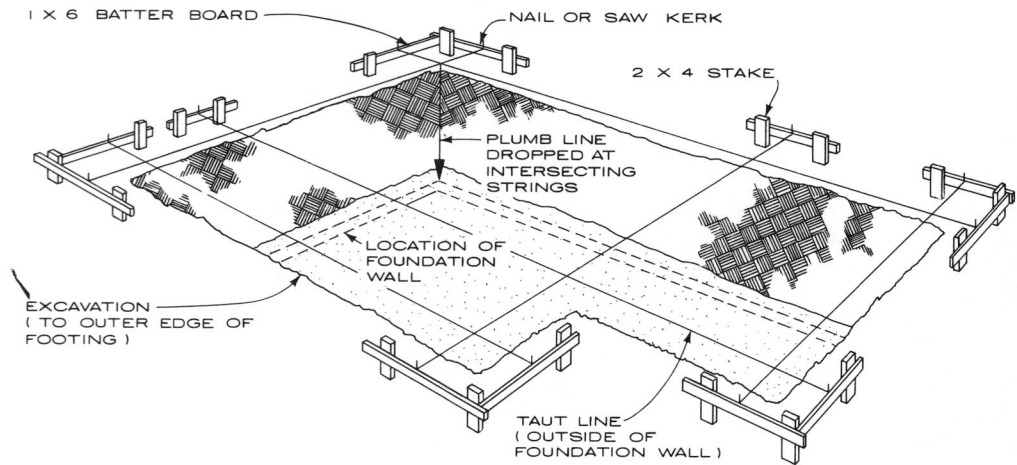

### NOTES

First locate the building in its correct relationship to the property lines. Set stakes at the building corners, using a transit to reestablish correct angles and steel tapes for distance measurements. Mark exact corner locations on the stake heads with finishing nails. Set offset stakes or batter boards 3 to 5 ft outside the corners to allow room for construction operations. Set batter boards at a predetermined elevation. Then project the location of the building corners to the tops of the batter boards and set nails. Stretch strings taut between nails to define the corners and outside wall lines. For small buildings, the elevation of the top of the footings can be located by measuring down from the strings. Strings sag over long distances and with changes in humidity, so for large buildings stakes indicating top of footings are set with the transit.

## BUILDING LAYOUT PROCEDURES

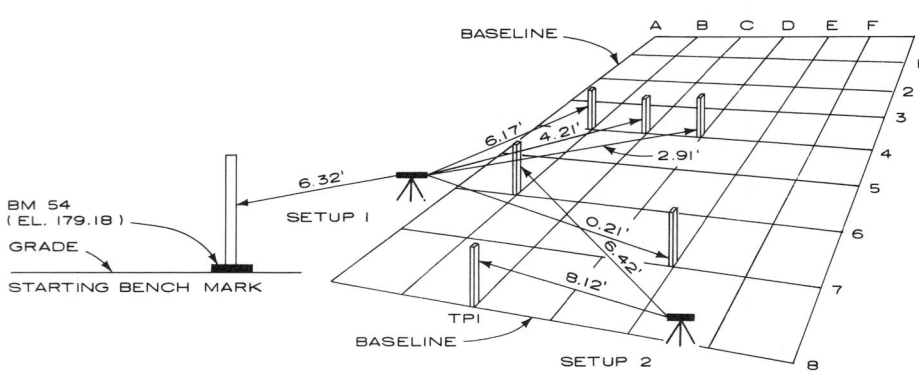

### NOTES

A grid system can be used for identifying those points whose elevation is required. The transit is set where both the BM and the points on the grid can be observed. Sighting on the BM determines HI. Elevations of grid points can then be found by sighting the rod held at each point. The rod reading is subtracted from the HI to obtain the elevation of the point sighted (HI − rod reading = elevation point). Resight the BM periodically to assure the instrument has not moved. Contour lines are then sketched between elevation points by interpolation.

## TOPOGRAPHIC SURVEY—GRID SYSTEM

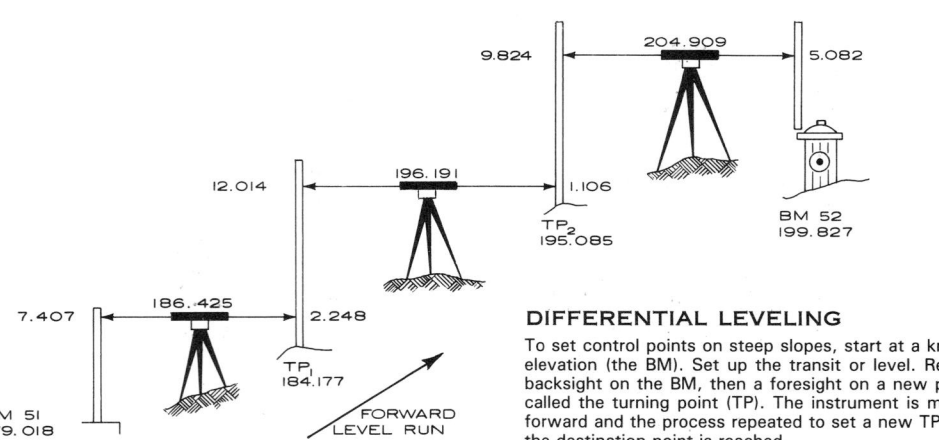

### DIFFERENTIAL LEVELING

To set control points on steep slopes, start at a known elevation (the BM). Set up the transit or level. Read a backsight on the BM, then a foresight on a new point, called the turning point (TP). The instrument is moved forward and the process repeated to set a new TP until the destination point is reached.

## DIFFERENTIAL LEVELING

# CHAPTER 3

# Concrete

# CAST-IN-PLACE CONCRETE CONSTRUCTION; PRELIMINARY DATA

## REINFORCED CONCRETE

Reinforced concrete consists of concrete and reinforcing steel; the concrete resists the compressive stresses and the reinforcing steel resists the tensile stresses.

Concrete is a mixture of hydraulic cement (usually portland cement), aggregate, admixtures, and water. The concrete strength develops by the hydration of the portland cement, which binds the aggregate together.

## TYPES OF CEMENT

Five types of portland cement are manufactured to meet ASTM standards.

Type I is a general purpose cement for all uses. It is the most commonly used type.

Type II cement provides moderate protection from sulfate attack for concrete in drainage structures and a lower heat of hydration for concrete use in heavy retaining walls, piers, and abutments where heat buildup in the concrete can cause problems.

Type III cement provides high strengths at an early age, a week or less. Type III is used when rapid removal of forms is desired and in cold weather to reduce time of controlled curing conditions.

Type IV cement has a low heat of hydration and is used for massive concrete structures such as gravity dams.

Type V cement is sulfate-resisting cement for use where the soil and groundwater have a high sulfate content.

Pozzolans such as fly ash can be used to reduce the amount of cement in a concrete mix. Fly ash is a powdery residue resulting from combustion in coal-fired electric generating plants. It reacts chemically with calcium hydroxide produced by hydration to form cementitious compounds.

## ADMIXTURES

Admixtures are various compounds, other than cement, water, and aggregates, added to a mixture to modify the fresh or hardened properties of concrete.

Air entraining admixtures disperse small air bubbles in the concrete, which improves the concrete's resistance to freezing and thawing and to scaling by deicing chemicals. Recommended total air contents are shown in Table 1 for different exposure conditions and for maximum size of aggregate.

Water reducing admixtures reduce the quantity of mixing water needed for a given consistency. Admixtures may delay the set time, and they also may entrain air.

Other mixtures are used to retard or to accelerate the set of concrete. Some accelerating admixtures contain chlorides that can cause corrosion of the reinforcing steel; therefore, they should be used with caution and only for very specific purposes. Some water reducing and accelerating admixtures may increase dry shrinkage.

Superplasticizers are high-range water reducers that can greatly affect the slump and strength of concrete. When used in concrete with normal water-cement ratios, they produce a high slump, flowable concrete that is easily placed. When used to reduce the water-cement ratio, the slump is not affected, but significantly higher than normal strengths are attained. When used to produce flowable concrete, the plasticizer's effect has a limited timespan.

## AGGREGATES

The aggregate portion of a concrete mix is divided into fine and coarse aggregates. The fine aggregate generally is sand of particles less than 3/8 in. large. The coarse aggregate is crushed rock or gravel. Concrete weighs 135 pcf to 165 pcf. Lightweight aggregate is manufactured from expanded shale, slate, clay, or slag, and the concrete weighs from 85 pcf to 115 pcf.

Normal weight aggregates must meet ASTM Specification C33. Lightweight aggregates must meet ASTM Specification C330.

The aggregate represents 60 percent to 80 percent of the concrete volume, and the gradation (range of particle sizes) affects the amount of cement and water required in the mix, the physical properties during placing and finishing, and the compressive strength. Aggregates should be clean, hard, strong, and free of surface materials.

## REINFORCING STEEL

Reinforcing steel, manufactured as round rods with raised deformations for adhesion and resistance to slip in the concrete, is available in several grades (yield strengths) and diameters manufactured to ASTM standards. Commonly used reinforcing rods have a yield strength of 60,000 psi available in sizes from #3 to #18, the size being the diameter in eighths of an inch. Reinforcing rods having a yield strength of 40,000 psi also are available in the smaller bar sizes. Welded wire mesh has yield strengths of 60,000 psi to 70,000 psi, and the wire is either plain or deformed.

Table 3 summarizes the various grades of reinforcing steel, and Figure 1 shows the system of reinforcing rod identification.

## SLUMP TEST

The ASTM standard slump cone test is to determine only the consistency among batches of concrete of the same mix design; it should not be used to compare mixes of greatly different mix proportions. A slump test mold is a funnel-shaped sheet metal form. The slump mold is filled from the top in three levels, each level being tamped 25 times with a 5/8 in. diameter rod. The mold is removed slowly, allowing the concrete to slump down from its original height. The difference from the top of the mold to the top of the slumped concrete is the slump. There is no "right" slump consistency for all concrete work. It can vary from 1 in. to 6 in., depending on the specific requirements of the job. Table 2 lists typical slumps for various types of construction.

Workability is the ease or difficulty of placing, consolidating, and finishing the concrete. Concrete should be workable, but it should not segregate or bleed excessively before finishing.

## CYLINDER TEST

A major problem with concrete tests is that the most important data, the compressive strength, cannot be determined until after curing has begun. This occasionally has caused the removal of deficient concrete several weeks after it was placed. A standard compression test is made in accordance with ASTM C39 by placing three layers of concrete in a cardboard cylinder 6 in. in diameter and 12 in. high. Each layer is rodded 25 times with a 5/8 in. diameter steel rod. The cylinder should be protected from damage but placed in the same temperature and humidity environment as the concrete from which the sample was obtained. At the end of the test curing time, usually 7 to 28 days, the concrete cylinder is removed from its form and tested in compression. The load at which the cylinder fails in compression is registered on a gauge in pounds, and the strength of the concrete is calculated in pounds per square inch.

## PLACING CONCRETE

Concrete should be placed as near its final position as possible, and it should not be moved horizontally in forms because segregation of the mortar from the coarser material may occur. Concrete should be placed in horizontal layers of uniform thickness, each layer being thoroughly consolidated before the next layer is positioned.

Consolidation of concrete can be achieved either by hand tamping and rodding or by mechanical internal or external vibration. The frequency and amplitude of an internal mechanical vibration should be appropriate for the plastic properties (stiffness or slump) and space in the forms to prevent segregation of the concrete during placing. External vibration can be accomplished by surface vibration for thin sections (slabs) that cannot be consolidated practically by internal vibration. Surface vibrators may be used directly on the surface of slab or with plates attached to the concrete form stiffeners. External vibration must be done for a longer time (1 to 2 min.) than for internal vibration (5 to 15 sec.) to achieve the same consolidation.

## TABLE 1. RECOMMENDED AIR CONTENT PERCENTAGE

| NOMINAL MAXIMUM SIZE OF COARSE AGGREGATE (IN.) | EXPOSURE | |
|---|---|---|
| | MILD | EXTREME |
| 3/8 (10 mm) | 4.5 | 7.5 |
| 1/2 (13 mm) | 4.0 | 6.0 |
| 3/4 (19 mm) | 3.5 | 6.0 |
| 1 (25 mm) | 3.0 | 6.0 |
| 1 1/2 (40 mm) | 2.5 | 5.5 |
| 2 (50 mm) | 2.0 | 5.0 |
| 3 (75 mm) | 1.5 | 4.5 |

## TABLE 2. RECOMMENDED SLUMPS FOR VARIOUS TYPES OF CONSTRUCTION

| CONCRETE CONSTRUCTION | SLUMP (IN.) | |
|---|---|---|
| | MAXIMUM* | MINIMUM |
| Reinforced foundation walls and footings | 3 | 1 |
| Plain footings, caissons, and substructure walls | 3 | 1 |
| Beams and reinforced walls | 4 | 1 |
| Building columns | 4 | 1 |
| Pavements and slabs | 3 | 1 |
| Mass concrete | 2 | 1 |

*May be increased 1 in. for consolidation by hand methods such as rodding and spading.

Quentin L. Reutershan, AIA, Architect; Potsdam, New York
Gordon B. Batson, P.E.; Potsdam, New York
Bob Cotton; W. E. Simpson Company Inc.; San Antonio, Texas

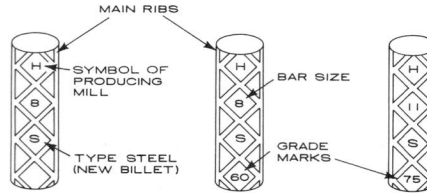

FIGURE 1. REINFORCING BAR IDENTIFICATION

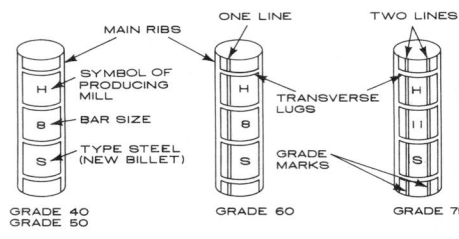

## TABLE 3. REINFORCING STEEL GRADES AND STRENGTHS

| ASTM SPEC | YIELD STRENGTH (PSI) | ULTIMATE STRENGTH (PSI) | STEEL TYPE |
|---|---|---|---|
| New billet ASTM A–615 | | | |
| Grade 40 | 40,000 | 70,000 | S |
| Grade 60 | 60,000 | 90,000 | |
| Rail steel ASTM A–616 | | | |
| Grade 50 | 50,000 | 80,000 | R |
| Grade 60 | 60,000 | 90,000 | |
| Axle steel ASTM A–617 | | | |
| Grade 40 | 40,000 | 70,000 | A |
| Grade 60 | 60,000 | 90,000 | |
| Deformed wire ASTM A–496 | | | |
| Welded fabric | 70,000 | 80,000 | — |
| Cold drawn wire ASTM A–82 | | | |
| Welded fabric | | | |
| W 1.2 | 56,000 | 70,000 | |
| Size | | | |
| W 1.2 | 65,000 | 75,000 | |

GENERAL INFORMATION

## PROPERTIES OF CONCRETE

Concrete design strength generally is stated as a minimum compressive strength at 28 days of age for concrete in various structural elements. The normal 28-day compressive strength for commercial-ready mix concrete is 3,000 psi to 4,000 psi; however, higher strengths of 5,000 psi to 7,000 psi generally are required for pre- or post-tensioned concrete. Higher strengths of 10,000 to 12,000 psi may be required for highrise concrete structures.

A typical design mix for 3,000 psi concrete would be 517 lb. of cement (5½ sacks), 1,300 lb. of sand, 1,800 lb. of gravel, and 34 gal. of water (6.2 gal. per sack), which would yield one cu. yd. of concrete, the standard unit of measure.

Compressive strength depends primarily on the type of cement, water-cement ratio, and aggregate quality; the most important is the water-cement ratio. The lower the water-cement ratio, the greater the compressive strength for workable mixes.

When cement, aggregate, and water are mixed, the water starts hydrating, a chemical reaction independent of drying. Concrete does not need air to cure. It can set under water. Concrete sets or becomes firm within hours after it has been mixed, but curing, the process of attaining strength, takes considerably longer. The majority of strength is achieved in the first days of curing. Approximately 50 percent of the total compressive strength is reached in 3 days; 70 percent is reached in 7 days. The remaining 30 percent occurs at a much slower rate in the last 21 days. The concrete's compressive strength may continue to increase beyond the designed strength, as shown in Figure 2.

### CURING AND PROTECTION

Two physical conditions profoundly affect concrete's final compressive strength and curing: temperature and the rate at which water used in mixing is allowed to leave the concrete. Optimum temperature for curing concrete is 73°F (22.8°C). Any great variance from this mark reduces its compressive strength. Freezing concrete during curing affects the compressive strength and reduces its weather resistance.

Proper curing is essential to obtain design strength. Moisture, at temperatures above 50°F, must be available for hydration, and the concrete must be protected against temperatures below 40°F during early curing. The longer the water is in the concrete, the longer the reaction takes place; hence, the stronger it becomes.

Moisture conditions can be maintained by spreading wet coverings of burlap or mats, waterproof paper, or plastic sheets over concrete; by placing plastic sheets on the ground before the slab is poured; by spraying liquid curing compound on the surface of fresh concrete; and by leaving the concrete in forms longer.

### HOT AND COLD WEATHER CONSTRUCTION

Additional precautions are needed in hot and cold weather to ensure proper curing of the concrete. High temperatures accelerate hardening. More water is needed to maintain the mix consistency; more cement is required to prevent reduced strength from the added water. Chilled water or ice reduces the temperature of the aggregates, and admixtures can retard the initial set. Temperatures ranging from 75°F to 90°F are hot weather construction conditions.

In cold weather the concrete must be heated to above 40°F during placing and early curing, the first 7 days. Protection against freezing may be necessary for up to 2 weeks. This is accomplished by covering the concrete with plastic sheets and heating the interior space with a portable heater. Concrete floors should be protected from carbon dioxide by using specially vented heaters that conduct the exhaust away from the concrete. The time the concrete must be protected can be reduced by using Type III and IIIA cement; a low water-cement ratio; accelerator admixtures; and steam curing. Concrete never should be placed directly on frozen ground. Fresh concrete that has frozen during curing should be removed and replaced because frozen concrete containing ice crystals has very little strength.

### PROPORTION OF STRUCTURAL ELEMENTS

Rules of thumb for approximating proportions of solid rectangular beams and slabs are one inch of depth for each foot of span, and the beam width is about two-thirds the depth. The area of steel varies from 1 percent to 2 percent of cross-sectional area of the beam or slab. Columns usually have higher steel percentages than beams. The maximum for columns is 8 percent of the cross-sectional area; however, common range is 3 percent to 6 percent.

### DEFLECTIONS

Deflection is affected by shrinkage, load duration, and creep. Creep is the tendency of concrete to continue to deform under sustained load. The more sustained load that a member supports, the more it creeps. The ACI-318 sets minimum length-to-depth ratios for concrete members as shown on Table 6. When members meet or exceed these minimums, deflections usually will not be a problem, and they do not need to be calculated.

### FORMWORK

Forming costs can account for 30 percent to 50 percent of a concrete structure. Economy can be gained through the repetitious use of forms. Usually it is cheaper to use one column size rather than to vary column sizes.

In sizing individual floor members, usually it is more economical to use wider girders that are the same depths as the joists or beams they support than to use narrow, deeper girders. Wall pilasters, lugs, and openings should be kept to a minimum since their use increases forming costs. All members should be sized so that readily available standard forms can be used instead of custom job-built forms.

### SHORING

Floor framing forms are supported by temporary columns and bracing called shoring. Concrete must be cured for a minimum time or reach a specified percentage of its design strength before shores and forms can be removed.

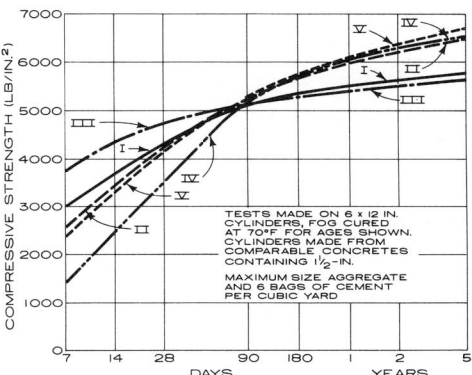

**FIGURE 2. RATES OF STRENGTH DEVELOPMENT FOR CONCRETE MADE WITH VARIOUS TYPES OF CEMENT**

## TABLE 4. MAXIMUM WATER-CEMENT RATIOS FOR VARIOUS EXPOSURE CONDITIONS

| EXPOSURE CONDITION | NORMAL WEIGHT CONCRETE, ABSOLUTE WATER-CEMENT RATIO BY WEIGHT |
|---|---|
| Concrete protected from exposure to freezing and thawing or application of deicer chemicals | Select water-cement ratio on basis of strength, workability, and finishing needs |
| Watertight concrete* In fresh water In seawater | 0.50 0.45 |
| Frost resistant concrete* Thin sections; any section with less than 2-in. cover over reinforcement and any concrete exposed to deicing salts All other structures | 0.45 0.50 |
| Exposure to sulfates* Moderate Severe | 0.50 0.45 |
| Placing concrete under water | Not less than 650 lb of cement per cubic yard (386 kg/m³) |
| Floors on grade | Select water-cement ratio for strength, plus minimum cement requirements |

*Contain entrained air within the limits of Table 1.

Bob Cotton; W. E. Simpson Company Inc.; San Antonio, Texas
Quentin L. Reutershan, AIA, Architect; Potsdam, New York
Gordon B. Batson, P.E.; Potsdam, New York

## TABLE 5. MAXIMUM PERMISSIBLE WATER-CEMENT RATIOS FOR CONCRETE WHEN STRENGTH DATA FROM TRIAL BATCHES OR FIELD EXPERIENCE ARE NOT AVAILABLE

| SPECIFIED COMPRESSIVE STRENGTH $F'_c$ (PSI*) | MAXIMUM ABSOLUTE PERMISSIBLE WATER-CEMENT RATIO, BY WEIGHT | |
|---|---|---|
| | NON-AIR ENTRAINED CONCRETE | AIR ENTRAINED CONCRETE |
| 2500 | 0.67 | 0.54 |
| 3000 | 0.58 | 0.46 |
| 3500 | 0.51 | 0.40 |
| 4000 | 0.44 | 0.35 |
| 4500 | 0.38 | † |
| 5000 | † | † |

NOTE: 1000 psi ≃ 7 MPa.
*28-day strength. With most materials, the water-cement ratios shown will provide average strengths greater than required.
†For strengths above 4500 psi (non-air entrained concrete) and 4000 psi (air entrained concrete), proportions should be established by the trial batch method.

ASTM, see data sources

## TABLE 6. MINIMUM THICKNESS OF NON-PRESTRESSED BEAMS OR ONE WAY SLABS

| | SIMPLY SUPPORTED | ONE END CONT. | BOTH ENDS CONT. | CANTILEVER |
|---|---|---|---|---|
| Solid One-Way Slabs | ℓ/20 | ℓ/24 | ℓ/28 | ℓ/10 |
| Beams or Ribbed One-Way Slabs | ℓ/16 | ℓ/18.5 | ℓ/21 | ℓ/8 |

### NOTE

Span length, l, is in inches. Values given are for members with normal weight concrete and Grade 60 reinforcement in construction not supporting or attached to partitions or other construction likely to be damaged by large deflection. For additional information, reference should be made to the American Concrete Institute Building Requirements for Reinforced Concrete (ACI 318).

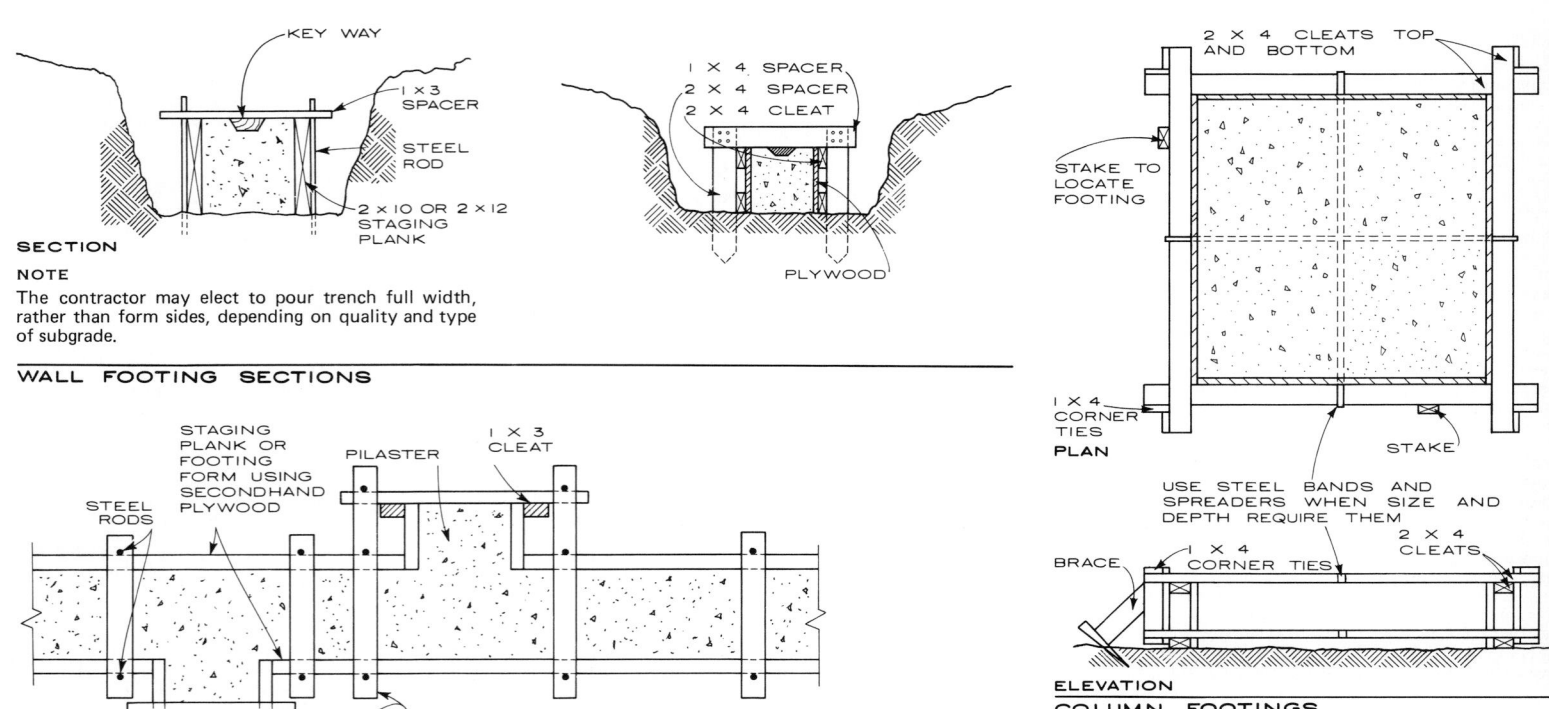

KEY WAY

1 X 3 SPACER

STEEL ROD

2 X 10 OR 2 X 12 STAGING PLANK

**SECTION**

**NOTE**

The contractor may elect to pour trench full width, rather than form sides, depending on quality and type of subgrade.

**WALL FOOTING SECTIONS**

1 X 4 SPACER
2 X 4 SPACER
2 X 4 CLEAT

PLYWOOD

2 X 4 CLEATS TOP AND BOTTOM

STAKE TO LOCATE FOOTING

1 X 4 CORNER TIES

STAKE

**PLAN**

USE STEEL BANDS AND SPREADERS WHEN SIZE AND DEPTH REQUIRE THEM

BRACE

1 X 4 CORNER TIES

2 X 4 CLEATS

**ELEVATION**
**COLUMN FOOTINGS**

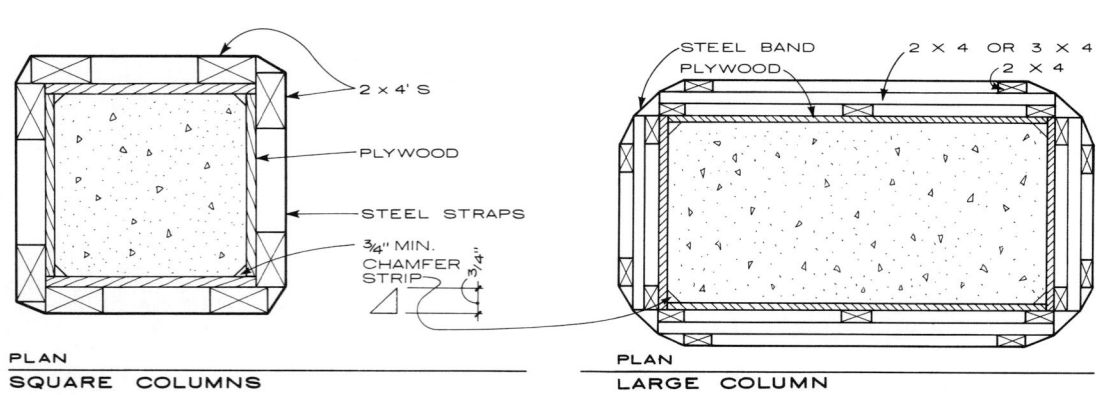

STAGING PLANK OR FOOTING FORM USING SECONDHAND PLYWOOD

PILASTER

1 X 3 CLEAT

STEEL RODS

SPACERS

**PLAN OF WALL FOOTINGS**

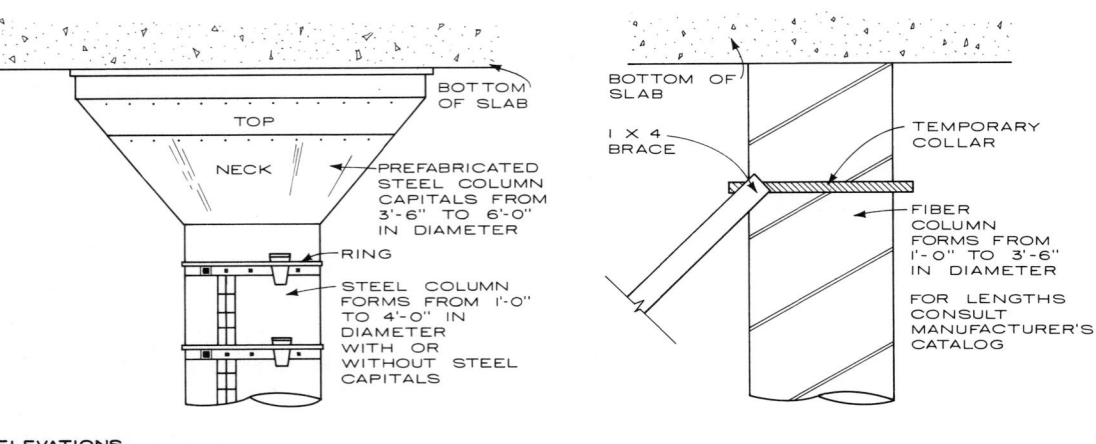

2 X 4'S

PLYWOOD

STEEL STRAPS

3/4" MIN. CHAMFER STRIP

**PLAN**
**SQUARE COLUMNS**

STEEL BAND
PLYWOOD

2 X 4 OR 3 X 4

2 X 4

**PLAN**
**LARGE COLUMN**

**NOTE**

Height of column will change thickness and spaces of steel bands. Consult manufacturers' catalogs. Selection of sheathing (or plywood), type of column clamps (job built or patented metal types), and their spacing will depend on column height, rate of concrete pour (ft/hr), and concrete temperature ($^\circ$F), as well as on whether the concrete is to be vibrated during pour. Consult design guides for correct selection of materials to ensure safe column forms.

It is recommended that chamfer strips be used at all outside corners to reduce damage to concrete when forms are removed.

BOTTOM OF SLAB

TOP

NECK

PREFABRICATED STEEL COLUMN CAPITALS FROM 3'-6" TO 6'-0" IN DIAMETER

RING

STEEL COLUMN FORMS FROM 1'-0" TO 4'-0" IN DIAMETER WITH OR WITHOUT STEEL CAPITALS

**ELEVATIONS**
**ROUND COLUMNS**

BOTTOM OF SLAB

1 X 4 BRACE

TEMPORARY COLLAR

FIBER COLUMN FORMS FROM 1'-0" TO 3'-6" IN DIAMETER

FOR LENGTHS CONSULT MANUFACTURER'S CATALOG

HINGE OR FIXED CORNER

BOARD OR 1 X 4

SHEATHING OR PLYWOOD

ADJUSTABLE CORNER, I.E., PATENTED LOCK OR DROP PINNED

**PLAN**
**TYPICAL PATENTED COLUMN CLAMP**

Tucker Concrete Form Co.; Malden, Massachusetts

**CONCRETE FORMWORK**

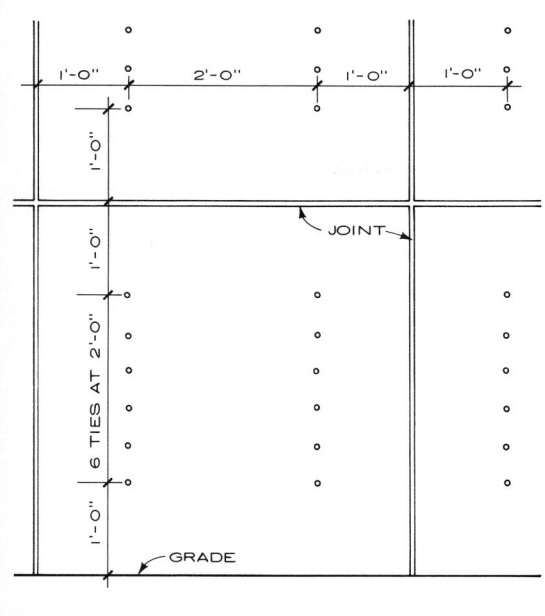

**ELEVATION**
**EXPOSED CONCRETE WITH RUSTICATION STRIP** ( IF DESIRED )

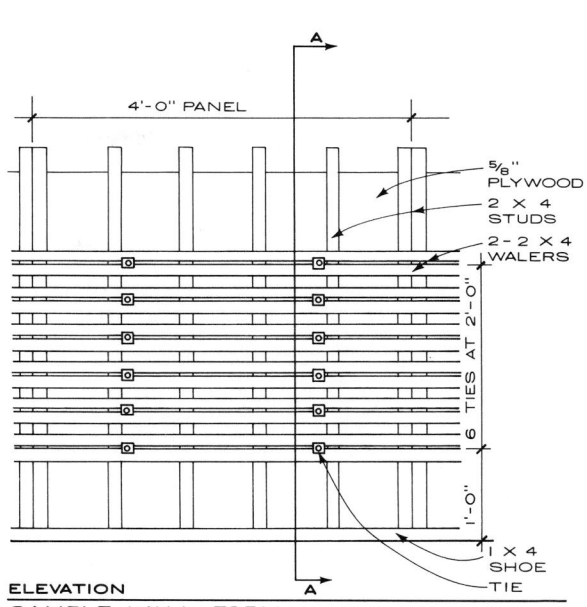

**ELEVATION**
**SAMPLE WALL FORM**

Mortar-tight forms are required for architectural exposed concrete. Consult manufacturers' literature on the proper use of metal forms or plywood forms with metal frames.

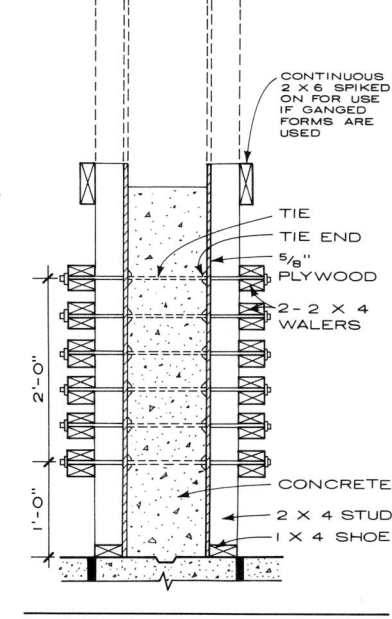

**SECTION A-A**

The section above will change if there are any variations in the thickness of plywood used, the type and strength of ties, or the size of studs and walers.

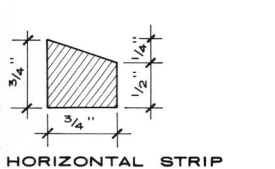 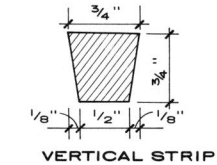

**HORIZONTAL STRIP**    **VERTICAL STRIP**

**RUSTICATION STRIPS**

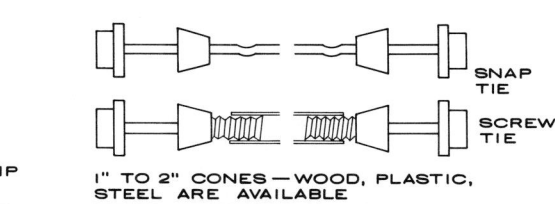

1" TO 2" CONES — WOOD, PLASTIC, STEEL ARE AVAILABLE

**TYPICAL TIES**

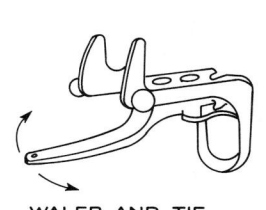

WALER AND TIE BRACKET    STRONG-BACK CAM

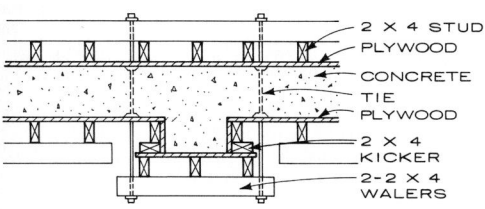

**PLAN**
**SMALL PILASTER**

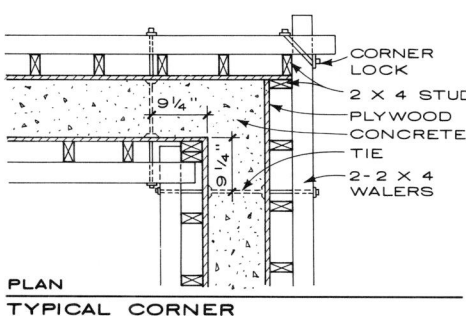

**PLAN**
**TYPICAL CORNER**

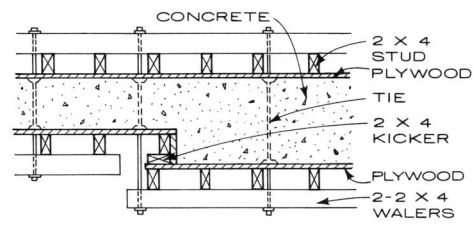

**PLAN**
**TYPICAL WALL WITH OFFSET**

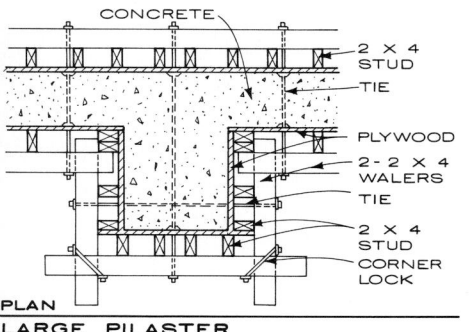

**PLAN**
**LARGE PILASTER**

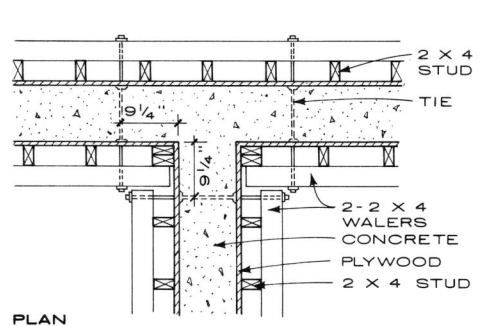

**PLAN**
**TYPICAL "T" WALL JUNCTION**

**FORM DESIGN NOTES**

1. Pressure depends on rate of pour (ft/hr) and concrete temperature (°F). Vibration of concrete is also a factor in form pressure.
2. Provide cleanout doors at bottom of wall forms.
3. Various types of form ties are on the market. Some are not suitable for architectural concrete work, i.e., they cannot be withdrawn from the concrete.
4. Various plastic cones 1½ in. in diameter and ½ in. deep can be used and the holes are left ungrouted to form a type of architectural feature.
5. Consult manufacturers' catalogs for form design and tie strength information.

Tucker Concrete Form Co.; Malden, Massachusetts

**CONCRETE FORMWORK**    3

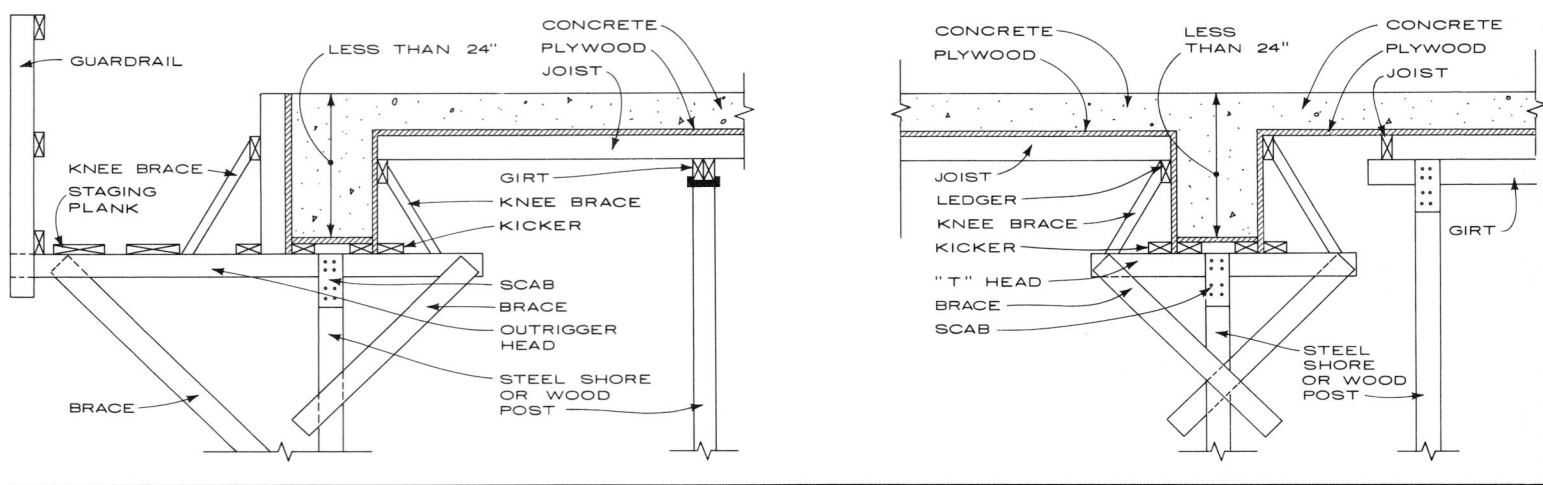

**TYPICAL SLAB AND SHALLOW BEAM FORMING**

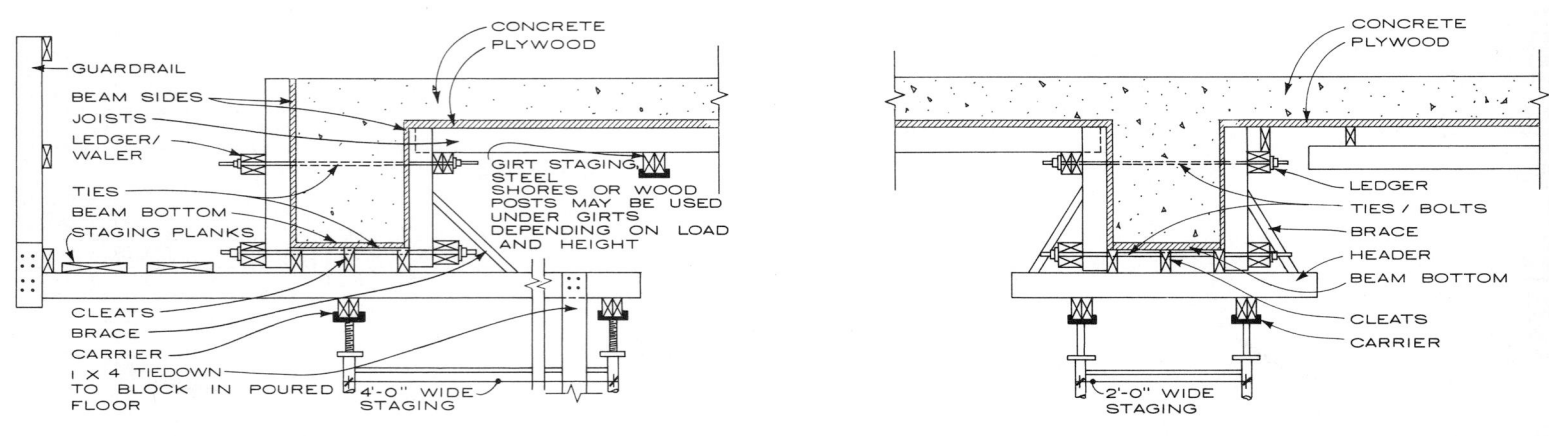

**TYPICAL SLAB AND HEAVY BEAM FORMING**

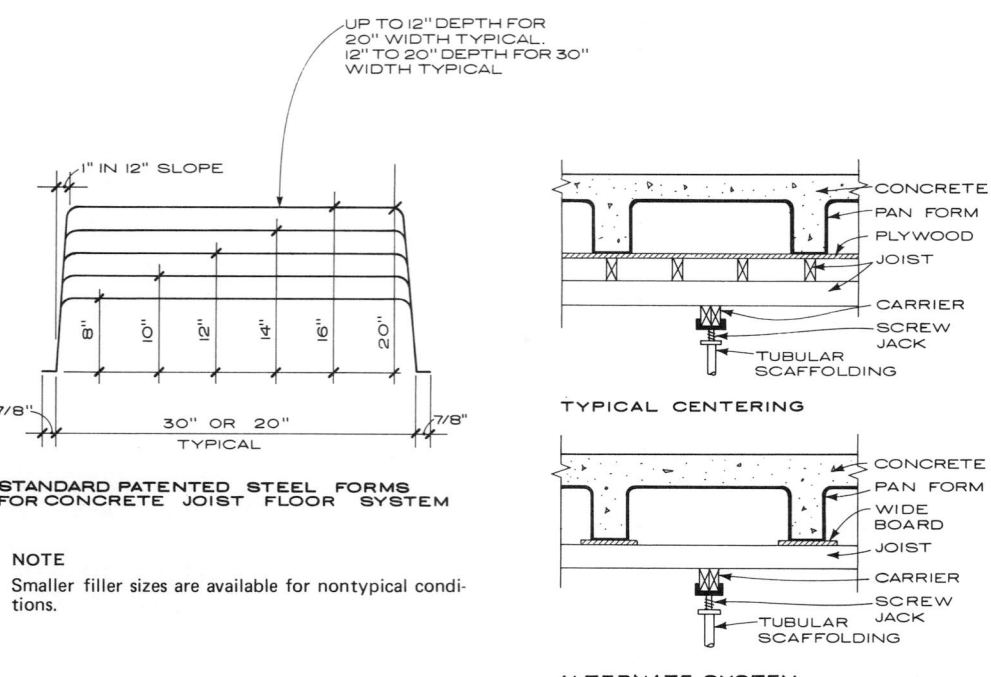

**STANDARD PATENTED STEEL FORMS FOR CONCRETE JOIST FLOOR SYSTEM**

**NOTE**
Smaller filler sizes are available for nontypical conditions.

**TYPICAL CENTERING**

**ALTERNATE SYSTEM**

**NOTES**
1. Staging, steel shores, or wood posts may be used under girts depending on loads and height requirements.
2. For flat slabs of flat plate forming, metal "flying forms" are commonly used.
3. Patented steel forms or fillers are also available for nontypical conditions on special order. See manufacturer's catalogs. Fiber forms, too, are on the market in similar sizes. Plywood deck is required for forming.
4. Plywood is usually $5/8''$ minimum thickness, Exposure 1.

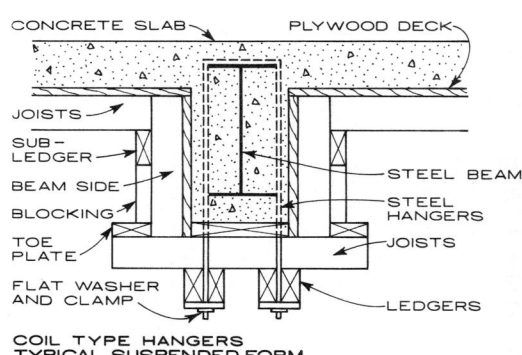

**COIL TYPE HANGERS TYPICAL SUSPENDED FORM**

Tucker Concrete Form Co.; Malden, Massachusetts

**CONCRETE FORMWORK**

## ASTM STANDARD REINFORCING BAR SIZES—
### NOMINAL DIAMETER

| BAR SIZE DESIGNATION | WEIGHT PER FOOT | | DIAMETER | | CROSS-SECTIONAL AREA SQUARED | |
|---|---|---|---|---|---|---|
| | LB | KG | IN. | CM | IN. | CM |
| #3 | 0.376 | 0.171 | 0.375 | 0.953 | 0.11 | 0.71 |
| #4 | 0.668 | 0.303 | 0.500 | 1.270 | 0.20 | 1.29 |
| #5 | 1.043 | 0.473 | 0.625 | 1.588 | 0.31 | 2.00 |
| #6 | 1.502 | 0.681 | 0.750 | 1.905 | 0.44 | 2.84 |
| #7 | 2.044 | 0.927 | 0.875 | 2.223 | 0.60 | 3.87 |
| #8 | 2.670 | 1.211 | 1.000 | 2.540 | 0.79 | 5.10 |
| #9 | 3.400 | 1.542 | 1.128 | 2.865 | 1.00 | 6.45 |
| #10 | 4.303 | 1.952 | 1.270 | 3.226 | 1.27 | 8.19 |
| #11 | 5.313 | 2.410 | 1.410 | 3.581 | 1.56 | 10.07 |
| #14 | 7.650 | 3.470 | 1.693 | 4.300 | 2.25 | 14.52 |
| #18 | 13.600 | 6.169 | 2.257 | 5.733 | 4.00 | 25.81 |

## COMMON STOCK STYLES OF WELDED WIRE FABRIC

| | NEW DESIGNATION SPACING—CROSS SECTIONAL AREA (IN.)—(SQ IN./100) | OLD DESIGNATION SPACING—WIRE GAUGE (IN.)—(AS & W) | STEEL AREA PER FOOT | | | | APPROXIMATE WEIGHT PER 100 SQ FT | |
|---|---|---|---|---|---|---|---|---|
| | | | LONGITUDINAL | | TRANSVERSE | | | |
| | | | IN. | CM | IN. | CM | LB | KG |
| Rolls | 6 x 6—W1.4 x W1.4 | 6 x 6—10 x 10 | 0.028 | 0.071 | 0.028 | 0.071 | 21 | 9.53 |
| | 6 x 6—W2.0 x W2.0 | 6 x 6—8 x 8 (1) | 0.040 | 0.102 | 0.040 | 0.102 | 29 | 13.15 |
| | 6 x 6—W2.9 x W2.9 | 6 x 6—6 x 6 | 0.058 | 0.147 | 0.058 | 0.147 | 42 | 19.05 |
| | 6 x 6—W4.0 x W4.0 | 6 x 6—4 x 4 | 0.080 | 0.203 | 0.080 | 0.203 | 58 | 26.31 |
| | 4 x 4—W1.4 x W1.4 | 4 x 4—10 x 10 | 0.042 | 0.107 | 0.042 | 0.107 | 31 | 14.06 |
| | 4 x 4—W2.0 x W2.0 | 4 x 4—8 x 8 (1) | 0.060 | 0.152 | 0.060 | 0.152 | 43 | 19.50 |
| | 4 x 4—W2.9 x W2.9 | 4 x 4—6 x 6 | 0.087 | 0.221 | 0.087 | 0.221 | 62 | 28.12 |
| | 4 x 4—W4.0 x W4.0 | 4 x 4—4 x 4 | 0.120 | 0.305 | 0.120 | 0.305 | 85 | 38.56 |
| Sheets | 6 x 6—W2.9 x W2.9 | 6 x 6—6 x 6 | 0.058 | 0.147 | 0.058 | 0.147 | 42 | 19.05 |
| | 6 x 6—W4.0 x W4.0 | 6 x 6—4 x 4 | 0.080 | 0.203 | 0.080 | 0.203 | 58 | 26.31 |
| | 6 x 6—W5.5 x W5.5 | 6 x 6—2 x 2 (2) | 0.110 | 0.279 | 0.110 | 0.279 | 80 | 36.29 |
| | 4 x 4—W4.0 x W4.0 | 4 x 4—4 x 4 | 0.120 | 0.305 | 0.120 | 0.305 | 85 | 38.56 |

### NOTES
1. Exact W-number size for 8 gauge is W2.1.
2. Exact W-number size for 2 gauge is W5.4.

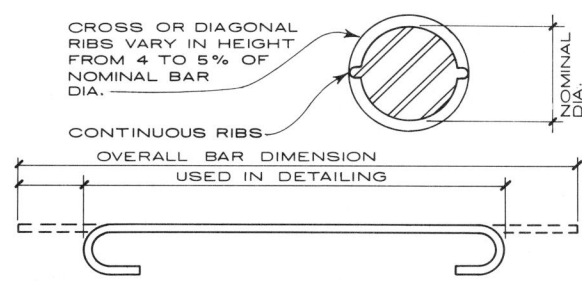

### REINFORCING BAR DIMENSIONING
## STANDARD STEEL WIRE SIZES AND GAUGES

| A.S.&W GAUGE | DIAMETER | | AREA SQUARED | | WEIGHT PER FOOT | |
|---|---|---|---|---|---|---|
| | IN. | CM | IN. | CM | LB | KG |
| 00 | 0.3310 | 0.8407 | 0.0860 | 0.5549 | 0.2922 | 0.1325 |
| 0 | 0.3065 | 0.7785 | 0.0738 | 0.4762 | 0.2506 | 0.1137 |
| 1 | 0.2830 | 0.7188 | 0.0629 | 0.4058 | 0.2136 | 0.0969 |
| 2 | 0.2625 | 0.6668 | 0.0541 | 0.3491 | 0.1829 | 0.0830 |
| — (1/4") | 0.2500 | 0.6350 | 0.0491 | 0.3168 | 0.1667 | 0.0756 |
| 3 | 0.2437 | 0.6190 | 0.0466 | 0.3007 | 0.1584 | 0.0718 |
| 4 | 0.2253 | 0.5723 | 0.0397 | 0.2561 | 0.1354 | 0.0614 |
| 5 | 0.2070 | 0.5258 | 0.0337 | 0.2174 | 0.1143 | 0.0518 |
| 6 | 0.1920 | 0.4877 | 0.0290 | 0.1871 | 0.0983 | 0.0446 |
| 7 | 0.1770 | 0.4496 | 0.0246 | 0.1587 | 0.0836 | 0.0379 |
| 8 | 0.1620 | 0.4115 | 0.0206 | 0.1329 | 0.0700 | 0.0318 |
| 9 | 0.1483 | 0.3767 | 0.0173 | 0.1116 | 0.0587 | 0.0266 |
| 10 | 0.1350 | 0.3429 | 0.0143 | 0.0922 | 0.0486 | 0.0220 |
| 11 (1/8") | 0.1250 | 0.3175 | 0.0114 | 0.0736 | 0.0387 | 0.0176 |
| 12 | 0.1055 | 0.2680 | 0.0087 | 0.0561 | 0.0297 | 0.0135 |
| 13 | 0.0915 | 0.2324 | 0.0066 | 0.0426 | 0.0223 | 0.0101 |
| 14 | 0.0800 | 0.2032 | 0.0050 | 0.0323 | 0.0171 | 0.0078 |
| 15 | 0.0720 | 0.1838 | 0.0041 | 0.0265 | 0.0138 | 0.0063 |
| 16 (1/16") | 0.0625 | 0.1588 | 0.0031 | 0.0200 | 0.0104 | 0.0047 |

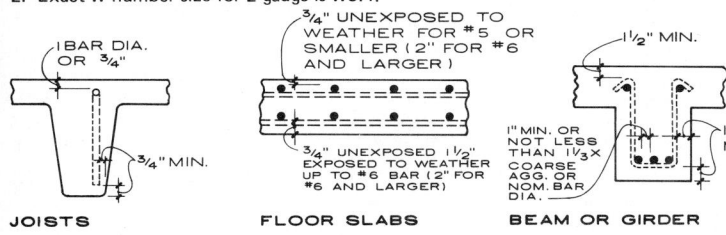

JOISTS     FLOOR SLABS     BEAM OR GIRDER

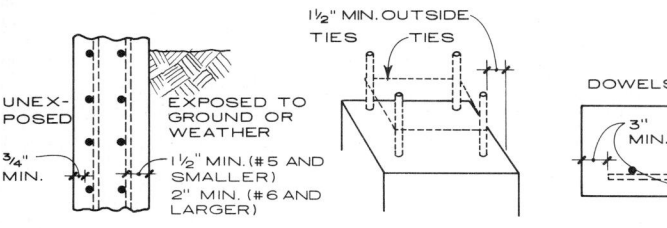

WALLS     COLUMNS     FOOTINGS

### PROTECTION FOR REINFORCEMENT

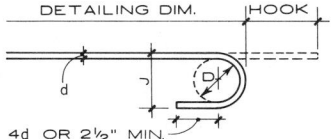

**180° HOOK**

d = (I) Bar Diameter
D = 6d for No. 3 to No. 8 Bars
D = 8d for No. 9 to No. 11 Bars
J = D + 2d
H = 5d + D/2 (or) 2 1/2" + d + D/2 minimum

**90° HOOK**

d = (1) Bar Diameter
D = 6d for No. 3 to No. 8 bars
D = 8d for No. 9 to No. 11 bars
J = 13d + D/2

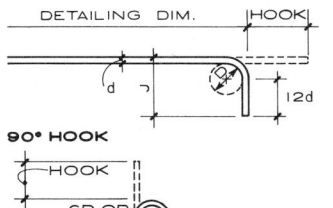

**135° HOOK STIRRUP — TIES SIMILAR**

d = (1) Bar Diameter
D = 1 1/2" for No. 3
D = 2" for No. 4
D = 2 1/2" for No. 5
D = 6d for No. 6 to No. 8

### STANDARD REINFORCING BAR HOOK DETAILS

## LAP SPLICE REQUIREMENTS
1983 CODE IN BAR DIAMETERS

| $f'_y$ (KSI) | SPIRAL COLUMN | TIED COLUMN | LOOSE |
|---|---|---|---|
| 40 | 15.0 | 16.6 | 20 |
| 50 | 18.75 | 20.75 | 25 |
| 60 | 22.5 | 24.9 | 30 |
| 75 | 32.6 | 36.2 | 43.5 |
| 80 | 36.0 | 39.9 | 48.0 |

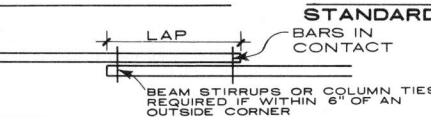

### NOTES
1. These requirements are for compression lap splices only.
2. Lap splice lengths are minimum for $f'_c \geq 3000$ psi.
3. Minimum lap is 12 in.
4. Maximum reinforcing bar size permitted in lap splice is No. 11.

## TEMPERATURE REINFORCEMENT FOR STRUCTURAL FLOOR AND ROOF SLAB (ONE WAY) (IN PERCENTAGE OF CROSS-SECTIONAL AREA OF CONCRETE)

| REINFORCEMENT | | CONCRETE SLABS | |
|---|---|---|---|
| GRADE | TYPE | | |
| 40/50 | Deformed bars | 0.20% | Max. spacing five times slab thickness |
| — | Welded wire fabric | 0.18% | |
| 60 | Deformed bars | 0.18% | |

Dave Keppler; Haver, Nunn and Collamer; Phoenix, Arizona

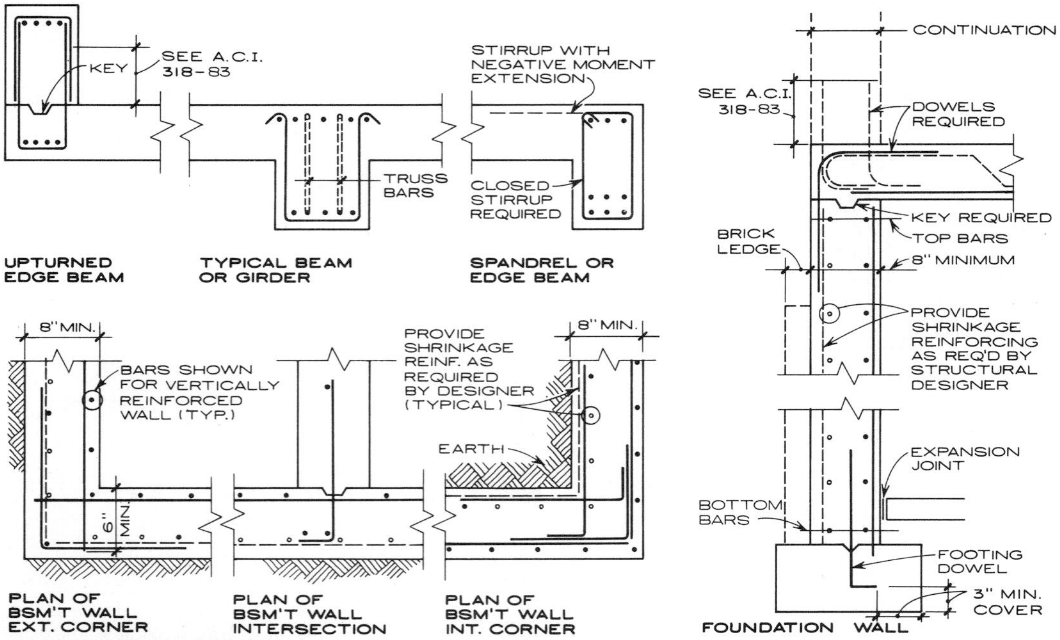

## REINFORCING DETAILS

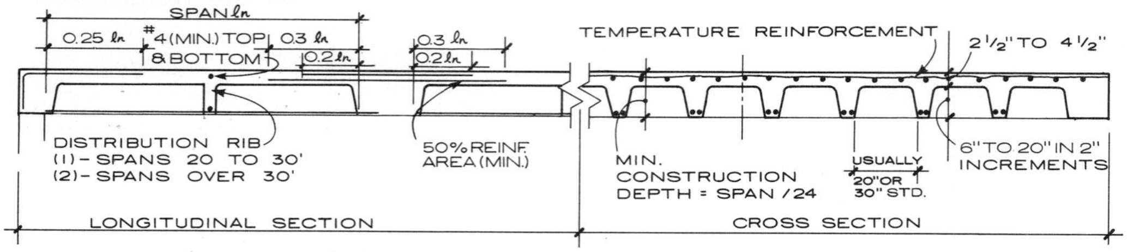

**UPTURNED EDGE BEAM**

KEY
SEE A.C.I. 318-83

**TYPICAL BEAM OR GIRDER**

STIRRUP WITH NEGATIVE MOMENT EXTENSION
TRUSS BARS

**SPANDREL OR EDGE BEAM**

CLOSED STIRRUP REQUIRED

**PLAN OF BSM'T WALL EXT. CORNER**

8" MIN.
BARS SHOWN FOR VERTICALLY REINFORCED WALL (TYP.)

**PLAN OF BSM'T WALL INTERSECTION**

PROVIDE SHRINKAGE REINF. AS REQUIRED BY DESIGNER (TYPICAL)
EARTH

**PLAN OF BSM'T WALL INT. CORNER**

8" MIN.

CONTINUATION
DOWELS REQUIRED
SEE A.C.I. 318-83
BRICK LEDGE
KEY REQUIRED TOP BARS
8" MINIMUM
PROVIDE SHRINKAGE REINFORCING AS REQ'D BY STRUCTURAL DESIGNER
BOTTOM BARS
EXPANSION JOINT
FOOTING DOWEL
3" MIN. COVER

**FOUNDATION WALL**

ROOF
DOWELS
SPIRAL
REBAR
1½ TURN FOR ANCHORAGE
VERTICAL REINF (6) BARS MIN. (ONLY 2 SHOWN)
CORE DIA.
10" MIN.

**PLAN**

SPIRAL TIE
MAX. 3" MIN. 1⅜" OR 1½" × AGG. SIZE
C. TO C. SPACING ⅙ CORE DIA. MAX.
1½" TURNS FOR ANCHORAGE

**6 TH. FL.**

6 (MIN.)
THRUST TIES REQUIRED
8" MIN.
REBAR
#4 TIES MIN.
MAXIMUM TIE SPACING 48 TIE DIA. 16 BAR DIA. LEAST COL. DIM.

**PLAN**

---

**SPAN** *l*n
0.25 *l*n
#4 (MIN.) TOP & BOTTOM
0.3 *l*n
0.2 *l*n
0.3 *l*n
0.2 *l*n
TEMPERATURE REINFORCEMENT
2½" TO 4½"

DISTRIBUTION RIB
(1) - SPANS 20 TO 30'
(2) - SPANS OVER 30'
50% REINF. AREA (MIN.)
MIN. CONSTRUCTION DEPTH = SPAN /24
USUALLY 20' OR 30' STD.
6" TO 20" IN 2" INCREMENTS

**LONGITUDINAL SECTION**

**CROSS SECTION**

### ONE-WAY CONCRETE JOIST CONSTRUCTION

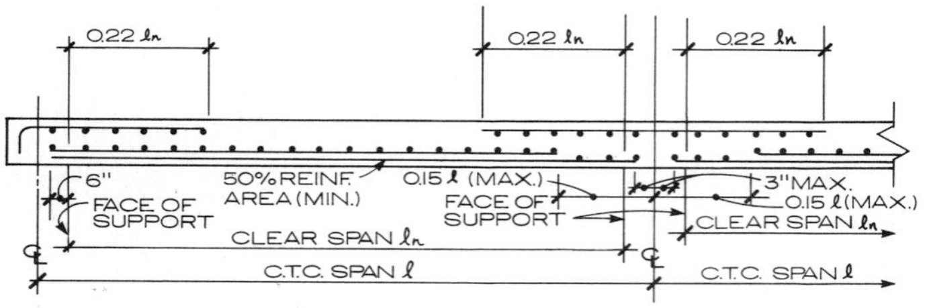

0.22 *l*n
0.22 *l*n
0.22 *l*n
6"
50% REINF. AREA (MIN.)
0.15 *l* (MAX.)
FACE OF SUPPORT
FACE OF SUPPORT
3" MAX.
0.15 *l* (MAX.)
CLEAR SPAN *l*n
CLEAR SPAN *l*n
C.T.C. SPAN *l*
C.T.C. SPAN *l*

### FLAT PLATE CONSTRUCTION - MIDDLE STRIP

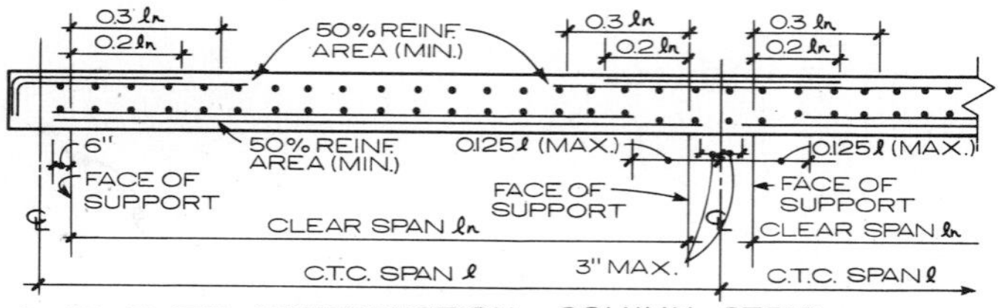

0.3 *l*n
0.2 *l*n
50% REINF. AREA (MIN.)
0.3 *l*n
0.2 *l*n
0.3 *l*n
0.2 *l*n
6"
50% REINF. AREA (MIN.)
0.125 *l* (MAX.)
0.125 *l* (MAX.)
FACE OF SUPPORT
FACE OF SUPPORT
FACE OF SUPPORT
CLEAR SPAN *l*n
CLEAR SPAN *l*n
C.T.C. SPAN *l*
3" MAX.
C.T.C. SPAN *l*

### FLAT PLATE CONSTRUCTION - COLUMN STRIP

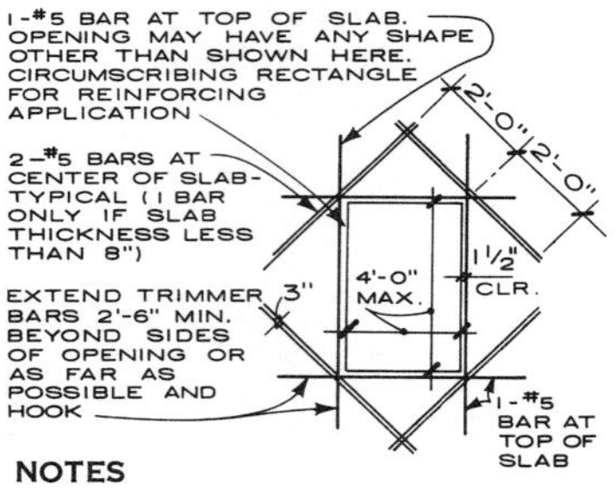

1-#5 BAR AT TOP OF SLAB. OPENING MAY HAVE ANY SHAPE OTHER THAN SHOWN HERE. CIRCUMSCRIBING RECTANGLE FOR REINFORCING APPLICATION

2-#5 BARS AT CENTER OF SLAB-TYPICAL (1 BAR ONLY IF SLAB THICKNESS LESS THAN 8")

EXTEND TRIMMER BARS 2'-6" MIN. BEYOND SIDES OF OPENING OR AS FAR AS POSSIBLE AND HOOK

2'-0"
2'-0"
4'-0" MAX.
1½ CLR.
1-#5 BAR AT TOP OF SLAB

### NOTES

1. Provide extra bars (not shown) parallel to sides of openings, equal to areas of interrupted slab bars. Extend full length of span or to top bars as applicable.
2. This detail is typical at openings up to 4 ft maximum dimensions except as otherwise shown.
3. Circular openings less than 18 in. diameter require no reinforcing.

### OPENING IN SLAB OR WALL

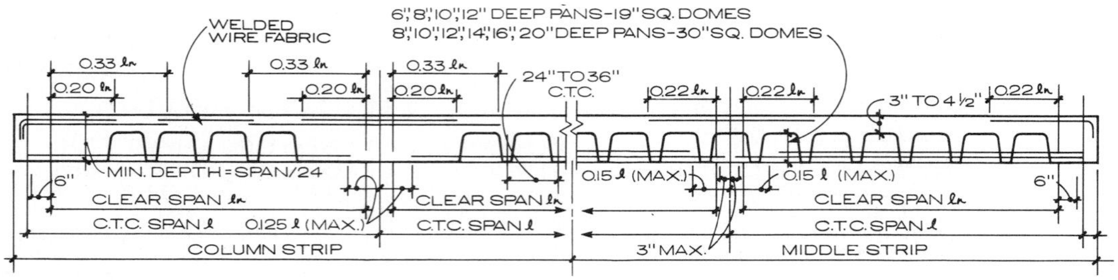

WELDED SPLICE
ANGLE
**SMALL BARS**
**4 TH. FL.**
WELDED SPLICE
DOUBLE TIE REQ'D
**LARGE BARS**
4'-0"
1'-6"

TIE
TENSION BAR
SLEEVE CLAMP
MIN. REBAR BOND DIM.
**COMPRESSION SPLICE**
**2 ND. FL.**

DOUBLE TIES
EXOTHERMIC OR SLEEVE WITH METAL FILLER
DOUBLE TIES REQUIRED
**COMPRESSION SPLICE** (TENSION WHERE APPROVED)
1'-6"

REBAR BUNDLES
TIES
DOUBLE TIES
BUNDLE OF BARS WHERE NECESSARY
**PLAN**

WELDED WIRE FABRIC
6", 8", 10", 12" DEEP PANS-19" SQ. DOMES
8", 10", 12", 14", 16", 20" DEEP PANS-30" SQ. DOMES
0.33 *l*n
0.20 *l*n
0.33 *l*n
0.20 *l*n
0.20 *l*n
24" TO 36" C.T.C.
0.22 *l*n
0.22 *l*n
3" TO 4½"
0.22 *l*n
6"
MIN. DEPTH = SPAN/24
CLEAR SPAN *l*n
C.T.C. SPAN *l*
0.125 *l* (MAX.)
CLEAR SPAN *l*n
C.T.C. SPAN *l*
0.15 *l* (MAX.)
0.15 *l* (MAX.)
CLEAR SPAN *l*n
C.T.C. SPAN *l*
3" MAX.
6"
**COLUMN STRIP**
**MIDDLE STRIP**

### WAFFLE FLAT SLAB - SQUARE BAY CONSTRUCTION

## CONCRETE FLOOR SYSTEMS

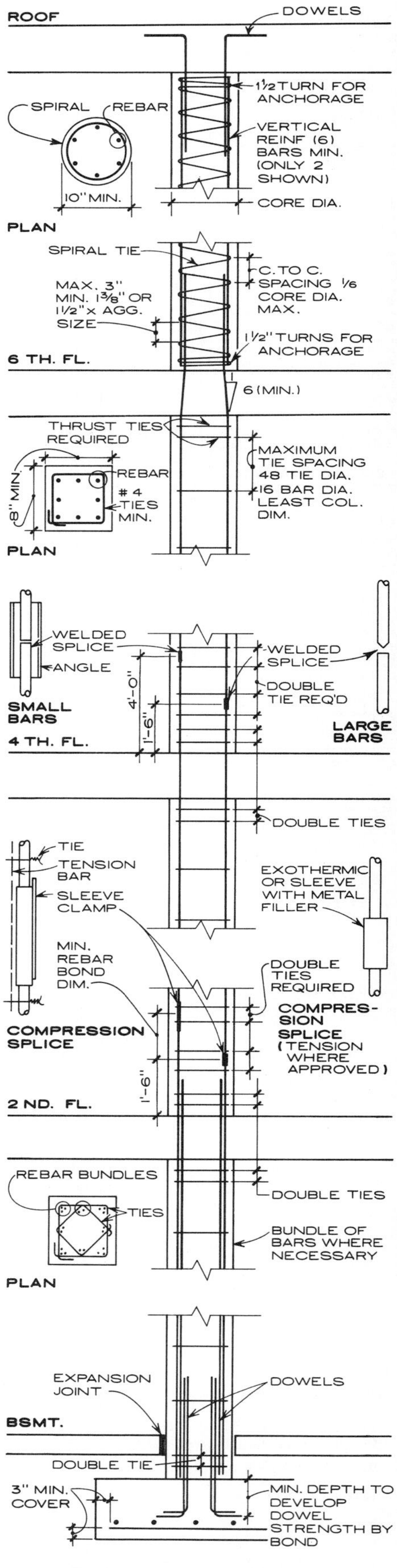

EXPANSION JOINT
DOWELS
**BSMT.**
DOUBLE TIE
3" MIN. COVER
MIN. DEPTH TO DEVELOP DOWEL STRENGTH BY BOND

### COMPOSITE OF MAJOR TYPES OF COLUMN REINFORCING BARS

Thomas A. Lines; Haver, Nunn and Collamer; Phoenix, Arizona
Kenneth D. Franch, AIA, PE; Phillips Swager Associates, Inc.; Dallas, Texas

**3**

# CONCRETE REINFORCEMENT

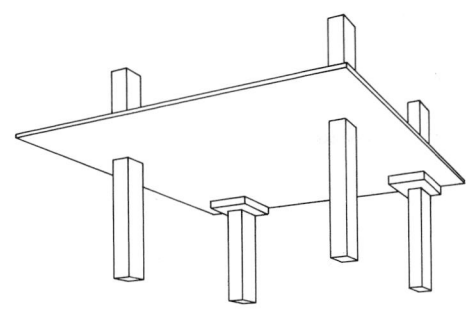

FLAT SLABS TO HAVE DROP
PANELS OR COLUMN CAPITALS.
FOR SUPERIMPOSED LOADS
OVER 100 PSF, USE BOTH DROP
PANELS AND COLUMN CAPITALS

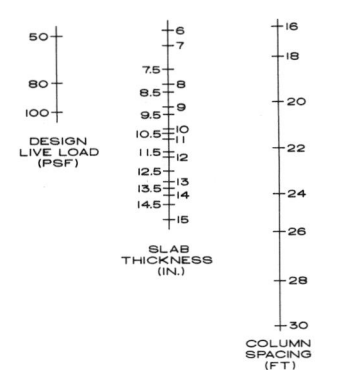

**FLAT PLATE**

**FLAT SLAB WITHOUT BEAMS**

**FLAT SLAB WITH BEAMS**

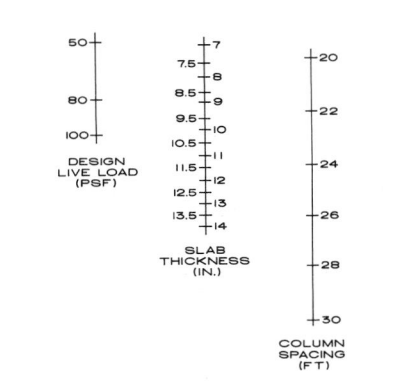

IF REQUIRED, USE
TAPERED PANS AT GIRDER TO
RESIST SHEAR FORCES

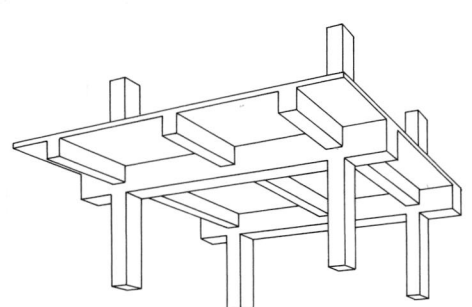

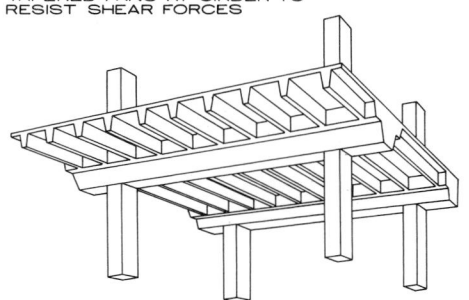

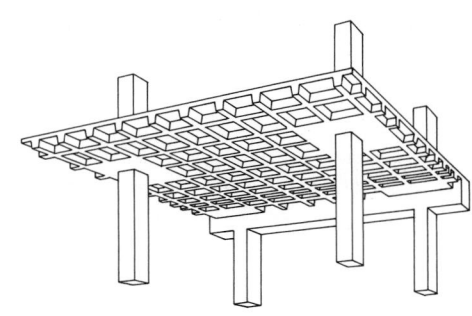

20" FORMS WITH
6" RIBS = 26" C. TO C.

19" x 19" FORMS WITH
5" RIBS = 24" C. TO C.

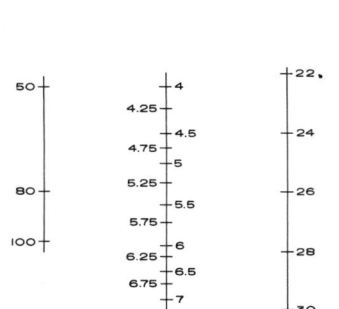

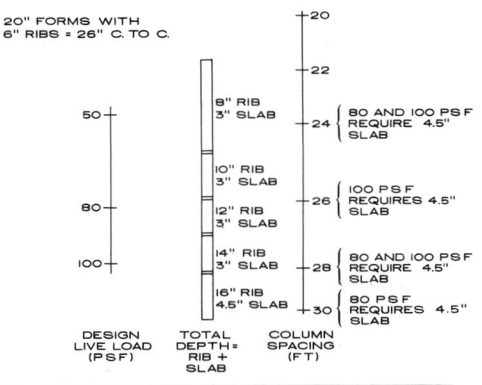

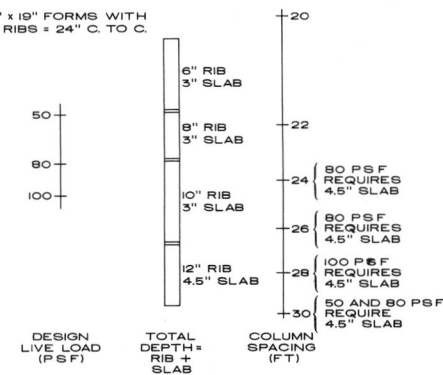

**ONE - WAY SLAB WITH BEAMS**
**(SPAN = ½ THE COLUMN SPACING)**

**ONE-WAY JOISTS WITH BEAMS**
**(METAL PAN CONSTRUCTION)**

**TWO-WAY JOISTS WITHOUT BEAMS**
**(WAFFLE FLAT PLATE**
**CONSTRUCTION)**

### GENERAL NOTES

To use bar graphs, lay straight edge across chart and line up with design live load required on left bar and with selected column spacing on right bar. Slab thickness required is indicated where straight edge intersects center bar.

The examples above are all calculated by the ultimate design strength method around the following parameters:

1. Concrete strength of 4000 psi at 28 days.
2. Steel reinforcing strength of 60,000 psi.
3. Steel to concrete ratio of minimum steel.

The information represented on this page is intended to be used as a preliminary design guide only and not to replace complete analysis and calculation of each project condition by a licensed professional engineer.

Killebrew/Rucker/Associates, Inc.; Architects/Planners/Engineers; Wichita Falls, Texas

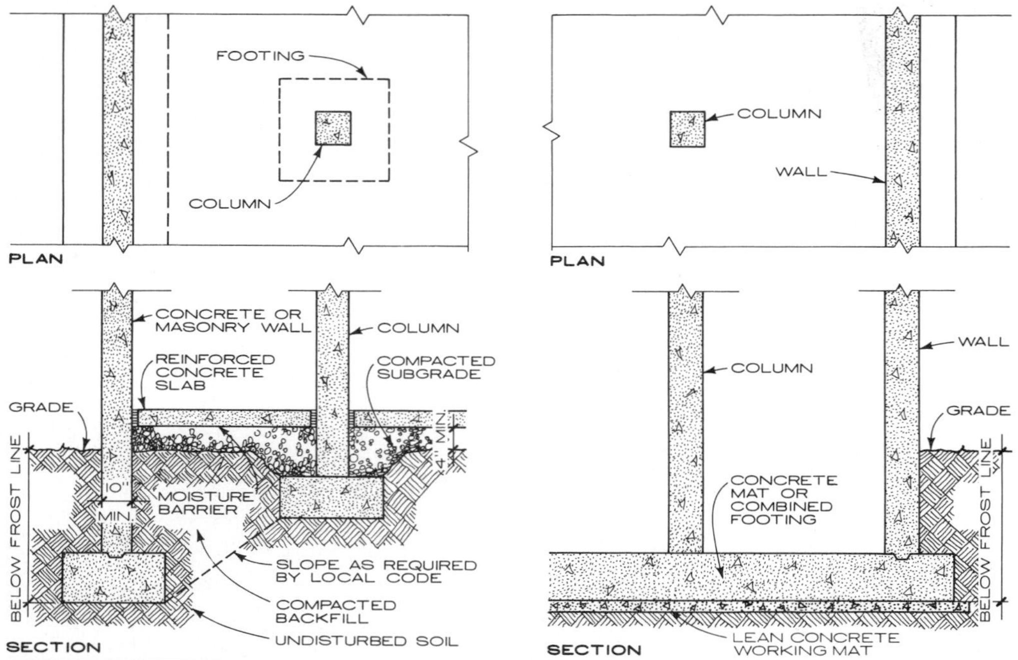

### SPREAD FOOTINGS

**PLAN** (left): FOOTING, COLUMN

**SECTION** (left): GRADE, CONCRETE OR MASONRY WALL, COLUMN, REINFORCED CONCRETE SLAB, COMPACTED SUBGRADE, BELOW FROST LINE, 10" MIN, MOISTURE BARRIER, 4" MIN, SLOPE AS REQUIRED BY LOCAL CODE, COMPACTED BACKFILL, UNDISTURBED SOIL

**PLAN** (middle): COLUMN, WALL

**SECTION** (middle): COLUMN, WALL, GRADE, CONCRETE MAT OR COMBINED FOOTING, BELOW FROST LINE, LEAN CONCRETE WORKING MAT

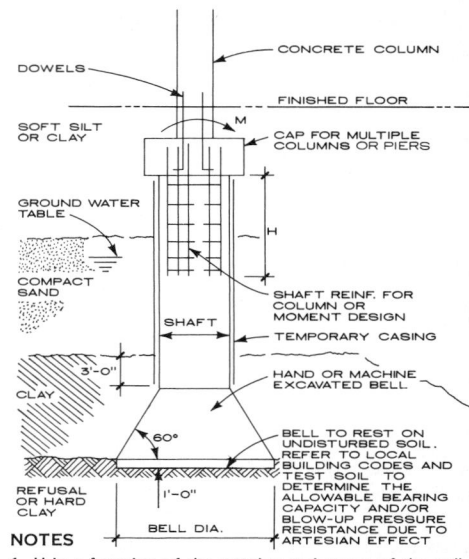

**BELL PIER FOUNDATION**

DOWELS, CONCRETE COLUMN, FINISHED FLOOR, SOFT SILT OR CLAY, M, CAP FOR MULTIPLE COLUMNS OR PIERS, GROUND WATER TABLE, H, COMPACT SAND, SHAFT, SHAFT REINF. FOR COLUMN OR MOMENT DESIGN, TEMPORARY CASING, CLAY, 3'-0", HAND OR MACHINE EXCAVATED BELL, 60°, BELL TO REST ON UNDISTURBED SOIL. REFER TO LOCAL BUILDING CODES AND TEST SOIL TO DETERMINE THE ALLOWABLE BEARING CAPACITY AND/OR BLOW-UP PRESSURE RESISTANCE DUE TO ARTESIAN EFFECT, REFUSAL OR HARD CLAY, 1'-0", BELL DIA.

**NOTES**
1. H is a function of the passive resistance of the soil, generated by the moment applied to the pier cap.
2. Piers may be used under grade beams or concrete walls. For very heavy loads, pier foundations may be more economical than piles.

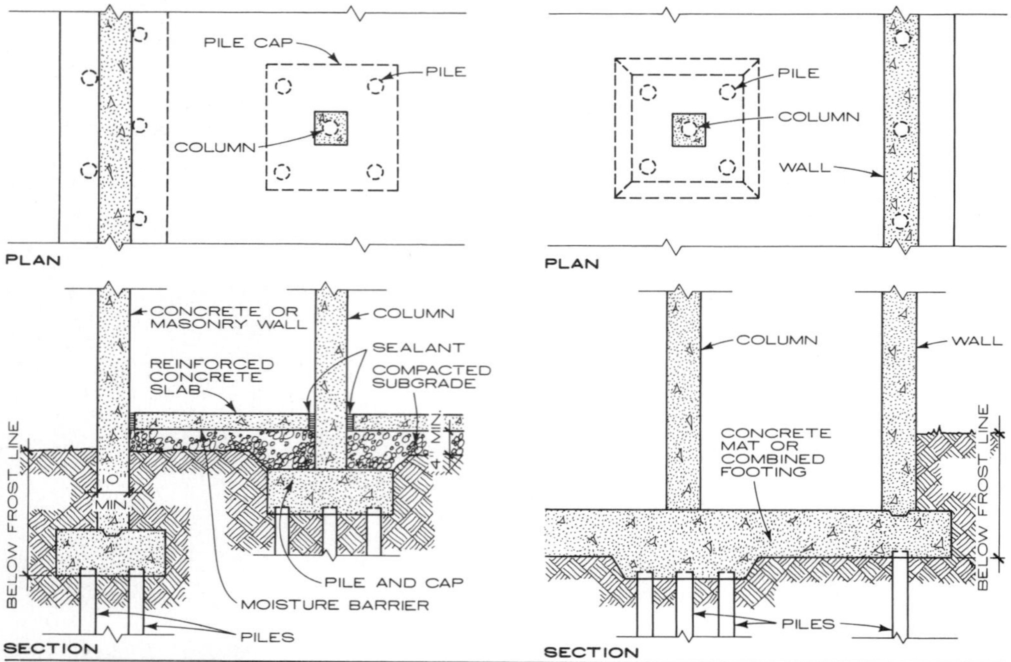

### PILE SUPPORTED FOUNDATIONS

**PLAN** (left): PILE CAP, PILE, COLUMN

**SECTION** (left): CONCRETE OR MASONRY WALL, COLUMN, REINFORCED CONCRETE SLAB, SEALANT, COMPACTED SUBGRADE, BELOW FROST LINE, 10" MIN, PILE AND CAP, MOISTURE BARRIER, PILES

**PLAN** (middle): PILE, COLUMN, WALL

**SECTION** (middle): COLUMN, WALL, CONCRETE MAT OR COMBINED FOOTING, BELOW FROST LINE, PILES

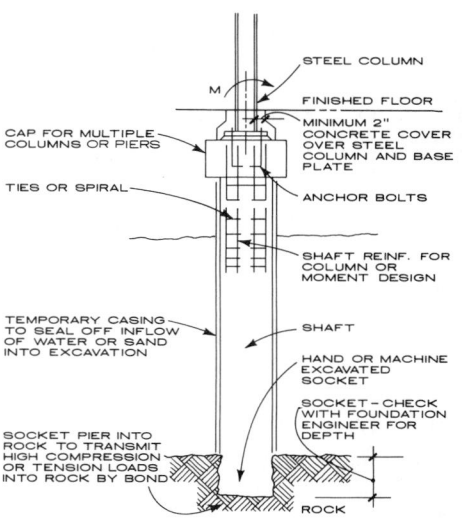

**SOCKET PIER FOUNDATION**

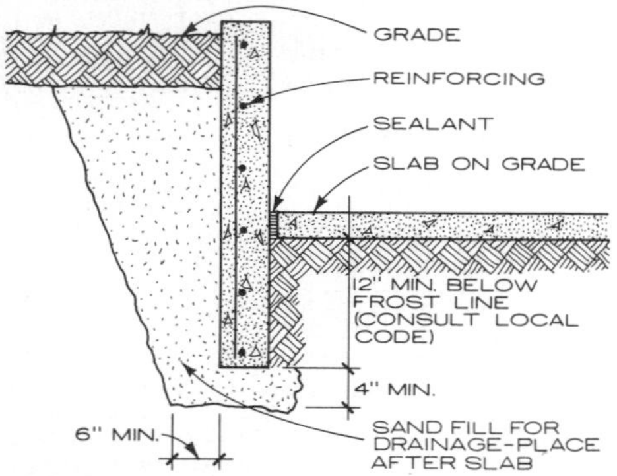

STEEL COLUMN, FINISHED FLOOR, M, MINIMUM 2" CONCRETE COVER OVER STEEL COLUMN AND BASE PLATE, CAP FOR MULTIPLE COLUMNS OR PIERS, ANCHOR BOLTS, TIES OR SPIRAL, SHAFT REINF. FOR COLUMN OR MOMENT DESIGN, TEMPORARY CASING TO SEAL OFF INFLOW OF WATER OR SAND INTO EXCAVATION, SHAFT, HAND OR MACHINE EXCAVATED SOCKET, SOCKET – CHECK WITH FOUNDATION ENGINEER FOR DEPTH, SOCKET PIER INTO ROCK TO TRANSMIT HIGH COMPRESSION OR TENSION LOADS INTO ROCK BY BOND, ROCK

**NOTES**
1. Pier shaft should be poured in the dry if possible, but tremie pours can be used with appropriate control.
2. Grout bottom of shaft against artesian water or sulphur gas intrusion into the excavation.

### AREAWAY WALL

GRADE, REINFORCING, SEALANT, SLAB ON GRADE, 12" MIN. BELOW FROST LINE (CONSULT LOCAL CODE), 4" MIN., 6" MIN., SAND FILL FOR DRAINAGE-PLACE AFTER SLAB

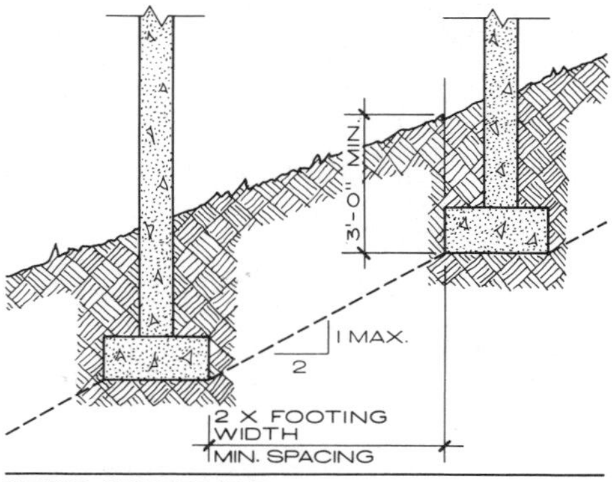

### STEP FOOTINGS
**MAX. STEEPNESS: 2 HORIZONTAL TO 1 VERTICAL**

3'-0" MIN., 1 MAX. / 2, 2 X FOOTING WIDTH MIN. SPACING

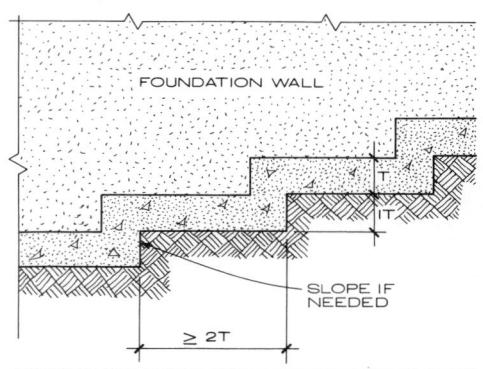

### STEP FOOTING (FOR CONTINUOUS WALL)
**MAX. STEEPNESS: 2 HORIZONTAL TO 1 VERTICAL**

FOUNDATION WALL, T, SLOPE IF NEEDED, ≥ 2T

Mueser, Rutledge, Johnston & DeSimone; New York, New York

## GENERAL NOTES

Factors to consider in construction of all concrete slabs on grade include assurance of uniform subgrade, quality of concrete, adequacy of structural capacity, type and spacing of joints, finishing, curing, and the application of special surfaces. It is vital to design and construct the subgrade as carefully as the floor slab itself. The subgrade support must be reasonably uniform, and the upper portion of the subgrade should be of uniform material and density. A subbase, a thin layer of granular material placed on the subgrade, should be used in most cases to cushion the slab.

Wear resistance is directly related to concrete strength. A low water-cement ratio improves the surface hardness and finishability as well as internal strength of concrete. Low water-cement ratio, low slump, and well graded aggregates with coarse aggregate size as large as placing and finishing requirements will permit and enhance the quality of concrete.

Exterior concrete subjected to freeze-thaw cycles should have 6 to 8% entrained air. Reinforcement is unnecessary where frequent joint spacing is used. Where less frequent joint spacing is necessary, reinforcement is put in the top one third depth to hold together any shrinkage cracks that form. Control joint spacing of 15 to 25 ft square is recommended. Checkerboard pouring patterns allow for some shrinkage between pours, but the process is more costly and is not recommended for large areas. The total shrinkage process takes up to one year. Strip pouring, allowing for a continuous pour with control joints cut after concrete has set, is a fast economical method, recommended for large areas.

Three types of joints are recommended:

1. ISOLATION JOINTS (also called expansion joints): Allow movement between slab and fixed parts of the building such as columns, walls, and machinery bases.
2. CONTROL JOINTS: Induce cracking at preselected locations.
3. CONSTRUCTION JOINTS: Provide stopping places during floor construction. Construction joints also function as control and isolation joints.
   Sawcut control joints should be made as early as is practical after finishing the slab and should be filled in areas with wet conditions, hygienic and dust control requirements, or considerable traffic

by hard wheeled vehicles, such as forklift trucks. A semirigid filler with Shore Hardness "A" of at least 80 should be used.

Concrete floor slabs are monolithically finished by floating and troweling the concrete to a smooth dense finish. Depressions of more than 1/8 in. in 10 ft or variations of more than 1/4 in. from a level plane are undesirable. Special finishes are available to improve appearance. These include sprinkled (shake) finishes and high strength concrete toppings, either monolithic or separate (two-stage floor).

A vaporproof barrier should be placed under all slabs on grade where the passage of water vapor through the floor is undesirable. Permeance of vapor barrier should not exceed 0.20 perms.

Generally the controlling factor in determining the thickness of a floor on ground is the heaviest concentrated load it will carry, usually the wheel load plus impact of an industrial truck. Because of practical considerations, the minimum recommended thickness for an industrial floor is about 5 in. For Class 1, 2, and 3 floors, the minimum thickness should be 4 in.

The floor thickness required for wheel loads on relatively small areas may be obtained from the table for concrete; an allowable flexural tensile stress (psi) can be estimated from the approximate formula $f_t = 4.6\sqrt{f'_c}$ in which $f'_c$ is the 28-day concrete compressive strength. If $f_t$ is not 300 psi, the table can be used by multiplying the actual total load by the ratio of 300 to the stress used and entering the chart with that value.

Assume that a 5000 psi concrete slab is to be designed for an industrial plant floor over which there will be considerable traffic—trucks with loads of 10,000 lb/wheel, each of which has a contact area of about 30 sq in. Assume that operating conditions are such that impact will be equivalent to about 25% of the load. The equivalent static load will then be 12,500 lb. The allowable flexural tensile stress for 5000 psi concrete is

$$4.6\sqrt{5000} = 325 \text{ psi}$$

The allowable loads in the table are based on a stress of 300 psi, so that the design load must be corrected by the factor 300/325. Thus 11,500 lb on an area of 30 sq in. requires a slab about 7 1/2 in. thick.

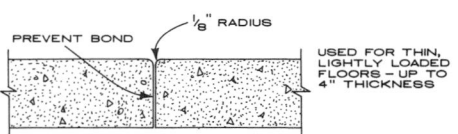

### BUTT TYPE CONSTRUCTION JOINT

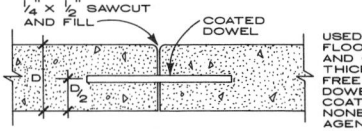

### BUTT TYPE CONSTRUCTION JOINT WITH DOWELS

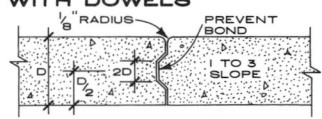

### TONGUE AND GROOVE CONSTRUCTION JOINT

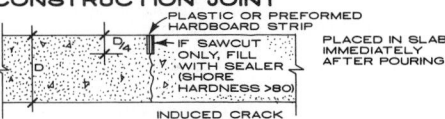

### SAWED OR PREMOLDED CONTROL JOINT FOR SLABS < 4"

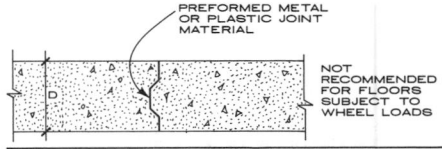

### TONGUE AND GROOVE CONTROL JOINT

### CONTROL JOINT WITH DOWELS

### ISOLATION JOINT

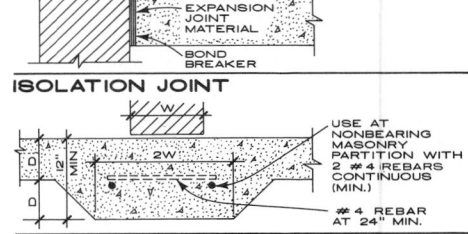

### THICKENED SLAB

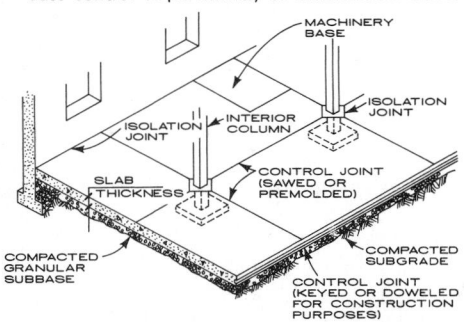

**CONTROL JOINTS FOR A SLAB ON GRADE**

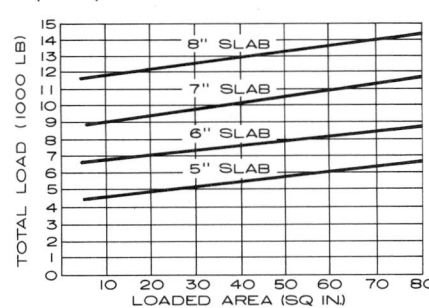

**MAXIMUM WHEEL LOADS FOR INDUSTRIAL FLOORS (FLEXURAL TENSILE STRESS = 300 PSI)**

## CLASSIFICATION OF CONCRETE SLABS ON GRADE

| CLASS | SLUMP RANGE (IN.) | MINIMUM COMPRESSIVE STRENGTH (PSI) | USUAL TRAFFIC | USE | SPECIAL CONSIDERATION | CONCRETE FINISHING TECHNIQUE |
|---|---|---|---|---|---|---|
| 1 | 2-4 | 3500 | Light foot | Residential or tile covered | Grade for drainage; plane smooth for tile | Medium steel trowel |
| 2 | 2-4 | 3500 | Foot | Offices, schools, hospitals, residential | Nonslip aggregate, mix in surface Color shake, special | Steel trowel; special finish for nonslip Steel trowel, color exposed aggregate |
| 3 | 2-4 | 3500 | Light foot and pneumatic wheels | Drives, garage floors, sidewalks for residences | Crown; pitch joints | Float, trowel, and broom |
| 4 | 1-3 | 4000 | Foot and pneumatic wheels | Light industrial, commercial | Careful curing | Hard steel trowel and brush for nonslip |
| 5 | 1-3 | 4500 | Foot and wheels— abrasive wear | Single course industrial, integral topping | Careful curing | Special hard aggregate, float and trowel |
| 6 | 2-4 | 3500 | Foot and steel tire vehicles—severe abrasion | Bonded two-course, heavy industrial | Base: textured surface and bond Top: special aggregate | Base: surface leveled by screeding Top: special power floats |
| 7 | 1-3 | 4000 | Same as Classes 3, 4, 5, 6 | Unbonded topping | Mesh reinforcing; bond breaker on old concrete surface | — |

Setter, Leach & Lindstrom, Inc.; Minneapolis, Minnesota

**EXPANSION AND CONSTRUCTION JOINTS** 3

## GENERAL CONSIDERATIONS

1. Concrete strength usually 5000 psi at 28 days and at least 3000 psi at time of prestressing. Hardrock aggregate or lightweight concrete used. Low slump controlled mix is required to reduce shrinkage. Shrinkage after prestressing increases prestress losses.

2. Post-tensioning systems can be divided into three categories depending on whether the tendon is wire, strand, or bar. Wire systems use 0.25 in. diameter wires that have a minimum strength of 240,000 psi and are usually cut to length in the shop. Strand systems use tendons composed of seven wires wrapped together that have a minimum strength of 270,000 psi and are cut in the field. Bar systems use bars ranging in diameter from $5/8$ to $1\,3/8$ in. in diameter, with a minimum strength of 145,000 psi; they may be smooth or deformed. The system used will determine the type of anchorage used, which in turn will affect the size of blockout required in the edge of slab or beam for the anchorage to be recessed.

3. Tendons are greased and wrapped, or placed in conduits to reduce frictional losses during stressing operations. Length of continuous tendons limited to about 100 ft if stressed from one end. Long tendons require simultaneous stressing from both ends to reduce friction losses. Tendons may be grouted after stressing or left unbonded. Bonded tendons have structural advantages that are more important for beams and primary structural members.

4. Minimum average prestress (net prestress force/area of concrete) = 150 to 250 psi for flat plates, 200 to 500 psi for beams. Exceeding these values very much will cause excessive prestress losses because of creep.

5. Field inspection of post-tensioned concrete is critical to ensure proper size and location of tendons and to monitor the tendon stress. Tendon stress should be checked by measuring elongation of the tendon, and by gauge pressures on the stressing jack.

6. Provisions must be made for the shortening of post-tensioned beams and slabs caused by elastic compression, shrinkage, and creep. Shearwalls, curtain walls, or other stiff elements that adjoin post-tensioned members should be built after the post-tensioning has been done or should be isolated from these members with an expansion joint. Otherwise, additional post-tensioning force will be required to overcome the stiffness of the walls; cracking of the walls may also occur.

7. Fire tests have been conducted on prestressed beam and slab assemblies according to ASTM E119 test procedures; they compare favorably with conventionally reinforced concrete. There is little difference between beams using grouted tendons and those using ungrouted tendons.

8. References for further study:
   a. Post-Tensioning Institute, "Post-Tensioning Manual."
   b. Prestressed Concrete Institute, "Design Handbook for Precast and Prestressed Concrete."
   c. Lin, T.Y., "Design of Prestressed Concrete Structures."
   d. American Concrete Institute, "Building Code Requirements for Reinforced Concrete" (ACI-318-83).

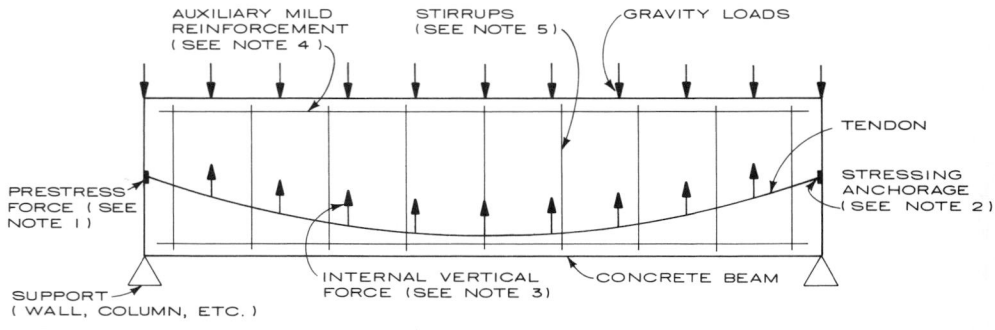

**PRESTRESSED OR POST-TENSIONED BEAM**

### NOTES

1. Prestressing force puts entire beam cross-section into compression, thereby reducing unwanted tension cracks.

2. Permanent tension is introduced into tendon and "locked in" with the stressing anchorage in one of two ways. In prestressed concrete, the tendon is elongated in a stressing bed before the concrete is poured. In post-tensioned concrete, the tendon is elongated after concrete has been poured and allowed to cure by means of hydraulic jacks pushing against the beam itself. The principle in both cases is the same. Post-tensioned beams permit casting at the site for members too large or heavy for transporting from factory to site.

3. Vertical internal force on beam is caused by tendency of tendon to "straighten out" under tension.

It reduces downward beam deflection and allows shallower beams and longer spans than in conventionally reinforced beams.

4. Auxiliary mild reinforcement provides additional strength, controls cracking, and produces more ductile behavior.

5. Stirrups are used to provide additional shear strength in the beam and to support the tendons and longitudinal mild reinforcement. Stirrups should be open at the top to allow the reinforcing to be fabricated and placed before the tendon is placed.

6. Shoring must be left in place until the post-tensioning operation is performed. After stressing, reshoring may be required to prevent overloading during additional construction.

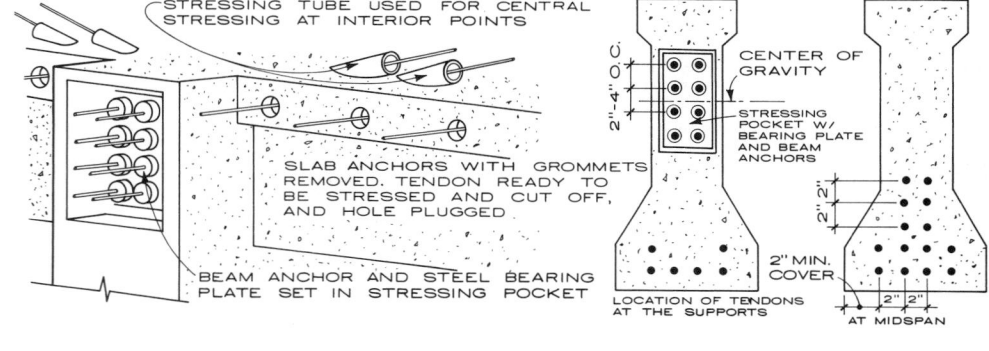

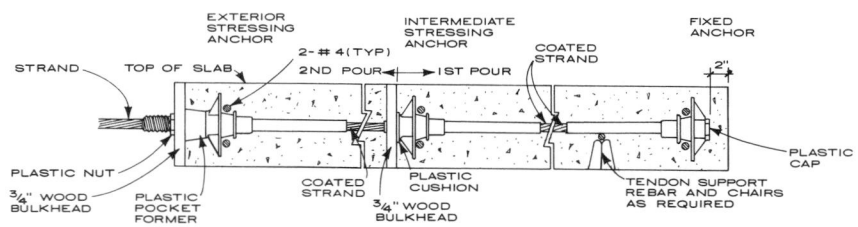

**TYPICAL UNBONDED SINGLE STRAND TENDON INSTALLATION**

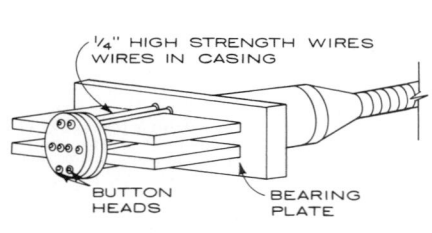

**8 WIRE BBRV POST-TENSIONING ANCHOR** (GROUTED)

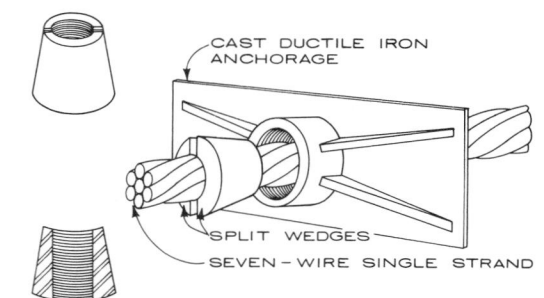

**SINGLE STRAND TENDON ANCHORAGE** (UNBONDED)

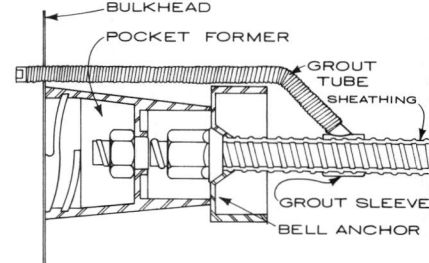

**THREAD BAR ANCHORAGE** (GROUTED)

Leo A. Daly, Architecture-Engineering-Planning; Omaha, Nebraska

**PRECAST CONCRETE**

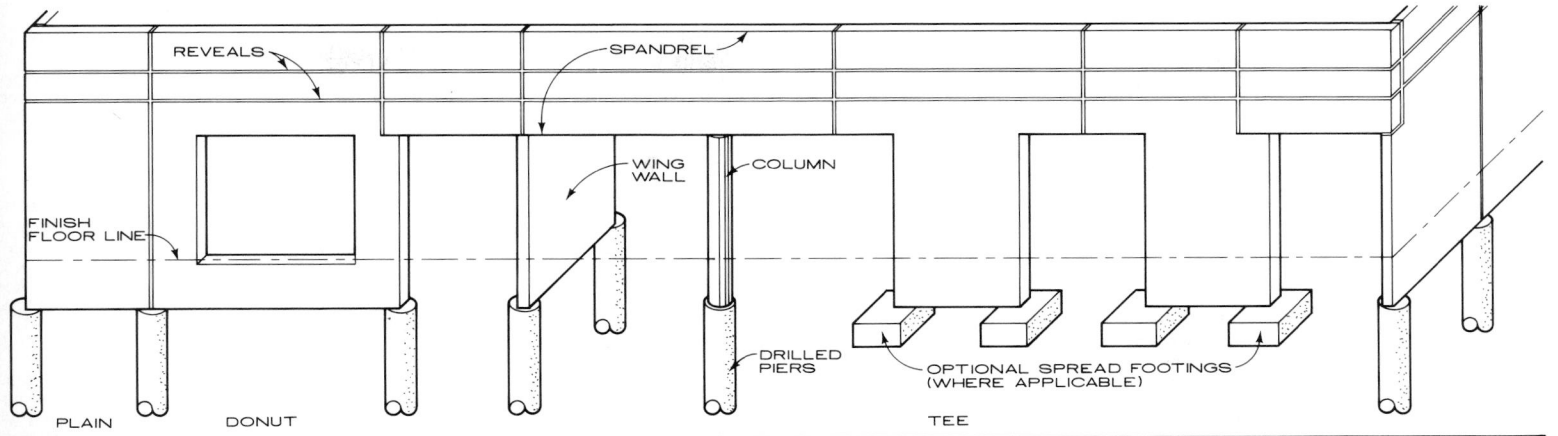

**PANEL TYPES**

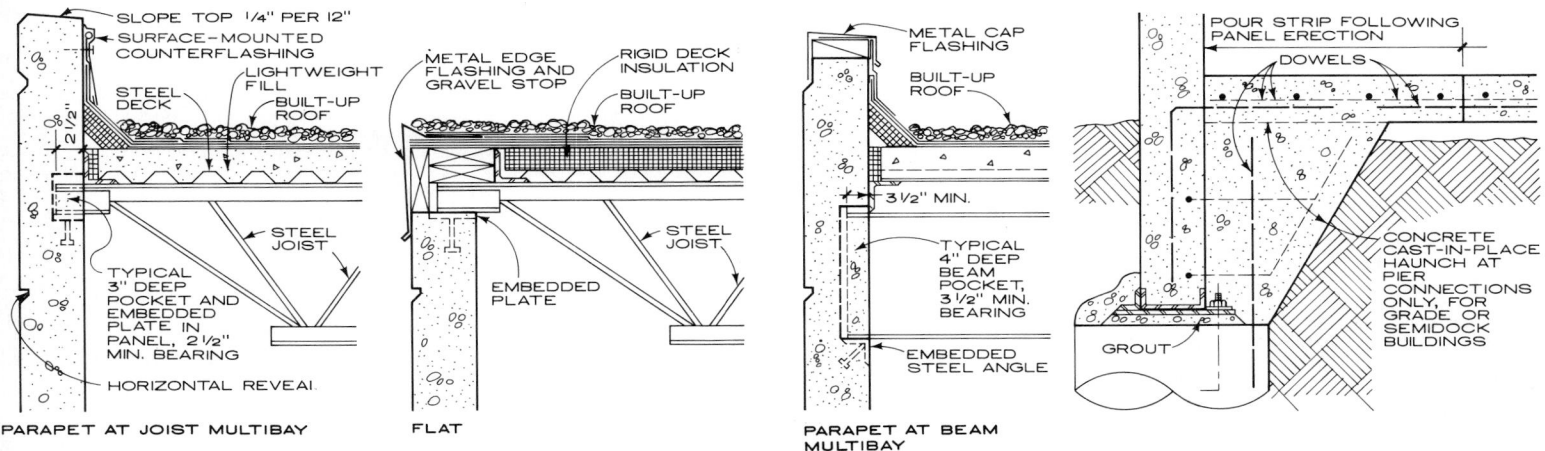

**LOADING BEARING PANEL CONNECTIONS AT ROOF**

**PIER CONNECTION**

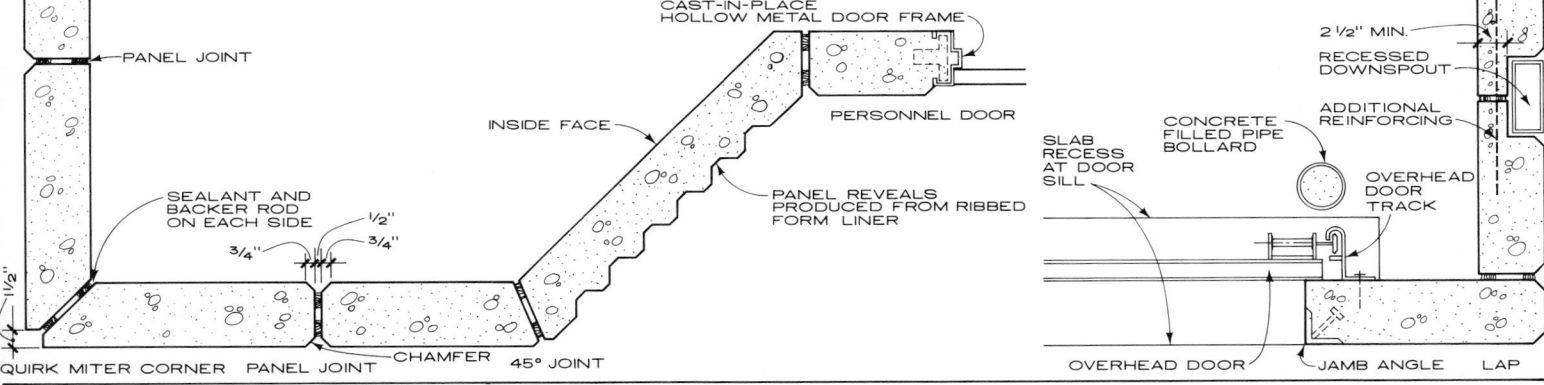

**PANEL DETAILS**

## GENERAL

Tilt-up concrete construction is a fast and economical method of enclosing a building with durable, load-bearing walls. Tilt-up concrete panels are cast horizontally on site utilizing the building's floor slab as a casting bed. Wood formwork is typically used to define the edges, reveals, details, and fenestrations of the panel. Once the concrete has reached sufficient strength, the panels are lifted, or "tilted up" by crane and placed on isolated footings where they are temporarily braced until they are attached to the interior structural framing system.

## DESIGN

Panel thickness varies from 5½ in. to 11¼ in., depending on height, span, depth of reveals, or surface finish, as well as local codes and construction practices. Full-height panel widths of 15 ft and weights of 30,000–50,000 lb are typical. Spans of 30 ft are common for spandrel panels, as are cantilevers of 10–15 ft. Panels are designed structurally to resist lifting stresses, which frequently exceed in-place loads. Floor slab design must accommodate panel and crane loads.

## FINISH

Most of the finishes used for factory precast concrete are possible in tilt-up construction. Panels can be cast either facedown or faceup, depending on desired finish and formwork methods. The facedown method, however, is usually easier to erect. Casting method, finish desired, and available aggregates will affect concrete mix design. Control of the concrete mix design and placement of the concrete in the forms are more difficult than with factory cast units. Discoloration will occur if cracks and joints in the casting bed are not sealed. Commonly used finishes are as follows:

Sandblast (light, medium, or heavy exposure)
Fractured (similar to bushhammer)
Form liner (metal deck, plastic, fiberglass, EPS)
Paint
Brick/tile veneer
Aggregate (cast facedown in sand bed)

Harry Gendel Architects; Houston, Texas
Haynes Whaley Associates, Inc., Structural Engineers; Houston, Texas

**PRECAST CONCRETE**    3

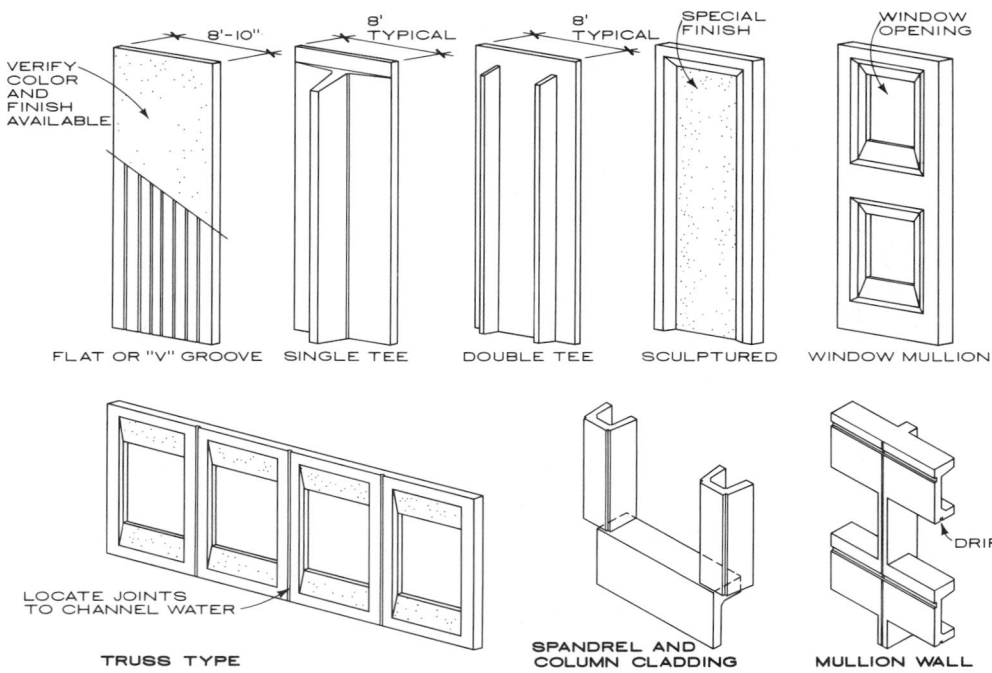

FLAT OR "V" GROOVE   SINGLE TEE   DOUBLE TEE   SCULPTURED   WINDOW MULLION

TRUSS TYPE   SPANDREL AND COLUMN CLADDING   MULLION WALL

**PANEL VARIATIONS**

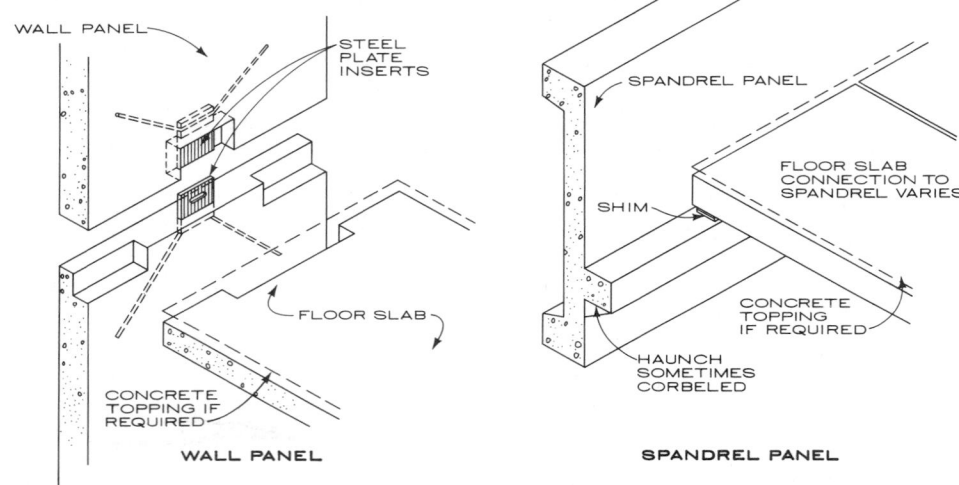

WALL PANEL   SPANDREL PANEL

**BEARING PANEL CONDITIONS**

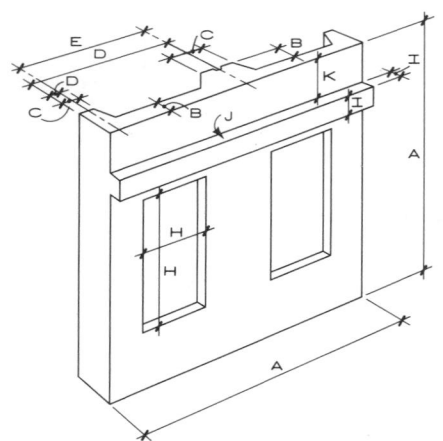

A. Overall height and width measured at face adjacent to mold at time of casting or neutral axis of ribbed member:
   10 ft or under: $\pm \frac{1}{8}$ in.
   10 ft to 20 ft: $\pm \frac{1}{8}$ in. to $\pm \frac{3}{16}$ in.
   20 ft to 30 ft: $\pm \frac{1}{8}$ in. to $\pm \frac{1}{4}$ in.
   Above 30 ft: $\pm \frac{1}{4}$ in.

B. Thickness, total or flange: $\frac{1}{4}$ in. to $\frac{1}{8}$ in.

C. Rib thickness: $\pm \frac{1}{8}$ in.

D. Rib to edge of flange: $\pm \frac{1}{8}$ in.

E. Distance between ribs: $\pm \frac{1}{8}$ in.

F. Angular deviation of plane of side mold: $\frac{1}{32}$ in. per 3 in. of depth or $\frac{1}{16}$ in. total, whichever is greater

G. Deviation from square or designated skew (difference in length of the two diagonal measurements): $\frac{1}{8}$ in. per 6 ft or $\frac{1}{4}$ in. total, whichever is greater

H. Length and width of blockouts and openings with one unit: $\pm \frac{1}{4}$ in.

I. Depth and width of haunches: $\pm \frac{1}{4}$ in.

J. Haunch-bearing surface deviation from specified plane: $\frac{1}{8}$ in.

K. Difference in relative position of adjacent haunch-bearing surfaces from specified relative position: $\frac{1}{4}$ in.

All other tolerances not defined above: $\pm \frac{1}{8}$ in.

**DIMENSIONAL TOLERANCES FOR FLAT AND VERTICAL RIBBED WALL PANELS**

## WALL PANELS

Carefully distinguish between the more specialized architectural wall panel and the structural wall panel which is a derivative of floor systems. Always work with manufacturers early in the design process. Careful attention must be given to manufacturing and joint tolerances during design. Thoroughly examine joint sealants for adhesion and expected joint movement.

## FINISHES

Form liner molds provide a wide variety of smooth and textured finishes. Finishes after casting but prior to hardening include exposed aggregate, broom, trowel, screed, float, or stippled. After hardening finishes include acid etching, sandblasting, honed, polished, or hammered rib.

## COLORS

Select a color range, as complete uniformity cannot be guaranteed. White cement offers the best color uniformity; gray cement is subject to color variations even when supplied from one source. Pigments require high-quality manufacturing and curing standards. Fine aggregate color requires control of the mixture graduation; coarse aggregate color should be chosen for durability and appearance.

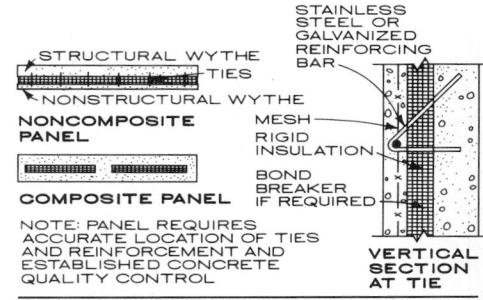

NONCOMPOSITE PANEL

COMPOSITE PANEL

NOTE: PANEL REQUIRES ACCURATE LOCATION OF TIES AND REINFORCEMENT AND ESTABLISHED CONCRETE QUALITY CONTROL

VERTICAL SECTION AT TIE

**SANDWICH WALL CONSTRUCTION**

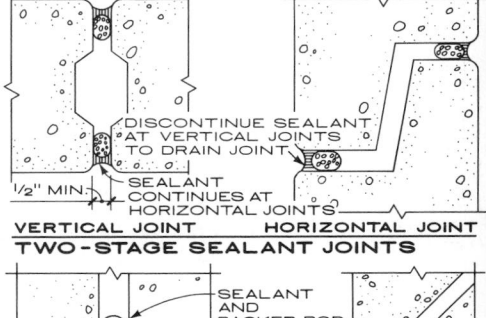

VERTICAL JOINT   HORIZONTAL JOINT

**TWO-STAGE SEALANT JOINTS**

RECESSED JOINT   QUIRK DETAIL

**JOINT DETAILS**

JOINT TAPER: $\frac{1}{40}$ IN. PER FT LENGTH (MAX. LENGTH OF TAPERING IN ONE DIRECTION OF 10 FT)

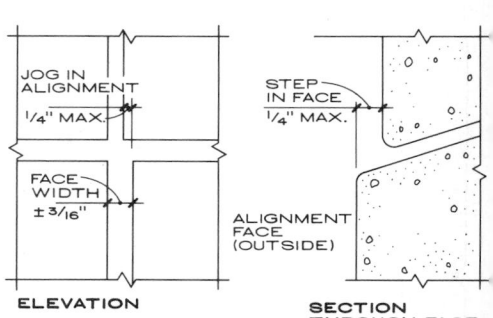

ELEVATION   SECTION THROUGH FACE

**JOINT TOLERANCES**

Bruce Lambert, AIA; Columbia, South Carolina

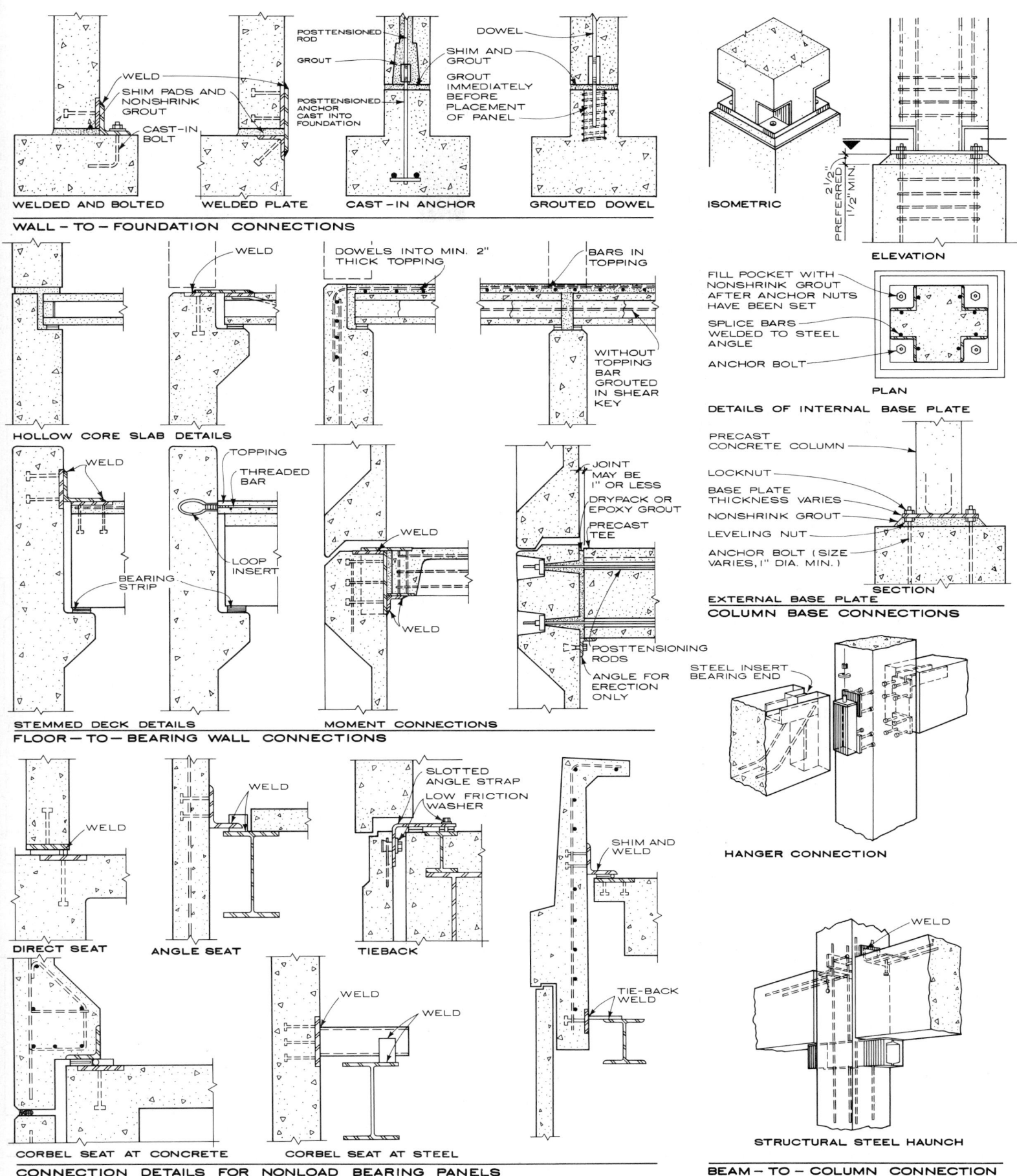

**WELDED AND BOLTED**

WELD
SHIM PADS AND NONSHRINK GROUT
CAST-IN BOLT

**WELDED PLATE**

WELD

**CAST-IN ANCHOR**

POSTTENSIONED ROD
GROUT
POSTTENSIONED ANCHOR CAST INTO FOUNDATION

**GROUTED DOWEL**

DOWEL
SHIM AND GROUT
GROUT IMMEDIATELY BEFORE PLACEMENT OF PANEL

## WALL-TO-FOUNDATION CONNECTIONS

WELD
DOWELS INTO MIN. 2" THICK TOPPING
BARS IN TOPPING
WITHOUT TOPPING BAR GROUTED IN SHEAR KEY

## HOLLOW CORE SLAB DETAILS

WELD
TOPPING
THREADED BAR
LOOP INSERT
BEARING STRIP

JOINT MAY BE 1" OR LESS
DRYPACK OR EPOXY GROUT
PRECAST TEE
WELD
WELD
POSTTENSIONING RODS
ANGLE FOR ERECTION ONLY

**STEMMED DECK DETAILS**     **MOMENT CONNECTIONS**

## FLOOR-TO-BEARING WALL CONNECTIONS

WELD

**DIRECT SEAT**

WELD

**ANGLE SEAT**

SLOTTED ANGLE STRAP
LOW FRICTION WASHER

**TIEBACK**

SHIM AND WELD

WELD

**CORBEL SEAT AT CONCRETE**

WELD
WELD

**CORBEL SEAT AT STEEL**

TIE-BACK WELD

## CONNECTION DETAILS FOR NONLOAD BEARING PANELS

**ISOMETRIC**

2 1/2" PREFERRED 1 1/2" MIN.

**ELEVATION**

FILL POCKET WITH NONSHRINK GROUT AFTER ANCHOR NUTS HAVE BEEN SET
SPLICE BARS WELDED TO STEEL ANGLE
ANCHOR BOLT

**PLAN**

**DETAILS OF INTERNAL BASE PLATE**

PRECAST CONCRETE COLUMN
LOCKNUT
BASE PLATE THICKNESS VARIES
NONSHRINK GROUT
LEVELING NUT
ANCHOR BOLT (SIZE VARIES, 1" DIA. MIN.)

**SECTION**

**EXTERNAL BASE PLATE**

## COLUMN BASE CONNECTIONS

STEEL INSERT BEARING END

**HANGER CONNECTION**

WELD

**STRUCTURAL STEEL HAUNCH**

## BEAM-TO-COLUMN CONNECTION

Bruce Lambert, AIA; Columbia, South Carolina

**PRECAST CONCRETE** 3

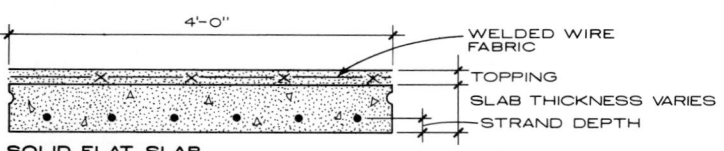
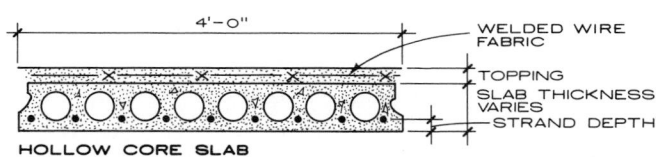

SOLID FLAT SLAB  HOLLOW CORE SLAB

## FLAT DECK MEMBERS

**TABLE 1** *
**SAFE SUPERIMPOSED SERVICE LOADS (PSF) FOR SOLID FLAT SLABS (4 FT WIDTH)**

| SLAB THICKNESS (IN.) | SLAB DESIGNATION | TOPPING THICKNESS (IN.) | SPAN (FT) | | | | | | | | | | | | | | |
|---|---|---|---|---|---|---|---|---|---|---|---|---|---|---|---|---|---|
| | | | 11 | 12 | 13 | 14 | 15 | 16 | 17 | 18 | 19 | 20 | 21 | 22 | 23 | 24 | 25 |
| 4" (STRAND DESIGNATION CODE: 58-S) | FS4 | NONE | 212 | 180 | 154 | 127 | 104 | 86 | 70 | | | | | | | | |
| | FS4+2 | 2 | | | 274 | 214 | 166 | 127 | 95 | | | | | | | | |
| 6" (STRAND DESIGNATION CODE: 78-S) | FS6 | NONE | 320 | 287 | 257 | 236 | 213 | 196 | 183 | 168 | 155 | 144 | 134 | 126 | 109 | 94 | 81 |
| | FS6+2 | 2 | | | | | 298 | 273 | 252 | 231 | 216 | 199 | 185 | 169 | 140 | 115 | 93 |
| 8" (STRAND DESIGNATION CODE: 68-S) | FS8 | NONE | | | | 318 | 291 | 266 | 245 | 227 | 209 | 196 | 181 | 169 | 155 | 136 | 119 |
| | FS8+2 | 2 | | | | | | | | 304 | 283 | 261 | 245 | 225 | 197 | 167 | 140 |

**TABLE 2** *
**SAFE SUPERIMPOSED SERVICE LOADS (PSF) FOR HOLLOW CORE SLABS (4 FT WIDTH)**

| SLAB THICKNESS (IN.) | SLAB DESIGNATION | TOPPING THICKNESS (IN.) | SPAN (FT) | | | | | | | | | | | | | | |
|---|---|---|---|---|---|---|---|---|---|---|---|---|---|---|---|---|---|
| | | | 12 | 14 | 16 | 18 | 20 | 22 | 24 | 26 | 28 | 30 | 32 | 34 | 36 | 38 | 40 |
| 6" (STRAND DESIGNATION CODE: 66-S) | 4HC6 | NONE | 257 | 197 | 154 | 113 | 84 | 63 | 47 | | | | | | | | |
| | 4HC6+2 | 2 | | 278 | 215 | 153 | 102 | 65 | | | | | | | | | |
| 8" (STRAND DESIGNATION CODE: 58-S) | 4HC8 | NONE | | | | 275 | 221 | 175 | 140 | 112 | 91 | 73 | 59 | | | | |
| | 4HC8+2 | 2 | | | | | 273 | 215 | 170 | 136 | 108 | 84 | 60 | | | | |
| 10" (STRAND DESIGNATION CODE: 78-S) | 4HC10 | NONE | | | | | 298 | 264 | 237 | 214 | 192 | 160 | 134 | 113 | 95 | 80 | 67 |
| | 4HC10+2 | 2 | | | | | | | 278 | 250 | 218 | 181 | 150 | 125 | 103 | 85 | 67 |
| 12" (STRAND DESIGNATION CODE: 68-S) | 4HC12 | NONE | | | | | | | | | 182 | 165 | 150 | 120 | 109 | 92 | 78 |
| | 4HC12+2 | 2 | | | | | | | 249 | 224 | 200 | 183 | 164 | 137 | 114 | 95 | 78 |

## LOAD TABLES FOR FLAT DECK MEMBERS

*NOTE: 1. NORMAL WEIGHT (150 PCF) CONCRETE SLAB AND TOPPING
2. SLABS $f_c$ = 5000 PSI
3. STRAND DESIGNATION CODE
7 8 - S
— STRAIGHT
— DIAMETER OF STRANDS IN 16THS
— NUMBER OF STRANDS

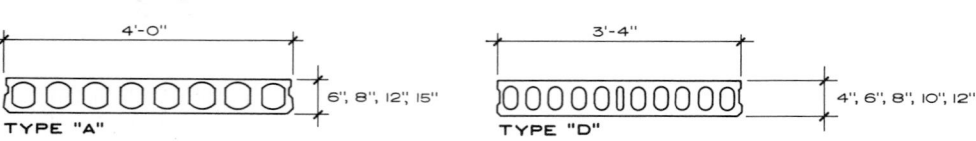

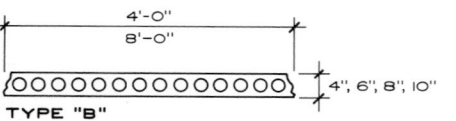

TYPE "A"  TYPE "D"

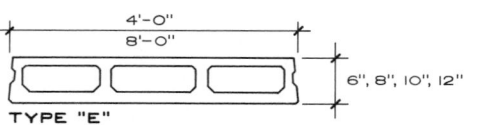

TYPE "B"  TYPE "E"

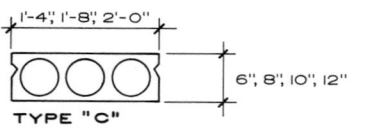

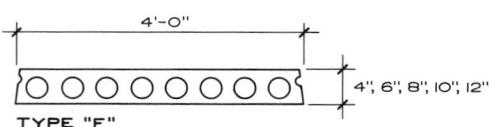

TYPE "C"  TYPE "F"

## HOLLOW CORE SLAB TYPES
**ALL SECTIONS ARE NOT AVAILABLE FROM ALL PRODUCERS
CHECK AVAILABILITY WITH LOCAL MANUFACTURERS**

### NOTES

1. Normal weight (150 pcf) or lightweight concrete (115 pcf) is used in standard slab construction. Topping concrete is usually normal weight concrete with a cylinder strength of 3000 psi. All units are prestressed with strand release when concrete strength is 3500 psi.

2. Strands are available in various sizes and strengths according to individual manufacturers. Strand placement may vary, which will change load capacity, camber values, and fire resistance. Contact the local supplier for strand placement and allowable loading.

3. Camber will vary substantially depending on slab design, span, and loading. Nonstructural components attached to members may be affected by camber variations. Calculations of topping quantities should recognize camber variations.

4. Safe superimposed service loads include a dead load of 10 psf for untopped concrete and 15 psf for topped concrete. The remainder is live load.

5. Smooth or textured soffits may be available in some types; check with the supplier.

Bruce Lambert, AIA; Columbia, South Carolina

## PRECAST CONCRETE

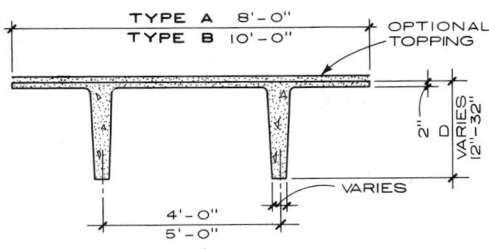

**DOUBLE TEE (DT)**

TYPE A  8'-0"
TYPE B  10'-0"
OPTIONAL TOPPING
2"
D VARIES (12"-32")
VARIES
4'-0"
5'-0"

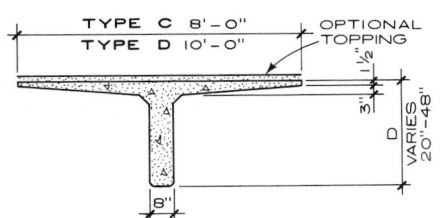

**SINGLE TEE (ST)**

TYPE C  8'-0"
TYPE D  10'-0"
OPTIONAL TOPPING
1½"
3"
D VARIES (20"-48")
8"

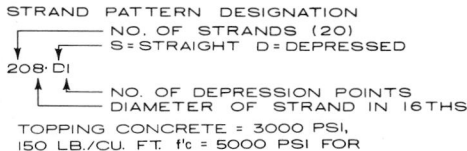

STRAND PATTERN DESIGNATION
NO. OF STRANDS (20)
S = STRAIGHT  D = DEPRESSED
208 · D1
NO. OF DEPRESSION POINTS
DIAMETER OF STRAND IN 16THS
TOPPING CONCRETE = 3000 PSI,
150 LB./CU. FT.  f'c = 5000 PSI FOR
NORMAL OR LIGHTWEIGHT DECK

**NOTES**

1. Safe loads shown indicate dead load of 10 psf for untopped members and 15 psf for topped members. Remainder is live load.
2. Designers should contact the manufacturers in the geographic area of the proposed structure to determine availability, exact dimensions, and load tables for various sections.
3. Camber should be checked for its effect on non-structural members (i.e., partitions, folding doors, etc.), which should be placed with adequate allowance for error. Calculations of topping quantities should also recognize camber variations.
4. Normal weight concrete is assumed to be 150 lb/cu ft; lightweight concrete is assumed to be 115 lb/cu ft.

**STEMMED DECK MEMBERS**
SEE CHART FOR APPROXIMATE MAX. SPANS

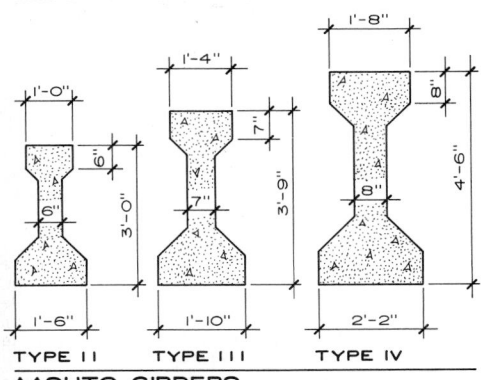

TYPE II        TYPE III        TYPE IV

**AASHTO GIRDERS**

**TABLE OF SAFE SUPERIMPOSED SERVICE LOAD\* (PLF) FOR AASHTO GIRDER**

| DESIG-NATION | NO. OF STRANDS | SPAN (FT) 36 | 40 | 44 | 48 | 52 | 56 | 60 |
|---|---|---|---|---|---|---|---|---|
| Type II | 14 | 3520 | 2785 | 2241 | 1826 | | | |
| Type III | 22 | 7231 | 5757 | 4667 | 3837 | 3192 | 2679 | 2266 |
| Type IV | 32 | | 9848 | 7996 | 6588 | 5492 | 4622 | 3920 |

Bruce Lambert, AIA; Columbia, South Carolina

## APPROXIMATE MAXIMUM SPAN FOR STEMMED DECK SECTIONS

| DECK TYPE | DEPTH D (IN.) | CONCRETE WEIGHT | DESIGNATION | TOPPING DEPTH (IN.) | STRAND DESIGNATION | MAX. SPAN (FT) | SAFE LOAD (PSF) |
|---|---|---|---|---|---|---|---|
| A | 12 | Normal weight | 8DT12 | 0 | 88 · D1 | 40 | 40 |
| | | | 8DT12 + 2 | 2 | 68 · D1 | 34 | 39 |
| | | Lightweight | 8LDT12 | 0 | 68 · D1 | 40 | 35 |
| | | | 8LDT12 + 2 | 2 | 68 · D1 | 36 | 36 |
| A | 18 | Normal weight | 8DT18 | 0 | 108 · D1 | 58 | 34 |
| | | | 8DT18 + 2 | 2 | 88 · D1 | 46 | 48 |
| | | Lightweight | 8LDT18 | 0 | 108 · D1 | 60 | 37 |
| | | | 8LDT18 + 2 | 2 | 88 · D1 | 50 | 39 |
| A | 24 | Normal weight | 8DT24 | 0 | 148 · D1 | 74 | 38 |
| | | | 8DT24 + 2 | 2 | 128 · D1 | 60 | 56 |
| | | Lightweight | 8LDT24 | 0 | 148 · D1 | 80 | 35 |
| | | | 8LDT24 + 2 | 2 | 108 · D1 | 62 | 44 |
| A | 32 | Normal weight | 8DT32 | 0 | 228 · D1 | 88 | 56 |
| | | | 8DT32 + 2 | 2 | 208 · D1 | 76 | 76 |
| | | Lightweight | 8LDT32 | 0 | 228 · D1 | 100 | 41 |
| | | | 8LDT32 + 2 | 2 | 208 · D1 | 82 | 67 |
| B | 32 | Normal weight | 10DT32 | 0 | 228 · D1 | 86 | 49 |
| | | | 10DT32 + 2 | 2 | 208 · D1 | 74 | 62 |
| | | Lightweight | 10LDT32 | 0 | 228 · D1 | 98 | 35 |
| | | | 10LDT32 + 2 | 2 | 208 · D1 | 78 | 59 |
| C | 36 | Normal weight | 8ST36 | 0 | 228 · D1 | 100 | 44 |
| | | | 8ST36 + 2 | 2 | 188 · D1 | 82 | 61 |
| | | Lightweight | 8LST36 | 0 | 228 · D1 | 110 | 38 |
| | | | 8LST36 + 2 | 2 | 168 · D1 | 86 | 50 |
| D | 48 | Normal weight | 10ST48 | 0 | 248 · D1 | 112 | 42 |
| | | Lightweight | 10LST48 | 0 | 248 · D1 | 120 | 41 |

## TABLE OF SAFE SUPERIMPOSED SERVICE LOAD\* (PLF) FOR PRECAST BEAM SECTIONS

| TYPE | DESIGNATION | NO. STRAND | H (IN.) | H1/H2 (IN.) | SPAN (FT) 18 | 22 | 26 | 30 | 34 | 38 | 42 | 46 | 50 |
|---|---|---|---|---|---|---|---|---|---|---|---|---|---|
| RECTANGULAR BEAM (B = 12" OR 16") | 12RB24 | 10 | 24 | | 6726 | 4413 | 3083 | 2248 | 1684 | 1288 | 1000 | | |
| | 12RB32 | 13 | 32 | | | 7858 | 5524 | 4059 | 3080 | 2394 | 1894 | 1519 | 1230 |
| | 16RB24 | 13 | 24 | | 8847 | 5803 | 4052 | 2954 | 2220 | 1705 | 1330 | | |
| | 16RB32 | 18 | 32 | | | 7434 | 5464 | 4147 | 3224 | 2549 | 2036 | 1642 | |
| | 16RB40 | 22 | 40 | | | | 8647 | 6599 | 5163 | 4117 | 3332 | 2728 | |
| L-SHAPED BEAM | 18LB20 | 9 | 20 | 12/8 | 5068 | 3303 | 2288 | 1650 | 1218 | | | | |
| | 18LB28 | 12 | 28 | 16/12 | | 6578 | 4600 | 3360 | 2531 | 1949 | 1524 | 1200 | |
| | 18LB36 | 16 | 36 | 24/12 | | | 7903 | 5807 | 4405 | 3422 | 2706 | 2168 | 1755 |
| | 18LB44 | 19 | 44 | 28/16 | | | 8729 | 6666 | 5219 | 4166 | 3370 | 2752 | |
| | 18LB52 | 23 | 52 | 36/16 | | | | 9538 | 7486 | 5992 | 4871 | 4007 | |
| | 18LB60 | 27 | 60 | 44/16 | | | | | 8116 | 6630 | 5481 | | |
| INVERTED TEE BEAM | 24IT20 | 9 | 20 | 12/8 | 5376 | 3494 | 2412 | 1726 | 1266 | | | | |
| | 24IT28 | 13 | 28 | 16/12 | | 6951 | 4848 | 3529 | 2648 | 2030 | | | |
| | 24IT36 | 16 | 36 | 24/12 | | | 8337 | 6127 | 4644 | 3598 | 2836 | 2265 | 1825 |
| | 24IT44 | 20 | 44 | 28/16 | | | 9300 | 7075 | 5514 | 4378 | 3525 | 2868 | |
| | 24IT52 | 24 | 52 | 36/16 | | | | 7916 | 6326 | 5132 | 4213 | | |
| | 24IT60 | 28 | 60 | 44/16 | | | | | 8616 | 7025 | 5800 | | |

\*Safe loads shown indicate 50% dead load and 50% live load; 800 psi top tension has been allowed, therefore additional top reinforcement is required.

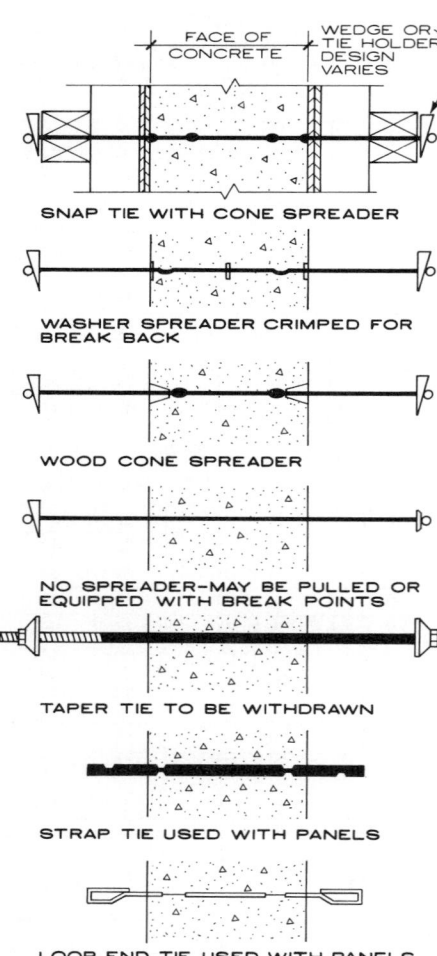

SNAP TIE WITH CONE SPREADER

WASHER SPREADER CRIMPED FOR BREAK BACK

WOOD CONE SPREADER

NO SPREADER—MAY BE PULLED OR EQUIPPED WITH BREAK POINTS

TAPER TIE TO BE WITHDRAWN

STRAP TIE USED WITH PANELS

LOOP END TIE USED WITH PANELS

**TYPICAL SINGLE MEMBER TIES**

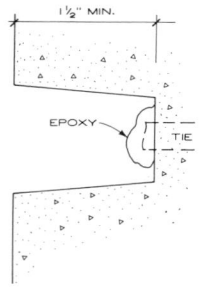
EPOXY OVER TIE

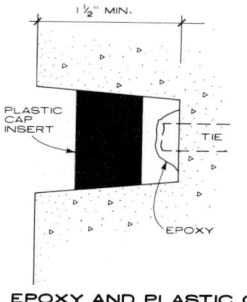
EPOXY AND PLASTIC CAP

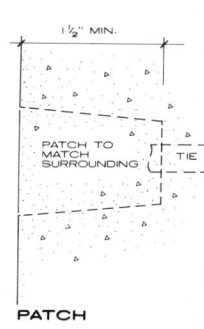
PATCH

**TIE HOLE TREATMENT OPTIONS**

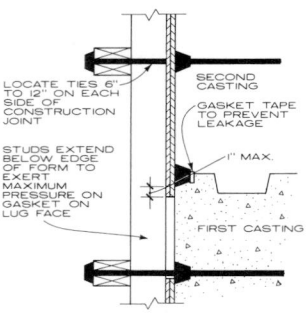
**TYPICAL CONSTRUCTION JOINT**

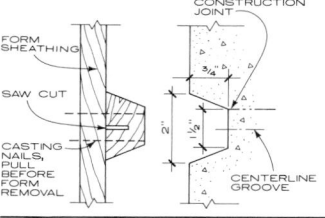
**RUSTICATION AT CONSTRUCTION JOINT**

## CONCRETE SURFACES—GENERAL

The variety of architectural finishes is as extensive as the cost and effort expended to achieve them. There are three basic ways to improve or change the appearance of concrete:

1. Changing materials, that is, using a colored matrix and exposed aggregates.
2. Changing the mold or form by such means as a form liner.
3. By treating or tooling the concrete surface in the final stages of hardening.

The aim is to obtain maximum benefit from one of three features—color, texture, and pattern—all of which are interrelated. Color is the easiest method of changing the appearance of concrete. It should not be used on a plain concrete surface with a series of panels, since color matches are difficult to achieve. The exception is possible when white cement is used, usually as a base for the pigment to help reduce changes of color variation. Since white cement is expensive, many effects are tried with gray cement to avoid an entire plain surface. Colored concrete is most effective when it is used with an exposed aggregate finish.

## FORM LINERS

1. Sandblasted Douglas fir or long leaf yellow pine dressed one side away from the concrete surface.
2. Flexible steel strip formwork adapted to curved surfaces (Schwellmer System).
3. Resin coated, striated, or sandblasted plywood.
4. Rubber mats.
5. Thermoplastic sheets with high gloss or texture laid over stone, for example.
6. Formed plastics.
7. Plaster of Paris molds for sculptured work.
8. Clay (sculpturing and staining concrete).
9. Hardboard (screen side).

10. Standard steel forms.
11. Wood boarding and reversed battens.
12. Square-edged lumber dressed one side.
13. Resawn wood boards.

## RELEASE AGENTS

1. Oils, petroleum based, used on wood, concrete, and steel forms.
2. Soft soaps.
3. Talcum.
4. Whitewash used on wood with tannin in conjunction with oils.
5. Calcium stearate powder.
6. Silicones used on steel forms.
7. Plastics used on wood forms.
8. Lacquers used on plywood and plaster forms.
9. Resins used on plywood forms.
10. Sodium silicate.
11. Membrane used over any form.
12. Grease used on plaster forms.
13. Epoxy resin plastic used on plywood.

## CATEGORIES OF COMMON AGGREGATE

1. QUARTZ: Clear, white, rose.
2. MARBLE: Green, yellow, red, pink, blue, gray, white, black.
3. GRANITE: Pink, gray, black, white.
4. CERAMIC: Full range.
5. VITREOUS/GLASS: Full range.

## CRITICAL FACTORS AFFECTING SURFACES

DESIGN DRAWINGS should show form details, including openings, control joints, construction joints, expansion joints, and other important specifics.

1. CEMENT: Types and brands.
2. AGGREGATES: Sources of coarse and fine aggregates.
3. TECHNIQUES: Uniformity in mixing and placing.
4. FORMS: Closure techniques or concealing joints in formwork materials.
5. SLUMP CONTROL: Ensure compliance with design.
6. CURING METHODS: Ensure compliance with design.

## TIES

A concrete tie is a tensile unit adapted to hold concrete forms secure against the lateral pressure of unhardened concrete. Two general types of concrete ties exist:

1. Continuous single member where the tensile unit is a single piece and the holding device engages the tensile unit against the exterior of the form. Standard types: working load = 2500 to 5000 lb.
2. Internal disconnecting where the tensile unit has an inner part with threaded connections to removable external members, which have suitable devices of securing them against the outside of the form. Working load = 6000 to 36,000 lb.

## GUIDELINES FOR PATCHING

1. Design the patch mix to match the original, with small amount of white cement; may eliminate coarse aggregate or hand place it. Trial and error is the only reliable match method.
2. Saturate area with water and apply bonding agent to base of hole and to water of patch mix.
3. Pack patch mix to density of original.
4. Place exposed aggregate by hand.
5. Bristle brush after setup to match existing material.
6. Moist cure to prevent shrinking.
7. Use form or finish to match original.

## CHECKLIST IN PLANNING FOR ARCHITECTURAL CONCRETE PLACING TECHNIQUES:

Pumping vs. bottom drop or other type of bucket.

1. FORMING SYSTEM: Evaluate whether architectural concrete forms can also be used for structural concrete.
2. SHOP DRAWINGS: Determine form quality and steel placement.
3. VIBRATORS: Verify that proper size, frequency, and power are used.
4. RELEASE AGENTS: Consider form material, color impact of agents, and possible use throughout job.
5. CURING COMPOUND: Determine how fast it wears off.
6. SAMPLES: Require approval of forms and finishes. Field mock-up is advised to evaluate appearance of panel and quality of workmanship.

D. Neil Rankins; SHWC, Inc.; Dallas, Texas

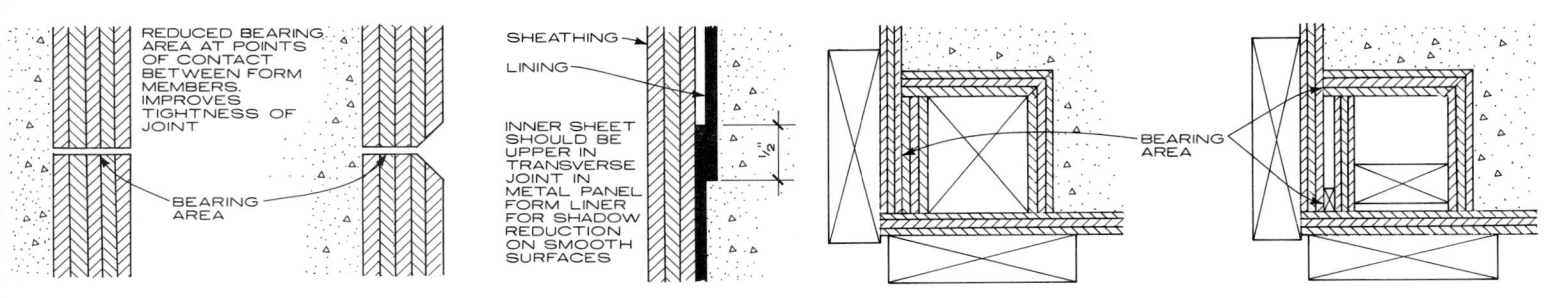

| USUAL | RECOMMENDED | LINER JOINT | USUAL | RECOMMENDED |

**FORM JOINTS**

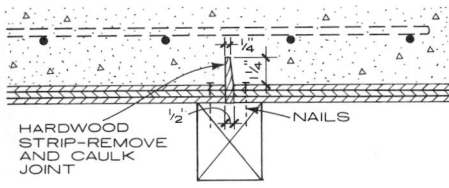

**RUBBER FORM INSERT**

HARDWOOD STRIP—REMOVE AND CAULK JOINT / NAILS

**WOOD FORM INSERT**

SHEET METAL WITH WOOD FILLER—REMOVE AND CAULK JOINT

**SHEET METAL FORM INSERT**

**CONTROL JOINTS**

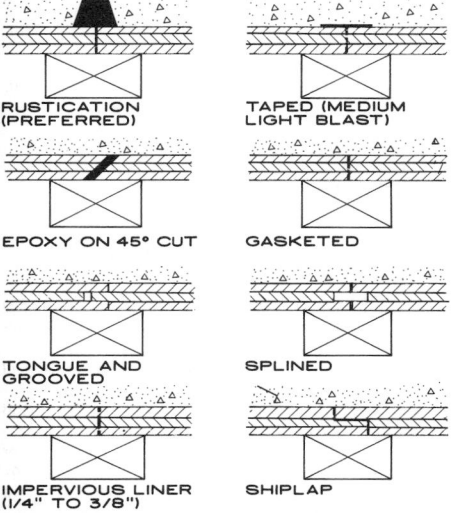

RUSTICATION (PREFERRED) | TAPED (MEDIUM LIGHT BLAST)

EPOXY ON 45° CUT | GASKETED

TONGUE AND GROOVED | SPLINED

IMPERVIOUS LINER (1/4" TO 3/8") | SHIPLAP

**PLYWOOD BUTT JOINTS FOR EXPOSED AGGREGATE FINISHES**

## CATEGORIES OF ARCHITECTURAL CONCRETE SURFACES

| CATEGORY | FINISH | COLOR | FORMS | CRITICAL DETAILS |
|---|---|---|---|---|
| 1. As cast | Remains as is after form removal—usually board marks or wood grain | Cement first influence, fine aggregate second influence | Plastic best<br>All others<br>• Wire-brushed plywood<br>• Sandblasted plywood<br>• Exposed-grain plywood<br>• Unfinished sheathing lumber<br>• Ammonia sprayed wood<br>• Tongue-and-groove bands spaced | Slump = 2½″ to 3½″<br><br>Joinery of forms<br><br>Proper release agent<br><br>Point form joints to avoid marks |
| 2. Abrasive blasted surfaces<br>A. Brush blast | Uniform scour cleaning | Cement plus fine aggregate have equal influence | All smooth | Scouring after 7 days<br><br>Slump = 2½″ to 3½″ |
| B. Light blast | Sandblast to expose fine and some coarse aggregate | Fine aggregate primary coarse aggregate plus cement secondary | All smooth | 10% more coarse aggregate<br><br>Slump = 2½″ to 3½″<br><br>Blasting between 7 and 45 days |
| C. Medium exposed aggregate | Sandblasted to expose coarse aggregate | Coarse aggregate | All smooth | Higher than normal coarse aggregate<br><br>Slump = 2″ to 3″<br><br>Blast before 7 days |
| D. Heavy exposed aggregate | Sandblasted to expose coarse aggregate<br><br>80% viable | Coarse aggregate | All smooth | Special mix coarse aggregate<br><br>Slump = 0″ to 2″<br><br>Blast within 24 hours<br><br>Use high frequency vibrator |
| 3. Chemical retardation of surface set | Chemicals expose aggregate<br><br>Aggregate can be adhered to surface | Coarse aggregate and cement | All smooth, glass fiber best | Chemical Grade determines etch depth<br><br>Stripping scheduled to prevent long drying between stripping and washoff |
| 4. Mechanically fractured surfaces, scaling, bush hammering, jackhammering, tooling | Varied | Cement, fine and coarse<br><br>Aggregate | Textured | Aggregate particles ⅜″ for scaling and tooling<br><br>Aggregate particles |
| 5. Combination/fluted | Striated/abrasive blasted/irregular pattern<br><br>Corrugated/abrasive<br><br>Vertical rusticated/abrasive blasted<br><br>Reeded and bush hammered<br><br>Reeded and hammered<br><br>Reeded and chiseled | The shallower the surface, the more influence aggregate fines and cement have | Wood or rubber strips, corrugated sheet metal or glass fiber | Depends on type of finish desired<br><br>Wood fluke kerfed and nailed loosely |

D. Neil Rankins; SHWC, Inc.; Dallas, Texas

**ARCHITECTURAL CONCRETE** 3

## NOTES

1. See page on stair dimensions for code requirements for stairs.
2. Structural designer to determine reinforcement and verify structural assumptions.

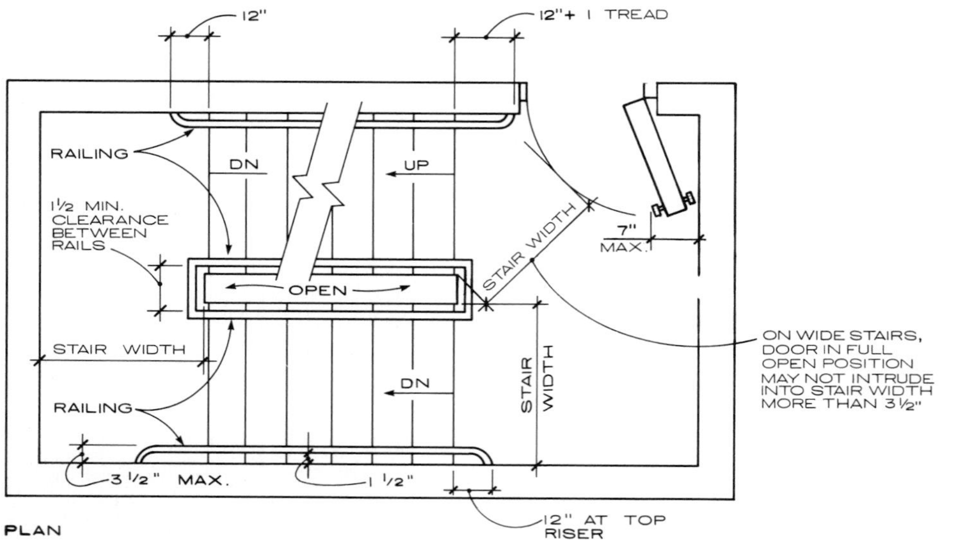

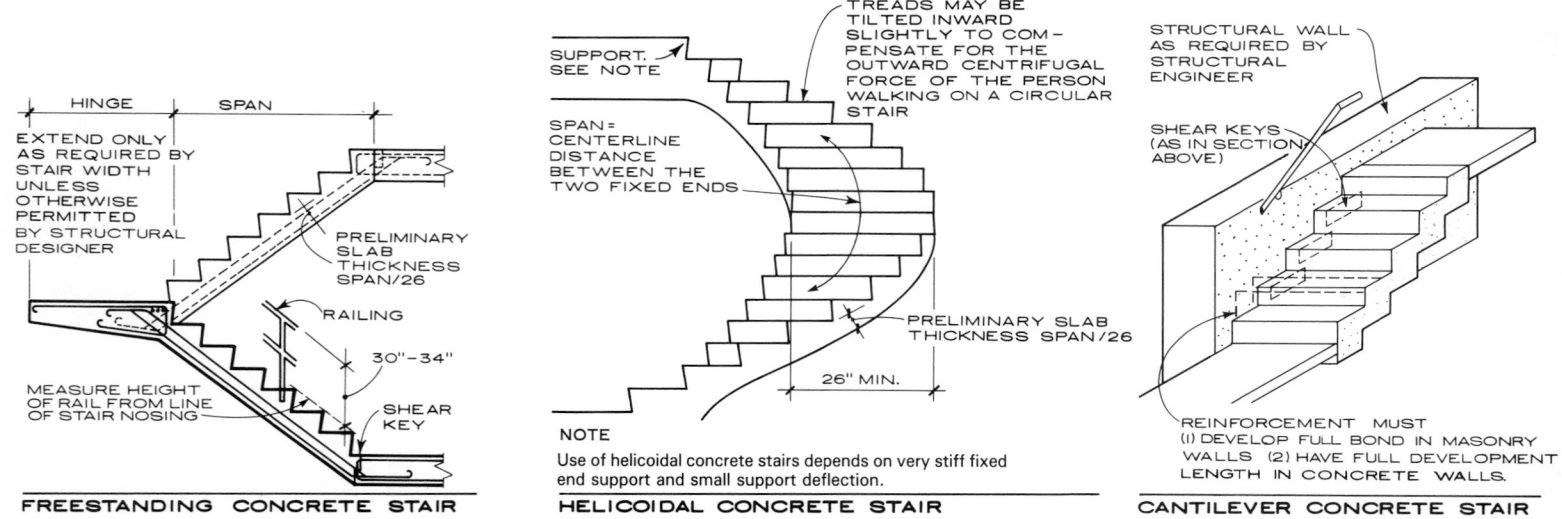

12"

12" + 1 TREAD

RAILING

DN

UP

1 1/2 MIN. CLEARANCE BETWEEN RAILS

OPEN

7" MAX.

STAIR WIDTH

STAIR WIDTH

STAIR WIDTH

RAILING

DN

ON WIDE STAIRS, DOOR IN FULL OPEN POSITION MAY NOT INTRUDE INTO STAIR WIDTH MORE THAN 3 1/2"

3 1/2" MAX.

1 1/2"

12" AT TOP RISER

PLAN

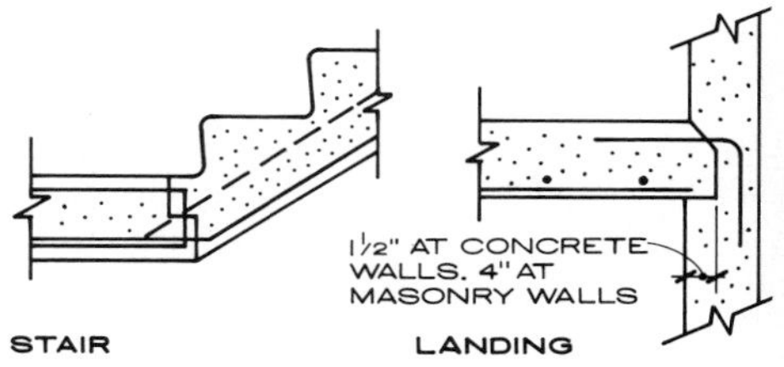

1 1/2" AT CONCRETE WALLS, 4" AT MASONRY WALLS

STAIR          LANDING

**SHEAR KEY DETAILS**

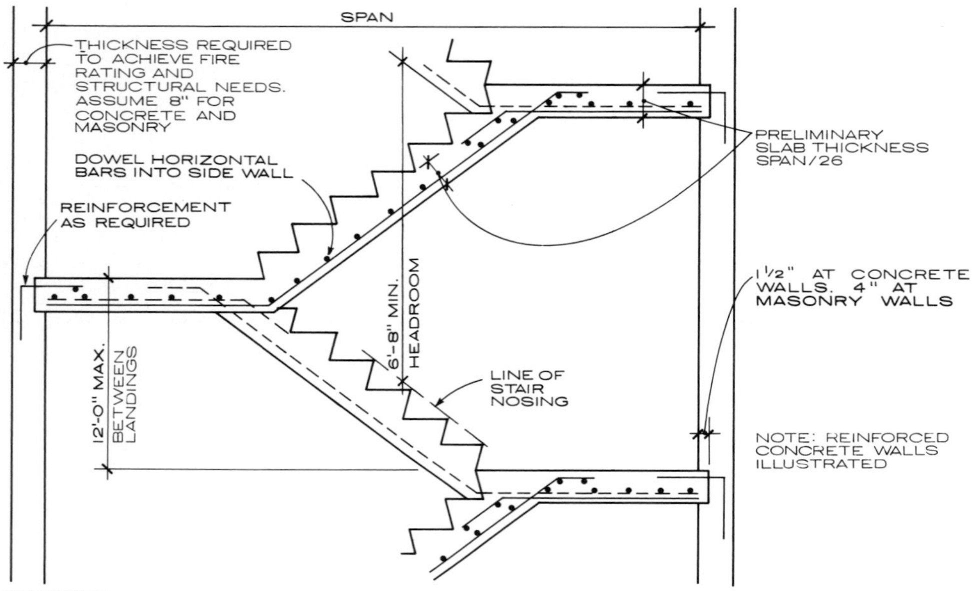

SPAN

THICKNESS REQUIRED TO ACHIEVE FIRE RATING AND STRUCTURAL NEEDS. ASSUME 8" FOR CONCRETE AND MASONRY

DOWEL HORIZONTAL BARS INTO SIDE WALL

REINFORCEMENT AS REQUIRED

12'-0" MAX. BETWEEN LANDINGS

6'-8" MIN. HEADROOM

PRELIMINARY SLAB THICKNESS SPAN/26

LINE OF STAIR NOSING

1 1/2" AT CONCRETE WALLS. 4" AT MASONRY WALLS

NOTE: REINFORCED CONCRETE WALLS ILLUSTRATED

SECTION

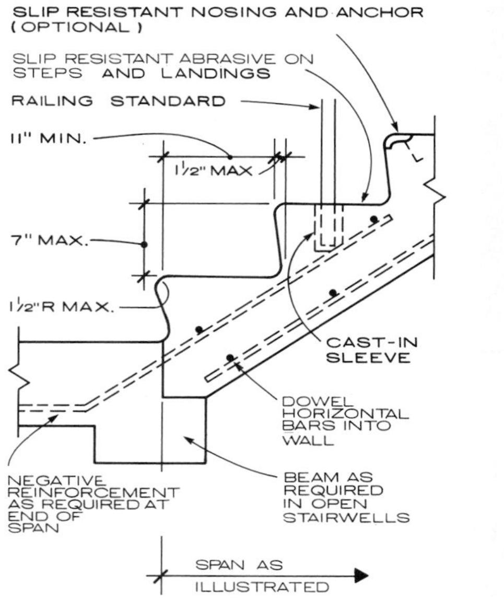

**U-TYPE CONCRETE STAIRS**

SLIP RESISTANT NOSING AND ANCHOR (OPTIONAL)

SLIP RESISTANT ABRASIVE ON STEPS AND LANDINGS

RAILING STANDARD

11" MIN.

1 1/2" MAX

7" MAX.

1 1/2"R MAX.

CAST-IN SLEEVE

DOWEL HORIZONTAL BARS INTO WALL

NEGATIVE REINFORCEMENT AS REQUIRED AT END OF SPAN

BEAM AS REQUIRED IN OPEN STAIRWELLS

SPAN AS ILLUSTRATED

**COMPOSITE DETAIL**

HINGE          SPAN

EXTEND ONLY AS REQUIRED BY STAIR WIDTH UNLESS OTHERWISE PERMITTED BY STRUCTURAL DESIGNER

PRELIMINARY SLAB THICKNESS SPAN/26

RAILING

30"–34"

MEASURE HEIGHT OF RAIL FROM LINE OF STAIR NOSING

SHEAR KEY

**FREESTANDING CONCRETE STAIR**

TREADS MAY BE TILTED INWARD SLIGHTLY TO COMPENSATE FOR THE OUTWARD CENTRIFUGAL FORCE OF THE PERSON WALKING ON A CIRCULAR STAIR

SUPPORT. SEE NOTE

SPAN = CENTERLINE DISTANCE BETWEEN THE TWO FIXED ENDS

PRELIMINARY SLAB THICKNESS SPAN/26

26" MIN.

NOTE

Use of helicoidal concrete stairs depends on very stiff fixed end support and small support deflection.

**HELICOIDAL CONCRETE STAIR**

STRUCTURAL WALL AS REQUIRED BY STRUCTURAL ENGINEER

SHEAR KEYS (AS IN SECTION ABOVE)

REINFORCEMENT MUST (1) DEVELOP FULL BOND IN MASONRY WALLS (2) HAVE FULL DEVELOPMENT LENGTH IN CONCRETE WALLS.

**CANTILEVER CONCRETE STAIR**

Krommenhoek/McKeown & Associates; San Diego, California
Karlsberger and Associates, Inc.; Columbus, Ohio

ARCHITECTURAL CONCRETE

# CHAPTER 4

## *Masonry*

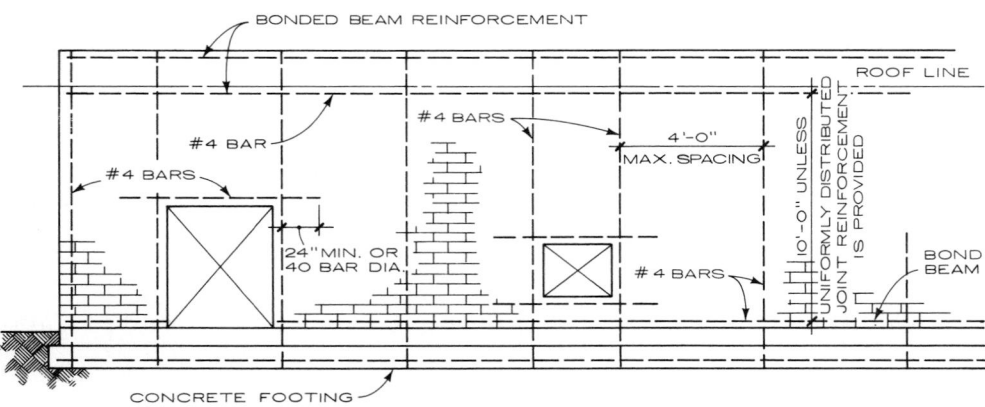

**PARTIALLY REINFORCED LOAD-BEARING BRICK OR CMU WALL (SEISMIC ZONES 0, 1, AND 2)**

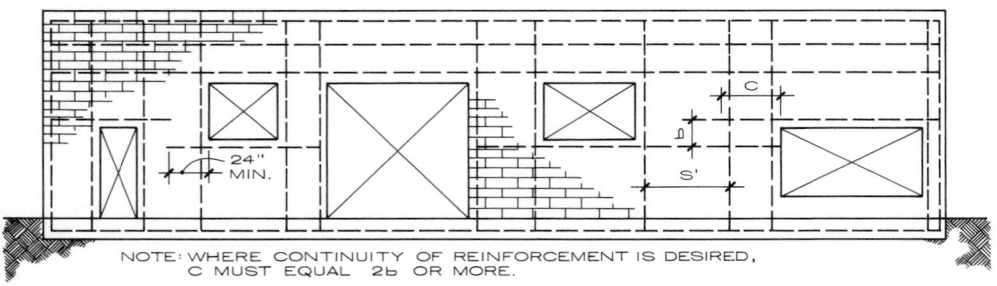

NOTE: WHERE CONTINUITY OF REINFORCEMENT IS DESIRED, C MUST EQUAL 2b OR MORE.

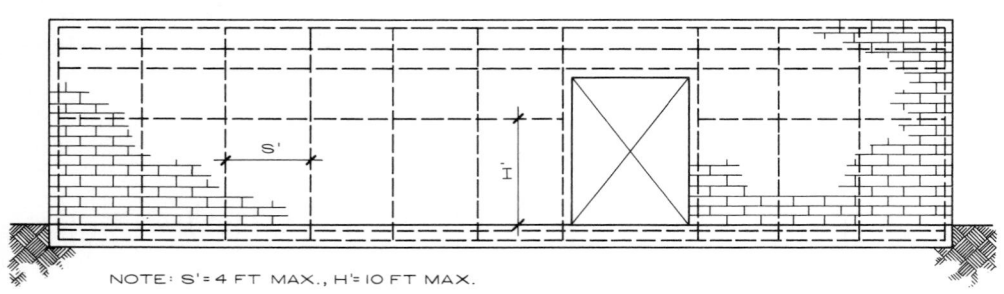

NOTE: S' = 4 FT MAX., H' = 10 FT MAX.

**REINFORCED LOAD-BEARING BRICK OR CMU WALLS (SEISMIC ZONES 3 AND 4)**

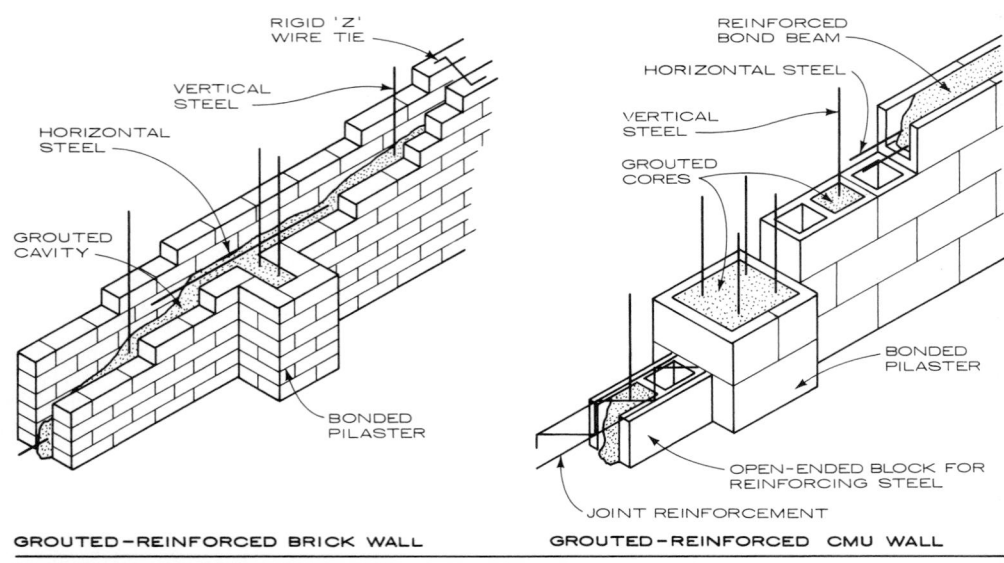

**GROUTED-REINFORCED BRICK WALL**      **GROUTED-REINFORCED CMU WALL**

**METHODS OF REINFORCING**

Christine Beall, AIA, CCS; Austin, Texas

## LOAD-BEARING MASONRY

Engineered load-bearing masonry walls may be plain (unreinforced), partially reinforced, or reinforced. They may be single-wythe CMU or structural clay tile, multiwythe brick, or combinations of these materials. Reinforcing steel increases resistance to lateral loads and to buckling. Single-wythe brick masonry may be reinforced to function as panel wall or curtain wall systems, with relatively long spans between lateral supports.

## ANCHORS AND REINFORCEMENT

Reinforced masonry uses standard deformed steel reinforcing bars, ASTM A615. Masonry wall ties should be rigid wire, minimum $3/16$ in. diameter, rectangular where open cavity occurs, rectangular or Z-ties where cavity is grouted. Do not used crimped ties with water drip, as strength is considerably reduced. Horizontal joint reinforcement is used to control shrinkage cracking in CMU construction. It may be ladder or truss type design with optional tabs for fixed or adjustable veneer anchorage. Standard widths are 2 in. less than nominal wall thickness to permit a minimum $5/8$ in. mortar cover at outside of joints. Longitudinal wires may be 10 gauge (light duty, interior only), 9 gauge (standard duty), 8 gauge (heavy duty), or $3/16$ in. diameter (extra heavy duty).

Cross wires may be a different size, generally 12 gauge minimum. For corrosion resistance, joint reinforcement and ties should be hot-dip galvanized, ASTM A153.

## HORIZONTAL AND VERTICAL STEEL

Some codes permit calculation of horizontal joint reinforcement as part of the steel required for certain types of load-bearing walls. Other codes require standard deformed reinforcing bars placed horizontally in bond beam courses or grouted cavities and vertically in grouted cores or cavities.

## PARTIALLY REINFORCED MASONRY (SEISMIC ZONE 2)

Partially reinforced masonry (not permitted in seismic zones 3 and 4) uses a certain minimum of code-required steel (check local requirements), plus an additional 0.2 sq in. in cross section horizontally and vertically wherever engineering design analysis indicated that tensile stress is developed. Maximum spacing of vertical steel is 4 ft 0 in. Vertical steel must also be placed at each side of window and door openings and at all corners. Bond beam courses must be provided at top of footings, bottom and top of wall openings, below roof and floor lines, and at top of parapet walls.

## REINFORCED MASONRY (SEISMIC ZONES 3 AND 4)

Walls designed as reinforced masonry must have a minimum area of steel equal to 0.002 times the cross-sectional area of the wall, not more than $2/3$ of which (0.0007) may be placed in either direction. Maximum spacing principal reinforcement may not exceed 6 times the wall thickness or 48 in. o.c. Horizontal reinforcement must be provided in bond beam courses at top of footings, bottom and top of wall openings, below roof and floor lines, and at top of parapet walls. There must also be one #4 bar vertically at all window and door openings, extending at least 24 in. beyond the opening to prevent diagonal cracking at these planes of weakness. Only continuous reinforcement may be considered in computing the minimum area of steel provided.

## PRECAUTIONS

Reinforcement must be lapped a minimum of 6 in. for continuity. Joint reinforcement, masonry ties, and steel wires located in mortar joints must be placed in the mortar bed and not directly on the masonry. CMU face shell bedding is acceptable except at grouted cores where cross-webs must also be bedded in mortar. Use spacers to hold vertical and horizontal reinforcement in proper alignment while grouting. Do not continue reinforcement through control or expansion joints. Do not place flashing in the same joint as reinforcement.

## REFERENCES

Consult a structural engineer and local code requirements for design of grouted-reinforced masonry. For further technical information:

Masonry Design and Detailing, 2d ed. Christine Beall. New York: McGraw-Hill, 1987.
Technical Notes Series. Brick Institute of America.
TEK Series. National Concrete Masonry Association.

4    **MASONRY ACCESSORIES**

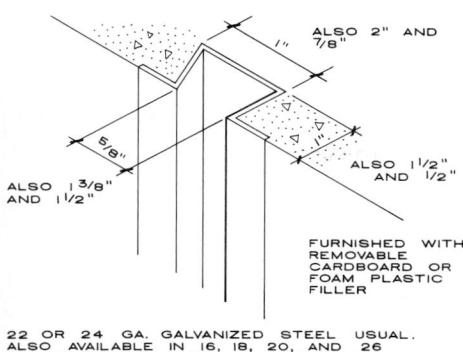

ALSO 2" AND 7/8"

1"

5/8"

ALSO 1 1/2" AND 1/2"

ALSO 1 3/8" AND 1 1/2"

FURNISHED WITH REMOVABLE CARDBOARD OR FOAM PLASTIC FILLER

22 OR 24 GA. GALVANIZED STEEL USUAL. ALSO AVAILABLE IN 16, 18, 20, AND 26 GA. GALVANIZED STEEL AND STAINLESS STEEL, COPPER AND ZINC ALLOY

## DOVETAIL SLOTS

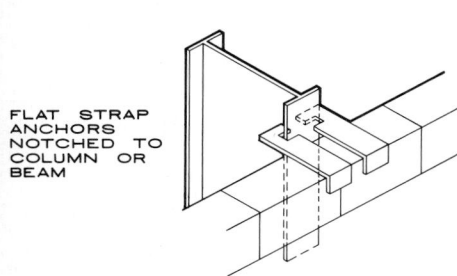

FLAT STRAP ANCHORS NOTCHED TO COLUMN OR BEAM

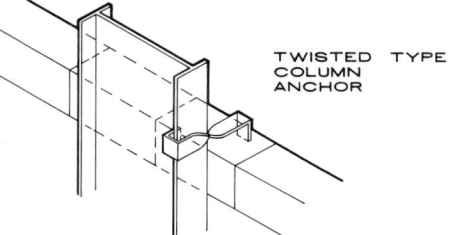

TWISTED TYPE COLUMN ANCHOR

Z-TYPE ANCHOR (MASONRY TO MASONRY)

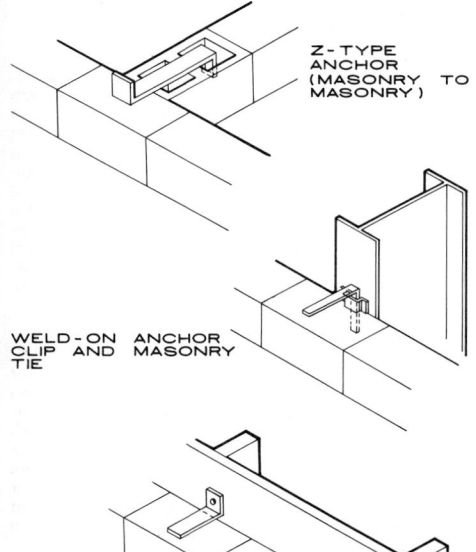

WELD-ON ANCHOR CLIP AND MASONRY TIE

VENEER ANCHORS (PLAIN AND CORRUGATED TYPES SHOWN)

## MISCELLANEOUS ANCHORS

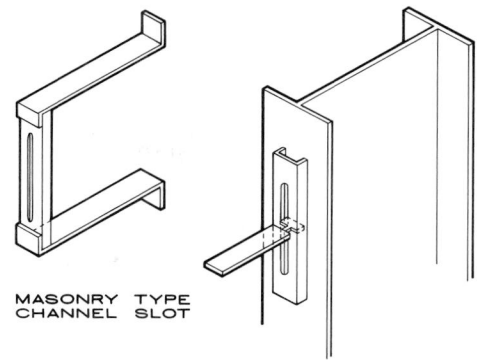

MASONRY TYPE CHANNEL SLOT

WELD-ON TYPE CHANNEL SLOT (WITH ANCHOR SHOWN)

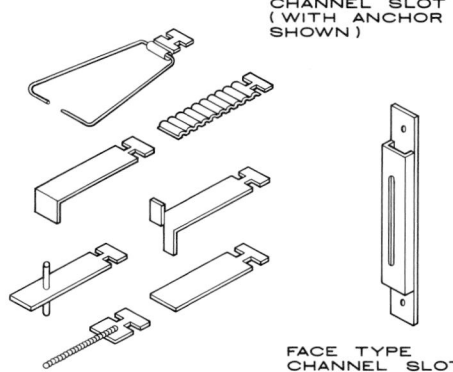

FACE TYPE CHANNEL SLOT

ANCHOR CONFIGURATIONS

## CHANNEL SLOTS AND ANCHORS

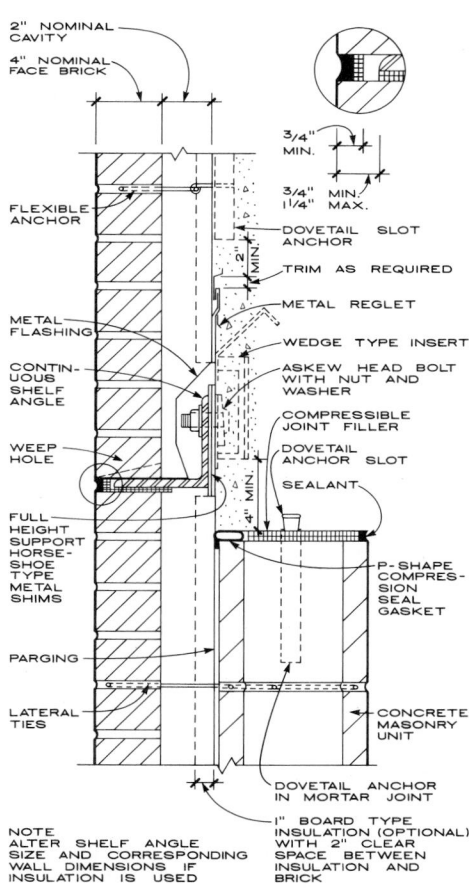

2" NOMINAL CAVITY

4" NOMINAL FACE BRICK

3/4" MIN.

3/4" MIN. 1 1/4" MAX.

FLEXIBLE ANCHOR

DOVETAIL SLOT ANCHOR

TRIM AS REQUIRED

METAL REGLET

METAL FLASHING

WEDGE TYPE INSERT

CONTINUOUS SHELF ANGLE

ASKEW HEAD BOLT WITH NUT AND WASHER

COMPRESSIBLE JOINT FILLER

WEEP HOLE

DOVETAIL ANCHOR SLOT

SEALANT

FULL HEIGHT SUPPORT HORSE-SHOE TYPE METAL SHIMS

P-SHAPE COMPRESSION SEAL GASKET

PARGING

LATERAL TIES

CONCRETE MASONRY UNIT

DOVETAIL ANCHOR IN MORTAR JOINT

1" BOARD TYPE INSULATION (OPTIONAL) WITH 2" CLEAR SPACE BETWEEN INSULATION AND BRICK

NOTE
ALTER SHELF ANGLE SIZE AND CORRESPONDING WALL DIMENSIONS IF INSULATION IS USED

## CAVITY WALL SHELF ANGLE SUPPORT

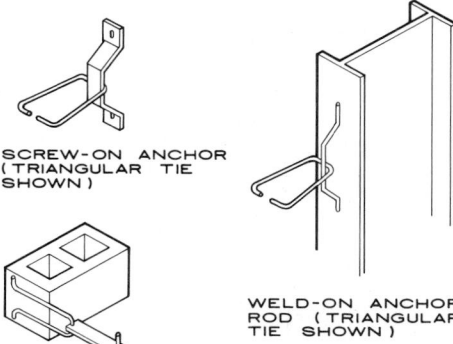

SCREW-ON ANCHOR (TRIANGULAR TIE SHOWN)

WELD-ON ANCHOR ROD (TRIANGULAR TIE SHOWN)

ADJUSTABLE U-BAR ANCHOR (FLAT TYPE PIN SHOWN)

| 1 | Rectangular | Available with or without moisture drip in 3/16 in. or 1/4 in. mill or hot dipped galvanized steel; conforms to ASTM (A-82); space 16 in. vertically and 24 in. horizontally |
| 2 | Z | |
| 3 | Adjustable Z | |
| 4 | Mesh | 1/2 in. mesh x 16 ga. hot dipped galvanized |
| 5 | Corrugated | mill or hot dipped galvanized steel 7/8 in. wide and 7 in. long; 12 to 28 ga. |

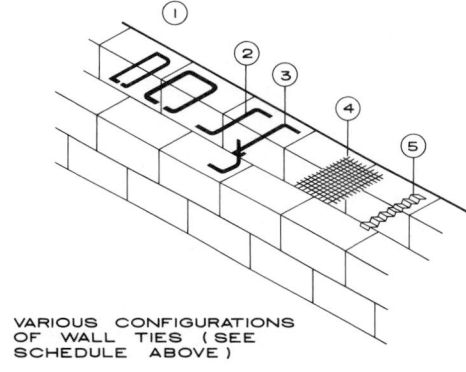

VARIOUS CONFIGURATIONS OF WALL TIES (SEE SCHEDULE ABOVE)

## WIRE TIES

Masonry veneer and facing must be anchored to back-up construction. Codes usually require one anchor for 3 sq. ft. of surface area. Inserts usually are spaced 2 ft. on center horizontally, and ties usually are spaced 16 to 18 in. on center vertically. Spandrel beams over 18 in. deep require inserts and anchors for tying masonry facing to the beam. Most anchor systems permit differential movement in one or two directions. An anchoring system that allows movement only in the intended direction should be selected. See ASTM STP 778.

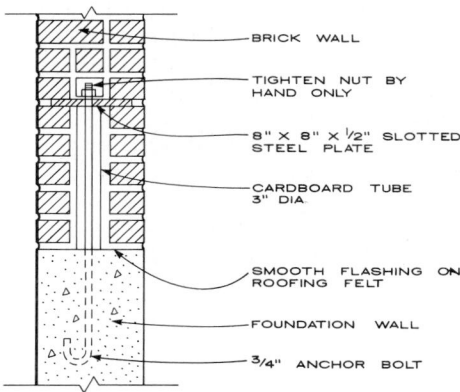

BRICK WALL

TIGHTEN NUT BY HAND ONLY

8" X 8" X 1/2" SLOTTED STEEL PLATE

CARDBOARD TUBE 3" DIA.

SMOOTH FLASHING ON ROOFING FELT

FOUNDATION WALL

3/4" ANCHOR BOLT

## WALL ANCHORAGE TO FOUNDATION

Narcisa P. Sanchez; Sanchez & Sanchez; Falls Church, Virginia
Metz Train Olson & Youngren, Inc.; Chicago, Illinois

## MASONRY ACCESSORIES

4

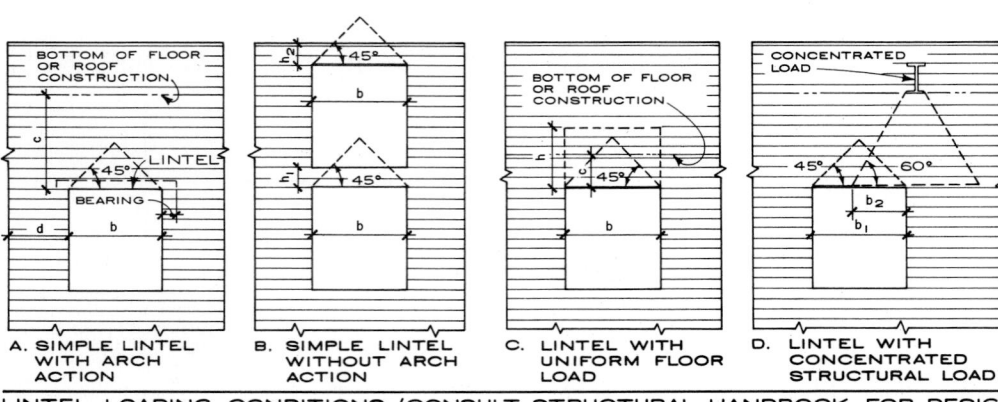

A. SIMPLE LINTEL WITH ARCH ACTION
B. SIMPLE LINTEL WITHOUT ARCH ACTION
C. LINTEL WITH UNIFORM FLOOR LOAD
D. LINTEL WITH CONCENTRATED STRUCTURAL LOAD

**NOTES FOR LINTEL CONDITIONS**

A. Simple lintel with arch action carries wall load only in triangle above opening:

$$c \geq b \quad \text{and} \quad d \geq b$$

B. Simple lintel without arch action carries less wall load than triangle above opening:

$$h_1 \text{ or } h_2 < 0.6b$$

C. Lintel with uniform floor load carries both wall and floor loads in rectangle above opening:

$$c < b$$

D. Lintel with concentrated load carries wall and portion of concentrated load distributed along length $b_2$.

**LINTEL LOADING CONDITIONS (CONSULT STRUCTURAL HANDBOOK FOR DESIGN FORMULAS)**

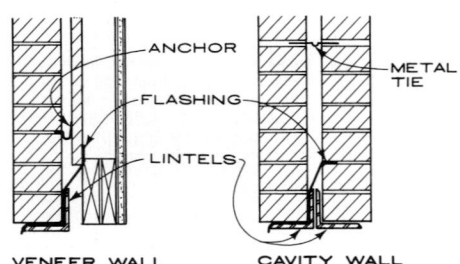

VENEER WALL    CAVITY WALL

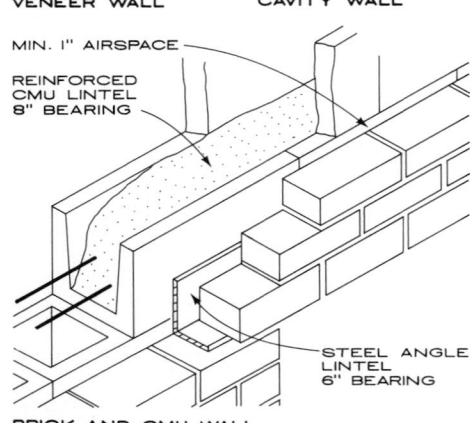

BRICK AND CMU WALL

**LOOSE STEEL LINTELS FOR MASONRY WALLS**

## ALLOWABLE UNIFORM SUPERIMPOSED LOAD (IN LB) PER LINEAR FOOT FOR STEEL ANGLE LINTELS

| HORIZONTAL LEG | ANGLE SIZE | WEIGHT PER FT. (LB) | SPAN IN FEET (CENTER TO CENTER OF REQUIRED BEARING) | | | | | | | | | |
|---|---|---|---|---|---|---|---|---|---|---|---|---|
| | | | 3 | 4 | 5 | 6 | 7 | 8 | 9 | 10 | 11 | 12 |
| 3½ | 3 x 3½ x ¼ | 5.4 | 956 | 517 | 262 | 149 | 91 | 59 | | | | |
| | x 5/16 | 6.6 | 1166 | 637 | 323 | 184 | 113 | 73 | | | | |
| | x 3/8 | 7.9 | 1377 | 756 | 384 | 218 | 134 | 87 | 59 | | | |
| 3½ | 3½ x 3½ x ¼ | 5.8 | 1281 | 718 | 406 | 232 | 144 | 94 | 65 | | | |
| | x 5/16 | 7.2 | 1589 | 891 | 507 | 290 | 179 | 118 | 80 | | | |
| | x 3/8 | 8.5 | 1947 | 1091 | 589 | 336 | 208 | 137 | 93 | 66 | | |
| 3½ | 4 x 3½ x ¼ | 6.2 | 1622 | 910 | 580 | 338 | 210 | 139 | 95 | 68 | | |
| | x 5/16 | 7.7 | 2110 | 1184 | 734 | 421 | 262 | 173 | 119 | 85 | 62 | |
| | x 3/8 | 9.1 | 2434 | 1365 | 855 | 490 | 305 | 201 | 138 | 98 | 71 | |
| | x 7/16 | 10.6 | 2760 | 1548 | 978 | 561 | 349 | 230 | 158 | 113 | 82 | 60 |
| 4 | 4 x 4 x 7/16 | 11.3 | 2920 | 1638 | 1018 | 584 | 363 | 239 | 164 | 116 | 85 | 62 |
| | x ½ | 12.8 | 3246 | 1820 | 1141 | 654 | 407 | 268 | 185 | 131 | 95 | 70 |
| 3½ | 5 x 3½ x ¼ | 7.0 | 2600 | 1460 | 932 | 636 | 398 | 264 | 184 | 132 | 97 | 73 |
| | x 5/16 | 8.7 | 3087 | 1733 | 1106 | 765 | 486 | 323 | 224 | 161 | 119 | 89 |
| | x 7/16 | 12.0 | 4224 | 2371 | 1513 | 1047 | 655 | 435 | 302 | 217 | 160 | 120 |
| | x ½ | 13.6 | 4875 | 2736 | 1746 | 1177 | 736 | 488 | 339 | 244 | 179 | 134 |
| 3½ | 6 x 3½ x ¼ | 7.9 | 3577 | 2009 | 1283 | 888 | 650 | 439 | 306 | 221 | 164 | 124 |
| | x 5/16 | 9.8 | 4390 | 2465 | 1574 | 1090 | 798 | 538 | 375 | 271 | 201 | 151 |
| | x 3/8 | 11.7 | 5200 | 2922 | 1865 | 1291 | 945 | 636 | 443 | 320 | 237 | 179 |
| | x ½ | 15.3 | 6828 | 3834 | 2448 | 1695 | 1228 | 818 | 570 | 412 | 305 | 230 |
| 4 | 6 x 4 x ¼ | 8.3 | 3739 | 2099 | 1340 | 928 | 679 | 458 | 319 | 231 | 171 | 129 |
| | x 5/16 | 10.3 | 4552 | 2556 | 1632 | 1129 | 827 | 562 | 391 | 283 | 209 | 158 |
| | x 3/8 | 12.3 | 5365 | 3012 | 1923 | 1331 | 974 | 665 | 463 | 335 | 248 | 187 |
| | x 7/16 | 14.3 | 6178 | 3469 | 2214 | 1533 | 1122 | 764 | 532 | 384 | 284 | 215 |
| | x ½ | 16.2 | 6990 | 3925 | 2506 | 1734 | 1270 | 857 | 597 | 431 | 319 | 241 |

NOTE: Allowable loads to the left of the heavy line are governed by moment, and to the right by deflection. $F_y$ = 36,000 psi. Maximum deflection $^1/_{700}$. Consult structural engineer for long spans.

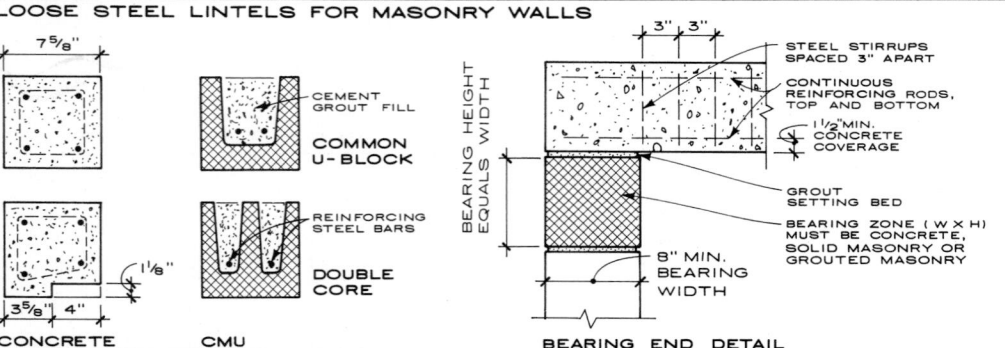

BEARING END DETAIL

**NUMBER AND SIZE OF REBARS REQUIRED**

Precast Concrete and Reinforced CMU Lintels (no superimposed loads)

| LINTEL TYPE | CLEAR SPAN (MAX) | 8'' BRICK WALL (80 LB/SQ FT) | 8'' CMU WALL (50 LB/SQ FT) |
|---|---|---|---|
| Reinforced concrete (7⅝'' square section) | 4'-0'' | 4-#3 | 4-#3 |
| | 6'-0'' | 4-#4 | 4-#3 |
| | 8'-0'' | 4-#5 | 4-#4 |
| CMU (7⅝'' square section) nominal 8 x 8 x 16 unit | 4'-0'' | 2-#4 | 2-#3 |
| | 6'-0'' | 2-#5 | 2-#4 |
| | 8'-0'' | 2-#6 | 2-#5 |

NOTE: fc' = 3000 psi concrete and grout
fy = 60,000 psi

**PRECAST CONCRETE AND CMU LINTELS**

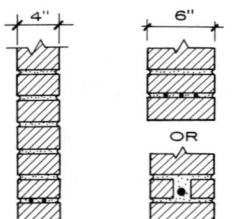

CONCRETE

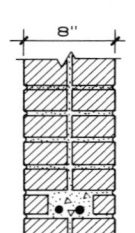

CMU

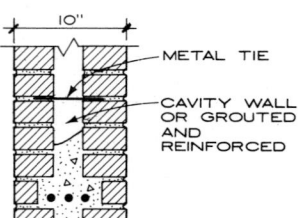

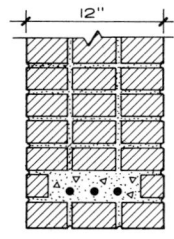

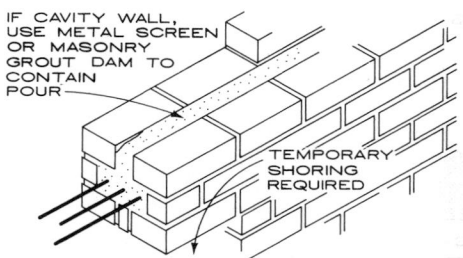

**REINFORCED BRICK LINTELS**

Christine Beall, AIA, CCS; Austin, Texas
Metz, Train, Olson and Youngren, Inc.; Chicago, Illinois

**UNIT MASONRY**

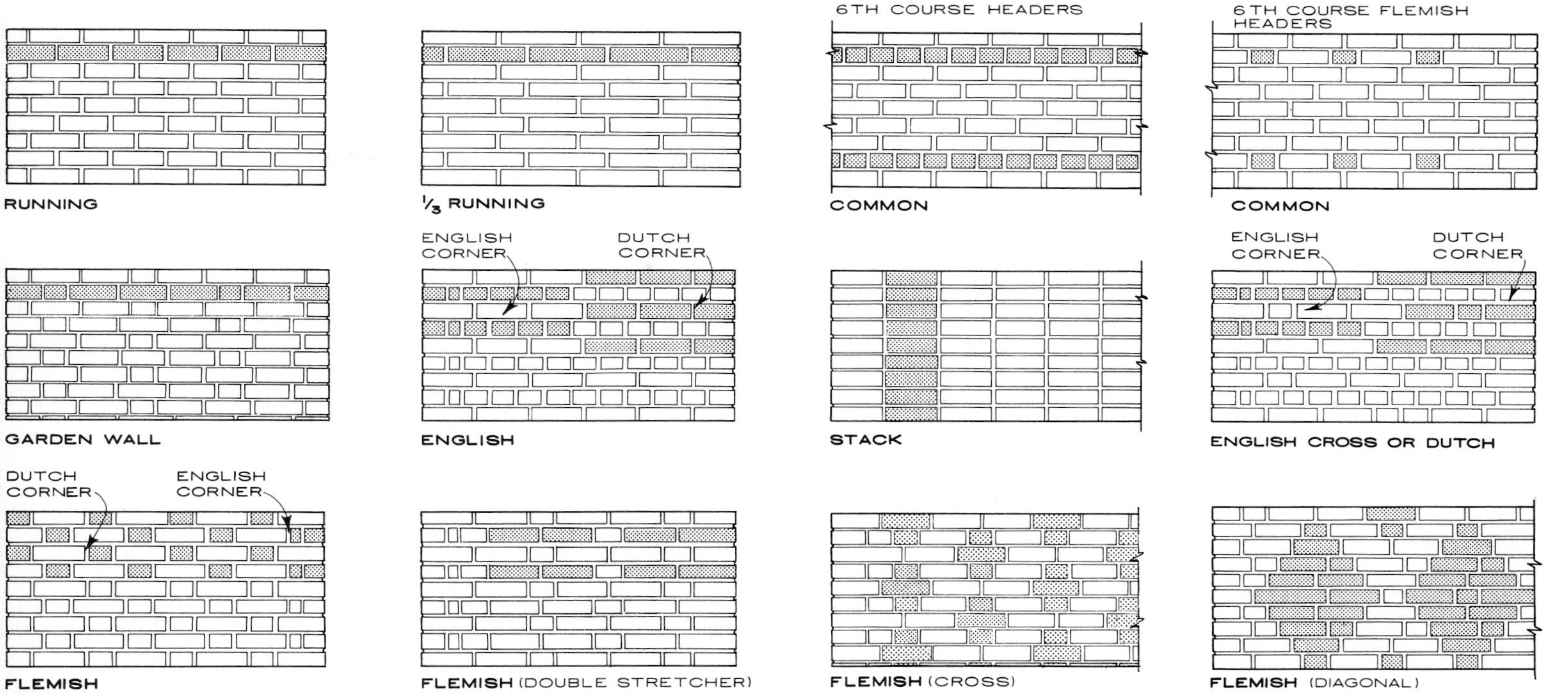

## BRICK BONDS

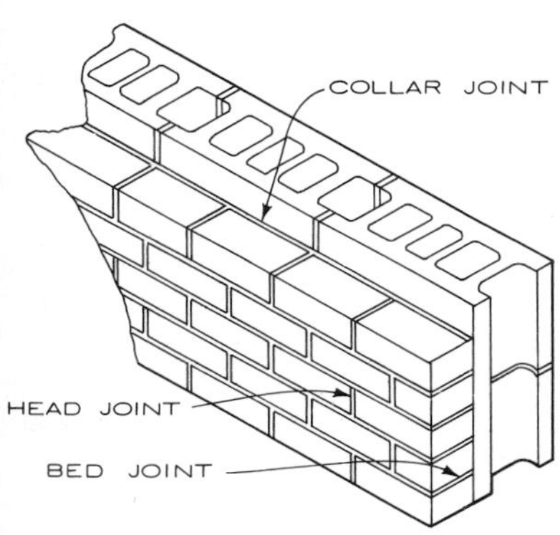

RUNNING

¹/₃ RUNNING

6TH COURSE HEADERS
COMMON

6TH COURSE FLEMISH HEADERS
COMMON

GARDEN WALL

ENGLISH
ENGLISH CORNER    DUTCH CORNER

STACK

ENGLISH CROSS OR DUTCH
ENGLISH CORNER    DUTCH CORNER

FLEMISH
DUTCH CORNER    ENGLISH CORNER

FLEMISH (DOUBLE STRETCHER)

FLEMISH (CROSS)

FLEMISH (DIAGONAL)

## BRICK JOINTS

COLLAR JOINT

HEAD JOINT

BED JOINT

TERMS APPLIED TO JOINTS

### TYPES OF JOINTS

Mortar serves multiple functions:

1. Joins and seals masonry units, allowing for dimensional variations in masonry units.
2. Affects overall appearance of wall color, texture, and patterns.
3. Bonds reinforcing steel to masonry, creating a composite assembly.

### MORTAR JOINT FINISH METHODS

1. Troweled—Excess mortar is struck off, the trowel is the only tool used for shaping and finishing.
2. Tooled—A special tool is used to compress and shape mortar in the joint.

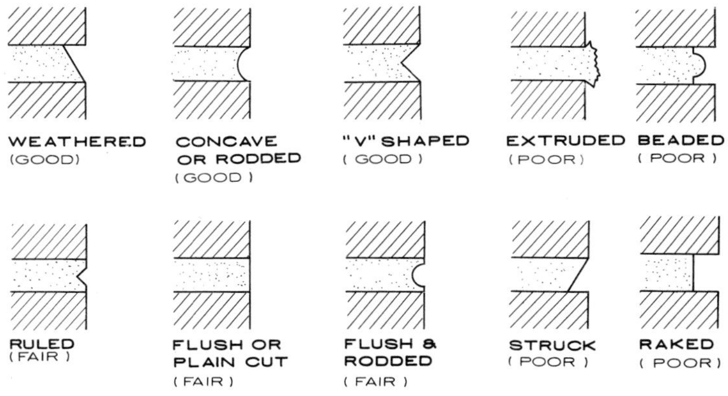

WEATHERED (GOOD)

CONCAVE OR RODDED (GOOD)

"V" SHAPED (GOOD)

EXTRUDED (POOR)

BEADED (POOR)

RULED (FAIR)

FLUSH OR PLAIN CUT (FAIR)

FLUSH & RODDED (FAIR)

STRUCK (POOR)

RAKED (POOR)

TYPES OF JOINTS (WEATHERABILITY)

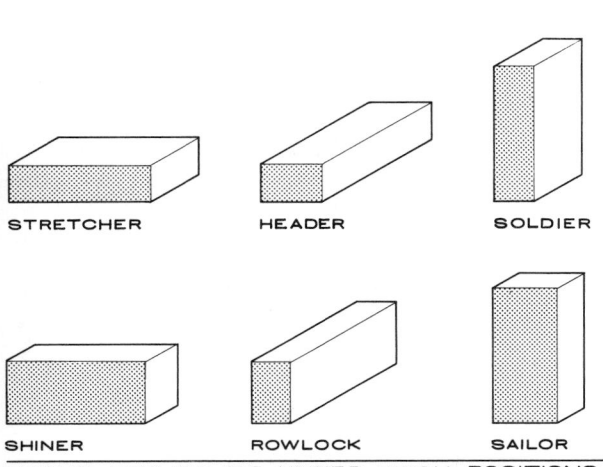

STRETCHER

HEADER

SOLDIER

SHINER

ROWLOCK

SAILOR

TERMS APPLIED TO VARIED BRICK POSITIONS

### SIZES OF MODULAR BRICK

| UNIT DESIGNATION | NOMINAL DIMENSIONS | | | MODULAR COURSING |
| --- | --- | --- | --- | --- |
| | THICKNESS | HEIGHT | LENGTH | |
| MODULAR | 4″ | 2²/₃″ | 8″ | 3C = 8″ |
| ENGINEER | 4″ | 3¹/₅″ | 8″ | 5C = 16″ |
| ECONOMY | 4″ | 4″ | 8″ | 1C = 4″ |
| DOUBLE | 4″ | 5¹/₃″ | 8″ | 3C = 16″ |
| ROMAN | 4″ | 2″ | 12″ | 2C = 4″ |
| NORMAN | 4″ | 2²/₃″ | 12″ | 3C = 8″ |
| NORWEGIAN | 4″ | 3¹/₅″ | 12″ | 5C = 16″ |
| UTILITY[1] | 4″ | 4″ | 12″ | 1C = 4″ |
| TRIPLE | 4″ | 5¹/₃″ | 12″ | 3C = 16″ |
| SCR BRICK | 6″ | 2²/₃″ | 12″ | 3C = 8″ |
| 6″ NORWEGIAN | 6″ | 3¹/₅″ | 12″ | 5C = 16″ |
| 6″ JUMBO | 6″ | 4″ | 12″ | 1C = 4″ |
| 8″ JUMBO | 8″ | 4″ | 12″ | 1C = 4″ |
| 8″ SQUARE | 4″ | 8″ | 8″ | 1C = 8″ |
| 12″ SQUARE | 4″ | 12″ | 12″ | 1C = 12″ |

[1] Also called Norman Economy, General and King Norman.
*For special shapes contact local brick manufacturers.

Brick Institute of America; Reston, Virginia
Raso·Greaves An Architecture Corporation; Waco, Texas

UNIT MASONRY   4

### STANDARD MODULAR
4″ x 2 2/3″ x 8″ NOMINAL

| | BRICK SIZES: | |
|---|---|---|
| * For 3/8″ Joint | | 3 5/8″ x 2 1/4″ x 7 5/8″ |
| ** For 1/2″ Joint | | 3 1/2″ x 2 3/16″ x 7 1/2″ |

### NORMAN
4″ x 2 2/3″ x 12″ NOMINAL

| | BRICK SIZES: | |
|---|---|---|
| * For 3/8″ Joint | | 3 5/8″ x 2 1/4″ x 11 5/8″ |
| ** For 1/2″ Joint | | 3 1/2″ x 2 3/16″ x 11 1/2″ |

### SCR BRICK
6″ x 2 2/3″ x 12″ NOMINAL

For 1/2″ Joint     5 1/2″ x 2 1/8″ x 11 1/2″

Joint selected determines brick size
3 courses = 2 modules (8″)

### NOMINAL HEIGHT OF 2 2/3″ COURSES

| | | | |
|---|---|---|---|
| 31 | 6′ – 10 2/3″ | 61 | 13′ – 6 2/3″ |
| 30 | 6′ – 8″ | 60 | 13′ – 4″ |
| 29 | 6′ – 5 1/3″ | 59 | 13′ – 1 1/3″ |
| 28 | 6′ – 2 2/3″ | 58 | 12′ – 10 2/3″ |
| 27 | 6′ – 0″ | 57 | 12′ – 8″ |
| 26 | 5′ – 9 1/3″ | 56 | 12′ – 5 1/3″ |
| 25 | 5′ – 6 2/3″ | 55 | 12′ – 2 2/3″ |
| 24 | 5′ – 4″ | 54 | 12′ – 0″ |
| 23 | 5′ – 1 1/3″ | 53 | 11′ – 9 1/3″ |
| 22 | 4′ – 10 2/3″ | 52 | 11′ – 6 2/3″ |
| 21 | 4′ – 8″ | 51 | 11′ – 4″ |
| 20 | 4′ – 5 1/3″ | 50 | 11′ – 1 1/3″ |
| 19 | 4′ – 2 2/3″ | 49 | 10′ – 10 2/3″ |
| 18 | 4′ – 0″ | 48 | 10′ – 8″ |
| 17 | 3′ – 9 1/3″ | 47 | 10′ – 5 1/3″ |
| 16 | 3′ – 6 2/3″ | 46 | 10′ – 2 2/3″ |
| 15 | 3′ – 4″ | 45 | 10′ – 0″ |
| 14 | 3′ – 1 1/3″ | 44 | 9′ – 9 1/3″ |
| 13 | 2′ – 10 2/3″ | 43 | 9′ – 6 2/3″ |
| 12 | 2′ – 8″ | 42 | 9′ – 4″ |
| 11 | 2′ – 5 1/3″ | 41 | 9′ – 1 1/3″ |
| 10 | 2′ – 2 1/3″ | 40 | 8′ – 10 2/3″ |
| 9 | 2′ – 0″ | 39 | 8′ – 8″ |
| 8 | 1′ – 9 1/3″ | 38 | 8′ – 5 1/3″ |
| 7 | 1′ – 6 2/3″ | 37 | 8′ – 2 2/3″ |
| 6 | 1′ – 4″ | 36 | 8′ – 0″ |
| 5 | 1′ – 1 1/3″ | 35 | 7′ – 9 1/3″ |
| 4 | 10 2/3″ | 34 | 7′ – 6 2/3″ |
| 3 | 8″ | 33 | 7′ – 4″ |
| 2 | 5 1/3″ | 32 | 7′ – 1 1/3″ |
| 1 | 2 2/3″ | | |

### ENGINEER
4″ x 3 1/5″ x 8″ NOMINAL

| | BRICK SIZES: | |
|---|---|---|
| * For 3/8″ Joint | | 3 5/8″ x 2 13/16″ x 7 5/8″ |
| For 1/2″ Joint | | 3 1/2″ x 2 11/16″ x 7 1/2″ |

Joint selected determines brick size.
5 courses = 4 modules (16″).

### NOMINAL HEIGHTS OF 3 1/5″ COURSES

| | | | |
|---|---|---|---|
| 29 | 7′ – 8 4/5″ | 59 | 15′ – 8 4/5″ |
| 28 | 7′ – 5 3/5″ | 58 | 15′ – 5 3/5″ |
| 27 | 7′ – 2 2/5″ | 57 | 15′ – 2 2/5″ |
| 26 | 6′ – 11 1/5″ | 56 | 14′ – 11 1/5″ |
| 25 | 6′ – 8″ | 55 | 14′ – 8″ |
| 24 | 6′ – 4 4/5″ | 54 | 14′ – 4 4/5″ |
| 23 | 6′ – 1 3/5″ | 53 | 14′ – 1 3/5″ |
| 22 | 5′ – 10 2/5″ | 52 | 13′ – 10 2/5″ |
| 21 | 5′ – 7 1/5″ | 51 | 13′ – 7 1/5″ |
| 20 | 5′ – 4″ | 50 | 13′ – 4″ |
| 19 | 5′ – 0 4/5″ | 49 | 13′ – 0 4/5″ |
| 18 | 4′ – 9 3/5″ | 48 | 12′ – 9 3/5″ |
| 17 | 4′ – 6 2/5″ | 47 | 12′ – 6 2/5″ |
| 16 | 4′ – 3 1/5″ | 46 | 12′ – 3 1/5″ |
| 15 | 4′ – 0″ | 45 | 12′ – 0″ |
| 14 | 3′ – 8 4/5″ | 44 | 11′ – 8 4/5″ |
| 13 | 3′ – 5 3/5″ | 43 | 11′ – 5 3/5″ |
| 12 | 3′ – 2 2/5″ | 42 | 11′ – 2 2/5″ |
| 11 | 2′ – 11 1/5″ | 41 | 10′ – 11 1/5″ |
| 10 | 2′ – 8″ | 40 | 10′ – 8″ |
| 9 | 2′ – 4 4/5″ | 39 | 10′ – 4 4/5″ |
| 8 | 2′ – 1 3/5″ | 38 | 10′ – 1 3/5″ |
| 7 | 1′ – 10 2/5″ | 37 | 9′ – 10 2/5″ |
| 6 | 1′ – 7 1/5″ | 36 | 9′ – 7 1/5″ |
| 5 | 1′ – 4″ | 35 | 9′ – 4″ |
| 4 | 1′ – 0 4/5″ | 34 | 9′ – 0 4/5″ |
| 3 | 9 3/5″ | 33 | 8′ – 9 3/5″ |
| 2 | 6 2/5″ | 32 | 8′ – 6 2/5″ |
| 1 | 3 1/5″ | 31 | 8′ – 3 1/5″ |
| | | 30 | 8′ – 0″ |

### ECONOMY
4″ x 4″ x 8″ NOMINAL

| | BRICK SIZES: | |
|---|---|---|
| * For 3/8″ Joint | | 3 5/8″ x 3 5/8″ x 7 5/8″ |
| ** For 1/2″ Joint | | 3 1/2″ x 3 1/2″ x 7 1/2″ |

### UTILITY
4″ x 4″ x 12″ NOMINAL

| | BRICK SIZES: | |
|---|---|---|
| For 3/8″ Joint | | 3 5/8″ x 3 5/8″ x 11 5/8″ |
| For 1/2″ Joint | | 3 1/2″ x 3 1/2″ x 11 1/2″ |

Joint selected determines brick size.
1 course = 1 module (4″)

### NOMINAL HEIGHTS OF 4″ COURSES

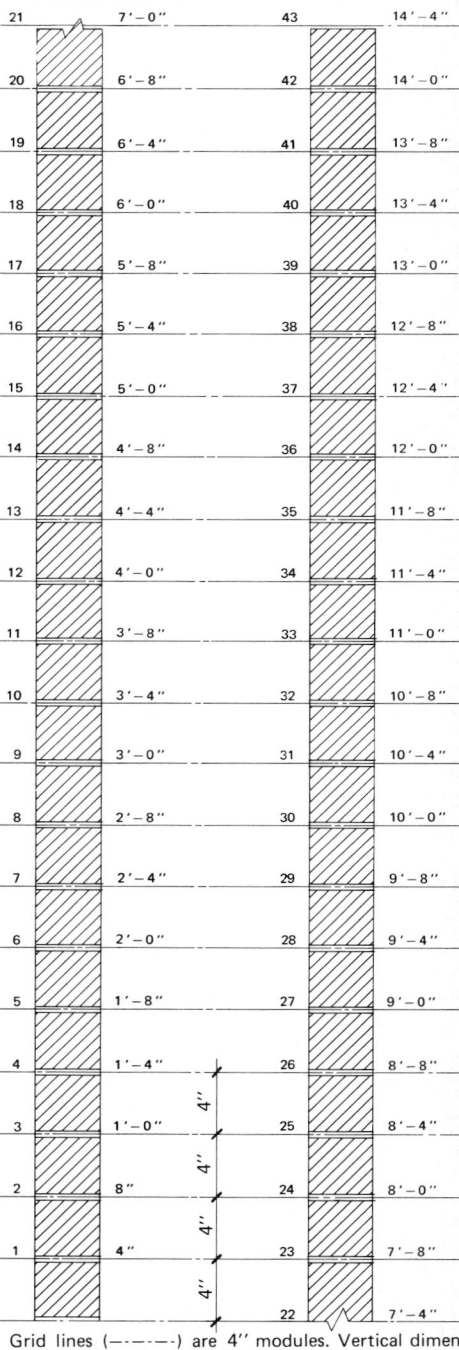

| | | | |
|---|---|---|---|
| 21 | 7′ – 0″ | 43 | 14′ – 4″ |
| 20 | 6′ – 8″ | 42 | 14′ – 0″ |
| 19 | 6′ – 4″ | 41 | 13′ – 8″ |
| 18 | 6′ – 0″ | 40 | 13′ – 4″ |
| 17 | 5′ – 8″ | 39 | 13′ – 0″ |
| 16 | 5′ – 4″ | 38 | 12′ – 8″ |
| 15 | 5′ – 0″ | 37 | 12′ – 4″ |
| 14 | 4′ – 8″ | 36 | 12′ – 0″ |
| 13 | 4′ – 4″ | 35 | 11′ – 8″ |
| 12 | 4′ – 0″ | 34 | 11′ – 4″ |
| 11 | 3′ – 8″ | 33 | 11′ – 0″ |
| 10 | 3′ – 4″ | 32 | 10′ – 8″ |
| 9 | 3′ – 0″ | 31 | 10′ – 4″ |
| 8 | 2′ – 8″ | 30 | 10′ – 0″ |
| 7 | 2′ – 4″ | 29 | 9′ – 8″ |
| 6 | 2′ – 0″ | 28 | 9′ – 4″ |
| 5 | 1′ – 8″ | 27 | 9′ – 0″ |
| 4 | 1′ – 4″ | 26 | 8′ – 8″ |
| 3 | 1′ – 0″ | 25 | 8′ – 4″ |
| 2 | 8″ | 24 | 8′ – 0″ |
| 1 | 4″ | 23 | 7′ – 8″ |
| | | 22 | 7′ – 4″ |

### NOTES
Not all sizes made in all sections of U.S.; check with local manufacturers for sizes available.

Brick Institute of America; Reston, Virginia

*3/8″ Joint used for facing brick.
**1/2″ Joint used for glazed and structural units and building brick.

Grid lines (—·—·—) are 4″ modules. Vertical dimensions are from bottom of mortar joint to bottom of mortar joint.

## UNIT MASONRY

## VERTICAL BRICK COURSES

| NUMBER OF BRICKS AND JOINTS | HEIGHT | |
|---|---|---|
| | 3/8" JOINTS | 1/2" JOINTS |
| 1 brk. & 1 jt. | 2 5/8" | 2 3/4" |
| 2 brks. & 2 jts. | 5 1/4" | 5 1/2" |
| 3 brks. & 3 jts. | 7 7/8" | 8 1/4" |
| 4 brks. & 4 jts. | 10 1/2" | 11" |
| 5 brks. & 5 jts. | 1'- 1 1/8" | 1'- 1 3/4" |
| 6 brks. & 6 jts. | 1'- 3 3/4" | 1'- 4 1/2" |
| 7 brks. & 7 jts. | 1'- 6 3/8" | 1'- 7 1/4" |
| 8 brks. & 8 jts. | 1'- 9" | 1'-10" |
| 9 brks. & 9 jts. | 1'-11 5/8" | 2'- 0 3/4" |
| 10 brks. & 10 jts. | 2'- 2 1/4" | 2'- 3 1/2" |
| 11 brks. & 11 jts. | 2'- 4 7/8" | 2'- 6 1/4" |
| 12 brks. & 12 jts. | 2'- 7 1/2" | 2'- 9" |
| 13 brks. & 13 jts. | 2'-10 1/8" | 2'-11 3/4" |
| 14 brks. & 14 jts. | 3'- 0 3/4" | 3'- 2 1/2" |
| 15 brks. & 15 jts. | 3'- 3 5/8" | 3'- 5 1/4" |
| 16 brks. & 16 jts. | 3'- 6" | 3'- 8" |
| 17 brks. & 17 jts. | 3'- 8 5/8" | 3'-10 3/4" |
| 18 brks. & 18 jts. | 3'-11 1/4" | 4'- 1 1/2" |
| 19 brks. & 19 jts. | 4'- 1 7/8" | 4'- 4 1/4" |
| 20 brks. & 20 jts. | 4'- 4 1/2" | 4'- 7" |
| 21 brks. & 21 jts. | 4'- 7 1/8" | 4'- 9 3/4" |
| 22 brks. & 22 jts. | 4'- 9 3/4" | 5'- 0 1/2" |
| 23 brks. & 23 jts. | 5'- 0 3/8" | 5'- 3 1/4" |
| 24 brks. & 24 jts. | 5'- 3" | 5'- 6" |
| 25 brks. & 25 jts. | 5'- 5 5/8" | 5'- 8 3/4" |
| 26 brks. & 26 jts. | 5'- 8 1/4" | 5'-11 1/2" |
| 27 brks. & 27 jts. | 5'-10 7/8" | 6'- 2 1/4" |
| 28 brks. & 28 jts. | 6'- 1 1/2" | 6'- 5" |
| 29 brks. & 29 jts. | 6'- 4 1/8" | 6'- 7 3/4" |
| 30 brks. & 30 jts. | 6'- 6 3/4" | 6'-10 1/2" |
| 31 brks. & 31 jts. | 6'- 9 3/8" | 7'- 1 1/4" |
| 32 brks. & 32 jts. | 7'- 0" | 7'- 4" |
| 33 brks. & 33 jts. | 7'- 2 5/8" | 7'- 6 3/4" |
| 34 brks. & 34 jts. | 7'- 5 1/4" | 7'- 9 1/2" |
| 35 brks. & 35 jts. | 7'- 7 7/8" | 8'- 0 1/4" |
| 36 brks. & 36 jts. | 7'-10 1/2" | 8'- 3" |
| 37 brks. & 37 jts. | 8'- 1 1/8" | 8'- 5 3/4" |
| 38 brks. & 38 jts. | 8'- 3 3/4" | 8'- 8 1/2" |
| 39 brks. & 39 jts. | 8'- 6 3/8" | 8'-11 1/4" |
| 40 brks. & 40 jts. | 8'- 9" | 9'- 2" |
| 41 brks. & 41 jts. | 8'-11 5/8" | 9'- 4 3/4" |
| 42 brks. & 42 jts. | 9'- 2 1/4" | 9'- 7 1/2" |
| 43 brks. & 43 jts. | 9'- 4 7/8" | 9'-10 1/4" |
| 44 brks. & 44 jts. | 9'- 7 1/2" | 10'- 1" |
| 45 brks. & 45 jts. | 9'-10 1/8" | 10'- 3 3/4" |
| 46 brks. & 46 jts. | 10'- 0 3/4" | 10'- 6 1/2" |
| 47 brks. & 47 jts. | 10'- 3 3/8" | 10'- 9 1/4" |
| 48 brks. & 48 jts. | 10'- 6" | 11'- 0" |
| 49 brks. & 49 jts. | 10'- 8 5/8" | 11'- 2 3/4" |
| 50 brks. & 50 jts. | 10'-11 1/4" | 11'- 5 1/2" |
| 51 brks. & 51 jts. | 11'- 1 7/8" | 11'- 8 1/4" |
| 52 brks. & 52 jts. | 11'- 4 1/2" | 11'-11" |
| 53 brks. & 53 jts. | 11'- 7 1/8" | 12'- 1 3/4" |
| 54 brks. & 54 jts. | 11'- 9 3/4" | 12'- 4 1/2" |
| 55 brks. & 55 jts. | 12'- 0 3/8" | 12'- 7 1/4" |
| 56 brks. & 56 jts. | 12'- 3" | 12'-10" |
| 57 brks. & 57 jts. | 12'- 5 5/8" | 13'- 0 3/4" |
| 58 brks. & 58 jts. | 12'- 8 1/4" | 13'- 3 1/2" |
| 59 brks. & 59 jts. | 12'-10 7/8" | 13'- 6 1/4" |
| 60 brks. & 60 jts. | 13'- 1 1/2" | 13'- 9" |
| 61 brks. & 61 jts. | 13'- 4 1/8" | 13'-11 3/4" |
| 62 brks. & 62 jts. | 13'- 6 3/4" | 14'- 2 1/2" |
| 63 brks. & 63 jts. | 13'- 9 3/8" | 14'- 5 1/4" |
| 64 brks. & 64 jts. | 14'- 0" | 14'- 8" |
| 65 brks. & 65 jts. | 14'- 2 5/8" | 14'-10 3/4" |
| 66 brks. & 66 jts. | 14'- 5 1/4" | 15'- 1 1/2" |
| 67 brks. & 67 jts. | 14'- 7 7/8" | 15'- 4 1/4" |
| 68 brks. & 68 jts. | 14'-10 1/2" | 15'- 7" |
| 69 brks. & 69 jts. | 15'- 1 1/8" | 15'- 9 3/4" |
| 70 brks. & 70 jts. | 15'- 3 3/4" | 16'- 0 1/2" |
| 71 brks. & 71 jts. | 15'- 6 3/8" | 16'- 3 1/4" |
| 72 brks. & 72 jts. | 15'- 9" | 16'- 6" |
| 73 brks. & 73 jts. | 15'-11 5/8" | 16'- 8 3/4" |
| 74 brks. & 74 jts. | 16'- 2 1/4" | 16'-11 1/2" |
| 75 brks. & 75 jts. | 16'- 4 7/8" | 17'- 2 1/4" |
| 76 brks. & 76 jts. | 16'- 7 1/2" | 17'- 5" |

Brick Institute of America; Reston, Virginia

## HORIZONTAL BRICK COURSES

| NUMBER OF BRICKS AND JOINTS | LENGTH OF COURSE | | NUMBER OF BRICKS AND JOINTS | LENGTH OF COURSE | |
|---|---|---|---|---|---|
| | 3/8" JOINTS | 1/2" JOINTS | | 3/8" JOINTS | 1/2" JOINTS |
| 1 brk. & 0 jt. | 0'- 8" | 0'- 8" | 39 brks. & 38 jts. | 27'- 2 1/4" | 27'- 7" |
| 1 1/2 brks. & 1 jt. | 1'- 0 3/8" | 1'- 0 1/2" | 39 1/2 brks. & 39 jts. | 27'- 6 5/8" | 27'-11 1/2" |
| 2 brks. & 1 jt. | 1'- 4 3/8" | 1'- 4 1/2" | 40 brks. & 39 jts. | 27'-10 5/8" | 28'- 3 1/2" |
| 2 1/2 brks. & 2 jts. | 1'- 8 3/4" | 1'- 9" | 40 1/2 brks. & 40 jts. | 28'- 3" | 28'- 8" |
| 3 brks. & 2 jts. | 2'- 0 3/4" | 2'- 1" | 41 brks. & 40 jts. | 28'- 7" | 29'- 0" |
| 3 1/2 brks. & 3 jts. | 2'- 5 1/8" | 2'- 5 1/2" | 41 1/2 brks. & 41 jts. | 28'-11 3/8" | 29'- 4 1/2" |
| 4 brks. & 3 jts. | 2'- 9 1/8" | 2'- 9 1/2" | 42 brks. & 41 jts. | 29'- 3 3/8" | 29'- 8 1/2" |
| 4 1/2 brks. & 4 jts. | 3'- 1 1/2" | 3'- 2" | 42 1/2 brks. & 42 jts. | 29'- 7 3/4" | 30'- 1" |
| 5 brks. & 4 jts. | 3'- 5 1/2" | 3'- 6" | 43 brks. & 42 jts. | 29'-11 3/4" | 30'- 5" |
| 5 1/2 brks. & 5 jts. | 3'- 9 7/8" | 3'-10 1/2" | 43 1/2 brks. & 43 jts. | 30'- 4 1/8" | 30'- 9 1/2" |
| 6 brks. & 5 jts. | 4'- 1 7/8" | 4'- 2 1/2" | 44 brks. & 43 jts. | 30'- 8 1/8" | 31'- 1 1/2" |
| 6 1/2 brks. & 6 jts. | 4'- 6 1/4" | 4'- 7" | 44 1/2 brks. & 44 jts. | 31'- 0 1/2" | 31'- 6" |
| 7 brks. & 6 jts. | 4'-10 1/4" | 4'-11" | 45 brks. & 44 jts. | 31'- 4 1/2" | 31'-10" |
| 7 1/2 brks. & 7 jts. | 5'- 2 5/8" | 5'- 3 1/2" | 45 1/2 brks. & 45 jts. | 31'- 8 7/8" | 32'- 2 1/2" |
| 8 brks. & 7 jts. | 5'- 6 5/8" | 5'- 7 1/2" | 46 brks. & 45 jts. | 32'- 0 7/8" | 32'- 6 1/2" |
| 8 1/2 brks. & 8 jts. | 5'-11" | 6'- 0" | 46 1/2 brks. & 46 jts. | 32'- 5 1/4" | 32'-11" |
| 9 brks. & 8 jts. | 6'- 3" | 6'- 4" | 47 brks. & 46 jts. | 32'- 9 1/4" | 33'- 3" |
| 9 1/2 brks. & 9 jts. | 6'- 7 3/8" | 6'- 8 1/2" | 47 1/2 brks. & 47 jts. | 33'- 1 5/8" | 33'- 7 1/2" |
| 10 brks. & 9 jts. | 6'-11 3/8" | 7'- 0 1/2" | 48 brks. & 47 jts. | 33'- 5 5/8" | 33'-11 1/2" |
| 10 1/2 brks. & 10 jts. | 7'- 3 3/4" | 7'- 5" | 48 1/2 brks. & 48 jts. | 33'-10" | 34'- 4" |
| 11 brks. & 10 jts. | 7'- 7 3/4" | 7'- 9" | 49 brks. & 48 jts. | 34'- 2" | 34'- 8" |
| 11 1/2 brks. & 11 jts. | 8'- 0 1/8" | 8'- 1 1/2" | 49 1/2 brks. & 49 jts. | 34'- 6 3/8" | 35'- 0 1/2" |
| 12 brks. & 11 jts. | 8'- 4 1/8" | 8'- 5 1/2" | 50 brks. & 49 jts. | 34'-10 3/8" | 35'- 4 1/2" |
| 12 1/2 brks. & 12 jts. | 8'- 8 1/2" | 8'-10" | 50 1/2 brks. & 50 jts. | 35'- 2 3/4" | 35'- 9" |
| 13 brks. & 12 jts. | 9'- 0 1/2" | 9'- 2" | 51 brks. & 50 jts. | 35'- 6 3/4" | 36'- 1" |
| 13 1/2 brks. & 13 jts. | 9'- 4 7/8" | 9'- 6 1/2" | 51 1/2 brks. & 51 jts. | 35'-11 1/8" | 36'- 5 1/2" |
| 14 brks. & 13 jts. | 9'- 8 7/8" | 9'-10 1/2" | 52 brks. & 51 jts. | 36'- 3 1/8" | 36'- 9 1/2" |
| 14 1/2 brks. & 14 jts. | 10'- 1 1/4" | 10'- 3" | 52 1/2 brks. & 52 jts. | 36'- 7 1/2" | 37'- 2" |
| 15 brks. & 14 jts. | 10'- 5 1/4" | 10'- 7" | 53 brks. & 52 jts. | 36'-11 1/2" | 37'- 6" |
| 15 1/2 brks. & 15 jts. | 10'- 9 5/8" | 10'-11 1/2" | 53 1/2 brks. & 53 jts. | 37'- 3 7/8" | 37'-10 1/2" |
| 16 brks. & 15 jts. | 11'- 1 5/8" | 11'- 3 1/2" | 54 brks. & 53 jts. | 37'- 7 7/8" | 38'- 2 1/2" |
| 16 1/2 brks. & 16 jts. | 11'- 6" | 11'- 8" | 54 1/2 brks. & 54 jts. | 38'- 0 1/4" | 38'- 7" |
| 17 brks. & 16 jts. | 11'-10" | 12'- 0" | 55 brks. & 54 jts. | 38'- 4 1/4" | 38'-11" |
| 17 1/2 brks. & 17 jts. | 12'- 2 3/8" | 12'- 4 1/2" | 55 1/2 brks. & 55 jts. | 38'- 8 5/8" | 39'- 3 1/2" |
| 18 brks. & 17 jts. | 12'- 6 3/8" | 12'- 8 1/2" | 56 brks. & 55 jts. | 39'- 0 5/8" | 39'- 7 1/2" |
| 18 1/2 brks. & 18 jts. | 12'-10 3/4" | 13'- 1" | 56 1/2 brks. & 56 jts. | 39'- 5" | 40'- 0" |
| 19 brks. & 18 jts. | 13'- 2 3/4" | 13'- 5" | 57 brks. & 56 jts. | 39'- 9" | 40'- 4" |
| 19 1/2 brks. & 19 jts. | 13'- 7 1/8" | 13'- 9 1/2" | 57 1/2 brks. & 57 jts. | 40'- 1 3/8" | 40'- 8 1/2" |
| 20 brks. & 19 jts. | 13'-11 1/8" | 14'- 1 1/2" | 58 brks. & 57 jts. | 40'- 5 3/8" | 41'- 0 1/2" |
| 20 1/2 brks. & 20 jts. | 14'- 3 1/2" | 14'- 6" | 58 1/2 brks. & 58 jts. | 40'- 9 3/4" | 41'- 5" |
| 21 brks. & 20 jts. | 14'- 7 1/2" | 14'-10" | 59 brks. & 58 jts. | 41'- 1 3/4" | 41'- 9" |
| 21 1/2 brks. & 21 jts. | 14'-11 7/8" | 15'- 2 1/2" | 59 1/2 brks. & 59 jts. | 41'- 6 1/8" | 42'- 1 1/2" |
| 22 brks. & 21 jts. | 15'- 3 7/8" | 15'- 6 1/2" | 60 brks. & 59 jts. | 41'-10 1/8" | 42'- 5 1/2" |
| 22 1/2 brks. & 22 jts. | 15'- 8 1/4" | 15'-11" | | | |
| 23 brks. & 22 jts. | 16'- 0 1/4" | 16'- 3" | | | |
| 23 1/2 brks. & 23 jts. | 16'- 4 5/8" | 16'- 7 1/2" | | | |
| 24 brks. & 23 jts. | 16'- 8 5/8" | 16'-11 1/2" | | | |
| 24 1/2 brks. & 24 jts. | 17'- 1" | 17'- 4" | | | |
| 25 brks. & 24 jts. | 17'- 5" | 17'- 8" | | | |
| 25 1/2 brks. & 25 jts. | 17'- 9 3/8" | 18'- 0 1/2" | | | |
| 26 brks. & 25 jts. | 18'- 1 3/8" | 18'- 4 1/2" | | | |
| 26 1/2 brks. & 26 jts. | 18'- 5 3/4" | 18'- 9" | | | |
| 27 brks. & 26 jts. | 18'- 9 3/4" | 19'- 1" | | | |
| 27 1/2 brks. & 27 jts. | 19'- 2 1/8" | 19'- 5 1/2" | | | |
| 28 brks. & 27 jts. | 19'- 6 1/8" | 19'- 9 1/2" | | | |
| 28 1/2 brks. & 28 jts. | 19'-10 1/2" | 20'- 2" | | | |
| 29 brks. & 28 jts. | 20'- 2 1/2" | 20'- 6" | | | |
| 29 1/2 brks. & 29 jts. | 20'- 6 7/8" | 20'-10 1/2" | | | |
| 30 brks. & 29 jts. | 20'-10 7/8" | 21'- 2 1/2" | | | |
| 30 1/2 brks. & 30 jts. | 21'- 3 1/4" | 21'- 7" | | | |
| 31 brks. & 30 jts. | 21'- 7 1/4" | 21'-11" | | | |
| 31 1/2 brks. & 31 jts. | 21'-11 5/8" | 22'- 3 1/2" | | | |
| 32 brks. & 31 jts. | 22'- 3 5/8" | 22'- 7 1/2" | | | |
| 32 1/2 brks. & 32 jts. | 22'- 8" | 23'- 0" | | | |
| 33 brks. & 32 jts. | 23'- 0" | 23'- 4" | | | |
| 33 1/2 brks. & 33 jts. | 23'- 4 3/8" | 23'- 8 1/2" | | | |
| 34 brks. & 33 jts. | 23'- 8 3/8" | 24'- 0 1/2" | | | |
| 34 1/2 brks. & 34 jts. | 24'- 0 3/4" | 24'- 5" | | | |
| 35 brks. & 34 jts. | 24'- 4 3/4" | 24'- 9" | | | |
| 35 1/2 brks. & 35 jts. | 24'- 9 1/8" | 25'- 1 1/2" | | | |
| 36 brks. & 35 jts. | 25'- 1 1/8" | 25'- 5 1/2" | | | |
| 36 1/2 brks. & 36 jts. | 25'- 5 1/2" | 25'-10" | | | |
| 37 brks. & 36 jts. | 25'- 9 1/2" | 26'- 2" | | | |
| 37 1/2 brks. & 37 jts. | 26'- 1 7/8" | 26'- 6 1/2" | | | |
| 38 brks. & 37 jts. | 26'- 5 7/8" | 26'-10 1/2" | | | |
| 38 1/2 brks. & 38 jts. | 26'-10 1/4" | 27'- 3" | | | |

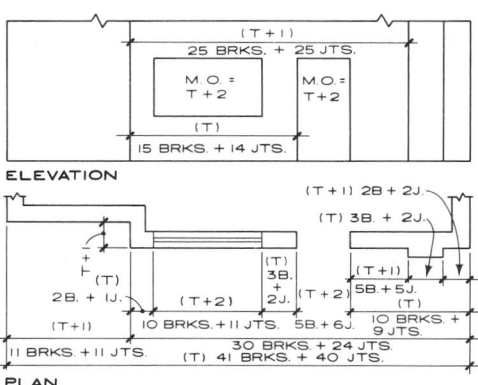

## EXAMPLE SHOWING USE OF TABLE

T:     Dimensions and number of joints as given in the table, that is, one joint less than the number of bricks.

T + 1:  One brick joint added to figure given in the table, that is, the number of bricks is equal to the number of joints.

T + 2:  Two brick joints added to figure given in the table, that is, one joint more than the number of bricks.

UNIT MASONRY

### GENERAL NOTES

1. Fire resistance ratings vary according to the ultimate composition of a masonry wall. Designers should refer to local codes to obtain this information.
2. Straight metal ties should be used in rigidly insulated masonry walls. Metal ties with drips should be used in noninsulated cavity masonry walls.
3. Water and vapor migration into a masonry wall may be controlled by designing a drainage-type wall or a barrier-type wall. Drainage walls are provided with damp course flashing and weep holes 24 in. o.c. just above the flashing. Barrier walls have a mortar-parged or fully grouted joint between wythes. Damp course flashing should also be used with the barrier-type wall. Most water migration occurs at mortar joints. Mortar

selection should be based on the "initial" rate of absorption of the brick selected, as well as on regional weather conditions; mortars containing air-entering agents should be avoided.
4. All anchors, ties, and attachments should be stainless steel or of corrosion-resistant metal or be coated with such metal.
5. Block and brick quality varies throughout the industry. Masonry units should be chosen on the basis of availability, historical product quality of the manufacturer, strength, cost, and appearance. As with most construction assemblies, the final product will only be as good as the design and installation.

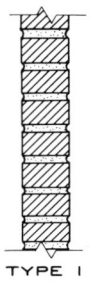

**TYPE 1**
4'' BRICK WALL
MODULAR BRICK
4'' x 2⅔'' x 8''

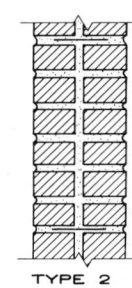

**TYPE 2**
8'' BRICK WALL
METAL TIED
4'' x 2⅔'' x 8''

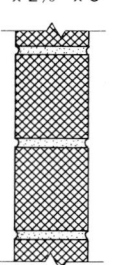

**TYPE 3**
CMU WALL

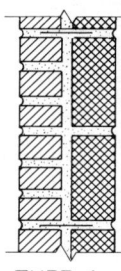

**TYPE 4**
4'' MODULAR BRICK
4'' CMU WALL
METAL TIED

### HEIGHT/THICKNESS RATIO OF MASONRY WALLS

| BEARING CONDITION | TYPE 1 | TYPE 2 | TYPE 3 |
|---|---|---|---|
| Maximum bearing wall height[1] | $\frac{H}{T} \leq 18$ | $\frac{H}{T} \leq 18$ | $\frac{H}{T} \leq 18$ |
| Maximum nonbearing wall height[1] | $\frac{H}{T} \leq 20$ | $\frac{H}{T} \leq 20$ | $\frac{H}{T} \leq 20$ |
| | TYPE 4 | TYPE 5 | TYPE 6 |
| Maximum bearing wall height[1] | $\frac{H}{T} \leq 18$ | $\frac{H}{T} \leq 25$ | $\frac{H}{T} \leq 25$ |
| Maximum nonbearing wall height[1] | $\frac{H}{T} \leq 20$ | $\frac{H}{T} \leq 48$ | $\frac{H}{T} \leq 48$ |
| | TYPE 7 | TYPE 8 | TYPE 9 |
| Maximum bearing wall height[1] | $\frac{H}{T} \leq 25$ | $\frac{H}{T} \leq 18^2$ | $\frac{H}{T} \leq 18^2$ |
| Maximum nonbearing wall height[1] | $\frac{H}{T} \leq 48$ | $\frac{H}{T} \leq 20^2$ | $\frac{H}{T} \leq 20^2$ |

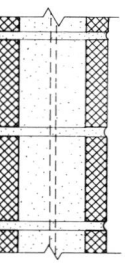

**TYPE 5**
REINFORCED
CMU WALL

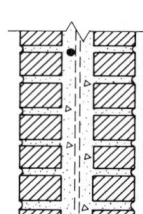

**TYPE 6**
REINFORCED
BRICK MASONRY
WALL (RBM)

### NOTES

1. Maximum unsupported wall heights should be determined by local codes. Formulas given are for planning purposes only and solutions should be verified by a structural engineer. In the formulas,
   H = height of wall (in feet)
   T = thickness of wall (in feet)
2. Resultant thickness is the net wall thickness of masonry units. Up to a 2 in. cavity may be used with this formula as long as the wythes are tied together with cavity wall ties.
3. Empirical formulas are taken from the 1982 Uniform Building Code.

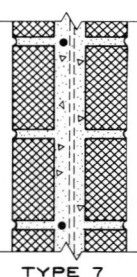

**TYPE 7**
REINFORCED
CMU WALL

**TYPE 8**
CAVITY WALL
SPLIT FACE CMU
AND CMU

### PROPERTIES OF MASONRY WALL COMPONENTS

| MATERIAL | WEIGHT (LB/SQ FT) | QUANTITY (100 SQ FT)[1] | U VALUE[2] | STC |
|---|---|---|---|---|
| 4 in. brick | 40 | 675 units | 2.27 | 39 |
| 4 in. CMU | 22 | 113 units | 0.71 | 40 |
| 6 in. CMU | 32 | 113 units | 0.65 | 44 |
| 8 in. CMU | 35 | 113 units | 0.57 | 45 |
| 10 in. CMU | 45 | 113 units | 0.50 | 50 |
| 12 in. CMU | 55 | 113 units | 0.47 | 55 |
| 2 in. vermiculite (loose) | 1.16 | 116 lb | 0.22 | — |
| 2 in. perlite (loose) | 1.08 | 108 lb | 0.18 | — |
| 2 in. polystyrene (rigid) | 0.58 | 100 sq ft | 0.09 | — |
| 2 in. polyurethane (rigid) | 0.25 | 100 sq ft | 0.08 | — |
| 2 in. Airspace | — | — | 0.40 | 4 |
| Air film exterior[3] | — | — | 4.76 | — |
| Air film interior[4] | — | — | 1.39 | — |

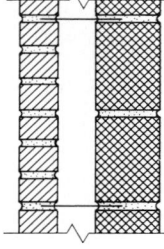

**TYPE 9**
CAVITY
WALL—BRICK
AND CMU

**WALL TYPES**

### NOTES

1. Waste is not included, as this will vary with the job. A waste factor of 2–5% is often applied for masonry units.
2. U values are tabulated from various sources and represent an average value for the given material. Check with manufacturers for actual U values.
3. U value given is an average of both winter and summer winds.
4. U value given is an average of still air on all surface positions and direction of heat flow.

Charles L. Goodman, AIA; Everett I. Brown Company; Indianapolis, Indiana
Robert Joseph Sangiamo, AIA; New York, New York
Davis, Brody & Associates; New York, New York

International Conference of Building Officials, see data sources

 **UNIT MASONRY**

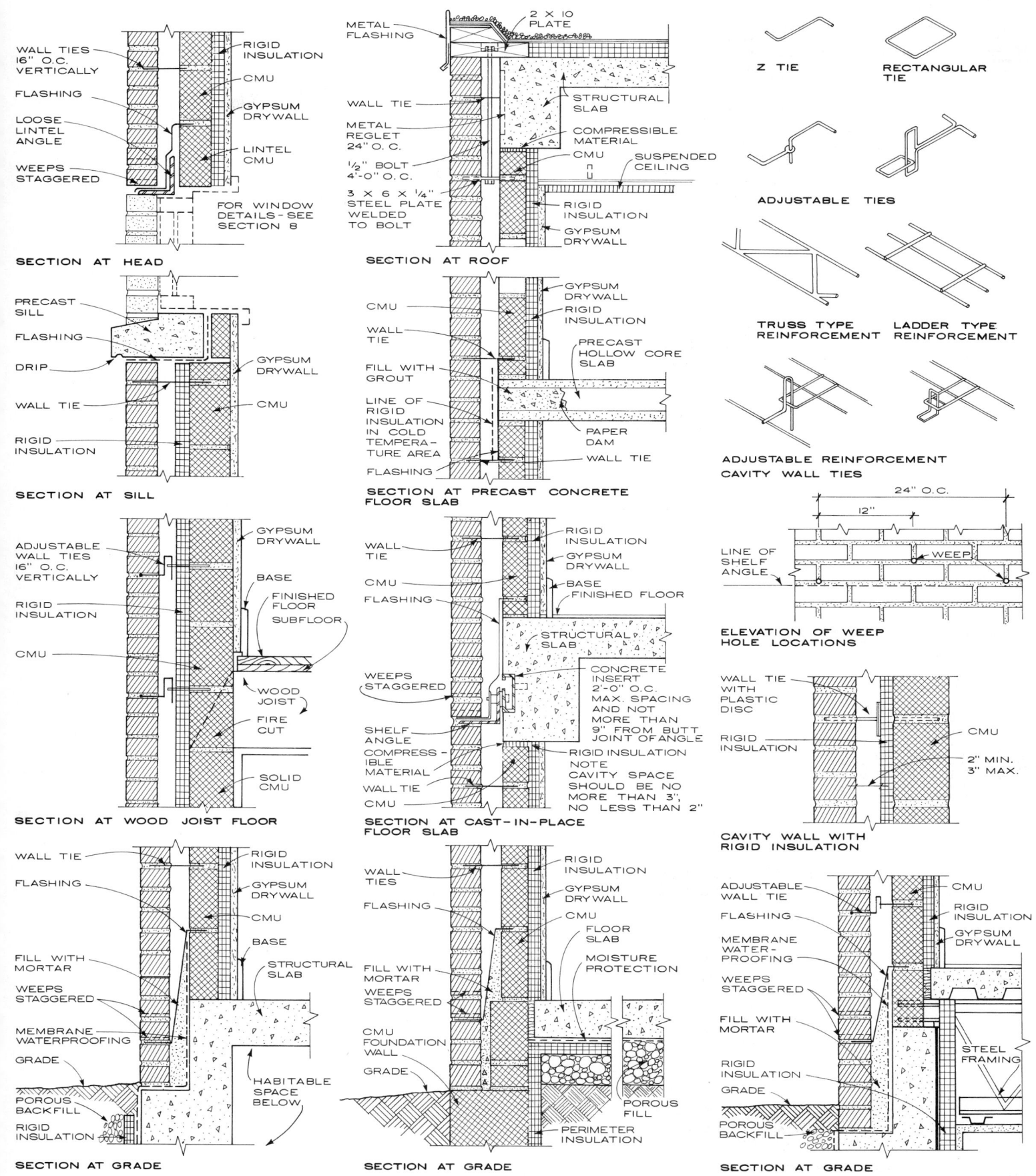

**SECTION AT HEAD**

WALL TIES 16" O.C. VERTICALLY
FLASHING
LOOSE LINTEL ANGLE
WEEPS STAGGERED
RIGID INSULATION
CMU
GYPSUM DRYWALL
LINTEL CMU
FOR WINDOW DETAILS—SEE SECTION 8

**SECTION AT SILL**

PRECAST SILL
FLASHING
DRIP
WALL TIE
RIGID INSULATION
GYPSUM DRYWALL
CMU

**SECTION AT WOOD JOIST FLOOR**

ADJUSTABLE WALL TIES 16" O.C. VERTICALLY
RIGID INSULATION
CMU
GYPSUM DRYWALL
BASE
FINISHED FLOOR
SUBFLOOR
WOOD JOIST
FIRE CUT
SOLID CMU

**SECTION AT GRADE**

WALL TIE
FLASHING
FILL WITH MORTAR
WEEPS STAGGERED
MEMBRANE WATERPROOFING
GRADE
POROUS BACKFILL
RIGID INSULATION
RIGID INSULATION
GYPSUM DRYWALL
CMU
BASE
STRUCTURAL SLAB
HABITABLE SPACE BELOW

**SECTION AT ROOF**

METAL FLASHING
2 X 10 PLATE
WALL TIE
METAL REGLET 24" O.C.
1/2" BOLT 4'-0" O.C.
3 X 6 X 1/4" STEEL PLATE WELDED TO BOLT
STRUCTURAL SLAB
COMPRESSIBLE MATERIAL
CMU
SUSPENDED CEILING
RIGID INSULATION
GYPSUM DRYWALL

**SECTION AT PRECAST CONCRETE FLOOR SLAB**

CMU
WALL TIE
FILL WITH GROUT
LINE OF RIGID INSULATION IN COLD TEMPERATURE AREA
FLASHING
GYPSUM DRYWALL
RIGID INSULATION
PRECAST HOLLOW CORE SLAB
PAPER DAM
WALL TIE

**SECTION AT CAST-IN-PLACE FLOOR SLAB**

WALL TIE
CMU
FLASHING
WEEPS STAGGERED
SHELF ANGLE
COMPRESSIBLE MATERIAL
WALL TIE
CMU
RIGID INSULATION
GYPSUM DRYWALL
BASE
FINISHED FLOOR
STRUCTURAL SLAB
CONCRETE INSERT 2'-0" O.C. MAX. SPACING AND NOT MORE THAN 9" FROM BUTT JOINT OF ANGLE
RIGID INSULATION
NOTE
CAVITY SPACE SHOULD BE NO MORE THAN 3", NO LESS THAN 2"

**SECTION AT GRADE**

WALL TIES
FLASHING
FILL WITH MORTAR
WEEPS STAGGERED
CMU FOUNDATION WALL
GRADE
RIGID INSULATION
GYPSUM DRYWALL
CMU
FLOOR SLAB
MOISTURE PROTECTION
POROUS FILL
PERIMETER INSULATION

**Z TIE**

**RECTANGULAR TIE**

**ADJUSTABLE TIES**

**TRUSS TYPE REINFORCEMENT**     **LADDER TYPE REINFORCEMENT**

**ADJUSTABLE REINFORCEMENT CAVITY WALL TIES**

LINE OF SHELF ANGLE
WEEP
24" O.C.
12"

**ELEVATION OF WEEP HOLE LOCATIONS**

WALL TIE WITH PLASTIC DISC
RIGID INSULATION
CMU
2" MIN.
3" MAX.

**CAVITY WALL WITH RIGID INSULATION**

**SECTION AT GRADE**

ADJUSTABLE WALL TIE
FLASHING
MEMBRANE WATERPROOFING
WEEPS STAGGERED
FILL WITH MORTAR
RIGID INSULATION
GRADE
POROUS BACKFILL
CMU
RIGID INSULATION
GYPSUM DRYWALL
STEEL FRAMING

Robert J. Sangiamo, AIA; New York, New York
Davis, Brody & Associates; New York, New York

**UNIT MASONRY**     4

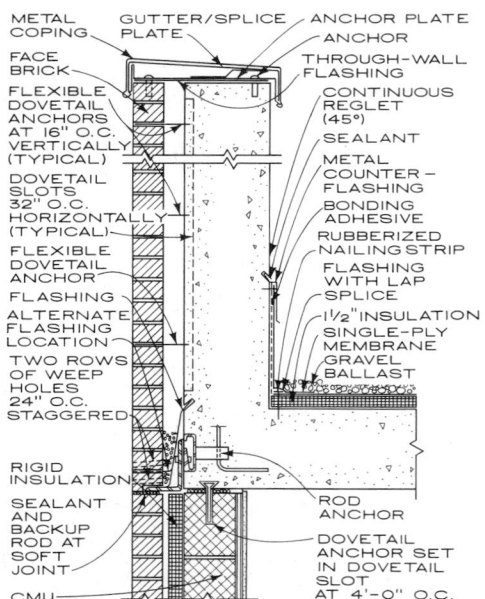

**CAVITY WALL AT CONCRETE PARAPET**

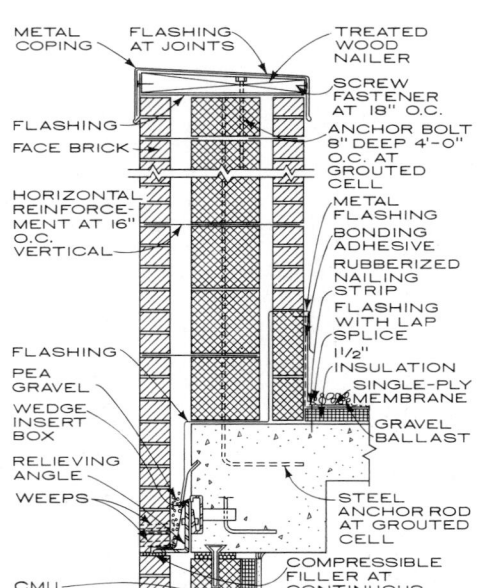

**PARAPET WALL WITH DOUBLE CAVITY**

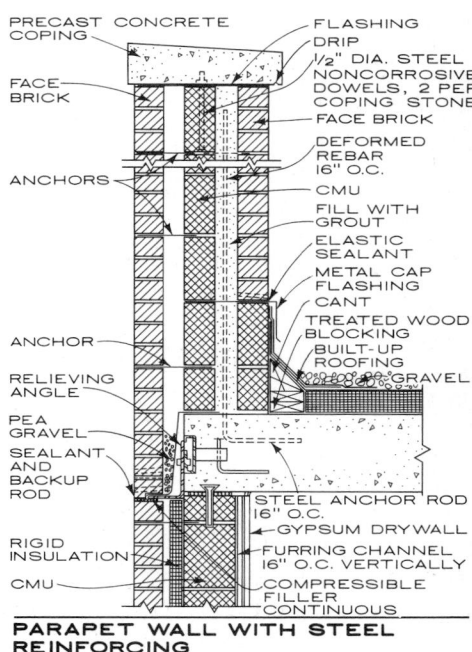

**PARAPET WALL WITH STEEL REINFORCING**

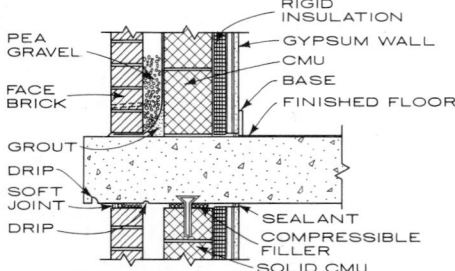

**EXPOSED SLAB DETAIL**

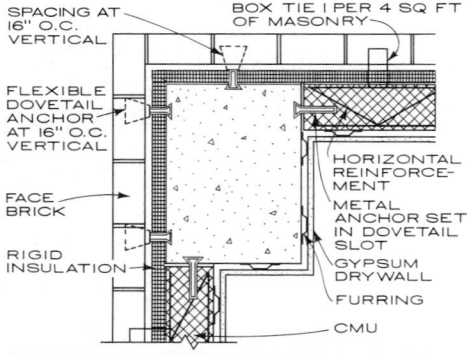

**DOVETAIL ANCHORS AT CORNER**

## GENERAL NOTES

1. Relieving angles should be designed to limit deflection to $1/700$ of span between wedge inset centerlines.

2. The horizontal reinforcing whose primary purposes are to prevent cracks in the mortar of the CMU wythe of masonry and aid in spanning wind load to supports should also be used to attach the brick masonry ties. The ties are required only to transfer forces due to positive and negative wind pressure on the brick wythe of the CMU wythe.

3. "Z" type masonry ties should not be used with hollow CMU masonry.

4. Type S mortar should be used where the winds are greater than 80 miles per hour.

5. Exterior brick should conform to the requirements of ASTM-216.

6. The exterior wythe of brick masonry should be panelized by the use of horizontal and vertical control joints.

7. Control joint sizes should accommodate the following Brick Institute of America Formula Technical Note 18A:

$$w = [0.0002 + 0.000004 \, (T \text{ max.} - T \text{ min.})] \, L$$

where: $L$ = length of wall in inches
$T$ max. = maximum mean wall temperature in degrees Fahrenheit
$T$ min. = minimum mean wall temperature in degrees Fahrenheit
$w$ = total expansion of wall in inches

Actual joint width in masonry is determined by anticipated movement times the limit of compressibility and expandability of the sealant. Typically for polysulfide sealants one multiplies anticipated movement by four, and for urethane sealants by two. Consult manufacturers' recommendations for the actual products proposed for use.

8. When the structural frame of a building is of reinforced concrete, horizontal control joints must also accommodate the dimensional change due to anticipated shrinkage and creep of the concrete columns.

9. Aligning vertical control joints with the window jambs is good practice for economy.

10. The number of vertical control joints required should be doubled at the parapet, and vertical control joints should also be added at 5 to 10 ft from each corner.

11. CMU masonry and brick masonry should not be exposed on the same parapet, as the CMU expands and contracts at different rates than the brick masonry, causing parapet cracking.

12. The spacing and size of the vertical reinforcing in a parapet are a function of parapet height wall and local wind pressure. For high-rise buildings, structural design is required.

13. For lateral support requirements consult local codes.

14. Refer to Brick Institute of America Technical Note 21, Brick Masonry Cavity Walls, for additional information.

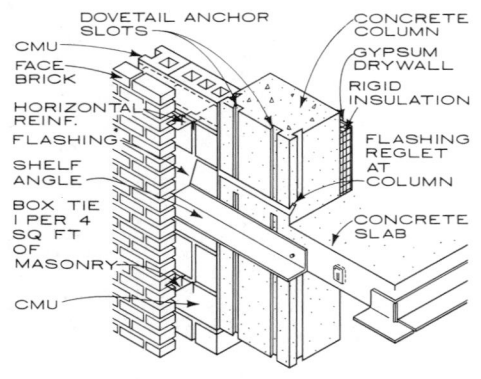

**SHELF ANGLE AT CORNER COLUMN**

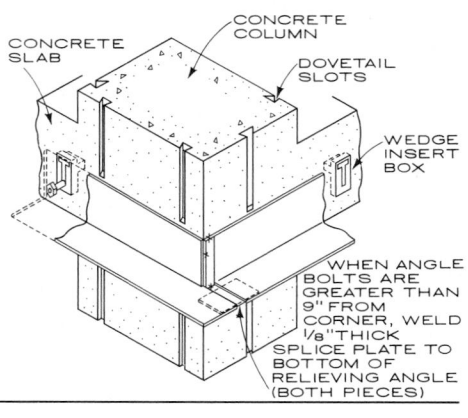

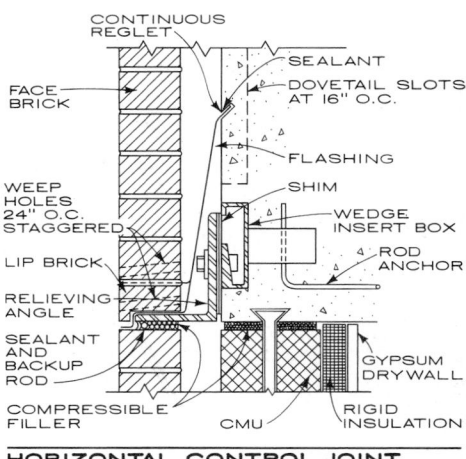

**HORIZONTAL CONTROL JOINT**

Theodore D. Sherman; Lev Zetlin Associates, Inc.; New York, New York
Robert J. Sangiamo, AIA; New York, New York
Davis, Brody & Associates; New York, New York

**UNIT MASONRY**

GENERAL NOTE : VERMICULITE SHOULD NOT BE USED TO FILL CAVITY WALLS

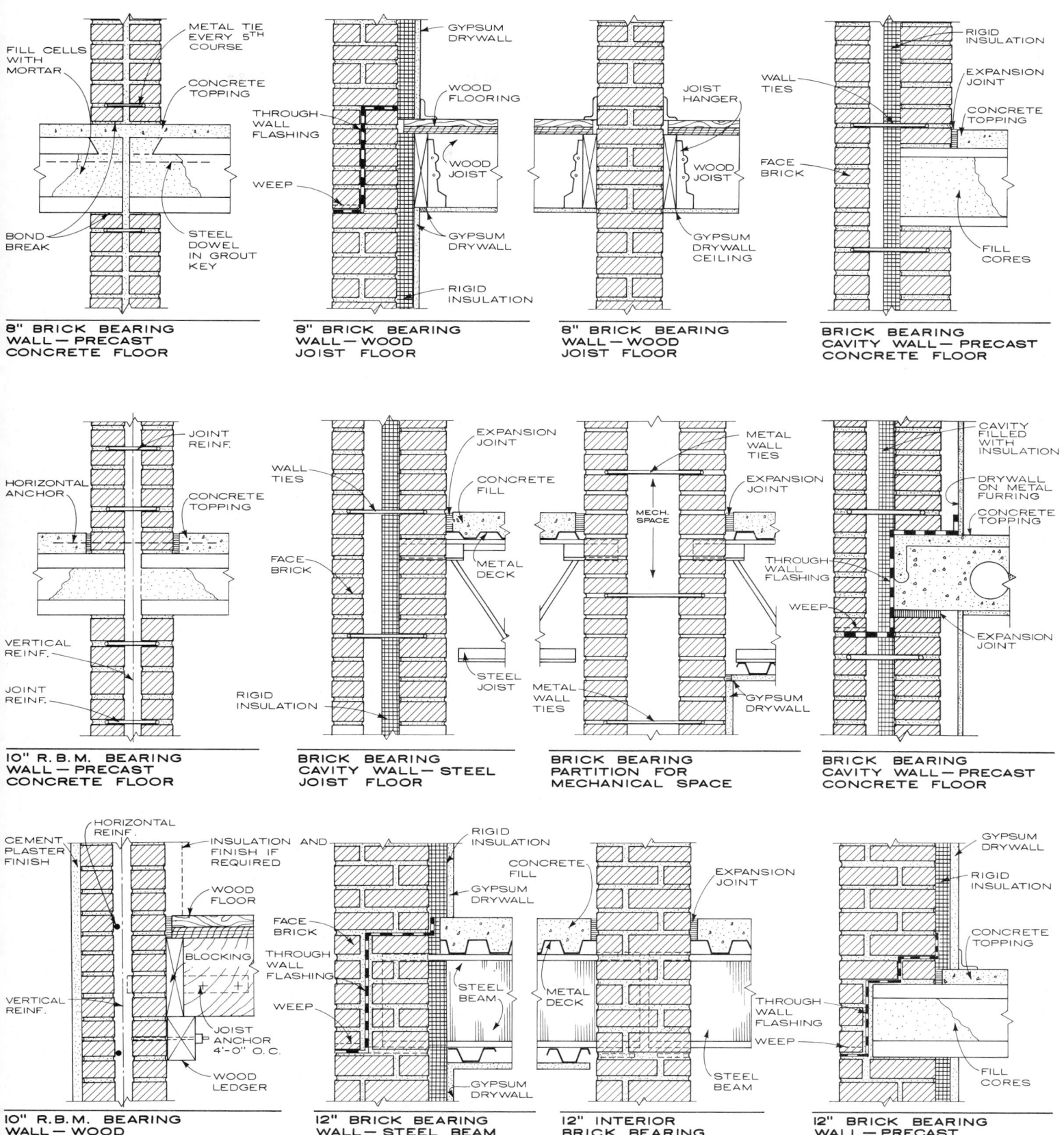

8" BRICK BEARING
WALL—PRECAST
CONCRETE FLOOR

8" BRICK BEARING
WALL—WOOD
JOIST FLOOR

8" BRICK BEARING
WALL—WOOD
JOIST FLOOR

BRICK BEARING
CAVITY WALL—PRECAST
CONCRETE FLOOR

10" R.B.M. BEARING
WALL—PRECAST
CONCRETE FLOOR

BRICK BEARING
CAVITY WALL—STEEL
JOIST FLOOR

BRICK BEARING
PARTITION FOR
MECHANICAL SPACE

BRICK BEARING
CAVITY WALL—PRECAST
CONCRETE FLOOR

10" R.B.M. BEARING
WALL—WOOD
JOIST FLOOR

12" BRICK BEARING
WALL—STEEL BEAM
AND METAL DECK
FLOOR

12" INTERIOR
BRICK BEARING
PARTITION

12" BRICK BEARING
WALL—PRECAST
CONCRETE FLOOR

Robert Joseph Sangiamo, AIA; New York, New York
Davis, Brody & Associates; New York, New York

UNIT MASONRY

4

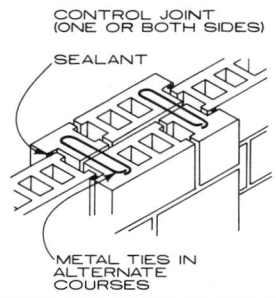

CONTROL JOINT (ONE OR BOTH SIDES)
SEALANT
METAL TIES IN ALTERNATE COURSES

**CONTROL JOINT AT PIER**

CONTROL JOINTS
TYPICAL HORIZONTAL JOINT REINFORCEMENT
FILLER ROD AND SEALANT

**FLUSH WALL AND PLASTER CONTROL JOINTS**

CONCRETE CONTROL BLOCK
FILLER ROD AND SEALANT

**CONTROL JOINT BLOCK**

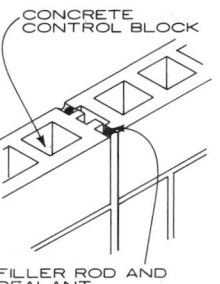

PREFORMED GASKET
SASH UNITS
RAKE JOINT ¾" (TYPICAL) AND SEALANT JOINT

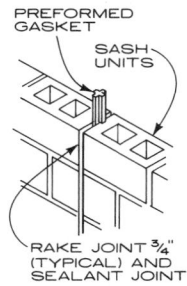

BUILDING FELT ON ONE SIDE ONLY OR COAT OF ASPHALT PAINT
CORE FILLED WITH MORTAR FOR LATERAL STABILITY AND SEALANT

**FLUSH WALL CONTROL JOINTS**

## PRINCIPLES

Masonry materials expand and contract in response to temperature changes. Dimensional changes also occur in masonry because of moisture variations. To compensate for these dimensional changes and thus control cracking in masonry, keep the following in mind:

1. Proper product specifications and construction procedures limit moisture related movements. For example, Type I moisture controlled concrete masonry units are manufactured to minimize moisture related movement.
2. Proper steel reinforcing, including horizontal joint reinforcing, increases the tensile resistance of masonry walls.
3. Properly placed expansion joints and control joints accommodate movement and provide for controlled crack locations.

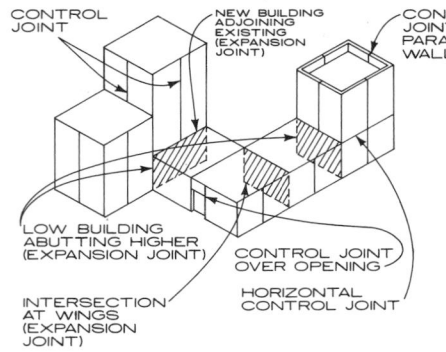
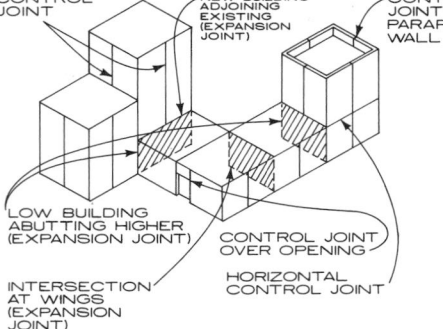

CONTROL JOINT
NEW BUILDING ADJOINING EXISTING (EXPANSION JOINT)
CONTROL JOINT THROUGH PARAPET WALL
LOW BUILDING ABUTTING HIGHER (EXPANSION JOINT)
CONTROL JOINT OVER OPENING
INTERSECTION AT WINGS (EXPANSION JOINT)
HORIZONTAL CONTROL JOINT

**LOCATION OF CONTROL AND EXPANSION JOINTS**

## CONTROL JOINT SPACING FOR MOISTURE CONTROLLED ASTM C90 TYPE I BLOCK UNITS

| RECOMMENDED SPACING OF CONTROL JOINTS | VERTICAL SPACING OF JOINT REINFORCEMENT | | | |
|---|---|---|---|---|
| | NONE | 24" | 16" | 8" |
| Expressed as ratio of panel length to height (L/H) | 2 | 2½ | 3 | 4 |
| Panel length (L) not to exceed (regardless of height (H)) | 40' | 45' | 50' | 60' |

## EXPANSION JOINTS

The purpose of expansion joints is to relieve tension and compression between separate portions of a masonry wall resulting from temperature and/or moisture induced dimensional movements.

Exterior and interior masonry wythes of cavity walls should be connected with flexible metal ties. Horizontal expansion joints should be located below shelf angles or structural frames supporting masonry walls or panels. Shelf angles should contain sufficient interruptions to accommodate thermal movement. Horizontal expansion joints (soft joints, slip channel, etc.) should also be provided above exterior masonry walls or panels abutting structural frames and at interior non-load-bearing masonry walls abutting the underside of floor or roof structures above.

## CONTROL JOINTS

The purpose of control joints is to provide tension relief between individual portions of a masonry wall that may change from their original dimensions. They must provide for lateral stability across the joint and contain a through wall seal.

Control joints should be located in long straight walls, at major changes in wall heights, at changes in wall thickness, above joints in foundations, at columns and pilasters, at one or both sides of wall openings, near wall intersections, and near junctions of walls in L, T, or U shaped buildings. Joints should continue through roof parapets.

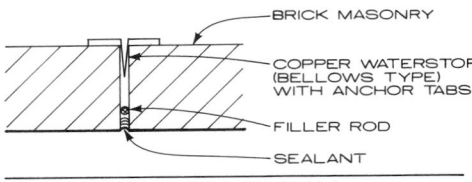

BRICK MASONRY
COPPER WATERSTOP (BELLOWS TYPE) WITH ANCHOR TABS
FILLER ROD
SEALANT

**EXPANSION JOINT AT WALL**

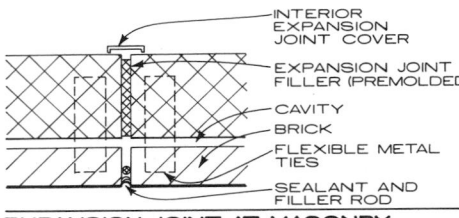

INTERIOR EXPANSION JOINT COVER
EXPANSION JOINT FILLER (PREMOLDED)
CAVITY
BRICK
FLEXIBLE METAL TIES
SEALANT AND FILLER ROD

**EXPANSION JOINT AT MASONRY CAVITY WALL**

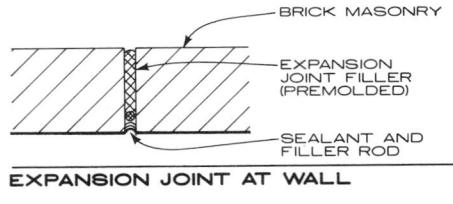

BRICK MASONRY
EXPANSION JOINT FILLER (PREMOLDED)
SEALANT AND FILLER ROD

**EXPANSION JOINT AT WALL**

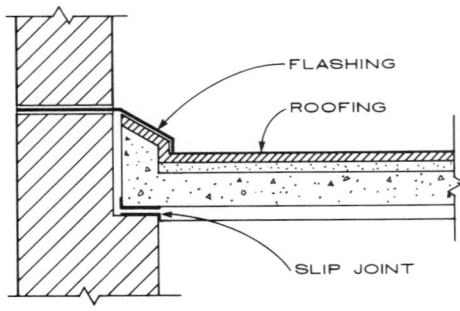

FLASHING
ROOFING
SLIP JOINT

**PARAPET AND RIGID ROOF SLAB**

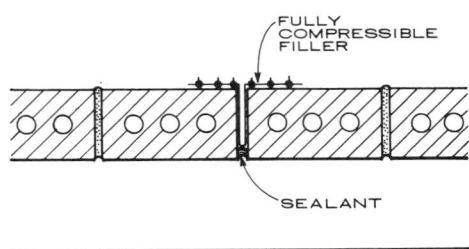

FULLY COMPRESSIBLE FILLER
SEALANT

**WALL EXPANSION JOINT**

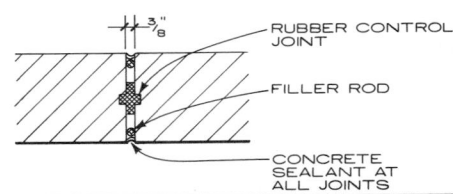

RUBBER CONTROL JOINT
FILLER ROD
CONCRETE SEALANT AT ALL JOINTS

**CONTROL JOINT AT STRAIGHT WALL**

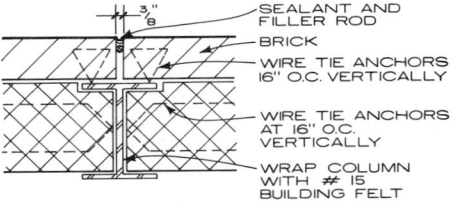

SEALANT AND FILLER ROD
BRICK
WIRE TIE ANCHORS 16" O.C. VERTICALLY
WIRE TIE ANCHORS AT 16" O.C. VERTICALLY
WRAP COLUMN WITH # 15 BUILDING FELT

**CONTROL JOINT AT STEEL COLUMN**

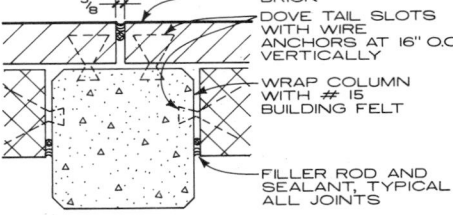

BRICK
DOVE TAIL SLOTS WITH WIRE ANCHORS AT 16" O.C. VERTICALLY
WRAP COLUMN WITH # 15 BUILDING FELT
FILLER ROD AND SEALANT, TYPICAL ALL JOINTS

**CONTROL JOINT AT CONCRETE COLUMN**

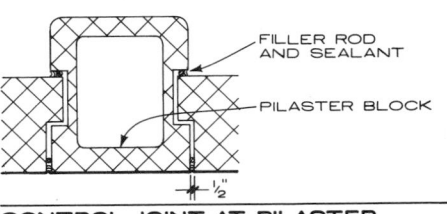

FILLER ROD AND SEALANT
PILASTER BLOCK

**CONTROL JOINT AT PILASTER**

Setter, Leach & Lindstrom, Inc.; Minneapolis, Minnesota

 **UNIT MASONRY**

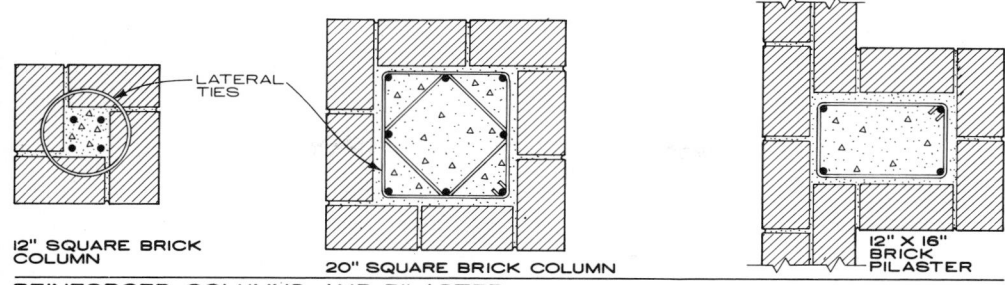

12" SQUARE BRICK COLUMN — LATERAL TIES

20" SQUARE BRICK COLUMN

12" X 16" BRICK PILASTER

**REINFORCED COLUMNS AND PILASTER**

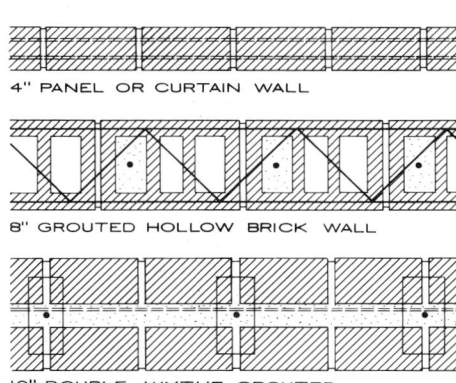

4" PANEL OR CURTAIN WALL

8" GROUTED HOLLOW BRICK WALL

10" DOUBLE-WYTHE GROUTED, REINFORCED BRICK WALL

**WALL TYPES**

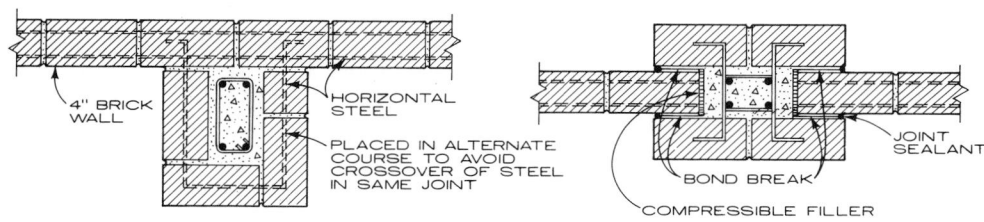

4" BRICK WALL — HORIZONTAL STEEL — PLACED IN ALTERNATE COURSE TO AVOID CROSSOVER OF STEEL IN SAME JOINT — BOND BREAK — COMPRESSIBLE FILLER — JOINT SEALANT

**REINFORCED BRICK MASONRY COLUMN**   **REINFORCED BRICK MASONRY PILASTER**

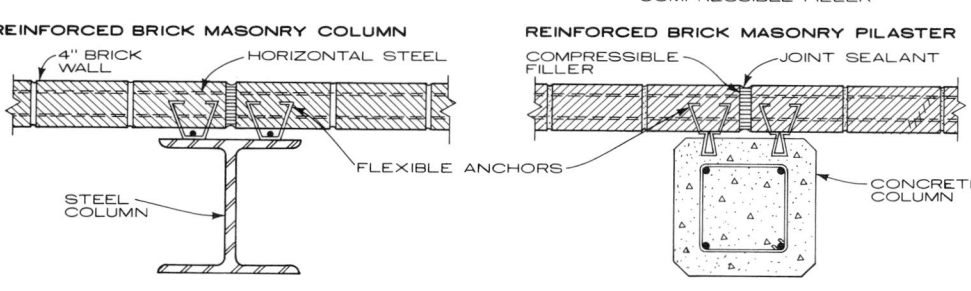

4" BRICK WALL — HORIZONTAL STEEL — FLEXIBLE ANCHORS — STEEL COLUMN — COMPRESSIBLE FILLER — JOINT SEALANT — CONCRETE COLUMN

**STEEL COLUMN**   **REINFORCED CONCRETE COLUMN**

**BRICK CURTAIN WALL AND PANEL WALL REINFORCEMENT AND ANCHORAGE**

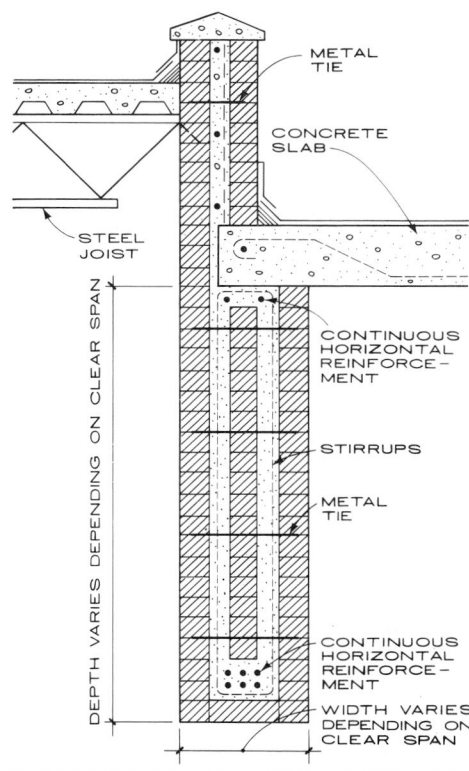

METAL TIE — CONCRETE SLAB — STEEL JOIST — DEPTH VARIES DEPENDING ON CLEAR SPAN — CONTINUOUS HORIZONTAL REINFORCEMENT — STIRRUPS — METAL TIE — CONTINUOUS HORIZONTAL REINFORCEMENT — WIDTH VARIES DEPENDING ON CLEAR SPAN

**REINFORCED BRICK BEAM**

## TYPICAL RETAINING WALL DESIGN VALUES

| H | B | L | D BARS | V BARS | F BARS |
|---|---|---|---|---|---|
| 2'-0" | 1'-9" | 1'-10" | #3 @ 40" | | #3 @ 40" |
| 2'-6" | 1'-9" | 2'-4" | #3 @ 40" | | #3 @ 40" |
| 3'-0" | 2'-0" | 2'-10" | #3 @ 40" | | #3 @ 40" |
| 3'-6" | 2'-0" | 3'-4" | #3 @ 40" | | #3 @ 40" |
| 4'-0" | 2'-4" | 1'-4" | #3 @ 27" #4 @ 40" | #3 @ 27" #3 @ 40" | #3 @ 27" #3 @ 40" |
| 4'-6" | 2'-8" | 1'-6" | #3 @ 19" #4 @ 35" | #3 @ 38" #3 @ 35" | #3 @ 19" #3 @ 35" |
| 5'-0" | 3'-0" | 1'-8" | #3 @ 14" #4 @ 25" #5 @ 40" | #3 @ 28" #3 @ 25" #4 @ 40" | #3 @ 14" #3 @ 25" #4 @ 40" |
| 5'-6" | 3'-3" | 1'-10" | #3 @ 11" #4 @ 20" #5 @ 31" | #3 @ 22" #4 @ 40" #4 @ 31" | #3 @ 11" #3 @ 20" #4 @ 31" |
| 6'-0" | 3'-6" | 2'-0" | #3 @ 8" #4 @ 14" #5 @ 20" | #3 @ 16" #4 @ 28" #5 @ 40" | #3 @ 8" #3 @ 14" #4 @ 20" |

NOTE: For convenience, this table was developed to aid the nondesigner in a typical application. However, materials must meet these additional minimum requirements:

1. Brick strength in excess of 6000 psi in compression.
2. Steel design tensile strength, $F_s$, of 20,000 psi.
3. No surcharge.

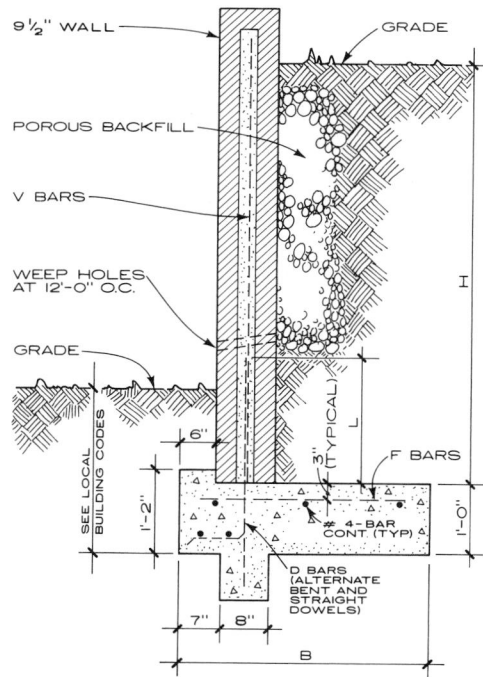

9½" WALL — GRADE — POROUS BACKFILL — V BARS — WEEP HOLES AT 12'-0" O.C. — GRADE — SEE LOCAL BUILDING CODES — F BARS — 4-BAR CONT. (TYP) — D BARS (ALTERNATE BENT AND STRAIGHT DOWELS)

**LOW BRICK MASONRY RETAINING WALL (LESS THAN 6'-0")**

NOTE

Consult a qualified engineer and local code requirements for design of all grouted, reinforced masonry construction.

The design of load-bearing masonry buildings is based on a rational analysis of the magnitude, line of action, and direction of all forces acting on the structure. Dead loads, live loads, lateral loads, and other forces such as those resulting from temperature changes, impact, and unequal settlement are considered. The combination of loads producing the greatest stresses is used to size the members. Reinforced masonry is used where compressive, flexural, and shear stresses are greater than those permitted for unreinforced or partially reinforced masonry. The minimum amount of steel reinforcing required by code is designed for seismic zones 3 and 4 where high winds or earthquake activity subject buildings to severe lateral dynamic loads. Reinforcing steel adds ductility and strength to the wall, which then bears the load with minimum deflection and maximum damping of the earthquake energy. For further technical information:

Masonry Design and Detailing, 2nd edition. Christine Beall. New York: McGraw-Hill, 1987.
Recommended Practice for Engineered Brick Masonry. Brick Institute of America. McLean, VA, 1969.
Reinforced Masonry Design. R. Schneider and W. Dickey. New York: Prentice-Hall, Inc., 1980.
Technical Notes Series. Brick Institute of America.

Christine Beall, AIA, CCS; Austin, Texas
John R. Hoke, Jr., AIA, Architect; Washington, D.C.

**UNIT MASONRY** 4

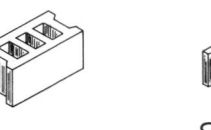

STRETCHER          CONTROL  JOINT          LINTEL          SCREEN

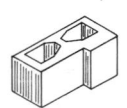
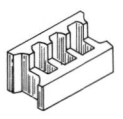
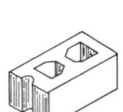
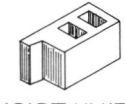
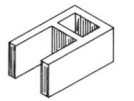

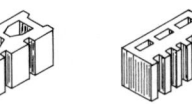
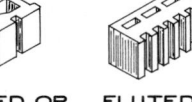

CORNER          BOND  BEAM          SILL          SPLIT  FACE

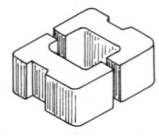
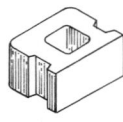
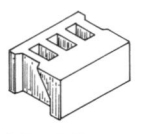
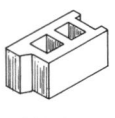
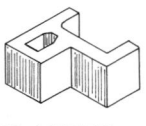

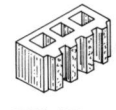

CORNER          HEADER          SASH          JOIST UNIT          OPEN-END  UNITS          RIBBED OR          FLUTED
RETURN                                                            PLUMBING    VERTICAL          SCORED
                                                                  STACK       STEEL

COLUMN          GRADE          JAMB          PILASTER          SCREEN          8 X 8          SPLIT
                                             INSERT                            SCORED         RIBBED
                                                                               FACE

TYPICAL  CONCRETE  MASONRY  UNIT  SHAPES

## CONCRETE MASONRY UNIT SPECIFICATIONS AND FIRE RESISTANCE DATA

1. A solid (load bearing) concrete block is a unit whose cross-sectional area in every plane parallel to the bearing surface is not less than 75% of the gross cross-sectional area measured in the same plane. (ASTM C145–75.)

2. A hollow concrete block is a unit whose cross-sectional area in every plane parallel to the bearing surface is less than 75% of the gross cross-sectional area measured in the same plane. (ASTM C90–75.)

3. Actual dimension is ⅜ in. less than nominal shown.

4. All shapes shown are available in all dimensions given in chart except for width (W) which may be otherwise noted.

5. Because the number of shapes and sizes for concrete masonry screen units is virtually unlimited, it is advisable for the designer to check on availability of any specific shape during early planning.

6. Screen units should be of high quality, even though they seldom are employed in load bearing construction. When tested with their hollow cells parallel to the direction of the load, screen units should have a compressive strength exceeding 1000 psi of gross area; a quality of concrete unit comparable to "Specifications for Hollow Load-Bearing Concrete Masonry Units" ASTM C90–75.

7. Building codes are quite specific in the degree of fire protection required in various areas of buildings. Local building regulations will govern the concrete masonry wall section best suited for specific applications. Fire resistance ratings of concrete masonry walls are based on fire tests made at Underwriters' Laboratories, Inc., National Bureau of Standards, Portland Cement Association, and other recognized laboratories. Methods of test are described in ASTM E119 "Standard Method of Fire Tests of Building Construction and Materials."

8. The fire resistance ratings of most concrete masonry walls are determined by heat transmission measured by temperature rise on the cold side. Fire endurance can be calculated as a function of the aggregate type used in the block unit,

and the solid thickness of the wall, or the equivalent solid thickness of the wall when working with hollow units.

9. Equivalent thickness of hollow units is calculated from actual thickness and the percentage of solid materials. Both needed items of information are normally reported by the testing laboratory using standard ASTM procedures, such as ASTM C140 "Methods of Sampling and Testing Concrete Masonry Units." When walls are plastered or otherwise faced with fire resistant materials, the thickness of these materials is included in calculating the equivalent thickness effective for fire resistance. Estimated fire resistance ratings shown in the table are for fully protected construction in which all structural members are of incombustible materials. Where combustible members are framed into walls, equivalent solid thickness protecting each such member should not be less than 93% of the thicknesses shown. Plaster is effective in increasing fire resistance when combustible members are framed into masonry walls, as is filling core spaces with various fire resistant materials.

10. Walls and partitions of 1- to 4-hr ratings are governed by code requirements for actual or equivalent solid thickness computed on the percent of core area in the unit. Increasing the wall thickness or filling the cores with grout increases the rating. Units with more than 25% core area are classified as hollow, and the equivalent solid thickness must first be computed in order to determine the fire rating. Since core size and shape will vary, either manufacturer's data or laboratory test data must be used to establish exact figures. A nominal 8 in. hollow unit reported to be 55% solid would be calculated as follows: equivalent solid thickness = 0.55 x 7.625 in. (actual thickness) = 4.19 in. Lightweight aggregates such as pumice, expanded slag, clay, or shale offer greater resistance to the transfer of heat in a fire because of their increased air content. Units made with these materials require less thickness to achieve the same fire rating as a heavyweight aggregate unit.

### NOMINAL DIMENSIONS OF TYPICAL CONCRETE MASONRY UNIT SHAPES

| | |
|---|---|
| Height (H) = | 4″, 8″ |
| Length (L) = | 8″, 12″, 16″, 24″ |
| Width (W) = | 4″, 6″, 8″, 10″, 12″ |

### EQUIVALENT THICKNESS FOR FIRE RATING

| | 1 HR | 2 HR | 3 HR | 4 HR |
|---|---|---|---|---|
| Expanded slag or pumice | 2.1 | 3.2 | 4.0 | 4.7 |
| Expanded clay or shale | 2.6 | 3.8 | 4.8 | 5.7 |
| Limestone, cinders, air-cooled slag | 2.7 | 4.0 | 5.0 | 5.9 |
| Calcareous gravel | 2.8 | 4.2 | 5.3 | 6.2 |
| Siliceous gravel | 3.0 | 4.5 | 5.7 | 6.7 |

### R VALUE OF SINGLE WYTHE CMU, EMPTY AND WITH LOOSE-FILL INSULATION*

| NOMINAL UNIT THICKNESS (IN.) | CORES | DENSITY OF CONCRETE IN CMU (PCF) | | | | |
|---|---|---|---|---|---|---|
| | | 60 | 80 | 100 | 120 | 140 |
| 4 | insul. | 3.36 | 2.79 | 2.33 | 1.92 | 1.14 |
| | empty | 2.07 | 1.68 | 1.40 | 1.17 | 0.77 |
| 6 | insul. | 5.59 | 4.59 | 3.72 | 2.95 | 1.59 |
| | empty | 2.25 | 1.83 | 1.53 | 1.29 | 0.86 |
| 8 | insul. | 7.46 | 6.06 | 4.85 | 3.79 | 1.98 |
| | empty | 2.30 | 2.12 | 1.75 | 1.46 | 0.98 |
| 10 | insul. | 9.35 | 7.45 | 5.92 | 4.59 | 2.35 |
| | empty | 3.00 | 2.40 | 1.97 | 1.63 | 1.08 |
| 12 | insul. | 10.98 | 8.70 | 6.80 | 5.18 | 2.59 |
| | empty | 3.29 | 2.62 | 2.14 | 1.81 | 1.16 |

*Vermiculite or perlite insulation.

Robert J. Sangiamo, AIA, and Davis, Brody & Associates; New York, New York
Christine Beall, AIA, CCS; Austin, Texas

 **UNIT MASONRY**

## NOTES

Concrete masonry unit walls are susceptible to cracking due to the differential or restrained movements of building elements. These stresses may be controlled through reinforcement in the form of bond beams and horizontal joint reinforcing and through separation, as in control joints which accommodate movement of the wall.

In seismic zones, concrete masonry unit walls should be reinforced horizontally and vertically to resist the lateral forces acting nonconcurrently in the direction of each of the main axes of the building.

Reference state and local building codes and The National Concrete Masonry Association for design requirements and recommendations.

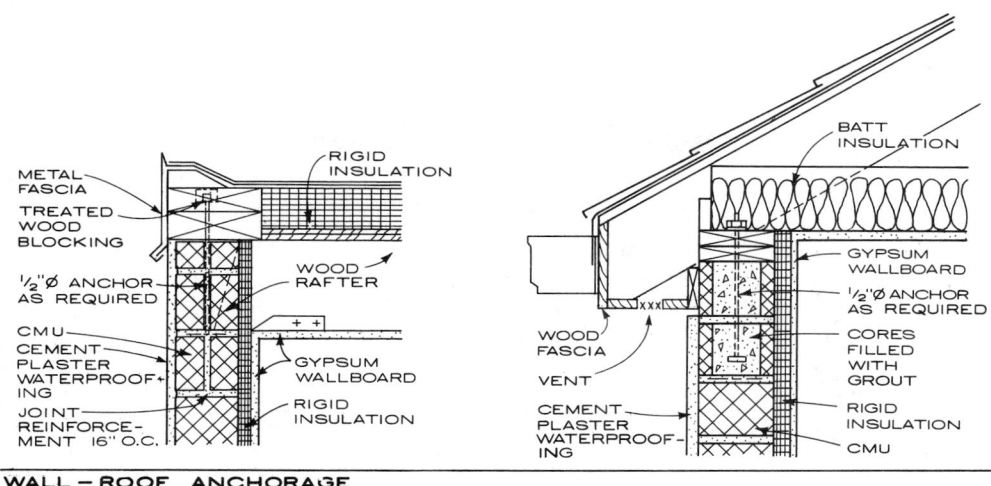

**WALL — ROOF ANCHORAGE**

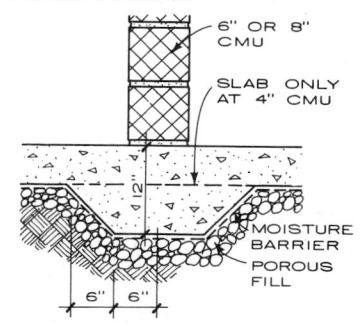

**NONBEARING WALL**

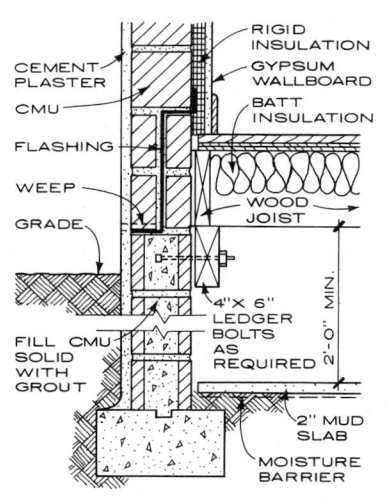

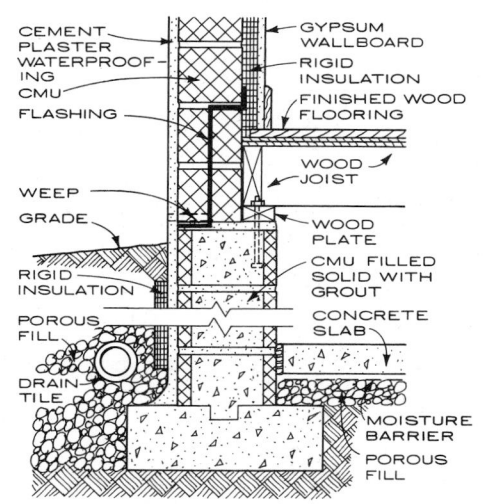

**FOUNDATION DETAILS**

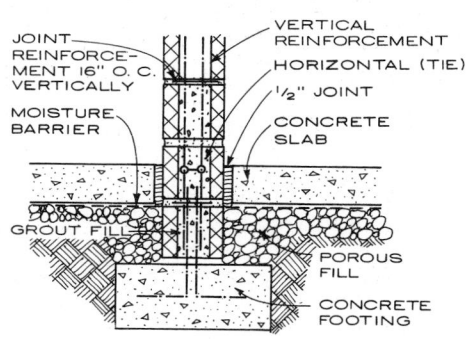

FOOTING DEPTH DETERMINED BY CODES

**BEARING WALL**

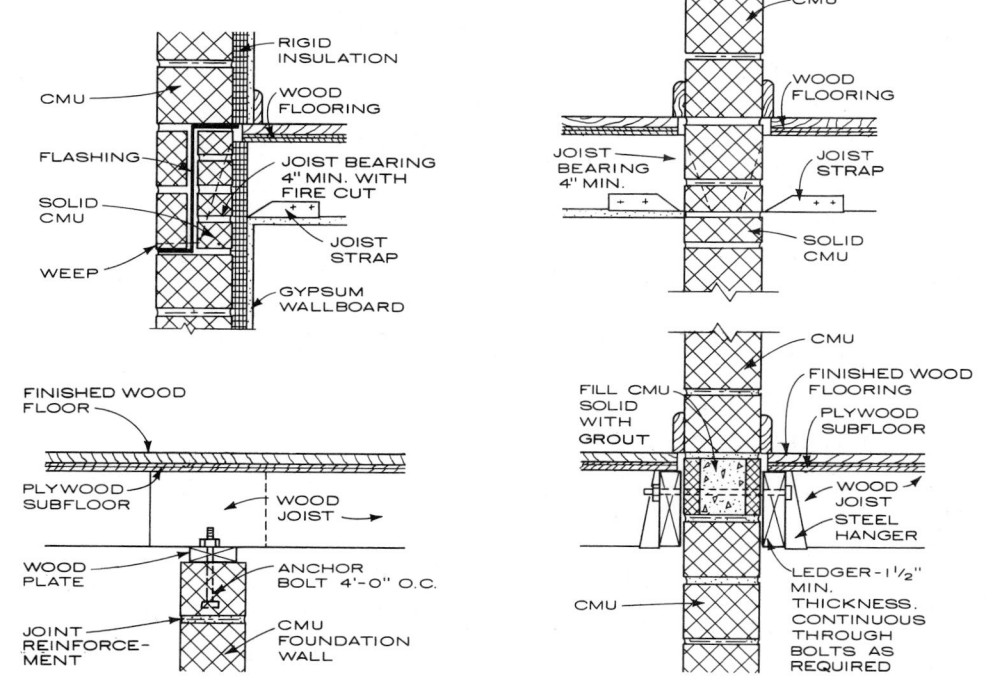

**WALL — FLOOR ANCHORAGE DETAILS**

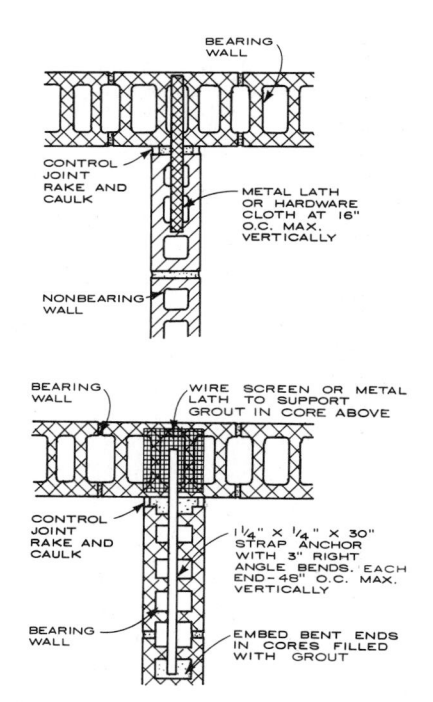

**INTERSECTING WALL DETAILS**

Robert J. Sangiamo, AIA; New York, New York
Davis, Brody & Associates; New York, New York
Ted B. Richey, AIA; The InterDesign Group; Indianapolis, Indiana

**UNIT MASONRY**    4

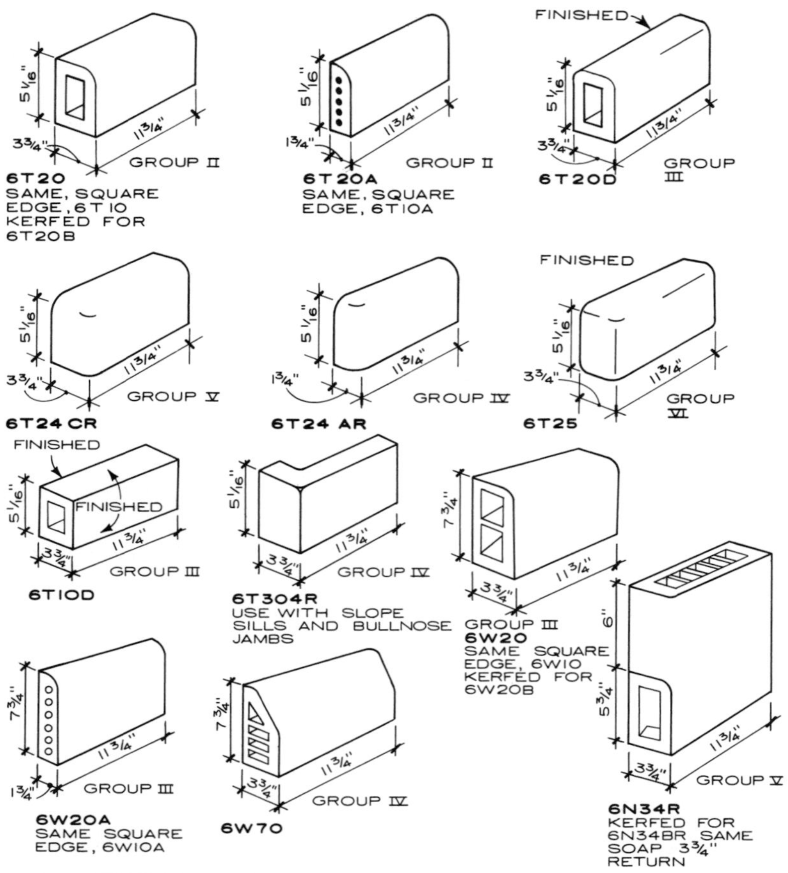

## SILLS, CAPS & MITERS

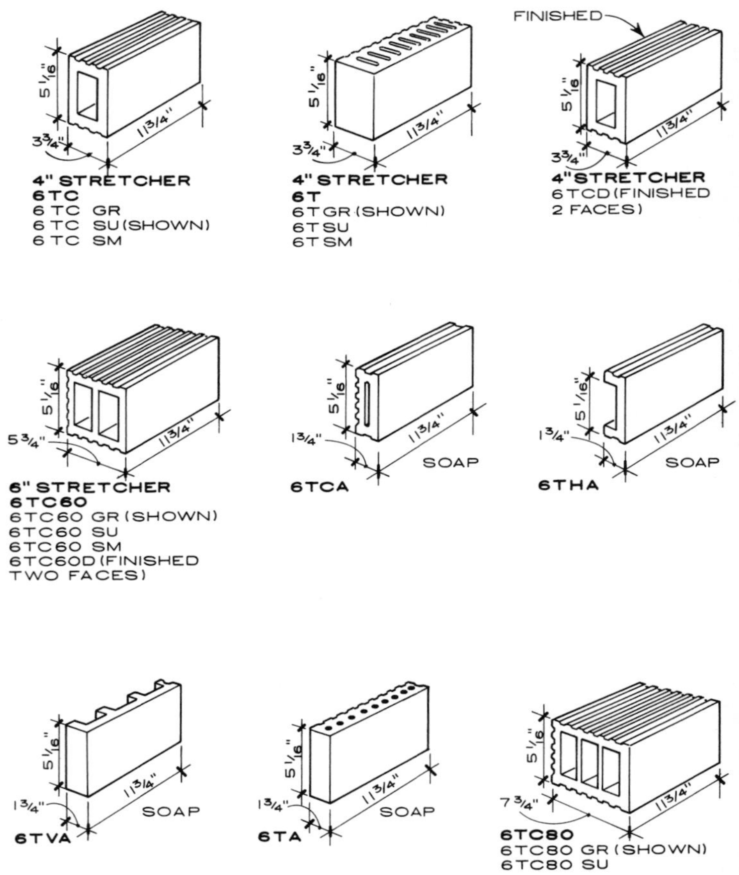

**6T20**
SAME, SQUARE EDGE, 6T10
KERFED FOR 6T20B
5 1/16"  1 3/4"  3 3/4"  GROUP II

**6T20A**
SAME, SQUARE EDGE, 6T10A
5 1/16"  1 3/4"  3 3/4"  GROUP II

**6T20D**
FINISHED
5 1/16"  1 3/4"  3 3/4"  GROUP III

**6T24 CR**
5 1/16"  1 3/4"  3 3/4"  GROUP V

**6T24 AR**
FINISHED
5 1/16"  1 3/4"  3 3/4"  GROUP IV

**6T25**
FINISHED
5 1/16"  1 3/4"  3 3/4"  GROUP VI

**6T10D**
FINISHED
5 1/16"  1 3/4"  3 3/4"  GROUP III

**6T304R**
USE WITH SLOPE SILLS AND BULLNOSE JAMBS
5 1/16"  1 3/4"  3 3/4"  GROUP IV

**6W20**
SAME SQUARE EDGE, 6W10 KERFED FOR 6W20B
7 1/4"  1 3/4"  3 3/4"  GROUP III

**6W20A**
SAME SQUARE EDGE, 6W10A
7 1/4"  1 3/4"  GROUP III

**6W70**
7 1/4"  1 3/4"  3 3/4"  GROUP IV

**6N34R**
KERFED FOR 6N34BR, SAME SOAP 3 3/4" RETURN
6"  5 3/4"  1 3/4"  3 3/4"  GROUP V

## STRETCHER GROUP

**4" STRETCHER 6TC**
6 TC GR
6 TC SU (SHOWN)
6 TC SM
5 1/16"  1 3/4"  3 3/4"

**4" STRETCHER 6T**
6 T GR (SHOWN)
6 T SU
6 T SM
5 1/16"  1 3/4"  3 3/4"

**4" STRETCHER 6TCD** (FINISHED 2 FACES)
FINISHED
5 1/16"  1 3/4"  3 3/4"

**6" STRETCHER 6TC60**
6TC60 GR (SHOWN)
6TC60 SU
6TC60 SM
6TC60D (FINISHED TWO FACES)
5 1/16"  5 3/4"  1 3/4"

**6TCA**
SOAP
5 1/16"  1 3/4"

**6THA**
SOAP
5 1/16"  1 3/4"

**6TVA**
SOAP
5 1/16"  1 3/4"

**6TA**
SOAP
5 1/16"  1 3/4"

**6TC80**
6TC80 GR (SHOWN)
6TC80 SU
5 1/16"  7 3/4"  1 3/4"

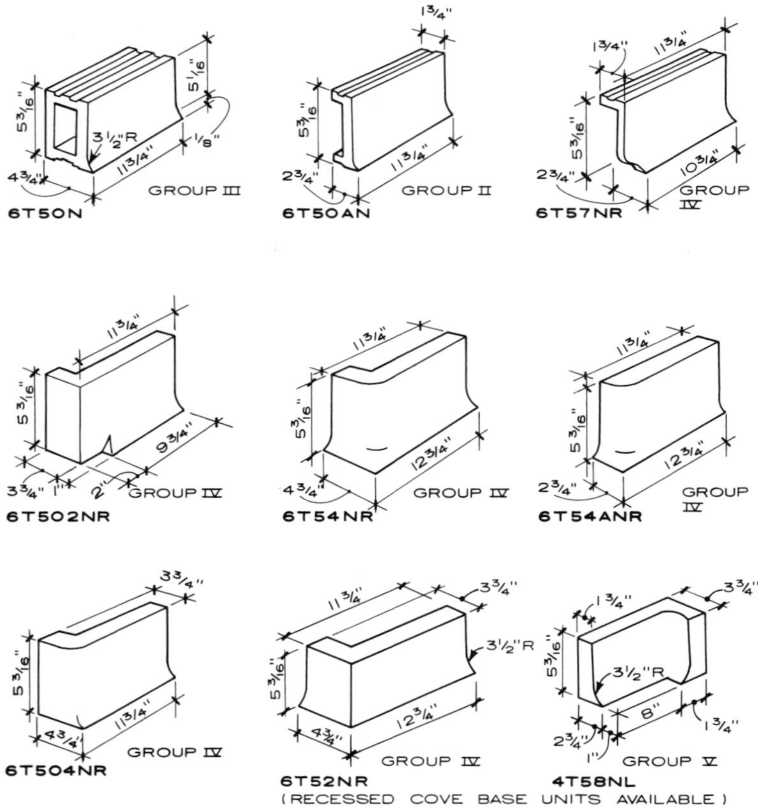

## COVE BASE  (NON RECESSED EXCEPT AS NOTED)

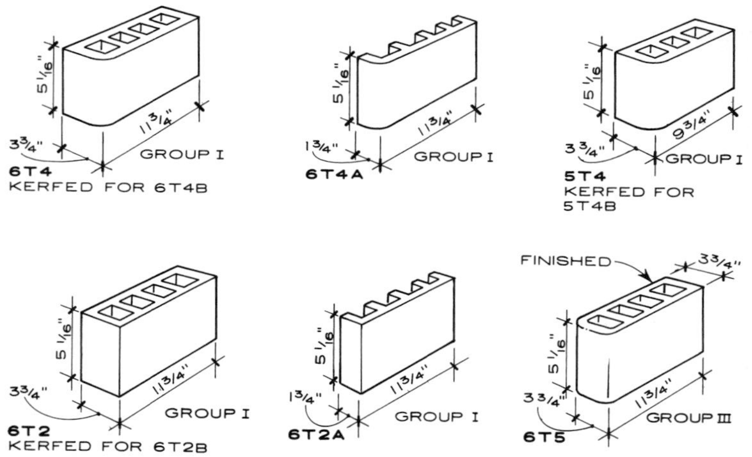

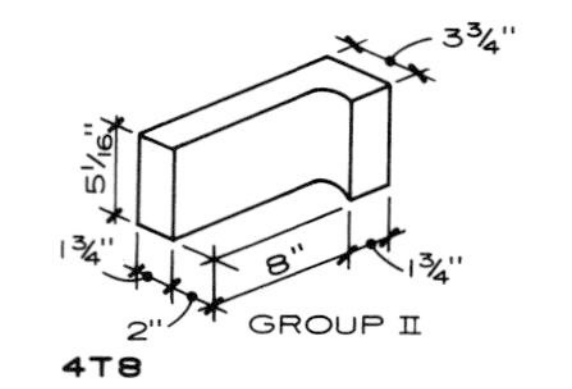

**6T50N**
5 3/16"  3 1/2"R  1/8"  1 3/4"  4 3/4"  GROUP III

**6T50AN**
5 3/16"  1 3/4"  2 3/4"  GROUP II

**6T57NR**
1 3/4"  1 1/3"  5 3/16"  2 3/4"  10 3/4"  GROUP IV

**6T502NR**
1 3/4"  5 3/16"  9 3/4"  3 3/4"  2"  GROUP IV

**6T54NR**
1 3/4"  5 3/16"  12 3/4"  4 3/4"  GROUP IV

**6T54ANR**
1 3/4"  5 3/16"  12 3/4"  2 3/4"  GROUP IV

**6T504NR**
3 3/4"  5 3/16"  1 3/4"  4 3/4"  GROUP IV

**6T52NR**
1 3/4"  3 3/4"  5 3/16"  3 1/2"R  12 3/4"  4 3/4"  GROUP IV

**4T58NL**
(RECESSED COVE BASE UNITS AVAILABLE)
3 3/4"  1 3/4"  5 3/16"  3 1/2"R  8"  2 3/4"  1"  1 3/4"  GROUP V

## CORNERS & JAMBS

**6T4**
KERFED FOR 6T4B
5 1/16"  1 3/4"  3 3/4"  GROUP I

**6T4A**
5 1/16"  1 3/4"  GROUP I

**5T4**
KERFED FOR 5T4B
5 1/16"  9 3/4"  3 3/4"  GROUP I

**6T2**
KERFED FOR 6T2B
5 1/16"  1 3/4"  3 3/4"  GROUP I

**6T2A**
5 1/16"  1 3/4"  1 3/4"  GROUP I

**6T5**
FINISHED
5 1/16"  3 3/4"  1 3/4"  3 3/4"  GROUP III

**4T8**
5 1/16"  8"  1 3/4"  1 3/4"  2"  GROUP II

## NOTES

1. Number with suffix R denotes right hand shape; left hand shape takes suffix L.
2. Type and direction of scoring and coring are optional with the manufacturer. In general, the manufacturer standardizes on either the horizontal or the vertical coring. This note also applies to 8W shapes shown on the preceding page.
3. Suffix B denotes soap with 3 3/4 in. reveal and return units designated by + are kerfed for soap with 3 3/4 in. reveal.
4. Suffix GR scored or grooved back.
5. Suffix SU unselected, unglazed back.
6. Suffix SM unselected, glazed back.

Facing Tile Institute; Washington, D.C.

 **UNIT MASONRY**

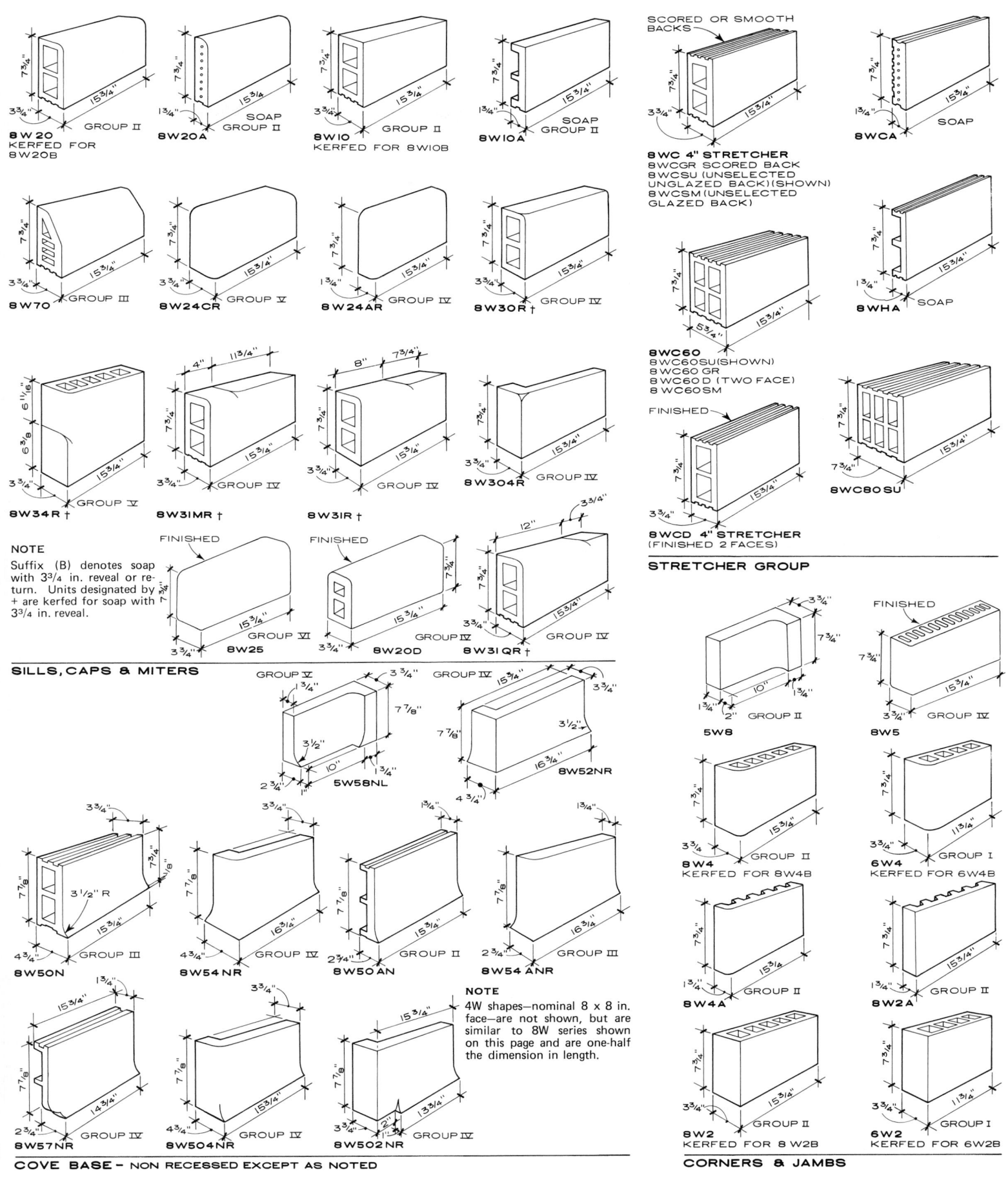

**8W20** KERFED FOR 8W20B — GROUP II

**8W20A** SOAP GROUP II

**8W10** KERFED FOR 8W10B — GROUP II

**8W10A** SOAP GROUP II

**8WC 4" STRETCHER**
8WCGR SCORED BACK
8WCSU (UNSELECTED UNGLAZED BACK)(SHOWN)
8WCSM (UNSELECTED GLAZED BACK)

**8WCA** SOAP

**8W70** GROUP III

**8W24CR** GROUP V

**8W24AR** GROUP IV

**8W30R †** GROUP IV

**8WC60**
8WC60SU(SHOWN)
8WC60 GR
8WC60 D (TWO FACE)
8WC60SM

**8WHA** SOAP

**8W34R †** GROUP V

**8W31MR †** GROUP IV

**8W31R †** GROUP IV

**8W304R** GROUP IV

**8WC80SU**

**NOTE**
Suffix (B) denotes soap with 3³/₄ in. reveal or return. Units designated by + are kerfed for soap with 3³/₄ in. reveal.

**8W25** FINISHED GROUP VI

**8W20D** FINISHED GROUP IV

**8W31QR †** GROUP IV

**8WCD 4" STRETCHER** (FINISHED 2 FACES)

## STRETCHER GROUP

**5W8** GROUP II

**8W5** FINISHED GROUP IV

### SILLS, CAPS & MITERS

**5W58NL** GROUP V

**8W52NR** GROUP IV

**8W4** KERFED FOR 8W4B — GROUP II

**6W4** KERFED FOR 6W4B — GROUP I

**8W50N** GROUP III

**8W54NR** GROUP IV

**8W50AN** GROUP II

**8W54ANR** GROUP III

**8W4A** GROUP II

**8W2A** GROUP II

**NOTE**
4W shapes—nominal 8 × 8 in. face—are not shown, but are similar to 8W series shown on this page and are one-half the dimension in length.

**8W57NR** GROUP IV

**8W504NR** GROUP IV

**8W502NR** GROUP IV

**8W2** KERFED FOR 8W2B — GROUP II

**6W2** KERFED FOR 6W2B — GROUP I

**COVE BASE** – NON RECESSED EXCEPT AS NOTED

**CORNERS & JAMBS**

Facing Tile Institute; Washington, D.C.

## VERTICAL COURSING

| NUMBER OF COURSES | 5 1/3" NOMINAL HEIGHT | 8" NOMINAL HEIGHT |
|---|---|---|
| 1 | 5 5/16" | 8" |
| 2 | 10 5/8" | 1' 4" |
| 3 | 1' 4" | 2' 0" |
| 4 | 1' 9 5/16" | 2' 8" |
| 5 | 2' 2 5/8" | 3' 4" |
| 6 | 2' 8" | 4' 0" |
| 7 | 3' 1 5/16" | 4' 8" |
| 8 | 3' 6 5/8" | 5' 4" |
| 9 | 4' 0" | 6' 0" |
| 10 | 4' 5 5/16" | 6' 8" |
| 11 | 4' 10 5/8" | 7' 4" |
| 12 | 5' 4" | 8' 0" |
| 13 | 5' 9 5/16" | 8' 8" |
| 14 | 6' 2 5/8" | 9' 4" |
| 15 | 6' 8" | 10' 0" |
| 16 | 7' 1 5/16" | 10' 8" |
| 17 | 7' 6 5/8" | 11' 4" |
| 18 | 8' 0" | 12' 0" |
| 19 | 8' 5 5/16" | 12' 8" |
| 20 | 8' 10 5/8" | 13' 4" |
| 21 | 9' 4" | 14' 0" |
| 22 | 9' 9 5/16" | 14' 8" |
| 23 | 10' 2 5/8" | 15' 4" |
| 24 | 10' 8" | 16' 0" |
| 25 | 11' 1 5/16" | 16' 8" |
| 26 | 11' 6 5/8" | 17' 4" |
| 27 | 12' 0" | 18' 0" |
| 28 | 12' 5 5/16" | 18' 8" |
| 29 | 12' 10 5/8" | 19' 4" |
| 30 | 13' 4" | 20' 0" |
| 31 | 13' 9 5/16" | 20' 8" |
| 32 | 14' 2 5/8" | 21' 4" |
| 33 | 14' 8" | 22' 0" |
| 34 | 15' 1 5/16" | 22' 8" |
| 35 | 15' 6 5/8" | 23' 4" |
| 36 | 16' 0" | 24' 0" |
| 37 | 16' 5 5/16" | 24' 8" |
| 38 | 16' 10 5/8" | 25' 4" |
| 39 | 17' 4" | 26' 0" |
| 40 | 17' 9 5/16" | 26' 8" |
| 41 | 18' 2 5/8" | 27' 4" |
| 42 | 18' 8" | 28' 0" |
| 43 | 19' 1 5/16" | 28' 8" |
| 44 | 19' 6 5/8" | 29' 4" |
| 45 | 20' 0" | 30' 0" |
| 46 | 20' 5 5/16" | 30' 8" |
| 47 | 20' 10 5/8" | 31' 4" |
| 48 | 21' 4" | 32' 0" |
| 49 | 21' 9 5/16" | 32' 8" |
| 50 | 22' 2 5/8" | 33' 4" |

Note: For convenience in using scale, 1/3" dimensions are changed to 5/16"

Bucks should be filled with mortar to provide sound attenuation

Panic-safe internal corners are possible using standard stretcher units in block bond with as few as 5 units, 3/8" joints producing a quarter circle with radius of 1' 1 1/8" or 9 units, 1/4" joints with a radius of 1'-11". See mfgrs data.

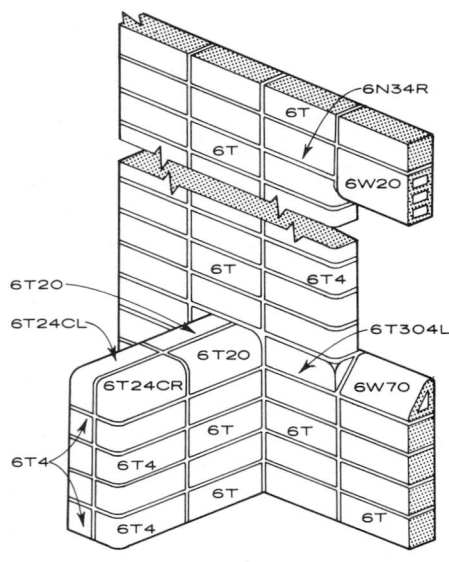

EIGHT INCH DOUBLE-FACED WING WALL BONDED TO MAIN WALL WITH TYPICAL BUTT JOINTS, STACK BOND

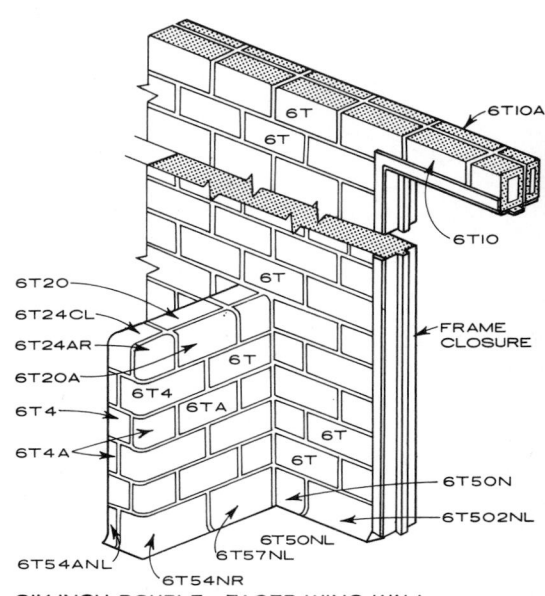

SIX INCH DOUBLE-FACED WING WALL BONDED TO MAIN WALL WITH TYPICAL BUTT JOINTS

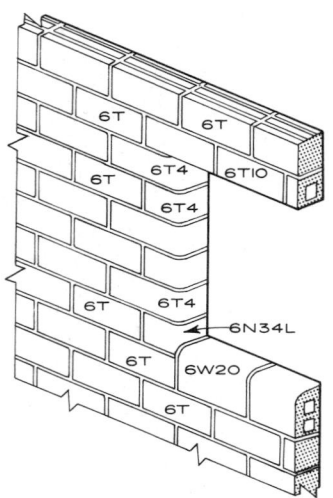

FOUR INCH SINGLE-FACED WALL WITH BULLNOSE SILL AND JAMB. SQUARE LINTEL RUNNING BOND

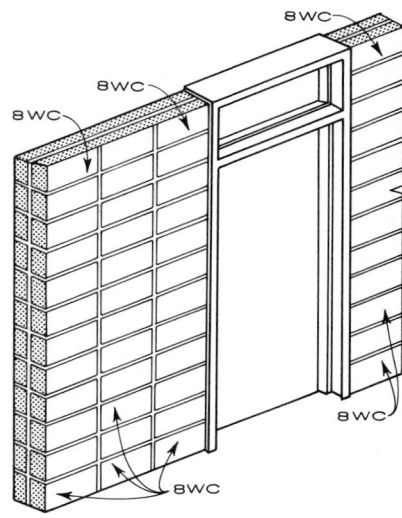

ECONOMY WALL CONSTRUCTION NO SHAPES REQUIRED FULL HEIGHT TRANSOM. 8W SERIES STACK BOND

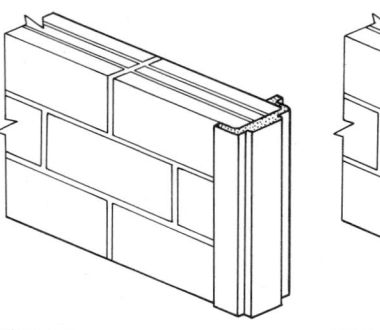
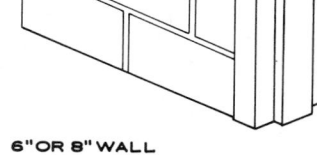
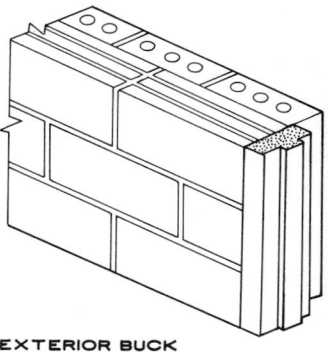

4" WALL          6" OR 8" WALL          EXTERIOR BUCK

**FRAME FITTINGS**

Facing Tile Institute; Washington, D.C.

 4 **UNIT MASONRY**

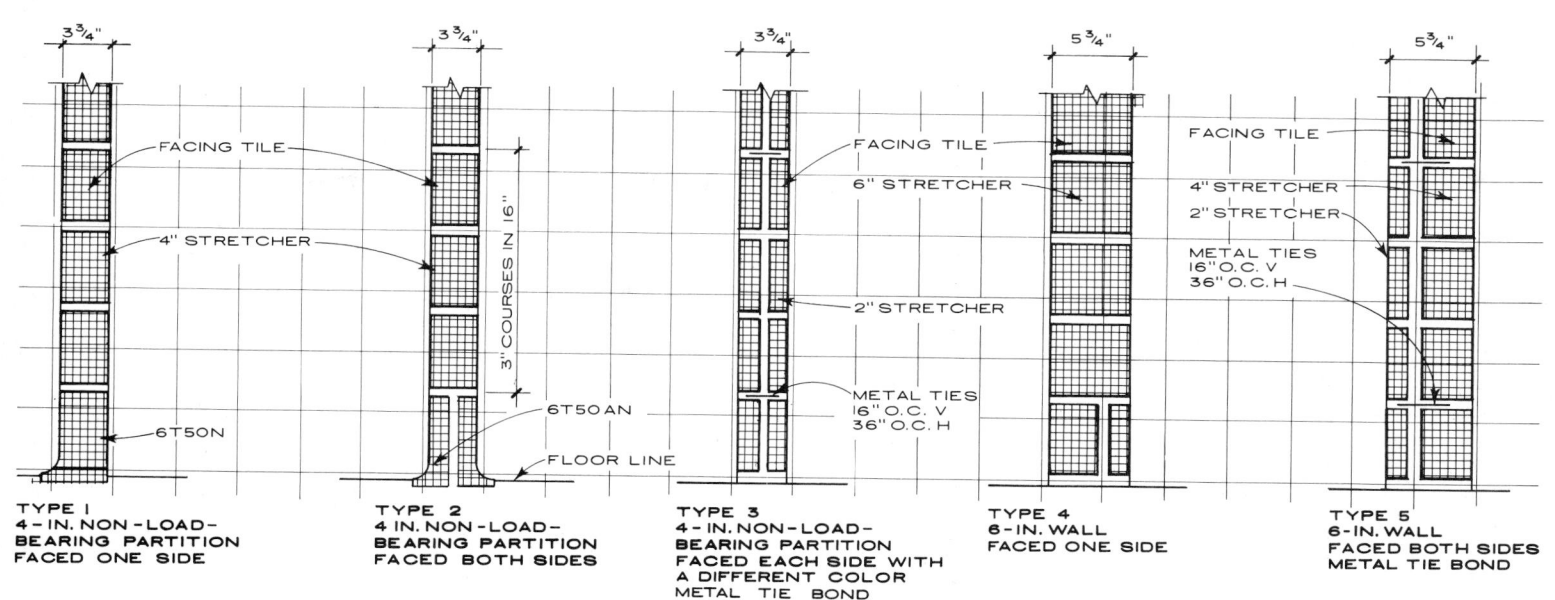

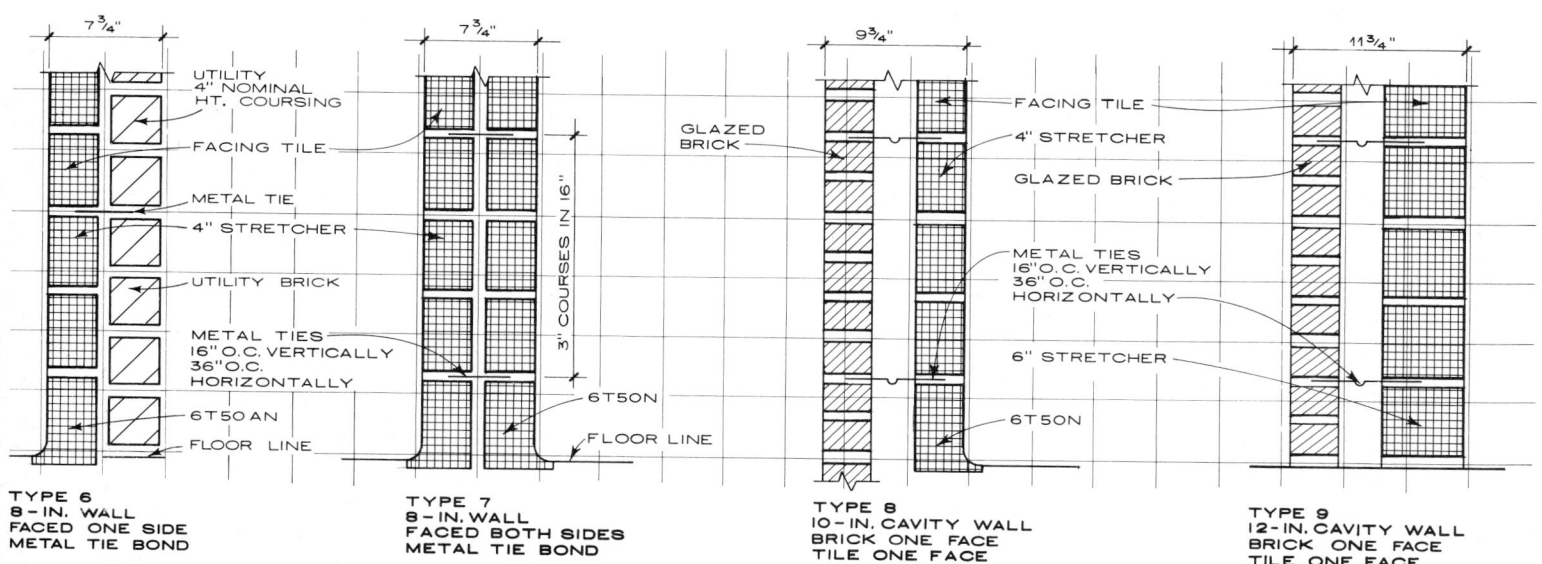

## WALL SECTIONS AND PROPERTIES

| WALL TYPE NUMBER | | 1 | 2 | 3 | 4 | 5 | 6 | 7 | 8 | 9 |
|---|---|---|---|---|---|---|---|---|---|---|
| Allowable load (lb/linear ft) | Type M mortar (85 psi) | | | | 5870 | 5870 | 5870 | 7900 | 6300[2] | 7970[2] |
| | Type S mortar (75 psi) | | | | 5180 | 5180 | 5180 | 6980 | 5400[2] | 6840[2] |
| | Type N mortar (70 psi) | | | | 4830 | 4830 | 4830 | 6510 | 4950[2] | 6270[2] |
| Material quantity (per 100 sq ft) | Mortar (cu ft) 25% waste added | 2.19 | 2.19 | 2.19 | 3.36 | 3.36[1] | 3.36 | 4.531[1] | 6.97 | 8.14 |
| | Facing tile      2% waste added | 230 | 230 | 460 | 230 | 230 | 230 | 460 | 230 | 230 |
| | Brick              5% waste added | | | | | | 230 | | 709 | 709 |
| | Metal ties       2% waste added | | | 25.5 | | 25.5 | 25.5 | 25.5 | 25.5 | 25.5 |
| U Values (BTU/sq ft · hr · °F) | Unplastered partition | 0.40 | 0.40 | 0.39 | 0.35 | 0.34 | 0.34 | 0.30 | | |
| | Exterior wall | | | | | | | | 0.30 | 0.23 |
| | With 2 in. insulation | | | | | | | | 0.08 | 0.08 |
| Lateral support spacing required (ft) | Non-load bearing | 12 | 12 | 12 | 18 | 18 | 18 | 24 | 24 | 30 |
| | Load-bearing | | | | 9 | 9 | 9 | 12 | 12 | 15 |
| Wall weight | Unplastered | 30 | 30 | 33 | 41 | 47 | 47 | 60 | 67 | 79 |
| Sound resistance (dB) | Unplastered | 45 | 45 | 46 | 47 | 48 | 48 | 50 | 54 | 58 |
| Fire resistance (hr) | Regular coring | * | * | 1 | 1 | 2 | | 2 | 3 | 4 |
| | Fire rated coring | 1 | 1 | 1 | 2 | 3 | | 4 | 4 | 4 |

NOTE

*3/4 in. plaster on back of these units will produce 1 hour fire rating.

[1] If collar joint is filled, add 2.6 cu ft per 100 sq ft of wall.     [2] Eccentrically loaded. For concentric loading increase allowable load 25 per cent.

Facing Tile Institute; Washington, D.C.

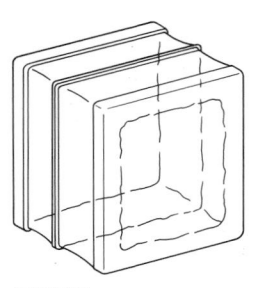
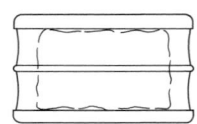

### SQUARE

4½ in. x 4½ in.
6 in. x 6 in. (5¾ in. x 5¾ in. actual)
7½ in. x 7½ in.
8 in. x 8 in. (7¾ in. x 7¾ in. actual)
9½ in. x 9½ in.
12 in. x 12 in. (11¾ in. x 11¾ in. actual)

115 mm x 115 mm
190 mm x 190 mm
240 mm x 240 mm
300 mm x 300 mm

Metric sizes are available from foreign manufacturers through distributors in the U.S.

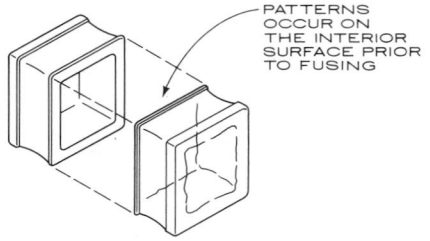

PATTERNS OCCUR ON THE INTERIOR SURFACE PRIOR TO FUSING

The basic glass block unit is made of two halves fused together with a partial vacuum inside. Faces may be clear, figured, or with integral relief forms.

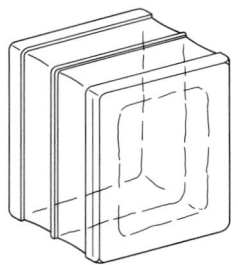

### RECTANGULAR

4 in. x 8 in. (3¾ in. x 7¾ in. actual)
6 in. x 8 in. (5¾ in. x 7¾ in. actual)
9½ in. x 4½ in. *

*240 mm x 115 mm

### THICKNESSES

Square and rectangular glass block are available in thicknesses ranging from a minimum of 3 in. for solid units to a maximum of 4 in. for hollow units. Metric thicknesses range from 80 mm to 100 mm.

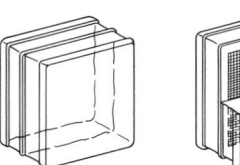

INSERT OR EXTERIOR COATING

Solid glass block units (glass bricks) are impact resistant and allow through vision.

Solar control units have either inserts or exterior coatings to reduce heat gain. Coated units require periodic cleaning to remove alkali and metal ions that can harm the surface coating. Edge drips are required to prevent moisture rundown on surface.

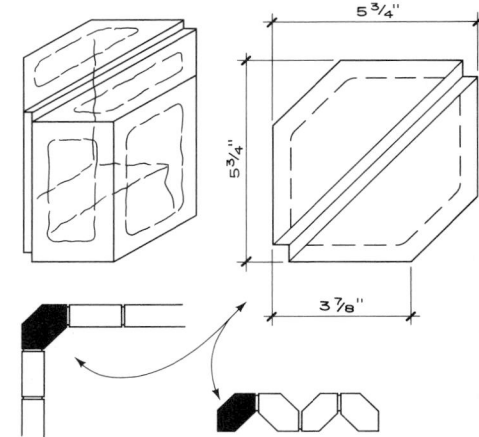

5¾"
5¾"
3⅞"

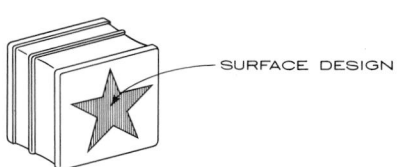

### SPECIAL SHAPES (CORNERS)

A limited number of manufacturers have special shapes to execute corner designs. These units also may be placed together for varying patterns and forms.

SURFACE DESIGN

Surface decoration may be achieved with fused-on ceramic, etching, or sandblasting. Glass block units may be split or shipped in halves in order to apply some decoration to the inside. Blocks then must be resealed. Resealed blocks will not perform the same under various stresses as factory sealed units. Placement in walls or panels should be limited to areas receiving minimum loading.

### STANDARD BLOCK DESIGN

12" GLASS BLOCK
9½" GLASS BLOCK
8" GLASS BLOCK
7½" GLASS BLOCK
6" GLASS BLOCK
4½" GLASS BLOCK
4" GLASS BLOCK

32"  38½"  48½"  63"  65"  80"  96½"

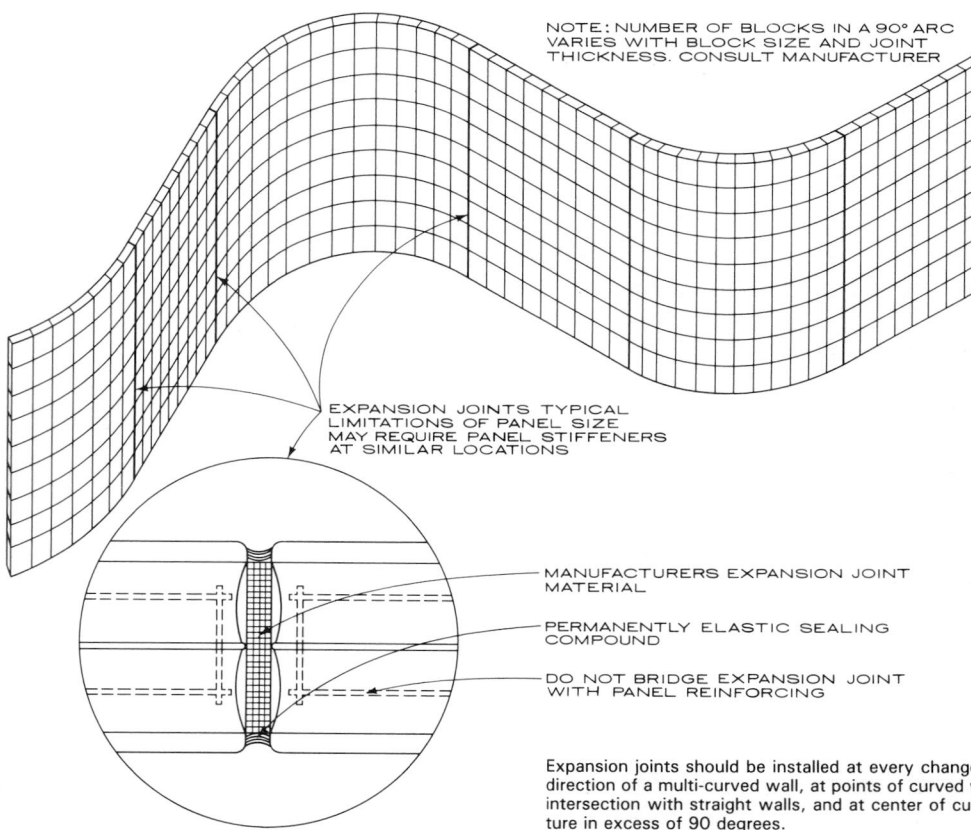

NOTE: NUMBER OF BLOCKS IN A 90° ARC VARIES WITH BLOCK SIZE AND JOINT THICKNESS. CONSULT MANUFACTURER

EXPANSION JOINTS TYPICAL LIMITATIONS OF PANEL SIZE MAY REQUIRE PANEL STIFFENERS AT SIMILAR LOCATIONS

⅝" OUTSIDE JOINT

⅛" OR 3/16" INSIDE JOINT

Curved walls may be constructed to the minimum radii (to the inside surface) indicated above. There are no maximum radii.

Table is based on an outside joint thickness of ⅝ in. and an inside joint thickness of ⅛ in. Some manufacturers prefer a minimum inside joint thickness of 3/16 in. Wider joints require a slightly larger radius.

MANUFACTURERS EXPANSION JOINT MATERIAL

PERMANENTLY ELASTIC SEALING COMPOUND

DO NOT BRIDGE EXPANSION JOINT WITH PANEL REINFORCING

Expansion joints should be installed at every change of direction of a multi-curved wall, at points of curved wall intersection with straight walls, and at center of curvature in excess of 90 degrees.

### CURVED WALL DESIGN

Raso·Greaves An Architecture Corporation; Waco, Texas

**4    UNIT MASONRY**

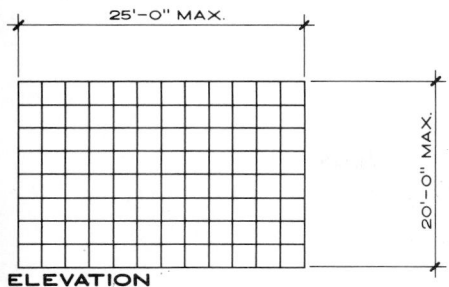

**ELEVATION**

**NOTES**

Area of exterior unbraced panel should not exceed 144 sq ft. Maximum size may be increased to 250 sq ft with the addition of mortared stiffeners.

Area of interior unbraced panel should not exceed 250 sq ft.

Panels are designed to be mortared at sill, with head and jambs providing for movement and settling. Deflection of lintel at head should be anticipated.

Consult manufacturers for specific design limitations of glass block panels. Thickness of block used also determines maximum panel size.

METAL ANCHORS SECURE GLASS BLOCK PANEL TO ADJACENT CONSTRUCTION (BEND WITHIN EXPANSION JOINT)

EXPANSION STRIP TO ALLOW FOR DIFFERENTIAL MOVEMENT

CLEAN SURFACES AFTER ERECTION WITH ORDINARY HOUSEHOLD SCRUB BRUSH WITH STIFF BRISTLES

HORIZONTAL JOINT REINFORCING AS REQUIRED FOR EACH INSTALLATION

FULL BED OF MORTAR TYPICALLY 1/4" WIDE AT FACE OF WALL MORTAR TO BE TYPE S OPTIMUM MIXTURE: 1 PART PORTLAND CEMENT 1/4 PART LIME 3 PARTS SAND

---

**GLASS BLOCK PANEL**

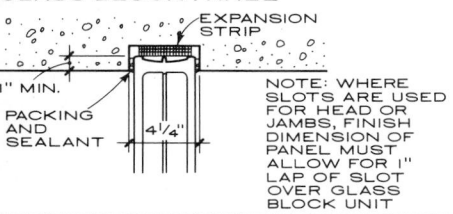

EXPANSION STRIP

1" MIN.

PACKING AND SEALANT

NOTE: WHERE SLOTS ARE USED FOR HEAD OR JAMBS, FINISH DIMENSION OF PANEL MUST ALLOW FOR 1" LAP OF SLOT OVER GLASS BLOCK UNIT

**GLASS BLOCK PANEL COMPONENTS**

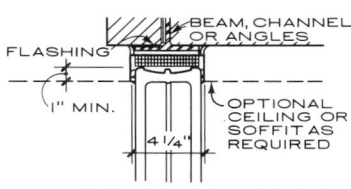

FLASHING

1" MIN.

BEAM, CHANNEL OR ANGLES

OPTIONAL CEILING OR SOFFIT AS REQUIRED

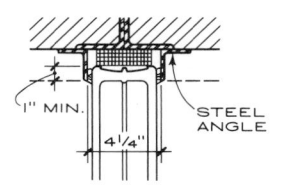

1" MIN.

STEEL ANGLE

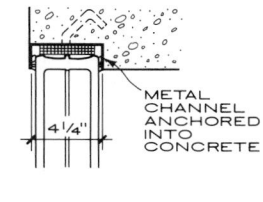

METAL CHANNEL ANCHORED INTO CONCRETE

---

**HEAD SECTIONS**

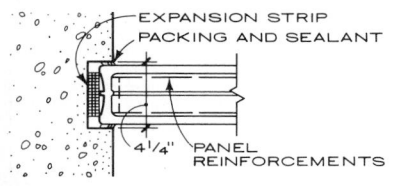

EXPANSION STRIP

PACKING AND SEALANT

PANEL REINFORCEMENTS

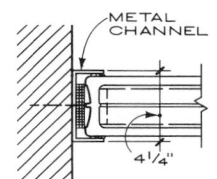

METAL CHANNEL

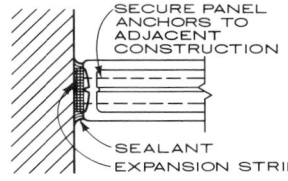

SECURE PANEL ANCHORS TO ADJACENT CONSTRUCTION

SEALANT

EXPANSION STRIP

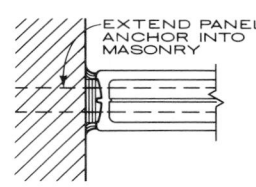

EXTEND PANEL ANCHOR INTO MASONRY

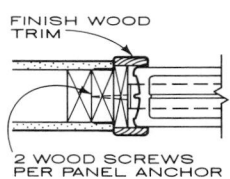

FINISH WOOD TRIM

2 WOOD SCREWS PER PANEL ANCHOR

---

**JAMB SECTIONS**

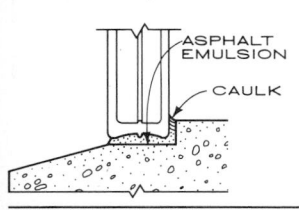

ASPHALT EMULSION

CAULK

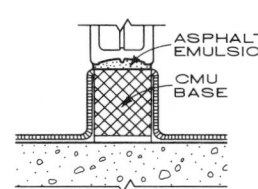

ASPHALT EMULSION

CMU BASE

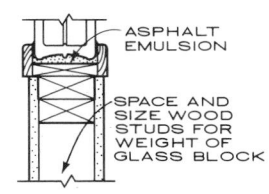

ASPHALT EMULSION

SPACE AND SIZE WOOD STUDS FOR WEIGHT OF GLASS BLOCK

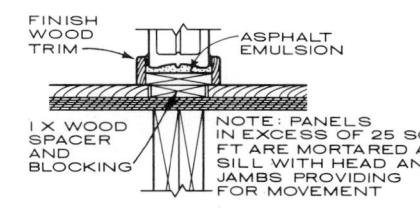

FINISH WOOD TRIM

ASPHALT EMULSION

1 X WOOD SPACER AND BLOCKING

NOTE: PANELS IN EXCESS OF 25 SQ FT ARE MORTARED AT SILL WITH HEAD AND JAMBS PROVIDING FOR MOVEMENT

---

**SILL SECTIONS**

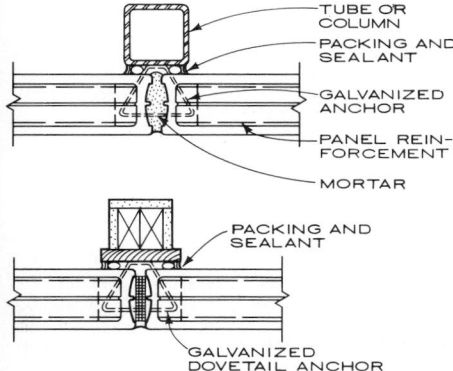

TUBE OR COLUMN

PACKING AND SEALANT

GALVANIZED ANCHOR

PANEL REIN-FORCEMENT

MORTAR

PACKING AND SEALANT

GALVANIZED DOVETAIL ANCHOR

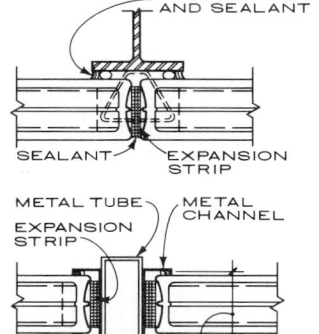

BACKER ROD AND SEALANT

SEALANT

EXPANSION STRIP

METAL TUBE

METAL CHANNEL

EXPANSION STRIP

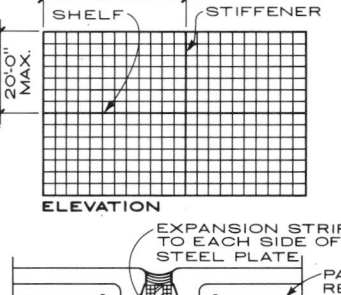

25'-0" MAX.

SHELF

STIFFENER

20'-0" MAX.

**ELEVATION**

EXPANSION STRIP TO EACH SIDE OF STEEL PLATE

PANEL REINFORCE-MENT

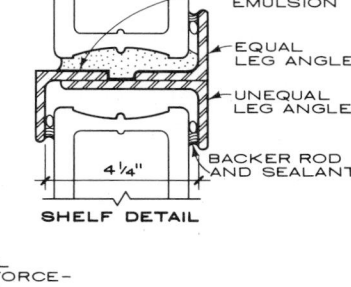

ASPHALT EMULSION

EQUAL LEG ANGLE

UNEQUAL LEG ANGLE

BACKER ROD AND SEALANT

**SHELF DETAIL**

NOTE: PANELS WITH AN EXPANSION JOINT STIFFENER INCORPORATING A CONCEALED VERTICAL PLATE SHOULD BE LIMITED TO 10 FT MAX. HEIGHT

**STIFFENER SECTIONS**

---

Raso·Greaves An Architecture Corporation; Waco, Texas

## GENERAL NOTES

Natural stone is used in building as a facing, veneer, and decoration. The major factors affecting the suitability and use of stone fall under two broad, but overlapping categories: physical and structural properties and aesthetic qualities. The three factors of building stone that most influence their selection by architects for aesthetic reasons are pattern, texture, and color. Consideration also should be given to costs, availability, weathering characteristics, physical properties, and size and thickness limitations.

Stone patterns are highly varied, and they provide special features that make building stone a unique material. Texture is varied, ranging from coarse fragments to fine grains and crystalline structures. Texture also varies with the hardness of minerals composing the stone. To accurately compare stone colors, the rock color chart published by the Geological Society of America (Boulder, CO) is recommended. Samples also may be used to establish acceptable color ranges for a particular installation.

Pattern, texture, and color all are affected by how the stone is fabricated and finished. Granites tend to hold their color and pattern, while limestone color and pattern changes with exposure. Textures may range from rough and flamed finishes to honed or polished surfaces. The harder the stone, the better it takes and holds a polish.

The three rock classes are igneous, sedimentary, and metamorphic. Common construction stones are marketed under the names given in the table below, although specialty stones such as soapstone and serpentine also are available. Each stone has various commercial grades. Limestone grades are A, statuary; B, select; C, standard; D, rustic; E, variegated; and F, old Gothic. Marble is graded A, B, C, or D on the basis of working qualities, uniformity, and flaws and imperfections. Only grade A highest quality stone should be used for exterior applications.

The physical characteristics of a particular stone must be suitable for its intended use. It is important to determine the physical properties of the actual stone being used rather than using values from a generic table, which can be very misleading. Considerations of the physical properties of the stone being selected include modulus of rupture, shear strength, coefficient of expansion, permanent irreversible growth and change in shape, creep deflection, compressive strength, modulus of elasticity, moisture resistance, and weatherability. Epoxy and polyester adhesives, often used with stone, are affected by cleanliness of surfaces to be bonded and ambient temperature. Curing time increases with cold temperatures and decreases with warmer temperatures.

With the introduction of new systems of fabrication and installation and recent developments in the design and detailing of stone cutting, support, and anchorage, costs are better controlled. Correct design of joints, selection of mortars, and use of sealants affect the quality and durability of installation. Adequate design and detailing of the anchorage of each piece of stone are required. The size and thickness of the stone should be established based on physical properties of the stone, its method of anchorage, and the loads it must resist. Appropriate safety factors should be developed based on the variability of the stone properties as well as other considerations such as imperfect workmanship, method of support and anchorage, and degree of exposure of the cladding installation. Relieving angles for stone support and anchorage may be necessary to preclude unacceptable compressive loading of the stone. The stone should be protected from staining and breakage during shipment, delivery, and installation.

Since stone cladding design and detailing vary with type of stone and installation, the designer should consult stone suppliers, stone-setting specialty contractors, industry standards (such as ASTM), and other publications to help select and implement a stone cladding system. Resource information is available in publications such as the Indiana Limestone Institute's Indiana Limestone Handbook and the Marble Institute of America's Dimensioned Stone, Volume 3.

## STONE CLASSIFIED ACCORDING TO QUALITIES AFFECTING USE

| CLASS | COLOR | TEXTURE | SPECIAL FEATURES | PARTINGS | HARDNESS | CHIEF USES |
|---|---|---|---|---|---|---|
| Sandstone | Very light buff to light chocolate brown or brick red; may tarnish to brown | Granular, showing sand grains, cemented together | Ripple marks; oblique color bands ("cross bedding") | Bedding planes; also fractures transverse to beds | Fairly hard if well cemented | General; walls; building; flagstone |
| Limestone | White, light gray to light buff | Fine to crystalline; may have fossils | May show fossils | Parallel to beds; also fractures across beds | Fairly soft; steel easily scratches | All building uses |
| Marble | Highly varied: snow white to black; also blue-gray and light to dark olive green; also pinkish | Finely granular to very coarsely crystalline showing flat-sided crystals | May show veins of different colors or angular rock pieces or fossils | Usually not along beds but may have irregular fractures | Slightly harder than limestone | May be used for building stone but usually in decorative panels |
| Granite (light igneous rock) | Almost white to pink-and-white or gray-and-white | Usually coarsely crystalline; crystals may be varicolored; may be fine grained | May be banded with pink, white or gray streaks and veins | Not necessarily any regular parting but fractures irregularly | Harder than limestone and marble; keeps cut shape well | Building stone, but also in paneling if attractively colored |
| Dark igneous rock | Gray, dark olive green to black; Laurvikite is beautifully crystalline | Usually coarsely crystalline if quarried but may be fine grained | May be banded with lighter and darker gray bands and veins | Not necessarily any regular parting but may fracture irregularly | About like granite; retains cut shape well | Building stone but also used in panels if nicely banded or crystalline |
| Lavas | Varies: pink, purple, black; if usable, rarely almost white | Fine grained; may have pores locally | Note rare porosity | Not necessarily any regular parting, as a rule, but some have parallel fractures | About as strong as granite; if light colored, usually softer | Good foundation and building stone; not decorative |
| Quartzite | Variable: white, buff, red, brown | Dense, almost glassy ideally | Very resistant to weather and impact | Usually no special parting | Very hard if well cemented, as usually the case | Excellent for building but hard to "shape" |
| Slate | Grayish-green, brick red or dark brown, usually gray; may be banded | Finely crystalline; flat crystals give slaty fracture | Some slates have color-fading with age | Splits along slate surface, often crossing color bands | Softer than granite or quartzite; scratches easily | Roofing; blackboards; paving |
| Gneiss | Usually gray with some pink, white or light gray bands | Crystalline, like granite, often with glassy bands (veins) | Banding is decorative; some bands very weak, however | No special parting; tends to break along banding | About like granite | Used for buildings; also may be decorative if banded |

## PHYSICAL PROPERTIES OF REPRESENTATIVE STONES

| PHYSICAL PROPERTY | | IGNEOUS ROCK | | SEDIMENTARY ROCK | | METAMORPHIC ROCK | |
|---|---|---|---|---|---|---|---|
| | | GRANITE | TRAPROCK | LIMESTONE | SANDSTONE | MARBLE | SLATE |
| Composition—ultimate strength | (psi) | 15,000–30,000 | 20,000 | 4,000–20,000 | 3,000–20,000 | 10,000–23,000 | 10,000–15,000 |
| Composition—allowable working stress (psi) | | 800–1,500 | | 500–1,000 | 400–700 | 500–900 | 1,000 |
| Shear—ultimate strength | (psi) | 1,800–2,700 | | 1,000–2,000 | 1,200–2,500 | 900–1,700 | |
| Shear—allowable working stress | (psi) | 200 | | 200 | 150 | 150 | |
| Tension—allowable working stress | (psi) | 150 | | 125 | 75 | 125 | |
| Weight | (psf) | 156–170 | 180–185 | 147–170 | 135–155 | 165–178 | 170–180 |
| Specific gravity | | 2.4–2.7 | 2.96 | 2.1–2.8 | 2.0–2.6 | 2.4–2.8 | 2.7–2.8 |
| Absorption of water (parts by weight) | | 1/750 | | 1/38 | 1/24 | 1/300 | 1/430 |
| Modulus of elasticity | (psi) | 6–10,000,000 | 12,000,000 | 4–14,000,000 | 1–7,500,000 | 4–13,500,000 | 12,000,000 |
| Coefficient of expansion | (psf) | 0.0000040 | | 0.0000045 | 0.0000055 | 0.0000045 | 0.0000058 |

NOTE: Particular stones may vary greatly from the average properties shown in this table. A particular stone's physical properties, as well as its allowable working values, always should be developed for each particular application.

The McGuire & Shook Corporation; Indianapolis, Indiana
Christine Beall, AIA, CCS; Austin, Texas

STONE

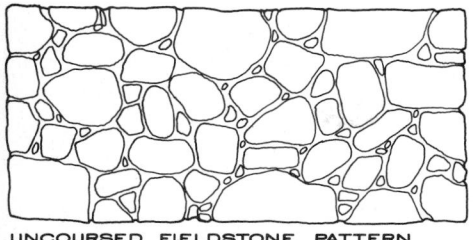

UNCOURSED FIELDSTONE PATTERN

COURSED ASHLAR-RUNNING BOND

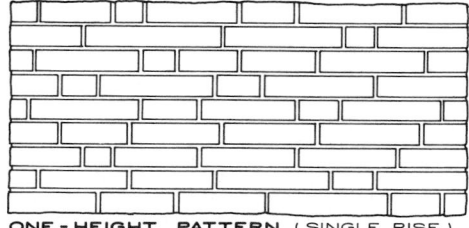

ONE-HEIGHT PATTERN (SINGLE RISE)

UNCOURSED LEDGEROCK PATTERN

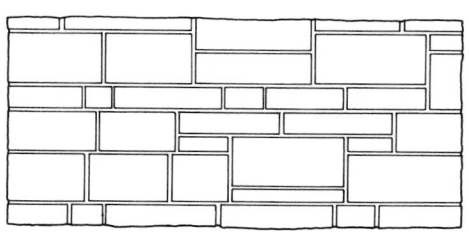

RANDOM COURSED ASHLAR

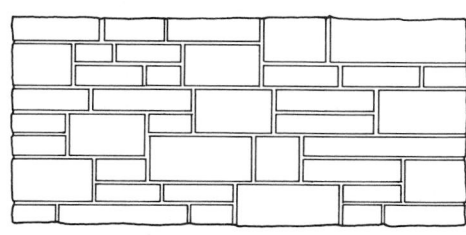

TWO-HEIGHT PATTERN (40% - 2 1/4"; 60% - 5")

UNCOURSED ROUGHLY SQUARED PATTERN

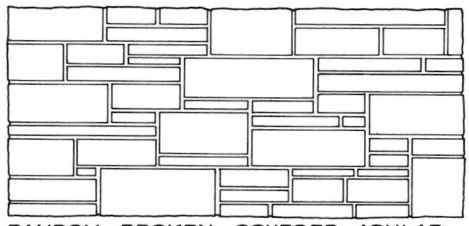

RANDOM BROKEN COURSED ASHLAR

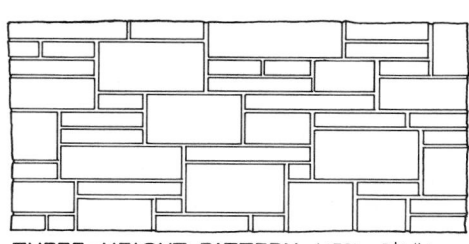

THREE-HEIGHT PATTERN (15% - 2 1/4"; 40% - 5"; 45% - 7 3/4")

RUBBLE STONE MASONRY PATTERNS — ELEVATIONS

SPLIT STONE MASONRY PATTERNS — ELEVATIONS

SPLIT STONE MASONRY HEIGHT PATTERNS — ELEVATIONS

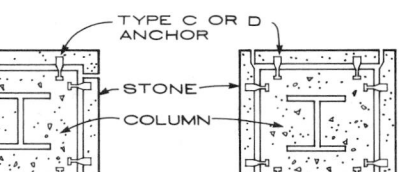

TYPE C OR D ANCHOR
STONE
COLUMN

SQUARE COLUMNS

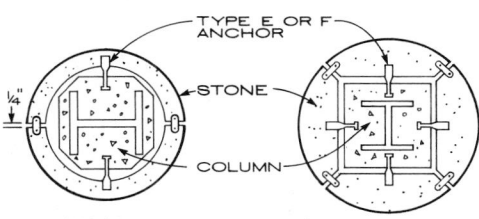

TYPE E OR F ANCHOR
STONE
COLUMN
1/4"

ROUND/QUADRANT COLUMNS

INSTALLATION DETAILS

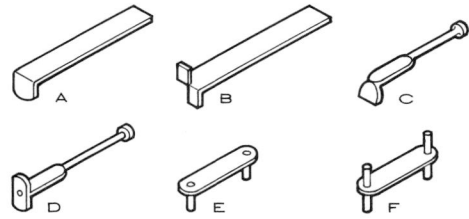

A    B    C
D    E    F

ANCHORS

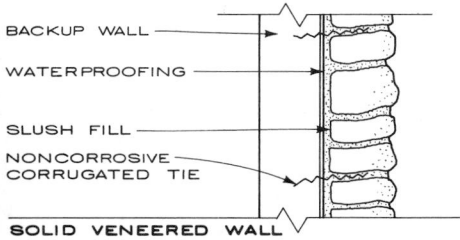

BACKUP WALL
WATERPROOFING
SLUSH FILL
NONCORROSIVE CORRUGATED TIE

SOLID VENEERED WALL

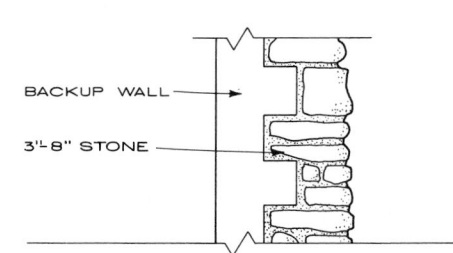

BACKUP WALL
3'L-8" STONE

BONDED VENEERED WALL
(TIES RECOMMENDED IN SOME CASES, E.G., LIMESTONE)

BACKUP WALL
AIRSPACE
NONCORROSIVE CORRUGATED TIE

CAVITY VENEERED WALL

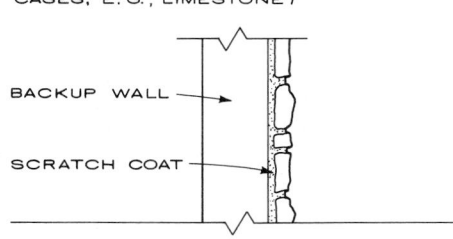

BACKUP WALL
SCRATCH COAT

THIN VENEERED WALL

TYPICAL WALL SECTIONS

### NOTES

1. A course is a horizontal row of stone. Bond pattern is described by the horizontal arrangement of vertical joints. (See also Brickwork.) Structural bond refers to the physical tying together of load bearing and veneer portions of a composite wall. Structural bond can be accomplished with metal ties or with stone units set as headers into the backup.

2. Ashlar masonry is composed of squared-off building stone units of various sizes. Cut Ashlar is dressed to specific design dimensions at the mill. Ashlar is often used in random lengths and heights, with jointing worked out on the job.

3. All ties and anchors must be made of noncorrosive material. Chromium-nickel stainless steel types 302 and 304 and eraydo alloy zinc are the most resistant to corrosion and staining. Hot dipped galvanized is widely used, but is not as resistant, hence is prohibited by some building codes. Copper, brass, and bronze will stain under some conditions. Local building codes often govern the types of metal that may be used for stone anchors.

4. Nonstaining cement mortar should be used on porous and light colored stones. At all corners use extra ties and, when possible, larger stones. Joints are usually 1/2 to 1 1/2 in. for rough work and 3/8 to 3/4 in. for Ashlar.

Building Stone Institute; New York, New York
George M. Whiteside, III, AIA, and James D. Lloyd; Kennett Square, Pennsylvania
Alexander Keyes; Darrel Downing Rippeteau, Architect; Washington, D.C.

STONE 4

**NOTES**

1. Throughout this section, flashing, sealants, and other ancillary materials necessary for sound weatherproof construction sometimes have been omitted for clarity. See flashing and sealant details elsewhere.
2. Earlier editions of *Architectural Graphic Standards* give examples of classical molding details.
3. Allow for tolerances by including correct shimming to prevent installation fitting problems or performance failure.

DOWELS
DRIP EDGE
FASCIA PANEL

**COPING**

BACKUP WALL
CLIP ANGLE WITH WELDED BAR TO RETAIN STONE
TWISTED STRAP
SELF-SUPPORTING STONE LINTEL

**WINDOW HEAD**

ROD ANCHOR
STONE VENEER
BACKUP WALL

**WINDOWSILL**

DOWEL
CLIP ANGLE

**RELIEF ANGLE**

CLIP ANGLE WITH WELDED BAR
HOOK ANCHOR

**SOFFIT**

SEALANT AND BACKER ROD
METAL ANCHOR

**COLUMN ANCHOR**

**STONE VENEER ON CONCRETE WITH MASONRY BACKUP**

CRAMP ANCHOR
BACKUP WALL

**COPING**

STRAP ANCHOR

**FASCIA**

EYE ROD AND DOWEL
CLIP ANGLE WITH WELDED BAR

**WINDOW HEAD**

EYE ROD AND DOWEL
STONE VENEER

**WINDOWSILL**

**GRIP STAY INSERT**

CLIP ANGLE WITH WELDED BAR
DOWEL

**SOFFIT**

ROD CRAMP
STRAP ANCHOR TURNED INTO STONE BOTH WAYS; WELD TO COLUMN

**COLUMN ANCHOR**

**STONE VENEER ON STEEL FRAME**

DISC AND ROD
SUPPORT ANGLE
DOWEL
VERTICAL FIN

**SUN SCREEN**

STONE VENEER
CRAMP ANCHOR
JAMB SHOULD ANCHOR TO WALL NOT TO ADJACENT STONE VENEER

**WINDOW JAMB**

ADJUSTABLE INSERT
ANGLE WITH WELDED BAR
CRAMP ANCHOR

**RELIEF ANGLE**

METAL "FEATHER" INSERT

**LEWIS BOLT**

DISC AND ROD

**BOND WALL AND BASE**

**STONE VENEER DETAILS; OPTIONS**

CLIP ANGLE

**EXPANSION BOLT**

HOOK ROD
T-SUPPORT
SETTING ROD

**HOOK ROD ANCHOR**

CLIP OR CONTINUOUS ANGLE

**ANGLE WITH WELDED BAR**

PLATE WITH WELDED TIE-BACK ROD

**PLATE WITH WELDED BAR**

DOWEL

**DOWEL PIN CONNECTION**

CLIP ANGLE

NOTE: EXPANSION BOLTS SHOULD BE STAINLESS STEEL

**EXPANSION BOLT**

**BASE DETAILS**

Building Stone Institute; New York, New York
George M. Whiteside, III, AIA, and James D. Lloyd; Kennett Square, Pennsylvania
Alexander Keyes; Darrel Downing Rippeteau, Architect; Washington, D.C.

**STONE**

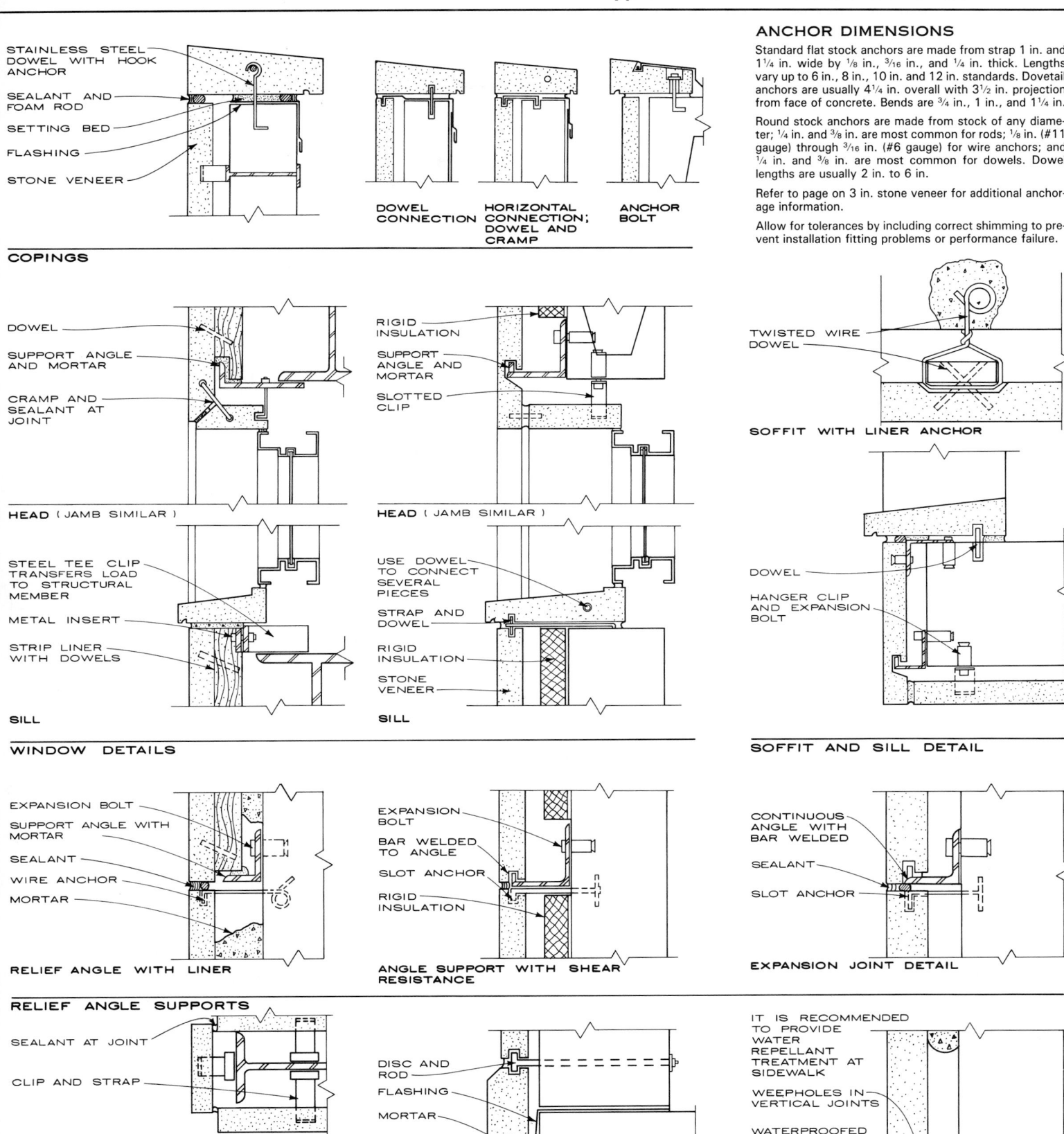

**COPINGS**

STAINLESS STEEL DOWEL WITH HOOK ANCHOR
SEALANT AND FOAM ROD
SETTING BED
FLASHING
STONE VENEER

DOWEL CONNECTION

HORIZONTAL CONNECTION; DOWEL AND CRAMP

ANCHOR BOLT

**ANCHOR DIMENSIONS**

Standard flat stock anchors are made from strap 1 in. and 1¼ in. wide by ⅛ in., ³⁄₁₆ in., and ¼ in. thick. Lengths vary up to 6 in., 8 in., 10 in. and 12 in. standards. Dovetail anchors are usually 4¼ in. overall with 3½ in. projection from face of concrete. Bends are ¾ in., 1 in., and 1¼ in.

Round stock anchors are made from stock of any diameter; ¼ in. and ⅜ in. are most common for rods; ⅛ in. (#11 gauge) through ³⁄₁₆ in. (#6 gauge) for wire anchors; and ¼ in. and ⅜ in. are most common for dowels. Dowel lengths are usually 2 in. to 6 in.

Refer to page on 3 in. stone veneer for additional anchorage information.

Allow for tolerances by including correct shimming to prevent installation fitting problems or performance failure.

DOWEL
SUPPORT ANGLE AND MORTAR
CRAMP AND SEALANT AT JOINT

HEAD (JAMB SIMILAR)

RIGID INSULATION
SUPPORT ANGLE AND MORTAR
SLOTTED CLIP

HEAD (JAMB SIMILAR)

TWISTED WIRE DOWEL

**SOFFIT WITH LINER ANCHOR**

STEEL TEE CLIP TRANSFERS LOAD TO STRUCTURAL MEMBER
METAL INSERT
STRIP LINER WITH DOWELS

**SILL**

USE DOWEL TO CONNECT SEVERAL PIECES
STRAP AND DOWEL
RIGID INSULATION
STONE VENEER

**SILL**

DOWEL
HANGER CLIP AND EXPANSION BOLT

**WINDOW DETAILS**

**SOFFIT AND SILL DETAIL**

EXPANSION BOLT
SUPPORT ANGLE WITH MORTAR
SEALANT
WIRE ANCHOR
MORTAR

**RELIEF ANGLE WITH LINER**

EXPANSION BOLT
BAR WELDED TO ANGLE
SLOT ANCHOR
RIGID INSULATION

**ANGLE SUPPORT WITH SHEAR RESISTANCE**

CONTINUOUS ANGLE WITH BAR WELDED
SEALANT
SLOT ANCHOR

**EXPANSION JOINT DETAIL**

**RELIEF ANGLE SUPPORTS**

SEALANT AT JOINT
CLIP AND STRAP

**STEEL**

SEALANT AT JOINT
DISC AND ROD

**CONCRETE**

**CORNER DETAILS**

DISC AND ROD
FLASHING
MORTAR
WEEPHOLE IN JOINT
GRADE

**BASE DETAILS**

IT IS RECOMMENDED TO PROVIDE WATER REPELLANT TREATMENT AT SIDEWALK
WEEPHOLES IN VERTICAL JOINTS
WATERPROOFED SURFACES
GRADE

Building Stone Institute; New York, New York
George M. Whiteside, III, AIA, and James D. Lloyd; Kennett Square, Pennsylvania
Alexander Keyes; Darrel Downing Rippeteau, Architect; Washington, D.C.

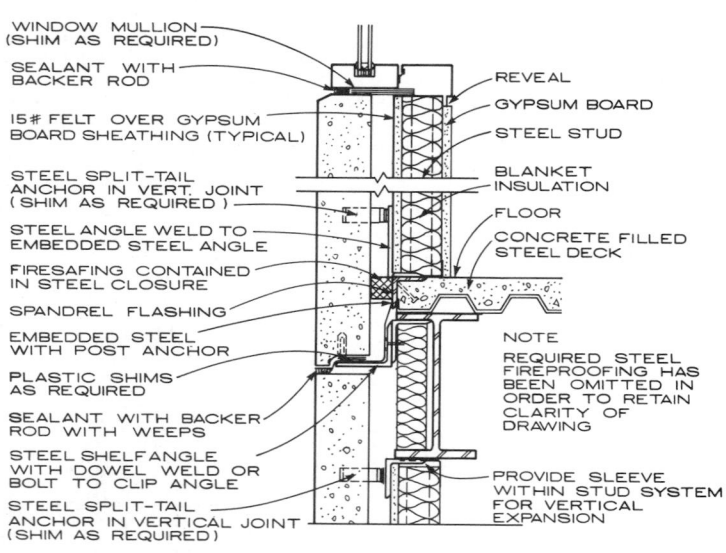

**SECTION THROUGH HARD STONE PANEL AT WINDOW WALL**

Labels (left to right):
- WINDOW MULLION (SHIM AS REQUIRED)
- SEALANT WITH BACKER ROD
- 15# FELT OVER GYPSUM BOARD SHEATHING (TYPICAL)
- STEEL SPLIT-TAIL ANCHOR IN VERT. JOINT (SHIM AS REQUIRED)
- STEEL ANGLE WELD TO EMBEDDED STEEL ANGLE
- FIRESAFING CONTAINED IN STEEL CLOSURE
- SPANDREL FLASHING
- EMBEDDED STEEL WITH POST ANCHOR
- PLASTIC SHIMS AS REQUIRED
- SEALANT WITH BACKER ROD WITH WEEPS
- STEEL SHELF ANGLE WITH DOWEL WELD OR BOLT TO CLIP ANGLE
- STEEL SPLIT-TAIL ANCHOR IN VERTICAL JOINT (SHIM AS REQUIRED)
- REVEAL
- GYPSUM BOARD
- STEEL STUD
- BLANKET INSULATION
- FLOOR
- CONCRETE FILLED STEEL DECK
- NOTE: REQUIRED STEEL FIREPROOFING HAS BEEN OMITTED IN ORDER TO RETAIN CLARITY OF DRAWING
- PROVIDE SLEEVE WITHIN STUD SYSTEM FOR VERTICAL EXPANSION

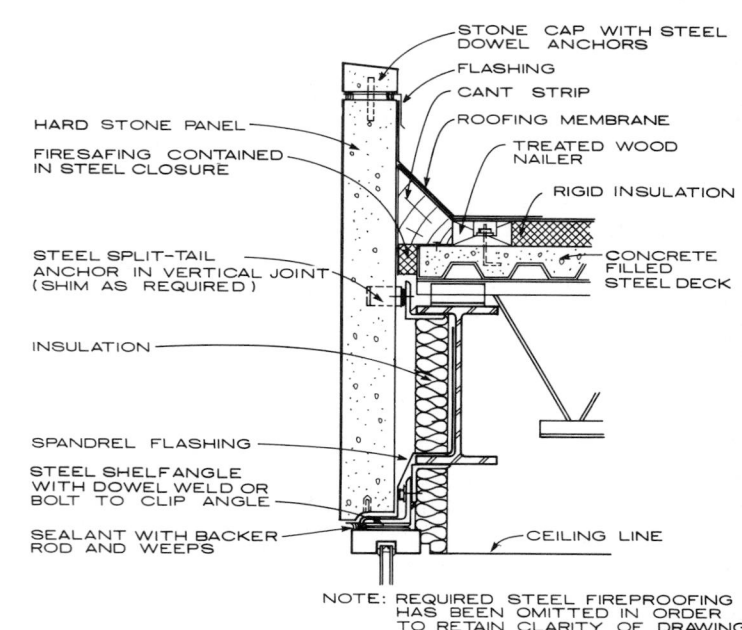

**SECTION THROUGH ROOF PARAPET AT HARD STONE PANEL**

Labels:
- STONE CAP WITH STEEL DOWEL ANCHORS
- FLASHING
- CANT STRIP
- ROOFING MEMBRANE
- TREATED WOOD NAILER
- RIGID INSULATION
- HARD STONE PANEL
- FIRESAFING CONTAINED IN STEEL CLOSURE
- STEEL SPLIT-TAIL ANCHOR IN VERTICAL JOINT (SHIM AS REQUIRED)
- INSULATION
- SPANDREL FLASHING
- STEEL SHELF ANGLE WITH DOWEL WELD OR BOLT TO CLIP ANGLE
- SEALANT WITH BACKER ROD AND WEEPS
- CONCRETE FILLED STEEL DECK
- CEILING LINE
- NOTE: REQUIRED STEEL FIREPROOFING HAS BEEN OMITTED IN ORDER TO RETAIN CLARITY OF DRAWING

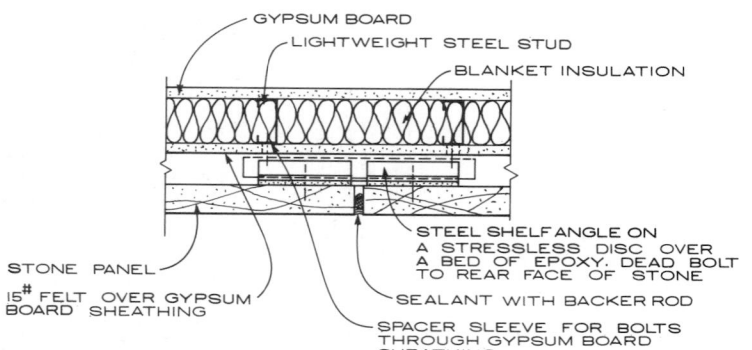

**SECTION AT VERTICAL JOINT**

Labels:
- GYPSUM BOARD
- LIGHTWEIGHT STEEL STUD
- BLANKET INSULATION
- STONE PANEL
- 15# FELT OVER GYPSUM BOARD SHEATHING
- STEEL SHELF ANGLE ON A STRESSLESS DISC OVER A BED OF EPOXY. DEAD BOLT TO REAR FACE OF STONE
- SEALANT WITH BACKER ROD
- SPACER SLEEVE FOR BOLTS THROUGH GYPSUM BOARD SHEATHING

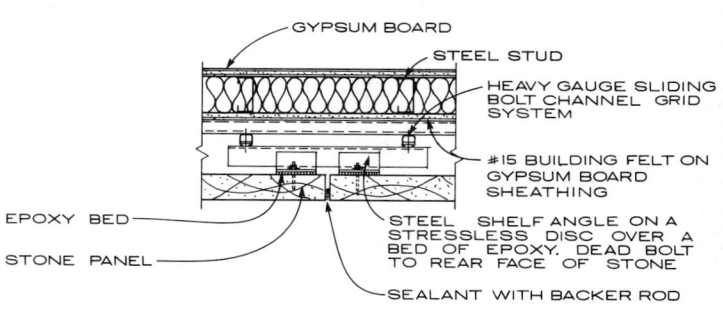

**SECTION AT VERTICAL JOINT**

Labels:
- GYPSUM BOARD
- STEEL STUD
- HEAVY GAUGE SLIDING BOLT CHANNEL GRID SYSTEM
- #15 BUILDING FELT ON GYPSUM BOARD SHEATHING
- EPOXY BED
- STONE PANEL
- STEEL SHELF ANGLE ON A STRESSLESS DISC OVER A BED OF EPOXY. DEAD BOLT TO REAR FACE OF STONE
- SEALANT WITH BACKER ROD

## NOTES

Use of the steel stud support system as shown requires an architect or engineer to develop adequate and realistic performance criteria, including thorough consideration of the long-term durability and corrosion resistance of light gauge members, mechanical fasteners, and other system components; provisions for adequate thermal movement; development of adequate system strength and stiffness; recognition of the structural interaction between the stone support system; and consideration of vapor retarders and flashing to control moisture migration. It also is important that adequate provisions be developed to ensure quality workmanship necessary to implement the system and to achieve the expected quality and durability.

The stone thickness depicted is a minimum of 1½ in. Thicker stone materials can use the same type of support system; however, engineering analyses of the system will be necessary to ensure proper performance and compliance with recommended design practices.

Design criteria for stone anchorage must include consideration of the particular stone's average as well as lowest strength values for safety, particularly at anchorage points. The proposed stone should be tested for adequate design properties and values. Stone anchorage size and location depend on establishing the particular stone's strength values, natural faults, and other properties; the stone's thickness and supported area; the expected lateral as well as gravity loading; and the amount of thermal movement to be accommodated.

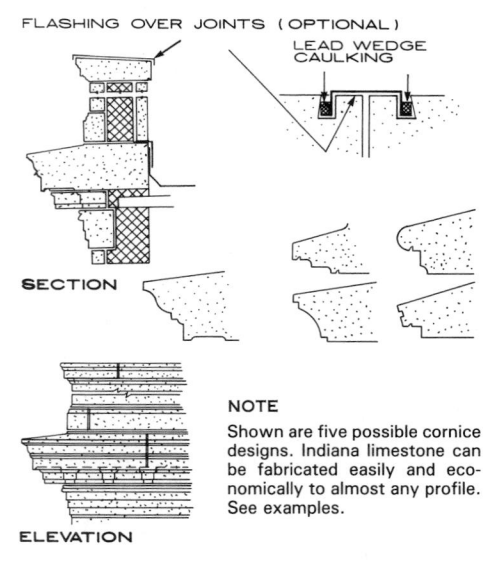

- FLASHING OVER JOINTS (OPTIONAL)
- LEAD WEDGE CAULKING
- SECTION
- ELEVATION

**NOTE**

Shown are five possible cornice designs. Indiana limestone can be fabricated easily and economically to almost any profile. See examples.

**TRADITIONAL CORNICES**

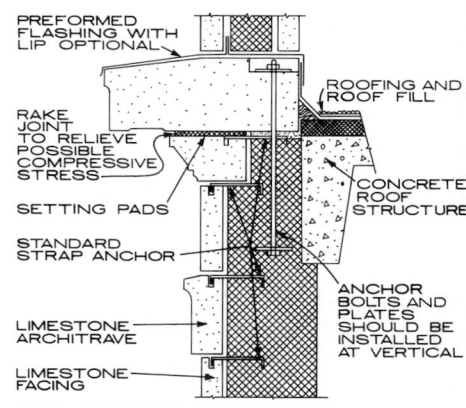

- PREFORMED FLASHING WITH LIP OPTIONAL
- ROOFING AND ROOF FILL
- RAKE JOINT TO RELIEVE POSSIBLE COMPRESSIVE STRESS
- SETTING PADS
- STANDARD STRAP ANCHOR
- LIMESTONE ARCHITRAVE
- LIMESTONE FACING
- CONCRETE ROOF STRUCTURE
- ANCHOR BOLTS AND PLATES SHOULD BE INSTALLED AT VERTICAL

**WALL SECTION**

Shown here is the most common method of anchoring a cornice, which has a large enough projection to be unbalanced in the wall.

The bed joint immediately below the heavy cornice is open far enough back to remove any compressive stress that would have a tendency to break off stone below.

The Spector Group; North Hills, New York

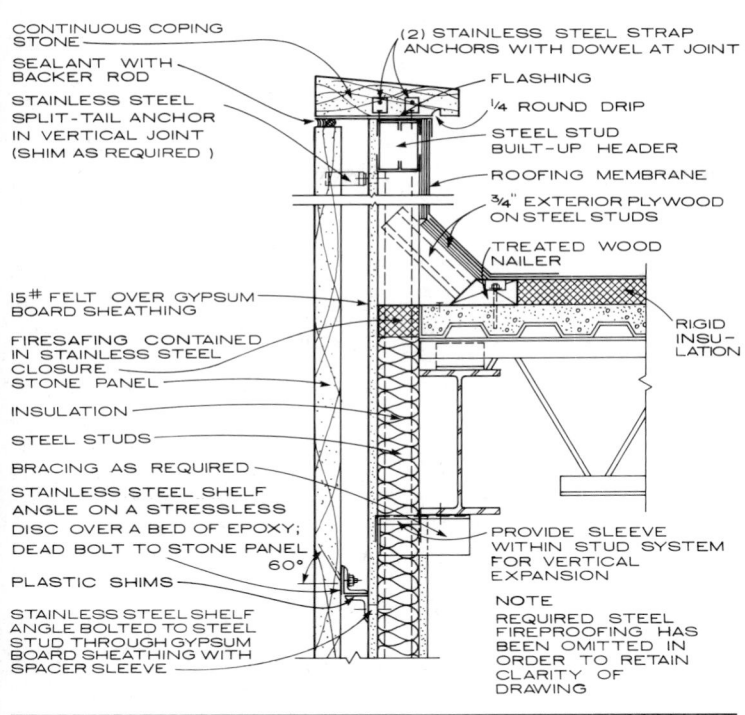

CONTINUOUS COPING STONE

SEALANT WITH BACKER ROD

STAINLESS STEEL SPLIT-TAIL ANCHOR IN VERTICAL JOINT (SHIM AS REQUIRED)

(2) STAINLESS STEEL STRAP ANCHORS WITH DOWEL AT JOINT

FLASHING

1/4 ROUND DRIP

STEEL STUD BUILT-UP HEADER

ROOFING MEMBRANE

3/4" EXTERIOR PLYWOOD ON STEEL STUDS

TREATED WOOD NAILER

15# FELT OVER GYPSUM BOARD SHEATHING

FIRESAFING CONTAINED IN STAINLESS STEEL CLOSURE

STONE PANEL

INSULATION

STEEL STUDS

BRACING AS REQUIRED

STAINLESS STEEL SHELF ANGLE ON A STRESSLESS DISC OVER A BED OF EPOXY; DEAD BOLT TO STONE PANEL

PLASTIC SHIMS

STAINLESS STEEL SHELF ANGLE BOLTED TO STEEL STUD THROUGH GYPSUM BOARD SHEATHING WITH SPACER SLEEVE

RIGID INSULATION

PROVIDE SLEEVE WITHIN STUD SYSTEM FOR VERTICAL EXPANSION

NOTE REQUIRED STEEL FIREPROOFING HAS BEEN OMITTED IN ORDER TO RETAIN CLARITY OF DRAWING

**SECTION AT ROOF PARAPET AND WINDOWLESS WALL**

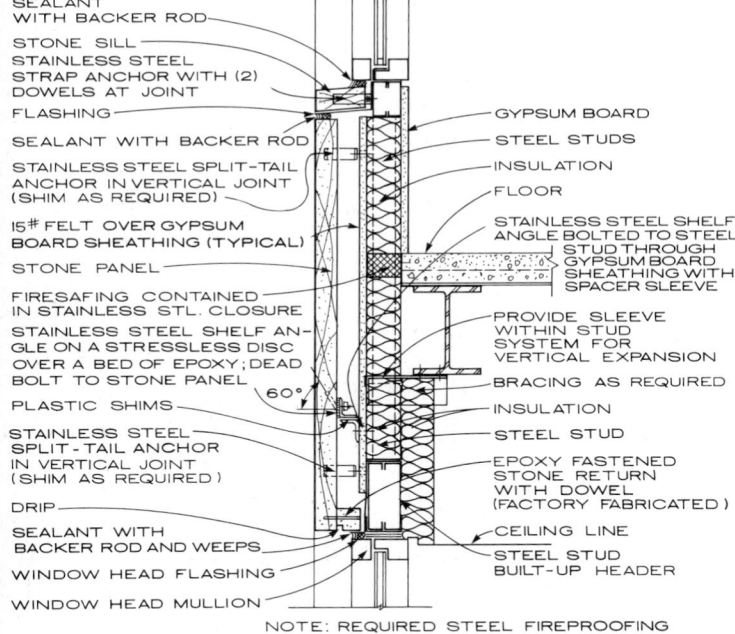

SEALANT WITH BACKER ROD

STONE SILL

STAINLESS STEEL STRAP ANCHOR WITH (2) DOWELS AT JOINT

FLASHING

SEALANT WITH BACKER ROD

STAINLESS STEEL SPLIT-TAIL ANCHOR IN VERTICAL JOINT (SHIM AS REQUIRED)

15# FELT OVER GYPSUM BOARD SHEATHING (TYPICAL)

STONE PANEL

FIRESAFING CONTAINED IN STAINLESS STL. CLOSURE

STAINLESS STEEL SHELF ANGLE ON A STRESSLESS DISC OVER A BED OF EPOXY; DEAD BOLT TO STONE PANEL

PLASTIC SHIMS

STAINLESS STEEL SPLIT-TAIL ANCHOR IN VERTICAL JOINT (SHIM AS REQUIRED)

DRIP

SEALANT WITH BACKER ROD AND WEEPS

WINDOW HEAD FLASHING

WINDOW HEAD MULLION

GYPSUM BOARD

STEEL STUDS

INSULATION

FLOOR

STAINLESS STEEL SHELF ANGLE BOLTED TO STEEL STUD THROUGH GYPSUM BOARD SHEATHING WITH SPACER SLEEVE

PROVIDE SLEEVE WITHIN STUD SYSTEM FOR VERTICAL EXPANSION

BRACING AS REQUIRED

INSULATION

STEEL STUD

EPOXY FASTENED STONE RETURN WITH DOWEL (FACTORY FABRICATED)

CEILING LINE

STEEL STUD BUILT-UP HEADER

NOTE: REQUIRED STEEL FIREPROOFING HAS BEEN OMITTED IN ORDER TO RETAIN CLARITY OF DRAWING

**STONE SPANDREL AT WINDOW HEAD AND SILL**

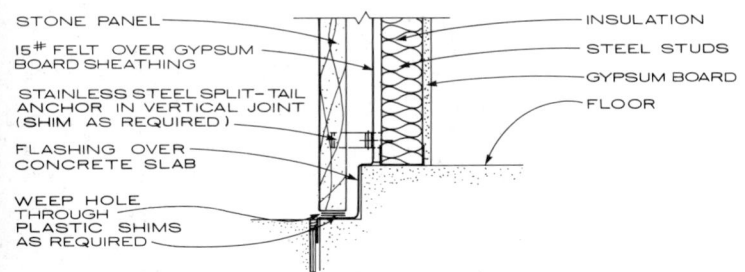

STONE PANEL

15# FELT OVER GYPSUM BOARD SHEATHING

STAINLESS STEEL SPLIT-TAIL ANCHOR IN VERTICAL JOINT (SHIM AS REQUIRED)

FLASHING OVER CONCRETE SLAB

WEEP HOLE THROUGH PLASTIC SHIMS AS REQUIRED

INSULATION

STEEL STUDS

GYPSUM BOARD

FLOOR

**STONE SPANDREL AT GRADE**

The Spector Group; North Hills, New York

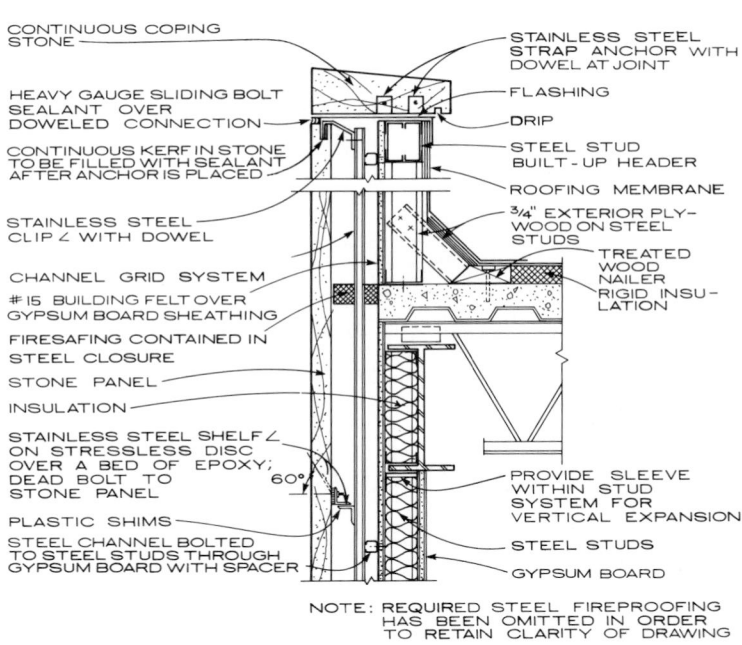

CONTINUOUS COPING STONE

HEAVY GAUGE SLIDING BOLT SEALANT OVER DOWELED CONNECTION

CONTINUOUS KERF IN STONE TO BE FILLED WITH SEALANT AFTER ANCHOR IS PLACED

STAINLESS STEEL CLIP ∠ WITH DOWEL

CHANNEL GRID SYSTEM

#15 BUILDING FELT OVER GYPSUM BOARD SHEATHING

FIRESAFING CONTAINED IN STEEL CLOSURE

STONE PANEL

INSULATION

STAINLESS STEEL SHELF ∠ ON STRESSLESS DISC OVER A BED OF EPOXY; DEAD BOLT TO STONE PANEL

PLASTIC SHIMS

STEEL CHANNEL BOLTED TO STEEL STUDS THROUGH GYPSUM BOARD WITH SPACER

STAINLESS STEEL STRAP ANCHOR WITH DOWEL AT JOINT

FLASHING

DRIP

STEEL STUD BUILT-UP HEADER

ROOFING MEMBRANE

3/4" EXTERIOR PLYWOOD ON STEEL STUDS

TREATED WOOD NAILER

RIGID INSULATION

60°

PROVIDE SLEEVE WITHIN STUD SYSTEM FOR VERTICAL EXPANSION

STEEL STUDS

GYPSUM BOARD

NOTE: REQUIRED STEEL FIREPROOFING HAS BEEN OMITTED IN ORDER TO RETAIN CLARITY OF DRAWING

**SECTION AT ROOF PARAPET AND WINDOWLESS WALL**

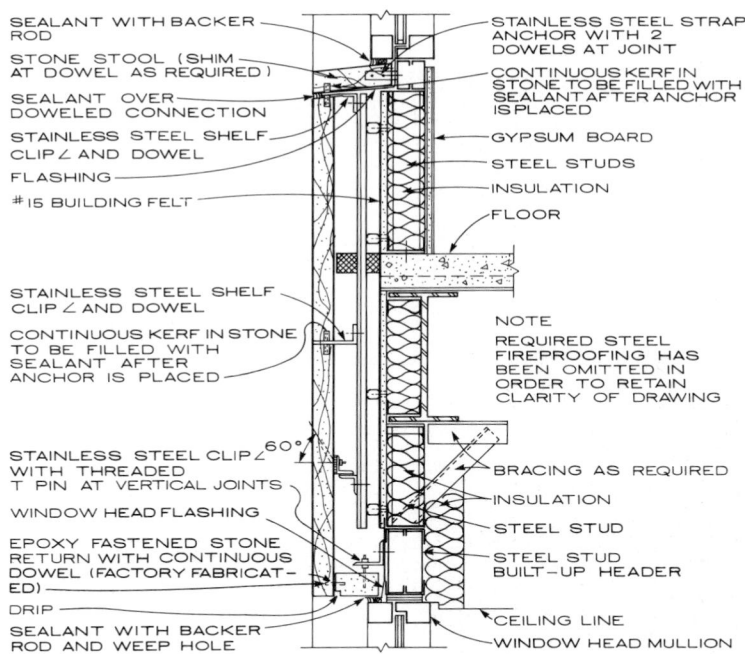

SEALANT WITH BACKER ROD

STONE STOOL (SHIM AT DOWEL AS REQUIRED)

SEALANT OVER DOWELED CONNECTION

STAINLESS STEEL SHELF CLIP ∠ AND DOWEL

FLASHING

#15 BUILDING FELT

STAINLESS STEEL SHELF CLIP ∠ AND DOWEL

CONTINUOUS KERF IN STONE TO BE FILLED WITH SEALANT AFTER ANCHOR IS PLACED

STAINLESS STEEL CLIP ∠ WITH THREADED T PIN AT VERTICAL JOINTS

WINDOW HEAD FLASHING

EPOXY FASTENED STONE RETURN WITH CONTINUOUS DOWEL (FACTORY FABRICATED)

DRIP

SEALANT WITH BACKER ROD AND WEEP HOLE

STAINLESS STEEL STRAP ANCHOR WITH 2 DOWELS AT JOINT

CONTINUOUS KERF IN STONE TO BE FILLED WITH SEALANT AFTER ANCHOR IS PLACED

GYPSUM BOARD

STEEL STUDS

INSULATION

FLOOR

NOTE REQUIRED STEEL FIREPROOFING HAS BEEN OMITTED IN ORDER TO RETAIN CLARITY OF DRAWING

60°

BRACING AS REQUIRED

INSULATION

STEEL STUD

STEEL STUD BUILT-UP HEADER

CEILING LINE

WINDOW HEAD MULLION

**STONE SPANDREL AT WINDOW HEAD AND SILL**

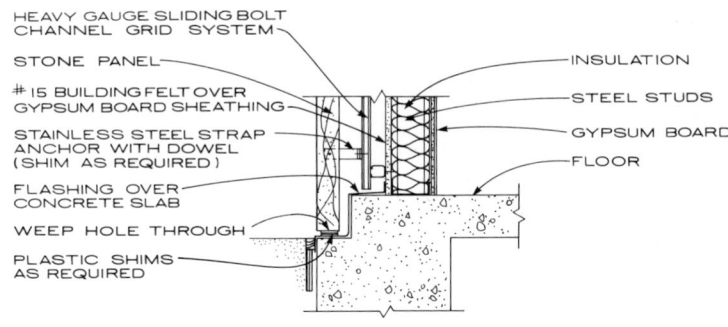

HEAVY GAUGE SLIDING BOLT CHANNEL GRID SYSTEM

STONE PANEL

#15 BUILDING FELT OVER GYPSUM BOARD SHEATHING

STAINLESS STEEL STRAP ANCHOR WITH DOWEL (SHIM AS REQUIRED)

FLASHING OVER CONCRETE SLAB

WEEP HOLE THROUGH

PLASTIC SHIMS AS REQUIRED

INSULATION

STEEL STUDS

GYPSUM BOARD

FLOOR

**STONE SPANDREL AT GRADE**

STONE    4

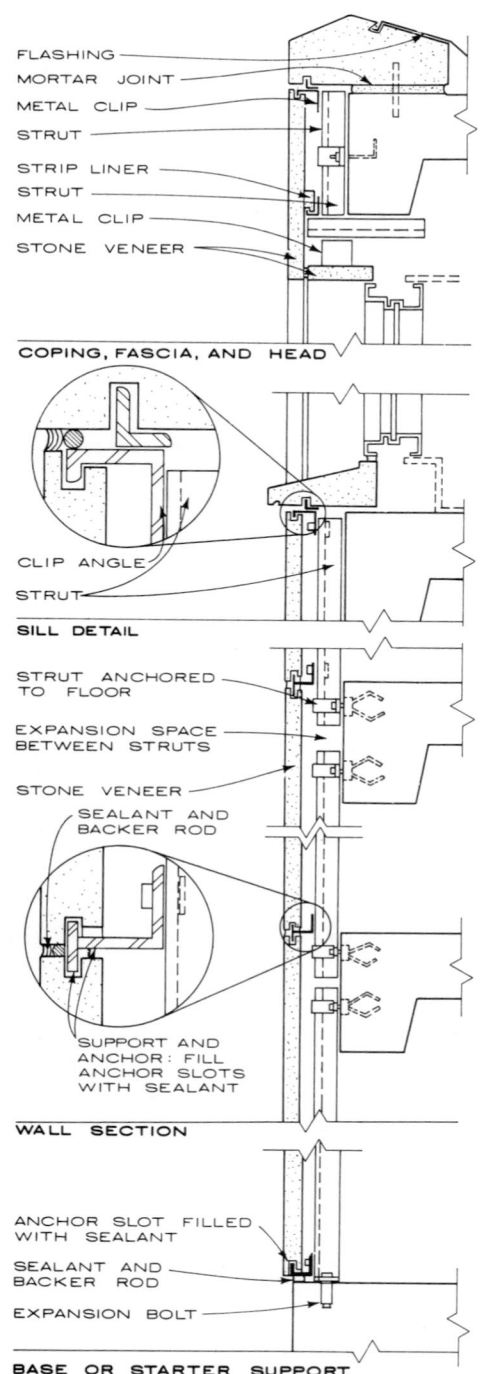

COPING, FASCIA, AND HEAD

- FLASHING
- MORTAR JOINT
- METAL CLIP
- STRUT
- STRIP LINER
- STRUT
- METAL CLIP
- STONE VENEER

SILL DETAIL

- CLIP ANGLE
- STRUT

WALL SECTION

- STRUT ANCHORED TO FLOOR
- EXPANSION SPACE BETWEEN STRUTS
- STONE VENEER
- SEALANT AND BACKER ROD
- SUPPORT AND ANCHOR: FILL ANCHOR SLOTS WITH SEALANT

BASE OR STARTER SUPPORT

- ANCHOR SLOT FILLED WITH SEALANT
- SEALANT AND BACKER ROD
- EXPANSION BOLT

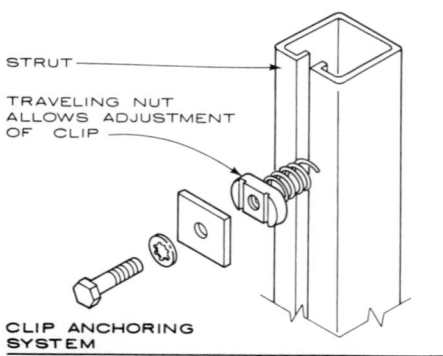

CLIP ANCHORING SYSTEM

- STRUT
- TRAVELING NUT ALLOWS ADJUSTMENT OF CLIP

**GRID STRUT SYSTEM — CONCRETE FRAME**

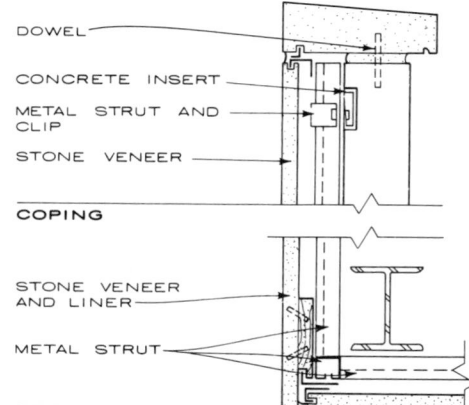

COPING

- DOWEL
- CONCRETE INSERT
- METAL STRUT AND CLIP
- STONE VENEER

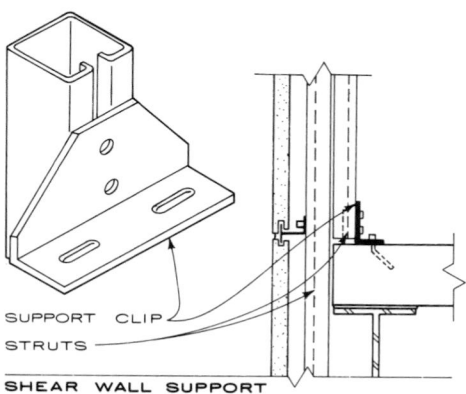

SOFFIT

- STONE VENEER AND LINER
- METAL STRUT

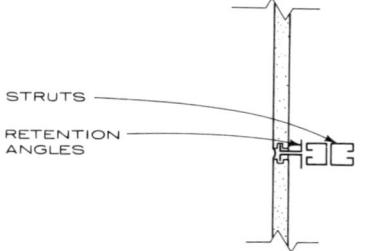

SHEAR WALL SUPPORT

- SUPPORT CLIP
- STRUTS

SHEAR WALL SIDE RETENTION (PLAN)

- STRUTS
- RETENTION ANGLES

**GRID STRUT SYSTEM — METAL FRAME**

### GRID STRUT SPACING RELATIVE TO SLAB HEIGHT—MARBLE

| HEIGHT OF SLAB UP TO | GRID STRUT SPACING | |
|---|---|---|
| | ⁷⁄₈" THICK | 1¼" THICK |
| 2'-6" | 4'-9" | 4'-0" |
| 3'-0" | 4'-6" | 3'-9" |
| 3'-6" | 4'-3" | 3'-6" |
| 4'-0" | 4'-0" | 3'-3" |
| 4'-6" | 3'-9" | 3'-0" |
| 5'-0"* | 3'-6" | 2'-9" |
| 5'-6"* | 3'-3" | 2'-6" |
| 6'-0"* | 3'-3" | 2'-3" |

*For slabs over 4'-6" height use intermediate vertical joint anchoring.

NOTE: Engineering design of all supports for this type of construction is essential.

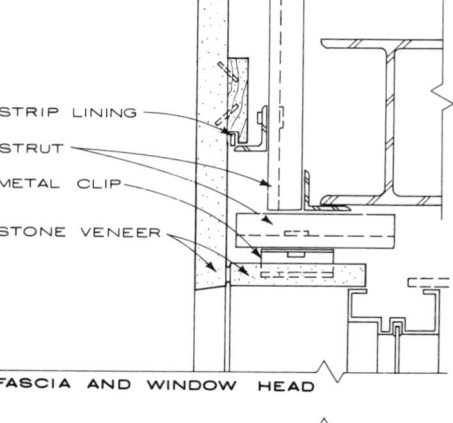

FASCIA AND WINDOW HEAD

- STRIP LINING
- STRUT
- METAL CLIP
- STONE VENEER

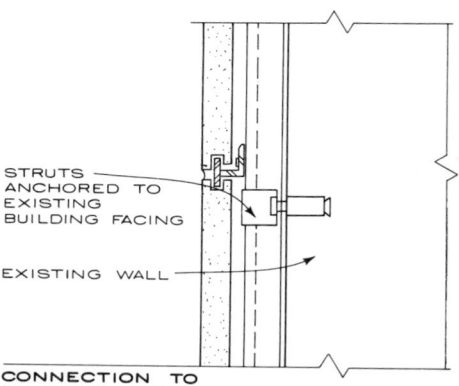

CONNECTION TO EXISTING FACING

- STRUTS ANCHORED TO EXISTING BUILDING FACING
- EXISTING WALL

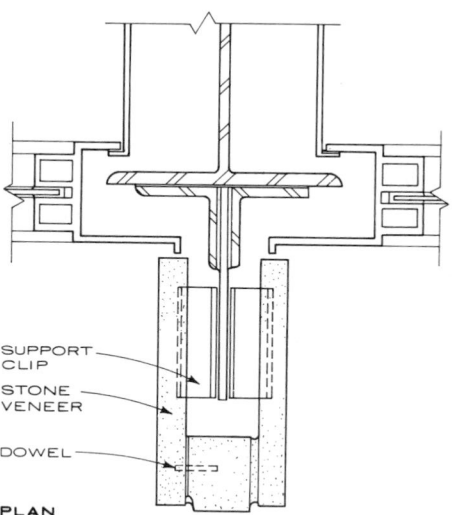

PLAN
COLUMN RETURN

- SUPPORT CLIP
- STONE VENEER
- DOWEL

### GRID ANCHOR SPACING AND STRUT SIZE—MARBLE

| MAXIMUM SPACING | | ANCHOR | STRUT SIZE |
|---|---|---|---|
| ⁷⁄₈" THICK | 1¼" THICK | | WIDTH, DEPTH, AND SHAPE |
| 4'-0" | 4'-0" | | 1⁵⁄₈" x 1⁵⁄₈" |
| 7'-0" | 6'-0" | | 1⁵⁄₈" x 2⁷⁄₁₆" |
| 10'-0" | 9'-0" | | 1⁵⁄₈" x 3¼" |
| 15'-0" | 13'-0" | | 1⁵⁄₈" x 4⁷⁄₈" |

NOTES
1. "X" = dimension between strut and outside face of stone.
2. "X" = 1⁵⁄₈" for ⁷⁄₈" marble.
3. "X" = 1¾" for 1¼" marble.

Building Stone Institute; New York, New York
George M. Whiteside, III, AIA, and James D. Lloyd; Kennett Square, Pennsylvania
Alexander Keyes; Darrel Downing Rippeteau, Architect; Washington, D.C.

 **STONE**

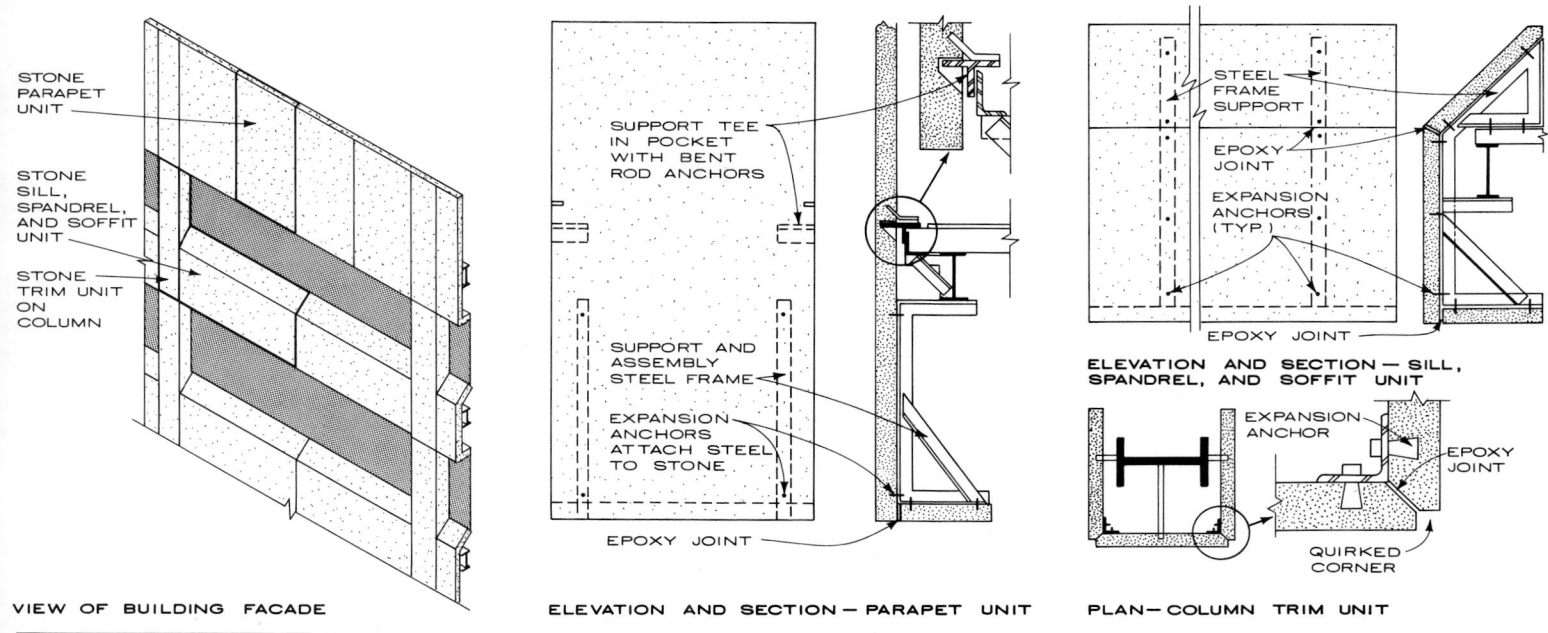

STONE PARAPET UNIT

STONE SILL, SPANDREL, AND SOFFIT UNIT

STONE TRIM UNIT ON COLUMN

**VIEW OF BUILDING FACADE**

SUPPORT TEE IN POCKET WITH BENT ROD ANCHORS

SUPPORT AND ASSEMBLY STEEL FRAME

EXPANSION ANCHORS ATTACH STEEL TO STONE

EPOXY JOINT

**ELEVATION AND SECTION — PARAPET UNIT**

STEEL FRAME SUPPORT

EPOXY JOINT

EXPANSION ANCHORS (TYP.)

EPOXY JOINT

**ELEVATION AND SECTION — SILL, SPANDREL, AND SOFFIT UNIT**

EXPANSION ANCHOR

EPOXY JOINT

QUIRKED CORNER

**PLAN — COLUMN TRIM UNIT**

## PREASSEMBLED STONE UNIT WITH EPOXY ON STEEL FRAME

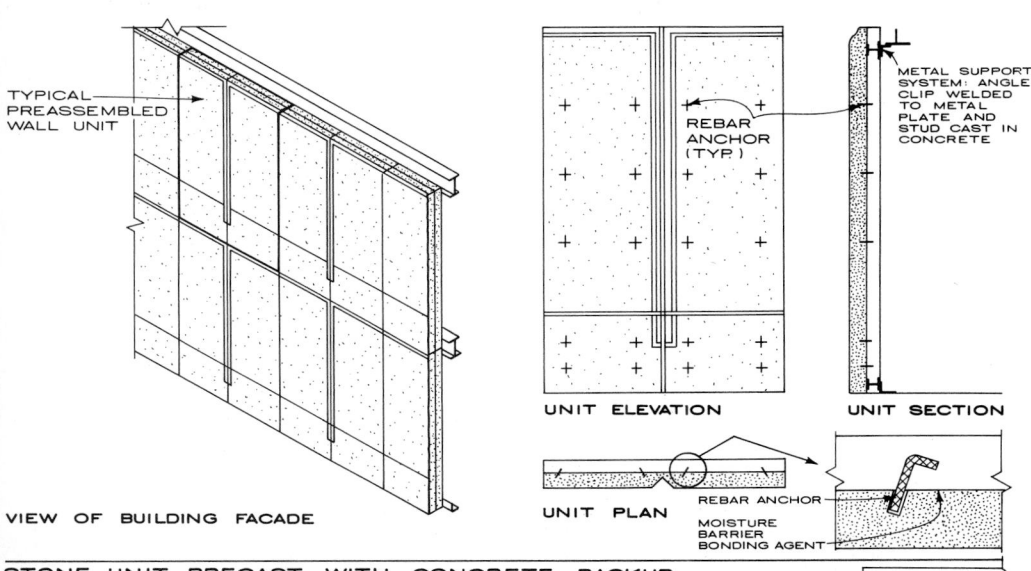

TYPICAL PREASSEMBLED WALL UNIT

**VIEW OF BUILDING FACADE**

REBAR ANCHOR (TYP.)

**UNIT ELEVATION**

METAL SUPPORT SYSTEM: ANGLE CLIP WELDED TO METAL PLATE AND STUD CAST IN CONCRETE

**UNIT SECTION**

**UNIT PLAN**

REBAR ANCHOR

MOISTURE BARRIER BONDING AGENT

## PREASSEMBLED PANELS

Savings in on-site labor and accurate component stone unit joining are available through preassembled stone panel technology.

Shipping and erection stresses on the stone panels and stone anchorage system to the preassembled units should be evaluated.

Design of sealant joints between preassembled units should include at least the following: thermal movement, fabrication and erection tolerances, irreversible material growth or shrinkage, and sealant movement potential.

### STONE ON STEEL FRAME WITH EPOXY JOINTS

Stone units are mounted on a steel frame with expansion bolts and dowel pins (as recommended by manufacturer). Joints in stone are epoxied and held to approximately ⅛ in. when finished for delivery. All stones in the assembly are anchored as a unit to the structure. Preassembled unit installation reduces individual leveling, plumbing, and aligning, and on-site joint sealing is not as extensive as with individual stone panels.

### COMPOSITE ASSEMBLIES OF STONE AND CONCRETE

Stone units are bonded to reinforced precast concrete panels with bent stainless steel anchors. A moisture barrier and a bonding agent are installed between the stone and concrete in conditions where concrete alkali salts may stain stone units.

### STONE AND STEEL ASSEMBLIES WITH SEALANT JOINTS

Stone units are shimmed and anchored to a steel frame using standard stone connecting hardware. Joints may be sealed on site, along with joints between assemblies.

## STONE UNIT PRECAST WITH CONCRETE BACKUP

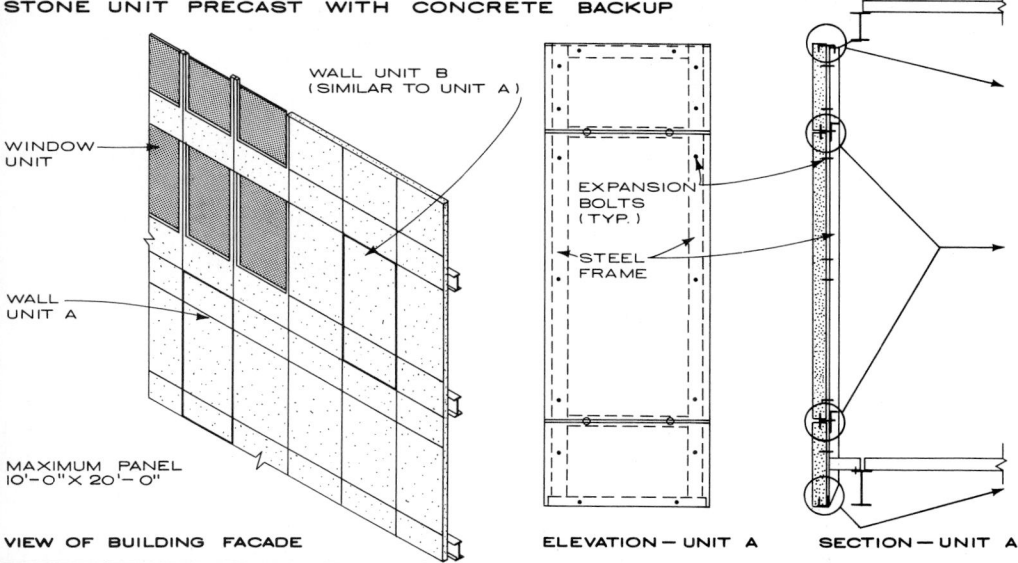

WALL UNIT B (SIMILAR TO UNIT A)

WINDOW UNIT

WALL UNIT A

MAXIMUM PANEL 10'-0" X 20'-0"

**VIEW OF BUILDING FACADE**

EXPANSION BOLTS (TYP.)

STEEL FRAME

**ELEVATION — UNIT A**

**SECTION — UNIT A**

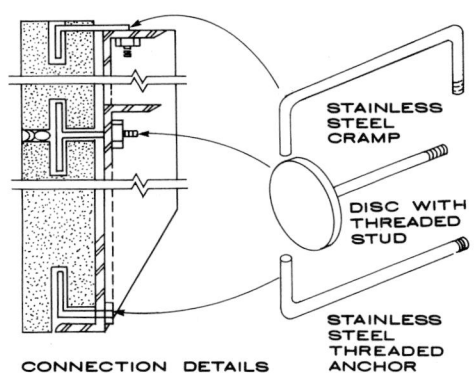

STAINLESS STEEL CRAMP

DISC WITH THREADED STUD

STAINLESS STEEL THREADED ANCHOR

**CONNECTION DETAILS**

**PREASSEMBLED STONE UNIT ON STEEL FRAME**
Building Stone Institute; New York, New York
George M. Whiteside, III, AIA, and James D. Lloyd; Kennett Square, Pennsylvania
Alexander Keyes; Darrel Downing Rippeteau, Architect; Washington, D.C.

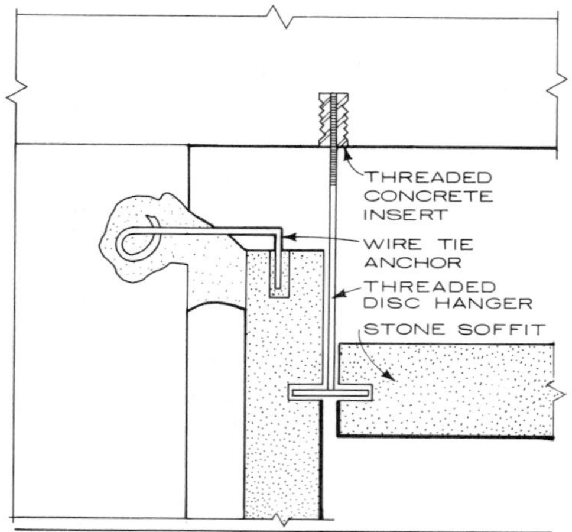

**SOFFIT DETAIL AT WALL**

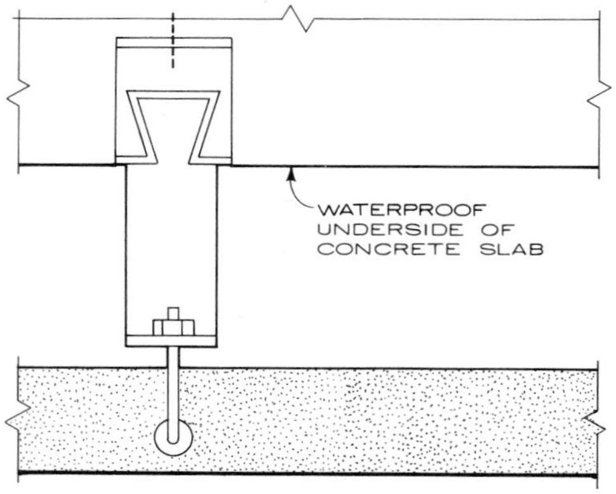

THREADED CONCRETE INSERT
WIRE TIE ANCHOR
THREADED DISC HANGER
STONE SOFFIT

**VERTICAL JOINT DETAIL - PLAN**

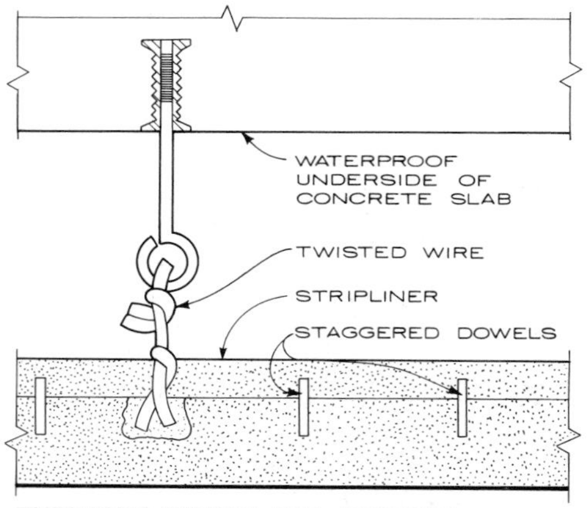

MORTAR
WIRE TIES
SEALANT

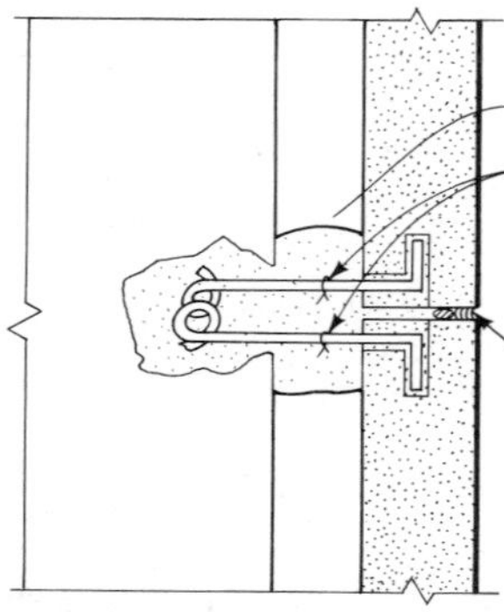

NOTE: WIRE ANCHORS CAN BE TIED AROUND A DOWEL INSERTED VERTICALLY INTO STONE

**BASE DETAIL**

WIRE ANCHOR
FLOOR

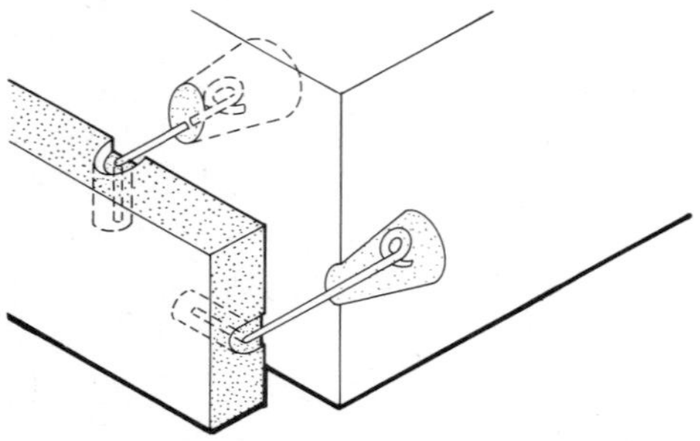

**SIMPLE WIRE ANCHOR CONNECTION**

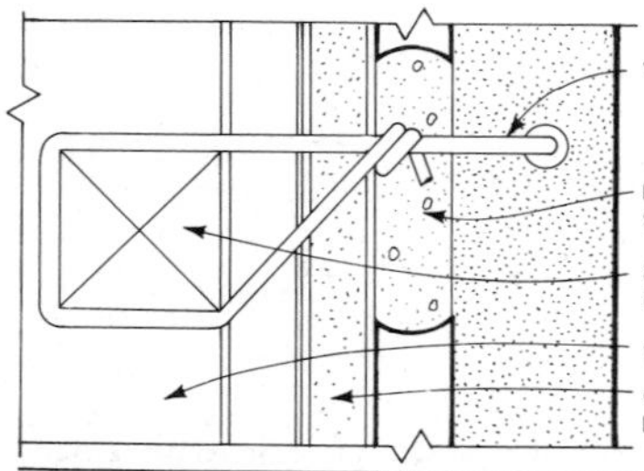

**STONE PANEL ON WOOD STUDS**

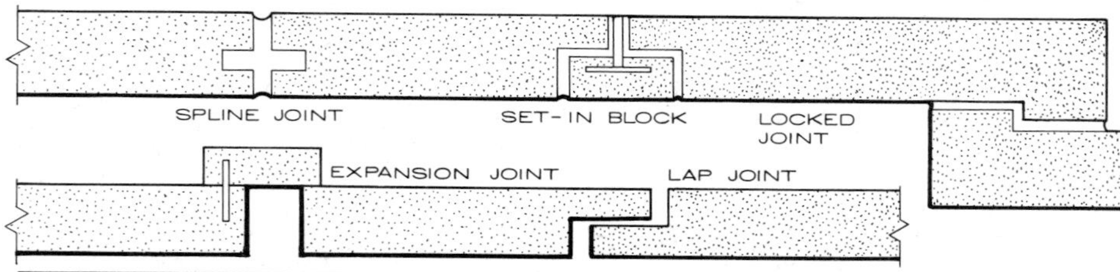

WIRE TIE
PLASTER SPOTS
2 X 2 BLOCKING
WOOD STUD
GYPSUM DRYWALL

**DOVETAIL STRAP WITH HOOK ROD ANCHOR**

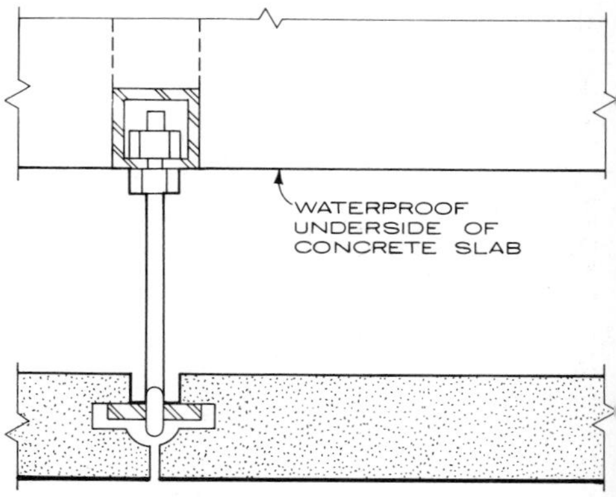

WATERPROOF UNDERSIDE OF CONCRETE SLAB

**EYEBOLT AND DOWEL BOLTED TO THREADED CONCRETE INSERT**

WATERPROOF UNDERSIDE OF CONCRETE SLAB

WATERPROOF UNDERSIDE OF CONCRETE SLAB
TWISTED WIRE
STRIPLINER
STAGGERED DOWELS

STEEL MEMBER

**THREADED INSERT AND EYEBOLT** 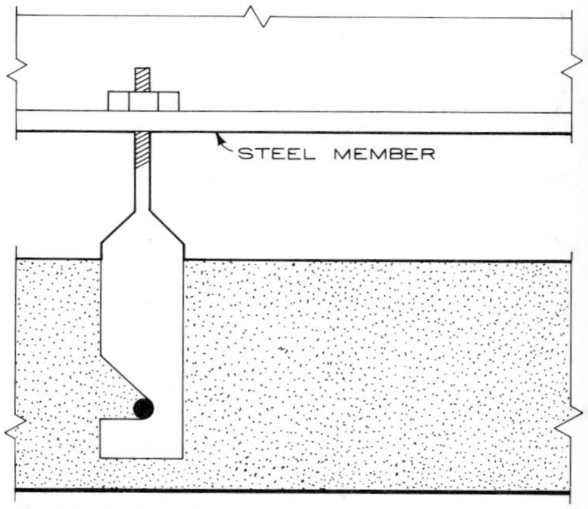         **FLAT HOOK ANCHOR AND DOWEL**

**TYPICAL SYSTEMS FOR HANGING INTERIOR VENEER STONE**

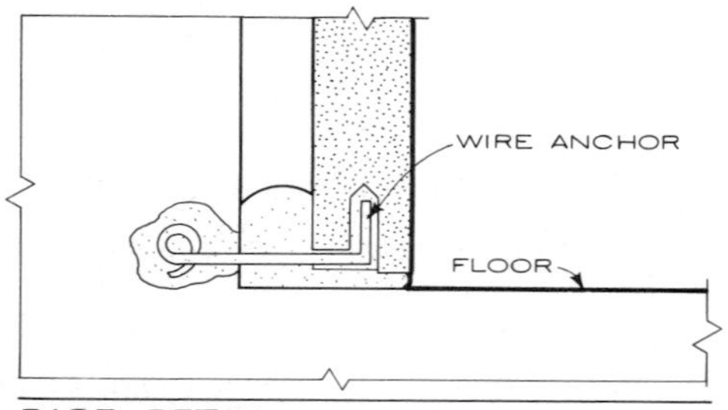

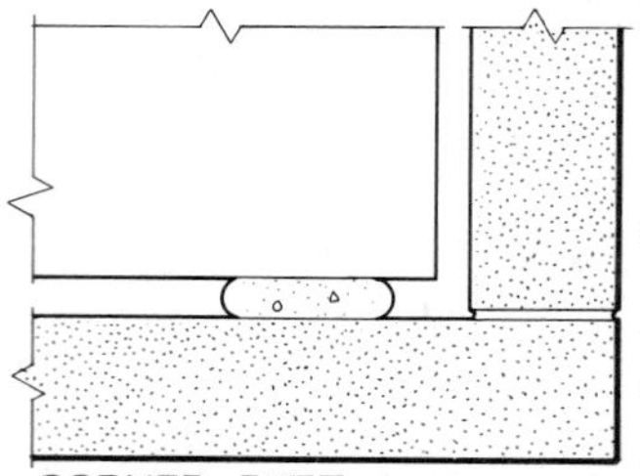

**CORNER BUTT** 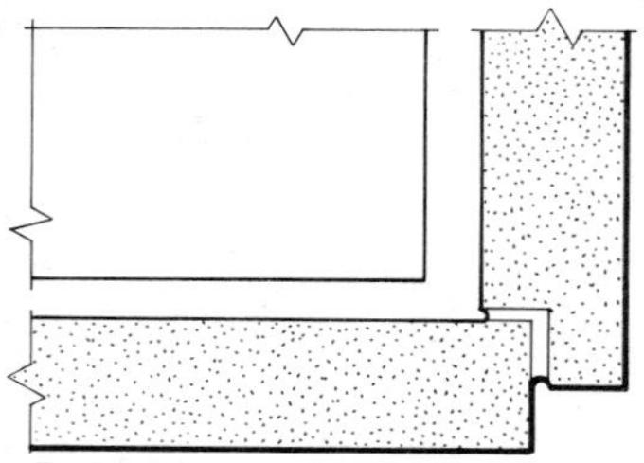          **RABBETED CORNER** 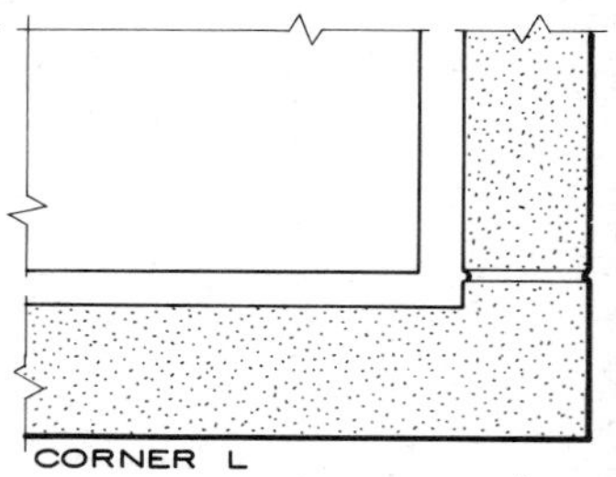          **CORNER L**

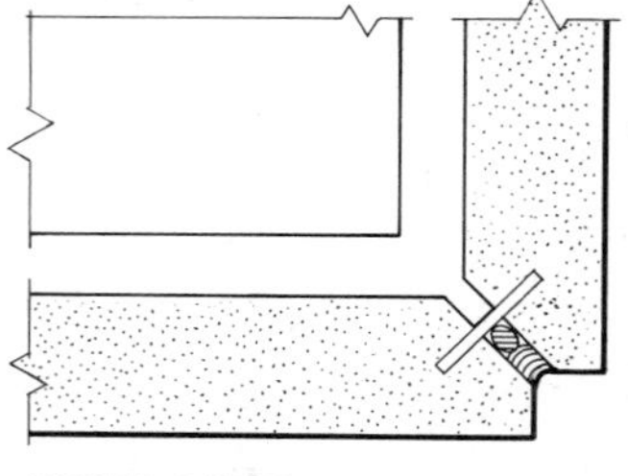

**QUIRK MITER** 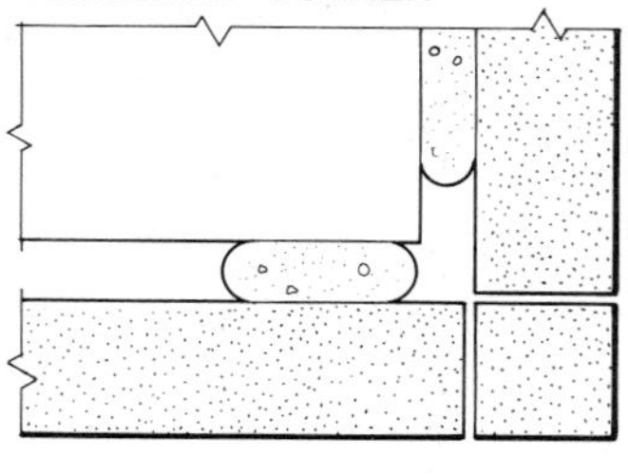          **CORNER BLOCK** 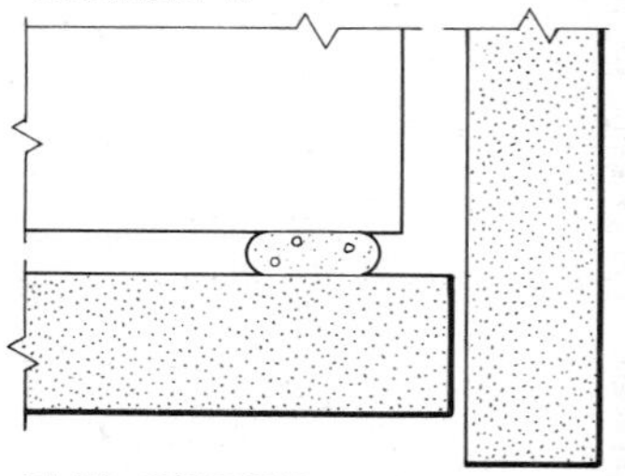          **SLIP CORNER**

**TYPICAL CORNER DETAILS**

SPLINE JOINT          SET-IN BLOCK          LOCKED JOINT

EXPANSION JOINT          LAP JOINT

**TYPICAL HORIZONTAL JOINTS**

Building Stone Institute; New York, New York
George M. Whiteside, III, AIA, and James D. Lloyd; Kennett Square, Pennsylvania
Alexander Keyes; Darrel Downing Rippeteau, Architect; Washington, D.C.

 **STONE**

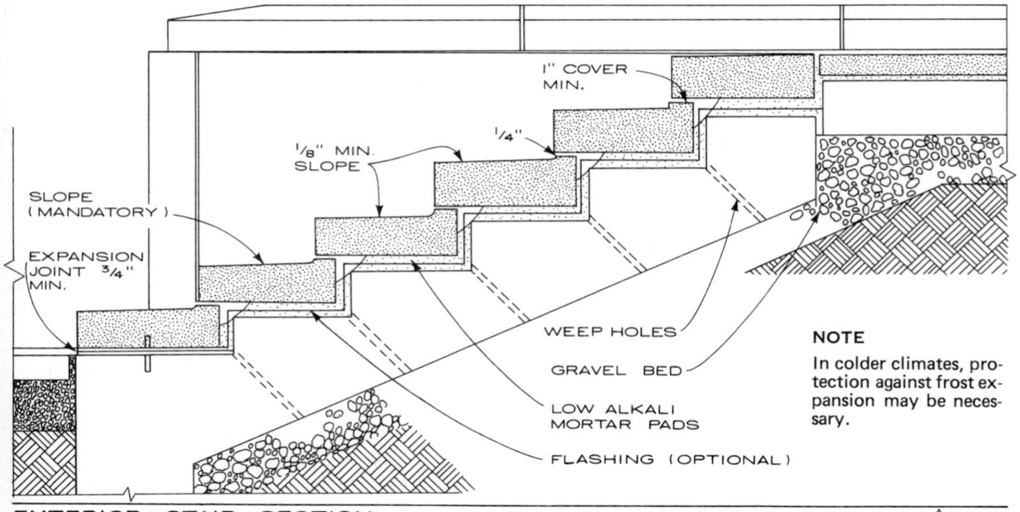

## EXTERIOR STAIR SECTION

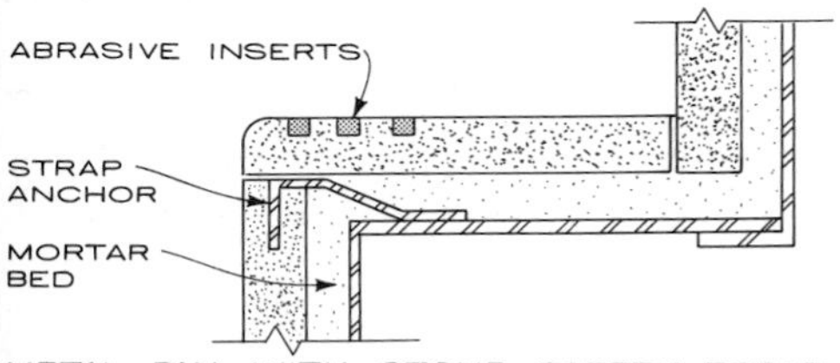

1" COVER MIN.

1/4"

1/8" MIN. SLOPE

SLOPE (MANDATORY)

EXPANSION JOINT 3/4" MIN.

WEEP HOLES

GRAVEL BED

LOW ALKALI MORTAR PADS

FLASHING (OPTIONAL)

**NOTE**
In colder climates, protection against frost expansion may be necessary.

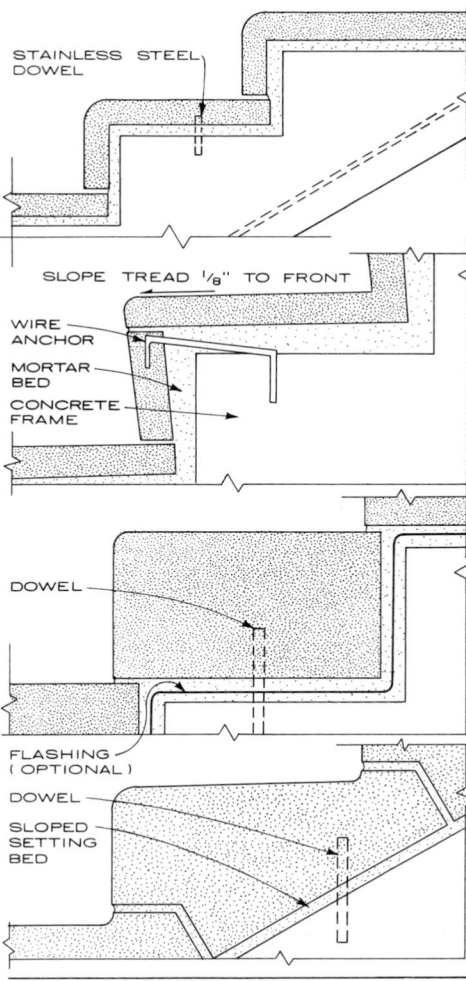

STAINLESS STEEL DOWEL

SLOPE TREAD 1/8" TO FRONT

WIRE ANCHOR

MORTAR BED

CONCRETE FRAME

DOWEL

FLASHING (OPTIONAL)

DOWEL

SLOPED SETTING BED

## STONE STAIRS WITH STEEL FRAME

ABRASIVE INSERTS

STRAP ANCHOR

MORTAR BED

**METAL PAN WITH STONE SAFETY TREAD**

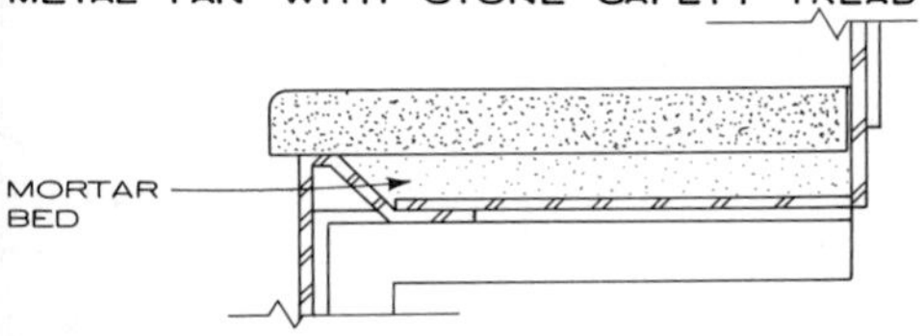

MORTAR BED

**STEEL SUBTREAD AND RISER WITH STONE TREAD**

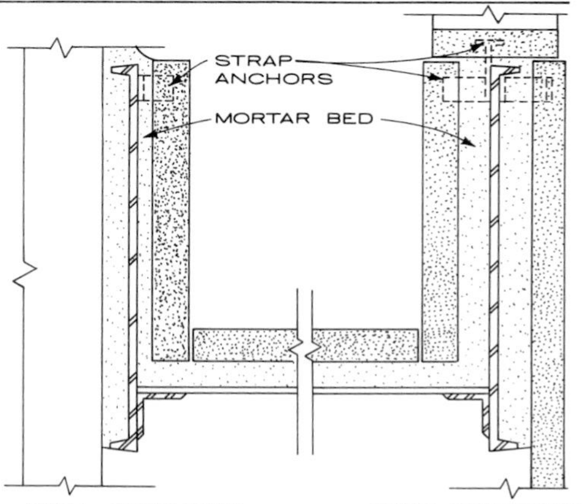

STRAP ANCHORS

MORTAR BED

**WALL STRINGER**　**OPEN STRINGER**

## STONE STAIRS WITH CONCRETE FRAME

### DESIGN FACTORS FOR STONE STAIRS

Stone used for steps should have an abrasive resistance of 10 (measured on a scale from a minimum of 6 to a maximum of 17). When different varieties of stone are used, their abrasive hardness should be similar to prevent uneven wear.

Dowels and anchoring devices should be noncorrosive.

If a safety tread is not used on stairs, a light bush hammered soft finish or nonslip finish is recommended.

To prevent future staining, dampproof the face of all concrete or concrete block, specify low alkali mortar, and provide adequate drainage (slopes and weepholes).

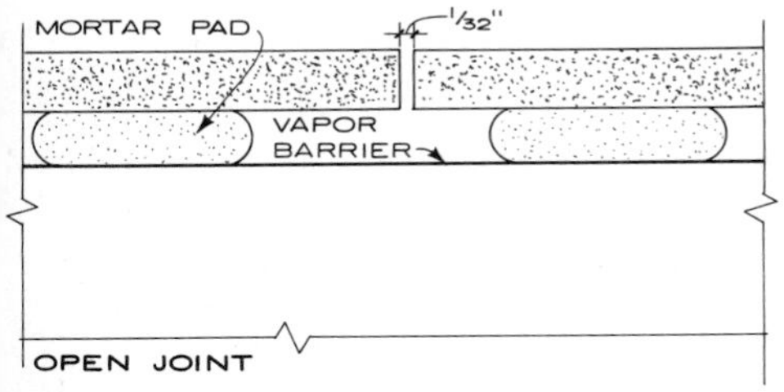

## STONE FLOORING

MORTAR PAD

1/32"

VAPOR BARRIER

**OPEN JOINT**

LATEX MORTAR

**THIN SET**

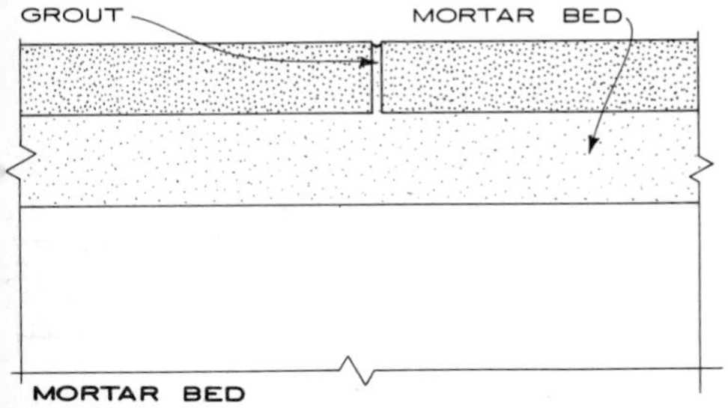

GROUT　MORTAR BED

**MORTAR BED**

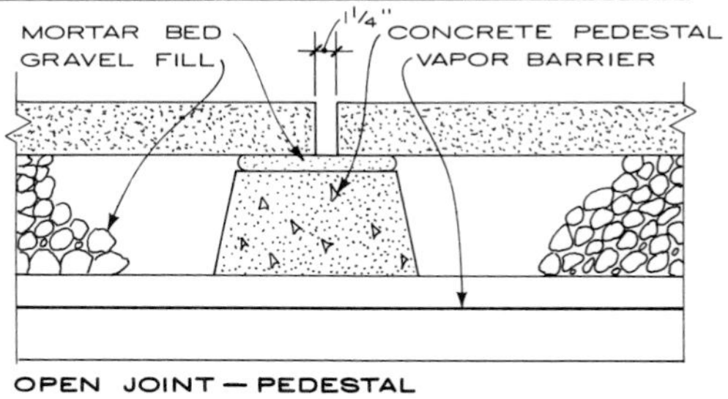

MORTAR BED GRAVEL FILL

1 1/4"

CONCRETE PEDESTAL

VAPOR BARRIER

**OPEN JOINT — PEDESTAL**

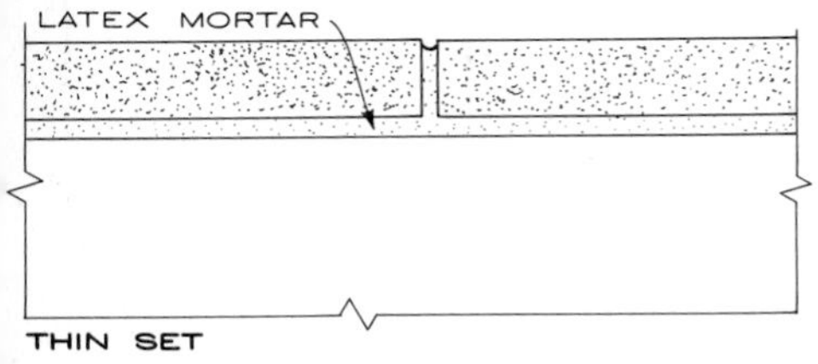

SEALANT

MORTAR BED

FILLER STRIP

CONCRETE

VAPOR BARRIER

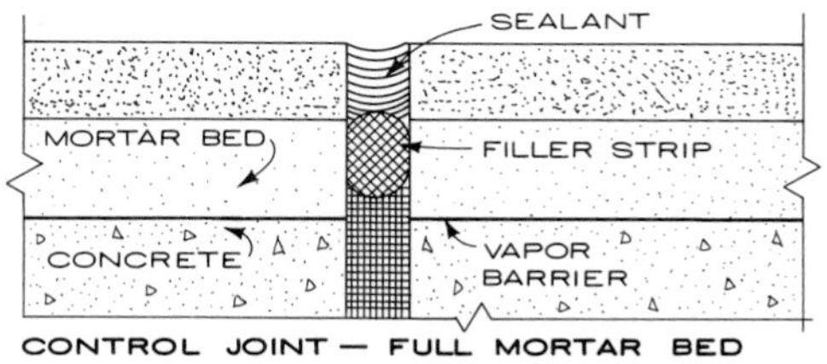

**CONTROL JOINT — FULL MORTAR BED**

MORTAR BED WITH REINFORCING

GROUT

ROOFING FELT OR POLYETHYLENE FILM

WOOD SUBFLOOR

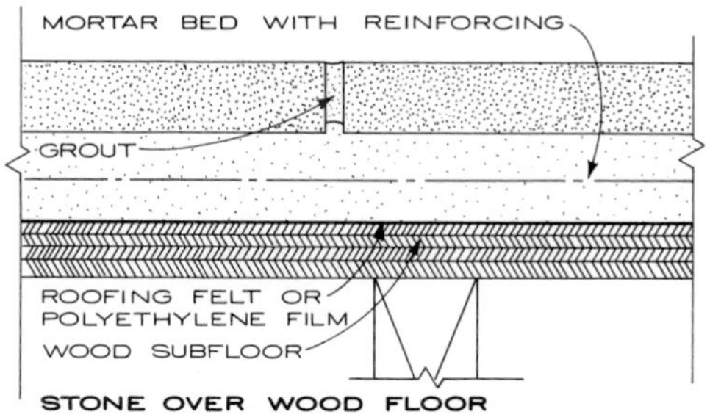

**STONE OVER WOOD FLOOR**

## STONE THRESHOLDS

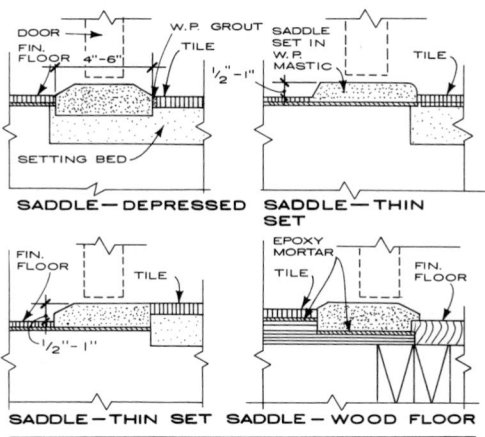

DOOR

FIN. FLOOR 4"-6"

W.P. GROUT

TILE

SADDLE SET IN W.P. MASTIC

1/2"-1"

TILE

SETTING BED

**SADDLE — DEPRESSED**　**SADDLE — THIN SET**

FIN. FLOOR

TILE

1/2"-1"

EPOXY MORTAR

TILE

FIN. FLOOR

**SADDLE — THIN SET**　**SADDLE — WOOD FLOOR**

Building Stone Institute; New York, New York
George M. Whiteside, III, AIA, and James D. Lloyd; Kennett Square, Pennsylvania
Alexander Keyes; Darrel Downing Rippeteau, Architect; Washington, D.C.

**STONE** 4

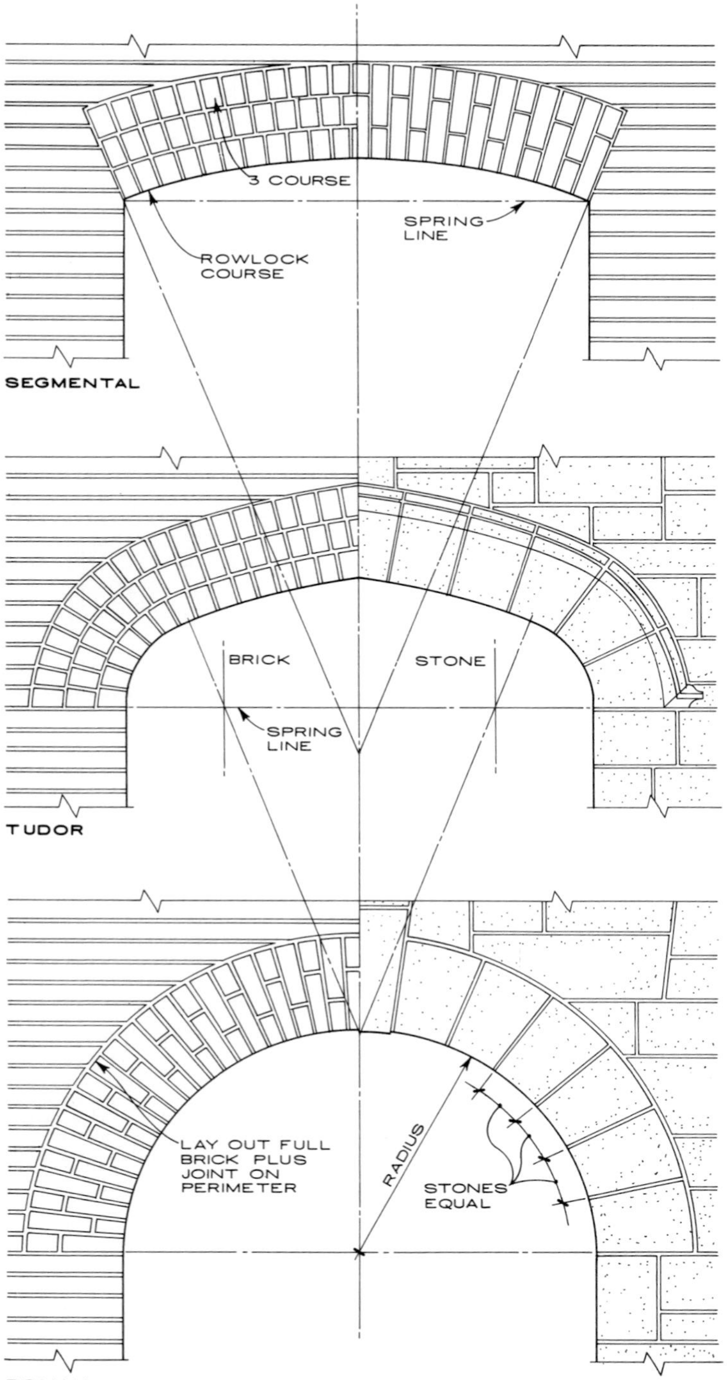

**SEGMENTAL**

3 COURSE

ROWLOCK COURSE

SPRING LINE

**JACK**

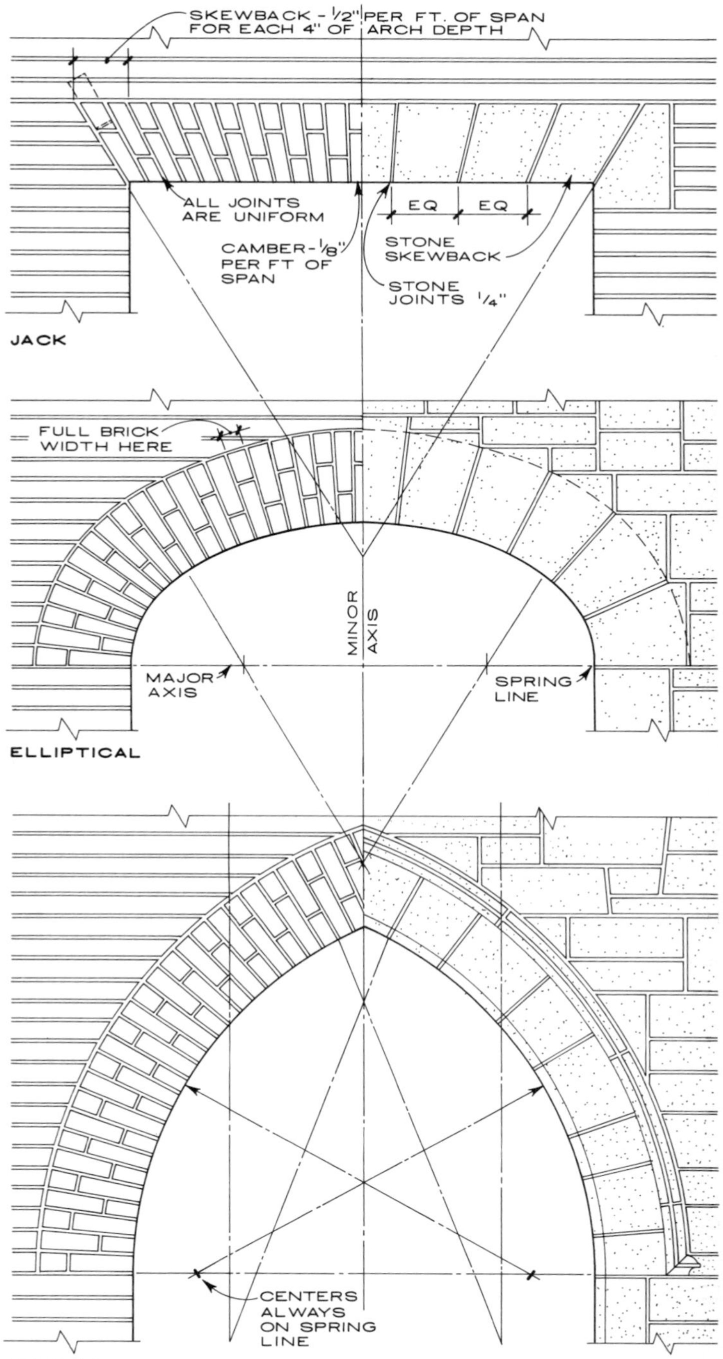

SKEWBACK - 1/2" PER FT. OF SPAN FOR EACH 4" OF ARCH DEPTH

ALL JOINTS ARE UNIFORM

CAMBER - 1/8" PER FT OF SPAN

EQ    EQ

STONE SKEWBACK

STONE JOINTS 1/4"

**TUDOR**

BRICK    STONE

SPRING LINE

**ELLIPTICAL**

FULL BRICK WIDTH HERE

MINOR AXIS

MAJOR AXIS

SPRING LINE

**ROMAN**

LAY OUT FULL BRICK PLUS JOINT ON PERIMETER

RADIUS

STONES EQUAL

**GOTHIC**

CENTERS ALWAYS ON SPRING LINE

NOTE: Walls, piers, or abutments adjacent to masonry arches must be of sufficient strength to resist horizontal thrusts.

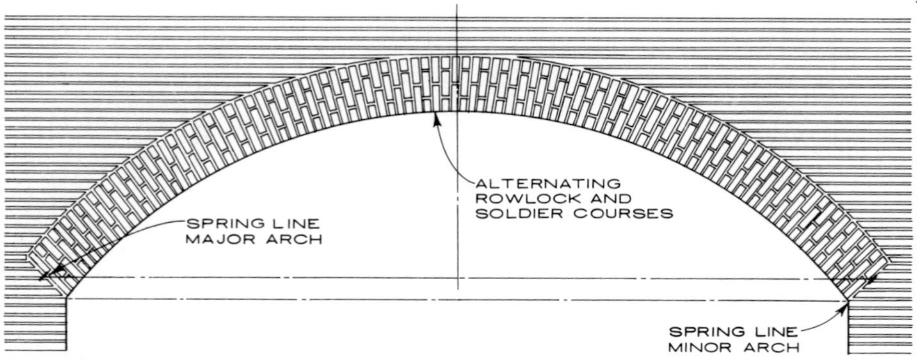

**PARABOLIC**

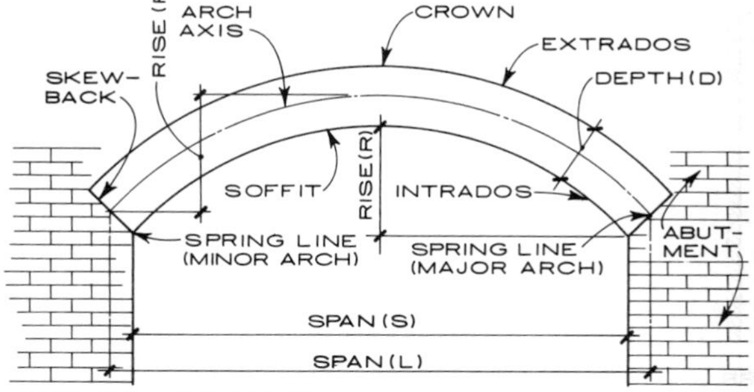

SPRING LINE MAJOR ARCH

ALTERNATING ROWLOCK AND SOLDIER COURSES

SPRING LINE MINOR ARCH

**ARCH TERMINOLOGY**

RISE (F)
ARCH AXIS
CROWN
EXTRADOS
DEPTH (D)
SKEW-BACK
RISE (R)
SOFFIT
INTRADOS
SPRING LINE (MINOR ARCH)
SPRING LINE (MAJOR ARCH)
ABUT-MENT
SPAN (S)
SPAN (L)

Brick Institute of America; Reston, Virginia

 **STONE**

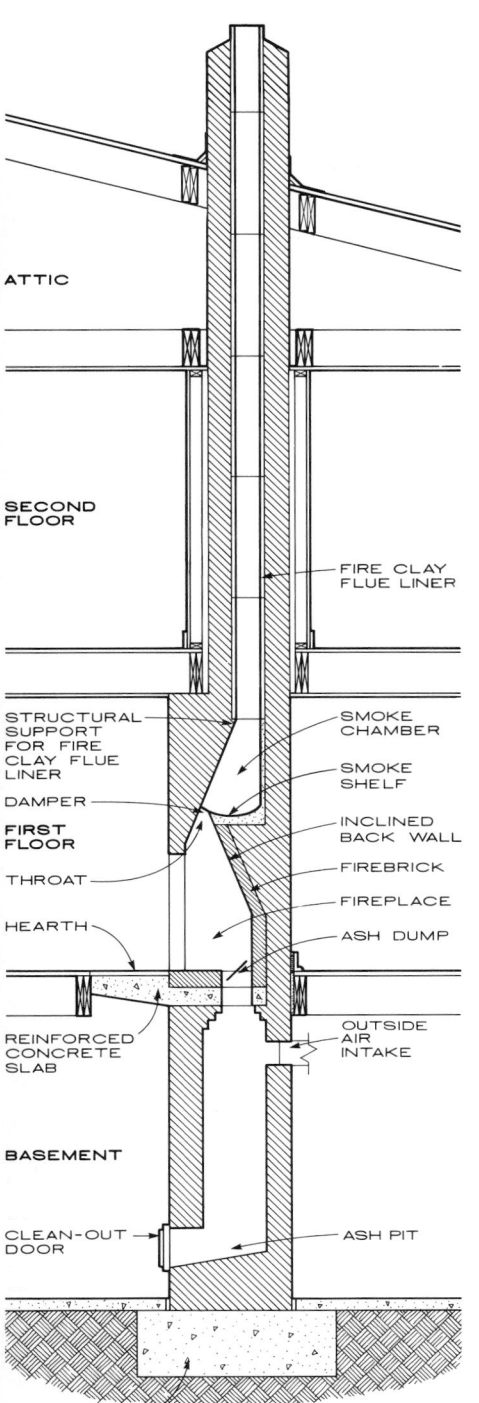

ATTIC

SECOND FLOOR

FIRE CLAY FLUE LINER

STRUCTURAL SUPPORT FOR FIRE CLAY FLUE LINER

DAMPER

FIRST FLOOR

THROAT

HEARTH

SMOKE CHAMBER

SMOKE SHELF

INCLINED BACK WALL

FIREBRICK

FIREPLACE

ASH DUMP

REINFORCED CONCRETE SLAB

OUTSIDE AIR INTAKE

BASEMENT

CLEAN-OUT DOOR

ASH PIT

REINFORCED CONCRETE FOOTING

**SECTION**

## INTRODUCTION

A masonry chimney is usually the heaviest single part of a wood frame structure; therefore, it requires a special foundation. The same is true for masonry buildings where walls are not thick enough to incorporate the chimney or where the chimney is not designed into a masonry wall. Beyond the structural requirements, a fireplace and chimney must be designed so spaces and relationships between spaces sustain combustion and carry smoke away safely. Fireplace design is bound by various building and mechanical codes. The internal diagram of a working fireplace shows the several required parts and their vertical organization. Each part is illustrated further on succeeding pages. Other pages describe more efficient prefabricated fireplace units that incorporate air heating and circulating devices.

Most important in fireplace design is the location of the fireplace and chimney. It is best located at the center of the house to prevent heat loss to the exterior. For best efficiency, a fireplace should not be located opposite an outside door, near an open stairway leading to an upper floor, near a forced-air furnace, or near a return air register. Two factors primarily affect the chimney draft: height of the flue above the fireplace, and the pressure differential between the heated exhaust and cooler outside air.

The even combustion of wood fuel is improved by providing a measured supply of air, independent of room air, to the firebox. This is done by: installing an air duct from the exterior access to the ash dump, letting the ash door serve as a damper; or by providing a separate chase directly to the firebox. When a separate chase to the firebox is coupled with operable doors in the fireplace opening, the user can control the rate of combustion and maintain positive room air pressure; air infiltration and drafts are avoided.

### DEFINITIONS

FLUE—Takes smoke from the smoke chamber to the outside. Flue area (in plan) is proportionally related to flue height and area of fireplace opening. A tight, lined flue is an important safety feature. Flue termination must be located according to codes. As an exterior building part, it requires weatherproofing.

SMOKE CHAMBER—Directs smoke into the flue by tapering up and in.

DAMPER—Allows throat size adjustment from fully open to tightly closed.

THROAT—Passes smoke from fireplace up into smoke chamber.

FIREPLACE—Where burning takes place. Size and proportions determine size of other components.

HEARTH—Extends fireplace floor beyond opening to protect room flooring from sparks, heat, and flames.

ASH DUMP—Operable louver in fireplace floor providing efficient ash removal. An air intake may be installed in the ash pit wall to introduce outside air into the fireplace via the ash dump.

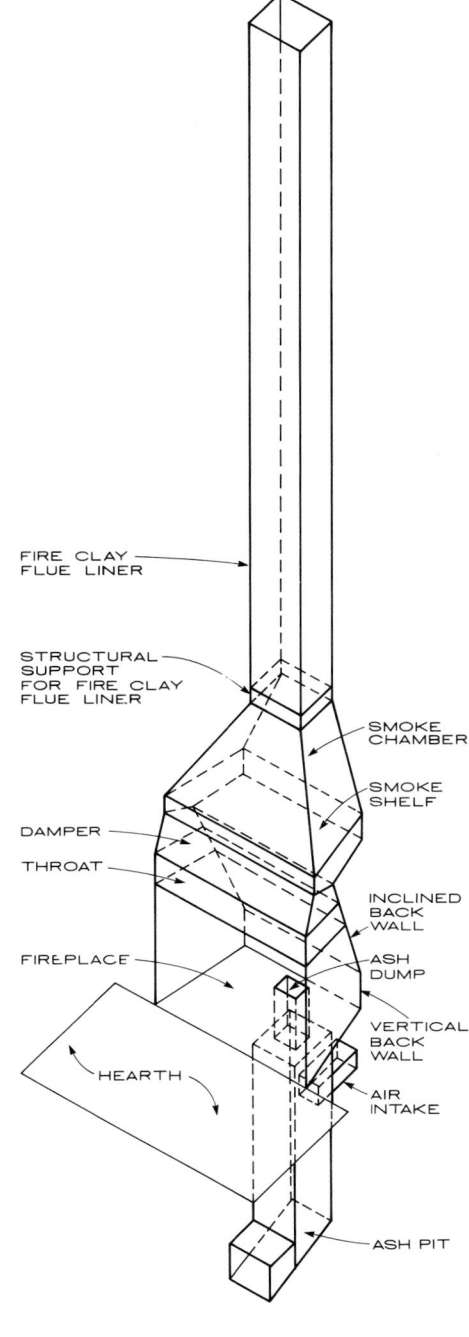

FIRE CLAY FLUE LINER

STRUCTURAL SUPPORT FOR FIRE CLAY FLUE LINER

DAMPER

THROAT

FIREPLACE

HEARTH

SMOKE CHAMBER

SMOKE SHELF

INCLINED BACK WALL

ASH DUMP

VERTICAL BACK WALL

AIR INTAKE

ASH PIT

**SCHEMATIC DIAGRAM**

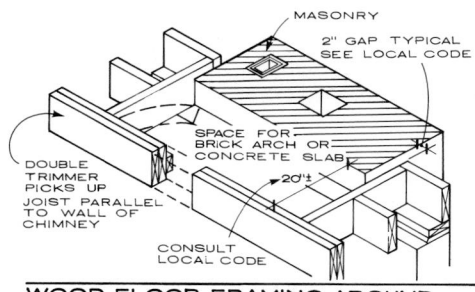

PLACE INCOMBUSTIBLE BOARD BETWEEN BASE AND BRICK

FIREPROOF FILL

½"

FLUE

GYPSUM DRYWALL CEILING

**BRICK CHIMNEY EXPOSED**

FLUE

STUD AND DRY WALL

POROUS NON-METALLIC, INCOMBUSTIBLE FILL

4"   2"

SHEET METAL OR LATH SUPPORT

**BRICK CHIMNEY CONCEALED BEHIND A STUD WALL**

**INSULATION OF WOOD FRAMING MEMBERS AT A CHIMNEY**

MASONRY

2" GAP TYPICAL SEE LOCAL CODE

SPACE FOR BRICK ARCH OR CONCRETE SLAB

20'±

DOUBLE TRIMMER PICKS UP JOIST PARALLEL TO WALL OF CHIMNEY

CONSULT LOCAL CODE

**WOOD FLOOR FRAMING AROUND CHIMNEY AND HEARTH**

Darrel Downing Rippeteau, Architect; Washington, D.C.
Timothy B. McDonald; Washington, D.C.

**FIREPLACES**

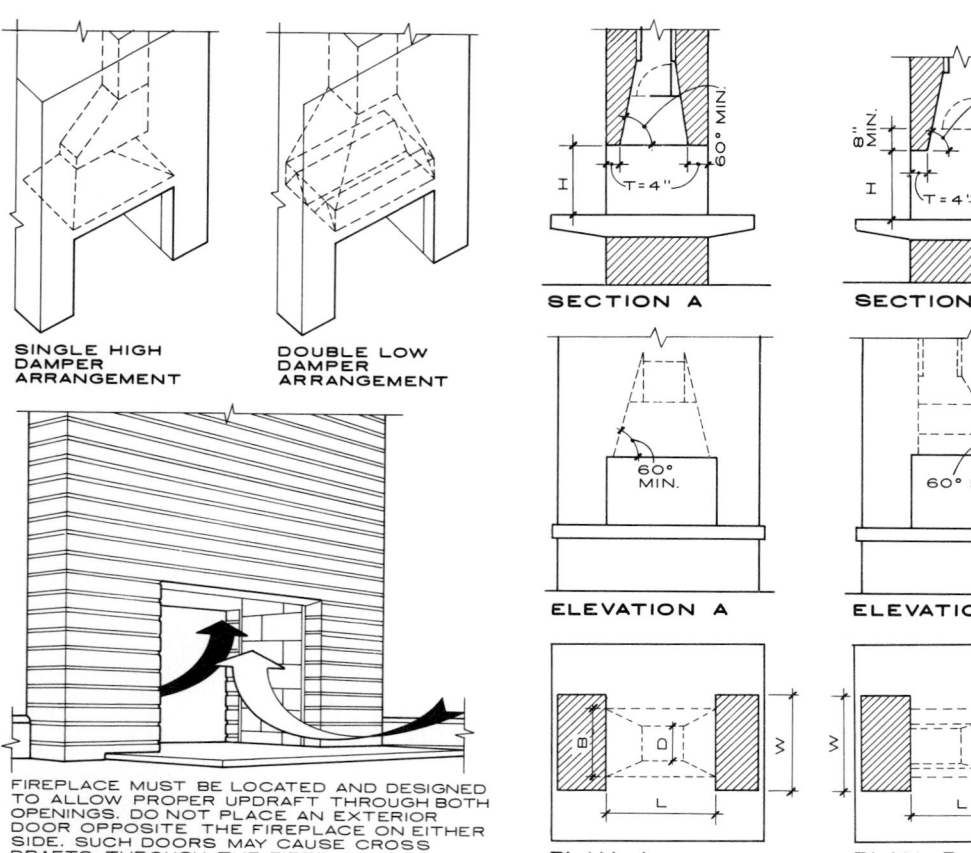

SINGLE HIGH DAMPER ARRANGEMENT

DOUBLE LOW DAMPER ARRANGEMENT

SECTION A

SECTION B

ELEVATION A

ELEVATION B

PLAN A

PLAN B

FIREPLACE MUST BE LOCATED AND DESIGNED TO ALLOW PROPER UPDRAFT THROUGH BOTH OPENINGS. DO NOT PLACE AN EXTERIOR DOOR OPPOSITE THE FIREPLACE ON EITHER SIDE. SUCH DOORS MAY CAUSE CROSS DRAFTS THROUGH THE FIREPLACE

FIREPLACE OPEN FRONT AND BACK

### FIREPLACE OPEN FRONT AND BACK

H    Height from top of hearth to bottom of facing.

B    (Depth of burning area) $5/8$ H minus 8 in. but never less than 16 in.

W    (Width of fireplace) B + 2T.

D    (Damper at bottom of flue, see Section A) equal to free area of flue.

D    (Damper closer to fire, see Section B) equal to twice the free area of flue. Set damper a minimum of 8 in. from bottom of smoke chamber. Open damper should extend entire length of smoke chamber.

### TYPICAL FIREPLACE DIMENSIONS

| L | H | B | FLUE |
|---|---|---|------|
| 28 | 24 | 16 | 13 x 13 |
| 30 | 28 | 16 | 13 x 18 |
| 36 | 30 | 17 | 18 x 18 |
| 48 | 32 | 19 | 20 x 24 |
| 54 | 36 | 22 | 24 x 24 |

NOTE: W should not be less than 24″.

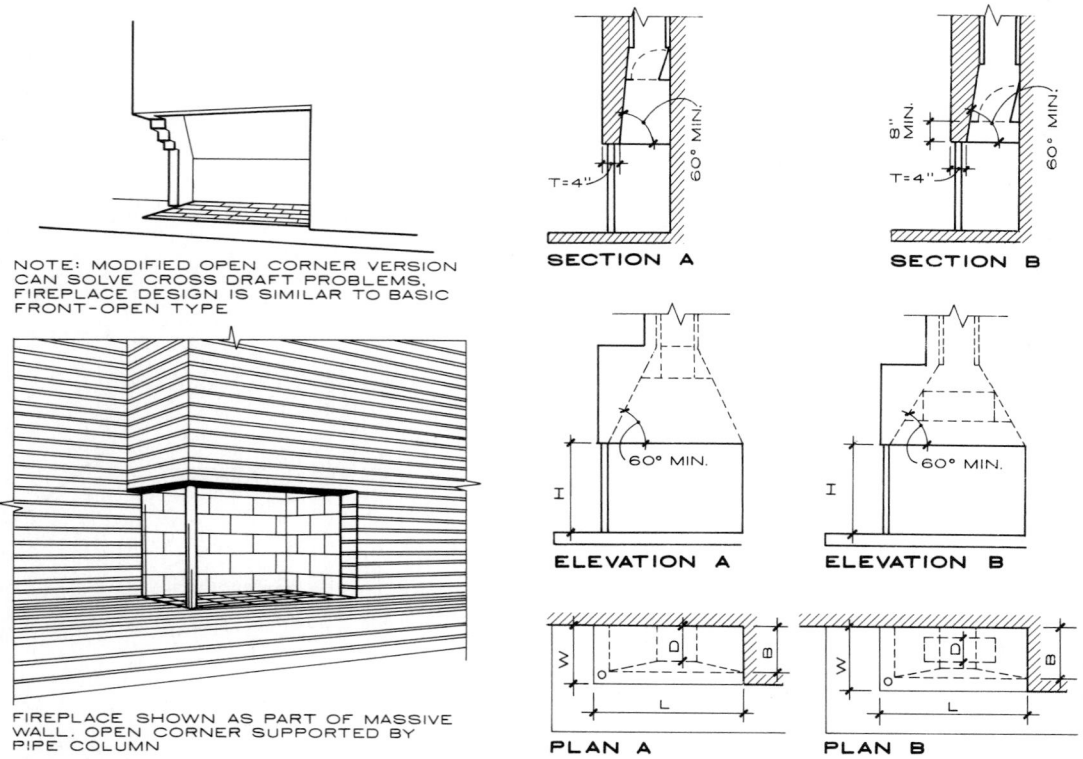

NOTE: MODIFIED OPEN CORNER VERSION CAN SOLVE CROSS DRAFT PROBLEMS. FIREPLACE DESIGN IS SIMILAR TO BASIC FRONT-OPEN TYPE

SECTION A

SECTION B

ELEVATION A

ELEVATION B

PLAN A

PLAN B

FIREPLACE SHOWN AS PART OF MASSIVE WALL. OPEN CORNER SUPPORTED BY PIPE COLUMN

FIREPLACE OPEN FRONT AND SIDE

### FIREPLACE OPEN FRONT AND SIDE

H    Height from top of hearth to bottom of facing.

B    (Depth of burning area) $2/3$ H minus 4 in.

W    (Width of fireplace) B + T.

D    (Damper at bottom of flue, see Section A) equal to twice the free area of the flue. Set damper a minimum of 8 in. from bottom of smoke chamber.

### TYPICAL FIREPLACE DIMENSIONS

| L | H | B | FLUE |
|---|---|---|------|
| 28 | 24 | 16 | 12 x 12 |
| 30 | 28 | 18 | 13 x 18 |
| 36 | 30 | 20 | 13 x 18 |
| 48 | 32 | 22 | 18 x 18 |

Darrel Downing Rippeteau, AIA, Architect; Washington, D.C.

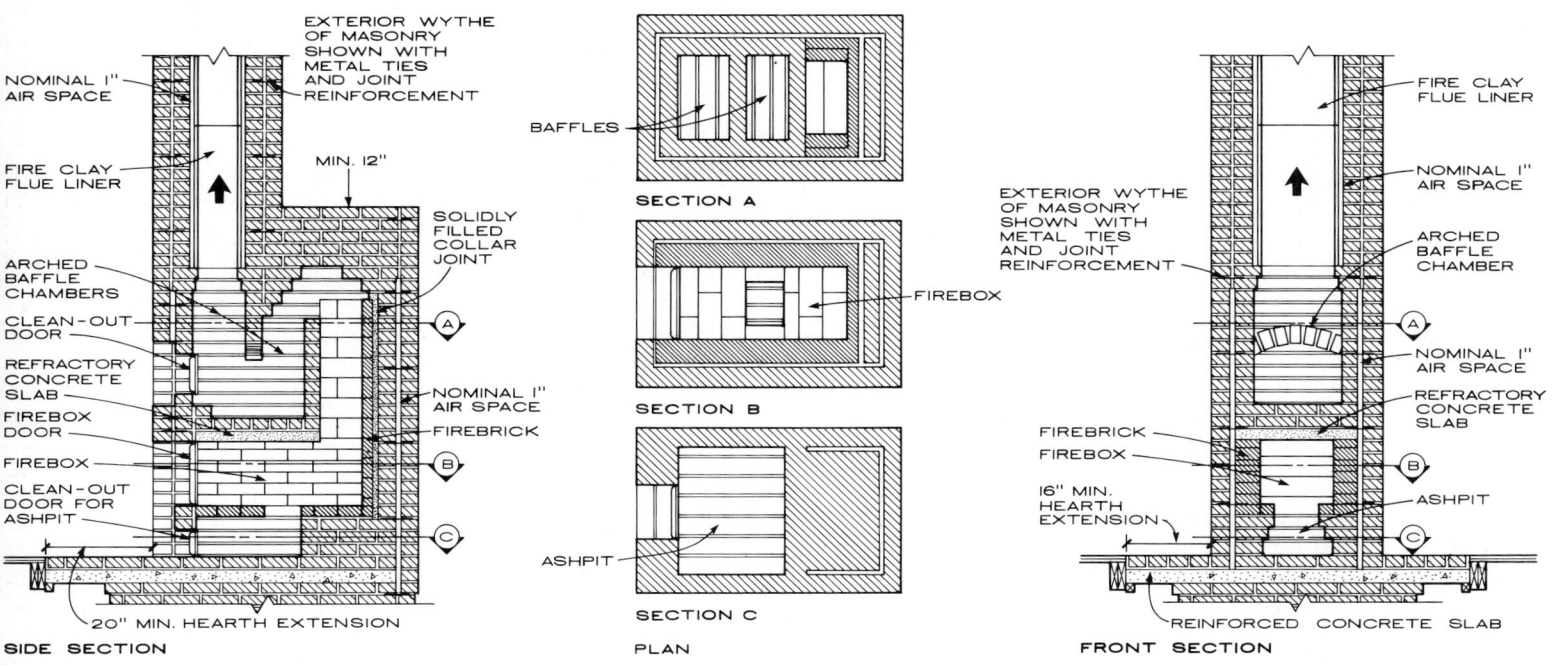

**RUSSIAN MASONRY STOVE**

## INTRODUCTION

Brick masonry stoves are adapted from prototypes used in northern and eastern Europe and were used for a number of heating functions, including cooking. Masonry stoves utilize two basic principles to obtain high combustion and heating efficiencies, namely, controlled air intake to the combustion chamber/firebox, and a heat exchange system of baffle chambers through which the combustion gases are circulated.

## FINNISH MASONRY STOVES

Finnish or contra-flow stoves are so called because heated air is forced from the top of the smoke chamber down through baffles on the sides of the stove while room air rises by convection along the exterior surface of the masonry. This allows for even heating of the masonry and efficient radiant heating of the room. The baffles converge below the firebox and open out to the flue from the base of the chimney.

## RUSSIAN MASONRY STOVES

Russian stoves are typically deep with a small opening to the firebox with a system of either vertically or horizontally aligned baffles above, which replace the smoke chamber. After circulating through the baffle system exhaust gases pass directly into the flue. There is no decided advantage to either baffle alignment, though the horizontal system is easier to construct. Clean-outs are optional on either system, but are recommended to observe creosote build-up.

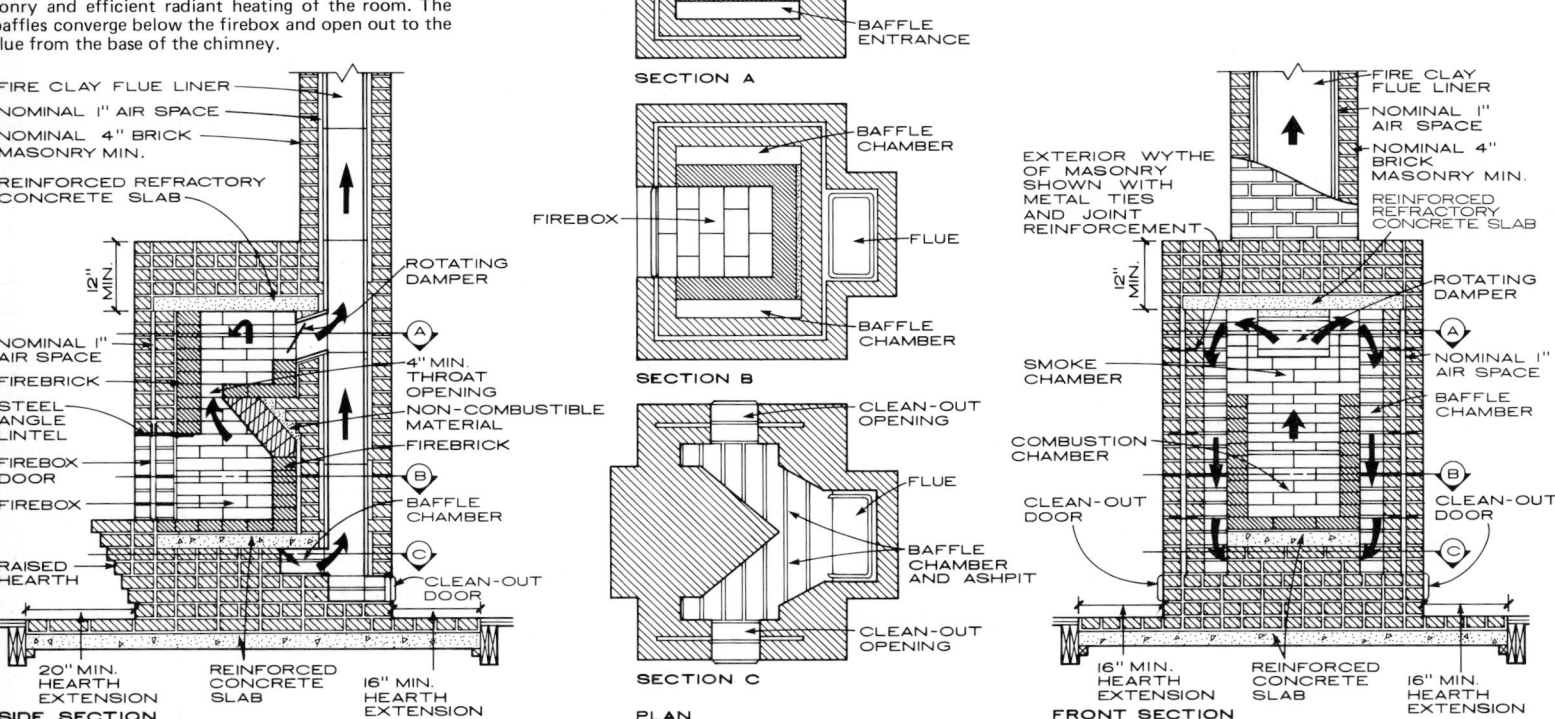

**FINNISH MASONRY STOVE**

Timothy B. McDonald; Washington, D.C.

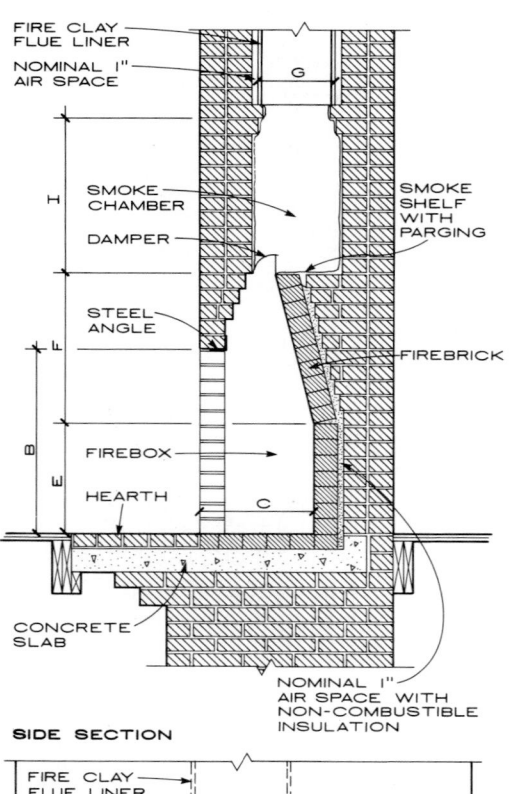

SIDE SECTION

FIRE CLAY FLUE LINER · NOMINAL 1" AIR SPACE · G · SMOKE CHAMBER · DAMPER · SMOKE SHELF WITH PARGING · STEEL ANGLE · FIREBRICK · FIREBOX · HEARTH · CONCRETE SLAB · NOMINAL 1" AIR SPACE WITH NON-COMBUSTIBLE INSULATION · H · F · B · E · C

SIDE SECTION

FIRE CLAY FLUE LINER · NOMINAL 1" AIR SPACE · G · MANTEL · HIGH FORMED DAMPER · STEEL ANGLE · FIREBRICK · FIREBOX · HEARTH · SMOKE CHAMBER · SMOKE SHELF WITH PARGING · FIREBRICK · AIR INLET GRILLE · CONCRETE SLAB · AIR PASSAGE · NOMINAL 1" AIR SPACE WITH NON-COMBUSTIBLE INSULATION · H · F · B · E · C

FRONT ELEVATION

FIRE CLAY FLUE LINER · G · I · SMOKE CHAMBER · DAMPER · STEEL ANGLE · H · J · D · A

FRONT ELEVATION

FIRE CLAY FLUE LINER · G · I · SMOKE CHAMBER · HIGH FORMED DAMPER · STEEL ANGLE · H · J · D · A

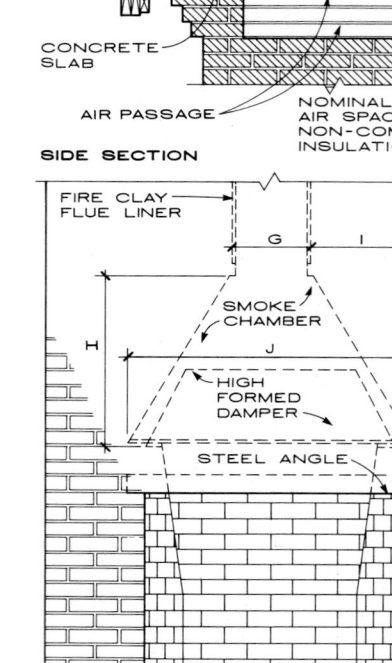

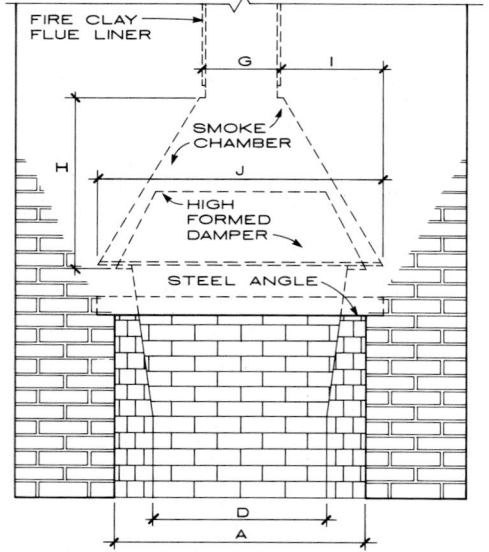

PLAN

RUMFORD FIREPLACE

FIREBRICK · NOMINAL 1" AIR SPACE · 16" MIN. · HEARTH · 20" MIN.

NOTE: IN SOME AREAS, THE FIREBOX IS SET 1" LOWER THAN THE HEARTH

PLAN

SINGLE FACE FIREPLACE

FIREBRICK · NOMINAL 1" AIR SPACE · 8" MIN. · 16" MIN. · HEARTH

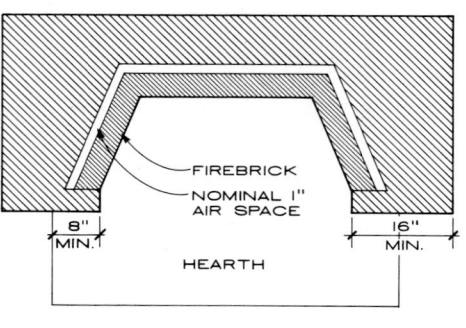

## SINGLE FACED FIREPLACES

The design of single faced fireplaces has been well documented, thus a reasonably accurate set of design dimensions of fireplace openings, dampers and flue linings has been developed.

Single faced fireplaces can be efficient radiant heaters. The amount of heat radiated and reflected into the room is directly proportional to the masonry surface area exposed to the fire. The Rumford fireplace is a variation of the single faced fireplace with a shallow firebox, a high throat, and widely splayed sides, all features for optimal direct radiant heating.

In addition, the energy efficiency of new fireplaces can be improved by:
1. Placing the fireplace on the interior of the house, preferably as close to the center as possible.
2. Supplying outside air for combustion and maintenance of positive room pressure.
3. Providing glass screens to prevent unwanted air infiltration.

## RECOMMENDED DIMENSIONS FOR WOOD BURNING FIREPLACES (IN.)

**TYPICAL FIREPLACES**

| FIREPLACE OPENINGS | BACKWALL (INCLINED) | | FLUE LINING (OUTSIDE DIM.) | SMOKE CHAMBER | | |
|---|---|---|---|---|---|---|
| A | B | C | D | E | F | G | H | I | J |
| 24 | 24 | 16 | 11 | 14 | 18 | 8 x 12 | 19 | 10 | 32 |
| 28 | 24 | 16 | 15 | 14 | 18 | 8 x 12 | 21 | 12 | 36 |
| 30 | 29 | 16 | 17 | 14 | 23 | 12 x 12 | 24 | 13 | 38 |
| 36 | 29 | 16 | 23 | 14 | 23 | 12 x 12 | 27 | 16 | 44 |
| 42 | 32 | 16 | 29 | 14 | 26 | 16 x 16 | 32 | 17 | 50 |
| 48 | 32 | 18 | 33 | 14 | 26 | 16 x 16 | 37 | 20 | 56 |
| 54 | 37 | 20 | 37 | 16 | 29 | 16 x 16 | 45 | 26 | 68 |
| 60 | 37 | 22 | 42 | 16 | 29 | 16 x 20 | 45 | 26 | 72 |
| 60 | 40 | 22 | 42 | 16 | 31 | 16 x 20 | 45 | 26 | 72 |
| 72 | 40 | 22 | 54 | 16 | 31 | 20 x 20 | 56 | 32 | 84 |

**RUMFORD FIREPLACES**

| A | B | C | D | E | F | G | H | I | J |
|---|---|---|---|---|---|---|---|---|---|
| 36 | 32 | 19 | 19 | 19 | 25 | 12 x 16 | 14 | 10 | 27 |
| 40 | 32 | 19 | 19 | 19 | 25 | 16 x 16 | 16 | 15 | 29 |
| 40 | 40 | 19 | 19 | 19 | 30 | 16 x 16 | 16 | 15 | 29 |
| 48 | 40 | 19 | 19 | 19 | 32 | 16 x 20 | 18 | 15 | 35 |
| 48 | 48 | 20 | 20 | 20 | 40 | 20 x 20 | 18 | 18 | 37 |
| 54 | 48 | 20 | 20 | 20 | 40 | 20 x 20 | 23 | 18 | 45 |
| 60 | 48 | 20 | 20 | 20 | 40 | 20 x 24 | 24 | 18 | 45 |

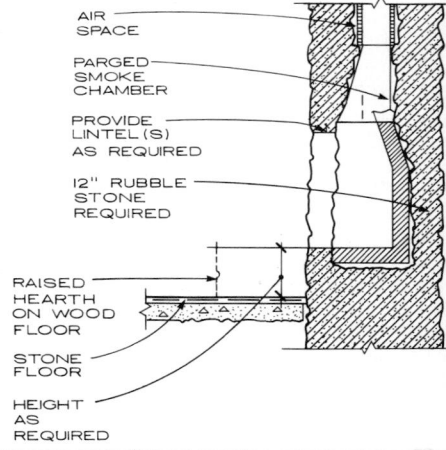

AIR SPACE · PARGED SMOKE CHAMBER · PROVIDE LINTEL(S) AS REQUIRED · 12" RUBBLE STONE REQUIRED · RAISED HEARTH ON WOOD FLOOR · STONE FLOOR · HEIGHT AS REQUIRED

SIDE SECTION

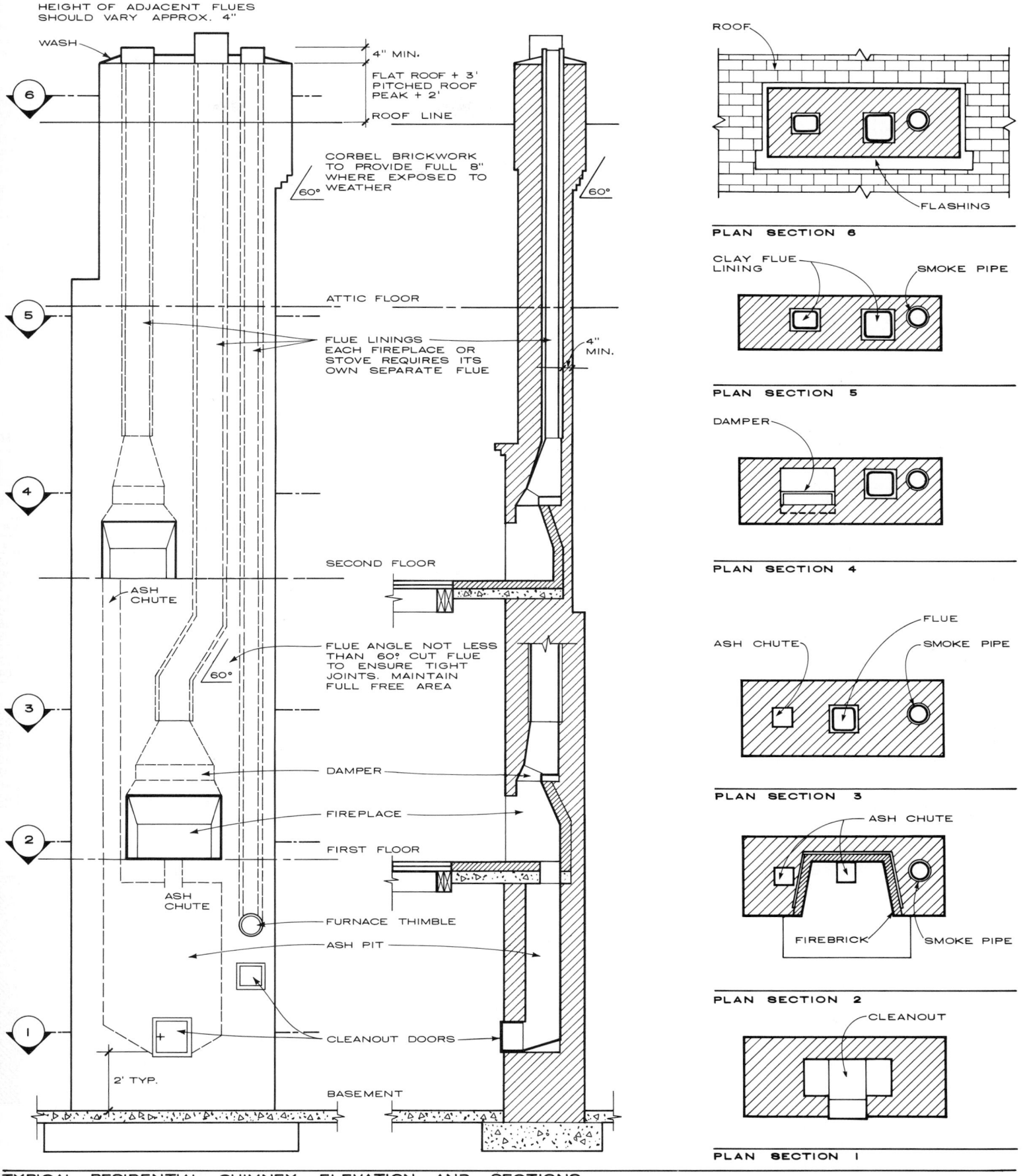

HEIGHT OF ADJACENT FLUES
SHOULD VARY APPROX. 4"

WASH

6

4" MIN.

FLAT ROOF + 3'
PITCHED ROOF
PEAK + 2'

ROOF LINE

CORBEL BRICKWORK
TO PROVIDE FULL 8"
WHERE EXPOSED TO
WEATHER

60°

60°

ATTIC FLOOR

5

FLUE LININGS
EACH FIREPLACE OR
STOVE REQUIRES ITS
OWN SEPARATE FLUE

4"
MIN.

4

ASH
CHUTE

SECOND FLOOR

FLUE ANGLE NOT LESS
THAN 60° CUT FLUE
TO ENSURE TIGHT
JOINTS. MAINTAIN
FULL FREE AREA

60°

3

DAMPER

FIREPLACE

2

FIRST FLOOR

ASH
CHUTE

FURNACE THIMBLE

ASH PIT

1

CLEANOUT DOORS

2' TYP.

BASEMENT

ROOF

FLASHING

**PLAN SECTION 6**

CLAY FLUE
LINING

SMOKE PIPE

**PLAN SECTION 5**

DAMPER

**PLAN SECTION 4**

ASH CHUTE

FLUE

SMOKE PIPE

**PLAN SECTION 3**

ASH CHUTE

FIREBRICK

SMOKE PIPE

**PLAN SECTION 2**

CLEANOUT

**PLAN SECTION 1**

**TYPICAL RESIDENTIAL CHIMNEY ELEVATION AND SECTIONS**

Darrel Downing Rippeteau, Architect; Washington, D.C.

**FIREPLACES** 4

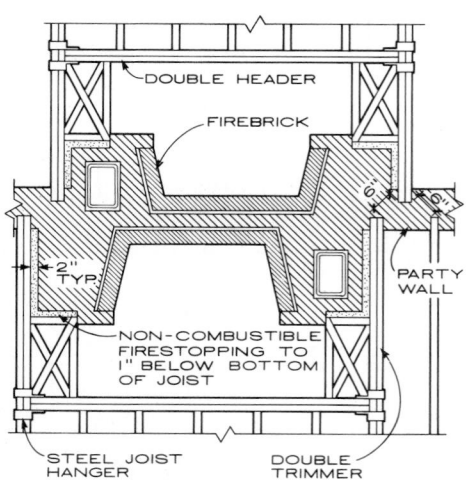

FIREPLACES BACK TO BACK IN PARTY WALL

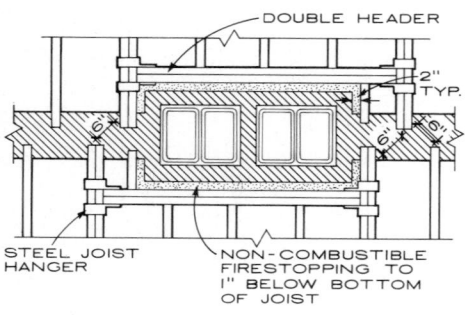

CHIMNEY IN PARTY WALL

**FIREPLACES CONSTRUCTED INTEGRALLY WITH BRICK PARTY WALL**

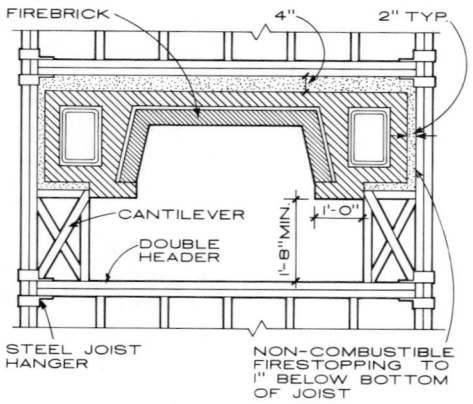

FLOOR FRAMING AT FIREPLACE

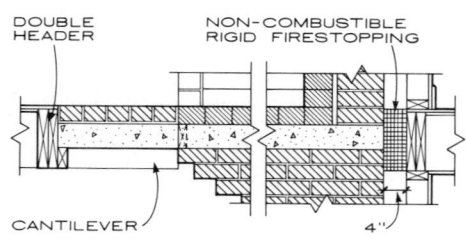

HEARTH FRAMING

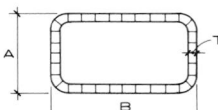

### RECTANGULAR FLUE LINING (STANDARD)

| AREA (SQ IN.) | A | B | T |
|---|---|---|---|
| 51 | 8½'' | 8½'' | ⅝'' |
| 79 | 8½'' | 13'' | ¾'' |
| 108 | 8½'' | 18'' | ⅞'' |
| 125 | 13'' | 13'' | ⅞'' |
| 168 | 13'' | 18'' | ⅞'' |
| 232 | 18'' | 18'' | 1⅛'' |
| 279 | 20'' | 20'' | 1⅜'' |
| 338 | 20'' | 24'' | 1½'' |
| 420 | 24'' | 24'' | 1½'' |

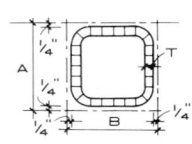

### RECTANGULAR FLUE LINING (MODULAR)

| AREA (SQ IN.) | A | B | T |
|---|---|---|---|
| 57 | 8'' | 12'' | ¾'' |
| 74 | 8'' | 16'' | ⅞'' |
| 87 | 12'' | 12'' | ⅞'' |
| 120 | 12'' | 16'' | 1'' |
| 162 | 16'' | 16'' | 1⅛'' |
| 208 | 16'' | 20'' | 1¼'' |
| 262 | 20'' | 20'' | 1⅜'' |
| 320 | 20'' | 24'' | 1½'' |
| 385 | 24'' | 24'' | 1⅝'' |

ACTUAL DIMENSION (INTERIOR DIAMETER)

### ROUND FLUE LINING

| AREA (SQ IN.) | A | T | LENGTH |
|---|---|---|---|
| 47 | 8'' | ¾'' | 2'-0'' |
| 74.5 | 10'' | ⅞'' | 2'-0'' |
| 108 | 12'' | 1'' | 2'-0'' |
| 171 | 15'' | 1⅛'' | 2'-0'' |
| 240 | 18'' | 1¼'' | 2'-0'' |
| 298 | 20'' | 1⅜'' | 2'-0'' |
| 433 | 24'' | 1⅝'' | 2'-0'' |

**CLAY FLUE LININGS**

**NOTES**

1. Availability of specific clay flue lining shapes varies according to location. Generally, oval and round flue linings, used in construction with steel reinforcing bars, are available in the western states, while rectangular flue linings are found commonly throughout the eastern states. Check with local manufacturers for available types and sizes.

2. U.L. approved lightweight concrete flues are available in the western states in modular sizes 8 x 8 in. and 16 x 16 in.

3. Nominal flue size for round flues is interior diameter; nominal flue sizes for standard rectangular flues are the exterior dimensions and, for modular flue linings, the outside dimensions plus ½ in.

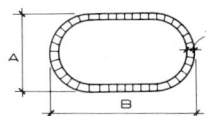

### OVAL FLUE LINING

| NOMINAL SIZE | AREA (SQ IN.) | A | B |
|---|---|---|---|
| 8½'' x 13'' | 69 | 8½'' | 12¾'' |
| 8½'' x 17'' | 87 | 8½'' | 16¾'' |
| 10'' x 18'' | 112 | 10'' | 17¾'' |
| 10'' x 21'' | 138 | 10'' | 21'' |
| 13'' x 17'' | 134 | 12¾'' | 16¾'' |
| 13'' x 21'' | 173 | 12¾'' | 21'' |
| 17'' x 17'' | 171 | 16¾'' | 16¾'' |
| 17'' x 21'' | 223 | 16¾'' | 21'' |
| 21'' x 21'' | 269 | 21'' | 21'' |

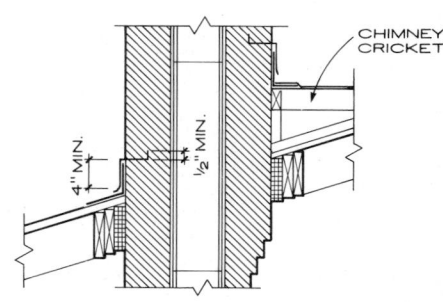

INSULATION OF WOOD FRAMING MEMBERS AT A CHIMNEY

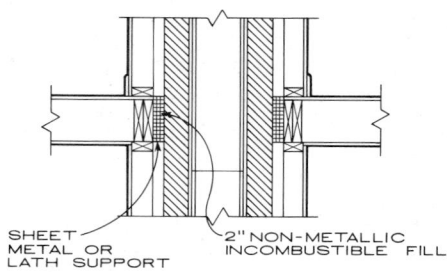

BRICK CHIMNEY CONCEALED BEHIND STUD WALL

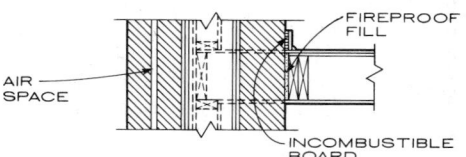

BRICK CHIMNEY EXPOSED

**CHIMNEY FRAMING AND INSULATION**

4. Areas shown are net minimum inside areas.

5. Wall thicknesses shown are minimum required. Flue dimensions vary ±½ in. about the nominal sizes shown.

6. All flue linings listed are generally available in 2 ft lengths. Verify other lengths with local supplier.

7. Fireplace flue sizes: One-tenth the area of fireplace opening recommended; one-eighth the area of opening recommended if chimney is higher than 20 ft and rectangular flues are used; one-twelfth the area is minimum required; verify with local codes.

8. Flue area should never be less than 70 sq in. for fireplace of 840 sq in. opening or smaller.

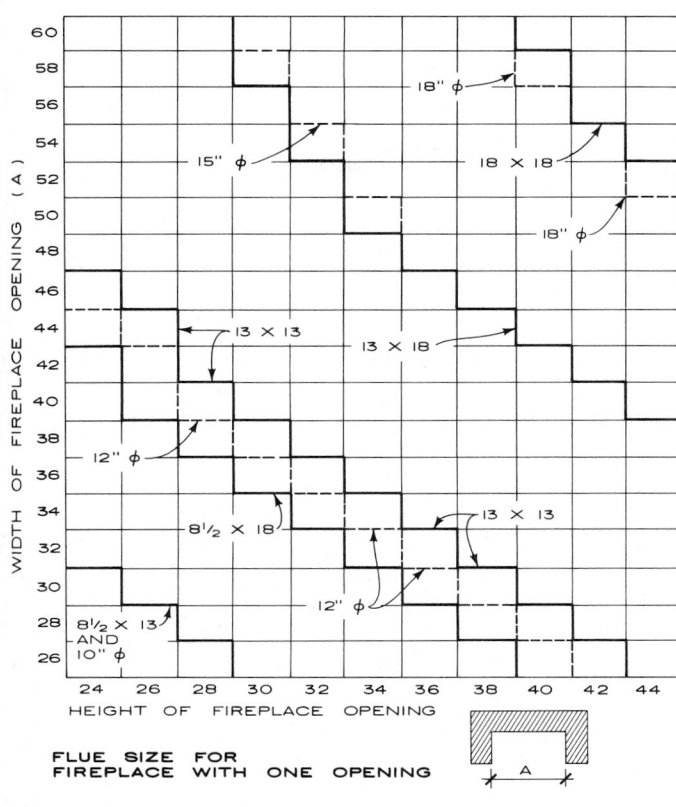

**FLUE SIZE FOR FIREPLACE WITH ONE OPENING**

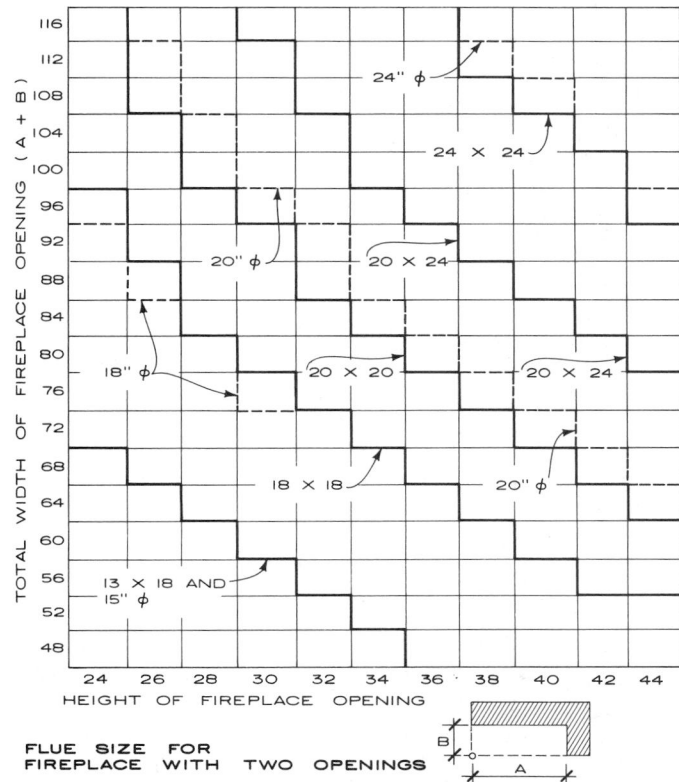

**FLUE SIZE FOR FIREPLACE WITH TWO OPENINGS**

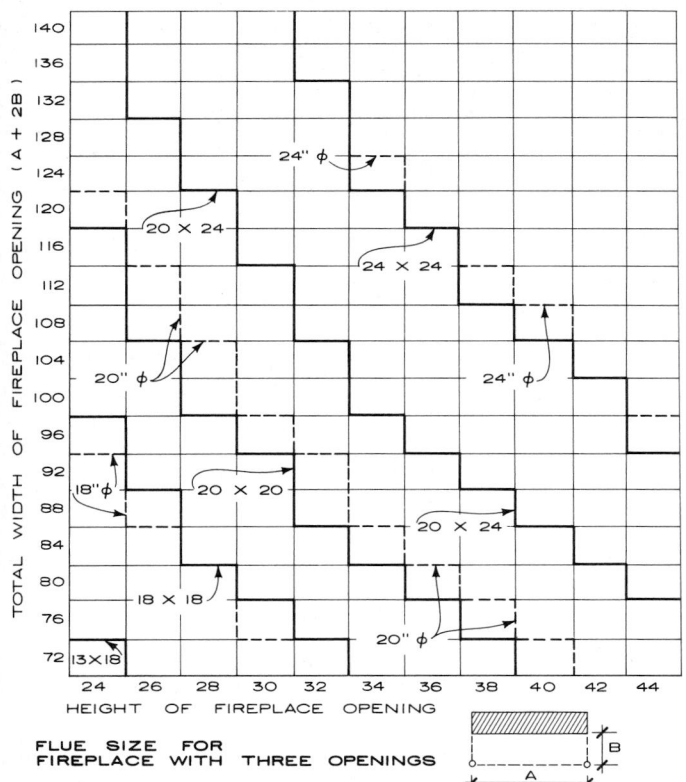

**FLUE SIZE FOR FIREPLACE WITH THREE OPENINGS**

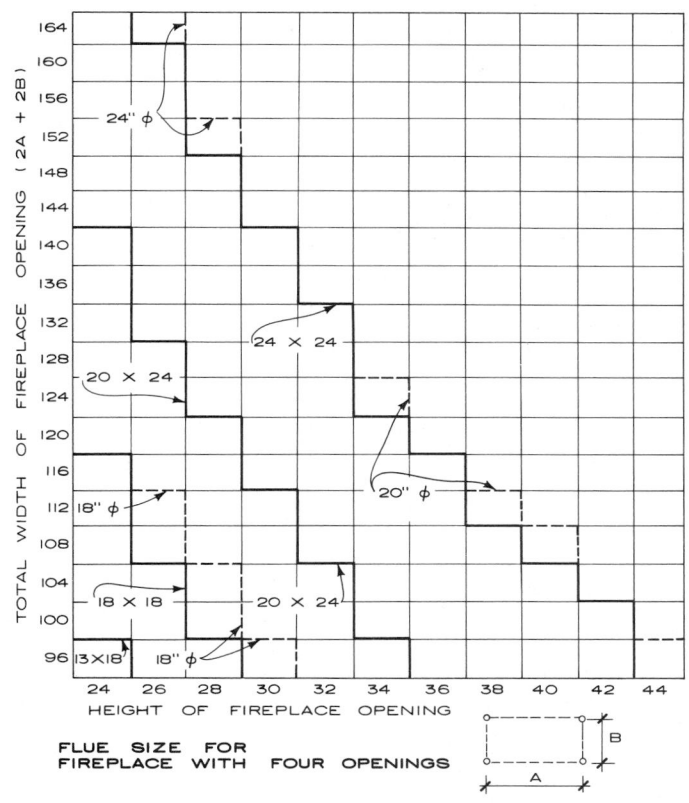

**FLUE SIZE FOR FIREPLACE WITH FOUR OPENINGS**

**KEY**

———— Rectangular flue.
- - - - Round flue.

Based on recommended sizes, ¹/₁₀ of fireplace area.

Alexander Keyes; Darrel Downing Rippeteau, Architect; Washington, D.C.

**EXPLANATION**

Flue size is indicated by the area of graph that lies within (or below) the designated solid or dashed line.

**NOTES**

Charts are based on minimum net inside area of standard rectangular and round terra cotta flue linings. Where rectangular (and round) flue designations coincide, the designation for rectangular flue is shown.

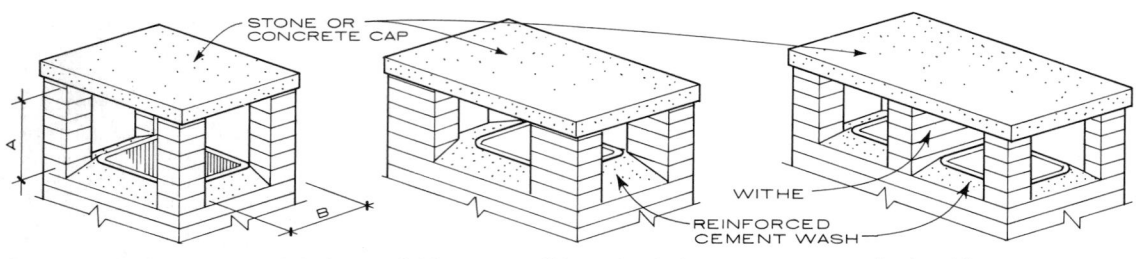

Chimney hoods to prevent downdraft due to adjoining hills, buildings, trees, etc.

A should be ¼ greater than B in all hooded chimneys

Chimney hoods also serve as water protection for seldom used flues

Withe between flues is the best method of preventing downdraft

**CHIMNEY HOODS**

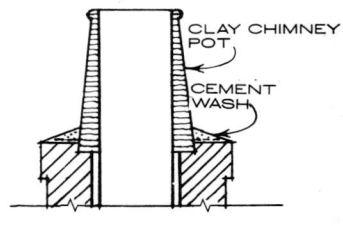

**CHIMNEY POT**

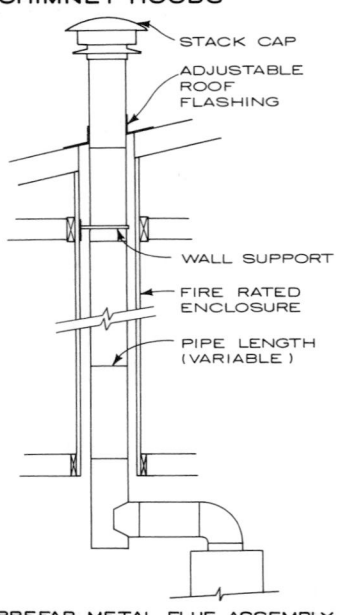

**PREFAB METAL FLUE ASSEMBLY**

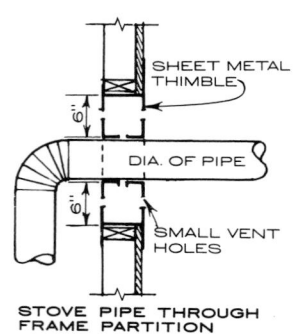

**STOVE PIPE THROUGH FRAME PARTITION**

Metal chimneys, connections, and flues are designed to be assembled with other pipes and accessory parts of the same model without requiring field construction. Pipes are single, double, or triple metal walls separated by ½ to 1 in. airspace. Sizes range from 3 to 14 in. I.D. round pipe and 4⅚ in. oval pipe for use in 2 x 6 stud walls. Provide 1 to 2 in. clearance from enclosure walls and roof structure. Verify with manufacturer's listings for approved uses and specifications.

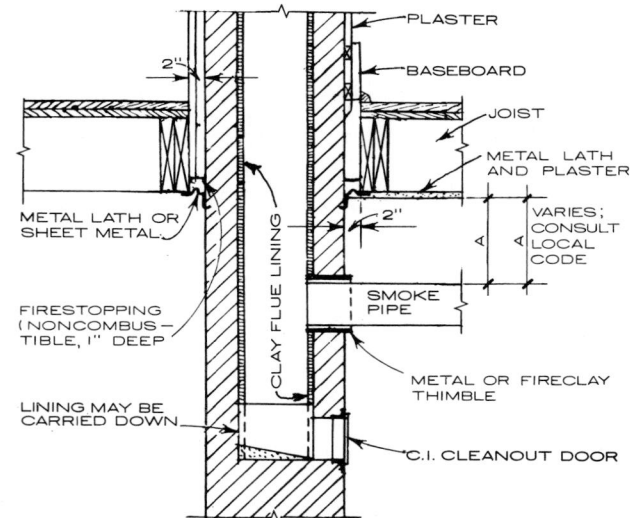

**SMOKE PIPE FOR STOVES, H.W. HEATERS AND SMALL RANGES—CONNECTIONS AND CLEARANCES**

**FLUES, VENTS, AND SMOKE CONNECTIONS—RESIDENTIAL**

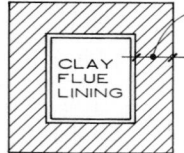

Chimneys for stoves, cooking ranges, warm air, hot water and low pressure steam heating furnaces, low heat industrial appliances, portable type incinerators, fireplaces.

**LOW HEAT APPLIANCES**

Chimneys for high pressure steam boilers, smokehouses, and other medium heat appliances other than incinerators. Continue firebrick up 25' min. N.Y.C. firebrick up 50' min.

**MEDIUM HEAT APPLIANCES**

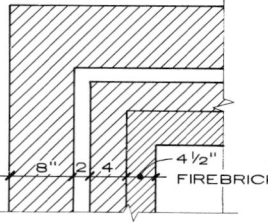

Chimneys for cupolas, brass furnaces, porcelain baking kilns, and other high heat appliances.

**HIGH HEAT APPLIANCES**

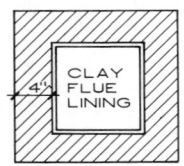

For domestic type incinerators where firebox or charging compartment is not larger than 5 cu ft

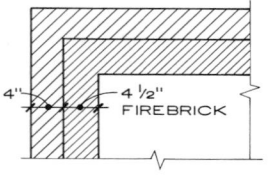

For apartment house type incinerators. Continue firebrick up 10' above roof of combustion chamber for grate area 7 sq ft or less; 40' above for grate area exceeding 7 sq ft.

FOR RESIDENCE BLDGS, INSTITUTIONAL BLDGS CHURCHES, SCHOOLS, & RESTAURANTS.

**CHIMNEYS FOR INCINERATORS**

**CHIMNEY REQUIREMENTS—VARIOUS USE TYPES**

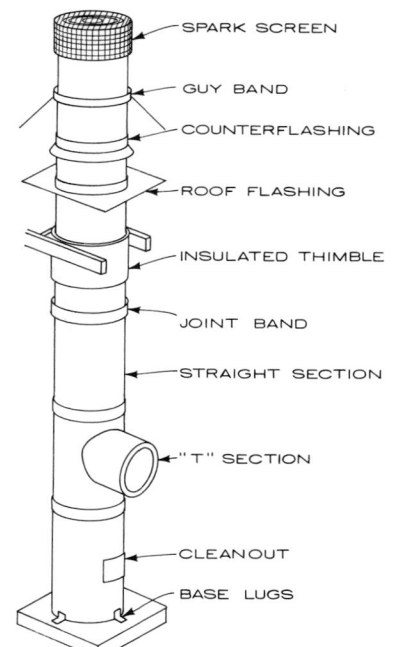

U.L. approved metal chimney systems with refractory linings are available in 10 to 60 in. I.D. in 4 ft lengths.

**INDUSTRIAL CHIMNEY SYSTEM**

Alexander Keyes; Darrel Downing Rippeteau, Architect; Washington, D.C.

 **FIREPLACES**

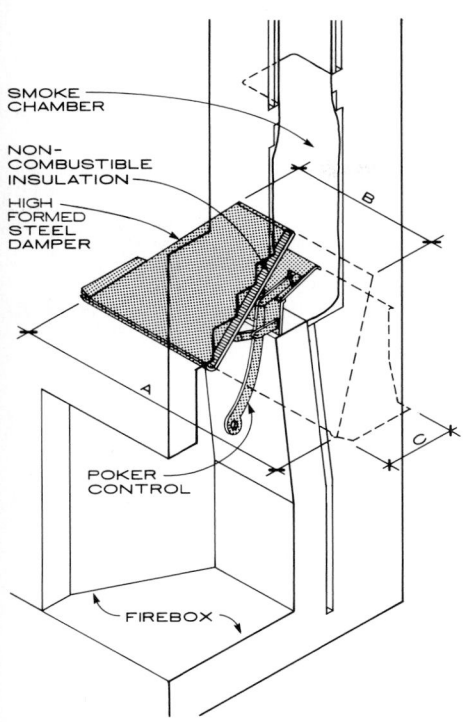

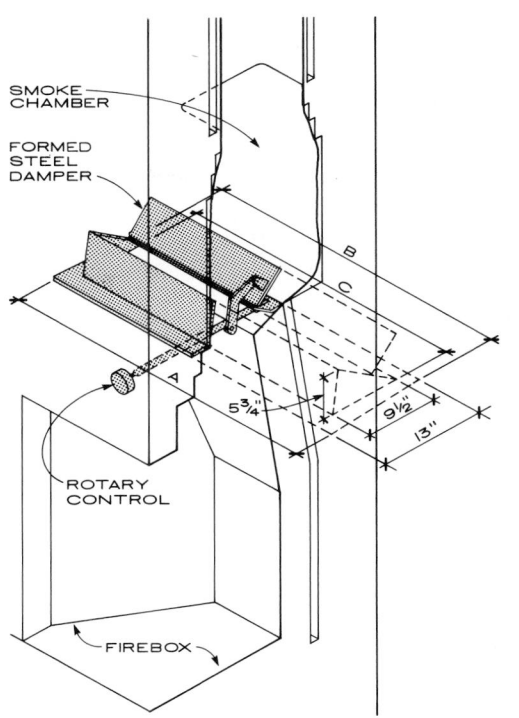

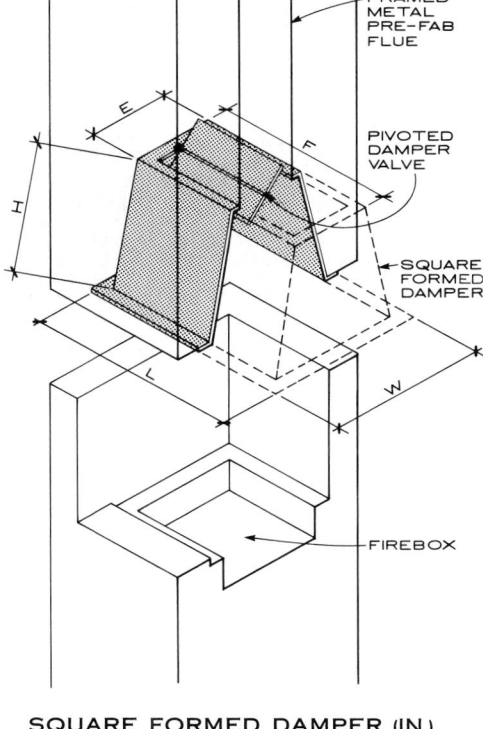

## HIGH FORMED DAMPER (IN.)

| A | B | C |
|---|---|---|
| 32 | 15¹/₄ | 9³/₄ |
| 36 | 19¹/₄ | 9³/₄ |
| 40 | 23¹/₄ | 9³/₄ |
| 44 | 27¹/₄ | 9³/₄ |
| 48 | 31¹/₄ | 9³/₄ |

HIGH FORMED DAMPERS provide correct ratio of throat-to-fireplace opening with an optional preformed smoke shelf, which can reduce material and labor requirements. They are useful for both single and multiple opening fireplaces.

## FORMED DAMPER (IN.)

| WIDTH OF OPENING | DAMPER DIMENSIONS (IN.) | | |
|---|---|---|---|
| | A | B | C |
| 24 to 26 | 28¹/₄ | 26³/₄ | 24 |
| 27 to 30 | 32¹/₄ | 30³/₄ | 28 |
| 31 to 34 | 36¹/₄ | 34³/₄ | 32 |
| 35 to 38 | 40¹/₄ | 38³/₄ | 36 |
| 39 to 42 | 44¹/₄ | 42³/₄ | 40 |
| 43 to 46 | 48¹/₄ | 46³/₄ | 44 |
| 47 to 50 | 52¹/₄ | 50³/₄ | 48 |

FORMED STEEL DAMPERS are designed to provide the correct ratio of throat-to-fireplace opening, producing maximum draft. These dampers are equipped with poker type control and are easily installed.

## SQUARE FORMED DAMPER (IN.)

| TOP OUTLET | | | OVERALL SIZE | |
|---|---|---|---|---|
| E | F | H | L | W |
| 17 | 17 | 17 | 41 | 27 |
| 17 | 17 | 25 | 45 | 27 |
| 17 | 23 | 25 | 49 | 27 |

SQUARE FORMED DAMPERS have high sloping sides that promote even draw on all sides of multiple opening fireplaces. They are properly proportioned for a strong draft and smokefree operation.

## FORMED STEEL DAMPERS

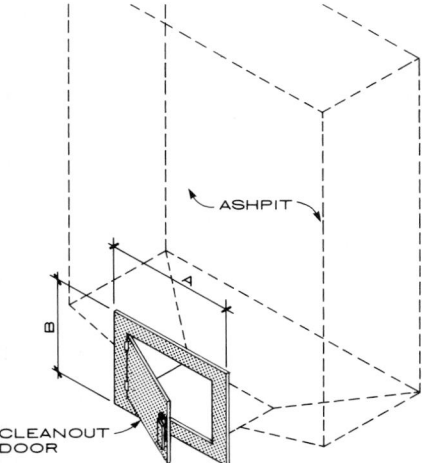

## DOOR DIMENSIONS (IN.)

| A | B |
|---|---|
| 6 | 8 |
| 8 | 8, 10 |
| 10 | 10, 12 |
| 12 | 8, 10, 12, 16, 18 |

### CLEANOUT OR ASHPIT DOOR

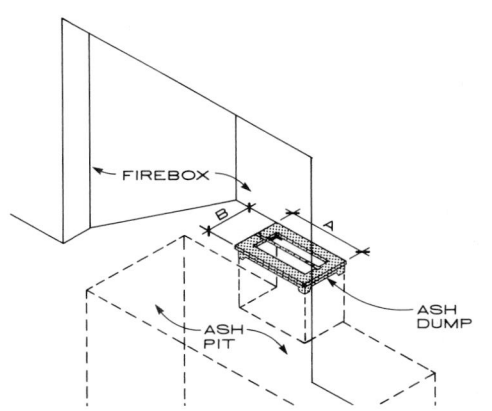

## DUMP DIMENSIONS (IN.)

| A | 3¹/₂ | 4¹/₂ | 7 |
|---|---|---|---|
| B | 7 | 9 | 10 |

NOTE

Ash dumps and cleanout doors are available in heavy gauge steel or cast iron. See local manufacturers for available types and sizes.

### ASH DUMP

## NOTES

1. Locate bottom of damper minimum 6 to 8 in. from top of fireplace opening.
2. Mineral wool blanket allows for expansion of metal damper walls.
3. Dampers are available in heavy gauge steel or cast iron. Check with local suppliers for specific forms and sizes.
4. A cord of wood consists of 128 cu. ft or a stack 4 ft. high and 8 ft. wide, with logs 4 ft. long.
5. A face cord of wood consists of 64 cu ft, or a stack 4 ft high and 8 ft wide, with logs 2 ft long.
6. Logs are cut to lengths of 1 ft 4 in., 2 ft 0 in., 2 ft 6 in., and 4 ft. Allow 3 in. minimum clearance between logs and each side of fireplace.

Timothy B. McDonald; Washington, D.C.

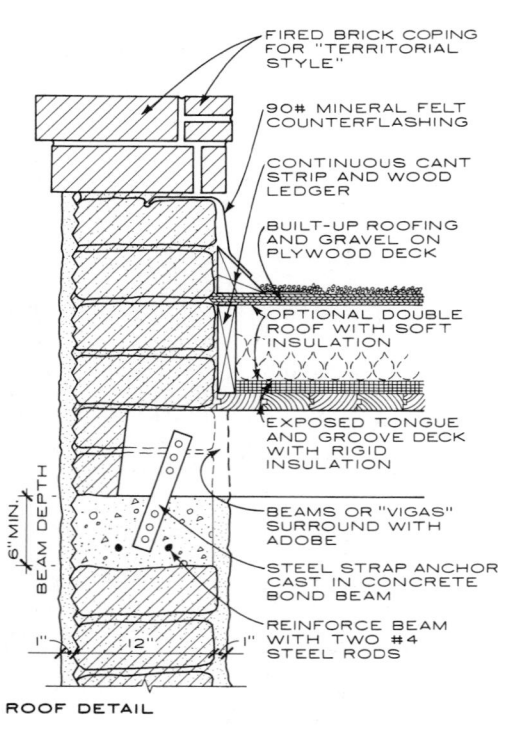

Labels for roof detail:
- FIRED BRICK COPING FOR "TERRITORIAL STYLE"
- 90# MINERAL FELT COUNTERFLASHING
- CONTINUOUS CANT STRIP AND WOOD LEDGER
- BUILT-UP ROOFING AND GRAVEL ON PLYWOOD DECK
- OPTIONAL DOUBLE ROOF WITH SOFT INSULATION
- EXPOSED TONGUE AND GROOVE DECK WITH RIGID INSULATION
- BEAMS OR "VIGAS" SURROUND WITH ADOBE
- STEEL STRAP ANCHOR CAST IN CONCRETE BOND BEAM
- REINFORCE BEAM WITH TWO #4 STEEL RODS
- 6" MIN. BEAM DEPTH
- 1"   12"   1"

**ROOF DETAIL**

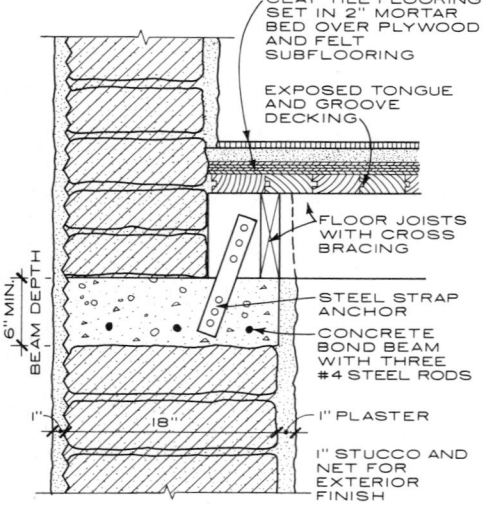

Labels for second floor detail:
- CLAY TILE FLOORING SET IN 2" MORTAR BED OVER PLYWOOD AND FELT SUBFLOORING
- EXPOSED TONGUE AND GROOVE DECKING
- FLOOR JOISTS WITH CROSS BRACING
- STEEL STRAP ANCHOR
- CONCRETE BOND BEAM WITH THREE #4 STEEL RODS
- 1" PLASTER
- 1" STUCCO AND NET FOR EXTERIOR FINISH
- 6" MIN. BEAM DEPTH
- 1"   18"   1"

**SECOND FLOOR DETAIL**

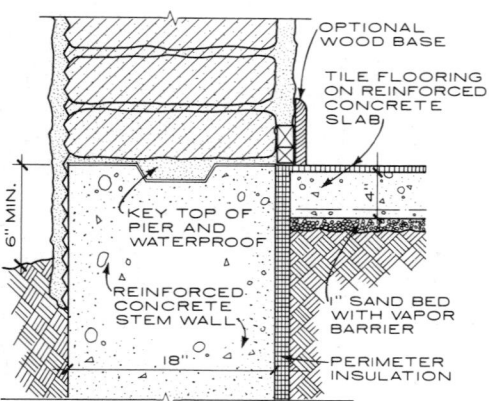

Labels for foundation detail:
- OPTIONAL WOOD BASE
- TILE FLOORING ON REINFORCED CONCRETE SLAB
- KEY TOP OF PIER AND WATERPROOF
- REINFORCED CONCRETE STEM WALL
- 1" SAND BED WITH VAPOR BARRIER
- PERIMETER INSULATION
- 6" MIN.
- 18"

**FOUNDATION DETAIL**

**WALL SECTIONS** (TERRITORIAL STYLE)

P. G. McHenry, Jr., AIA; Albuquerque, New Mexico

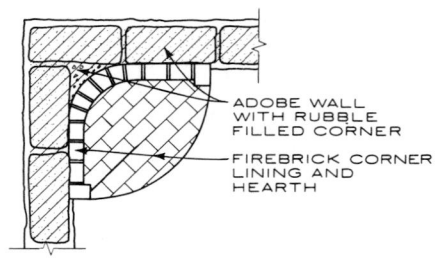

Labels:
- ADOBE WALL WITH RUBBLE FILLED CORNER
- FIREBRICK CORNER LINING AND HEARTH

**PLAN**

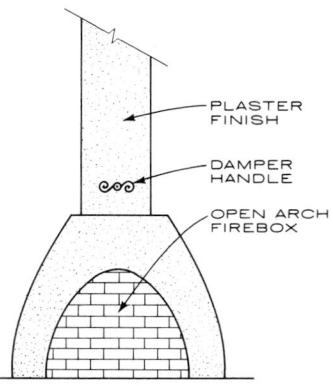

Labels:
- PLASTER FINISH
- DAMPER HANDLE
- OPEN ARCH FIREBOX

**ELEVATION**

**"HORNO" FIREPLACES**

### TYPICAL SIZES OF ADOBE BRICK

| HEIGHT | LENGTH | WIDTH |
|--------|--------|-------|
| 4" | 8" | 16" |
| 4" | 10" | 16" |
| 4" | 9" | 18" |
| 4" | 12" | 18" |
| 5" | 12" | 16" |
| 5" | 10" | 20" |
| 5" | 12" | 18" |
| 6" | 12" | 24" |

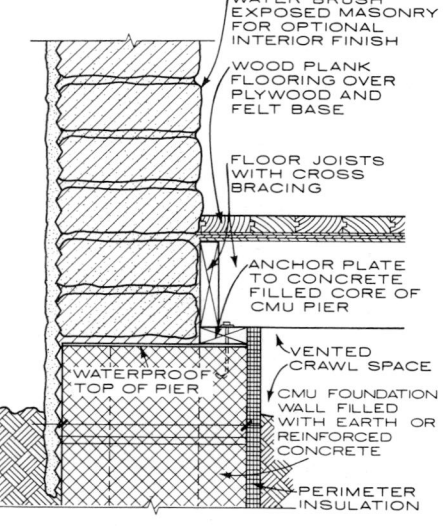

Labels:
- WATER BRUSH EXPOSED MASONRY FOR OPTIONAL INTERIOR FINISH
- WOOD PLANK FLOORING OVER PLYWOOD AND FELT BASE
- FLOOR JOISTS WITH CROSS BRACING
- ANCHOR PLATE TO CONCRETE FILLED CORE OF CMU PIER
- VENTED CRAWL SPACE
- WATERPROOF TOP OF PIER
- CMU FOUNDATION WALL FILLED WITH EARTH OR REINFORCED CONCRETE
- PERIMETER INSULATION

## FIREPLACES

A traditional feature of most adobe homes is one or more corner "Kiva" or "Horno" fireplaces. The main masonry structure is provided by the adobe wall at a corner. If a corner is not available, sometimes a "Padercita" (little wall) is projected from another wall to provide a corner. The corner is lined with firebrick, and a masonry shell encloses the firebox and fireplace flue. A vitreous flue liner or masonry flue is projected through the roof. The curved back wall and open firebox reflect heat efficiently into the room, and the curve provides a smoke shelf. A butterfly damper in the flue or throat is controlled by a decorative wrought iron handle.

New seismic requirements in some areas require vertical steel reinforcement in the masonry of fireplaces.

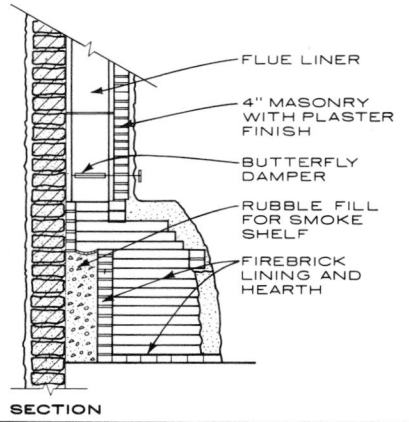

Labels:
- FLUE LINER
- 4" MASONRY WITH PLASTER FINISH
- BUTTERFLY DAMPER
- RUBBLE FILL FOR SMOKE SHELF
- FIREBRICK LINING AND HEARTH

**SECTION**

## ADOBE WALL CONSTRUCTION

The strength of an adobe wall lies in its mass and homogeneous nature, using the same material, mud, for mortar. The addition of reinforcing bars or anchor bolts may weaken joints. An international use standard for adobe wall thickness-height ratio is approximately 1:10. Uniform sizes for sundried bricks vary widely with different locales. The bricks should be made near the point of use and will vary with tradition and the standards of the manufacturer. Larger sizes of great weight will increase the labor cost. Minimum bonding distance is approximately 4 in.

One story walls should be 12 in. thick in Arizona and 10 in. in New Mexico and should not exceed 12 ft in height. Two story walls should be 18 in. thick at first floor and 12 in. at second and not over 22 ft in height.

Avoidance of flowing water on mud surfaces is the most important detail consideration. Rising damp is of no consequence if the site immediately adjacent is well drained and moisture is not trapped by waterproofing materials. Unstabilized mud brick or plaster (without the addition of waterproofing compounds) bonds well to itself and to wood without the use of normal lathing reinforcement. Rain erosion of unstabilized mud surfaces will only approximate 1 in. in 20 years in rainfall areas of 10 to 25 in. per year. Monolithic slab/foundations are not desirable with mud adobe because possible concentrations of rainwater on the slab during construction may damage lower courses.

"Effective" U values for insulation are more significant than the ASHRAE "steady-state" values in common use. The "effective" values take into account the thermal mass, storage, insulation gains in various climate zones, wall compass orientation, and color.

"Burned adobe," which is merely a low fired brick, should be dealt with in the manner normal for brick masonry. Its use is not recommended in climate zones where high daily temperature fluctuations can cause severe freeze-thaw cycle damage. Mud bricks can be stabilized (waterproofed) by the addition of cement, asphalt emulsion, or other compounds. These materials often do not bond well with themselves in repeated layers and may accelerate the deterioration at the point of contact with the mud material.

**4**    **ADOBE**

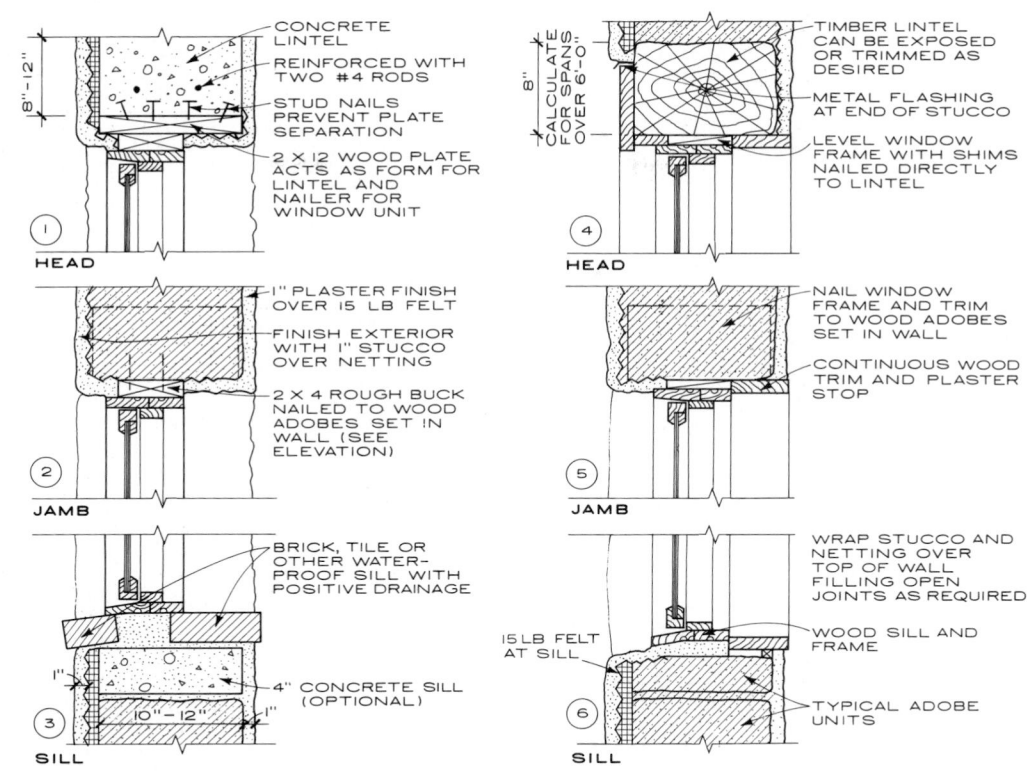

**1 HEAD**
- CONCRETE LINTEL
- 8"–12"
- REINFORCED WITH TWO #4 RODS
- STUD NAILS PREVENT PLATE SEPARATION
- 2 × 12 WOOD PLATE ACTS AS FORM FOR LINTEL AND NAILER FOR WINDOW UNIT

**2 JAMB**
- 1" PLASTER FINISH OVER 15 LB FELT
- FINISH EXTERIOR WITH 1" STUCCO OVER NETTING
- 2 × 4 ROUGH BUCK NAILED TO WOOD ADOBES SET IN WALL (SEE ELEVATION)

**3 SILL**
- BRICK, TILE OR OTHER WATER-PROOF SILL WITH POSITIVE DRAINAGE
- 1"
- 4" CONCRETE SILL (OPTIONAL)
- 10"–12"
- 1"

**4 HEAD**
- 8" CALCULATE FOR SPANS OVER 6'-0"
- TIMBER LINTEL CAN BE EXPOSED OR TRIMMED AS DESIRED
- METAL FLASHING AT END OF STUCCO
- LEVEL WINDOW FRAME WITH SHIMS NAILED DIRECTLY TO LINTEL

**5 JAMB**
- NAIL WINDOW FRAME AND TRIM TO WOOD ADOBES SET IN WALL
- CONTINUOUS WOOD TRIM AND PLASTER STOP

**6 SILL**
- WRAP STUCCO AND NETTING OVER TOP OF WALL FILLING OPEN JOINTS AS REQUIRED
- 15 LB FELT AT SILL
- WOOD SILL AND FRAME
- TYPICAL ADOBE UNITS

**WINDOW DETAILS** (SEE ELEVATION FOR ANCHORAGE OF FRAME)

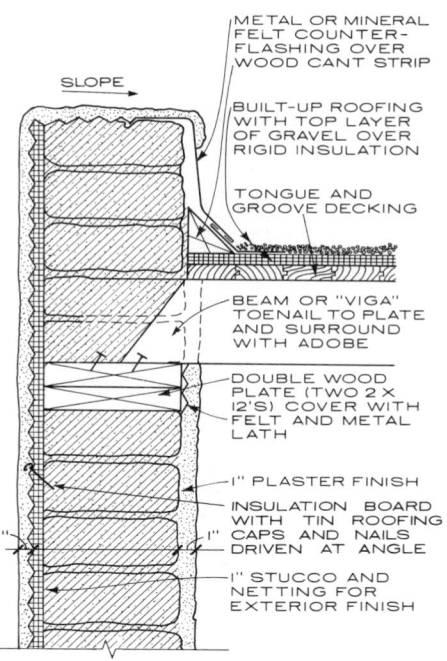

**PARAPET WITH WOOD COLLAR**
- METAL OR MINERAL FELT COUNTER-FLASHING OVER WOOD CANT STRIP
- SLOPE
- BUILT-UP ROOFING WITH TOP LAYER OF GRAVEL OVER RIGID INSULATION
- TONGUE AND GROOVE DECKING
- BEAM OR "VIGA" TOENAIL TO PLATE AND SURROUND WITH ADOBE
- DOUBLE WOOD PLATE (TWO 2 × 12'S) COVER WITH FELT AND METAL LATH
- 1" PLASTER FINISH
- INSULATION BOARD WITH TIN ROOFING CAPS AND NAILS DRIVEN AT ANGLE
- 1"    1"
- 1" STUCCO AND NETTING FOR EXTERIOR FINISH

## NOTES

Details deal with the use of sundried mud bricks. They may be stabilized with additives or simply made of mud. Proportions for the mud mixture of sand, silt, and clay normally are not critical. Gravel and small stones can also be present if they do not exceed 50% of the volume. Adobe is approved by local building officials in areas where adobe use is traditional or familiar to builders or construction officials. Information concerning local codes should be sought.

Nailing anchors are best provided by the use of wood adobes ("Gringo blocks"), either solid or made of scrap lumber, laid up with the wall in locations where door and window jambs may require attachment. Nails will not hold permanently when nailed into adobe bricks unless additionally secured by plaster or other material. Later attachments can be made by the use of wooden triple wedges driven into a pilot hole. Channels for wiring, pipes, and decorative features may be easily cut in the wall after it is in place.

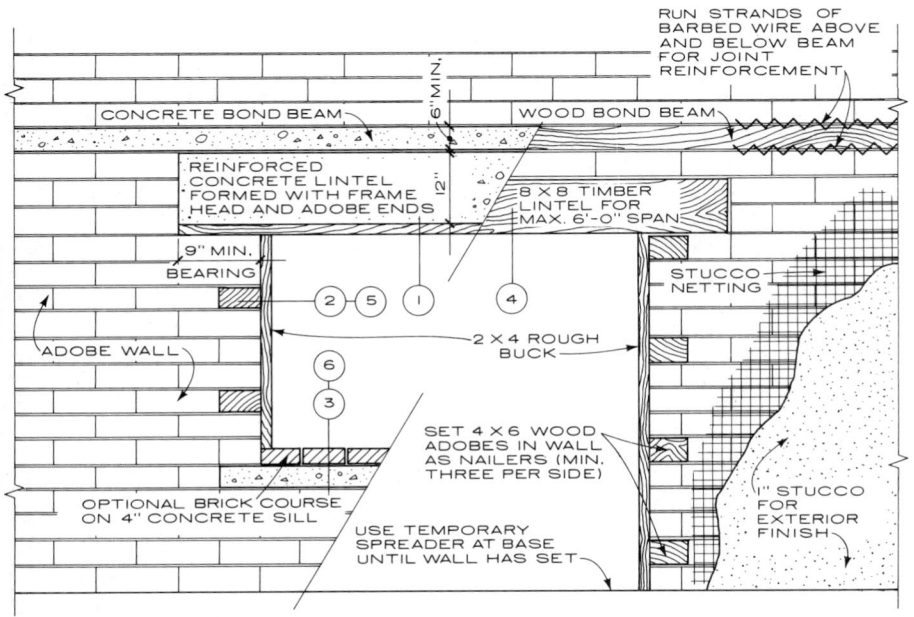

**ELEVATION OF TYPICAL FRAMED OPENINGS**
- CONCRETE BOND BEAM
- 6" MIN.
- WOOD BOND BEAM
- RUN STRANDS OF BARBED WIRE ABOVE AND BELOW BEAM FOR JOINT REINFORCEMENT
- 12"
- REINFORCED CONCRETE LINTEL FORMED WITH FRAME HEAD AND ADOBE ENDS
- 8 × 8 TIMBER LINTEL FOR MAX. 6'-0" SPAN
- STUCCO NETTING
- 9" MIN. BEARING
- ② ⑤ ① ④
- ⑥ ③
- 2 × 4 ROUGH BUCK
- ADOBE WALL
- OPTIONAL BRICK COURSE ON 4" CONCRETE SILL
- SET 4 × 6 WOOD ADOBES IN WALL AS NAILERS (MIN. THREE PER SIDE)
- USE TEMPORARY SPREADER AT BASE UNTIL WALL HAS SET
- 1" STUCCO FOR EXTERIOR FINISH

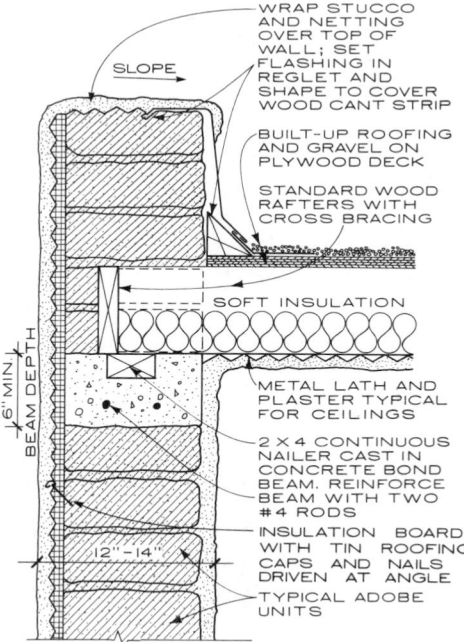

**PARAPET WITH CONCRETE COLLAR**
- WRAP STUCCO AND NETTING OVER TOP OF WALL; SET FLASHING IN REGLET AND SHAPE TO COVER WOOD CANT STRIP
- SLOPE
- BUILT-UP ROOFING AND GRAVEL ON PLYWOOD DECK
- STANDARD WOOD RAFTERS WITH CROSS BRACING
- SOFT INSULATION
- 6" MIN.    BEAM DEPTH    6" MIN.
- METAL LATH AND PLASTER TYPICAL FOR CEILINGS
- 2 × 4 CONTINUOUS NAILER CAST IN CONCRETE BOND BEAM. REINFORCE BEAM WITH TWO #4 RODS
- INSULATION BOARD WITH TIN ROOFING CAPS AND NAILS DRIVEN AT ANGLE
- 12"–14"
- TYPICAL ADOBE UNITS

## GENERAL NOTE

Some building codes may require additional thicknesses and reinforcement of concrete bond beams. The anchorage of pitched roof structures may be done by normal attachment to the bond beams shown.

P. G. McHenry, Jr., AIA; Albuquerque, New Mexico

**ADOBE**   **4**

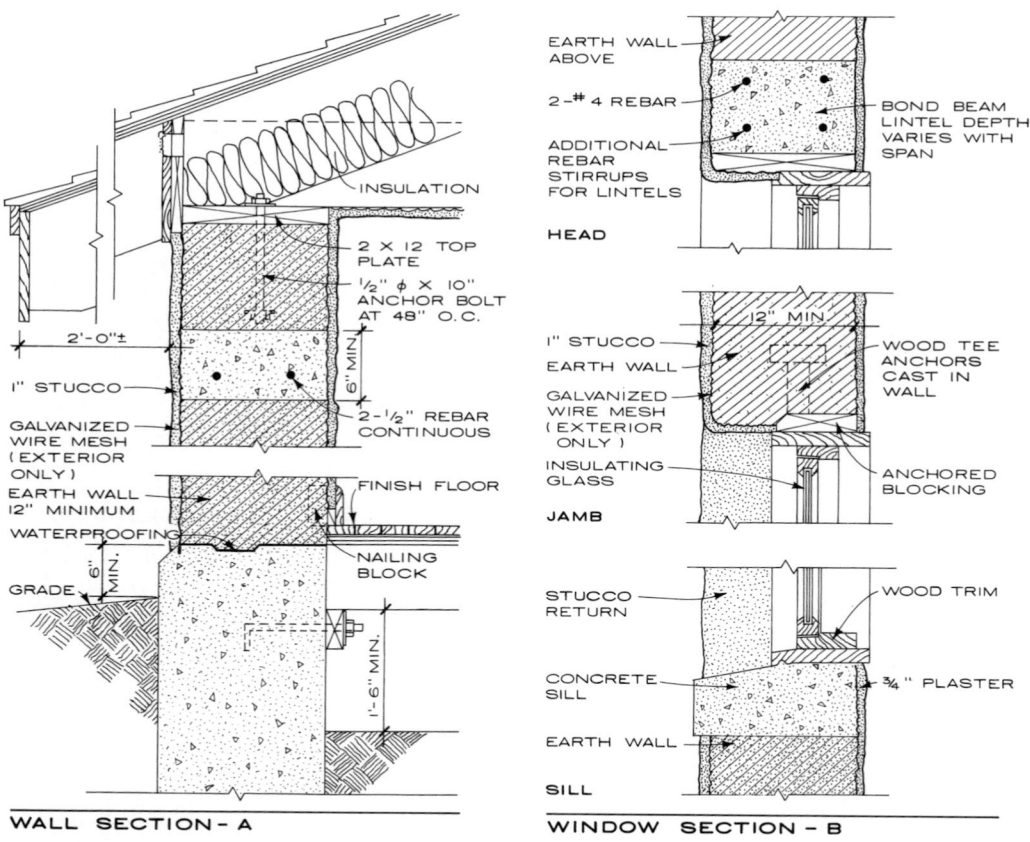

**WALL SECTION - A**

INSULATION

2 X 12 TOP PLATE

½" φ X 10" ANCHOR BOLT AT 48" O.C.

2'-0"±

1" STUCCO

2-½" REBAR CONTINUOUS

GALVANIZED WIRE MESH (EXTERIOR ONLY)

EARTH WALL 12" MINIMUM

WATERPROOFING

FINISH FLOOR

NAILING BLOCK

GRADE

6" MIN.

1'-6" MIN.

**WINDOW SECTION - B**

EARTH WALL ABOVE

2 -# 4 REBAR

ADDITIONAL REBAR STIRRUPS FOR LINTELS

BOND BEAM LINTEL DEPTH VARIES WITH SPAN

**HEAD**

1" STUCCO

EARTH WALL

GALVANIZED WIRE MESH (EXTERIOR ONLY)

INSULATING GLASS

12" MIN

WOOD TEE ANCHORS CAST IN WALL

ANCHORED BLOCKING

**JAMB**

STUCCO RETURN

CONCRETE SILL

EARTH WALL

WOOD TRIM

¾" PLASTER

**SILL**

### NOTES

1. Rammed earth wall construction is an old technique used effectively in many parts of the world. The basic material is earth, with allowable proportions of clay, silt, and aggregate, commonly found almost everywhere. The soil in most locations has naturally usable proportions that do not require further tempering. The ideal soil mixture will have less than 50% clay and silt, and a maximum aggregate size of ¼ in. The solid is dampened to a moisture content of approximately 10% by weight, of dry soil. Saltwater should not be used under any circumstances.

2. The walls are constructed by the use of slip forms, (24 to 36 in. high x 8 to 12 ft long) placed level and secure. The forms are filled with damp (not wet) earth in 4 in. lifts. Each lift is rammed with a tamper until full compaction is reached. The tamp should be flat, approximately 6 x 6 in., weighing 18 to 25 lb, tamped by hand or mechanically. Full compaction can be determined by a ringing sound when the tamp compacts the fill. When the form is full and compacted, it is moved to a new location and secured and the process is repeated. The corners should be placed first, with special corner forms. When the full circumference is completed, the next course is started. The form heights (courses) are best coordinated with heights of window and door lintels. Form replacement can begin as soon as compaction is reached, without further drying.

3. Exterior wall thickness should be a minimum of 12 in. for one story, 18 in. to support a second story, and interior walls of not less than 9 in. Wall thickness can be increased as appropriate to the design. Basic rammed earth walls have many of the same characteristics of sundried adobe. The insulation value of the walls is not as great as more efficient insulating materials, but will provide thermal mass for heat storage, sound control, and other benefits.

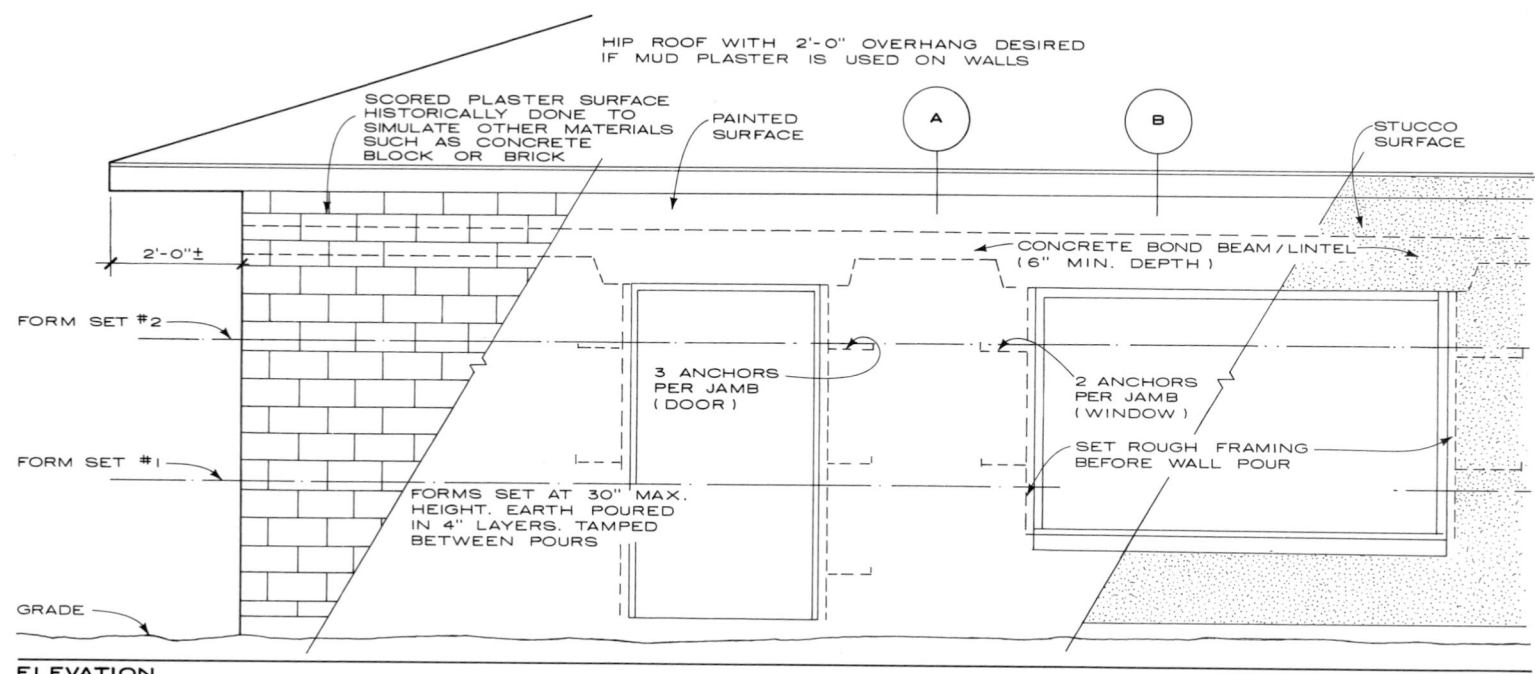

HIP ROOF WITH 2'-0" OVERHANG DESIRED IF MUD PLASTER IS USED ON WALLS

SCORED PLASTER SURFACE HISTORICALLY DONE TO SIMULATE OTHER MATERIALS SUCH AS CONCRETE BLOCK OR BRICK

PAINTED SURFACE

A

B

STUCCO SURFACE

2'-0"±

FORM SET #2

FORM SET #1

GRADE

CONCRETE BOND BEAM / LINTEL (6" MIN. DEPTH)

3 ANCHORS PER JAMB (DOOR)

2 ANCHORS PER JAMB (WINDOW)

SET ROUGH FRAMING BEFORE WALL POUR

FORMS SET AT 30" MAX. HEIGHT. EARTH POURED IN 4" LAYERS. TAMPED BETWEEN POURS

**ELEVATION**

### NOTES

1. Foundations are normally conventional spread footings of sufficient width to support the heavy (3000 # per lin ft) walls. The foundation wall should be of a waterproof material, topped with a vapor barrier to prevent capillary moisture rise. Attachment anchors in the form of wood tees or plugs are placed in the wall as it is erected, in the positions required to secure window and door frames. A continuous steel reinforced concrete beam (6 in. thick) is placed as a continuous lintel beam to support walls above the openings.

2. A top plate of wood is secured by means of anchor bolts cast in the top of the walls. The plate provides load distribution and an attachment point for the roof structure. Interior and exterior walls can be finished by the application of conventional stucco or plaster. Simpler treatment can be achieved by smoothing or texturing the earth wall with a sponge rubber float, wet burlap, or sheepskin, and painting it. Sealing and preparation of the surface before painting is the same as for plaster. If waterproof stucco is not used, roof overhangs should be of sufficient width to protect the walls from rain erosion.

P. G. McHenry, Jr., AIA; Albuquerque, New Mexico

 **RAMMED EARTH**

# CHAPTER 5

# *Metals*

## TYPES OF METALS

There are two general types of metals, ferrous and non-ferrous. Ferrous metals contain iron, nonferrous do not.

### FERROUS METALS

Iron, which contains no trace amount of carbon, is soft, ductile, easily worked, oxidizes rapidly, but is susceptible to most acids. It is the main element in steel.

Cast iron and gray cast iron both are brittle metals with high compressive strength and capacity to absorb vibration, which makes them ideal for gratings, stair components and manhole covers. Neither should be hammered or beaten because they lack ductility. Both are relatively corrosion resistant.

Malleable iron, often used for the same purposes, is a low carbon iron that is cast, reheated and slowly cooled, or annealed, to improve its workability.

Wrought iron is soft, corrosion and fatigue resistant, and machinable. It is easily worked, making it ideal for railings, grilles, fences, screens, and various types of ornamental work. It often is cast or worked into bars, sheets or pipes. Because of its corrosion resistance, wrought iron until recently was used for below grade applications. Other metals are now preferred.

Steel is iron with low to medium amounts of carbon; carbon content is the measure used to categorize carbon steel. Greater carbon content increases strength and hardness but reduces ductility and welding capability. Its corrosion resistance is increased when a finish such as galvanizing or an organic coating is applied. Some architectural uses are as structural shapes, castings, studs, joists, fasteners, wall grilles, and ceiling suspension grids.

Steel alloys are produced when other elements are combined with carbon steel to modify steel properties. For example, high strength, low alloy steels (HSLA) improve corrosion resistance and are chosen where weight is a consideration and high strength is required. They are used infrequently in architectural applications because water runoff tends to stain adjacent materials. Below are a number of modifying alloy elements:

1. Aluminum for surface hardening.
2. Chromium for corrosion resistance.
3. Copper for resistance to atmospheric corrosion.
4. Manganese in small amounts for hardening; in larger amounts for wear resistance.
5. Molybdenum, combined with other alloying metals such as chromium and nickel, to increase corrosion resistance and to raise tensile strength without reducing ductility.
6. Nickel to increase tensile strength without reducing ductility; in high concentrations, to improve corrosion resistance.
7. Silicon to strengthen low-alloy steels and improve oxidation resistance; in larger amounts to provide hard, brittle castings resistant to corrosive chemicals.
8. Sulfur for free machining, especially in mild steels.
9. Titanium to prevent intergranular corrosion of stainless steels.
10. Tungsten, vanadium, and cobalt for hardness and abrasion resistance.

Stainless steel contains a minimum of 11.5 percent chromium. Nickel is added to boost atmospheric corrosion resistance. Where maximum corrosion resistance is required, such as resistance to pitting by sea water, molybdenum is added. Stainless steel is used in construction for flashing, coping, fasciae, wall panels, floor plates, gratings, handrails, hardware, fasteners and anchors.

### NONFERROUS METALS

Nonferrous metals (those containing no iron) used in construction are:

Aluminum: High-purity aluminum is soft and ductile, highly corrosion resistant, but lacking in strength. Aluminum alloys are identified by numbers that distinguish each by its relative properties. For example, the identification number of pure aluminum is 1100. The manganese-based aluminum alloy, 3003, is used for roofing, sheet metal, siding, and conduit.

Lead: Extremely dense metal, easily worked, and corrosion resistant. Alloys are added to improve its properties such as hardness and strength. Lead is used for waterproofing, sound and vibration isolation, and radiation shielding. It can be combined with a tin alloy to plate iron or steel, commonly called "terneplate." Care should be taken where and how lead is used because lead vapors or dust are toxic if ingested.

Zinc, although corrosion resistant in water and air, is brittle and low in strength. Its major use is in galvanizing (dipping hot iron or steel in molten zinc), but it also is used for roofing, flashing, hardware, die casting and as an alloying element.

Chromium and nickel also are used primarily as alloying elements; however, both can take a bright polish and do not tarnish in air, making them ideal for use in plating.

Monel, a nickel-copper alloy, most commonly is used to make fasteners and anchors, and is excellent where high corrosion resistance is required.

Copper is resistant to corrosion, impact and fatigue, yet it is ductile. It is used primarily in construction as electrical wiring, roofing, flashing, and piping.

Bronze originally was a copper-tin alloy; however, today copper is alloyed with various elements such as aluminum or silicon. In fact, the term "bronze" seldom is used without a modifying adjective giving the name of at least one of its alloying components, such as phosphor bronze, a copper-tin-phosphorus alloy, or leaded phosphor bronze composed of copper-lead-tin and phosphorus; aluminum bronze containing copper and aluminum; and silicon bronze, a copper-silicon alloy.

Brass is copper with zinc as its principal alloying element; however, some types of brass alloys often are called bronze even though they are not. Some nonbronze, brass alloys are: commercial bronze, 90 percent copper, 10 percent zinc; naval brass, 60 percent copper, 29 percent zinc, one percent tin; and manganese bronze, 58 percent copper, 39 percent zinc, one percent tin and iron. When a metal is identified as bronze, the alloy cannot contain zinc or nickel; if it does, it probably is brass. Architectural and commercial bronze are really brass, and are used for doors, windows, door and window frames, railings, trim and grilles and for finish hardware.

## THE GALVANIC SERIES

| | |
|---|---|
| Anode (least noble) | Magnesium, magnesium alloys |
| | Zinc |
| + | Aluminum 1100 |
| | Cadmium |
| | Aluminum 2024-T4 |
| | Steel or Iron, Cast iron |
| | Chromium iron (active) |
| | Ni-Resist |
| | Type 304, 316 stainless (active) |
| | Hastelloy "C" |
| | Lead, Tin |
| | Nickel (Inconel) (active) |
| | Hastelloy "B" |
| electric current flows from positive (+) to negative (−) | Brasses, Copper, Bronzes, Copper-Nickel alloys, Monel |
| | Silver solder |
| | Nickel (Inconel) (passive) |
| | Chromium iron (passive) |
| | Type 304, 316 stainless (passive) |
| − | Silver |
| | Titanium |
| Cathode (most noble) | Graphite, Gold, Platinum |

## CORROSION TO METALS

Galvanic action, or corrosion, occurs between dissimilar metals or metals and other materials when sufficient moisture is present to carry an electrical current. The galvanic series, a list of metals arranged in order from "least noble, most reactive to corrosion" to "most noble, least reactive to corrosion," is a good indicator of corrosion susceptibility due to galvanic action. The farther apart two metals are on the list, the greater the deterioration of the least noble one.

Metal deterioration also occurs when metals come in contact with chemically active materials, particularly when moisture is present. For example, aluminum in direct contact with concrete or mortar corrodes, or steel in contact with certain types of treated wood corrodes.

Other types of corrosion are pitting and concentration cell corrosion. Pitting corrosion occurs when particles or bubbles of gas are deposited on a metal surface. Oxygen deficiency under the deposit sets up anodic areas causing pitting. Concentration cell corrosion is similar to galvanic corrosion; the difference is in electrolytes. Concentration cell corrosion may be produced by differences in ion concentration, oxygen concentration, or foreign matter adhering to the surface.

## FABRICATION ON METALS

Fabrication is a process applied to metal to obtain a shape. Following are various types of fabrication.

Rolling hot or cold metal between rollers under pressure produces most of the primary shapes available. The metal's temperature determines the properties of the end product. This method is applicable to most metals except iron.

In the extruding process metal is pushed under pressure through a die orifice producing various complex shapes limited only by the size or capability of the die. This process is applicable to all metals except iron.

Casting is a process in which molten metal is poured into molds and allowed to solidify into the shape of the mold. Casting is applicable to aluminum, copper, iron, steel, bronze, and other metals; however, surface quality and physical characteristics are affected by metal type, casting technique, and the molten metal's temperature.

In the drawing process either hot or cold metal is pulled through dies that alter or reduce its cross-sectional shape to attain three-dimensional shapes. Common extrusions are sheets, tubes, pipes, rods, bars, and wires. Drawing is applicable to all metals except iron.

Forging is a process of hammering or pressing hot or cold metal to a desired shape. It usually improves the strength and surface characteristics of the metal. Forging is applicable to aluminum, copper and steel.

Forming shapes metals by mechanical operations, excluding machining.

Bending produces curved shapes, and generally is applied to tubes, rods, and extrusions.

Brake forming, usually applied to plates or metal sheets, is a process of successive pressings to achieve specific shapes.

In the spinning process metal is shaped with tools while it is spun on an axis.

Embossing and coining are processes usually performed on flat shapes to achieve textured or raised patterns.

Blanking is shearing, sawing or cutting metal sheets with a punch press to achieve an outline.

Perforating is achieved by punching or drilling holes usually in flat shapes.

Piercing is a process that punches holes through metal without removing any of the metal.

Welding is the fusion of metals above the molten point with or without the aid of a metal filler. Gas welding is the most portable and economical. It can be used on site. The heat for fusion is provided by a torch using oxygen and acetylene gases.

Shielded metal arc welding, sometimes called manual, hand, or stick welding, can be performed in the shop or the field. An electric arc between a coated metal electrode and the components to be welded heat them both to a point where a molten pool forms on the surface of the components. As the arc is moved along the joint between the components, the pool solidifies, forming a homogeneous weld.

Gas metal arc welding also can be done on site or in a shop; however, provisions must be made on a job site to screen from any winds. This process uses an uncoated solid wire electrode and a stream of gas to provide shielding for the arc and welded metal. Several other types of welding are confined to the shop. Further information on welding is available from the American Welding Society.

## FINISHES, MECHANICAL AND CHEMICAL

An as-fabricated finish is the texture and surface appearance given to a metal by the fabrication process.

A brightened finish is produced by electrolytic brightening or dipping the metal in acid solutions.

A buffed finish is produced by successive polishing and buffing operations using fine abrasives, lubricants, and soft fabric wheels.

A chemical finish produces a physical change on the metal's surface depending on the type of metal and chemical used.

Directional textured finishes have a smooth satiny sheen produced by making tiny parallel scratches on the metal surface using a belt or wheel and fine abrasive, or by hand rubbing with steel wool. Non-directional textured finishes are produced by blasting the metal under controlled conditions with sand, glass beads, or metal shot.

An etched finish produces a matte, frosted surface with varying degrees of roughness by treating the metal with an acid or alkaline solution.

Metallic finishes are created by applying one metal to another by electrolysis, hot dipping, electroplating, or other techniques.

Galvanizing is an example of metal coating where zinc is applied to steel. Zinc may be applied by electrolysis, peening, hot zinc spray, hot dip or paint. Hot dip galvanizing is used for nails, nuts and bolts, and structural members. Thickness of the zinc coating may be varied depending on the corrosive nature of the atmosphere at the place of use. Galvanized steel may be painted with special formulated coatings to substantially extend the life of the galvanized coating.

Patterned finishes, mechanically produced, are available in various textures and designs. They are produced by passing an as-fabricated sheet either between two machine matched-design rollers, embossing patterns on both sides of the sheet, or between a smooth roll and a design roll, embossing or coining on one side of the sheet only.

## APPLIED COATINGS

Applied coatings are surface coverings over metal. They may be inorganic, such as porcelain enamel, or organic, like most commonly used fluorocarbons. Both can be applied over suitable primers (although not always necessary) for added corrosion resistance and to improve adhesion. Generally they are applied and baked on at the factory. Air-dry formulas usually are available for touch-ups.

Fluorocarbons generally are based on resins and are applied over primers such as epoxy-zinc chromate primers. They are available in a wide range of colors and in low to medium ranges of gloss.

Siliconized polymers, a combination of organic polymers and silicone intermediates, are applied in combination with a primer or alone. They are available in a wide range of colors and low to high gloss. The silicone extends gloss retention and improves resistance to color change and weathering. The two principal types are siliconized acrylic and siliconized polyester.

Plastisols are the top coat of a two-coat system. They require a special primer to bond to the metal surface. The top coat thickness can vary from 3 mils to 15 mils.

Conversion coatings for aluminum are amorphous chrome phosphate; for steel, a phosphate or various strong salt solutions generally is used.

Vitreous coatings are composed of inorganic glossy materials such as porcelain enamels. They are one of the hardest and most durable finishes, but they are brittle. Deformation of metal may cause cracking and spalling. These coatings are available in a wide range of colors and finishes from matte to high gloss.

Anodic finishes for coating aluminum consist of a mechanical finish, then a preanodic treatment to remove all foreign matter, and finally an oxide coating. Aluminum alloys must be suitable for anodizing. Fabrication, such as welding, can show when anodized.

## REPRESENTATIVE ARCHITECTURAL USES AND COMPARATIVE PROPERTIES OF COATINGS

| BINDER TYPE | TYPICAL USES | APPLICATION SHOP | FIELD | COST | OUT-DOOR LIFE (YEARS) | COLOR STABLE, EX-TERIOR | GLOSS RETEN-TION, EX-TERIOR | STAIN RESIS-TANCE | WEATHER RESIS-TANCE | ABRA-SION AND IM-PACT RESIS-TANCE | FLEXI-BILITY | WATER-REDU-CIBLE AVAIL-ABLE | CLEAR AVAIL-ABLE | WELD-ABLE AS PRIMER |
|---|---|---|---|---|---|---|---|---|---|---|---|---|---|---|
| Acrylics—<br>Solvent reducible | Residential siding and similar products; cabinets and implements; clear top coats | yes | no | M | 10 | yes | G | F | G | G | G | — | yes | yes* |
| Water reducible:<br>air dried | | yes | yes | M | 5–10 | yes | F | F | G | G | G | yes | yes | yes* |
| baked | | yes | no | M | 15–20 | yes | G–E | F | G–E | G | G | yes | yes | yes* |
| Alkyds | Exterior primers and enamels | yes | yes | L–M | 5–9 | no | G | F | F | F | F–G | yes | yes | yes* |
| Cellulose Acetate Butyrate | Decorative high gloss finishes | yes | no | M | NA | yes | G | F | G | G | G | no | yes | no |
| Chlorinated rubber | Corrosion-resistant paints; swimming pool coatings; protection of dissimilar metals | yes | yes | M | 10 | yes | F | F | G | G | G | no | no | no |
| Chloro-sulfonated polyethylene | Paints for piping, tanks, valves, etc. | yes | yes | VH | 15 | yes | NA | F | E | F–G | E | no | no | no |
| Epoxy | Moisture- and alkali-resistant coatings; nondecorative interior uses requiring high chemical resistance | yes | yes | H–VH | 15–20 | no | P | G | G–E | E | G | no | no | yes* |
| Fluorocarbons | High performance exterior coatings; industrial siding; curtain walls | yes | no | VH | 20+ | yes | E | E | E | E | G | no | no | no |
| Phenol formaldehyde | Chemical- and moisture-resistant coatings | yes | yes | M | 10 | no | F | F | G–E | G–E | G | no | yes | yes* |
| Polyester | Cabinets and furniture; ceiling tile; piping | yes | yes | H | 15 | some versions | G–E | G–E | G–E | G | G–E | yes | yes | no |
| Polyvinyl chloride | Residential siding; rain-carrying equipment; metal wall tile; baseboard heating covers, etc. Plastisols: industrial siding; curtain walls | yes | yes | H | 15 | yes | G | F | G–E | G | G–E | yes | no | yes* |
| Silicates (inorganic) | Corrosion-inhibitive primers; solvent-resistant coatings | yes | yes | H | NA | NA | NA | NA | NA | G | G | no | no | yes |
| Silicone-modified polymers | High performance exterior coatings; industrial siding; curtain walls | yes | yes | H–VH | 15–20 | yes | G–E | G | G–E | G–E | G | yes | no | no |
| Urethane (aliphatic-cured) | Heavy duty coatings for stain, chemical, abrasion, and corrosion resistance | yes | yes | VH | 20+ | some versions | E | G–E | G–E | G–E | E | yes | yes | yes* |

KEY: L = Low; M = Moderate; H = High; VH = Very High; NA = not applicable or not available; P = Poor; F = Fair; G = Good; E = Excellent          *For light welding only

## STRUCTURAL ECONOMY—STEEL FRAMING

The most commonly used strength grade of structural steel is 36,000 psi yield strength (ASTM A36). For heavily loaded members such as columns, girders, or trusses where buckling, lateral stability, deflection, or vibration does not control member selection, higher yield strength steels may be economically utilized. A 50,000 psi yield strength is most frequently used among high strength, low alloy steels.

The Manual of Steel Construction of the AISC contains column and beam load tables for both 36,000 and 50,000 psi yield strengths.

High strength, low alloy steels are available in several grades, and some possess superior corrosion resistance to such a degree that they are classified as "weathering steel." Table 1 contains data for several ASTM alloys used for structural members.

### TABLE 1   STRUCTURAL STEEL DATA

| ATSM DESIGNATION | STRENGTH GRADES (KSI) | ATMOSPHERIC CORROSION RESISTANCE | REMARKS |
|---|---|---|---|
| A572 | 42, 45, 50, 55, 60, 65 | Same as carbon steel | Most commonly used of low alloy steels |
| A441 | 40, 42, 46, 50 | Twice the resistance of carbon steel | Primarily for welded structures—not frequently used |
| A242 | 42, 46, 50* | 5 to 8 times the resistance of carbon steel | Used exposed as "weathering steel" or painted |
| A588 | 42, 46, 50* | 4 times the resistance of carbon steel | Used exposed as "weathering steel" or painted |

*50 KSI normally provided, but reduced for thicker material.

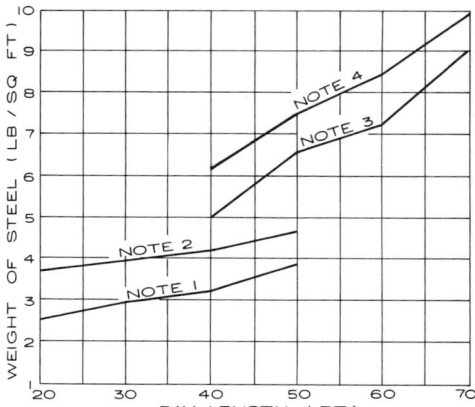

Figure above shows approximate weight of noncomposite structural steel floor or roof framing versus bay size.

### NOTES

1. Roof of 15 ft high one-story structure, H-series open web joists on continuous A36 girders (weight of A36 columns included). Joist span = 30 ft.
2. Same as (1) except that joist span = 45 ft.
3. Typical level of five-story garage, V-50 steel throughout (weight of columns included) bay width = 20 ft.
4. Same as (3) except that bay width = 30 ft.

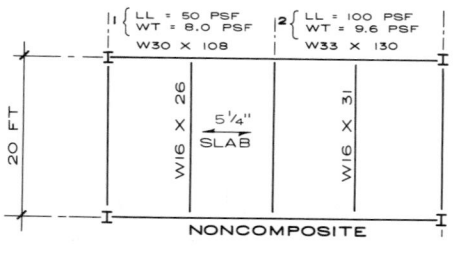

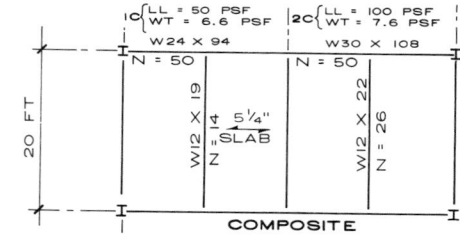

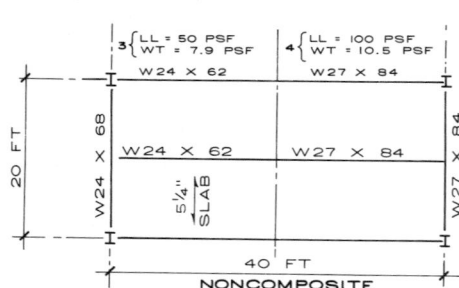

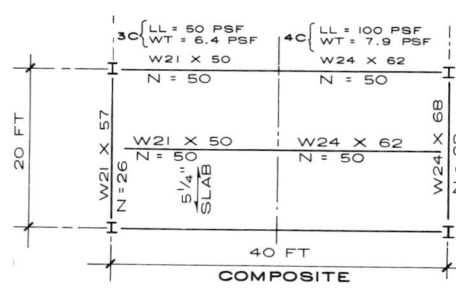

### TABLE 2   ALTERNATE FRAMING

| | SHORT BEAMS, LONG GIRDERS | | | | LONG BEAMS, SHORT GIRDERS | | | |
|---|---|---|---|---|---|---|---|---|
| | LL = 50 PSF | | LL = 100 PSF | | LL = 50 PSF | | LL = 100 PSF | |
| | 1 | 1C | 2 | 2C | 3 | 3C | 4 | 4C |
| Girder depth | 30″ | 24″ | 33″ | 30″ | 24″ | 21″ | 27″ | 24″ |
| Steel weight per bay (lb) | 6400 | 5280 | 7680 | 6080 | 6320 | 5140 | 8400 | 6320 |
| Weight ratio—Noncomposite : composite | 1.21 : 1 | | 1.26 : 1 | | 1.23 : 1 | | 1.33 : 1 | |
| No. shear studs | 0 | 106 | 0 | 154 | 0 | 126 | 0 | 128 |
| Cost ratio (see Note 5) | 1.16 : 1 | | 1.19 : 1 | | 1.16 : 1 | | 1.27 : 1 | |

### NOTES

1. Floor slab: 5¼ in. total thickness—3¼ in. lightweight concrete over 2 in. composite metal deck, all schemes. This provides a 2 hr fire rating without spraying the deck.
2. Additional dead load allowance for finishes, etc.: 30 psf, all schemes.
3. All steel ASTM A36.
4. Shear studs: ¾ in. dia. x 3½ in. long. N = 50 indicates total number of studs per beam.
5. The cost ratio between noncomposite and composite floor steel is approximately 95% of the weight ratio. The cost of studs accounts for the difference.
6. Vibration of floor beams should be analyzed.

Walter D. Shapiro, P.E.; Tor, Shapiro & Associates; New York, New York

### NOTES

The weight of structural steel per square foot of floor area increases with bay size, as does the depth of the structure. Cost of structural steel may not rise as rapidly as weight if savings can be realized by reducing the number of pieces to be fabricated and erected. Improved space utilization afforded by larger bay sizes is offset by increases in wall area and building volume resulting from increased structure depth.

Steel frame economy can be improved by incorporating as many of these cost reducing factors into the structure layout and design as architectural requirements permit:

1. Keep columns in line in both directions and avoid offsets or omission of columns.
2. Design for maximum repetition of member sizes within each level and from floor to floor.
3. Reduce the number of beams and girders per level to reduce fabrication and erection time and cost.
4. Maximize the use of simple beam connections by bracing the structure at a limited number of moment resisting bents or by the most efficient method, cross-bracing.
5. Utilize high strength steels for columns and floor members where studies indicate that cost can be reduced while meeting other design parameters.
6. Use composite design, but consider effect of in-slab electric raceways or other discontinuities.
7. Consider open web steel joists, especially for large roofs of one-story structures, and for floor framing in many applications.

An analysis of alternate framing schemes for a 20 x 40 ft interior floor bay appears in Table 2.

One constant relationship that may be noted in the analysis is the decrease in girder depth when using long beams and short girders. The weight of steel for roofs or lightly loaded floors is generally least when long beams and short girders are used. For heavier loadings long girders and short filler beams should result in less steel weight. The most economical framing type (composite, noncomposite, continuous, simple spans, etc.) and arrangement must be determined for each structure, considering such factors as structure depth, building volume, wall area, mechanical system requirements, deflection or vibration limitations, wind or seismic load interaction between floor system, and columns or shear walls.

## GENERAL INFORMATION

Composite construction combines two different materials or two different grades of a material to form a structural member that utilizes the most desirable properties of each material. Examples of composite construction are all around us but may go unrecognized as such. Perhaps the earliest composite structural unit was the mud brick reinforced with straw. Other common examples are: nineteenth century trusses of wood and iron; modern trusses and open web joists of wood and steel; reinforced concrete, which combines the tensile strength of steel with the compressive strength of concrete; cable supported concrete roofs and bridges; fiberglass reinforced plastics; wire reinforced safety glass; plywood; glued laminated wood beams.

Composite systems currently used in building construction include:

1. Concrete topped composite steel decks.
2. Steel beams acting compositely with concrete slabs.
3. Steel columns encased by or filled with concrete.
4. Open web joists of wood and steel or joists with plywood webs and wood chords.
5. Trusses combining wood and steel.
6. Hybrid girders utilizing steels of different strengths.
7. Cast-in-place concrete slab on precast concrete joists or beams.

To make two different materials act compositely as one unit they must be joined at their interface by one or a combination of these means:

1. Chemical bonding (concrete).
2. Gluing (plywood, glulam).
3. Welding (steel, aluminum).
4. Screws (sheet metal, wood).
5. Bolts (steel, wood).
6. Shear studs (steel to concrete).
7. Keys or embossments (steel deck to concrete, concrete to concrete).
8. Dowels (concrete to concrete).
9. Friction (positive clamping force must be present).

Individual elements of the composite unit must be securely fastened to prevent slippage with respect to one another. This principle can be demonstrated by bending a telephone book at its free edges and then trying to bend the book at its binding—the binding makes all the pages resist bending in a combined effort, unlike the free edges where pages slip and slide, offering little resistance.

The illustrations of composite systems show points of potential slippage, which occur where load is transferred from one element of the composite member to another.

Comparative designs are shown below for a floor beam and a roof joist to demonstrate possible reductions in structure weight and cost savings through use of composite design. Additional information on structural economy is presented in this chapter.

```
FLOOR:  DEAD LOAD = 80 PSF    ROOF: D.L. = 20 PSF
        LIVE LOAD = 100 PSF         L.L. = 30 PSF
        TOTAL = 180 PSF             TOTAL = 50 PSF
```

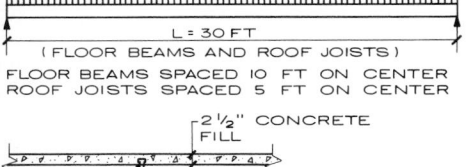

L = 30 FT
( FLOOR BEAMS AND ROOF JOISTS )
FLOOR BEAMS SPACED 10 FT ON CENTER
ROOF JOISTS SPACED 5 FT ON CENTER

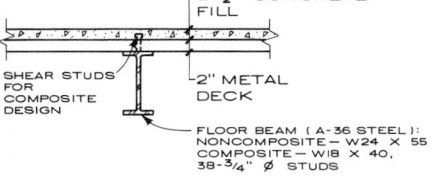

2 1/2" CONCRETE FILL
SHEAR STUDS FOR COMPOSITE DESIGN
2" METAL DECK
FLOOR BEAM ( A-36 STEEL): NONCOMPOSITE—W24 X 55 COMPOSITE—W18 X 40, 38-3/4" Ø STUDS

ROOF JOIST:
STEEL BEAM ( A-36 )—W14 X 22 #/FT
STEEL JOIST—24J6 (9.9 #/FT) OR 20H5 (8.4 #/FT)
WOOD-STEEL JOIST—26" DEEP(5#/FT) DOUBLE 1.5" X 2.3"
( SEE DET. 4B ABOVE )  MICRO-LAM CHORDS, STEEL TUBE DIAGONALS - 1 1/2" TO 1" DIA.

**COMPARATIVE  DESIGN  EXAMPLE**

Walter D. Shapiro, P.E.; Tor, Shapiro & Associates; New York, New York

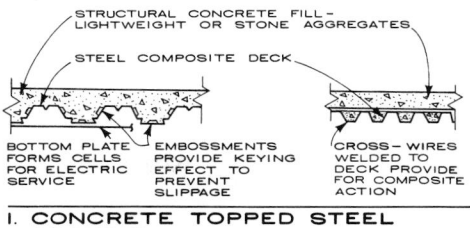

STRUCTURAL CONCRETE FILL—LIGHTWEIGHT OR STONE AGGREGATES
STEEL COMPOSITE DECK
BOTTOM PLATE FORMS CELLS FOR ELECTRIC SERVICE
EMBOSSMENTS PROVIDE KEYING EFFECT TO PREVENT SLIPPAGE
CROSS-WIRES WELDED TO DECK PROVIDE FOR COMPOSITE ACTION

**1. CONCRETE TOPPED STEEL DECKING**

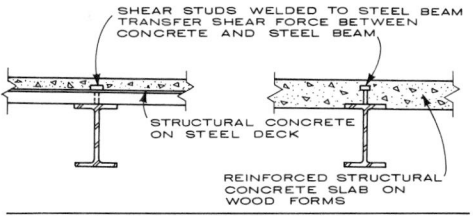

SHEAR STUDS WELDED TO STEEL BEAM TRANSFER SHEAR FORCE BETWEEN CONCRETE AND STEEL BEAM
STRUCTURAL CONCRETE ON STEEL DECK
REINFORCED STRUCTURAL CONCRETE SLAB ON WOOD FORMS

**2. STEEL BEAM WITH STUD IN CONCRETE SLAB**

WOOD TOP AND BOTTOM CHORDS AND COMPRESSION DIAGONALS

STEEL TENSION MEMBERS

**HOWE TRUSS**

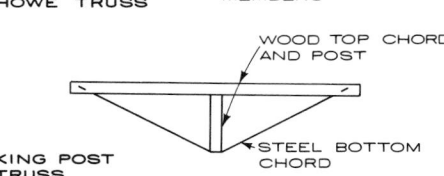

WOOD TOP CHORD AND POST
STEEL BOTTOM CHORD

**KING POST TRUSS**

**5. WOOD AND STEEL TRUSSES**

TOP AND BOTTOM FLANGE PLATES: YIELD STRESS = 50,000 PSI OR MORE
FILLET WELDS TO TRANSFER SHEAR FORCES BETWEEN FLANGES AND WEB
WEB: YIELD STRESS = 36,000 PSI

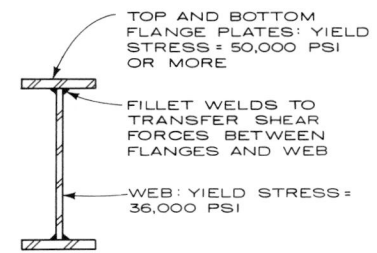

**6A. HYBRID GIRDERS** (USING DIFFERENT STRENGTH STEELS)

CUT LINE FOR CASTELLATED BEAM

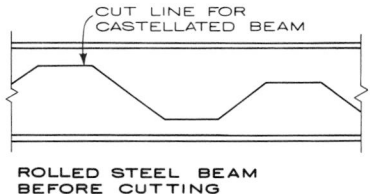

ROLLED STEEL BEAM BEFORE CUTTING

TOP CHORD CUT FROM STEEL BEAM: YIELD STRESS = 36,000 PSI
WELD

FINISHED BEAM
BOTTOM CHORD CUT FROM DIFFERENT WEIGHT STEEL BEAM: YIELD STRESS SAME AS OR HIGHER THAN THAT FOR TOP CHORD

**6 CASTELLATED BEAMS**

CONCRETE FILL BONDS TO STEEL PIPE OR TUBE
CONCRETE ENCASEMENT BONDS TO STRUCTURAL STEEL COLUMN AND REBARS FOR COMPOSITE ACTION

**3. STEEL AND CONCRETE COLUMNS**

STRESS RATED WOOD TOP CHORD ( DECK CAN BE NAILED DIRECTLY TO TOP CHORD)
WEB MEMBERS OF STEEL TUBING
STRESS RATED WOOD BOTTOM CHORD
PIN CONNECTIONS TRANSFER LOADS BETWEEN WEB MEMBERS AND CHORDS

**4A. WOOD AND STEEL JOIST**

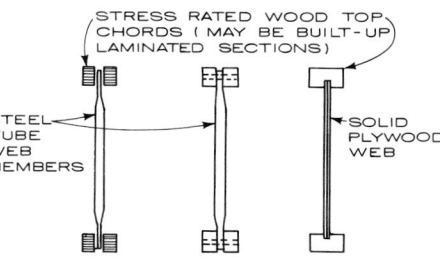

STRESS RATED WOOD TOP CHORDS ( MAY BE BUILT-UP LAMINATED SECTIONS)
STEEL TUBE WEB MEMBERS
SOLID PLYWOOD WEB

**4. TYPICAL COMPOSITE JOISTS**

STRUCTURAL CONCRETE SLAB ACTS AS COMPRESSION FLANGE OF COMPOSITE MEMBER
SHEAR STUDS
HEAVY TEE: YIELD STRESS SAME AS TOP TEE OR HIGHER
LIGHT TEE: YIELD STRESS = 36,000 PSI
WELD TO TRANSFER SHEAR FORCES BETWEEN TEES

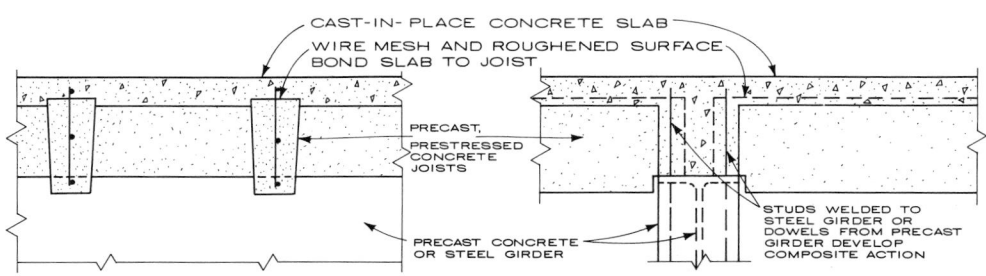

CAST-IN-PLACE CONCRETE SLAB
WIRE MESH AND ROUGHENED SURFACE BOND SLAB TO JOIST
PRECAST, PRESTRESSED CONCRETE JOISTS
PRECAST CONCRETE OR STEEL GIRDER
STUDS WELDED TO STEEL GIRDER OR DOWELS FROM PRECAST GIRDER DEVELOP COMPOSITE ACTION

**7. REINFORCED CONCRETE SLAB AND PRECAST JOIST**

NOTE: ALL WOOD SIZES ARE NOMINAL

| ROUGH CARPENTRY | PENNY | INCHES | TYPE OF NAIL |
|---|---|---|---|
| 1 in. thick stock | 8 | 2½ | Common nails |
| 2 in. thick stock | 16 to 20 | 3½ to 4 | Common nails |
| 3 in. thick stock | 40 to 60 | 5 to 6 | Common nails or spikes |
| Concrete forms | variable | | Common or double-headed nails |
| Framing for general use and for large members | 10, 16, 20, 60 | 3, 3½, 4, 6 | Common nails or spikes depending on size of members |
| Toenailing studs, joists, etc. | 10 | 3 | Common nails |
| Spiking usual plates and sills | 16 | 3½ | Common nails |
| Toenailing rafters and plates | 10 | 3 | Common nails |
| Sheathing—roof and wall | 8 | 2½ | Common nails, may be zinc coated |
| Finished rough flooring | 8 | 2½ | Common nails, may be zinc coated |
| **FINISH CARPENTRY** | | | |
| Moldings—Sizes as required | | 7/8 to 1¼ | Molding nails (brads) |
| Carpet strips, shoes | 8 | 2½ | Finishing or casing nails |
| Door window stops and members ¼ in. to ½ in. thick | 4 | 1½ | Finishing or casing nails |
| Ceiling, trim, casing, picture mold, base balusters and members ½ in. to ¾ in. thick | 6 | 2 | Finishing or casing nails |
| Ceiling, trim, casing, base, jambs, trim and members ¾ in. to 1 in. thick | 8 | 2½ | Finishing or casing nails |
| Doors and window trim, boards and other members 1 in. to 1¼ in. thick | 10 | 3 | Finishing or casing nails |
| Drop siding, 1 in. thick | 7 or 9 | 2¼ or 2¾ | Siding nails (7d), Casing nails (9d) |
| Bevel siding, ½ in. thick | 6 or 8 | 2 or 2½ | Finishing nails (6d), Siding nails (8d) |
| **WOOD FLOORING** | | | |
| See wood flooring page for nail sizes and types recommended | | | Cut steel, wire, finishing, wire casing, flooring brads, parquet and flooring nails |
| **LATHING** | | | |
| Wood lath | 3 | 1¼ | Blued lath nail |
| Gypsum lath | 3 | 1¼ | Blued common |
| Fiber lath | | | |
| Metal lath, interior | | 1 | Blued lath nails, staples or offset head nails |
| Metal lath, exterior | 3 | 1¼ | Self-furring nails (double heads). Staple or cement coated |
| **SHEATHING OR SIDING** | | | |
| Fiber board ½ in. and 25/32 in. | | 1½ to 2 | Galvanized roofing nail with 7/16 in. diameter head |
| Gypsum board ½ in. | | 1¾ | Galvanized roofing nail 7/16 in. diameter head |
| Plywood 5/16 in. and 3/8 in. thick | 6 | 2 | Common nails |
| Plywood ½ in. and 5/8 in. thick | 8 | 2½ | Common nails |
| **ROOFING & SHEET METAL** | | | |
| Aluminum roofing | 1 | 1¾ to 2½ | Aluminum nail, neoprene washer optional |
| Asphalt shingles | | | Galvanized large head roofing |
| Copper cleats and flashing to wood | | | Copper wire or cut slating nails |
| Copper cleats and flashing to prevent joints | | | Barbed copper nails |
| Clay tile | 4 to 6 | 1½ to 2 | Copper nails |
| Prepared felt roofing | | 1 to 1¼ | Zinc roofing nails or large head roofing nails (barbed preferred). Heads may be reinforced |
| Shingles, wood usual size<br>for heavy butts | 3 to 4<br>4 to 8 | 1¼ to 1½<br>1½ to 2½ | Zinc-coated, copper wire shingle, copper clad shingle, cut iron or cut steel |
| Slate | Use nails 1 in. larger than thickness of slate | | Copper wire slating nail (large head). In dry climates zinc-coated or copper-clad nails may be used. |
| Tin, zinc roofing | | | Zinc-coated nails (roofing or slating) |
| Monel roofing | | | Monel nail |
| Nailing to sheet metal | | | Self-tapping screws, helical drive screws |
| **TO CONCRETE OR CEMENT MORTAR** | | | |
| See following pages of fastening devices | | | Concrete or cement nails (hardened), helical drive nails or drive bolts |

NOTES

1. Thread sizes and lengths vary.
2. Hammer and powder-driven studs are intended for connections to concrete and steel. Refer to manufacturers' literature for specific applications.
3. Refer to building code provisions covering the use of powder-actuated devices. Some jurisdictions do not approve their use.
4. See ANSI A10.3 "Safety Requirements for Powder Actuated Fastening Systems" and OSHA regulations.

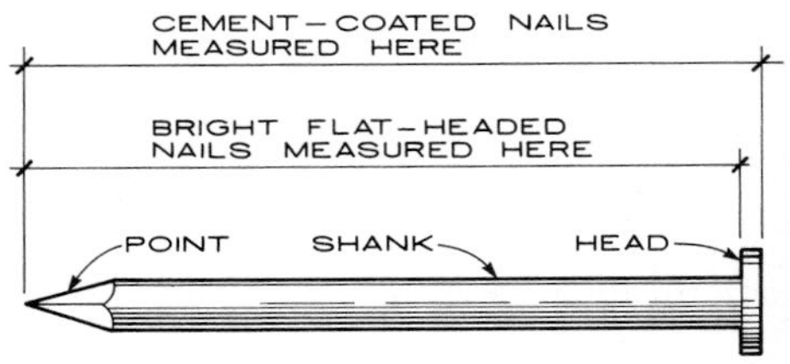

COMMON NAIL (STEEL WIRE)

**COMMON NAIL (STEEL WIRE)**

| LENGTH | PENNY | GAUGE | DIAM. OF HEAD (IN.) | NAILS/ LB. | SAFE WORKING RESISTANCE TO LATERAL SHEAR LB. |
|---|---|---|---|---|---|
| 1 | 2 | 15 | 11/64 | 847 | |
| 1¼ | 3 | 14 | 13/64 | 543 | |
| 1½ | 4 | 12½ | ¼ | 296 | |
| 1¾ | 5 | 12½ | ¼ | 254 | |
| 2 | 6 | 11½ | 17/64 | 167 | 48 |
| 2¼ | 7 | 11½ | 17/64 | 150 | |
| 2½ | 8 | 10¼ | 9/32 | 101 | 64 |
| 2¾ | 9 | 10¼ | 9/32 | 92.1 | |
| 3 | 10 | 9 | 5/16 | 66 | 80 |
| 3¼ | 12 | 9 | 5/16 | 66.1 | 96 |
| 3½ | 16 | 8 | 11/32 | 47.4 | 128 |
| 4 | 20 | 6 | 13/32 | 29.7 | 160 |
| 4½ | 30 | 5 | 7/16 | 22.7 | |
| 5 | 40 | 4 | 15/32 | 17.3 | |
| 5½ | 50 | 3 | ½ | 13.5 | |
| 6 | 60 | 2 | 17/32 | 10.7 | |

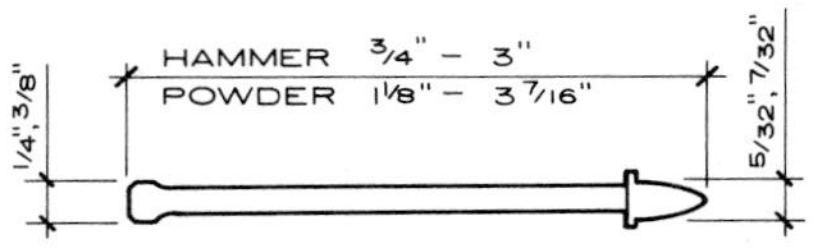

HAMMER–DRIVEN OR POWDER–DRIVEN PIN

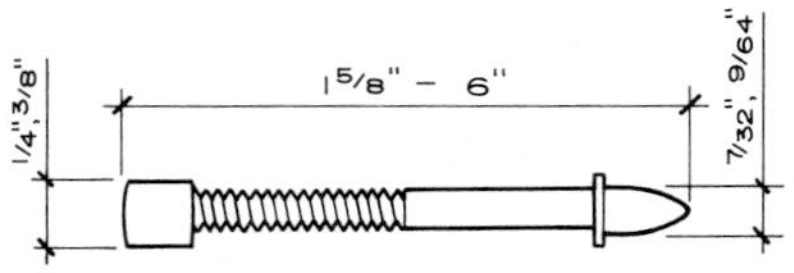

POWDER–DRIVEN UTILITY HEAD THREADED STUD

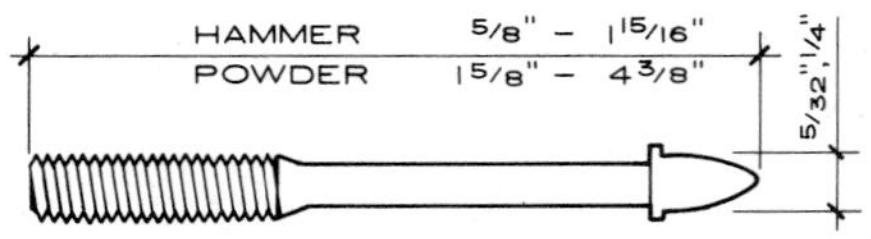

HAMMER–DRIVEN OR POWDER–DRIVEN HEADLESS THREADED STUD

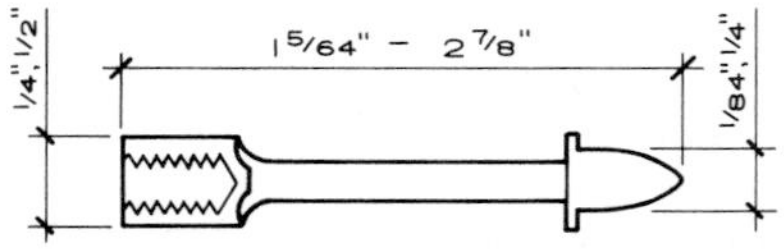

POWDER–DRIVEN INTERNALLY THREADED STUD

HAMMER– AND POWDER–DRIVEN FASTENERS

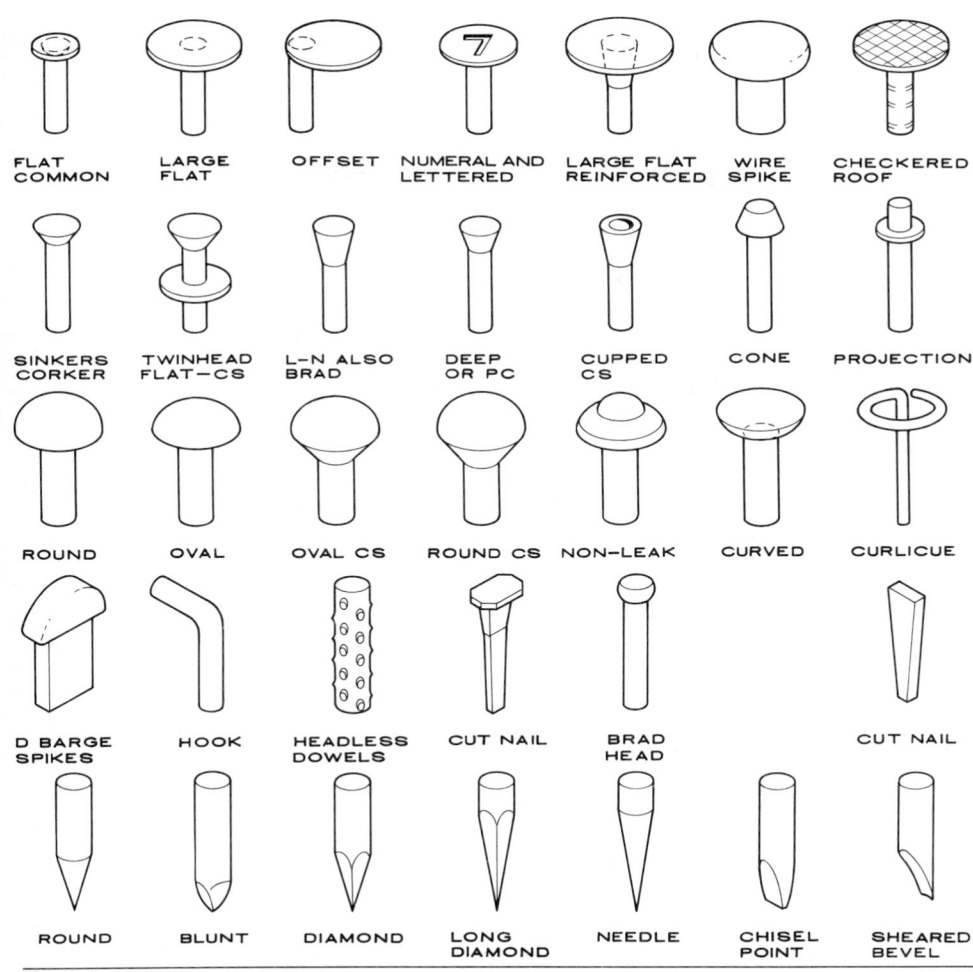

FLAT COMMON   LARGE FLAT   OFFSET   NUMERAL AND LETTERED   LARGE FLAT REINFORCED   WIRE SPIKE   CHECKERED ROOF

SINKERS CORKER   TWINHEAD FLAT—CS   L—N ALSO BRAD   DEEP OR PC   CUPPED CS   CONE   PROJECTION

ROUND   OVAL   OVAL CS   ROUND CS   NON-LEAK   CURVED   CURLICUE

D BARGE SPIKES   HOOK   HEADLESS DOWELS   CUT NAIL   BRAD HEAD   CUT NAIL

ROUND   BLUNT   DIAMOND   LONG DIAMOND   NEEDLE   CHISEL POINT   SHEARED BEVEL

## TYPES OF NAIL HEADS AND NAIL POINTS

### NOTES

1. Nail diameter, length, shape and surface affect holding power (withdrawal resistance and lateral resistance). See NFPA publications.

2. Materials: Zinc, brass, monel, copper, aluminum, iron or steel, stainless steel, copper bearing steel, muntz metal.

3. Coatings: Tin, copper, cement, brass plated, zinc, nickel, chrome, cadmium, etched acid, parkerized.

4. Forms: Smooth, barbed, helical, annular-ring.

5. Colors: Blue, bright, coppered, black (annealed).

6. Gauges shown are for steel wire (Washburn and Moen).

7. Abbreviations (for the following pages of nails only):

| | | |
|---|---|---|
| B = blunt | F = flat | O = oval |
| CS = countersunk | L = long | PC = pointing cone |
| D = diamond | N = narrow | R = round |

## FASTENER FINISHES AND COATINGS

| COATINGS OR FINISH | USED ON: | COMMENTS |
|---|---|---|
| Anodizing | Aluminum | Excellent corrosion protection |
| Chromate: black, clear, colored | Zinc and cadmium plated | Colors usually offer better protection than clear |
| Cadmiumplate | Most metals | |
| Copperplate | Most metals | Electroplated, fair protection |
| Copper, brass, bronze | Most metals | Indoor, decorative finishes |
| Lacquering | All metals | Some specially designed for humid conditions |
| Lead-tin | Steel | Applied by hot-dip. Gives good lubrication to tapping screws. |
| Nickel, bright and dull | Most metals | Indoor; outdoor if at least .0005 in. thick |
| Phosphate rust preventative | Steel | Rustproofs steel. Oils increase corrosion resistance |
| Phosphate paint-base preparations | Steel, aluminum zinc plate | Chemical process for painting or lacquering |
| Colored phosphate coatings | Steel | Superior to regular phosphated or oiled surfaces |
| Rust preventatives | All metals | Usually applied to phosphate and black oxide finishes |
| Electroplated zinc or tin; electrogalvanized zinc; hot-dip zinc or tin | All metals | Zinc or Tin |
| Hot-dip aluminum | Steel | Maximum corrosion protection, withstands high temperatures |

Timothy B. McDonald; Washington, D.C.

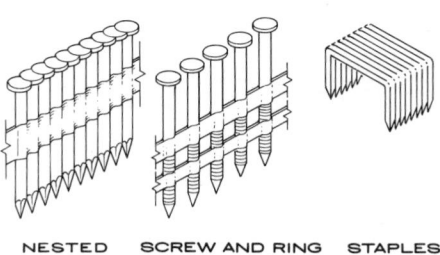

NESTED HEADED NAILS   SCREW AND RING SHANK NAILS   STAPLES

## STAPLES AND NAILS FOR PNEUMATIC FASTENERS
## ALLOWABLE LOADS FOR DESIGNED STRUCTURES

| FAS-TENER | WIRE DIAM-ETER | WIRE GAUGE | PENE-TRA-TION INTO MAIN MEM-BER | ALLOWABLE LOAD (LBS.) (6,7) | |
|---|---|---|---|---|---|
| | | | | LAT-ERAL (4,5) | WITH-DRAWAL |
| T-nail | .097 | 12½ | 1⅛ | 52 | 29 |
| T-nail | .113 | 11½ | 1¼ | 63 | 34 |
| T-nail | .131 | 10¼ | 1½ | 78 | 39 |
| T-nail | .148 | 9 | 1⅝ | 94 | 44 |
| staple | .0625 | 16 | 1 | 52 | 36 |
| staple | .072 | 15 | 1 | 64 | 42 |
| staple | .080 | 14 | 1 | 75 | 46 |
| staple | .0915 | 13 | 1 | 92 | 53 |
| staple | .1055 | 12 | 1⅛ | 113 | 62 |

### NOTES

1. Refer to Industrial Stapling and Nailing Technical Association, HUD-FHA Bulletin No. UM-25d (1973), for complete data.

2. Crown widths range from ³/₁₆ in. to 1 in. Leg lengths vary from ⁵/₃₂ in. to 3½ in. Gauge should be chosen for shear value needed.

3. Screw shank and ring shank nails have the same allowable loads as common nails.

4. Nested nails are manufactured with a crescent-shaped piece missing in the head.

5. For wood diaphragms resisting wind or seismic loading these values may be increased 30 percent in addition to the 33⅓ percent increase permitted for duration of load.

6. The tabulated allowable lateral values are for fasteners installed in Douglas Fir-Larch or Southern Pine.

7. Allowable values shall be adjusted for duration of load in accordance with standard engineering practices. Where metal side plates are used, lateral strength values may be increased 25 percent.

8. Withdrawal values are for fasteners inserted perpendicular to the grain in pounds per linear inch of penetration into the main member based on a specific gravity of approximately 0.545.

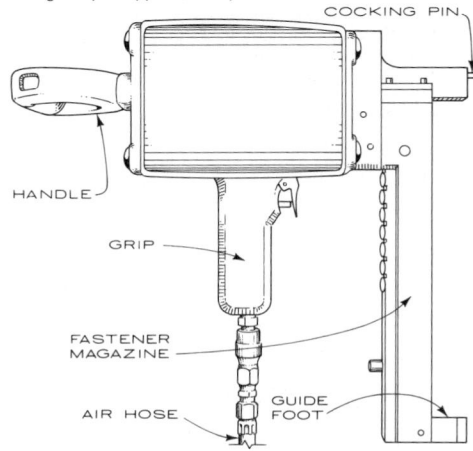

COCKING PIN

HANDLE

GRIP

FASTENER MAGAZINE

AIR HOSE   GUIDE FOOT

## PNEUMATIC NAILERS AND STAPLERS

Pneumatic nailers and staplers, connected to compressors or $CO_2$ bottles, are capable of attaching a variety of fasteners to concrete and steel as well as wood. Consult manufacturer for special features and interchangeability of fasteners.

| NAIL TYPE | SIZE | MATERIAL |
|---|---|---|
| BARBED NAILS (#14 GAUGE) | 1/4" TO 1 1/2" | CEMENT COATED, BRASS, STEEL |
| CASING NAILS (#14 GAUGE) | 2d TO 40d <br> 6d TO 10d | BRIGHT, CEMENT COATED <br> CUPPED HEADS AVAILABLE IN ALUMINUM |
| CEMENT NAILS ALSO CALLED CONCRETE NAILS AND HARDENED NAILS (ALSO FLAT HEAD CS, #5 TO #10 GAUGE) | 1/2" TO 3" | SMOOTH, BRIGHT <br> OIL QUENCHED |
| COMMON BRAD (CUP HEAD AVAILABLE, #15 TO #2 GAUGE) | 2d TO 60d | BRIGHT—MAY BE SECURED WITH CUPPED HEAD, CEMENT COATED—USUALLY MADE IN HEAVY GAUGES |
| CUT COMMON NAILS OR CUT COMMON SPIKE | 2d TO 60d <br> 20d TO 100d | STEEL OR IRON <br> PLAIN OR ZINC COATED |
| COMMON NAILS (SHINGLE NAILS) (GAUGE) | 2d TO 60d | COPPER-CLAD |
| COMMON BRASS WIRE NAILS (LIGHT GAUGE .095", HEAVY GAUGE .120") | LIGHT GAUGE 1/2" 1" TO 3 1/2" <br> HEAVY GAUGE 3/4"—6" | BRASS, ALUMINUM |
| COMMON NAILS (SHINGLE NAILS) (.109 ABOUT 12 GAUGE) | 5/8" TO 6" | COPPER WIRE, ALUMINUM |
| STANDARD CUT NAILS (NON-FERROUS) | 5/8" TO 6" | COPPER, MUNTZ METAL OR ZINC |
| DOUBLE HEADED (2" LONG, #11 1/2 GAUGE) | 1 3/4", 2", 2 1/4", 2 1/2", 2 3/4", 3", 3 1/2", 4", 4 1/2" | BRIGHT, CEMENT COATED, MADE IN SEVERAL DESIGNS |
| DOWEL PINS (CUPPED HEAD AVAILABLE, MADE IN 5 DIAMETERS) | 5/8" TO 2" | BARBED—CUPPED HEAD AVAILABLE |
| ESCUTCHEON PINS (MADE IN 3 GAUGES) | 1/4" TO 2" | BRIGHT STEEL, BRASS PLATED, BRASS, ALSO NICKEL, SILVER, COPPER, ALUMINUM |
| FENCE NAILS (6d—2", #10 GAUGE) | 5d TO 20d | SMOOTH; BRIGHT, CEMENT COATED (GAUGE HEAVIER THAN COMMON) |
| FINISHING NAIL, WIRE (#15 GAUGE) | 2d TO 20d | SMOOTH; CUPPED HEADS AVAILABLE (SMALLER GAUGE THAN USUAL COMMON BRAD) |
| FINISHING NAILS | STANDARD 3d TO 20d <br> FINE 6d TO 10d | CUT IRON AND STEEL |
| FINE NAILS (3d—1 1/8", #15 & #16 GAUGE) | 2d & 2d EX. FINE <br> 3d & 3d EX. FINE | BRIGHT—SMALLER GAUGE AND HEADS THAN COMMON NAILS |
| FLOORING NAILS (#14 GAUGE, ALSO WITH D. POINT) | 3d TO 20d <br> 6d TO 20d | BRIGHT AND CEMENT COATED (DIFFERENT GAUGE) CUPPED HEADS AVAILABLE |
| FLOORING BRAD (6d—2", #11 GAUGE, D OR BLUNT D) | 6d TO 20d | SMOOTH; BRIGHT AND CEMENT COATED CUPPED HEADS AVAILABLE |

5    **METAL FASTENING**

| NAIL TYPE | | SIZE | | MATERIAL |
|---|---|---|---|---|
| 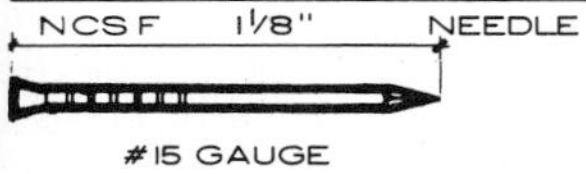 NCSF 1⅛" NEEDLE<br>#15 GAUGE | PARQUET FLOORING<br>NAIL OR BRAD | 1", 1⅛", 1¼" | | SMOOTH OR BARBED |
|  | FLOORING NAILS | 4d TO 10d | | IRON OR STEEL (CUT) |
| 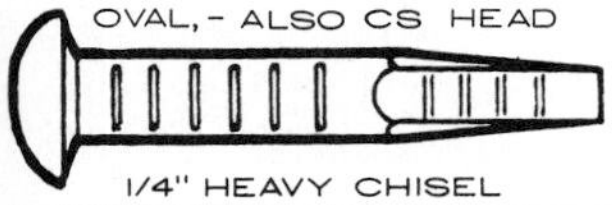 OVAL, - ALSO CS HEAD<br>1/4" HEAVY CHISEL | HINGE NAILS | HEAVY: 1/4"<br>TO 3/8" DIA.<br>LIGHT–3/16"<br>TO 1/4" DIA | 1½" TO<br>4" LONG | SMOOTH, BRIGHT OR ANNEALED |
| 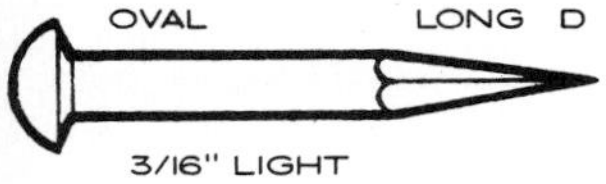 OVAL LONG D<br>3/16" LIGHT | HINGE NAILS | HEAVY-1/4"<br>DIA.<br>LIGHT -<br>3/16" DIA. | 1½" TO<br>3" ALSO<br>TO 4" | SMOOTH, BRIGHT OR ANNEALED |
| 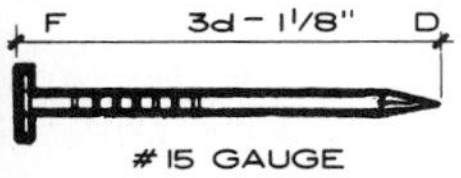 F 3d – 1⅛" D<br>#15 GAUGE | LATH NAILS<br>(WOOD) | 2d, 2d LIGHT, 3d,<br>3d LIGHT, 3d HEAVY<br>4d. | | BRIGHT (NOT RECOMMENDED), BLUED OR<br>CEMENT COATED |
| 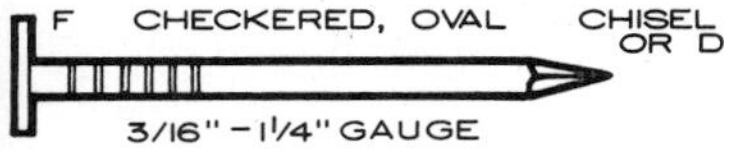 F CHECKERED, OVAL CHISEL<br>OR D<br>3/16" – 1¼" GAUGE | GUTTER SPIKES | 6" TO 10" | | STEEL, ZINC COATED |
| O R<br>#6½" GAUGE | HINGE NAILS | 1½" TO 3" | | STEEL, ZINC COATED |
|  HOOK<br>1⅛" #12 GAUGE | LATH NAILS<br>(METAL) | 1⅛" | | BRIGHT, BLUED, ZINC COATED, ANNEALED |
| 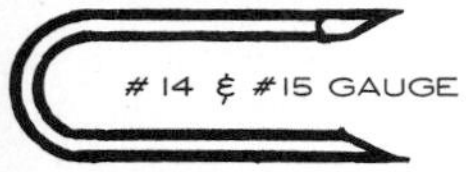 #14 & #15 GAUGE | LATH STAPLES | 1" TO 1½" | | BRIGHT, BLUED, ZINC COATED, ANNEALED |
|  OFFSET F D<br>#10 GAUGE | LATH OFFSET<br>HEAD NAILS<br>FOR SELF FURRING METAL<br>LATH | 1¼" TO 1¾" | | BRIGHT, ZINC COATED |
|  F<br>#7 - #9 GAUGE | MASONRY NAILS<br>USED FOR FURRING STRIPS<br>CLEATS, PLATES | 1/2" TO 4" | | HIGH CARBON STEEL, HEATED & TEMPERED |
|  NCSF NEEDLE<br>#14 GAUGE | MOLDING NAILS (BRADS) | 7/8" TO 1¼" | | SMOOTH, BRIGHT OR CEMENT COATED |
| 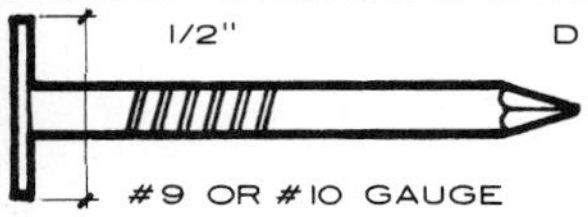 1/2" D<br>#9 OR #10 GAUGE | PLASTER-BOARD NAILS<br>USED ALSO FOR WALL-<br>BOARD<br>ROCK LATH (5/16" HEAD) | 1" TO 1¾"<br>1⅛" TO 1½" | | SMOOTH, BRIGHT OR CEMENT COATED, BLUED<br>ALUMINUM |
|  F D<br>#10 GAUGE | ROOFING NAILS<br>(STANDARD) | 3/4" TO 2" | | BRIGHT, CEMENT COATED, ZINC COATED<br>BARBED |
| 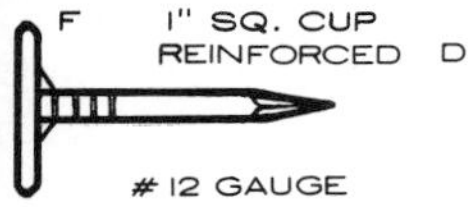 F 1" SQ. CUP<br>REINFORCED D<br>#12 GAUGE | ROOFING NAILS<br>FOR BUILT-UP ROOFING | 3/8" TO 2" | | STEEL, ZINC COATED |
| 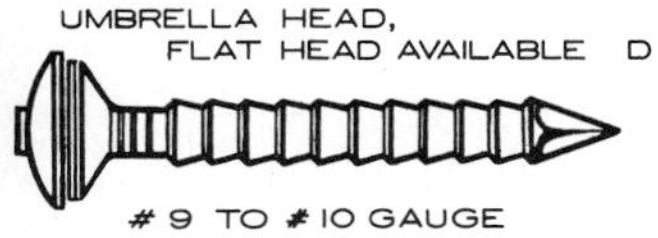 UMBRELLA HEAD,<br>FLAT HEAD AVAILABLE D<br>#9 TO #10 GAUGE | NEOPRENE WASHER<br>ROOFING NAILS | 1½" TO 2½" | | STEEL, ZINC COATED |
| 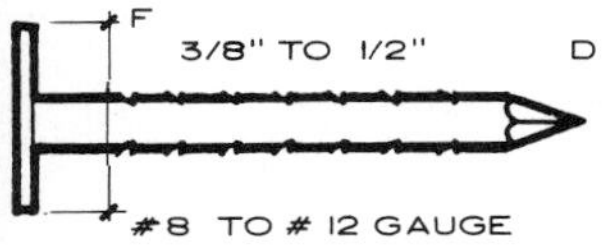 F 3/8" TO 1/2" D<br>#8 TO #12 GAUGE | ROOFING NAILS<br>LARGE HEAD | 3/4" TO 1¾"<br>ALSO 2"<br>3/4" TO 2½" | | BARBED, BRIGHT OR ZINC COATED<br>CHECKERED HEAD AVAILABLE<br>ALUMINUM (ETCHED) NEOPRENE WASHER OPTIONAL |

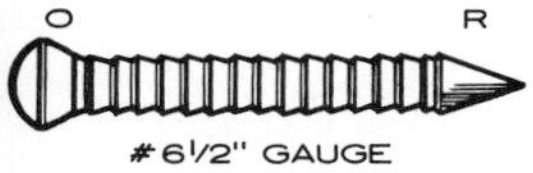

**METAL FASTENING** 5

| NAIL TYPE | SIZE | MATERIAL |
|---|---|---|
| 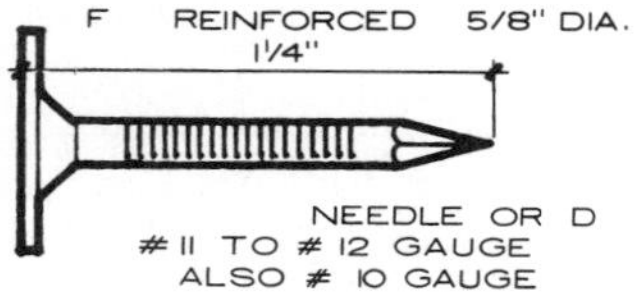 F    REINFORCED   5/8" DIA.<br>1¼"<br>ROOFING NAILS<br>LARGE HEAD<br>NEEDLE OR D<br># 11 TO # 12 GAUGE<br>ALSO # 10 GAUGE | 3/4" TO 1¼" | BRIGHT OR ZINC COATED |
| 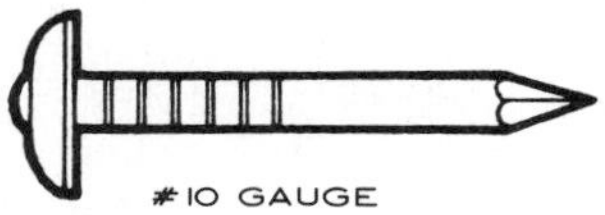 NON-LEAKING<br>ROOFING NAIL<br># 10 GAUGE | 1¾" TO 2" | ZINC COATED, ALSO WITH LEAD HEADS |
|  CUT SHEATHING NAILS | 3/4" TO 3" | COPPER OR MUNTZ METAL |
| 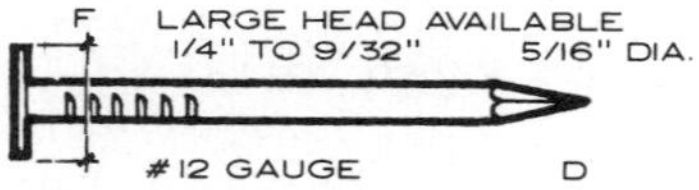 F   LARGE HEAD AVAILABLE<br>1/4" TO 9/32"   5/16" DIA.<br>SHINGLE NAILS<br># 12 GAUGE        D | 3d TO 6d<br>2d TO 6d | SMOOTH, BRIGHT, ZINC,<br>CEMENT COATED, LIGHT AND HEAVY<br>ALUMINUM |
|  CUT SHINGLE NAILS | 2d TO 6d | IRON OR STEEL (CUT)<br>PLAIN OR ZINC COATED |
| 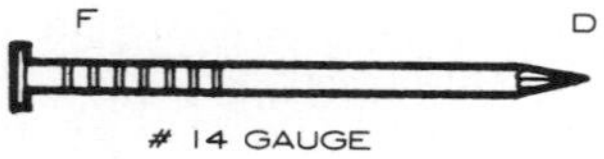 F                D<br>SIDING NAILS<br># 14 GAUGE | 2d TO 40d<br>6d TO 10d | SMOOTH, BRIGHT OR CEMENT COATED<br>SMALLER DIAMETER THAN COMMON NAILS<br>ALUMINUM |
|  F                    D<br>SIDING NAILS<br>USED FOR FENCES,<br>TANKS, GATES, ETC.<br># 11 GAUGE | 2½" TO 3" | STEEL ZINC COATED |
| F<br>5/16" TO 3/8"<br>SLATING NAILS<br>SEVERAL GAUGES | 3/8" HEAD \| 1"TO 2"<br>SMALL HEADS \| 1"TO 2"<br>COPPER WIRE \| 7/8"-1½" | ZINC COATED, BRIGHT, CEMENT COATED,<br>COPPER CLAD, COPPER |
| 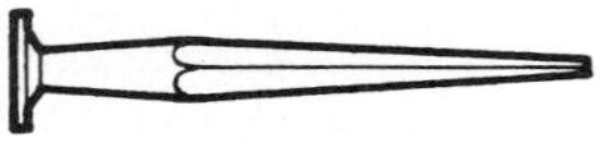 CUT SLATING NAILS,<br>NON-FERROUS | 1¼" TO 2" | COPPER, ZINC OR MUNTZ METAL |
| 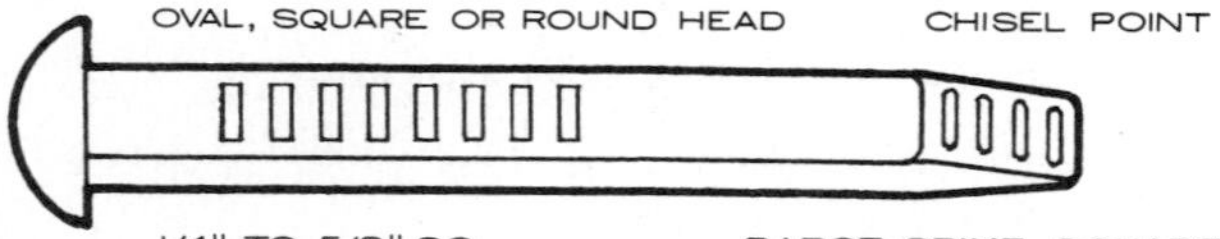 OVAL, SQUARE OR ROUND HEAD    CHISEL POINT<br>1/4" TO 5/8" SQ.    BARGE SPIKE, SQUARE | 3" TO 12"<br>ALSO 16" | PLAIN AND ZINC COATED<br>USED FOR HARDWOOD |
| 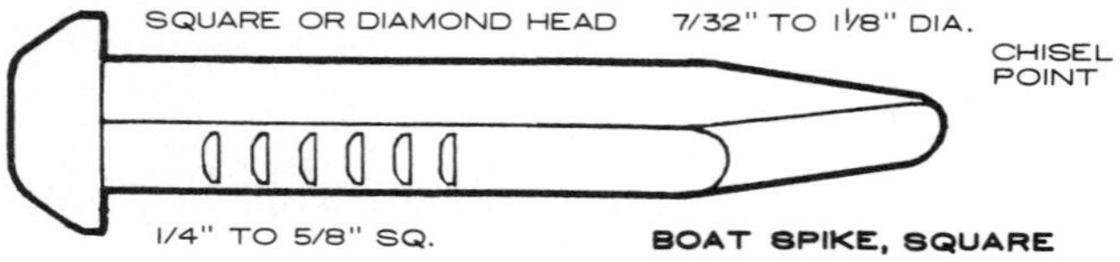 SQUARE OR DIAMOND HEAD    7/32" TO 1⅛" DIA.<br>CHISEL POINT<br>1/4" TO 5/8" SQ.    BOAT SPIKE, SQUARE | 3" TO 12" | PLAIN AND ZINC COATED<br>USED FOR HARD WOOD |
|  1" HEAD<br>ROOF DECK NAILS | 1" AND 1¾" | GALVANIZED – NAILS STEEL TUBE |
| 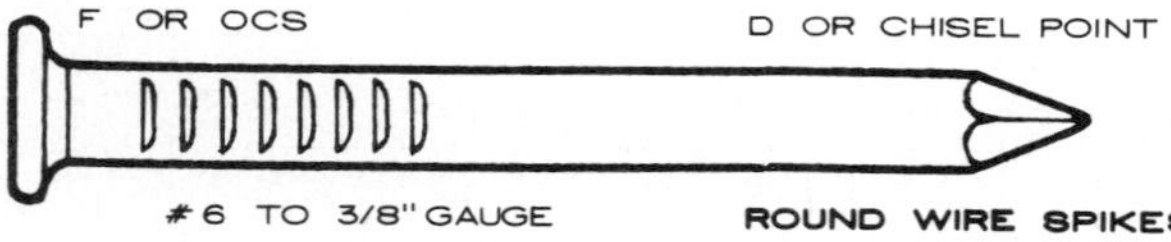 F OR OCS         D OR CHISEL POINT<br># 6 TO 3/8" GAUGE    ROUND WIRE SPIKES | 10d TO 60d<br>& 7" TO 12"<br>ALSO 16" | SMOOTH, BRIGHT OR ZINC COATED |

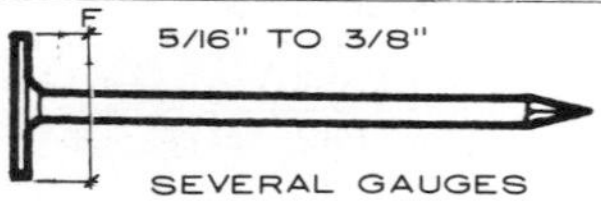

5   METAL FASTENING

## MACHINE BOLT ANCHORS AND SHIELDS (IN.)

| BOLT DIA. | THPS PER INCH | DECIMAL EQUIV. (IN.) | SINGLE EXPANDING ANCHOR (CAULKING) | | SINGLE EXPANDING ANCHOR (NONCAULKING) | | MULTIPLE EXPANDING ANCHOR (PLAIN STYLE) | | | MULTIPLE EXPANDING ANCHOR (THREADED STYLE) | | | DOUBLE ACTING SHIELD | |
|---|---|---|---|---|---|---|---|---|---|---|---|---|---|---|
| | | | A | L | A | L | A | L UNITS 2 | 3 | A | L UNITS 2 | 3 | A | L |
| 6 | 32 | .138 | 5/16 | 1/2 | | | | | | | | | | |
| 8 | 32 | .164 | 5/16 | 1/2 | | | | | | | | | | |
| 10 | 24 | .190 | 3/8 | 5/8 | | | | | | | | | | |
| 12 | 24 | .216 | 1/2 | 7/8 | | | | | | | | | | |
| 1/4 | 20 | .250 | 1/2 | 7/8 | 1/2 | 1 3/8 | 1/2" | 1 1/8 | | 1/2 | 1 | | 1/2 | 1 1/4 |
| 5/16 | 18 | .312 | 5/8 | 1 | 5/8 | 1 5/8 | | | | | | | 5/8 | 1 1/2 |
| 3/8 | 16 | .375 | 3/4 | 1 1/4 | 5/8 | 1 5/8 | 3/4 | 1 1/2 | | 3/4 | 1 1/2 | | 3/4 | 1 3/4 |
| 1/2 | 13 | .500 | 7/8 | 1 1/2 | 7/8 | 2 1/2 | 1 | 1 3/4 | 2 3/8 | 1 | 1 3/4 | 2 1/4 | 7/8 | 2 1/4 |
| 5/8 | 11 | .625 | 1 1/8 | 2 | 1 | 2 3/4 | 1 1/8 | * | 2 5/8 | 1 1/8 | * | 2 1/2 | 1 | 2 1/2 |
| 3/4 | 10 | .750 | 1 1/4 | 2 1/4 | 1 1/4 | 2 7/8 | 1 3/8 | * | 3 | 1 3/8 | * | 3 1/8 | 1 1/4 | 3 1/2 |
| 7/8 | 9 | .875 | | | | | 1 1/2 | * | 3 1/2 | 1 1/2 | * | 3 5/8 | 1 5/8 | 4" |
| 1 | 8 | 1.00 | | | | | 1 5/8 | * | 3 7/8 | 1 5/8 | * | 3 3/4 | 1 3/4 | 4 1/4 |

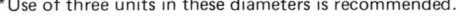

*Use of three units in these diameters is recommended.

NOTE
1. Extension sleeve for deep setting.
2. Expansion shields and anchors shown are representative of many types, some of which may be used in single or multiple units.
3. Many are threaded for use with the head of the screw outside, some with the head inside and some types require setting tools to install.
4. In light construction plastic expansion shields are used frequently.

### SELF-DRILLING EXPANSION ANCHOR (SNAP-OFF TYPE)

NOTE
1. Refer to manufacturers for size variations within the limits shown, and for different types of bolts.
2. The anchor is made of case hardened steel and drawn carburizing steel.

## HOLLOW WALL ANCHORS

| ANCHOR DIA. (IN.) | A | L | A | L |
|---|---|---|---|---|
| 1/8 | 5/16 | 1-2 9/16 | | XS-L |
| 3/16 | 7/16 | 2 1/4-3 1/2 | | |
| 1/4 | 1/2 | 2 1/4-3 1/2 | | |

## SHIELDS FOR LAG BOLTS AND WOOD SCREWS (IN.)

| LAG SCREW DIA. (IN.) | WOOD SCREW SIZES | DECIMAL EQUIV. (IN.) | LAG BOLT EXPANSION SHIELD A | L SHORT | L LONG | LEAD SHIELD FOR LAG BOLT OR WOOD SCREW A | L |
|---|---|---|---|---|---|---|---|
| | 6 | .138 | | | | 1/4 | 3/4-1 1/2 |
| | 8 | .164 | | | | 1/4 | 3/4-1 1/2 |
| | 10 | .190 | | | | 5/16 | 1-1 1/2 |
| | 12 | .216 | | | | 5/16 | 1-1 1/2 |
| 1/4 | 14 | .250 | 1/2 | 1 | 1 1/2 | 5/16 | 1-1 1/2 |
| | 16 | .268 | | | | 3/8 | 1 1/2 |
| | 18 | .294 | | | | 3/8 | 1 1/2 |
| 5/16 | 20 | .320 | 1/2 | 1 1/4 | 1 3/4 | 7/16 | 1 3/4 |
| 3/8 | 24 | .372 | 5/8 | 1 3/4 | 2 1/2 | 7/16 | 1 3/4 |
| 1/2 | | .500 | 3/4 | 2 | 3 | | |
| 5/8 | | .625 | 7/8 | 2 | 3 1/2 | | |
| 3/4 | | .750 | 1 | 2 | 3 1/2 | | |

## ONE PIECE ANCHORS (IN.)

| ANCHOR SIZE AND DRILL SIZE | DECIMAL EQUIV. (IN.) | WEDGE ANCHOR L | MIN. HOLE DEPTH D | STUD ANCHOR L | MIN. HOLE DEPTH D | SLEEVE ANCHOR L | MIN. HOLE DEPTH D | HEAD STYLE |
|---|---|---|---|---|---|---|---|---|
| 1/4 | .250 | 1 3/4-3 1/4 | 1 3/8 | 1 3/4-3 1/4 | 1 3/8 | 5/8-2 1/4 | 1/2-1 1/8 | Acorn nut |
| 5/16 | .320 | | | | | 1 1/2-2 1/2 | 1 1/8 | Hex nut |
| 3/8 | .375 | 2 1/4-5 | 1 3/4 | 2 1/4-6 | 1 5/8 | 1 7/8-3 | 1 1/2 | " |
| 1/2 | .500 | 2 3/4-7 | 2 1/8 | 2 3/4-5 1/4 | 1 7/8 | 2 1/4-4 | 1 7/8 | " |
| 5/8 | .625 | 3 1/2-8 1/2 | 2 5/8 | 3 3/8-7 | 2 3/8 | 2 1/4-6 | 2 | " |
| 3/4 | .750 | 4 1/4-10 | 3 1/4 | 4 1/4-8 1/2 | 2 7/8 | 2 1/2-8 | 2 1/4-5 1/2 | " |
| 7/8 | .875 | 6-10 | 3 3/4 | | | | | |
| 1 | 1.00 | 6-12 | 4 1/2 | | | | | |
| 1 1/4 | 1.25 | 9-12 | 5 1/2 | | | | | |

Sleeve anchors available in acorn nut, hex nut, flat head, round head, Phillips round head, and tie wire head styles.

## MACHINE SCREW AND STOVE BOLT (INS.)

| STOVE BOLT DIAM. | MACHINE SCREW DIAM. | ROUND HEAD | FLAT HEAD | FILLISTER HEAD | OVAL HEAD | OVEN HEAD |
|---|---|---|---|---|---|---|
| | 2 | 1/8-7/8 | | 1/8-7/8 | | |
| | 3 | 1/8-7/8 | | 1/8-7/8 | | |
| | 4 | 1/8-1 1/2 | 40 N.C. | 1/8-1 1/2 | | |
| | 4 | 1/8-1 1/2 | 36 N.C. | 1/8-1 1/2 | | 1/8-3/4 |
| 1/8 | 5 | 1/8-2 | | 1/8-2 | | 3/8-2 |
| | 6 | 1/8-2 | | 1/8-2 | | 1/8-1 |
| 5/32 | 8 | 3/16-3 | | 3/16-3 | | 3/16-2 |
| 3/16 | 10 | 3/16-6 | | 3/16-3 | | 1/4-6 |
| | 12 | 1/4-3 | | 1/4-3 | | |
| 1/4 | 1/4 | 5/16-6 | | 5/16-3 | | 3/8-6 |
| 5/16 | 5/16 | 3/8-6 | | 3/8-3 | | 3/4-6 |
| 3/8 | 3/8 | 1/2-5 | | 1/2-3 | | 3/4-5 |
| 1/2 | 1/2 | 1-4 | | | | |

Length intervals = 1/16 in. increments up to 1/2 in., 1/8 in. increments from 5/8 in. to 1 1/4 in., 1/4 in. increments from 1 1/2 in. to 3 in., 1/2 in. increments from 3 1/2 in. to 6 in.
NOTE: N.C. = Course thread

## SCREW AND BOLT LENGTHS (INS.)

| DIAMETER (INS.) | CAP SCREWS | | | | BOLTS | | |
|---|---|---|---|---|---|---|---|
| | BUTTON HEAD | FLAT HEAD | HEXAGON HEAD | FILLISTER HEAD | MACHINE BOLT | CARRIAGE BOLT | LAG BOLT |
| 1/4 | 1/2-2 1/4 | 1/2-3 1/2 | 3/4-3 | | 1/2-8 | 3/4-8 | 1-6 |
| 5/16 | 1/2-2 3/4 | 1/2-3 1/2 | 3/4-3 3/4 | | 1/2-8 | 3/4-8 | 1-10 |
| 3/8 | 5/8-3 | 1/2-4 | 3/4-3 1/2 | | 3/4-12 | 3/4-12 | 1-12 |
| 7/16 | 3/4-3 | 3/4-4 | 3/4-3 3/4 | | 3/4-12 | 1-12 | 1-12 |
| 1/2 | 3/4-4 | 3/4-4 1/2 | 3/4-4 | | 3/4-24 | 1-20 | 1-12 |
| 9/16 | 1-4 | 1-4 1/2 | 1-4 | | 1-30 | 1-20 | |
| 5/8 | 1-4 | 1-5 | 1 1/4-4 1/2 | | 1-30 | 1-20 | 1 1/2-16 |
| 3/4 | 1-4 | 1 1/4-5 | 1 1/2-4 1/2 | | 1-30 | 1-20 | 1 1/2-16 |
| 7/8 | | | 2-6 | 1 3/4-5 | 1 1/2-30 | | 2-16 |
| 1 | | | 2-6 | 2-5 | 1 1/2-30 | | 2-16 |

Length intervals = 1/8 in. increments up to 1 in., 1/4 in. increments from 1 1/4 in. to 4 in., 1/2 in. increments from 4 1/2 in. to 6 in.

Length intervals = 1/4 in. increments up to 6 in., 1/2 in. increments from 6 1/2 in. to 12 in., 1 in. increments over 12 in.

Length intervals = 1/2 in. increments up to 8 in., 1 in. increments over 8 in.

ROUND   FLAT   OVAL   PAN   FILLISTER   TRUSS   HEX   WASHER

**HEAD TYPES**

 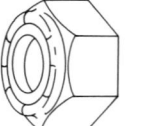 

SQUARE   HEX   LOCK

CASTELLATED   CAP

WING

Self-locking nuts have a pin that acts as a ratchet, sliding down the thread as the bolt is tightened, to prevent loosening from shock and vibration.

**NUTS**

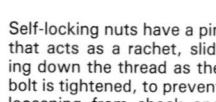

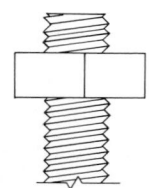

Interference body bolts are driven into reamed or drilled holes to create a joint in full bearing.

**INTERFERENCE BODY BOLTS**

Fiberglass nuts and bolts are noncorrosive and nonconductive. Bolts are available in 3/8 in., 1/2 in., 5/8 in., 3/4 in., and 1 in. standard diameters.

**FIBERGLASS NUTS AND BOLTS**

 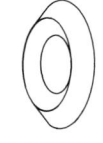

FLAT   LOCK (SPRING)   COUNTERSUNK

TOOTHLOCK (INTERNAL)   (EXTERNAL)

LOAD INDICATOR

**WASHERS**

The bolt's clamping force causes protrusions on the washer to flatten partially, closing the gap between the washer and the bolt head. Measurement of the gap indicates whether the bolt has been tightened adequately.

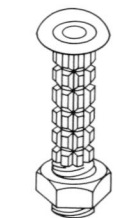

High tension, stainless steel helical inserts are held in place by spring-like pressure, and they are used to salvage damaged threads. They also eliminate thread failure due to stress conditions.

**HELICAL INSERTS**

**NOTES**
1. Bent bolts are specialty items made to order.
2. D = bolt diameter; C = inside opening width; T = thread length; L = inside length of bolt; A = inside depth.

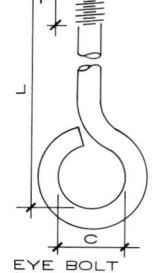 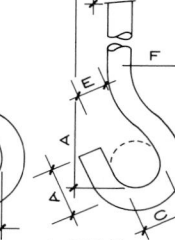

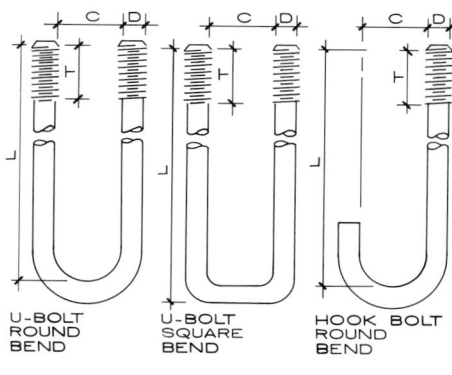

EYE BOLT (CLOSED)   EYE BOLT (OPEN)   J-BOLT

U-BOLT ROUND BEND   U-BOLT SQUARE BEND   HOOK BOLT ROUND BEND

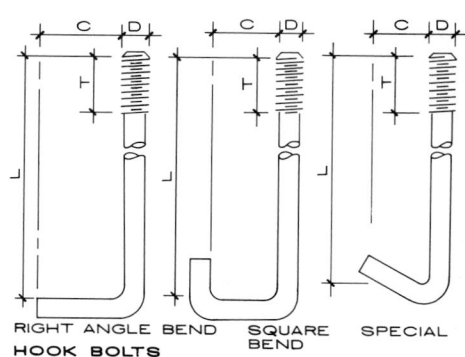

RIGHT ANGLE BEND   SQUARE BEND   SPECIAL

**HOOK BOLTS**

Timothy B. McDonald; Washington, D.C.

 **METAL FASTENING**

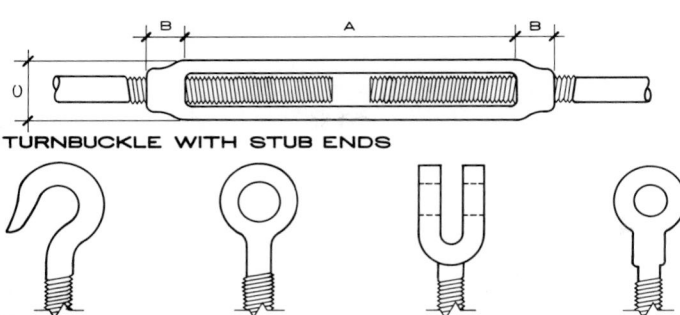

## TURNBUCKLE WITH STUB ENDS

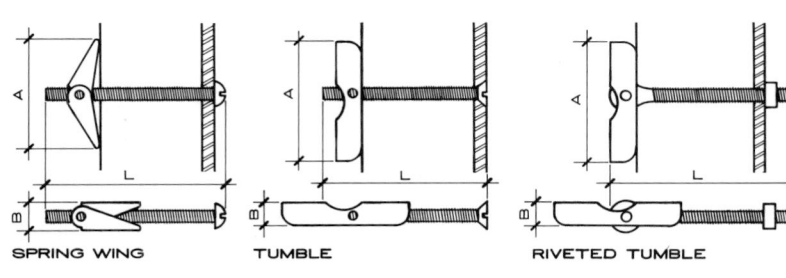

SPRING WING    TUMBLE    RIVETED TUMBLE

HOOK    EYE    CLEVIS

### TURNBUCKLES (IN INCHES)

| DIAMETER | 1/4 | 5/16 | 3/8 | 1/2 | 5/8 | 3/4 | 7/8 | 1 |
|---|---|---|---|---|---|---|---|---|
| DECI. EQUIV. | .250 | .313 | .375 | .500 | .625 | .750 | .875 | 1.00 |
| | 4 | 4 1/2 | 6" | 6" | 6" | 6" | 6" | 6" |
| A | | | | 9" | 9" | 9" | | |
| | | | | 12" | 12" | 12" | 12" | 12" |
| B | 7/16 | 1/2 | 9/16 | 3/4 | 29/32 | 1 1/16 | 1 7/32 | 1 3/8 |
| C | 3/4 | 7/8 | 31/32 | 1 7/32 | 1 1/2 | 1 23/32 | 1 7/8 | 2 1/32 |

DIAMETERS OVER 1" AVAILABLE, NOT ALWAYS STOCKED.

### TOGGLE BOLTS (IN INCHES)

| DIAMETER | | 1/8 | 5/32 | 3/16 | 1/4 | 5/16 | 3/8 | 1/2 |
|---|---|---|---|---|---|---|---|---|
| DECIMAL EQUIV. | | .138 | .164 | .190 | .250 | .313 | .375 | .500 |
| SPRING WING | A | 1.438 | 1.875 | 1.875 | 2.063 | 2.750 | 2.875 | 4.625 |
| | B | .375 | .500 | .500 | .688 | .875 | 1.000 | 1.250 |
| | L | 2 - 4 | 2 1/2 - 4 | 2 - 6 | 2 1/2 - 6 | 3 - 6 | 3 - 6 | 4 - 6 |
| TUMBLE | A | 1.250 | 2.000 | 2.000 | 2.250 | 2.750 | 2.750 | |
| | B | .375 | .500 | .500 | .688 | .875 | .875 | |
| | L | 2 - 4 | 2 1/2 - 4 | 3 - 6 | 3 - 6 | 3 - 6 | 3 - 6 | |
| RIVETED TUMBLE | A | | 2.000 | 2.000 | 2.250 | 2.750 | 2.750 | 3.375 |
| | B | | .375 | .375 | .500 | .625 | .688 | .875 |
| | L | | | 2 1/2 - 4 | 3 - 6 | 3 - 6 | 3 - 6 | 3 - 6 |

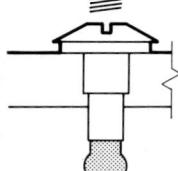 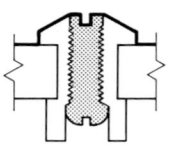 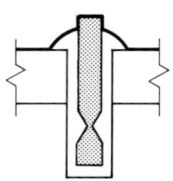 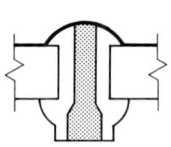 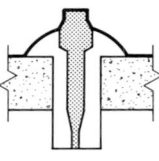 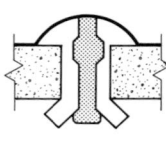 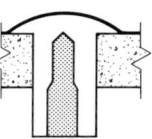 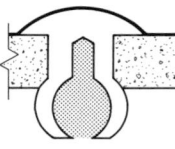

THREADED        PULL MANDREL        DRIVE PIN        CHEMICALLY EXPANDED

**BLIND RIVETS** FOR USE IN A JOINT THAT IS ACCESSIBLE FROM ONLY ONE SIDE

 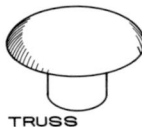 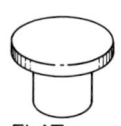  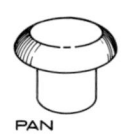

ROUND    TRUSS    FLAT    COUNTERSUNK    PAN

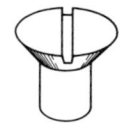 

SLOTTED    OVAL HEAD / ROUND HEAD

## RIVETS
STANDARD RIVETS AVAILABLE WITH SOLID, TUBULAR AND SPLIT SHANKS OF STEEL, BRASS, COPPER, ALUMINUM, MONEL METAL AND STAINLESS STEEL; IN DIAMETERS OF 1/8" TO 7/16" AND LENGTHS OF 3/16" TO 4 IN.

 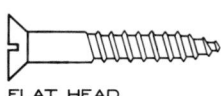

FLAT HEAD

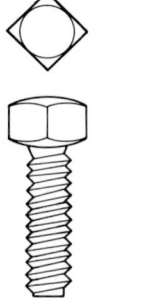

Self-drilling fasteners: used to attach metal to metal, wood, and concrete. Consult manufacturer for sizes and drilling capabilities.

### SHEET METAL GIMLET POINT

Sheet metal gimlet point: hardened, self-tapping. Used in 28 gauge to 6 gauge sheet metal; aluminum, plastic, slate, etc. Usual head types.

PHILLIPS

### WOOD SCREWS (IN IN.)

| DIA. | DECI. EQUIV. | LENGTH |
|---|---|---|
| 0 | .060 | 1/4 - 3/8 |
| 1 | .073 | 1/4 - 1/2 |
| 2 | .086 | 1/4 - 3/4 |
| 3 | .099 | 1/4 - 1 |
| 4 | .112 | 1/4 - 1 1/2 |
| 5 | .125 | 3/8 - 1 1/2 |
| 6 | .138 | 3/8 - 2 1/2 |
| 7 | .151 | 3/8 - 2 1/2 |
| 8 | .164 | 3/8 - 3 |
| 9 | .177 | 1/2 - 3 |
| 10 | .190 | 1/2 - 3 1/2 |
| 11 | .203 | 5/8 - 3 1/2 |
| 12 | .216 | 5/8 - 4 |
| 14 | .242 | 3/4 - 5 |
| 16 | .268 | 1 - 5 |
| 18 | .294 | 1 1/4 - 5 |
| 20 | .320 | 1 1/2 - 5 |
| 24 | .372 | 3 - 5 |

FREARSON

## SELF-DRILLING FASTENERS

   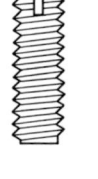   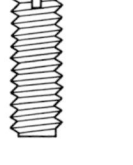 

### SHEET METAL BLUNT POINT

Sheet metal blunt point: hardened, self-tapping. Used in 28 to 18 gauge sheet metal. Made in sizes 4 to 14 in usual head types.

### THREAD CUTTING- CUTTING SLOT

Thread cutting, cutting slot: hardened. Used in metals up to 1/4 in. thick in sizes 4 in. to 5/16 in. in usual head types.

SQUARE HEAD    SLOTTED    HEX SOCKET

Set Screws: headless with socket or slotted top; made in sizes 4 in. to 1/2 in., and in lengths 1/2 in. to 5 in. Square head sizes 1/4 in. to 1 in., and lengths 1/2 in. to 5 in.

## SET SCREWS

## SHEET METAL & THREADING SCREWS

## DRIVE TYPES

Timothy B. McDonald; Washington, D.C.

## MAXIMUM ALLOWABLE FORM LOAD (KIPS) FOR BEAMS LATERALLY SUPPORTED—ASTM A-36 STEEL*

| LENGTH (FT) | DEPTH† WEIGHT | w6 9 | 12 | 16 | w8 10 | 12 | 15 | 18 | 21 | 24 | 28 | 31 | w10 12 | 15 | 17 | 19 | 22 | 26 | 30 | 33 | w12 14 | 16 | 19 | 22 | 26 | 30 | 35 | M14 40 | w14 18 | 22 | 26 |
|---|---|---|---|---|---|---|---|---|---|---|---|---|---|---|---|---|---|---|---|---|---|---|---|---|---|---|---|---|---|---|---|
| 6 | | 15 | 20 | 27 | 21 | 27 | 32 | 41 | 49 | 56 | 65 | 73 | 29 | 37 | 43 | 50 | 62 | 74 | 86 | 93 | 40 | 46 | 57 | 68 | 89 | 103 | 122 | 138 | 56 | 77 | 94 |
| 8 | | 11 | 15 | 20 | 16 | 20 | 24 | 30 | 36 | 42 | 49 | 55 | 22 | 28 | 32 | 38 | 46 | 56 | 65 | 70 | 30 | 34 | 43 | 51 | 67 | 77 | 91 | 104 | 42 | 58 | 71 |
| 10 | | 9 | 12 | 16 | 13 | 16 | 19 | 24 | 29 | 33 | 39 | 44 | 17 | 22 | 26 | 30 | 37 | 45 | 52 | 56 | 24 | 27 | 34 | 41 | 53 | 62 | 73 | 83 | 34 | 46 | 57 |
| 12 | | 7 | 10 | 14 | 10 | 13 | 16 | 20 | 24 | 28 | 32 | 37 | 15 | 18 | 22 | 25 | 31 | 37 | 43 | 47 | 20 | 23 | 28 | 34 | 45 | 52 | 61 | 69 | 28 | 39 | 47 |
| 14 | | | | | 9 | 11 | 14 | 17 | 21 | 24 | 28 | 31 | 12 | 16 | 19 | 22 | 27 | 32 | 37 | 40 | 17 | 20 | 24 | 29 | 38 | 44 | 52 | 59 | 24 | 33 | 40 |
| 16 | | | | | 8 | 10 | 12 | 15 | 18 | 21 | 24 | 28 | 11 | 14 | 16 | 19 | 23 | 28 | 32 | 35 | 15 | 17 | 21 | 25 | 33 | 39 | 46 | 52 | 21 | 29 | 35 |
| 18 | | | | | | | | | | | | | 10 | 12 | 14 | 17 | 21 | 25 | 29 | 31 | 13 | 15 | 19 | 23 | 30 | 34 | 41 | 46 | 19 | 26 | 31 |
| 20 | | | | | | | | | | | | | 9 | 11 | 13 | 15 | 19 | 22 | 26 | 28 | 12 | 14 | 17 | 20 | 27 | 31 | 37 | 42 | 17 | 23 | 28 |
| 22 | | | | | | | | | | | | | | | | | | | | | 11 | 12 | 16 | 18 | 24 | 28 | 33 | 38 | 15 | 21 | 26 |
| 24 | | | | | | | | | | | | | | | | | | | | | 10 | 11 | 14 | 17 | 22 | 26 | 30 | 35 | 14 | 19 | 24 |

NOTE: Verify lateral support with structural engineering consultant.

*For capacity of beams that are not shown see "AISC Manual of Steel Construction."
†Depth = steel designation (in.); weight = lb/ft; Kip = 1000 lb.

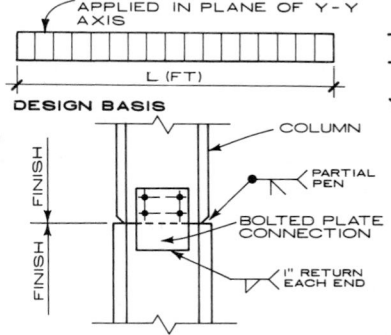

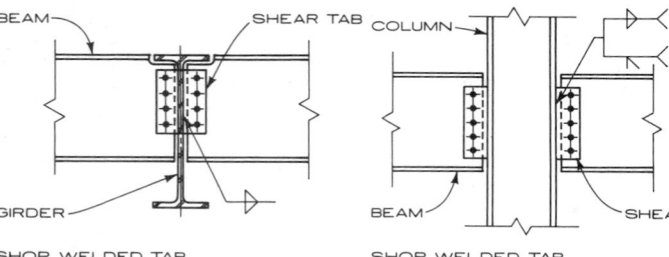

| SHEAR CONNECTION BEAM TO GIRDER | NONMOMENT CONNECTION BEAM TO COLUMN FLANGE | NONMOMENT CONNECTION BEAM TO COLUMN WEB | COLUMN SPLICE FLANGE AND WEB |
|---|---|---|---|
| SHOP WELDED TAB FIELD HIGH STRENGTH BOLTED | SHOP WELDED TAB FIELD H.S. BOLTED | SHOP WELD TAB TO COLUMN WEB AND PLATES FIELD H.S. BOLTED | WEB-FIELD H.S. BOLTED FLANGE-PARTIAL PENETRATION |

## MAXIMUM ALLOWABLE CONCENTRIC LOAD (KIPS) FOR COLUMNS ASTM A-36 STEEL (W SHAPES AND PIPE) A-46 STEEL (TUBING)

| DESIGNATION | * | 6 | 7 | 8 | 9 | 10 | 11 | 12 | 13 | 14 | 15 | 16 | 17 | 18 | 19 | 20 | 22 | 24 |
|---|---|---|---|---|---|---|---|---|---|---|---|---|---|---|---|---|---|---|
| W4 | 13 | 62 | 57 | 52 | 46 | 39 | 33 | 28 | 24 | 20 | 18 | 16 | | | | | | |
| W6 | 15 | 81 | 78 | 75 | 71 | 67 | 62 | 58 | 53 | 48 | 43 | 38 | 33 | 30 | 27 | 24 | 20 | 17 |
| | 20 | 109 | 105 | 100 | 95 | 90 | 85 | 79 | 73 | 67 | 60 | 54 | 47 | 42 | 38 | 34 | 28 | 24 |
| | 25 | 136 | 131 | 126 | 120 | 114 | 107 | 100 | 93 | 85 | 77 | 69 | 61 | 54 | 49 | 44 | 36 | 31 |
| W8 | 24 | 133 | 129 | 124 | 118 | 113 | 107 | 101 | 95 | 88 | 81 | 74 | 66 | 59 | 53 | 48 | 39 | 33 |
| | 28 | 155 | 150 | 144 | 138 | 132 | 125 | 118 | 111 | 103 | 95 | 87 | 78 | 69 | 62 | 56 | 46 | 39 |
| | 31 | 178 | 174 | 170 | 165 | 160 | 154 | 149 | 143 | 137 | 131 | 124 | 117 | 110 | 103 | 95 | 80 | 67 |
| pipe 3" 3.5" OD | 0.216 | 38 | 36 | 34 | 31 | 28 | 25 | 22 | 19 | 16 | 14 | 12 | 11 | 10 | 9 | | | |
| | 0.300 | 52 | 48 | 45 | 41 | 37 | 33 | 28 | 24 | 21 | 18 | 16 | 14 | 12 | 11 | | | |
| | 0.600 | 91 | 84 | 77 | 69 | 60 | 51 | 43 | 37 | 32 | 28 | 24 | 22 | | | | | |
| pipe 3½" 4" OD | 0.226 | 48 | 46 | 44 | 41 | 38 | 35 | 32 | 29 | 25 | 22 | 19 | 17 | 15 | 14 | 12 | 10 | |
| | 0.318 | 66 | 63 | 59 | 55 | 51 | 47 | 43 | 38 | 33 | 29 | 25 | 23 | 20 | 18 | 16 | | |
| pipe 4" 4½" OD | 0.237 | 59 | 57 | 54 | 52 | 49 | 46 | 43 | 40 | 36 | 33 | 29 | 26 | 23 | 21 | 19 | 15 | 13 |
| | 0.337 | 81 | 78 | 75 | 71 | 67 | 63 | 59 | 54 | 49 | 44 | 39 | 35 | 31 | 28 | 25 | 21 | 17 |
| | 0.674 | 147 | 140 | 133 | 126 | 118 | 109 | 100 | 91 | 81 | 70 | 62 | 55 | 49 | 44 | 40 | 33 | |
| pipe 5" 5.563" OD | 0.258 | 83 | 81 | 78 | 76 | 73 | 71 | 68 | 65 | 61 | 58 | 55 | 51 | 47 | 43 | 39 | 32 | 27 |
| | 0.375 | 118 | 114 | 111 | 107 | 103 | 99 | 95 | 91 | 86 | 81 | 76 | 70 | 65 | 59 | 54 | 44 | 37 |
| | 0.750 | 216 | 209 | 202 | 195 | 187 | 178 | 170 | 160 | 151 | 141 | 130 | 119 | 108 | 97 | 87 | 72 | 61 |
| pipe 6" 6.625" OD | 0.280 | 110 | 108 | 106 | 103 | 101 | 98 | 95 | 92 | 89 | 86 | 82 | 79 | 75 | 71 | 67 | 59 | 51 |
| | 0.432 | 166 | 162 | 159 | 155 | 151 | 146 | 142 | 137 | 132 | 127 | 122 | 117 | 111 | 105 | 99 | 86 | 73 |
| | 0.864 | 306 | 299 | 292 | 284 | 275 | 266 | 257 | 247 | 237 | 227 | 216 | 205 | 193 | 181 | 168 | 142 | 119 |
| TS 4 x 4 | 0.250 | 83 | 79 | 75 | 70 | 65 | 60 | 55 | 49 | 43 | 38 | 33 | 29 | 26 | 24 | 21 | 18 | 15 |
| TS 5 x 5 | 0.250 | 111 | 108 | 104 | 100 | 96 | 92 | 87 | 82 | 77 | 72 | 66 | 60 | 54 | 49 | 44 | 36 | 31 |
| TS 6 x 6 | 0.250 | 140 | 137 | 133 | 130 | 126 | 122 | 117 | 113 | 108 | 104 | 99 | 94 | 88 | 83 | 77 | 65 | 55 |
| TS 5 x 3 | 0.250 | 76 | 70 | 64 | 58 | 51 | 43 | 36 | 31 | 27 | 23 | 20 | 18 | 16 | 15 | | | |
| TS 6 x 4 | 0.250 | 107 | 103 | 98 | 92 | 87 | 81 | 75 | 68 | 61 | 54 | 48 | 42 | 38 | 34 | 30 | 25 | 21 |
| TS 8 x 4 | 0.250 | 132 | 126 | 120 | 114 | 108 | 101 | 94 | 86 | 79 | 70 | 62 | 55 | 49 | 40 | 33 | | |

NOTE: For additional columns and actual dimensions of tubing see "AISC Manual of Steel Construction."

*Weight per foot for w columns. Wall thickness for tubing. KIP = 1000 lb; K = effective length factor (verify with structural engineering consultant).

All data on this page derived from "AISC Manual of Steel Construction 8th edition."

H. Thompson, P.E.; Thompson & Czark; Hempstead, Long Island, New York

**STRUCTURAL METAL FRAMING**

## W SHAPES—DIMENSIONS FOR DETAILING

| DESIGNATION | DEPTH d (IN.) | FLANGE WIDTH b_f (IN.) | FLANGE THICKNESS t_f (IN.) | WEB THICKNESS t_w (IN.) |
|---|---|---|---|---|
| W36 x 300 | 36 3/4 | 16 5/8 | 1 11/16 | 15/16 |
| x 280 | 36 1/2 | 16 5/8 | 1 9/16 | 7/8 |
| x 260 | 36 1/4 | 16 1/2 | 1 7/16 | 13/16 |
| x 245 | 36 1/8 | 16 1/2 | 1 3/8 | 13/16 |
| x 230 | 35 7/8 | 16 1/2 | 1 1/4 | 3/4 |
| W36 x 210 | 36 3/4 | 12 1/8 | 1 3/8 | 13/16 |
| x 194 | 36 1/2 | 12 1/8 | 1 1/4 | 3/4 |
| x 182 | 36 3/8 | 12 1/8 | 1 3/16 | 3/4 |
| x 170 | 36 1/8 | 12 | 1 1/8 | 11/16 |
| x 160 | 36 | 12 | 1 | 5/8 |
| x 150 | 35 7/8 | 12 | 15/16 | 5/8 |
| x 135 | 35 1/2 | 12 | 13/16 | 5/8 |
| W33 x 241 | 34 1/8 | 15 7/8 | 1 3/8 | 13/16 |
| x 221 | 33 7/8 | 15 3/4 | 1 1/4 | 3/4 |
| x 201 | 33 5/8 | 15 3/4 | 1 1/8 | 11/16 |
| W33 x 152 | 33 1/2 | 11 5/8 | 1 1/16 | 5/8 |
| x 141 | 33 1/4 | 11 1/2 | 15/16 | 5/8 |
| x 130 | 33 1/8 | 11 1/2 | 7/8 | 9/16 |
| x 118 | 32 7/8 | 11 1/2 | 3/4 | 9/16 |
| W30 x 211 | 31 | 15 1/8 | 1 5/16 | 3/4 |
| x 191 | 30 5/8 | 15 | 1 3/16 | 11/16 |
| x 173 | 30 1/2 | 15 | 1 1/16 | 5/8 |
| W30 x 132 | 30 1/8 | 10 1/2 | 1 | 5/8 |
| x 124 | 30 1/8 | 10 1/2 | 15/16 | 9/16 |
| x 116 | 30 | 10 1/2 | 7/8 | 9/16 |
| x 108 | 29 7/8 | 10 1/2 | 3/4 | 9/16 |
| x 99 | 29 5/8 | 10 1/2 | 11/16 | 1/2 |
| W27 x 178 | 27 3/4 | 14 1/8 | 1 3/16 | 3/4 |
| x 161 | 27 5/8 | 14 | 1 1/16 | 11/16 |
| x 146 | 27 3/8 | 14 | 1 | 5/8 |
| W27 x 114 | 27 1/4 | 10 1/8 | 15/16 | 9/16 |
| x 102 | 27 1/8 | 10 | 13/16 | 1/2 |
| x 94 | 26 7/8 | 10 | 3/4 | 1/2 |
| x 84 | 26 3/4 | 10 | 5/8 | 7/16 |
| W24 x 162 | 25 | 13 | 1 1/4 | 11/16 |
| x 146 | 24 3/4 | 12 7/8 | 1 1/16 | 5/8 |
| x 131 | 24 1/2 | 12 7/8 | 15/16 | 5/8 |
| x 117 | 24 1/4 | 12 3/4 | 7/8 | 9/16 |
| x 104 | 24 | 12 3/4 | 3/4 | 1/2 |
| W24 x 94 | 24 1/4 | 9 1/8 | 7/8 | 1/2 |
| x 84 | 24 1/8 | 9 | 3/4 | 1/2 |
| x 76 | 23 7/8 | 9 | 11/16 | 7/16 |
| x 68 | 23 3/4 | 9 | 9/16 | 7/16 |
| W24 x 62 | 23 3/4 | 7 | 9/16 | 7/16 |
| x 55 | 23 5/8 | 7 | 1/2 | 3/8 |
| W21 x 147 | 22 | 12 1/2 | 1 1/8 | 3/4 |
| x 132 | 21 7/8 | 12 1/2 | 1 1/16 | 5/8 |
| x 122 | 21 5/8 | 12 3/8 | 15/16 | 5/8 |
| x 111 | 21 1/2 | 12 3/8 | 7/8 | 9/16 |
| x 101 | 21 3/8 | 12 1/4 | 13/16 | 1/2 |
| W21 x 93 | 21 5/8 | 8 3/8 | 15/16 | 9/16 |
| x 83 | 21 3/8 | 8 3/8 | 13/16 | 1/2 |
| x 73 | 21 1/4 | 8 1/4 | 3/4 | 7/16 |
| x 68 | 21 1/8 | 8 1/4 | 11/16 | 7/16 |
| x 62 | 21 | 8 1/4 | 5/8 | 3/8 |
| W21 x 57 | 21 | 6 1/2 | 5/8 | 3/8 |
| x 50 | 20 7/8 | 6 1/2 | 9/16 | 3/8 |
| x 44 | 20 5/8 | 6 1/2 | 7/16 | 3/8 |
| W18 x 119 | 19 | 11 1/4 | 1 1/16 | 5/8 |
| x 106 | 18 3/4 | 11 1/4 | 15/16 | 9/16 |
| x 97 | 18 5/8 | 11 1/8 | 7/8 | 9/16 |
| x 86 | 18 3/8 | 11 1/8 | 3/4 | 1/2 |
| x 76 | 18 1/4 | 11 | 11/16 | 7/16 |
| W18 x 71 | 18 1/2 | 7 5/8 | 13/16 | 1/2 |
| x 65 | 18 3/8 | 7 5/8 | 3/4 | 7/16 |
| x 60 | 18 1/4 | 7 1/2 | 11/16 | 7/16 |
| x 55 | 18 1/8 | 7 1/2 | 5/8 | 3/8 |
| x 50 | 18 | 7 1/2 | 9/16 | 3/8 |
| W18 x 46 | 18 | 6 | 5/8 | 3/8 |
| x 40 | 17 7/8 | 6 | 1/2 | 5/16 |
| x 35 | 17 3/4 | 6 | 7/16 | 5/16 |
| W16 x 100 | 17 | 10 3/8 | 1 | 9/16 |
| x 89 | 16 3/4 | 10 3/8 | 7/8 | 1/2 |
| x 77 | 16 1/2 | 10 1/4 | 3/4 | 7/16 |
| x 67 | 16 3/8 | 10 1/4 | 11/16 | 3/8 |
| W16 x 57 | 16 3/8 | 7 1/8 | 11/16 | 7/16 |
| x 50 | 16 1/4 | 7 1/8 | 5/8 | 3/8 |
| x 45 | 16 1/8 | 7 | 9/16 | 3/8 |
| x 40 | 16 | 7 | 1/2 | 5/16 |
| x 36 | 15 7/8 | 7 | 7/16 | 5/16 |
| W16 x 31 | 15 7/8 | 5 1/2 | 7/16 | 1/4 |
| x 26 | 15 3/4 | 5 1/2 | 3/8 | 1/4 |
| W14 x 730 | 22 3/8 | 17 7/8 | 4 15/16 | 3 1/16 |
| x 665 | 21 5/8 | 17 7/8 | 4 1/2 | 2 13/16 |
| x 605 | 20 7/8 | 17 3/8 | 4 3/16 | 2 5/8 |
| x 550 | 20 1/4 | 17 1/4 | 3 13/16 | 2 3/8 |
| x 500 | 19 5/8 | 17 | 3 1/2 | 2 3/16 |
| x 455 | 19 | 16 7/8 | 3 3/16 | 2 |
| W14 x 426 | 18 5/8 | 16 3/4 | 3 1/16 | 1 7/8 |
| x 398 | 18 1/4 | 16 5/8 | 2 7/8 | 1 3/4 |
| x 370 | 17 7/8 | 16 1/2 | 2 11/16 | 1 5/8 |
| x 342 | 17 1/2 | 16 3/8 | 2 1/2 | 1 9/16 |
| x 311 | 17 1/8 | 16 1/4 | 2 1/4 | 1 7/16 |
| x 283 | 16 3/4 | 16 1/8 | 2 1/16 | 1 5/16 |
| x 257 | 16 3/8 | 16 | 1 7/8 | 1 3/16 |
| x 233 | 16 | 15 7/8 | 1 3/4 | 1 1/16 |
| x 211 | 15 3/4 | 15 3/4 | 1 9/16 | 1 |
| x 193 | 15 1/2 | 15 3/4 | 1 7/16 | 7/8 |
| x 176 | 15 1/4 | 15 5/8 | 1 5/16 | 13/16 |
| x 159 | 15 | 15 5/8 | 1 3/16 | 3/4 |
| x 145 | 14 3/4 | 15 1/2 | 1 1/16 | 11/16 |
| W14 x 132 | 14 5/8 | 14 3/4 | 1 | 5/8 |
| x 120 | 14 1/2 | 14 5/8 | 15/16 | 9/16 |
| x 109 | 14 3/8 | 14 5/8 | 7/8 | 1/2 |
| x 99 | 14 1/8 | 14 5/8 | 3/4 | 1/2 |
| x 90 | 14 | 14 1/2 | 11/16 | 7/16 |
| W14 x 82 | 14 1/4 | 10 1/8 | 7/8 | 1/2 |
| x 74 | 14 1/4 | 10 1/8 | 13/16 | 1/2 |
| x 68 | 14 | 10 | 3/4 | 7/16 |
| x 61 | 13 7/8 | 10 | 5/8 | 3/8 |
| W14 x 53 | 13 7/8 | 8 | 11/16 | 3/8 |
| x 48 | 13 3/4 | 8 | 5/8 | 5/16 |
| x 43 | 13 5/8 | 8 | 1/2 | 5/16 |
| W14 x 38 | 14 1/8 | 6 3/4 | 1/2 | 5/16 |
| x 34 | 14 | 6 3/4 | 7/16 | 5/16 |
| x 30 | 13 7/8 | 6 3/4 | 3/8 | 1/4 |
| W14 x 26 | 13 7/8 | 5 | 7/16 | 1/4 |
| x 22 | 13 3/4 | 5 | 5/16 | 1/4 |
| W12 x 336 | 16 7/8 | 13 3/8 | 2 15/16 | 1 3/4 |
| x 305 | 16 3/8 | 13 1/4 | 2 11/16 | 1 5/8 |
| x 279 | 15 7/8 | 13 1/8 | 2 1/2 | 1 1/2 |
| x 252 | 15 3/8 | 13 | 2 1/4 | 1 3/8 |
| x 230 | 15 | 12 7/8 | 2 1/16 | 1 5/16 |
| x 210 | 14 3/4 | 12 3/4 | 1 7/8 | 1 3/16 |
| W12 x 190 | 14 3/8 | 12 5/8 | 1 3/4 | 1 1/16 |
| x 170 | 14 | 12 5/8 | 1 9/16 | 15/16 |
| x 152 | 13 3/4 | 12 1/2 | 1 3/8 | 7/8 |
| x 136 | 13 3/8 | 12 3/8 | 1 1/4 | 13/16 |
| x 120 | 13 1/8 | 12 3/8 | 1 1/8 | 11/16 |
| x 106 | 12 7/8 | 12 1/4 | 1 | 5/8 |
| x 96 | 12 3/4 | 12 1/8 | 7/8 | 9/16 |
| x 87 | 12 1/2 | 12 1/8 | 13/16 | 1/2 |
| x 79 | 12 3/8 | 12 1/8 | 3/4 | 1/2 |
| x 72 | 12 1/4 | 12 | 11/16 | 7/16 |
| x 65 | 12 1/8 | 12 | 5/8 | 3/8 |
| W12 x 58 | 12 1/4 | 10 | 5/8 | 3/8 |
| x 53 | 12 | 10 | 9/16 | 3/8 |
| W12 x 50 | 12 1/4 | 8 1/8 | 5/8 | 3/8 |
| x 45 | 12 | 8 | 9/16 | 3/8 |
| x 40 | 12 | 8 | 1/2 | 5/16 |
| W12 x 35 | 12 1/2 | 6 1/2 | 1/2 | 5/16 |
| x 30 | 12 3/8 | 6 1/2 | 7/16 | 1/4 |
| x 26 | 12 1/4 | 6 1/2 | 3/8 | 1/4 |
| W12 x 22 | 12 1/4 | 4 | 7/16 | 1/4 |
| x 19 | 12 1/8 | 4 | 3/8 | 1/4 |
| x 16 | 12 | 4 | 1/4 | 1/4 |
| x 14 | 11 7/8 | 4 | 3/16 | 1/4 |
| W10 x 112 | 11 3/8 | 10 3/8 | 1 1/4 | 3/4 |
| x 100 | 11 1/8 | 10 3/8 | 1 1/8 | 11/16 |
| x 88 | 10 7/8 | 10 1/4 | 1 | 5/8 |
| x 77 | 10 5/8 | 10 1/4 | 7/8 | 1/2 |
| x 68 | 10 3/8 | 10 1/8 | 3/4 | 1/2 |
| x 60 | 10 1/4 | 10 1/8 | 11/16 | 7/16 |
| x 54 | 10 1/8 | 10 | 5/8 | 3/8 |
| x 49 | 10 | 10 | 9/16 | 5/16 |
| W10 x 45 | 10 1/8 | 8 | 5/8 | 3/8 |
| x 39 | 9 7/8 | 8 | 1/2 | 5/16 |
| x 33 | 9 3/4 | 8 | 7/16 | 5/16 |
| W10 x 30 | 10 1/2 | 5 3/4 | 1/2 | 5/16 |
| x 26 | 10 3/8 | 5 3/4 | 7/16 | 1/4 |
| x 22 | 10 1/8 | 5 3/4 | 3/8 | 1/4 |
| W10 x 19 | 10 1/4 | 4 | 3/8 | 1/4 |
| x 17 | 10 1/8 | 4 | 5/16 | 1/4 |
| x 15 | 10 | 4 | 1/4 | 1/4 |
| x 12 | 9 7/8 | 4 | 3/16 | 3/16 |
| W8 x 67 | 9 | 8 1/4 | 15/16 | 9/16 |
| x 58 | 8 3/4 | 8 1/4 | 13/16 | 1/2 |
| x 48 | 8 1/2 | 8 1/8 | 11/16 | 3/8 |
| x 40 | 8 1/4 | 8 1/8 | 9/16 | 3/8 |
| x 35 | 8 1/8 | 8 | 1/2 | 5/16 |
| x 31 | 8 | 8 | 7/16 | 5/16 |
| W8 x 28 | 8 | 6 1/2 | 7/16 | 5/16 |
| x 24 | 7 7/8 | 6 1/2 | 3/8 | 1/4 |
| W8 x 21 | 8 1/4 | 5 1/4 | 3/8 | 1/4 |
| x 18 | 8 1/8 | 5 1/4 | 5/16 | 1/4 |
| W8 x 15 | 8 1/8 | 4 | 5/16 | 1/4 |
| x 13 | 8 | 4 | 1/4 | 1/4 |
| x 10 | 7 7/8 | 4 | 3/16 | 3/16 |
| W6 x 25 | 6 3/8 | 6 1/8 | 7/16 | 5/16 |
| x 20 | 6 1/4 | 6 | 3/8 | 1/4 |
| x 15 | 6 | 6 | 1/4 | 1/4 |
| W6 x 16 | 6 1/4 | 4 | 3/8 | 1/4 |
| x 12 | 6 | 4 | 1/4 | 1/4 |
| x 9 | 5 7/8 | 4 | 3/16 | 3/16 |
| W5 x 19 | 5 1/8 | 5 | 7/16 | 1/4 |
| x 16 | 5 | 5 | 3/8 | 1/4 |
| W4 x 13 | 4 1/8 | 4 | 3/8 | 1/4 |

## M SHAPES—DIMENSIONS FOR DETAILING

| DESIGNATION | DEPTH d (IN.) | FLANGE WIDTH b_f (IN.) | FLANGE THICKNESS t_f (IN.) | WEB THICKNESS t_w (IN.) |
|---|---|---|---|---|
| M 14 x 17.2 | 14 | 4 | 1/4 | 3/16 |
| M 12 x 11.8 | 12 | 3 1/8 | 1/4 | 3/16 |
| M 10 x 29.1 | 9 7/8 | 5 7/8 | 3/8 | 7/16 |
| x 22.9 | 9 7/8 | 5 3/4 | 3/8 | 1/4 |
| M 10 x 9 | 10 | 2 3/4 | 3/16 | 3/16 |
| M 8 x 37.7 | 8 1/8 | 8 | 1/2 | 3/8 |
| x 34.3 | 8 | 8 | 7/16 | 3/8 |
| x 32.6 | 8 | 8 | 7/16 | 5/16 |
| M 8 x 22.5 | 8 | 5 3/8 | 3/8 | 3/8 |
| x 18.5 | 8 | 5 1/4 | 3/8 | 1/4 |
| M 8 x 6.5 | 8 | 2 1/4 | 3/16 | 1/8 |
| M 7 x 5.5 | 7 | 2 1/8 | 3/16 | 1/8 |
| M 6 x 33.75 | 6 1/4 | 6 1/8 | 5/8 | 1/2 |
| x 22.5 | 6 | 6 | 3/8 | 3/8 |
| x 20 | 6 | 6 | 3/8 | 1/4 |
| M 6 x 4.4 | 6 | 1 7/8 | 3/16 | 1/8 |
| M 5 x 18.9 | 5 | 5 | 7/16 | 5/16 |
| M 4 x 16.3 | 4 1/4 | 4 | 1/2 | 5/16 |
| x 13.8 | 4 | 4 | 3/8 | 5/16 |
| x 13 | 4 | 4 | 3/8 | 1/4 |

## S SHAPES— DIMENSIONS FOR DETAILING

| DESIGNA-TION | DEPTH d (IN.) | FLANGE WIDTH $b_f$ (IN.) | FLANGE AVERAGE THICKNESS $t_f$ (IN.) | WEB THICKNESS $t_w$ (IN.) |
|---|---|---|---|---|
| S 24 x 120 | 24 | 8 | $1\frac{1}{8}$ | $\frac{13}{16}$ |
| x 105.9 | 24 | $7\frac{7}{8}$ | $1\frac{1}{8}$ | $\frac{5}{8}$ |
| S 24 x 100 | 24 | $7\frac{1}{4}$ | $\frac{7}{8}$ | $\frac{3}{4}$ |
| x 90 | 24 | $7\frac{1}{8}$ | $\frac{7}{8}$ | $\frac{5}{8}$ |
| x 79.9 | 24 | 7 | $\frac{7}{8}$ | $\frac{1}{2}$ |
| S 20 x 95 | 20 | $7\frac{1}{4}$ | $\frac{15}{16}$ | $\frac{13}{16}$ |
| x 85 | 20 | 7 | $\frac{15}{16}$ | $\frac{5}{8}$ |
| S 20 x 75 | 20 | $6\frac{3}{8}$ | $\frac{13}{16}$ | $\frac{5}{8}$ |
| x 65.4 | 20 | $6\frac{1}{4}$ | $\frac{13}{16}$ | $\frac{1}{2}$ |
| S 18 x 70 | 18 | $6\frac{1}{4}$ | $\frac{11}{16}$ | $\frac{11}{16}$ |
| x 54.7 | 18 | 6 | $\frac{11}{16}$ | $\frac{7}{16}$ |
| S 15 x 50 | 15 | $5\frac{5}{8}$ | $\frac{5}{8}$ | $\frac{9}{16}$ |
| x 42.9 | 15 | $5\frac{1}{2}$ | $\frac{5}{8}$ | $\frac{7}{16}$ |
| S 12 x 50 | 12 | $5\frac{1}{2}$ | $\frac{11}{16}$ | $\frac{11}{16}$ |
| x 40.8 | 12 | $5\frac{1}{4}$ | $\frac{11}{16}$ | $\frac{7}{16}$ |
| S 12 x 35 | 12 | $5\frac{1}{8}$ | $\frac{9}{16}$ | $\frac{7}{16}$ |
| x 31.8 | 12 | 5 | $\frac{9}{16}$ | $\frac{3}{8}$ |
| S 10 x 35 | 10 | 5 | $\frac{1}{2}$ | $\frac{5}{8}$ |
| x 25.4 | 10 | $4\frac{5}{8}$ | $\frac{1}{2}$ | $\frac{5}{16}$ |
| S 8 x 23 | 8 | $4\frac{1}{8}$ | $\frac{7}{16}$ | $\frac{7}{16}$ |
| x 18.4 | 8 | 4 | $\frac{7}{16}$ | $\frac{1}{4}$ |
| S 7 x 20 | 7 | $3\frac{7}{8}$ | $\frac{3}{8}$ | $\frac{7}{16}$ |
| x 15.3 | 7 | $3\frac{5}{8}$ | $\frac{3}{8}$ | $\frac{1}{4}$ |
| S 6 x 17.25 | 6 | $3\frac{5}{8}$ | $\frac{3}{8}$ | $\frac{7}{16}$ |
| x 12.5 | 6 | $3\frac{5}{8}$ | $\frac{3}{8}$ | $\frac{1}{4}$ |
| S 5 x 14.75 | 5 | $3\frac{1}{4}$ | $\frac{5}{16}$ | $\frac{1}{2}$ |
| x 10 | 5 | 3 | $\frac{5}{16}$ | $\frac{3}{16}$ |
| S 4 x 9.5 | 4 | $2\frac{3}{4}$ | $\frac{5}{16}$ | $\frac{5}{16}$ |
| x 7.7 | 4 | $2\frac{5}{8}$ | $\frac{5}{16}$ | $\frac{3}{16}$ |
| S 3 x 7.5 | 3 | $2\frac{1}{2}$ | $\frac{1}{4}$ | $\frac{3}{8}$ |
| x 5.7 | 3 | $2\frac{3}{8}$ | $\frac{1}{4}$ | $\frac{3}{16}$ |

## HP SHAPES— DIMENSIONS FOR DETAILING

| DESIGNA-TION | DEPTH d (IN.) | FLANGE WIDTH $b_f$ (IN.) | FLANGE AVERAGE THICKNESS $t_f$ (IN.) | WEB THICKNESS $t_w$ (IN.) |
|---|---|---|---|---|
| HP14 x 117 | $14\frac{1}{4}$ | $14\frac{7}{8}$ | $\frac{13}{16}$ | $\frac{13}{16}$ |
| x 102 | 14 | $14\frac{3}{4}$ | $\frac{11}{16}$ | $\frac{11}{16}$ |
| x 89 | $13\frac{7}{8}$ | $14\frac{3}{4}$ | $\frac{5}{8}$ | $\frac{5}{8}$ |
| x 73 | $13\frac{5}{8}$ | $14\frac{5}{8}$ | $\frac{1}{2}$ | $\frac{1}{2}$ |
| HP12 x 74 | $12\frac{1}{8}$ | $12\frac{1}{4}$ | $\frac{5}{8}$ | $\frac{5}{8}$ |
| x 53 | $11\frac{3}{4}$ | 12 | $\frac{7}{16}$ | $\frac{7}{16}$ |
| HP10 x 57 | 10 | $10\frac{1}{4}$ | $\frac{9}{16}$ | $\frac{9}{16}$ |
| x 42 | $9\frac{3}{4}$ | $10\frac{1}{8}$ | $\frac{7}{16}$ | $\frac{7}{16}$ |
| HP8 x 36 | 8 | $8\frac{1}{8}$ | $\frac{7}{16}$ | $\frac{7}{16}$ |

## AMERICAN STANDARD CHANNELS

| | | | | |
|---|---|---|---|---|
| C 15 x 50 | 15 | $3\frac{3}{4}$ | $\frac{5}{8}$ | $\frac{11}{16}$ |
| x 40 | 15 | $3\frac{1}{2}$ | $\frac{5}{8}$ | $\frac{1}{2}$ |
| x 33.9 | 15 | $3\frac{3}{8}$ | $\frac{5}{8}$ | $\frac{3}{8}$ |
| C 12 x 30 | 12 | $3\frac{1}{8}$ | $\frac{1}{2}$ | $\frac{1}{2}$ |
| x 25 | 12 | 3 | $\frac{1}{2}$ | $\frac{3}{8}$ |
| x 20.7 | 12 | 3 | $\frac{1}{2}$ | $\frac{5}{16}$ |
| C 10 x 30 | 10 | 3 | $\frac{7}{16}$ | $\frac{11}{16}$ |
| x 25 | 10 | $2\frac{7}{8}$ | $\frac{7}{16}$ | $\frac{1}{2}$ |
| x 20 | 10 | $2\frac{3}{4}$ | $\frac{7}{16}$ | $\frac{3}{8}$ |
| x 15.3 | 10 | $2\frac{5}{8}$ | $\frac{7}{16}$ | $\frac{1}{4}$ |
| C 9 x 20 | 9 | $2\frac{5}{8}$ | $\frac{7}{16}$ | $\frac{7}{16}$ |
| x 15 | 9 | $2\frac{1}{2}$ | $\frac{7}{16}$ | $\frac{5}{16}$ |
| x 13.4 | 9 | $2\frac{3}{8}$ | $\frac{7}{16}$ | $\frac{1}{4}$ |
| C 8 x 18.75 | 8 | $2\frac{1}{2}$ | $\frac{3}{8}$ | $\frac{1}{2}$ |
| x 13.75 | 8 | $2\frac{3}{8}$ | $\frac{3}{8}$ | $\frac{5}{16}$ |
| x 11.5 | 8 | $2\frac{1}{4}$ | $\frac{3}{8}$ | $\frac{1}{4}$ |
| C 7 x 14.75 | 7 | $2\frac{1}{4}$ | $\frac{3}{8}$ | $\frac{1}{2}$ |
| x 12.25 | 7 | $2\frac{1}{4}$ | $\frac{3}{8}$ | $\frac{5}{16}$ |
| x 9.8 | 7 | $2\frac{1}{8}$ | $\frac{3}{8}$ | $\frac{3}{16}$ |
| C 6 x 13 | 6 | $2\frac{1}{8}$ | $\frac{5}{16}$ | $\frac{7}{16}$ |
| x 10.5 | 6 | 2 | $\frac{5}{16}$ | $\frac{5}{16}$ |
| x 8.2 | 6 | $1\frac{7}{8}$ | $\frac{5}{16}$ | $\frac{3}{16}$ |
| C 5 x 9 | 5 | $1\frac{7}{8}$ | $\frac{5}{16}$ | $\frac{5}{16}$ |
| x 6.7 | 5 | $1\frac{3}{4}$ | $\frac{5}{16}$ | $\frac{3}{16}$ |
| C 4 x 7.25 | 4 | $1\frac{3}{4}$ | $\frac{5}{16}$ | $\frac{5}{16}$ |
| x 5.4 | 4 | $1\frac{5}{8}$ | $\frac{5}{16}$ | $\frac{3}{16}$ |
| C 3 x 6 | 3 | $1\frac{5}{8}$ | $\frac{1}{4}$ | $\frac{3}{8}$ |
| x 5 | 3 | $1\frac{1}{2}$ | $\frac{1}{4}$ | $\frac{1}{4}$ |
| x 4.1 | 3 | $1\frac{3}{8}$ | $\frac{1}{4}$ | $\frac{3}{16}$ |

## MISCELLANEOUS CHANNELS— DIMENSIONS FOR DETAILING

| DESIG-NATION | DEPTH d (IN.) | FLANGE WIDTH $b_f$ (IN.) | FLANGE AVERAGE THICKNESS $t_f$ (IN.) | WEB THICKNESS $t_w$ (IN.) |
|---|---|---|---|---|
| MC 18 x 58 | 18 | $4\frac{1}{4}$ | $\frac{11}{16}$ | $\frac{5}{8}$ |
| x 51.9 | 18 | $4\frac{1}{8}$ | $\frac{5}{8}$ | $\frac{5}{8}$ |
| x 45.8 | 18 | 4 | $\frac{1}{2}$ | $\frac{5}{8}$ |
| x 42.7 | 18 | 4 | $\frac{1}{2}$ | $\frac{7}{16}$ |
| MC 13 x 50 | 13 | $4\frac{3}{8}$ | $\frac{13}{16}$ | $\frac{5}{8}$ |
| x 40 | 13 | $4\frac{1}{8}$ | $\frac{9}{16}$ | $\frac{5}{8}$ |
| x 35 | 13 | $4\frac{1}{8}$ | $\frac{7}{16}$ | $\frac{5}{8}$ |
| x 31.8 | 13 | 4 | $\frac{3}{8}$ | $\frac{5}{8}$ |
| MC 12 x 50 | 12 | $4\frac{1}{8}$ | $\frac{13}{16}$ | $\frac{11}{16}$ |
| x 45 | 12 | 4 | $\frac{11}{16}$ | $\frac{11}{16}$ |
| x 40 | 12 | $3\frac{7}{8}$ | $\frac{9}{16}$ | $\frac{11}{16}$ |
| x 35 | 12 | $3\frac{3}{4}$ | $\frac{7}{16}$ | $\frac{11}{16}$ |
| MC 12 x 37 | 12 | $3\frac{5}{8}$ | $\frac{5}{8}$ | $\frac{5}{8}$ |
| x 32.9 | 12 | $3\frac{1}{2}$ | $\frac{1}{2}$ | $\frac{5}{8}$ |
| x 30.9 | 12 | $3\frac{1}{2}$ | $\frac{7}{16}$ | $\frac{5}{8}$ |
| MC 12 x 10.6 | 12 | $1\frac{1}{2}$ | $\frac{3}{16}$ | $\frac{5}{16}$ |
| MC 10 x 41.1 | 10 | $4\frac{3}{8}$ | $\frac{13}{16}$ | $\frac{9}{16}$ |
| x 33.6 | 10 | $4\frac{1}{8}$ | $\frac{9}{16}$ | $\frac{9}{16}$ |
| x 28.5 | 10 | 4 | $\frac{7}{16}$ | $\frac{9}{16}$ |
| MC 10 x 28.3 | 10 | $3\frac{1}{2}$ | $\frac{1}{2}$ | $\frac{9}{16}$ |
| x 25.3 | 10 | $3\frac{1}{2}$ | $\frac{7}{16}$ | $\frac{1}{2}$ |
| x 24.9 | 10 | $3\frac{3}{8}$ | $\frac{3}{8}$ | $\frac{9}{16}$ |
| x 21.9 | 10 | $3\frac{1}{2}$ | $\frac{5}{16}$ | $\frac{1}{2}$ |
| MC 10 x 8.4 | 10 | $1\frac{1}{2}$ | $\frac{3}{16}$ | $\frac{1}{4}$ |
| MC 10 x 6.5 | 10 | $1\frac{1}{8}$ | $\frac{1}{8}$ | $\frac{3}{16}$ |
| MC 9 x 25.4 | 9 | $3\frac{1}{2}$ | $\frac{9}{16}$ | $\frac{7}{16}$ |
| 9 x 23.9 | 9 | $3\frac{1}{2}$ | $\frac{9}{16}$ | $\frac{3}{8}$ |
| MC 8 x 22.8 | 8 | $3\frac{1}{2}$ | $\frac{1}{2}$ | $\frac{7}{16}$ |
| x 21.4 | 8 | $3\frac{1}{2}$ | $\frac{1}{2}$ | $\frac{3}{8}$ |
| MC 8 x 20 | 8 | 3 | $\frac{1}{2}$ | $\frac{3}{8}$ |
| x 18.7 | 8 | 3 | $\frac{1}{2}$ | $\frac{3}{8}$ |
| MC 8 x 8.5 | 8 | $1\frac{7}{8}$ | $\frac{5}{16}$ | $\frac{3}{16}$ |
| MC 7 x 22.7 | 7 | $3\frac{5}{8}$ | $\frac{1}{2}$ | $\frac{1}{2}$ |
| x 19.1 | 7 | $3\frac{1}{2}$ | $\frac{1}{2}$ | $\frac{3}{8}$ |
| MC 7 x 17.6 | 7 | 3 | $\frac{1}{2}$ | $\frac{3}{8}$ |
| MC 6 x 18 | 6 | $3\frac{1}{2}$ | $\frac{1}{2}$ | $\frac{3}{8}$ |
| x 15.3 | 6 | $3\frac{1}{2}$ | $\frac{1}{2}$ | $\frac{5}{16}$ |
| MC 6 x 16.3 | 6 | 3 | $\frac{1}{2}$ | $\frac{3}{8}$ |
| x 15.1 | 6 | 3 | $\frac{1}{2}$ | $\frac{5}{16}$ |
| MC 6 x 12 | 6 | $2\frac{1}{2}$ | $\frac{3}{8}$ | $\frac{5}{16}$ |

## ANGLES (EQUAL LEGS)— DIMENSIONS FOR DETAILING

| SIZE AND THICKNESS (IN.) | SIZE AND THICKNESS (IN.) |
|---|---|
| L 8 x 8 x $1\frac{1}{8}$ | L $3\frac{1}{2}$ x $3\frac{1}{2}$ x $\frac{1}{2}$ |
| 1 | $\frac{7}{16}$ |
| $\frac{7}{8}$ | $\frac{3}{8}$ |
| $\frac{3}{4}$ | $\frac{5}{16}$ |
| $\frac{5}{8}$ | $\frac{1}{4}$ |
| $\frac{9}{16}$ | |
| $\frac{1}{2}$ | L 3 x 3 x $\frac{1}{2}$ |
| L 6 x 6 x 1 | $\frac{7}{16}$ |
| $\frac{7}{8}$ | $\frac{3}{8}$ |
| $\frac{3}{4}$ | $\frac{5}{16}$ |
| $\frac{5}{8}$ | $\frac{1}{4}$ |
| $\frac{9}{16}$ | $\frac{3}{16}$ |
| $\frac{1}{2}$ | L $2\frac{1}{2}$ x $2\frac{1}{2}$ x $\frac{1}{2}$ |
| $\frac{7}{16}$ | $\frac{3}{8}$ |
| $\frac{3}{8}$ | $\frac{5}{16}$ |
| $\frac{5}{16}$ | $\frac{1}{4}$ |
| L 5 x 5 x $\frac{7}{8}$ | $\frac{3}{16}$ |
| $\frac{3}{4}$ | L 2 x 2 x $\frac{3}{8}$ |
| $\frac{5}{8}$ | $\frac{5}{16}$ |
| $\frac{1}{2}$ | $\frac{1}{4}$ |
| $\frac{7}{16}$ | $\frac{3}{16}$ |
| $\frac{3}{8}$ | $\frac{1}{8}$ |
| $\frac{5}{16}$ | L $1\frac{3}{4}$ x $1\frac{3}{4}$ x $\frac{1}{4}$ |
| L 4 x 4 x $\frac{3}{4}$ | $\frac{3}{16}$ |
| $\frac{5}{8}$ | $\frac{1}{8}$ |
| $\frac{1}{2}$ | L $1\frac{1}{2}$ x $1\frac{1}{2}$ x $\frac{1}{4}$ |
| $\frac{7}{16}$ | $\frac{3}{16}$ |
| $\frac{3}{8}$ | $\frac{5}{32}$ |
| $\frac{5}{16}$ | $\frac{1}{8}$ |
| $\frac{1}{4}$ | L $1\frac{1}{4}$ x $1\frac{1}{4}$ x $\frac{1}{4}$ |
| | $\frac{3}{16}$ |
| | $\frac{1}{8}$ |
| | L 1 x 1 x $\frac{1}{4}$ |
| | $\frac{3}{16}$ |
| | $\frac{1}{8}$ |

## ANGLES (UNEQUAL LEGS)—DIMENSIONS FOR DETAILING

| SIZE AND THICKNESS (IN.) | SIZE AND THICKNESS (IN.) | SIZE AND THICKNESS (IN.) | SIZE AND THICKNESS (IN.) |
|---|---|---|---|
| L 9 x 4 x 1 | L 6 x 4 x $\frac{7}{8}$ | L 4 x $3\frac{1}{2}$ x $\frac{5}{8}$ | L 3 x 2 x $\frac{1}{2}$ |
| $\frac{3}{4}$ | $\frac{3}{4}$ | $\frac{1}{2}$ | $\frac{7}{16}$ |
| $\frac{5}{8}$ | $\frac{9}{16}$ | $\frac{7}{16}$ | $\frac{3}{8}$ |
| $\frac{9}{16}$ | $\frac{1}{2}$ | $\frac{3}{8}$ | $\frac{5}{16}$ |
| $\frac{1}{2}$ | $\frac{7}{16}$ | $\frac{5}{16}$ | $\frac{1}{4}$ |
| L 8 x 6 x 1 | $\frac{3}{8}$ | $\frac{1}{4}$ | $\frac{3}{16}$ |
| $\frac{7}{8}$ | $\frac{5}{16}$ | L 4 x 3 x $\frac{5}{8}$ | L $2\frac{1}{2}$ x 2 x $\frac{3}{8}$ |
| $\frac{3}{4}$ | L 6 x $3\frac{1}{2}$ x $\frac{1}{2}$ | $\frac{1}{2}$ | $\frac{5}{16}$ |
| $\frac{5}{8}$ | $\frac{3}{8}$ | $\frac{7}{16}$ | $\frac{1}{4}$ |
| $\frac{9}{16}$ | $\frac{5}{16}$ | $\frac{3}{8}$ | $\frac{3}{16}$ |
| $\frac{1}{2}$ | $\frac{1}{4}$ | $\frac{5}{16}$ | L $2\frac{1}{2}$ x $1\frac{1}{2}$ x $\frac{5}{16}$ |
| $\frac{7}{16}$ | L 5 x $3\frac{1}{2}$ x $\frac{3}{4}$ | $\frac{1}{4}$ | $\frac{1}{4}$ |
| L 8 x 4 x 1 | $\frac{5}{8}$ | L $3\frac{1}{2}$ x 3 x $\frac{1}{2}$ | $\frac{3}{16}$ |
| $\frac{7}{8}$ | $\frac{1}{2}$ | $\frac{7}{16}$ | L 2 x $1\frac{1}{2}$ x $\frac{1}{4}$ |
| $\frac{3}{4}$ | $\frac{7}{16}$ | $\frac{3}{8}$ | $\frac{3}{16}$ |
| $\frac{5}{8}$ | $\frac{3}{8}$ | $\frac{5}{16}$ | $\frac{1}{8}$ |
| $\frac{9}{16}$ | $\frac{5}{16}$ | $\frac{1}{4}$ | L 2 x $1\frac{1}{4}$ x $\frac{1}{4}$ |
| $\frac{1}{2}$ | $\frac{1}{4}$ | L $3\frac{1}{2}$ x $2\frac{1}{2}$ x $\frac{1}{2}$ | $\frac{3}{16}$ |
| $\frac{7}{16}$ | L 5 x 3 x $\frac{1}{2}$ | $\frac{7}{16}$ | $\frac{1}{8}$ |
| L 7 x 4 x $\frac{7}{8}$ | $\frac{7}{16}$ | $\frac{3}{8}$ | L $1\frac{3}{4}$ x $1\frac{1}{4}$ x $\frac{1}{4}$ |
| $\frac{3}{4}$ | $\frac{3}{8}$ | $\frac{5}{16}$ | $\frac{3}{16}$ |
| $\frac{5}{8}$ | $\frac{5}{16}$ | $\frac{1}{4}$ | $\frac{1}{8}$ |
| $\frac{9}{16}$ | $\frac{1}{4}$ | L 3 x $2\frac{1}{2}$ x $\frac{1}{2}$ | |
| $\frac{1}{2}$ | | $\frac{7}{16}$ | |
| $\frac{7}{16}$ | | $\frac{3}{8}$ | |
| $\frac{3}{8}$ | | $\frac{5}{16}$ | |
| | | $\frac{1}{4}$ | |
| | | $\frac{3}{16}$ | |

## STRUCTURAL TEES CUT FROM W SHAPES—DIMENSIONS FOR DETAILING

| DESIGNATION | DEPTH OF SECTION d (IN.) | FLANGE WIDTH b_f (IN.) | FLANGE AVERAGE THICKNESS t_f (IN.) | STEM THICKNESS t_w (IN.) |
|---|---|---|---|---|
| WT18 x 150 | 18.370 | 16.655 | 1.680 | 0.945 |
| x 140 | 18.260 | 16.595 | 1.570 | 0.885 |
| x 130 | 18.130 | 16.550 | 1.440 | 0.840 |
| x 122.5 | 18.040 | 16.510 | 1.350 | 0.800 |
| x 115 | 17.950 | 16.470 | 1.260 | 0.760 |
| WT18 x 105 | 18.345 | 12.180 | 1.360 | 0.830 |
| x 97 | 18.245 | 12.115 | 1.260 | 0.765 |
| x 91 | 18.165 | 12.075 | 1.180 | 0.725 |
| x 85 | 18.085 | 12.030 | 1.100 | 0.680 |
| x 80 | 18.005 | 12.000 | 1.020 | 0.650 |
| x 75 | 17.925 | 11.975 | 0.940 | 0.625 |
| x 67.5 | 17.775 | 11.950 | 0.790 | 0.600 |
| WT16.5 x 120.5 | 17.090 | 15.860 | 1.400 | 0.830 |
| x 110.5 | 16.965 | 15.805 | 1.275 | 0.775 |
| x 100.5 | 16.840 | 15.745 | 1.150 | 0.715 |
| WT16.5 x 76 | 16.745 | 11.565 | 1.055 | 0.635 |
| x 70.5 | 16.650 | 11.530 | 0.960 | 0.605 |
| x 65 | 16.545 | 11.510 | 0.855 | 0.580 |
| x 59 | 16.430 | 11.480 | 0.740 | 0.550 |
| WT15 x 105.5 | 15.470 | 15.105 | 1.315 | 0.775 |
| x 95.5 | 15.340 | 15.040 | 1.185 | 0.710 |
| x 86.5 | 15.220 | 14.985 | 1.065 | 0.655 |
| WT15 x 66 | 15.155 | 10.545 | 1.000 | 0.615 |
| x 62 | 15.085 | 10.515 | 0.930 | 0.585 |
| x 58 | 15.005 | 10.485 | 0.850 | 0.565 |
| x 54 | 14.915 | 10.475 | 0.760 | 0.545 |
| x 49.5 | 14.825 | 10.450 | 0.670 | 0.520 |
| WT13.5 x 89 | 13.905 | 14.085 | 1.190 | 0.725 |
| x 80.5 | 13.795 | 14.020 | 1.080 | 0.660 |
| x 73 | 13.690 | 13.965 | 0.975 | 0.605 |
| WT13.5 x 57 | 13.645 | 10.070 | 0.930 | 0.570 |
| x 51 | 13.545 | 10.015 | 0.830 | 0.515 |
| x 47 | 13.460 | 9.990 | 0.745 | 0.490 |
| x 42 | 13.355 | 9.960 | 0.640 | 0.460 |
| WT12 x 81 | 12.500 | 12.955 | 1.220 | 0.705 |
| x 73 | 12.370 | 12.900 | 1.090 | 0.650 |
| x 65.5 | 12.240 | 12.855 | 0.960 | 0.605 |
| x 58.5 | 12.130 | 12.800 | 0.850 | 0.550 |
| x 52 | 12.030 | 12.750 | 0.750 | 0.500 |
| WT12 x 47 | 12.155 | 9.065 | 0.875 | 0.515 |
| x 42 | 12.050 | 9.020 | 0.770 | 0.470 |
| x 38 | 11.960 | 8.990 | 0.680 | 0.440 |
| x 34 | 11.865 | 8.965 | 0.585 | 0.415 |
| WT12 x 31 | 11.870 | 7.040 | 0.590 | 0.430 |
| x 27.5 | 11.785 | 7.005 | 0.505 | 0.395 |
| WT10.5 x 73.5 | 11.030 | 12.510 | 1.150 | 0.720 |
| x 66 | 10.915 | 12.440 | 1.035 | 0.650 |
| x 61 | 10.840 | 12.390 | 0.960 | 0.600 |
| x 55.5 | 10.755 | 12.340 | 0.875 | 0.550 |
| x 50.5 | 10.680 | 12.290 | 0.800 | 0.500 |
| WT10.5 x 46.5 | 10.810 | 8.420 | 0.930 | 0.580 |
| x 41.5 | 10.715 | 8.355 | 0.835 | 0.515 |
| x 36.5 | 10.620 | 8.295 | 0.740 | 0.455 |
| x 34 | 10.565 | 8.270 | 0.685 | 0.430 |
| x 31 | 10.495 | 8.240 | 0.615 | 0.400 |
| WT10.5 x 28.5 | 10.530 | 6.555 | 0.650 | 0.405 |
| x 25 | 10.415 | 6.530 | 0.535 | 0.380 |
| x 22 | 10.330 | 6.500 | 0.450 | 0.350 |
| WT9 x 59.5 | 9.485 | 11.265 | 1.060 | 0.655 |
| x 53 | 9.365 | 11.200 | 0.940 | 0.590 |
| x 48.5 | 9.295 | 11.145 | 0.870 | 0.535 |
| x 43 | 9.195 | 11.090 | 0.770 | 0.480 |
| x 38 | 9.105 | 11.035 | 0.680 | 0.425 |
| WT9 x 35.5 | 9.235 | 7.635 | 0.810 | 0.495 |
| x 32.5 | 9.175 | 7.590 | 0.750 | 0.450 |
| x 30 | 9.120 | 7.555 | 0.695 | 0.415 |
| x 27.5 | 9.055 | 7.530 | 0.630 | 0.390 |
| x 25 | 8.995 | 7.495 | 0.570 | 0.355 |
| WT9 x 23 | 9.030 | 6.060 | 0.605 | 0.360 |
| x 20 | 8.950 | 6.015 | 0.525 | 0.315 |
| x 17.5 | 8.850 | 6.000 | 0.425 | 0.300 |
| WT8 x 50 | 8.485 | 10.425 | 0.985 | 0.585 |
| x 44.5 | 8.375 | 10.365 | 0.875 | 0.525 |
| x 38.5 | 8.260 | 10.295 | 0.760 | 0.455 |
| x 33.5 | 8.165 | 10.235 | 0.665 | 0.395 |
| WT8 x 28.5 | 8.215 | 7.120 | 0.715 | 0.430 |
| x 25 | 8.130 | 7.070 | 0.630 | 0.380 |
| x 22.5 | 8.065 | 7.035 | 0.565 | 0.345 |
| x 20 | 8.005 | 6.995 | 0.505 | 0.305 |
| x 18 | 7.930 | 6.985 | 0.430 | 0.295 |
| WT8 x 15.5 | 7.940 | 5.525 | 0.440 | 0.275 |
| x 13 | 7.845 | 5.500 | 0.345 | 0.250 |
| WT7 x 365 | 11.210 | 17.890 | 4.910 | 3.070 |
| x 332.5 | 10.820 | 17.650 | 4.520 | 2.830 |
| x 302.5 | 10.460 | 17.415 | 4.160 | 2.595 |
| x 275 | 10.120 | 17.200 | 3.820 | 2.380 |
| x 250 | 9.800 | 17.010 | 3.500 | 2.190 |
| x 227.5 | 9.510 | 16.835 | 3.210 | 2.015 |
| WT7 x 213 | 9.335 | 16.695 | 3.035 | 1.875 |
| x 199 | 9.145 | 16.590 | 2.845 | 1.770 |
| x 185 | 8.960 | 16.475 | 2.660 | 1.655 |
| x 171 | 8.770 | 16.360 | 2.470 | 1.540 |
| x 155.5 | 8.560 | 16.230 | 2.260 | 1.410 |
| x 141.5 | 8.370 | 16.110 | 2.070 | 1.290 |
| x 128.5 | 8.190 | 15.995 | 1.890 | 1.175 |
| x 116.5 | 8.020 | 15.890 | 1.720 | 1.070 |
| x 105.5 | 7.860 | 15.800 | 1.560 | 0.980 |
| x 96.5 | 7.740 | 15.710 | 1.440 | 0.890 |
| x 88 | 7.610 | 15.650 | 1.310 | 0.830 |
| x 79.5 | 7.490 | 15.565 | 1.190 | 0.745 |
| x 72.5 | 7.390 | 15.500 | 1.090 | 0.680 |
| WT7 x 66 | 7.330 | 14.725 | 1.030 | 0.645 |
| x 60 | 7.240 | 14.670 | 0.940 | 0.590 |
| x 54.5 | 7.160 | 14.605 | 0.860 | 0.525 |
| x 49.5 | 7.080 | 14.565 | 0.780 | 0.485 |
| x 45 | 7.010 | 14.520 | 0.710 | 0.440 |
| WT7 x 41 | 7.155 | 10.130 | 0.855 | 0.510 |
| x 37 | 7.085 | 10.070 | 0.785 | 0.450 |
| x 34 | 7.020 | 10.035 | 0.720 | 0.415 |
| x 30.5 | 6.945 | 9.995 | 0.645 | 0.375 |
| WT7 x 26.5 | 6.960 | 8.060 | 0.660 | 0.370 |
| x 24 | 6.895 | 8.030 | 0.595 | 0.340 |
| x 21.5 | 6.830 | 7.995 | 0.530 | 0.305 |
| WT7 x 19 | 7.050 | 6.770 | 0.515 | 0.310 |
| x 17 | 6.990 | 6.745 | 0.455 | 0.285 |
| x 15 | 6.920 | 6.730 | 0.385 | 0.270 |
| WT7 x 13 | 6.955 | 5.025 | 0.420 | 0.255 |
| x 11 | 6.870 | 5.000 | 0.335 | 0.230 |
| WT6 x 95 | 7.190 | 12.670 | 1.735 | 1.060 |
| x 85 | 7.015 | 12.570 | 1.560 | 0.960 |
| x 76 | 6.855 | 12.480 | 1.400 | 0.870 |
| x 68 | 6.705 | 12.400 | 1.250 | 0.790 |
| x 60 | 6.560 | 12.320 | 1.105 | 0.710 |
| x 53 | 6.445 | 12.220 | 0.990 | 0.610 |
| x 48 | 6.355 | 12.160 | 0.900 | 0.550 |
| x 43.5 | 6.265 | 12.125 | 0.810 | 0.515 |
| x 39.5 | 6.190 | 12.080 | 0.735 | 0.470 |
| x 36 | 6.125 | 12.040 | 0.670 | 0.430 |
| x 32.5 | 6.060 | 12.000 | 0.605 | 0.390 |
| WT6 x 29 | 6.095 | 10.010 | 0.640 | 0.360 |
| x 26.5 | 6.030 | 9.995 | 0.575 | 0.345 |
| WT6 x 25 | 6.095 | 8.080 | 0.640 | 0.370 |
| x 22.5 | 6.030 | 8.045 | 0.575 | 0.335 |
| x 20 | 5.970 | 8.005 | 0.515 | 0.295 |
| WT6 x 17.5 | 6.250 | 6.560 | 0.520 | 0.300 |
| x 15 | 6.170 | 6.520 | 0.440 | 0.260 |
| x 13 | 6.110 | 6.490 | 0.380 | 0.230 |
| WT6 x 11 | 6.155 | 4.030 | 0.425 | 0.260 |
| x 9.5 | 6.080 | 4.005 | 0.350 | 0.235 |
| x 8 | 5.995 | 3.990 | 0.265 | 0.220 |
| x 7 | 5.955 | 3.970 | 0.225 | 0.200 |
| WT5 x 56 | 5.680 | 10.415 | 1.250 | 0.755 |
| x 50 | 5.550 | 10.340 | 1.120 | 0.680 |
| x 44 | 5.420 | 10.265 | 0.990 | 0.605 |
| x 38.5 | 5.300 | 10.190 | 0.870 | 0.530 |
| x 34 | 5.200 | 10.130 | 0.770 | 0.470 |
| x 30 | 5.110 | 10.080 | 0.680 | 0.420 |
| x 27 | 5.045 | 10.030 | 0.615 | 0.370 |
| x 24.5 | 4.990 | 10.000 | 0.560 | 0.340 |
| WT5 x 22.5 | 5.050 | 8.020 | 0.620 | 0.350 |
| x 19.5 | 4.960 | 7.985 | 0.530 | 0.315 |
| x 16.5 | 4.865 | 7.960 | 0.435 | 0.290 |
| WT5 x 15 | 5.235 | 5.810 | 0.510 | 0.300 |
| x 13 | 5.165 | 5.770 | 0.440 | 0.260 |
| x 11 | 5.085 | 5.750 | 0.360 | 0.240 |
| WT5 x 9.5 | 5.120 | 4.020 | 0.395 | 0.250 |
| x 8.5 | 5.055 | 4.010 | 0.330 | 0.240 |
| x 7.5 | 4.995 | 4.000 | 0.270 | 0.230 |
| x 6 | 4.935 | 3.960 | 0.210 | 0.190 |
| WT4 x 33.5 | 4.500 | 8.280 | 0.935 | 0.570 |
| x 29 | 4.375 | 8.220 | 0.810 | 0.510 |
| x 24 | 4.250 | 8.110 | 0.685 | 0.400 |
| x 20 | 4.125 | 8.070 | 0.560 | 0.360 |
| x 17.5 | 4.060 | 8.020 | 0.495 | 0.310 |
| x 15.5 | 4.000 | 7.995 | 0.435 | 0.285 |
| WT4 x 14 | 4.030 | 6.535 | 0.465 | 0.285 |
| x 12 | 3.965 | 6.495 | 0.400 | 0.245 |
| WT4 x 10.5 | 4.140 | 5.270 | 0.400 | 0.250 |
| x 9 | 4.070 | 5.250 | 0.330 | 0.230 |
| WT4 x 7.5 | 4.055 | 4.015 | 0.315 | 0.245 |
| x 6.5 | 3.995 | 4.000 | 0.255 | 0.230 |
| x 5 | 3.945 | 3.940 | 0.205 | 0.170 |
| WT3 x 12.5 | 3.190 | 6.080 | 0.455 | 0.320 |
| x 10 | 3.100 | 6.020 | 0.365 | 0.260 |
| x 7.5 | 2.995 | 5.990 | 0.260 | 0.230 |
| WT3 x 8 | 3.140 | 4.030 | 0.405 | 0.260 |
| x 6 | 3.015 | 4.000 | 0.280 | 0.230 |
| x 4.5 | 2.950 | 3.940 | 0.215 | 0.170 |

## STRUCTURAL TEES CUT FROM S SHAPES—DIMENSIONS FOR DETAILING

| DESIGNATION | DEPTH OF SECTION d (IN.) | FLANGE WIDTH b_f (IN.) | FLANGE AVERAGE THICKNESS t_f (IN.) | STEM THICKNESS t_w (IN.) |
|---|---|---|---|---|
| ST12 x 60 | 12.00 | 8.048 | 1.102 | 0.798 |
| x 52.95 | 12.00 | 7.875 | 1.102 | 0.625 |
| ST12 x 50 | 12.00 | 7.247 | 0.871 | 0.747 |
| x 45 | 12.00 | 7.124 | 0.871 | 0.624 |
| x 39.95 | 12.00 | 7.001 | 0.871 | 0.501 |
| ST10 x 47.5 | 10.00 | 7.200 | 0.916 | 0.800 |
| x 42.5 | 10.00 | 7.053 | 0.916 | 0.653 |
| ST10 x 37.5 | 10.00 | 6.391 | 0.789 | 0.641 |
| x 32.7 | 10.00 | 6.250 | 0.789 | 0.500 |
| ST9 x 35 | 9.00 | 6.251 | 0.691 | 0.711 |
| x 27.35 | 9.00 | 6.001 | 0.691 | 0.461 |
| ST7.5 x 25 | 7.50 | 5.640 | 0.622 | 0.550 |
| x 21.45 | 7.50 | 5.501 | 0.622 | 0.411 |
| ST6 x 25 | 6.00 | 5.477 | 0.659 | 0.687 |
| x 20.4 | 6.00 | 5.252 | 0.659 | 0.462 |
| ST6 x 17.5 | 6.00 | 5.078 | 0.544 | 0.428 |
| x 15.9 | 6.00 | 5.000 | 0.544 | 0.350 |
| ST5 x 17.5 | 5.00 | 4.944 | 0.491 | 0.594 |
| x 12.7 | 5.00 | 4.661 | 0.491 | 0.311 |
| ST4 x 11.5 | 4.00 | 4.171 | 0.425 | 0.441 |
| x 9.2 | 4.00 | 4.001 | 0.425 | 0.271 |
| ST3.5 x 10 | 3.50 | 3.860 | 0.392 | 0.450 |
| x 7.65 | 3.50 | 3.662 | 0.392 | 0.252 |
| ST3 x 8.625 | 3.00 | 3.565 | 0.359 | 0.465 |
| x 6.25 | 3.00 | 3.332 | 0.359 | 0.232 |
| ST2.5 x 7.375 | 2.50 | 3.284 | 0.326 | 0.494 |
| x 5 | 2.50 | 3.004 | 0.326 | 0.214 |
| ST2 x 4.75 | 2.00 | 2.796 | 0.293 | 0.326 |
| x 3.85 | 2.00 | 2.663 | 0.293 | 0.193 |
| ST1.5 x 3.75 | 1.50 | 2.509 | 0.260 | 0.349 |
| x 2.85 | 1.50 | 2.330 | 0.260 | 0.170 |

NOTE

The following tables show sizes and shapes usually stocked or readily available. Manufacturers' data should be checked for availability of sizes other than those in these tables. Where necessary, and where extra cost is warranted, other sections may be produced by welding, cutting, or other methods.

STEEL CHANNEL

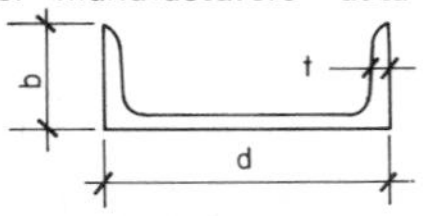


## STEEL CHANNELS—BAR SIZE (IN.)

| d x b x t | d x b x t | d x b x t |
|---|---|---|
| 3/4 x 5/16 x 1/8 | 1 1/4 x 1/2 x 1/8 | 2 x 9/16 x 3/16 |
| 3/4 x 3/8 x 1/8 | 1 1/2 x 1/2 x 1/8 | 2 x 5/8 x 1/4 |
| 7/8 x 3/8 x 1/8 | 1 1/2 x 9/16 x 3/16 | 2 x 1 x 1/8 |
| 7/8 x 7/16 x 1/8 | 1 1/2 x 3/4 x 1/8 | 2 x 1 x 3/16 |
| 1 x 3/8 x 1/8 | 1 1/2 x 1 1/2 x 3/16 | 2 1/2 x 5/8 x 3/16 |
| 1 x 1/2 x 1/8 | 1 3/4 x 1/2 x 3/16 | |
| 1 1/8 x 9/16 x 3/16 | 2 x 1/2 x 1/8 | |

NOTE: For structural channel sizes (d = 3 in. and larger) see Dimensions of Channel Shapes in this chapter.

STEEL TEES

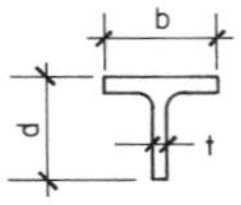


## STEEL TEES—BAR SIZE (IN.)

| b x d x t | b x d x t | b x d x t |
|---|---|---|
| 3/4 x 3/4 x 1/8 | 1 1/2 x 1 1/2 x 3/16 | 2 x 2 x 5/16 |
| 1 x 1 x 1/8 | 1 1/2 x 1 1/2 x 1/4 | 2 1/4 x 2 1/4 x 1/4 |
| 1 x 1 x 3/16 | 1 3/4 x 1 3/4 x 3/16 | 2 1/2 x 2 1/4 x 1/4 |
| 1 1/4 x 1 1/4 x 1/8 | 1 3/4 x 1 3/4 x 1/4 | 2 1/2 x 2 1/2 x 5/16 |
| 1 1/4 x 1 1/4 x 3/16 | 2 x 1 1/2 x 1/4 | 2 1/2 x 2 1/2 x 3/8 |
| 1 1/4 x 1 1/4 x 1/4 | 2 x 2 x 1/4 | |
| STRUCTURAL | | |
| 3 x 2 1/2 x 5/16 | 3 x 3 x 3/8 | 4 x 4 x 1/2 |
| 3 x 3 x 5/16 | 4 x 3 x 3/8 | 5 x 3 1/8 x 1/2 |

ALUMINUM ANGLE STRUCTURAL

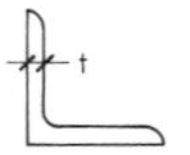


## ALUMINUM ANGLES—STRUCTURAL —EQUAL LEGS (IN.)

| SIZE x t | SIZE x t | SIZE x t |
|---|---|---|
| 3/4 x 3/4 x 1/8 | 2 x 2 x 3/16 | 3 1/2 x 3 1/2 x 1/4 |
| 1 x 1 x 1/8 | 2 x 2 x 1/4 | 3 1/2 x 3 1/2 x 3/8 |
| 1 x 1 x 3/16 | 2 x 2 x 5/16 | 3 1/2 x 3 1/2 x 1/2 |
| 1 x 1 x 1/4 | 2 x 2 x 3/8 | 4 x 4 x 1/4 |
| 1 1/4 x 1 1/4 x 1/8 | 2 1/2 x 2 1/2 x 1/8 | 4 x 4 x 5/16 |
| 1 1/4 x 1 1/4 x 3/16 | 2 1/2 x 2 1/2 x 3/16 | 4 x 4 x 3/8 |
| 1 1/4 x 1 1/4 x 1/4 | 2 1/2 x 2 1/2 x 1/4 | 4 x 4 x 1/2 |
| 1 1/2 x 1 1/2 x 1/8 | 2 1/2 x 2 1/2 x 5/16 | 4 x 4 x 3/4 |
| 1 1/2 x 1 1/2 x 3/16 | 2 1/2 x 2 1/2 x 3/8 | 5 x 5 x 3/8 |
| 1 1/2 x 1 1/2 x 1/4 | 3 x 3 x 3/16 | 5 x 5 x 1/2 |
| 1 3/4 x 1 3/4 x 1/8 | 3 x 3 x 1/4 | 6 x 6 x 3/8 |
| 1 3/4 x 1 3/4 x 3/16 | 3 x 3 x 5/16 | 6 x 6 x 1/2 |
| 1 3/4 x 1 3/4 x 1/4 | 3 x 3 x 3/8 | 8 x 8 x 1/2 |
| 2 x 2 x 1/8 | 3 x 3 x 1/2 | |
| UNEQUAL LEGS (IN.) | | |
| 1 1/2 x 1 1/4 x 1/8 | 2 1/2 x 2 x 5/16 | 4 x 3 x 1/2 |
| 1 1/2 x 1 1/4 x 3/16 | 2 1/2 x 2 x 3/8 | 5 x 3 x 3/8 |
| 1 1/2 x 1 1/4 x 1/4 | 3 x 2 x 3/16 | 5 x 3 x 1/2 |
| 1 3/4 x 1 1/4 x 1/8 | 3 x 2 x 1/4 | 5 x 3 1/2 x 5/16 |
| 1 3/4 x 1 1/4 x 3/16 | 3 x 2 x 3/8 | 5 x 3 1/2 x 3/8 |
| 1 3/4 x 1 1/4 x 1/4 | 3 x 2 1/2 x 1/4 | 5 x 3 1/2 x 1/2 |
| 2 x 1 1/2 x 1/8 | 3 x 2 1/2 x 3/8 | 6 x 3 1/2 x 5/16 |
| 2 x 1 1/2 x 3/16 | 3 1/2 x 2 1/2 x 1/4 | 6 x 3 1/2 x 1/2 |
| 2 x 1 1/2 x 1/4 | 3 1/2 x 2 1/2 x 3/8 | 6 x 4 x 3/8 |
| 2 1/2 x 1 1/2 x 1/4 | 3 1/2 x 3 x 1/4 | 6 x 4 x 1/2 |
| 2 1/2 x 2 x 3/16 | 4 x 3 x 1/4 | 6 x 4 x 5/8 |
| 2 1/2 x 2 x 1/4 | 4 x 3 x 3/8 | 8 x 6 x 3/4 |

STEEL ANGLES UNEQUAL LEGS

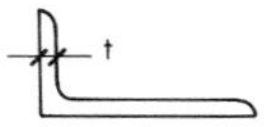


## STEEL ANGLES —UNEQUAL LEGS—BAR SIZE (IN.)

| SIZE x t | SIZE x t | SIZE x t |
|---|---|---|
| 1 x 5/8 x 1/8 | 2 x 1 1/4 x 1/4 | 2 1/2 x 1 1/2 x 5/16 |
| 1 x 3/4 x 1/8 | 2 x 1 1/2 x 1/8 | 2 1/2 x 2 x 3/16 |
| 1 3/8 x 7/8 x 1/8 | 2 x 1 1/2 x 3/16 | 2 1/2 x 2 x 1/4 |
| 1 3/8 x 7/8 x 3/16 | 2 x 1 1/2 x 1/4 | 2 1/2 x 2 x 5/16 |
| 1 1/2 x 1 1/4 x 3/16 | 2 1/4 x 1 1/2 x 3/16 | 2 1/2 x 2 x 1/8 |
| 1 3/4 x 1 1/4 x 1/8 | 2 1/2 x 1 1/2 x 3/16 | |
| 2 x 1 1/4 x 3/16 | 2 1/2 x 1 1/2 x 1/4 | |

NOTE: For structural angle sizes (3 x 2 x 3/16 in. and larger) see Dimensions of Angle Shapes in this chapter.

STEEL ZEES

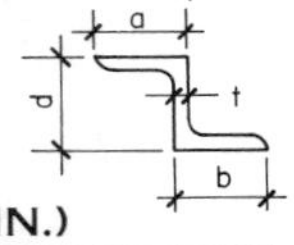


## STEEL ZEES—BAR SIZE (IN.)

| d x a x b x t | d x a x b x t |
|---|---|
| 1 x 1/2 x 5/8 x 1/8 | 1 3/8 x 3/4 x 1 3/16 x 1/8 |
| 1 3/16 x 5/8 x 3/4 x 1/8 | 1 3/4 x 1 1/4 x 3/4 x 3/16 |
| STRUCTURAL | |
| 3 x 2 11/16 x 2 11/16 x 1/4 | 4 1/8 x 3 3/16 x 3 3/16 x 3/8 |
| 3 x 2 11/16 x 2 11/16 x 3/8 | 5 x 3 1/4 x 3 1/4 x 5/16 |
| 3 x 2 11/16 x 2 11/16 x 1/2 | 5 x 3 1/4 x 3 1/4 x 1/2 |
| 4 x 3 1/16 x 3 1/16 x 1/4 | 5 1/16 x 3 5/16 x 3 5/16 x 3/8 |
| 4 1/16 x 3 1/8 x 3 1/8 x 5/16 | 6 x 3 1/2 x 3 1/2 x 3/8 |

ALUMINUM ANGLE SQUARE CORNERS

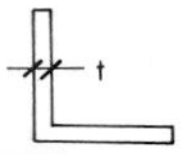


## ALUMINUM ANGLES—SQUARE CORNERS—EQUAL LEGS (IN.)

| SIZE x t | SIZE x t | SIZE x t |
|---|---|---|
| 1/2 x 1/2 x 1/16 | 1 1/8 x 1 1/8 x 3/16 | 2 x 2 x 3/16 |
| 1/2 x 1/2 x 1/8 | 1 1/4 x 1 1/4 x 1/8 | 2 x 2 x 1/4 |
| 5/8 x 5/8 x 1/8 | 1 1/4 x 1 1/4 x 3/16 | 2 1/2 x 2 1/2 x 1/8 |
| 3/4 x 3/4 x 1/16 | 1 1/2 x 1 1/2 x 1/8 | 3 x 3 x 1/8 |
| 3/4 x 3/4 x 1/8 | 1 1/2 x 1 1/2 x 3/16 | 3 x 3 x 3/16 |
| 1 x 1 x 1/16 | 1 1/2 x 1 1/2 x 1/4 | 3 1/2 x 3 1/2 x 1/8 |
| 1 x 1 x 1/8 | 1 3/4 x 1 3/4 x 1/8 | 4 x 4 x 1/8 |
| 1 x 1 x 3/16 | 2 x 2 x 1/8 | |
| UNEQUAL LEGS (IN.) | | |
| 3/4 x 3/8 x 3/32 | 2 x 3/4 x 1/8 | 3 1/2 x 2 x 1/8 |
| 1 x 1/2 x 1/8 | 2 x 1 x 1/8 | 3 1/2 x 2 1/2 x 1/8 |
| 1 x 3/4 x 1/8 | 2 x 1 x 3/16 | 3 1/2 x 3 x 1/8 |
| 1 1/4 x 1/2 x 1/8 | 2 x 1 1/2 x 1/8 | 4 x 2 x 1/8 |
| 1 1/2 x 1/2 x 1/8 | 2 1/2 x 1 x 1/8 | 4 x 3 x 1/8 |
| 1 1/2 x 3/4 x 1/8 | 2 1/2 x 1 1/2 x 1/8 | 5 x 3 x 1/8 |
| 1 1/2 x 1 x 1/8 | 2 1/2 x 2 x 1/8 | 5 x 4 x 1/8 |
| 1 3/4 x 1 x 1/8 | 3 x 1 x 1/8 | 5 1/4 x 2 1/4 x 1/8 |
| 1 3/4 x 1 1/2 x 1/8 | 3 x 2 x 1/8 | |
| 2 x 1/2 x 1/8 | 3 1/2 x 1 1/4 x 1/8 | |

ALUMINUM ZEES SQUARE CORNERS

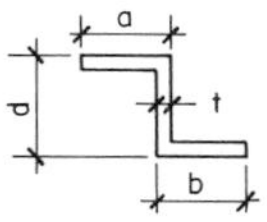


## ALUMINUM ZEES— SQUARE CORNERS (IN.)

| d x a x b x t | d x a x b x t |
|---|---|
| 1/2 x 1/2 x 1/2 x 3/32 | 1 x 1 1/8 x 1 1/8 x 1/8 |
| 3/4 x 3/4 x 3/4 x 1/8 | 1 x 5/8 x 7/8 x 1/8 |
| 7/8 x 3/4 x 3/4 x 1/8 | |

STEEL ANGLES EQUAL LEGS

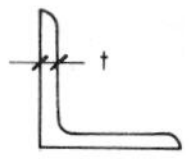


## STEEL ANGLES —EQUAL LEGS—BAR SIZE (IN.)

| SIZE x t | SIZE x t | SIZE x t |
|---|---|---|
| 1/2 x 1/2 x 1/8 | 1 1/4 x 1 1/4 x 3/16 | 2 x 2 x 3/16 |
| 5/8 x 5/8 x 1/8 | 1 1/4 x 1 1/4 x 1/4 | 2 x 2 x 1/4 |
| 3/4 x 3/4 x 1/8 | 1 1/2 x 1 1/2 x 1/8 | 2 x 2 x 5/16 |
| 7/8 x 7/8 x 1/8 | 1 1/2 x 1 1/2 x 3/16 | 2 x 2 x 3/8 |
| 1 x 1 x 1/8 | 1 1/2 x 1 1/2 x 1/4 | 2 1/2 x 2 1/2 x 3/16 |
| 1 x 1 x 3/16 | 1 3/4 x 1 3/4 x 1/8 | 2 1/2 x 2 1/2 x 1/4 |
| 1 x 1 x 1/4 | 1 3/4 x 1 3/4 x 3/16 | 2 1/2 x 2 1/2 x 5/16 |
| 1 1/8 x 1 1/8 x 1/8 | 1 3/4 x 1 3/4 x 1/4 | 2 1/2 x 2 1/2 x 3/8 |
| 1 1/4 x 1 1/4 x 1/8 | 2 x 2 x 1/8 | 2 1/2 x 2 1/2 x 1/2 |

NOTE: For structural angle sizes (3 x 3 x 3/16 in. and larger) see Dimensions of Angle Shapes in this chapter.

ALUMINUM CHANNEL SQUARE CORNERS

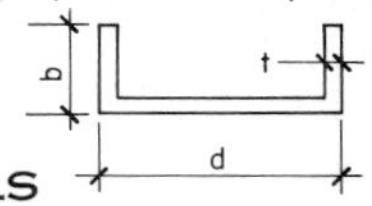


## ALUMINUM CHANNELS —SQUARE CORNERS (IN.)

| d x b x t | d x b x t | d x b x t |
|---|---|---|
| 3/8 x 3/8 x 7/64 | 1 1/4 x 3/4 x 1/8 | 2 1/2 x 3/4 x 1/8 |
| 1/2 x 3/8 x 1/8 | 1 1/4 x 1 1/4 x 1/8 | 2 1/2 x 1 1/2 x 1/8 |
| 1/2 x 1/2 x 3/32 | 1 1/2 x 1/2 x 1/8 | 2 1/2 x 2 1/2 x 1/8 |
| 1/2 x 3/4 x 1/8 | 1 1/2 x 5/8 x 1/8 | 3 x 1/2 x 1/8 |
| 5/8 x 5/8 x 1/8 | 1 1/2 x 3/4 x 1/8 | 3 x 1 x 1/8 |
| 5/8 x 1 x 1/8 | 1 1/2 x 1 x 1/8 | 3 x 2 x 1/8 |
| 3/4 x 3/8 x 1/8 | 1 1/2 x 1 1/2 x 1/8 | 3 x 3 x 1/8 |
| 3/4 x 1/2 x 1/8 | 1 3/4 x 1/2 x 1/8 | 4 x 1 1/2 x 1/8 |
| 3/4 x 3/4 x 1/8 | 1 3/4 x 3/4 x 1/8 | 4 1/2 x 2 x 1/8 |
| 1 x 1/2 x 1/8 | 1 3/4 x 1 x 1/8 | 5 x 2 x 3/16 |
| 1 x 3/4 x 1/8 | 2 x 1/2 x 1/8 | |
| 1 x 1 x 1/8 | 2 x 1 x 1/8 | |
| 1 1/4 x 1/2 x 1/8 | 2 x 2 x 1/8 | |
| 1 1/4 x 5/8 x 1/8 | 2 1/4 x 7/8 x 1/8 | |

NOTE: For aluminum channels in American Standard sizes and Aluminum Association Standard sizes, see Dimensions of Channel Shapes in this chapter.

ALUMINUM TEES SQUARE CORNERS

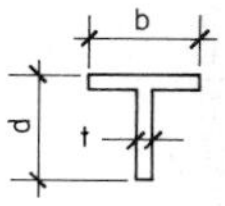


## ALUMINUM TEES— SQUARE CORNERS (IN.)

| b x d x t | b x d x t | b x d x t |
|---|---|---|
| 3/4 x 3/4 x 1/8 | 1 1/8 x 1/2 x 3/8 | 2 x 3/4 x 1/8 |
| 3/4 x 1 1/4 x 1/8 | 1 1/8 x 1 1/8 x 1/8 | 2 x 2 x 3/16 |
| 1 x 3/4 x 1/8 | 1 1/4 x 7/8 x 1/8 | |
| 1 x 1 x 1/8 | 1 1/2 x 1 1/2 x 1/8 | |

ALUMINUM TEES SQUARE CORNERS

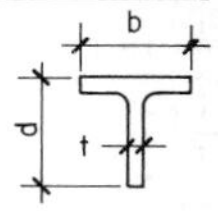


## STRUCTURAL (IN.)

| | | |
|---|---|---|
| 1 1/2 x 1 1/2 x 1/4 | 2 1/4 x 2 1/4 x 1/4 | 4 x 4 x 3/8 |
| 2 x 2 x 1/4 | 3 x 3 x 3/8 | |

STAINLESS STEEL ANGLES

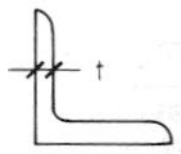


## STAINLESS STEEL ANGLES (IN.)

| SIZE x t | SIZE x t | SIZE x t |
|---|---|---|
| 3/4 x 3/4 x 1/8 | 1 1/2 x 1 1/2 x 3/16 | 2 1/2 x 2 1/2 x 1/4 |
| 1 x 1 x 1/8 | 1 1/2 x 1 1/2 x 1/4 | 3 x 3 x 1/4 |
| 1 x 1 x 3/16 | 2 x 2 x 1/8 | 3 x 3 x 5/16 |
| 1 1/4 x 1 1/4 x 1/8 | 2 x 2 x 3/16 | 3 x 3 x 3/8 |
| 1 1/4 x 1 1/4 x 3/16 | 2 x 2 x 1/4 | |
| 1 1/2 x 1 1/2 x 1/8 | 2 1/2 x 2 1/2 x 3/16 | |

Harnish, Morgan, and Causey, Architects; Ontario, California

**RECTANGULAR TUBING**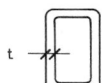

## RECTANGULAR TUBING—STEEL

| SIZE (IN.) | T = WALL THICKNESS (BW GAUGE OR IN.) | | | | |
|---|---|---|---|---|---|
| 1¹/₂ x ³/₄ | 0.073 | | | | |
| 1¹/₂ x 1 | 16 | 14 | 11 | | |
| 2 x 1 | 16 | 14 | 11 | | |
| 2 x 1¹/₄ | 14 | | | | |
| 2 x 1¹/₂ | 11 | | | | |
| 2¹/₂ x 1 | 14 | | | | |
| 2¹/₂ x 1¹/₄ | 14 | | | | |
| 2¹/₂ x 1¹/₂ | 14 | 0.145 | 7 | 5 | ¹/₄″ |
| 3 x 1 | 14 | | | | |
| 3 x 1¹/₂ | 16 | 14 | 11 | 7 | |
| 3 x 2 | 14 | 11 | ⁹/₆₄″ | ³/₁₆″ | ¹/₄″ |
| 4 x 2 | 14 | 11 | ⁵/₃₂″ | ³/₁₆″ | ¹/₄″ |
| 4 x 2¹/₂ | 11 | | | | |
| 4 x 3 | 11 | ⁵/₃₂″ | ³/₁₆″ | ¹/₄″ | ⁵/₁₆″ |
| 5 x 2 | ³/₁₆″ | ¹/₄″ | | | |
| 5 x 2¹/₂ | 11 | 7 | | | |
| 5 x 3 | ³/₁₆″ | ¹/₄″ | ⁵/₁₆″ | ³/₈″ | ¹/₂″ |
| 6 x 2 | ³/₁₆″ | ¹/₄″ | | | |
| 6 x 3 | ³/₁₆″ | ¹/₄″ | ⁵/₁₆″ | ³/₈″ | ¹/₂″ |
| 6 x 4 | ³/₁₆″ | ¹/₄″ | ⁵/₁₆″ | ³/₈″ | ¹/₂″ |
| 7 x 4 | ¹/₄″ | ³/₈″ | | | |
| 7 x 5 | ¹/₄″ | ⁵/₁₆″ | ³/₈″ | ¹/₂″ | |
| 8 x 2 | ³/₁₆″ | | | | |
| 8 x 3 | ³/₁₆″ | ¹/₄″ | | | |
| 8 x 4 | ³/₁₆″ | ¹/₄″ | ⁵/₁₆″ | ³/₈″ | ¹/₂″ |
| 8 x 6 | ³/₁₆″ | ¹/₄″ | ⁵/₁₆″ | ³/₈″ | ¹/₂″ |
| 10 x 2 | ³/₁₆″ | | | | |
| 10 x 4 | ³/₁₆″ | ¹/₄″ | | | |
| 10 x 5 | ¹/₄″ | | | | |
| 10 x 6 | ¹/₄″ | ⁵/₁₆″ | ³/₈″ | ¹/₂″ | |
| 10 x 8 | ¹/₄″ | ³/₈″ | ¹/₂″ | | |
| 12 x 2 | ³/₁₆″ | | | | |
| 12 x 4 | ¹/₄″ | ³/₈″ | | | |
| 12 x 6 | ¹/₄″ | ³/₈″ | ¹/₂″ | | |

**ALUMINUM**

| 2 x 3 | ³/₁₆″ |
|---|---|
| 2 x 4 | ³/₁₆″ |
| 2 x 6 | ³/₁₆″ |

**STAINLESS STEEL**

| ¹/₂ x 1¹/₂ | 0.065 |
|---|---|
| ³/₄ x 1¹/₄ | 0.065 |
| ³/₄ x 1¹/₂ | 0.065 |
| 1 x 1¹/₂ | 0.065 |
| 1 x 2 | 0.065 |
| 1¹/₄ x 2¹/₂ | 0.065 |
| 1³/₄ x 3 | 0.065 |
| 1³/₄ x 4 | 0.065 |

## ROUND TUBING—COPPER

| SIZE (IN.) NOMINAL INSIDE DIA. | OUTSIDE DIA. (BW GAUGE) | INSIDE DIAMETER (BW GAUGE) | | | |
|---|---|---|---|---|---|
| | | TYPE K | TYPE L | TYPE M | TYPE DWV |
| ¹/₄ | 0.375 | 0.305 | 0.315 | | |
| ¹/₂ | 0.625 | 0.527 | 0.545 | 0.569 | |
| ³/₄ | 0.875 | 0.745 | 0.785 | 0.811 | |
| 1 | 1.125 | 0.995 | 1.025 | 1.055 | |
| 1¹/₂ | 1.625 | 1.481 | 1.505 | 1.527 | 1.541 |
| 2 | 2.125 | 1.959 | 1.985 | 2.009 | 2.041 |
| 4 | 4.125 | 3.857 | 3.905 | 3.935 | 4.009 |

**RECTANGULAR ALUMINUM TUBING**

## RECTANGULAR ALUMINUM TUBING (IN.)

| SIZE x T | SIZE x T | SIZE x T |
|---|---|---|
| ¹/₂ x 1 x ¹/₈ | 1¹/₂ x 2¹/₂ x ¹/₈ | 2 x 3 x ¹/₈ |
| ³/₄ x 1¹/₂ x ¹/₈ | 1¹/₂ x 6 x ¹/₈ | 2 x 4 x ¹/₈ |
| 1 x 1¹/₂ x ¹/₈ | 1³/₄ x 2¹/₄ x ¹/₈ | 2 x 5 x ¹/₈ |
| 1 x 2 x ¹/₈ | 1³/₄ x 3 x ¹/₈ | 2 x 6 x ¹/₈ |
| 1 x 3 x ¹/₈ | 1³/₄ x 3¹/₂ x ¹/₈ | 3 x 5 x ¹/₈ |
| 1¹/₄ x 2¹/₂ x ¹/₈ | 1³/₄ x 4 x ¹/₈ | 3 x 5 x ¹/₈ |
| 1¹/₄ x 3 x ¹/₈ | 1³/₄ x 4¹/₂ x ¹/₈ | |
| 1¹/₂ x 2 x ¹/₈ | 1³/₄ x 5 x ¹/₈ | |

**SQUARE ALUMINUM TUBING**

## SQUARE ALUMINUM TUBING (IN.)

| SIZE x T | SIZE x T | SIZE x T |
|---|---|---|
| ¹/₂ x ¹/₂ x ¹/₁₆ | 1¹/₄ x 1¹/₄ x ⁵/₆₄ | 2 x 2 x ¹/₈ |
| ⁵/₈ x ⁵/₈ x ¹/₁₆ | 1¹/₄ x 1¹/₄ x ¹/₈ | 2¹/₂ x 2¹/₂ x ¹/₈ |
| ³/₄ x ³/₄ x ¹/₁₆ | 1¹/₂ x 1¹/₂ x ⁵/₆₄ | 3 x 3 x ¹/₈ |
| ³/₄ x ³/₄ x ¹/₈ | 1¹/₂ x 1¹/₂ x ¹/₈ | 4 x 4 x ¹/₈ |
| 1 x 1 x ¹/₁₆ | 1³/₄ x 1³/₄ x ¹/₈ | |
| 1 x 1 x ¹/₈ | 2 x 2 x ⁵/₆₄ | |

NOTE: Rectangular and square aluminum tubing with sharp corners is usually used for miscellaneous architectural metalwork.

**NOTE**

Round tubing, usually manufactured for mechanical purposes, is used for architectural metalwork to supplement round pipe. Round tubing is measured by the outside diameter and the wall thickness by gauge, fractions, or decimals of an inch. Round tubing is used where a high grade finish is required and exact diameters are necessary.

Round tubing is available in steel, aluminum, copper, stainless steel, and other metals. Individual manufacturers' catalogs should be consulted for availability of materials and sizes.

DMV  
M  
L  
K  
ROUND TUBING COPPER

**ROUND PIPE**

## ROUND PIPE—STEEL

| SIZE (IN.) NOMINAL INSIDE DIA. | OUTSIDE DIA. (BW GAUGE) | INSIDE DIAMETER (BW GAUGE) | | |
|---|---|---|---|---|
| | | STANDARD | EXTRA STRONG | DOUBLE EXTRA STRONG |
| ¹/₈ | 0.405 | 0.269 | 0.215 | |
| ¹/₄ | 0.540 | 0.364 | 0.302 | |
| ³/₈ | 0.675 | 0.493 | 0.423 | |
| ¹/₂ | 0.840 | 0.622 | 0.546 | 0.252 |
| ³/₄ | 1.050 | 0.824 | 0.742 | 0.434 |
| 1 | 1.315 | 1.049 | 0.957 | 0.599 |
| 1¹/₄ | 1.660 | 1.380 | 1.278 | 0.896 |
| 1¹/₂ | 1.900 | 1.610 | 1.500 | 1.100 |
| 2 | 2.375 | 2.067 | 1.939 | 1.503 |
| 2¹/₂ | 2.875 | 2.469 | 2.323 | 1.771 |
| 3 | 3.500 | 3.068 | 2.900 | 2.300 |
| 3¹/₂ | 4.000 | 3.548 | 3.364 | 2.728 |
| 4 | 4.500 | 4.026 | 3.826 | 3.152 |
| 5 | 5.563 | 5.047 | 4.813 | 4.063 |
| 6 | 6.625 | 6.065 | 5.761 | 4.897 |
| 8 | 8.625 | 7.981 | 7.625 | 6.875 |
| 10 | 10.750 | 10.020 | 9.750 | 8.750 |
| 12 | 12.750 | 12.000 | 11.750 | 10.750 |

**NOTE**

Round pipe is made in primarily three weights: Standard, Extra Strong (or Extra Heavy), and Double Extra Strong (or Double Extra Heavy). Outside diameters of the three weights of pipe in each size are always the same, extra thickness always being on the inside and therefore reducing the inside diameter of the heavier pipe. All sizes are specified by what is known as the "nominal inside diameter."

Round pipe is also available in aluminum and stainless steel. Individual manufacturers' catalogs should be consulted for sizes.

**SQUARE TUBING**

## SQUARE TUBING—STEEL

| SIZE (IN.) | T = WALL THICKNESS (BW GAUGE OR IN.) | | | | | | | | | | SIZE (IN.) | T |
|---|---|---|---|---|---|---|---|---|---|---|---|---|
| ¹/₂ x ¹/₂ | 18 | 16 | | | | | | | | | **ALUMINUM** | |
| ⁵/₈ x ⁵/₈ | 18 | 0.060 | 16 | | | | | | | | 2 x 2 | 0.120 |
| ³/₄ x ³/₄ | 20 | 18 | 0.060 | 16 | 11 | | | | | | 3 x 3 | ³/₁₆″ |
| ⁷/₈ x ⁷/₈ | 18 | 16 | | | | | | | | | 4 x 4 | ³/₁₆″ |
| 1 x 1 | 20 | 18 | 0.060 | 16 | 14 | 13 | 0.102 | 12 | 11 | | **STAINLESS STEEL** | |
| 1¹/₈ x 1¹/₈ | 18 | 16 | | | | | | | | | ³/₄ x ³/₄ | 0.049 |
| 1¹/₄ x 1¹/₄ | 18 | 0.060 | 16 | 0.075 | 0.090 | 11 | ³/₁₆″ | | | | 1 x 1 | 0.049 | 0.065 |
| 1¹/₂ x 1¹/₂ | 18 | 0.060 | 16 | 14 | 11 | 0.140 | 7 | ³/₁₆″ | ¹/₄″ | | 1¹/₄ x 1¹/₄ | 0.065 |
| 1³/₄ x 1³/₄ | 16 | 14 | 13 | 11 | | | | | | | 1¹/₂ x 1¹/₂ | 0.065 |
| 2 x 2 | 0.060 | 18 | 16 | 14 | 11 | ¹/₈″ | 0.145 | ³/₁₆″ | ¹/₄″ | | 1³/₄ x 1³/₄ | 0.065 |
| 2¹/₂ x 2¹/₂ | 16 | 14 | 11 | 0.141 | ¹/₄″ | | | | | | 2 x 2 | 0.065 |
| 3 x 3 | 16 | 14 | 13 | 11 | ³/₁₆″ | ¹/₄″ | | | | | | |
| 3¹/₂ x 3¹/₂ | 11 | ⁵/₃₂″ | 5 | ¹/₄″ | | | | | | | | |
| 4 x 4 | 14 | 11 | ³/₁₆″ | ¹/₄″ | ³/₈″ | ¹/₂″ | | | | | | |
| 4¹/₂ x 4¹/₂ | ³/₁₆″ | ¹/₄″ | | | | | | | | | | |
| 5 x 5 | ³/₁₆″ | ¹/₄″ | ⁵/₁₆″ | ³/₈″ | | | | | | | | |
| 6 x 6 | ³/₁₆″ | ¹/₄″ | ⁵/₁₆″ | ³/₈″ | | | | | | | | |
| 7 x 7 | ³/₁₆″ | ¹/₄″ | ⁵/₁₆″ | ³/₈″ | | | | | | | | |
| 8 x 8 | ¹/₄″ | ⁵/₁₆″ | ³/₈″ | ¹/₂″ | | | | | | | | |
| 10 x 10 | ¹/₄″ | ⁵/₁₆″ | ³/₈″ | ¹/₂″ | | | | | | | | |

Harnish, Morgan, and Causey, Architects; Ontario, California

**STRUCTURAL METAL FRAMING**  5

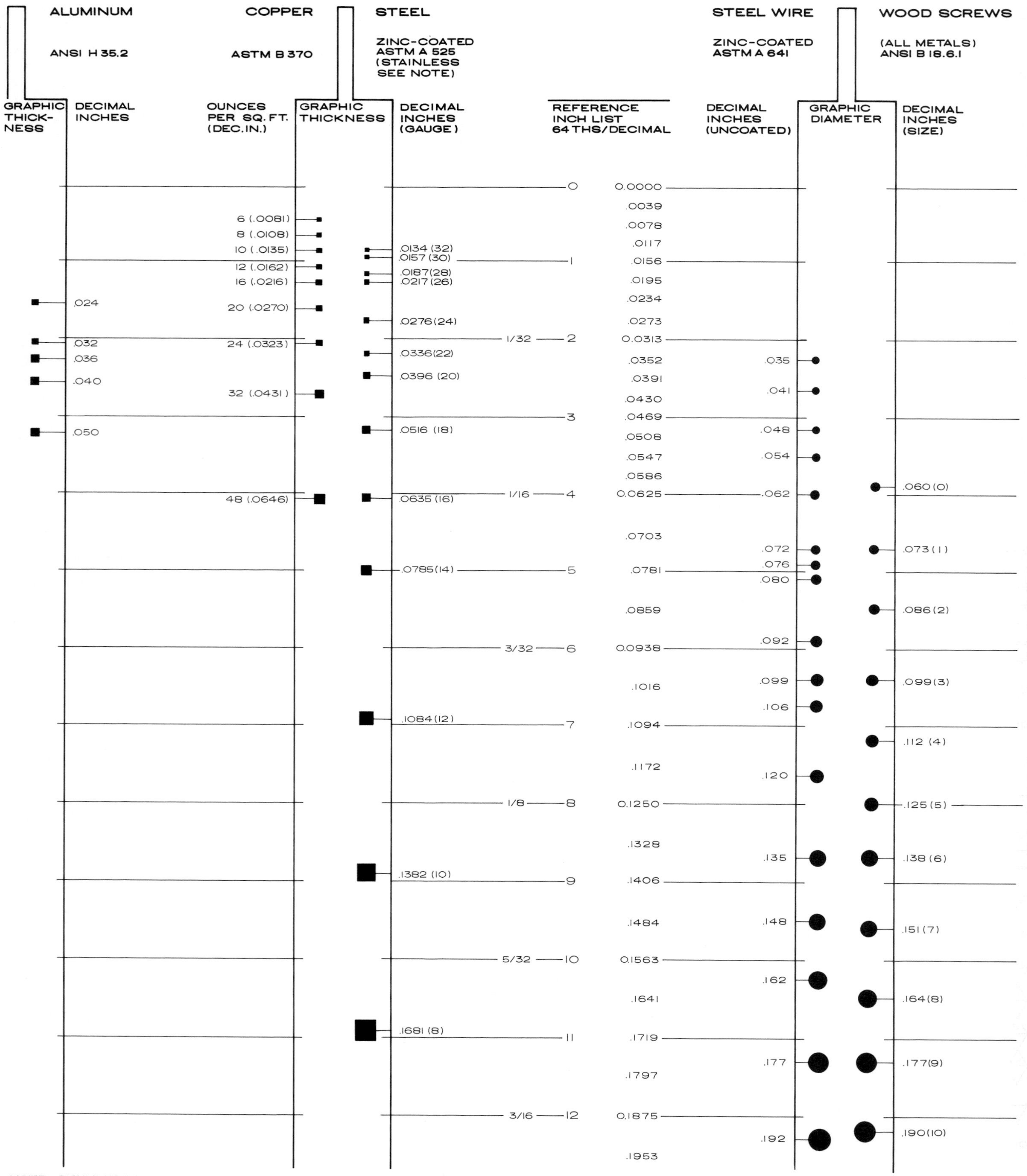

| ALUMINUM | | COPPER | STEEL | | | STEEL WIRE | WOOD SCREWS |
|---|---|---|---|---|---|---|---|
| ANSI H 35.2 | | ASTM B 370 | ZINC-COATED ASTM A 525 (STAINLESS SEE NOTE) | | | ZINC-COATED ASTM A 641 | (ALL METALS) ANSI B 18.6.1 |
| GRAPHIC THICK-NESS | DECIMAL INCHES | OUNCES PER SQ. FT. (DEC. IN.) | GRAPHIC THICKNESS | DECIMAL INCHES (GAUGE) | REFERENCE INCH LIST 64 THS/DECIMAL | DECIMAL INCHES (UNCOATED) | GRAPHIC DIAMETER | DECIMAL INCHES (SIZE) |

Reference inch list / decimal values:

| | | | | | REFERENCE | | | |
|---|---|---|---|---|---|---|---|---|
| | | 6 (.0081) | | | O  0.0000 | | | |
| | | 8 (.0108) | | | .0039 | | | |
| | | 10 (.0135) | | .0134 (32) | .0078 | | | |
| | | 12 (.0162) | | .0157 (30) —— 1 | .0117 | | | |
| | | 16 (.0216) | | .0187 (28) | .0156 | | | |
| | .024 | | | .0217 (26) | .0195 | | | |
| | | 20 (.0270) | | | .0234 | | | |
| | | | | .0276 (24) | .0273 | | | |
| | .032 | 24 (.0323) | | | 1/32 — 2  0.0313 | | | |
| | .036 | | | .0336 (22) | .0352 | .035 | | |
| | .040 | | | .0396 (20) | .0391 | | | |
| | | 32 (.0431) | | | .0430 | .041 | | |
| | | | | | 3  .0469 | | | |
| | .050 | | | .0516 (18) | .0508 | .048 | | |
| | | | | | .0547 | .054 | | |
| | | | | | .0586 | | | |
| | | 48 (.0646) | | .0635 (16) | 1/16 — 4  0.0625 | .062 | | .060 (O) |
| | | | | | .0703 | | | |
| | | | | .0785 (14) — 5 | .0781 | .072 | | .073 (1) |
| | | | | | | .076 | | |
| | | | | | | .080 | | |
| | | | | | .0859 | | | .086 (2) |
| | | | | | 3/32 — 6  0.0938 | .092 | | |
| | | | | | .1016 | .099 | | .099 (3) |
| | | | | | | .106 | | |
| | | | | .1084 (12) — 7 | .1094 | | | |
| | | | | | .1172 | .120 | | .112 (4) |
| | | | | 1/8 — 8  0.1250 | | | | .125 (5) |
| | | | | | .1328 | .135 | | .138 (6) |
| | | | | .1382 (10) — 9 | .1406 | | | |
| | | | | | .1484 | .148 | | .151 (7) |
| | | | | 5/32 — 10  0.1563 | | .162 | | .164 (8) |
| | | | | | .1641 | | | |
| | | | | .1681 (8) — 11 | .1719 | .177 | | .177 (9) |
| | | | | | .1797 | | | |
| | | | | 3/16 — 12  0.1875 | | .192 | | .190 (10) |
| | | | | | .1953 | | | |

NOTE: STAINLESS NOMINALLY SAME AS ZINC-COATED BUT VARIES SLIGHTLY BETWEEN MANUFACTURERS.

E. E. Gene Emery; University of Oklahoma; Norman, Oklahoma
ASME; ASTM; see data sources

5

**STRUCTURAL METAL FRAMING**

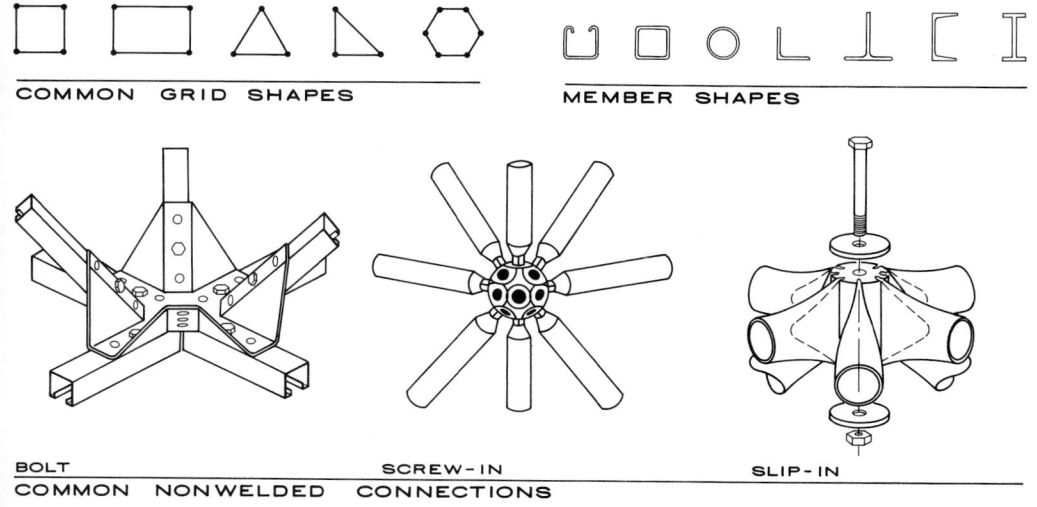

COMMON GRID SHAPES

MEMBER SHAPES

BOLT  SCREW-IN  SLIP-IN

COMMON NONWELDED CONNECTIONS

## MODULE SELECTION CRITERIA

Select a space frame module that (a) is compatible with the building planning module in shape (e.g., square module with orthogonal plan) and size (multiple of planning module); (b) is consistent with the limitations of the interfacing systems (e.g., maximum span of roof deck or mullion spacing of glazing system); and (c) satisfies the desired spatial and aesthetic effect in scale and form.

## OPTIMIZATION

1. SUPPORT LOCATION: Two- or three-way symmetry with cantilever of 15 to 30% of span.
2. MODULE SIZE: As large as possible with a minimum number of joints (dependent on interfacing system); 1:3 to 7:10 depth:width ratio (in general, shallower modules are more economical).
3. DEPTH-TO-SPAN RATIO: Roof—1:18 (column support), 1:20 to 1:25 (edge support); floor—1:16 to 1:20.
4. MEMBER SHAPE: Square tubes or angles within their span range are often the most economical.
5. INFILL SYSTEM: Two- or three-way system or one-way system applied in checkerboard pattern.
6. SHOP VS. FIELD CONNECTIONS: Keep field and, in particular, in-place connections to a minimum; welded connections often eliminate joint pieces.

## NOTES

1. The prime attributes of space frame structural systems are their light weight, inherent rigidity, extensive capabilities in form, size, and span, and compatible interaction with other building support systems, primarily HVAC.
2. Most systems are designed for specific applications and a structural engineer with space frame experience should always be consulted. Consult also manufacturers for full range of capabilities: loading, spans, shapes, specific details. Standardized systems in 4 and 5 ft modules are available.
3. Metal space frames are classified as noncombustible construction and can usually be exposed when 20 ft above the floor. However, an automatic fire extinguishing system or a rated ceiling may be required. Consult applicable building and fire codes.
4. Roof drainage is achieved by locating drains in natural low points, sloping the entire frame, changing the interface depth, or cambering the system.
5. The finishes commonly available are painted and galvanized.

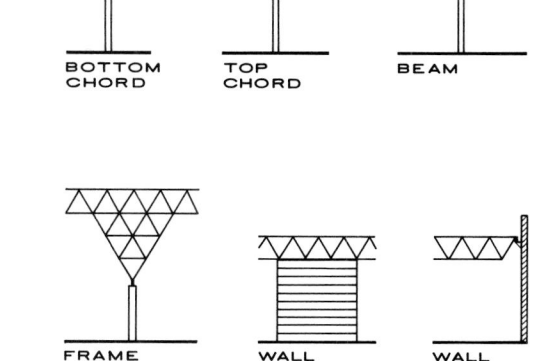

BOTTOM CHORD  TOP CHORD  BEAM

FRAME CAPITAL  WALL  WALL

SUPPORT METHODS

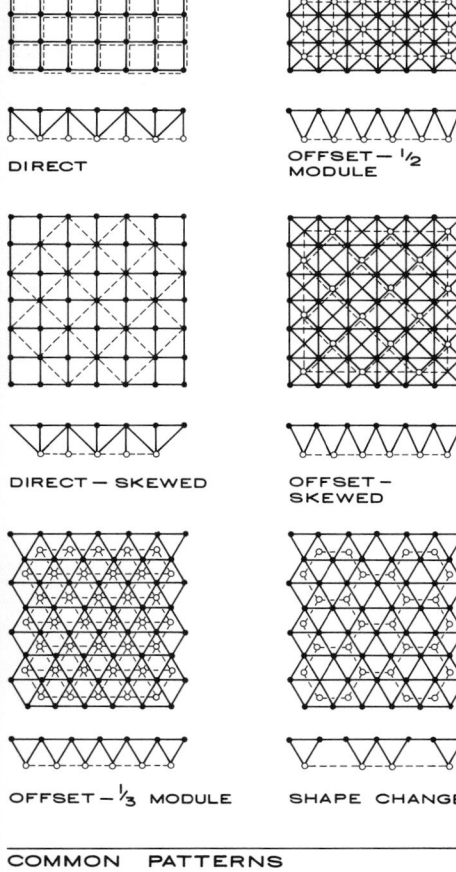

DIRECT  OFFSET—1/2 MODULE

DIRECT — SKEWED  OFFSET— SKEWED

OFFSET—1/3 MODULE  SHAPE CHANGE

COMMON PATTERNS

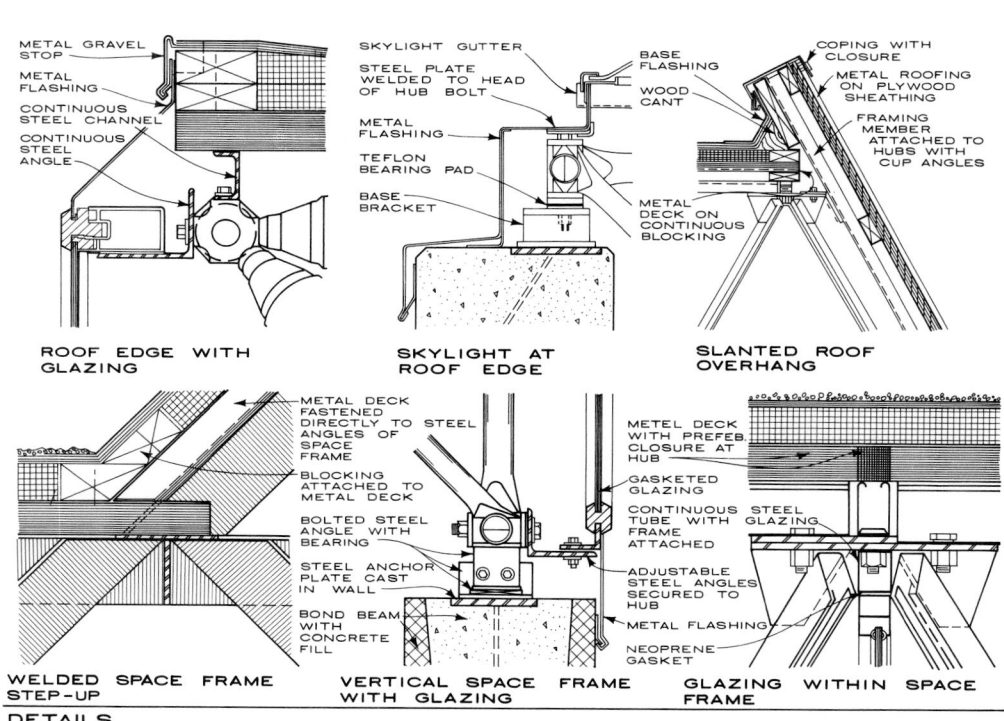
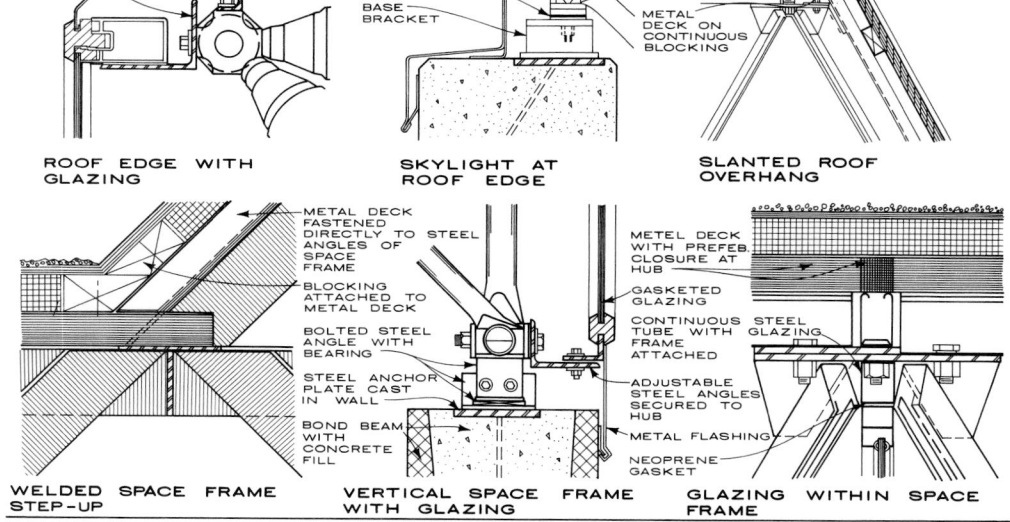

ROOF EDGE WITH GLAZING  SKYLIGHT AT ROOF EDGE  SLANTED ROOF OVERHANG

WELDED SPACE FRAME STEP-UP  VERTICAL SPACE FRAME WITH GLAZING  GLAZING WITHIN SPACE FRAME

DETAILS

Steven W. Henkelman, R.A.; Cope, Linder, Walmsley; Philadelphia, Pennsylvania

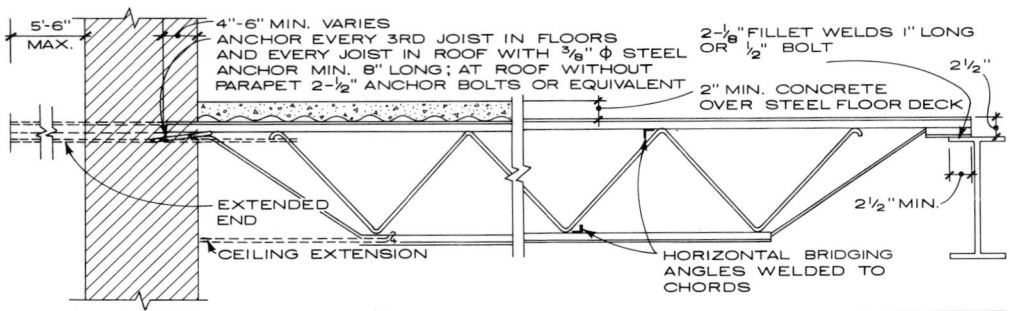

**SECTION THROUGH JOIST BEARING**

**SECTION THROUGH JOISTS**

**NOTES**

The following information applies to both open web and long span steel joists.

JOIST DESIGNATION:

25 LH 10 ← Chord
└── Type of steel
└── Longspan (DL-deep longspan)
└── Nominal depth (in.)

For greater economy, the K-series joist replaced the H-series joist in 1986.

1. ROOF CONSTRUCTION: Joists are usually covered by steel deck topped with either rigid insulation board or lightweight concrete fill and built-up felt and gravel roof. Plywood, poured gypsum, or structural wood fiber deck systems can also be used with built-up roof.

2. CEILINGS: Ceiling supports can be suspended from or mounted directly to bottom chords of joists, although suspended systems are recommended because of dimensional variations in actual joist depths.

3. FLOOR CONSTRUCTION: Joists usually covered by 2 to $2\frac{1}{2}$ in. concrete on steel centering. Concrete thickness may be increased for electrical conduit or electrical/communications raceways. Precast concrete, gypsum planks, or plywood can also be used for the floor system.

4. VIBRATION: Objectionable vibrations can occur in open web joist and $2\frac{1}{2}$ in. concrete slab designs for open floor areas at spans between 24 and 40 ft, especially at 28 ft. When a floor area cannot have partitions, objectionable vibrations can be prevented or reduced by increasing slab thickness, joist spacing, or floor spans. Attention should also be given to support framing beams which can magnify a vibration problem.

5. OPENINGS IN FLOOR OR ROOF SYSTEMS: Small openings between joists are framed with angles of channel supported on the adjoining two joists. Larger openings necessitating interruption of joists are framed with steel angle or channel headers spanning the adjoining two joists. The interrupted joists bear on the headers.

6. ROOF DRAINAGE: Roof drainage should be carefully considered on level or near level roofs especially with parapet walls. Roof insulation can be sloped, joists can be sloped or obtained with sloping top chords in one or both directions, and overflow scuppers should be provided in parapet walls.

---

**PRELIMINARY JOIST SELECTION:** The tables below are not to be used for final joist design but are intended as an aid in speeding selection of steel joists for preliminary design and planning. The final design must be a separate and thorough process, involving a complete investigation of the pertinent conditions. This page is not for that purpose. Consult structural engineer.

**EXAMPLE:** Assume a particular clear span. By assuming a joist spacing and estimating the total load a joist can immediately be selected from the table. Then proceed with preliminary design studies.

**NOTES**
1. Total safe load = live load + dead load. Dead load includes weight of joist. For dead loads and recommended live loads, see pages on weights of materials. Local codes will govern.
2. Span not to exceed a depth 24 times that of a nominal joist.
3. For more detailed information refer to standard specifications and load tables adopted by the Steel Joist Institute.

**NUMBER OF ROWS OF BRIDGING (FT)**
**DISTANCES ARE CLEAR SPAN DIMENSIONS**

| CHORD SIZE[1] | 1 ROW | 2 ROWS | 3 ROWS | 4 ROWS[2] | 5 ROWS[2] |
|---|---|---|---|---|---|
| #1 | Up to 16 | 16–24 | 24–28 | — | — |
| #2 | Up to 17 | 17–25 | 25–32 | — | — |
| #3 | Up to 18 | 18–28 | 28–38 | 38–40 | — |
| #4 | Up to 19 | 19–28 | 28–38 | 38–48 | — |
| #5 | Up to 19 | 19–29 | 29–39 | 39–50 | 50–52 |
| #6 | Up to 19 | 19–29 | 29–39 | 39–51 | 51–56 |
| #7 | Up to 20 | 20–33 | 33–45 | 45–58 | 58–60 |
| #8 | Up to 20 | 20–33 | 33–45 | 45–58 | 58–60 |
| #9 | Up to 20 | 20–33 | 33–46 | 46–59 | 59–60 |
| #10 | Up to 20 | 20–37 | 37–51 | 51–60 | |
| #11 | Up to 20 | 20–38 | 38–53 | 53–60 | |
| #12 | Up to 20 | 20–39 | 39–53 | 53–60 | |

1. Last digit(s) of joist designation shown in load table below.
2. Where four or five rows of bridging are required, a row nearest the midspan of the joist shall be diagonal bridging with bolted connections at chords and intersections.

---

**SELECTED LOAD TABLES: K SERIES**—TOTAL SAFE UNIFORMLY DISTRIBUTED LOAD (LB/FT)

| JOIST DESIGNATION | | 8 | 12 | 16 | 20 | 24 | 28 | 32 | 36 | 42 | 48 | 54 | 60 |
|---|---|---|---|---|---|---|---|---|---|---|---|---|---|
| K SERIES $f_s$ = 30,000 psi | 8K1 | 550 | 444 | 246 | | | | | | | | | |
| | 10K1 | | 550 | 313 | 199 | | | | | | | | |
| | 12K3 | | 550 | 476 | 302 | 208 | | | | | | | |
| | 14K4 | | | 550 | 428 | 295 | 216 | | | | | | |
| | 16K5 | | | 550 | 550 | 384 | 281 | 214 | | | | | |
| | 18K6 | | | | 550 | 473 | 346 | 264 | 208 | | | | |
| | 20K7 | | | | 550 | 550 | 430 | 328 | 259 | | | | |
| | 22K9 | | | | | 550 | 550 | 436 | 344 | 252 | | | |
| | 24K9 | | | | | 550 | 550 | 478 | 377 | 276 | 211 | | |
| | 26K10 | | | | | | 550 | 549 | 486 | 356 | 272 | | |
| | 28K10 | | | | | | 550 | 549 | 487 | 384 | 294 | 232 | |
| | 30K11 | | | | | | | 549 | 487 | 417 | 362 | 285 | 231 |
| | 30K12 | | | | | | | 549 | 487 | 417 | 365 | 324 | 262 |

Note: Number preceding letter is joist depth; 14K4 is 14 in. deep.

Kenneth D. Franch, AIA, PE; Phillips Swager Associates, Inc.; Dallas, Texas
Setter, Leach & Lindstrom, Inc.; Minneapolis, Minnesota

**5**    **METAL JOISTS**

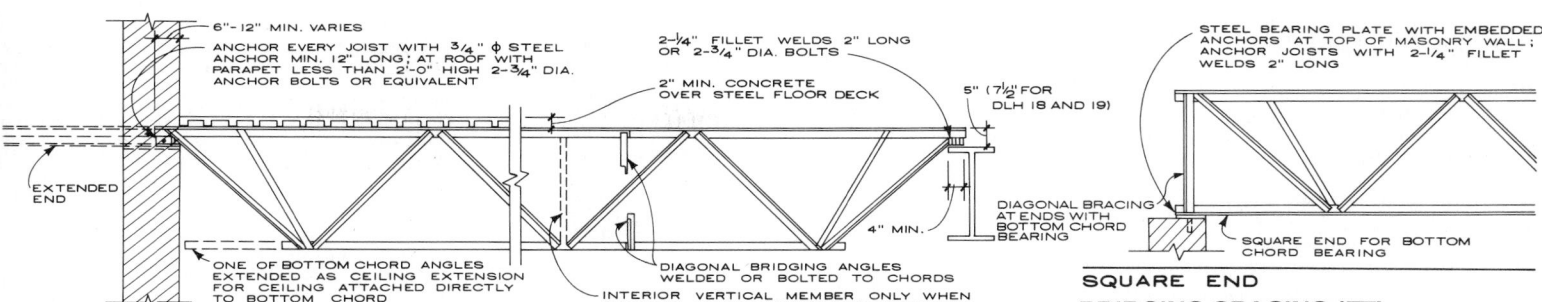

## SECTION THROUGH JOIST BEARING

6"-12" MIN. VARIES

ANCHOR EVERY JOIST WITH 3/4" φ STEEL ANCHOR MIN. 12" LONG; AT ROOF WITH PARAPET LESS THAN 2'-0" HIGH 2-3/4" DIA. ANCHOR BOLTS OR EQUIVALENT

EXTENDED END

ONE OF BOTTOM CHORD ANGLES EXTENDED AS CEILING EXTENSION FOR CEILING ATTACHED DIRECTLY TO BOTTOM CHORD

2-1/4" FILLET WELDS 2" LONG OR 2-3/4" DIA. BOLTS

2" MIN. CONCRETE OVER STEEL FLOOR DECK

5" (7 1/2" FOR DLH 18 AND 19)

4" MIN.

DIAGONAL BRIDGING ANGLES WELDED OR BOLTED TO CHORDS

INTERIOR VERTICAL MEMBER ONLY WHEN REQUIRED BY TOP CHORD STRESSES

STEEL BEARING PLATE WITH EMBEDDED ANCHORS AT TOP OF MASONRY WALL; ANCHOR JOISTS WITH 2-1/4" FILLET WELDS 2" LONG

DIAGONAL BRACING AT ENDS WITH BOTTOM CHORD BEARING

SQUARE END FOR BOTTOM CHORD BEARING

## SQUARE END BRIDGING SPACING (FT)

| LH CHORD SIZE† | MAXIMUM SPACING (FT) |
|---|---|
| 02–09 | 11 |
| 10–14 | 16 |
| 15–17 | 21 |
| DLH CHORD SIZE† | MAXIMUM SPACING (FT) |
| 10 | 14 |
| 11–14 | 16 |
| 15–17 | 21 |
| 18–19 | 26 |

†Last two digits of joist designation shown in load tables.

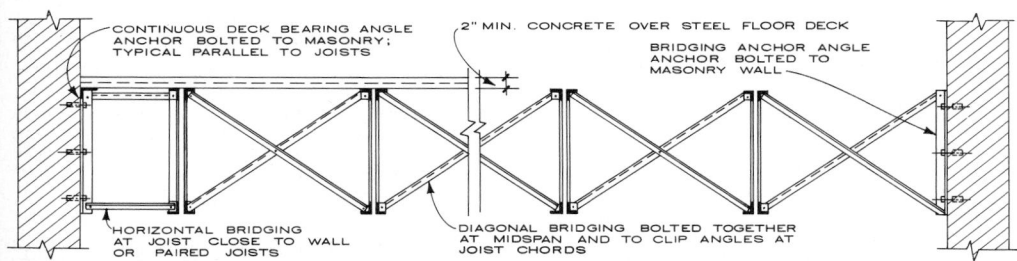

## SECTION THROUGH JOISTS

CONTINUOUS DECK BEARING ANGLE ANCHOR BOLTED TO MASONRY; TYPICAL PARALLEL TO JOISTS

2" MIN. CONCRETE OVER STEEL FLOOR DECK

BRIDGING ANCHOR ANGLE ANCHOR BOLTED TO MASONRY WALL

HORIZONTAL BRIDGING AT JOIST CLOSE TO WALL OR PAIRED JOISTS

DIAGONAL BRIDGING BOLTED TOGETHER AT MIDSPAN AND TO CLIP ANGLES AT JOIST CHORDS

## PRELIMINARY JOIST SELECTION

The tables below are not to be used for final joist design but are intended as an aid in speeding selection of steel joists for preliminary design and planning.

The final design must be a separate thorough process, involving a complete investigation of the pertinent conditions. This page is not for that purpose. Consult a structural engineer.

### EXAMPLE

Assume a particular clear span. By assuming a joist spacing and estimating the total load a joist can immediately be selected from the table. Then proceed with preliminary design studies.

### NOTES

1. Total safe load = live load + dead load. Dead load includes weight of joist. For dead loads and recommended live loads, see pages on weights of materials. Local codes will govern.
2. Span not to exceed 24 times depth of a nominal joist for roofs; 20 times depth for floors.
3. For more detailed information refer to standard specifications and load tables adopted by the Steel Joist Institute.

## FIRE RESISTANCE RATINGS

| TIME (HR) | FLOOR ASSEMBLIES | TIME (HR) | ROOF ASSEMBLIES |
|---|---|---|---|
| 1 or 1 1/2 | 2" reinforced concrete, listed 1/2" (5/8" for 1 1/2 hr) acoustical tile ceiling, concealed ceiling grid suspended from joists | 1 | Built-up roofing on 2" structural wood fiber units, listed 3/4" acoustical ceiling tiles, concealed ceiling grid suspended from joists |
| | 2" reinforced concrete, listed 1/2" acoustical board ceiling, listed exposed ceiling grid suspended from joists | | Built-up roofing and insulation on 26 gauge min. steel deck, listed 5/8" acoustical ceiling boards, listed exposed ceiling grid suspended from joists |
| | 2" reinforced concrete, listed 1/2" gypsum board ceiling fastened to joists | | Built-up roofing over 2" vermiculite on centering, listed 1/2" acoustical ceiling boards, listed exposed ceiling grid suspended from joists |
| 2 | 2 1/2" reinforced concrete, listed 5/8" acoustical tile ceiling, listed concealed ceiling grid suspended from joists | | |
| | 2 1/2" reinforced concrete, listed 1/2" acoustical board ceiling, listed exposed ceiling grid suspended from joists | 2 | Built-up roofing on 2" listed gypsum building units, listed 5/8" acoustical ceiling boards, listed exposed ceiling grid suspended from joists |
| | 2" reinforced concrete, listed 5/8" gypsum board ceiling fastened to joists | | Built-up roofing on 22 gauge min. steel deck, suspended 7/8" metal lath and plaster ceiling |
| | 2 1/2" reinforced concrete, listed 1/2" gypsum board ceiling fastened to joists | | |

NOTE: Listed by Underwriters Laboratories or Factory Mutual approved, as appropriate. Ratings are the result of tests made in accordance with ASTM Standard E 119. A more complete list can be obtained from the SJI Technical Digest concerning the design of fire resistive assemblies with steel joists.

## SELECTED LOAD TABLES: LH AND DLH SERIES—TOTAL SAFE UNIFORMLY DISTRIBUTED LOAD (LB/FT)

| JOIST DESIGNATION | | CLEAR SPAN (FT) | | | | | | | | | | | | |
|---|---|---|---|---|---|---|---|---|---|---|---|---|---|---|
| | | 28 | 32 | 36 | 42 | 48 | 54 | 60 | 66 | 72 | 78 | 84 | 90 | 96 |
| LH Series $f_s$ = 30,000 psi | 18LH05 | 581 | 448 | 355 | | | | | | | | | | |
| | 20LH06 | 723 | 560 | 444 | | | | | | | | | | |
| | 24LH07 | | | 588 | 446 | 343 | | | | | | | | |
| | 28LH09 | | | | 639 | 499 | 401 | | | | | | | |
| | 32LH10 | | | | | 478 | 389 | | | | | | | |
| | 36LH11 | | | | | | 451 | 378 | 322 | | | | | |
| | 40LH12 | | | | | | | 472 | 402 | 346 | | | | |
| | 44LH13 | | | | | | | | | 423 | 369 | | | |
| | 48LH14 | | | | | | | | | | 444 | 390 | 346 | |
| | | 90 | 96 | 102 | 108 | 114 | 120 | 126 | 132 | 138 | 144 | | | |
| DLH Series $f_s$ = 30,000 psi | 52DLH13 | 433 | 381 | 338 | | | | | | | | | | |
| | 56DLH14 | | | 411 | 368 | | | | | | | | | |
| | 60DLH15 | | | 442 | 398 | 361 | | | | | | | | |
| | 64DLH16 | | | | 466 | 421 | 382 | | | | | | | |
| | 68DLH17 | | | | | 460 | 420 | | | | | | | |
| | 72DLH18 | | | | | | 505 | 463 | 426 | | | | | |

NOTE: Number preceding letter is joist depth; 32LH10 is 32 in. deep.

Setter, Leach & Lindstrom, Inc.; Minneapolis, Minnesota

## EXAMPLES OF THE MANY TYPES OF DECK AVAILABLE (SEE TABLES)

1. Roof deck.
2. Floor deck (noncomposite).
3. Composite floor deck interacting with concrete.
4. Permanent forms for self-supporting concrete slabs.
5. Cellular deck (composite or noncomposite).
6. Acoustical roof deck.
7. Acoustic cellular deck (composite or noncomposite).
8. Electric raceway cellular deck.
9. Prevented roof deck (used with lightweight insulating concrete fill).

All metal floor and roof decks must be secured to all supports, generally by means of "puddle welds" made through the deck to supporting steel. Steel sheet lighter than 22 gauge (0.0295 in. thick) should be secured by use of welding washers (see illustration).

Shear studs welded through floor deck also serve to secure the deck to supporting steel. Power actuated and pneumatically driven fasteners may also be used in certain applications.

Side laps between adjacent sheets of deck must be secured by button-punching standing seams, welding, or screws, in accordance with manufacturer's recommendations.

Decks used as lateral diaphragms must be welded to steel supports around their entire perimeter to ensure development of diaphragm action. More stringent requirements may govern the size and/or spacing of attachments to supports and side lap fasteners or welds.

Roof deck selection must take into consideration construction and maintenance loads as well as the capacity to support uniformly distributed live loads. Consult current Steel Deck Institute recommendations and Factory Mutual requirements.

Floor deck loadings are virtually unlimited in scope, ranging from light residential and institutional loads to heavy duty industrial floors utilizing composite deck with slabs up to 24 in. thick. The designer can select the deck type, depth, and gauge most suitable for the application.

Fire resistance ratings for roof deck assemblies are published by Underwriters Laboratories and Factory Mutual. Ratings of 1 to 2 hr are achieved with spray-on insulation: a 1 hr rating with suspended acoustical ceiling and a 2 hr rating with a metal lath and plaster ceiling.

Floor deck assembly fire resistive ratings are available both with and without spray-applied fireproofing, and with regular weight or lightweight concrete fill. From 1 to 3 hr ratings are possible using only concrete fill—consult Underwriters Laboratory Fire Resistance Index for assembly ratings.

Consult manufacturer's literature and technical representatives for additional information. Consult "Steel Deck Institute Design Manual for Floor Decks and Roof Decks" and "Tentative Recommendations for the Design of Steel Deck Diaphragms" by the Steel Deck Institute.

## ADVANTAGES OF METAL ROOF DECKS

1. High strength-to-weight ratio reduces roof dead load.
2. Can be erected in most weather conditions.
3. Variety of depths and rib patterns available.
4. Acoustical treatment is possible.
5. Serve as base for insulation and roofing.
6. Fire ratings can be obtained with standard assemblies.
7. Provide lateral diaphragm.
8. Can be erected quickly.
9. Can be erected economically.

The use of vapor barriers on metal deck roofs is not customary for normal building occupancies. For high relative humidity exposure a vapor barrier may be provided as part of the roofing system, but the user should be aware of the great difficulties encountered in installing a vapor barrier on metal deck. Punctures of the vapor barrier over valleys might reduce or negate entirely the effectiveness of the vapor barrier.

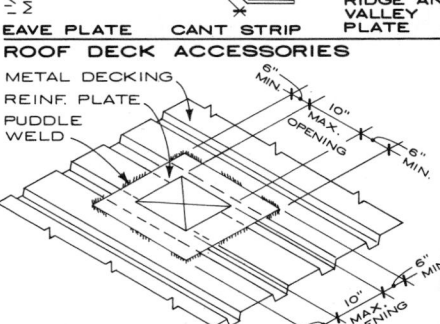

**ROOF DECK ACCESSORIES**

**REINFORCING PLATE**

Small openings (up to 6 x 6 in. or 6 in. dia.) may usually be cut in roof or floor deck without reinforcing the deck. Openings up to 10 x 10 in. or 10 in. dia. require reinforcing of the deck by either welding a reinforcing plate to the deck all around the opening, or by providing channel shaped headers and/or supplementary reinforcing parallel to the deck span. Reinforcing plates should be 14 gauge sheets with a minimum projection of 6 in. beyond all sides of the opening, and they should be welded to each cell of the deck.

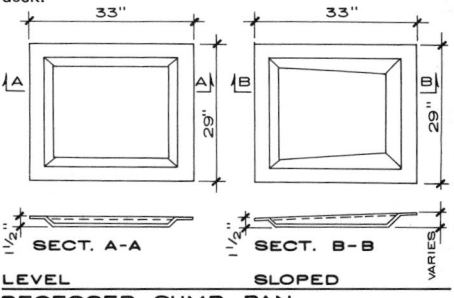

**RECESSED SUMP PAN**

Preformed recessed sump pans are available from deck manufacturers for use at roof drains.

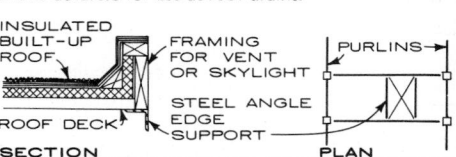

**FRAMED OPENING**

Larger openings should be framed with supplementary steel members so that all free edges of deck are supported.

Roof-mounted mechanical equipment should not be placed directly on metal roof deck. Equipment on built-up or prefabricated curbs should be supported directly on main and supplementary structural members and the deck must also be supported along all free edges (see illustration). Heavy items such as cooling towers which must be elevated should be supported by posts extending through pitch pockets directly onto structural members below the deck. Openings through the deck may be handled as previously discussed.

## ROOF DECK (ACOUSTICAL ROOF DECKS ARE AVAILABLE IN MANY OF THESE PROFILES – CONSULT MANUFACTURERS)

| TYPICAL EXAMPLES | ECONOMICAL SPANS | USUAL WIDTH | MAX. LENGTH AVAILABLE |
|---|---|---|---|
| 1½" NARROW RIB | 4'- 6' | 24" – 36" | 36'– 42' |
| 1½" INTERMEDIATE RIB | 5'- 7' | 24"– 36" | 40'– 42' |
| 1½" WIDE RIB | 6'- 9' | 24" – 30" | 32'– 42' |
| 3" | 8'- 16' | 24" | 40' |
| 4½" | 15'- 18' | 12" | 32' |
| 1½" | 7'- 11' | 24" | 32' |
| 3/16" | 10'- 20' | 24" | 40' |
| 7½" | 12'- 30' | 12" | 40'- 42' |
| 7½" | 13'- 33' | 24" | 40' |

Walter D. Shapiro, P.E.; Tor, Shapiro & Associates; New York, New York

# 5   METAL DECKING

## FLOOR DECK – COMPOSITE WITH CONCRETE FILL

| TYPICAL EXAMPLES | ECONOMICAL SPANS | USUAL WIDTH | MAX. LENGTH AVAILABLE |
|---|---|---|---|
| 1½" | 4'– 9' | 30" | 36' |
| 2" | 8'– 12' | 30" | 40'– 45' |
| 3" | 8'– 15' | 24" | 40' |
| 7½" 6" 4½" 3" | 8'– 24' | 12" | 40' |

## FLOOR DECK – COMPOSITE CELLULAR (ACOUSTIC DECK AVAILABLE IN SOME PROFILES; CONSULT MANUFACTURERS )

| | ECONOMICAL SPANS | USUAL WIDTH | MAX. LENGTH AVAILABLE |
|---|---|---|---|
| 1½" 6" | 6'– 12' | 24" | 40' |
| ⅝" | 6'– 12' | 24" | 40' |
| 2" | 6'– 12' | 30" | 36'– 45' |
| 3" | 10'– 16' | 24" | 40' |
| 7½" 6" 4½" 3" | 8'– 24' | 24" | 40' |

## CORRUGATED FORMS FOR CONCRETE SLABS – NONCOMPOSITE

| | ECONOMICAL SPANS | USUAL WIDTH | MAX. LENGTH AVAILABLE |
|---|---|---|---|
| ½" | 1'– 2' | 96" | 2'– 6' |
| 9/16" | 1'– 6"– 3' | 30" | 40' |
| 15/16" | 3'– 5' | 29" | 40' |
| 1" 4" | 3'– 5' | 28" | 30'– 40' |
| 1⅝" 4½" | 4'– 9' | 27" | 30'– 40' |
| 2" 6" | 7'– 12' | 24" | 30'– 40' |

Walter D. Shapiro, P.E.; Tor, Shapiro & Associates; New York, New York

---

### ADVANTAGES OF METAL FLOOR DECKS:

1. Provide a working platform, eliminating temporary wood planking in highrise use.
2. Composite decks provide positive reinforcement for concrete slabs.
3. Noncomposite and composite decks serve as forms for concrete, eliminate forming and stripping.
4. Fire ratings can be achieved without spray-on fire-proofing or rated ceilings.
5. Acoustical treatment is possible.
6. Electric raceways may be built into floor slab.
7. Economical floor assemblies.

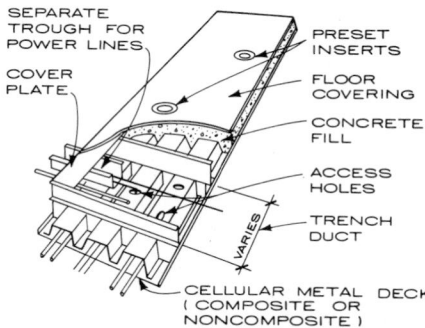

### ELECTRICAL TRENCH DUCT

Electric raceways may be built into floor slabs by use of cellular deck or special units that are blended with plain deck. Two-way distribution is achieved by use of trench ducts that sit astride the cellular units at right angles. Use of trench ducts with composite floor deck may reduce or eliminate entirely the effectiveness of composite action at the trench duct. This is also true for composite action between steel floor beams and concrete fill. Trench duct locations must be taken into account in deciding whether composite action is possible.

Openings in composite deck may be blocked out on top of the deck and the deck can be burned out after the concrete has set and become self-supporting. Reinforcing bars can be added alongside openings to replace positive moment deck steel area lost at openings.

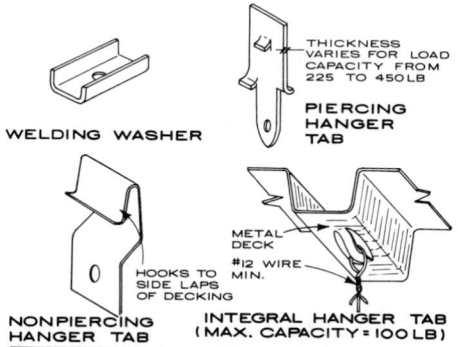

### DECKING ATTACHMENTS

A convenient and economical means for supporting lightweight acoustical ceilings is by attaching suspension system to hanger tabs at side laps, piercing tabs driven through deck, or prepunched tabs in roof deck (see illustrations above). These tabs and metal decks must not be used to support plaster ceilings, piping, ductwork, electric equipment, or other heavy loads. Such elements must be supported directly from structural joists, beams, girders, and so on, or from supplementary subframing, and not from metal deck.

## ALLOWABLE LOADS FOR SIMPLE SPAN STEEL "C" JOISTS (LB/LINEAR FOOT) MADE OF 40 KSI MATERIAL

| SPAN | SECTION (DEPTH/GAUGE) | SINGLE MEMBER | | DOUBLE MEMBER | |
|---|---|---|---|---|---|
| | | TOTAL ALLOWABLE LOAD | ALLOWABLE LIVE LOAD | TOTAL ALLOWABLE LOAD | ALLOWABLE LIVE LOAD |
| 8' | 6"/18 | 201 | 189 | 402* | 378 |
| | 6"/16 | 245 | 230 | 490 | 460 |
| | 6"/14 | 301 | 283 | 602 | 566 |
| | 8"/18 | 295 | 295 | 590* | 590 |
| | 8"/16 | 359 | 359 | 718* | 718 |
| | 8"/14 | 442 | 442 | 884* | 884 |
| | 10"/16 | 506 | 506 | 1012* | 1012 |
| | 10"/14 | 627 | 627 | 1254* | 1254 |
| 10' | 6"/18 | 129 | 97 | 258 | 194 |
| | 6"/16 | 157 | 118 | 314 | 236 |
| | 6"/14 | 193 | 144 | 386 | 288 |
| | 8"/18 | 188 | 186 | 376* | 372 |
| | 8"/16 | 230 | 228 | 460* | 456 |
| | 8"/14 | 283 | 280 | 566 | 560 |
| | 10"/16 | 326 | 326 | 652* | 652 |
| | 10"/14 | 401 | 401 | 802* | 802 |
| 12' | 6"/18 | 89 | 56 | 178 | 112 |
| | 6"/16 | 109 | 68 | 218 | 136 |
| | 6"/14 | 134 | 83 | 268 | 166 |
| | 8"/18 | 131 | 108 | 262* | 216 |
| | 8"/16 | 159 | 131 | 318 | 262 |
| | 8"/14 | 196 | 162 | 392 | 324 |
| | 10"/16 | 226 | 226 | 452* | 452 |
| | 10"/14 | 278 | 278 | 556* | 556 |
| 14' | 6"/18 | 65 | 35 | 130 | 70 |
| | 6"/16 | 80 | 43 | 160 | 86 |
| | 6"/14 | 98 | 52 | 196 | 204 |
| | 8"/18 | 96 | 68 | 192 | 136 |
| | 8"/16 | 117 | 83 | 234 | 166 |
| | 8"/14 | 144 | 102 | 288 | 204 |
| | 10"/16 | 166 | 150 | 332* | 300 |
| | 10"/14 | 204 | 184 | 408 | 368 |
| 16' | 6"/18 | 50 | 23 | 100 | 46 |
| | 6"/16 | 61 | 28 | 122 | 56 |
| | 6"/14 | 75 | 35 | 150 | 70 |
| | 8"/18 | 73 | 45 | 146 | 90 |
| | 8"/16 | 89 | 55 | 178 | 110 |
| | 8"/14 | 110 | 68 | 220 | 136 |
| | 10"/16 | 127 | 100 | 254 | 200 |
| | 10"/14 | 156 | 123 | 312 | 246 |
| 18' | 8"/18 | 58 | 32 | 116 | 64 |
| | 8"/16 | 71 | 39 | 142 | 78 |
| | 8"/14 | 87 | 48 | 174 | 96 |
| | 10"/16 | 100 | 70 | 200 | 140 |
| | 10"/14 | 123 | 86 | 246 | 172 |
| 20' | 8"/18 | 47 | 23 | 94 | 46 |
| | 8"/16 | 57 | 28 | 114 | 56 |
| | 8"/14 | 70 | 35 | 140 | 70 |
| | 10"/16 | 81 | 51 | 162 | 102 |
| | 10"/14 | 100 | 63 | 200 | 126 |
| 22' | 8"/18 | 39 | 17 | 78 | 34 |
| | 8"/16 | 47 | 21 | 94 | 42 |
| | 8"/14 | 58 | 26 | 116 | 52 |
| | 10"/16 | 67 | 38 | 134 | 76 |
| | 10"/14 | 82 | 47 | 164 | 94 |
| 24' | 10"/16 | 56 | 29 | 112 | 58 |
| | 10"/14 | 69 | 36 | 138 | 72 |

### NOTES
The tables on this page are not to be used for final design.
They are intended to serve only as aids in the preliminary selection of members.
Consult appropriate manufacturers' literature for final and/or additional information.
*Ends of members require additional reinforcing, such as by end clips.

Ed Hesner; Rasmussen & Hobbs Architects; Tacoma, Washington

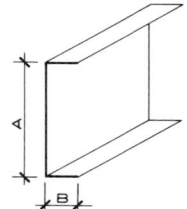 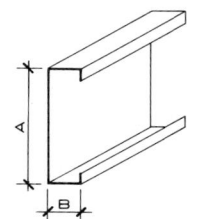 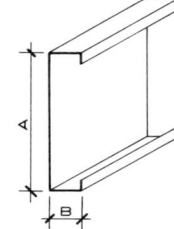

| CHANNEL STUDS | | "C" STUDS | | "C" JOISTS | |
|---|---|---|---|---|---|
| A | B | A | B | A | B |
| 2½" | 1" | 2½" | 1¼" | 5½" | 1⅞" |
| 3¼" | 1⅜" | 3" | 1⅜" | 6" | 1⅝" |
| 3⅝" | | 3⅝" | 1½" | 7¼" | 1¾" |
| 4" | | 3¼" | 1⅝" | 8" | 2" |
| 6" | | 3½" | | 9¼" | 2½" |
| | | 4" | | 10" | |
| | | 5½" | | 12" | |
| | | 6" | | | |
| | | 7½" | | | |
| | | 8" | | | |

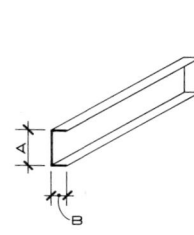 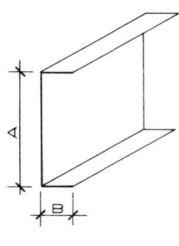 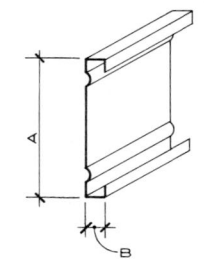

| FURRING CHANNEL | | "C" JOIST CLOSURE | | NESTABLE JOIST | |
|---|---|---|---|---|---|
| A | B | A | B | A | B |
| ¾" | ½" | 5½" | 1¼" | 7¼" | 1¾" |
| 1½" | 17/32" | 6" | | 7½" | |
| | | 7¼" | | 8" | |
| | | 8" | | 9¼" | |
| | | 9¼" | | 9½" | |
| | | 10" | | 11½" | |
| | | 12" | | 13½" | |

Normally available in all joist sizes

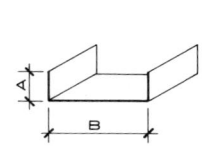 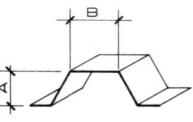 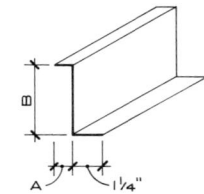

| RUNNER CHANNEL | | FURRING HAT CHANNEL | | "Z" FURRING | |
|---|---|---|---|---|---|
| A | B | A | B | A | B |
| ¾" | 2 11/16" | ⅞" | 1⅜" | ¾" | 1" |
| 1" | 3 13/16" | 1½" | 1¼" | | 1½" |
| 1⅜" | 3 7/16" | | | | 2" |
| 1¼" | 4 3/16" | | | | 3" |
| 1½" | 6 3/16" | | | | |
| 1¾" | 8 3/16" | | | | |
| 3½" | | | | | |

## LIGHT GAUGE FRAMING MEMBERS
MEMBERS AVAILABLE IN 14, 16, 18, 20 & 22 GAUGE MATERIAL

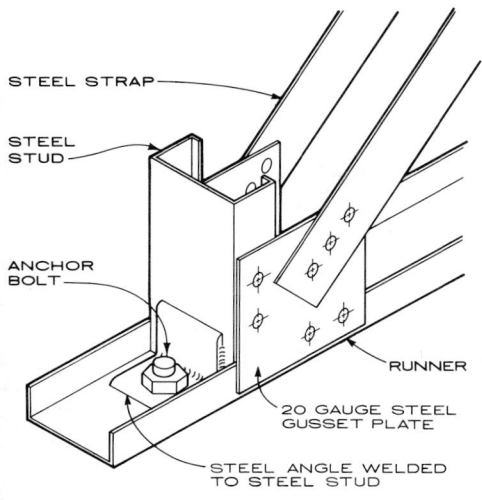

**DIAGONAL STEEL STRAPPING**

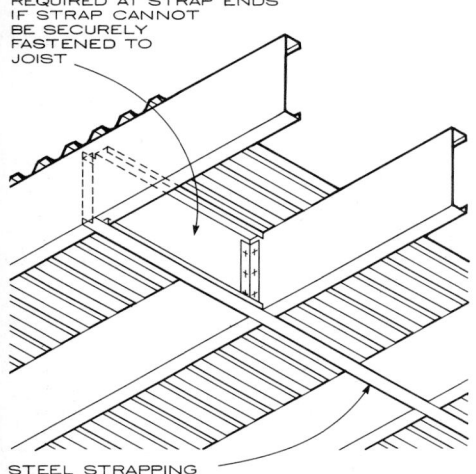

**JOIST BRACING**

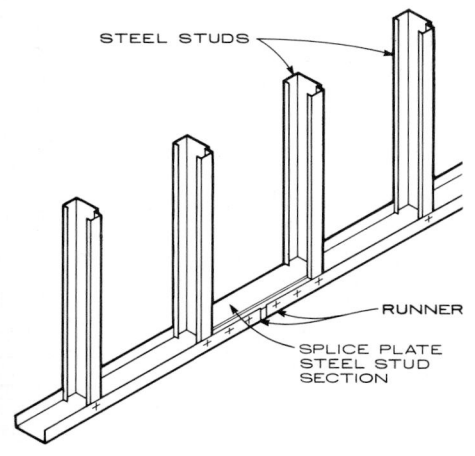

**RUNNER SPLICE**

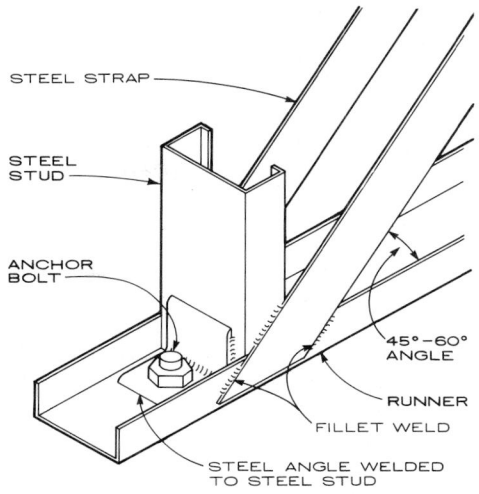

**DIAGONAL STEEL STRAPPING**

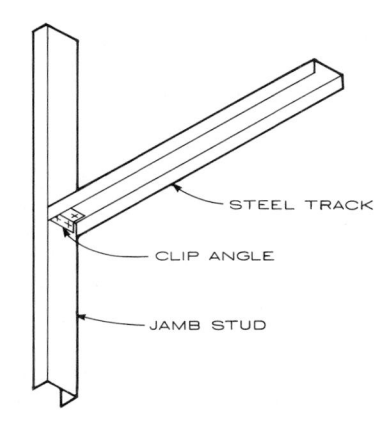

**SILL ATTACHMENT**

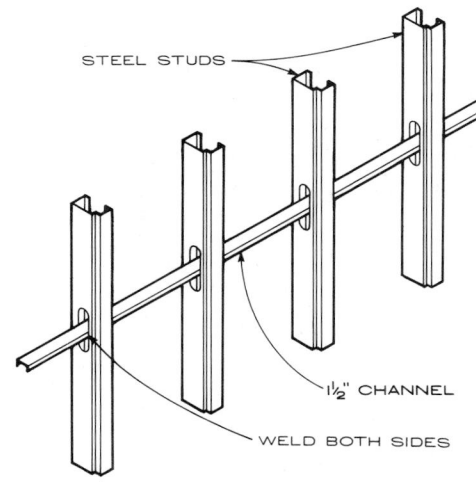

**HORIZONTAL BRACING**

## LIMITING HEIGHT TABLES FOR INTERIOR PARTITIONS AND CHASE WALL PARTITIONS

| STUD WIDTH | STUD SPACING | ALLOW. DEFL. | PARTITION ONE LAYER | PARTITION TWO LAYERS | FURRING ONE LAYER |
|---|---|---|---|---|---|
| **LIMITING HEIGHTS 25 GAUGE STEEL STUD ASSEMBLIES** | | | | | |
| 1 5/8" | 16" | 1/120 | 10'9"f | 10'9"d | 10'3"d |
|  |  | 1/240 | 9'6"d | 10'6"d | 8'3"d |
| | 24" | 1/120 | 8'9"f | 8'9"f | 8'9"f |
|  |  | 1/240 | 8'3"d | 8'9"f | 7'3"d |
| 2 1/2" | 16" | 1/120 | 14'3"f | 14'3"f | 14'0"d |
|  |  | 1/240 | 12'6"d | 13'6"d | 11'0"d |
| | 24" | 1/120 | 11'6"f | 11'6"f | 11'6"f |
|  |  | 1/240 | 10'9"d | 11'6"f | 9'9"d |
| 3 5/8" | 16" | 1/120 | 18'3"f | 18'3"f | 18'3"f |
|  |  | 1/240 | 16'0"d | 17'0"d | 14'6"d |
| | 24" | 1/120 | 15'0"f | 15'0"f | 15'0"f |
|  |  | 1/240 | 14'0"d | 14'9"d | 12'9"d |
| 4" | 16" | 1/120 | 19'6"f | 19'6"f | 19'6"f |
|  |  | 1/240 | 17'3"d | 18'3"d | 15'9"d |
| | 24" | 1/120 | 16'0"f | 16'0"f | 16'0"f |
|  |  | 1/240 | 15'0"d | 15'9"d | 13'9"d |
| 6" | 16" | 1/120 | 26'0"f | 26'0"f | 26'0"f |
|  |  | 1/240 | 23'0"d | 24'0"d | 21'6"d |
| | 24" | 1/120 | 21'3"f | 21'3"f | 21'3"f |
|  |  | 1/240 | 20'3"d | 21'0"d | 18'9"d |
| **20 GAUGE STEEL STUDS ASSEMBLIES** | | | | | |
| 2 1/2" | 16" | 1/120 | 17'9"d | 18'6"d | 16'6"d |
|  |  | 1/240 | 14'0"d | 14'9"d | 13'0"d |
| | 24" | 1/120 | 15'6"d | 16'3"f | 14'6"d |
|  |  | 1/240 | 12'3"d | 13'0"d | 11'6"d |
| 3 5/8" | 16" | 1/120 | 23'0"d | 24'0"d | 21'9"d |
|  |  | 1/240 | 18'3"d | 19'0"d | 17'3"d |
| | 24" | 1/120 | 20'0"d | 20'9"f | 19'0"d |
|  |  | 1/240 | 16'0"d | 16'6"d | 15'0"d |
| 4" | 16" | 1/120 | 24'9"d | 25'9"d | 23'6"d |
|  |  | 1/240 | 19'6"d | 20'3"d | 18'9"d |
| | 24" | 1/120 | 21'6"d | 22'0"f | 20'6"d |
|  |  | 1/240 | 17'3"d | 17'9"d | 16'3"d |
| 6" | 16" | 1/120 | 33'6"d | 34'6"d | 32'3"d |
|  |  | 1/240 | 26'6"d | 27'6"d | 25'6"d |
| | 24" | 1/120 | 29'3"d | 29'6"d | 28'0"d |
|  |  | 1/240 | 23'3"d | 24'0"d | 22'3"d |
| **LIMITING HEIGHT 25 GAUGE CHASE WALL PARTITIONS** | | | | | |
| 1 5/8" | 16" | 1/120 | 15'3"f | 15'3"f | |
|  |  | 1/240 | 13'3"d | 14'6"d | |
| | 24" | 1/120 | 12'6"f | 12'6"f | |
|  |  | 1/240 | 11'6"d | 12'6"f | |
| 2 1/2" | 16" | 1/120 | 20'3"f | 20'3"f | |
|  |  | 1/240 | 17'6"d | 19'0"d | |
| | 24" | 1/120 | 16'6"f | 16'6"f | |
|  |  | 1/240 | 15'6"d | 16'6"f | |
| 3 5/8" | 16" | 1/120 | 25'9"f | 25'9"f | |
|  |  | 1/240 | 22'9"d | 24'3"d | |
| | 24" | 1/120 | 21'0"d | 21'0"f | |
|  |  | 1/240 | 19'9"d | 21'0"f | |
| 2 1/2" * | 16" | 1/120 | 24'3"d | 25'9"d | |
|  |  | 1/240 | 19'3"d | 20'6"d | |
| | 24" | 1/120 | 21'3"d | 22'6"f | |
|  |  | 1/240 | 17'0"d | 18'0"d | |

**NOTE**

1. Limiting height for 1/2 in. or 5/8 in. thick panels and 5 psf uniform load perpendicular to partition or furring. Use one-layer heights for unbalanced assemblies. Limiting criteria: d-deflection, f-bending stress. Consult local code authority for limiting criteria.

\* 20 Gauge chase wall partitions

Timothy B. McDonald; Washington, D.C.

**COLD-FORMED METAL FRAMING**   5

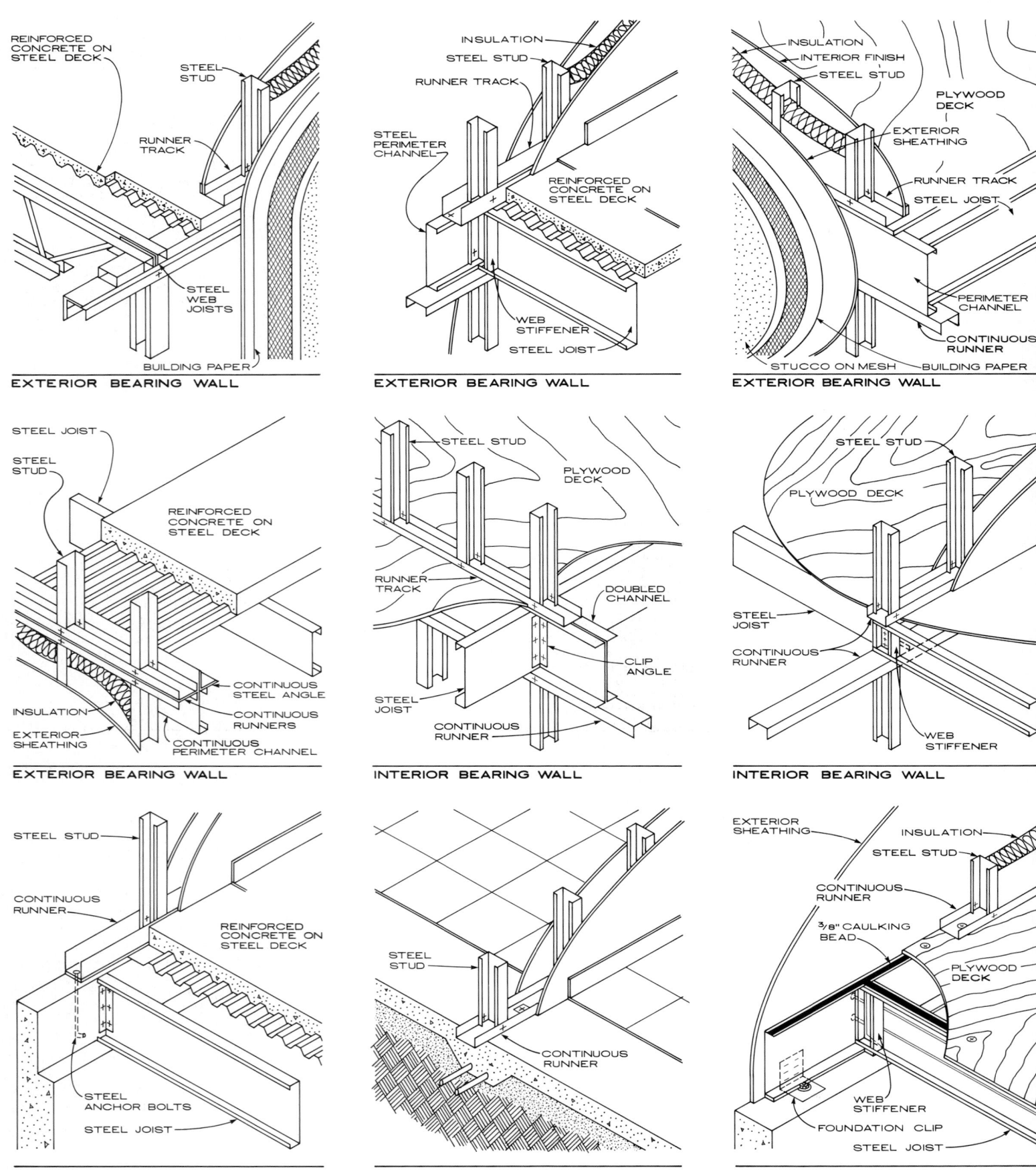

REINFORCED CONCRETE ON STEEL DECK

STEEL STUD

RUNNER TRACK

STEEL WEB JOISTS

BUILDING PAPER

EXTERIOR BEARING WALL

INSULATION

STEEL STUD

RUNNER TRACK

STEEL PERIMETER CHANNEL

REINFORCED CONCRETE ON STEEL DECK

WEB STIFFENER

STEEL JOIST

EXTERIOR BEARING WALL

INSULATION

INTERIOR FINISH

STEEL STUD

PLYWOOD DECK

EXTERIOR SHEATHING

RUNNER TRACK

STEEL JOIST

PERIMETER CHANNEL

CONTINUOUS RUNNER

STUCCO ON MESH   BUILDING PAPER

EXTERIOR BEARING WALL

STEEL JOIST

STEEL STUD

REINFORCED CONCRETE ON STEEL DECK

CONTINUOUS STEEL ANGLE

CONTINUOUS RUNNERS

INSULATION

EXTERIOR SHEATHING

CONTINUOUS PERIMETER CHANNEL

EXTERIOR BEARING WALL

STEEL STUD

PLYWOOD DECK

RUNNER TRACK

DOUBLED CHANNEL

CLIP ANGLE

STEEL JOIST

CONTINUOUS RUNNER

INTERIOR BEARING WALL

STEEL STUD

PLYWOOD DECK

STEEL JOIST

CONTINUOUS RUNNER

WEB STIFFENER

INTERIOR BEARING WALL

STEEL STUD

CONTINUOUS RUNNER

REINFORCED CONCRETE ON STEEL DECK

STEEL ANCHOR BOLTS

STEEL JOIST

EXTERIOR FOUNDATION

STEEL STUD

CONTINUOUS RUNNER

INTERIOR BEARING WALL

EXTERIOR SHEATHING

INSULATION

STEEL STUD

CONTINUOUS RUNNER

3/8" CAULKING BEAD

PLYWOOD DECK

WEB STIFFENER

FOUNDATION CLIP

STEEL JOIST

EXTERIOR FOUNDATION

Timothy B. McDonald; Washington, D.C.

5   **COLD-FORMED METAL FRAMING**

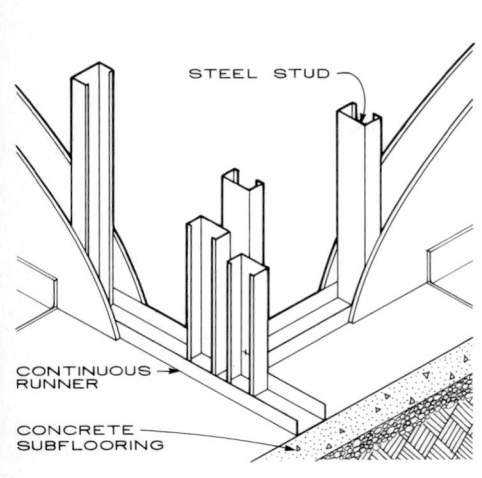

**PARTITION INTERSECTION**

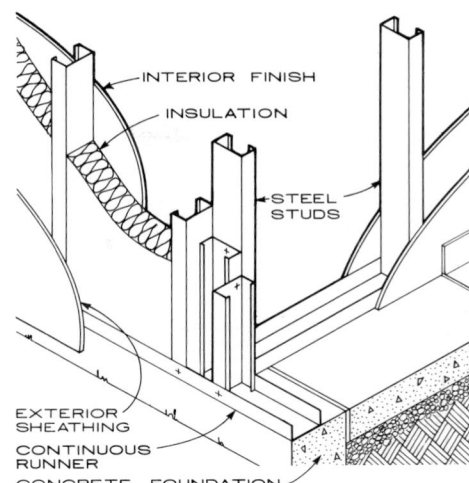

**PARTITION / EXTERIOR WALL**

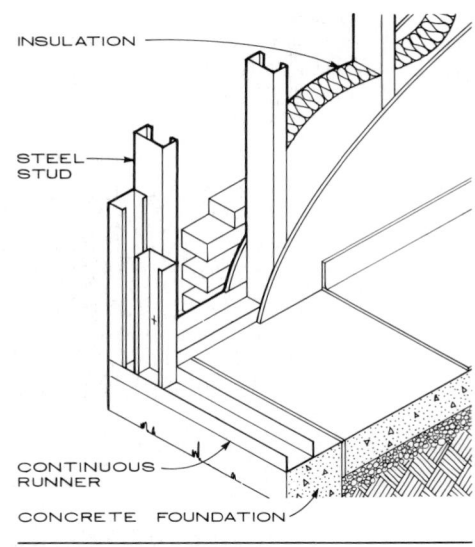

**EXTERIOR CORNER**

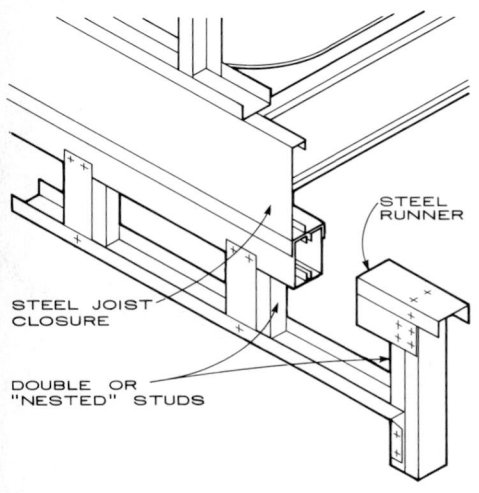

**TWO MEMBER LINTEL**

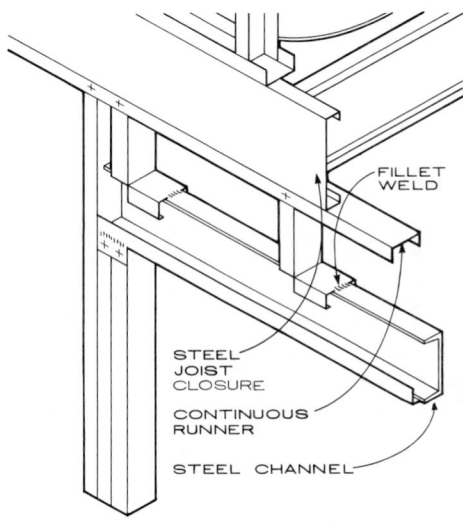

**LONG SPAN LINTEL**

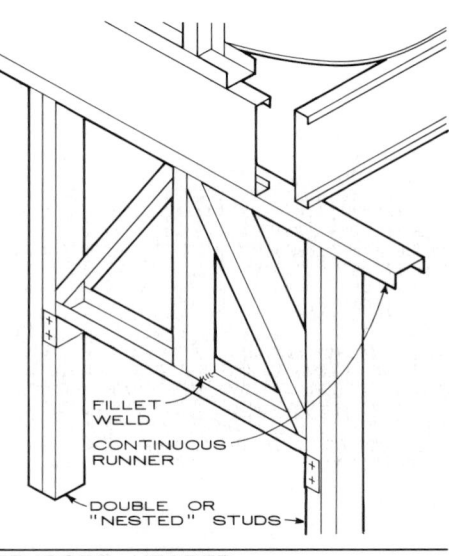

**TRUSSED HEADER**

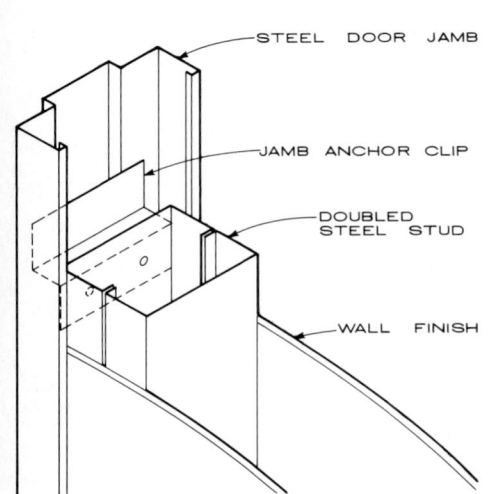

**STUD-TO-DOOR BUCK**

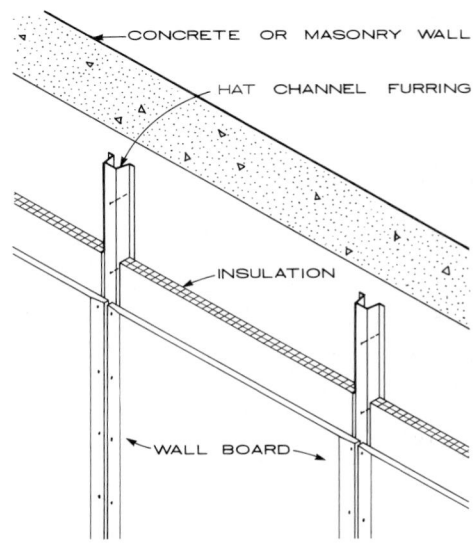

**FURRING**

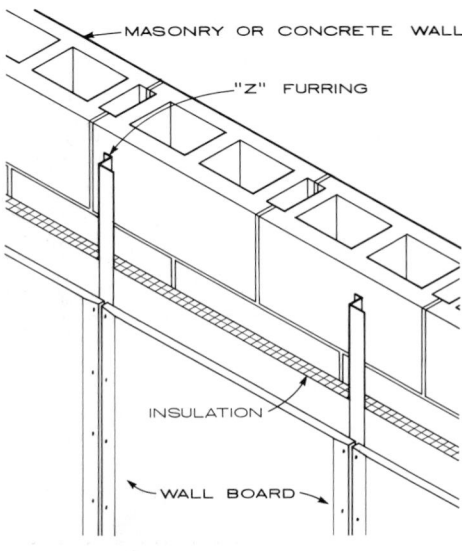

**FURRING**

Timothy B. McDonald; Washington, D.C.

**COLD-FORMED METAL FRAMING**    5

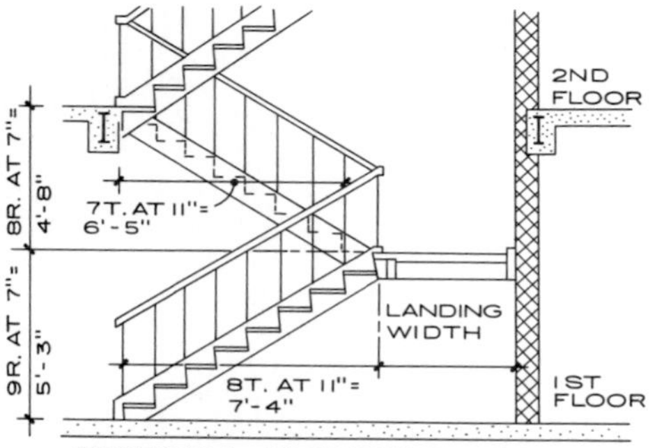

**SECTION A** - DIMENSIONS ARE SHOWN ONLY AS A GUIDE

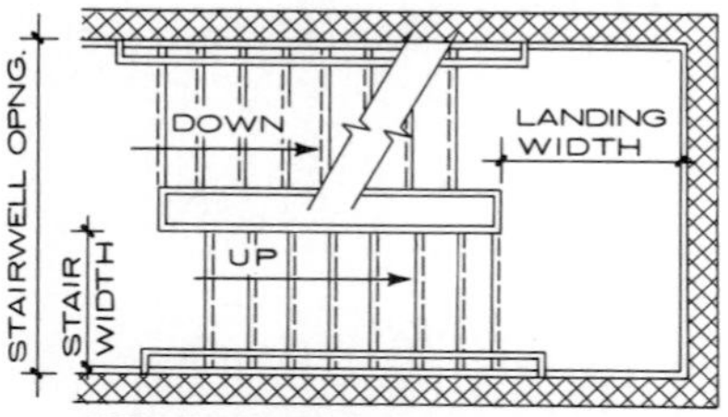

2ND FLOOR

1ST FLOOR

9R. AT 7" = 5'-3"
8R. AT 7" = 4'-8"
7T. AT 11" = 6'-5"
8T. AT 11" = 7'-4"

LANDING WIDTH

**UPPER FLOOR PLAN** - WIDTHS AND CLEARANCES AS PER CODE

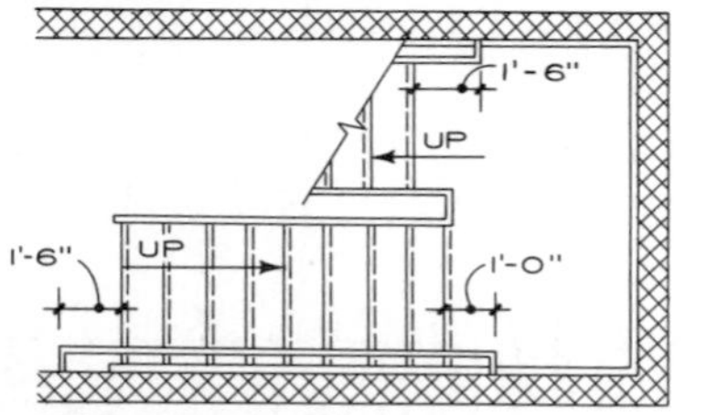

STAIRWELL OPNG.
STAIR WIDTH
DOWN
UP
LANDING WIDTH

**GROUND FLOOR PLAN** - SHOWING HANDRAIL EXTENSIONS

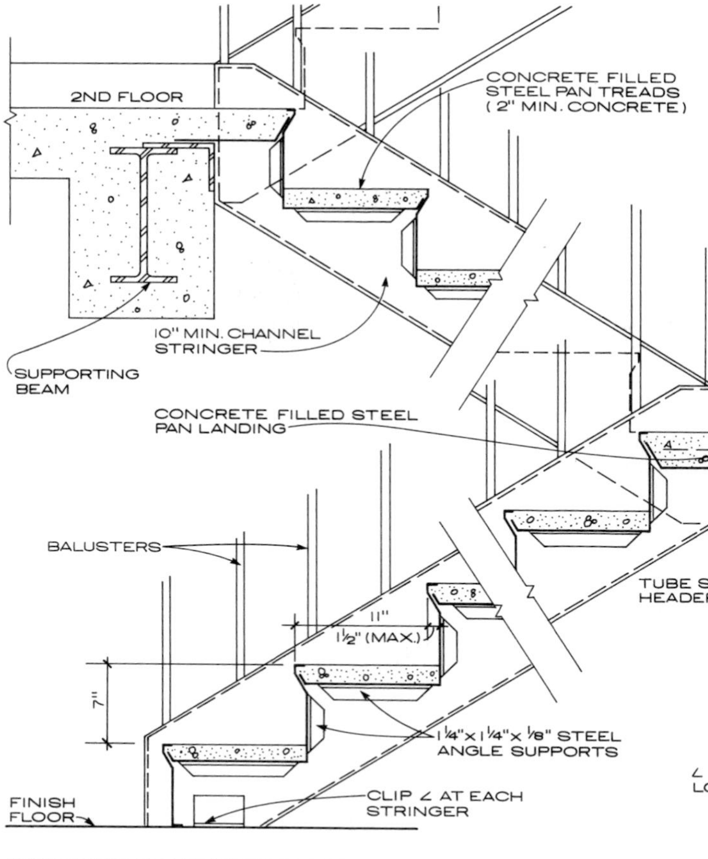

1'-6"
UP
UP
1'-6"
1'-0"

**TYPICAL PAN TYPE CONSTRUCTION**

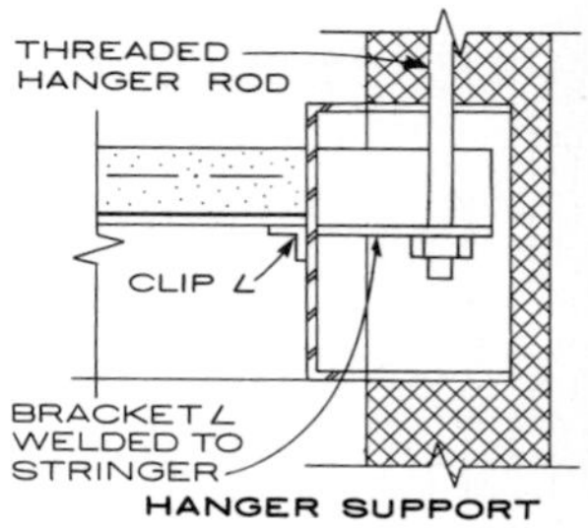

2ND FLOOR

CONCRETE FILLED STEEL PAN TREADS (2" MIN. CONCRETE)

SUPPORTING BEAM

10" MIN. CHANNEL STRINGER

CONCRETE FILLED STEEL PAN LANDING

BALUSTERS

11"
1½" (MAX.)
7"

TUBE STEEL HEADER

FINISH FLOOR

1¼" x 1¼" x ⅛" STEEL ANGLE SUPPORTS

CLIP ∠ AT EACH STRINGER

**HANGER SUPPORT**

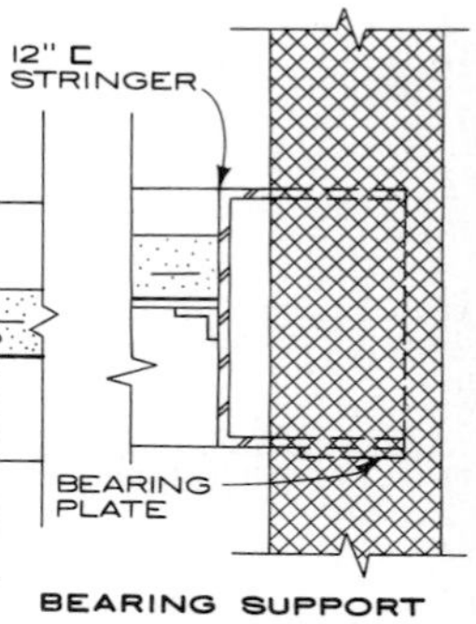

THREADED HANGER ROD
CLIP ∠
BRACKET ∠ WELDED TO STRINGER

**BEARING SUPPORT**

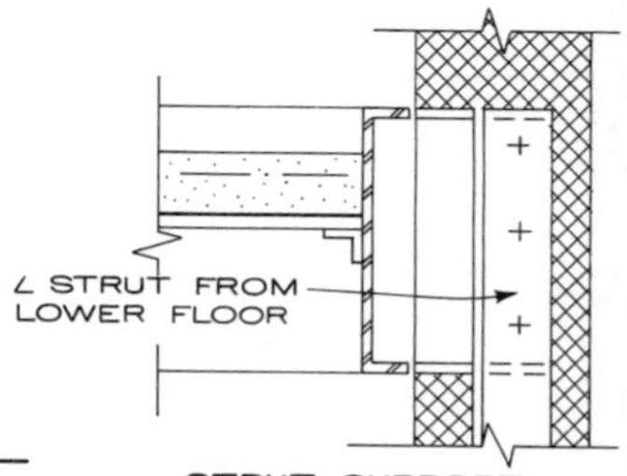

12" C STRINGER
BEARING PLATE

**STRUT SUPPORT**

∠ STRUT FROM LOWER FLOOR

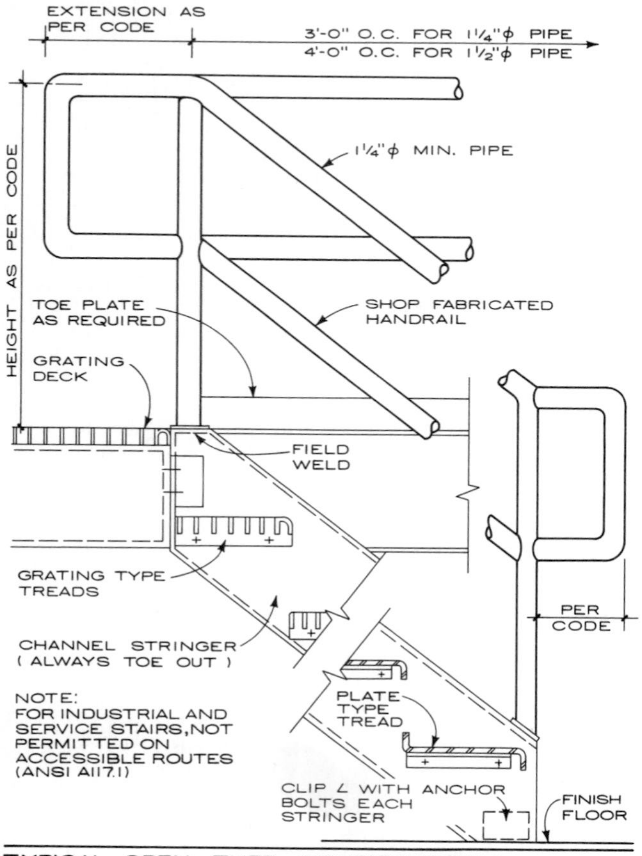

**TYPICAL OPEN TYPE CONSTRUCTION**

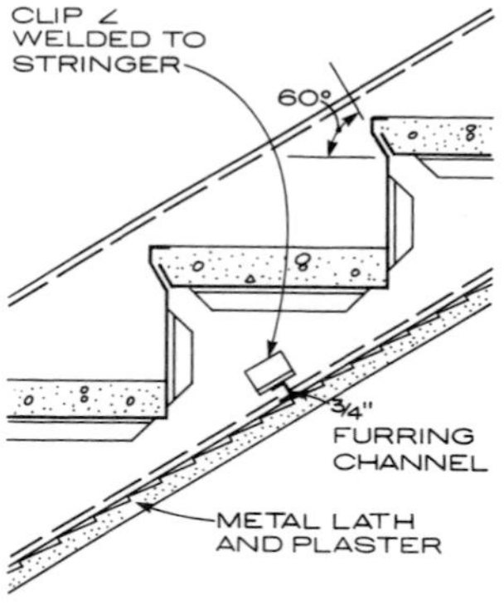

EXTENSION AS PER CODE

3'-0" O.C. FOR 1¼"φ PIPE
4'-0" O.C. FOR 1½"φ PIPE

1¼"φ MIN. PIPE

HEIGHT AS PER CODE

SHOP FABRICATED HANDRAIL

TOE PLATE AS REQUIRED

GRATING DECK

FIELD WELD

GRATING TYPE TREADS

PER CODE

CHANNEL STRINGER (ALWAYS TOE OUT)

NOTE: FOR INDUSTRIAL AND SERVICE STAIRS, NOT PERMITTED ON ACCESSIBLE ROUTES (ANSI A117.1)

PLATE TYPE TREAD

CLIP ∠ WITH ANCHOR BOLTS EACH STRINGER

FINISH FLOOR

**SOFFIT DETAILS**

CLIP ∠ WELDED TO STRINGER
60°
¾" FURRING CHANNEL
METAL LATH AND PLASTER

**PLASTER**

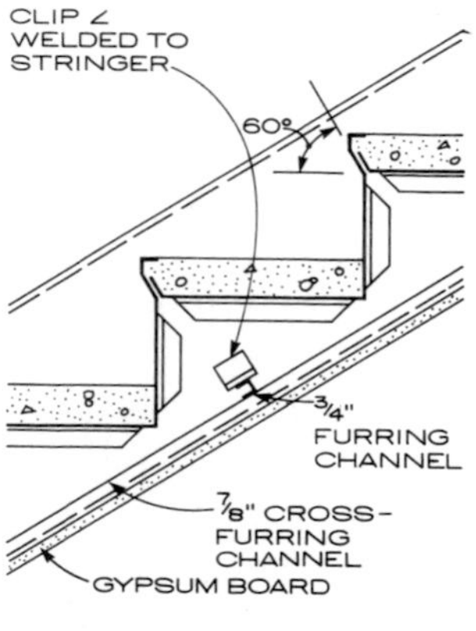

CLIP ∠ WELDED TO STRINGER
60°
¾" FURRING CHANNEL
⅞" CROSS-FURRING CHANNEL
GYPSUM BOARD

**GYPSUM BOARD**

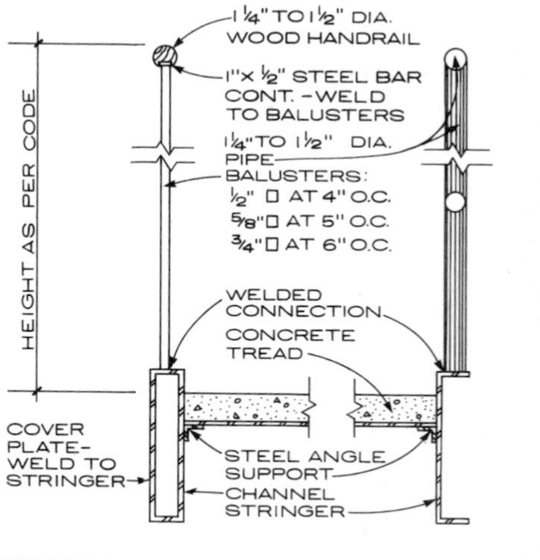

**STRINGER AND HANDRAIL SECTIONS**

1¼" TO 1½" DIA. WOOD HANDRAIL
1" x ½" STEEL BAR CONT. - WELD TO BALUSTERS
1¼" TO 1½" DIA. PIPE

BALUSTERS:
½" □ AT 4" O.C.
⅝" □ AT 5" O.C.
¾" □ AT 6" O.C.

HEIGHT AS PER CODE

WELDED CONNECTION
CONCRETE TREAD

COVER PLATE- WELD TO STRINGER

STEEL ANGLE SUPPORT- CHANNEL STRINGER

**NOTE**

Refer to applicable national, state, and local building codes for specific requirements as well as the standards established by ANSI 117.1, OSHA, and NFPA 1010 (Life Safety Code). Beyond these standards, special consideration should be given to stair surface texture, color, and lighting to improve stair safety. Further information may be obtained from the "Metal Stairs Manual" (National Association of Architectural Metal Manufacturers) and AIA's "Design for Aging: An Architect's Guide" (AIA Press, Washington, D.C., 1986).

Ted B. Richey, AIA; The InterDesign Group; Indianapolis, Indiana
John D. Harvey, AIA; Wheatley Associates; Charlotte, North Carolina

**5** **METAL FABRICATIONS**

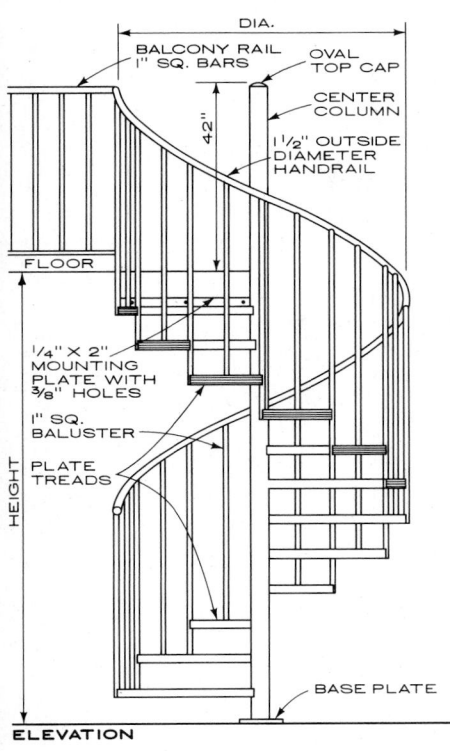

**ELEVATION**

*Labels on diagram:*
DIA.
BALCONY RAIL 1" SQ. BARS
OVAL TOP CAP
CENTER COLUMN
42"
1 1/2" OUTSIDE DIAMETER HANDRAIL
FLOOR
1/4" X 2" MOUNTING PLATE WITH 3/8" HOLES
1" SQ. BALUSTER
HEIGHT
PLATE TREADS
BASE PLATE

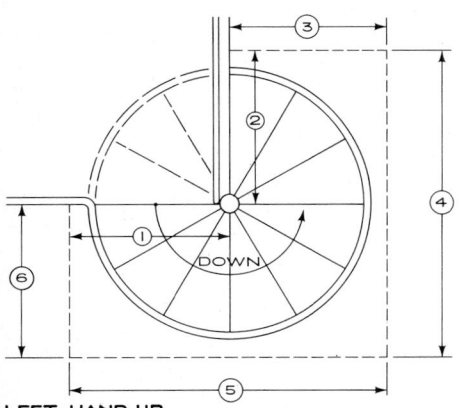

**LEFT-HAND UP**
12 TREADS/CIRCLE 8" TO 9 1/2" RISERS MAY BE RIGHT-HAND UP

DOWN

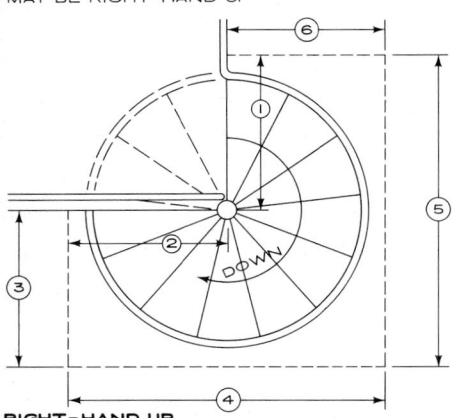

**RIGHT-HAND UP**
13 TREADS/CIRCLE 7 1/2" TO 8" RISERS MAY BE LEFT-HAND UP

DOWN

Framing dimensions are used when the stair passes through the flooring. The opening is "L" shaped, not square. For maximum head room, taper joist #2 45°. For standard 27° treads and 10 in. or over joist, delete one step to increase head room.

**SPIRAL STAIRS**

David W. Johnson; Washington, D.C.

## NOTES

1. Dimensions: Spiral stairs are manufactured in a variety of diameters. Larger diameters increase perceived comfort, ease of use, and safety.
2. Tread and platform materials: The most common materials are steel, aluminum, and wood. Steel and aluminum can be smooth plate, checker plate, pan type, and bar. A variety of hardwoods can be used, although many manufacturers use steel substructures to support the finish wood surface. Plywood usually is used under carpeting.
3. Factory finishes: Standard for exterior and wet area interiors are zinc-chromated rust inhibitor or hot-dipped galvanized. Other coatings are black acrylic enamel and black epoxy.
4. Handrails and balusters: A large variety of materials are available, including steel, aluminum, brass, bronze, wood, glass, and plastic laminate.
5. Platform dimensions usually are 2 in. larger than the stair radius. Various anchorage connections are available to suit the floor structure.
6. Refer to local and national codes for dimension and construction requirements and allowable uses.

## SPECIFICATIONS (IN.)

| Diameter | 40 | 48 | 52 | 60 | 64 | 72 | 76 | 88 | 96 |
|---|---|---|---|---|---|---|---|---|---|
| Center Column | 4 | 4 | 4 | 4 | 4 | 4 | 4 | 6 5/8 | 6 5/8 |
| Lb per 9 ft | 205 | 220 | 235 | 250 | 265 | 310 | 325 | 435 | 485 |
| Tread Detail A | 4 | 4 | 4 | 4 | 4 | 4 | 4 | 6 5/8 | 6 5/8 |
| Tread Detail B | 18 | 22 | 24 | 28 | 32 | 34 | 36 | 42 | 48 |
| 27° Tread Detail C | 9 1/4 | 11 1/8 | 12 1/8 | 13 15/16 | 14 7/8 | 16 3/4 | 17 5/8 | 20 1/2 | 22 5/16 |
| 27° Tread Detail D | 7 5/8 | 8 | 8 1/4 | 8 3/8 | 8 1/2 | 8 5/8 | 8 3/4 | 10 | 10 1/2 |
| 30° Tread Detail C | 10 1/2 | 12 9/16 | 13 5/8 | 15 3/4 | 16 3/4 | 18 7/8 | 19 7/8 | 23 | 25 1/8 |
| 30° Tread Detail D | 8 1/2 | 8 5/8 | 8 3/4 | 8 7/8 | 9 | 9 1/4 | 9 3/8 | 11 3/8 | 11 1/2 |
| Landing Size | 22 | 26 | 28 | 32 | 34 | 38 | 40 | 46 | 52 |

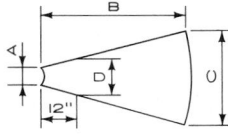
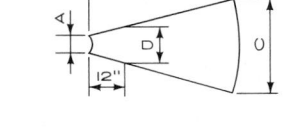

**TREAD DETAIL**

## 27° RISER TABLE

| FINISH FLOOR HEIGHT (IN.) | NUMBER OF STEPS | CIRCLE DEGREE |
|---|---|---|
| 90 to 96 | 11 | 297° |
| 97 to 104 | 12 | 324° |
| 105 to 112 | 13 | 351° |
| 113 to 120 | 14 | 375° |
| 121 to 128 | 15 | 405° |
| 129 to 136 | 16 | 432° |
| 137 to 144 | 17 | 459° |
| 145 to 152 | 18 | 486° |
| 153 to 160 | 19 | 513° |
| 161 to 168 | 20 | 540° |

## 30° RISER TABLE

| FINISH FLOOR HEIGHT (IN.) | NUMBER OF STEPS | CIRCLE DEGREE |
|---|---|---|
| 85 to 95 | 9 | 270° |
| 96 to 104 | 10 | 300° |
| 105 to 114 | 11 | 330° |
| 115 to 123 | 12 | 360° |
| 124 to 133 | 13 | 390° |
| 134 to 142 | 14 | 420° |
| 143 to 152 | 15 | 450° |
| 153 to 161 | 16 | 480° |
| 162 to 171 | 17 | 510° |
| 172 to 180 | 18 | 540° |

## FRAMING DIMENSIONS (IN.)

| STAIR DIAMETER | 1 | 2 | 3 | 4 | 5 | 6 |
|---|---|---|---|---|---|---|
| 40 | 20 | 20 | 24 | 44 | 44 | 24 |
| 48 | 24 | 24 | 28 | 52 | 52 | 28 |
| 52 | 26 | 26 | 30 | 56 | 56 | 30 |
| 60 | 30 | 30 | 34 | 64 | 64 | 34 |
| 64 | 32 | 32 | 36 | 68 | 68 | 36 |
| 72 | 36 | 36 | 40 | 76 | 76 | 40 |
| 76 | 38 | 38 | 42 | 80 | 80 | 42 |
| 88 | 44 | 44 | 48 | 92 | 92 | 48 |
| 96 | 48 | 48 | 52 | 100 | 100 | 52 |

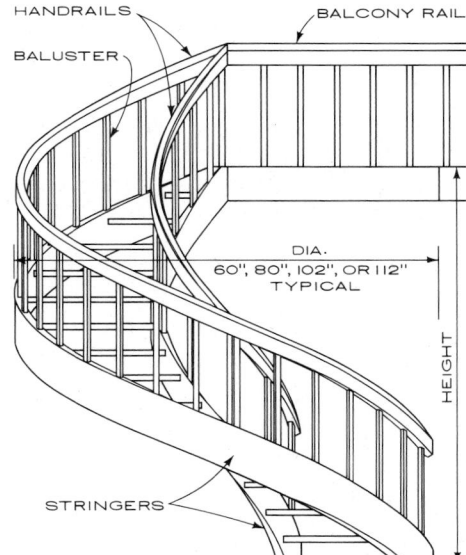

**ELEVATION**

*Labels on diagram:*
HANDRAILS
BALCONY RAIL
BALUSTER
DIA. 60", 80", 102", OR 112" TYPICAL
HEIGHT
STRINGERS

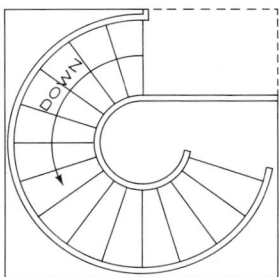

**PLAN**

DOWN

Design considerations are similar to those for spiral stairs. Made of fabricated steel tube one-piece stringer with treads bolted or welded to the stringer. Treads also are made of laminated wood. Numerous finishes are available, with wood the most common. Risers can be open or closed, and they can be carpeted.

**CIRCULAR STAIRS**

**METAL FABRICATIONS** 5

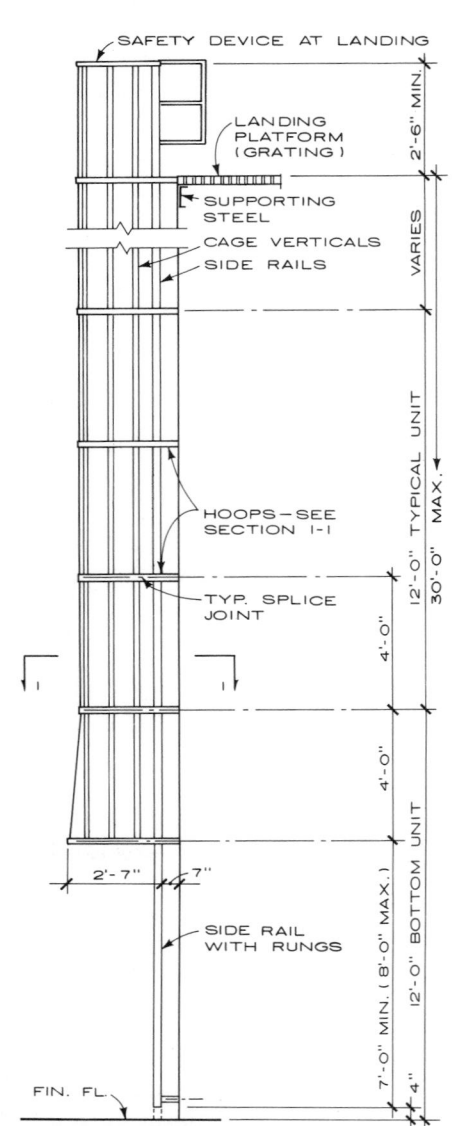

**TYPICAL SIDE ELEVATION**
( EXTRUDED ALUMINUM LADDER )
**MEETS OSHA REQUIREMENTS AND ANSI SPECIFICATIONS A 14.3**

**NOTE**

All ladder safety devices such as those that incorporate lifebelts, friction brakes, and sliding attachments shall meet the design requirements of fire escape ladders; by U.S. Department of Labor-Occupational Safety and Health Administration.

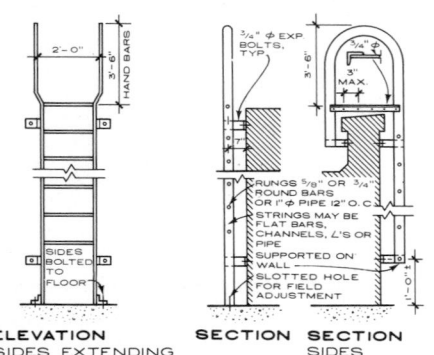

**ELEVATION**
SIDES EXTENDING ABOVE LANDING

**SECTION**
SIDES OVER PARAPET

**VERTICAL AND SHIPS LADDERS**

Jan M. Sprawka; Symmes, Maini and McKee Associates, Inc.; Cambridge, Massachusetts
Max O. Urbahn Associates, Inc.; New York, New York
NFPA, see data sources

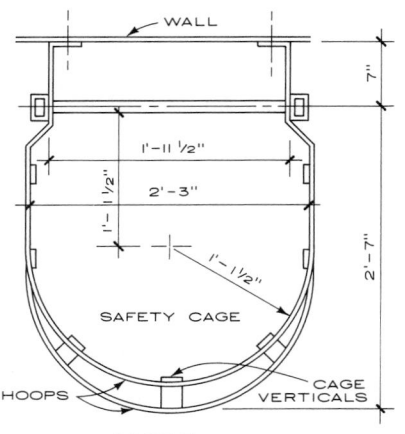

**SECTION 1-1**

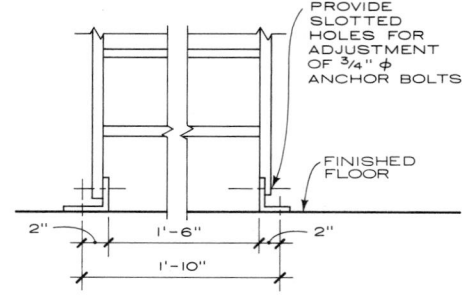

**TYPICAL LADDER FOOTING CONNECTIONS**

**SHIPS LADDER HEAD CONNECTION**

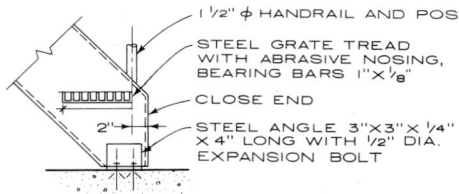

**FIRE ESCAPE FOOTING CONNECTION**

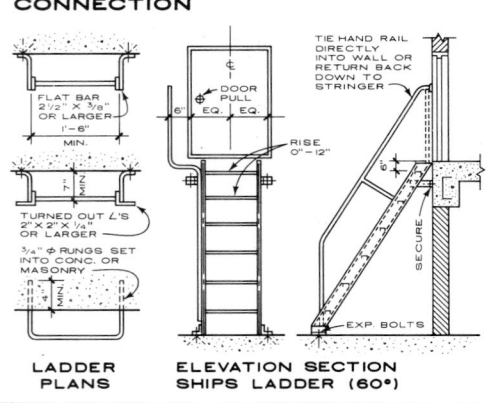

**LADDER PLANS**

**ELEVATION SECTION SHIPS LADDER (60°)**

**PLAN**

**ELEVATION**

NOTE: WEATHER PROTECTION FROM ICE AND SNOW IS REQUIRED IN SOME AREAS

**NOTES**

1. Freestanding stairways that are independently supported on steel columns with platforms at exits can be used on new and existing buildings. This type of exterior stair is subject to height limitations, occupancy classifications, and fire separation ratings.

2. Stairways supported on brackets attached to building walls with platforms at exits may be used for existing buildings, but only when outside stairways are not practical. This type of fire escape stair is subject to occupancy provisions: "Fire escape stairs may be used in existing buildings as permitted in applicable existing occupancy chapters but shall not constitute more than 50 percent of the required exit capacity" (NFPA 101 National Fire Code 1985, 5-2.8.1.4).

3. Slide fire escapes, used chiefly in institutional buildings, must be designed in accordance with state or local laws and ordinances. Frames for platforms can be angles or channels bolted to brackets; grating can be bolted or welded to the frame. Alternate brackets may be round or square steel, sized by a structural engineer.

4. Ships' ladder railings are ¾ in., 1 in., or larger pipe railing on one or both sides, bolted or welded to strings. Tread may be channels, angles, bent plates, grating, or cast metals, with or without abrasives. Brackets are to be 2½ in. x ⅜ in. or larger, and may be welded, bolted, or clamped to strings, but spaced not over 10 ft. Fastening to wall should be through bolts, bolts set in wall, or by expansion bolts. Rungs, ⅝ in. or ¼ in. diameter bars, usually are set into holes in string and welded together.

5. Galvanic corrosion (electrolysis) potential between common flashing materials and selected construction materials should be considered.

6. Portable ladders, rope fire escapes, and similar emergency escape devices may be useful in buildings that lack adequate standard exits. Their use is not recognized by the Life Safety Code as satisfying requirements for means of egress. Many such devices are unsuited for use by aged or infirm persons or small children. Such devices may give a false sense of security and should not substitute for standard exit facilities.

 **METAL FABRICATIONS**

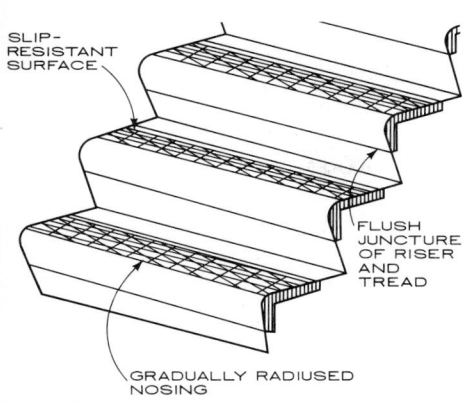

"SAFE" STAIR ELEMENTS

## TREAD AND RISER SIZES

Riser and tread dimensions must be uniform for the length of the stair. ANSI specifications recommend a minimum tread dimension of 11 in. nosing to nosing and a riser height of 7 in. maximum. Open risers are not permitted on stairs accessible to the handicapped.

## TREAD COVERING

OSHA standards require finishes to be "reasonably slip resistant" with nosings of slip-resistant finish. Treads without nosings are acceptable provided that the tread is serrated or is of a definite slip-resistant design. Uniform color and texture are recommended for clear delineation of edges.

## NOSING DESIGN

ANSI specifications recommend nosings without abrupt edges that project no more than 1½ in. beyond the edge of the riser. A safe stair uses a ½ in. radius abrasive nosing firmly anchored to the tread, with no overhangs and a clearly visible edge.

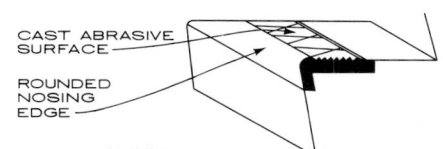

PREFERRED CAST METAL ABRASIVE NOSING

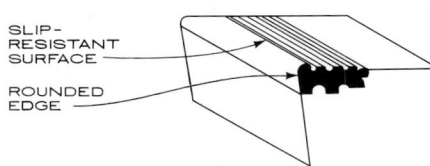

PREFERRED CAST METAL NOSING FOR CONCRETE STAIR

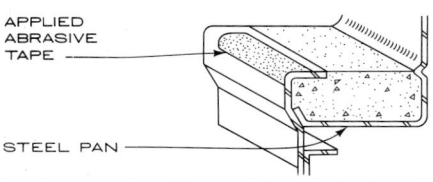

PREFERRED ABRASIVE TAPE NOSING

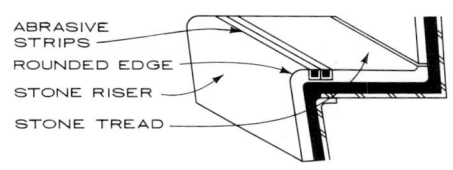

PREFERRED STONE TREAD

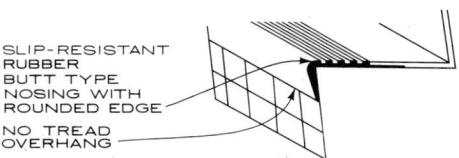

PREFERRED VINYL OR RUBBER NOSING

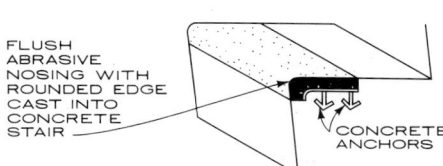

PREFERRED ABRASIVE EPOXY

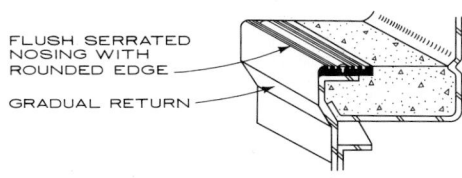

PREFERRED STEEL SUBTREAD

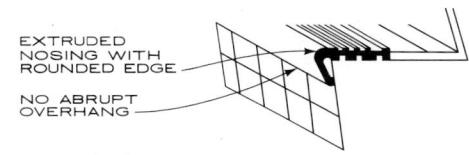

PREFERRED ALUMINUM NOSING

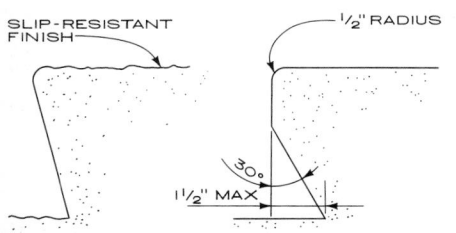

ACCEPTABLE NOSING PROFILES

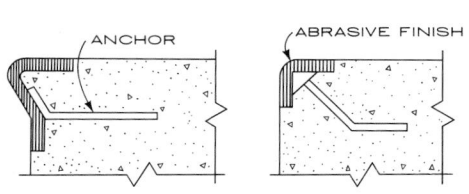

PREFERRED CAST NOSINGS FOR CONCRETE

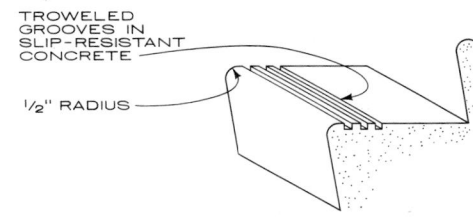

PREFERRED CONCRETE TREAD

DESIGN OF A "SAFE" STAIR, USABLE BY THE PHYSICALLY HANDICAPPED

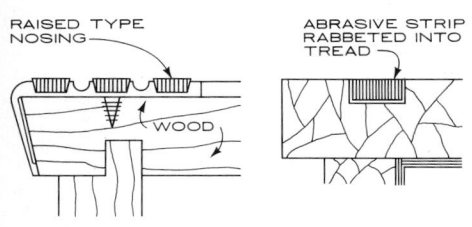

OTHER ALUMINUM NOSINGS WITH ABRASIVE FILLER

NOTE

Cast nosings for concrete stairs are iron, aluminum, or bronze, custom-made to exact size. Nosings and treads come with factory-drilled countersunk holes, with riveted strap anchors, or with wing-type anchors.

NOTE

Abrasive materials are used as treads, nosings, or inlay strips for new work and as surface-mounted replacement treads for old work. A homogeneous epoxy abrasive is cured on an extruded aluminum base for a smoother surface, or it is used as a filler between aluminum ribs.

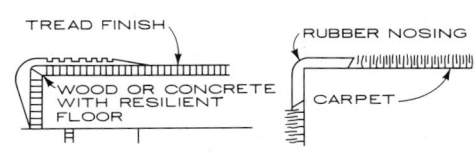

OTHER SLIP-RESISTANT VINYL AND RUBBER NOSINGS

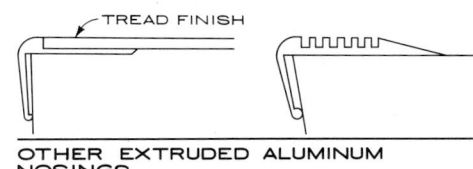

OTHER EXTRUDED ALUMINUM NOSINGS

Olga Barmine; Darrel Downing Rippeteau, Architect; Washington, D.C.
Krommenhoek/McKeown & Associates; San Diego, California

METAL FABRICATIONS    5

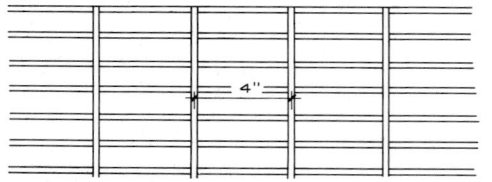

**WITH SPACER BARS WELDED 4" O.C.**

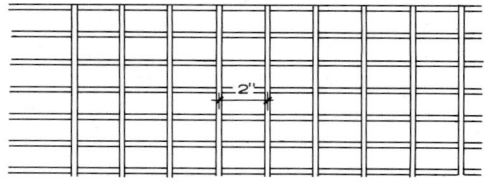

**WITH SPACER BARS WELDED 2" O.C.**

## RECTANGULAR (WELDED OR PRESSURE LOCKED)

### NOTES

Constructed of flat bearing bars of steel or aluminum I-bars, with spacer bars at right angles. Spacer bars may be square, rectangular, or of another shape. Spacer bars are connected to bearing bars by pressing them into prepared slots or by welding. They have open ends or perhaps ends banded with flat bars that are of about the same size as welded bearing bars. Standard bar spacings are $^{15}/_{16}$ and $1^3/_{16}$ in.

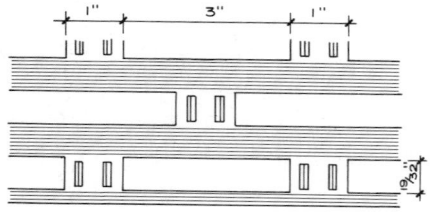

**WITH SPACER BARS RIVETED APPROX. 7"O.C. USED FOR AVERAGE INSTALLATION**

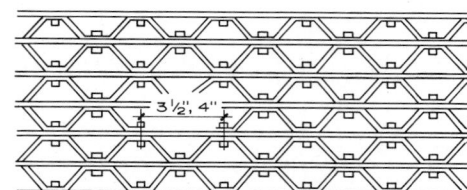

**WITH SPACER BARS RIVETED 3½" OR 4" USED FOR HEAVY TRAFFIC AND WHERE WHEELED EQUIPMENT IS USED**

## RETICULATED (RIVETED)

### NOTES

Flat bearing bars are made of steel or aluminum, and continuous bent spacer or reticulate bars are riveted to the bearing bars. Usually they have open ends or ends that are banded with flat bars of the same size as bearing bars, welded across the ends. Normal spacing of bars: $^3/_4$, $1^1/_8$, or $2^5/_{16}$ in. Many bar gratings cannot be used in areas of public pedestrian traffic (crutches, canes, pogo sticks, women's shoes, etc.). Close mesh grating ($^1/_4$ in.) is available in steel and aluminum, for use in pedestrian traffic areas.

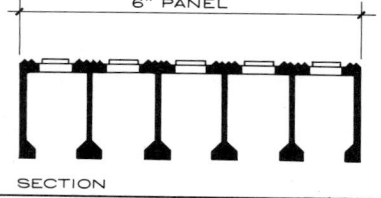

**ALUMINUM PLANK**

### NOTES

Grating is extruded from aluminum alloy in one piece with integral I-beam ribs and can have a natural finish or be anodized. Top of surface may be solid or punched. Standard panel width is 6 in.

**NOSING OF ANGLE AND ABRASIVE STRIP AND BAR ENDS**

**HEAVY FRONT AND BACK BEARING BARS AND BAR END PLATES**

**FLOOR PLATE NOSING, BAR END PLATES**

**NOSING OF CLOSELY SPACED BARS, ANGLE ENDS**

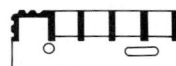

**CHECKER PLATE NOSING, BAR END PLATES**

**EXTRUDED ALUMINUM CORRUGATED NOSING, BAR END PLATES**

## TREADS

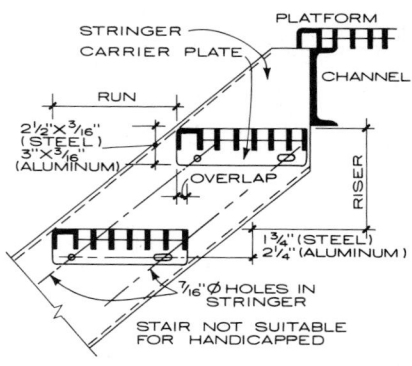

**STAIR STRINGER AND TREAD CARRIER**

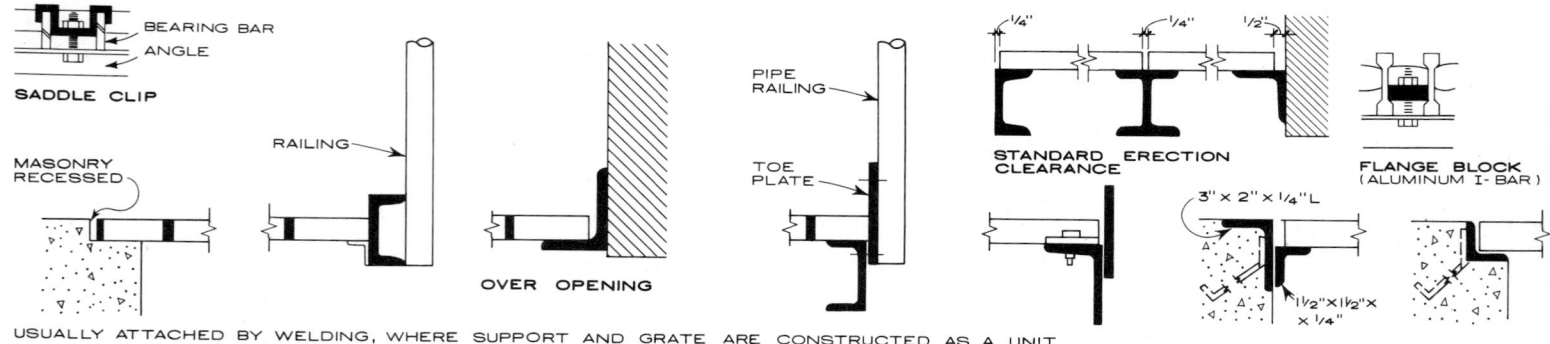

**USUALLY ATTACHED BY WELDING, WHERE SUPPORT AND GRATE ARE CONSTRUCTED AS A UNIT**

## FIXED OR LOOSE GRATINGS

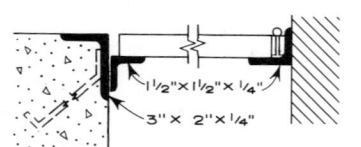
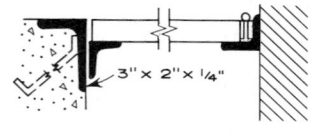
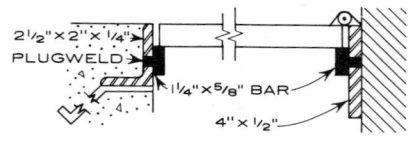
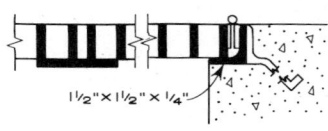

**SIZES OF ANGLES SUPPORTING GRATING DEPEND ON DEPTH OF GRATING BARS**

## HINGED AREA GRATINGS

Vicente Cordero, AIA; Arlington, Virginia

# METAL FABRICATIONS

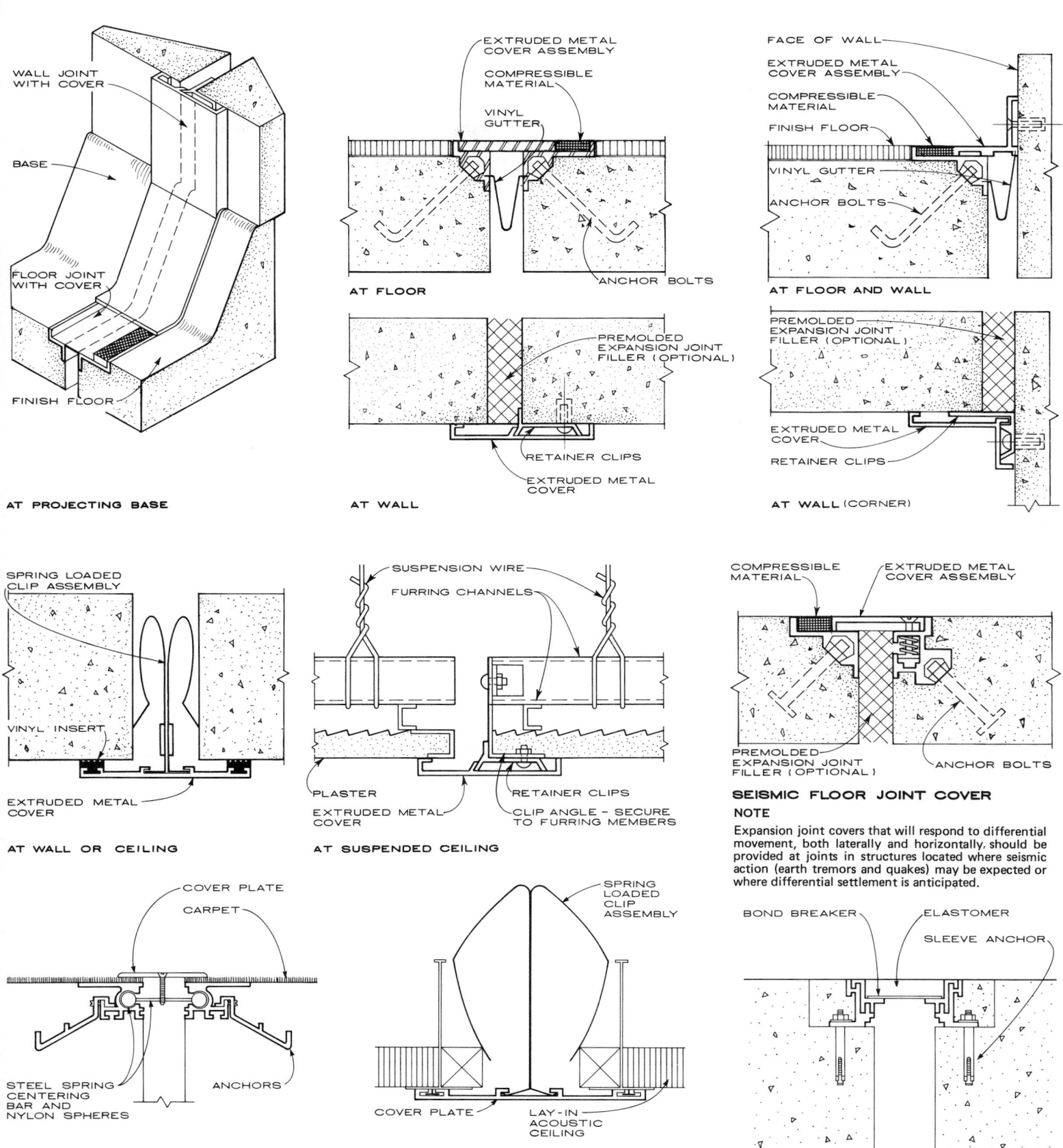

WALL JOINT WITH COVER

BASE

FLOOR JOINT WITH COVER

FINISH FLOOR

**AT PROJECTING BASE**

EXTRUDED METAL COVER ASSEMBLY

COMPRESSIBLE MATERIAL

VINYL GUTTER

ANCHOR BOLTS

**AT FLOOR**

PREMOLDED EXPANSION JOINT FILLER (OPTIONAL)

RETAINER CLIPS

EXTRUDED METAL COVER

**AT WALL**

FACE OF WALL

EXTRUDED METAL COVER ASSEMBLY

COMPRESSIBLE MATERIAL

FINISH FLOOR

VINYL GUTTER

ANCHOR BOLTS

**AT FLOOR AND WALL**

PREMOLDED EXPANSION JOINT FILLER (OPTIONAL)

EXTRUDED METAL COVER

RETAINER CLIPS

**AT WALL** (CORNER)

SPRING LOADED CLIP ASSEMBLY

VINYL INSERT

EXTRUDED METAL COVER

**AT WALL OR CEILING**

SUSPENSION WIRE

FURRING CHANNELS

PLASTER

EXTRUDED METAL COVER

RETAINER CLIPS

CLIP ANGLE – SECURE TO FURRING MEMBERS

**AT SUSPENDED CEILING**

COMPRESSIBLE MATERIAL

EXTRUDED METAL COVER ASSEMBLY

PREMOLDED EXPANSION JOINT FILLER (OPTIONAL)

ANCHOR BOLTS

**SEISMIC FLOOR JOINT COVER**

**NOTE**

Expansion joint covers that will respond to differential movement, both laterally and horizontally, should be provided at joints in structures located where seismic action (earth tremors and quakes) may be expected or where differential settlement is anticipated.

COVER PLATE

CARPET

STEEL SPRING CENTERING BAR AND NYLON SPHERES

ANCHORS

**FLEXIBLE FLOOR JOINT COVER**

SPRING LOADED CLIP ASSEMBLY

COVER PLATE

LAY-IN ACOUSTIC CEILING

**SUSPENDED ACOUSTIC CEILING**

BOND BREAKER

ELASTOMER

SLEEVE ANCHOR

**ELASTOMERIC JOINT COVER** (REMOVABLE)

**NOTE**

A large selection of prefabricated assemblies to cover interior expansion joints are available from various manufacturers to satisfy most joint and finish conditions.

**PREFABRICATED INTERIOR EXPANSION JOINT COVERS**

Robert D. Abernathy; J. N. Pease Associates; Charlotte, North Carolina

GENERAL NOTES

Many variations of the typical types shown are available such as slanted, rounded, or tapered tops and ends; grooved, ribbed, fluted and shaped faces; as well as other decorative treatment.

| Refer to | a) Standard | b) Metal |
|---|---|---|
| the following | Metal | Stair |
| sections for: | Shapes | Nosings |

D.O.F. = DEPTH OF FACE

LEGEND

⬜ INDICATES BACK-UP MATERIAL (PLYWOOD, PLASTER OR OTHER DENSE SURFACE)

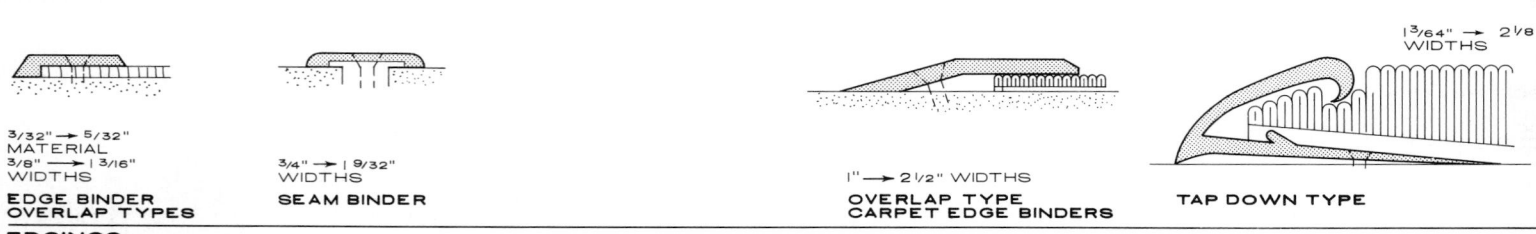

13/32" AND 11/16" OVERLAP
7/8" → 1 3/8"
D.O.F.

1/4" OVERLAP
3/4" → 1 1/4"
D.O.F.

1/16" → 1/8" MATERIAL
5/8" → 1 1/2" D.O.F.

BUTT TYPE

5/64" → 1/8" MATERIAL
13/16" → 1 3/32" D.O.F.

OVERLAP TYPE

1/16" → 1/8" MATERIAL
3/4" → 1 1/16" D.O.F.

ROLL DOWN TYPE

CONCEALED FLANGES: TAPERED OR STRAIGHT

1/2" AND 5/8" OVERLAP
13/16" → 1 1/2" D.O.F.

3/16" AND 1/4" OVERLAP
5/16" → 2" D.O.F.

APPLIED AFTER TYPES

1/8" AND 3/16" OVERLAP
5/16" → 1/2" INSERT
3/4" → 1 1/4" D.O.F.

5/16" → 1 25/32" FACE

TEE TYPE

NOSINGS

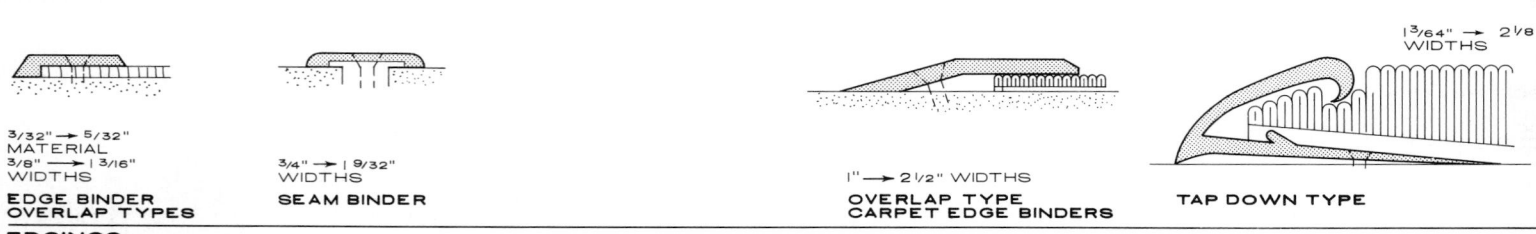

5/64" → 1/8" MATERIAL

1/8" AND 1/4" UNDER FLANGE

1/16" → 3/16" MATERIAL

1/16" → 1/8" MATERIAL

1/8" AND 3/16" MATERIAL

1/8" AND 3/16" MATERIAL

SINK (FLAT RIM) OR DOORWAY: BUTT & ROLL DOWN TYPES
CONCEALED FLANGES: TAPERED OR STRAIGHT

BUTT TYPES

EDGINGS

3/32" → 5/32" MATERIAL
3/8" → 1 3/16" WIDTHS

EDGE BINDER
OVERLAP TYPES

3/4" → 1 9/32" WIDTHS

SEAM BINDER

1" → 2 1/2" WIDTHS

OVERLAP TYPE
CARPET EDGE BINDERS

13/64" → 2 1/8" WIDTHS

TAP DOWN TYPE

EDGINGS

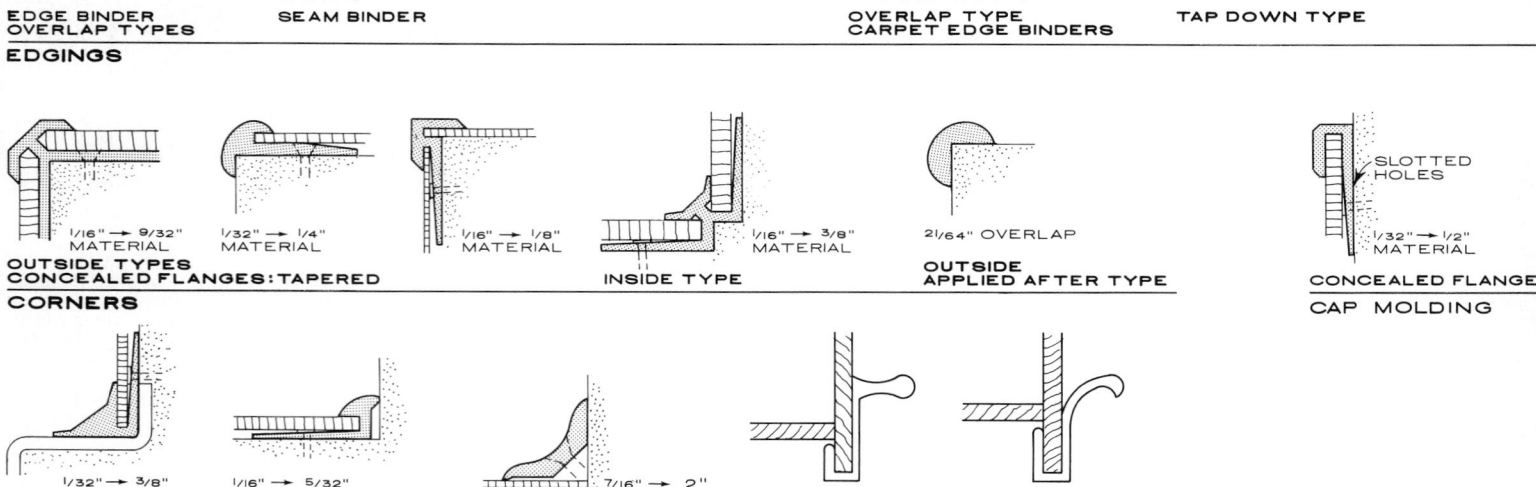

1/16" → 9/32" MATERIAL

OUTSIDE TYPES
CONCEALED FLANGES: TAPERED

1/32" → 1/4" MATERIAL

1/16" → 1/8" MATERIAL

1/16" → 3/8" MATERIAL

INSIDE TYPE

21/64" OVERLAP

OUTSIDE
APPLIED AFTER TYPE

SLOTTED HOLES
1/32" → 1/2" MATERIAL

CONCEALED FLANGE

CORNERS

CAP MOLDING

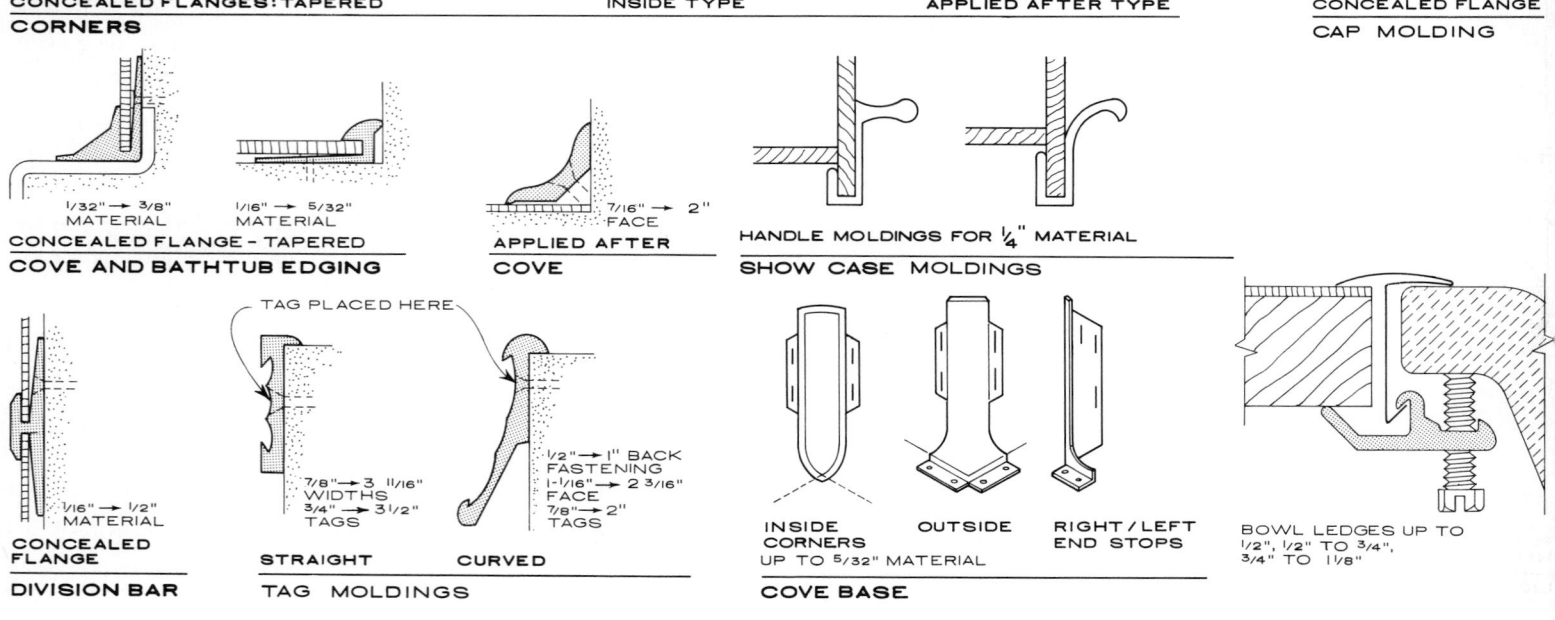

1/32" → 3/8" MATERIAL

CONCEALED FLANGE - TAPERED

1/16" → 5/32" MATERIAL

COVE AND BATHTUB EDGING

7/16" → 2" FACE

APPLIED AFTER

COVE

HANDLE MOLDINGS FOR 1/4" MATERIAL

SHOW CASE MOLDINGS

1/16" → 1/2" MATERIAL

CONCEALED FLANGE

DIVISION BAR

TAG PLACED HERE

7/8" → 3 11/16" WIDTHS
3/4" → 3 1/2" TAGS

STRAIGHT

1/2" → 1" BACK FASTENING
1-1/16" → 2 3/16" FACE
7/8" → 2" TAGS

CURVED

TAG MOLDINGS

INSIDE CORNERS
UP TO 5/32" MATERIAL

OUTSIDE

RIGHT/LEFT END STOPS

COVE BASE

BOWL LEDGES UP TO 1/2", 1/2" TO 3/4", 3/4" TO 1 1/8"

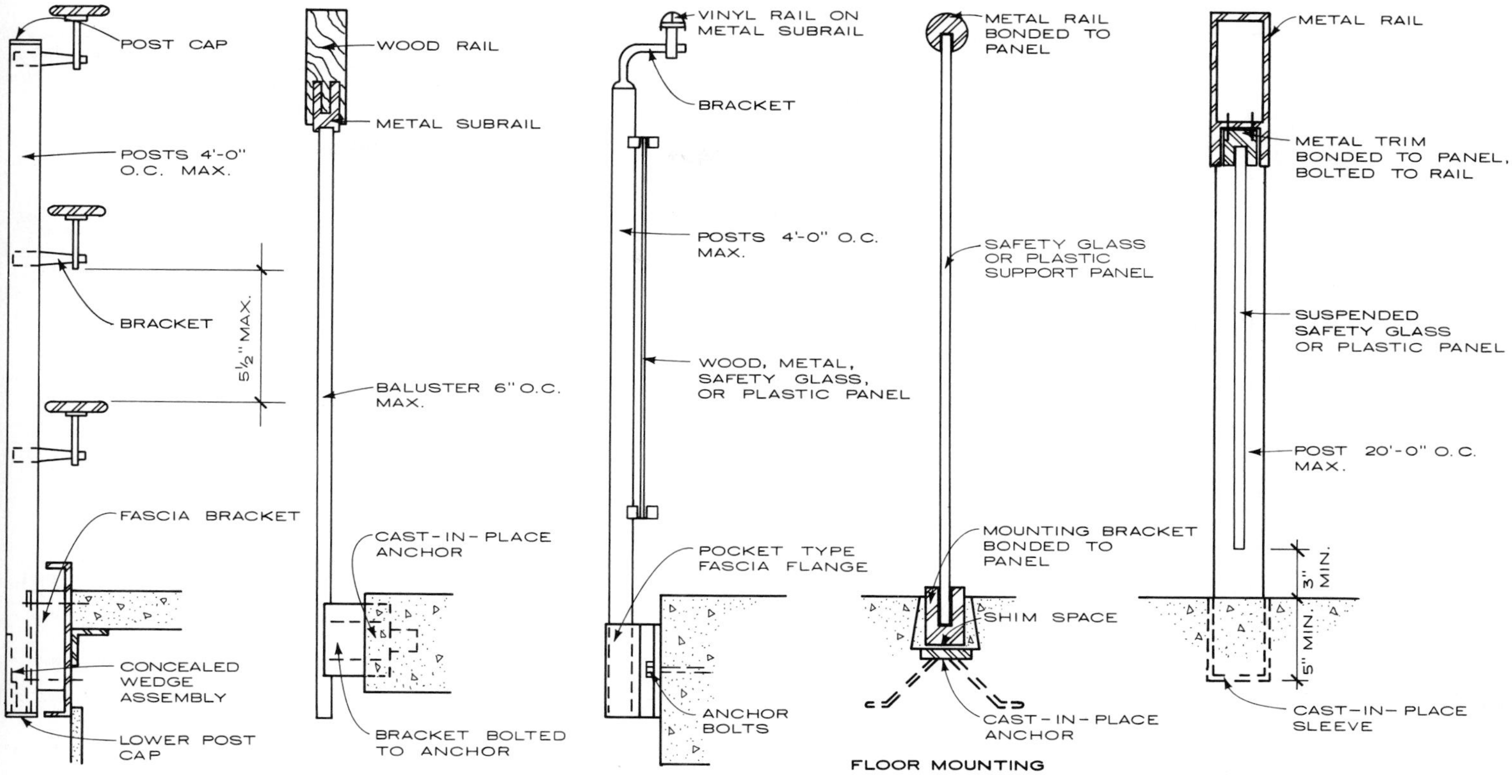

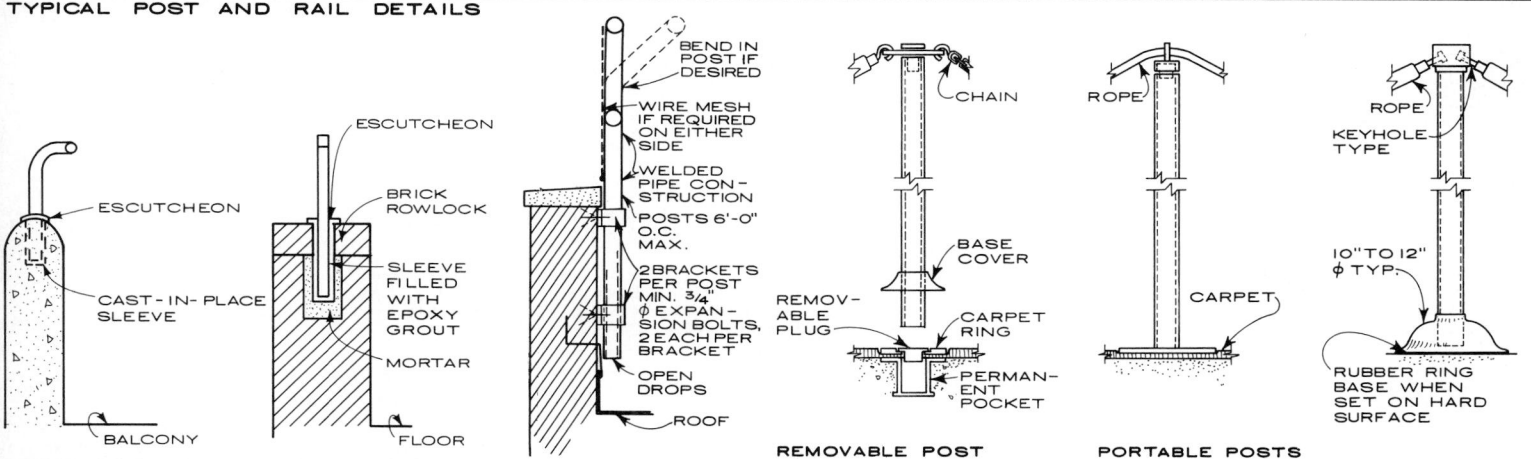

POST CAP

WOOD RAIL

VINYL RAIL ON METAL SUBRAIL

METAL RAIL BONDED TO PANEL

METAL RAIL

POSTS 4'-0" O.C. MAX.

METAL SUBRAIL

BRACKET

METAL TRIM BONDED TO PANEL, BOLTED TO RAIL

BRACKET

5½" MAX.

POSTS 4'-0" O.C. MAX.

SAFETY GLASS OR PLASTIC SUPPORT PANEL

SUSPENDED SAFETY GLASS OR PLASTIC PANEL

BALUSTER 6" O.C. MAX.

WOOD, METAL, SAFETY GLASS, OR PLASTIC PANEL

POST 20'-0" O.C. MAX.

FASCIA BRACKET

CAST-IN-PLACE ANCHOR

POCKET TYPE FASCIA FLANGE

MOUNTING BRACKET BONDED TO PANEL

3" MIN.

SHIM SPACE

CONCEALED WEDGE ASSEMBLY

5" MIN.

LOWER POST CAP

BRACKET BOLTED TO ANCHOR

ANCHOR BOLTS

CAST-IN-PLACE ANCHOR

CAST-IN-PLACE SLEEVE

**FLOOR MOUNTING**
SEE MANUFACTURER'S DETAILS FOR CLEARANCE BETWEEN FLOOR EDGE AND RAIL

**SIDE MOUTING**

CONSULT CODE FOR RAILING HEIGHT, POST RAIL, AND BALUSTER SPACING, AND LOADING REQUIREMENTS

**TYPICAL POST AND RAIL DETAILS**

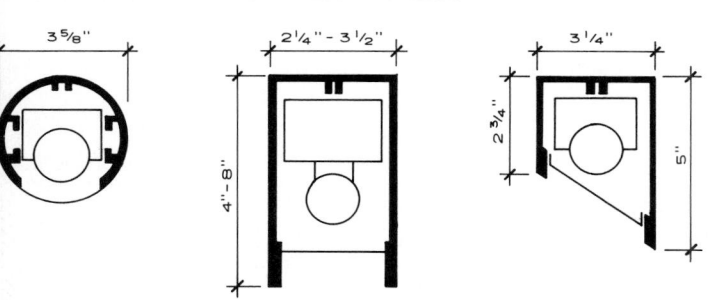

BEND IN POST IF DESIRED

ESCUTCHEON

WIRE MESH IF REQUIRED ON EITHER SIDE

BRICK ROWLOCK

WELDED PIPE CONSTRUCTION

ESCUTCHEON

POSTS 6'-0" O.C. MAX.

CHAIN

ROPE

ROPE

KEYHOLE TYPE

SLEEVE FILLED WITH EPOXY GROUT

2 BRACKETS PER POST MIN. ¾" φ EXPANSION BOLTS, 2 EACH PER BRACKET

BASE COVER

CAST-IN-PLACE SLEEVE

MORTAR

REMOVABLE PLUG

CARPET RING

CARPET

10" TO 12" φ TYP.

OPEN DROPS

BALCONY

FLOOR

ROOF

PERMANENT POCKET

RUBBER RING BASE WHEN SET ON HARD SURFACE

**REMOVABLE POST**

**PORTABLE POSTS**

**TYPICAL RAILING ON LOW WALLS**

**CONTROL POSTS**

3⅝"

2¼" – 3½"

3¼"

2¾"

4" – 8"

5"

FLUORESCENT FIXTURES AND PLASTIC DIFFUSERS, SMALLER HANDRAILS AVAILABLE WITH INCANDESCENT FIXTURES

**LIGHTED HANDRAILS**

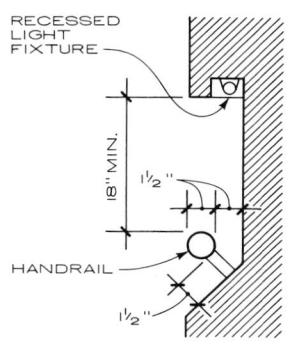

RECESSED LIGHT FIXTURE

18" MIN.

1½"

HANDRAIL

1½"

**RECESSED HANDRAIL**

## GUIDELINES

Factors to consider for railing design include:

1. Follow all local code requirements, especially as they relate to handicap requirements, ramps, rail diameter, and rail clearances.
2. Verify allowable design stresses of rails, posts, and panels.
3. Verify the structural value of fasteners and anchorage to building structure for both vertical and lateral (horizontal) forces.
4. Requirements for uniform loading may vary from 100 to 200 lb/linear foot.
5. Requirements for concentrated loads, at any point along the rail, may vary from 200 to 300 lb.
6. Horizontal guardrail or rail at ramps is 42 in. above floor surface.
7. Guardrails and rails at stairs should be designed to prevent passage of a 6 in. diameter sphere, at any opening, in areas accessible to the public.
8. Refer to ASTM E-985 for additional information.

John McCartney, AIA; Washington, D.C.

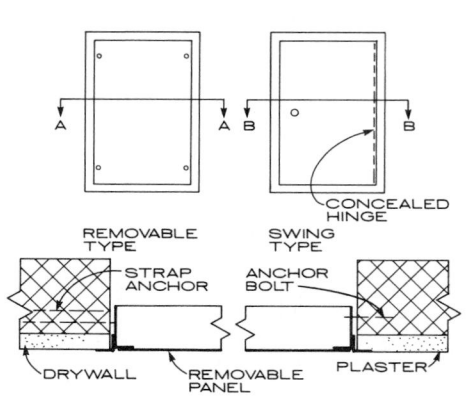

### SECTION A-A

### NOTES

1. Frames usually are set into building construction; doors are constructed to fit later. Doors may be hinged, set in with clips, or fastened with screws. Hinges may be butt or pivot, separate or continuous, surface or concealed. Assorted stock sizes range from 8 in. x 8 in. to 24 in. x 36 in.
2. Access panels should have a fire rating similar to the wall in which they occur. Access panels of more than 144 sq. ins. require automatic closers.
3. Minimum size for attic and crawl space access often is specified by building code.

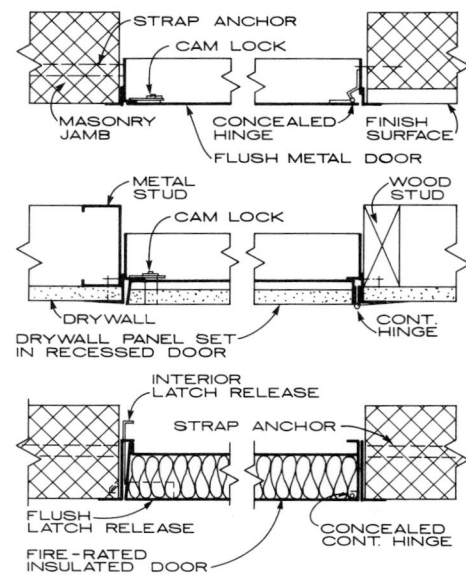

### SECTION B-B

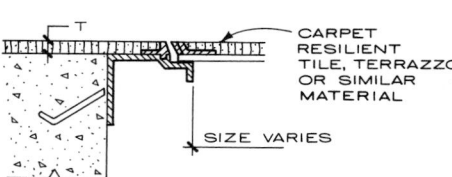

### PLASTER

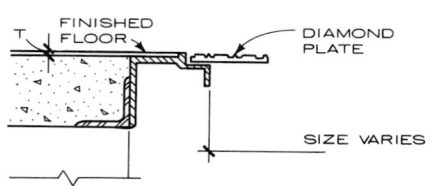

### ACOUSTICAL PLASTER

### ACOUSTICAL TILE

### NOTES

1. Spring-operated, swingdown panels and swingup panels frequently are used for ceiling access.
2. Standard sizes range from 12 in. x 12 in. to 24 in. x 36 in.
3. Other finish ceiling panels are detailed similar to acoustical tiles.

### ACCESS DOORS

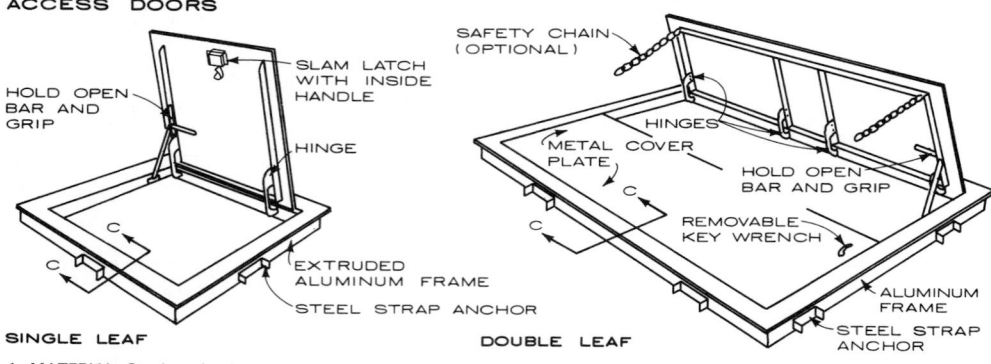

### SINGLE LEAF

1. MATERIAL: Steel or aluminum.
2. SIZES: Single leaf—2 ft. x 2 ft., 2 ft. 6 in. x 2 ft. 6 in., 2 ft. 6 in. x 3 ft., 3 ft. x 3 ft. Double leaf—3 ft. 6 in. x 3 ft. 6 in., 4 ft. x 4 ft., 4 ft. x 6 ft., 5 ft. x 5 ft.

### DOUBLE LEAF

Thickness "T" varies from ⅛ in. for resilient flooring to 3/16 in. for carpet; some manufacturers offer ¾ in. for terrazzo and tile floor.

Double-leaf floor hatch is recommended for areas where there is danger a person could fall into the opening. Safety codes require that floor openings be protected. Check local codes for special requirements.

### CEILING ACCESS PANELS

### FLOOR HATCH - SECTION C-C

### FLOOR HATCH - SECTION C-C

### LIGHT-DUTY TRENCH COVERS

1. MATERIAL: Extruded aluminum.
2. SIZE: 2 in. to 36 in. wide. Side frames are available in cut length of 20 ft. stocks that can be spliced to any length. Recessed cover plates are available in 20 ft. stock; other covers are available in 10 ft. and 12 ft. stock.
3. Side frames normally are cast in concrete around trough form.

### HEAVY-DUTY TRENCH COVERS

1. MATERIAL: Cast iron or ductile iron.
2. SIZES: Heavy duty cast iron trench covers should be planned carefully to use standard stock length to avoid cutting, or special length casting should be ordered.
3. STOCK COVER SIZE: To 48 in. wide and 24 in. long. Frames are manufactured in standard lengths of 24 in. or 36 in. depending on size and manufacturer. Cast iron troughs are 8 in. deep, 6 in. to 24 in. wide, and 48 in. in stock lengths.
4. Minimum grating size in walkways is specified in ANSI A117.1-1986.

### FLOOR HATCHES

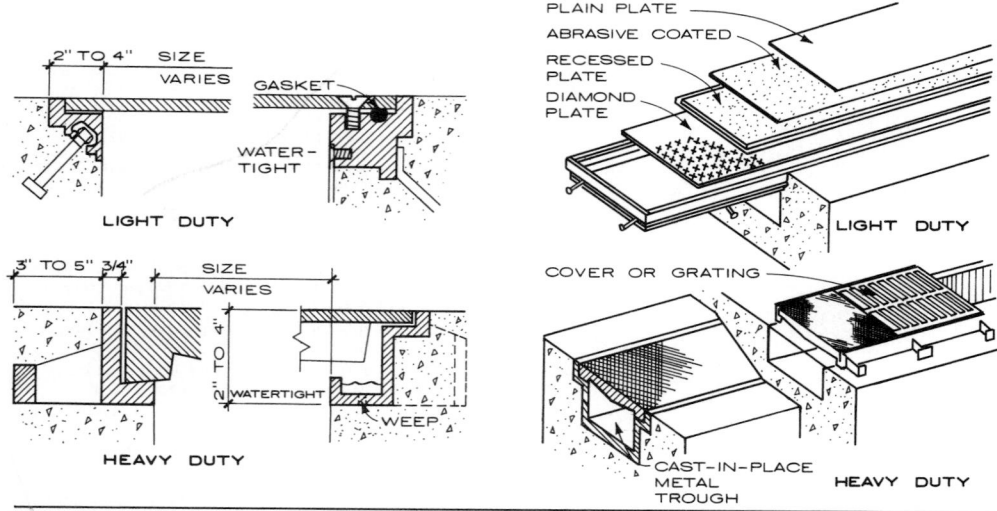

### LIGHT DUTY

### HEAVY DUTY

### LIGHT DUTY

### HEAVY DUTY

### TRENCH COVERS

Cohen, Karydas & Associates, Chartered; Washington, D.C.
Harold C. Munger, FAIA; Munger Munger + Associates Architects, Inc.; Toledo, Ohio

 **ORNAMENTAL METAL**

# CHAPTER 6

## DESIGN VALUES FOR VISUALLY GRADED STRUCTURAL LUMBER—DESIGN VALUES LISTED FOR NORMAL LOADING CONDITIONS.

DESIGN VALUES IN POUNDS PER SQUARE INCH

| SPECIES AND COMMERCIAL GRADE | SIZE CLASSIFICATION | EXTREME FIBER IN BENDING "$F_b$" SINGLE-MEMBER USES | EXTREME FIBER IN BENDING "$F_b$" REPETITIVE-MEMBER USES | TENSION PARALLEL TO GRAIN "$F_t$" | HORIZONTAL SHEAR "$F_v$" | COMPRESSION PERPENDICULAR TO GRAIN "$F_{c\perp}$" | COMPRESSION PARALLEL TO GRAIN "$F_c$" | MODULUS OF ELASTICITY "E" | GRADING RULES AGENCY |
|---|---|---|---|---|---|---|---|---|---|
| **BALSAM FIR** (Surfaced dry or surfaced green. Used at 19% max. m.c.) | | | | | | | | | |
| Select Structural | 2" to 4" | 1750 | 2000 | 1000 | 70 | 305 | 1350 | 1,500,000 | |
| No. 1 | thick | 1450 | 1700 | 850 | 70 | 305 | 1050 | 1,500,000 | |
| No. 2 | 2" to 4" | 1200 | 1400 | 700 | 70 | 305 | 850 | 1,300,000 | |
| No. 3 | wide | 675 | 775 | 400 | 70 | 305 | 525 | 1,200,000 | |
| Appearance | | 1450 | 1700 | 850 | 70 | 305 | 1250 | 1,500,000 | |
| Stud | | 675 | 775 | 400 | 70 | 305 | 525 | 1,200,000 | NELMA NHPMA (see notes 1 through 6, 8 through 13, and 19) |
| Construction | 2" to 4" | 875 | 1000 | 525 | 70 | 305 | 950 | 1,200,000 | |
| Standard | thick | 500 | 575 | 275 | 70 | 305 | 775 | 1,200,000 | |
| Utility | 4" wide | 225 | 275 | 125 | 70 | 305 | 525 | 1,200,000 | |
| Select Structural | 2" to 4" | 1500 | 1700 | 1000 | 70 | 305 | 1200 | 1,500,000 | |
| No. 1 | thick | 1250 | 1450 | 850 | 70 | 305 | 1050 | 1,500,000 | |
| No. 2 | 5" and | 1050 | 1200 | 550 (See note 8) | 70 | 305 | 900 | 1,300,000 | |
| No. 3 | wider | 600 | 700 | 325 | 70 | 305 | 575 | 1,200,000 | |
| Appearance | | 1250 | 1450 | 850 | 70 | 305 | 1250 | 1,500,000 | |
| Stud | | 600 | 700 | 325 | 70 | 305 | 575 | 1,200,000 | |
| **CALIFORNIA REDWOOD** (Surfaced dry or surfaced green. Used at 19% max. m.c.) | | | | | | | | | |
| Select Decking, Close grain | Decking 2" thick | 1850 | 2150 | — | — | — | — | 1,400,000 | RIS (see notes 1, 2, 9, and 10) |
| Select Decking | 6" and | 1450 | 1700 | — | — | — | — | 1,100,000 | |
| Commercial Decking | wider | 1200 | 1350 | — | — | — | — | 1,000,000 | |
| **DOUGLAS FIR-LARCH** (Surfaced dry or surfaced green. Used at 19% max. m.c.) | | | | | | | | | |
| Dense Select Structural | 2" to 4" | 1850 | 2800 | 1100 | 95 | 730 | 1850 | 1,900,000 | |
| Select Structural | thick | 2100 | 2400 | 950 | 95 | 625 | 1600 | 1,800,000 | |
| Dense No. 1 | 2" to 4" | 2050 | 2400 | 775 | 95 | 730 | 1450 | 1,900,000 | |
| No. 1 | wide | 1750 | 2050 | 675 | 95 | 625 | 1250 | 1,800,000 | |
| Dense No. 2 | | 1700 | 1950 | 1000 | 95 | 730 | 1150 | 1,700,000 | |
| No. 2 | | 1450 | 1650 | 850 | 95 | 625 | 1000 | 1,700,000 | |
| No. 3 | | 800 | 925 | 475 | 95 | 625 | 600 | 1,500,000 | |
| Appearance | | 1750 | 2050 | 1050 | 95 | 625 | 1500 | 1,800,000 | |
| Stud | | 800 | 925 | 475 | 95 | 625 | 600 | 1,500,000 | WCLIB WWPA (see notes 1 through 6, 8 through 13, and 19) |
| Construction | 2" to 4" | 1050 | 1200 | 625 | 95 | 625 | 1150 | 1,500,000 | |
| Standard | thick | 600 | 675 | 350 | 95 | 625 | 925 | 1,500,000 | |
| Utility | 4" wide | 275 | 325 | 175 | 95 | 625 | 600 | 1,500,000 | |
| Dense Select Structural | 2" to 4" | 2100 | 2400 | 1400 | 95 | 730 | 1650 | 1,900,000 | |
| Select Structural | thick | 1800 | 2050 | 1200 | 95 | 625 | 1400 | 1,800,000 | |
| Dense No. 1 | 5" and | 1800 | 2050 | 1200 | 95 | 730 | 1450 | 1,900,000 | |
| No. 1 | wider | 1500 | 1750 | 1000 (See note 8) | 95 | 625 | 1250 | 1,800,000 | |
| Dense No. 2 | | 1450 | 1700 | 775 | 95 | 730 | 1250 | 1,700,000 | |
| No. 2 | | 1250 | 1450 | 650 | 95 | 625 | 1050 | 1,700,000 | |
| No. 3 | | 725 | 850 | 375 | 95 | 625 | 675 | 1,500,000 | |
| Appearance | | 1500 | 1750 | 1000 | 95 | 625 | 1500 | 1,800,000 | |
| Stud | | 725 | 850 | 375 | 95 | 625 | 675 | 1,500,000 | |
| Dense Select Structural | Beams and | 1900 | — | 1100 | 85 | 730 | 1300 | 1,700,000 | |
| Select Structural | Stringers | 1600 | — | 950 | 85 | 625 | 1100 | 1,600,000 | |
| Dense No. 1 | | 1550 | — | 775 | 85 | 730 | 1100 | 1,700,000 | |
| No. 1 | | 1300 | — | 675 | 85 | 625 | 925 | 1,600,000 | |
| Dense Select Structural | Posts and | 1750 | — | 1150 | 85 | 730 | 1350 | 1,700,000 | WCLIB (see notes 1 through 6, 8 through 13, and 19) |
| Select Structural | Timbers | 1500 | — | 1000 | 85 | 625 | 1150 | 1,600,000 | |
| Dense No. 1 | | 1400 | — | 950 | 85 | 730 | 1200 | 1,700,000 | |
| No. 1 | | 1200 | — | 825 | 85 | 625 | 1000 | 1,600,000 | |
| Select Dex | Decking | 1750 | 2000 | — | — | 625 | — | 1,800,000 | |
| Commercial Dex | | 1450 | 1650 | — | — | 625 | — | 1,700,000 | |
| Dense Select Structural | Beams and | 1900 | — | 1250 | 85 | 730 | 1300 | 1,700,000 | |
| Select Structural | Stringers | 1600 | — | 1050 | 85 | 625 | 1100 | 1,600,000 | |
| Dense No. 1 | | 1550 | — | 1050 | 85 | 730 | 1100 | 1,700,000 | |
| No. 1 | | 1350 | — | 900 | 85 | 625 | 925 | 1,600,000 | |
| Dense Select Structural | Posts and | 1750 | — | 1150 | 85 | 730 | 1350 | 1,700,000 | WWPA (see notes 1 through 13, and 19) |
| Select Structural | Timbers | 1500 | — | 1000 | 85 | 625 | 1150 | 1,600,000 | |
| Dense No. 1 | | 1400 | — | 950 | 85 | 730 | 1200 | 1,700,000 | |
| No. 1 | | 1200 | — | 825 | 85 | 625 | 1000 | 1,600,000 | |
| Selected Decking | Decking | — | 2000 | — | — | — | — | 1,800,000 | |
| Commercial Decking | | — | 1650 | — | — | — | — | 1,700,000 | |
| Selected Decking | Decking | — | 2150 | (Surfaced at 15% max. m.c. and used at 15% max. m.c.) | | | — | 1,900,000 | |
| Commercial Decking | | — | 1800 | | | | — | 1,700,000 | |
| **ENGELMANN SPRUCE—ALPINE FIR (ENGELMANN SPRUCE—LODGEPOLE PINE)** (Surfaced dry or surfaced green. Used at 19% max. m.c.) | | | | | | | | | |
| Select Structural | 2" to 4" | 1350 | 1550 | 625 | 70 | 320 | 950 | 1,300,000 | |
| No. 1 | thick | 1150 | 1350 | 450 | 70 | 320 | 750 | 1,300,000 | |
| No. 2 | 2" to 4" | 950 | 1100 | 550 | 70 | 320 | 600 | 1,100,000 | WWPA (see notes 1 through 13) |
| No. 3 | wide | 525 | 600 | 300 | 70 | 320 | 375 | 1,000,000 | |
| Appearance | | 1150 | 1350 | 675 | 70 | 320 | 900 | 1,300,000 | |
| Stud | | 525 | 600 | 300 | 70 | 320 | 375 | 1,000,000 | |
| Construction | 2" to 4" | 700 | 800 | 400 | 70 | 320 | 675 | 1,000,000 | |
| Standard | thick | 375 | 450 | 225 | 70 | 320 | 550 | 1,000,000 | |
| Utility | 4" wide | 175 | 200 | 100 | 70 | 320 | 375 | 1,000,000 | |

m.c.—moisture content based on oven-dry weight of wood, percent.

National Forest Products Association; Washington, D.C.

## GENERAL INFORMATION

## DESIGN VALUES FOR VISUALLY GRADED STRUCTURAL LUMBER—DESIGN VALUES LISTED FOR NORMAL LOADING CONDITIONS.

| SPECIES AND COMMERCIAL GRADE | SIZE CLASSIFICATION | DESIGN VALUES IN POUNDS PER SQUARE INCH | | | | | | | GRADING RULES AGENCY |
|---|---|---|---|---|---|---|---|---|---|
| | | EXTREME FIBER IN BENDING "$F_b$" | | TENSION PARALLEL TO GRAIN "$F_t$" | HORIZONTAL SHEAR "$F_v$" | COMPRESSION PERPENDICULAR TO GRAIN "$F_{c\perp}$" | COMPRESSION PARALLEL TO GRAIN "$F_c$" | MODULUS OF ELASTICITY "E" | |
| | | SINGLE-MEMBER USES | REPETITIVE-MEMBER USES | | | | | | |
| **ENGELMANN SPRUCE—ALPINE FIR (ENGELMANN SPRUCE—LODGEPOLE PINE)** (Surfaced dry or surfaced green. Used at 19% max. m.c.) | | | | | | | | | |
| Select Structural | 2" to 4" | 1200 | 1350 | 775 | 70 | 320 | 850 | 1,300,000 | WWPA (see notes 1 through 13 and 19) |
| No. 1 | thick | 1000 | 1150 | 675 | 70 | 320 | 750 | 1,300,000 | |
| No. 2 | 5" and | 825 | 950 | 425 | 70 | 320 | 625 | 1,100,000 | |
| No. 3 | wider | 475 | 550 | 250 | 70 | 320 | 400 | 1,000,000 | |
| Appearance | | 1000 | 1150 | 675 | 70 | 320 | 900 | 1,300,000 | |
| Stud | | 475 | 550 | 250 | 70 | 320 | 400 | 1,000,000 | |
| Select Structural | Beams and | 1050 | — | 700 | 65 | 320 | 675 | 1,100,000 | |
| No. 1 | Stringers | 875 | — | 600 | 65 | 320 | 550 | 1,100,000 | |
| Select Structural | Posts and | 975 | — | 650 | 65 | 320 | 700 | 1,100,000 | |
| No. 1 | Timbers | 800 | — | 525 | 65 | 320 | 625 | 1,100,000 | |
| Selected Decking | Decking | — | 1300 | — | — | — | — | 1,300,000 | |
| Commercial Decking | | — | 1100 | — | — | — | — | 1,100,000 | |
| Selected Decking | Decking | — | 1400 | (Surfaced at 15% max. m.c. and used at 15% max. m.c.) | | | — | 1,300,000 | |
| Commercial Decking | | — | 1200 | | | | — | 1,200,000 | |
| **HEM-FIR** (Surfaced dry or surfaced green. Used at 19% max. m.c.) | | | | | | | | | |
| Select Structural | 2" to 4" | 1650 | 1900 | 725 | 75 | 405 | 1300 | 1,500,000 | |
| No. 1 | thick | 1400 | 1600 | 525 | 75 | 405 | 1050 | 1,500,000 | |
| No. 2 | 2" to 4" | 1150 | 1350 | 675 | 75 | 405 | 825 | 1,400,000 | |
| No. 3 | wide | 650 | 725 | 375 | 75 | 405 | 500 | 1,200,000 | |
| Appearance | | 1400 | 1600 | 825 | 75 | 405 | 1250 | 1,500,000 | |
| Stud | | 650 | 725 | 375 | 75 | 405 | 500 | 1,200,000 | |
| Construction | 2" to 4" | 825 | 975 | 500 | 75 | 405 | 925 | 1,200,000 | WCLIB WWPA (see notes 1 through 6, 8 through 13, and 19) |
| Standard | thick | 475 | 550 | 275 | 75 | 405 | 775 | 1,200,000 | |
| Utility | 4" wide | 225 | 250 | 125 | 75 | 405 | 500 | 1,200,000 | |
| Select Structural | 2" to 4" | 1400 | 1650 | 950 | 75 | 405 | 1150 | 1,500,000 | |
| No. 1 | thick | 1200 | 1400 | 800 | 75 | 405 | 1050 | 1,500,000 | |
| No. 2 | 5" and | 1000 | 1150 | 525 | 75 | 405 | 875 | 1,400,000 | |
| No. 3 | wider | 575 | 675 | 300 | 75 | 405 | 550 | 1,200,000 | |
| Appearance | | 1200 | 1400 | 800 | 75 | 405 | 1250 | 1,500,000 | |
| Stud | | 575 | 675 | 300 | 75 | 405 | 550 | 1,200,000 | |
| Select Structural | Beams and | 1300 | — | 750 | 70 | 405 | 925 | 1,300,000 | WCLIB (see notes 1 through 6, 8 through 13, and 19) |
| No. 1 | Stringers | 1050 | — | 525 | 70 | 405 | 750 | 1,300,000 | |
| Select Structural | Posts and | 1200 | — | 800 | 70 | 405 | 975 | 1,300,000 | |
| No. 1 | Timbers | 975 | — | 650 | 70 | 405 | 850 | 1,300,000 | |
| Select Dex | Decking | 1400 | 1600 | — | — | 405 | — | 1,500,000 | |
| Commercial Dex | | 1150 | 1350 | — | — | 405 | — | 1,400,000 | |
| Select Structural | Beams and | 1250 | — | 850 | 70 | 405 | 925 | 1,300,000 | WWPA (see notes 1 through 13 and 19) |
| No. 1 | Stringers | 1050 | — | 725 | 70 | 405 | 775 | 1,300,000 | |
| Select Structural | Posts and | 1200 | — | 800 | 70 | 405 | 975 | 1,300,000 | |
| No. 1 | Timbers | 950 | — | 650 | 70 | 405 | 850 | 1,300,000 | |
| Selected Decking | Decking | — | 1600 | — | — | — | — | 1,500,000 | |
| Commercial Decking | | — | 1350 | — | — | — | — | 1,400,000 | |
| Selected Decking | Decking | — | 1700 | (Surfaced at 15% max. m.c. and used at 15% max. m.c.) | | | — | 1,600,000 | |
| Commercial Decking | | — | 1450 | | | | — | 1,400,000 | |
| **IDAHO WHITE PINE** (Surfaced dry or surfaced green. Used at 19% max. m.c.) | | | | | | | | | |
| Selected Decking | Decking | — | 1300 | — | — | — | — | 1,400,000 | WWPA (see notes 1 through 13) |
| Commercial Decking | | — | 1050 | — | — | — | — | 1,300,000 | |
| Selected Decking | Decking | — | 1400 | (Surfaced at 15% max. m.c. and used at 15% max. m.c.) | | | — | 1,500,000 | |
| Commercial Decking | | — | 1150 | | | | — | 1,400,000 | |
| **NORTHERN PINE** (Surfaced dry or surfaced green. Used at 19% max. m.c.) | | | | | | | | | |
| Select Structural | 2" to 4" | 1650 | 1850 | 950 | 70 | 435 | 1200 | 1,400,000 | |
| No. 1 | thick | 1400 | 1600 | 825 | 70 | 435 | 975 | 1,400,000 | |
| No. 2 | 2" to 4" | 1150 | 1300 | 675 | 70 | 435 | 775 | 1,300,000 | |
| No. 3 | wide | 625 | 725 | 375 | 70 | 435 | 475 | 1,100,000 | |
| Appearance | | 1200 | 1400 | 800 | 70 | 435 | 1150 | 1,400,000 | |
| Stud | | 625 | 725 | 375 | 70 | 435 | 475 | 1,100,000 | |
| Construction | 2" to 4" | 825 | 950 | 475 | 70 | 435 | 875 | 1,100,000 | NELMA NHPMA (see notes 1 through 6, 8 through 13, and 19) |
| Standard | thick | 450 | 525 | 275 | 70 | 435 | 725 | 1,100,000 | |
| Utility | 4" wide | 225 | 250 | 125 | 70 | 435 | 475 | 1,100,000 | |
| Select Structural | 2" to 4" | 1400 | 1600 | 950 | 70 | 435 | 1100 | 1,400,000 | |
| No. 1 | thick | 1200 | 1400 | 800 | 70 | 435 | 975 | 1,400,000 | |
| No. 2 | 5" and | 950 | 1100 | 525 | 70 | 435 | 825 | 1,300,000 | |
| No. 3 | wider | 575 | 650 | 300 | 70 | 435 | 525 | 1,100,000 | |
| Appearance | | 1200 | 1400 | 800 | 70 | 435 | 1150 | 1,400,000 | |
| Stud | | 575 | 650 | 300 | 70 | 435 | 525 | 1,100,000 | |
| Select Structural | Beams and | 1250 | — | 850 | 65 | 435 | 850 | 1,300,000 | NHPMA (see notes 1 through 6, 8 through 13, and 19) |
| No. 1 | Stringers | 1050 | — | 700 | 65 | 435 | 725 | 1,300,000 | |
| Select Structural | Posts and | 1150 | — | 800 | 65 | 435 | 900 | 1,300,000 | |
| No. 1 | Timbers | 950 | — | 650 | 65 | 435 | 800 | 1,300,000 | |
| Select | Decking | 1350 | 1550 | — | — | — | — | 1,400,000 | NELMA (see notes 1-6, 8-13, and 19) |
| Commercial | | 1150 | 1300 | — | — | — | — | 1,300,000 | |

m.c.—moisture content based on oven-dry weight of wood, percent.

National Forest Products Association; Washington, D.C.

GENERAL INFORMATION

## DESIGN VALUES FOR VISUALLY GRADED STRUCTURAL LUMBER—DESIGN VALUES LISTED FOR NORMAL LOADING CONDITIONS.

| SPECIES AND COMMERCIAL GRADE | SIZE CLASSIFICATION | DESIGN VALUES IN POUNDS PER SQUARE INCH: EXTREME FIBER IN BENDING "$F_b$" SINGLE-MEMBER USES | EXTREME FIBER IN BENDING "$F_b$" REPETITIVE-MEMBER USES | TENSION PARALLEL TO GRAIN "$F_t$" | HORIZONTAL SHEAR "$F_v$" | COMPRESSION PERPENDICULAR TO GRAIN "$F_{c\perp}$" | COMPRESSION PARALLEL TO GRAIN "$F_c$" | MODULUS OF ELASTICITY "E" | GRADING RULES AGENCY |
|---|---|---|---|---|---|---|---|---|---|
| **PONDEROSA PINE—SUGAR PINE (PONDEROSA PINE—LODGEPOLE PINE)** (Surfaced dry or surfaced green. Used at 19% max. m.c.) | | | | | | | | | |
| Select Structural | 2″ to 4″ | 1400 | 1650 | 825 | 70 | 375 | 1050 | 1,200,000 | WWPA (see notes 1 through 13 and 19) |
| No. 1 | thick | 1200 | 1400 | 700 | 70 | 375 | 850 | 1,200,000 | |
| No. 2 | 2″ to 4″ | 1000 | 1150 | 575 | 70 | 375 | 675 | 1,100,000 | |
| No. 3 | wide | 550 | 625 | 325 | 70 | 375 | 400 | 1,000,000 | |
| Appearance | | 1200 | 1400 | 700 | 70 | 375 | 1000 | 1,200,000 | |
| Stud | | 550 | 625 | 325 | 70 | 375 | 400 | 1,000,000 | |
| Construction | 2″ to 4″ | 725 | 825 | 425 | 70 | 375 | 775 | 1,000,000 | |
| Standard | thick | 400 | 450 | 225 | 70 | 375 | 625 | 1,000,000 | |
| Utility | 4″ wide | 200 | 225 | 100 | 70 | 375 | 400 | 1,000,000 | |
| Select Structural | 2″ to 4″ | 1200 | 1400 | 825 | 70 | 375 | 950 | 1,200,000 | |
| No. 1 | thick | 1050 | 1200 | 700 | 70 | 375 | 850 | 1,200,000 | |
| No. 2 | 5″ and | 850 | 975 | 450 (See note 8) | 70 | 375 | 700 | 1,100,000 | |
| No. 3 | wider | 500 | 575 | 250 | 70 | 375 | 450 | 1,000,000 | |
| Appearance | | 1050 | 1200 | 700 | 70 | 375 | 1000 | 1,200,000 | |
| Stud | | 500 | 575 | 250 | 70 | 375 | 450 | 1,000,000 | |
| Select Structural | Beams and | 1100 | — | 725 | 65 | 375 | 750 | 1,100,000 | |
| No. 1 | Stringers | 925 | — | 625 | 65 | 375 | 625 | 1,100,000 | |
| Select Structural | Posts and | 1000 | — | 675 | 65 | 375 | 800 | 1,100,000 | |
| No. 1 | Timbers | 825 | — | 550 | 65 | 375 | 700 | 1,100,000 | |
| Selected Decking | Decking | — | 1350 | — | — | — | — | 1,200,000 | |
| Commercial Decking | | — | 1150 | — | — | — | — | 1,100,000 | |
| Selected Decking | Decking | — | 1450 | (Surfaced at 15% max. m.c. and used at 15% max. m.c.) | | | — | 1,300,000 | |
| Commercial Decking | | — | 1250 | | | | — | 1,100,000 | |
| **SOUTHERN PINE** (Surfaced at 15% maximum moisture content, KD-15. Used at 15% max. m.c.) | | | | | | | | | |
| Select Structural | 2″ to 4″ thick | 2150 | 2500 | 1250 | 105 | 565 | 1800 | 1,800,000 | SPIB (see notes 1, 3, 4, 6, 8, 12, 13, and 16 through 19) |
| Dense Select Structural | 2″ to 4″ wide | 2500 | 2900 | 1500 | 105 | 660 | 2100 | 1,900,000 | |
| No. 1 | | 1850 | 2100 | 1050 | 105 | 565 | 1450 | 1,800,000 | |
| No. 1 Dense | | 2150 | 2450 | 1250 | 105 | 660 | 1700 | 1,900,000 | |
| No. 2 | | 1550 | 1750 | 900 | 95 | 565 | 1150 | 1,600,000 | |
| No. 2 Dense | | 1800 | 2050 | 1050 | 95 | 660 | 1350 | 1,700,000 | |
| No. 3 | | 850 | 975 | 500 | 95 | 565 | 675 | 1,500,000 | |
| No. 3 Dense | | 1000 | 1150 | 575 | 95 | 660 | 800 | 1,500,000 | |
| Stud | | 850 | 975 | 500 | 95 | 565 | 675 | 1,500,000 | |
| Construction | 2″ to 4″ | 1100 | 1250 | 650 | 105 | 565 | 1300 | 1,500,000 | |
| Standard | thick | 625 | 725 | 375 | 95 | 565 | 1050 | 1,500,000 | |
| Utility | 4″ wide | 275 | 300 | 175 | 95 | 565 | 675 | 1,500,000 | |
| Select Structural | 2″ to 4″ thick | 1850 | 2150 | 1200 | 95 | 565 | 1600 | 1,800,000 | |
| Dense Select Structural | 5″ and | 2200 | 2500 | 1450 | 95 | 660 | 1850 | 1,900,000 | |
| No. 1 | wider | 1600 | 1850 | 1050 | 95 | 565 | 1450 | 1,800,000 | |
| No. 1 Dense | | 1850 | 2150 | 1250 | 95 | 660 | 1700 | 1,900,000 | |
| No. 2 | | 1300 | 1500 | 675 (See note 8) | 95 | 565 | 1200 | 1,600,000 | |
| No. 2 Dense | | 1550 | 1750 | 800 | 95 | 660 | 1400 | 1,700,000 | |
| No. 3 | | 750 | 875 | 400 | 95 | 565 | 725 | 1,500,000 | |
| No. 3 Dense | | 875 | 1000 | 450 | 95 | 660 | 850 | 1,500,000 | |
| Stud | | 800 | 900 | 400 | 95 | 565 | 725 | 1,500,000 | |
| Dense Standard Decking | 2″ to 4″ | 2150 | 2450 | — | — | 660 | — | 1,900,000 | |
| Select Decking | thick | 1550 | 1750 | — | — | 565 | — | 1,600,000 | |
| Dense Select Decking | 2″ and | 1800 | 2050 | — | — | 660 | — | 1,700,000 | |
| Commercial Decking | wider | 1550 | 1750 | — | — | 565 | — | 1,600,000 | |
| Dense Commercial Decking | Decking | 1800 | 2050 | — | — | 660 | — | 1,700,000 | |
| Dense Structural 86 | 2″ to 4″ | 2800 | 3250 | 1900 | 165 | 660 | 2300 | 1,900,000 | |
| Dense Structural 72 | thick | 2400 | 2750 | 1600 | 135 | 660 | 1950 | 1,900,000 | |
| Dense Structural 65 | | 2150 | 2450 | 1450 | 125 | 660 | 1750 | 1,900,000 | |
| **SOUTHERN PINE** (Surfaced dry. Used at 19% max. m.c.) | | | | | | | | | |
| Select Structural | 2″ to 4″ thick | 2000 | 2300 | 1150 | 100 | 565 | 1550 | 1,700,000 | SPIB (see notes 1, 3, 4, 6, 8, 12, 13, and 16 through 19) |
| Dense Select Structural | 2″ to 4″ | 2350 | 2700 | 1350 | 100 | 660 | 1800 | 1,800,000 | |
| No. 1 | wide | 1700 | 1950 | 1000 | 100 | 565 | 1250 | 1,700,000 | |
| No. 1 Dense | | 2000 | 2300 | 1150 | 100 | 660 | 1450 | 1,800,000 | |
| No. 2 | | 1400 | 1650 | 825 | 90 | 565 | 975 | 1,600,000 | |
| No. 2 Dense | | 1650 | 1900 | 975 | 90 | 660 | 1150 | 1,600,000 | |
| No. 3 | | 775 | 900 | 450 | 90 | 565 | 575 | 1,400,000 | |
| No. 3 Dense | | 925 | 1050 | 525 | 90 | 660 | 675 | 1,500,000 | |
| Stud | | 775 | 900 | 450 | 90 | 565 | 575 | 1,400,000 | |
| Construction | 2″ to 4″ | 1000 | 1150 | 600 | 100 | 565 | 1100 | 1,400,000 | |
| Standard | thick | 575 | 675 | 350 | 90 | 565 | 900 | 1,400,000 | |
| Utility | 4″ wide | 275 | 300 | 150 | 90 | 565 | 575 | 1,400,000 | |
| Select Structural | 2″ to 4″ thick | 1750 | 2000 | 1150 | 90 | 565 | 1350 | 1,700,000 | |
| Dense Select Structural | 5″ and | 2050 | 2350 | 1300 | 90 | 660 | 1600 | 1,800,000 | |
| No. 1 | wider | 1450 | 1700 | 975 | 90 | 565 | 1250 | 1,700,000 | |
| No. 1 Dense | | 1700 | 2000 | 1150 | 90 | 660 | 1450 | 1,800,000 | |
| No. 2 | | 1200 | 1400 | 625 (See note 8) | 90 | 565 | 1000 | 1,600,000 | |
| No. 2 Dense | | 1400 | 1650 | 725 | 90 | 660 | 1200 | 1,600,000 | |
| No. 3 | | 700 | 800 | 350 | 90 | 565 | 625 | 1,400,000 | |
| No. 3 Dense | | 825 | 925 | 425 | 90 | 660 | 725 | 1,500,000 | |
| Stud | | 725 | 850 | 350 | 90 | 565 | 625 | 1,400,000 | |

m.c.—moisture content based on oven-dry weight of wood, percent.

National Forest Products Association; Washington, D.C.

## DESIGN VALUES FOR VISUALLY GRADED STRUCTURAL LUMBER—DESIGN VALUES LISTED FOR NORMAL LOADING CONDITIONS.

| SPECIES AND COMMERCIAL GRADE | SIZE CLASSIFICATION | DESIGN VALUES IN POUNDS PER SQUARE INCH | | | | | | | |
|---|---|---|---|---|---|---|---|---|---|
| | | EXTREME FIBER IN BENDING "Fb" | | TENSION PARALLEL TO GRAIN "Ft" | HORIZONTAL SHEAR "Fv" | COMPRESSION PERPENDICULAR TO GRAIN "Fc⊥" | COMPRESSION PARALLEL TO GRAIN "Fc" | MODULUS OF ELASTICITY "E" | GRADING RULES AGENCY |
| | | SINGLE-MEMBER USES | REPETITIVE-MEMBER USES | | | | | | |
| **SOUTHERN PINE** (Surfaced dry. Used at 19% max. m.c.) | | | | | | | | | |
| Dense Standard Decking | 2″ to 4″ thick | 2000 | 2300 | — | — | 660 | — | 1,800,000 | |
| Select Decking | thick | 1400 | 1650 | — | — | 565 | — | 1,600,000 | |
| Dense Select Decking | 2″ and | 1650 | 1900 | — | — | 660 | — | 1,600,000 | |
| Commercial Decking | wider | 1400 | 1650 | — | — | 565 | — | 1,600,000 | |
| Dense Commercial Decking | Decking | 1650 | 1900 | — | — | 660 | — | 1,600,000 | |
| Dense Structural 86 | 2″ to 4″ | 2600 | 3000 | 1750 | 155 | 660 | 2000 | 1,800,000 | |
| Dense Structural 72 | thick | 2200 | 2550 | 1450 | 130 | 660 | 1650 | 1,800,000 | |
| Dense Structural 65 | | 2000 | 2300 | 1300 | 115 | 660 | 1500 | 1,800,000 | |
| **SOUTHERN PINE** (Surfaced green. Used any condition.) | | | | | | | | | |
| Select Structural | 2½″ to 4″ thick | 1600 | 1850 | 925 | 95 | 375 | 1050 | 1,500,000 | |
| Dense Select Structural | 2½″ to 4″ wide | 1850 | 2150 | 1100 | 95 | 440 | 1200 | 1,600,000 | |
| No. 1 | | 1350 | 1550 | 800 | 95 | 375 | 825 | 1,500,000 | |
| No. 1 Dense | | 1600 | 1800 | 925 | 95 | 440 | 950 | 1,600,000 | |
| No. 2 | | 1150 | 1300 | 675 | 85 | 375 | 650 | 1,400,000 | |
| No. 2 Dense | | 1350 | 1500 | 775 | 85 | 440 | 750 | 1,400,000 | |
| No. 3 | | 625 | 725 | 375 | 85 | 375 | 400 | 1,200,000 | |
| No. 3 Dense | | 725 | 850 | 425 | 85 | 440 | 450 | 1,300,000 | |
| Stud | | 625 | 725 | 375 | 85 | 375 | 400 | 1,200,000 | |
| Construction | 2½″ to 4″ | 825 | 925 | 475 | 95 | 375 | 725 | 1,200,000 | |
| Standard | thick | 475 | 525 | 275 | 85 | 375 | 600 | 1,200,000 | |
| Utility | 4″ wide | 200 | 250 | 125 | 85 | 375 | 400 | 1,200,000 | |
| Select Structural | 2½″ to 4″ thick | 1400 | 1600 | 900 | 85 | 375 | 900 | 1,500,000 | SPIB (see notes 1, 3, 4, 6, 8, 12, 13, and 16 through 19) |
| Dense Select Structural | 5″ and | 1600 | 1850 | 1050 | 85 | 440 | 1050 | 1,600,000 | |
| No. 1 | wider | 1200 | 1350 | 775 | 85 | 375 | 825 | 1,500,000 | |
| No. 1 Dense | | 1400 | 1600 | 925 | 85 | 440 | 950 | 1,600,000 | |
| No. 2 | | 975 | 1100 | 500 | 85 | 375 | 675 | 1,400,000 | |
| No. 2 Dense | | 1150 | 1300 | 600 | 85 | 440 | 800 | 1,400,000 | |
| No. 3 | | 550 | 650 | 300 | 85 | 375 | 425 | 1,200,000 | |
| No. 3 Dense | | 650 | 750 | 350 | 85 | 440 | 475 | 1,300,000 | |
| Stud | | 575 | 675 | 300 | 85 | 375 | 425 | 1,200,000 | |
| Dense Standard Decking | 2½″ to 4″ | 1600 | 1800 | — | — | 440 | — | 1,600,000 | |
| Select Decking | thick | 1150 | 1300 | — | — | 375 | — | 1,400,000 | |
| Dense Select Decking | 2″ and | 1350 | 1500 | — | — | 440 | — | 1,400,000 | |
| Commercial Decking | wider | 1150 | 1300 | — | — | 375 | — | 1,400,000 | |
| Dense Commercial Decking | Decking | 1350 | 1500 | — | — | 440 | — | 1,400,000 | |
| No. 1 SR | 5″ and | 1350 | — | 875 | 110 | 375 | 775 | 1,500,000 | |
| No. 1 Dense SR | thicker | 1550 | — | 1050 | 110 | 440 | 925 | 1,600,000 | |
| No. 2 SR | | 1100 | — | 725 | 95 | 375 | 625 | 1,400,000 | |
| No. 2 Dense SR | | 1250 | — | 850 | 95 | 440 | 725 | 1,400,000 | |
| Dense Structural 86 | 2½″ and | 2100 | 2400 | 1400 | 145 | 440 | 1300 | 1,600,000 | |
| Dense Structural 72 | thicker | 1750 | 2050 | 1200 | 120 | 440 | 1100 | 1,600,000 | |
| Dense Structural 65 | | 1600 | 1800 | 1050 | 110 | 440 | 1000 | 1,600,000 | |
| **SPRUCE—PINE—FIR** (Surfaced dry or surfaced green. Used at 19% max. m.c.) | | | | | | | | | |
| Select Structural | 2″ to 3″ | 1450 | 1650 | 850 | 70 | 425 | 1100 | 1,500,000 | NLGA (A Canadian agency. See notes 1 through 6, 8 through 15, and 19) |
| No. 1 | thick | 1200 | 1400 | 725 | 70 | 425 | 875 | 1,500,000 | |
| No. 2 | 2″ to 4″ | 1000 | 1150 | 600 | 70 | 425 | 675 | 1,300,000 | |
| No. 3 | wide | 550 | 650 | 325 | 70 | 425 | 425 | 1,200,000 | |
| Appearance | | 1200 | 1400 | 725 | 70 | 425 | 1050 | 1,500,000 | |
| Stud | | 550 | 650 | 325 | 70 | 425 | 425 | 1,200,000 | |
| Construction | 2″ to 4″ | 725 | 850 | 425 | 70 | 425 | 775 | 1,200,000 | |
| Standard | thick | 400 | 475 | 225 | 70 | 425 | 650 | 1,200,000 | |
| Utility | 4″ wide | 175 | 225 | 100 | 70 | 425 | 425 | 1,200,000 | |
| Select Structural | 2″ to 4″ | 1250 | 1450 | 825 | 70 | 425 | 975 | 1,500,000 | |
| No. 1 | thick | 1050 | 1200 | 700 | 70 | 425 | 875 | 1,500,000 | |
| No. 2 | 5″ and | 875 | 1000 | 450 | 70 | 425 | 725 | 1,300,000 | |
| No. 3 | wider | 500 | 575 | 275 | 70 | 425 | 450 | 1,200,000 | |
| Appearance | | 1050 | 1200 | 700 | 70 | 425 | 1050 | 1,500,000 | |
| Stud | | 500 | 575 | 275 | 70 | 425 | 450 | 1,200,000 | |
| Select Structural | Beams and | 1100 | — | 650 | 65 | 425 | 775 | 1,300,000 | |
| No. 1 | Stringers | 900 | — | 450 | 65 | 425 | 625 | 1,300,000 | |
| Select Structural | Posts and | 1050 | — | 700 | 65 | 425 | 800 | 1,300,000 | |
| No. 1 | Timbers | 850 | — | 550 | 65 | 425 | 700 | 1,300,000 | |
| Select | Decking | 1200 | 1400 | — | — | 425 | — | 1,500,000 | |
| Commercial | | 1000 | 1150 | — | — | 425 | — | 1,300,000 | |
| **WESTERN CEDARS** (Surfaced dry or surfaced green. Used at 19% max. m.c.) | | | | | | | | | |
| Selected Decking | Decking | — | 1450 | — | — | — | — | 1,100,000 | WWPA (see notes 1 through 13 and 19) |
| Commercial Decking | | — | 1200 | — | — | — | — | 1,000,000 | |
| Selected Decking | Decking | — | 1550 | (Surfaced at 15% max. m.c. and used at 15% max. m.c.) | | | — | 1,100,000 | |
| Commercial Decking | | — | 1300 | | | | — | 1,000,000 | |
| **WESTERN HEMLOCK** (Surfaced dry or surfaced green. Used at 19% max. m.c.) | | | | | | | | | |
| Select Structural | 2″ to 4″ | 1800 | 2100 | 825 | 90 | 410 | 1450 | 1,600,000 | WCLIB WWPA (see notes 1-6, 8-13, and 19) |
| No. 1 | thick | 1550 | 1800 | 575 | 90 | 410 | 1150 | 1,600,000 | |
| No. 2 | 2″ to 4″ | 1300 | 1450 | 750 | 90 | 410 | 900 | 1,400,000 | |
| No. 3 | wide | 700 | 800 | 425 | 90 | 410 | 550 | 1,300,000 | |
| Appearance | | 1550 | 1800 | 900 | 90 | 410 | 1350 | 1,600,000 | |
| Stud | | 700 | 800 | 425 | 90 | 410 | 550 | 1,300,000 | |

National Forest Products Association; Washington, D.C.

## DESIGN VALUES FOR VISUALLY GRADED STRUCTURAL LUMBER—DESIGN VALUES LISTED FOR NORMAL LOADING CONDITIONS.

| SPECIES AND COMMERCIAL GRADE | SIZE CLASSIFICATION | EXTREME FIBER IN BENDING "$F_b$" SINGLE-MEMBER USES | EXTREME FIBER IN BENDING "$F_b$" REPETITIVE-MEMBER USES | TENSION PARALLEL TO GRAIN "$F_t$" | HORIZONTAL SHEAR "$F_v$" | COMPRESSION PERPENDICULAR TO GRAIN "$F_{c\perp}$" | COMPRESSION PARALLEL TO GRAIN "$F_c$" | MODULUS OF ELASTICITY "$E$" | GRADING RULES AGENCY |
|---|---|---|---|---|---|---|---|---|---|
| **WESTERN HEMLOCK** (Surfaced dry or surfaced green. Used at 19% max. m.c.) | | | | | | | | | |
| Construction | 2" to 4" thick | 925 | 1050 | 550 | 90 | 410 | 1050 | 1,300,000 | WCLIB WWPA (see notes 1 through 6, 8 through 13, and 19) |
| Standard | 4" wide | 525 | 600 | 300 | 90 | 410 | 850 | 1,300,000 | |
| Utility | | 250 | 275 | 150 | 90 | 410 | 550 | 1,300,000 | |
| Select Structural | 2" to 4" thick | 1550 | 1800 | 1050 | 90 | 410 | 1300 | 1,600,000 | |
| No. 1 | 5" and wider | 1350 | 1550 | 900 | 90 | 410 | 1150 | 1,600,000 | |
| No. 2 | | 1100 | 1250 | 575 (See note 8) | 90 | 410 | 975 | 1,400,000 | |
| No. 3 | | 650 | 750 | 325 | 90 | 410 | 625 | 1,300,000 | |
| Appearance | | 1350 | 1550 | 900 | 90 | 410 | 1350 | 1,600,000 | |
| Stud | | 650 | 750 | 325 | 90 | 410 | 625 | 1,300,000 | |
| Select Structural | Beams and Stringers | 1400 | — | 825 | 85 | 410 | 1000 | 1,400,000 | WCLIB (see notes 1 through 6, 8 through 13, and 19) |
| No. 1 | | 1150 | — | 575 | 85 | 410 | 850 | 1,400,000 | |
| Select Structural | Posts and Timbers | 1300 | — | 875 | 85 | 410 | 1100 | 1,400,000 | |
| No. 1 | | 1050 | — | 700 | 85 | 410 | 950 | 1,400,000 | |
| Select Dex | Decking | 1500 | 1750 | — | — | 410 | — | 1,600,000 | |
| Commercial Dex | | 1300 | 1450 | — | — | 410 | — | 1,400,000 | |
| Select Structural | Beams and Stringers | 1400 | — | 950 | 85 | 410 | 1000 | 1,400,000 | WWPA (see notes 1 through 6, 8 through 13, and 19) |
| No. 1 | | 1150 | — | 775 | 85 | 410 | 850 | 1,400,000 | |
| Select Structural | Posts and Timbers | 1300 | — | 875 | 85 | 410 | 1100 | 1,400,000 | |
| No. 1 | | 1050 | — | 700 | 85 | 410 | 950 | 1,400,000 | |
| Selected Decking | Decking | — | 1750 | — | — | — | — | 1,600,000 | |
| Commercial Decking | | — | 1450 | — | — | — | — | 1,400,000 | |
| Selected Decking | Decking | — | 1900 | (Surfaced at 15% max. m.c. and used at 15% max. m.c.) | | | — | 1,700,000 | |
| Commercial Decking | | — | 1600 | | | | — | 1,500,000 | |
| **WHITE WOODS (WESTERN WOODS)** (Surfaced dry or surfaced green. Used at 19% max. m.c.) | | | | | | | | | |
| Select Structural | 2" to 4" thick | 1350 | 1550 | 600 | 70 | 315 | 950 | 1,100,000 | WWPA (see notes 1 through 13 and 19) |
| No. 1 | 2" to 4" wide | 1150 | 1300 | 425 | 70 | 315 | 750 | 1,100,000 | |
| No. 2 | | 925 | 1050 | 550 | 70 | 315 | 600 | 1,000,000 | |
| No. 3 | | 525 | 600 | 300 | 70 | 315 | 375 | 900,000 | |
| Appearance | | 1150 | 1300 | 650 | 70 | 315 | 900 | 1,100,000 | |
| Stud | | 525 | 600 | 300 | 70 | 315 | 375 | 900,000 | |
| Construction | 2" to 4" thick | 675 | 775 | 400 | 70 | 315 | 675 | 900,000 | |
| Standard | 4" wide | 375 | 425 | 225 | 70 | 315 | 550 | 900,000 | |
| Utility | | 175 | 200 | 100 | 70 | 315 | 375 | 900,000 | |
| Select Structural | 2" to 4" thick | 1150 | 1300 | 775 | 70 | 315 | 850 | 1,100,000 | |
| No. 1 | 5" and wider | 975 | 1100 | 650 | 70 | 315 | 750 | 1,100,000 | |
| No. 2 | | 800 | 925 | 425 (See note 8) | 70 | 315 | 625 | 1,000,000 | |
| No. 3 | | 475 | 550 | 250 | 70 | 315 | 400 | 900,000 | |
| Appearance | | 975 | 1100 | 650 | 70 | 315 | 900 | 1,100,000 | |
| Stud | | 475 | 550 | 250 | 70 | 315 | 400 | 900,000 | |
| Select Structural | Beams and Stringers | 1000 | — | 700 | 65 | 315 | 675 | 1,000,000 | |
| No. 1 | | 850 | — | 575 | 65 | 315 | 550 | 1,000,000 | |
| Select Structural | Posts and Timbers | 950 | — | 650 | 65 | 315 | 700 | 1,000,000 | |
| No. 1 | | 775 | — | 525 | 65 | 315 | 625 | 1,000,000 | |
| Selected Decking | Decking | — | 1300 | — | — | — | — | 1,100,000 | |
| Commercial Decking | | — | 1050 | — | — | — | — | 1,000,000 | |
| Selected Decking | Decking | — | 1400 | (Surfaced at 15% max. m.c. and used at 15% max. m.c.) | | | — | 1,100,000 | |
| Commercial Decking | | — | 1150 | | | | — | 1,000,000 | |

m.c.—moisture content based on oven-dry weight of wood, percent.

### NOTES ON VISUALLY GRADED LUMBER

1. Grading rules agencies listed include the following:
   NELMA—Northeastern Lumber Manufacturers Association
   NHPMA—Northern Hardwood and Pine Manufacturers Association
   NLGA—National Lumber Grades Authority (Canada)
   RIS—Redwood Inspection Service
   SPIB—Southern Pine Inspection Bureau
   WCLIB—West Coast Lumber Inspection Bureau
   WWPA—Western Wood Products Association

   The grading rules promulgated by these agencies, including design values, have been approved by the Board of Review of the American Lumber Standards Committee and certified for conformance with U.S. Department of Commerce Voluntary Product Standard PS 20-70, "American Softwood Lumber Standard."

2. The design values herein are applicable to lumber that will be used under dry conditions such as in most covered structures. For 2 in. to 4 in. thick lumber the DRY surfaced size shall be used. In calculating design values, the natural gain in strength and stiffness that occurs as lumber dries has been taken into consideration as well as the reduction in size that occurs when unseasoned lumber shrinks. The gain in load carrying capacity due to increased strength and stiffness resulting from drying more than offsets the design effect of size reductions due to shrinkage. For 5 in. and thicker lumber, the surfaced sizes also may be used because design values have been adjusted to compensate for any loss in size by shrinkage which may occur.

3. Design values for all species of Stud grade in 5 in. and wider size classifications apply to 5 in. and 6 in. widths only.

4. Values for "$F_b$", "$F_t$", and "$F_c$" for all species of the grades of Construction, Standard and Utility apply only to 4 in. widths. Design values for 2 in. and 3 in. widths of these grades are available from the grading rules agencies (see Note 1).

5. The design values for extreme fiber in bending for decking may be increased by 10 percent for 2 in. thick decking and by 4 percent for 3 in. thick decking. (Not applicable to California Redwood.)

6. Stress-rated boards of nominal 1 in., 1¼ in. and 1½ in. thickness, 2 in. and wider, of most species are permitted the design values shown for Select Structural, No. 1, No. 2, No. 3, Construction, Standard, Utility, Appearance, and Clear Structural grades as shown in the 2 in. to 4 in. thick categories herein, when graded in accordance with the stress-rated board provisions in the applicable grading rules. Information on stress rated board grades applicable to the various species is available from the respective grading rules agencies. Information on additional design values also may be available from the respective grading agencies.

7. When Decking graded to WWPA rules is surfaced at 15 percent maximum moisture content and used where the moisture content will exceed 15 percent for an extended period of time, the tabulated design values for Decking surfaced at 15 percent maximum moisture content shall be multiplied by the following factors: Extreme Fiber in Bending "$F_b$", 0.79; Modulus of Elasticity "$E$", 0.92.

National Forest Products Association; Washington, D.C.

## GENERAL INFORMATION

8. Tabulated tension parallel to grain values for all species for 5 in. and wider, 2 in. to 4 in. thick (and 2½ in. to 4 in. thick) size classifications apply to 5 in. and 6 in. widths only, for grades of Select Structural, No. 1, No. 2, No. 3, Appearance and Stud (including dense grades). For lumber wider than 6 in. in these grades, the tabulated "Fₜ" values shall be multiplied by the following factors:

### GRADE

| (2 IN. TO 4 IN. THICK, 5 IN. AND WIDER) (2 ½ IN. TO 4 IN. THICK, 5 IN. AND WIDER) (INCLUDES "DENSE" GRADES) | MULTIPLY TABULATED "Fₜ" VALUES BY | | |
|---|---|---|---|
| | 5 IN. AND 6 IN. WIDE | 8 IN. WIDE | 10 IN. AND WIDER |
| Select Structural | 1.00 | 0.90 | 0.80 |
| No. 1, No. 2, No. 3 and Appearance | 1.00 | 0.80 | 0.60 |
| Stud | 1.00 | — | — |

9. When 2 in. to 4 in. thick lumber is manufactured at a maximum moisture content of 15 percent and used in a condition where the moisture content does not exceed 15 percent, the design values for surfaced dry or surfaced green lumber may be multiplied by the following factors (for Southern Pine use tabulated design values without adjustment):

### 2 IN. TO 4 IN. THICK LUMBER MANUFACTURED AND USED AT 15% MAXIMUM MOISTURE CONTENT (MC15)

| EXTREME FIBER IN BENDING "Fᵦ" | TENSION PARALLEL TO GRAIN "Fₜ" | HORIZONTAL SHEAR "Fᵥ" | COMPRESSION PERPENDICULAR TO GRAIN "Fₒ⊥" | COMPRESSION* PARALLEL TO GRAIN "Fₒ" | MODULUS* OF ELASTICITY "E" |
|---|---|---|---|---|---|
| 1.08 | 1.08 | 1.05 | 1.00 | 1.17 | 1.05 |
| | | | | 1.15 | 1.04 |

*For Redwood use only.

10. When 2 in. to 4 in. thick lumber is designed for use where the moisture content will exceed 19 percent for an extended period of time, the design values shown herein shall be multiplied by the following factors, except that for Southern Pine note 17 applies:

### 2 IN. TO 4 IN. THICK LUMBER USED WHERE MOISTURE CONTENT WILL EXCEED 19%

| EXTREME FIBER IN BENDING "Fᵦ" | TENSION PARALLEL TO GRAIN "Fₜ" | HORIZONTAL SHEAR "Fᵥ" | COMPRESSION PERPENDICULAR TO GRAIN "Fₒ⊥" | COMPRESSION PARALLEL TO GRAIN "Fₒ" | MODULUS OF ELASTICITY "E" |
|---|---|---|---|---|---|
| 0.86 | 0.84 | 0.97 | 0.67 | 0.70 | 0.97 |

11. When lumber 5 in. and thicker is designed for use where the moisture content will exceed 19 percent for an extended period of time, the design values (except those for Southern Pine) shall be multiplied by the following factors:

### 5 IN. AND THICKER LUMBER USED WHERE MOISTURE CONTENT WILL EXCEED 19%

| EXTREME FIBER IN BENDING "Fᵦ" | TENSION PARALLEL TO GRAIN "Fₜ" | HORIZONTAL SHEAR "Fᵥ" | COMPRESSION PERPENDICULAR TO GRAIN "Fₒ⊥" | COMPRESSION PARALLEL TO GRAIN "Fₒ" | MODULUS OF ELASTICITY "E" |
|---|---|---|---|---|---|
| 1.00 | 1.00 | 1.00 | 0.67 | 0.91 | 1.00 |

12. Specific horizontal shear values may be established by use of the following table when length of split, or size of check or shake is known and no increase in them is anticipated. For California Redwood or Southern Pine, the provisions in this note apply only to the following Fᵥ Values: 80 psi, California Redwood; 95 psi, Southern Pine (KD-15); 90 psi, Southern Pine (S-DRY); 85 psi, Southern Pine (S-Green).

### SHEAR STRESS MODIFICATION FACTOR

| LENGTH OF SPLIT ON WIDE FACE OF 2 IN. LUMBER (NOMINAL): | MULTIPLY TABULATED "Fᵥ" VALUE BY: | LENGTH OF SPLIT ON WIDE FACE OF 3 IN. AND THICKER LUMBER (NOMINAL): | MULTIPLY TABULATED "Fᵥ" VALUE BY: | SIZE OF SHAKE* IN 3 IN. AND THICKER LUMBER (NOMINAL): | MULTIPLY TABULATED "Fᵥ" VALUE BY: |
|---|---|---|---|---|---|
| no split | 2.00 | no split | 2.00 | no shake | 2.00 |
| ½ x wide face | 1.67 | ½ x narrow face | 1.67 | ⅙ x narrow face | 1.67 |
| ¾ x wide face | 1.50 | 1 x narrow face | 1.33 | ⅓ x narrow face | 1.33 |
| 1 x wide face | 1.33 | 1 ½ x narrow face or more | 1.00 | ½ x narrow face or more | 1.00 |
| 1 ½ x wide face or more | 1.00 | | | | |

*Shake is measured at the end between lines enclosing the shake and parallel to the wide face.

13. The values for dimension lumber 2 in. to 4 in. in thickness are based on edgewise use. When such lumber is used flat, the design values for extreme fiber in bending for all species may be multiplied by the following factors:

### DIMENSION LUMBER USED FLAT

| WIDTH | THICKNESS | | |
|---|---|---|---|
| | 2 in. | 3 in. | 4 in. |
| 2 in. to 4 in. | 1.10 | 1.04 | 1.00 |
| 5 in. and wider | 1.22 | 1.16 | 1.11 |

14. National Lumber Grades Authority is the Canadian rules writing agency responsible for preparation, maintenance and dissemination of a uniform softwood lumber grading rule for all Canadian species.

15. For species graded to NLGA rules, values shown in the Table for Select Structural, No. 1, No. 2, No. 3 and Stud grades are not applicable to 3 in. x 4 in. and 4 in. x 4 in. sizes.

16. Repetitive member design values for extreme fiber in bending for Southern Pine grades of Dense Structural 86, 72 and 65 apply to 2 in. to 4 in. thicknesses only.

17. When 2 in. to 4 in. thick Southern Pine lumber is surfaced dry or at 15 percent maximum moisture content (KD-15) and is designed for use where the moisture content will exceed 19 percent for an extended period of time, the design values in the Table for the corresponding grades of 2½ in. to 4 in. thick surfaced green Southern Pine lumber shall be used. The net green size may be used in such designs.

18. When 2 in. to 4 in. thick Southern Pine lumber is surfaced dry or at 15 percent maximum moisture content (KD-15) and is designed for use under dry conditions, such as in most covered structures, the net DRY size shall be used in design. For other sizes and conditions of use, the net green size may be used in design.

19. When the depth of a beam, stringer, post, timber, or other rectangular sawn lumber member 5 in. or thicker exceeds 12 in., the design value for the extreme fiber in bending, Fᵦ, shall be multiplied by the size factor, C_F, as determined by the following formula:

$$C_F = \left(\frac{12}{d}\right)^{1/9}$$

National Forest Products Association; Washington, D.C.

## NOMINAL AND MINIMUM DRESSED SIZES OF LUMBER PRODUCTS (IN.)
The thicknesses apply to all widths and all widths to all thicknesses.

| LUMBER PRODUCT | THICKNESSES | | | FACE WIDTHS | | |
|---|---|---|---|---|---|---|
| | NOMINAL | MINIMUM DRESSED DRY | MINIMUM DRESSED GREEN | NOMINAL | MINIMUM DRESSED DRY | MINIMUM DRESSED GREEN |
| Boards | 1 | $3/4$ | $25/32$ | 2 | $1\,1/2$ | $1\,9/16$ |
| | | | | 3 | $2\,1/2$ | $2\,9/16$ |
| | | | | 4 | $3\,1/2$ | $3\,9/16$ |
| | | | | 5 | $4\,1/2$ | $4\,5/8$ |
| | 1 1/4 | 1 | $1\,1/32$ | 6 | $5\,1/2$ | $5\,5/8$ |
| | | | | 7 | $6\,1/2$ | $6\,5/8$ |
| | 1 1/2 | 1 1/4 | $1\,9/32$ | 8 | $7\,1/4$ | $7\,1/2$ |
| | | | | 9 | $8\,1/4$ | $8\,1/2$ |
| | | | | 10 | $9\,1/4$ | $9\,1/2$ |
| | | | | 11 | $10\,1/4$ | $10\,1/2$ |
| | | | | 12 | $11\,1/4$ | $11\,1/2$ |
| | | | | 14 | $13\,1/4$ | $13\,1/2$ |
| | | | | 16 | $15\,1/4$ | $15\,1/2$ |
| Dimension lumber | 2 | 1 1/2 | $1\,9/16$ | 2 | $1\,1/2$ | $1\,9/16$ |
| | 2 1/2 | 2 | $2\,1/16$ | 3 | $2\,1/2$ | $2\,9/16$ |
| | 3 | 2 1/2 | $2\,9/16$ | 4 | $3\,1/2$ | $3\,9/16$ |
| | 3 1/2 | 3 | $3\,1/16$ | 5 | $4\,1/2$ | $4\,5/8$ |
| | | | | 6 | $5\,1/2$ | $5\,5/8$ |
| | | | | 8 | $7\,1/4$ | $7\,1/2$ |
| | | | | 10 | $9\,1/4$ | $9\,1/2$ |
| | | | | 12 | $11\,1/4$ | $11\,1/2$ |
| | | | | 14 | $13\,1/4$ | $13\,1/2$ |
| | | | | 16 | $15\,1/4$ | $15\,1/2$ |
| | 4 | 3 1/2 | $3\,9/16$ | 2 | $1\,1/2$ | $1\,9/16$ |
| | 4 1/2 | 4 | $4\,1/16$ | 3 | $2\,1/2$ | $2\,9/16$ |
| | | | | 4 | $3\,1/2$ | $3\,9/16$ |
| | | | | 5 | $4\,1/2$ | $4\,5/8$ |
| | | | | 6 | $5\,1/2$ | $5\,5/8$ |
| | | | | 8 | $7\,1/4$ | $7\,1/2$ |
| | | | | 10 | $9\,1/4$ | $9\,1/2$ |
| | | | | 12 | $11\,1/4$ | $11\,1/2$ |
| | | | | 14 | | $13\,1/2$ |
| | | | | 16 | | $15\,1/2$ |
| Timbers | 5 and thicker | | $1/2$ off | 5 and wider | | $1/2$ off |
| Shiplap $3/8''$ lap | 1 | $3/4$ | $25/32$ | 4 | $3\,1/8$ | $3\,3/16$ |
| | | | | 6 | $5\,1/8$ | $5\,1/4$ |
| | | | | 8 | $6\,7/8$ | $7\,1/8$ |
| | | | | 10 | $8\,7/8$ | $9\,1/8$ |
| | | | | 12 | $10\,7/8$ | $11\,1/8$ |
| | | | | 14 | $12\,7/8$ | $13\,1/8$ |
| | | | | 16 | $14\,7/8$ | $15\,1/8$ |
| Shiplap $1/2''$ lap | 1 | $3/4$ | $25/32$ | 4 | 3 | $3\,1/16$ |
| | | | | 6 | 5 | $5\,1/8$ |
| | | | | 8 | $6\,3/4$ | 7 |
| | | | | 10 | $8\,3/4$ | 9 |
| | | | | 12 | $10\,3/4$ | 11 |
| | | | | 14 | $12\,3/4$ | 13 |
| | | | | 16 | $14\,3/4$ | 15 |
| Centermatch $1/4''$ tongue | 1 | $3/4$ | $25/32$ | 4 | $3\,1/8$ | $3\,3/16$ |
| | 1 1/4 | 1 | $1\,1/32$ | 5 | $4\,1/8$ | $4\,1/4$ |
| | 1 1/2 | 1 1/4 | $1\,9/32$ | 6 | $5\,1/8$ | $5\,1/4$ |
| | | | | 8 | $6\,7/8$ | $7\,1/8$ |
| | | | | 10 | $8\,7/8$ | $9\,1/8$ |
| | | | | 12 | $10\,7/8$ | $11\,1/8$ |
| 2'' dressed and matched $3/8''$ tongue | 2 | 1 1/2 | $1\,9/16$ | 4 | 3 | $3\,1/16$ |
| | | | | 6 | 5 | $5\,1/8$ |
| | | | | 8 | $6\,3/4$ | 7 |
| | | | | 10 | $8\,3/4$ | 9 |
| | | | | 12 | $10\,3/4$ | 11 |
| 2'' shiplap $1/2''$ lap | 2 | 1 1/2 | $1\,9/16$ | 4 | 3 | $3\,1/16$ |
| | | | | 6 | 5 | $5\,1/8$ |
| | | | | 8 | $6\,3/4$ | 7 |
| | | | | 10 | $8\,3/4$ | 9 |
| | | | | 12 | $10\,3/4$ | 11 |

NOTE: For dry lumber moisture content is 19% or less and for green lumber moisture content is in excess of 19%.

## NOMINAL AND MINIMUM DRESSED DRY SIZES OF LUMBER PRODUCTS (IN.)
The thicknesses apply to all widths and all widths to all thicknesses.

| LUMBER PRODUCT | THICKNESSES | | FACE WIDTHS | |
|---|---|---|---|---|
| | NOMINAL | MINIMUM DRESSED | NOMINAL | MINIMUM DRESSED |
| Finish | $3/8$ | $5/16$ | 2 | $1\,1/2$ |
| | $1/2$ | $7/16$ | 3 | $2\,1/2$ |
| | $5/8$ | $9/16$ | 4 | $3\,1/2$ |
| | $3/4$ | $5/8$ | 5 | $4\,1/2$ |
| | 1 | $3/4$ | 6 | $5\,1/2$ |
| | $1\,1/4$ | 1 | 7 | $6\,1/2$ |
| | $1\,1/2$ | $1\,1/4$ | 8 | $7\,1/4$ |
| | $1\,3/4$ | $1\,3/8$ | 9 | $8\,1/4$ |
| | 2 | $1\,1/2$ | 10 | $9\,1/4$ |
| | $2\,1/2$ | 2 | 11 | $10\,1/4$ |
| | 3 | $2\,1/2$ | 12 | $11\,1/4$ |
| | $3\,1/2$ | 3 | 14 | $13\,1/4$ |
| | 4 | $3\,1/2$ | 16 | $15\,1/4$ |
| Flooring; dimension is face dimension excluding tongue | $3/8$ | $5/16$ | 2 | $1\,1/8$ |
| | $1/2$ | $7/16$ | 3 | $2\,1/8$ |
| | $5/8$ | $9/16$ | 4 | $3\,1/8$ |
| | 1 | $3/4$ | 5 | $4\,1/8$ |
| | $1\,1/4$ | 1 | 6 | $5\,1/8$ |
| | $1\,1/2$ | $1\,1/4$ | | |
| Ceiling | $3/8$ | $5/16$ | 3 | $2\,1/8$ |
| | $1/2$ | $7/16$ | 4 | $3\,1/8$ |
| | $5/8$ | $9/16$ | 5 | $4\,1/8$ |
| | $3/4$ | $11/16$ | 6 | $5\,1/8$ |
| Partition | 1 | $23/32$ | 3 | $2\,1/8$ |
| | | | 4 | $3\,1/8$ |
| | | | 5 | $4\,1/8$ |
| | | | 6 | $5\,1/8$ |
| Stepping | 1 | $3/4$ | 8 | $7\,1/4$ |
| | $1\,1/4$ | 1 | 10 | $9\,1/4$ |
| | $1\,1/2$ | $1\,1/4$ | 12 | $11\,1/4$ |
| | 2 | $1\,1/2$ | | |
| Bevel siding | $1/2$ | $7/16$ butt, $3/16$ tip | 4 | $3\,1/2$ |
| | $9/16$ | $15/32$ butt, $3/16$ tip | 5 | $4\,1/2$ |
| | $5/8$ | $9/16$ butt, $3/16$ tip | 6 | $5\,1/2$ |
| | $3/4$ | $11/16$ butt, $3/16$ tip | 8 | $7\,1/4$ |
| | 1 | $3/4$ butt, $3/16$ tip | 10 | $9\,1/4$ |
| | | | 12 | $11\,1/4$ |
| Bungalow siding | $3/4$ | $11/16$ butt, $3/16$ tip | 8 | $7\,1/4$ |
| | | | 10 | $9\,1/4$ |
| | | | 12 | $11\,1/4$ |
| Rustic and drop siding shiplapped $3/8''$ | $5/8$ | $9/16$ | 4 | 3 |
| | 1 | $23/32$ | 5 | 4 |
| | | | 6 | 5 |
| Rustic and drop siding shiplapped $1/2''$ | $5/8$ | $9/16$ | 4 | $2\,7/8$ |
| | 1 | $23/32$ | 5 | $3\,7/8$ |
| | | | 6 | $4\,7/8$ |
| | | | 8 | $6\,5/8$ |
| | | | 10 | $8\,5/8$ |
| | | | 12 | $10\,5/8$ |
| Rustic and drop siding dressed and matched | $5/8$ | $9/16$ | 4 | $3\,1/8$ |
| | 1 | $23/32$ | 5 | $4\,1/8$ |
| | | | 6 | $5\,1/8$ |
| | | | 8 | $6\,7/8$ |
| | | | 10 | $8\,7/8$ |

NOTE: Maximum moisture content is 19%.

**NOTE**

For additional information reference should be made to the National Bureau of Standards, Product Standard PS20-70 American Softwood Lumber Standard. Available through U.S. Government Printing Office.

## DESIGN VALUES FOR MACHINE STRESS RATED STRUCTURAL LUMBER (1)

DESIGN VALUES LISTED ARE FOR NORMAL LOADING CONDITIONS. SEE NOTES BELOW, AND OTHER PROVISIONS IN THE NATIONAL DESIGN SPECIFICATION, FOR ADJUSTMENTS OF TABULATED VALUES (2)

| | | | DESIGN VALUES (PSI) | | | | |
|---|---|---|---|---|---|---|---|
| | | | EXTREME FIBER IN BENDING, $F_b$ | | | | |
| GRADE DESIGNATION | GRADING RULES AGENCY (SEE NOTES 3–6) | SIZE CLASSIFICATION | SINGLE MEMBER USES | REPETITIVE MEMBER USES | TENSION PARALLEL TO GRAIN, $F_t$ | COMPRESSION PARALLEL TO GRAIN, $F_c$ | MODULUS OF ELASTICITY, E |
| 900f-1.0E | 5, 6 | | 900 | 1050 | 350 | 725 | 1,000,000 |
| 1200f-1.2E | 3, 4, 5, 6 | | 1200 | 1400 | | 950 | 1,200,000 |
| 1350f-1.3E | 4, 5, 6 | | 1350 | 1550 | 750 | | 1,300,000 |
| 1450f-1.3E | 3, 5, 6 | | 1450 | 1650 | 800 | 1150 | 1,300,000 |
| 1500f-1.3E | 4 | | 1500 | 1750 | 900 | 1200 | 1,300,000 |
| 1500f-1.4E | 3, 4, 5, 6 | | 1500 | 1750 | 900 | 1200 | 1,400,000 |
| 1650f-1.4E | 4 | | 1650 | 1900 | 1020 | 1320 | 1,400,000 |
| 1650f-1.5E | 3, 4, 5, 6 | Machine rated lumber, 2 in. thick or less, all widths | 1650 | 1900 | 1020 | 1320 | 1,500,000 |
| 1800f-1.6E | 3, 4, 5, 6 | | 1800 | 2050 | 1175 | 1450 | 1,600,000 |
| 1950f-1.5E | 4 | | 1950 | 2250 | 1375 | 1550 | 1,500,000 |
| 1950f-1.7E | 3, 4, 6 | | 1950 | 2250 | 1375 | 1550 | 1,700,000 |
| 2100f-1.8E | 3, 4, 5, 6 | | 2100 | 2400 | 1575 | 1700 | 1,800,000 |
| 2250f-1.6E | 4 | | 2250 | 2600 | 1750 | 1800 | 1,600,000 |
| 2250f-1.9E | 3, 4, 6 | | 2250 | 2600 | 1750 | 1800 | 1,900,000 |
| 2400f-1.7E | 4 | | 2400 | 2750 | 1925 | 1925 | 1,700,000 |
| 2400f-2.0E | 3, 4, 5, 6 | | 2400 | 2750 | 1925 | 1925 | 2,000,000 |
| 2550f-2.1E | 3, 4, 6 | | 2550 | 2950 | 2050 | 2050 | 2,100,000 |
| 2700f-2.2E | 3, 4, 5, 6 | | 2700 | 3100 | 2150 | 2150 | 2,200,000 |
| 2850f-2.3E | 4 | | 2850 | 3300 | 2300 | 2300 | 2,300,000 |
| 3000f-2.4E | 3, 4 | | 3000 | 3450 | 2400 | 2400 | 2,400,000 |
| 3150f-2.5E | 4 | | 3150 | 3600 | 2500 | 2500 | 2,500,000 |
| 3300f-2.6E | 4 | | 3300 | 3800 | 2650 | 2650 | 2,600,000 |
| 900f-1.0E | 3, 4, 5 | | 900 | 1050 | 350 | 725 | 1,000,000 |
| 900f-1.2E | 3, 4, 5 | | 900 | 1050 | 350 | 725 | 1,200,000 |
| 1200f-1.5E | 3, 4, 5 | See note 7 | 1200 | 1400 | 600 | 950 | 1,500,000 |
| 1350f-1.8E | 3, 4 | | 1350 | 1550 | 750 | 1075 | 1,800,000 |
| 1500f-1.8E | 5 | | 1500 | 1750 | 900 | 1200 | 1,800,000 |
| 1800f-2.1E | 3, 4, 5 | | 1800 | 2050 | 1175 | 1450 | 2,100,000 |

When lumber 2 in. thick or less is designed for use where the moisture content will exceed 19% for an extended period of time, the design values shown herein shall be multiplied by the following factors:

| EXTREME FIBER IN BENDING IN "$F_b$" | TENSION PARALLEL TO GRAIN "$F_t$" | HORIZONTAL SHEAR "$F_v$" | COMPRESSION PERPENDICULAR TO GRAIN "$F_{c\perp}$" | COMPRESSION PARALLEL TO GRAIN "$F_c$" | MODULUS OF ELASTICITY "E" |
|---|---|---|---|---|---|
| 0.86 | 0.84 | 0.97 | 0.67 | 0.70 | 0.97 |

Tabulated extreme fiber values in bending values $F_b$ are applicable to lumber loaded on edge. When loaded flat, these values may be increased by multiplying by the following factors:

| Nominal width (in.) | 3 | 4 | 5 | 6 | 8 | 10 | 12 | 14 |
|---|---|---|---|---|---|---|---|---|
| Factor | 1.06 | 1.10 | 1.12 | 1.15 | 1.19 | 1.22 | 1.25 | 1.28 |

### NOTES

1. Stresses apply at 19% maximum moisture content.
2. Design values for compression perpendicular to grain ($F_{c\perp}$) and horizontal shear ($F_v$) are the same as assigned to visually graded lumber of the appropriate species.
3. National Lumber Grades Authority grading rules.
4. Southern Pine Inspection Bureau grading rules.
5. West Coast Lumber Inspection Bureau grading rules.
6. Western Wood Products Association grading rules.
7. Size classifications for these grades are:
   NLGA—machine rated lumber; 2 in. thick or less; all widths.
   SPIB—machine rated lumber; 2 in. thick or less; all widths.
   WCLIB—machine rated joists; 2 in. thick or less; 6 in. and wider.
   WWPA—machine rated lumber; 2 in. thick or less; all widths.

Design values for horizontal shear $F_v$ (DRY) and compression perpendicular to grain $F_{c\perp}$ (DRY) are:

| | CEDAR (WWPA/WCLIB) | DOUGLAS FIR-LARCH (WWPA/WCLIB/NLGA) | DOUGLAS FIR SOUTH (WWPA) | ENGLEMANN SPRUCE (WWPA) | HEM-FIR (WWPA/WCLIB/NLGA) | MIXED SPECIES (WCLIB) | PINE (WWPA) | SOUTHERN PINE (SPIB) | SPRUCE PINE-FIR (NLGA) | WESTERN HEMLOCK (WWPA/WCLIB) |
|---|---|---|---|---|---|---|---|---|---|---|
| **HORIZONTAL SHEAR $F_v$ (DRY)** | | | | | | | | | | |
| | 75 | 95 | 90 | 70 | 75 | 70 | 70 | 90 / 95 For Southern pine KD | 70 | 90 |
| **COMPRESSION PERPENDICULAR TO GRAIN $F_{c\perp}$ (DRY)** | | | | | | | | | | |
| | 265 | 385 | 335 | 195 | 245 | 190 | 190 | 405 | 265 | 280 |

NOTE: Cedar includes incense or Western red cedar. Pine includes Idaho white pine, lodgepole pine, ponderosa pine, or sugar pine.

National Forest Products Association; Washington, D.C.

## CEILING JOISTS—10 LB/SQ FT LIVE LOAD (GYPSUM WALLBOARD CEILING)
No attic storage and roof slope not steeper than 3 IN 12.

### MAXIMUM ALLOWABLE LENGTHS L BETWEEN SUPPORTS

| JOIST SIZE (NOMINAL) (IN.) | JOIST SPACING (NOMINAL) (IN.) | | SPAN L LIMITED BY DEFLECTION AND $F_b$ IS EXTREME FIBER STRESS | | | |
|---|---|---|---|---|---|---|
| | | E = | 1,000,000 | 1,200,000 | 1,400,000 | 1,600,000 |
| 2 x 4 | 12 | L = | 10-7 | 11-3 | 11-10 | 12-5 |
| | | $F_b$ = | 830 | 930 | 1030 | 1130 |
| | 16 | L = | 9-8 | 10-3 | 10-9 | 11-3 |
| | | $F_b$ = | 910 | 1030 | 1140 | 1240 |
| | 24 | L = | 8-5 | 8-11 | 9-5 | 9-10 |
| | | $F_b$ = | 1040 | 1170 | 1300 | 1420 |
| 2 x 6 | 12 | L = | 16-8 | 17-8 | 18-8 | 19-6 |
| | | $F_b$ = | 830 | 930 | 1030 | 1130 |
| | 16 | L = | 15-2 | 16-1 | 16-11 | 17-8 |
| | | $F_b$ = | 910 | 1030 | 1140 | 1240 |
| | 24 | L = | 13-3 | 14-1 | 14-9 | 15-6 |
| | | $F_b$ = | 1040 | 1170 | 1300 | 1420 |
| 2 x 8 | 12 | L = | 21-11 | 23-4 | 24-7 | 25-8 |
| | | $F_b$ = | 830 | 930 | 1030 | 1130 |
| | 16 | L = | 19-11 | 21-2 | 22-4 | 23-4 |
| | | $F_b$ = | 910 | 1030 | 1140 | 1240 |
| | 24 | L = | 17-5 | 18-6 | 19-6 | 20-5 |
| | | $F_b$ = | 1040 | 1170 | 1300 | 1420 |
| 2 x 10 | 12 | L = | 28-0 | 29-9 | 31-4 | 32-9 |
| | | $F_b$ = | 830 | 930 | 1030 | 1130 |
| | 16 | L = | 25-5 | 27-1 | 28-6 | 29-9 |
| | | $F_b$ = | 910 | 1030 | 1140 | 1240 |
| | 24 | L = | 22-3 | 23-8 | 24-10 | 26-0 |
| | | $F_b$ = | 1040 | 1170 | 1300 | 1420 |

NOTE: L in feet and inches; E and $F_b$ in pounds per square inch as shown above.

### DESIGN CRITERIA
1. Maximum allowable deflection = 1/240 of span length.
2. Live load of 10 lb/sq ft plus dead load of 5 lb/sq ft determine required fiber stress value.

## CEILING JOISTS—20 LB/SQ FT LIVE LOAD (GYPSUM WALLBOARD CEILING)
Limited attic storage where development of future rooms is not possible.

### MAXIMUM ALLOWABLE LENGTHS L BETWEEN SUPPORTS

| JOIST SIZE (NOMINAL) (IN.) | JOIST SPACING (NOMINAL) (IN.) | | SPAN L LIMITED BY DEFLECTION AND $F_b$ IS EXTREME FIBER STRESS | | | |
|---|---|---|---|---|---|---|
| | | E = | 1,000,000 | 1,200,000 | 1,400,000 | 1,600,000 |
| 2 x 4 | 12 | L = | 8-5 | 8-11 | 9-5 | 9-10 |
| | | $F_b$ = | 1040 | 1170 | 1300 | 1420 |
| | 16 | L = | 7-8 | 8-1 | 8-7 | 8-11 |
| | | $F_b$ = | 1140 | 1290 | 1430 | 1570 |
| | 24 | L = | 6-8 | 7-1 | 7-6 | 7-10 |
| | | $F_b$ = | 1310 | 1480 | 1640 | 1790 |
| 2 x 6 | 12 | L = | 13-3 | 14-1 | 14-9 | 15-6 |
| | | $F_b$ = | 1040 | 1170 | 1300 | 1420 |
| | 16 | L = | 12-0 | 12-9 | 13-5 | 14-1 |
| | | $F_b$ = | 1140 | 1290 | 1430 | 1570 |
| | 24 | L = | 10-6 | 11-2 | 11-9 | 12-3 |
| | | $F_b$ = | 1310 | 1480 | 1640 | 1790 |
| 2 x 8 | 12 | L = | 17-5 | 18-6 | 19-6 | 20-5 |
| | | $F_b$ = | 1040 | 1170 | 1300 | 1420 |
| | 16 | L = | 15-10 | 16-10 | 17-9 | 18-6 |
| | | $F_b$ = | 1140 | 1290 | 1430 | 1570 |
| | 24 | L = | 13-10 | 14-8 | 15-6 | 16-2 |
| | | $F_b$ = | 1310 | 1480 | 1640 | 1790 |
| 2 x 10 | 12 | L = | 22-3 | 23-8 | 24-10 | 26-0 |
| | | $F_b$ = | 1040 | 1170 | 1300 | 1420 |
| | 16 | L = | 20-2 | 21-6 | 22-7 | 23-8 |
| | | $F_b$ = | 1140 | 1290 | 1430 | 1570 |
| | 24 | L = | 17-8 | 18-9 | 19-9 | 20-8 |
| | | $F_b$ = | 1310 | 1480 | 1640 | 1790 |

NOTE: L in feet and inches; E and $F_b$ in pounds per square inch as shown above.

### DESIGN CRITERIA
1. Maximum allowable deflection = 1/240 of span length.
2. Live load of 20 lb/sq ft plus dead load of 10 lb/sq ft determine required fiber stress value.

### NOTE
For rafters, design values in $F_b$ may be greater than the design values for normal duration of load, by the following amounts:
15% for 2 months' duration, as for snow.
25% for 7 days' duration, as for construction loading.

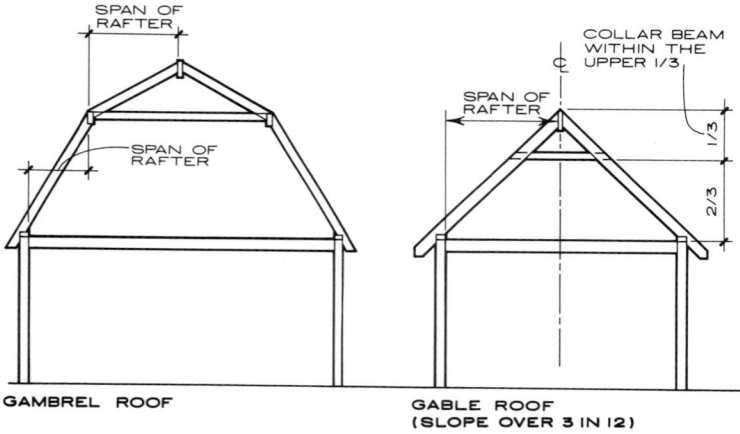

GAMBREL ROOF

GABLE ROOF (SLOPE OVER 3 IN 12)

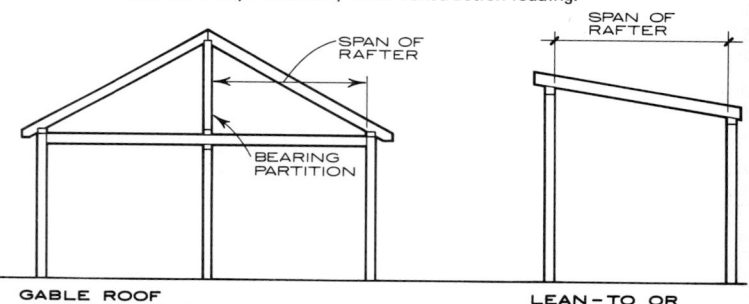

GABLE ROOF (SLOPE UNDER 3 IN 12)

LEAN-TO OR SHED ROOF

### NOTE

(Applicable to this and the following pages on joist and rafter sizes.)

SPANS LIMITED BY DEFLECTION: Computed for the assumed loads to cause a deflection not exceeding 1/360 of the span. The weight of plaster itself was ignored in the assumed loads for the deflection computations, because the initial deflection from the dead load occurs before plaster sets. The influence of live loads, rather than dead loads, when the ratio of live to dead loads is relatively high, is the principal factor to be considered. Also with joisted floors, flooring and bridging serve to distribute moving or concentrated loads to adjoining members. The omission of the plaster weight in load assumption applies to deflection computations only; the full dead and live load is considered when computing for strength.

SPANS LIMITED BY BENDING STRENGTH OF PIECE: May be used where ceilings are not plastered and deflection is not objectionable.

E = modulus of elasticity
$F_b$ = extreme fiber stress in bending
L = span length between supports

LIVE LOAD ASSUMPTIONS: Uniformly distributed.

PARTITIONS: Spans shown are computed for the given live load plus the dead load and do not provide for additional loads such as partitions. Where concentrated loads are imposed the spans should be recomputed to provide for them.

### SECTION MODULUS

| LUMBER SIZES (NOMINAL) | S (INCHES³) |
|---|---|
| 2 x 3 | 1.56 |
| 2 x 4 | 3.06 |
| 2 x 6 | 7.56 |
| 2 x 8 | 13.41 |
| 2 x 10 | 21.39 |
| 2 x 12 | 31.64 |
| 3 x 6 | 12.60 |
| 3 x 8 | 21.90 |
| 3 x 10 | 35.65 |
| 3 x 12 | 52.73 |
| 3 x 14 | 73.15 |
| 4 x 4 | 7.15 |
| 4 x 6 | 17.65 |
| 4 x 8 | 30.66 |
| 4 x 10 | 49.91 |
| 4 x 12 | 73.82 |

**SECTION MODULUS**

$$S = \frac{bd^2}{6} \text{ (INCHES}^3)$$

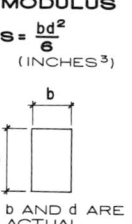

b AND d ARE ACTUAL DIMENSIONS

National Forest Products Association; Washington, D.C.

## DESIGN LOAD TABLES

**DESIGN CRITERIA**

STRENGTH: 15 psf dead load plus 20 psf live load determines required fiber stress.

DEFLECTION: For 20 psf live load. Limited to span in inches divided by 240.

RAFTERS: Spans are measured along the horizontal projection, and loads are considered as applied on the horizontal projection.

## FLAT OR SLOPED RAFTERS—20 LB LIVE LOAD
### FLAT ROOF OR CATHEDRAL CEILING WITH NO ATTIC SPACE—SUPPORTING GYPSUM WALLBOARD CEILING

| RAFTER SIZE, SPACING (IN.) | | EXTREME FIBER STRESS IN BENDING, $F_b$ (PSI) | | | | | | | | | | | | | | |
|---|---|---|---|---|---|---|---|---|---|---|---|---|---|---|---|---|
| | | 500 | 600 | 700 | 800 | 900 | 1000 | 1100 | 1200 | 1300 | 1400 | 1500 | 1600 | 1700 | 1800 | 1900 |
| 2 x 6 | 12 | 8-6 / 0.26 | 9-4 / 0.35 | 10-0 / 0.44 | 10-9 / 0.54 | 11-5 / 0.64 | 12-0 / 0.75 | 12-7 / 0.86 | 13-2 / 0.98 | 13-8 / 1.11 | 14-2 / 1.24 | 14-8 / 1.37 | 15-2 / 1.51 | 15-8 / 1.66 | 16-1 / 1.81 | 16-7 / 1.96 |
| | 16 | 7-4 / 0.23 | 8-1 / 0.30 | 8-8 / 0.38 | 9-4 / 0.46 | 9-10 / 0.55 | 10-5 / 0.65 | 10-11 / 0.75 | 11-5 / 0.85 | 11-10 / 0.96 | 12-4 / 1.24 | 12-9 / 1.19 | 13-2 / 1.31 | 13-7 / 1.44 | 13-11 / 1.56 | 14-4 / 1.70 |
| | 24 | 6-0 / 0.19 | 6-7 / 0.25 | 7-1 / 0.31 | 7-7 / 0.38 | 8-1 / 0.45 | 8-6 / 0.53 | 8-11 / 0.61 | 9-4 / 0.70 | 9-8 / 0.78 | 10-0 / 0.88 | 10-5 / 0.97 | 10-9 / 1.07 | 11-1 / 1.17 | 11-5 / 1.28 | 11.8 / 1.39 |
| 2 x 8 | 12 | 11-2 / 0.26 | 12-3 / 0.35 | 13-3 / 0.44 | 14-2 / 0.54 | 15-0 / 0.64 | 15-10 / 0.75 | 16-7 / 0.86 | 17-4 / 0.98 | 18-0 / 1.11 | 18-9 / 1.24 | 19-5 / 1.37 | 20-0 / 1.51 | 20-8 / 1.66 | 21-3 / 1.81 | 21-10 / 1.96 |
| | 16 | 9-8 / 0.23 | 10-7 / 0.30 | 11-6 / 0.38 | 12-3 / 0.46 | 13-0 / 0.55 | 13-8 / 0.65 | 14-4 / 0.75 | 15-0 / 0.85 | 15-7 / 0.96 | 16-3 / 1.07 | 16-9 / 1.19 | 17-4 / 1.31 | 17-10 / 1.44 | 18-5 / 1.56 | 18-11 / 1.70 |
| | 24 | 7-11 / 0.19 | 8-8 / 0.25 | 9-4 / 0.31 | 10-0 / 0.38 | 10-7 / 0.45 | 11-2 / 0.53 | 11-9 / 0.61 | 12-3 / 0.70 | 12-9 / 0.78 | 13-3 / 0.88 | 13-8 / 0.97 | 14-2 / 1.07 | 14-7 / 1.17 | 15-0 / 1.28 | 15-5 / 1.39 |
| 2 x 10 | 12 | 14-3 / 0.26 | 15-8 / 0.35 | 16-11 / 0.44 | 18-1 / 0.54 | 19-2 / 0.64 | 20-2 / 0.75 | 21-2 / 0.86 | 22-1 / 0.98 | 23-0 / 1.11 | 23-11 / 1.24 | 24-9 / 1.37 | 25-6 / 1.51 | 26-4 / 1.66 | 27-1 / 1.81 | 27.10 / 1.96 |
| | 16 | 12-4 / 0.23 | 13-6 / 0.30 | 14-8 / 0.38 | 15-8 / 0.46 | 16-7 / 0.55 | 17-6 / 0.65 | 18-4 / 0.75 | 19-2 / 0.85 | 19-11 / 0.96 | 20-8 / 1.07 | 21-5 / 1.19 | 22-1 / 1.31 | 22-10 / 1.44 | 23-5 / 1.56 | 24.1 / 1.70 |
| | 24 | 10-1 / 0.19 | 11-1 / 0.25 | 11-11 / 0.31 | 12-9 / 0.38 | 13-6 / 0.45 | 14-3 / 0.53 | 15-0 / 0.61 | 15-8 / 0.70 | 16-3 / 0.78 | 16-11 / 0.88 | 17-6 / 0.97 | 81-1 / 1.07 | 18-7 / 1.17 | 19-2 / 1.28 | 19-8 / 1.39 |
| 2 x 12 | 12 | 17-4 / 0.26 | 19-0 / 0.35 | 20-6 / 0.44 | 21-11 / 0.54 | 23-3 / 0.64 | 24-7 / 0.75 | 25-9 / 0.86 | 26-11 / 0.98 | 28-0 / 1.11 | 29-1 / 1.24 | 30-1 / 1.37 | 31-1 / 1.51 | 32-0 / 1.66 | 32-11 / 1.81 | 33-10 / 1.96 |
| | 16 | 15-0 / 0.23 | 16-6 / 0.30 | 17-9 / 0.38 | 19-0 / 0.46 | 20-2 / 0.55 | 21-3 / 0.65 | 22-4 / 0.75 | 23-3 / 0.85 | 24-3 / 0.96 | 25-2 / 1.07 | 26-0 / 1.19 | 26-11 / 1.31 | 27-9 / 1.44 | 28.6 / 1.56 | 29-4 / 1.70 |
| | 24 | 12-3 / 0.19 | 13-5 / 0.25 | 14-6 / 0.31 | 15-6 / 0.38 | 16-6 / 0.45 | 17-4 / 0.53 | 18-2 / 0.61 | 19-0 / 0.70 | 19-10 / 0.78 | 20-6 / 0.88 | 21-3 / 0.97 | 21-11 / 1.07 | 22-8 / 1.17 | 23-3 / 1.28 | 23-11 / 1.39 |

NOTE: The required modulus of elasticity, E, in 1,000,000 psi is shown below each span.

**DESIGN CRITERIA**

STRENGTH: 15 psf dead load plus 30 psf live load determines required fiber stress.

DEFLECTION: For 30 psf live load. Limited to span in inches divided by 240.

RAFTERS: Spans are measured along the horizontal projection, and loads are considered as applied on the horizontal projection.

## FLAT OR SLOPED RAFTERS—30 LB LIVE LOAD
### FLAT ROOF OR CATHEDRAL CEILING WITH NO ATTIC SPACE—SUPPORTING GYPSUM WALLBOARD CEILING

| RAFTER SIZE, SPACING (IN.) | | EXTREME FIBER STRESS IN BENDING, $F_b$ (PSI) | | | | | | | | | | | | | | |
|---|---|---|---|---|---|---|---|---|---|---|---|---|---|---|---|---|---|
| | | 500 | 600 | 700 | 800 | 900 | 1000 | 1100 | 1200 | 1300 | 1400 | 1500 | 1600 | 1700 | 1800 | 1900 |
| 2 x 6 | 12 | 7-6 / 0.27 | 8-2 / 0.36 | 8-10 / 0.45 | 9-6 / 0.55 | 10-0 / 0.66 | 10-7 / 0.77 | 11-1 / 0.89 | 11-7 / 1.01 | 12-1 / 1.14 | 12-6 / 1.28 | 13-0 / 1.41 | 13-5 / 1.56 | 13-10 / 1.71 | 14-2 / 1.86 | 14-7 / 2.02 |
| | 16 | 6-6 / 0.24 | 7-1 / 0.31 | 7-8 / 0.39 | 8-2 / 0.48 | 8-8 / 0.57 | 9-2 / 0.67 | 9-7 / 0.77 | 10-0 / 0.88 | 10-5 / 0.99 | 10-10 / 1.10 | 11-3 / 1.22 | 11-7 / 1.35 | 11-11 / 1.48 | 12-4 / 1.61 | 12-8 / 1.75 |
| | 24 | 5-4 / 0.19 | 5-10 / 0.25 | 6-3 / 0.32 | 6-8 / 0.39 | 7-1 / 0.46 | 7-6 / 0.54 | 7-10 / 0.63 | 8-2 / 0.72 | 8-6 / 0.81 | 8-10 / 0.90 | 9-2 / 1.00 | 9-6 / 1.10 | 9-9 / 1.21 | 10-0 / 1.31 | 10-4 / 1.43 |
| 2 x 8 | 12 | 9-10 / 0.27 | 10-10 / 0.36 | 11-8 / 0.45 | 12-6 / 0.55 | 13-3 / 0.66 | 13-11 / 0.77 | 14-8 / 0.89 | 15-3 / 1.01 | 15-11 / 1.14 | 16-6 / 1.28 | 17-1 / 1.41 | 17-8 / 1.56 | 18-2 / 1.71 | 18-9 / 1.86 | 19-3 / 2.02 |
| | 16 | 8-7 / 0.24 | 9-4 / 0.31 | 10-1 / 0.39 | 10-10 / 0.48 | 11-6 / 0.57 | 12-1 / 0.67 | 12-8 / 0.77 | 13-3 / 0.88 | 13-9 / 0.99 | 14-4 / 1.10 | 14-10 / 1.22 | 15-3 / 1.35 | 15-9 / 1.48 | 16-3 / 1.61 | 16-8 / 1.75 |
| | 24 | 7-0 / 0.19 | 7-8 / 0.25 | 8-3 / 0.32 | 8-10 / 0.39 | 9-4 / 0.46 | 9-10 / 0.54 | 10-4 / 0.63 | 10-10 / 0.72 | 11-3 / 0.81 | 11-8 / 0.90 | 12-1 / 1.00 | 12-6 / 1.10 | 12-10 / 1.21 | 13-3 / 1.31 | 13-7 / 1.43 |
| 2 x 10 | 12 | 12-7 / 0.27 | 13-9 / 0.36 | 14-11 / 0.45 | 15-11 / 0.55 | 16-11 / 0.66 | 17-10 / 0.77 | 18-8 / 0.89 | 19-6 / 1.01 | 20-4 / 1.14 | 21-1 / 1.28 | 21-10 / 1.41 | 22-6 / 1.56 | 23-3 / 1.71 | 23-11 / 1.86 | 24-6 / 2.02 |
| | 16 | 10-11 / 0.24 | 11-11 / 0.31 | 12-11 / 0.39 | 13-9 / 0.48 | 14-8 / 0.57 | 15-5 / 0.67 | 16-2 / 0.77 | 16-11 / 0.88 | 17-7 / 0.99 | 18-3 / 1.10 | 18-11 / 1.22 | 19-6 / 1.35 | 20-1 / 1.48 | 20-8 / 1.61 | 21-3 / 1.75 |
| | 24 | 8-11 / 0.19 | 9-9 / 0.25 | 10-6 / 0.32 | 11-3 / 0.39 | 11-11 / 0.46 | 12-7 / 0.54 | 13-2 / 0.63 | 13-9 / 0.72 | 14-4 / 0.81 | 14-11 / 0.90 | 15-5 / 1.00 | 15-11 / 1.10 | 16-5 / 1.21 | 16-11 / 1.31 | 17-4 / 1.43 |
| 2 x 12 | 12 | 15-4 / 0.27 | 16-9 / 0.36 | 18-1 / 0.45 | 19-4 / 0.55 | 20-6 / 0.66 | 21-8 / 0.77 | 22-8 / 0.89 | 23-9 / 1.01 | 24-8 / 1.14 | 25-7 / 1.28 | 26-6 / 1.41 | 27-5 / 1.56 | 28-3 / 1.71 | 29-1 / 1.86 | 29-10 / 2.02 |
| | 16 | 13-3 / 0.24 | 14-6 / 0.31 | 15-8 / 0.39 | 16-9 / 0.48 | 17-9 / 0.57 | 18-9 / 0.67 | 19-8 / 0.77 | 20-6 / 0.88 | 21-5 / 0.99 | 22-2 / 1.10 | 23-0 / 1.22 | 23-9 / 1.35 | 24-5 / 1.48 | 25-2 / 1.61 | 25-10 / 1.75 |
| | 24 | 10-10 / 0.19 | 11-10 / 0.25 | 12-10 / 0.32 | 13-8 / 0.39 | 14-6 / 0.46 | 15-4 / 0.54 | 16-1 / 0.63 | 16-9 / 0.72 | 17-5 / 0.81 | 18-1 / 0.90 | 18-9 / 1.00 | 19-4 / 1.10 | 20-0 / 1.21 | 20-6 / 1.31 | 12-1 / 1.43 |

NOTE: The required modulus of elasticity, E, in 1,000,000 psi is shown below each span.

National Forest Products Association; Washington, D.C.

**DESIGN LOAD TABLES**

DESIGN CRITERIA

STRENGTH: 10 psf dead load plus 20 psf live load determines required fiber stress.

DEFLECTION: For 20 psf live load. Limited to span in inches divided by 240.

RAFTERS: Spans are measured along the horizontal projection, and loads are considered as applied on the horizontal projection.

## FLAT OR LOW SLOPE RAFTERS—20 LB LIVE LOAD
NO CEILING LOAD—SLOPE 3 IN 12 OR LESS

| RAFTER SIZE, SPACING (IN.) | | EXTREME FIBER STRESS IN BENDING, $F_b$ (PSI) | | | | | | | | | | | | | | |
|---|---|---|---|---|---|---|---|---|---|---|---|---|---|---|---|---|
| | | 500 | 600 | 700 | 800 | 900 | 1000 | 1100 | 1200 | 1300 | 1400 | 1500 | 1600 | 1700 | 1800 | 1900 |
| 2 x 6 | 12 | 9-2 0.33 | 10-0 0.44 | 10-10 0.55 | 11-7 0.67 | 12-4 0.80 | 13-0 0.94 | 13-7 1.09 | 14-2 1.24 | 14-9 1.40 | 15-4 1.56 | 15-11 1.73 | 16-5 1.91 | 16-11 2.09 | 17-5 2.28 | 17-10 2.47 |
| | 16 | 7-11 0.29 | 8-8 0.38 | 9-5 0.48 | 10-0 0.58 | 10-8 0.70 | 11-3 0.82 | 11-9 0.94 | 12-4 1.07 | 12-10 1.21 | 13-3 1.35 | 13-9 1.50 | 14-2 1.65 | 14-8 1.81 | 15-1 1.97 | 15-6 2.14 |
| | 24 | 6-6 0.24 | 7-1 0.31 | 7-8 0.39 | 8-2 0.48 | 8-8 0.57 | 9-2 0.67 | 9-7 0.77 | 10-0 0.88 | 10-5 0.99 | 10-10 1.10 | 11-3 1.22 | 11-7 1.35 | 11-11 1.48 | 12-4 1.61 | 12-8 1.75 |
| 2 x 8 | 12 | 12-1 0.33 | 13-3 0.44 | 14-4 0.55 | 15-3 0.67 | 16-3 0.80 | 17-1 0.94 | 17-11 1.09 | 18-9 1.24 | 19-6 1.40 | 20-3 1.56 | 20-11 1.73 | 21-7 1.91 | 22-3 2.09 | 22-11 2.28 | 23-7 2.47 |
| | 16 | 10-6 0.29 | 11-6 0.38 | 12-5 0.48 | 13-3 0.58 | 14-0 0.70 | 14-10 0.82 | 15-6 0.94 | 16-3 1.07 | 16-10 1.21 | 17-6 1.35 | 18-2 1.50 | 18-9 1.65 | 19-4 1.81 | 19-10 1.97 | 20-5 2.14 |
| | 24 | 8-7 0.24 | 9-4 0.31 | 10-1 0.39 | 10-10 0.48 | 11-6 0.57 | 12-1 0.67 | 12-8 0.77 | 13-3 0.88 | 13-9 0.99 | 14-4 1.10 | 14-10 1.22 | 15-3 1.35 | 15-9 1.48 | 16-3 1.61 | 16-8 1.75 |
| 2 x 10 | 12 | 15-5 0.33 | 16-11 0.44 | 18-3 0.55 | 19-6 0.67 | 20-8 0.80 | 21-10 0.94 | 22-10 1.09 | 23-11 1.24 | 24-10 1.40 | 25-10 1.56 | 26-8 1.73 | 27-7 1.91 | 28-5 2.09 | 29-3 2.28 | 30-1 2.47 |
| | 16 | 13-4 0.29 | 14-8 0.38 | 15-10 0.48 | 16-11 0.58 | 17-11 0.70 | 18-11 0.82 | 19-10 0.94 | 20-8 1.07 | 21-6 1.21 | 22-4 1.35 | 23-2 1.50 | 23-11 1.65 | 24-7 1.81 | 25-4 1.97 | 26-0 2.14 |
| | 24 | 10-11 0.24 | 11-11 0.31 | 12-11 0.39 | 13-9 0.48 | 14-8 0.57 | 15-5 0.67 | 16-2 0.77 | 16-11 0.88 | 17-7 0.99 | 18-3 1.10 | 18-11 1.22 | 19-6 1.35 | 20-1 1.48 | 20-8 1.61 | 21-3 1.75 |
| 2 x 12 | 12 | 18-9 0.33 | 20-6 0.44 | 22-2 0.55 | 23-9 0.67 | 25-2 0.80 | 26-6 0.94 | 27-10 1.09 | 29-1 1.24 | 30-3 1.40 | 31-4 1.56 | 32-6 1.73 | 33-6 1.91 | 34-7 2.09 | 35-7 2.28 | 36-7 2.47 |
| | 16 | 16-3 0.29 | 17-9 0.38 | 19-3 0.48 | 20-6 0.58 | 21-9 0.70 | 23-0 0.82 | 24-1 0.94 | 25-2 1.07 | 26-2 1.21 | 27-2 1.35 | 28-2 1.50 | 29-1 1.65 | 29-11 1.81 | 30-10 1.97 | 31-8 2.14 |
| | 24 | 13-3 0.24 | 14-6 0.31 | 15-8 0.39 | 16-9 0.48 | 17-9 0.57 | 18-9 0.67 | 19-8 0.77 | 20-6 0.88 | 21-5 0.99 | 22-2 1.10 | 23-0 1.22 | 23-9 1.35 | 24-5 1.48 | 25-2 1.61 | 25-10 1.75 |

NOTE: The required modulus of elasticity, E, in 1,000,000 psi is shown below each span.

DESIGN CRITERIA

STRENGTH: 10 psf dead load plus 30 psf live load determines required fiber stress.

DEFLECTION: For 30 psf live load. Limited to span in inches divided by 240.

RAFTERS: Spans are measured along the horizontal projection, and loads are considered as applied on the horizontal projection.

## FLAT OR LOW SLOPE RAFTERS—30 LB LIVE LOAD
NO CEILING LOAD—SLOPE 3 IN 12 OR LESS

| RAFTER SIZE, SPACING (IN.) | | EXTREME FIBER STRESS IN BENDING, $F_b$ (PSI) | | | | | | | | | | | | | | |
|---|---|---|---|---|---|---|---|---|---|---|---|---|---|---|---|---|
| | | 500 | 600 | 700 | 800 | 900 | 1000 | 1100 | 1200 | 1300 | 1400 | 1500 | 1600 | 1700 | 1800 | 1900 |
| 2 x 6 | 12 | 7-11 0.32 | 8-8 0.43 | 9-5 0.54 | 10-0 0.66 | 10-8 0.78 | 11-3 0.92 | 11-9 1.06 | 12-4 1.21 | 12-10 1.36 | 13-3 1.52 | 13-9 1.69 | 14-2 1.86 | 14-8 2.04 | 15-1 2.22 | 15-6 2.41 |
| | 16 | 6-11 0.28 | 7-6 0.37 | 8-2 0.47 | 8-8 0.57 | 9-3 0.68 | 9-9 0.80 | 10-2 0.92 | 10-8 1.05 | 11-1 1.18 | 11-6 1.32 | 11-11 1.46 | 12-4 1.61 | 12-8 1.76 | 13-1 1.92 | 13-5 2.08 |
| | 24 | 5-7 0.23 | 6-2 0.30 | 6-8 0.38 | 7-1 0.46 | 7-6 0.55 | 7-11 0.65 | 8-4 0.75 | 8-8 0.85 | 9-1 0.96 | 9-5 1.08 | 9-9 1.19 | 10-0 1.31 | 10-4 1.44 | 10-8 1.57 | 10-11 1.70 |
| 2 x 8 | 12 | 10-6 0.32 | 11-6 0.43 | 12-5 0.54 | 13-3 0.66 | 14-0 0.78 | 14-10 0.92 | 15-6 1.06 | 16-3 1.21 | 16-10 1.36 | 17-6 1.52 | 18-2 1.69 | 18-9 1.86 | 19-4 2.04 | 19-10 2.22 | 20-5 2.41 |
| | 16 | 9-1 0.28 | 9-11 0.37 | 10-9 0.47 | 11-6 0.57 | 12-2 0.68 | 12-10 0.80 | 13-5 0.92 | 14-0 1.05 | 14-7 1.18 | 15-2 1.32 | 15-8 1.46 | 16-3 1.61 | 16-9 1.76 | 17-2 1.92 | 17-8 2.08 |
| | 24 | 7-5 0.23 | 8-1 0.30 | 8-9 0.38 | 9-4 0.46 | 9-11 0.55 | 10-6 0.65 | 11-0 0.75 | 11-6 0.85 | 11-11 0.96 | 12-5 1.08 | 12-10 1.19 | 13-3 1.31 | 13-8 1.44 | 14-0 1.57 | 14-5 1.70 |
| 2 x 10 | 12 | 13-4 0.32 | 14-8 0.43 | 15-10 0.54 | 16-11 0.66 | 17-11 0.78 | 18-11 0.92 | 19-10 1.06 | 20-8 1.21 | 21-6 1.36 | 22-4 1.52 | 23-2 1.69 | 23-11 1.86 | 24-7 2.04 | 25-4 2.22 | 26-0 2.41 |
| | 16 | 11-7 0.28 | 12-8 0.37 | 13-8 0.47 | 14-8 0.57 | 15-6 0.68 | 16-4 0.80 | 17-2 0.92 | 17-11 1.05 | 18-8 1.18 | 19-4 1.32 | 20-0 1.46 | 20-8 1.61 | 21-4 1.76 | 21-11 1.92 | 22-6 2.08 |
| | 24 | 9-5 0.23 | 10-4 0.30 | 11-2 0.38 | 11-11 0.46 | 12-8 0.55 | 13-4 0.65 | 14-0 0.75 | 14-8 0.85 | 15-3 0.96 | 15-10 1.08 | 16-4 1.19 | 16-11 1.31 | 17-5 1.44 | 17-11 1.57 | 18-5 1.70 |
| 2 x 12 | 12 | 16-3 0.32 | 17-9 0.43 | 19-3 0.54 | 20-6 0.66 | 21-9 0.78 | 23-0 0.92 | 24-1 1.06 | 25-2 1.21 | 26-2 1.36 | 27-2 1.52 | 28-2 1.69 | 29-1 1.86 | 29-11 2.04 | 30-10 2.22 | 31-8 2.41 |
| | 16 | 14-1 0.28 | 15-5 0.37 | 16-8 0.47 | 17-9 0.57 | 18-10 0.68 | 19-11 0.80 | 20-10 0.92 | 21-9 1.05 | 22-8 1.18 | 23-6 1.32 | 24-4 1.46 | 25-2 1.61 | 25-11 1.76 | 26-8 1.92 | 27-5 2.08 |
| | 24 | 11-6 0.23 | 12-7 0.30 | 13-7 0.38 | 14-6 0.46 | 15-5 0.55 | 16-3 0.65 | 17-0 0.75 | 17-9 0.85 | 18-6 0.96 | 19-2 1.08 | 19-11 1.19 | 20-6 1.31 | 21-2 1.44 | 21-9 1.57 | 22-5 1.70 |

NOTE: The required modulus of elasticity, E, in 1,000,000 psi is shown below each span.

National Forest Products Association; Washington, D.C.

 **DESIGN LOAD TABLES**

DESIGN CRITERIA

STRENGTH: 15 psf dead load plus 20 psf live load determines required fiber stress.

DEFLECTION: For 20 psf live load. Limited to span in inches divided by 180.

RAFTERS: Spans are measured along the horizontal projection, and loads are considered as applied on the horizontal projection.

### MEDIUM OR HIGH SLOPE RAFTERS—20 LB LIVE LOAD
HEAVY ROOF COVERING—NO CEILING LOAD—SLOPE OVER 3 IN 12

| RAFTER SIZE, SPACING (IN.) | | EXTREME FIBER STRESS IN BENDING, $F_b$ (PSI) | | | | | | | | | | | | | | |
|---|---|---|---|---|---|---|---|---|---|---|---|---|---|---|---|---|
| | | 500 | 600 | 700 | 800 | 900 | 1000 | 1100 | 1200 | 1300 | 1400 | 1500 | 1600 | 1700 | 1800 | 1900 |
| 2 x 4 | 12 | 5-5 | 5-11 | 6-5 | 6-10 | 7-3 | 7-8 | 8-0 | 8-4 | 8-8 | 9-0 | 9-4 | 9-8 | 9-11 | 10-3 | 10-6 |
| | | 0.20 | 0.26 | 0.33 | 0.40 | 0.48 | 0.56 | 0.65 | 0.74 | 0.83 | 0.93 | 1.03 | 1.14 | 1.24 | 1.36 | 1.47 |
| | 16 | 4-8 | 5-1 | 5-6 | 5-11 | 6-3 | 6-7 | 6-11 | 7-3 | 7-6 | 7-10 | 8-1 | 8-4 | 8-7 | 8-10 | 9-1 |
| | | 0.17 | 0.23 | 0.28 | 0.35 | 0.41 | 0.49 | 0.56 | 0.64 | 0.72 | 0.80 | 0.89 | 0.98 | 1.08 | 1.17 | 1.27 |
| | 24 | 3-10 | 4-2 | 4-6 | 4-10 | 5-1 | 5-5 | 5-8 | 5-11 | 6-2 | 6-5 | 6-7 | 6-10 | 7-0 | 7-3 | 7-5 |
| | | 0.14 | 0.18 | 0.23 | 0.28 | 0.34 | 0.40 | 0.46 | 0.52 | 0.59 | 0.66 | 0.73 | 0.80 | 0.88 | 0.96 | 1.04 |
| 2 x 6 | 12 | 8-6 | 9-4 | 10-0 | 10-9 | 11-5 | 12-0 | 12-7 | 13-2 | 13-8 | 14-2 | 14-8 | 15-2 | 15-8 | 16-1 | 16-7 |
| | | 0.20 | 0.26 | 0.33 | 0.40 | 0.48 | 0.56 | 0.65 | 0.74 | 0.83 | 0.93 | 1.03 | 1.14 | 1.24 | 1.36 | 1.47 |
| | 16 | 7-4 | 8-1 | 8-8 | 9-4 | 9-10 | 10-5 | 10-11 | 11-5 | 11-10 | 12-4 | 12-9 | 13-2 | 13-7 | 13-11 | 14-4 |
| | | 0.17 | 0.23 | 0.28 | 0.35 | 0.41 | 0.49 | 0.56 | 0.64 | 0.72 | 0.80 | 0.89 | 0.98 | 1.08 | 1.17 | 1.27 |
| | 24 | 6-0 | 6-7 | 7-1 | 7-7 | 8-1 | 8-6 | 8-11 | 9-4 | 9-8 | 10-0 | 10-5 | 10-9 | 11-1 | 11-5 | 11-8 |
| | | 0.14 | 0.18 | 0.23 | 0.28 | 0.34 | 0.40 | 0.46 | 0.52 | 0.59 | 0.66 | 0.73 | 0.80 | 0.88 | 0.96 | 1.04 |
| 2 x 8 | 12 | 11-12 | 12-3 | 13-3 | 14-2 | 15-0 | 15-10 | 16-7 | 17-4 | 18-0 | 18-9 | 19-5 | 20-0 | 20-8 | 21-3 | 21-10 |
| | | 0.20 | 0.26 | 0.33 | 0.40 | 0.48 | 0.56 | 0.65 | 0.74 | 0.83 | 0.93 | 1.03 | 1.14 | 1.24 | 1.36 | 1.47 |
| | 16 | 9-8 | 10-7 | 11-6 | 12-3 | 13-0 | 13-8 | 14-4 | 15-0 | 15-7 | 16-3 | 16-9 | 17-4 | 17-10 | 18-5 | 18-11 |
| | | 0.17 | 0.23 | 0.28 | 0.35 | 0.41 | 0.49 | 0.56 | 0.64 | 0.72 | 0.80 | 0.89 | 0.98 | 1.08 | 1.17 | 1.27 |
| | 24 | 7-11 | 8-8 | 9-4 | 10-0 | 10-7 | 11-2 | 11-9 | 12-3 | 12-9 | 13-3 | 13-8 | 14-2 | 14-7 | 15-0 | 15-5 |
| | | 0.14 | 0.18 | 0.23 | 0.28 | 0.34 | 0.40 | 0.46 | 0.52 | 0.59 | 0.66 | 0.73 | 0.80 | 0.88 | 0.96 | 1.04 |
| 2 x 10 | 12 | 14-3 | 15-8 | 16-11 | 18-1 | 19-2 | 20-2 | 21-2 | 22-1 | 23-0 | 23-11 | 24-9 | 25-6 | 26-4 | 27-1 | 27-10 |
| | | 0.20 | 0.26 | 0.33 | 0.40 | 0.48 | 0.56 | 0.65 | 0.74 | 0.83 | 0.93 | 1.03 | 1.14 | 1.24 | 1.36 | 1.47 |
| | 16 | 12-4 | 13-6 | 14-8 | 15-8 | 16-7 | 17-6 | 18-4 | 19-2 | 19-11 | 20-8 | 21-5 | 22-1 | 22-10 | 23-5 | 24-1 |
| | | 0.17 | 0.23 | 0.28 | 0.35 | 0.41 | 0.49 | 0.56 | 0.64 | 0.72 | 0.80 | 0.89 | 0.98 | 1.08 | 1.17 | 1.27 |
| | 24 | 10-1 | 11-1 | 11-11 | 12-9 | 13-6 | 14-3 | 15-0 | 15-8 | 16-3 | 16-11 | 17-6 | 18-1 | 18-7 | 19-2 | 19-8 |
| | | 0.14 | 0.18 | 0.23 | 0.28 | 0.34 | 0.40 | 0.46 | 0.52 | 0.59 | 0.66 | 0.73 | 0.80 | 0.88 | 0.96 | 1.04 |

NOTE: The required modulus of elasticity, E, in 1,000,000 psi is shown below each span.

DESIGN CRITERIA

STRENGTH: 15 psf dead load plus 30 psf live load determines required fiber stress.

DEFLECTION: For 30 psf live load. Limited to span in inches divided by 180.

RAFTERS: Spans are measured along the horizontal projection, and loads are considered as applied on the horizontal projection.

### MEDIUM OR HIGH SLOPE RAFTERS—30 LB LIVE LOAD
HEAVY ROOF COVERING—NO CEILING LOAD—SLOPE OVER 3 IN 12

| RAFTER SIZE, SPACING (IN.) | | EXTREME FIBER STRESS IN BENDING, $F_b$ (PSI) | | | | | | | | | | | | | | |
|---|---|---|---|---|---|---|---|---|---|---|---|---|---|---|---|---|
| | | 500 | 600 | 700 | 800 | 900 | 1000 | 1100 | 1200 | 1300 | 1400 | 1500 | 1600 | 1700 | 1800 | 1900 |
| 2 x 4 | 12 | 4-9 | 5-3 | 5-8 | 6-0 | 6-5 | 6-9 | 7-1 | 7-5 | 7-8 | 8-0 | 8-3 | 8-6 | 8-9 | 9-0 | 9-3 |
| | | 0.20 | 0.27 | 0.34 | 0.41 | 0.49 | 0.58 | 0.67 | 0.76 | 0.86 | 0.96 | 1.06 | 1.17 | 1.28 | 1.39 | 1.51 |
| | 16 | 4-1 | 4-6 | 4-11 | 5-3 | 5-6 | 5-10 | 6-1 | 6-5 | 6-8 | 6-11 | 7-2 | 7-5 | 7-7 | 7-10 | 8-0 |
| | | 0.18 | 0.23 | 0.29 | 0.36 | 0.43 | 0.50 | 0.58 | 0.66 | 0.74 | 0.83 | 0.92 | 1.01 | 1.11 | 1.21 | 1.31 |
| | 24 | 3-4 | 3-8 | 4-0 | 4-3 | 4-6 | 4-9 | 5-0 | 5-3 | 5-5 | 5-8 | 5-10 | 6-0 | 6-3 | 6-5 | 6-7 |
| | | 0.14 | 0.19 | 0.24 | 0.29 | 0.35 | 0.41 | 0.47 | 0.54 | 0.61 | 0.68 | 0.75 | 0.83 | 0.90 | 0.99 | 1.07 |
| 2 x 6 | 12 | 7-6 | 8-2 | 8-10 | 9-6 | 10-0 | 10-7 | 11-1 | 11-7 | 12-1 | 12-6 | 13-0 | 13-5 | 13-10 | 14-2 | 14-7 |
| | | 0.20 | 0.27 | 0.34 | 0.41 | 0.49 | 0.58 | 0.67 | 0.76 | 0.86 | 0.96 | 1.06 | 1.17 | 1.28 | 1.39 | 1.51 |
| | 16 | 6-6 | 7-1 | 7-8 | 8-2 | 8-8 | 9-2 | 9-7 | 10-0 | 10-5 | 10-10 | 11-3 | 11-7 | 11-11 | 12-4 | 12-8 |
| | | 0.18 | 0.23 | 0.29 | 0.36 | 0.43 | 0.50 | 0.58 | 0.66 | 0.74 | 0.83 | 0.92 | 1.01 | 1.11 | 1.21 | 1.31 |
| | 24 | 5-4 | 5-10 | 6-3 | 6-8 | 7-1 | 7-6 | 7-10 | 8-2 | 8-6 | 8-10 | 9-2 | 9-6 | 9-9 | 10-0 | 10-4 |
| | | 0.14 | 0.19 | 0.24 | 0.29 | 0.35 | 0.41 | 0.47 | 0.54 | 0.61 | 0.68 | 0.75 | 0.83 | 0.90 | 0.99 | 1.07 |
| 2 x 8 | 12 | 9-10 | 10-10 | 11-8 | 12-6 | 13-3 | 13-11 | 14-8 | 15-3 | 15-11 | 16-6 | 17-1 | 17-8 | 18-2 | 18-9 | 19-3 |
| | | 0.20 | 0.27 | 0.34 | 0.41 | 0.49 | 0.58 | 0.67 | 0.76 | 0.86 | 0.96 | 1.06 | 1.17 | 1.28 | 1.39 | 1.51 |
| | 16 | 8-7 | 9-4 | 10-1 | 10-10 | 11-6 | 12-1 | 12-8 | 13-3 | 13-9 | 14-4 | 14-10 | 15-3 | 15-9 | 16-3 | 16-8 |
| | | 0.18 | 0.23 | 0.29 | 0.36 | 0.43 | 0.50 | 0.58 | 0.66 | 0.74 | 0.83 | 0.92 | 1.01 | 1.11 | 1.21 | 1.31 |
| | 24 | 7-0 | 7-8 | 8-3 | 8-10 | 9-4 | 9-10 | 10-4 | 10-10 | 11-3 | 11-8 | 21-1 | 12-6 | 12-10 | 13-3 | 13-7 |
| | | 0.14 | 0.19 | 0.24 | 0.29 | 0.35 | 0.41 | 0.47 | 0.54 | 0.61 | 0.68 | 0.75 | 0.83 | 0.90 | 0.99 | 1.07 |
| 2 x 10 | 12 | 12-7 | 13-9 | 14-11 | 15-11 | 15-11 | 17-10 | 18-8 | 19-6 | 20-4 | 21-1 | 21-10 | 22-6 | 23-3 | 23-11 | 24-6 |
| | | 0.20 | 0.27 | 0.34 | 0.41 | 0.49 | 0.58 | 0.67 | 0.76 | 0.86 | 0.96 | 1.06 | 1.17 | 1.28 | 1.39 | 1.51 |
| | 16 | 10-11 | 11-11 | 12-11 | 13-9 | 14-8 | 15-5 | 16-2 | 16-11 | 17-7 | 18-3 | 18-11 | 19-6 | 20-1 | 20-8 | 21-3 |
| | | 0.18 | 0.23 | 0.29 | 0.36 | 0.43 | 0.50 | 0.58 | 0.66 | 0.74 | 0.83 | 0.92 | 1.01 | 1.11 | 1.21 | 1.31 |
| | 24 | 8-11 | 9-9 | 10-6 | 11-3 | 11-11 | 12-7 | 13-2 | 13-9 | 14-4 | 14-11 | 15-5 | 15-11 | 16-5 | 16-11 | 17-4 |
| | | 0.14 | 0.19 | 0.24 | 0.29 | 0.35 | 0.41 | 0.47 | 0.54 | 0.61 | 0.68 | 0.75 | 0.83 | 0.90 | 0.99 | 1.07 |

NOTE: The required modulus of elasticity, E, in 1,000,000 psi is shown below each span.

National Forest Products Association; Washington, D.C.

DESIGN LOAD TABLES 6

DESIGN CRITERIA

STRENGTH: 7 psf dead load plus 20 psf live load determines required fiber stress.

DEFLECTION: For 20 psf live load. Limited to span in inches divided by 180.

RAFTERS: Spans are measured along the horizontal projection, and loads are considered as applied on the horizontal projection.

## MEDIUM OR HIGH SLOPE RAFTERS—20 LB LIVE LOAD
LIGHT ROOF COVERING—NO CEILING LOAD—SLOPE OVER 3 IN 12

| RAFTER SIZE, SPACING (IN.) | | EXTREME FIBER STRESS IN BENDING, $F_b$ (PSI) | | | | | | | | | | | | | | |
|---|---|---|---|---|---|---|---|---|---|---|---|---|---|---|---|---|
| | | 500 | 600 | 700 | 800 | 900 | 1000 | 1100 | 1200 | 1300 | 1400 | 1500 | 1600 | 1700 | 1800 | 1900 |
| 2 x 4 | 12 | 6-2 0.29 | 6-9 0.38 | 7-3 0.49 | 7-9 0.59 | 8-3 0.71 | 8-8 0.83 | 9-1 0.96 | 9-6 1.06 | 9-11 1.23 | 10-3 1.37 | 10-8 1.52 | 11-0 1.68 | 11-4 1.84 | 11-8 2.00 | 12-0 1.17 |
| | 16 | 5-4 0.25 | 5-10 0.33 | 6-4 0.42 | 6-9 0.51 | 7-2 0.61 | 7-6 0.72 | 7-11 0.83 | 8-3 0.94 | 8-7 1.06 | 8-11 1.19 | 9-3 1.32 | 9-6 1.45 | 9-10 1.59 | 10-1 1.73 | 10-5 1.88 |
| | 24 | 4-4 0.21 | 4-9 0.27 | 5-2 0.34 | 5-6 0.42 | 5-10 0.50 | 6-2 0.59 | 6-5 0.68 | 6-9 0.77 | 7-0 0.87 | 7-3 0.97 | 7-6 1.08 | 7-9 1.19 | 8-0 1.30 | 8-3 1.41 | 8-6 1.53 |
| 2 x 6 | 12 | 9-8 0.29 | 10-7 0.38 | 11-5 0.49 | 12-3 0.59 | 13-0 0.71 | 13-8 0.83 | 14-4 0.96 | 15-0 1.09 | 15-7 1.23 | 16-2 1.37 | 16-9 1.52 | 17-3 1.68 | 17-10 1.84 | 18-4 2.00 | 18-10 2.17 |
| | 16 | 8-4 0.25 | 9-2 0.33 | 9-11 0.42 | 10-7 0.51 | 11-3 0.61 | 11-10 0.72 | 12-5 0.83 | 13-0 0.94 | 13-6 1.06 | 14-0 1.19 | 14-6 1.32 | 15-0 1.45 | 15-5 1.59 | 15-11 1.73 | 16-4 1.88 |
| | 24 | 6-10 0.21 | 7-6 0.27 | 8-1 0.34 | 8-8 0.42 | 9-2 0.50 | 9-8 0.59 | 10-2 0.68 | 10-7 0.77 | 11-0 0.87 | 11-5 0.97 | 11-10 1.08 | 12-3 1.19 | 12-7 1.30 | 13-0 1.41 | 13-4 1.53 |
| 2 x 8 | 12 | 12-9 0.29 | 13-11 0.38 | 15-1 0.49 | 16-1 0.59 | 17-1 0.71 | 18-0 0.83 | 18-11 0.96 | 19-9 1.09 | 20-6 1.23 | 21-4 1.37 | 22-1 1.52 | 22-9 1.68 | 23-6 1.84 | 24-2 2.00 | 24-10 2.17 |
| | 16 | 11-0 0.25 | 12-1 0.33 | 13-1 0.42 | 13-11 0.51 | 14-10 0.61 | 15-7 0.72 | 16-4 0.83 | 17-1 0.94 | 17-9 1.06 | 18-5 1.19 | 19-1 1.32 | 19-9 1.45 | 20-4 1.59 | 20-11 1.73 | 21-6 1.88 |
| | 24 | 9-0 0.21 | 9-10 0.27 | 10-8 0.34 | 11-5 0.42 | 12-1 0.50 | 12-9 0.59 | 13-4 0.68 | 13-11 0.77 | 14-6 0.87 | 15-1 0.97 | 15-7 1.08 | 16-1 1.19 | 16-7 1.30 | 17-1 1.41 | 17-7 1.53 |
| 2 x 10 | 12 | 16-3 0.29 | 17-10 0.38 | 19-3 0.49 | 20-7 0.59 | 21-10 0.71 | 23-0 0.83 | 24-1 0.96 | 25-2 1.09 | 26-2 1.23 | 27-2 1.37 | 28-2 1.52 | 29-1 1.68 | 30-0 1.84 | 30-10 2.00 | 31-8 2.17 |
| | 16 | 14-1 0.25 | 15-5 0.33 | 16-8 0.42 | 17-10 0.51 | 18-11 0.61 | 19-11 0.72 | 20-10 0.83 | 21-10 0.94 | 22-8 1.06 | 23-7 1.19 | 24-5 1.32 | 25-2 1.45 | 25-11 1.59 | 26-8 1.73 | 27-5 1.88 |
| | 24 | 11-6 0.21 | 12-7 0.27 | 13-7 0.34 | 14-6 0.42 | 15-5 0.50 | 16-3 0.59 | 17-1 0.68 | 17-10 0.77 | 18-6 0.87 | 19-3 0.97 | 19-11 1.08 | 20-7 1.19 | 21-2 1.30 | 21-10 1.41 | 22-5 1.53 |

NOTE: The required modulus of elasticity, E, in 1,000,000 psi is shown below each span.

DESIGN CRITERIA

STRENGTH: 7 psf dead load plus 30 psf live load determines required fiber stress.

DEFLECTION: For 30 psf live load. Limited to span in inches divided by 180.

RAFTERS: Spans are measured along the horizontal projection, and loads are considered as applied on the horizontal projection.

## MEDIUM OR HIGH SLOPE RAFTERS—30 LB LIVE LOAD
LIGHT ROOF COVERING—NO CEILING LOAD—SLOPE OVER 3 IN 12

| RAFTER SIZE, SPACING (IN.) | | EXTREME FIBER STRESS IN BENDING, $F_b$ (PSI) | | | | | | | | | | | | | | |
|---|---|---|---|---|---|---|---|---|---|---|---|---|---|---|---|---|
| | | 500 | 600 | 700 | 800 | 900 | 1000 | 1100 | 1200 | 1300 | 1400 | 1500 | 1600 | 1700 | 1800 | 1900 |
| 2 x 4 | 12 | 5-3 0.27 | 5-9 0.36 | 6-3 0.45 | 6-8 0.55 | 7-1 0.66 | 7-5 0.77 | 7-9 0.89 | 8-2 1.02 | 8-6 1.15 | 8-9 1.28 | 9-1 1.42 | 9-5 1.57 | 9-8 1.72 | 10-0 1.87 | 10-3 2.03 |
| | 16 | 4-7 0.24 | 5-0 0.31 | 5-5 0.39 | 5-9 0.48 | 6-1 0.57 | 6-5 0.67 | 6-9 0.77 | 7-1 0.88 | 7-4 0.99 | 7-7 1.11 | 7-11 1.23 | 8-2 1.36 | 8-5 1.49 | 8-8 1.62 | 8-10 1.76 |
| | 24 | 3-9 0.19 | 4-1 0.25 | 4-5 0.32 | 4-8 0.39 | 5-0 0.47 | 5-3 0.55 | 5-6 0.63 | 5-9 0.72 | 6-0 0.81 | 6-3 0.91 | 6-5 1.01 | 6-8 1.11 | 6-10 1.21 | 7-1 1.32 | 7-3 1.43 |
| 2 x 6 | 12 | 8-3 0.27 | 9-1 0.36 | 9-9 0.45 | 10-5 0.55 | 11-1 0.66 | 11-8 0.77 | 12-3 0.89 | 12-9 1.02 | 13-4 1.15 | 13-10 1.28 | 14-4 1.42 | 14-9 1.57 | 15-3 1.72 | 15-8 1.87 | 16-1 2.03 |
| | 16 | 7-2 0.24 | 7-10 0.31 | 8-5 0.39 | 9-1 0.48 | 9-7 0.57 | 10-1 0.67 | 10-7 0.77 | 11-1 0.88 | 11-6 0.99 | 12-0 1.11 | 12-5 1.23 | 12-9 1.36 | 13-2 1.49 | 13-7 1.62 | 13-11 1.76 |
| | 24 | 5-10 0.19 | 6-5 0.25 | 6-11 0.32 | 7-5 0.39 | 7-10 0.47 | 8-3 0.55 | 8-8 0.63 | 9-1 0.72 | 9-5 0.81 | 9-9 0.91 | 10-1 1.01 | 10-5 1.11 | 10-9 1.21 | 11-1 1.32 | 11-5 1.43 |
| 2 x 8 | 12 | 10-11 0.27 | 11-11 0.36 | 12-10 0.45 | 13-9 0.55 | 14-7 0.66 | 15-5 0.77 | 16-2 0.89 | 16-10 1.02 | 17-7 1.15 | 18-2 1.28 | 18-10 1.42 | 19-6 1.57 | 20-1 1.72 | 20-8 1.87 | 21-3 2.03 |
| | 16 | 9-5 0.24 | 10-4 0.31 | 11-2 0.39 | 11-11 0.48 | 12-8 0.57 | 13-4 0.67 | 14-0 0.77 | 14-7 0.88 | 15-2 0.99 | 15-9 1.11 | 16-4 1.23 | 16-10 1.36 | 17-4 1.49 | 17-11 1.62 | 18-4 1.76 |
| | 24 | 7-8 0.19 | 8-5 0.25 | 9-1 0.32 | 9-9 0.39 | 10-4 0.47 | 10-11 0.55 | 11-5 0.63 | 11-11 0.72 | 12-5 0.81 | 12-10 0.91 | 13-4 1.01 | 13-9 1.11 | 14-2 1.21 | 14-7 1.32 | 15-0 1.43 |
| 2 x 10 | 12 | 13-11 0.27 | 15-2 0.36 | 16-5 0.45 | 17-7 0.55 | 18-7 0.66 | 19-8 0.77 | 20-7 0.89 | 21-6 1.02 | 22-5 1.15 | 23-3 1.28 | 24-1 1.42 | 24-10 1.57 | 25-7 1.72 | 26-4 1.87 | 27-1 2.03 |
| | 16 | 12-0 0.26 | 13-2 0.34 | 14-3 0.43 | 15-2 0.53 | 16-2 0.63 | 17-0 0.74 | 17-10 0.85 | 18-7 0.97 | 19-5 1.09 | 20-1 1.22 | 20-10 1.35 | 21-6 1.49 | 22-2 1.63 | 22-10 1.78 | 23-5 1.93 |
| | 24 | 9-10 0.19 | 10-9 0.25 | 11-7 0.32 | 12-5 0.39 | 13-2 0.47 | 13-11 0.55 | 14-7 0.63 | 15-2 0.72 | 15-10 0.81 | 16-5 0.91 | 17-0 1.01 | 17-7 1.11 | 18-1 1.21 | 18-7 1.32 | 19-2 1.43 |

NOTE: The required modulus of elasticity, E, in 1,000,000 psi is shown below each span.

National Forest Products Association; Washington, D.C.

**DESIGN LOAD TABLES**

**DESIGN CRITERIA**

STRENGTH: Live load of 30 psf plus dead load of 10 psf determines the required fiber stress value.
DEFLECTION: For 30 psf live load. Limited to span in inches divided by 360.

## FLOOR JOISTS—30 LB LIVE LOAD

**ALL ROOMS USED FOR SLEEPING AREAS AND ATTIC FLOORS**

| JOIST (IN.) SIZE | SPACING | MODULUS OF ELASTICITY, E, IN 1,000,000 PSI | | | | | | | | | | | | | | |
|---|---|---|---|---|---|---|---|---|---|---|---|---|---|---|---|---|
| | | 0.5 | 0.6 | 0.7 | 0.8 | 0.9 | 1.0 | 1.1 | 1.2 | 1.3 | 1.4 | 1.5 | 1.6 | 1.7 | 1.8 | 1.9 |
| 2 x 6 | 12 | 8-0 / 510 | 8-6 / 570 | 8-11 / 640 | 9-4 / 700 | 9-9 / 750 | 10-1 / 810 | 10-5 / 860 | 10-9 / 910 | 11-0 / 960 | 11-3 / 1010 | 11-7 / 1060 | 11-10 / 1100 | 12-0 / 1150 | 12-3 / 1200 | 12-6 / 1240 |
| | 16 | 7-3 / 560 | 7-9 / 630 | 8-2 / 700 | 8-6 / 770 | 8-10 / 830 | 9-2 / 890 | 9-6 / 950 | 9-9 / 1000 | 10-0 / 1060 | 10-3 / 1110 | 10-6 / 1160 | 10-9 / 1220 | 10-11 / 1270 | 11-2 / 1320 | 11-4 / 1360 |
| | 24 | 6-4 / 640 | 6-9 / 720 | 7-1 / 800 | 7-5 / 880 | 7-9 / 950 | 8-0 / 1020 | 8-3 / 1080 | 8-6 / 1150 | 8-9 / 1210 | 8-11 / 1270 | 9-2 / 1330 | 9-4 / 1390 | 9-7 / 1450 | 9-9 / 1510 | 9-11 / 1560 |
| 2 x 8 | 12 | 10-7 / 510 | 11-3 / 570 | 11-10 / 640 | 12-4 / 700 | 12-10 / 750 | 13-4 / 810 | 13-9 / 860 | 14-2 / 910 | 14-6 / 960 | 14-11 / 1010 | 15-3 / 1060 | 15-7 / 1100 | 15-10 / 1150 | 16-2 / 1200 | 16-6 / 1240 |
| | 16 | 9-7 / 560 | 10-2 / 630 | 10-9 / 700 | 11-13 / 770 | 11-8 / 830 | 12-1 / 890 | 12-6 / 950 | 12-10 / 1000 | 13-2 / 1060 | 13-6 / 1110 | 13-10 / 1160 | 14-2 / 1220 | 14-5 / 1270 | 14-8 / 1320 | 15-0 / 1360 |
| | 24 | 8-5 / 640 | 8-11 / 720 | 9-4 / 800 | 9-10 / 880 | 10-2 / 950 | 10-7 / 1020 | 10-11 / 1080 | 11-3 / 1150 | 11-6 / 1210 | 11-10 / 1270 | 12-1 / 1330 | 12-4 / 1390 | 12-7 / 1450 | 12-10 / 1510 | 13-1 / 1560 |
| 2 x 10 | 12 | 13-6 / 510 | 14-4 / 570 | 15-1 / 640 | 15-9 / 700 | 16-5 / 750 | 17-0 / 810 | 17-6 / 860 | 18-0 / 910 | 18-6 / 960 | 19-0 / 1010 | 19-5 / 1060 | 19-10 / 1100 | 20-3 / 1150 | 20-8 / 1200 | 21-0 / 1240 |
| | 16 | 12-3 / 560 | 13-0 / 630 | 13-8 / 700 | 14-4 / 770 | 14-11 / 830 | 15-5 / 890 | 15-11 / 950 | 16-5 / 1000 | 16-10 / 1060 | 17-3 / 1110 | 17-8 / 1160 | 18-0 / 1220 | 18-5 / 1270 | 18-9 / 1320 | 19-1 / 1360 |
| | 24 | 10-8 / 640 | 11-4 / 720 | 11-11 / 800 | 12-6 / 880 | 13-0 / 950 | 13-6 / 1020 | 13-11 / 1080 | 14-4 / 1150 | 14-8 / 1210 | 15-1 / 1270 | 15-5 / 1330 | 15-9 / 1390 | 16-1 / 1450 | 16-5 / 1510 | 16-8 / 1560 |
| 2 x 12 | 12 | 16-5 / 510 | 17-5 / 570 | 18-4 / 640 | 19-2 / 700 | 19-11 / 750 | 20-8 / 810 | 21-4 / 860 | 21-11 / 910 | 22-6 / 960 | 23-1 / 1010 | 23-7 / 1060 | 24-2 / 1100 | 24-8 / 1150 | 25-1 / 1200 | 25-7 / 1240 |
| | 16 | 14-11 / 560 | 15-10 / 630 | 16-8 / 700 | 17-5 / 770 | 18-1 / 830 | 18-9 / 890 | 19-4 / 950 | 19-11 / 1000 | 20-6 / 1060 | 21-0 / 1110 | 21-6 / 1160 | 21-11 / 1220 | 22-5 / 1270 | 22-10 / 1320 | 23-3 / 1360 |
| | 24 | 13-0 / 640 | 13-10 / 720 | 14-7 / 800 | 15-2 / 880 | 15-10 / 950 | 16-5 / 1020 | 16-11 / 1080 | 17-5 / 1150 | 17-11 / 1210 | 18-4 / 1270 | 18-9 / 1330 | 19-2 / 1390 | 19-7 / 1450 | 19-11 / 1510 | 20-3 / 1560 |

NOTE: The required extreme fiber stress in bending, $F_b$, in psi is shown below each span.

**DESIGN CRITERIA**

STRENGTH: Live load of 40 psf plus dead load of 10 psf determines the required fiber stress value.
DEFLECTION: For 40 psf live load. Limited to span in inches divided by 360.

## FLOOR JOISTS—40 LB LIVE LOAD

**ALL ROOMS EXCEPT THOSE USED FOR SLEEPING AREAS AND ATTIC FLOORS**

| JOIST (IN.) SIZE | SPACING | MODULUS OF ELASTICITY, E, IN 1,000,000 PSI | | | | | | | | | | | | | | |
|---|---|---|---|---|---|---|---|---|---|---|---|---|---|---|---|---|
| | | 0.5 | 0.6 | 0.7 | 0.8 | 0.9 | 1.0 | 1.1 | 1.2 | 1.3 | 1.4 | 1.5 | 1.6 | 1.7 | 1.8 | 1.9 |
| 2 x 6 | 12 | 7-3 / 520 | 7-9 / 590 | 8-2 / 660 | 8-6 / 720 | 8-10 / 780 | 9-2 / 830 | 9-6 / 890 | 9-9 / 940 | 10-0 / 990 | 10-3 / 1040 | 10-6 / 1090 | 10-9 / 1140 | 10-11 / 1190 | 11-2 / 1230 | 11-4 / 1280 |
| | 16 | 6-7 / 580 | 7-0 / 650 | 7-5 / 720 | 7-9 / 790 | 8-0 / 860 | 8-4 / 920 | 8-7 / 980 | 8-10 / 1040 | 9-1 / 1090 | 9-4 / 1150 | 9-6 / 1200 | 9-9 / 1250 | 9-11 / 1310 | 10-2 / 1360 | 10-4 / 1410 |
| | 24 | 5-9 / 660 | 6-2 / 750 | 6-6 / 830 | 6-9 / 900 | 7-0 / 980 | 7-3 / 1050 | 7-6 / 1120 | 7-9 / 1190 | 7-11 / 1250 | 8-2 / 1310 | 8-4 / 1380 | 8-6 / 1440 | 8-8 / 1500 | 8-10 / 1550 | 9-0 / 1610 |
| 2 x 8 | 12 | 9-7 / 520 | 10-2 / 590 | 10-9 / 660 | 11-3 / 720 | 11-8 / 780 | 12-1 / 830 | 12-6 / 890 | 12-10 / 940 | 13-2 / 990 | 13-6 / 1040 | 13-10 / 1090 | 14-2 / 1140 | 14-5 / 1190 | 14-8 / 1230 | 15-0 / 1280 |
| | 16 | 8-9 / 580 | 9-3 / 650 | 9-9 / 720 | 10-2 / 790 | 10-7 / 850 | 11-0 / 920 | 11-4 / 980 | 11-8 / 1040 | 12-0 / 1090 | 12-3 / 1150 | 12-7 / 1200 | 12-10 / 1250 | 13-1 / 1310 | 13-4 / 1360 | 13-7 / 1410 |
| | 24 | 7-7 / 660 | 8-1 / 750 | 8-6 / 830 | 8-11 / 900 | 9-3 / 980 | 9-7 / 1050 | 9-11 / 1120 | 10-2 / 1190 | 10-6 / 1250 | 10-9 / 1310 | 11-0 / 1380 | 11-3 / 1440 | 11-5 / 1500 | 11-8 / 1550 | 11-11 / 1610 |
| 2 x 10 | 12 | 12-3 / 520 | 13-0 / 590 | 13-8 / 660 | 14-4 / 720 | 14-11 / 780 | 15-5 / 830 | 15-11 / 890 | 16-5 / 940 | 16-10 / 990 | 17-3 / 1040 | 17-8 / 1090 | 18-0 / 1140 | 18-5 / 1190 | 18-9 / 1230 | 19-1 / 1280 |
| | 16 | 11-1 / 580 | 11-10 / 650 | 12-5 / 720 | 13-0 / 790 | 13-6 / 850 | 14-0 / 920 | 14-6 / 980 | 14-11 / 1040 | 15-3 / 1090 | 15-8 / 1150 | 16-0 / 1200 | 16-5 / 1250 | 16-9 / 1310 | 17-0 / 1360 | 17-4 / 1410 |
| | 24 | 9-9 / 660 | 10-4 / 750 | 10-10 / 830 | 11-4 / 900 | 11-10 / 980 | 12-3 / 1050 | 12-8 / 1120 | 13-0 / 1190 | 13-4 / 1250 | 13-8 / 1310 | 14-0 / 1380 | 14-4 / 1440 | 14-7 / 1500 | 14-11 / 1550 | 15-2 / 1610 |
| 2 x 12 | 12 | 14-11 / 520 | 15-10 / 590 | 16-8 / 660 | 17-5 / 720 | 18-1 / 780 | 18-9 / 830 | 19-4 / 890 | 19-11 / 940 | 20-6 / 990 | 21-0 / 1040 | 21-6 / 1090 | 21-11 / 1140 | 22-5 / 1190 | 22-10 / 1230 | 23-3 / 1280 |
| | 16 | 13-6 / 580 | 14-4 / 650 | 15-2 / 720 | 15-10 / 790 | 16-5 / 860 | 17-0 / 920 | 17-7 / 980 | 18-1 / 1040 | 18-7 / 1090 | 19-1 / 1150 | 19-6 / 1200 | 19-11 / 1250 | 20-4 / 1310 | 20-9 / 1360 | 21-1 / 1410 |
| | 24 | 11-10 / 660 | 12-7 / 750 | 13-3 / 830 | 13-10 / 900 | 14-4 / 980 | 14-11 / 1050 | 15-4 / 1120 | 15-10 / 1190 | 16-3 / 1250 | 16-8 / 1310 | 17-0 / 1380 | 17-5 / 1440 | 17-9 / 1500 | 18-1 / 1550 | 18-5 / 1610 |

NOTE: The required extreme fiber stress in bending, $F_b$, in psi is shown below each span.

National Forest Products Association; Washington, D.C.

DESIGN LOAD TABLES  6

## GENERAL DESIGN INFORMATION

For floor construction where live loading is heavier than customarily found in residential occupancies, tabular data are provided.

The tabulated spans are based on bending strength using the live load indicated in each table heading plus a dead load of 10 psf. In calculating the required modulus of elasticity for the tabulated span, the live load only was used, since this is in accordance with established practice for design of floor joists.

### SPAN

While the effective span length for an isolated beam is customarily taken as the distance from face to face of supports plus one-half the required length of bearing at each end, it is the practice in designing joists spaced not over 24 in. apart to consider the span as the clear distance between supports.

### NET SIZES OF LUMBER

Joists are customarily specified in terms of nominal sizes, but calculations to determine the allowable span and required modulus of elasticity are based on actual sizes.

### DESIGN STRESSES

Unit design values for design of wood joists are given in the National Design Specification for Wood Construc-tion, available from the National Forest Products Association.

### ADJUSTMENT OF MODULUS OF ELASTICITY

The modulus of elasticity values listed in the span tables are those required for the tabulated spans if deflection under the live load is limited to $\ell/360$. Where other deflection limits are acceptable, the tabular E values may be adjusted by multiplying them by the following factors:

For limit of $\ell/300$: 0.833
For limit of $\ell/240$: 0.667
For limit of $\ell/180$: 0.500

## FLOOR JOISTS—50 LB LIVE LOAD

| JOIST (IN.) SIZE, SPACING | | EXTREME FIBER STRESS IN BENDING, $F_b$ (PSI) | | | | | | | | | |
|---|---|---|---|---|---|---|---|---|---|---|---|
| | | 900 | 1000 | 1100 | 1200 | 1300 | 1400 | 1500 | 1600 | 1800 | 2000 |
| 2 x 6 | 12 | 8-8 1.063 | 9-2 1.246 | 9-7 1.437 | 10-0 1.637 | 10-5 1.846 | 10-10 2.063 | 11-3 2.289 | 11-7 2.521 | 12-3 3.007 | 12-11 3.522 |
| | 16 | 7-6 0.924 | 7-11 1.083 | 8-4 1.249 | 8-8 1.423 | 9-1 1.605 | 9-5 1.794 | 9-9 1.989 | 10-0 2.191 | 10-7 2.614 | 11-2 3.062 |
| | 24 | 6-1 0.744 | 6-5 0.871 | 6-9 1.005 | 7-1 1.144 | 7-4 1.291 | 7-7 1.443 | 7-11 1.600 | 8-2 1.762 | 8-7 2.103 | 9-1 2.463 |
| 2 x 8 | 12 | 11-5 1.063 | 12-1 1.246 | 12-7 1.437 | 13-3 1.631 | 13-9 1.846 | 14-3 2.063 | 14-9 2.289 | 15-3 2.521 | 16-2 3.007 | 17-1 3.522 |
| | 16 | 9-11 0.924 | 10-5 1.083 | 11-0 1.249 | 11-6 1.423 | 11-11 1.605 | 12-5 1.794 | 12-10 1.989 | 13-3 2.191 | 14-0 2.614 | 14-10 3.062 |
| | 24 | 8-1 0.744 | 8-6 0.871 | 8-11 1.005 | 9-4 1.144 | 9-8 1.291 | 10-1 1.443 | 10-5 1.600 | 10-9 1.762 | 11-5 2.103 | 12-0 2.463 |
| 2 x 10 | 12 | 14-7 1.063 | 15-5 1.246 | 16-2 1.437 | 16-10 1.637 | 17-6 1.846 | 18-2 2.063 | 18-10 2.289 | 19-5 2.521 | 20-7 3.007 | 21-9 3.522 |
| | 16 | 12-7 0.924 | 13-4 1.083 | 14-0 1.249 | 14-7 1.423 | 15-3 1.605 | 15-10 1.794 | 16-4 1.989 | 16-10 2.191 | 17-11 2.614 | 18-11 3.062 |
| | 24 | 10-3 0.744 | 10-10 0.871 | 11-4 1.005 | 11-10 1.144 | 12-4 1.291 | 12-10 1.443 | 13-3 1.600 | 13-9 1.762 | 14-7 2.103 | 15-4 2.463 |
| 2 x 12 | 12 | 17-9 1.063 | 18-9 1.246 | 19-7 1.437 | 20-6 1.637 | 21-4 1.846 | 22-2 2.063 | 22-11 2.289 | 23-8 2.521 | 25-1 3.007 | 26-6 3.522 |
| | 16 | 15-5 0.924 | 16-3 1.083 | 17-1 1.249 | 17-10 1.423 | 18-6 1.605 | 19-2 1.794 | 19-10 1.989 | 20-6 2.191 | 21-9 2.614 | 23-0 3.062 |
| | 24 | 12-6 0.744 | 13-2 0.871 | 13-10 1.005 | 14-5 1.144 | 15-0 1.291 | 15-7 1.443 | 16-2 1.600 | 16-7 1.762 | 17-8 2.103 | 18-10 2.463 |
| 2 x 14 | 12 | 20-11 1.063 | 22-1 1.246 | 23-2 1.437 | 24-2 1.637 | 25-2 1.846 | 26-1 2.063 | 27-0 2.289 | 27-11 2.521 | 29-7 3.007 | 31-2 3.522 |
| | 16 | 18-2 0.924 | 19-2 1.083 | 20-1 1.249 | 20-11 1.423 | 21-9 1.605 | 22-7 1.794 | 23-5 1.989 | 24-2 2.191 | 25-7 2.614 | 27-0 3.062 |
| | 24 | 14-9 0.744 | 15-6 0.871 | 16-3 1.005 | 17-0 1.144 | 17-8 1.291 | 18-4 1.443 | 19-0 1.600 | 19-7 1.762 | 20-10 2.103 | 22-0 2.463 |
| 3 x 6 | 12 | 11-2 1.373 | 11-10 1.608 | 12-5 1.855 | 12-11 2.113 | 13-6 2.383 | 14-0 2.663 | 14-6 2.953 | 14-11 3.254 | 15-10 3.882 | 16-9 4.547 |
| | 16 | 9-9 1.193 | 10-3 1.397 | 10-9 1.612 | 11-3 1.836 | 11-8 2.071 | 12-2 2.314 | 12-7 2.567 | 12-11 2.827 | 13-9 3.374 | 14-6 3.952 |
| | 24 | 7-11 0.960 | 8-4 1.124 | 8-9 1.297 | 9-2 1.478 | 9-6 1.666 | 9-10 1.862 | 10-2 2.065 | 10-6 2.275 | 11-2 2.714 | 11-9 3.179 |
| 3 x 8 | 12 | 14-9 1.373 | 15-7 1.608 | 16-4 1.855 | 17-1 2.113 | 17-9 2.383 | 18-5 2.663 | 19-1 2.953 | 19-9 3.254 | 20-11 3.882 | 22-1 4.537 |
| | 16 | 12-10 1.193 | 13-6 1.397 | 14-2 1.612 | 14-10 1.836 | 15-5 2.071 | 16-0 2.314 | 16-7 2.567 | 17-1 2.827 | 18-1 3.374 | 19-1 3.952 |
| | 24 | 10-5 0.960 | 11-0 1.124 | 11-6 1.297 | 12-0 1.478 | 12-6 1.666 | 13-0 1.862 | 13-5 2.065 | 13-10 2.275 | 14-8 2.714 | 15-6 3.179 |
| 3 x 10 | 12 | 18-10 1.373 | 19-10 1.608 | 20-10 1.855 | 21-9 2.113 | 22-7 2.383 | 23-6 2.663 | 24-4 2.953 | 25-1 3.254 | 26-7 3.882 | 28-1 4.547 |
| | 16 | 16-4 1.193 | 17-3 1.397 | 18-1 1.612 | 18-10 1.836 | 19-7 2.071 | 20-5 2.314 | 21-1 2.567 | 21-10 2.827 | 23-2 3.374 | 24-5 3.952 |
| | 24 | 13-3 0.960 | 14-0 1.124 | 14-8 1.297 | 15-4 1.478 | 16-0 1.666 | 16-7 1.862 | 17-2 2.065 | 17-8 2.275 | 18-9 2.714 | 19-10 3.179 |
| 3 x 12 | 12 | 22-11 1.373 | 24-2 1.608 | 25-4 1.855 | 26-5 2.113 | 27-6 2.383 | 28-7 2.663 | 29-7 2.953 | 30-7 3.254 | 32-5 3.882 | 34-2 4.547 |
| | 16 | 19-11 1.193 | 20-11 1.397 | 21-11 1.612 | 22-11 1.836 | 23-11 2.071 | 24-10 2.314 | 25-8 2.567 | 26-6 2.827 | 28-1 3.374 | 29-7 3.952 |
| | 24 | 16-2 0.960 | 17-0 1.124 | 17-10 1.297 | 18-8 1.478 | 19-5 1.666 | 20-2 1.862 | 20-10 2.065 | 21-6 2.275 | 22-10 2.714 | 24-1 3.179 |
| 3 x 14 | 12 | 27-0 1.373 | 28-5 1.608 | 29-10 1.855 | 31-2 2.113 | 32-5 2.383 | 33-8 2.663 | 34-10 2.953 | 36-0 3.254 | 38-2 3.882 | 40-3 4.547 |
| | 16 | 23-5 1.193 | 24-8 1.397 | 25-11 1.612 | 27-1 1.836 | 28-2 2.071 | 29-3 2.314 | 30-3 2.567 | 31-3 2.827 | 33-1 3.374 | 34-11 3.952 |
| | 24 | 19-0 0.960 | 20-0 1.124 | 21-0 1.297 | 22-0 1.478 | 22-11 1.666 | 23-9 1.862 | 24-7 2.065 | 25-5 2.275 | 26-11 2.714 | 28-4 3.179 |

NOTE: The required modulus of elasticity, E, in 1,000,000 psi is shown below each span, if deflection under the live load is limited to $\ell/360$.

National Forest Products Association; Washington, D.C.

## DESIGN LOAD TABLES

## GENERAL DESIGN INFORMATION

For floor construction where live loading is heavier than customarily found in residential occupancies, tabular data are provided.

The tabulated spans are based on bending strength using the live load indicated in each table heading plus a dead load of 10 psf. In calculating the required modulus of elasticity for the tabulated span, the live load only was used, since this is in accordance with established practice for design of floor joists.

## SPAN

While the effective span length for an isolated beam is customarily taken as the distance from face to face of supports plus one-half the required length of bearing at each end, it is the practice in designing joists spaced not over 24 in. apart to consider the span as the clear distance between supports.

## NET SIZES OF LUMBER

Joists are customarily specified in terms of nominal sizes, but calculations to determine the allowable span and required modulus of elasticity are based on actual sizes.

## DESIGN STRESSES

Unit design values for design of wood joists are given in the National Design Specification for Wood Construc-tion, available from the National Forest Products Association.

## ADJUSTMENT OF MODULUS OF ELASTICITY

The modulus of elasticity values listed in the span tables for joists are those required for the tabulated spans if deflection under the live load is limited to $\ell/360$. Where other deflection limits are acceptable, the tabular E values may be adjusted by multiplying them by the following factors:

For limit of $\ell/300$: 0.833
For limit of $\ell/240$: 0.667
For limit of $\ell/180$: 0.500

## FLOOR JOISTS— 60 LB LIVE LOAD

| JOIST (IN.) SIZE, SPACING | | EXTREME FIBER STRESS IN BENDING, $F_b$ (PSI) | | | | | | | | | |
|---|---|---|---|---|---|---|---|---|---|---|---|
| | | 900 | 1000 | 1100 | 1200 | 1300 | 1400 | 1500 | 1600 | 1800 | 2000 |
| 2 x 6 | 12 | 8-1 / 1.012 | 8-6 / 1.186 | 8-11 / 1.368 | 9-3 / 1.558 | 9-8 / 1.757 | 10-0 / 1.964 | 10-5 / 2.179 | 10-9 / 2.400 | 11-5 / 2.863 | 12-0 / 3.353 |
| | 16 | 7-0 / 0.880 | 7-4 / 1.031 | 7-9 / 1.189 | 8-1 / 1.355 | 8-5 / 1.528 | 8-8 / 1.708 | 9-0 / 1.894 | 9-4 / 2.191 | 9-10 / 2.489 | 10-5 / 2.915 |
| | 24 | 5-8 / 0.708 | 6-0 / 0.829 | 6-4 / 0.957 | 6-7 / 1.089 | 6-10 / 1.229 | 7-1 / 1.374 | 7-4 / 1.523 | 7-7 / 1.677 | 8-0 / 2.002 | 8-5 / 2.345 |
| 2 x 8 | 12 | 10-7 / 1.012 | 11-2 / 1.186 | 11-9 / 1.368 | 12-3 / 1.558 | 12-9 / 1.757 | 13-3 / 1.964 | 13-8 / 2.179 | 14-1 / 2.400 | 15-0 / 2.863 | 15-10 / 3.353 |
| | 16 | 9-2 / 0.880 | 9-8 / 1.031 | 10-2 / 1.189 | 10-7 / 1.355 | 11-0 / 1.528 | 11-5 / 1.708 | 11-10 / 1.894 | 12-3 / 2.191 | 13-0 / 2.489 | 13-8 / 2.915 |
| | 24 | 7-6 / 0.708 | 7-11 / 0.829 | 8-3 / 0.957 | 8-7 / 1.089 | 9-0 / 1.229 | 9-4 / 1.374 | 9-7 / 1.523 | 9-11 / 1.677 | 10-7 / 2.002 | 11-2 / 2.345 |
| 2 x 10 | 12 | 13-6 / 1.012 | 14-3 / 1.186 | 14-11 / 1.368 | 15-7 / 1.558 | 16-3 / 1.757 | 16-10 / 1.964 | 17-5 / 2.179 | 18-0 / 2.400 | 19-1 / 2.863 | 20-2 / 3.353 |
| | 16 | 11-9 / 0.880 | 12-3 / 1.031 | 13-0 / 1.189 | 13-6 / 1.355 | 14-0 / 1.528 | 14-6 / 1.708 | 15-1 / 1.894 | 15-7 / 2.191 | 16-7 / 2.489 | 17-6 / 2.915 |
| | 24 | 9-6 / 0.708 | 10-0 / 0.829 | 10-6 / 0.957 | 11-0 / 1.089 | 11-6 / 1.229 | 11-11 / 1.374 | 12-4 / 1.523 | 12-9 / 1.677 | 13-6 / 2.002 | 14-3 / 2.345 |
| 2 x 12 | 12 | 16-6 / 1.012 | 17-4 / 1.186 | 18-2 / 1.368 | 19-0 / 1.558 | 19-9 / 1.757 | 20-6 / 1.964 | 21-3 / 2.179 | 21-11 / 2.400 | 23-3 / 2.863 | 24-6 / 3.353 |
| | 16 | 14-3 / 0.880 | 15-0 / 1.031 | 15-9 / 1.189 | 16-6 / 1.355 | 17-2 / 1.528 | 17-10 / 1.708 | 18-5 / 1.894 | 19-0 / 2.191 | 20-2 / 2.489 | 21-3 / 2.915 |
| | 24 | 11-7 / 0.708 | 12-3 / 0.829 | 12-10 / 0.957 | 13-5 / 1.089 | 13-11 / 1.229 | 14-5 / 1.374 | 14-11 / 1.523 | 15-5 / 1.677 | 16-5 / 2.002 | 17-5 / 2.345 |
| 2 x 14 | 12 | 19-5 / 1.012 | 20-5 / 1.186 | 21-5 / 1.368 | 22-4 / 1.558 | 23-3 / 1.757 | 24-2 / 1.964 | 25-0 / 2.179 | 25-10 / 2.400 | 27-5 / 2.863 | 28-11 / 3.353 |
| | 16 | 16-10 / 0.880 | 17-8 / 1.031 | 18-6 / 1.189 | 19-4 / 1.355 | 20-2 / 1.528 | 20-11 / 1.708 | 21-8 / 1.894 | 22-5 / 2.191 | 23-9 / 2.489 | 25-1 / 2.915 |
| | 24 | 13-8 / 0.708 | 14-5 / 0.829 | 15-1 / 0.957 | 15-9 / 1.089 | 16-5 / 1.229 | 17-0 / 1.374 | 17-7 / 1.523 | 18-2 / 1.677 | 19-3 / 2.002 | 20-4 / 2.345 |
| 3 x 6 | 12 | 10-4 / 1.037 | 10-11 / 1.531 | 11-6 / 1.766 | 12-0 / 2.012 | 12-6 / 2.269 | 13-0 / 2.535 | 13-5 / 2.811 | 13-10 / 3.098 | 14-8 / 3.696 | 15-6 / 4.329 |
| | 16 | 9-0 / 1.136 | 9-6 / 1.330 | 10-0 / 1.535 | 10-5 / 1.748 | 10-10 / 1.972 | 11-3 / 2.203 | 11-8 / 2.444 | 12-0 / 2.691 | 12-9 / 3.212 | 13-5 / 3.762 |
| | 24 | 7-4 / 0.914 | 7-9 / 1.070 | 8-1 / 1.235 | 8-5 / 1.406 | 8-9 / 1.586 | 9-1 / 1.773 | 9-5 / 1.966 | 9-9 / 2.166 | 10-4 / 2.584 | 10-11 / 3.026 |
| 3 x 8 | 12 | 13-8 / 1.307 | 14-5 / 1.531 | 15-2 / 1.766 | 15-10 / 2.012 | 16-6 / 2.269 | 17-1 / 2.535 | 17-8 / 2.811 | 18-3 / 3.098 | 19-4 / 3.696 | 20-5 / 4.329 |
| | 16 | 11-10 / 1.136 | 12-6 / 1.330 | 13-1 / 1.535 | 13-8 / 1.748 | 14-3 / 1.972 | 14-10 / 2.203 | 15-4 / 2.444 | 15-10 / 2.691 | 16-9 / 3.212 | 17-8 / 3.762 |
| | 24 | 9-7 / 0.914 | 10-1 / 1.070 | 10-7 / 1.235 | 11-1 / 1.406 | 11-7 / 1.586 | 12-0 / 1.773 | 12-5 / 1.966 | 12-10 / 2.166 | 13-7 / 2.584 | 14-4 / 3.026 |
| 3 x 10 | 12 | 17-5 / 1.307 | 18-5 / 1.531 | 19-4 / 1.766 | 20-2 / 2.012 | 21-0 / 2.269 | 21-9 / 2.535 | 22-7 / 2.811 | 23-4 / 3.098 | 24-9 / 3.696 | 26-1 / 4.329 |
| | 16 | 15-2 / 1.136 | 16-0 / 1.330 | 16-9 / 1.535 | 17-6 / 1.748 | 18-2 / 1.972 | 18-10 / 2.203 | 19-6 / 2.444 | 20-2 / 2.691 | 21-5 / 3.212 | 22-7 / 3.762 |
| | 24 | 12-4 / 0.914 | 13-0 / 1.070 | 13-7 / 1.235 | 14-2 / 1.406 | 14-9 / 1.586 | 15-4 / 1.773 | 15-10 / 1.966 | 16-4 / 2.166 | 17-5 / 2.584 | 18-4 / 3.026 |
| 3 x 12 | 12 | 21-3 / 1.307 | 22-4 / 1.531 | 23-5 / 1.766 | 24-6 / 2.012 | 25-6 / 1.269 | 26-6 / 2.535 | 27-5 / 2.811 | 28-4 / 3.098 | 30-0 / 3.696 | 31-7 / 4.329 |
| | 16 | 18-5 / 1.136 | 19-5 / 1.330 | 20-4 / 1.535 | 21-3 / 1.748 | 22-2 / 1.972 | 23-0 / 2.203 | 23-9 / 2.444 | 24-6 / 2.691 | 26-0 / 3.212 | 27-5 / 3.762 |
| | 24 | 15-0 / 0.914 | 15-9 / 1.070 | 16-6 / 1.235 | 17-3 / 1.406 | 18-0 / 1.586 | 18-8 / 1.773 | 19-4 / 1.966 | 20-0 / 2.166 | 21-2 / 2.584 | 22-4 / 3.036 |
| 3 x 14 | 12 | 25-0 / 1.307 | 26-4 / 1.531 | 27-7 / 1.766 | 28-10 / 2.012 | 30-1 / 2.269 | 31-3 / 2.535 | 32-4 / 2.811 | 33-4 / 3.098 | 35-4 / 3.696 | 37-4 / 4.329 |
| | 16 | 21-8 / 1.136 | 22-10 / 1.330 | 24-0 / 1.535 | 25-1 / 1.748 | 26-1 / 1.972 | 27-1 / 2.203 | 28-0 / 2.444 | 28-11 / 2.691 | 30-8 / 3.212 | 32-4 / 3.762 |
| | 24 | 17-7 / 0.914 | 18-7 / 1.070 | 19-6 / 1.235 | 20-4 / 1.406 | 21-2 / 1.586 | 22-0 / 1.773 | 22-9 / 1.966 | 23-6 / 2.166 | 24-11 / 2.584 | 26-3 / 3.026 |

NOTE: The required modulus of elasticity, E, in 1,000,000 psi is shown below each span, if deflection under the live load is limited to $\ell/360$.

National Forest Products Association; Washington, D.C.

DESIGN LOAD TABLES

## GENERAL DESIGN INFORMATION

For floor construction where live loading is heavier than customarily found in residential occupancies, tabular data are provided.

The tabulated spans are based on bending strength using the live load indicated in each table heading plus a dead load of 10 psf. In calculating the required modulus of elasticity for the tabulated span, the live load only was used, since this is in accordance with established practice for design of floor joists.

## SPAN

While the effective span length for an isolated beam is customarily taken as the distance from face to face of supports plus one-half the required length of bearing at each end, it is the practice in designing joists spaced not over 24 in. apart to consider the span as the clear distance between supports.

## NET SIZES OF LUMBER

Joists are customarily specified in terms of nominal sizes, but calculations to determine the allowable span and required modulus of elasticity are based on actual sizes.

## DESIGN STRESSES

Unit design values for design of wood joists are given in the National Design Specification for Wood Construction, available from the National Forest Products Association.

## ADJUSTMENT OF MODULUS OF ELASTICITY

The modulus of elasticity values listed in the span tables for joists are those required for the tabulated spans if deflection under the live load is limited to $\ell/360$. Where other deflection limits are acceptable, the tabular E values may be adjusted by multiplying them by the following factors:

For limit of $\ell/300$: 0.833
For limit of $\ell/240$: 0.667
For limit of $\ell/180$: 0.500

## FLOOR JOISTS— 70 LB LIVE LOAD

| JOIST (IN.) SIZE, SPACING | | EXTREME FIBER STRESS IN BENDING, $F_b$ (PSI) | | | | | | | | | |
|---|---|---|---|---|---|---|---|---|---|---|---|
| | | 900 | 1000 | 1100 | 1200 | 1300 | 1400 | 1500 | 1600 | 1800 | 2000 |
| 2 x 10 | 12 | 12-8 / 0.963 | 13-4 / 1.133 | 14-0 / 1.306 | 14-7 / 1.488 | 15-2 / 1.678 | 15-9 / 1.875 | 16-4 / 2.081 | 16-10 / 2.292 | 17-11 / 2.733 | 18-10 / 3.201 |
| | 16 | 11-1 / 0.840 | 11-7 / 0.984 | 12-1 / 1.135 | 12-7 / 1.294 | 13-2 / 1.459 | 13-8 / 1.631 | 14-2 / 1.808 | 14-7 / 1.992 | 15-6 / 2.376 | 16-4 / 2.783 |
| | 24 | 8-11 / 0.676 | 9-5 / 0.792 | 9-10 / 0.914 | 10-3 / 1.040 | 10-8 / 1.174 | 11-1 / 1.312 | 11-6 / 1.454 | 11-11 / 1.602 | 12-7 / 1.912 | 13-3 / 2.239 |
| 2 x 12 | 12 | 15-5 / 0.963 | 16-3 / 1.133 | 17-0 / 1.306 | 17-9 / 1.488 | 18-6 / 1.678 | 19-2 / 1.875 | 19-10 / 2.081 | 20-6 / 2.292 | 21-9 / 2.733 | 22-11 / 3.201 |
| | 16 | 13-4 / 0.840 | 14-1 / 0.984 | 14-9 / 1.135 | 15-5 / 1.294 | 16-0 / 1.459 | 16-7 / 1.631 | 17-3 / 1.808 | 17-10 / 1.992 | 18-10 / 2.376 | 19-11 / 2.783 |
| | 24 | 10-10 / 0.676 | 11-5 / 0.792 | 12-0 / 0.914 | 12-6 / 1.040 | 13-0 / 1.174 | 13-6 / 1.312 | 14-0 / 1.454 | 14-5 / 1.602 | 15-4 / 1.912 | 16-4 / 2.239 |
| 2 x 14 | 12 | 18-2 / 0.963 | 19-1 / 1.133 | 20-0 / 1.306 | 20-11 / 1.488 | 21-9 / 1.678 | 22-7 / 1.875 | 23-5 / 2.081 | 24-2 / 2.292 | 25-7 / 2.733 | 27-0 / 3.201 |
| | 16 | 15-9 / 0.840 | 16-7 / 0.984 | 17-5 / 1.135 | 18-2 / 1.294 | 18-11 / 1.459 | 19-7 / 1.631 | 20-3 / 1.808 | 20-11 / 1.992 | 22-3 / 2.376 | 23-5 / 2.783 |
| | 24 | 12-9 / 0.676 | 13-6 / 0.792 | 14-2 / 0.914 | 14-9 / 1.040 | 15-4 / 1.174 | 15-11 / 1.312 | 16-6 / 1.454 | 17-0 / 1.602 | 18-1 / 1.912 | 19-1 / 2.239 |
| 3 x 8 | 12 | 12-10 / 1.248 | 13-6 / 1.462 | 14-2 / 1.686 | 14-9 / 1.921 | 15-4 / 2.166 | 15-11 / 2.421 | 16-6 / 2.684 | 17-1 / 2.958 | 18-1 / 3.529 | 19-1 / 4.133 |
| | 16 | 11-1 / 1.084 | 11-8 / 1.270 | 12-3 / 1.465 | 12-10 / 1.669 | 13-4 / 1.883 | 13-10 / 2.103 | 14-4 / 2.333 | 14-10 / 2.570 | 15-8 / 3.067 | 16-7 / 3.592 |
| | 24 | 9-0 / 0.873 | 9-6 / 1.022 | 10-0 / 1.179 | 10-5 / 1.344 | 10-10 / 1.514 | 11-3 / 1.693 | 11-8 / 1.877 | 12-0 / 2.068 | 12-9 / 2.467 | 13-5 / 2.900 |
| 3 x 10 | 12 | 16-4 / 1.248 | 17-3 / 1.462 | 18-1 / 1.686 | 18-10 / 1.921 | 19-7 / 2.166 | 20-4 / 2.421 | 21-1 / 2.684 | 21-9 / 2.958 | 23-1 / 3.529 | 24-4 / 4.133 |
| | 16 | 14-2 / 1.084 | 14-11 / 1.270 | 15-8 / 1.465 | 16-4 / 1.669 | 17-0 / 1.883 | 17-8 / 2.103 | 18-3 / 2.333 | 18-11 / 2.570 | 20-1 / 3.067 | 21-1 / 3.592 |
| | 24 | 11-6 / 0.873 | 12-2 / 1.022 | 12-9 / 1.179 | 13-3 / 1.344 | 13-10 / 1.514 | 14-4 / 1.693 | 14-10 / 1.877 | 15-4 / 2.068 | 16-3 / 2.467 | 17-2 / 2.900 |
| 3 x 12 | 12 | 19-11 / 1.248 | 20-11 / 1.462 | 21-11 / 1.686 | 22-22 / 1.921 | 23-10 / 2.166 | 24-9 / 2.421 | 25-8 / 2.684 | 26-6 / 2.958 | 28-1 / 3.529 | 29-7 / 4.133 |
| | 16 | 17-3 / 1.084 | 18-2 / 1.270 | 19-1 / 1.465 | 19-11 / 1.669 | 20-9 / 1.883 | 21-6 / 2.103 | 22-3 / 2.333 | 23-0 / 2.570 | 24-4 / 3.067 | 25-8 / 3.592 |
| | 24 | 14-0 / 0.873 | 14-9 / 1.022 | 15-6 / 1.179 | 16-2 / 1.344 | 16-10 / 1.514 | 17-6 / 1.693 | 18-1 / 1.877 | 18-7 / 2.068 | 19-9 / 2.467 | 20-10 / 2.900 |
| 3 x 14 | 12 | 23-4 / 1.248 | 24-7 / 1.462 | 25-10 / 1.686 | 27-0 / 1.921 | 28-1 / 2.166 | 29-2 / 2.421 | 30-2 / 2.684 | 21-2 / 2.958 | 33-1 / 3.529 | 34-11 / 4.133 |
| | 16 | 20-3 / 1.084 | 21-4 / 1.270 | 22-5 / 1.465 | 23-5 / 1.669 | 24-5 / 1.883 | 25-4 / 2.103 | 26-2 / 2.333 | 27-0 / 2.570 | 28-8 / 3.067 | 30-3 / 3.592 |
| | 24 | 16-6 / 0.873 | 17-4 / 1.022 | 18-7 / 1.179 | 19-0 / 1.344 | 19-9 / 1.514 | 20-6 / 1.693 | 21-3 / 1.877 | 22-0 / 2.068 | 23-4 / 2.467 | 24-7 / 2.900 |
| 4 x 8 | 12 | 15-2 / 1.490 | 16-0 / 1.745 | 16-10 / 2.015 | 17-7 / 2.295 | 18-3 / 2.588 | 18-11 / 2.891 | 19-7 / 3.207 | 20-3 / 3.533 | 21-6 / 4.217 | 22-7 / 4.939 |
| | 16 | 13-2 / 1.300 | 13-11 / 1.533 | 14-7 / 1.757 | 15-3 / 2.002 | 15-11 / 2.257 | 16-6 / 2.522 | 17-1 / 2.799 | 17-7 / 3.082 | 18-7 / 3.676 | 19-7 / 4.306 |
| | 24 | 10-9 / 1.054 | 11-4 / 1.234 | 11-11 / 1.425 | 12-5 / 1.625 | 12-11 / 1.831 | 13-5 / 2.046 | 13-11 / 2.268 | 14-4 / 2.500 | 15-2 / 2.922 | 16-0 / 3.492 |
| 4 x 10 | 12 | 19-5 / 1.490 | 20-5 / 1.745 | 21-5 / 2.015 | 22-5 / 2.295 | 22-4 / 2.588 | 24-2 / 2.891 | 25-0 / 3.207 | 25-10 / 3.533 | 27-5 / 4.217 | 28-9 / 4.939 |
| | 16 | 16-10 / 1.300 | 17-9 / 1.533 | 18-7 / 1.757 | 19-5 / 2.002 | 20-3 / 2.257 | 21-0 / 2.522 | 21-9 / 2.799 | 22-5 / 3.082 | 23-10 / 3.676 | 25-1 / 4.306 |
| | 24 | 13-8 / 1.054 | 14-5 / 1.234 | 15-2 / 1.425 | 15-10 / 1.625 | 16-6 / 1.831 | 17-1 / 2.046 | 17-8 / 2.268 | 18-3 / 2.500 | 19-3 / 2.922 | 20-5 / 3.492 |
| 4 x 12 | 12 | 23-7 / 1.490 | 24-10 / 1.745 | 26-1 / 2.015 | 27-3 / 2.295 | 28-4 / 2.588 | 29-5 / 2.891 | 20-5 / 2.533 | 31-5 / 2.533 | 33-4 / 4.217 | 35-2 / 4.939 |
| | 16 | 20-6 / 1.300 | 21-7 / 1.533 | 22-7 / 1.757 | 23-7 / 2.002 | 24-7 / 2.257 | 25-6 / 2.522 | 26-5 / 2.799 | 27-4 / 3.082 | 28-5 / 3.676 | 30-6 / 4.306 |
| | 24 | 16-8 / 1.054 | 17-7 / 1.234 | 18-5 / 1.425 | 19-3 / 1.625 | 20-1 / 1.831 | 20-10 / 2.046 | 21-6 / 2.268 | 22-2 / 2.500 | 23-6 / 2.922 | 24-10 / 3.492 |

NOTE: The required modulus of elasticity, E, in 1,000,000 psi is shown below each span, if deflection under the live load is limited to $\ell/360$.

National Forest Products Association; Washington, D.C.

DESIGN LOAD TABLES

## GENERAL DESIGN INFORMATION

For floor construction where live loading is heavier than customarily found in residential occupancies, tabular data are provided.

The tabulated spans are based on bending strength using the live load indicated in each table heading plus a dead load of 10 psf. In calculating the required modulus of elasticity for the tabulated span, the live load only was used, since this is in accordance with established practice for design of floor joists.

## SPAN

While the effective span length for an isolated beam is customarily taken as the distance from face to face of supports plus one-half the required length of bearing at each end, it is the practice in designing joists spaced not over 24 in. apart to consider the span as the clear distance between supports.

## NET SIZES OF LUMBER

Joists are customarily specified in terms of nominal sizes, but calculations to determine the allowable span and required modulus of elasticity are based on actual sizes.

## DESIGN STRESSES

Unit design values for design of wood joists are given in the National Design Specification for Wood Construction, available from the National Forest Products Association.

## ADJUSTMENT OF MODULUS OF ELASTICITY

The modulus of elasticity values listed in the span tables for joists are those required for the tabulated spans if deflection under the live load is limited to ℓ/360. Where other deflection limits are acceptable, the tabular E values may be adjusted by multiplying them by the following factors:

For limit of ℓ/300: 0.833
For limit of ℓ/240: 0.667
For limit of ℓ/180: 0.500

## FLOOR JOISTS—80 LB LIVE LOAD

| JOIST (IN.) SIZE, SPACING | | EXTREME FIBER STRESS IN BENDING, $F_b$ (PSI) | | | | | | | | | |
|---|---|---|---|---|---|---|---|---|---|---|---|
| | | 900 | 1000 | 1100 | 1200 | 1300 | 1400 | 1500 | 1600 | 1800 | 2000 |
| 2 x 10 | 12 | 11-11 0.926 | 12-7 1.084 | 13-2 1.250 | 13-9 1.423 | 14-4 1.604 | 14-11 1.795 | 15-5 1.988 | 15-11 2.191 | 16-10 2.617 | 17-9 3.062 |
| | 16 | 10-4 0.803 | 10-11 0.941 | 11-5 1.086 | 11-11 1.236 | 12-5 1.395 | 12-11 1.561 | 13-4 1.730 | 13-9 1.903 | 14-7 2.273 | 15-5 2.662 |
| | 24 | 8-5 0.646 | 8-10 0.758 | 9-3 0.873 | 9-8 0.995 | 10-1 1.124 | 10-6 1.254 | 10-10 1.390 | 11-2 1.533 | 11-10 1.829 | 12-6 2.143 |
| 2 x 12 | 12 | 14-6 0.926 | 15-4 1.084 | 16-1 1.250 | 16-9 1.423 | 17-5 1.604 | 18-1 1.795 | 18-9 1.988 | 19-4 2.191 | 20-6 2.617 | 21-7 3.062 |
| | 16 | 11-3 0.803 | 12-7 0.947 | 13-11 1.089 | 14-6 1.236 | 15-1 1.395 | 15-8 1.561 | 16-3 1.730 | 16-9 1.903 | 17-9 2.273 | 18-9 2.662 |
| | 24 | 10-3 0.646 | 10-9 0.758 | 11-3 0.873 | 11-9 0.995 | 12-3 1.124 | 12-9 1.254 | 13-2 1.390 | 13-7 1.533 | 14-5 1.829 | 15-5 2.143 |
| 2 x 14 | 12 | 17-1 0.926 | 18-0 1.084 | 18-10 1.250 | 19-8 1.423 | 20-6 1.604 | 21-4 1.795 | 22-1 1.988 | 22-9 2.191 | 24-2 2.617 | 25-5 3.062 |
| | 16 | 14-10 0.803 | 15-7 0.941 | 16-4 1.086 | 17-1 1.236 | 17-10 1.395 | 18-6 1.561 | 19-2 1.730 | 19-9 1.903 | 20-11 2.273 | 22-1 2.662 |
| | 24 | 12-0 0.646 | 12-8 0.758 | 13-4 0.873 | 13-11 0.995 | 14-5 1.124 | 15-0 1.254 | 15-6 1.390 | 16-0 1.533 | 17-0 1.829 | 18-0 2.143 |
| 3 x 8 | 12 | 12-0 1.195 | 12-8 1.399 | 13-4 1.614 | 13-11 1.838 | 14-6 2.073 | 15-1 2.317 | 15-7 2.569 | 16-1 2.831 | 17-1 3.377 | 18-0 3.956 |
| | 16 | 10-6 1.038 | 11-0 1.215 | 11-7 1.402 | 12-1 1.597 | 12-7 1.802 | 13-1 2.013 | 13-6 2.233 | 13-11 2.459 | 14-9 2.935 | 15-7 3.438 |
| | 24 | 8-6 0.835 | 9-0 0.978 | 9-5 1.128 | 9-10 1.286 | 10-3 1.449 | 10-7 1.620 | 11-0 1.797 | 11-4 1.979 | 12-0 2.361 | 12-8 2.766 |
| 3 x 10 | 12 | 15-5 1.195 | 16-3 1.399 | 17-0 1.614 | 17-9 1.838 | 18-6 2.073 | 19-2 2.317 | 19-10 2.569 | 20-6 2.831 | 21-8 3.377 | 22-11 3.956 |
| | 16 | 13-4 1.038 | 14-1 1.215 | 14-9 1.402 | 15-5 1.597 | 16-0 1.802 | 16-7 2.013 | 17-3 2.233 | 17-9 2.459 | 18-10 2.935 | 19-11 3.438 |
| | 24 | 10-10 0.835 | 11-5 0.978 | 12-0 1.128 | 12-6 1.286 | 13-0 1.446 | 13-6 1.620 | 14-0 1.797 | 14-5 1.979 | 15-4 2.361 | 16-2 2.766 |
| 3 x 12 | 12 | 18-9 1.195 | 19-9 1.399 | 20-8 1.614 | 21-7 1.838 | 22-6 2.073 | 23-4 2.317 | 24-2 2.569 | 25-0 2.831 | 26-5 3.377 | 27-11 3.956 |
| | 16 | 16-3 1.038 | 17-1 1.215 | 17-11 1.402 | 18-9 1.597 | 19-6 1.802 | 20-3 2.013 | 20-11 2.233 | 21-7 2.459 | 22-11 2.935 | 24-2 3.438 |
| | 24 | 13-2 0.835 | 13-11 0.978 | 14-7 1.128 | 15-3 1.286 | 15-10 1.449 | 16-5 1.620 | 17-0 1.797 | 17-7 1.979 | 18-7 2.361 | 19-7 2.766 |
| 3 x 14 | 12 | 22-1 1.195 | 23-3 1.399 | 24-4 1.614 | 25-5 1.838 | 26-6 2.073 | 27-6 2.317 | 28-6 2.569 | 29-5 2.831 | 31-2 3.377 | 32-10 3.956 |
| | 16 | 19-2 1.038 | 20-2 1.215 | 21-2 1.402 | 22-1 1.597 | 23-0 1.802 | 23-10 2.013 | 24-8 2.233 | 25-6 2.459 | 27-1 2.935 | 28-6 3.438 |
| | 24 | 15-6 0.835 | 16-4 0.978 | 17-2 1.128 | 17-11 1.286 | 18-8 1.449 | 19-5 1.620 | 20-1 1.797 | 20-9 1.979 | 22-0 2.361 | 23-2 2.776 |
| 4 x 8 | 12 | 14-4 1.426 | 15-1 1.670 | 15-10 1.928 | 16-6 2.196 | 17-2 2.475 | 17-10 2.766 | 18-5 3.068 | 19-0 3.379 | 20-3 4.034 | 21-4 4.725 |
| | 16 | 12-5 1.243 | 13-1 1.457 | 13-9 1.681 | 14-4 1.915 | 14-11 2.159 | 15-6 2.413 | 16-1 2.677 | 16-7 2.948 | 17-7 3.516 | 18-6 4.119 |
| | 24 | 10-2 1.009 | 10-8 1.180 | 11-2 1.363 | 11-8 1.554 | 12-2 1.752 | 12-6 1.957 | 13-1 2.170 | 13-6 2.391 | 14-4 2.795 | 15-1 3.340 |
| 4 x 10 | 12 | 18-3 1.426 | 19-3 1.670 | 20-2 1.928 | 21-1 2.196 | 21-11 2.475 | 22-9 2.766 | 23-7 3.068 | 24-4 3.379 | 25-10 4.034 | 27-3 4.725 |
| | 16 | 15-10 1.243 | 16-8 1.457 | 17-6 1.681 | 18-4 1.915 | 19-1 2.159 | 19-10 2.413 | 20-6 2.677 | 21-2 2.948 | 22-5 3.516 | 23-7 4.119 |
| | 24 | 12-11 1.009 | 13-7 1.180 | 14-3 1.363 | 14-11 1.554 | 15-6 1.752 | 16-1 1.957 | 16-8 2.170 | 17-2 2.391 | 18-2 2.795 | 19-3 3.340 |
| 4 x 12 | 12 | 22-3 1.426 | 23-5 1.670 | 25-6 1.928 | 25-7 2.196 | 26-8 2.475 | 27-8 2.766 | 28-8 3.068 | 29-7 3.379 | 31-5 4.034 | 33-2 4.725 |
| | 16 | 19-3 1.243 | 20-4 1.457 | 21-4 1.681 | 22-3 1.915 | 23-2 2.159 | 24-1 2.413 | 24-11 2.677 | 25-9 2.948 | 27-3 3.516 | 28-9 4.119 |
| | 24 | 15-9 1.009 | 16-7 1.180 | 17-4 1.363 | 18-1 1.554 | 18-10 1.752 | 19-7 1.957 | 20-3 2.170 | 20-11 2.391 | 22-2 2.795 | 23-5 3.340 |

NOTE: The required modulus of elasticity, E, in 1,000,000 psi is shown below each span, if deflection under the live load is limited to ℓ/360.

National Forest Products Association; Washington, D.C.

**DESIGN LOAD TABLES**

## UNIT AXIAL STRESSES: SIMPLE SOLID COLUMNS—ℓ/d FROM 11 TO 30

| E | $F_c$ | 11+ | 12 | 13 | 14 | 15 | 16 | 17 | 18 | 19 | 20 | 21 | 22 | 23 | 24 | 25 | 26 | 27 | 28 | 29 | 30 |
|---|---|---|---|---|---|---|---|---|---|---|---|---|---|---|---|---|---|---|---|---|---|
| 1,800,000 | 1500 | 1475 | 1464 | 1451 | 1434 | 1413 | 1388 | 1357 | 1320 | 1277 | 1226 | 1167 | 1098 | 1020 | 938 | 864 | 799 | 741 | 689 | 642 | 600 |
|  | 1400 | 1380 | 1371 | 1360 | 1346 | 1329 | 1309 | 1284 | 1254 | 1218 | 1177 | 1129 | 1073 | 1010 | 937 | 864 | 799 | 741 | 689 | 642 | 600 |
|  | 1300 | 1284 | 1277 | 1268 | 1257 | 1243 | 1227 | 1207 | 1188 | 1155 | 1121 | 1083 | 1039 | 988 | 930 | 864 | 799 | 741 | 689 | 642 | 600 |
|  | 1200 | 1187 | 1182 | 1175 | 1166 | 1156 | 1142 | 1127 | 1108 | 1086 | 1060 | 1029 | 994 | 954 | 909 | 857 | 799 | 741 | 689 | 642 | 600 |
| 1,700,000 | 1500 | 1472 | 1460 | 1445 | 1426 | 1403 | 1374 | 1339 | 1298 | 1249 | 1192 | 1126 | 1050 | 964 | 885 | 816 | 754 | 700 | 651 | 606 | 567 |
|  | 1400 | 1377 | 1368 | 1355 | 1340 | 1321 | 1298 | 1269 | 1236 | 1196 | 1150 | 1096 | 1034 | 963 | 885 | 816 | 754 | 700 | 651 | 606 | 567 |
|  | 1300 | 1282 | 1274 | 1264 | 1252 | 1237 | 1218 | 1195 | 1169 | 1137 | 1100 | 1057 | 1007 | 950 | 885 | 816 | 754 | 700 | 651 | 606 | 567 |
|  | 1200 | 1186 | 1180 | 1172 | 1162 | 1150 | 1135 | 1118 | 1097 | 1072 | 1043 | 1009 | 969 | 925 | 873 | 816 | 754 | 700 | 651 | 606 | 567 |
| 1,600,000 | 1500 | 1468 | 1455 | 1438 | 1417 | 1390 | 1358 | 1319 | 1272 | 1217 | 1153 | 1078 | 992 | 907 | 833 | 768 | 710 | 658 | 612 | 571 | 533 |
|  | 1400 | 1374 | 1363 | 1350 | 1332 | 1311 | 1284 | 1253 | 1215 | 1170 | 1118 | 1057 | 987 | 907 | 833 | 768 | 710 | 658 | 612 | 571 | 533 |
|  | 1300 | 1279 | 1271 | 1260 | 1246 | 1228 | 1207 | 1182 | 1152 | 1116 | 1074 | 1025 | 969 | 905 | 833 | 768 | 710 | 658 | 612 | 571 | 533 |
|  | 1200 | 1184 | 1177 | 1168 | 1157 | 1144 | 1127 | 1107 | 1083 | 1055 | 1022 | 984 | 940 | 889 | 831 | 768 | 710 | 658 | 612 | 571 | 533 |
|  | 1100 | 1087 | 1082 | 1076 | 1067 | 1057 | 1044 | 1029 | 1010 | 988 | 963 | 934 | 900 | 861 | 816 | 766 | 710 | 658 | 612 | 571 | 533 |
|  | 1000 | 991 | 987 | 982 | 975 | 967 | 958 | 946 | 933 | 916 | 897 | 875 | 849 | 820 | 787 | 749 | 706 | 658 | 612 | 571 | 533 |
|  | 900 | 893 | 890 | 887 | 882 | 876 | 869 | 861 | 851 | 839 | 825 | 809 | 790 | 769 | 744 | 717 | 686 | 651 | 612 | 571 | 533 |
| 1,500,000 | 1400 | 1371 | 1358 | 1343 | 1323 | 1298 | 1268 | 1232 | 1189 | 1138 | 1079 | 1010 | 930 | 851 | 781 | 720 | 666 | 617 | 574 | 535 | 500 |
|  | 1300 | 1276 | 1267 | 1254 | 1238 | 1219 | 1195 | 1166 | 1131 | 1091 | 1043 | 987 | 923 | 851 | 781 | 720 | 666 | 617 | 574 | 535 | 500 |
|  | 1200 | 1181 | 1174 | 1164 | 1151 | 1136 | 1117 | 1094 | 1067 | 1035 | 998 | 954 | 904 | 846 | 781 | 720 | 666 | 617 | 574 | 535 | 500 |
|  | 1100 | 1086 | 1080 | 1072 | 1063 | 1051 | 1036 | 1019 | 998 | 973 | 944 | 911 | 872 | 828 | 777 | 720 | 666 | 617 | 574 | 535 | 500 |
|  | 1000 | 989 | 985 | 979 | 972 | 963 | 952 | 939 | 923 | 905 | 883 | 858 | 829 | 795 | 757 | 714 | 666 | 617 | 574 | 535 | 500 |
|  | 900 | 892 | 889 | 885 | 880 | 873 | 865 | 855 | 844 | 830 | 815 | 796 | 775 | 751 | 723 | 692 | 656 | 617 | 574 | 535 | 500 |
|  | 800 | 795 | 792 | 789 | 786 | 781 | 775 | 769 | 761 | 751 | 740 | 727 | 712 | 695 | 676 | 654 | 629 | 601 | 570 | 535 | 500 |
|  | 700 | 696 | 695 | 693 | 690 | 687 | 684 | 679 | 674 | 667 | 660 | 651 | 641 | 630 | 617 | 602 | 585 | 567 | 546 | 523 | 497 |
|  | 600 | 598 | 597 | 595 | 594 | 592 | 590 | 587 | 583 | 579 | 575 | 569 | 563 | 556 | 548 | 538 | 528 | 516 | 503 | 488 | 472 |
| 1,400,000 | 1200 | 1179 | 1170 | 1159 | 1144 | 1127 | 1105 | 1079 | 1048 | 1011 | 968 | 918 | 860 | 794 | 729 | 672 | 621 | 576 | 536 | 499 | 467 |
|  | 1100 | 1084 | 1077 | 1068 | 1057 | 1043 | 1027 | 1007 | 983 | 954 | 921 | 883 | 838 | 787 | 729 | 672 | 621 | 576 | 536 | 499 | 467 |
|  | 1000 | 988 | 983 | 976 | 968 | 957 | 945 | 930 | 912 | 891 | 866 | 837 | 803 | 765 | 721 | 672 | 621 | 576 | 536 | 499 | 467 |
|  | 900 | 891 | 887 | 883 | 876 | 869 | 860 | 849 | 836 | 820 | 802 | 781 | 757 | 729 | 697 | 661 | 620 | 576 | 536 | 499 | 467 |
|  | 800 | 794 | 791 | 788 | 783 | 778 | 772 | 764 | 755 | 744 | 731 | 716 | 699 | 680 | 657 | 632 | 604 | 571 | 536 | 499 | 467 |
|  | 700 | 696 | 694 | 692 | 689 | 685 | 681 | 676 | 670 | 662 | 654 | 644 | 633 | 619 | 604 | 587 | 568 | 547 | 523 | 496 | 467 |
| 1,300,000 | 1100 | 1081 | 1073 | 1063 | 1050 | 1034 | 1015 | 992 | 964 | 931 | 893 | 848 | 796 | 737 | 677 | 624 | 577 | 535 | 497 | 464 | 433 |
|  | 1000 | 986 | 980 | 972 | 963 | 951 | 936 | 919 | 898 | 873 | 844 | 811 | 772 | 727 | 677 | 624 | 577 | 535 | 497 | 464 | 433 |
|  | 900 | 890 | 885 | 880 | 873 | 864 | 853 | 841 | 825 | 807 | 786 | 762 | 734 | 701 | 664 | 623 | 577 | 535 | 497 | 464 | 433 |
|  | 800 | 793 | 790 | 786 | 781 | 775 | 767 | 758 | 748 | 735 | 720 | 703 | 683 | 660 | 635 | 605 | 572 | 535 | 497 | 464 | 433 |
|  | 700 | 695 | 693 | 690 | 687 | 683 | 678 | 672 | 665 | 656 | 647 | 635 | 622 | 607 | 589 | 569 | 547 | 522 | 495 | 464 | 433 |
| 1,200,000 | 1100 | 1078 | 1068 | 1057 | 1042 | 1023 | 1000 | 973 | 940 | 902 | 857 | 804 | 744 | 681 | 625 | 576 | 533 | 444 | 459 | 428 | 400 |
|  | 1000 | 983 | 976 | 967 | 956 | 942 | 925 | 905 | 880 | 851 | 817 | 778 | 732 | 680 | 625 | 576 | 533 | 444 | 459 | 428 | 400 |
|  | 900 | 888 | 883 | 876 | 868 | 858 | 845 | 830 | 813 | 791 | 767 | 738 | 705 | 667 | 624 | 576 | 533 | 444 | 459 | 428 | 400 |
|  | 800 | 791 | 788 | 783 | 778 | 770 | 762 | 751 | 739 | 724 | 706 | 686 | 663 | 636 | 606 | 571 | 533 | 444 | 459 | 428 | 400 |
|  | 700 | 694 | 692 | 689 | 685 | 680 | 674 | 667 | 659 | 649 | 637 | 624 | 608 | 590 | 570 | 547 | 521 | 492 | 459 | 428 | 400 |
|  | 600 | 596 | 595 | 593 | 591 | 588 | 584 | 579 | 574 | 568 | 560 | 552 | 542 | 531 | 518 | 504 | 487 | 469 | 448 | 425 | 400 |
|  | 500 | 498 | 497 | 496 | 495 | 493 | 491 | 488 | 485 | 481 | 477 | 472 | 467 | 460 | 453 | 444 | 435 | 424 | 412 | 399 | 384 |
|  | 400 | 399 | 398 | 398 | 397 | 396 | 395 | 394 | 392 | 390 | 388 | 386 | 383 | 380 | 376 | 371 | 367 | 361 | 355 | 348 | 341 |
| 1,100,000 | 900 | 885 | 879 | 872 | 862 | 850 | 835 | 817 | 796 | 771 | 741 | 707 | 668 | 622 | 573 | 528 | 488 | 453 | 421 | 392 | 397 |
|  | 800 | 790 | 786 | 780 | 773 | 765 | 754 | 742 | 727 | 709 | 689 | 665 | 637 | 605 | 569 | 528 | 488 | 453 | 421 | 392 | 397 |
|  | 700 | 693 | 690 | 687 | 682 | 676 | 669 | 661 | 651 | 639 | 625 | 609 | 591 | 569 | 545 | 518 | 487 | 453 | 421 | 392 | 397 |
|  | 600 | 596 | 594 | 592 | 589 | 585 | 581 | 575 | 569 | 562 | 553 | 543 | 531 | 518 | 503 | 485 | 466 | 444 | 419 | 392 | 397 |
|  | 500 | 498 | 496 | 495 | 493 | 491 | 489 | 486 | 482 | 478 | 473 | 467 | 460 | 452 | 444 | 434 | 422 | 410 | 395 | 380 | 362 |
|  | 400 | 399 | 398 | 398 | 397 | 396 | 394 | 393 | 391 | 389 | 386 | 383 | 380 | 376 | 371 | 366 | 360 | 354 | 346 | 338 | 329 |
| 1,000,000 | 700 | 692 | 688 | 684 | 678 | 671 | 663 | 653 | 641 | 626 | 610 | 590 | 568 | 542 | 513 | 479 | 444 | 412 | 383 | 357 | 333 |
|  | 600 | 595 | 593 | 590 | 586 | 582 | 577 | 570 | 563 | 554 | 543 | 531 | 517 | 501 | 482 | 461 | 438 | 411 | 383 | 357 | 333 |
|  | 500 | 497 | 496 | 494 | 492 | 490 | 487 | 483 | 478 | 473 | 467 | 460 | 452 | 442 | 432 | 420 | 406 | 391 | 374 | 354 | 333 |
|  | 400 | 398 | 398 | 397 | 396 | 395 | 393 | 391 | 389 | 386 | 383 | 380 | 375 | 371 | 365 | 359 | 352 | 344 | 335 | 325 | 315 |
|  | 300 | 299 | 299 | 299 | 298 | 298 | 297 | 296 | 295 | 294 | 293 | 291 | 290 | 288 | 285 | 283 | 280 | 276 | 273 | 269 | 264 |

## UNIT AXIAL STRESSES: SIMPLE SOLID COLUMNS—ℓ/d FROM 30 TO 50

| E | $F_c$ | 30 | 31 | 32 | 33 | 34 | 35 | 36 | 37 | 38 | 39 | 40 | 41 | 42 | 43 | 44 | 45 | 46 | 47 | 48 | 49 | 50 |
|---|---|---|---|---|---|---|---|---|---|---|---|---|---|---|---|---|---|---|---|---|---|---|
| 1,800,000 | 900 or more | 600 | 562 | 527 | 496 | 467 | 441 | 417 | 394 | 374 | 355 | 338 | 321 | 306 | 292 | 279 | 267 | 255 | 244 | 234 | 225 | 216 |
| 1,700,000 | 900 or more | 567 | 531 | 498 | 468 | 441 | 416 | 394 | 373 | 353 | 335 | 319 | 303 | 289 | 276 | 263 | 252 | 241 | 231 | 221 | 212 | 204 |
| 1,600,000 | 800 or more | 533 | 499 | 469 | 441 | 415 | 392 | 370 | 351 | 332 | 316 | 300 | 286 | 272 | 260 | 248 | 237 | 227 | 217 | 208 | 200 | 192 |
| 1,500,000 | 800 or more | 500 | 468 | 439 | 413 | 389 | 367 | 347 | 329 | 312 | 296 | 281 | 268 | 255 | 243 | 232 | 222 | 213 | 204 | 195 | 187 | 180 |
| 1,400,000 | 700 or more | 467 | 437 | 410 | 386 | 363 | 343 | 324 | 307 | 291 | 276 | 263 | 250 | 238 | 227 | 217 | 207 | 198 | 190 | 182 | 175 | 168 |
| 1,300,000 | 700 or more | 433 | 406 | 381 | 358 | 337 | 318 | 301 | 285 | 270 | 256 | 244 | 232 | 221 | 211 | 201 | 193 | 184 | 177 | 169 | 162 | 156 |
| 1,200,000 | 600 or more | 400 | 375 | 352 | 331 | 311 | 294 | 278 | 263 | 249 | 237 | 225 | 214 | 204 | 195 | 186 | 178 | 170 | 163 | 156 | 150 | 144 |
| 1,100,000 | 600 or more | 367 | 343 | 322 | 303 | 285 | 269 | 255 | 241 | 229 | 217 | 206 | 196 | 187 | 178 | 170 | 163 | 156 | 149 | 143 | 137 | 132 |
| 1,000,000 | 500 or more | 333 | 312 | 293 | 275 | 260 | 245 | 231 | 219 | 208 | 197 | 188 | 178 | 170 | 162 | 155 | 148 | 142 | 136 | 130 | 125 | 120 |

**NOTES**

1. Obtain design values for E and $F_C$ from the National Design Specification for Wood Construction.
2. Modify $F_C$ for different load duration, if applicable.
3. Calculate ℓ/d where ℓ = unsupported length of column (in.) and d = applicable least actual dimension of column cross section.
4. Determine value of $F_C'$ from table.
5. Total design load on column = cross-sectional area (sq in.) x $F_C'$ value.

National Forest Products Association; Washington, D.C.

**DESIGN LOAD TABLES**

## FLOOR AND ROOF BEAMS—DESIGN TABLES 20 POUNDS PSF

REQUIRED VALUES FOR FIBER STRESS IN BENDING (f) AND MODULUS OF ELASTICITY (E) FOR THE SIZES SHOWN TO SUPPORT SAFELY A LIVE LOAD OF 20 POUNDS PER SQUARE FOOT WITH A DEFLECTION LIMITATION OF $1/300$ 1 = SPAN IN INCHES.

| SPAN OF BEAM | NOMINAL SIZE OF BEAM | 6'-0" f | 6'-0" E | 7'-0" f | 7'-0" E | 8'-0" f | 8'-0" E |
|---|---|---|---|---|---|---|---|
| 10' | 2-3 x 6 | 1070 | 975000 | 1250 | 1138000 | 1430 | 1300000 |
| | 1-3 x 8 | 1235 | 850000 | 1440 | 992000 | 1645 | 1133000 |
| | 2-2 x 8 | 1030 | 712000 | 1200 | 831000 | 1370 | 949000 |
| | 1-4 x 8 | 880 | 606000 | 1030 | 707000 | 1175 | 808000 |
| | 3-2 x 8 | 685 | 475000 | 800 | 554000 | 915 | 633000 |
| | 2-3 x 8 | 615 | 425000 | 720 | 496000 | 820 | 566000 |
| | 2-2 x 10 | 630 | 341000 | 735 | 398000 | 840 | 455000 |
| 11' | 2-3 x 6 | 1295 | 1296000 | 1510 | 1512000 | 1730 | 1727000 |
| | 1-3 x 8 | 1490 | 1131000 | 1740 | 1320000 | 1990 | 1508000 |
| | 2-2 x 8 | 1245 | 942000 | 1450 | 1099000 | 1660 | 1256000 |
| | 1-4 x 8 | 1065 | 809000 | 1245 | 944000 | 1420 | 1078000 |
| | 3-2 x 8 | 830 | 629000 | 970 | 734000 | 1105 | 838000 |
| | 2-3 x 8 | 745 | 566000 | 870 | 660000 | 995 | 754000 |
| | 2-2 x 10 | 765 | 454000 | 890 | 530000 | 1020 | 605000 |
| 12' | 2-3 x 6 | 1545 | 1682000 | 1800 | 1963000 | 2060 | 2242000 |
| | 1-3 x 8 | 1775 | 1469000 | 2070 | 1714000 | 2370 | 1958000 |
| | 2-2 x 8 | 1480 | 1225000 | 1725 | 1429000 | 1970 | 1633000 |
| | 1-4 x 8 | 1270 | 1050000 | 1480 | 1225000 | 1690 | 1400000 |
| | 3-2 x 8 | 985 | 816000 | 1150 | 952000 | 1315 | 1088000 |
| | 2-3 x 8 | 890 | 735000 | 1035 | 858000 | 1185 | 980000 |
| | 1-6 x 8 | 755 | 604000 | 880 | 705000 | 1005 | 805000 |
| | 2-2 x 10 | 910 | 590000 | 1060 | 688000 | 1210 | 786000 |
| 13' | 1-3 x 8 | 2085 | 1867000 | 2430 | 2179000 | 2780 | 2489000 |
| | 2-2 x 8 | 1740 | 1556000 | 2025 | 1816000 | 2315 | 2074000 |
| | 1-4 x 8 | 1490 | 1334000 | 1735 | 1557000 | 1985 | 1778000 |
| | 3-2 x 8 | 1160 | 1037000 | 1350 | 1210000 | 1545 | 1382000 |
| | 2-3 x 8 | 1045 | 934000 | 1215 | 1090000 | 1390 | 1245000 |
| | 1-6 x 8 | 885 | 767000 | 1040 | 895000 | 1185 | 1022000 |
| | 2-2 x 10 | 1070 | 750000 | 1245 | 875000 | 1420 | 1000000 |
| | 1-3 x 10 | 1280 | 899000 | 1495 | 1049000 | 1710 | 1198000 |
| | 1-4 x 10 | 915 | 642000 | 1070 | 749000 | 1220 | 856000 |
| 14' | 3-2 x 8 | 1340 | 1296000 | 1570 | 1512000 | 1790 | 1727000 |
| | 2-3 x 8 | 1210 | 1166000 | 1410 | 1361000 | 1610 | 1554000 |
| | 1-6 x 8 | 1025 | 957000 | 1200 | 1117000 | 1370 | 1276000 |
| | 1-3 x 10 | 1485 | 1124000 | 1730 | 1312000 | 1980 | 1498000 |
| | 2-2 x 10 | 1235 | 936000 | 1445 | 1092000 | 1650 | 1248000 |
| | 1-4 x 10 | 1060 | 802000 | 1240 | 936000 | 1415 | 1069000 |
| | 3-2 x 10 | 825 | 624000 | 965 | 728000 | 1100 | 832000 |
| | 2-3 x 10 | 740 | 561000 | 865 | 655000 | 990 | 748000 |
| | 1-6 x 10 | 640 | 471000 | 745 | 550000 | 850 | 628000 |
| | 4-2 x 10 | 620 | 468000 | 720 | 546000 | 825 | 624000 |
| | 2-2 x 12 | 835 | 520000 | 975 | 607000 | 1115 | 693000 |
| 15' | 3-2 x 8 | 1540 | 1594000 | 1800 | 1860000 | 2055 | 2125000 |
| | 2-3 x 8 | 1390 | 1435000 | 1620 | 1675000 | 1850 | 1913000 |
| | 1-6 x 8 | 1180 | 1179000 | 1375 | 1376000 | 1570 | 1572000 |
| | 1-3 x 10 | 1705 | 1381000 | 1990 | 1612000 | 2270 | 1841000 |
| | 2-2 x 10 | 1420 | 1151000 | 1660 | 1343000 | 1895 | 1534000 |
| | 1-4 x 10 | 1220 | 986000 | 1420 | 1151000 | 1625 | 1314000 |
| | 3-2 x 10 | 950 | 767000 | 1105 | 895000 | 1265 | 1022000 |
| | 2-3 x 10 | 850 | 691000 | 995 | 806000 | 1135 | 921000 |
| | 1-6 x 10 | 735 | 580000 | 855 | 677000 | 980 | 773000 |
| | 4-2 x 10 | 710 | 576000 | 830 | 672000 | 945 | 768000 |
| | 2-2 x 12 | 960 | 640000 | 1120 | 747000 | 1280 | 853000 |
| | 1-4 x 12 | 825 | 549000 | 960 | 641000 | 1100 | 732000 |
| 16' | 2-3 x 8 | 1580 | 1741000 | 1840 | 2032000 | 2105 | 2321000 |
| | 2-2 x 10 | 1615 | 1397000 | 1890 | 1630000 | 2155 | 1862000 |
| | 1-4 x 10 | 1385 | 1197000 | 1615 | 1397000 | 1845 | 1596000 |
| | 3-2 x 10 | 1075 | 931000 | 1260 | 1086000 | 1435 | 1241000 |
| | 2-3 x 10 | 970 | 839000 | 1130 | 979000 | 1290 | 1118000 |
| | 1-6 x 10 | 835 | 704000 | 975 | 821000 | 1130 | 938000 |
| | 4-2 x 10 | 810 | 699000 | 945 | 816000 | 1080 | 932000 |
| | 1-8 x 10 | 615 | 516000 | 715 | 602000 | 815 | 688000 |
| | 1-3 x 12 | 1310 | 932000 | 1530 | 1087000 | 1750 | 1242000 |
| | 2-2 x 12 | 1090 | 776000 | 1275 | 905000 | 1455 | 1034000 |
| | 1-4 x 12 | 935 | 666000 | 1090 | 777000 | 1250 | 888000 |
| | 3-2 x 12 | 730 | 518000 | 850 | 604000 | 970 | 690000 |

| SPAN OF BEAM | NOMINAL SIZE OF BEAM | 6'-0" f | 6'-0" E | 7'-0" f | 7'-0" E | 8'-0" f | 8'-0" E |
|---|---|---|---|---|---|---|---|
| 17' | 2-2 x 10 | 1825 | 1676000 | 2130 | 1956000 | 2435 | 2234000 |
| | 1-4 x 10 | 1565 | 1437000 | 1825 | 1677000 | 2085 | 1915000 |
| | 3-2 x 10 | 1215 | 1117000 | 1420 | 1303000 | 1625 | 1489000 |
| | 2-3 x 10 | 1095 | 1005000 | 1280 | 1173000 | 1460 | 1340000 |
| | 1-6 x 10 | 945 | 844000 | 1100 | 985000 | 1260 | 1125000 |
| | 4-2 x 10 | 910 | 837000 | 1065 | 977000 | 1215 | 1116000 |
| | 1-8 x 10 | 690 | 619000 | 805 | 722000 | 910 | 825000 |
| | 1-3 x 12 | 1480 | 1117000 | 1725 | 1303000 | 1975 | 1489000 |
| | 2-2 x 12 | 1235 | 931000 | 1440 | 1086000 | 1645 | 1241000 |
| | 1-4 x 12 | 1060 | 799000 | 1230 | 932000 | 1410 | 1065000 |
| | 3-2 x 12 | 820 | 621000 | 960 | 725000 | 1095 | 828000 |
| | 2-3 x 12 | 740 | 559000 | 865 | 652000 | 990 | 745000 |
| 18' | 1-4 x 10 | 1755 | 1705000 | 2045 | 1990000 | 2340 | 2273000 |
| | 3-2 x 10 | 1365 | 1326000 | 1590 | 1547000 | 1815 | 1767000 |
| | 2-3 x 10 | 1270 | 1194000 | 1480 | 1393000 | 1695 | 1592000 |
| | 1-6 x 10 | 1060 | 1001000 | 1235 | 1168000 | 1415 | 1334000 |
| | 4-2 x 10 | 1020 | 995000 | 1195 | 1161000 | 1365 | 1326000 |
| | 1-8 x 10 | 780 | 735000 | 910 | 858000 | 1040 | 980000 |
| | 1-3 x 12 | 1660 | 1327000 | 1935 | 1549000 | 2210 | 1769000 |
| | 2-2 x 12 | 1380 | 1106000 | 1615 | 1291000 | 1845 | 1474000 |
| | 1-4 x 12 | 1185 | 947000 | 1385 | 1105000 | 1580 | 1262000 |
| | 3-2 x 12 | 920 | 737000 | 1075 | 860000 | 1230 | 982000 |
| | 2-3 x 12 | 830 | 664000 | 970 | 775000 | 1105 | 885000 |
| | 1-6 x 12 | 720 | 565000 | 840 | 659000 | 960 | 753000 |
| 19' | 3-2 x 10 | 1520 | 1560000 | 1775 | 1820000 | 2025 | 2079000 |
| | 2-3 x 10 | 1365 | 1404000 | 1595 | 1638000 | 1825 | 1871000 |
| | 1-6 x 10 | 1170 | 1179000 | 1365 | 1376000 | 1560 | 1572000 |
| | 4-2 x 10 | 1140 | 1170000 | 1330 | 1365000 | 1520 | 1560000 |
| | 2-4 x 10 | 975 | 1002000 | 1140 | 1169000 | 1300 | 1336000 |
| | 1-8 x 10 | 860 | 864000 | 1005 | 1008000 | 1145 | 1152000 |
| | 1-3 x 12 | 1850 | 1561000 | 2155 | 1822000 | 2465 | 2081000 |
| | 2-2 x 12 | 1540 | 1301000 | 1800 | 1518000 | 2055 | 1734000 |
| | 1-4 x 12 | 1320 | 1115000 | 1540 | 1301000 | 1760 | 1486000 |
| | 3-2 x 12 | 1025 | 867000 | 1200 | 1012000 | 1370 | 1156000 |
| | 2-3 x 12 | 925 | 780000 | 1080 | 910000 | 1230 | 1040000 |
| | 1-6 x 12 | 805 | 664000 | 940 | 775000 | 1070 | 885000 |
| 20' | 3-2 x 10 | 1685 | 1820000 | 1965 | 2124000 | 2245 | 2426000 |
| | 2-3 x 10 | 1515 | 1637000 | 1770 | 1910000 | 2020 | 2182000 |
| | 1-6 x 10 | 1300 | 1374000 | 1515 | 1603000 | 1735 | 1831000 |
| | 4-2 x 10 | 1260 | 1365000 | 1475 | 1593000 | 1685 | 1819000 |
| | 2-4 x 10 | 1080 | 1170000 | 1265 | 1365000 | 1445 | 1560000 |
| | 1-8 x 10 | 960 | 1007000 | 1120 | 1175000 | 1280 | 1342000 |
| | 2-2 x 12 | 1705 | 1517000 | 1990 | 1770000 | 2275 | 2022000 |
| | 1-4 x 12 | 1465 | 1300000 | 1710 | 1517000 | 1950 | 1733000 |
| | 3-2 x 12 | 1140 | 1011000 | 1330 | 1180000 | 1520 | 1348000 |
| | 2-3 x 12 | 1025 | 910000 | 1195 | 1062000 | 1365 | 1213000 |
| | 1-6 x 12 | 970 | 775000 | 1130 | 904000 | 1295 | 1003000 |
| | 4-2 x 12 | 855 | 759000 | 995 | 886000 | 1135 | 1012000 |
| 21' | 2-3 x 10 | 1670 | 1895000 | 1950 | 2211000 | 2225 | 2526000 |
| | 1-6 x 10 | 1430 | 1591000 | 1670 | 1857000 | 1905 | 2121000 |
| | 4-2 x 10 | 1390 | 1580000 | 1625 | 1844000 | 1855 | 2106000 |
| | 2-4 x 10 | 1195 | 1354000 | 1390 | 1580000 | 1590 | 1805000 |
| | 1-8 x 10 | 1050 | 1166000 | 1225 | 1361000 | 1400 | 1554000 |
| | 2-2 x 12 | 1880 | 1756000 | 2195 | 2049000 | 2510 | 2341000 |
| | 1-4 x 12 | 1615 | 1505000 | 1880 | 1756000 | 2150 | 2006000 |
| | 3-2 x 12 | 1255 | 1171000 | 1465 | 1366000 | 1670 | 1561000 |
| | 2-3 x 12 | 1130 | 1054000 | 1320 | 1230000 | 1505 | 1405000 |
| | 1-6 x 12 | 970 | 896000 | 1130 | 1046000 | 1295 | 1194000 |
| | 4-2 x 12 | 940 | 878000 | 1100 | 1025000 | 1255 | 1170000 |
| | 2-4 x 12 | 805 | 752000 | 940 | 877000 | 1075 | 1002000 |
| 22' | 4-2 x 10 | 1525 | 1816000 | 1780 | 2119000 | 2035 | 2421000 |
| | 2-4 x 10 | 1310 | 1556000 | 1530 | 1816000 | 1745 | 2074000 |
| | 1-8 x 10 | 1160 | 1341000 | 1355 | 1565000 | 1545 | 1787000 |
| | 1-4 x 12 | 1770 | 1730000 | 2065 | 2019000 | 2360 | 2306000 |
| | 3-2 x 12 | 1375 | 1346000 | 1605 | 1571000 | 1835 | 1794000 |
| | 2-3 x 12 | 1240 | 1211000 | 1445 | 1413000 | 1655 | 1614000 |
| | 1-6 x 12 | 1080 | 1031000 | 1260 | 1203000 | 1440 | 1374000 |
| | 4-2 x 12 | 1030 | 1010000 | 1205 | 1179000 | 1375 | 1346000 |
| | 2-4 x 12 | 885 | 865000 | 1035 | 1009000 | 1180 | 1153000 |
| | 5-2 x 12 | 825 | 807000 | 965 | 942000 | 1105 | 1076000 |
| | 3-3 x 12 | 825 | 799000 | 965 | 932000 | 1105 | 1065000 |

National Forest Products Association; Washington, D.C.

DESIGN LOAD TABLES   6

**FLOOR AND ROOF BEAMS**—DESIGN TABLES 30 POUNDS PSF

REQUIRED VALUES FOR FIBER STRESS IN BENDING (f) AND MODULUS OF ELASTICITY (E) FOR THE SIZES SHOWN TO SUPPORT SAFELY A LIVE LOAD OF 30 POUNDS PER SQUARE FOOT WITH A DEFLECTION LIMITATION OF 1/300 1 = SPAN IN INCHES.

| SPAN OF BEAM | NOMINAL SIZE OF BEAM | MINIMUM "f" & "E" IN PSI FOR BEAMS SPACED: | | | | | |
| --- | --- | --- | --- | --- | --- | --- | --- |
| | | 6'-0" | | 7'-0" | | 8'-0" | |
| | | f | E | f | E | f | E |
| 10' | 2-3 x 6 | 1430 | 1462000 | 1670 | 1706000 | 1905 | 1948000 |
| | 1-3 x 8 | 1645 | 1275000 | 1920 | 1488000 | 2195 | 1699000 |
| | 1-4 x 8 | 1175 | 909000 | 1370 | 1061000 | 1565 | 1212000 |
| | 3-2 x 8 | 915 | 712000 | 1070 | 831000 | 1220 | 949000 |
| | 2-3 x 8 | 820 | 637000 | 955 | 743000 | 1095 | 849000 |
| | 2-4 x 8 | 590 | 455000 | 690 | 531000 | 785 | 606000 |
| | 2-2 x 10 | 840 | 511000 | 980 | 596000 | 1120 | 681000 |
| 11' | 1-3 x 8 | 1990 | 1696000 | 2320 | 1979000 | 2655 | 2261000 |
| | 1-4 x 8 | 1420 | 1212000 | 1660 | 1414000 | 1895 | 1615000 |
| | 3-2 x 8 | 1105 | 942000 | 1290 | 1099000 | 1475 | 1255000 |
| | 2-3 x 8 | 995 | 849000 | 1160 | 991000 | 1325 | 1132000 |
| | 2-4 x 8 | 710 | 606000 | 830 | 707000 | 945 | 808000 |
| | 2-2 x 10 | 1020 | 680000 | 1190 | 793000 | 1360 | 906000 |
| | 1-3 x 10 | 1220 | 817000 | 1425 | 953000 | 1625 | 1089000 |
| 12' | 1-4 x 8 | 1690 | 1575000 | 1970 | 1838000 | 2255 | 2099000 |
| | 3-2 x 8 | 1315 | 1224000 | 1535 | 1428000 | 1755 | 1631000 |
| | 2-3 x 8 | 1185 | 1102000 | 1385 | 1286000 | 1580 | 1469000 |
| | 2-4 x 8 | 845 | 787000 | 985 | 918000 | 1125 | 1049000 |
| | 1-6 x 8 | 1005 | 905000 | 1175 | 1056000 | 1340 | 1206000 |
| | 2-2 x 10 | 1210 | 885000 | 1410 | 1033000 | 1615 | 1180000 |
| | 3-2 x 10 | 810 | 590000 | 945 | 688000 | 1080 | 786000 |
| | 2-3 x 10 | 725 | 530000 | 845 | 618000 | 965 | 706000 |
| 13' | 1-4 x 8 | 1985 | 2000000 | 2315 | 2334000 | 2645 | 2666000 |
| | 3-2 x 8 | 1545 | 1556000 | 1805 | 1816000 | 2060 | 2074000 |
| | 2-3 x 8 | 1390 | 1400000 | 1620 | 1634000 | 1855 | 1866000 |
| | 2-4 x 8 | 990 | 1001000 | 1155 | 1168000 | 1320 | 1334000 |
| | 1-6 x 8 | 1180 | 1151000 | 1375 | 1343000 | 1575 | 1534000 |
| | 2-2 x 10 | 1425 | 1125000 | 1665 | 1313000 | 1900 | 1500000 |
| | 3-2 x 10 | 950 | 750000 | 1110 | 875000 | 1265 | 1000000 |
| | 2-3 x 10 | 855 | 675000 | 1000 | 788000 | 1140 | 900000 |
| | 1-4 x 10 | 1220 | 1154000 | 1425 | 1347000 | 1625 | 1538000 |
| 14' | 3-2 x 8 | 1790 | 1944000 | 2090 | 2268000 | 2385 | 2591000 |
| | 2-3 x 8 | 1610 | 1750000 | 1880 | 2042000 | 2145 | 2333000 |
| | 2-4 x 8 | 1150 | 1250000 | 1340 | 1459000 | 1535 | 1666000 |
| | 1-6 x 8 | 1370 | 1436000 | 1600 | 1676000 | 1825 | 1914000 |
| | 2-2 x 10 | 1650 | 1404000 | 1925 | 1638000 | 2200 | 1871000 |
| | 3-2 x 10 | 1100 | 935000 | 1285 | 1091000 | 1465 | 1246000 |
| | 2-3 x 10 | 990 | 841000 | 1155 | 981000 | 1320 | 1121000 |
| | 1-4 x 10 | 1415 | 1204000 | 1650 | 1405000 | 1885 | 1605000 |
| | 1-6 x 10 | 915 | 1179000 | 1070 | 1376000 | 1220 | 1572000 |
| | 2-4 x 10 | 705 | 601000 | 825 | 701000 | 940 | 801000 |
| 15' | 2-4 x 8 | 1320 | 1537000 | 1540 | 1794000 | 1760 | 2049000 |
| | 1-6 x 8 | 1570 | 1767000 | 1830 | 2062000 | 2095 | 2355000 |
| | 2-2 x 10 | 1895 | 1726000 | 2210 | 2014000 | 2525 | 2301000 |
| | 3-2 x 10 | 1260 | 1151000 | 1470 | 1343000 | 1680 | 1534000 |
| | 2-3 x 10 | 1135 | 1036000 | 1325 | 1209000 | 1515 | 1381000 |
| | 1-4 x 10 | 1620 | 1479000 | 1890 | 1726000 | 2160 | 1971000 |
| | 1-6 x 10 | 980 | 870000 | 1145 | 1015000 | 1305 | 1160000 |
| | 2-4 x 10 | 810 | 740000 | 945 | 863000 | 1080 | 986000 |
| | 4-2 x 10 | 945 | 864000 | 1105 | 1008000 | 1260 | 1152000 |
| | 1-8 x 10 | 720 | 637000 | 840 | 743000 | 960 | 849000 |
| | 2-2 x 12 | 1280 | 960000 | 1495 | 1120000 | 1705 | 1280000 |
| | 1-4 x 12 | 1095 | 822000 | 1280 | 959000 | 1460 | 1096000 |
| 16' | 2-2 x 10 | 2155 | 2096000 | 2515 | 2446000 | 2875 | 2794000 |
| | 3-2 x 10 | 1435 | 1396000 | 1675 | 1629000 | 1915 | 1861000 |
| | 2-3 x 10 | 1290 | 1257000 | 1505 | 1467000 | 1720 | 1675000 |
| | 1-4 x 10 | 1845 | 1796000 | 2155 | 2096000 | 2460 | 2394000 |
| | 1-6 x 10 | 1115 | 1055000 | 1300 | 1231000 | 1485 | 1406000 |
| | 2-4 x 10 | 925 | 899000 | 1080 | 1049000 | 1235 | 1198000 |
| | 4-2 x 10 | 1075 | 1047000 | 1255 | 1222000 | 1435 | 1395000 |
| | 1-8 x 10 | 815 | 774000 | 950 | 903000 | 1085 | 1032000 |
| | 2-2 x 12 | 1455 | 1164000 | 1700 | 1358000 | 1940 | 1552000 |
| | 1-4 x 12 | 1250 | 999000 | 1460 | 1166000 | 1665 | 1332000 |
| | 3-2 x 12 | 970 | 776000 | 1130 | 905000 | 1295 | 1034000 |
| | 2-3 x 12 | 875 | 699000 | 1020 | 816000 | 1165 | 932000 |

| SPAN OF BEAM | NOMINAL SIZE OF BEAM | MINIMUM "f" & "E" IN PSI FOR BEAMS SPACED: | | | | | |
| --- | --- | --- | --- | --- | --- | --- | --- |
| | | 6'-0" | | 7'-0" | | 8'-0" | |
| | | f | E | f | E | f | E |
| 17' | 3-2 x 10 | 1620 | 1676000 | 1890 | 1956000 | 2160 | 2234000 |
| | 2-3 x 10 | 1460 | 1507000 | 1705 | 1759000 | 1945 | 2009000 |
| | 1-6 x 10 | 1255 | 1265000 | 1465 | 1476000 | 1675 | 1686000 |
| | 2-4 x 10 | 1040 | 1077000 | 1215 | 1257000 | 1385 | 1435000 |
| | 4-2 x 10 | 1215 | 1256000 | 1420 | 1466000 | 1620 | 1674000 |
| | 1-8 x 10 | 920 | 927000 | 1075 | 1082000 | 1225 | 1236000 |
| | 2-2 x 12 | 1645 | 1396000 | 1920 | 1629000 | 2195 | 1861000 |
| | 1-4 x 12 | 1410 | 1197000 | 1645 | 1397000 | 1880 | 1596000 |
| | 3-2 x 12 | 1095 | 931000 | 1280 | 1086000 | 1460 | 1241000 |
| | 2-3 x 12 | 985 | 839000 | 1150 | 979000 | 1315 | 1118000 |
| | 4-2 x 12 | 820 | 699000 | 955 | 816000 | 1095 | 932000 |
| | 2-4 x 12 | 705 | 599000 | 820 | 699000 | 940 | 799000 |
| 18' | 2-3 x 10 | 1695 | 1790000 | 1980 | 2089000 | 2260 | 2386000 |
| | 1-6 x 10 | 1415 | 1501000 | 1650 | 1752000 | 1885 | 2000000 |
| | 2-4 x 10 | 1170 | 1279000 | 1365 | 1492000 | 1560 | 1705000 |
| | 4-2 x 10 | 1360 | 1492000 | 1590 | 1741000 | 1815 | 1989000 |
| | 1-8 x 10 | 1040 | 1102000 | 1215 | 1286000 | 1385 | 1469000 |
| | 2-2 x 12 | 1840 | 1659000 | 2150 | 1936000 | 2455 | 2211000 |
| | 1-4 x 12 | 1580 | 1421000 | 1845 | 1658000 | 2105 | 1894000 |
| | 3-2 x 12 | 1230 | 1106000 | 1435 | 1291000 | 1640 | 1474000 |
| | 2-3 x 12 | 1105 | 995000 | 1290 | 1161000 | 1475 | 1326000 |
| | 4-2 x 12 | 920 | 829000 | 1075 | 967000 | 1225 | 1105000 |
| | 2-4 x 12 | 790 | 711000 | 920 | 830000 | 1055 | 948000 |
| | 5-2 x 12 | 735 | 664000 | 860 | 775000 | 980 | 885000 |
| 19' | 1-6 x 10 | 1570 | 1767000 | 1830 | 2062000 | 2095 | 2355000 |
| | 2-4 x 10 | 1300 | 1504000 | 1515 | 1755000 | 1735 | 2005000 |
| | 4-2 x 10 | 1520 | 1755000 | 1775 | 2048000 | 2025 | 2339000 |
| | 1-8 x 10 | 1145 | 1295000 | 1335 | 1511000 | 1525 | 1726000 |
| | 1-4 x 12 | 1760 | 1672000 | 2055 | 1951000 | 2345 | 2229000 |
| | 3-2 x 12 | 1370 | 1301000 | 1600 | 1518000 | 1825 | 1734000 |
| | 2-3 x 12 | 1230 | 1170000 | 1435 | 1365000 | 1640 | 1560000 |
| | 4-2 x 12 | 1025 | 975000 | 1195 | 1138000 | 1365 | 1300000 |
| | 2-4 x 12 | 880 | 836000 | 1025 | 976000 | 1175 | 1114000 |
| | 5-2 x 12 | 820 | 780000 | 955 | 910000 | 1095 | 1040000 |
| | 1-6 x 12 | 1070 | 995000 | 1250 | 1161000 | 1425 | 1326000 |
| | 3-3 x 12 | 820 | 771000 | 955 | 900000 | 1095 | 1028000 |
| 20' | 1-8 x 10 | 1280 | 1511000 | 1495 | 1763000 | 1705 | 2014000 |
| | 3-2 x 12 | 1520 | 1516000 | 1775 | 1769000 | 2025 | 2021000 |
| | 2-3 x 12 | 1365 | 1365000 | 1595 | 1593000 | 1820 | 1819000 |
| | 4-2 x 12 | 1025 | 1137000 | 1195 | 1327000 | 1365 | 1516000 |
| | 2-4 x 12 | 975 | 975000 | 1140 | 1138000 | 1300 | 1300000 |
| | 5-2 x 12 | 910 | 910000 | 1060 | 1062000 | 1215 | 1213000 |
| | 1-6 x 12 | 1295 | 1162000 | 1510 | 1356000 | 1725 | 1549000 |
| | 3-3 x 12 | 910 | 900000 | 1060 | 1050000 | 1215 | 1200000 |
| | 1-8 x 12 | 870 | 852000 | 1015 | 994000 | 1160 | 1136000 |
| | 1-10 x 12 | 690 | 672000 | 805 | 784000 | 920 | 896000 |
| | 4-3 x 12 | 680 | 682000 | 795 | 796000 | 905 | 909000 |
| | 2-3 x 14 | 985 | 836000 | 1150 | 976000 | 1315 | 1114000 |
| 21' | 3-2 x 12 | 1670 | 1756000 | 1950 | 2049000 | 2225 | 2341000 |
| | 2-3 x 12 | 1505 | 1580000 | 1755 | 1844000 | 2005 | 2106000 |
| | 4-2 x 12 | 1255 | 1317000 | 1465 | 1537000 | 1675 | 1755000 |
| | 2-4 x 12 | 1075 | 1129000 | 1255 | 1317000 | 1435 | 1505000 |
| | 5-2 x 12 | 1005 | 1054000 | 1175 | 1230000 | 1340 | 1405000 |
| | 1-6 x 12 | 1295 | 1344000 | 1510 | 1568000 | 1725 | 1791000 |
| | 3-3 x 12 | 1005 | 1041000 | 1175 | 1215000 | 1340 | 1388000 |
| | 1-8 x 12 | 960 | 986000 | 1120 | 1151000 | 1280 | 1314000 |
| | 1-10 x 12 | 760 | 779000 | 885 | 909000 | 1015 | 1038000 |
| | 4-3 x 12 | 750 | 790000 | 875 | 922000 | 1000 | 1053000 |
| | 2-3 x 14 | 1085 | 967000 | 1265 | 1128000 | 1445 | 1289000 |
| | 1-6 x 14 | 950 | 832000 | 1110 | 971000 | 1265 | 1109000 |
| 22' | 4-2 x 12 | 1375 | 1515000 | 1605 | 1768000 | 1835 | 2019000 |
| | 2-4 x 12 | 1180 | 1297000 | 1380 | 1513000 | 1575 | 1729000 |
| | 5-2 x 12 | 1100 | 1211000 | 1285 | 1413000 | 1465 | 1614000 |
| | 1-6 x 12 | 1440 | 1546000 | 1680 | 1804000 | 1920 | 2061000 |
| | 3-3 x 12 | 1100 | 1197000 | 1285 | 1397000 | 1465 | 1596000 |
| | 1-8 x 12 | 1055 | 1134000 | 1230 | 1323000 | 1405 | 1511000 |
| | 1-10 x 12 | 830 | 895000 | 970 | 1044000 | 1105 | 1193000 |
| | 4-3 x 12 | 825 | 909000 | 965 | 1061000 | 1100 | 1212000 |
| | 2-3 x 14 | 1190 | 1112000 | 1390 | 1298000 | 1585 | 1482000 |
| | 1-6 x 14 | 1045 | 956000 | 1220 | 1116000 | 1395 | 1274000 |
| | 3-3 x 14 | 795 | 736000 | 930 | 859000 | 1060 | 981000 |
| | 2-4 x 14 | 820 | 751000 | 955 | 1114000 | 1095 | 1001000 |

**FLOOR AND ROOF BEAMS**—DESIGN TABLES 40 POUNDS PSF

REQUIRED VALUES FOR FIBER STRESS IN BENDING (f) AND MODULUS OF ELASTICITY (E) FOR THE SIZES SHOWN TO SUPPORT SAFELY A LIVE LOAD OF 40 POUNDS PER SQUARE FOOT WITHIN A DEFLECTION LIMITATION OF $1/300$  $1 =$ SPAN IN INCHES.

| SPAN OF BEAM | NOMINAL SIZE OF BEAM | MINIMUM "f" & "E" IN PSI FOR BEAMS SPACED: | | | | | |
| --- | --- | --- | --- | --- | --- | --- | --- |
| | | 6'-0" f | 6'-0" E | 7'-0" f | 7'-0" E | 8'-0" f | 8'-0" E |
| 10' | 1-3 x 8 | 2055 | 1700000 | 2400 | 1984000 | 2740 | 2266000 |
| | 2-2 x 8 | 1710 | 1417000 | 1995 | 1654000 | 2280 | 1889000 |
| | 1-4 x 8 | 1470 | 1211000 | 1715 | 1413000 | 1960 | 1614000 |
| | 1-6 x 8 | 875 | 697000 | 1020 | 813000 | 1165 | 929000 |
| | 2-2 x 10 | 1050 | 681000 | 1225 | 795000 | 1400 | 908000 |
| | 1-3 x 10 | 1260 | 819000 | 1470 | 956000 | 1680 | 1092000 |
| | 1-4 x 10 | 900 | 585000 | 1050 | 683000 | 1200 | 780000 |
| 11' | 2-2 x 8 | 2070 | 1886000 | 2415 | 2201000 | 2760 | 2514000 |
| | 1-4 x 8 | 1775 | 1616000 | 2070 | 1886000 | 2365 | 2154000 |
| | 1-6 x 8 | 1055 | 929000 | 1230 | 1084000 | 1405 | 1238000 |
| | 2-2 x 10 | 1275 | 906000 | 1490 | 1057000 | 1700 | 1208000 |
| | 1-3 x 10 | 1525 | 1090000 | 1780 | 1272000 | 2030 | 1453000 |
| | 1-4 x 10 | 1090 | 779000 | 1270 | 909000 | 1455 | 1038000 |
| | 3-2 x 10 | 850 | 605000 | 990 | 706000 | 1135 | 806000 |
| 12' | 1-6 x 8 | 1255 | 1206000 | 1465 | 1407000 | 1670 | 1607000 |
| | 3-2 x 8 | 1645 | 1631000 | 1920 | 1903000 | 2190 | 2174000 |
| | 2-2 x 10 | 1510 | 1180000 | 1760 | 1377000 | 2010 | 1573000 |
| | 1-3 x 10 | 1820 | 1415000 | 2125 | 1651000 | 2425 | 1886000 |
| | 1-4 x 10 | 1300 | 1010000 | 1515 | 1179000 | 1735 | 1346000 |
| | 3-2 x 10 | 1010 | 786000 | 1180 | 917000 | 1345 | 1048000 |
| | 2-3 x 10 | 905 | 706000 | 1055 | 824000 | 1205 | 941000 |
| | 1-6 x 10 | 785 | 594000 | 915 | 693000 | 1045 | 792000 |
| | 2-4 x 10 | 650 | 505000 | 760 | 589000 | 865 | 673000 |
| 13' | 1-6 x 8 | 1475 | 1535000 | 1720 | 1791000 | 1965 | 2046000 |
| | 2-3 x 8 | 1735 | 1866000 | 2025 | 2178000 | 2315 | 2487000 |
| | 2-4 x 8 | 1235 | 1335000 | 1440 | 1558000 | 1645 | 1779000 |
| | 3-2 x 10 | 1185 | 1000000 | 1380 | 1167000 | 1580 | 1333000 |
| | 2-2 x 10 | 1780 | 1500000 | 2075 | 1750000 | 2370 | 2000000 |
| | 1-3 x 10 | 2130 | 1799000 | 2485 | 2099000 | 2840 | 2398000 |
| | 2-3 x 10 | 1070 | 900000 | 1250 | 1050000 | 1425 | 1200000 |
| | 1-4 x 10 | 1525 | 1537000 | 1780 | 1794000 | 2035 | 2049000 |
| | 2-4 x 10 | 760 | 642000 | 890 | 749000 | 1015 | 856000 |
| 14' | 2-4 x 8 | 1435 | 1666000 | 1675 | 1944000 | 1915 | 2221000 |
| | 3-2 x 10 | 1375 | 1246000 | 1605 | 1454000 | 1830 | 1661000 |
| | 2-3 x 10 | 1235 | 1121000 | 1440 | 1308000 | 1645 | 1494000 |
| | 1-4 x 10 | 1770 | 1605000 | 2065 | 1873000 | 2360 | 2139000 |
| | 2-4 x 10 | 880 | 801000 | 1025 | 935000 | 1175 | 1068000 |
| | 3-3 x 10 | 825 | 749000 | 960 | 874000 | 1100 | 998000 |
| | 1-6 x 10 | 1145 | 1571000 | 1335 | 1833000 | 1525 | 2094000 |
| | 1-8 x 10 | 780 | 691000 | 910 | 806000 | 1040 | 921000 |
| | 4-2 x 10 | 1030 | 936000 | 1200 | 1092000 | 1375 | 1248000 |
| | 2-2 x 12 | 1395 | 1040000 | 1630 | 1214000 | 1860 | 1386000 |
| 15' | 3-2 x 10 | 1575 | 1535000 | 1840 | 1791000 | 2100 | 2046000 |
| | 2-3 x 10 | 1420 | 1381000 | 1655 | 1612000 | 1890 | 1841000 |
| | 2-4 x 10 | 1010 | 986000 | 1175 | 1151000 | 1345 | 1314000 |
| | 3-3 x 10 | 945 | 921000 | 1100 | 1075000 | 1260 | 1228000 |
| | 1-6 x 10 | 1225 | 1160000 | 1430 | 1354000 | 1635 | 1546000 |
| | 1-8 x 10 | 900 | 850000 | 1050 | 992000 | 1200 | 1133000 |
| | 4-2 x 10 | 1180 | 1151000 | 1375 | 1343000 | 1575 | 1534000 |
| | 2-2 x 12 | 1600 | 1280000 | 1865 | 1494000 | 2130 | 1706000 |
| | 3-2 x 12 | 1065 | 854000 | 1240 | 997000 | 1420 | 1138000 |
| | 1-3 x 12 | 1920 | 1536000 | 2240 | 1792000 | 2560 | 2047000 |
| | 4-2 x 12 | 800 | 640000 | 935 | 747000 | 1065 | 853000 |
| | 2-3 x 12 | 960 | 767000 | 1120 | 895000 | 1280 | 1022000 |
| 16' | 3-2 x 10 | 1795 | 1861000 | 2095 | 2172000 | 2395 | 2481000 |
| | 2-3 x 10 | 1610 | 1676000 | 1880 | 1956000 | 2145 | 2234000 |
| | 2-4 x 10 | 1155 | 1199000 | 1350 | 1399000 | 1540 | 1598000 |
| | 3-3 x 10 | 1075 | 1117000 | 1255 | 1303000 | 1435 | 1489000 |
| | 1-6 x 10 | 1395 | 1406000 | 1625 | 1641000 | 1860 | 1874000 |
| | 1-8 x 10 | 1020 | 1031000 | 1190 | 1203000 | 1360 | 1374000 |
| | 4-2 x 10 | 1345 | 1396000 | 1570 | 1629000 | 1790 | 1861000 |
| | 2-2 x 12 | 1820 | 1551000 | 2120 | 1810000 | 2425 | 2067000 |
| | 3-2 x 12 | 1210 | 1035000 | 1410 | 1208000 | 1610 | 1380000 |
| | 4-2 x 12 | 910 | 776000 | 1060 | 905000 | 1215 | 1034000 |
| | 5-2 x 12 | 730 | 621000 | 850 | 725000 | 975 | 828000 |
| | 2-3 x 12 | 1095 | 931000 | 1280 | 1086000 | 1460 | 1241000 |

| SPAN OF BEAM | NOMINAL SIZE OF BEAM | MINIMUM "f" & "E" IN PSI FOR BEAMS SPACED: | | | | | |
| --- | --- | --- | --- | --- | --- | --- | --- |
| | | 6'-0" f | 6'-0" E | 7'-0" f | 7'-0" E | 8'-0" f | 8'-0" E |
| 17' | 2-3 x 10 | 1825 | 2010000 | 2310 | 2345000 | 2430 | 2679000 |
| | 2-4 x 10 | 1300 | 1436000 | 1520 | 1676000 | 1735 | 1914000 |
| | 3-3 x 10 | 1215 | 1341000 | 1420 | 1565000 | 1620 | 1787000 |
| | 1-8 x 10 | 1150 | 1236000 | 1340 | 1442000 | 1535 | 1647000 |
| | 3-2 x 12 | 1370 | 1241000 | 1600 | 1448000 | 1825 | 1654000 |
| | 4-2 x 12 | 1025 | 931000 | 1195 | 1086000 | 1365 | 1241000 |
| | 5-2 x 12 | 820 | 745000 | 955 | 869000 | 1095 | 993000 |
| | 2-3 x 12 | 1230 | 1119000 | 1435 | 1306000 | 1640 | 1492000 |
| | 3-3 x 12 | 820 | 737000 | 955 | 860000 | 1095 | 982000 |
| | 2-4 x 12 | 880 | 799000 | 1025 | 932000 | 1175 | 1065000 |
| | 1-6 x 12 | 1070 | 951000 | 1250 | 1110000 | 1425 | 1268000 |
| | 1-8 x 12 | 785 | 697000 | 915 | 813000 | 1045 | 929000 |
| 18' | 2-4 x 10 | 1460 | 1705000 | 1705 | 1990000 | 1945 | 2273000 |
| | 3-3 x 10 | 1365 | 1591000 | 1595 | 1857000 | 1820 | 2121000 |
| | 1-8 x 10 | 1300 | 1470000 | 1515 | 1715000 | 1730 | 1959000 |
| | 3-2 x 12 | 1540 | 1475000 | 1800 | 1721000 | 2050 | 1966000 |
| | 4-2 x 12 | 1150 | 1105000 | 1340 | 1289000 | 1530 | 1473000 |
| | 5-2 x 12 | 920 | 885000 | 1075 | 1033000 | 1225 | 1180000 |
| | 2-3 x 12 | 1380 | 1326000 | 1610 | 1547000 | 1840 | 1767000 |
| | 3-3 x 12 | 920 | 875000 | 1075 | 1021000 | 1225 | 1166000 |
| | 2-4 x 12 | 990 | 949000 | 1155 | 1107000 | 1320 | 1265000 |
| | 1-6 x 12 | 1200 | 1129000 | 1400 | 1317000 | 1600 | 1505000 |
| | 1-8 x 12 | 880 | 829000 | 1025 | 967000 | 1175 | 1105000 |
| | 3-4 x 12 | 660 | 632000 | 770 | 737000 | 880 | 842000 |
| 19' | 3-3 x 10 | 1520 | 1872000 | 1775 | 2184000 | 2025 | 2495000 |
| | 3-2 x 12 | 1710 | 1735000 | 1995 | 2025000 | 2280 | 2313000 |
| | 4-2 x 12 | 1280 | 1300000 | 1495 | 1517000 | 1705 | 1733000 |
| | 5-2 x 12 | 1025 | 1040000 | 1195 | 1214000 | 1365 | 1386000 |
| | 2-3 x 12 | 1540 | 1560000 | 1795 | 1820000 | 2050 | 2079000 |
| | 3-3 x 12 | 1025 | 1029000 | 1195 | 1201000 | 1365 | 1372000 |
| | 2-4 x 12 | 1100 | 1115000 | 1280 | 1301000 | 1465 | 1486000 |
| | 1-6 x 12 | 1335 | 1326000 | 1560 | 1547000 | 1780 | 1767000 |
| | 1-8 x 12 | 980 | 973000 | 1145 | 1135000 | 1305 | 1297000 |
| | 3-4 x 12 | 735 | 744000 | 860 | 868000 | 980 | 992000 |
| | 4-3 x 12 | 770 | 780000 | 900 | 910000 | 1025 | 1040000 |
| | 2-6 x 12 | 670 | 1329000 | 780 | 1551000 | 895 | 1771000 |
| 20' | 3-2 x 12 | 1900 | 2021000 | 2220 | 2358000 | 2530 | 2694000 |
| | 4-2 x 12 | 1280 | 1516000 | 1495 | 1769000 | 1705 | 2021000 |
| | 5-2 x 12 | 1135 | 1214000 | 1325 | 1417000 | 1515 | 1618000 |
| | 3-3 x 12 | 1135 | 1200000 | 1325 | 1400000 | 1515 | 1600000 |
| | 2-4 x 12 | 1220 | 1300000 | 1425 | 1517000 | 1625 | 1733000 |
| | 1-6 x 12 | 1620 | 1550000 | 1890 | 1809000 | 2160 | 2066000 |
| | 1-8 x 12 | 1085 | 1136000 | 1265 | 1326000 | 1445 | 1514000 |
| | 3-4 x 12 | 810 | 866000 | 945 | 1011000 | 1080 | 1154000 |
| | 4-3 x 12 | 850 | 910000 | 990 | 1062000 | 1135 | 1213000 |
| | 2-6 x 12 | 740 | 775000 | 865 | 904000 | 985 | 1033000 |
| | 1-10 x 12 | 860 | 896000 | 1005 | 1046000 | 1145 | 1194000 |
| | 2-3 x 14 | 1230 | 1114000 | 1435 | 1300000 | 1640 | 1485000 |
| 21' | 4-2 x 12 | 1570 | 1756000 | 1830 | 2049000 | 2095 | 2341000 |
| | 5-2 x 12 | 1255 | 1405000 | 1465 | 1640000 | 1675 | 1873000 |
| | 3-3 x 12 | 1255 | 1389000 | 1465 | 1621000 | 1675 | 1851000 |
| | 2-4 x 12 | 1345 | 1505000 | 1570 | 1756000 | 1795 | 2006000 |
| | 1-8 x 12 | 1200 | 1315000 | 1400 | 1535000 | 1600 | 1753000 |
| | 3-4 x 12 | 895 | 1004000 | 1045 | 1172000 | 1195 | 1338000 |
| | 4-3 x 12 | 935 | 1054000 | 1090 | 1230000 | 1245 | 1405000 |
| | 2-6 x 12 | 820 | 896000 | 955 | 1046000 | 1095 | 1194000 |
| | 1-10 x 12 | 950 | 1039000 | 1110 | 1212000 | 1265 | 1385000 |
| | 2-3 x 14 | 1355 | 1290000 | 1580 | 1505000 | 1805 | 1719000 |
| | 1-6 x 14 | 1190 | 1109000 | 1390 | 1294000 | 1585 | 1478000 |
| | 2-4 x 14 | 930 | 871000 | 1085 | 1016000 | 1240 | 1161000 |
| 22' | 4-2 x 12 | 1720 | 2020000 | 2005 | 2357000 | 2295 | 2693000 |
| | 5-2 x 12 | 1375 | 1615000 | 1605 | 1885000 | 1830 | 2153000 |
| | 3-3 x 12 | 1375 | 1596000 | 1605 | 1862000 | 1830 | 2127000 |
| | 3-4 x 12 | 985 | 1154000 | 1150 | 1347000 | 1315 | 1538000 |
| | 4-3 x 12 | 1030 | 1211000 | 1200 | 1413000 | 1375 | 1614000 |
| | 2-6 x 12 | 900 | 1031000 | 1050 | 1203000 | 1200 | 1374000 |
| | 1-10 x 12 | 1035 | 1194000 | 1205 | 1393000 | 1380 | 1592000 |
| | 2-3 x 14 | 1485 | 1484000 | 1730 | 1732000 | 1980 | 1978000 |
| | 1-6 x 14 | 1305 | 1275000 | 1525 | 1488000 | 1740 | 1700000 |
| | 2-4 x 14 | 1025 | 1001000 | 1195 | 1168000 | 1365 | 1334000 |
| | 3-3 x 14 | 995 | 981000 | 1160 | 1145000 | 1325 | 1308000 |
| | 3-4 x 14 | 680 | 667000 | 795 | 778000 | 905 | 889000 |

National Forest Products Association; Washington, D.C.

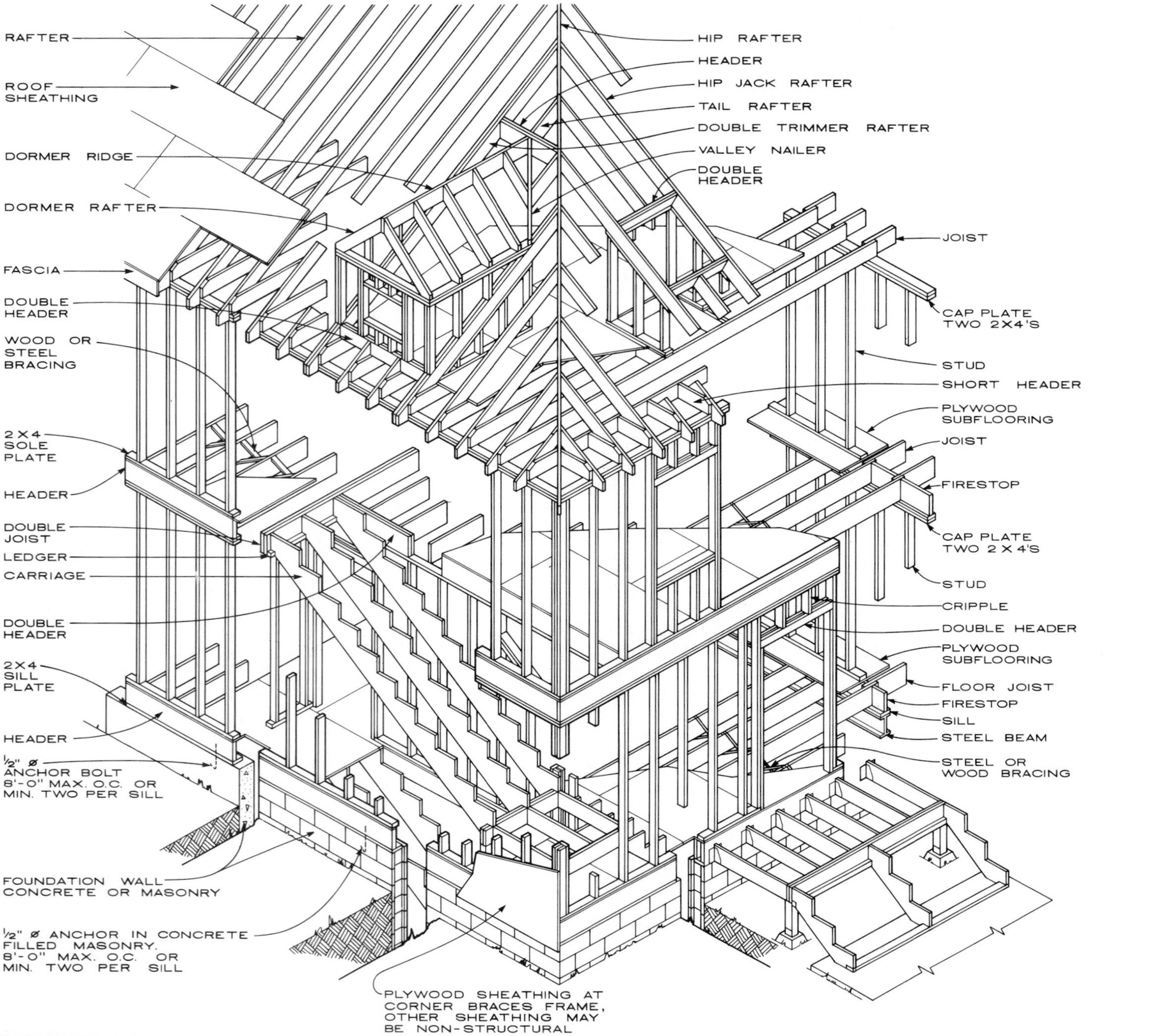

RAFTER

ROOF
SHEATHING

DORMER RIDGE

DORMER RAFTER

FASCIA

DOUBLE
HEADER

WOOD OR
STEEL
BRACING

2×4
SOLE
PLATE

HEADER

DOUBLE
JOIST

LEDGER

CARRIAGE

DOUBLE
HEADER

2×4
SILL
PLATE

HEADER

½" ∅
ANCHOR BOLT
8'-0" MAX. O.C. OR
MIN. TWO PER SILL

FOUNDATION WALL
CONCRETE OR MASONRY

½" ∅ ANCHOR IN CONCRETE
FILLED MASONRY.
8'-0" MAX. O.C. OR
MIN. TWO PER SILL

HIP RAFTER

HEADER

HIP JACK RAFTER

TAIL RAFTER

DOUBLE TRIMMER RAFTER

VALLEY NAILER

DOUBLE
HEADER

JOIST

CAP PLATE
TWO 2X4'S

STUD

SHORT HEADER

PLYWOOD
SUBFLOORING

JOIST

FIRESTOP

CAP PLATE
TWO 2 X 4'S

STUD

CRIPPLE

DOUBLE HEADER

PLYWOOD
SUBFLOORING

FLOOR JOIST

FIRESTOP

SILL

STEEL BEAM

STEEL OR
WOOD BRACING

PLYWOOD SHEATHING AT
CORNER BRACES FRAME,
OTHER SHEATHING MAY
BE NON-STRUCTURAL

## PLATFORM FRAMING

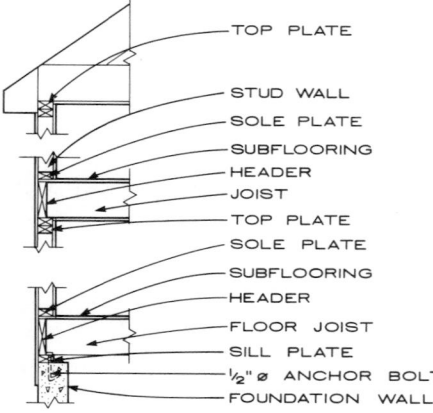

TOP PLATE
STUD WALL
SOLE PLATE
SUBFLOORING
HEADER
JOIST
TOP PLATE
SOLE PLATE
SUBFLOORING
HEADER
FLOOR JOIST
SILL PLATE
½" ∅ ANCHOR BOLT
FOUNDATION WALL

### NOTES

#### WESTERN OR PLATFORM FRAMING

Before any of the superstructure is erected, the first floor subflooring is put down making a platform on which the walls and partitions can be assembled and tilted into place. The process is repeated for each story of the building. This framing system is used frequently .

#### FIRESTOPPING

All concealed spaces in framing, with the exception of areas around flues and chimneys, are to be fitted with 2 in. blocking arranged to prevent drafts between spaces.

#### EXTERIOR WALL FRAMING

One story buildings: 2 x 4's, 16 in. or 24 in. o.c.;
2 x 6's, 24 in. o.c.
Two and three stories: 2 x 4's, 16 in. o.c.;
2 x 6's, 24 in. o.c.

#### BRACING EXTERIOR WALLS

Because floor framing and wall frames do not interlock, adequate sheathing must act as bracing and provide the necessary lateral resistance. Where required for additional stiffness or bracing, 1 x 4's may be let into outer face of studs at 45° angle secured at top, bottom, and to studs.

#### BRIDGING FOR FLOOR JOISTS

May be omitted when flooring is nailed adequately to joist; however, where nominal depth-to-thickness ratio of joists exceeds 6, bridging would be installed at 8 ft. 0 in. intervals. Building codes may allow omission of bridging under certain conditions.

Steel bridging is available. Some types do not require nails.

Timothy B. McDonald; Washington, D.C.

**ROUGH CARPENTRY**

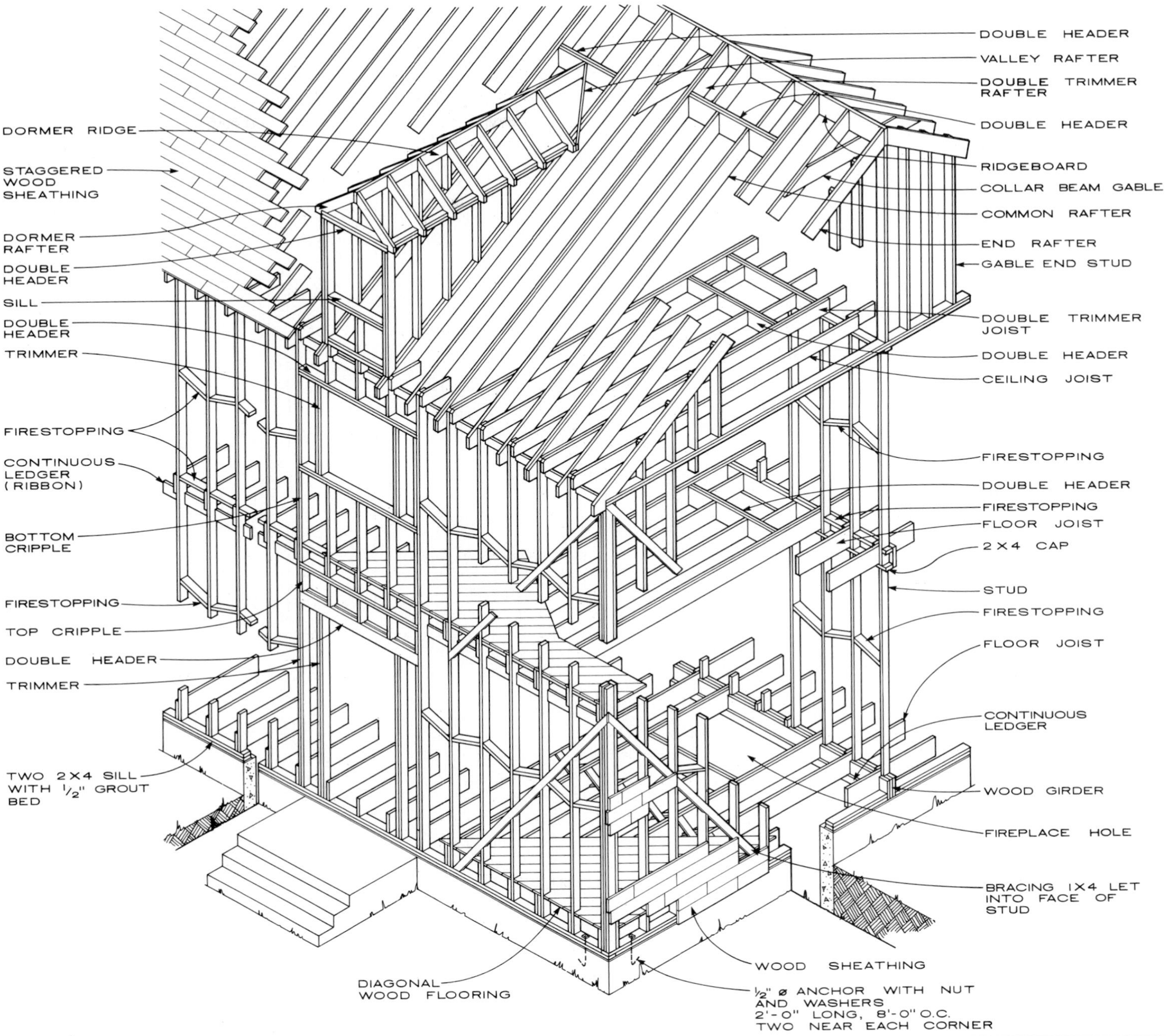

DORMER RIDGE

STAGGERED WOOD SHEATHING

DORMER RAFTER

DOUBLE HEADER

SILL

DOUBLE HEADER

TRIMMER

FIRESTOPPING

CONTINUOUS LEDGER (RIBBON)

BOTTOM CRIPPLE

FIRESTOPPING

TOP CRIPPLE

DOUBLE HEADER

TRIMMER

TWO 2×4 SILL WITH ½" GROUT BED

DIAGONAL WOOD FLOORING

DOUBLE HEADER

VALLEY RAFTER

DOUBLE TRIMMER RAFTER

DOUBLE HEADER

RIDGEBOARD

COLLAR BEAM GABLE

COMMON RAFTER

END RAFTER

GABLE END STUD

DOUBLE TRIMMER JOIST

DOUBLE HEADER

CEILING JOIST

FIRESTOPPING

DOUBLE HEADER

FIRESTOPPING

FLOOR JOIST

2×4 CAP

STUD

FIRESTOPPING

FLOOR JOIST

CONTINUOUS LEDGER

WOOD GIRDER

FIREPLACE HOLE

BRACING 1×4 LET INTO FACE OF STUD

WOOD SHEATHING

½" ⌀ ANCHOR WITH NUT AND WASHERS 2'-0" LONG, 8'-0" O.C. TWO NEAR EACH CORNER

## BALLOON FRAMING

### NOTES

### BALLOON FRAMING

Balloon Framing's principal characteristics are that wall studs and joists rest on an anchored sill, with the studs extending in one continuous piece from sill to roof. At the second floor level a ribbon is let into the studs. The floor joists rest on the ribbon and are fastened to the studs: supporting and tying the structure together. This type of framing can be found in older structures and is generally not used today.

### FIRESTOPPING

The flue effect created by continuous studs from sill to roof make firestopping mandatory in this type of framing. Firestopping is provided at each floor level and at the mid wall level.

### TYPICAL EXTERIOR WALL FRAMING

One story: 2 x 4's 16 in. o.c.
Two story: 2 x 4's 16 in. o.c.

Timothy B. McDonald; Washington, D.C.

### BRACING EXTERIOR WALLS

There are no braces in the balloon frame itself; hence, two methods are used to provide lateral rigidity. Previously diagonal sheathing was used. The other method, sometimes used in conjunction with diagonal sheathing, is to let continuous 1 x 4's into the outer face of corner studs at a 45° angle, and fastened top, bottom, and to the studs.

### BRIDGING FOR FLOOR JOISTS

May be omitted when flooring is properly nailed to joists. However, where nominal depth-to-thickness ratio of joists exceeds 6 bridging should be installed at 8 ft 0 in. intervals. (F.H.A. also allows omission of bridging under certain conditions—see F.H.A. publication No. 300, revised 1965.)

Steel bridging is available. Some types do not require nails.

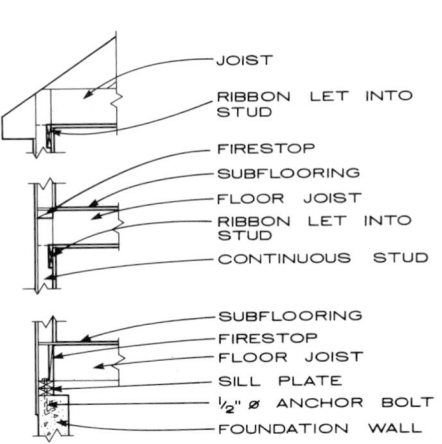

JOIST

RIBBON LET INTO STUD

FIRESTOP

SUBFLOORING

FLOOR JOIST

RIBBON LET INTO STUD

CONTINUOUS STUD

SUBFLOORING

FIRESTOP

FLOOR JOIST

SILL PLATE

½" ⌀ ANCHOR BOLT

FOUNDATION WALL

## ROUGH CARPENTRY

6

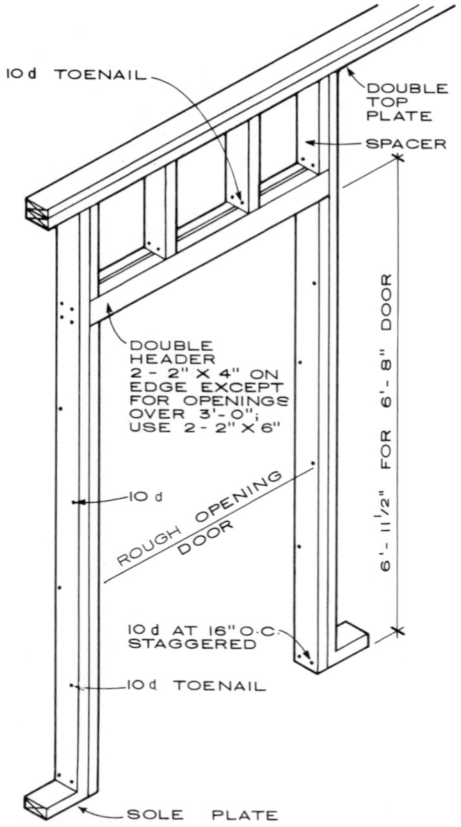

10 d TOENAIL

DOUBLE TOP PLATE

SPACER

DOUBLE HEADER 2 - 2" X 4" ON EDGE EXCEPT FOR OPENINGS OVER 3'- 0"; USE 2 - 2" X 6"

6'- 11 1/2" FOR 6'- 8" DOOR

10 d

ROUGH OPENING DOOR

10 d AT 16" O.C. STAGGERED

10 d TOENAIL

SOLE PLATE

**DOOR OPENING**

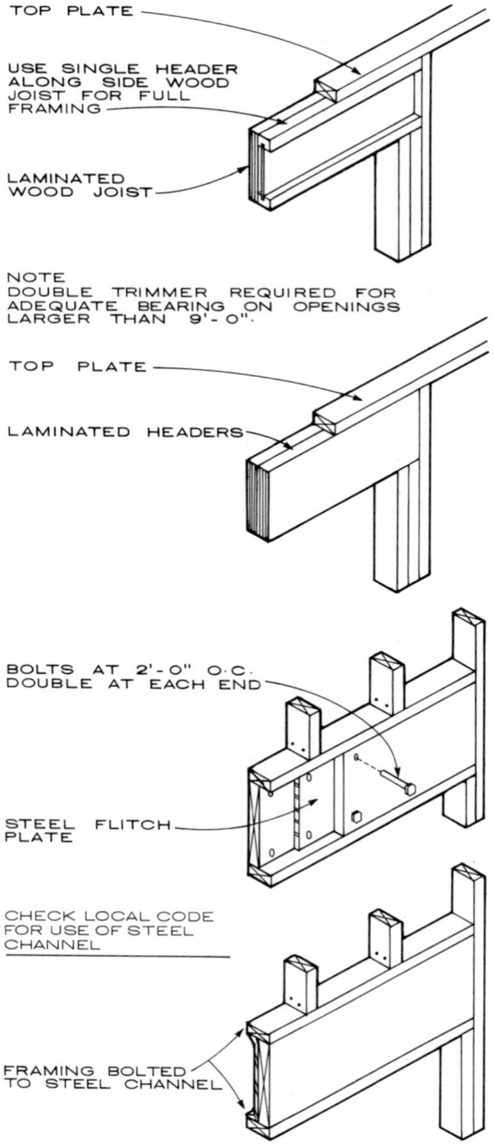

TOP PLATE

USE SINGLE HEADER ALONG SIDE WOOD JOIST FOR FULL FRAMING

LAMINATED WOOD JOIST

NOTE
DOUBLE TRIMMER REQUIRED FOR ADEQUATE BEARING ON OPENINGS LARGER THAN 9'- 0".

TOP PLATE

LAMINATED HEADERS

BOLTS AT 2'- 0" O.C. DOUBLE AT EACH END

STEEL FLITCH PLATE

CHECK LOCAL CODE FOR USE OF STEEL CHANNEL

FRAMING BOLTED TO STEEL CHANNEL

**LINTELS FOR WIDE OPENINGS**

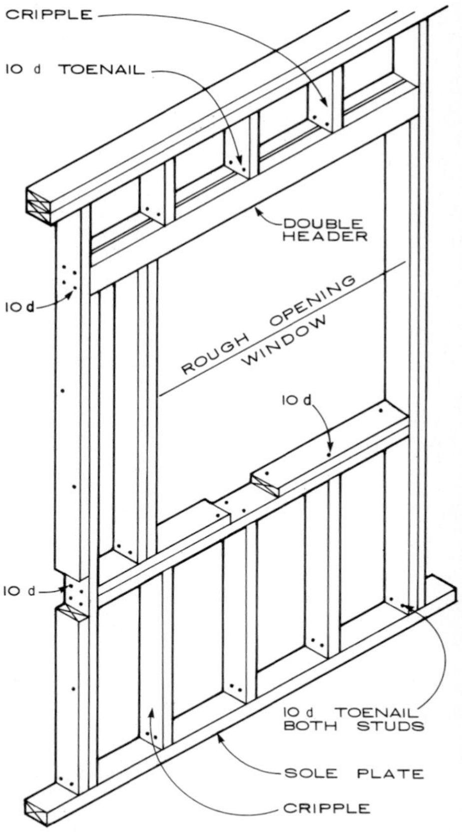

CRIPPLE

10 d TOENAIL

DOUBLE HEADER

10 d

ROUGH OPENING WINDOW

10 d

10 d

10 d TOENAIL BOTH STUDS

SOLE PLATE

CRIPPLE

**WINDOW OPENING**

**NOTES**

1. Steel lintels are selected from steel beam design tables on the basis of floor, wall, and roof openings.
2. Wood lintels over openings in bearing walls may be engineered as beams.
3. Composite beams, such as glued laminated beams, also are appropriate in some applications. Plywood box beams are used for garage doors. Steel flitch plates can add strength without adding extra width to a composite beam.
4. Check with local codes and standards for fire resistance requirements.

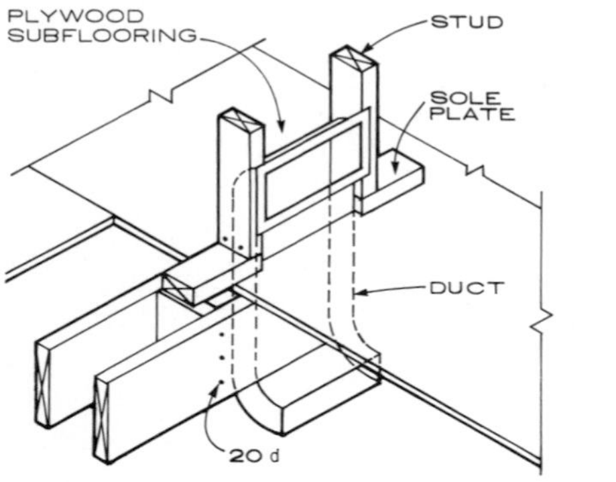

PLYWOOD SUBFLOORING

STUD

SOLE PLATE

DUCT

20 d

**SMALL OPENING**

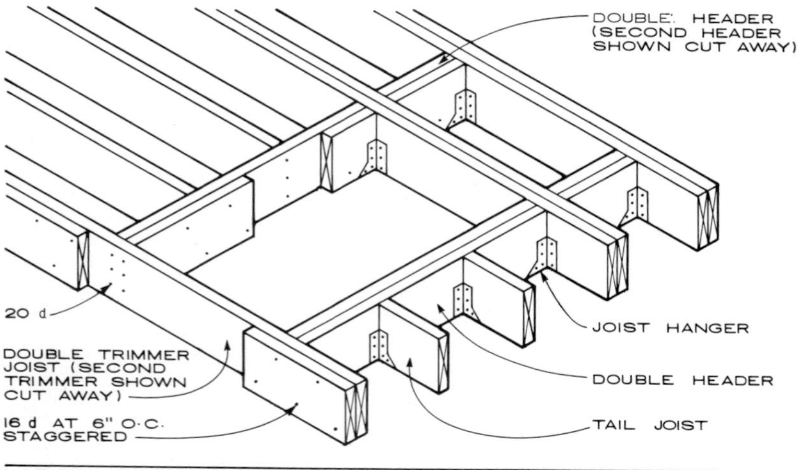

DOUBLE HEADER (SECOND HEADER SHOWN CUT AWAY)

20 d

DOUBLE TRIMMER JOIST (SECOND TRIMMER SHOWN CUT AWAY)

16 d AT 6" O.C. STAGGERED

JOIST HANGER

DOUBLE HEADER

TAIL JOIST

**LARGE OPENING REMOVED FROM BEARING WALLS**

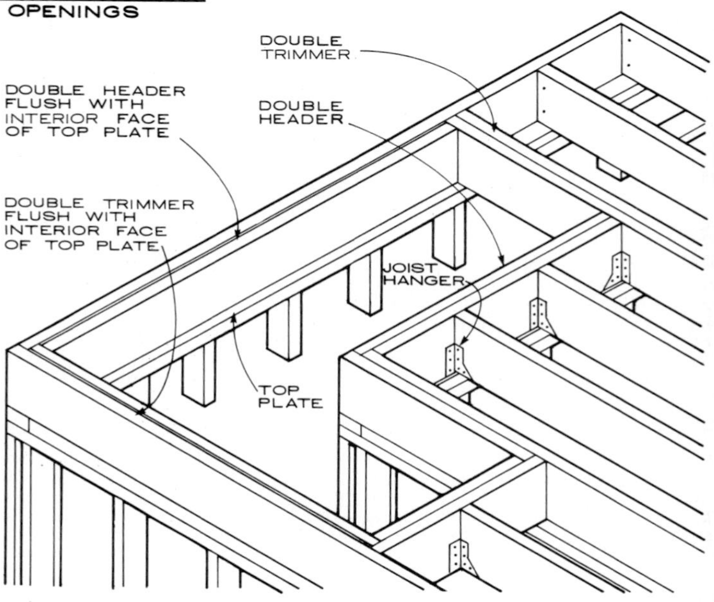

DOUBLE TRIMMER

DOUBLE HEADER

DOUBLE HEADER FLUSH WITH INTERIOR FACE OF TOP PLATE

DOUBLE TRIMMER FLUSH WITH INTERIOR FACE OF TOP PLATE

JOIST HANGER

TOP PLATE

**STAIR OPENING AT EXTERIOR WALL**

Joseph A. Wilkes, FAIA; Wilkes and Faulkner; Washington, D.C.

**6    ROUGH CARPENTRY**

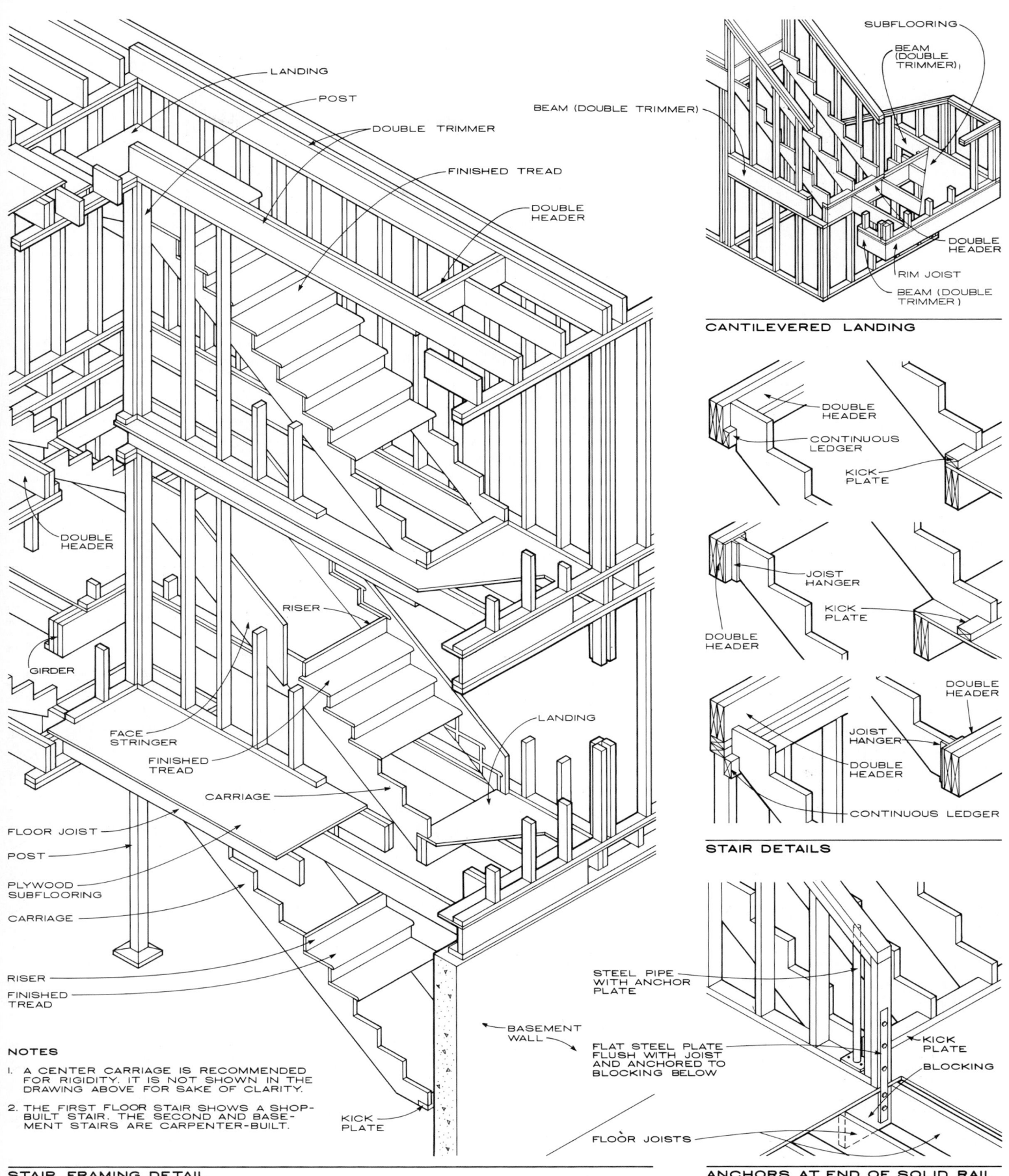

SUBFLOORING

BEAM (DOUBLE TRIMMER)

BEAM (DOUBLE TRIMMER)

DOUBLE HEADER

RIM JOIST

BEAM (DOUBLE TRIMMER)

**CANTILEVERED LANDING**

DOUBLE HEADER

CONTINUOUS LEDGER

KICK PLATE

JOIST HANGER

KICK PLATE

DOUBLE HEADER

DOUBLE HEADER

JOIST HANGER

DOUBLE HEADER

CONTINUOUS LEDGER

**STAIR DETAILS**

STEEL PIPE WITH ANCHOR PLATE

FLAT STEEL PLATE FLUSH WITH JOIST AND ANCHORED TO BLOCKING BELOW

KICK PLATE

BLOCKING

FLOOR JOISTS

**ANCHORS AT END OF SOLID RAIL**

LANDING

POST

DOUBLE TRIMMER

FINISHED TREAD

DOUBLE HEADER

DOUBLE HEADER

RISER

GIRDER

FACE STRINGER

FINISHED TREAD

CARRIAGE

LANDING

FLOOR JOIST

POST

PLYWOOD SUBFLOORING

CARRIAGE

RISER

FINISHED TREAD

BASEMENT WALL

KICK PLATE

**NOTES**

1. A CENTER CARRIAGE IS RECOMMENDED FOR RIGIDITY. IT IS NOT SHOWN IN THE DRAWING ABOVE FOR SAKE OF CLARITY.

2. THE FIRST FLOOR STAIR SHOWS A SHOP-BUILT STAIR. THE SECOND AND BASE-MENT STAIRS ARE CARPENTER-BUILT.

**STAIR FRAMING DETAIL**

Timothy B. McDonald; Washington, D.C.

**ROUGH CARPENTRY**    6

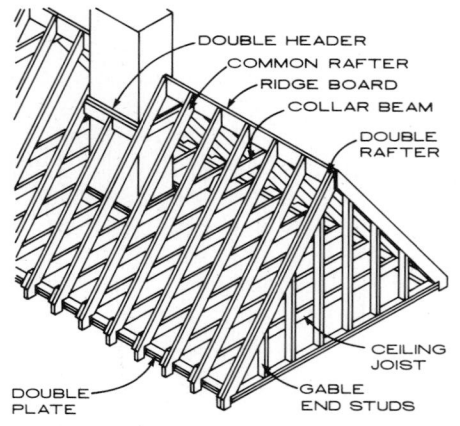

**GABLE ROOF**

DOUBLE HEADER
COMMON RAFTER
RIDGE BOARD
COLLAR BEAM
DOUBLE RAFTER
CEILING JOIST
DOUBLE PLATE
GABLE END STUDS

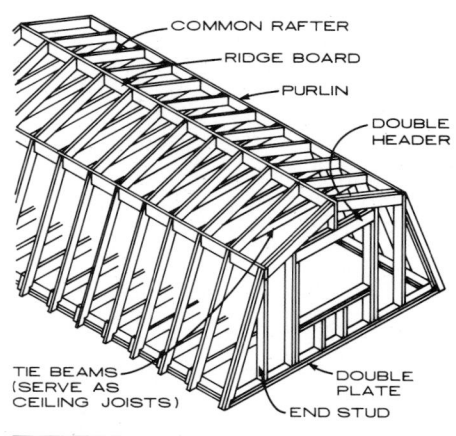

**GAMBREL ROOF**

COMMON RAFTER
RIDGE BOARD
PURLIN
DOUBLE HEADER
TIE BEAMS (SERVE AS CEILING JOISTS)
DOUBLE PLATE
END STUD

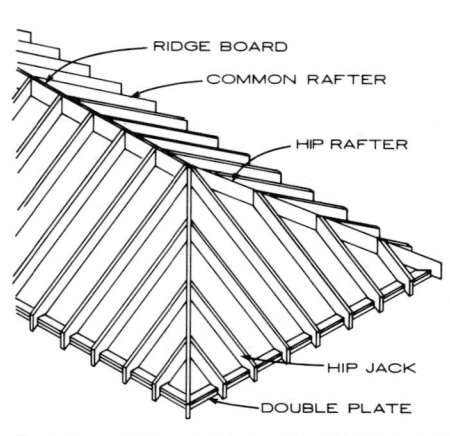

**HIP ROOF**

RIDGE BOARD
COMMON RAFTER
HIP RAFTER
HIP JACK
DOUBLE PLATE

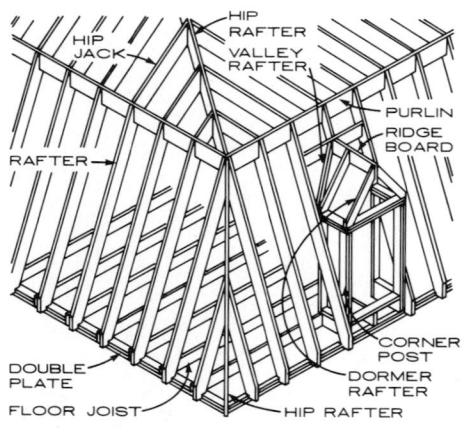

**MANSARD ROOF**

HIP RAFTER
HIP JACK
VALLEY RAFTER
PURLIN
RIDGE BOARD
RAFTER
CORNER POST
DORMER RAFTER
DOUBLE PLATE
FLOOR JOIST
HIP RAFTER

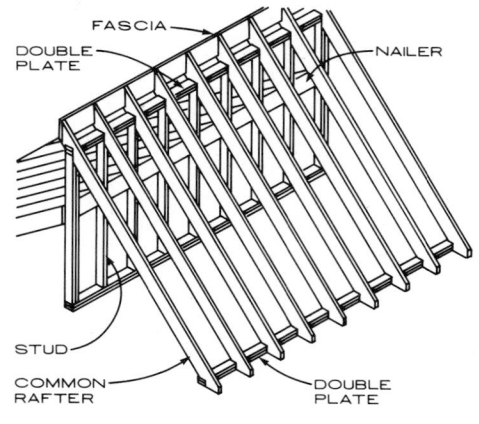

**SHED ROOF**

FASCIA
DOUBLE PLATE
NAILER
STUD
COMMON RAFTER
DOUBLE PLATE

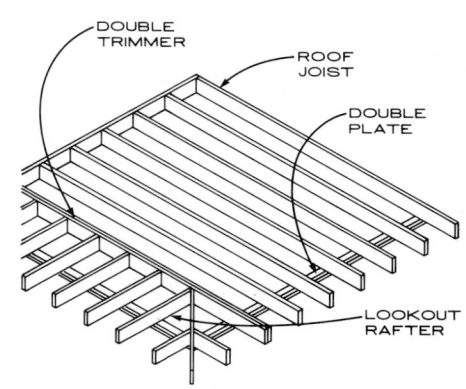

**FLAT ROOF**

DOUBLE TRIMMER
ROOF JOIST
DOUBLE PLATE
LOOKOUT RAFTER

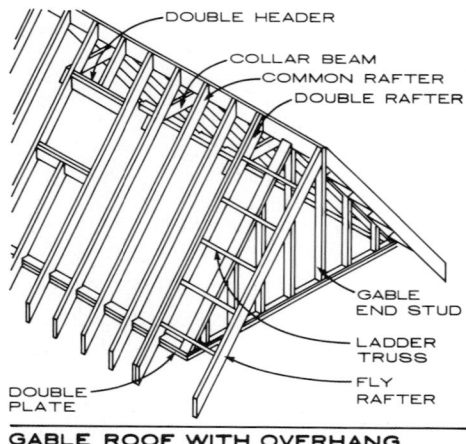

**GABLE ROOF WITH OVERHANG**

DOUBLE HEADER
COLLAR BEAM
COMMON RAFTER
DOUBLE RAFTER
GABLE END STUD
LADDER TRUSS
DOUBLE PLATE
FLY RAFTER

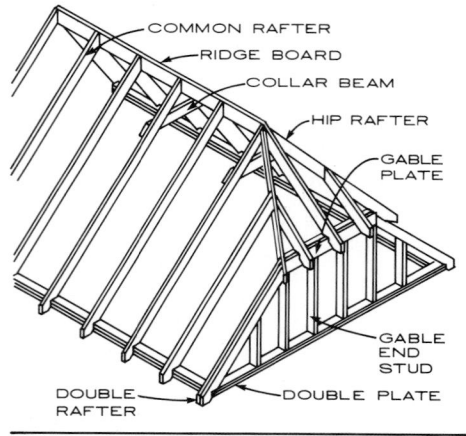

**HIP GABLE ROOF**

COMMON RAFTER
RIDGE BOARD
COLLAR BEAM
HIP RAFTER
GABLE PLATE
GABLE END STUD
DOUBLE RAFTER
DOUBLE PLATE

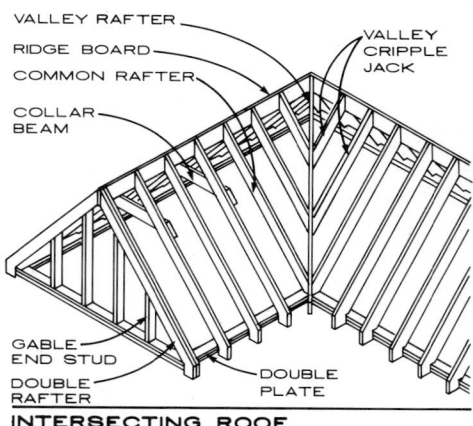

**INTERSECTING ROOF**

VALLEY RAFTER
RIDGE BOARD
COMMON RAFTER
COLLAR BEAM
VALLEY CRIPPLE JACK
GABLE END STUD
DOUBLE RAFTER
DOUBLE PLATE

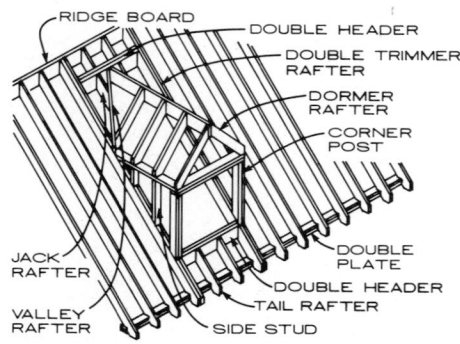

**DORMER**

RIDGE BOARD
DOUBLE HEADER
DOUBLE TRIMMER RAFTER
DORMER RAFTER
CORNER POST
JACK RAFTER
DOUBLE PLATE
DOUBLE HEADER
VALLEY RAFTER
TAIL RAFTER
SIDE STUD

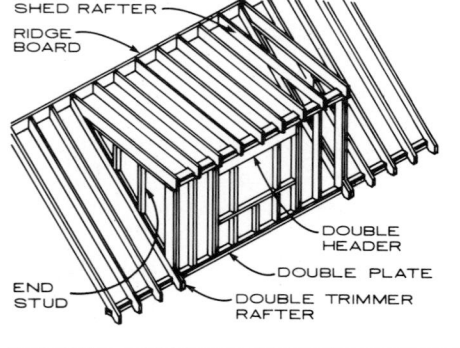

**SMALL SHED DORMER**

SHED RAFTER
RIDGE BOARD
DOUBLE HEADER
DOUBLE PLATE
END STUD
DOUBLE TRIMMER RAFTER

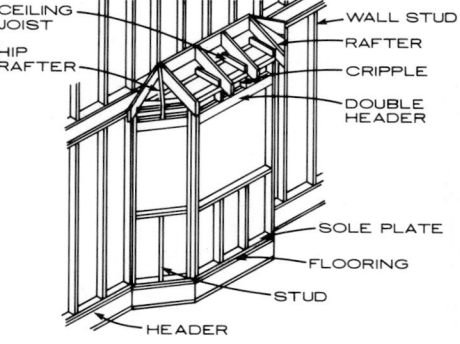

**BAY WINDOW**

CEILING JOIST
HIP RAFTER
WALL STUD
RAFTER
CRIPPLE
DOUBLE HEADER
SOLE PLATE
FLOORING
STUD
HEADER

Timothy B. McDonald; Washington, D.C.

 **ROUGH CARPENTRY**

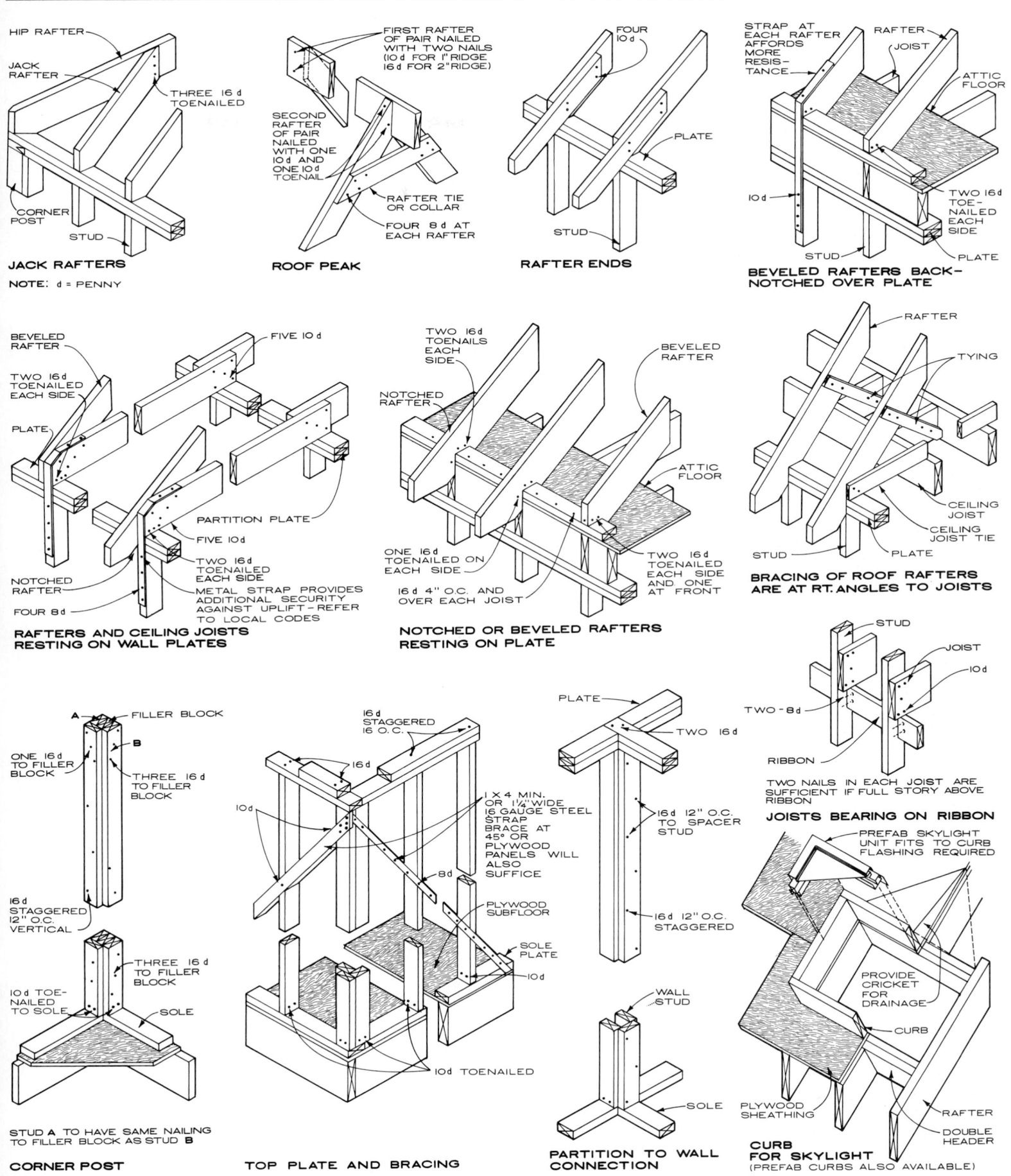

**JACK RAFTERS**

HIP RAFTER
JACK RAFTER
THREE 16 d TOENAILED
CORNER POST
STUD

NOTE: d = PENNY

**ROOF PEAK**

FIRST RAFTER OF PAIR NAILED WITH TWO NAILS (10 d FOR 1" RIDGE 16 d FOR 2" RIDGE)
SECOND RAFTER OF PAIR NAILED WITH ONE 10 d AND ONE 10 d TOENAIL
RAFTER TIE OR COLLAR
FOUR 8 d AT EACH RAFTER

**RAFTER ENDS**

FOUR 10 d
PLATE
STUD

**BEVELED RAFTERS BACK-NOTCHED OVER PLATE**

STRAP AT EACH RAFTER AFFORDS MORE RESISTANCE
RAFTER
JOIST
ATTIC FLOOR
10 d
TWO 16 d TOE-NAILED EACH SIDE
STUD
PLATE

**RAFTERS AND CEILING JOISTS RESTING ON WALL PLATES**

BEVELED RAFTER
TWO 16 d TOENAILED EACH SIDE
PLATE
NOTCHED RAFTER
FOUR 8 d
FIVE 10 d
PARTITION PLATE
FIVE 10 d
TWO 16 d TOENAILED EACH SIDE
METAL STRAP PROVIDES ADDITIONAL SECURITY AGAINST UPLIFT - REFER TO LOCAL CODES

**NOTCHED OR BEVELED RAFTERS RESTING ON PLATE**

TWO 16 d TOENAILS EACH SIDE
NOTCHED RAFTER
BEVELED RAFTER
ATTIC FLOOR
ONE 16 d TOENAILED ON EACH SIDE
16 d 4" O.C. AND OVER EACH JOIST
TWO 16 d TOENAILED EACH SIDE AND ONE AT FRONT

**BRACING OF ROOF RAFTERS ARE AT RT. ANGLES TO JOISTS**

RAFTER
TYING
CEILING JOIST
CEILING JOIST TIE
STUD
PLATE

**CORNER POST**

A
FILLER BLOCK
B
ONE 16 d TO FILLER BLOCK
THREE 16 d TO FILLER BLOCK
16 d STAGGERED 12" O.C. VERTICAL
THREE 16 d TO FILLER BLOCK
10 d TOE-NAILED TO SOLE
SOLE

STUD **A** TO HAVE SAME NAILING TO FILLER BLOCK AS STUD **B**

**TOP PLATE AND BRACING**

16 d STAGGERED 16 O.C.
16 d
10 d
1 X 4 MIN. OR 1¼ WIDE 16 GAUGE STEEL STRAP BRACE AT 45° OR PLYWOOD PANELS WILL ALSO SUFFICE
8 d
PLYWOOD SUBFLOOR
SOLE PLATE
10 d
10 d TOENAILED

**PARTITION TO WALL CONNECTION**

PLATE
TWO 16 d
16 d 12" O.C. TO SPACER STUD
16 d 12" O.C. STAGGERED
WALL STUD
SOLE

**JOISTS BEARING ON RIBBON**

STUD
JOIST
10 d
TWO - 8 d
RIBBON
TWO NAILS IN EACH JOIST ARE SUFFICIENT IF FULL STORY ABOVE RIBBON

**CURB FOR SKYLIGHT**
(PREFAB CURBS ALSO AVAILABLE)

PREFAB SKYLIGHT UNIT FITS TO CURB FLASHING REQUIRED
PROVIDE CRICKET FOR DRAINAGE
CURB
PLYWOOD SHEATHING
RAFTER
DOUBLE HEADER

Joseph A. Wilkes, FAIA; Wilkes and Faulkner; Washington, D.C.

**ROUGH CARPENTRY**     6

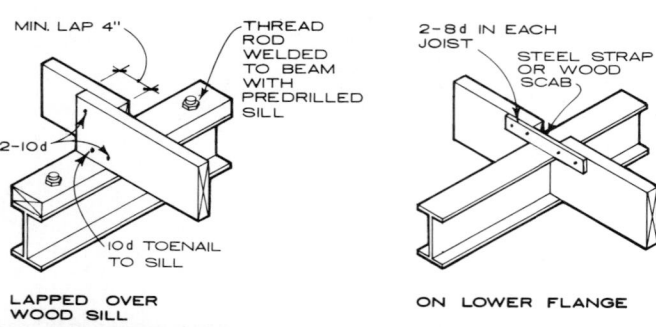

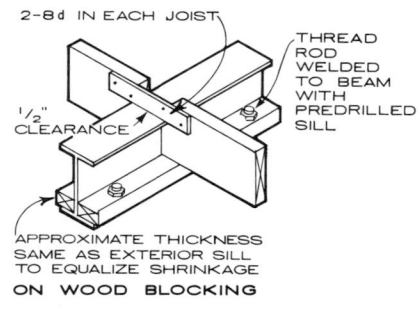

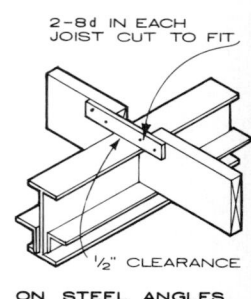

LAPPED OVER
WOOD SILL

ON LOWER FLANGE

ON WOOD BLOCKING

ON STEEL ANGLES

## WOOD JOISTS SUPPORTED ON STEEL GIRDERS

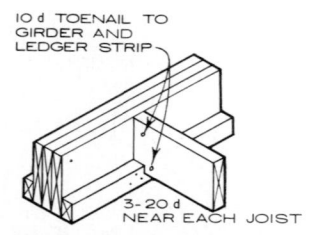

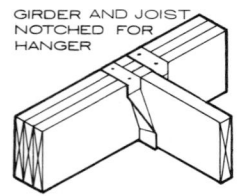

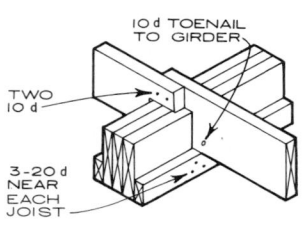

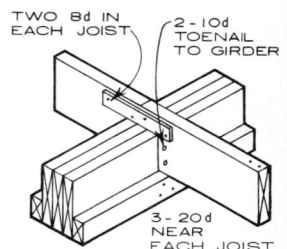

JOIST NOTCHED OVER
LEDGER STRIP
NOTCHING OVER BEARING
NOT RECOMMENDED

JOIST IN JOIST
HANGER IRON
ALSO CALLED STIRRUP
OR BRIDLE IRON

OVERLAPPING JOISTS
NOTCHED OVER GIRDER
BEARING ONLY ON LEDGER,
NOT ON TOP OF GIRDER

JOISTS NOTCHED
OVER GIRDER
BEARING ONLY ON
LEDGER, NOT ON TOP
OF GIRDER

## WOOD JOISTS SUPPORTED ON WOOD GIRDERS

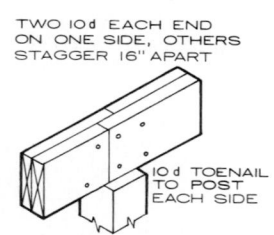

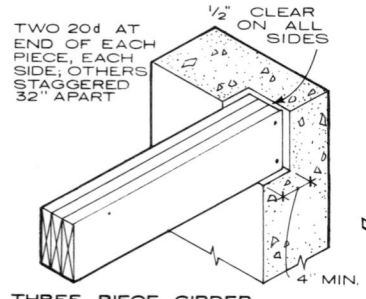

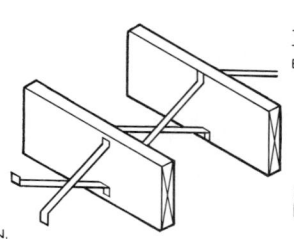

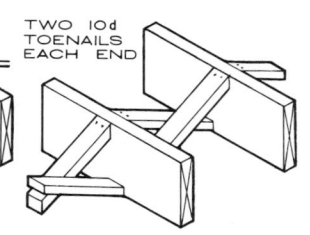

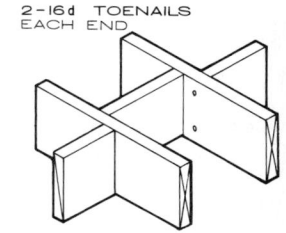

TWO PIECE GIRDER
GIRDER JOINTS ONLY
AT SUPPORTS
STAGGER JOINTS

THREE PIECE GIRDER
FOR FOUR PIECE GIRDER: ADD
NAILS

STEEL BRIDGING
SOME HAVE BUILT-IN
TEETH, NEEDS NO
NAILS

1" X 3" CROSS BRIDGING
LOWER ENDS NOT NAILED,
UNTIL SUBFLOORING
IS LAYED

SOLID BRIDGING
USED UNDER PARTITIONS
FOR HEAVY LOADING
STAGGER BOARDS FOR
EASE OF NAILING

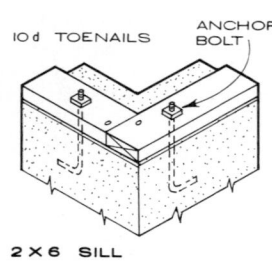

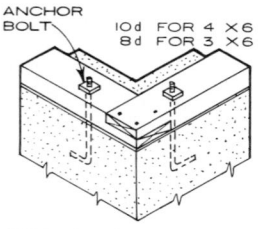

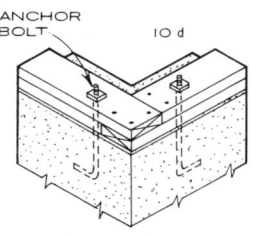

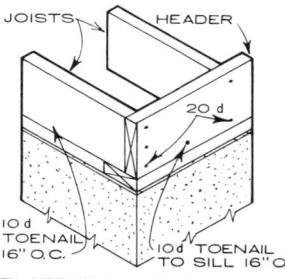

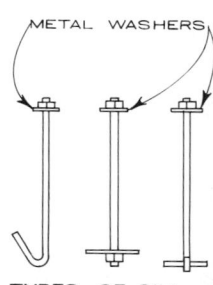

2 X 6 SILL

3 X 6, 4 X 6 SILL
HALVED AT CORNERS

4 X 6 DOUBLE SILL
NAILS STAGGERED ALONG
SILL 24" ON CENTER

PLATFORM FRAMING
TOENAIL TO SILL NOT
REQUIRED IF DIAGONAL
SHEATHING USED

TYPES OF SILL
ANCHOR BOLTS

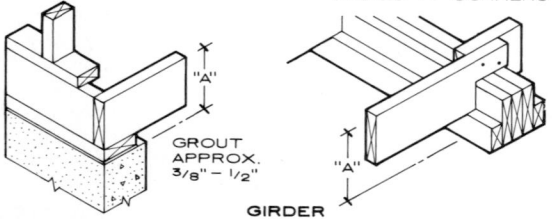

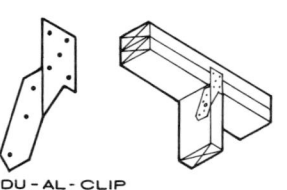

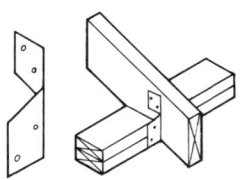

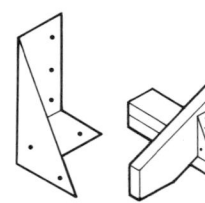

SHRINKAGE
SELECT JOIST-GIRDER DETAIL THAT HAS
APPROXIMATE SAME SHRINKAGE "A" AS THE
SILL DETAIL USED

DU-AL-CLIP
METAL FRAMING DEVICES

TY-DOWN ANCHOR

TRIP-L-GRIP
16-18 GAUGE ZINC COATED STEEL

Joseph A. Wilkes, FAIA; Wilkes and Faulkner; Washington, D.C.

 **ROUGH CARPENTRY**

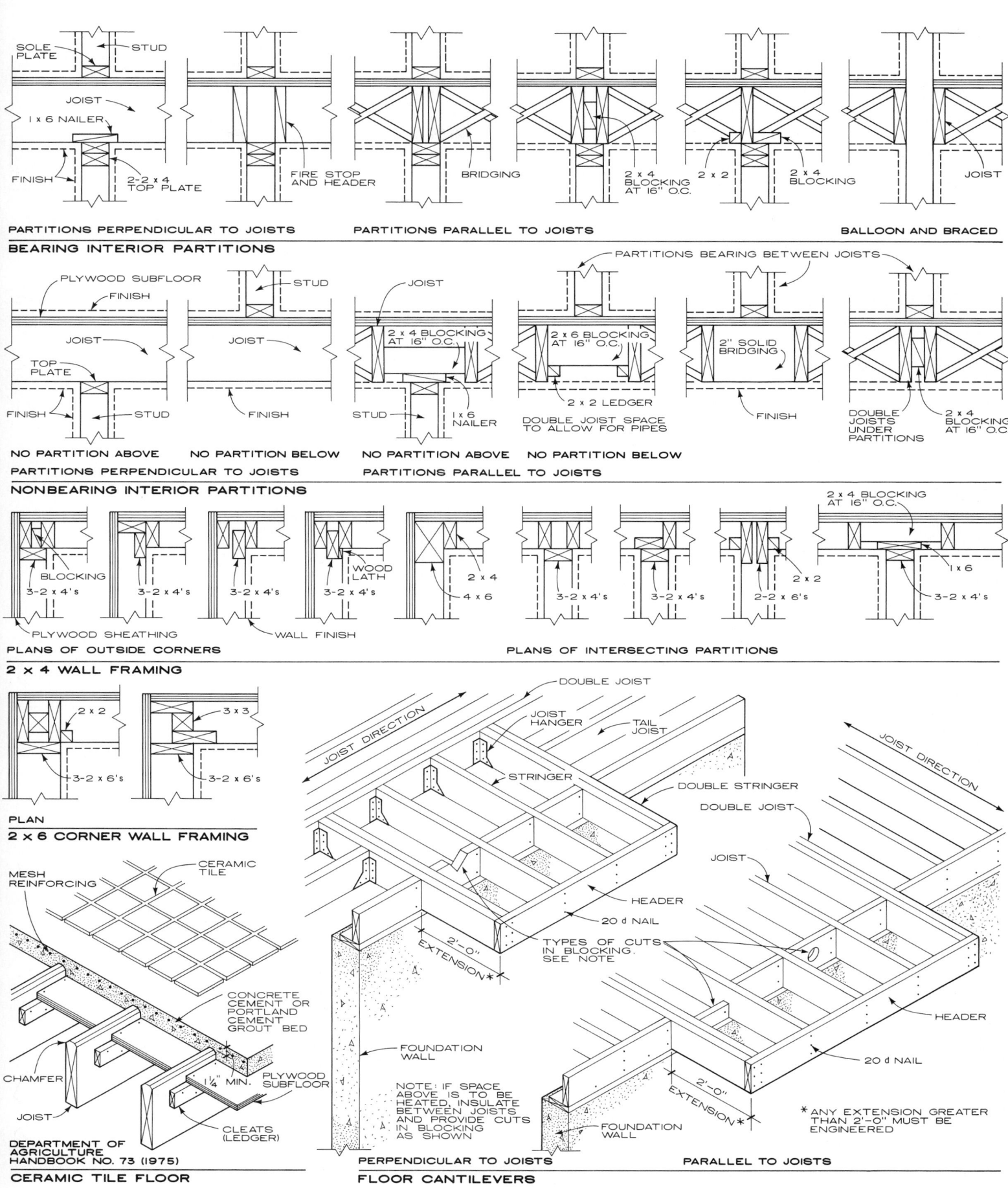

### BEARING INTERIOR PARTITIONS

SOLE PLATE — STUD — JOIST — 1 x 6 NAILER — FINISH — 2-2 x 4 TOP PLATE — FIRE STOP AND HEADER — BRIDGING — 2 x 4 BLOCKING AT 16" O.C. — 2 x 2 — 2 x 4 BLOCKING — JOIST

PARTITIONS PERPENDICULAR TO JOISTS     PARTITIONS PARALLEL TO JOISTS     BALLOON AND BRACED

### NONBEARING INTERIOR PARTITIONS

PLYWOOD SUBFLOOR — FINISH — STUD — JOIST — JOIST — JOIST — PARTITIONS BEARING BETWEEN JOISTS — TOP PLATE — FINISH — STUD — FINISH — STUD — 1 x 6 NAILER — 2 x 4 BLOCKING AT 16" O.C. — 2 x 6 BLOCKING AT 16" O.C. — 2" SOLID BRIDGING — FINISH — 2 x 2 LEDGER — DOUBLE JOIST SPACE TO ALLOW FOR PIPES — DOUBLE JOISTS UNDER PARTITIONS — 2 x 4 BLOCKING AT 16" O.C.

NO PARTITION ABOVE    NO PARTITION BELOW     NO PARTITION ABOVE    NO PARTITION BELOW

PARTITIONS PERPENDICULAR TO JOISTS     PARTITIONS PARALLEL TO JOISTS

### 2 x 4 WALL FRAMING

BLOCKING — 3-2 x 4's — 3-2 x 4's — 3-2 x 4's — 3-2 x 4's — WOOD LATH — 2 x 4 — 4 x 6 — 3-2 x 4's — 3-2 x 4's — 2-2 x 6's — 2 x 2 — 1 x 6 — 3-2 x 4's — 2 x 4 BLOCKING AT 16" O.C. — PLYWOOD SHEATHING — WALL FINISH

PLANS OF OUTSIDE CORNERS     PLANS OF INTERSECTING PARTITIONS

### 2 x 6 CORNER WALL FRAMING

2 x 2 — 3 x 3 — 3-2 x 6's — 3-2 x 6's

PLAN

### CERAMIC TILE FLOOR

MESH REINFORCING — CERAMIC TILE — CONCRETE CEMENT OR PORTLAND CEMENT GROUT BED — PLYWOOD SUBFLOOR — 1¼" MIN. — CHAMFER — JOIST — CLEATS (LEDGER)

DEPARTMENT OF AGRICULTURE HANDBOOK NO. 73 (1975)

### FLOOR CANTILEVERS

DOUBLE JOIST — JOIST DIRECTION — JOIST HANGER — TAIL JOIST — STRINGER — DOUBLE STRINGER — DOUBLE JOIST — JOIST — JOIST DIRECTION — HEADER — 20 d NAIL — TYPES OF CUTS IN BLOCKING. SEE NOTE — EXTENSION* — 2'-0" — FOUNDATION WALL — HEADER — 20 d NAIL — 2'-0" EXTENSION* — FOUNDATION WALL

NOTE: IF SPACE ABOVE IS TO BE HEATED, INSULATE BETWEEN JOISTS AND PROVIDE CUTS IN BLOCKING AS SHOWN

* ANY EXTENSION GREATER THAN 2'-0" MUST BE ENGINEERED

PERPENDICULAR TO JOISTS     PARALLEL TO JOISTS

John Ray Hoke, Jr., AIA; Washington, D.C.

**ROUGH CARPENTRY**    6

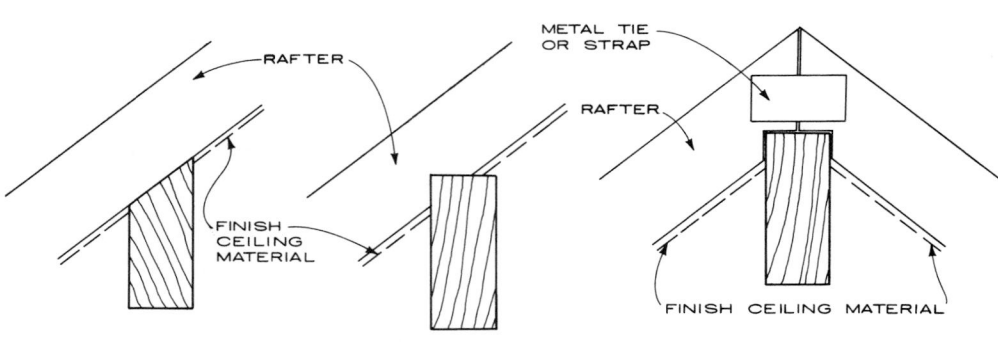

SLOPED BEAM          BIRD'S MOUTH          RIDGE BEAM

## EXPOSED BEAMS AT SLOPING RAFTERS

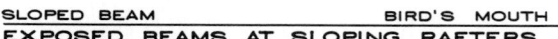

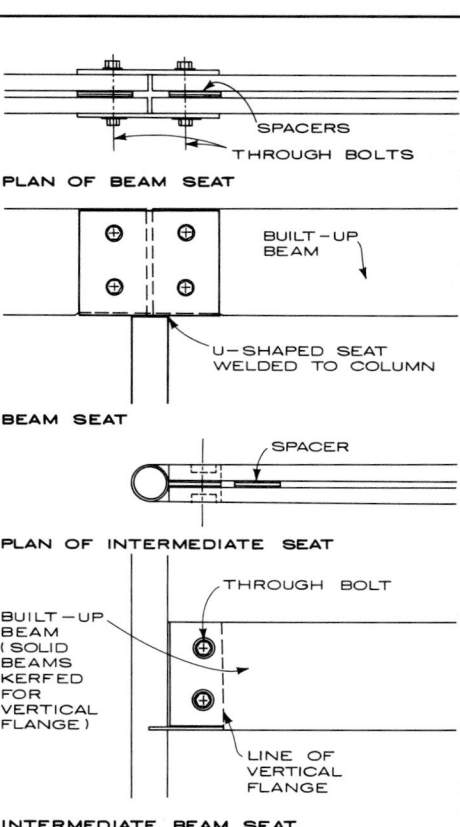

PLAN OF BEAM SEAT

SPACERS
THROUGH BOLTS

BUILT—UP BEAM

BEAM SEAT

U—SHAPED SEAT WELDED TO COLUMN

SPACER

PLAN OF INTERMEDIATE SEAT

THROUGH BOLT

BUILT—UP BEAM (SOLID BEAMS KERFED FOR VERTICAL FLANGE)

LINE OF VERTICAL FLANGE

INTERMEDIATE BEAM SEAT

SIZE OF BASE PLATE MAY BE LIMITED TO FIT WITHIN STUD WALLS

PLAN OF BASE

BASE PLATE WELDED TO PIPE AND BOLTED TO STRUCTURE BELOW

BASE

### STEEL PIPE COLUMNS

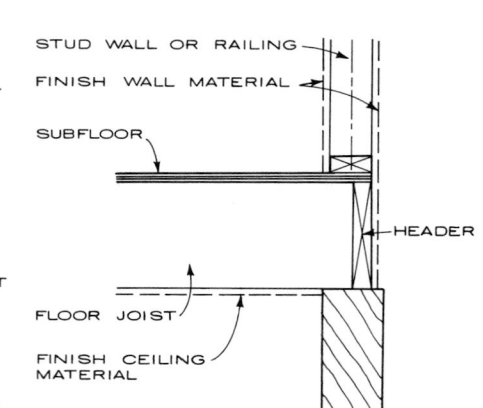

## EXPOSED BEAMS AT FLOORS

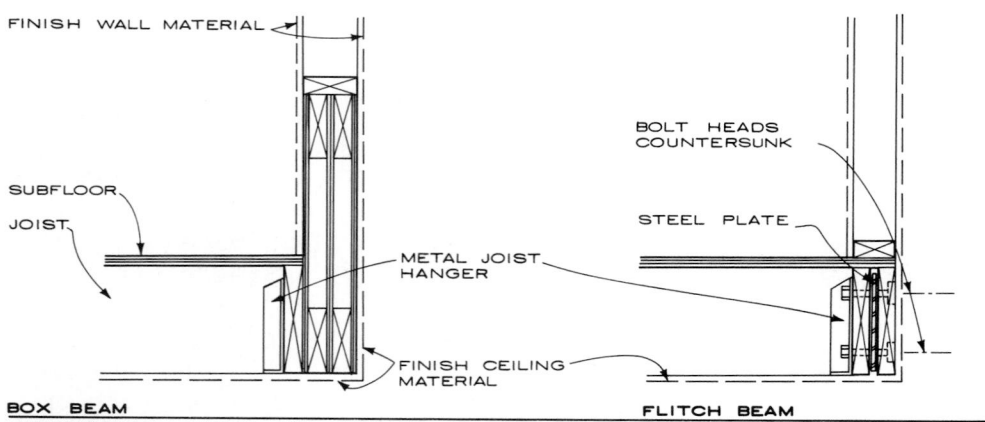

BOX BEAM          FLITCH BEAM

## CONCEALED BUILT—UP BEAMS AT FLOORS

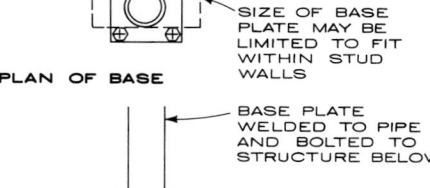

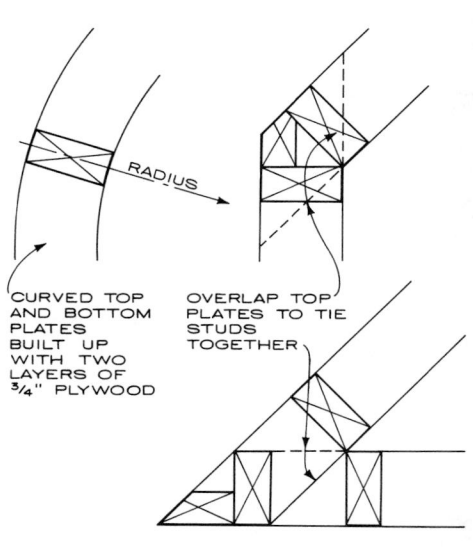

RADIUS

CURVED TOP AND BOTTOM PLATES BUILT UP WITH TWO LAYERS OF ¾" PLYWOOD

OVERLAP TOP PLATES TO TIE STUDS TOGETHER

## NON—RIGHT ANGLE WALL CORNERS

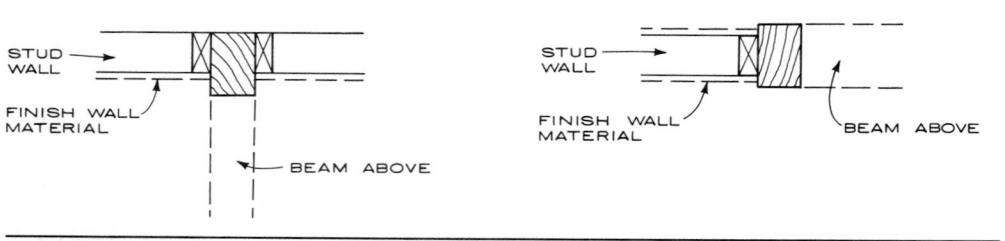

## EXPOSED POSTS AT STUD WALLS

The Bumgardner Partnership/Architects; Seattle, Washington

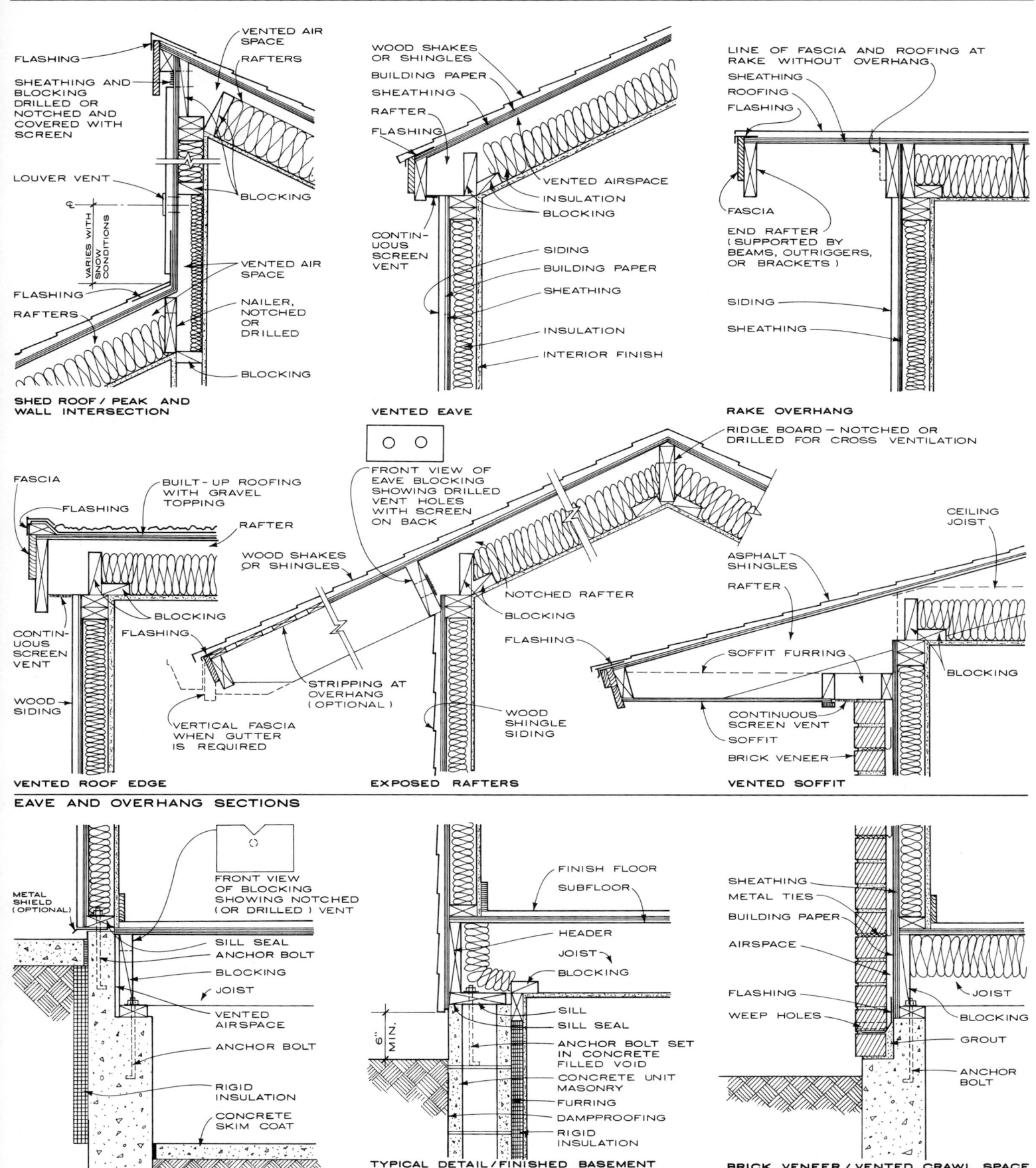

EAVE AND OVERHANG SECTIONS

FOUNDATION WALL SECTIONS

The Bumgardner Partnership/Architects; Seattle, Washington

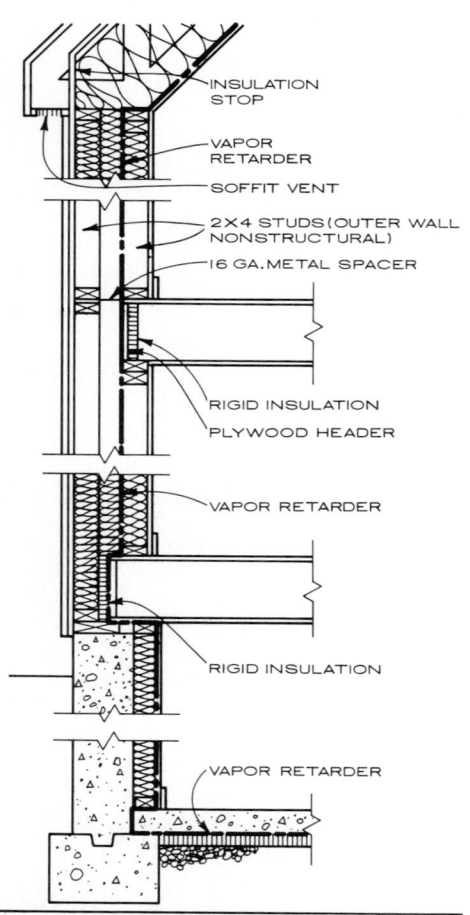

- INSULATION STOP
- VAPOR RETARDER
- SOFFIT VENT
- 2×4 STUDS (OUTER WALL NONSTRUCTURAL)
- 16 GA. METAL SPACER
- RIGID INSULATION
- PLYWOOD HEADER
- VAPOR RETARDER
- RIGID INSULATION
- VAPOR RETARDER

**DOUBLE WALL (SECTION)**

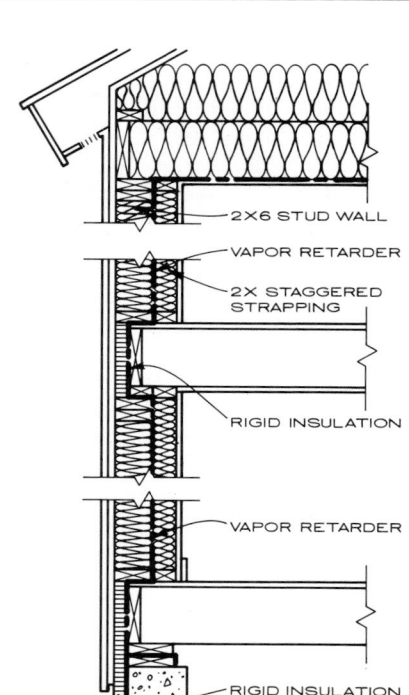

- 2×6 STUD WALL
- VAPOR RETARDER
- 2× STAGGERED STRAPPING
- RIGID INSULATION
- VAPOR RETARDER
- RIGID INSULATION
- RIGID INSULATION & VAPOR RETARDER

**STRAPPED WALL (SECTION)**

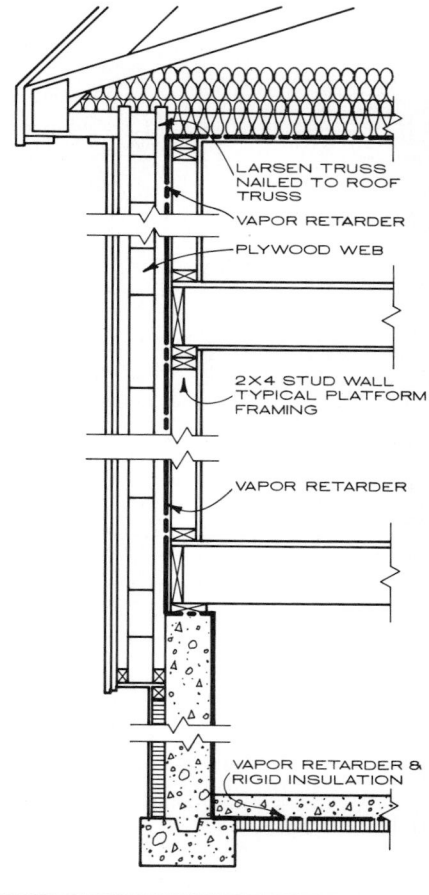

- LARSEN TRUSS NAILED TO ROOF TRUSS
- VAPOR RETARDER
- PLYWOOD WEB
- 2×4 STUD WALL TYPICAL PLATFORM FRAMING
- VAPOR RETARDER
- VAPOR RETARDER & RIGID INSULATION

**LARSEN TRUSS (SECTION)**

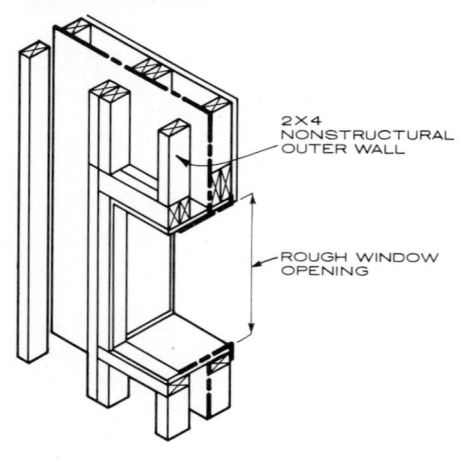

- 2×4 NONSTRUCTURAL OUTER WALL
- ROUGH WINDOW OPENING

**WINDOW DETAIL**

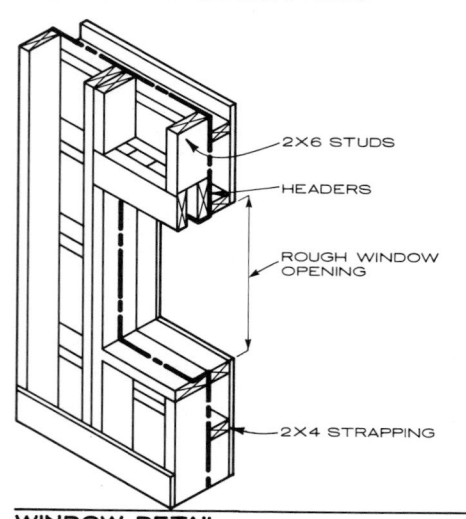

- 2×6 STUDS
- HEADERS
- ROUGH WINDOW OPENING
- 2×4 STRAPPING

**WINDOW DETAIL**

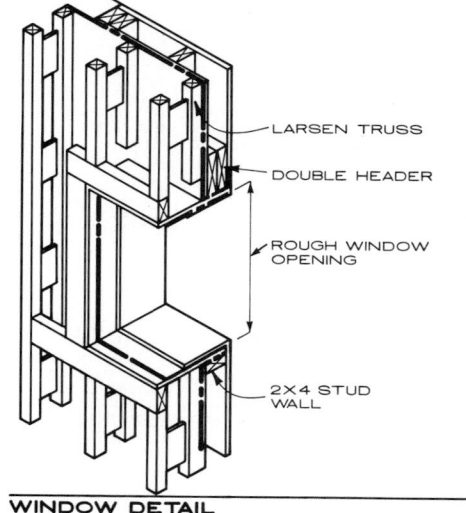

- LARSEN TRUSS
- DOUBLE HEADER
- ROUGH WINDOW OPENING
- 2×4 STUD WALL

**WINDOW DETAIL**

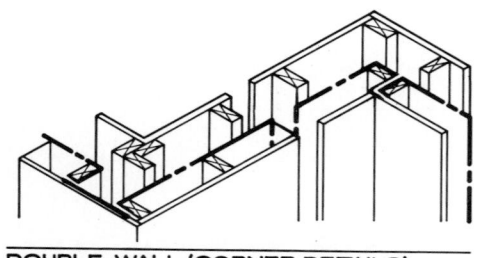

**DOUBLE WALL (CORNER DETAILS)**

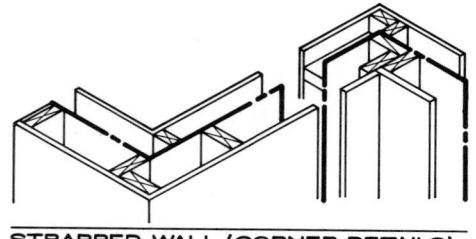

**STRAPPED WALL (CORNER DETAILS)**

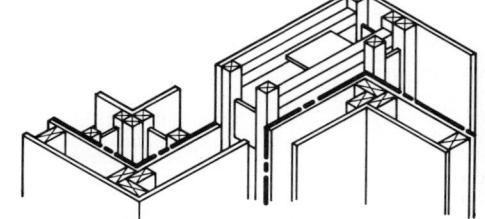

**LARSEN TRUSS (CORNER DETAILS)**

Timothy B. McDonald; Washington, D.C.

**ROUGH CARPENTRY**

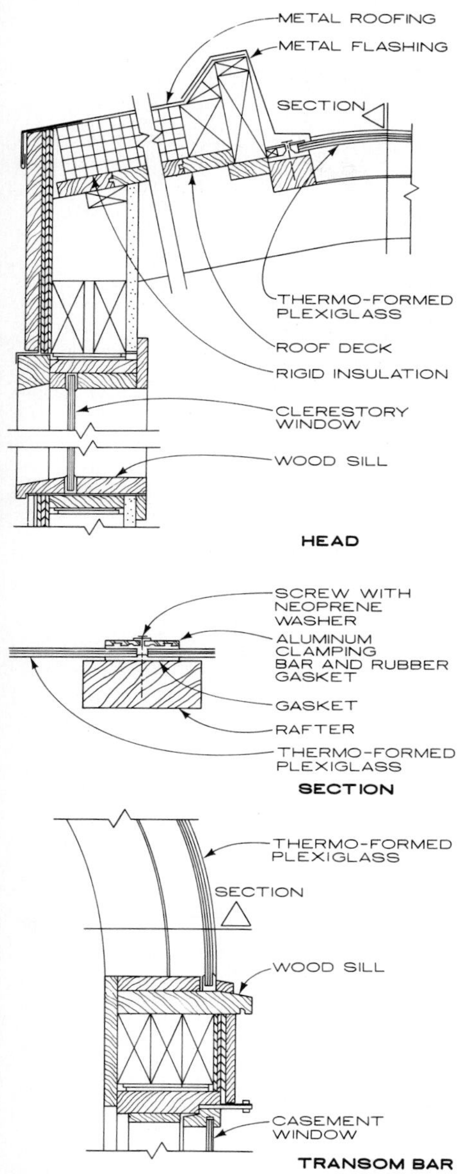

METAL ROOFING
METAL FLASHING
SECTION ◁
THERMO-FORMED PLEXIGLASS
ROOF DECK
RIGID INSULATION
CLERESTORY WINDOW
WOOD SILL

**HEAD**

SCREW WITH NEOPRENE WASHER
ALUMINUM CLAMPING BAR AND RUBBER GASKET
GASKET
RAFTER
THERMO-FORMED PLEXIGLASS

**SECTION**

THERMO-FORMED PLEXIGLASS
SECTION △
WOOD SILL
CASEMENT WINDOW

**TRANSOM BAR**

**SUNSPACE DETAILS**

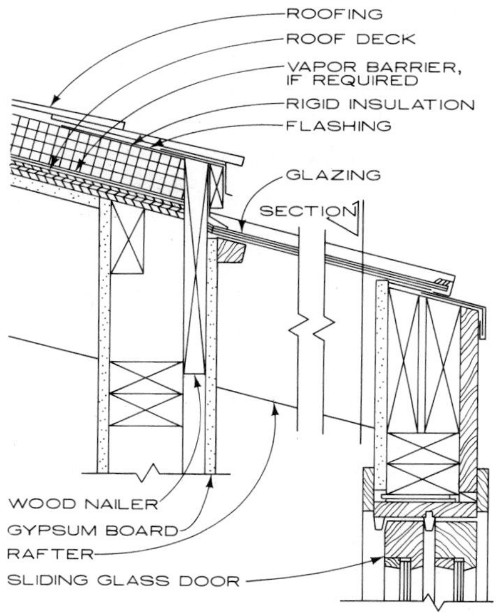

ROOFING
ROOF DECK
VAPOR BARRIER, IF REQUIRED
RIGID INSULATION
FLASHING
GLAZING
SECTION
WOOD NAILER
GYPSUM BOARD
RAFTER
SLIDING GLASS DOOR

**SLOPING GLASS**

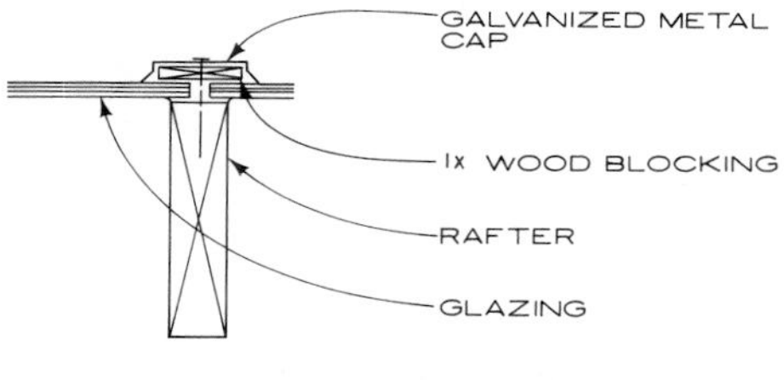

GALVANIZED METAL CAP
1x WOOD BLOCKING
RAFTER
GLAZING

**SECTION**
**FIXED GLASS AT RAFTERS**

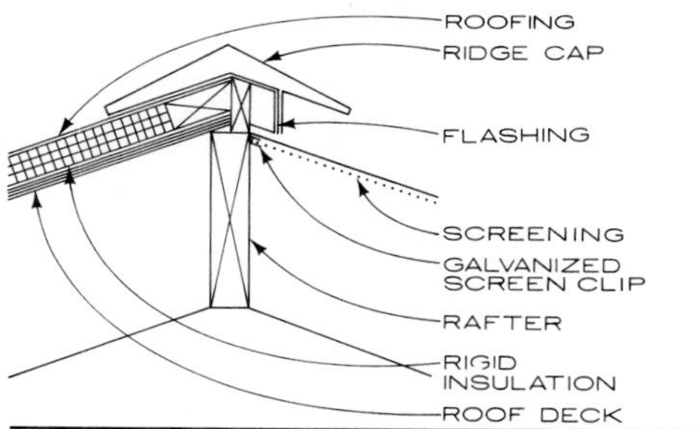

ROOFING
RIDGE CAP
FLASHING
SCREENING
GALVANIZED SCREEN CLIP
RAFTER
RIGID INSULATION
ROOF DECK

**SCREENED ROOF**

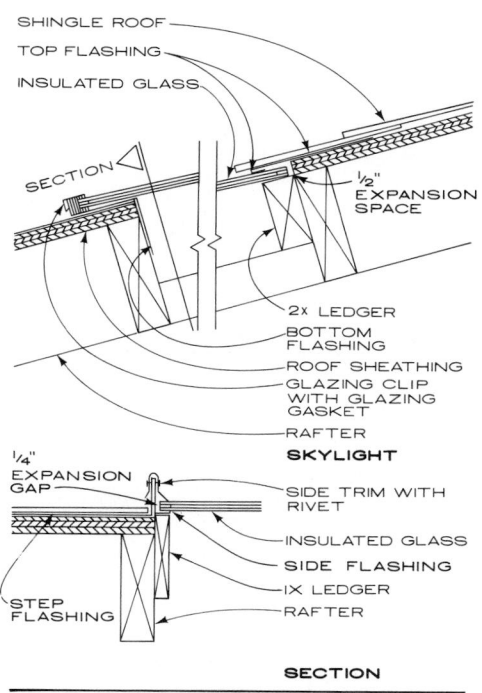

SHINGLE ROOF
TOP FLASHING
INSULATED GLASS
SECTION ◁
½" EXPANSION SPACE
2x LEDGER
BOTTOM FLASHING
ROOF SHEATHING
GLAZING CLIP WITH GLAZING GASKET
RAFTER

**SKYLIGHT**

¼" EXPANSION GAP
STEP FLASHING
SIDE TRIM WITH RIVET
INSULATED GLASS
SIDE FLASHING
1X LEDGER
RAFTER

**SECTION**
**CURBLESS SKYLIGHT INSTALLATION**

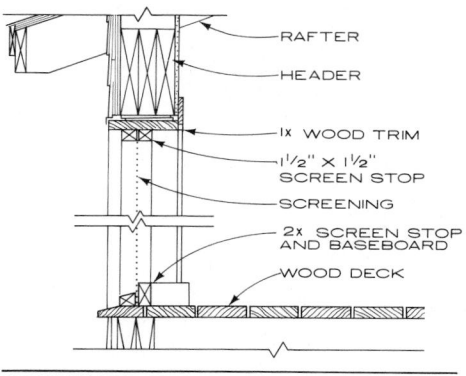

RAFTER
HEADER
1x WOOD TRIM
1½" × 1½" SCREEN STOP
SCREENING
2x SCREEN STOP AND BASEBOARD
WOOD DECK

**SCREENED DECK**

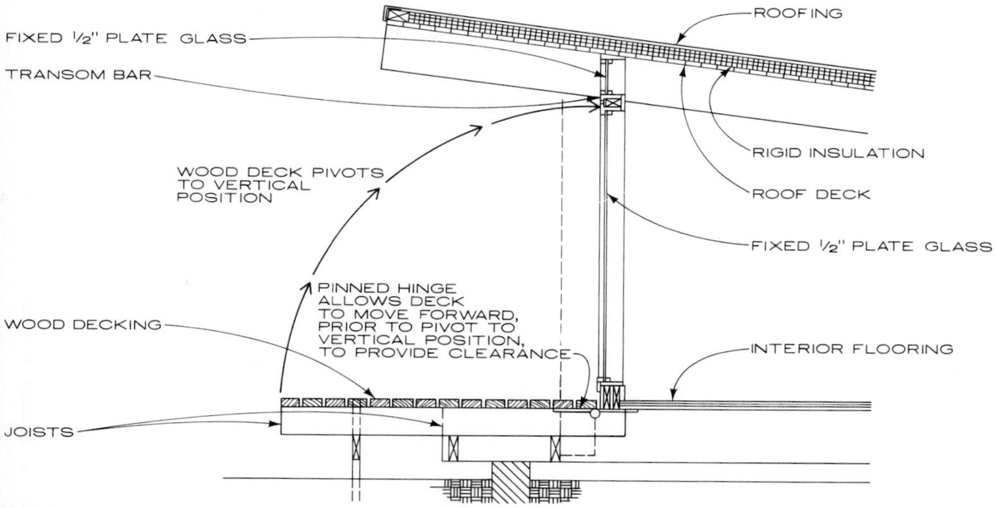

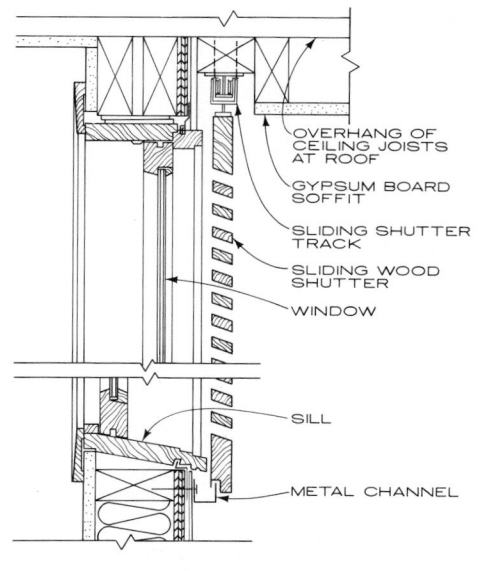

OVERHANG OF CEILING JOISTS AT ROOF
GYPSUM BOARD SOFFIT
SLIDING SHUTTER TRACK
SLIDING WOOD SHUTTER
WINDOW
SILL
METAL CHANNEL

**SLIDING WOOD SHUTTERS**

FIXED ½" PLATE GLASS
TRANSOM BAR
WOOD DECK PIVOTS TO VERTICAL POSITION
WOOD DECKING
JOISTS
PINNED HINGE ALLOWS DECK TO MOVE FORWARD, PRIOR TO PIVOT TO VERTICAL POSITION, TO PROVIDE CLEARANCE
ROOFING
RIGID INSULATION
ROOF DECK
FIXED ½" PLATE GLASS
INTERIOR FLOORING

**WINDOW PROTECTION**

Daniel Tinney, AIA; The Russell Partnership, Inc.
Hoffman, see data sources

**ROUGH CARPENTRY** 6

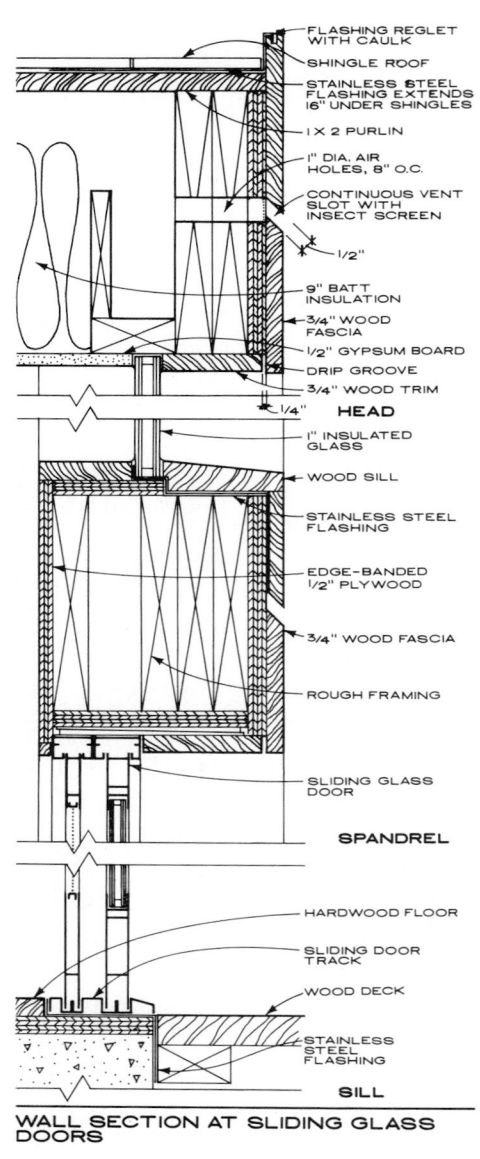

FLASHING REGLET WITH CAULK
SHINGLE ROOF
STAINLESS STEEL FLASHING EXTENDS 16" UNDER SHINGLES
1 X 2 PURLIN
1" DIA. AIR HOLES, 8" O.C.
CONTINUOUS VENT SLOT WITH INSECT SCREEN
1/2"
9" BATT INSULATION
3/4" WOOD FASCIA
1/2" GYPSUM BOARD
DRIP GROOVE
3/4" WOOD TRIM
1/4"
**HEAD**

1" INSULATED GLASS
WOOD SILL
STAINLESS STEEL FLASHING
EDGE-BANDED 1/2" PLYWOOD
3/4" WOOD FASCIA
ROUGH FRAMING
SLIDING GLASS DOOR

**SPANDREL**

HARDWOOD FLOOR
SLIDING DOOR TRACK
WOOD DECK
STAINLESS STEEL FLASHING

**SILL**

**WALL SECTION AT SLIDING GLASS DOORS**

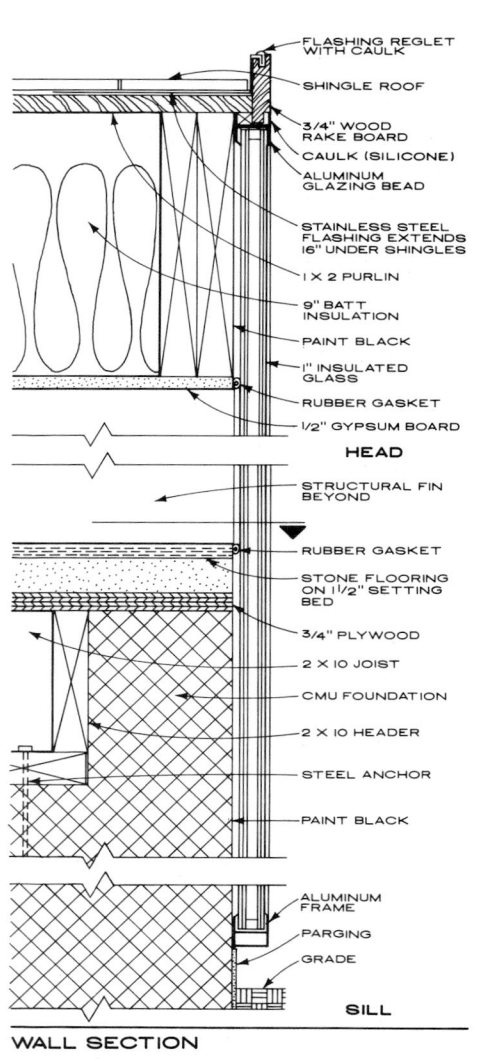

FLASHING REGLET WITH CAULK
SHINGLE ROOF
3/4" WOOD RAKE BOARD
CAULK (SILICONE)
ALUMINUM GLAZING BEAD
STAINLESS STEEL FLASHING EXTENDS 16" UNDER SHINGLES
1 X 2 PURLIN
9" BATT INSULATION
PAINT BLACK
1" INSULATED GLASS
RUBBER GASKET
1/2" GYPSUM BOARD

**HEAD**

STRUCTURAL FIN BEYOND
RUBBER GASKET
STONE FLOORING ON 1 1/2" SETTING BED
3/4" PLYWOOD
2 X 10 JOIST
CMU FOUNDATION
2 X 10 HEADER
STEEL ANCHOR
PAINT BLACK
ALUMINUM FRAME
PARGING
GRADE

**SILL**

**WALL SECTION**

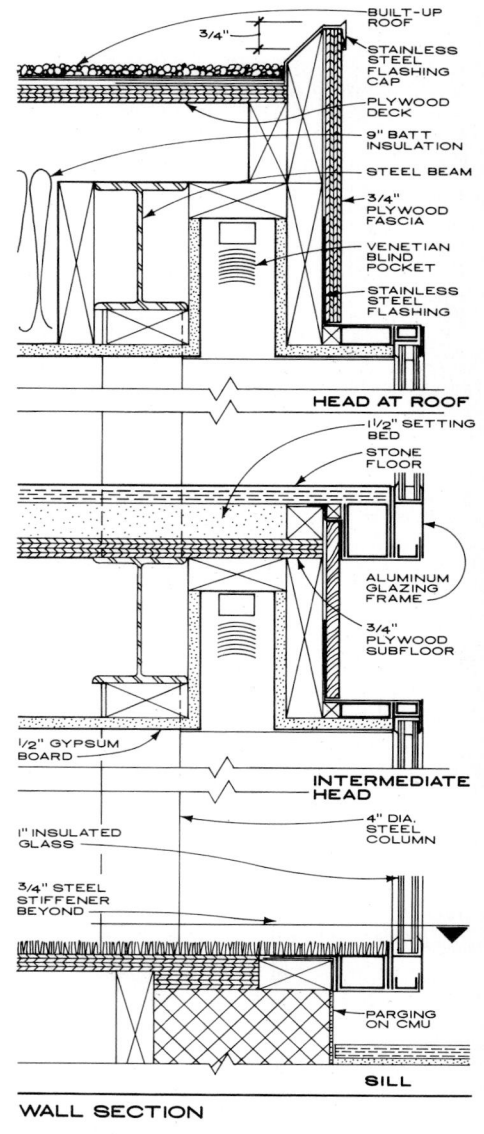

BUILT-UP ROOF
3/4"
STAINLESS STEEL FLASHING CAP
PLYWOOD DECK
9" BATT INSULATION
STEEL BEAM
3/4" PLYWOOD FASCIA
VENETIAN BLIND POCKET
STAINLESS STEEL FLASHING

**HEAD AT ROOF**

1 1/2" SETTING BED
STONE FLOOR
ALUMINUM GLAZING FRAME
3/4" PLYWOOD SUBFLOOR
1/2" GYPSUM BOARD

**INTERMEDIATE HEAD**

1" INSULATED GLASS
4" DIA. STEEL COLUMN
3/4" STEEL STIFFENER BEYOND
PARGING ON CMU

**SILL**

**WALL SECTION**

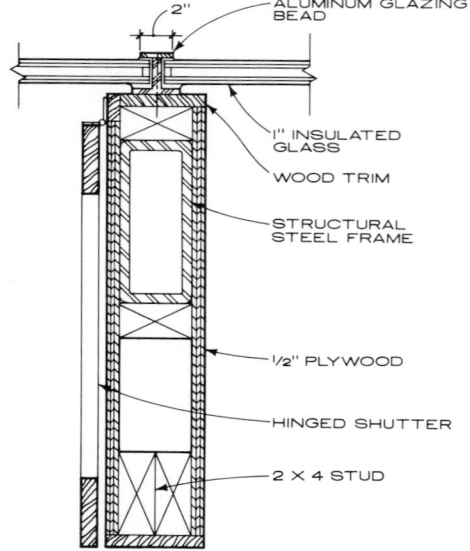

2"
ALUMINUM GLAZING BEAD
1" INSULATED GLASS
WOOD TRIM
STRUCTURAL STEEL FRAME
1/2" PLYWOOD
HINGED SHUTTER
2 X 4 STUD

**CURTAIN WALL STRUCTURAL FIN**

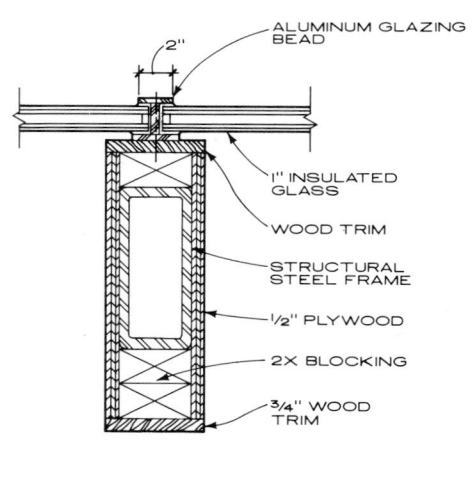

2"
ALUMINUM GLAZING BEAD
1" INSULATED GLASS
WOOD TRIM
STRUCTURAL STEEL FRAME
1/2" PLYWOOD
2X BLOCKING
3/4" WOOD TRIM

**CURTAIN WALL STRUCTURAL FIN**

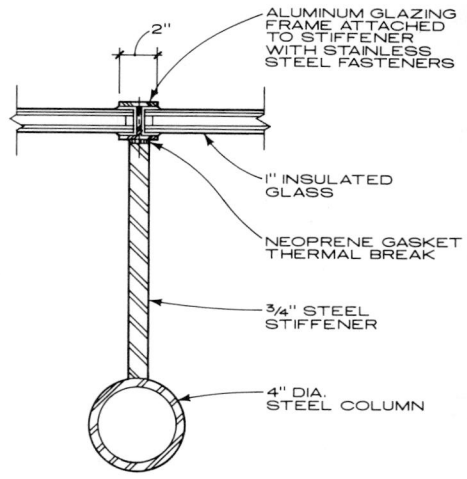

2"
ALUMINUM GLAZING FRAME ATTACHED TO STIFFENER WITH STAINLESS STEEL FASTENERS
1" INSULATED GLASS
NEOPRENE GASKET THERMAL BREAK
3/4" STEEL STIFFENER
4" DIA. STEEL COLUMN

**COLUMN WITH STIFFENER AT WINDOW WALL**

Hugh Newell Jacobsen, FAIA; Washington, D.C.

 **ROUGH CARPENTRY**

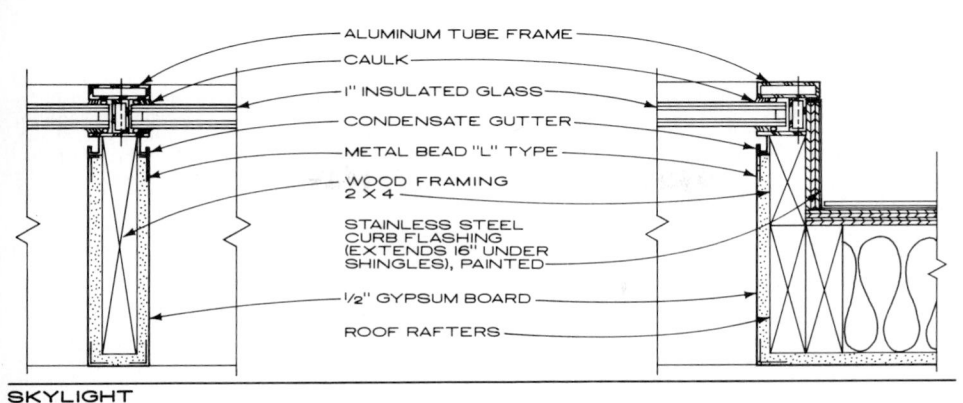

ALUMINUM TUBE FRAME
CAULK
1" INSULATED GLASS
CONDENSATE GUTTER
METAL BEAD "L" TYPE
WOOD FRAMING 2 X 4
STAINLESS STEEL CURB FLASHING (EXTENDS 16" UNDER SHINGLES), PAINTED
1/2" GYPSUM BOARD
ROOF RAFTERS

**SKYLIGHT**

SHINGLE ROOF
9" FOIL-ENCASED INSULATION
INBOARD STAINLESS STEEL GUTTER
CAULK    VARIES
VARIES
1/2" GYPSUM BOARD
ALIGN TRIM AT FASCIA BOTTOM
SPRING FLASHING
1 X 12 WOOD FASCIA

**HEAD AT GUTTER**

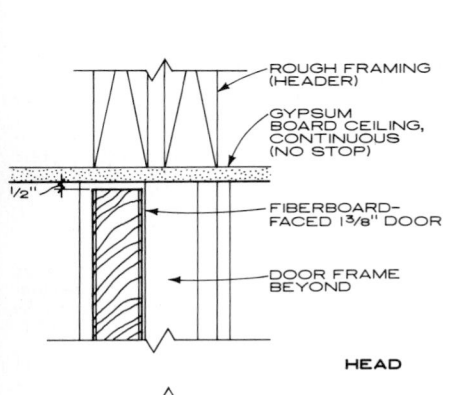

ROUGH FRAMING (HEADER)
GYPSUM BOARD CEILING, CONTINUOUS (NO STOP)
1/2"
FIBERBOARD-FACED 1 3/8" DOOR
DOOR FRAME BEYOND

**HEAD**

ASPHALT SHINGLE
5/8" PLYWOOD ROOF DECK
VENT SPACE
9" FOIL-ENCLOSED INSULATION
GUTTER STRAP 24" O.C.
CAULK
VARIES
VARIES

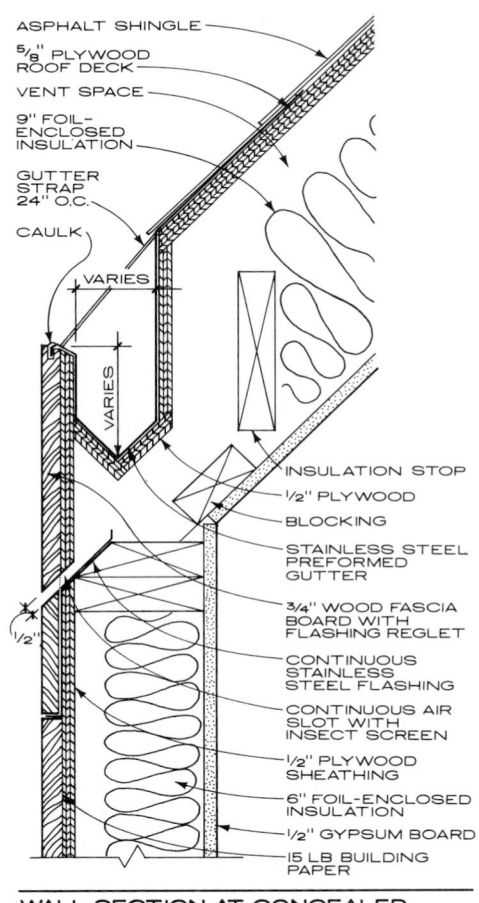

INSULATION STOP
1/2" PLYWOOD
BLOCKING
STAINLESS STEEL PREFORMED GUTTER
3/4" WOOD FASCIA BOARD WITH FLASHING REGLET
CONTINUOUS STAINLESS STEEL FLASHING
CONTINUOUS AIR SLOT WITH INSECT SCREEN
1/2" PLYWOOD SHEATHING
6" FOIL-ENCLOSED INSULATION
1/2" GYPSUM BOARD
15 LB BUILDING PAPER

**WALL SECTION AT CONCEALED GUTTER**

3/8" CLEAR ACRYLIC, CONFORM TO ROOF SLOPE
1/4" POLISHED PLATE MIRROR

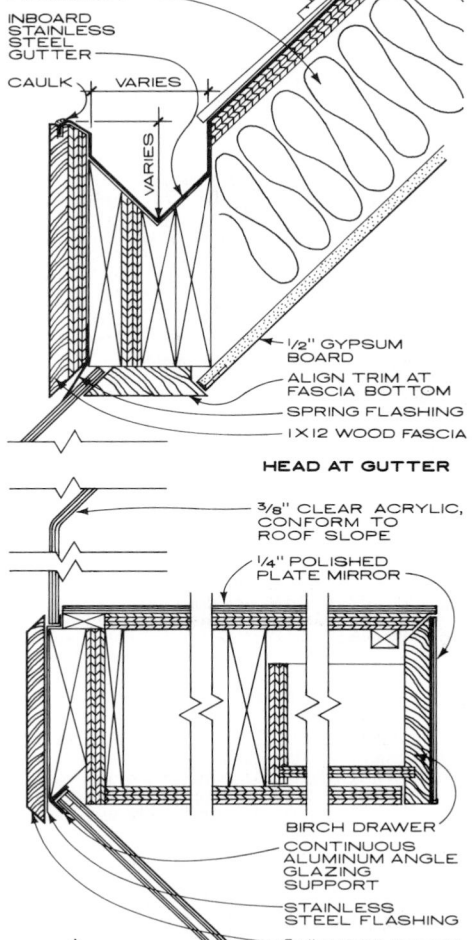

BIRCH DRAWER
CONTINUOUS ALUMINUM ANGLE GLAZING SUPPORT
STAINLESS STEEL FLASHING
3/4" WOOD FASCIA

**PLYWOOD BUFFET**

5/8" INSULATED GLASS
WOOD FLOORING ON 3/4" PLYWOOD SUBFLOOR
3/4" WOOD TRIM
STAINLESS STEEL FLASHING
15 LB BUILDING PAPER
1/2" PLYWOOD SHEATHING

**SILL**

**WALL SECTION AT ORIEL**

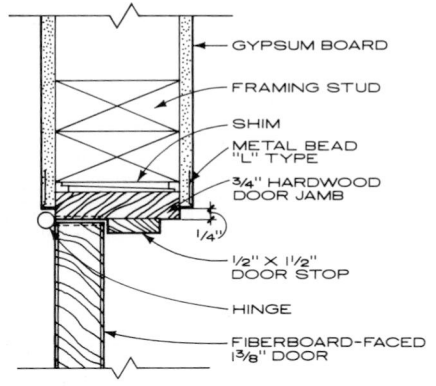

GYPSUM BOARD
FRAMING STUD
SHIM
METAL BEAD "L" TYPE
3/4" HARDWOOD DOOR JAMB
1/4"
1/2" X 1 1/2" DOOR STOP
HINGE
FIBERBOARD-FACED 1 3/8" DOOR

**JAMB**

**TYPICAL INTERIOR DOOR**

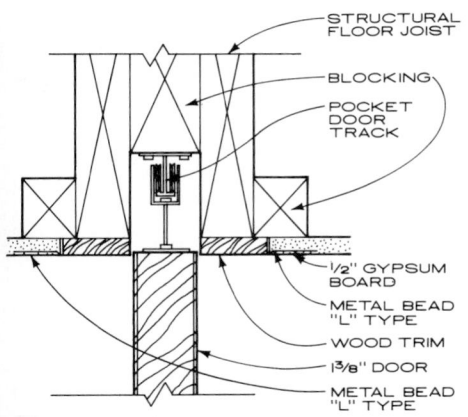

STRUCTURAL FLOOR JOIST
BLOCKING
POCKET DOOR TRACK
1/2" GYPSUM BOARD
METAL BEAD "L" TYPE
WOOD TRIM
1 3/8" DOOR
METAL BEAD "L" TYPE

**CONCEALED POCKET DOOR HEAD**

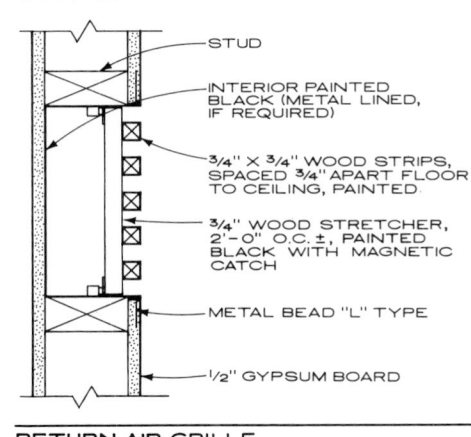

STUD
INTERIOR PAINTED BLACK (METAL LINED, IF REQUIRED)
3/4" X 3/4" WOOD STRIPS, SPACED 3/4" APART FLOOR TO CEILING, PAINTED
3/4" WOOD STRETCHER, 2'-0" O.C.±, PAINTED BLACK WITH MAGNETIC CATCH
METAL BEAD "L" TYPE
1/2" GYPSUM BOARD

**RETURN AIR GRILLE**

CONTINUOUS METAL RIDGE ROOF VENT, SLOPE TO CONFORM TO ROOF
RIDGE BEAM
ROOFING MATERIAL (SHINGLE, METAL, ETC.)
PLYWOOD DECK
VENT SPACE
BUILDING PAPER
FOIL-ENCLOSED INSULATION
1/2" GYPSUM BOARD
METAL BEAD "L" TYPE
1/4"
WOOD BLOCKING

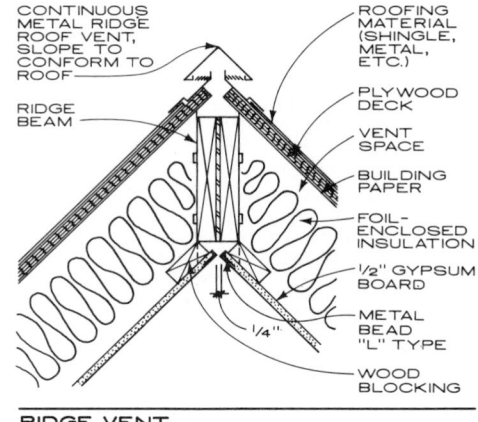

**RIDGE VENT**

Hugh Newell Jacobsen, FAIA; Washington, D.C.

**ROUGH CARPENTRY**

6

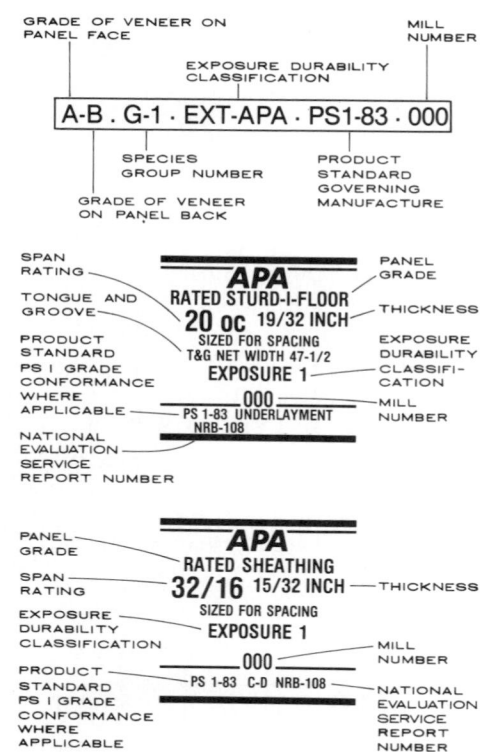

## APA TRADEMARKS

### GRADE DESIGNATIONS

Construction and industrial panel grades are generally identified in terms of the veneer grade used on the face and back of the panel (e.g., A-B, B-C, etc.), or by a name suggesting the panel's intended end-use (e.g., APA RATED SHEATHING, APA RATED STURD-I-FLOOR, etc.).

Veneer grades define veneer appearance in terms of natural unrepaired growth characteristics and allowable number and size of repairs that may be made during manufacture. The highest quality veneer grades are N and A. The minimum grade of veneer permitted in Exterior plywood is C-grade. D-grade veneer is used only for backs and inner plies of panels intended for interior use or applications protected from exposure to permanent or severe moisture.

### VENEER GRADES

**N**    Smooth surface "natural finish" veneer. Select, all heartwood or all sapwood. Free of open defects. Allows not more than 6 repairs, wood only, per 4 x 8 panel, made parallel to grain and well matched for grain and color.

**A**    Smooth, paintable. Not more than 18 neatly made repairs, boat, sled, or router type, and parallel to grain, permitted. May be used for natural finish in less demanding applications.

**B**    Solid surface. Shims, circular repair plugs and tight knots to 1 inch across grain permitted. Some minor splits permitted.

**C Plugged**    Improved C veneer with splits limited to $1/8$ inch width and knotholes and borer holes limited to $1/4$ x $1/2$ inch. Admits some broken grain. Synthetic repairs permitted.

**C**    Tight knots to 1-$1/2$ inch. Knotholes to 1 inch across grain and some to 1-$1/2$ inch if total width of knots and knotholes is within specified limits. Synthetic or wood repairs. Discoloration and sanding defects that do not impair strength permitted. Limited splits allowed. Stitching permitted.

**D**    Knots and knotholes to 2-$1/2$ inch width across grain and $1/2$ inch larger within specified limits. Limited splits allowed. Stitching permitted. Limited to Interior, Exposure 1 and Exposure 2 panels.

John D. Bloodgood, Architects, P.C.; Des Moines, Iowa
American Plywood Association

**ROUGH CARPENTRY**

## SPAN RATINGS

APA RATED SHEATHING, APA RATED STURD-I-FLOOR and APA 303 SIDING panels carry numbers in their trademarks called Span Ratings. These denote the maximum recommended center-to-center spacing in inches of supports over which the panels should be placed in construction applications.

The Span Rating in the trademark on APA RATED SHEATHING panels appears as two numbers separated by a slash, such as 32/16, 48/24, etc. The left-hand number denotes the maximum recommended spacing of supports when the panel is used for roof sheathing with the long dimension of the panel across three or more supports. The right-hand number indicates the maximum recommended spacing of supports when the panel is used for subflooring with the long dimension of the panel across three or more supports. A panel marked 32/16, for example, may be used for roof sheathing over supports 32 inches on center or for subflooring over supports 16 inches on center.

The Span Ratings in the trademarks on APA RATED STURD-I-FLOOR and 303 SIDING panels appear as a single number. APA RATED STURD-I-FLOOR panels are designed specifically for residential or other light-frame single-floor (combined subfloor-underlayment) applications and are manufactured with Span Ratings of 16, 20, 24 and 48 inches. These ratings, like those for APA RATED SHEATHING, are based on application of the panel with the long dimension across three or more supports.

APA 303 SIDINGS are manufactured with Span Ratings of 16 and 24 inches and may be used direct to studs or over nonstructural wall sheathing (Sturd-I-Wall construction), or over nailable panel or lumber sheathing (double-wall construction). Panels with a Span Rating of 16 inches may be applied vertically direct to studs spaced 16 inches on center. Panels bearing a Span Rating of 24 inches may be used vertically direct to studs spaced 24 inches on center. All 303 SIDING panels may be applied horizontally direct to studs 16 or 24 inches on center provided horizontal joints are blocked. When used over nailable structural panel or lumber sheathing, the 303 SIDING Span Rating refers to the maximum recommended spacing of vertical rows of nails rather than to stud spacing.

## GROUP NUMBER

Plywood can be manufactured from over 70 species of wood. These species are divided on the basis of bending strength and stiffness into five Groups under U.S. Product Standard PS 1. Stiffest species are in Group 1, the next stiffest in Group 2, and so on. The Group number that appears in the trademark on some APA trademarked panels—primarily sanded grades—is based on the species of face and back veneers. Where face and back veneers are not from the same species Group, the higher Group number is used, except for sanded and decorative panels $3/8$ inch thick or less. These are identified by face species because they are chosen primarily for appearance and used in applications where structural integrity is not critical. Sanded panels greater than $3/8$ inch are identified by face species if C or D grade backs are at least $1/8$ in. and are no more than one species group number larger. Some species are used widely in plywood manufacture; others rarely. Check local availability before specifying if a particular species is desired.

## EXPOSURE DURABILITY

Plywood manufactured under Product Standard PS1-83 is produced in two basic types: Exterior type with 100 percent waterproof glueline and Interior type with highly moisture resistant glueline. Interior type panels can be manufactured with exterior, intermediate or interior glue, although most Interior type plywood today is manufactured with exterior glue (Exposure 1). Exposure 1 panels are suitable for applications where ability to resist moisture during long construction delays or where exposure to conditions of similar severity is required. However, because the lower grade of veneer permitted for backs and inner plies of Interior type panels may affect glueline performance, only Exterior type plywood should be used for permanent exposure to the weather or moisture.

APA Performance-Rated Panels can be manufactured in three exposure durability classifications—Exterior, Exposure 1 and Exposure 2. Panels marked Exterior are designed for applications subject to continuous exposure to the weather or moisture and are comparable to panels designated under PS 1 as Exterior type. Panels with an Exposure 1 designation are intended for protected construction applications where ability to resist moisture during long construction delays or where exposure to conditions of similar severity is required. Exposure 1 panels are comparable to panels designated under PS 1 as Exposure 1 or Interior type with exterior glue. Panels with an Exposure 2 designation are intended for protected construction applications where moderate delays in providing protection from moisture may be expected or where water leakage or conditions of high humidity may exist. Exposure 2 panels are comparable to panels designated under PS 1 as Interior type with intermediate glue.

## SANDED, UNSANDED AND TOUCH-SANDED PANELS

Panels with B-grade or better veneer faces are always sanded smooth in manufacture to fulfill the requirements of their intended end-use—applications such as cabinets, shelving, furniture, built-ins, etc. APA RATED SHEATHING panels are unsanded since a smooth surface is not a requirement of their intended end-use. Still other panels—APA UNDERLAYMENT, APA RATED STURD-I-FLOOR, APA C-D PLUGGED, and APA C-C PLUGGED—require only touch-sanding for "sizing" to make the panel thickness more uniform.

## CLASSIFICATION

| GROUP 1 | GROUP 2 | | GROUP 3 | GROUP 4 | GROUP 5 |
|---|---|---|---|---|---|
| Apitong | Cedar, Port | Maple, Black | Alder, Red | Aspen | Basswood |
| Beech, | Orford | Mengkulang | Birch, Paper | Bigtooth | Poplar, |
| American | Cypress | Meranti, | Cedar, Alaska | Quaking | Balsam |
| Birch | Douglas | Red[b] | Fir, | Cativo | |
| Sweet | Fir 2[a] | Mersawa | Subalpine | Cedar | |
| Yellow | Fir | Pine | Hemlock, | Incense | |
| Douglas | Balsam | Pond | Eastern | Western | |
| Fir 1[a] | California | Red | Maple | Red | |
| Kapur | Red | Virginia | Bigleaf | Cottonwood | |
| Keruing | Grand | Western | Pine | Eastern | |
| Larch, | Noble | White | Jack | Black | |
| Western | Pacific | Spruce | Lodgepole | (Western | |
| Maple, Sugar | Silver | Black | Ponderosa | Poplar) | |
| Pine | White | Red | Spruce | Pine | |
| Caribbean | Hemlock, | Sitka | Redwood | Eastern | |
| Ocote | Western | Sweetgum | Spruce | White | |
| Pine, South. | Lauan | Tamarack | Engelmann | Sugar | |
| Loblolly | Almon | Yellow- | White | | |
| Longleaf | Bagtikan | Poplar | | | |
| Shortleaf | Mayapis | | | | |
| Slash | Red | | | | |
| Tanoak | Tangile | | | | |
| | White | | | | |

**NOTES**

a.   Douglas Fir from trees grown in the states of Washington, Oregon, California, Idaho, Montana, Wyoming, and the Canadian Provinces of Alberta and British Columbia shall be classed as Douglas Fir No. 1. Douglas Fir from trees grown in the states of Nevada, Utah, Colorado, Arizona and New Mexico shall be classed as Douglas Fir No. 2.

b.   Red Meranti shall be limited to species having a specific gravity of 0.41 or more based on green volume and oven dry weight.

Unsanded and touch-sanded panels, and panels with B-grade or better veneer on one side only, usually carry the APA trademark on the panel back. Panels with both sides of B-grade or better veneer, or with special overlaid surfaces (such as Medium Density Overlay), carry the APA trademark on the panel edge.

#### APA 303 SIDING FACE GRADES

APA 303 plywood siding products are manufactured in four basic classes—Special Series 303, 303-6, 303-18 and 303-30. Each class, as shown below, is further divided into grades according to categories of repair and appearance characteristics. The grade designations appear within the APA trademark on panels so graded, thus making it easy to select and specify the siding appropriate for any particular project. Depending on species, type of repair, finishing, etc., premium products can be found in all grades.

### 303 SIDING FACE GRADES

| | | PATCHES | |
|---|---|---|---|
| CLASS | GRADE[1] | WOOD | SYNTHETIC |
| | 303-OC[2,3] | Not permitted | Not permitted |
| Special Series 303 | 303-OL[4] | Not applicable for overlays | |
| | 303-NR[5] | Not permitted | Not permitted |
| | 303-SR[6] | Not permitted | Permitted as natural-defect shape only |
| | 303-6-W | Limit 6 | Not permitted |
| 303-6 | 303-6-S | Not permitted | Limit 6 |
| | 303-6-S/W | Limit 6—any combination | |
| | 303-18-W | Limit 18 | Not permitted |
| 303-18 | 303-18-S | Not permitted | Limit 18 |
| | 303-18-S/W | Limit 18—any combination | |
| | 303-30-W | Limit 30 | Not permitted |
| 303-30 | 303-30-S | Not permitted | Limit 30 |
| | 303-30-S/W | Limit 30—any combination | |

NOTES

1. Limitations on grade characteristics are based on 4 ft. x 8 ft. panel size. Limits on other sizes vary in proportion. All panels except 303-NR allow restricted minor repairs such as shims. These and such other face appearance characteristics as knots, knotholes, splits, etc., are limited by both size and number in accordance with panel grades, 303-OC being most restrictive and 303-30 being least. Multiple repairs are permitted only on 303-18 and 303-30 panels. Patch size is restricted on all panel grades. For additional information, including finishing recommendations, see *APA Product Guide: 303 Plywood Siding, E300.*
2. Check local availability.
3. "Clear"
4. "Overlaid" (e.g., Medium Density Overlay siding)
5. "Natural Rustic"
6. "Synthetic Rustic"

### APA SANDED & TOUCH-SANDED PANEL[3][4][6]

#### APA A-A

Use where appearance of both sides is important for interior applications such as built-ins, cabinets, furniture, partitions; and exterior applications such as fences, signs, boats, shipping containers, tanks, ducts, etc. Smooth surfaces suitable for painting. EDC: Interior, Exposure 1, Exterior. COMMON THICKNESSES: 1/4, 3/8, 1/2, 5/8, 3/4.[7]

#### APA A-B

For use where appearance of one side is less important but where two solid surfaces are necessary. EDC: Interior, Exposure 1, Exterior. COMMON THICKNESSES: 1/4, 3/8, 1/2, 5/8, 3/4.[7]

#### APA A-C

For use where appearance of only one side is important in exterior applications, such as soffits, fences, structural uses, boxcar and truck linings, farm buildings, tanks, trays, commercial refrigerators, etc. EDC: Exterior. COMMON THICKNESSES: 1/4, 3/8, 1/2, 5/8, 3/4.[7]

#### APA A-D

For use where appearance of only one side is important in interior applications, such as paneling, built-ins, shelving, partitions, flow racks, etc. EDC: Interior, Exposure 1. COMMON THICKNESSES: 1/4, 3/8, 1/2, 5/8, 3/4.[7]

Bloodgood Architects, PC; Des Moines and New York
American Plywood Association

#### APA B-B

Utility panels with two solid sides. EDC: Interior, Exposure 1, Exterior. COMMON THICKNESSES: 1/4, 3/8, 1/2, 5/8, 3/4.[7]

#### APA B-C

Utility panel for farm service and work buildings, boxcar and truck linings, concrete forms, containers, tanks, agricultural equipment, as a base for exterior coatings and other exterior uses or applications subject to high or continuous moisture. EDC: Exterior. COMMON THICKNESSES: 1/4, 3/8, 1/2, 5/8, 3/4.[7]

#### APA B-D

Utility panel for backing, sides of built-ins, industry shelving, slip sheets, separator boards, bins and other interior or protected applications. EDC: Interior, Exposure 1. COMMON THICKNESSES: 1/4, 3/8, 1/2, 5/8, 3/4.[7]

#### APA UNDERLAYMENT

For application over structural subfloor. Provides smooth surface for application of carpet and pad and possesses high concentrated and impact load resistance. EDC: Interior, Exposure 1. COMMON THICKNESSES: 3/8, 1/2, 19/32, 5/8, 23/32, 3/4, 11/32.

#### APA C-C PLUGGED

For use as an underlayment over structural subfloor, refrigerated or controlled atmosphere storage rooms, pallet fruit bins, tanks, boxcar and truck floors and linings, open soffits, tile backing and other similar applications where continuous or severe moisture may be present. Provides smooth surface for application of carpet and pad and possesses high concentrated and impact load resistance. EDC: Exterior. COMMON THICKNESSES: 3/8, 1/2, 19/32, 5/8, 23/32, 3/4, 11/32.

#### APA C-D PLUGGED

For built-ins, wall and ceiling tile backing, cable reels, walkways, separator boards and other interior or protected applications. Not a substitute for Underlayment or APA Rated Sturd-I-Floor as it lacks their puncture resistance. EDC: Interior, Exposure 1. COMMON THICKNESSES: 3/8, 1/2, 19/32, 5/8, 23/32, 3/4.

### APA SPECIALTY PANELS[6]

#### APA 303 SIDING

Proprietary plywood products for exterior siding, fencing, etc. Special surface treatment such as V-groove, channel groove, striated, brushed, rough-sawn and texture-embossed (MDO). Stud spacing (Span Rating) and face grade classification indicated in trademark. EDC: Exterior. COMMON THICKNESSES: 11/32, 3/8, 15/32, 1/2, 19/32, 5/8.

#### APA TEXTURE 1-11

Special 303 Siding panel with grooves 1/4" deep, 3/8" wide, spaced 4" or 8" o.c. Other spacings may be available on special order. Edges shiplapped. Available unsanded, textured and MDO. EDC: Exterior. THICKNESSES: 19/32 and 5/8 only.

#### APA DECORATIVE

Rough-sawn, brushed, grooved, or striated faces. For paneling, interior accent walls, built-ins, counter facing, exhibit displays. Can also be made by some manufacturers in Exterior for siding, gable ends, fences, etc. Use recommendations for Exterior panels vary with the particular product. Check with manufacturer. EDC: Interior, Exposure 1, Exterior. COMMON THICKNESSES: 5/16, 3/8, 1/2, 5/8.

#### APA HIGH DENSITY OVERLAY (HDO)[5]

Has a hard semi-opaque resin-fiber overlay both sides. Abrasion resistant. For concrete forms, cabinets, countertops, signs, tanks. Also available with skid-resistant screen-grid surface. EDC: Exterior. COMMON THICKNESSES: 3/8, 1/2, 5/8, 3/4.

#### APA MEDIUM DENSITY OVERLAY (MDO)[5]

Smooth, opaque, resin-fiber overlay one or both sides. Ideal base for paint, indoors and outdoors. Also available as a 303 Siding. EDC: Exterior. COMMON THICKNESSES: 11/32, 3/8, 1/2, 5/8, 3/4, 15/32, 19/32, 23/32.

#### APA MARINE

Ideal for boat hulls. Made only with Douglas fir or western larch. Special solid jointed core construction. Subject to special limitations on core gaps and face repairs. Also available with HDO or MDO faces. EDC: Exterior. COMMON THICKNESSES: 1/4, 3/8, 1/2, 5/8, 3/4.

#### APA B-B PLYFORM CLASS I AND CLASS II

Concrete form grades with high reuse factor. Sanded both sides and mill-oiled unless otherwise specified. Special restrictions on species. Class I panels are stiffest, strongest and most commonly available. Also available in HDO for very smooth concrete finish, in Structural I (all plies limited to Group 1 species), and with special overlays. EDC: Exterior. COMMON THICKNESSES: 5/8, 3/4, 19/32, 23/32.

#### APA PLYRON

Hardboard face on both sides. Faces tempered, untempered, smooth or screened. For countertops, shelving, cabinet doors, flooring. EDC: Interior, Exposure 1, Exterior. COMMON THICKNESSES: 1/2, 5/8, 3/4.

### APA PERFORMANCE-RATED PANELS[1][2][6]

#### APA RATED SHEATHING

Specially designed for subflooring and wall and roof sheathing. Also good for broad range of other construction and industrial applications. Can be manufactured as conventional veneered plywood, as a composite, or as a nonveneered panel. For special engineered applications, veneered panels conforming to PS 1 may be required. EDC: Exterior, Exposure 1, Exposure 2. COMMON THICKNESSES: 5/16, 3/8, 7/16, 1/2, 5/8, 3/4, 15/32, 19/32, 23/32.

#### APA STRUCTURAL I AND II RATED SHEATHING[3]

Unsanded all-veneer PS 1 plywood grades for use where strength properties are of maximum importance, such as box beams, gusset plates, stressed-skin panels, containers, pallet bins. Structural I more commonly available. EDC: Exterior, Exposure 1. COMMON THICKNESSES: 5/16, 3/8, 1/2, 5/8, 3/4, 15/32, 19/32, 23/32.

#### APA RATED STURD-I-FLOOR

Specially designed as combination subfloor-underlayment. Provides smooth surface for application of carpet and pad and possesses high concentrated and impact load resistance. Can be manufactured as conventional veneered plywood, as a composite, or as a nonveneered panel. Available square edge or tongue-and-groove. EDC: Exterior, Exposure 1, Exposure 2. COMMON THICKNESSES: 19/32, 5/8, 23/32, 3/4.

#### APA RATED STURD-I-FLOOR 48 OC (2-4-1)

For combination subfloor-underlayment on 32- and 48-inch spans and for heavy timber roof construction. Manufactured only as conventional veneered plywood. Available square edge or tongue-and-groove. EDC: Exposure 1. THICKNESS: 1 1/8.

NOTES

1. Specify Performance-Rated Panels by thickness and Span Rating. Span Ratings are based on panel strength and stiffness. Since these properties are a function of panel composition and configuration as well as thickness, the same Span Rating may appear on panels of different thickness. Conversely, panels of the same thickness may be marked with different Span Ratings.
2. All plies in Structural I panels are special improved grades and limited to Group 1 species. All plies in Structural II panels are special improved grades and limited to Group 1, 2, or 3 species.
3. Exterior sanded panels, C-C Plugged, C-D Plugged and Underlayment grades can also be manufactured in Structural I (all plies limited to Group 1 species) and Structural II (all plies limited to Group 1, 2 or 3 species).
4. Some manufacturers also produce panels with premium N-grade veneer on one or both faces. Available only by special order.
5. Can also be manufactured in Structural I (all plies limited to Group 1 species) and Structural II (all plies limited to Group 1, 2 or 3 species).
6. EDC: Exposure Durability Classifications (typical).
7. Also available in 11/32, 15/32, 19/32, 23/32.

## EXTERIOR TYPE PANELS

### APPEARANCE (1, 3)

| GRADE (2) | COMMON USES | F | M | B | 1/4 | 5/16 | 11/32 3/8 | 15/32 1/2 | 19/32 5/8 | 23/32 3/4 |
|---|---|---|---|---|---|---|---|---|---|---|
| A-A EXT APA (5) | Use where both sides are visible | A | C | A | • | | • | • | • | • |
| A-B EXT APA (5) | Use where view of one side is less important | A | C | B | • | | • | • | • | • |
| A-C EXT APA (5) | Use where only one side is visible | A | C | C | • | | • | • | • | • |
| B-B EXT APA (5) | Utility panel with two solid faces | B | C | B | • | | • | • | • | • |
| B-C EXT APA (5) | Utility panel. Also used as base for exterior coatings on walls and roofs | B | C | C | • | | • | • | • | • |
| HDO EXT-APA (5) | High density overlay plywood has a hard, semi-opaque resin fiber overlay on both faces. Abrasion resistant. Use for concrete forms, cabinets, and countertops | A/B | C | A/B | | | • | • | • | • |
| MDO EXT APA (5) | Medium density overlay with smooth resin fiber overlay on one or two faces. Recommended for siding and other outdoor applications. Ideal base for paint | B | C | B/C | | | • | • | • | • |
| 303 SIDING EXT-APA (7) | Special surface treatment such as V-groove, channel groove, striated, brushed, rough sawn | (6) | C | C | | | • | • | • | |
| T1-11 EXT-APA (7) | Special 303 panel having grooves 1/4 in. deep, 3/8 in. wide, spaced 4 in. or 8 in. o.c. Other spacing optional. Edges shiplapped. Available unsanded, textured, and medium density overlay | A/B/C | C | C | | | | | • | |
| PLYRON EXT-APA | Hardboard faces both sides, tempered, smooth or screened | HB | C | HB | | | | • | • | • |
| UNDER-LAYMENT C-C PLUGGED EXT-APA (5) | For application over structural subfloor. Provides smooth surface for application of resilient floor coverings where severe moisture conditions may be present. Touch-sanded | C | C | C | | | | • | • | • |
| C-C PLUGGED EXT-APA (5) | For refrigerated or controlled atmosphere rooms. Touch-sanded | C | C | C | | | | • | • | • |
| B-B PLYFORM CLASS I and CLASS II EXT-APA (4) | Concrete form grades with high reuse factor. Sanded both sides and mill-oiled unless otherwise specified. Special restrictions on species. Also available in HDO for very smooth concrete finish | B | C | B | | | | | • | • |

### PERFORMANCE RATED (3)

| GRADE | COMMON USES | F | M | B | 1/4 | 5/16 | 3/8 | 15/32 1/2 | 19/32 5/8 | 23/32 3/4 |
|---|---|---|---|---|---|---|---|---|---|---|
| SHEATHING EXT-APA | Exterior sheathing panel for subflooring and wall and roof sheathing, siding on service and farm buildings. Manufactured as conventional veneered plywood | C | C | C | | | • | • | • | • |
| STRUCTURAL I and II SHEATHING EXT-APA | For engineered applications in construction and industry where full exterior type panels are required. Unsanded. See Note 5 for species group requirements | C | C | C | | | • | • | • | • |
| STURDI-I-FLOOR EXT-APA | For combination subfloor underlayment under carpet and pad where severe moisture conditions exist, as in balcony decks. Touch-sanded and tongue and groove | C | C (11) | C | | | | | • | • |

## INTERIOR TYPE PANELS

### APPEARANCE (1, 3)

| GRADE (2) (12) | COMMON USES | F | M | B | 1/4 | 5/16 | 11/32 3/8 | 15/32 1/2 | 19/32 5/8 | 23/32 3/4 |
|---|---|---|---|---|---|---|---|---|---|---|
| N-N, N-A, N-B INT-APA | Cabinet quality. For natural finish furniture. Special order items | N | C | NA / B | | | | | | • |
| N-D INT-APA | For natural finish paneling. Special orders | N | D | D | • | | | | | |
| A-A INT-APA | For applications where both sides are visible. Smooth face; suitable for painting | A | D | A | • | | • | • | • | • |
| A-B INT-APA | Use where view of one side is less important but two solid surfaces are needed | A | D | B | • | | • | • | • | • |
| A-D INT-APA | Use where only one side is visible | A | D | D | • | | • | • | • | • |
| B-B INT-APA | Utility panel with two solid sides | B | D | B | • | | • | • | • | • |
| B-D INT-APA | Utility panel with one solid side | B | D | D | • | | • | • | • | • |
| Decorative panels-INT-APA | Rough sawn, brushed, grooved, or striated faces for walls and built-ins | A/B/C | D | D | | • | • | • | • | |
| PLYRON INT-APA | Hardboard face on both sides, tempered smooth or screened for counters and doors | HB | C/D | HB | | | | • | • | • |
| UNDER-LAYMENT INT-APA (5) | For application over structural subfloor. Provides smooth surface for application of resilient floor coverings. Touch-sanded. Also available with exterior glue | C | C/D | D | | | | • | • | • |
| C-D PLUGGED INT-APA (5) | For built-ins, wall and ceiling tile backing, cable reels, walkways, separator boards. Not a substitute for UNDERLAYMENT or STURD-I-FLOOR as it lacks their indentation resistance. Touch-sanded. Also made with exterior glue | C | D | D | | | | • | • | • |

### PERFORMANCE RATED (3, 8)

VENEER (13)

| GRADE | COMMON USES | F | M | B | 1/4 | 5/16 | 3/8 | 15/32 1/2 | 19/32 5/8 | 23/32 3/4 |
|---|---|---|---|---|---|---|---|---|---|---|
| SHEATHING EXP 1 and 2-APA | Commonly available with exterior glue for sheathing and subflooring. Specify Exposure 1 treated wood foundations | C | D | D | | | • | • | • | • |
| STRUCTURAL I and II SHEATHING EXP 1-APA | Unsanded structural grades where plywood strength properties are of maximum importance. Made only with exterior glue for beams, gusset plates, and stressed-skin panels | C (10) | D (10) | D (10) | | | • | • | • | • |
| STURD-I-FLOOR EXP 1 and 2-APA | For combination subfloor and underlayment under carpet and pad. Specify Exposure 1 where moisture is present. Available in tongue and groove | C | C/D (11) | D | | | | | • | • |
| STURD-I-FLOOR 48 o.c. (2, 4, 1) EXP 1-APA (9) | Combination subfloor underlayment on 32 and 48 in. spans and for heavy timber roofs. Use in areas subject to moisture; or if construction may be delayed as in site built floors. Unsanded or touch-sanded as specified | C | C/D | D | | | | | | 1⅛ |

## GENERAL NOTES

1. Sanded on both sides except where decorative or other surfaces specified.
2. Available in Group 1, 2, 3, 4, or 5 unless otherwise noted.
3. Standard 4 × 8 panel sizes; other sizes available.
4. Also available in Structural I.
5. Also available in Structural I (all plies limited to Group I species) and Structural II (all plies limited to Group 1, 2, or 3 species).
6. C or better for five plies; C Plugged or better for three-ply panels.
7. Stud spacing is shown on grade stamp.
8. Exposure 1 made with exterior glue, Exposure 2 with intermediate glue.
9. Made only in woods of certain species to conform to APA specifications.
10. Special improved grade for structural panels.
11. Special construction to resist indentation from concentrated loads.
12. Interior type panels with exterior glue are identified as Exposure 1.
13. Also available as nonveneer or composite panels.

Bloodgood Architects, PC; Des Moines and New York
American Plywood Association

 **ROUGH CARPENTRY**

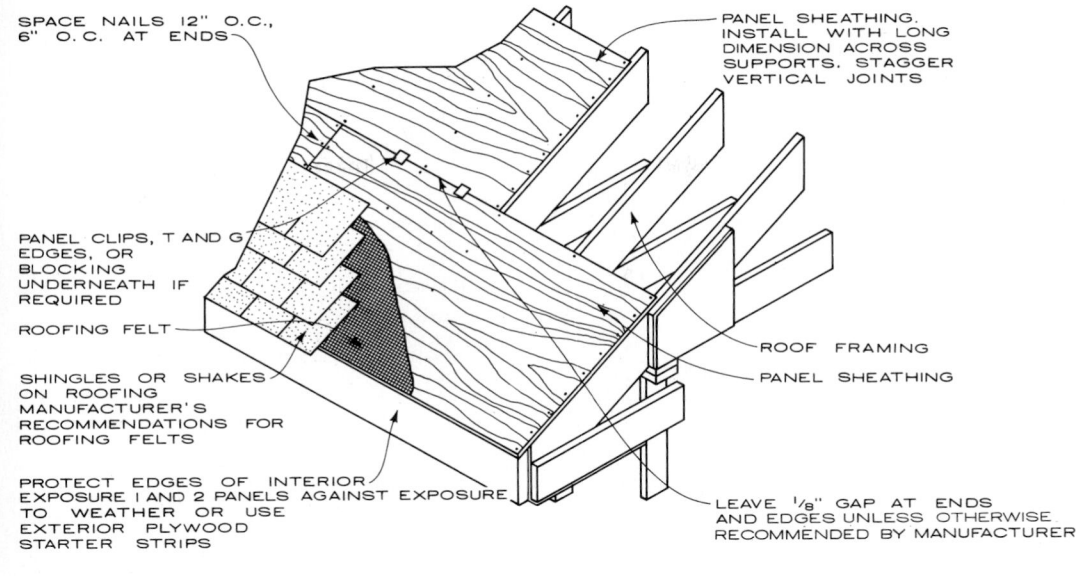

SPACE NAILS 12" O.C.,
6" O.C. AT ENDS

PANEL SHEATHING.
INSTALL WITH LONG
DIMENSION ACROSS
SUPPORTS. STAGGER
VERTICAL JOINTS

PANEL CLIPS, T AND G
EDGES, OR
BLOCKING
UNDERNEATH IF
REQUIRED

ROOFING FELT

ROOF FRAMING

PANEL SHEATHING

SHINGLES OR SHAKES
ON ROOFING
MANUFACTURER'S
RECOMMENDATIONS FOR
ROOFING FELTS

PROTECT EDGES OF INTERIOR
EXPOSURE 1 AND 2 PANELS AGAINST EXPOSURE
TO WEATHER OR USE
EXTERIOR PLYWOOD
STARTER STRIPS

LEAVE 1/8" GAP AT ENDS
AND EDGES UNLESS OTHERWISE
RECOMMENDED BY MANUFACTURER

**STRUCTURAL-USE PANEL ROOF SHEATHING**

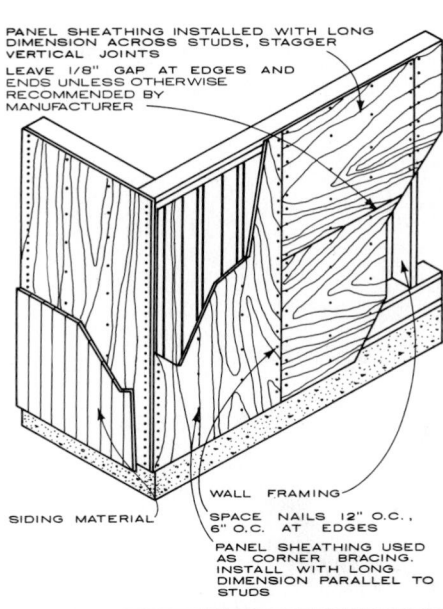

PANEL SHEATHING INSTALLED WITH LONG
DIMENSION ACROSS STUDS, STAGGER
VERTICAL JOINTS

LEAVE 1/8" GAP AT EDGES AND
ENDS UNLESS OTHERWISE
RECOMMENDED BY
MANUFACTURER

WALL FRAMING

SIDING MATERIAL

SPACE NAILS 12" O.C.,
6" O.C. AT EDGES

PANEL SHEATHING USED
AS CORNER BRACING.
INSTALL WITH LONG
DIMENSION PARALLEL TO
STUDS

**STRUCTURAL-USE PANEL WALL SHEATHING**

## PLYWOOD ROOF SHEATHING

Plywood grades commonly used for roof (and wall) sheathing are A.P.A. rated sheathing with span ratings: 16/0, 20/0, 24/0, 24/16, 32/16, 40/20, 48/20; exposure durability classifications: Exterior, Exposure 1, Exposure 2. Refer to American Plywood Association recommendations for unsupported edges.

## PLYWOOD WALL SHEATHING

Common grade is same as used in roof sheathing. Refer to American Plywood Association recommendations for unsupported edges.

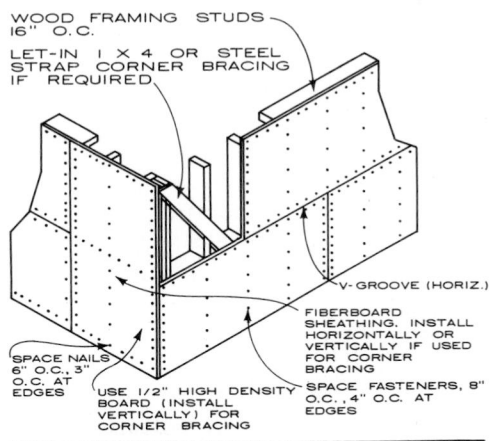

FOR HORIZONTAL
SHEATHING SPACE
NAILS 8" O.C. IF
USED FOR CORNER
BRACING SPACE
NAILS 12" O.C.
AND USE ADHESIVE

SPACE STUDS 24"
O.C. MAX. 16" O.C.
IF USED FOR
CORNER
BRACING

NAIL SIDING TO STUDS
NOT TO GYPSUM BOARD

GYPSUM SHEATHING.
INSTALL
HORIZONTALLY. IF
USED FOR
CORNER BRACING
INSTALL
VERTICALLY

NOTE: REFER TO MANUFACTURER'S
RECOMMENDATIONS FOR SPECIFIC
INSTALLATION INSTRUCTIONS

**GYPSUM WALL SHEATHING**

WOOD FRAMING STUDS
16" O.C.

LET-IN 1 X 4 OR STEEL
STRAP CORNER BRACING
IF REQUIRED

V-GROOVE (HORIZ.)

FIBERBOARD
SHEATHING. INSTALL
HORIZONTALLY OR
VERTICALLY IF USED
FOR CORNER
BRACING

SPACE NAILS
6" O.C. 3"
O.C. AT
EDGES

USE 1/2" HIGH DENSITY
BOARD (INSTALL
VERTICALLY) FOR
CORNER BRACING

SPACE FASTENERS, 8"
O.C., 4" O.C. AT
EDGES

**FIBERBOARD SHEATHING**

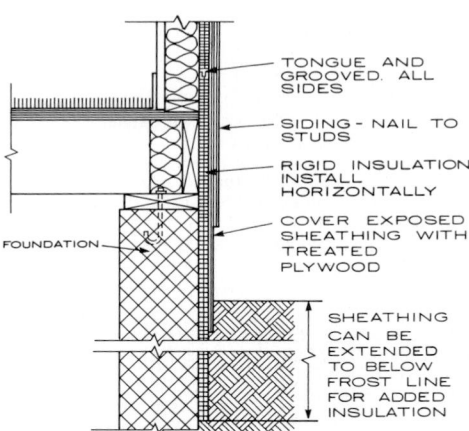

TONGUE AND
GROOVED. ALL
SIDES

SIDING - NAIL TO
STUDS

RIGID INSULATION.
INSTALL
HORIZONTALLY

COVER EXPOSED
SHEATHING WITH
TREATED
PLYWOOD

FOUNDATION

SHEATHING
CAN BE
EXTENDED
TO BELOW
FROST LINE
FOR ADDED
INSULATION

**PLASTIC SHEATHING**

## GYPSUM WALL SHEATHING

Fire rated panels are available in 1/2 and 5/8 in. thicknesses. Gypsum board is not an effective vapor barrier.

## FIBERBOARD SHEATHING

Also called insulation board. Can be treated or impregnated with asphalt. Available in regular or 1/2 in. high density panels.

## PLASTIC SHEATHING

Usually made of polyurethane or polystyrene. Can be considered an effective vapor barrier, hence wall must be effectively vented. All edges are usually tongue and groove.

## SHEATHING MATERIALS

| CHARACTERISTICS | PLYWOOD | GYPSUM | FIBERBOARD | PLASTIC |
|---|---|---|---|---|
| Nailable base | Yes | No | Only high density | No |
| Vapor barrier | No | No | If asphalt treated | Yes |
| Insulation R value (1/2 in. thickness) | 1.2 | 0.7 | 2.6 | 6.25 |
| Corner bracing provided | Yes | Yes (see manufacturer's recommendation) | Only high density | No |
| Panel sizes (ft.) | 4 x 8, 4 x 9, 4 x 10 | 4 x 8, 4 x 10, 4 x 12, 4 x 14 | 4 x 8, 4 x 9, 4 x 10, 4 x 12 | 16 x 96, 24 x 48, 24 x 96 |
| Panel thickness (in.) | 5/16, 3/8, 7/16, 15/32, 1/2, 19/32, 5/8, 23/32, 3/4 | 1/4, 3/8, 1/2, 5/8 | 1/2, 25/32 | 3/4 to 6 (for roof) |

Timothy B. McDonald; Washington, D.C.
John D. Bloodgood, Architects, P.C.; Des Moines, Iowa
American Plywood Association

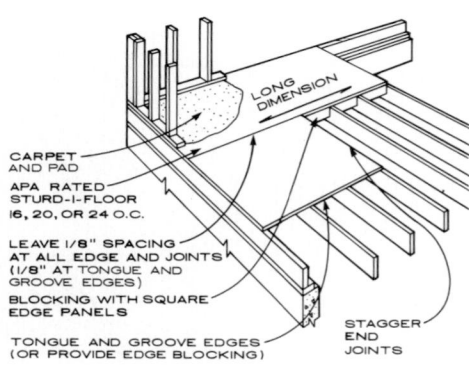

LONG DIMENSION

CARPET AND PAD

APA RATED STURD-I-FLOOR 16, 20, OR 24 O.C.

LEAVE 1/8" SPACING AT ALL EDGE AND JOINTS (1/8" AT TONGUE AND GROOVE EDGES)

BLOCKING WITH SQUARE EDGE PANELS

TONGUE AND GROOVE EDGES (OR PROVIDE EDGE BLOCKING)

STAGGER END JOINTS

## APA RATED STURD-I-FLOOR

### APA RATED STURD-I-FLOOR (1)

| SPAN RATING (MAXIMUM JOIST SPACING) (IN.) | PANEL THICKNESS (2) (IN.) | FASTENING NAIL SIZE AND TYPE | GLUE-NAILED (3) | | NAILED ONLY | |
|---|---|---|---|---|---|---|
| | | | SPACING (IN.) | | | |
| | | | PANEL EDGE | INTERMEDIATE | PANEL EDGE | INTERMEDIATE |
| 16 | 19/32, 5/8, 21/32 | 6d Ring or Screw-Shank (4) | 12 / 6 | 12 / 10 | | |
| 20 | 19/32, 5/8, 23/32, 3/4 | 6d Ring or Screw-Shank (4) | 12 / 6 | 12 / 10 | | |
| 24 | 11/16, 23/32, 3/4 | 6d Ring or Screw-Shank (4) | 12 / 6 | 12 / 10 | | |
| | 7/8, 1 | 8d Ring or Screw-Shank (4) | 12 / 6 | 12 / 10 | | |
| 48 (2-4-1 Panels) | 1 1/8 | 8d Ring or Screw-Shank (5) | 6 / 6 | (6) / (6) | | |

### STURD-I-FLOOR NOTES

1. For conditions not listed, see APA literature.
2. Use only APA Specification AFG-01 adhesives, properly applied. Use only solvent-based glues on non-veneered panels with sealed surfaces and edges.
3. 8d common nails may be substituted if ring- or screw-shank nails are not available.
4. 10d common nails may be substituted with 1 1/8 in. panels if supports are well seasoned.
5. Space nails 6 in. for 48 in. spans and 10 in. for 32 in. spans.

## ALLOWABLE CLEAR SPANS FOR APA: GLUED FLOOR SYSTEM (1,4,5)

| | | APA GLUED FLOOR SPANS | | | |
|---|---|---|---|---|---|
| | | JOIST SPACING | | | |
| | | 16" o.c. | | 19.2" o.c. | 24" o.c. |
| | | APA RATED STURD-I-FLOOR | | | |
| SPECIES GRADE | JOIST SIZE | 16" OR 20" o.c. | 24" o.c. | 20" o.c. | 24" o.c. |
| Douglas fir Larch-No. 2 | 2 x 6 | 10'-5" | 10'-6" | 9'-7" | 8'-7" |
| | 2 x 8 | 13'-7" | 13'-10" | 12'-7" | 11'-3" |
| | 2 x 10 | 17'-2" | 17'-7" | 16'-1" | 14'-5" |
| | 2 x 12 | 20'-9" | 21'-5" | 19'-7" | 17'-6" |
| Douglas fir South-No. 1 | 2 x 6 | 9'-10" | 10'-8" | 9'-11" | 9'-1" |
| | 2 x 8 | 12'-9" | 13'-8" | 12'-8" | 12'-0" |
| | 2 x 10 | 16'-2" | 17'-0" | 15'-11" | 15'-4" |
| | 2 x 12 | 19'-7" | 20'-5" | 19'-1" | 18'-4" |
| Hem-fir No. 1 | 2 x 6 | 10'-0" | 10'-3" | 9'-5" | 8'-5" |
| | 2 x 8 | 13'-1" | 13'-7" | 12'-5" | 11'-1" |
| | 2 x 10 | 16'-6" | 17'-4" | 15'-10" | 14'-2" |
| | 2 x 12 | 20'-0" | 20'-10" | 19'-3" | 17'-2" |
| Mountain hemlock No. 2 | 2 x 6 | 9'-2" | 9'-6" | 8'-8" | 7'-9" |
| | 2 x 8 | 11'-11" | 12'-7" | 11'-6" | 10'-3" |
| | 2 x 10 | 15'-0" | 16'-0" | 14'-8" | 13'-1" |
| | 2 x 12 | 18'-2" | 19'-2" | 17'-9" | 15'-11" |
| Southern pine KD No. 2 | 2 x 6 | 10'-2" | 10'-8" | 9'-9" | 8'-8" |
| | 2 x 8 | 13'-4" | 14'-0" | 12'-10" | 11'-6" |
| | 2 x 10 | 16'-10" | 17'-8" | 16'-4" | 14'-8" |
| | 2 x 12 | 20'-5" | 21'-2" | 19'-10" | 17'-9" |

John D. Bloodgood, Architects, P.C.; Des Moines, Iowa
American Plywood Association

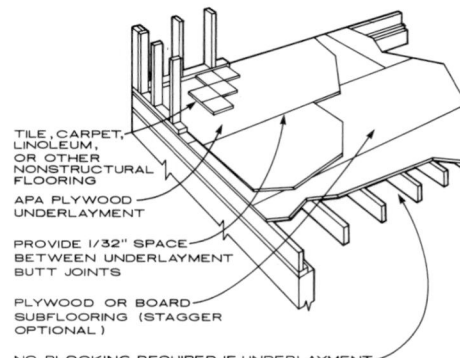

TILE, CARPET, LINOLEUM, OR OTHER NONSTRUCTURAL FLOORING

APA PLYWOOD UNDERLAYMENT

PROVIDE 1/32" SPACE BETWEEN UNDERLAYMENT BUTT JOINTS

PLYWOOD OR BOARD SUBFLOORING (STAGGER OPTIONAL)

NO BLOCKING REQUIRED IF UNDERLAYMENT JOINTS ARE OFFSET FROM SUBFLOOR JOINTS

## PLYWOOD UNDERLAYMENT

### PLYWOOD UNDERLAYMENT (1)

| PLYWOOD GRADES AND SPECIES GROUP | APPLICATION (2) | MINIMUM PLYWOOD THICKNESS (IN.) |
|---|---|---|
| Groups 1, 2, 3, 4, 5 UNDERLAYMENT INT-APA (with interior or exterior glue), or UNDERLAYMENT EXT-APA (C-C plugged) EXT | Over smooth subfloor | 1/4 |
| | Over lumber subfloor or other uneven surfaces | 11/32 |
| Same grades as above, but Group 1 only | Over lumber floor up to 4 in. wide. Face grain must be perpendicular to boards | 1/4 |

### UNDERLAYMENT NOTES

1. For tile, carpeting, linoleum, or other nonstructural flooring. (Ceramic tile not recommended.)
2. Where floors may be subject to unusual moisture conditions, use panels with exterior glue (Exposure 1) or UNDERLAYMENT C-C Plugged EXT-APA. C-D Plugged is not an adequate substitute for underlayment grade, since it does not ensure equivalent dent resistance.
3. Recommended grades have a solid surface backed with a special inner ply construction that resists punch-through, dents, and concentrated loads.

### UNDERLAYMENT NAILING SCHEDULE

Use 3d ring shank nails for underlayment up to 1/2 in. thickness, 4d for 5/8 in. and thicker. Use 16 gauge staples, except that 18 gauge may be used with 1/4 in. thick underlayment. Crown width should be 3/8 in. for 16 gauge staples, 3/16 in. for 18 gauge. Length should be sufficient to penetrate subflooring at least 5/8 in. or extend completely through. Space fasteners at 3 in. along panel edges and at 6 in. each way in the panel interior, except for 3/8 in. or thicker underlayment applied with ring shank nails. In this case, use 6 in. spacing along edges and 8 in. spacing each way in the panel interior. Unless subfloor and joists are of thoroughly seasoned material and have remained dry during construction, countersink nail heads below surface of the underlayment just prior to laying finish floors to avoid nail popping. If thin resilient flooring is to be applied, fill and thoroughly sand joints.

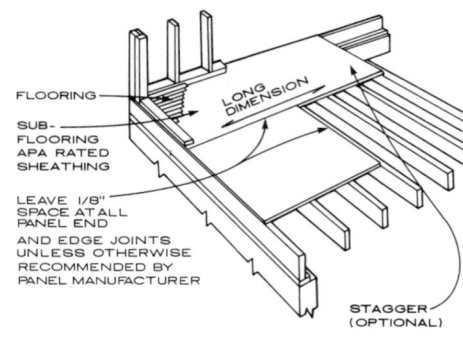

LONG DIMENSION

FLOORING

SUB-FLOORING APA RATED SHEATHING

LEAVE 1/8" SPACE AT ALL PANEL END AND EDGE JOINTS UNLESS OTHERWISE RECOMMENDED BY PANEL MANUFACTURER

STAGGER (OPTIONAL)

**APA PANEL SUBFLOOR**

## APA PANEL SUBFLOORING (1)

| PANEL SPAN RATING (OR GROUP NUMBER) | PANEL THICKNESS (IN.) | MAXIMUM SPACING (2, 3, 5) (IN.) |
|---|---|---|
| 24/16 | 7/16, 1/2 | 16 |
| 32/16 | 15/32, 1/2, 5/8 | 16(4) |
| 40/20 | 19/32, 5/8, 3/4, 7/8 | 20(4) |
| 48/24 | 23/32, 3/4, 7/8 | 24 |
| 1 1/8 in. groups (1, 2) | 1 1/8 | 32 (2x joists) 48 (4x joists) |

### SUBFLOORING NOTES

1. Applies to APA rated sheathing grades only.
2. The spans assume plywood continuous over two or more spans with long dimension across supports.
3. In some nonresidential buildings special conditions may require construction in excess of minimums given.
4. May be 24 in. if 25/32 in. wood strip flooring is installed at right angles to joists.
5. Spans are limited to the values shown because of the possible effect of concentrated loads.

### SUBFLOORING NAILING SCHEDULE

For 7/16 in. panel, 16 in. span, use 6d common nails at 6 in. o.c. at panel edges, 10 in. o.c. at intermediate supports. For 15/32 in. to 7/8 in. panels, 16 in. to 24 in. spans, use 8d common nails at 6 in. o.c. at panel edges, 10 in. o.c. at intermediate supports. For 1 1/8 in. and 1 1/4 in. panels up to 48 in. span, use 10d common nails 6 in. o.c. at panel edges, and 6 in. at intermediate supports.

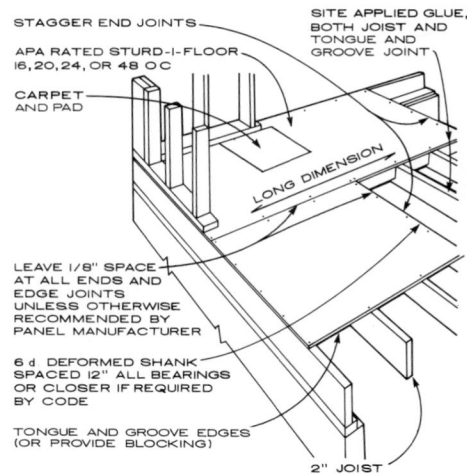

STAGGER END JOINTS

SITE APPLIED GLUE, BOTH JOIST AND TONGUE AND GROOVE JOINT

APA RATED STURD-I-FLOOR 16, 20, 24, OR 48 O.C.

CARPET AND PAD

LONG DIMENSION

LEAVE 1/8" SPACE AT ALL ENDS AND EDGE JOINTS UNLESS OTHERWISE RECOMMENDED BY PANEL MANUFACTURER

6d DEFORMED SHANK SPACED 12" ALL BEARINGS OR CLOSER IF REQUIRED BY CODE

TONGUE AND GROOVE EDGES (OR PROVIDE BLOCKING)

2" JOIST

### APA GLUED FLOOR SYSTEM

### GLUED FLOOR NOTES

1. For complete information on glued floors, including joist span tables (based on building code criteria and lumber sizes), application sequence, and a list of recommended adhesives, contact the American Plywood Association.
2. Place APA STURD-I-FLOOR T&G across the joists with end joints staggered. Leave 1/8 in. space at all end and edge joints.
3. Although T&G is used most often, square edge may be used if 2 x 4 blocking is placed under panel edge joints between joists.
4. Based on live load of 40 psf, total load of 50 psf, deflection limited to 1/360 at 40 psf.
5. Glue tongue and groove joints. If square edge panels are used, block panel edges and glue between panels and between panels and blocking.

### GLUED FLOOR NAILING SCHEDULE

Panels should be secured with power driven fasteners or nailed with 6d deformed shank nails, spaced 12 in. at supports. (8d common smooth nails may be substituted.)

**ROUGH CARPENTRY**

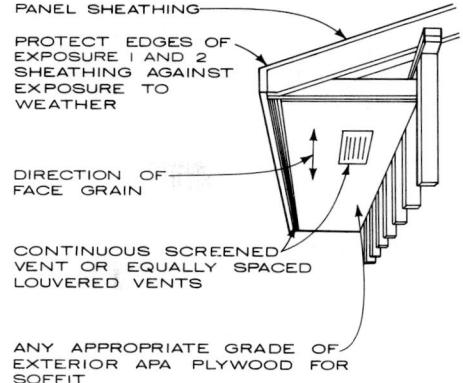

PANEL SHEATHING

PROTECT EDGES OF EXPOSURE 1 AND 2 SHEATHING AGAINST EXPOSURE TO WEATHER

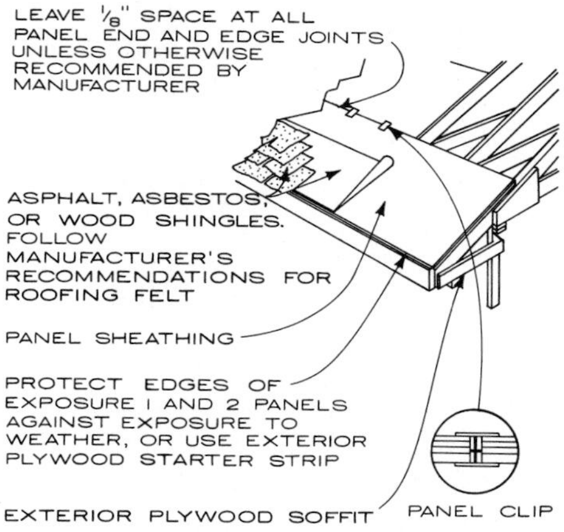

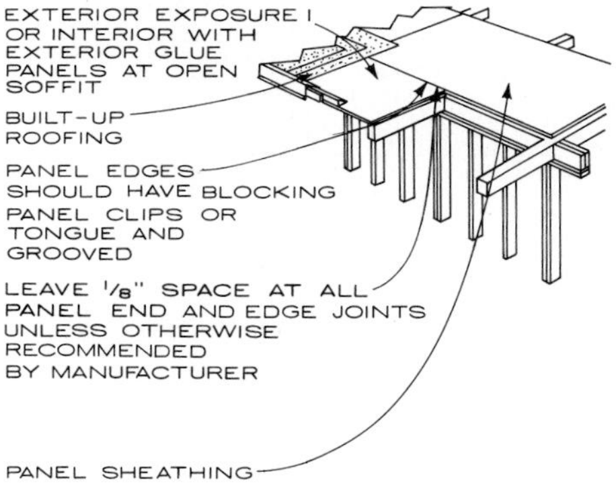

DIRECTION OF FACE GRAIN

CONTINUOUS SCREENED VENT OR EQUALLY SPACED LOUVERED VENTS

ANY APPROPRIATE GRADE OF EXTERIOR APA PLYWOOD FOR SOFFIT

LEAVE ⅛" SPACE AT ALL PANEL END AND EDGE JOINTS UNLESS OTHERWISE RECOMMENDED BY MANUFACTURER

ASPHALT, ASBESTOS, OR WOOD SHINGLES. FOLLOW MANUFACTURER'S RECOMMENDATIONS FOR ROOFING FELT

PANEL SHEATHING

PROTECT EDGES OF EXPOSURE 1 AND 2 PANELS AGAINST EXPOSURE TO WEATHER, OR USE EXTERIOR PLYWOOD STARTER STRIP

EXTERIOR PLYWOOD SOFFIT

PANEL CLIP

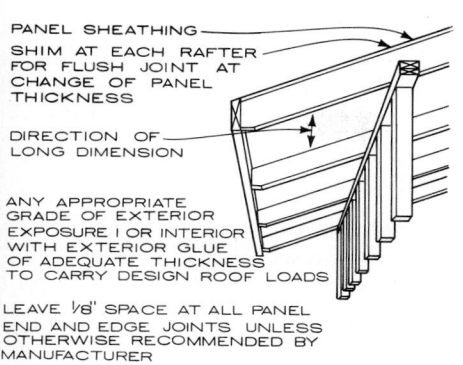

PANEL SHEATHING

SHIM AT EACH RAFTER FOR FLUSH JOINT AT CHANGE OF PANEL THICKNESS

DIRECTION OF LONG DIMENSION

ANY APPROPRIATE GRADE OF EXTERIOR EXPOSURE 1 OR INTERIOR WITH EXTERIOR GLUE OF ADEQUATE THICKNESS TO CARRY DESIGN ROOF LOADS

LEAVE ⅛" SPACE AT ALL PANEL END AND EDGE JOINTS UNLESS OTHERWISE RECOMMENDED BY MANUFACTURER

## OPEN SOFFIT
### EXTERIOR OPEN SOFFITS/COMBINED CEILING DECKING (1)

| PANEL DESCRIPTIONS, MINIMUM RECOMMENDATIONS | GROUP | MAXIMUM SPAN (IN.) |
|---|---|---|
| ¹⁵/₃₂″ APA 303 siding | 1, 2, 3, 4 | 16 |
| ¹⁵/₃₂″ APA sanded | 1, 2, 3, 4 | |
| ¹⁵/₃₂″ APA 303 siding | 1 | 24 |
| ¹⁵/₃₂″ APA sanded | 1, 2, 3 | |
| ¹⁹/₃₂″ APA 303 siding | 1, 2, 3, 4 | |
| ¹⁹/₃₂″ APA sanded | 1, 2, 3, 4 | |
| ¹⁹/₃₂″ APA 303 siding | 1 | |
| ¹⁹/₃₂″ APA sanded | 1 | 32 (2) |
| ²³/₃₂″ APA 303 siding | 1, 2, 3, 4 | |
| ²³/₃₂″ APA sanded | 1, 2, 3, 4 | |
| 1⅛″ APA textured | 1, 2, 3, 4 | 48 (2) |

### NOTES
1. Plywood is assumed to be continuous across two or more spans with face grain across supports.
2. For spans of 32 or 48 in. in open soffit construction, provide adequate blocking, tongue-and-groove edges, or other support such as panel clips. Minimum loads are at least 30 psf live load, plus 10 psf dead load.

NAILING SCHEDULE: For open soffits, use 6d common smooth, ring shank, or spiral thread nails for ½ in. or smaller thicknesses; use 8d nails for plywood ⅝ in. to 1 in. thick. Use 8d ring shank or spiral thread or 10d common smooth shank nails for 1⅛ in. textured panels. Space nails 6 in. at panel edges, 12 in. at intermediate supports, except for 48 in. spans where nails should be spaced 6 in. at all supports.

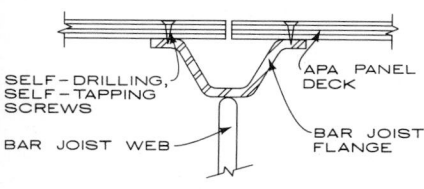

SELF-DRILLING, SELF-TAPPING SCREWS

APA PANEL DECK

BAR JOIST WEB

BAR JOIST FLANGE

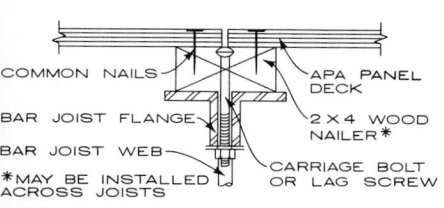

COMMON NAILS

APA PANEL DECK

BAR JOIST FLANGE

BAR JOIST WEB

2 × 4 WOOD NAILER *

CARRIAGE BOLT OR LAG SCREW

*MAY BE INSTALLED ACROSS JOISTS

## CONNECTIONS TO OPEN WEB STEEL JOISTS

## CLOSED SOFFIT
### EXTERIOR CLOSED PLYWOOD SOFFITS

| NOMINAL PLYWOOD THICKNESS | GROUP | MAXIMUM SPAN (IN.) ALL EDGES SUPPORTED |
|---|---|---|
| ¹¹/₃₂″ APA 303 siding or APA sanded | | 24 |
| ¹⁵/₃₂″ APA 303 siding or APA sanded | 1, 2, 3, 4 | 32 |
| ¹⁹/₃₂″ APA 303 siding or APA sanded | | 48 |

NOTE: Plywood is assumed to be continuous across two or more spans with face grain across supports.

NAILING SCHEDULE: For closed soffits, use nonstaining box or casing nails, 6d for ¹¹/₃₂ and ¹⁵/₃₂ in. panels and 8d for ¹⁹/₃₂ in. panels. Space nails 6 in. at panel edges and 12 in. along intermediate supports.

### APA PANEL ROOF DECKING (1)

| PANEL SPAN RATING | PANEL THICKNESS (IN.) | MAXIMUM SPAN (IN.) | | NAIL SIZE AND TYPE | NAIL SPACING (IN.) | |
|---|---|---|---|---|---|---|
| | | WITH EDGE SUPPORT | WITHOUT EDGE SUPPORT | | PANEL EDGES | INTERMEDIATE |
| 12/0 | ⁵/₁₆ | 12 | 12 | 6d common | 6 | 12 |
| 16/0 | ⁵/₁₆ ³/₈ | 16 | 16 | | | |
| 20/0 | ⁵/₁₆ ³/₈ | 20 | 20 | | | |
| 24/0 | ³/₈ ⁷/₁₆ ½ | 24 | 20 | | | |
| 24/16 | ⁷/₁₆ ½ | 24 | 24 | | | |
| 32/16 | ¹⁵/₃₂, ½ | 32 | 28 | | | |
| 32/16 | ⁵/₈ | 32 | 28 | 8d common | | |
| 40/20 | ⁵/₈ ¹⁹/₃₂, ³/₄ ⁷/₈ | 40 | 32 | | | |
| 48/24 | ²³/₃₂, ³/₄ ⁷/₈ | 48 | 36 | | | |

| | | | | STAPLING SPACES (IN.) | | |
|---|---|---|---|---|---|---|
| | | | | LEG LENGTH | PANEL EDGES | INTERMEDIATE |
| (see above) | ⁵/₁₆″ | (see above) | | 1¼″ | 4 | 8 |
| | ³/₈″ | | | 1⅜″ | | |
| | ⁷/₁₆″, ¹⁵/₃₂″, ½″ | | | 1½″ | | |

### NAILING SCHEDULE
Use 6d common smooth, ring shank, or spiral thread nails for plywood ½ in. thick or thinner and 8d for plywood to 1 in. thick. Use 8d ring shank or spiral thread or 10d common smooth for 2-4-1, and 1⅛ in. panels. Space nails 6 in. at panel edges and 12 in. at intermediate supports, except for 48 in. or longer spans where nails should be spaced 6 in. at all supports.

LEAVE ⅛" SPACE AT ALL PANEL END AND EDGE JOINTS UNLESS OTHERWISE RECOMMENDED BY MANUFACTURER

## GABLE ROOF
EXTERIOR EXPOSURE 1 OR INTERIOR WITH EXTERIOR GLUE PANELS AT OPEN SOFFIT

BUILT-UP ROOFING

PANEL EDGES SHOULD HAVE BLOCKING PANEL CLIPS OR TONGUE AND GROOVED

LEAVE ⅛" SPACE AT ALL PANEL END AND EDGE JOINTS UNLESS OTHERWISE RECOMMENDED BY MANUFACTURER

PANEL SHEATHING

## FLAT - LOW PITCHED ROOF

### NOTES
1. Apply to APA rated panel sheathing.
2. All panels will support at least 30 psf live load plus 10 psf dead load at maximum span. Uniform load deflection limit is 1/180 span under live load plus dead load, or 1/240 under live load only.
3. Special conditions may require construction in excess of the given minimums.
4. Panel is assumed to be continuous across two or more spans with long dimension across supports.

John D. Bloodgood, Architects, P.C.; Des Moines, Iowa
American Plywood Association

**ROUGH CARPENTRY** 6

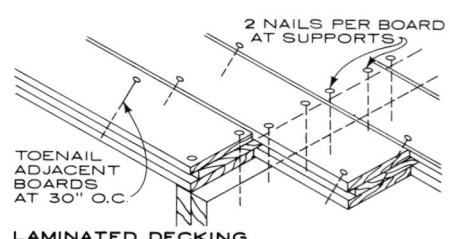

**LAMINATED DECKING**

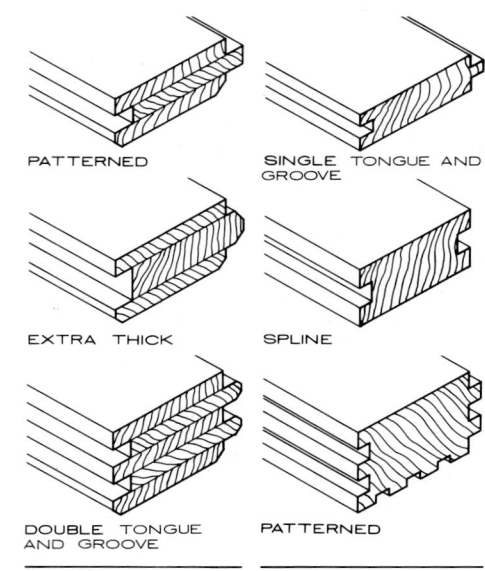

PATTERNED

SINGLE TONGUE AND GROOVE

EXTRA THICK

SPLINE

DOUBLE TONGUE AND GROOVE

PATTERNED

**GLUED LAMINATED**

**MACHINE SHAPED**

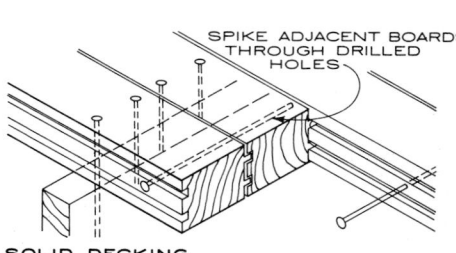

**SOLID DECKING**

## LAMINATED SIZES (IN.)

| THICKNESS | | WIDTH | |
|---|---|---|---|
| NOMINAL | ACTUAL | NOMINAL | ACTUAL |
| 3 | $2^{3}/_{16}$, $2^{1}/_{4}$ | 6,8 | $5^{1}/_{4}$, 7 |
| 3 STX | $2^{7}/_{8}$ | | |
| 5 | $3^{21}/_{32}$, $3^{13}/_{16}$ | | |

## MACHINE SHAPED SIZES (IN.)

| THICKNESS | | WIDTH | |
|---|---|---|---|
| NOMINAL | ACTUAL | NOMINAL | ACTUAL |
| 2 | $1^{1}/_{2}$ | 5,6,8,10,12 | 4, 5, $6^{3}/_{4}$ $8^{3}/_{4}$, $10^{3}/_{4}$ |
| 3 | $2^{1}/_{2}$ | 6 | $5^{1}/_{4}$ |
| 4 | $3^{1}/_{2}$ | 6 | $5^{1}/_{4}$ |

## WEIGHT AND INSULATION VALUES

| SPECIES | DECKING THICKNESS NOMINAL IN. | DECKING WEIGHTS PSF | DECKING ONLY R |
|---|---|---|---|
| Inland Red Cedar | 3 | 4 | 4.00 |
| | 3 STX | 5 | 5.02 |
| | 5 | 7 | 6.16 |
| Cedar Face IWP/W Fir Core & Back | 3 | 5 | 3.70 |
| | 3 STX | 7 | 4.58 |
| | 5 | 8 | 5.59 |
| White Fir Idaho White & Ponderosa Pine | 3 | 5 | 3.58 |
| | 3 STX | 7 | 4.47 |
| | 5 | 9 | 5.48 |
| Douglas Fir | 3 | 6 | 3.08 |
| | 3 STX | 8 | 3.81 |
| | 5 | 11 | 4.63 |
| Southern Pine | 3 | 7 | 3.05 |
| | 3 STX | 9 | 3.69 |
| | 5 | 12 | 4.63 |

### NOTES

1. Insulation value may be increased with added rigid insulation.
2. Use of random lengths reduces waste.

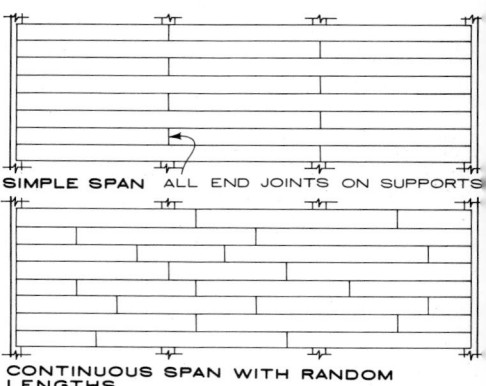

**SIMPLE SPAN**   ALL END JOINTS ON SUPPORTS

**CONTINUOUS SPAN WITH RANDOM LENGTHS**

## LAMINATED DECK—ALLOWABLE UNIFORMLY DISTRIBUTED TOTAL ROOF LOADS GOVERNED BY DEFLECTION (1)

| | SPAN IN FEET (2) | SOUTHERN PINE—E1.8 (3) F = 2640 SIMPLE SPAN END-JOINTS OVER SUPPORTS 1/180 PSF | 1/240 PSF | RANDOM LENGTH CONTINUOUS OVER THREE OR MORE SPANS 1/180 PSF | 1/240 PSF | INLAND RED CEDAR—E1.2 (INLAND RED CEDAR FACE AND BACK) F = 1590 SIMPLE SPAN END-JOINTS OVER SUPPORTS 1/180 PSF | 1/240 PSF | RANDOM LENGTH CONTINUOUS OVER THREE OR MORE SPANS 1/180 PSF | 1/240 PSF | PONDEROSA PINE—E1.3 INLAND RED CEDAR—E1.3 (IDAHO WHITE PINE OR WHITE FIR BACK) F = 1590 SIMPLE SPAN END-JOINTS OVER SUPPORTS 1/180 PSF | 1/240 PSF | RANDOM LENGTH CONTINUOUS OVER THREE OR MORE SPANS 1/180 PSF | 1/240 PSF | IDAHO WHITE PINE—E1.5 IDAHO WHITE FIR—E1.5 F = 1850 SIMPLE SPAN END-JOINTS OVER SUPPORTS 1/180 PSF | 1/240 PSF | RANDOM LENGTH CONTINUOUS OVER THREE OR MORE SPANS 1/180 PSF | 1/240 PSF | DOUGLAS FIR/LARCH—E1.8 F = 2640 SIMPLE SPAN END-JOINTS OVER SUPPORTS 1/180 PSF | 1/240 PSF | RANDOM LENGTH CONTINUOUS OVER THREE OR MORE SPANS 1/180 PSF | 1/240 PSF |
|---|---|---|---|---|---|---|---|---|---|---|---|---|---|---|---|---|---|---|---|---|---|
| 3 IN. NOMINAL | 8 | — | — | — | — | 71 | 54 | 121 | 91 | 77 | 58 | 127(F) | 98 | 89 | 67 | 151 | 113 | 107 | 80 | 181 | 136 |
| | 9 | 80 | 60 | 136 | 101 | 50 | 38 | 85 | 64 | 54 | 41 | 92 | 69 | 63 | 47 | 106 | 80 | 75 | 56 | 127 | 96 |
| | 10 | 59 | 44 | 99 | 74 | 37 | 27 | 62 | 46 | 40 | 30 | 67 | 50 | 46 | 34 | 77 | 58 | 55 | 41 | 93 | 70 |
| | 11 | 44 | 32 | 74 | 56 | 27 | 21 | 47 | 35 | 30 | 22 | 50 | 38 | 34 | 26 | 58 | 44 | 41 | 31 | 70 | 52 |
| | 12 | 33 | 25 | 57 | 42 | 21 | 16 | 36 | 27 | 23 | 17 | 39 | 29 | 26 | 20 | 45 | 34 | 32 | 24 | 54 | 40 |
| | 13 | 26 | 20 | 45 | 33 | 17 | 12 | 28 | 21 | 18 | 14 | 31 | 23 | 21 | 16 | 35 | 26 | 25 | 19 | 42 | 32 |
| 3 IN. STX | 10 | 125 | 94 | 212 | 159 | 83 | 63 | 141 | 106 | 90 | 68 | 144(F) | 115 | 104 | 78 | 168(F) | 132 | 125 | 94 | 212 | 159 |
| | 11 | 94 | 70 | 159 | 119 | 63 | 47 | 106 | 79 | 68 | 51 | 115 | 86 | 78 | 59 | 132(F) | 99 | 94 | 70 | 159 | 119 |
| | 12 | 72 | 54 | 122 | 92 | 48 | 36 | 82 | 61 | 52 | 39 | 88 | 66 | 60 | 45 | 102 | 77 | 72 | 54 | 122 | 92 |
| | 13 | 57 | 43 | 96 | 72 | 38 | 28 | 64 | 48 | 41 | 31 | 70 | 52 | 47 | 36 | 80 | 60 | 57 | 43 | 96 | 72 |
| | 14 | 46 | 34 | 77 | 58 | 30 | 23 | 51 | 39 | 33 | 25 | 56 | 42 | 38 | 28 | 64 | 48 | 46 | 34 | 77 | 58 |
| | 15 | 37 | 28 | 63 | 47 | 25 | 19 | 42 | 31 | 27 | 20 | 45 | 34 | 31 | 23 | 52 | 39 | 37 | 28 | 63 | 47 |
| | 16 | 31 | 23 | 52 | 39 | 20 | 15 | 34 | 26 | 22 | 17 | 37 | 28 | 25 | 19 | 43 | 32 | 31 | 23 | 52 | 39 |
| | 17 | 25 | 19 | 43 | 32 | 17 | 13 | 29 | 22 | 18 | 14 | 31 | 23 | 21 | 16 | 36 | 27 | 25 | 19 | 43 | 32 |
| 5 IN. NOMINAL | 15 | 89 | 66 | 150 | 113 | 51 | 38 | 86 | 64 | 55 | 41 | 93 | 70 | 63 | 47 | 107 | 80 | | | | |
| | 16 | 73 | 55 | 124 | 93 | 42 | 31 | 71 | 53 | 45 | 34 | 76 | 57 | 52 | 39 | 88 | 66 | | | | |
| | 17 | 61 | 46 | 103 | 77 | 35 | 26 | 59 | 44 | 38 | 28 | 64 | 48 | 43 | 33 | 74 | 55 | | | | |
| | 18 | 51 | 38 | 87 | 65 | 29 | 22 | 50 | 37 | 32 | 24 | 54 | 40 | 37 | 27 | 62 | 46 | | | | |
| | 19 | 44 | 33 | 74 | 55 | 25 | 19 | 42 | 32 | 27 | 20 | 46 | 34 | 31 | 23 | 53 | 40 | | | | |
| | 20 | 37 | 28 | 63 | 47 | 21 | 16 | 36 | 27 | 23 | 17 | 39 | 29 | 27 | 20 | 45 | 34 | | | | |
| | 21 | 32 | 24 | 55 | 41 | 18 | 14 | 31 | 23 | 20 | 15 | 34 | 25 | 23 | 17 | 39 | 29 | | | | |

### SPAN TABLE NOTES

1. Values followed by (f) are governed by stress. Allowable loads for floors when governed by deflection are half of those listed in the 1/180 columns.
2. Span loads shown assume compliance to layup rules. Longer spans may require specific lengths differing from the standard shipment.
3. Custom Grade 3 in. and 5 in. Southern Pine deflection values are 83% of the E1.8 values shown. 3 in. STX Southern Pine values are equal to E1.5 Idaho White Pine values except when bending governs.
4. E = Modulus of elasticity psi.
5. Information derived from data supplied by the Potlatch Corporation.

Timothy B. McDonald; Washington, D.C.

**ROUGH CARPENTRY**

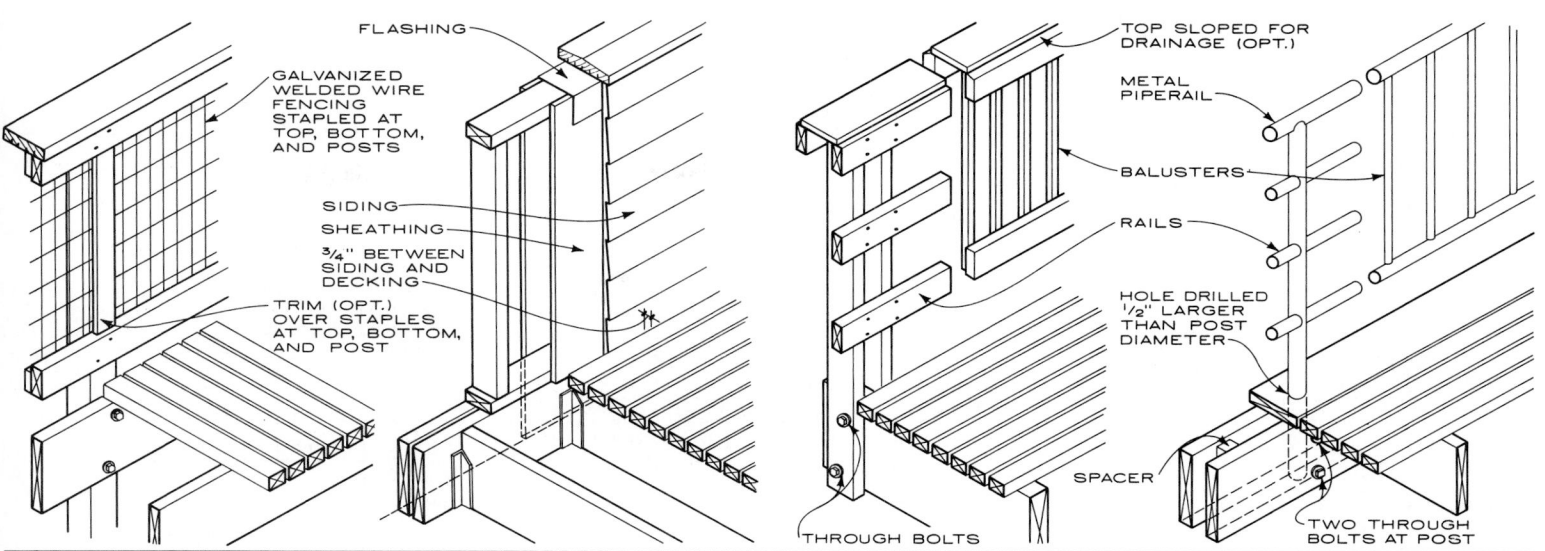

**RAILINGS**

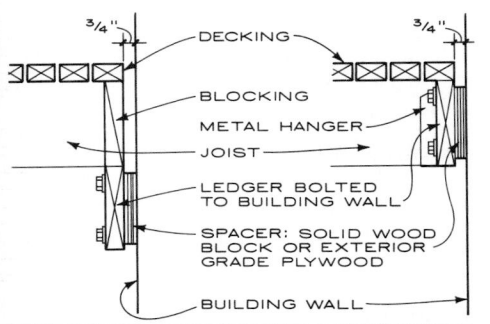

**CONNECTIONS AT BUILDING WALL**

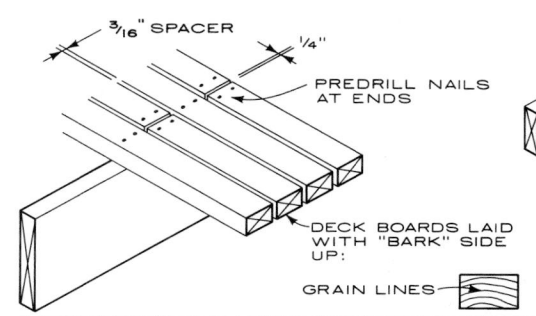

**DECKING APPLICATIONS**

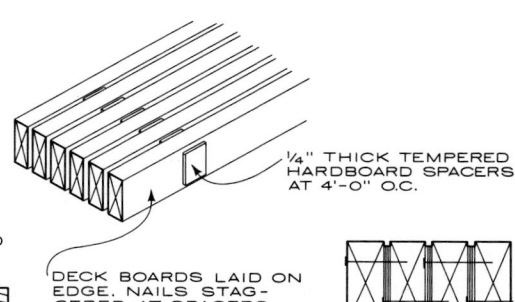

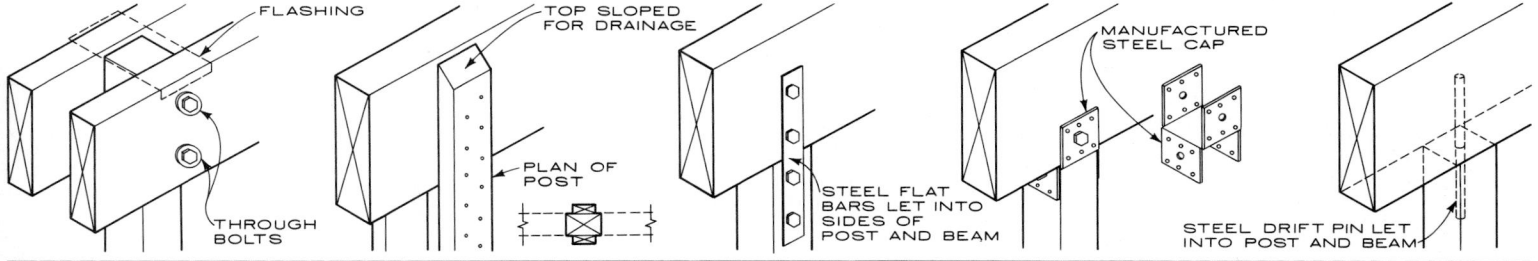

**POST AND BEAM CONNECTIONS**

## RELATIVE COMPARISON OF VARIOUS QUALITIES OF WOOD USED IN DECK CONSTRUCTION

| | DOUGLAS FIR— LARCH | SOUTHERN PINE | HEMLOCK FIR* | SOFT PINES[†] | WESTERN RED CEDAR | REDWOOD | SPRUCE | CYPRESS |
|---|---|---|---|---|---|---|---|---|
| Hardness | Fair | Fair | Poor | Poor | Poor | Fair | Poor | Fair |
| Warp resistance | Fair | Fair | Fair | Good | Good | Good | Fair | Fair |
| Ease of working | Poor | Fair | Fair | Good | Good | Fair | Fair | Fair |
| Paint holding | Poor | Poor | Poor | Good | Good | Good | Fair | Good |
| Stain acceptance[†] | Fair | Fair | Fair | Fair | Good | Good | Fair | Fair |
| Nail holding | Good | Good | Poor | Poor | Poor | Fair | Fair | Fair |
| Heartwood decay resistance | Fair | Fair | Poor | Poor | Good | Good | Poor | Good |
| Proportion of heartwood | Good | Poor | Poor | Fair | Good | Good | Poor | Good |
| Bending strength | Good | Good | Fair | Poor | Poor | Fair | Fair | Fair |
| Stiffness | Good | Good | Good | Poor | Poor | Fair | Fair | Fair |
| Strength as a post | Good | Good | Fair | Poor | Fair | Good | Fair | Fair |
| Freedom from pitch | Fair | Poor | Good | Fair | Good | Good | Good | Good |

*Includes West Coast and eastern hemlocks.
[†]Includes western and northeastern pines.
[‡]Categories refer to semitransparent oil base stain.

The Bumgardner Partnership/Architects; Seattle, Washington

## MAXIMUM SPAN OF DECK BOARDS

| | FLAT | | ON EDGE | |
|---|---|---|---|---|
| | 1 x 4 | 2 x 2 (x3)(x4) | 2 x 3 | 2 x 4 |
| Douglas fir, larch, and southern pine | 1'-4'' | 5'-0'' | 7'-6'' | 12'-0'' |
| Hemlock-fir, Douglas-fir, southern | 1'-2'' | 4'-0'' | 6'-6'' | 10'-0'' |
| Western pines and cedars, redwoods, spruce | 1'-0'' | 3'-6'' | 5'-6'' | 9'-0'' |

**NOTES**

Size and spacing of joists, posts, and beams may be selected according to other pages in chapter.

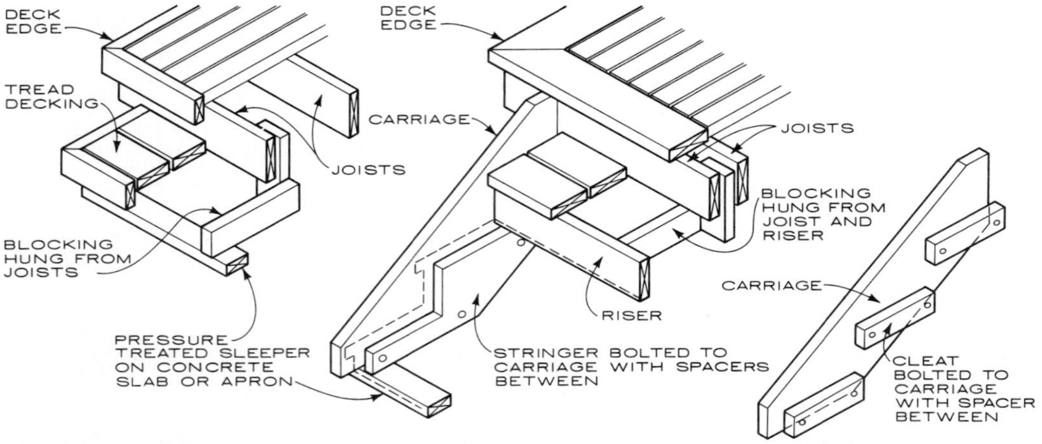

## STEPS AND STAIRS

DECK EDGE

TREAD DECKING

BLOCKING HUNG FROM JOISTS

JOISTS

PRESSURE TREATED SLEEPER ON CONCRETE SLAB OR APRON

**STEP PLATFORM**

DECK EDGE

CARRIAGE

JOISTS

RISER

STRINGER BOLTED TO CARRIAGE WITH SPACERS BETWEEN

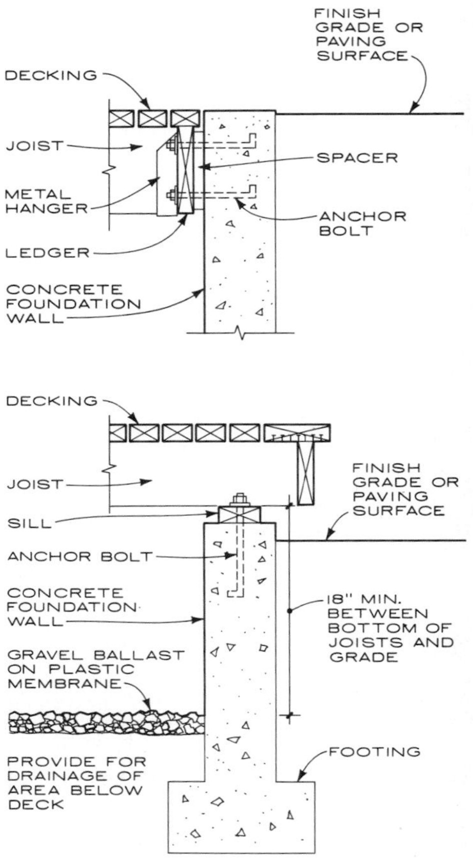

BLOCKING HUNG FROM JOIST AND RISER

CARRIAGE

CLEAT BOLTED TO CARRIAGE WITH SPACER BETWEEN

**STAIR CARRIAGE WITH STRINGER**

**CARRIAGE WITH CLEATS**

## STEEL POST ANCHORS

POST AND ANCHOR BOLT HOLES SHOULD BE SHOP DRILLED TO ENSURE ALIGNMENT

POST KERFED FOR ANCHOR

PIPE OR BAR WELDED TO ANCHOR

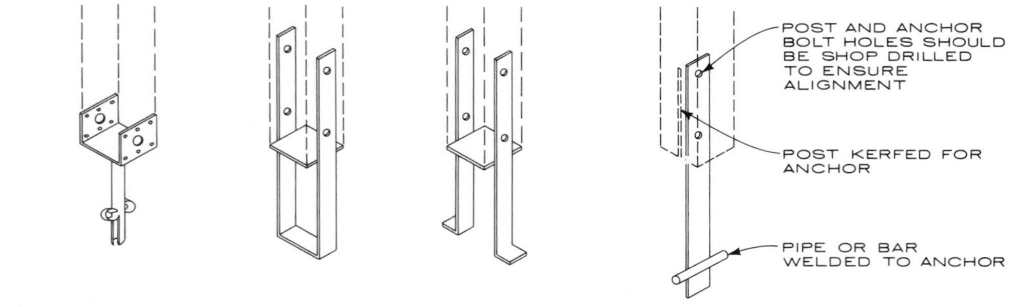

**STANDARD MANUFACTURED**

**SHOP FABRICATED**

## POSTS AND FOOTINGS

STEEL DRIFT PIN

BUILDING PAPER

FINISH GRADE

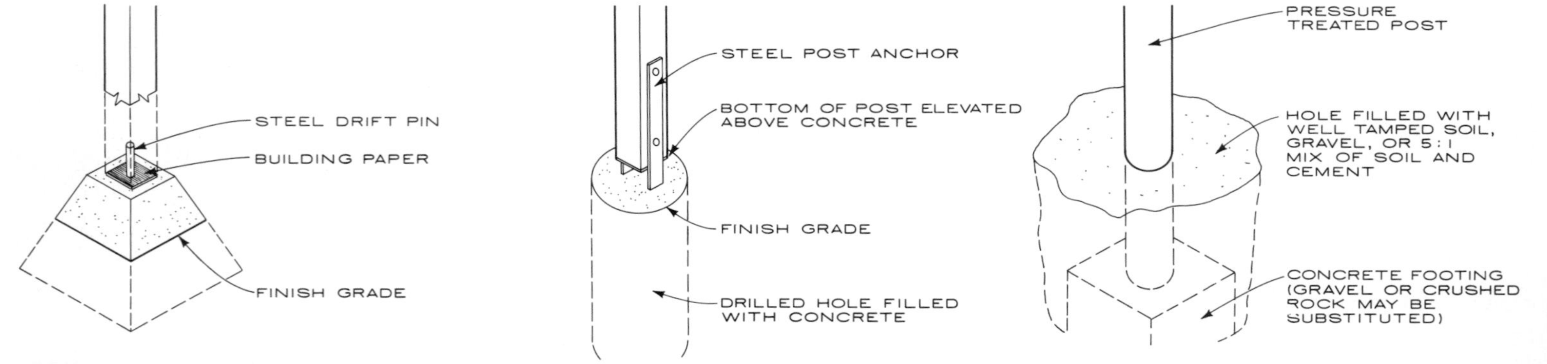

**PRECAST CONCRETE PLINTH/UNTREATED POST**

STEEL POST ANCHOR

BOTTOM OF POST ELEVATED ABOVE CONCRETE

FINISH GRADE

DRILLED HOLE FILLED WITH CONCRETE

**POURED FOOTING/UNTREATED POST**

PRESSURE TREATED POST

HOLE FILLED WITH WELL TAMPED SOIL, GRAVEL, OR 5:1 MIX OF SOIL AND CEMENT

CONCRETE FOOTING (GRAVEL OR CRUSHED ROCK MAY BE SUBSTITUTED)

**POURED OR PRECAST FOOTING/TREATED POST**

## LOW DECK EDGES

FINISH GRADE OR PAVING SURFACE

DECKING

JOIST

METAL HANGER

LEDGER

CONCRETE FOUNDATION WALL

SPACER

ANCHOR BOLT

DECKING

JOIST

SILL

ANCHOR BOLT

CONCRETE FOUNDATION WALL

GRAVEL BALLAST ON PLASTIC MEMBRANE

PROVIDE FOR DRAINAGE OF AREA BELOW DECK

FINISH GRADE OR PAVING SURFACE

18" MIN. BETWEEN BOTTOM OF JOISTS AND GRADE

FOOTING

## FASTENERS

1. Smooth shank nails lose holding strength after repeated wet/dry cycles. Ring or spiral grooved shank nails are preferable.
2. Use galvanized or plated fasteners to avoid corrosion and staining.
3. To reduce board splitting by nailing: blunt nail points; predrill (3/4 of nail diameter); stagger nailing; place nails no closer to edge than one half of board thickness.
4. Avoid end grain nailing and toenailing if possible.
5. Use flat washers under heads of lag screws and bolts, and under nuts.

## MOISTURE PROTECTION

1. All wood members should be protected from weather by pressure treatment or field application of preservatives, stains, or paints.
2. All wood in direct contact with soil must be pressure treated.
3. Bottoms of posts on piers should be 6 in. above grade.
4. Sterilize or cover soil with membrane to keep plant growth away from wood members so as to minimize moisture exchange.
5. Treat all ends, cuts, holes, and so on with preservative prior to placement.
6. Decking and flat trim boards, 2 x 6 and wider, should be kerfed on the underside with 3/4 in. deep saw cuts at 1 in. on center to prevent cupping.
7. Avoid horizontal exposure of endgrain or provide adequate protection by flashing or sealing. Avoid or minimize joint situations where moisture may be trapped by using spacers and/or flashing, caulking, sealant, plastic roofing cement.

## CONSTRUCTION

1. WOOD SELECTION: Usual requirements are good decay resistance, nonsplintering, fair stiffness, strength, hardness, and warp resistance. Selection varies according to local climate and exposure.
2. BRACING: On large decks, or decks where post heights exceed 5 ft, lateral stability should be achieved with horizontal bracing (metal or wood diagonal ties on top or bottom of joists, or diagonal application of decking) in combination with vertical bracing (rigid bolted or gusseted connections at top of posts, knee bracing, or "X" bracing between posts), and/or connection to a braced building wall. Lateral stability should be checked by a structural engineer.

The Bumgardner Partnership/Architects; Seattle, Washington

**ROUGH CARPENTRY**

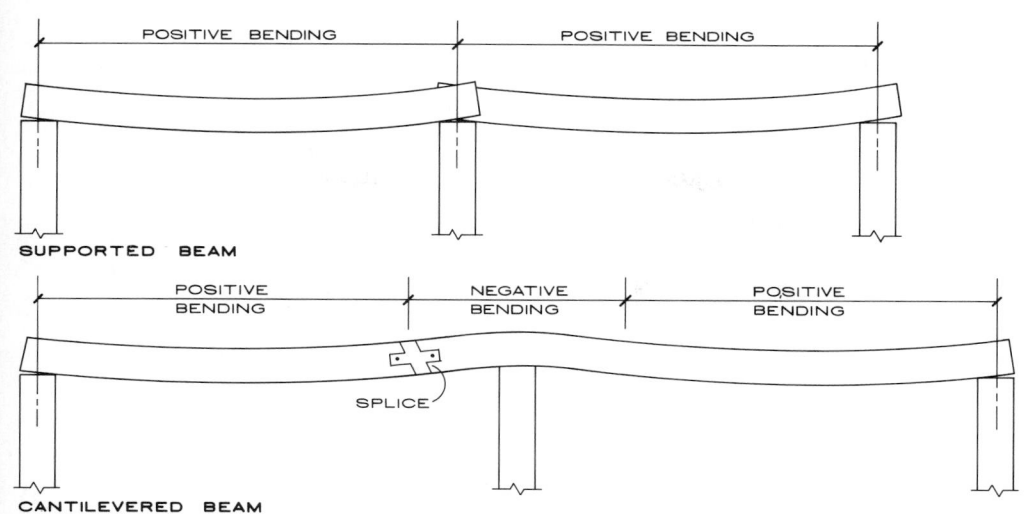

POSITIVE BENDING    POSITIVE BENDING

SUPPORTED BEAM

POSITIVE BENDING    NEGATIVE BENDING    POSITIVE BENDING

SPLICE

CANTILEVERED BEAM

**SIMPLE AND CANTILEVERED FRAMING**

**SIMPLE FRAMING:** This illustration shows the "positive" or downward bending that occurs in conventional framing with simple spans.

**CANTILEVERED FRAMING:** This illustration shows the combination of "positive" (downward) and "negative" (upward) bending that occurs with beams spliced at quarterpoint producing supported beam and cantilevered beam. The two types of bending counterbalance each other, which produces more uniform stresses and uses material more efficiently. In-line joists simplify plywood subflooring.

**MOMENT SPLICE:** Compression stress is taken in bearing on the wood through a steel compression plate. Tension is taken across the splice by means of steel straps and sheer plates. Side plates and straps are used to hold sides and tops of members in position. Shear is taken by shear plates in end grain. Bolts and shear plates are used as design and construction considerations require.

GROOVED PLANK MOLDED SPLINE

RABBETED PLANK BATTEN INSERT

GROOVED PLANK WITH SPLINE

GROOVED PLANK WITH EXPOSED SPLINE

SQUARE EDGE

TONGUE AND GROOVE

**JOINT TYPES IN EXPOSED PLANK CEILINGS**

**DESIGN TABLE FOR NOMINAL 2 IN. PLANK**

REQUIRED VALUES FOR FIBER STRESS IN BENDING (f) AND MODULUS OF ELASTICITY (E) TO SUPPORT SAFELY A LIVE LOAD OF 20, 30, OR 40 LB/SQ FT WITHIN A DEFLECTION LIMITATION OF ℓ/240, ℓ/300, OR ℓ/360.

| SPAN (FT) | LIVE LOAD (PSF) | DEFLECTION LIMIT | TYPE A SINGLE SPAN f (PSI) | TYPE A E (PSI) | TYPE B DOUBLE SPAN f (PSI) | TYPE B E (PSI) | TYPE C THREE SPAN f (PSI) | TYPE C E (PSI) | TYPE D COMBINATION SINGLE AND DOUBLE SPAN f (PSI) | TYPE D E (PSI) | TYPE E RANDOM LAYUP f (PSI) | TYPE E E (PSI) |
|---|---|---|---|---|---|---|---|---|---|---|---|---|
| 6 | 20 | ℓ/240 | 360 | 576,000 | 360 | 239,000 | 288 | 305,000 | 360 | 408,000 | 360 | 442,000 |
| | | ℓ/300 | 360 | 720,000 | 360 | 299,000 | 288 | 381,000 | 360 | 509,000 | 360 | 553,000 |
| | | ℓ/360 | 360 | 864,000 | 360 | 359,000 | 288 | 457,000 | 360 | 611,000 | 360 | 664,000 |
| | 30 | ℓ/240 | 480 | 864,000 | 480 | 359,000 | 384 | 457,000 | 480 | 611,000 | 480 | 664,000 |
| | | ℓ/300 | 480 | 1,080,000 | 480 | 448,000 | 384 | 571,000 | 480 | 764,000 | 480 | 829,000 |
| | | ℓ/360 | 480 | 1,296,000 | 480 | 538,000 | 384 | 685,000 | 480 | 917,000 | 480 | 995,000 |
| | 40 | ℓ/240 | 600 | 1,152,000 | 600 | 478,000 | 480 | 609,000 | 600 | 815,000 | 600 | 885,000 |
| | | ℓ/300 | 600 | 1,440,000 | 600 | 598,000 | 480 | 762,000 | 600 | 1,019,000 | 600 | 1,106,000 |
| | | ℓ/360 | 600 | 1,728,000 | 600 | 717,000 | 480 | 914,000 | 600 | 1,223,000 | 600 | 1,327,000 |
| 7 | 20 | ℓ/240 | 490 | 915,000 | 490 | 380,000 | 392 | 484,000 | 490 | 647,000 | 490 | 702,000 |
| | | ℓ/300 | 490 | 1,143,000 | 490 | 475,000 | 392 | 605,000 | 490 | 809,000 | 490 | 878,000 |
| | | ℓ/360 | 490 | 1,372,000 | 490 | 570,000 | 392 | 726,000 | 490 | 971,000 | 490 | 1,054,000 |
| | 30 | ℓ/240 | 653 | 1,372,000 | 653 | 570,000 | 522 | 726,000 | 653 | 971,000 | 653 | 1,054,000 |
| | | ℓ/300 | 653 | 1,715,000 | 653 | 712,000 | 522 | 907,000 | 653 | 1,213,000 | 653 | 1,317,000 |
| | | ℓ/360 | 653 | 2,058,000 | 653 | 854,000 | 522 | 1,088,000 | 653 | 1,456,000 | 653 | 1,581,000 |
| | 40 | ℓ/240 | 817 | 1,829,000 | 817 | 759,000 | 653 | 968,000 | 817 | 1,294,000 | 817 | 1,405,000 |
| | | ℓ/300 | 817 | 1,187,000 | 817 | 949,000 | 653 | 1,209,000 | 817 | 1,618,000 | 817 | 1,756,000 |
| | | ℓ/360 | 817 | 2,744,000 | 817 | 1,139,000 | 653 | 1,451,000 | 817 | 1,941,000 | 817 | 2,107,000 |
| 8 | 20 | ℓ/240 | 640 | 1,365,000 | 640 | 567,000 | 512 | 722,000 | 640 | 966,000 | 640 | 1,049,000 |
| | | ℓ/300 | 640 | 1,707,000 | 640 | 708,000 | 512 | 903,000 | 640 | 1,208,000 | 640 | 1,311,000 |
| | | ℓ/360 | 640 | 2,048,000 | 640 | 850,000 | 512 | 1,083,000 | 640 | 1,449,000 | 640 | 1,573,000 |
| | 30 | ℓ/240 | 853 | 2,048,000 | 853 | 850,000 | 682 | 1,083,000 | 853 | 1,449,000 | 853 | 1,573,000 |
| | | ℓ/300 | 853 | 2,560,000 | 853 | 1,063,000 | 682 | 1,345,000 | 853 | 1,811,000 | 853 | 1,966,000 |
| | | ℓ/360 | 853 | 3,072,000 | 853 | 1,275,000 | 682 | 1,625,000 | 853 | 2,174,000 | 853 | 2,359,000 |
| | 40 | ℓ/240 | 1,067 | 2,731,000 | 1,067 | 1,134,000 | 853 | 1,144,000 | 1,067 | 1,932,000 | 1,067 | 2,097,000 |
| | | ℓ/300 | 1,067 | 3,413,000 | 1,067 | 1,417,000 | 853 | 1,805,000 | 1,067 | 2,145,000 | 1,067 | 2,621,000 |
| | | ℓ/360 | 1,067 | 4,096,000 | 1,067 | 1,700,000 | 853 | 2,166,000 | 1,067 | 2,898,000 | 1,067 | 3,146,000 |

Timothy B. McDonald; Washington, D.C.

**HEAVY TIMBER CONSTRUCTION**

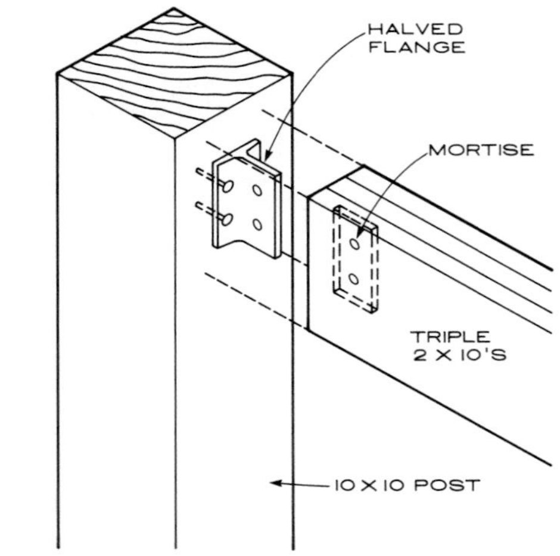

HALVED
FLANGE

MORTISE

TRIPLE
2 × 10'S

10 × 10 POST

**BEAM AND COLUMN CONNECTION**

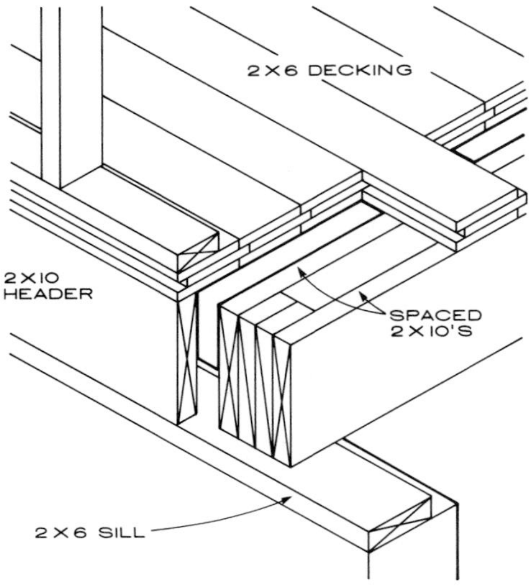

2 × 6 DECKING

2 × 10
HEADER

SPACED
2 × 10'S

2 × 6 SILL

**SPACED BEAM AT FOUNDATION**

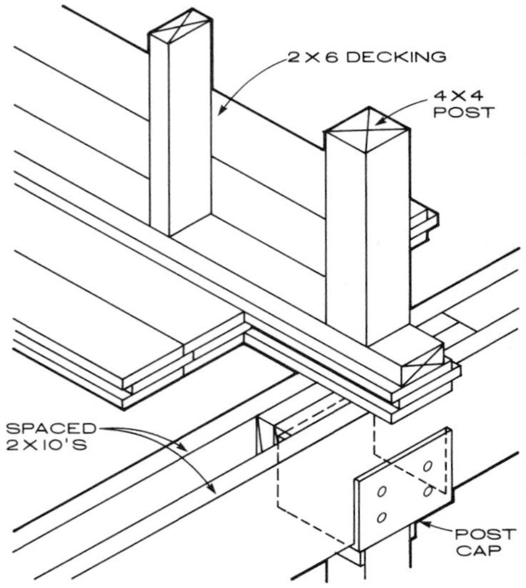

2 × 6 DECKING

4 × 4
POST

SPACED
2 × 10'S

POST
CAP

**SPACED BEAM BEARING ON
INTERIOR COLUMN**

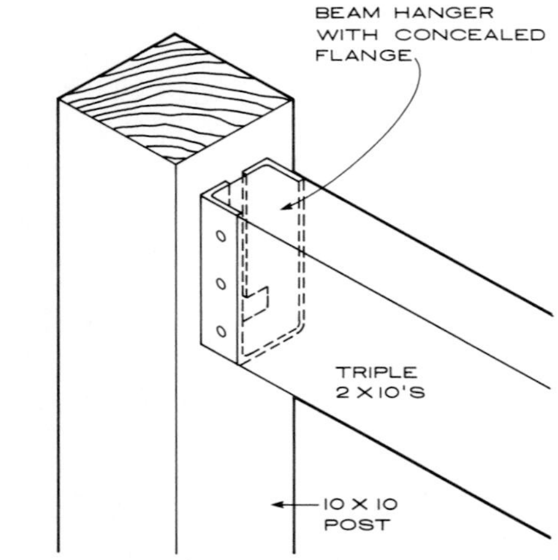

BEAM HANGER
WITH CONCEALED
FLANGE

TRIPLE
2 × 10'S

10 × 10
POST

**BEAM HANGER CONNECTION**

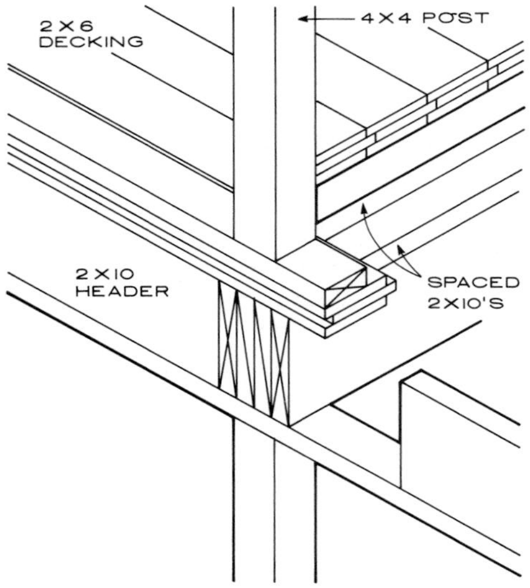

2 × 6
DECKING

4 × 4 POST

2 × 10
HEADER

SPACED
2 × 10'S

**SPACED BEAM BEARING AT
EXTERIOR WALL**

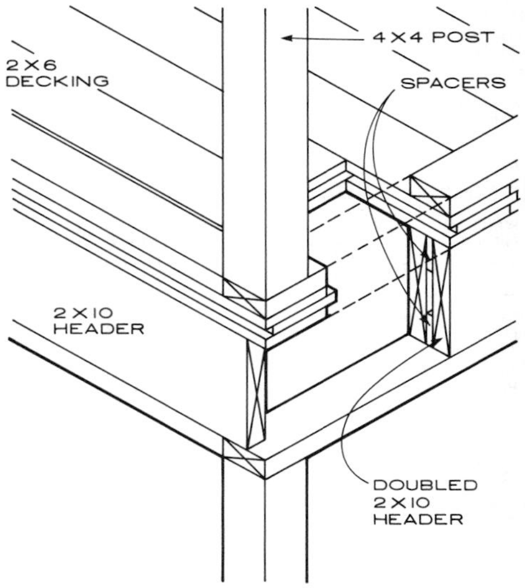

2 × 6
DECKING

4 × 4 POST

SPACERS

2 × 10
HEADER

DOUBLED
2 × 10
HEADER

**CORNER CONNECTION**

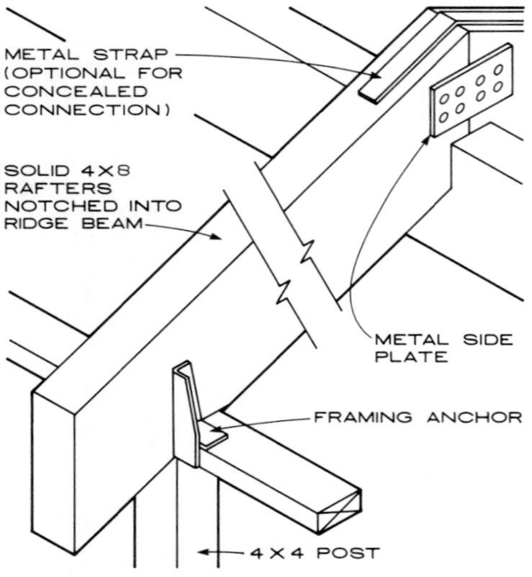

METAL STRAP
(OPTIONAL FOR
CONCEALED
CONNECTION)

SOLID 4 × 8
RAFTERS
NOTCHED INTO
RIDGE BEAM

METAL SIDE
PLATE

FRAMING ANCHOR

4 × 4 POST

**ROOF BEAM AT COLUMN AND RIDGE**

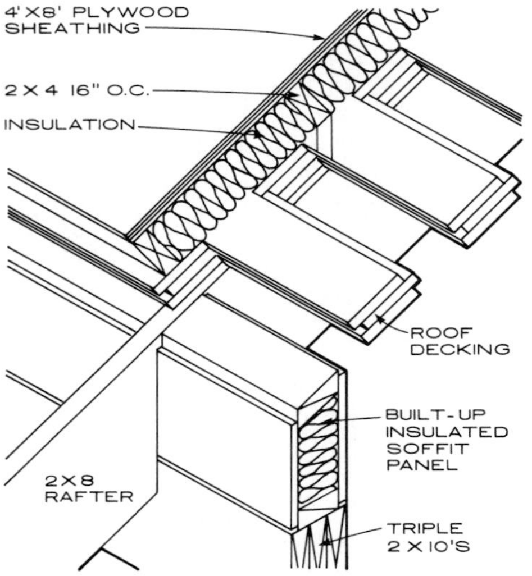

4' X 8' PLYWOOD
SHEATHING

2 × 4 16" O.C.

INSULATION

ROOF
DECKING

2 × 8
RAFTER

BUILT-UP
INSULATED
SOFFIT
PANEL

TRIPLE
2 × 10'S

**RAFTER AND PLATE DETAIL**

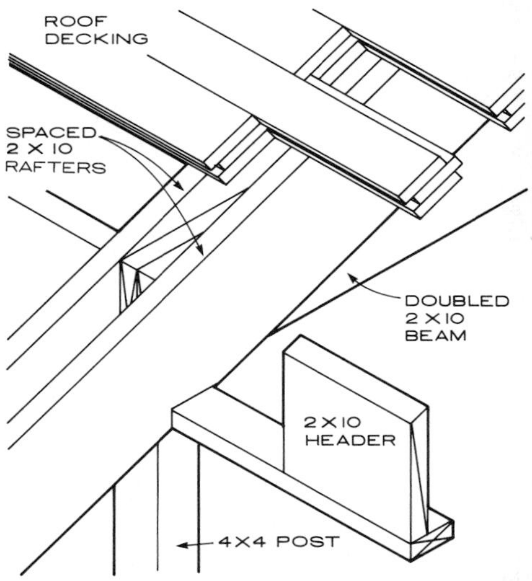

ROOF
DECKING

SPACED
2 × 10
RAFTERS

DOUBLED
2 × 10
BEAM

2 × 10
HEADER

4 × 4 POST

**SPACED ROOF BEAM AT EXTERIOR
COLUMN**

Timothy B. McDonald; Washington, D.C.

**HEAVY TIMBER CONSTRUCTION**

### NOTES

1. Pole embedment depth depends on soil, slope and seismic zone.
2. Cross-bracing between poles may be required to resist lateral loads if shallow embedment. Treat all exposed surfaces with approved pressure treatment.
3. Pole notching for major beams can help align beams and walls that otherwise would be out of plumb due to pole warp. Notching improves bearing of major beams but weakens poles.
4. Roofs, walls and floors should be insulated to suit local climatic conditions. Wall and soffit insulation should meet continuously at the joint. Penetration of insulation should be minimal.
5. Various siding types can be used.
6. Dapping is a U.S. carpentry term for cutting wood to receive timber connectors.

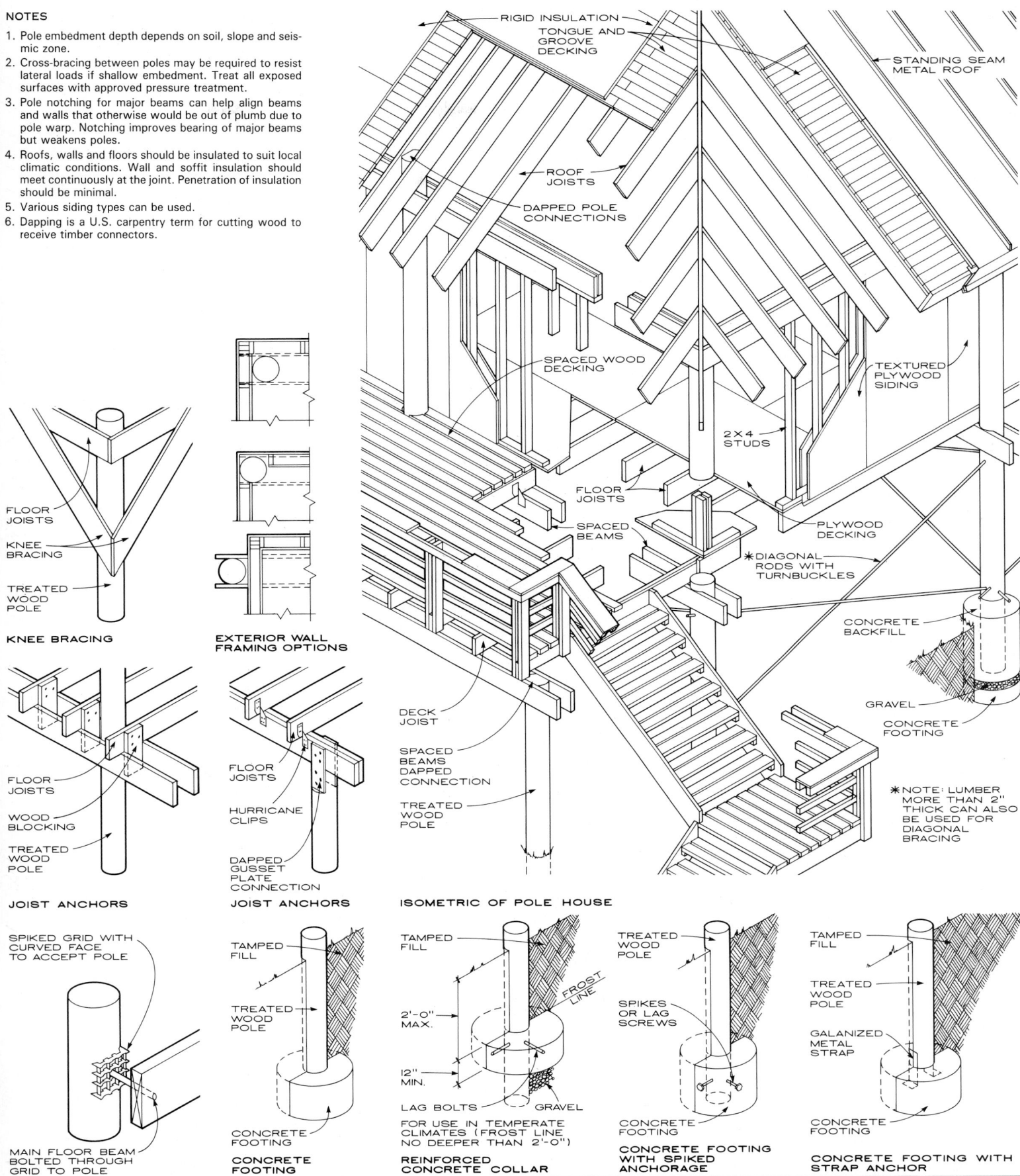

**KNEE BRACING**

**EXTERIOR WALL FRAMING OPTIONS**

**JOIST ANCHORS**

**JOIST ANCHORS**

**ISOMETRIC OF POLE HOUSE**

**CONCRETE FOOTING**

**REINFORCED CONCRETE COLLAR**

**CONCRETE FOOTING WITH SPIKED ANCHORAGE**

**CONCRETE FOOTING WITH STRAP ANCHOR**

**POLE CONSTRUCTION**

Timothy B. McDonald; Washington, D.C.

## HEAVY TIMBER CONSTRUCTION    6

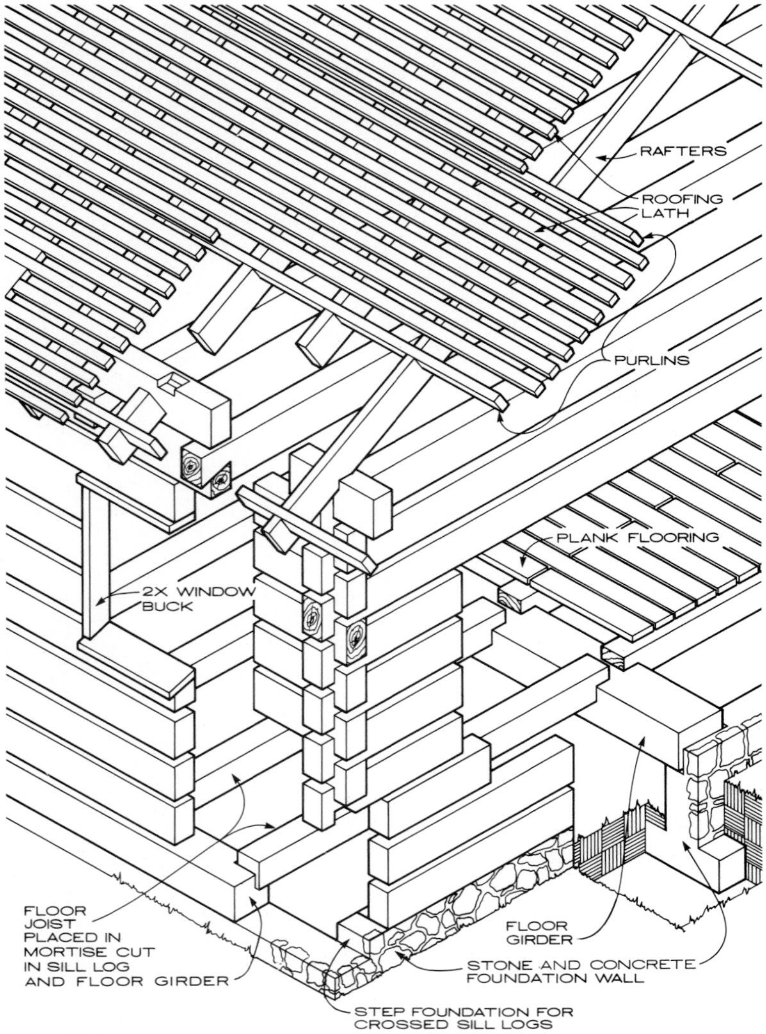

**RAFTER AT RIDGE**

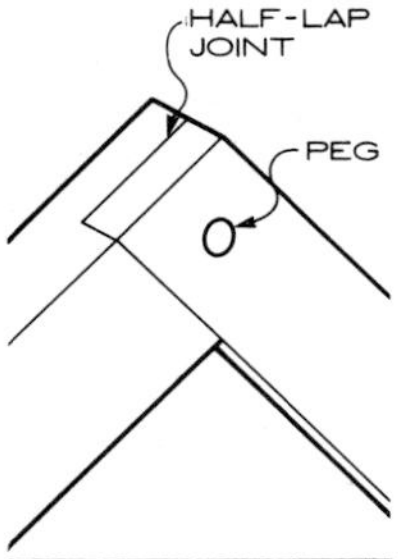

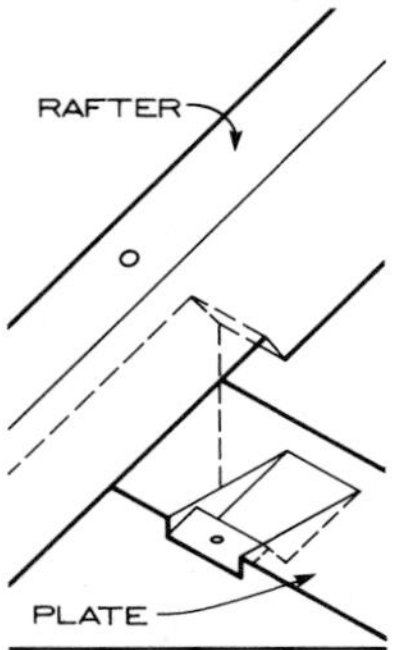

HALF-LAP JOINT

PEG

RAFTERS

ROOFING LATH

PURLINS

**NOTCHING FOR RAFTER**

RAFTER

PLATE

2X WINDOW BUCK

PLANK FLOORING

FLOOR JOIST PLACED IN MORTISE CUT IN SILL LOG AND FLOOR GIRDER

FLOOR GIRDER

STONE AND CONCRETE FOUNDATION WALL

STEP FOUNDATION FOR CROSSED SILL LOGS

**LOG FRAMING**

**SHINGLING**

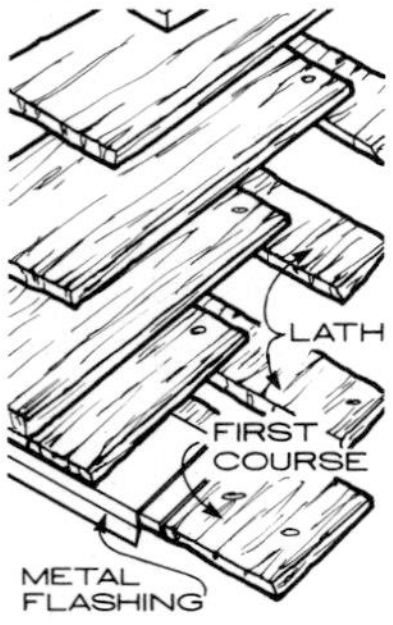

LATH

FIRST COURSE

METAL FLASHING

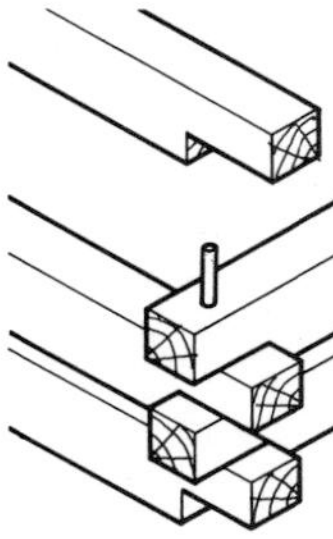

**HALF-LAPPED NOTCHES**

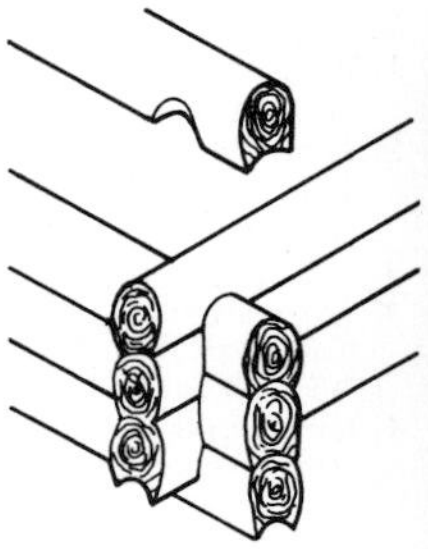

**SADDLE NOTCHES**

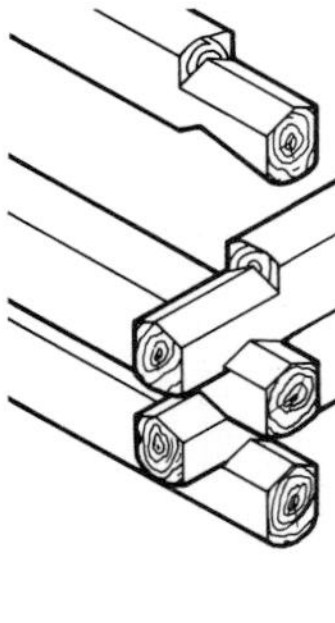

**V-NOTCHES**

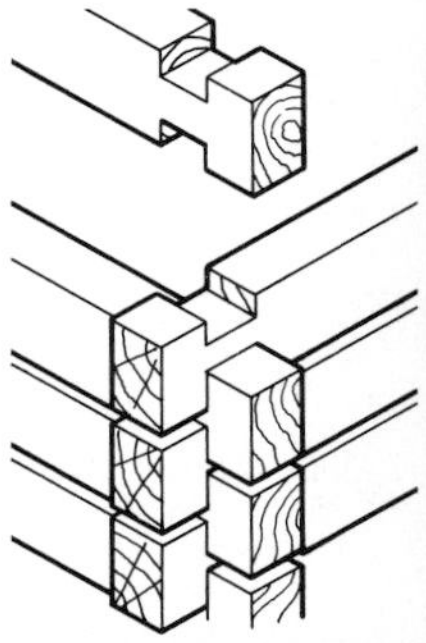

**LOCK-NOTCHES**

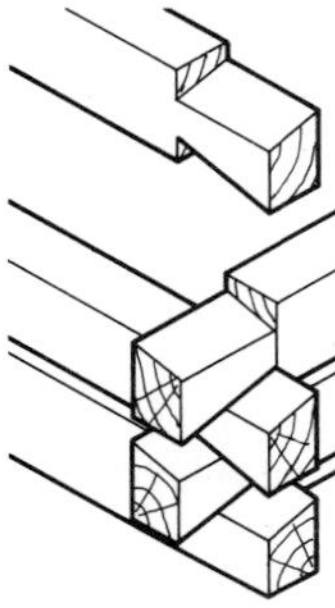

**FULL DOVETAIL**

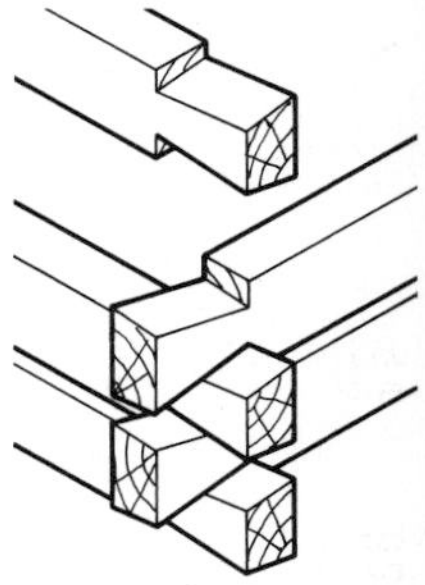

**HALF-DOVETAIL**

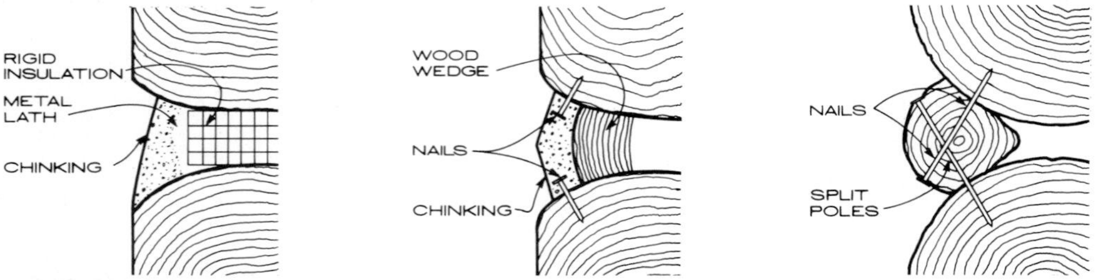

RIGID INSULATION

METAL LATH

CHINKING

WOOD WEDGE

NAILS

CHINKING

NAILS

SPLIT POLES

**CHINKING DETAILS**

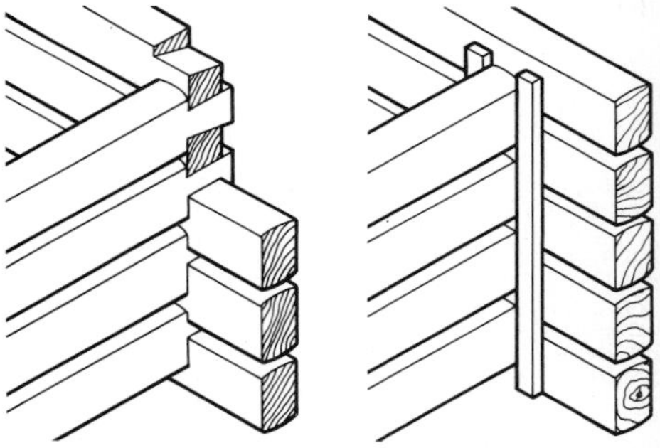

**INTERSECTING WALLS**

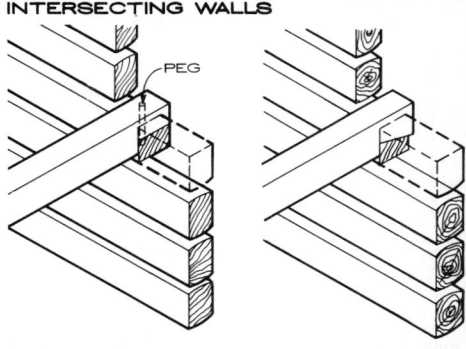

PEG

**SECOND FLOOR JOISTS**

### GENERAL NOTES

1. Hewing logs square removes most of the sapwood, which reduces the log weight and its susceptibility to insect damage and rot. It also leaves flat surfaces that are easier to work from.

2. Damage from rot (fungi decay) can be prevented or controlled in several ways: removing sapwood, which is high in cellulose and lignum on which fungi feed; reducing the log's moisture content to 20 percent or less by air or kiln drying; and by providing proper air circulation under floors and around foundations. Generous roof overhangs and properly maintained gutters help keep water off the sides of the building.

3. Insect damage from termites, beetles, and carpenter ants can be prevented by properly seasoning the wood (kiln or air drying), and by providing continuous vapor barriers under ground floors. Also, good air circulation can help prevent infestations.

4. Exposed interior logs must be coordinated carefully with placement of plumbing, electrical wiring, and mechanical equipment.

5. Good drainage around the building is important, since log buildings are susceptible to rot.

6. Manufacturers of prefabricated log structures offer milled log details to reduce air leakage and to improve weatherability of the wall. Such details include tongue-and-groove joints, dovetailing use of steel splines, and butyl gaskets.

7. Spaces between individual logs (chink area) are filled with chinking, which varies from ½ to 10 in. thick.

### COMMON CHINKING FORMULAS

Chinking formulas that use large amounts of cement are not porous enough to let moisture trapped between the logs migrate to the surface. High-lime formulas are more porous, allowing the surface to dry more quickly. They are more elastic.

1. 1 part portland cement, 4–8 parts lime, 7–10 parts sand.

2. ¼ part cement, 11 parts lime, 4 parts sand, ⅛ part dry color, excelsior.

3. 1 part cement, 4 parts lime, 6 parts sand.

Timothy B. McDonald; Washington, D.C.

 **HEAVY TIMBER CONSTRUCTION**

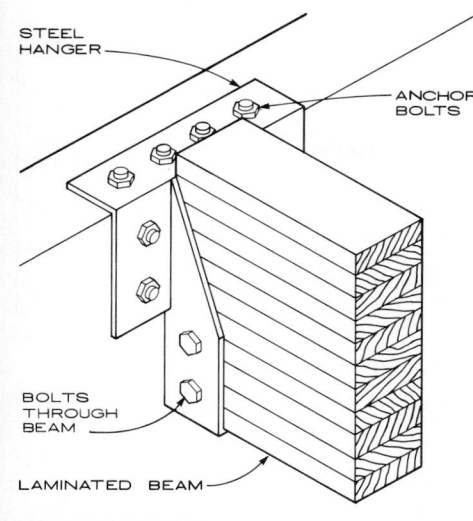

**BEAM HANGER**

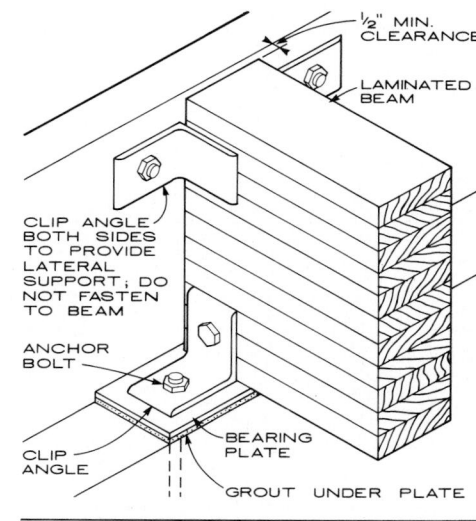

**BEAM ANCHOR**

**BEAM ANCHOR**

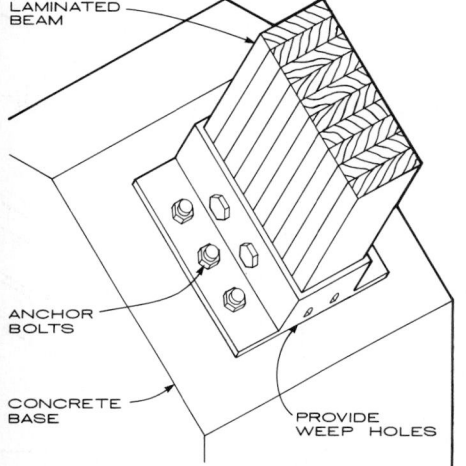

**FIXED ARCH ANCHORAGE**

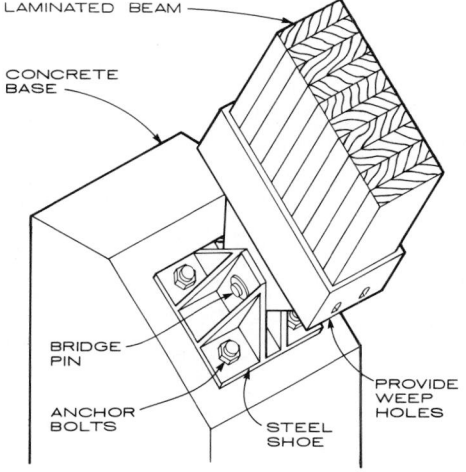

**TRUE HINGE ANCHORAGE FOR ARCHES**

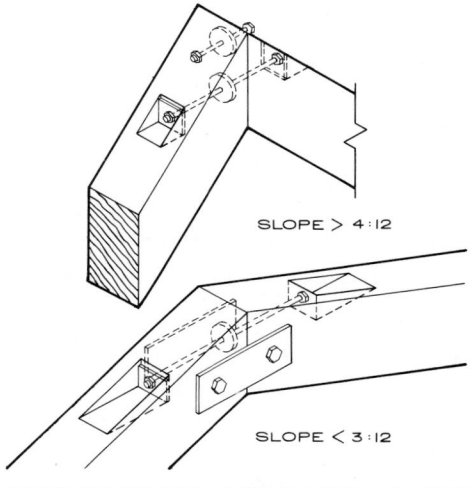

**ARCH PEAK CONNECTION**

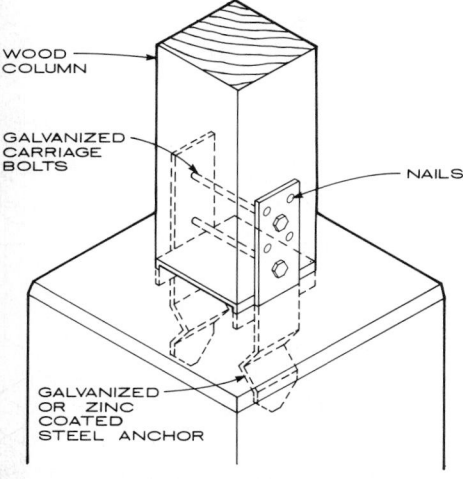

**WET POST ANCHORAGE TO CONCRETE BASE**

This detail is recommended for heavy duty use where moisture protection is desired. Anchor is set and leveled in wet concrete after screeding.

Timothy B. McDonald; Washington, D.C.

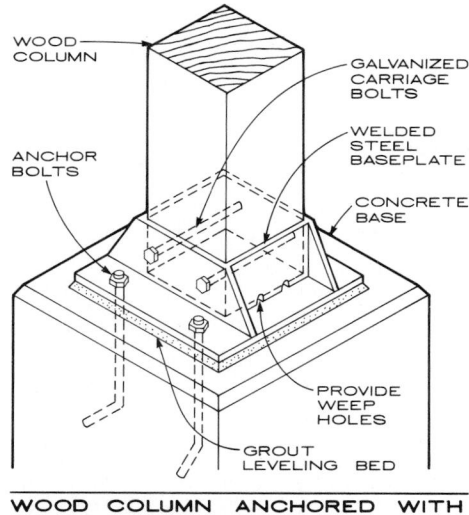

**WOOD COLUMN ANCHORED WITH STEEL BASEPLATE**

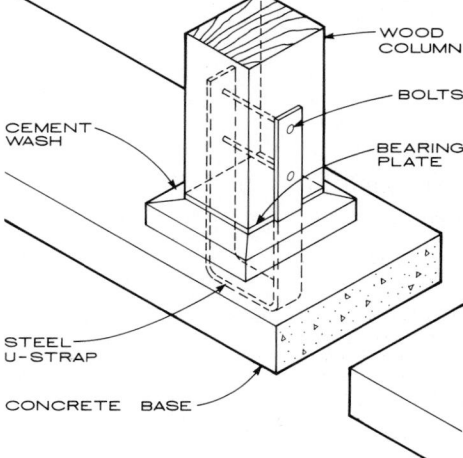

**U-STRAP COLUMN ANCHORAGE TO CONCRETE BASE**

This detail is recommended for industrial buildings and warehouses to resist both horizontal forces and uplift. Moisture barrier is recommended. It may be used with shear plates.

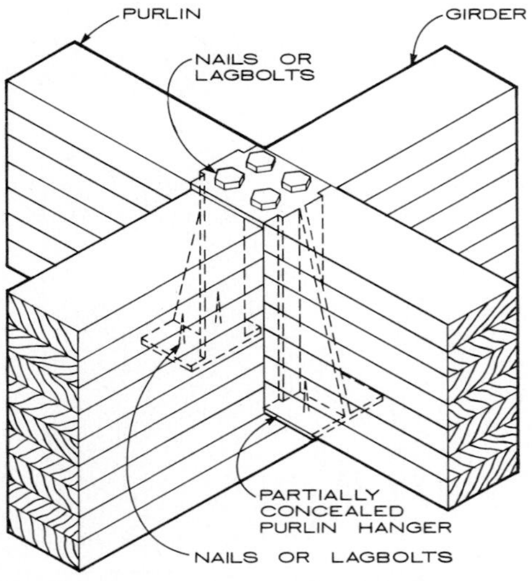

PURLIN

GIRDER

NAILS OR
LAGBOLTS

PARTIALLY
CONCEALED
PURLIN HANGER

NAILS OR LAGBOLTS

**BEAM TO PURLIN CONNECTION**

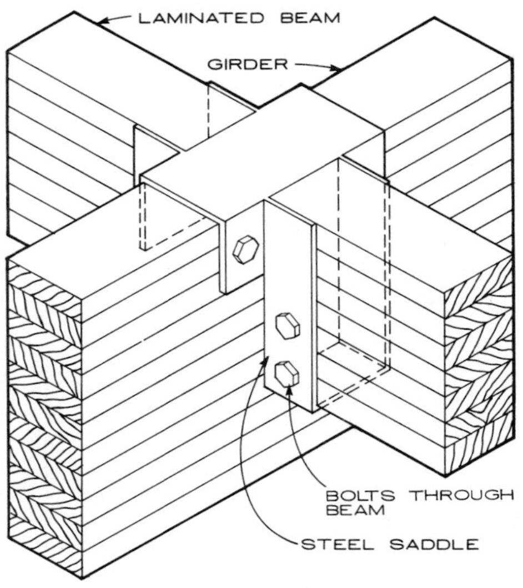

LAMINATED BEAM

GIRDER

BOLTS THROUGH
BEAM

STEEL SADDLE

**BEAM TO GIRDER CONNECTION**

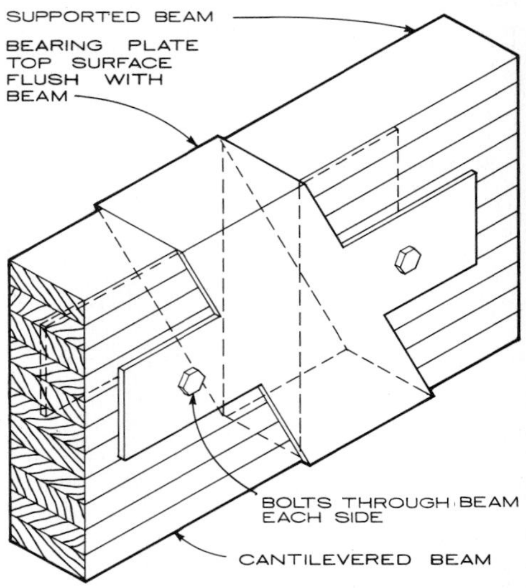

SUPPORTED BEAM

BEARING PLATE
TOP SURFACE
FLUSH WITH
BEAM

BOLTS THROUGH BEAM
EACH SIDE

CANTILEVERED BEAM

**BEAM SPLICING**

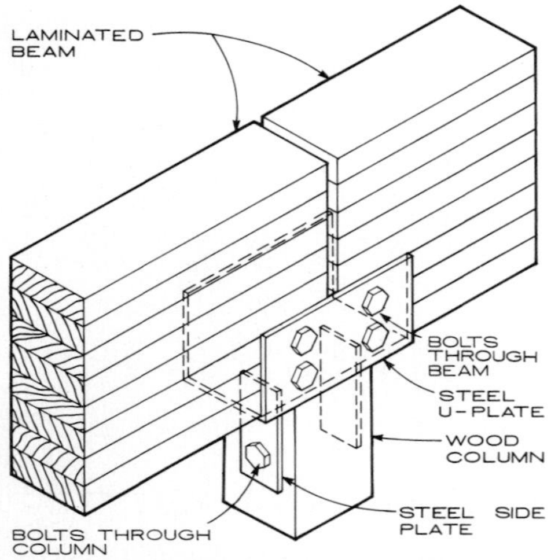

LAMINATED
BEAM

BOLTS
THROUGH
BEAM

STEEL
U-PLATE

WOOD
COLUMN

STEEL SIDE
PLATE

BOLTS THROUGH
COLUMN

**BEAM TO COLUMN CONNECTION**

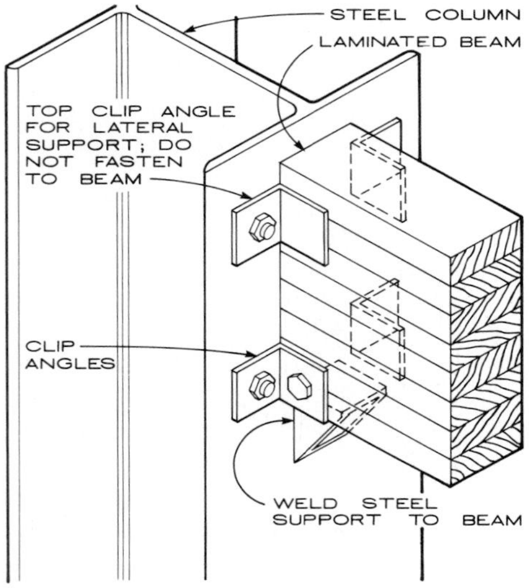

STEEL COLUMN

LAMINATED BEAM

TOP CLIP ANGLE
FOR LATERAL
SUPPORT; DO
NOT FASTEN
TO BEAM

CLIP
ANGLES

WELD STEEL
SUPPORT TO BEAM

**BEAM TO COLUMN CONNECTION**

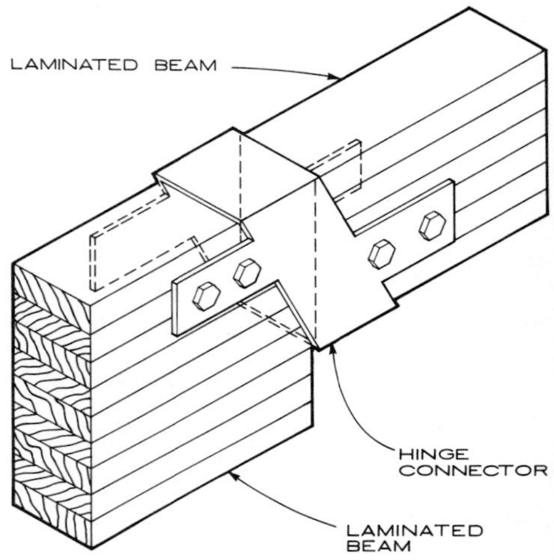

LAMINATED BEAM

HINGE
CONNECTOR

LAMINATED
BEAM

**BEAM SPLICING**

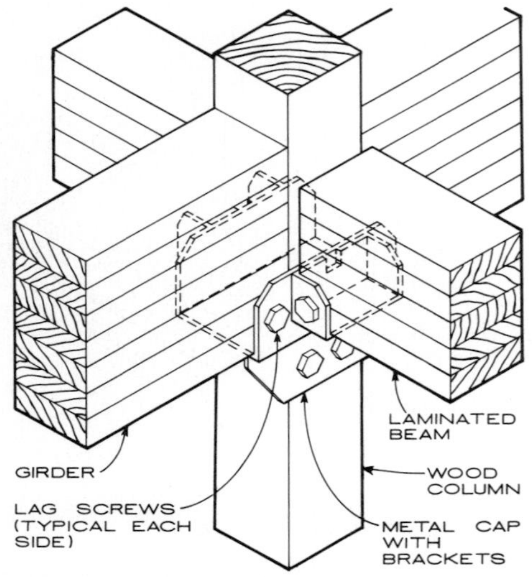

GIRDER

LAMINATED
BEAM

LAG SCREWS
(TYPICAL EACH
SIDE)

WOOD
COLUMN

METAL CAP
WITH
BRACKETS

**METAL COLUMN CAP WITH
BEAM SEATS**

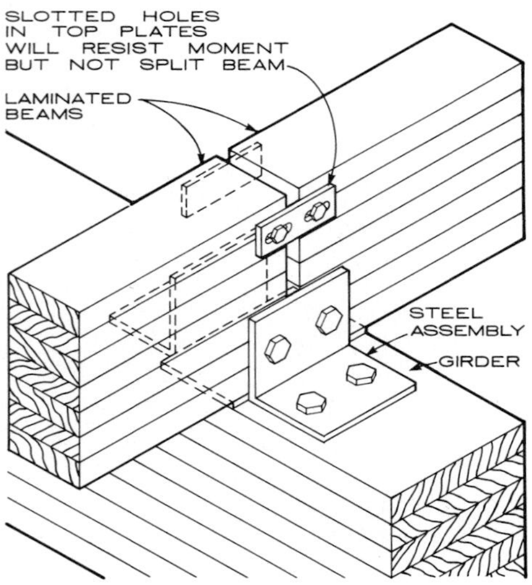

SLOTTED HOLES
IN TOP PLATES
WILL RESIST MOMENT
BUT NOT SPLIT BEAM

LAMINATED
BEAMS

STEEL
ASSEMBLY

GIRDER

**BEAM CONNECTION**

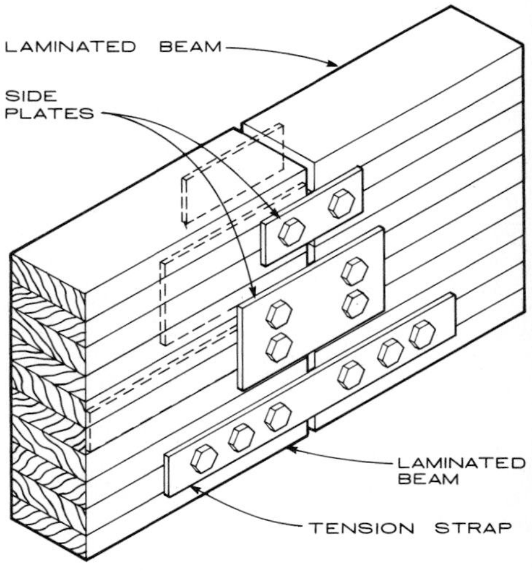

LAMINATED BEAM

SIDE
PLATES

LAMINATED
BEAM

TENSION STRAP

**MOMENT SPLICING**

Timothy B. McDonald; Washington, D.C.

 **HEAVY TIMBER CONSTRUCTION**

NOTES

1. For light trusses (trussed rafters), average spacing is 2 ft. o.c., but varies up to 4 ft. o.c. The average combined dead and live loads is 45 lbs. per sq.ft. Spans, usually 20 ft. to 32 ft., can be up to 50 ft. in some applications.

2. Early in the design process, consult engineer or truss supplier for preengineered truss designs to establish the most economical and efficient truss proportions. Supplier may provide final truss engineering design.

3. Permanent and temporary erection bracing must be installed as specified to prevent failure of properly designed trusses.

4. Some locales require an engineer's stamp when prefab trusses are used. Check local codes.

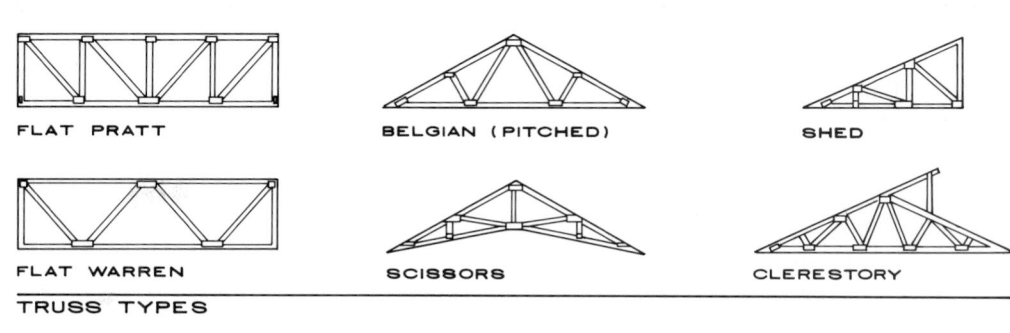

FLAT PRATT     BELGIAN (PITCHED)     SHED

FLAT WARREN     SCISSORS     CLERESTORY

**TRUSS TYPES**

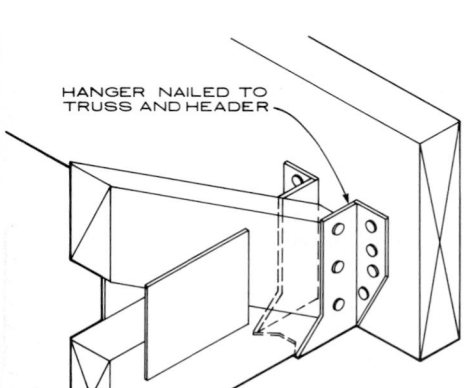

**TRUSS HANGER (DETAIL)**

HANGER NAILED TO TRUSS AND HEADER

HANGER NAILED TO BOTH TRUSSES

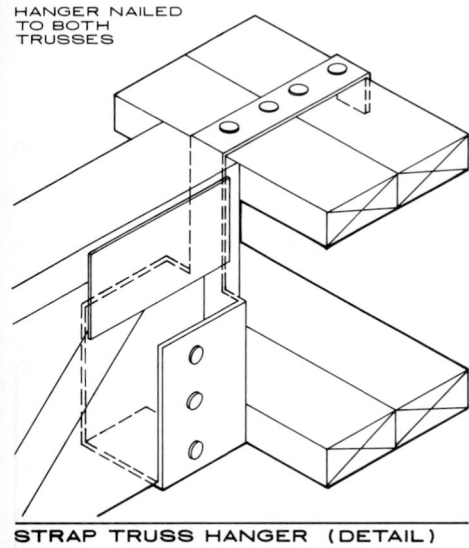

**STRAP TRUSS HANGER (DETAIL)**

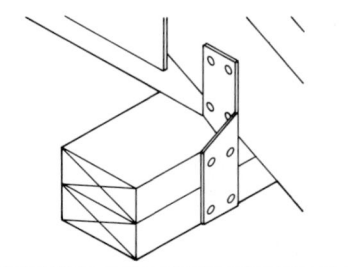

**FRAMING ANCHOR (DETAIL)**

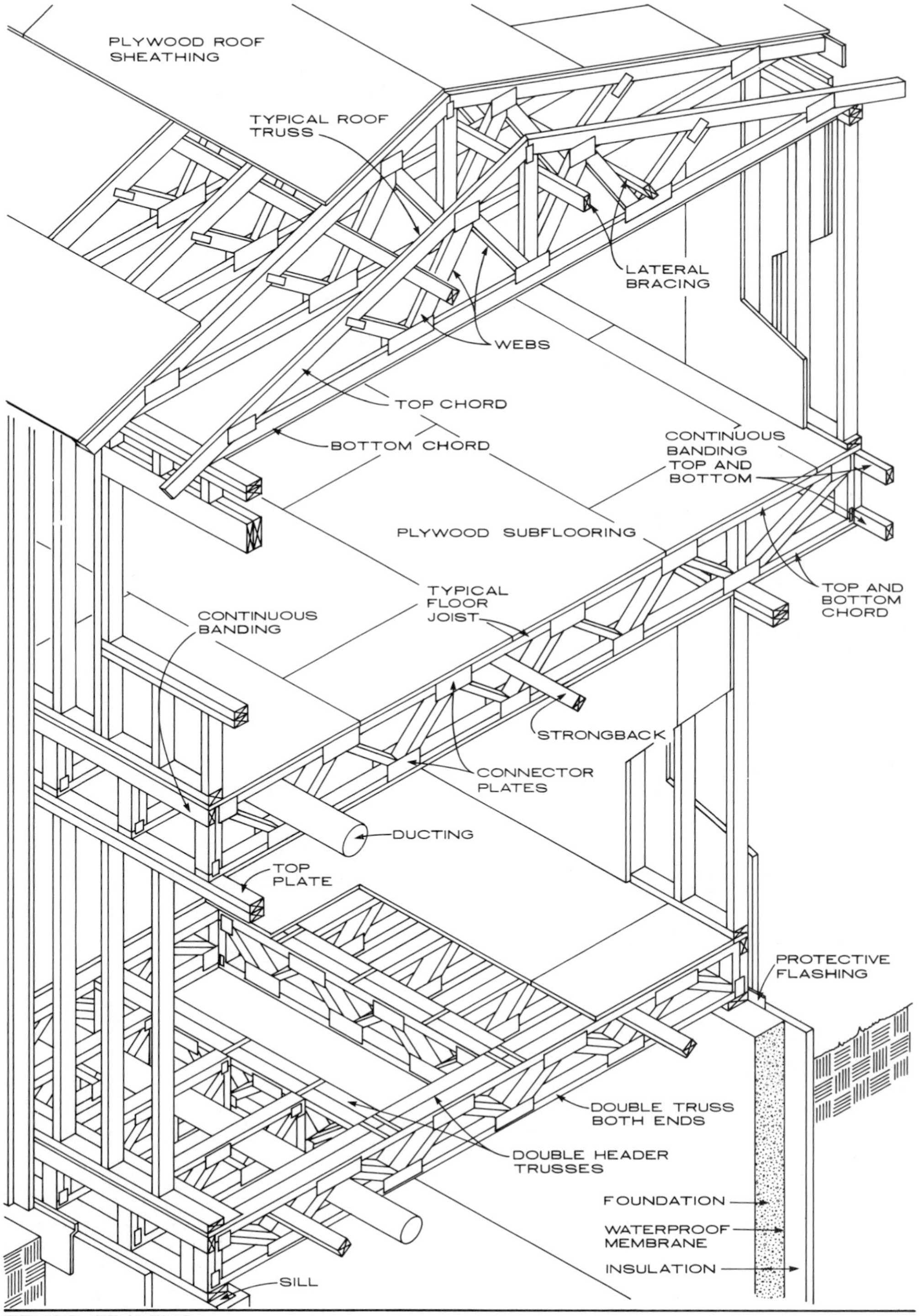

PLYWOOD ROOF SHEATHING

TYPICAL ROOF TRUSS

LATERAL BRACING

WEBS

TOP CHORD

BOTTOM CHORD

CONTINUOUS BANDING TOP AND BOTTOM

PLYWOOD SUBFLOORING

TOP AND BOTTOM CHORD

TYPICAL FLOOR JOIST

CONTINUOUS BANDING

STRONGBACK

CONNECTOR PLATES

DUCTING

TOP PLATE

PROTECTIVE FLASHING

DOUBLE TRUSS BOTH ENDS

DOUBLE HEADER TRUSSES

FOUNDATION

WATERPROOF MEMBRANE

INSULATION

SILL

**TRUSS FRAMING**

Timothy B. McDonald; Washington, D.C.

**PREFABRICATED STRUCTURAL WOOD** 6

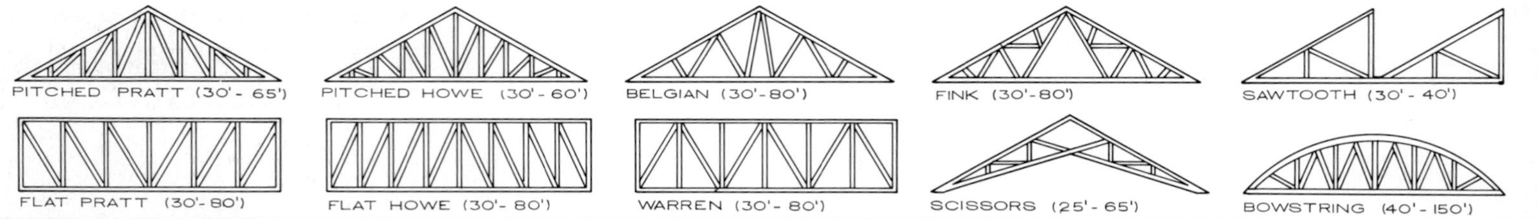

PITCHED PRATT (30'- 65')    PITCHED HOWE (30'- 60')    BELGIAN (30'-80')    FINK (30'-80')    SAWTOOTH (30'- 40')

FLAT PRATT (30'- 80')    FLAT HOWE (30'- 80')    WARREN (30'- 80')    SCISSORS (25'- 65')    BOWSTRING (40'- 150')

## HEAVY WOOD TRUSSES

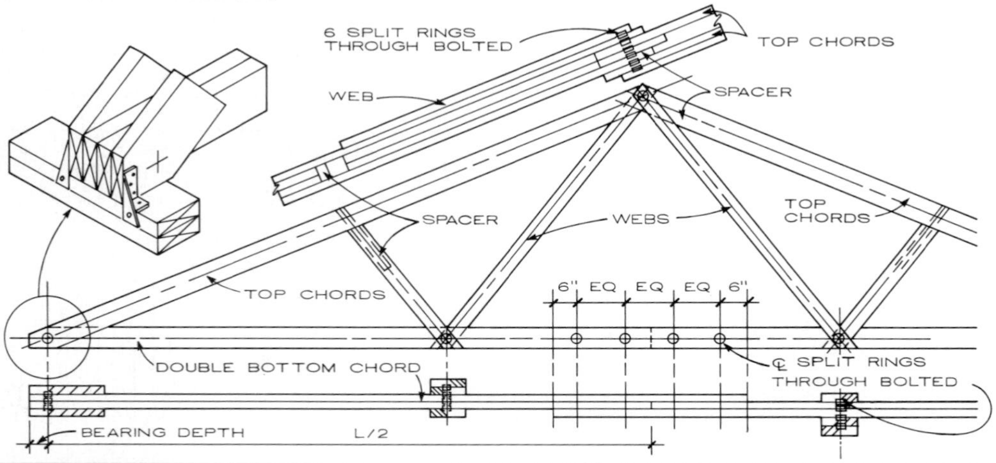

6 SPLIT RINGS THROUGH BOLTED

WEB

TOP CHORDS

SPACER

SPACER

WEBS

TOP CHORDS

TOP CHORDS

6" EQ EQ EQ 6"

DOUBLE BOTTOM CHORD

℄ SPLIT RINGS THROUGH BOLTED

BEARING DEPTH    L/2

### PITCHED TRUSS

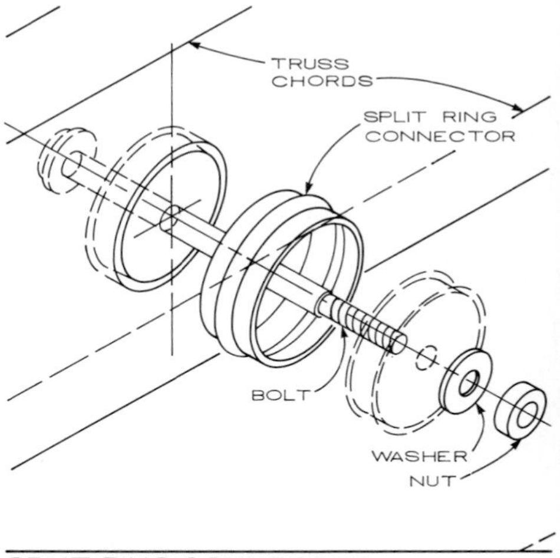

TRUSS CHORDS

SPLIT RING CONNECTOR

BOLT

WASHER

NUT

### SPLIT RING CONNECTOR

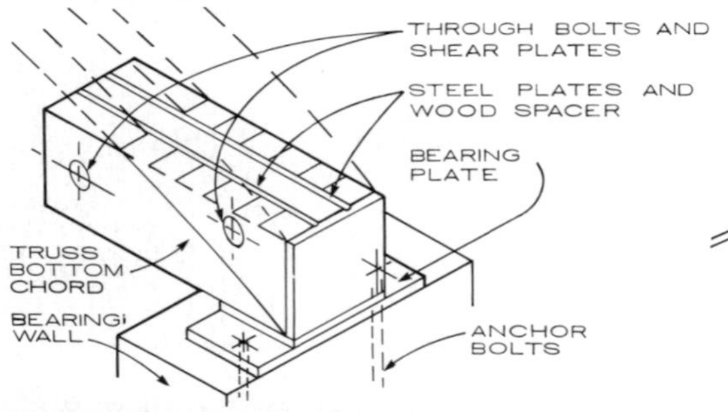

THROUGH BOLTS AND SHEAR PLATES

STEEL PLATES AND WOOD SPACER

BEARING PLATE

TRUSS BOTTOM CHORD

BEARING WALL

ANCHOR BOLTS

### BOWSTRING TRUSS DETAIL

| INSIDE DIAME-TER | STEEL SIZE | BOLT SIZE | MINIMUM LUMBER SIZES | |
|---|---|---|---|---|
| | | | RING 1 SIDE | RING IN BOTH SIDES |
| 2½" | ¾" x ⁵⁄₃₂" | ½" | 1" x 3½" | 1½" x 3½" |
| 4" | 1" x ³⁄₁₆" | ¾" | 1" x 5½" | 1½" x 5½" |

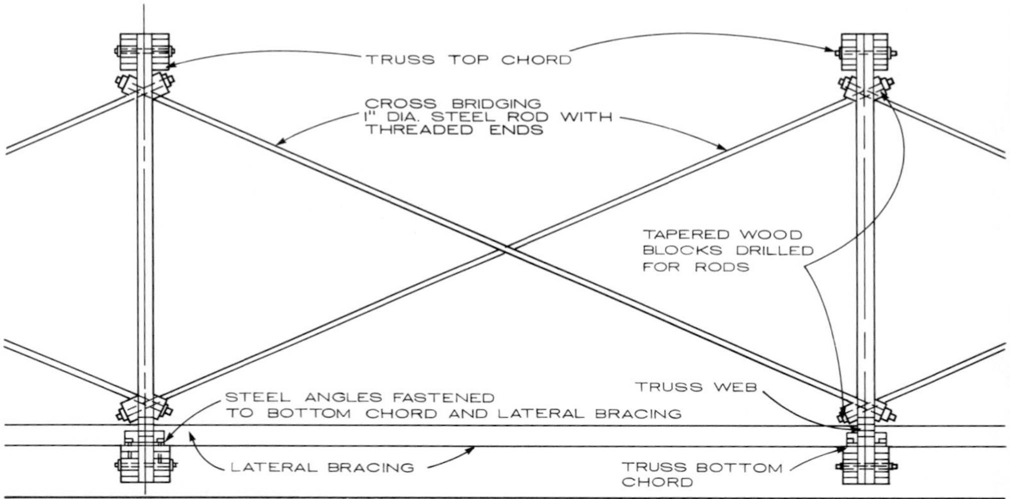

TRUSS TOP CHORD

CROSS BRIDGING 1" DIA. STEEL ROD WITH THREADED ENDS

TAPERED WOOD BLOCKS DRILLED FOR RODS

TRUSS WEB

STEEL ANGLES FASTENED TO BOTTOM CHORD AND LATERAL BRACING

LATERAL BRACING

TRUSS BOTTOM CHORD

### SECTION—CROSS BRIDGING AND LATERAL BRACING

SHEAR PLATE

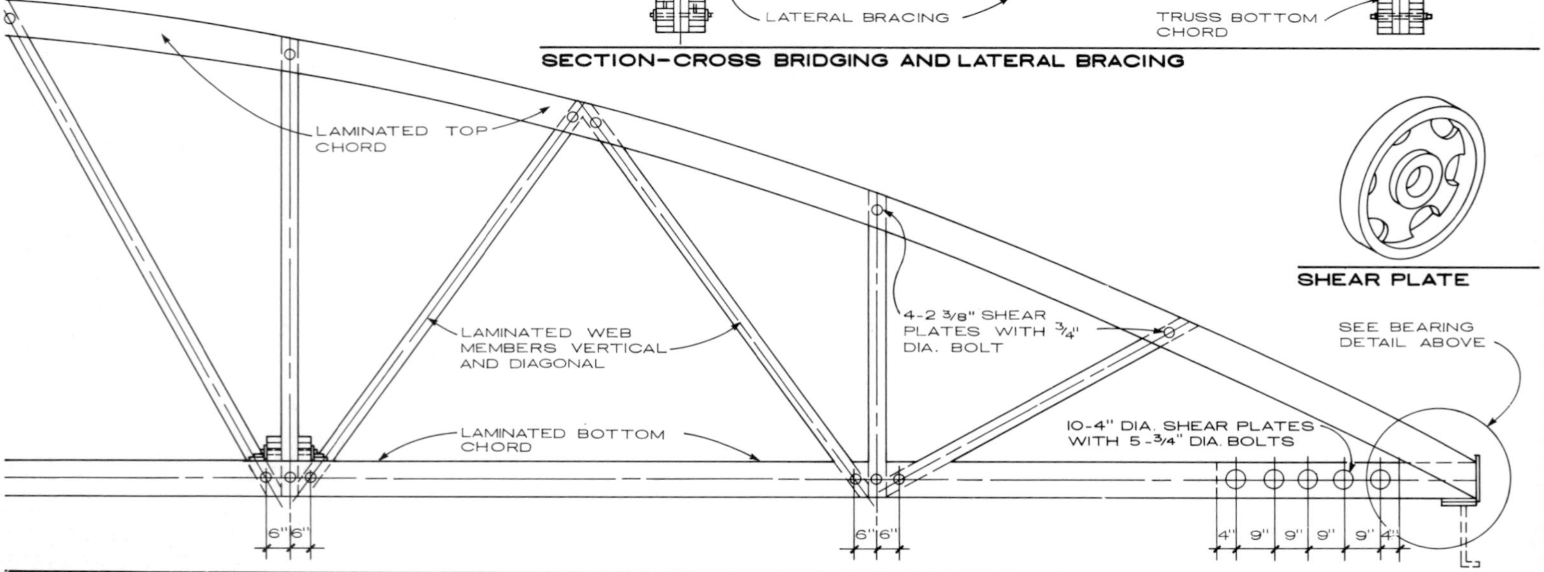

LAMINATED TOP CHORD

LAMINATED WEB MEMBERS VERTICAL AND DIAGONAL

LAMINATED BOTTOM CHORD

4-2 ³⁄₈" SHEAR PLATES WITH ¾" DIA. BOLT

SEE BEARING DETAIL ABOVE

10-4" DIA. SHEAR PLATES WITH 5 -¾" DIA. BOLTS

6" 6"    6" 6"    4" 9" 9" 9" 9" 4"

### BOWSTRING TRUSS

Timothy B. McDonald; Washington, D.C.

**6**  **PREFABRICATED STRUCTURAL WOOD**

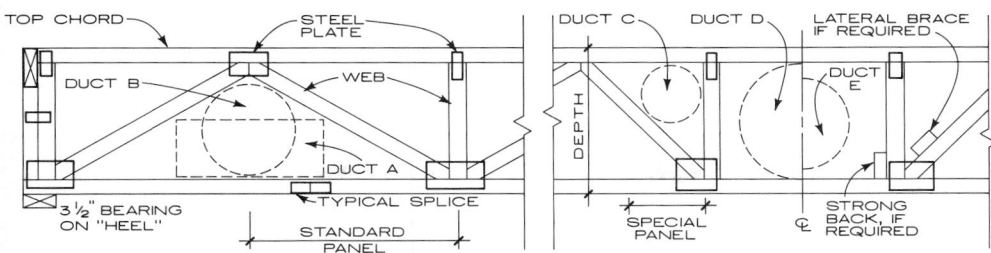

**RESIDENTIAL TYPE TRUSSED FLOOR JOIST STEEL PLATE CONNECTED**

## GENERAL

Monoplaner trusses are usually made up from 2 x 4 or 2 x 6 lumber. Spacing, normally 24 in. o.c., varies for special uses, especially in agriculture. Camber is designed for dead load only. Bottom chord furring generally is not required for drywall ceiling. Joints in plywood floor or roof should be staggered. Many trusses are approved by model codes, such as BOCA, ICBO, FHA, and SBC.

$$\text{CAMBER (USUAL)} = \frac{L(FT)}{60}$$

## BRACING

Adequate bracing of trusses is vital. Sufficient support at right angles to plane of truss must be provided to hold each truss member in its designated position. Consider bracing during design, fabrication, and erection. In addition, provide permanent bracing/anchorage as an integral part of the building. Strongbacks are often used.

## DUCT SIZES

Ease of running electrical and mechanical services through framing is a major advantage of trussed joists. Most manufacturers provide a large rectangular open panel at midspan; this void will generally accommodate a trunk line.

Sizes given here are approximations. Because web size and angles vary with different brands, the designer is cautioned to verify individual sizes carefully. Note that shape E is the duct that will fit in a flat truss with double chords top and bottom.

## DEPTH OF TRUSS AND SIZE OF DUCTWORK

| DEPTH | 12" | 16" | 20" | 24" |
|---|---|---|---|---|
| SHAPE | | | | |
| A | 4 x 9 | 6 x 12 | 7 x 13 | 8 x 14 |
| B | 7" | 10" | 12" | 14" |
| C | 5" | 7" | 8" | 9" |
| D | 9" | 13" | 17" | 21" |
| E | 6" | 10" | 14" | 18" |

## WOOD TRUSSED RAFTERS SPANS FOR PRELIMINARY DESIGN

### RESIDENTIAL LIVE LOADS

| | FLOORS 55 PSF (A) | | | ROOFS 40 PSF (B) | | 55 PSF (C) | | (DOUBLE CHORDS) 55 PSF (C) | |
|---|---|---|---|---|---|---|---|---|---|
| | TRUSSED RAFTERS SPACING (C TO C) | | | | | | | | |
| DEPTH | 12" | 16" | 24" | 16" | 24" | 16" | 24" | 16" | 24" |
| 12" | 23-6 | 21-0 | 17-1 | 24-0 | 21-4 | 21-11 | 18-2 | | |
| 13" | 24-11 | 22-0 | 17-11 | | | | | | |
| 14" | 26-4 | 22-11 | 18-8 | 27-5 | 23-3 | 24-5 | 19-10 | | |
| 15" | 27-7 | 23-10 | 19-5 | | | | | | |
| 16" | 28-7 | 24-9 | 20-1 | 30-3 | 25-0 | 26-4 | 21-4 | 31-10 | 27-10 |
| 18" | 30-6 | 26-4 | 21-5 | 32-11 | 26-9 | 28-1 | 22-9 | 35-1 | 30-7 |
| 20" | 32-4 | 27-11 | 22-8 | 34-8 | 28-0 | 29-7 | 23-11 | 38-1 | 33-1 |
| 22" | 34-0 | 26-9 | 23-11 | | | | | | |
| 24" | 35-8 | 30-10 | 25-0 | 38-3 | 30-11 | 32-7 | 26-4 | 43-10 | 36-7 |
| 28" | | | | 41-6 | 33-6 | 35-5 | 28-7 | 49-2 | 39-11 |
| 32" | | | | 44-3 | 35-7 | 37-8 | 30-4 | 52-9 | 42-9 |
| 36" | | | | 47-0 | 37-10 | 40-1 | 32-3 | 56-3 | 45-7 |
| 48" | | | | | | | | 60-0 | 53-3 |

### COMMERCIAL LIVE LOADS

| | FLOORS 80 PSF (D) | | | 100 PSF (E) | | | 120 PSF (F) | | |
|---|---|---|---|---|---|---|---|---|---|
| | TRUSSED RAFTERS SPACING (C TO C) | | | | | | | | |
| DEPTH | 12" | 16" | 24" | 12" | 16" | 24" | 12" | 16" | 24" |
| 12" | 19-0 | 17-3 | 15-1 | 17-3 | 15-8 | 13-7 | 16-0 | 14-7 | 12-4 |
| 14" | 21-4 | 19-4 | 16-6 | 19-4 | 17-7 | 14-9 | 18-0 | 16-4 | 13-6 |
| 16" | 23-6 | 21-5 | 17-10 | 21-5 | 19-5 | 15-11 | 19-10 | 17-11 | 14-6 |
| 18" | 25-8 | 23-4 | 19-0 | 23-4 | 21-0 | 17-0 | 21-8 | 19-2 | 15-6 |
| 20" | 27-8 | 24-10 | 20-2 | 25-2 | 22-3 | 18-0 | 23-4 | 20-3 | 16-7 |
| 24" | 31-6 | 27-5 | 22-2 | 28-5 | 24-6 | 19-10 | 25-11 | 22-4 | 18-1 |
| 16"* | 27-7 | 25-1 | 21-11 | 25-1 | 22-9 | 19-11 | 23-2 | 21-2 | 18-5 |
| 24"* | 38-0 | 34-6 | 30-1 | 34-6 | 31-4 | 27-4 | 32-0 | 29-1 | 25-1 |
| 32"* | 47-1 | 42-9 | 36-1 | 42-9 | 38-10 | 32-3 | 39-8 | 36-1 | 29-5 |

| | | | | | | | | |
|---|---|---|---|---|---|---|---|---|
| Top chord live load | 40 psf | 20 psf | 35 psf | 60 psf | 80 psf | 100 psf |
| Top chord dead load | 10 psf | 10 psf | 10 psf | 10 psf | 10 psf | 10 psf |
| Bottom chord dead load | 5 psf | 10 psf | 10 psf | 10 psf | 10 psf | 10 psf |
| Total load | (A) 55 psf | (B) 40 psf | (C) 55 psf | (D) 80 psf | (E) 100 psf | (F) 120 psf |

## NOTES

1. Spans are clear, inside to inside, for bottom chord bearing. Values shown would vary very slightly for a truss with top chord loading.
2. Spans should not exceed 24 x depth of truss.
3. Designed deflection limit under total load is ℓ/240 for roofs, ℓ/360 for residential floors, and ℓ/480 for commercial floors.
4. Roof spans include a +15% short term stress.

5. Asterisk (*) indicates that truss has double chords, top and bottom.
6. Spans shown are for only one type of lumber; in this case—#2 Southern pine, with an $f_b$ value of 1550. Charts are available for other grades and species. Lumber and grades may be mixed in the same truss, but chord size must be identical. Repetitive member bending stress is used in this chart.

Michael Bengis, AIA; Hopatcong, New Jersey

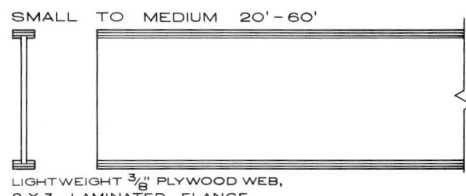

LIGHTWEIGHT 3/8" PLYWOOD WEB, 2 x 3 LAMINATED FLANGE

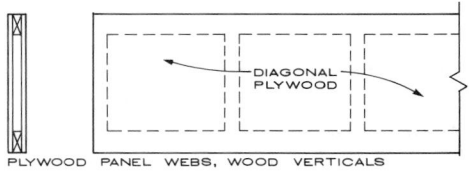

PLYWOOD PANEL WEBS, WOOD VERTICALS

MEDIUM 40'-60'

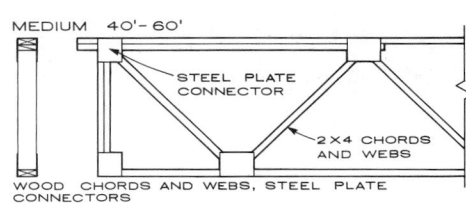

WOOD CHORDS AND WEBS, STEEL PLATE CONNECTORS

MEDIUM TO LONG 40'-80'

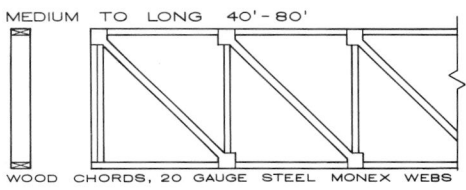

WOOD CHORDS, 20 GAUGE STEEL MONEX WEBS

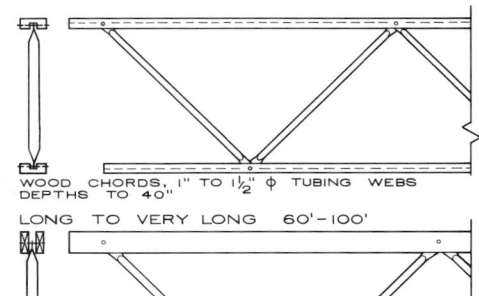

WOOD CHORDS, 1" TO 1½" φ TUBING WEBS DEPTHS TO 40"

LONG TO VERY LONG 60'-100'

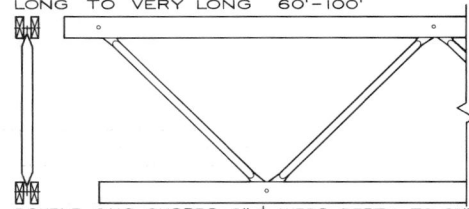

DOUBLE 2x6 CHORDS, 2" φ WEBS DEPTH TO 63"

**TYPES OF FABRICATED TRUSSES**

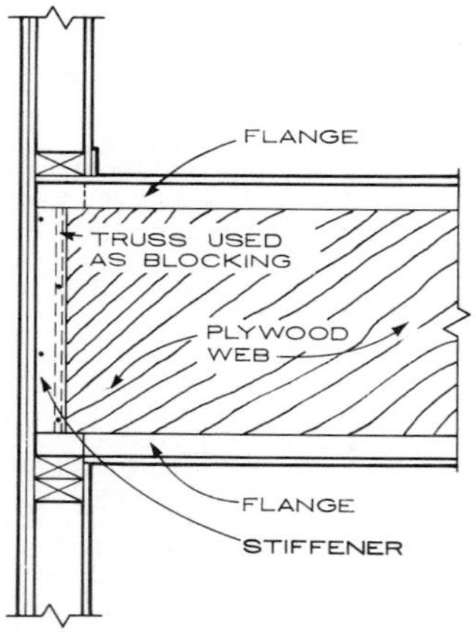

FLANGE

TRUSS USED
AS BLOCKING

PLYWOOD
WEB

FLANGE

STIFFENER

**BEARING ON STUD WALL**

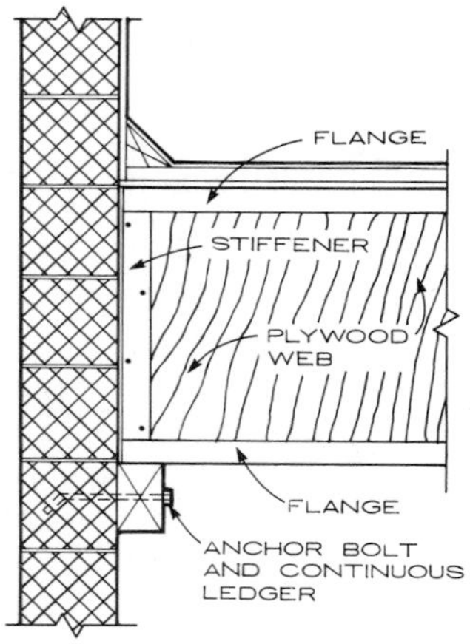

FLANGE

STIFFENER

PLYWOOD
WEB

FLANGE

ANCHOR BOLT
AND CONTINUOUS
LEDGER

**BEARING ON LEDGER**

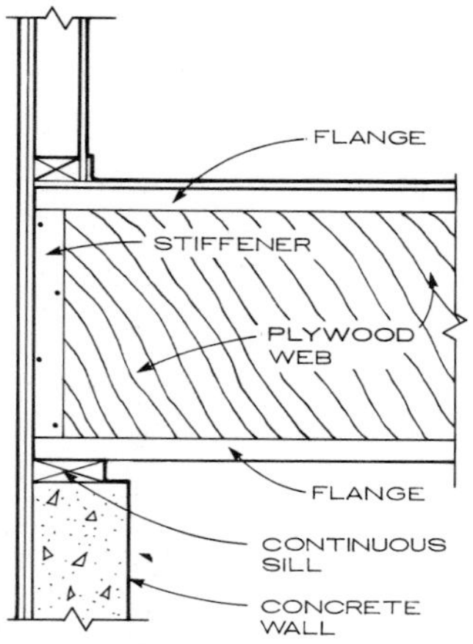

FLANGE

STIFFENER

PLYWOOD
WEB

FLANGE

CONTINUOUS
SILL

CONCRETE
WALL

**FOUNDATION**

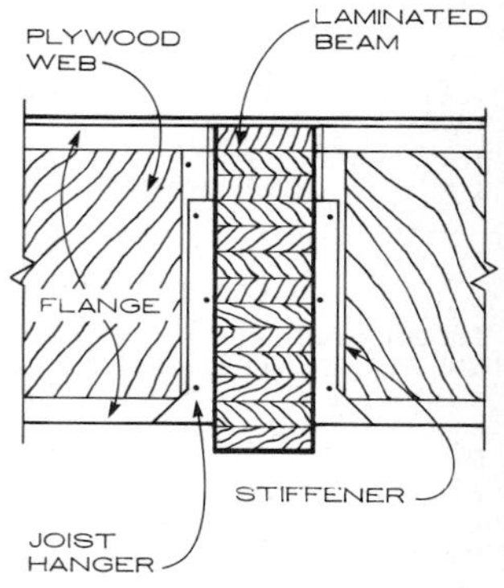

PLYWOOD
WEB

LAMINATED
BEAM

FLANGE

JOIST
HANGER

STIFFENER

**BOTTOM CHORD BEAM**

**PLYWOOD WEB TRUSS**    (WOOD CHORDS AND FLANGES)

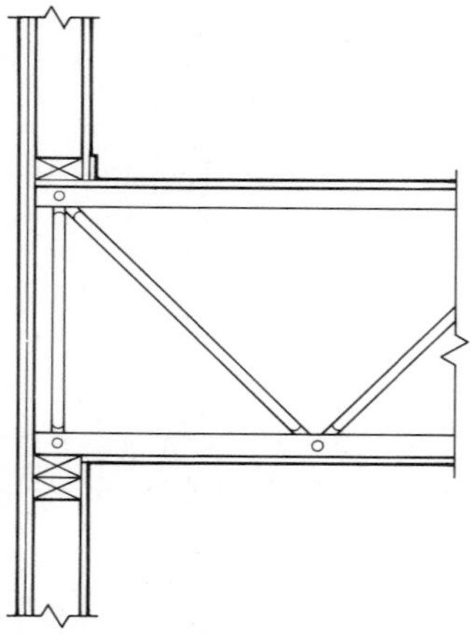

**BOTTOM CHORD
BEARING ON STUD WALL**

CONTINUOUS
NAILER FOR
LATERAL
SUPPORT

½" TYPICAL

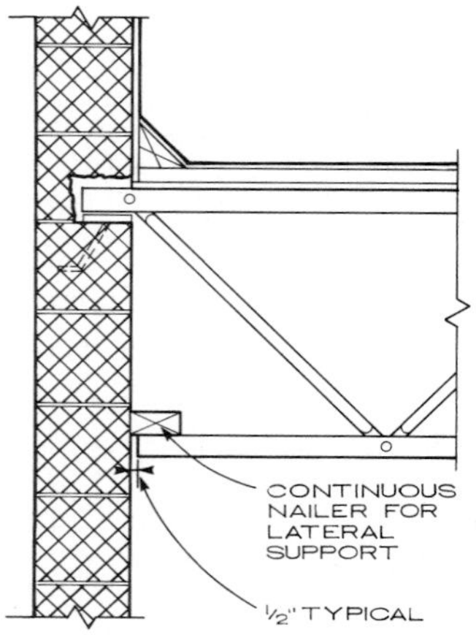

**TOP CHORD BEARING –
MASONRY WALL**

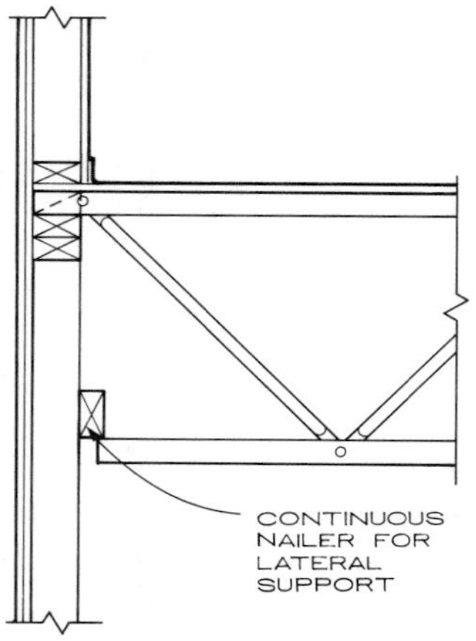

CONTINUOUS
NAILER FOR
LATERAL
SUPPORT

**TOP CHORD BEARING ON
STUD WALL**

CONTINUOUS
NAILER FOR
LATERAL
SUPPORT

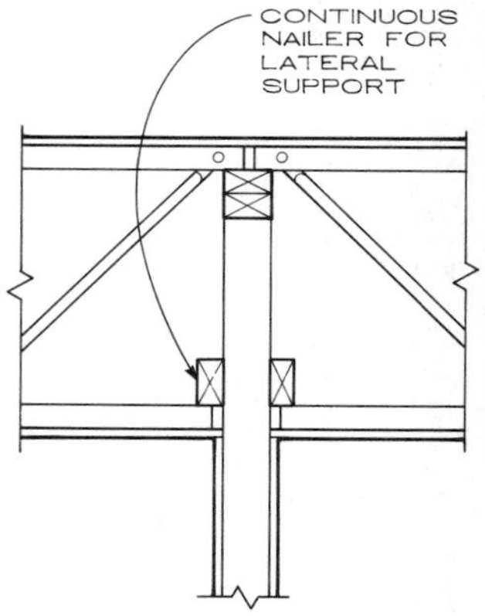

**TOP CHORD BEARING**

**OPEN WEB TRUSS**    (STEEL WEB WOOD CHORD)

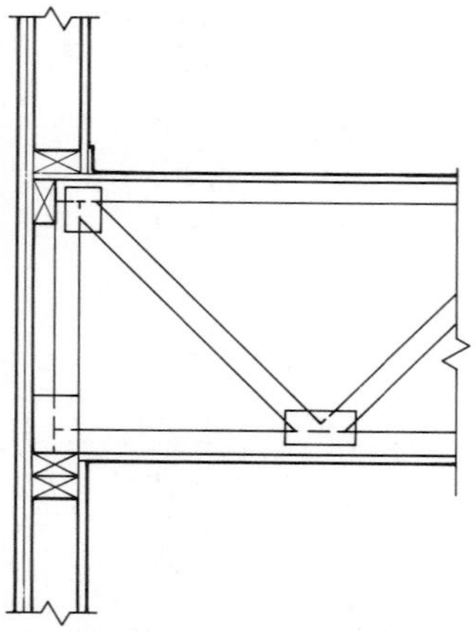

**BOTTOM CHORD
BEARING ON STUD WALL**

CONTINUOUS
NAILER FOR
LATERAL
SUPPORT

½" TYPICAL

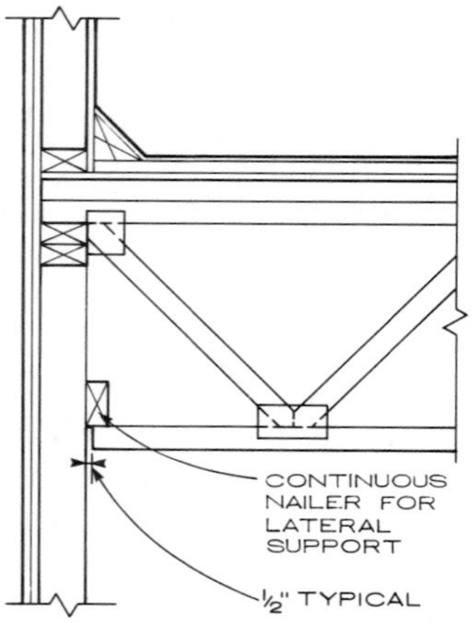

**TOP CHORD BEARING ON
MASONRY WALL**

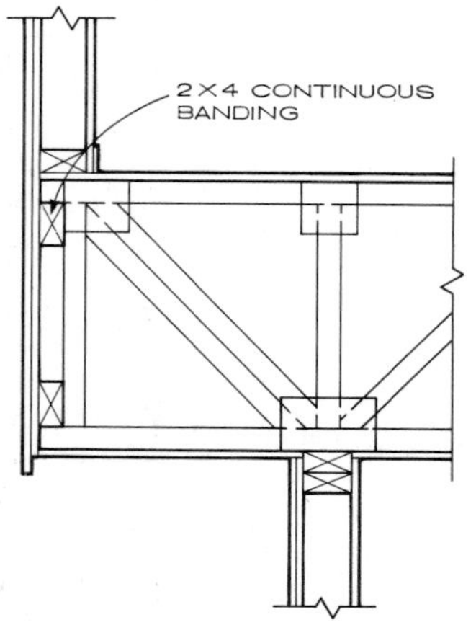

2×4 CONTINUOUS
BANDING

**CANTILEVERED
FLOOR TRUSS**

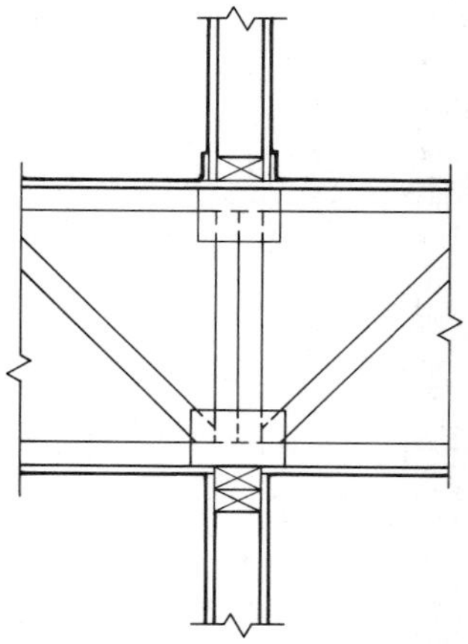

**BOTTOM CHORD
BEARING**

**OPEN WEB TRUSS**    (WOOD CHORDS AND WEB, METAL PLATE CONNECTORS)

Timothy B. McDonald; Washington, D.C.

**PREFABRICATED STRUCTURAL WOOD**

## STRUCTURAL GLUED LAMINATED TIMBER

The term "structural glued laminated timber" refers to an engineered, stress-rated product made of appropriately selected and prepared wood laminations bonded with adhesives. The grain of all laminations is approximately parallel lengthwise. Laminations can be made of pieces end-joined to form any length, of pieces placed or glued edge-to-edge to make wider ones, or of bent pieces curved during gluing.

## STANDARD DEPTHS

Dimensional lumber, surfaced to 1½ in. (38 mm), normally is used to laminate straight members and those curved members that have radii of curvature within the bending radius limitations for the species. Boards, surfaced to ¾ in. (19 mm), are recommended for laminating curved members when the bending radius is too short to permit the use of dimension lumber, provided that the bending radius limitations for the species are observed. Other lamination thicknesses may be used to meet special requirements.

## STANDARD WIDTHS

| Nominal width | in. | 3 | 4 | 6 | 8 | 10 | 12 | 14 | 16 |
|---|---|---|---|---|---|---|---|---|---|
| Net finished width | in. | 2⅛ | 3⅛* | 5⅛* | 6¾ | 8¾ | 10¾ | 12¼ | 14¼ |
| | mm | 57 | 79 | 130 | 171 | 222 | 273 | 311 | 362 |

* 3 in. and 5 in. for Southern pine.

## CAMBER

Camber is curvature (circular or parabolic) made into structural glued laminated beams opposite the anticipated deflection movement. The recommended minimum camber is one and one-half times dead load deflection which, after plastic deformation has taken place, usually will produce a near level floor or roof beam under dead load conditions. Additional camber of slope may be provided to insure adequate drainage of roof beams. On level, long-span roof beams and floor beams of multistory buildings, additional camber may be needed to counter the optical illusion of the beam sagging.

## FIRE SAFETY

The self-insulating qualities of heavy timber sizes create a slow burning characteristic. Good structural details, elimination of concealed spaces, and use of fire stops to interfere with the vertical passage of flames contribute to the fire performance of heavy timber construction in fire. While timber will burn, it retains its strength under fire longer than unprotected metals, which lose their strength quickly under extreme heat.

Building codes generally classify glued laminated timber as heavy timber construction if certain minimum dimensional requirements are met.

Fire retardant treatments may be applied to glued laminated timber but they do not substantially increase the fire resistance of heavy timber construction. When fire retardant treatments are used, the reduction of strength as related to type and penetration of treatment, the compatibility of treatment and adhesive, the use of special gluing procedures, the difficulty of application, and the effect on wood color and on fabricating procedures should be investigated.

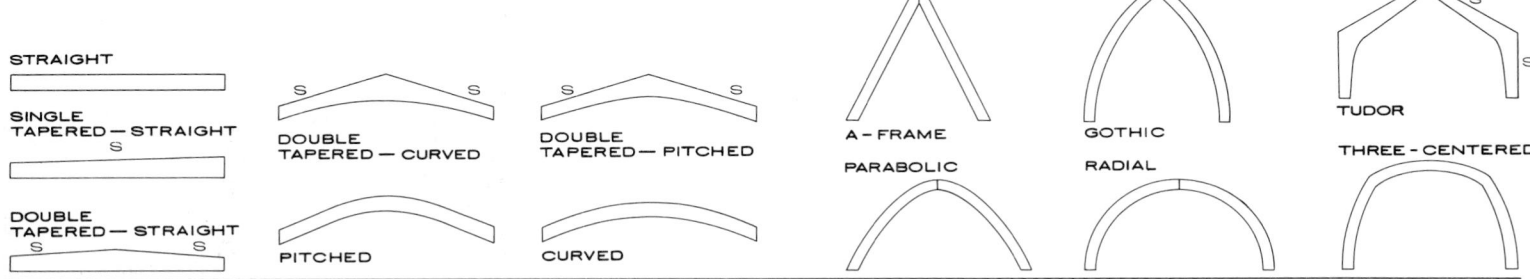

## STRUCTURAL GLUED LAMINATED TIMBER SHAPES

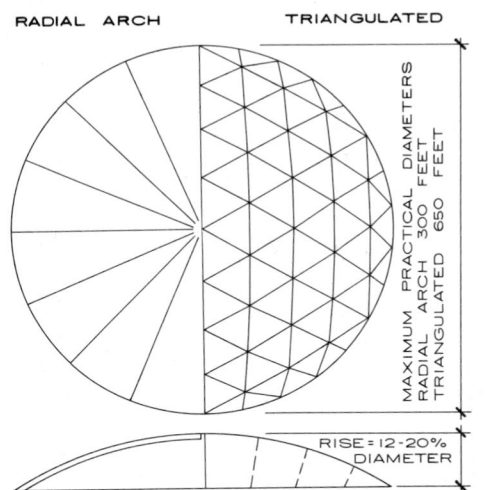

RADIAL ARCH   TRIANGULATED

MAXIMUM PRACTICAL DIAMETERS RADIAL ARCH 300 FEET TRIANGULATED 650 FEET

RISE = 12-20% DIAMETER

## NOTES ON SHAPES

1. Beam names describe top and bottom surfaces of the beam. "S" designates a sawn or tapered surface. Sloped or pitched surfaces should be used on the tension side of the beam.

2. The three hinged arches and frames shown at right produce horizontal reactions requiring horizontal ties or modified foundations.

3. More complex shapes may be fabricated. Contact the American Institute of Timber Construction (AITC).

## LAMINATED DOME SYSTEMS

The triangulated and the radial arch are the two basic types of structural glued laminated wood dome systems available. Both systems require a tension ring at the dome spring line to convert axial thrusts to vertical loads. Consideration must be given to the perimeter bond beam design since wind forces will produce loads in this member. The length of main members of the radial arch system, which must span a distance greater than half the dome diameter, limit the maximum practical dome diameter. The far smaller members of the triangulated dome result in the greater diameters. The triangulated system can be designed for five or more segments with an equal number of peripheral supports at each segment.

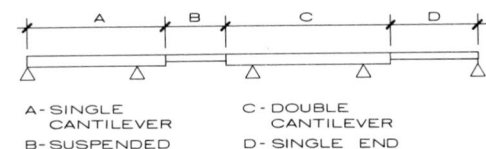

A - SINGLE CANTILEVER
B - SUSPENDED
C - DOUBLE CANTILEVER
D - SINGLE END SUSPENDED

## CANTILEVERED AND CONTINUOUS SPAN SYSTEMS

Cantilever beam systems may be composed of any of the various types and combinations of beams shown above. Cantilever systems generally permit longer spans or larger loads per a given size member than do simple span systems. For economy, the negative bending moment at the support of a cantilevered beam should be equal in magnitude to the positive moment.

## ALLOWABLE UNIT STRESS RANGES FOR STRUCTURAL GLUED LAMINATED - NORMAL DURATION OF LOADING

| SPECIES | EXTREME FIBER IN BENDING | TENSION PARALLEL TO GRAIN | COMPRESSION PARALLEL TO GRAIN | HORIZONTAL SHEAR | COMPRESSION PERPENDICULAR TO GRAIN | MODULUS OF ELASTICITY |
|---|---|---|---|---|---|---|
| DRY CONDITIONS OF USE - MOISTURE CONTENT IN SERVICE LESS THAT 16% | | | | | | |
| Douglas fir - larch | 1600 to 2400 | 900 to 1600 | 1200 to 2400 | 165 | 560 to 650 | 1.5 to 1.8 |
| Hem fir | 1600 to 2400 | 800 to 1400 | 975 to 1750 | 155 | 375 to 500 | 1.4 to 1.5 |
| Southern pine | 1600 to 2400 | 900 to 1550 | 675 to 2300 | 200 | 560 to 650 | 1.4 to 1.8 |
| California redwood | 1600 | 875 to 1000 | 1350 to 1600 | 125 | 315 | 1.1 |
| WET CONDITIONS OF USE FACTORS - MOISTURE CONTENT IN SERVICE 16% OR MORE (REQUIRES WET USE ADHESIVES) | | | | | | |
| | 0.800 | 0.800 | 0.730 | 0.875 | 0.530 | 0.833 |

Note: Multiply dry condition of use stress ranges by the above factors for corresponding wet conditions of use values

*For complete information see current American Institute of Timber Construction Publication AITC 117 - Design.

Thomas Hodne/Roger Kipp Architects, Planners, Inc.; Minneapolis, Minnesota

## APPEARANCE GRADES

Structural glued laminated timber is produced in three appearance grades:

1. Industrial: For use where appearance is not a primary concern.
2. Architectural: For use where appearance is a factor.
3. Premium: For uses that demand the finest appearance.

These appearance grades do not modify design stresses, fabrication controls, grades of lumber used, or other provisions of the applicable standards. Descriptions of the three grades follow. A textured (rough sawn) surface may be called for instead of the surfacing described. In all grades, lamination will possess the natural growth characteristics of the lumber grade.

### INDUSTRIAL APPEARANCE GRADE

Void filling on the edge of laminations is not required. The wide face of laminations exposed to view will be free of loose knots and open knot holes. Edge joints on the wide face will not be filled. Members will be surfaced two sides only, an occasional miss being permitted along individual laminations.

### ARCHITECTURAL APPEARANCE GRADE

In exposed surfaces, knot holes and other voids measuring more than ¾ in. (19 mm) will be replaced with clear wood inserts or a wood-tone colored filler. Inserts will be selected with reasonable care for similarity of the grain and color to the adjacent wood in the lamination. The wide face of laminations exposed to view will be free of loose knots and open knot holes. Voids greater than ¹⁄₁₆ in. (2 mm) wide in edge joints appearing on the wide face of laminations exposed to view will be filled. Exposed faces will be surfaced smooth. Misses are not permitted. The corners on the wide face of laminations exposed to view will be eased. Current practice for eased edges is for a radius between ⅛ in. (3 mm) and ½ in. (13 mm).

### PREMIUM APPEARANCE GRADE

Similar to architectural grade except that in exposed surfaces, all knot holes and other voids will be replaced with wood inserts or a wood-tone colored filler as described for architectural grade. In addition, knots will be limited in size to 20 percent of the net face width of the lamination, with no more than two maximum size knots occurring in a

6 ft. (1.8 M) length of the exposed wide face of the laminations.

## FINISHES

Available finishes for glued laminated timber include sealers, stains and paints.

End sealers retard moisture transmission and minimize checking and normally are applied to the ends of all members.

Surface sealers increase resistance to soiling, control grain raising, minimize checking, and serve as a moisture retardant. They fall within two classifications. Penetrating sealers provide limited protection and are suitable for use when the final finish requires staining or a natural finish. Primer and sealer coats provide maximum protection by sealing the surface of the wood, but should not be specified when the final finish requires a natural or stained finish. Wood color is modified by any sealer application. Wood sealers followed by staining will look different from stained untreated wood.

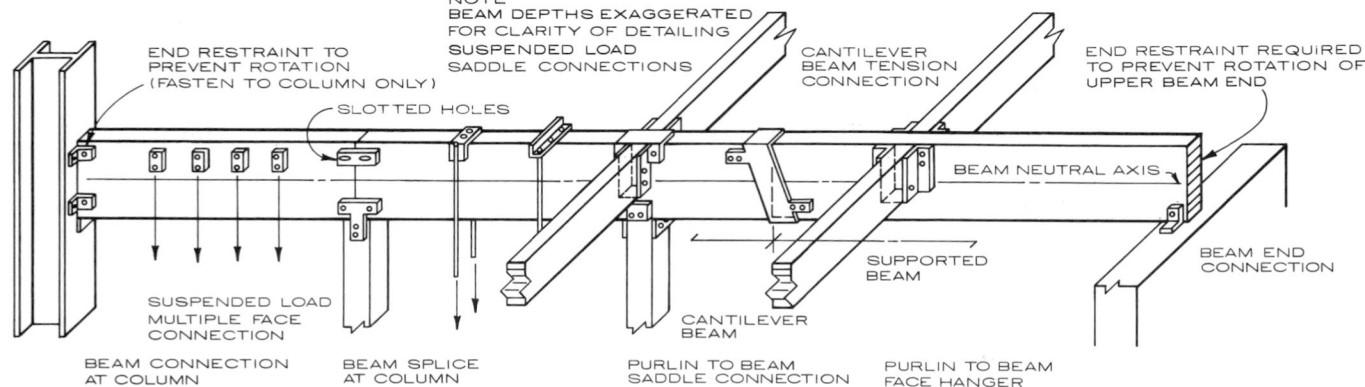

## CONNECTION DESIGN

The design of connections for glued laminated timbers is similar to the design of connections for sawn lumber. Since glued laminated timbers often are much larger than sawn lumber and the loads transferred also are larger, the effect of increased size should be taken into account in the design of connections. In addition to being designed for strength to transfer loads, connections also should be designed to avoid splitting of the member and to accommodate swelling and shrinking of the wood.

### BEAM END CONNECTIONS

Beam end connections should be designed to carry both induced horizontal and vertical loads. Bolts or fastenings at the end of the beam should be located toward the bottom of the beam so that the effect of shrinkage between the bottom of the beam and the fastening is minimized. Bolts or connectors located near or above the beam's neutral axis should not be used on large glued laminated beams

or girders since the concentration of the tension perpendicular to grain due to restraint of shrinkage, and shear stresses acting at fasteners located in these beam areas tend to cause splitting of the member.

### SUSPENDED LOADS

In cases where it is not possible for the suspending system to be carried on top of the beam, it is good practice to place the fastener above the neutral axis, particularly when other than light loading is involved or when a number of loads are to be suspended from the member. For heavy loads, a saddle detail placing loads directly on top of the beam is recommended.

Very light loads may be suspended near the bottom of a glued laminated timber. The distance above the beam bottom must be at least equal to the specified edge distance of the fastener used.

### PURLIN TO BEAM CONNECTIONS

The preferred purlin to beam connection method is to transfer the end reaction by bearing perpendicular to grain in a saddle type connection extending over the beam top.

When the end reaction of the beam or purlin is relatively small, the hanger can be fastened to the face of the girder. The bolts or connectors in the main carrying beam or girder should be placed above the neutral axis of the member, and in the supported member should be placed near the bottom to avoid potential splitting.

### SPLICE CONNECTIONS

At beam splice connections occurring over columns, it is important to allow for movement in the upper portions of the beam due to end rotation. Slotted connections will help to reduce the problem by allowing for some beam movement.

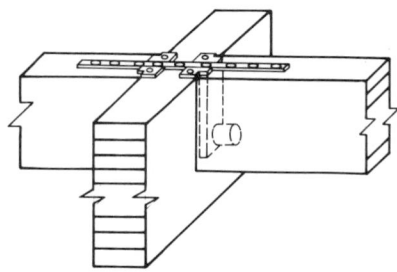

### CONCEALED AND PARTIALLY CONCEALED PURLIN HANGERS

Partially concealed purlin hangers of the type shown to the left are used for normal loads. The center arrangement and the concealed hanger at the right are appropriate for relatively light loads. The concealed hanger at the right,

as well as connections where the support plate at the base is notched into the beam, should be designed as notched beam reactions.

It is recommended that the support for the purlin be close to the bottom of the member to utilize the maximum ef-

fective area for shear. End fastenings should not include rows of bolts or other fasteners perpendicular to the grain. Glued laminated timbers, although relatively dry at the time of manufacture, may shrink when the members reach equilibrium moisture content in place. This may cause tension perpendicular to the grain and result in splitting.

Thomas Hodne/Roger Kipp Architects, Planners, Inc.; Minneapolis, Minnesota

## PREFABRICATED STRUCTURAL WOOD

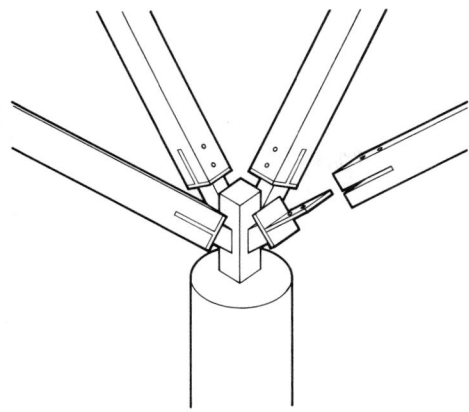

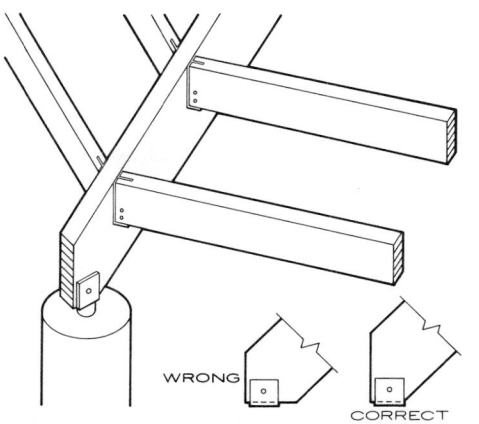

WRONG    CORRECT

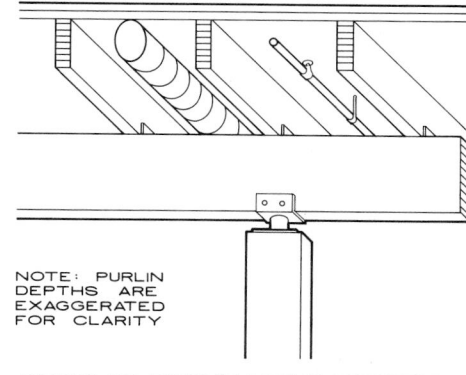

NOTE: PURLIN
DEPTHS ARE
EXAGGERATED
FOR CLARITY

## SPECIAL CONNECTIONS

The detail above is just one of a large variety of special connections and connection assemblies possible using structural glued laminated timber. It is critical that connections be designed carefully in accordance with good engineering practice.

## GLUED LAMINATED COLUMNS

Structural glued laminated timber columns offer higher allowable stresses, controlled appearance, and the ability to fabricate variable sections. For simple rectangular columns, the slenderness ratio, or the ratio of the unsupported length between points of lateral support to the least column dimension, may not exceed 50. The least dimension for tapered columns is taken as the sum of the smaller dimension and one-third the difference between the smaller and greater dimensions. Spaced columns consist of two or more members with their longitudinal axes parallel, separated at the ends and at the midpoint by blocking, and joined at the ends by shear fastenings. The members are considered to act together to carry the total column load, and because of the end fixity developed, a greater slenderness ratio than that allowed for solid columns is permitted.

## NOTCHED BEARING CONDITIONS

An abrupt notch in the end of a wood member reduces the effective shear strength of the member and may permit a more rapid migration of moisture in the lower portion of the member causing potential splitting. This condition is similar to the incorrect detail above, but perhaps is not as evident. The shear strength of the end of the member is reduced and the exposed end grain also may result in splitting because of drying. At inclined beams, the taper cut should be loaded in bearing.

## NOTES ON BEAM DESIGN CHART

1. Total load carrying capacity includes beam weight. Floor beams are designed for uniform loads of 40 psf live load and 10 psf dead load.
2. Allowable stresses: $F_b$ = 2400 psi (reduced by size factor), $F_v$ = 165 psi, E = 1,800,000 psi.
3. Deflection limits: roof = $1/180$, floor = $1/360$.
4. Values are for preliminary design purposes only. For more complete information see the AITC *Timber Construction Manual.*

## OVERLAY PURLIN-BEAM SYSTEM

The design of a structural glued laminated system in which the purlins frame over the top of the beams has the advantage of more easily accommodating the distribution of heating, cooling, and fire protection components. As with any timber structural design, beam and purlin end restraint, as well as overall system lateral stability, must be provided for.

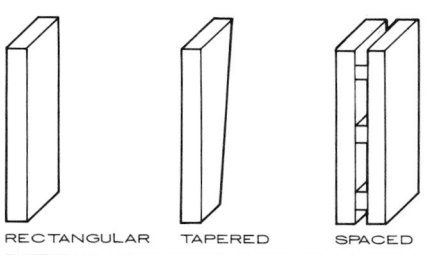

RECTANGULAR    TAPERED    SPACED

**COLUMNS**

## LAMINATED FLOOR, ROOF BEAM, AND PURLIN DESIGN CHART—
## TYPICAL SINGLE SPAN SIMPLY SUPPORTED GLUED LAMINATED BEAMS (MEMBER SIZES IN INCHES)

| SPAN (FT) | SPACING (FT) | TOTAL LOAD CARRYING CAPACITY (PSF) | | | | | | FLOOR BEAMS 50 PSF |
|---|---|---|---|---|---|---|---|---|
| | | 30 PSF | 35 PSF | 40 PSF | 45 PSF | 50 PSF | 55 PSF | |
| 12 | 6 | $3^1/8$ x 6 | $3^1/8$ x 6 | $3^1/8$ x $7^1/2$ | $3^1/8$ x $7^1/2$ | $3^1/8$ x $7^1/2$ | $3^1/8$ x $7^1/2$ | $3^1/8$ x 9 |
| | 8 | $3^1/8$ x 6 | $3^1/8$ x $7^1/2$ | $3^1/8$ x 9 | $3^1/8$ x 9 | $3^1/8$ x 9 | $3^1/8$ x 9 | $3^1/8$ x $10^1/2$ |
| | 10 | $3^1/8$ x $7^1/2$ | $3^1/8$ x $7^1/2$ | $3^1/8$ x 9 | $3^1/8$ x 9 | $3^1/8$ x 9 | $3^1/8$ x $10^1/2$ | $3^1/8$ x $10^1/2$ |
| | 12 | $3^1/8$ x $7^1/2$ | $3^1/8$ x 9 | $3^1/8$ x 9 | $3^1/8$ x 9 | $3^1/8$ x $10^1/2$ | $3^1/8$ x $10^1/2$ | $3^1/8$ x 12 |
| 16 | 8 | $3^1/8$ x 9 | $3^1/8$ x 9 | $3^1/8$ x $10^1/2$ | $3^1/8$ x $10^1/2$ | $3^1/8$ x 12 | $3^1/8$ x 12 | $3^1/8$ x $13^1/2$ |
| | 12 | $3^1/8$ x $10^1/2$ | $3^1/8$ x 12 | $3^1/8$ x 12 | $3^1/8$ x 12 | $3^1/8$ x $13^1/2$ | $3^1/8$ x $13^1/2$ | $3^1/8$ x 15 |
| | 14 | $3^1/8$ x 12 | $3^1/8$ x 12 | $3^1/8$ x $13^1/2$ | $3^1/8$ x $13^1/2$ | $3^1/8$ x 15 | $3^1/8$ x 15 | $3^1/8$ x 15 |
| | 16 | $3^1/8$ x 12 | $3^1/8$ x $13^1/2$ | $3^1/8$ x $13^1/2$ | $3^1/8$ x 15 | $3^1/8$ x 15 | $3^1/8$ x $16^1/2$ | $3^1/8$ x 15 |
| 20 | 8 | $3^1/8$ x 12 | $3^1/8$ x 12 | $3^1/8$ x $13^1/2$ | $3^1/8$ x $13^1/2$ | $3^1/8$ x $13^1/2$ | $3^1/8$ x 15 | $3^1/8$ x $16^1/2$ |
| | 12 | $3^1/8$ x $13^1/2$ | $3^1/8$ x $13^1/2$ | $3^1/8$ x 15 | $3^1/8$ x $16^1/2$ | $3^1/8$ x $16^1/2$ | $5^1/8$ x $13^1/2$ | $5^1/8$ x 15 |
| | 16 | $3^1/8$ x 15 | $3^1/8$ x $16^1/2$ | $3^1/8$ x 18 | $3^1/8$ x 18 | $5^1/8$ x 15 | $5^1/8$ x $16^1/2$ | $5^1/8$ x 18 |
| | 20 | $3^1/8$ x 16 | $3^1/8$ x 18 | $5^1/8$ x 15 | $5^1/8$ x $16^1/2$ | $5^1/8$ x $16^1/2$ | $5^1/8$ x 18 | $5^1/8$ x 18 |
| 24 | 8 | $3^1/8$ x $13^1/2$ | $3^1/8$ x 15 | $3^1/8$ x 15 | $3^1/8$ x $16^1/2$ | $3^1/8$ x $16^1/2$ | $3^1/8$ x 18 | $5^1/8$ x $19^1/2$ |
| | 12 | $3^1/8$ x $16^1/2$ | $3^1/8$ x $16^1/2$ | $3^1/8$ x 18 | $5^1/8$ x 15 | $5^1/8$ x $16^1/2$ | $5^1/8$ x $16^1/2$ | $5^1/8$ x 21 |
| | 16 | $3^1/8$ x 18 | $5^1/8$ x $16^1/2$ | $5^1/8$ x $16^1/2$ | $5^1/8$ x 18 | $5^1/8$ x 18 | $5^1/8$ x $19^1/2$ | $5^1/8$ x 24 |
| | 20 | $5^1/8$ x $16^1/2$ | $5^1/8$ x $16^1/2$ | $5^1/8$ x 18 | $5^1/8$ x $19^1/2$ | $5^1/8$ x $19^1/2$ | $5^1/8$ x 21 | $5^1/8$ x $25^1/2$ |
| 28 | 8 | $3^1/8$ x $16^1/2$ | $3^1/8$ x $16^1/2$ | $3^1/8$ x 18 | $3^1/8$ x 18 | $5^1/8$ x $16^1/2$ | $5^1/8$ x $16^1/2$ | $5^1/8$ x $19^1/2$ |
| | 12 | $3^1/8$ x 18 | $5^1/8$ x $16^1/2$ | $5^1/8$ x 18 | $5^1/8$ x 18 | $5^1/8$ x 18 | $5^1/8$ x $19^1/2$ | $5^1/8$ x 21 |
| | 16 | $5^1/8$ x 18 | $5^1/8$ x 18 | $5^1/8$ x $19^1/2$ | $5^1/8$ x $19^1/2$ | $5^1/8$ x 21 | $5^1/8$ x $22^1/2$ | $5^1/8$ x 24 |
| | 20 | $5^1/8$ x 18 | $5^1/8$ x $19^1/2$ | $5^1/8$ x 21 | $5^1/8$ x $22^1/2$ | $5^1/8$ x 24 | $5^1/8$ x $25^1/2$ | $5^1/8$ x $25^1/2$ |
| 32 | 8 | $3^1/8$ x 18 | $5^1/8$ x $16^1/2$ | $5^1/8$ x 18 | $5^1/8$ x 18 | $5^1/8$ x 18 | $5^1/8$ x $19^1/2$ | $5^1/8$ x 21 |
| | 12 | $5^1/8$ x 18 | $5^1/8$ x $19^1/2$ | $5^1/8$ x $19^1/2$ | $5^1/8$ x 21 | $5^1/8$ x 21 | $5^1/8$ x $22^1/2$ | $5^1/8$ x 24 |
| | 16 | $5^1/8$ x $19^1/2$ | $5^1/8$ x 21 | $5^1/8$ x $22^1/2$ | $5^1/8$ x $22^1/2$ | $5^1/8$ x 24 | $5^1/8$ x $25^1/2$ | $5^1/8$ x 27 |
| | 20 | $5^1/8$ x 21 | $5^1/8$ x $22^1/2$ | $5^1/8$ x 24 | $5^1/8$ x $25^1/2$ | $5^1/8$ x 27 | $5^1/8$ x $28^1/2$ | $6^3/4$ x 24 |
| 40 | 12 | $5^1/8$ x $22^1/2$ | $5^1/8$ x 24 | $5^1/8$ x 24 | $5^1/8$ x $25^1/2$ | $5^1/8$ x 27 | $6^3/4$ x $25^1/2$ | $6^3/4$ x $28^1/2$ |
| | 16 | $5^1/8$ x 24 | $5^1/8$ x $25^1/2$ | $5^1/8$ x 27 | $5^1/8$ x $28^1/2$ | $6^3/4$ x 27 | $6^3/4$ x $28^1/2$ | $6^3/4$ x $31^1/2$ |
| | 20 | $5^1/8$ x 27 | $5^1/8$ x $28^1/2$ | $6^3/4$ x 27 | $6^3/4$ x $28^1/2$ | $6^3/4$ x 30 | $6^3/4$ x $31^1/2$ | $6^3/4$ x 33 |
| | 24 | $5^1/8$ x $28^1/2$ | $6^3/4$ x 27 | $6^3/4$ x $28^1/2$ | $6^3/4$ x $31^1/2$ | $6^3/4$ x 33 | $6^3/4$ x $34^1/2$ | $6^3/4$ x 36 |
| 48 | 12 | $5^1/8$ x 27 | $5^1/8$ x $28^1/2$ | $5^1/8$ x 30 | $5^1/8$ x 30 | $6^3/4$ x $28^1/2$ | $6^3/4$ x 30 | $6^3/4$ x 33 |
| | 16 | $5^1/8$ x 30 | $6^3/4$ x $28^1/2$ | $6^3/4$ x 30 | $6^3/4$ x 30 | $6^3/4$ x $31^1/2$ | $6^3/4$ x $34^1/2$ | $6^3/4$ x $37^1/2$ |
| | 20 | $6^3/4$ x $28^1/2$ | $6^3/4$ x 30 | $6^3/4$ x $31^1/2$ | $6^3/4$ x $34^1/2$ | $6^3/4$ x 36 | $6^3/4$ x $37^1/2$ | $8^3/4$ x 36 |
| | 24 | $6^3/4$ x 30 | $6^3/4$ x 33 | $6^3/4$ x $34^1/2$ | $6^3/4$ x $37^1/2$ | $6^3/4$ x 39 | $8^3/4$ x 36 | $8^3/4$ x 39 |
| 60 | 12 | $6^3/4$ x 30 | $6^3/4$ x $31^1/2$ | $6^3/4$ x 33 | $6^3/4$ x $34^1/2$ | $6^3/4$ x 36 | $6^3/4$ x $37^1/2$ | $8^3/4$ x 39 |
| | 16 | $6^3/4$ x 33 | $6^3/4$ x $34^1/2$ | $6^3/4$ x 36 | $6^3/4$ x 39 | $8^3/4$ x 36 | $8^3/4$ x $37^1/2$ | $8^3/4$ x 42 |
| | 20 | $6^3/4$ x 36 | $6^3/4$ x $37^1/2$ | $8^3/4$ x 36 | $8^3/4$ x $37^1/2$ | $8^3/4$ x $40^1/2$ | $8^3/4$ x 42 | $8^3/4$ x 45 |
| | 24 | $6^3/4$ x 39 | $8^3/4$ x 36 | $8^3/4$ x 39 | $8^3/4$ x 42 | $8^3/4$ x $43^1/2$ | $8^3/4$ x 45 | $8^3/4$ x 48 |

Thomas Hodne/Roger Kipp Architects, Planners, Inc.; Minneapolis, Minnesota

**COMPARATIVE TABLE FOR SELECTION OF WOOD SPECIES**—CONSULT WITH THE ARCHITECTURAL WOODWORK INSTITUTE

| SPECIES | HARDNESS | PRINCIPAL USES | APPEARANCE | | | REMARKS |
|---------|----------|----------------|------------|--|--|---------|
| | | | COLOR | FIGURE | GRAIN | |
| Ash, white | Hard | Trim, cabinetry | Creamy white to light brown | High | Open | Excellent strength; bold grain |
| Basswood | Soft | Decorative moldings and carvings | Creamy white | No figure | Closed | Good for moldings; uniform grain |
| Beech | Hard | Semiexposed cabinet parts | White to reddish brown | Medium | Closed | Good utility hardwood |
| Birch, yellow–"natural" | Hard | Trim, paneling and cabinetry | White to dark red | Medium | Closed | Excellent architectural wood, plentiful supply |
| Birch, yellow–"select red" (heartwood) | Hard | Trim, paneling and cabinetry | Dark red | Medium | Closed | Rich color |
| Birch, yellow–"select white" (sapwood) | Hard | Trim, paneling and cabinetry | Creamy white | Medium | Closed | Uniform appearance |
| Butternut | Medium | Trim, paneling and cabinetry | Pale brown | High | Open | Beautiful wood |
| Cedar, western red | Soft | Trim, paneling exterior and interior | Reddish brown to nearly white sapwood | Medium | Closed | Decay resistant; rough texture |
| Cherry, American black | Hard | Trim, paneling and cabinetry | Reddish brown | High | Closed | Beautiful wood |
| Chestnut–wormy | Medium | Paneling and trim | Greyish brown | High | Open with wormholes | Very limited supply |
| Cypress, yellow | Medium | Trim, frames and special siding | Yellowish brown | High | Closed | Subject to regional availability |
| Fir, Douglas–flat grain | Medium | Trim, frames and paneling | Reddish tan | High | Closed | Good supply |
| Fir, Douglas–vertical grain | Medium | Trim, frames and paneling | Reddish tan | Low | Closed | Very limited supply |
| Mahogany, African–plain sawn | Medium | Trim, frames, paneling, and cabinetry | Reddish brown | Medium | Open | Fine hardwood |
| Mahogany, African–quarter sawn | Medium | Trim, frames, paneling, and cabinetry | Reddish brown | Low | Open | Limited supply |
| Mahogany, tropical American–"Honduras" | Medium | Trim, frames, paneling, and cabinetry | Rich golden brown | Medium | Open | One of the world's finest cabinet woods |
| Maple, hard–natural | Very hard | Trim, paneling and cabinetry | White to reddish brown | Medium | Closed | Plentiful supply; excellent properties |
| Maple, hard–select white (sapwood) | Very hard | Trim, paneling and cabinetry | White | Medium | Closed | Uniform appearance |
| Maple, soft–natural | Medium | Trim, semiexposed cabinet parts | White to reddish brown | Low | Closed | Good utility hardwood |
| Oak, English brown | Hard | Veneered paneling and cabinetry | Leathery brown | High | Open | Distinctive appearance; high cost |
| Oak, red–plain sawn | Hard | Trim, paneling and cabinetry | Reddish tan to brown | High | Open | Excellent architectural wood; plentiful supply |
| Oak, red–rift sawn | Hard | Trim, paneling and cabinetry | Reddish tan to brown | Low | Open | Closer grain pattern; limited supply |
| Oak, red–quarter sawn | Hard | Trim, paneling and cabinetry | Reddish tan to brown | Low | Open | Shows flakes; limited supply |
| Oak, white–plain sawn | Hard | Trim, paneling and cabinetry | Greyish tan | High | Open | Excellent architectural wood; moderate supply |
| Oak, white–rift sawn | Hard | Trim, paneling and cabinetry | Greyish tan | Low | Open | Close grain pattern; limited supply |
| Oak, white–quarter sawn | Hard | Trim, paneling and cabinetry | Greyish tan | Low figure accented with flakes | Open | Shows flakes; limited supply |
| Pecan | Hard | Trim, paneling and cabinetry | Reddish brown with brown stripes | Medium | Open | Subject to regional availability; attractive |
| Pine, eastern or northern white | Soft | Trim, frames, paneling, and cabinetry | Creamy white to pink | Medium | Closed | True white pine, wide range of applications for general use |
| Pine, Idaho, sugar | Soft | Trim, frames, paneling, and cabinetry | Creamy white | Low | Closed | True white pine, wide range of applications for general use |
| Pine, ponderosa | Soft | Trim, frames, paneling, and cabinetry | White to pale yellow | Medium | Closed | Most widely used pine, wide range of application for general use |
| Pine, southern yellow–shortleaf | Soft | Trim, frames, paneling, and cabinetry | White to pale yellow | High | Closed | Wide range of applications for general use |
| Poplar, yellow | Medium | Trim, paneling and cabinetry | White to brown with green cast | Medium | Closed | Good utility hardwood; excellent paintability |
| Redwood, flat grain (heartwood) | Soft | Trim, frames and paneling | Deep red | High | Closed | Superior exterior wood, high natural decay resistance |
| Redwood, vertical grain (heartwood) | Soft | Trim, frames and paneling | Deep red | Low | Closed | Superior exterior wood, high natural decay resistance |
| Rosewood, Brazilian | Very hard | Veneered paneling and cabinetry | Mixed reds, browns, and blacks | High | Open | Exotic figure; high cost |
| Spruce, Sitka | Soft | Trim, frames | Light yellowish tan | High | Closed | Limited general availability |

Architectural Woodwork Institute; Arlington, Virginia

**6    FINISH CARPENTRY**

## COMPARATIVE TABLE FOR SELECTION OF WOOD SPECIES—CONSULT WITH THE ARCHITECTURAL WOODWORK INSTITUTE

| SPECIES | HARDNESS | PRINCIPAL USES | APPEARANCE | | | REMARKS |
|---|---|---|---|---|---|---|
| | | | COLOR | FIGURE | GRAIN | |
| Teak | Hard | Trim, paneling and cabinetry | Tawny yellow to dark brown | High | Open | Outstanding wood for decorative applications; high cost |
| Walnut, American black | Hard | Trim, paneling and cabinetry | Chocolate brown | High | Open | Fine domestic hardwood; extremely limited width/length; readily available veneer |
| Zebrawood, African-quarter sawn | Hard | Trim, paneling and cabinetry | Light gold color/streaked and dark brown to black | High | Closed | Highly decorative |

## COMPARATIVE TABLE OF WOOD SPECIES FOR DESIGN CRITERIA—CONSULT WITH THE ARCHITECTURAL WOODWORK INSTITUTE

| SPECIES | BOTANICAL NAME | FINISHING | | PRACTICAL SIZE LIMITATIONS | | | AVAILABILITY OF MATCHING PLYWOOD (A) | DIMENSIONAL STABILITY (B) |
|---|---|---|---|---|---|---|---|---|
| | | PAINT | TRANSPARENT | MAX. PRACTICAL THICKNESS WITHOUT LAMINATION | MAX. PRACTICAL WIDTH | MAX. PRACTICAL LENGTH | | |
| Ash, white | Fraxinus americana | Not normally used | Excellent | $1\frac{1}{2}''$ | $7\frac{1}{2}''$ | 12' | 3 | $^{10}/_{64}''$ |
| Basswood | Tilia, americana | Excellent | Excellent | $1\frac{1}{2}''$ | $7\frac{1}{2}''$ | 10' | 4 | $^{10}/_{64}''$ |
| Beech | Fagus grandifolia | Excellent | Good | $1\frac{1}{2}''$ | $7\frac{1}{2}''$ | 12' | 4 | $^{14}/_{64}''$ |
| Birch, yellow–"natural" | Betula alleghaniensis | Excellent | Good | $1\frac{1}{2}''$ | $7\frac{1}{2}''$ | 12' | 1 | $^{12}/_{64}''$ |
| Birch, yellow–"select red" (heartwood) | Betula alleghaniensis | Not normally used | Excellent | $1\frac{1}{2}''$ | $5\frac{1}{2}''$ | 11' | 2 | $^{12}/_{64}''$ |
| Birch, yellow–"select white" (sapwood) | Betula alleghaniensis | Not normally used | Excellent | $1\frac{1}{2}''$ | $5''$ | 11' | 2 | $^{12}/_{64}''$ |
| Butternut | Juglans cinerea | Not normally used | Excellent | $1\frac{1}{2}''$ | $5\frac{1}{2}''$ | 8' | 3 | $^{8}/_{64}''$ |
| Cedar, western red | Thuja plicata | Not normally used | Good | $3\frac{1}{4}''$ | $11''$ | 16' | 1 & 3 | $^{10}/_{64}''$ |
| Cherry, American black | Prunus serotina | Not normally used | Excellent | $1\frac{1}{2}''$ | $5\frac{1}{2}''$ | 7' | 2 | $^{9}/_{64}''$ |
| Chestnut-wormy | Castanea dentata | Not normally used | Excellent | $3/4''$ | $7\frac{1}{2}''$ | 10' | 4 | $^{9}/_{64}''$ |
| Cypress, yellow | Taxodium distichum | Good | Good | $2\frac{1}{2}''$ | $9\frac{1}{2}''$ | 16' | 4 | $^{8}/_{64}''$ |
| Fir, Douglas–flat grain | Pseudotsuga taxifolia | Fair | Fair | $3\frac{1}{4}''$ | $11''$ | 16' | 1 | $^{10}/_{64}''$ |
| Fir, Douglas–vertical grain | Pseudotsuga taxifolia | Good | Good | $1\frac{1}{2}''$ | $11''$ | 16' | 4 | $^{6}/_{64}''$ |
| Mahogany, African–plain sawn | Khaya ivorensis | Good | Excellent | $2\frac{1}{2}''$ | $11''$ | 15' | 3 | $^{7}/_{64}''$ |
| Mahogany, African–quarter sawn | Khaya ivorensis | Not normally used | Excellent | $2\frac{1}{2}''$ | $7\frac{1}{2}''$ | 15' | 3 | $^{5}/_{64}''$ |
| Mahogany, tropical American–"Honduras" | Sweitenia macrophylla | Not normally used | Excellent | $2\frac{1}{2}''$ | $11''$ | 15' | 3 | $^{6}/_{64}''$ |
| Maple, hard-natural | Acer saccharum | Excellent | Good | $3\frac{1}{2}''$ | $9\frac{1}{2}''$ | 12' | 3 | $^{12}/_{64}''$ |
| Maple, hard-select white (sapwood) | Acer saccharum | Not normally used | Excellent | $2\frac{1}{2}''$ | $9\frac{1}{2}''$ | 12' | 3 | $^{12}/_{64}''$ |
| Maple, soft-natural | Acer saccharum | Excellent | Not normally used | $3\frac{1}{4}''$ | $9\frac{1}{2}''$ | 12' | 4 | $^{9}/_{64}''$ |
| Oak, English brown | Quercus robur | Not normally used | Excellent | $1\frac{1}{2}''$ | $5\frac{1}{2}''$ | 8' | 3 | |
| Oak, red-plain sawn | Quercus rubra | Not normally used | Excellent | $1\frac{1}{2}''$ | $7\frac{1}{4}''$ | 12' | 1 | $^{11}/_{64}''$ |
| Oak, red-rift sawn | Quercus rubra | Not normally used | Excellent | $1^{1}/_{16}''$ | $5\frac{1}{2}''$ | 10' | 3 | $^{7}/_{64}''$ |
| Oak, red-quarter sawn | Quercus rubra | Not normally used | Excellent | $1^{1}/_{6}''$ | $5\frac{1}{2}''$ | 8' | 3 | $^{7}/_{64}''$ |
| Oak, white-plain sawn | Quercus alba | Not normally used | Excellent | $1\frac{1}{2}''$ | $5\frac{1}{2}''$ | 10' | 2 | $^{11}/_{64}''$ |
| Oak, white-rift sawn | Quercus alba | Not normally used | Excellent | $3/4''$ | $4\frac{1}{2}''$ | 10' | 3 | $^{7}/_{64}''$ |
| Oak, white-quarter sawn | Quercus alba | Not normally used | Excellent | $3/4''$ | $4\frac{1}{2}''$ | 10' | 3 | $^{7}/_{64}''$ |
| Pecan | Carya species | Not normally used | Good | $1\frac{1}{2}''$ | $5\frac{1}{2}''$ | 12' | 3 | $^{11}/_{64}''$ |
| Pine, eastern or northern white | Pinus strobus | Good | Good | $1\frac{1}{2}''$ | $9\frac{1}{2}''$ | 14' | 3 | $^{8}/_{64}''$ |
| Pine, Idaho, sugar | Pinus monticola | Good | Good | $1\frac{1}{2}''$ | $9\frac{1}{2}''$ | 14' | 4 | $^{8}/_{64}''$ |
| Pine, ponderosa | Pinus ponderosa | Good | Good | $1\frac{1}{2}''$ | $9\frac{1}{2}''$ | 16' | 3 | $^{8}/_{64}''$ |
| Pine, southern yellow-shortleaf | Pinus echinata | Fair | Good | $1\frac{1}{2}''$ | $7\frac{1}{2}''$ | 16' | 3 | $^{10}/_{64}''$ |
| Poplar, yellow | Liriodendron tulipfera | Excellent | Good | $2\frac{1}{2}''$ | $7\frac{1}{2}''$ | 12' | 3 | $^{9}/_{64}''$ |
| Redwood, flat grain (heartwood) | Sequoia sempervirens | Good | Good | $2\frac{1}{2}''$ | $11''$ | 16' | 1 & 3 | $^{6}/_{64}''$ |
| Redwood, vertical grain (heartwood) | Sequoia sempervirens | Excellent | Excellent | $2\frac{1}{2}''$ | $11''$ | 16' | 3 | $^{3}/_{64}''$ |
| Rosewood, Brazilian | Dalbergia nigra | Not normally used | Excellent | | | | 3 | |
| Spruce, Sitka | Picea sitchensis | Fair | Fair | $3\frac{1}{4}''$ | $9\frac{1}{2}''$ | 16' | 4 | $^{10}/_{64}''$ |
| Teak | Tectona grandis | Not normally used | Excellent | $1\frac{1}{2}''$ | $7\frac{1}{2}''$ | 10' | 2 | $^{6}/_{64}''$ |
| Walnut, American black | Juglans | Not normally used | Excellent | $1\frac{1}{2}''$ | $4\frac{1}{2}''$ | 6' | 1 | $^{10}/_{64}''$ |
| Zebrawood, African-quarter sawn | Brachystegea fleuryana | Not normally used | Excellent | $1\frac{1}{2}''$ | $9''$ | 16' | 3 | $^{7}/_{64}''$ |

(A) Rated from 1 to 4 as follows:

1. Warehouse stock in good quantities and fair assortment of thicknesses and lengths.
2. Warehouse stock in fair quantity but not in thicknesses other than 1/4 and 3/4 in.; or sizes other than 4 x 8 feet.

3. Produced on a special order only.
4. Not generally available.

(B) These figures represent possible width change in a 12 in. board when moisture content is reduced from 10 to 5%. Figures are for plain sawn unless indicated otherwise in species column.

Architectural Woodwork Institute; Arlington, Virginia

**FINISH CARPENTRY**    6

## GUIDELINES

1. Check current local building code regulations for requirements that may differ from the general recommendations shown or stated on this page.
2. Interior stair width: 3 ft (36 in.) minimum.
3. Minimum headroom should be 6 ft 8 in. as measured vertically from a diagonal line connecting tread nosings to the underside of the finished ceiling or stair landing directly above the stair run. Recommended headroom is 7 ft.
4. Only handrails and stair stringers may project into the required width of a stair.
   Handrail projection: 3½ in. maximum.
   Stringer projection: 1½ in. maximum.
5. The width of a landing or platform should be the same as the actual width of the stair.
6. Maximum vertical rise of stair between landings: 12 ft.
7. Maximum riser height: 7 in.
   Minimum riser height: 4 in.
   Minimum tread width: 11 in.

Tolerances for variation in tread or riser dimension should not exceed 3/16 in. for adjacent tread width or riser height. The maximum difference between the largest and smallest tread width or riser height for an entire flight of stairs should be 3/8 in.

8. Height of handrail: 2 ft 6 in. to 2 ft 10 in. (at stair and landings). Handrails should be designed to be easily gripped and to fit the hand. Recommended diameter is 1½ in. for round handrail and similar size for elliptical or rounded edge square section. Handrails should be structurally designed so that both downward (vertical) and lateral (horizontal) thrust loads are considered.
9. Extensions of handrail at top and bottom of stair may affect total length of required run. Verify extensions required by local code before starting stair design.
10. Construction details on this page are for shop-built stairs reflecting Architectural Woodwork Institute Premium Grade Standards.

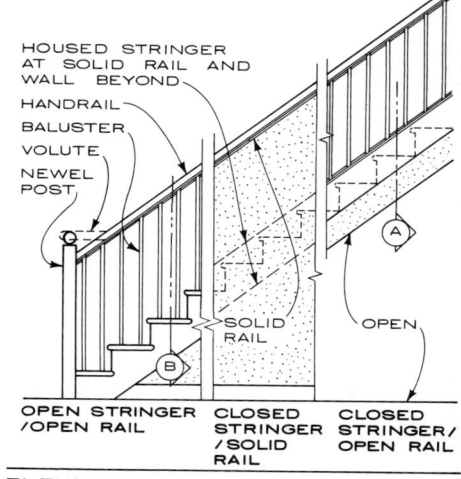

**ELEVATION OF FACE STRINGER**

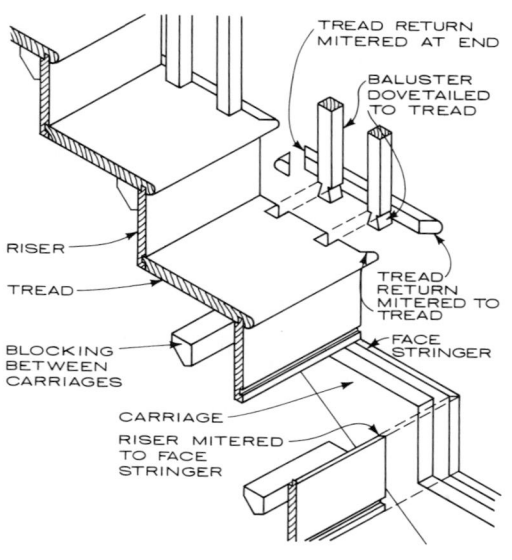

**BALUSTERS AND TRIM AT FACE STRINGER**

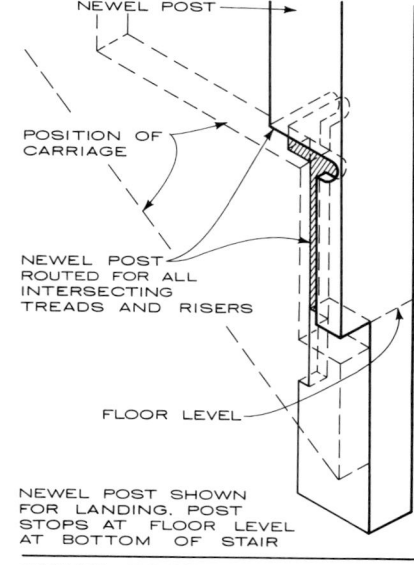

**NEWEL POST**

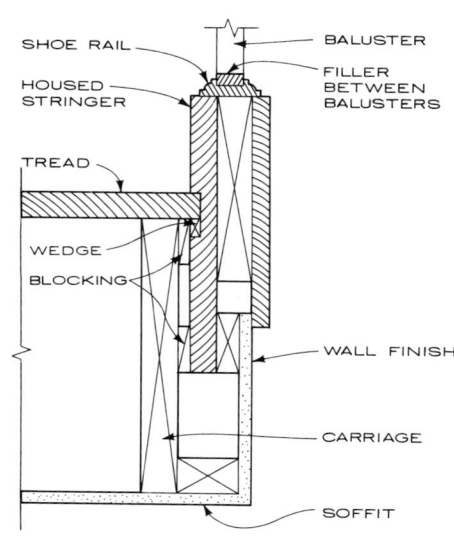

**SECTION A**

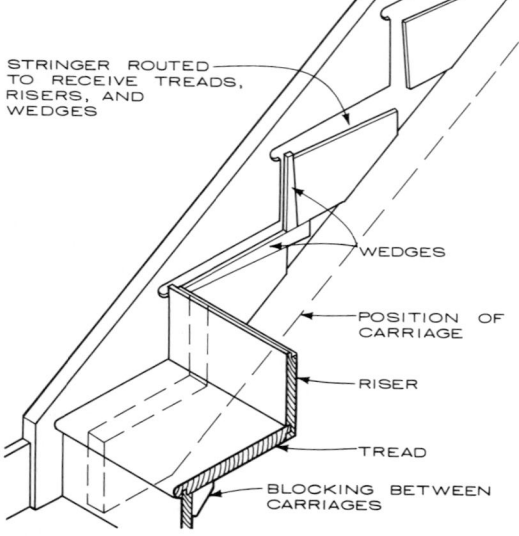

**TREADS AND RISERS AT HOUSED STRINGER**

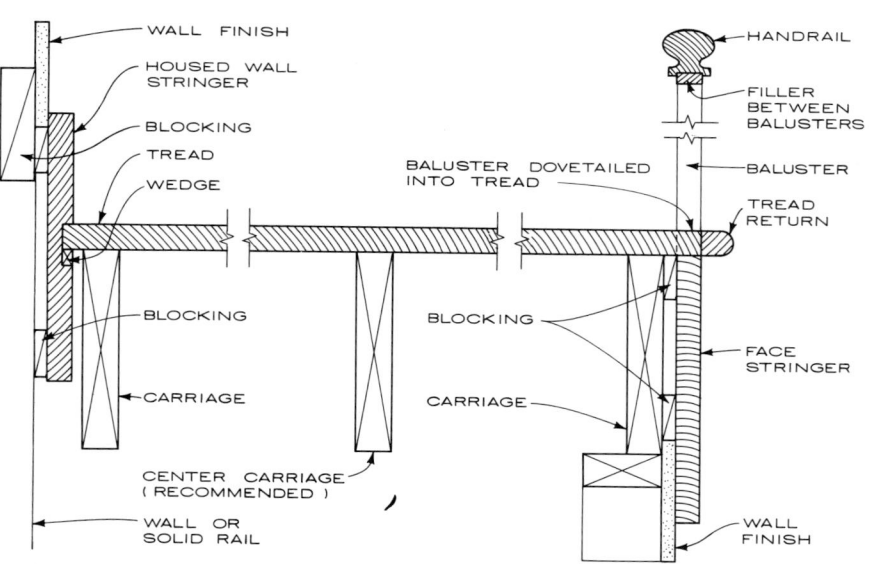

**SECTION B**

The Bumgardner Partnership/Architects; Seattle, Washington

**FINISH CARPENTRY**

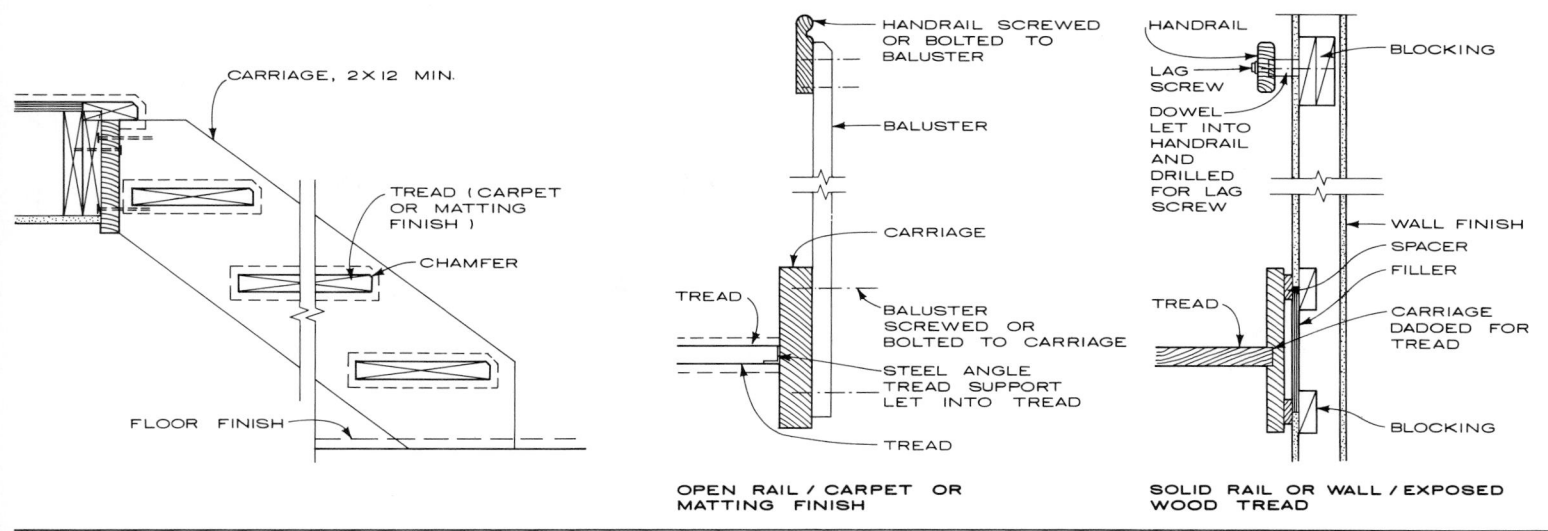

OPEN RISER STAIR

OPEN RAIL / CARPET OR MATTING FINISH

SOLID RAIL OR WALL / EXPOSED WOOD TREAD

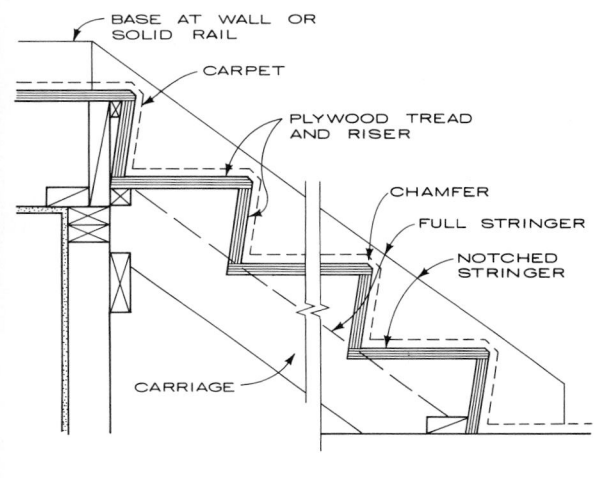

CLOSED RISER STAIR/CARPET FINISH

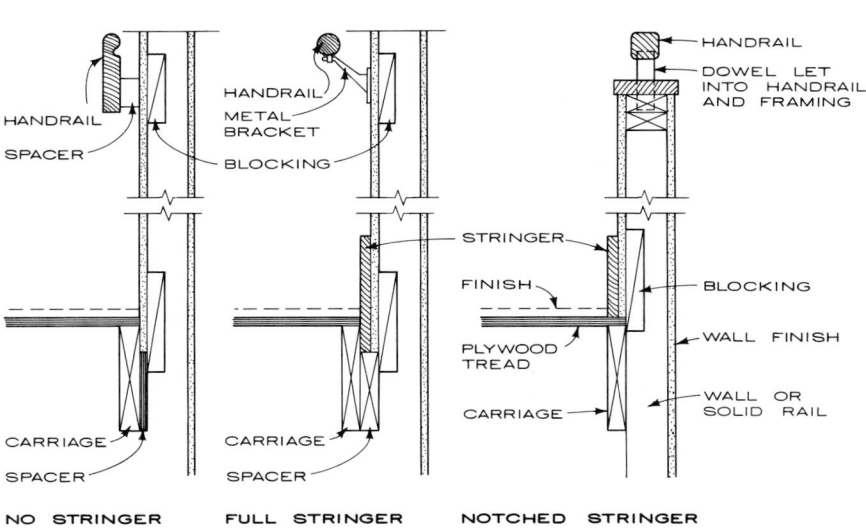

NO STRINGER   FULL STRINGER   NOTCHED STRINGER

CLOSED RISER STAIRS AT WALLS AND SOLID RAILING WALLS

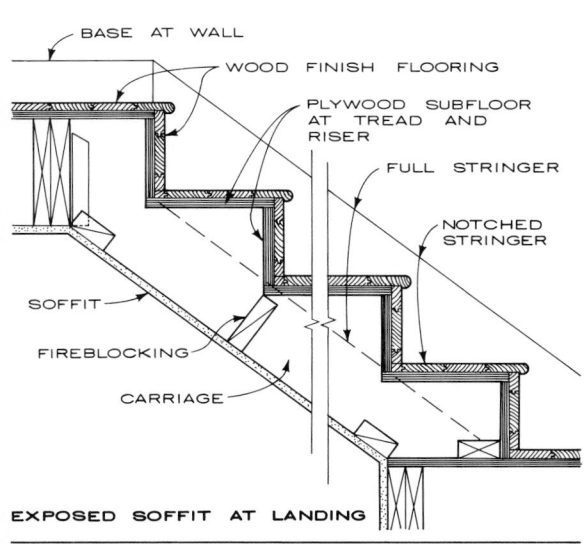

EXPOSED SOFFIT AT LANDING

CLOSED RISER STAIR/WOOD FINISH

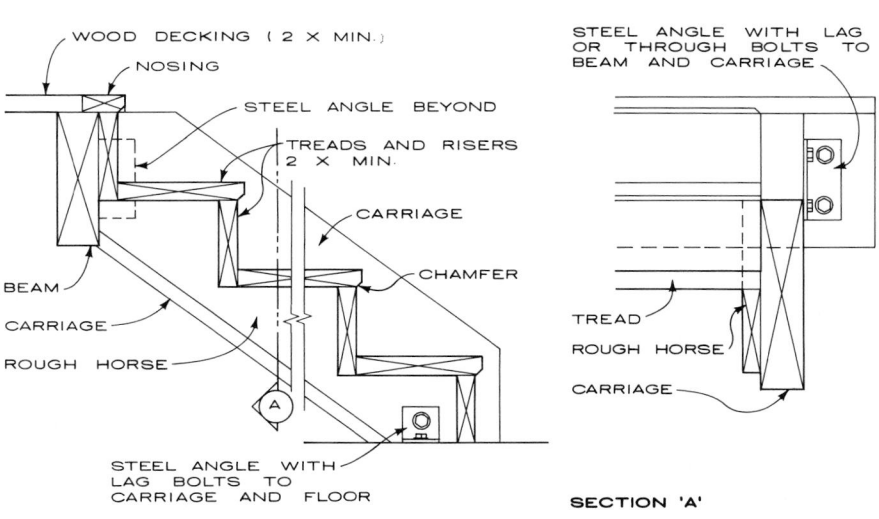

SECTION 'A'

HEAVY TIMBER STAIR

The Bumgardner Partnership/Architects; Seattle, Washington

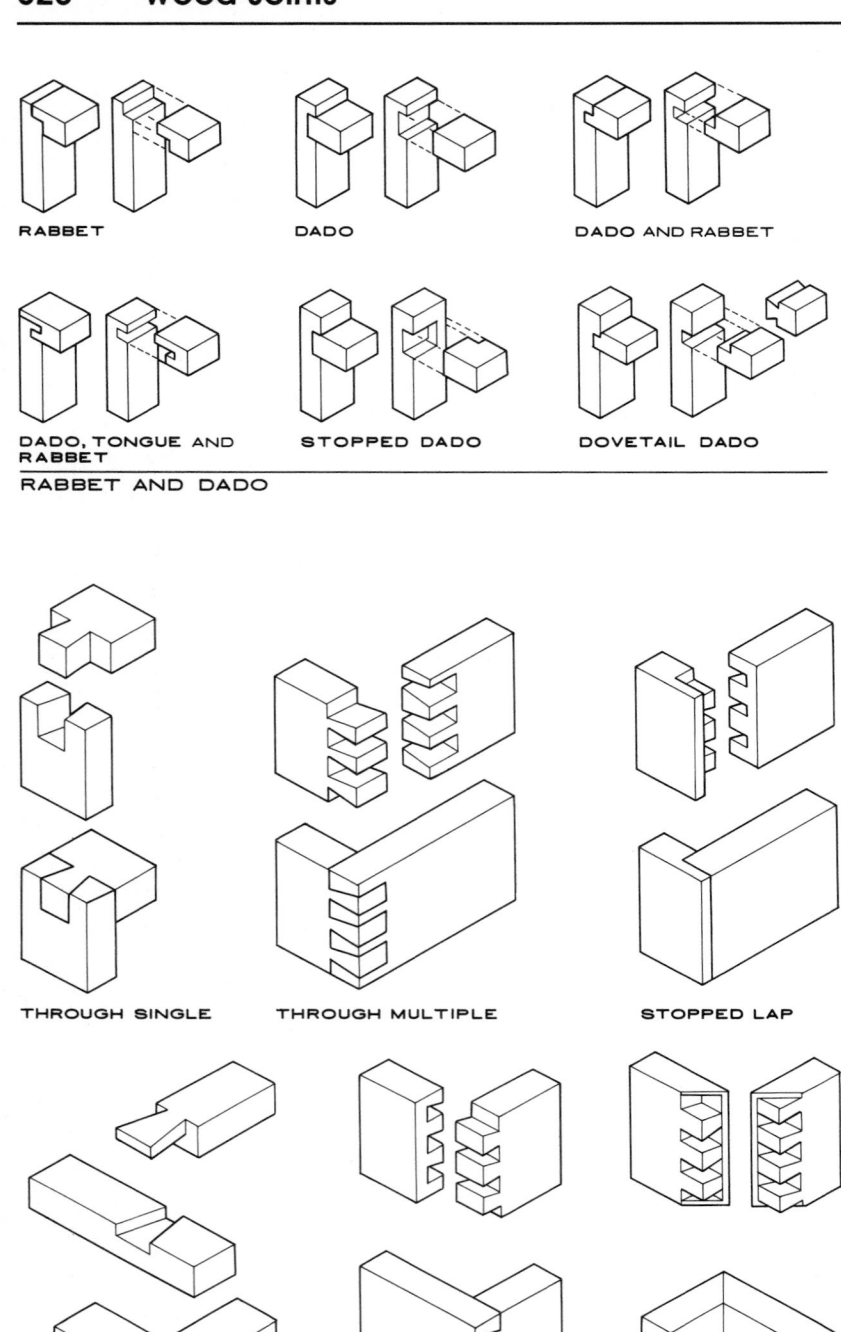

**RABBET**

**DADO**

**DADO AND RABBET**

**DADO, TONGUE AND RABBET**

**STOPPED DADO**

**DOVETAIL DADO**

**RABBET AND DADO**

**THROUGH SINGLE**

**THROUGH MULTIPLE**

**STOPPED LAP**

**HALF LAP**

**LAP (OR HALF BLIND)**

**BLIND MITER**

**DOVETAIL**

**NOTES**

1. Wood joints may be grouped into three classes: (1) right angle joints, (2) end joints, and (3) edge joints.

2. End joints are used to increase the length of a wood member. By proper utilization of end joints short lengths can be used which might otherwise have been wasted.

3. Edge joints are used to increase the width of a wood member. By giving narrow widths greater use of narrow stock may result.

4. A rabbet (rebate) is a right angle cut made along a corner edge of a wood member. A dado is a rectangular groove cut across the grain of a wood member. If this groove extends along the edge or face of a wood member (being cut parallel to the grain) it is known as a plough (plow).

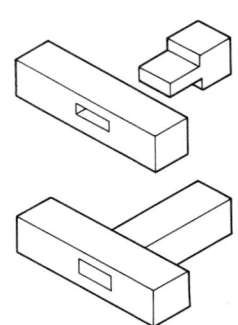

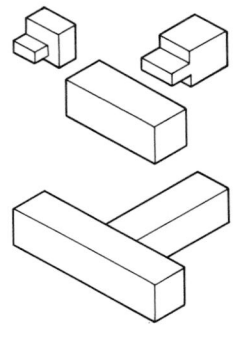

**FULL (OR THROUGH)**

**BLIND AND STUB**

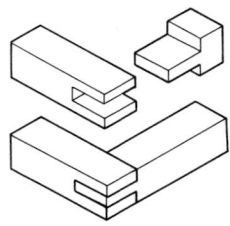
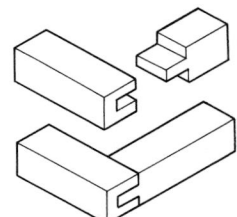

**SHIP (OR OPEN)**

**HALF BLIND**

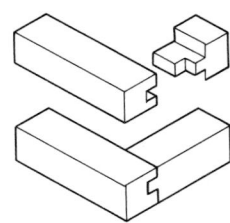
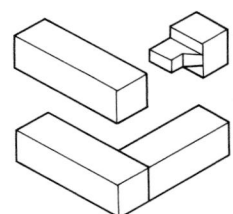

**HAUNCH**

**HAUNCH — BLIND**

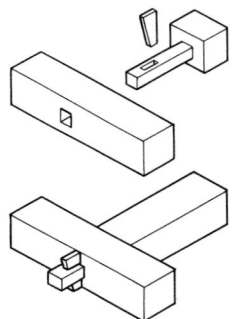
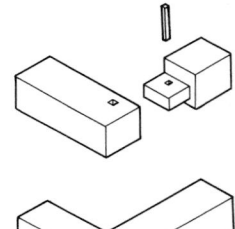

**KEYED**

**PINNED BLIND**

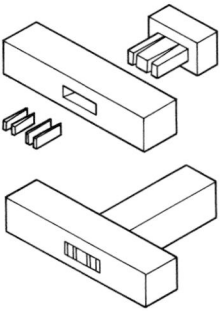

**WEDGED**

**MORTISE AND TENON**

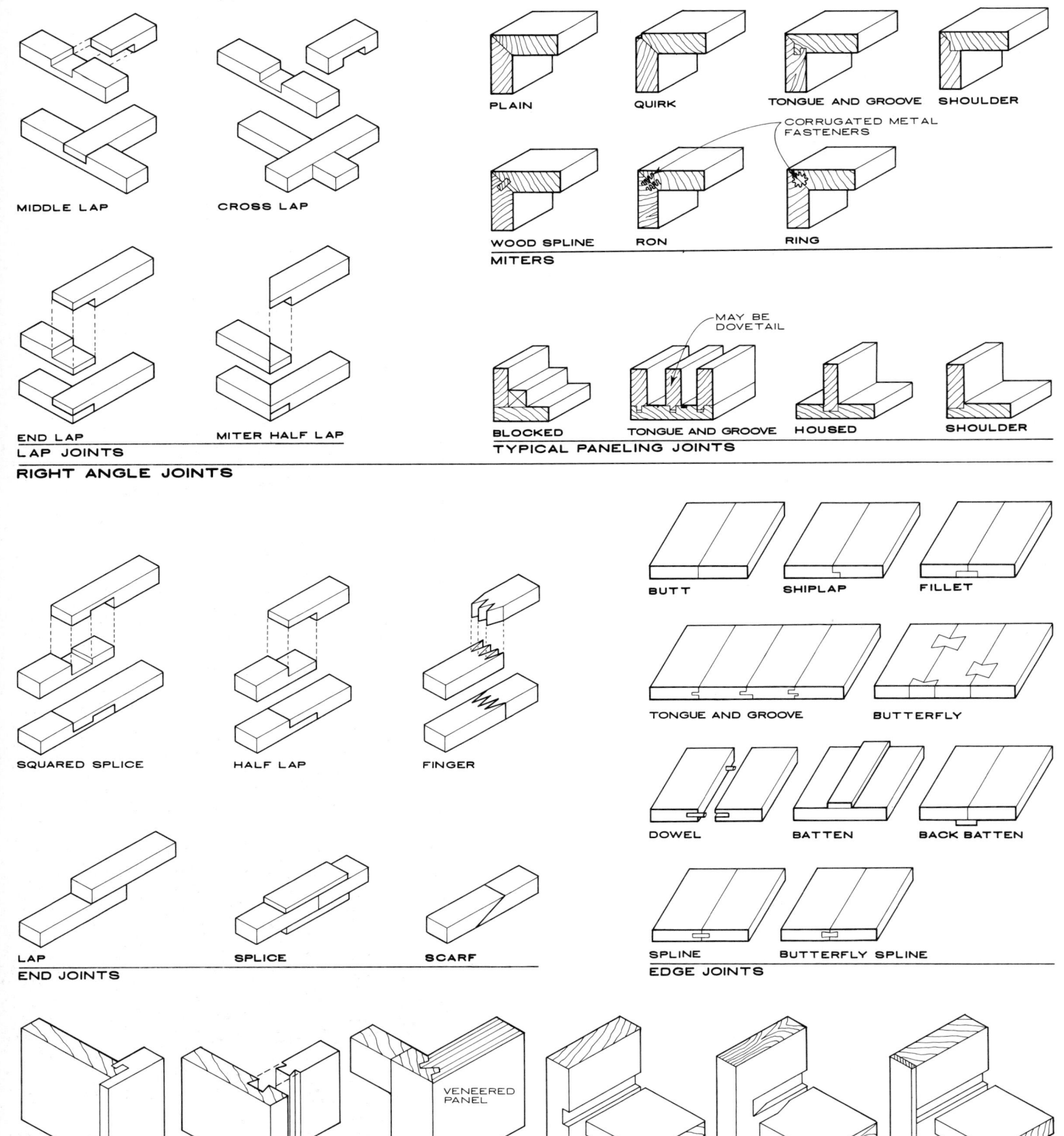

MIDDLE LAP     CROSS LAP

PLAIN    QUIRK    TONGUE AND GROOVE    SHOULDER

CORRUGATED METAL FASTENERS

WOOD SPLINE    RON    RING

**MITERS**

END LAP     MITER HALF LAP

**LAP JOINTS**

**RIGHT ANGLE JOINTS**

MAY BE DOVETAIL

BLOCKED    TONGUE AND GROOVE    HOUSED    SHOULDER

**TYPICAL PANELING JOINTS**

SQUARED SPLICE    HALF LAP    FINGER

BUTT    SHIPLAP    FILLET

TONGUE AND GROOVE    BUTTERFLY

DOWEL    BATTEN    BACK BATTEN

LAP    SPLICE    SCARF

**END JOINTS**

SPLINE    BUTTERFLY SPLINE

**EDGE JOINTS**

DRAWER LOCK JOINT    FRENCH DOVETAIL JOINT    MILLWORK CORNER

VENEERED PANEL

**CORNER DETAILS**

THROUGH DADO    STOP DADO    BLIND DADO

**SHELF DETAILS**

**ARCHITECTURAL WOODWORK**    6

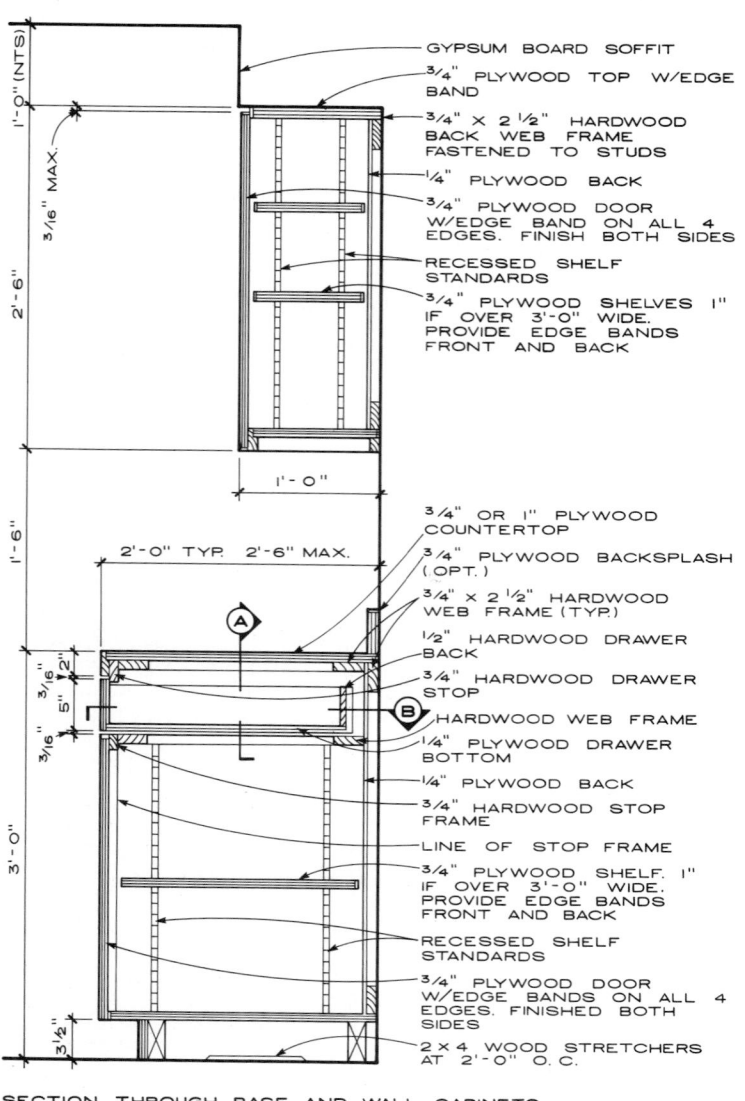

1'-0" (NTS)

3/16" MAX.

2'-6"

GYPSUM BOARD SOFFIT

3/4" PLYWOOD TOP W/EDGE BAND

3/4" X 2 1/2" HARDWOOD BACK WEB FRAME FASTENED TO STUDS

1/4" PLYWOOD BACK

3/4" PLYWOOD DOOR W/EDGE BAND ON ALL 4 EDGES. FINISH BOTH SIDES

RECESSED SHELF STANDARDS

3/4" PLYWOOD SHELVES I" IF OVER 3'-0" WIDE. PROVIDE EDGE BANDS FRONT AND BACK

1'-0"

1'-6"

2'-0" TYP. 2'-6" MAX.

3/4" OR I" PLYWOOD COUNTERTOP

3/4" PLYWOOD BACKSPLASH (OPT.)

3/4" X 2 1/2" HARDWOOD WEB FRAME (TYP.)

1/2" HARDWOOD DRAWER BACK

3/4" HARDWOOD DRAWER STOP

HARDWOOD WEB FRAME

1/4" PLYWOOD DRAWER BOTTOM

1/4" PLYWOOD BACK

3/4" HARDWOOD STOP FRAME

LINE OF STOP FRAME

3/4" PLYWOOD SHELF. I" IF OVER 3'-0" WIDE. PROVIDE EDGE BANDS FRONT AND BACK

RECESSED SHELF STANDARDS

3/4" PLYWOOD DOOR W/EDGE BANDS ON ALL 4 EDGES. FINISHED BOTH SIDES

2 x 4 WOOD STRETCHERS AT 2'-0" O.C.

3/16"  2"
5"
3/16"

3'-0"

3 1/2"

(A) (B)

**SECTION THROUGH BASE AND WALL CABINETS**

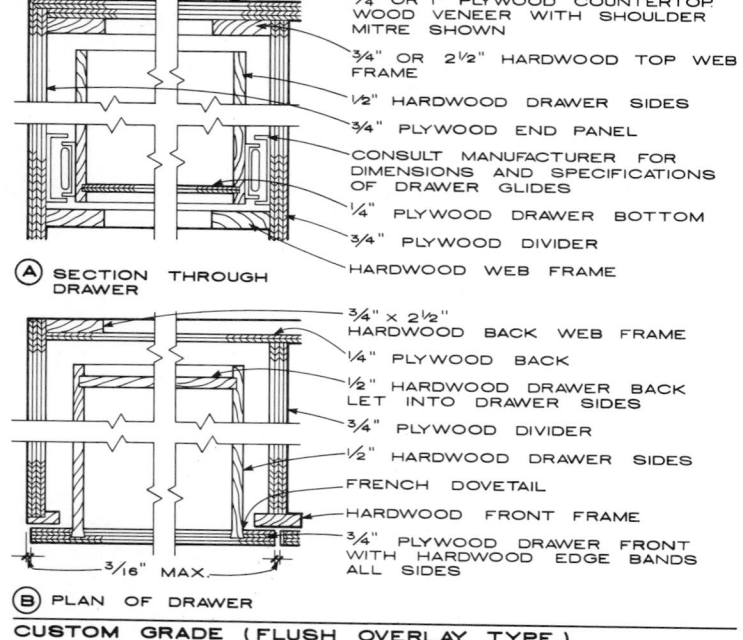

3/4" OR I" PLYWOOD COUNTERTOP WOOD VENEER WITH SHOULDER MITRE SHOWN

3/4" OR 2 1/2" HARDWOOD TOP WEB FRAME

1/2" HARDWOOD DRAWER SIDES

3/4" PLYWOOD END PANEL

CONSULT MANUFACTURER FOR DIMENSIONS AND SPECIFICATIONS OF DRAWER GLIDES

1/4" PLYWOOD DRAWER BOTTOM

3/4" PLYWOOD DIVIDER

HARDWOOD WEB FRAME

(A) SECTION THROUGH DRAWER

3/4" X 2 1/2" HARDWOOD BACK WEB FRAME

1/4" PLYWOOD BACK

1/2" HARDWOOD DRAWER BACK LET INTO DRAWER SIDES

3/4" PLYWOOD DIVIDER

1/2" HARDWOOD DRAWER SIDES

FRENCH DOVETAIL

HARDWOOD FRONT FRAME

3/4" PLYWOOD DRAWER FRONT WITH HARDWOOD EDGE BANDS ALL SIDES

3/16" MAX.

(B) PLAN OF DRAWER

**CUSTOM GRADE (FLUSH OVERLAY TYPE)**

---

1'-0" (NTS)

3/32"  2"
3/32" MAX.
3"

2'-6"

GYPSUM BOARD SOFFIT

SCRIBE FACE FRAME TO FIT SOFFIT

3/4" PLYWOOD TOP LET INTO FACE FRAME

HARDWOOD STOP FRAME FINISHED TO MATCH EXTERIOR

3/4" X 2 1/2" BACK WEB FRAME FASTENED TO STUDS

LINE OF STOP FRAME

3/4" PLYWOOD DOOR W/EDGE BANDS ALL 4 EDGES. FINISH BOTH SIDES

1/4" PLYWOOD BACK

3/4" PLYWOOD SHELVES. I" IF OVER 3'-0" WIDE. PROVIDE EDGE BANDS ON ALL 4 EDGES

UNDERCABINET LIGHT (OPT.) FURNISHED AND INSTALLED BY ELECTRICIAN TYPICALLY. CONSULT MANUFACTURER FOR DIMENSIONS AND SPECIFICATIONS

1'-0"

1'-6"

2'-0" TYP. 2'-6" MAX.

3/32"
5"
2"
2"

3/32" MAX.

3'-0"

2 1/2"

3/4" OR I" PLYWOOD COUNTERTOP

3/4" PLYWOOD BACKSPLASH (OPT.)

3/4" X 2 1/2" HARDWOOD WEB FRAME (TYP.)

1/2" HARDWOOD DRAWER BACK

HARDWOOD DRAWER STOP

HARDWOOD WEB FRAME

1/4" PLYWD. DRAWER BOTTOM

1/4" HARDBOARD DUST PANEL

1/4" PLYWOOD BACK

3/4" X 2" HDWD. STOP FRAME

LINE OF STOP FRAME

3/4" PLYWD. SHELF. I" IF OVER 3'-0" WIDE. PROVIDE EDGE BANDS ON ALL 4 EDGES

RECESSED SHELF STDS.

3/4" PLYWOOD DOOR W/EDGE BANDS ON ALL 4 EDGES. FINISHED BOTH SIDES

2 x 4 WOOD STRETCHERS AT 2'-0" O.C.

(C) (D)

**SECTION THROUGH BASE AND WALL CABINETS**

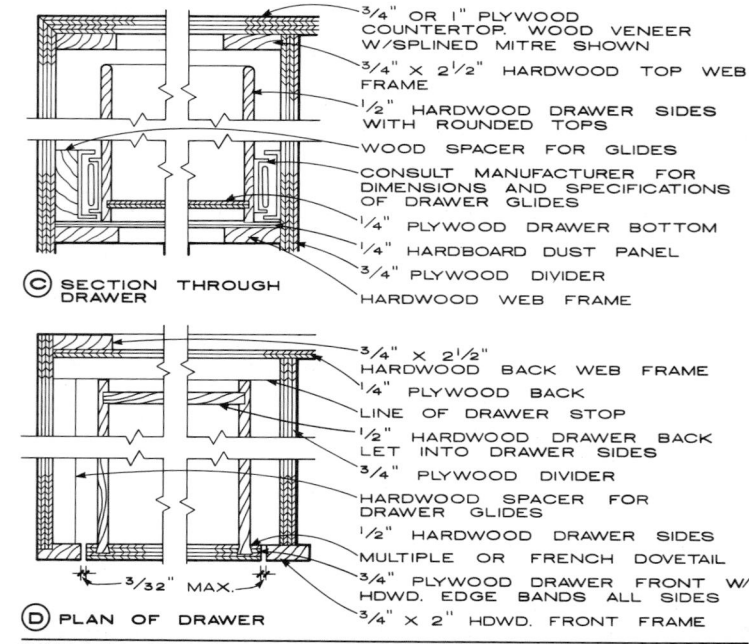

3/4" OR I" PLYWOOD COUNTERTOP. WOOD VENEER W/SPLINED MITRE SHOWN

3/4" X 2 1/2" HARDWOOD TOP WEB FRAME

1/2" HARDWOOD DRAWER SIDES WITH ROUNDED TOPS

WOOD SPACER FOR GLIDES

CONSULT MANUFACTURER FOR DIMENSIONS AND SPECIFICATIONS OF DRAWER GLIDES

1/4" PLYWOOD DRAWER BOTTOM

1/4" HARDBOARD DUST PANEL

3/4" PLYWOOD DIVIDER

HARDWOOD WEB FRAME

(C) SECTION THROUGH DRAWER

3/4" X 2 1/2" HARDWOOD BACK WEB FRAME

1/4" PLYWOOD BACK

LINE OF DRAWER STOP

1/2" HARDWOOD DRAWER BACK LET INTO DRAWER SIDES

3/4" PLYWOOD DIVIDER

HARDWOOD SPACER FOR DRAWER GLIDES

1/2" HARDWOOD DRAWER SIDES

MULTIPLE OR FRENCH DOVETAIL

3/4" PLYWOOD DRAWER FRONT W/ HDWD. EDGE BANDS ALL SIDES

3/4" X 2" HDWD. FRONT FRAME

3/32" MAX.

(D) PLAN OF DRAWER

**PREMIUM GRADE (EXPOSED FRONT FRAME TYPE)**

John S. Fornaro, AIA; Columbia, Virginia

**ARCHITECTURAL WOODWORK**

## CABINET CLASSIFICATIONS

The Architectural Woodworking Institute classifies cabinets in three groups: economy, the lowest grade; custom, the average grade; and premium, the best grade. These details show the progression to higher quality and generally follow the AWI standards, but do not show all possible variations of cabinet details. Woodworking shops frequently set their own quality standards; thus many higher quality details can be found in lower quality work, and vice versa. Also, an architect's design may require crossover of details between the different quality groups.

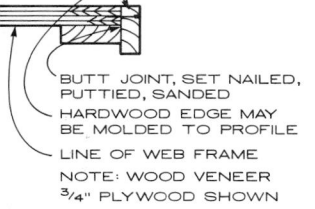

- BUTT JOINT, SET NAILED, PUTTIED, SANDED
- HARDWOOD EDGE MAY BE MOLDED TO PROFILE
- LINE OF WEB FRAME
- NOTE: WOOD VENEER ³/₄" PLYWOOD SHOWN

**ECONOMY GRADE**

**EDGE DETAIL**

- SHOULDER MITER SHOWN, TONGUE AND GROOVE MITER AND WOOD SPLINE MITER ALSO USED
- LINE OF WEB FRAME
- NOTE: WOOD VENEER ³/₄" PLYWOOD SHOWN

**CUSTOM GRADE**

**EDGE DETAIL**

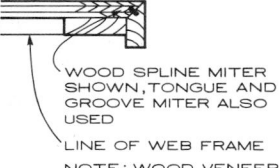
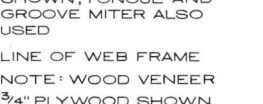

- WOOD SPLINE MITER SHOWN, TONGUE AND GROOVE MITER ALSO USED
- LINE OF WEB FRAME
- NOTE: WOOD VENEER ³/₄" PLYWOOD SHOWN

**PREMIUM GRADE**

**EDGE DETAIL**

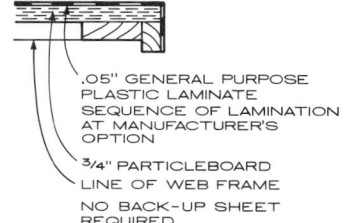

- .05" GENERAL PURPOSE PLASTIC LAMINATE SEQUENCE OF LAMINATION AT MANUFACTURER'S OPTION
- ³/₄" PARTICLEBOARD LINE OF WEB FRAME
- NO BACK-UP SHEET REQUIRED

**ECONOMY GRADE**

**EDGE DETAIL**

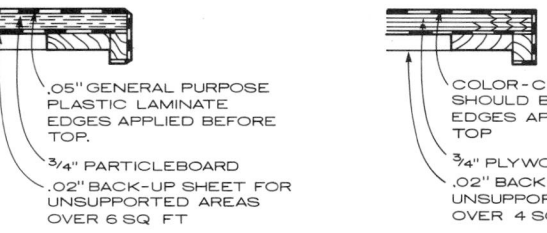

- .05" GENERAL PURPOSE PLASTIC LAMINATE EDGES APPLIED BEFORE TOP.
- ³/₄" PARTICLEBOARD
- .02" BACK-UP SHEET FOR UNSUPPORTED AREAS OVER 6 SQ FT

**CUSTOM GRADE**

**EDGE DETAIL**

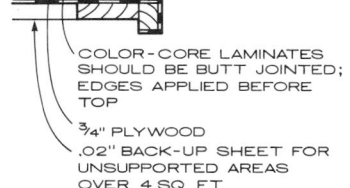

- COLOR-CORE LAMINATES SHOULD BE BUTT JOINTED; EDGES APPLIED BEFORE TOP
- ³/₄" PLYWOOD
- .02" BACK-UP SHEET FOR UNSUPPORTED AREAS OVER 4 SQ FT

**PREMIUM GRADE**

**EDGE DETAIL**

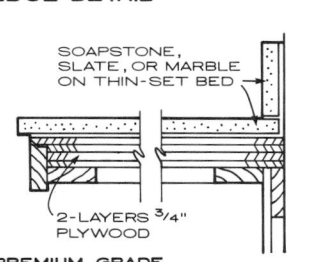

- SOAPSTONE, SLATE, OR MARBLE ON THIN-SET BED
- 2-LAYERS ³/₄" PLYWOOD

**PREMIUM GRADE**

**STONE COUNTER**

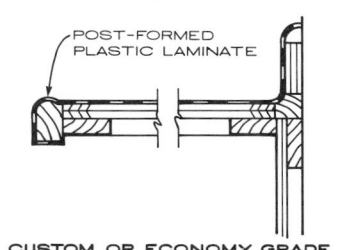

- POST-FORMED PLASTIC LAMINATE

**CUSTOM OR ECONOMY GRADE**

**POST-FORMED COUNTER**

### SECTION THROUGH BASE AND WALL CABINETS

- GYPSUM BOARD SOFFIT (OPTIONAL)
- ³/₄"X 2¹/₂" HARDWOOD CLEAT FASTENED TO STUDS
- II PLY PLYWOOD LIPPED DOOR WITHOUT EDGE BANDING
- ³/₄" PLYWOOD WITH NAILED AND GLUED EDGE BAND ON FRONT
- ¹/₈"-³/₁₆" φ HOLES FOR SHELF SUPPORTS, CONSULT MANUFACTURER FOR DIMENSIONS

- ³/₄" PLYWOOD COUNTERTOP
- ³/₄" PLYWOOD BACKSPLASH (OPTIONAL)
- ³/₄"X 2¹/₂" HARDWOOD WEB FRAME
- HARDWOOD TILT STRIP
- ¹/₂" HARDWOOD DRAWER BACK
- ¹/₈" HARDBOARD DRAWER BOTTOM. ¹/₄" IF OVER I'-0" WIDE
- ³/₄" THICK HARDWOOD DRAWER SUPPORT
- ³/₄" PLYWOOD SHELF WITH NAILED AND GLUED EDGE BAND ON FRONT
- HOLES FOR SHELF SUPPORT; SPACING OPTIONAL I" TYPICAL
- II PLY PLYWOOD LIPPED DOOR WITHOUT EDGE BANDING
- 2X4 WOOD SLEEPER AT 2'-8" O.C.

**ECONOMY GRADE**

### SECTION THROUGH BASE AND WALL CABINETS

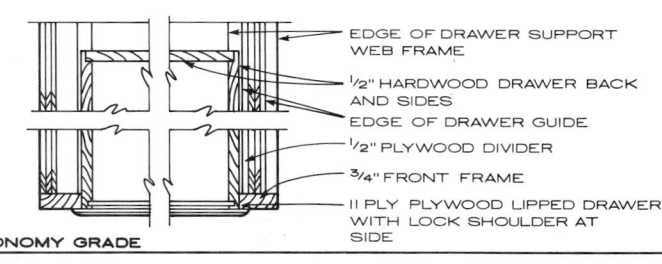

- EDGE OF DRAWER SUPPORT WEB FRAME
- ¹/₂" HARDWOOD DRAWER BACK AND SIDES
- EDGE OF DRAWER GUIDE
- ¹/₂" PLYWOOD DIVIDER
- ³/₄" FRONT FRAME
- II PLY PLYWOOD LIPPED DRAWER WITH LOCK SHOULDER AT SIDE

**ECONOMY GRADE**

### PLAN OF DRAWER (LIPPED DRAWER TYPE)

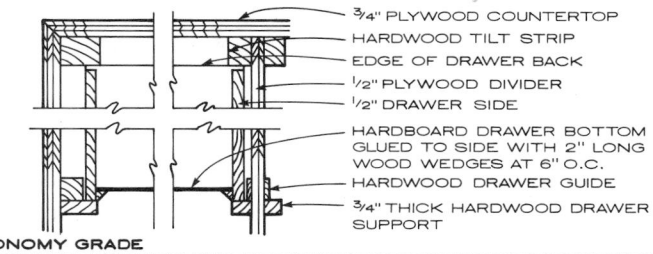

- ³/₄" PLYWOOD COUNTERTOP
- HARDWOOD TILT STRIP
- EDGE OF DRAWER BACK
- ¹/₂" PLYWOOD DIVIDER
- ¹/₂" DRAWER SIDE
- HARDBOARD DRAWER BOTTOM GLUED TO SIDE WITH 2" LONG WOOD WEDGES AT 6" O.C.
- HARDWOOD DRAWER GUIDE
- ³/₄" THICK HARDWOOD DRAWER SUPPORT

**ECONOMY GRADE**

### SECTION THROUGH DRAWER

John S. Fornaro, AIA; Columbia, Virginia

**ARCHITECTURAL WOODWORK**

6

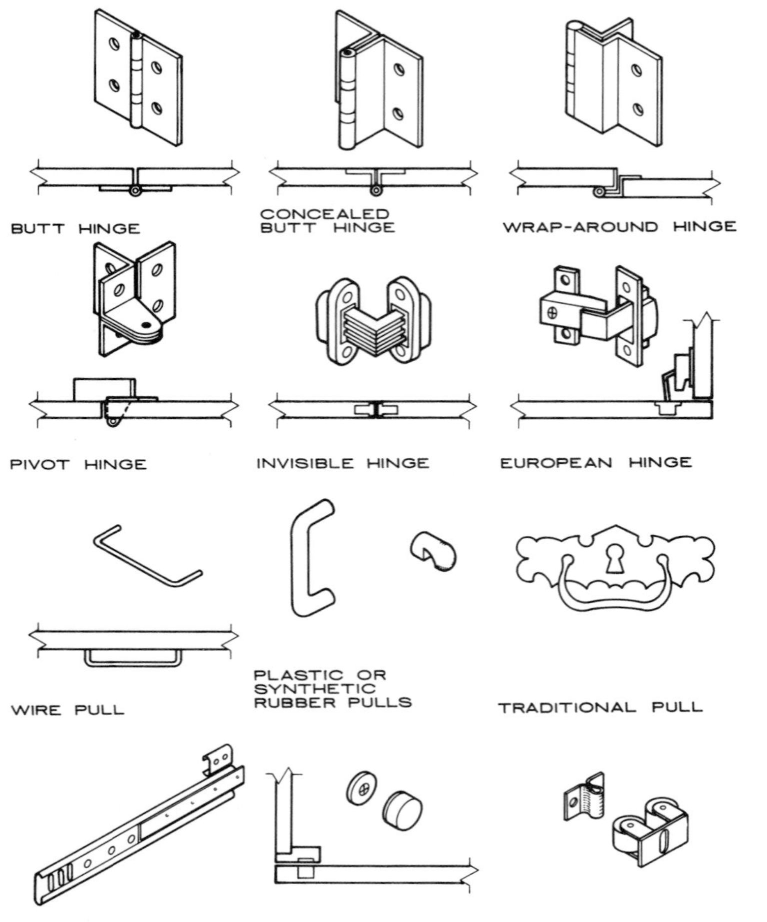

**BUTT HINGE**

**CONCEALED BUTT HINGE**

**WRAP-AROUND HINGE**

**PIVOT HINGE**

**INVISIBLE HINGE**

**EUROPEAN HINGE**

**WIRE PULL**

**PLASTIC OR SYNTHETIC RUBBER PULLS**

**TRADITIONAL PULL**

**DRAWER GLIDE**

**MAGNETIC CATCH**

**FRICTION CATCH**

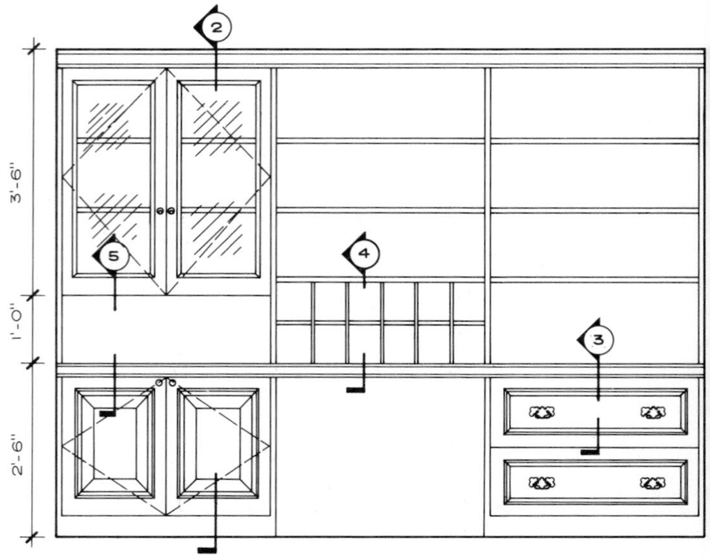

3/4" PLYWOOD SHELF WITH DECORATIVE HARDWOOD EDGE

1/2" HARDWOOD SHELF STOP DADOED INTO VERTICAL DIVIDER. PROVIDE ROUNDED EDGE

1" PLYWOOD COUNTERTOP

HARDWOOD TRIM

**CUSTOM GRADE**

**① TRADITIONAL BUILT-IN CABINETRY**

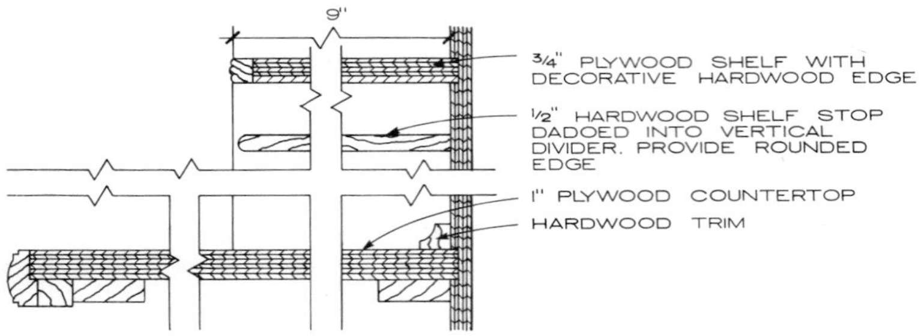

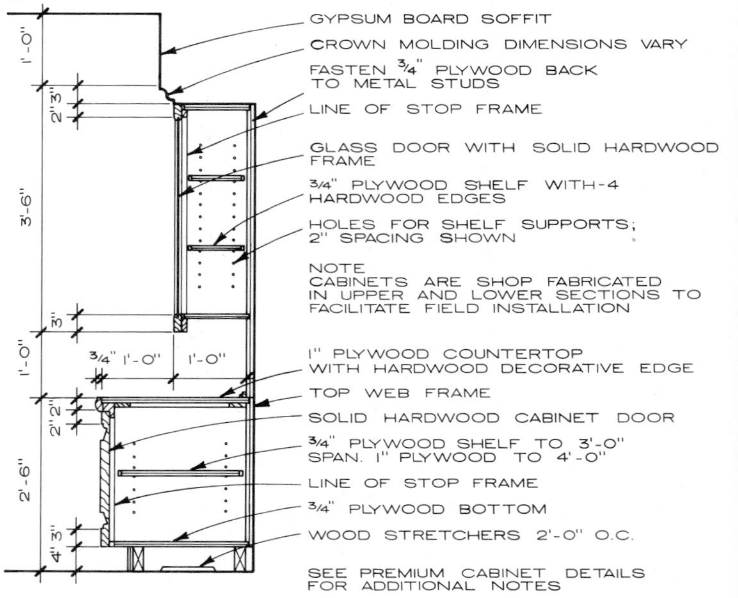

GYPSUM BOARD SOFFIT

CROWN MOLDING DIMENSIONS VARY

FASTEN 3/4" PLYWOOD BACK TO METAL STUDS

LINE OF STOP FRAME

GLASS DOOR WITH SOLID HARDWOOD FRAME

3/4" PLYWOOD SHELF WITH 4 HARDWOOD EDGES

HOLES FOR SHELF SUPPORTS; 2" SPACING SHOWN

NOTE
CABINETS ARE SHOP FABRICATED IN UPPER AND LOWER SECTIONS TO FACILITATE FIELD INSTALLATION

1" PLYWOOD COUNTERTOP WITH HARDWOOD DECORATIVE EDGE

TOP WEB FRAME

SOLID HARDWOOD CABINET DOOR

3/4" PLYWOOD SHELF TO 3'-0" SPAN. 1" PLYWOOD TO 4'-0"

LINE OF STOP FRAME

3/4" PLYWOOD BOTTOM

WOOD STRETCHERS 2'-0" O.C.

SEE PREMIUM CABINET DETAILS FOR ADDITIONAL NOTES

**④ SECTION THROUGH PIGEONHOLE**

LINE OF STOP FRAME

1/8" FLOAT OR NON-GLARE GLASS

REMOVABLE HARDWOOD STOP

SOLID HARDWOOD DOOR FRAME. DIMENSIONS AND PROFILES VARY

SOLID HARDWOOD RAISED PANEL CABINET DOOR SHOWN. CONSULT A.W.I STANDARDS FOR OTHER TYPES OF RAISED PANEL DOOR CONSTRUCTION. DIMENSIONS AND PROFILES OF DOOR VARY

**② SECTION THROUGH CABINETRY**

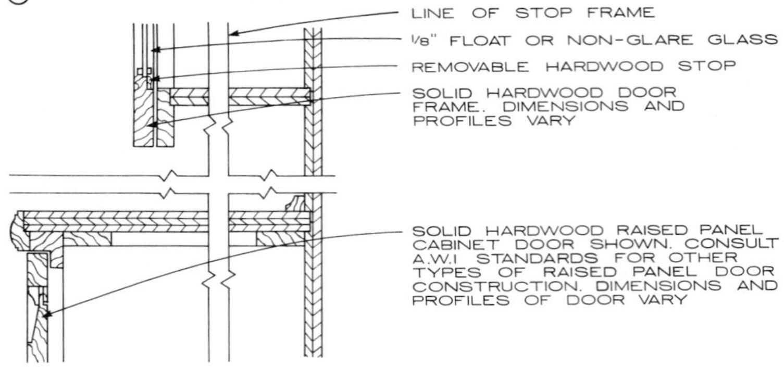

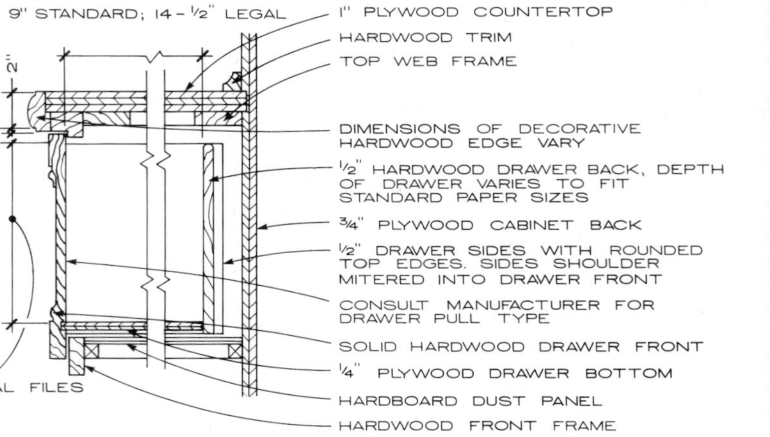

9" STANDARD; 14-1/2" LEGAL

1" PLYWOOD COUNTERTOP

HARDWOOD TRIM

TOP WEB FRAME

DIMENSIONS OF DECORATIVE HARDWOOD EDGE VARY

1/2" HARDWOOD DRAWER BACK, DEPTH OF DRAWER VARIES TO FIT STANDARD PAPER SIZES

3/4" PLYWOOD CABINET BACK

1/2" DRAWER SIDES WITH ROUNDED TOP EDGES. SIDES SHOULDER MITERED INTO DRAWER FRONT

CONSULT MANUFACTURER FOR DRAWER PULL TYPE

SOLID HARDWOOD DRAWER FRONT

1/4" PLYWOOD DRAWER BOTTOM

HARDBOARD DUST PANEL

HARDWOOD FRONT FRAME

10" FOR LATERAL FILES

**⑤ SECTION THROUGH GLASS AND WOOD DOOR**

John S. Fornaro, AIA; Columbia, Virginia

**③ SECTION THROUGH LATERAL FILE**

**ARCHITECTURAL WOODWORK**

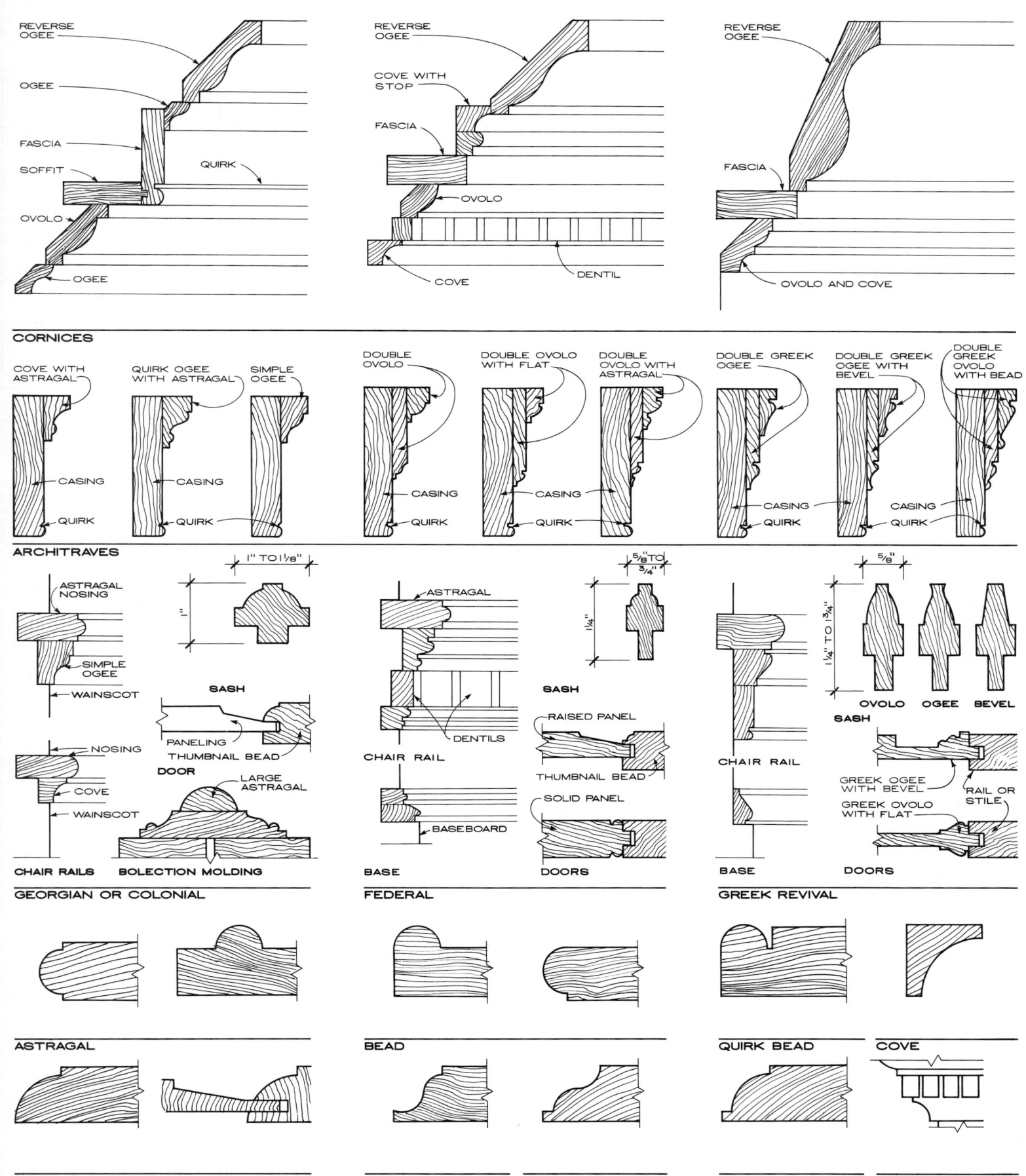

**CORNICES**

**ARCHITRAVES**

GEORGIAN OR COLONIAL

FEDERAL

GREEK REVIVAL

ASTRAGAL

BEAD

QUIRK BEAD    COVE

THUMBNAIL BEAD

OGEE    REVERSE OGEE

OVOLO    DENTIL

Timothy B. McDonald; Washington, D.C.

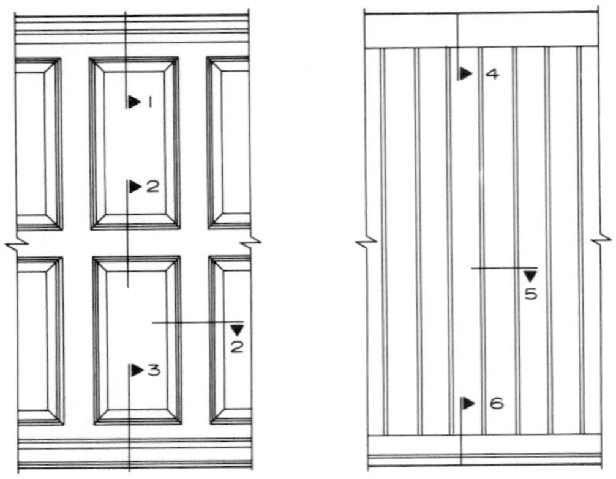

## NOTES

1. For flush plywood paneling, refer to interior plywood detail page and plywood pages.
2. For fire retardant performance requirements, refer to applicable building codes. Fire retardant classifications are based on both "flame spread" and "smoke developed" and are determined by ASTM E-84 tunnel test.
3. Since treated lumber may discolor, treated core veneered construction with untreated face veneers is preferred.
4. For specification of architectural woodwork, refer to Architectural Woodworking Institute (AWI) Architectural Woodwork Quality Standards, Guide to Wood Species, Building Code Flame Spread Classifications, and Building Code Applications for Miscellaneous Exterior and Interior Wood Uses.

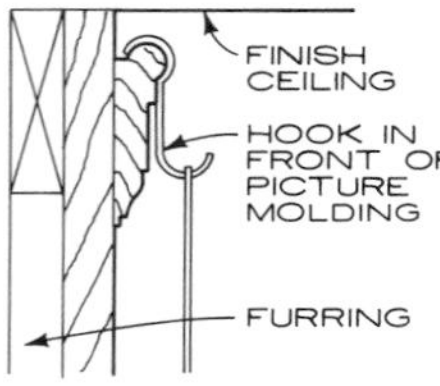

**WOOD PANELING ELEVATIONS**

**PICTURE MOLDING DETAILS**

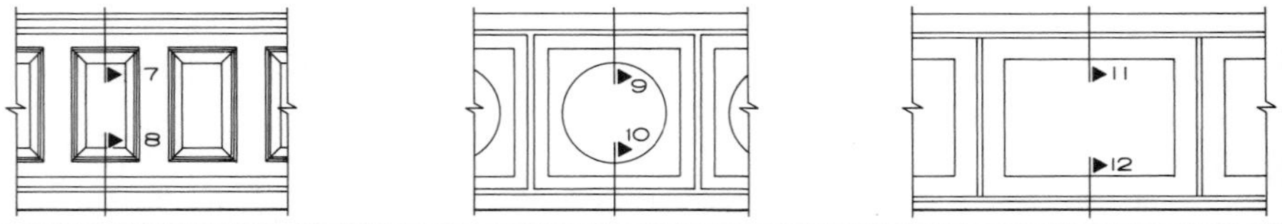

EXPOSED HOOK 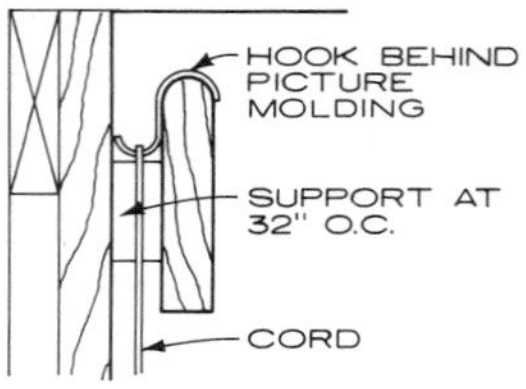    CONCEALED HOOK 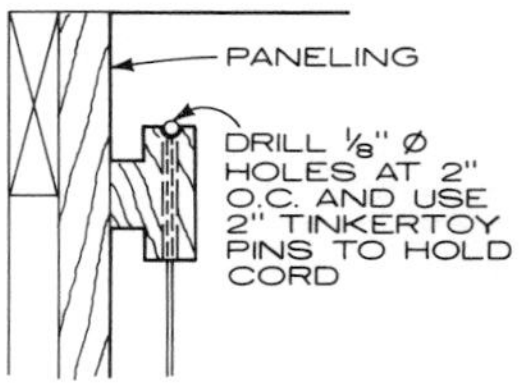    CONCEALED PIN

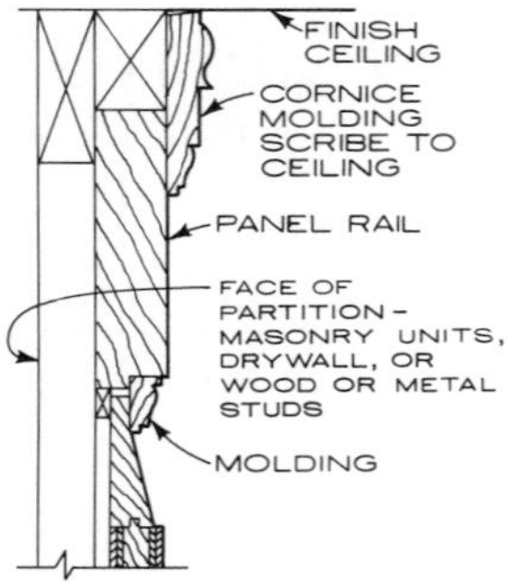

① CEILING CLOSURE 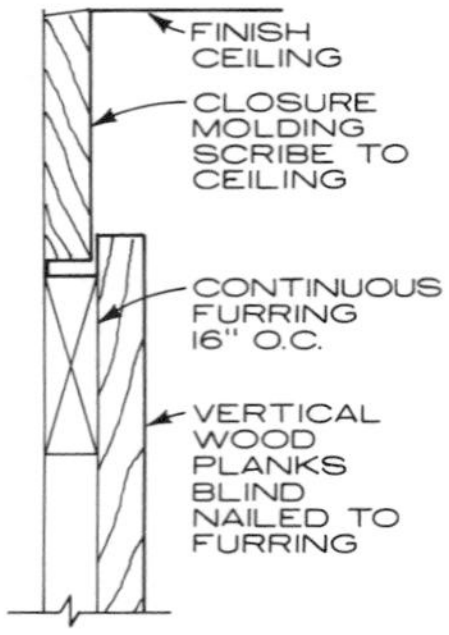    ④ RECESSED CEILING CLOSURE

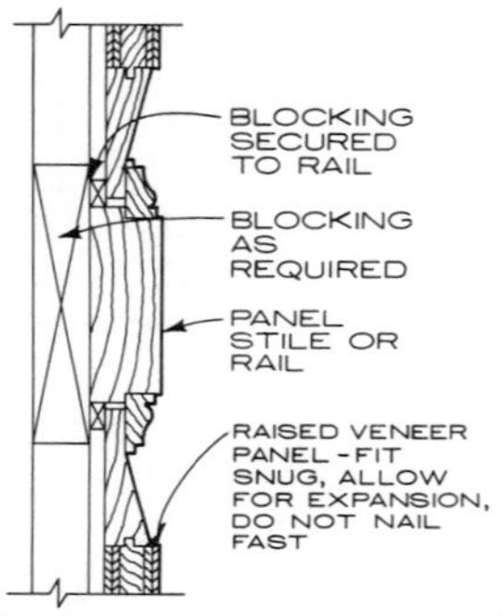

**WOOD RAILING ELEVATIONS**

② RAIL OR STILE 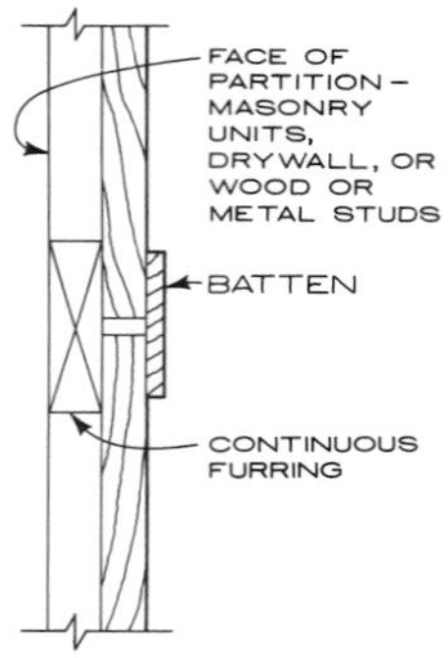    ⑤ BATTEN    ⑦ CAP 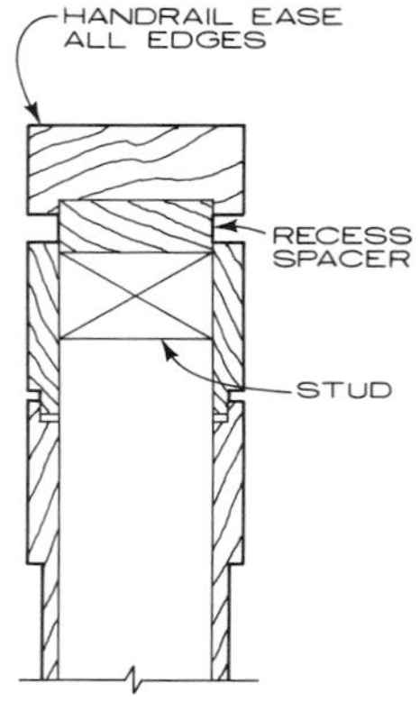    ⑨ CAP 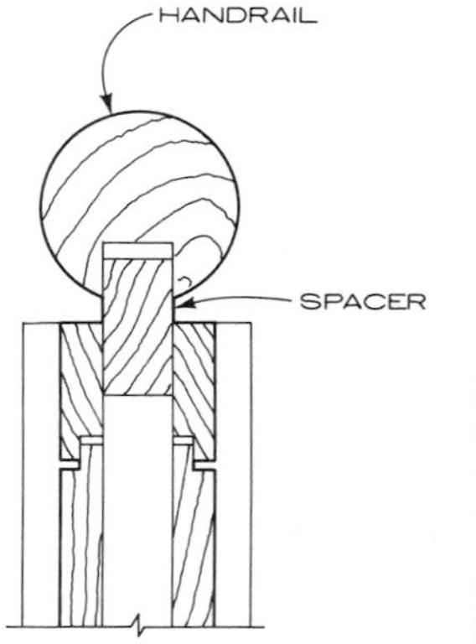    ⑪ CAP

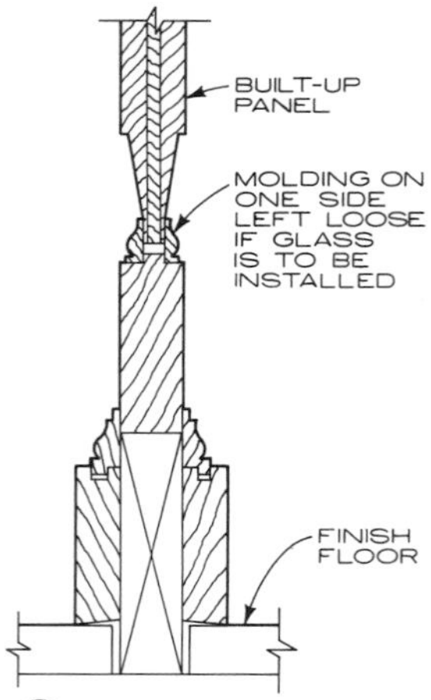

③ BASE    ⑥ RECESSED BASE    ⑧ BASE 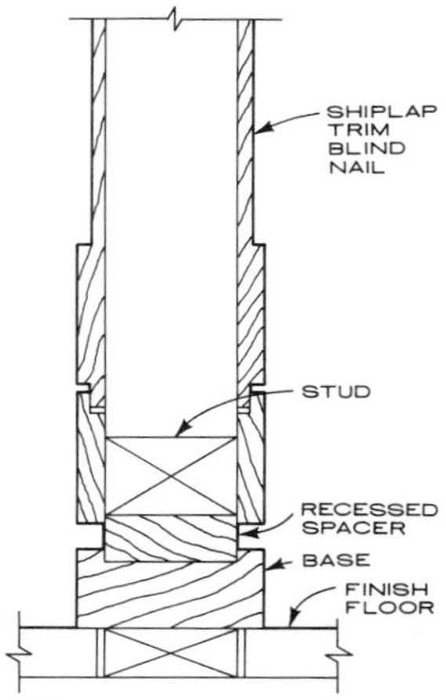    ⑩ BASE 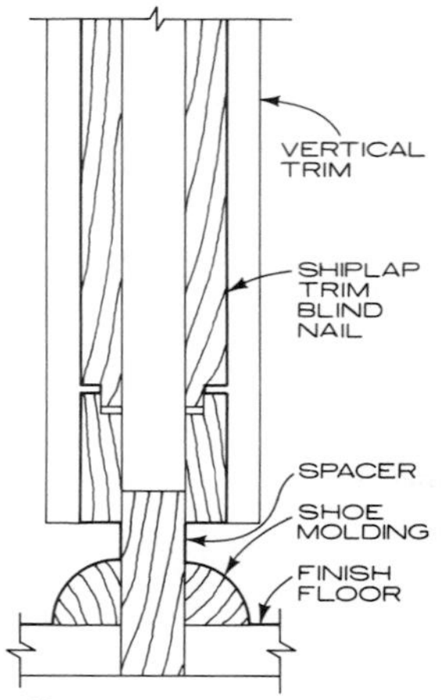    ⑫ BASE

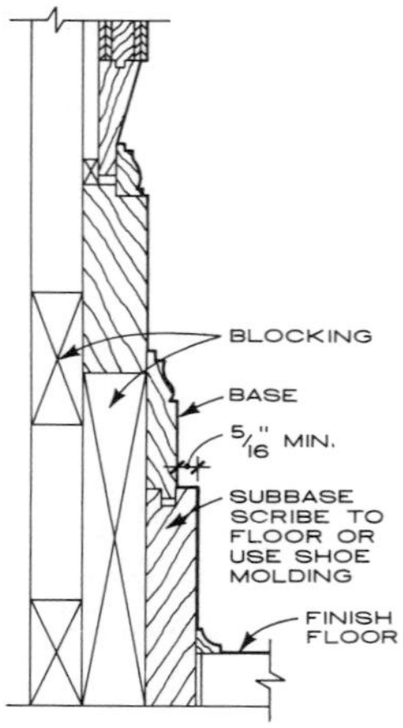

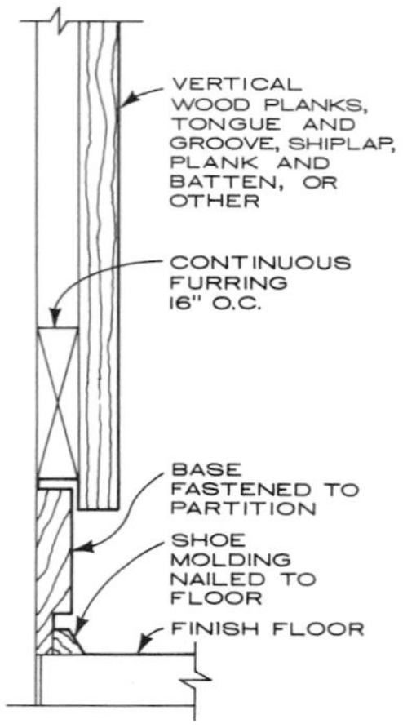

SECTIONS
**WOOD PANELING DETAILS**

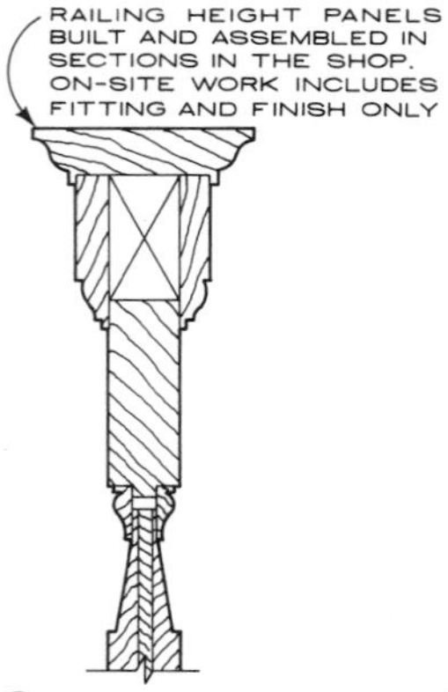

SECTIONS
**WOOD RAILING DETAILS**

Charles Szoradi, AIA; Washington, D.C.

## ARCHITECTURAL WOODWORK

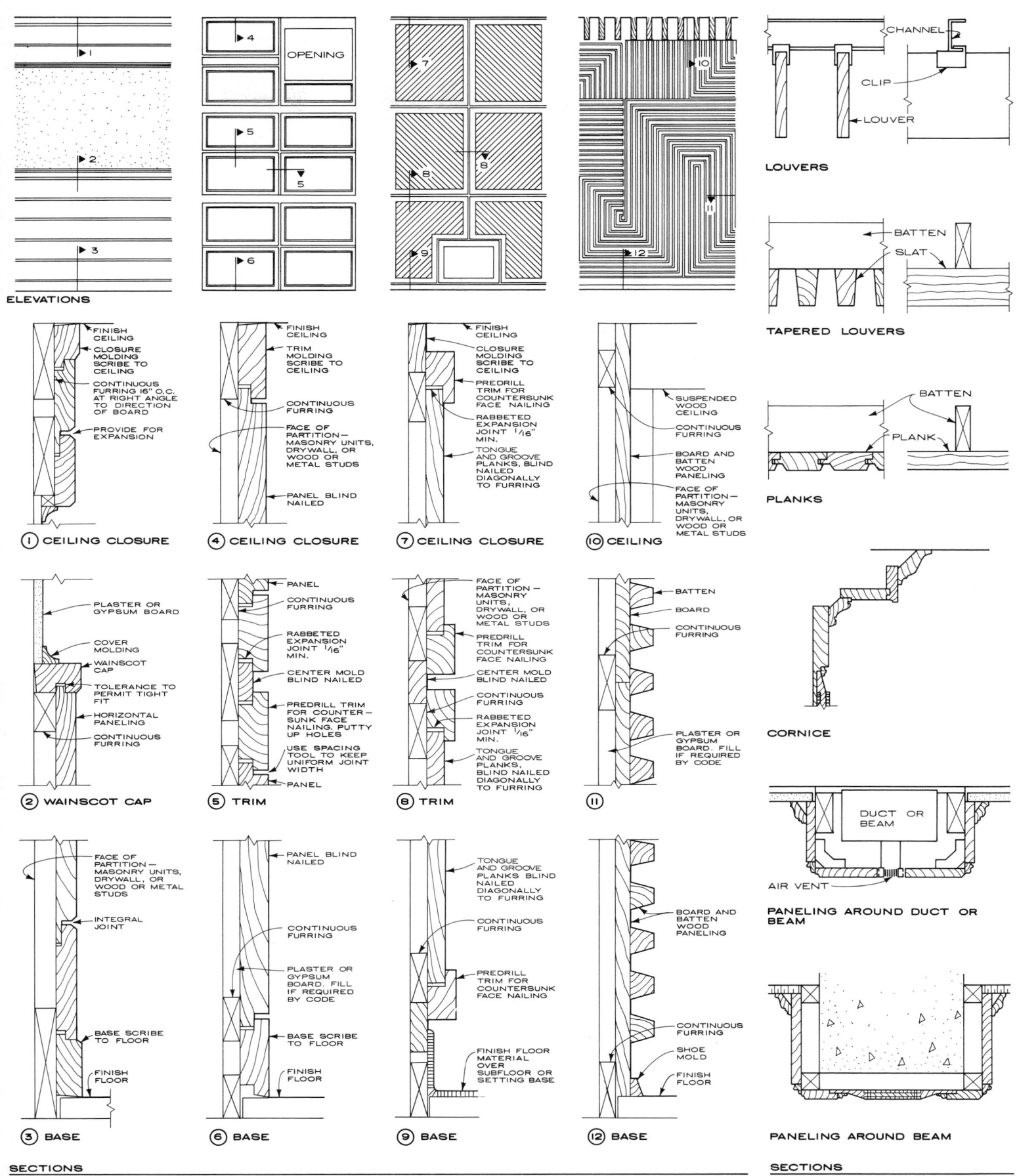

ELEVATIONS

① CEILING CLOSURE

FINISH CEILING
CLOSURE MOLDING SCRIBE TO CEILING
CONTINUOUS FURRING 16" O.C. AT RIGHT ANGLE TO DIRECTION OF BOARD
PROVIDE FOR EXPANSION

② WAINSCOT CAP

PLASTER OR GYPSUM BOARD
COVER MOLDING
WAINSCOT CAP
TOLERANCE TO PERMIT TIGHT FIT
HORIZONTAL PANELING
CONTINUOUS FURRING

③ BASE

FACE OF PARTITION — MASONRY UNITS, DRYWALL, OR WOOD OR METAL STUDS
INTEGRAL JOINT
BASE SCRIBE TO FLOOR
FINISH FLOOR

④ CEILING CLOSURE

FINISH CEILING
TRIM MOLDING SCRIBE TO CEILING
CONTINUOUS FURRING
FACE OF PARTITION — MASONRY UNITS, DRYWALL, OR WOOD OR METAL STUDS
PANEL BLIND NAILED

⑤ TRIM

PANEL
CONTINUOUS FURRING
RABBETED EXPANSION JOINT 1/16" MIN.
CENTER MOLD BLIND NAILED
PREDRILL TRIM FOR COUNTER-SUNK FACE NAILING. PUTTY UP HOLES
USE SPACING TOOL TO KEEP UNIFORM JOINT WIDTH
PANEL

⑥ BASE

PANEL BLIND NAILED
CONTINUOUS FURRING
PLASTER OR GYPSUM BOARD. FILL IF REQUIRED BY CODE
BASE SCRIBE TO FLOOR
FINISH FLOOR

⑦ CEILING CLOSURE

FINISH CEILING
CLOSURE MOLDING SCRIBE TO CEILING
PREDRILL TRIM FOR COUNTERSUNK FACE NAILING
RABBETED EXPANSION JOINT 1/16" MIN.
TONGUE AND GROOVE PLANKS, BLIND NAILED DIAGONALLY TO FURRING

⑧ TRIM

FACE OF PARTITION — MASONRY UNITS, DRYWALL, OR WOOD OR METAL STUDS
PREDRILL TRIM FOR COUNTERSUNK FACE NAILING
CENTER MOLD BLIND NAILED
CONTINUOUS FURRING
RABBETED EXPANSION JOINT 1/16" MIN.
TONGUE AND GROOVE PLANKS, BLIND NAILED DIAGONALLY TO FURRING

⑨ BASE

TONGUE AND GROOVE PLANKS BLIND NAILED DIAGONALLY TO FURRING
CONTINUOUS FURRING
PREDRILL TRIM FOR COUNTERSUNK FACE NAILING
FINISH FLOOR MATERIAL OVER SUBFLOOR OR SETTING BASE

⑩ CEILING

SUSPENDED WOOD CEILING
CONTINUOUS FURRING
BOARD AND BATTEN WOOD PANELING
FACE OF PARTITION — MASONRY UNITS, DRYWALL, OR WOOD OR METAL STUDS

⑪

BATTEN
BOARD
CONTINUOUS FURRING
PLASTER OR GYPSUM BOARD. FILL IF REQUIRED BY CODE

⑫ BASE

BOARD AND BATTEN WOOD PANELING
CONTINUOUS FURRING
SHOE MOLD
FINISH FLOOR

SECTIONS
WOOD PANEL DETAILS

LOUVERS

CHANNEL
CLIP
LOUVER

TAPERED LOUVERS

BATTEN
SLAT

PLANKS

BATTEN
PLANK

CORNICE

PANELING AROUND DUCT OR BEAM

DUCT OR BEAM
AIR VENT

PANELING AROUND BEAM

SECTIONS
WOOD CEILING DETAILS

Charles Szoradi, AIA; Washington, D.C.

## NOTE

Wood is preserved by pressure treatment with an EPA registered pesticide to protect it from insect attack and decay. Treated wood should be used only where such protection is required. Exposure to preservatives may present certain hazards. Precautions should be taken in handling, using, and disposing of treated wood. Refer to local codes.

## DECAY AND INSECT RESISTANT WOOD

### WOLMANIZED PRESSURE TREATED WOOD AND OUTDOOR BRAND WOOD

Wolmanized wood has been pressure treated with a water solution of preservative chemicals. Has outstanding durability under any condition of exposure. Use is limited to the treatment of fully air seasoned or kiln dried material. Wolman salts, the preservative used, impart a light green, blue-green, or brownish color to the wood, depending on the species. Wolmanized wood weathers to a silver gray.

1. GENERAL USE: In the ground; in water; in contact with masonry, or when the wood will be exposed to wetting.
2. SPECIFIC USE: Decks, patios, walkways, fences, boat docks, sill plates, soffits, fascia, all weather wood foundations, pole houses, and pole buildings.
3. ADVANTAGES: Provides lasting protection against decay producing fungi and insects. Clean, oil free. Odorless. Can be painted or stained. Preservative chemicals are fiberfixed in the wood to prevent leaching. Harmless to people, plants, and animals.
4. LIMITATIONS: Air seasoning or kiln drying is required after treatment to make Wolmanized lumber paintable and to guard further against shrinkage in service. Moisture content should be 19% or less. Because undercoated steel rusts quickly, nails or bolts should be galvanized.

### CELLON PRESSURE TREATED WOOD

The Cellon pressure treatment process utilizes liquefied butane gas as a solvent to carry pentachlorophenol, the preservative, deep into the wood. After treatment, the solvent is evaporated. Particularly suitable for treating hardwoods and all plywoods.

1. GENERAL USE: Ground contact, in contact with masonry, or when the wood will be exposed to wetting.
2. SPECIFIC USE: Glued laminated beams, lighting standards, pole houses and pole buildings, decking.
3. ADVANTAGES: Provides lasting protection against decay producing fungi and insects. Clean and dry to the touch. Can be painted, stained, and glued. Since neither water nor oil is used in the Cellon process, air seasoning and kiln drying are not required after treatment. Retains the wood's original texture and color. Weathers naturally.
4. LIMITATIONS: Will not protect against attack from marine organisms. Certain species such as Douglas fir, southern pine, and ponderosa pine may exude resin from knots and heartwood after treatment. Wood rich in tannin, such as redwood and oak, may develop a blue-black surface stain if the lumber has not been well seasoned prior to treatment; however, the sun's rays will bleach out the stain in several months.

### PENTACHLOROPHENOL PRESSURE TREATED WOOD

Pentachlorophenol is the principal preservative in the "oil borne" category. Toxic to insects and fungi.

1. GENERAL USE: In the ground.
2. SPECIFIC USE: Industrial and farm buildings; fence posts.
3. ADVANTAGES: Protects against fungi and insect attack. Seasoned hardwoods and softwoods can be treated without fear of grain raising, checking, or splitting.
4. LIMITATIONS: Penta treated forest products may become blotchy when exposed to the weather; this condition disappears after extended service. Penta-in-oil treated wood would NOT be used as a subflooring, or in contact with materials subject to staining (plaster, wallboard). Not readily paintable; would not be used in direct contact with roofing felt, since it can cause the tar to drip. Not recommended for use in saltwater.

## CREOSOTE

Creosote is the oldest commercial wood preservative currently being used. It has demonstrated, through years of actual service, outstanding durability, dependability, and general utility. Creosote contains a multitude of chemical compounds which are toxic to fungi, insects, and most marine organisms. Average life expectancy of a creosoted wood pole in the ground is 35 to 40 years, but some creosoted poles are still standing fast after more than 75 years of rugged service.

1. GENERAL USE: In the ground and in water.
2. SPECIFIC USE: Foundation piles, landscape ties, fence posts, highway guard rails, marine piling, and bulkheads.
3. ADVANTAGES: Creosote is a coal tar product that derives its effectiveness from its persistent high toxicity to wood destroying insects and fungi. Creosote effectively protects wood from the ravages of most marine organisms.
4. LIMITATIONS: Pressure creosoted lumber should NOT be used as a subflooring or in contact with materials subject to staining (plaster, wallboard). It is not readily paintable, and should not be used in direct contact with roofing felt, since it can cause the tar to drip.

## CORROSION RESISTANT WOOD

### KP RESIN IMPREGNATED WOOD

KP resin impregnated wood has been impregnated with a phenolic resin solution to obtain a high degree of acid resistance and excellent dimensional stability. The treatment is limited to southern pine, hard maple, cativo, and kempas. Natural wood color.

1. GENERAL USE: Where corrosion resistance or dimensional stability is required.
2. SPECIFIC USE: Filter press plates and frames, flumes, stacks, tank covers, tanks, troughs and trays, die models.
3. ADVANTAGES: High degree of acid resistance. Dimensional stability far greater than untreated wood. Can be machined. Gouging the surface does not reduce the protection.
4. LIMITATIONS: Should not be exposed to alkaline solutions, aniline, chlorine gas, strong bleaching solutions, strong oxidizing acids.

### ASIDBAR IMPREGNATED WOOD

Asidbar impregnated wood has been impregnated with topped coal tar material that provides the natural structural properties of wood as well as the chemical resistant properties of coal tar composites. Color is coal-tar black. Treatment is for southern pine lumber, and southern pine and Douglas fir plywood.

1. GENERAL USE: Where corrosion resistance is required.
2. SPECIFIC USE: Beams, interior wall cladding, decking, effluent systems, platforms, roof systems, walkways.
3. ADVANTAGES: High degree of acid resistance. Gouging of surface does not reduce the protection.
4. LIMITATIONS: Tends to soften and expand in severe temperatures above 130°F. Not suitable for use with acetate solvents, benzene or benzol, ethers, trichloroethylene, xylene, or xylol.

## FIRE RETARDANT TREATED WOOD

### NON-COM FIRE RETARDANT TREATED WOOD

Non-Com fire retardant treated wood is used indoors where the relative humidity is normally below 80%. The wood is pressure impregnated with inorganic salts that react chemically at temperatures below the ignition point of untreated wood. This chemical reaction reduces the flammable vapors emitted by wood subjected to fire. A protective char is formed and wood underneath remains structurally sound longer than untreated and surface treated wood.

1. CLASSIFIED: Non-Com fire retardant treated lumber and plywood have an Underwriters' Laboratories designated rating of FRS, which means that the material has a fire hazard classification of 25 or less for flame spread, fuel contributed, and smoke developed, and shows no sign of progressive combustion when the 10 minute fire hazard classification test is continued for an additional 20 minutes.
2. APPROVED: The Factory Mutual Engineering Division, the Factory Insurance Association, all state insurance rating bureaus, and all branches of the Insurance Services Office frequently permit the use of Non-Com fire retardant treated wood as an alternative to materials classified as noncombustible.
3. GENERAL USE: In buildings (interior).
4. SPECIFIC USE: Studs, wall plates, and fire stops with metal lath and plaster or drywall construction of interior nonbearing walls and partitions in fire resistive buildings. Roof systems including deck, purlins, and joists.
5. ADVANTAGES: Reduces flame spread and fuel contributed. Requires no maintenance to retain its fire retardant properties. Can be installed by regular carpenter crews. Low sound transmission makes it an excellent product for remodeling as well as for new construction.
6. LIMITATIONS: If Non-Com is to be painted, sealed, or varnished, it must be kiln dried to a maximum moisture content of 12%. Not recommended for use in the ground or for exposed locations that are subject to weathering or humidity normally above 80%. At jobsite, dry lumber should be stored indoors if possible. Otherwise, it should be stored on raised platforms and covered with suitable weatherproof protective covering such as tarpaulins or polyethylene film. NOTE: NCX fire retardant treated wood is recommended for architectural appearance applications.

### NCX FIRE RETARDANT TREATED WOOD

NCX fire retardant treated wood is used outside or where the relative humidity is frequently above 80%. The wood is pressure impregnated with a fire retardant monomeric resin solution. After impregnation, the wood is kiln dried to cure the chemicals in the wood. The cured chemicals in the wood are not affected by direct outdoor weather exposure and high humidity.

1. CLASSIFIED: NCX fire retardant treated lumber and plywood have an Underwriters' Laboratories designated rating of FRS, which means that the material has a fire hazard classification of 25 or less for flame spread, fuel contributed, and smoke developed, and shows no sign of progressive combustion when the 10 minute fire hazard classification test is continued for an additional 20 minutes.
2. APPROVED: The Factory Mutual Engineering Division, the Factory Insurance Association, all state insurance rating bureaus, and all branches of the Insurance Services Office frequently permit the use of NCX as an alternative to materials classified as noncombustible.
3. RECOGNIZED: For certain applications by numerous state and city building codes. Also by BOCA, ICBO, SBCC, Southern Standard, AIA, and American Insurance Association.
4. GENERAL USE: Exterior use and where humidity is frequently above 80%. Also, interior appearance applications.
5. SPECIFIC USE: Balconies and steps. Roof systems. Soffit and fascia. Architectural hardwood molding and paneling. Western red cedar shingles and shakes.
6. ADVANTAGES: Suitable for exposure to the weather or high humidity conditions. Clear architectural finishes can be applied without causing below-film blushes.
7. LIMITATIONS: Although NCX wood has excellent weathering characteristics, it is not recommended for use in the ground or in ground contact. Treatment may darken wood slightly, but basic tone or hue remains almost unchanged. Treated wood may show sticker marks after drying. Underwriters' Laboratories permits milling of some species after drying. Where marks are objectionable, milling is recommended.

Derek Martin, FAIA; Pittsburgh, Pennsylvania
Domenic F. Valente, AIA; D. F. Valente, Architect & Planner; Medford, Massachusetts

**WOOD TREATMENT**

# CHAPTER 7

# Thermal and Moisture Protection

## BUILT-UP ROOFING

| DECK OR SUBSTRATE | SURFACING | SLOPE (IN./FT) | BASE SHEET | PLYSHEETS | PLY BITUMEN (LB/SQ/PLY) | SURFACING BITUMEN (LB/SQ) | NOTES TO DESIGNER/SPECIFIER |
|---|---|---|---|---|---|---|---|
| Nonnailable decks or roof insulations<br><br>(Consult manufacturer for approved types of roof insulation and recommendations for venting)[6] | Aggregate surface:<br><br>Gravel: 400 lb/sq<br><br>OR<br><br>Slag: 300 lb/sq<br><br>OR<br><br>White marble chips: 400 lb/sq | Inclines up to ½:12 | 43 lb coated base spot mopped in asphalt to deck or solid mopped in asphalt to insulation[2] | 3 coal tar saturated felts (perforated) | Coal tar @ 20–25 | Coal tar @ 70–75 | UL Class A on most deck and insulation types[1]<br>Requires complete surfacing daily<br>For ponded roofs, add 4th ply of felt and double flood and double gravel surface<br>Base flashings must be installed in flashing cement<br>Same configuration possible on slopes of ½-3 in./ft using Type III asphalt[5] |
| | | | Organic base felts 43 lb mopped. 43 lb coated base spot mopped in asphalt to deck or solid mopped in asphalt to insulation | 3 organic felts (perforated) | Type II asphalt[3] @ 25 | Type I asphalt[4] @ 60 | |
| | | Inclines up to ½:12 | Fiberglass base spot mopped to deck or solid mopped to insulation | 3 fiberglass plysheets, ASTM D2178 Type IV | Coal tar @ 25–30 | Coal tar @ 75 | UL Class A on most deck and insulation types[1]<br>Roofing may be left up to 6 months before surfacing<br>For ponded roofs, add plysheet and double flood and double gravel surface<br>Base flashings must be installed in flashing cement<br>Same configuration possible on slopes of ½-3 in./ft using Type III asphalt[5] |
| | | | | 3 fiberglass plysheets[7] | Type II asphalt @ 25 | Type I asphalt @ 60 | |
| | Mineral surface cap sheet<br><br>(72–80 lb) | ¼:12[5] | Fiberglass base spot mopped to deck or solid mopped to insulation | 2 fiberglass plysheets | Type III asphalt @ 25–30 | Asphalt @ 25–30 for cap sheet | UL Class A, B, or C depending on deck substrate, slope, and manufacturer[1]<br>Consult manufacturer for specific regional requirements<br>Proper application of mineral cap sheet requires warm weather<br>Cold process fiberglass systems also possible; consult manufacturer |
| | Smooth surface | ¼:12[5] | Fiberglass base spot mopped to deck or solid mopped to insulation | 3 fiberglass plysheets | Type II asphalt @ 25–30 | Asphalt/clay emulsion @ 6 gal/sq | UL Class A, B, or C depending on deck/substrate, slope, and manufacturer[1]<br>Consult manufacturer for specific regional requirements<br>Reflective coatings are recommended over smooth surface systems |

### NOTES

1. Underwriter's Laboratories test for Fire-Hazard Classification by assembling particular constructions using specific products of stated manufacturers; consult UL or the manufacturer to verify classifications for specific roofing systems for given project conditions.
   Class A: Not readily flammable under severe fire exposure and protects roof deck to high degree.
   Class B: Not readily flammable under moderate fire exposure and protects roof deck to moderate degree.
   Class C: Not readily flammable under light fire exposure and protects roof deck to slight degree.
   Only classes A and B are fire retardant.

2. On slopes up to ½ in./ft, apply asphalt and combine with felts to comply with ASTM D312.
3. For hot climates, use Type III instead of Type II, for higher softening point.
4. For hot climates, use Type III.
5. On slopes of 1 in./ft or greater, plies should be strapped (laid parallel to slope) and back nailed to prevent slippage, and Type III or Type IV asphalt should be used; if roofing is on roof insulation, wood insulation stops/nailers should be provided.
6. Vapor retarder under roof insulation is advisable for conditions having low outdoor temperatures (below 40°F) combined with high indoor relative humidity (above 44%). Allow vapor pressure to escape from between vapor retarder and roofing membrane by use of venting base sheets, vent stacks, or other methods recommended by manufacturer.
7. Three-ply or four-ply membrane system may be used. Number of plysheets to suit system selected.

## ROLL ROOFING

| TYPE | DESCRIPTION | SLOPE (IN./FT) MIN. | SLOPE (IN./FT) MAX. | WEIGHT (LB/SQ) | SIZE | UNDERLAY | FASTENERS | EXPOSURE | COLOR AND TEXTURE | U.L. RATING |
|---|---|---|---|---|---|---|---|---|---|---|
| Asphalt Roll Roofing | Smooth surface | 0 | 6 | 50 | 36" x 36' | | Nails and cement | 33" | Black | C-wind resistant |
| | | | | 65 | | | | | | |
| | Mineral surface | | | 90 | 36" x 36' | | | | | |
| | Double coverage fiberglass | ½ | 4 | 60 | 36" x 36' | | | 17" | Various color blends | A-wind resistant |
| | Fiberglass reinforced mineral fiber | ⅛ | 4 | 75 | 36" x 72' | | | | Black | B-wind resistant |

Walter H. Sobel, FAIA, & Associates; Chicago, Illinois
Kent Wong; Hewlett, Jamison, Atkinson & Luey; Portland, Oregon; from data furnished by A. Larry Brown; Owens/Corning Fiberglas Corporation

GENERAL INFORMATION

## BUILT-UP ROOFING (CONT.)

| DECK OR SUBSTRATE | SURFACING | SLOPE (IN./FT) | BASE SHEET | PLYSHEETS | PLY BITUMEN (LB/SQ/PLY) | SURFACING BITUMEN (LB/SQ) | NOTES TO DESIGNER/SPECIFIER |
|---|---|---|---|---|---|---|---|
| Wood or other nailable decking (Over wood board decks, one ply of sheathing paper should be applied under base felt next to deck) (Consult manufacturers for approved decks and fasteners) | Gravel: 400 lb/sq OR Slag: 300 lb/sq OR White marble chips: 400 lb/sq | Inclines up to 1/2 | 43 lb coated base mechanically attached | 3 coal tar saturated felts (perforated) | Coal tar @ 25 | Coal tar @ 75 | • U.L. Class A on most deck types (1)<br>• Requires complete surfacing daily<br>• For ponded roofs, add a 4th ply of felt and double flood and double gravel surface<br>• Base flashings must be installed in flashing cement |
| | | | 43 lb organic base felt mechanically attached | 3 asphalt saturated felts | Type II asphalt @ 25 | Type I asphalt @ 60 | • Same configuration possible on slopes of 1/2–3 in./ft (2) using Type III asphalt |
| | | Inclines up to 1/2 | Fiberglas® base mechanically attached (3) | 3 fiberglass plysheets ASTM D2178 Type IV (3) | Coal tar @ 25–30 | Coal tar @ 75 | • U.L. Class A on most deck types (1)<br>• Roofing may be left up to 6 months before surfacing<br>• For ponded roofs, add a 3rd ply of Perma-Ply R and double flood and double gravel surface<br>• Base flashings must be installed in flashing cement |
| | | | Fiberglas® base mechanically attached (3) | 3 fiberglass plysheets ASTM D2178 Type IV (3) | Type II asphalt @ 25 | Type I asphalt @ 60–70 | • Same configuration possible on slopes of 1/2–3 in./ft (2) using Type III asphalt |
| | Mineral surface cap sheet (72–80 lb) | 1/4-12 (2) | Fiberglass base mechanically attached | 2 fiberglass plysheets, ASTM D2178 Type III or IV | Asphalt @ 25 | Asphalt @ 30 for cap sheet | • U.L. Class A, B, or C depending on deck type, slope, and manufacturer (1)<br>• Consult manufacturer for specific regional requirements for various types of plysheets<br>• Fiberglass roofing may be left up to 6 months before surfacing<br>• Proper application of mineral cap sheet requires warm weather |
| | | | 43 lb organic base mechanically attached | 2 fiberglass plysheets, ASTM D2178 Type III or IV | Asphalt @ 30 | Asphalt @ 30 for cap sheet | |
| | Smooth surface | 1/4-12 (2) | Fiberglass base mechanically attached | 3 fiberglass plysheets, ASTM D2178 Type III or IV; ASTM D250 Type II | Asphalt @ 25–30 | Asphalt/clay emulsion @ 6 gal/sq | • U.L. Class A, B, or C depending on deck type, slope, and manufacturer (1)<br>• Consult manufacturer for specific regional requirements<br>• Reflective coatings are recommended over smooth surface systems |

## SHINGLES

| TYPE | DESCRIPTION | SLOPE (IN./FT) MIN. | SLOPE (IN./FT) MAX. | WEIGHT (LB/SQ)[3] | SIZE | UNDERLAY | FASTENERS | EXPOSURE | COLOR AND TEXTURE | U.L. RATING |
|---|---|---|---|---|---|---|---|---|---|---|
| Asphalt Organic Felt[1,2] | 3 tab | 4 | 12 | 235 | 12″ x 36″ | 15 lb asphalt felt | Galvanized steel or aluminum roofing nails, or zinc-coated staples | 5″ | Various colors; granular texture | Class C fire resistant, wind resistant |
| | 2 tab | 4 | 12 | 300 | 12″ x 36″ | | | | | |
| | Random edged | 4 | 12 | 345 | 12″ x 36″ | | | | Varied; smooth | |
| | No cutout | 2 | 12 | 290 | 12″ x 36″ | | | | | |
| | Interlocking | | | 180 | 19¾″ x 20½″ | | | — | Varied; smooth | Class C fire resistant, wind resistant |
| | Basketweave | | | 245 | 18½″ x 20″ | | | | | |
| Fiberglass | Random edged Laminated Overlay | 4 | 12 | 300 | 14″ x 35⁹⁄₁₆″ | 15 lb asphalt felt | Galvanized steel or aluminum roofing nails, or zinc-coated staples | 6″ | Varied; smooth | Class A fire resistant, wind resistant |
| | 3 tab | 4 | 12 | 225 | 12″ x 36″ | | | 5″ | | |
| | 2 tab | 4 | 12 | 260 | 12″ x 36″ | | | 5″ | Varied; granular texture | |
| | No cutout Random edged | 4 | 12 | 225 | 12″ x 36¼″ | | | 5″ | Varied; smooth | |

### NOTES

1. These shingles may be used on slopes down to 2 in./ft when over a two ply felt underlayment.

2. All shingles are self-sealing.

3. A SQUARE is a term used to describe 100 sq ft of roof area.

Walter H. Sobel, FAIA & Associates; Chicago, Illinois
Kent Wong; Hewlett, Jamison, Atkinson & Luey; Portland, Oregon; from data furnished by A. Larry Brown; Owens/Corning Fiberglas Corporation

## SHINGLES AND ROOFING TILES

| TYPE | DESCRIPTION | APPLICATION | SLOPE MINIMUM (IN./FT) | WEIGHT (LB/SQ) | UNDERLAY | FASTENERS | COLOR AND TEXTURE | SIZE (IN.) L X W | BUTT THICKNESS | EXPOSURE DATA |
|---|---|---|---|---|---|---|---|---|---|---|
| Wood: red cedar; most types and sizes available in cypress, redwood, white cedar; shakes | Handsplit and resawn | Roofs and sidewall panels for institutional, commercial, residential use | 4 | 200–450 | Spaced sheathing 30 lb felt interlayment with shakes | Corrosion resistant nails | Natural or various stains  Various textures | Length 15–24 Width random | 1/2–3/4 in. | 5–7 1/2 in. |
|  | Taper split |  |  | 260 |  |  |  | Length 24 Width random | 1/2 in. | 10 in. |
|  | Straight split |  |  | 200–260 |  |  |  | Length 18–24 Width random | 3/8 in. | 3 in. overlap |
| Wood: red cedar; most types and sizes available in cypress, redwood, white cedar; shingles | No. 1 Blue Label No. 2 Red Label No. 3 Black Label | Roofs and sidewall panels for institutional, commercial, residential use | 4 | None given | Open or solid sheathing  Open sheathing shall be 1 x 4 or 1 x 6 in. boards | Corrosion resistant nails | Natural or various stains  Various textures | Length 16 | 3/8 in. | 5 in. |
|  |  |  |  |  |  |  |  | 18 |  | 5 1/2 in. |
|  |  |  |  |  |  |  |  | 24 |  | 7 1/2 in. |
|  | No. 4 |  |  |  |  |  |  | 16 |  |  |
|  | Undercoursing |  |  |  |  |  |  | 18 |  |  |
|  | No. 1 or No. 2 Rebutted-rejointed |  |  |  |  |  |  | 16 18 24 Width random |  |  |
| Clay tile | Shingle—flat | Institutional, commercial, residential | 3 | 800–1600 | One layer 30 lb or 45 lb felt over plywood | Noncorrosive copper nails | Various finishes | l w 15 x 7 | 3/8 in. minimum | Exposed length 6 1/2 in. Exposed width 7 in. |
|  | Interlocking flat |  |  | 800 |  |  |  | 14 x 9 | 7/8 in. minimum | Exposed length 11 in. Exposed width 8 1/4 in. |
|  | French |  |  | 940–1000 |  |  |  | 16 1/4 x 9 | 2 in. | Exposed length 13 1/8 in. Exposed width 8 1/8 in. |
|  | Spanish |  | 4 | 850 |  |  |  | 13 1/4 x 9 3/4 | 1/2 in. | Exposed length 10 1/2 in. Exposed width 8 1/4 in. |
| Concrete[1] | Shingle—flat | Institutional, commercial, residential | 4 | 950 | One layer 30 lb felt over plywood | 10 penny corrosion resistant galvanized copper, or colors stainless steel box nail | Various colors | 13 x 16 | 1 in. | 3 in. overlap |
|  | Barreled mission curved |  |  |  |  |  |  |  |  |  |
| Slate | Commercial grade—smooth | Institutional, commercial, residential | 4 | 700–800 | One layer 30 lb asphalt saturated rag felt over plywood | Slaters hard copper wire nails cut copper, cut brass, or cut yellow metal slat nails | Blue-black | Various sizes | 3/16, 1/4 in. | 3 in. overlap |
|  | Quarry—run rough |  |  | 825–3600 |  |  |  |  | 3/8, 1/2, 3/4 in. |  |

### NOTES

1. Specifier should ask for concrete tile freeze-thaw test.
2. Underwriters Laboratories Standard UL 580 classifies roof deck assemblies as Class 30, Class 60, and Class 90. The nominal uplift pressures and wind velocities commonly related in technical studies and literature are the following:

| RATING | NOMINAL UPLIFT PRESSURE | NOMINAL WIND VELOCITY |
|---|---|---|
| Class 30 | 30 psf | 100 mph |
| Class 60 | 60 psf | 142 mph |
| Class 90 | 90 psf | 174 mph |

Consult local manufacturer or agent for roofing system rating.

3. Underwriters Laboratories classifies prepared roof covering materials as Class A, B, or C.  CLASS A includes roof coverings that are effective against severe fire exposure.  Roof coverings of this class are then not readily flammable and do not carry or communicate fire; afford a fairly high degree of fire protection to the roof deck; do not slip from position; possess no flying brand hazard; and do not require frequent repairs in order to maintain their fire resisting properties.

Walter H. Sobel, FAIA, & Associates; Chicago, Illinois

## GENERAL INFORMATION

## SEAMED METAL ROOFING

| TYPE | DESCRIPTION | MIN. SLOPE (IN./FT) | SIZE | THICKNESS | WEIGHT (LB/SQ) | UNDERLAY | FASTENER |
|---|---|---|---|---|---|---|---|
| Aluminum coated steel | Polyurethane insulation sandwiched between two layers of steel[1] standing seam | 1/4 | 40" x 32' | 2 1/2" | 250 | None | Panels are clipped to structurals, and interlocking seams sealed |
| Copper coated galvanized steel | Standing seam, pan, or roll method | 3 | 20" x 30' max. / 22" x 30' max. | 24 gauge | 130 | 30 lb felt | Anchor clips and galvanized nails or screws |
| Prepainted galvanized steel | Batten seam pan method | 3 | 24" x 30' max. | | | | |
| Zinc-copper titanium alloy | Batten or standing seam pan method | 3 | 20", 24", or 28" x 8', 10', 12', or 14' | 0.027" | 100 | Roofing felt | Galvanized U channel or L seam support spacer with screw or nails |
| Terne coated stainless[2,3,5] | Standing or batten seam | 3 | 20", 24", 28", or 36" x 96", or 120" | 0.015" or 0.018" | 89 | Roofing felt and rosin paper | TCS cleats and stainless steel nails |
| | Flat locked seam | 1/2 | 20" x 28" | | | | |
| Terne plate[4-6] | Batten seam | 3 | 20" x 120" max. | 26 gauge | 62 | Rosin paper | Terne cleats and roofing nails |
| | Standing seam | 3 | 14", 20" | 28 gauge | | | |
| | | | 24" x 120" max. | 30 gauge | | | |
| | Flat locked seam (wood deck only) | 1/2 | 14" x 20" | 28 gauge | | | |
| | | | 20" x 28" | 30 gauge | | | |
| | Horizontal seam (wood deck only) | 3 1/2 | 24" x 96" max. | 26 gauge | | | |
| | | | | 28 gauge | | | |
| Painted aluminum | Standing seam | 1/2 | 12" x 60"–80" | 0.032" | 72.5 | None | Anchor clips |
| | | | 16" x 60"–80" | 0.040" | 90.4 | | |

### NOTES

1. This is a composite section providing structural deck, insulation, and weathertight roof. U value is 0.50; class I fire rating.
2. Terne coated steel is 304 nickel-chrome stainless steel covered on both sides with terne alloy (80% lead, 20% tin).
3. Terne coated steel can be painted without special preparation of the surface.
4. Terne plate is prime copper bearing steel coated with lead-tin alloy.
5. Expansion seams must be provided on runs exceeding 30 ft where both ends are free to move or exceeding 15 ft where ends are securely fastened.
6. Terne must be shop coated or painted one coat underside and primed and painted two coats on exposed side.

## METAL SHINGLES AND TILES

| TYPE | DESCRIPTION | APPLICATION | SLOPE MINIMUM (IN./FT) | WEIGHT (LB/SQ) | UNDERLAY | FASTENERS | COLOR AND TEXTURE | SIZE (IN.) L X W | BUTT THICKNESS | EXPOSURE DATA |
|---|---|---|---|---|---|---|---|---|---|---|
| Aluminum | California mission tile | Institutional, commercial, residential | 3 | 48 | One layer 30 lb asphalt saturated rag felt over plywood | Aluminum nails, screws | Tile red, Burnt red | 10 1/2 x 17, 5 x 14 | 30 gauge aluminum | 2 in. overlap |
| | Shake—shingle | Institutional, commercial, residential | 4 | 36–88 | One layer 30 lb felt over plywood | Anchor clip nailed | Various baked enamel finishes | 12 x 48 | Variable up to 1 3/16 in. | 12 in. |
| Porcelain enamel on aluminum | Individual American method | Institutional, commercial, residential | 3 | 225 | One layer 30 lb felt plus 18 in. felt strips between tile | Special sealing nails supplied with tile | Various finishes | 10 x 10 | Prefinish for tiles custom fabricated to fit roof | |

Walter H. Sobel, FAIA, & Associates; Chicago, Illinois

## CORRUGATED AND CRIMPED ROOFING

| TYPE | | SLOPE MIN. (IN./FT) | MAX. SPAN (IN.) | WEIGHT (LB/SQUARE) | SIZE | WEIGHT OR THICKNESS | EXPOSURE OR LAP | COLOR AND TEXTURE | FASTENER |
|---|---|---|---|---|---|---|---|---|---|
| Iron and steel or galvanized iron | 2.67" corrugations with ⅞, ¾, or ½" depth | 3 | 81-51[1] | Uncoated from 548 to 69. Coated from 568 to 90. Add approx. 10% for 3" corrugations | Width 34-⅝", 39-⅛", length 2-45' | Gauges 18-26 | 31½, 36", End lap 6" min. | Uncoated galvanized or several colors of coatings | Corrosion resistant self-tapping screws, bolts, welded studs, power driven fasteners or nails in wood. All use neoprene washers |
| Protected metal (steel)[3] | Corrugated sheet 2.67" corrugations with ¾ or ½" depth | (4) | 88-44[1] | From 244 to 147 | Width 33" length to 12' | Gauges 18-24 | 29-¾" wide. End lap 6" min. | Smooth black or several colors | Same as corrugated steel |
| | Mansard sheet, 6 beads per sheet | | | | Width 30" length to 12' | | | | |
| | V-beam sheet, 5.4" pitch and 1⅝" deep, 5 vees per sheet | | | From 278 to 167 | | | | | |
| Aluminum | Corrugated sheet, 2.67" corrugations, ⅞" depth | 3[6,7] | 77-55[1] 91-64 102-72 | 42 56 70 | Widths 35 or 48", length 3-39'[1] | 0.024 0.032 0.040 0.050 | 1½" corrugation side lap. 6" min. end lap. 1 vee side lap[6] | Plain mill or stucco in natural and various colors of baked-on or porcelain enamel | Same as for corrugated steel, except use aluminum nails and sheet metal screws |
| | Curved corrugated sheet, same corrugations[5] | | | 55.2 | Width 33¾", length 3-39'[1] | 0.032 | | | |
| | V-beam sheet, 4⅞" pitch and 1⅝" deep, top and bottom flats ¾" | | 130-92[1] 152-107 173-122 | 58.4 72.2 90.3 | Width 41⅝", length 3-39'[1] | 0.032 0.040 0.050 | | | |
| | Concealed clip panels (Reynolds Metals Co.)[7] | | | 68.9 86.1 107.7 | Width 13.35", length 3-39'[1] | 0.032 0.040 0.050 | Width 12", End lap 6" min. | Stucco only; same colors as above | Clips with sheets locked at side laps |
| Corrugated fiberglass, wire-reinforced plastic | 1¼" corrugations, ¼" deep | 3[6,7] | 40-22[2] | Approx. 40 | Width 26" (max. 50") length 4-39' | 5, 6, 8 oz/sq ft | 1, 1½ or 2 corrugation side lap. 6" min. end lap | Many colors, translucent opaque; or smooth or pebble finish. | Self-tapping screws, drive screws and nails. All with neoprene washers |
| | 2½" corrugations, ½" deep | | 65-32[2] | | Widths 26" (max. 50") length 4-39' | 4, 5, 6, 8, 10, 12 oz/sq ft | | | |
| | 4.2" corrugations, 1¹⁄₁₆" deep | | 72-50[2] | | Widths 42, 50⅜", length 4-39' | 5-12 oz/sq ft | | | |
| | 2.67" corrugations, ⅞" deep | | 70-42[2] | | Width 50", length 4-39' | 5-12 oz/sq ft | | | |
| | 5-V crimp, ½" deep | | 65-32[2] | | Width 26", length 4-39' | 5-8 oz/sq ft | | | |
| | 5.3-V crimp, 1" deep | | 84-60[2] | | Width 41⅝, 45", length 4-39' | 5-12 oz/sq ft | | | |
| Corrugated glass or plastic, nonreinforced plastic[9] | 2.67" corrugations, ⁹⁄₁₆" deep | 1 | 70-42[2] | Approx. 40 | Width 50½", length 8, 10, 12, 15, 20' | 5-8 oz/sq ft ¼" thick | 1 corrugation side lap, 8" min. end lap | Same as for reinforced plastic | Same as for reinforced plastic |

**NOTES**

1. For 20 to 40 psf.
2. For 15 to 40 psf.
3. For use in chemical atmospheres. Panels are made of steel core, with both sides covered by a dry film at least 4 mils thick. The film has a special liquid resin coating, which is fused under high heat to a special corrosion resistant bond coat over chemically treated galvanized steel.
4. Corrugated and mansard sheets may be used on 4 in. min. slope with laps unsealed and on 3 in. min. slope with laps sealed. V-beam sheets may be used on 3 in. min. slope with laps unsealed and on 1½ in. min. slope with laps sealed.
5. Minimum curvature radius 18 in.
6. Use 9 in. min. side laps on slopes from 2 to 3 in. Use 6 in. min. side laps on slopes above 3 in.
7. May be used on min. ½ in. slope only when one course used on slope. When more than one slope, the min. slope is 4 in.
8. Available in General Purpose, Type I, and Fire Retardant, Type II, except Type I has 5 oz weight only.
9. Used where economy and light weight are major considerations. Corrugated glass also available with installation requiring no side lap.

## INSULATION

Many roof panel systems are available with foamed-in-place insulation. Their applications are subject to temperature limitations and various building codes, however. Check codes and manufacturers' fire ratings. Certain applications of roofing systems can also be applied directly over fiberglass batts.

## VAPOR BARRIERS

To control a moderate level of relative humidity in living spaces, vapor resistant membranes must be utilized:

1. To control the moisture level within the structure.
2. To prevent moisture from passing through the insulation to a cold point where it can condense into water, possibly causing structural damage or rot. Provide condensate drainage.

Walter H. Sobel, FAIA, & Associates; Chicago, Illinois

## GENERAL INFORMATION

# WATER VAPOR MIGRATION

Water is present as vapor in indoor and outdoor air and as absorbed moisture in many building materials. Within the range of temperatures encountered in buildings water may exist in the liquid, vapor, or solid states. Moisture related problems may arise from changes in moisture content, from the presence of excessive moisture, or from the effects of changes of state such as freezing within wall insulation.

In the design and construction of buildings the behavior of moisture must be considered, including particularly the change from vapor to liquid (condensation). Such problems generally arise when moisture in relatively humid indoor air comes in contact with a cold surface such as a window or when the moisture migrates under the influence of vapor pressure differences through walls to enter a region of relatively low temperature where condensation can occur.

Moisture problems in residences generally occur in winter when the outdoor temperature and vapor pressure are low and there are many indoor vapor sources. These may include cooking, laundering, bathing, breathing, and perspiration from the occupants, as well as automatic washers and driers, dishwashers and humidifiers. All of these sources combine to cause vapor pressure indoors to be much higher than outdoors, so that the vapor tends to migrate outward through the building envelope. Vapor cannot permeate glazed windows or metal doors, but most other building materials are permeable to some extent. Walls are particularly susceptible to this phenomenon, and such migration must be prevented or at least minimized by the use of low permeability membranes known as vapor barriers, which should be installed as close as possible to the indoor surface of the building.

Water vapor migration is relatively independent of air motion within the building, since such migration depends primarily on vapor pressure differences. Migration always takes place from regions of higher vapor pressure toward spaces such as wall cavities where the vapor pressure will be lower. When surfaces below the local dewpoint temperature are encountered, condensation will occur and moisture droplets will form. If the local drybulb temperature is at or below 32°F, freezing will occur, which may lead to permanent structural damage.

Moisture in building materials usually increases their thermal conductance to a significant and unpredictable extent. Porous materials that become saturated with moisture lose most of their insulating capability and may not regain it when they dry out. Dust, which usually settles in airspaces, may become permanently affixed to originally reflective surfaces. Moisture migration by evaporation, vapor flow, and condensation can transport significant quantities of latent heat, particularly through fibrous insulating materials.

Positive steps should be taken to prevent migration of moisture in the form of vapor and accumulation in the form of water or ice within building components. Vapor barriers, correctly located near the source of the moisture, are the most effective means of preventing such migration. Venting of moisture laden air from bathrooms, laundry rooms, and kitchens will reduce indoor vapor pressure, as will the introduction of outdoor air with low moisture content.

## BUILDING SECTION ANALYSIS FOR POTENTIAL CONDENSATION

Any building section may be analyzed by simple calculations to determine where condensation might occur and what might be done in selecting materials or their method of assembly to eliminate that possibility. The section may or may not contain a vapor barrier or it may contain a relatively imperfect barrier; the building section may include cold side materials of comparatively high resistance to the passage of vapor (which is highly undesirable and is to be avoided). With few exceptions, the vapor resistance at or near the warm surface should be five times that of any components. The table above gives permeances and permeability of building and vapor barrier materials. These values can be used in analyzing building sections by the following simple method:

- List the materials, without surface films or airspaces, in the order of their appearance in the building section, beginning with the inside surface material and working to the outside.
- Against each material list the permeance (or permeability) value from the table or a more accurate value if available from tests or manufacturers' data.

Where a range is given, select an average value or use judgment in assigning a value based on the character and potential installation method of the material proposed for use.

- Start at the top of the list and note any material that has less permeance than the materials above it on the list. At that point the possibility exists that vapor leaking through the first material may condense on the second, provided the dew point (condensation point) is reached and the movement is considerable. In that case, provide ventilation through the cold side material or modify the design to eliminate or change the material to one of greater permeance.

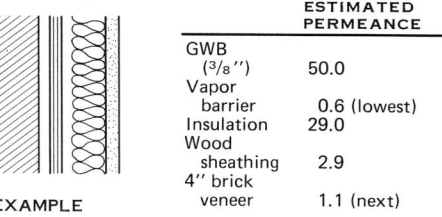

| | ESTIMATED PERMEANCE |
|---|---|
| GWB (3/8'') | 50.0 |
| Vapor barrier | 0.6 (lowest) |
| Insulation | 29.0 |
| Wood sheathing | 2.9 |
| 4'' brick veneer | 1.1 (next) |

**EXAMPLE**

In this example the vapor barrier transmits 1 grain of moisture per square foot per hour for each unit of vapor pressure difference, and nothing else transmits less. However, since the cold brick veneer is nearly as low in permeance it is advisable to make certain that the vapor barrier is expertly installed, with all openings at pipes and with outlet boxes or joints carefully fitted or sealed. Alternatively, the brick veneer may have open mortar joints near the top and bottom to serve both as weep holes and as vapor release openings. They will also ventilate the wall and help to reduce heat gain in summer.

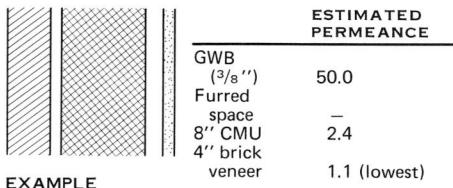

| | ESTIMATED PERMEANCE |
|---|---|
| GWB (3/8'') | 50.0 |
| Furred space | — |
| 8'' CMU | 2.4 |
| 4'' brick veneer | 1.1 (lowest) |

**EXAMPLE**

Vapor (under pressure) would easily pass through the interior finish, be slowed up by the concrete masonry unit, and be nearly stopped by the cold brick veneer. Unless this design is radically improved, the masonry will become saturated and may cause serious water stains or apparent "leaks" in cold weather. In addition, alternating freezing and thawing of condensation within the masonry wall can physically damage the construction.

## PERMEANCE AND PERMEABILITY OF MATERIALS TO WATER VAPOR

| MATERIAL | PERMEANCE (PERM) | MATERIAL | PERMEANCE (PERM) |
|---|---|---|---|
| **MATERIALS USED IN CONSTRUCTION** | | **BUILDING PAPERS, FELTS, ROOFING PAPERS[3]** | |
| Concrete (1:2:4 mix) | 3.2[5] | Duplex sheet, asphalt laminated, aluminum foil one side (43)[4] | 0.176 |
| Brick-masonry (4 in. thick) | 0.8-1.1 | Saturated and coated roll roofing (326)[4] | 0.24 |
| Concrete masonry (8 in. cored, limestone aggregate) | 2.4 | Kraft paper and asphalt laminated, reinforced 30-120-30 (34)[4] | 1.8 |
| Plaster on metal lath (3/4 in.) | 15 | Asphalt-saturated, coated vapor-barrier paper (43)[4] | 0.6 |
| Plaster on plain gypsum lath (with studs) | 20 | Asphalt-saturated, not coated sheathing paper (22)[4] | 20.2 |
| Gypsum wallboard (3/8 in. plain) | 50 | 15-lb asphalt felt (70)[4] | 5.6 |
| Structural insulating board (sheathing quality) | 20-50[5] | 15-lb tar felt (70)[4] | 18.2 |
| Structural insulating board (interior, uncoated, 1/2 in.) | 50-90 | Single kraft, double infused (16)[4] | 42 |
| Hardboard (1/8 in. standard) | 11 | | |
| Hardboard (1/8 in. tempered) | 5 | **LIQUID APPLIED COATING MATERIALS** | |
| Built-up roofing (hot mopped) | 0.0 | | |
| Wood, fir sheathing, 3/4 in. | 2.9 | Paint—two coats | |
| Plywood (Douglas fir, exterior glue, 1/4 in.) | 0.7 | Aluminum varnish on wood | 0.3-0.5 |
| Plywood (Douglas fir, interior, glue, 1/4 in.) | 1.9 | Enamels on smooth plaster | 0.5-1.5 |
| Acrylic, glass fiber reinforced sheet, 56 mil | 0.12 | Primers and sealers on interior insulation board | 0.9-2.1 |
| Polyester, glass fiber reinforced sheet, 48 mil | 0.05 | Miscellaneous primers plus one coat flat oil paint on plastic | 1.6-3.0 |
| | | Flat paint on interior insulation board | 4 |
| | | Water emulsion on interior insulation board | 30-85 |
| **THERMAL INSULATIONS** | | Paint—three coats | |
| Cellular glass | 0.0[5] | Exterior paint, white lead and oil on wood siding | 0.3-1.0 |
| Mineral wool, unprotected | 29.0 | Exterior paint, white lead-zinc oxide and oil on wood | 0.9 |
| Expanded polyurethane (R-11 blown) | 0.4-1.6[5] | Styrene-butadiene latex coating, 2 oz/sq ft | 11 |
| Expanded polystyrene—extruded | 1.2[5] | Polyvinyl acetate latex coating, 4 oz/sq ft | 5.5 |
| Expanded polystyrene—bead | 2.0-5.8[5] | | |
| | | Asphalt cutback bastic | |
| **PLASTIC AND METAL FOILS AND FILMS[2]** | | 1/16 in. dry | 0.14 |
| | | 3/16 in. dry | 0.0 |
| Aluminum foil (1 mil) | 0.0 | Hot melt asphalt | |
| Polyethylene (4 mil) | 0.08 | 2 oz/sq ft | 0.5 |
| Polyethylene (6 mil) | 0.06 | 3.5 oz/sq ft | 0.1 |
| Polyethylene (8 mil) | 0.04 | | |
| Polyester (1 mil) | 0.7 | | |
| Polyvinylchloride, unplasticized (2 mil) | 0.68 | | |
| Polyvinylchloride, plasticized (4 mil) | 0.8-1.4 | | |

**NOTES**

1. The vapor transmission rates listed will permit comparisons of materials, but selection of vapor barrier materials should be based on rates obtained from the manufacturer or from laboratory tests. The range of values shown indicates variation among mean values for materials that are similar but of different density. Values are intended for design guidance only.

2. Usually installed as vapor barriers. If used as exterior finish and elsewhere near cold side, special considerations are required.

3. Low permeance sheets used as vapor barriers. High permeance use elsewhere in construction.

4. Bases (weight in lb/500 sq ft).

5. Permeability (PERM-in.).

Based on data from "ASHRAE Handbook of Fundamentals," 1981, Chapter 20.

Owen J. Delevante, AIA; Glen Rock, New Jersey
E. C. Shuman, P.E.; Consulting Engineer; State College, Pennsylvania

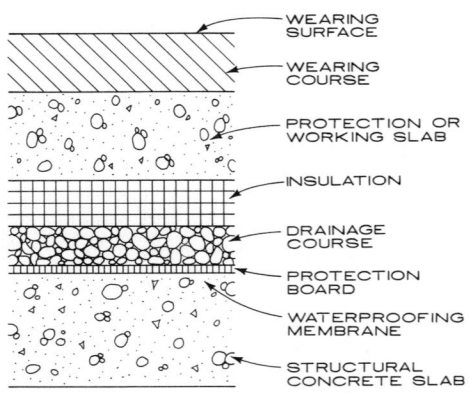

WEARING SURFACE
WEARING COURSE
PROTECTION OR WORKING SLAB
INSULATION
DRAINAGE COURSE
PROTECTION BOARD
WATERPROOFING MEMBRANE
STRUCTURAL CONCRETE SLAB

## BASIC COMPONENTS OF WATERPROOFING SYSTEMS

### GENERAL

The basic components, subsystems, and features for a building deck waterproofing system are the structural building deck or substrate to be waterproofed, waterproofing membrane, protection of membrane, drainage, insulation, and wearing course. See following pages for generic membrane applications.

### SUBSTRATE

The substrate referred to is reinforced cast-in-place structural concrete. Precast concrete slabs pose more technical problems than cast-in-place concrete and the probability of lasting watertightness is greatly diminished and difficult to achieve because of the multitude of joints which have the capability of movement and must be treated accordingly.

The concrete used for the substrate should have a minimum density of 1762 kg/m³ (110 lb/ft³) and have a maximum moisture content of 8% when cured.

### SLOPE FOR DRAINAGE

A monolithic concrete substrate slope of a minimum 11 mm/m (⅛ in./ft) should be maintained. Slope is best achieved with a monolithic structural slab and not with a separate concrete fill layer.

### MEMBRANE

Detection of leakage can be a significant problem when the membrane is not bonded to the structural slab or when additional layers of materials separate it from the structural slab. Therefore, only membranes that can be bonded to the substrate should be used.

The membrane should be applied under dry, frost-free conditions on the surface as well as throughout the depth of the concrete slab.

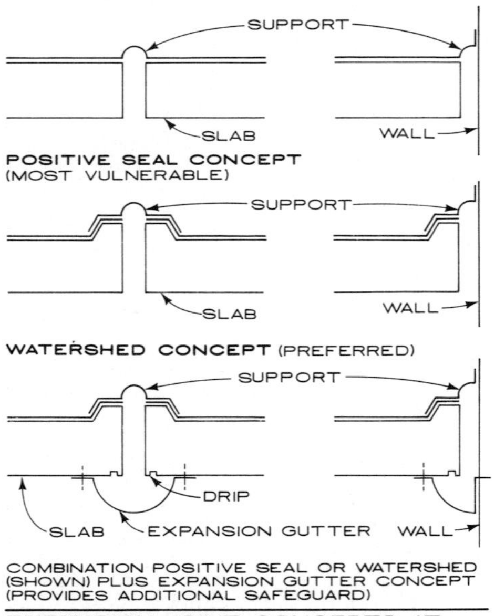

When the membrane is turned up on a wall, it is preferable to terminate it above the wearing surface to eliminate the possibility of ponded surface water penetrating the wall above the membrane and running down behind it into the building.

Penetrations should be avoided wherever possible. For protection at such critical locations, pipe sleeves should be cast into the structural slab against which the membrane can be terminated.

Treatment at reinforced and nonreinforced joints depends on the membrane used. See following pages.

There are basically two concepts that could be considered in the detailing of expansion joints at the membrane level. These are the positive seal concept directly at the membrane level and the watershed concept with the seal at a higher lever than the membrane. Where additional safeguards are desired, a drainage gutter under the joint could be considered. Flexible support of the membrane is required in each case. Expansion joint details should be considered and used in accordance with their movement capability.

The positive seal concept entails a greater risk than the watershed concept, since it relies fully on positive seal joinery of materials at the membrane level, where the membrane is most vulnerable to water penetration. Since the precision required is not always attainable, this concept is best avoided.

The watershed concept, although requiring a greater height and more costly concrete forming, is superior in safeguarding against leakage, having the advantage of providing a water dam at the membrane level. However, if a head of water rises to the height of the materials joinery, this concept becomes almost as vulnerable as the positive seal concept. Therefore, drainage is recommended at the membrane level.

### PROTECTION BOARD

The membrane should be protected from damage prior to and during the remainder of construction. Protection board should be applied after the membrane is installed. The proper timing of application after placement of the membrane is important and could vary with the type of membrane used. The manufacturer's printed instructions should be followed.

### DRAINAGE SYSTEM

Drainage should be considered as a total system from the wearing surface down to the membrane, including use of multilevel drains.

Drainage at the wearing surface is generally accomplished in one of two ways:

1. By an open joint and pedestal system permitting most of the rainwater to penetrate rapidly down to the membrane level and subsurface drainage system, and

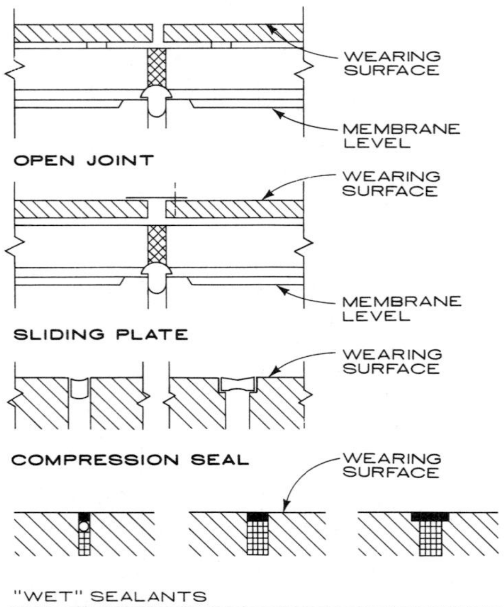

2. By a closed-joint system designed to remove most of the rainwater rapidly by slope to surface drains and to allow a minor portion to infiltrate to membrane.

A drainage course of washed, round gravel should be provided above the protection board, over the membrane. This permits water to filter to the drain and provides a place where it can collect and freeze without potential damage to the wearing course.

### INSULATION

When required, insulation should be located above the membrane, but not in direct contact with it.

### PROTECTION OR WORKING SLAB

A concrete slab could be placed soon after the membrane, protection board, drainage course, and insulation, if required, have been installed. It would serve as protection for the permanent waterproofing materials and insulation below, provide a working platform for construction traffic and storage of materials (within weight limits), and provide a substantial substrate for the placement of the finish wearing course materials near the completion of the project.

### WEARING COURSE

The major requirements for the wearing course are a stable support of sufficient strength, resistance against lateral thrust, adequate drainage to avoid ponding of water, and proper treatment of joints.

Joints in which movement is anticipated should be treated as expansion joints.

Various proprietary compression seals are available that can be inserted into a formed joint under compression. Most of these, however, are not flush at the top surface and could fill up with sand or dirt.

Wet sealants are the materials most commonly used in moving joints at the wearing surface level. Dimension A is the design width dimension or the dimension at which the joint will be formed. The criterion normally used for determining this dimension with sealants capable of ±25% movement is to multiply the maximum expected movement in one direction by 4. Generally, this is expected to be about three-fourths of the total anticipated joint movement, but if there is any doubt, multiply the total anticipated joint movement by 4. It is better to have the joint too wide than too narrow. Dimension B (sealant depth) is related to dimension A and is best established by the sealant manufacturer. Generally, B is equal to A for widths up to 13 mm (½ in.), 15 mm (⁹⁄₁₆ in.) for a 16 mm (⅝ in.) width, and 16 mm (⅝ in.) for 19 mm (¾ in.) and greater widths. This allows some tolerance for self-leveling sealants.

Reference: ASTM C 898 and C 981. Highlights of text and figures are reprinted with permission from ASTM Committee C-24 of the American Society for Testing Materials.

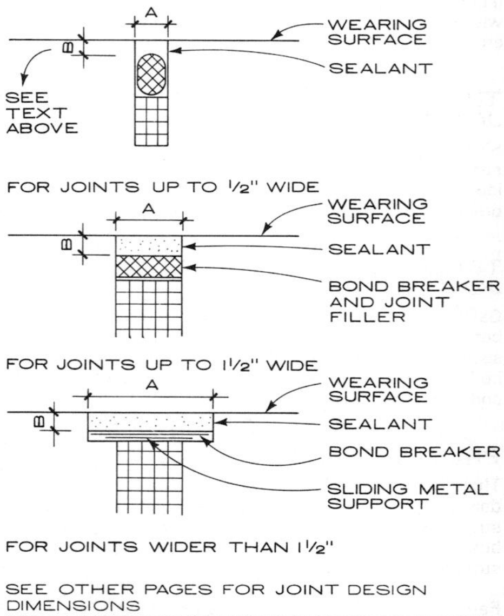

---

SUPPORT
SLAB    WALL

**POSITIVE SEAL CONCEPT** (MOST VULNERABLE)

SUPPORT
SLAB    WALL

**WATERSHED CONCEPT** (PREFERRED)

SUPPORT
DRIP
SLAB    EXPANSION GUTTER    WALL

COMBINATION POSITIVE SEAL OR WATERSHED (SHOWN) PLUS EXPANSION GUTTER CONCEPT (PROVIDES ADDITIONAL SAFEGUARD)

### EXPANSION JOINT CONCEPTS AT MEMBRANE LEVEL

---

WEARING SURFACE
MEMBRANE LEVEL

**OPEN JOINT**

WEARING SURFACE
MEMBRANE LEVEL

**SLIDING PLATE**

WEARING SURFACE

**COMPRESSION SEAL**

WEARING SURFACE

"WET" SEALANTS

### EXPANSION JOINT CONCEPTS AT WEARING SURFACE LEVEL

---

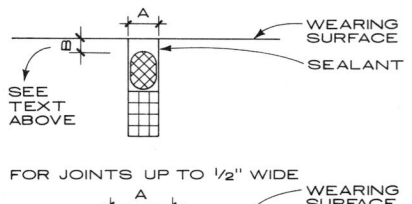

A
WEARING SURFACE
SEALANT
SEE TEXT ABOVE

FOR JOINTS UP TO ½" WIDE

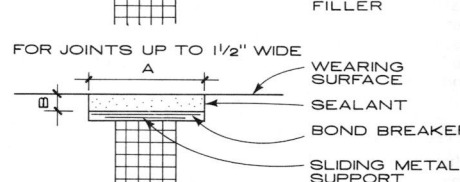

A
WEARING SURFACE
SEALANT
BOND BREAKER AND JOINT FILLER

FOR JOINTS UP TO 1½" WIDE

A
WEARING SURFACE
SEALANT
BOND BREAKER
SLIDING METAL SUPPORT

FOR JOINTS WIDER THAN 1½"

SEE OTHER PAGES FOR JOINT DESIGN DIMENSIONS

### WET SEALANT DETAILS AT WEARING SURFACE

---

Charles J. Parise, FAIA, FASTM; Smith, Hinchman & Grylls Associates, Inc.; Detroit, Michigan

## SUBSTRATE

The building deck or substrate referred to is reinforced cast-in-place structural concrete.

Polymeric, latex, or other organic chemical-based admixtures or modifiers can coat the concrete particles and reduce the ability of the membrane to bond to the substrate. Admixtures should not be used in the concrete unless determined that they are acceptable for use with the membrane.

The underside of the concrete deck should not have an impermeable barrier. A metal liner or coating that forms a vapor barrier on the underside traps moisture in the concrete and destroys or prevents the adhesive bond of the membrane to the upper surface of the concrete.

The surface should be of sufficiently rough texture to provide a mechanical bond for the membrane, but not so rough as to preclude achieving continuity of the membrane of the specified thickness across the surface.

The concrete should be cured a minimum of 7 days and aged a minimum of 28 days, including curing time, before application of the liquid-applied membrane. Curing is accomplished chemically with moisture and should not be construed as drying. Liquid or chemical curing compounds should not be used unless approved by the manufacturer of the liquid-applied membrane as the material may interfere with the bond of the membrane to the structural slab.

## MEMBRANE

The membrane should be applied under dry, frost-free conditions on the surface as well as throughout the depth of the concrete slab. Use manufacturer's requirements for the particular membrane.

## TERMINATION ON WALLS

A liquid-applied membrane, because of its inherent adhesive properties, may be terminated flush on the wall without the use of a reglet. However, the use of a reglet in a concrete wall has the advantage of providing greater depth protection at the terminal.

## TERMINATION AT DRAINS

Drains should be designed with a wide flange or base as an integral part. The drain base should be set flush with the structural slab.

## TREATMENT AT REINFORCED JOINTS

One recommended treatment of reinforced concrete joints in the structural slab is to apply a double layer of membrane over the crack. This type of detail is quite limited and implicitly relies on the membrane's crack-bridging ability. An alternative approach is to prevent the membrane from adhering to the substrate for a finite width centered on the joint or crack by means of a properly designed compatible bond-breaker tape.

## TREATMENT AT NONREINFORCED JOINTS

Since the joints are not held together with reinforcing steel, some movement, however slight, should be anticipated and provided for, since the liquid-applied membrane has limited ability to take movement.

## TREATMENT AT EXPANSION JOINTS

Gaskets and flexible preformed sheets lend themselves better to absorbing large amounts of movement. Since such materials, when used at an expansion joint, must be joined to the liquid-applied membrane, the watershed concept should be used.

## PROTECTION BOARD

The liquid-applied membrane should be protected from damage prior to and during the remainder of deck construction. The proper timing of the application of the board is important and the manufacturer's printed instructions should be followed.

Reference: ASTM C 898. Highlights of text and figures are reprinted with permission from ASTM Committee C-24 of the American Society for Testing and Materials.

Charles J. Parise, FAIA, FASTM; Smith, Hinchman & Grylls Associates, Inc.; Detroit, Michigan

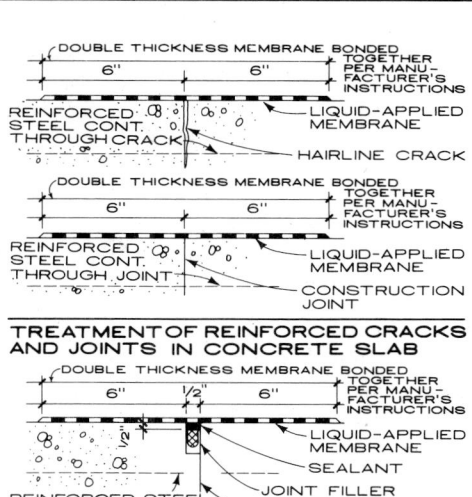

**TREATMENT OF REINFORCED CRACKS AND JOINTS IN CONCRETE SLAB**

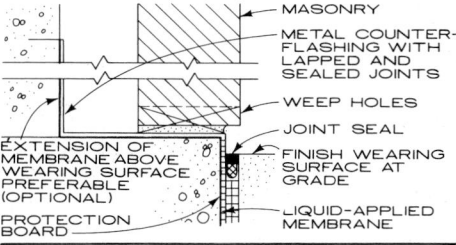

**TREATMENT OF NONREINFORCED BUTTED JOINT IN CONCRETE SLAB**

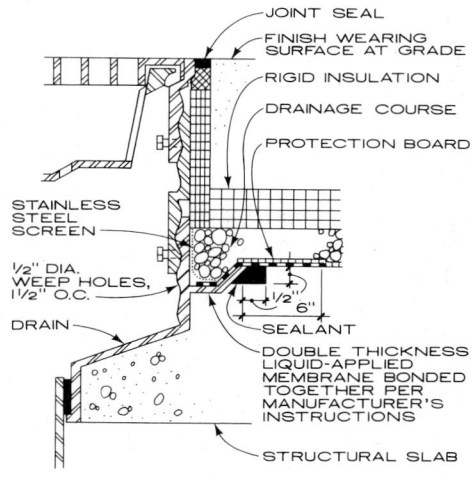

**TERMINAL CONDITION WITH MASONRY ABOVE FINISH WEARING SURFACE AT GRADE**

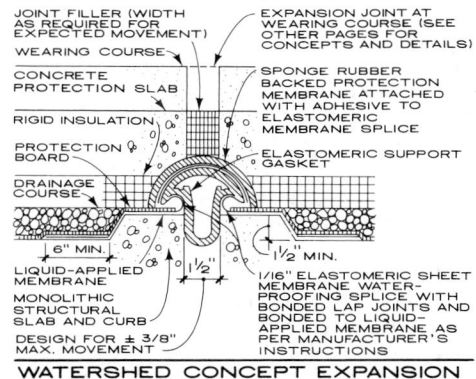

**WATERSHED CONCEPT EXPANSION JOINT**

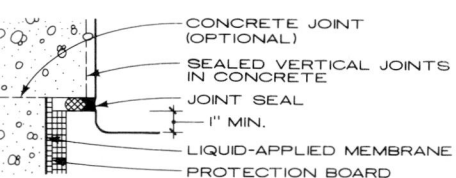

**TERMINAL CONDITION ABOVE FINISH GRADE ON CONCRETE WALL**

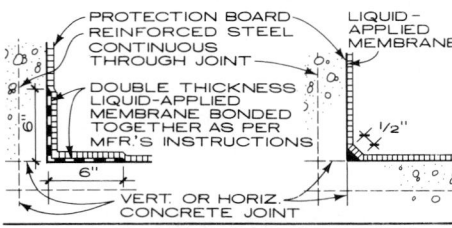

**TURNUP DETAILS AT REINFORCED JOINT**

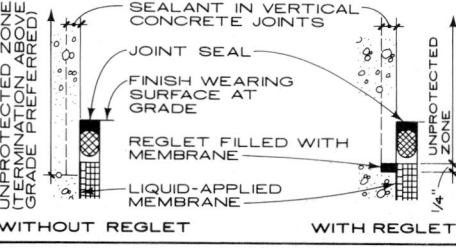

**TERMINAL CONDITIONS ON CONCRETE WALL BELOW FINISH WEARING SURFACE AT GRADE**

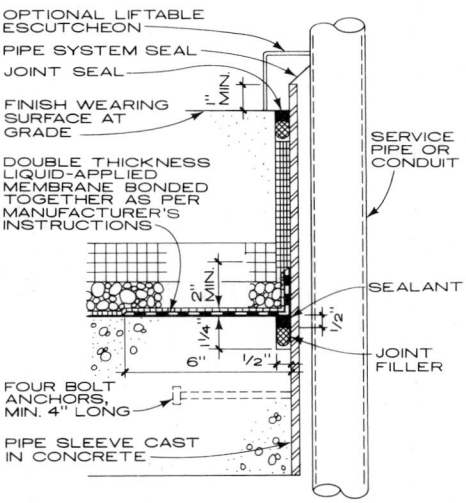

**TERMINATION AT PIPE PENETRATIONS**

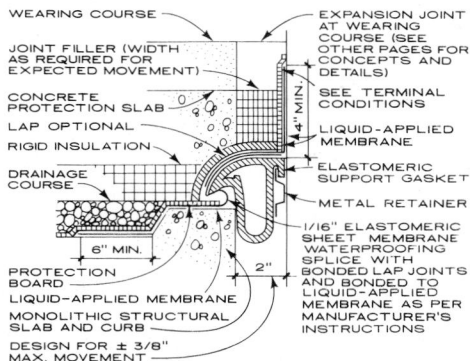

**WATERSHED CONCEPT EXPANSION JOINT**

## SUBSTRATE

The building deck or substrate referred to is reinforced cast-in-place structural concrete.

The structural slab should have a finish of sufficiently rough texture to provide a mechanical bond for the membrane, but not so rough to preclude achieving continuity of the membrane across the surface.

The concrete should be cured a minimum of 7 days and aged a minimum of 28 days, including curing time, before application of the bituminous membrane. Curing is accomplished chemically with moisture and should not be construed as drying. Liquid or chemical curing compounds should not be used unless approved by the manufacturer of the built-up bituminous membrane as the material may interfere with the bond of the membrane to the structural slab.

## MEMBRANE

A built-up bituminous waterproofing membrane consists of components joined together and bonded to its substrate at the site. The major membrane components include primers, bitumens, reinforcements, and flashing materials.

Surfaces to receive waterproofing must be clean, dry, reasonably smooth, and free of dust, dirt, voids, cracks, laitance, or sharp projections before application of materials.

Concrete surfaces should be uniformly primed to enhance the bond between the membrane and the substrate, so as to inhibit lateral movement of water.

The number of plies of membrane reinforcement required is dependent upon the head of water and strength required by the design function of the wearing surface. Plaza deck membranes should be composed of not less than three plies. The composition of the membrane is normally of a "shingle" or "ply-on-ply" (phased) construction.

For application temperatures, follow the recommendations of the manufacturers of the membrane materials.

Over reinforced structural slab joints, one ply of 6-in.-wide membrane reinforcement should be applied before application of the bituminous membrane.

Nonreinforced joints should receive a bead of compatible sealant in a recessed joint before application of the membrane.

At expansion joints, gaskets and flexible preformed sheets are required inasmuch as bituminous membranes have little or no movement capability. Since such materials must be joined to the bituminous membrane, the watershed concept should be used.

Reinforce all intersections with walls and corners with two layers of woven fabric embedded in hot bitumen.

Flashing membranes should extend above the wearing surface and the highest possible water level and not less than 150 mm (6 in.) onto the deck membrane.

The flashing should extend over the wall dampproofing or membrane waterproofing not less than 100 mm (4 in.).

Drains must be provided with a wide metal flange or base and set slightly below the drainage level. Metal flashing for the drain, if required, and the clamping ring should be set on the membrane in bituminous plastic cement. The metal flashing should be stripped in with a minimum of two plies of membrane reinforcement and three applications of bituminous plastic cement.

Penetrations through the membrane such as conduits and pipes should be avoided whenever possible. Penetrations must be flashed to a height above the anticipated water table that may extend above the wearing surface.

The built-up bituminous membrane should be protected from damage. Protection board should be placed on the waterproofing membrane when the final mopping is being placed. It will then be adhered to the membrane.

Reference: ASTM C 981. Highlights of text and figures are reprinted with permission from ASTM Committee C-24 of the American Society for Testing and Materials.

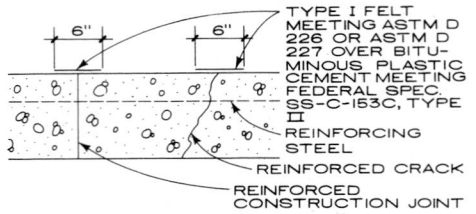

**TREATMENT AT REINFORCED JOINTS**

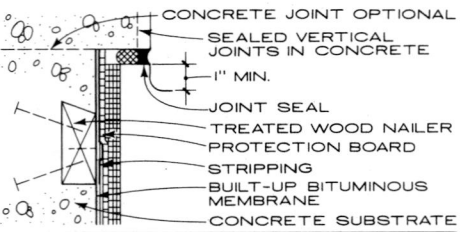

**TERMINAL CONDITION ABOVE FINISH GRADE ON CONCRETE WALL**

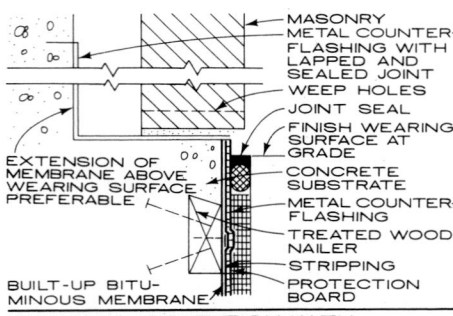

**TERMINAL CONDITION WITH MASONRY ABOVE FINISH WEARING SURFACE AT GRADE**

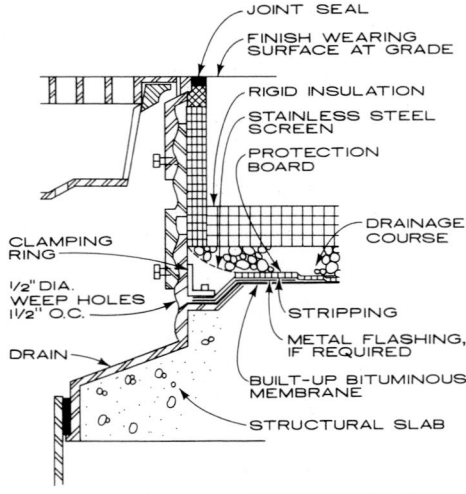

**TERMINATION AT DRAIN**

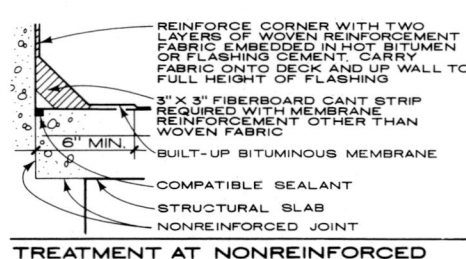

**TREATMENT AT NONREINFORCED JOINTS**

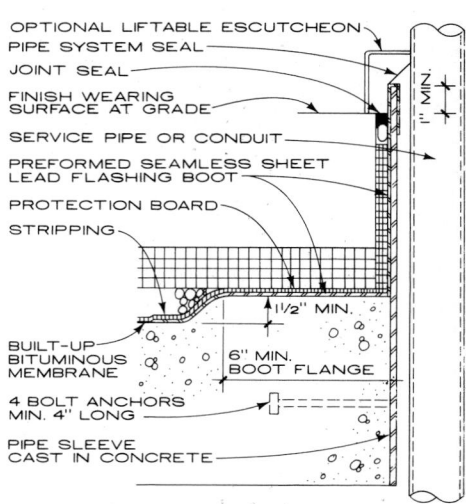

**TERMINAL CONDITIONS ON CONCRETE WALL BELOW FINISH WEARING SURFACE AT GRADE**

**TERMINATION AT PIPE PENETRATIONS**

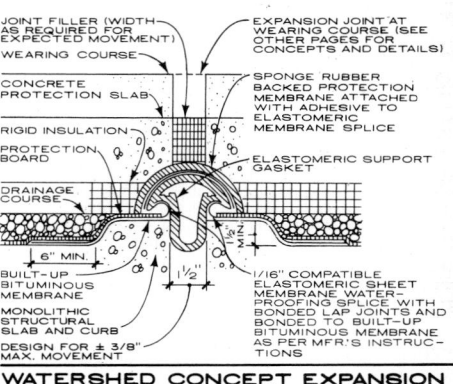

**WATERSHED CONCEPT EXPANSION JOINT**

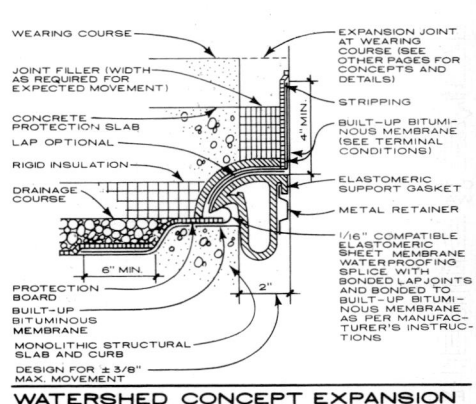

**WATERSHED CONCEPT EXPANSION JOINT**

Charles J. Parise, FAIA, FASTM; Smith, Hinchman & Grylls Associates, Inc.; Detroit, Michigan

**NOTES**

1. Consult a soils engineer to determine soil types and groundwater levels and their effect on selection of drainage and waterproofing methods.

2. Most membranes require a stable, rigid, and level substrate for their application. Generally a subslab (mudslab) is used when the membrane is below the structural slab. When placed on the structural slab, a protective cover, such as another concrete slab, is required.

3. Bentonite panels may be placed over level, well-compacted fill. Cover them with polyethylene film to prevent premature expansion from wet concrete placed over them. Note: Bentonite forms an impermeable barrier when confined by foundation backfill or by lagging or sheet piling. The material may swell, exerting pressure on adjacent construction. Consult with structural engineer and manufacturer to assure appropriate use and structural adequacy.

4. Protect the water-resistant membrane during construction and backfill operations by covering it with a protection course of parging or solid sheets of protection boards.

5. Some drainage membranes or composites may also serve as the protection course.

6. Footing drains recommended when groundwater level may rise above top of floor slab or when subject to hydrostatic pressure after heavy rain. The drainage composite conveys water to the drain, thus reducing hydrostatic pressure.

7. Water-resistant membrane of interior face of foundation wall only recommended when outside is not accessible.

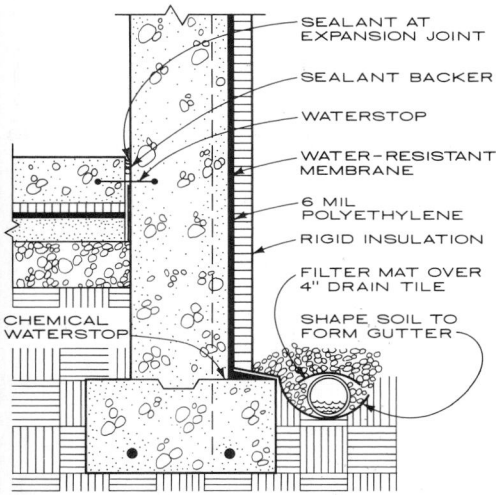

**FOOTING WATER RESISTANCE – TYPE 1**

- SEALANT AT EXPANSION JOINT
- SEALANT BACKER
- WATERSTOP
- WATER-RESISTANT MEMBRANE
- 6 MIL POLYETHYLENE
- RIGID INSULATION
- FILTER MAT OVER 4" DRAIN TILE
- SHAPE SOIL TO FORM GUTTER
- CHEMICAL WATERSTOP

**FOUNDATION CONDITIONS**

- KEY WATERSTOP
- WATER-RESISTANT BENTONITE
- DRAINAGE MEMBRANE
- SHEET PILING
- NEOPRENE WATERSTOP
- MUDSLAB
- WATER-RESISTANT MEMBRANE
- PROTECTION BOARD
- CONCRETE SLAB

**WATER RESISTANCE APPLICATIONS**

- KEY WATERSTOP
- WATER-RESISTANT BENTONITE
- DRAINAGE MEMBRANE
- TIMBER LAGGING
- WATER-RESISTANT MEMBRANE
- DRAINAGE MEMBRANE
- PROTECTION BOARD
- DRAIN TILE
- GRAVEL DRAIN BACKFILL
- FILTER FABRIC

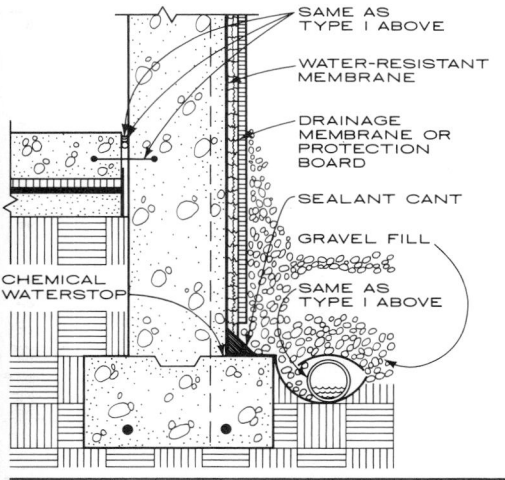

**FOOTING WATER RESISTANCE – TYPE 2**

- SAME AS TYPE 1 ABOVE
- WATER-RESISTANT MEMBRANE
- DRAINAGE MEMBRANE OR PROTECTION BOARD
- SEALANT CANT
- GRAVEL FILL
- SAME AS TYPE 1 ABOVE
- CHEMICAL WATERSTOP

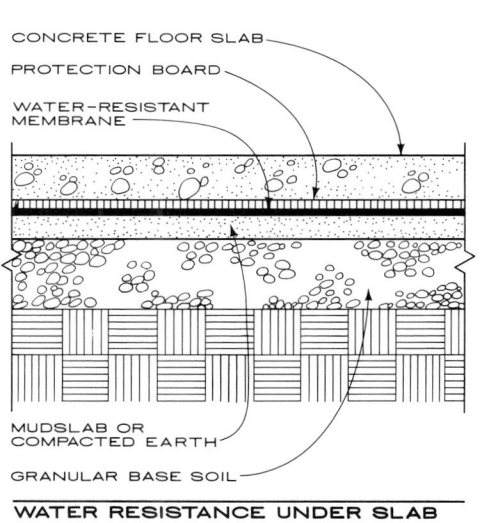

**WATER RESISTANCE UNDER SLAB**

- CONCRETE FLOOR SLAB
- PROTECTION BOARD
- WATER-RESISTANT MEMBRANE
- MUDSLAB OR COMPACTED EARTH
- GRANULAR BASE SOIL

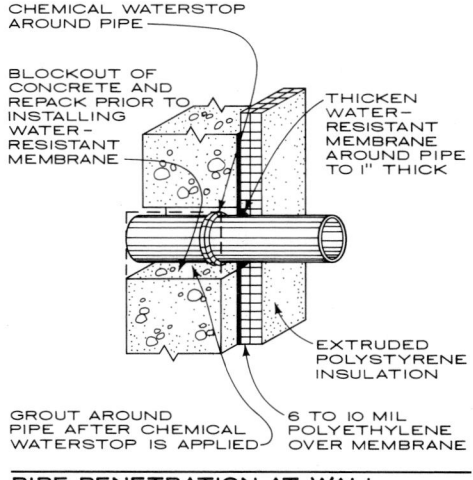

**PIPE PENETRATION AT WALL**

- CHEMICAL WATERSTOP AROUND PIPE
- BLOCKOUT OF CONCRETE AND REPACK PRIOR TO INSTALLING WATER-RESISTANT MEMBRANE
- THICKEN WATER-RESISTANT MEMBRANE AROUND PIPE TO 1" THICK
- EXTRUDED POLYSTYRENE INSULATION
- 6 TO 10 MIL POLYETHYLENE OVER MEMBRANE
- GROUT AROUND PIPE AFTER CHEMICAL WATERSTOP IS APPLIED

Krommenhoek/McKeown & Associates; San Diego, California

## RED CEDAR HANDSPLIT SHAKES

| GRADE | LENGTH AND THICKNESS | DESCRIPTION |
|---|---|---|
| No. 1 handsplit and resawn | 15" starter-finish<br>18 x ½" medium<br>18 x ¾" heavy<br>24 x ⅜" medium<br>24 x ½" medium<br>24 x ¾" heavy | These shakes have split faces and sawn backs. Cedar logs are first cut into desired lengths. Blanks or boards of proper thickness are split and then run diagonally through a bandsaw to produce two tapered shakes from each blank |
| No. 1 tapersplit | 24 x ½" | Produced largely by hand, using a sharp bladed steel froe and a wooden mallet. The natural shinglelike taper is achieved by reversing the block, end-for-end, with each split |
| No. 1 straight | 18 x ⅜" side wall<br>18 x ⅜"<br>24 x ⅜" | Produced in the same manner as tapersplit shakes except that by splitting from the same end of the block, the shakes acquire the same thickness throughout |

## RED CEDAR SHINGLES

| | NO. 1 BLUE LABEL* | | | NO. 2 RED LABEL† | | | NO. 3 BLACK LABEL‡ | | |
|---|---|---|---|---|---|---|---|---|---|
| | MAXIMUM EXPOSURE RECOMMENDED FOR ROOFS | | | | | | | | |
| ROOF PITCH | 16" | 18" | 24" | 16" | 18" | 24" | 16" | 18" | 24" |
| 3 in 12 to 4 in 12 | 3¾" | 4¼" | 5¾" | 3½" | 4" | 5½" | 3" | 3½" | 5" |
| 4 in 12 and steeper | 5" | 5½" | 7½" | 4" | 4½" | 6½" | 3½" | 4" | 5½" |

*Premium Grade: 100% heartwood, 100% clear, 100% edge grain, for highest quality.
†Intermediate Grade: not less then 10" clear on 16" shingles, 11" clear on 18" shingles, 16" clear on 24" shingles. Flat grain and limited sapwood permitted.
‡Utility Grade: 6" clear on 16" and 18" shingles, 10" clear on 24" shingles. For economy applications.

## UNDERLAYMENT AND SHEATHING

| ROOFING TYPE | SHEATHING | UNDERLAYMENT | NORMAL SLOPE | | LOW SLOPE | |
|---|---|---|---|---|---|---|
| Wood shakes and shingles | Solid or spaced | No. 30 asphalt saturated felt (interlayment) | 4 in 12 and up | Underlayment starter course; interlayment over entire roof | 3 in 12 to 4 in 12 | Single layer underlayment over entire roof; interlayment over entire roof |

### NOTES
1. Shakes not recommended on slopes less than 4 in 12.
2. Breathing type building paper—such as deadening felt—may be applied over either type of sheating, although paper is not used in most applications.

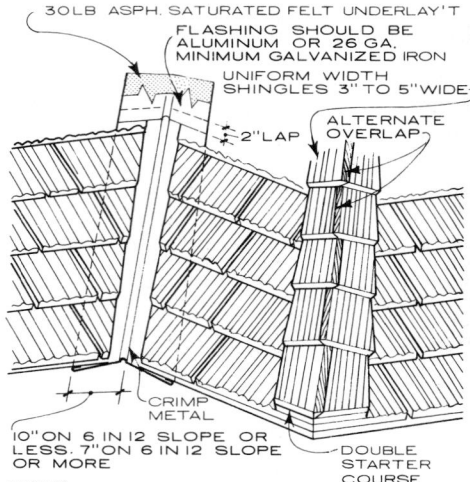

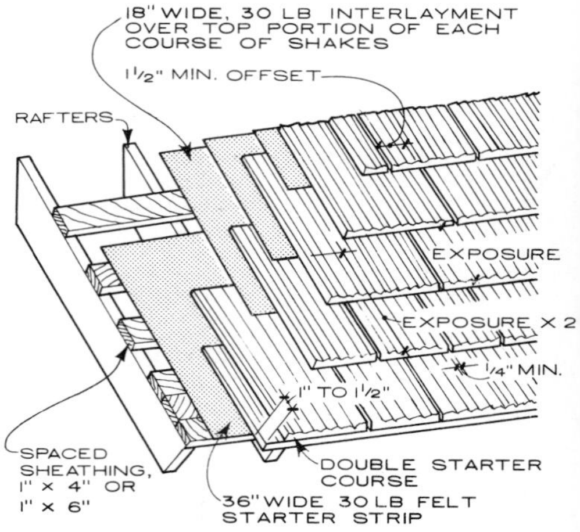

INSTALLATION OF SHAKES OVER SPACED SHEATHING ( 4 IN 12 MIN.)

VALLEY HIP AND RIDGE APPLICATION OF SHAKES AND SHINGLES

**NOTE**
Copper flashing should not be used with red cedar.

---

## SHINGLES AND SHAKES USED FOR ROOFING

### EXPOSURE FOR SHINGLES AND SHAKES USED FOR SIDING

| SHINGLE LENGTH | EXPOSURE OF SHINGLES | |
|---|---|---|
| | SGL. COURSE | DBL. COURSE |
| 16" | 6" TO 7½" | 8" TO 12" |
| 18" | 6" TO 8½" | 9" TO 14" |
| 24" | 8" TO 11½" | 12" TO 20" |

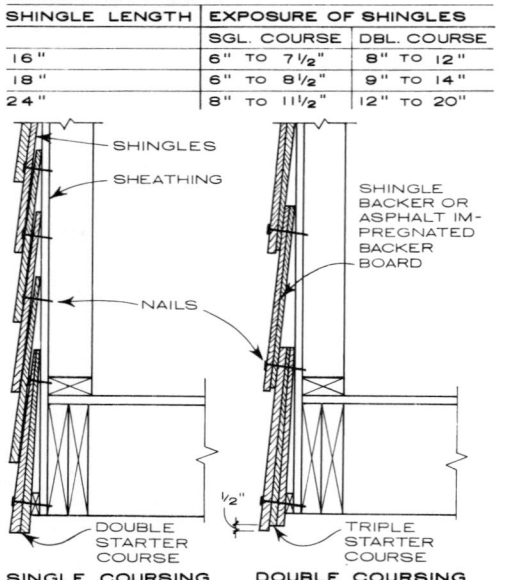

SINGLE COURSING APPLICATION

DOUBLE COURSING APPLICATION

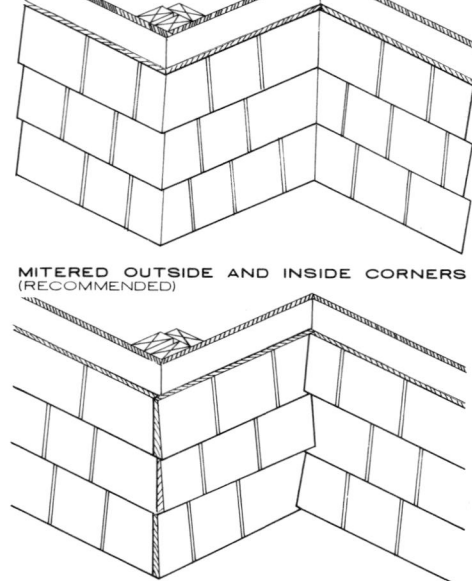

MITERED OUTSIDE AND INSIDE CORNERS (RECOMMENDED)

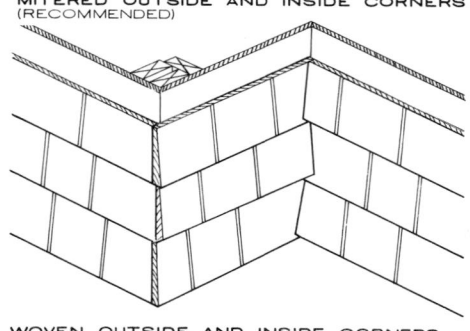

WOVEN OUTSIDE AND INSIDE CORNERS (MORE ECONOMICAL)

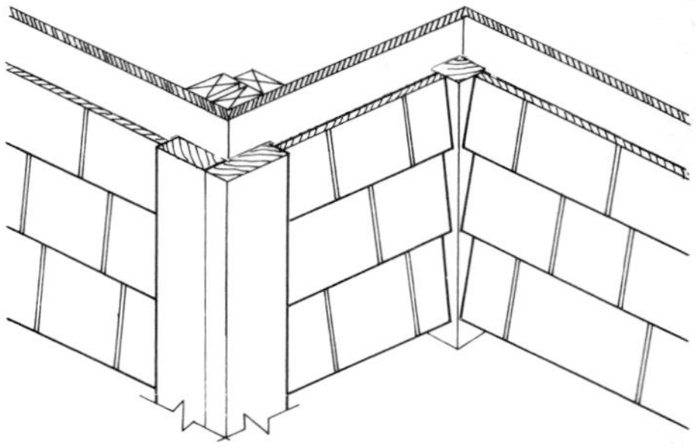

WOOD SHINGLES AND SHAKES FOR SIDING

CORNER BOARDS OUTSIDE AND INSIDE CORNERS

**NAILING** (DEFORMED SHANK NON-FERROUS)
THICKNESS AND NAILS

| 16" long | 5 butts = 2" | 3d |
|---|---|---|
| 18" long | 5 butts = 2 ¼" | 3d |
| 24" long | 4 butts = 2" | 4d |
| 25" to 27" | 1 butt = ½" | 5 or 6d |
| 25" to 27" | 1 butt = ⅝" to 1¼" | 7 or 8d |

**SHEATHING NOTES**

Sheathing may be strip-type, solid 1" x 6" diagonal type, plywood, fiberboard or gypsum. Horizontal wood nailing strips, 1" x 2", should be used over fiberboard and gypsum sheathing. Space strips equal to shingle exposure.

---

Developed by Holroyd and Gray, Architects; Charlotte, North Carolina; from data furnished by Robert M. Stafford, P.E.; Consulting Engineer; Charlotte, North Carolina

 **SHINGLES AND ROOFING TILES**

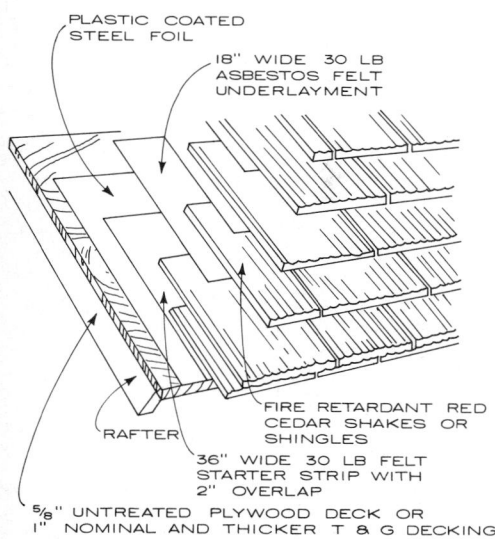

**FIRE RATED ROOF CONSTRUCTION**

**NOTES**

In treating shakes, fire retardant chemicals are pressure impregnated into the wood cells, and chemicals are then fixed in the wood to prevent leaching. Treatment does not alter appearance. Fire retardant red cedar shakes are classified as Class C by U.L. With the addition of the deck constructed of 5/8 in. plywood with exterior glue or 1 in. nominal T&G boards, overlaid with a layer of approved asbestos felt lapped 2 in. on all joints and between each shake is an 18 in. wide strip of approved asbestos felt not exposed to the weather, Class B classification by U.L. is used. Decorative stains may be applied.

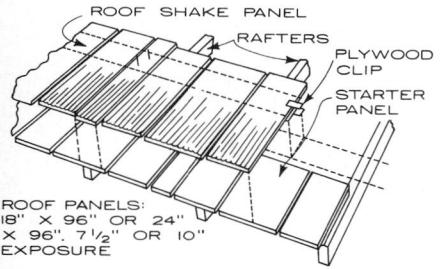

ROOF PANELS:
18" X 96" OR 24"
X 96". 7 1/2" OR 10"
EXPOSURE

**ROOF PANEL**

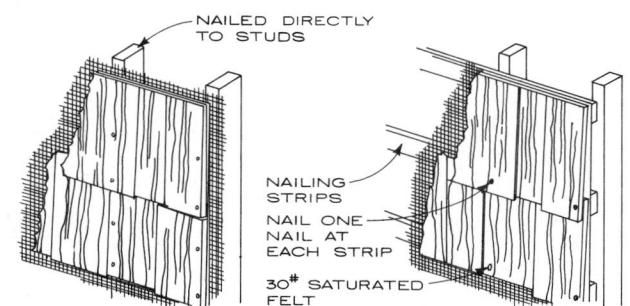

**WOOD SHAKES APPLIED TO EXISTING ROOF**

**NOTES**

Shakes can also be applied over any existing wall or roof. Brick or other masonry requires vertical frameboards and horizontal nailing strips.

Over stucco, horizontal nailing strips are attached directly to wall. Nails should penetrate shading or studs. Over wood, apply shakes directly just as if on new sheathing.

**NOTES**

Shakes and shingles plus sheathing go up in one operation. 8 ft roof panels have 16 individual handsplit shakes bonded to 6 in. wide 1/2 in. plywood strip, which form a solid deck when the panels are nailed. A 4 to 12 in. or steeper roof pitch is recommended.

After application of starter panels, attach panels directly to rafters. Although designed to center on 16 or 24 in. spacing, they may meet between rafters. Use two 6d nails at each rafter.

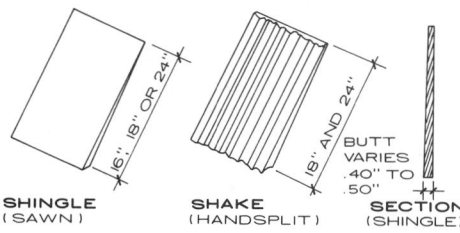

**NOMENCLATURE**

SHINGLE (SAWN)  SHAKE (HANDSPLIT)  SECTION (SHINGLE)

Species: Shingles and shakes are available in red cedar, redwood, and tidewater red cypress.

**GENERAL NOTES**

1. Wood shingles and shakes are manufactured from wood species that are naturally resistant to water, sunlight, rot, and hail. They are typically installed in the natural state, although stains, primers, and paint may be applied.

2. Nails must be hot dipped in zinc or aluminum. Nail heads should be driven flush with the surface of the shingle or shake, but never into the wood.

3. Underlayment and sheathing should be designed to augment the protection provided by the shingles or shakes, depending on roof pitch and climate. For instance, a low pitched roof in an area subject to wind driven snow should have solid sheathing and an additional underlayment.

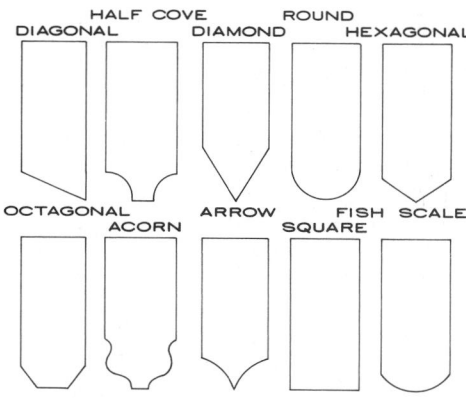

HALF COVE    ROUND
DIAGONAL    DIAMOND    HEXAGONAL

OCTAGONAL    ARROW    FISH SCALE
ACORN    SQUARE

**NOTE**

Fancy butt shingles are 5 in. wide and 7 1/2 in. long. Custom produced to individual orders.

**FANCY BUTT RED CEDAR SHINGLES**

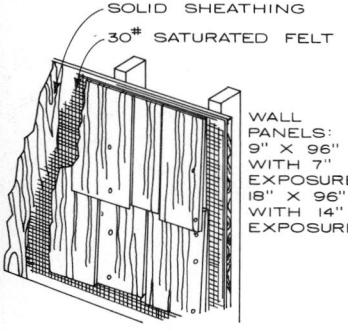

**APPLIED TO SHEATHING**    **APPLIED DIRECTLY TO STUD**    **APPLIED TO NAILING STRIPS**

**NOTES**

8 ft sidewall panels are of three-ply construction.

1. Surface layer of individual #1 grade shingles or shakes.
2. Cross binder core of plywood veneer.

3. Undercourse layer of shingle backing panels.

Panels can be applied to nailing strips or directly to studs where Code permits. Use 30 lb saturated fill lapped 3 in. vertically and horizontally. Stagger joints between panels. Matching sidewall or mansard style corners are available.

**SIDEWALL PANELS**

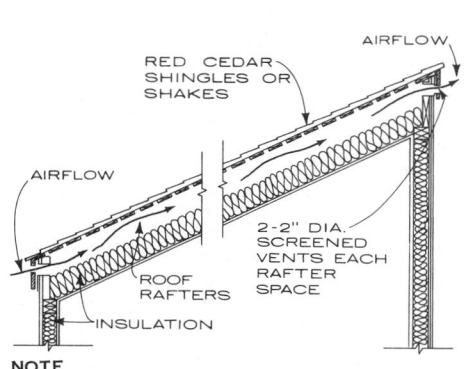

**NOTE**

A recommended ratio of total free area to adding area should not be less than 1 : 150 for adequate ventilation.

**SECTION**

**VENTILATION OF ROOF**

Robert E. Fehlberg, FAIA; CTA Architects Engineers; Billings, Montana

**SHINGLES AND ROOFING TILES**    7

## SCHEDULE OF UNDERLAYMENT

| SLOPE | TYPE OF UNDERLAYMENT |
|---|---|
| Normal slope: 4 in 12 and up | Single layer of 15 lb asphalt saturated felt over entire roof |
| Low slope: 3 in 12 to 4 in 12 | Two layers of 15 lb asphalt saturated felt over entire roof |

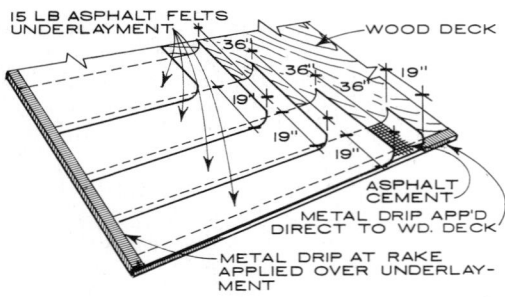

Use only enough nails to hold underlayment in place until shingles are laid.

## APPLICATION OF UNDERLAYMENT ON LOW SLOPE ROOFS

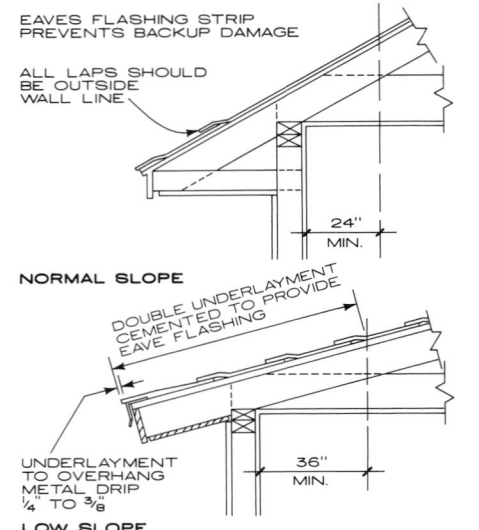

**NORMAL SLOPE**

**LOW SLOPE**

## EAVE FLASHING

## SCHEDULE OF SHINGLE TYPES (1)

| DESCRIPTION | DESIGN | MATERIAL | U.L. RATING | WEIGHT | SIZE |
|---|---|---|---|---|---|
| Three-tab square butt | | Fiberglass / Organic felts | A (4) / C | 205–225 lb/sq / 235–300 lb/sq | 36'' x 12'' |
| Two-tab square butt | | Fiberglass / Organic felts | A (4) / C | 260–325 lb/sq / 300 lb/sq | 36'' x 12'' |
| Laminated overlay (2) | | Fiberglass / Organic felts | A (3) / C | 300 lb/sq / 330–380 lb/sq | 36'' x 14'' |
| Random edge cut | | Fiberglass / Organic felts | A (3) / C | 225–260 lb/sq / 250 lb/sq | 36'' x 12'' |

NOTE: Exposure 5'', edge lap 2''.

### NOTES

1. Exposure 5 in., edge lap 2 in., for all designs.
2. More than one thickness for varying surface texture.
3. Many rated as wind resistant.
4. All rated as wind resistant.

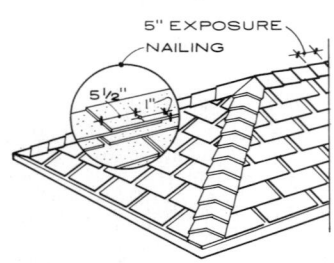

**HIP AND RIDGE**

**THREE TAB SQUARE BUTT STRIP SHINGLES**

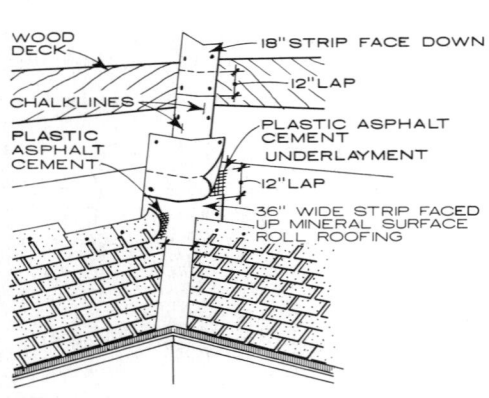

**OPEN VALLEY**

*Valley width should be 6'' wide at ridge and spread wider at the rate of $^1/_8$''/foot downward to eave. Establish valley width using chalkline from ridge to cove.

## APPLICATION DIAGRAMS

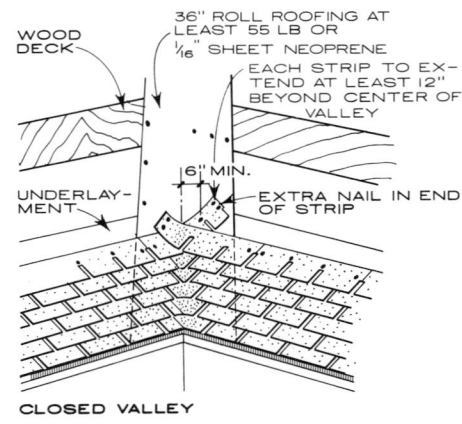

**CLOSED VALLEY**

## EAVE FLASHING
Eave flashing is required wherever the January daily average temperature is 30°F or less or where there is a possibility of ice forming along the eaves.

### NORMAL SLOPE—4 IN./FT OR OVER
A course of 90 lb mineral surfaced roll roofing or a course of 50 lb smooth roll roofing is installed to overhang the underlay and metal edge from $^1/_4$ to $^3/_8$ in. Extend up the roof far enough to cover a point at least 24 in. inside the interior wall line of the building. When the overhang requires flashing wider than 36 in., the horizontal lap joint is cemented and located on the roof deck extending beyond the exterior line of the building.

### LOW SLOPE—3 TO 4 IN./FT
Cover the deck with two layers of 15# asphalt saturated felt. Begin with a 19 in. starter course laid along the eaves, followed by a 36 in. wide sheet laid even with the eaves and completely overlapping the starter course. The starter course is covered with asphalt cement. Thereafter, 36 in. sheets are laid in asphalt cement, each to overlap the preceding course 19 in., exposing 17 in. of the underlying sheet.

The plies are placed in asphalt cement to a point at least 36 in. inside the interior wall line of the building.

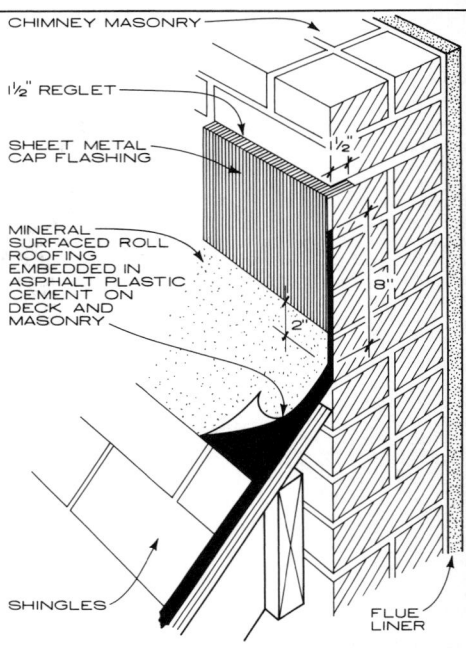

## METHOD OF SECURING CAP FLASHING TO CHIMNEY MASONRY

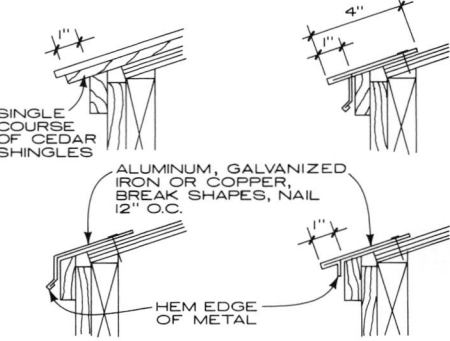

## DRIP EDGE DETAILS

**NAIL TYPES**
- SMOOTH
- ANNULAR THREADED
- SCREW THREADED

### NAILING OF SHINGLES RECOMMENDATION

| DECK TYPE | NAIL LENGTH |
|---|---|
| 1'' Wood sheathing | 1 $^1/_4$'' |
| $^3/_8$'' Plywood | $^7/_8$'' |
| $^1/_2$'' Plywood | 1'' |
| Reroofing over asphalt shingles | 1 $^3/_4$'' |

Robert E. Fehlberg, FAIA; CTA Architects Engineers; Billings, Montana

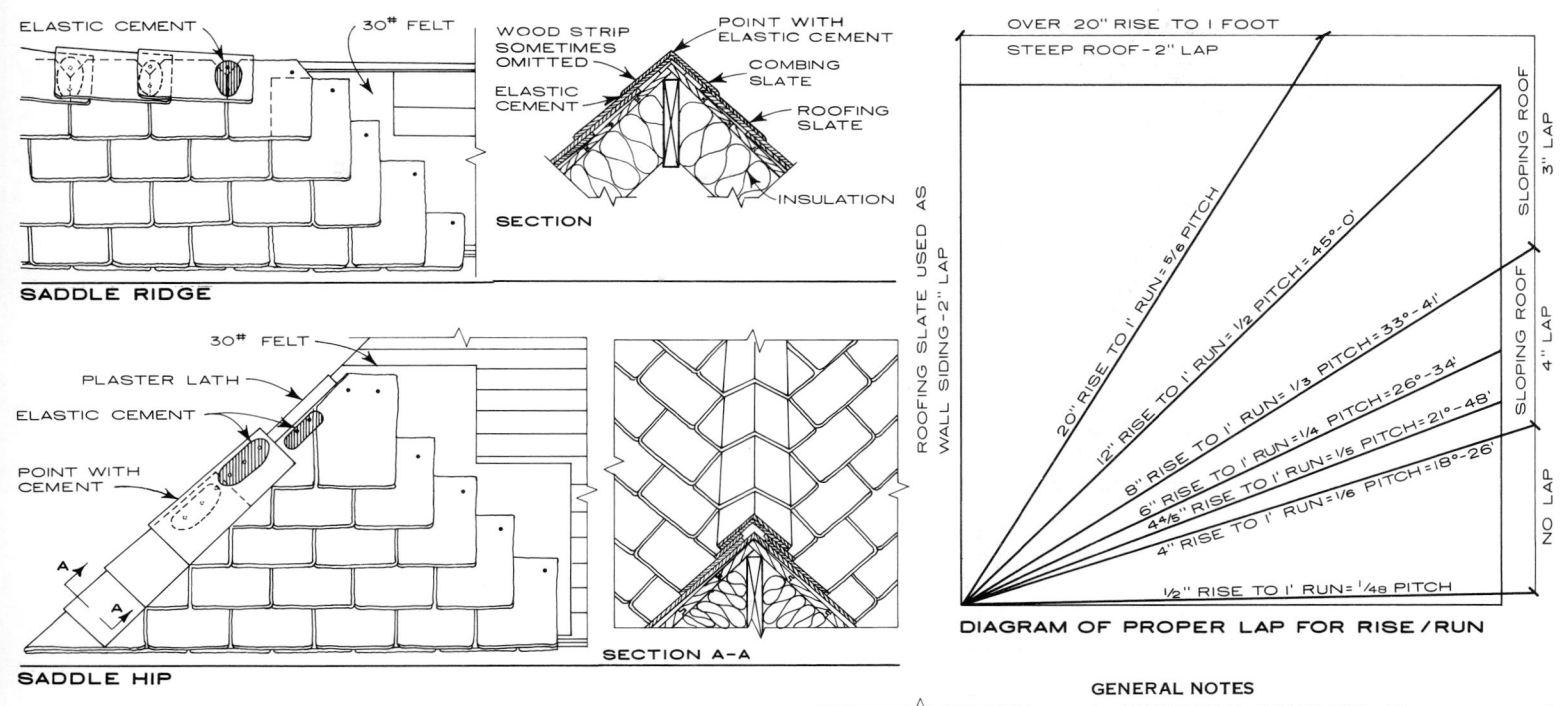

**SADDLE RIDGE**

ELASTIC CEMENT · 30# FELT · WOOD STRIP SOMETIMES OMITTED · ELASTIC CEMENT · POINT WITH ELASTIC CEMENT · COMBING SLATE · ROOFING SLATE · INSULATION · **SECTION**

**SADDLE HIP**

30# FELT · PLASTER LATH · ELASTIC CEMENT · POINT WITH CEMENT · **SECTION A-A**

ROOFING SLATE USED AS WALL SIDING—2" LAP

OVER 20" RISE TO 1 FOOT · STEEP ROOF—2" LAP

20" RISE TO 1' RUN = 5/6 PITCH
12" RISE TO 1' RUN = 1/2 PITCH = 45°-0'
8" RISE TO 1' RUN = 1/3 PITCH = 33°-4'
6" RISE TO 1' RUN = 1/4 PITCH = 26°-34'
4⅘" RISE TO 1' RUN = 1/5 PITCH = 21°-48'
4" RISE TO 1' RUN = 1/6 PITCH = 18°-26'
½" RISE TO 1' RUN = 1/48 PITCH

SLOPING ROOF 3" LAP · SLOPING ROOF 4" LAP · NO LAP

**DIAGRAM OF PROPER LAP FOR RISE / RUN**

**BOSTON HIP**

30# FELT · ELASTIC CEMENT · POINT WITH CEMENT · A · B

**MITERED HIP**

30# FELT · ELASTIC CEMENT · POINT WITH CEMENT

## GENERAL NOTES

1. COMMERCIAL STANDARD: The quarry run of $3/16$ in. thickness; includes tolerable variations above and below $3/16$ in.
2. TEXTURAL: A rough textured slate roof with uneven butts; the slates vary in thickness and size, which is generally not true of slate more than $3/8$ in. thick.
3. GRADUATED: A textural roof of large slates; more variation in thickness, size, and color.
4. A SQUARE OF ROOFING SLATE: A number of slates of any size sufficient to cover 100 ft$^2$ with a 3 in. lap. Weight per square: $3/16$ in.—800 lb; $1/4$ in.—900 lb; $3/8$ in.—1100 lb; $1/2$ in.—1700 lb; $3/4$ in.—2600 lb.
5. STANDARD NOMENCLATURE FOR SLATE COLOR: Black, blue black, mottled gray, purple, green, mottled purple and green, purple variegated, red; to be preceded by the word "Unfading" or "Weathering." Other colors and combinations are available.
6. PROPER JOINTING FOR PITCHED ROOFS: Requires a 3 in. minimum vertical overlap. Overlap varies with pitch; see graph above.
7. FELT: With Commercial Standard Slate use 30# saturated felt. With graduated roofs use 30# for $1/4$ in. slate and 45#, 50#, or 65# prepared roll roofing for heavier slate.
8. NAIL FASTENING: Use large head, slaters' hard copper wire nails, cut copper, cut brass, or cut yellow metal slating nails. Each slate punched with two nail holes. Use nails that are 1 in. longer than thickness of slate. Cover all exposed heads with elastic cement. In dry climates hot dip galvanized nails may be used.

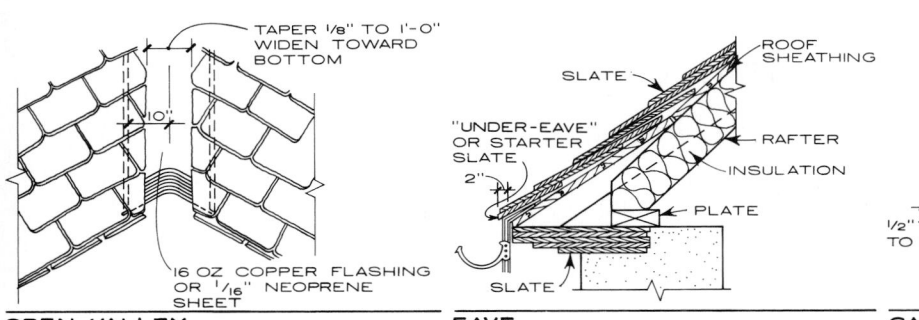

**OPEN VALLEY**

TAPER ⅛" TO 1'-0" WIDEN TOWARD BOTTOM · 10" · 16 OZ COPPER FLASHING OR 1/16" NEOPRENE SHEET

**EAVE**

ROOF SHEATHING · SLATE · "UNDER-EAVE" OR STARTER SLATE · 2" · RAFTER · INSULATION · PLATE · SLATE

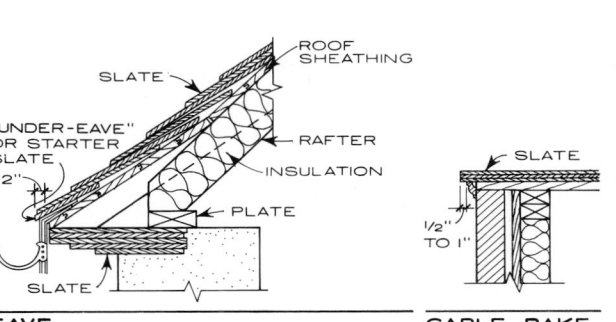

**GABLE RAKE**

SLATE · ½" TO 1"

**NAILING CONCRETE ON CONCRETE SLAB**

NAILING CONCRETE TO RECEIVE SLATE—USUALLY 2" THICK · 30# FELT · CONCRETE SLAB · THICKNESS OF SLAB TO DEPEND ON SPAN, ETC.

**WOOD RAFTER TO RECEIVE SLATE**

30# FELT · TWO NAILS TO A SLATE · RAFTER · INSULATION · 7/8" ROOFERS T. & G. 6" OR 8"

**ROOFING SLATE**

¼" TO ⅓" · 1¼" MIN. · LENGTH · PREDRILLED NAIL HOLES, 2 PER SLATE · THICKNESS · WIDTH

## STANDARD SLATE DIMENSIONS*

| LENGTH (IN.) | WIDTH (IN.) |
|---|---|
| 10† | 6, 7, 8, 9, 10 |
| 12† | 6, 7, 8, 9, 10, 12 |
| 14† | 7, 8, 9, 10, 11, 12 |
| 16 | 8, 9, 10, 11, 12, 14 |
| 18 | 9, 10, 11, 12, 13, 14 |
| 20 | 9, 10, 11, 12, 13, 14 |
| 22 | 10, 11, 12, 13, 14 |
| 24 | 11, 12, 13, 14, 16 |

*The slates are split in these thicknesses: $3/16$, $1/4$, $3/8$, $1/2$, $3/4$, 1, $1 1/4$, and $1 1/2$ in.
†$1/2$ in. and larger slates are not often used in these sizes. Random widths are usually used.

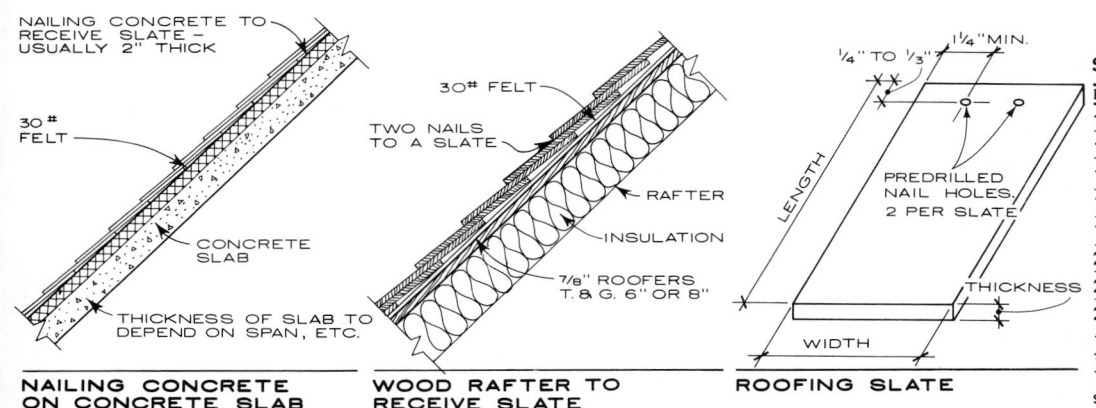

Domenic F. Valente, AIA, Architect & Planner; Medford, Massachusetts

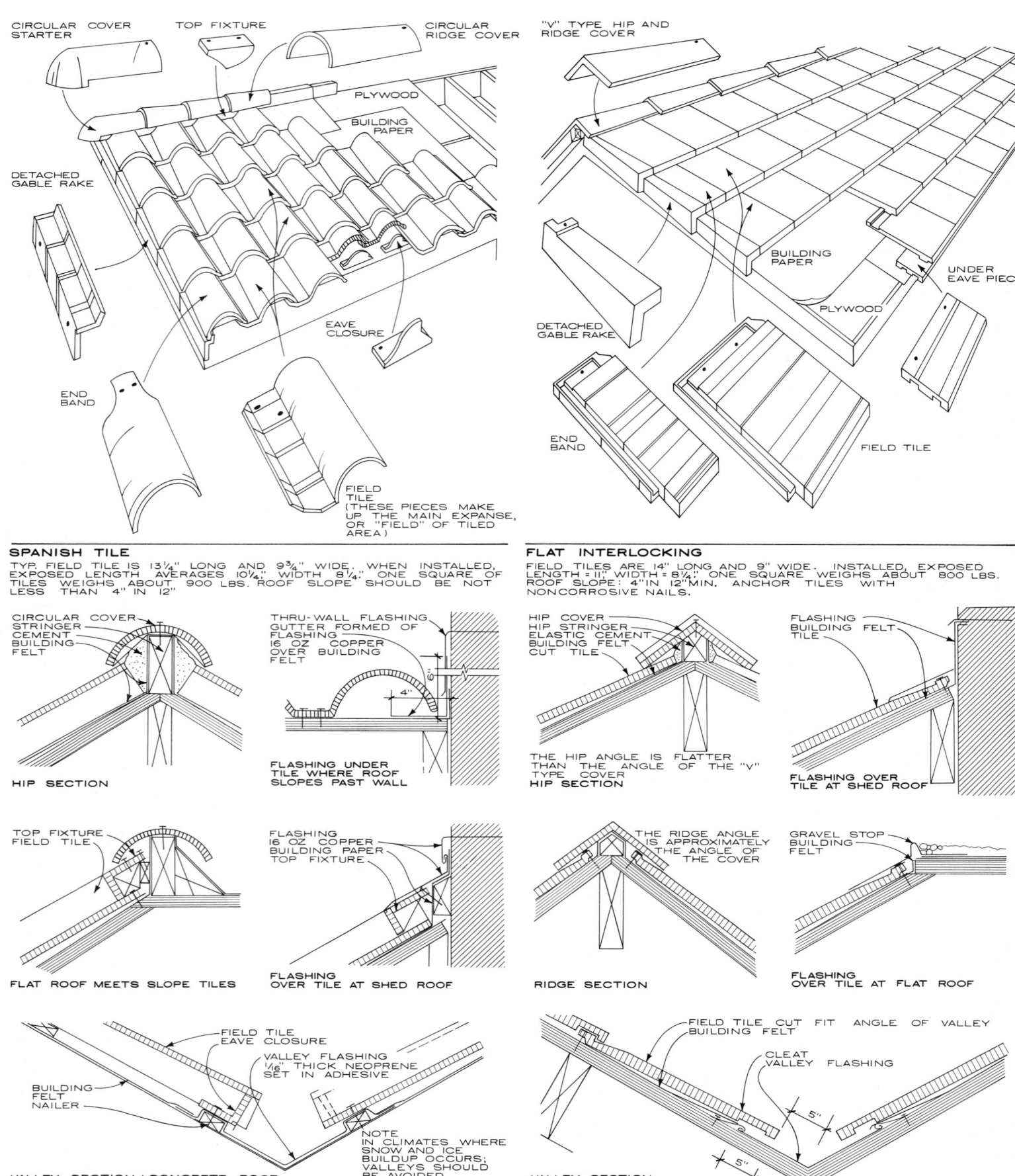

CIRCULAR COVER STARTER

TOP FIXTURE

CIRCULAR RIDGE COVER

PLYWOOD

BUILDING PAPER

DETACHED GABLE RAKE

EAVE CLOSURE

END BAND

FIELD TILE (THESE PIECES MAKE UP THE MAIN EXPANSE, OR "FIELD" OF TILED AREA)

"V" TYPE HIP AND RIDGE COVER

BUILDING PAPER

PLYWOOD

UNDER EAVE PIECE

DETACHED GABLE RAKE

END BAND

FIELD TILE

## SPANISH TILE

TYP. FIELD TILE IS 13¼" LONG AND 9¾" WIDE. WHEN INSTALLED, EXPOSED LENGTH AVERAGES 10¼," WIDTH 8¼." ONE SQUARE OF TILES WEIGHS ABOUT 900 LBS. ROOF SLOPE SHOULD BE NOT LESS THAN 4" IN 12"

CIRCULAR COVER STRINGER
CEMENT
BUILDING FELT

**HIP SECTION**

THRU-WALL FLASHING GUTTER FORMED OF FLASHING 16 OZ COPPER OVER BUILDING FELT

**FLASHING UNDER TILE WHERE ROOF SLOPES PAST WALL**

TOP FIXTURE FIELD TILE

**FLAT ROOF MEETS SLOPE TILES**

FLASHING 16 OZ COPPER BUILDING PAPER TOP FIXTURE

**FLASHING OVER TILE AT SHED ROOF**

FIELD TILE EAVE CLOSURE

VALLEY FLASHING ⅟₁₆" THICK NEOPRENE SET IN ADHESIVE

BUILDING FELT NAILER

NOTE IN CLIMATES WHERE SNOW AND ICE BUILDUP OCCURS; VALLEYS SHOULD BE AVOIDED

**VALLEY SECTION/CONCRETE ROOF**

## FLAT INTERLOCKING

FIELD TILES ARE 14" LONG AND 9" WIDE. INSTALLED, EXPOSED LENGTH = 11", WIDTH = 8¼." ONE SQUARE WEIGHS ABOUT 800 LBS. ROOF SLOPE: 4" IN 12" MIN. ANCHOR TILES WITH NONCORROSIVE NAILS.

HIP COVER
HIP STRINGER
ELASTIC CEMENT
BUILDING FELT
CUT TILE

THE HIP ANGLE IS FLATTER THAN THE ANGLE OF THE "V" TYPE COVER
**HIP SECTION**

FLASHING BUILDING FELT TILE

**FLASHING OVER TILE AT SHED ROOF**

THE RIDGE ANGLE IS APPROXIMATELY THE ANGLE OF THE COVER

**RIDGE SECTION**

GRAVEL STOP BUILDING FELT

**FLASHING OVER TILE AT FLAT ROOF**

FIELD TILE CUT FIT ANGLE OF VALLEY
BUILDING FELT

CLEAT
VALLEY FLASHING

5"

5"

**VALLEY SECTION**

Darrel Downing Rippeteau, Architect; Washington, D.C.

**7**

## SHINGLES AND ROOFING TILES

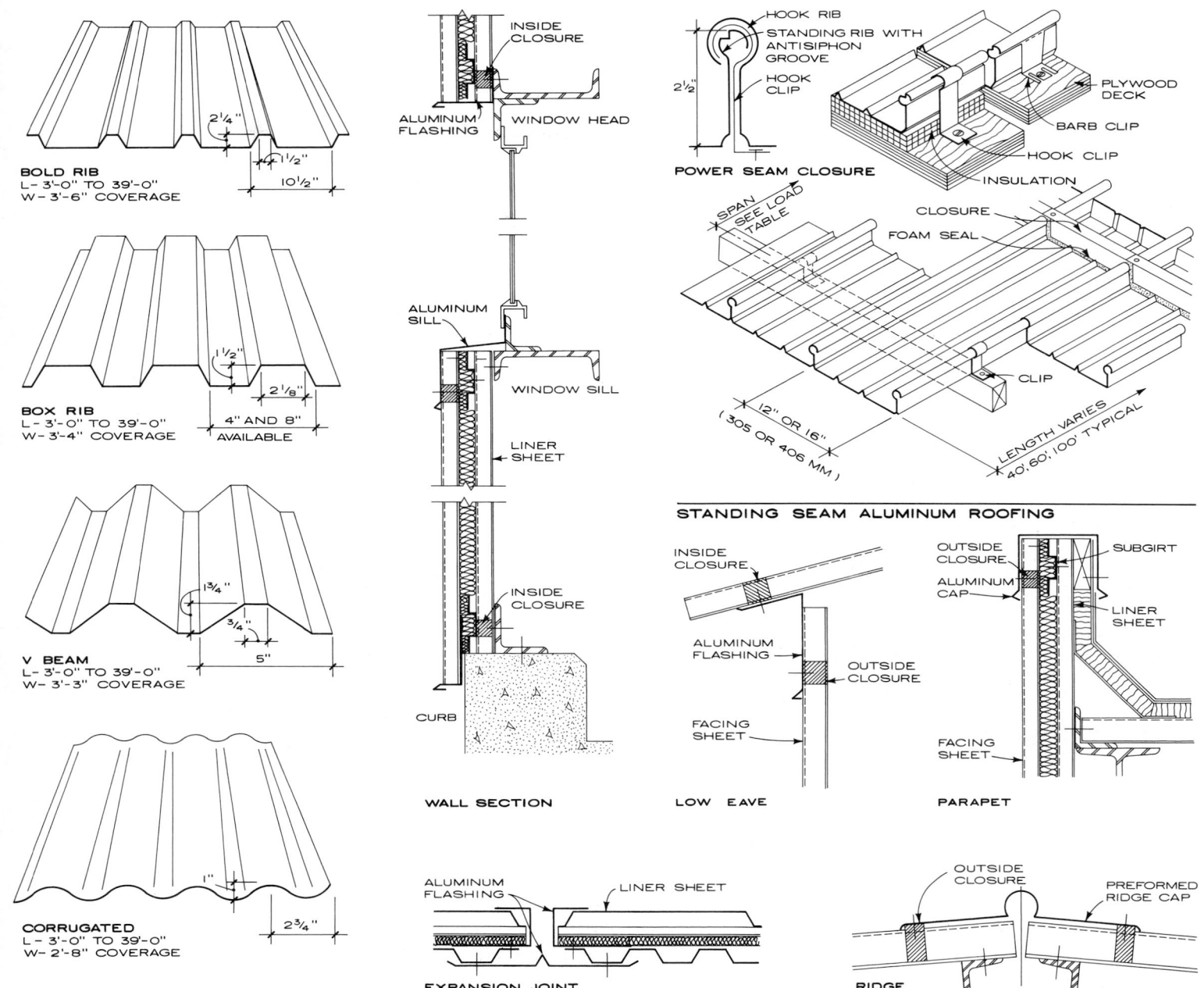

**BOLD RIB**
L – 3'-0" TO 39'-0"
W – 3'-6" COVERAGE

**BOX RIB**
L – 3'-0" TO 39'-0"
W – 3'-4" COVERAGE
4" AND 8" AVAILABLE

**V BEAM**
L – 3'-0" TO 39'-0"
W – 3'-3" COVERAGE

**CORRUGATED**
L – 3'-0" TO 39'-0"
W – 2'-8" COVERAGE

INSIDE CLOSURE
ALUMINUM FLASHING
WINDOW HEAD
ALUMINUM SILL
WINDOW SILL
LINER SHEET
INSIDE CLOSURE
CURB
**WALL SECTION**

HOOK RIB
STANDING RIB WITH ANTISIPHON GROOVE
HOOK CLIP
**POWER SEAM CLOSURE**
PLYWOOD DECK
BARB CLIP
HOOK CLIP
INSULATION
SPAN SEE LOAD TABLE
CLOSURE
FOAM SEAL
CLIP
12" OR 16" (305 OR 406 MM)
LENGTH VARIES 40', 60', 100' TYPICAL

**STANDING SEAM ALUMINUM ROOFING**

INSIDE CLOSURE
ALUMINUM FLASHING
OUTSIDE CLOSURE
FACING SHEET
**LOW EAVE**

OUTSIDE CLOSURE
ALUMINUM CAP
SUBGIRT
LINER SHEET
FACING SHEET
**PARAPET**

ALUMINUM FLASHING
LINER SHEET
**EXPANSION JOINT**

OUTSIDE CLOSURE
PREFORMED RIDGE CAP
**RIDGE**

**FORMED ALUMINUM ROOFING AND SIDING**

**NOTES**

1. Endlaps for roofing and siding shall be at least 6 in. and fastened at every rib. Two fasteners may be required when designing for a negative (uplift) loading condition.
2. Minimum sidelaps shall be equal to one rib or corrugation and laid away from prevailing wind. Fasteners shall be spaced a maximum of 12 in. on center for all types of roofing and siding.
3. For roofing, fasteners shall pierce only the high corrugation. For siding, fasteners shall pierce either the high or low corrugation. Consult manufacturer for proper sheet metal fasteners and accessories.
4. Minimum slopes for sheet roofing are as follows:
   a. 1 in. depth corrugated—3 in 12.
   b. 1½ in. depth ribbed—2 in 12.
   c. 1¾ in. v-corrugated—2 in 12.
5. See page on Metal Walls for insulation details and fire rated wall assemblies.

**MAXIMUM SPAN TABLE FOR FORMED ALUMINUM ROOFING AND SIDING (IN.)**

| DESIGN LOAD (PSF) | BOLD RIB | | 4" BOX RIB | | V BEAM | | CORRUGATED | | STANDING SEAM | |
|---|---|---|---|---|---|---|---|---|---|---|
| | 0.032 IN. THICK | 0.040 IN. THICK | 0.032 IN. THICK | 0.040 IN. THICK | 0.032 IN. THICK | 0.040 IN. THICK | 0.032 IN. THICK | 0.040 IN. THICK | 0.032 IN. THICK | 0.040 IN. THICK |
| 20 | 95 | 123 | 100 | 120 | 131 | 151 | 90 | 98 | 103 | 124 |
| 30 | 77 | 100 | 82 | 98 | 107 | 124 | 73 | 80 | 86 | 104 |
| 40 | 67 | 87 | 71 | 85 | 92 | 107 | 64 | 69 | 77 | 92 |
| 50 | 60 | 76 | 63 | 76 | 83 | 96 | 57 | 62 | 70 | 83 |

NOTE: Values are based on uniform positive (downward) and walking loads on single span only.

John A. Schulte; Hellmuth, Obata & Kassabaum, Inc.; St. Louis, Missouri

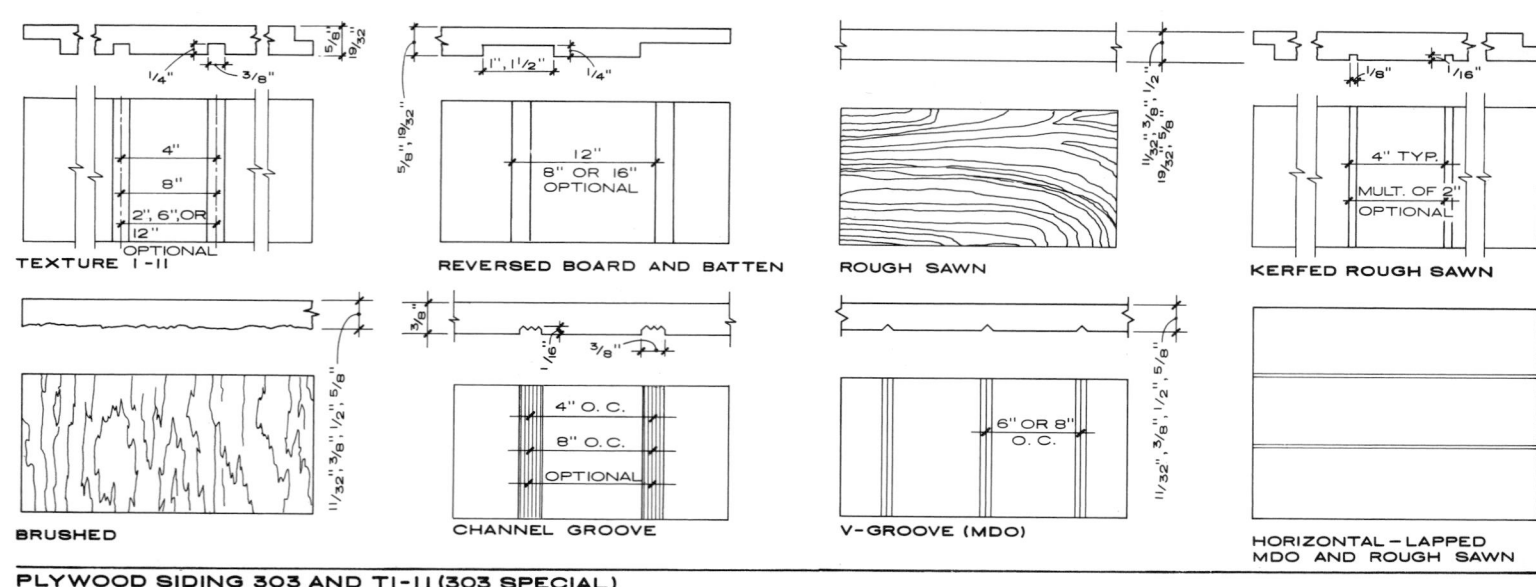

**TEXTURE 1-11**

**REVERSED BOARD AND BATTEN**

**ROUGH SAWN**

**KERFED ROUGH SAWN**

**BRUSHED**

**CHANNEL GROOVE**

**V-GROOVE (MDO)**

**HORIZONTAL – LAPPED MDO AND ROUGH SAWN**

## PLYWOOD SIDING 303 AND T1-11 (303 SPECIAL)

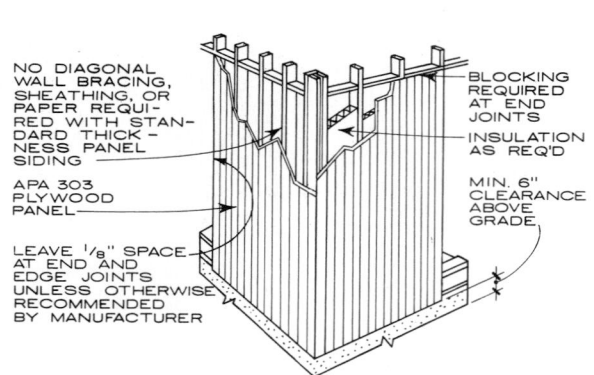

Medium density overlay (MDO) plywood lap siding: standard thickness is 3/8 in. in lengths to 16 ft on order; standard widths are 12 or 16 in.

**PANEL SIDING VERTICAL APPLICATION**

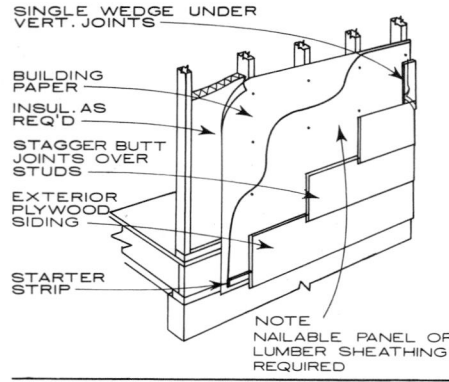

**PLYWOOD LAP SIDING APPLICATION**

**PANEL SIDING HORIZONTAL**

**VERTICAL JOINTS**

BUTT AND CAULK

VERTICAL BATTEN

SHIPLAP

**HORIZONTAL JOINTS**

BUTT AND FLASH

SHIPLAP

OVERLAP

## APA STURD-I-WALL CONSTRUCTION RECOMMENDATIONS (SIDING DIRECT TO STUDS AND OVER NONSTRUCTURAL SHEATHING)

| PLYWOOD PANEL SIDING DESCRIPTION (ALL SPECIES GROUPS) | NOMINAL THICKNESS (IN.) | MAX. STUD SPACING (IN.) | | NAIL SIZE (USE NONSTAINING BOX, SIDING, OR CASING NAILS (1)(2) | NAIL SPACING (IN.) | |
|---|---|---|---|---|---|---|
| | | FACE GRAIN VERTICAL | FACE GRAIN HORIZONTAL | | PANEL EDGES | INTER-MEDIATE |
| APA MDO EXT | $^{11}/_{32}$ and $^3/_8$ | 16 | 24 | 6d for panels $^1/_2$" thick or less 8d for thicker panels | 6(4) | 12 |
| | $^1/_2$ and thicker | 24 | 24 | | | |
| APA 303 siding—16 o.c. EXT (including T1-11) | $^{11}/_{32}$ and thicker | 16 | 24 | | | |
| APA 303 siding— 24 o.c. EXT | $^{15}/_{32}$ and thicker (3) | 24 | 24 | | | |

**NOTES**

1. If siding is applied over sheathing thicker than $^1/_2$ in. use next regular nail size. Use nonstaining box nails for siding installed over foam insulation sheathing.

2. Hot-dipped or hot-tumbled galvanized steel nails are recommended for most siding applications. For best performance, stainless steel nails or aluminum nails should be considered. APA tests also show that electrically or mechanically galvanized steel nails appear satisfactory when plating meets or exceeds thickness requirements of ASTM A641 Class 2 coatings and is further protected by yellow chromate coating.

3. Only panels $^{15}/_{32}$ in. and thicker which have certain groove depths and spacings qualify for 24 in. o.c. Span Rating.

4. For braced wall section with $^{11}/_{32}$ in. or $^3/_8$ in. siding applied horizontally over studs 24 in. o.c.

| MINIMUM BENDING RADII FOR PLYWOOD PANELS PANEL THICKNESS (IN.) | $^1/_4$ | $^3/_8$ | $^1/_2$ | $^5/_8$ | $^3/_4$ |
|---|---|---|---|---|---|
| Across grain (ft) | 2 | 3 | 6 | 8 | 12 |
| Parallel to grain (ft) | 5 | 8 | 12 | 16 | 20 |

**NOTES**

The types of plywood recommended for exterior siding are: A.P.A. grade trademarked medium density overlay (MDO), Type 303 siding or Texture 1-11 (T1-11 special 303 siding). T1-11 plywood siding is manufactured with $^3/_8$ in. wide parallel grooves and shiplapped edges. MDO is recommended for paint finishes and is available in variety of surfaces. 303 plywood panels are also available in a wide variety of surfaces. The most common A.P.A. plywood siding panel dimensions are 4 x 8 ft but the panels are also available in 9 and 10 ft lengths, lap siding to 16 ft.

John D. Bloodgood, Architect, P.C.; Des Moines, Iowa
American Plywood Association

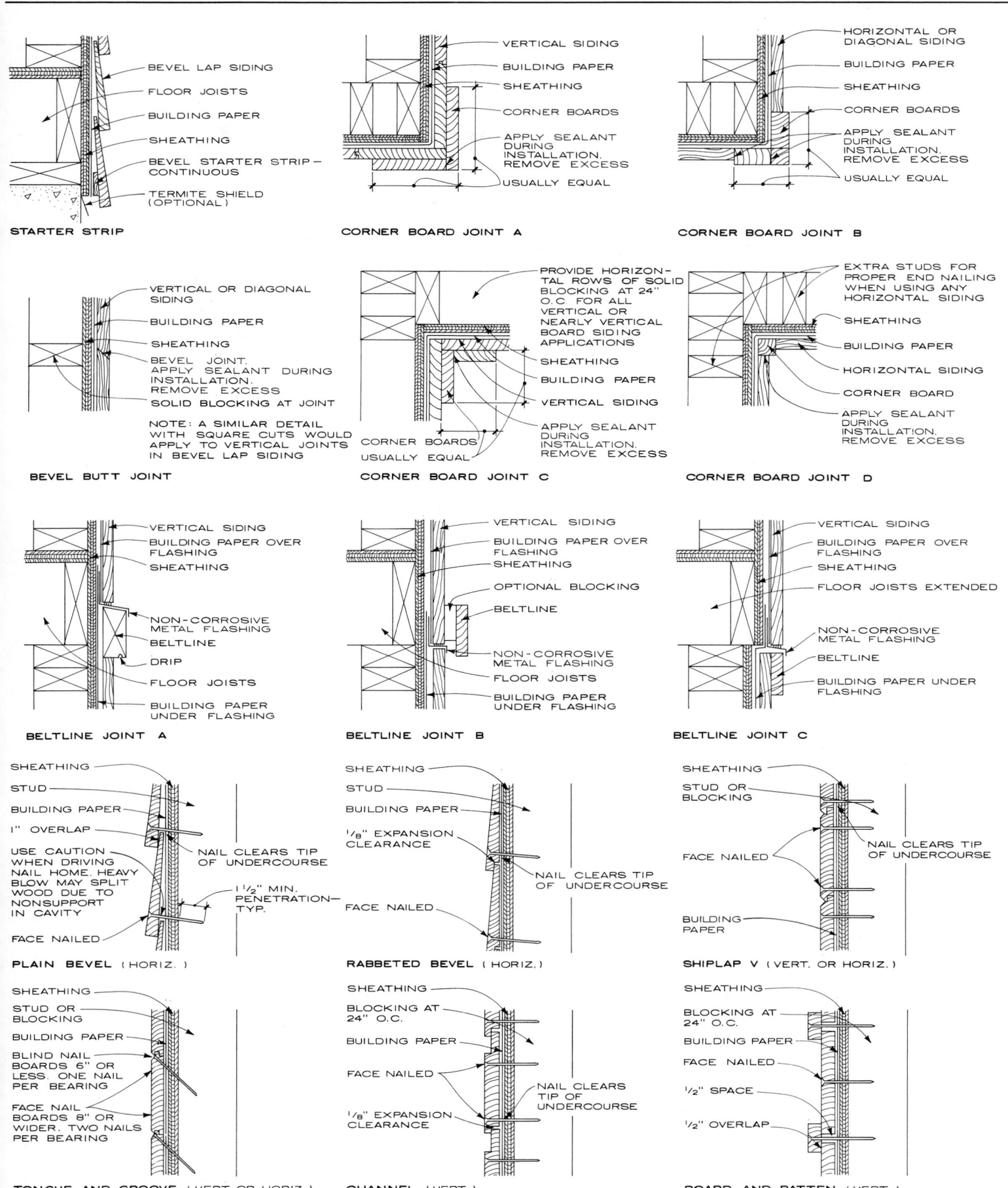

Gerald D. Graham; CTA Architects Engineers; Billings, Montana

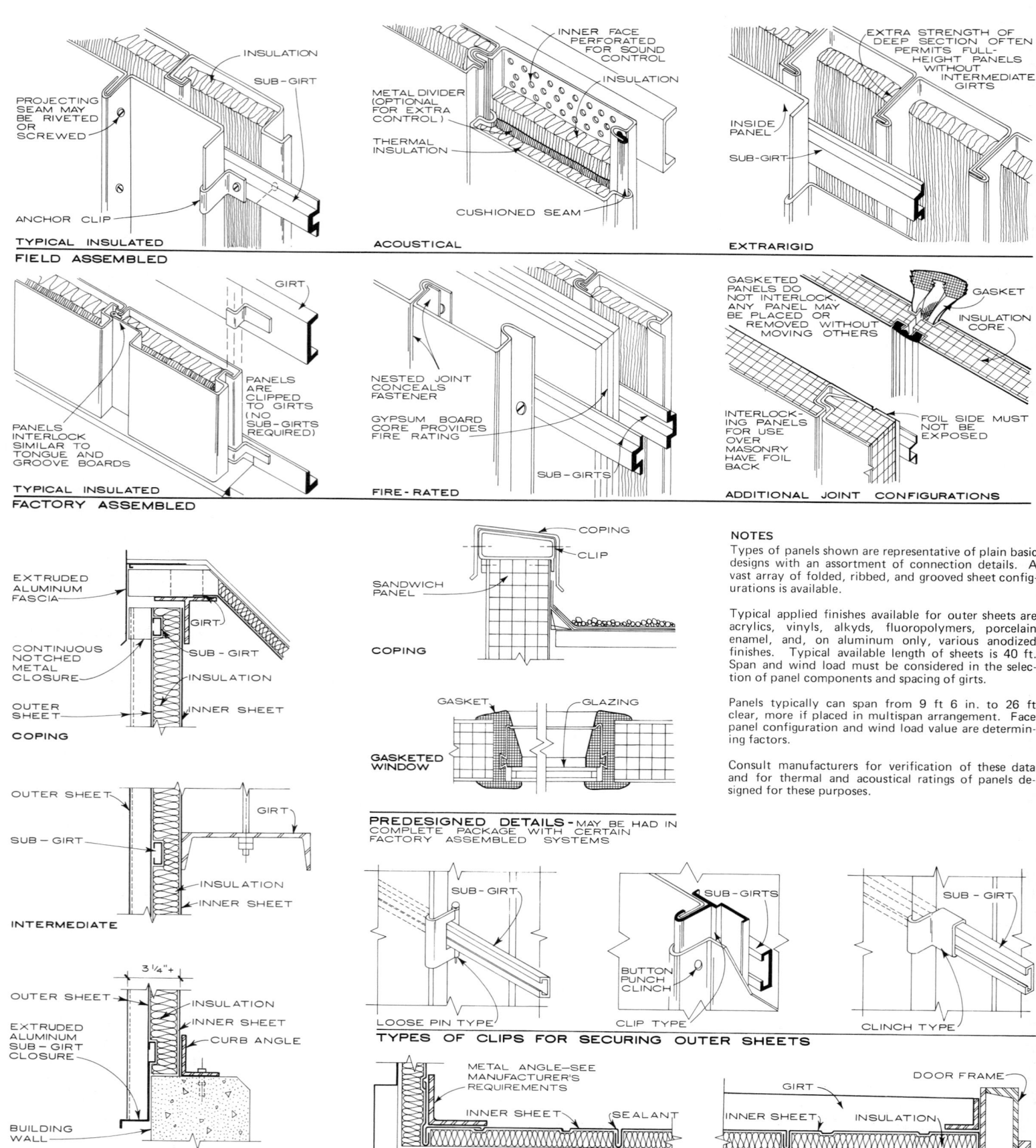

**TYPICAL INSULATED FIELD ASSEMBLED**

- PROJECTING SEAM MAY BE RIVETED OR SCREWED
- INSULATION
- SUB-GIRT
- ANCHOR CLIP

**ACOUSTICAL**

- INNER FACE PERFORATED FOR SOUND CONTROL
- INSULATION
- METAL DIVIDER (OPTIONAL FOR EXTRA CONTROL)
- THERMAL INSULATION
- CUSHIONED SEAM

**EXTRARIGID**

- EXTRA STRENGTH OF DEEP SECTION OFTEN PERMITS FULL-HEIGHT PANELS WITHOUT INTERMEDIATE GIRTS
- INSIDE PANEL
- SUB-GIRT

**TYPICAL INSULATED FACTORY ASSEMBLED**

- GIRT
- PANELS ARE CLIPPED TO GIRTS (NO SUB-GIRTS REQUIRED)
- PANELS INTERLOCK SIMILAR TO TONGUE AND GROOVE BOARDS

**FIRE-RATED**

- NESTED JOINT CONCEALS FASTENER
- GYPSUM BOARD CORE PROVIDES FIRE RATING
- SUB-GIRTS

**ADDITIONAL JOINT CONFIGURATIONS**

- GASKETED PANELS DO NOT INTERLOCK. ANY PANEL MAY BE PLACED OR REMOVED WITHOUT MOVING OTHERS
- GASKET
- INSULATION CORE
- INTERLOCKING PANELS FOR USE OVER MASONRY HAVE FOIL BACK
- FOIL SIDE MUST NOT BE EXPOSED

**COPING**

- EXTRUDED ALUMINUM FASCIA
- GIRT
- SUB-GIRT
- INSULATION
- INNER SHEET
- CONTINUOUS NOTCHED METAL CLOSURE
- OUTER SHEET

**INTERMEDIATE**

- OUTER SHEET
- GIRT
- SUB-GIRT
- INSULATION
- INNER SHEET

**SILL**

- 3 1/4"+
- OUTER SHEET
- INSULATION
- INNER SHEET
- CURB ANGLE
- EXTRUDED ALUMINUM SUB-GIRT CLOSURE
- BUILDING WALL

**CONSTRUCTION DETAILS OF FIELD-ASSEMBLED INSULATED METAL WALLS**

**COPING**

- COPING
- CLIP
- SANDWICH PANEL

**GASKETED WINDOW**

- GASKET
- GLAZING

**PREDESIGNED DETAILS** - MAY BE HAD IN COMPLETE PACKAGE WITH CERTAIN FACTORY ASSEMBLED SYSTEMS

**TYPES OF CLIPS FOR SECURING OUTER SHEETS**

- SUB-GIRT
- LOOSE PIN TYPE
- SUB-GIRTS
- BUTTON PUNCH CLINCH
- CLIP TYPE
- SUB-GIRT
- CLINCH TYPE

**OUTSIDE CORNER**

- METAL ANGLE—SEE MANUFACTURER'S REQUIREMENTS
- INNER SHEET
- SEALANT
- METAL CORNER
- SEALANT AND BUTTON PUNCH

**JAMB AT DOOR**

- GIRT
- DOOR FRAME
- INNER SHEET
- INSULATION
- SUB-GIRT
- SEALANT AND BUTTON PUNCH
- SEALANT

**NOTES**

Types of panels shown are representative of plain basic designs with an assortment of connection details. A vast array of folded, ribbed, and grooved sheet configurations is available.

Typical applied finishes available for outer sheets are acrylics, vinyls, alkyds, fluoropolymers, porcelain enamel, and, on aluminum only, various anodized finishes. Typical available length of sheets is 40 ft. Span and wind load must be considered in the selection of panel components and spacing of girts.

Panels typically can span from 9 ft 6 in. to 26 ft clear, more if placed in multispan arrangement. Face panel configuration and wind load value are determining factors.

Consult manufacturers for verification of these data and for thermal and acoustical ratings of panels designed for these purposes.

## FACING MATERIALS AVAILABLE

1. Aluminum.
2. Aluminized steel.
3. Galvanized steel.

## FINISHES AVAILABLE

1. Anodized aluminum.
2. 50% silicone—modified polyester baked enamel paint.
3. Fluorocarbon baked enamel paint.
4. Porcelain enamel on aluminized steel.

| INSULATING VALUES | MAX. U FACTOR |
|---|---|
| 2 in. urethane core | 0.065 |
| 3 in. honeycomb core | 0.41 |
| 2 in. honeycomb with fill | 0.107 |

## NOTE

Some codes restrict the use of the urethane core panel. The honeycomb panels are more acceptable.

Urethane panel = 25 flame spread rating
Honeycomb panel = 15 flame spread rating
See manufacturer for span tables.

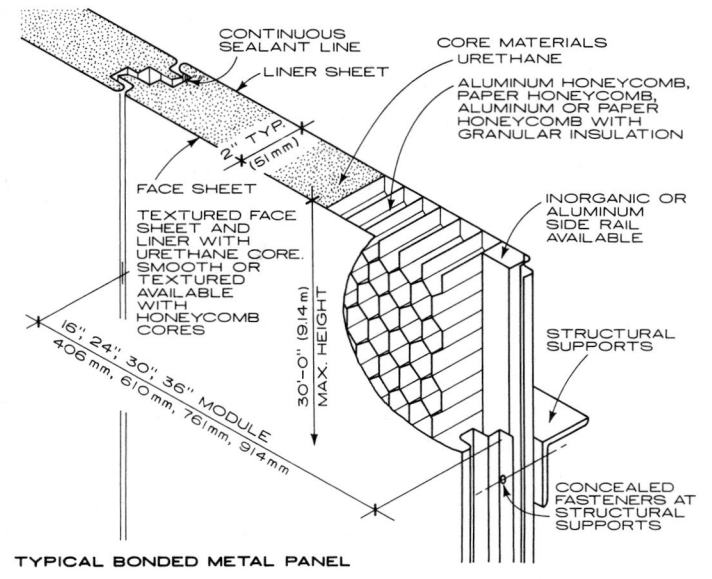

**TYPICAL BONDED METAL PANEL**

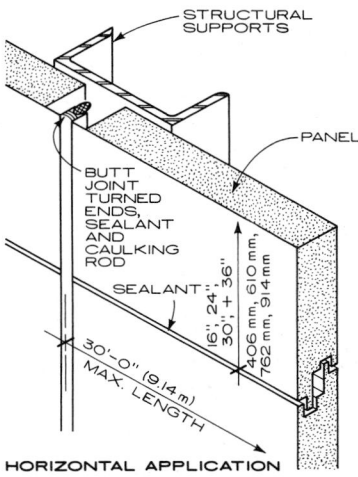

**HORIZONTAL APPLICATION**

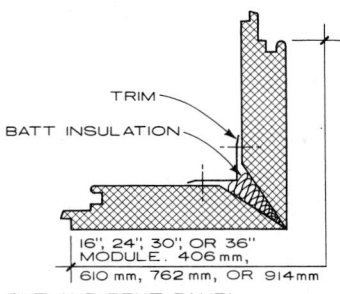

**CUT AND BENT PANEL**

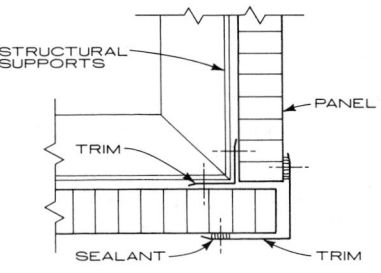

**EXPOSED TRIM**

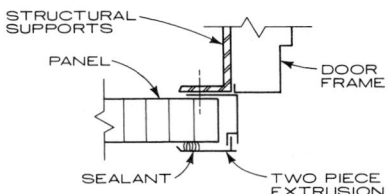

**DOOR JAMB**

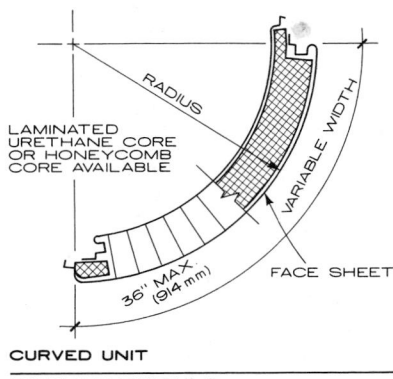

**CURVED UNIT**

**CORNER DETAILS**

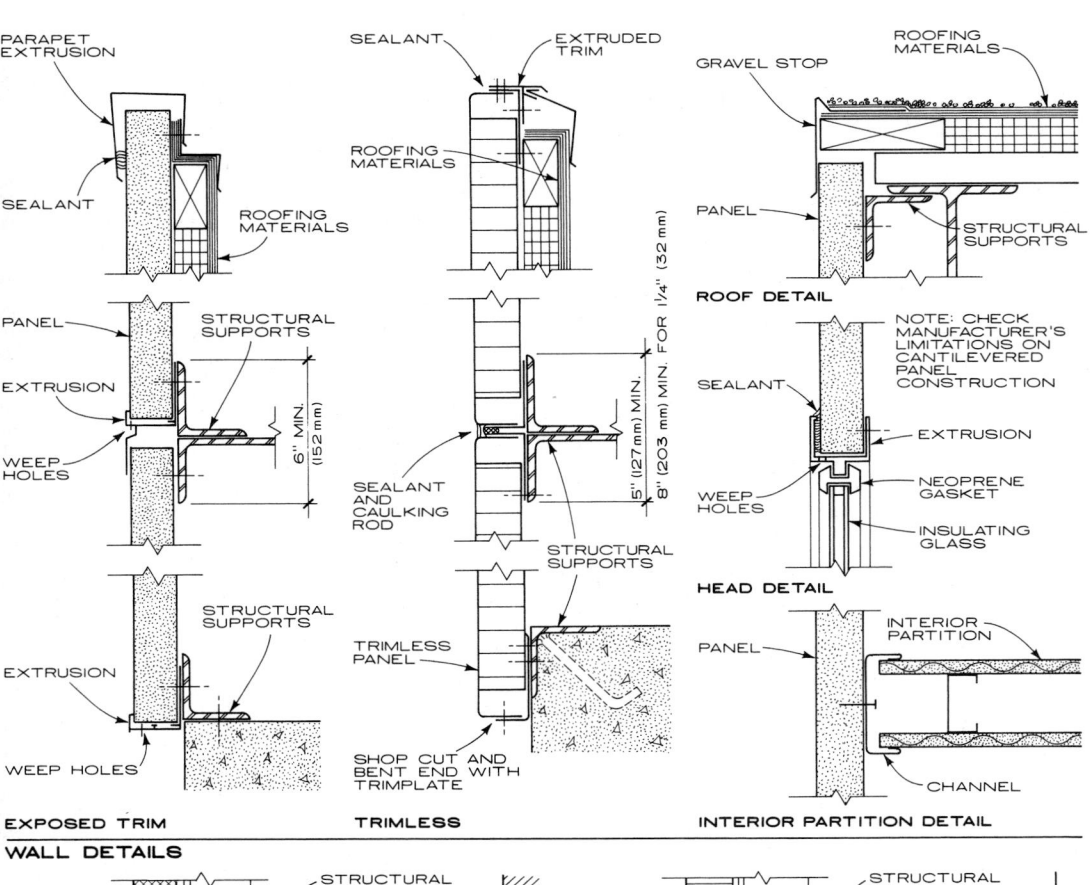

**WALL DETAILS**

**ROOF DETAIL**

**HEAD DETAIL**

**INTERIOR PARTITION DETAIL**

**EXPOSED TRIM**    **TRIMLESS**

**EXPOSED TRIM**    **TRIMLESS**

**SOFFIT DETAILS**

John A. Schulte; Hellmuth, Obata, & Kassabaum, Inc.; St. Louis, Missouri

## NOTE

Polyvinyl chloride (PVC) is a semirigid material that requires the addition of plasticizers to fabricate a flexible roofing membrane. PVC exhibits excellent weldability for making lap joints or attaching to PVC clad metal flashing.

## TYPES OF MEMBRANE

Unreinforced sheet
Sheet reinforced with fiberglass or polyester

## METHOD OF MANUFACTURE

Calendering
Spread coating
Extruding

## GENERAL

Single ply roofing systems are also referred to as flexible sheet roofing systems. Consult manufacturers for specific requirements regarding materials selection and installation requirements. Compatibility of materials comprising total roofing system is essential.

## MATERIAL PROPERTIES

Thickness: Typically 48 and 60 mil; 45 mil minimum

Color: Typically gray; other colors available

Contaminants to avoid: Bitumen, oils, animal fats, and coal tar pitch. See manufacturer's chemical resistance list.

Minimum standards: ASTM has developed standard test methods to evaluate the materials properties of PVC roof membranes. These test results form a useful basis for comparing various PVC membranes. ASTM's standard specification establishes minimum performance criteria for tensile strength, elongation, tear resistance, heat aging, weathering, and water absorption.

## INSTALLATION

General guidelines: It is recommended that all roofing materials be installed on roofs with positive slope to drainage. Check with manufacturers regarding their specific requirements.

Lap joining methods: Hot air or solvent weld

Flashing methods: Membrane or PVC coated metal

Types of preformed accessories available: Inside and outside corners; pipe stacks

Weather restrictions during installation: 0°–120°F temperature range. Substrates and welding/bonding surfaces must be dry.

Method of repair: Clean surface; hot air or solvent weld of PVC patch

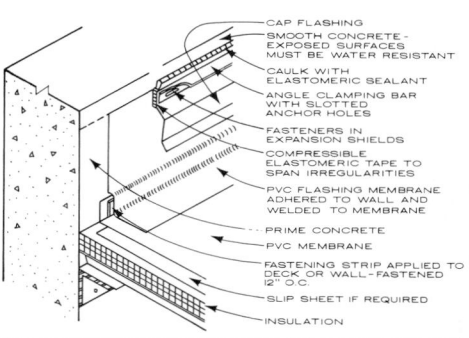

**TYPICAL PARAPET FLASHING**

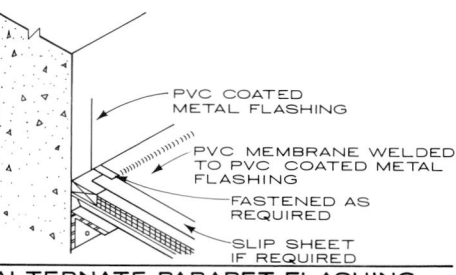

**ALTERNATE PARAPET FLASHING**

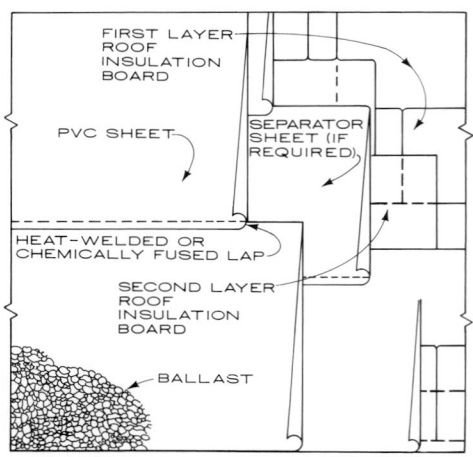

Membrane sheets are laid loose over roof insulation (also laid loose) and secured at the perimeter and around penetrations only. The membrane is then covered with a ballast of river-washed stones (typically 10 lb/sq ft) or appropriate pavers.

This system works efficiently with insulation approved by the membrane manufacturer and on roofs with a slope not exceeding 2 in 12.

**LOOSE-LAID BALLASTED SHEETS**

Membrane sheets are laid loose over a sloped roof deck and with the insulation on top of it. When the roof deck is dead level, tapered roof insulation is either loose laid or mechanically attached under the membrane to achieve positive slope to drainage. In either instance, a layer of insulation is placed over the membrane and held in place by one of two methods: Either a loose fabric is laid over the insulation, with a minimum of 10 lb/sq ft of ballast laid over the fabric, or insulation with an integrally bonded concrete facing is used in place of the fabric and loose ballast. Membrane manufacturers should be consulted for their approved insulation list. In this roofing system, the membrane is protected from year-round temperature extremes, direct exposure to weather, and damage from other sources. The heat gain or loss is just the same as if the insulation were installed under the membrane. Since the waterproofing membrane is placed on the warm side of the insulation, it functions as a vapor retarder. For high humidity conditions with a dead level roof deck utilizing tapered insulation, a separate vapor barrier should be placed directly beneath the tapered insulation to prevent condensation.

**PROTECTED MEMBRANE SHEET**

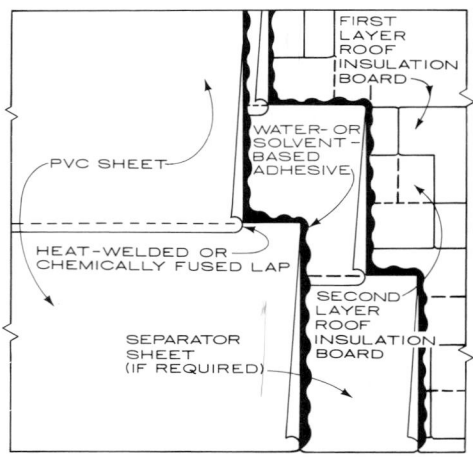

For system with no slope limitations which secures membrane to substrate with bonding adhesive and by mechanically fastening the membrane to perimeter and penetrations. System is appropriate for contoured roofs and roofs that cannot withstand weight of ballasted system.

Membrane can be directly applied to deck surface of concrete, wood surfaces, or be applied to compatible insulation that is mechanically fastened to the deck.

**FULLY ADHERED SHEETS**

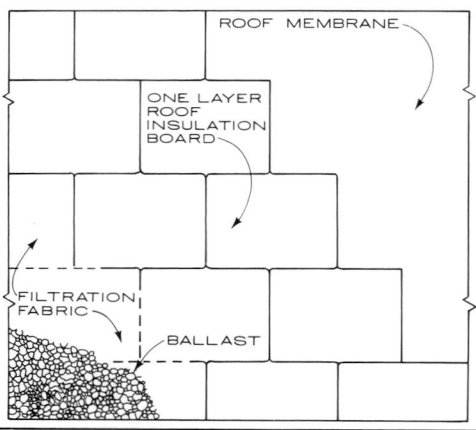

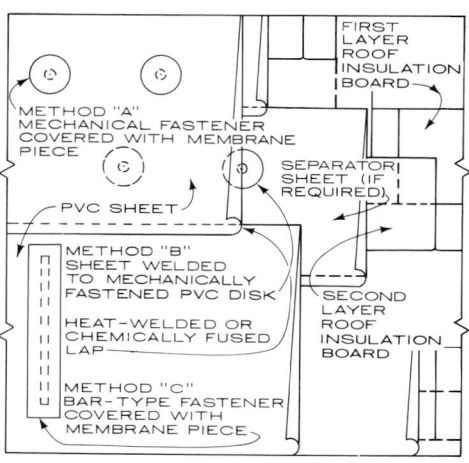

A mechanically anchored roof system is appropriate for roofs that cannot carry the additional load of ballasted roof systems. Systems are available with fasteners that penetrate the membrane or that require no membrane penetration.

The membrane is anchored to the roof using metal bars or individual clips, and it may be installed over concrete, wood, metal, or compatible insulation.

**MECHANICALLY ATTACHED SHEETS**

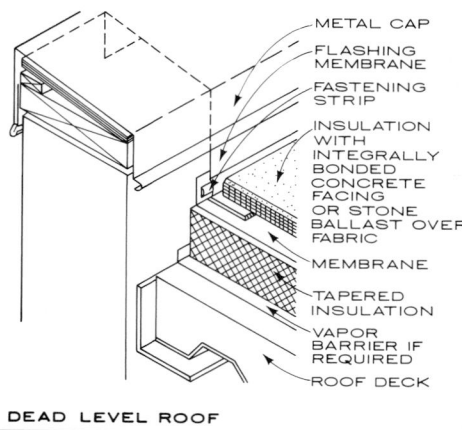

**DEAD LEVEL ROOF**

CTA Architects Engineers; Billings, Montana

**7 MEMBRANE ROOFING**

## NOTES

There are three generic installation methods for EPDM roofing:

1. Fully Adhered: Membrane roofing is rolled onto the substrate and allowed to relax. Underside is then fully coated with bonding adhesive. After both surfaces are tacky, the membrane is pressed onto the substrate with a push broom. Adjoining sheets must overlap at least 3 in., with laps spliced and cemented. Membrane is mechanically secured at perimeter and penetration edges. Flashing protects all edges, openings, and penetrations.

2. Loose Laid: Roofing in this application is laid loose over the substrate, either deck or rigid insulation, and ballasted in place. It is positioned without stretching, allowed to attain its natural shape, and adjacent sheets spliced with adjoining sheets overlapping at least 3 in. Sheets are cemented and rolled together to seal seams. The membrane is mechanically secured at perimeter and penetration edges, and flashing is installed. For ballast, a sufficient amount of river-washed gravel is laid over the membrane to provide 10 lb/sq ft of weight. As an alternate, a precast roof paver system is applied to hold the roofing membrane.

3. Mechanically Fastened: Membrane roof is directly attached to the roof deck with mechanical fasteners. The substrate is anchored to the roof deck, and the fasteners either go through both membrane and insulation or only go through the insulation and deck, with the membrane held down by retainer and cap over the base. Sealant protects against moisture.

Many EPDM membranes are field surfaced to improve resistance to weathering and fire, or to enhance appearance.

## GENERAL NOTES

EPDM elastomeric roofing is synthesized from ethylene, propylene, and a small amount of diene monomer. Manufactured sheets range in thickness from 30 to 60 mils.

Advantages: EPDM roofing exhibits a high degree of resistance to ozone, ultraviolet, extreme temperature and other elements, and degradation from abrasion. It is resilient, strong, elastic, and less prone to cracking and tearing when compared to other forms of membrane roofing.

Disadvantages: Application methods, specific formulas and configurations for adhesives, fasteners, and coatings are unique with each system manufactured. Materials, design, and appropriate use vary widely. Close supervision and regular inspection by manufacturer are a requirement. Labor cost and time allotted for installation may vary.

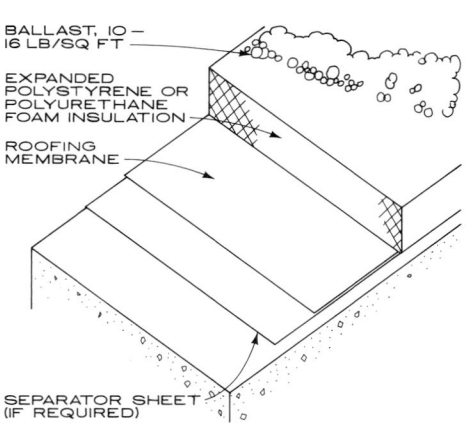

**INSULATED ROOF MEMBRANE APPLICATION**

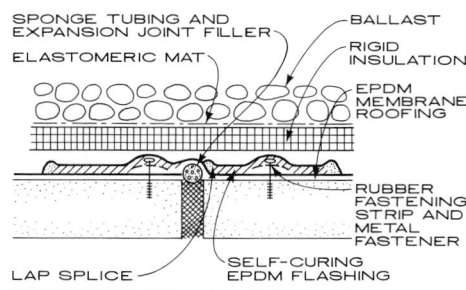

**EXPANSION JOINT: INSULATED ROOF MEMBRANE BALLASTED**

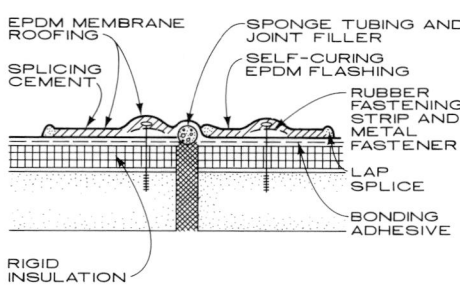

**EXPANSION JOINT: FULLY ADHERED ROOF MEMBRANE**

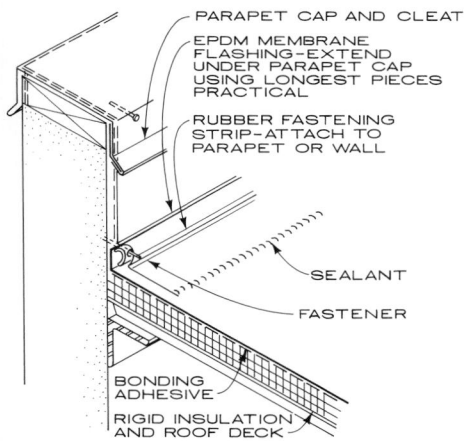

**FULLY ADHERED ROOF AT PARAPET OR WALL**

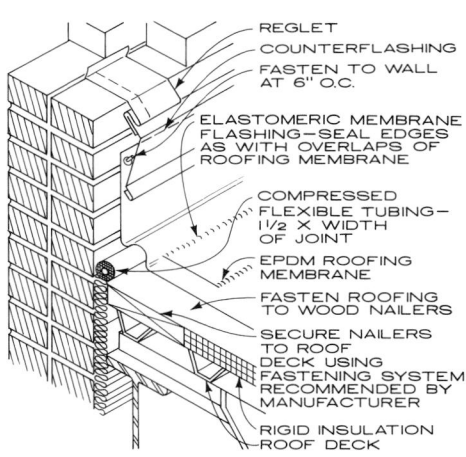

**ROOF EDGE AT NONSUPPORTING WALL**

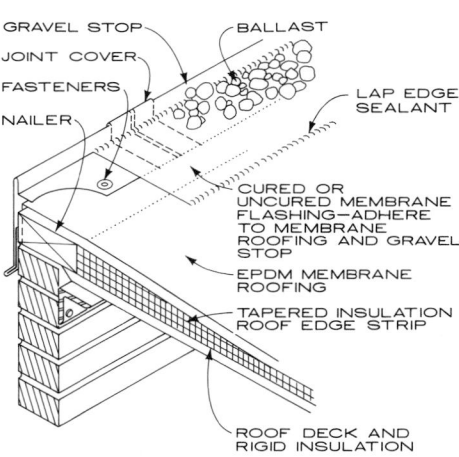

**LIGHT METAL ROOF EDGE**

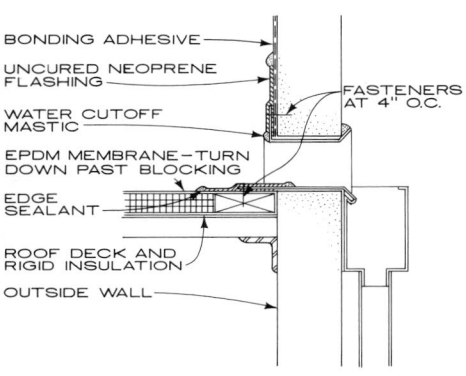

**FULLY ADHERED ROOF SCUPPER**

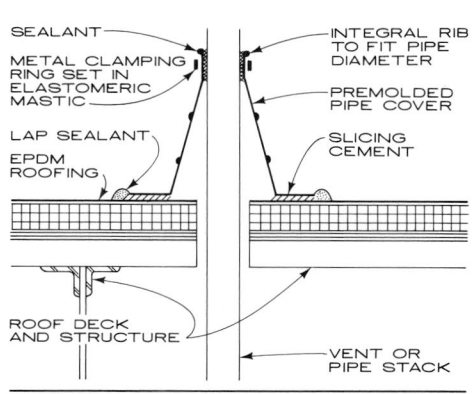

**PREMOLDED VENT PIPE FLASHING**

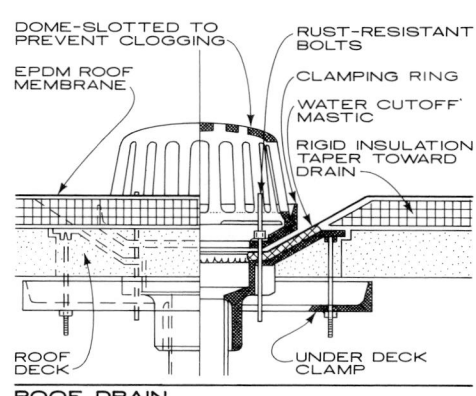

**ROOF DRAIN**

Catherine A. Broad; Washington, D.C.

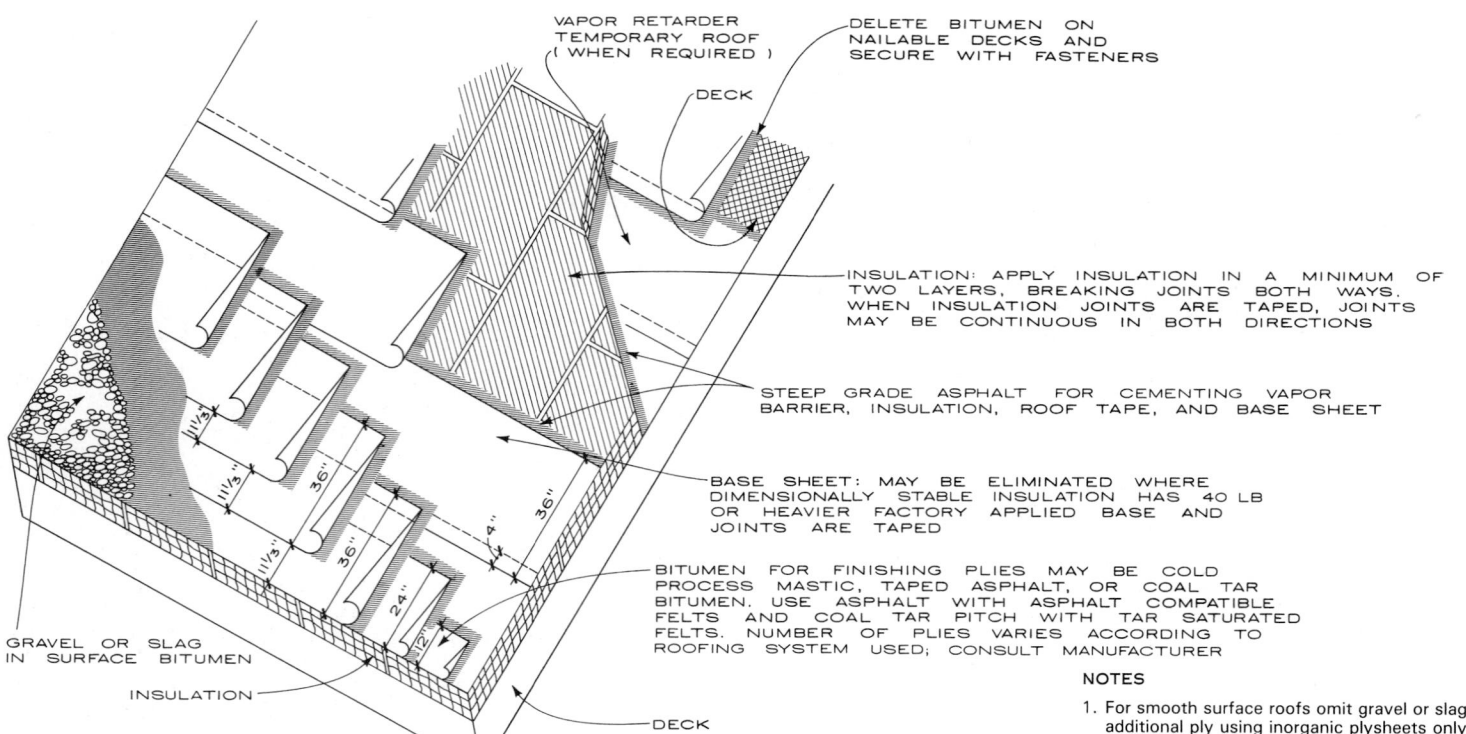

VAPOR RETARDER
TEMPORARY ROOF
(WHEN REQUIRED)

DELETE BITUMEN ON
NAILABLE DECKS AND
SECURE WITH FASTENERS

DECK

INSULATION: APPLY INSULATION IN A MINIMUM OF
TWO LAYERS, BREAKING JOINTS BOTH WAYS.
WHEN INSULATION JOINTS ARE TAPED, JOINTS
MAY BE CONTINUOUS IN BOTH DIRECTIONS

STEEP GRADE ASPHALT FOR CEMENTING VAPOR
BARRIER, INSULATION, ROOF TAPE, AND BASE SHEET

BASE SHEET: MAY BE ELIMINATED WHERE
DIMENSIONALLY STABLE INSULATION HAS 40 LB
OR HEAVIER FACTORY APPLIED BASE AND
JOINTS ARE TAPED

BITUMEN FOR FINISHING PLIES MAY BE COLD
PROCESS MASTIC, TAPED ASPHALT, OR COAL TAR
BITUMEN. USE ASPHALT WITH ASPHALT COMPATIBLE
FELTS AND COAL TAR PITCH WITH TAR SATURATED
FELTS. NUMBER OF PLIES VARIES ACCORDING TO
ROOFING SYSTEM USED; CONSULT MANUFACTURER

GRAVEL OR SLAG
IN SURFACE BITUMEN

INSULATION

DECK

**20 YEAR TYPE BUILT-UP ROOF OVER INSULATION**

### NOTES

1. For smooth surface roofs omit gravel or slag and add additional ply using inorganic plysheets only.
2. On slopes over 1 in./ft all felts along top edge must usually be strapped and back-nailed.
3. When vapor retarder is used, edges of felt should be turned up to a height of 2 in. above cant strip at vertical surfaces. Felts should overlap all roof edges a minimum of 6 in. before application of roofing. 6 in. of felt must be re-turned over the insulation and mopped solidly.

### NOTES

1. Over nonnailable deck or insulation omit rosin paper and cement with asphalt. Nailing strips must be provided.
2. Minimum slope for organic felt: ½ in./ft.
3. Minimum slope for fiberglass felt: 0 in./ft.
4. Consult manufacturer for spacing of nails for particular roofing system.

### SCHEDULE OF FELT OVERLAP (INCHES)

| | |
|---|---|
| Organic base sheet | 4 |
| Fiberglass or base sheet | 2 |
| 2-ply felts/plysheets | 19 |
| 3-ply felts/plysheets | 24²/₃ |
| 4-ply felts/plysheets | 27½ |
| Fiberglass mineral | 3 if selvage granulated |
| Surface cap sheet | 2 if selvage granulated |

STAGGER NAILS AT 12" O.C.

NAILABLE DECK

ROSIN PAPER
(OVER WOOD,
EXCEPT PLYWOOD)

MINERAL SURFACE
ROOFING. 2" SIDE LAPS IF
SELVAGE IS UNGRANULATED;
3" SIDE LAPS IF SELVAGE
IS GRANULATED

STEEP GRADE ASPHALT

ASPHALT BETWEEN
PLIES OF 15 LB FELT.
ASPHALT TYPE (I, II,
III, OR IV)
DETERMINED BY
ROOF SLOPE

**MINERAL SURFACE BUILT-UP ROOF**

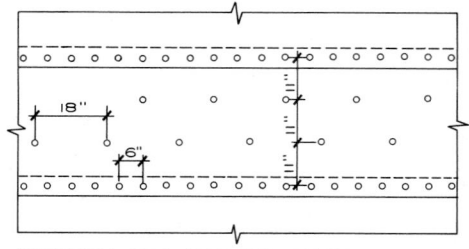

PATTERN FOR NAILING BASE
SHEET OR VAPOR RETARDER OVER
NAILABLE DECK

Kent Wong; Hewlett, Jamison, Atkinson & Luey; Portland, Oregon
Developed by Angelo J. Forlidas, AIA; Charlotte, North Carolina; from data furnished by Robert M. Stafford, P.E., Consulting
Engineer; Charlotte, North Carolina

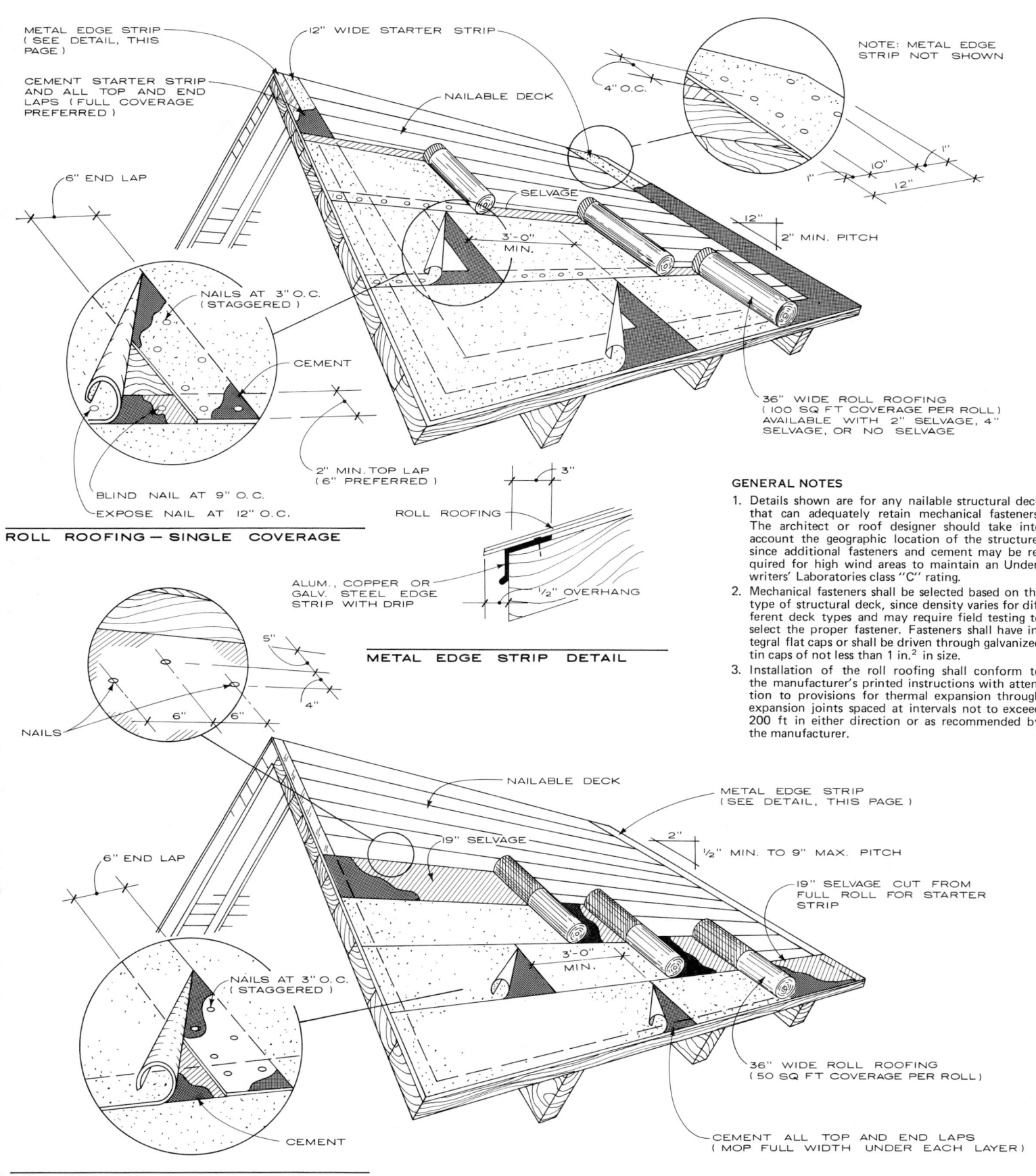

METAL EDGE STRIP
( SEE DETAIL, THIS
PAGE )

CEMENT STARTER STRIP
AND ALL TOP AND END
LAPS ( FULL COVERAGE
PREFERRED )

12" WIDE STARTER STRIP

NAILABLE DECK

NOTE: METAL EDGE
STRIP NOT SHOWN

4" O.C.

1"

10"

1"

12"

SELVAGE

6" END LAP

3'-0"
MIN.

12"

2" MIN. PITCH

NAILS AT 3" O.C.
( STAGGERED )

CEMENT

36" WIDE ROLL ROOFING
( 100 SQ FT COVERAGE PER ROLL )
AVAILABLE WITH 2" SELVAGE, 4"
SELVAGE, OR NO SELVAGE

BLIND NAIL AT 9" O.C.

EXPOSE NAIL AT 12" O.C.

2" MIN. TOP LAP
( 6" PREFERRED )

**ROLL ROOFING — SINGLE COVERAGE**

3"

ROLL ROOFING

ALUM., COPPER OR
GALV. STEEL EDGE
STRIP WITH DRIP

1/2" OVERHANG

**METAL EDGE STRIP DETAIL**

5"

4"

NAILS

6"

6"

**GENERAL NOTES**

1. Details shown are for any nailable structural deck that can adequately retain mechanical fasteners. The architect or roof designer should take into account the geographic location of the structure, since additional fasteners and cement may be required for high wind areas to maintain an Underwriters' Laboratories class "C" rating.

2. Mechanical fasteners shall be selected based on the type of structural deck, since density varies for different deck types and may require field testing to select the proper fastener. Fasteners shall have integral flat caps or shall be driven through galvanized tin caps of not less than 1 in.$^2$ in size.

3. Installation of the roll roofing shall conform to the manufacturer's printed instructions with attention to provisions for thermal expansion through expansion joints spaced at intervals not to exceed 200 ft in either direction or as recommended by the manufacturer.

NAILABLE DECK

METAL EDGE STRIP
( SEE DETAIL, THIS PAGE )

2"

1/2" MIN. TO 9" MAX. PITCH

19" SELVAGE

19" SELVAGE CUT FROM
FULL ROLL FOR STARTER
STRIP

6" END LAP

3'-0"
MIN.

NAILS AT 3" O.C.
( STAGGERED )

36" WIDE ROLL ROOFING
( 50 SQ FT COVERAGE PER ROLL )

CEMENT

CEMENT ALL TOP AND END LAPS
( MOP FULL WIDTH UNDER EACH LAYER )

**ROLL ROOFING — DOUBLE COVERAGE
CONCEALED NAILING**

James E. Phillips; AIA, Liles/Associates/Architects; Greenville, South Carolina

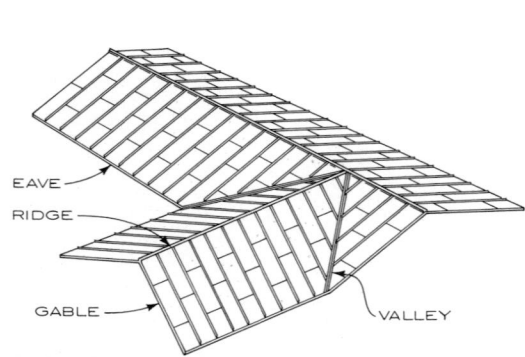

**STANDING SEAM METAL ROOF**

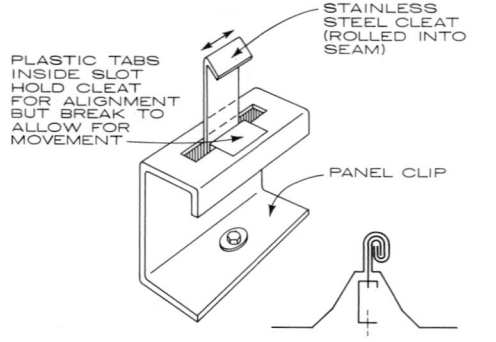

STAINLESS STEEL CLEAT (ROLLED INTO SEAM)

PLASTIC TABS INSIDE SLOT HOLD CLEAT FOR ALIGNMENT BUT BREAK TO ALLOW FOR MOVEMENT

PANEL CLIP

**NOTES**

To allow for expansion and contraction movement in roof panels, some manufacturers set movable cleats into a stationary panel clip system. The cleat is held in position in the center of a slot in the panel clip by two temporary plastic tabs. This allows for correct alignment of the cleat with the roof panel. Once the cleat has been rolled into the panel seam, it will move with the roof panel by forcing the plastic tabs to break under movement pressure.

**MOVABLE CLEAT**

**NOTES**

Roof panels secured at the eave expand up the slope of the roof. Depending on the length of the roof panel, an engineered distance should be left between the end of roof panels on each side of the ridge, thereby allowing for expansion at the ridge. In cases of a very long run of roof panels (usually in excess of 200 ft), expansion joints will be required at other points in addition to the ridge. Any blocking at the ridge should be cut at an angle to provide a space for the panels to bend into when expanding (as in ridge detail A). Ridge coverings can be formed or bowed to move with the expansion of the roof panels (as in ridge details B and C). In addition, the seams can either be flattened or left upright. Upright seams require a closing gasket or panel between seams.

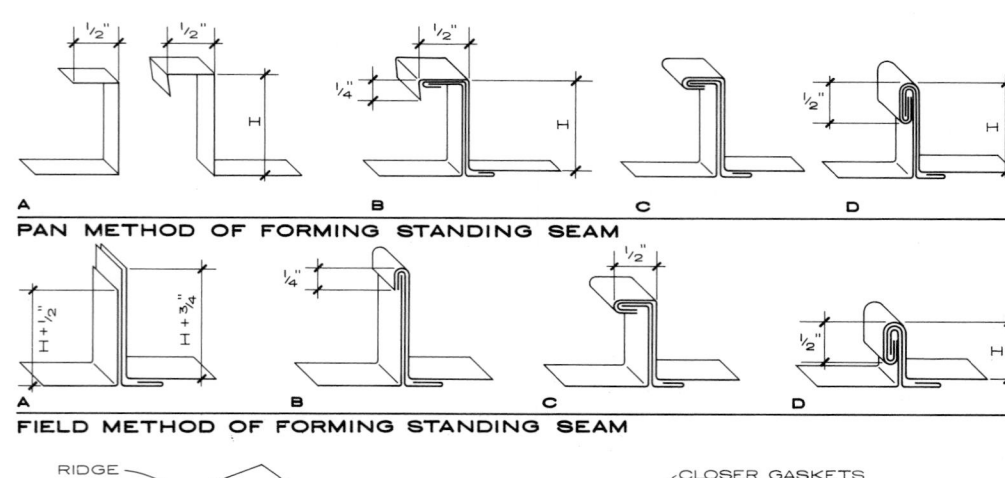

**PAN METHOD OF FORMING STANDING SEAM**

**FIELD METHOD OF FORMING STANDING SEAM**

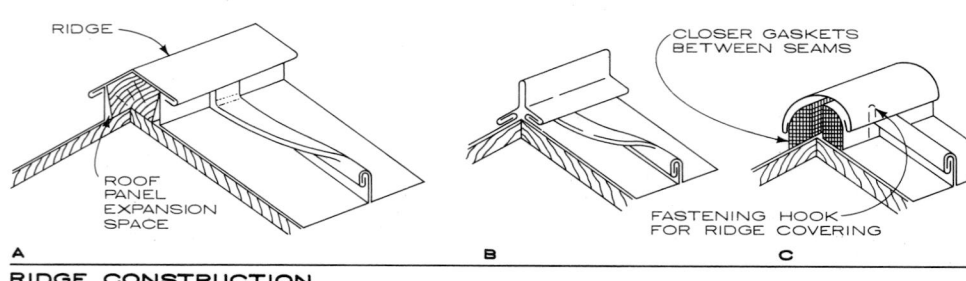

**RIDGE CONSTRUCTION**

END SPLICES SHOULD BE STAGGERED FROM ADJACENT SHEETS SPLICES ARE COVERED WITH A CLAMPING PLATE WITH INTEGRAL CHANNELS TO DIVERT WATER AROUND FASTENERS

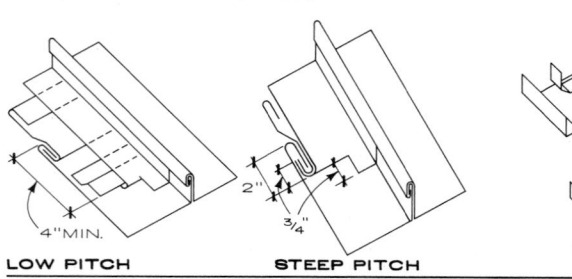

LOW PITCH    STEEP PITCH

**TRANSVERSE SEAM AND PANEL SPLICE**

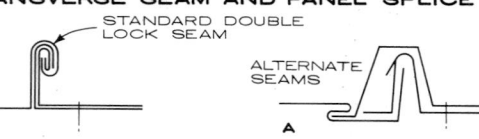

STANDARD DOUBLE LOCK SEAM

ALTERNATE SEAMS

Standing seam roofing may be installed on slopes as gentle as ¼ in./ft. Because of the architectural appearance of the roof system, it is more commonly used on steeper roof slopes, allowing the panels to be seen as part of the overall design.

The spacing of seams may vary within reasonable limits to suit the architectural style of a given building. Preformed sheets (as used with preengineered metal buildings) have seam locations set by locations of prepunched holes in the structural framing members.

The two methods of forming a standing seam are the pan method and the roll method. In the pan method, the

top, bottom, and sides of the individual sheets are preformed to allow locking together at each edge. Seams at the top and bottom of each sheet are called transverse seams. In the roll method, a series of long sheets are joined together at their ends with double flat lock seams. These field-formed seams can be executed either manually or with a seaming machine (a wheeled electronic device which runs along the sheet joint forming the seam).

In either method, cleats (spaced as recommended by the manufacturer) are formed into the standing seam. Seam terminations are usually soldered.

**STANDING SEAM METHODS AND SHAPES**

**GABLE DETAILS**

**EAVE DETAILS**

**VALLEY DETAIL**

Raso-Greaves An Architecture Corporation; Waco, Texas
Straub, VanDine, Dziurman/Architects; Troy, Michigan
Emory E. Hinkel, Jr.; A. G. Odell, Jr. and Associates; Charlotte, North Carolina

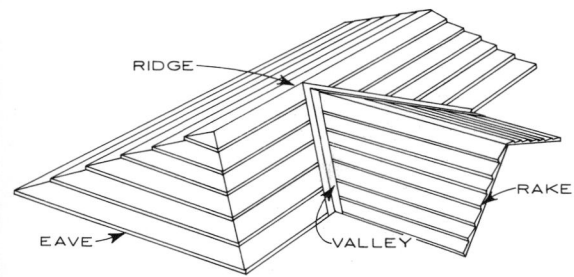

**BERMUDA TYPE METAL ROOF**

### RECOMMENDED GAUGES OR WEIGHTS FOR PAN WIDTHS

| WIDTH OF SHEET (IN.) | WIDTH OF PAN "D" (IN.) | COPPER (OZ) | GALVANIZED STEEL (GAUGE) | STAINLESS STEEL (GAUGE) | PAINTED TERNE 40 LB COATING |
|---|---|---|---|---|---|
| 20 | 16½ | 16 | 26 | 28 | 0.015 IN. |
| 22 | 18½ | 16 | 26 | 28 | 0.015 IN. |
| 24 | 20½ | 16 | 26 | 26 | 0.015 IN. |
| 26 | 22½ | 20 | 24 | 26 | 0.0178 IN. |
| 28 | 24½ | 20 | 24 | 26 | 0.0178 IN. |

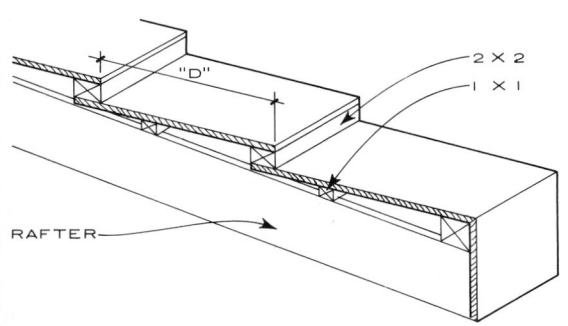

**DETAIL I-WOOD FRAMING**

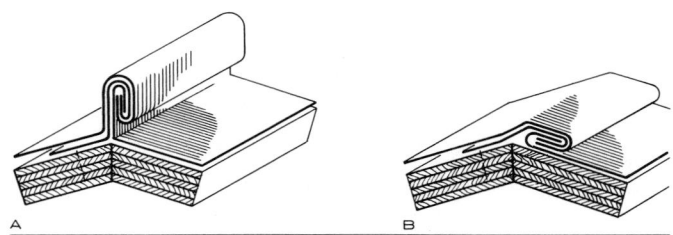

**DETAIL 2-SEAM TYPES AT HIP OR RIDGE**

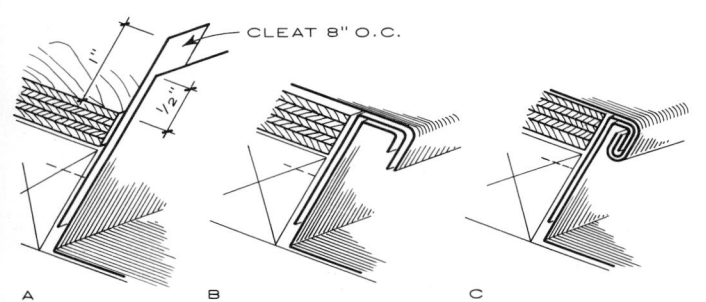

**DETAIL 3-CONSTRUCTION AT BATTEN**

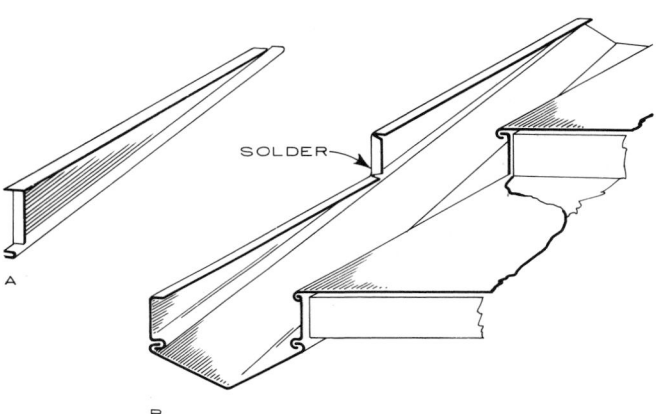

**DETAIL 4-CONSTRUCTION AT CLOSURE AND VALLEY**

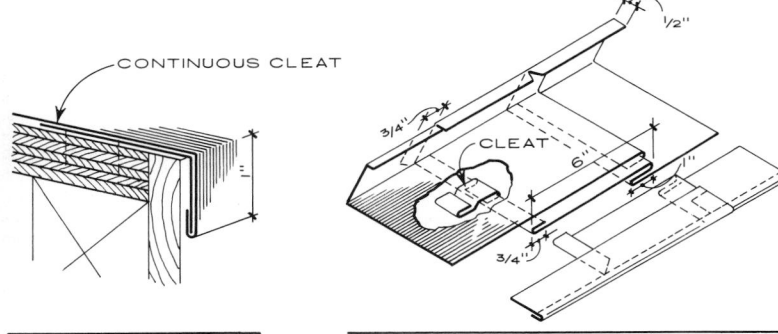

**DETAIL 5-EAVE**   **DETAIL 6-EXPANSION JOINT**

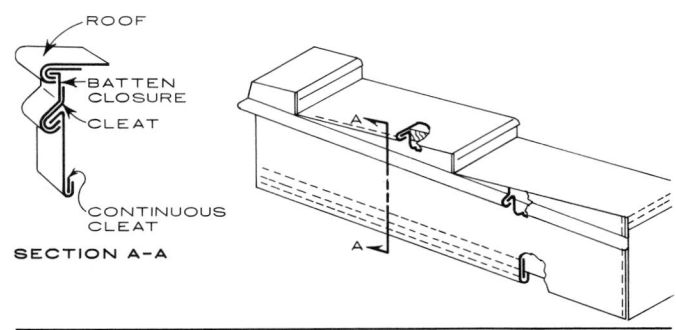

**SECTION A-A**

**DETAIL 7-CONSTRUCTION AT RAKE**

## NOTES

1. The Bermuda roof may be used for roofs having a slope greater than 2½ in./ft. Wood framing must be provided as shown in detail 1. Dimension "D" and gauge of metal will depend on the size of sheet used. See chart. Consult general notes on metal roofs for recommended surface preparation.

2. Bermuda roof is applied beginning at the eave. The first pan is hooked over a continuous cleat as shown in detail 5. The upper portion of the first and each succeeding pan is attached as shown in detail 3. Cleats spaced on 8 in. centers are nailed to batten as in A of detail 3. Joint is developed as shown in B of detail 3 and malleted against batten as shown in C of detail 3. All cross seams are single locked and soldered except at expansion joints. Cross seams should be staggered. Expansion joints should be used at least every 25 ft and formed as shown in detail 6. Roofing is joined at hip or ridge by use of a standing seam as shown in A of detail 2. Seam may be malleted down as shown in B of detail 2.

3. Detail 4 shows the method of forming valleys. Valley sections are lapped 8 in. in direction of flow.

Individual closures for sides of valley are formed as shown in A of detail 4 and must be soldered as indicated in B of detail 4. A method of terminating the roof at rake is shown in detail 7. The face plate (optional) is held in place by continuous cleats at both top and bottom. The batten closure is formed as a cleat to hold edge of roof pan as shown in section A-A of detail 7.

See also Metal Roofs for general notes.

Straub, VanDine, Dziurman/Architects; Troy, Michigan
Emory E. Hinkel, Jr.; A. G. Odell, Jr. and Associates; Charlotte, North Carolina

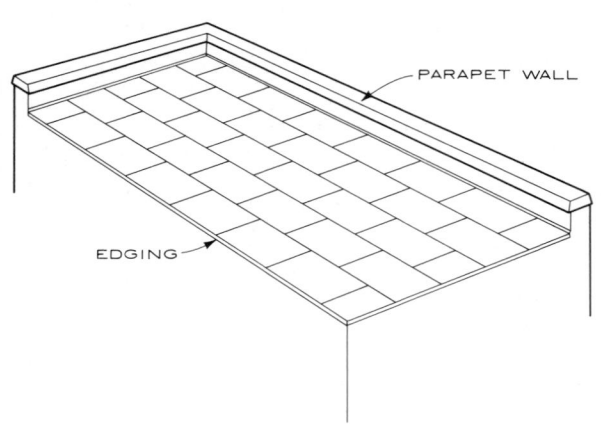

FLAT SEAM ROOF

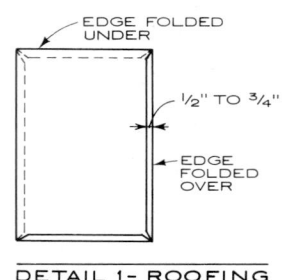

DETAIL 1- ROOFING
SHEET

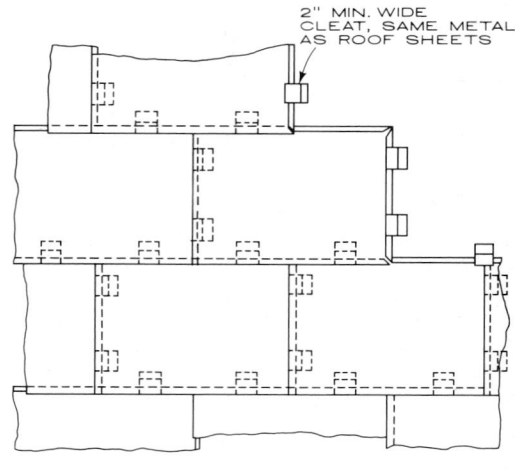

DETAIL 2- FLAT SEAM ROOF

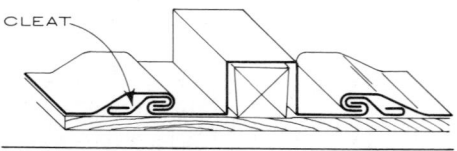

DETAIL 3- EXPANSION BATTEN

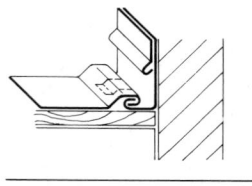

DETAIL 4- JUNCTION AT
PARAPET WALL

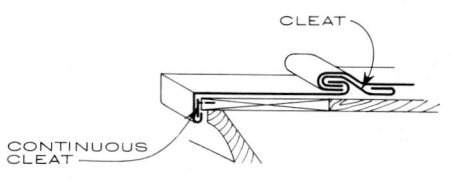

DETAIL 5- ROOF EDGE

## NOTES

1. The flat seam method of roofing as illustrated is most commonly used on roofs of slight pitch or for the covering of curved surfaces such as towers or domes.
2. The joints connecting the sheets of roofs having a pitch greater than $1/2$ in./ft may be sealed with caulking compound or white lead. The joints of roofs having a pitch of less than $1/2$ in./ft must be malleted and thoroughly sweated full with solder.
3. Roofs of slight pitch should be divided by expansion batten as shown in detail 3, into sections not

exceeding maximum total areas of 30 ft$^2$.
4. Consult general notes on metal roofs for recommended surface preparation.
5. The metal sheets may be pretinned if required, $1^{1}/_{2}$ in. back from all edges and on both sides of the sheet. Pans are formed by notching and folding the sheets as shown in detail 1.
6. The pans are held in place by cleating as shown. After pans are in place, all seams are malleted and soldered or sealed.

7. Detail 4 shows the junction of a roof and a parapet wall. Metal base flashing is cleated to deck on 2 ft centers and extended up wall; 8 in. pans are locked and soldered to base flashing. Metal counter flashing covers 4 in. of the base flashing. Detail 5 illustrates the installation of flashing at edge of roof. Flashing is formed as shown and attached to the face by a continuous cleat nailed on 1 ft centers and cleated to the roof deck. Pans are locked and soldered or sealed to the flashing. See also general notes below.

## GENERAL NOTES

1. Detail drawings for metal roof types are diagrammatic only. The indication of adjoining construction is included merely to establish its relation to the sheet metal work and is not intended as a recommendation of architectural design. Any details that may suggest an architectural period do not limit the application of sheet metal to that or any other architectural style.
2. For weights of metals and roof slopes, see data of the Sheet Metal and Air Conditioning Contractors' National Association and recommendations of manufacturers.

3. Metals used must be of a thickness or gauge heavy enough and in correct proportion to the breadth and scale of the work. Provide expansion joints for freedom of movement.
4. Prevent direct contact of metal roofing with dissimilar metals that cause electrolysis.
5. A wide range of metals, alloys, and finishes are available for metal roofing. The durability as well as the maintenance requirements of each should be taken into consideration when selecting roofing.

6. The surface to receive the metal roofing should be thoroughly dry and covered by a saturated roofing felt in case of leakage due to construction error or wind driven moisture. A rosin paper should be applied over the felt to avoid bonding between felt and metal.
7. Many of the prefabricated batten and standing seam devices are not as watertight as with conventional methods and are therefore more suitable for steeply pitched roofs and mansards.

Straub, VanDine, Dziurman/Architects; Troy, Michigan
Emory E. Hinkel, Jr.; A. G. Odell, Jr. and Associates; Charlotte, North Carolina

**FLASHING AND SHEET METAL**

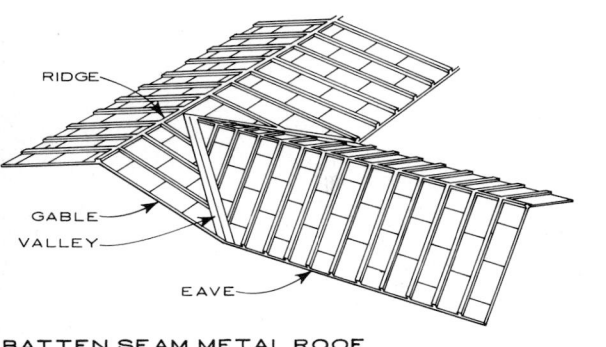

BATTEN SEAM METAL ROOF

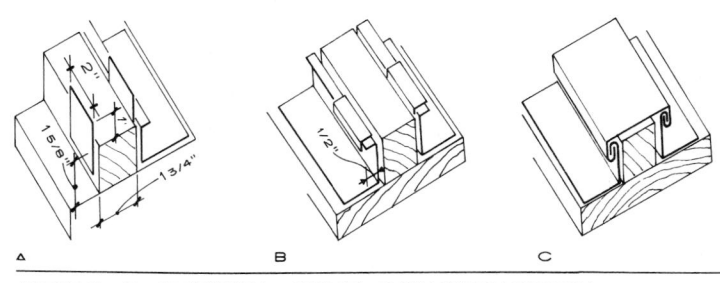

DETAIL 1-BATTEN ALTERNATES FOR METAL ROOFING

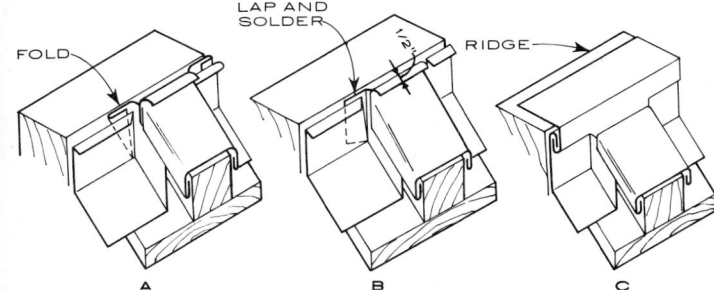

DETAIL 2 - RIDGE CONSTRUCTION

DETAIL 3-BATTEN JOINT CONSTRUCTION

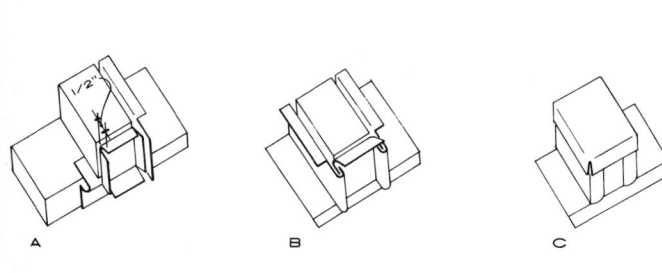

DETAIL 4 - BATTEN CAP CONSTRUCTION

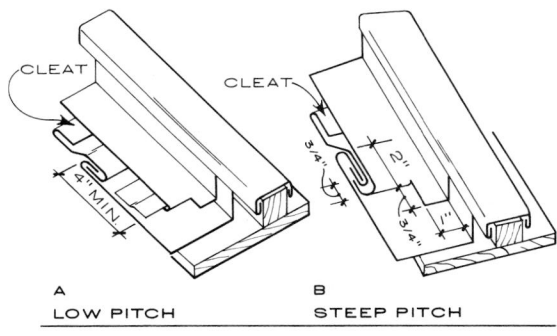

DETAIL 5 - TRANSVERSE SEAM

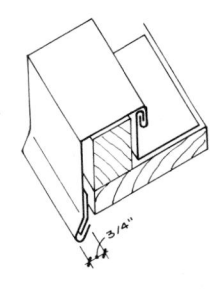

DETAIL 6 - GABLE

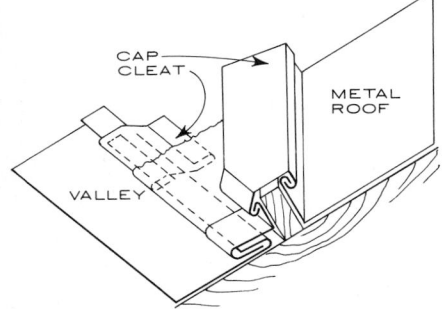

DETAIL 7 - VALLEY

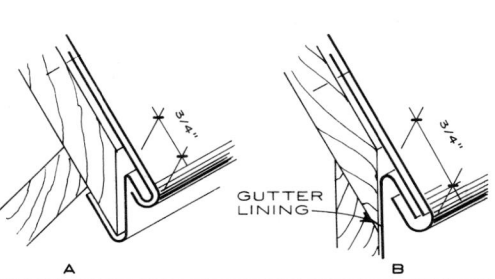

DETAIL 8 - EAVES

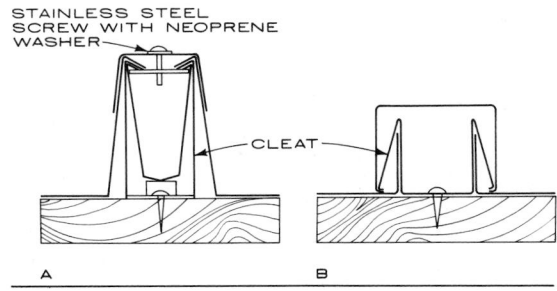

DETAIL 9 - PREFABRICATED BATTENS

## NOTES

1. Batten seam roofing may be applied on slopes of 3 in./ft or greater. If the surface to receive the roofing is other than wood, the battens should be bolted into place. All batten fasteners must be countersunk into battens. See general notes on Metal Roofs for recommended surface preparation.

2. The spacing of the wood battens may vary within reasonable limits to suit the architectural style and scale of the building, but the recommended maximum distance is 20 in. between battens. Care should be taken to space the battens in such a manner that waste of metal is held to a minimum. Battens may be shaped as shown in A or B of detail 1.

A is preferred, since it automatically makes allowance for expansion. When battens shown in B are used, care must be taken to provide for expansion by bending the metal where it meets the batten at greater than 90°.

3. Sheets are formed into pans with each side turned up 2 1/8 in. A 1/2 in. flange is turned toward the center of the pan as shown in B of detail 3. At lower end of the pan, the sheet is notched and a hook edge is formed as in A or B of detail 5. For low pitched roofs the upper end of the sheet is formed as in A of detail 5. On steeper roofs the upper end is formed as shown in B of detail 5. Pans

are installed, starting at the eave, and held in place with cleats spaced not over 12 in. on center as shown in A of detail 3. Each pan is hooked to the one below it and cleated into place. After pans are in place, a cap is installed over the batten as shown in B and C of detail 3.

4. A number of manufacturers have developed metal roofing systems using several prefabricated devices. A and B of detail 9 show two common prefabricated battens in use.

5. See also Standing Seam Metal Roofing for details on combination batten and standing or flat seam roofing. See also Metal Roofs for general notes.

Straub, VanDine, Dziurman/Architects; Troy, Michigan
Emory E. Hinkel, Jr.; A. G. Odell, Jr. and Associates; Charlotte, North Carolina

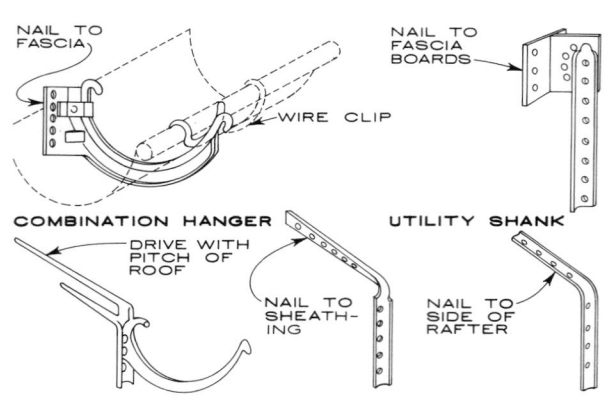

COMBINATION HANGER    UTILITY SHANK

NAIL TO FASCIA

WIRE CLIP

NAIL TO FASCIA BOARDS

DRIVE WITH PITCH OF ROOF

NAIL TO SHEATH-ING

NAIL TO SIDE OF RAFTER

### DRIVE HANGER    VARIOUS SHANKS

**SHANK AND CIRCLE HANGERS**
Available in malleable and wrought copper, bronze, stainless steel and aluminum. Only a sampling of the wide variety of shapes available is shown. See mfrs. literature.

### GUTTER HANGERS

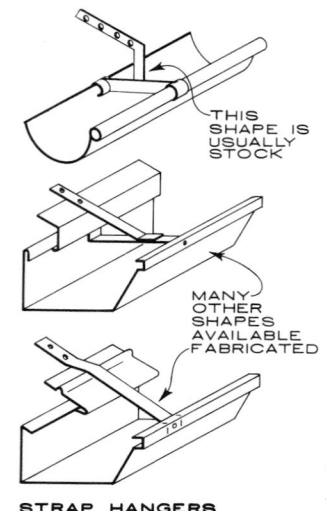

THIS SHAPE IS USUALLY STOCK

MANY OTHER SHAPES AVAILABLE FABRICATED

**STRAP HANGERS**

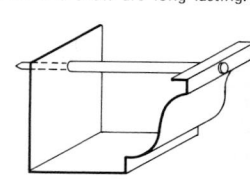

**BRACKET HANGER**
Various shapes are available.

**SPIKE AND FERRULE**
Not recommended if girth is over 15 in.

NOTE: Gutter hangers are normally spaced 3'-0" O.C. Reduce to 1'-6" O.C. where ice and snow are long lasting.

### GUTTER BRACKET OR STRAP SIZES

| GIRTH INCHES | GALV. STEEL INCHES | COPPER INCHES | ALUM. INCHES | STAINLESS INCHES |
|---|---|---|---|---|
| UP TO 15 | 1/8 x 1 | 1/8 x 1 | 3/16 x 1 | 1/8 x 1 |
| 15 TO 20 | 3/16 x 1 | 1/4 x 1 | 1/4 x 1 | 1/8 x 1 1/2 |
| 20 TO 24 | 1/4 x 1 1/2 | 1/4 x 1 1/2 | 1/4 x 2 | 1/8 x 2 |

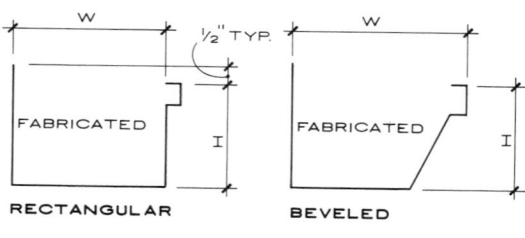

RECTANGULAR    BEVELED    OGEE OR STYLE "K"    SEMICIRCULAR OR HALF-ROUND

FABRICATED    FABRICATED    STOCK    STOCK

1/2" TYP.

**METAL GUTTER NOTES**

Various sizes and other shapes available.

Always keep front 1/2 in. lower than back of gutter.

Do not use width less than 4 in. except for canopies and small porches. Minimum ratio of depth to width should be 3 to 4.

| OGEE OR STYLE "K" | | SEMICIRCULAR OR HALF-ROUND | |
|---|---|---|---|
| 2 1/2" H x 3" W | | 4" W | G |
| 2 3/4" H x 4" W | G A | 5" W | G A |
| 3 3/4" H x 5" W | G A | 6" W | G A |
| 4 3/4" H x 6" W | G | 7" W | G |
| 5 1/4" H x 7" W | | 8" W | G |
| 6" H x 8" W | | | |

NOTE: Stock sizes—G = galvanized, A = aluminum.

### METAL GUTTER SHAPES AND SIZES

### NOTES

1. Continuous gutters may be formed at the installation site with cold forming equipment, thus eliminating joints in long runs of gutter.
2. Girth is width of sheet metal from which gutter is fabricated.
3. Sizes listed in table to the left but not marked stock are available on special order.
4. Aluminum and galvanized steel are more commonly used, whereas copper and especially stainless steel are least used.
5. All jointing methods are applicable to most gutter shapes. Lap joints are more commonly used. Seal all joints with mastic or by soldering. Lock, slip, or lap joints do not provide expansion.
6. See SMACNA Architectural Sheet Metal Manual for gutter sizing and details.

### EXPANSION JOINTS

Expansion joints should be used on all straight runs over 40 ft. In a 10 ft section of gutter and a 100° temperature change linear expansion will be:

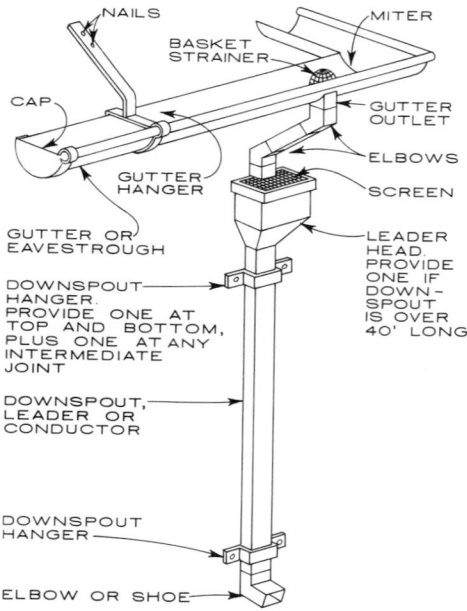

NAILS    MITER
BASKET STRAINER
CAP
GUTTER OUTLET
ELBOWS
GUTTER HANGER
SCREEN
GUTTER OR EAVESTROUGH
LEADER HEAD. PROVIDE ONE IF DOWN-SPOUT IS OVER 40' LONG
DOWNSPOUT HANGER. PROVIDE ONE AT TOP AND BOTTOM, PLUS ONE AT ANY INTERMEDIATE JOINT
DOWNSPOUT, LEADER OR CONDUCTOR
DOWNSPOUT HANGER
ELBOW OR SHOE

### PARTS OF A GUTTER

**NOTE**
PVC plastic gutter and downspout parts are similar to metal. See manufacturers' data for shapes and sizes.

Jones/Richards and Associates; Ogden, Utah
Lawrence W. Cobb; Columbia, South Carolina

DASH LINE INDICATES ROOF SLOPE

PITCH 12:12    12:7    12:5    12:0

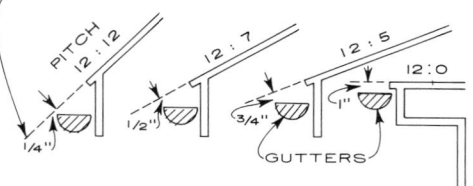

1/4"   1/2"   3/4"   1"   GUTTERS

Gutters should be placed below slope line so that snow and ice can slide clear. Steeper pitch requires less clearance.

### PLACING OF GUTTERS

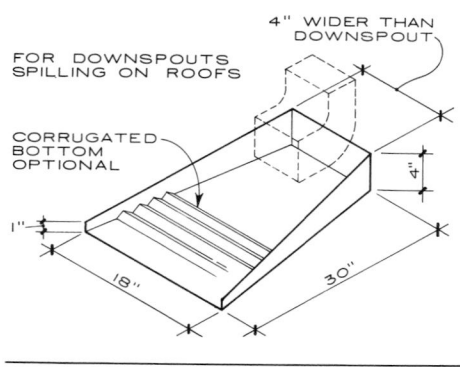

4" WIDER THAN DOWNSPOUT

FOR DOWNSPOUTS SPILLING ON ROOFS

CORRUGATED BOTTOM OPTIONAL

1"   18"   30"   4"

### SPLASH PAN

### EXPANSION OF METAL GUTTERS IN 40 FT

| METAL | COEFFICIENT OF EXPANSION | MOVEMENT |
|---|---|---|
| Aluminum | .00128 | .15 in. |
| Copper | .00093 | .11 in. |
| Galvanized steel | .0065 | .08 in. |

STOCK    STOCK
CORRUGATED ROUND    PLAIN ROUND
FABRI-CATED    STOCK
PLAIN RECTANGULAR    CORRUGATED RECTANGULAR

### NOTES

Space downspouts 20 ft min., 50 ft max., generally. Extreme max. 60 ft.

Do not use size smaller than 7.00 in area except for canopies.

Corrugated shapes resist freezing better than plain shapes.

Elbows available: 45°, 60°, 75°, 90°.

# WIDTH OF RECTANGULAR GUTTERS FOR GIVEN ROOF AREAS AND RAINFALL INTENSITIES

NOTE

The terms "leader," "conductor," and "downspout" all mean the same thing.

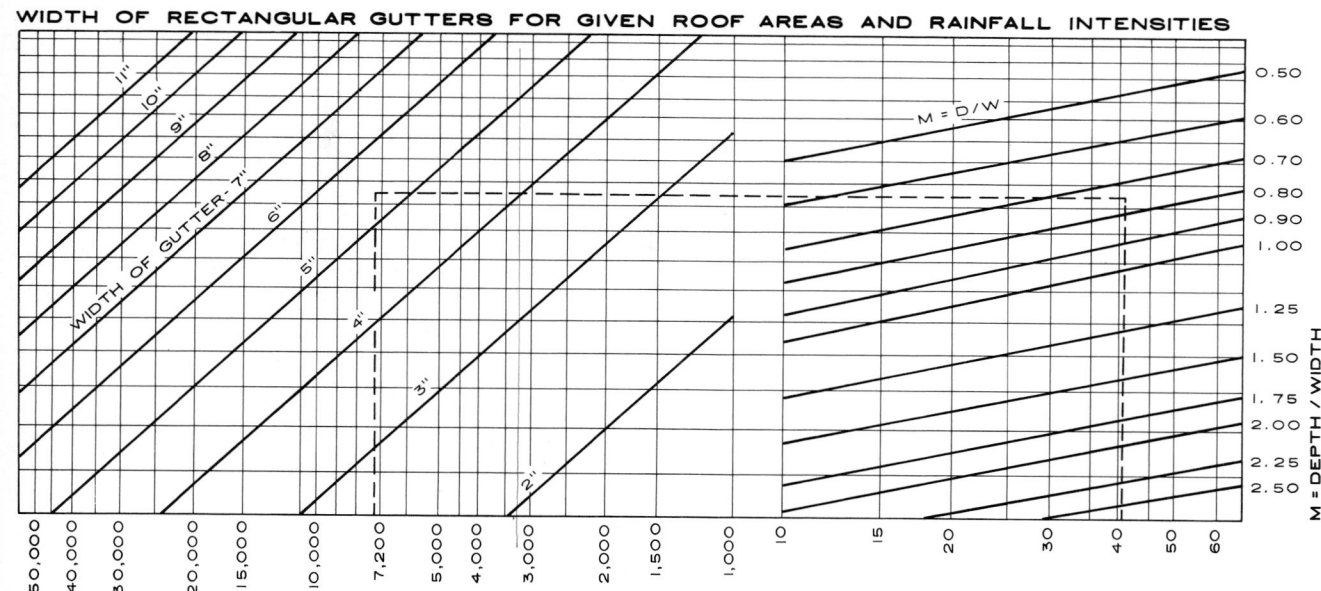

IA = RAINFALL INTENSITY × AREA

L = LENGTH OF GUTTER IN FEET

## SAMPLE PROBLEM

To size rectangular gutter for a building 120 x 30 ft. located in New York City. This building has a flat roof with a raised roof edge on three sides. A gutter is to be located on one of the 120 ft. sides. So that each section of gutter will not exceed 50 ft., three downspouts will be used with 2 gutter expansion joints. The area to be drained by each section of gutter will be 1200 sq. ft., the rainfall intensity from map below is 6 in., the length of each gutter section is 40 ft., and the ratio of gutter depth to width is 0.75. On chart above find the vertical line representing L = 40. Proceed vertically along this line to its intersection with the oblique line representing M = 0.75. Pass horizontally to the left to intersect the vertical line representing IA = 7200. The point of intersection occurs between the oblique line representing gutter widths of 5 and 6 in. The required width of gutter is, therefore, 6 in. and its depth need be only 4 $\frac{1}{2}$ in.

## DESIGN AREAS FOR PITCHED ROOFS

| PITCH | FACTOR |
|---|---|
| LEVEL TO 3 IN./FT. | 1.00 |
| 4 TO 5 IN./FT. | 1.05 |
| 6 TO 8 IN./FT. | 1.10 |
| 9 TO 11 IN./FT. | 1.20 |
| 12 IN./FT. | 1.30 |

NOTE: When a roof is sloped neither the plan nor actual area should be used in sizing drainage. Multiply the plan area by the factor shown above to obtain design area.

## INFLUENCE OF GUTTER SHAPE ON DESIGN

### 1. RECTANGULAR GUTTERS

Use graph at top of page.

### 2. IRREGULAR SHAPES

Determine equivalent rectangular size and use same method.

### 3. SEMICIRCULAR GUTTERS

First size downspout from tables below. Then use gutter 1 inch larger in diameter.

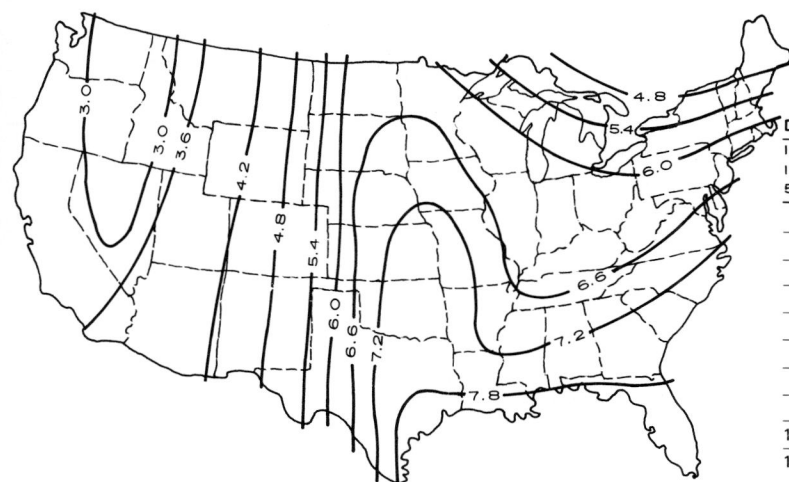

## RAINFALL INTENSITY MAP

NOTE

Map shows hourly rainfall intensity in inches per hour for 5 minute periods to be expected once in 10 years. Normally this is adequate for design, but some storms have been twice as intense in some areas. See local records.

Lawrence W. Cobb; Columbia, South Carolina

## DOWNSPOUT CAPACITY

| INTENSITY IN IN./HR. LASTING 5 MIN. | SQ.FT. ROOF/ SQ.IN. DOWN-SPOUT |
|---|---|
| 2 | 600 |
| 3 | 400 |
| 4 | 300 |
| 5 | 240 |
| 6 | 200 |
| 7 | 175 |
| 8 | 150 |
| 9 | 130 |
| 10 | 120 |
| 11 | 110 |

## GENERAL NOTES

Most gutters are run level for appearance. However, a slope of $\frac{1}{16}$ in. per foot is desirable for drainage.

For residential work allow 100 sq. ft. of roof area per 1 sq. in. of downspout.

## DOWNSPOUT SIZES

| TYPE | AREA SQ. IN. | NOM. SIZE IN. | ACT. SIZE IN. |
|---|---|---|---|
| PLAIN ROUND | 7.07 | 3 | 3 |
| | 12.57 | 4 | 4 |
| | 19.63 | 5 | 5 |
| | 28.27 | 6 | 6 |
| CORR. ROUND | 5.94 | 3 | 3 |
| | 11.04 | 4 | 4 |
| | 17.72 | 5 | 5 |
| | 25.97 | 6 | 6 |
| CORR. RECT. | 3.80 | 2 | 1$\frac{3}{4}$ x 2$\frac{1}{4}$ |
| | 7.73 | 3 | 2$\frac{1}{8}$ x 3$\frac{1}{4}$ |
| | 11.70 | 4 | 2$\frac{3}{4}$ x 4$\frac{1}{4}$ |
| | 18.75 | 5 | 3$\frac{3}{4}$ x 5 |
| PLAIN RECT. | 3.94 | 2 | 1$\frac{3}{4}$ x 2$\frac{1}{4}$ |
| | 6.00 | 3 | 2 x 3 |
| | 12.00 | 4 | 3 x 4 |
| | 20.00 | 5 | 3$\frac{3}{4}$ x 4$\frac{3}{4}$ |
| | 24.00 | 6 | 4 x 6 |

## MINIMUM THICKNESS (GAUGES OR WEIGHT) FOR COMMON FLASHING CONDITIONS

| MATERIALS | BASE COURSE | WALL OPENINGS HEAD AND SILL | THROUGH WALL AND SPANDREL | CAP AND BASE FLASHING | VERTICAL AND HORIZONTAL SURFACES | ROOF EDGE RIDGES AND HIPS | CRICKETS VALLEY OR GUTTER | CHIMNEY PAN | LEDGE FLASHING | ROOF PENETRATIONS | COPING WIDTH UP TO 12" | COPING WIDTH ABOVE 12" | EDGE STRIPS | CLEATS | NOTE |
|---|---|---|---|---|---|---|---|---|---|---|---|---|---|---|---|
| Copper | 10 oz | 10 oz | 10 oz | 16 oz | 16 oz | 16 oz | 16 oz | 16 oz | 16 oz | 16 oz | 16 oz | 20 oz | 20 oz | 16 oz | |
| Aluminum | 0.019″ | 0.019″ | 0.019″ | 0.019″ | 0.019″ | 0.019″ | 0.019″ | 0.019″ | 0.019″ | 0.040″ | 0.032″ | 0.040″ | 0.024″ | ✕ | Note 6 |
| Stainless steel | 30 GA | 30 GA | 30 GA | 26 GA | 30 GA | 26 GA | 26 GA | 30 GA | 26 GA | 26 GA | 26 GA | 24 GA | 24 GA | ✕ | Note 5 |
| Galvanized steel | 26 GA | 26 GA | 26 GA | 26 GA | 26 GA | 24 GA | 24 GA | 26 GA | 24 GA | 24 GA | 24 GA | 22 GA | 26 GA | 22 GA | Note 2 |
| Zinc alloy | 0.027″ | 0.027″ | 0.027″ | 0.027″ | 0.027″ | 0.027″ | 0.027″ | 0.027″ | 0.027″ | 0.027″ | 0.027″ | 0.032″ | 0.040″ | 0.027″ | Note 4 |
| Lead | 3# | 2½# | 2½# | 2½# | 3# | 3# | 3# | 3# | 3# | 3# | 3# | 3# | 3# | 3# | Note 3 |
| Painted terne | 40# | 40# | 40# | 20# | 40# | 20# | 40# | 20# | 40# | 40# | ✕ | ✕ | 20# | 40# | Note 8 |
| elastomeric sheet; fabric-coated metal | See Note 7 | | | ✕ | ✕ | ✕ | ✕ | ✕ | See Note 7 | | ✕ | ✕ | ✕ | | Note 7 |

### GENERAL NOTES

1. All sizes and weights of material given in chart are minimum. Actual conditions may require greater strength.
2. All galvanized steel must be painted.
3. With lead flashing use 16 oz copper cleats. If any part is exposed, use 3# lead cleats.
4. Coat zinc with asphaltum paint when in contact with redwood or cedar. High acid content (in these woods only) develops stains.
5. Type 302 stainless steel is an all purpose flashing type.
6. Use only aluminum manufactured for the purpose of flashing.
7. See manufacturer's literature for use and types of flashing.
8. In general, cleats will be of the same material as flashing, but heavier weight or thicker gauge.
9. In selecting metal flashing, precaution must be taken not to place flashing in direct contact with dissimilar metals that cause electrolysis.
10. Spaces marked ✕ in the table are uses not recommended for that material.

## GALVANIC CORROSION (ELECTROLYSIS) POTENTIAL BETWEEN COMMON FLASHING MATERIALS AND SELECTED CONSTRUCTION MATERIALS

| FLASHING MATERIALS | COPPER | ALUMINUM | STAINLESS STEEL | GALVANIZED STEEL | ZINC | LEAD | BRASS | BRONZE | MONEL | UNCURED MORTAR OR CEMENT | WOODS WITH ACID (REDWOOD AND RED CEDAR) | IRON/STEEL |
|---|---|---|---|---|---|---|---|---|---|---|---|---|
| Copper | | ● | ● | ◗ | ● | ◗ | ◗ | ◗ | ◗ | ○ | ○ | ● |
| Aluminum | | | ○ | ○ | ◗ | ● | ● | ● | ○ | ● | ● | ● |
| Stainless steel | | | | ● | ● | ○ | ● | ● | ● | ○ | ● | ◗ |
| Galvanized steel | | | | | ○ | ○ | ◗ | ◗ | ● | ● | ● | ● |
| Zinc alloy | | | | | | ○ | ● | ● | ● | ● | ● | ● |
| Lead | | | | | | | ◗ | ◗ | ◗ | ● | ◗ | ○ |

● Galvanic action will occur, hence direct contact should be avoided.
◗ Galvanic action may occur under certain circumstances and/or over a period of time.
○ Galvanic action is insignificant, metals may come into direct contact under normal circumstances.

GENERAL NOTE: Galvanic corrosion is apt to occur when water runoff from one material comes in contact with a potentially reactive material.

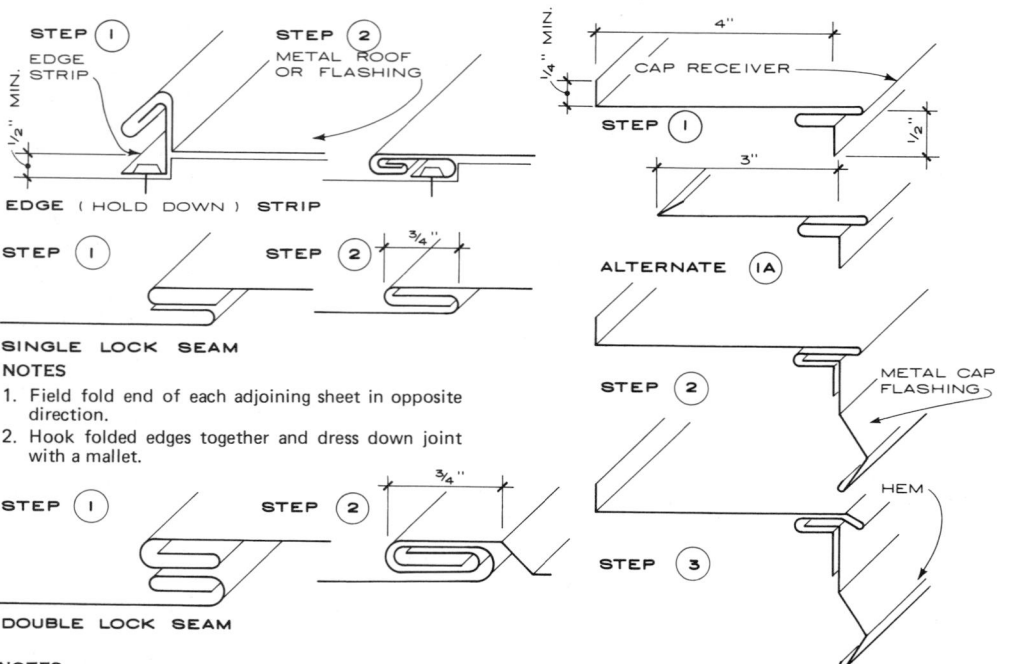

**SINGLE LOCK SEAM**

NOTES
1. Field fold end of each adjoining sheet in opposite direction.
2. Hook folded edges together and dress down joint with a mallet.

**DOUBLE LOCK SEAM**

NOTES
1. Double fold end of each adjoining sheet in opposite direction with bar folder.
2. Slide edges together and dress down joint with a mallet.

**DEVELOPMENT OF CAP FLASHING**

NOTE
Hem in cap flashing recommended for stiffness; but may be omitted if heavier gauge material used.

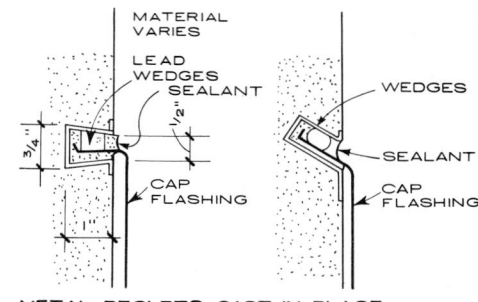

**METAL REGLETS CAST IN PLACE**

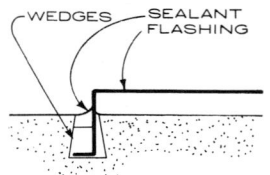

**REGLET SAWED IN MATERIAL**

**TYPICAL REGLETS**

NOTE
Various types of metal reglets are available for cast in place and masonry work; see manufacturer's literature. Where material permits, reglets may be sawn. Flashing is secured in reglets with lead wedges at max. 12″ o.c., fill reglet with nonhardening water-resistant compound.

Michael Scott Rudden, The Stephens Associates P.C.—Architects; Albany, New York

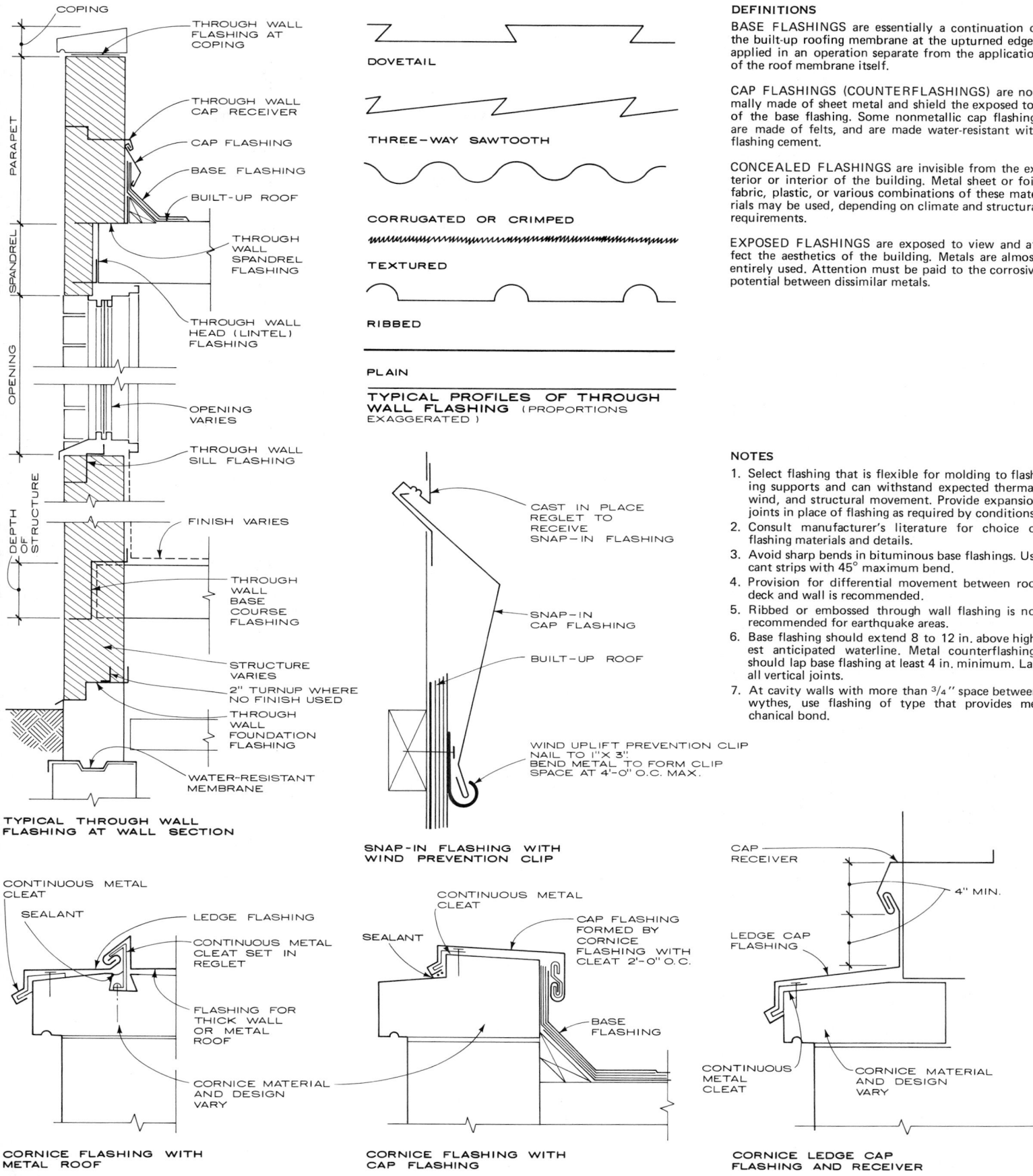

## DEFINITIONS

**BASE FLASHINGS** are essentially a continuation of the built-up roofing membrane at the upturned edges, applied in an operation separate from the application of the roof membrane itself.

**CAP FLASHINGS (COUNTERFLASHINGS)** are normally made of sheet metal and shield the exposed top of the base flashing. Some nonmetallic cap flashings are made of felts, and are made water-resistant with flashing cement.

**CONCEALED FLASHINGS** are invisible from the exterior or interior of the building. Metal sheet or foil, fabric, plastic, or various combinations of these materials may be used, depending on climate and structural requirements.

**EXPOSED FLASHINGS** are exposed to view and affect the aesthetics of the building. Metals are almost entirely used. Attention must be paid to the corrosive potential between dissimilar metals.

## NOTES

1. Select flashing that is flexible for molding to flashing supports and can withstand expected thermal, wind, and structural movement. Provide expansion joints in place of flashing as required by conditions.
2. Consult manufacturer's literature for choice of flashing materials and details.
3. Avoid sharp bends in bituminous base flashings. Use cant strips with 45° maximum bend.
4. Provision for differential movement between roof deck and wall is recommended.
5. Ribbed or embossed through wall flashing is not recommended for earthquake areas.
6. Base flashing should extend 8 to 12 in. above highest anticipated waterline. Metal counterflashings should lap base flashing at least 4 in. minimum. Lap all vertical joints.
7. At cavity walls with more than 3/4" space between wythes, use flashing of type that provides mechanical bond.

### Labels within figures

COPING

THROUGH WALL FLASHING AT COPING

THROUGH WALL CAP RECEIVER

CAP FLASHING

BASE FLASHING

BUILT-UP ROOF

THROUGH WALL SPANDREL FLASHING

THROUGH WALL HEAD (LINTEL) FLASHING

OPENING VARIES

THROUGH WALL SILL FLASHING

FINISH VARIES

THROUGH WALL BASE COURSE FLASHING

STRUCTURE VARIES

2" TURNUP WHERE NO FINISH USED

THROUGH WALL FOUNDATION FLASHING

WATER-RESISTANT MEMBRANE

PARAPET

SPANDREL

OPENING

DEPTH OF STRUCTURE

**TYPICAL THROUGH WALL FLASHING AT WALL SECTION**

DOVETAIL

THREE-WAY SAWTOOTH

CORRUGATED OR CRIMPED

TEXTURED

RIBBED

PLAIN

**TYPICAL PROFILES OF THROUGH WALL FLASHING** (PROPORTIONS EXAGGERATED)

CAST IN PLACE REGLET TO RECEIVE SNAP-IN FLASHING

SNAP-IN CAP FLASHING

BUILT-UP ROOF

WIND UPLIFT PREVENTION CLIP NAIL TO 1" X 3". BEND METAL TO FORM CLIP SPACE AT 4'-0" O.C. MAX.

**SNAP-IN FLASHING WITH WIND PREVENTION CLIP**

CONTINUOUS METAL CLEAT

SEALANT

LEDGE FLASHING

CONTINUOUS METAL CLEAT SET IN REGLET

FLASHING FOR THICK WALL OR METAL ROOF

CORNICE MATERIAL AND DESIGN VARY

**CORNICE FLASHING WITH METAL ROOF**

CONTINUOUS METAL CLEAT

SEALANT

CAP FLASHING FORMED BY CORNICE FLASHING WITH CLEAT 2'-0" O.C.

BASE FLASHING

CORNICE MATERIAL AND DESIGN VARY

**CORNICE FLASHING WITH CAP FLASHING**

CAP RECEIVER

4" MIN.

LEDGE CAP FLASHING

CONTINUOUS METAL CLEAT

CORNICE MATERIAL AND DESIGN VARY

**CORNICE LEDGE CAP FLASHING AND RECEIVER**

**CORNICE FLASHING**

Michael Scott Rudden, The Stephens Associates P.C.—Architects; Albany, New York

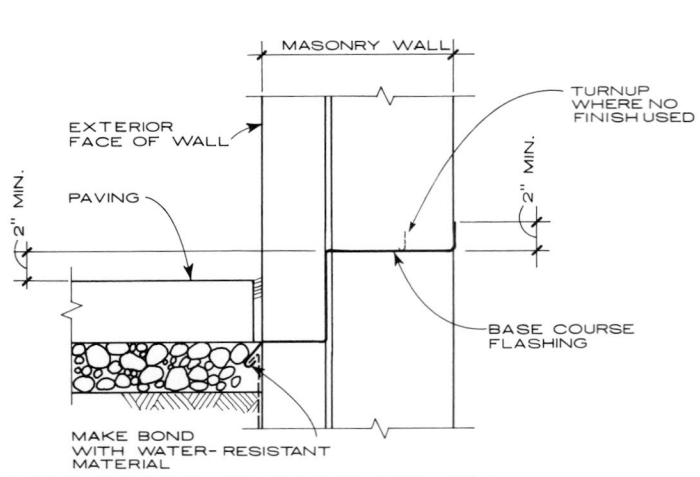

**BASE COURSE AT PAVING AND WALL**

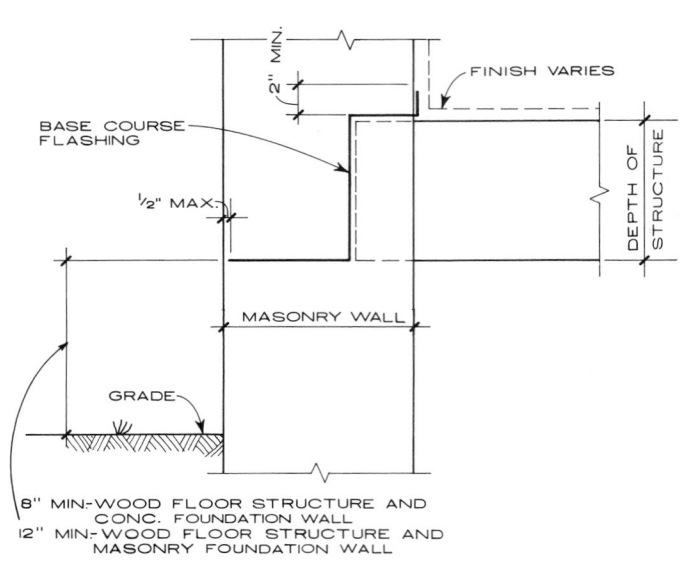

**BASE COURSE AT FLOOR CONSTRUCTION**

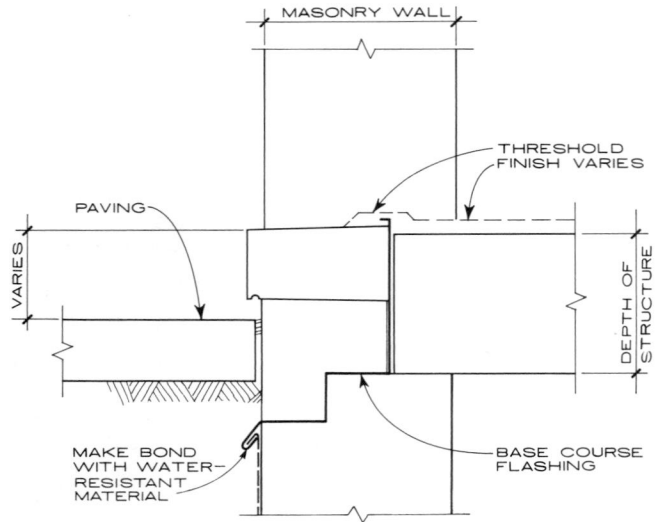

**BASE COURSE AT SILL OF MASONRY CONSTRUCTION**

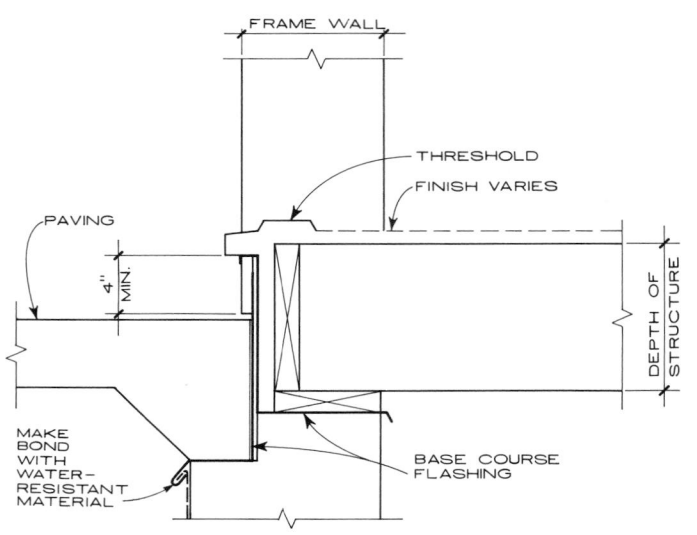

**BASE COURSE AT SILL OF FRAME CONSTRUCTION**

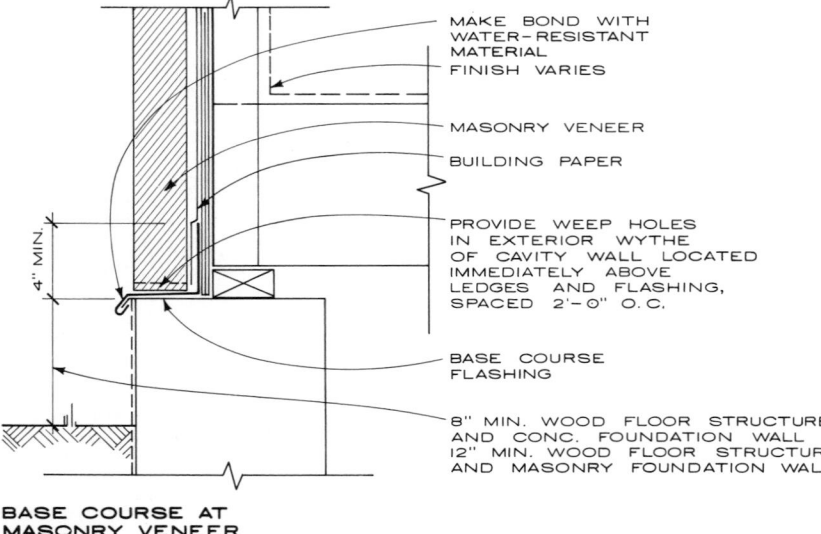

**BASE COURSE AT MASONRY VENEER**

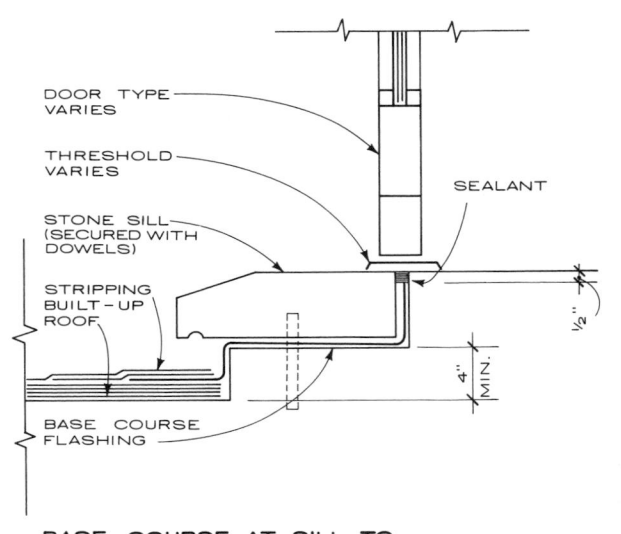

**BASE COURSE AT SILL TO BUILT-UP ROOF**

Michael Scott Rudden, The Stephens Associates P.C.—Architects; Albany, New York

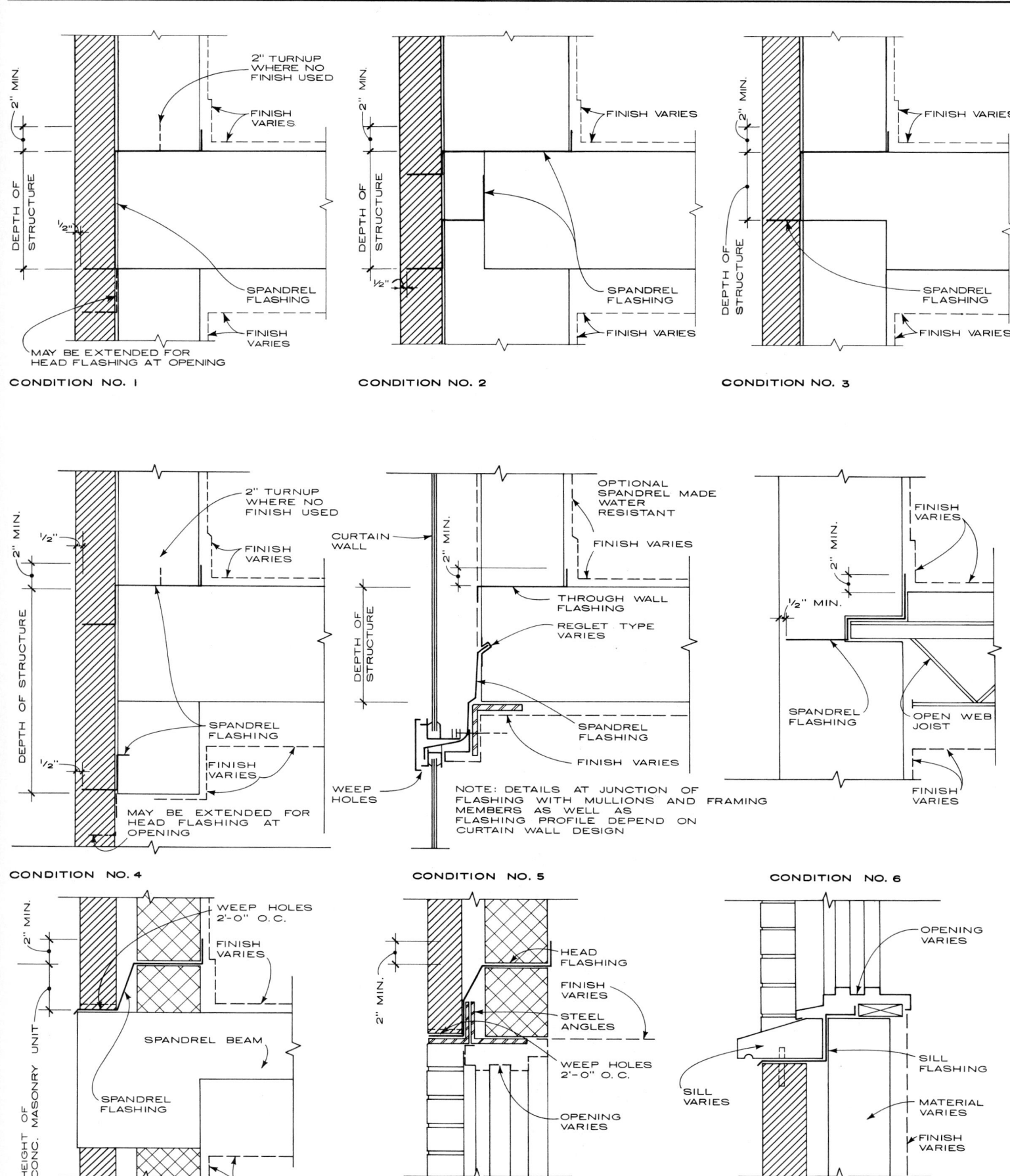

CONDITION NO. 1

CONDITION NO. 2

CONDITION NO. 3

CONDITION NO. 4

CONDITION NO. 5

NOTE: DETAILS AT JUNCTION OF FLASHING WITH MULLIONS AND FRAMING MEMBERS AS WELL AS FLASHING PROFILE DEPEND ON CURTAIN WALL DESIGN

CONDITION NO. 6

CONDITION NO. 7

HEAD FLASHING

SILL FLASHING

Michael Scott Rudden, The Stephens Associates P.C.—Architects; Albany, New York

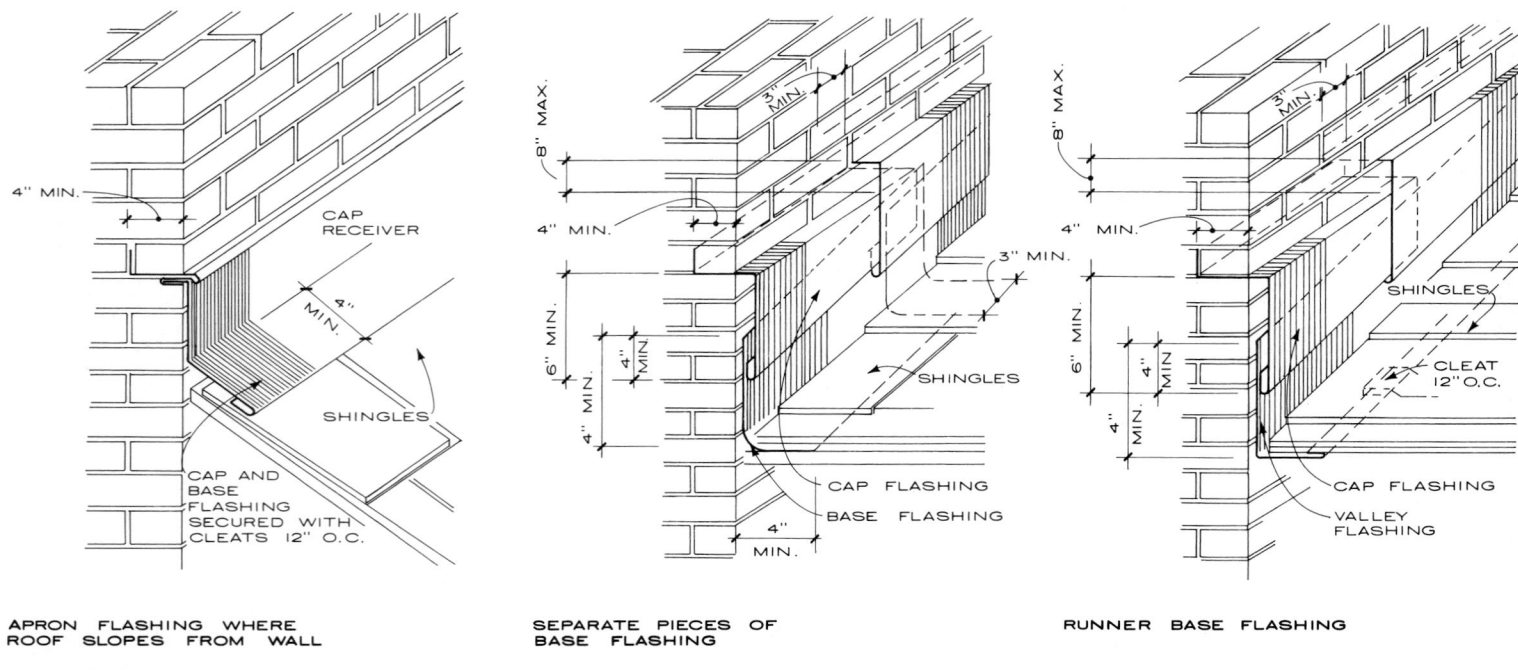

4" MIN.

CAP RECEIVER

4" MIN.

SHINGLES

CAP AND BASE FLASHING SECURED WITH CLEATS 12" O.C.

**APRON FLASHING WHERE ROOF SLOPES FROM WALL**

8" MAX.

3" MIN.

4" MIN.

6" MIN.

4" MIN.

3" MIN.

SHINGLES

CAP FLASHING

BASE FLASHING

4" MIN.

**SEPARATE PIECES OF BASE FLASHING**

8" MAX.

3" MIN.

4" MIN.

6" MIN.

4" MIN.

SHINGLES

CLEAT 12" O.C.

CAP FLASHING

VALLEY FLASHING

**RUNNER BASE FLASHING**

**PITCHED ROOF WITH WALL FLASHING**

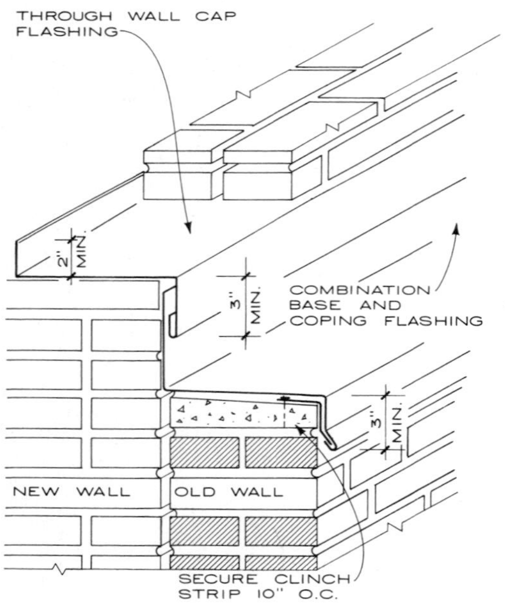

THROUGH WALL CAP FLASHING

2" MIN.

3" MIN.

COMBINATION BASE AND COPING FLASHING

3" MIN.

NEW WALL    OLD WALL

SECURE CLINCH STRIP 10" O.C.

**NEW WALL HIGHER THAN OLD WALL**

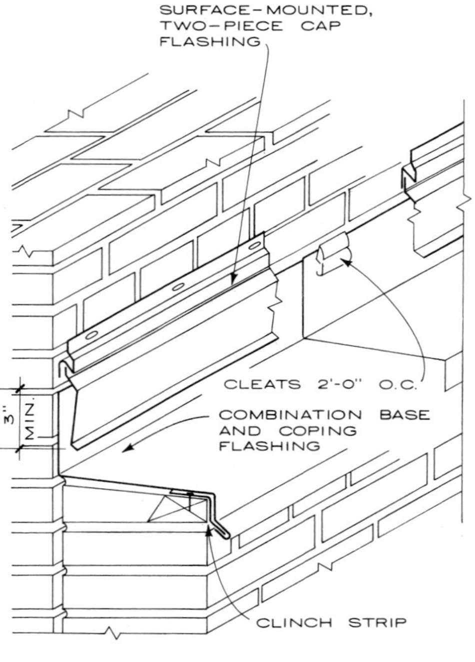

SURFACE-MOUNTED, TWO-PIECE CAP FLASHING

3" MIN.

CLEATS 2'-0" O.C.

COMBINATION BASE AND COPING FLASHING

CLINCH STRIP

**NEW WALL LOWER THAN OLD WALL**

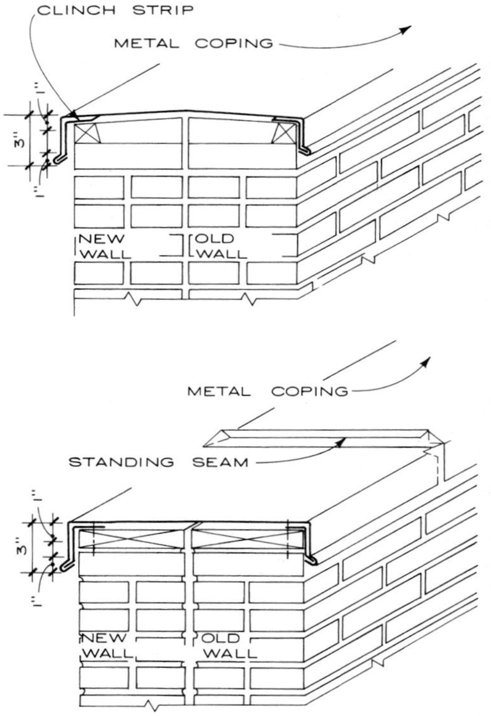

CLINCH STRIP

METAL COPING

3"

1"

NEW WALL    OLD WALL

METAL COPING

STANDING SEAM

3"

1"

NEW WALL    OLD WALL

**COPING FLASHING**

**NEW WALL TO OLD WALL FLASHING**

NOTE

Through wall flashing not recommended in earthquake areas.

Michael Scott Rudden, The Stephens Associates P.C.—Architects; Albany, New York

**7**    **FLASHING AND SHEET METAL**

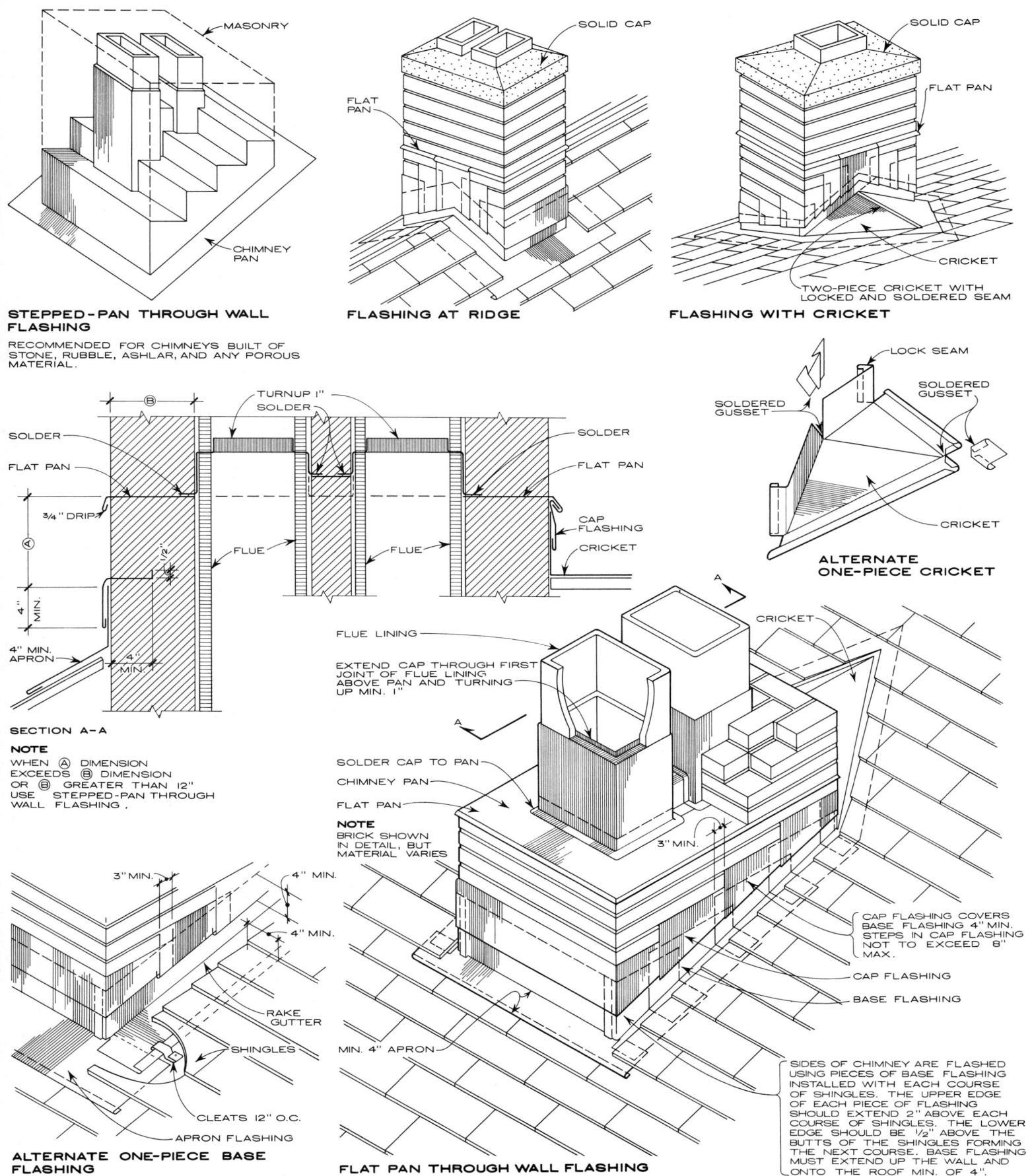

**STEPPED-PAN THROUGH WALL FLASHING**

RECOMMENDED FOR CHIMNEYS BUILT OF STONE, RUBBLE, ASHLAR, AND ANY POROUS MATERIAL.

MASONRY

CHIMNEY PAN

**FLASHING AT RIDGE**

SOLID CAP

FLAT PAN

**FLASHING WITH CRICKET**

SOLID CAP

FLAT PAN

CRICKET

TWO-PIECE CRICKET WITH LOCKED AND SOLDERED SEAM

**SECTION A-A**

TURNUP 1"
SOLDER
SOLDER
SOLDER
FLAT PAN
FLAT PAN
3/4" DRIP
1/2"
FLUE
FLUE
CAP FLASHING
CRICKET
4" MIN.
4" MIN. APRON
4" MIN.
Ⓐ
Ⓑ

**NOTE**
WHEN Ⓐ DIMENSION EXCEEDS Ⓑ DIMENSION OR Ⓑ GREATER THAN 12" USE STEPPED-PAN THROUGH WALL FLASHING.

**ALTERNATE ONE-PIECE CRICKET**

LOCK SEAM
SOLDERED GUSSET
SOLDERED GUSSET
CRICKET

**ALTERNATE ONE-PIECE BASE FLASHING**

3" MIN.
4" MIN.
4" MIN.
RAKE GUTTER
SHINGLES
CLEATS 12" O.C.
APRON FLASHING

**FLAT PAN THROUGH WALL FLASHING**

FLUE LINING

EXTEND CAP THROUGH FIRST JOINT OF FLUE LINING ABOVE PAN AND TURNING UP MIN. 1"

SOLDER CAP TO PAN
CHIMNEY PAN
FLAT PAN

**NOTE**
BRICK SHOWN IN DETAIL, BUT MATERIAL VARIES

CRICKET
A
A
3" MIN.
CAP FLASHING COVERS BASE FLASHING 4" MIN. STEPS IN CAP FLASHING NOT TO EXCEED 8" MAX.
CAP FLASHING
BASE FLASHING
MIN. 4" APRON

SIDES OF CHIMNEY ARE FLASHED USING PIECES OF BASE FLASHING INSTALLED WITH EACH COURSE OF SHINGLES. THE UPPER EDGE OF EACH PIECE OF FLASHING SHOULD EXTEND 2" ABOVE EACH COURSE OF SHINGLES. THE LOWER EDGE SHOULD BE 1/2" ABOVE THE BUTTS OF THE SHINGLES FORMING THE NEXT COURSE. BASE FLASHING MUST EXTEND UP THE WALL AND ONTO THE ROOF MIN. OF 4".

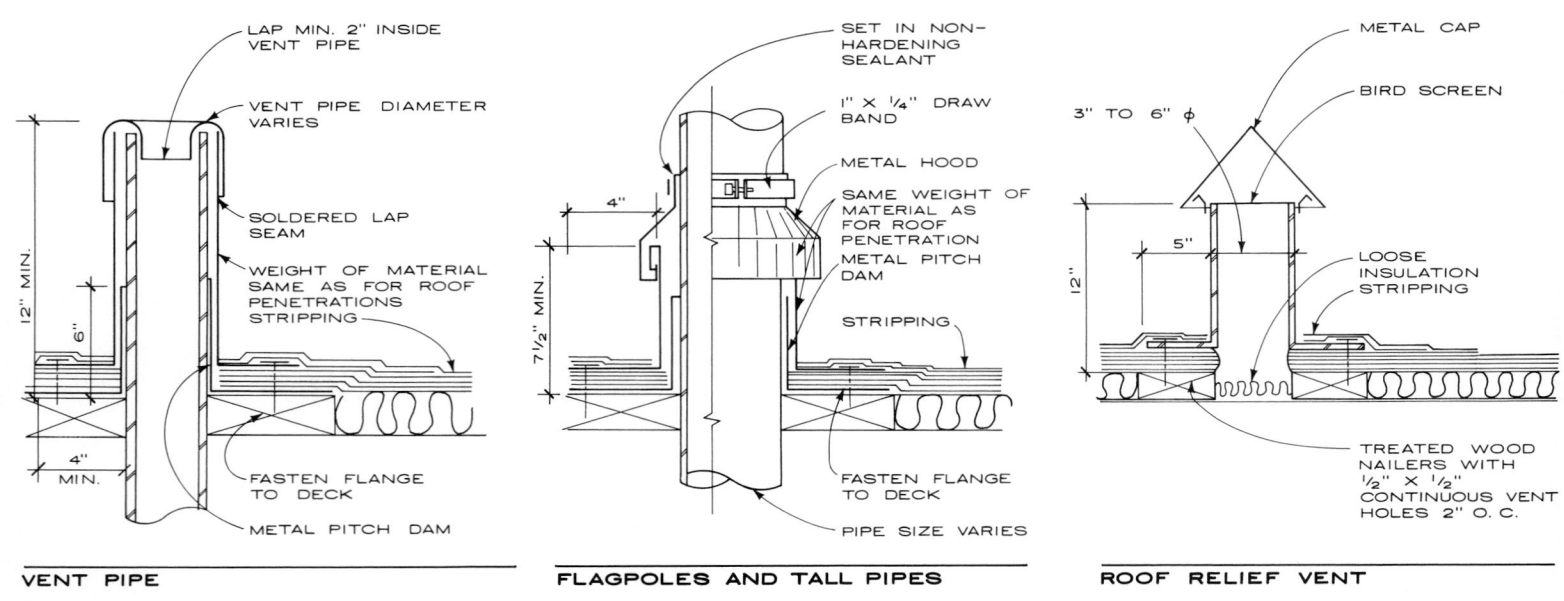

LAP MIN. 2" INSIDE VENT PIPE

VENT PIPE DIAMETER VARIES

SOLDERED LAP SEAM

WEIGHT OF MATERIAL SAME AS FOR ROOF PENETRATIONS STRIPPING

12" MIN.

6"

4" MIN.

FASTEN FLANGE TO DECK

METAL PITCH DAM

**VENT PIPE**

SET IN NON-HARDENING SEALANT

1" X ¼" DRAW BAND

METAL HOOD

SAME WEIGHT OF MATERIAL AS FOR ROOF PENETRATION METAL PITCH DAM

STRIPPING

4"

7½" MIN.

FASTEN FLANGE TO DECK

PIPE SIZE VARIES

**FLAGPOLES AND TALL PIPES**

METAL CAP

BIRD SCREEN

3" TO 6" φ

LOOSE INSULATION STRIPPING

12"

5"

TREATED WOOD NAILERS WITH ½" X ½" CONTINUOUS VENT HOLES 2" O.C.

**ROOF RELIEF VENT**

METAL COPING

STRUCTURAL ATTACHMENTS WITH WEATHERSEAL WASHERS

NEOPRENE PAD

2 PLY MEMBRANE IN FLASHING CEMENT TURNED DOWN OVER BASE.

CLINCH STRIP OR FASTENERS 24" O.C. WITH WEATHERSEAL WASHERS

STRIPPING

7½" MIN.

STUB COLUMN ATTACHED TO STRUCTURAL FRAMING

TREATED WOOD NAILER SURROUNDING COLUMN

**FUTURE COLUMNS, SIGN SUPPORTS, AND STEEL ANGLES**

STRUCTURAL SECTION THROUGH ROOF DECK

WELD PLATE WATERTIGHT

2" X CURB

SEAL TOP OF BASE FLASHING WITH FABRIC TAPE AND MASTIC

BASE FLASHING

10"

TREATED WOOD NAILER

INSULATION

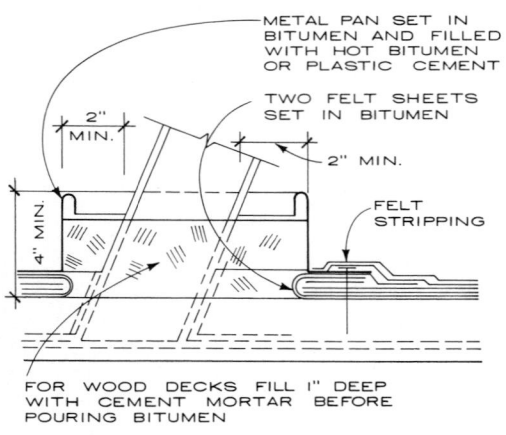

METAL PAN SET IN BITUMEN AND FILLED WITH HOT BITUMEN OR PLASTIC CEMENT

TWO FELT SHEETS SET IN BITUMEN

2" MIN.

FELT STRIPPING

2" MIN.

4" MIN.

FOR WOOD DECKS FILL 1" DEEP WITH CEMENT MORTAR BEFORE POURING BITUMEN

**NOTE**

Whenever possible avoid the use of pitch pockets in favor of curbs with base and cap flashing around the penetrating member.

**PITCH POCKET**

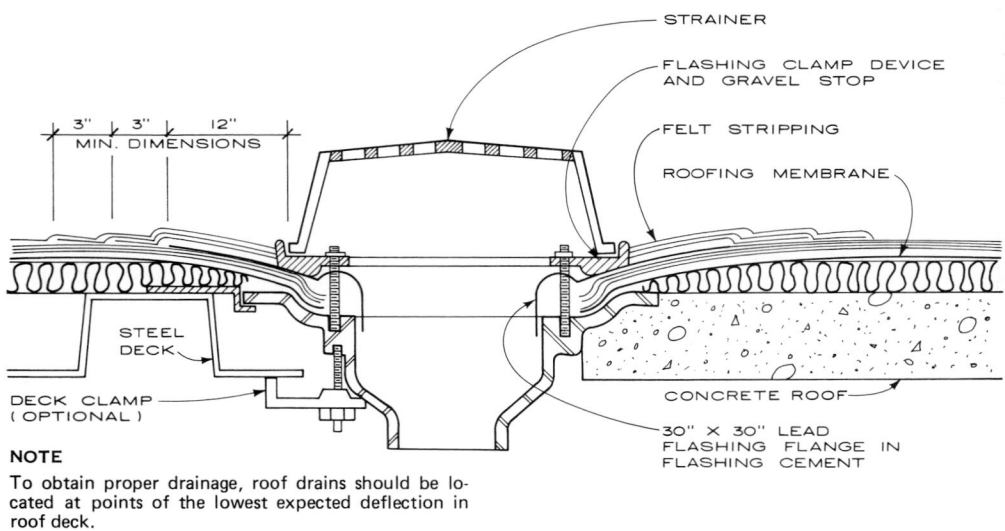

STRAINER

FLASHING CLAMP DEVICE AND GRAVEL STOP

FELT STRIPPING

ROOFING MEMBRANE

3" 3" 12"
MIN. DIMENSIONS

STEEL DECK

DECK CLAMP (OPTIONAL)

CONCRETE ROOF

30" X 30" LEAD FLASHING FLANGE IN FLASHING CEMENT

**NOTE**

To obtain proper drainage, roof drains should be located at points of the lowest expected deflection in roof deck.

**ROOF DRAIN**

Michael Scott Rudden, The Stephens Associates P.C.—Architects; Albany, New York

**7**    **FLASHING AND SHEET METAL**

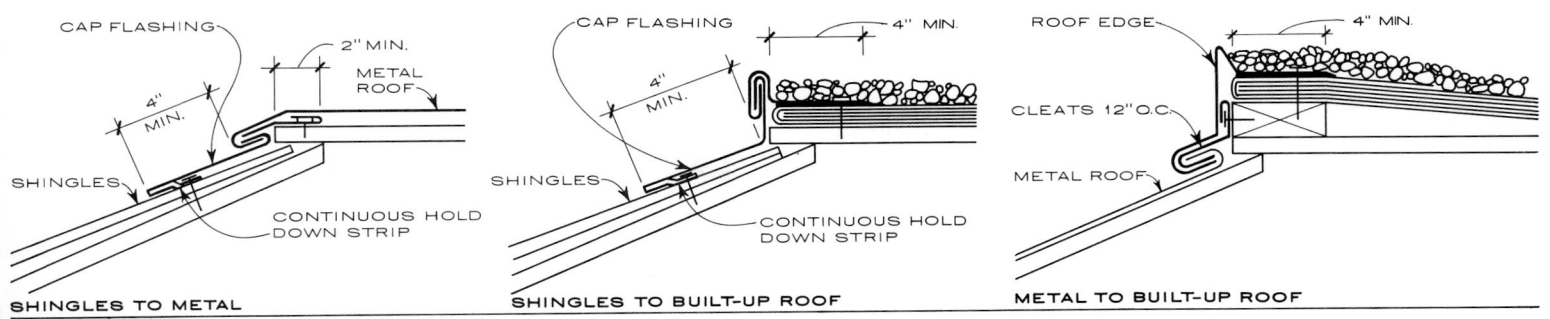

**FLASHING AT CHANGE IN ROOF MATERIAL**

SHINGLES TO METAL

SHINGLES TO BUILT-UP ROOF

METAL TO BUILT-UP ROOF

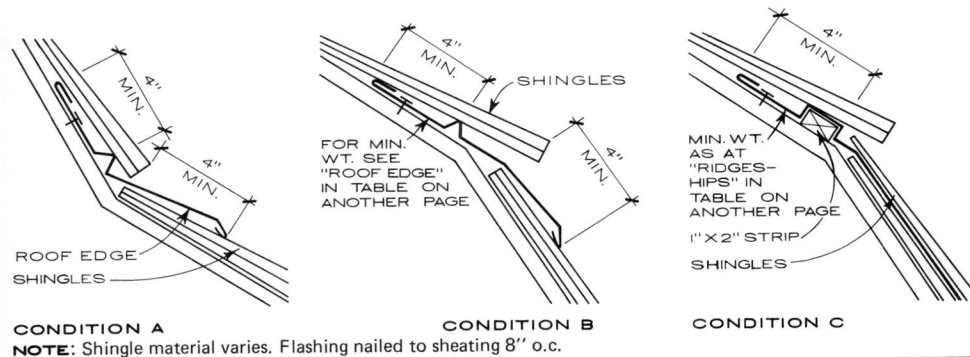

CONDITION A

CONDITION B

CONDITION C

**NOTE:** Shingle material varies. Flashing nailed to sheating 8″ o.c.

**FLASHING OF BREAK IN SLOPE OF SHINGLE ROOFS**

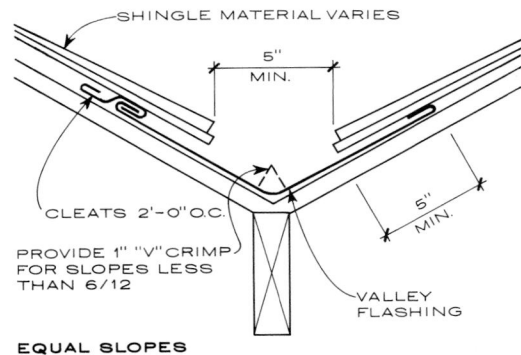

**EQUAL SLOPES**

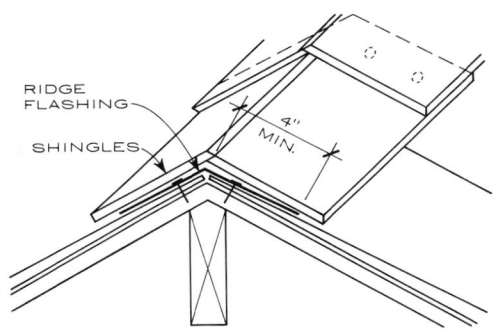

**CONCEALED RIDGE FLASHING**
NOTE

Ridge flashing formed in 10′ lengths and lapped 4″. Flashing is nailed to sheathing after shingles are installed, then flashing is covered with ridge shingles.

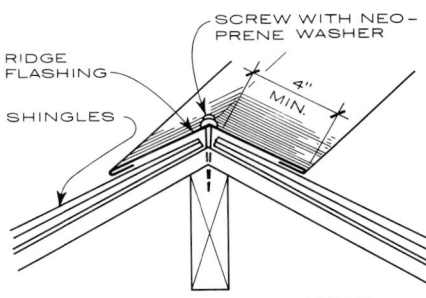

**EXPOSED RIDGE FLASHING**
NOTE

Ridge flashing formed in 10′ lengths and lapped 4″.

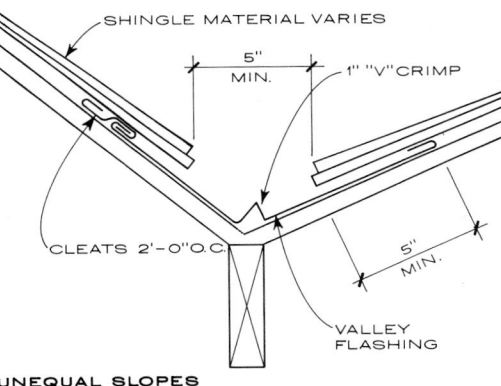

**UNEQUAL SLOPES**
**OPEN VALLEY FLASHING**

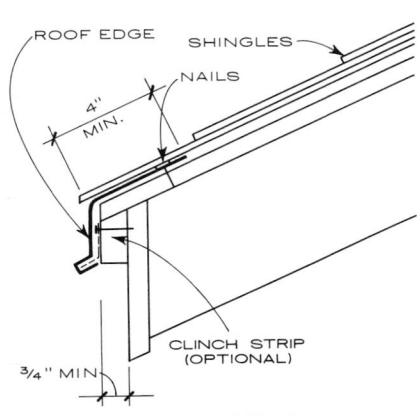

**ROOF EDGE FLASHING**

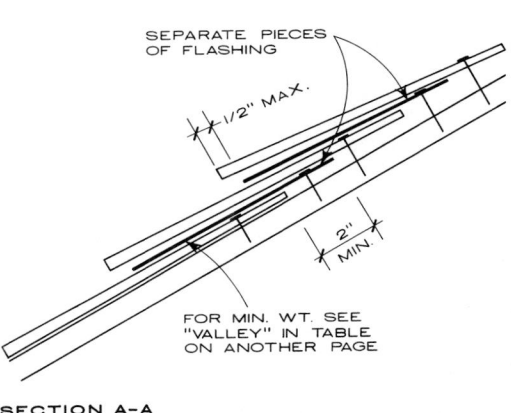

**SECTION A-A**
**CONCEALED VALLEY FLASHING**

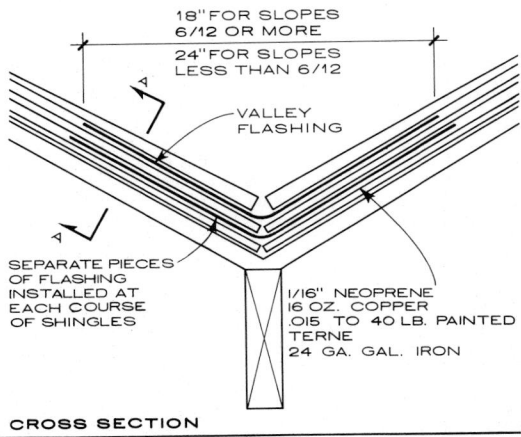

**CROSS SECTION**

Michael Scott Rudden, The Stephens Associates P.C.—Architects; Albany, New York

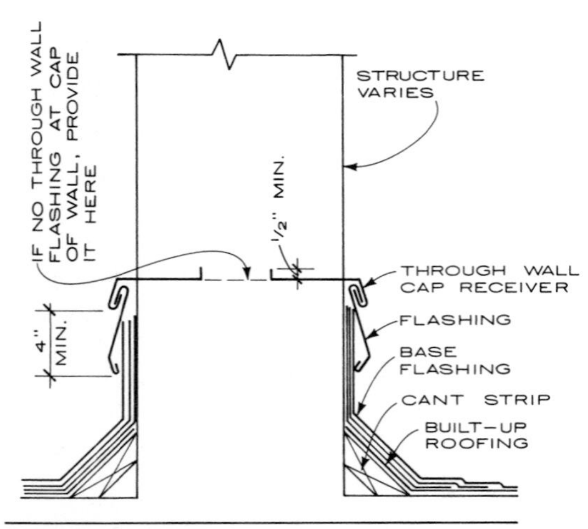

**FIRE WALL**

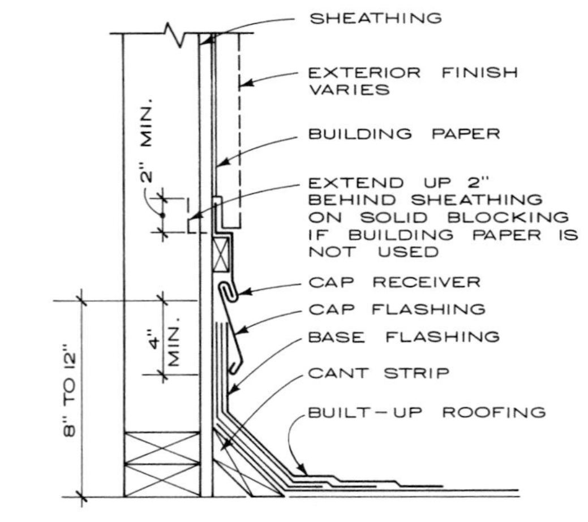

- IF NO THROUGH WALL FLASHING AT CAP OF WALL, PROVIDE IT HERE
- STRUCTURE VARIES
- ½" MIN.
- 4" MIN.
- THROUGH WALL CAP RECEIVER
- FLASHING
- BASE FLASHING
- CANT STRIP
- BUILT-UP ROOFING

**FRAME WALL**

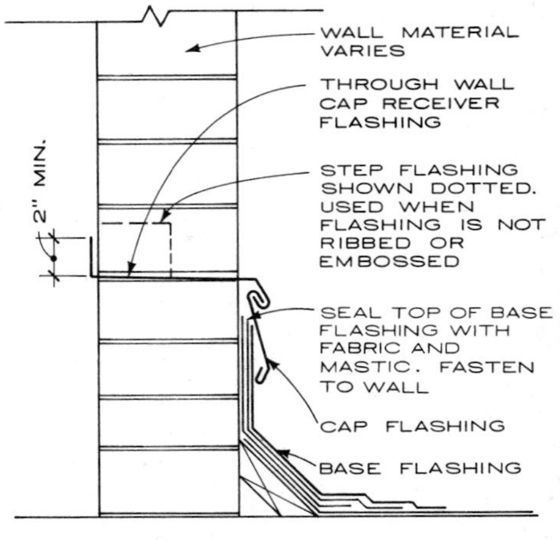

- SHEATHING
- EXTERIOR FINISH VARIES
- BUILDING PAPER
- EXTEND UP 2" BEHIND SHEATHING ON SOLID BLOCKING IF BUILDING PAPER IS NOT USED
- CAP RECEIVER
- CAP FLASHING
- BASE FLASHING
- CANT STRIP
- BUILT-UP ROOFING
- 2" MIN.
- 4" MIN.
- 8" TO 12"

**MASONRY WALL**

- WALL MATERIAL VARIES
- THROUGH WALL CAP RECEIVER FLASHING
- STEP FLASHING SHOWN DOTTED. USED WHEN FLASHING IS NOT RIBBED OR EMBOSSED
- SEAL TOP OF BASE FLASHING WITH FABRIC AND MASTIC. FASTEN TO WALL
- CAP FLASHING
- BASE FLASHING
- 2" MIN.

**CAST IN PLACE CONC. WALL**

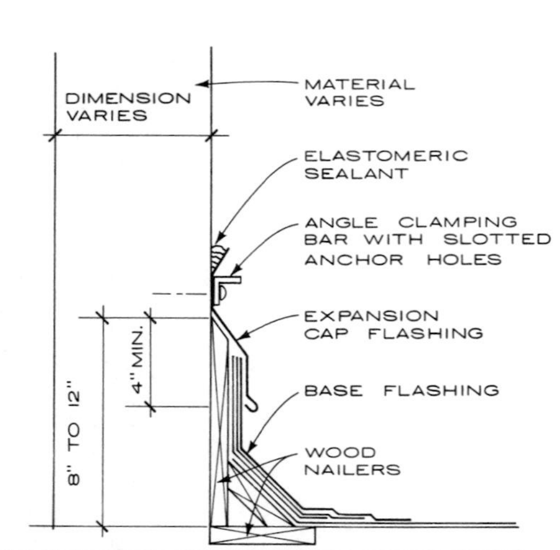

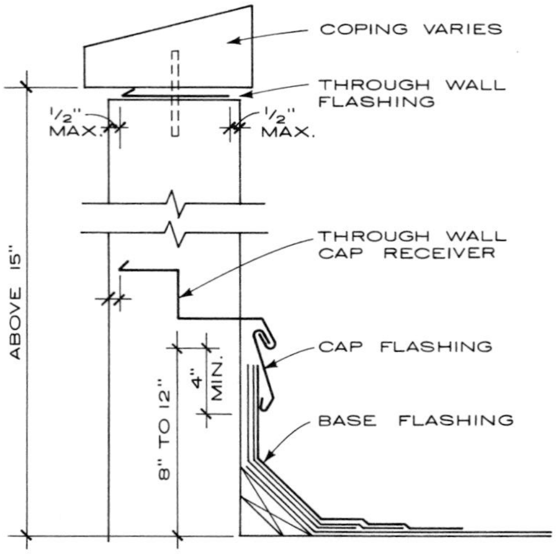

- DIMENSION VARIES
- MATERIAL VARIES
- ELASTOMERIC SEALANT
- ANGLE CLAMPING BAR WITH SLOTTED ANCHOR HOLES
- EXPANSION CAP FLASHING
- BASE FLASHING
- WOOD NAILERS
- 4" MIN.
- 8" TO 12"

**HIGH PARAPET FLASHING**

- COPING VARIES
- THROUGH WALL FLASHING
- ½" MAX.
- ½" MAX.
- THROUGH WALL CAP RECEIVER
- CAP FLASHING
- BASE FLASHING
- ABOVE 15"
- 8" TO 12"
- 4" MIN.

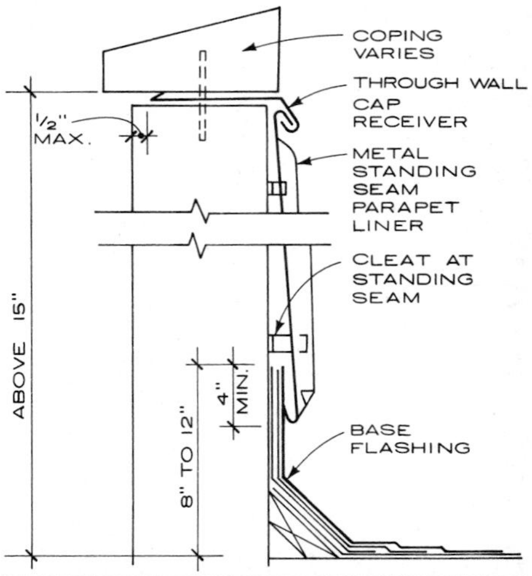

**HIGH PARAPET WITH LINING**

- COPING VARIES
- THROUGH WALL CAP RECEIVER
- ½" MAX.
- METAL STANDING SEAM PARAPET LINER
- CLEAT AT STANDING SEAM
- BASE FLASHING
- ABOVE 15"
- 8" TO 12"
- 4" MIN.

**LOW PARAPET FLASHING**

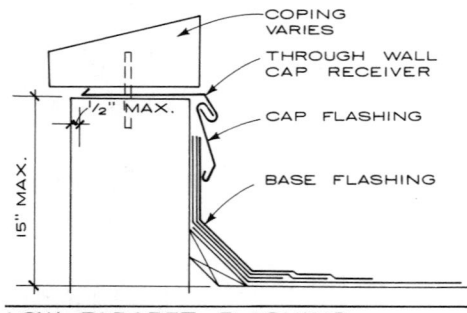

- COPING VARIES
- THROUGH WALL CAP RECEIVER
- ½" MAX.
- CAP FLASHING
- BASE FLASHING
- 15" MAX.

**GENERAL NOTES**

1. Select flashing that is flexible for molding to flashing supports and that can withstand expected thermal, wind, and structural movement. Provide expansion joints in place of flashing as required by conditions.
2. Consult manufacturer's literature for choice of flashing materials and details.
3. Avoid sharp bends in bituminous base flashings. Use cant strips with 45° maximum bend.
4. Provision for differential movement between roof deck and wall is recommended.
5. A ribbed or embossed pattern should be used for all through wall flashing. Through wall flashing is not recommended for earthquake areas.
6. Base flashing should extend 8 to 12 in. above highest anticipated waterline. Metal counterflashing should lap base flashing by at least 4 in. Lap all vertical joints.

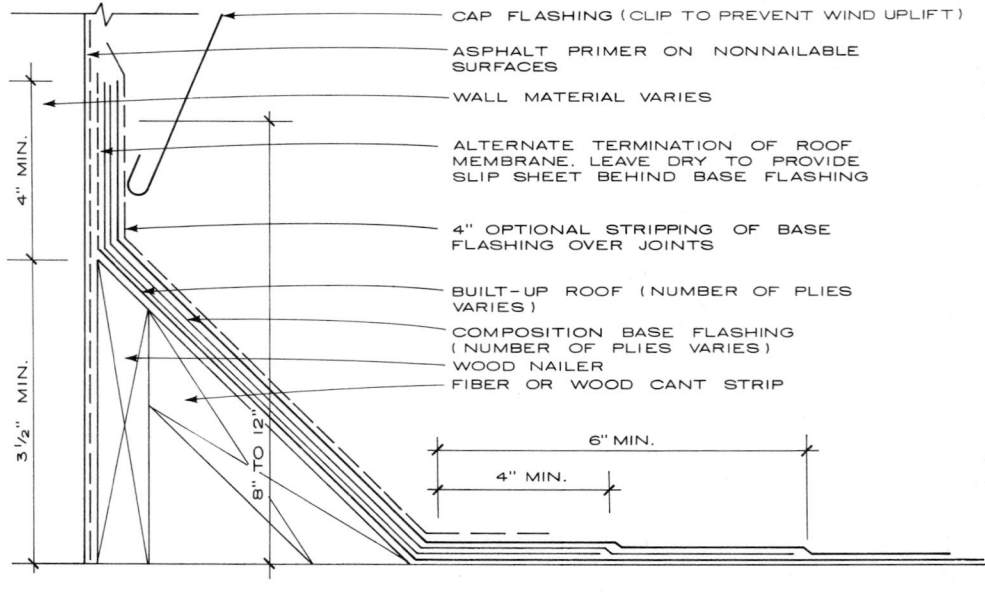

- CAP FLASHING (CLIP TO PREVENT WIND UPLIFT)
- ASPHALT PRIMER ON NONNAILABLE SURFACES
- WALL MATERIAL VARIES
- ALTERNATE TERMINATION OF ROOF MEMBRANE. LEAVE DRY TO PROVIDE SLIP SHEET BEHIND BASE FLASHING
- 4" OPTIONAL STRIPPING OF BASE FLASHING OVER JOINTS
- BUILT-UP ROOF (NUMBER OF PLIES VARIES)
- COMPOSITION BASE FLASHING (NUMBER OF PLIES VARIES)
- WOOD NAILER
- FIBER OR WOOD CANT STRIP
- 4" MIN.
- 3½" MIN.
- 8" TO 12"
- 6" MIN.
- 4" MIN.

**TYPICAL BASE FLASHING**

Michael Scott Rudden, The Stephens Associates P.C.—Architects; Albany, New York

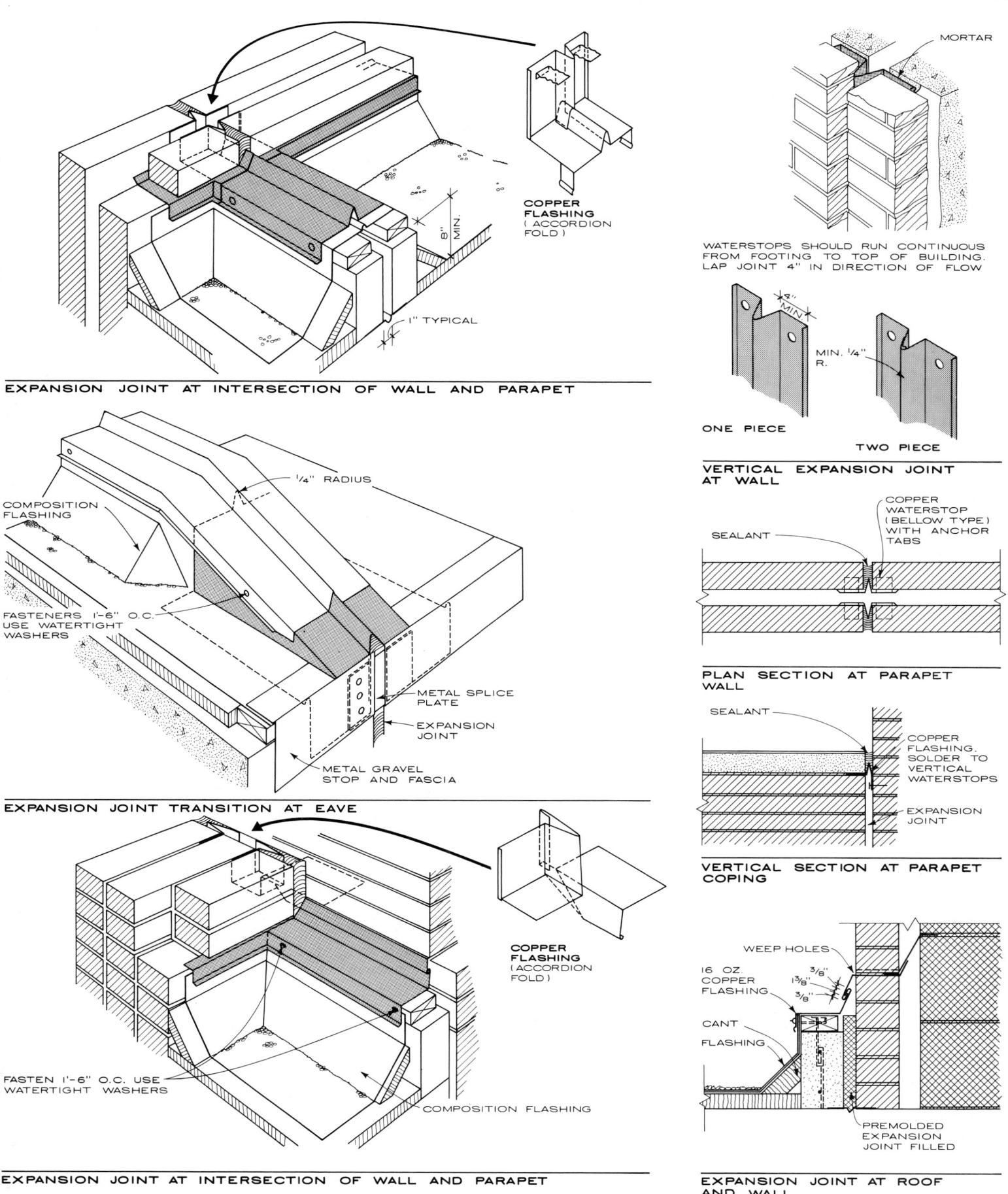

EXPANSION JOINT AT INTERSECTION OF WALL AND PARAPET

COPPER FLASHING (ACCORDION FOLD)

8" MIN.

1" TYPICAL

COMPOSITION FLASHING

1/4" RADIUS

FASTENERS 1'-6" O.C. USE WATERTIGHT WASHERS

METAL SPLICE PLATE

EXPANSION JOINT

METAL GRAVEL STOP AND FASCIA

EXPANSION JOINT TRANSITION AT EAVE

COPPER FLASHING (ACCORDION FOLD)

FASTEN 1'-6" O.C. USE WATERTIGHT WASHERS

COMPOSITION FLASHING

EXPANSION JOINT AT INTERSECTION OF WALL AND PARAPET

MORTAR

WATERSTOPS SHOULD RUN CONTINUOUS FROM FOOTING TO TOP OF BUILDING. LAP JOINT 4" IN DIRECTION OF FLOW.

4" MIN.

MIN. 1/4" R.

ONE PIECE

TWO PIECE

VERTICAL EXPANSION JOINT AT WALL

SEALANT

COPPER WATERSTOP (BELLOW TYPE) WITH ANCHOR TABS

PLAN SECTION AT PARAPET WALL

SEALANT

COPPER FLASHING. SOLDER TO VERTICAL WATERSTOPS

EXPANSION JOINT

VERTICAL SECTION AT PARAPET COPING

WEEP HOLES

16 OZ. COPPER FLASHING

3/8"
1 3/8"
3/8"

CANT

FLASHING

PREMOLDED EXPANSION JOINT FILLED

EXPANSION JOINT AT ROOF AND WALL

CTA Architects Engineers; Billings, Montana

ROOF SPECIALTIES AND ACCESSORIES    7

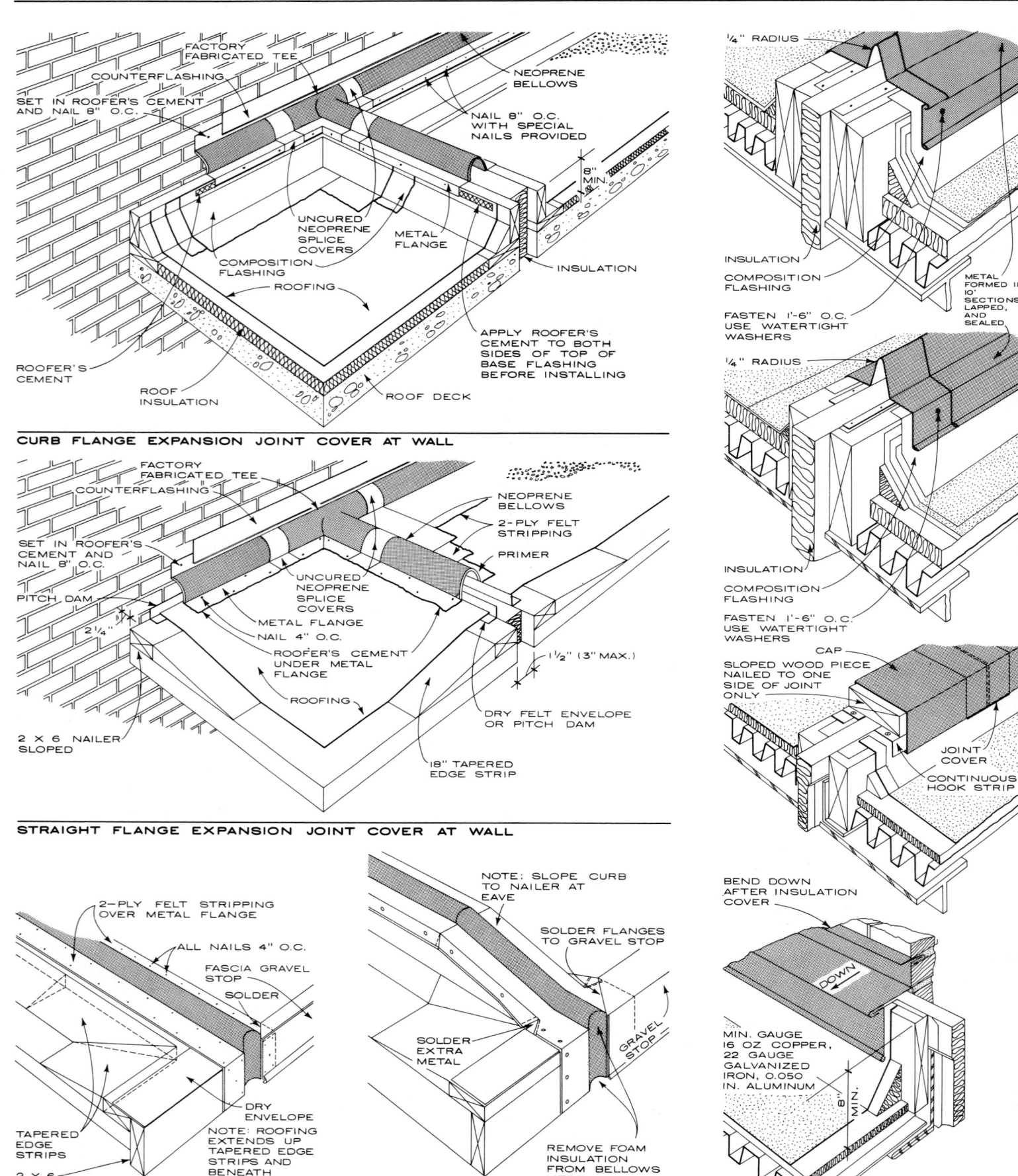

**CURB FLANGE EXPANSION JOINT COVER AT WALL**

- FACTORY FABRICATED TEE
- COUNTERFLASHING
- SET IN ROOFER'S CEMENT AND NAIL 8" O.C.
- NEOPRENE BELLOWS
- NAIL 8" O.C. WITH SPECIAL NAILS PROVIDED
- 8" MIN.
- UNCURED NEOPRENE SPLICE COVERS
- METAL FLANGE
- COMPOSITION FLASHING
- ROOFING
- INSULATION
- ROOFER'S CEMENT
- ROOF INSULATION
- ROOF DECK
- APPLY ROOFER'S CEMENT TO BOTH SIDES OF TOP OF BASE FLASHING BEFORE INSTALLING

**STRAIGHT FLANGE EXPANSION JOINT COVER AT WALL**

- FACTORY FABRICATED TEE
- COUNTERFLASHING
- SET IN ROOFER'S CEMENT AND NAIL 8" O.C.
- NEOPRENE BELLOWS
- 2-PLY FELT STRIPPING
- PRIMER
- PITCH DAM
- $2\frac{1}{4}$"
- UNCURED NEOPRENE SPLICE COVERS
- METAL FLANGE
- NAIL 4" O.C.
- ROOFER'S CEMENT UNDER METAL FLANGE
- ROOFING
- $1\frac{1}{2}$" (3" MAX.)
- DRY FELT ENVELOPE OR PITCH DAM
- 2 X 6 NAILER SLOPED
- 18" TAPERED EDGE STRIP

**STRAIGHT FLANGE AT GRAVEL STOP**

- 2-PLY FELT STRIPPING OVER METAL FLANGE
- ALL NAILS 4" O.C.
- FASCIA GRAVEL STOP
- SOLDER
- DRY ENVELOPE
- TAPERED EDGE STRIPS
- 2 X 6 NAILER
- NOTE: ROOFING EXTENDS UP TAPERED EDGE STRIPS AND BENEATH FLANGE AND DRY ENVELOPE

**CURB FLANGE AT GRAVEL STOP**

- NOTE: SLOPE CURB TO NAILER AT EAVE
- SOLDER FLANGES TO GRAVEL STOP
- SOLDER EXTRA METAL
- GRAVEL STOP
- REMOVE FOAM INSULATION FROM BELLOWS HERE

**BUILDING EXPANSION JOINTS**

- $\frac{1}{4}$" RADIUS
- INSULATION
- COMPOSITION FLASHING
- METAL FORMED IN 10' SECTIONS, LAPPED, AND SEALED
- FASTEN 1'-6" O.C. USE WATERTIGHT WASHERS
- $\frac{1}{4}$" RADIUS
- INSULATION
- COMPOSITION FLASHING
- FASTEN 1'-6" O.C. USE WATERTIGHT WASHERS
- CAP
- SLOPED WOOD PIECE NAILED TO ONE SIDE OF JOINT ONLY
- JOINT COVER
- CONTINUOUS HOOK STRIP
- BEND DOWN AFTER INSULATION COVER
- DOWN
- MIN. GAUGE 16 OZ COPPER, 22 GAUGE GALVANIZED IRON, 0.050 IN. ALUMINUM
- 8" MIN.

CTA Architects Engineers; Billings, Montana

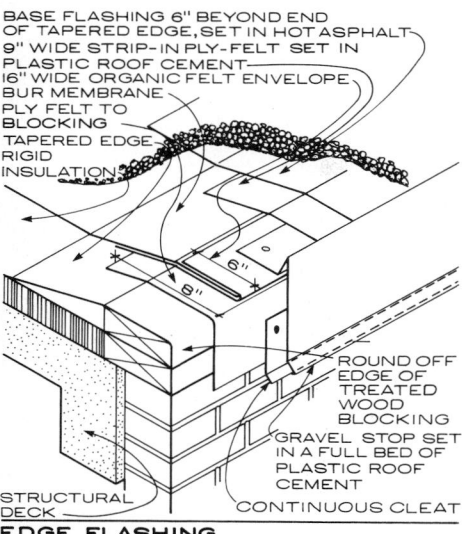

**EDGE FLASHING**

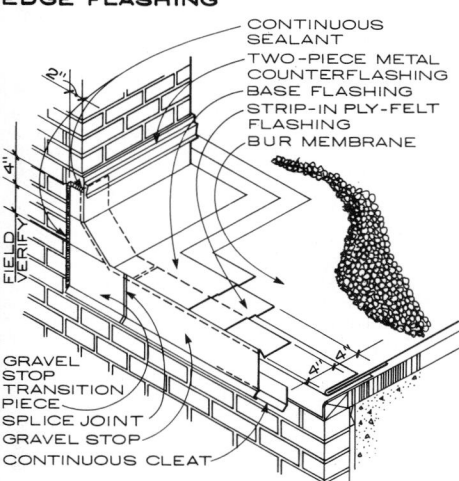

**GRAVEL STOP TRANSITION**

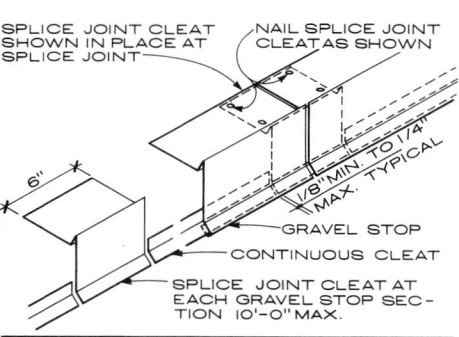

**GRAVEL STOP SPLICE JOINT**

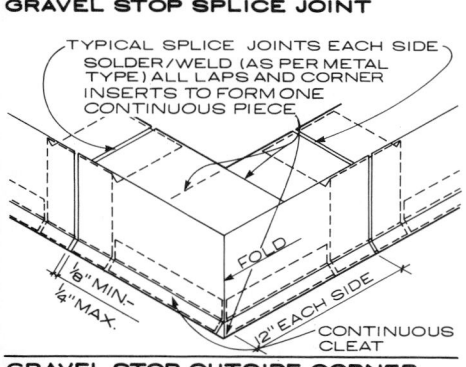

**GRAVEL STOP OUTSIDE CORNER FABRICATION**

Joseph J. Williams, AIA; A/R/C Associates Inc.; Orlando, Florida

## RECOMMENDED MINIMUM GAUGES GRAVEL STOP—FASCIA

| D (MAX.) (IN.) | GALVANIZED STEEL (GAUGE) | COPPER (OZ.) | ALUMINUM (IN.) | ZINC ALLOY (IN.) | STAINLESS STEEL (GAUGE) |
|---|---|---|---|---|---|
| 4 | 24 | 16 | 0.025 | 0.020 | 26 |
| 5 | 24 | 16 | 0.032 | 0.027 | 26 |
| 6 | 22 | 20 | 0.040 | 0.027 | 24 |
| 7 | 22 | 20 | 0.040 | — | 22 |
| 8 | 20 | 20 | 0.050 | — | 20 |

## RECOMMENDED MINIMUM GAUGES FOR COPING

| WIDTH OF COPING TOP (IN.) | GALVANIZED STEEL (GAUGE) | STAINLESS STEEL (GAUGE) | ALUMINUM (IN.) | COPPER (OZ.) |
|---|---|---|---|---|
| Through 12 | 24 | 26 | 0.232 | 16 |
| 13 to 18 | 22 | 24 | 0.040 | 20 |

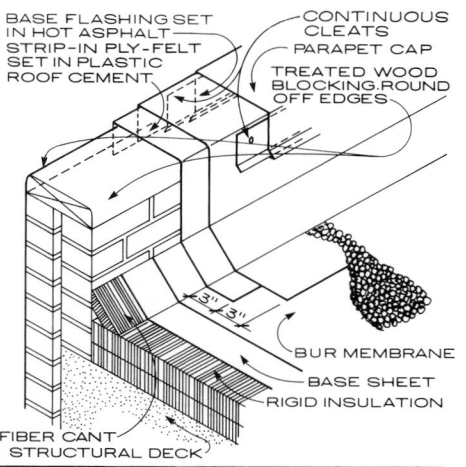

**PARAPET EDGE DETAIL**

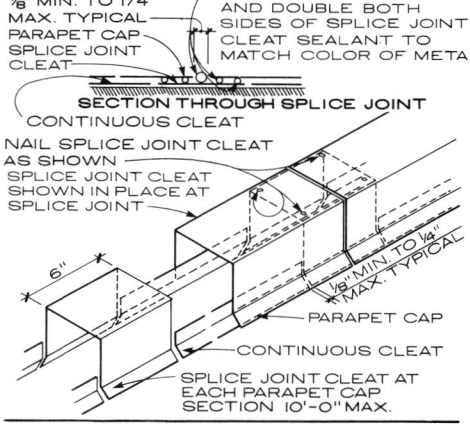

**PARAPET CAP SPLICE JOINT**

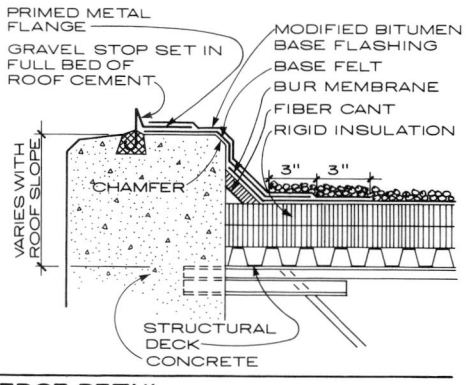

**EDGE DETAIL**

## USER GUIDES TO FLASHING METAL SELECTION

Each commonly used flashing metal has distinctive characteristics, uses, and limitations. Thickness of materials is a function of material size, aesthetic consideration (prevention of oil-canning), and wind uplift due to metal movement during violent storms.

### GALVANIZED STEEL

Galvanized steel flashings should be a minimum of 24 gauge with a G-90 galvanized coating. Of commonly used flashing metals, galvanized steel probably is the most common and least expensive. Although galvanized flashing metal may be left exposed, generally it is painted to further protect the steel from corrosion. Before it is painted, galvanized metal must be prepared. Plain galvanized material chemically etched in the field is preferred for surfaces to be painted. Factory etching, in which the metal is dipped in an acid bath, etches it on all sides. As a result, exposed edges often rust. Field etching is preferred because only the surfaces to be painted are etched. After etching, the surface should be primed and finish painted, preferably with two coats.

Galvanized steel is easy to solder, low in cost, and easy to work. All flashing metal transitions and terminations should be soldered fully for permanent installation; however, this should not be done at metal flashing joints where movement caused by thermal expansion is expected or at building expansion joints.

### STAINLESS STEEL

Stainless steel has many advantages of other steel products, yet generally is corrosion resistant and can be field soldered to accommodate difficult transitions and terminations. If the mill finish appearance is unacceptable, stainless steel may be painted after installation with primer and finish coat.

### COPPER

Copper also is a lifetime, relatively maintenance-free material. It can be soldered and molded easily, making it adaptable to complicated transitions and plane changes. Its terminations should be soldered fully. Runoff from the metal can stain adjoining building materials. Generally, copper is softer than other flashing metals and has a moderate expansion coefficient higher than steel, but less than aluminum.

### ALUMINUM

Aluminum is a permanent material that corrodes slowly; however, it oxidizes and pits over time, depending on exposure. Since aluminum only can be welded, field connections can be difficult. Although corners can be prefabricated, some plane changes may be difficult. Aluminum has a high expansion and contraction coefficient compared with other flashing metals.

## FRAMING

Skylights are available as preassembled units, stock or custom designed, shipped to the site ready to be installed, as assemblies of units, or framed assemblies of stock components, prefabricated off site and then site assembled. Skylight framing systems should provide complete control of both condensation and water infiltration.

Exterior gutter systems should be as simple and functional as possible. Design must take into account compatibility of materials and provision of positive slope for drainage.

The supporting structure, as well as the enclosure itself, must be engineered to carry the total resultant forces of the particular live load, wind load, and dead load in accordance with all building codes.

Framed skylights require somewhat greater mullion widths when glazed with acrylics, due to the expansion and contraction characteristics of plastics that must be taken up at the glazing connection.

Mullion spacing for framed skylights and dimensional limitations on skylight assemblies are governed by building codes responding to the glazing material specified. Maximum widths of glass vary with type:

1. Wire glass—60 in.
2. Laminated glass—48 in.
3. Tempered glass—72 in.

Other factors limiting size are

1. Requirements for positive drainage of rain water
2. Snow and wind loading
3. Condensate gutters in the body of the skylight assembly as well as at its perimeter

Mount on built-up curb with frame and counterflashing. Curb minimum height is 8 in. above roof structure. Prefabricated curbs are available with or without insulation.

Energy efficiency may be increased by use of double and triple glazing and with frames that have thermal breaks. These items will also reduce the probability of condensation.

All skylight units must be securely attached to the roof assembly which may require structural or miscellaneous steel frames at openings in deck.

## GLAZING

The thickness, size, and geometric profile of all glass and acrylic glazing material should be carefully selected for compliance with building codes and manufacturer's recommendations.

The following glazing materials are available:

1. Formed acrylic with mar-resistant finish
2. Formed acrylic or flat acrylic
3. Polycarbonates
4. Tempered glass or laminated glass
5. Clear polished wire glass
6. Textured, obscure wire glass

Excessive expansion and contraction of acrylic glazing may cause "rolling" of the sealant between metal framing, causing shifting of glazing material out of the joint.

LOW RISE     MEDIUM RISE     HIGH RISE

The minimum rise to span on curved structures of framed skylights for vaulted and dome shapes is 22%.

Tinted acrylics should be limited to ¼ in. thickness for economy. A combination fiberglass sheet and aluminum frame system which has high insulating and excessive light diffusion may be an economic consideration.

Proper glazing methods have an important influence. Exposed gasketing is subject to material breakdown due to ultraviolet rays of the sun. Small valleys created at the bottom of sloped glazing and horizontal glazing cap will hold water.

Mar-resistant coatings for plastics should be specified if frequent cleaning or heavy pedestrian contact is anticipated.

Glazing with high-performance insulated glass units provides important energy savings and offers the architect numerous functional and aesthetic design choices, but initial cost may be high.

CTA Architects Engineers; Billings, Montana

## FINISHES

Finishes for aluminum components are available in the following:

1. Mill finish
2. Clear anodized
3. Duranodic bronze or black
4. Acrylic enamel
5. Fluorocarbons

## CONDENSATION

Double glazing and thermal break framing will minimize condensation.

Usually a separation is made where the glazing member is bolted into the framing member by use of a nonheat conductive material.

Insulated assemblies reduce condensation and energy losses.

Thermalized design will help in preventing excessive condensation buildup on the frame of domed skylight units, minimizing corrosion, staining, and general maintenance.

Incorporate a continuous condensation gutter to collect and store moisture until it evaporates.

## BUILDING SECURITY

Resistance to forced entry through skylight should include

1. Provision to prevent disassembly of framing from the exterior
2. Elimination of snap-on materials
3. Melting point of glazing: Acrylics can be easily burned through with a torch
4. Use of metal security screens or burglar bars welded to steel angle frame directly below skylight

## ENVIRONMENTAL CONTROL

In determining the desired form and size of the skylight unit/assembly, consideration should be given to

1. Environmental conditions, including orientation and the resulting winter and summer solar penetration angles in the given geographic location.
2. Prevailing wind's direction and force
3. Precipitation quantity and patterns
4. Topography and landscaping (trees/shades/leaves)
5. Coordination of the area of skylight with the HVAC system

Views into and out of the building through clear skylights are affected by

1. Overhanging trees and adjacent buildings
2. Nearby street lights
3. Other parts of the same building
4. Views into building from adjacent higher areas (privacy).

The more a formed plastic dome is raised, the greater its ability to refract light of the low early morning and late afternoon sun, which maximizes the use of natural light, but increases the solar heat gain.

AVAILABLE LIGHT ZONES

## PERCENTAGE OF ROOF AREA REQUIRED FOR SKYLIGHTING

| LIGHT ZONE | LIGHT DESIGN LEVELS | | |
|---|---|---|---|
| | 30 FT-C | 60 FT-C | 120 FT-C |
| 1 | 3.3 | 5.2 | 13.3 |
| 2 | 2.8 | 4.3 | 10.8 |
| 3 | 1.8 | 3.2 | 6.9 |
| 4 | 1.5 | 2.8 | 4.0 |

## SKYLIGHTS WITH MOVABLE SECTIONS

Skylights can be designed with movable sections for those locations where a combination indoor–outdoor open-to-the-sky condition is desired. The movable sections are of two basic designs:

1. Complete skylight assemblies of double pitch or barrel vault configurations that roll open horizontally along a track.
2. Individual skylight roof panels of an overall double-pitched enclosure which are normally designed so that the top half slides down over the lower half to open the upper portion of roof.

Consideration should be given to motors, tracks, and other operating parts.

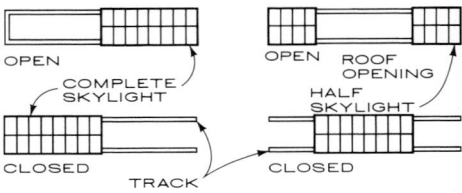

SINGLE UNIT       DOUBLE UNIT
DESIGN 1       DESIGN 2
**MOVABLE SKYLIGHT PLANS**

## GLASS AND PLASTIC STRUCTURES

Greenhouses, pool enclosures, and covered walkways are applications of skylight assemblies as complete envelopes. Available forms are domes, arches, barrel vaults, and single and double pitch. Lean-to enclosures are available with straight eaves, curved eaves, vertical sides, or slanted sides.

Framing may be of steel, aluminum, or wood, with a variety of glazing options. Secondary component options include doors, operable sash, louvers, shades, blinds, and ventilators. Envelopes are preengineered for specific live and wind loads, which should be checked against requirements of building codes.

## FIRE AND SMOKE VENTING

In certain building types and occupancies fire and smoke units that open automatically due to fire-induced temperature increase are required. Their function is to permit the smoke to escape and lower temperatures at floor level.

A sufficient number of vents must be distributed over the entire roof area to assure reasonably early venting of a fire regardless of its location. The size and spacing of the vents must be determined for each building, depending upon

1. Size of building
2. Its particular use or combination of uses
3. The degree of hazard involved

Smoke venting is based upon movement of a specific number of cubic feet of air per minute through the fire vents. Building codes give required capacities, size, and spacing for various types of vents.

Typical roof vent area requirements are:

0.67% of roof area for low heat release occupancies
1% of roof area for moderate heat release occupancies
2% of roof area for high heat release occupancies

Roof vents may be required over stairs, elevator hoistways, atriums, and high hazard occupancies to offer explosion relief, as well as for stages and areas behind the proscenium in theaters.

In determining the number of vents to be used to satisfy the total required venting area, recognize that venting can be better accomplished by several small units than by a few larger ones (NFPA #204). The size of the vent required is based upon its opened area, about equal to its frame size.

Consider also the spacing of vents in relation to interior spaces and their uses, proximity to exits, and their use in providing daylighting. Fire vents may also function as skylights when glazed.

Fire vents may also function as skylights when glazed.

**SKYLIGHTS**

**SIZES AND SPANS**

2 ft 6 in. to 7 ft 7 in., with dome rise from 10 to 24 in.

**GLAZING**

1. Generally acrylic, but other glazing available.
2. Single and double glazed normal, triple available.
3. Clear, tinted transparent, and white translucent.
4. Scratches are difficult to remove from acrylic.

**FRAMING**

1. Self-flashing, with or without integral curb.
2. Insulated curbs available.
3. Areas where excessive snow loading occurs may require additional reinforcement. Consult manufacturer.
4. Skylight—No structural framing within unit.

**REMARKS**

1. Circular shape may make roofing seal more difficult.
2. Some visual distortion due to curvature of glazing.
3. Side wall installation possible.

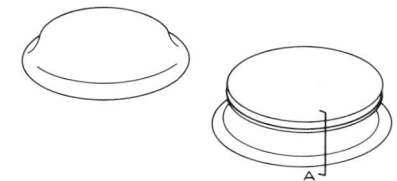

## DOME-CIRCULAR

**SIZES AND SPANS**

Square from 2 ft 0 in. to 10 ft 0 in.; rectangular from 2 ft 0 in. to 5 ft 0 in. wide by 4 ft 0 in. to 8 ft 0 in. long, with dome rise from 8 to 22 in.

**GLAZING**

1. Acrylic, polycarbonate, glass fiber reinforced.
2. Single and double normal, triple glazing available.
3. Clear, tinted transparent, and white translucent.

**FRAMING**

1. See framing notes for circular dome skylight.
2. Self-flashing flanged available for pitched roof.

**REMARKS**

1. Steel security grill inserts available.
2. Explosion relief domes are available.
3. Louvered curbs available to allow skylight to act as ventilator without being opened.

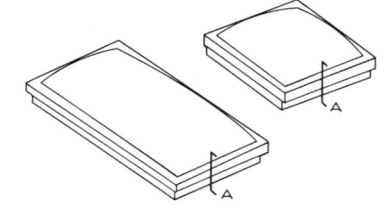

## DOME-SQUARE AND RECTANGULAR

**SIZES AND SPANS**

2 ft 6 in. to 8 ft 0 in., with dome rise from 8 to 22 in.

**GLAZING**

1. Acrylic and polycarbonate typical.
2. Clear, tinted transparent, and white translucent.
3. Single and double normal.
4. Low visual distortion.

**FRAMING**

1. See framing notes for circular dome skylight.
2. Triangular base frame available.
3. Octagonal frame with curved dome glazing possible.
4. Normally designed for level roof application.

**REMARKS**

1. Sealed double domes available from some manufacturers.
2. Secondary dome under pyramid is normally curved.

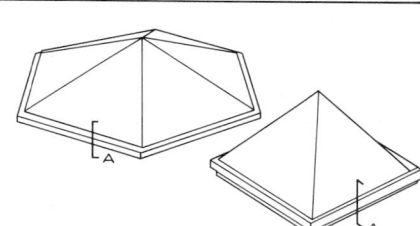

## DOME-POLYGON AND PYRAMID

**SIZES AND SPANS**

Square 1 ft 2 in. to 4 ft 0 in.; rectangular from 2 ft 0 in. to 4 ft 0 in. wide to 4 ft 8 in. long.

**GLAZING**

1. Double glazed, insulating glass typical.
2. Tempered, laminated, and wire glass available.
3. Clear and tinted transparent normal.
4. Minimum visual distortion.

**FRAMING**

1. Operable sash: Hinged, pivoted, or sliding types.
2. Lockable frames available.
3. Aluminum and wood frames commonly available.
4. Skylight—No structural framing within unit.

**REMARKS**

1. Premanufactured screens and shades available.
2. Electric remote control opening operation optional.

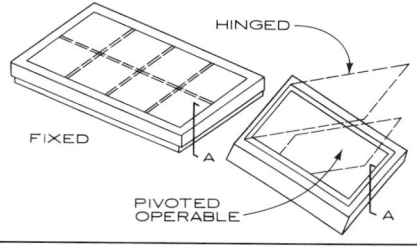

## FLAT PANEL-FIXED AND OPERABLE

**SIZES AND SPANS**

1. 2 ft 0 in. to 10 ft 0 in. wide by any length; rise from 6 to 14 in. or higher as width increases.
2. Larger widths available with vertical ends only.

**GLAZING**

1. Acrylic and polycarbonate typical.
2. Single or double available.
3. Clear, tinted, and white transluscent.

**FRAMING**

1. May be installed in series (with structural supports).
2. Expansion and contraction clearances must be considered at frame as size of unit increases.
3. Skylight—No structural framing within unit.

**REMARKS**

1. Quarter round vault (lean-to) available.
2. May also be used as exterior entry canopy.

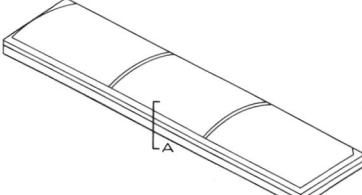

## VAULT

**SIZES AND SPANS**

1. Length and width—almost any design requirement.
2. Variable pitch; up to 4 ft 0 in. along single slope.

**GLAZING**

1. Generally acrylic, but polycarbonate available.
2. Single or double.
3. Clear, tinted, or white transluscent.
4. Ends may be vertical glazed or hipped.

**FRAMING**

1. Integral condensation gutters with frame.
2. Expansion and contraction clearances may be needed.
3. Skylight—No structural framing within unit.

**REMARKS**

Normally used to provide natural light to interior spaces. May be used as exterior entry canopy and walkway protection.

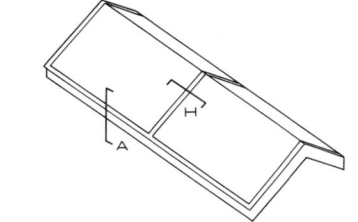

## RIDGE

**SIZES AND SPANS**

Vertical wall and slope to 28 ft 0 in.; rafter spacing of 2, 3, and 4 ft, with glazing lengths of 4, 6, and 8 ft typical.

**GLAZING**

1. All types of glazing for flat panels; cold formed or thermoplastic for curved shapes.
2. Safety glass or plastic recommended.

**FRAMING**

1. Tubular or I-beam construction available.
2. May be custom sized to meet retrofit requirements.
3. Glazed structure—Framing within unit is structural to support glazed panels.

**REMARKS**

1. Shop drawings desirable for these structures.
2. Check local code for requirements of all glazing.

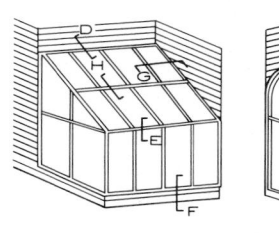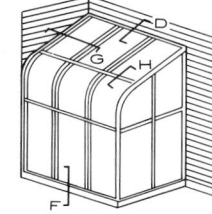

## SHED

CTA Architects Engineers; Billings, Montana
Wheeler & Guay Architects PC; Alexandria, Virginia

### SIZES AND SPANS

Custom sizes from 3 to 10 ft square, factory assembled. Grid more economical with larger units. Uninterrupted spans of 60 by 90 ft not unusual. Long-span grid networks require a perimeter gutter system to control watersheds.

### GLAZING

All types of glazing for flat panels; cold-formed or thermoformed plastic for curved shapes.

### FORMS

1. Flat panels used typically for low-pitched roof.
2. Domed units available from most manufacturers.

### FRAMING

1. Tubular or I-beam construction available.
2. Glazed structure—framing within unit is structural to support glazed panels.

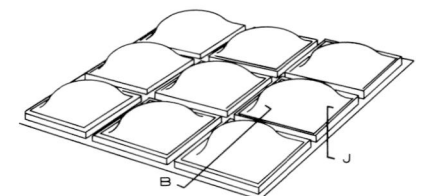

## MULTIPLE GRID

### SIZES AND SPANS

45 ft across, maximum used. Consult manufacturer before designing custom polygons.

### GLAZING

1. All types applicable. Metal panel inserts available.
2. Thickness determined by load and environmental factors.

### FORMS

A variety obtainable with varying facets constructed by joining straight framing sections.

### FRAMING

1. Tubular and I-beam construction available.
2. Glazed structure—framing within unit is structural to support glazed panels.

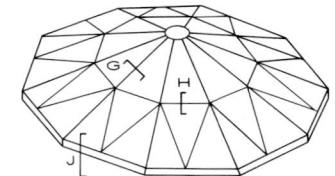

## POLYGON

### SIZES AND SPANS

10–24 ft usual; available in spans to 300 ft in both static and rollaway structures.

### GLAZING

Only plastic glazing materials used. Cold-formed or thermoformed plastic, depending on strength requirements.

### FORMS

Can be fabricated to most radii provided rise/span ratio is minimum 22%.

### FRAMING

1. Number of curved framing sections can vary within same loading conditions.
2. Glazed structure—framing is structural.

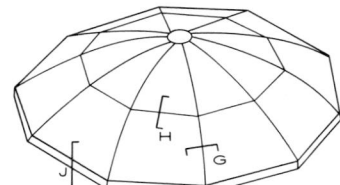

## DOME

### SIZES AND SPANS

1. Lean-to most economical for up to 20 ft 0 in. common. Slopes vary from 10° to 60°.
2. 40 ft spans possible if rafter depth increased.

### GLAZING

1. All types applicable. Insulated glass is tempered.
2. Plastic or safety glass most common.

### FORMS

1. Lean-to most commonly used.
2. For double pitch, hip (ridge) detail may vary.
3. Vertical or hip end possible.

### FRAMING

1. Tubular or I-beam construction available.
2. Glazed structure—framing within units is structural.

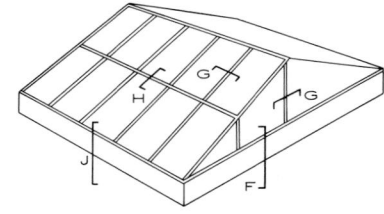

## SINGLE OR DOUBLE PITCH

### SIZES AND SPANS

1. Common sizes—10–40 ft, standard; one piece thermoformed units up to 10 by 10 ft available.
2. Curb load increases as size increases.

### GLAZING

1. All types applicable. Insulated glass is tempered.
2. Plastic or safety glass most common.

### FORMS

Three and four sided; standard slopes up to 45°. Maintain minimum rise of 15°.

### FRAMING

1. Standard aluminum framing.
2. Many custom framing configurations possible.
3. Glazed structure—framing within unit is structural.

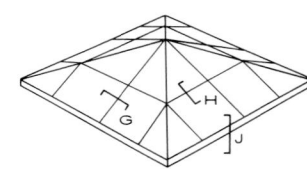

## PYRAMID

### SIZES AND SPANS

1. 15–25 ft most economical. Up to 40 ft used.
2. Height and width can be customized.

### GLAZING

1. All types applicable.
2. Plastic or safety glass most common.
3. Insulated glass usually tempered.

### FORMS

Can be used as single or multiple units; hipped gable ends also available.

### FRAMING

1. Tubular or I-beam construction available.
2. Use structural gutter network with multiple units.
3. Glazed structure—framing is structural.

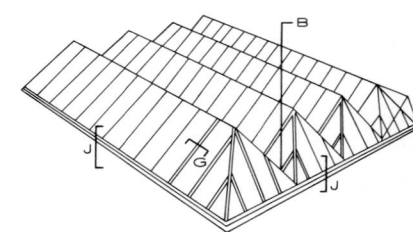

## MULTIPLE RIDGE

### SIZES AND SPANS

1. 10–40 ft most common. Up to 60 ft available.
2. As width increases, cross purlins become necessary.

### GLAZING

1. Plastic glazing materials typical. Glass available in segmented vaults.
2. Glazed panel normally 4 ft wide maximum.

### FORMS

Rises from 10 to 50%; 22% most economical.

### FRAMING

1. Tubular or I-beam construction available.
2. Glazed structure—framing within unit is structural to support glazed panels.

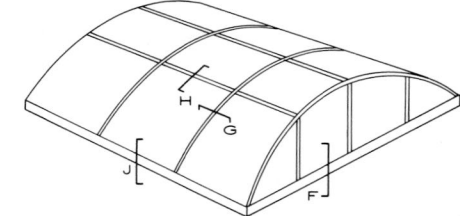

## BARREL VAULT

CTA Architects Engineers; Billings, Montana
Wheeler & Guay Architects PC; Alexandria, Virginia

**SKYLIGHTS**

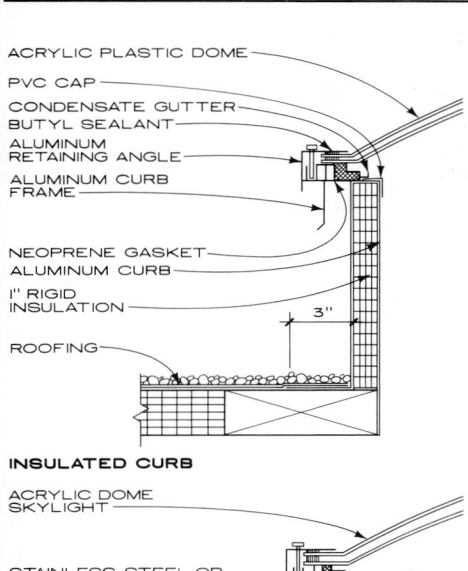

ACRYLIC PLASTIC DOME
PVC CAP
CONDENSATE GUTTER
BUTYL SEALANT
ALUMINUM RETAINING ANGLE
ALUMINUM CURB FRAME

NEOPRENE GASKET
ALUMINUM CURB
I" RIGID INSULATION
ROOFING

3"

**INSULATED CURB**

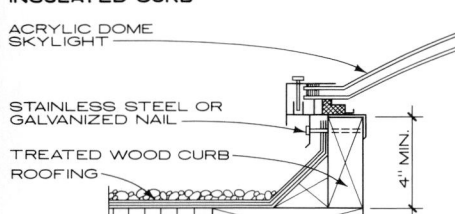

ACRYLIC DOME SKYLIGHT

STAINLESS STEEL OR GALVANIZED NAIL

TREATED WOOD CURB
ROOFING

4" MIN.

**WOOD CURB**

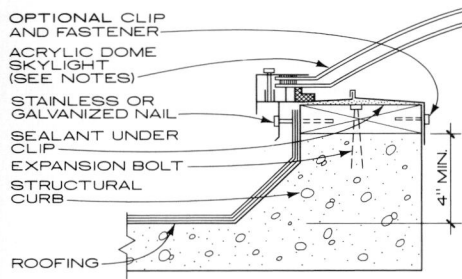

OPTIONAL CLIP AND FASTENER
ACRYLIC DOME SKYLIGHT (SEE NOTES)
STAINLESS OR GALVANIZED NAIL
SEALANT UNDER CLIP
EXPANSION BOLT
STRUCTURAL CURB

ROOFING

4" MIN.

**CONCRETE CURB**

**DETAIL A: CURB TYPES**

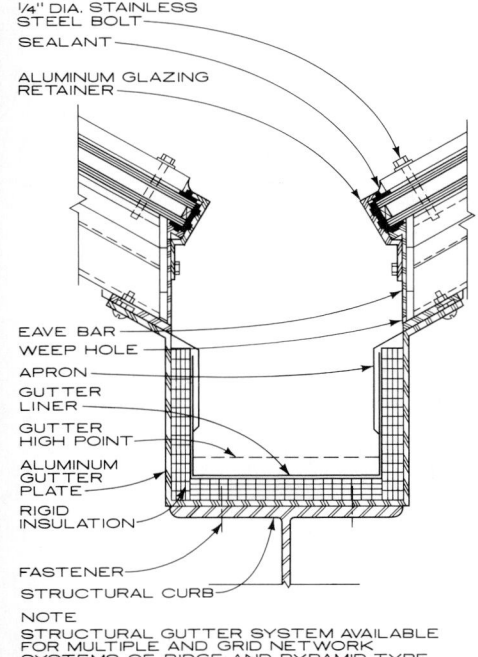

1/4" DIA. STAINLESS STEEL BOLT
SEALANT
ALUMINUM GLAZING RETAINER

EAVE BAR
WEEP HOLE
APRON
GUTTER LINER
GUTTER HIGH POINT
ALUMINUM GUTTER PLATE
RIGID INSULATION

FASTENER
STRUCTURAL CURB
NOTE
STRUCTURAL GUTTER SYSTEM AVAILABLE FOR MULTIPLE AND GRID NETWORK SYSTEMS OF RIDGE AND PYRAMID TYPE ENCLOSURES

**DETAIL B: GUTTER**

CTA Architects Engineers; Billings, Montana
Wheeler & Guay Architects PC; Alexandria, Virginia

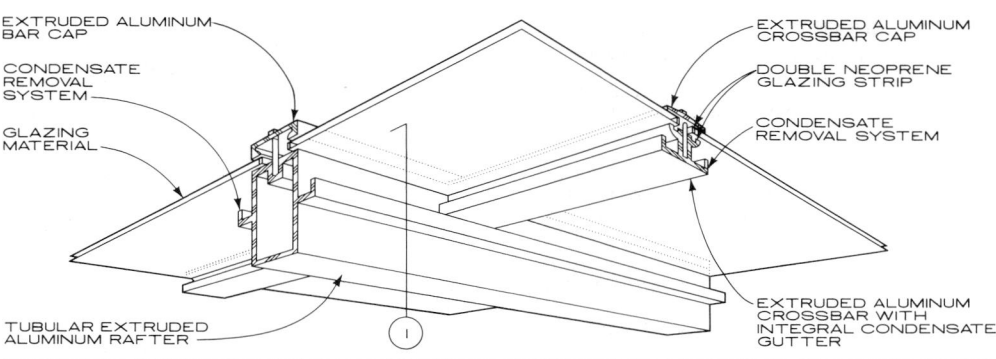

EXTRUDED ALUMINUM BAR CAP
CONDENSATE REMOVAL SYSTEM
GLAZING MATERIAL

EXTRUDED ALUMINUM CROSSBAR CAP
DOUBLE NEOPRENE GLAZING STRIP
CONDENSATE REMOVAL SYSTEM

TUBULAR EXTRUDED ALUMINUM RAFTER

EXTRUDED ALUMINUM CROSSBAR WITH INTEGRAL CONDENSATE GUTTER

1

**DETAIL C: TYPICAL TUBULAR ALUMINUM FRAMING**

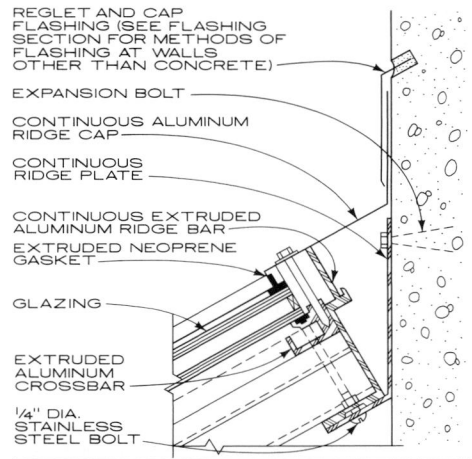

REGLET AND CAP FLASHING (SEE FLASHING SECTION FOR METHODS OF FLASHING AT WALLS OTHER THAN CONCRETE)
EXPANSION BOLT
CONTINUOUS ALUMINUM RIDGE CAP
CONTINUOUS RIDGE PLATE
CONTINUOUS EXTRUDED ALUMINUM RIDGE BAR
EXTRUDED NEOPRENE GASKET
GLAZING
EXTRUDED ALUMINUM CROSSBAR
1/4" DIA. STAINLESS STEEL BOLT

**DETAIL D: RIDGE AT SHED**

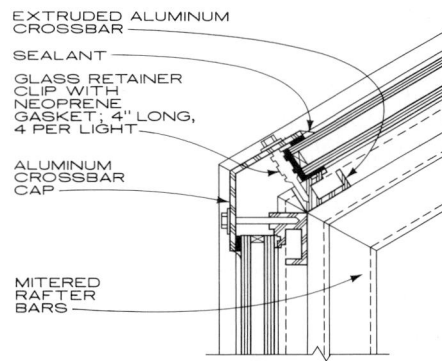

EXTRUDED ALUMINUM CROSSBAR
SEALANT
GLASS RETAINER CLIP WITH NEOPRENE GASKET; 4" LONG, 4 PER LIGHT
ALUMINUM CROSSBAR CAP

MITERED RAFTER BARS

**DETAIL E: KNEE EDGE**

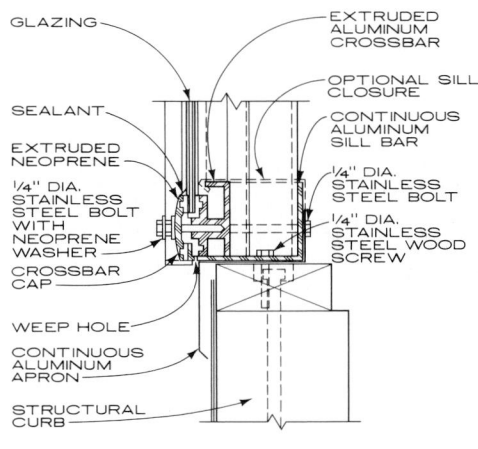

GLAZING
SEALANT
EXTRUDED NEOPRENE
1/4" DIA. STAINLESS STEEL BOLT WITH NEOPRENE WASHER
CROSSBAR CAP
WEEP HOLE
CONTINUOUS ALUMINUM APRON
STRUCTURAL CURB

EXTRUDED ALUMINUM CROSSBAR
OPTIONAL SILL CLOSURE
CONTINUOUS ALUMINUM SILL BAR
1/4" DIA. STAINLESS STEEL BOLT
1/4" DIA. STAINLESS STEEL WOOD SCREW

**DETAIL F: VERTICAL SILL**

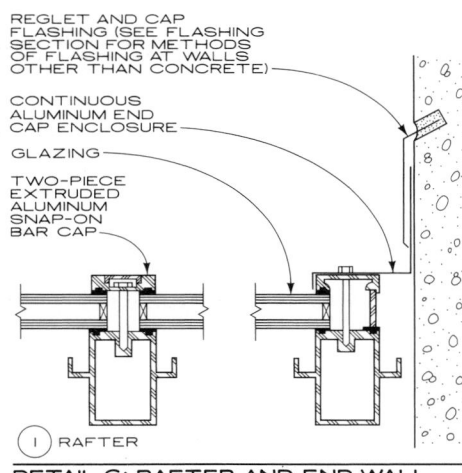

REGLET AND CAP FLASHING (SEE FLASHING SECTION FOR METHODS OF FLASHING AT WALLS OTHER THAN CONCRETE)
CONTINUOUS ALUMINUM END CAP ENCLOSURE
GLAZING
TWO-PIECE EXTRUDED ALUMINUM SNAP-ON BAR CAP

1 RAFTER

**DETAIL G: RAFTER AND END WALL**

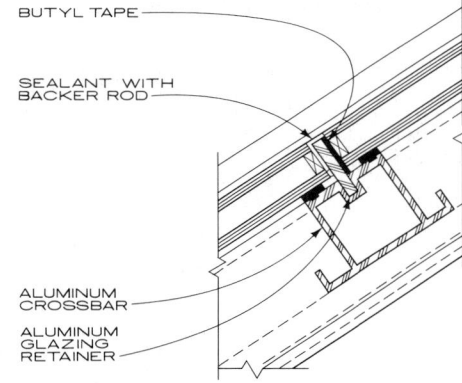

BUTYL TAPE
SEALANT WITH BACKER ROD

ALUMINUM CROSSBAR
ALUMINUM GLAZING RETAINER

**DETAIL H: BUTT GLAZING**

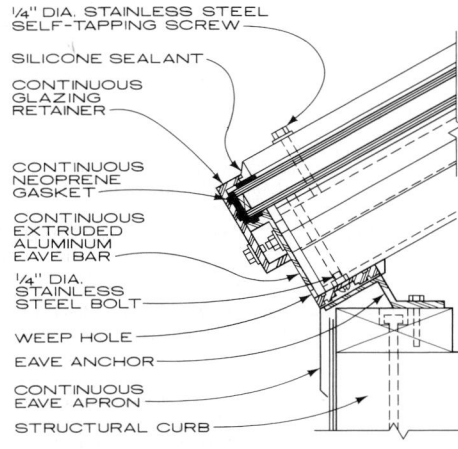

1/4" DIA. STAINLESS STEEL SELF-TAPPING SCREW
SILICONE SEALANT
CONTINUOUS GLAZING RETAINER
CONTINUOUS NEOPRENE GASKET
CONTINUOUS EXTRUDED ALUMINUM EAVE BAR
1/4" DIA. STAINLESS STEEL BOLT
WEEP HOLE
EAVE ANCHOR
CONTINUOUS EAVE APRON
STRUCTURAL CURB

**DETAIL J: EAVE OR SILL**

## MAJOR COMPONENTS

The major components of a good joint seal are the substrate, primer, joint filler, bond breaker, and sealant.

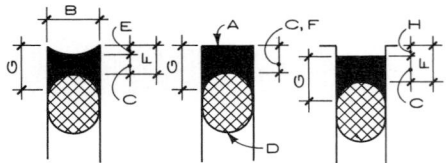

A — sealant
B — sealant width
C — sealant depth
D — joint-filler
E — tooling depth
F — joint-filler depth
G — sealant contact depth
H — sealant recess depth

**TYPICAL VERTICAL APPLICATIONS, PROFILES, AND TERMINOLOGY**

### SUBSTRATE

The more common substrates are masonry concrete, metal, and glass. These are generally classified as porous or nonporous.

Some substrates may not be suitable for achieving a bond unless treated mechanically, chemically, or both.

When the substrate has a coating, the coating must be compatible with the sealant and its bond to the substrate and sealant must be adequate.

Proprietary treatments or protective coatings on metal and waterproofing or water-repellent treatments on concrete may inhibit bonding. Consult both substrate and sealant manufacturers for suitable joint preparation methods and the primers to be used before applying joint materials. Adhesion testing of trial applications in the field is recommended.

Surface laitance and incompatible or bond-inhibiting form release agents on concrete surfaces must be removed.

Substrates must be clean, dry, sound, and free of loose particles, contaminants, foreign matter, water-soluble material, and frost.

Joints in masonry and concrete should be sealed before cleaning exposed surfaces and applying required protective barriers.

### PRIMER

The purpose of a primer is to improve the adhesion of a sealant to a substrate. Many sealants require primers on all substrates, some on only certain substrates or on none at all. Most require a primer for maximum adhesion to concrete and masonry surfaces.

### JOINT FILLERS

A joint filler is used to control the depth of sealant in the joint and permit full wetting of the intended interface when tooled.

Some joint fillers may be incompatible with the substrate and sealant, causing stains on either one of them or both. Some may be factory coated with a suitable material that provides a barrier to staining. To confirm its suitability, the barrier coating should be acceptable to both the sealant and joint filler manufacturers.

Joint fillers for vertical application may be flexible, compatible, closed cell plastic foam or sponge rubber rod stock and elastomeric tubing of such materials as neoprene, butyl, and EPDM. They should resist permanent deformation before and during sealant application, be nonabsorbent to water or gas, and resist flowing upon mild heating, since this can cause bubbling of the sealant. Open cell sponge type materials such as urethane foam may be satisfactory provided that their water absorption characteristics are recognized. The sealant should be applied immediately after joint filler placement to prevent water absorption from rain. Elastomeric tubing of neoprene, butyl, or EPDM may be applied immediately as a temporary seal until the primary sealant is

put in place, after which they serve to a limited degree as a secondary water barrier. When used as temporary seals, joint fillers should be able to remain resilient at temperatures down to −15°F and have low compression set.

Joint fillers for horizontal application for floors, pavements, sidewalks, patios, and other light-traffic areas may be compatible, extruded, closed cell, high density, flexible foams, corkboard, resin-impregnated fiberboard, or elastomeric tubing or rods. These joint fillers should remain resilient down to −15°F, exhibit good recovery, not cause the sealant to bubble in the joint because of heat, and be capable of supporting the sealant in traffic areas. They should not exude liquids under compression, which could hydraulically cause sealant failure by forcing the sealant from the joint. Combinations of joint filler may be used to form a joint in concrete, and an additional joint filler material may be installed under compression across the width and to the proper depth just before the sealant is applied to provide a clean, dry, compatible backup.

### BOND BREAKER

A bond breaker may be necessary to prevent adhesion of the sealant to any surface or material where such adhesion would be detrimental to the performance of the sealant.

The use of a joint filler to which the sealant will not adhere may preclude the need for a bond breaker.

The bond breaker may be a polyethylene tape with pressure-sensitive adhesive on one side or various liquid applied compounds, as recommended by the sealant manufacturer.

### SEALANT

Sealants are classified as single component or multicomponent, nonsag or self-leveling, and traffic or nontraffic use, as well as according to movement capability. Characteristics of some generic types are listed in the accompanying table.

## CHARACTERISTICS OF COMMON ELASTOMERIC SEALANTS

| | ACRYLIC (SOLVENT RELEASES) (ONE-PART) | POLYSULFIDE | | POLYURETHANE | | SILICONE (ONE-PART) |
|---|---|---|---|---|---|---|
| | | TWO-PART | ONE-PART | TWO-PART | ONE-PART | |
| Chief ingredients | Acrylic terpolymer, inert pigments, stabilizer, and selected fillers | Polysulfide polymers, activators, pigments, plasticizers, inert fillers, gelling, and curing agents | | Polyurethane prepolymer, inert fillers, pigment, plasticizers, accelerators, activators, and extenders | Polyurethane prepolymer, inert fillers, pigment, and plasticizers | Siloxane polymer, pigment, and selected fillers |
| Percent solids | 85–95 | 95–100 | 95–100 | 95–100 | 95–100 | 95–100 |
| Curing process | Solvent release and very slow chemical cure | Chemical reaction with curing agent | Chemical reaction with moisture in the air | Chemical reaction with curing agent | Chemical reaction with moisture in air, also oxygen | Chemical reaction with moisture in air |
| Curing characteristics | Skins on exposed surface; interior remains soft and tacky | Cures uniformly throughout; rate affected by temperature and humidity | Skins over, cures progressively inward; final cure uniform throughout | Cures uniformly throughout; rate affected by temperature and humidity | Skins over, cures progressively inward; final cure uniform throughout | Cures progressively inward; final cure uniform throughout |
| Primer | Generally not required | Manufacturer's approved primer required for porous surfaces, sometimes for other surfaces | | Manufacturer's approved primer required for most surfaces | | Required for most surfaces |
| Application temperature (°F) | 40–120 | 40–100 | 60–100 | 40–120 | 40–120 | 0–120 |
| Tackfree time | 1–7 days | 6–24 hr | 6–72 hr | 1–24 hr | Slightly tacky until weathered | 1 hr or less |
| Hardness, Shore A Cured 1 to 6 months Aged 5 years | 0–25 45–55 | 15–45 30–60 | 25–35 40–50 | 20–40 35–55 | 25–45 30–50 | 20–40 35–55 |
| Toxicity | Nontoxic | Curing agent is toxic | Contains toxic ingredients | Toxic; gloves recommended for handling | | Nontoxic |
| Cure time (days) | 14 | 7 | 14–21 | 3–5 | 14 | 5 |
| Joint movement capability (max.) | ±12.5% | ±25% | ±15% | ±25% | ±15% | ±25% high modulus ±50% low modulus |
| Ultraviolet resistance (direct) | Very good | Poor to good | Good | Poor to good | Poor to good | Excellent |
| Dirt resistance cured | Good | Good | Good | Good | Good | Poor |
| Use characteristics | Excellent adhesion; poor low-temperature flexibility; not usable in traffic areas; unpleasant odor 5–12 days | Wide range of appropriate applications; curing time depends on temperature and humidity | Unpleasant odor; broad range of cured hardnesses available | Sets very fast; broad range of cured hardnesses; excellent for concrete joints and traffic areas | Excellent for concrete joints and traffic areas, but substrate must be absolutely dry; short package stability | Requires contact with air for curing; low abrasion resistance; not tough enough for use in traffic areas |

Charles J. Parise, FAIA, FASTM; Smith, Hinchman & Grylls Associates, Inc.; Detroit, Michigan

# 7    JOINT SEALER

## JOINT DESIGN

The design geometry of a joint seal is related to numerous factors including desired appearance, spacing of joints, anticipated movement in joint, movement capability of sealant to be used, required sealant width to accommodate anticipated movement, and tooling method.

## SEALANT WIDTH

The required width of the sealant relative to thermal movement is determined by the application temperature range of the sealant, the temperature extremes anticipated at the site location, the temperature at the time of sealant application, and the movement capability of the sealant to be used. In the absence of specific application temperature knowledge, an ambient application temperature from 4 to 38°C (40 to 100°F) should be assumed in determining the anticipated amount of joint movement in the design of joints. Although affected by ambient temperatures, anticipated joint movement must be determined from anticipated building material temperature extremes rather than ambient temperature extremes.

The accompanying graph provides an average working relationship of recommended joint widths for sealants with various movement capabilities based only on thermal expansion of the more common substrates. These joint widths should be considered as minimal. They do not take into consideration variations in joint dimensions encountered during construction or temperature extremes at the time of sealant application. It is advisable to consider these variables and to also incorporate a safety factor (s.f.) into the joint design by only using a percentage of the stated sealant movement capability, since sealants do not always perform at their stated maximum capabilities.

Many other factors can be involved in building joint movement including, but not limited to, material mass, color, insulation, wind loads, settlement, thermal conductivity, differential thermal stress (bowing), residual growth or shrinkage of materials, building sway, and seismic forces. Of particular importance are material and construction tolerances that can produce joints on the job site smaller than anticipated. The design joint width should be calculated taking all possible movement and tolerance factors into consideration, as shown with the following examples:

$$J = \text{minimum joint width (inches)}$$
$$= \frac{100}{X}(M_t + M_o) + T$$

$X$ = percentage of stated movement capability of the sealant by ASTM Test Method C719

$M_t$ = joint movement due to thermal expansion of substrates (inches)

$\quad = (E_c)\,(\Delta_t)\,(L)$

where $E_c$ = coefficient of expansion of substrate from accompanying table (in./in./°F)

$\quad \Delta_t$ = temperature change of substrate (°F)

$\quad L$ = substrate length (inches)

$M_o$ = joint movement due to other factors (inches)

$T$ = tolerances for construction (inches)

A sample calculation for joint width between concrete panels of 10 ft lengths, expecting a temperature change in the concrete of 120°F, construction tolerances of 0.25 in., and sealed with a sealant capable of a maximum ±25% (reduced to 20% for s.f.) movement is

$$J = \frac{100}{X}M_t + T$$
$$= \frac{100}{X}(E_c)\,(\Delta_t)\,(L) + T$$
$$= \frac{100}{20}(6 \times 10^{-6}\ \text{in./in./°F})\,(120°F)\,(120\ \text{in.})$$
$$\quad + 0.25\ \text{in.}$$
$$= 0.68\ \text{in.}$$

A more simplified method (but not as accurate) is to use the accompanying graph as follows:

$$J = (\text{joint width scaled}) + T$$
$$= (0.5\ \text{in./in./°F})\left(\frac{120°F}{130°F}\right) + 0.25\ \text{in.}$$
$$= 0.71\ \text{in.}$$

## SEALANT DEPTH

The sealant depth, when applied, depends on the sealant width. The following guidelines are normally accepted practice.

1. For a recommended minimum width of ¼ in., the depth should by ¼ in.

2. For joints in concrete, masonry, or stone, the depth of the sealant may be equal to the sealant width in joints up to ½ in. For joints ½ to 1 in. wide, the sealant depth should be one-half the width. For joints 1 to 2 in. wide, the sealant depth should not be greater than ½ in. For widths exceeding 2 in., the depth should be determined by the sealant manufacturer.

3. For sealant widths over ¼ in. and up to ½ in. in metal, glass, and other nonporous surface joints, the minimum of ¼ in. in depth applies, and over ½ in. in width the sealant depth shold be one-half the sealant width and should in no case exceed ½ in.

When determining location of the joint filler in the joint, consideration should be given to the reduction in sealant depth with concave and recessed tooled joints, and the joint should be designed accordingly.

## COEFFICIENTS OF EXPANSION

| MATERIALS | AVERAGE COEFFICIENT OF LINEAR EXPANSION (MULTIPLY BY 10⁻⁶) | |
|---|---|---|
| | CENTIGRADE (MM/MM/°C) | FAHRENHEIT (IN./IN./°F) |
| Aluminum: | | |
|   5005 or 6061 alloy | 23.8 | 13.2 |
| Brass: | | |
|   230 alloy | 18.7 | 10.4 |
| Bronze: | | |
|   220 alloy | 18.4 | 10.2 |
|   385 alloy | 20.9 | 11.6 |
| Clay masonry: | | |
|   Clay or shale brick | 6.5 | 3.6 |
|   Fire clay brick or tile | 4.5 | 2.5 |
| Concrete masonry: | | |
|   Dense aggregate | 9.4 | 5.2 |
|   Lightweight aggregate | 7.7 | 4.3 |
| Concrete: | | |
|   Calcareous aggregate | 9.0 | 5.0 |
|   Siliceous aggregate | 10.8 | 6.0 |
|   Quartzite aggregate | 12.6 | 7.0 |
| Copper: | | |
|   110 alloy | 16.9 | 9.4 |
|   122 alloy | 16.9 | 9.4 |
| Glass | 8.8 | 4.9 |
| Iron: | | |
|   Cast, gray | 10.6 | 5.9 |
|   Wrought | 12.1 | 6.7 |
| Lead | 28.6 | 15.9 |
| Plastic: | | |
|   Acrylic sheet | 74.0 | 41.0 |
|   High-impact acrylic sheet | 50.0 | 82.0 |
|   Polycarbonate sheet | 68.4 | 38.0 |
| Steel, Carbon | 12.1 | 6.7 |
| Steel, Stainless: | | |
|   301 alloy | 16.9 | 9.4 |
|   302 alloy | 17.3 | 9.6 |
|   304 alloy | 17.3 | 9.6 |
|   316 alloy | 16.0 | 8.9 |
| Stone: | | |
|   Granite | 5.0–11.0 | 2.8– 6.1 |
|   Limestone | 4.0–12.0 | 2.2– 6.7 |
|   Marble | 6.7–22.1 | 3.7–12.3 |
|   Sandstone | 8.0–12.0 | 4.4– 6.7 |
|   Slate | 8.0–10.0 | 4.4– 5.6 |
|   Travertine | 6.0–10.0 | 3.3– 5.6 |
| Zinc | 32.4 | 18.0 |

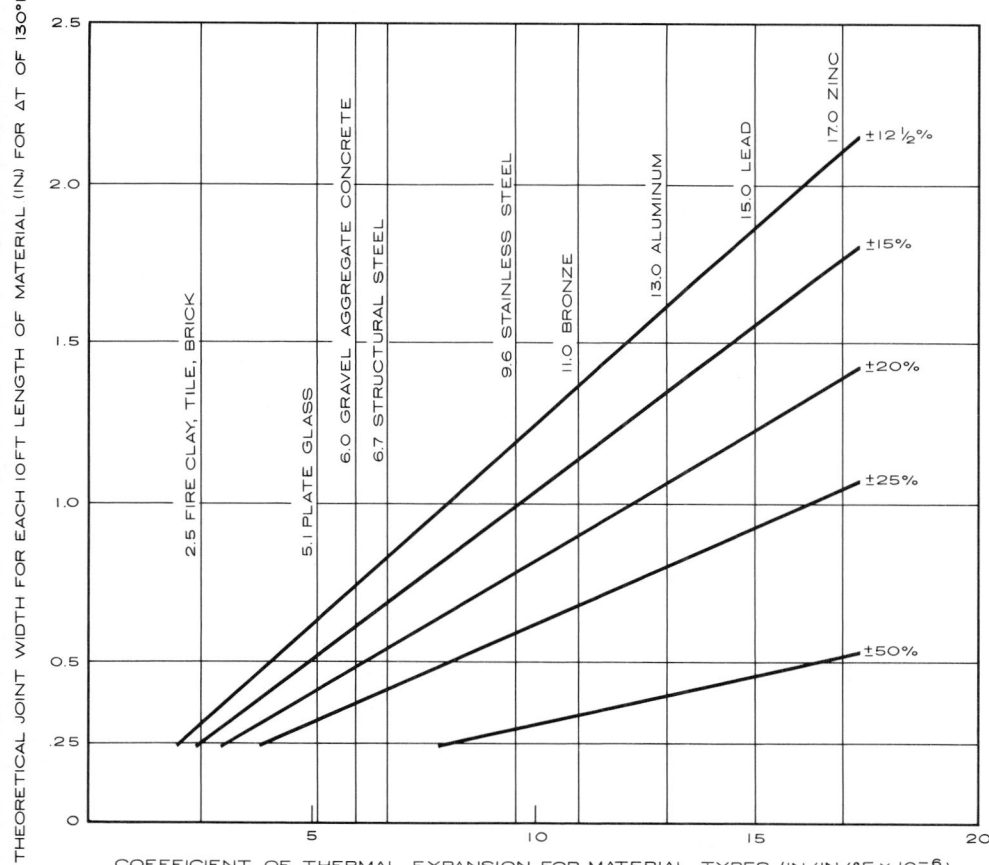

**RECOMMENDED JOINT WIDTH FOR SEALANTS WITH VARIOUS MOVEMENT CAPABILITIES**

Charles J. Parise, FAIA, FASTM; Smith, Hinchman & Grylls Associates, Inc.; Detroit, Michigan

## APPLICATION

To obtain proper adhesion, it is essential that the sealant come in direct contact with the substrate, that the sealant wet the surface of the substrate, and that the substrate be strong enough to provide a firm anchor for the sealant. If any of these conditions is not met, poor adhesion will usually result. The sealant should be installed in such a manner as to completely fill the recess provided in the joint.

Against a porous material, the sealant must enter the pores if good adhesion is to be obtained. Sealants used for this application are thixotropic and will resist flow into the pores unless an external force is applied. Proper filling of the recess accomplishes this, in part, and proper tooling ensures it.

### JOINT PREPARATION

Joints to receive sealant should be cleaned out and raked to full width and depth required for installation of joint seal materials. Thoroughly clean all joints, removing all foreign matter such as dust, paint (unless it is a permanent protective coating), oil, grease, waterproofing or water-repellent treatments, water, surface dirt, and frost. Clean porous materials such as concrete, masonry, and unglazed surfaces of ceramic tile by brushing, grinding, blast cleaning, mechanical abrading, acid washing, or a combination of these methods to provide a clean, sound substrate for optimum sealant adhesion. The surface of concrete may be cut back to remove contaminants and expose a clean surface when acceptable to the purchaser.

Remove laitance from concrete by acid washing, grinding, or mechanical abrading and remove form oils from concrete by blast cleaning. Remove loose particles originally present or resulting from grinding, abrading, or blast cleaning by blowing out joints with oil-free compressed air (or vacuuming) prior to application of primer or sealant.

Clean nonporous surfaces, such as metal, glass, porcelain enamel, and glazed surfaces of ceramic tile chemically or by other means that are not harmful to the substrate and are acceptable to the substrate manufacturer.

Remove temporary protective coatings on metallic surfaces by a solvent that leaves no residue. Apply the solvent with clean oil-free cloths or lintless paper towels. Do not dip cleaning cloths into solvent. Always pour the solvent on the cloth to eliminate the possibility of contaminating the solvent. Do not allow the solvent to air-dry without wiping. Wipe dry with a clean dry cloth or lintless paper towels. Permanent coatings that are to remain must not be removed or damaged.

### MASKING TAPE

Install masking tape at joint edges when necessary to avoid undesirable sealant smears on exposed visible surfaces. Use a nonstaining, nonabsorbent, compatible type.

### PRIMER AND JOINT FILLER

Install primer when and as recommended by the sealant manufacturer for optimum adhesion.

Install compatible joint filler uniformly to proper depth without twisting and braiding.

### SEALANT

Install sealant in strict accordance with the manufacturer's recommendations and precautions. Completely fill the recess provided in the joint. Sealants are more safely applied at temperatures above 40°F. Joints must be dry.

### TOOLING

Tooling nonsag sealants is essential to force the sealant into the joint and eliminate air pockets and should be done as soon as possible after application and before

skinning or curing begins. Tooling also ensures contact of the sealant to the sides of a joint.

Plastic or metal tools may be used. Most applicators use dry tools, but they may be surface-treated to prevent adhesion to the sealant and may be shaped as desired to produce the desired joint profile. Dipping tools in certain liquids decreases adhesion of the sealant to the tool. All liquids should first be tested and accepted for use by the manufacturer. The use of some liquids may result in surface discoloration. In using tooling liquids, care should be taken to ensure that the liquid does not contact joint surfaces prior to the sealant contacting the joint surface. If the sealant overlaps the area contaminated with the liquid, the sealant bond may be adversely affected.

Tool sealant so as to force it into the joint, eliminating air pockets and ensuring contact of the sealant with the sides of the joint. Use appropriate tool to provide a concave, flush, or recessed joint as required.

Immediately after tooling the joint, remove masking tape carefully, if used, without disturbing the sealant.

### FIELD TESTING

In cases where the building joints are ready to receive sealant and the question of adhesion of the sealant to novel or untried surfaces arises, it is advisable to install the sealant in a 1.5-m (5 ft) length of joint as a test. It would be good practice to do this as a matter of standard procedure on most projects, even though unusual conditions are not suspected. Following instructions of the sealant manufacturer and using primer as and when recommended, install the sealant in the joint and examine for adhesion after cure to determine whether proper adhesion has been obtained.

Reference: ASTM C-962 "Standard Guide for Use of Elastomeric Joint Sealants." Highlights of text, graph, and figures are reprinted with permission from ASTM Committee C-24 of the American Society for Testing and Materials.

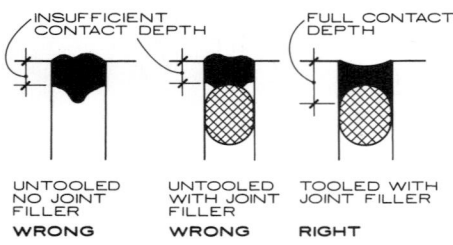

**PURPOSE FOR JOINT FILLER AND TOOLING**

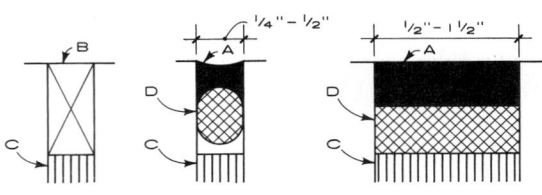
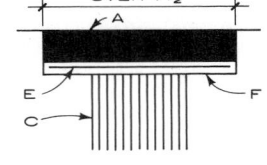

A — sealant
B — removable joint filler
C — premolded joint filler cast in concrete
D — joint filler installed under compression

E — bond breaker (use over sliding metal support in relatively wide joints)
F — concrete shoulder provides vertical support

**USE OF MULTIPLE JOINT FILLERS IN HORIZONTAL APPLICATIONS IN CAST-IN-PLACE CONCRETE**

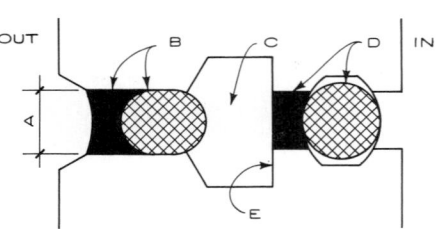

A — 1" minimum for access to interior air seal
B — sealant and joint filler preferred for rain screen; preformed compression seal also used
C — pressure equalization chamber; vent to outside, and chamber baffles at every second floor vertically and same distance horizontally
D — sealant and joint filler installed from outside to facilitate continuity of air seal; building framework hinders application of continuous air seal from interior
E — concrete shoulders required for tooling screed

**TWO-STAGE PRESSURE EQUALIZED JOINT SEAL**

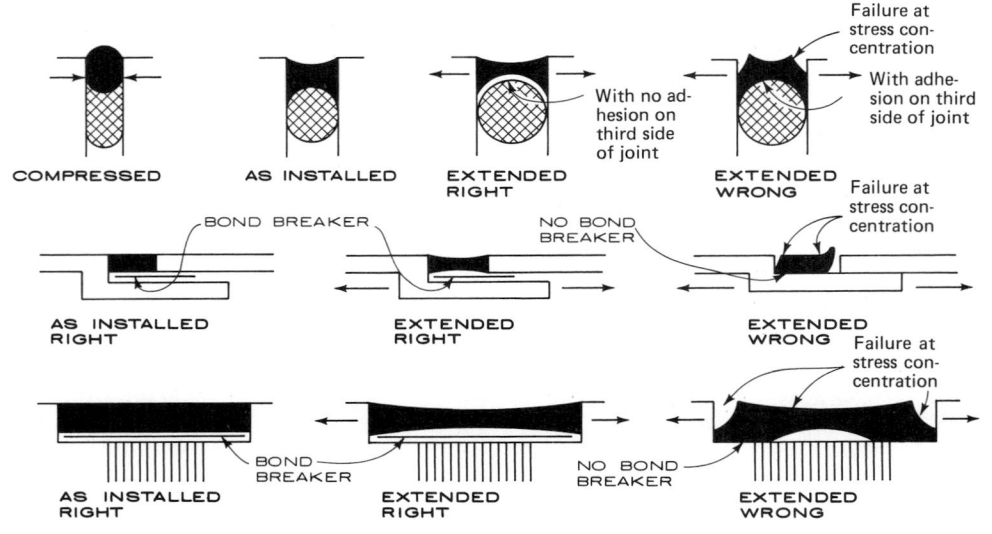

**SEALANT CONFIGURATIONS WITH MOVEMENT AND EFFECT OF THREE-SIDED ADHESION**

Charles J. Parise, FAIA, FASTM; Smith, Hinchman & Grylls Associates, Inc.; Detroit, Michigan

# CHAPTER 8

## Doors and Windows

## INTRODUCTION:

The following is a selection of hollow metal details from various manufacturers. They are in no way intended to favor a manufacturer or a product. Details vary. Consult manufacturers literature.

Hollow metal is divided into a frame section and a door section. The frame section can be used with wood doors. Both sections are complete in themselves.

## NOMENCLATURE

|  |  |
|---|---|
| Active Leaf | The door leaf of a pair in which the lock is normally installed. |
| Astragal (overlapping) | A vertical molding attached to the meeting edge of one leaf of a pair of doors for protection against weather conditions and to retard passage of smoke, flame and gasses. |
| Astragal (split) | A vertical molding attached to both leaves at a pair of doors at the meeting edge for protection against weather conditions. |
| Barrier Screen | See Smoke Screen. |
| Beveled Edge | The edge at a door that is not at a 90° angle to the face of the door (std. bevel is 1/8" in 2"). |
| Blank Jamb | Vertical member of frame without hardware preparation. Used when doors are furnished with push and pull hardware or surface mounted strikes and single active floor hinges. |
| Borrowed Light | Four-sided frame prepared for glass installation in field. |
| Bullnose Trim | The face & jamb width joined by a radius rather than a 90° break. |
| Cabinet Jamb | Frame in three or more pieces applied as the finished frame over rough buck. |
| Cap | See Soffit. |
| Cased Opening | Frame section which does not have any stops. |
| Covemold Frame | Frame having contour faces (exposed) simulating contour of wood frame. |
| Cut-Out | A preparation for hardware and/or accessories. |
| Double Acting Door | Type of door prepared for pivot or spring type hinge permitting the door to swing 90° in either direction. |
| Double Egress Frame | Double rabbeted double frame prepared to receive two single-acting doors swinging in opposite directions. |
| Dutch Door | Door having two separate leaves, one hung above the other. Shelf on lower leaf, optional. |

|  |  |
|---|---|
| Face | Exposed part of frame parallel to face of wall. |
| Filler Plate | A blank plate used to fill mortised cutouts. |
| Flat Frame | Frame having flat faces exposed. |
| Floor Clearance | Distance between bottom of door and finished floor. |
| Glass Stop | Fixed trim on a glass tight door against which glass is set. |
| Glazing Bead | A removable trim at glazing opening to hold glass securely in place. |
| Hand | Term used to designate direction in which door swings. |
| Handing | The swinging of the door e.g., right hand or left hand. To determine the hand of a door, view the door from the outside. The side that the hinges are on is the hand of the door. If the door swings away from the viewer, the hand is a regular hand, i.e. right or left hand. If the door swings to the viewer, the door is reverse swing, i.e. right hand reverse swing or left hand reverse swing. |
| Head | Horizontal frame member at top of door opening or top member of transom frames. |
| Header | See Head. |
| Hinge Backset | Distance from edge to hinge to stop on frame. |
| Hinge Filler Plate | Plate installed for a hinge cut-out when no hinge is required. |
| Inactive Leaf | The door leaf in a pair of doors which is normally held closed by top and bottom bolts. |
| Jamb | Vertical frame member; between door and glass or wall; between glass and door or wall. See also Mullion. |
| Jamb Depth | Over-all width of frame section. |
| Knock Down (KD) Frame | Door frame furnished by manufacturer in three or more basic parts for assembly in field. |
| Lock Backset | Distance from edge of door to centerline of cylinder or knob. |
| Masonry Box | See Plaster Guard. |
| Mortise Preparation | Reinforcing drilling and tapping for hardware which is to be mortised into door or frame. |
| Mullion | Vertical or horizontal frame member; between glass and glass, or door and door. |
| Muntin | Non-structural member used to subdivide an open area in frame or door. |

|  |  |
|---|---|
| Opening Size | Size of frame opening measured between rabbets and finished floor. |
| Plaster Guard | Metal shield attached behind hinge and strike reinforcement to prevent mortar or plaster from entering mounting holes. |
| Reveal | That part of the backband which extends beyond finished wall. |
| Reveal | Distance from face of frame to surface of finished wall. |
| Reversing Channel | See End Channel. |
| Reverse Bevel | Refers to hand of door or lock when doors swing to outside. |
| Rough Opening | Size of wall opening into which frame is installed. |
| Rubber Silencer | A part attached to the stop of a frame to cushion the closing of door. |
| Section Width | See Jamb Depth. |
| Single Acting Door | Type of door prepared for a pivot type or spring-type single-acting hinge permitting the door to swing 90° in one direction only. |
| Smoke Screen | A door frame combined with sidelights on either or both sides of door openings, including transom opening when and if required. |
| Soffit | Underside of stop on frame. |
| Split Jambs | Frames with jamb width in two pieces. |
| Stilts | See Floor Struts. |
| Stop | Part of frame against which door closes or glass rests. |
| Strike Stile | Vertical member of an inactive door leaf which receives the strike. |
| Strut Guide | Metal piece attached inside throat of frame which guides and holds ceiling strut to frame (usually incorporated in clip). |
| Sub Buck | See Rough Buck. |
| Surface Hardware Preparation | Reinforcing or machining or both, for hardware which is applied to surface of door or frame in field. |
| Top & Bottom Cap | Horizontal channel used in doors which do not have a flush top or bottom. |
| Transom Bar | The part of a transom frame which separates the top of the door from the transom. |
| Trim | (1) See face. (2) An applied face. |
| Trimmed Opening | See Cased Opening. |

James W. G. Watson, AIA; Ronald A. Spahn and Associates; Cleveland Heights, Ohio

## METAL DOORS AND FRAMES

## GENERAL

Fire door assemblies are used for the protection of openings in fire-rated walls. The assembly consists of a fire door, frame, and hardware. Each component is crucial to the overall performance of the assembly as a fire barrier.

NFPA 80 is a national standard to establish the degree of fire protection required at a given opening. Fire doors and frames are classified by the duration of test exposure (hourly rating) and the class of opening the assembly is intended for (letter designation).

Additional information is available in Chapter 7 of the NFPA ''Fire Protection Handbook.''

## TYPES OF OPENINGS

1. CLASS A (3-hour doors): Openings in fire walls and in walls that divide a single building into fire areas.
2. CLASS B (1- or 1½-hour doors): Openings in enclosures of vertical communications through buildings and in 2-hour rated partitions providing horizontal fire separations.
3. CLASS C (¾-hour door): Openings in walls or partitions between rooms and corridors having a fire resistance rating of 1 hour or less.
4. CLASS D (1½-hour door): Openings in exterior walls subject to severe fire exposure from outside of the building.
5. CLASS E (¾-hour door): Openings in exterior walls subject to moderate or light fire exposure from outside of the building.

½- and ⅓-hour doors are used for smoke control in corridor walls.

## TYPES OF DOORS

Typical construction for swinging fire doors:

1. COMPOSITE fire doors consist of wood, steel, or plastic sheets bonded to and supported by a solid core material.
2. HOLLOW METAL fire doors are of flush or panel design with not less than 20 gauge steel face.
3. METAL CLAD fire doors are of flush or panel design consisting of metal covered wood cores or stiles and rails and insulated panels covered with steel of 24 gauge or lighter.
4. SHEET METAL fire doors are formed of 22 gauge or lighter steel and are corrugated, flush sheet, or panel design.
5. TINCLAD fire doors consist of a wood core with a terne plate or galvanized steel facing (#30 or #24 gauge).
6. WOOD core-type doors consist of wood, hardboard, or plastic face sheets bonded to a wood block or wood particleboard core material with untreated wood edges.

## TYPES OF FRAMES

Fire-rated door frames can be factory or field assembled. All frames must be adequately anchored at the jambs and floor per the manufacturers' specifications.

1. WOOD: Head and jamb members, with or without solid transom panel (20 minute maximum rating).
2. LIGHT GAUGE METAL FRAME: Head and jamb members with or without transom panel made from aluminum (45 minute maximum rating) or light gauge steel (1½ hour maximum rating). Frame is installed over finished wall.
3. PRESSED STEEL (HOLLOW METAL): Head and jamb members, with or without solid or glazed transoms or sidelights made from 18 gauge or heavier steel (3 hour maximum rating). This frame is required for most metal doors.

## HARDWARE

Door hardware is either provided by the builder or furnished by the manufacturer. Generally the door and frame must be prepared to receive hardware by the manufacturer to insure that the integrity of the fire-rated assembly is maintained.

Fire doors are hung on steel ball bearing hinges. A fire door must close and latch at the time of a fire. Labeled automatic latches and door closers can be self-operated or controlled by failsafe devices that activate in a fire situation. Pairs of doors require coordinators with astragals to ensure both doors close. Gasketing to seal the head and jambs should be provided where smoke control is required.

Thomas Emme, AIA; Albert C. Martin & Associates; Los Angeles, California
William G. Miner, AIA; Architect; Washington, D.C.
NFPA, see data sources

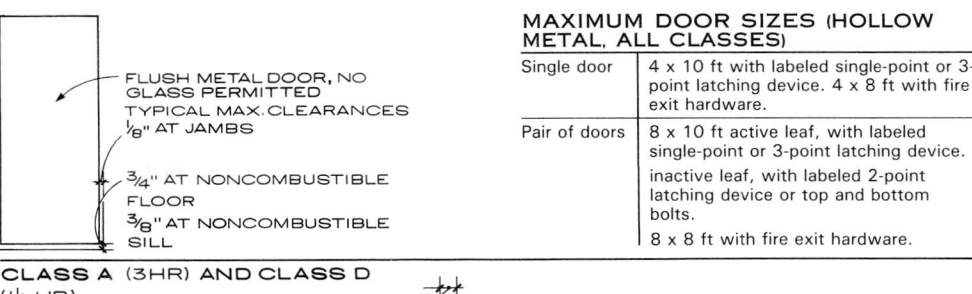

### MAXIMUM DOOR SIZES (HOLLOW METAL, ALL CLASSES)

| Single door | 4 x 10 ft with labeled single-point or 3-point latching device. 4 x 8 ft with fire exit hardware. |
| --- | --- |
| Pair of doors | 8 x 10 ft active leaf, with labeled single-point or 3-point latching device. inactive leaf, with labeled 2-point latching device or top and bottom bolts. 8 x 8 ft with fire exit hardware. |

**CLASS A (3HR) AND CLASS D (1½ HR)**

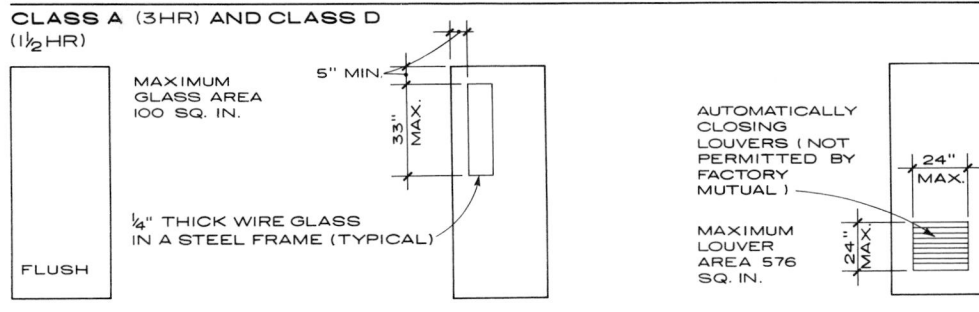

**CLASS B (1 OR 1½ HR)**

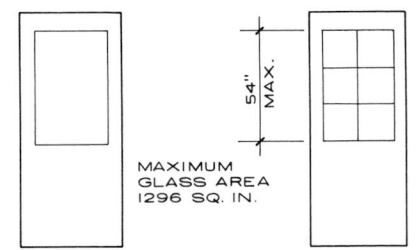

### HINGE REQUIREMENTS (ALL CLASSES)

All hinges or pivots must be steel. Two hinges are required on doors up to 5 ft in height and an additional hinge is required for each additional 2 ft 6 in. of door height or fraction thereof. The same requirement holds for pivots.

**CLASS C (¾ HR), CLASS E (¾HR) AND SMOKE CONTROL DOORS (½ AND ⅓ HR)**

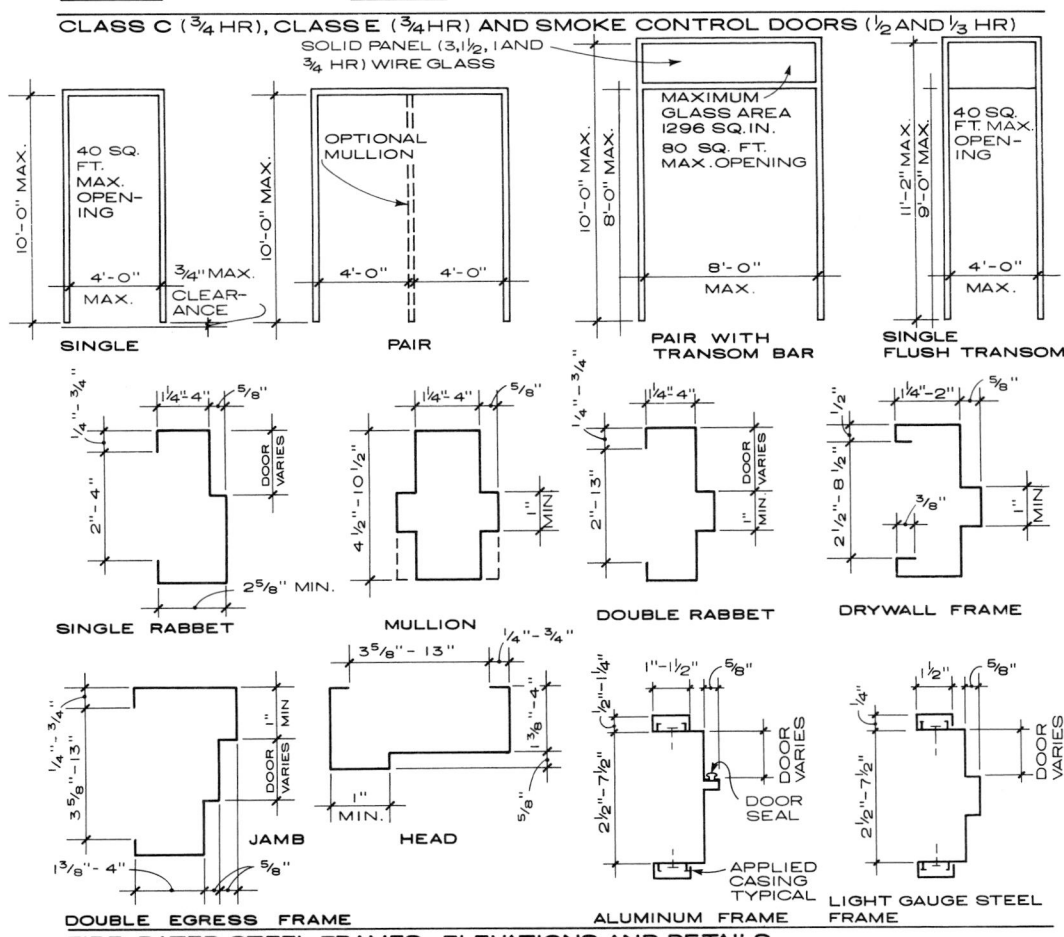

**FIRE-RATED STEEL FRAMES—ELEVATIONS AND DETAILS**

## METAL DOORS AND FRAMES

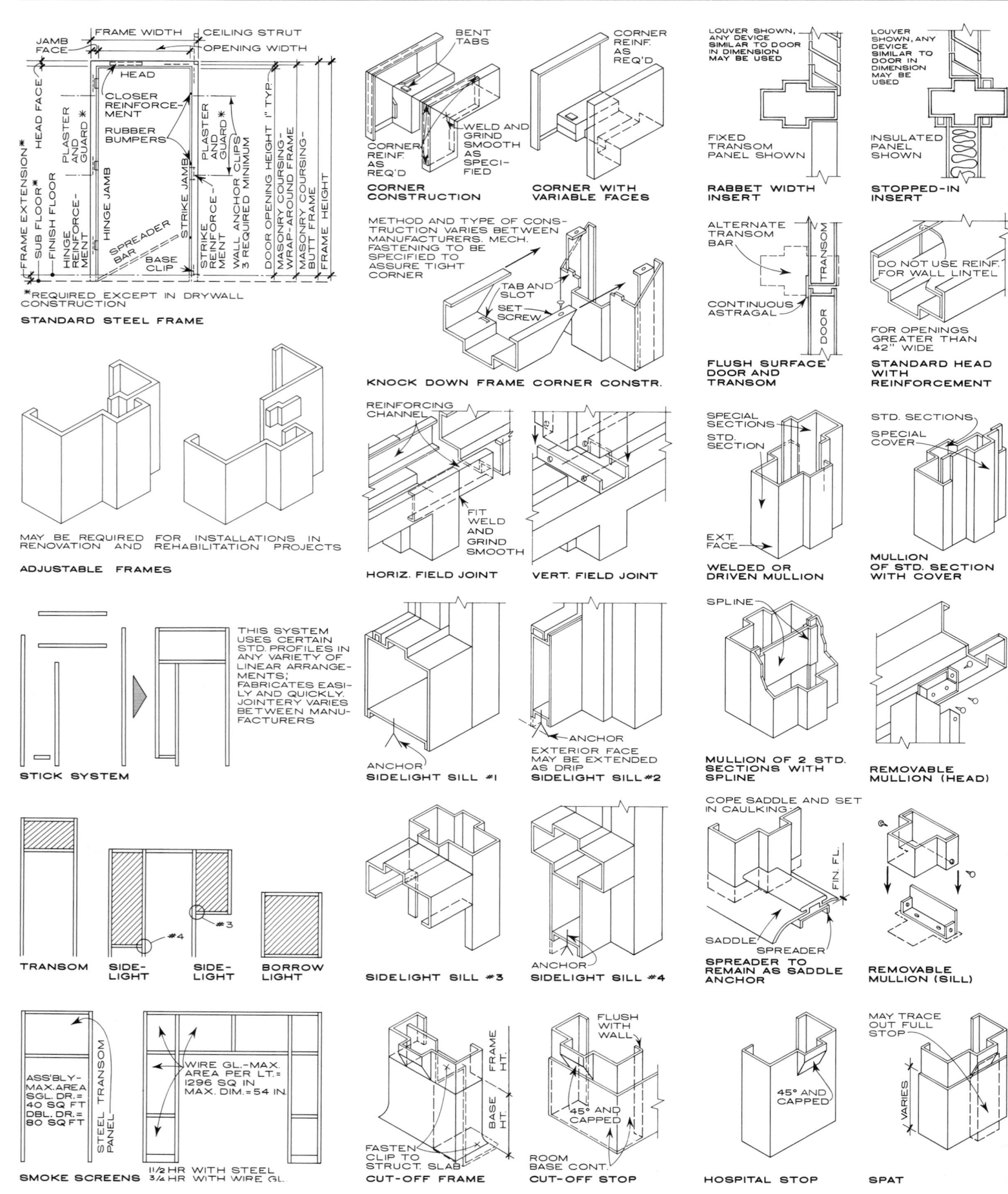

STANDARD STEEL FRAME

*REQUIRED EXCEPT IN DRYWALL CONSTRUCTION

ADJUSTABLE FRAMES

MAY BE REQUIRED FOR INSTALLATIONS IN RENOVATION AND REHABILITATION PROJECTS

STICK SYSTEM

THIS SYSTEM USES CERTAIN STD. PROFILES IN ANY VARIETY OF LINEAR ARRANGEMENTS; FABRICATES EASILY AND QUICKLY. JOINTERY VARIES BETWEEN MANUFACTURERS

TRANSOM    SIDELIGHT    SIDELIGHT    BORROW LIGHT

SMOKE SCREENS
1½ HR WITH STEEL
¾ HR WITH WIRE GL.

ASS'BLY - MAX. AREA SGL. DR. = 40 SQ FT DBL. DR. = 80 SQ FT

WIRE GL.-MAX. AREA PER LT.= 1296 SQ IN MAX. DIM.= 54 IN.

CORNER CONSTRUCTION

CORNER WITH VARIABLE FACES

KNOCK DOWN FRAME CORNER CONSTR.

METHOD AND TYPE OF CONSTRUCTION VARIES BETWEEN MANUFACTURERS. MECH. FASTENING TO BE SPECIFIED TO ASSURE TIGHT CORNER

HORIZ. FIELD JOINT

VERT. FIELD JOINT

SIDELIGHT SILL #1

SIDELIGHT SILL #2

EXTERIOR FACE MAY BE EXTENDED AS DRIP

SIDELIGHT SILL #3

SIDELIGHT SILL #4

CUT-OFF FRAME

CUT-OFF STOP

RABBET WIDTH INSERT

STOPPED-IN INSERT

FLUSH SURFACE DOOR AND TRANSOM

STANDARD HEAD WITH REINFORCEMENT

DO NOT USE REINF. FOR WALL LINTEL

FOR OPENINGS GREATER THAN 42" WIDE

WELDED OR DRIVEN MULLION

MULLION OF STD. SECTION WITH COVER

MULLION OF 2 STD. SECTIONS WITH SPLINE

REMOVABLE MULLION (HEAD)

SPREADER TO REMAIN AS SADDLE ANCHOR

REMOVABLE MULLION (SILL)

HOSPITAL STOP

SPAT

James W. G. Watson, AIA; Ronald A. Spahn and Associates; Cleveland Heights, Ohio

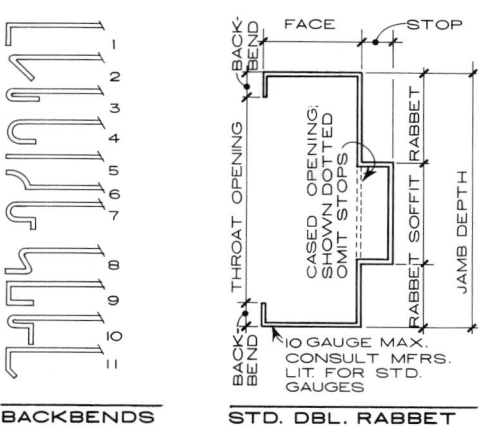

**BACKBENDS**

**STD. DBL. RABBET**

Labels in the right diagram: BACK-BEND, FACE, STOP, THROAT OPENING, CASED OPENING, SHOWN DOTTED OMIT STOPS, RABBET, SOFFIT, RABBET, JAMB DEPTH, BACK BEND, 10 GAUGE MAX. CONSULT MFRS. LIT. FOR STD. GAUGES

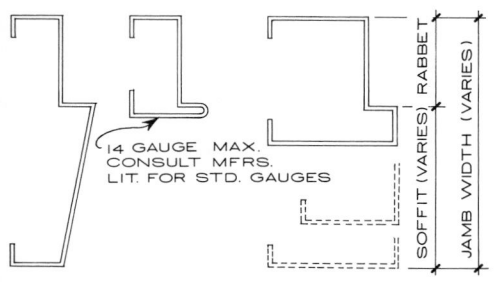

14 GAUGE MAX. CONSULT MFRS. LIT. FOR STD. GAUGES

SOFFIT (VARIES) RABBET, RABBET (VARIES), JAMB WIDTH (VARIES)

**VARIOUS SINGLE RABBETS**

## VARIOUS STANDARD PROFILES

| JAMB DEPTH | 2¾ | 3 | 3¾ | 4¾ | 5½ | 5¾ | 6¾ | 7¾ | 8¾ | 12¾ |
|---|---|---|---|---|---|---|---|---|---|---|
| RABBET ³ | SINGLE | | 1 15/16 STD. FOR 1¾" DOOR | | | | | | | |
| SOFFIT ³ | RABBET ONLY | | | | | | | | | |
| RABBET ³ | | | 1 9/16 STD. FOR 1⅜" DOOR | | | | | | | |
| BACKBEND | ½ | 7/16 | ½ | ½ | ¾ | ½ | ½ | ½ | ½ | ½ |
| THROAT | 1¾ | 2⅛ | 2 | 3¾ | 4 | 4¾ | 5¾ | 6¾ | 7¾ | 11¾ |

### NOTES
1. Many others available. Consult mfrs. list for dimensions and options.
2. Depths vary in ⅛" increments to 12 ¾" max.
3. Omit stops for cased opening frames.
4. Std. stop ⅝", ½" min. + std. face 2", 1" min.

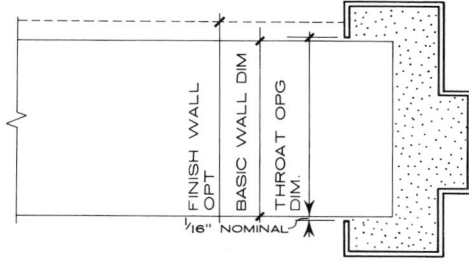

Labels: FINISH WALL OPT, BASIC WALL DIM, THROAT OPG DIM., ¹⁄₁₆" NOMINAL

1. Basic wall dim. < throat opening dim. Fin wall mat'l (dotted may encroach on backbend).
2. Anchors appropriate for wall constr. Req'd min. 3 per jamb.
3. Fill frame w/mortar or plaster as used in wall.
4. Grout frame, backbend at masonry wall.
5. Backbend may vary as selected.

**WRAP-AROUND FRAMES**

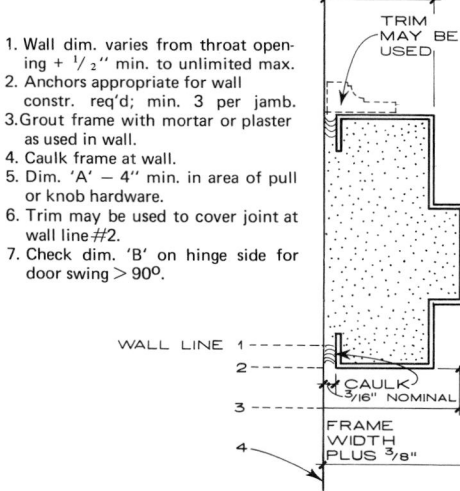

1. Wall dim. varies from throat opening + ½" min. to unlimited max.
2. Anchors appropriate for wall constr. req'd; min. 3 per jamb.
3. Grout frame with mortar or plaster as used in wall.
4. Caulk frame at wall.
5. Dim. 'A' — 4" min. in area of pull or knob hardware.
6. Trim may be used to cover joint at wall line #2.
7. Check dim. 'B' on hinge side for door swing > 90°.

Labels: A, TRIM MAY BE USED, WALL LINE 1, 2, 3, 4, CAULK ³⁄₁₆" NOMINAL, B, FRAME WIDTH PLUS ⅜"

**BUTT FRAME**

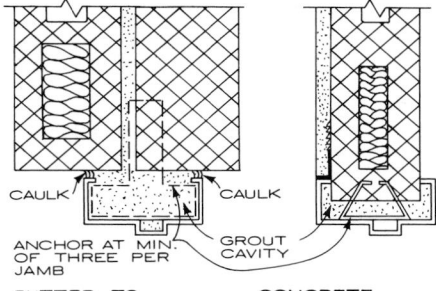

Labels: CAULK, CAULK, ANCHOR AT MIN. OF THREE PER JAMB, GROUT CAVITY

**BUTTED TO MASONRY**

**CONCRETE MASONRY UNIT WITH PLASTER FINISH**

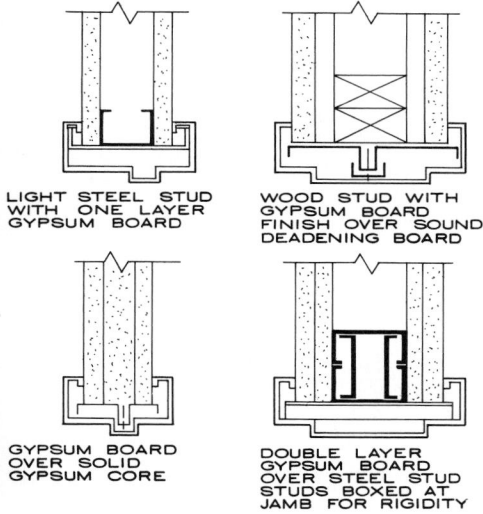

**LIGHT STEEL STUD WITH ONE LAYER GYPSUM BOARD**

**WOOD STUD WITH GYPSUM BOARD FINISH OVER SOUND DEADENING BOARD**

**GYPSUM BOARD OVER SOLID GYPSUM CORE**

**DOUBLE LAYER GYPSUM BOARD OVER STEEL STUD STUDS BOXED AT JAMB FOR RIGIDITY**

**DRYWALL INSTALLATIONS**

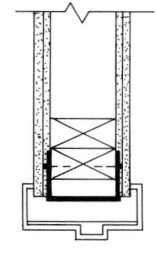 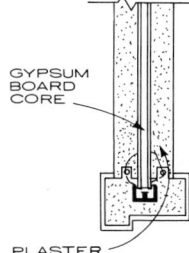

Labels: GYPSUM BOARD CORE, PLASTER

**WOOD STUD WITH PLASTER ON PLASTER LATH**

**SOLID PLASTER**

**VARIOUS INSTALLATIONS**

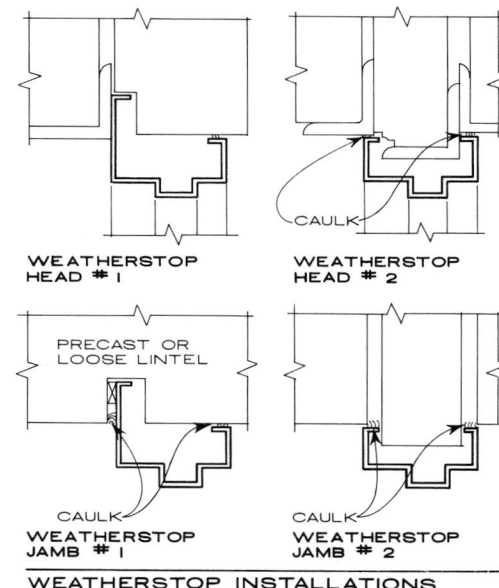

**WEATHERSTOP HEAD # 1**

**WEATHERSTOP HEAD # 2** — CAULK

**PRECAST OR LOOSE LINTEL** — CAULK

CAULK

**WEATHERSTOP JAMB # 1**

**WEATHERSTOP JAMB # 2**

**WEATHERSTOP INSTALLATIONS**

### NOTES
1. Some details vary between manufacturers.
2. Stock frames stocked in warehouse prior to receipt of order. Certain profiles are warehoused locally.
3. Standard frames manufactured from existing jigs and tooling upon receipt of order. Certain profiles are readily available.
4. Custom frames manufactured in response to specific dimensional requirements of a particular customer. Custom profiles are available with relative delay.
5. Selection should reflect anticipated requirements of construction schedule.
6. Certain detail features will constitute a custom frame, verify with manufacturer.

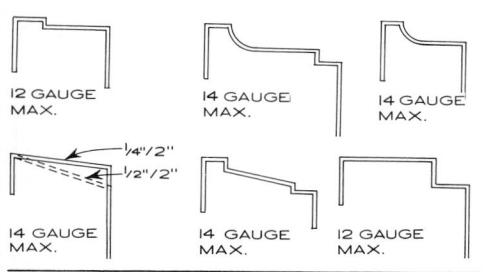

12 GAUGE MAX.   14 GAUGE MAX.   14 GAUGE MAX.

¼"/2"   ½"/2"

14 GAUGE MAX.   14 GAUGE MAX.   12 GAUGE MAX.

**VARIOUS FACES**

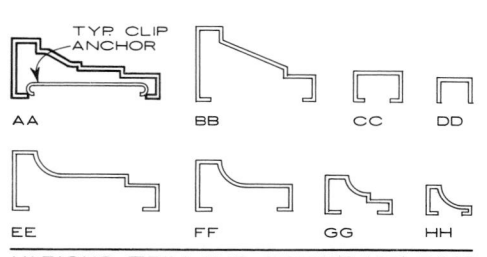

TYP CLIP ANCHOR

AA   BB   CC   DD

EE   FF   GG   HH

**VARIOUS TRIM AND SCRIBE MOLDING**

James W. G. Watson, AIA; Ronald A. Spahn and Associates; Cleveland Heights, Ohio

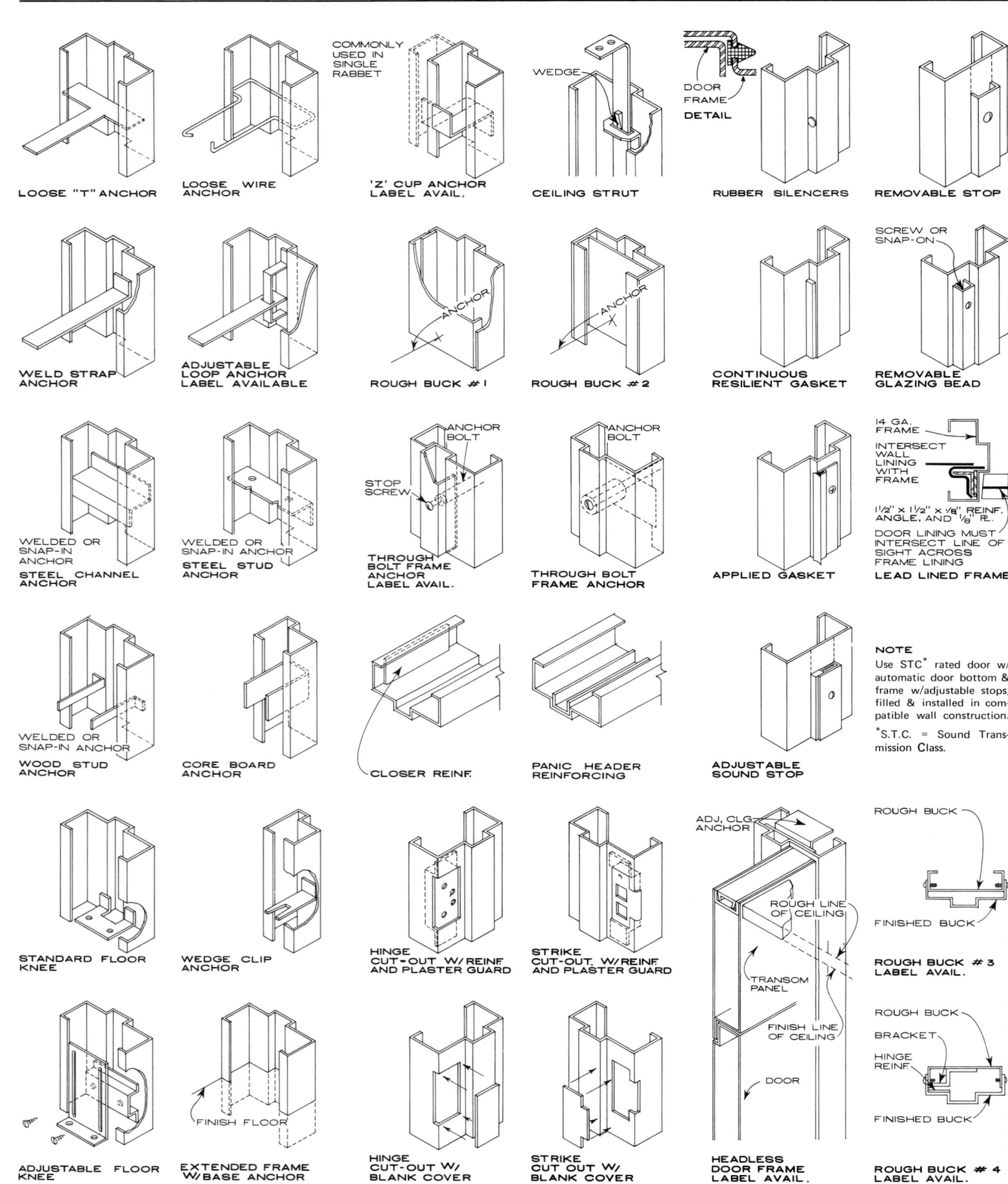

LOOSE "T" ANCHOR

LOOSE WIRE ANCHOR

COMMONLY USED IN SINGLE RABBET

'Z' CUP ANCHOR LABEL AVAIL.

WEDGE

CEILING STRUT

DOOR FRAME DETAIL

RUBBER SILENCERS

REMOVABLE STOP

WELD STRAP ANCHOR

ADJUSTABLE LOOP ANCHOR LABEL AVAILABLE

ANCHOR

ROUGH BUCK #1

ANCHOR

ROUGH BUCK #2

CONTINUOUS RESILIENT GASKET

SCREW OR SNAP-ON

REMOVABLE GLAZING BEAD

WELDED OR SNAP-IN ANCHOR
STEEL CHANNEL ANCHOR

WELDED OR SNAP-IN ANCHOR
STEEL STUD ANCHOR

ANCHOR BOLT
STOP SCREW
THROUGH BOLT FRAME ANCHOR LABEL AVAIL.

ANCHOR BOLT
THROUGH BOLT FRAME ANCHOR

APPLIED GASKET

14 GA. FRAME
INTERSECT WALL LINING WITH FRAME
1½" x 1½" x ⅛" REINF. ANGLE, AND ⅛" PL.
DOOR LINING MUST INTERSECT LINE OF SIGHT ACROSS FRAME LINING
LEAD LINED FRAME

WELDED OR SNAP-IN ANCHOR
WOOD STUD ANCHOR

CORE BOARD ANCHOR

CLOSER REINF.

PANIC HEADER REINFORCING

ADJUSTABLE SOUND STOP

NOTE
Use STC* rated door w/ automatic door bottom & frame w/adjustable stops; filled & installed in compatible wall construction.
*S.T.C. = Sound Transmission Class.

STANDARD FLOOR KNEE

WEDGE CLIP ANCHOR

HINGE CUT-OUT W/REINF. AND PLASTER GUARD

STRIKE CUT-OUT. W/REINF. AND PLASTER GUARD

ADJ. CLG. ANCHOR
ROUGH LINE OF CEILING
TRANSOM PANEL
FINISH LINE OF CEILING
DOOR

ROUGH BUCK
FINISHED BUCK
ROUGH BUCK #3 LABEL AVAIL.

ADJUSTABLE FLOOR KNEE

EXTENDED FRAME W/BASE ANCHOR
FINISH FLOOR

HINGE CUT-OUT W/ BLANK COVER

STRIKE CUT OUT W/ BLANK COVER

HEADLESS DOOR FRAME LABEL AVAIL.

ROUGH BUCK
BRACKET
HINGE REINF.
FINISHED BUCK
ROUGH BUCK #4 LABEL AVAIL.

James W. G. Watson, AIA; Ronald A. Spahn and Associates; Cleveland Heights, Ohio

⑧ **METAL DOORS AND FRAMES**

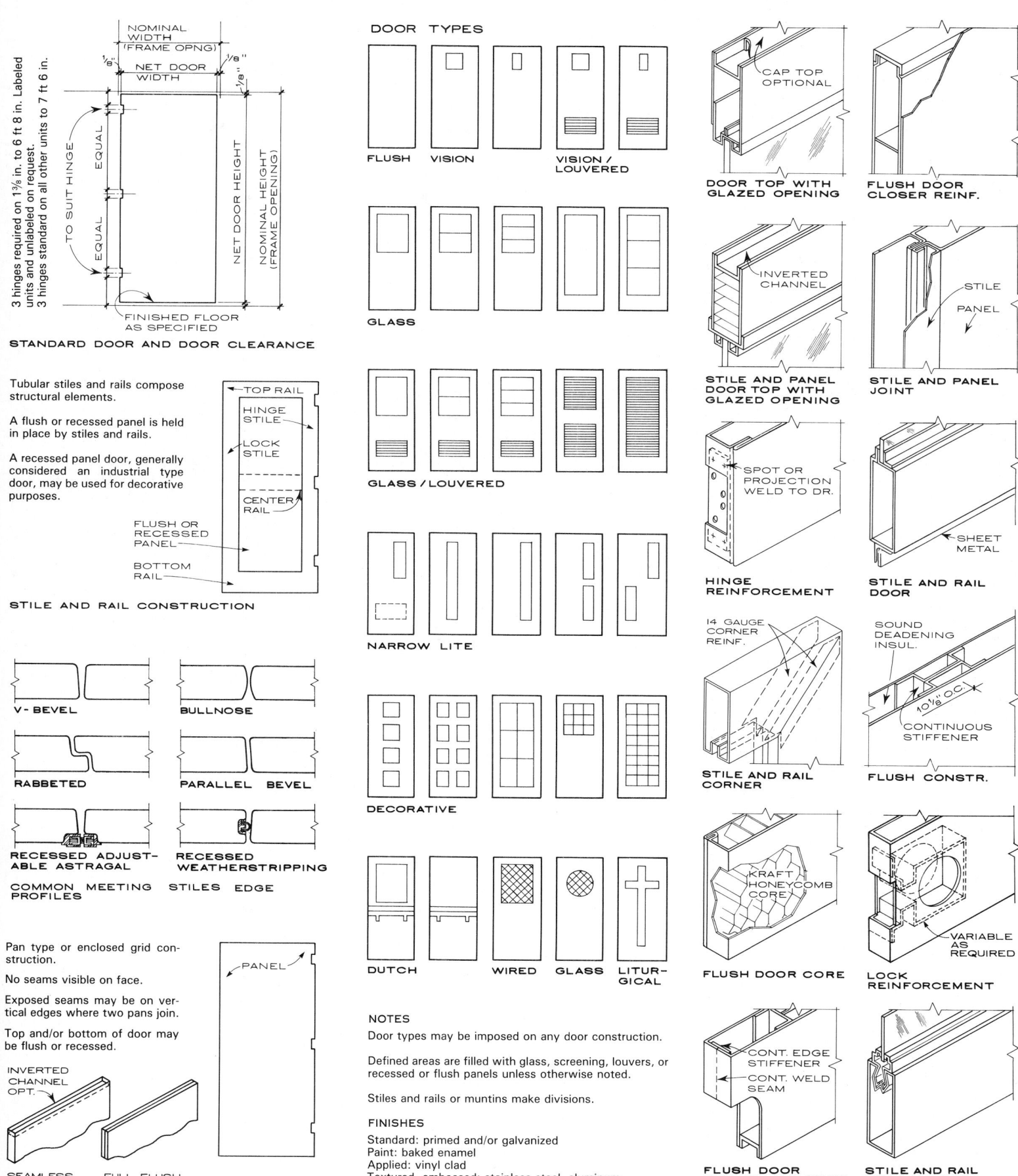

STANDARD DOOR AND DOOR CLEARANCE

3 hinges required on 1⅜ in. to 6 ft 8 in. Labeled units and unlabeled on request.
3 hinges standard on all other units to 7 ft 6 in.

NOMINAL WIDTH (FRAME OPNG)
NET DOOR WIDTH
TO SUIT HINGE
EQUAL
EQUAL
EQUAL
NET DOOR HEIGHT
NOMINAL HEIGHT (FRAME OPENING)
FINISHED FLOOR AS SPECIFIED

Tubular stiles and rails compose structural elements.

A flush or recessed panel is held in place by stiles and rails.

A recessed panel door, generally considered an industrial type door, may be used for decorative purposes.

STILE AND RAIL CONSTRUCTION

TOP RAIL
HINGE STILE
LOCK STILE
CENTER RAIL
FLUSH OR RECESSED PANEL
BOTTOM RAIL

V - BEVEL
BULLNOSE
RABBETED
PARALLEL BEVEL
RECESSED ADJUSTABLE ASTRAGAL
RECESSED WEATHERSTRIPPING
COMMON MEETING STILES EDGE PROFILES

Pan type or enclosed grid construction.

No seams visible on face.

Exposed seams may be on vertical edges where two pans join.

Top and/or bottom of door may be flush or recessed.

INVERTED CHANNEL OPT.
PANEL

SEAMLESS     FULL FLUSH
FLUSH CONSTRUCTION

DOOR TYPES

FLUSH     VISION     VISION / LOUVERED

GLASS

GLASS / LOUVERED

NARROW LITE

DECORATIVE

DUTCH     WIRED     GLASS     LITURGICAL

NOTES

Door types may be imposed on any door construction.

Defined areas are filled with glass, screening, louvers, or recessed or flush panels unless otherwise noted.

Stiles and rails or muntins make divisions.

FINISHES

Standard: primed and/or galvanized
Paint: baked enamel
Applied: vinyl clad
Textured, embossed: stainless steel, aluminum
Polished: stainless steel

CAP TOP OPTIONAL
DOOR TOP WITH GLAZED OPENING

FLUSH DOOR CLOSER REINF.

INVERTED CHANNEL
STILE AND PANEL DOOR TOP WITH GLAZED OPENING

STILE
PANEL
STILE AND PANEL JOINT

SPOT OR PROJECTION WELD TO DR.
HINGE REINFORCEMENT

SHEET METAL
STILE AND RAIL DOOR

14 GAUGE CORNER REINF.
STILE AND RAIL CORNER

SOUND DEADENING INSUL.
10⅛ O.C.
CONTINUOUS STIFFENER
FLUSH CONSTR.

KRAFT HONEYCOMB CORE
FLUSH DOOR CORE

VARIABLE AS REQUIRED
LOCK REINFORCEMENT

CONT. EDGE STIFFENER
CONT. WELD SEAM
FLUSH DOOR BOTTOM AND EDGE CONST.

STILE AND RAIL DOOR BOTTOM CONST.

James W. G. Watson, AIA; Ronald A. Spahn and Associates; Cleveland Heights, Ohio

## MINIMUM GAUGES FOR COMMERCIAL STEEL DOORS

| ITEM | GAUGE NO. | EQUIVALENT THICKNESS (IN.) |
|---|---|---|
| Door frames | 16 | 0.0598 |
| Surface applied hardware reinforcement | 16 | 0.0598 |
| Doors—hollow steel construction | | |
| Panels and stile | 18 | 0.0478 |
| Doors—composite construction | | |
| Perimeter channel | 18 | 0.0478 |
| Surface sheets | 22 | 0.0299 |
| Reinforcement | | |
| Surface applied hardware | 16 | 0.0598 |
| Lock and strike | 16 | 0.0598 |
| Hinge | 10 | 0.1345 |
| Flush bolt | 16 | 0.0598 |
| Glass molding | 20 | 0.0359 |
| Glass muntins | 22 | 0.0299 |

**NOTES**

1. The steel door tables represent minimum standards published by the U.S. Department of Commerce for standard stock commercial, 1¾ in. thick steel doors and frames, and flush type interior steel doors and frames (doors not more than 3 ft in width).

2. Specifications for custom hollow metal doors and frames are published by the National Association of Architectural Metal Manufacturers. Standards may also vary according to location or the agency—always consult with the local authorities and/or agencies to determine what they require. Doors must be selected according to the project requirements such as frequency of usage, type of traffic, conditions required by the enclosed space, and environmental conditions.

## MINIMUM GAUGES FOR INTERIOR STEEL DOORS

| ITEM | GAUGE NO. | EQUIVALENT THICKNESS (IN.) |
|---|---|---|
| Door frames, 1⅜ in. thick | 18 | 0.0478 |
| Door frames, 1¾ in. thick | 16 | 0.0598 |
| Stiles and panels | 20 | 0.0359 |
| Reinforcement | | |
| Lock and strike | 16 | 0.0598 |
| Hinge | 11 | 0.1196 |
| Closer | 14 | 0.0747 |

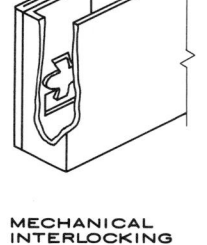

**MECHANICAL INTERLOCKING**

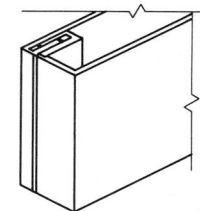

**HEMMED**

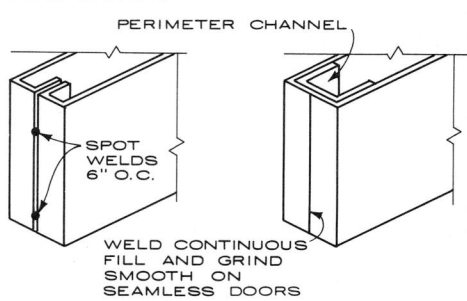

**SPOT WELDED SEAM**      **EXPOSED SEAM OR SEAMLESS**

**DOOR EDGES**

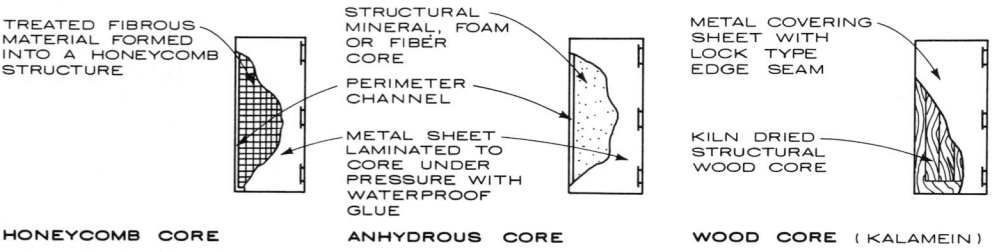
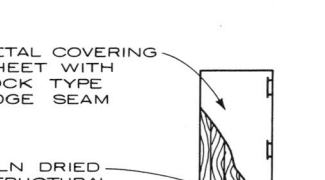

**HONEYCOMB CORE      ANHYDROUS CORE      WOOD CORE** (KALAMEIN)

**NONMETALLIC CORE DOORS**

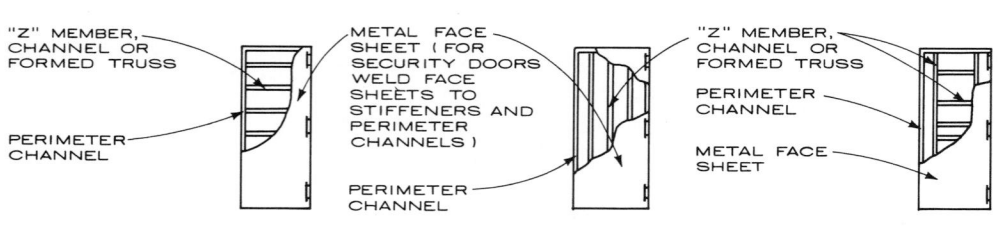

**HORIZONTAL STIFFENERS      VERTICAL STIFFENERS      GRID STIFFENERS**

**STIFFENED CORE DOORS** (HEAVY DOORS) **NORMALLY SOUND DEADENED OR INSULATED**

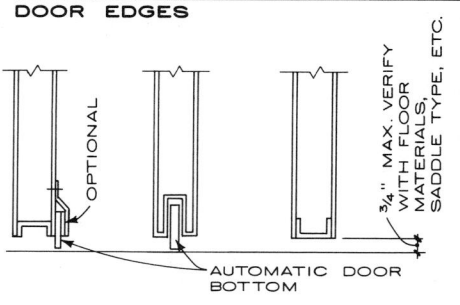

**DOOR BOTTOMS**

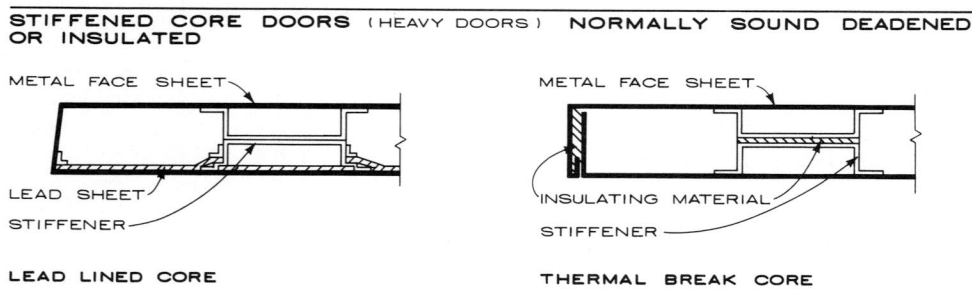

**LEAD LINED CORE          THERMAL BREAK CORE**

**SPECIAL CORE DOORS**

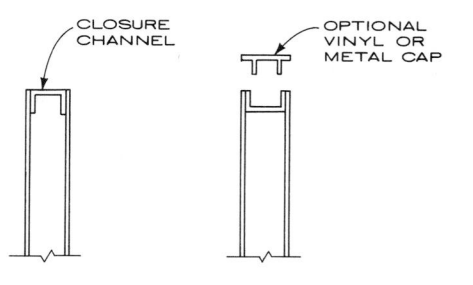

**DOOR TOPS**

Kelly Sacher & Associates; Architects Engineers Planners; N. Babylon, New York

## METAL DOORS AND FRAMES

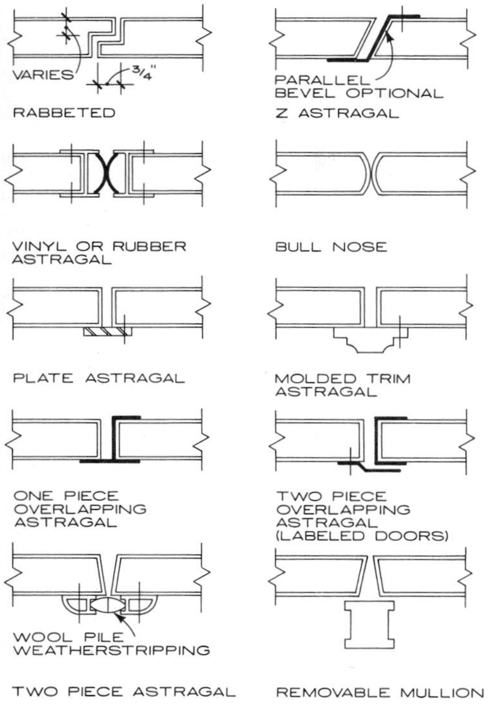

## MEETING STILES

VARIES · 3/4"
RABBETED

PARALLEL BEVEL OPTIONAL
Z ASTRAGAL

VINYL OR RUBBER ASTRAGAL

BULL NOSE

PLATE ASTRAGAL

MOLDED TRIM ASTRAGAL

ONE PIECE OVERLAPPING ASTRAGAL

TWO PIECE OVERLAPPING ASTRAGAL (LABELED DOORS)

WOOL PILE WEATHERSTRIPPING

TWO PIECE ASTRAGAL

REMOVABLE MULLION

NOTE: V BEVELS ARE OPTIONAL

## GLAZING DETAILS

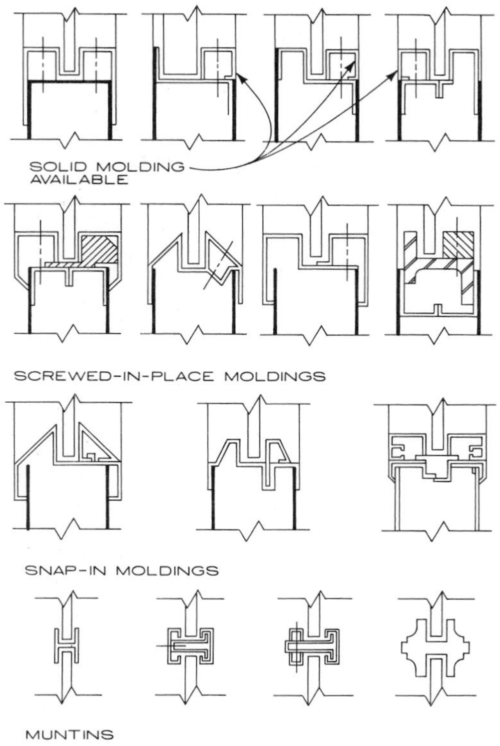

SOLID MOLDING AVAILABLE

SCREWED-IN-PLACE MOLDINGS

SNAP-IN MOLDINGS

MUNTINS

## LOUVERS AND VENTS

INVERTED V LOUVERS

INVERTED Y LOUVERS

Z LOUVER

BAR GRILLES

LIGHTPROOF LOUVERS

USED WITH AIR CONDITIONING (I.E. PRESSURE DROP)

AIR CONDITIONING LOUVER

PUNCHED GRILLE

STAMPED LOUVERS

DOOR LOUVER MOLDINGS

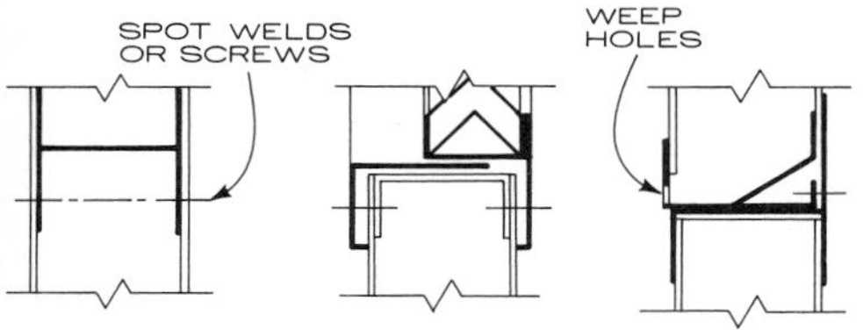

SPOT WELDS OR SCREWS

WEEP HOLES

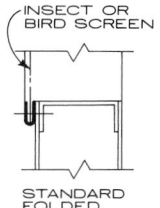
INSECT OR BIRD SCREEN

STANDARD FOLDED

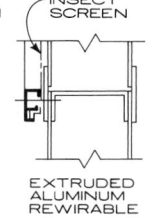
INSECT SCREEN

EXTRUDED ALUMINUM REWIRABLE

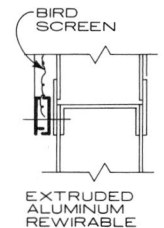
BIRD SCREEN

EXTRUDED ALUMINUM REWIRABLE

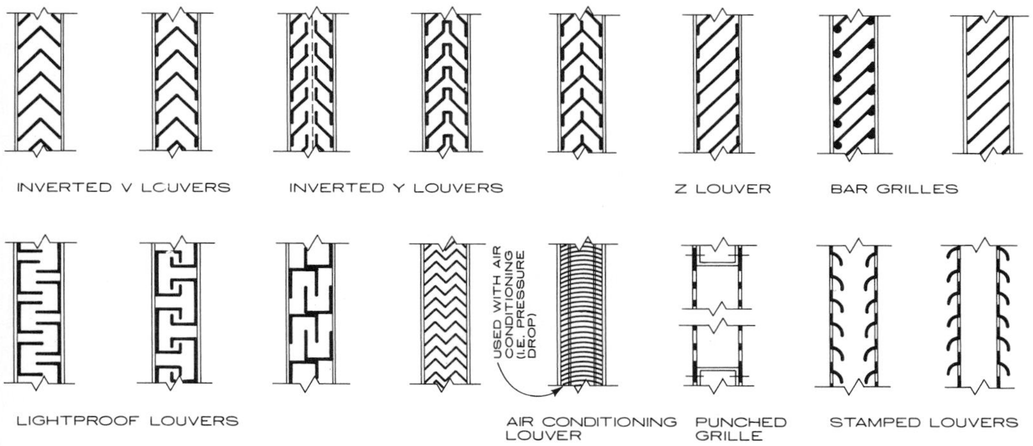

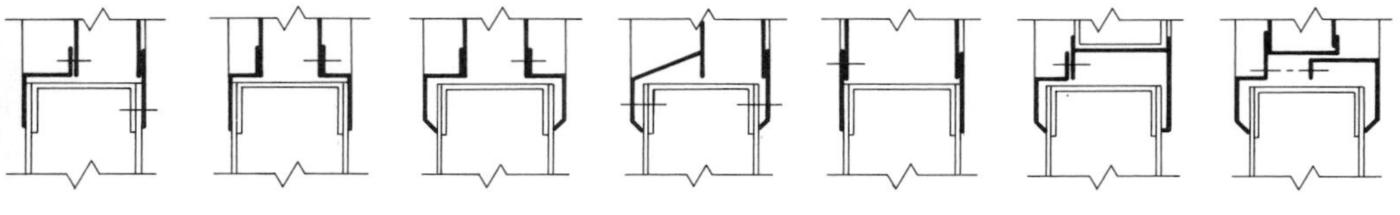

DOOR LOUVER MOLDINGS

### DOOR SCREENS

Kelly Sacher & Associates; Architects Engineers Planners; N. Babylon, New York

## MATERIALS

Hollow metal doors are available in various steel gauges according to where and how they will be used. The following gradings should be used only as guidelines in selecting doors for a particular project. Local codes and governing authorities establish minimum gauges, which should always be consulted.

| GRADE | GAUGE |
|---|---|
| Residential | 20 gauge and lighter |
| Commercial | 16 and 18 gauge |
| Institutional | 12 and 14 gauge |
| High security | Steel plate |

Some manufacturers will custom make moldings and muntins to meet a specific design, as long as there is sufficient quantity involved.

For security, the exterior moldings on exterior doors should be welded into the door and all exposed fasteners should be tamperproof.

For fire ratings of hollow metal doors and requirements for fire doors see other pages in this series.

## FINISH

Hollow metal doors should receive at least one shop coat of rust inhibitive primer before they are delivered to the job site. In very corrosive atmospheres, such as saltwater beach locations, it is advisable to have the doors and frames hot dipped galvanized for additional protection.

Doors are available from several manufacturers, with factory applied paint finishes in various colors.

## GLAZING

The size and type of glass permitted in fire rated doors is determined by local building codes and governing authorities having jurisdiction. The following table should only be used as a guide:

| DOOR RATING | GLAZING REQUIREMENTS |
|---|---|
| *A—3 hr | No glazing permitted |
| *B—1 1/2 hr | 100 sq in. of glazing per door leaf |
| C—3/4 hr | Max. 1296 sq in. of glazing per light. Max. dim. per light = 54 in. Min. dim. per light = 3 in. |
| *D—1 1/2 hr | No glazing permitted |
| E—3/4 hr | Max. 720 sq in. of glazing per light. Max. dim. per light = 54 in. |

NOTE: Available on composite doors only. A, B, and D doors are available with Heat Transmission Ratings of 250°F or 650°F, or are not rated.

## LOUVERS AND VENTS

Door louvers are available extruded, formed, and stamped in various metals and configurations; operable with or without a fusible link. Punched, stamped, and bar grilles are also available.

The percentage of free area for louvers depends on the louver blade thickness, spacing, and type. For this information consult the manufacturer's catalogs.

Door louvers and grilles are available prefinished, without moldings, and with moldings attached at the factory on one or both sides.

Insert screens are often used in conjunction with louvers or grilles; they may be used by themselves as well, however, in some applications. Screen material is available in various grid and wire sizes and materials.

## GENERAL NOTES FOR ALL WOOD DOORS

Kiln dried wood, moisture content @ 6–12%.

Type 1 doors:   Fully waterproof bond ext. and int.
Type 11 doors:  Water resistant bond. Interior only.

Tolerances: Height, width, thickness, squareness and warp per NWMA STANDARDS and vary with solid vs. built-up construction.

Prefit: Doors @ 3/16″ less in width and 1/8″ less in height than nominal size, ± 1/32″ tolerance, with vertical edges eased.

Premachining: Doors mortised for locks and cut out for hinges when so specified.

Premium: For transparent finish. Good/custom: For paint or transparent finish. Sound: For paint, with 2 coats completely covering defects.

## FLUSH WOOD DOORS
### CORE MATERIAL
### SOLID CORES

Wood block, single specie, @ 2 1/2″ max. width, surfaced two sides, without spaces or defects impairing strength or visible thru hdwd. veneer facing.

### HOLLOW CORES

Wood, wood derivative, or class A insulation board.

### TYPES OF WOOD FACES

Standard thickness face veneers @ 1/16″–1/32″, bonded to hardwood, crossband @ 1/10″–1/16″. Most economical and widely used, inhibits checking, difficult to refinish or repair face damage, for use on all cores.

1/8″ Sawn veneers, bonded to crossband, easily refinished and repaired.

For use on staved block and stile and rail solid cores. 1/4″ Sawn veneers: same as 1/8″ but without crossband on stile and rail solid cores with horizontal blocks. Decorative grooves can be cut into faces.

### LIGHT & LOUVER OPENINGS

Custom made to specifications. Wood beads and slats to match face veneer. 5″ min. between opening and edge of door.

Hollow core: Cut-out area max. 1/2 height of door. Door not guaranteed with openings greater than 40%. Exterior doors: Weatherproofing required to prevent moisture from leaking into core.

### FACTORY FINISHING

Partial: Sealing coats applied, final job finish.
Complete: Requires prefit and premachining.

### SPECIAL FACING

High or medium-low density overlay faces of phenolic resins and cellulose fibers fused to inner faces of hardwood in lieu of final veneers as base for final opaque finish only.

1/16″ min. laminated plastic bonded to 1/16″ min. wood back of two or more piles.

1/8″ hardboard, smooth one or two sides.

### SPECIAL CORES
### SOUND INSULATING DOORS

Thicknesses 1 3/4″, 2 1/4″. Transmission loss rating C Stc 36 for 1 3/4″, 42 for 2 1/4″. Barrier faces separated by a void or damping compound to keep faces from vibrating in unison. Special stops, gaskets, and threshold devices required. Mfrs. requirements as to wd. frames and wall specs.

### FIRE RATED DOORS

3/4 hr "C" label and 1 hr "B" label-maximum size 4'0" x 10'0".
1 1/2 hr "B" label-maximum size 4'0" x 9'0". All doors 1 3/4″ minimum thickness.

### LEAD LINED DOORS

See U/L requirements. Optional location within door construction of 1/32″ to 1/2″ continuous lead sheet from edge to edge which may be reinforced with lead bolts or glued.

### GROUNDED DOORS

Wire mesh located at center of core, grounded with copper wire through hinges to frame.

## TYPES OF HOLLOW CORE DOORS

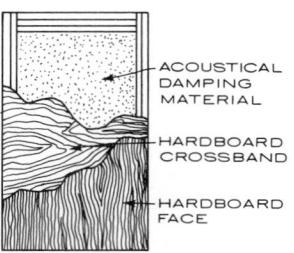

**ACOUSTICAL DOOR**
Uses gasketed stops and neoprene bottom seals to cut sound transmission.

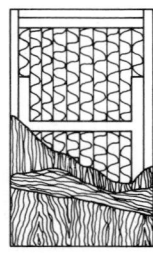

**HONEYCOMB FIBER**
**INSTITU-**
**TIONAL:**
With cross rail.
**INTERIOR:**
Without cross rail. Uniform core of honeycomb fiber to form 1/2″ air cells.

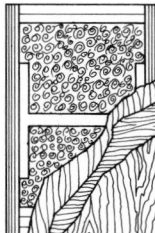

**IMPLANTED BLANKS**
Spirals or other forms separated or joined, implanted between & supporting outer faces of door.

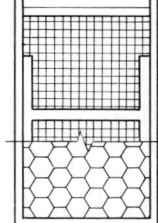

**MESH**
Interlocked, horizontal & vertical strips, equally spaced, notched into stiles, or expandable cellular or honey-comb core.

## TYPES OF SOLID CORES

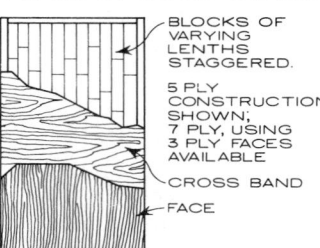

**CONTINUOUS BLOCK STAVED CORE**
Bonded staggered blocks bonded to face panels. Most widely used & economical solid core.

**FRAMED BLOCK STAVED CORE**
Non-bonded staggered blocks laid up within stile rail frame, bonded to face panels.

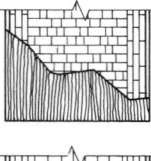

**STILE AND RAIL**
Horizontal blocks when cross banding is not used. Vertical panel blocks when cross banding is used.

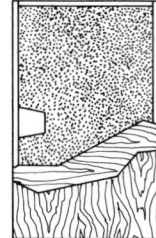

**PARTICLE BOARD**
Extremely heavy, more soundproof, economical door, available in hardwood face veneer or high pressure laminate face.

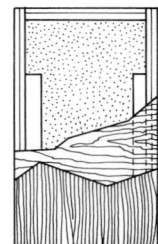

**MINERAL COMPOSITION**
Lightest weight of all cores. Details, as cut-outs, difficult. Low screw holding strength.

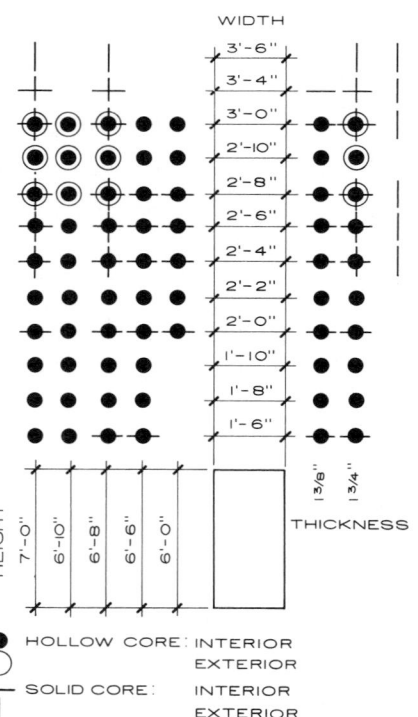

**STANDARD SIZES**

● HOLLOW CORE:  INTERIOR
○                EXTERIOR
— SOLID CORE:   INTERIOR
|                EXTERIOR

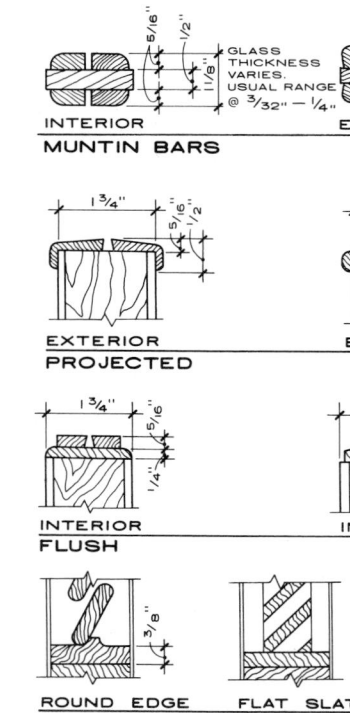

**MUNTIN BARS**
GLASS THICKNESS VARIES. USUAL RANGE @ 3/32″ – 1/4″

INTERIOR          EXTERIOR

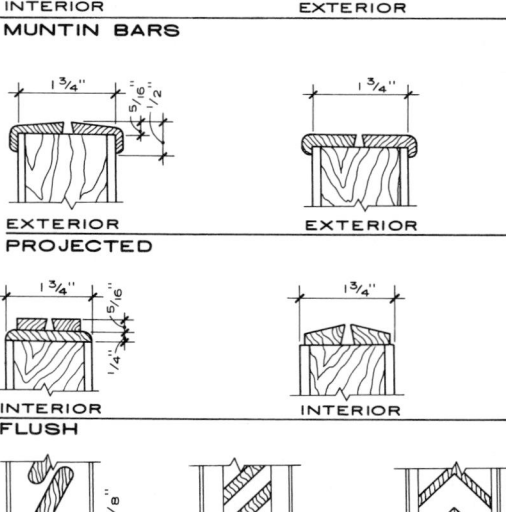

EXTERIOR          EXTERIOR
**PROJECTED**

INTERIOR          INTERIOR
**FLUSH**

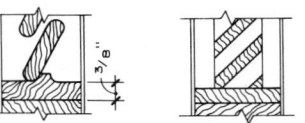

ROUND EDGE     FLAT SLAT     SIGHTPROOF
**LOUVERS · METAL LOUVERS ALSO AVAILABLE**
**STOCK OPENING AND LOUVER DETAIL**

## NOTES

### CONSTRUCTION

Solid or built-up stiles, rails, and vertical members or mullions, doweled as in NWWDA standard. Stock material includes ponderosa pine or other Western pine, fir, hemlock, and spruce, and hardwood veneers. Hardboard, metal, and plastic facings available in patterns simulating panel doors.

### GRADES

Premium (select) grade: for natural, clear, or stained finish. Exposed wood free of defects that affect appearance.

Standard grade: for opaque finishes. Defects, discoloration, mixed species, and finger joints permitted if undetectable after finishing.

### BUILT-UP MEMBERS

Core as in solid core of flush doors. Edge and end strips as in flush doors. Face veneer: hardwood at 1/8 in. minimum.

### PANELS

Flat: 3-ply hardwood or softwood. Raised—two sides: solid hardwood or softwood built-up of two or more plies. Doors 1 ft 6 in. wide and narrower are one panel wide.

### STICKING, GLASS STOPS, AND MUNTINS

Cove, bead, or ovolo; solid, matching face.

### GLAZING

Must be safety glazing. Insulated (dual) glazing is available.

### THICKNESS

Interior doors: 1 3/8 in.
Exterior doors: 1 3/8 in. or 1 3/4 in.
Storm and screen doors: 1 1/8 in.

See index for other door types and door hardware.

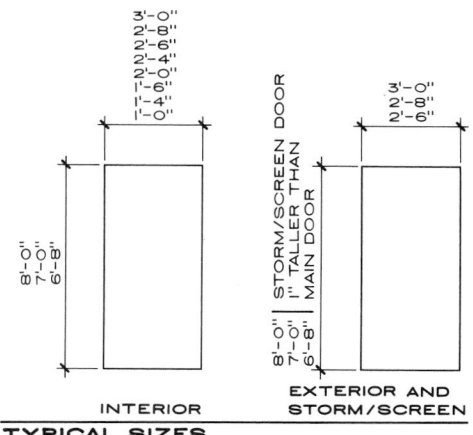

**TYPICAL SIZES**

**EXTERIOR**

182-575 2031-615 5118 5571-000 000-567 2020-600 2130-110 1501-602 2060-113 000-514

000-758 5001-733 82-000 30-000 44-106 55-107 66-108 88-109

DIVIDED LIGHTS FOR INTERIOR AND EXTERIOR DOORS

**SCREEN/STORM**      **INTERIOR**

## SELECTED STANDARD DOOR TYPES (NUMBERS CORRESPOND TO NWWDA STANDARD)

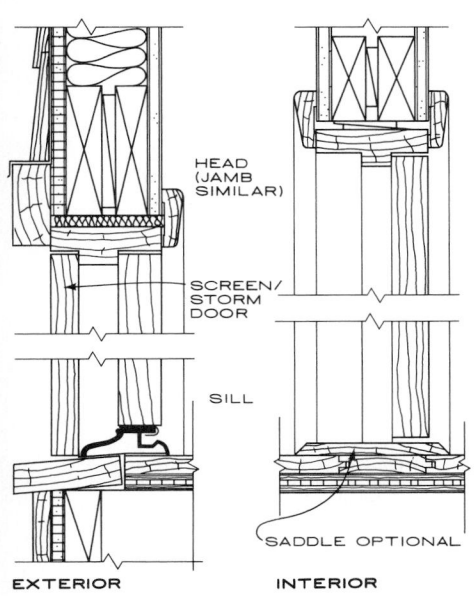

**DOOR FRAMES**

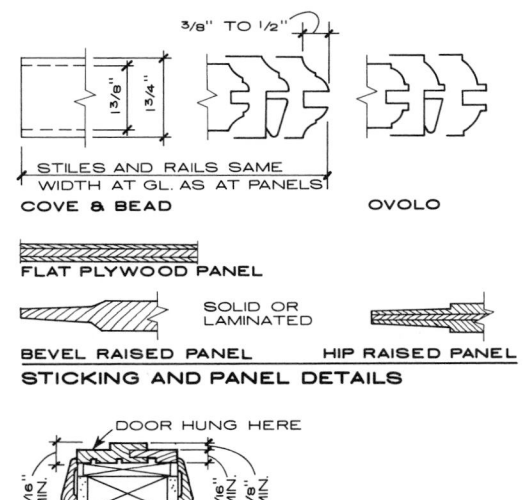

STILES AND RAILS SAME WIDTH AT GL. AS AT PANELS

COVE & BEAD      OVOLO

FLAT PLYWOOD PANEL

SOLID OR LAMINATED

BEVEL RAISED PANEL      HIP RAISED PANEL

**STICKING AND PANEL DETAILS**

DOOR HUNG HERE

**ADJUSTABLE DOOR FRAME**

### NOTES

Top operable alone or with bottom using joining hardware.

Can swing in or out.

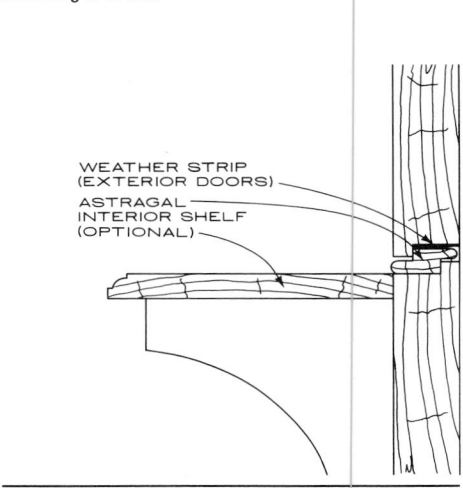

WEATHER STRIP (EXTERIOR DOORS)
ASTRAGAL
INTERIOR SHELF (OPTIONAL)

**DUTCH DOOR MEETING RAIL**

Jeffrey R. Vandevoort; Talbott Wilson Associates, Inc.; Houston, Texas

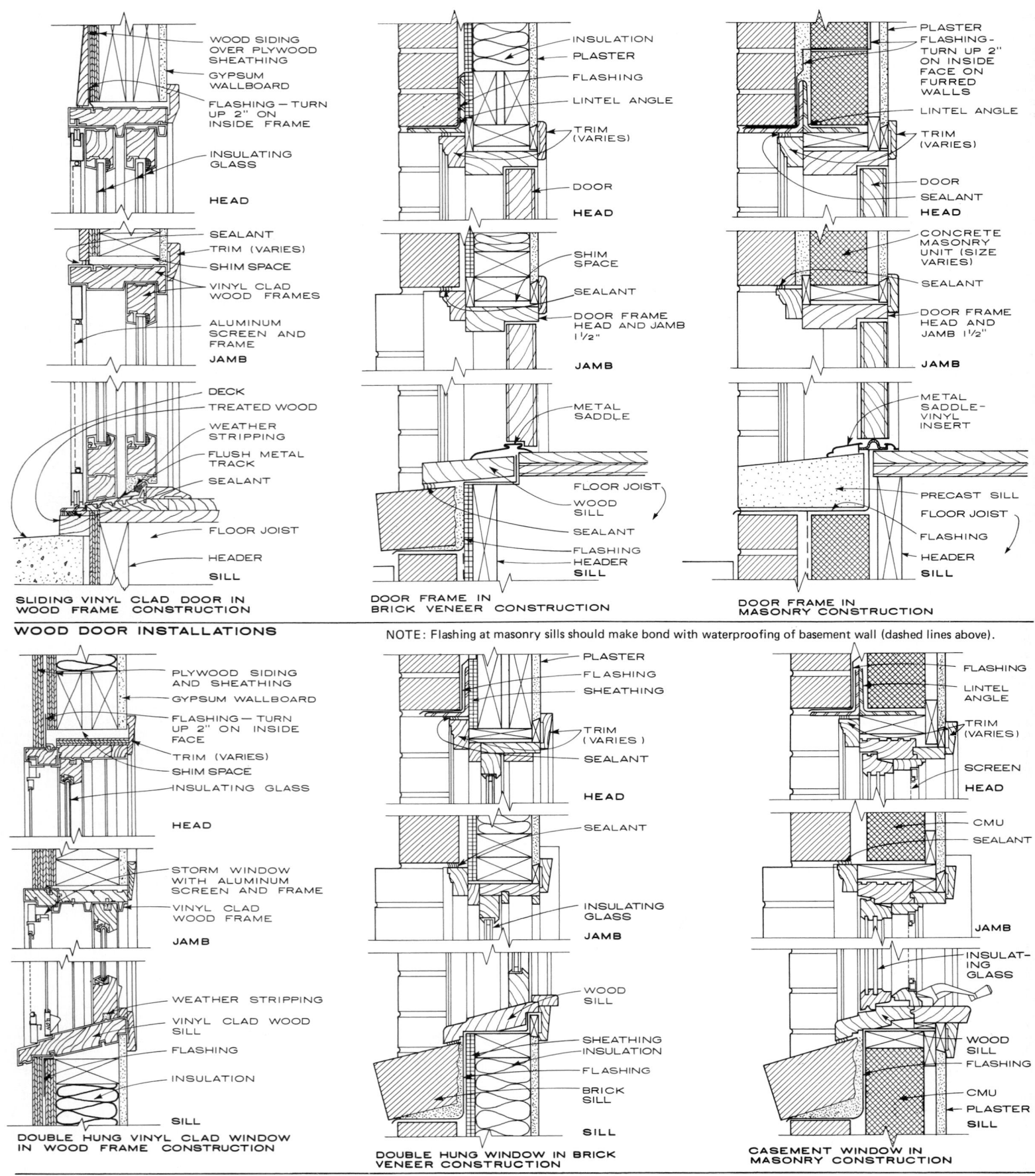

**WOOD DOOR INSTALLATIONS**

*Top row — labels (left to right groupings):*

Left diagram (SLIDING VINYL CLAD DOOR IN WOOD FRAME CONSTRUCTION):
- WOOD SIDING OVER PLYWOOD SHEATHING
- GYPSUM WALLBOARD
- FLASHING — TURN UP 2" ON INSIDE FRAME
- INSULATING GLASS
- **HEAD**
- SEALANT
- TRIM (VARIES)
- SHIM SPACE
- VINYL CLAD WOOD FRAMES
- ALUMINUM SCREEN AND FRAME
- **JAMB**
- DECK
- TREATED WOOD
- WEATHER STRIPPING
- FLUSH METAL TRACK
- SEALANT
- FLOOR JOIST
- HEADER
- **SILL**

Middle diagram (DOOR FRAME IN BRICK VENEER CONSTRUCTION):
- INSULATION
- PLASTER
- FLASHING
- LINTEL ANGLE
- TRIM (VARIES)
- DOOR
- **HEAD**
- SHIM SPACE
- SEALANT
- DOOR FRAME HEAD AND JAMB 1 1/2"
- **JAMB**
- METAL SADDLE
- FLOOR JOIST
- WOOD SILL
- SEALANT
- FLASHING
- HEADER
- **SILL**

Right diagram (DOOR FRAME IN MASONRY CONSTRUCTION):
- PLASTER
- FLASHING — TURN UP 2" ON INSIDE FACE ON FURRED WALLS
- LINTEL ANGLE
- TRIM (VARIES)
- DOOR
- SEALANT
- **HEAD**
- CONCRETE MASONRY UNIT (SIZE VARIES)
- SEALANT
- DOOR FRAME HEAD AND JAMB 1 1/2"
- **JAMB**
- METAL SADDLE - VINYL INSERT
- PRECAST SILL
- FLOOR JOIST
- FLASHING
- HEADER
- **SILL**

NOTE: Flashing at masonry sills should make bond with waterproofing of basement wall (dashed lines above).

**WOOD WINDOW INSTALLATIONS**

Left diagram (DOUBLE HUNG VINYL CLAD WINDOW IN WOOD FRAME CONSTRUCTION):
- PLYWOOD SIDING AND SHEATHING
- GYPSUM WALLBOARD
- FLASHING — TURN UP 2" ON INSIDE FACE
- TRIM (VARIES)
- SHIM SPACE
- INSULATING GLASS
- **HEAD**
- STORM WINDOW WITH ALUMINUM SCREEN AND FRAME
- VINYL CLAD WOOD FRAME
- **JAMB**
- WEATHER STRIPPING
- VINYL CLAD WOOD SILL
- FLASHING
- INSULATION
- **SILL**

Middle diagram (DOUBLE HUNG WINDOW IN BRICK VENEER CONSTRUCTION):
- PLASTER
- FLASHING
- SHEATHING
- TRIM (VARIES)
- SEALANT
- **HEAD**
- SEALANT
- INSULATING GLASS
- **JAMB**
- WOOD SILL
- SHEATHING
- INSULATION
- FLASHING
- BRICK SILL
- **SILL**

Right diagram (CASEMENT WINDOW IN MASONRY CONSTRUCTION):
- FLASHING
- LINTEL ANGLE
- TRIM (VARIES)
- SCREEN
- **HEAD**
- CMU
- SEALANT
- **JAMB**
- INSULATING GLASS
- WOOD SILL
- FLASHING
- CMU
- PLASTER
- **SILL**

## SWINGING DOOR ASSEMBLIES

A door, in addition to providing a portal for entry, should resist unwanted intruders. This resistance can be accommodated by requiring that all exterior doors comply with ANSI/ASTM standard F476-76 Standard Test Methods for Security of Swinging Door Assemblies. The security of a door assembly depends not only on the lock but also on the strike, buck, hinge, door, and even the surrounding wall.

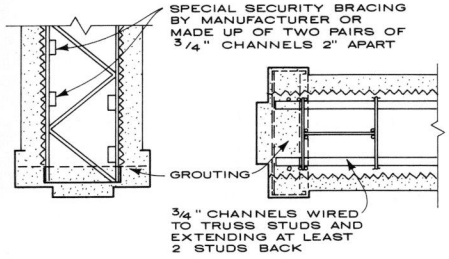

SPECIAL SECURITY BRACING BY MANUFACTURER OR MADE UP OF TWO PAIRS OF 3/4" CHANNELS 2" APART

GROUTING

3/4" CHANNELS WIRED TO TRUSS STUDS AND EXTENDING AT LEAST 2 STUDS BACK

HEAD          JAMB

**DOOR BUCK DETAIL**

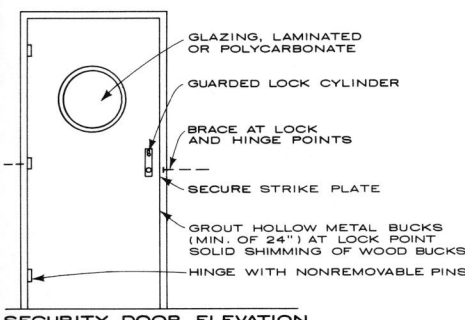

GLAZING, LAMINATED OR POLYCARBONATE

GUARDED LOCK CYLINDER

BRACE AT LOCK AND HINGE POINTS

SECURE STRIKE PLATE

GROUT HOLLOW METAL BUCKS (MIN. OF 24") AT LOCK POINT SOLID SHIMMING OF WOOD BUCKS

HINGE WITH NONREMOVABLE PINS

**SECURITY DOOR ELEVATION**

NOTE: Brace at lock point is essential; brace at hinge points for additional security. If two hinges, braces required at both; if three hinges, brace only at middle hinge. Braces should extend two studs back.

## SUGGESTED MATERIALS AND METHODS FOR DOORS

1. GRADE 40: Hollow metal steel doors, 16 gauge.
2. GRADE 30: Hollow metal, 18 gauge; flush wood, lumber core, 1 3/4 in. thick.
3. GRADE 20: Flush wood, particle core, 1 3/4 in. thick, lock block of dense solid wood at least 6 in. wide x 24 in. high. Hinge blocks, 6 in. wide, x 12 in. high.
4. GRADE 10: Flush wood, particle core, 1 3/4 in. thick; wood panel door with minimum thickness of panel at 1/2 in. including rebate, stiles minimum dimension 1 3/4 x 6 in.

### FRAME

The stiffness of the bucks is critical; wood bucks should be a minimum of 2 in. thick and have solid, secure shims for 24 in. at the locking point and 12 in. at each hinge point; stops should be milled integral with the buck; wood bucks for Grade 20 should be of hard wood premium grade; Grade 20 bucks should be 16 gauge steel; Grade 40 bucks should be 15 gauge steel; all steel bucks should be grouted full.

### WALL

Fire stops or braces should be located at the lock point and each hinge point—for one stud space at Grade 10, two stud spaces for Grade 20 and above; if wood studs appear, plywood sheathing should be used on both sides of the studs for two stud spaces to each side of the doorway; if it is a masonry wall, grout all space between frame and wall.

## GRADE SELECTION FACTORS

The following items should be considered when designing and selecting components for an entrance door:

1. LOCATION: If the doorway is hidden from public view, or if security lighting is not provided, a higher grade is required than that normally used in the area.
2. ACCESS: If entry is controlled by a guard or protected by a detection device, a lower grade should be adequate.
3. USE: If the doorway provides access to particularly valuable or desirable property, a higher grade is required.
4. TYPE: In a double door, each door should be tested. If the door has solid or glazed panels make sure they meet the test requirements; mail slots are not recommended in the door.

### GRADE 10

Minimum security level; adequate for single family residential buildings located in stable, comparatively low crime areas.

### GRADE 20

Low to medium security level; provides security for residential buildings located in average crime rate areas or for apartments in both low and average crime rate areas.

### GRADE 30

Medium to high security level; provides security for residential buildings located in higher than average crime rate areas or for small commercial buildings in average or low crime rate areas.

### GRADE 40

High security level; provides security for commercial buildings located in medium to high crime rate areas.

## SLIDING DOOR UNITS

Sliding glass doors are a particular concern in securing a building. Performance requirements specified in the NILECJ-STD-0318, Physical Security of Sliding Glass Door Units should be complied with.

The locking devices should include vertical rod, or lever bolts, at top and bottom; the frame should be solid or reinforced at the locking points; the stile must also be reinforced at the lock points. The operating panels should be designed so that they cannot be lifted out of their tracks when in the locked position.

Glazing and other components should be installed from the inside so that entry cannot be gained by disassembly. As with windows and other doors, a hidden location requires a higher grade.

PROVIDE LEVER BOLT AT TOP AND BOTTOM WITH 1" MINIMUM THROW

INTERLOCKING MEETING STILE

HEAVY DUTY LOCK WITH HOOK TYPE HARDENED DEAD BOLT

FIXED PANEL SECURED ON THE INSIDE

OPERABLE DOOR SECURED AGAINST LIFTOUT

GROUT FRAME FULL OR BRACE SOLID FROM FLOOR TO 12" ABOVE LOCK

POLYCARBONATE OR LAMINATED GLASS

**SLIDING GLASS DOOR**

## WINDOW FORCED ENTRY DESIGN CRITERIA

### EXTERIOR DESIGN ELEMENTS

1. The following items should be considered when designing and selecting windows:
   LOCATION: If accessible (residential: 12 ft vertical, 6 ft horizontal; commercial: 18 ft vertical, 10 ft horizontal) and hidden from public view, a higher grade is required.
   PROTECTED: If windows are protected by a detection device (such as shutters, security screens, or bars), the window grade could be irrelevant. If security screens, bars, or shutters are used, requirements for fire exiting must be met.
2. The existence of windbreaks near a building may provide cover for intruders.
3. The use of shades and window coverings may deter intruders, depending on the ease of removal of these devices or the noise from breakage. The use of lockable shutters or rolldown blinds is very effective.
4. WINDOW UNITS: Window units should at least comply with ANSI/ASTM F 588-79 Standard Test Methods for Resistance of Window Assemblies to Forced Entry for a minimum grade performance and with NILECJ-STD-0316, Physical Security of Window Units, for higher grade performance.
5. As with a door assembly, the security of a window does not rely on the lock alone.

### FRAME DESIGN ELEMENTS

1. A rigid frame and sash is important to resist prying and should be removable from the inside only.
2. The quality of the hardware and its placement and anchorage are critical to security. Exposed removable hinges should not be used.
3. Special attention must be given to the use of weather stripping, since this can permit insertion of wires to unlock windows.

### GLAZING DESIGN ELEMENTS

1. Multiple glazing systems provide a greater hazard to entry/exit through broken-out windows.
2. Reflective glazing impedes outside daytime surveillance.

## MATERIALS AND METHODS FOR WINDOWS

1. Grade 40: Very heavy fixed frames with laminated glass over 1/4 in. thick or security screen, bars, or shutters with special locking device.
2. Grade 30: Heavy duty sash with laminated glass over 1/4 in. thick or polycarbonate glazing 1/4 in. thick. Lock should include at least two heavy duty dead locking bolts.
3. Grade 20: Heavy duty sash with laminated glass or polycarbonate glazing; if wood, sash must be reinforced or heavy; double locks required.
4. Grade 10: Regular glazing in commercial sash with double locks; can be wood frame.

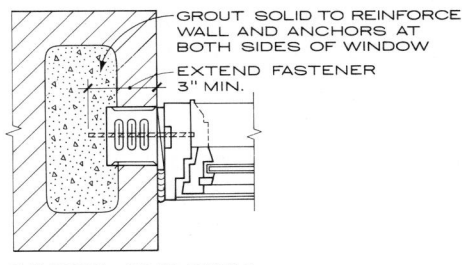

GROUT SOLID TO REINFORCE WALL AND ANCHORS AT BOTH SIDES OF WINDOW

EXTEND FASTENER 3" MIN.

**WINDOW JAMB DETAIL**

John Stroik, Architect, and Porter Driscoll, AIA, Architect; Center for Building Technology, National Bureau of Standards; Washington, D.C. William G. Miner, AIA; Washington, D.C.

**SPECIAL DOORS**   8

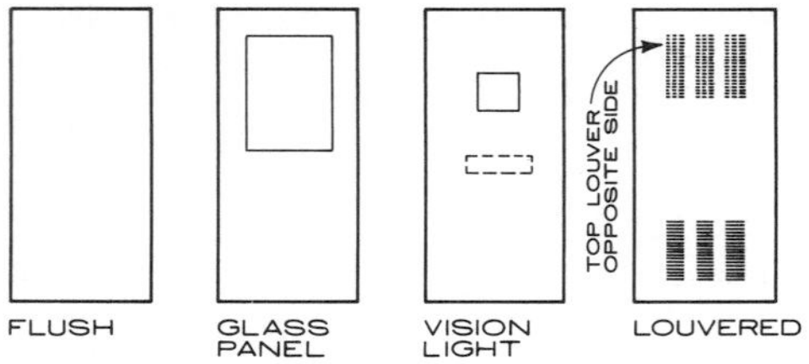

## DOOR TYPES

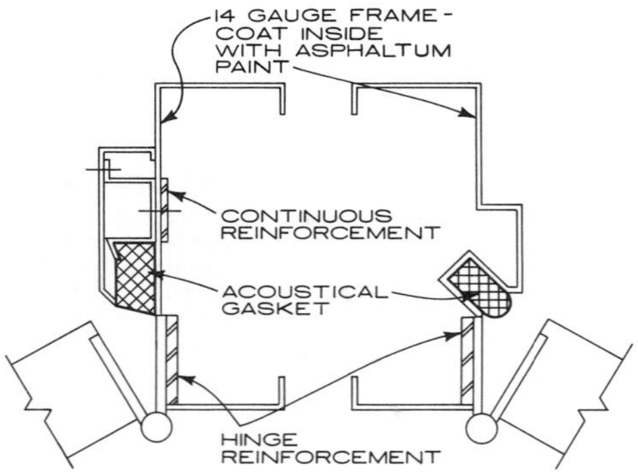

FLUSH    GLASS PANEL    VISION LIGHT    LOUVERED

TOP LOUVER OPPOSITE SIDE

## DOOR FRAMES

14 GAUGE FRAME - COAT INSIDE WITH ASPHALTUM PAINT

CONTINUOUS REINFORCEMENT

ACOUSTICAL GASKET

HINGE REINFORCEMENT

## ACOUSTIC DOORS AND FRAMES

ACOUSTICAL DROP SEAL

FLOOR OR SADDLE

SOUND ATTENUATION DUCT INSIDE DOOR

ACOUSTICAL DROP SEAL - MORTISED DOOR

FLOOR OR SADDLE

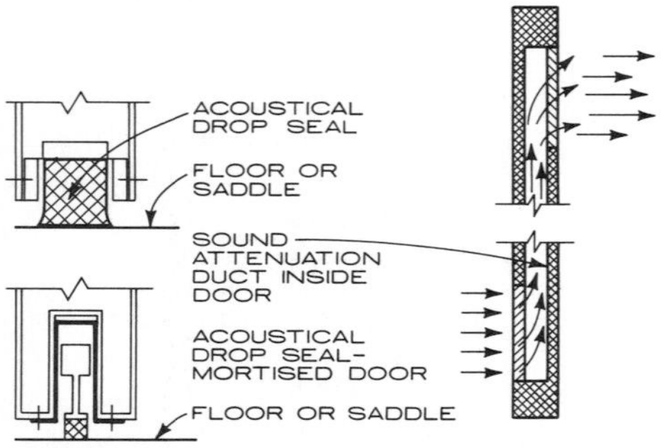

DOOR BOTTOMS    LOUVERED DOOR

NOTE: SURFACE MOUNTED DROP SEALS ARE AVAILABLE

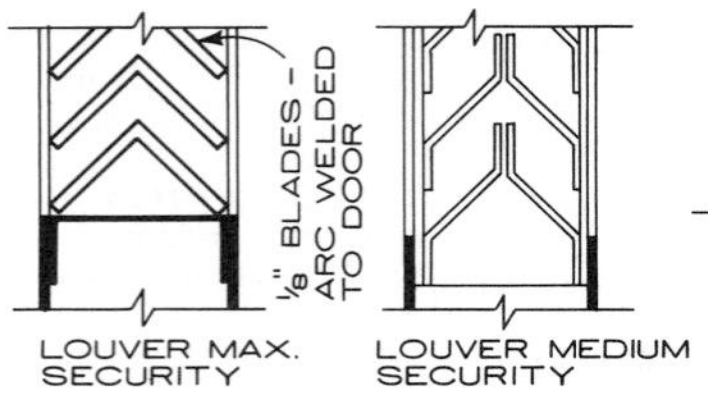

LOUVER MAX. SECURITY    LOUVER MEDIUM SECURITY

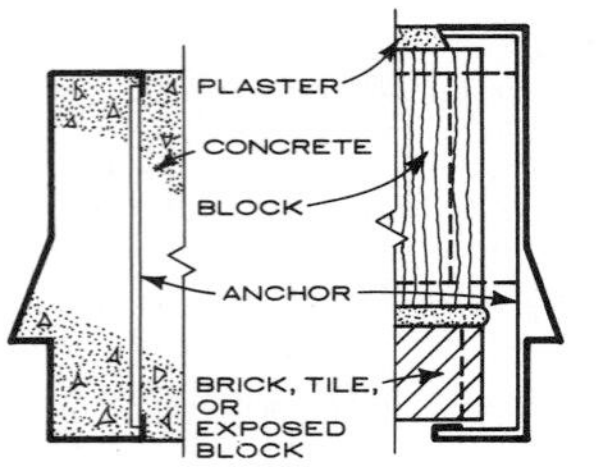

⅛" BLADES - ARC WELDED TO DOOR

PLASTER
CONCRETE
BLOCK
ANCHOR
BRICK, TILE, OR EXPOSED BLOCK

HINGED DOOR JAMBS 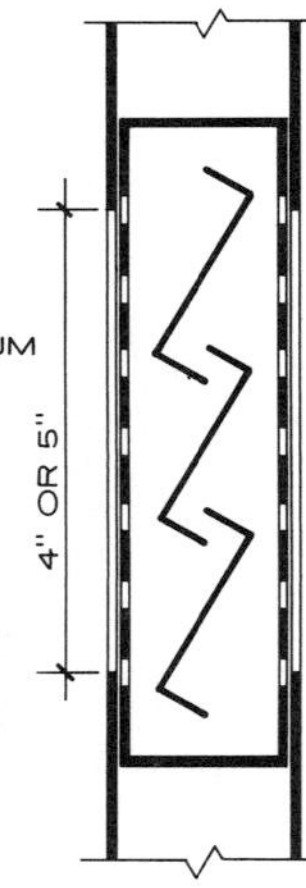    SPEAKER

4" OR 5"

ROLLER ASSEMBLY
SHEET STEEL COVER
STEEL TRACK
STEEL ANGLE - ARC WELDED TO DOOR
STEEL GUIDE
WELDED TO DOOR

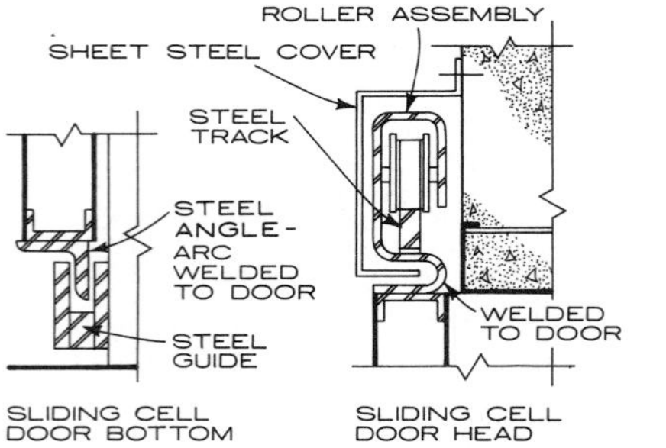

SLIDING CELL DOOR BOTTOM    SLIDING CELL DOOR HEAD

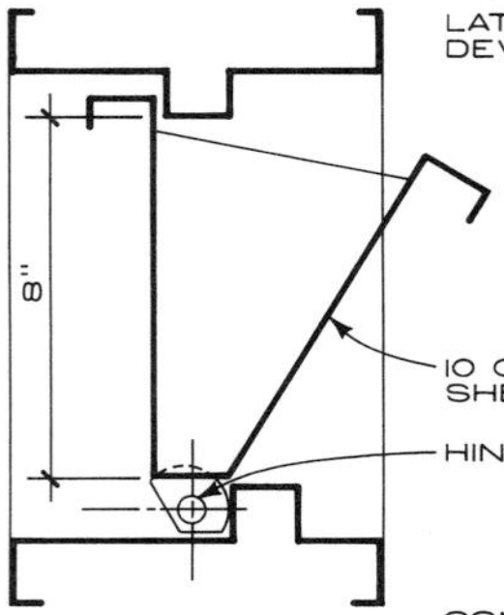

MULLION
ANCHOR
GUIDE AND ANGLE - SEE SLIDING CELL DOOR DETAIL THIS PAGE

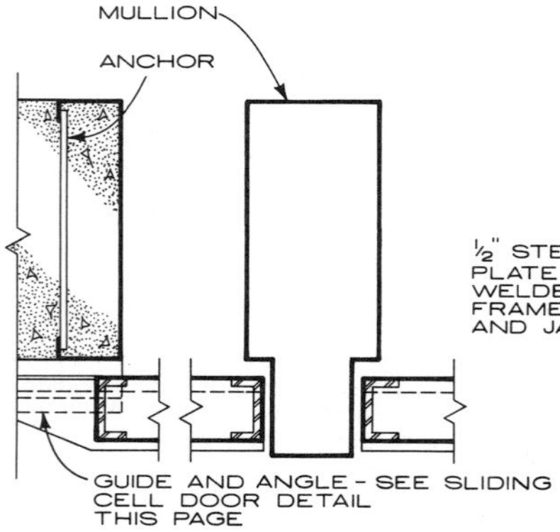

PLAN OF SLIDING CELL DOORS

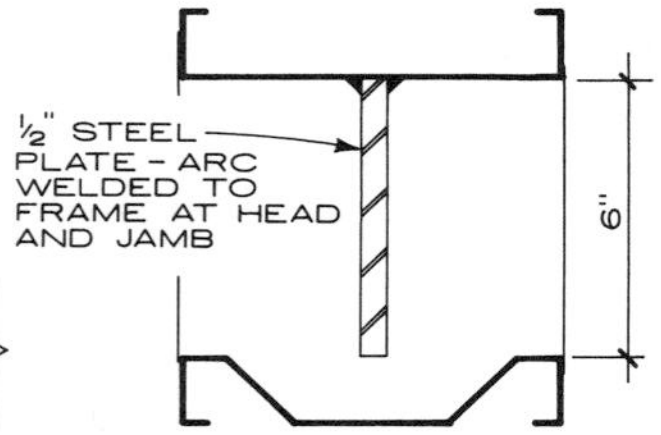

½" STEEL PLATE - ARC WELDED TO FRAME AT HEAD AND JAMB

KEY PASS

## NOTES

1. Security doors must have a minimum nominal thickness of 2 in. so that security locks can be fitted in them. The required door thickness should always be coordinated with the type of security hardware being used.
2. All locking devices should be protected with a ⅛ in. steel plate at the detention side and door edge.
3. Pressed steel security frames should be a minimum of 14 gauge and are made up to 7 gauge. The frame gauge should be selected according to the desired performance. This information is available from the manufacturers.
4. All joints in security frames should be mitered and arc welded.
5. The following hardware reinforcement information should only be used as a guide:

   | | |
   |---|---|
   | Surface hinges | 10 gauge steel channel and a ⅜ in. steel plate |
   | Mortise hinges | 10 gauge steel channel and a 3/16 in. steel plate |
   | Surface pull | ⅜ x 1 x 12 in. steel plate |
   | Surface closer | 12 gauge channel x 2½ x 14 in. |

6. Frames are available for single and double door units. Double door units must have a fixed mullion.

LATCHING DEVICE
8"
10 GAUGE SHEET STEEL
HINGE

GUN PASS

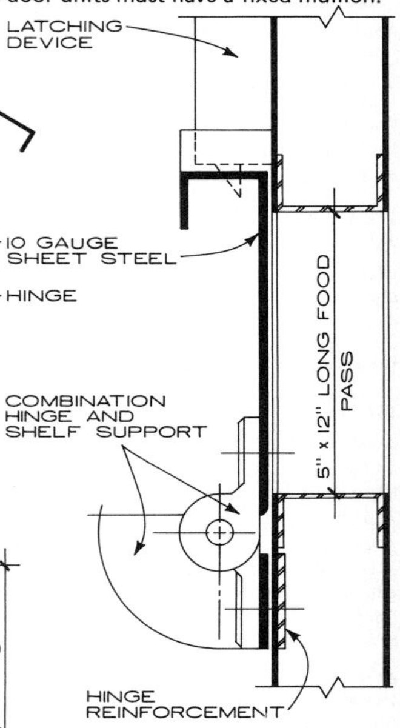

COMBINATION HINGE AND SHELF SUPPORT
5" x 12" LONG FOOD PASS
HINGE REINFORCEMENT

FOOD PASS WITH COVER SHELF

HINGE REINFORCEMENT

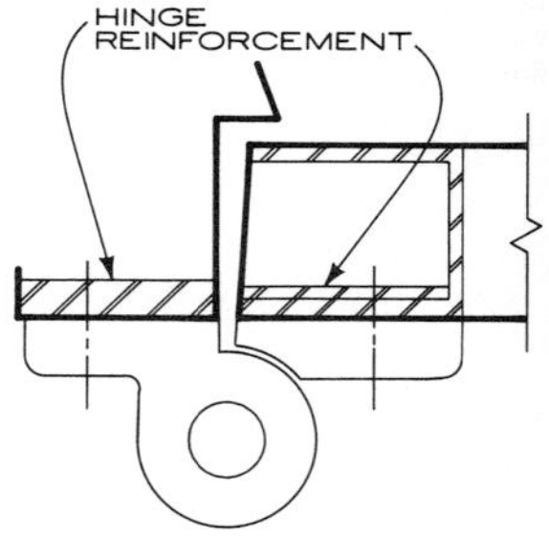

FULL SURFACE HINGE

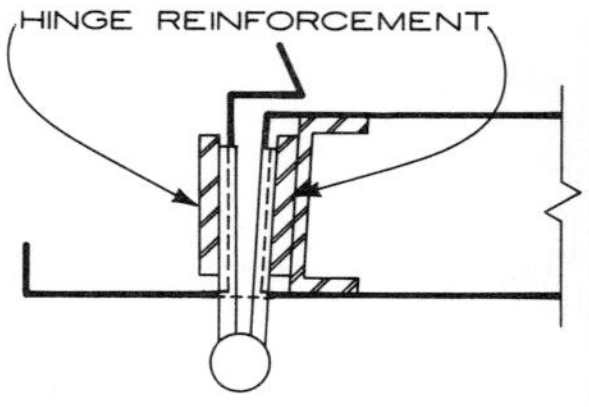

HINGE REINFORCEMENT

FULL MORTISE HINGE

## DOOR TYPES

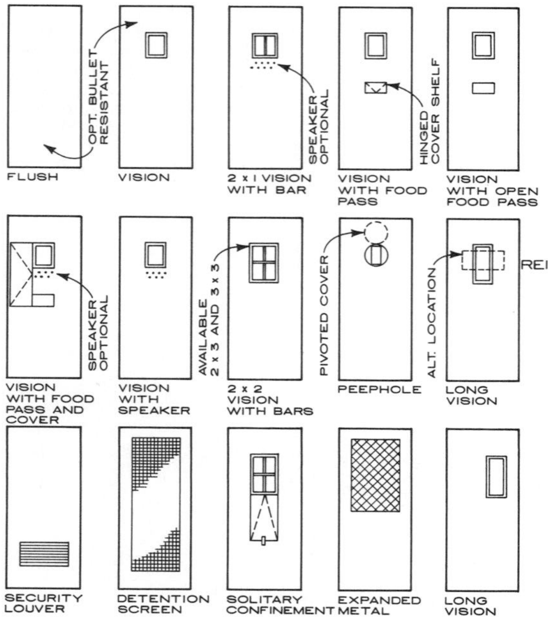

FLUSH
OPT. BULLET RESISTANT

VISION

2 x 1 VISION WITH BAR
SPEAKER OPTIONAL

VISION WITH FOOD PASS

VISION WITH OPEN FOOD PASS
HINGED COVER SHELF

VISION WITH FOOD PASS AND COVER
SPEAKER OPTIONAL

VISION WITH SPEAKER

2 x 2 VISION WITH BARS
AVAILABLE 2 x 3 AND 3 x 3

PEEPHOLE
PIVOTED COVER

LONG VISION
ALT. LOCATION

SECURITY LOUVER

DETENTION SCREEN

SOLITARY CONFINEMENT

EXPANDED METAL

LONG VISION

## DOOR DETAILS

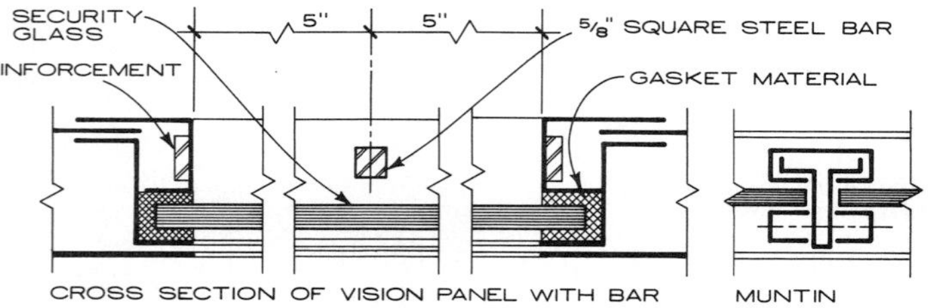

SECURITY GLASS
REINFORCEMENT
5"    5"
5/8" SQUARE STEEL BAR
GASKET MATERIAL

CROSS SECTION OF VISION PANEL WITH BAR    MUNTIN

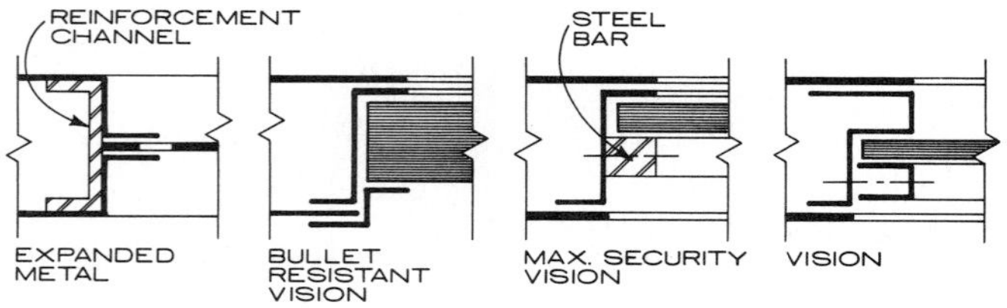

REINFORCEMENT CHANNEL

STEEL BAR

EXPANDED METAL    BULLET RESISTANT VISION    MAX. SECURITY VISION    VISION

## DETENTION DOORS AND DETAILS

Kelly Sacher & Associates; Architects Engineers Planners; N. Babylon, New York

**SPECIAL DOORS**

## GENERAL

Comprehensive, effective site security provides deterrents to hostile acts, barriers to unauthorized entry, access/egress control, detection of unauthorized entry or exit, and positions for security personnel. Design of the system includes:

1. Perimeter physical barriers preventing penetration by intruders and vehicles
2. Entry/exit control
3. Protective lighting
4. Standoff distance from blasts
5. Intrusion detection, alert, and notification
6. Guard posts and guard walls

Perimeter and site security are augmented by a comprehensive building security system.

## SITE ACCESS

A screening facility at perimeter access points should be considered in high risk areas to detect explosives, firearms, and other weapons. A sally port detains vehicles for inspection and prevents other vehicles from gaining access by tailgating.

A protected guard booth should be located so that the guard can control entry/exit of pedestrians and vehicles. Guard booths in high risk areas should be constructed to appropriate ballistic and forced entry resistant standards. Where extensive vehicle inspection is required, a roving guard should augment guards in the booth.

## PERIMETER PROTECTION

Perimeter security addresses issues of protection against forced entry by unauthorized personnel and vehicles, and against explosive blast.

## PERSONNEL BARRIERS: FENCES AND WALLS

Walls and opaque fences to deter and resist intruders should be smooth-faced with no easy foot or handholds, and be a minimum 9 ft high. Open fencing should be constructed of vertical elements with 9 ft minimum between horizontal elements.

## SITE SECURITY LIGHTING

A comprehensive system of security lighting should include illumination of the perimeter, structures within, and site passageways.

Continuous lighting using fixed luminaires to flood an area with overlapping cones of light is most common. Lighting across an area makes it difficult for intruders to see inside the area. Controlled lighting, which adjusts light to fit a particular strip inside and/or outside the perimeter, is less intrusive to adjacent properties.

Auxiliary standby lighting is turned on if suspicious activity is detected. Movable lighting supplements continuous or standby lighting.

## EXPLOSIVE BLAST RESISTANCE

The most effective protective measure against explosive blast is to maximize the standoff distance from perimeter barriers to buildings or other assets. Blast walls are of limited effectiveness.

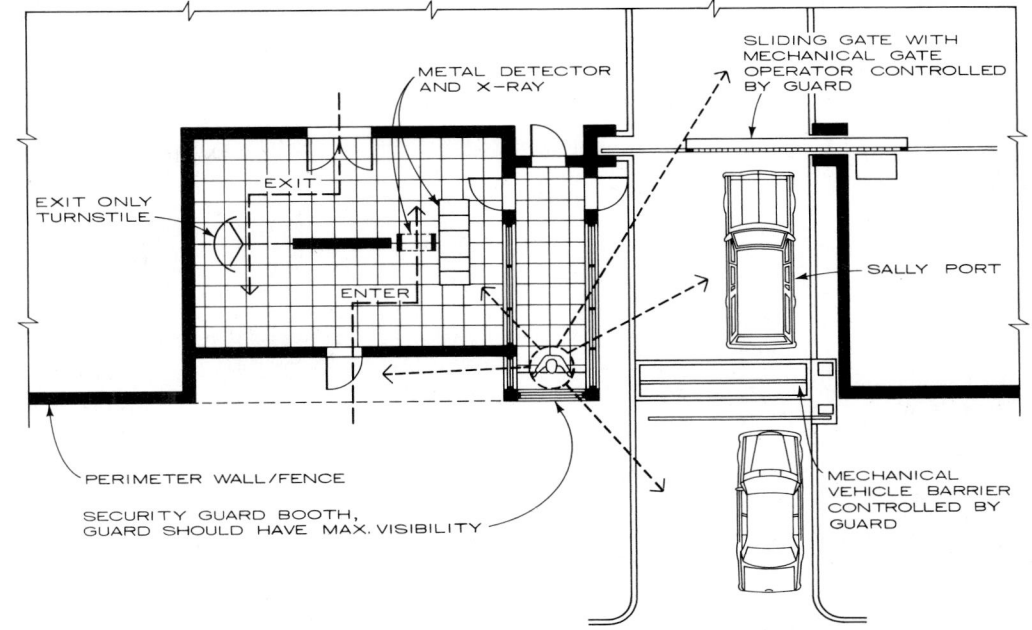

**SITE ACCESS DIAGRAM**

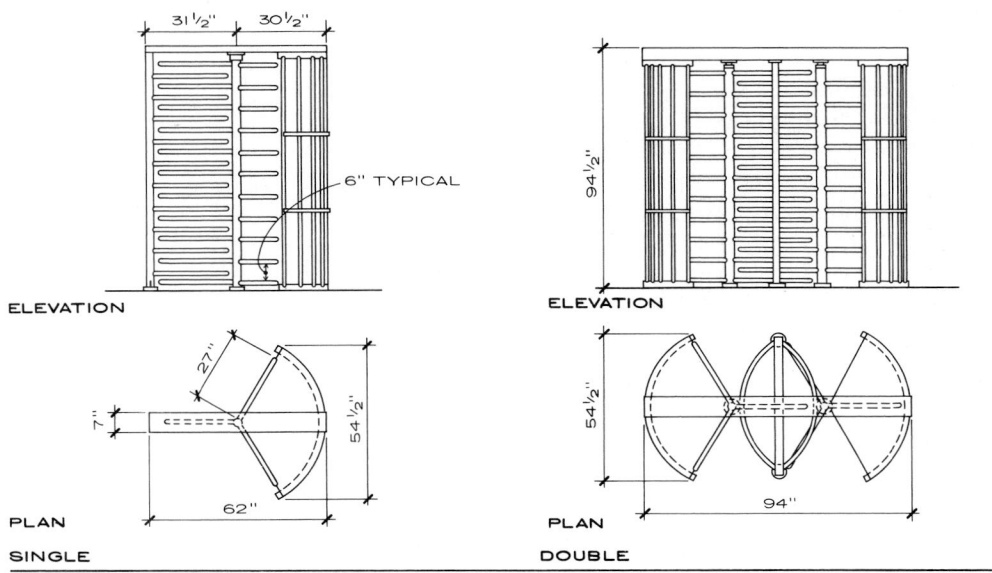

SINGLE       DOUBLE

**TURNSTILES**

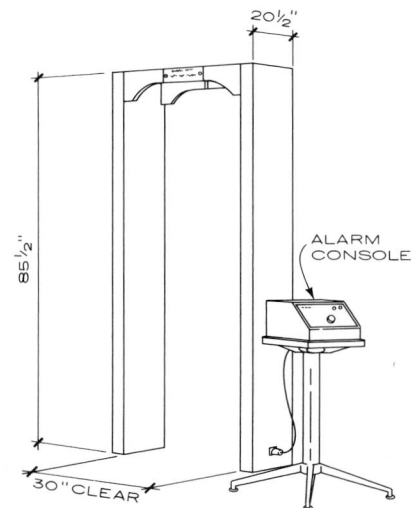

**WALK THROUGH METAL DETECTOR**

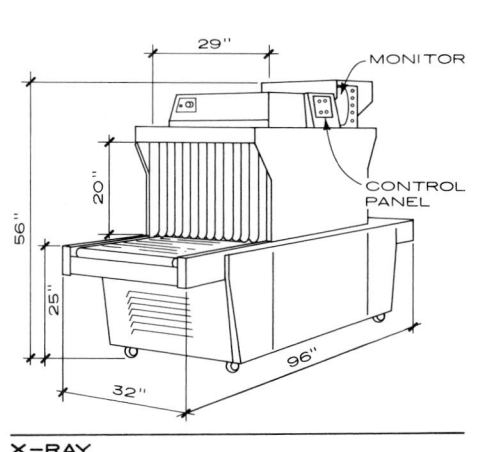

**X-RAY**

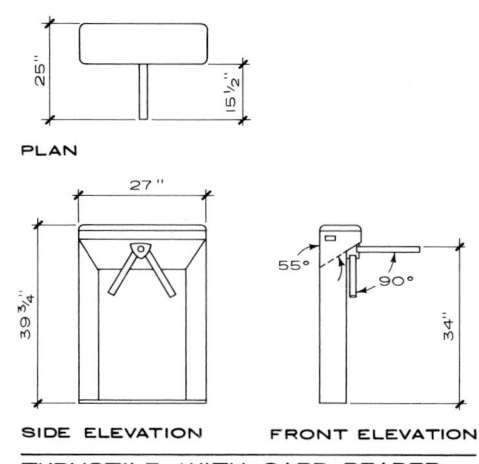

**TURNSTILE WITH CARD READER**

Edwin Daly, AIA; Joseph Handwerger, Architects; Washington, D.C.
William G. Miner, AIA; Washington, D.C.

**SPECIAL DOORS**       8

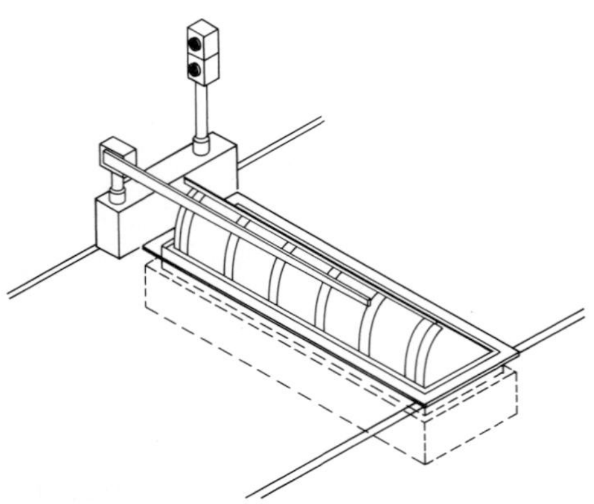

RETRACTABLE BARRIER

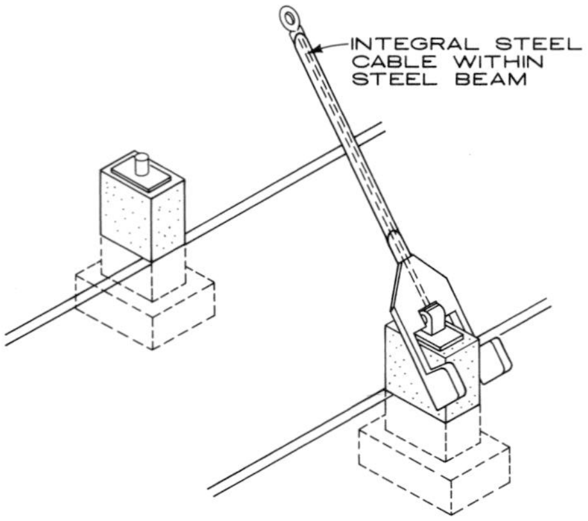

INTEGRAL STEEL CABLE WITHIN STEEL BEAM

CABLE CRASH BEAM

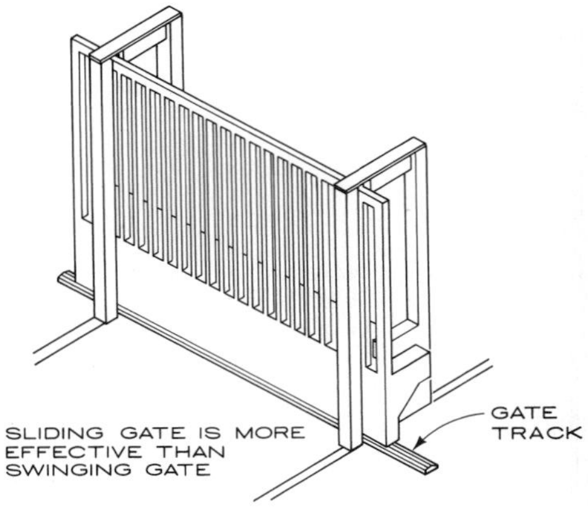

SLIDING GATE IS MORE EFFECTIVE THAN SWINGING GATE

GATE TRACK

SLIDING CRASH GATE

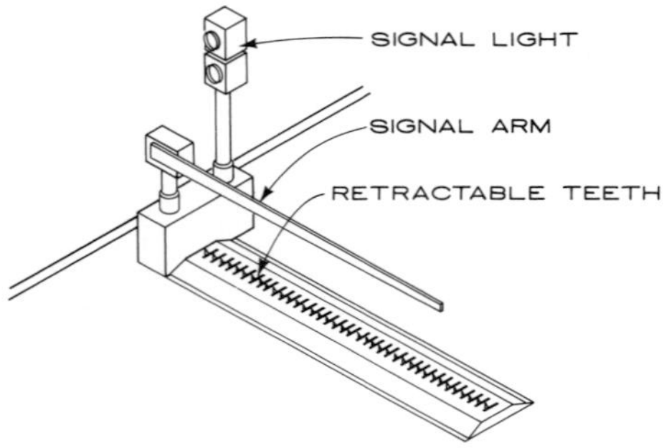

SIGNAL LIGHT

SIGNAL ARM

RETRACTABLE TEETH

TRAFFIC CONTROLLER

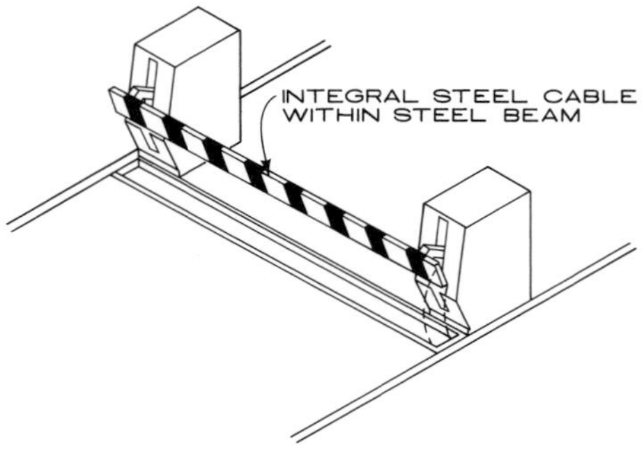

INTEGRAL STEEL CABLE WITHIN STEEL BEAM

LIFT CRASH GATE

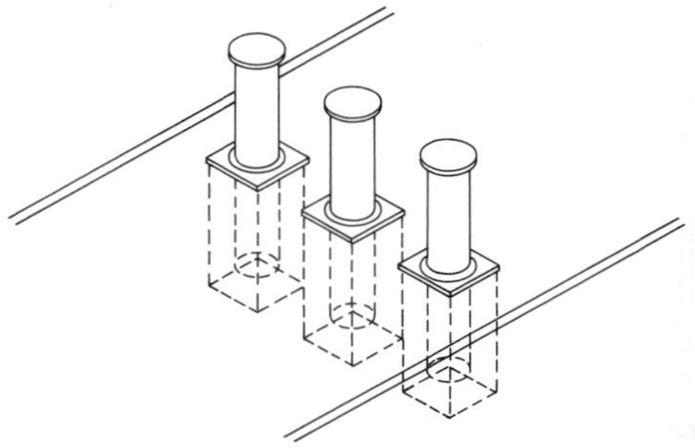

RETRACTABLE BOLLARDS

## MECHANICAL BARRIERS

## VEHICLE BARRIERS

1. Active barriers at access/egress points in high security areas should be fully engaged until vehicle is cleared for passage. A visible signal light or drop arm should indicate the barrier's status to approaching vehicles. Operating time should not exceed 3–4 sec. The barrier system must maintain its position, preventing access in case of power failure, be capable of manual operation, and should be connected to emergency power. Remote controls should include a status indicator.

2. Passive vehicle barriers (walls, bollards, planters, trench/berms, and ponds) can enhance site design and be inexpensive, low-maintenance vehicle barriers.

3. Concrete bollards and walls require heavy reinforcement tied into massive continuously reinforced concrete footings.

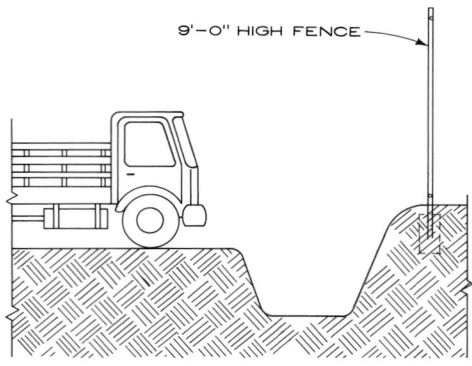

9'-0" HIGH FENCE

TRENCH/BERM/FENCE

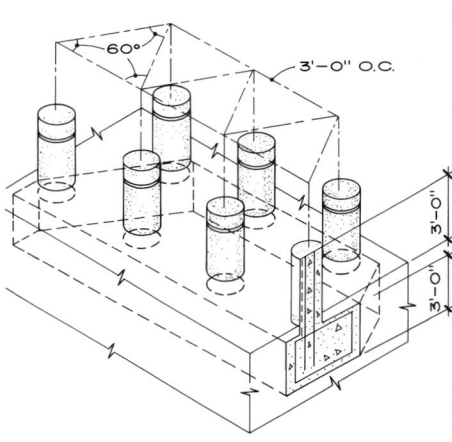

60°    3'-0" O.C.

CONCRETE BOLLARDS WITH CONTINUOUS FOOTING

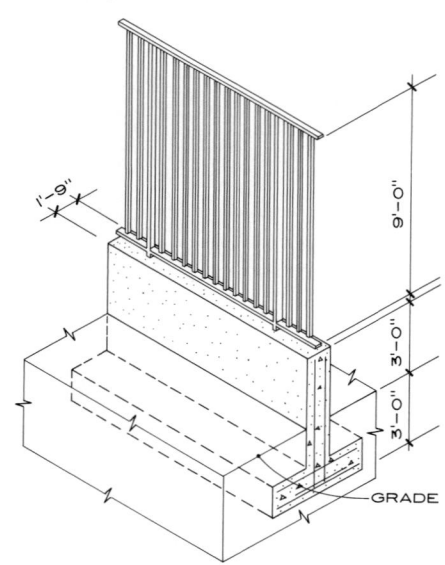

9'-0"

3'-0"

1'-9"

GRADE

FENCE ON BARRIER WALL

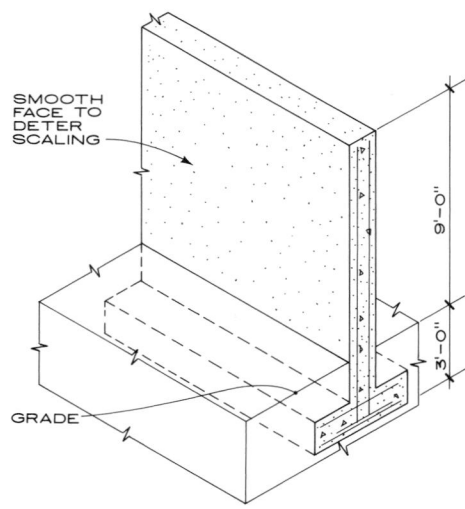

SMOOTH FACE TO DETER SCALING

9'-0"

3'-0"

GRADE

CONCRETE BARRIER WALL

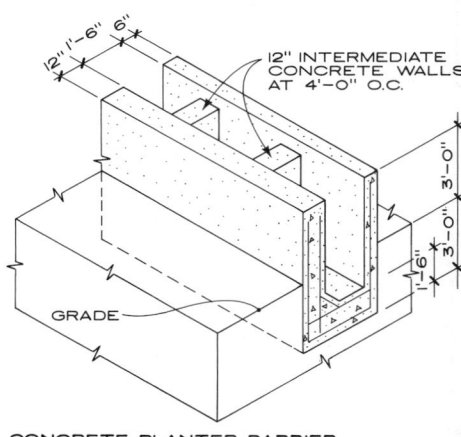

12"    1'-6"    6"

12" INTERMEDIATE CONCRETE WALLS AT 4'-0" O.C.

3'-0"

1'-6"

GRADE

CONCRETE PLANTER BARRIER

## FIXED BARRIERS

Edwin Daly, AIA, and Ellen Delaney; Joseph Handwerger, Architects; Washington, D.C.
William G. Miner, AIA; Washington, D.C.

# SPECIAL DOORS

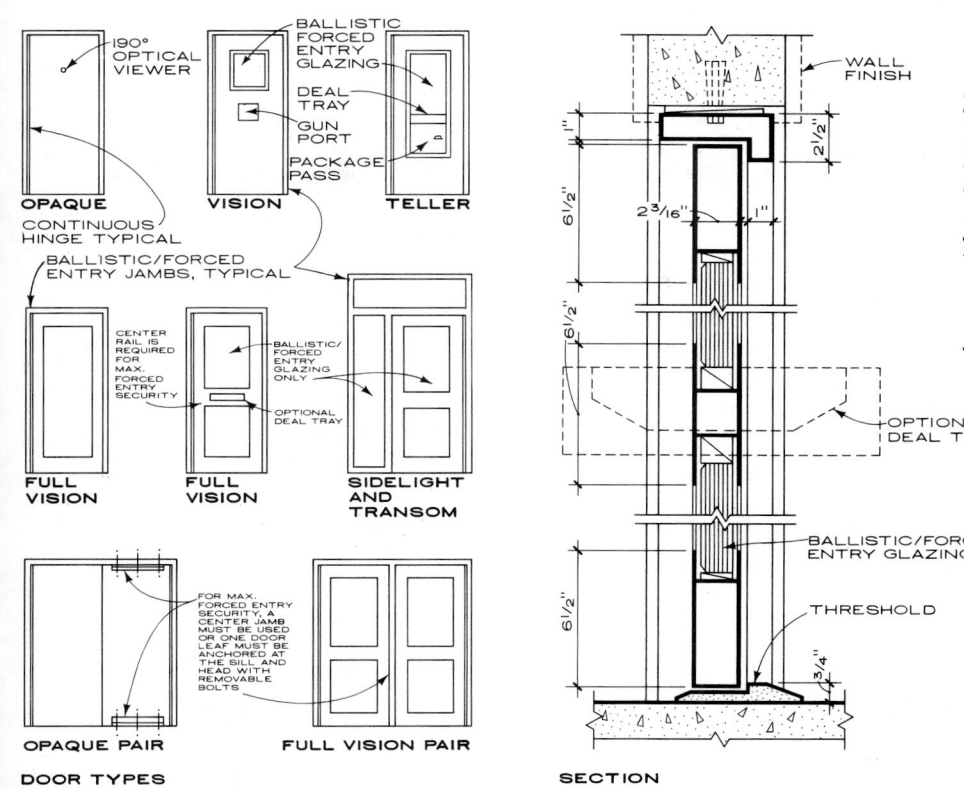

**DOOR TYPES**

**BALLISTIC/FORCED ENTRY DOORS**

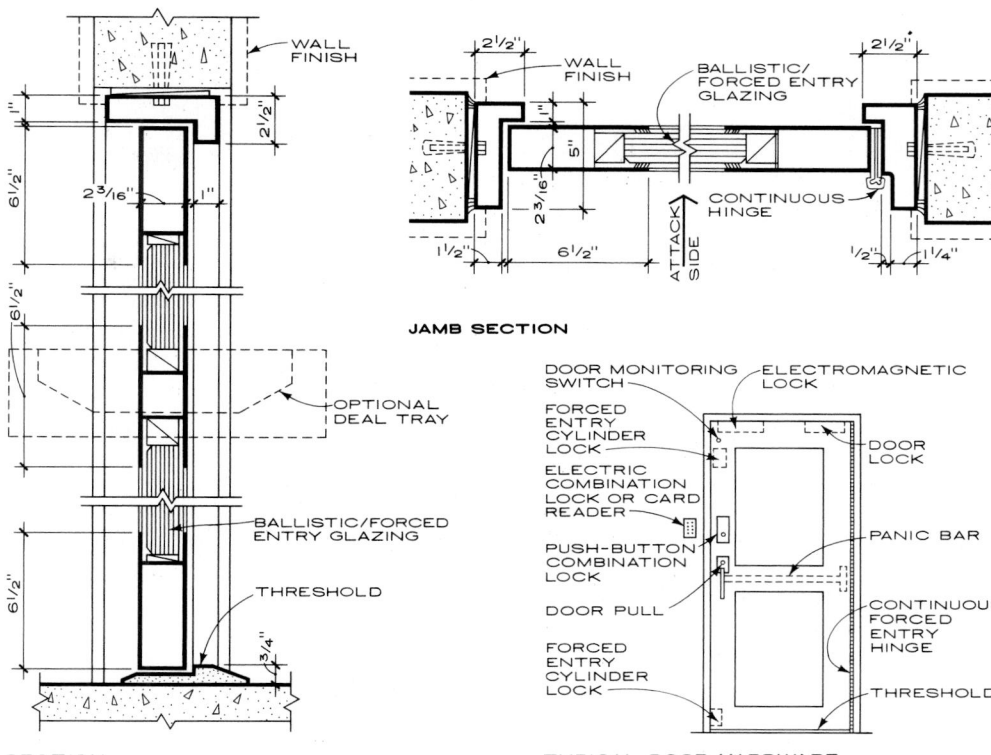

**JAMB SECTION**

**SECTION**

**TYPICAL DOOR HARDWARE**

## NOTES

1. Ballistic/forced entry modular units from manufacturers can be combined to form a wall or room.

2. Fire-rated opaque security doors are available.

3. Ballistic resistant glazing is manufactured in various thicknesses to attain required levels of resistant standards; e.g., 9 mm, high-powered rifle.

4. To maximize forced entry resistance, security doors must swing toward the attack side.

5. Custom doors can be fabricated when designed within manufacturers' parameters.

6. Walls must be constructed to meet the same level of resistance as the windows and doors installed in them.

7. Doors and windows must be anchored in strict accordance with manufacturers' directions to attain resistant standards.

8. Ballistic/forced entry windows for use in exterior building openings are similar to the teller windows detailed on this page.

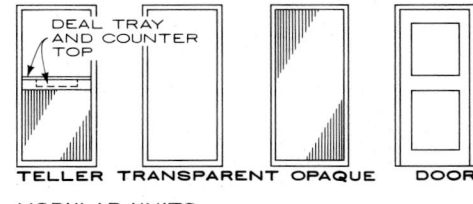

**MODULAR UNITS**

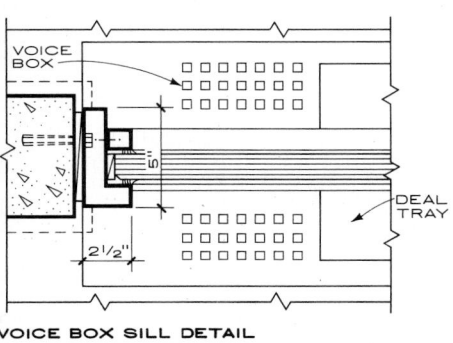

**VOICE BOX SILL DETAIL**

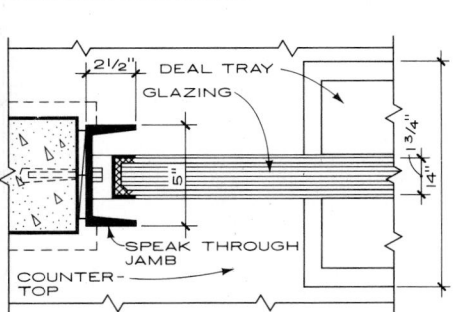

**SPEAK THROUGH JAMB DETAIL**

**BALLISTIC/FORCED ENTRY TELLER WINDOWS**

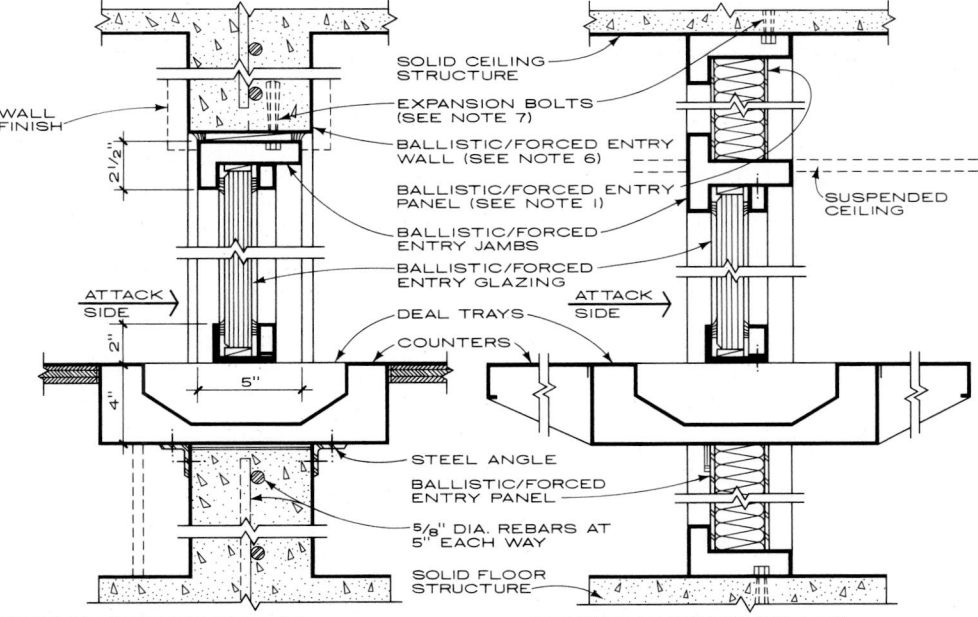

SECTION THROUGH TELLER WINDOW MOUNTED IN BALLISTIC/FORCED ENTRY CONCRETE WALL

SECTION THROUGH TELLER WINDOW MODULAR UNIT

Edwin Daly, AIA; Joseph Handwerger, Architects; Washington, D.C.
William G. Miner, AIA; Washington, D.C.

**SPECIAL DOORS** 8

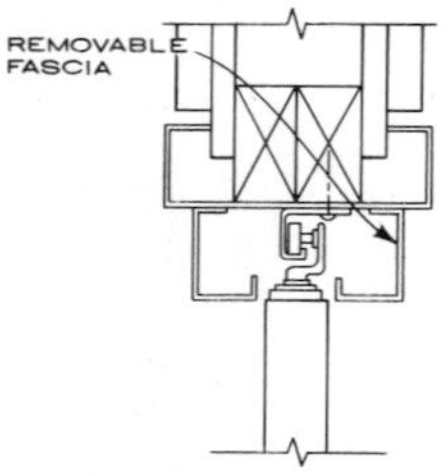

REMOVABLE FASCIA

**POCKET SLIDE DOOR HEAD**

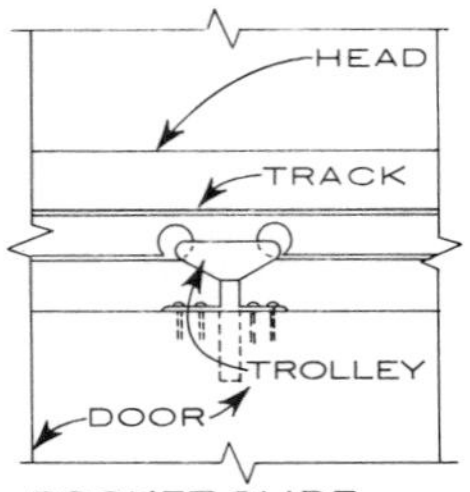

HEAD
TRACK
TROLLEY
DOOR

**POCKET SLIDE DOOR TRACK**

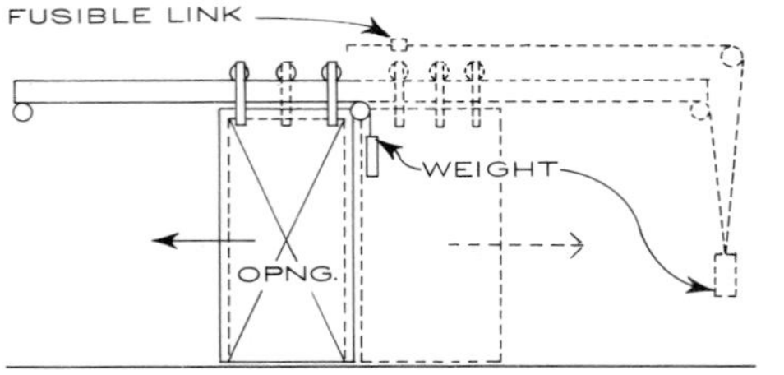

FUSIBLE LINK
WEIGHT
OPNG.

**INDUSTRIAL DOOR--HORIZONTAL TRACK**

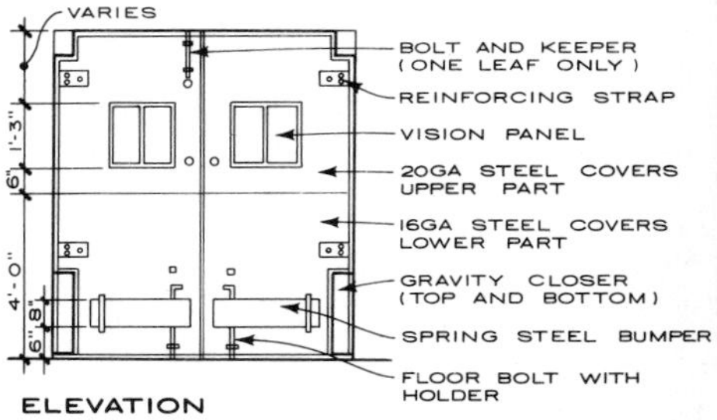

VARIES
1'-3"
6"
4'-0"
6'-8"

BOLT AND KEEPER (ONE LEAF ONLY)
REINFORCING STRAP
VISION PANEL
20GA STEEL COVERS UPPER PART
16GA STEEL COVERS LOWER PART
GRAVITY CLOSER (TOP AND BOTTOM)
SPRING STEEL BUMPER
FLOOR BOLT WITH HOLDER

**ELEVATION**

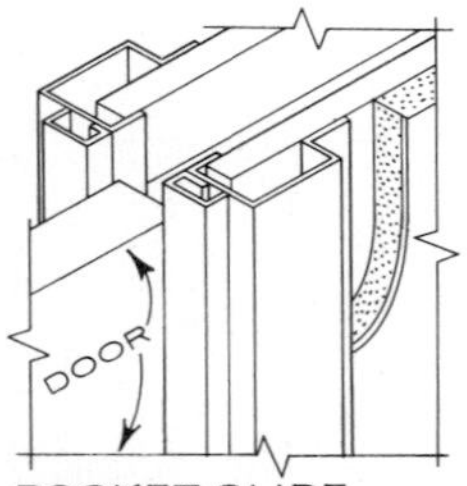

DOOR

**POCKET SLIDE DOOR JAMB**

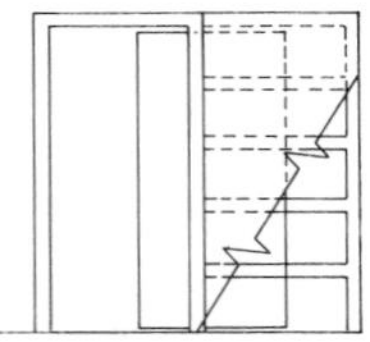

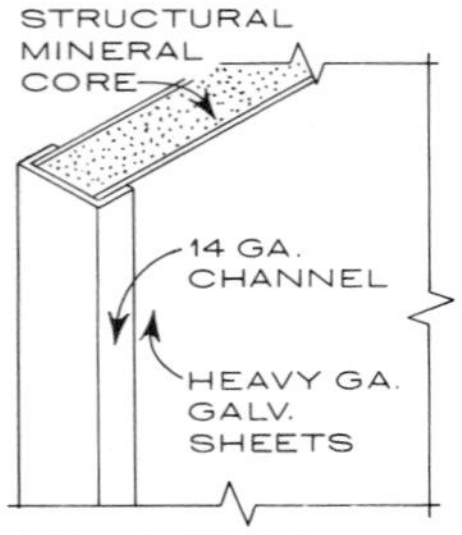

**POCKET SLIDE DOOR ELEVATION**

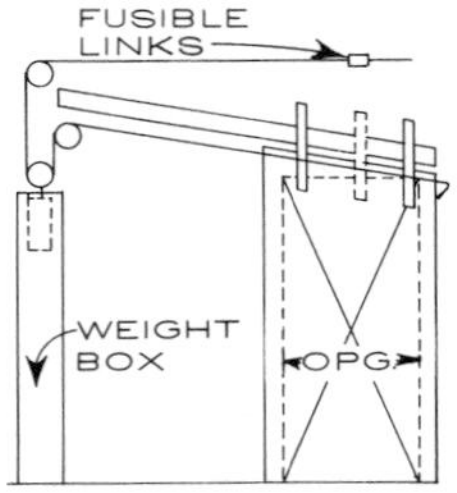

FUSIBLE LINKS
WEIGHT BOX
OPG.

**SLOPED TRACK**

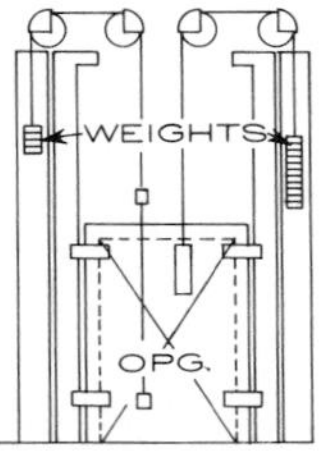

WEIGHTS
OPG.

**VERTICAL TRACK**

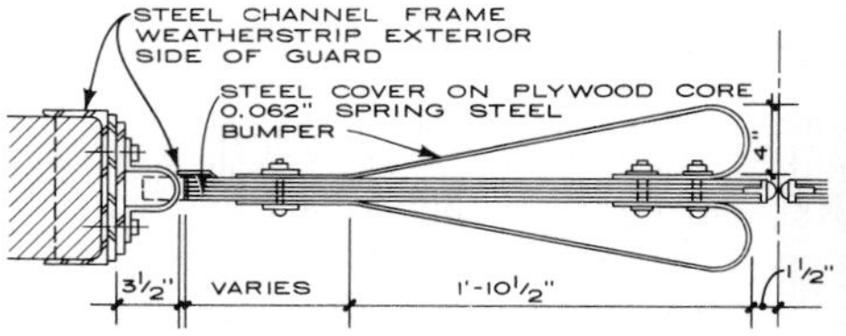

STEEL CHANNEL FRAME WEATHERSTRIP EXTERIOR SIDE OF GUARD
STEEL COVER ON PLYWOOD CORE 0.062" SPRING STEEL BUMPER
3½"
VARIES
1'-10½"
1½"

**PLAN THROUGH BUMPER**

**DOUBLE ACTING DOOR** (POSTAL SERVICE TYPE)

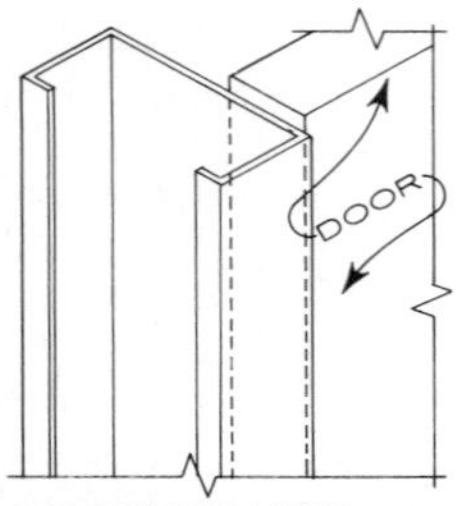

STRUCTURAL MINERAL CORE
DOOR
14 GA. CHANNEL
HEAVY GA. GALV. SHEETS

**POCKET SLIDE DOOR JAMB**

**METAL CLAD CONSTRUCTION**

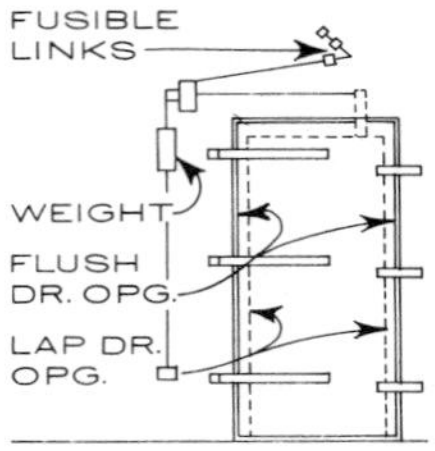

FUSIBLE LINKS
WEIGHT
FLUSH DR. OPG.
LAP DR. OPG.

**FLUSH OR LAP SWING DOOR**

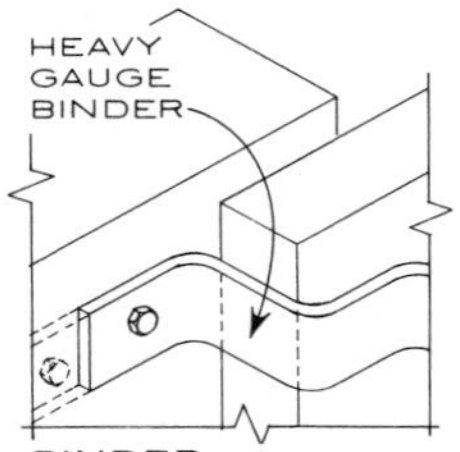

HEAVY GAUGE BINDER

**BINDER**

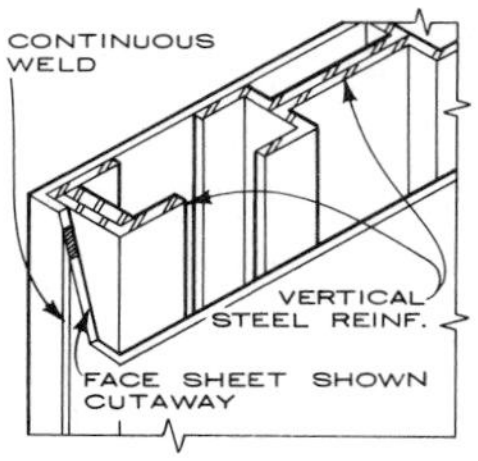

CONTINUOUS WELD
VERTICAL STEEL REINF.
FACE SHEET SHOWN CUTAWAY
TYPICAL CONSTRUCTION WITH STIFFENERS

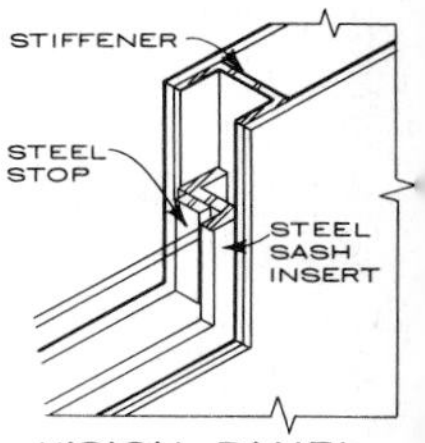

STIFFENER
STEEL STOP
STEEL SASH INSERT

**VISION PANEL**

**SECURITY DOOR DETAILS**

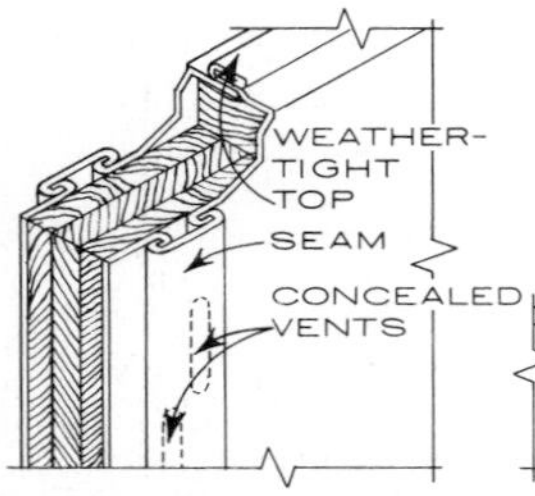

WEATHER-TIGHT TOP
SEAM
CONCEALED VENTS

**METAL CLAD CONSTRUCTION**

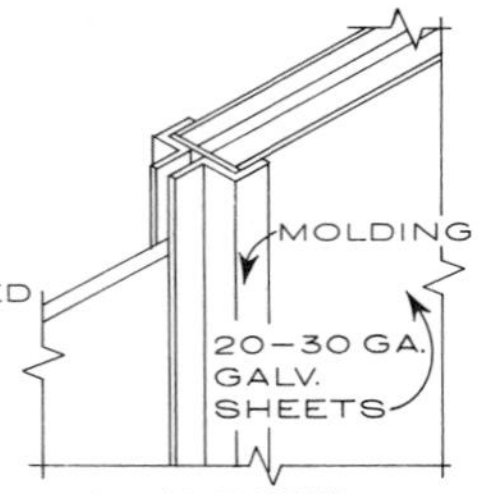

MOLDING
20-30 GA. GALV. SHEETS

**VISION PANEL**

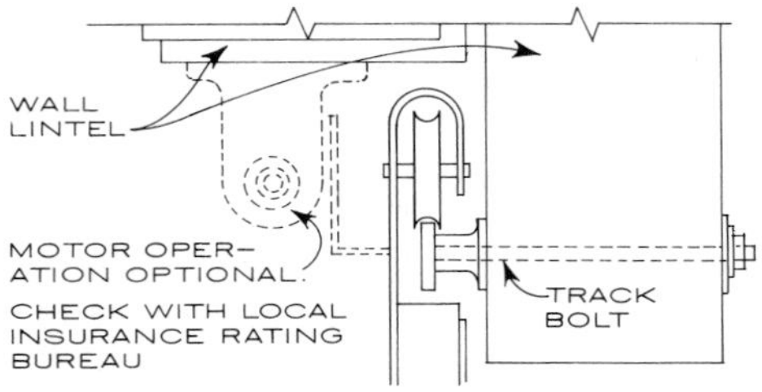

WALL LINTEL
MOTOR OPER-ATION OPTIONAL
CHECK WITH LOCAL INSURANCE RATING BUREAU
TRACK BOLT

**INDUSTRIAL SLIDING DOOR--HEAD**

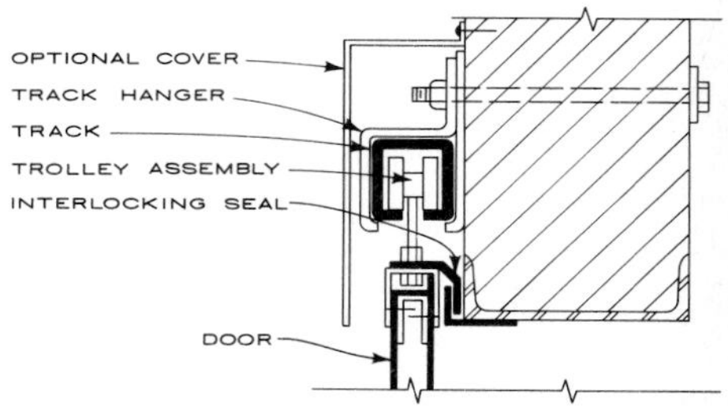

OPTIONAL COVER
TRACK HANGER
TRACK
TROLLEY ASSEMBLY
INTERLOCKING SEAL
DOOR

**FIRE RATED SLIDING DOOR HEAD**

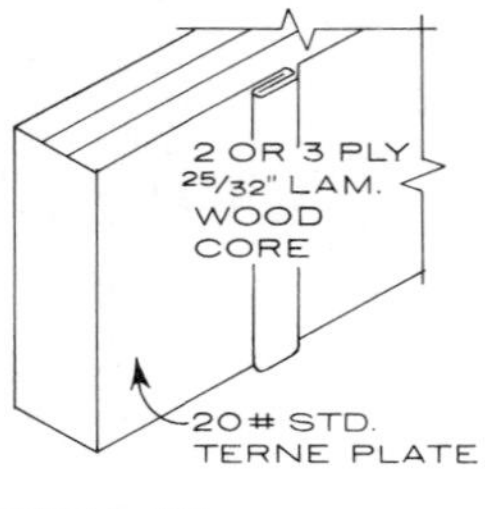

2 OR 3 PLY 25/32" LAM. WOOD CORE
20# STD. TERNE PLATE

**TIN CLAD CONSTRUCTION**

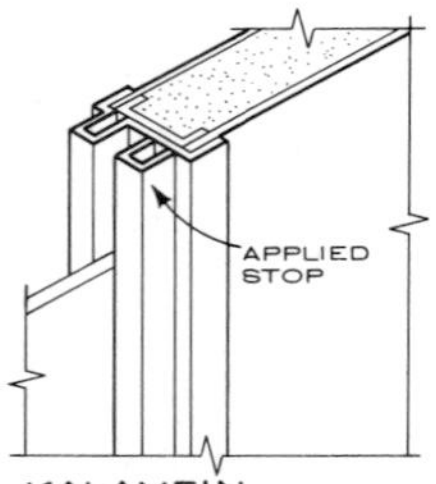

APPLIED STOP

**KALAMEIN GLAZING**

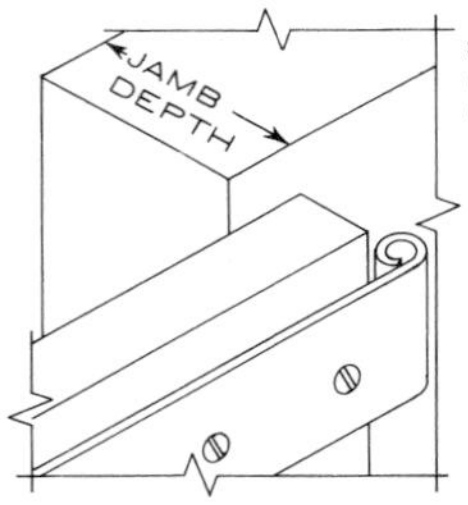

JAMB DEPTH
STRUCT. STEEL CHANNEL

**SWING LAP JAMB**

USE WITH APPROVED ANCHOR

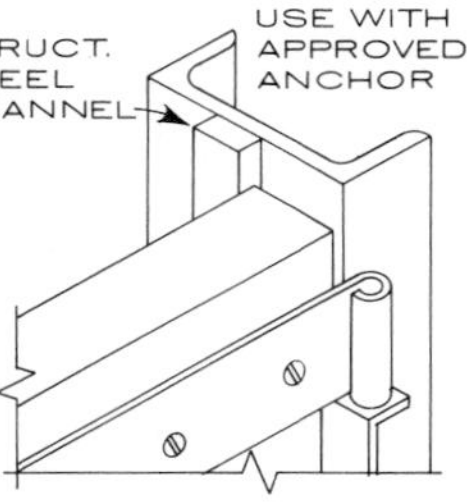

**U.L. APPROVED JAMB**

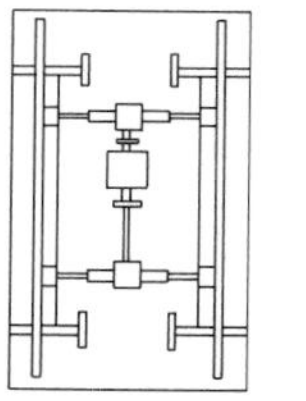

**INSIDE ELEVATION**

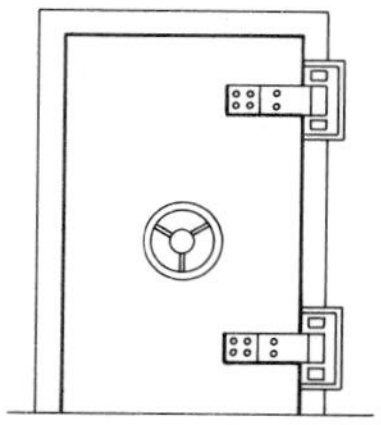

**OUTSIDE ELEVATION**

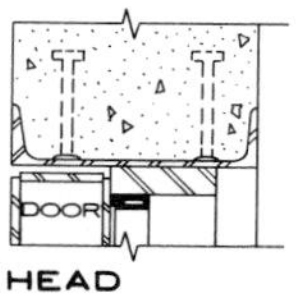

DOOR

**HEAD**

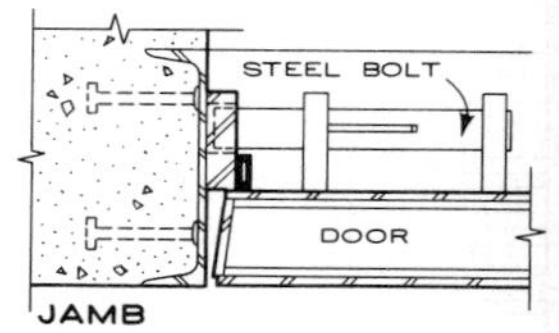

STEEL BOLT
DOOR

**JAMB**

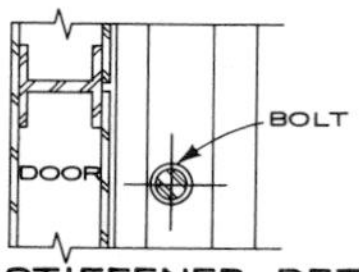

ROLLER STRIP

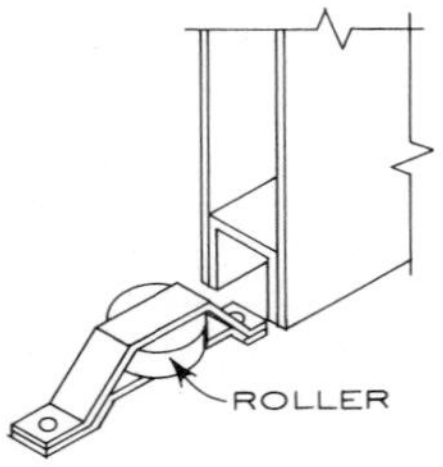

ROLLER

**FLOOR GUIDE #1**

ROLLER

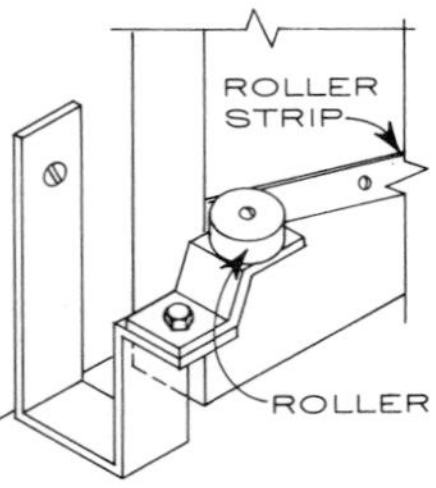

**FLOOR GUIDE #2**

**NOTE**

Specifications for metal door assemblies used as fire doors vary from code to code. Most requirements are based on ASTM E-152 or Underwriters Laboratories (UL- 36) standards. Requirements vary for openings in exterior walls, in fire walls, by building occupancy, and by amount of glass in the door itself.

Salts used for deicing may cause corrosion of aluminum frames and walls.

BOLT
DOOR

**STIFFENER DETAIL**

BLAST DOORS ARE USED TO ISOLATE HAZARDOUS SECTIONS OF BUILDINGS TO PROTECT HUMANS AND PROPERTY. DOOR MUST BE ABLE TO CONTAIN BLAST, BUT REMAIN OPERABLE AFTERWARD. SOLID PLATE ALSO AVAILABLE.

**BLAST DOOR - COMPOSITE STEEL CONSTRUCTION**

Darrel Downing Rippeteau, Architect; Washington, D.C.
James W. G. Watson, AIA; Ronald A. Spahn and Associates; Cleveland Heights, Ohio

**SPECIAL DOORS**

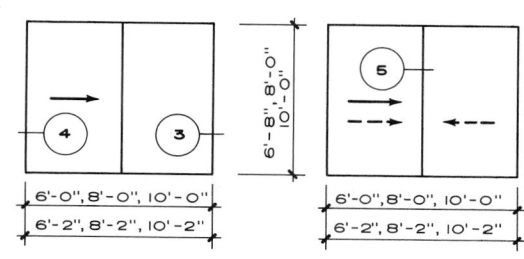
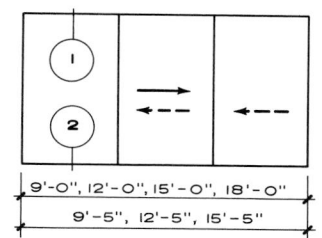
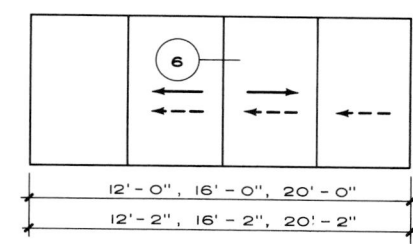

| ALUM. | 6'-0", 8'-0", 10'-0" | 6'-0", 8'-0", 10'-0" | 9'-0", 12'-0", 15'-0", 18'-0" | 12'-0", 16'-0", 20'-0" |
|---|---|---|---|---|
| WOOD | 6'-2", 8'-2", 10'-2" | 6'-2", 8'-2", 10'-2" | 9'-5", 12'-5", 15'-5" | 12'-2", 16'-2", 20'-2" |

## RESIDENTIAL SLIDING DOOR DIMENSIONS
DIMENSIONS SHOWN ARE NOMINAL STOCK SIZES

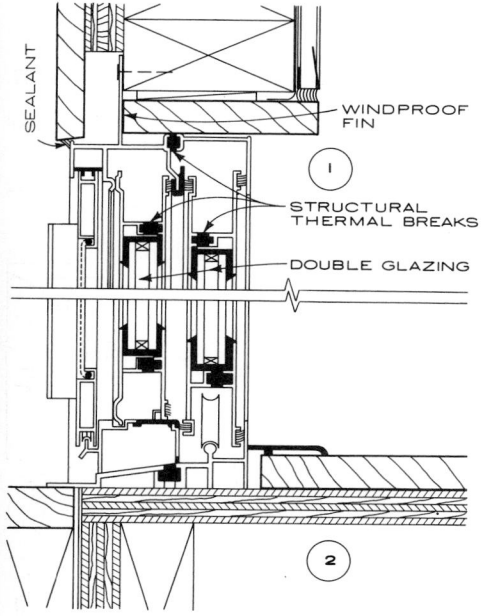

**NOTES**

1. Residential sliding door dimensions shown are nominal stock sizes. Custom sizes are available in accordance with individual manufacturing limitations and availability of glass sizes.
2. Details shown are for wood frame construction. Interior and exterior finishes and trim are optional. See manufacturer's data for typical installation details.
3. Tempered glass should always be used to reduce the chance of breakage and to avoid dangerous glass shards if breakage occurs.
4. Screens are available for all doors. Details show screens on the exterior for both the metal and wood doors. Consult individual manufacturer's literature to determine if screens are interior only, exterior only, or available either way.
5. Energy conservation is enhanced through the use of structural thermal breaks in aluminum sliding doors along with windproof mounting fins and double glazing. Standard aluminum sliding doors are also available.
6. See manufacturer's data for special sizes, locking devices, finishes, and specific limitations.

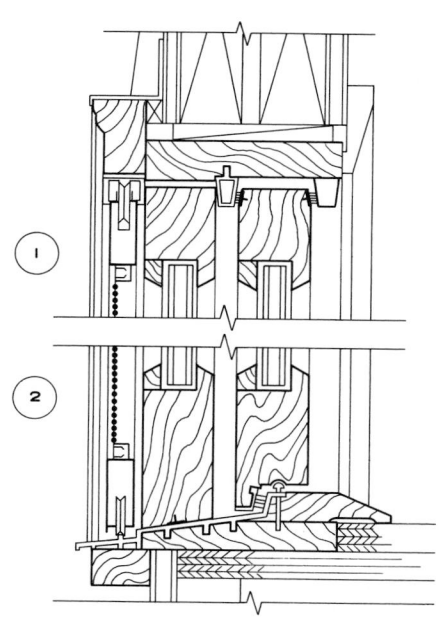

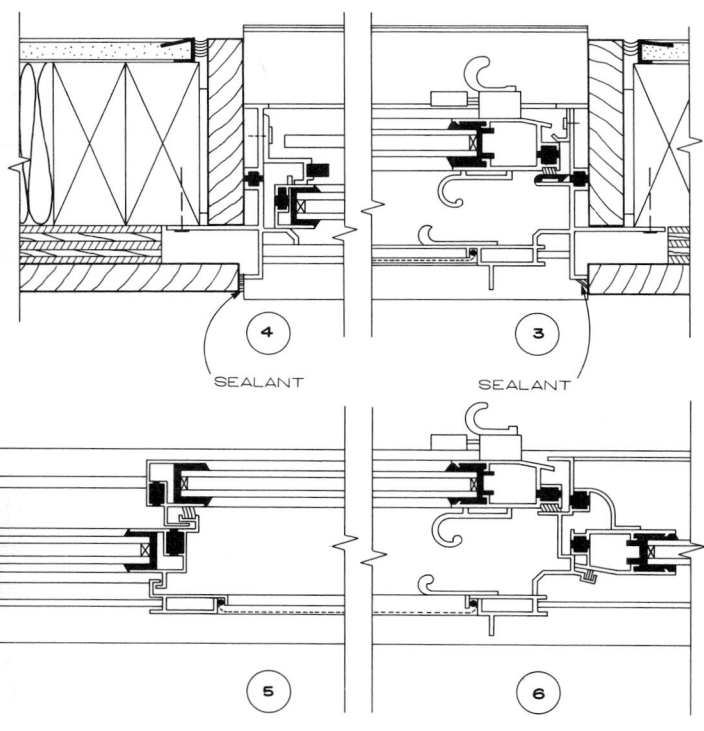

## ALUMINUM SLIDING DOOR DETAILS WITH ENERGY CONSERVATION FEATURES

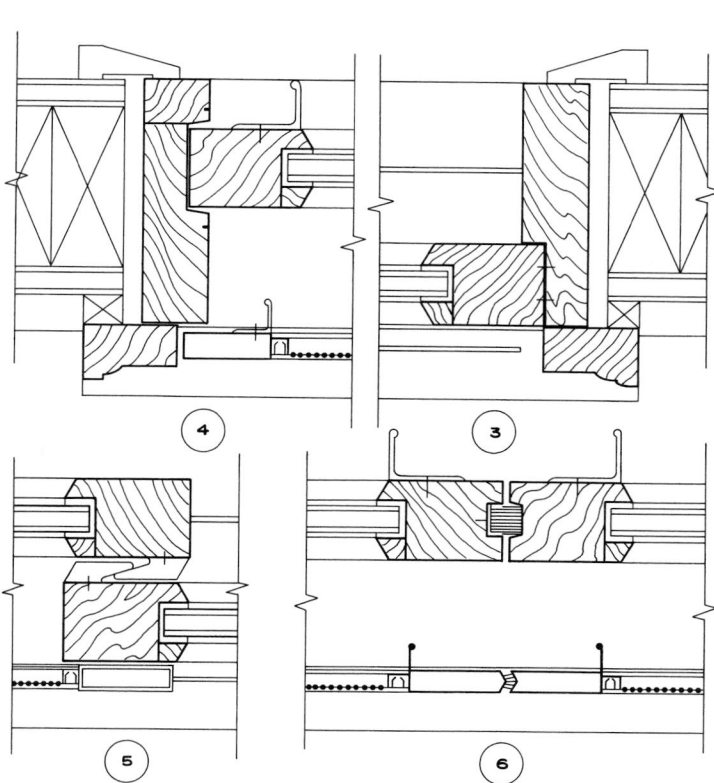

## WOOD SLIDING DOOR DETAILS

Leo A. Daly; Architecture-Engineering-Planning; Omaha, Nebraska

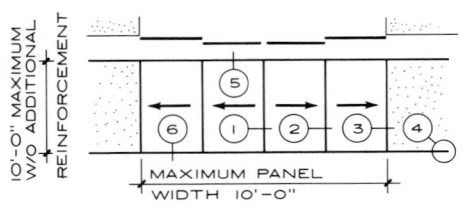

**BYPASS DOOR ELEVATION**

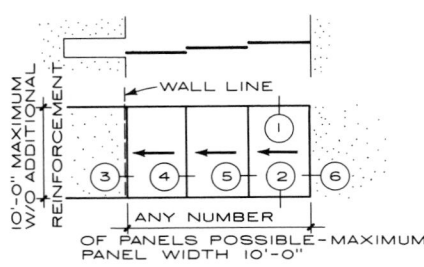

**POCKET DOOR ELEVATION**

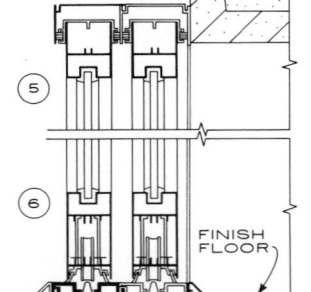

**MULTIPLE SLIDING DOOR ELEVATION**

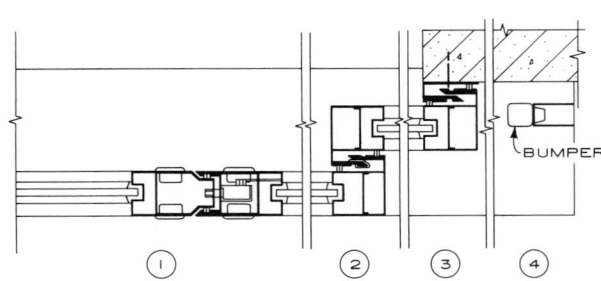

**BYPASS DOOR DETAILS**

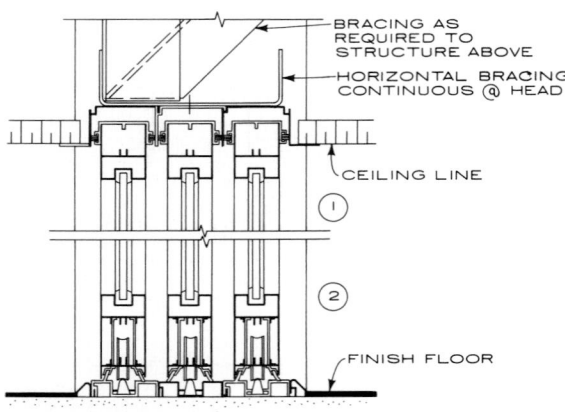

**POCKET DOOR DETAILS**

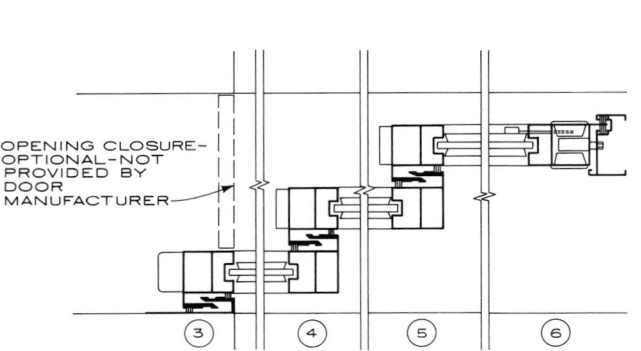

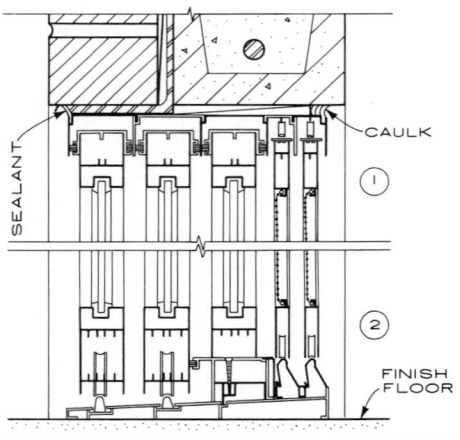

**MULTIPLE SLIDING DOOR DETAILS**

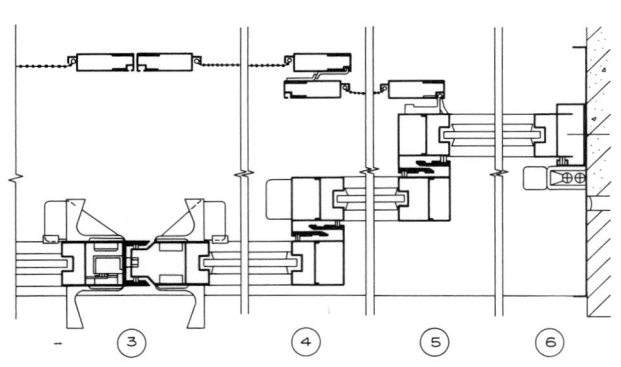

**NOTES**

1. Details shown are for masonry construction. Interior and exterior finishes are optional. Consult manufacturer's data for typical installation details.
2. Screens are available for all doors if required. Where shown, the details indicate screens on the interior. Consult specific manufacturer's literature to determine if screens are available for interior only, exterior only, or both. Glazing should be of safety glass, tempered, or insulating glass. Maximum manufacturable sizes of individual glass types will be the governing factor in determining maximum panel sizes. Consult industry standards for applicable data.
3. Consult manufacturer's data for available sizes, locking devices, and finishes.

Leo A. Daly; Architecture-Engineering-Planning; Omaha, Nebraska

**SPECIAL DOORS**

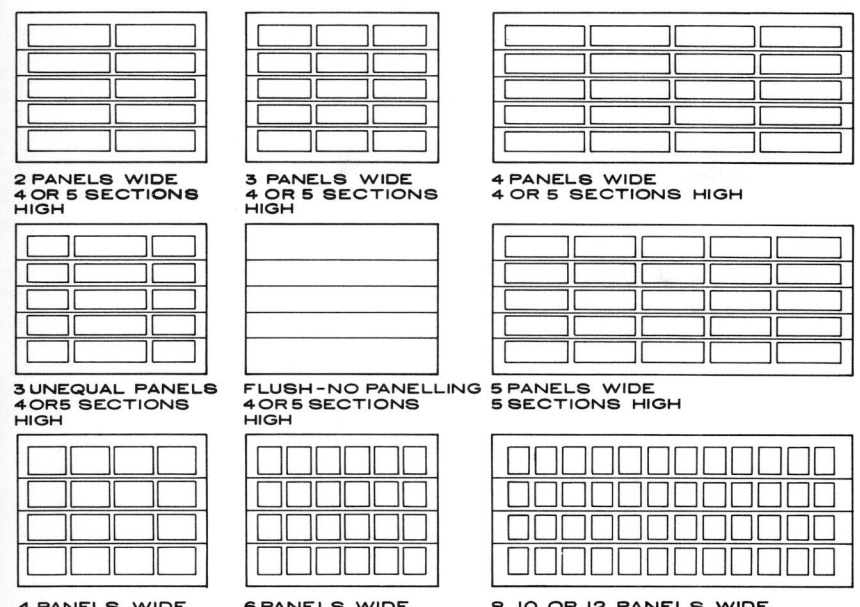

**2 PANELS WIDE 4 OR 5 SECTIONS HIGH**

**3 PANELS WIDE 4 OR 5 SECTIONS HIGH**

**4 PANELS WIDE 4 OR 5 SECTIONS HIGH**

**3 UNEQUAL PANELS 4 OR 5 SECTIONS HIGH**

**FLUSH—NO PANELLING 4 OR 5 SECTIONS HIGH**

**5 PANELS WIDE 5 SECTIONS HIGH**

**4 PANELS WIDE 4 SECTIONS HIGH**

**6 PANELS WIDE 4 SECTIONS HIGH**

**8, 10, OR 12 PANELS WIDE 4 SECTIONS HIGH**

Panel and section dimensions are set in the factory to provide overall door dimensions that meet the design requirements. Manufacturers will recommend the optimum number of panels and sections to best accommodate specific dimensional ranges. Heights range up to 20 ft, widths to 30 ft (approximate).

## WOOD DOORS STANDARD STOCK DESIGNS

**NOTE**

Glazed panels may be located as desired. 3 section doors also available. Other stock designs and sizes available varying with manufacturers.

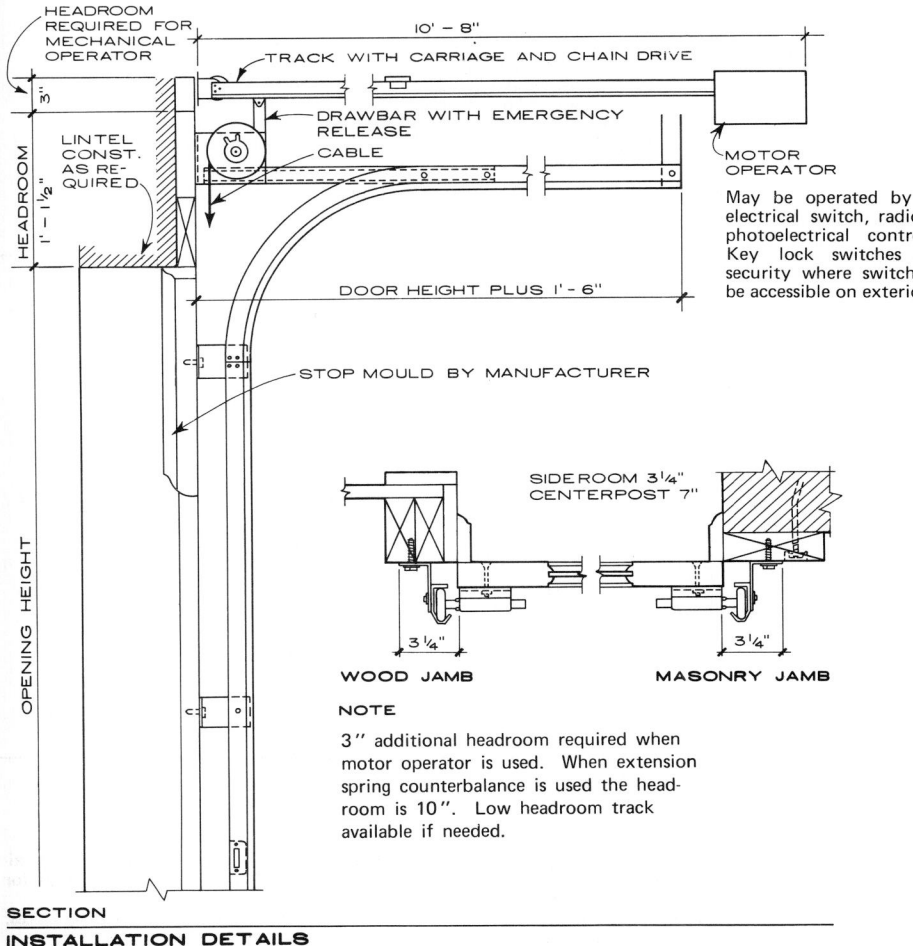

May be operated by remote electrical switch, radio signal, photoelectrical control, etc. Key lock switches provide security where switches must be accessible on exterior.

SIDEROOM 3¼"
CENTERPOST 7"

**WOOD JAMB**    **MASONRY JAMB**

**NOTE**

3" additional headroom required when motor operator is used. When extension spring counterbalance is used the headroom is 10". Low headroom track available if needed.

**SECTION**
**INSTALLATION DETAILS**

Eugene Patrick Holden, AIA; Dale E. Selzer, AIA, Architect; Dallas, Texas

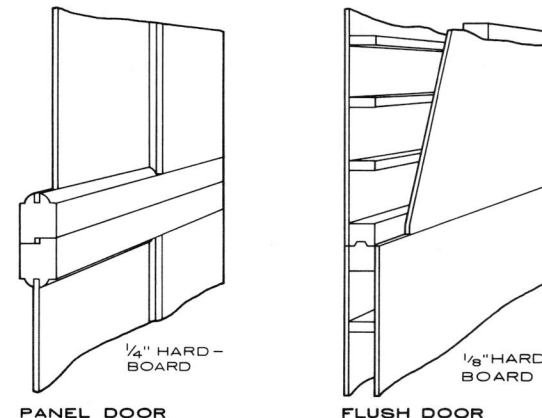

¼" HARD-BOARD

⅛" HARD-BOARD

**PANEL DOOR**    **FLUSH DOOR**

**TYPICAL DETAILS OF WOOD DOORS**
All doors available with torsion or extension spring counterbalance.

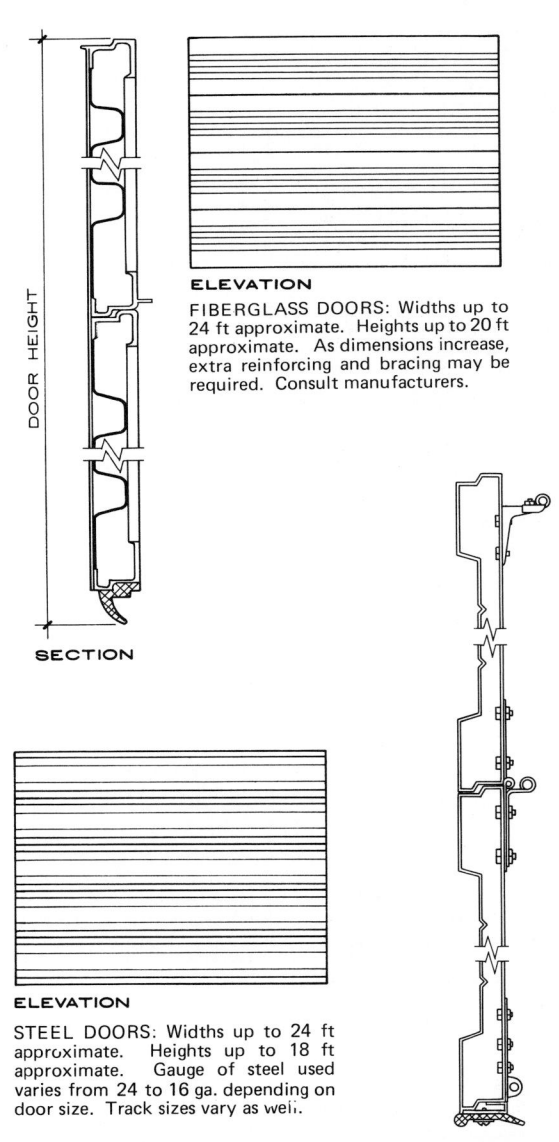

**ELEVATION**

FIBERGLASS DOORS: Widths up to 24 ft approximate. Heights up to 20 ft approximate. As dimensions increase, extra reinforcing and bracing may be required. Consult manufacturers.

**ELEVATION**

STEEL DOORS: Widths up to 24 ft approximate. Heights up to 18 ft approximate. Gauge of steel used varies from 24 to 16 ga. depending on door size. Track sizes vary as well.

**SECTION**

**FIBERGLASS AND STEEL DOORS**

**SPECIAL DOORS** 8

## WOOD PANEL DOOR

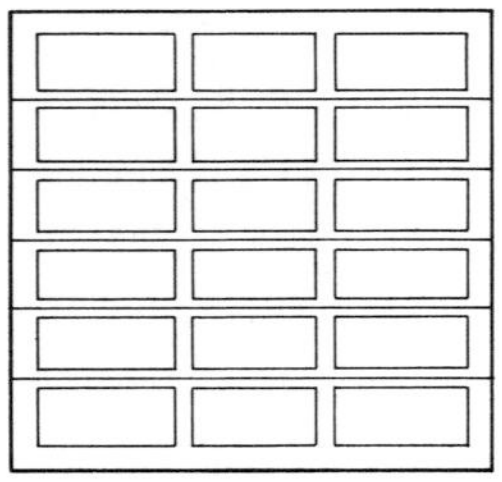

**SIZE LIMITATIONS**

2" Track—not to exceed 240 sq. ft., 24'—2" wide or 16'—1" high.

3" Track—not to exceed 600 sq. ft., 33'—2" wide or 25'—1" high.

Wood doors are easily repaired, but are more susceptible to moisture and heat damage than are metal and fiberglass doors.

**ELEVATION**

**NOTE**

Number of panels varies from 2 for an 8'—6" wide door, through 14 for widths from 30'—4" to 33'—3"; number of vertical sections varies from 4 for doors up to 8'—6" high through 13 sections for doors from 24'—2" to 25'—1" high. Number of panels and sections depends on increments in height and width established by manufacturer.

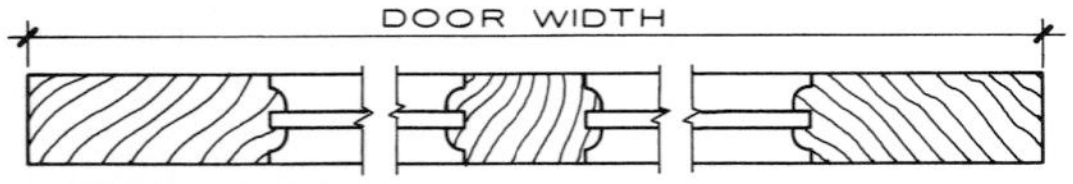

**HORIZONTAL SECTION** 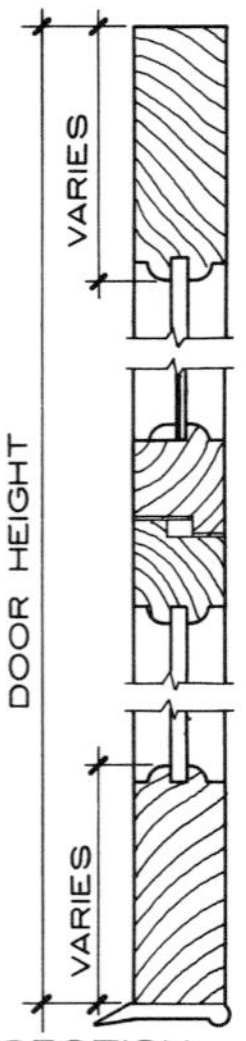    **SECTION**

## FLUSH WOOD DOOR

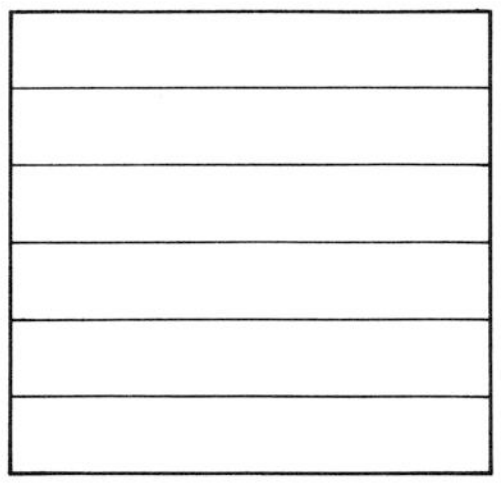

**SIZE LIMITATIONS**

2" Track—not to exceed 240 sq. ft., 24'—2" wide or 16'—1" high.

3" Track—not to exceed 600 sq. ft., 33'—2" wide or 25'—1" high.

**MATERIAL**

1/8" hardboard secured with waterproof adhesive on both sides of 1 1/2" wood frame. Pressure bonded between the hardboard walls are thick, tough waterproof core strips of styrofoam.

**ELEVATION**

**NOTE**

Number of vertical sections varies from 4 for doors up to 7'—0" high through 15 sections for doors from 24'—7" to 25'—1" high, depending on increments in height established by particular manufacturers.

**HORIZONTAL SECTION** 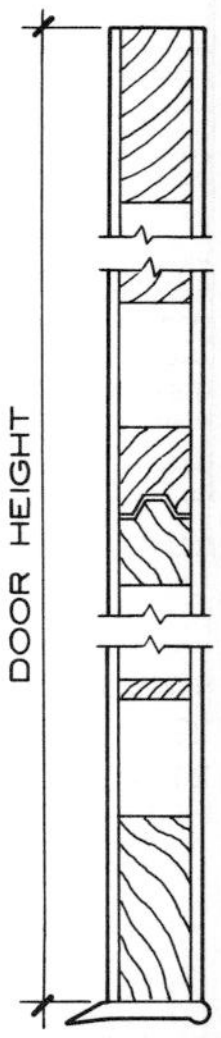    **SECTION**

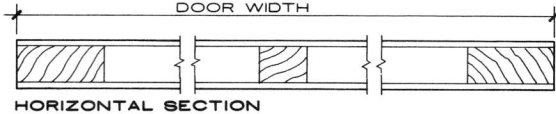

## PANORAMIC ALUMINUM

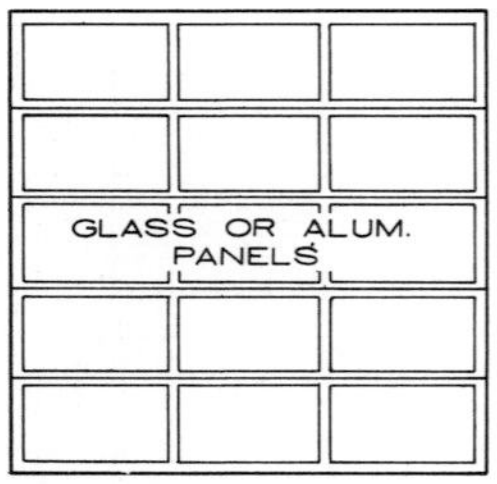

**SIZE LIMITATIONS**

2 in. track is not to exceed 240 sq. ft. or 20 ft. 2 in. wide or 16 ft. 1 in. high. Rails and stiles are of extruded aluminum. Stiles and rails are bolted with 1/4 in. rods for the length of the stile.

This and other doors are available with slats. Check manufacturer's literature.

GLASS OR ALUM. PANELS

**ELEVATION**

**NOTE**

Number of panels varies from 2 for doors up to 8'—11" wide, through 6 for widths from 18'—0" to 20'—2"; number of vertical sections varies from 4 for doors up to 8'—6" high, through 8 sections for doors from 14'—2" to 16'—1" high. Number of panels and sections depends on increments in height and width established by manufacturer.

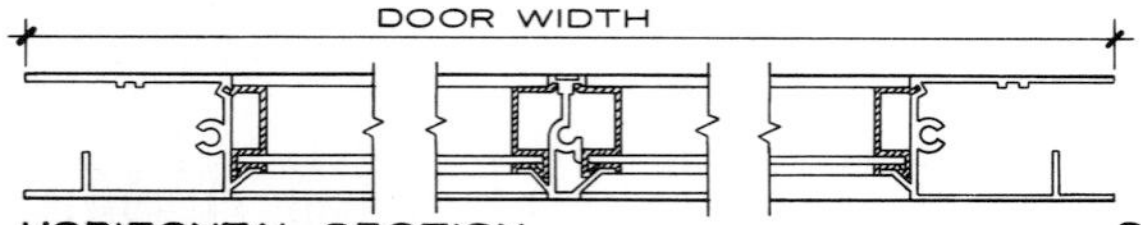

**HORIZONTAL SECTION** 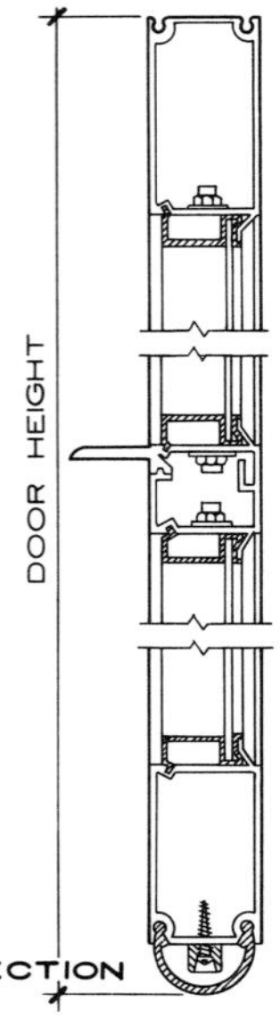    **SECTION**

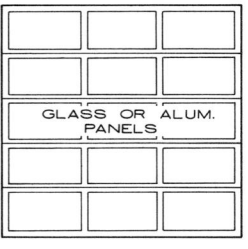

## HEAVY DUTY ALUMINUM

**SIZE LIMITATIONS**

2" Track—not to exceed 336 sq. ft. 24'—2" wide or 16'—1" high.

3" Track—not to exceed 384 sq. ft. 24'—2" wide or 16'—1" high.

Stiles and rails of extruded aluminum. Stiles are bolted to rails with 1/4" rods the length of the stile.

GLASS OR ALUM. PANELS

**ELEVATION**

**NOTE**

Number of panels varies from 2 for doors up to 8'—11" wide through 8 for widths from 21'—0" to 23'—11"; number of vertical sections varies from 4 for doors up to 8'—6" high, through 8 sections for doors from 14'—2" to 16'—1" high. Number of panels and sections depends on increments in height and width established by manufactures.

**HORIZONTAL SECTION** 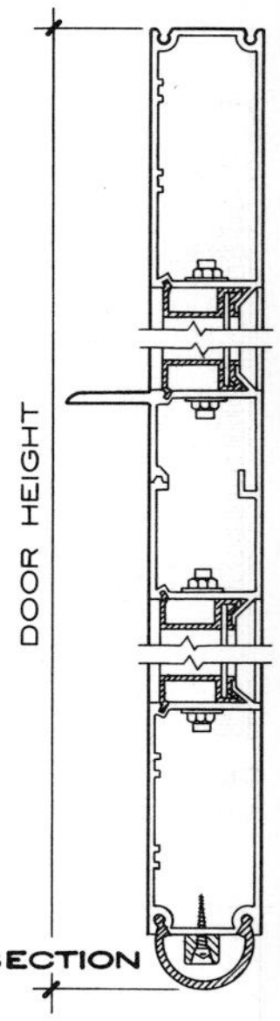    **SECTION**

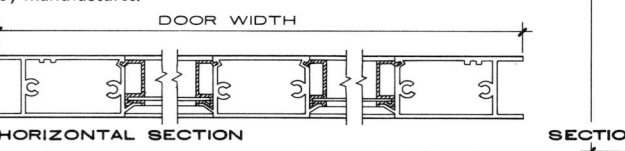

## 16 GAUGE STEEL DOOR

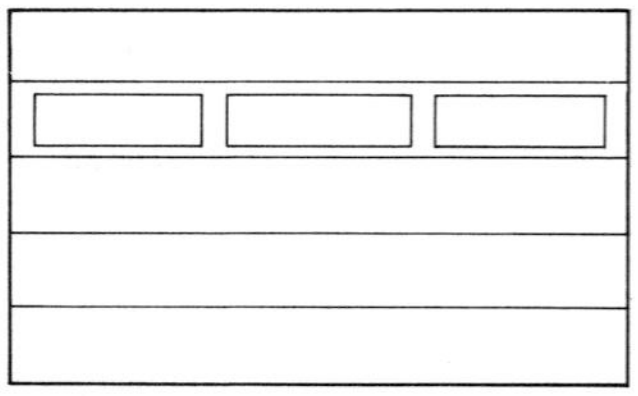

**SIZE LIMITATIONS**

2 in. track is not to exceed 180 sq. ft. or 16 ft. 2 in. wide or 14 ft. 1 in. high. 3 in. track is not to exceed 450 sq. ft. or 33 ft. 2 in. wide or 22 ft. 1 in. high.

This and other doors are available with varying amounts of insulation. Check manufacturer's literature.

**ELEVATION**

**NOTE**

Number of panels varies from 2 for doors up to 9'—11" wide through 10 for widths from 31'—11" to 33'—2"; number of vertical sections varies from 5 for doors up to 8'—0" high, through 14 sections for doors from 20'—11" to 22'—1" high. Number of panels and sections depends on increments in height and width established by particular manufacturers.

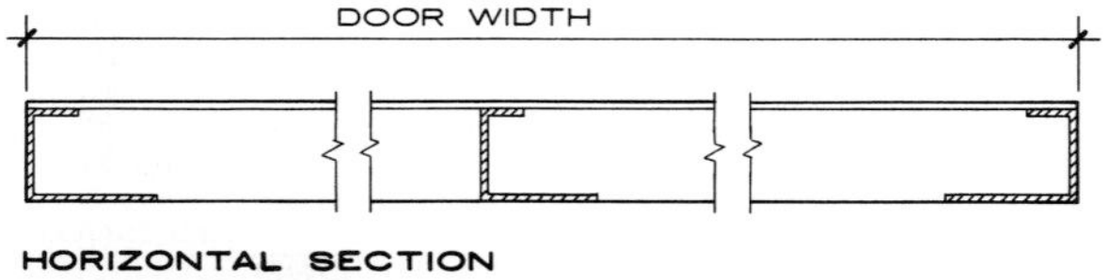

**HORIZONTAL SECTION** 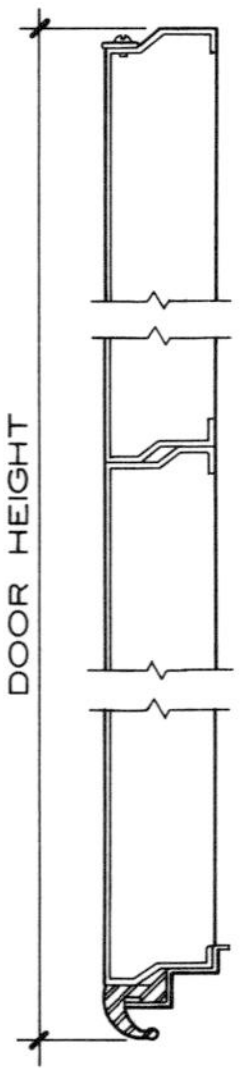    **SECTION**

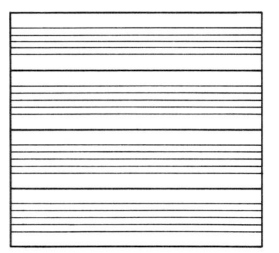

## FIBERGLASS

**SIZE LIMITATIONS**

2" Track—not to exceed 340 sq. ft., 26'—2" wide or 16'—1" high.

3" Track—optional.

Stiles and rails made of extruded aluminum.

Doors made of fiberglass fastened to both the rails and stiles.

**ELEVATION**

**NOTE**

Number of stiles varies from 2 for doors up to 12'—2" wide, through 7 for widths from 22'—3" to 26'—2"; number of vertical sections varies from 4 for doors up to 8'—1" high, through 8 sections for doors from 14'—2" to 16'—1" high. Number of stiles and sections depends on increments in height and width established by particular manufacturers.

STILE

**HORIZONTAL SECTION** 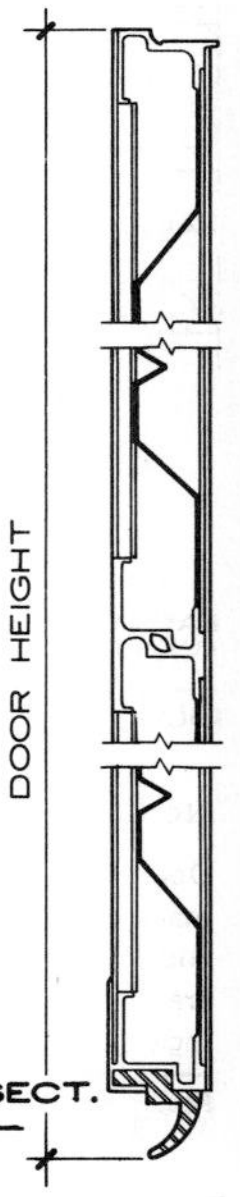    **SECT.**

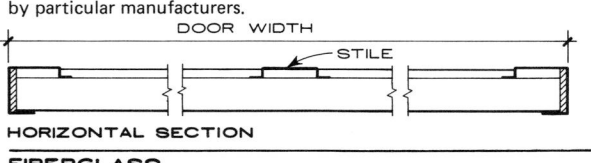

Eugene Patrick Holden, AIA; Dale E. Selzer, AIA, Architect; Dallas, Texas

**SPECIAL DOORS**

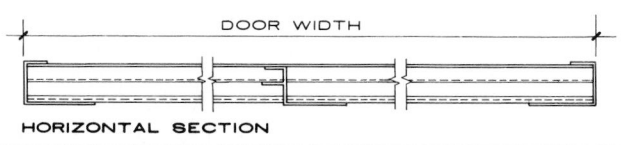

ELEVATION

| CENTER STILE | | SECTION | |
|---|---|---|---|
| DOOR WIDTH | NO. OF STILES | DOOR HEIGHT | NO. OF SECTIONS |
| to 8'-2'' | 2 | to 8'-1'' | 4 |
| 8'-3'' to 12'-2'' | 3 | 8'-2'' to 10'-1'' | 5 |
| 12'-3'' to 16'-2'' | 4 | 10'-2'' to 12'-1'' | 6 |
| 16'-3'' to 19'-2'' | 5 | 12'-2'' to 14'-1'' | 7 |
| 19'-3'' to 22'-2'' | 6 | 14'-2'' to 16'-1'' | 8 |
| 22'-3'' to 26'-2'' | 7 | 16'-2'' to 18'-1'' | 9 |
| | | 18'-2'' to 20'-1'' | 10 |
| | | 20'-2'' to 22'-1'' | 11 |
| | | 22'-2'' to 24'-1'' | 12 |

SIZE LIMITATIONS FOR STANDARD SIZES ON STANDARD TRACK:
20 gauge, 3 in. track—not to exceed 600 sq. ft., 33 ft. 2 in. wide or 24 ft. 1 in. high.
24 gauge, 2 in. track—not to exceed 340 sq. ft., 26 ft. 2 in. wide or 16 ft. 1 in. high.

DOOR WIDTH

HORIZONTAL SECTION

DOOR HEIGHT

SECTION

## GENERAL INFORMATION

1. Standard commercial doors are designed to 20 lbs. per sq. ft. wind load.
2. All doors are available with sash sections or sash openings in standard section.
3. Doors are available using 20 gauge or 24 gauge steel sections on the top and bottom and intermediate fiberglass sections.
4. Larger openings can be enclosed by using 2 or more doors with removable or swing-up center posts. When the center posts are removed or raised, the entire opening is clear.
5. Larger size doors can be manufactured with special engineering.
6. Consider the range of energy-conscious options now available, such as weatherstripping and anti-infiltration hoods.
7. In some applications doors may require specific fire ratings. Check local building codes.
8. Doors are available with built-in pass-through doors, vision panels, insulation, and many other options. Check manufacturers' literature for availability.

**COMBINED DOOR - 20 AND 24 GAUGE STEEL AND FIBERGLASS**

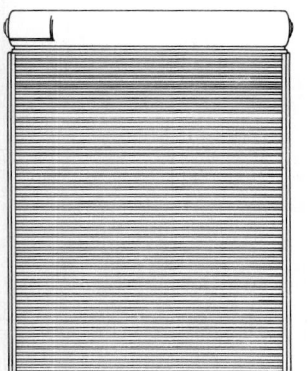

CURTAIN
Available in sizes listed below.

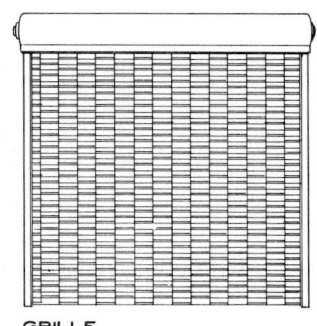

GRILLE
Maximum push-up grille sizes: 95 sq. ft. in steel, 130 sq. ft. in aluminum.

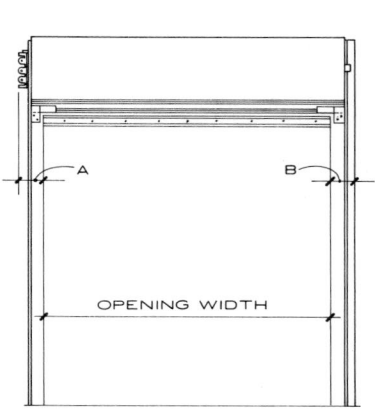

FRAME ELEVATION

OPENING WIDTH

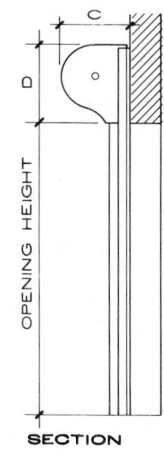

SECTION

OPENING HEIGHT

JAMB MOUNTED, STEEL

JAMB MOUNTED, ALUMINUM PREFAB.
OPTIONAL LINE OF FINISHED WALL OPENING

FLAT SLAT
Provides best weather protection.

ROLLED SLAT
Available in galvanized, stainless steel and aluminum.

FRONT OF HOOD MOUNTED OPERATOR
Refer to manufacturers' literature for dimensions.

FACE MOUNTED, WEATHER STRIPPED

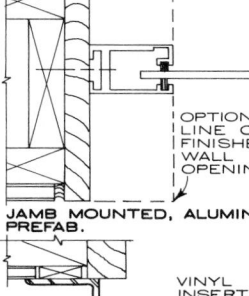

FACE MOUNTED WITH VINYL INSERTS TO EASE OPERATION
VINYL INSERTS

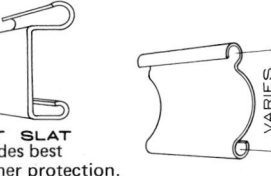

ROLLING GRILLE

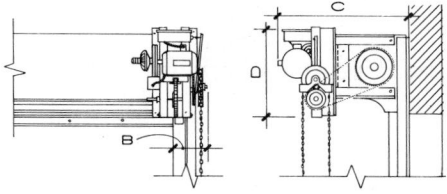

EXTRUDED ALUMINUM SLAT
For use with rolling counter doors.

WALL MOUNTED OPERATOR
Refer to manufacturers' literature for dimensions.

**GUIDE DETAILS (THESE VARY AMONG MANUFACTURERS)**

NOTE

Doors and grilles are manufactured in a wide range of sizes. Many makers provide standard products up to approximately 30 ft high and 33 ft wide. Larger items may require special engineering. Operator dimensions A, B, C, D, and E vary with size and type of rolling door. Small units may be obtained in preassembled form.

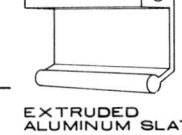

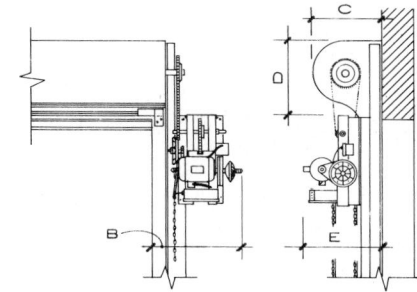

**ROLLING METAL DOORS & GRILLES**

Eugene Patrick Holden, AIA; Dale E. Selzer, AIA, Architect; Dallas, Texas

## SPECIAL DOORS

8

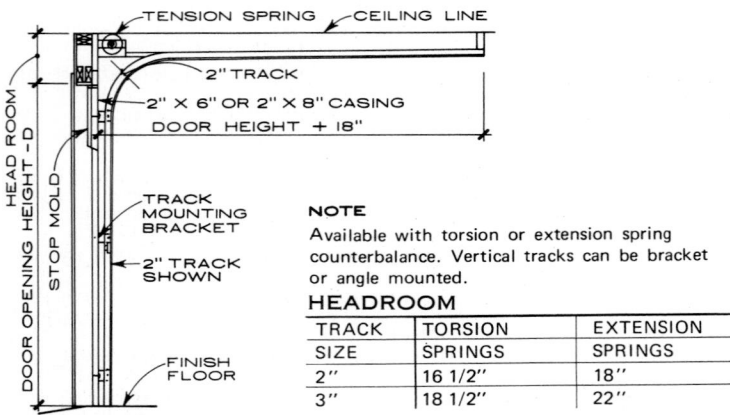

**STANDARD HEADROOM TRACK - 2" OR 3"**

NOTE

Available with torsion or extension spring counterbalance. Vertical tracks can be bracket or angle mounted.

### HEADROOM

| TRACK SIZE | TORSION SPRINGS | EXTENSION SPRINGS |
|---|---|---|
| 2" | 16 1/2" | 18" |
| 3" | 18 1/2" | 22" |

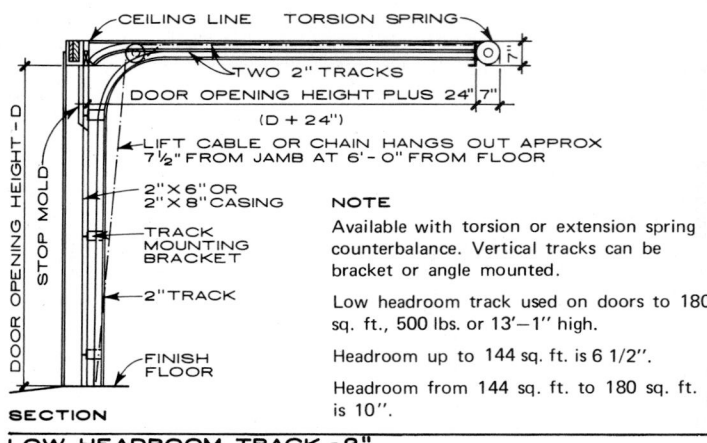

**LOW HEADROOM TRACK - 2"**

NOTE

Available with torsion or extension spring counterbalance. Vertical tracks can be bracket or angle mounted.

Low headroom track used on doors to 180 sq. ft., 500 lbs. or 13'-1" high.

Headroom up to 144 sq. ft. is 6 1/2".

Headroom from 144 sq. ft. to 180 sq. ft. is 10".

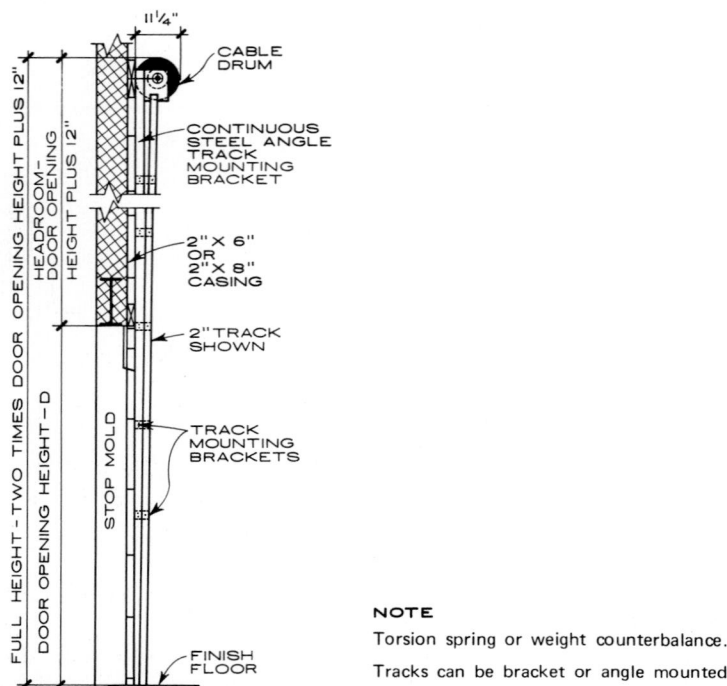

**FULL VERTICAL TRACK - 2" OR 3"**

NOTE

Torsion spring or weight counterbalance.

Tracks can be bracket or angle mounted.

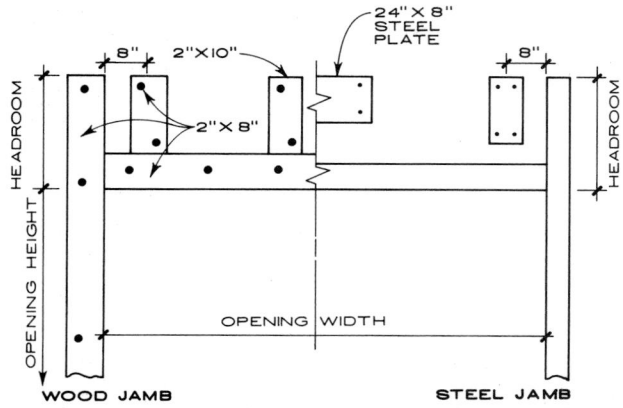

All pads and plates to be flush with wood or steel jambs.

Wide or heavy doors which require more than two springs will require pads additional to those shown in the above detail.

**INTERIOR ELEVATION OF DOOR OPENING**

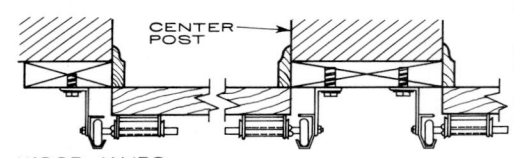

**WOOD JAMBS**

NOTE

For weight counterbalance doors, additional sideroom is required.

See note for asterisk at Table for Steel Jamb sideroom below.

### SIDEROOM

| TRACK SIZE | SIDEROOM | FOR DOORS | | CENTER POST |
|---|---|---|---|---|
| 2" | 3" | to 12'-1" high | | 6" |
| 2" | 3 1/2" | 12'-2" to 14'-1" | * | 7" |
| 2" | 4 1/2" | 14'-2" to 16'-1" | * | 9" |
| 3" | 5" | to 320 sq. ft. | * | 10" |
| 3" | 5 1/2" | over 320 sq. ft. | * | 11" |

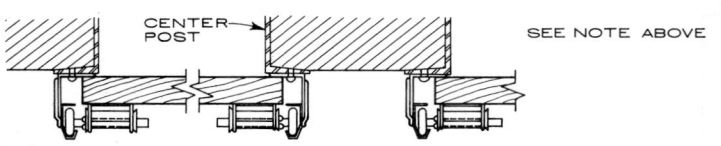

**STEEL JAMBS**

SEE NOTE ABOVE

### SIDEROOM

| TRACK SIZE | SIDEROOM | FOR DOORS | | CENTER POST |
|---|---|---|---|---|
| 2" | 4" | to 12'-1" high | | 8" |
| 2" | 4 1/2" | 12'-2" to 14'-1" | * | 9" |
| 2" | 5 1/2" | 14'-2" to 16'-1" | * | 11" |
| 3" | 6" | to 320 sq. ft. | * | 12" |
| 3" | 7" | over 320 sq. ft. | * | 14" |

\* 16 ga. steel doors over 168 sq. ft. Use 3" angle mounted track with 7" sideroom, 14" center post.

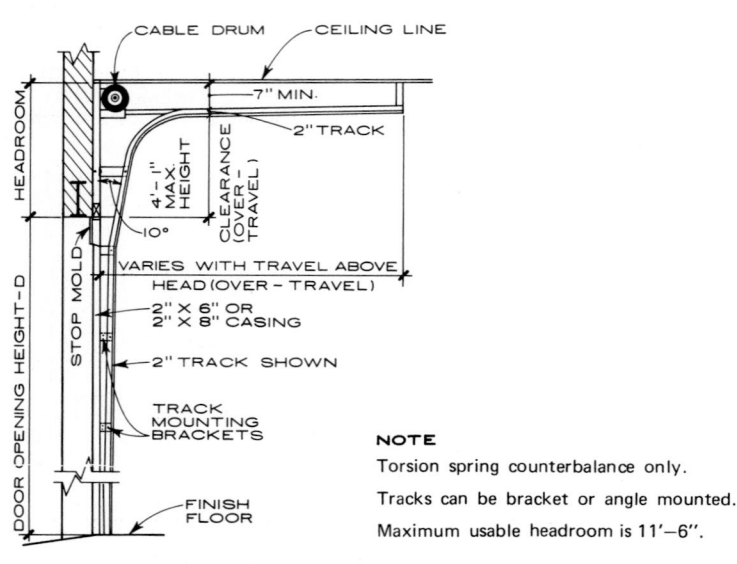

**LIFT CLEARANCE TRACK - 2" OR 3"**

NOTE

Torsion spring counterbalance only.

Tracks can be bracket or angle mounted.

Maximum usable headroom is 11'-6".

Eugene Patrick Holden, AIA; Dale E. Selzer, AIA, Architect; Dallas, Texas

 **SPECIAL DOORS**

NOTE

If door is not electric operated, a chain hoist is recommended for all doors exceeding 160 sq. ft. or 13'-0" high. For 16 ga. steel use chain hoist on doors exceeding 120 sq. ft. or 12'-0" high.

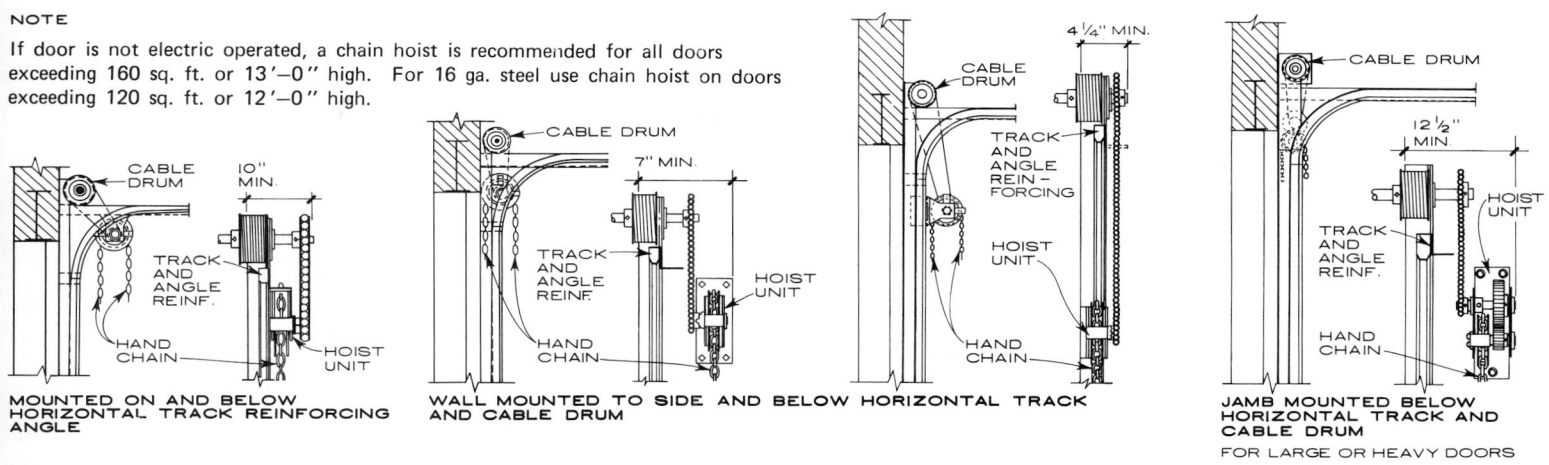

**MOUNTED ON AND BELOW HORIZONTAL TRACK REINFORCING ANGLE**

**WALL MOUNTED TO SIDE AND BELOW HORIZONTAL TRACK AND CABLE DRUM**

**JAMB MOUNTED BELOW HORIZONTAL TRACK AND CABLE DRUM**
FOR LARGE OR HEAVY DOORS

## CHAIN HOIST OPERATORS - MINIMUM SIDE ROOM CLEARANCE

NOTE: All chain hoist operators require additional sideroom clearance. Operator may be mounted on left or right side as shown; on the left greater sideroom is required. Dimensions shown are from door jamb to projection of operator.

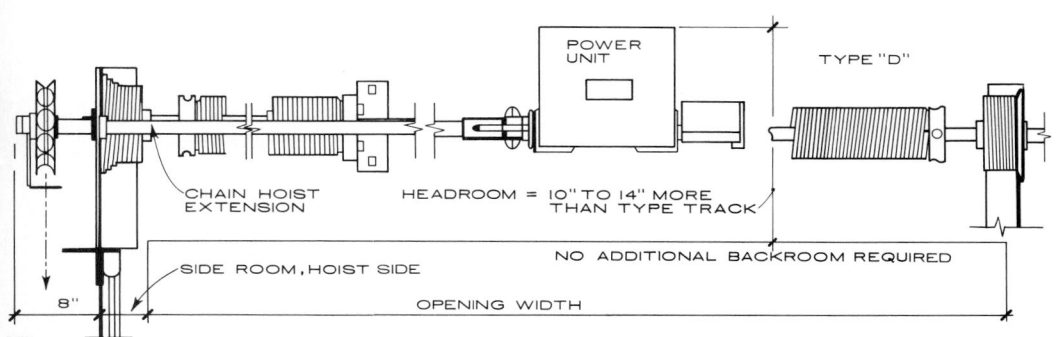

**CENTER MOUNTED OPERATOR**

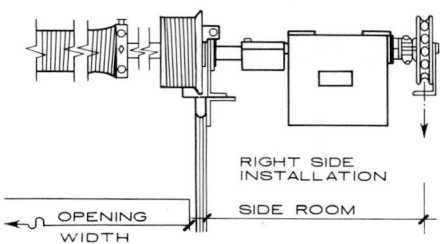

**SIDE MOUNTED OPERATOR**

NOTES
CENTER MOUNTED
Same principle as side mounted operator except power unit is located on front wall above door opening. No additional sideroom is needed. Needs from 10" to 18" additional headroom; 3" additional sideroom on chain hoist side.

NOTES
SIDE MOUNTED
Power unit is mounted on inside front wall to the right or left of the door and is connected to the crosshead shaft with a drive chain and sprockets or an adjustable coupling. Power is applied to the shaft to raise the door. The door closes by its own weight with the speed controlled by the operator.

No extra headroom required. Needs 20" to 24" of sideroom on mounting side.
Side mounted operators are available with direct coupled or chain drive, depending on installation condition.

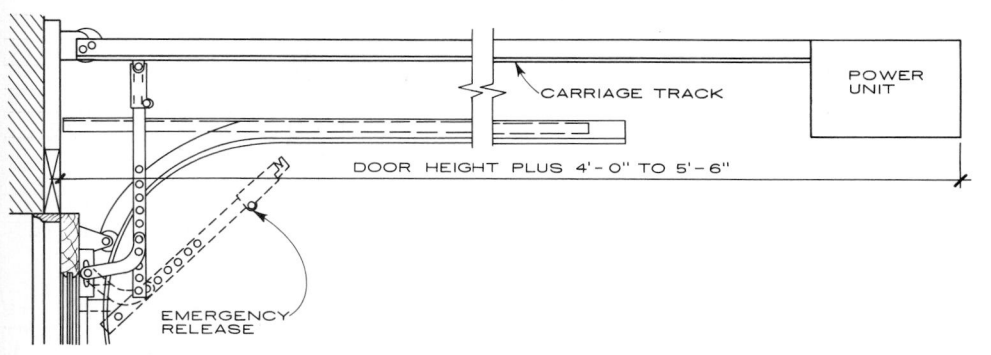

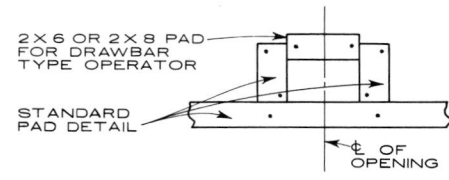

**PAD DETAIL FOR DRAWBAR TYPE OPERATORS**

**DRAWBAR TYPE OPERATOR**
NOTE
Power unit is mounted between, above and to the rear of horizontal tracks of door. A chain-driven carriage slides forward and back in its own tracks, which run from power unit to front wall above door. An arm linking the carriage and the door applies force to open and close the door as the carriage moves backward and forward. Door requires a minimum of 2" additional head room above tracks plus 1" to 3 1/2" more at power unit. No additional sideroom is required.

Drawbar type is not recommended for use on extra large doors nor with lift clearance track installations. Emergency chain hoists are not normally used on drawbar type operators.

## ELECTRIC MOTOR OPERATORS

Available in all standard voltages, frequency and phase. Control can be by 2 or 3 button push button station, pull switches, photoelectric, radio control (single or multiple), time delay closing and/or reversing or stop only safety switch. For Operator Selector chart see manufacturers data.

Eugene Patrick Holden, AIA; Dale E. Selzer, AIA, Architect; Dallas, Texas

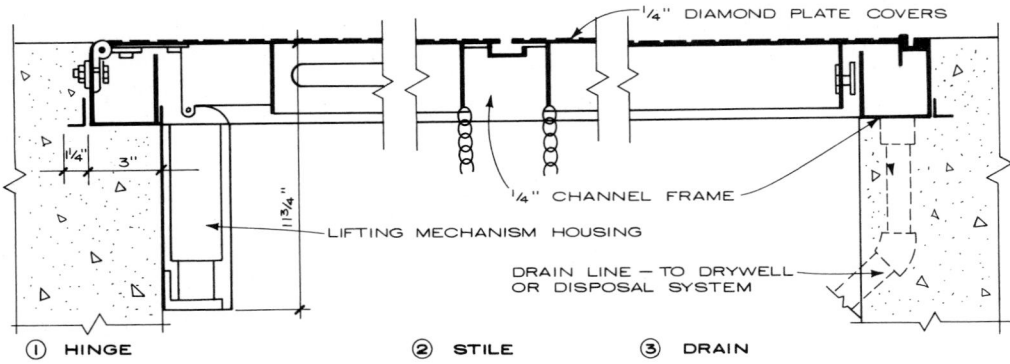

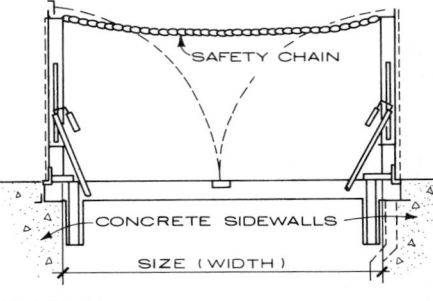

**SECTION**

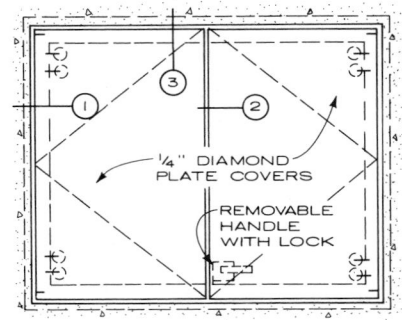

**PLAN**

**DETAILS**

## SIDEWALK DOOR

SIDEWALK DOORS are available in single and double leaf openings. Single leaf doors range in size from 2 ft to 3 ft 6 in. in 6 in. increments. Double leaf doors range in size from 4 to 6 ft in 1 ft increments. Special sizes are available.

Units are constructed in steel or aluminum. The door leafs are made of 1/4 in. diamond plate and are reinforced to withstand 300 psf of live load. Doors can be reinforced for greater loading conditions. The channel frames are made of 1/4 in. steel or aluminum with an anchor flange around the perimeter. Each door leaf is equipped with forged brass hinges, stainless steel pins, spring operators, and an automatic hold-open arm with release handle and is locked with a concealed snap lock. A drain coupling is provided to drain the internal gutter system. Safety chains are required to protect the opening.

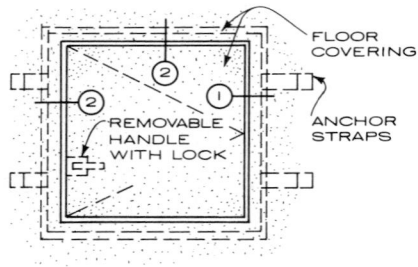

**PLAN**

## FLOOR DOOR

FLOOR DOORS are available in single and double leaf openings. Single leaf doors range in size from 2 ft to 3 ft 6 in. in 6 in. increments. Double leaf doors range in size from 4 to 6 ft in 1 ft increments. Special sizes are available. Units are constructed in aluminum.

The door leafs are made of 1/4 in. extruded aluminum. Doors are made to accept 1/8 or 3/16 in. flooring. Each leaf has cast steel hinges and torsion bars. Doors open by a removable handle and are locked with a concealed snap lock.

## CELLAR DOOR

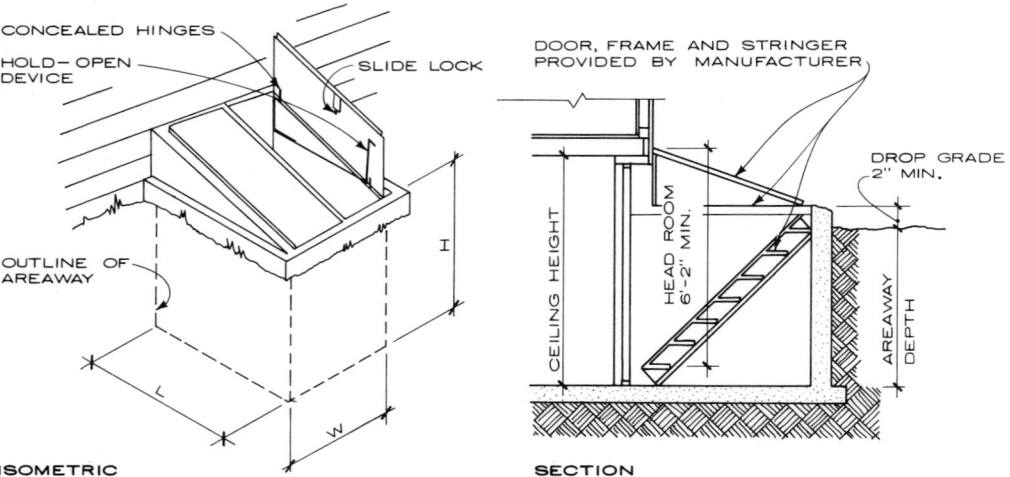

**ISOMETRIC**

**SECTION**

### CELLAR DOOR DIMENSIONS

| TYPE | LENGTH | WIDTH | HEIGHT |
|------|--------|-------|--------|
| S/L | 3'-7 1/4" | 4'-3" | 4'-4" |
| O | 4'-10" | 3'-11" | 2'-6" |
| B | 5'-4" | 4'-3" | 1'-10" |
| C | 6'-0" | 4'-7" | 1'-7 1/2" |

### AREAWAY DIMENSIONS (INSIDE)

| TYPE | LENGTH | WIDTH | HEIGHT |
|------|--------|-------|--------|
| S/L | 3'-4" | 3'-8" | 3'-5 1/4" |
| O | 4'-6" | 3'-4" | 4'-9 3/4" |
| B | 5'-0" | 3'-8" | 5'-6" |
| C* | 5'-8" | 4'-0" | 6'-2 1/4" |

*Type C door can have a deeper areaway dimension with the use of stringer extensions.

Ronald C. Olech; SRGF, Inc., Architects; Champaign, Illinois

**SPECIAL DOORS**

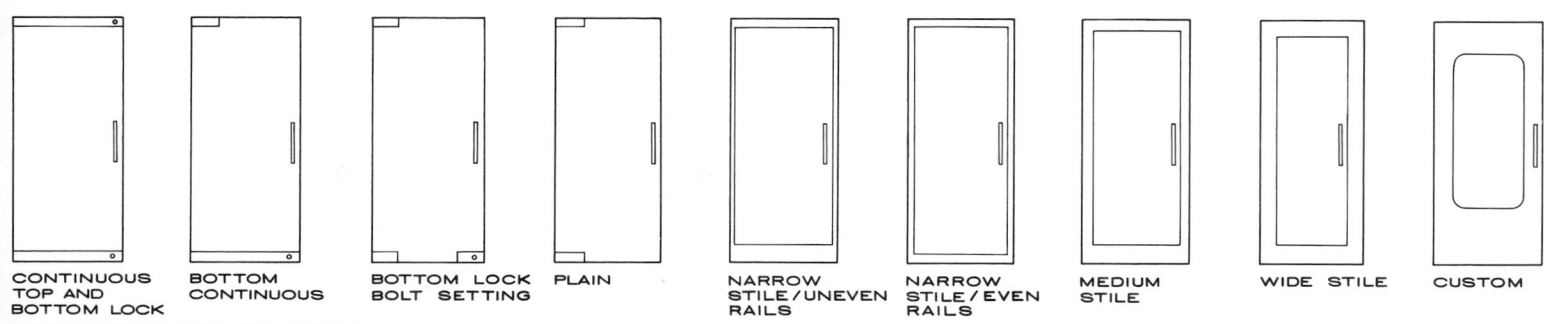

CONTINUOUS TOP AND BOTTOM LOCK  |  BOTTOM CONTINUOUS  |  BOTTOM LOCK BOLT SETTING  |  PLAIN  |  NARROW STILE/UNEVEN RAILS  |  NARROW STILE/EVEN RAILS  |  MEDIUM STILE  |  WIDE STILE  |  CUSTOM

**DOOR TYPES** – NOTE: DOORS WITH NARROW STILES SHOULD NOT BE USED IN HEAVILY TRAFFICKED AREAS.

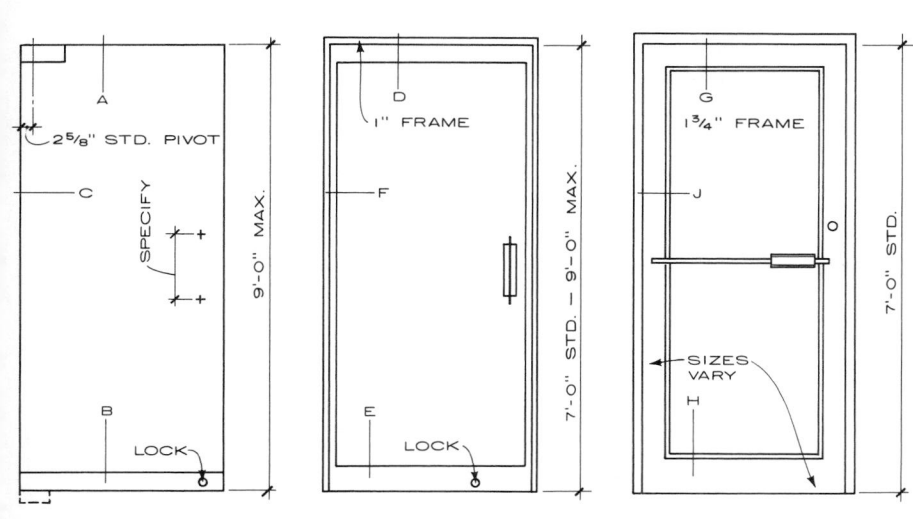

2⅝" STD. PIVOT

SPECIFY

9'-0" MAX.

A

C

B

LOCK

FRAMELESS DOOR

1" FRAME

D

F

E

LOCK

7'-0" STD. – 9'-0" MAX.

NARROW FRAMED DOOR

1¾" FRAME

G

J

O

SIZES VARY

H

7'-0" STD.

STANDARD FRAMED DOOR

**ELEVATION – TYPICAL GLASS DOORS**

CLOSED POSITION  |  PARTLY OPEN  |  COMPLETELY OPEN

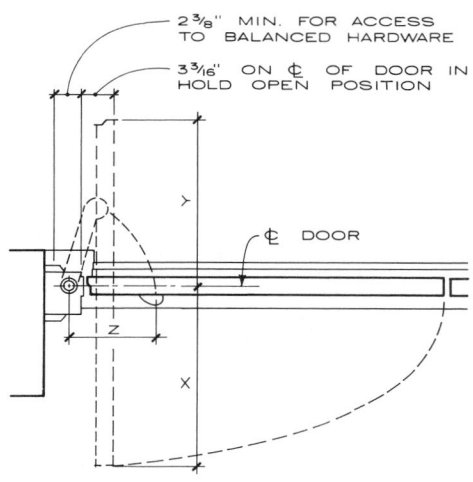

2⅜" MIN. FOR ACCESS TO BALANCED HARDWARE

3 3/16" ON ℄ OF DOOR IN HOLD OPEN POSITION

℄ DOOR

Y

Z

X

**PLAN**

**BALANCED DOOR**

## SPACE REQUIREMENTS—VARIOUS DOOR WIDTHS (IN.)

|   | 34 | 36 | 38 | 40 | 42 | 44 |
|---|----|----|----|----|----|----|
| X | 21¼ | 23¼ | 25¼ | 23¼ | 25¼ | 27¼ |
| Y | 12¾ | | | 16¼ | | |
| Z | 7⅛ | | | 8⅞ | | |

### NOTES

1. Consult applicable codes for safety requirements, glass size, thickness, and tempering.
2. Frameless ½ in. glass doors are available in clear, grey, or bronze tints in sizes up to 60 in. x 108 in. Frameless ¾ in. glass doors are available only in clear tint in sizes up to 48 in. x 108 in.
3. Consult manufacturer's data on structural adequacy for required loads and for frames and transom bars reinforcement.
4. Aluminum doors and frames are available in all standard aluminum finishes in sizes up to 6 ft. x 7 ft.
5. Frameless doors may not permit adequate weatherstripping. The use of frameless doors in exterior walls in northern climates should be evaluated for energy efficiency and comfort.

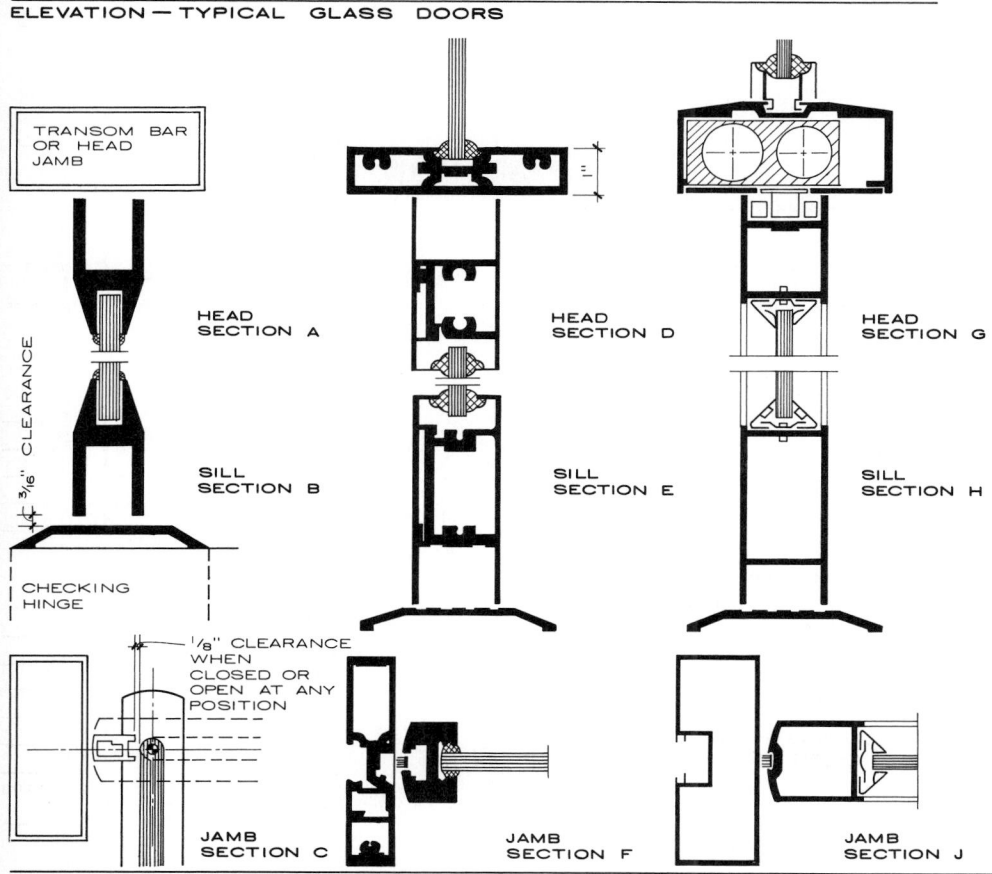

TRANSOM BAR OR HEAD JAMB

3/16" CLEARANCE

CHECKING HINGE

HEAD SECTION A

SILL SECTION B

1"

HEAD SECTION D

SILL SECTION E

HEAD SECTION G

SILL SECTION H

⅛" CLEARANCE WHEN CLOSED OR OPEN AT ANY POSITION

JAMB SECTION C

JAMB SECTION F

JAMB SECTION J

**DETAILS—TYPICAL GLASS DOORS**

G. Lawson Drinkard, III, AIA; The Vickery Partnership, Architects; Charlottesville, Virginia

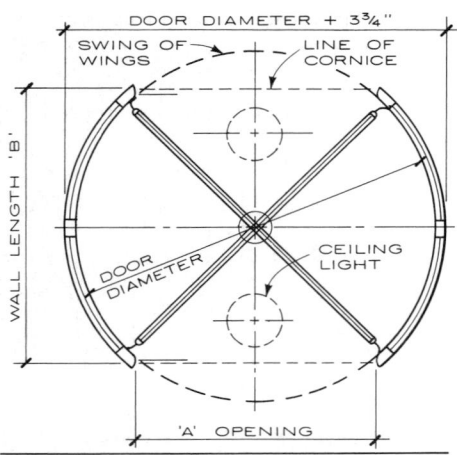

KEY TO TABLE DIMENSIONS

## STANDARD DOOR DIMENSIONS

| DIAMETER | A (OPENING) | B (WALL LENGTH) |
|---|---|---|
| 6'-6'' | 4'-5$\frac{1}{4}$'' | 4'-11$\frac{5}{8}$'' |
| 6'-8'' | 4'-6$\frac{11}{16}$'' | 5'-1$\frac{1}{16}$'' |
| 6'-10'' | 4'-8$\frac{1}{8}$'' | 5'-2$\frac{1}{2}$'' |
| 7'-0'' | 4'-9$\frac{1}{2}$'' | 5'-3$\frac{7}{8}$'' |
| 7'-2'' | 4'-10$\frac{15}{16}$'' | 5'-5$\frac{5}{16}$'' |
| 7'-4'' | 5'-0$\frac{3}{8}$'' | 5'-6$\frac{3}{4}$'' |
| 7'-6'' | 5'-1$\frac{3}{4}$'' | 5'-8$\frac{1}{8}$'' |

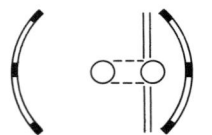
LOCKED 45° (COMMON)

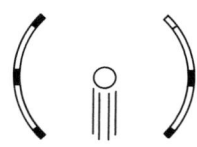
LOCKED 90° (RARE)

CENTRAL OPEN

ONE WING COLLAPSED FOR NIGHT SWING DOOR (RARE)

SIDE OPEN (NOTE: REQUIRES OVERHEAD SPEED CONTROL)

FULL PANIC COLLAPSED POSITION (ALL DOORS)

Curved sliding night door available for security if code permits. Enclosure walls and wings may be designed to roll aside.

**PLANS SHOWING LOCKED AND FOLDED WING POSITIONS**

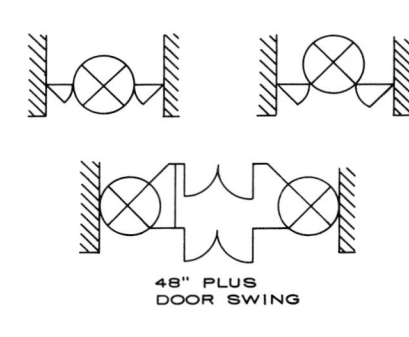
48" PLUS DOOR SWING

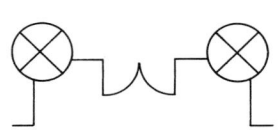

CURVED SLIDING NIGHT DOORS (IF CODE PERMITS)

48" PLUS DOOR SWING

**LAYOUT TYPES**

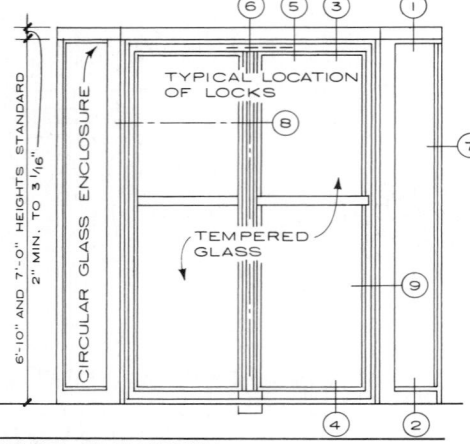

**DOOR ELEVATION**

## NOTES

1. Circular glass enclosure walls may be simply annealed $\frac{1}{4}$ in. glass. However, this varies with different government bodies. Some jurisdictions require laminated or wire glass. Tempered glass is not available for this use. Refer to Consumer Products Safety Commission Standards for Glazing.
2. Theoretical capacity each way = 2880 per hour. Practical capacity = 2000 per hour.
3. Doors fabricated from stainless steel, aluminum, or bronze sections are available. Wall enclosure may be all metal, all glass, partial glass, or housed-in construction.
4. Provide heating and cooling source integral with or immediately adjacent to enclosure.
5. Motor drive recommended with constant low speed.
6. For general use, use 6 ft 6 in. diameter. For hotels, department stores, or other large traffic areas, use 7 ft or greater diameter.
7. Codes may allow 50% of legal exiting requirements by means of revolving doors. Some do not credit any and require hinged doors adjacent. Verify with local authorities.

① SECTION—ENCLOSURE HEAD AT CEILING  ③ SECTION—WING HEAD AT CEILING  ⑤ DETAIL AT PIVOT HEAD  ⑥ CEILING LIGHT DETAIL

② SECTION—ENCLOSURE SILL AT FLOOR  ④ SECTION—WING SILL AT FLOOR

⑦ PLAN—ENCLOSURE AT MULLION

⑧ SECTION—WING AT CENTER SHAFT  ⑨ SECTION—WING AT ENCLOSURE TERMINAL

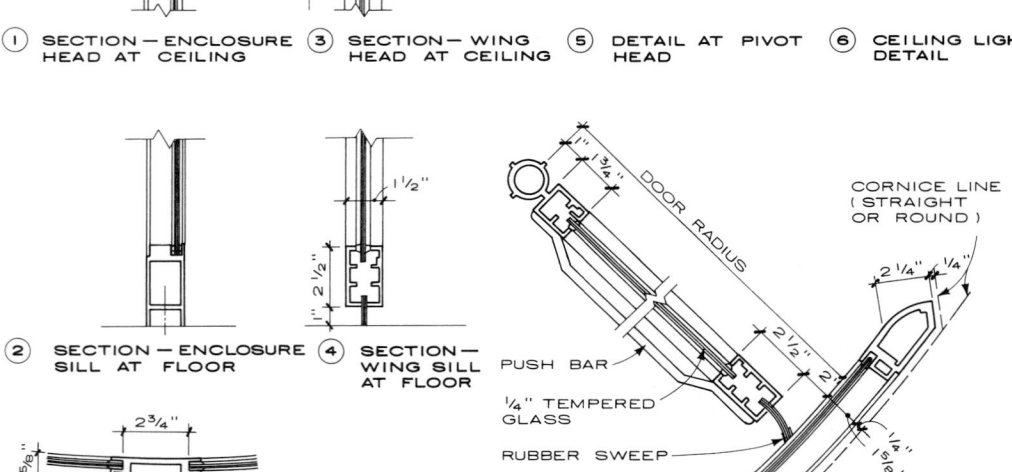

**TYPICAL DOOR DETAILS**

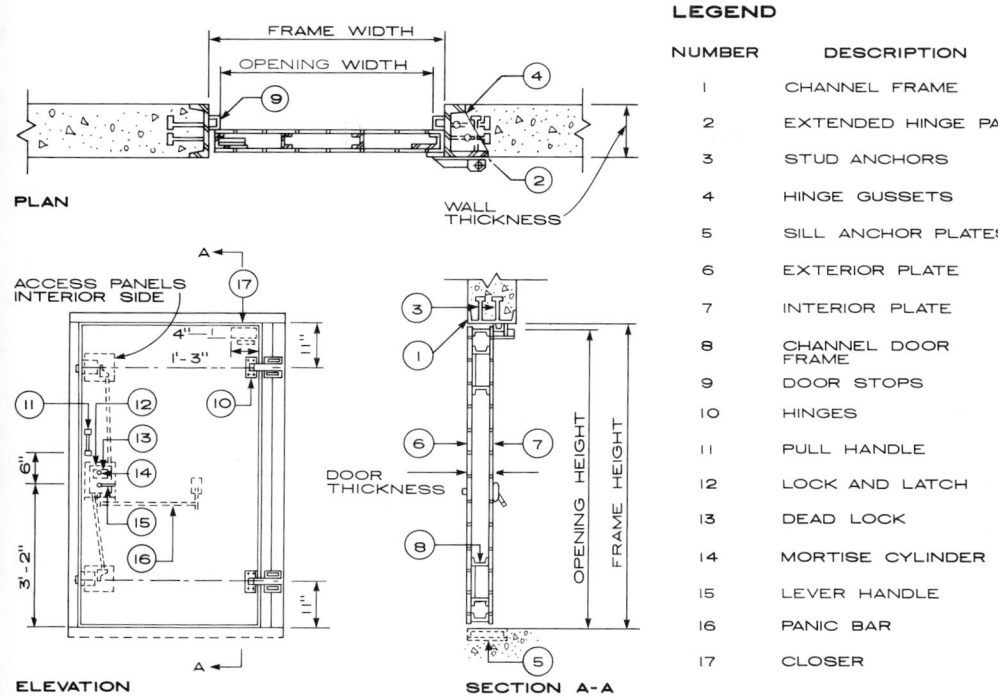

**LEGEND**

| NUMBER | DESCRIPTION |
|--------|-------------|
| I | CHANNEL FRAME |
| 2 | EXTENDED HINGE PAD |
| 3 | STUD ANCHORS |
| 4 | HINGE GUSSETS |
| 5 | SILL ANCHOR PLATES |
| 6 | EXTERIOR PLATE |
| 7 | INTERIOR PLATE |
| 8 | CHANNEL DOOR FRAME |
| 9 | DOOR STOPS |
| 10 | HINGES |
| 11 | PULL HANDLE |
| 12 | LOCK AND LATCH |
| 13 | DEAD LOCK |
| 14 | MORTISE CYLINDER |
| 15 | LEVER HANDLE |
| 16 | PANIC BAR |
| 17 | CLOSER |

**BLAST-RESISTANT DOOR DETAILS**

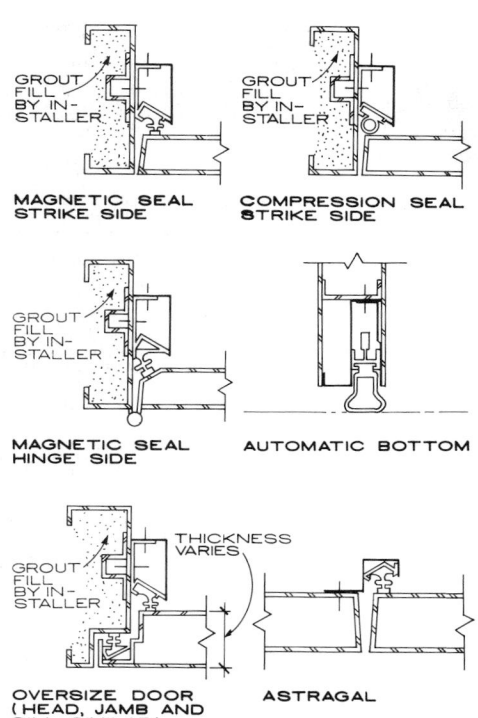

**SOUND-RESISTANT DOOR COMPONENTS**

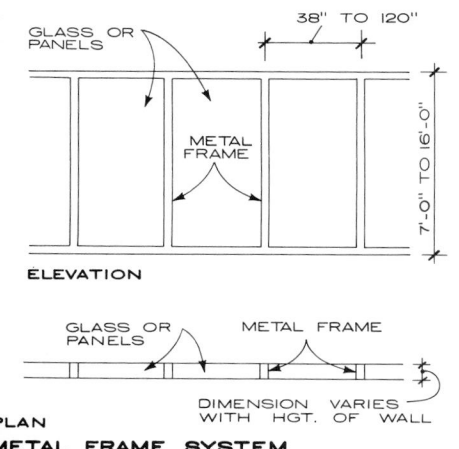

**METAL FRAME SYSTEM**

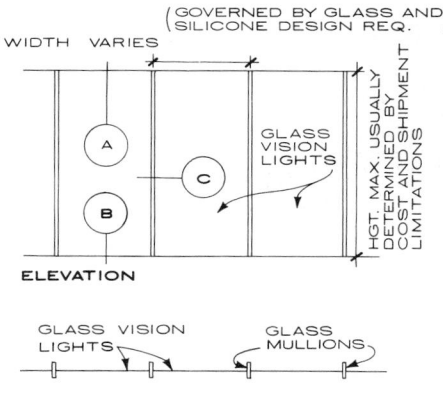

**ALL GLASS SYSTEM**

**NOTES**

All glass wall systems are engineered, custom fabricated combinations of clear glass vertical mullion lights with silicone structural sealant at the mullion and vision light interfaces.

Glass mullion systems replace conventional masonry, wood, or metal supports for large glass walls, and they may be used inside or out. No opaque materials are used except for simple metal sections at the head and sill. Engineers usually rely on ¾ in. thick mullions as the principal supporting element. The thickness and width of large vision lights for clear glass (or, under special conditions, tinted glass) are governed by glass and silicone design requirements at the design wind load or other loading requirements. When an all-glass system is proposed, reputable glass manufacturers with expertise in this type of construction should be consulted from the beginning.

Glass thickness varies with width, height, and loading conditions. Consult glass manufacturer for glass sizing recommendations for vision lights and glass mullions.

Local, state, and federal regulations regarding use and application of safety glazing materials and glass walls must be heeded.

Each component (other than glass) should be designed so that deflections normal to the wall plane at required loading will not exceed ¹⁄₂₀₀ of the component's clear span; but the deflection of glass-supporting members is limited to ¹⁄₃₀₀ of the distance over which such glass is supported. Deflections parallel to the wall plane must not exceed 75 percent of the glass edge clearances or other clearances provided between component parts. Calculations for such deflections are based on the combination of maximum direct loading, building deflections, thermal stresses, and fabrication and erection tolerances. Permanent deflections in this type of work are not permitted.

**AUTOMATIC DOORS (POWER OPERATED)**

Hand- or floor-mat-activated and pneumatic, hydraulic, or electric-powered automatic doors are available from various sources. This type of door is either horizontally sliding (both single and biparting) or pivotal (single or double). Both types usually have break out features from inside that allow them to be used as exit doors. Power-off safety features can be provided to ensure safe public passage, including for the handicapped. Minimum clear opening width for the handicapped is 32 in.

All glass used in doors, sidelights, and vestibule return lights must comply with safety glazing requirements. See "Glass Doors: Entrances."

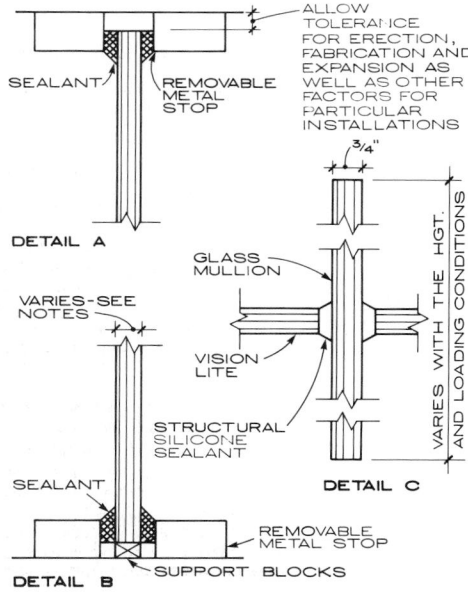

**ALL GLASS DETAILS**

**LARGE GLASS WALLS**

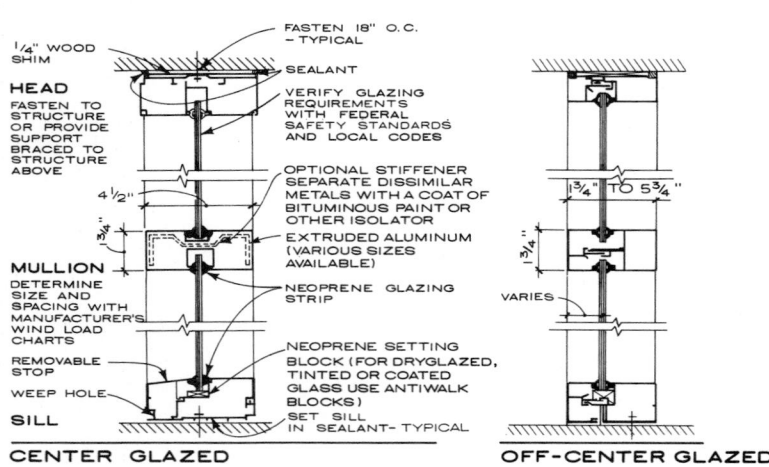

CENTER GLAZED

OFF-CENTER GLAZED

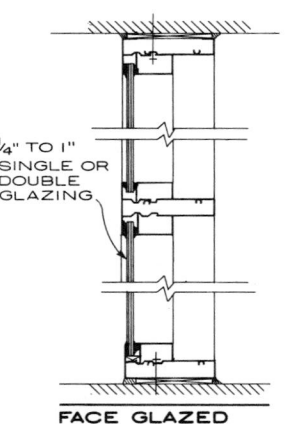

FACE GLAZED

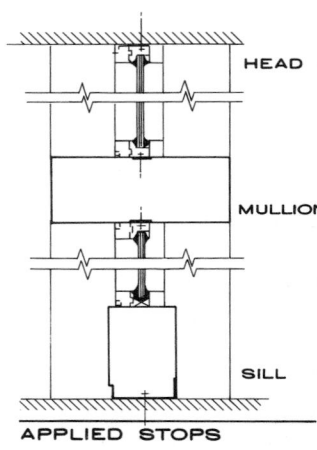

APPLIED STOPS

NOTES

1. Review tinted and coated glass applications and details to eliminate possibility of thermal breakage due to shading devices and shadow patterns.
2. Review setting block spacing, size, and hardness to prevent glass slippage and breakage.
3. Weep holes are required at sill for double glazing.
4. Refer to manufacturer's current recommendations for specific applications.
5. Other materials such as hollow metal or wood can be used for custom work and in saltwater atmospheres where aluminum will corrode.

6. Various aluminum anodized color finishes are available. Class I (0.7 mil) or Class II (0.4 mil) in black, bronze, or clear are standard with most manufacturers.
7. To extend life of aluminum and to reduce tendency of surface pitting, wash aluminum periodically with water and mild detergent.
8. Glass edges mitered at corners are not recommended. Maximum vertical span for butt glazing is 10 ft. x 8 ft. wide.
9. Mullions are clear glass. Tinted or coated glass lights may be considered for small areas. Maximum vertical span is 30 ft.

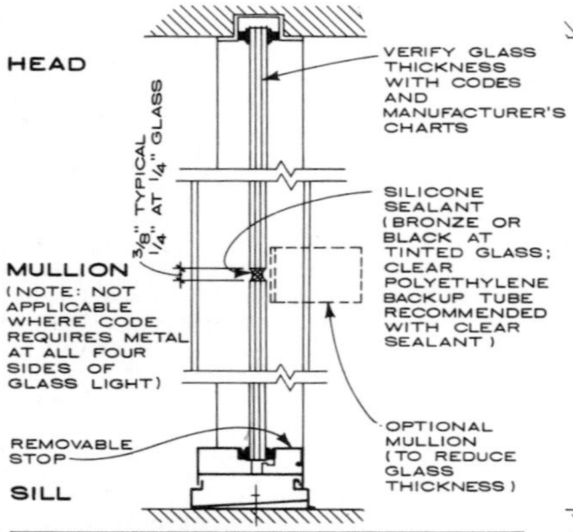

BUTT GLAZED WITH FLUSH HEAD AND JAMB

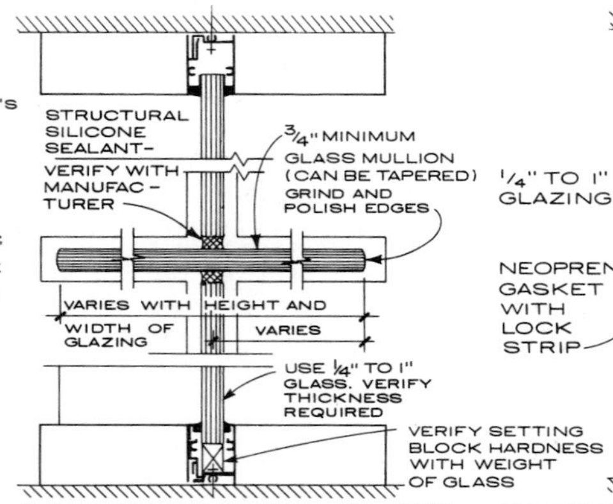

GLASS MULLION

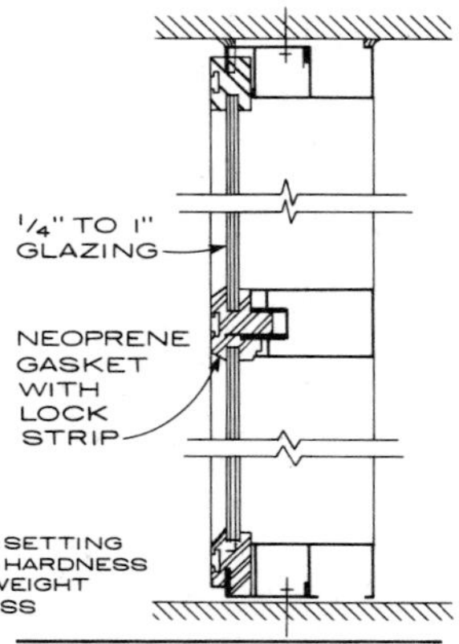

GASKET GLAZED

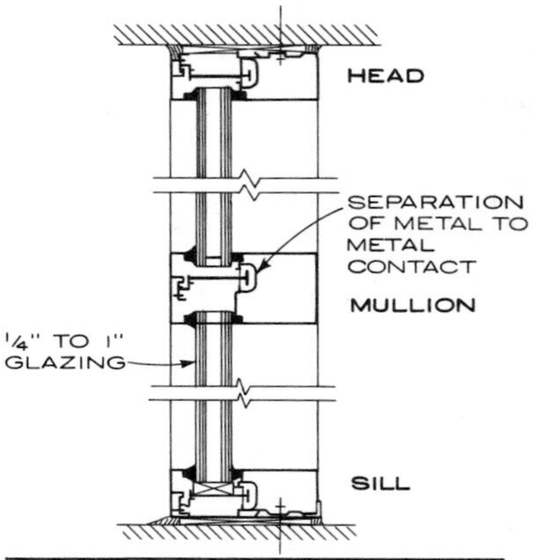

THERMAL GLAZING

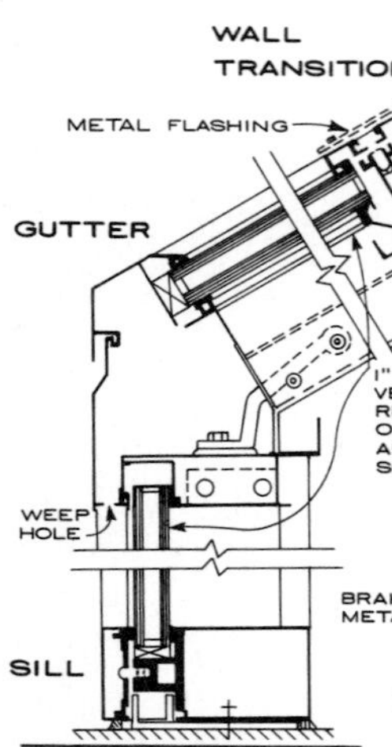

SLOPED GLAZING

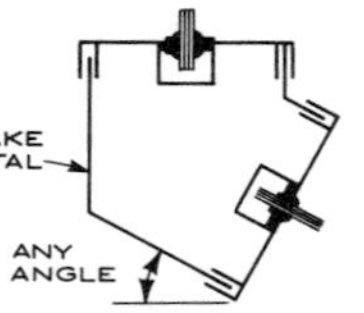

Care should be taken to protect the public from the possibility of overhead glass breakage.

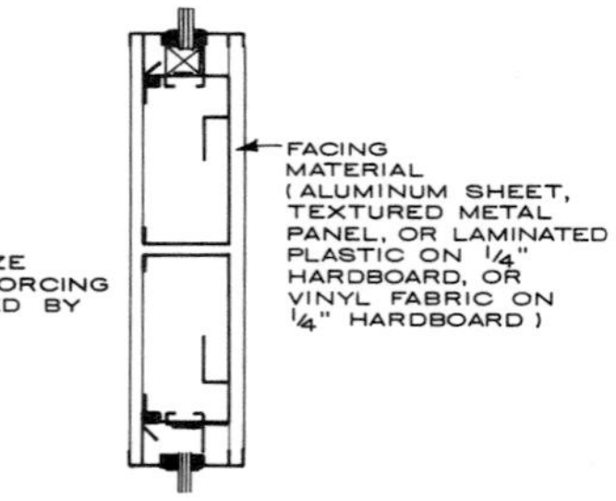

ANGLED CORNER

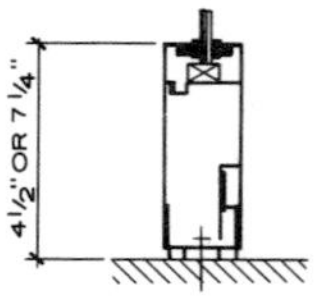

BULKHEAD SILL

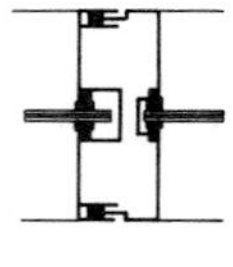

EXPANSION MULLION

HORIZONTAL MUNTIN

Higher bulkheads can be built up with aluminum tubing and applied stops. Locate expansion mullions 20 ft o.c.

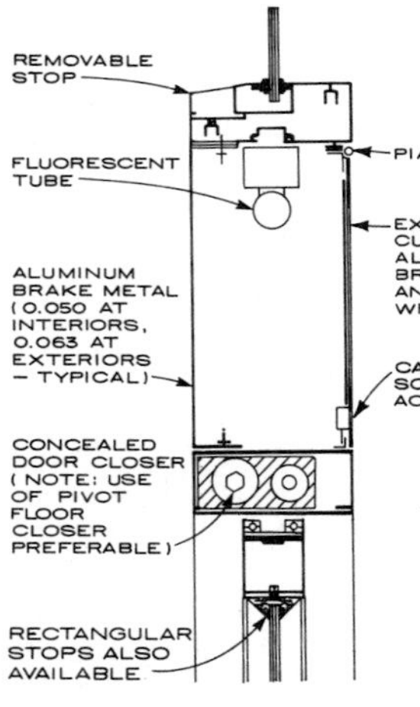

DOOR TRANSOM WITH CLOSER AND ILLUMINATED EXIT SIGN

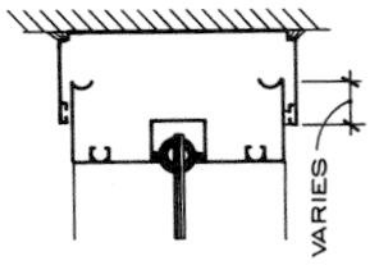

HEAD WITH RECEPTOR

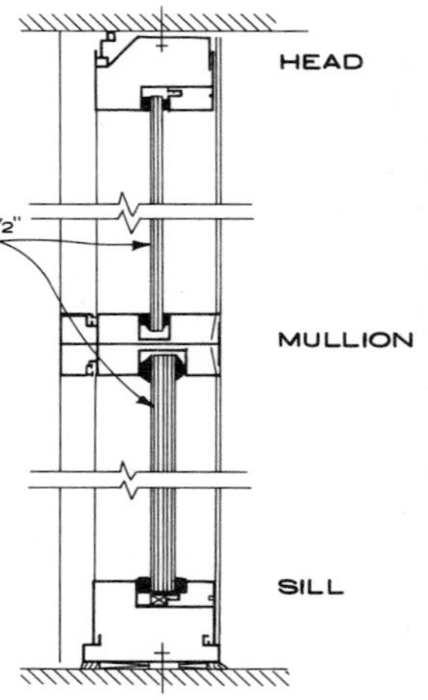

VARIABLE POCKET GLAZING

Use receptor for deflection or dimensional tolerance problems.

O'Leary Terasawa Takahashi DeChellis & Chaffin, AIA Architects; Los Angeles, California

 **ENTRANCES AND STOREFRONTS**

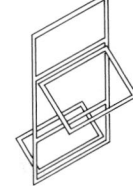

## PROJECTED

This is the workhorse of metal windows, available in many combinations of fixed and operating sash. Usually the lowest light will project in and the upper vents project out for maximum comfort and convenience. However, the flexibility of substituting fixed lights for vents and omitting muntins permits a variety of configurations.

Available in various weights, these windows are frequently used in institutional, commercial, and industrial projects. They will receive single or double glazing, from inside or outside. A wide assortment of hardware has been developed to meet almost every need, including special accessories for manual or mechanical operation of sash above normal reach.

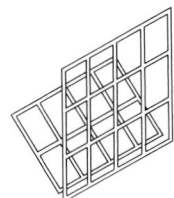

## SECURITY

Another variation of the projected sash, this window provides an integral grill permitting ventilation but restricting the size of an object that can pass through the window. Used in institutions requiring detention or tight security against outside entry, this sash minimizes the psychological, installation, and maintenance problems associated with a separate grill.

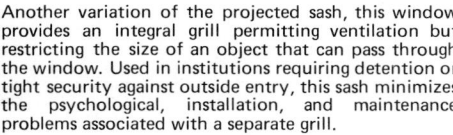

## DOUBLE HUNG

The traditional window of the United States wood window industry, metal double hung windows are finding wide application in projects where economy and flush window treatment are paramount. Single hung windows, which provide a fixed light in lieu of the top sash, are employed where economy is particularly critical. Triple hung windows are another variation, providing three operating sash for ease of operation in tall windows.

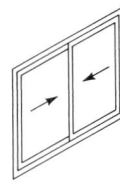

## SLIDING

Horizontally sliding or rolling sash provide flush interior and exterior wall surfaces without the need for counterbalancing hardware intrinsic in the double hung window. Initially they were popular as economical sash in residential applications. The sliding window industry has subsequently made substantial product improvements. Their inherent weatherproofing problems have been overcome with careful engineering and workmanship utilizing heavier members. Generally speaking, horizontally or squarely proportioned sash will operate more smoothly than tall, narrow sash. Most manufacturers apply full width insect screens on the exterior.

William A. Klene, AIA, Architect; Herndon, Virginia

## COMBINATION

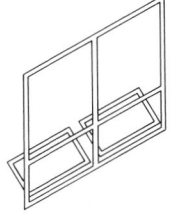

An economical variation of the projected sash that is used where light more than ventilation is desired. Size and height of this type of window will determine its usability as a fire escape in dwelling units and small offices. It may not be used as a fire escape in buildings classified for public assembly such as schools. Operating vents may be designed to project in or out. Insect screens pose different problems in both situations.

## CASEMENT

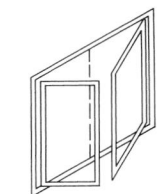

Consisting of vertically proportioned sash that swing outward, somewhat like a door, casement windows offer an aesthetic appeal not furnished by other window types. Insect screens are necessarily placed on the inside. Thus underscreen mechanical operators are usually provided. Otherwise the screen would have to be hinged or equipped with wickets for access to manual pulls.

## AWNING

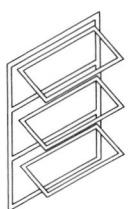

A window that has grown in popularity from its Southern residential origins, an awning window offers 100% ventilation combined with a degree of rain protection not attainable with casement sash. Awning sash can be fully weatherstripped and will readily receive double glazing or storm sash. Since their inherent horizontal proportions are not currently in vogue, their use has diminished recently. Insect screens are mounted in the interior, and rotary operators are standard.

## JALOUSIE

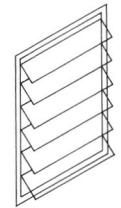

When the individual sash depth of the awning window is reduced to the point where it becomes, in effect, an operating louver, horizontal sash members are unnecessary. This has a profound effect on appearance and the ability to provide weatherstripping. Most often found in residences and commercial work, particularly where ventilation is most desirable, jalousie windows are not as widely used as most other sash. Sash widths are limited to the free span capability of the blade materials (usually glass, wood, or metal). Storm sash are readily available and, in some instances, are an integral part of the jalousie. Insect screens are necessarily placed on the interior, with operating hardware usually placed at normal hand height.

## PIVOTED

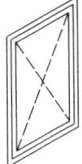

Popular in multistory, air-conditioned commercial buildings, horizontally or vertically pivoting sash are used only for maintenance. Though they usually rotate 90°, some manufacturers produce a sash that rotates 180°. Effective weatherstripping is mandatory in both cases. Wind action on walls of highrise structures must be considered in sash design. Top or side hung sash are also produced by some manufacturers for occasional opening of fixed sash.

## GENERAL NOTES

1. Most types are readily available in steel or aluminum. Steel sash tend to be more rigid and have thinner sight lines. They will be galvanized and/or bonderized and primed prior to finishing if so specified. While aluminum sash may be more economical and may offer greater inherent corrosion resistance, they have greater thermal expansion and conductance. Both are available in a variety of finishes.

2. All operating sash are regularly mulled to fixed sash, thus providing for economy, appearance, and a variety of functions.

3. Thoughtful selection of glazing material is as important as window type selection. Plastic glazing materials generally have greater coefficients of thermal expansion than glass, requiring deeper glazing legs and stops.

4. Effective thermal isolation requires double glazing (some manufacturers offer triple glazing or dual sash), continuous weatherstripping, and a "thermal break" in aluminum sash for colder climates.

5. Many manufacturers produce more than one quality window. SWI criteria for various weights of steel sash are useful in making comparisons. Current criteria for aluminum sash are based on performance of a tested specimen, hence require careful consideration unless the manufacturer has a well established reputation.

6. Many manufacturers have ceased using "stock sizes" and produce only custom work. Consequently, special shapes and configurations are easier to obtain, particularly in monumental or commercial grades. Some manufacturers also produce specialized windows that are sound resistant, contain venetian blinds, and so on. Since there is little correlation between the manufacturers' dimensioning systems, individual consultation is imperative where dimensions are critical.

7. Residential grades are somewhat more standardized, generally based on available dimensions of welded edge insulating glass.

8. Muntins, either simulating or forming small glass lights, are usually available for residential sash, if desired.

9. Installation details must take into account internal condensation in most climates. Hardware selection must consider insect screens as well as mounting heights, operating convenience, security, and so on.

10. Most codes have a minimum light and ventilation, minimum wind load resistance, and maximum thermal transmittance requirements, as well as minimum egress provisions from residential sleeping space. All these factors may affect window selection.

11. Prefinished window frames are generally installed after contiguous masonry rather than being built in.

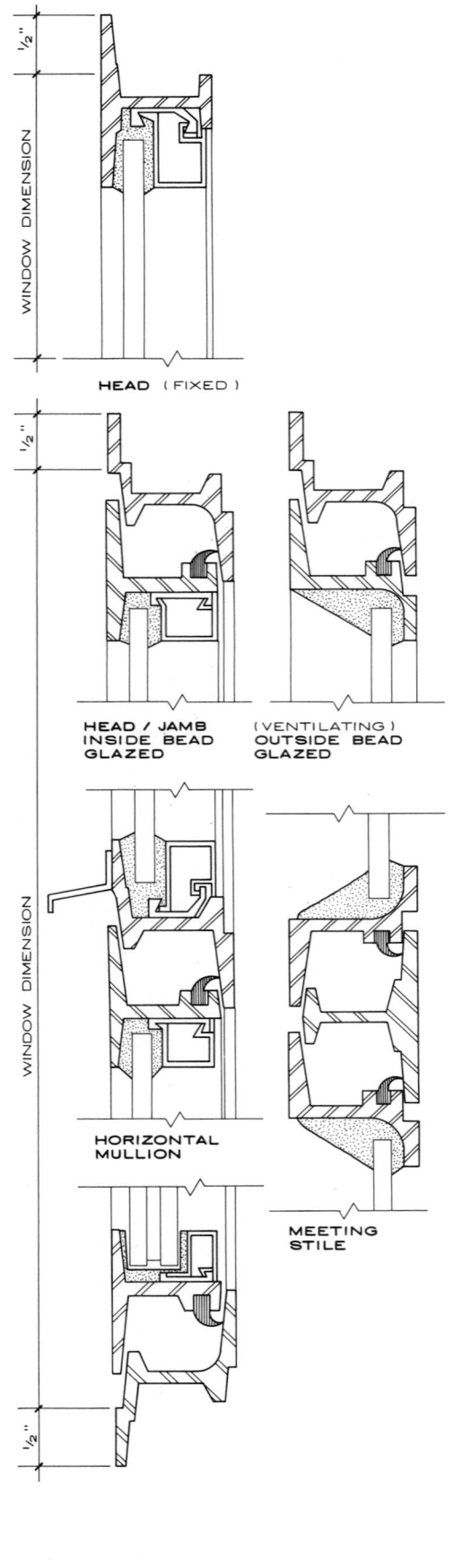

HEAD (FIXED)

HEAD / JAMB INSIDE BEAD GLAZED

(VENTILATING) OUTSIDE BEAD GLAZED

HORIZONTAL MULLION

MEETING STILE

**STEEL SASH CONSTRUCTION**

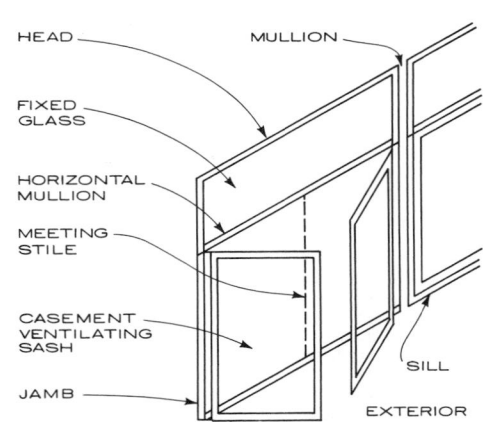

HEAD — MULLION
FIXED GLASS
HORIZONTAL MULLION
MEETING STILE
CASEMENT VENTILATING SASH
JAMB
SILL
EXTERIOR

**WINDOW NOMENCLATURE**

## NOTES

1. Window sizes and dimensioning methods, as listed, are not uniform for all manufacturers. Some manufacturers have no stock sizes, producing only custom work. Check with those who supply sash for each geographical area.
2. In general, heavier grades of windows offer greater configuration flexibility. Larger operating sash can be produced with heavier members than with lighter members. Thus the fixed lights shown for taller steel sash can be avoided, if desired.
3. Insect screens are necessarily installed on the interior and must be taken into account when selecting hardware.
4. The raindrip indicated on the horizontal mullion may be required at ventilating heads if sash is placed flush with exterior face of wall.
5. Drawings or specification must contain the following information: window size and location, installation details, sills, stools, flashing, sealing, and anchors; sash material and finish; glazing material; glazing method (tape, putty, or bead, inside or outside); weatherstripping, insect screen material, and hardware.

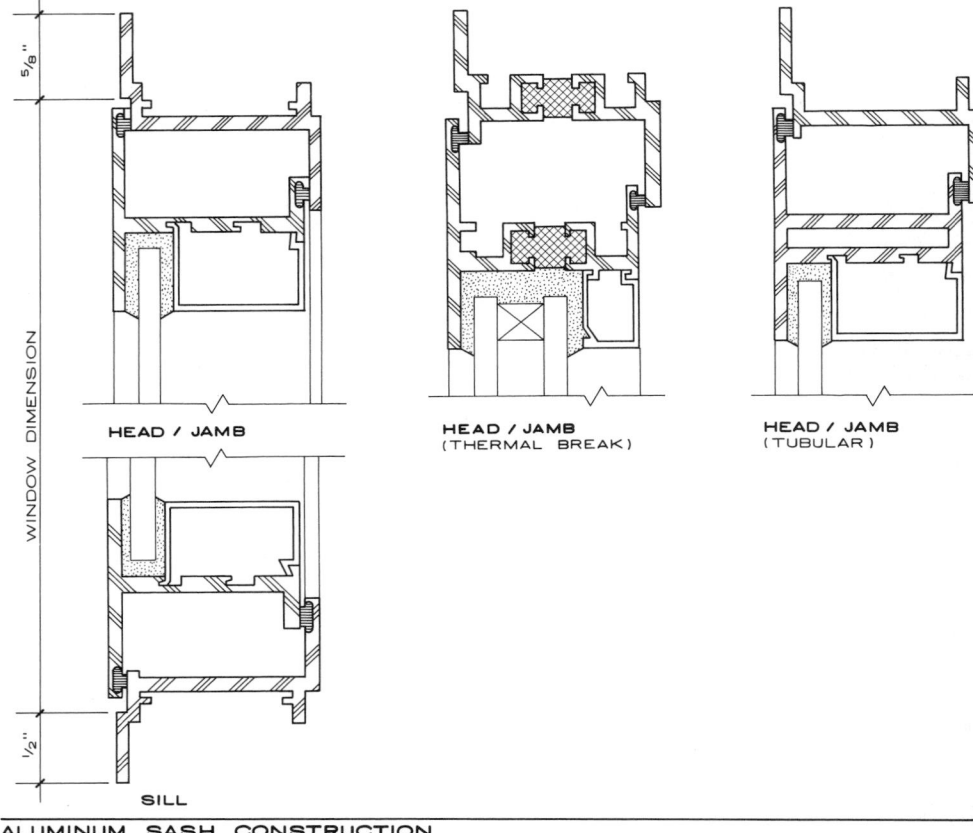

HEAD / JAMB

SILL

HEAD / JAMB (THERMAL BREAK)

HEAD / JAMB (TUBULAR)

**ALUMINUM SASH CONSTRUCTION**

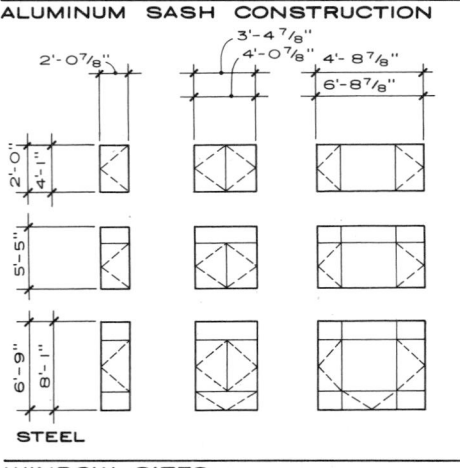
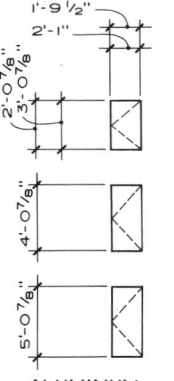
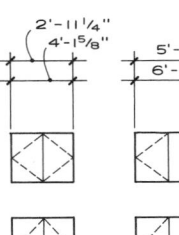
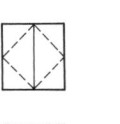
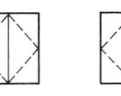
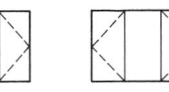

STEEL

ALUMINUM

**WINDOW SIZES**

William A. Klene, AIA, Architect; Herndon, Virginia

**METAL WINDOWS**

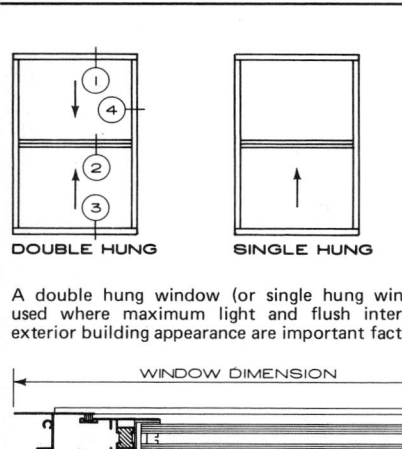

**DOUBLE HUNG**    **SINGLE HUNG**

A double hung window (or single hung window) is used where maximum light and flush interior and exterior building appearance are important factors.

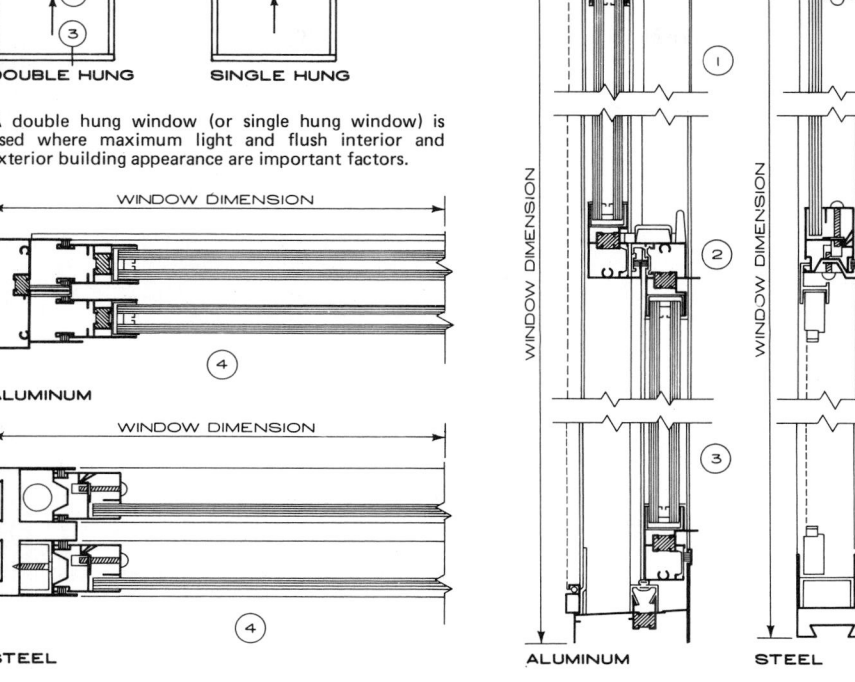

WINDOW DIMENSION

**ALUMINUM**

WINDOW DIMENSION

**STEEL**

**JAMB SECTIONS**

**VERTICAL SECTIONS**

WINDOW DIMENSION    WINDOW DIMENSION

**ALUMINUM**    **STEEL**

**SINGLE AND DOUBLE HUNG WINDOWS**

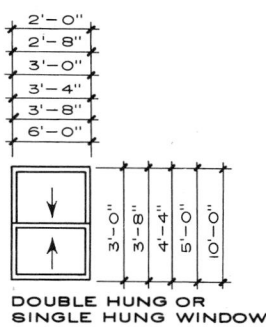

2'-0"
2'-8"
3'-0"
3'-4"
3'-8"
6'-0"

3'-0"  3'-8"  4'-4"  5'-0"  10'-0"

**DOUBLE HUNG OR SINGLE HUNG WINDOW**
Alum: Residential
Steel: No std. by SWI

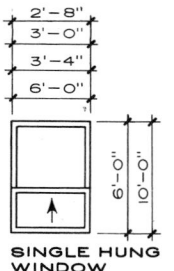

2'-8"
3'-0"
3'-4"
6'-0"

6'-0"  10'-0"

**SINGLE HUNG WINDOW**
Alum: Residential
Steel: No std. by SWI

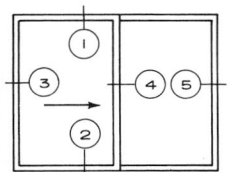

**SLIDING**

A horizontal sliding glass window (single or double) is used where maximum light, flush interior and exterior building appearance, simple manual operation, and accessibility are important factors.

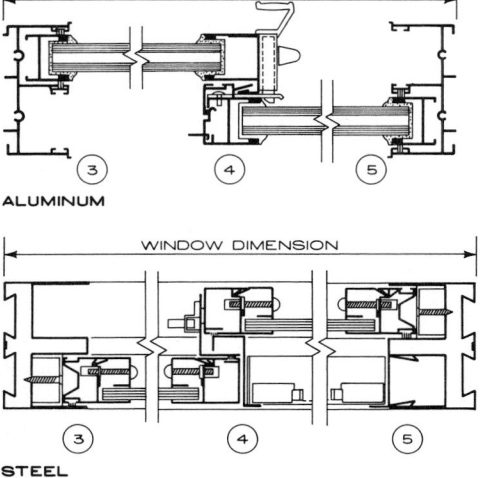

WINDOW DIMENSION

**ALUMINUM**

WINDOW DIMENSION

**STEEL**

**JAMB SECTIONS**

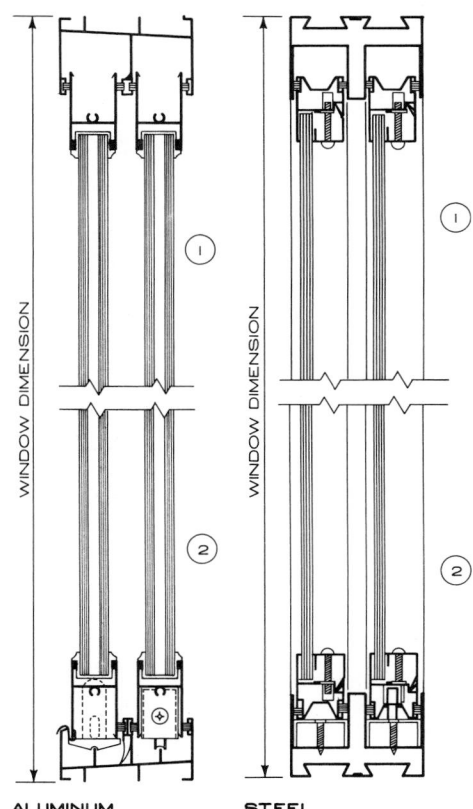

WINDOW DIMENSION    WINDOW DIMENSION

**ALUMINUM**    **STEEL**

**VERTICAL SECTIONS**

**SLIDING WINDOWS**

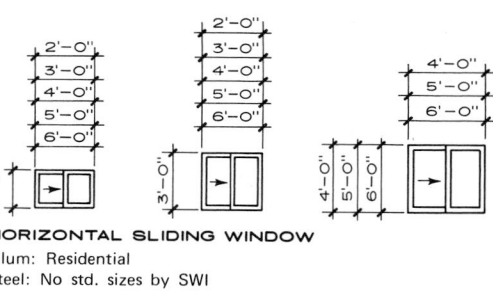

2'-0"    2'-0"    4'-0"
3'-0"    3'-0"    5'-0"
4'-0"    4'-0"    6'-0"
5'-0"    5'-0"
6'-0"    6'-0"

2'-0"    3'-0"    4'-0" 5'-0" 6'-0"

**HORIZONTAL SLIDING WINDOW**
Alum: Residential
Steel: No std. sizes by SWI

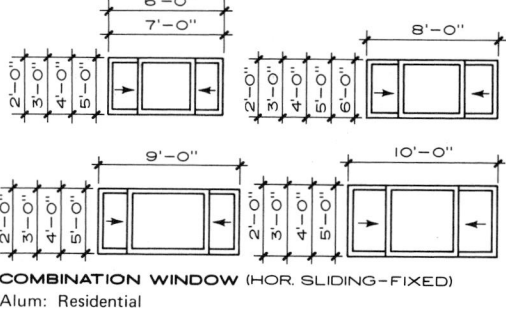

6'-0"    8'-0"
7'-0"

2'-0" 3'-0" 4'-0" 5'-0"    2'-0" 3'-0" 4'-0" 5'-0" 6'-0"

9'-0"    10'-0"

2'-0" 3'-0" 4'-0" 5'-0"    2'-0" 3'-0" 4'-0" 5'-0"

**COMBINATION WINDOW (HOR. SLIDING–FIXED)**
Alum: Residential
Steel: No std. sizes by SWI

David W. Johnson; Washington, D.C.

**METAL WINDOWS**    8

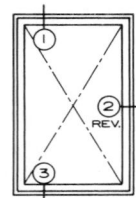

**ELEVATION**

**NOTE**

A reversible window is used mostly in multistory, air conditioned buildings where window washing from the interior is desired. It is normally opened for cleaning only; however, it may be combined with a hopper if ventilation is required.

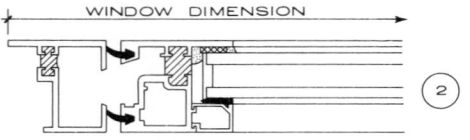

ALUMINUM

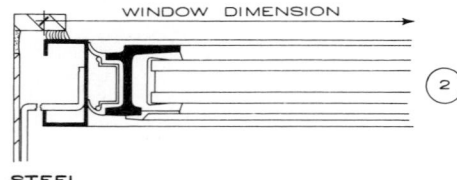

STEEL

JAMB SECTIONS

**REVERSIBLE WINDOWS**

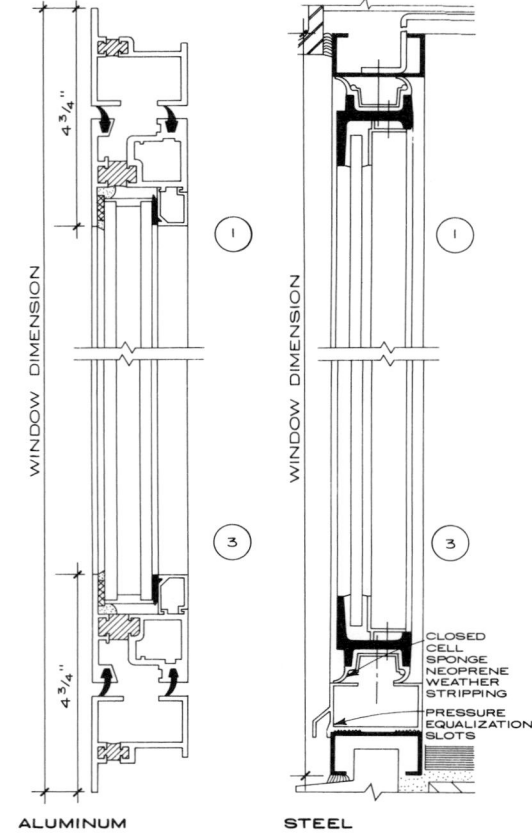

ALUMINUM          STEEL

CLOSED CELL SPONGE NEOPRENE WEATHER STRIPPING

PRESSURE EQUALIZATION SLOTS

VERTICAL SECTIONS

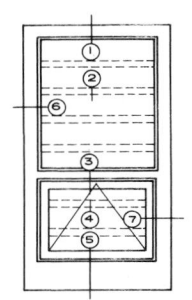

**ELEVATIONS**

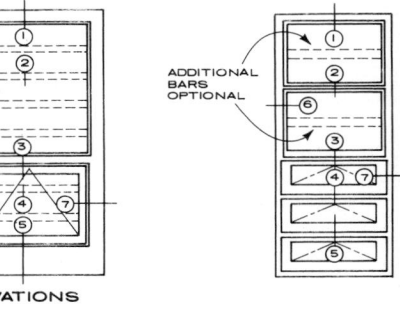

ADDITIONAL BARS OPTIONAL

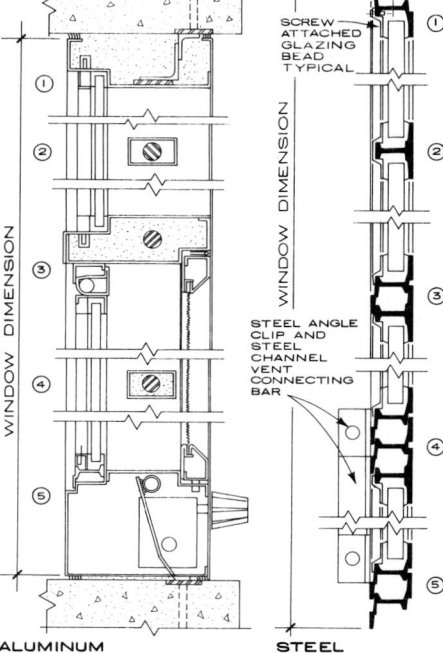

SCREW ATTACHED GLAZING BEAD TYPICAL

STEEL ANGLE CLIP AND STEEL CHANNEL VENT CONNECTING BAR

ALUMINUM          STEEL

**VERTICAL SECTIONS**

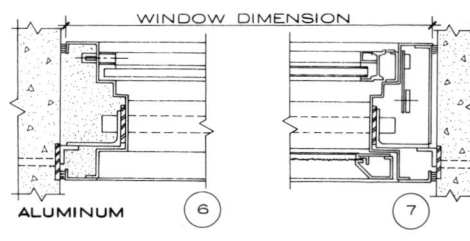

ALUMINUM

WINDOW DIMENSION

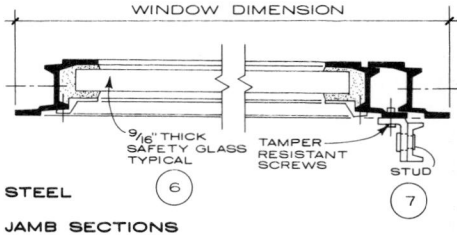

STEEL

9/16" THICK SAFETY GLASS TYPICAL

TAMPER RESISTANT SCREWS

STUD

**JAMB SECTIONS**

**NOTES**

1. Housing sill frame size varies with manufacturer of window operator.
2. Muntin and mullion tubes are 12 gauge maximum and 14 gauge medium security, grouted full, and contain a $7/8$ in. diameter tamper resistant bar.
3. Tempered glass is $1/2$ in. on exterior side.
4. Horizontal tube/bars to have maximum spacing of 5 in.

**SECURITY WINDOWS**

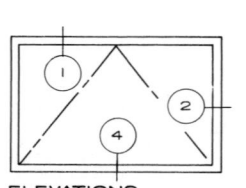

**ELEVATIONS**
**NOTE**

A projected (special) window is used mostly in multistory, air conditioned buildings where window washing from the interior is desired. It is normally opened for cleaning only; however, it may be combined with a hopper if ventilation is required. For such use see alternate above.

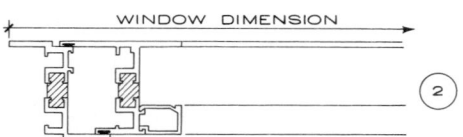

ALUMINUM

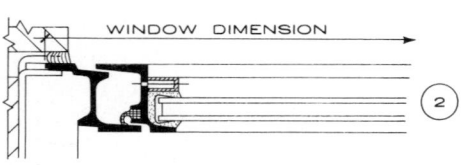

STEEL

JAMB SECTIONS

**PROJECTED WINDOWS**

ALUMINUM          STEEL

VERTICAL SECTIONS

David W. Johnson; Washington, D.C.

**METAL WINDOWS**

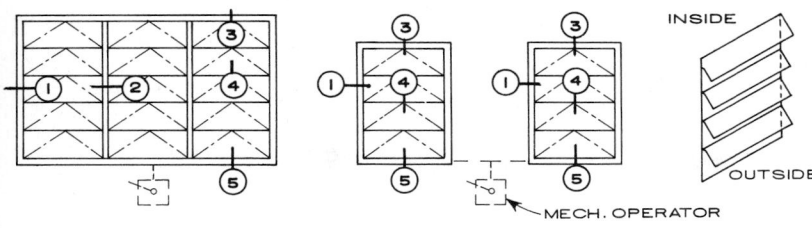

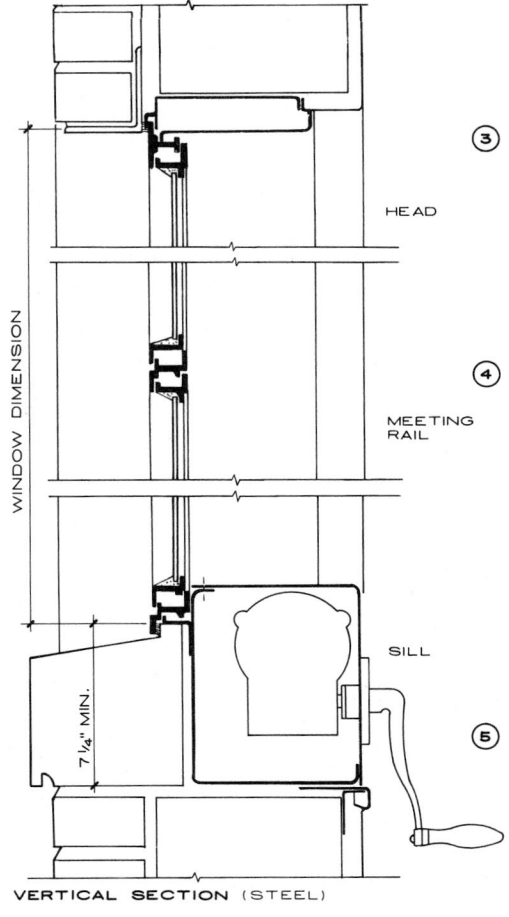

HEAD

WINDOW DIMENSION

③

④

MEETING RAIL

SILL

⑤

7¼" MIN.

MECH. OPERATOR

INSIDE

OUTSIDE

## AWNING

AN AWNING WINDOW is one whose movable units consist of a group of hand operated or gear operated outward projecting ventilators, all of which move in unison. It is used where maximum height and ventilation is required in inaccessible areas such as upper parts of gymnasiums or auditoriums. Hand operation is limited to one window only, while a single gear operator may be connected to two or more awning windows, and may be motorized.

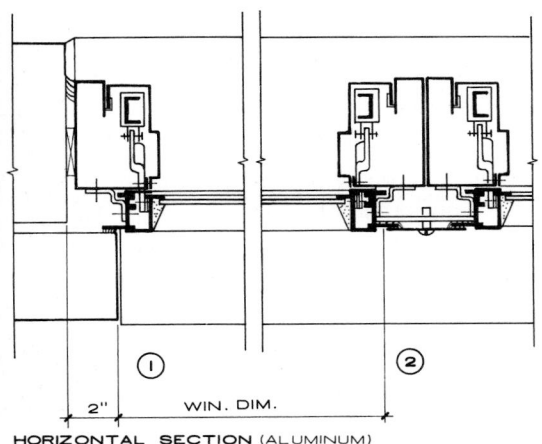

2"   WIN. DIM.

**HORIZONTAL SECTION (ALUMINUM)**

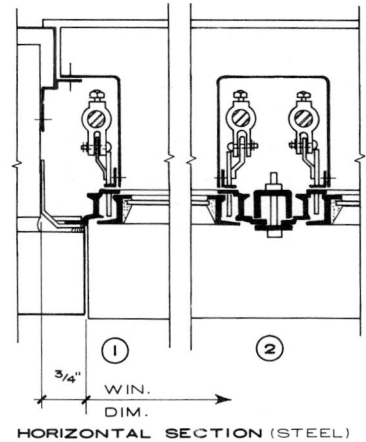

3/4"   WIN. DIM.

**HORIZONTAL SECTION (STEEL)**

**VERTICAL SECTION (STEEL)**

## AWNING WINDOWS

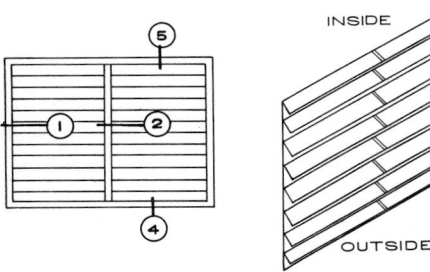

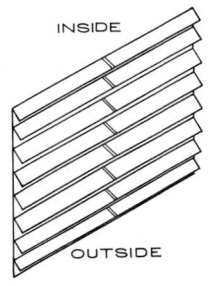

INSIDE

OUTSIDE

## JALOUSIE

A JALOUSIE WINDOW (ALUMINUM) consists of a series of operable overlapping glass louvers which pivot in unison. It may be combined in the same frame with a series of operable opaque louvers for climate control. It is used mostly in residential type constructions in southern climates, where maximum ventilation and flush exterior and interior appearance is desired.

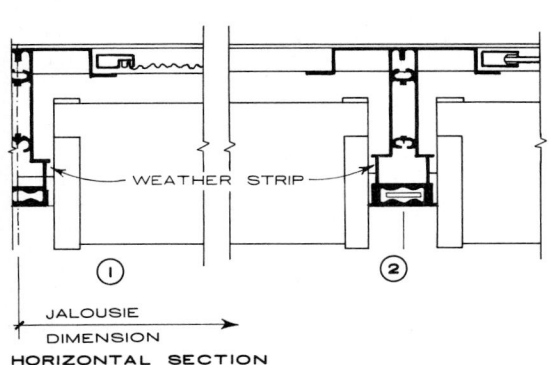

WEATHER STRIP

JALOUSIE DIMENSION

**HORIZONTAL SECTION**

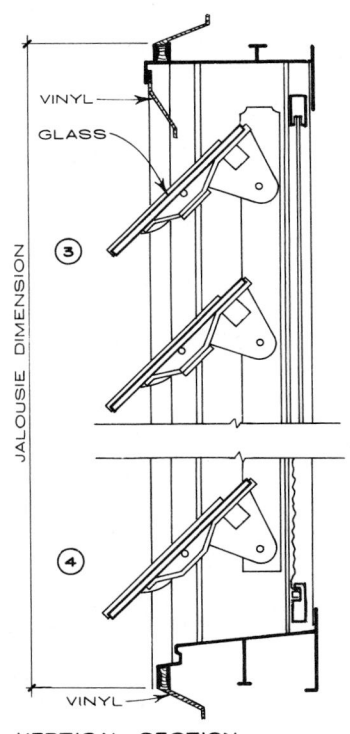

VINYL

GLASS

JALOUSIE DIMENSION

③

④

VINYL

**VERTICAL SECTION**

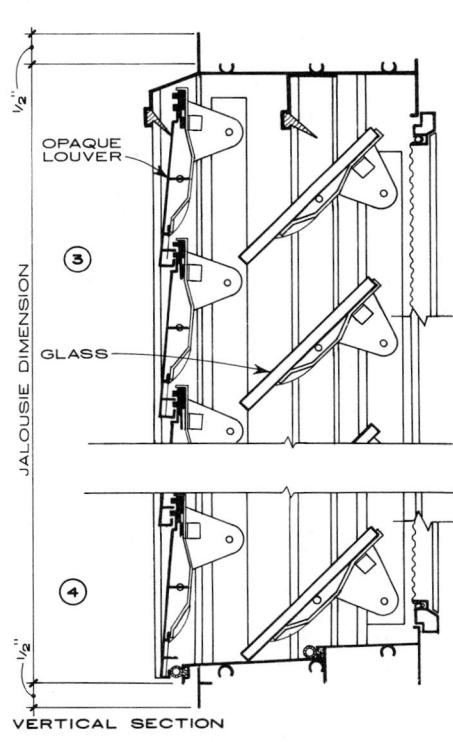

½"

OPAQUE LOUVER

JALOUSIE DIMENSION

③

GLASS

④

½"

**VERTICAL SECTION**

## JALOUSIE WINDOWS

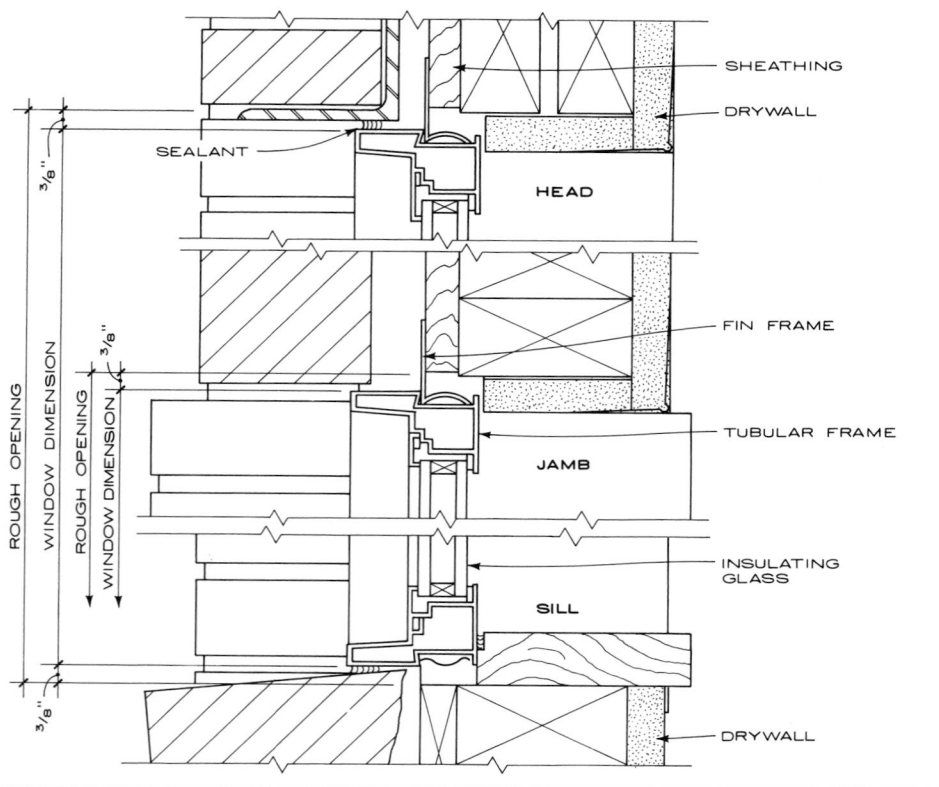

**BRICK VENEER ON WOOD FRAME WALL**

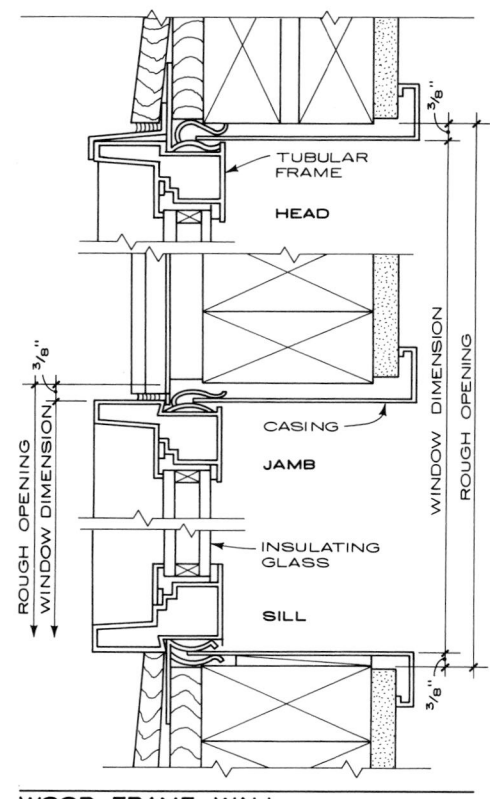

**WOOD FRAME WALL**

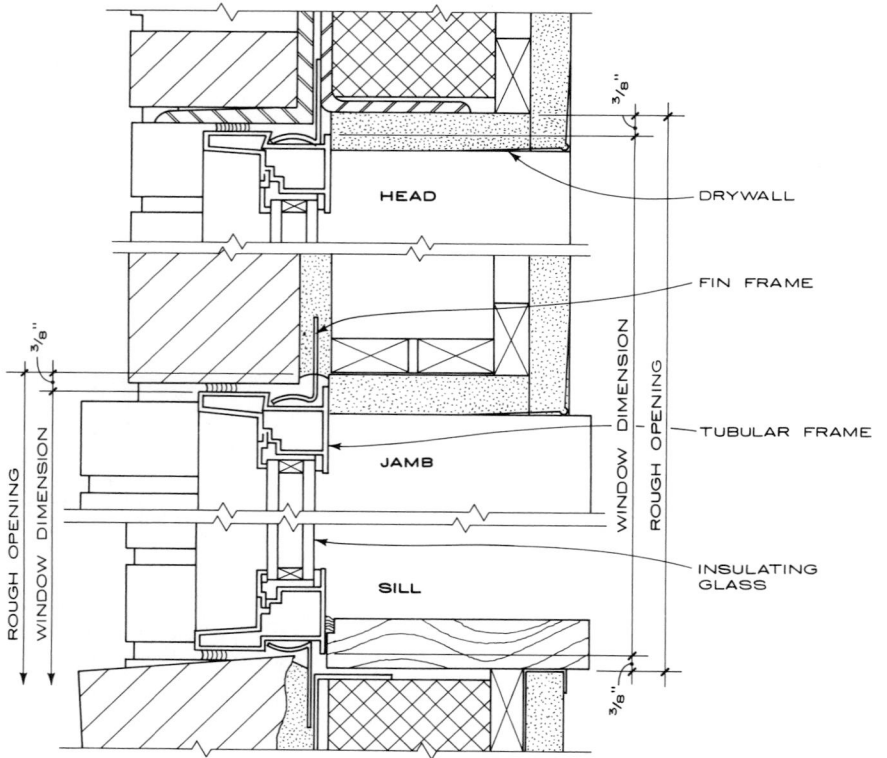

**MASONRY WALL**

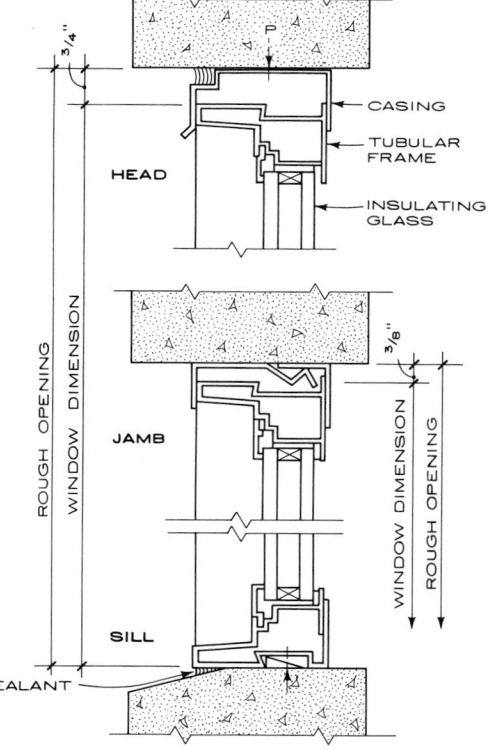

**CONCRETE WALL**

**NOTES**

1. Fins and interior casings are available to meet various installation requirements. Interior trims are available in depths of 2 to 10 in., in 1/2 in. increments.

2. Thermal-break type extrusions are available. Consult with manufacturers for sizes and shapes.

Nicanor A. Alano, Architect; Tacoma, Washington

**METAL WINDOWS**

## TYPICAL OPERATING HARDWARE FOR METAL WINDOWS

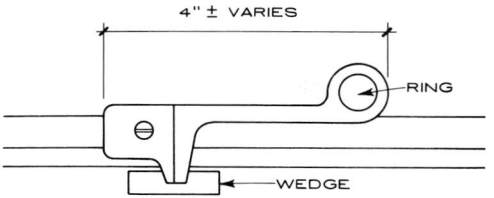

TYPICAL (CAM) LOCKING HANDLE

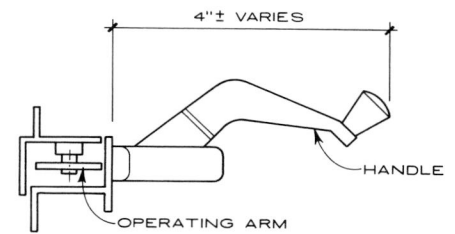

TYPICAL CRANK (ROTO) OPERATOR

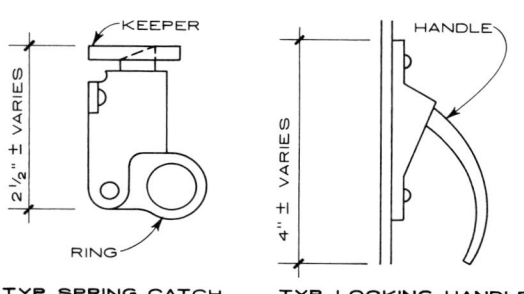

TYP. SPRING CATCH　　TYP. LOCKING HANDLE

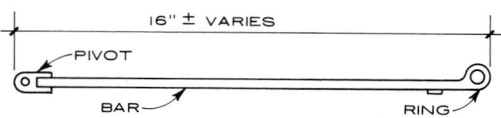

TYPICAL STAY BAR (PUSH BAR)

### OTHER TYPES OF HARDWARE

1. Concealed cam hardware.
2. Hardware with removable handles for A.C. buildings. Also key locks.
3. Sliding window hardware.
4. D. H. window hardware (sweeplock).
5. Telescoping adjuster.
6. Chain, pole & cord operated hardware.
7. Hardware for security windows.
8. Heavy duty, electrical powered hardware for group window control.

### FINISHES INCLUDE

1. Steel: diecast, lacquered & painted.
2. Aluminum: wide range of finishes and colors. Generally match window finish.
3. Bronze
4. White bronze & nickel bronze

Charles F. D. Egbert, AIA, Architect; Washington, D.C.

## EXTRUDED ALUMINUM SILLS

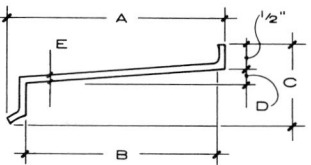

For Lug Sills
　　Extend into brick joints at window jambs and allow 1/4" space for expansion at ends.

For Continuous Sills
　　At joints allow 1/4" to 3/8" expansion and flash joints.

| A | B | C | D | E | Std. No.* |
|---|---|---|---|---|---|
| 3 7/16" | 3" | 1 9/16" | 3/16" | 3/32" | 37734 |
| 3 29/32" | | 1 1/2" | | | P-3684 |
| 3 15/16" | 3 1/2" | 1 19/32" | 7/32" | 3/32" | 37735 |
| 4 13/32" | | 1 17/32" | | | P-3683 |
| 4 7/16" | 4" | 1 5/8" | 1/4" | 3/32" | 37736 |
| 4 7/8" | | 1 9/16" | | | 3686 |
| 4 15/16" | 4 1/2" | 1 21/32" | 9/32" | 3/32" | 37737 |
| 5 3/8" | | 1 9/16" | | | 3687 |
| 5 7/16" | 5" | 1 11/16" | 5/16" | 3/32" | 37738 |
| 5 7/8" | | 1 5/8" | | | 3685 |
| 5 15/16" | 5 1/2" | 1 23/32" | 11/32" | 3/32" | 37739 |
| 9 1/16" | 8 1/2" | 1 31/32" | 7/32" | 5/32" | 37745 |
| | | | | | |
| | | | | | |
| 3 1/2" | 2 3/4" | 1 13/16" | 3/16" | 1/8" | 54684 |
| 4" | 3 1/4" | 1 27/32" | 7/32" | 1/8" | 54685 |
| 4 1/2" | 3 3/4" | 1 7/8" | 1/4" | 1/8" | 54686 |
| | | | | | 9558 |
| 5" | 4 1/4" | 1 29/32" | 9/32" | 1/8" | 54687 |
| | | | | | 13008 |
| 5 1/2" | 4 3/4" | 1 15/16" | 5/16" | 1/8" | 54688 |
| | | | | | 13009 |
| 6" | 5 1/4" | 1 31/32" | 11/32" | 1/8" | 54689 |
| 6 9/16" | 5 3/4" | 2" | 3/8" | 5/32" | 54690 |
| 7 9/16" | 6 3/4 | 2 1/16" | 7/16" | 5/32" | 54691 |
| 8 1/8" | 7 1/4" | 2 5/32" | 15/32" | 3/16" | 54692 |
| 9 1/8" | 8 1/4" | 2 7/32" | 17/32" | 3/16" | 54693 |
| | | | | | |
| | | | | | |
| 3 1/2" | | 1 9/16" | | | P-3692 |
| 4" | | 1 19/32" | | | P-3691 |
| 4 1/2" | | 1 5/8" | | | P-3690 |
| 5" | | 1 21/32" | | | P-3126 |
| 5 1/2" | | 1 11/16" | | | P-3127 |
| 6" | | 1 23/32" | | | P-3128 |
| 9 1/16" | | 1 29/32" | | | P-3230 |

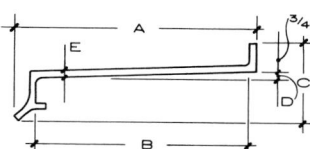

Used for continuous line of windows. Provide 1/4" to 3/8" expansion space at jamb or butt joints of continuous sills.

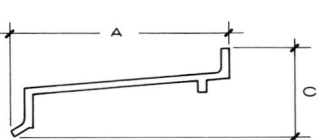

Sills may be made to fit posts or mullions, and may be mitered at corners. Sills over eight feet in length should have central anchorage to keep them in proper position.

* Non-warehouse items

Refer to aluminum manufacturers catalogs.

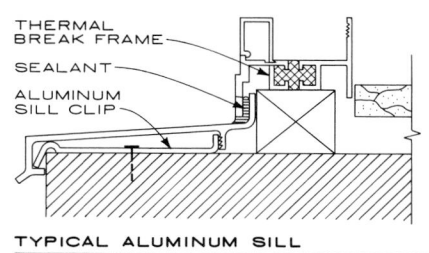

TYPICAL ALUMINUM SILL　　REPLACEMENT SILL

**INSTALLATION DETAILS**

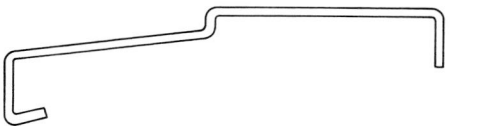
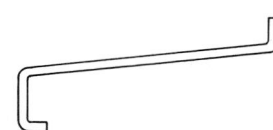

TYPICAL FORMED METAL SILLS
SHAPES MADE TO ORDER

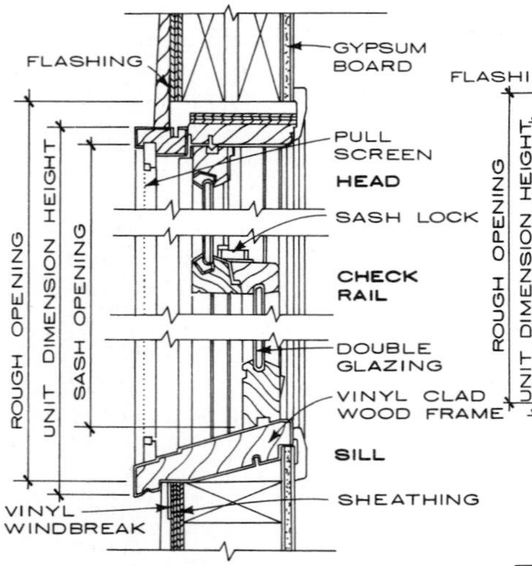

## VERTICAL SECTION

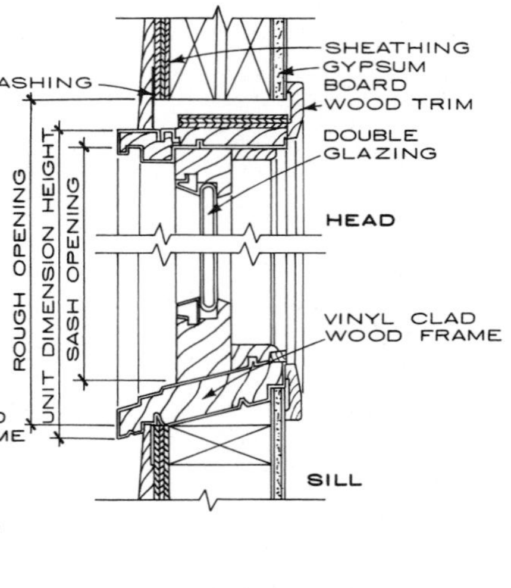

FLASHING
GYPSUM BOARD
PULL SCREEN
**HEAD**
SASH LOCK
**CHECK RAIL**
DOUBLE GLAZING
VINYL CLAD WOOD FRAME
**SILL**
VINYL WINDBREAK
SHEATHING
ROUGH OPENING
UNIT DIMENSION HEIGHT
SASH OPENING

## PICTURE WINDOW DETAIL

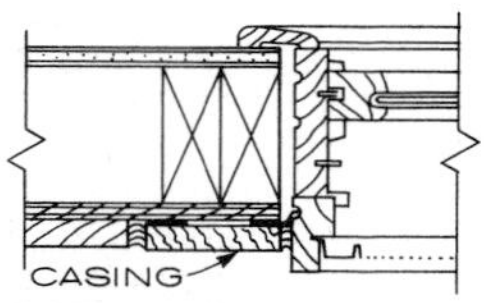

FLASHING
SHEATHING
GYPSUM BOARD
WOOD TRIM
DOUBLE GLAZING
**HEAD**
VINYL CLAD WOOD FRAME
**SILL**
ROUGH OPENING
UNIT DIMENSION HEIGHT
SASH OPENING

## PLAN SECTION

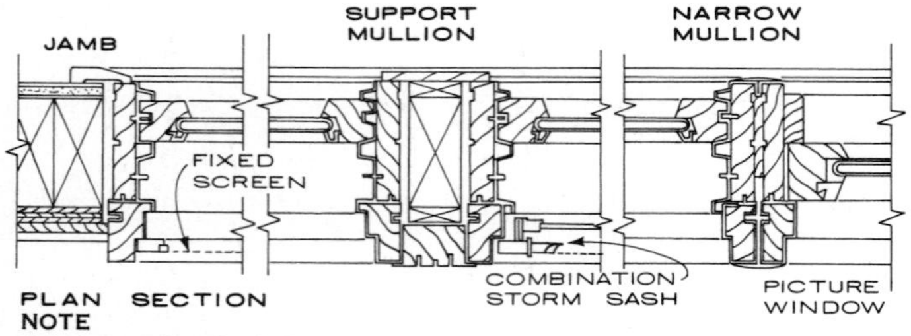

JAMB
SUPPORT MULLION
NARROW MULLION
FIXED SCREEN
COMBINATION STORM SASH
PICTURE WINDOW

### NOTE
Spiral or reel spring balances or pressure weatherstrip operation. Glass size 12 x 12 in. to 44 x 40 in. for 1-light sash.

PLAIN RAIL WINDOW: No parting stop; movable sash slides against fixed sash with hold-open jamb bolts.

## DOUBLE HUNG WINDOWS
### NOTE
CASEMENT WINDOWS: Stiles and top rail 1 to 2 in., bottom rail 3 in. nominal. Outswinging: screen inside, regular or self-storing flexible type with operation similar to window shade. Sash opening range for 1 sash per frame 1 ft 4 in. x 2 ft 2 in. to 2 x 6 ft. Extension hinges, friction arms, folding push bar or roto worm gear operator.

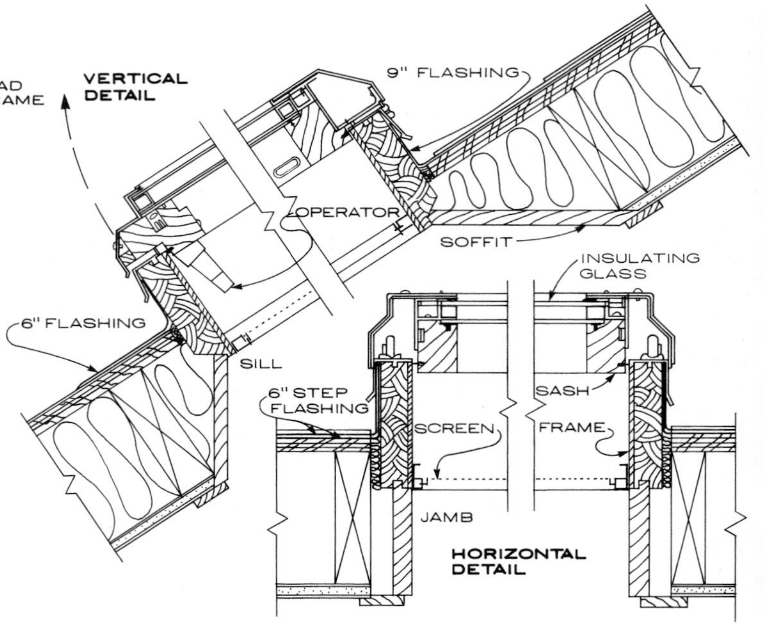

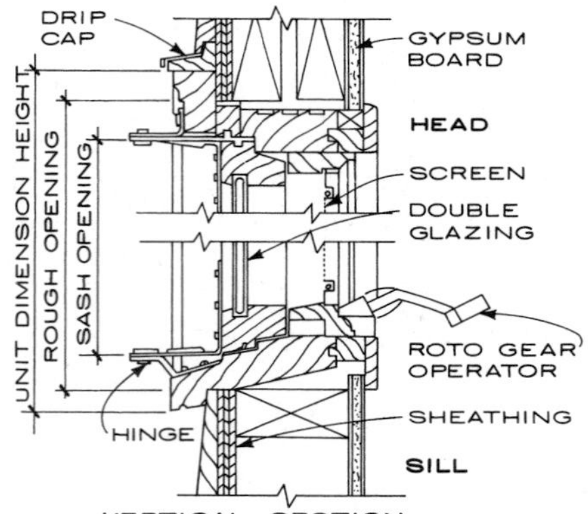

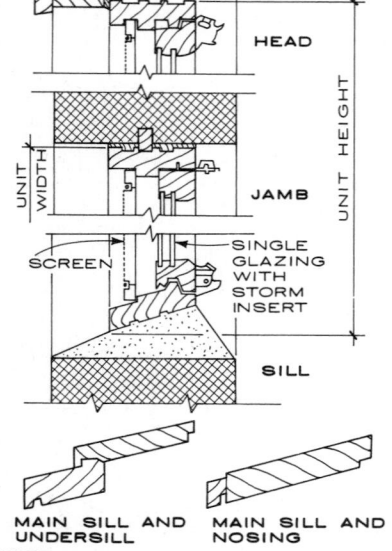

FLOOR JOIST
**HEAD**
**JAMB**
SCREEN
SINGLE GLAZING WITH STORM INSERT
**SILL**
UNIT WIDTH
UNIT HEIGHT

MAIN SILL AND UNDERSILL
MAIN SILL AND NOSING

### NOTE
Removable sash and dual purpose hinges for opening from top or bottom.

## BASEMENT WINDOWS

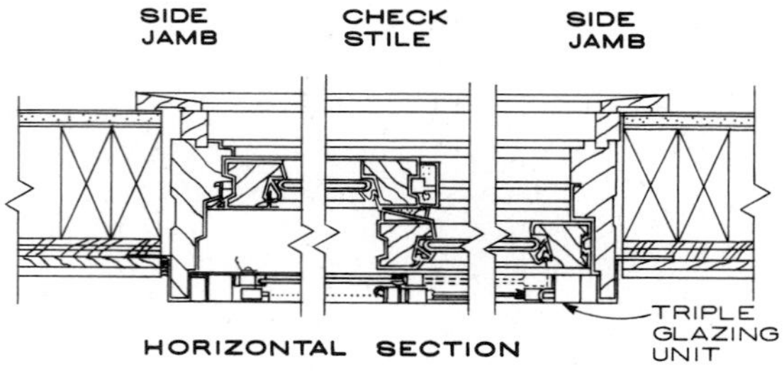

## REPLACEMENT WINDOW

REMODELING AND REPLACEMENT WINDOWS: Stock window sizes of all standard types are available as replacement units with metal or vinyl clad adapter casings added to perimeter to fit existing openings in renovation work.

CASING

## ROOF WINDOW

VERTICAL DETAIL
9" FLASHING
OPERATOR
SOFFIT
6" FLASHING
SILL
INSULATING GLASS
6" STEP FLASHING
SCREEN
SASH FRAME
JAMB
**HORIZONTAL DETAIL**

Sash openings approximately 2 to 4 ft wide, 3 to 6 ft high. Awning or pivot. Optional equipment includes shades, blinds, screens, electric operators. May be equipped with automatic closer activated by rain sensor. Weep holes to retard condensation.

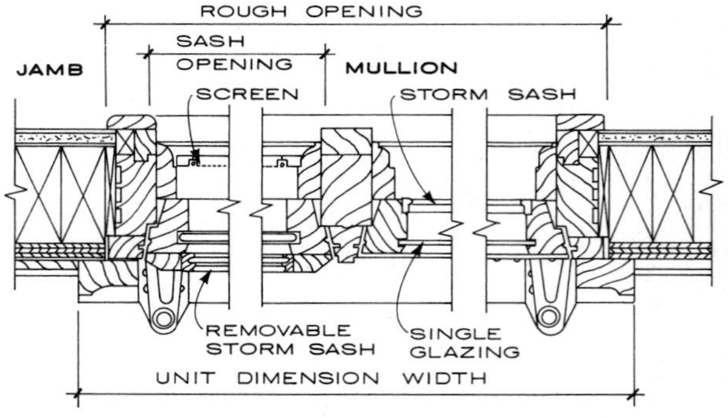

## CASEMENT WINDOWS

### VERTICAL SECTION
DRIP CAP
GYPSUM BOARD
**HEAD**
SCREEN
DOUBLE GLAZING
ROTO GEAR OPERATOR
HINGE
SHEATHING
**SILL**
UNIT DIMENSION HEIGHT
ROUGH OPENING
SASH OPENING

### PLAN SECTION
JAMB
ROUGH OPENING
SASH OPENING
SCREEN
MULLION
STORM SASH
REMOVABLE STORM SASH
SINGLE GLAZING
UNIT DIMENSION WIDTH

## HORIZONTAL SLIDING WINDOWS

### HORIZONTAL SECTION
SIDE JAMB
CHECK STILE
SIDE JAMB
TRIPLE GLAZING UNIT

### VERTICAL SECTION
SEALANT
SHIM
**HEAD**
ROUGH OPENING
**SILL**
SEALANT
TRIM

Sash opening for 2 sash per frame approximately 3 to 6 ft wide by 3 to 5 ft high. Plastic weatherstrip track top and bottom, center lock with handle.

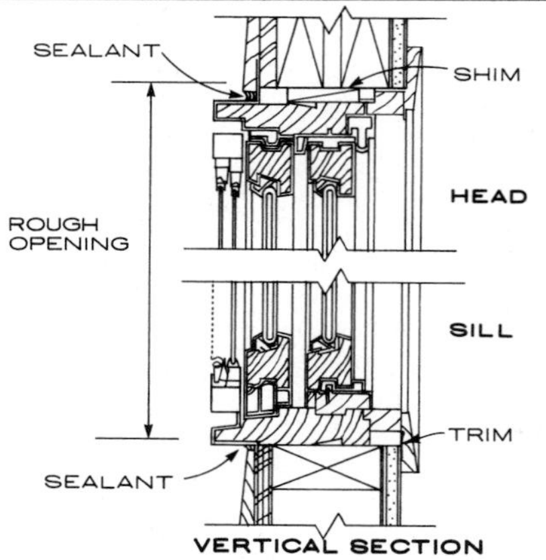

Carleton Granbery, FAIA; Guilford, Connecticut

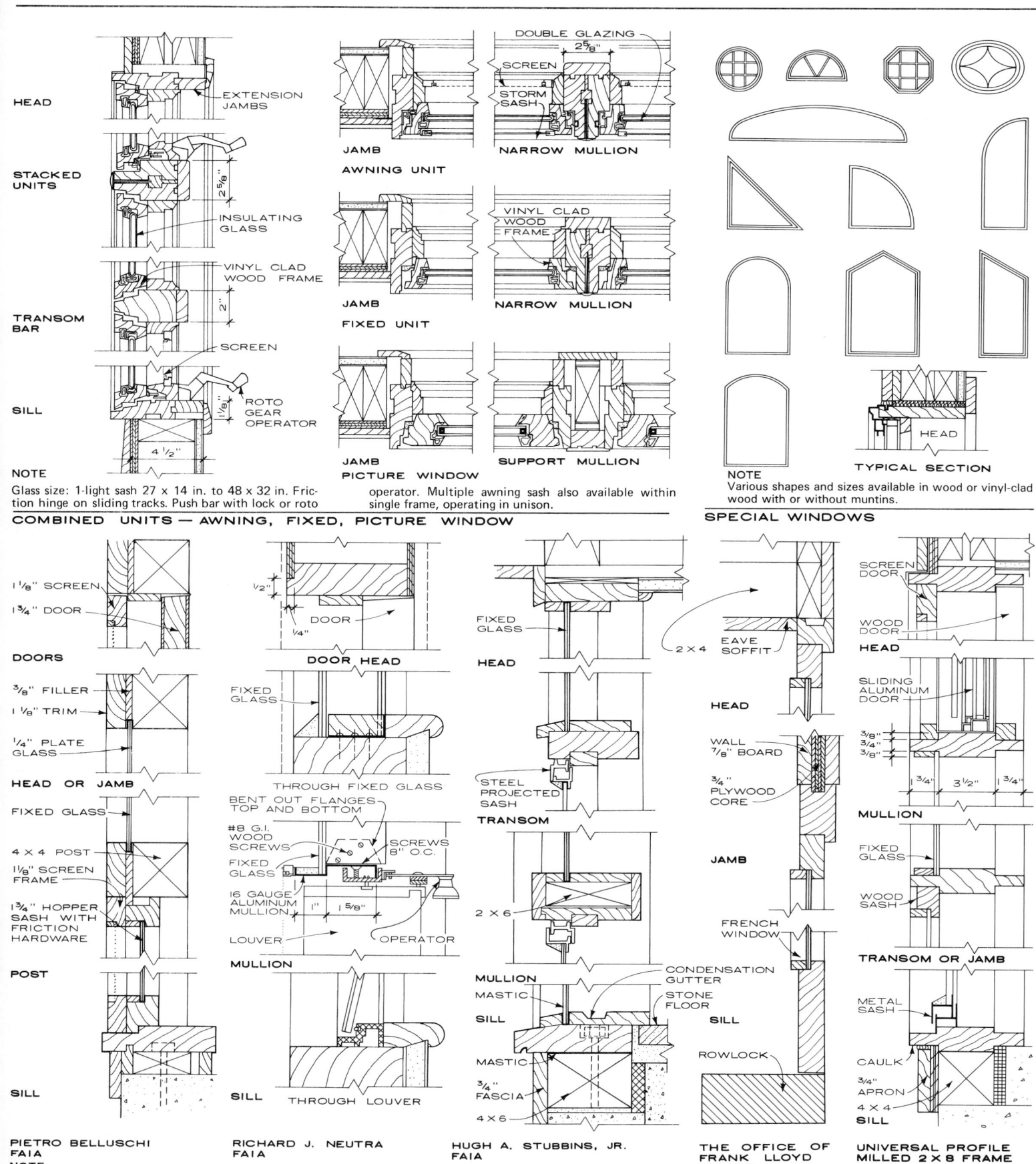

**HEAD** — EXTENSION JAMBS

**STACKED UNITS** — $2\frac{5}{8}''$ — INSULATING GLASS — VINYL CLAD WOOD FRAME

**TRANSOM BAR** — $2''$ — SCREEN

**SILL** — $1\frac{1}{8}''$ — ROTO GEAR OPERATOR — $4\frac{1}{2}''$

**NOTE**
Glass size: 1-light sash 27 x 14 in. to 48 x 32 in. Friction hinge on sliding tracks. Push bar with lock or roto operator. Multiple awning sash also available within single frame, operating in unison.

DOUBLE GLAZING — $2\frac{5}{8}''$ — SCREEN — STORM SASH

**JAMB**    **NARROW MULLION**
**AWNING UNIT**

VINYL CLAD WOOD FRAME

**JAMB**    **NARROW MULLION**
**FIXED UNIT**

**JAMB**    **SUPPORT MULLION**
**PICTURE WINDOW**

**COMBINED UNITS — AWNING, FIXED, PICTURE WINDOW**

**NOTE**
Various shapes and sizes available in wood or vinyl-clad wood with or without muntins.

HEAD — **TYPICAL SECTION**

**SPECIAL WINDOWS**

$1\frac{1}{8}''$ SCREEN — $1\frac{3}{4}''$ DOOR

**DOORS**

$\frac{3}{8}''$ FILLER — $1\frac{1}{8}''$ TRIM — $\frac{1}{4}''$ PLATE GLASS

**HEAD OR JAMB**

FIXED GLASS — 4 X 4 POST — $1\frac{1}{8}''$ SCREEN FRAME — $1\frac{3}{4}''$ HOPPER SASH WITH FRICTION HARDWARE

**POST**

**SILL**

**PIETRO BELLUSCHI FAIA**

$\frac{1}{2}''$ — DOOR — $\frac{1}{4}''$

**DOOR HEAD**

FIXED GLASS

**THROUGH FIXED GLASS**

BENT OUT FLANGES TOP AND BOTTOM — #8 G.I. WOOD SCREWS — SCREWS 8" O.C. — FIXED GLASS — 16 GAUGE ALUMINUM MULLION — $1''$ — $1\frac{5}{8}''$ — LOUVER — OPERATOR

**MULLION**

**SILL**

**THROUGH LOUVER**

**RICHARD J. NEUTRA FAIA**

FIXED GLASS

**HEAD**

STEEL PROJECTED SASH

**TRANSOM**

2 X 6

**MULLION**
MASTIC — CONDENSATION GUTTER — STONE FLOOR

**SILL**
MASTIC — $\frac{3}{4}''$ FASCIA — 4 X 6

**HUGH A. STUBBINS, JR. FAIA**

2 X 4 — EAVE SOFFIT

**HEAD**

WALL $\frac{7}{8}''$ BOARD — $\frac{3}{4}''$ PLYWOOD CORE

**JAMB**

FRENCH WINDOW

**SILL**
ROWLOCK

**THE OFFICE OF FRANK LLOYD WRIGHT**

SCREEN DOOR — WOOD DOOR

**HEAD**

SLIDING ALUMINUM DOOR — $\frac{3}{8}''$ — $\frac{3}{4}''$ — $\frac{3}{8}''$ — $1\frac{3}{4}''$ — $3\frac{1}{2}''$ — $1\frac{3}{4}''$

**MULLION**

FIXED GLASS — WOOD SASH

**TRANSOM OR JAMB**

METAL SASH — CAULK — $\frac{3}{4}''$ APRON — 4 X 4

**SILL**

**UNIVERSAL PROFILE MILLED 2 X 8 FRAME**

**NOTE**
Selected examples indicating joinery to achieve weathertight narrow profiles. Adaptable to insulating glass for energy conservation where dictated by local conditions. See also pages on metal windows.

**CUSTOM DETAILS — FIXED GLASS, HOPPER, CASEMENTS, JALOUSIE, AWNING, AND TRANSOM SASH**

Carleton Granbery, FAIA; Guilford, Connecticut

## FREQUENCY OF DOOR OPERATION

| TYPE OF BUILDING AND DOOR | ESTIMATED FREQUENCY | | HINGE TYPE |
| | DAILY | YEARLY | |
|---|---|---|---|
| **HIGH FREQUENCY** | | | |
| Large department store entrance | 5,000 | 1,500,000 | |
| Large office building entrance | 4,000 | 1,200,000 | |
| School entrance | 1,250 | 225,000 | Heavy Weight |
| School toilet door | 1,250 | 225,000 | |
| Store or bank entrance | 500 | 150,000 | |
| Office building toilet door | 400 | 118,000 | |
| **AVERAGE FREQUENCY** | | | |
| School corridor door | 80 | 15,000 | Standard Weight |
| Office building corridor door | 75 | 22,000 | Antifriction Bearing |
| Store toilet door | 60 | 18,000 | (except on heavy doors) |
| Dwelling entrance | 40 | 15,000 | |
| **LOW FREQUENCY** | | | |
| Dwelling toilet door | 25 | 9,000 | Plain Bearing Hinges |
| Dwelling corridor door | 10 | 3,600 | may be used |
| Dwelling closet door | 6 | 2,200 | on light doors |

TOP HINGE 5" FROM JAMB RABBET TO TOP EDGE OF BARREL

THIRD HINGE CENTERED BETWEEN TOP AND BOTTOM HINGES

BOTTOM HINGE 10" FROM BOTTOM EDGE OF BARREL TO FINISHED FLOOR

NOTE: THE ABOVE IS U.S. STANDARD PROCEDURE. CERTAIN WESTERN STATES USE AS STANDARD 7" FROM TOP AND 11" FROM THE BOTTOM

### LOCATION OF HINGES ON DOORS

### HINGE WIDTH

| THICKNESS OF DOOR (IN.) | CLEARANCE REQUIRED* (IN.) | OPEN WIDTH OF HINGES (IN.) |
|---|---|---|
| $1\frac{3}{8}$ | $1\frac{1}{4}$ | $3\frac{1}{2}$ |
| | $1\frac{3}{4}$ | 4 |
| $1\frac{3}{4}$ | 1 | 4 |
| | $1\frac{1}{2}$ | $4\frac{1}{2}$ |
| | 2 | 5 |
| | 3 | 6 |
| 2 | 1 | $4\frac{1}{2}$ |
| | $1\frac{1}{2}$ | 5 |
| | $2\frac{1}{2}$ | 6 |
| $2\frac{1}{4}$ | 1 | 5 |
| | 2 | 6 |
| $2\frac{1}{2}$ | $\frac{3}{4}$ | 5 |
| | $1\frac{3}{4}$ | 6 |
| 3 | $\frac{3}{4}$ | 6 |
| | $2\frac{3}{4}$ | 8 |
| | $4\frac{3}{4}$ | 10 |

*Note: Clearance is computed for door flush with casing.

### HINGE HEIGHT

| THICKNESS (IN.) | WIDTH OF DOORS (IN.) | HEIGHT OF HINGES (IN.) |
|---|---|---|
| Doors $\frac{3}{4}$ to $1\frac{1}{8}$ cabinet | to 24 | $2\frac{1}{2}$ |
| $\frac{7}{8}$ and $1\frac{1}{8}$ screen or combination | to 36 | 3 |
| $1\frac{3}{8}$ | to 32 | $3\frac{1}{2}$ – 4 |
| | over 32 | 4 – $4\frac{1}{2}$ |
| $1\frac{3}{4}$ | to 36 | *$4\frac{1}{2}$ |
| | over 36 to 48 | *5 |
| | over 48 | *6 |
| 2, $2\frac{1}{4}$ and $2\frac{1}{2}$ | to 42 | 5 heavy |
| | over 42 | 6 weight |
| Transoms $1\frac{1}{4}$ and $1\frac{3}{8}$ | .................. | 3 |
| $1\frac{3}{4}$ | .................. | $3\frac{1}{2}$ |
| 2, $2\frac{1}{4}$ and $2\frac{1}{2}$ | .................. | 4 |

*Note: Heavy weight hinges should be specified for heavy doors and for doors where high frequency service is expected. The heavy weight hinges should be of $4\frac{1}{2}$ in., 5 in. and 6 in. sizes as shown in table.

### HINGE SELECTION DESIGN FACTORS

1. Material of door and frame
2. Size, thickness and weight of door with all hardware accessories
3. Clearance required
4. Use—exterior or interior exposure; frequency
5. Exposure to corrosive atmospheric elements (such as sea air, dust, etc.)
6. Quality desired
7. Special application or use (e.g., schools)
8. Door accessories (overhead holders, closers, stops, kick plates, etc.), which affect hinge performance
9. Hinge edge of door—beveled or squared

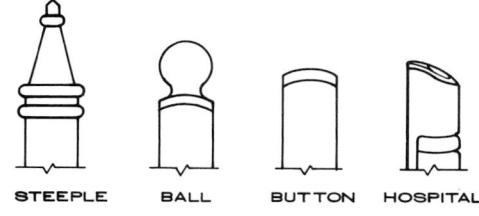

STEEPLE     BALL     BUTTON     HOSPITAL

NOTES
1. HOSPITAL TIPS ARE ROUNDED FOR EASE OF CLEANING.

2. CONSULT MANUFACTURERS FOR A WIDE VARIETY OF ORNAMENTAL TIPS

### TYPES OF TIPS

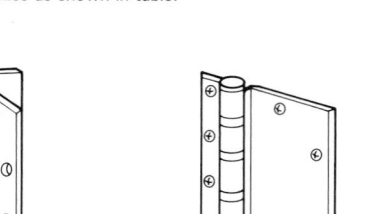
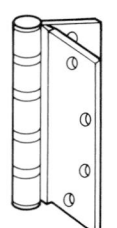
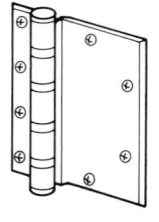

FULL MORTISE     HALF MORTISE     HALF SURFACE     FULL SURFACE

### TYPES OF HINGES

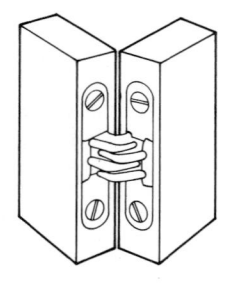

MINIMUM DIMENSION

### INVISIBLE HINGE

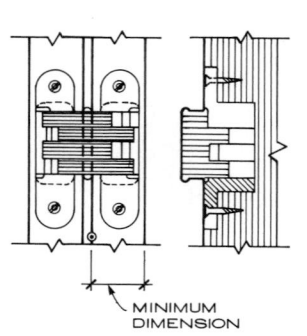

DOOR LEAF
JAMB LEAF
BALL BEARING OR WASHER
CL OF LEAF USUALLY ON CL OF DOOR
HEIGHT VARIES
CLEARANCE
LEAF WIDTH
WIDTH MAY VARY INDEPENDENT OF HEIGHT
RIGHT HAND HINGE SHOWN

### OLIVE KNUCKLE HINGE

Narcisa P. Sanchez; Sanchez & Sanchez; Falls Church, Virginia

**HARDWARE**

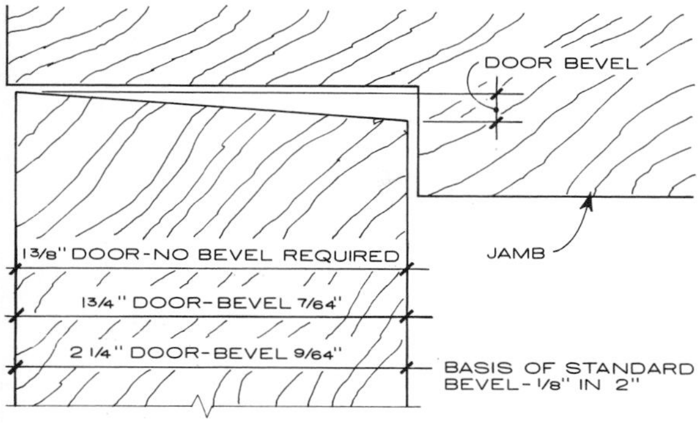

## DOOR BEVELS

DOOR BEVEL

JAMB

1 3/8" DOOR-NO BEVEL REQUIRED

1 3/4" DOOR-BEVEL 7/64"

2 1/4" DOOR-BEVEL 9/64"

BASIS OF STANDARD BEVEL- 1/8" IN 2"

**DOOR BEVELS**

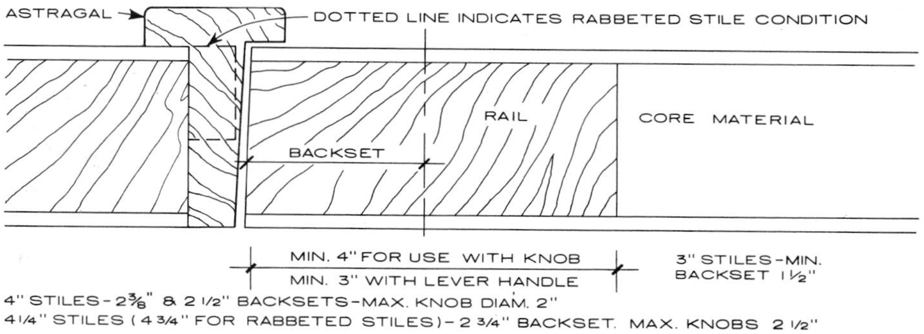

---

ASTRAGAL

DOTTED LINE INDICATES RABBETED STILE CONDITION

RAIL

CORE MATERIAL

BACKSET

MIN. 4" FOR USE WITH KNOB
MIN. 3" WITH LEVER HANDLE

3" STILES-MIN.
BACKSET 1 1/2"

4" STILES- 2 3/8" & 2 1/2" BACKSETS-MAX. KNOB DIAM. 2"
4 1/4" STILES (4 3/4" FOR RABBETED STILES)- 2 3/4" BACKSET. MAX. KNOBS 2 1/2"

**DOUBLE DOORS WITH FLAT ASTRAGAL** (ALSO APPLIES TO DOORS WITH RABBETED MEETING STILES)

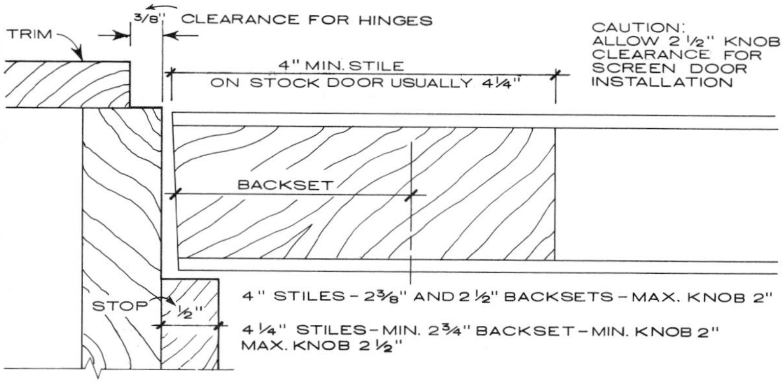

---

TRIM

3/8" CLEARANCE FOR HINGES

4" MIN. STILE
ON STOCK DOOR USUALLY 4 1/4"

CAUTION:
ALLOW 2 1/2" KNOB CLEARANCE FOR SCREEN DOOR INSTALLATION

BACKSET

STOP 1/2"

4" STILES - 2 3/8" AND 2 1/2" BACKSETS - MAX. KNOB 2"
4 1/4" STILES-MIN. 2 3/4" BACKSET - MIN. KNOB 2" MAX. KNOB 2 1/2"

**DOOR WITH KNOB USING CYLINDER LOCK**

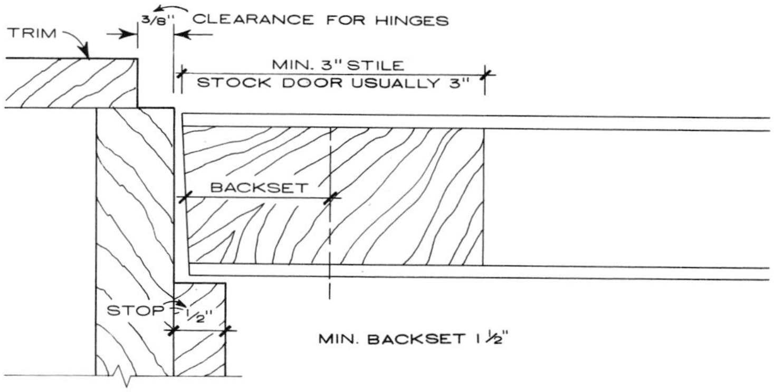

---

TRIM

3/8" CLEARANCE FOR HINGES

MIN. 3" STILE
STOCK DOOR USUALLY 3"

BACKSET

STOP 1/2"

MIN. BACKSET 1 1/2"

**DOOR WITH LEVER HANDLE USING CYLINDER LOCK**

**DOOR STILES**

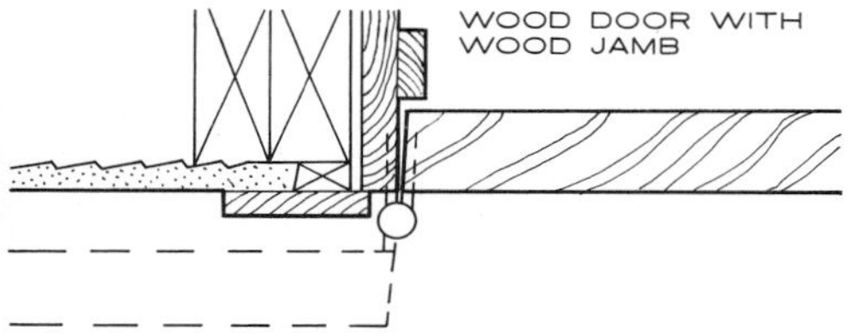

---

WOOD DOOR WITH WOOD JAMB

**FULL MORTISE NON-TEMPLATE**

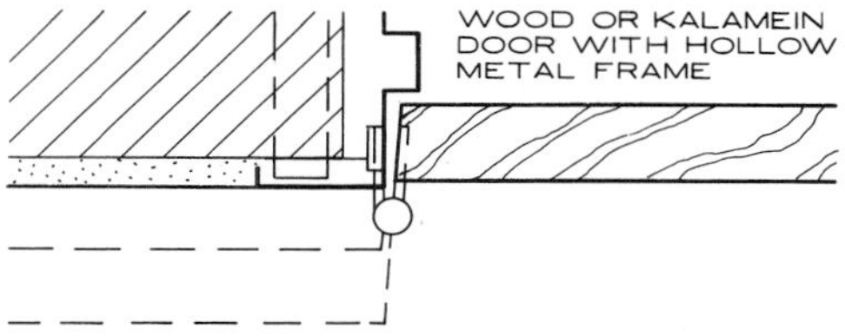

WOOD OR KALAMEIN DOOR WITH HOLLOW METAL FRAME

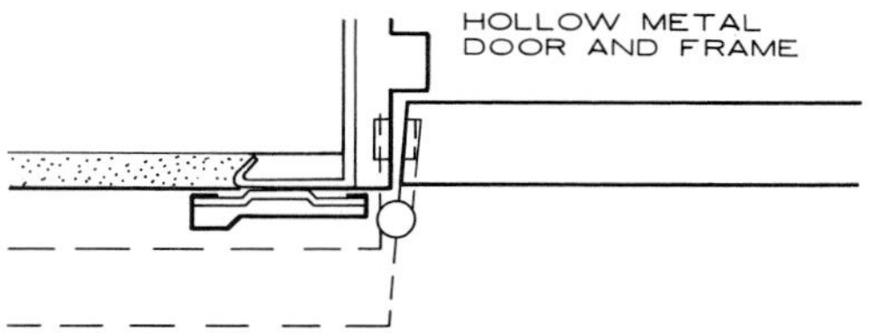

**FULL MORTISE TEMPLATE**

HOLLOW METAL DOOR AND FRAME

**FULL MORTISE TEMPLATE**

---

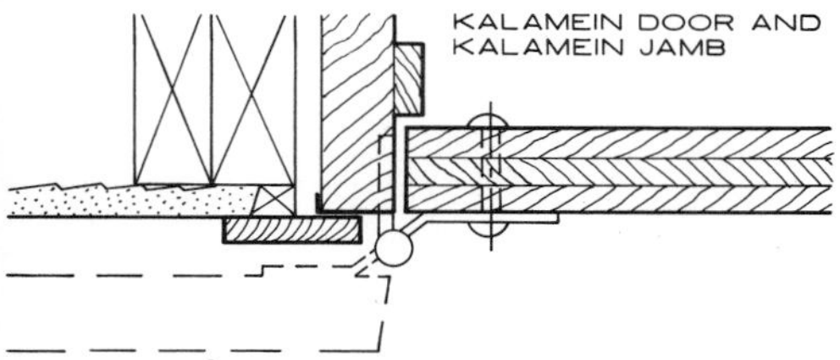

KALAMEIN DOOR AND KALAMEIN JAMB

**HALF SURFACE TEMPLATE**

KALAMEIN DOOR WITH HOLLOW METAL FRAME

**HALF SURFACE TEMPLATE**

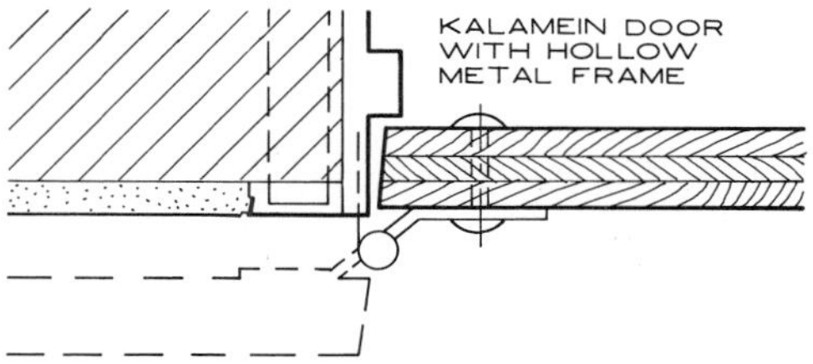

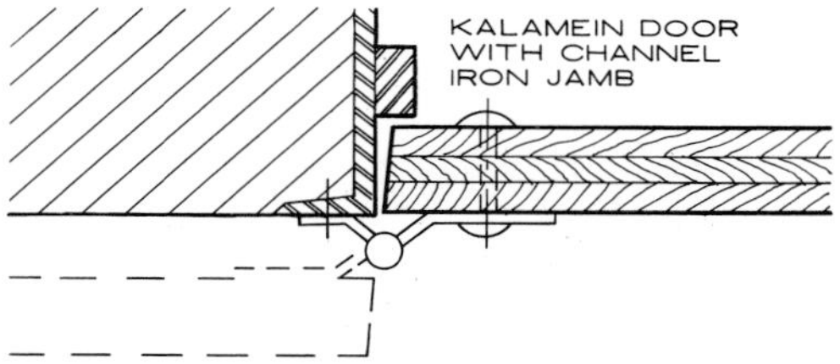

KALAMEIN DOOR WITH CHANNEL IRON JAMB

**FULL SURFACE TEMPLATE**

---

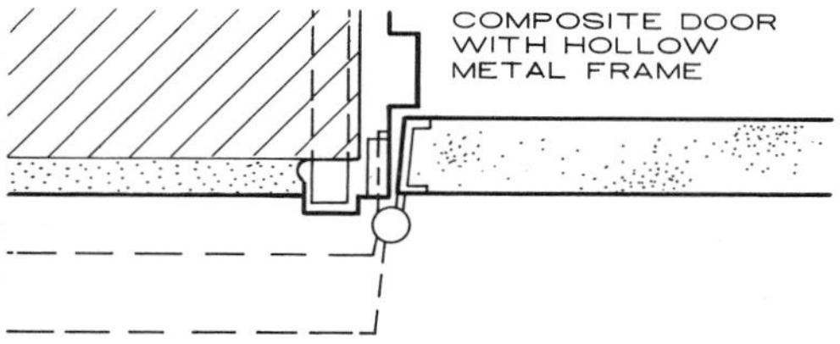

COMPOSITE DOOR WITH HOLLOW METAL FRAME

**FULL MORTISE TEMPLATE**

TUBULAR STEEL DOOR WITH CHANNEL IRON JAMB

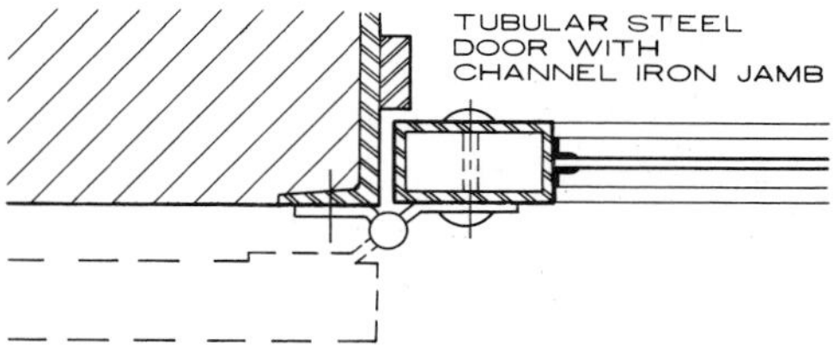

**FULL SURFACE TEMPLATE**

HOLLOW METAL DOOR WITH CHANNEL IRON JAMB

**HALF MORTISE TEMPLATE**

**MORTISE TEMPLATES**

---

F. J. Trost, SMS Architects; New Canaan, Connecticut
Door and Hardware Institute; Arlington, Virginia

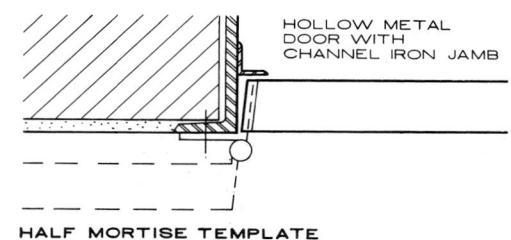

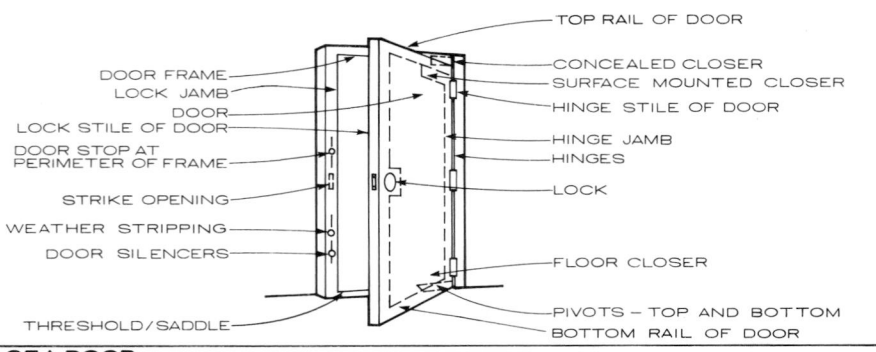

**PARTS OF A DOOR**

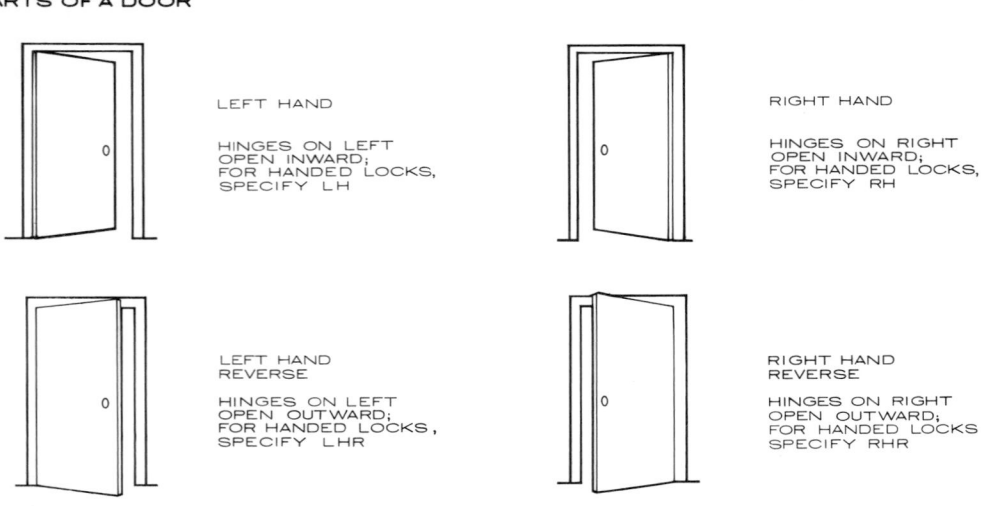

**HANDS OF DOORS**

## DOOR FINISHES

| NEAREST U.S. EQUIVALENT | BHMA CODE | FINISH DESCRIPTION | BASE MATERIAL |
|---|---|---|---|
| USP | 600 | Primed for painting | Steel |
| US1B | 601 | Bright japanned | Steel |
| US2C | 602 | Cadmium plated | Steel |
| US2G | 603 | Zinc plated | Steel |
| US3 | 605 | Bright brass, clear coated | Brass* |
| US4 | 606 | Satin brass, clear coated | Brass* |
| US9 | 611 | Bright bronze, clear coated | Bronze* |
| US10 | 612 | Satin bronze, clear coated | Bronze* |
| US10B | 613 | Oxidized satin bronze, oil rubbed | Bronze* |
| US14 | 618 | Bright nickel plated, clear coated | Brass, Bronze* |
| US15 | 619 | Satin nickel plated, clear coated | Brass, Bronze* |
| US19 | 622 | Flat black coated | Brass, Bronze* |
| US20A | 624 | Dark oxidized, statuary bronze, clear coated | Bronze* |
| US26 | 625 | Bright chromium plated | Brass, Bronze* |
| US26D | 626 | Satin chromium plated | Brass, Bronze* |
| US27 | 627 | Satin aluminum, clear coated | Aluminum |
| US28 | 628 | Satin aluminum, clear anodized | Aluminum |
| US32 | 629 | Bright stainless steel | Stainless steel 300 series |
| US32D | 630 | Satin, stainless steel | Stainless steel 300 series |
| — | 684 | Black chrome, bright | Brass, Bronze* |
| — | 685 | Black chrome, satin | Brass, Bronze* |

*Also applicable to other base metals under a different BHMA code number.
Note: BHMA—Builders' Hardware Manufacturers Association

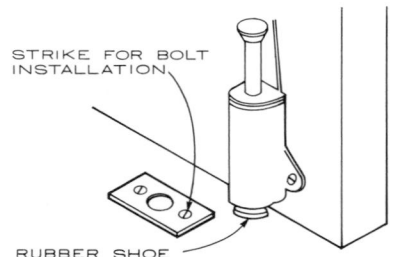

**PLUNGER TYPE HOLDER OR BOLT**

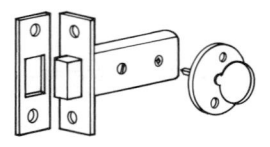

**MORTISE BOLT**

F. J. Trost, SMS Architects; New Canaan, Connecticut
Door and Hardware Institute; Arlington, Virginia

## GLOSSARY

**Coordinator**—A device used on a pair of doors to insure that the inactive leaf is permitted to close before the active leaf.

**Cylinder (of a lock)**—The cylindrical shaped assembly containing the tumbler mechanism and the keyway, which can be actuated only by the correct keys.

**Cylinder Lock**—A lock in which the locking mechanism is controlled by a cylinder.

**Deadbolt (of a lock)**—A lock bolt having no spring action or bevel, and which is operated by a key or a turn piece.

**Door Bolt**—A manually operated rod or bar attached to a door providing means of locking.

**Door Holder**—A device to hold a door open at selected positions.

**Door Stop**—A device to stop the swing or movement of a door at a certain point.

**Electric Strike**—An electrical device that permits releasing of the door from a remote control.

**Exit Device**—A door locking device which grants instant exit by pressing on a crossbar to release the locking bolt or latch.

**Flush Bolt**—A door bolt set flush with the face or edge of the door.

**Hand (of a lock, etc.)**—A term used to indicate the direction of swing or movement, and locking security side of a door.

**Lock Set**—A lock, complete with trim, such as knobs, escutcheons, or handles.

**Mortise**—A cavity made to receive a lock or other hardware; also the act of making such a cavity.

**Mortise Lock (or Latch)**—A lock designed to be installed in a mortise rather than applied to the door's surface.

**Rabbet**—The abutting edges of a pair of doors or windows, shaped to provide a tight fit.

**Reversible Lock**—A lock which, by reversing the latch bolt, may be used by any hand. On certain types of locks, other parts must also be changed.

**Rose**—A trim plate attached to the door under the knob. It sometimes acts as a knob bearing.

**Shank (of a knob)**—The projecting stem of knob into which the spindle is fastened.

**Spindle (of a knob)**—The bar or tube connected with the knob or lever handle that passes through the hub of the lock or otherwise engages the mechanism to transmit the knob action to the bolt(s).

**Stop (of a lock)**—The button, or other small device, which serves to lock the latch bolt against the outside knob or thumb piece or unlock it if locked. Another type holds the bolt retracted.

**Strike**—A metal plate or box which is pierced or recessed to receive the bolt or latch when projected. Sometimes called "keeper."

**Three-Point Lock**—A device sometimes required on three-hour fire doors to lock the active leaf of a pair of doors at three points.

## NOTES

1. See also Hollow Metal Frames and Doors: Glossary.
2. Face the outside of the door to determine its hand. The outside of the door is the "key side" or that side which would be secured should a lock be used. This would usually be the exterior of an entrance or the corridor side of an office door.

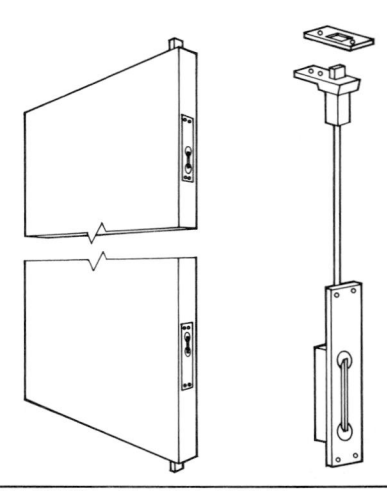

**EXTENSION FLUSH BOLT**

**HARDWARE**

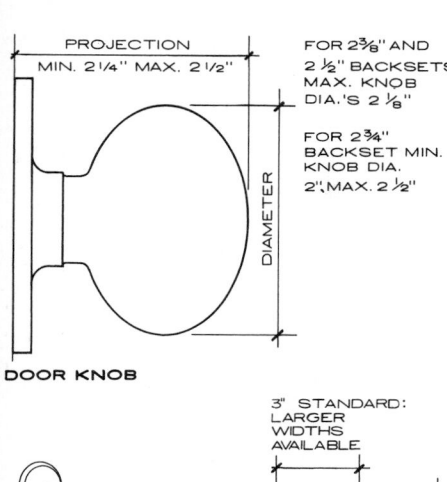

**DOOR KNOB**

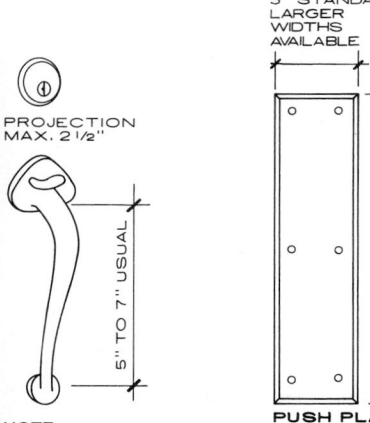

**NOTE**

Entrance door handle complete lockset includes mortise lock, handle outside, and knob and rose inside.

**ENTRANCE HANDLE**

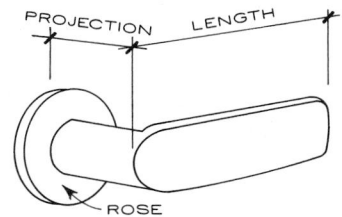

**NOTES**

Projection—$1\frac{3}{4}$ in. to $2\frac{1}{2}$ in.
Length—2 in. to 4 in.
Rose—max. diameter $1\frac{1}{2}$ in. for 3 in.
Stile—larger stile takes larger rose.

**LEVER HANDLE**

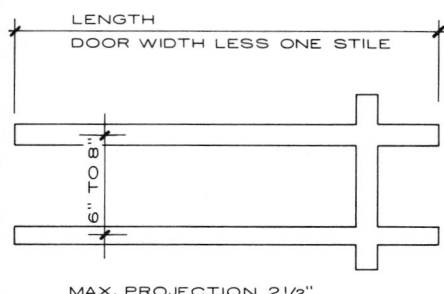

**NOTE**

Double push-pull bars may be used on the pull side of single acting doors or on either side of double acting doors.

**PUSH—PULL BAR**

**KNOB, HANDLES, PLATE AND BAR**

F. J. Trost, SMS Architects; New Canaan, Connecticut
Door and Hardware Institute; Arlington, Virginia

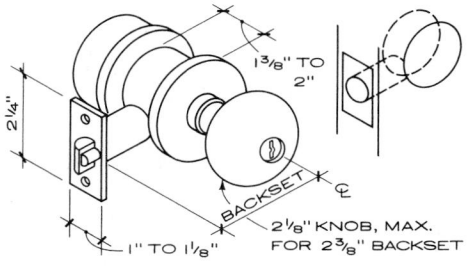

**NOTES**

1. Installation requires $2\frac{1}{8}$ in. hole in door face. Door edge requires $\frac{7}{8}$ in. or $\frac{15}{16}$ in. hole for standard lock, 1 in. hole for heavy duty lock.
2. Backsets: standard lock—$2\frac{3}{8}$ in. (regular), 2 in., $2\frac{3}{4}$ in., $3\frac{3}{4}$ in., 5 in., 7 in., 8 in., 10 in., 18 in. Heavy duty lock $2\frac{3}{4}$ in. (regular), $3\frac{3}{4}$ in., 5 in., 6 in., 7 in., 8 in., 18 in., 19 in. (42 in. special).

**CYLINDER**

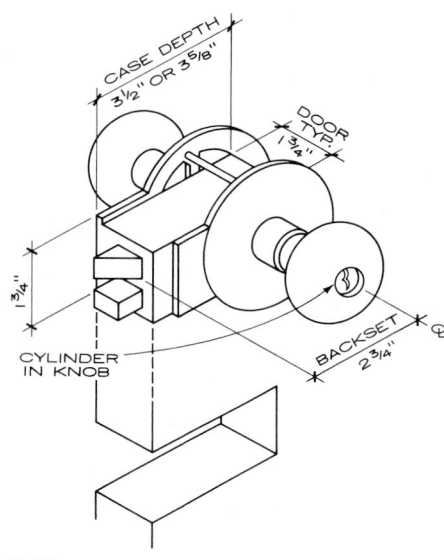

**NOTES**

1. Also available for other door thicknesses.
2. Also available without deadbolt for use as latch.
3. Installation requires notch cut in lock side of door to suit case size. Complete factory assembly eliminates much adjustment on the job.

**UNIT**

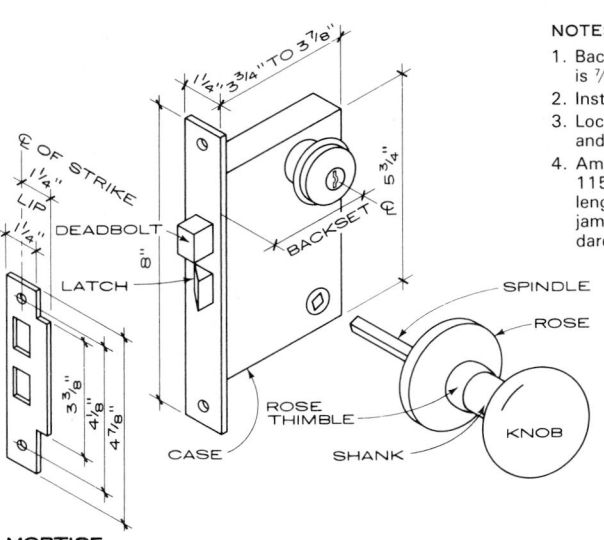

**MORTISE**

**LOCK TYPES**

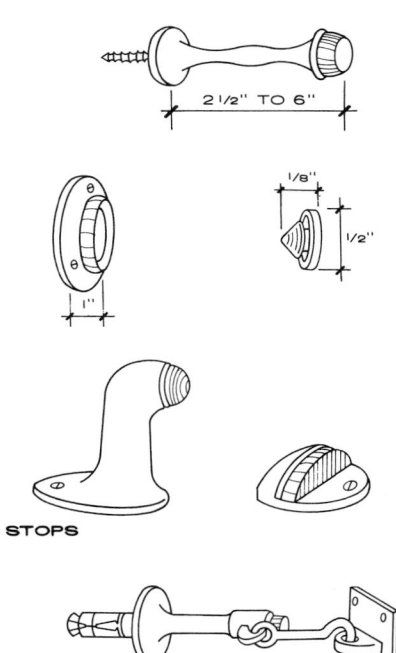

**STOPS**

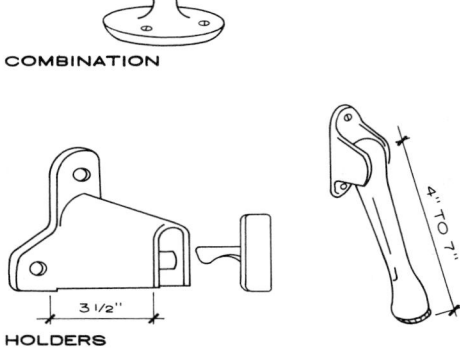

**COMBINATION**

**HOLDERS**

**STOPS AND HOLDERS**

**NOTES**

1. Backset $2\frac{3}{4}$ in. for $1\frac{3}{4}$ in. door. For $1\frac{3}{8}$ in. door, front is $\frac{7}{8}$ in. or 1 in. and backset $2\frac{1}{2}$ in. or $2\frac{3}{4}$ in.
2. Installation requires mortise opening in door.
3. Locks available with rabbeted fronts and many key and latch functions.
4. American Standards Association Lock Strikes A-115V-1959 for metal door frames. To determine lip length measure from centerline of strike to edge of jamb and add $\frac{1}{4}$ in. Outside strike dimensions standard for all lock types shown.

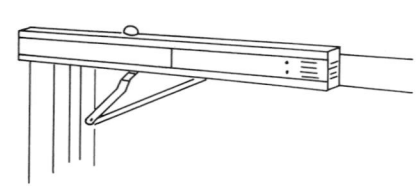

CLOSER, HOLDER, AND DETECTOR
PUSH-SIDE MOUNTED

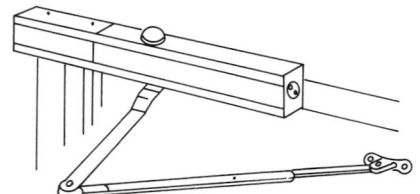

CLOSER AND HOLDER ONLY
PUSH-SIDE MOUNTED

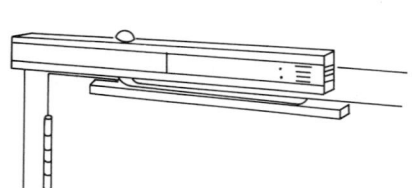

CLOSER, HOLDER, AND DETECTOR
PULL-SIDE MOUNTED

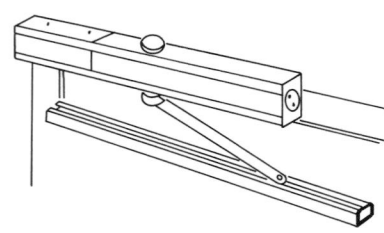

CLOSER AND HOLDER ONLY
PULL-SIDE MOUNTED

## FIRE AND SMOKE DETECTION SYSTEMS

1. Heat sensing detectors operate on the basis of fixed temperature or a rate of temperature rise. Door closers are activated upon release of a heat activated device such as a fusible link. Closing mechanisms may consist of gravity operated weights or wound steel springs.
2. Smoke sensing detectors detect both visible and invisible airborne particles. Various operating principles include ionization, photoelectric, resistance, sampling, and cloud chamber detection.
3. Ionization detection closers contain a small quantity of radioactive material within the sensing chamber. The resulting ionized air permits an electric current flow between electrodes. When smoke particles reduce the flow of ionized air between electrodes to a certain level, the detection circuit responds. Closing mechanisms usually consist of a detector, electromechanical holding device, and a door closer.
4. Ionization detectors sense ordinary products of combustion from sources such as kitchens, motors, power tools, and automobile exhausts.
5. Photoelectric detection closers consist of a light source and a photoelectric cell. They activate when smoke becomes dense enough to change the reflectance of light reaching the photoelectric device. Photoelectric detectors may be spot or beam type. Closing mechanisms consist of a detector, electromechanical holding device, and a door closer.
6. Other types of smoke detectors include electrical bridging, sampling, and cloud chambers. Each has operating characteristics similar to ionization and photoelectric detectors.
7. Requirements for closers and detectors vary by code and governing jurisdiction. Refer to local building codes, the National Fire Protection Association's life safety code (NFPA) and other applicable regulations.

A COMBINATION DOOR CLOSER, HOLDER, AND FIRE AND SMOKE DETECTOR is available with ionization, photoelectric, or heat sensing detectors for smoke or any combustion products and for holding the door open.

A COMBINATION CLOSER AND HOLDER (only) will hold door in open position when incorporated with an independent detector or when wired into any type of fire detecting system.

All these units have unlimited hold-open from 0° to approximately 170°, or limited hold-open from 85° to 170° for cross-corridor doors.

## SURFACE MOUNTED COMBINATION CLOSERS, HOLDERS, AND DETECTORS

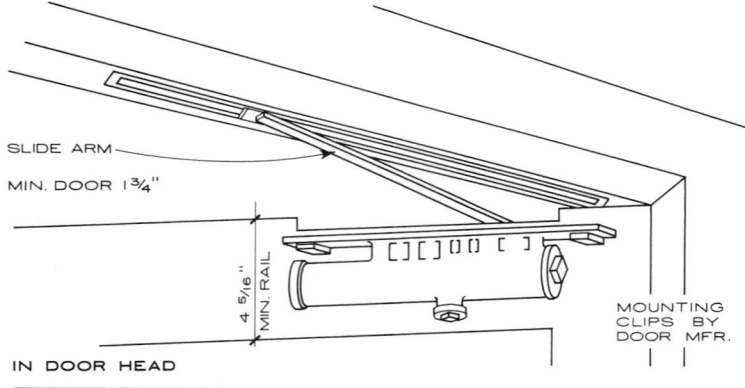

SLIDE ARM
MIN. DOOR 1¾"
4 5/16" MIN. RAIL
IN DOOR HEAD
MOUNTING CLIPS BY DOOR MFR.

CONSULT MANUFACTURERS FOR MIN. SIZES
4½" MAX.
LEVER ARM
SLIDING SHOE IN DOOR HEAD
IN FRAME HEAD

## CONCEALED CLOSERS

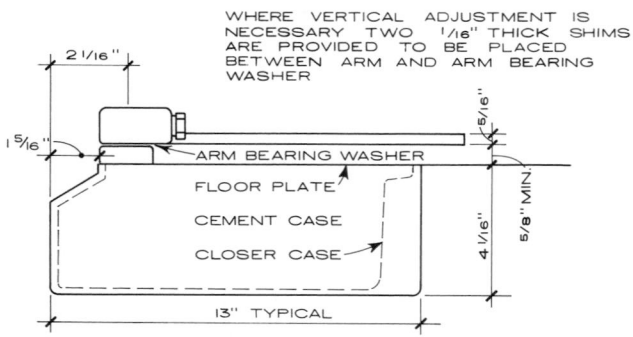

WHERE VERTICAL ADJUSTMENT IS NECESSARY TWO 1/16" THICK SHIMS ARE PROVIDED TO BE PLACED BETWEEN ARM AND ARM BEARING WASHER

2 1/16"
1 5/16"
5/16"
ARM BEARING WASHER
FLOOR PLATE
CEMENT CASE
CLOSER CASE
4 1/16"
5/8" MIN.
13" TYPICAL

EXTERIOR DOOR CLOSER CONCEALED IN FLOOR

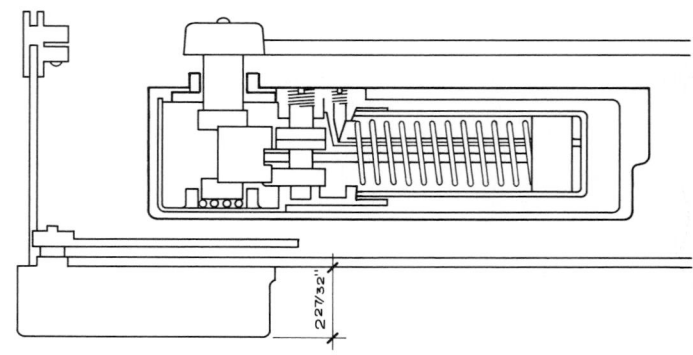

22 7/32"

CHECKING FLOOR HINGE FOR INTERIOR DOORS

Lee A. Anderson; SRGF, Inc., Architects; Champaign, Illinois
Sam A. Buzbee, AIA; Mott, Mobley, Richter, McGowan & Griffin; Fort Smith, Arkansas

## HARDWARE

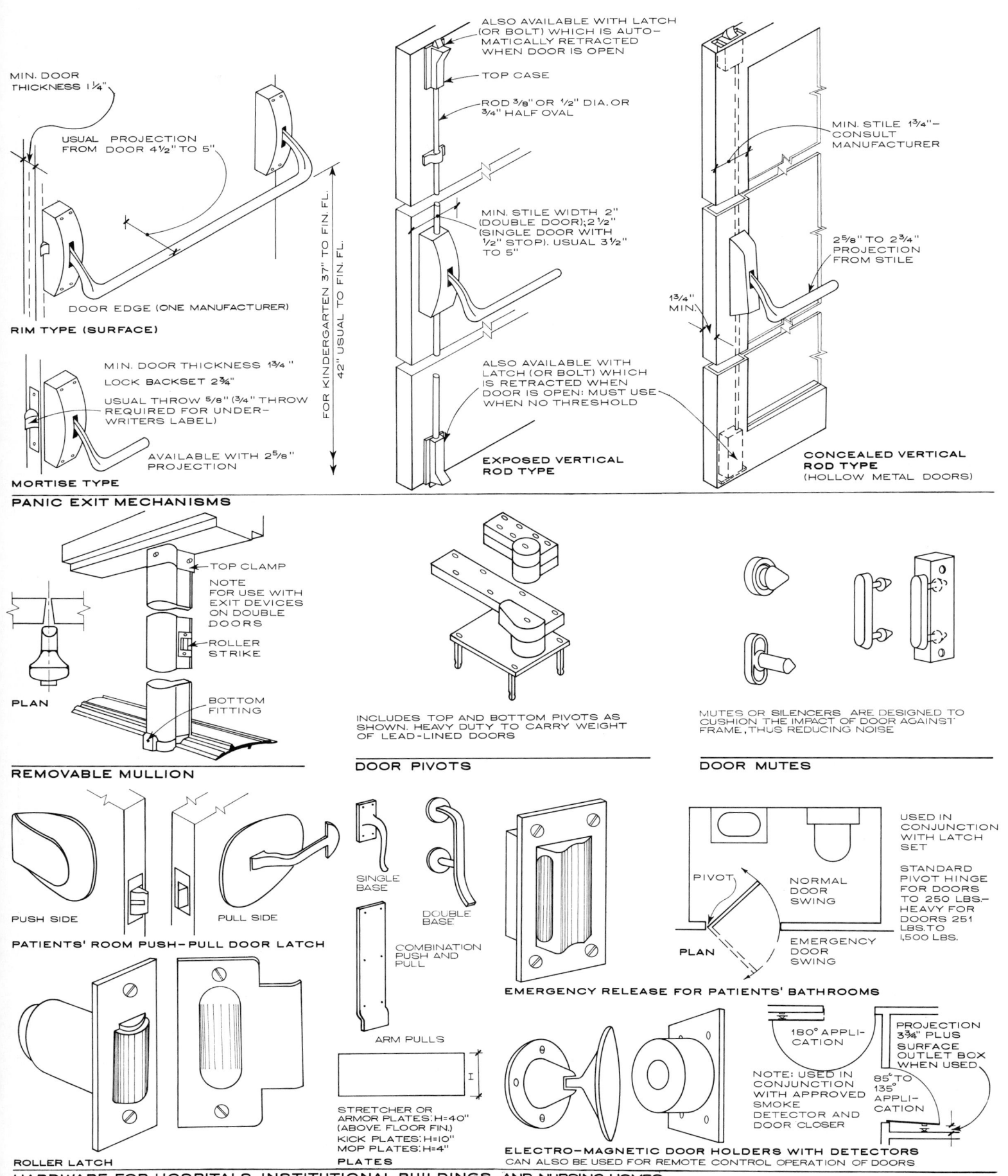

MIN. DOOR THICKNESS 1¼"

USUAL PROJECTION FROM DOOR 4½" TO 5"

DOOR EDGE (ONE MANUFACTURER)

**RIM TYPE (SURFACE)**

MIN. DOOR THICKNESS 1¾"

LOCK BACKSET 2¾"

USUAL THROW ⅝" (¾" THROW REQUIRED FOR UNDER-WRITERS LABEL)

AVAILABLE WITH 2⅝" PROJECTION

**MORTISE TYPE**

FOR KINDERGARTEN 37" TO FIN. FL.
42" USUAL TO FIN. FL.

ALSO AVAILABLE WITH LATCH (OR BOLT) WHICH IS AUTO-MATICALLY RETRACTED WHEN DOOR IS OPEN

TOP CASE

ROD ⅜" OR ½" DIA. OR ¾" HALF OVAL

MIN. STILE WIDTH 2" (DOUBLE DOOR); 2½" (SINGLE DOOR WITH ½" STOP). USUAL 3½" TO 5"

ALSO AVAILABLE WITH LATCH (OR BOLT) WHICH IS RETRACTED WHEN DOOR IS OPEN; MUST USE WHEN NO THRESHOLD

**EXPOSED VERTICAL ROD TYPE**

MIN. STILE 1¾"—CONSULT MANUFACTURER

2⅝" TO 2¾" PROJECTION FROM STILE

1¾" MIN.

**CONCEALED VERTICAL ROD TYPE** (HOLLOW METAL DOORS)

**PANIC EXIT MECHANISMS**

TOP CLAMP

NOTE FOR USE WITH EXIT DEVICES ON DOUBLE DOORS

ROLLER STRIKE

BOTTOM FITTING

**PLAN**

**REMOVABLE MULLION**

INCLUDES TOP AND BOTTOM PIVOTS AS SHOWN. HEAVY DUTY TO CARRY WEIGHT OF LEAD-LINED DOORS

**DOOR PIVOTS**

MUTES OR SILENCERS ARE DESIGNED TO CUSHION THE IMPACT OF DOOR AGAINST FRAME, THUS REDUCING NOISE

**DOOR MUTES**

PUSH SIDE          PULL SIDE

**PATIENTS' ROOM PUSH-PULL DOOR LATCH**

SINGLE BASE

DOUBLE BASE

COMBINATION PUSH AND PULL

**ARM PULLS**

STRETCHER OR ARMOR PLATES: H=40" (ABOVE FLOOR FIN.)
KICK PLATES: H=10"
MOP PLATES: H=4"

**PLATES**

**ROLLER LATCH**

**EMERGENCY RELEASE FOR PATIENTS' BATHROOMS**

USED IN CONJUNCTION WITH LATCH SET

STANDARD PIVOT HINGE FOR DOORS TO 250 LBS.—HEAVY FOR DOORS 251 LBS. TO 1,500 LBS.

PIVOT

NORMAL DOOR SWING

EMERGENCY DOOR SWING

**PLAN**

NOTE: USED IN CONJUNCTION WITH APPROVED SMOKE DETECTOR AND DOOR CLOSER

180° APPLI-CATION

85° TO 135° APPLI-CATION

PROJECTION 3¾" PLUS SURFACE OUTLET BOX WHEN USED

**ELECTRO-MAGNETIC DOOR HOLDERS WITH DETECTORS**
CAN ALSO BE USED FOR REMOTE CONTROL OPERATION OF DOORS

## HARDWARE FOR HOSPITALS, INSTITUTIONAL BUILDINGS, AND NURSING HOMES

F. J. Trost, SMS Architects; New Canaan, Connecticut
Door and Hardware Institute; Arlington, Virginia

**HARDWARE**   8

**NOTE**

Threshold profiles vary from mfr. to mfr. Consult mfr. catalog for additional sizes. Std. length is 18' to 20' or saddles may be cut to size. Anchors to wood floors are screws; to terrazzo or cement floors, screws in fiber plugs or expansive metal anchors; to concrete, screws tapped to clips set in concrete.

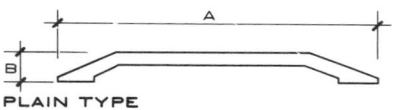

**PLAIN TYPE**

| BRASS | | ALUMINUM | | | | BRONZE | |
|---|---|---|---|---|---|---|---|
| A | B | A | B | A | B | A | B |
| 3" | 1/4" | 4 5/64" | 3/32" | 4" | | 2 1/2 & 3 | 1/4" |
| 2 1/4" | 3/16" | 2 1/4" | 3/16" | 4 5/64" | 1/2" | 4, 5 | |
| 4,5 & 6 | 1/2" | 2 1/2, 3" | 1/4" | 5 & 6 | | & 6 | 1/2" |
| | | 2 1/4" | 3/16" | 4" | 7/16" | | |

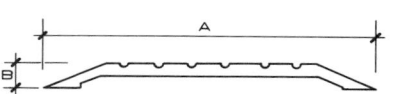

**FLUTED TYPES**

| BRASS | | ALUM. | | BRONZE | | STEEL | |
|---|---|---|---|---|---|---|---|
| A | B | A | B | A | B | A | B |
| 3, 3 1/2 | | 3, 4 | | 3 | 5/16" | 3 & 4 | 1/2" |
| 4,5 | 1/2" | 5,6 | | 3 | 3/8" | 5 1/2" | 9/16" |
| & 6 | | 6 1/4" | 1/2" | 4, 4 1/2 | | 5 1/2 | |
| | | 7 | | 5, 6 | 1/2" | & 7 | 5/8" |
| | | 7 1/2 | | & 7 | | | |
| | | 3, 4 | | 6 & 7 | 5/8" | | |
| | | 5 & 6 | 5/8" | | | | |

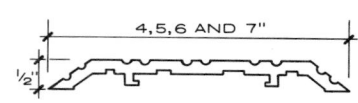

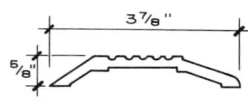

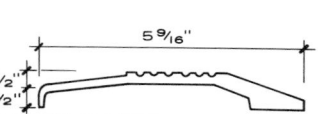

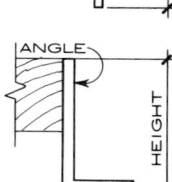

**JOINT STRIP**

Used for division of floors of different materials

**PLAIN AND FLUTED SADDLES AND JOINT STRIPS FOR INTERIORS**

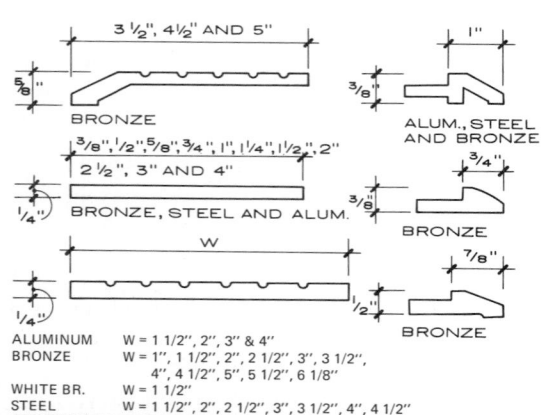

ALUMINUM    W = 1 1/2", 2", 3" & 4"
BRONZE      W = 1", 1 1/2", 2", 2 1/2", 3", 3 1/2", 4", 4 1/2", 5", 5 1/2", 6 1/8"
WHITE BR.   W = 1 1/2"
STEEL       W = 1 1/2", 2", 2 1/2", 3", 3 1/2", 4", 4 1/2"

**ASSEMBLED SADDLE COMPONENTS**

**SLIDING DOOR SADDLE COMPONENTS**

**ROOF DOOR**

**SLIDING DOOR**

**TYPICAL ASSEMBLED SADDLES**

By combining components saddles may be made to any width, joints will not show as fluting pattern is identical.

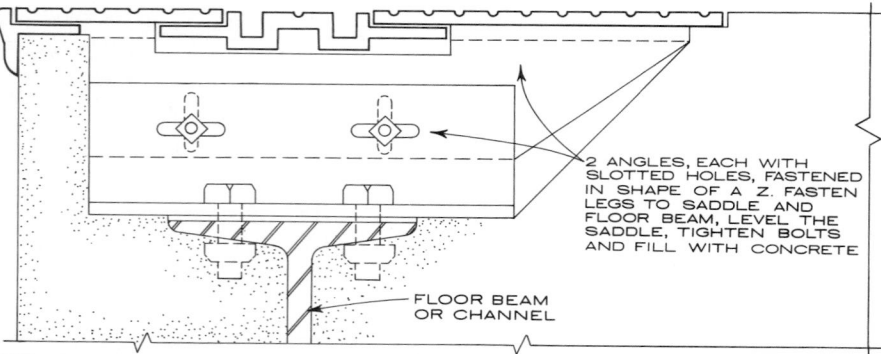

2 ANGLES, EACH WITH SLOTTED HOLES, FASTENED IN SHAPE OF A Z. FASTEN LEGS TO SADDLE AND FLOOR BEAM, LEVEL THE SADDLE, TIGHTEN BOLTS AND FILL WITH CONCRETE

FLOOR BEAM OR CHANNEL

**ELEVATOR SADDLE CONSTRUCTION**

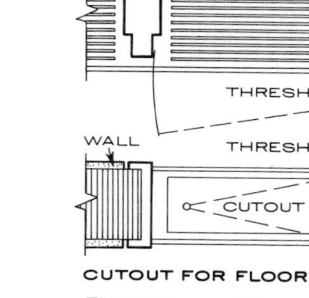

THRESHOLD

WALL

CUTOUT

THRESHOLD

WALL

CUTOUT

**CUTOUT FOR FLOOR HINGES**

Threshold assemblies may also be cut or notched to fit mullions or columns.

NOTE: STANDARD WIDTH = 4", 5" AND 6"

1" TYP.

**RECOMMENDED PRACTICE**

| TH. | IRON | BRONZE | ALUMINUM | NICKEL |
|---|---|---|---|---|
| 1/4 | | to 6" wide | to 10" wide | to 6" wide |
| 5/16 | to 6" wide | to 10" wide | to 18" wide | to 10" wide |
| 3/8 | to 12" wide | to 18" wide | to 24" wide | to 14" wide |
| 7/16 | to 24" wide | to 24" wide | to 36" wide | to 18" wide |
| 1/2 | to 30" wide | to 30" wide | to 42" wide | to 24" wide |
| 5/8 | to 42" wide | to 42" wide | to 42" wide | to 30" wide |
| 3/4 | to 42" wide | to 42" wide | to 42" wide | to 30" wide |

Length, to 9'-6". When width exceeds 32", length should not exceed 7'-6".

**CAST METAL ABRASIVE SURFACE SADDLES**

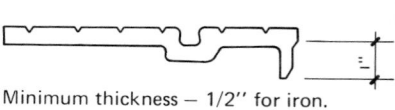

Minimum thickness — 1/2" for iron. 3/8" for bronze, aluminum and nickel

**ELEVATOR DOOR SADDLE**

Saddles with floor hinge cut-outs, as shown above also available.

Dan Cowling and Associates, Inc.; Little Rock, Arkansas

**HARDWARE**

## GLASS: DEFINITION

A hard, brittle amorphous substance made by fusing silica (sometimes combined with oxides of boron or phosphorus) with certain basic oxides (notably sodium, potassium, calcium, magnesium, and lead) and cooling rapidly to prevent crystallization or devitrification. Most glasses melt at 800°C to 950°C. Heat-resisting glass usually contains a high proportion of boric oxide. The brittleness of glass is such that minute surface scratches in manufacturing greatly reduce its strength.

## INDUSTRY QUALITY STANDARDS

FEDERAL SPECIFICATION DD-G-451: Establishes thickness and dimensional tolerances and quality characteristics of flat glass products.

FEDERAL SPECIFICATION DD-G-1403: Establishes standards for tempered glass, heat strengthened glass, and spandrel glass.

AMERICAN NATIONAL STANDARD 2971: Establishes standards for testing safety glazing material.

INSULATING GLASS CERTIFICATION COUNCIL (IGCC): Conducts periodic inspection and independent laboratory tests of insulating glass products.

ASTM STANDARD E546: Test method for frost point of sealed insulating glass units (horizontal position).

ASTM STANDARD E576: Dew/frost point of sealed insulating glass units in vertical position.

ASTM STANDARD E773: Test method for seal durability of sealed insulating glass units.

ASTM STANDARD E774: Specification for sealed insulating glass units.

### NOTE

Consult glass manufacturers for current information because processes, qualities, finishes, colors, sizes, thicknesses, and limitations are revised continuously. The following information represents one or more manufacturers' guidelines.

## BASIC TYPES OF GLASS (CLEAR GLASS)

### WINDOW AND SHEET GLASS

Manufactured by a horizontally flat or vertical draw process, then annealed slowly to produce natural flat fired, high gloss surfaces. Generally has residential and industrial applications. Inherent surface waves are noticeable in sizes larger than 4 sq. ft. For minimum distortion, larger sizes are installed with the wave running horizontally. The width is listed first when specifying.

### FLOAT GLASS

Generally accepted as the successor to polished plate glass, float glass has become the quality standard of the glass industry in architectural, mirror, and specialty applications. It is manufactured by floating on a surface of molten tin, then annealing slowly to produce a transparent flat glass, thus eliminating grinding and polishing.

### PLATE GLASS

Transparent flat glass is ground and polished after rolling. Within limits, cylindrical and conic shapes can be bent to desired curvature.

## VARIATIONS OF BASIC TYPES OF GLASS

### PATTERNED GLASS

Known also as rolled or figured glass, it is made by passing molten glass through rollers that are etched to produce the appropriate design. Most often only one side of the glass is imprinted with a pattern; however, it is possible to imprint both sides.

### WIRE GLASS

Available as clear polished glass or in various patterns, most commonly with embedded welded square or diamond wire. Some distortion, wire discoloration, and misalignment are inherent. Some 1/4 in. (6 mm) wired glass products are recognized as certified safety glazing materials for use in hazardous locations. For applicable fire and safety codes that govern their use, refer to ANSI Z97.1.

### CATHEDRAL GLASS

Known also as art glass, stained glass, or opalescent glass. It is produced in many colors, textures, and patterns, is usually 1/8 in. thick, and is used primarily in decorating leaded glass windows. Specialty firms usually contract this highly exacting art.

### OBSCURE GLASS

To obscure a view or create a design, the entire surface on one or both sides of the glass can be sandblasted, acid etched, or both. When a glass surface is altered by any of these methods, the glass is weakened and may be difficult to clean.

### HEAT-ABSORBING OR TINTED GLASS

The glass absorbs a portion of the sun's energy because of admixture contents and thickness. It then dissipates the heat to both the exterior and interior. The exterior glass surface reflects a portion of energy depending on the sun's position. Heat-absorbing glass has a higher temperature when exposed to the sun than clear glass does; thus the central area expands more than the cooler shaded edges, causing edge tensile stress buildup.

### DESIGN CONSIDERATIONS

1. To avoid shading problems, provide conditions so glass edges warm as rapidly as other lights. An example is framing systems with low heat capacity and minimal glass grip or stops. Structural rubber gaskets can be used.
2. The thicker the glass, the greater the solar energy absorption.
3. Indoor shading devices such as blinds and draperies reflect energy back through the glass, thus increasing the glass temperature. Spaces between indoor shading and the glass, including ceiling pockets, should be vented adequately. Heating elements always should be located on the interior side of shading devices, directing warm air away from the glass.

### REFLECTIVE COATED GLASS

Reflective glass coatings may be applied to float plate, heat strengthened, tempered, laminated, insulated, or spandrel glass; the number is vast. Design considerations for heat absorbing glass also apply to reflective coated glass.

Reflective coating glass falls in three basic classifications:

1. Single glazing with a coating on one surface.
2. Laminated glass coated between the glass plies or on the exterior surface.
3. Insulating glass units with coating on the exterior surface or on either of the interior surfaces.

Application of a reflective coating on the exterior surface creates a visually uniform surface on any or all these glass classifications. Extreme care must be taken in handling, glazing, and cleaning this type of glass to avoid scratching the coating. Some reflective coatings are available only with insulating units.

### HEAT STRENGTHENED AND TEMPERED GLASS

Produced by reheating and rapidly cooling annealed glass, it has greatly increased mechanical strength and resistance to thermal stresses. Neither type can be altered after fabrication; the manufacturer must furnish the exact size and shape. The inherent warpage may cause glazing problems. Refer to Federal Specifications DD-G-1404 for allowable tolerances.

### HEAT STRENGTHENED GLASS

Twice as strong as annealed glass. Unlike tempered glass, it does not pulverize into crystal-like form when broken.

### TEMPERED GLASS

Four to five times the strength of annealed glass; it breaks into innumerable small, cubed fragments. It can be much safer than annealed glass. Shallow patterned glass also may be tempered. Tong marks are visible near the edge on the short side when the glass is held vertically during tempering. Some manufacturers temper horizontally to eliminate these marks. Strain patterns are inherent and can be seen under some lighting conditions or through polarized eyeglasses.

### SPANDREL GLASS

Heat strengthened by firefusing an opaque ceramic color to the interior surface of sheet, plate, or float glass. May be tempered fully if it conforms with GSA guide specification No. PBS-4-0885.

A variety of colors and special finishes are available. Supplied with a reflective coating, color frit, or opacifier film and with insulation or as part of an insulating glass unit. Pinholes and nonuniformity of color are apparent if used without solid opaque backup. If monolithic spandrel glass is supplied without integral insulation, at least 2 in. air space is required between glass back and insulation material.

### SOUND CONTROL GLASS

Laminated, insulating, laminated insulating, and double laminated insulating glass products commonly are used for sound control. STC ratings from 31 to 51 are available depending on glass thicknesses, air space size, polyvinyl butyl film thickness, and number of laminated units used in insulating products.

### LAMINATED GLASS

#### SAFETY GLASS
(See also Wire Glass, Mirrors)

A tough, clear plastic film sheet (interlayer) 0.015 in. (0.636 mm) thick minimum is sandwiched, under heat and pressure, between plies of sheet, plate, float, wired, heat absorbing, tinted, reflective, heat strengthened, full-tempered glass, or combinations of each.

When fractured, particles tend to adhere to the plastic film. Always weep the glazing cavity to the exterior.

#### SECURITY GLASS

Safety glass with a plastic film of 0.060 in. (1.5 mm) minimum thickness for bullet resistant and burglar resistant glass. Bullet resisting glass consists of three to five plies of glass and, in some cases, high performance plastics, with an overall 3/4 in. to 3 in. thickness. Avoid sealants with organic solvents or oil, which can react with the plastic film. (See Plastics in Glazing.)

## GENERAL CONSIDERATIONS FOR GLAZING ASSEMBLIES

1. Thermal movement in frame and glass.
2. Deflection, vertical framing members.
3. Deflection, horizontal framing members.
4. Clearances, shims, drainage.

Expansion and contraction of the glazing material and the resulting movement and stresses the glazing system must cope with are determined by:

1. Size of light to be glazed.
2. Maximum exposure temperatures for glazing materials.
3. Sealed insulating units (hotter trapped air.)

Consult manufacturer for load capacities.

Some factors impacting transfer of wind loads to surrounding structure are:

1. Proportion and size of opening, span between supports, and thickness and deflection of glass.
2. Method of support for the glass pane.
3. Movement of the surrounding structure.
4. Setting blocks placed under bottom edge of glass.
5. Spacer shims—to assure proper clearances between face of glazing material and framing channels.
6. Squareness, flatness tolerances surrounding channel.

## INSULATING GLASS

Insulating glass, with high performance in thermal resistance and shading coefficient, is used primarily to control heat transfer. Insulating glass units are manufactured from two or more pieces of glass separated by a hermetically sealed air space. Two unit types are available:

1. GLASS EDGE OR GLASS SEAL UNIT: Primarily for residential use. Constructed by fusing edges of two glass lights together with ³⁄₁₆ in. (5 mm) space filled with a dry gas at atmospheric pressure. Use at high altitudes is not recommended. Do not glaze with lockstrip structural gaskets.
2. ORGANIC SEALED EDGE UNIT: Primarily for commercial and industrial use, as well as for some residential

applications. Constructed with two sheets of glass separated by a metal or organic spacer (filled with a moisture absorbing material) around the edges and hermetically sealed. Insulating units should be fabricated to IGCC AND ASTM E546, E576, E773, and E774 standards.

Available with ¼ in. and ½ in. air space in float, patterned, heat absorbing, tinted, reflective coated, annealed, heat-strengthened, tempered, and laminated glass. The thickness of the two glass panes, however, should not differ by more than ¹⁄₁₆ in. Performance characteristics, glass thickness, maximum fabricated sizes, and a multitude of various combinations may be found in the manufacturer's literature.

The heat absorbing glass of a heat absorbing unit should be to the exterior. When sloped insulated glazing is used over occupied areas, heat-strengthened, laminated glass is advisable as the interior light; however, the glass manufacturer and governing codes and authorities on fire and safety should be consulted. Triple glazing units are available for special application. Moisture drainage that might collect in the glazing pocket, destroying the organic seal, must be provided for.

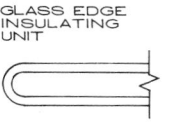

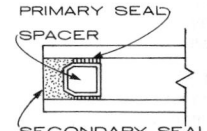

GLASS EDGE INSULATING UNIT — INSULATING GLASS UNITS

PRIMARY SEAL / SPACER / SECONDARY SEAL — ORGANIC SEALED EDGE INSULATING UNIT

**INSULATING GLASS**

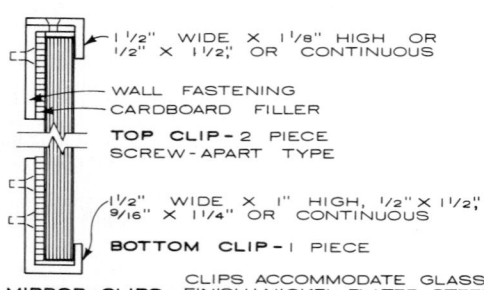

1½" WIDE × 1⅛" HIGH OR ½" × 1½", OR CONTINUOUS
WALL FASTENING
CARDBOARD FILLER
TOP CLIP — 2 PIECE SCREW — APART TYPE
1½" WIDE × 1" HIGH, ½" × 1½", ⁹⁄₁₆" × 1¼" OR CONTINUOUS
BOTTOM CLIP — 1 PIECE

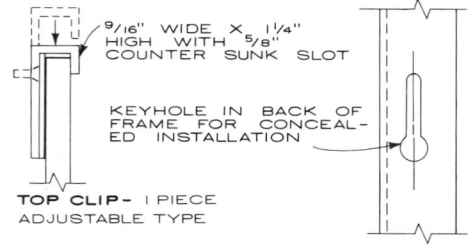

⁹⁄₁₆" WIDE × 1¼" HIGH WITH ⅝" COUNTER SUNK SLOT
KEYHOLE IN BACK OF FRAME FOR CONCEALED INSTALLATION
TOP CLIP — 1 PIECE ADJUSTABLE TYPE

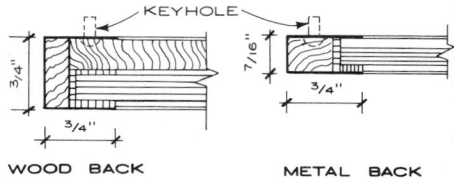

KEYHOLE
¾" / ⁷⁄₁₆" / ¾"
WOOD BACK    METAL BACK
MIRROR WITH METAL FRAME AVAILABLE IN BRASS, BRONZE AND NICKEL SILVER WITH ANY POLISHED OR PLATED FINISH

**MIRROR CLIPS** — CLIPS ACCOMMODATE GLASS FROM 1/4" TO 3/8". AVAILABLE IN BRASS-BRIGHT CHROME FINISH; NICKEL PLATED STEEL; BRASS, NICKEL SILVER, BRONZE-ANY FINISH, BRASS-NICKEL PLATED

**MIRROR GLAZING DETAILS**

## MIRRORS

Most commonly manufactured from surfacing sheet, float, or plate glass, hermetically sealing a silver coating with a uniform film of electrolytic copper plating. A protective coating of paint is then applied to seal out moisture from the silver. When sheet glass is used, the quality should be A-silvering or B-silvering. Float or plate glass should be selected for mirror glazing quality. Incidental applications include safety, observation (two-way), and institutional uses.

For applications of mirrored acrylic plastics, see Glazing with Plastics.

### CONVEX AND CONCAVE MIRRORS

Mirrors can be used to provide both security and safety for "blind spots" from visual vantage points. Twisted or bent mirrors are used to create distorted images.

### SAFETY MIRRORS

Used for cladding full height, hinged, pivoted, or sliding doors. Commonly manufactured by one of the following methods:

1. Silvering fully tempered glass—visually inferior to regular glass mirrors because of inherent warpage of tempered glass.
2. Silvering the back of laminated glass—visually inferior.
3. Silvering a light of glass and laminating it to another glass light with the silvering inside the unit—visually the best of the three.

### OBSERVATION (ONE-WAY OR TWO-WAY) MIRRORS

Commonly used for research and security in observation areas. Designed to provide vision through one side while reflecting images when viewed from the opposite side. To facilitate this function, the observers' area should have dull, subdued colors and low lighting levels with controlled dimming. The area to be observed should have light colors and a high illumination level, as suggested in the light ratio table.

Light ratio = observed area : viewing area.

## LIGHT RATIO TABLE

| BASE | | LIGHT RATIO | |
|---|---|---|---|
| GLASS | DESCRIP- TION | PRE- FERRED | ACCEPT- ABLE |
| Float | Clear | 10:1 | 5:1 |
| | Laminated | 10:1 | 5:1 |
| | Gray | 4:1 | 2:1 |

Observation mirrors can be manufactured in the following forms (for comments, see Safety Mirrors):

1. Single glazed, for interior applications. Extreme care must be taken to avoid damaging the reflective coating through abrasion.
2. Safety tempered.
3. Safety laminated. The mirror coating is usually located between the two bonded plys of glass, thus protecting it against abrasion.
4. Security laminated. A single light of observation mirror glass that is laminated between two lights of clear glass with a plastic film interlayer.

### INSTITUTIONAL MIRRORS

Used in detention or security areas and in areas involving high risk to personal safety. Often made of highly polished noncorrosive metal with reinforced rounded corners and edges. Commonly made for attachment to masonry walls with flat head spanner screws.

### MOUNTING APPLICATIONS

Mirrors can be mounted by way of frames or they can be surface mounted frameless by any of the following methods:

1. MASTIC: Mastic specifically made for mirrors is not generally recommended for use without clips, channels, or other auxiliary supportive devices. Certain design considerations, mirror sizes, and weights may, however, make this type of installation desirable. Mounting surfaces should be clean, dry, smooth, and plumb. Avoid applying to papered surfaces. Paint the back of the mirror with an extra coat of water resistant paint. Spot apply mastic to dry mirror back; it should not cover more than approximately 25% of the mirror area or exceed ½ to ⅝ in. in thickness, so as to allow for trueing the

mirror and adequate ventilation. Always provide support along the bottom edge and brace the mirror until the mastic sets.

2. DOUBLE FACED TAPE: The tape must be compatible with the mirror backing and supportive surface. Thicknesses and quantities depend on adhesive qualities of the tape. A tape with a capability of 1 lb for every ½ sq in. is recommended. To prevent moisture collection, install tape vertically, cutting the top edge to a point. Provide a bottom edge support that allows for drainage.

3. BOTTOM CHANNEL AND CLIPS.

4. WOOD FRAME BACK: Used to level a single mirror or multiple mirrors in a uniform plane. Paint the surface facing the mirror back to prevent wood resins from spoiling the silver. All mechanical fastening devices should be countersunk into the frame. Use clips at the bottom edge; provide paper padding to prevent metal contact.

5. ROSETTES OR SCREWS: Only experienced glaziers should undertake this type of work, since extreme care is needed. To prevent the glass from coming in contact with the metal screw anchor, make the hole in the mirror of adequate size to accommodate a rubber sleeve fitting around the screw. A felt cushion should be placed behind the rosette on the face of the glass. It is recommended that mirrors up to 10 sq ft in area be supported at each corner, 4 in. in from the edges; mirrors over 10 sq ft in area should have holes about 36 in. on centers.

Surface mounted, frameless mirrors should have all exposed edges ground and polished. If a continuous bottom channel is used, the bottom edge should be ground and painted to protect it from possible moisture intrusion. The paint must be water resistant and compatible with the coating on the mirror's back, as it must overlap the back to seal the edge. To avoid moisture penetration, mirrors should not be mounted directly against felt or felt paper and unpainted plaster, wood, or plywood.

When walls are entirely covered with mirrors, either in vertical panels or rectilinear stacked panels, the mirror edges must be flat polished with an appropriate thin ¹⁄₁₆ in. divider strip placed between all butt joints. In working with large areas, use a wood frame system, with members behind each vertical and horizontal joint, to allow for proper leveling.

Skidmore, Owings & Merrill

**GLAZING**

# STRUCTURAL SEALANT CURTAIN WALL SYSTEMS

Structural sealant glazing is a system of retaining glass or other materials to the aluminum members of curtain walls using a structural quality sealant specifically designed, tested, and recommended for structural sealant glazing. In structural glazing applications, wind-induced and other loadings are transferred by the structural sealant from the glass to the aluminum curtain wall system. There are no mechanical fasteners. Presently only certain silicone sealants are suitable for use in these systems, and reference in the balance of the text is to silicone materials.

The design, testing, fabrication, erection, and maintenance of these systems require utmost care and meticulous detailing by the design professional. If the design professional is not fully knowledgeable of structural sealant glazing, then a curtain wall consultant should be retained to be responsible for development and implementation. All parties from the owner to the glazier should be aware of the serious potential liabilities of structural sealant glazing and should be willing to assume their appropriate share of responsibility.

The applicable codes and regulations that apply to the jurisdiction where the structural sealant glazed curtain wall will be erected should be consulted early in the development of the system. Some jurisdictions have regulations that can impact the design as well as the subsequent development and implementation of the system.

Preference should be given to those curtain wall systems, whether 2-side or 4-side structurally glazed, that permit as part of their design the ability to apply the structural silicone sealant in the factory rather than at the construction site. Factory glazing of the structural silicone sealant has fewer variables to control and permits better quality assurance procedures to obtain the high level of sealant workmanship that is necessary for these systems. Construction site glazing is often subject to a multitude of conditions (e.g., rain, dust, storage condition) that can be very detrimental to achieving a quality installation of structural silicone sealant.

The following text includes concerns that need to be resolved when developing structurally glazed curtain walls. It is not all inclusive; additional issues may need resolving for each curtain wall system and its particular performance criteria.

# QUALITY ASSURANCE

## FABRICATION OF COMPONENTS

A quality assurance program should be implemented that adequately monitors and checks the fabrication of the system components, whether in a factory or at the construction site. This type of quality assurance is best performed by an independent inspection agency that has been properly trained to perform this service.

The objectives of the program are to periodically monitor the materials and workmanship to ensure that no undesirable changes occur which would be detrimental to the performance of the system. For example, the quality of materials would be verified (i.e., cleaning solvents for purity, structural sealants for proper mixing or storage life, adhesion of structural sealants to the intended substrates, and lack of adhesion of sealants to joint fillers and backing) as well as workmanship (i.e., substrate cleaning procedures, sealant application, and that the parts of the system are being installed correctly). This monitoring could also include periodic static load testing of assembled components as a statistical check of the fabrication process.

## ERECTION OF COMPONENTS

Quality assurance during this part of the process is equally important, particularly if construction site structural sealant glazing is to be performed. A program should be developed that adequately addresses the training of workmen to the system requirements, monitors the initial installation to fine tune procedures, and then periodically monitors the continuing installation.

# COMPONENTS

Developing a structurally glazed curtain wall system requires careful, conservative design and consideration of all system components and their interaction, including structural silicone sealant, insulating glass, monolithic glass, aluminum finishes, spacer gaskets, and setting blocks.

## STRUCTURAL SILICONE SEALANT

The structural silicone sealant should be chosen by the professional designer, sealant manufacturer, and curtain wall contractor and glazier, all working together to establish the necessary strength, adhesive and cohesive properties, curing characteristics, and fabrication concerns for the intended sealant. An appropriate design factor should be established which includes consideration of the above and also indeterminate variables such as application procedures, whether factory or field installed, and secondary stresses induced in the structural sealant by thermal movement, wind-induced building movement, gravity loads, and other factors.

## INSULATING GLASS

Insulating glass units should be dual seal units, with a secondary seal of structural quality silicone sealant, certified by the Insulating Glass Certification Council (IGCC) to a CBA quality level. Compatibility of the structural silicone sealant with the secondary insulating glass structural sealant should be verified by the sealant manufacturer and the insulating glass manufacturer. If the structural silicone sealant used with the insulating glass units is acetoxy curing (acetic acid liberating), the sealant details must be approved for compatibility by the sealant and insulating glass manufacturers. Caution should be exercised when choosing the structural silicone sealant if it is being used with insulating glass.

Design considerations for the secondary structural silicone seal of insulating glass units include adequate dimensions to resist wind loading and other secondary stresses previously described. The surfaces of insulating glass units should be tested by the sealant and insulating glass manufacturers for compatibility and adhesion of the intended structural silicone sealant. The insulating glass units should be certified by the manufacturer for use in structural silicone sealant glazing.

## MONOLITHIC GLASS

Compatibility and adhesion of the structural silicone sealant to the coated or uncoated glass surface should be tested by the sealant manufacturer. Certain silicone sealants may not develop adequate adhesion to some reflective and low emissivity coated glasses. Monolithic glass used for a spandrel area may require an opacifier applied to the interior glass surface. The opacifier should be cut back for the full contact area on all sides where structural adhesion is required. The sealant manufacturer should test for compatibility of the structural silicone sealant with the opacifier and any other adjacent materials that may come in contact with or be in close proximity to the structural silicone sealant.

## ALUMINUM FINISHES

The finish of aluminum framing members and trim pieces where structural adhesion will occur should be tested for compatibility and adhesion with the intended structural silicone sealant. The sealant manufacturer should verify this by laboratory tests performed before the components are fabricated and also periodically on samples of production run components. If factory applied organic coatings are used, then the adhesion and fatigue resistance of the organic coating to the aluminum is as important as the adhesion and fatigue resistance of the structural sealant to the organic coating and should be laboratory tested to verify the coating's suitability for use in structural sealant glazing. Only high-quality coatings with proven durability, applied by licensed applicators, should be considered.

## SPACER GASKETS AND SETTING BLOCKS

Compatibility with the structural silicone sealant of spacer gaskets, setting blocks, glazing gaskets, and other accessories should be established before those components are fabricated and also verified periodically on samples of production run components, with laboratory testing by the sealant manufacturer. Preference should be given to the use of silicone rubber for most of these components.

## SILICONE WEATHER SEALANTS

Silicone sealants used as a weather seal should be laboratory tested by the sealant manufacturer for adhesion to substrates and for compatibility and stain resistance with adjacent materials before component fabrication and also periodically on samples of production run components.

## TESTING OF ASSEMBLED COMPONENTS

Realistic, comprehensive testing criteria for a mock-up of the assembled curtain wall system should be developed by the design professional or curtain wall consultant and the testing laboratory. Performance criteria that should be considered for testing include static air infiltration; static and dynamic water infiltration; wind loading structural adequacy at design loads, at 1.5 times design loads, and perhaps to destruction; deflection characteristics; seismic or racking load resistance; cyclic structural loading; steady state thermal performance; verification of reglazing procedures; verification of fabrication and erection techniques; condensation resistance; and aesthetic evaluation.

Mock-up testing helps to verify the curtain wall system design adequacy; it does not predict long-term durability.

The mock-up must be of sufficient size. It also must be representative of the building conditions and should be constructed using the actual production run materials and components, as well as fabrication and erection methods to be used for the building. The mock-up should be erected by the personnel, both supervisory and production, who will fabricate and erect the system. More than one mock-up may be necessary.

Any changes or modifications resulting from mock-up testing may require additional laboratory testing of components as well as the mock-up. Any changes or modifications after mock-up testing has been completed should be carefully evaluated. Certain aspects of the mock-up testing and perhaps the curtain wall system design could be invalidated by the changes or modifications.

Production and fabrication of the system for erection on the building should not begin until successful mock-up performance is achieved.

## MAINTENANCE

The structural sealant curtain wall system design must be capable of being maintained without the need for elaborate or expensive procedures or methods. Glass will break or insulating glass seals will fail, leaks may develop, and the surface will be cleaned periodically. These basic needs should be resolved by the system design. The reglazing of glass is of particular importance, and procedures should be developed in advance of the need. Reglazing may necessitate the use of a different structural sealant from that used for the original work. If this occurs, then this sealant will also have to be tested for compatibility and adhesion during the system design. Factory glazed systems can be designed to greatly ease the field reglazing process.

Consideration should be given to a periodic inspection of the system (particularly a 4-side structurally glazed system) by a qualified professional after installation to verify the continuing performance of the curtain wall system.

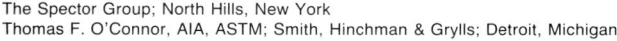
The Spector Group; North Hills, New York
Thomas F. O'Connor, AIA, ASTM; Smith, Hinchman & Grylls; Detroit, Michigan

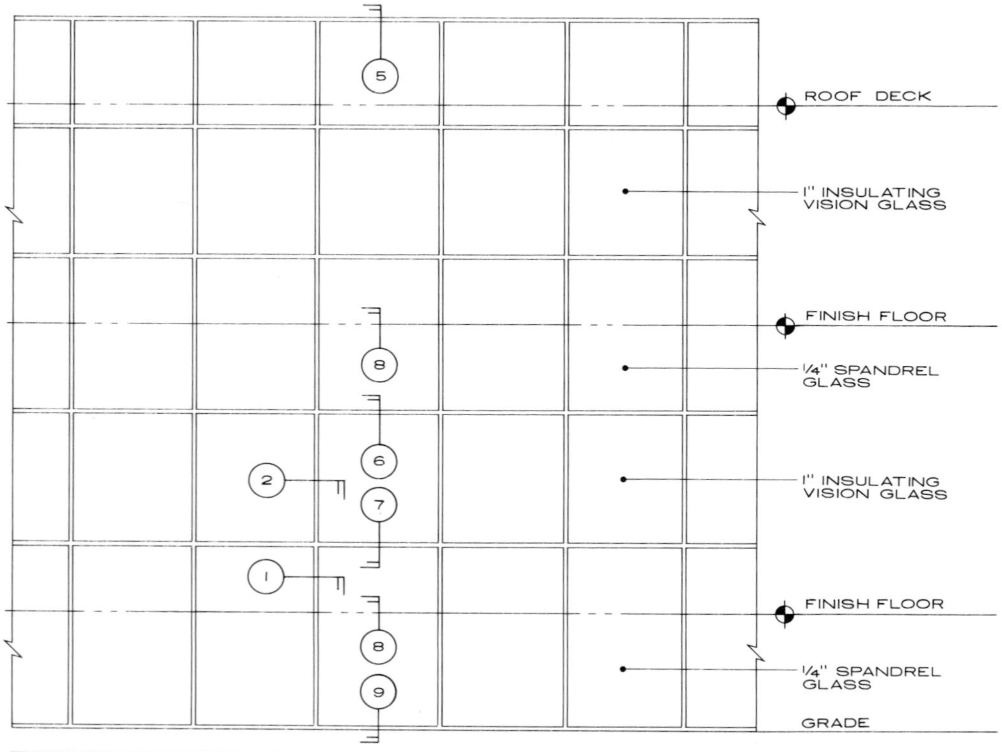

5
ROOF DECK
1" INSULATING VISION GLASS
FINISH FLOOR
8
1/4" SPANDREL GLASS
6
2
7
1" INSULATING VISION GLASS
1
FINISH FLOOR
8
9
1/4" SPANDREL GLASS
GRADE


CURTAIN WALL ELEVATION

NOTE

Detail section cut number 8 is for insulation with sheet metal vapor barrier and insulation against glass. If foil vapor barrier is used, then insulation must be of same material and rating as fire-safing material, and if insulation is 2 in. from glass, then a sheet metal vapor barrier with stiffeners is necessary.

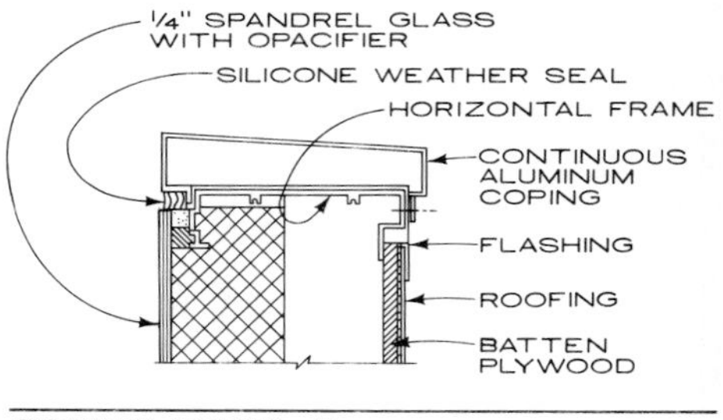

1/4" SPANDREL GLASS WITH OPACIFIER
SILICONE WEATHER SEAL
HORIZONTAL FRAME
CONTINUOUS ALUMINUM COPING
FLASHING
ROOFING
BATTEN PLYWOOD


COPING DETAIL 5

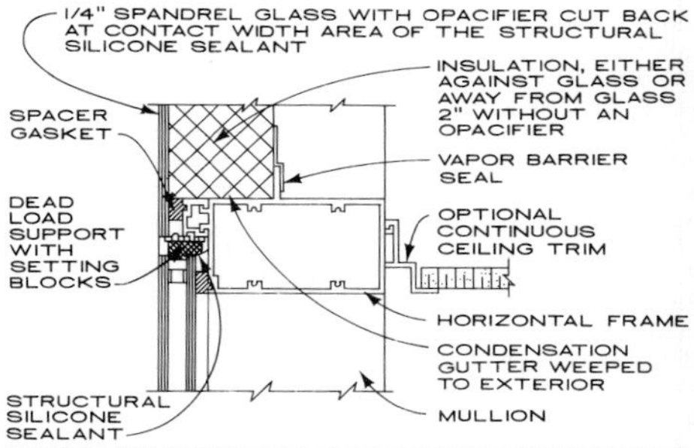

1/4" SPANDREL GLASS WITH OPACIFIER CUT BACK AT CONTACT WIDTH AREA OF THE STRUCTURAL SILICONE SEALANT
INSULATION, EITHER AGAINST GLASS OR AWAY FROM GLASS 2" WITHOUT AN OPACIFIER
SPACER GASKET
VAPOR BARRIER SEAL
DEAD LOAD SUPPORT WITH SETTING BLOCKS
OPTIONAL CONTINUOUS CEILING TRIM
HORIZONTAL FRAME
CONDENSATION GUTTER WEEPED TO EXTERIOR
STRUCTURAL SILICONE SEALANT
MULLION


HEAD DETAIL 6

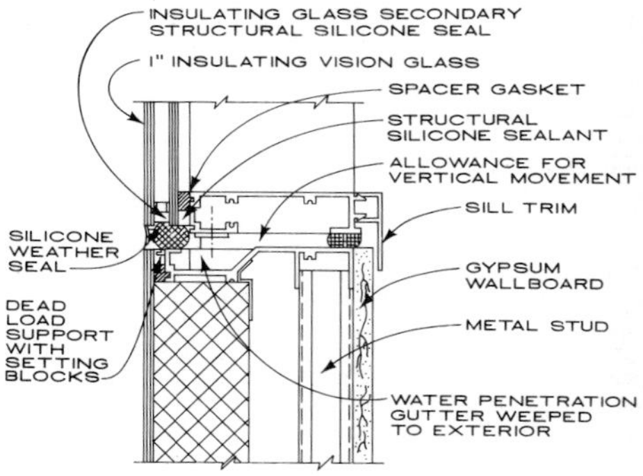

INSULATING GLASS SECONDARY STRUCTURAL SILICONE SEAL
1" INSULATING VISION GLASS
SPACER GASKET
STRUCTURAL SILICONE SEALANT
ALLOWANCE FOR VERTICAL MOVEMENT
SILL TRIM
SILICONE WEATHER SEAL
GYPSUM WALLBOARD
DEAD LOAD SUPPORT WITH SETTING BLOCKS
METAL STUD
WATER PENETRATION GUTTER WEEPED TO EXTERIOR


SILL DETAIL 7

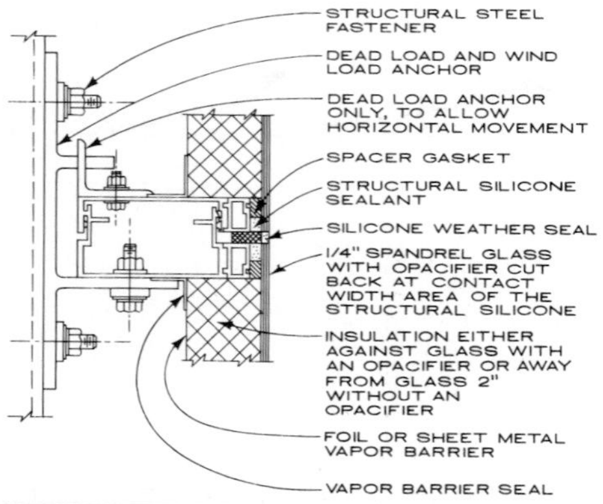

STRUCTURAL STEEL FASTENER
DEAD LOAD AND WIND LOAD ANCHOR
DEAD LOAD ANCHOR ONLY, TO ALLOW HORIZONTAL MOVEMENT
SPACER GASKET
STRUCTURAL SILICONE SEALANT
SILICONE WEATHER SEAL
1/4" SPANDREL GLASS WITH OPACIFIER CUT BACK AT CONTACT WIDTH AREA OF THE STRUCTURAL SILICONE
INSULATION EITHER AGAINST GLASS WITH AN OPACIFIER OR AWAY FROM GLASS 2" WITHOUT AN OPACIFIER
FOIL OR SHEET METAL VAPOR BARRIER
VAPOR BARRIER SEAL


MULLION DETAIL 1 AT SPANDREL GLASS

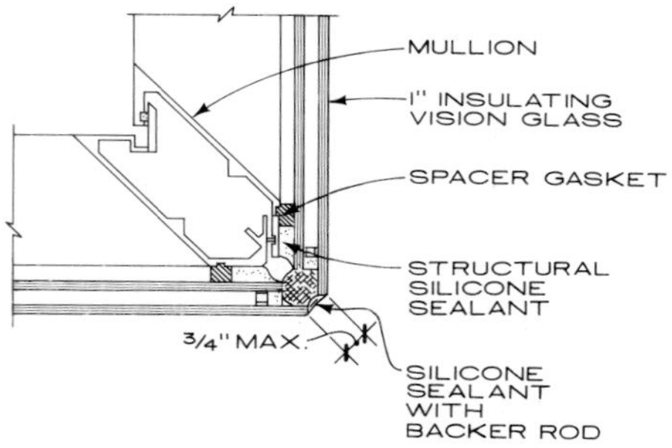

MULLION
1" INSULATING VISION GLASS
SPACER GASKET
STRUCTURAL SILICONE SEALANT
3/4" MAX.
SILICONE SEALANT WITH BACKER ROD


MULLION DETAIL 3 AT OUTSIDE CORNER

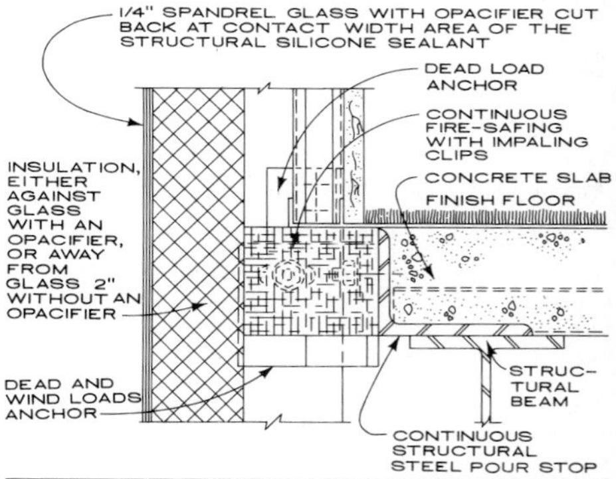

1/4" SPANDREL GLASS WITH OPACIFIER CUT BACK AT CONTACT WIDTH AREA OF THE STRUCTURAL SILICONE SEALANT
DEAD LOAD ANCHOR
CONTINUOUS FIRE-SAFING WITH IMPALING CLIPS
INSULATION, EITHER AGAINST GLASS WITH AN OPACIFIER, OR AWAY FROM GLASS 2" WITHOUT AN OPACIFIER
CONCRETE SLAB
FINISH FLOOR
STRUC-TURAL BEAM
DEAD AND WIND LOADS ANCHOR
CONTINUOUS STRUCTURAL STEEL POUR STOP


FLOOR SLAB DETAIL 8

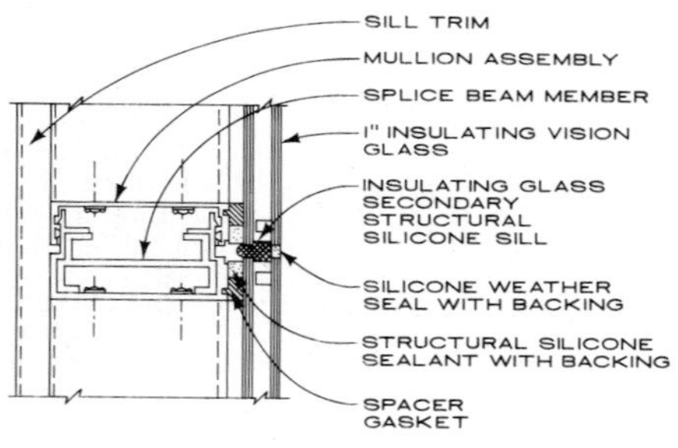

SILL TRIM
MULLION ASSEMBLY
SPLICE BEAM MEMBER
1" INSULATING VISION GLASS
INSULATING GLASS SECONDARY STRUCTURAL SILICONE SILL
SILICONE WEATHER SEAL WITH BACKING
STRUCTURAL SILICONE SEALANT WITH BACKING
SPACER GASKET


MULLION DETAIL 2 AT VISION GLASS

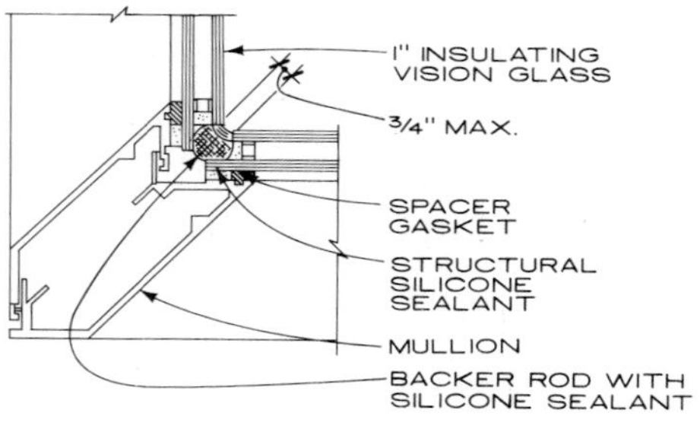

1" INSULATING VISION GLASS
3/4" MAX.
SPACER GASKET
STRUCTURAL SILICONE SEALANT
MULLION
BACKER ROD WITH SILICONE SEALANT


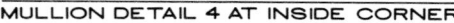

MULLION DETAIL 4 AT INSIDE CORNER

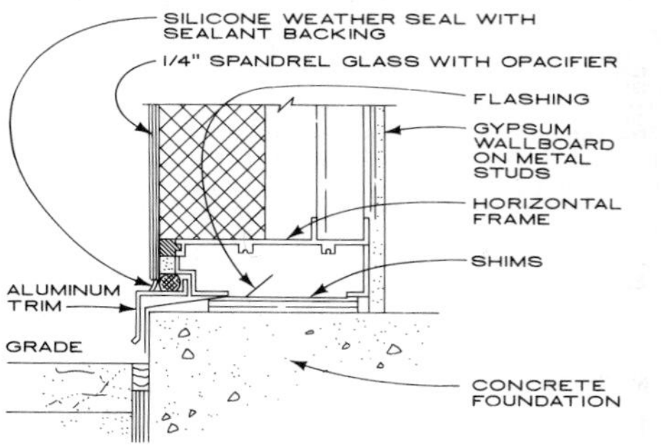

SILICONE WEATHER SEAL WITH SEALANT BACKING
1/4" SPANDREL GLASS WITH OPACIFIER
FLASHING
GYPSUM WALLBOARD ON METAL STUDS
HORIZONTAL FRAME
SHIMS
ALUMINUM TRIM
GRADE
CONCRETE FOUNDATION


GRADE DETAIL 9

The Spector Group; North Hills, New York
Thomas F. O'Connor, AIA, ASTM; Smith, Hinchman & Grylls; Detroit, Michigan

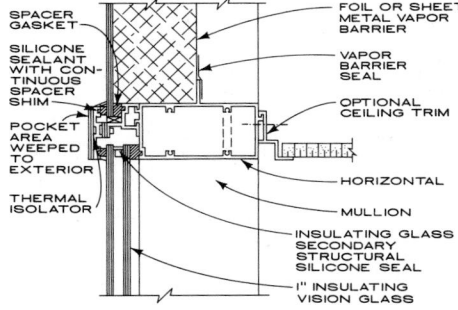

**FLOOR SLAB DETAIL 5**

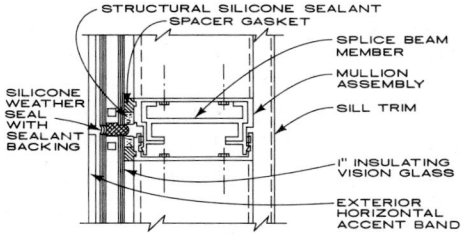

**HEAD DETAIL 6**

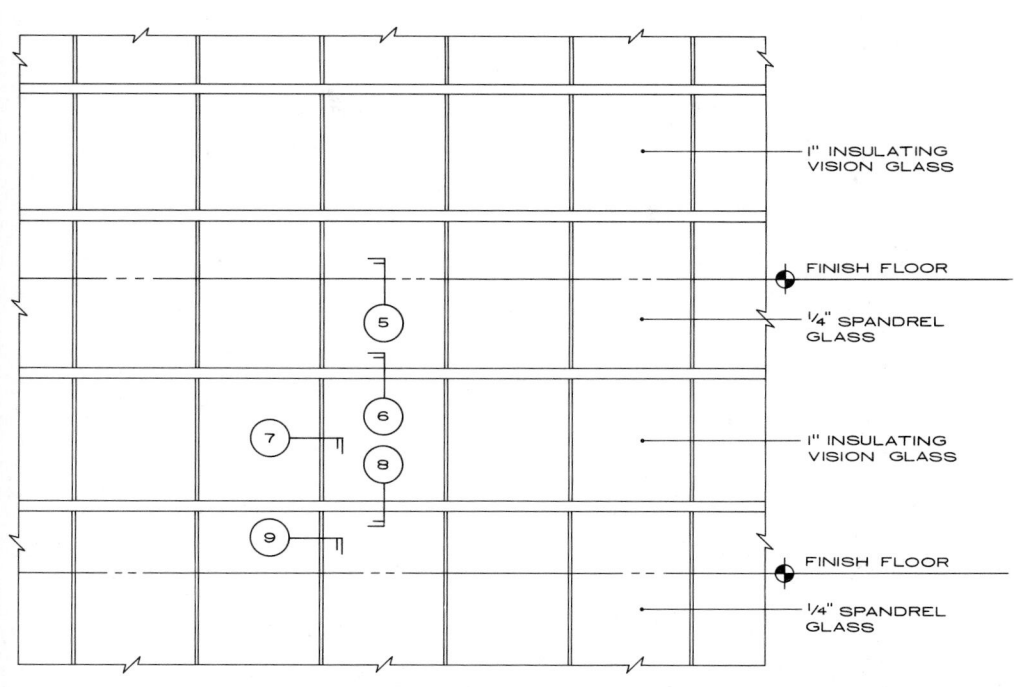

**CURTAIN WALL ELEVATION**

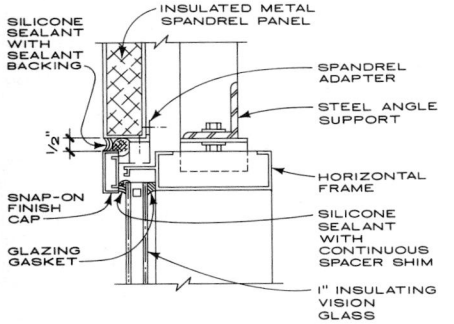

**HEAD DETAIL 1 AT METAL SPANDREL**

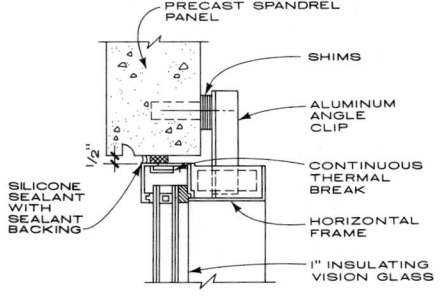

**HEAD DETAIL 3 AT PRECAST SPANDREL**

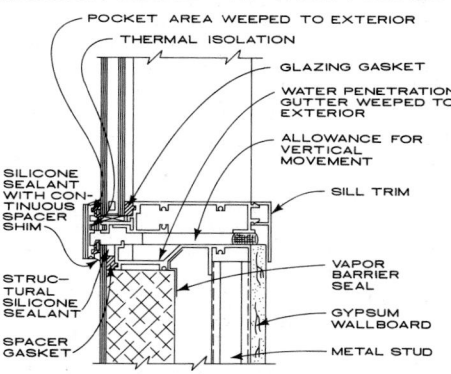

**MULLION DETAIL 7 AT VISION GLASS**

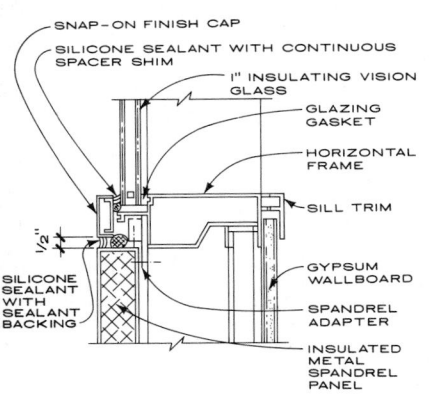

**SILL DETAIL 2 AT METAL SPANDREL**

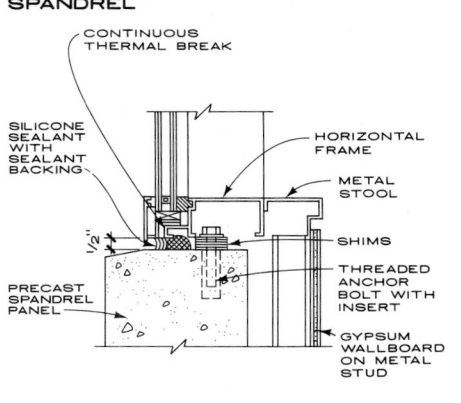

**SILL DETAIL 4 AT PRECAST SPANDREL**

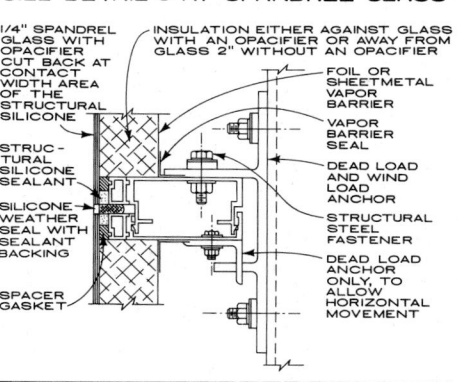

**MULLION DETAIL 9 AT SPANDREL GLASS**

**SILL DETAIL 8 AT SPANDREL GLASS**

**NOTES**

1. Coping detail and base detail similar to details 5 and 9 of four-sided structural curtain wall system.
2. Detail section cut numbers 1–4 are not shown on elevation, but represent its intended use for two-sided structural curtain wall system with precast and metal spandrel panel at the head and sill.
3. Detail section cut number 5 refers to note on four-sided structural sealant glazing system.

The Spector Group; North Hills, New York
Thomas F. O'Connor, AIA, ASTM; Smith, Hinchman & Grylls; Detroit, Michigan

**GLAZING** 8

## GENERAL NOTES

1. Information on this page is representative of industry recommendations for vertical glazing applications (within 15° of vertical). Consult with the applicable manufacturers and fabricators for specific applications or for applications at greater than 15° from vertical.

2. It is good practice to glaze at temperatures above 40°F (4°C) to preclude condensation and frost contamination of surfaces that will receive sealants. For sealant glazing below 40°F (4°C), consult the glazing sealant manufacturer.

3. Glazing materials should not be installed more than one day in advance of glass placement to avoid potential damage to the glazing materials by other trades or contamination of the materials.

4. Glazing materials used with high-performance reflective coated glass may require the consideration of additional factors for the glazing materials.

5. Glass should always be cushioned in the glazing opening by resilient glazing materials and should also be free to "float in the opening" so there is no direct contact of the glass with the perimeter framing system.

6. For glazing of polycarbonate and acrylic plastic sheet, particular attention should be given to thermal movement of the sheet and adhesion and compatibility of the sheet with glazing materials, as well as proper preparation of the glazing opening. Consult the manufacturer or fabricator for glazing recommendations.

7. Insulating, wired, and laminated glass must be installed in glazing pockets that are weeped to the exterior to preclude the detrimental effects of moisture.

8. For large glass lites the deflection characteristics of the glass should be investigated to preclude detrimental deflection which can cause glazing seal failure and glass breakage by contact of an edge or corner with the framing.

9. For setting and edge block requirements for casement, vertically pivoted and horizontally pivoted windows refer to the Flat Glass Marketing Association (FGMA) Glazing Manual.

## SETTING BLOCK NOTES

1. Blocks should always be wider than the thickness of glass or panel, no more or less than two per glass or panel, and be of identical material.

2. For glass using the alternate method, verify acceptability of method with glass manufacturer or fabricator.

3. Setting block length per block
   a. Neoprene, EPDM, or silicone block = 0.1 in./sq ft of glass area; never less than 4 in. long.
   b. Lead block = 0.05 in./sq ft of glass area; never less than 4 in. long.
   c. Lock-strip gasket block = 0.5 in./sq ft of glass area; never less than 6 in. long.

4. For neoprene, EPDM, silicone, or lead blocks, the material should be 85 ± 5 shore A durometer.

5. Lead blocks should never be used with laminated, insulating, or wired glass or in lock-strip gaskets, nor should they be used with glass less than ½ in. thick.

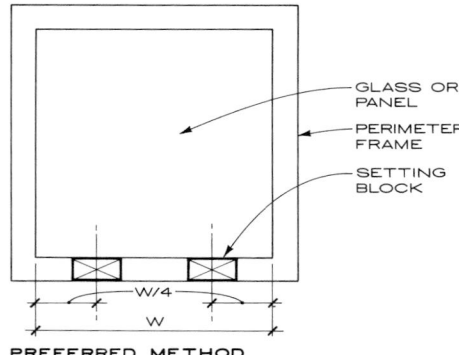

PREFERRED METHOD

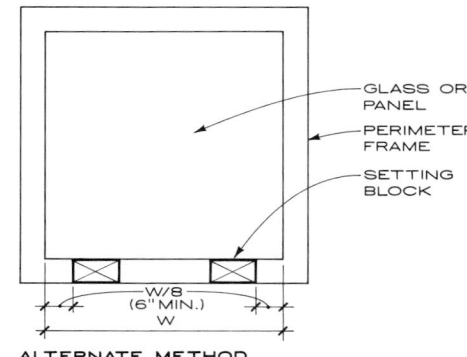

ALTERNATE METHOD

**SETTING BLOCK LOCATIONS**

## EDGE BLOCK NOTES

1. Edge blocking is used to limit lateral movement of the glass or panel caused by horizontal thermal movement, building vibration, and other causes.

2. Method A is preferred.

3. Material should be neoprene, EPDM, or silicone rubber.

4. Hardness should be 65 ± 5 shore A durometer.

5. Blocks should be a minimum of 4 in. long.

6. Blocks should be placed in vertical frame spaces.

7. Blocks should be sized to permit a nominal ⅛ in. of clearance between the edge of the glass or panel and the block.

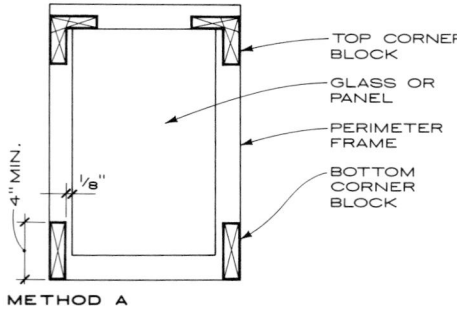

METHOD A

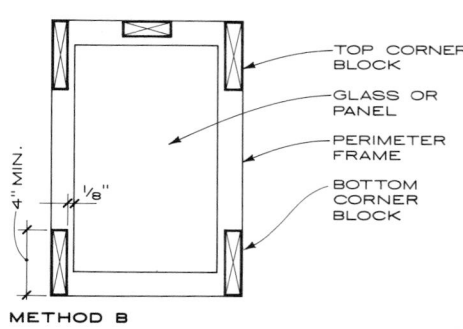

METHOD B

**EDGE BLOCK LOCATIONS**

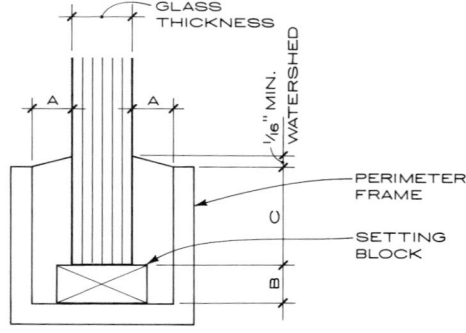

## NOTES

1. The typical clearances indicated in the adjacent table may vary by glass manufacturer or fabricator, particularly for special products or applications. Consult the glass manufacturer, fabricator, and sealing material supplier for those conditions.

2. The permissible bow and warp of large lites of heat-strengthened and tempered glass can be substantial, which may require extra face clearance.

## TYPICAL FACE AND EDGE CLEARANCE AND BITE

| GLASS THICKNESS | | MINIMUM CLEARANCES | | |
|---|---|---|---|---|
| IN. | MM | A = FACE | B = EDGE | C = BITE |
| MONOLITHIC GLASS | | | | |
| SS* | 2.5 | ¹⁄₁₆ | ⅛ | ¼ |
| ⅛—DS† | 3 | ⅛ | ⅛ | ¼ |
| ⅛—DS‡ | 3 | ⅛ | ¼ | ⅜ |
| ³⁄₁₆† | 5 | ⅛ | ³⁄₁₆ | ⁵⁄₁₆ |
| ³⁄₁₆‡ | 5 | ⅛ | ¼ | ⅜ |
| ¼ | 6 | ⅛ | ¼ | ⅜ |
| ⁵⁄₁₆ | 8 | ³⁄₁₆ | ⁵⁄₁₆ | ⁷⁄₁₆ |
| ⅜ | 10 | ³⁄₁₆ | ⁵⁄₁₆ | ⁷⁄₁₆ |
| ½ | 12 | ¼ | ⅜ | ⁷⁄₁₆ |
| ⅝ | 15 | ¼ | ⅜ | ½ |
| ¾ | 19 | ¼ | ½ | ⅝ |
| ⅞ | 22 | ¼ | ½ | ¾ |
| INSULATING GLASS | | | | |
| ½ | 12 | ⅛ | ⅛ | ½ |
| ⅝ | 15 | ⅛ | ⅛ | ½ |
| ¾ | 19 | ³⁄₁₆ | ¼ | ½ |
| 1 | 25 | ³⁄₁₆ | ¼ | ½ |
| CERAMIC COATED SPANDREL GLASS | | | | |
| ¼ | 6 | ³⁄₁₆ | ¼ | ½ |

*SS, Single strength; DS, double strength.
†Annealed glass only.
‡Tempered glass only.

**FACE AND EDGE CLEARANCE AND BITE**

Thomas F. O'Connor, AIA, ASTM; Smith, Hinchman & Grylls; Detroit, Michigan

# GLAZING

## GLAZING SYSTEMS NOTES

1. Only rubber materials formulated to recognized standards and of proven durability such as neoprene, EPDM; and silicone should be used for gaskets and blocking.
2. At least two ¼ to ⅜ in. diameter weep holes for the glazing pocket per glass lite or panel are necessary with access to weep holes not prevented by setting blocks or sealants.
3. Glazing compound or putty should not be used to glaze laminated or insulating glass in openings.
4. Sealants in contact or close proximity to gaskets, rubber blocking, and other sealants must be compatible with those materials to preclude loss of adhesion or lessened durability. Consult with the sealant manufacturer.
5. Sealant must be compatible with the insulating glass edge seal and the butyral laminate of laminated glass to preclude failure of the edge seal or delamination and discoloration of the laminate.
6. The dry glazing method requires careful design and control of tolerances of the frame opening and glazing materials to ensure the development of adequate compression sealing pressure (generally 4–10 lb/lin in. to achieve weathertightness.
7. Closed cell gaskets for dry glazing should have molded or vulcanized corners as the preferred method so as to form a continuous, joint-free glazing material around all sides of the opening.
8. The following table lists sources for specifications and installation practices for glazing materials which should be consulted when designing and specifying.

## LOCK-STRIP GASKET NOTES

1. Lock-strip gasket glazing requires careful design and control of framing, gasket, and glazing tolerances to achieve the anticipated weather sealing pressures and structural capacity to resist lateral loads.
2. The best weather sealing performance is achieved with a continuous gasket having factory-formed, injection-molded joints.
3. Concrete gasket lugs require a draft on some surface of the lug to facilitate mold removal. Draft is permissible either on the sides or on top (preferred), not both. Draft on top should slope to the exterior.

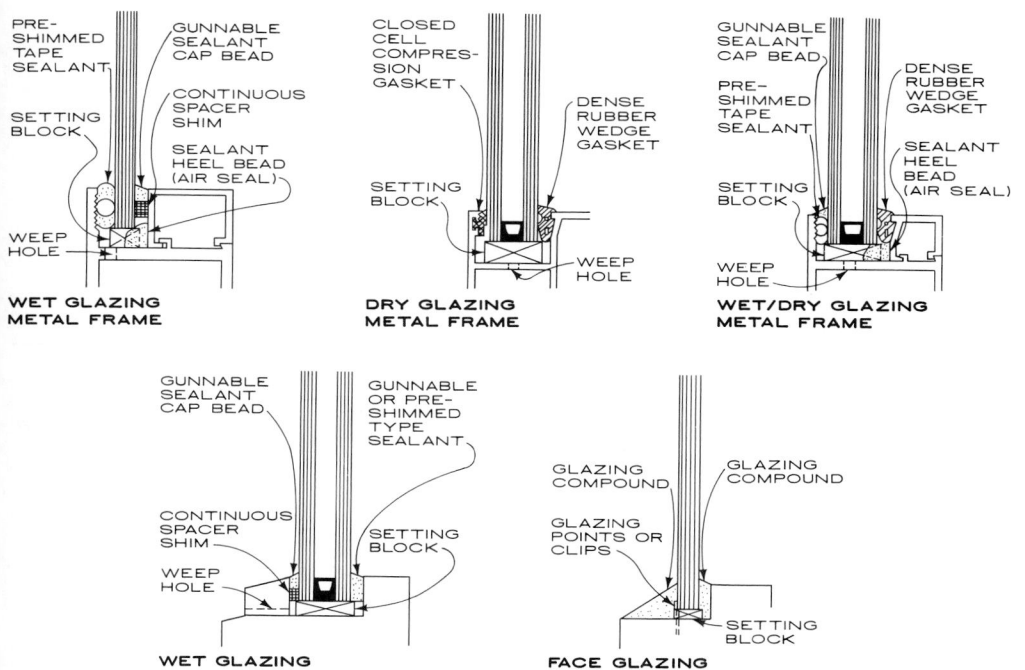

**TYPICAL GLAZING SYSTEMS**

## GLAZING SPECIFICATIONS*

| PART | MATERIAL | SPECIFICATION | INSTALLATION PRACTICE |
|---|---|---|---|
| Closed cell rubber gasket | Neoprene Silicone EPDM | ASTM C0509 | FGMA Glazing Manual |
| Dense wedge rubber gasket | Neoprene Silicone EPDM | ASTM C0864 | FGMA Glazing Manual |
| Gunnable sealant | Silicone Polyurethane Polysulfide | ASTM C0920 | ASTM C0962 |
| Tape sealant | Butyl Polyisobutylene | AAMA 804.1, 806.1, 807.1 | FGMA Glazing Manual |
| Lock-strip gasket | Neoprene EPDM | ASTM C0542 | ASTM C0716, C0963, C0964 |
| Setting and edge blocks | Neoprene Silicone EPDM | ASTM C0864 | See setting block and edge block location details and FGMA Glazing Manual |
| Glazing compound | Oil or resin based | ASTM C0570, C0669 | ASTM C0797 |

*AAMA, Architectural Aluminum Manufacturers Association.
ASTM, American Society for Testing and Materials.
FGMA, Flat Glass Marketing Association.

Thomas F. O'Connor, AIA, ASTM; Smith, Hinchman & Grylls; Detroit, Michigan

**GASKET MOUNTING ON METAL FRAME**

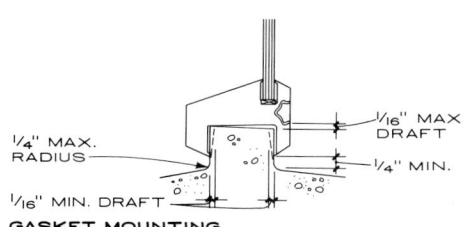

**REGLET TYPE GASKET IN CONCRETE**

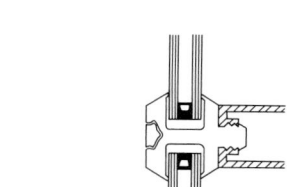

**GASKET MOUNTING ON CONCRETE LUG**

**GASKET MOUNTING ON VERTICAL MULLION**

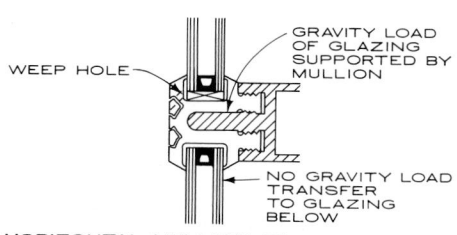

**HORIZONTAL MULLION AT VERTICALLY STACKED GLAZING**

**LOCK-STRIP GASKETS**

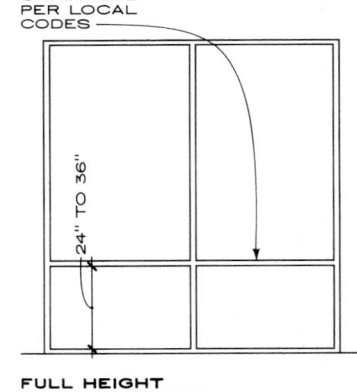

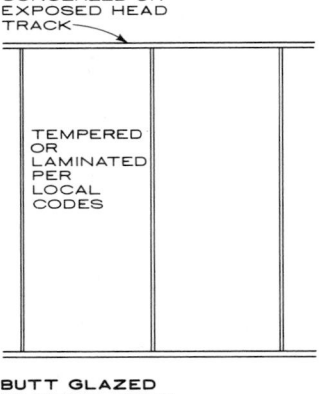

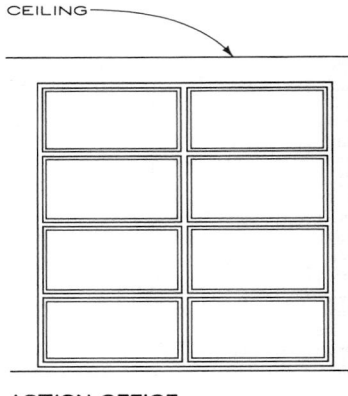

**FULL HEIGHT WITH TRANSOM**     **FULL HEIGHT WITH CHAIR RAIL**     **BUTT GLAZED SILICONE JOINT**     **ACTION OFFICE MODULAR SYSTEM**

## GLASS PARTITION ELEVATIONS

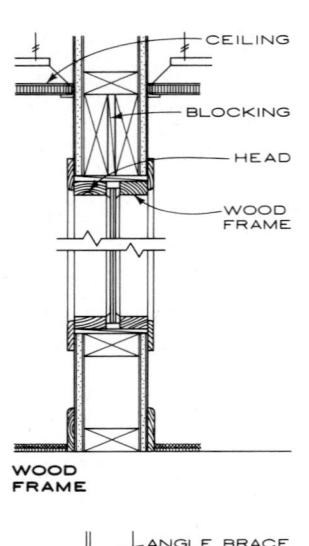

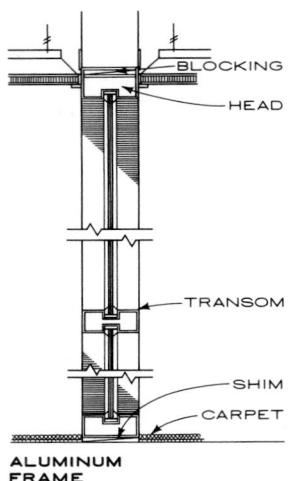

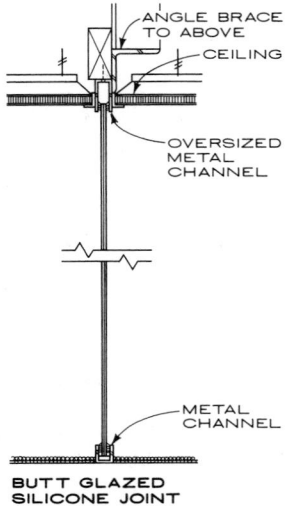

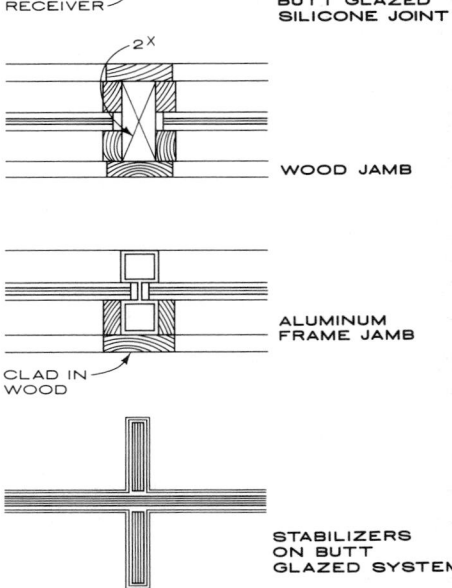

**WOOD FRAME**     **ALUMINUM FRAME**     **BUTT GLAZED SILICONE JOINT**

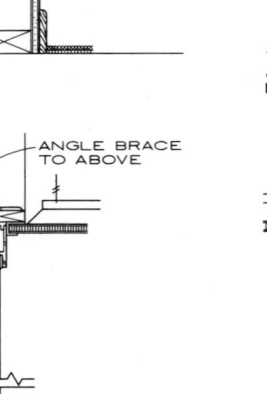

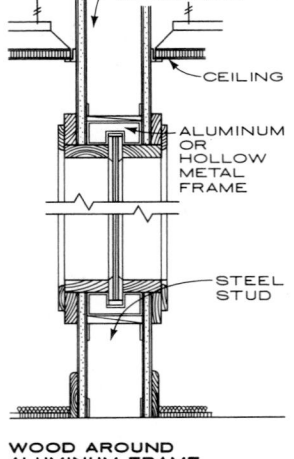

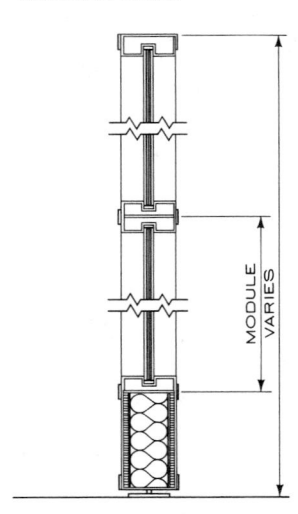

**ENTRANCE SYSTEM (FIXED)**     **WOOD AROUND ALUMINUM FRAME**     **ACTION OFFICE SYSTEM**

## GLASS PARTITION SECTIONS

**PLAN SECTIONS**

### GLAZED PARTITION NOTES

1. Interior glazed partitions are available in a variety of standard sizes, materials, and colors. Many manufacturers accommodate special or custom designs.
2. Finishes: Aluminum frames usually come in standard anodized or painted finishes. Many manufacturers now offer rich colors as well. Wood and hollow metal frames can be painted or finished in any tone or color. Action office systems are available in a wide array of colors and finishes, trimmed in wood, metal, or plastic.
3. Silicone glazing (butt glazing) partitions are framed at the top and bottom with either exposed or concealed frames. It is important that the glass thickness be in correct proportion to the unbraced length. If thickness alone cannot handle the span, then glass stabilizers should be used (see diagram).
4. Most manufacturers of action office systems offer a variety of glazed units to be incorporated in their system. Many systems are available with patterned, etched, or tinted glass for safety and privacy.

### DRAPERIES

Draperies usually are custom made to specification. Drapery length is unlimited. Fabric width, usually 48 to 118 in. wide, does not limit final drapery width, but affects fabrication only. Considerations in drapery selection include: fabric weight, pleating (fullness), number of seams, track capacity, type of mounting track, type of draw, and control cords location.

### SHADES

In addition to the common opaque shade, many shades with excellent shading coefficients that retain a high degree of transparency are available. Single shades usually are limited to 72 in. wide x 198 in. long (manual) or 312 in. long (motorized).

### SHUTTERS

Interior shutters are available with fixed or operable vanes in all sizes up to 18 x 78 in. for ¾ in. thick units and 48 x 96 in. for 1¼ in. thick units. Frames usually are painted or stained wood. Some styles use panels of cane, metal, plastic, or solid wood in lieu of vanes.

### GLASS COATINGS

A full array of shading films and screens is available for use in new and existing glazing. Films range from totally reflective to slightly tinted. Many also provide excellent shading coefficients.

Sterling Thompson, AIA, and Larry Gawloski, AIA; ARCHIFORMS; Waco, Texas

⑧   **GLAZING**

## ACRYLIC PLASTIC AND POLYCARBONATE SHEETS

Both materials are relatively tough, break, shatter, or crack resistant thermoplastics. They are commonly used in the clear transparent form for glazing in schools, factories, skylights, domes, display cases, and protective shields for stained glass assemblies. Certain conditions of varying temperatures and/or humidity on opposing surfaces of a single light may cause it to bow in the direction of the higher temperature and/or humidity. Though this does not affect visibility, it may cause distorted reflections. The surfaces of these materials are susceptible to scratching and abrasions. Progress is being made in developing abrasion resistant coatings. As compared with clear glass of equal size and thickness, they maintain greater resistance to impact and breakage and are lighter in weight. Polycarbonates have softer surfaces and are more impact resistant than acrylics. Acrylics generally weather better than polycarbonates. Because of a somewhat higher coefficient of thermal expansion than in clear glass and other materials with which they are used in construction, acrylics and polycarbonates are subject to a greater degree of dimensional change. In applications that must allow for wide ranges of thermal expansion, avoid inflexible installation methods. Both may be produced with or without light absorbing properties. The allowable continuous service temperature for polycarbonates is slightly higher than that for acrylics. Both may be cold formed to a smooth arc if the resulting radius of curvature is at least 100 times the thickness of the sheet for polycarbonates (180 times for acrylics) and both are supported by curved channel supports following this radius.

Mirrored coatings applied to acrylic sheets are available for interior applications and may be installed with recommended contact cements, double faced tape, clip and channel mounting, and through fastening. Distortion problems indicate that they should not be used for precise image reflectance requirements.

Certain polycarbonate sheets may be used in some bullet resisting and burglar resisting applications.

Consult the manufacturers for current information. Refer to and adhere to all applicable codes and governing authorities on fire and safety.

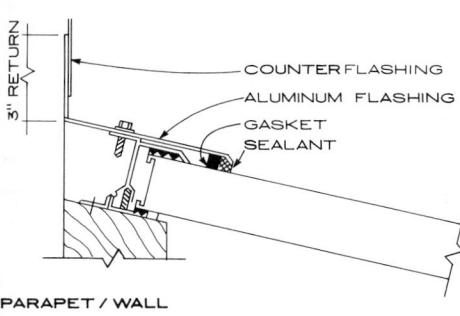

**PARAPET / WALL**

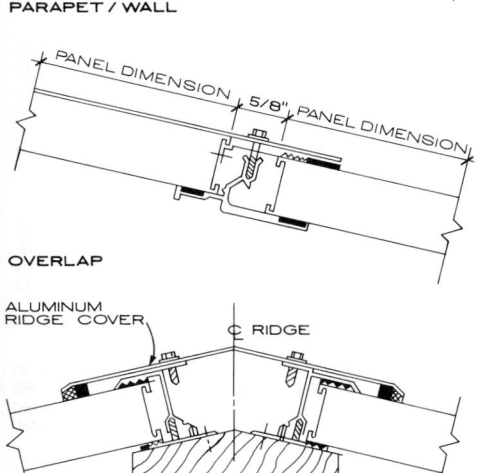

**OVERLAP**

**RIDGE**

**SKYROOF SYSTEM DETAILS**

Skidmore, Owings & Merrill

## POLYCARBONATE GLAZING

| | POLY-CARBONATE SHEET THICKNESS | SHORT DIMEN-SION | RABBET DEPTH |
|---|---|---|---|
| Small lights | 1/8'' | 24'' | 1/2'' |
| Intermediate lights | 3/16'' | 36'' | 3/4'' |
| | 1/4'' | 48'' | 3/4'' |
| Large lights | 3/8'' | 60'' | 1'' |
| | 1/2'' | 72'' | 1'' |

### NOTES

1. Rabbet width is determined by sheet thickness plus sealant and tape as recommended by sealant tape manufacturers.
2. To select polycarbonate sheet thickness based on wind loads refer to manufacturers' information.

## SMALL ACRYLIC LIGHTS

Maximum dimension to 24''
Minimum thickness—0.100''
Minimum rabbet depth 9/32''

## INTERMEDIATE ACRYLIC LIGHTS

| ACRYLIC THICK-NESS | MAXIMUM SASH OPENING | | RABBET DIMENSIONS | |
|---|---|---|---|---|
| | SQUARE | RECTAN-GULAR | DEPTH | WIDTH |
| 0.125'' | 40'' x 40'' | 30'' x 42'' | 1/2'' | 3/8'' |
| 0.125'' | 55'' x 55'' | 36'' x 68'' | 3/4'' | 3/8'' |
| 0.187'' | 42'' x 42'' | 30'' x 45'' | 1/2'' | 7/16'' |
| 0.187'' | 63'' x 63'' | 36'' x 72'' | 3/4'' | 7/16'' |
| 0.250'' | 44'' x 44'' | 30'' x 46'' | 1/2'' | 1/2'' |
| 0.250'' | 69'' x 69'' | 36'' x 72'' | 3/4'' | 1/2'' |

## LARGE ACRYLIC LIGHTS

| ACRYLIC THICKNESS | LONG DIMENSIONS | RABBET DIMENSIONS* | |
|---|---|---|---|
| | | DEPTH | WIDTH |
| 0.187 | 57'' to 85'' | 3/4'' | 7/16'' |
| 0.250 | 78'' to 96'' | 1'' | 5/8'' |
| 0.250 | 108'' to 144'' | 1 1/8'' | 3/4'' |
| 0.375 | 72'' to 108'' | 1'' | 3/4'' |
| 0.375 | 108'' to 144'' | 1 1/8'' | 7/8'' |
| 0.500 | 114'' to 144'' | 1 1/8'' | 1'' |

\* When darker (less than 60% light transmittance) transparent tints of acrylic plastic are used, rabbet depth shown above should be increased by 1/4'' to allow for greater thermal expansion resulting from solar energy absorption.

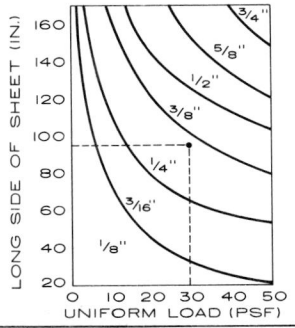

### ACRYLIC GLAZING GRAPH
Design load data—large area acrylic glazing

Problem:
Size = 48 x 96 in.
Design load = 30 psf

Solution:
Select 1/4 in.
Sheet thickness

Data apply to square and rectangular lights of acrylic sheets when the length is no more than three times the width. All edges continuously held.

Sheet thickness section is based on total deflection under uniform load limited to 5% of the short side, or 3 in., whichever is smaller.

## ACRYLIC SHEET EXPANSION ALLOWANCE

| SASH LENGTH OR HEIGHT (IN.) | REDUCE ACRYLIC GLAZING LENGTH OR HEIGHT | |
|---|---|---|
| | CLEAR ACRYLIC (IN.) | TINTED ACRYLIC (IN.) |
| 0 to 36 | 1/16 | 1/16 |
| 36 to 60 | 1/8 | 3/16 |
| 60 to 96 | 3/16 | 5/16 |
| 96 to 132 | 1/4 | 3/8 |
| 132 to 144 | 5/16 | 1/2 |

Note: Both length and height must be reduced according to this table. For polycarbonate glazing expansion allowance, refer to manufacturer's literature.

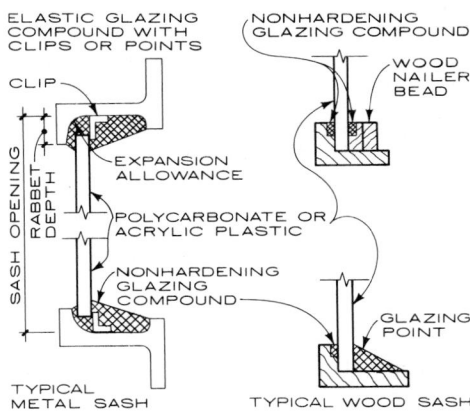

**SMALL LIGHTS**

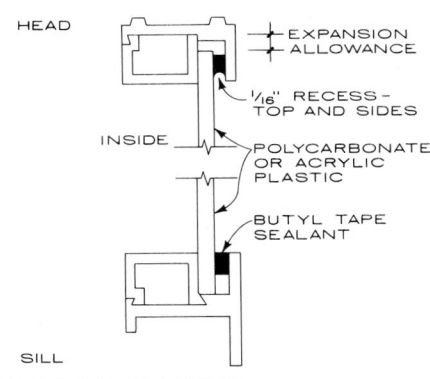

**INTERMEDIATE LIGHTS**

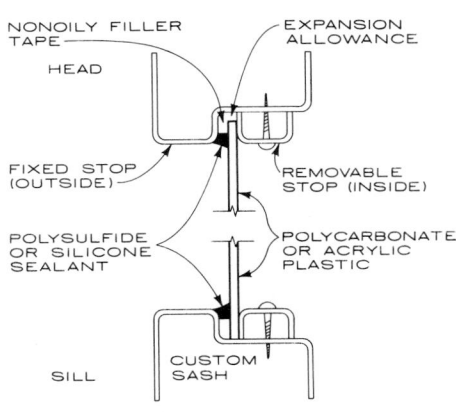

**LARGE LIGHTS**

**PLASTIC GLAZING DETAILS**

## METAL CURTAIN WALLS

Exterior metal and glass enclosure walls require more careful development and skilled erection than traditional wall construction. Because metal and glass react differently to environmental conditions than do other wall materials, the technology is different from all other enclosure systems.

Errors in judgment can be avoided if behavior of the wall is understood. Some of the important considerations for successful curtain wall development are delineated below. Further in-depth material is available from the Architectural Aluminum Manufacturers Association (AAMA), the Flat Glass Marketing Association (FGMA), and standards developed by American Society for Testing and Materials (ASTM) committees C24 on building seals and sealants and EO6 on performance of building constructions. See index under "Structural Sealant Glazing" for additional information that should be considered when developing a structural sealant curtain wall system.

## FUNCTION OF THE WALL

The metal and glass curtain wall functions as an "enclosure system" which, when properly developed, can serve multiple functions: (1) withstand the action of the elements; (2) control the passage inward and outward of heat, light, air, and sound; (3) prevent or control access from outside.

## NATURAL FORCES

Curtain wall development is determined in part by the impact of natural forces. Natural forces that cause the most concern and failures are (1) water, (2) wind, (3) sunlight, (4) temperature, (5) gravity, and (6) seismic forces. To understand the impact of these forces on curtain wall development, the effects of each should be separately examined.

### WATER

The most frequent cause of problems with all enclosures is leakage from rain, snow, vapor, or condensate. Wind driven moisture can enter very small openings and may move within the wall, appearing far from its point of entry. Water vapor can penetrate microscopic pores and will condense on cool surfaces. Such moisture trapped within a wall can result in lessened durability of the wall which can result in serious damage that is difficult to detect. Leaks are usually limited to joints and openings, which must be designed to provide a weathertight enclosure.

### WIND

Structural design development of the wall must take into account both positive and negative pressures caused by wind action, increasing in effect depending on the height and shape of the building. Increases in wind loading will occur in corner areas of the building and must be considered accordingly. Framing members, panels, and glass thicknesses should be determined by maximum wind load anticipated and permissible deflection allowable. Winds contribute to the movement of the wall, affecting joint seals and wall anchorage. The effect of positive or negative wind pressure can cause stress reversal on framing members and glass and will cause water to travel in any direction (including upward) across the face of the wall. The state of the art is to conduct scale model wind studies in a boundary layer wind tunnel to more realistically establish expected prevailing wind patterns and their effects on the building cladding. Wind is a major factor in potential water leakage.

### SUNLIGHT

The ultraviolet spectrum of sunlight will cause breakdown of organic materials such as color pigments, various rubber gaskets, plastics, and sealants. Fading and failure of these materials will cause problems with the appearance and weathertightness of the curtain wall. Only quality organic materials should be used, and they should be tested for resistance to ultraviolet radiation and ozone attack.

Sunlight passing through glass can cause excessive brightness and glare and will cause fading of interior furnishings and finishes. Shading devices and the use of glare-reducing or high-performance types of glass should be considered in development of the wall.

### TEMPERATURE

Change in temperature causes the expansion and contraction of materials. Control of the passage of heat or cold through the wall is also required. Thermal movement as a result of solar heating is one of the major problems in curtain wall development. Minimum outdoor temperatures vary about 80°F. Throughout the country, the maximum surface temperature of the darker colored surfaces on buildings can range as high as 170°F. This temperature fluctuation, both daily and seasonally, critically affects wall development. Thermal expansion and contraction is much greater in metals than in wood or masonry.

Heat passage through the wall causes heat gain in hot weather and heat loss in cold weather, the relative importance of the two varying with geographic location. Thermal insulation of opaque wall areas becomes an extremely important consideration, especially whenever these areas constitute a large portion of the total wall area. When vision glass areas predominate, the use of high-performance glasses and the minimizing of through metal or "cold bridges" (usually by inserting continuous nonmetallic breaks in the metal assembly) are more effective in lowering the heat transfer (U-value) through the wall.

### GRAVITY

Because gravity is constant and static rather than variable and dynamic, gravity is a less critical force affecting the development of a window wall design, but is important in that it should be recognized. It causes deflection in horizontal load-carrying members, particularly under the weight of large sheets of heavy glass. However, because the weight of the wall is transferred at frequent intervals to the building frame, the structural effect of gravity is small in comparison with that imposed by wind action. Far greater gravity forces, in the form of floor and roof loads, are acting on the building frame to which the wall is attached. As these loads may cause deflections and displacements of the frame, connections of the wall to this frame must be designed to provide sufficient relative movement to ensure that the displacements do not impose vertical loads on the wall itself.

### SEISMIC

Seismic (earthquake) loadings will produce additional static and dynamic loadings to the window wall system. Seismic loadings will produce both vertical and horizontal deflections of the wall. This will necessitate special energy absorption considerations in the detail of all wall anchorages and adequate consideration of the joints between curtain wall members.

## DESIGN DEVELOPMENT CONSIDERATIONS: STRUCTURAL INTEGRITY

Structural integrity of the curtain wall is a prime concern involving the same design procedures used in any other exterior wall. However, deficiencies of weathertightness and temperature movements are more prevalent than deficiencies in strength, which will be elaborated upon further.

The structural integrity of the window wall must be evaluated using two criteria: strength and deflection. Based on numerous window wall tests, it has been found that the ultimate performance of the system is usually dependent on the elastic and inelastic deflections of the system rather than on just the strength of component parts.

Curtain wall fabrication and erection tolerances must be carefully reviewed in conjunction with structural frame tolerances. Many window wall failures have been caused by inadequate anchorage details and inadequate consideration of tolerances.

### WEATHERTIGHTNESS

Weathertightness ensures protection against the penetration of water and an excessive amount of air through the wall. This depends on adequate provision for movement and is closely related to proper joint design. A major share of the problems experienced over the years has been due to the lack of weathertightness.

## PROVISION FOR MOVEMENT

Development of the wall must accommodate relative movements of the wall components and also differential movements between the wall assembly and the building structure. Relative movements of the wall components will primarily be affected by thermal movements of the wall elements and erection tolerances of the individual wall elements. Erection tolerances may exceed the tolerance for thermal movement. The differential movements between the wall components and the building structure will be a direct function of the dead and live load deflections of the structure and also the creep, shrinkage, thermal, wind, and seismic deformations of the building structure. These differential movements may be of considerable magnitude, and the effects of such differential movements must not be transferred from the structure directly to the window wall system. Usually provisions for such differential movement are provided at the head and jamb anchorage locations between the wall jointery and/or joints between wall and adjacent cladding. Behavior of sealants must be considered. Current recommendations from sealant manufacturers are to limit movement of the joint to a percentage of the sealant's rated movement capacity. This will provide a safety factor to help prevent sealant failure. Temperature of metal parts at time of erection, as well as the anticipated design temperature range, will aid in predicting the extent of movement in a joint. Fabrication and erection tolerances must also be considered when establishing the joint opening width.

## MOISTURE CONTROL

Control of condensation is essential because metal and glass are not only impermeable to moisture, but have low heat retention capacity. A vapor barrier should be provided on or near the room side wall face. Impervious surfaces within the wall should be insulated to keep them warmer than the dew point of the air contacting them. Provision should be made for the escape of water vapor to the outside. The wall should be detailed so that any condensation occurring within it will be collected and drained away via weeps to the exterior.

## THERMAL INSULATION

High thermal and condensation resistance of the wall is a good long-term investment to minimize heat loss in cold weather or heat gain in hot weather. Such devices as minimizing the exposure of the framing members by using thermal breaks, employing high-performance glass, and insulating opaque surfaces are recommended.

## SOUND TRANSMISSION

By careful selection of details and materials, sound transmission characteristics of the metal and glass wall can be made equal to traditional construction.

Use of insulating and laminated glass separately and in combination as well as increasing the mass of the wall will reduce the transmission of sound.

## FIRE AND SMOKE STOPS

Prevention of the spread of fire and smoke by continuous firestopping between the curtain wall and the edge of each floor is necessary. Proper detailing and installation of a quality safing material not subject to breakdown by fire will help to avoid what can become an extremely dangerous condition.

## CONCLUSION

The following items can be utilized to further refine the techniques of good curtain wall development and construction: It is very beneficial to work with contractors or manufacturers who have specialized for a period of not less than 5 years in the fabrication and installation of curtain walls. Visits to and interviews with owners and managers of buildings will help give an overall view of the performance of curtain wall systems. It is important at the start of design to work with the metal, glass, and sealant manufacturers' technical personnel when developing a metal curtain wall system. Before fabrication and construction starts, wall and component testing should be done under both laboratory and field conditions.

Skidmore, Owings & Merrill
Thomas F. O'Connor, AIA, ASTM; Smith, Hinchman & Grylls; Detroit, Michigan

# GLAZED CURTAIN WALLS

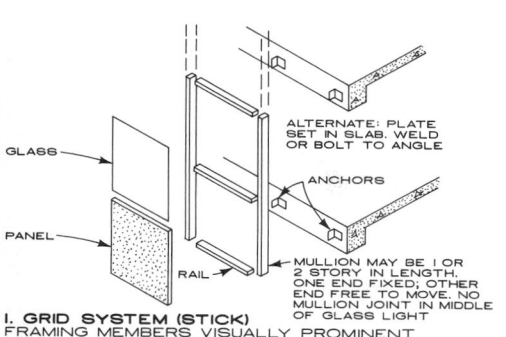

**1. GRID SYSTEM (STICK)** FRAMING MEMBERS VISUALLY PROMINENT COMPONENTS INSTALLED PIECE BY PIECE

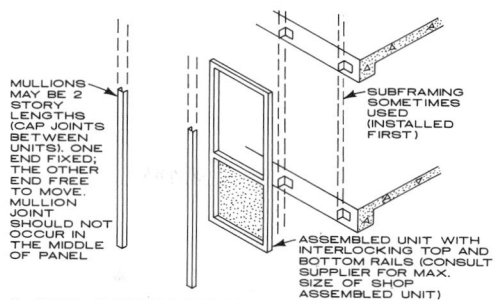

**2. GRID SYSTEM (PANEL AND MULLION)** FRAMING MEMBERS VISUALLY PROMINENT PANEL PREASSEMBLED AND INSTALLED AS SHOWN

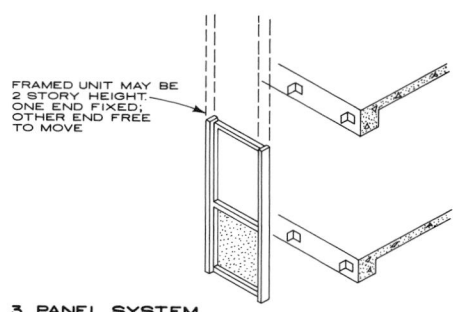

**3. PANEL SYSTEM** COMPLETELY PREASSEMBLED UNITS; MAY OR MAY NOT INCLUDE INTERIOR FINISH

## CUSTOM TYPE

Walls designed specifically for one project, using specially designed parts and details. Such walls may be used on buildings of any height, but are more typical of multistoried structures. Included in this category are the highly publicized (and often more expensive) walls that serve as design pacesetters. Methods 1, 2, and 3 above are used for custom-type walls.

## COMMERCIAL TYPE

Walls made up principally of parts and details standardized by the manufacturer and assembled either in the manufacturer's stock patterns or in accord with the architect's design. This type is commonly used on one- and two-story buildings and on taller structures. Commercial walls cost less because of quantity production and also offer the advantages of proven performance. Methods 1 and 2 above are used for commercial-type walls.

## INDUSTRIAL TYPE

Walls in which ribbed, fluted, or otherwise preformed metal sheets in stock sizes are used along with standard metal sash as the principal components. This type of metal curtain wall has a long history of satisfactory performance and, in its insulated form, is used in buildings other than industrial use-type buildings.

## CLASSIFICATION BY CONSTRUCTION AND TYPE

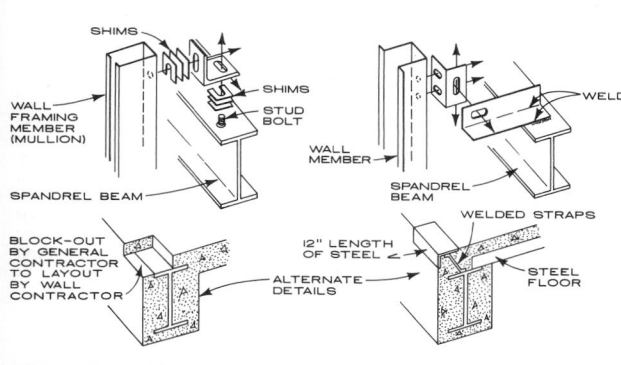

STEEL STRUCTURE

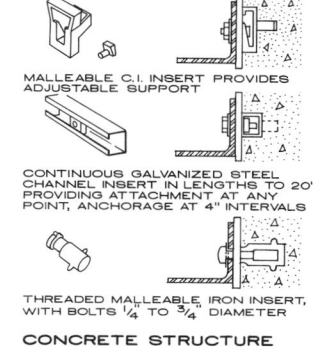

CONCRETE STRUCTURE

### NOTES

1. Anchorage devices must permit three-dimensional adjustment. Metal-to-metal connections subject to intentional movement should be designed to eliminate noise caused by movement due to temperature change.
2. Anchors must be designed to withstand wind loads acting outward and inward as well as other required loads.
3. Anchors must be permanently secured in position after final assembly and adjustment of wall components.
4. All anchorage members must be corrosion resistant or protected against corrosive forces.
5. Shim plates may be installed between vertical leg of angle anchor and concrete structure, as required, for proper anchor alignment.

## ATTACHMENT AND ANCHORAGE DETAILS

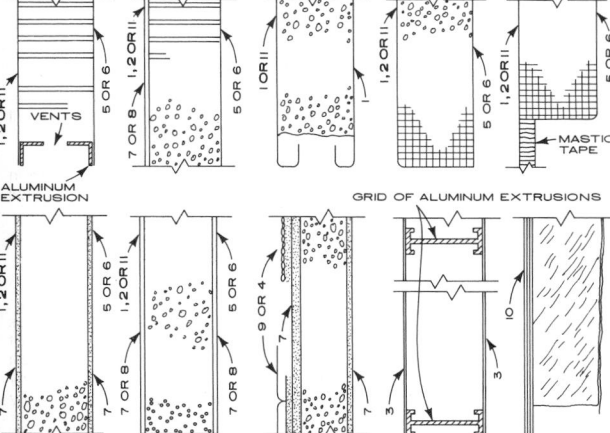

**REPRESENTATIVE INSULATING PANEL TYPES** (EXTERIOR FACE ON LEFT)

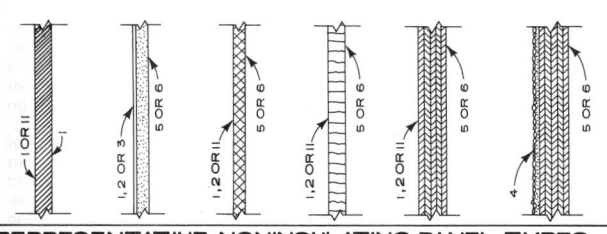

**REPRESENTATIVE NONINSULATING PANEL TYPES** (EXTERIOR FACE ON LEFT)

### TYPICAL CORE MATERIALS

- FIBER CEMENT
- TEMPERED HARDBOARD
- ALUMINUM HONEYCOMB
- EXTERIOR GRADE PLYWOOD
- PAPER HONEYCOMB
- FOAMED PLASTIC
- CELLULAR GLASS
- POLYETHYLENE
- PERLITE BEADS IN MINERAL BINDER
- FIBERGLASS — ALUMINUM FOIL

### TYPICAL FACING MATERIALS

1. Aluminum or stainless-steel sheet.
2. Porcelain enameled metal.
3. Glass-reinforced plastic sheet.
4. Stone chips in plastic matrix.
5. Galvanized bonderized steel sheet.
6. Aluminum sheet.
7. Fiber cementboard.
8. Tempered hardboard.
9. Ceramic tile in plastic matrix.
10. Opaque tinted glass.
11. Organic color coating on aluminum.

## PROPERTIES OF COMMON INSULATING CORE MATERIALS

| MATERIAL | DENSITY (LB/CU FT) | APPROXIMATE K VALUE | GENERAL REMARKS |
|---|---|---|---|
| Paper honeycomb | 2.5–7.0 | 0.45–0.55 | 1. Local codes and ordinances should be consulted for fire resistance requirements of panel construction. This depends, in part, on conditions of use, degree of fire exposure, and core material type. |
| Paper honeycomb, with foamed plastic fill | 4.5–10.0 | 0.20–0.35 | |
| Paper honeycomb, with vermiculite fill | 5–14 | 0.35–0.40 | |
| Polystyrene foam, extruded | 1.7–3.5 | 0.20–0.26 | |
| Polyurethane foam | 1.5–3.0 | 0.18 | 2. Choice of core material should be made with consideration of potential thermal bowing of panel, flatness of facing materials, oil-canning of facing materials, moisture resistance of panel, and thermal resistance aging characteristics of the core material. |
| Polyisocyanurate foam | 2.0 | 0.18 | |
| Phenolic foam | 2.5 | 0.12 | |
| Fiberglass | 0.3–2.0 | 0.23–0.27 | |
| Cellular glass | 8.5 | 0.35 | |
| Perlite beads in mineral binder | 11 | 0.36 | |

Skidmore, Owings & Merrill
Thomas F. O'Connor, AIA, ASTM; Smith, Hinchman & Grylls; Detroit, Michigan

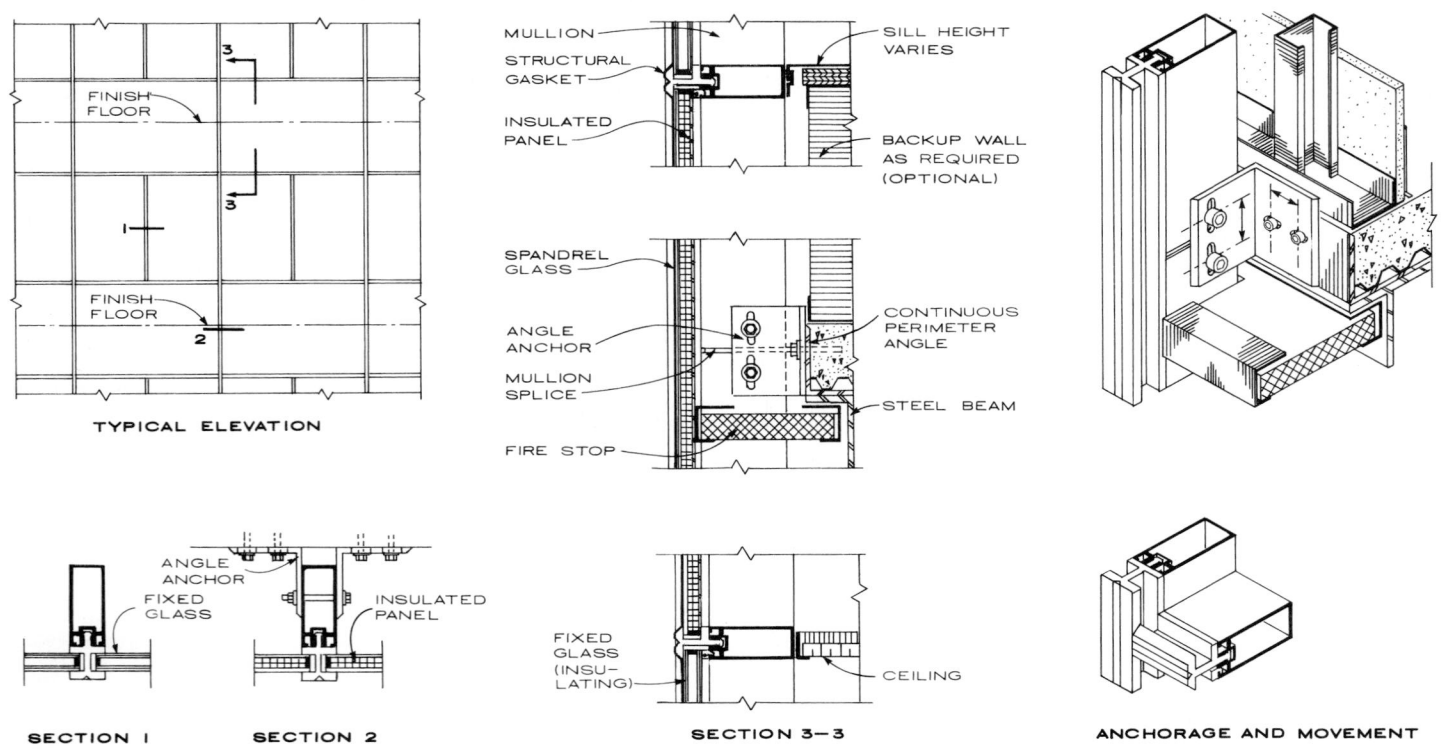

TYPICAL ELEVATION

MULLION
STRUCTURAL GASKET
INSULATED PANEL
SILL HEIGHT VARIES
BACKUP WALL AS REQUIRED (OPTIONAL)

SPANDREL GLASS
ANGLE ANCHOR
MULLION SPLICE
FIRE STOP
CONTINUOUS PERIMETER ANGLE
STEEL BEAM

ANGLE ANCHOR
FIXED GLASS
INSULATED PANEL

SECTION 1   SECTION 2

FIXED GLASS (INSULATING)
CEILING

SECTION 3-3

ANCHORAGE AND MOVEMENT

**GRID SYSTEM (STICK OR STUD)—COMMERCIAL TYPE—ALUMINUM—GASKETED**
MULTISTORY STICK OR STUD SYSTEM USING STRUCTURAL RUBBER GASKETS

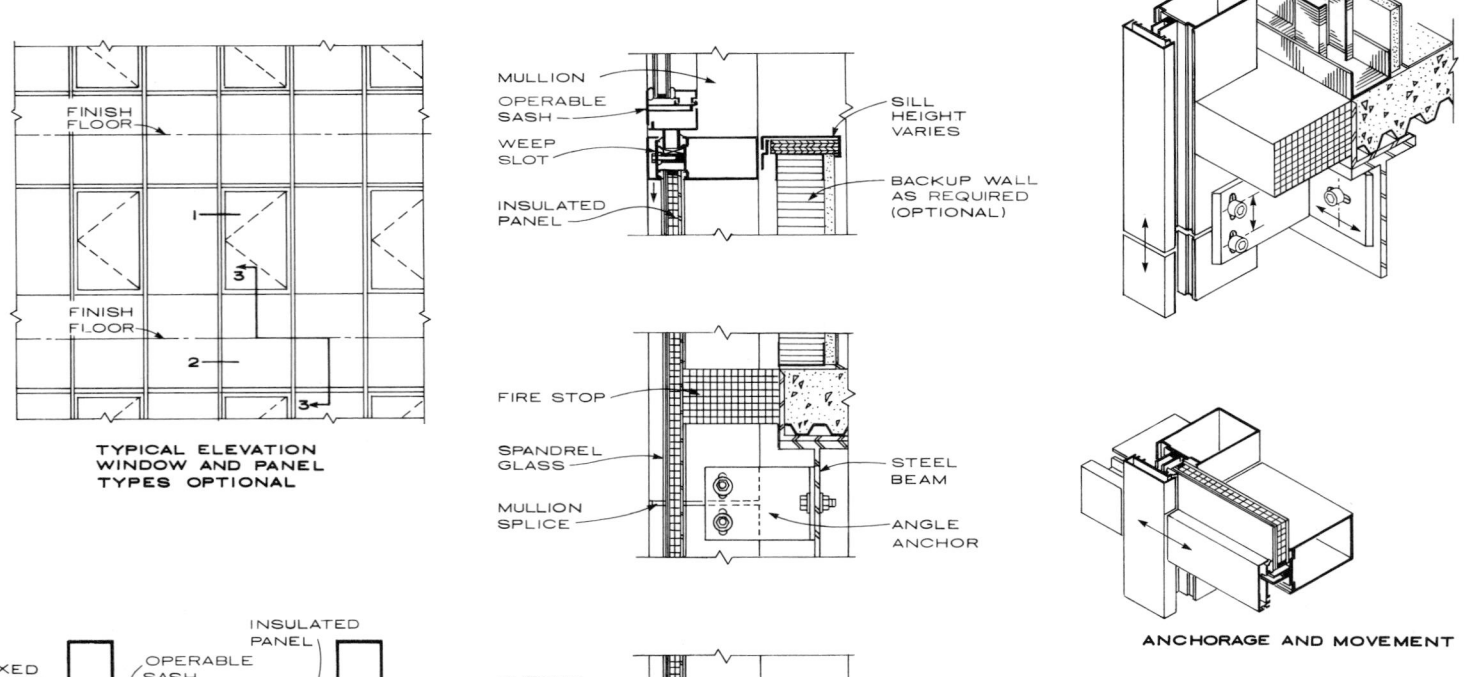

TYPICAL ELEVATION
WINDOW AND PANEL TYPES OPTIONAL

MULLION
OPERABLE SASH
WEEP SLOT
INSULATED PANEL
SILL HEIGHT VARIES
BACKUP WALL AS REQUIRED (OPTIONAL)

FIRE STOP
SPANDREL GLASS
MULLION SPLICE
STEEL BEAM
ANGLE ANCHOR

FIXED GLASS
OPERABLE SASH
INSULATED PANEL
PRESSURE BAR
SNAP-ON COVER
PRESSURE BAR
SNAP-ON COVER

SECTION 1   SECTION 2

THERMAL BREAK
WEEP HOLE
CEILING

SECTION 3-3

ANCHORAGE AND MOVEMENT

**NOTES**
1. Horizontals are weeped for positive performance against water infiltration with slots at glazing pressure plate and holes at cover.
2. See index under "Structural Sealant Glazing" for additional information that should be considered when developing a structural sealant curtainwall system.

**GRID SYSTEM (STICK OR STUD)—COMMERCIAL TYPE—ALUMINUM—PRESSURE BAR**
TYPICAL MULTISTORY STICK OR STUD SYSTEM USING PRESSURE BARS

Bullock Tice Associates Architects, Inc.; Pensacola, Florida

**GLAZED CURTAIN WALLS**

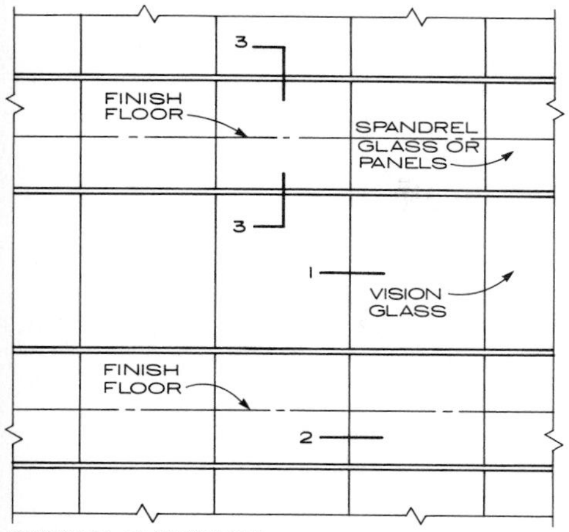

## STRUCTURAL GLAZING SYSTEM (STRIP WINDOW)—COMMERCIAL TYPE—ALUMINUM
### SYSTEM WITH STRUCTURAL SILICONE SEALANT ATTACHMENT ON TWO SIDES

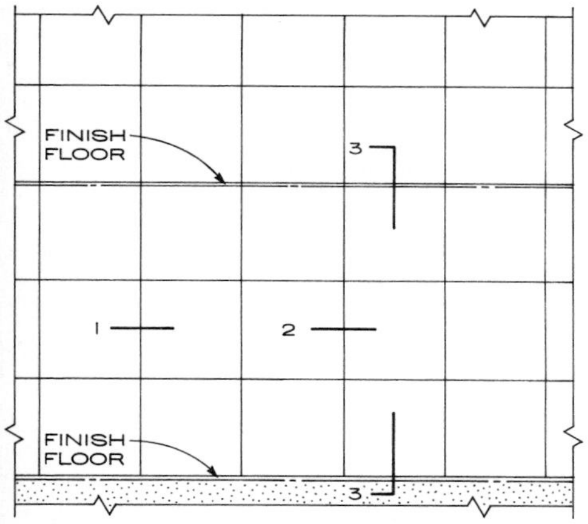

**TYPICAL ELEVATION**

FINISH FLOOR

SPANDREL GLASS OR PANELS

VISION GLASS

FINISH FLOOR

**SECTION 1**

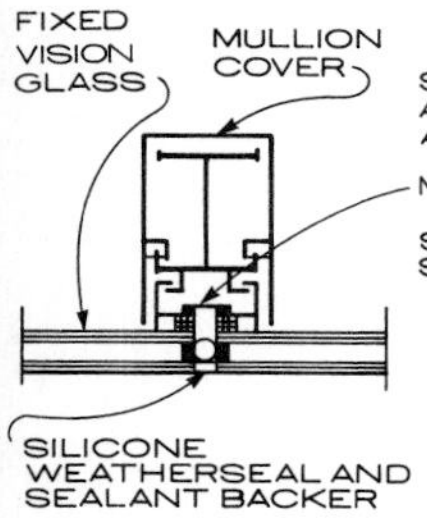

FIXED VISION GLASS

MULLION COVER

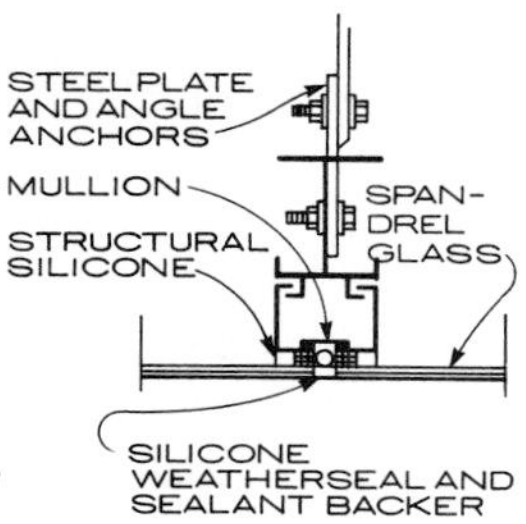

STEEL PLATE AND ANGLE ANCHORS

MULLION

STRUCTURAL SILICONE

SILICONE WEATHERSEAL AND SEALANT BACKER

**SECTION 2**

SPANDREL GLASS

SILICONE WEATHERSEAL AND SEALANT BACKER

**SECTION 3-3**

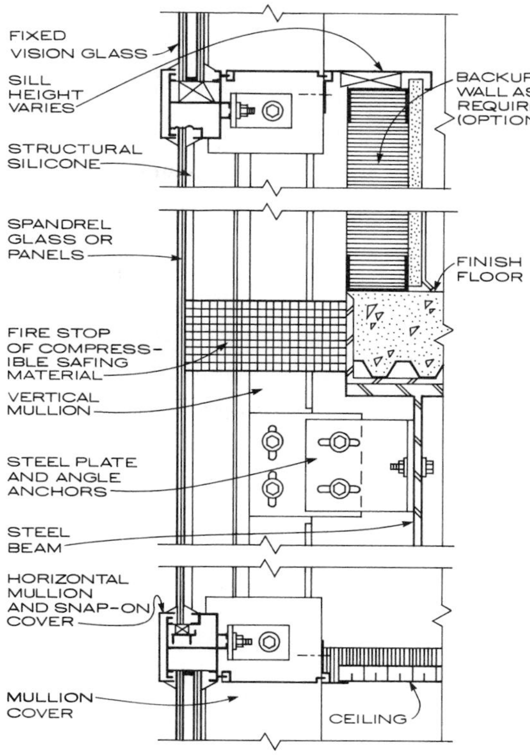

FIXED VISION GLASS

SILL HEIGHT VARIES

STRUCTURAL SILICONE

SPANDREL GLASS OR PANELS

FIRE STOP OF COMPRESSIBLE SAFING MATERIAL

VERTICAL MULLION

STEEL PLATE AND ANGLE ANCHORS

STEEL BEAM

HORIZONTAL MULLION AND SNAP-ON COVER

MULLION COVER

BACKUP WALL AS REQUIRED (OPTIONAL)

FINISH FLOOR

CEILING

**ANCHORAGE AND MOVEMENT**

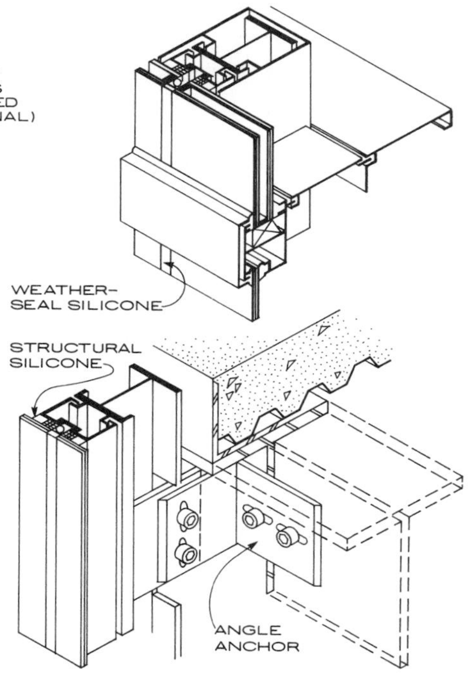

WEATHER-SEAL SILICONE

STRUCTURAL SILICONE

ANGLE ANCHOR

## STRUCTURAL GLAZING SYSTEM (STOPLESS)—COMMERCIAL TYPE—ALUMINUM
### SYSTEM WITH STRUCTURAL SILICONE SEALANT ATTACHMENT ON FOUR SIDES

**TYPICAL ELEVATION**

FINISH FLOOR

FINISH FLOOR

**NOTE**

See index under "Structural Sealant Glazing" for additional information that should be considered when developing a structural sealant curtainwall system.

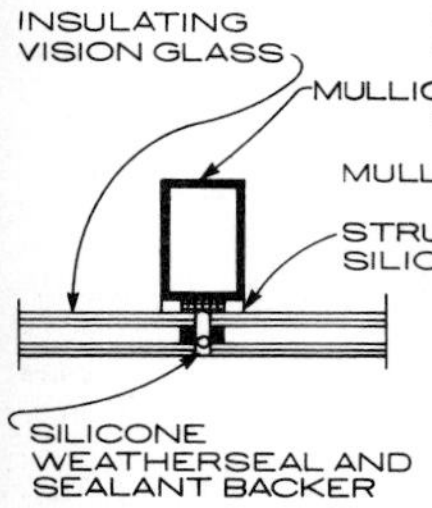

INSULATING VISION GLASS

MULLION

ANGLE ANCHOR

MULLION STIFFENER

MULLION

STRUCTURAL SILICONE

SILICONE WEATHERSEAL AND SEALANT BACKER

**SECTION 1**

SILICONE WEATHERSEAL AND SEALANT BACKER

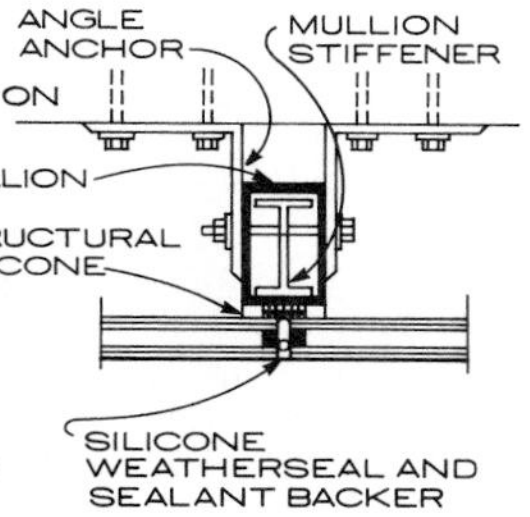

**SECTION 2**

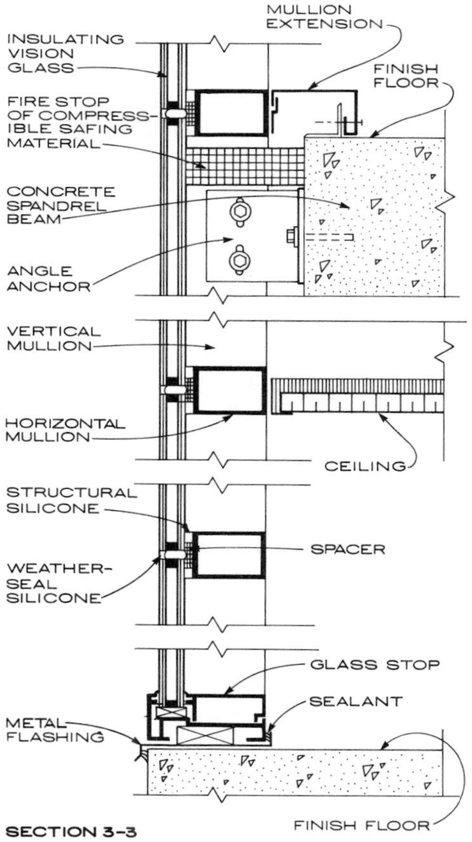

INSULATING VISION GLASS

FIRE STOP OF COMPRESSIBLE SAFING MATERIAL

CONCRETE SPANDREL BEAM

ANGLE ANCHOR

VERTICAL MULLION

HORIZONTAL MULLION

STRUCTURAL SILICONE

WEATHER-SEAL SILICONE

METAL FLASHING

**SECTION 3-3**

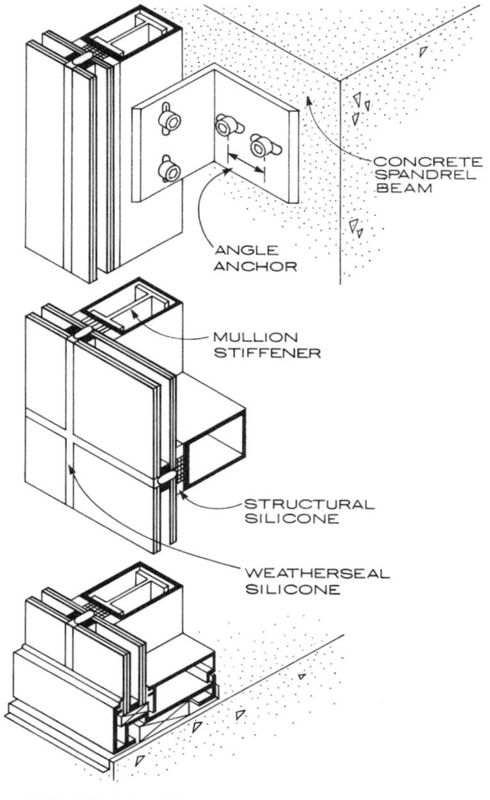

MULLION EXTENSION

FINISH FLOOR

CEILING

SPACER

GLASS STOP

SEALANT

FINISH FLOOR

**ANCHORAGE AND MOVEMENT**

CONCRETE SPANDREL BEAM

ANGLE ANCHOR

MULLION STIFFENER

STRUCTURAL SILICONE

WEATHERSEAL SILICONE

Bullock Tice Associates Architects, Inc.; Pensacola, Florida

## GLAZED CURTAIN WALLS

8

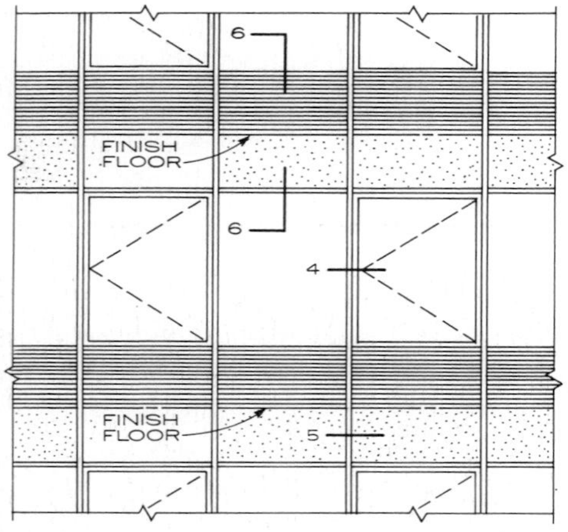

## TYPICAL ELEVATION

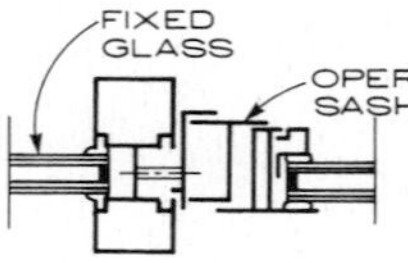

FINISH FLOOR

FINISH FLOOR

SECTION 4

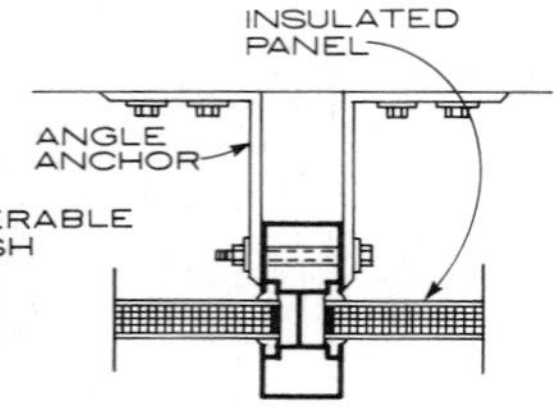

SECTION 5

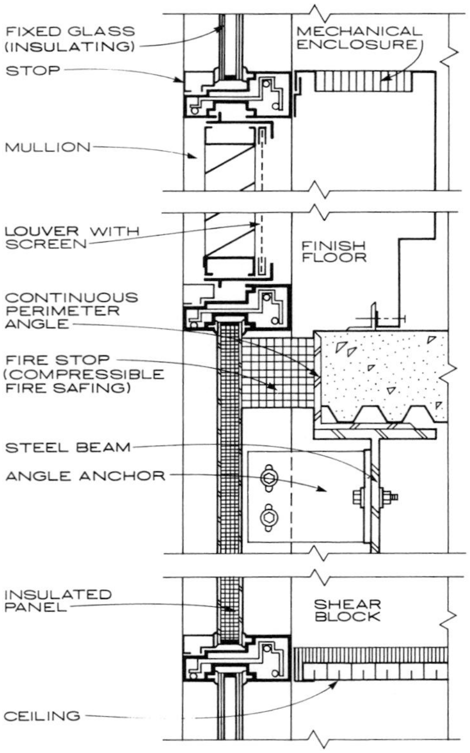

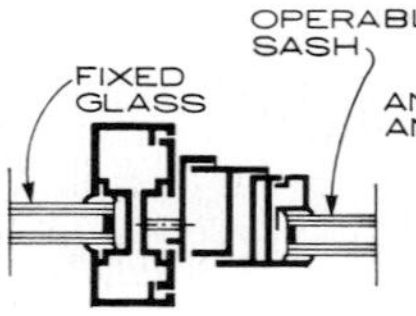

FIXED GLASS
OPERABLE SASH
ANGLE ANCHOR
INSULATED PANEL

FIXED GLASS (INSULATING)
STOP
MECHANICAL ENCLOSURE
MULLION
LOUVER WITH SCREEN
FINISH FLOOR
CONTINUOUS PERIMETER ANGLE
FIRE STOP (COMPRESSIBLE FIRE SAFING)
STEEL BEAM
ANGLE ANCHOR
INSULATED PANEL
SHEAR BLOCK
CEILING

SECTION 6-6

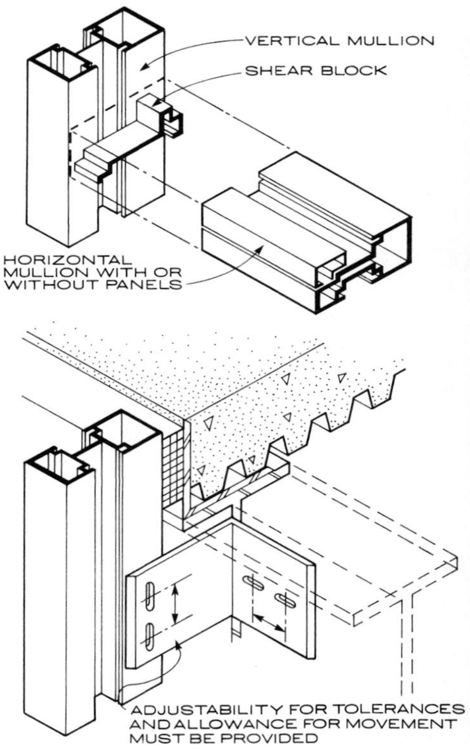

VERTICAL MULLION
SHEAR BLOCK
HORIZONTAL MULLION WITH OR WITHOUT PANELS
ADJUSTABILITY FOR TOLERANCES AND ALLOWANCE FOR MOVEMENT MUST BE PROVIDED

ANCHORAGE

## GRID SYSTEM (PANEL AND MULLION)—COMMERCIAL TYPE—ALUMINUM
LOW-RISE APPLICATION USING SHEAR BLOCK FABRICATION

ADJUSTABILITY FOR TOLERANCES AND ALLOW-ANCE FOR MOVEMENT MUST BE PROVIDED

## TYPICAL ELEVATION

METAL COPING
OPER-ABLE SASH
FINISH FLOOR
FIXED GLASS
FINISH FLOOR

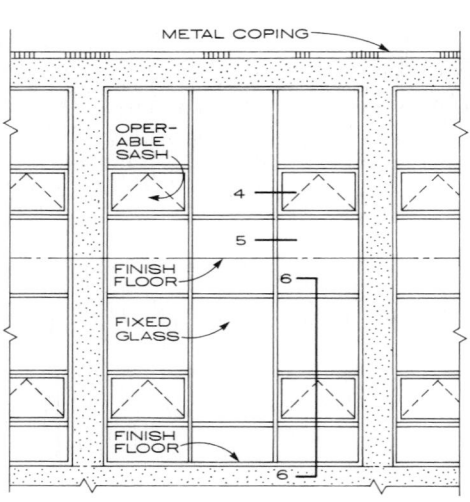

INSULATED PANEL
OPERABLE SASH
FIXED GLASS
ANGLE ANCHOR

SECTION 4

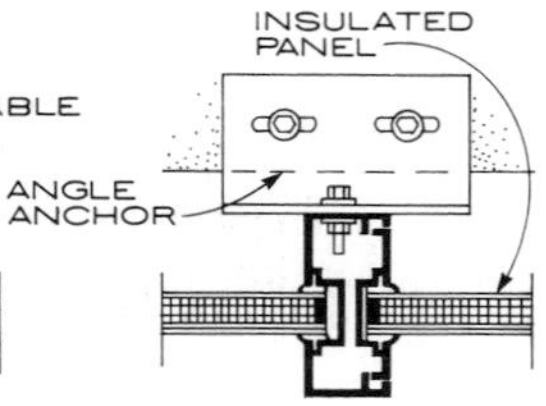

SECTION 5

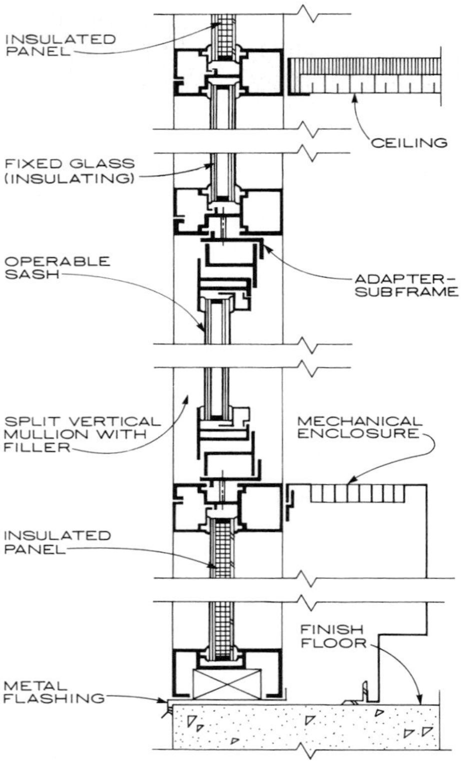

INSULATED PANEL
FIXED GLASS (INSULATING)
OPERABLE SASH
SPLIT VERTICAL MULLION WITH FILLER
INSULATED PANEL
METAL FLASHING
CEILING
ADAPTER-SUBFRAME
MECHANICAL ENCLOSURE
FINISH FLOOR

SECTION 6-6

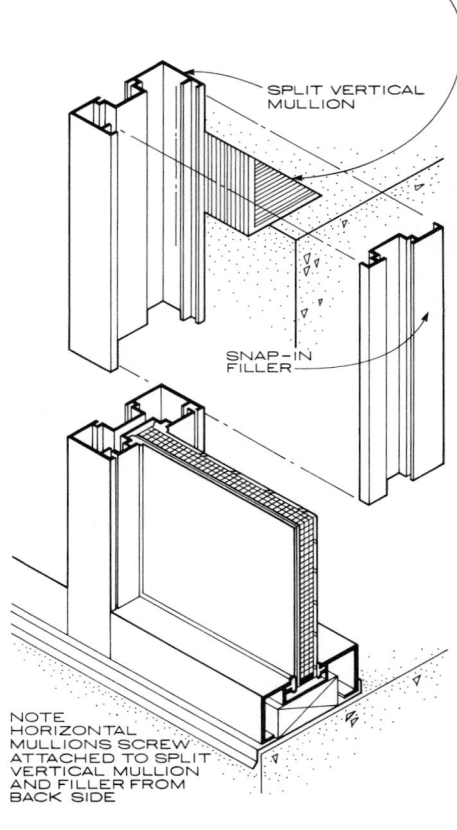

SPLIT VERTICAL MULLION
SNAP-IN FILLER
NOTE HORIZONTAL MULLIONS SCREW ATTACHED TO SPLIT VERTICAL MULLION AND FILLER FROM BACK SIDE

ANCHORAGE

## PANEL SYSTEM—COMMERCIAL TYPE—ALUMINUM
LOW-RISE APPLICATION USING SCREW SPLINE FABRICATION

Bullock Tice Associates Architects, Inc.; Pensacola, Florida

# GLAZED CURTAIN WALLS

# CHAPTER 9

# *Finishes*

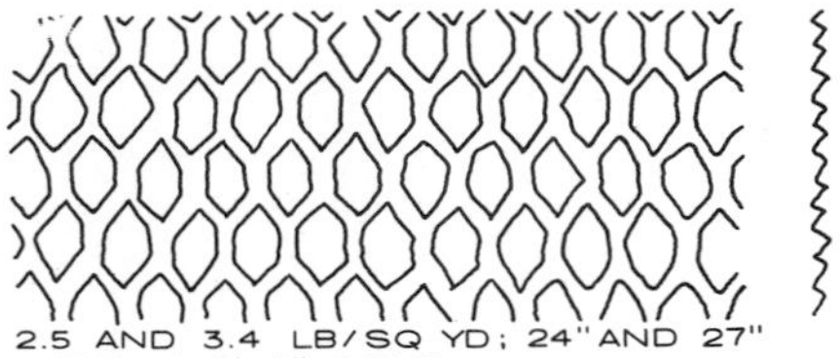

2.5 AND 3.4 LB/SQ YD; 24" AND 27" WIDE × 8'-0" LONG

DIAMOND MESH EXPANDED METAL

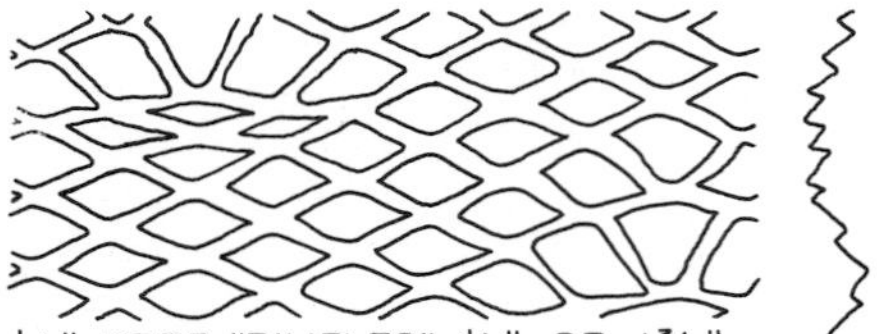

1/4" DEEP "DIMPLES" 1½" OR 1¾" O.C.; 24" AND 24" WIDE × 8'-0" LONG

SELF-FURRING DIAMOND MESH

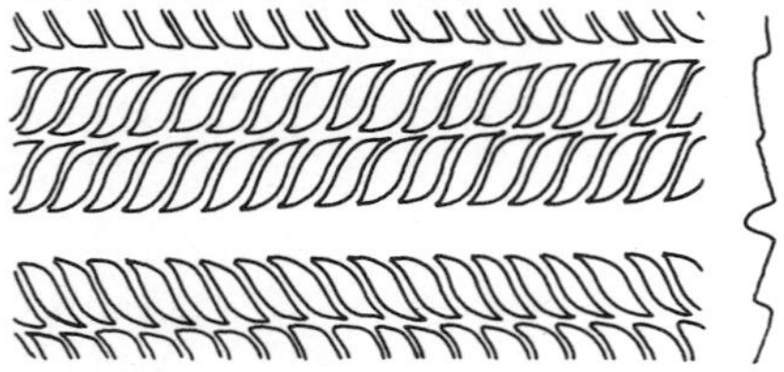

RIB EXPANDED METAL

LATHING SYSTEMS

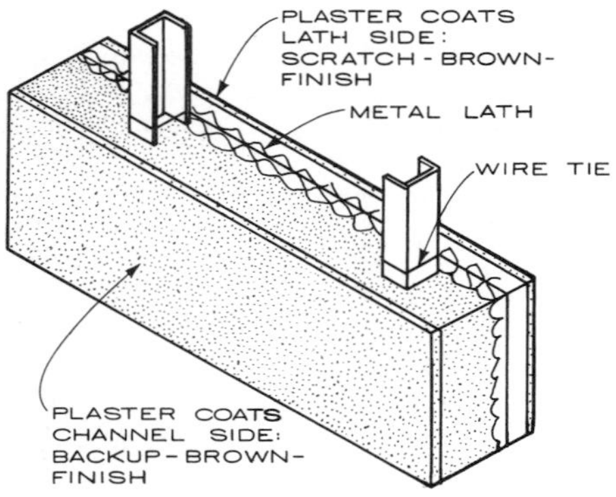


SOLID PARTITION SYSTEMS

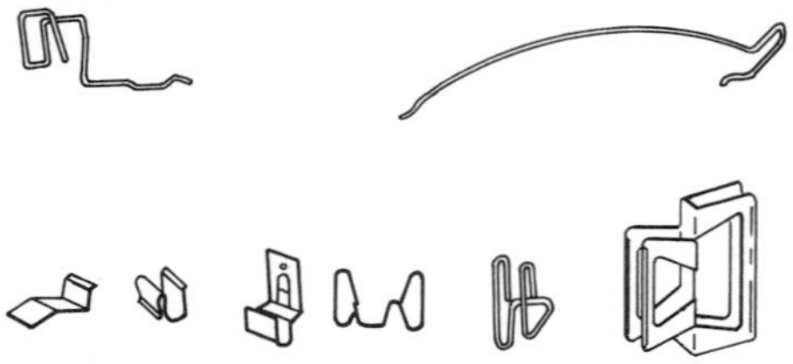

FIELD CLIPS

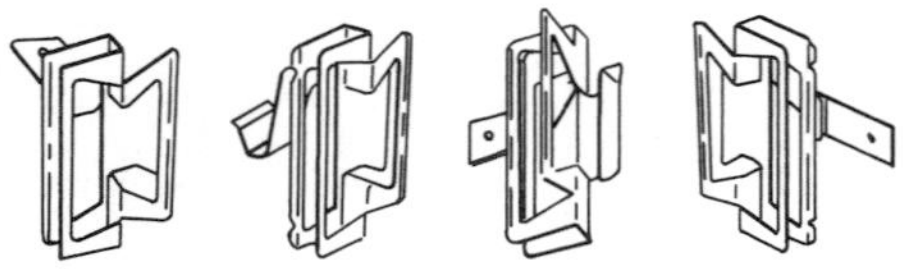

CORNER CLIPS

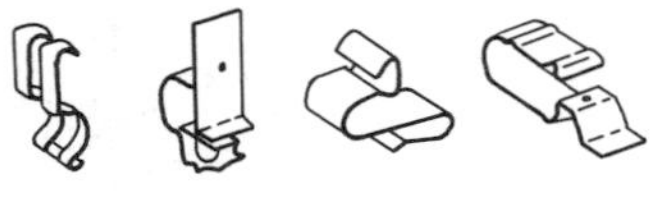

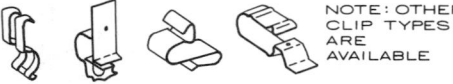

NOTE: OTHER CLIP TYPES ARE AVAILABLE

MISCELLANEOUS

CLIPS FOR GYPSUM LATH SYSTEM

NOTES

Self-furring paperbacked reinforcing is available in diamond mesh, welded wire, and hexagonal woven wire. Paperbacks are available to conform to Federal Specifications UU-B-790, Type 1, Grade A, Style 2 for highly water-vapor resistant paper.

Metal lath is also manufactured in large diamond mesh 27 x 96 in., 2.5 or 3.4 lb/sq yd, painted steel or galvanized; 1/8 in. flat rib 27 x 96 in., 2.75 or 3.4 lb/sq yd painted or galvanized; 3/8 in. rib expanded 27 x 96 in., 3.4 lb/sq yd painted or galvanized and 3/4 in. rib expanded 24 x 96 in., 5.4 lb/sq yd painted.

Other types of lath are available from some manufacturers.

## GYPSUM LATH

Gypsum lath is composed of an air entrained gypsum core sandwiched between two sheets of fibrous absorbent paper and used as a basecoat for gypsum plaster.

1. PLAIN GYPSUM LATH: 3/8 and 1/2 in. thick, 48 in. long, and 16 in. wide (16 1/5 in. in the Western U.S.).
2. PERFORATED GYPSUM LATH: Plain gypsum lath with 3/4 in. diameter holes punched 4 in. o.c. in both directions to provide mechanical key to plaster.
3. INSULATING GYPSUM LATH: Plain gypsum lath with aluminum foil laminated to the backside as insulator or vapor barrier.
4. LONG LENGTH GYPSUM LATH: 16 and 24 in. wide, in lengths up to 12 ft, available insulated or plain with square or vee-jointed Tongue and Groove edges or interlocking as ship-lap edge.

## SOLID PLASTER PARTITION CONSTRUCTION

| PARTITION CONSTRUCTION | THICKNESS | MAXIMUM HEIGHT |
|---|---|---|
| 3/4″ cold-rolled channels Diamond mesh lath and plaster | 2″ | 12′-0″ |
| 3/4″ cold-rolled channels Diamond mesh lath and plaster | 2 1/2″ | 16′-0″ |
| 1 1/2″ cold-rolled channels Diamond mesh lath and plaster | 3″ | 20′-0″ |
| 1 1/2″ cold-rolled channels Diamond mesh lath and plaster | 3 1/2″ | 22′-0″ |

NOTE: Maximum partition length is unrestricted if less than 10 ft tall. Twice the height if over 10 ft tall; one and one half the height if over 14 ft tall and equal to the height if over 20 ft tall.

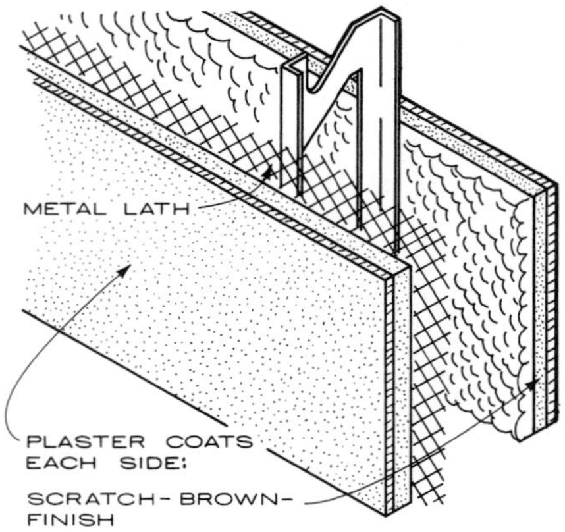


NOTES

Prefabricated metal studs are used as the supporting elements of lath and plaster hollow partitions. They are available in 1 5/8, 2, 2 1/2, 3 1/4, 4, and 6 in. widths. Lengths are available in various increments up to 24 ft. Prefabricated studs are usually of the nonload bearing type, but load bearing metal studs also are manufactured. Designs vary with the manufacturer, and most manufacturers produce a line of related accessories, such as clips, runners, stud shoes, and similar articles.

HOLLOW PARTITION SYSTEMS

DEFINITIONS

AGGREGATE: Inert material used as filler with a cementitious material and water to produce plaster or concrete. Usually implies sand, perlite, or vermiculite.

BASECOAT: Any plaster coat applied before the finish coat.

BEAD: Light gauge metal strip with one or more expanded or short perforated flanges and variously shaped noses; used at the perimeter of plastered surfaces.

BROWN COAT: In three-coat plaster, the brown coat is the second coat; in two-coat plaster, the base coat.

CALCINED GYPSUM: Gypsum that has been partially dehydrated by heating.

CLIP: A device made of wire or sheet metal for attaching various types of lath to the substructure and lath sheets to one another.

FIBERED PLASTER: Gypsum plaster containing fibers of hair, glass, nylon, or sisal.

FINISH COAT: The final coat of plaster, which provides the decorative surface.

FURRING: Grillage for the attachment of gypsum or metal lath.

GAUGING: Cementitious material, usually calcined gypsum or portland cement combined with lime putty to control set.

GROUND: A formed metal shape or wood strip that acts as a combined edge and gauge for various thicknesses of plaster to be applied to a plaster base.

GYPSUM: Hydrous calcium sulphate, a natural mineral in crystalline form.

GYPSUM LATH: A base for plaster; a sheet having a gypsum core, faced with paper.

GYPSUM READY MIX PLASTER: Ground gypsum that has been calcined and then mixed with various additives to control its setting and working qualities; used, with the addition of aggregate and water, for basecoat plaster.

HYDRATED LIME: Quicklime mixed with water, on the job, to form a lime putty.

LIME: Obtained by burning various types of limestone, consisting of oxides or hydroxides of calcium and magnesium.

LIME PLASTER: Basecoat plaster of hydrated lime and an aggregate.

NEAT PLASTER: Basecoat plaster, fibered or unfibered, used for job mixing with aggregates.

PERLITE: Siliceous volcanic glass containing silica and alumina expanded by heat for use as a lightweight plaster aggregate.

PLASTER: Cementitious material or combination of cementitious materials and aggregate that, when mixed with water, forms a plastic mass that sets and hardens when applied to a surface.

PORTLAND CEMENT: Manufactured combination of limestone and an argillaceous substance.

SCRATCH COAT: In three-coat plastering, the first coat, which is then scratched to provide a bond for second or brown coat.

SCREED: A device secured to a surface which serves as a guide for subsequent applications of plaster. Thicknesses and widths vary with the thicknesses desired for each operation.

STUCCO PORTLAND CEMENT: Plaster used in exterior application.

VERMICULITE: Micaceous mineral of silica, magnesium, and alumina oxides made up in a series of parallel plates or laminae and expanded by heat for use as a lightweight plaster aggregate.

NOTES

Keene's cement plaster is a specialty finish coat of gypsum plaster primarily used where a smooth, dense, white finish is desired.

Thickness, proportions of mixes of various plastering materials, and finishes vary. Systems and methods of application vary widely depending on local traditions and innovations promoted by the industry.

The Marmon Mok Partnership; San Antonio, Texas

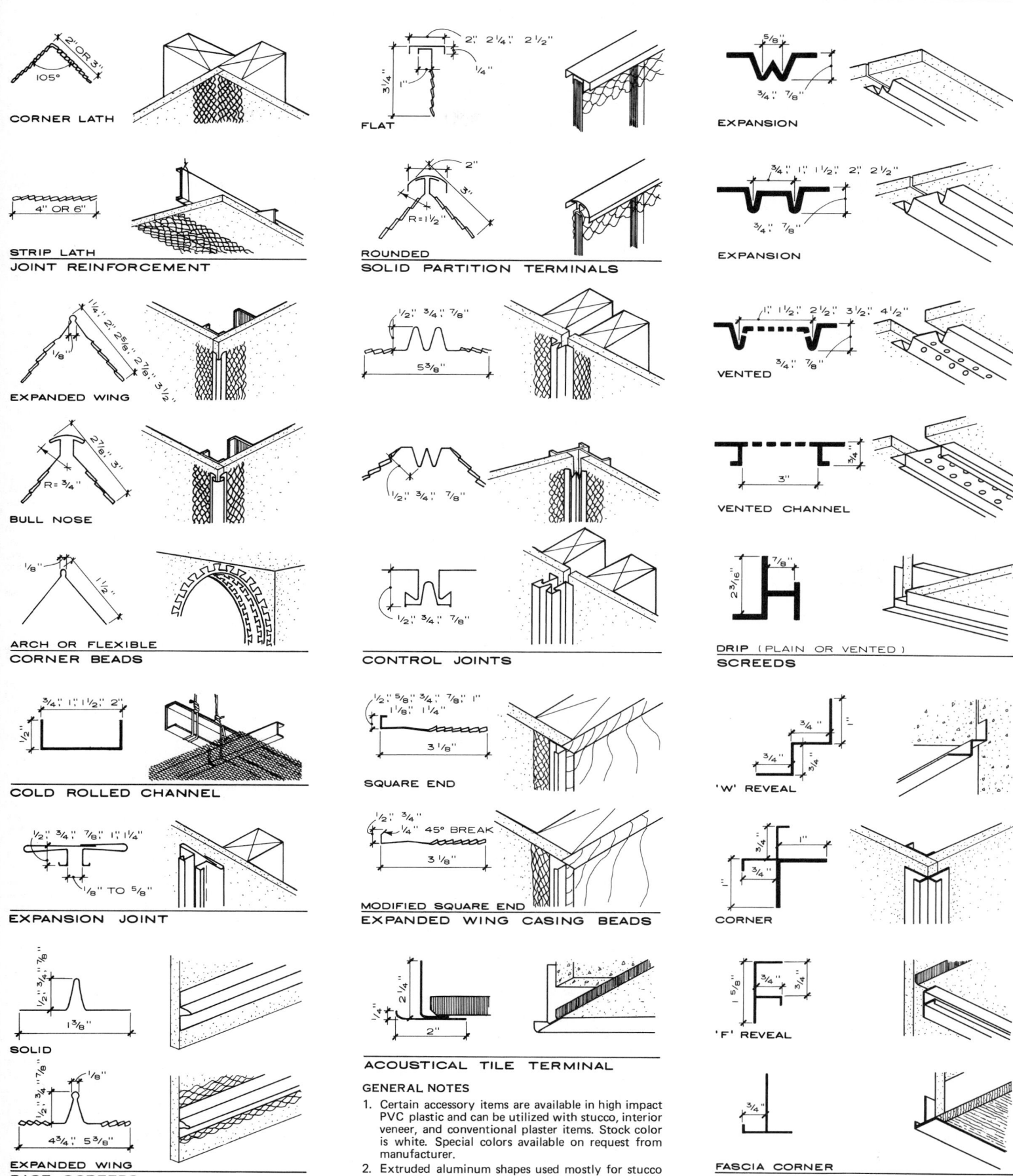

CORNER LATH

STRIP LATH
JOINT REINFORCEMENT

EXPANDED WING

BULL NOSE

ARCH OR FLEXIBLE
CORNER BEADS

COLD ROLLED CHANNEL

EXPANSION JOINT

SOLID

EXPANDED WING
BASE SCREEDS

FLAT

ROUNDED
SOLID PARTITION TERMINALS

CONTROL JOINTS

SQUARE END

MODIFIED SQUARE END
EXPANDED WING CASING BEADS

ACOUSTICAL TILE TERMINAL

EXPANSION

EXPANSION

VENTED

VENTED CHANNEL

DRIP (PLAIN OR VENTED)
SCREEDS

'W' REVEAL

CORNER

'F' REVEAL

FASCIA CORNER
MOLDING

**GENERAL NOTES**

1. Certain accessory items are available in high impact PVC plastic and can be utilized with stucco, interior veneer, and conventional plaster items. Stock color is white. Special colors available on request from manufacturer.

2. Extruded aluminum shapes used mostly for stucco are available in a variety of anodized finishes.

The Marmon Mok Partnership; San Antonio, Texas

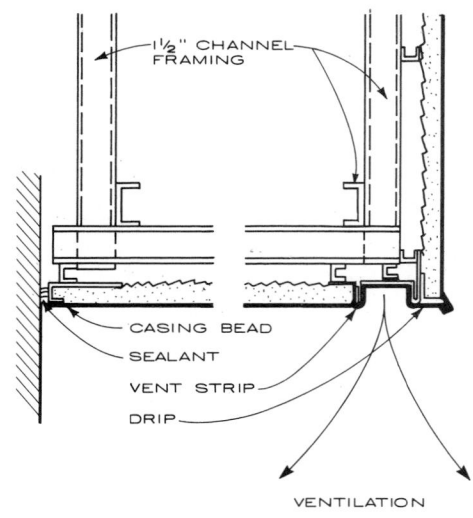

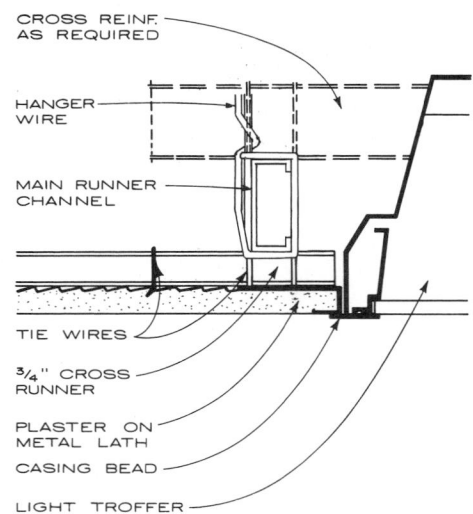

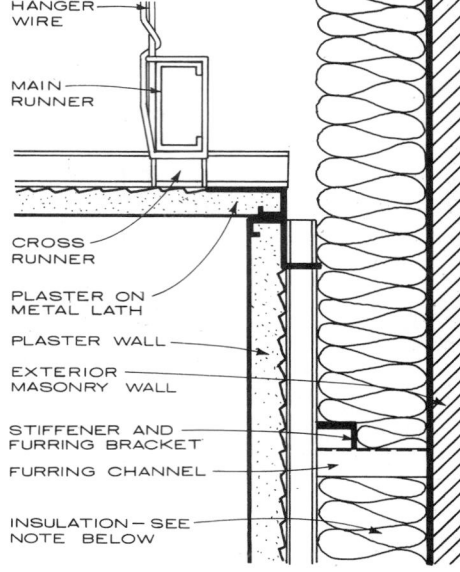

## SOFFIT DETAIL

**NOTE**

Framing details for exterior cement plaster (stucco) are similar to details shown. Wind loads must be considered in designing framing systems for exterior stucco work. Galvanized mesh is available for exterior applications and use in humid areas. Ventilation strips should be used for ventilating all dead airspaces. Where plenum or attic spaces are closed off by ceiling installation, ventilation shall be provided with a minimum of $\frac{1}{2}$ sq. in./sq. ft. of horizontal surface.

## SUSPENDED PLASTER CEILING AT RECESSED LIGHT FIXTURE

**NOTE**

Penetrations of the lath and plaster ceiling—at borrowed light openings, vents, grilles, access panels, and light troffers, for example—require additional reinforcement to distribute concentrated stresses if a control joint is not used. Where a plaster surface is flush with metal, as at metal access panels, grilles, or light troffers, the plaster should be grooved between the two materials.

## SUSPENDED PLASTER CEILING AT FURRED MASONRY WALL

**NOTE**

When interior walls are furred from an exterior masonry wall and insulated, the ceiling should stop short of the furred space. This allows wall insulation to continue above the ceiling line to ceiling or roof insulation, thus forming a complete insulation envelope. In a suspension system that abuts masonry wall, provide 1 in. clearance between ends of main runners or furring channels and wall face.

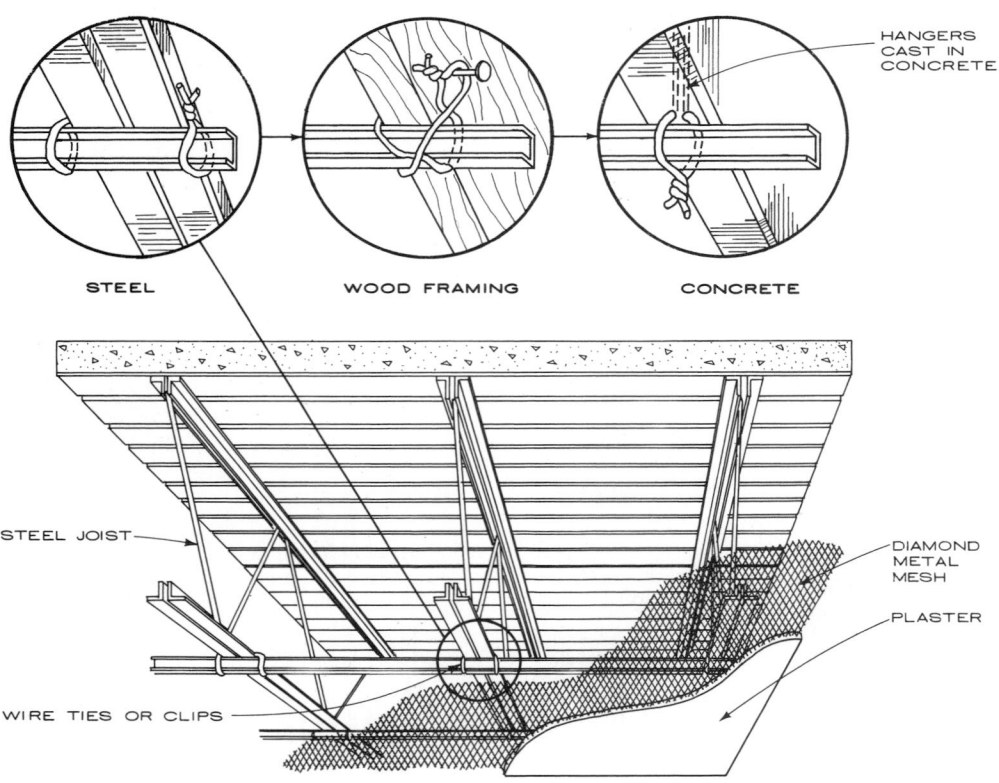

**NOTE**
RIB METAL LATH MAY BE USED IN LIEU OF DIAMOND MESH LATH AND FURRING CHANNELS IF LATH SPANS DO NOT EXCEED ALLOWABLE MAXIMUM. SEE TABLE I

## FURRED METAL LATH ON STEEL JOIST

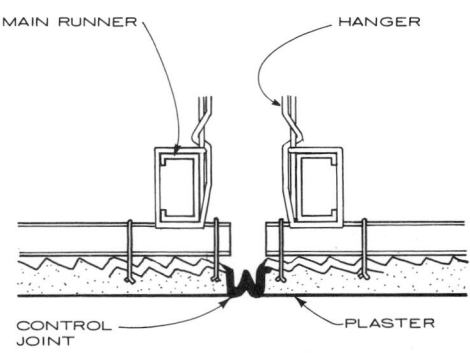

## CONTROL JOINT DETAIL

**NOTE**

Control joints shall be spaced no further than 30 ft on center in each direction for large plastered ceiling areas. Area shall not exceed 900 sq ft without provision for expansion control. Exterior plaster soffits should have control joints spaced no further than 25 ft on center. For portland cement plaster (stucco) areas, interior or exterior, control joints should be placed at 10 ft on center and areas should not exceed 100 sq ft without provisions for expansion/contraction control. Control joints are spaced closer for cement plaster because of its inherent shrinkage during curing.

**NOTE**

Details shown are for furred (contact) ceilings that are attached directly to the structural members. The architect or ceiling designer should give consideration to the deflection and movement of the structure, since movement and deflection of more than $\frac{1}{360}$ of the span will cause cracking of plaster ceilings. If spacing of structural members exceeds the maximum span of furring members shown in the span charts, the addition of suspended main runners between structural members will be required. Flat rib lath may be attached directly to wood framing members, but is subjected to stresses created by the inherent properties of wood members.

James E. Phillips, AIA; Enwright Associates, Inc.; Greenville, South Carolina

**LATH AND PLASTER**

## DIRECTIONS FOR USING TABLES

1. Select lath and plaster system.
2. Determine spacing of cross furring channels from Table 1—Lath Span.
3. Determine spacing of main runners from Table 2—Maximum Spacing between Runners.
4. Determine hanger support spacing for main runner from Table 3—Maximum Spacing between Hangers.
5. Calculate area of ceiling supported per hanger.
6. Select hanger type from Table 4—Hanger Selection.
7. Select tie wire size from Table 5—Tie Wire Selection.

## TABLE 1. LATH SPAN

|  | LATH TYPE | WEIGHT/SQ. FT. | SPAN (IN.) |
|---|---|---|---|
| Gypsum lath | 3/8" plain | 1.5# | 16 |
| | 1/2" plain | 2.0# | 16 |
| | 1/2" veneer | 1.8# | 16 |
| | 5/8" veneer | 2.25# | 16 |
| | 3/8" perforated | 1.4# | 16 |
| Metal lath | Diamond mesh | 0.27# | 12 |
| | Diamond mesh | 0.38# | 16 |
| | 1/8" flat rib | 0.31# | 12 |
| | 1/8" flat rib | 0.38# | 19 |
| | 3/8" flat rib | 0.38# | 24 |

## TABLE 2. MAXIMUM SPACING BETWEEN RUNNERS

| CROSS FURRING TYPE | CROSS FURRING SPACING | | | |
|---|---|---|---|---|
| | 12" | 16" | 19" | 24" |
| 1/4" diam. pencil rod | 2'-0" | — | — | — |
| 3/8" diam. pencil rod | 2'-6" | — | 2'-0" | — |
| 3/4" CRC, HRC (0.3 lb/ft) | — | 4'-6" | 3'-6" | 3'-0" |
| 1" HRC (0.41 lb/ft) | 5'-0" | — | 4'-6" | 4'-0" |

CRC = Cold rolled channel
HRC = Hot rolled channel

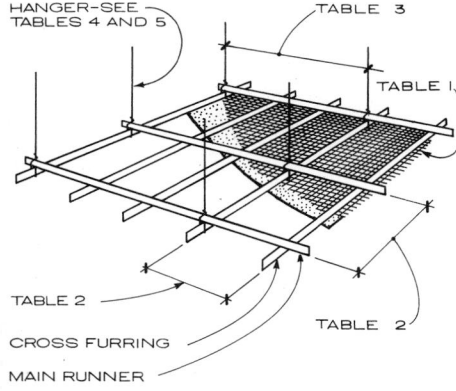

FURRED AND SUSPENSION SYSTEM COMPONENT SELECTION DETAIL

HANGER-SEE TABLES 4 AND 5
TABLE 3
TABLE 1
TABLE 2
TABLE 2
CROSS FURRING
MAIN RUNNER

SUSPENSION SYSTEM TIE WIRES AS REQUIRED
MAIN RUNNER CHANNEL
3/4" CROSS FURRING CHANNEL
SUSPENSION SYSTEM HANGER WIRE FROM STRUCTURE ABOVE

## NOTE

Dimensional requirements for support spacing, runner spacing, hanger spacing, hanger type selection, and tie wire selection are given in tables on this page.

James E. Phillips, AIA; Enwright Associates, Inc.; Greenville, South Carolina

## TABLE 3. MAXIMUM SPACING BETWEEN HANGERS

| MAIN RUNNER TYPE | MAIN RUNNER SPACING | | | | |
|---|---|---|---|---|---|
| | 3'-0" | 3'-6" | 4'-0" | 4'-6" | 5'-0" |
| 3/4" CRC (0.3 lb/ft) | 2'-0" | — | — | — | — |
| 1 1/2" CRC (0.3 lb/ft) | 3'-0"* | — | — | — | — |
| 1 1/2" CRC (0.875 lb/ft) | 4'-0" | 3'-6" | 3'-0" | — | — |
| 1 1/2" HRC (1.12 lb/ft) | — | — | — | 4'-0" | — |
| 2" CRC (0.59 lb/ft) | — | — | 5'-0" | — | — |
| 2" HRC (1.26 lb/ft) | — | — | — | — | 5'-0" |
| 1/2" x 1/2" x 3/16" ST1 | — | 5'-0" | — | — | — |

*For concrete construction only—a 10-gauge wire may be inserted in the joint before concrete is poured.

## TABLE 4. HANGER SELECTION

| MAX. CEILING AREA | MIN. HANGER SIZE |
|---|---|
| 12 sq. ft. | 9-gauge galvanized wire |
| 16 sq. ft. | 8-gauge galvanized wire |
| 18 sq. ft. | 3/16" mild steel rod* |
| 25 sq. ft. | 1/4" mild steel rod* |
| 25 sq. ft. | 3/16" x 1" steel flat* |

*Rods galvanized or painted with rust inhibitive paint and galvanized straps are recommended under severe moisture conditions.

## TABLE 5. TIE WIRE SELECTION

| SUPPORT | | MAX. CEILING AREA | MIN. HANGER SIZE |
|---|---|---|---|
| Cross furring | | 8 sq. ft. | 14-gauge wire |
| | | 8 sq. ft. | 16-gauge wire (two loops) |
| Main runners | Single hangers between beams | 8 sq. ft. | 12-gauge wire |
| | | 12 sq. ft. | 10-gauge wire |
| | | 16 sq. ft. | 8-gauge wire |
| | Double wire loops at supports | 8 sq. ft. | 14-gauge wire |
| | | 12 sq. ft. | 12-gauge wire |
| | | 16 sq. ft. | 11-gauge wire |

## ERECTION OF METAL LATH SUSPENSIONS

Metal lath suspensions commonly are made below all types of construction for fire rated plaster ceilings. The lath is supported by framing channels and furring channels suspended with wire hangers from the floor or roof structure above. Framing channels normally are spaced up to 4 ft. o.c. perpendicular to joists and should be erected to conform with the contour of the finished ceiling. Framing channels normally are furred with 3/4 in. channels placed at right angles to the framing. Spacing varies by lath types and weights. The lath should be lapped at both sides and ends and secured to the 3/4 in. channels with wire ties every 6 in. Where plaster on metal lath ceilings abuts masonry walls, partitions, or arch soffits, galvanized casing beads should be installed at the periphery.

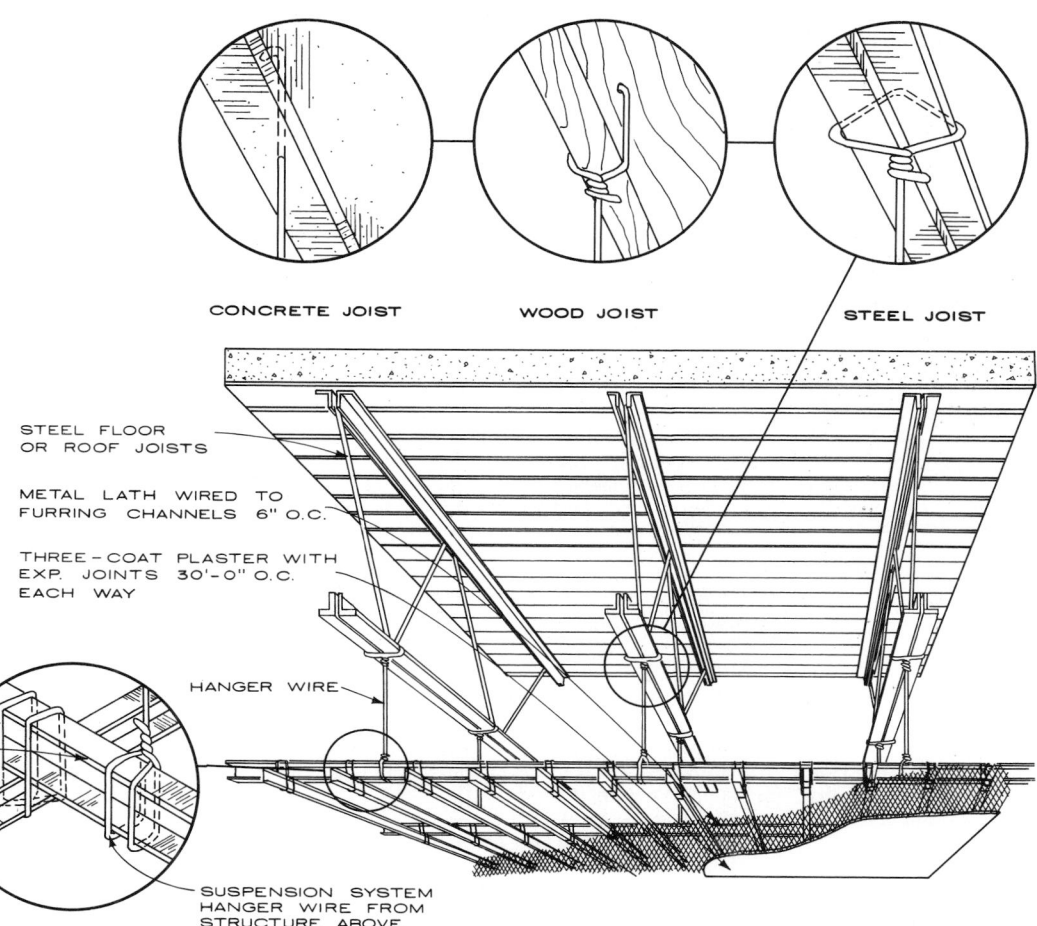

CONCRETE JOIST    WOOD JOIST    STEEL JOIST

STEEL FLOOR OR ROOF JOISTS
METAL LATH WIRED TO FURRING CHANNELS 6" O.C.
THREE-COAT PLASTER WITH EXP. JOINTS 30'-0" O.C. EACH WAY
HANGER WIRE

METAL LATH SUSPENDED FROM STEEL JOISTS

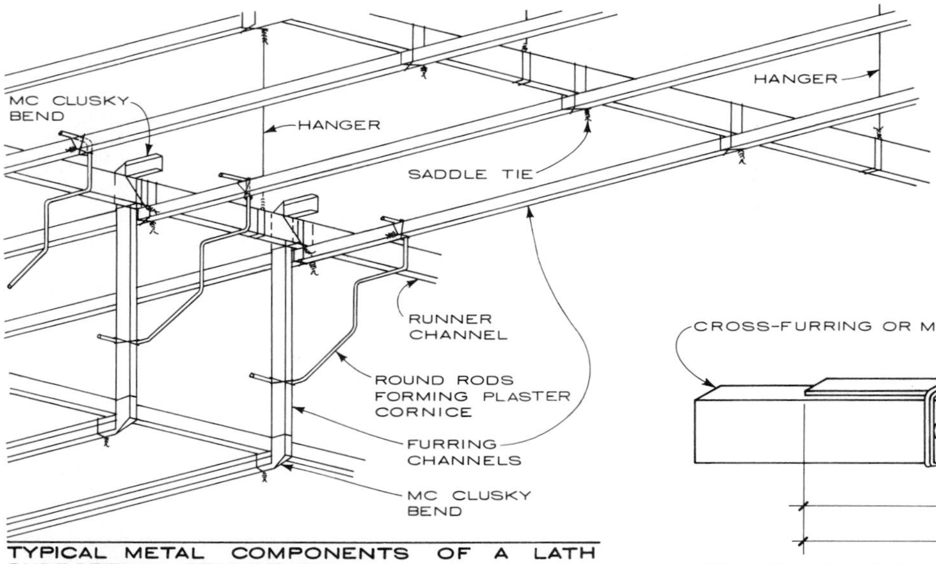

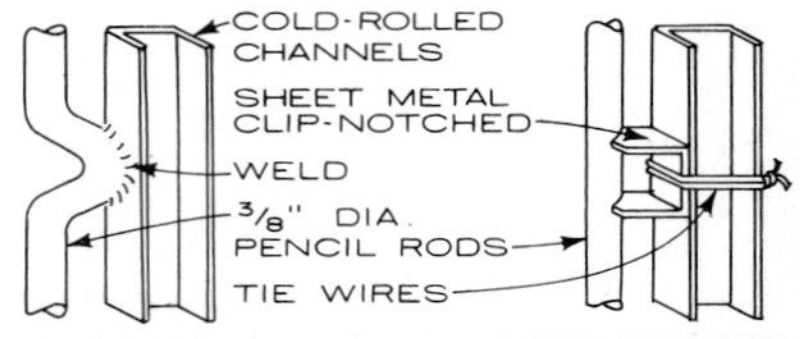

COLD-ROLLED CHANNELS
SHEET METAL CLIP-NOTCHED
WELD
3/8" DIA. PENCIL RODS
TIE WIRES

**SHIM DETAILS**

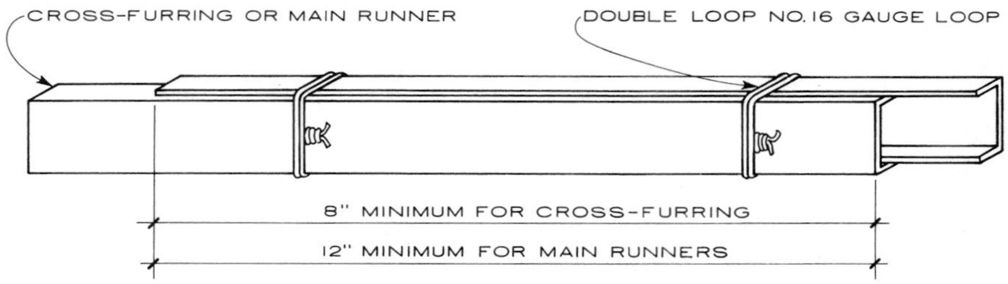

MC CLUSKY BEND
HANGER
HANGER
SADDLE TIE
RUNNER CHANNEL
ROUND RODS FORMING PLASTER CORNICE
FURRING CHANNELS
MC CLUSKY BEND

**TYPICAL METAL COMPONENTS OF A LATH SUPPORTING STRUCTURE**

CROSS-FURRING OR MAIN RUNNER
DOUBLE LOOP NO. 16 GAUGE LOOP
8" MINIMUM FOR CROSS-FURRING
12" MINIMUM FOR MAIN RUNNERS

**CHANNEL SPLICE**

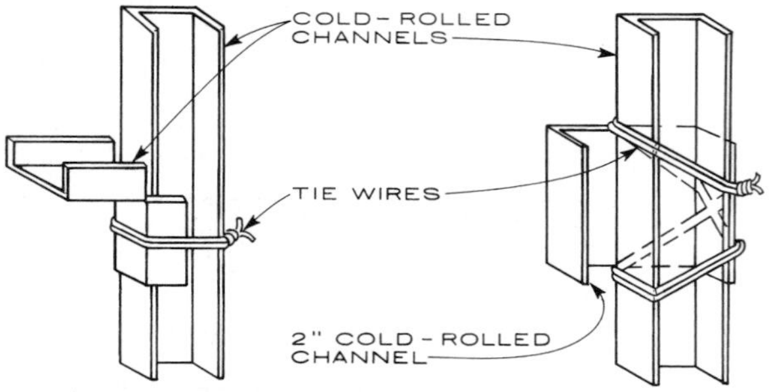

COLD-ROLLED CHANNELS
TIE WIRES
2" COLD-ROLLED CHANNEL

**SPACER DETAILS**

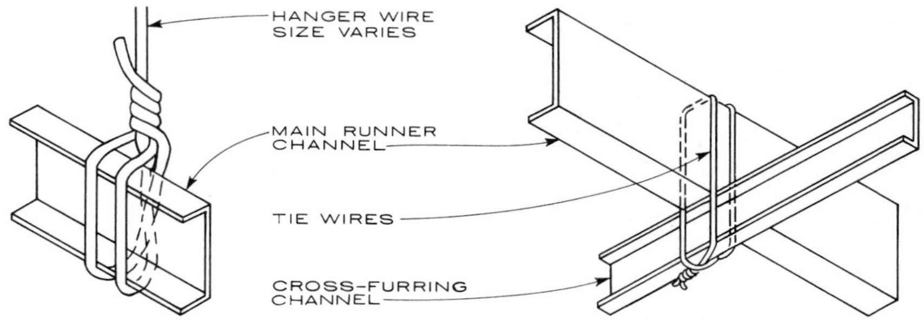

HANGER WIRE SIZE VARIES
MAIN RUNNER CHANNEL
TIE WIRES
CROSS-FURRING CHANNEL

**SADDLE TIES**

**TYPICAL METAL CHANNEL SUSPENSION AND FURRING DETAILS**

MAIN RUNNER CHANNEL
3/4" FRAMING CHANNEL EXTENDS TO RUNNERS
BOLT
CATCH
METAL LATH
VARIES
PLASTER
HINGE
8" X 8" TO 30"X36" DOORS ADD 3/8" FOR CLEAR OPENING
METAL CASING

**FLUSH METAL FACE**

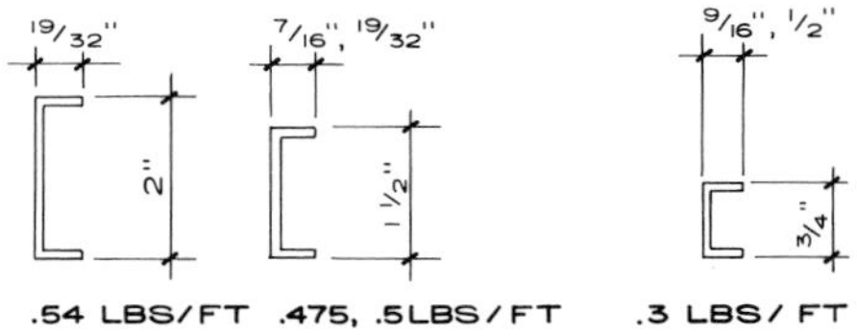

19/32"
7/16", 19/32"
9/16", 1/2"
2"
1 1/2"
3/4"
.54 LBS/FT
.475, .5 LBS/FT
.3 LBS/FT

**RUNNERS**          **FURRING**

FRAMING CHANNELS
TYPICAL MAIN RUNNER
VARIES
VARIES
HINGE SIDE
12" X 12" TO 24" X 24" DOORS ADD 3/8" FOR CLEAR OPENING
METAL CASING

**FLUSH PLASTER FACE**

**METAL ACCESS DOORS AND FRAMES**

NOTE
GAUGE OF METAL, NO. OF LOCKS, HINGES VARY. FIRE-RATED DOORS AVAILABLE

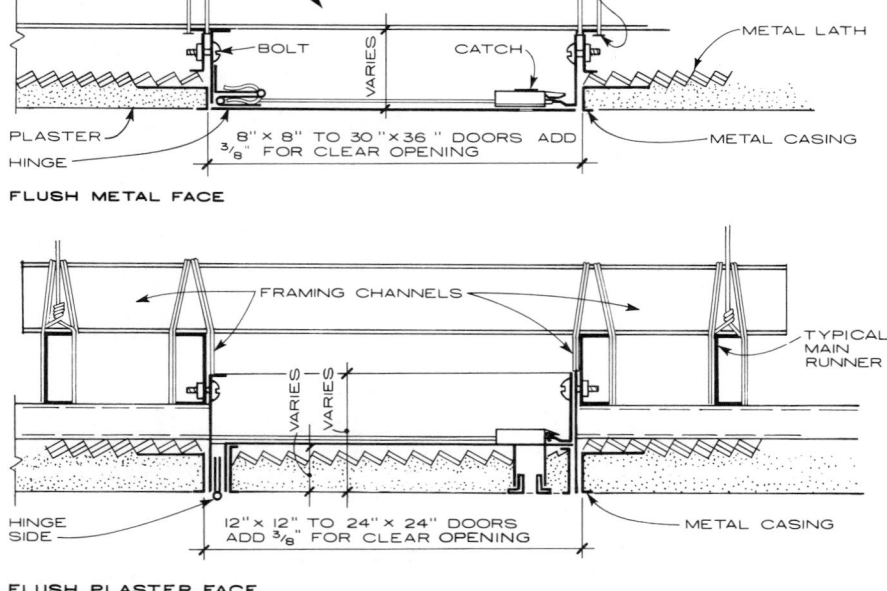

## TYPICAL COLD-ROLLED CHANNEL SHAPES

Heat-rolled channels (HRC) generally run heavier than cold-rolled channels (CRC). Shapes illustrated are available in 16 gauge, 16 ft. and 20 ft. standard lengths.

Galvanizing of all components is recommended where moisture is a factor. Extra heavy galvanizing is required for swimming pools.

See Suspended Ceiling Systems for instructions for selection of components.

Douglas S. Stenhouse, AIA; Los Angeles, California

**LATH AND PLASTER**

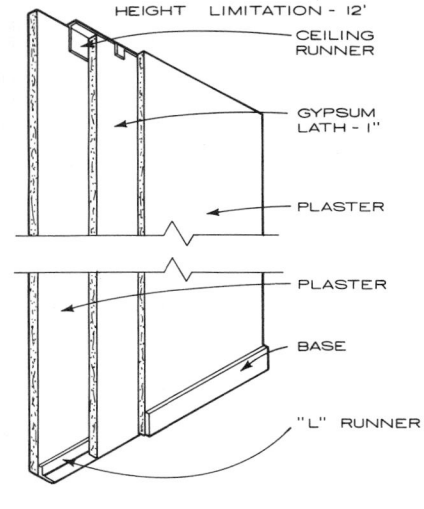

SECTION THROUGH TYPICAL WALL

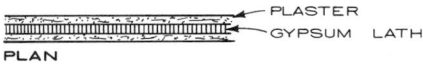

PLAN

**2 IN. SOLID GYPSUM LATH**

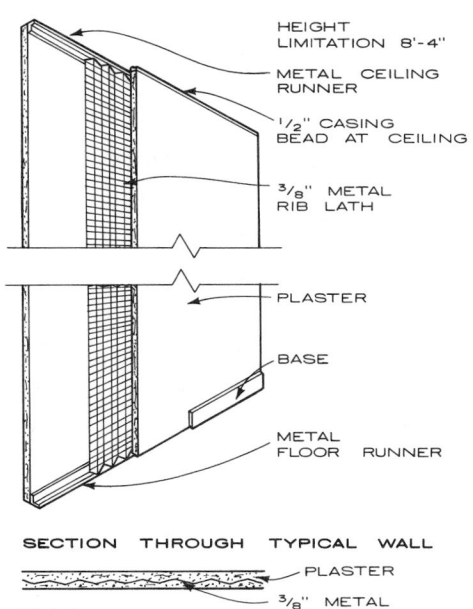

SECTION THROUGH TYPICAL WALL

PLAN

**2 IN. SOLID METAL LATH AND PLASTER**

## CHANNEL STUD SPACING

| TYPE OF LATH | WEIGHT #/SQ YD | SPACING OF SUPPORTS |
|---|---|---|
| Diamond mesh | 2.5 | 16 |
|  | 3.4 | 16 |
| Flat rib | 2.75 | 16 |
|  | 3.4 | 24* |

*Spacing for solid partitions not to exceed 16'-0" in height.

## CHANNEL STUD SIZE

| PARTITION HEIGHT | PARTITION THICKNESS | CHANNEL |
|---|---|---|
| 12' | 2" |  |
| 14' | 2¼" | ¾ in. 300 lb per 1000 ft |
| 16' | 2½" |  |
| 18' | 2¾" | 1½ in. 475 lb per 1000 ft |

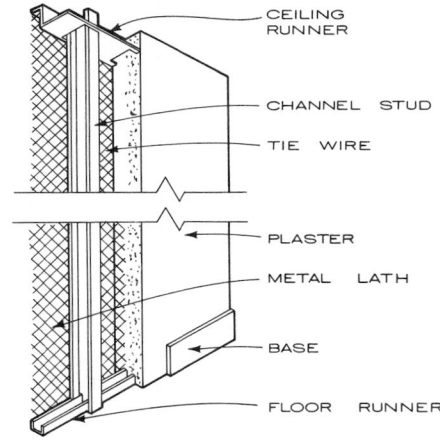

SECTION THROUGH TYPICAL WALL

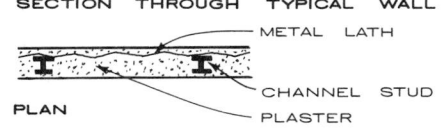

PLAN

**METAL LATH-CHANNEL STUD-PLASTER**

## METAL STUD WITH METAL LATH STUD SPACING AND HEIGHT LIMITATION*

| STUD WIDTH | THICKNESS | MAXIMUM HEIGHT | | |
|---|---|---|---|---|
|  |  | 16" OC. | 19" OC. | 24" OC. |
| 2½" | 4" | 15' | 14' | 9' |
| 3¼" | 4¾" | 21' | 18' | 13' |
| 4" | 5½" | 22' | 20' | 16' |
| 6" | 7½" | 26' | 24' | 20' |

*For length not exceeding 1½ times height; for lengths exceeding this, reduce 20%.

## METAL STUD WITH ⅜" GYPSUM LATH HEIGHT LIMITATIONS

| STUD WIDTH | THICKNESS STANDARD SYSTEM | MAX. HEIGHT STUDS 16" OC. |
|---|---|---|
| 2½" | 4¼" | 15' |
| 3¼" | 5" | 21' |
| 4" | 5¾" | 22' |
| 6" | 7¾" | 26' |

Walter H. Sobel, FAIA & Associates; Chicago, Illinois

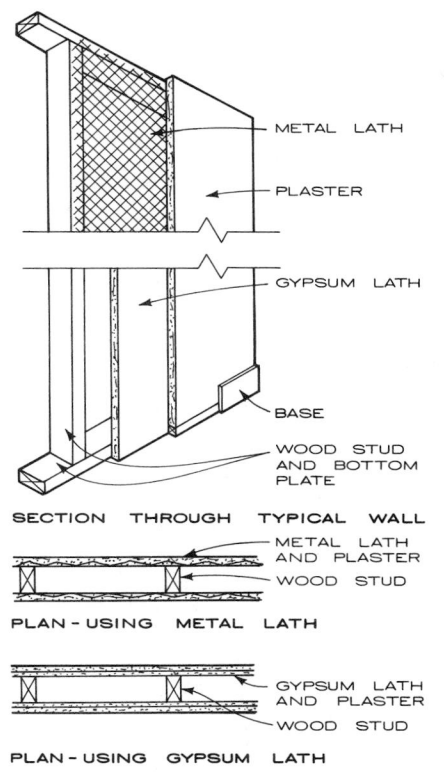

SECTION THROUGH TYPICAL WALL

PLAN - USING METAL LATH

PLAN - USING GYPSUM LATH

**WOOD STUD AND LATH**

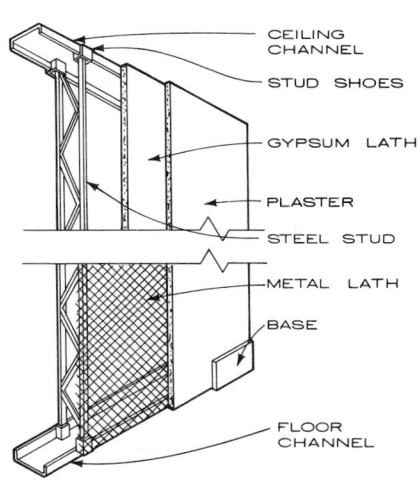

SECTION THROUGH TYPICAL WALL

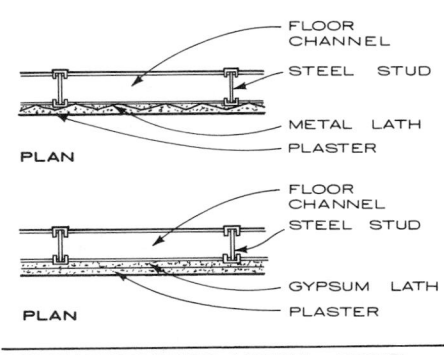

PLAN

PLAN

**PREFABRICATED METAL STUD**

## TYPES OF GYPSUM PANEL PRODUCTS

| DESCRIPTION | THICKNESS (IN.) | WIDTH/EDGE (FT) | STOCK LENGTH (FT) |
|---|---|---|---|
| Regular gypsum wallboard used as a base layer for improving sound control; repair and remodeling | $1/4$ | 4, square or tapered | 8-10 |
| Regular gypsum wallboard used in a double wall system over wood framing; repair and remodeling | $3/8$ | 4, square or tapered | 8-14 |
| Regular gypsum wallboard for use in single layer construction | $1/2$, $5/8$ | 4, square or tapered | 8-16 |
| Rounded taper edge system offers maximum joint strength and minimizes joint deformity problems | $3/8$ $1/2$, $5/8$ | 4, rounded taper | 8-16 |
| Type X gypsum wallboard with core containing special additives to give increased fire resistance ratings. Consult manufacturer for approved assemblies | $1/2$, $5/8$ | 4, tapered, rounded taper, or rounded | 8-16 |
| Aluminum foil backed board effective as a vapor barrier for exterior walls and ceilings and as a thermal insulator when foil faces $3/4''$ minimum air space. Not for use as a tile base or in air conditioned buildings in hot, humid climates (Southern Atlantic and Gulf Coasts) | $3/8$ $1/2$, $5/8$ | 4, square or tapered | 8-16 |
| Water resistant board for use as a base for ceramic and other nonabsorbant wall tiles in bath and shower areas. Type X core is available | $1/2$, $5/8$ | 4, tapered | 8, 10, 12 |
| Prefinished vinyl surface gypsum board in standard and special colors | $1/2$, $5/8$ | 2, $2 1/2$, 4, square and beveled | 8, 9, 10 |
| Prefinished board available in many colors and textures. See manufacturers' literature | $5/16$ | 4, square | 8 |
| Coreboard for use to enclose vent shafts and laminated gypsum partitions | 1 | 2, tongue and groove or square | 4-16 |
| Shaft wall liner core board type X with gypsum core used to enclose elevator shafts and other vertical chases | 1, 2 | 2, square or beveled | 6-16 |
| Sound underlayment gypsum wallboard attached to plywood subfloor acts as a base for any durable floor covering. When used with resiliently attached gypsum panel ceiling, the assembly meets HUD requirements for sound control in multifamily dwellings | $3/4$ | 4, square | 6-8 |
| Exterior ceiling/soffit panel for use on surfaces with indirect exposure to the weather | $1/2$ | 4, rounded taper | 8, 12 |
| Sheathing used as underlayment on exterior walls with type X or regular core | $1/2$ | 2, tongue and groove | 8 |
| | $1/2$, $5/8$ | 4, square | 8, 9, 10 |

NOTE: A large range of adhesives, sealants, joint treatments, and texture products are available from the manufacturers of most gypsum board products. Consult available literature for current recommendations and products.

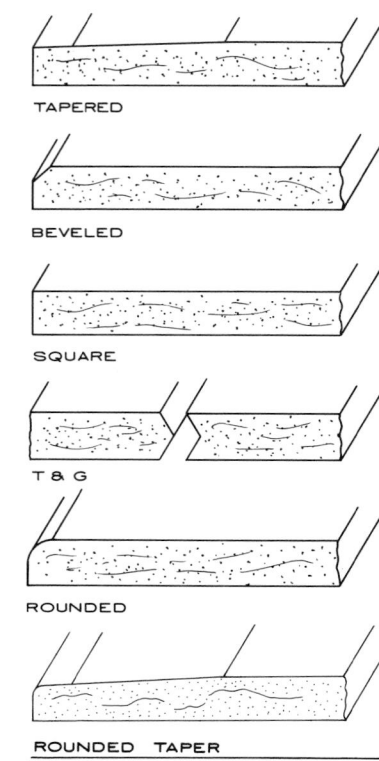

TAPERED

BEVELED

SQUARE

T & G

ROUNDED

ROUNDED TAPER
**TYPES OF EDGES**

### MAX. BENDING FOR DRYWALL

| | BENDING RADII | |
|---|---|---|
| THICKNESS | LENGTHWISE | WIDTH |
| $1/4''$ | 5'-0'' | 15'-0'' |
| $3/8''$ | 7'-6'' | 25'-0'' |
| $1/2''$ | 20'-0'' | — |

Shorter radii may be obtained by moistening face and back so that water will soak well into core of board.

### MAXIMUM ALLOWABLE PARTITION HEIGHT

| STUD SPACING (IN.) (FACING ON EACH SIDE) | STUD DEPTH (IN.) | | | | |
|---|---|---|---|---|---|
| | $1 5/8$ * | $2 1/2$ | $3 1/4$ | $3 5/8$ | 4 |
| | MAXIMUM ALLOWABLE HEIGHT | | | | |
| 16 ($1/2$ one-ply) | 11'-0'' | 14'-8'' | 17'-10'' | 19'-5'' | 20'-8'' |
| 24 ($1/2$ one-ply) | 10'-0'' | 13'-5'' | 16'-0'' | 17'-3'' | 18'-5'' |
| 24 ($1/2$ two-ply) | 12'-4'' | 15'-10'' | 18'-3'' | 19'-5'' | 20'-8'' |

*$1 5/8''$ stud with single layer of gypsum wallboard recommended for chase walls and closets only.

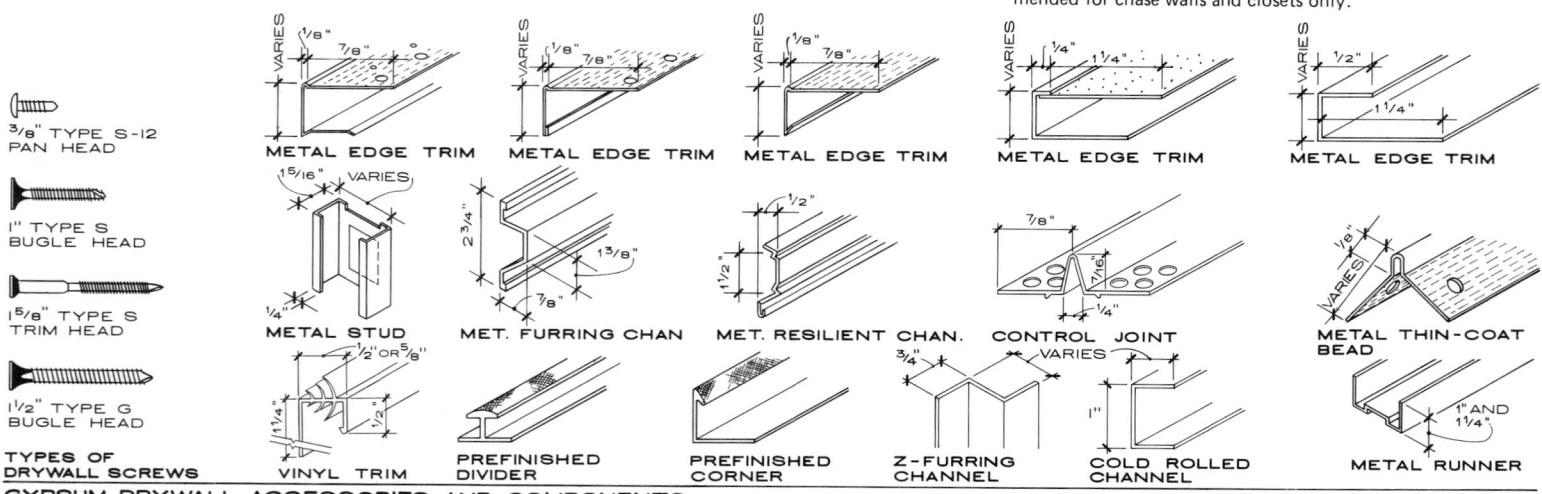

$3/8''$ TYPE S-12 PAN HEAD

1'' TYPE S BUGLE HEAD

$1 5/8''$ TYPE S TRIM HEAD

$1 1/2''$ TYPE G BUGLE HEAD

**TYPES OF DRYWALL SCREWS**

METAL EDGE TRIM    METAL EDGE TRIM    METAL EDGE TRIM    METAL EDGE TRIM    METAL EDGE TRIM

METAL STUD    MET. FURRING CHAN    MET. RESILIENT CHAN.    CONTROL JOINT    METAL THIN-COAT BEAD

VINYL TRIM    PREFINISHED DIVIDER    PREFINISHED CORNER    Z-FURRING CHANNEL    COLD ROLLED CHANNEL    METAL RUNNER

**GYPSUM DRYWALL ACCESSORIES AND COMPONENTS**

Ferdinand R. Scheeler, AIA; Skidmore, Owings & Merrill; Chicago, Illinois
James Lloyd; Kennett Square, Pennsylvania

  **GYPSUM WALLBOARD**

| FIRE RATING | STC | WALL THICKNESS | CONSTRUCTION DESCRIPTION | WALL SECTIONS |
|---|---|---|---|---|
| 1 HOUR | 30 TO 34 | 4 7/8" | One layer 1/2 in. type X veneer base nailed to each side of 2 x 4 in. wood studs 16 in. o.c. with 5d coated nails 8 in. o.c. Minimum 3/32 in. gypsum veneer plaster. Joints staggered vertically 16 in. and horizontal joints each side at 12 in. | |
| | | 4 7/8" | One layer 5/8 in. type X gypsum wallboard or veneer base nailed to each side of 2 x 4 in. wood studs 16 in. o.c. with 6d coated nails 7 in. o.c. Stagger joints 24 in. on each side. | |
| | 35 TO 39 | 5 1/8" | Two layers 3/8 in. regular gypsum wallboard or veneer base nailed to each side of 2 x 4 in. wood studs 16 in. o.c. First layer attached with 4d coated nails, second layer applied with laminating compound and nailed with 5d coated nails 8 in. o.c. Stagger joints 16 in. o.c. each side. | |
| | 45 TO 49 | 5 3/8" | Base layer 3/8 in. regular gypsum wallboard or veneer base nailed to each side of 2 x 4 in. wood studs 16 in. o.c. Face layer 1/2 in. (same as base layer). Use 5d coated nails 24 in. o.c. for base layer and 8d coated nails 12 in. o.c. to edge and 24 in. o.c. to intermediate studs. Stagger joints 16 in. o.c. each layer and side. | |
| | | 5 7/8" | Base layer 1/2 in. wood fiberboard to each side of 2 x 4 in. wood studs 16 in. o.c. with 5d coated nails 24 in. o.c. on vertical joints and 16 in. o.c. to top and bottom plates. Face layer 5/8 in. type X gypsum wallboard or veneer base applied to each side with laminating compound and nailed with 8d coated nails 24 in. o.c. on vertical joints and 16 in. o.c. to top and bottom plates. Stagger joints 24 in. o.c. each layer and side. | |
| | | 5 7/8" | Both sides resilient channels 24 in. o.c. attached with GWB 54 drywall nails to each side of 2 x 4 in. wood studs 16 in. o.c. One layer 5/8 in. type X gypsum wallboard or veneer base attached with 1 in. type S drywall screws 12 in. o.c. to each side and vertical joints back-blocked. GWB filler strips along floor and ceiling both sides. Stagger joints 24 in. o.c. each side. | |
| | 50 TO 54 | 5 3/8" | Base layer 1/4 in. proprietary gypsum wallboard applied to each side of 2 x 4 in. wood studs 16 in. o.c. with 4d coated nails 12 in. o.c. Face layer 5/8 in. type X gypsum wallboard or veneer base applied with laminating compound and nailed with 6d coated nails 16 in. o.c. to each side. 1 1/2 in. mineral fiber insulation in cavity. Stagger joints 24 in. o.c. each side. | |
| | | 5 3/8" | One side resilient channel 24 in. o.c. with 1 1/4 in. type S drywall screws to 2 x 4 in. wood studs 16 in. o.c. Both sides 5/8 in. gypsum wallboard or veneer base attached to resilient channel with 1 in. type S drywall screws 12 in. o.c. and GWB to stud with 1 1/4 in. type W drywall screws. 1 1/2 in. mineral fiber insulation in cavity. Stagger joints 48 in. o.c. each side. | |
| | 60 TO 64 | 6 7/8" | One side resilient channels 24 in. o.c. attached with 1 in. type S drywall screws to 2 x 4 in. wood studs 16 in. o.c. Two layers of 5/8 in. type X gypsum wallboard or veneer base. First layer attached with 1 in. type S drywall screws, second layer applied with laminating compound. Other side one layer each of 5/8 in. and 1/2 in. gypsum wallboard or veneer base plus top 3/8 in. gypsum wallboard applied with laminating compound. Use 5d coated nails 32 in. o.c. for base, 8d for 1/2 in. center layer. 2 in. glass fiber insulation in cavity. Stagger all joints 16 in. o.c. | |
| 2 HOUR | 40 TO 44 | 6 1/8" | Two layers 5/8 in. type X gypsum wallboard or veneer base applied to each side of 2 x 4 in. wood studs 24 in. o.c. Use 6d coated nails 24 in. o.c. for base layer and 8d coated nails 8 in. o.c. for face layer. Stagger joints 24 in. o.c. each layer and side. | |
| | 50 TO 54 | 8" | Two layers 5/8 in. type X gypsum wallboard or veneer base applied to each side of 2 x 4 in. wood studs 16 in. o.c. staggered 8 in. o.c. on 2 x 6 in. wood plates. Use 6d coated nails 24 in. o.c. for base layer and 8d coated nails 8 in. o.c. for face layer. Stagger vertical joints 16 in. o.c. each layer and side. | |
| | 55 TO 59 | 10 3/4" | Two layers 5/8 in. type X gypsum wallboard or veneer base applied to each side of double row of 2 x 4 in. wood studs 16 in. o.c. on separate plates 1 in. apart. Use 6d coated nails 24 in. o.c. for base layer and 8d coated nails 8 in. o.c. for face layer. 3 1/2 in. glass fiber insulation in cavity. Stagger joints 16 in. o.c. each layer and side. GWB fire stop continuous in space between plates. | |

**CONSULT MANUFACTURER OR GYPSUM ASSOCIATION FOR ADDITIONAL INFORMATION**

| FIRE RATING | STC | WALL THICKNESS | CONSTRUCTION DESCRIPTION | WALL SECTIONS |
|---|---|---|---|---|
| 1 HOUR | 35 TO 39 | 2 7/8" | One layer 5/8 in. type X gypsum wallboard or veneer base applied to each side of 1 5/8 in. metal studs 24 in. o.c. with 1 in. type S drywall screws 8 in. o.c. to edges and 12 in. o.c. to intermediate studs. Stagger joints 24 in. o.c. each side. | |
| | 40 TO 44 | 3 3/8" | Base layer 3/8 in. regular gypsum wallboard or veneer base applied to each side of 1 5/8 in. metal studs 24 in. o.c. with 1 in. type S drywall screws 27 in. o.c. to edges and 54 in. o.c. to intermediate studs. Face layer 1/2 in. attached on each side to studs with 1 5/8 in. type S drywall screws 12 in. o.c. to perimeter and 24 in. o.c. to intermediate studs. Stagger joints 24 in. o.c. each layer and side. | |
| | | 4 7/8" | One layer 5/8 in. type X gypsum wallboard or veneer base applied to each side of 3 5/8 in. metal studs 24 in. o.c. with 1 in. type S drywall screws 8 in. o.c. to vertical edges and 12 in. o.c. to intermediate studs. Stagger joints 24 in. o.c. each side. | |
| | 45 TO 49 | 3 1/8" | Two layers 1/2 in. regular gypsum wallboard or veneer base applied to each side of 1 5/8 in. metal studs 24 in. o.c. Use 1 in. type S drywall screws 12 in. o.c. for base layer and 1 5/8 in. type S drywall screws 12 in. o.c. for face layer. Stagger joints 24 in. o.c. each layer and side. | |
| | | 3 1/8" | Base layer 1/4 in. gypsum wallboard applied to each side of 1 5/8 in. metal studs 24 in. o.c. with 1 in. type S drywall screws 24 in. o.c. to edges and 36 in. o.c. to intermediate studs. Face layer 1/2 in. type X gypsum wallboard or veneer base applied to each side of studs with 1 5/8 in. type S drywall screws 12 in. o.c. Stagger joints 24 in. o.c. each layer and side. | |
| | | 5 1/2" | One layer 5/8 in. type X gypsum wallboard or veneer base applied to each side of 3 5/8 in. metal studs 24 in. o.c. with 1 in. type S drywall screws 8 in. o.c. to edge and vertical joints and 12 in. o.c. to intermediate stud. Face layer 5/8 in. (same as other layer) applied on one side to stud with laminating compound and attached with 1 5/8 in. type S drywall screws 8 in. o.c. to edges and sides and 12 in. o.c. to intermediate studs. 3 1/2 in. glass fiber insulation in cavity. Stagger joints 24 in. o.c. each layer and side. | |
| | 50 TO 54 | 4" | Base layer 1/4 in. regular gypsum wallboard applied to each side of 2 1/2 in. metal studs 24 in. o.c. with 1 in. type S drywall screws 12 in. o.c. Face layer 1/2 in. type X gypsum wallboard or veneer base applied to each side of studs with laminating compound and with 1 5/8 in. type S drywall screws in top and bottom runners 8 in. o.c. 2 in. glass fiber insulation in cavity. Stagger joints 24 in. o.c. each layer and side. | |
| | | 4" | Two layers 1/2 in. type X gypsum wallboard or veneer base applied to one side of 2 1/2 in. metal studs 24 in. o.c. Base layer 1 in. and face layer 1 5/8 in. type S drywall screws 8 in. o.c. to edge and adhesive beads to intermediate studs. Opposite side layer 1/2 in. type X gypsum wallboard or veneer base applied with 1 in. type S drywall screws 8 in. o.c. to vertical edges and 12 in. o.c. to intermediate studs. 3 in. glass fiber insulation in cavity. Stagger joints 24 in. o.c. each layer and face. | |
| | 55 TO 59 | 4 1/4" | Base layer 1/4 in. gypsum wallboard applied to each side of 2 1/2 in. metal studs 24 in. o.c. with 7/8 in. type S drywall screws 12 in. o.c. Face layer 5/8 in. type X gypsum wallboard or veneer base applied on each side of studs with 1 5/16 in. type S drywall screws 12 in. o.c. 1 1/2 in. glass fiber insulation in cavity. Stagger joints 24 in. o.c. each layer and side. | |
| 2 HOUR | 40 TO 44 | 5" | Two layers 5/8 in. type X gypsum wallboard or veneer base applied to each side of 2 1/2 in. metal studs 16 in. o.c. braced laterally. Use 1 in. for base layer and 1 5/8 in. for facelayer type S-12 drywall screws 12 in. o.c. Stagger joints 16 in. o.c. each layer and side. | |
| | 50 TO 54 | 3 5/8" | Base layer 1/2 in. type X gypsum wallboard or veneer base applied to each side of 1 5/8 in. metal studs 24 in. o.c. Use 1 in. type S drywall screws 12 in. o.c. for base layer and 1 5/8 in. type S drywall screws 12 in. o.c. for face layer. 1 1/2 in. glass fiber insulation in cavity. Stagger joints 24 in. o.c. each layer and side. | |
| | 55 TO 59 | 6 1/4" | Two layers 5/8 in. type X gypsum wallboard or veneer base applied to each side of 3 5/8 in. metal studs 24 in. o.c. Use 1 in. type S drywall screws 32 in. o.c. for base layer and 1 5/8 in. type S drywall screws 12 in. o.c. to edge and 24 in. o.c. to intermediate studs. One side third layer 1/4 or 3/8 in. gypsum wallboard or veneer base applied with laminating compound. Stagger joints 24 in. o.c. each layer and side. | |

CONSULT MANUFACTURER OR GYPSUM ASSOCIATION FOR ADDITIONAL INFORMATION

 **GYPSUM WALLBOARD**

| FIRE RATING | STC | WALL THICKNESS | CONSTRUCTION DESCRIPTION | WALL SECTIONS |
|---|---|---|---|---|
| 1 HOUR | 35 TO 39 | 3 1/8" | 1 in. x 24 in. proprietary type X gypsum panels inserted between 2 1/2 in. floor and ceiling J runners with 2 1/2 in. proprietary vented C-H studs between panels. One layer 5/8 in. proprietary type X gypsum wallboard or veneer base applied parallel to studs on side opposite proprietary gypsum panels with 1 in. type S drywall screws spaced 12 in. o.c. in studs and runners. STC estimate based on 1 in. mineral fiber in cavity. (NLB) | FIRE SIDE / FIRE SIDE |
| | 40 TO 44 | 2 7/8" | 3/4 in. x 24 in. proprietary type X gypsum panels inserted between 2 1/4 in. floor and ceiling track and fitted to proprietary 2 1/4 in. slotted metal I studs with tab-flange. Face layer 5/8 in. type X gypsum board applied at right angles to studs, with 1 in. type S drywall screws, 12 in. o.c. Sound tested with 1 in. glass fiber friction fit in stud space. (NLB) | FIRE SIDE / FIRE SIDE |
| 2 HOURS | 30 TO 34 | 2 1/4" | One layer 5/8 in. type X gypsum wallboard or veneer base applied vertically to each side of 1 in. gypsum board panels (solid or laminated) with laminating compound combed over entire contact surface. Panel supported by metal runners at top and bottom and horizontal bracing angles of No. 22 gauge galvanized steel 3/4 in. x 1 1/4 in. spaced 5 ft. 0 in. o.c. or less on shaft side. (NLB)<br><br>*Limiting height shown is based on interior partition exposure conditions. Shaft wall exposure conditions may require reduction of limiting height. | FIRE SIDE |
| | 35 TO 39 | 4 1/8" | Four layers 5/8 in. type X gypsum wallboard or veneer base applied at right angles to one side of 1 5/8 in. metal studs 24 in. o.c. Base layer attached to studs with 1 in. type S drywall screws 12 in. o.c. Second layer attached to studs with 1 5/8 in. type S drywall screws using only two screws per board. Third layer attached with 2 5/8 in. type S drywall screws similar to second layer. Steel strips 1 1/2 in. wide vertically applied over third layer at stud lines and attached 12 in. o.c. to studs with 2 5/8 in. type S drywall screws. Third layer also attached to top and bottom track with 2 5/8 in. type S drywall screws placed midway between studs. Face layer attached to steel strips with 1 in. type S drywall screws 8 in. o.c. at each stud. Stagger joints of each layer. (NLB) | FIRE SIDE / FIRE SIDE |
| | 40 TO 44 | 3 1/2" | 1 in. x 24 in. proprietary type X gypsum panels inserted between 2 1/2 in. floor and ceiling J track with T section of 2 1/2 in. proprietary C-T metal studs between proprietary gypsum panels. Two layers of 1/2 in. type X gypsum wallboard applied to face of C-T studs. Base layer applied at right angles to studs with 1 in. type S drywall screws 24 in. o.c. and face layer applied at right angles to studs with 1 5/8 in. type S drywall screws 8 in. o.c. Stagger joints 24 in. o.c. each layer. (NLB) | FIRE SIDE / FIRE SIDE |
| | 45 TO 49 | 3 1/2" | 1 in. x 24 in. proprietary type X gypsum panels inserted between 2 1/2 in. floor and ceiling track with tab-flange section of 2 1/2 in. metal I studs between proprietary gypsum panels. One layer of 1/2 in. proprietary type X gypsum wallboard or veneer base applied at right angles to each side of metal I studs with 1 in. type S drywall screws 12 in. o.c. Sound tested using 1 1/2 in. glass fiber friction fit in stud space. (NLB) | FIRE SIDE / FIRE SIDE |
| | 50 TO 54 | 4" | 1 in. x 24 in. proprietary type X gypsum panels inserted between 2 1/2 in. floor and ceiling track with tab-flange section of 2 1/2 in. metal I studs between proprietary gypsum panels. One layer of 1/2 in. proprietary type X gypsum wallboard or veneer base applied at right angles to flanges of I studs adjacent to proprietary gypsum panels with 1 in. type S drywall screws 12 in. o.c. Resilient channels spaced 24 in. o.c. horizontally, screw attached to opposite flanges of I studs with 3/8 in. type S screws, one per channel-stud intersection. 1/2 in. proprietary type X gypsum wallboard or veneer base applied parallel to resilient furring channels with 1 in. type S drywall screws 12 in. o.c. Sound tested using 1 in. glass fiber friction fit in stud space. (NLB) | FIRE SIDE / FIRE SIDE |
| 3 HOURS | 40 TO 44 | 4 1/8" | 2 in. x 24 in. laminated gypsum board panels installed vertically between floor and ceiling 20 gauge J runners with 25 gauge steel H members between panels. Panels attached at midpoint to 2 1/2 in. leg of J runners with 2 3/8 in. type S-12 drywall screws. H studs formed from 20 or 25 gauge 2 in. x 1 in. channels placed back to back and spot welded 24 in. o.c. Base layer 5/8 in. gypsum wallboard or veneer base applied parallel to one side of panels, with 1 in. type S drywall screws 12 in. o.c. to H studs. Rigid furring channels horizontally attached 24 in. o.c. to H studs with 1 in. type S drywall screws. Face layer 5/8 in. gypsum wallboard or veneer base attached at right angles to furring channels with 1 in. type S drywall screws 12 in. o.c. Stagger joints 24 in. o.c. each layer and side. (NLB) | FIRE SIDE |
| | 45 TO 49 | 5 1/4" | 3/4 in. x 24 in. proprietary type X gypsum panels inserted between 2 1/4 in. floor and ceiling tracks and fitted to 2 1/4 in. slotted metal I studs with tab-flange. First layer 5/8 in. type X gypsum board applied at right angles to studs with 1 in. type S drywall screws 24 in. o.c. Second layer 5/8 in. type X gypsum board applied parallel to studs with 1 5/8 in. type S drywall screws 42 in. o.c. starting 12 in. from bottom. Third layer 5/8 in. type X gypsum board applied parallel to studs with 2 1/4 in. type S drywall screws 24 in. o.c. Resilient channels applied 24 in. o.c. at right angles to studs with 2 1/4 in. type S drywall screws. Fourth layer 5/8 in. type X gypsum board applied at right angles to resilient channels with 1 in. type S drywall screws 12 in. o.c. Sound tested with 1 in. glass fiber friction fit in stud space. (NLB) | FIRE SIDE / FIRE SIDE |

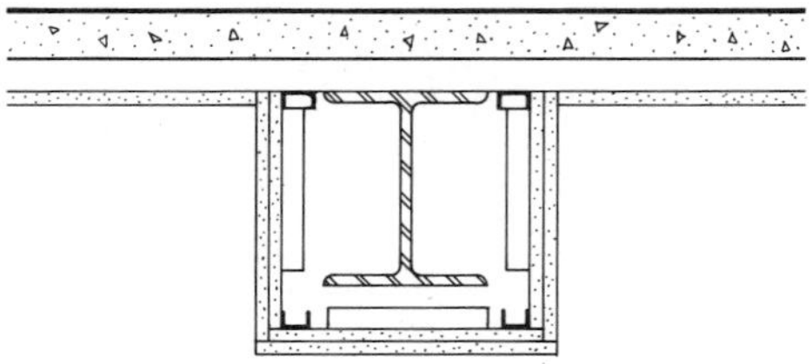

2 HOUR FIRE RATING

Two layers of 5/8 in. type X gypsum wallboard or veneer base around beam. Base layer attached with 1 1/4 in. type S drywall screws 16 in. o.c., face layer attached with 1 3/4 in. type S drywall screws 8 in. o.c. to horizontally installed U-shaped steel channels (25 gauge steel 1 11/16 in. wide and 1 in. legs) located not less than 1/2 in. from beam flanges. Upper channels secured to steel deck units with 1/2 in. type S pan head screws spaced 12 in. o.c. U-shaped brackets formed of steel channels spaced 24 in. o.c. suspended from the upper channels with 1/2 in. type S pan head screws and supported steel channels installed at lower corners of brackets. Outside corners of gypsum board protected by 0.020-in.-thick steel corner beads crimped or nailed. (2 hour restrained or unrestrained beam)

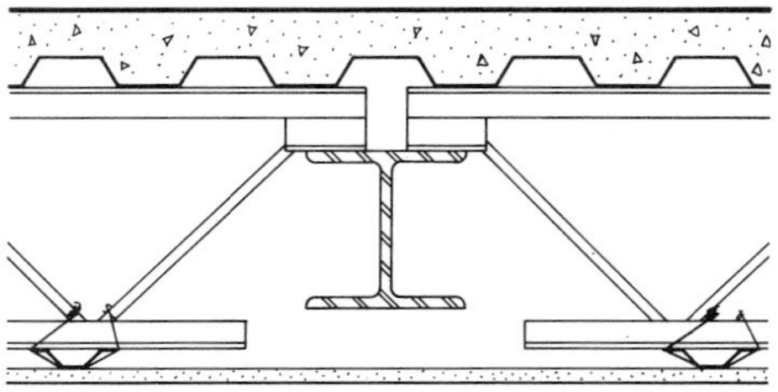

3 HOUR FIRE RATING

One layer 1/2 in. type X gypsum wallboard or veneer base applied at right angles to rigid furring channels with 1 in. type S drywall screws 12 in. o.c. Wallboard end joints located midway between continuous channels and attached to additional pieces of channel 54 in. long with screws at 12 in. o.c. Furring channels 24 in. o.c. attached with 18 gauge wire ties 48 in. o.c. to open web steel joists 24 in. o.c. supporting 3/8 in. rib metal lath or 9/16 in. deep, 28 gauge corrugated steel and 2 1/2 in. concrete slab measured from top of flute. Furring channels may be attached to 1 1/2 in. cold-rolled carrying channels 48 in. o.c. suspended from joists by 8 gauge wire hangers not over 48 in. o.c. (3 hour unrestrained beam)

BEAMS, GIRDERS AND TRUSSES

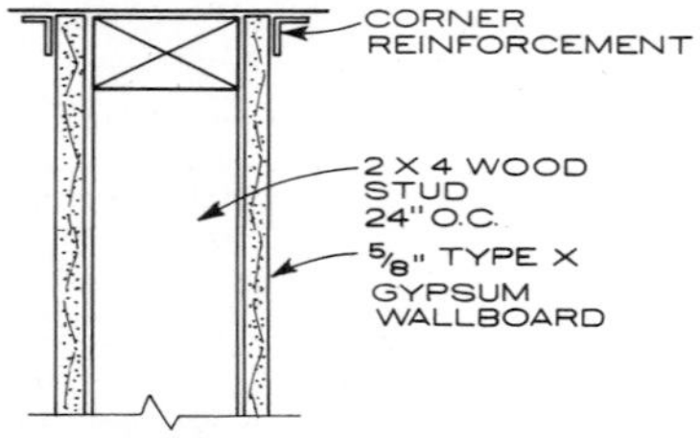
CORNER REINFORCEMENT
2 X 4 WOOD STUD 24" O.C.
5/8" TYPE X GYPSUM WALLBOARD

CEILING CONDITION

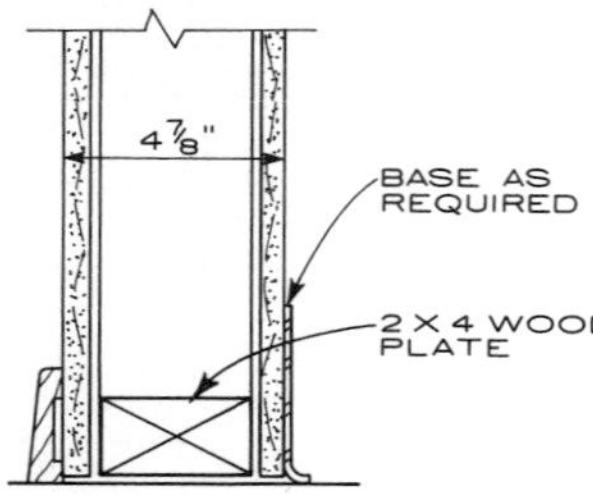
4 7/8"
BASE AS REQUIRED
2 X 4 WOOD PLATE

FLOOR CONDITION

FIRE RATING 1 HR STC 35 TO 39

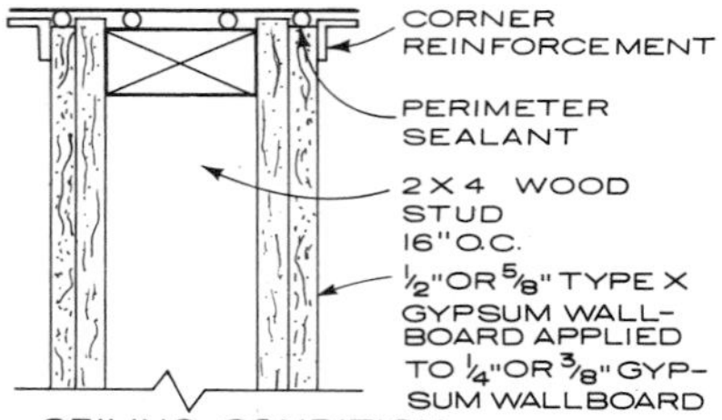
CORNER REINFORCEMENT
PERIMETER SEALANT
2 X 4 WOOD STUD 16" O.C.
1/2" OR 5/8" TYPE X GYPSUM WALLBOARD APPLIED TO 1/4" OR 3/8" GYPSUM WALLBOARD

CEILING CONDITION

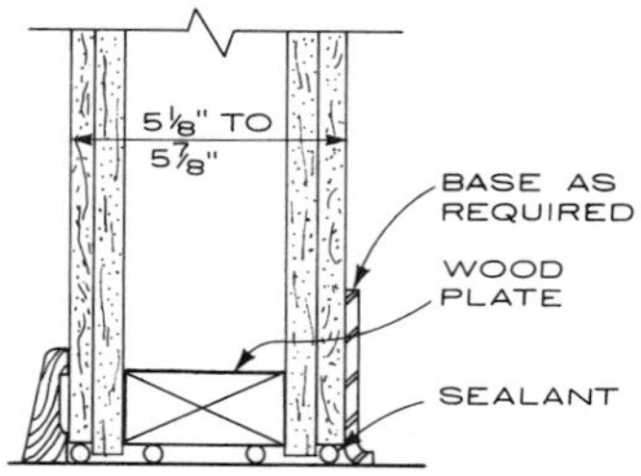
5 1/8" TO 5 7/8"
BASE AS REQUIRED
WOOD PLATE
SEALANT

FLOOR CONDITION

FIRE RATING 1 HR STC 45 TO 49

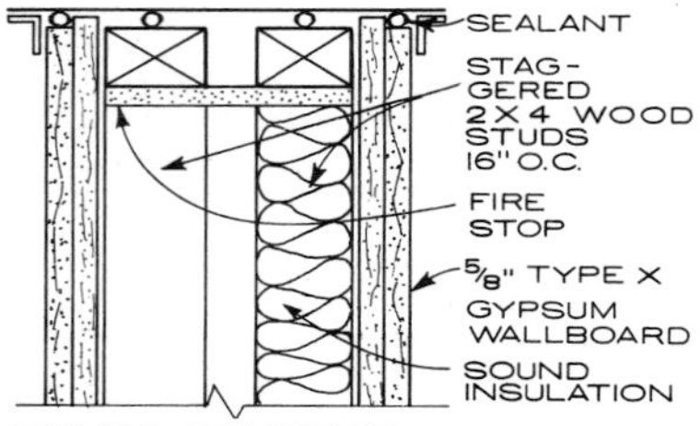
SEALANT
STAGGERED 2 X 4 WOOD STUDS 16" O.C.
FIRE STOP
5/8" TYPE X GYPSUM WALLBOARD
SOUND INSULATION

CEILING CONDITION

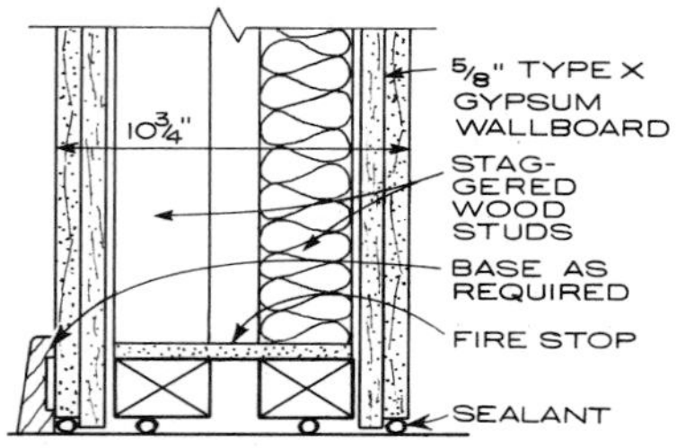
10 3/4"
5/8" TYPE X GYPSUM WALLBOARD
STAGGERED WOOD STUDS
BASE AS REQUIRED
FIRE STOP
SEALANT

FLOOR CONDITION

FIRE RATING 2 HR STC 55 TO 59

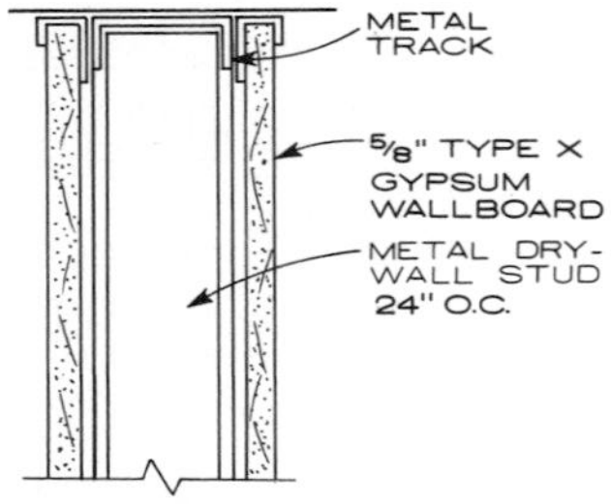
METAL TRACK
5/8" TYPE X GYPSUM WALLBOARD
METAL DRYWALL STUD 24" O.C.

CEILING CONDITION

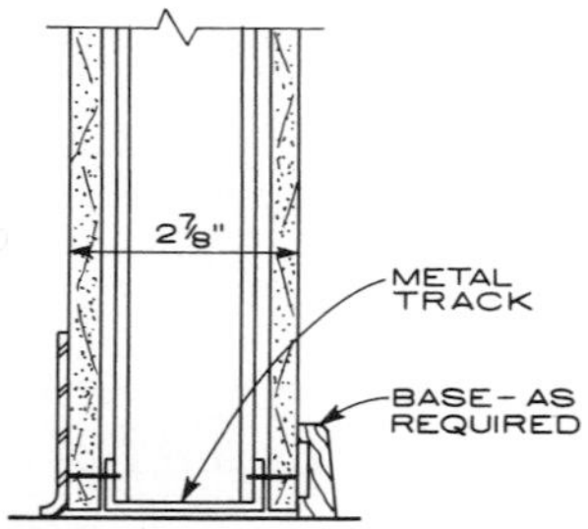
2 7/8"
METAL TRACK
BASE-AS REQUIRED

FLOOR CONDITION

FIRE RATING 1 HR STC 35 TO 39

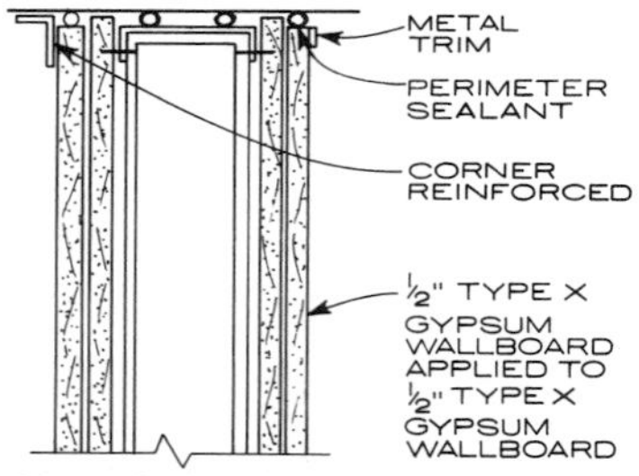
METAL TRIM
PERIMETER SEALANT
CORNER REINFORCED
1/2" TYPE X GYPSUM WALLBOARD APPLIED TO 1/2" TYPE X GYPSUM WALLBOARD

CEILING CONDITION

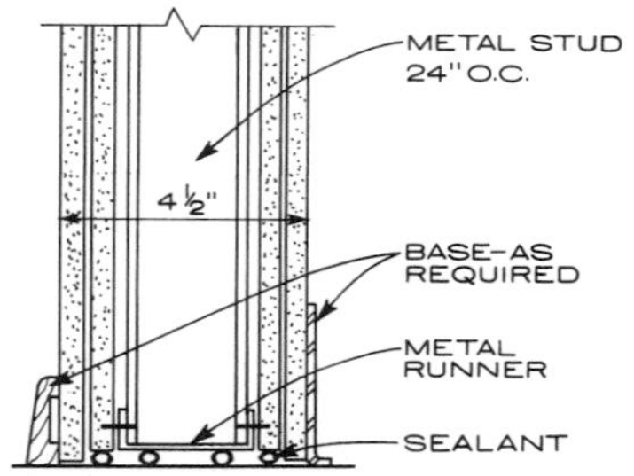
METAL STUD 24" O.C.
4 1/2"
BASE-AS REQUIRED
METAL RUNNER
SEALANT

FLOOR CONDITION

FIRE RATING 2 HR STC 45 TO 49

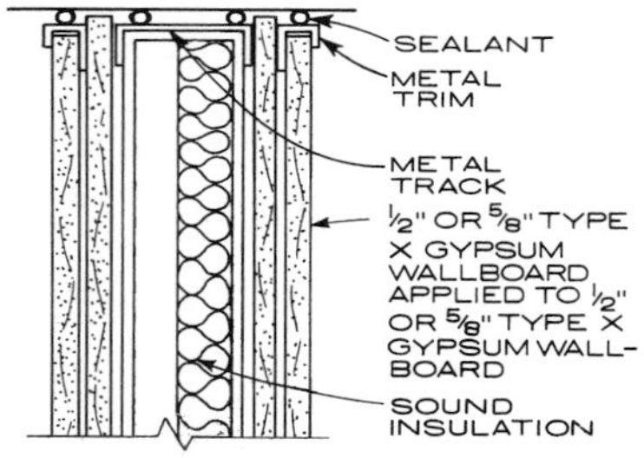
SEALANT
METAL TRIM
METAL TRACK
1/2" OR 5/8" TYPE X GYPSUM WALLBOARD APPLIED TO 1/2" OR 5/8" TYPE X GYPSUM WALLBOARD
SOUND INSULATION

CEILING CONDITION

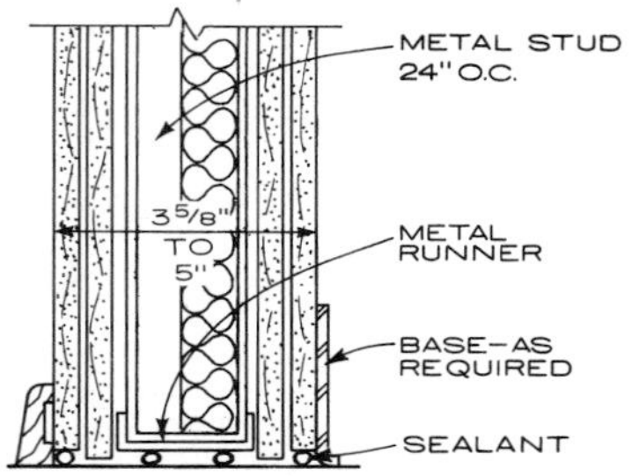
METAL STUD 24" O.C.
3 5/8" TO 5"
METAL RUNNER
BASE-AS REQUIRED
SEALANT

FLOOR CONDITION

FIRE RATING 2 HR STC 50 TO 54

GYPSUM WOOD AND METAL FRAMED TYPE PARTITIONS

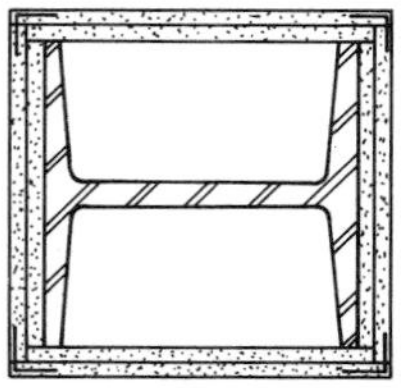

1 HOUR FIRE RATING

Base layer 1/2 in. gypsum wallboard or veneer base tied to column with 18 gauge wire 15 in. o.c. Face layer 1/2 in. gypsum wallboard or veneer base applied with laminating compound over entire contact surface.

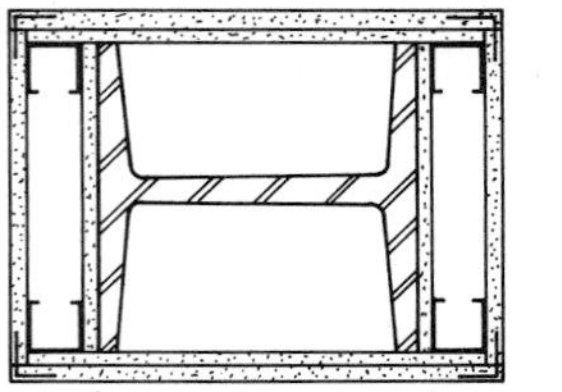

2 HOUR FIRE RATING

Base layer 1/2 in. type X gypsum wallboard or veneer base against flanges and across web openings fastened to 1 5/8 in. metal studs with 1 in. type S drywall screws 24 in. o.c. at corners. Face layers 1/2 in. type X gypsum wallboard or veneer base screw-attached to studs with 1 in. type S drywall screws 12 in. o.c. to provide a cavity between boards on the flange. Face layers across the web opening laid flat across the base layer and screw attached with 1 5/8 in. type S drywall screws 12 in. o.c. Metal corner beads nailed to outer layer with 4d nails 1 3/8 in. long, 0.067 in. shank, 13/64 in. heads, 12 in. o.c.

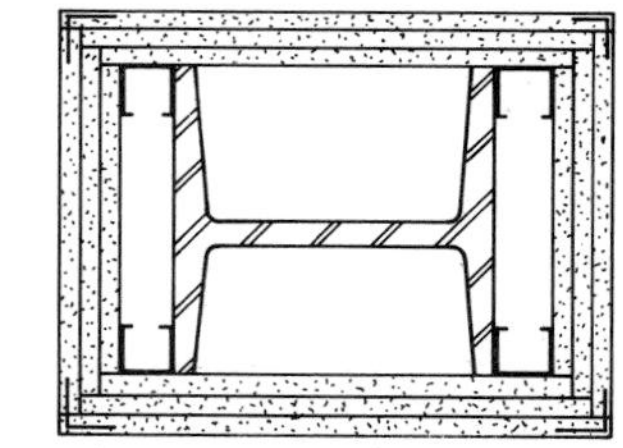

3 HOUR FIRE RATING

Three layers of 5/8 in. type X gypsum wallboard or veneer base screw attached to 1 5/8 in. metal studs located at each corner of column. Base layer attached with 1 in. type S drywall screws 24 in. o.c. Second layer with 1 5/8 in. type S drywall screws 12 in. o.c. and 18 gauge wire tied 24 in. o.c. Face layer attached with 2 1/4 in. type S drywall screws 12 in. o.c. and 1 1/4 in. corner bead at each corner nailed with 6d coated nails, 1 7/8 in. long, 0.0915 in. shank, 1/4 in. heads, 12 in. o.c.

COLUMNS FIRE-RESISTIVE CONSTRUCTION

Ferdinand R. Scheeler, AIA; Skidmore, Owings & Merrill; Chicago, Illinois
James Lloyd; Kennett Square, Pennsylvania

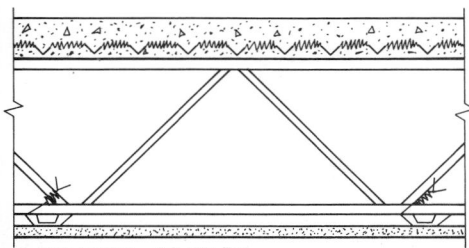

**2 HR / STC 50 TO 54**

1/2 in. type X gypsum wallboard or veneer base applied to drywall furring channels. Furring channels 24 in. o.c. attached with 18 gauge wire ties 48 in. o.c. to open web steel joists 24 in. o.c. supporting 3/8 in. rib metal lath or 9/16 in. deep, 28 gauge corrugated steel and 2 1/2 in. concrete slab measured from top of flute. Double channel at wallboard end joints.

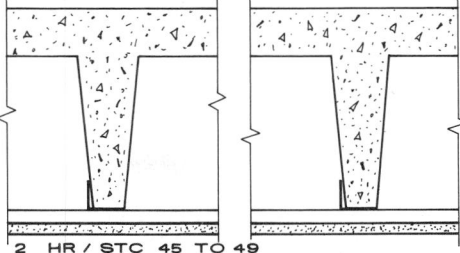

**2 HR / STC 45 TO 49**

5/8 in. type X gypsum wallboard or veneer base screw attached to drywall furring channels. Furring channels 24 in. o.c. suspended from 2 1/2 in. precast reinforced concrete joists 35 in. o.c. with 21 gauge galvanized steel hanger straps fastened to sides of joists. Joist leg depth, 10 in. Double channel at wallboard end joints.

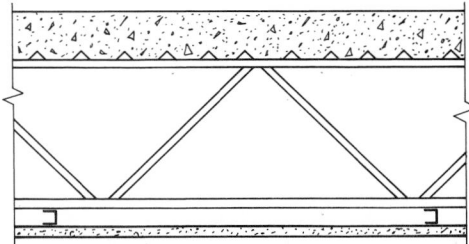

**3 HR / STC 45 TO 49**

5/8 in. proprietary type X gypsum wallboard or veneer base screw attached to furring channels 24 in. o.c. (double channels at end joints). Furring channel wire tied to open web steel joist 24 in. o.c. supporting 3 in. concrete slab over 3/8 in. rib metal lath. 5/8 x 2 3/4 in. type X gypsum wallboard strips over butt joints.

## FLOOR/CEILING ASSEMBLIES, NONCOMBUSTIBLE

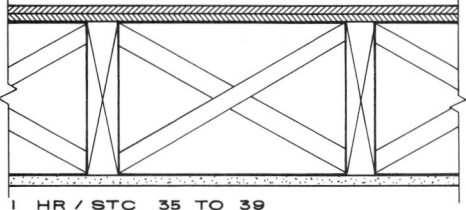

**I HR / STC 35 TO 39**

5/8 in. type X gypsum wallboard or veneer base applied to wood joists 16 in. o.c. Joists supporting 1 in. nominal wood sub and finish floor, or 5/8 in. plywood finished floor with long edges T & G and 1/2 in. interior plywood with exterior glue subfloor perpendicular to joists with joints staggered.

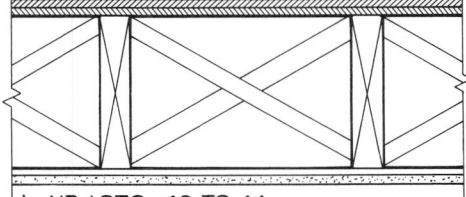

**I HR / STC 40 TO 44**

1/2 in. type X gypsum wallboard or veneer base applied to drywall resilient furring channels 24 in. o.c. and nailed to wood joists 16 in. o.c. Wood joists supporting 1 in. nominal T & G wood sub and finish floor, or 5/8 in. plywood finished floor with long edges T & G and 1/2 in. interior plywood with exterior glue subfloor perpendicular to joists with joints staggered.

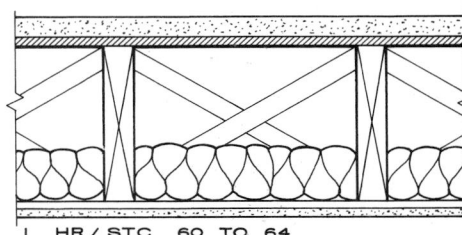

**I HR / STC 60 TO 64**

1/2 in. type X gypsum wallboard or veneer base applied to resilient furring channels. Resilient channels applied 24 in. o.c. to wood joists 16 in. o.c. Wood joists support 1/2 in. plywood subfloor and 1 1/2 in. cellular or lightweight concrete over felt. 3 1/2 in. glass fiber batts in joist spaces. Sound tested with carpet and pad over 5/8 in. plywood subfloor.

## FLOOR/CEILING ASSEMBLIES, WOOD FRAMED

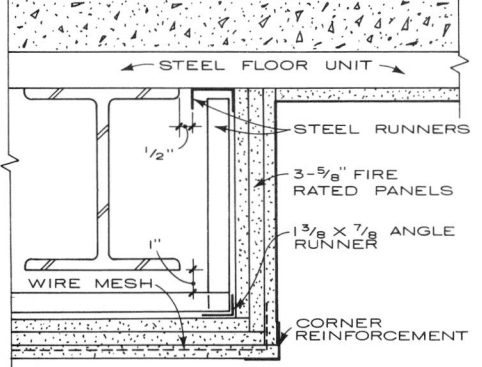

**BEAM PROTECTION**
3 HR. RESTRAINED    2 HR. UNRESTRAINED

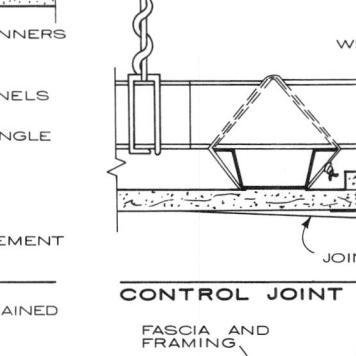

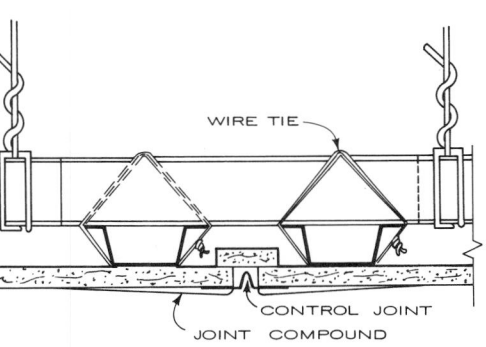

**CONTROL JOINT**

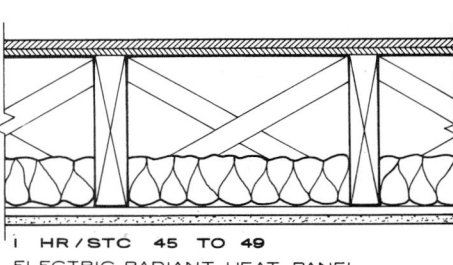

**I HR / STC 45 TO 49**
ELECTRIC RADIANT HEAT PANEL

5/8 in. proprietary type X gypsum board electrical radiant heating panels attached to resilient furring channels spaced 24 in. o.c. installed to 2 x 10 in. wood joists 16 in. o.c. 3/12 in. glass fiber insulation friction fit in joist space. Wood floor of nominal 1 in. T & G or 1/2 in. plywood subfloor and nominal 1 in. T & G 5/8 in. plywood finish floor.

## FLOOR/CEILING ASSEMBLIES, WOOD FRAMED

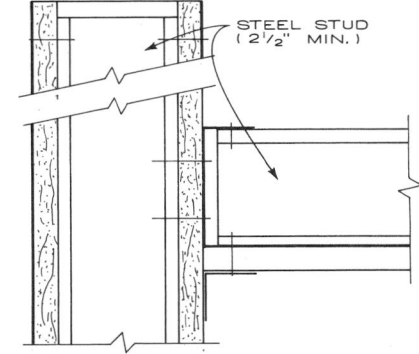

**PARTITION ATTACHMENT**
(SCREW ATTACHED)

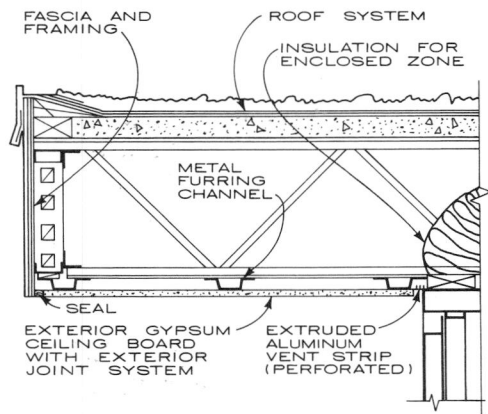

**EXTERIOR SOFFIT**

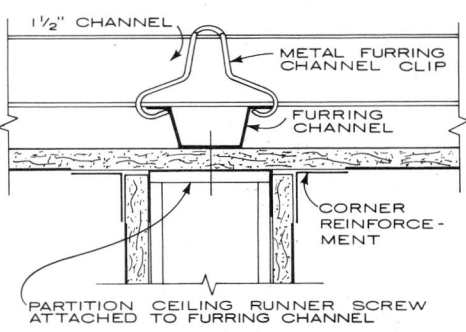

**CONTINUOUS CEILING**

James Lloyd; Kennett Square, Pennsylvania

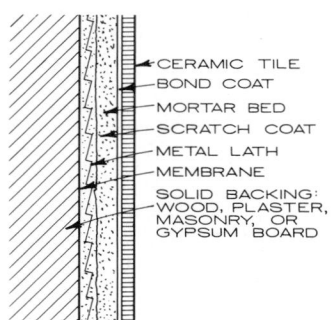

**CEMENT MORTAR**

Use over solid backing, over wood or metal studs. Preferred method for showers and tub enclosures. Ideal for remodeling.

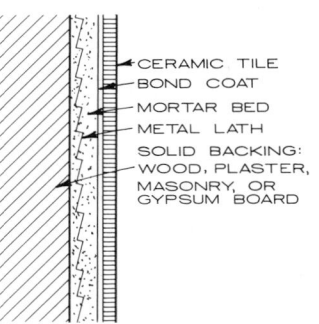

**ONE COAT METHOD**

Use for remodeling or on surfaces that present bonding problems. Preferred method of applying tile over gypsum plaster or gypsum board in showers and tub enclosures.

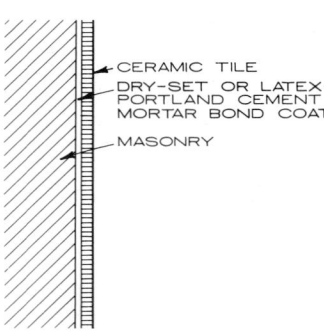

**DRY-SET MORTAR**

Use over gypsum board, plaster, exterior plywood, or other smooth, dimensionally stable surfaces. Use water-resistant gypsum board in wet areas.

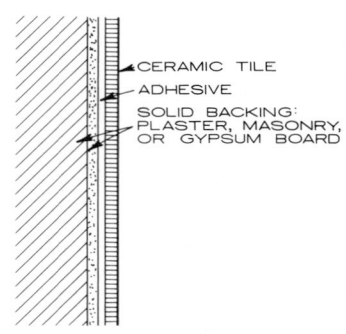

**ORGANIC ADHESIVE**

Use over gypsum board, plaster, exterior plywood, or other smooth, dimensionally stable surfaces. Use water-resistant gypsum board in wet areas.

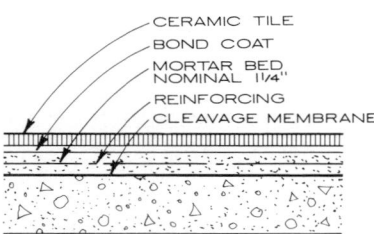

**CEMENT MORTAR**

Use over structural floors subject to bending and deflection. Reinforcing mesh mandatory; mortar bed nominal 1¼ in. thick and uniform.

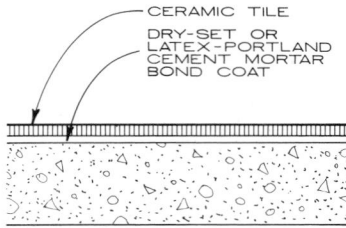

**DRY-SET MORTAR**

Use on level clean concrete where bending stresses do not exceed 1/360 of span and expansion joints are installed. Scarify existing concrete floors before installing tile.

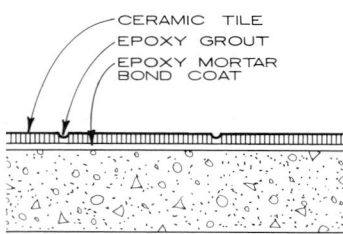

**EPOXY MORTAR & GROUT**

Use where moderate chemical exposure and severe cleaning methods are used, such as in commercial kitchens, dairies, breweries and food plants.

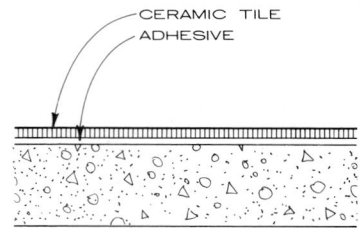

**ORGANIC OR EPOXY ADHESIVE**

Use over concrete floors in residential construction only. Will not withstand high impact or wheel loads. Not recommended in areas where temperatures exceed 140°F.

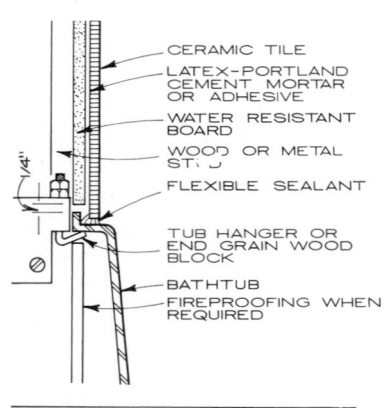

**CERAMIC TILE TUB ENCLOSURE**

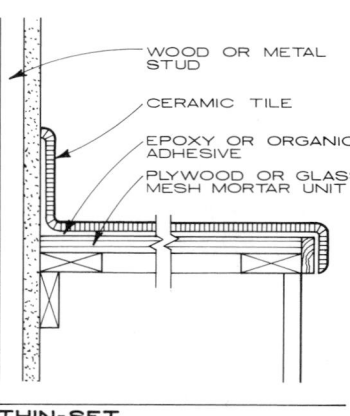

**THIN-SET COUNTERTOP**

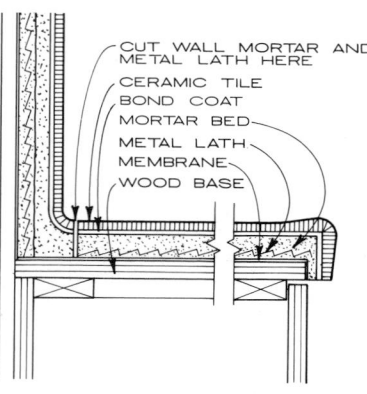

**CEMENT MORTAR COUNTERTOP**

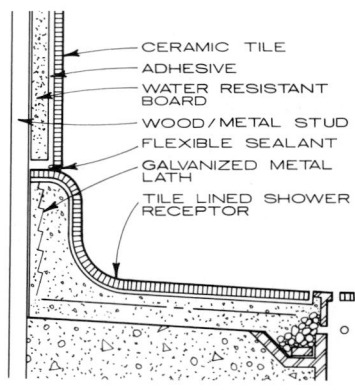

**CERAMIC TILE SHOWER RECEPTOR AND WALL**

## TYPES OF MORTAR

### PORTLAND CEMENT MORTAR

A mixture of portland cement and sand (for floor) or sand and lime (for walls) used for thick-bed installation.

### DRY-SET MORTAR

A mixture of portland cement with sand and additives, imparting water retention that eliminates the need to soak tiles.

### LATEX-PORTLAND CEMENT MORTAR

A mixture similar to dry-set but with latex (an emulsion of rubber or resin particles in water) added to replace all or part of the water in the mortar. It provides better adhesion, density and impact strength than dry-set mortar, and it is more flexible and resistant to frost damage.

### MODIFIED EPOXY EMULSION MORTAR

As with epoxy mortars, this mixture contains a resin and hardener along with portland cement and sand. Although

Tile Council of America, Inc.

it is not as chemically resistant as epoxy mortar, it binds well. Compared with straight portland cement, it allows little or no shrinkage.

## METHODS OF INSTALLATION

In a thick-bed process, tiles usually are applied over a portland cement mortar bed ¾ in. to 1¼ in. thick. The thick-bed allows for accurate slopes or planes in the finished tile work and is not affected by prolonged contact with water. If the backing surface is damaged, cracked or unstable, a membrane should be used between the surface and the tile.

In a thin-set process, tiles are set or bonded to the surface with a thin coat of material varying from 1/32 in. to 1/8 in. thickness. Bonding materials used include dry-set mortar, latex-portland cement mortar, organic adhesive, and modified epoxy emulsion mortar. Thin-set application requires a continuous, stable and undamaged surface.

## THIN-SET MORTAR WITHOUT PORTLAND CEMENT

### EPOXY MORTAR

A two- or three-part mixture (resin and hardener with silica filler) used where chemical resistance is important. It has high bond strength and high resistance to impact. This mortar and furan mortar are the only two that can be recommended for use over steel plates.

### EPOXY ADHESIVE

Mixture similar to epoxy mortar in bonding capability, but not as chemical or solvent resistant.

### ORGANIC ADHESIVE

A one-part mastic mixture that requires no mixing. It remains somewhat flexible (as compared with portland cement mortar), and has good bond strength but should not be used for exterior or wet applications.

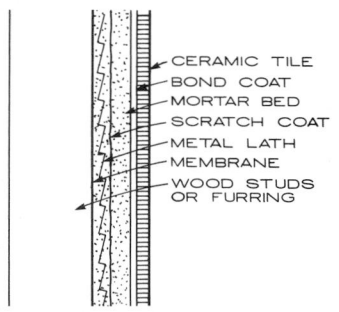

## CEMENT MORTAR

Use over dry, well-braced wood studs or furring. Preferred method of installation in showers and tub or enclosures.

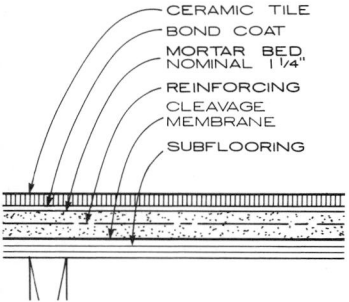

## CEMENT MORTAR

Use over wood floors that are structurally sound and where deflection, including live and dead loads, does not exceed 1/360 of span.

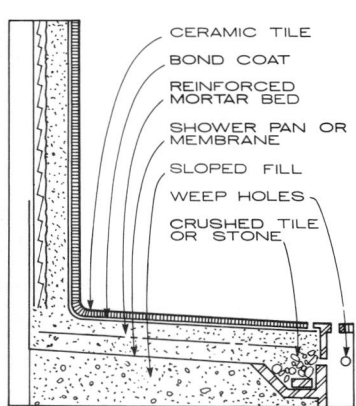

## TILE SHOWER RECEPTOR

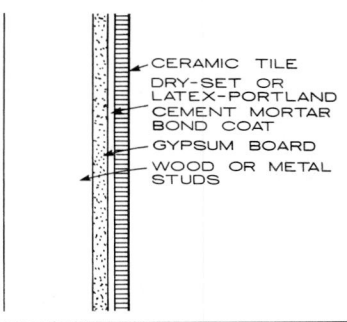

## DRY-SET MORTAR

Use in dry interior areas in schools, institutions and commercial buildings. Do not use in areas where temperatures exceed 125° F.

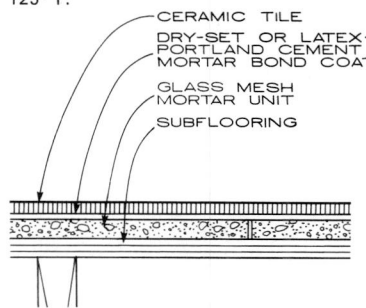

## DRY-SET MORTAR

Use in light commercial and residential construction, deflection not to exceed 1/360, including live and dead loads. Waterproof membrane is required in wet areas.

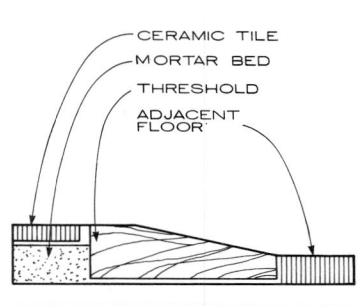

## THRESHOLDS, SADDLES

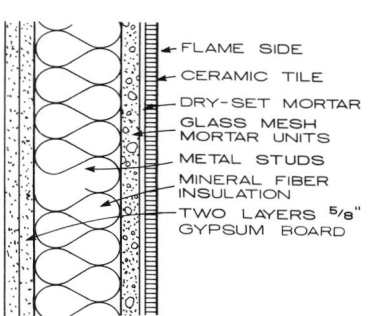

## DRY-SET MORTAR WITH GLASS MESH MORTAR UNIT

Use in wet areas over well-braced wood or metal studs. Stud spacing should not exceed 16 in. o.c., and metal studs should be 20 ga. or heavier.

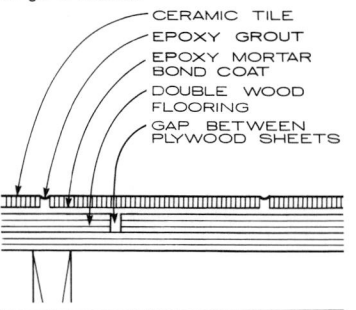

## EPOXY MORTAR AND GROUT

Use in residential, normal commercial and light institutional construction. Recommended where resistance to water, chemicals or staining is needed.

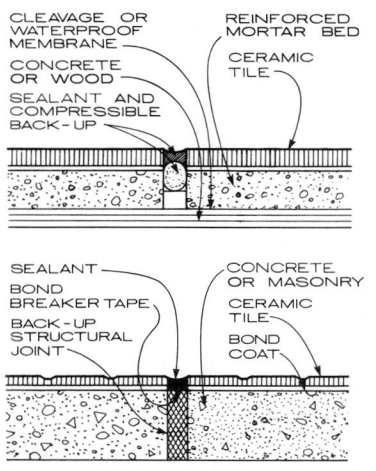

## DRY-SET MORTAR (FIRE-RATED WALL)

Use where a fire resistance rating of 2 hours is required with tile face exposed to flame. Stud spacing not to exceed 16 in. o.c. and mortar bed min. thickness 3/32 in.

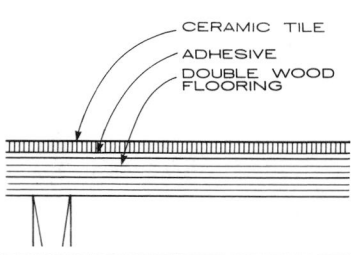

## ORGANIC ADHESIVE

Use over wood or concrete floors in residential construction only. Not recommended in wet areas.

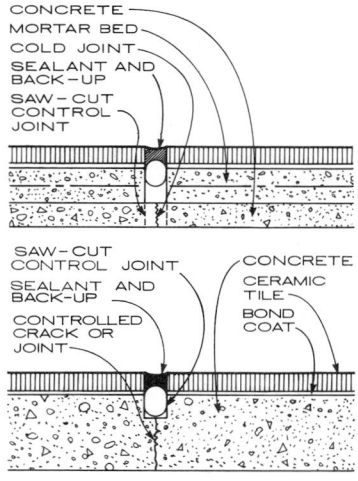

## VERTICAL AND HORIZONTAL EXPANSION JOINTS

## FURAN MORTAR

A two-part mixture (furan resin and hardener) excellent for chemical resistant uses and its high temperatures (350°F.) tolerance.

## GROUT

Grout is used to fill joints between tiles and is selected with a compatible mortar. Types include:

## PORTLAND CEMENT BASED GROUTS

Include commercial portland cement grout, sand-portland cement grout, dry-set grout and latex-portland cement grout.

## EPOXY GROUT

A two- or three-part mixture (epoxy resin hardener with silica sand filler) highly resistant to chemicals. It has great bond strength. This grout and furan grout are made for different chemical and solvent resistance.

## FURAN RESIN GROUT

A two-part furan mixture (similar to furan mortar) that resists high temperatures and solvents.

## MASTIC GROUT

A flexible one-part mixture.

## SILICONE RUBBER GROUT

An elastomeric mixture based on silicone rubber. It has high bond strength, is resistant to water and staining, and remains flexible under freezing conditions.

Tile Council of America, Inc.

## CERAMIC MOSAIC TILE

Ceramic mosaic tile may be either natural clay or porcelain in composition. Special abrasive or slip-resistant surfaces and conductive tile are available only in 1 in. x 1 in. size. Nominal thickness is ¼ in.

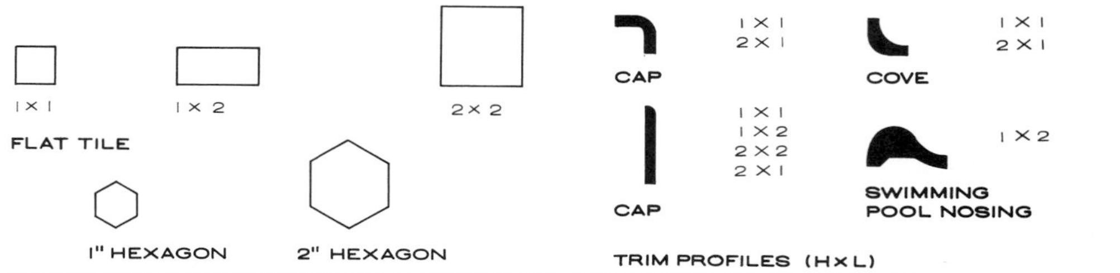
1 × 1
1 × 2
2 × 2
FLAT TILE
1" HEXAGON
2" HEXAGON
CAP
1 × 1
2 × 1
COVE
1 × 1
2 × 1
CAP
1 × 1
1 × 2
2 × 2
2 × 1
SWIMMING POOL NOSING
1 × 2
TRIM PROFILES (H×L)

CERAMIC MOSAIC TILE

## GLAZED WALL TILE

Traditional bright and matte glazed wall tile has been supplemented with tile of variegated appearance. Textured, sculptured, embossed, and engraved surface characteristics are coupled with accent designs. Imported tile has increased in availability, and it offers a wide range of variation from the native materials used in the manufacturing process as well as the process itself. Tile from Germany, France, Italy, Mexico, Switzerland, Austria, Brazil, and Spain currently are represented in manufacturer's literature. Nominal thickness is 5/16 in.

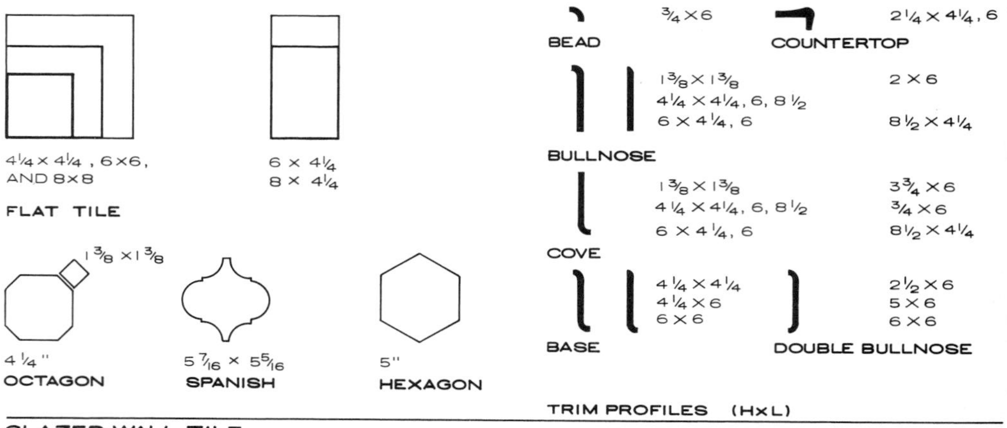
4¼ × 4¼ , 6×6, AND 8×8
6 × 4¼
8 × 4¼
FLAT TILE
1⅜ × 1⅜
4¼"
OCTAGON
5 7/16 × 5 5/16
SPANISH
5"
HEXAGON
BEAD
¾ × 6
COUNTERTOP
2¼ × 4¼, 6
BULLNOSE
1⅜ × 1⅜
4¼ × 4¼, 6, 8½
6 × 4¼, 6
2 × 6
8½ × 4¼
COVE
1⅜ × 1⅜
4¼ × 4¼, 6, 8½
6 × 4¼, 6
3¾ × 6
¾ × 6
8½ × 4¼
BASE
4¼ × 4¼
4¼ × 6
6 × 6
DOUBLE BULLNOSE
2½ × 6
5 × 6
6 × 6
TRIM PROFILES (H×L)

GLAZED WALL TILE

## QUARRY AND PAVER TILE

Quarry and paver tile may be natural clay, shale, or porcelain in composition. These tile are characterized by their natural earth-tone coloration, high compressive strength, and slip and stain resistance. They are recommended for interior and exterior applications. Nominal thicknesses are ½ in. and ¾ in. for quarry tile and ⅜ in. and ½ in. for paver tile.

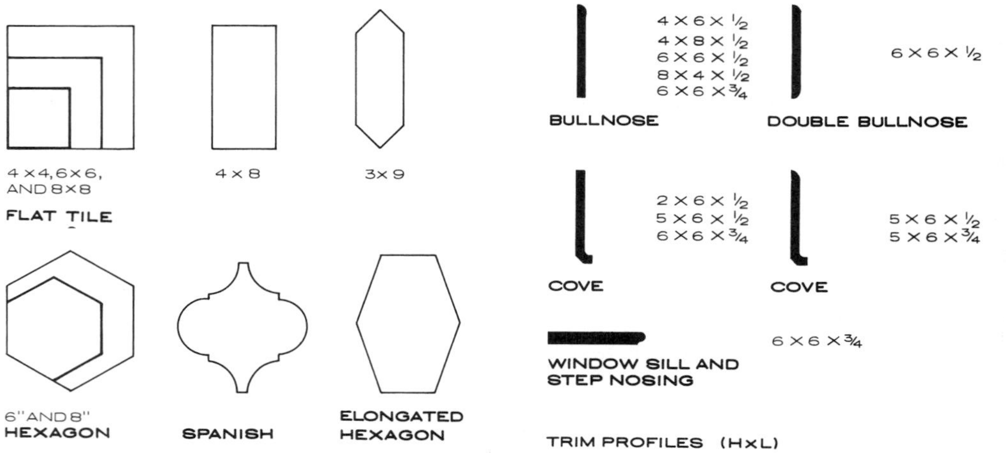
4 × 4, 6 × 6, AND 8 × 8
4 × 8
3 × 9
FLAT TILE
6" AND 8"
HEXAGON
SPANISH
ELONGATED
HEXAGON
BULLNOSE
4 × 6 × ½
4 × 8 × ½
6 × 6 × ½
8 × 4 × ½
6 × 6 × ¾
DOUBLE BULLNOSE
6 × 6 × ½
COVE
2 × 6 × ½
5 × 6 × ½
6 × 6 × ¾
COVE
5 × 6 × ½
5 × 6 × ¾
WINDOW SILL AND STEP NOSING
6 × 6 × ¾
TRIM PROFILES (H×L)

QUARRY TILE AND PAVER TILE

NOTES

1. The trim diagram shows typical shapes available for portland cement mortar installations of glazed wall tile. Similar types are available for thin-set installations and for ceramic mosaic tile, quarry tile, and paver tile. See manufacturer's literature for exact shapes, colors, and glazes available.
2. Mounted tile assemblies (sometimes referred to as ready-set systems) are available for glazed tile and ceramic mosaic applications. These assemblies consist of either pregrouted sheets using flexible silicone grout or backmounted sheets that are finished with dry-set grout after installation. Both provide approximately 2 sq ft of coverage per sheet. They are designed to simplify installation and improve uniformity.
3. Ceramic bathroom accessories usually are supplied in sets that include bath and lavatory soap holders, roll-paper holder, towel post, and toothbrush tumbler holder. Designs include surface-mounted and fully recessed models. They may be used with both conventional mortar and thin-set tile installations. Colors and glazes are available to match or harmonize with glazed wall tiles.

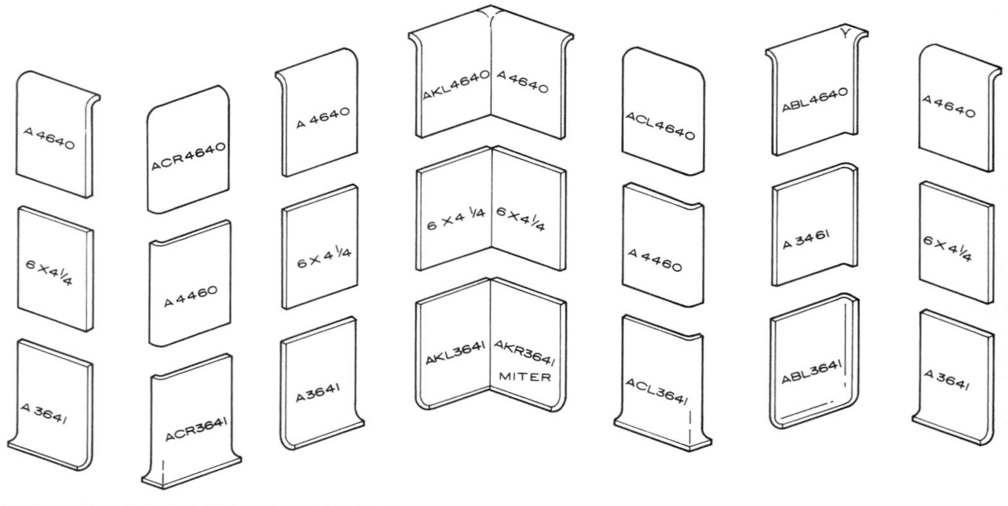
A 4640
6×4¼
A 3641
ACR4640
A 4460
ACR3641
A 4640
6×4¼
A3641
AKL4640
A 4640
6 × 4¼
6×4¼
AKL3641
AKR3641
MITER
ACL4640
A 4460
ACL3641
ABL4640
A 3461
ABL3641
A4640
6×4¼
A 3641

PORTLAND CEMENT MORTAR TRIM SHAPES
VERTICAL INSTALLATION 6" × 4¼" GLAZED WALL TILE

Ted B. Richey, AIA; The InterDesign Group; Indianapolis, Indiana

Terrazzo is a material composed of stone chips and cement matrix and is usually polished. There are four generally accepted types, classified by appearance:

1. STANDARD TERRAZZO: The most common type; relatively small chip sizes (#1 and #2 size chips).

2. VENETIAN TERRAZZO: Larger chips (size #3 through #8), with smaller chips filling the spaces between.

3. PALLADIANA: Random fractured slabs of marble up to approximately 15 in. greatest dimension, $3/8$ to 1 in. thick, with smaller chips filling spaces between.

4. RUSTIC TERRAZZO: Uniformly textured terrazzo in which matrix is depressed to expose chips, not ground or only slightly ground.

## MATRIX DATA

Two basic types exist: portland cement and chemical binders. Color pigments are added to create special effects. Limeproof mineral pigments or synthetic mineral pigments compatible with portland cement are required. Both white and grey portland cement is used depending on final color.

## CHEMICAL BINDERS

All five types of chemical binders provide excellent chemical and abrasion resistance, except for latex, which is rated good.

1. EPOXY MATRIX: Two component resinous matrix.

2. POLYESTER MATRIX: Two component resinous matrix.

3. POLYACRYLATE MATRIX: Composite resinous matrix.

4. LATEX MATRIX: Synthetic latex matrix.

5. CONDUCTIVE MATRIX: Special formulated matrix to conduct electricity with regulated resistance, use in surgical areas and where explosive gases are a hazard.

## PRECAST TERRAZZO

Several units are routinely available and almost any shape can be produced. Examples include: straight, coved, and splayed bases; window sills; stair treads and risers; shower receptors; floor tiles; and wall facings.

## STONE CHIPS

Stone used in terrazzo includes all calcareous serpentine and other rocks capable of taking a good polish. Marble and onyx are the preferred materials. Quartz, granite, quartzite, and silica pebbles are used for rustic terrazzo and textured mosaics not requiring polishing.

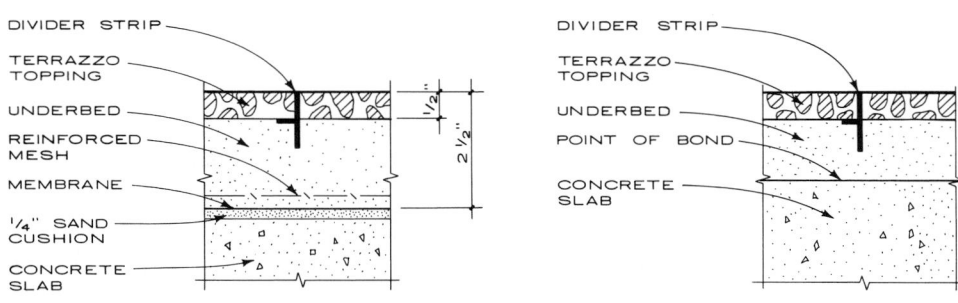

SAND CUSHION TERRAZZO

BONDED TERRAZZO

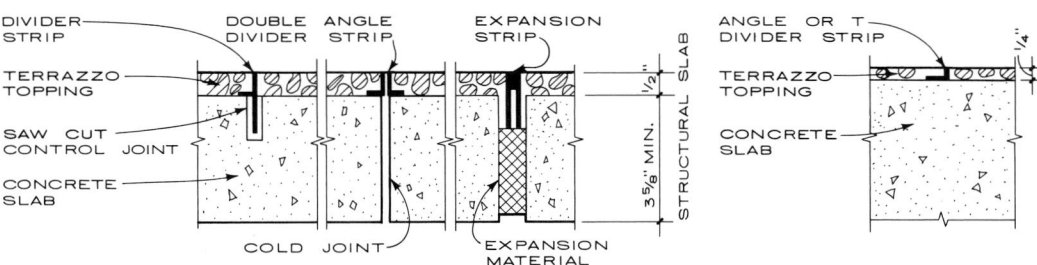

MONOLITHIC TERRAZZO

THIN-SET TERRAZZO

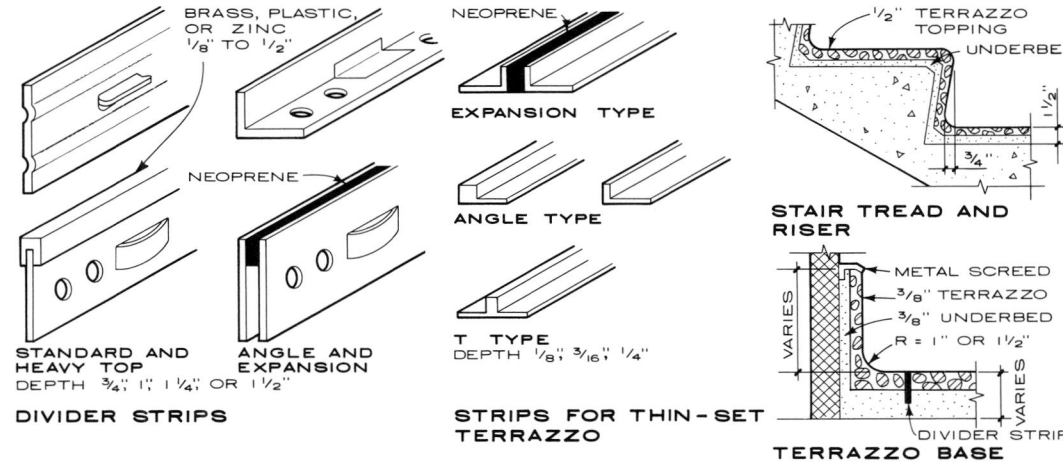

DIVIDER STRIPS

STRIPS FOR THIN-SET TERRAZZO

STAIR TREAD AND RISER

TERRAZZO BASE

## TERRAZZO SYSTEMS

| TERRAZZO SYSTEM | MINIMUM ALLOWANCE FOR FINISH | MINIMUM WEIGHT/ SQ FT | CONTROL JOINT STRIP LOCATION | SUGGESTED PANEL SIZE AND DIVIDER STRIP LOCATION | COMMENTS |
|---|---|---|---|---|---|
| Sand cushion terrazzo | $2\frac{1}{2}$'' | 27 lb | At all control joints in structure | 9 to 36 sq ft | Avoid narrow proportions (length no more than twice the width) and acute angles |
| Bonded underbed or strip terrazzo | $1\frac{3}{4}$'' | 18 lb | At all control joints in structure | 16 to 36 sq ft | Avoid narrow proportions as in sand cushion |
| Monolithic terrazzo | $\frac{1}{2}$'' | 7 lb | At all control joints in structure and at column centers or over grade beams where spans are great | At column centers in sawn or recessed slots maximum 24 x 24 ft | T or L strips usually provide decorative feature only |
| Thin-set terrazzo (chemical binders) | $\frac{1}{4}$'' | 3 lb | At all control joints | Only where structural crack can be anticipated | |
| Modified thin-set terrazzo | $\frac{3}{8}$'' | $4\frac{1}{2}$ lb | At all control joints | Only where structural crack can be anticipated | |
| Terrazzo over permanent metal forms | Varies, 3'' minimum | Varies | Directly over beam | Directly over joist centers and at 3 to 5 ft on center in the opposite direction | |
| Structural terrazzo | Varies, 4'' minimum | Varies | At all control joints at columns and at perimeter of floor | Deep strip ($1\frac{1}{2}$ in. min.) at all column centers and over grade beams | Use divider strip at any location where structural crack can be anticipated |

### NOTES

1. Venetian and Palladiana require greater depth due to larger chip size; $2\frac{3}{4}$ in. minimum allowance for finish 28 lb/sq ft.

2. Divider and control joint strips are made of white alloy of zinc, brass, aluminum, or plastic. Aluminum is not satisfactory for portland cement matrix terrazzo; use brass and plastic in chemical binder matrix only with approval of binder manufacturer.

3. In exterior terrazzo, brass will tarnish and white alloy of zinc will deteriorate.

John C. Lunsford, AIA, Varney Sexton Sydnor Architects; Phoenix, Arizona

## ACOUSTICAL CEILING SYSTEMS

| CEILING TYPE | MAIN, CROSS T | ACCESS T's | Z CHANNEL | H CHANNEL | T SPLINE | FLAT SPLINE | SPACER | MODULAR T | METAL PAN T | SPECIAL | BENT STEEL | BENT STEEL ALUM. CAP | BENT ALUMINUM | EXTRUDED ALUMINUM | GALVANIZED | PAINTED | ANODIZED | EMBOSSED PATTERN | FIRE RATING AVAILABLE | 12×12 | 12×24 | 24×24 | 24×48 | 24×60 | 20×60 | 30×60 | 60×60 | 48×48 | NOTES |
|---|---|---|---|---|---|---|---|---|---|---|---|---|---|---|---|---|---|---|---|---|---|---|---|---|---|---|---|---|---|
| **GYPSUM WALLBOARD** | | | | | | | | | | | | | | | | | | | | | | | | | | | | | |
| Suspended | ● | | | | | | | | | | ● | | | | ● | ● | | | ● | | | | | | | | | | |
| Exposed grid | ● | | | | | | | | | | ● | ● | ● | ● | ● | ● | ● | ● | ● | | | ● | ● | | | | | | |
| Semiconcealed grid | ● | | | | ● | | ● | | | | ● | | | | ● | ● | | | ● | | | ● | ● | | | | | | |
| Concealed H & T | | | | ● | ● | ● | | | | | ● | | | | ● | ● | | | ● | ● | ● | | | | | | | | |
| Concealed T & G | | | ● | | | | | | | | ● | | | | ● | ● | | | ● | ● | | | | | | | | | |
| Concealed Z | | | ● | | | ● | | | | | ● | | | | ● | ● | | | ● | ● | | | | | | | | | |
| Concealed access | ● | ● | | | ● | ● | ● | | | | ● | | | | ● | ● | | | ● | ● | | ● | | | | | | | |
| Modular | ● | | | | ● | ● | | ● | | | ● | | | | | ● | | | ● | | | | ● | ● | ● | ● | ● | ● | 50 or 60″ sq main grid |
| Metal pan | | | | | | | | | ● | | ● | | ● | | ● | | ● | | | ● | ● | | | | | | | | 12″ sq pattern |
| Linear metal | | | | | | | | | ● | | ● | | | | | ● | | | | | | | | | | | | | 4″ o.c. typical |
| Perforated metal | ● | | | | ● | | | | | | ● | | ● | | | ● | | | | | | | | | | | | | 1 way grid 4′–8′ o.c. |
| Luminous ceiling | | | | | | | | | ● | | | | ● | | | ● | ● | | | | | | | | | | | | 1″ to 4″ sq grid |

## ACOUSTICAL CEILING MATERIALS

| MATERIALS | 12×12 | 12×24 | 24×24 | 24×48 | 24×60 | 20×60 | 30×60 | 60×60 | 48×48 | CUSTOM SIZES | 1/2 | 5/8 | 3/4 | 1 | 1 1/2 | 3 | SQUARE | TEGULAR | T & G | KERFED AND RABBETED | .45–.60 | .60–.70 | .70–.80 | .80–.90 | .90–.95 | HIGH HUMIDITY | EXTERIOR SOFFIT | HIGH ABUSE/IMPACT | SCRUBBABLE | FIRE RATING AVAILABLE |
|---|---|---|---|---|---|---|---|---|---|---|---|---|---|---|---|---|---|---|---|---|---|---|---|---|---|---|---|---|---|---|
| **Mineral fiber:** | | | | | | | | | | | | | | | | | | | | | | | | | | | | | | |
| Painted | ● | ● | ● | ● | ● | ● | ● | | ● | | ● | ● | ● | | | | ● | ● | ● | ● | ● | ● | ● | ● | | | | | | ● |
| Plastic face | | ● | ● | | | | | | | | | ● | | | | | ● | | | | | ● | | | | | | ● | ● | ● |
| Aluminum face | ● | ● | ● | | | | | | | | | ● | | | | | ● | | | | ● | ● | | | | ● | | | ● | |
| Ceramic face | | ● | ● | | | | | | | | | ● | | | | | ● | | | | ● | | | | | ● | ● | | | |
| Mineral face | ● | ● | ● | | | | | | | | | ● | ● | | | | ● | | | | ● | | | | | | | | ● | |
| **Glass fiber:** | | | | | | | | | | | | | | | | | | | | | | | | | | | | | | |
| Painted | | ● | ● | ● | | ● | | | | | | | | ● | | | ● | | | | | | ● | | | | ● | | | |
| Film face | | ● | ● | ● | | | | | | ● | | | | ● | | | ● | | | | | | | ● | | ● | ● | | | |
| Glass cloth face | | ● | ● | ● | ● | ● | ● | | | | | | ● | ● | ● | | ● | | | | | | | ● | | | ● | ● | | |
| Molded | | ● | ● | | | | | | | | | | ● | ● | ● | | Varies | | | | ● | | | | | | | | | |
| Gypsum | | ● | ● | | | | | | | | ● | | | | | | ● | | | | ● | | | | | | | | ● | ● |
| Mylar face | ● | ● | ● | | | | | | | | | | ● | ● | | | ● | ● | | | ● | | | | | | | | | |
| Tectum | | ● | ● | | ● | | ● | ● | | | 1–3 | | | | | | ● | ● | | | ● | | | | | | | | ● | |

## SPECIAL ACOUSTICAL SYSTEMS

SOUND ISOLATION: When it is necessary to isolate a high noise area from a building or a "quiet room" from a high surrounding noise level; floors, walls, and ceilings should be built free of rigid contact with the building structure to reduce sound and vibration transmission.

CUSTOM WALLS: Auditoriums, concert halls, and other special acoustically conditioned space may require both absorptive and reflective surfaces and in some cases surfaces that can be adjusted for varying absorption coefficients to "tune" the space.

## LOOSE BATTS

USE: Reduce sound transmission through or over partitions; installed over suspended acoustical tile. Also used between gypsum wall partitions.

MATERIALS: Expanded fiberglass or mineral fiber.

S.T.C.: Based on total designed system, can range from 40 to 60.

Setter, Leach & Lindstrom, Inc.; Minneapolis, Minnesota

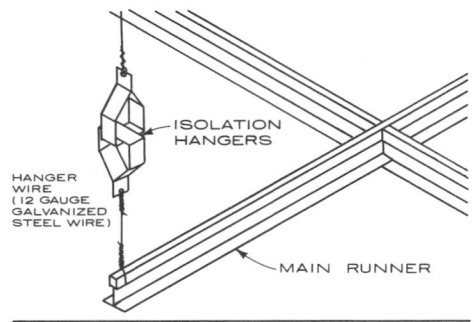

### ISOLATION HANGER
### CEILING ISOLATION HANGER

Isolates ceilings from noise traveling through the building structure. Hangers also available for isolating ceiling systems to shield spaces from mechanical equipment and/or aircraft noise.

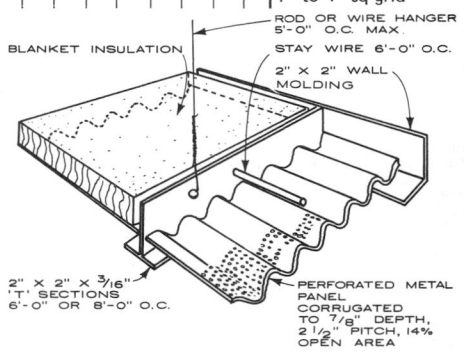

PERFORATED METAL CEILING

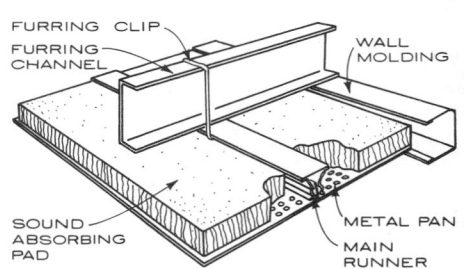

METAL PAN CEILING

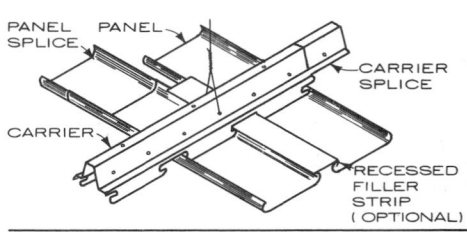

LINEAR METAL CEILING

### METAL CEILINGS

USE: Sound absorption depends on batt insulation.

MATERIALS: Bent steel, aluminum, or stainless steel.

N.R.C.: 0.70 to 0.90.

FINISH: Painted, anodized, or stainless steel.

# ACOUSTICAL TREATMENT

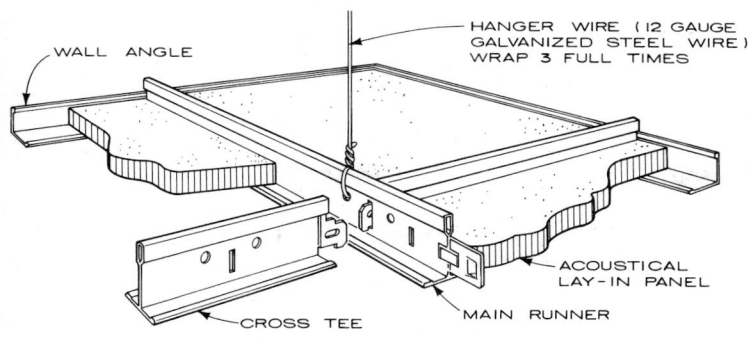

**EXPOSED GRID**

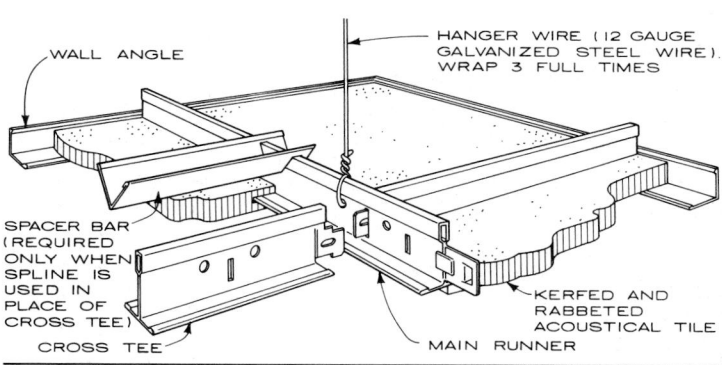

**CONCEALED GRID**

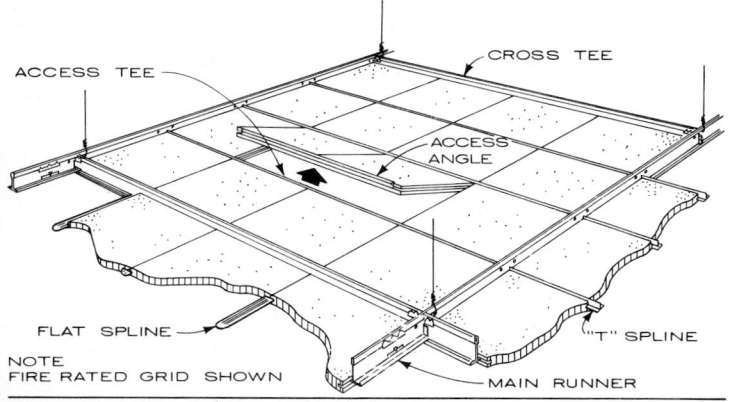

**CONCEALED GRID – UPWARD ACCESS** ( SIDE PIVOT SHOWN — END PIVOT AVAILABLE )

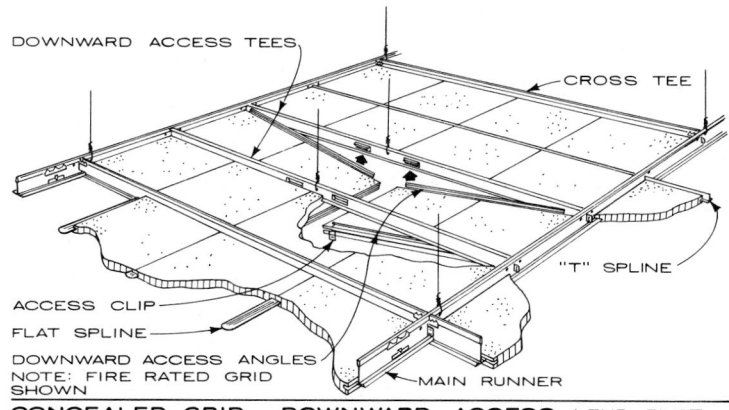

**CONCEALED GRID – DOWNWARD ACCESS** ( END PIVOT SHOWN — SIDE PIVOT AVAILABLE )

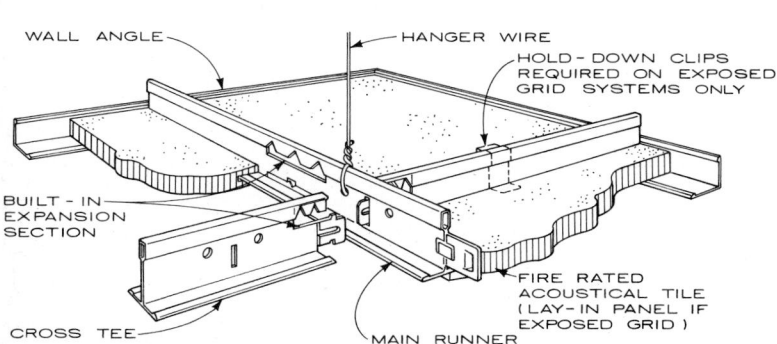

**FIRE RATED GRID** ( CONCEALED GRID SHOWN )

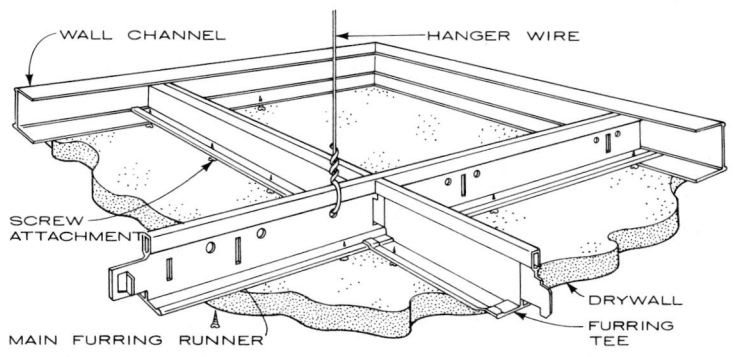

**DRYWALL FURRING SYSTEM**

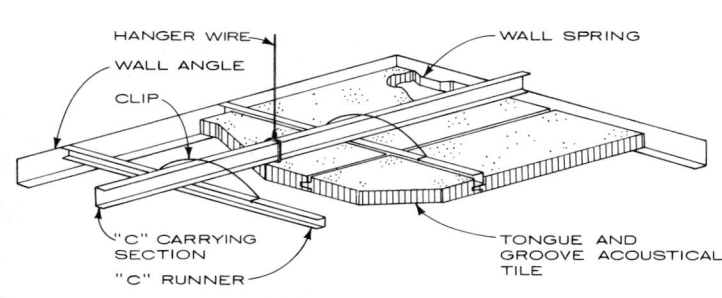

**TONGUE AND GROOVE**

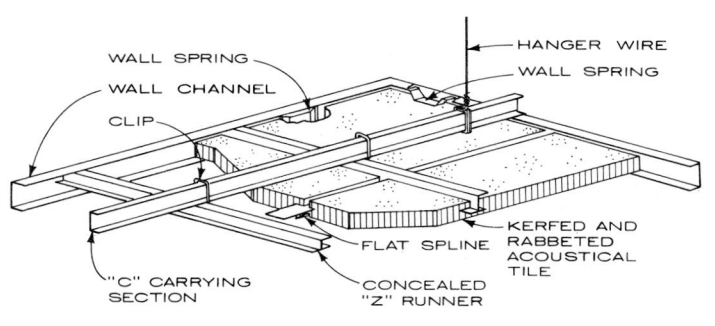

**CONCEALED "Z" SYSTEM**

Setter, Leach & Lindstrom, Inc.; Minneapolis, Minnesota

**ACOUSTICAL TREATMENT**    9

## NOTES

1. Flooring can be manufactured from practically every commercially available species of wood. In the United States wood flooring is grouped for marketing purposes roughly according to species and region. There are various grading systems used with various species, and often different specifications for different sized boards in a given species. For instance, nail size and spacing varies among the several board sizes typically available in oak.

2. Information given here should be used for preliminary decision making only. Precise specifications must be obtained from the supplier or from the appropriate industry organization named below.

3. Several considerations in wood flooring selection and installation are applicable industrywide. These are shown graphically at right.

4. The table below includes typical grades and sizes of boards for each species or regional group. Grade classifications vary, but in each case one can assume that the first grade listed is the highest quality, and that the quality decreases with each succeeding grade. The best grade will typically minimize or exclude features such as knots, streaks, spots, checks, and torn grain and will contain the highest percentage of longer boards. Grade standards have been reduced in recent years for practically all commercially produced flooring, hence a thorough review of exact grade specifications is in order when selecting wood flooring.

5. End matching gives a complete tongue and grooved joint all around each board. Board length is reduced as required to obtain the matched ends.

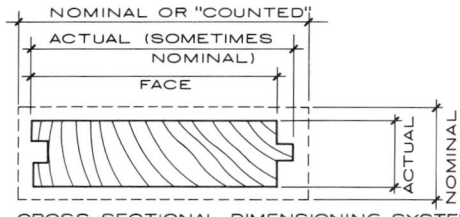

CROSS SECTIONAL DIMENSIONING SYSTEMS VARY AMONG SPECIES, PATTERNS, MANUFACTURERS. TRADE ORGANIZATIONS PROVIDE PERCENTAGE MULTIPLIERS FOR COMPUTING COVERAGE

### CROSS SECTIONAL DIMENSIONS

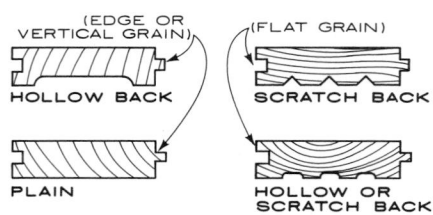

THE UNDERSIDE OF FLOORING BOARDS MAY BE PATTERNED AND OFTEN WILL CONTAIN MORE DEFECTS THAN ARE ALLOWED IN THE TOP FACE. GRAIN IS OFTEN MIXED IN ANY GIVEN RUN OF BOARDS

### BOARD CHARACTERISTICS

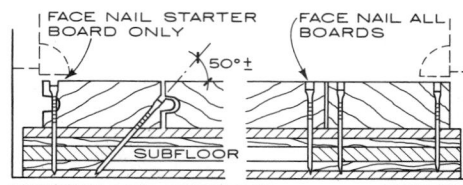

MOST FLOORING MAY BE HAD IN VARYING THICKNESSES TO SUIT WEAR REQUIREMENTS. ACTUAL DIMENSIONS SHOWN ARE AVAILABLE IN MAPLE

### VARIOUS THICKNESSES

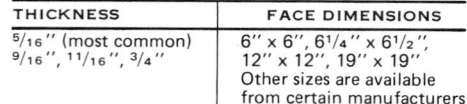

JOINTED FLOORING MUST BE FACE NAILED, USUALLY WITH FULLY BARBED FLOORING BRADS
TONGUE AND GROOVED BOARDS ARE BLIND NAILED WITH SPIRAL FLOOR SCREWS, CEMENT COATED NAILS, CUT NAILS, MACHINE DRIVEN FASTENERS, USE MANUFACTURER'S RECOMMENDATIONS

### FASTENING

### PARQUET FLOORING—SQUARE PANELS

| THICKNESS | FACE DIMENSIONS |
|---|---|
| $5/16''$ (most common) $9/16''$, $11/16''$, $3/4''$ | 6'' x 6'', $6^{1}/_4''$ x $6^{1}/_2''$, 12'' x 12'', 19'' x 19'' Other sizes are available from certain manufacturers |

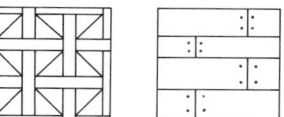 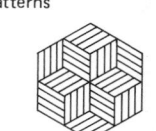

### PARQUET FLOORING—INDIVIDUAL STRIPS

| THICKNESS | FACE DIMENSIONS |
|---|---|
| $5/16''$ | 2'' x 12'' typical strips can be cut, mitered, etc., to obtain pieces required for special patterns |

## TYPICAL GRADES AND SIZES OF BOARDS BY SPECIES OR REGIONAL GROUP

| GROUP | INDUSTRY ORGANIZATION | GRADE | THICKNESS | WIDTH | | NOTES |
|---|---|---|---|---|---|---|
| Oak (also beech, birch, pecan, and hard maple) | National Oak Flooring Manufacturers' Assoc. | Quarter Sawn: Clear Select Plain Sawn: Clear Select No. 1 Common No. 2 Common | $3/4''$, $1/2''$ Standard; also $3/8''$ $5/16''$ | Face $1^{1}/_2''$ 2'' $2^{1}/_4''$ | | This association grades birch, beech, and hard maple. First Grade, Second Grade, Third Grade, and "Special Grades." Pecan is graded: First Grade, First Grade Red, Second Grade, Second Grade Red, Third Grade. |
| Hard maple (also beech and birch) (acer saccharum—not soft maple) | Maple Flooring Manufacturers' Assoc. Inc. | First Grade Second Grade Third Grade Fourth Grade Combinations | $3/8''$, $12/32''$ $41/32''$, $1/2''$ $33/32''$ $53/32''$, $5/8''$ | Face $1^{1}/_2''$ 2'' $2^{1}/_4''$ $3^{1}/_4''$ | | Association states that beech and birch have physical properties that make them fully suitable as substitutes for hard maple. See manufacturer for available width and thickness combinations. |
| Southern pine | Southern Pine Inspection Bureau | B & B C C & Btr D No. 2 | $3/8''$, $1/2''$ $5/8''$, 1'' $1^{1}/_4''$, $1^{1}/_2''$ | Nom. 2'' 3'' 4'' 5'' 6'' | Face $1^{1}/_8''$ $2^{1}/_8''$ $3^{1}/_8''$ $4^{1}/_8''$ $5^{1}/_8''$ | Grain may be specified as edge (rift), near-rift, or flat. If not specified, manufacturer will ship flat or mixed grain boards. See manufacturer for available width and thickness combinations. |
| Western woods (Douglas fir, hemlock, Englemann spruce, Idaho pine, incense cedar, lodgepole pine, Ponderosa pine, sugar pine, Western larch, Western red cedar) | Western Wood Products Association | Select: 1 & 2 clear- B & Btr C Select D Select Finish: Superior Prime E | 2'' and thinner | Nominal 3'' 4'' 6'' | | Flooring is machined tongue and groove and may be furnished in any grade agreeable to buyer and seller. Grain may be specified as vertical (VG), flat (FG), or mixed (MG). Basic size for flooring is 1'' x 4'' x 12'; standard lengths 4' and above. |
| Eastern white pine Norway pine Jack pine Eastern spruce Balsam fir Eastern hemlock Tamarack | Northern Hardwood & Pine Manufacturers' Association | C & Btr Select D Select Stained Select | $3/8''$, $1/2''$ $5/8''$, 1'', $1^{1}/_4''$, $1^{1}/_2''$ | Nom. 2'' 3'' 4'' 5'' 6'' | Face $1^{1}/_8''$ $2^{1}/_8''$ $3^{1}/_8''$ $4^{1}/_8''$ $5^{1}/_8''$ | The various species included in this "Lake States Region" group provide different visual features. Consult manufacturer or local supplier to determine precisely what is available in terms of species and appearance. |

Darrel Downing Rippeteau, Architect; Washington, D.C.

 WOOD FLOORING

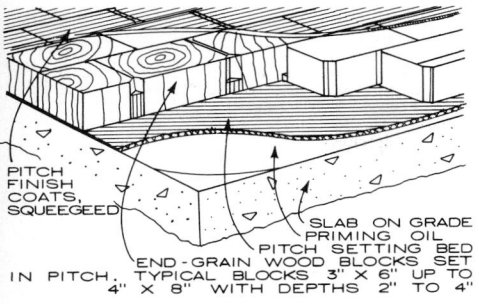

PITCH FINISH COATS, SQUEEGEED

SLAB ON GRADE
PRIMING OIL
PITCH SETTING BED
END-GRAIN WOOD BLOCKS SET IN PITCH. TYPICAL BLOCKS 3" X 6" UP TO 4" X 8" WITH DEPTHS 2" TO 4"

**INDUSTRIAL WOOD BLOCK** URETHANE FINISH COATS AVAILABLE FOR NONINDUSTRIAL USES

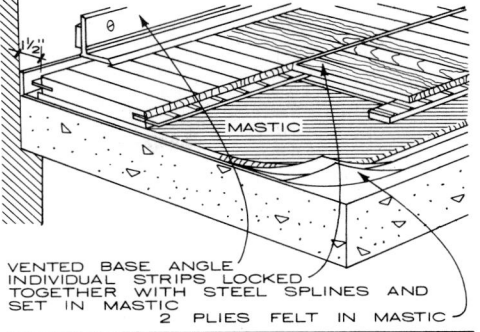

MASTIC

VENTED BASE ANGLE
INDIVIDUAL STRIPS LOCKED TOGETHER WITH STEEL SPLINES AND SET IN MASTIC
2 PLIES FELT IN MASTIC

**STEEL SPLINED ROWS OF STRIPS** CORK UNDERLAYMENT ADDED FOR NON-INDUSTRIAL USE

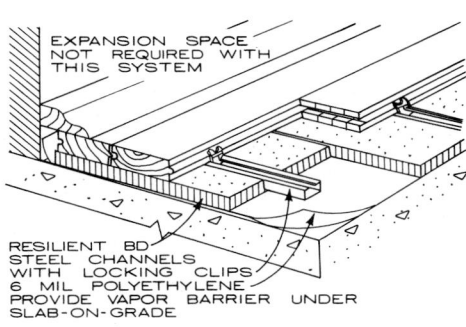

EXPANSION SPACE NOT REQUIRED WITH THIS SYSTEM

RESILIENT BD STEEL CHANNELS WITH LOCKING CLIPS
6 MIL POLYETHYLENE PROVIDE VAPOR BARRIER UNDER SLAB-ON-GRADE

**METAL CHANNEL RUNNERS WITH CLIPS**

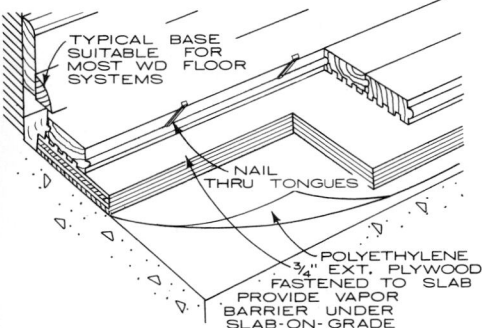

TYPICAL BASE SUITABLE FOR MOST WD FLOOR SYSTEMS

NAIL THRU TONGUES

POLYETHYLENE
¾" EXT. PLYWOOD FASTENED TO SLAB PROVIDE VAPOR BARRIER UNDER SLAB-ON-GRADE

**STRIPS OVER PLYWOOD UNDERLAYMENT** A NOFMA STANDARD

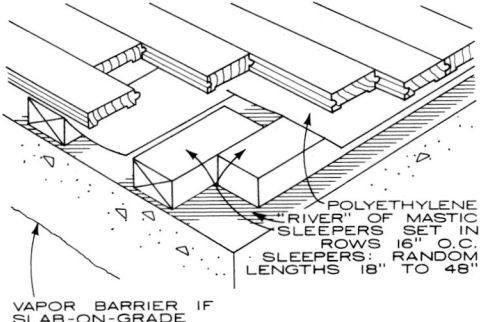

POLYETHYLENE
"RIVER" OF MASTIC SLEEPERS SET IN ROWS 16" O.C. SLEEPERS: RANDOM LENGTHS 18" TO 48"

VAPOR BARRIER IF SLAB-ON-GRADE

**STRIPS OVER STAGGERED 2 X 4 SLEEPERS** A NOFMA STANDARD

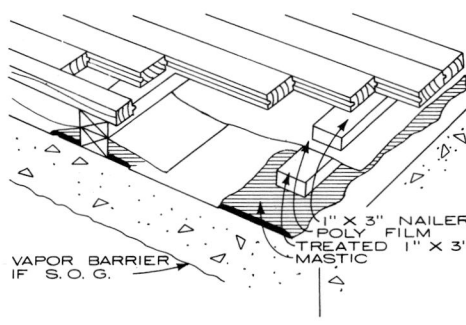

1" X 3" NAILER POLY FILM TREATED 1" X 3" MASTIC

VAPOR BARRIER IF S.O.G.

**DOUBLE COURSE OF SLEEPER STRIPS** A NOFMA STANDARD

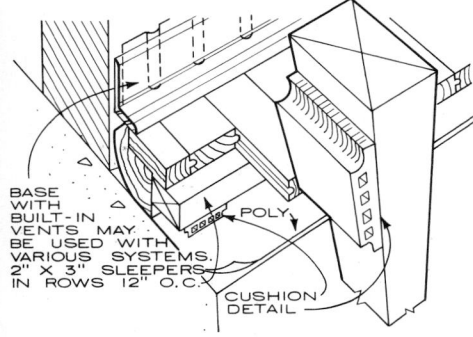

BASE WITH BUILT-IN VENTS MAY BE USED WITH VARIOUS SYSTEMS.
2" X 3" SLEEPERS IN ROWS 12" O.C.

POLY

CUSHION DETAIL

**STRIPS OVER CUSHIONED SLEEPERS**

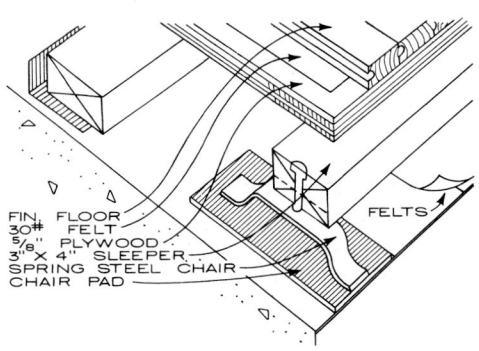

FIN. FLOOR
30# FELT
⅝" PLYWOOD
3" X 4" SLEEPER
SPRING STEEL CHAIR
CHAIR PAD

FELTS

**STRIPS OVER SLEEPERS MOUNTED ON SPRING-STEEL CHAIRS**

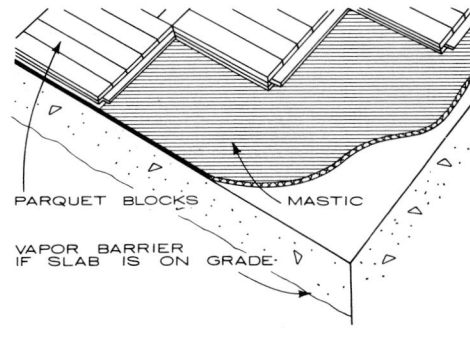

PARQUET BLOCKS

MASTIC

VAPOR BARRIER IF SLAB IS ON GRADE.

**PARQUET BLOCKS SET IN MASTIC**

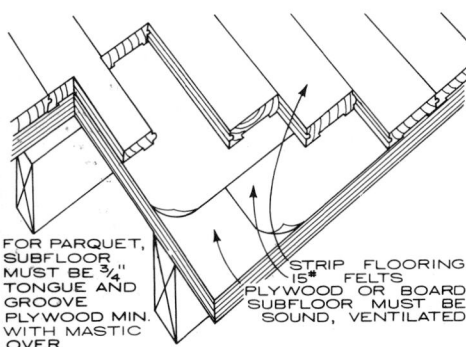

FOR PARQUET, SUBFLOOR MUST BE ¾" TONGUE AND GROOVE PLYWOOD MIN. WITH MASTIC OVER

STRIP FLOORING
15# FELTS
PLYWOOD OR BOARD SUBFLOOR MUST BE SOUND, VENTILATED

**STRIPS OVER SUBFLOOR ON WOOD JOISTS**

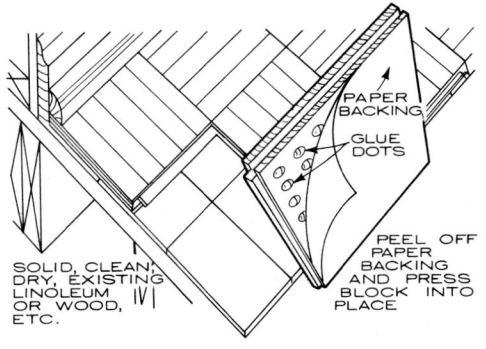

PAPER BACKING

GLUE DOTS

SOLID, CLEAN, DRY, EXISTING LINOLEUM OR WOOD, ETC.

PEEL OFF PAPER BACKING AND PRESS BLOCK INTO PLACE

**PRESSURE-SENSITIVE "DO-IT-YOURSELF" PANELS (PRE-FINISHED)**

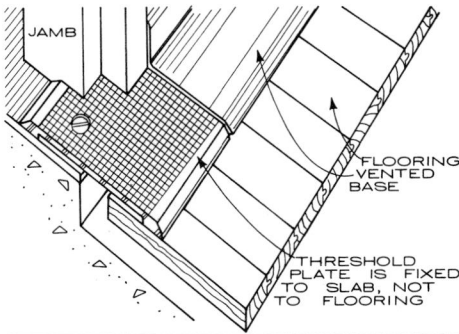

JAMB

FLOORING VENTED BASE

THRESHOLD PLATE IS FIXED TO SLAB, NOT TO FLOORING

**EXPANSION PLATE AT DOORWAY /JOINT WITH DISSIMILAR CONSTRUCTION**

Wood flooring is visually attractive and provides an excellent wearing surface. However, wood requires particular care in handling and installation to prevent moisture attack. Minimize moisture attack on wood floors by avoiding proximity to wet areas. Installation should occur after all "wet" jobs are completed. All the permanent lighting and heating plant should be installed to ensure constant temperature and humidity.

Darrel Downing Rippeteau, Architect; Washington, D.C.

Expansion and contraction is a fact of life with most wood flooring. Perimeter base details that allow for movement and ventilation are included in the details above. Moisture control is further enhanced by use of a vapor barrier under a slab on or below grade. This provision should be carefully considered for each installation. Wood structures require adequate ventilation in basement and crawl space.

Wearing properties vary from species to species in wood flooring and should be considered along with appearance. In addition, grain pattern will affect a given species wearability. For instance, industrial wood blocks are typically placed with the end grain exposed because it presents the toughest wearing surface. The thickness of the wood above tongues in T & G flooring may be increased for extra service.

## RESILIENT FLOORING CHARACTERISTICS

| TYPE OF RESILIENT FLOORING | BASIC COMPONENTS | SUBFLOOR APPLICATION* | | | RECOMMENDED LOAD LIMIT (PSI) | DURA-BILITY† | RESIS-TANCE TO HEEL DAMAGE | EASE OF MAINTE-NANCE | GREASE RESIS-TANCE | SURFACE ALKALI RESIS-TANCE | RESIS-TANCE TO STAINING | CIGARETTE BURN RESISTANCE | RESIL-IENCE | QUIET-NESS |
|---|---|---|---|---|---|---|---|---|---|---|---|---|---|---|
| Vinyl sheet | Vinyl resins with fiber back | B | O | S | 75–100 | 2–3 | 2–5 | 1–2 | 1 | 1–3 | 3–4 | 4 | 4 | 4 |
| Homogeneous vinyl tile | Vinyl resins | B | O | S | 150–200 | 1–3 | 1–4 | 2–4 | 1 | 1–2 | 1–5 | 2–5 | 2–5 | 2–5 |
| Vinyl composition tile | Vinyl resins and fillers | B | O | S | 25–50 | 2 | 4–5 | 2–3 | 2 | 4 | 2 | 6 | 6 | 6 |
| Cork tile with vinyl coating | Raw cork and vinyl resins | | | S | 150 | 4 | 3 | 2 | 1 | 1 | 5 | 3 | 3 | 3 |
| Cork tile | Raw cork and resins | | | S | 75 | 5 | 4 | 4 | 4 | 5 | 4 | 1 | 1 | 1 |
| Rubber tile | Rubber compound | B | O | S | 200 | 2 | 4 | 4 | 3 | 2 | 1 | 2 | 2 | 2 |
| Linoleum | Cork, wood, floor, and oleoresins | | | S | 75 | 3 | 4–5 | 4–5 | 1 | 4 | 2 | 4 | 4 | 4 |

*B: below grade; O: on grade; S: suspended.
†Numerals indicate subjective ratings (relative rank of each floor to others listed above), "1" indicating highest.
 Bruce A. Kenan, AIA, Pederson, Hueber, Hares & Glavin; Syracuse, New York.

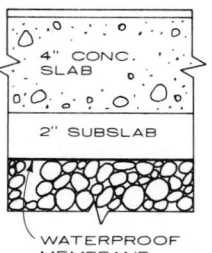
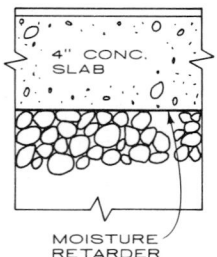
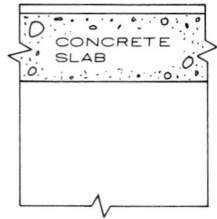
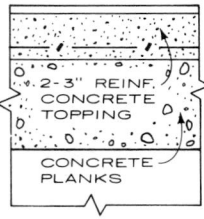
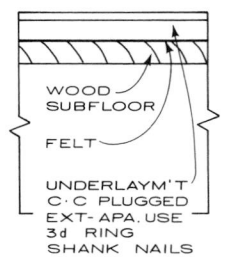
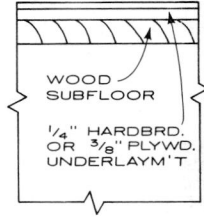

| SLAB BELOW GRADE | SLAB ON GRADE | SLAB ABOVE GRADE | SLAB OVER PRECAST | WOOD SUBFLOOR | WOOD SUBFLOOR |

**RESILIENT FLOORING**

### PREPARING OLD WOOD FLOORS

| TYPE OF SUBFLOOR | | COVER WITH |
|---|---|---|
| Single wood floor | Tongue and groove not over 3″ | Hardboard or plywood, ¼″ or heavier |
| | Not tongue and groove | Plywood ½″ or heavier |
| Double wood floor | Strips 3″ or more | Hardboard or plywood 1″ or heavier |
| | Strips less than 3″ tongue and groove | Renail or replace loose boards, remove surface irregularities |

### PREPARING OLD CONCRETE FLOORS

1. Check for dampness.
2. Remove all existing surface coatings.
3. Wirebrush and sweep dusty, porous surfaces. Apply primer.

### PREPARING LIFT SLABS

Remove curing compounds prior to resilient flooring installation.

### CONCRETE SLABS BY DENSITY

| Density | | | |
|---|---|---|---|
| | Light | Medium | Heavy |
| Pounds per cubic foot | | | |
| | 20/40 | 60/90    90/120 | 120/150 |
| Type of concrete | | | |
| | Expanded perlite, vermiculite, and others | Expanded slag shale, and clay | Standard concrete of sand, gravel, or stone |
| Recommendations | | | |
| | Top with 1″ thickness of standard concrete mix | Approved for use of resilient flooring if troweled smooth and even | |

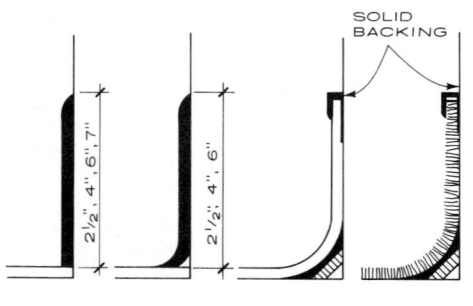
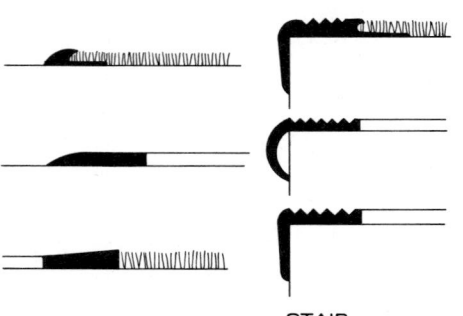
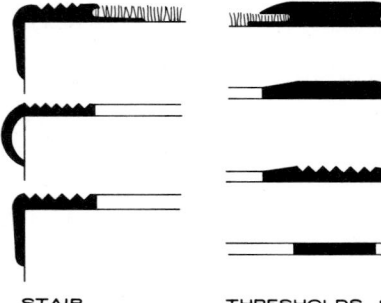
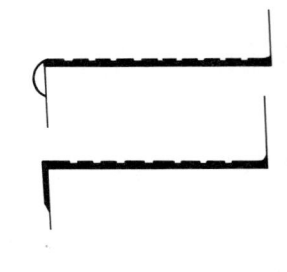

| BASES - STRAIGHT OR COVED | COVE STRIP AND CAP STRIP | REDUCERS | STAIR NOSINGS | THRESHOLDS, SADDLES FEATURE STRIP | STAIR TREAD |

**RESILIENT FLOORING ACCESSORIES, CARPET ACCESSORIES**

Broome, Oringdulph, O'Toole, Rudolf & Associates; Portland, Oregon

**RESILIENT FLOORING**

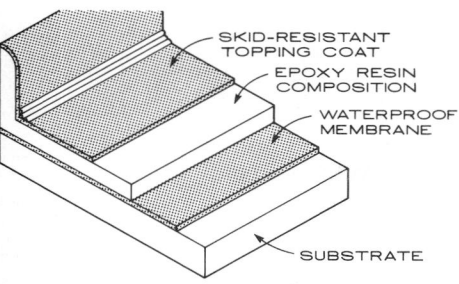

An epoxy resin composition flooring resistant to a large number of corrosive materials, $3/16$ in. to $1/4$ in. thickness, weight 3 psf. Used in manufacturing areas, food processing, hotel and restaurant kitchens, beverage bottling plants and loading docks.

### EPOXY RESIN COMPOSITION FLOORING

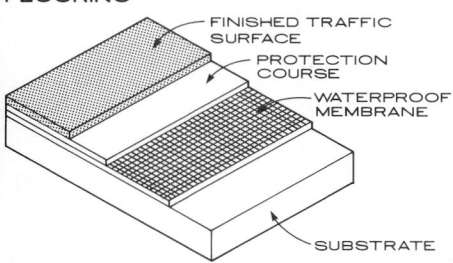

A multicolored installation consisting of a fabric reinforced latex membrane, a neoprene-cement protection course, and a flexible, oil-resistant finish. Thickness $3/16$ in., weight 1.5 psf. Used on interior or exterior auto parking facilities.

### REINFORCED LATEX MEMBRANE

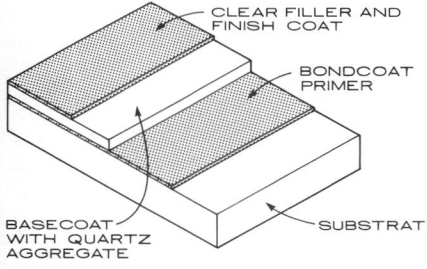

A jointless flooring in which quartz aggregates are embedded either by trowel or broadcast into a wet epoxy binding coat followed by clear filler coat. Used in laboratories, pollution control facilities, locker rooms, light manufacturing.

### EPOXY / QUARTZ AGGREGATE

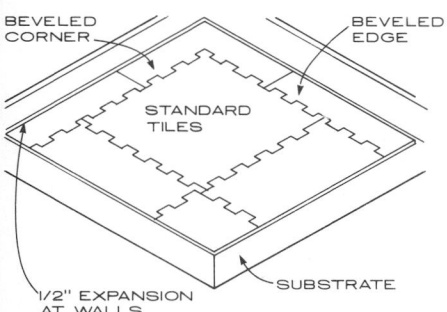

An interlocking rubber tile flooring system made in various thicknesses and types according to user requirements. Can be used in saunas, deck areas, weight, exercise, and locker rooms, on assembly lines, in industrial art rooms.

### INTERLOCKING RUBBER FLOORING

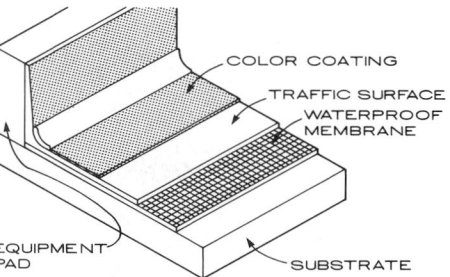

A troweled surface over a fabric reinforced latex-type waterproof membrane. Flooring thickness $3/16$ in., weight $2\frac{1}{2}$ psf. Used in mechanical equipment rooms and plenum rooms.

### WATERPROOF LATEX MEMBRANE FLOORING

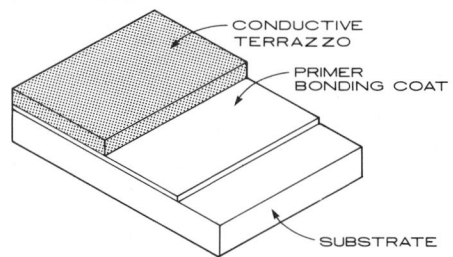

Static-dissipating, nonsparking trowel-applied jointless flooring of elastomeric resin terrazzo, incorporating marble chips. Thickness $1/4$ in. to $1/2$ in., weighing 3 psf ($1/4$ in. thick). Used in hospital operating suites.

### CONDUCTIVE FLOORING

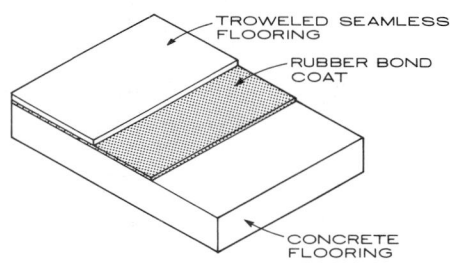

A trowel-applied cupric oxychloride flooring that is nonsparking and solvent resistant, weighing 3.2 psf at $3/8$ in. thick. Used in hospitals, arsenals and ammunition plants, light manufacturing areas, warehouses, laboratories.

### CUPRIC OXYCHLORIDE FLOORING

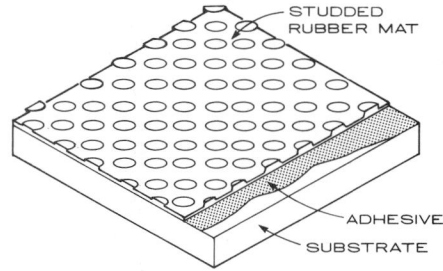

A solid, nonconductive rubber flooring with a raised circular, square, "H" or ribbed pattern. Applied to substrate by use of an adhesive. Used in terminals, malls, recreation facilities, elevators and offices.

### STUDDED RUBBER FLOORING

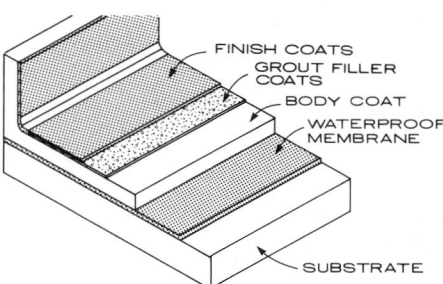

A trowel-applied elastomeric latex resin forming a jointless floor with good chemical resistance, is waterproof in conjunction with membrane. Thickness $1/4$ in., weight 3 psf. Used in showers and locker rooms, laboratories, pollution control facilities, TV studios.

### ELASTOMERIC LATEX RESIN FLOORING

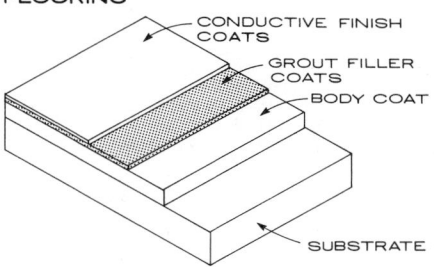

Static-dissipating and nonsparking trowel-applied jointless flooring, $1/4$ in. thick, weighing 3 psf. Used in arsenals and ammunition plants, flammable materials storage areas and explosion-hazardous industrial locations.

### CONDUCTIVE FLOORING

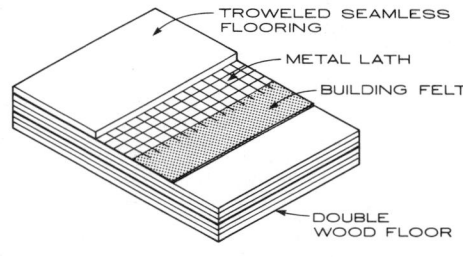

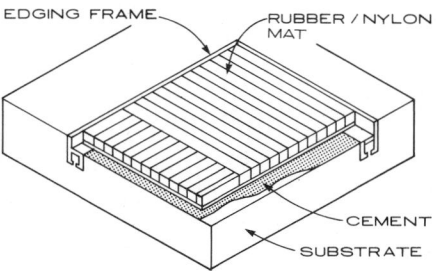

Manufactured from recycled synthetic rubber tires containing nylon fibers for strength and bonded to a glass-cloth backing. Applied to substrate cement adhesive. Used in golf clubs, stores, malls, and air terminals.

### RUBBER / NYLON FLOORING

Timothy B. McDonald; Washington, D.C.

# BACKGROUND

The word "carpet" comes from the Latin *carpere*, "to card wool." Carpet production in the U.S. has grown from 100 million square yards in 1910 to over 1 billion square yards per year in the 1980s. Three events account for the major increases:

1. Development of man-made fibers in the 1930s.
2. Replacement of weaving by tufting in the 1950s.
3. Combining of the tufting machine with piece dyeable bulked continuous filament (BCF) nylon in the period beginning 1960. This gave the industry the ability to produce carpet styles with long color lines of up to 50 or more colors without large inventory costs.

# CARPET FIBERS

Nature accounted for 100% of face fiber production for floor coverings. The uncertainties of supply of desirable wools from about 20 countries, plus variation in fiber length and increasing costs of scouring and processing encouraged development of man-made fibers. Man-made fibers are easy to clean, mildew resistant, mothproof, and nonallergenic.

Wool: Of 1986 U.S.-produced carpet production, 1% was wool. Its qualities have been copied but never quite duplicated. The natural tendency of animal fibers to stretch and return to their original length makes wool carpet resilient, with excellent recovery from crushing. Problems of supply make it the most expensive fiber and the only one requiring antimoth treatment.

Cotton: Negligible current usage. Early tufted carpet was an offshoot of the "turfed" bedspread cottage industry in the South and had single color, loop, or cut pile fibers made of cotton.

Nylon: Of 1986 carpet production, 80% was nylon—a petrochemical engineered for carpet use, with easy dying characteristics. First successfully introduced into carpet in continuous filament, it was later cut and processed in staple lengths (like wool) to give more natural qualities to the finished product. Recent developments have combined topical treatments with modified extrusions to give antisoil properties to the fibers. Adequate maintenance provisions should accompany specifications for these products, since soil that remains hidden will cause fiber damage unless properly removed by regular vacuuming and cleaning.

Acrylic: Negligible current usage. This hydrocarbon synthetic is considered to be the most wool-like of all man-made fibers.

Polypropylene (olefin): Of 1986 production, 12% and growing. This man-made hydrocarbon normally lacks resilience and the ability to be post dyed. Its simplified extrusion capabilities plus the ability to be solution dyed prior to extrusion have encouraged many carpet makers to install their own polypropylene fiber-making facilities.

Polyester: Of 1986 production, 7%. A high tensile strength synthetic made by the esterification of ethyl glycol, having easy care and water-repellent qualities.

# CARPET CONSTRUCTION

Woven carpet represents 2% of the total carpet production in the U.S. today. Whether hand-knotted, loomed, or mechanically produced, there are many similarities in production methods. The side-to-side progression in hand-knotted is accelerated in a loom as the shuttle propels the weft (or woof) yarn back and forth over the 12 or 15 ft width of the finished carpet. This is missing in tufted and later methods. Common to all, however, is a progression of the leading edge of this 12–15 ft finished width in the direction of manufacture. This sets up the direction of lay of the finished face fibers, always in the opposite direction. The exception is in hand-knotted,

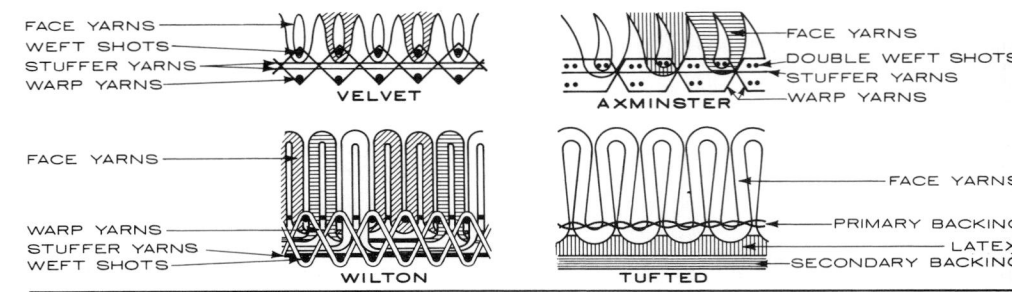

FACE YARNS — WEFT SHOTS — STUFFER YARNS — WARP YARNS — **VELVET**

FACE YARNS — DOUBLE WEFT SHOTS — STUFFER YARNS — WARP YARNS — **AXMINSTER**

FACE YARNS — WARP YARNS — STUFFER YARNS — WEFT SHOTS — **WILTON**

FACE YARNS — PRIMARY BACKING — LATEX — SECONDARY BACKING — **TUFTED**

**CONSTRUCTION MODES**

where the direction of lay of the face fibers falls to one side or the other, depending on the style of knot. In hand-knotted, it will also change after cleaning to follow the direction of brushing.

In all tufted or woven broadloom, it is imperative that the direction of lay be made to run in the same direction on all components of every installation. Otherwise, adjacent widths, although perfectly seamed, will appear to mismatch in perceived color and texture.

Oriental rugs: Defined by the Oriental Rug Retailers of America as "a rug of either wool or silk, knotted entirely by hand by native craftsmen in some parts of Asia, from the shores of the Persian Gulf, North to the Caspian Sea, and Eastward through Iran, the Soviet Union, Afghanistan, Pakistan, India, China, and Japan." An Oriental rug is classed an antique if it is over 75 years old, semiantique if less than 75 years old, and new if made in the past 15 years.

More than 60% of the hand-knotted rugs imported by the U.S. come from China and India. Most machine-made rugs are manufactured in the U.S. or imported from Belgium or Spain. They are available in traditional (floral or curvilinear) and contemporary (geometric) colors and designs.

Dhurrie and Kilim rugs are flat weaves costing less than hand-knotted Orientals. They can be either machine- or hand-made and have primitive as well as modern designs. Other types of rugs are ryas from Scandinavia, American Indian woven rugs, and Greek flotakis. Braided and rag rugs are also finding a niche in the market. Many carpet and rug makers offer custom designs (some computer aided) in a variety of fiber construction.

# CONSTRUCTION MODES

Velvet: Simplest of all carpet weaves. Although the simplicity of the loom does not permit patterned designs, beautiful yarn color combinations can be used to produce tweed effects. Pile is formed as the warp yarns are looped over removable "wires" inserted consecutively across the loom (weft-wise). Requires additional space equal to the width of the loom for this rapid operation. Alternate height wires can be used to create high–low loop texture, while wires with a raised knife blade at the trailing end are used to create cut pile upon retraction.

Axminster: Has a smooth cut pile surface, with almost all of the yarn appearing on the surface. Colors and patterns are limited only by the number of tufts in the carpet. Identifying feature is the heavy ribbed backing that only allows the carpet to be rolled lengthwise.

Wilton: Basic velvet loom, improved in the early 1800s by the addition of a Jacquard mechanism to feed yarn through as many as six separate punched hole patterns to vary the texture or colored design. Uses only one color at a time on the surface; the other yarns remain buried; thus the reputation that Wiltons have a hidden quality because of the extra "hand" or feel that this gives to the finished carpet.

Tufted: This technique developed from an early method for making tufted bedspreads. Spacing of as many as 2000 needles on a huge sewing machine (12–15 ft wide) determines the carpet gauge. Face yarn is stitched through the primary backing, where it is bonded to a secondary backing with latex before curing in a drying oven. For energy saving, hot-melt adhesive is substituted for latex by some mills, though this results in a loss of ability to pass flammability tests. Some "single-needle" tufting machines exist having a small stitching head that moves from side to side during carpet construction. They are mainly used for special orders for multiple odd-shaped spaces to eliminate installation waste.

Knitted: Resembles weaving in that knitted carpet is a warp-knitted fabric comprised of warp chains, weft-forming yarns, and face yarns and is knitted in a single operation. Warp-chain stitches run longitudinally and parallel to each other. The backing yarns are laid weftwise into the warp stitches and pass over 3 or 4 rows of warp stitches overlapping in the back of the carpet for strength and stiffness. As in tufted carpet, latex is applied to the back for stability and tuft lock. An additional backing may also be attached. Knitted carpets usually have solid or tweed colors, with level-loop textures.

Flocked: Made by propelling short strands of pile fiber (usually nylon) electrostatically against an adhesive-coated (usually jute), prefabricated backing sheet. As many as 18,000 pile fibers per inch become vertically embedded in the adhesive before a secondary backing is laminated to the fabric and the adhesive cured. The pile fibers can either be dyed prior to flocking or the finished surface can be printed after fabrication.

Needlepunched: First made of polypropylene fibers in solid colors for outdoor use (patios and swimming pools), they are now made for indoor and automotive use as well, using wool, nylon, acrylic, and/or olefin fibers in variegated colors and designs. They are made by impinging loose layers of random, staple carpet fibers into a solid sheet of polypropylene, from both sides, by means of thousands of barbed needles until the entire mass is compressed to a solid bonded fiber mass of indoor/outdoor carpet.

Fusion bonded: This process produces dense cut pile or level-loop carpet in solid or moresque colors. For cut pile, the face yarn, fed simultaneously from the total width of the supply roll, or "beam," is folded back and forth between two vertically emerging primary backings as they are coated with a viscous vinyl paste that hardens, binding the folded face yarns alternately to the vertical backing sheet on each side. Final operation is a mid-line cutting that separates the vertical "sandwich" into two identical cut pile finished rolls. To make loop pile fusion-bonded carpet, one primary backing and the cutting operation are omitted. Fusion bonding is especially suited to making carpet tiles.

# SELECTION CRITERIA

| FIBER | DURABILITY | SOIL RESISTANCE | RESILIENCE | ABRASION RESISTANCE | CLEANABILITY |
|---|---|---|---|---|---|
| Nylon | Excellent | Good | Good to excellent | Excellent | Very good |
| Polyester | Very good | Fair | Good | Excellent | Very good |
| Polypropylene | Excellent | Fair | Poor | Excellent | Very good |
| Acrylic | Good | Fair | Fair | Good | Very good |
| Wool | Very good | Good to excellent | Excellent | Good | Very good |

Neil Spencer, AIA; North Canton, Ohio

# DEFINITIONS

Carpet tiles: Square (from 18 to 36 in.) modules, dense cut pile or loop, heavy backed. Can be made to cover flat, regular wiring; low-voltage lighting systems ("safelites"); or underfloor utilities.

Carpet wear: As defined by fiber manufacturers refers to percent of face fiber lost over the life of a guarantee.

Commercial: Includes all contract, institutional, transportation; any use where carpet is specified by other than the end user.

Residential: Includes all carpet specified and purchased for residential use by the owner.

Life-cycle costing: Permits comparison of diverse flooring methods by totaling initial cost, installation, and detailed predictable maintenance expenses over the expected life of the carpet.

Traffic: Usage expressed in terms of foot traffics (person) per unit of time or as light, medium, or heavy, to define need for matching carpet construction, which normally increases in density as traffic increases. See recommendations below.

Pile height: Height of loop or tuft from the surface of the backing to the top of the pile, measured in fractions, or decimals, of an inch.

Pile weight (face weight): total weight of pile yarns in the carpet (measured in oz/sq yd, excluding backing).

Pile density: D = 36 times the finished pile weight, in oz/yd, divided by the average pile height.

$$\text{Weight density (WD)} = \frac{(\text{Face weight})^2 \times 36}{\text{Pile height}}$$

Pitch (in woven carpet): The number of yarn ends in a 27 in. finished width of carpet.

Gauge: In tufted carpet, the number of needles per inch across the width of the finished carpet.

Stitches: Number of rows of yarn ends per inch, finished carpet. Tufts per sq in.: Calculation made by multiplying pitch x wires for woven carpet, or gauge x stitches per in. for tufted.

Denier: Weight in grams of 9000 meters (9750 yd) of a single extruded filament of nylon. Based on the standard weight of 450 meters of silk weighing 5 centigrams.

Filament: Continuous strand of extruded synthetic fiber, combined into a "singles" yarn by simply twisting, without the need for spinning.

Ply: Refers to the number of strands of "singles" yarn twisted together for color or texture reasons to create a two-ply or three-ply yarn system.

Point: A single tuft of carpet pile.

BCF: Bulked continuous filament.

Cut pile pattern: Plush or saxony type carpet with woven, tufted, or printed design or pattern.

Level loop: Carpet made from uncut tufts in looped form and having all tufts the same pile height.

Cut pile velvet: Solid color, tweed, or heather blend yarns which give smooth velvety or velour texture.

Cut and loop: Carpet with areas of both cut pile and loop pile, most often with the cut pile being higher than the loop.

Frieze: Cut pile carpet made from highly twisted yarns that are heat set to give a curled random configuration to the pile yarns.

Primary backing: The matrix used in making tufted carpet, consisting of woven or nonwoven fabric, usually jute or polypropylene, into which pile yarn tufts are stitched.

Secondary backing: The woven or nonwoven material adhered to the underside of a carpet during construction to provide additional tuft bind for tufted carpet and dimensional stability and body. Usually jute, or polypropylene, latex foam, or vinyl.

Neil Spencer, AIA; North Canton, Ohio

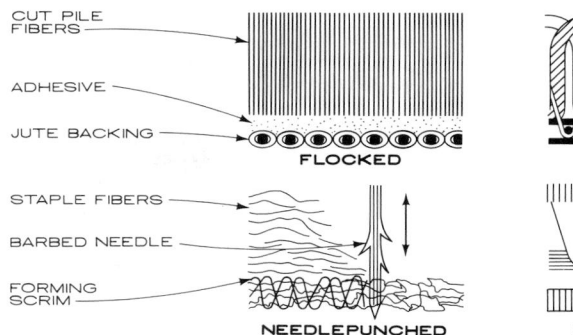

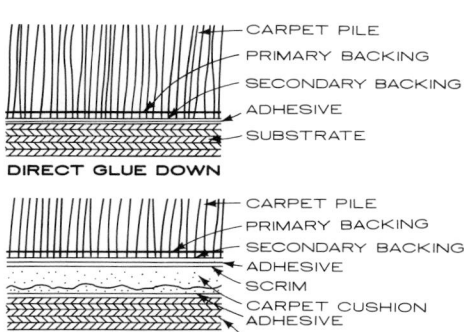

## CONSTRUCTION MODES

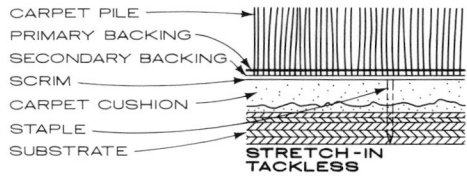

## INSTALLATION (THREE TYPES)

1. Stretch-in (tackless). Over separate cushion. Best condition for maximum carpet wear and most effective cleaning.
2. Direct glue down. For large surface areas which make power-stretching and tackless installations prohibitive. Adhesive must be tailored to match carpet backing and substrate, as recommended by carpet manufacturer.
3. Double glue down. Developed to counter early fiber failure, occurring in direct glue-down carpets in heavy traffic areas, due to lower than normal resilience level of man-made fibers. Provides ease of large area coverage plus benefits of separate pad.

## INSTALLATION

### CARPET CUSHION OR UNDERLAYMENT

Four reasons for considering separate carpet cushion in wall-to-wall installations are:

1. Adds as much as 50% to the life of the carpet.
2. Absorbs as much as 90% of the traffic noise.
3. Can reduce installation costs by eliminating need for repairs to less than perfect substrate.
4. Improves thermal environment by insulation, which varies depending on material.

Four major categories of carpet cushion are:

1. Felt padding
2. Sponge rubber
3. Urethane foam
4. Foam rubber

### TRAFFIC CLASSIFICATION

| CARPETED AREAS | TRAFFIC RATING | | |
|---|---|---|---|
| | LIGHT | MEDIUM | HEAVY |
| Educational | | | |
| Schools and colleges | | | |
| Administration | | • | • |
| Classroom | | | • |
| Dormitory | | | • |
| Corridor | | | • |
| Libraries | | • | |
| Museums and art galleries | | | |
| Display room | | | • |
| Lobby | | | • |
| Medical | | | |
| Health care | | | |
| Executive | • | • | |
| Patient's room | | | • |
| Lounge | | | • |
| Nurses' station | | | • |
| Corridor | | | • |
| Lobby | | | • |
| Commercial | | | |
| Retail establishments | | | |
| Aisle | | | • |
| Sales counter | | | • |
| Smaller boutiques, etc. | | | • |

### TRAFFIC CLASSIFICATION (CONTINUED)

| CARPETED AREAS | TRAFFIC RATING | | |
|---|---|---|---|
| | LIGHT | MEDIUM | HEAVY |
| Office buildings | | | |
| Executive | | • | |
| Clerical | | | • |
| Corridor | | | • |
| Cafeteria | | | • |
| Supermarkets | | | • |
| Food services | | | • |
| Recreational | | | |
| Recreation areas | | | • |
| Club house | | | • |
| Locker room | | | • |
| Convention centers | | | |
| Auditorium | | | • |
| Corridor and lobby | | | • |
| Religious | | | |
| Churches/temples | | | |
| Worship | • | • | |
| Meeting room | | | • |
| Lobby | | | • |

NOTE: If rolling traffic is a factor, carpet may be of maximum density for minimum resistance to rollers. Select only level loop or dense low cut pile for safety.

## MAINTENANCE PROGRAMMING

The following maintenance-related factors should be considered in the selection of carpet:

Color: Carpets in the mid-value range show less soil than very dark or very light colors. Consider the typical regional soil color. Specify patterned or multicolored carpets for heavy traffic areas in hotels, hospitals, theaters, and restaurants.

Traffic: The heavier the traffic, the heavier the density of carpet construction.

Topical treatment: Note that the soil-hiding qualities of advanced generation fibers do not reduce the need for regular maintenance. They do make soil removal easier, but by disguising the presence of dirt, make it easier for the dirt that remains hidden to contribute to earlier fiber failure unless regularly removed.

Placement: The location of carpeted areas within a building affects the maintenance expense. Walk-off carpet areas can contribute effectively to reducing tracked-in soil near entrances.

## COATINGS

Coatings, thin surface facings, protect components from harmful exposure. Selection of appropriate coatings is dictated by conditions under which the coating must perform: exposure to sun, rain, wind, temperature extremes, salt spray, pollution, and chemicals. Another consideration is the rate at which the coated matter deteriorates if the coating fails. Coatings consist of the surface prepared to receive the coating; the prime coat, or undercoat, when needed; and the finish coating, or topcoat. Each must be compatible from layer to layer. Incompatibilities between layers reduce adhesion and accelerate deterioration.

### DESIGN CONSIDERATIONS

1. Flow: ease with which a coating can be applied.
2. Leveling: ability of a coating to smooth out after application.
3. Film thickness: amount of protection a coating provides.
4. Drying time: set-to-touch, or surface drying, when the surface resists surface contaminants. Through-dry, when drying is complete through all layers and may be recoated.
5. Permeability: moisture migration through the coating.
6. Wetting: a coating's degree of penetration to a lower level. The lower a coating's wetting ability, the more surface preparation required for adequate adhesion.
7. Adhesion: attachment between layers.
8. Flexibility: accommodation to temperature and moisture changes in the uncoated base.
9. Abrasion and impact resistance; stain resistance; and cleaning.

### TYPES

Coatings, classified by composition and appearance,are liquid vehicles (alone when clear, or with pigments when opaque), consisting of a nonvolatile part (binder) and a volatile part (solvent). Pigments and binders are coating solids. Binders form the coating film. Solvents dilute the binder to facilitate application.

Solvent-based coatings contain binders in organic solvents. Water-based coatings contain binders that are soluble or dispersed in water. Clear coatings usually contain the vehicle only. They are used to preserve the base material's appearance. Semi-transparent coatings, with limited pigment in a vehicle, modify but do not change completely a base material's appearance, as in wood stains. Opaque coatings with sufficient pigment to obscure the base material's surface are used when the coating's color or texture is preferable to the base material's appearance.

Paint finishes are available in a range of gloss levels—flat, eggshell, semi-gloss, and gloss. Gloss level is determined by the pigment in the paint. More pigment provides a flatter, rougher finish. Less pigment increases gloss. Following are standard gloss ranges developed by the Consumerism Subcommittee of the NPCA Scientific Committee:

#### TEST METHOD

| NAME | (ASTM D-523) | GLOSS RANGE |
|---|---|---|
| Flat | 85° meter | Below 15 |
| Eggshell | 60° meter | 5 to 20 |
| Satin | 60° meter | 15 to 35 |
| Semi-Gloss | 60° meter | 30 to 65 |
| Gloss | 60° meter | Over 65 |

### PIGMENTS

Pigments add color to the coating film. Depending on type and concentration, they also may increase a coating's durability and protectiveness by screening out ultraviolet radiation, controlling transmission of moisture and gases, and inhibiting corrosion.

### BINDERS

Binders are fundamental in film-forming coatings. They bond to the base material and incorporate special ingredients such as driers to speed up curing; plasticizers to add flexibility or moisture resistance; stabilizers to control the effects of heat and solar radiation; and thinners to facilitate application.

## SOLVENT-BASED COATINGS

Solvent-based coatings may be transparent, translucent, or opaque. Binders determine clearness or opaqueness. Many binders are available in both formulations.

Binders used for clear coatings include drying oils combined with a resin, drier, and solvent. Clear coatings usually are referred to as varnishes. Clear finishes over wood exposed at length to sunlight generally will not last more than two years.

Phenolic resins have good water and weather resistance. Spar varnish with phenolic resin and tung oil is durable for exterior exposures, including marine environment, but it is a relatively dark color, and it tends to darken with age.

Shellac resin or other resins or gums dissolved in a volatile solvent are referred to as spirit varnish, a sealer for porous surfaces.

Cellulose derivations in volatile spirits are lacquers. They have limited use in building construction, but they are used as furniture finishes.

Silicon resin in a solvent solution of mineral spirits containing about five percent silicone by weight can be used as a clear coating to seal masonry and concrete walls. Life expectancy generally is five to ten years. Silicone is not applicable in all situations.

Urethane, one-component, moisture-cure, solvent-based formulations, is used as a clear floor coating when superior wear resistance is required. Some formulations yellow and chalk with age under exterior exposure.

Stains are pigmented clear coatings used over wood.

Pigmented stains are recommended for exterior exposure. Dyes are not sufficiently light-fast and allow ultraviolet radiation to pass through, degrading the wood.

## OPAQUE, SOLVENT-BASED COATINGS

Opaque coatings provide the greatest property choices. Alkyds are the principal binders used in solvent-based opaque, or pigmented, coatings. They are derived from polyhydric alcohols and polybasic acids, and they are available in water dispersion as well as solvent-based.

Alkyd-oil coatings can be flat, semigloss, gloss, and clear with various properties: fast drying, hardness, flexible, durable, chalk resistant, and gloss and color retentive.

Alkyds are not resistant to strong alkali, and they are not compatible with previous coatings containing zinc or lead. Since an impermeable layer over ferrous metals is desirable, alkyd-zinc formulations are used as primers. Alkyds can be modified with other binders such as phenolics for improved resistance to water and alkali salts; vinyl-chloride acetate to improve gloss and resistance to chalking; and silicone for good color and gloss retention.

Alkyds also are used in shop-applied baked-on coatings.

Chlorinated rubber is resistant to microorganism attacks, to alkali, and to acids. It is impervious to water and water vapor and adheres to wood and concrete surfaces.

Chlorosulfonated polyethylene is used in severe corrosive conditions. It is resistant to halogens such as chlorine and bromine, and to action of hot water, oxygen, ozone, and ultraviolet radiation. It is available clear or pigmented.

Epoxy-ester is an epoxy resin reacted with drying oil. It has similar properties to alkyd resins and phenolic varnishes, except that its gloss retention is poorer and its resistance to chemical fumes and marine environment is better. Usually it can be applied over previous coatings without lifting or blistering.

Epoxy, specifically the polyamide-cured type, has excellent resistance to corrosion and chemicals such as solvents, oils, acids, and alkalies. It resists abrasion, strong detergents, and the frequent scrubbing necessary in hospitals, dairies, and chemical plants. Epoxy has excellent adhesion to concrete, wood, and metal substrates; 100% solid types will adhere and cure when applied underwater. Bitumen-epoxy, both coal tar and asphalt, is available. It generally is used for heavy-duty immersion service such as buried structural steel, underground piping, and oil storage tanks.

Oil, or oleoresinous coatings, contain pigments in drying oil, varnish, or an oleoresinous vehicle. Oil degrades by surface erosion under sunlight and water. It is permeable to water vapor and minimizes blistering over porous surfaces such as wood. It should not be used in corrosive, especially alkaline, environments. Oil is used frequently as a primer because it wets the surface and adheres well to steel.

Phenolic coatings, polymerized with formaldehyde reactant through polyamide catalysts, are used where resistance to acids, alkalies, and solvents is required. Phenolic coatings withstand continuous immersion in hot distilled water.

Polyester is available in a wide range of durability and flexibility. It also is available modified with amine and silicone. It is used more frequently in glass fiber reinforced structural plastics than as a coating.

Silicone is used mainly in heat resistant coatings where surface temperatures reach up to 1200°F. It also is used with alkyds, acrylics, polyesters, epoxies, and urethanes to improve their weathering and color retention properties. Also see clear coatings.

Vinyl is polyvinyl chloride copolymerized with polyvinyl acetate. Its adherence is poor, and special primers must be used. Vinyl-mastics, available for high-build coatings, tend to be porous. Polyvinyl chloride commonly is used in water-based coatings. Vinyls have excellent durability and resistance to acids, alkalies, salt water, oils, and fats.

## WATER-BASED COATINGS

Water-based coatings first were developed as interior coatings for plaster and gypsum board surfaces, and are commonly, but incorrectly, known as latex paints. The term "latex" applies only to styrene, or styrene butadiene, the binder first used. 'Latex" generally is used only as interior coating or as primer for porous masonry surfaces. On the exterior it oxidizes, leading to yellowing and brittleness.

Other binders include acrylic, or acrylic ester resin, which is best suited for exterior exposure. Acrylic is available pigmented and clear. The clear acrylic based on methyl methacrylate has been found to offer the best protection for concrete against weathering.

Vinyl, or polyvinyl acetate, is available as homopolymer for interior application and copolymer for exterior use.

All water-based opaque coatings have high permeability to water vapor, making them suitable for use over moist porous surfaces such as concrete, masonry, or wood. They should not be used directly over chalking or previous coatings.

Cement is a water-soluble rather than a water-dispersed coating, composed of portland cement, some hydrated lime, and silica aggregate. They are mixed on-site with water for application and require moist curing like any other cement-based product that resists alkali and moisture and may be pigmented, but color retention is poor.

## SPECIAL PURPOSE COATINGS

Fire-retardant insulating, or intumescent, coatings are formulated to bubble and swell on heating to form an insulating cover over the base material. The degree of protection afforded depends on the film thickness and the nature of the substrate. A heat barrier is provided for incombustible surfaces. On combustible base materials, the coating provides an additional, more fire resistant surface layer. It should not be applied over previous coatings.

Reflective coatings will absorb the ultraviolet band of solar radiation and reflect it as visible light. The life expectancy of reflective coatings is about one year when subjected to sunlight.

Bituminous coatings are water emulsions or solvent cutbacks of coal tar pitch or asphalt. They are used as low-cost coatings under corrosive and high humidity conditions, such as for buried structural steel, piping, and below-grade concrete.

## PRIMERS

Primers generally are used to improve adhesion of the finish coating to a substrate. Primers also may be used to impart other desirable properties to a coating system, such as resistance to corrosion in the substrate, while the finish coating provides resistance to impact and abrasion. Primers are critical for the proper performance of a coating, especially for exterior exposure, where the substrate and the coating may be subject to heat, to chemicals, and to changes in, or high levels of, humidity. The condition of any substrate is an important consideration with any type of coating.

### PRIMERS FOR WOOD BASES

Wood base material presents the following problems: it may exhibit different degrees of absorption, and it may contain water soluble dyes, such as in redwood and cedar, which may be released by moisture penetrating the substrate.

Preparation of wood base material should include the following: the wood must be dry before the coating is applied and be sanded smooth; knots and resin streaks should be sealed. Redwood and cedar must be primed with an oil primer to keep soluble dyes within them from bleeding through an opaque coating.

Primers for wood should seal the surface against moisture penetration and have controlled penetration to obtain good adhesion. Flexibility and adhesion should be sufficient to resist movement (especially across the grain) caused by variations in temperature, and the internal moisture content of the wood.

Oil-based primers are used for uncoated wooden surfaces such as vertical siding, smooth surface shingles, and trim. They provide good penetration, adhesion, and flexibility. Alkyd-oil primers are used for rough siding and shakes. The thin-bodied exterior coating is self-priming, and it also can be used as a top coat. Drying oil and/or varnish can be used as a filler for open grain wood to minimize absorption of the top coat. It can be used over stain and a shellac-type of wash coat. Shellac is used as a sealer for surface knots to prevent resin bleeding.

Timothy B. McDonald; Washington, D.C.

## PRIMERS FOR CEMENT BASES

Concrete, masonry, stucco and other base materials which incorporate portland cement tend to be alkaline, especially when fresh, and they are relatively porous. Coatings used on such surfaces should be alkali-resistant and have low water sensitivity as the surfaces also may be damp.

For surface preparation, surfaces should be damp for cement-water coatings; surfaces can be damp when water-based coatings, such as acrylic, are applied, but they must be dry for application of solvent-based coatings, such as alkyd. Smooth-trowelled surfaces should be acid etched for better coating adhesion.

Salts contained in the base material also can be dissolved after the coating is applied.

Curing agents, binder breakers, and antifreeze compounds can remain on the surface or in a cement base material that impairs a coating's adhesion.

Generally, coatings for alkaline surfaces should be alkali resistant and thus self-priming. Primers are required for coatings that are not resistant to alkali when there is moisture in the base material or if there is a possibility moisture will penetrate into a dry base material.

Concrete and masonry primers usually are water-based acrylic or polyvinyl acetate, which also can be used as a top coat. Chlorinated rubber is used as a primer for high humidity or wet conditions, and also can be used as a top coat. For corrosive conditions, vinyl resin can be used as a primer and as a top coat.

Plaster should be allowed to age at least 30 days if an oil-based coating is to be applied. Water-based coatings can be applied sooner. Most conditions applicable to concrete also apply to plaster.

Gypsum board is porous. Only nonpenetrating primers or sealers should be used. Oil-based primers or coatings such as alkyd, penetrate and tend to raise the nap of the facing. Water-based primers or coatings generally are recommended.

## PRIMERS FOR METAL BASES

The effects of a metallic base on coatings generally is not a factor; however, metals may have oil, grease, or chemicals remaining on their surfaces. Ferrous metals may have, in addition, rust and mill scale, and they usually require more preparation than other base metals. The degree of surface preparation required and the methods used vary for different primers and top coats from a simple manual wire brushing to remove loose rust and mill scale to extensive chemical treatments, grinding, or blast cleaning.

Primers for ferrous metal bases, which are subject to rapid corrosion in moisture, must include corrosion inhibiting pigments. Red lead is such a reactive primer. It chemically combines with some vehicles to form resistive films particularly suited for protecting surfaces that cannot be cleaned thoroughly of rust. It is used with binders such as oil and alkyd.

Basic lead–silico-chromate has excellent anticorrosive and weather resistant properties. It may be tinted to match some top coats, and the top coats also may contain the same pigment.

Zinc dust provides galvanic protection because the zinc slowly is sacrificed as a cathode in the presence of moisture, while the ferrous surface serves as the anode and remains intact. Zinc dust is used under severe conditions with organic binders such as acrylics, epoxies, alkyds, and chlorinated rubber.

Zinc chromate or zinc yellow has a low sodium content and provides inhibiting chromate ions.

Zinc dust–zinc oxide, usually 80 percent zinc dust, provides excellent rust-inhibiting properties as well as adhesion, elasticity, and abrasion resistance. Primers containing zinc dust–zinc oxide can be applied over moderately cleaned or galvanized surfaces.

Commonly used binders and vehicles for metal primers include:

Oil, which often is added to other vehicles to penetrate rust and to promote adhesion. Linseed oil, often combined with alkyd, is used with red lead. When a surface is poorly prepared, oil and straight red lead are used.

Alkyd is usable with most corrosion inhibiting pigments. It serves as a binder for primers of intermediate durability where meticulous surface preparation is not practical.

Phenolic is used with zinc chromate or basic silicon lead chromate. It provides good protection from excessive dampness or from immersion in water. It can be used with red lead also.

Epoxy has excellent adhesion to carefully prepared surfaces. It can be combined with polyamide resins and zinc dust or lead pigments for high performance primers. Epoxy esters also are used under less demanding conditions.

Chlorinated rubber has excellent resistance to water vapor transmission, acids, alkalies, and various salts.

Vinyl with zinc chromate or iron oxide provides excellent resistance to chemicals.

Silicate with zinc dust offers excellent resistance to weather, chemicals, and salt spray.

Polyesters and acrylics are used mostly with factory-applied coatings.

Nonferrous metals do not have serious corrosion problems. When coated, aluminum and other nonferrous metals (such as tin and copper) generally are pretreated with a wash primer followed by a zinc chromate primer.

## APPLICATION PROPERTIES

| | ALKYD | 2-CAN EPOXY | ACRYLIC LATEX | LINSEED OIL | PHENOLIC | CHLORINATED RUBBER | ALIPHATIC URETHANE | VINYL |
|---|---|---|---|---|---|---|---|---|
| Solvents | Aliphatic or Aromatic | Lacquer | Water | Aliphatic | Aromatic | Aromatic | Lacquer | Lacquer |
| Min. surface preparation* | SP 3 | SP 6 | SP 6 | SP 2 | SP 6 | SP 6 | *** | SP 6 |
| Stability during use | EX | F | EX | EX | EX | EX | F | EX |
| Brushability | G | F | EX | VG | G | F | G | P |
| Method of cure | Oxid. | Chem. | Coal. | Oxid. | Oxid. | Evap. | Chem. | Evap. |
| Speed of cure | | | | | | | | |
| 50°F–90°F** | G | G | EX | F | G | EX | EX | EX |
| 35°F–50°F** | F | NR | NR | P | F | G | G | G |
| Film build per coat | G | VG | F | G | G | G | VG | G |
| Use in primers | G | EX | F | EX | G | G | G | G |
| Use on damp surfaces | P | G | VG | P | P | P | G | G |

## APPEARANCE PROPERTIES

| | ALKYD | 2-CAN EPOXY | ACRYLIC LATEX | LINSEED OIL | PHENOLIC | CHLORINATED RUBBER | ALIPHATIC URETHANE | VINYL |
|---|---|---|---|---|---|---|---|---|
| Use as clear finish (varnish) | VG | F | P | NR | VG | NR | EX | NR |
| Use in ready mixed aluminum paint | G | F | NR | F | EX | F | F | G |
| Pale color | VG | G | EX | G | P | VG | EX | EX |
| Ability to produce high gloss | EX | EX | F | G | EX | VG | EX | F |

## PERFORMANCE PROPERTIES

| | ALKYD | 2-CAN EPOXY | ACRYLIC LATEX | LINSEED OIL | PHENOLIC | CHLORINATED RUBBER | ALIPHATIC URETHANE | VINYL |
|---|---|---|---|---|---|---|---|---|
| Hardness | G | VG | F | P | VG | VG | EX | G |
| Adhesion | G | EX | F | VG | G | VG | VG | F |
| Flexibility | G | G | EX | VG | F | VG | VG | EX |
| Resistance to: | | | | | | | | |
| Abrasion | F | VG | F | P | G | VG | EX | VG |
| Water | G | EX | F | P | EX | EX | VG | EX |
| Strong Solvents | P | EX | F | P | G | P | EX | P |
| Acid | F | VG | F | P | EX | EX | EX | EX |
| Alkali | P | EX | G | P | G | EX | VG | EX |
| Heat—200°F | G | G | F | F | G | NR | G | NR |

## DURABILITY

| | ALKYD | 2-CAN EPOXY | ACRYLIC LATEX | LINSEED OIL | PHENOLIC | CHLORINATED RUBBER | ALIPHATIC URETHANE | VINYL |
|---|---|---|---|---|---|---|---|---|
| Moisture permeability | Mod | Low | High | Mod | Low | Low | Low | Low |
| Normal exposure | VG | VG | VG | G | VG | EX | EX | EX |
| Marine exposure | F | EX | F | F | G | EX | EX | EX |
| Corrosive exposure | F | EX | F | NR | G | VG | EX | EX |
| Color retention | G | P | VG | F | P | G | EX | VG |
| Gloss retention | G | P | EX | P | G | G | EX | VG |
| Chalk resistance | G | P | VG | P | G | G | EX | VG |

*SSPC Surface Preparation Specifications
**Painting should not be done above 90°F or below 34°F
***Usually used in topcoats

**CODES**
EX—Excellent
VG—Very Good
G—Good
F—Fair
P—Poor
NR—Not Recommended

**SOLVENTS**
Aliphatic—Mineral spirits
Aromatic—Xylene, toluene, etc.
Lacquer—Aromatic plus kétone, ester, or ether solvents (See Solvents)

**ABBREVIATIONS**
Oxid.—Oxidative polymerization or oxidation
Chem.—Chemical reaction (two component)
Coal.—Coalescence (latex)
Evap.—Solvent evaporation (lacquer)
Min.—Minimum

Timothy B. McDonald; Washington, D.C.

## TYPICAL COVERINGS AND AVAILABLE SIZES

| DESCRIPTION | WIDTH | LENGTH PER SINGLE ROLL | MINIMUM[1] UNIT SOLD | FLAME SPREAD RATING | ADHESIVE USED[2] | GENERAL WEARABILITY |
|---|---|---|---|---|---|---|
| Burlap<br>Vinyl backed<br>Paper backed | 30″, 36″ | 4 yards | Single roll | Class A-25 | Premixed vinyl adhesive | Durable |
| Canvas<br>Paper backed | 24″, 27″, 48″ | 5 yards | Single roll | Class A-25 | Premixed vinyl adhesive | Durable |
| Cork<br>Paper backed<br>Cloth backed | 30″, 36″ | 4 yards<br>5 yards | Single roll | Class A-25<br>Class B-35 | Nonstaining paste<br>Wheat paste<br>Premixed vinyl | Less durable |
| Fabric<br>(wool, linen, cotton, rayon, jute, etc.)<br>Paper backed<br>Acrylic backed<br>Polyfoam backed | 36″, 54″ | 4 yards<br>Continuous rolls | Single roll | Class A-25, 15 | Premixed vinyl adhesive | Variable |
| Felt<br>Paper backed | 20½″, 24″, 30″, 36″, 54″ | 5 yards | Single roll | Class A-25 | Premixed adhesive | Less durable |
| Grass cloth<br>Paper backed | 30″, 36″ | 4 yards | Single roll | Class A-25 | Wheat paste<br>Cellulose paste | Less durable |
| Paper<br>American | 18″<br>20½″<br>27″ | 8 yards<br>7 yards<br>5 yards | Single roll | Class A-25<br>Class B-35 | Vinyl adhesive | Less durable |
| European | 18″<br>20½″<br>27″ | 12½ yards<br>11 yards<br>8½ yards | Single roll | Class A-25<br>Class B-35 | Vinyl adhesive | Less durable |
| Flocked | 27″ | 5 yards | Single roll | Class A-25<br>Class B-35 | Vinyl adhesive | Less durable |
| Foil | 27″, 30″ | 5 yards | Single roll | Class A-25 | Vinyl adhesive | Less durable |
| Handprinted sheets | 30″ | 5 yards | Single roll | Class A-25 | Vinyl adhesive | Less durable |
| Murals (variable) | 28″ Variations | Variable | Single panel | Class A-25 | Vinyl adhesive | Less durable |
| Scenic (variable) | 11″, 28″ Variations | 5 yards | Single roll | Class A-25 | Vinyl adhesive | Less durable |
| Silk<br>Paper backed | 30″, 36″ | 5 yards | Single roll | Class A-25 | Cellulose paste | Less durable |
| Textures (sand, etc.)<br>Plastic coated<br>Paper backed | 3′, 4′ | 5 yards | Single roll | Class A-25 | Premixed vinyl nonstaining paste | Durable |
| Vinyl<br>Cloth backed<br>Paper backed<br>Felt polyester Backed | 27″, 54″ | Variable | Variable | Class A-25, 15<br>Class B-35 | Vinyl adhesive | Durable |
| Wood veneer | Up to 24″ flitch | 12′ flitch | Single flitch | Class A-25 | Premixed adhesive | Durable |
| Substrate Indian/Bangladesh jute with a stainless jute backing | 48″ | 5 yards | Single roll | Class A-15 | Nonstaining and nonbleeding type that causes a crystallization and forms a bond | Very durable |

**NOTES**
1. Large quantities are available in multiple rolls or continuous yardages.
2. Consult manufacturers concerning proper adhesive to be used for specific applications.
3. Consult manufacturers to obtain specific test results for a product's typical flame spread rating.

K. Shahid Rab, AIA; Friesen International; Washington, D.C.

## FORMULA FOR COVERAGE

1. Determine number of panels required: total lineal feet of wall divided by width of fabric.
2. Find number of rolls required: number of full (floor to ceiling) panels per roll times number of panels required.
3. Window and door areas may be deducted, but only to the extent that no horizontal seaming occurs.

## TYPICAL ROOM COVERAGE

| ROOM SIZE (FT) | SINGLE ROLLS REQUIRED USING 30 SQ FT/ROLL | | | SINGLE ROLLS FOR CEILING |
|---|---|---|---|---|
| | 8-FT CEILING | 10-FT CEILING | 12-FT CEILING | |
| 9 x 12 | 11 | 14 | 17 | 4 |
| 12 x 14 | 14 | 17 | 21 | 6 |
| 14 x 16 | 16 | 20 | 24 | 8 |
| 16 x 18 | 18 | 22 | 27 | 10 |
| 18 x 20 | 21 | 25 | 30 | 12 |

NOTE: Deduct approximately two thirds of the roll for each door and window opening.

## CLASSIFICATION OF VINYL WALL COVERINGS

Type I, Light Duty (7 oz/sq yd). For use on surfaces not subjected to abrasion or wear.

Type II, Medium Duty (13 oz/sq yd). For general use in areas of average traffic and scuffing.

TYPE III, Heavy Duty (22 oz/sq yd). For use as wainscot or wall protection for areas exposed to damage, or for decorative effect.

## REGULAR FINISH (CLASS I) AND MILDEW RESISTANT FINISH (CLASS II)

Composition may be of three layers, the first being a supporting material of cotton cloth, nonwoven fiberglass, asbestos, or other suitable material. Supporting material for Class II must be mildew resistant. The second layer is a coating compound of specialized vinyl chloride resin which is laminated to the supporting material in a continuous film. This layer is embossed, color printed, or integrally pigmented. A clear coating may be added as a third layer if needed to meet the physical requirements noted in the specification.

## AVAILABLE SIZES OF VINYL WALL COVERINGS

| TYPE | PIECES PER ROLL | WIDTH PER ROLL | YARDAGE PER ROLL (3 YD LENGTH OR MULTIPLES) |
|---|---|---|---|
| Type I | 1 piece | 27″, 54″ | Not less than 72 sq ft plus 1 ft-tolerance |
| Type II | 2 pieces | 54″ | Not less than 15 yd or more than 45 yd |
| Type III | 4 pieces | 54″ | 15 to 30 yd |
| | 6 pieces | | Over 30 yd |

Manufacturers should be able to supply all information concerning specification requirements and test data on the covering's breaking strength, tear strength, hydrostatic resistance, abrasion resistance, flame resistance, char length, colorfastness to light, shrinkage, cold crack, blocking, heat aging, and crocking.

## SUBSTRATE FABRICS

The material that lies between the wallcovering and the wall itself becomes a substrate which performs a wide variety of functions such as reducing noise, increasing flame retardancy, and allowing a smoother application of a wall covering over surfaces that are imperfect. Manufacturers can supply information on types of substrates they carry and the qualities of each.

THE GYPSUM SUBSTRATE consists of fabric impregnated with uncrystallized gypsum. The gypsum is formulated so that when it is applied to a substrate with an adhesive, it will crystallize and form a secure bond with the substrate. The fabric can be used in many cases as a finished surface over rough walls as well as a surface prepared for an additional covering.

## PREFINISHED PANELS

| MATERIAL TYPE | USE | THICKNESS | | | | | | | | | |
|---|---|---|---|---|---|---|---|---|---|---|---|
| | | 1/32 | 1/16 | 1/8 | 3/16 | 1/4 | 5/16 | 3/8 | 1/2 | 5/8 | 3/4 |
| **PLYWOOD** | | | | | | | | | | | |
| Hardwood veneer | Cabinets, interior paneling, protective surfaces | | | | | ● | | ● | ● | | ● |
| Softwood veneer | Interior paneling | | | | | ● | | ● | ● | ● | ● |
| Printed/embossed | Interior paneling | | | | | ● | | ● | ● | ● | ● |
| Textured | Interior paneling, siding | | | | | | | ● | ● | ● | ● |
| Printed vinyl faced | Decorative interior finish | | | | | | | ● | ● | ● | |
| **HARDBOARD** | | | | | | | | | | | |
| Standard | Interior use, cabinet liner | | | ● | ● | ● | ● | ● | ● | | |
| Tempered | Interior and exterior use, underlayment where strength and wear count | | | ● | ● | ● | ● | ● | ● | | |
| Plastic finished | Interior paneling, wearing surfaces | | | ● | | ● | | ● | | ● | |
| Embossed factory finish | Interior decorative paneling | | | | ● | ● | | | | | |
| **FIBERBOARD** | | | | | | | | | | | |
| Vinyl covered | Tackboard—interior decorative paneling | | | | | | | | ● | | |
| Fabric covered | Acoustic, panels, tackboard | | | | | | | | ● | | |
| **LAMINATES** | | | | | | | | | | | |
| Plastic laminates | Cabinets, countertops, protective wall finish | ● | ● | ● | | | | | | | |
| Metal faced | Decorative paneling | ● | ● | ● | | | | | | | |
| **GYPSUM** | | | | | | | | | | | |
| Vinyl covered | Interior walls | | | | | ● | | ● | ● | ● | |
| Fabric covered | Interior walls | | | | | ● | | ● | ● | ● | |

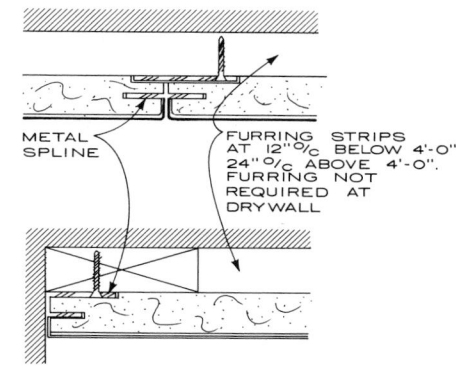

METAL SPLINE

FURRING STRIPS AT 12" O/C BELOW 4'-0" 24" O/C ABOVE 4'-0". FURRING NOT REQUIRED AT DRYWALL

**FABRIC COVERED FIBERBOARD**

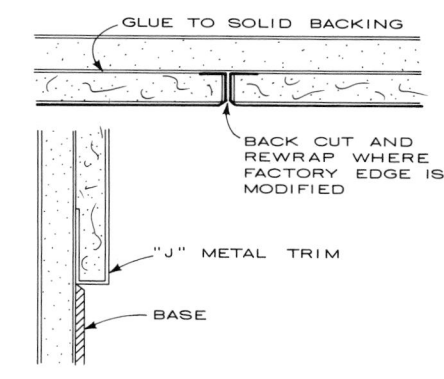

GLUE TO SOLID BACKING

BACK CUT AND REWRAP WHERE FACTORY EDGE IS MODIFIED

"J" METAL TRIM

BASE

**VINYL COVERED FIBERBOARD**

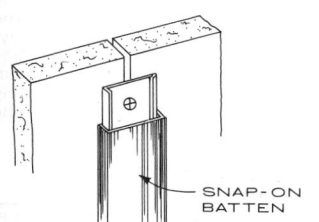

SNAP-ON BATTEN

**VINYL COVERED GYPSUM BOARD**

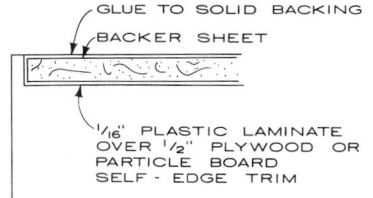

GLUE TO SOLID BACKING

BACKER SHEET

1/16" PLASTIC LAMINATE OVER 1/2" PLYWOOD OR PARTICLE BOARD SELF-EDGE TRIM

**PLASTIC LAMINATE PANELS**

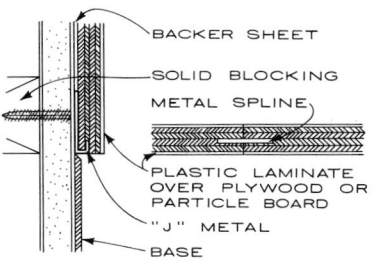

BACKER SHEET

SOLID BLOCKING

METAL SPLINE

PLASTIC LAMINATE OVER PLYWOOD OR PARTICLE BOARD

"J" METAL

BASE

**PLASTIC LAMINATE PANELS**

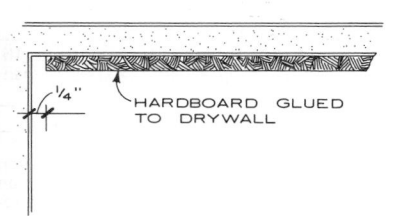

1/4"

HARDBOARD GLUED TO DRYWALL

**TEMPERED HARDBOARD**

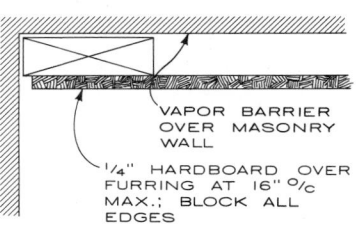

VAPOR BARRIER OVER MASONRY WALL

1/4" HARDBOARD OVER FURRING AT 16" O/C MAX.; BLOCK ALL EDGES

**TEMPERED HARDBOARD**

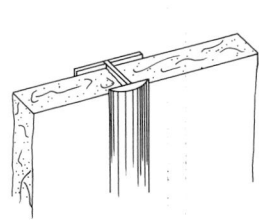

**DIVIDER**

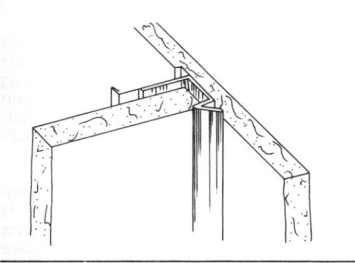

**INSIDE CORNER TRIM**

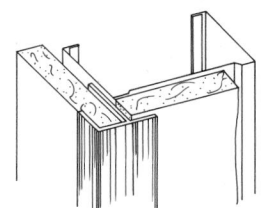

**OUTSIDE CORNER TRIM**

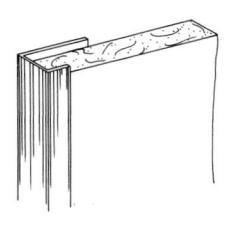

**END CAP**

Broome, Oringdulph, O'Toole, Rudolf & Associates; Portland, Oregon

**WALL COVERING**   9

## WALL TREATMENT

1. USE: Sound absorption.
2. MATERIALS: Fabric-wrapped glass fiber or mineral wool.
3. N.R.C.: .55–.85
4. NOTES: Wall panels may be used individually or grouped to form an entire wall system. Noise reduction coefficient varies with material thickness and acoustical transparency of fabric facing. Maximum panel sizes vary with manufacturer up to 4 x 12 ft.

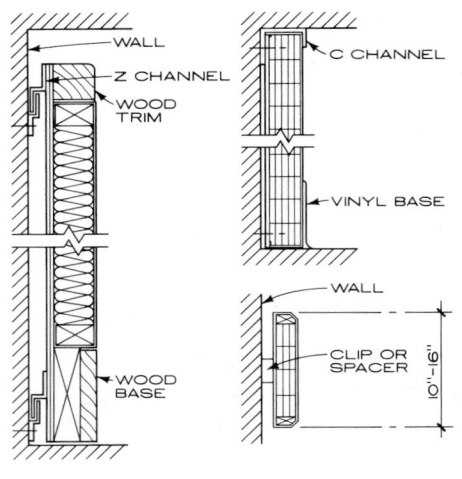

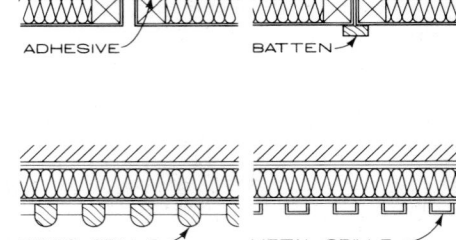

**SECTIONS**

**PLAN SECTIONS**

## WALL TREATMENT

### PLENUM BARRIER

1. USE: Reduce sound transmission through plenum above partitions.
2. MATERIALS: 1/64 in. sheet lead, lead-loaded vinyl, perforated aluminum, or foil-wrapped glass fiber.
3. S.T.C.: 18–41 dB improvement.
4. NOTES: All openings through barrier for pipes, ducts, etc., must be sealed airtight for maximum effectiveness.

### SUSPENDED PANELS

1. USE: Sound absorption.
2. MATERIALS: Vertical suspension–glass fiber blanket wrapped with perforated aluminum foil or fabric stretched over frame. Horizontal suspension–perforated steel or aluminum with glass fiber blanket, or similar to vertical.
3. N.R.C.: .55–.85
4. NOTES: Panels may be suspended from structure or attached directly to ceiling grid. May be arranged in a variety of patterns including linear, square, zigzag vertical, or regular or random spaced horizontal panels.

### ACOUSTICAL MASONRY UNITS

1. USE: Sound absorption
2. MATERIALS: Concrete masonry unit, 4, 6, or 8 in. thick, with metal baffle and/or fibrous filler in slotted areas.
   Structural glazed facing tile, 4, 6, or 8 in. thick; 8 x 8 in. or 8 x 16 in. (nominal) face dimensions, with fibrous filler in cores.
3. N.R.C.: .45–.65

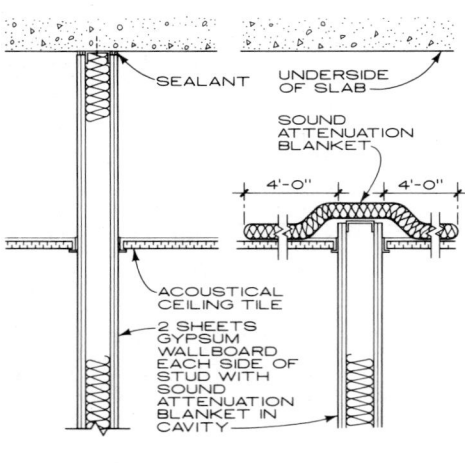

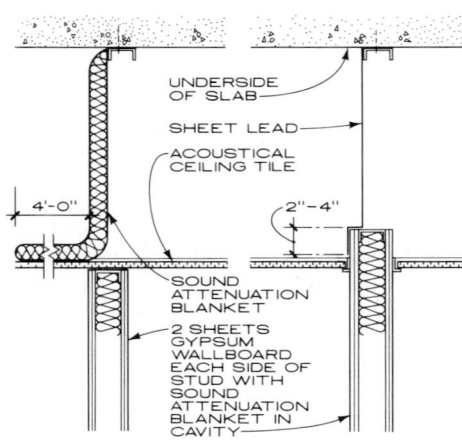

**PLENUM BARRIERS**

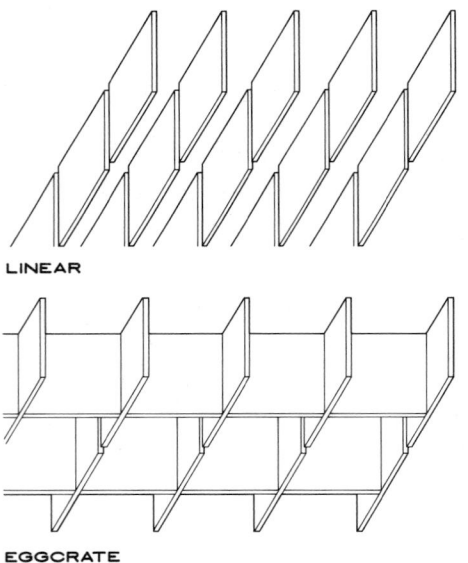

**LINEAR**

**EGGCRATE**

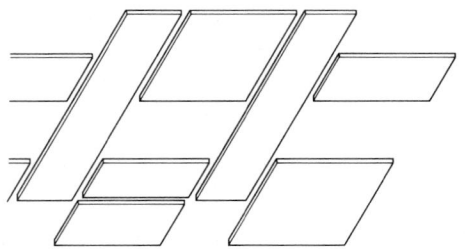

**CLOUD**

**SUSPENDED PANELS**

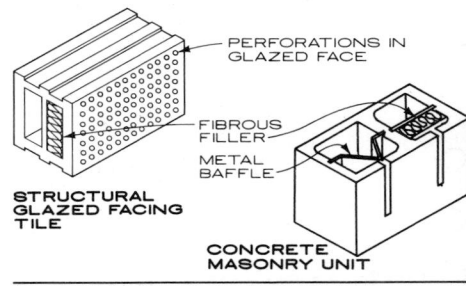

**ACOUSTICAL MASONRY UNITS**

### SPRAY-ON ACOUSTICAL MATERIAL

1. USE: Sound absorption.
2. MATERIALS: Mineral or cellulose fibers spray applied to metal lath or directly to hard surfaces such as concrete, steel, masonry, or gypsum wallboard.
3. N.R.C.: .50–.95
4. NOTES: Application to metal lath provides slightly better sound absorption and permits irregular shapes. Available with a hard surface for wall applications. Available with fire protection rating.

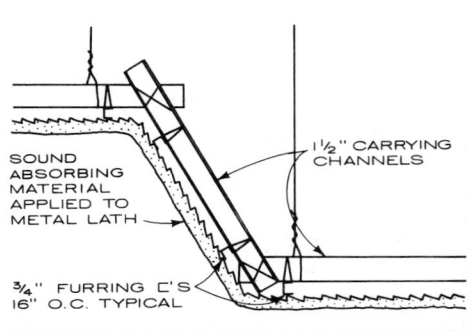

**SPRAY-ON ACOUSTICAL MATERIAL**

Setter, Leach & Lindstrom, Inc.; Minneapolis, Minnesota
Blythe + Nazdin Architects, Ltd.; Bethesda, Maryland

 **WALL COVERING**

# CHAPTER 10

# Specialties

## TACKBOARD TYPES AND SIZES

| TYPE | VARIATIONS | BACKING | THICKNESS | MAXIMUM SIZE WITHOUT JOINTS |
|---|---|---|---|---|
| Cork | Unfaced cork, plain or burlap backed | Unmounted | 1/8″, 1/4″ | 4′ x 130′, 6′ x 90′ |
| | | Particle board | 1/2″ | 4′ x 16′ |
| | | Hardboard | | |
| | Vinyl covered cork | Unmounted | 1/4″ | 4′ x 100′ |
| | | Particle board | 1/2″ | 4′ x 16′ |
| | | Hardboard | | 4 x 12′ fire rated |
| | Vinyl impregnated cork | Unmounted | 1/8″, 1/4″ | 6′ x 90′ |
| | | Hardboard | 1/2″ | 4′ x 12′ |
| Fiber-board | Vinyl covered | | 1/2″ | 4′ x 12′ |
| | Burlap covered | | | 4′ x 8′, 4′ x 14′ spec. |

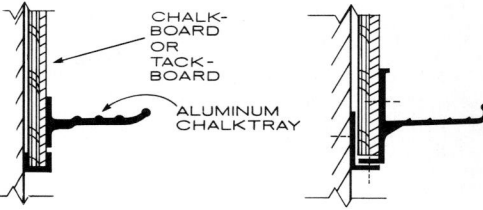

ADDITIONAL VARIETIES
OF TRIM AND CHALKTRAYS
ARE AVAILABLE

## CHALKBOARD TYPES AND SIZES

| TYPE | CORE | THICKNESS | MAXIMUM SIZE WITHOUT JOINTS |
|---|---|---|---|
| Porcelain enamel steel (18-28 gauge)* | None | 1/32″ | 4′ x 12′ |
| | Plywood | 1/4″ - 7/16″ | 4′ x 12′ |
| | Hardboard | 1/4″, 7/16″ | 5′ x 12′, 4′ x 16′ |
| | Fiberboard | 7/16″, 1/2″ | 4′ x 12′ |
| | Particle board | 3/8″ - 1/2″ | 4′ x 16′ |
| | Gypsum board | 3/8″, 1/2″ | 4′ x 12′ |
| | Honeycomb | 3/8″, 7/16″ | 4′ x 16′ |
| Painted-on composition | Hardboard | 1/4″, 1/2″ | 4′ x 16′ |
| | Gypsum board | 1/4″, 1/2″ | 4′ x 12′ |
| Natural slate | | 1/4″ - 3/8″ | 4′ x 6′ |

* Available in either chalkboard or liquid marker board.

CHALKRAILS

**CHALKBOARDS WITH
ALUMINUM FRAMING**

### AVERAGE RECOMMENDED CHALKBOARD MOUNTING HEIGHT
(Chalkrail to Floor)

| | |
|---|---|
| Nursery | 20″ |
| Kindergarten | 24″ |
| 1st–3rd grade | 30″ |
| 4th–6th grade | 32″ |
| Junior high | 36″ |
| Senior high | 36″ |
| Adult | 36″ |

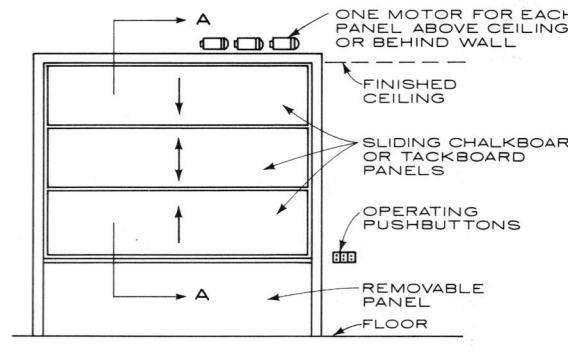

**VERTICAL SLIDING PANELS**
(MANUAL OR MOTOR OPERATED)

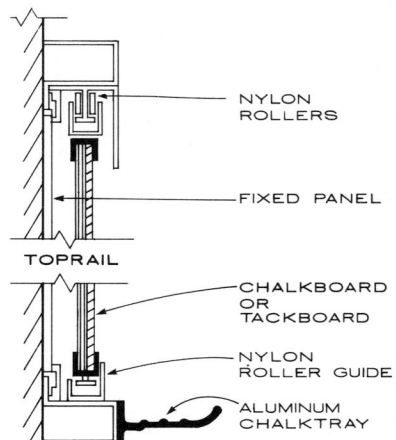

CHALKRAIL     SECTION A

CHALKRAIL     SECTION B

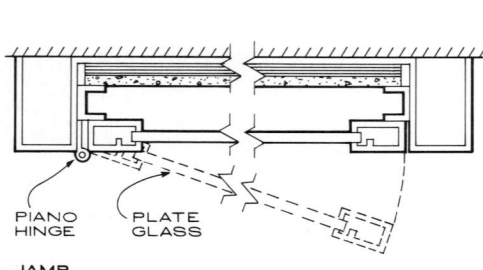

JAMB

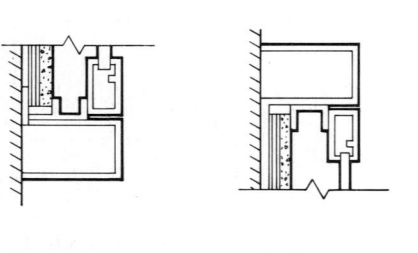

SILL          HEAD

**BULLETIN BOARD**

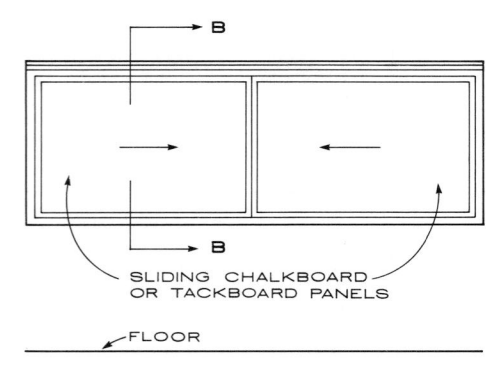

**HORIZONTAL SLIDING PANELS**

**SLIDING CHALKBOARDS AND TACKBOARDS**

## NOTES

1. Compartment types: ceiling hung (marble or metal), overhead braced, wall hung (metal only).
2. Metal finishes: baked-on enamel, porcelain enamel, stainless steel. Phenolic core, plastic laminate, solid polyethylene, tempered glass, and marble panels also are available.
3. A = standard compartment widths: 2 ft. 6 in., 2 ft. 8 in., 2 ft. 10 in., 3 ft. 0 in. (2 ft. 10 in. is used most frequently).
4. B = standard door widths: 1 ft. 8 in., 1 ft. 10 in., 2 ft. 0 in., 2 ft. 2 in., 2 ft. 4 in., 2 ft. 6 in. (2 ft. 0 in. metal doors are standard with marble compartments). Non-standard sizes that sometimes are used: 1 ft. 11 in., 2 ft. 3 in., 2 ft. 5 in.
5. C = standard pilaster widths: 3 in., 4 in., 5 in., 6 in., 8 in., 10 in., 1 ft. 0 in. Nonstandard sizes that sometimes are used: 2 in., 7 in., 1 ft. 2 in.
6. D = standard panel widths: 18 in. to 57 in. in 1 in. increments. All panels are 58 in. high.
7. Wall hung models apply only to metal partitions.
8. Accessories include such items as paper holders, coat hooks, and purse shelves.

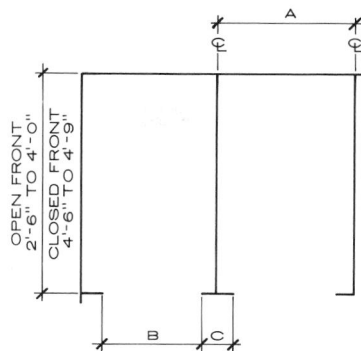

PLAN OF STANDARD W.C. COMPARTMENT
(TYPICAL FOR METAL OR PLASTIC LAMINATE)

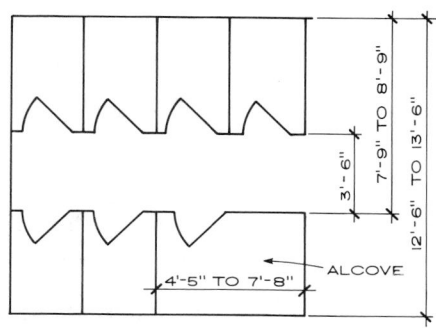

SPACE REQUIREMENTS

---

## GENERAL PLANNING DATA

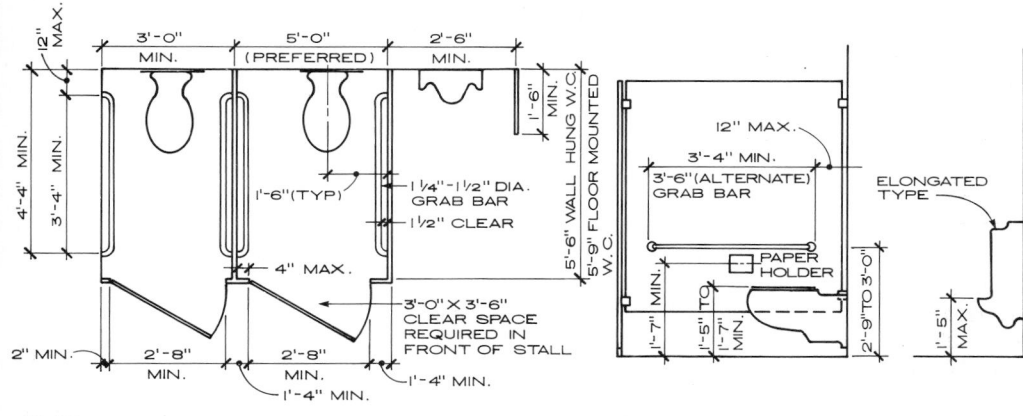

PLAN

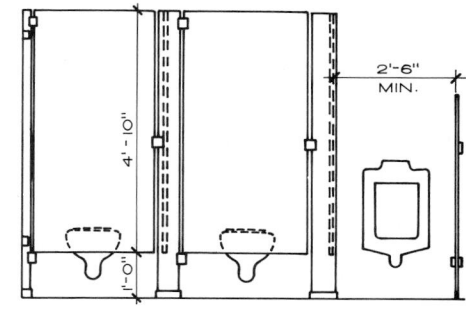

SECTION

SECTION AT URINAL

FRONT ELEVATION

---

## HANDICAPPED TOILET LAYOUT

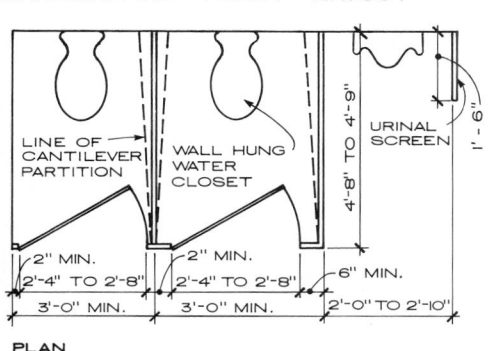

PLAN

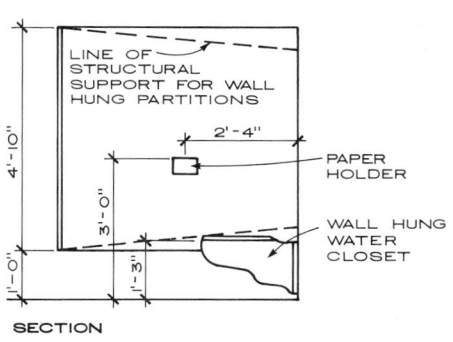

SECTION

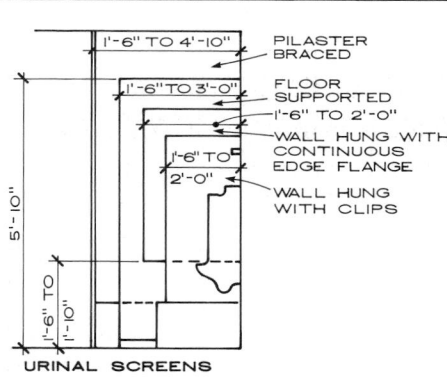

URINAL SCREENS

---

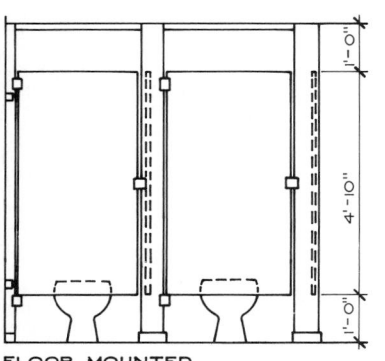

FLOOR MOUNTED

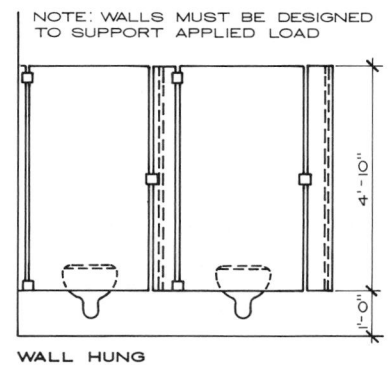

WALL HUNG

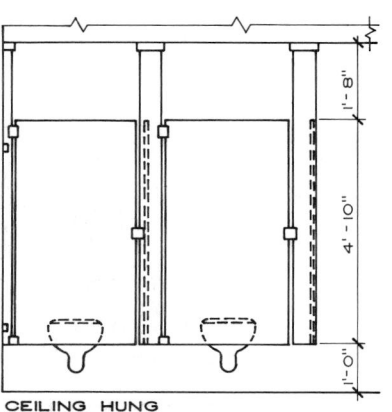

CEILING HUNG

METAL AND PLASTIC LAMINATE TOILET PARTITIONS

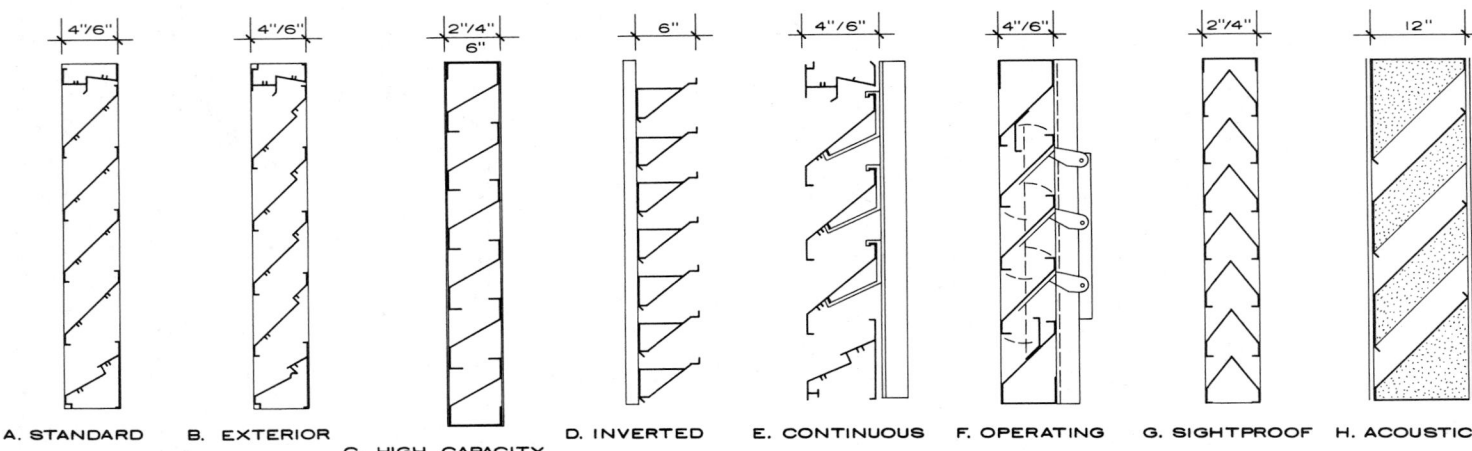

**A. STANDARD  B. EXTERIOR  C. HIGH CAPACITY  D. INVERTED  E. CONTINUOUS  F. OPERATING  G. SIGHTPROOF  H. ACOUSTIC**

## TYPICAL LOUVER AND VENT PROFILES

A. For use in single louver application in small openings or in multiple louver applications where vertical mullion or horizontal joint appearance is desired.

B. Exterior blades provide superior weather protection but reduce free area.
Maximum standard width is 6 ft; minimum width is 1 ft.

C. Used in situations where high velocity and maximum free area are of primary importance.

D. Used primarily as a cooling tower screen where water spray should be contained. They are field assembled and are available in unlimited widths.

E. Used for large openings where continuous horizontal line appearance is desired. Unlimited widths are available; they are field assembled.

F. This permits maximum ventilation capacity when open as well as resistance against weather penetration when closed. Airflow is easily controlled. Recommended maximum blade span is 5 ft; minimum width is 1 ft.

G. This is 100% sightproof from all angles with horizontal blade lines. Maximum recommended width is 7 ft.

H. Used to reduce ambient noise and noise transmission. Blades are backed with mineral fiber. Maximum recommended blade span is 7 ft.

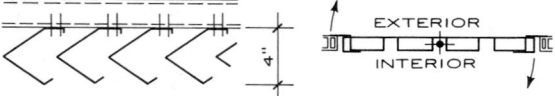
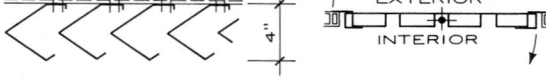

**J. "V" BLADE  K. PIVOTED DOOR LOUVER  L. VERTICAL LINE**

J. Used for soffit, vertical, continuous horizontal, or sightproof louvers. Blades are field assembled to any desired length or width. They must have horizontal supports at 5 ft maximum.

K. Vertically pivoted intake device provides large volumes of air. It may be individually or gang operated. Units are 24 in. wide and maximum height is 8 ft 5 in.

L. Vertical louver matches standard exterior metal building panel profiles. Maximum recommended blade width is 16 ft; additional length is lapped.

M. Vents for use in foundations, chimney flues, or crawl spaces are made from cast or extruded aluminum and are available with anodic, baked enamel, lacquer, or sandblasted finish. They are made to be compatible with standard, modular, speed, or fuel brick sizes in 4, 6, or 8 in. depths and in lengths to 20 ft.

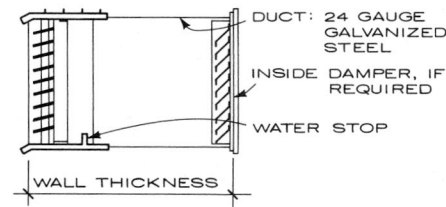

DUCT: 24 GAUGE GALVANIZED STEEL

INSIDE DAMPER, IF REQUIRED

WATER STOP

WALL THICKNESS

**M. BRICK VENT**

### GENERAL NOTES

1. The dimensions shown are the most common; others are available.

2. Horizontal louvers can be of unlimited height. Larger louver depths provide more free area per square foot and better weather penetration resistance than smaller depths.

3. Standard materials are 16 gauge galvanized or cold rolled steel and 14 or 12 gauge extruded aluminum alloy. Other metals can be used for special applications. Translucent fiberglass is also a standard blade material where daylighting is desirable.

4. A welded assembly of louvers is preferred to mechanical assembly. This eliminates blade/frame loosening, wear, and vibration noise, as well as providing a better assembly for finishing.

5. Factory finishing is recommended for maximum control of color and durability. The finish for steel louvers is baked enamel in a variety of colors. Aluminum finishes include mill, clear lacquer, baked enamel, and anodic.

6. Screens may be used for protection from insects, birds, or vandalism. Supplied in frames, typical screening for insects is 16 x 18 mesh aluminum or fiberglass; for birds or vandalism 1/2 in. square mesh 14 or 16 gauge aluminum or 1/4 in. square mesh 16 or 18 gauge aluminum.

7. Other options available with louvers include mullions, blank-off plates or insulated panels, frame extensions, sill pieces, sealant stops, and fusible links.

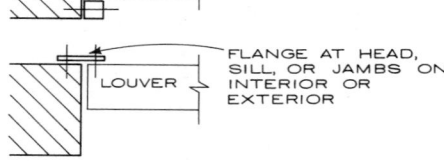

STOPS OR MOLDING HOLD LOUVER IN PLACE

LOUVER

FLANGE AT HEAD, SILL, OR JAMBS ON INTERIOR OR EXTERIOR

LOUVER

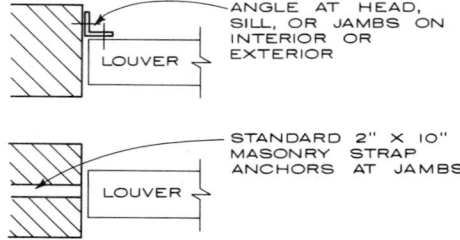

ANGLE AT HEAD, SILL, OR JAMBS ON INTERIOR OR EXTERIOR

LOUVER

STANDARD 2" X 10" MASONRY STRAP ANCHORS AT JAMBS

LOUVER

SCREW OR ANCHOR BOLT AT JAMBS

LOUVER

## METHODS OF INSTALLATION

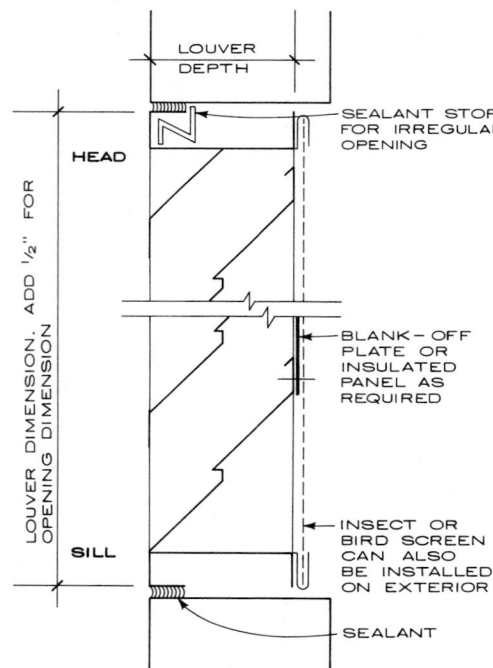

LOUVER DEPTH

HEAD

SEALANT STOP FOR IRREGULAR OPENING

LOUVER DIMENSION, ADD 1/2" FOR OPENING DIMENSION

BLANK-OFF PLATE OR INSULATED PANEL AS REQUIRED

INSECT OR BIRD SCREEN CAN ALSO BE INSTALLED ON EXTERIOR

SILL

SEALANT

## LOUVER ACCESSORIES

Graham Davidson, Architect; Washington, D.C.

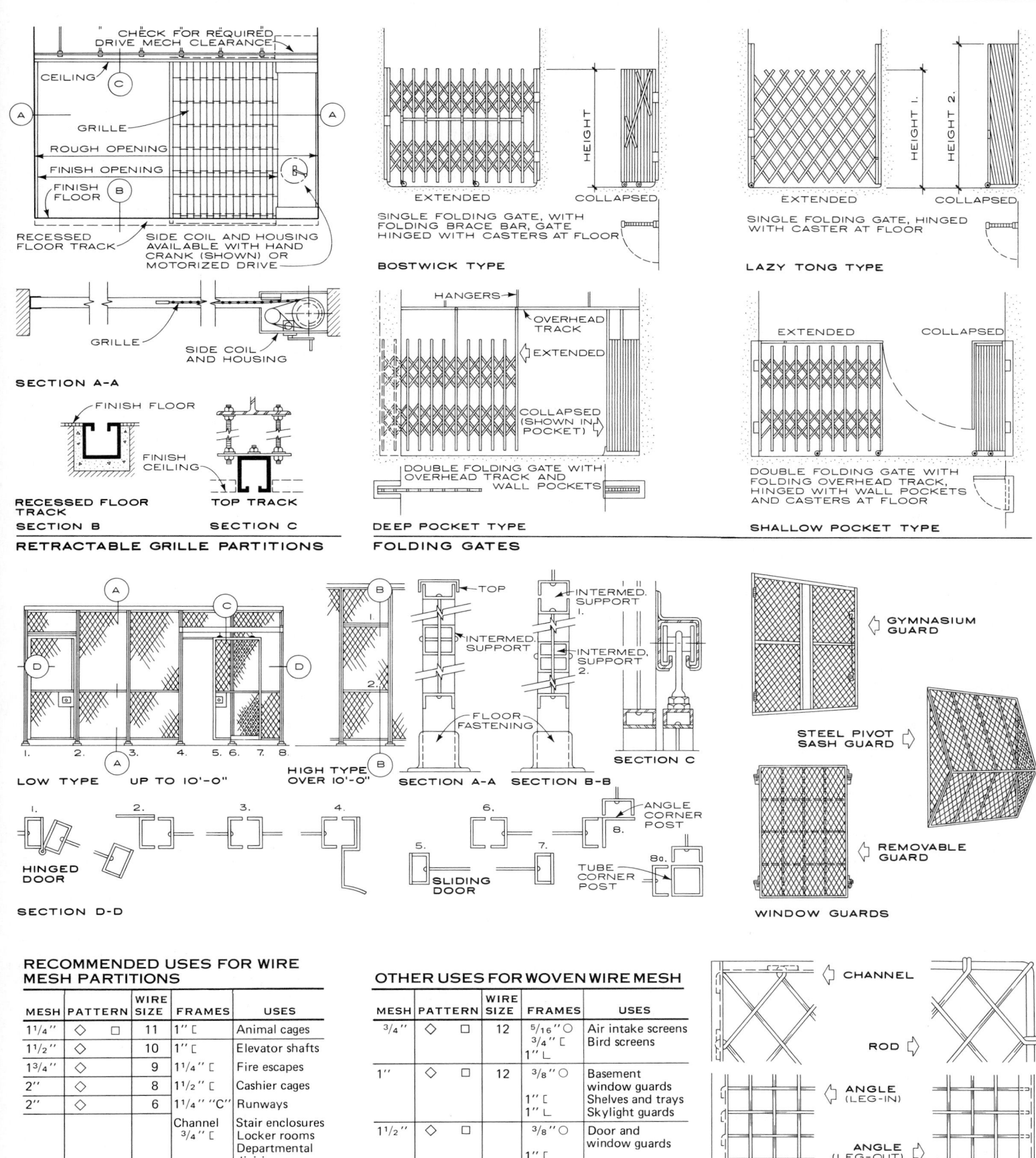

**RETRACTABLE GRILLE PARTITIONS**

**FOLDING GATES**

**WIRE MESH PARTITIONS**

## RECOMMENDED USES FOR WIRE MESH PARTITIONS

| MESH | PATTERN | | WIRE SIZE | FRAMES | USES |
|------|---------|---|-----------|--------|------|
| 1 1/4″ | ◇ | □ | 11 | 1″ ⊏ | Animal cages |
| 1 1/2″ | ◇ | | 10 | 1″ ⊏ | Elevator shafts |
| 1 3/4″ | ◇ | | 9 | 1 1/4″ ⊏ | Fire escapes |
| 2″ | ◇ | | 8 | 1 1/2″ ⊏ | Cashier cages |
| 2″ | ◇ | | 6 | 1 1/4″ "C" | Runways |
| | | | | Channel 3/4″ ⊏ | Stair enclosures Locker rooms Departmental divisions Stock rooms Tool rooms |

## OTHER USES FOR WOVEN WIRE MESH

| MESH | PATTERN | | WIRE SIZE | FRAMES | USES |
|------|---------|---|-----------|--------|------|
| 3/4″ | ◇ | □ | 12 | 5/16″ ○ 3/4″ ⊏ 1″ ∟ | Air intake screens Bird screens |
| 1″ | ◇ | □ | 12 | 3/8″ ○ 1″ ⊏ 1″ ∟ | Basement window guards Shelves and trays Skylight guards |
| 1 1/2″ | ◇ | □ | | 3/8″ ○ 1″ ⊏ | Door and window guards |
| 2 1/4″ | ◇ | □ | 7 | 7/16″ ○ | Wire roof signs |
| 2 1/2″ | ◇ | | 6 | 1 1/2″ ⊏ | Fencing gratings |

**TYPES OF FRAMES AND WOVEN WIRE MESH**

**WIRE MESH PARTITIONS**

Harnish, Morgan & Causey, Architects; Ontario, California

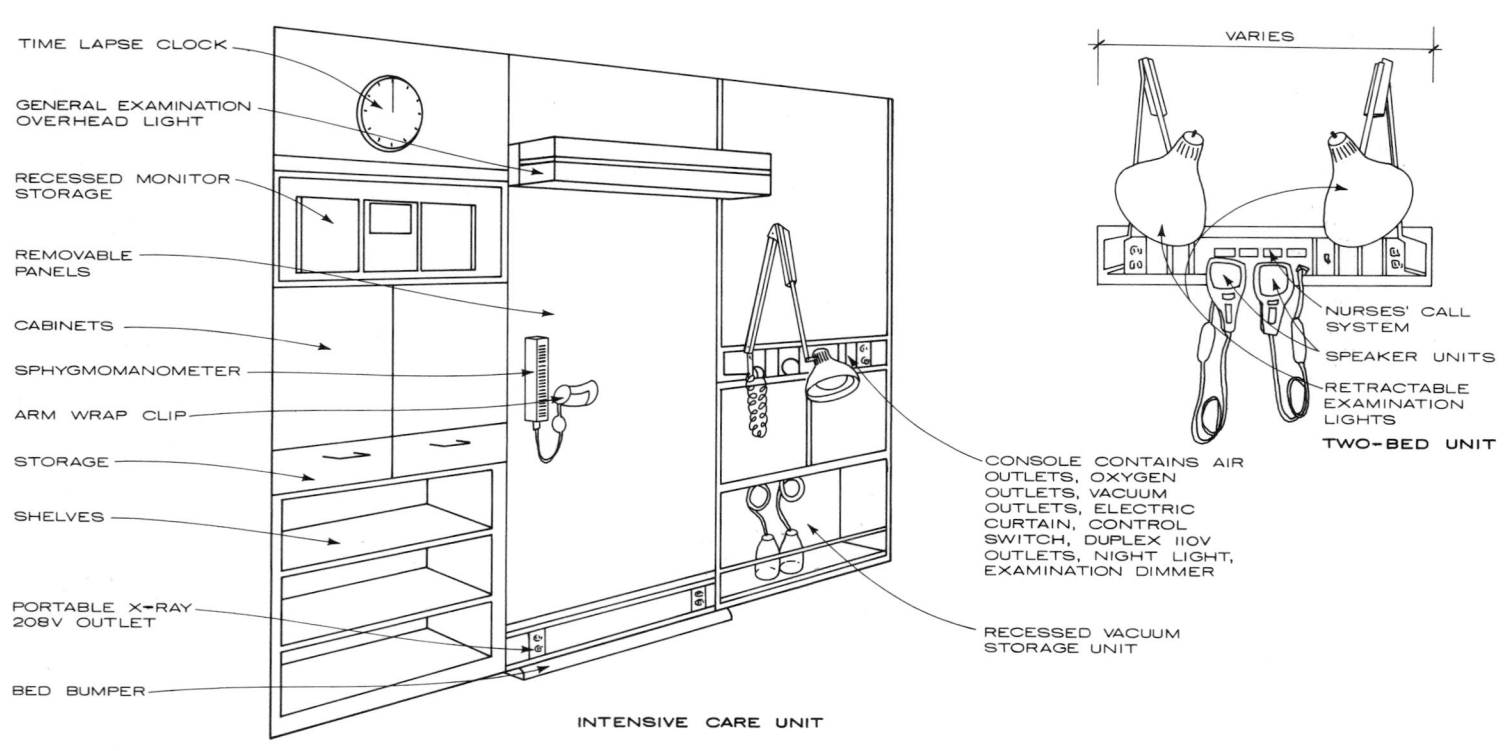

## HOSPITAL SERVICE MODULES

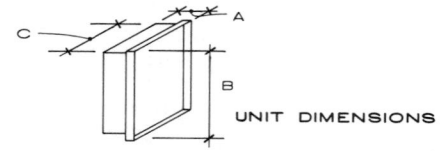

**UNIT DIMENSIONS**

| UNIT | A | B | C |
|---|---|---|---|
| Fire hose cabinet | 10" | 30" | 30" |
| Fire extinguisher | 10" | 30" | 14" |
| Fountain | 10" | 30" | 14" |
| Waste receptacle | 7" | 30" | 14" |
| Louvers | 11" | 30" | 14" |
| Speaker | 3" | 15" | 15" |
| Clock | 3" | 15" | 15" |
| Fire pull | 7" | 14" | 6" |
| Electric outlet | 3" | 30" | 6" |

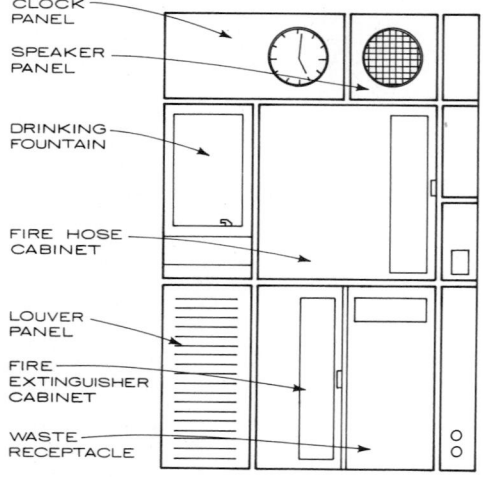

**CORRIDOR SERVICE MODULE**

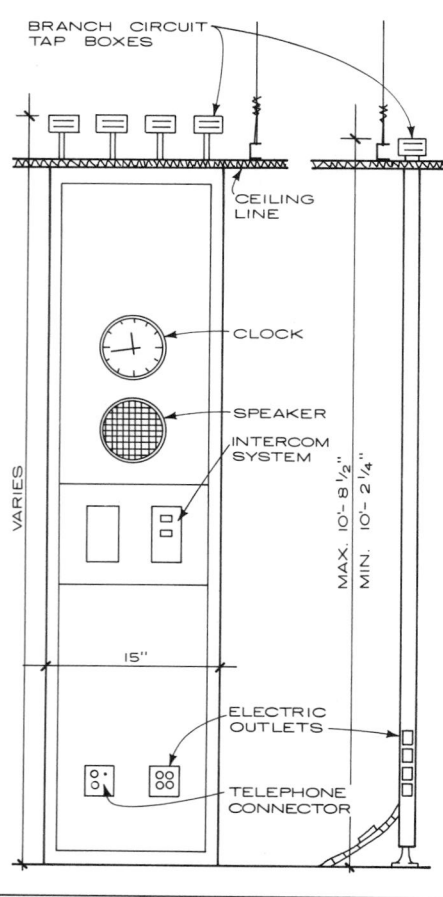

**COMMUNICATION AND POWER COLUMNS**

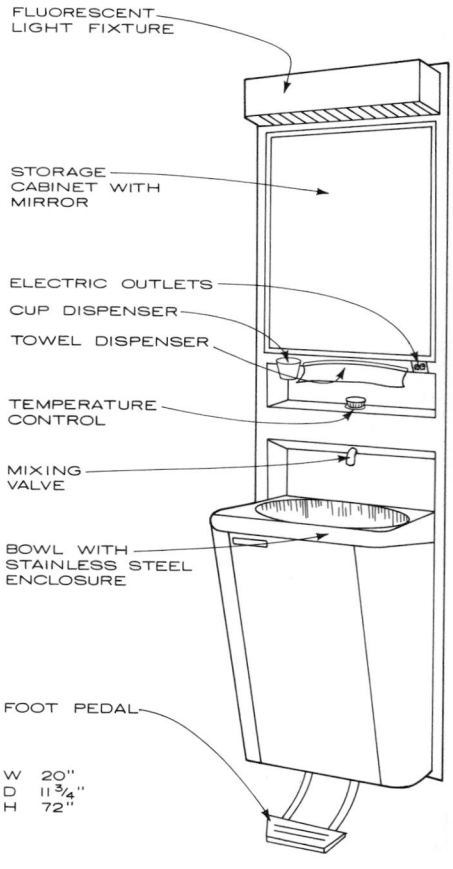

**WASH CENTER**

John Sava; The Architects Collaborative, Inc.; Cambridge, Massachusetts

**SPECIALTY MODULES**

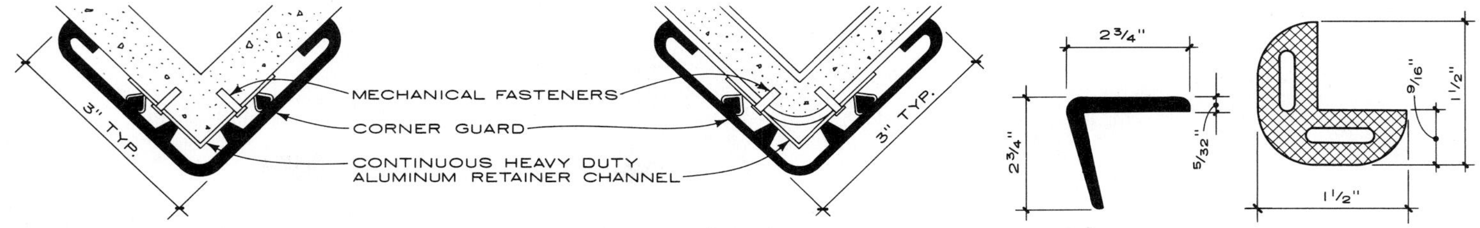

**MECHANICAL FASTENERS**

**CORNER GUARD**

**CONTINUOUS HEAVY DUTY ALUMINUM RETAINER CHANNEL**

3" TYP.

NONADHESIVE — SQUARE CORNER

3" TYP.

NONADHESIVE — ROUND CORNER

2¾"

2¾"

5/32"

9/16"

1½"

1½"

ADHESIVE CORNER GUARDS

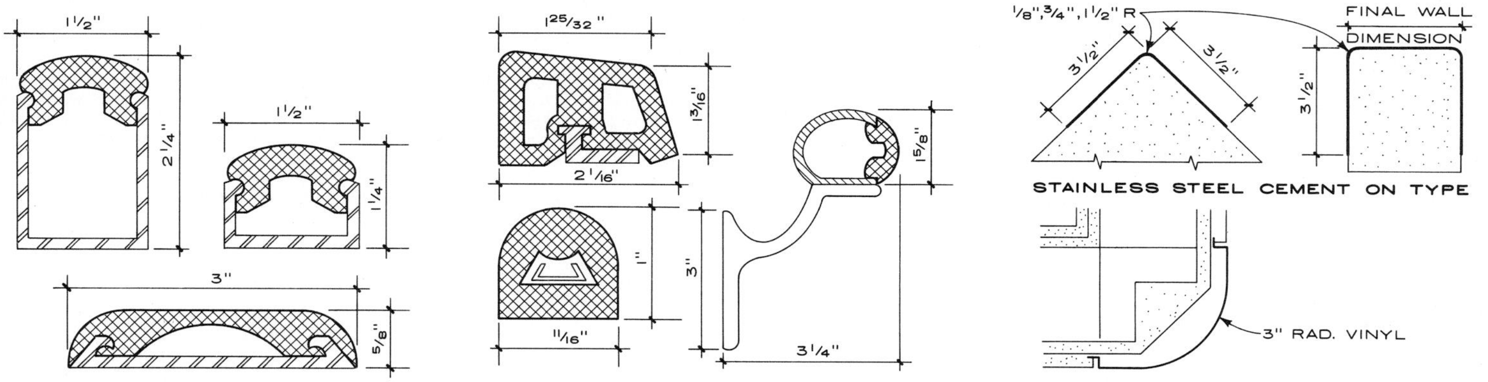

1½"

2¼"

1½"

1¼"

3"

5/8"

WALL GUARDS — VINYL

1²⁵/₃₂"

3/16"

2 1/16"

11/16"

1"

RUBBER

1 5/8"

3"

3¼"

WALL BRACKET

⅛", ¾", 1½" R

3½"

3½"

STAINLESS STEEL

FINAL WALL DIMENSION

3½"

CEMENT ON TYPE

3" RAD. VINYL

ROUNDED

## INTERIOR WALL AND CORNER GUARDS

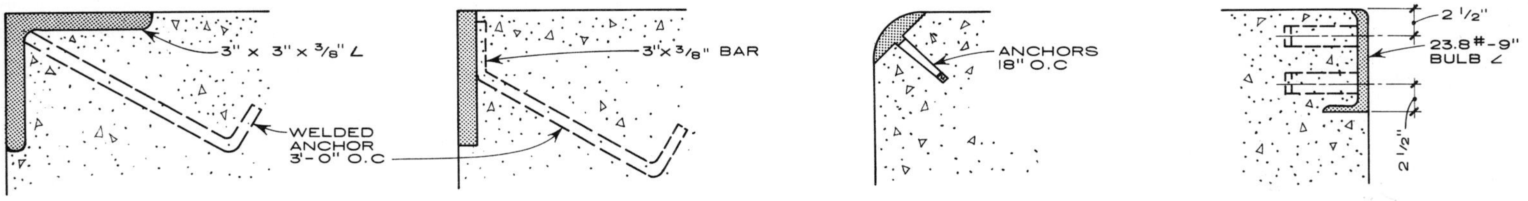

3" × 3" × ⅜" ∠

WELDED ANCHOR 3'-0" O.C.

ANGLE (FOR LIGHT DUTY)

3" × ⅜" BAR

FLAT BAR (LIGHT DUTY)

ANCHORS 18" O.C.

ROLLED BAR (LIGHT DUTY)

2½"

23.8 #-9" BULB ∠

2½"

SHIPBUILDERS BULB ANGLE (FOR HEAVY DUTY)

## CURB GUARDS

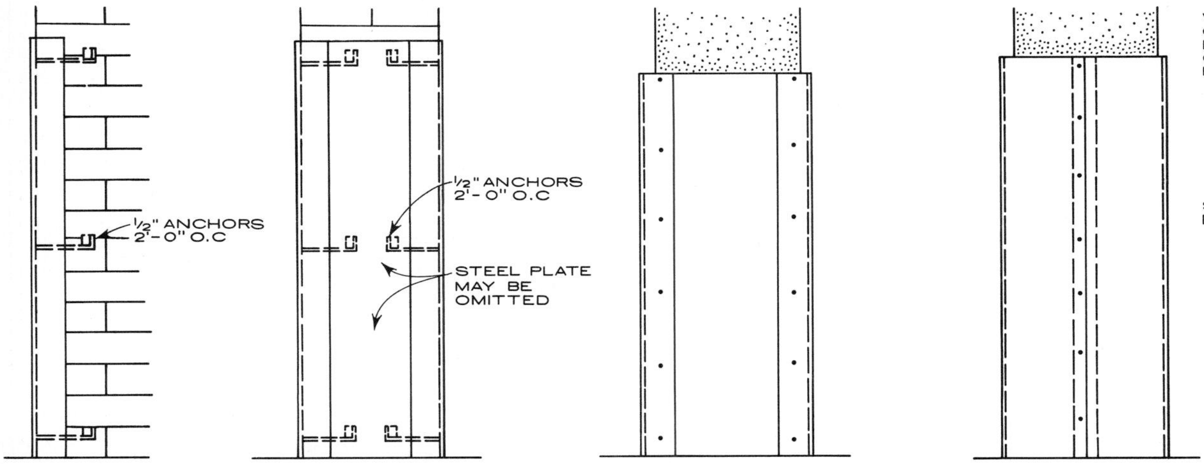

½" ANCHORS 2'-0" O.C.

½" ANCHORS 2'-0" O.C.

STEEL PLATE MAY BE OMITTED

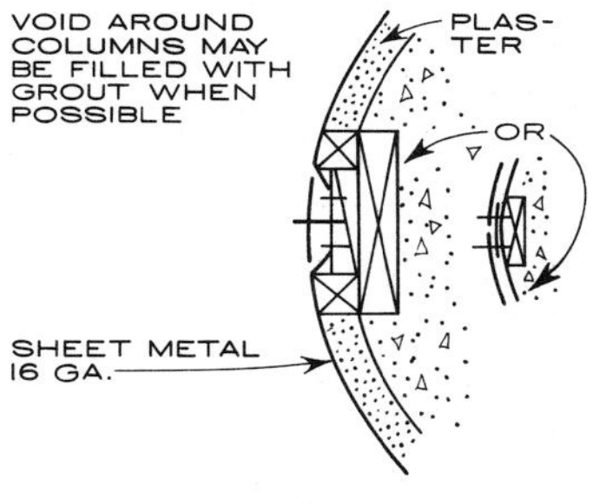

VOID AROUND COLUMNS MAY BE FILLED WITH GROUT WHEN POSSIBLE

PLASTER

OR

SHEET METAL 16 GA.

INTERIOR COL.

COLUMN GUARD COMPONENTS BOLTED TOGETHER ON JOB

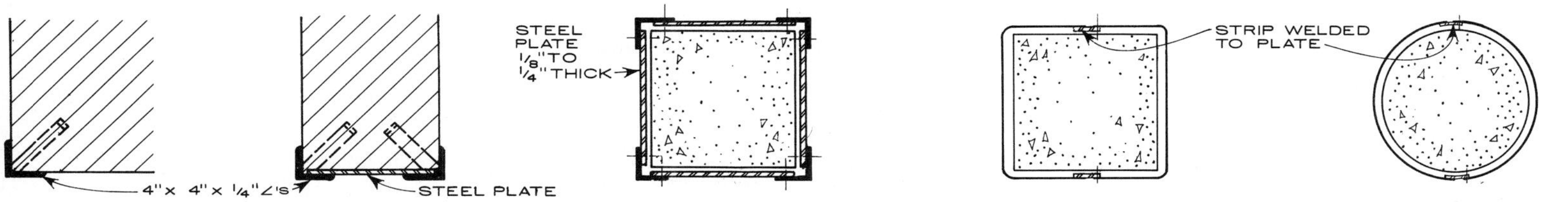

4" × 4" × ¼" ∠'s

SINGLE CORNER

STEEL PLATE

DOUBLE CORNER

STEEL PLATE ⅛" TO ¼" THICK

COL. WITH ∠s & PLATES

STRIP WELDED TO PLATE

COLUMNS WITH FORMED PLATE

## CORNER AND COLUMN GUARDS

John Sava; The Architects Collaborative, Inc.; Cambridge, Massachusetts
Vicente Cordero, AIA; Arlington, Virginia

**WALL AND CORNER GUARDS**

**10**

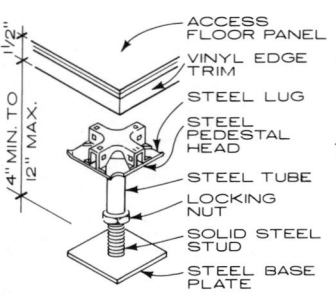

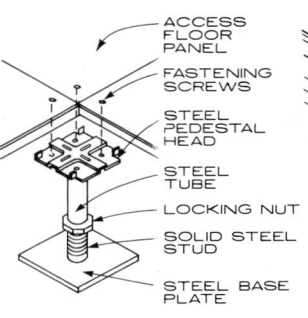

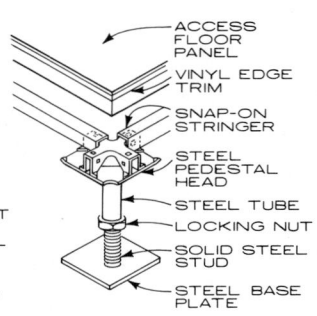

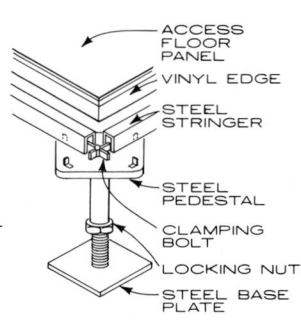

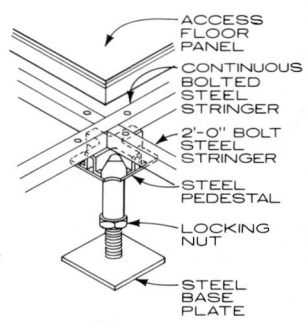

### STRINGERLESS

This system is used in general construction or small computer rooms. It provides maximum accessibility, optimum underfloor space, and electrical continuity. Note that it is dependent on panels being restrained by perimeter walls. Maximum load: 150 psf. Concentrated load: 400 lb.

### PANEL LOCK

This system is used in general construction and is designed without a stringer connection at the edge. Bolted at the corner, it provides added rigidity over stringerless systems and maximum access and flexibility.

### SNAP-ON-GRID

This system is used in computer rooms and in general construction where frequent access is required. It provides improved lateral stability when compared to stringerless systems, electrical continuity, and plenum seal.

### CLAMPED STRINGER

This system is used in computer rooms and provides high lateral stability, complete access to the below-floor cavity, electrical continuity for grounding, and static control. The system's contact between panel edge and stringer provides a plenum seal.

### RIGID GRID

This system is used in computer rooms and areas of heavy loading. It provides maximum rigidity for seismic or dynamic loading, electrical continuity for grounding or static control, and plenum seal. Maximum load: 400 psf. Concentrated load: 1250 lb.

## TYPES OF SUPPORT SYSTEMS – LEAST STABLE TO MOST STABLE

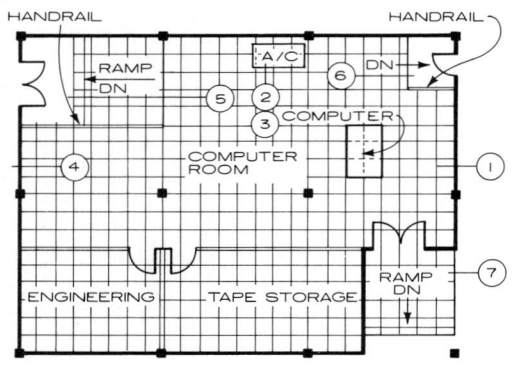

**TYPICAL COMPUTER ROOM PLAN**

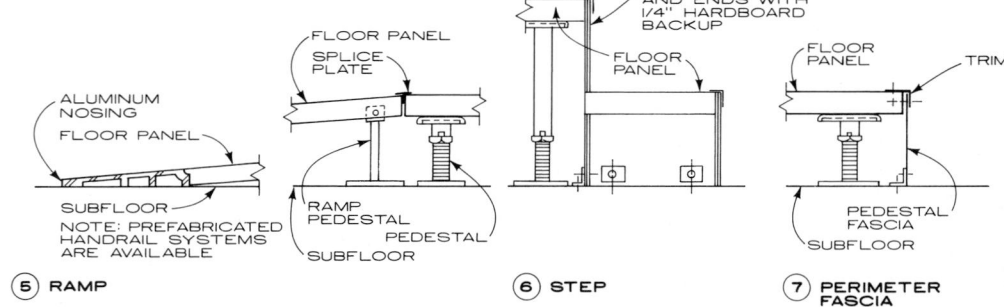

**TYPICAL ACCESS FLOOR CONDITIONS**

## COMPUTER ROOMS

Computers place high demands on electrical, mechanical and floor systems. The floor surface must be conductive and grounded to avoid static electricity and dust accumulation. An automatic fire detection system should be installed in below-floor plenums. Plenums may not exceed 10,000 sq. ft., and they must be divided by noncombustible bulkheads. Computer rooms should be separated from all other occupancies within buildings by fire-resistant walls, floors, and ceilings with a resistance rating of not less than 1 hour. Structural floors beneath access floors should provide for water drainage to reduce damage to computer systems. All access floor openings should be protected from debris. Computer rooms require precision temperature and humidity control. Package air-conditioning units suitable for computer rooms can supply air within a tolerance of ±1.5° and ±5% humidity.

Computer room heat gains often are concentrated. For minimum room temperature gradients, supply air distribution should match closely the load distribution. The distribution system should be flexible enough to accommodate location changes and heat gain with minimum change in the basic distribution system. Supply air systems require about 74 litres per second per kilowatt of cooling to satisfy computer room conditions. This provides enough air change rate for even air temperature distribution. Packaged air-conditioning systems using the underfloor air supply plenum should supply the large computer area adequately. The zoning area is controlled by various floor registers and perforated floor panels.

Setter, Leach and Lindstrom, Inc.; Minneapolis, Minnesota

## ACCESS FLOORS

Access floor systems are used in business offices, hospitals, laboratories, open area schools, television systems, computer rooms, and telephone-communication centers. They provide mechanical and electrical accessibility and flexibility in placing desks, telephone services, machines, and general office equipment. Equipment can be moved and reconnected quickly. Raised access floors in large areas offer maximum flexibility for future change. They also can be used in a recessed structural floor area.

Reinforced steel panels, aluminum, steel-encased wood core, and cementitious fill are available with finish surfaces of vinyl tile, plastic laminate, and carpet. Basic panel sizes are 24 in. x 24 in. Panel systems rely on gravity-held connections, but they can be held mechanically, increasing rigidity. Wraparound, butt, and protective plastic edge carpet systems are available; some are available with Class A flame-spread ratings. Panels are available in structural grades ranging from general office to light industrial construction.

Using modular wiring increases installation speed and simplifies panel variation. Space beneath floors can be used as an air-conditioning plenum. Special panels provide perforation for air distribution, cable slots, and sound and thermal insulation. Various support systems can be provided in steel. Possible difficulties encountered with access floor systems are restricted minimal floor heights and structural integrity of older buildings. Wet washing techniques cannot be used, and poor placement of exceedingly heavy loads can damage floor systems.

## DOUBLE-ACCESS FIREPLACE

- DOUBLE-WALL METAL CHIMNEY
- INSULATED FIREBOX
- REFRACTORY BRICK LINING
- MESH SCREEN (GLASS DOORS OPTIONAL)
- GAS STARTER ACCESS
- WALL CONSTRUCTION
- OUTSIDE AIR ACCESS
- INTEGRAL STEEL GRATE
- FLUSH HEARTH, TWO SIDES

45"
37"
24"

## CORNER FIREPLACE

- DOUBLE-WALL METAL CHIMNEY
- OUTSIDE AIR ACCESS
- GAS STARTER ACCESS
- INSULATED FIREBOX
- REFRACTORY BRICK LINING
- MESH SCREEN (GLASS DOORS OPTIONAL)
- INTEGRAL STEEL GRATE
- FLUSH HEARTH, TWO SIDES

41 1/2"
37"
22"

## GENERAL NOTES

1. Verify local/state codes for maximum and minimum chimney height clearances above roof deck.
2. Chimney pipe requires a 2-in. clearance to combustible surfaces. In a multichase installation, chimney pipes should be 20 in. apart, center to center. Chase top must be constructed of noncombustible material.
3. See manufacturer's specifications for chimney joint band and stabilizer locations.
4. Fire-stop spacer must be used whenever a ceiling, floor, or sidewall is penetrated.
5. No special floor support is usually necessary for prefabricated fireplaces; however, local/state codes should be checked to determine exact requirements.
6. Facing material must not obstruct louvered or screened area at sides, top, or bottom of fireplace opening; however, noncombustible finishing material may be used over the black metal on fireplace fronts. See manufacturer's specifications.
7. Inadequate ventilation can occur from air conditioning, heating, or other mechanical systems that generate negative air pressures in the fireplace room. Plan for proper ventilation to ensure smoke-free operation.
8. There is no minimum or maximum horizontal distance for outside air access line.
9. A noncombustible hearth extension must extend at least 8 in. on either side of firebox openings and 16–20 in. in front of firebox.
10. Distances from combustible walls perpendicular to the front of the fireplace—including mantles—vary. Consult manufacturer's specifications.
11. Outlet grilles must be at least 10 in. below ceiling for ducted heat-circulating fireplace.
12. Room furnishings such as drapes, curtains, and chairs must be at least 4 ft 0 in. from firebox opening.

## HEAT-CIRCULATING FIREPLACE

- DOUBLE-WALL METAL CHIMNEY
- HEATED AIR RETURN
- EXTERNAL DAMPER CONTROL
- INSULATED FIREBOX
- REFRACTORY BRICK LINING
- MESH SCREEN (OPTIONAL GLASS DOORS)
- INTEGRAL TIP-UP GRATE
- GAS STARTER ACCESS
- OUTSIDE AIR ACCESS
- ROOM AIR ENTRY WITH OPTIONAL FANS
- HEARTH

41 1/2"
48 1/2"
24"

## DUCTED HEAT-CIRCULATING FIREPLACE

- DOUBLE-WALL METAL CHIMNEY
- HEATED AIR RETURN-TWIN DUCTS
- HEATED AIR RETURN
- INSULATED FIREBOX
- EXTERNAL DAMPER CONTROL
- REFRACTORY BRICK LINING
- MESH SCREEN (OPTIONAL GLASS DOORS)
- GAS STARTER ACCESS
- OUTSIDE AIR ACCESS
- ROOM AIR ENTRY WITH OPTIONAL FANS
- INTEGRAL TIP-UP GRATE
- FLUSH HEARTH

38 1/2"
46"
24 1/2"

## TRADITIONAL FIREPLACE

- DOUBLE-WALL METAL CHIMNEY
- MESH SCREEN (OPTIONAL GLASS DOORS)
- REFRACTORY BRICK LINING
- INSULATED FIREBOX
- OUTSIDE AIR ACCESS
- GAS STARTER ACCESS
- INTEGRAL STEEL GRATE
- FLUSH HEARTH

41 1/2"
50"
22"

## INSTALLATION CONDITIONS FOR PREFABRICATED FIREPLACES

**INTERIOR WALL CONDITION CHASE CONSTRUCTED ON ROOF**

- TYPICAL INTERIOR STUD WALL CONSTRUCTION
- DOUBLE-ACCESS FIREPLACE
- CORNER FIREPLACE

**EXTERIOR WALL CONDITION CHASE CONSTRUCTED ON ROOF**

- FRONT-FACING FIREPLACE (TYP.)
- BRICK VENEER
- CORNER INSTALLATION
- BATT INSULATION IN EXTERIOR WALL (TYP.)

**EXTERIOR WALL CONDITION CHIMNEY OFFSET THROUGH EXTERIOR WALL AND ENCLOSED IN CHASE**

- 2" MIN. (TYP.)
- CORNER INSTALLATION
- BATT INSULATION IN EXTERIOR WALL AND AROUND CHASE (TYP.)

**EXTERIOR WALL CONDITION FIREPLACE AND CHIMNEY ENCLOSED IN CHASE**

- GYPSUM WALLBOARD OR PLYWOOD TO HOLD CHASE INSULATION IN PLACE (TYP.)

Richard J. Vitullo; Washington Grove, Maryland

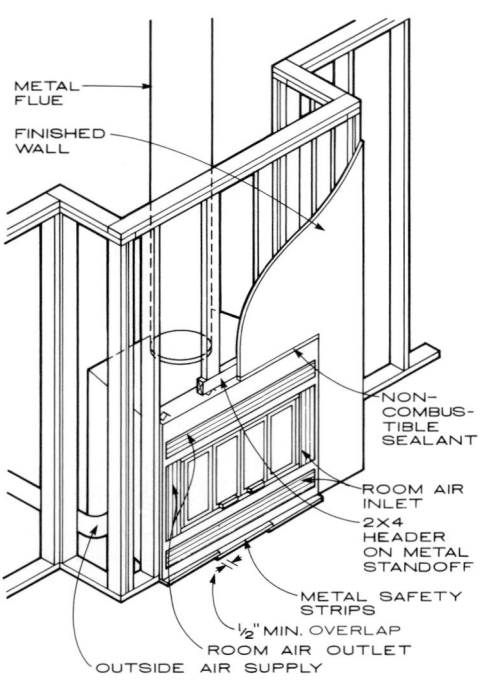

- METAL FLUE
- FINISHED WALL
- NON-COMBUSTIBLE SEALANT
- ROOM AIR INLET
- 2×4 HEADER ON METAL STANDOFF
- METAL SAFETY STRIPS
- 1/2" MIN. OVERLAP
- ROOM AIR OUTLET
- OUTSIDE AIR SUPPLY

## HEAT CIRCULATING FIREPLACE

Specially constructed steel fireplaces must be properly enclosed in masonry to obtain a complete wood burning unit. When placed on a firebrick hearth, a steel fireplace includes all essential combustion and smoke handling spaces. A circulator provides a heat transfer chamber with inlets and outlets that draw in cool air, heat it, and expel warm air by natural convection. The air heating cycle can be augmented with electric fans in the intakes (not in the outlets). A steel shell provides a form for the masonry enclosure, but it is not a structural element. Enclosing masonry must be held at least 1/2 in. away from the shell to allow for expansion and contraction in the metal. The 1/2 in. space is taken up with fireproof insulation that covers the entire circulator. The fireplace rear wall should be at least 8 in. thick if exposed to the exterior. Placing the fireplace within the exterior stud wall gives better thermal insulation in exchange for some lost indoor floor space.

Steel circulatory fireplaces are manufactured in various sizes with proportions set for proper burning action and air heating. An incorrect flue size may negate the fireplace design. The flue must be independently supported.

### NOTES

Circulator must be entirely wrapped in insulation to control heat and to help space the masonry away from the steel shell.

1. Some manufacturers recommend using a chimney cap with a heat-circulating fireplace.
2. Check local codes for minimum clearance requirements to combustible materials such as walls and mantles.

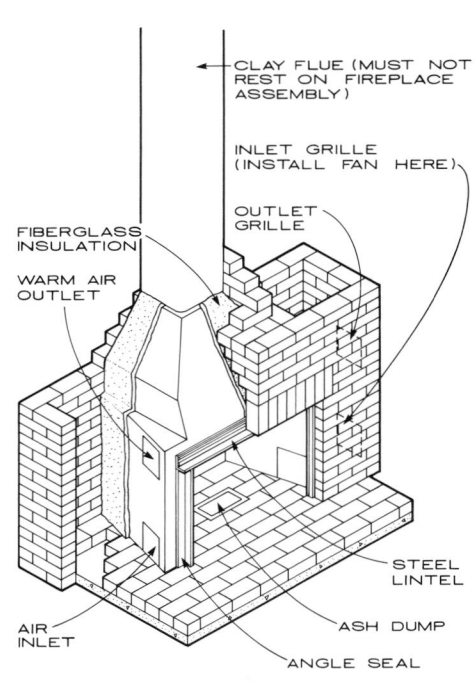

- CLAY FLUE (MUST NOT REST ON FIREPLACE ASSEMBLY)
- INLET GRILLE (INSTALL FAN HERE)
- OUTLET GRILLE
- FIBERGLASS INSULATION
- WARM AIR OUTLET
- STEEL LINTEL
- AIR INLET
- ASH DUMP
- ANGLE SEAL

**HEAT CIRCULATING FIREPLACE SET IN STUD WALL**

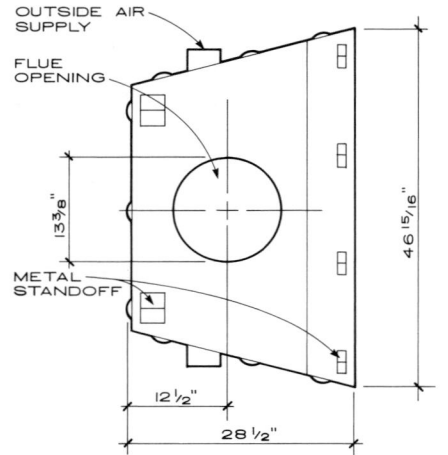

- OUTSIDE AIR SUPPLY
- FLUE OPENING
- METAL STANDOFF
- 13 3/8"
- 46 15/16"
- 12 1/2"
- 28 1/2"

**PLAN**

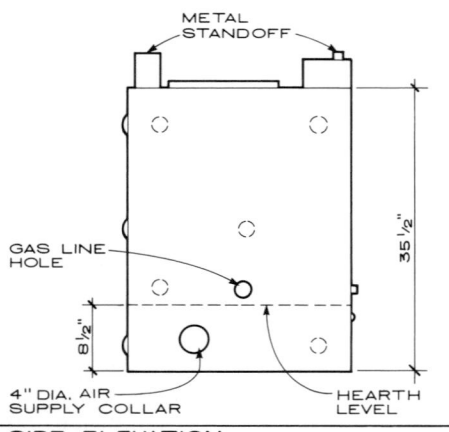

- METAL STANDOFF
- GAS LINE HOLE
- 4" DIA. AIR SUPPLY COLLAR
- HEARTH LEVEL
- 35 1/2"
- 8 1/2"

**SIDE ELEVATION**

Timothy B. McDonald; Washington, D.C.

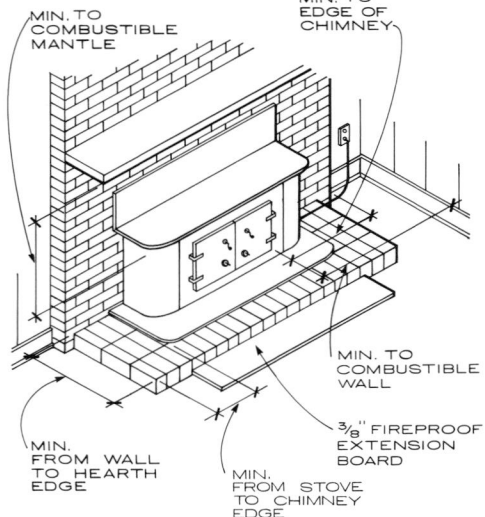

- MIN. TO COMBUSTIBLE MANTLE
- MIN. TO EDGE OF CHIMNEY
- MIN. TO COMBUSTIBLE WALL
- 3/8" FIREPROOF EXTENSION BOARD
- MIN. FROM WALL TO HEARTH EDGE
- MIN. FROM STOVE TO CHIMNEY EDGE

**HEAT CIRCULATING FIREPLACE**

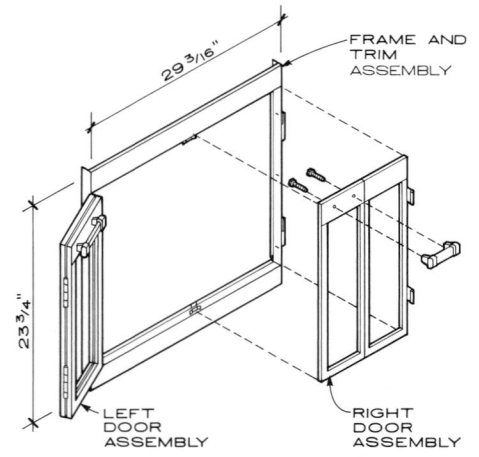

- 29 3/16"
- FRAME AND TRIM ASSEMBLY
- 23 3/4"
- LEFT DOOR ASSEMBLY
- RIGHT DOOR ASSEMBLY

**FIREPLACE DOOR ASSEMBLY**

**HEAT CIRCULATING FIREPLACE SET IN MASONRY**

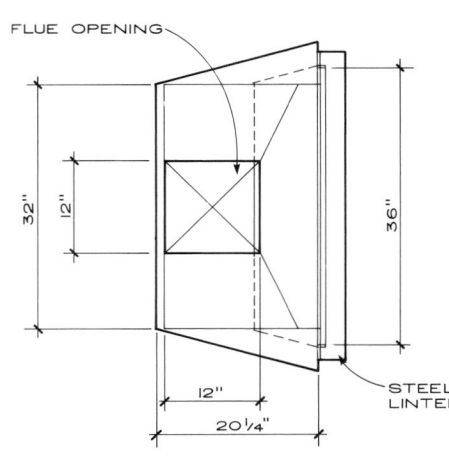

- FLUE OPENING
- 32"
- 12"
- 36"
- 12"
- 20 1/4"
- STEEL LINTEL

**PLAN**

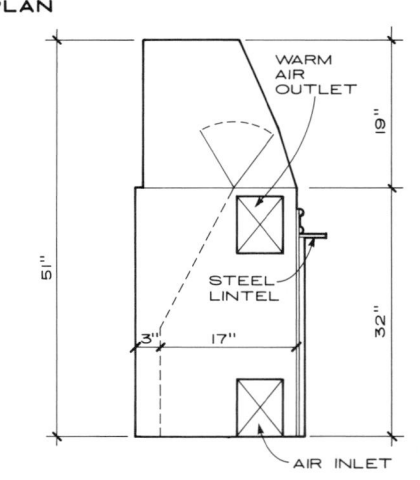

- WARM AIR OUTLET
- 19"
- 51"
- STEEL LINTEL
- 32"
- 3"
- 17"
- AIR INLET

**SIDE ELEVATION**

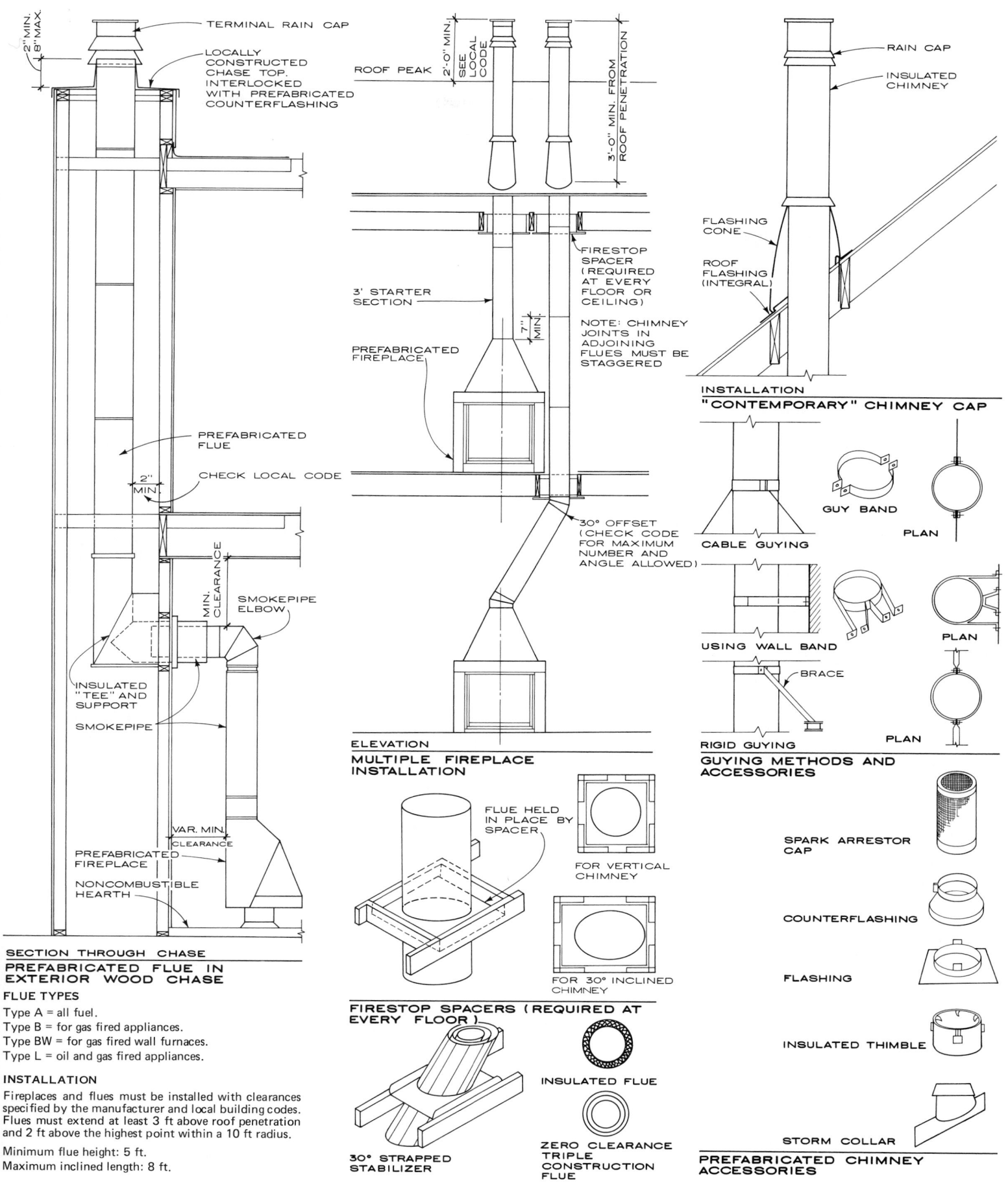

TERMINAL RAIN CAP

2" MIN.
8" MAX.

LOCALLY CONSTRUCTED CHASE TOP, INTERLOCKED WITH PREFABRICATED COUNTERFLASHING

PREFABRICATED FLUE

2" MIN

CHECK LOCAL CODE

MIN. CLEARANCE

SMOKEPIPE ELBOW

INSULATED "TEE" AND SUPPORT

SMOKEPIPE

VAR. MIN. CLEARANCE

PREFABRICATED FIREPLACE

NONCOMBUSTIBLE HEARTH

**SECTION THROUGH CHASE**
**PREFABRICATED FLUE IN EXTERIOR WOOD CHASE**

**FLUE TYPES**

Type A = all fuel.
Type B = for gas fired appliances.
Type BW = for gas fired wall furnaces.
Type L = oil and gas fired appliances.

**INSTALLATION**

Fireplaces and flues must be installed with clearances specified by the manufacturer and local building codes. Flues must extend at least 3 ft above roof penetration and 2 ft above the highest point within a 10 ft radius.

Minimum flue height: 5 ft.
Maximum inclined length: 8 ft.

ROOF PEAK

2'-0" MIN. SEE LOCAL CODE

3'-0" MIN. FROM ROOF PENETRATION

FIRESTOP SPACER (REQUIRED AT EVERY FLOOR OR CEILING)

3' STARTER SECTION

PREFABRICATED FIREPLACE

7" MIN.

NOTE: CHIMNEY JOINTS IN ADJOINING FLUES MUST BE STAGGERED

30° OFFSET (CHECK CODE FOR MAXIMUM NUMBER AND ANGLE ALLOWED)

**ELEVATION**
**MULTIPLE FIREPLACE INSTALLATION**

FLUE HELD IN PLACE BY SPACER

FOR VERTICAL CHIMNEY

FOR 30° INCLINED CHIMNEY

**FIRESTOP SPACERS (REQUIRED AT EVERY FLOOR)**

30° STRAPPED STABILIZER

INSULATED FLUE

ZERO CLEARANCE TRIPLE CONSTRUCTION FLUE

RAIN CAP

INSULATED CHIMNEY

FLASHING CONE

ROOF FLASHING (INTEGRAL)

**INSTALLATION**
**"CONTEMPORARY" CHIMNEY CAP**

GUY BAND

PLAN

CABLE GUYING

USING WALL BAND

BRACE

PLAN

RIGID GUYING

PLAN

**GUYING METHODS AND ACCESSORIES**

SPARK ARRESTOR CAP

COUNTERFLASHING

FLASHING

INSULATED THIMBLE

STORM COLLAR

**PREFABRICATED CHIMNEY ACCESSORIES**

Olga Barmine; Darrel Downing Rippeteau, Architect; Washington, D.C.

**FIREPLACES AND STOVES**

10

     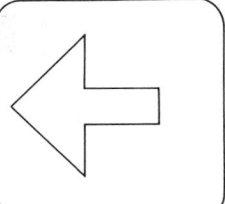

**SYMBOLS**

emergency
exit
only

In case of fire
do not use elevators

Use stairways

30" X 30"
RECOMMENDED SIZE          24" X 24"
RECOMMENDED SIZE          24" X 24"
RECOMMENDED SIZE

**WARNING/PROHIBITORY SIGNS**

PARKING
FOR
HANDICAPPED
ONLY

MEN

EXIT
STAIRS

1

HANDICAPPED

PARKING

12" X 24"
RECOMMENDED SIZE

12" X 12" RECOMMENDED
SIZE          12" X 18" RECOMMENDED
SIZE

**HANDICAPPED ACCESS SIGNS**

Marr Knapp Crawfis Associates, Inc.; Mansfield, Ohio
Richard J. Vitullo; Washington Grove, Maryland

 **IDENTIFYING DEVICES**

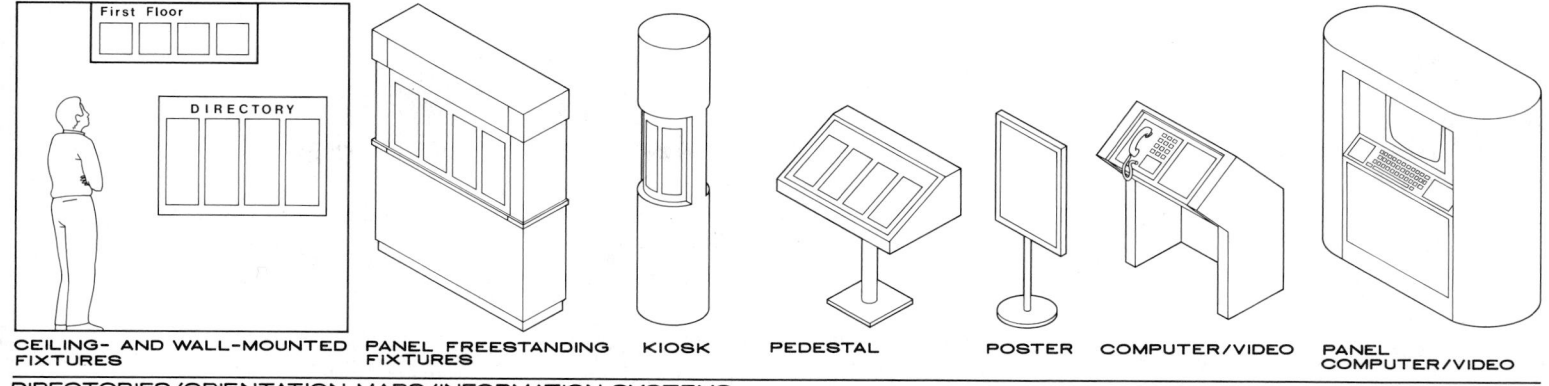

CEILING- AND WALL-MOUNTED FIXTURES    PANEL FREESTANDING FIXTURES    KIOSK    PEDESTAL    POSTER    COMPUTER/VIDEO    PANEL COMPUTER/VIDEO

## DIRECTORIES/ORIENTATION MAPS/INFORMATION SYSTEMS

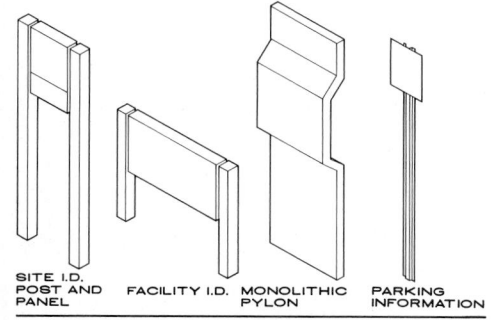

SITE I.D. POST AND PANEL    FACILITY I.D.    MONOLITHIC PYLON    PARKING INFORMATION

## EXTERIOR SIGN TYPES

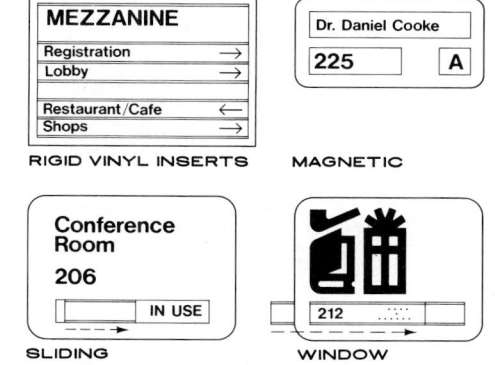

RIGID VINYL INSERTS    MAGNETIC

SLIDING    WINDOW

## INTERIOR SIGN TYPES

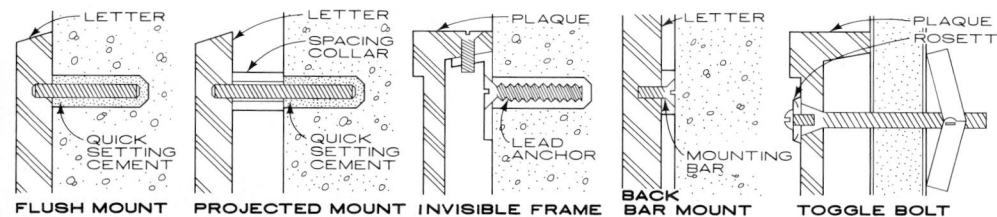

FLUSH MOUNT    PROJECTED MOUNT    INVISIBLE FRAME    BACK BAR MOUNT    TOGGLE BOLT

## MOUNTING METHODS/MATERIALS

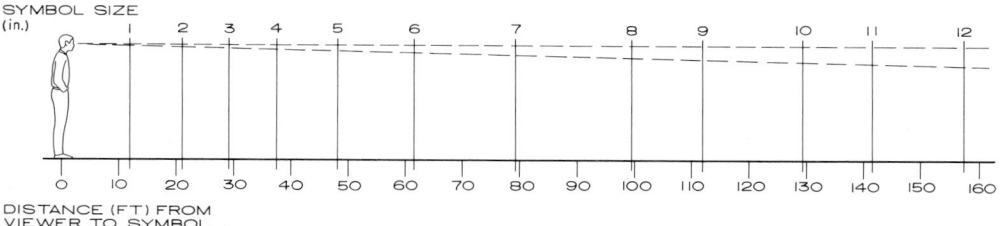

SYMBOL SIZE (in.)

DISTANCE (FT) FROM VIEWER TO SYMBOL

## SYMBOL READABILITY

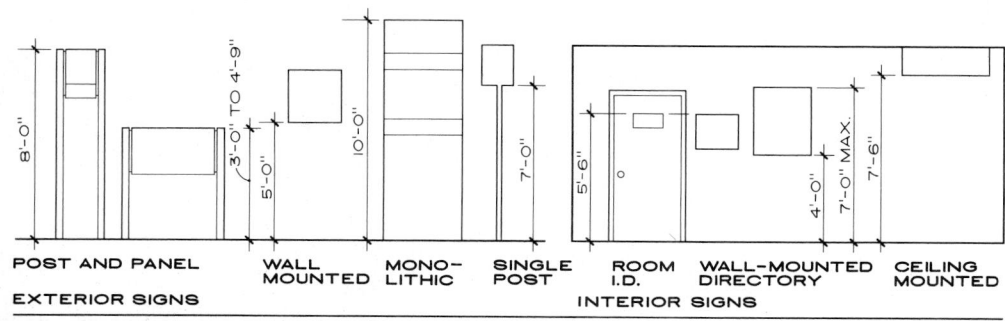

POST AND PANEL    WALL MOUNTED    MONO-LITHIC    SINGLE POST    ROOM I.D.    WALL-MOUNTED DIRECTORY    CEILING MOUNTED

EXTERIOR SIGNS    INTERIOR SIGNS

## MOUNTING HEIGHTS

Marr Knapp Crawfis Associates, Inc.; Mansfield, Ohio
Richard J. Vitullo; Washington Grove, Maryland

## GENERAL NOTES

### EXTERIOR SIGNS

1. Identify entrance and exit of site and building, handicapped information, parking lot location, and facility identification.
2. Signs should be 6 ft 0 in. min. from face of curb, 7 ft 0 in. from grade to bottom of sign, and 100–200 ft from intersections.
3. Building signage materials: fabricated aluminum, illuminated plastic face, back lighted, cast aluminum, applied letter, die raised, engraved, and hot stamped.
4. Plaque and sign materials: cast bronze, cast aluminum, plastic/acrylic, stone (cornerstone), masonry, and wood.
5. For handicapped signage, designate building entrance access, identify parking areas, and direction to facilities. See ANSI 117.1 or state regulations for specific headings.

### DIRECTORIES AND MAPS

1. Locate these in main entrances and/or lobbies with appropriate information for the handicapped.
2. Place directory information adjacent to "You are here" information.
3. Directories should be placed in stair/elevator lobbies of each floor.
4. Mounting choices: surface mounted, semirecessed, full recessed (flush), cantilevered, chain suspended, rigidly suspended, mechanically fastened, or track mounted.

### INTERIOR SIGNS

1. Lightweight freestanding signs should not be used in high-traffic areas. Use when specific location/information maneuverability is required.
2. Electronic, computer, and videotex technologies can provide an innovative and highly flexible directory/sign display system for mapping and/or routing, information (facility and local), advertisement and messages, and management tie-in capabilities.
3. Where changeability and flexibility is a design priority, a modular system is recommended. Rigid vinyl, aluminum, and acrylic inserts as well as magnetic systems may be used.
4. For maximum ease of reading interior signs, any given line in a sign should not exceed 30 characters in width, including upper and lower case letters and spaces between words. To accommodate the visually handicapped, room numbers should be raised or accompanied with braille.
5. Choose the height and "weight" of letter styles and symbols for readability. Consider background materials and contrast when choosing a color scheme.
6. Permanent mounting:
   a. Vinyl tape/adhesive backing, usually factory applied.
   b. Silastic adhesive, usually supplied with vinyl tape strips to hold sign in place until adhesive cures.
   c. Mechanically fastened; specify hole locations.
7. Semipermanent: vinyl tape square can be used on inserts.
8. Changeable: dual-lock mating fasteners, magnets, magnetic tape, or tracks may be used.

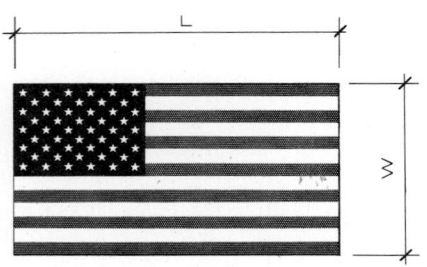

U.S. GOVERNMENT STANDARD L=1.9 W.

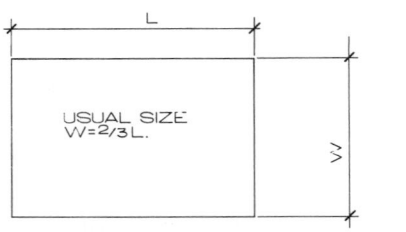

USUAL SIZE
W=2/3 L.

**PROPORTIONS OF U.S. FLAG**

**U.S. FLAG SIZES AS MANUFACTURED AND USED**

| WIDTH | LENGTH | WIDTH | LENGTH |
|---|---|---|---|
| 3'— 0'' | 5'— 0'' | 10'— 0'' | 18'— 0'' |
| 4'— 0'' | 6'— 0'' | 10'— 0'' | 19'— 0'' |
| 4'— 4'' | 5'— 6'' | 12'— 0'' | 20'— 0'' |
| 5'— 0'' | 8'— 0'' | 15'— 0'' | 25'— 0'' |
| 5'— 0'' | 9'— 6'' | 20'— 0'' | 30'— 0'' |
| 6'— 0'' | 10'— 0'' | 20'— 0'' | 38'— 0'' |
| 8'— 0'' | 12'— 0'' | 26'— 0'' | 45'— 0'' |
| 10'— 0'' | 15'— 0'' | | |

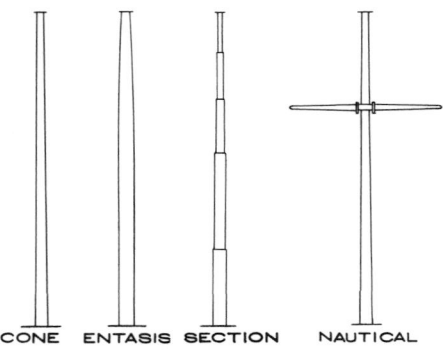

CONE     ENTASIS   SECTION     NAUTICAL

Poles are manufactured in steel, aluminum, bronze, and fiberglass.

Flagpoles must be designed to withstand wind loads while the flag is flying. Design dimensions are dictated by the maximum wind load a pole is exposed to depending on geographical location, whether it is located in a city or open country, whether it is mounted at ground or on top of a building, and size of the flag to be flown. The combination wind load on pole and flag should always be considered. Refer to wind load tests conducted by the National Association of Architectural Metal Manufacturers. (NAAMM)

**POLE STYLES**

**RELATION OF HEIGHT OF POLE TO HEIGHT OF BLDG.**

| HEIGHT OF POLE | HEIGHT OF BLDG. |
|---|---|
| 20'— 0'' | 1 to 2 stories |
| 25'— 0'' | 3 to 5 stories |
| 33'— 0'' to 35'— 0'' | 6 to 10 stories |
| 40'— 0'' to 50'— 0'' | 11 to 15 stories |
| 60'— 0'' to 75'— 0'' | over 15 stories |

**NOTE**

This rule serves for preliminary assumptions.

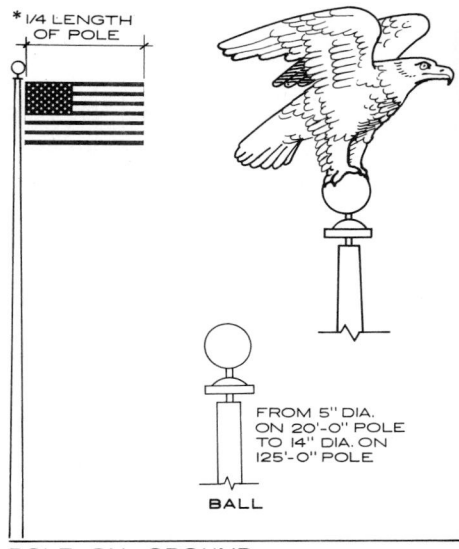

\* 1/4 LENGTH OF POLE

FROM 5'' DIA. ON 20'-0'' POLE TO 14'' DIA. ON 125'-0'' POLE

BALL

**POLE ON GROUND**

**SIZE OF FLAG IN RELATION TO POLE
RECOMMENDED FLAG SIZES**

| POLE | FLAG SIZE | POLE | FLAG SIZE |
|---|---|---|---|
| 15'— 0'' | 3'— 0'' x 5'— 0'' | 50'— 0'' | 8'— 0'' x 12'— 0'' |
| 20'— 0'' | 4'— 0'' x 6'— 0'' | 60'— 0'' | 8'— 0'' x 12'— 0'' |
| 25'— 0'' | 4'— 0'' x 6'— 0'' | 65'— 0'' | 9'— 0'' x 15'— 0'' |
| 30'— 0'' | 5'— 0'' x 8'— 0'' | 70'— 0'' | 9'— 0'' x 15'— 0'' |
| 35'— 0'' | 5'— 0'' x 8'— 0'' | 80'— 0'' | 10'— 0'' x 15'-- 0'' |
| 40'— 0'' | 6'— 0'' x 10'— 0'' | 90'— 0'' | 10'— 0'' x 15'— 0'' |
| 45'— 0'' | 6'— 0'' x 10'— 0'' | 100'— 0'' | 12'— 0'' x 18'— 0'' |

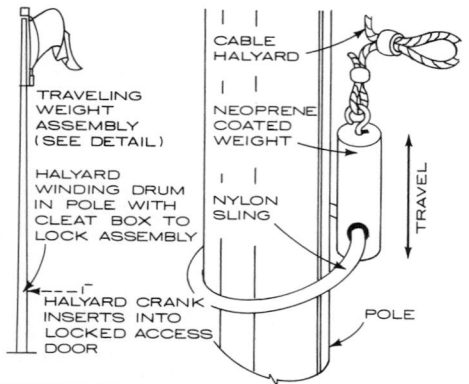

CABLE HALYARD

TRAVELING WEIGHT ASSEMBLY (SEE DETAIL)

NEOPRENE COATED WEIGHT

HALYARD WINDING DRUM IN POLE WITH CLEAT BOX TO LOCK ASSEMBLY

NYLON SLING

TRAVEL

HALYARD CRANK INSERTS INTO LOCKED ACCESS DOOR

POLE

**CONCEALED HALYARD SYSTEM**
(HALYARD INACCESSIBLE WHEN STORED OR CARRYING FLAG)

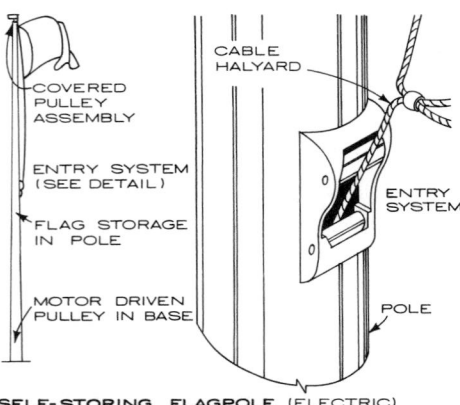

CABLE HALYARD

COVERED PULLEY ASSEMBLY

ENTRY SYSTEM (SEE DETAIL)

FLAG STORAGE IN POLE

ENTRY SYSTEM

MOTOR DRIVEN PULLEY IN BASE

POLE

**SELF-STORING FLAGPOLE** (ELECTRIC)
AUTOMATIC SOLAR CELL OR REMOTE SWITCH OPERATION

**SPECIAL MECHANISMS FOR REMOTE OR VANDAL – PROOF OPERATION**

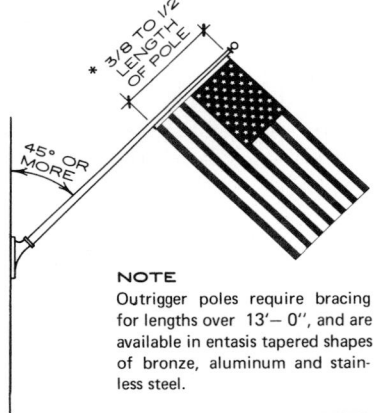

\* 3/8 TO 1/2 LENGTH OF POLE

45° OR MORE

**NOTE**

Outrigger poles require bracing for lengths over 13'— 0'', and are available in entasis tapered shapes of bronze, aluminum and stainless steel.

**OUTRIGGER POLES FOR FLAGS ON BUILDING FRONTS**

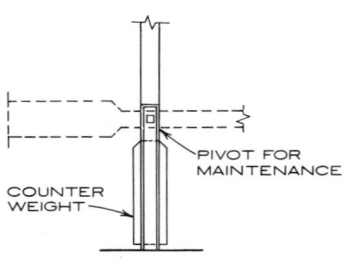

PIVOT FOR MAINTENANCE

COUNTER WEIGHT

**TILTING POLE UNIT**

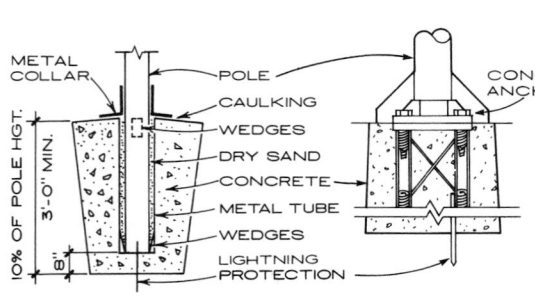

METAL COLLAR

POLE

CAULKING

WEDGES

DRY SAND

CONCRETE

METAL TUBE

WEDGES

LIGHTNING PROTECTION

10% OF POLE HGT.

3'-0'' MIN.

8''

CONCRETE ANCHORS

EXPANSION BOLT

**FOUNDATION FOR GROUND SET POLES**      **WALL MOUNTING FLAGPOLES**

**FOUNDATION AND SURFACE MOUNTING DETAILS**

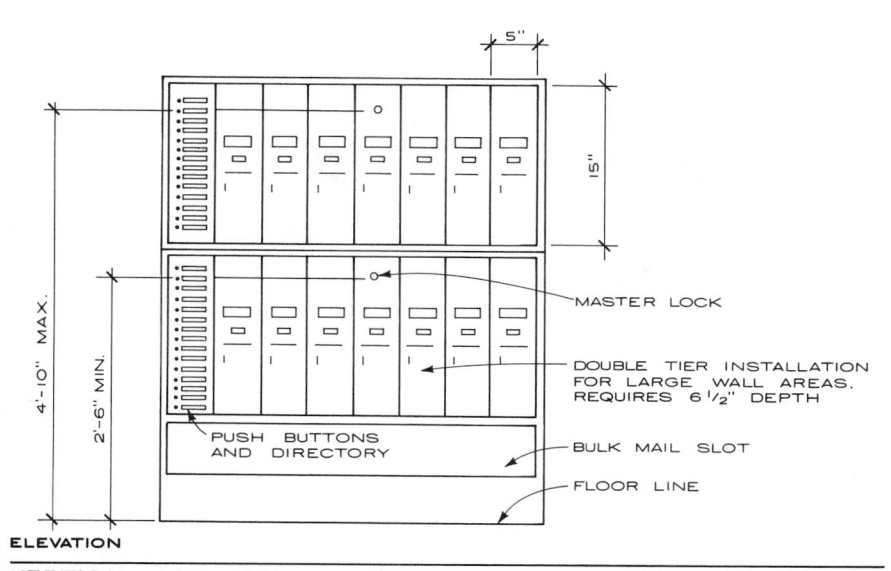

**ELEVATION**

## VERTICAL COMPARTMENT TYPE
FRONT LOADING

Labels in figure:
- 5"
- 15"
- 4'-10" MAX.
- 2'-6" MIN.
- MASTER LOCK
- DOUBLE TIER INSTALLATION FOR LARGE WALL AREAS. REQUIRES 6 1/2" DEPTH
- PUSH BUTTONS AND DIRECTORY
- BULK MAIL SLOT
- FLOOR LINE

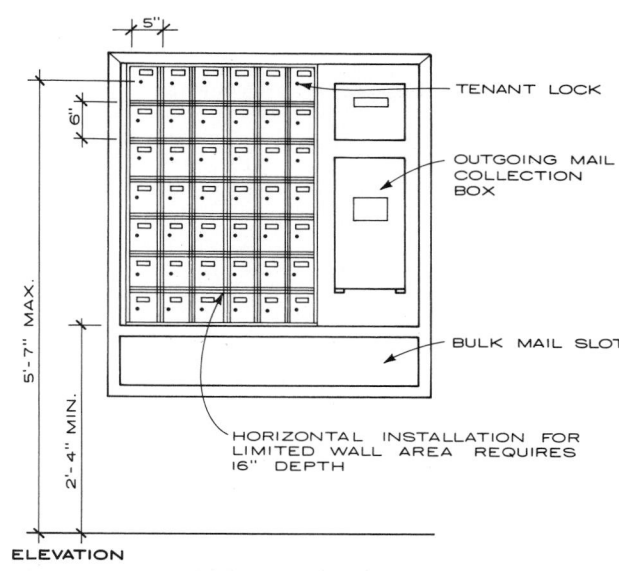

**ELEVATION**

## HORIZONTAL COMPARTMENT TYPE
FRONT OR REAR LOADING

Labels in figure:
- 5"
- 6"
- 5'-7" MAX.
- 2'-4" MIN.
- TENANT LOCK
- OUTGOING MAIL COLLECTION BOX
- BULK MAIL SLOT
- HORIZONTAL INSTALLATION FOR LIMITED WALL AREA REQUIRES 16" DEPTH

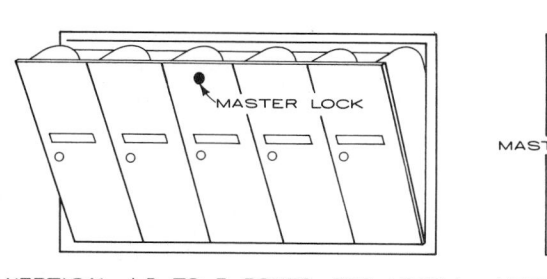

VERTICAL ( 3 TO 7 BOXES PER LOCK )

MASTER LOCK

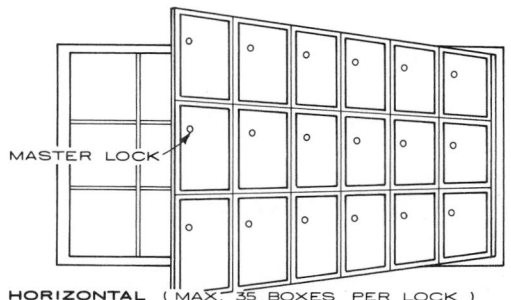

HORIZONTAL ( MAX. 35 BOXES PER LOCK )

MASTER LOCK

## FRONT LOADING COMPARTMENTS WITH MASTER LOCK

**PEDESTAL MOUNTED TYPE**

Labels in pedestal figure:
- 2'-0"
- 5'-0"
- 16", 23", OR 30 1/2"

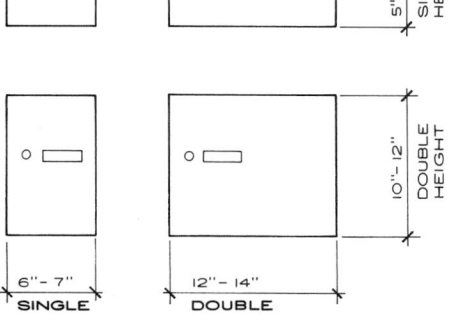

- 5'-6" SINGLE HEIGHT
- 10"-12" DOUBLE HEIGHT
- 6"-7" SINGLE
- 12"-14" DOUBLE

## COMPARTMENT SIZES

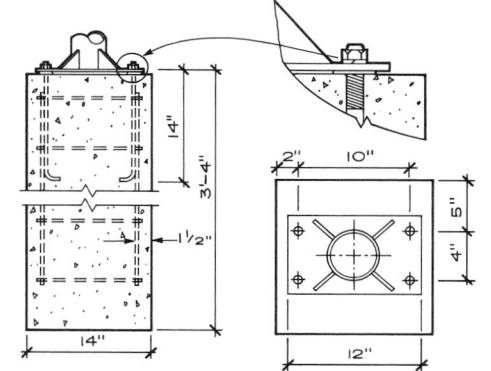

## FOUNDATION DETAILS OF PEDESTAL MOUNTED TYPE

Labels: 14", 3'-4", 1 1/2", 2", 10", 5", 4", 12"

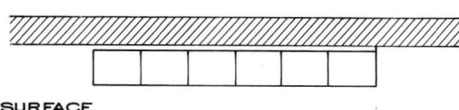

SURFACE

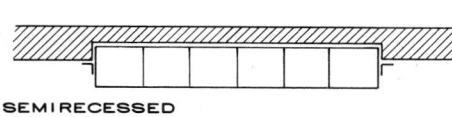

SEMIRECESSED

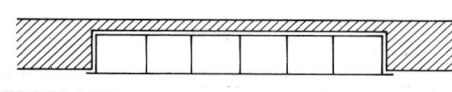

RECESSED

## MOUNTING TYPES
FRONT LOADED COMPARTMENTS

- REMOVABLE COVER
- 3'-0" MIN.
- COMPARTMENTS
- COLLECTION BOX

## MAILROOM PLAN
REAR LOADED COMPARTMENTS

### GENERAL NOTES

1. Postal Service approved mail receptacles are required for apartment houses containing three or more apartments with a common building entrance and street number.
2. Individual compartments should be large enough to receive long letter mail 4 1/2 in. wide and bulky magazines 14 1/2 in. long and 3 1/2 in. in diameter.
3. An outdoor installation should preferably be at least 15 ft from a street or public sidewalk, protected from driving rain, and visible from at least one apartment window.
4. All installations must be adequately lighted to afford better protection to the mail and enable carriers to read addresses on mail and names on boxes.
5. A directory, in alphabetical order, is required for installations with more than 15 compartments.
6. Each compartment group is supplied with mounting hardware for master lock.
7. Call buttons with telephone can be integrated into frame with mailboxes.
8. Depending on occupancy, a certain number of compartments shall be assigned to handicapped tenants. Key slots shall be no more than 48 in. from floor.
9. Use of collection boxes is subject to approval by local offices of the United States Postal Service.

Cohen, Karydas & Associates, Chartered; Washington, D.C.

## FIRE CLASSIFICATION

### CLASS Ⓐ

Incipient fires on which quenching or the cooling effect of water is of primary importance. Fires of wood, paper, textile, and rubbish.

### CLASS Ⓑ

Incipient fires on which blanketing or smothering effect of extinguishing is of primary importance. Fires of gasoline, oil, grease, and fat.

### CLASS Ⓒ

Incipient fires in electrical equipment where a non-conducting extinguishing agent is needed.

## OCCUPANCY CLASSIFICATION

Light hazard occupancies (schools, offices, and public buildings) require one unit of extinguishing capacity for every 3000 sq ft of floor area for use on Class A fires.

Ordinary hazard occupancies (dry goods shops and warehouses) require one unit of extinguishing capacity for every 1500 sq ft of floor space for use on Class A fires.

Extra hazard occupancies (paint shops, etc.) require one unit of extinguishing capacity for every 1000 sq ft of floor area for use on Class A fires.

Class A fire extinguishers, regardless of occupancy, shall be located so that maximum travel distance from any point to the nearest extinguisher is less than 75 ft.

The maximum travel distance to a Class B extinguisher is 50 ft (smaller rated extinguishers shall be placed no more than 30 ft from the hazard).

### NOTES

1. These classifications are taken from the National Fire Protection Association, Publication #10, Portable Extinguishers, 1978.
2. In all cases check the requirements of local codes.

## WATER BASE EXTINGUISHERS

|  | PRESSURIZED | CARTRIDGE | PUMP TANK | | LOADED STREAM |
|---|---|---|---|---|---|
|  | CLASS A ONLY | CLASS A ONLY | CLASS A ONLY | | CLASS A & B |
| Capacity (gal) | 2½ | 2½ | 2½ | 5 | 2½ |
| Height | 25″ | 25″ | 26″ | 28″ | 27″ |
| Diameter | 8″ | 8″ | 8″ | 11″ | 8″ |
| Weight (lb) | 28 | 26 | 36 | 55 | 42 |
| Class | 2A | 2A | 2A | 4A | 2A, ½B |
| Recharge | Weigh cylinder and check annually. In all cases, follow instructions on extinguisher label | | | | |
| Effective range | 45-55 ft | | 30-40 ft | | 35-40 ft |
| Pressure source | Compressed air | Gas cartridge | Hand pump | | Pressure |
| Temperature effect | Will freeze | Will freeze | Will freeze | | Will operate at -40°F |
| Method of extinguishing | Quenches, cools | Quenches, cools | Quenches, cools | | Alkametal salt quenches, cools, and fireproofs |

NOTE: All water base extinguishing agents are electrical conductors.

## CARBON DIOXIDE

### CLASS B & C FIRES

| CAPACITY (LB) | 2½ | 5 | 10 | 15 | 20 |
|---|---|---|---|---|---|
| Height | 18″ | 17″ | 22″ | 26″ | 26″ |
| Diameter | 4″ | 6″ | 7″ | 7″ | 8″ |
| Weight (lb) | 10 | 18 | 35 | 44 | 55 |
| Class | 2 B, C | 2 B, C | 5 B, C | 10 B, C | 10 B, C |
| Height | 16″ | 15″ | 26″ | 30″ | 37″ |
| Diameter | 7″ | 10″ | 13″ | 12″ | 11″ |
| Weight (lb) | 12 | 17 | 34 | 44 | 55 |
| Class | 2 B, C | 5 B, C | 10 B, C | 10 B, C | 10 B, C |
| Height | 18″ | 17″ | 26″ | 33″ | 33″ |
| Diameter | 9″ | 9″ | 11″ | 11″ | 12″ |
| Weight (lb) | 9 | 17 | 34 | 42 | 55 |
| Class | 2 B, C | 5 B, C | 10 B, C | 10 B, C | 10 B, C |

**EFFECTIVE RANGE**
3 to 8 ft
**DISCHARGE TIME**
2½ lb, 12 sec; 5 lb, 22 sec; 10 lb, 23 sec; 15 lb, 26 sec; 20 lb, 25 sec
**RECHARGE**
after use
**PRESSURE SOURCE**
compressed gas
**TEMPERATURE EFFECT**
will operate at minus 40°F
**ELECTRICAL CONDUCTIVITY**
will not conduct

PRESSURIZED

## HALOGENATED AGENT

### CLASS B & C FIRES

| CAPACITY (LB) | 2½ | 5 |
|---|---|---|
| Height | 14″ | 15″ |
| Diameter | 3″ | 3½″ |
| Weight (lb) | 7½ | 9½ |
| Class | 5 B, C | 10 B, C |
| Height | 15″ | 15½″ |
| Diameter | 3″ | 4½″ |
| Weight (lb) | 5 | 10 |
| Class | 5 B, C | 10 B, C |

**EFFECTIVE RANGE**
25 to 30 ft
**DISCHARGE TIME**
2½ lb, 11 sec; 5 lb, 11 sec
**RECHARGE**
after use
**PRESSURE SOURCE**
pump or pressurized
**TEMPERATURE EFFECT**
will operate at minus 40°F
**ELECTRICAL CONDUCTIVITY**
will not conduct

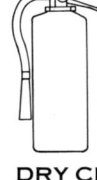

Dimensions below are for two makes of extinguisher to show relative sizes

## DRY CHEMICAL

### CLASS A, B, & C

| CAPACITY (LB) | 5 | 10 | 20 | 30 |
|---|---|---|---|---|
| Height | 19″ | 21″ | 22″ | 30″ |
| Diameter | 5″ | 6″ | 8″ | 8″ |
| Weight (lb) | 15 | 33 | 48 | 70 |
| Class | 2A,10B,C | 2A,20B,C | 2A,80B,C | 2A,80B,C |
| Height | 13″ | 22″ | 21″ | 25″ |
| Diameter | 5″ | 7″ | 9″ | 9″ |
| Weight (lb) | 12 | 21 | 35 | 50 |
| Class | 2A,10B,C | 2A,20B,C | 2A,80B,C | 2A,80B,C |

**EFFECTIVE RANGE**
10 to 20 ft
**DISCHARGE TIME**
5 lb, 10 sec; 10 lb, 11 sec; 20 lb, 15 sec; 30 lb, 34 sec
**RECHARGE**
after use
**PRESSURE SOURCE**
compressed gas
**TEMPERATURE EFFECT**
will operate at minus 40°F
**ELECTRICAL CONDUCTIVITY**
will not conduct

Dimensions below are for three makes of extinguisher to show relative sizes

William G. Miner, AIA, Architect; Washington, D.C.

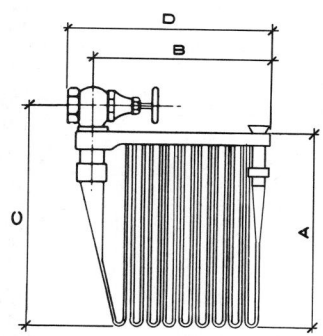

**SWING RACK SEMIAUTOMATIC**
1½" LINED HOSE

| HOSE CAPACITY | 25 | 50 | 75 | 100 |
|---|---|---|---|---|
| A | 10" | 20" | 24" | 27" |
| B | 15" | 16" | 19" | 20" |
| C | 14" | 23" | 27" | 32" |
| D | 17" | 18" | 20" | 22" |
| WIDTH | 4" | 4" | 4" | 4" |

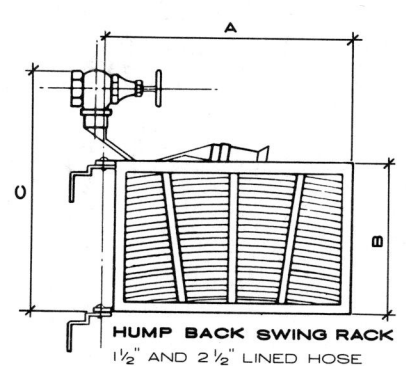

**HUMP BACK SWING RACK**
1½" AND 2½" LINED HOSE

| HOSE CAPACITY | 50 | 100 | 150 | 200 |
|---|---|---|---|---|
| A | 30" | 30" | 34" | 40" |
| B | 17" | 21" | 28" | 39" |
| C | 30" | 33" | 40" | 50" |
| WIDTH 1½" HOSE | 4" | 4" | 4" | 4" |
| WIDTH 2½" HOSE | 6" | 6" | 6" | 6" |

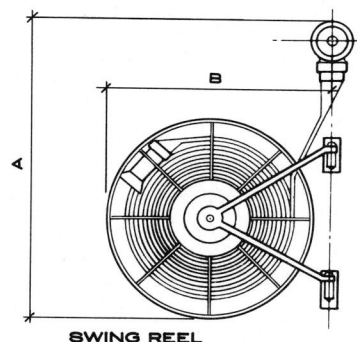

**SWING REEL**
1½" AND 2½" LINED HOSE

| HOSE CAPACITY | 50 | 100 | 150 |
|---|---|---|---|
| A | 38" | 38" | 36" |
| B | 21" | 27" | 31" |
| WIDTH 1½" HOSE | 4" | 4" | 4" |
| WIDTH 2½" HOSE | 6" | 6" | 6" |

## FIRE HOSE RACK AND REELS
**NOTE**

Recommended hose size for use with building standpipes should not exceed 1½ in. in diameter and 100 ft in length. A larger hose used by amateurs is likely to tangle, cause excessive water damage, and create injuries.

A connection for 2½ in. hose should be available to each station for the use of firemen. Many codes require 2½ in. outlets at all standpipes.

By using a reducing coupling 1½ in. hose can be attached. When a 2½ in. stream is required the coupling may be removed. Industrial installations use 2½ in. hoses and train personnel in the use of the heavier equipment. Valves may be located 5 ft 6 in. above floor (check local code).

Lined synthetic fiber plastic hose is recommended for use on standpipe installations. Cotton rubber lined hose is standard for fire department and heavy equipment hose.

Tables show rack and reels for 1½ and 2½ in. lined hose only. Consult manufacturer's literature for rack and reel dimensions when other types and sizes of hose are used.

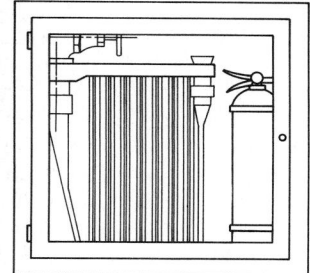

**75' 1½" LINED HOSE, RACK, AND ANGLE VALVE; 2½ GAL EXTINGUISHER**
2'-9" x 2'-9" x 8½" TO 2'-11" x 2'-11" x 9"

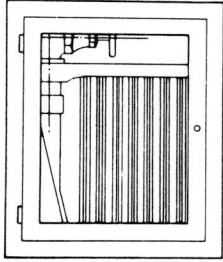

**75' 1½" LINED HOSE, RACK, AND ANGLE VALVE**
1'-9" x 2'-5" x 8" TO 1'-4" x 2'-7" x 8½"

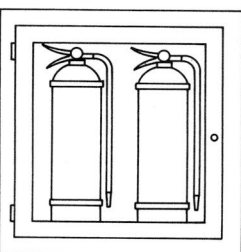

**TWO 2½ GAL EXTINGUISHERS**
1'-11"X2'-9"X7" TO 2'-2"X2'-11"X8"

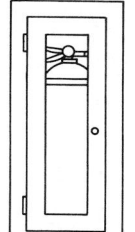

**ONE 2½ GAL EXTINGUISHER**
1'-0"X2'-6"X8" TO 1'-4"X2'-7"X8½"
NOTE: RESIDENTIAL EXTINGUISHER CABINET 1'-5"X7"X2"

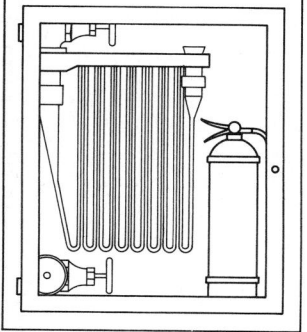

**75' 1½" LINED HOSE AND RACK; 1½" AND 2½" ANGLE VALVE; 2½ GAL EXTINGUISHER**
2'-9" x 3'-4" x 8½" TO 2'-10" x 3'-7" x 9"

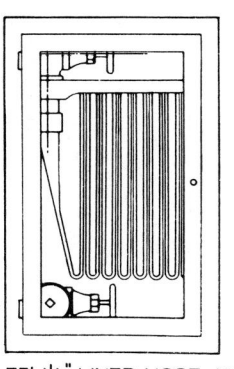

**75' 1½" LINED HOSE AND RACK; 1½" AND 2½" ANGLE VALVE**
1'-11" x 3'-3" x 8½" TO 2'-4" x 3'-4" x 9"

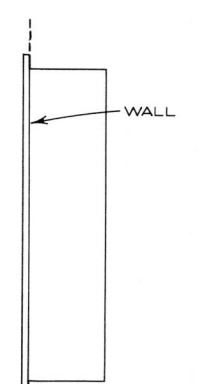

**RECESSED**

**SEMIRECESSED**

**SURFACE MOUNTED**

## FIRE HOSE AND EXTINGUISHER CABINETS
**NOTE**

Cabinets are #18 gauge steel with glass doors as shown or with doors of metal, wood, mirror, and so on.

Consult manufacturer's literature for cabinets with special features such as revolving door, twin doors, pivoting door with attached extinguisher, and curved door.

Cabinets are obtainable for 25, 50, 75, and 100 ft hose racks. Rough dimensions are shown.

William G. Miner, AIA, Architect; Washington, D.C.

## GENERAL NOTES

1. Construction of locker frame and door typically is of 16 gauge steel for sides and back. Top and bottom are typically 20 to 24 gauge steel. Finishes vary. Number plates, a shelf, and coat hooks on back and side walls are generally included. Other construction such as plastic laminate and wood is also used for club facilities.

2. Door types may be solid, perforated (all or part), or louvered (all or part), and ordered in a variety of steel mesh patterns or in special finishes. Doors and locks may be provided with noise-deadening de-vices. Locking mechanisms include built-in adjustable combination lock, built-in flat or grooved key, and latching locker handle (for padlock use). All locking mechanisms are available for surface or recessed applications.

3. Optional locker equipment includes sloping top for nonrecessed locations with corner miters available, 6 in. legs for open base installation, interior partitions (some models), multiple shelves, coat rods (for models over 18 in. deep), closed base and closed-end base for legs, and attachable bench elements.

4. Ventilation within locker spaces should provide 15 cu ft/min. air movement for locker.

5. Handicapped user access may suggest use of some multiple tier lockers; shelf and coat hooks on single tier lockers are out of reach of most handicapped.

6. Bench arrangements may be attached to locker front or may be freestanding and require a raised installation. Finishes of lockers may be varied as conditions dictate such as stainless steel bottoms or sides when used in areas where long-term chemical contamination may affect finishes.

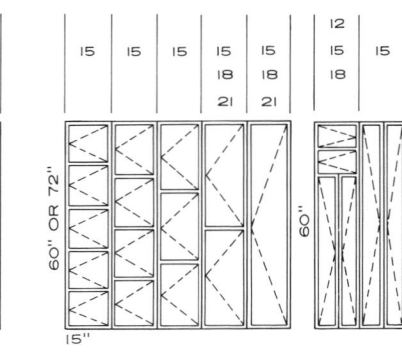
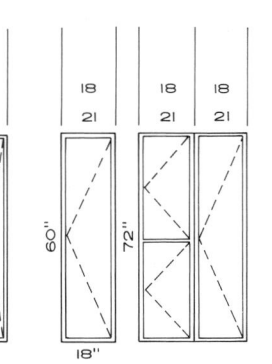
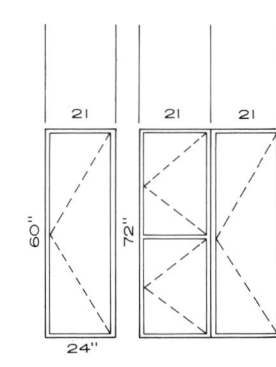

**ELEVATIONS**

## LOCKERS

Checking lockers for heavy duty use are available in enameled steel or stainless steel. Locks are provided with built-in multiple coin selector, which is owner adjustable for coins, tokens, or "free" operation. They may be installed on legs or recessed and may be made movable. Overall height is 6 ft 0 in. on most models, 5 ft 0 in. on some.

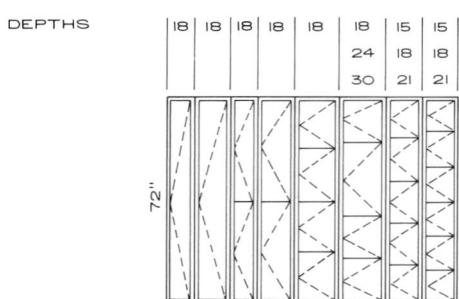

**ELEVATION**

## CHECKING LOCKERS

**LOCKER SECTION**

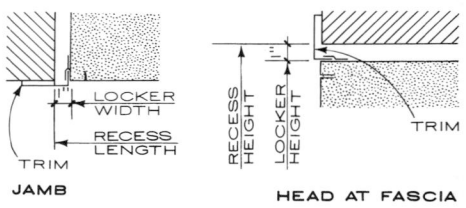

**FILLER PIECE**     **FLUSH WALL JOINT**

**JAMB**     **HEAD AT FASCIA**

**RECESSED/FLUSH BASE AT WALL**

2 WOOD SLEEPERS REQUIRED FOR ISLAND INSTALLATION

**RECESSED/FLUSH BASE AT ISLAND**

**INSTALLATION DETAILS**

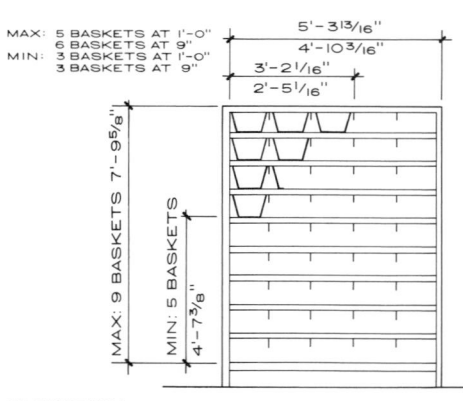

**ELEVATION**

## BASKET RACKS

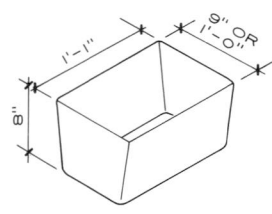

**LOCKER BASKET**

Basket racks may be arranged in single tier or back to back. Single tier depth is 1 ft 1¼ in. Optional pilfer guards may be installed on sides, top, and bottom, preventing access into adjacent baskets, and should be considered at the back as well. Basket materials include wire mesh (all surfaces), perforated steel ends and mesh sides and bottom, and louvered ends with perforated steel sides and bottom.

Frederick C. Krenson, AIA; Rosser Fabrap International; Atlanta, Georgia

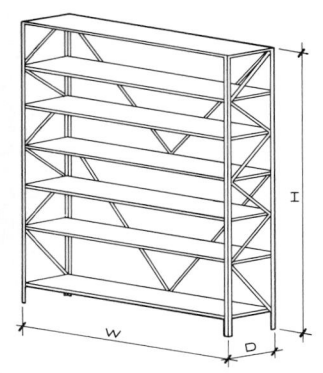

**TYPICAL BASIC UNIT**

## AVAILABLE SIZES

| W | D | H |
|---|---|---|
| 24″ | 9″ | 3′-3″ |
| 30″ | 12″ | 6′-3″ |
| 36″ | 15″ | 7′-3″ |
| 42″ | 18″ | 8′-3″ |
| 48″ | 24″ | 10′-3″ |
| | 30″ | |
| | 36″ | |

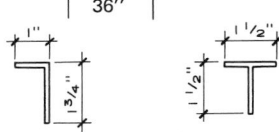

**TYPICAL UPRIGHTS**

**CLASS 1 — STANDARD**

**CLASS 2 — REINFORCED**

**CLASS 3 — HEAVY DUTY**

**LOAD CAPACITY CLASSES**

## TYPICAL SHELF CAPACITIES

| SHELF WIDTH | UNIFORM LOAD (LB) | | |
|---|---|---|---|
| | CLASS 1 | CLASS 2 | CLASS 3 |
| 24″ | 900 | 1500 | 2000 |
| 30″ | 800 | 1300 | 1800 |
| 36″ | 700 | 1200 | 1500 |
| 42″ | 350 | 800 | 1200 |
| 48″ | 300 | 700 | 1000 |

### NOTES
1. Shelving is available in two types. When bolted, the separate movable units are more permanent. When clipped, the shelving is continuous, but more easily set up and dismantled.
2. Shelves are adjustable at 1 in. increments.
3. Diagonal bracing may be eliminated when solid backs or ends are used.

## SOLID SHELVING SYSTEM

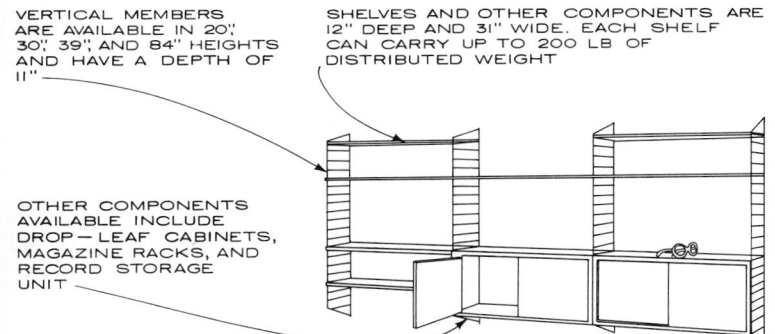

UPRIGHTS — STANDARD OR REINFORCED — 12″, 18″, AND 24″ WIDE AND 53″, 63″, 73″, AND 88″ HIGH

SHELVES — 12″ AND 18″ DEEP AND 24″, 30″, 36″, 42″, 48″, AND 60″ LONG. USE TWO 12″ SHELVES WITH 24″ UPRIGHTS. SHELVES ADJUST ON 5″ CENTERS

### NOTES
1. Approved by National Sanitation Foundation for food storage.
2. Available accessories include corner braces, dividers, bottle shelves, back, and side ledges.
3. Finishes may be nickel plated, chrome, stainless steel, and brass.

**FLOOR MOUNTED — ERECTA SHELVING**

## WIRE SHELVING SYSTEM — FOR FOOD AND RESIDENTIAL STORAGE — METROPOLITAN WIRE CORPORATION

VERTICAL MEMBERS ARE AVAILABLE IN 20″, 30″, 39″, AND 84″ HEIGHTS AND HAVE A DEPTH OF 11″

SHELVES AND OTHER COMPONENTS ARE 12″ DEEP AND 31″ WIDE. EACH SHELF CAN CARRY UP TO 200 LB OF DISTRIBUTED WEIGHT

OTHER COMPONENTS AVAILABLE INCLUDE DROP — LEAF CABINETS, MAGAZINE RACKS, AND RECORD STORAGE UNIT

**WALL MOUNTED — EUROWALL 73 STORAGE SYSTEM**

## METAL AND WOOD SHELVING SYSTEM ARCHITECTURAL SUPPLEMENTS INCORPORATED

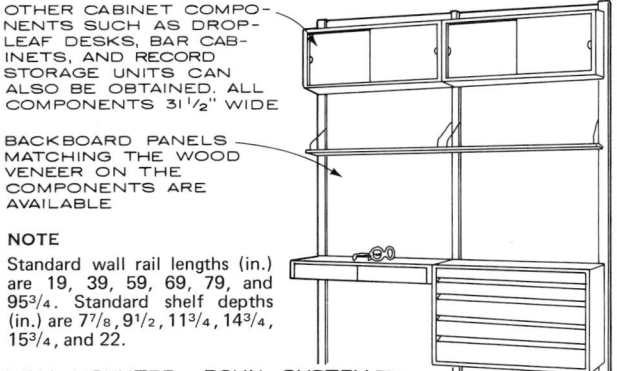

OTHER CABINET COMPONENTS SUCH AS DROP-LEAF DESKS, BAR CABINETS, AND RECORD STORAGE UNITS CAN ALSO BE OBTAINED. ALL COMPONENTS 31½″ WIDE

BACKBOARD PANELS MATCHING THE WOOD VENEER ON THE COMPONENTS ARE AVAILABLE

### NOTE
Standard wall rail lengths (in.) are 19, 39, 59, 69, 79, and 95¾. Standard shelf depths (in.) are 7⅞, 9½, 11¾, 14¾, 15¾, and 22.

**WALL MOUNTED — ROYAL SYSTEM**

## WOOD SHELVING SYSTEM ROYAL SYSTEM INC.

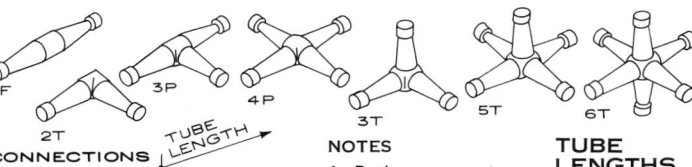

**2T**  **CONNECTIONS**  TUBE LENGTH

### NOTES
1. Both connectors and tubes are available in chrome and matte black finishes.
2. Tubes are manufactured in heavy gauge stainless steel ½ in. o.d.

### TUBE LENGTHS

| CM | IN. |
|---|---|
| 65 | 2.09 |
| 130 | 4.68 |
| 275 | 10.39 |
| 395 | 15.08 |
| 460 | 17.68 |
| 530 | 20.27 |
| 595 | 22.87 |
| 805 | 31.18 |

**FLOOR MOUNTED — ABSTRACTA SHELVING**

## TUBULAR STEEL SHELVING SYSTEM — FOR DISPLAYS AND EXHIBITS — ABSTRACTA STRUCTURES, INC.

### NOTES
Shelves are hung from a steel truss; thus tension is transferred to metal members, increasing load capacity.
**TYPICAL DIMENSIONS:**
Height: 81⅞ in.
Depth: 15 in.
Length: 85, 119¼, 121⅝ in.

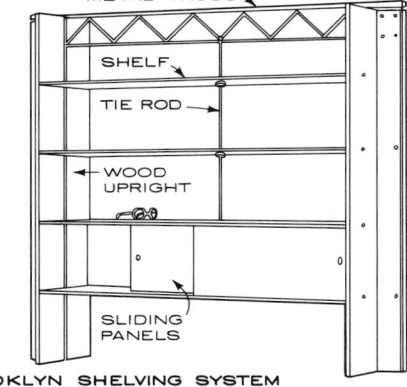

METAL TRUSS

SHELF

TIE ROD

WOOD UPRIGHT

SLIDING PANELS

**FLOOR MOUNTED — BROOKLYN SHELVING SYSTEM**

## METAL AND WOOD SHELVING SYSTEM ACERBIS INTERNATIONAL

### NOTES
This storage system can be entirely assembled from the front. Available components include fold-down bar units, desk tops, drawer chests, and hideaway beds. Walk-in closets are also available. All units come in 15¾ and 24 in. depths.

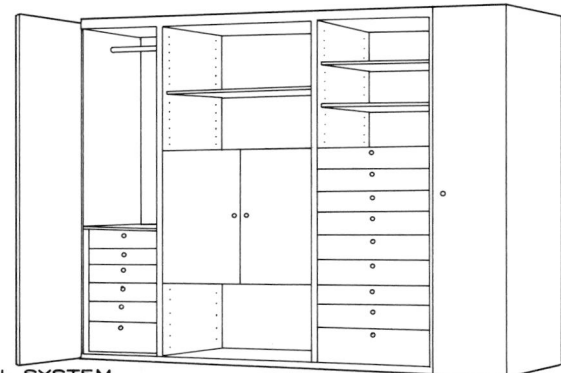

**FLOOR MOUNTED — WALL SYSTEM**

## PANEL AND COMPONENT SHELVING SYSTEM INTERLUBKE - ICF

Charles Szoradi, AIA, and F. Menendez; Washington, D.C.

**STORAGE SHELVING**  **10**

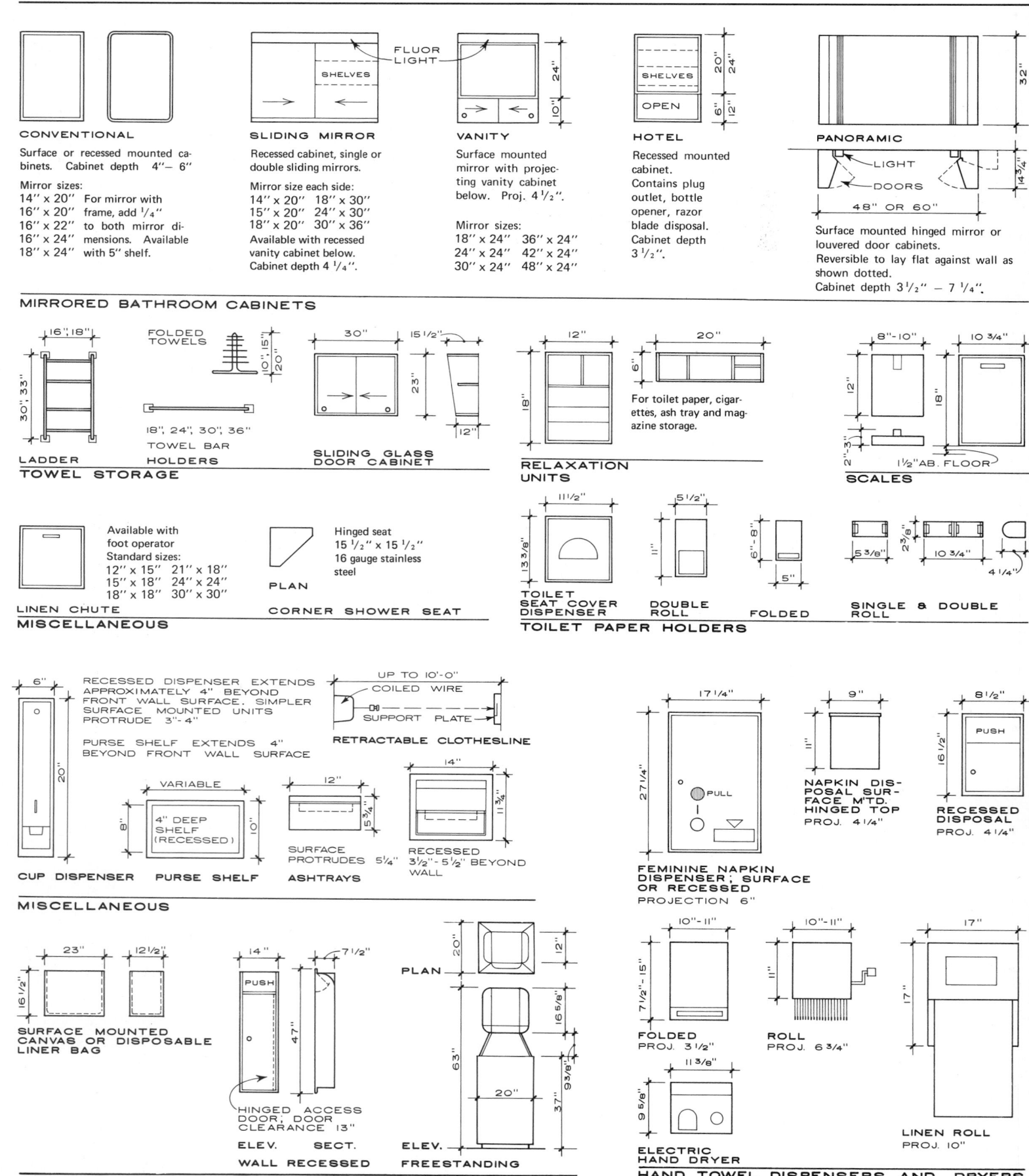

## MIRRORED BATHROOM CABINETS

### CONVENTIONAL

Surface or recessed mounted cabinets. Cabinet depth 4″– 6″

Mirror sizes:
14″ x 20″  For mirror with
16″ x 20″  frame, add ¼″
16″ x 22″  to both mirror dimensions. Available
16″ x 24″  mensions. Available
18″ x 24″  with 5″ shelf.

### SLIDING MIRROR

Recessed cabinet, single or double sliding mirrors.

Mirror size each side:
14″ x 20″   18″ x 30″
15″ x 20″   24″ x 30″
18″ x 20″   30″ x 36″
Available with recessed vanity cabinet below.
Cabinet depth 4 ¼″.

### VANITY

Surface mounted mirror with projecting vanity cabinet below. Proj. 4 ½″.

Mirror sizes:
18″ x 24″   36″ x 24″
24″ x 24″   42″ x 24″
30″ x 24″   48″ x 24″

### HOTEL

Recessed mounted cabinet. Contains plug outlet, bottle opener, razor blade disposal. Cabinet depth 3 ½″.

### PANORAMIC

Surface mounted hinged mirror or louvered door cabinets. Reversible to lay flat against wall as shown dotted. Cabinet depth 3 ½″ – 7 ¼″.

## TOWEL STORAGE

LADDER

FOLDED TOWELS

TOWEL BAR HOLDERS
18″, 24″, 30″, 36″

SLIDING GLASS DOOR CABINET

### RELAXATION UNITS
For toilet paper, cigarettes, ash tray and magazine storage.

### SCALES

## MISCELLANEOUS

LINEN CHUTE
Available with foot operator
Standard sizes:
12″ x 15″   21″ x 18″
15″ x 18″   24″ x 24″
18″ x 18″   30″ x 30″

CORNER SHOWER SEAT
Hinged seat
15 ½″ x 15 ½″
16 gauge stainless steel

## TOILET PAPER HOLDERS

TOILET SEAT COVER DISPENSER

DOUBLE ROLL

FOLDED

SINGLE & DOUBLE ROLL

## MISCELLANEOUS

CUP DISPENSER

PURSE SHELF

ASHTRAYS

RECESSED DISPENSER EXTENDS APPROXIMATELY 4″ BEYOND FRONT WALL SURFACE. SIMPLER SURFACE MOUNTED UNITS PROTRUDE 3″- 4″.

PURSE SHELF EXTENDS 4″ BEYOND FRONT WALL SURFACE

RETRACTABLE CLOTHESLINE
UP TO 10′-0″
COILED WIRE
SUPPORT PLATE

4″ DEEP SHELF (RECESSED)

SURFACE PROTRUDES 5¼″

RECESSED 3½″-5½″ BEYOND WALL

FEMININE NAPKIN DISPENSER; SURFACE OR RECESSED
PROJECTION 6″

NAPKIN DISPOSAL SURFACE M'TD. HINGED TOP
PROJ. 4¼″

RECESSED DISPOSAL
PROJ. 4¼″

## WASTE RECEPTACLES

SURFACE MOUNTED CANVAS OR DISPOSABLE LINER BAG

HINGED ACCESS DOOR; DOOR CLEARANCE 13″

ELEV.   SECT.
WALL RECESSED

PLAN

ELEV.
FREESTANDING

## HAND TOWEL DISPENSERS AND DRYERS

FOLDED
PROJ. 3½″

ROLL
PROJ. 6¾″

ELECTRIC HAND DRYER

LINEN ROLL
PROJ. 10″

H. E. Hallenbeck, Capuccilli-Bell Architects, AIA; Syracuse, New York

# 10   TOILET AND BATH ACCESSORIES

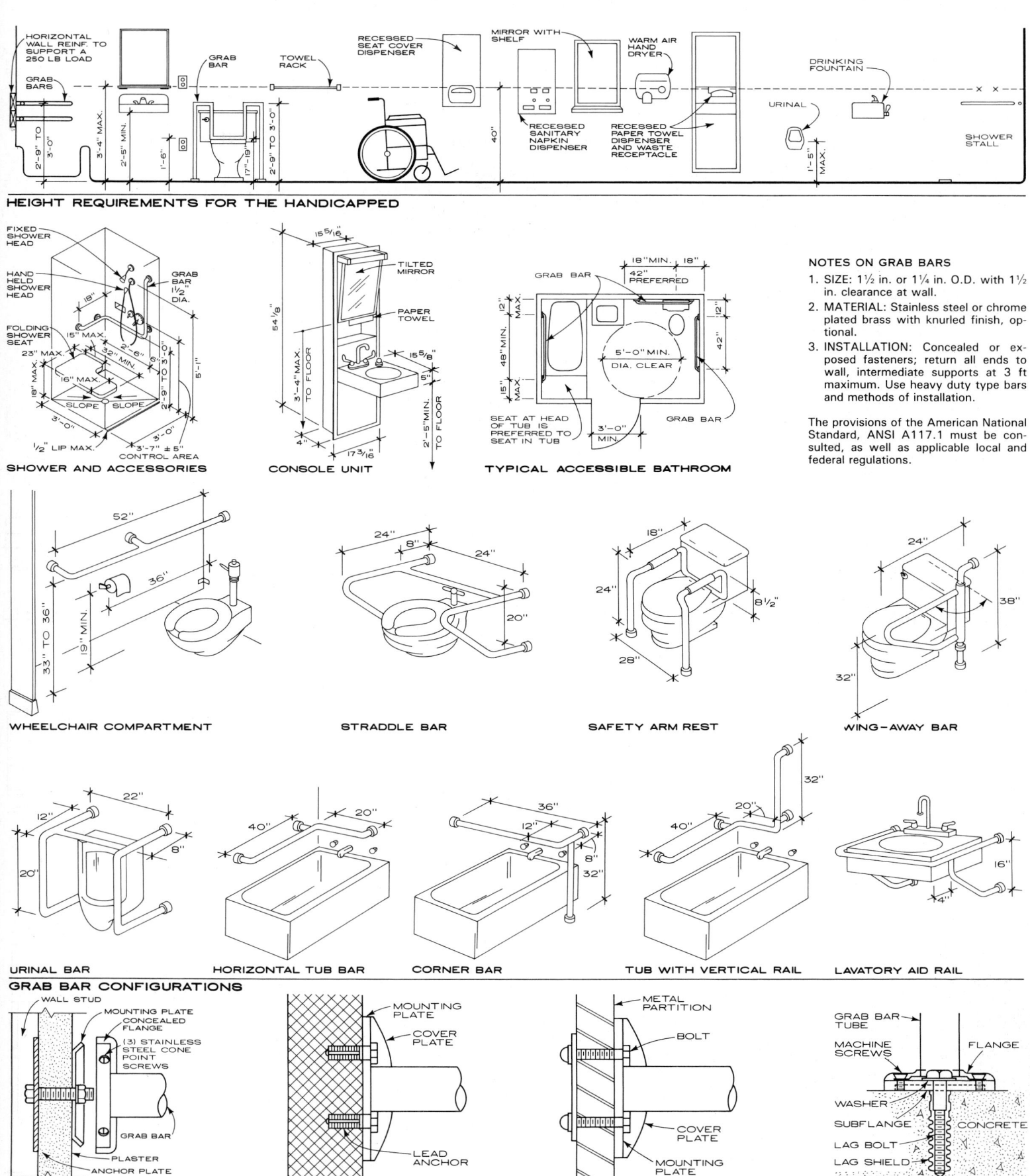

HORIZONTAL WALL REINF. TO SUPPORT A 250 LB LOAD

GRAB BARS

GRAB BAR

TOWEL RACK

RECESSED SEAT COVER DISPENSER

MIRROR WITH SHELF

WARM AIR HAND DRYER

DRINKING FOUNTAIN

URINAL

SHOWER STALL

2'-9" TO 3'-0"

3'-4" MAX.

2'-5" MIN.

1'-6"

17"-19"

2'-9" TO 3'-0"

40"

RECESSED SANITARY NAPKIN DISPENSER

RECESSED PAPER TOWEL DISPENSER AND WASTE RECEPTACLE

1'-5" MAX.

## HEIGHT REQUIREMENTS FOR THE HANDICAPPED

FIXED SHOWER HEAD

HAND HELD SHOWER HEAD

FOLDING SHOWER SEAT

GRAB BAR 1½" DIA.

18"

15" MAX.

23" MAX.

32" MIN.

16" MAX.

18" MAX.

SLOPE   SLOPE

3'-0"

½" LIP MAX.

3'-7" ± 5"

CONTROL AREA

### SHOWER AND ACCESSORIES

TILTED MIRROR

PAPER TOWEL

15 5/16"

54 1/8"

3'-4" MAX TO FLOOR

4"

17 3/16"

15 5/8"

5"

2'-5" MIN. TO FLOOR

### CONSOLE UNIT

GRAB BAR

18" MIN.   18"

42" PREFERRED

12" MAX.

48" MIN.

15" MAX.

5'-0" MIN. DIA. CLEAR

42"

12"

GRAB BAR

SEAT AT HEAD OF TUB IS PREFERRED TO SEAT IN TUB

3'-0" MIN.

### TYPICAL ACCESSIBLE BATHROOM

### NOTES ON GRAB BARS

1. SIZE: 1½ in. or 1¼ in. O.D. with 1½ in. clearance at wall.
2. MATERIAL: Stainless steel or chrome plated brass with knurled finish, optional.
3. INSTALLATION: Concealed or exposed fasteners; return all ends to wall, intermediate supports at 3 ft maximum. Use heavy duty type bars and methods of installation.

The provisions of the American National Standard, ANSI A117.1 must be consulted, as well as applicable local and federal regulations.

52"

36"

33" TO 36"

19" MIN.

### WHEELCHAIR COMPARTMENT

24"   8"

24"

20"

### STRADDLE BAR

18"

24"

28"

8½"

### SAFETY ARM REST

24"

38"

32"

### WING—AWAY BAR

22"

12"

20"

8"

### URINAL BAR

40"

20"

### HORIZONTAL TUB BAR

36"

12"

8"

32"

### CORNER BAR

40"

20"

32"

### TUB WITH VERTICAL RAIL

16"

4"

### LAVATORY AID RAIL

## GRAB BAR CONFIGURATIONS

WALL STUD

MOUNTING PLATE CONCEALED FLANGE

(3) STAINLESS STEEL CONE POINT SCREWS

GRAB BAR

PLASTER

ANCHOR PLATE

### STUD WALL

MOUNTING PLATE

COVER PLATE

LEAD ANCHOR

### MASONRY WALL

METAL PARTITION

BOLT

COVER PLATE

MOUNTING PLATE

### METAL PARTITION

GRAB BAR TUBE

MACHINE SCREWS

FLANGE

WASHER

SUBFLANGE

LAG BOLT

LAG SHIELD

CONCRETE

### SLAB

## ATTACHMENT DETAILS

Jones/Richards and Associates; Ogden, Utah

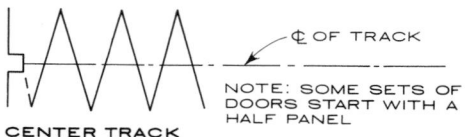

**CENTER TRACK**

Center track—supported at either the floor or ceiling. Panels are connected to each other and are either manually or power operated.

NOTE: SOME SETS OF DOORS START WITH A HALF PANEL

⊄ OF TRACK

**EDGE TRACK**

Edge track—supported at either the floor or ceiling. Panels are connected to each other and are either manually or power operated.

⊄ OF TRACK

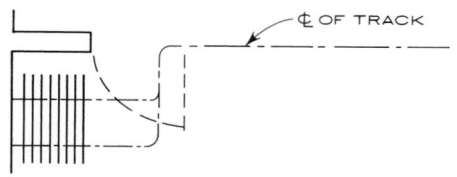

**STACKING POCKET**

Ceiling suspended, unconnected panels, manually operated only.

⊄ OF TRACK

**STACKING WITH SWITCHES**

SWITCH

SUPPORT
ADJUSTABLE SPACERS SECURED TO SUPPORT
TRACK
DOOR CARRIER
SOUND BAFFLE (OPT)
CEILING
STEEL OR WOOD SOFFIT
TOP SEAL
PANEL

HEAD

RETRACTABLE BOTTOM SEAL
FINISHED FLOOR
FIXED SEAL

**SILL TYPES**

**TOP HUNG**

BLOCKING AS REQUIRED FOR SUPPORT
CHANNEL TRACK
SOUND SEAL (OPTIONAL)
LINE OF FINISHED CEILING FOR CONCEALED INSTALLATION (CEILING HEIGHT MAY VARY)

**HEAD**

ADJUSTABLE ROLLERS
GUIDE
STEEL TRACK
STEEL PLATE SECURED FIRMLY
FELT SWEEP STRIPS (OPTIONAL)
FINISHED FLOOR
**SILL**

**FLOOR—SUPPORTED**

**LARGE PANEL FOLDING PARTITIONS**

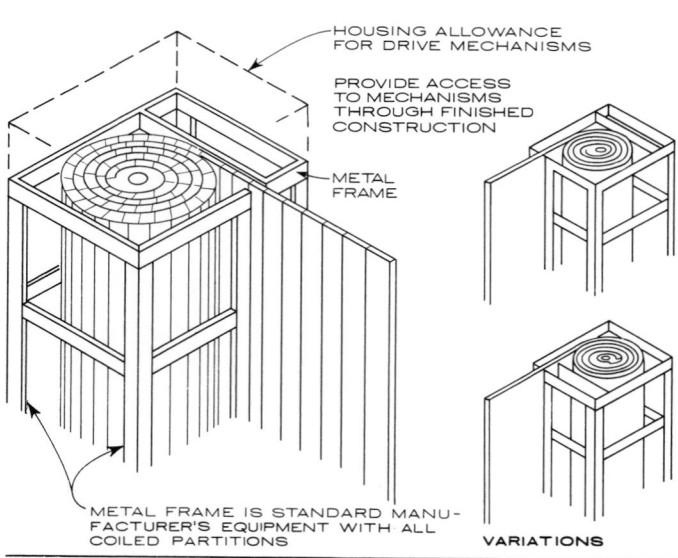

HOUSING ALLOWANCE FOR DRIVE MECHANISMS
PROVIDE ACCESS TO MECHANISMS THROUGH FINISHED CONSTRUCTION
METAL FRAME
METAL FRAME IS STANDARD MANUFACTURER'S EQUIPMENT WITH ALL COILED PARTITIONS

**VARIATIONS**

**COILED FOLDING PARTITIONS**

REQUIRED CLEARANCES VARY CONSULT MANUFACTURER
SECURE TO ADEQUATE SUPPORT
TRACK
CEILING

**TRACK (HEAD)**          **TRACK (HEAD)**

METAL COVER PLATE
FINISHED FLOOR
VARIES 3" – 6½"
7"±
**GUIDE (SILL) SINGLE**

OPTIONAL SOUND ABSORBENT MATERIAL
GROUT
12"±
**GUIDE (SILL) DOUBLE**

**SECTIONS**

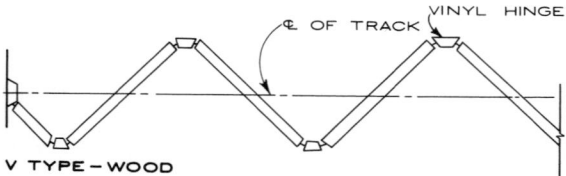

⊄ OF TRACK     VINYL HINGE

**V TYPE – WOOD**

"V" Type door is available in metal with fabric covering or in solid wood panels.

**TYPICAL ACCORDION PARTITIONS**

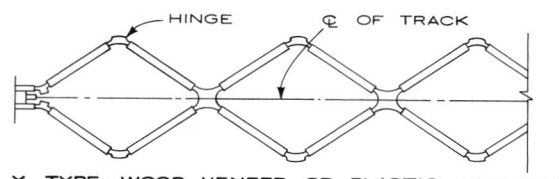

HINGE      ⊄ OF TRACK

**X TYPE – WOOD VENEER OR PLASTIC LAMINATE HINGES ARE EXTRUDED VINYL**

# CHAPTER 11

# Equipment

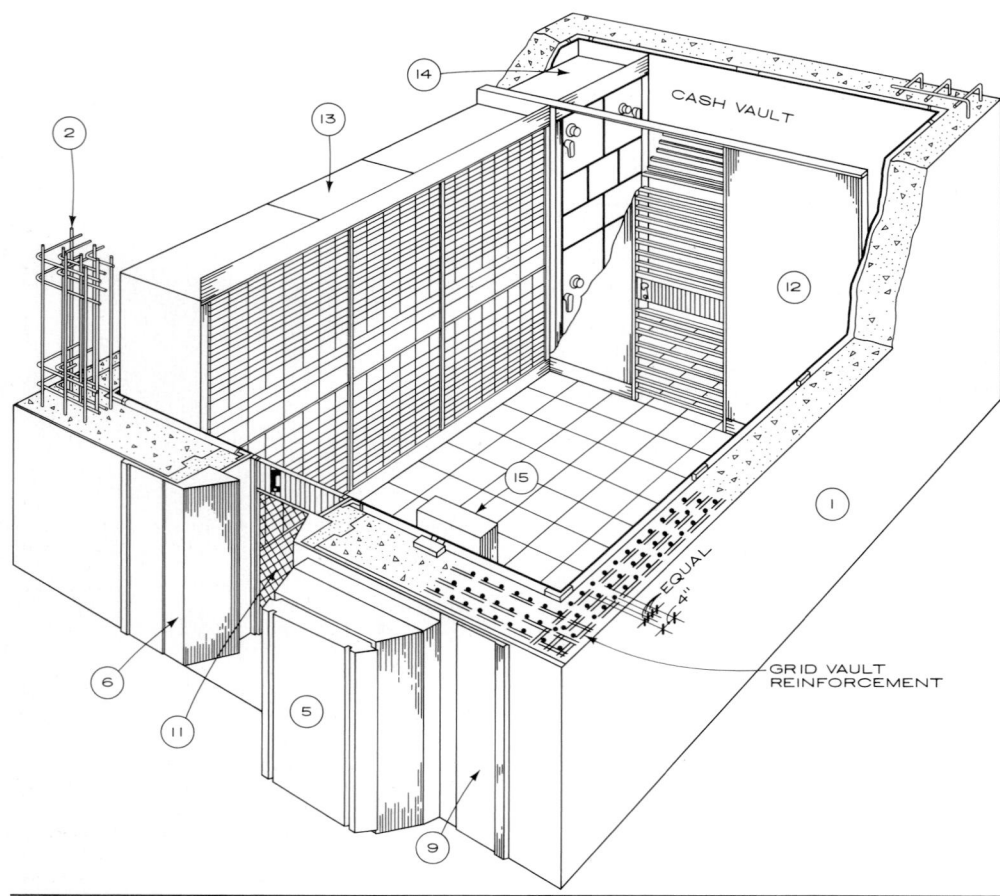

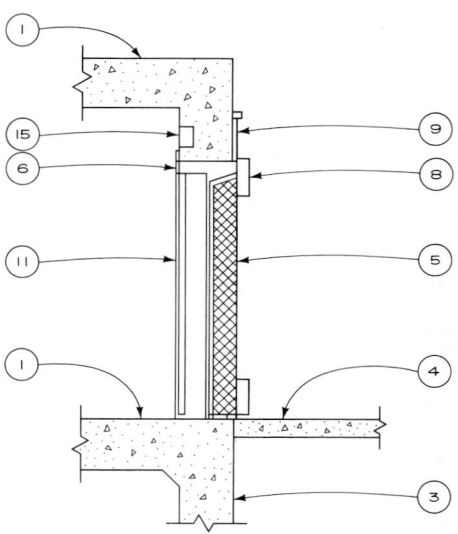

## VAULT DOOR SECTION

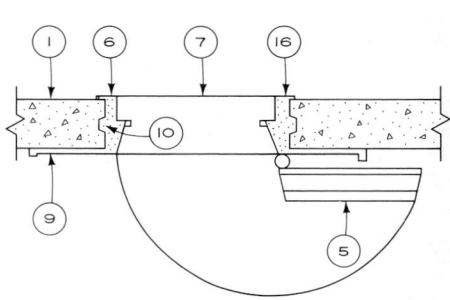

## VAULT DOOR OPENING

## SAFE DEPOSIT VAULT

### NOTE KEY

1. Reinforced concrete walls, floor, and ceiling
2. Steel reinforcing bars
3. Supporting foundation
4. Bank hall finished floor
5. Vault door
6. Vault door frame
7. Vault door sill
8. Vault door hinge beyond
9. Extended architrave
10. Tapered key—grout solid after door installation
11. Day gate
12. Partition and grille gate
13. Safe deposit box sections
14. Cash locker sections
15. Alarm junction box and required electrical service
16. Emergency vault ventilator in jamb of vault door

## INSURANCE SERVICES OFFICE (ISO)

| STEEL DOORS | WALL SPECIFICATIONS EFFECTIVE OCTOBER 30, 1974 | ISO CLASSI-FICATION |
|---|---|---|
| 3½ in. | A. ½ in. steel lining[3]<br>B. 12 in. reinforced concrete | 5R |
| 3½ in. | A. 1 in. steel lining[3]<br>B. ½ in. steel lining and 12 in. reinforced concrete<br>C. 18 in. reinforced concrete | 6R |
| 7 in. | A. 1 in. steel lining[3]<br>B. ½ in. steel lining and 12 in. reinforced concrete<br>C. 18 in. reinforced concrete | 9R |
| 9½ in. | A. 1½ in. steel lining[3]<br>B. ½ in. steel lining and 12 in. reinforced concrete<br>C. ½ in. steel lining and 18 in. reinforced concrete<br>D. 27 in. reinforced concrete or 18 in. listed reinforced concrete | 10R |

## UNDERWRITER'S LABORATORIES (UL) PERFORMANCE VAULTS

| | |
|---|---|
| Class 1 (½ hr) | Not shown—available for application only in existing buildings where structural support (floor load) is critical (does not comply with Bank Protection Act). |
| Class 2 (1 hr) | A. 18 in. reinforced concrete<br>B. 8 in. UL listed modular panel |
| Class 3 (2 hr) | A. 27 in. reinforced concrete<br>B. 13 in. UL listed modular panel |

### NOTES

1. The size, configuration, and specific requirements of all equipment and alarm systems that might be included in a bank will vary with different manufacturers and design considerations.

### GENERAL

Federally insured banks and savings institutions are regulated under the Bank Protection Act of 1968 as revised in 1973 which only recognizes vaults with walls, floor, and ceiling of reinforced concrete at least 12 in. thick. The following comparative classifications charts are used to rate security vaults:

Krommenhoek/McKeown & Associates; San Diego, California

2. Concrete used in vault construction should develop an ultimate compression strength of at least 3000 lb/in.$^2$

3. With fire-resistive materials to meet local building codes. Steel lining is not considered acceptable as burglary-resistant material equivalencies for UL vault construction and does not meet the Bank Protection Act requirements. Special approval required.

4. Class 2 UL listed vault is positioned as superior to the 9R vault classification.

5. Class 3 UL listed vault is positioned as superior to the 10R vault classification.

6. The above UL listed vaults are superior to traditional ISO and Bank Protection Act construction.

7. The Class 2 UL listed vault is recommended throughout the industry as minimum protection for safe deposit vault operations. A 2-hr, Class 3, is preferable.

### REINFORCING

No. 5 (⅝ in. diameter) deformed steel reinforcing bars located on 4 in. centers in horizontal and vertical rows to form a grid, or expanded steel bank vault mesh weighing 6 lb/ft$^2$ per grid and having a diamond pattern of 3 x 8 in.

Grids are to be located not less than 4 in. apart and shall be staggered in each direction. The number of grids required depends on the thickness of the wall, floor and ceiling (and specific insurance requirements).

#### MINIMUM NUMBER OF GRIDS FOR DEFORMED BARS

| | |
|---|---|
| 12 in. concrete thickness | 3 grids |
| 18 in. concrete thickness | 4 grids |
| 27 in. concrete thickness or over | 5 grids |

#### MINIMUM NUMBER OF GRIDS FOR #6 EXPANDED STEEL

| | |
|---|---|
| 12 in. concrete thickness | 2 grids |
| 18 in. concrete thickness | 3 grids |
| 27 in. concrete thickness or over | 4 grids |

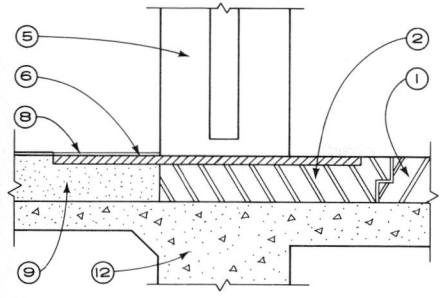

**VAULT DOOR SECTION AT STEEL PANEL FLOOR**

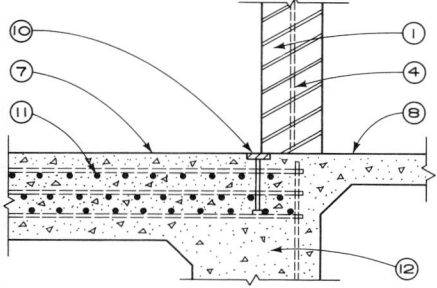

**STEEL WALL PANEL AT REINFORCED CONCRETE FLOOR**

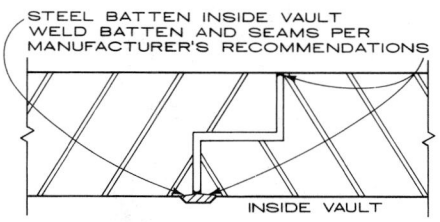

STEEL BATTEN INSIDE VAULT WELD BATTEN AND SEAMS PER MANUFACTURER'S RECOMMENDATIONS

INSIDE VAULT

**PANEL INTERSECTION DETAIL**

The vault floor construction may be either horizontal modular panels or reinforced concrete of varying thicknesses. If floor panels are used, the wall panels are welded directly to them at both sides.

## TYPICAL PANEL CONFIGURATION

### NOTE KEY

1. Modular vault panel
2. Special recessed floor panel
3. Welded steel batten inside vault
4. Vertical panel joint
5. Vault door jamb
6. ½ in. thick steel sill plate
7. Vault room floor (varies)

8. Bank hall floor
9. Bank hall subfloor
10. ½ in. thick x 3 in. wide continuous steel plate at finish floor with ½ in. diameter welded anchor studs set in concrete
11. #5 staggered, horizontal reinforcing bars at 4 in. o.c. each way typical
12. Supporting foundation

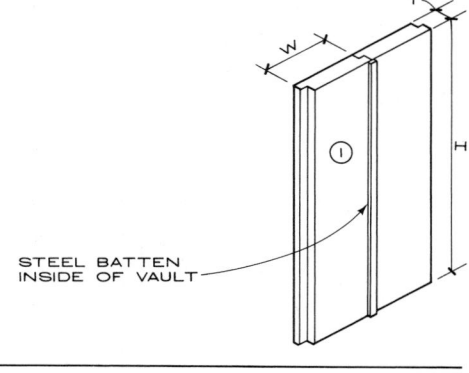

STEEL BATTEN INSIDE OF VAULT

## PANEL COMPARISON SCHEDULE

| PANEL TYPE | WEIGHT APPROXIMATE (PER SQ FT) | T THICKNESS | EQUIVALENT ISO WALL CONSTRUCTION | H HEIGHT MIN. | H HEIGHT MAX. | W WIDTH MIN. | W WIDTH MAX. |
|---|---|---|---|---|---|---|---|
| UL Class 1 | 29.5 lb | 6″ | 12″ R.C. — 3 Grids | 7′-6″ | 14′ | 2′ | 4′ |
| UL Class 2 | 39.5 lb | 8″ | 18″ R.C. — 4 Grids | 7′-6″ | 14′ | 2′ | 4′ |
| UL Class 3 | 60.0 lb | 13″ | 27″ R.C. — 5 Grids | 7′-6″ | 14′ | 2′ | 4′ |

### MODULAR VAULT SYSTEMS

Advantages over reinforced concrete vaults:

1. Comprise ⅓ to ⅕ the weight of concrete vaults
2. Can be installed virtually anywhere including high-rise buildings or where floor loading is critical
3. Structural reinforcement is reduced or eliminated
4. Faster installation time and reduced initial investment
5. Flexibility in disassembly, relocation, and future expansion purposes
6. Thin wall design uses less floor area and has superior torch and tool attack resistance

### STEEL LINING FOR RETROFIT

Typically, ½ in. thick steel vault linings are used in remodel or retrofit applications. Advantages include:

1. Meets ISO 5R classification
2. Lightweight construction
3. Less floor area required
4. Quicker installation time
5. Flexibility in disassembly, relocation, and future expansion purposes
6. Least expensive vault system overall

Disadvantages:

1. Highly susceptible to torch and tool attack
2. Consequently subject to higher insurance costs

### SAFE DEPOSIT BOXES

The standard design module for safe deposit boxes is 22¼ in. high x 32⅝ in. wide x 24 in. deep. Typical opening sizes include 2 x 5 in., 3 x 5 in., 5 x 5 in., 3 x 10 in., 5 x 10 in., and 10 x 10 in. with right- or left-hand swings. Available in steel or aluminum construction.

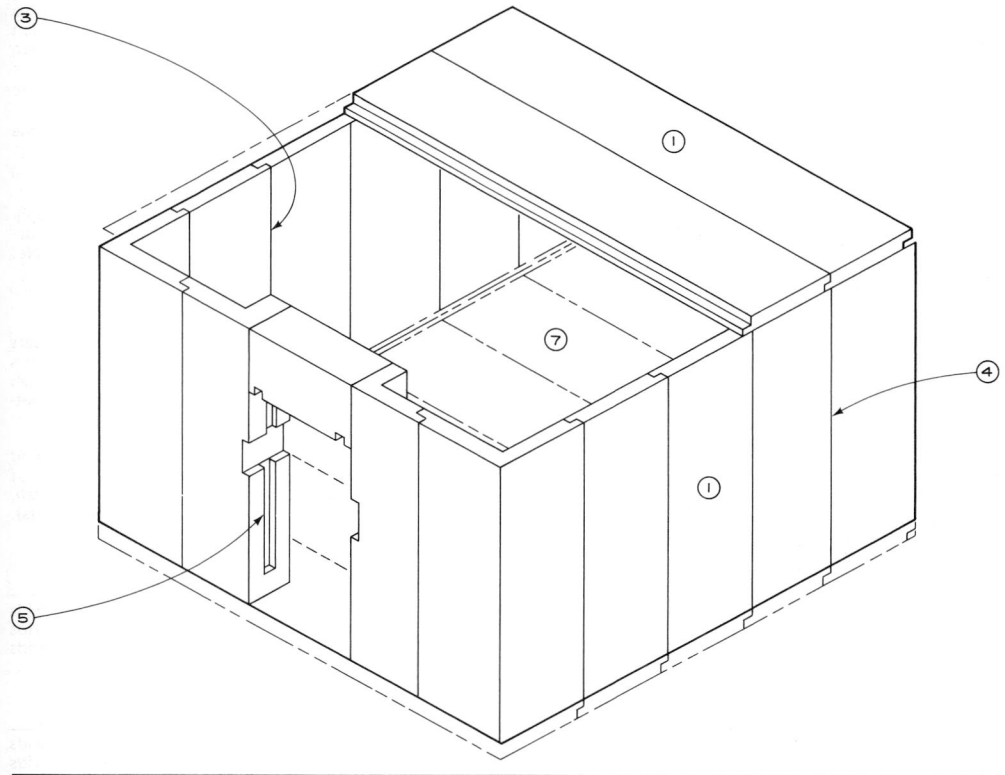

**MODULAR VAULT**

Krommenhoek/McKeown & Associates; San Diego, California

### ELECTRICAL

All electrical conduit for the alarm system, security equipment, lighting, telephone, etc., shall be in accordance with the National Electric Code. All conduit entering the walls, ceiling, or floor shall have at least one offset within the vault structure. Arrangement of bends shall be so that drainage is to the exterior. Conduit shall not exceed 1½ in. diameter.

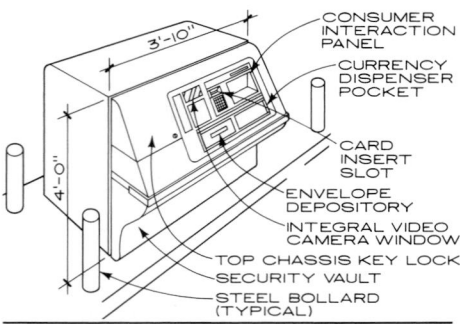

**DRIVE-UP AUTOMATIC TELLER MACHINE (ATM)**

Labels: CONSUMER INTERACTION PANEL; CURRENCY DISPENSER POCKET; CARD INSERT SLOT; ENVELOPE DEPOSITORY; INTEGRAL VIDEO CAMERA WINDOW; TOP CHASSIS KEY LOCK; SECURITY VAULT; STEEL BOLLARD (TYPICAL); 3'-10"; 4'-0"

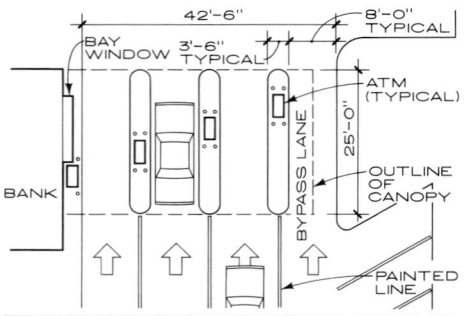

**PLAN OF DRIVE-UP TELLERS**

Labels: BAY WINDOW; BANK; 42'-6"; 3'-6" TYPICAL; 8'-0" TYPICAL; ATM (TYPICAL); 25'-0"; BYPASS LANE; OUTLINE OF CANOPY; PAINTED LINE

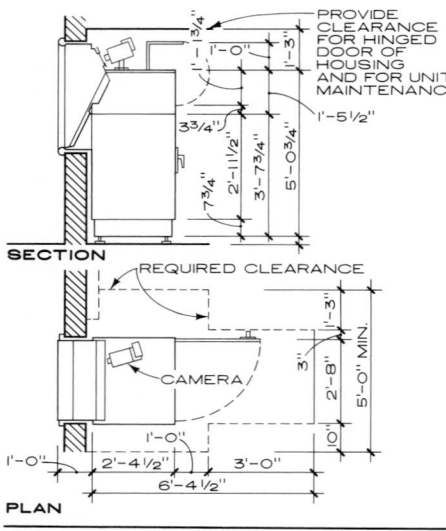

**SECTION**

**PLAN**

**AUTOMATIC TELLER MACHINE (ATM)**

Labels: PROVIDE CLEARANCE FOR HINGED DOOR OF HOUSING AND FOR UNIT MAINTENANCE; REQUIRED CLEARANCE; CAMERA; 3¾; 1'-0"; 1'-3"; 1'-5½"; 3¾"; 7¾"; 2'-11½"; 3'-7¾"; 5'-0¾"; 1'-3"; 3"; 2'-8"; 5'-0" MIN.; 1'-0"; 2'-4½"; 3'-0"; 6'-4½"

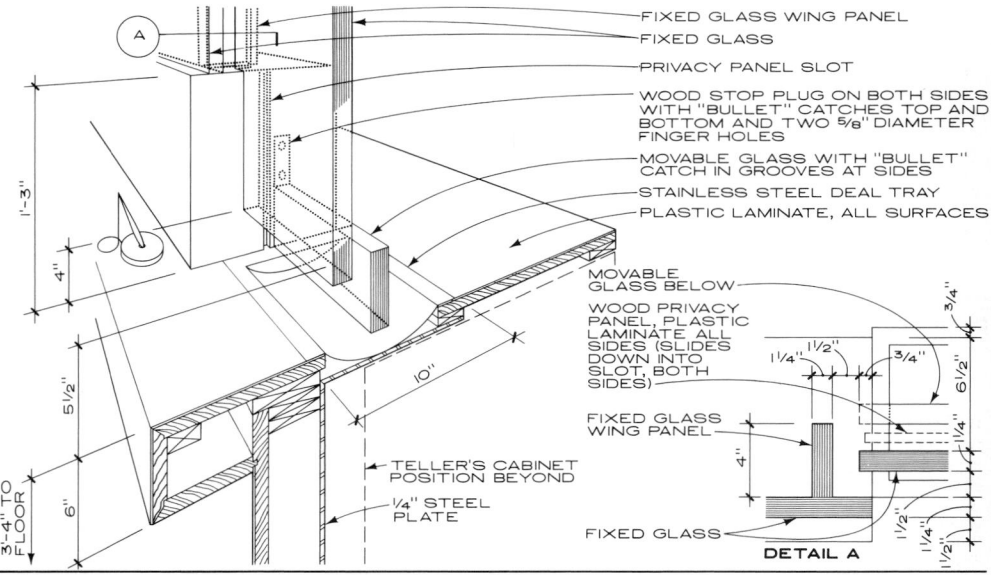

**BULLETPROOF GLASS AT TELLER'S STATION**

Labels: FIXED GLASS WING PANEL; FIXED GLASS; PRIVACY PANEL SLOT; WOOD STOP PLUG ON BOTH SIDES WITH "BULLET" CATCHES TOP AND BOTTOM AND TWO ⅝" DIAMETER FINGER HOLES; MOVABLE GLASS WITH "BULLET" CATCH IN GROOVES AT SIDES; STAINLESS STEEL DEAL TRAY; PLASTIC LAMINATE, ALL SURFACES; MOVABLE GLASS BELOW; WOOD PRIVACY PANEL, PLASTIC LAMINATE ALL SIDES (SLIDES DOWN INTO SLOT, BOTH SIDES); FIXED GLASS WING PANEL; FIXED GLASS; TELLER'S CABINET POSITION BEYOND; ¼" STEEL PLATE; DETAIL A; A; 1'-3"; 4"; 5½"; 6"; 3'-4" TO FLOOR; 10"; 4"; ¾; 1¼; 1½; ¾; 6½; 4"; ½; 1¼; 1½

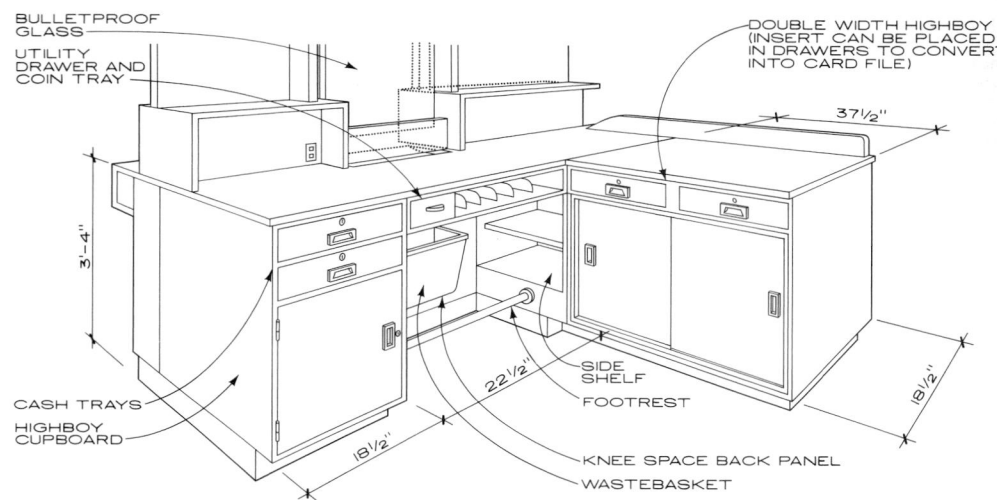

**TELLER STATION**

Labels: BULLETPROOF GLASS; UTILITY DRAWER AND COIN TRAY; CASH TRAYS; HIGHBOY CUPBOARD; DOUBLE WIDTH HIGHBOY (INSERT CAN BE PLACED IN DRAWERS TO CONVERT INTO CARD FILE); SIDE SHELF; FOOTREST; KNEE SPACE BACK PANEL; WASTEBASKET; 37½"; 3'-4"; 22½"; 18½"; 18½"

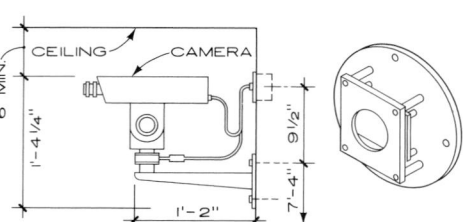

**SURVEILLANCE CAMERA AND VOICE PORT (TELLER SIDE)**

Labels: CEILING; CAMERA; 6" MIN.; 1'-4¼"; 9½"; 7'-4"; 1'-2"

## GENERAL NOTES

1. STANDARDS: Comply with the latest edition of "Comptroller's Manual for National Banks, Minimum Security Devices and Procedures" except when higher standards are shown in the construction documents.

2. SURVEILLANCE SYSTEM:
   a. 35 mm hold-up stile cameras.
   b. Device should be capable of enlarging images of persons to produce a 1 in. vertical head size.
   c. Device should be reasonably silent in operation.
   d. Capable of taking at least one picture every 2 sec.
   e. Capable of operating not less than 3 min.
   f. Surveillance devices other than at teller's station or window should be located so as to reproduce identifiable images of persons either leaving the banking office or in a position to transact business at each such station or window, and capable of actuation by initiating devices located at each teller's station or window.
   g. Surveillance devices for teller stations or windows should be located in such a manner as to reproduce

identifiable images of persons in a position to transact business at each such station or window and areas of such station or window that are vulnerable to robbery or larceny. Such devices should be capable of actuation by one or more initiating devices located within or in close proximity to such station or window. The teller should have access to a device to actuate a surveillance system that covers the area of vulnerability or the exits to the banking office.

3. ROBBERY ALARM SYSTEM:
   a. Four wire interphase control box.
   b. Money clip.
   c. Designated to transmit to the police through an intermediary, a signal indicating that a crime against the banking office has occurred or is in progress.

d. Capable of actuation by initiating devices located at each teller's station or window.
   e. Safeguarded against accidental transmission.
   f. Equipped with a visual and audible signal capable of indicating improper functioning of or tampering with the system.
   g. Equipped with an independent source of power sufficient to assure continuously reliable operation of the system for at least 24 hr.

4. BURGLARY ALARM SYSTEM:
   a. Capable of detecting promptly an attack on the outer door, walls, floor, or ceiling of each vault and each safe not stored in a vault, each Night Depository (ND) and each Automated Teller Machine (ATM) in which currency, negotiable securities, or similar valuables are stored when the office is closed, and any attempt to move any such safe.
   b. Designed to transmit to the police, through an intermediary, a signal indicating that any such attempt is in progress.
   c. Safeguarded against accidental transmission of an alarm.
   d. Equipped with a visual and audible signal capable of indicating improper functioning of or tampering with the system.
   e. Equipped with an independent source of power (such as a battery) sufficient to assure continuously reliable operation of the system for at least 80 hr in the event of failure of the usual source of power.

5. Equipment information was furnished by Diebold, Inc., Canton, OH.

Charles Szoradi, AIA; Washington, D.C.

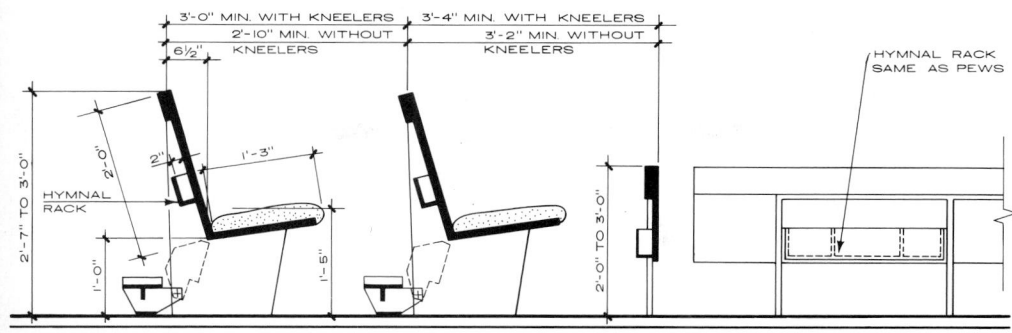

**PEW AND FRONTAL**

## PEW SPACING

| BACK-TO-BACK BETWEEN PEWS | | | PEW LENGTH* | | |
|---|---|---|---|---|---|
| NO. OF SPACES | 2'-10'' SPAC-ING | 3'-0'' SPAC-ING | NO. OF PER-SONS | 1'-8'' PER PER-SON | 1'-10'' PER PER-SON |
| 5 | 14'-2'' | 15'-0'' | 3 | 5'-0'' | 5'-6'' |
| 10 | 28'-4'' | 30'-0'' | 5 | 8'-4'' | 9'-2'' |
| 20 | 56'-8'' | 60'-0'' | 7 | 11'-8'' | 12'-10'' |
| 30 | 85'-0'' | 90'-0'' | 9 | 15'-0'' | 16'-6'' |
| | | | 11 | 18'-4'' | 20'-0'' |
| | | | 12 | 20'-0'' | |

*Minimum space allowed per person is 1 ft 6 in. Based on NFPA 101 Life Safety Code (1985), the maximum number of seats allowed in a row with aisles at both ends of the row is 14; maximum length allowed for a row is 21 ft 0 in.

## INTRODUCTION

Ecclesiastical furnishings are as much or more a part of the ambiance, symbolism, and meaning of a worship environment as the structure and architecture itself. Virtually all ecclesiastical furnishings are available from various manufacturers in predesigned, prefabricated form. In many cases, especially with regard to pews and chairs, such stock or semicustom items can be highly satisfactory and economical. Where special scale, material, or symbolism is desired, custom-designed and custom-built furnishings may be more appropriate, as is often true of chancel/sanctuary furnishings including pulpit, table, font, and clergy chairs. The illustrations on these pages provide information concerning the general size and character of such furnishings. The theology and liturgical attitudes of each church should provide primary guidance in the design and execution of ecclesiastical furnishings.

## PEWS

Most pew manufacturers offer a diverse selection of styles, materials, and finishes, and many will custom build special designs prepared by the architect. Pew ends contribute most to style and are available in numerous designs from closed to semiopen to fully open. Kneelers are optional and some are available with hydraulic pistons to govern the speed (and noise) with which they are lowered and raised. Other options include book, card, pencil, and communion cup holders.

## PULPIT/AMBO

The pulpit (Protestant) or ambo (Roman Catholic) has historically been a fixed chancel/sanctuary furnishing. However, with increasing demands for multiple uses of worship spaces, the need for flexibility often requires that all furnishings be movable.

Among the most important features of a pulpit/ambo is an adjustable top to accommodate the physical variations of speakers. A drop-down step may also be desirable. A pulpit should include a concealed reading lamp (especially where A/V darkening is employed) and a built-in clock. Although extensive use is being made of lavalier or wireless microphones, a concealed microphone cable raceway should be provided and the pulpit top padded to minimize the noise of rustling notes that sensitive microphones may amplify.

## LECTERN

The lectern is almost always movable. In small churches or chapels, a lectern may be used as a pulpit. Features similar to those required of the pulpit should be provided.

## COMMUNION RAIL

Communion rails should provide for comfortable kneeling. The rail may need to provide for the disposition of individual communion cups (as illustrated below). In worship spaces also used for concerts or drama, communion rails may need to be easily removable.

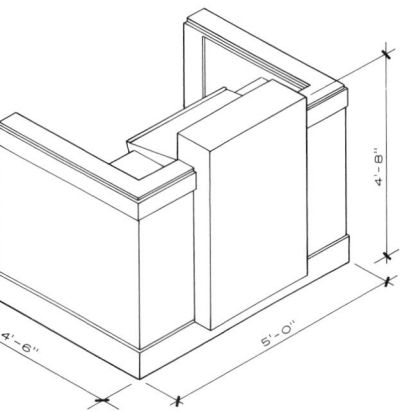

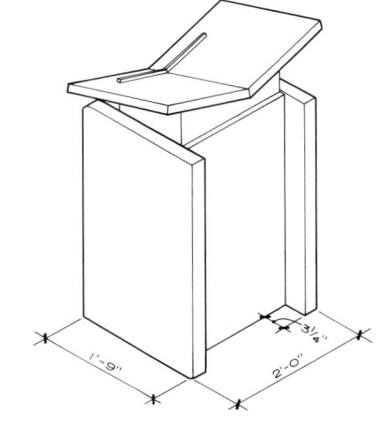

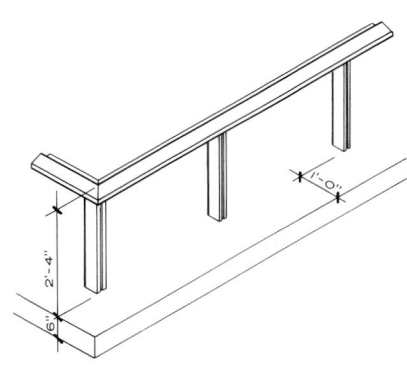

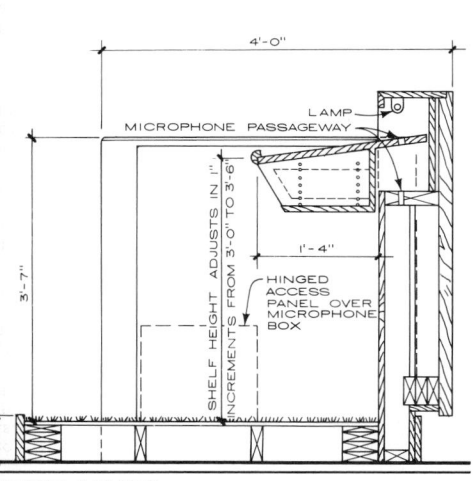

**PULPIT / AMBO**

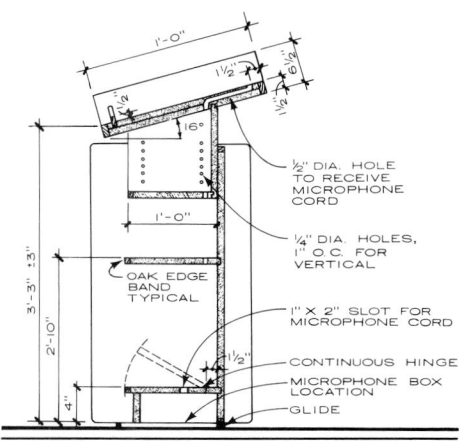

**LECTERN**

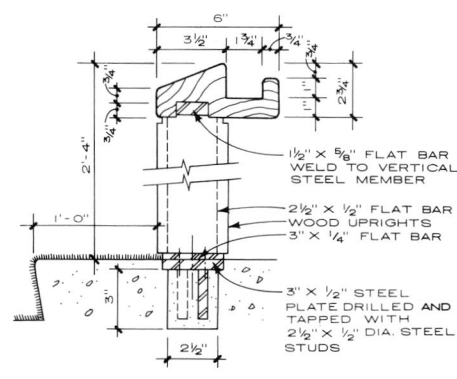

**COMMUNION RAIL**

Ware Associates, Inc.; Rockford, Illinois/Chicago/Los Angeles

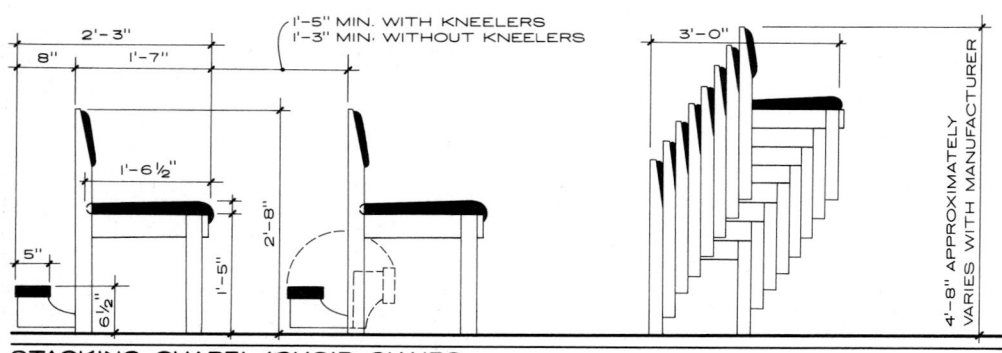

STACKING CHAPEL/CHOIR CHAIRS

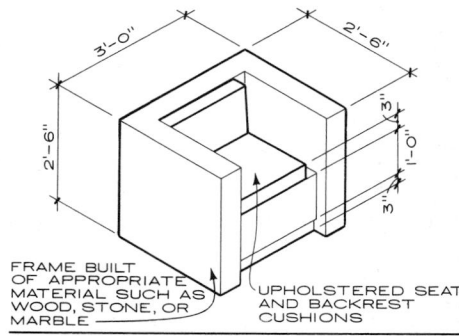

CLERGY/PRESIDER CHAIR

## STACK CHAIRS

A variety of stacking or modular chairs are available and well suited to uses such as small churches, chapels, and choir areas where flexibility of arrangement or complete removal is desired. Like pews, these chairs may be upholstered in differing degrees and equipped with kneelers, book holders, and other features. In addition, most manufacturers offer an interlocking device that enables the user to join rows of chairs together for temporarily fixed arrangements. Stacking capability allows efficient storage of chairs. When worship spaces become large enough to require a sloped floor for proper sight and sound lines, chairs are generally not advisable.

## ALTAR/COMMUNION TABLE

In most churches, the altar or communion table is the primary focus and therefore the most visually prominent

furnishing. Style and symbolism of the altar/table are deeply rooted in the liturgy of individual churches and usually require the participation and theological direction of both clergy and laity during design. Appropriateness of scale and material are particularly important and widely variable. The altar/table is among the most suitable furnishings for artist collaboration in design and execution.

## BAPTISMAL FONT

A font for ceremonial sprinkling of infants and/or adults may be placed in various locations including at the chancel/sanctuary or at the entrance to the church in the narthex. In some cases, the font may be alternately moved between these locations. Usually space for gathering of family and friends is required around the font and, in many churches, the font is required to be in a position that permits general viewing of a baptism by the entire congregation. Churches practicing baptism by im-

mersion or submersion require an altogether different style of baptistry involving a pool or tank that allows full entry by laity and clergy. Prefabricated baptistry tanks are available and custom installations possible.

## TABERNACLE

The tabernacle generally associated with Roman Catholic, Orthodox, and Episcopalian ("ambry" rather than tabernacle) churches is a very significant element in the worship environment, acting as the place of repose for the consecrated Host—the body of Christ. It is often a highly artistic and custom furnishing. Careful attention to the liturgical attitudes of the individual church and review of the document "*Environment and Art in Catholic Worship*" (for Roman Catholic churches) should guide the design and placement of the tabernacle.

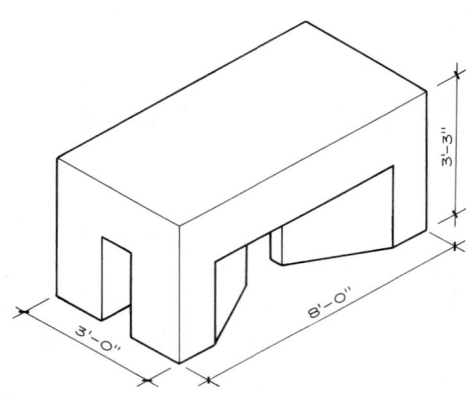

ALTAR

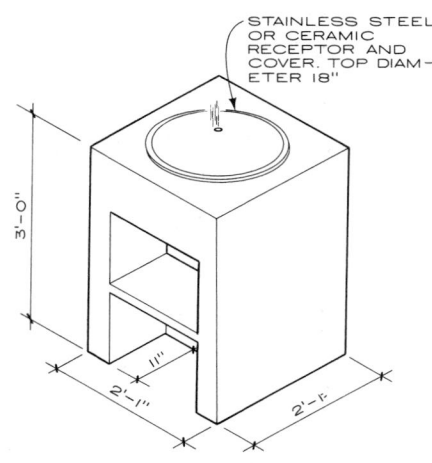

BAPTISMAL FONT

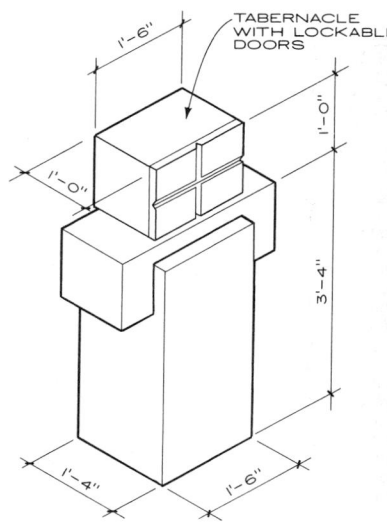

TABERNACLE

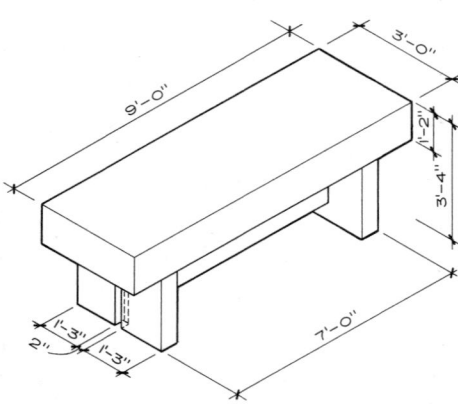

COMMUNION TABLE

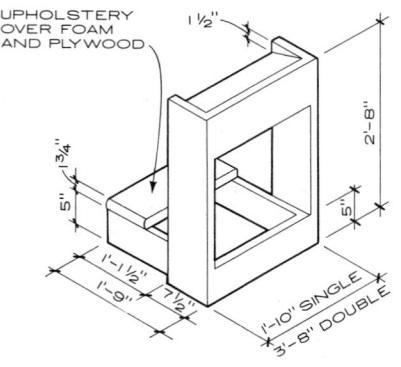

INDIVIDUAL KNEELER

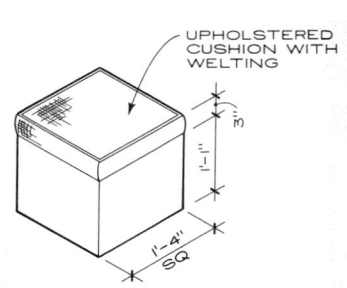

ACOLYTE STOOL

Ware Associates, Inc.; Rockford, Illinois/Chicago/Los Angeles

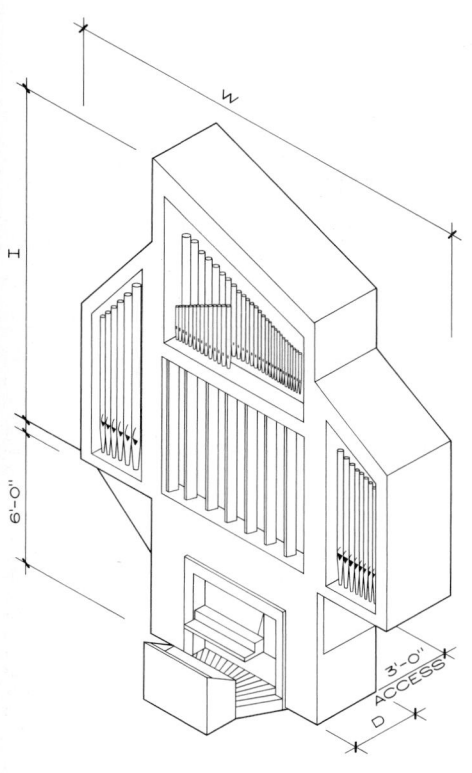

**MECHANICAL ACTIONED ORGAN (TRACKER)**

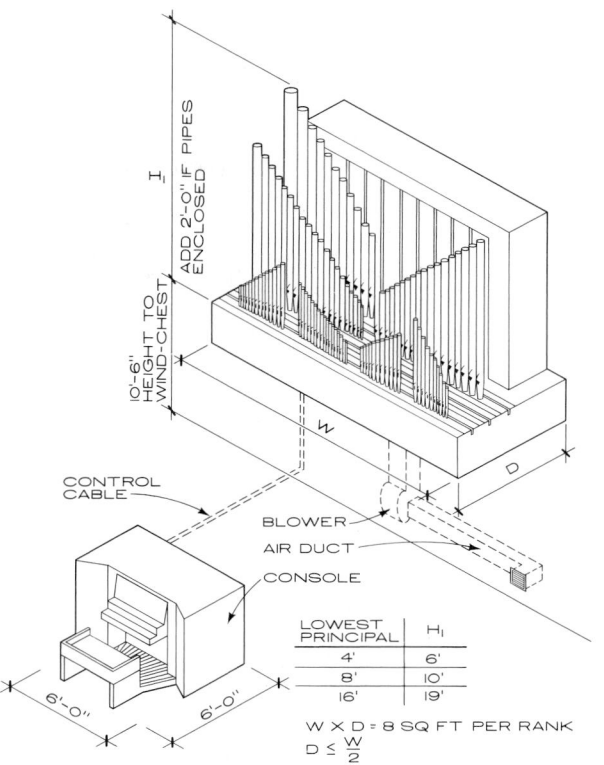

**ELECTROMECHANICAL OR ELECTROPNEUMATIC ORGAN**

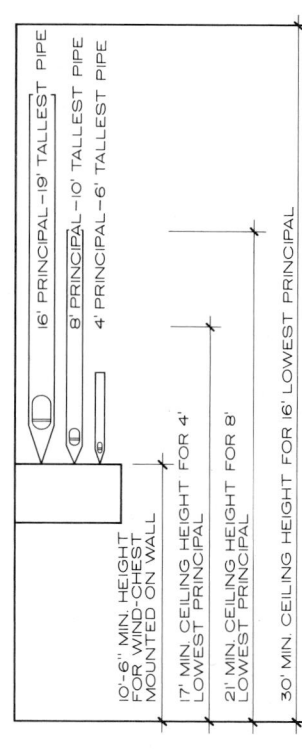

| LOWEST PRINCIPAL | $H_1$ |
|---|---|
| 4' | 6' |
| 8' | 10' |
| 16' | 19' |

$$W \times D = 8 \text{ SQ FT PER RANK}$$
$$D \leq \frac{W}{2}$$

## PIPE ORGANS

Organ builders recommend that the pipes and casework be located within the space they are to serve, not in an organ chamber. Organ and console, located in proximity to one another, should be placed so that sound can travel freely and directly to the listeners. No furnishings, people, or other barriers should be located in front of the organ pipes. Drafts and sudden temperature changes to the pipes may necessitate more frequent tuning.

While blowers may be built in to the organ casework, quieter operation can be achieved placing the blower in a remote space. However, air for the blower should be drawn from the room in which the organ is located to avoid tuning changes. Sound isolation, power requirements, serviceability, and need for a large duct chase to the organ must be considered when designing the blower room.

The number of stops or ranks required for an organ installation is related to musical flexibility rather than the loudness of an organ. The number of manuals will also vary depending on need for flexibility in the musical program. The table below outlines general guidelines to select the number of ranks for an organ installation.

## ELECTROMECHANICAL AND ELECTROPNEUMATIC ORGANS

In these types of instruments, air that passes from the wind-chests into the pipes is controlled by either electromechanical or electropneumatic means. The required size of the organ pipe space will vary depending on the organ builder, but 8 sq ft per rank may be used as a general rule of thumb. If height is available, divisions may be stacked, reducing the floor area required by approximately 25%. All pipes must be accessible for tuning.

Weight of the organ will also vary. A general average is 450 lb per rank. If the organ is enclosed in a case, 50 lb per rank should be added. A stacked arrangement of pipe divisions will increase the floor loading proportionally.

## MECHANICAL ACTIONED ORGANS

Commonly know as tracker organs, these instruments introduce air into the pipes through a valve mechanically attached to the keys on the console. The size of tracker organs is measured in terms of stops rather than ranks. Tracker organs are self-contained in wooden cases that house pipes, wind-chests, manuals, and mechanical

components. Such wooden cases may be designed to complement the architecture of the surrounding space. Compared to electromechanical and electropneumatic organs, a tracker organ will usually require more height for pipe cases but consequently less floor area. Often used in chapels because of their compactness, tracker organs are not limited to use in small worship spaces. In larger installations the console may be separated from the pipe chests by a limited distance, but must nonetheless be fixed, due to the mechanical connections between manuals and pipes.

Blowers for this type of instrument are built into the organ casework. Electrical power for the blower must be provided.

Mechanical actioned organs have an average weight of 400–500 lb per stop. A 3 ft 0 in. minimum access space behind the instrument is required for servicing and tuning.

Additional information is available through the Associated Pipe Organ Builders of America.

## GENERAL SIZE REQUIREMENTS BASED UPON VARIOUS SEATING CAPACITIES

| NO. OF SEATS | NO. OF STOPS | NO. OF RANKS | NO. OF DIVISIONS (1) | LOWEST PRINCIPAL (2) |
|---|---|---|---|---|
| 150 | 4–9 | 6–12 | 2–3 | 4' |
| 200 | 9–13 | 12–16 | 3 | 8' |
| 250 | 12–18 | 16–23 | 3 | 8' |
| 300 | 15–25 | 18–34 | 3 | 8' |
| 400 | 20–30 | 26–44 | 3 | 16' |
| 500 | 25–35 | 34–50 | 3–4 | 16' |
| 750 | 30–45 | 44–64 | 4 | 16' |
| 1000 | 35–50 | 50–78 | 4 | 16' |

## MINIMUM DIMENSIONS FOR A TRACKER ORGAN CASE BASED UPON VARIOUS NUMBERS OF STOPS

| NO. OF SEATS | NO. OF STOPS | NO. OF RANKS | NO. OF DIVISIONS | LOWEST PRINCIPAL | W WIDTH | D DEPTH | H HEIGHT |
|---|---|---|---|---|---|---|---|
| 150 | 4–9 | 6–12 | 2–3 | 4 | 10' | 28'' | 10' |
| 200 | 9–13 | 12–16 | 3 | 8 | 12' | 28'' | 12' |
| 250 | 12–18 | 16–23 | 3 | 8 | 15' | 36'' | 14' |
| 300 | 15–25 | 18–34 | 3 | 8 | 18' | 42'' | 17' |
| 400 | 20–30 | 26–44 | 3 | 16 | 20' | 48'' | 23' |
| 500 | 25–55 | 34–50 | 3–4 | 16 | 22' | 52'' | 25' |
| 750 | 30–45 | 44–64 | 4 | 16 | 22' | 56'' | 25' |
| 1000 | 35–50 | 50–78 | 4 | 16 | 22' | 60'' | 25' |

Ware Associates, Inc.; Rockford, Illinois/Chicago/Los Angeles

**ECCLESIASTICAL EQUIPMENT**    11

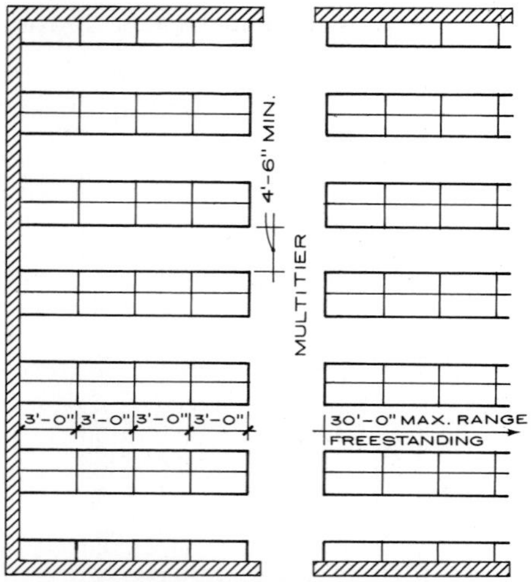

## SHELF CAPACITY AND DEPTH

| TYPE OF BOOK | VOLUMES PER LINEAR FT | SHELF DEPTH (IN.) |
|---|---|---|
| Children's | 10-12 | 8 |
| Fiction and economics | 7 | 8 |
| History and General Literature | 7 | 8 |
| Reference | 7 | 10 |
| Technical and Scientific | 6 | 8 |
| Medical | 5 | 10 |
| Law and public documents | 4-5 | 8 |
| Bound periodicals | 5 | 10-12 |
| U.S. Patent spec. | 2 | 8 |

### BOOK CAPACITY PER GROSS FLOOR AREA

Many variables must be considered: size and kind of books, book lifts, carrels, number and width of aisles, ultimate capacity, and so on. Variances run from 13½ to 19 books/sq ft. For a rule of thumb allow 16 books/sq ft of gross area. The average dead load of books is 25 lb/cu ft.

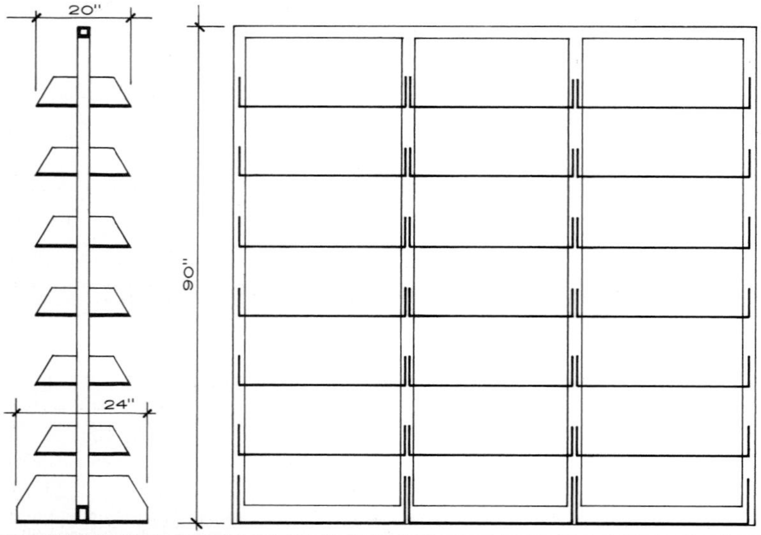

**4'-6" MIN.**

**MULTITIER**

**3'-0" 3'-0" 3'-0" 3'-0"**

**30'-0" MAX. RANGE FREESTANDING**

**PLAN—WOOD OR STEEL**

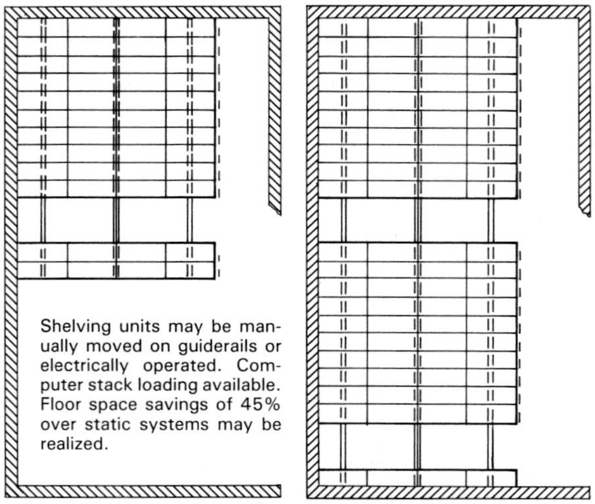

Shelving units may be manually moved on guiderails or electrically operated. Computer stack loading available. Floor space savings of 45% over static systems may be realized.

**PLAN—TRACK OR STACK SHELVING**

**20"**

**90"**

**24"**

**ADJUSTABLE SHELF UNIT, STEEL**

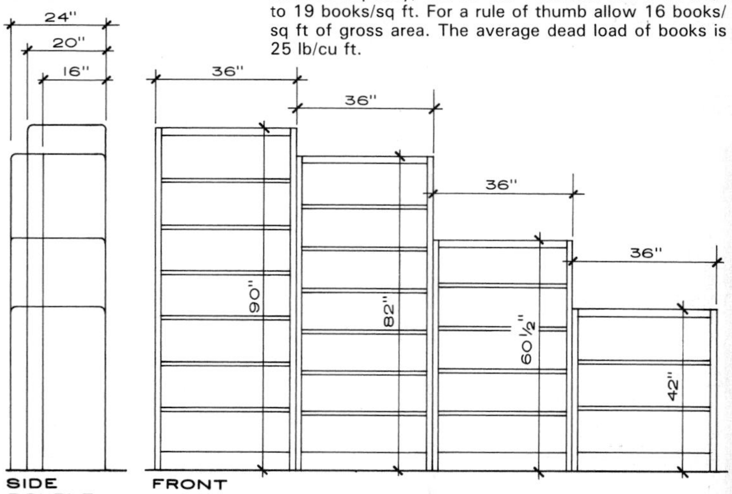

**24"** **20"** **16"**

**SIDE DOUBLE FACED**

**36" 36" 36" 36"**

**90" 82" 60½" 42"**

**FRONT**

SINGLE FACED 8", 10", 12" DEPTH. 90" HEIGHT ONLY 10" DEPTH. DOUBLE FACED 16", 20", 24" DEPTH. 90" HEIGHT ONLY, 20" DEPTH

**ADJUSTABLE SHELF UNIT, WOOD**

SHELF

DESK TOP

ELECTRICAL OUTLET, THIN LINE, OPTIONAL

**48½"**

**35¾"**

**FRONT**

SHELF

LIGHT OPTIONAL

DESK TOP

**¾"**

**24"**

**SIDE, SINGLE FACED**

**46¼"**

**SIDE, DOUBLE FACED**

**CARRELS**

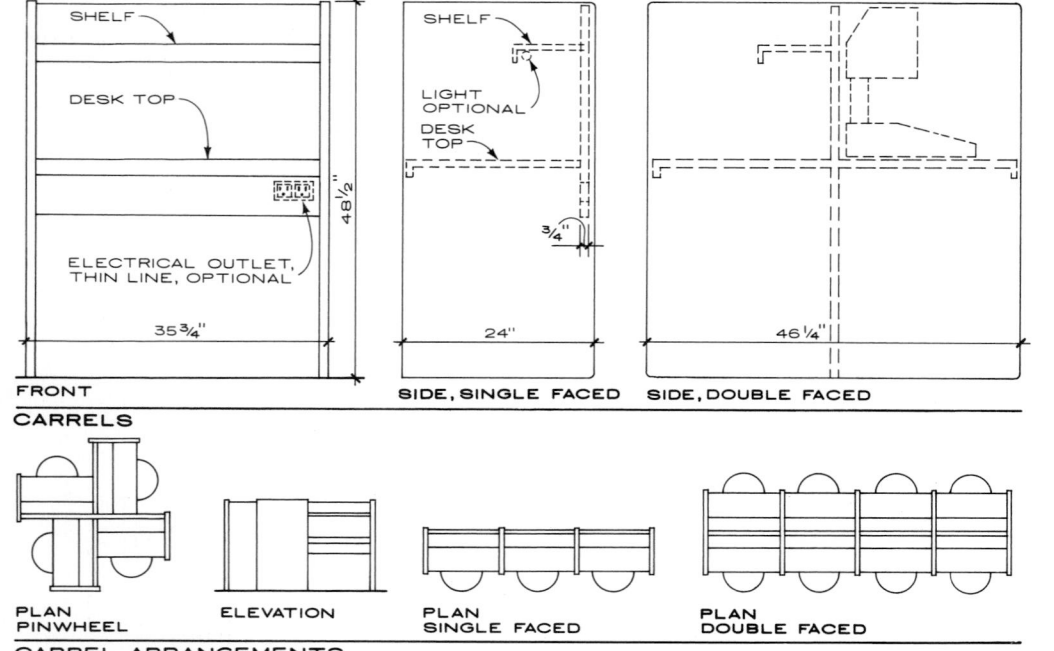

**PLAN PINWHEEL**    **ELEVATION**    **PLAN SINGLE FACED**    **PLAN DOUBLE FACED**

**CARREL ARRANGEMENTS**

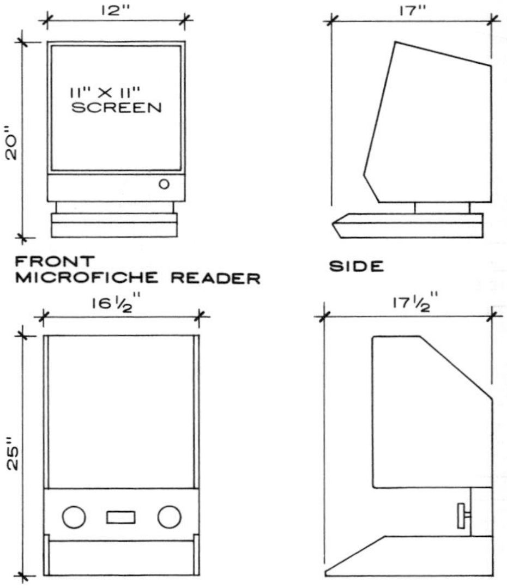

**12"**

**20"**

**11" X 11" SCREEN**

**FRONT MICROFICHE READER**

**17"**

**SIDE**

**16½"**

**25"**

**FRONT MICROREADER FOR FICHE OR FILM**

**17½"**

**SIDE**

**NOTE**

Generally microfilm and microfiche readers and video display terminals (VDT) are positioned on tables.

**LIBRARY EQUIPMENT**

Walter Hart Associates, AIA; White Plains, New York

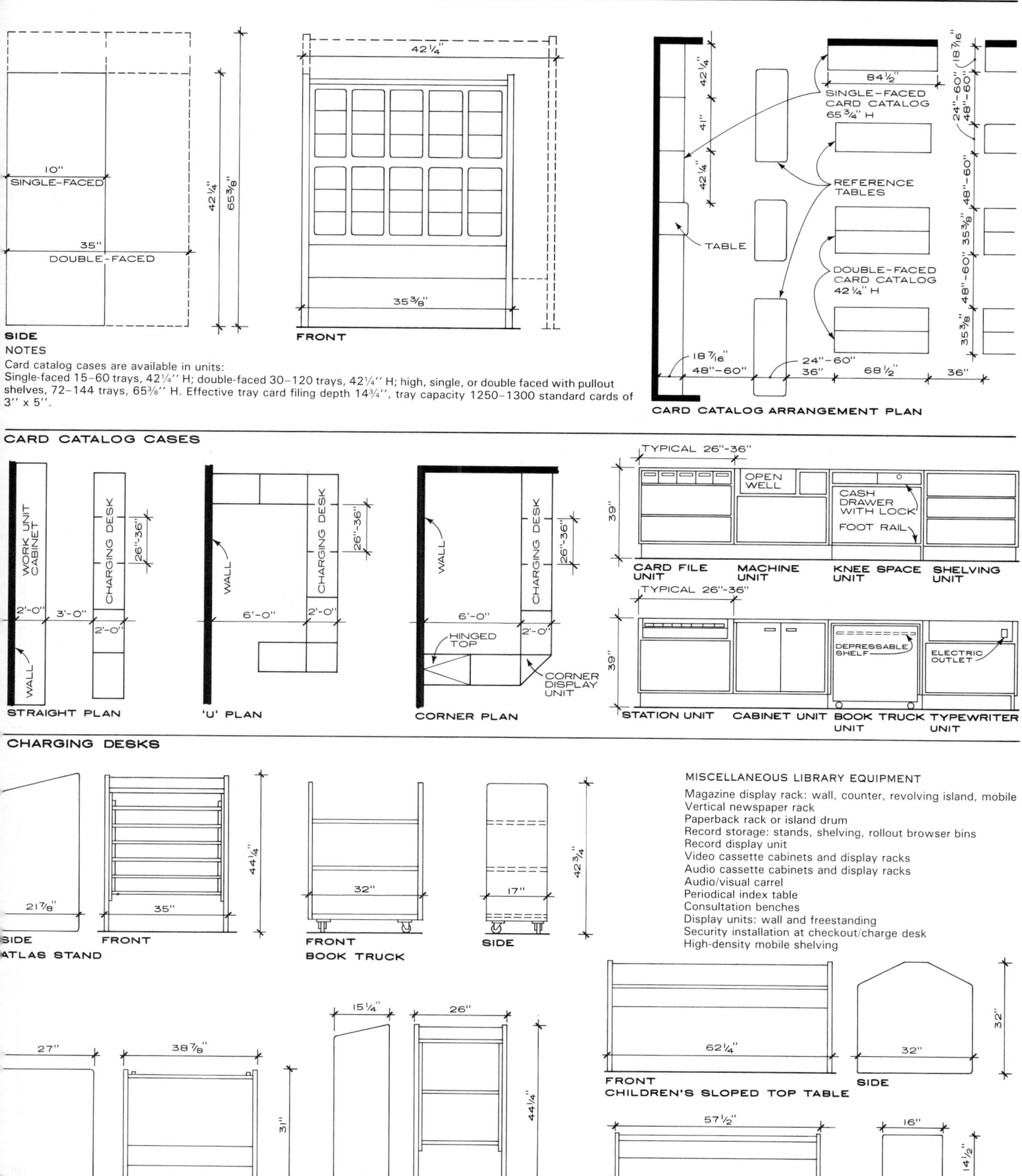

**SIDE**

10" SINGLE-FACED

35" DOUBLE-FACED

42 1/4"

65 3/8"

**FRONT**

42 1/4"

35 3/8"

**NOTES**

Card catalog cases are available in units:
Single-faced 15–60 trays, 42 1/4" H; double-faced 30–120 trays, 42 1/4" H; high, single, or double faced with pullout shelves, 72–144 trays, 65 3/8" H. Effective tray card filing depth 14 3/4", tray capacity 1250–1300 standard cards of 3" x 5".

**CARD CATALOG ARRANGEMENT PLAN**

SINGLE-FACED CARD CATALOG 65 3/4" H

REFERENCE TABLES

TABLE

DOUBLE-FACED CARD CATALOG 42 1/4" H

84 1/2"

42 1/4"

41"

42 1/4"

18 7/16"  48"–60"

24"–60"  36"

68 1/2"

36"

24"–60"  (18 7/16")
48"–60"
48"–60"  48"–60"  35 3/8"  48"–60"
35 3/8"

## CARD CATALOG CASES

**STRAIGHT PLAN**

WORK UNIT CABINET

CHARGING DESK

WALL

2'-0"  3'-0"  2'-0"  26"-36"

**'U' PLAN**

WALL

CHARGING DESK

6'-0"  2'-0"  26"-36"

**CORNER PLAN**

WALL

CHARGING DESK

HINGED TOP

CORNER DISPLAY UNIT

6'-0"  2'-0"  26"-36"

**CARD FILE UNIT**  **MACHINE UNIT**  **KNEE SPACE UNIT**  **SHELVING UNIT**

TYPICAL 26"-36"

OPEN WELL

CASH DRAWER WITH LOCK

FOOT RAIL

39"

**STATION UNIT**  **CABINET UNIT**  **BOOK TRUCK UNIT**  **TYPEWRITER UNIT**

TYPICAL 26"-36"

DEPRESSABLE SHELF

ELECTRIC OUTLET

39"

## CHARGING DESKS

**ATLAS STAND**

SIDE  FRONT

21 7/8"  35"  44 1/4"

**BOOK TRUCK**

FRONT  SIDE

32"  17"  42 3/4"

**NEWSPAPER STAND**

SIDE  FRONT

27"  38 7/8"  31"

SIDE  FRONT

15 1/4"  26"  44 1/4"

### MISCELLANEOUS LIBRARY EQUIPMENT

Magazine display rack: wall, counter, revolving island, mobile
Vertical newspaper rack
Paperback rack or island drum
Record storage: stands, shelving, rollout browser bins
Record display unit
Video cassette cabinets and display racks
Audio cassette cabinets and display racks
Audio/visual carrel
Periodical index table
Consultation benches
Display units: wall and freestanding
Security installation at checkout/charge desk
High-density mobile shelving

**CHILDREN'S SLOPED TOP TABLE**

FRONT  SIDE

62 1/4"  32"  32"

**CHILDREN'S BENCH**

FRONT  SIDE

57 1/2"  16"  14 1/2"

## MISCELLANEOUS LIBRARY EQUIPMENT

Walter Hart Associates, AIA; White Plains, New York

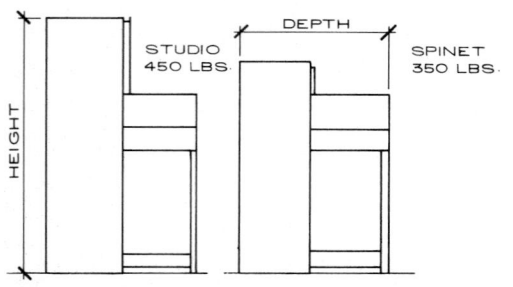

**SIDE ELEVATIONS – UPRIGHT PIANOS**

## PIANO SIZES

| TYPE | DEPTH | WIDTH | HEIGHT | HEIGHT WITH LID RAISED |
|---|---|---|---|---|
| Concert grand | 9'-8'' | 5'-4'' | 3'-3'' | 6'-1'' |
| Music room grand | 7' | 5' | 3'-4'' | 6'-1'' |
| Parlor grand | 6'-3'' | 4'-10'' | 3'-4'' | 5'-10'' |
| Baby grand | 4'-5'' | 4'-7'' | 3' | 4'-4'' |
| Spinet | 2'-1'' | 4'-10'' | 3'-4'' | — |
| Studio | 2'-1'' | 4'-9'' | 3'-10'' | — |

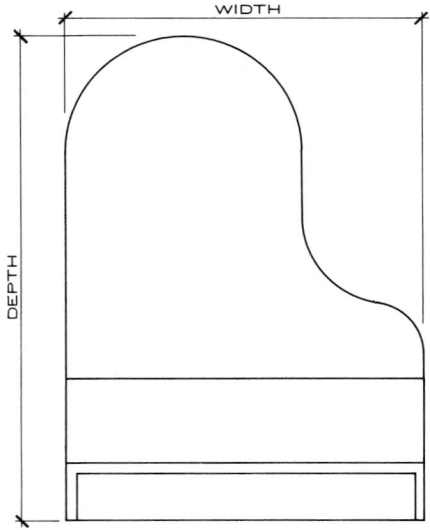

**PLAN: GRAND PIANO** 600-1200 LBS.

## PIANOS

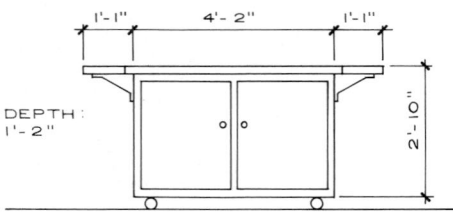

**FRONT ELEVATION**

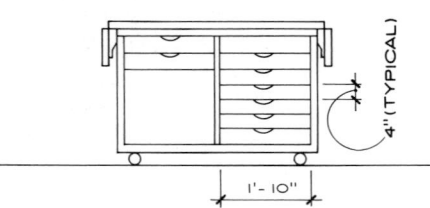

**FRONT ELEVATION**
(SHOWING DOORS REMOVED AND THE LEAVES DOWN)

**PERCUSSION CABINET**

**ELECTRONIC SYNTHESIZERS**

NOTE

Shown are the typical elements of synthesizers: keyboard, amplifier, and speakers. Many different models, combining two or more of the standard elements, are available as small portable or large sophisticated units.

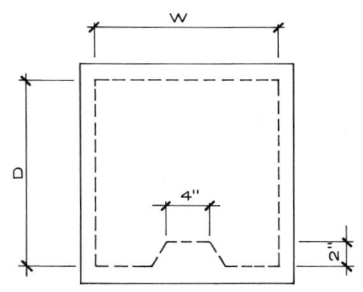

**ELEVATION**

**PLAN**

## FOLIO MUSIC STORAGE

| | D | W |
|---|---|---|
| Choral folio music | 14¼'' | 10½'' |
| Band folio music | 16'' | 14¾'' |
| Orchestra folio music | 16'' | 14¾'' |
| Marching band folio music | 8¼'' | 7'' |

NOTE

Music folio, uniform and choral robe, and other music storage components are available commercially. Consult manufacturer for additional information.

Doors may be added for security and to keep out dust. Shelves should be adjustable to accommodate thicker material when required.

**FOLIO MUSIC STORAGE**

**ELEVATION**

NOTE

Consider storage space for amplifiers, synthesizers, microphones, and other electronic equipment. School music rooms also may require storage space for choral risers, music stands, etc. Individual instrument cabinets should be lockable by key or combination lock.

**MUSICAL INSTRUMENT STORAGE CABINETS**

## STORAGE CABINET SIZES

| INSTRUMENT TYPE | CABINET SIZE (IN.)* | | |
|---|---|---|---|
| | H | W | D |
| A. Clarinet, alto clarinet, bass clarinet, flute, oboe, piccolo, soprano saxophone, trumpet | 12 | 12 | 30 |
| B. Cornet, flugel horn, double trumpet | 20 | 12 | 30 |
| C. Bassoon, alto saxophone, tenor saxophone, brass trumpet, violin, viola, trombone | 40 | 12 | 30 |
| D. Alto horn, French horn, baritone horn, tenor horn | 40 | 18 | 30 |
| E. Valve trombone, parade drum, snare drum | 20 | 24 | 30 |
| F. Bass drum, concert drum, scotch drum | 40 | 36 | 30 |
| G. Tuba, sousaphone, baritone saxophone | 40 | 48 | 30 |

*General sizes only. Actual instrument and case sizes may vary in size requirements. Commercially manufactured cabinets, which can be stacked together as units, are shown to the left.

Leland D. Blackledge, AIA; South St. Paul, Minnesota

**NOTE**
Dimensions given are the maximum length, height, and width found if several models and styles exist.

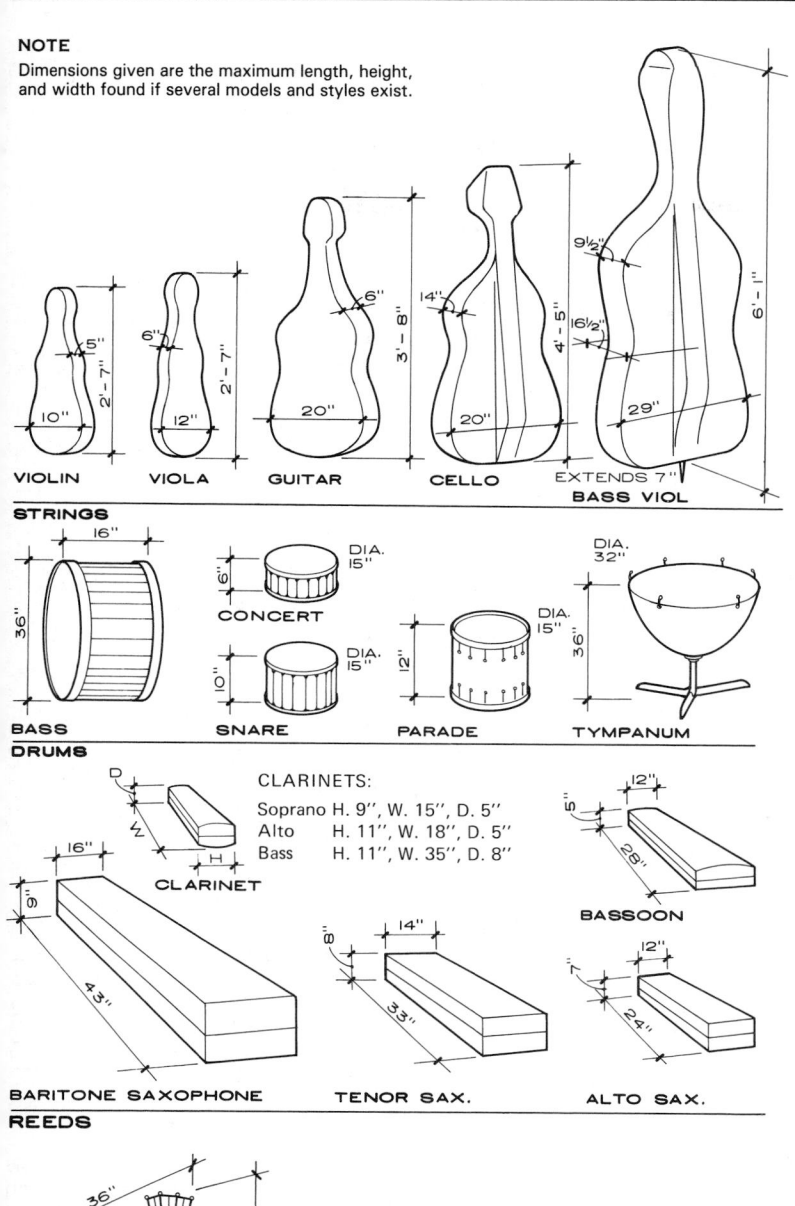

**STRINGS**

**DRUMS**

CLARINETS:
Soprano H. 9″, W. 15″, D. 5″
Alto H. 11″, W. 18″, D. 5″
Bass H. 11″, W. 35″, D. 8″

**REEDS**

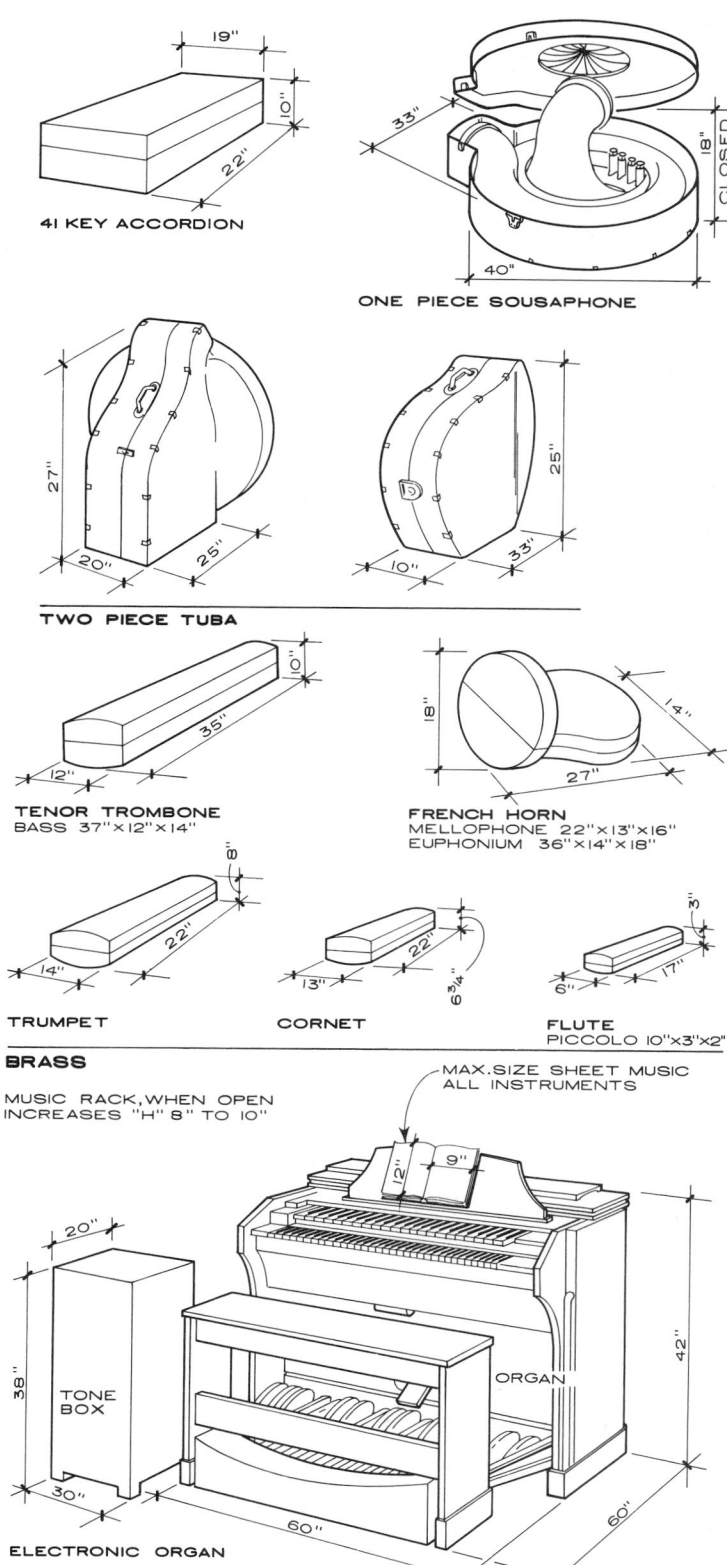

41 KEY ACCORDION

ONE PIECE SOUSAPHONE

TWO PIECE TUBA

TENOR TROMBONE
BASS 37″x12″x14″

FRENCH HORN
MELLOPHONE 22″x13″x16″
EUPHONIUM 36″x14″x18″

TRUMPET    CORNET    FLUTE
PICCOLO 10″x3″x2″

**BRASS**

MUSIC RACK, WHEN OPEN
INCREASES "H" 8" TO 10"

MAX. SIZE SHEET MUSIC
ALL INSTRUMENTS

ELECTRONIC ORGAN

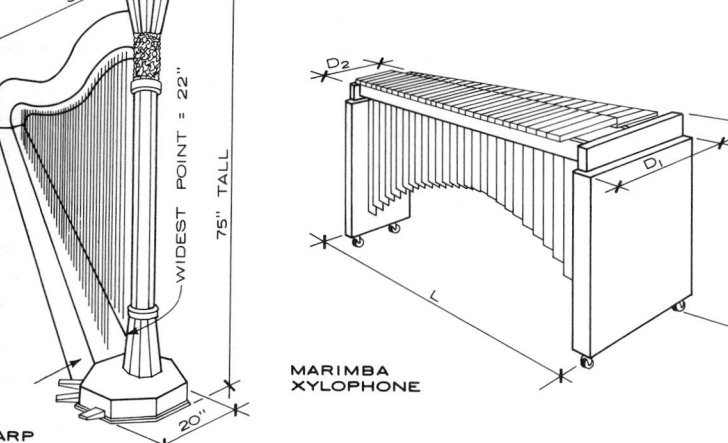

MARIMBA
XYLOPHONE

**HARP**

**NOTE**
Harps are made in various sizes. A typical larger model is shown. The widest dimension is at the "soundboard" and equals 22 in. A harp case is 25 in. wide x 84 in. deep. Total weight, including harp and case, is approximately 200 lb.

| | L | H | D₁ | D₂ | WEIGHT |
|---|---|---|---|---|---|
| Marimba | 87 | 36 | 33 | 16 | 175 lb |
| Xylophone | 54 | 34 | 32 | 13 | 70 lb |

NOTE: All dimensions are in inches. Many sizes are manufactured. The sizes given above are typical larger size that are available.

**NOTE**
Electronic organs are manufactured in many different types, styles, and models. Much smaller units than that shown are available as well as models weighing several tons. In general, allow space 72 in. wide x 72 in. long x 72 in. high. Also required is a clearance of approximately 50 in. to rear of unit for servicing. Consult organ manufacturers for exact details and models available.

Pipe organs are designed to fit the building in which they are to be used. After factory assembly and testing, they are disassembled and shipped. Pipes may vary from less than 1 in. to more than 30 ft in length. A single organ may have thousands of pipes. Basic components are the pipes, wind chest, blower, valve mechanism, and keyboards.

Leland D. Blackledge, AIA; South St. Paul, Minnesota
John A. Lesire, AIA; Arlington, Virginia

## WARDROBE AND STORAGE UNITS (IN.)

| W | H | D |
|---|---|---|
| 18, 24, 36 | $64\frac{1}{2}$–$80\frac{1}{2}$ | 18 |
| 18, 24, 36 | $41\frac{1}{4}$–$52\frac{1}{4}$ | 18 |
| 18, 24, 36 | $64\frac{1}{2}$–$80\frac{1}{2}$ | 24 |
| 18, 24, 36 | $41\frac{1}{4}$–$52\frac{1}{4}$ | 24 |

NOTE: Capacity depends on type of coats stored.

## SHELVING UNITS (IN.)

| | W | D | H |
|---|---|---|---|
| 2 shelves | 18, 24, 36 | 18 | 29 |
| 3 shelves | 18, 24, 36 | 18 | 42 |
| 4 shelves | 18, 24, 36 | 18 | 60 |
| 5 shelves | 18, 24, 36 | 18 | 78 |
| 6 shelves | 18, 24, 36 | 18 | 84 |

NOTE: Heights vary with manufacturer.

### NOTES

1. Files, wardrobe, and storage shelving units if used together should be compatible in dimension and design. If possible, one manufacturer should be selected to furnish all items.
2. If storage units are used as space dividers in an open plan, some acoustical corrections can be gained by applying acoustical panels to the back of the units.

CABINET      WARDROBE      WARDROBE/STORAGE      STORAGE      SHELVES

**TYPICAL METAL STORAGE UNITS**

### NOTES

Cabinets are available in multiple widths and heights and with or without doors. The basic cabinet can accept a variety of interchangeable filing components.

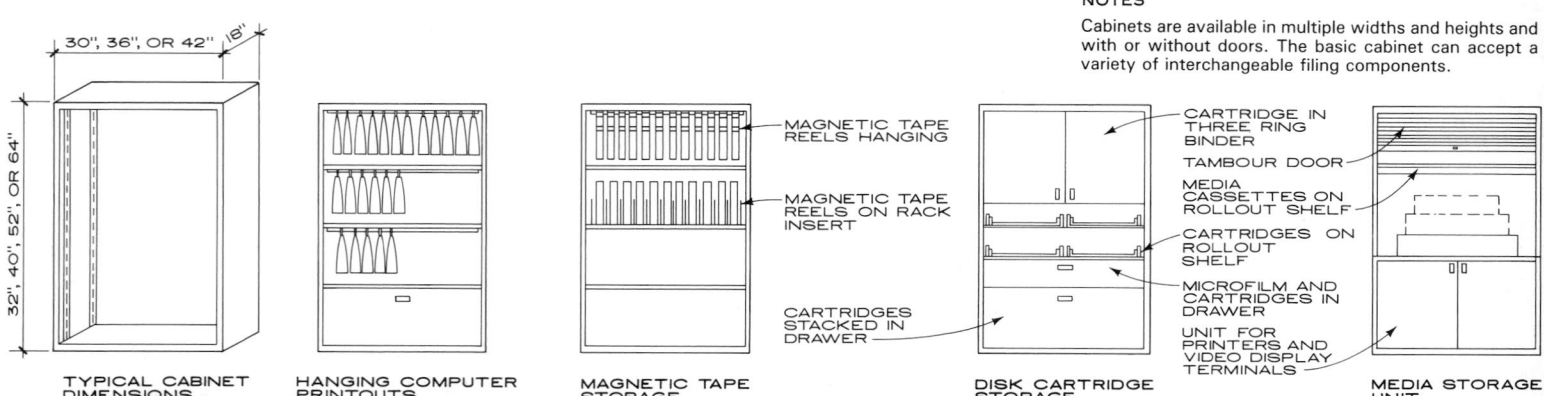

TYPICAL CABINET DIMENSIONS — HANGING COMPUTER PRINTOUTS — MAGNETIC TAPE STORAGE — DISK CARTRIDGE STORAGE — MEDIA STORAGE UNIT

MAGNETIC TAPE REELS HANGING
MAGNETIC TAPE REELS ON RACK INSERT
CARTRIDGES STACKED IN DRAWER
CARTRIDGE IN THREE RING BINDER
TAMBOUR DOOR
MEDIA CASSETTES ON ROLLOUT SHELF
CARTRIDGES ON ROLLOUT SHELF
MICROFILM AND CARTRIDGES IN DRAWER
UNIT FOR PRINTERS AND VIDEO DISPLAY TERMINALS

**DATA PROCESSING/MEDIA STORAGE METAL CABINETS**

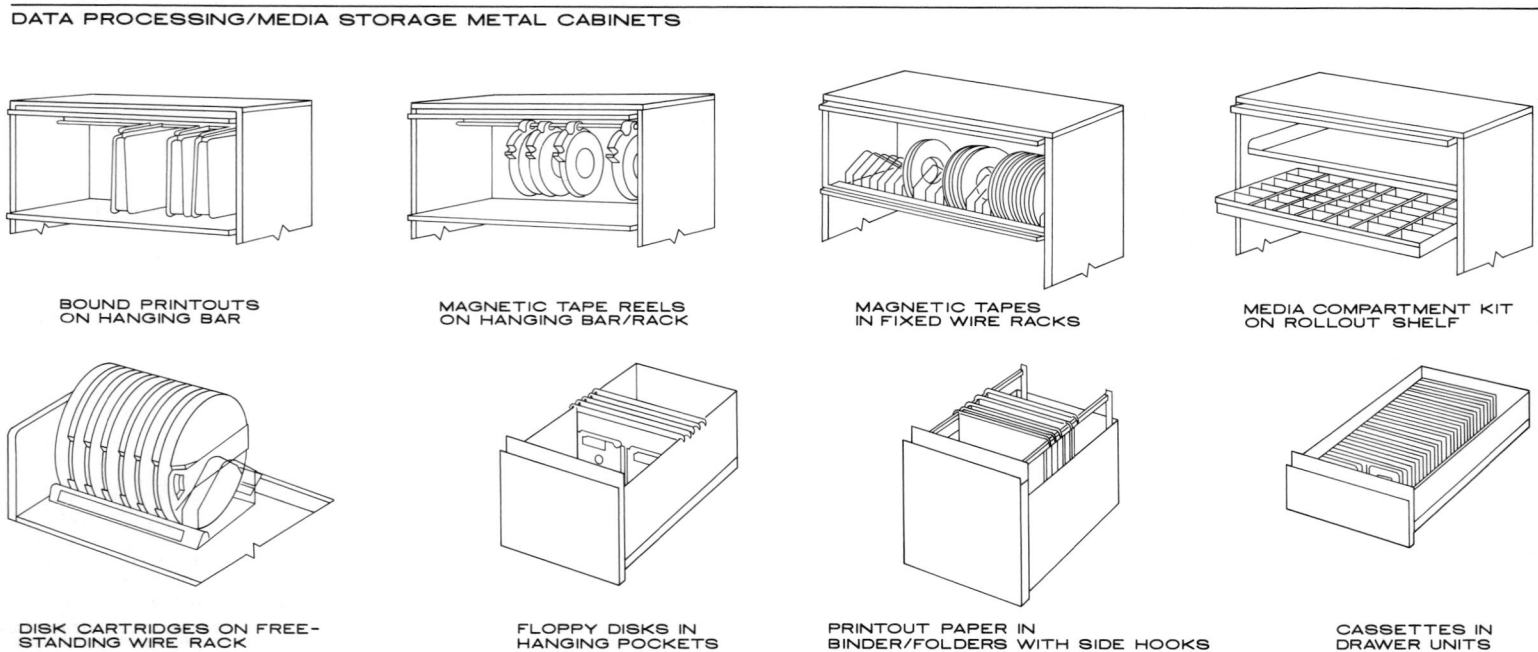

BOUND PRINTOUTS ON HANGING BAR      MAGNETIC TAPE REELS ON HANGING BAR/RACK      MAGNETIC TAPES IN FIXED WIRE RACKS      MEDIA COMPARTMENT KIT ON ROLLOUT SHELF

DISK CARTRIDGES ON FREE-STANDING WIRE RACK      FLOPPY DISKS IN HANGING POCKETS      PRINTOUT PAPER IN BINDER/FOLDERS WITH SIDE HOOKS      CASSETTES IN DRAWER UNITS

**CABINET INSERTS FOR DATA PROCESSING/MEDIA STORAGE**

Associated Space Design, Inc.; Atlanta, Tampa, Washington, D.C.
Blythe + Nazdin Architects, Ltd.; Bethesda, Maryland

# 11    CHECKROOM EQUIPMENT

## GENERAL NOTES

Coatrooms should be adjacent to and have line-of-sight connections with lobby or with circulation path between building entry and destination (auditorium, gallery, etc). Care should be taken to provide ample space for orderly queuing out of the mainstream of circulation. This is of particular importance in theaters, concert halls, and similar facilities where check in and out of massive numbers of people occurs in a very brief period of time. In galleries, museums, and restaurants, the flow of people is more even, resulting in a diminished need for queuing space and a smaller staffing requirement for the checkroom itself.

For general planning purposes, allow between 1.1 and 1.5 in. of rack space per garment, depending on climate. Hats, umbrellas, and packages should be stored with the garment rather than segregating items by type. Most racks contain from one to three overhead shelves for this purpose. For ease of access, these shelves should not extend above 6 ft 8 in.

For small to medium size facilities, conventional coatrooms are adequate. In large facilities where hundreds of garments will be accommodated, the designer should consider using automated conveyors. These systems save a great deal of time by eliminating the need to access aisles searching for a garment. In addition, the aisles are eliminated, resulting in a more efficient use of space. These systems function as follows:

The coatroom attendant hangs incoming garments on a conveyor in prenumbered slots that correspond to the claim check number. Hats and other items are placed in bins over the patron's garments. When departing patrons present their claim check, the attendant keys in the number on a control panel, and the conveyor revolves until it automatically stops at the correct number.

### COATROOM AREA REQUIREMENTS

| CAPACITY | AREA, CONVENTIONAL | AREA, AUTOMATED |
|---|---|---|
| 100 | 75 | N.A. |
| 200 | 140 | 100 |
| 300 | 200 | 130 |
| 400 | 240 | 150 |
| 500 | 310 | 180 |
| 1000 | 575 | 320 |
| 1500 | 760 | 460 |
| 2000 | 1025 | 600 |

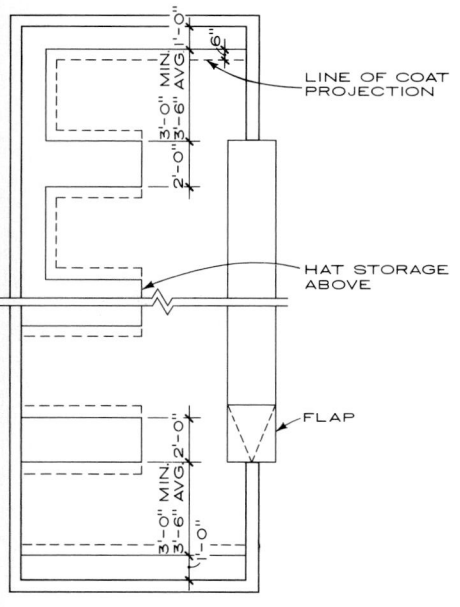

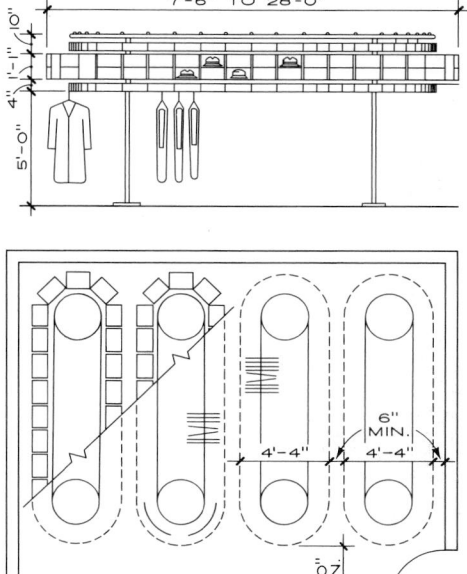

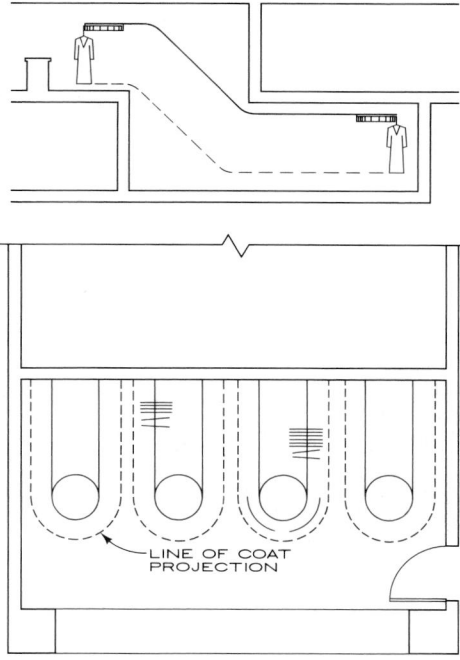

## CONVENTIONAL COATROOM

## AUTOMATED COATROOMS

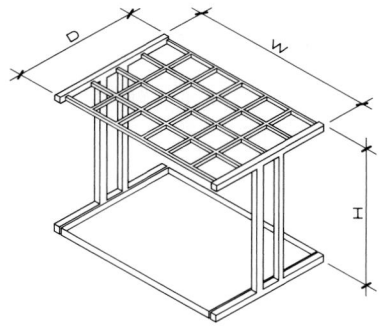

| UMBRELLAS | HEIGHT | DEPTH | WIDTH |
|---|---|---|---|
| 12 | 18″ | 12″ | 10″ |
| 18 | 18″ | 9″ | 18″ |
| 24 | 18″ | 12″ | 18″ |

**UMBRELLA RACK**

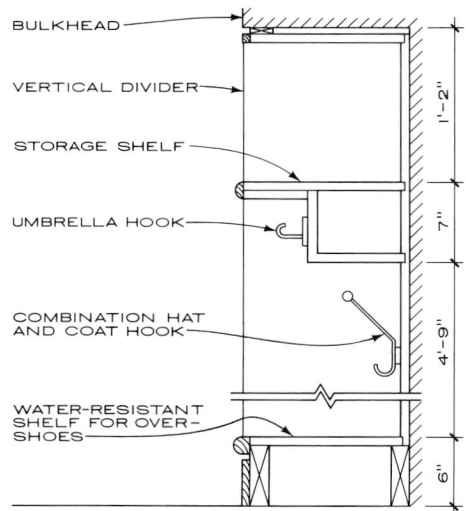

**"CUSTOM" COATROOM RACK**

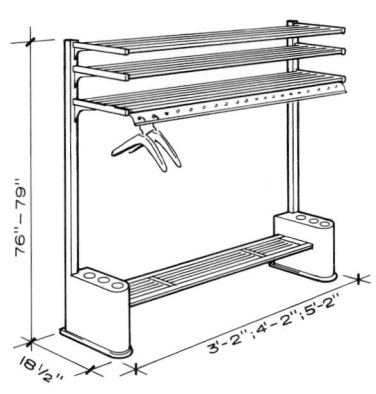

**COMBINATION COAT, HAT, UMBRELLA, OVERSHOE RACK**

Above model may be mounted back-to-back. Portable models are mounted on casters. Models available with or without umbrella and overshoe racks, and some are collapsible.

---

## COATROOM EQUIPMENT

Blythe + Nazdin Architects, Ltd.; Bethesda, Maryland

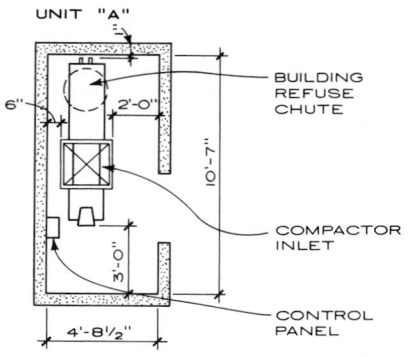

ROOM PLAN

## WASTE COMPACTORS AND CONTAINERS

| UNIT TYPE | SIZE | CAPACITY OF CONTAINER |
|---|---|---|
| Average household compactor | 12″ W, 24″ D, 33½″–34½″ H | 1.3 cu ft |
| Small industrial | See units A, B, and C | 4 cu ft per bag |
| Industrial | See unit D | 2 cu yd per container |
| Schools, offices, restaurants | 26″ W, 53″ H, 31″ D | 6 cu ft |
| Apartment house stationary compactor with roll away containers | Units vary | 2 to 8 cu yd |
| Industrial waste containers | 95″ W, 36″ H, 62″ D to 95″ W, 102″ H, 92″ D | 3 to 15 cu yd |
| Heavy duty industrial waste containers | 8′ ± W, 8′-10″ H, 23′-2″ L | Up to 43 cu yd |
| Combination shredder/compactor | 45″ W, 29″ D, 78″ H See unit "E" | 5.25 cu ft per bag |

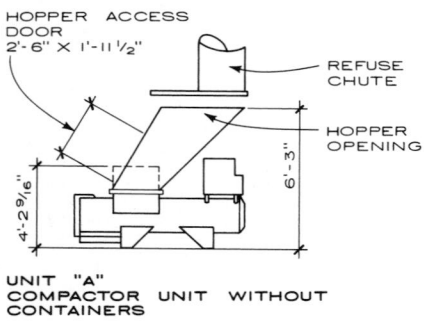

UNIT "A"
COMPACTOR UNIT WITHOUT CONTAINERS

## APARTMENT SELECTION GUIDE

The daily refuse output of 15 to 30 apartments is approximately ½ cu yd (13½ cu ft) weighing about 75 lb. At standard compaction ratios of 4 or 5 to 1, a compactor will reduce the refuse to an approximate volume of 3 cu ft.

If the apartments are large, averaging two or three bedrooms, use the figure of 15 apartments per bag. If apartments average one or two bedrooms, use 20 to 25 apartments per compacted bag, and if the units are small efficiency apartments or one-bedroom apartments occupied by young working people or the elderly, use the figure of 30 apartments per compacted bag per day.

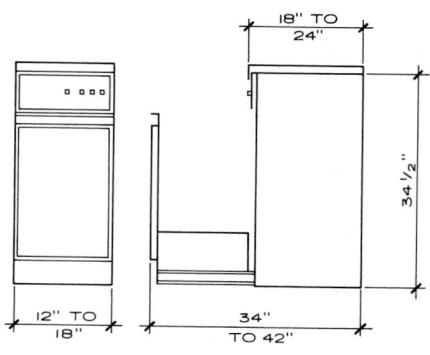

AVERAGE   HOUSEHOLD   COMPACTOR

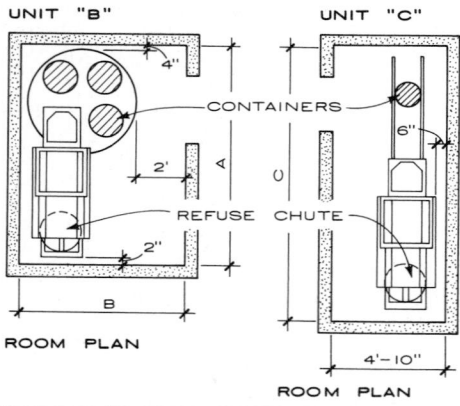

UNIT "B"          UNIT "C"

ROOM PLAN          ROOM PLAN

| NO. OF CONTAINERS | A | B | C |
|---|---|---|---|
| 3 | | | 11′-10″ |
| 4 | 9′-8″ | 7′-0″ | 13′-5″ |
| 5 | | | 17′-1″ |
| 6 | 10′-6″ | 8′-0″ | |
| 8 | 11′-6″ | 9′-1″ | |
| 10 | 12′-6″ | 10′-9″ | |

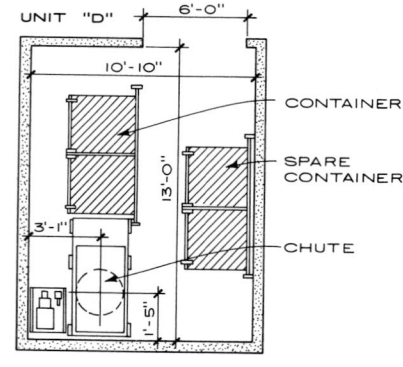

UNIT "D"

ROOM PLAN

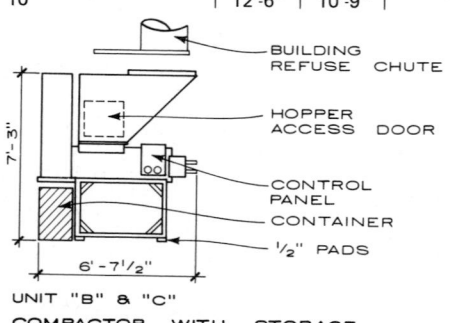

UNIT "B" & "C"
COMPACTOR WITH STORAGE CONTAINERS

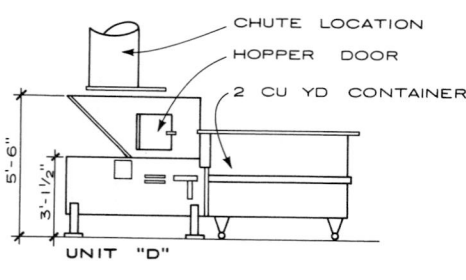

UNIT "D"
INDUSTRIAL COMPACTOR

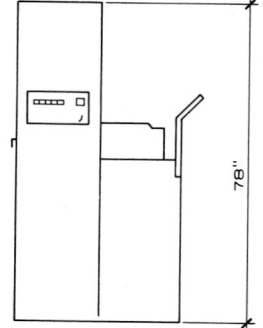

PLAN

UNIT "E"
COMBINATION SHREDDER
COMPACTOR

Walter H. Sobel, FAIA, & Associates; Chicago, Illinois

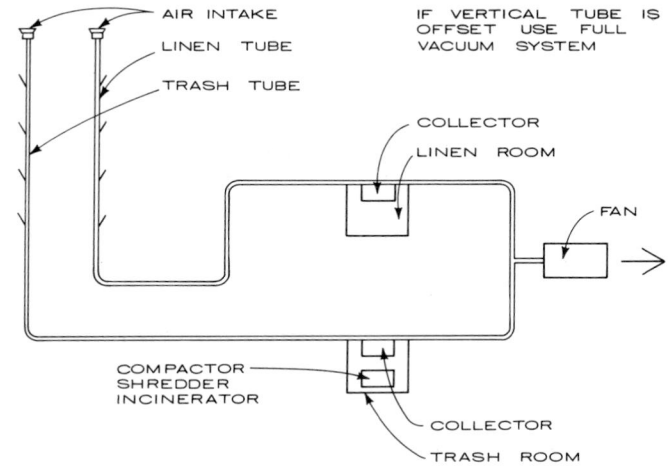

**DUAL TUBE FULL VACUUM SYSTEM**

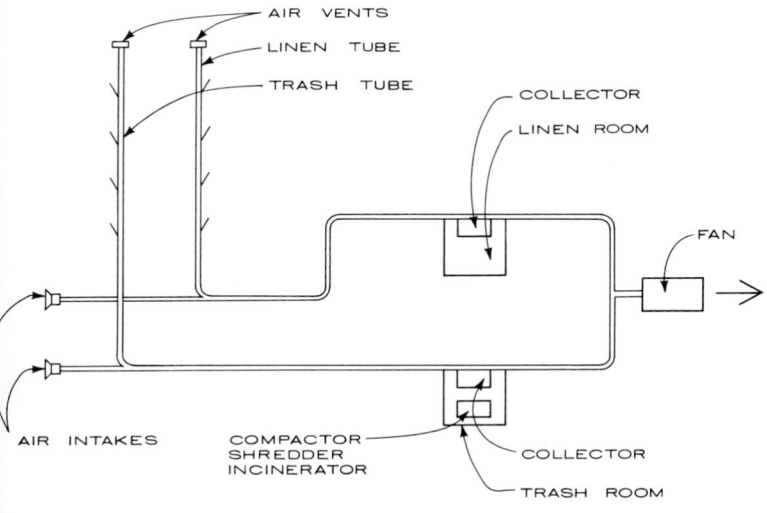

**DUAL TUBE GRAVITY / VACUUM SYSTEM**

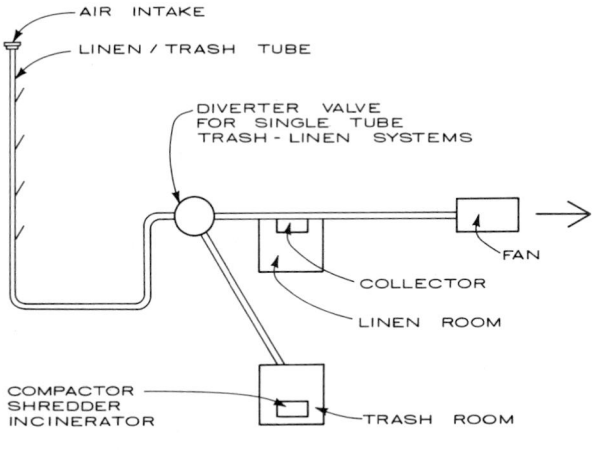

**SINGLE TUBE FULL VACUUM SYSTEM**

## DUAL TUBE FULL VACUUM

The two-tube fully pneumatic system offers flexibility in design and improved sanitation. A two-tube system eliminates the need to place trash and linen depositories at the same location. The vertical tubes can be offset, adding to the flexibility of the system. Horizontal tubes dispose at a central point, eliminating manually operated collections.

## DUAL TUBE GRAVITY/VACUUM SYSTEM

The two-tube gravity/pneumatic system consists of gravity vertical chutes and pneumatic horizontal collection, leading to centralized collection point. The gravity/pneumatic system does not permit offsets in vertical tubes.

## SINGLE TUBE FULL VACUUM SYSTEM

The single tube fully pneumatic system offers the advantage of centralized collection of linen and trash. The system is limited in flexibility. Sanitation is somewhat compromised by having trash and linen using the same tubes. Manufacturers do not recommend this situation. A diverter valve controlled from loading station directs material to proper central receiving room.

## SPECIFICS

### GRAVITY TYPE VERTICAL CHUTES

Recommended 24 in. minimum diameter tube with air vent above roof and flushing spray and sprinkler head above top loading door.

### PNEUMATIC TYPE VERTICAL CHUTES

Recommended 16 in. diameter tube with air intake above roof. Fire rated tube enclosure at each floor with electricity, air, and sprinkler at each enclosure.

## CAPACITY

Uniform or variable size/regular or irregular in shape, a waste/linen handling system can accommodate a wide variety of materials. A standard 16 in. system can convey individual units weighing up to 50 lb.

## AVERAGE PER DAY SOILED LINEN QUANTITIES

| BUILDING TYPE | LINEN IN POUNDS* |
|---|---|
| Apartments | N/A |
| Hospitals | 15 per room, double occupancy |
| Nurses' or interns' homes | 8 per person |
| Rest homes | 10–12 per person |
| Homes for the aged | 10–12 per person |
| Hotels | 15 per room |
| Motels | 15 per room |
| Schools | N/A |
| Office building | N/A |

*Pounds will vary per use of disposable linens.

Walter H. Sobel, FAIA, & Associates; Chicago, Illinois

**SOLID WASTE HANDLING EQUIPMENT** 11

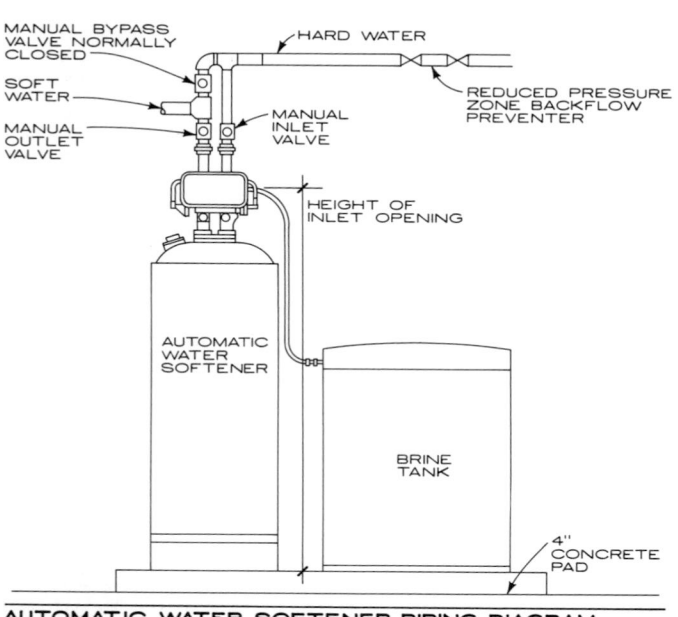

**AUTOMATIC WATER SOFTENER PIPING DIAGRAM**

### GENERAL

Water hardness is caused by calcium and magnesium salts and is usually expressed in grains per gallon. For example: New York City 1-5 grains (low); Grand Rapids, Mich., 9 grains (5-9 moderate); Jacksonville, Fla., 18 grains (over 9 high); well water 0-50 grains.

A water softener is typically one tank for manual operation and two adjacent or concentric tanks with automatic controls. To determine the proper size softener for a residence, use this formula:

No. of people x 50 gal (75 if 3 or more baths) = gal water used/day

Gal water/day x no. of days of service = gal soft water needed

Gal soft water x hardness (grains/gal = capacity of softener needed

If the capacity found necessary by this formula is too large, reduce the number of days of service; the softener will need to be regenerated more often. The table lists data for residential size softeners. If a softener is needed for use in another building type, consult a manufacturer. Rental equipment with service plans is available in some areas, and responsibility for design adequacy should be assumed by the renting company.

When water supplies contain suspended matter, a filter should be placed at the hard water inlet. The softening process often removes any taste the water may have, but filters can also correct bad taste, acidity, or odor problems caused by other salts and minerals.

### AUTOMATIC WATER SOFTENER SCHEDULE—FLOW RATE—17 TO 40 GPM

| GRAIN CAPACITY AND SALT DOSAGE PER POUND | SERVICE FLOW RATE (GPM) | | PIPE SIZE (IN.) | RESIN QUANTITY (CU FT) | TANK SIZE (IN.) | |
|---|---|---|---|---|---|---|
| | PEAK | CONTINUOUS | | | SOFTENER | BRINE |
| 14,000 grains/5 lb | 25 | 12 | 1 1/2 | 1.5 | 12 x 40 | 18 x 38 |
| 28,000 grains/10 lb | 17 | 13 | 1 | 3 | 16 x 48 | 24 x 38 |
| 43,000 grains/15 lb | 17 | 13 | 1 | 4 | 16 x 60 | 24 x 38 |
| 45,000 grains/22 lb | 25 | 12 | 1 1/2 | 1.5 | 12 x 40 | 18 x 38 |
| 90,000 grains/45 lb | 40 | 20 | 1 1/2 | 3 | 16 x 48 | 24 x 38 |
| 120,000 grains/60 lb | 40 | 20 | 1 1/2 | 4 | 16 x 60 | 24 x 38 |

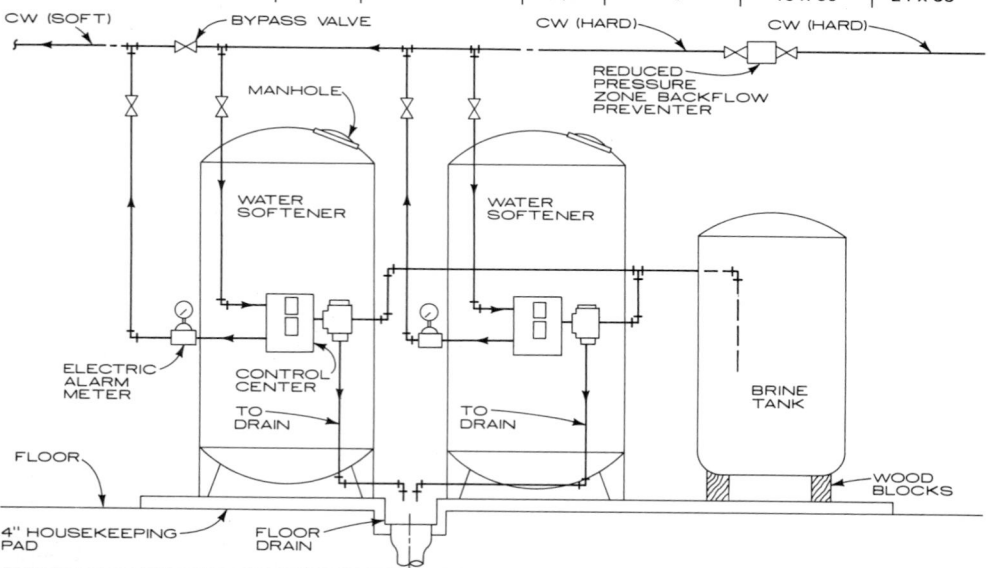

**INDUSTRIAL WATER SOFTENER PIPING DIAGRAM**

### INDUSTRIAL WATER SOFTENER—FLOW RATE—60 TO 200 GPM

| GRAIN CAPACITY AND SALT DOSAGE PER POUND | SERVICE FLOW RATE (GPM) | | PIPE SIZE (IN.) | RESIN QUANTITY (CU FT) | TANK SIZE (IN.) | |
|---|---|---|---|---|---|---|
| | PEAK | CONTINUOUS | | | SOFTENER | BRINE |
| 80,000 grains/20 lb | 60 | 35 | 1 1/2 | 5 | 24 x 54 | 24 x 48 |
| 116,000 grains/30 lb | 75 | 50 | 1 1/2 | 6.75 | 24 x 54 | 24 x 48 |
| 250,000 grains/125 lb | 75 | 50 | 1 1/2 | 8.5 | 24 x 54 | 24 x 48 |
| 300,000 grains/150 lb | 110 | 80 | 2 | 10 | 30 x 60 | 30 x 48 |
| 450,000 grains/225 lb | 110 | 80 | 2 | 15 | 30 x 60 | 30 x 48 |
| 600,000 grains/300 lb | 150 | 110 | 2 1/2 | 20 | 36 x 60 | 36 x 48 |
| 800,000 grains/405 lb | 200 | 150 | 3 | 27 | 42 x 60 | 42 x 48 |

DiClemente-Siegel Engineering, Inc.; Southfield, Michigan

### TYPICAL MANUFACTURERS' DATA

| CHARACTERISTICS | MODELS | | |
|---|---|---|---|
| REGENERATION METHOD | FULLY AUTOMATIC[1] | SEMI-AUTOMATIC[2] | MANUAL[3] |
| Capacity (grains) | 18,000 | 25,000 | 50,000 |
| Service flow rate (gal) | 10 | 7.5 | 8 |
| Rinse flow rate (gal) | 0.7 | 0.5 | 1.0 |
| Ion exchanger (cu ft) | 1.0 | 0.85 | 1.7 |
| Salt per regeneration (lb) | 5.5 | 10 | 30 |
| Regeneration time (min) | 60 | 120 | 90 |
| Service piping (in.) | 1 | 3/4 | 3/4 |
| Waste piping (in.) | 3/8 | 3/4 | 1/2 |
| Pressure range (lb) | 25-100 | 25-100 | 25-100 |
| Electric current (V) | 110-60 capacity | 110-60 capacity | — |
| Resin tank diameter (in.) | 9 3/16 | 9 | 12 |
| Bed area (sq ft) | 0.442 | 0.44 | 0.78 |
| Shipping weight (lb) | 100 | 116 | 197 |
| Floor space (in.) | 22 x 30 | 11 x 15 | 13 x 18 |
| Overall height (in.) | 43 3/4 | 44 3/4 | 54 |

1. Complete regeneration by time clock.
2. Manually operated switch to start regeneration.
3. Complete manual regeneration by adding dry pellet type salt directly to the softener.

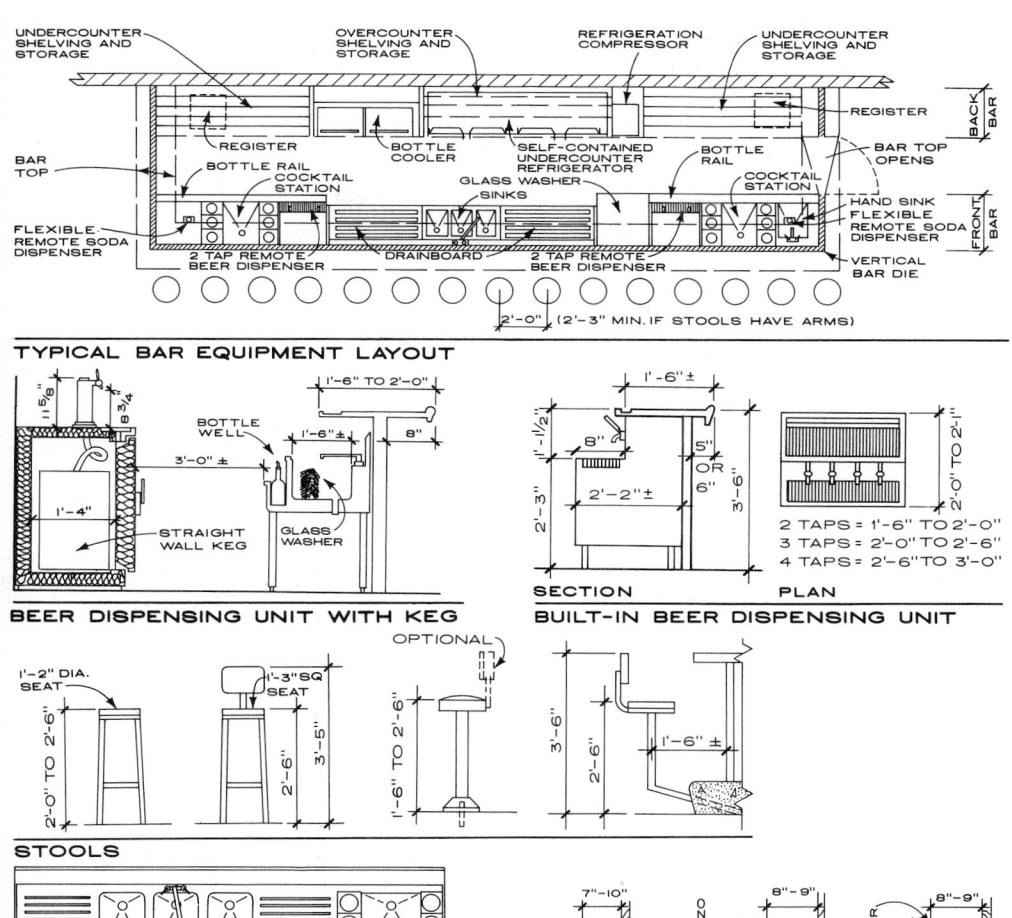

**TYPICAL BAR EQUIPMENT LAYOUT**

**BEER DISPENSING UNIT WITH KEG**

**BUILT-IN BEER DISPENSING UNIT**

2 TAPS = 1'-6" TO 2'-0"
3 TAPS = 2'-0" TO 2'-6"
4 TAPS = 2'-6" TO 3'-0"

SECTION    PLAN

**STOOLS**

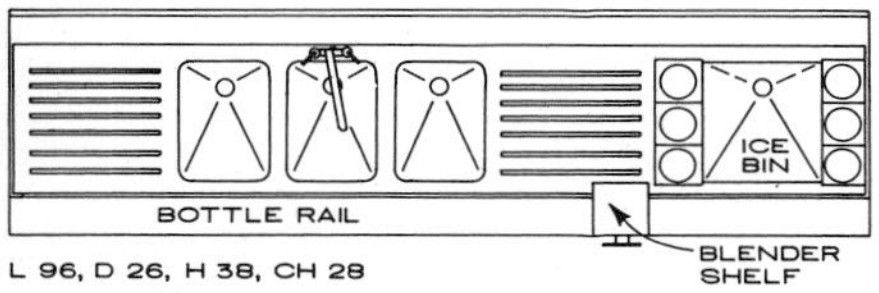

**UNDERBAR WORKBOARD**

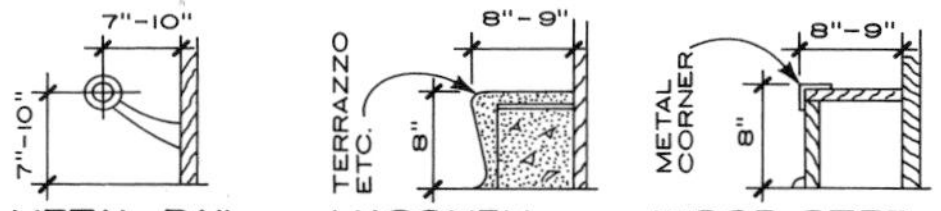

L 96, D 26, H 38, CH 28

**FOOT RAIL AND STEPS**

METAL RAIL    MASONRY STEP    WOOD STEP

## GENERAL DESIGN CRITERIA

1. In beverage service situations only, smaller tables may be used in comparison to food service size requirements. 1 ft 6 in. square minimum. Refer to section on counters and seating for additional dimensional requirements.
2. If beverage service from cocktail lounge to dining room is planned, convenient access between service areas should be provided.
3. Most health codes require a hand sink in the underbar area.
4. Service bar should not interfere with regular bar service and seating. Refer to section on seating.
5. The most common surface material for carpentry is plastic laminate. It is very durable and easily cleaned. Wood is often used, but requires coating or sealer for greater protection, longer life, and good sanitation. Other materials are glass, plexiglass, mirrors, and metals. All must fill local code requirements for cleaning, safety, and fire resistance.

### NOTES

1. Other commonly found beverage service equipment includes glass froster, ice machine, automatic liquor dispensing system, blender, mixer, bottle disposal devices, condiment trays, and preparation tools. Service stations on outside of bar may include equipment such as ice bin, soda dispenser, water, cash register access, glass storage, glass washer access, coffee urn, condiments, and tabletop accessories.
2. BACK BAR: Above—space allocated for register, glass storage, beer keg dispenser, and wine and liquor storage and dispensing. Under—generally refrigerated cases for wine, beer, mixer, and condiment storage and shelving for glass and liquor storage and display.
3. WORKBOARD: Corrugated metal top, stainless steel preferred, for clean glass drainage and storage.
4. SINKS: Three compartments or as required by codes; includes glass washer if not located elsewhere.
5. Underbar options include blender shelf, cutting board, condiment trays, and utility outlets, built in. Bottle and glass chillers are available; check utility requirements and space available. Drainage and waste disposal required. Check local codes for hand sink requirements.

## BAR EQUIPMENT

GLASS WASHER

| UNITS | WIDTH (IN.) | DEPTH (IN.) | HEIGHT (IN.) | OPTIONS AND NOTES |
|---|---|---|---|---|
| Back bar storage cabinets | 23⅞–111½ | 23⁹⁄₁₆ | 32 or 37 | Beverage dispensers; enamel, laminate or stainless steel finishes; refrigeration; stepped or stacked display shelves |
| Cocktail stations | 24–96 | 24¾ | 34⅞ | Adjustable dividers; beverage dispensers; bottle rails and wells; condiment trays; cutting board; drainers; dump tank; drop-in ice-cream cabinet; glass storage shelves; ice chest; sink; towel rings; utility outlets; and waste chutes |
| Coolers | | | | Bottle opener with cap catcher; locking or sliding doors; interior light |
| Bottle Flat top | 24–96 | 24¾ | 34⁷⁄₁₆ | Condensing unit adds 12'' to height Enamel or stainless steel finish |
| Roll top | 54⅜–118³⁄₁₆ | 29½ | 39⅞ | |
| Keg | 45¹¹⁄₁₆–84⅝ | 45½ | 66⅞ | Keg shelf available; remote location; walk-in |
| Frosters or glass chillers | 24 or 48 | 24¾ | 33¹⁵⁄₁₆ | Racks |

**BACK BAR STORAGE CABINET**

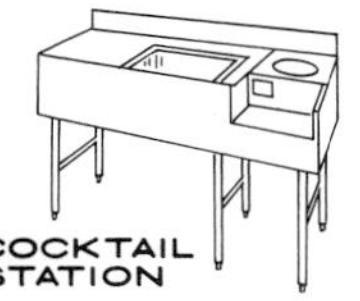

**COCKTAIL STATION**

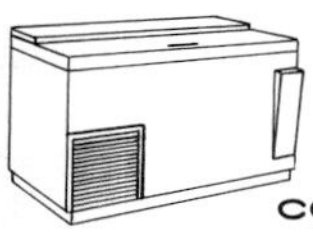

**COOLER**

**COOLER**

**BEER (KEG) DISPENSER**

ICE CHEST

ICE CREAM

ICE CREAM CABINET

SINK

STORAGE UNITS

## BAR EQUIPMENT (CONTINUED)

| UNITS | WIDTH (IN.) | DEPTH (IN.) | HEIGHT (IN.) | OPTIONS AND NOTES |
|---|---|---|---|---|
| Glass washers | 24 or 30 | 24 or 30 | 36–38 | Includes controlled chemical and sanitizing system |
| Ice chests | 24–36 | 18⁹⁄₁₆ | 37½–38½ | Bottle rails and wells; condiment trays; glass storage shelf; ice dividers; separate bottle rack compartments |
| Ice-cream cabinets | 24 | 18⁹⁄₁₆ | 37½–38½ | 3 gal capacity |
| Sinks | 12–144 | 18⁹⁄₁₆ or 24 | 36½–38½ | Blender shelf; bottle rail; corrugated stainless steel drainboards; glass storage shelf; towel rings; utility outlets; waste chutes. (Brush type glass washers may be installed in sinks on site.) |
| Storage units | 30 or 48 | 23⁹⁄₁₆ | 37½–38½ | Sliding or swinging doors |

### NOTES

1. Modular stainless steel units may be factory connected to form a continuous surface, at any angle, up to 12 ft maximum length.
2. All sizes are approximate. Check codes and sanitary and utility requirements.

Carole Harrison Martinie; Whitefish Bay, Wisconsin
Cini-Grissom Associates, Inc.; Food Service Consultants; Washington, D.C.

## BAR GLASSWARE

| BEVERAGE | TYPE | VOLUME (OZ) | DIAMETER (IN.) | HEIGHT (IN.) | *NUMBER PER LINEAR SHELF FOOT |
|---|---|---|---|---|---|
| Beer  | Goblet | 10–14 | 3–3⅝ | 6½–7⅜ | *3 |
| | Tulip | 10–14 | 3–3⅝ | 6½–7⅜ | *3 |
| | Mug, stein, or tankard | 8.5–33.8 (1 L) | 4⅝–6 | 5⅜–8 | 2–*1 |
| | Pilsner | 10–12 | 3⅛–3¼ | 6¾–7¼ | 3 |
| | Hourglass | 8.5–15 | 2⅞–3¼ | 5⅝–6⅝ | 4–3 |
| | Sham | 6–12 | 2⅝–3⅛ | 5–6¼ | 4–3 |
| | Stemmed | 7–12 | 2¾–3 | 7½–8⅝ | 4–*3 |
| | Schooner | 10–60 | 4–6¼ | 6⅛–7⅛ | 2–1 |
| | Pitcher | 33.8 (1 L), 40, 55, 60, 80 | 6¼–6¾ | 8–9¼ | 1 |
| Liquor  | Brandy | 2–34 | 1⅝–5 | 4⅛–6⅜ | 7–2 |
| | Cocktail | 3–6 | 2⅞–4¼ | 4½–6 | 4–2 |
| | Collins: stemmed | 10–12 | 2⅜–2⅞ | 4⅝–5½ | 4 |
| | Cordial | 1–2.5 | 1½–1¾ | 4⅛–4¼ | 7–6 |
| | Dutch | 1.5 | 2 | 6⅛ | 5 |
| | Stemmed | .75–1.75 | 1½–1⅞ | 3½–3⅞ | 7–6 |
| | Demitasse | 4.5 | 3¼ | 4⅜ | 3 |
| | Highball | 7–10.5 | 2½–2¾ | 4⅛–6 | 4 |
| | Stemmed | 8–10 | 2⅜–3 | 5¼–5⅞ | 4–*3 |
| | Hurricane | 8–23.5 | 2⅜–3⅜ | 6⅝–10 | 5–3 |
| | Irish coffee | 6–8.5 | 2⅞–4⅛ | 5⅜–6 | 4–2 |
| | Jigger | 1.5 | 2–2¼ | 2⅜–2⅞ | 5 |
| | Margarita: coupette | 5–9 | 3⅞–4½ | 4½–6⅛ | 3–2 |
| | Fiesta | 8.5–16.75 | 4–5 | 5⅜–6¼ | 2 |
| | Old-fashioned | 5–10.25 | 2⅞–3¼ | 2⅞–3⅜ | 4–3 |
| | Double | 12.25–15 | 3¼–3⅝ | 3⅞–4⅜ | 3 |
| | Rocks | 5.5–10.5 | 2¾–3⅛ | 3⅛–4⅛ | 4–3 |
| | Double | 11–13 | 3½–3¾ | 3¼–4 | 3 |
| | Stemmed | 5–7 | 3–3¼ | 3¾–4⅜ | 3 |
| | Shot | 1.5–3 | 1⅞–2 | 2⅜–2⅝ | 6–5 |
| | Thistle | 6.5–21 | 3¼–3⅞ | 8½ | 3 |
| | Whiskey | .5–3 | 1¾–2 | 2⅜–2⅝ | 6–*5 |
| | Sour/stemmed | 4.5–5.25 | 2½–2⅝ | 5¾–6¼ | 4 |
| | Zombie | 10–24 | 2½–2⅞ | 5¼–9 | 4 |
| Wine  | Champagne | 4.5–10 | 3½–3⅞ | 4¼–5 | 3 |
| | Tulip | 4.5–12 | 2¼–3⅛ | 7½–9 | 5–3 |
| | Cooler | 15–22 | 3–3⅜ | 6–6⅝ | 3 |
| | Flute | 6–8 | 2–3 | 7–9¼ | *5–3 |
| | Goblet | 8–12 | 3–3⅝ | 5⅞–6⅛ | 3 |
| | Sherry | 2–3 | 2⅜–2½ | 4⅞ | 5–4 |
| | Wine | 3–14 | 2½–4 | 4⅝–7⅞ | 4–2 |
| | Hock or round | 4–14 | 2½–4 | 4⅞–7⅞ | 4–3 |
| | Decanter or carafe | 1.5–48 | 2–5 | 3½–10⅞ | *5–2 |

NOTES

1. Options include colors, crests, lettering, and/or logos: Some styles are frosted, heat treated, lined, of various strengths, and/or available with specialty rims. (Allow a 2 in. minimum clearance above glassware on shelves.)
2. *Based on glassware avoiding contact with each other.

Carole Harrison Martinie; Whitefish Bay, Wisconsin

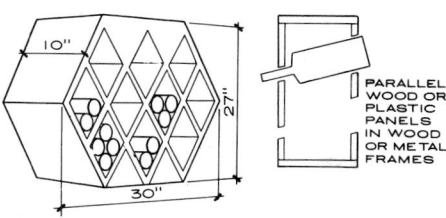

**WINE BIN**

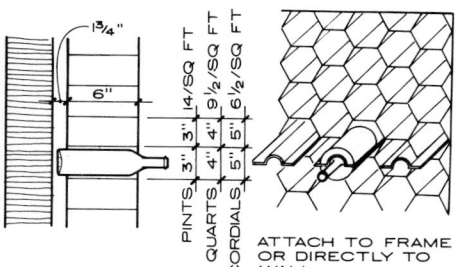

**METAL RACKS**

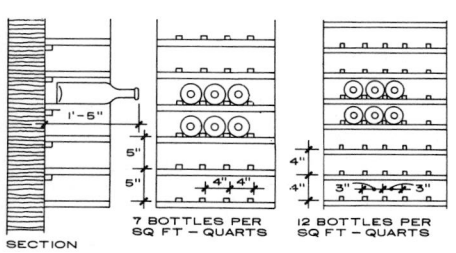

**WOOD BOARD SHELVES**

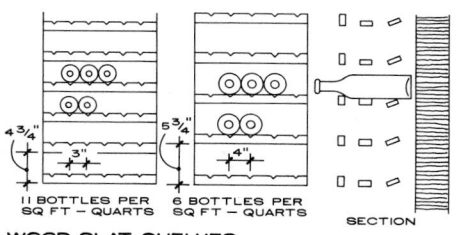

**WOOD SLAT SHELVES**

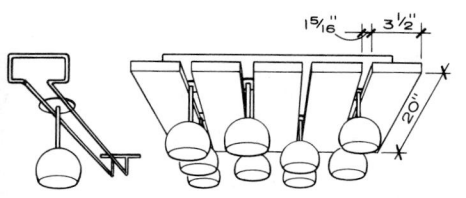

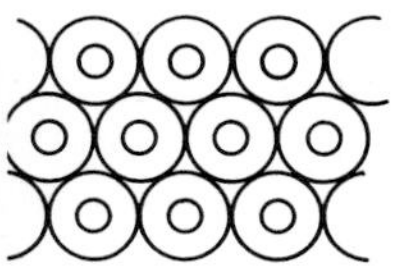

| Bottle Size | Number per sq ft |
|---|---|
| 2 1/2" d. | 20 |
| 2 3/4 d. | 18 |
| 3" d. | 14 |
| 3 1/2" d. | 9 |

These figures also for standing bottles

**STANDING OR STACKED BOTTLES**

**BOTTLE STORAGE**

## CONTAINERS

| BEVERAGE | TYPE | VOLUME (OZ) | DIAMETER (OR L x W)(IN.) | HEIGHT (IN.) |
|---|---|---|---|---|
| Beer | Bottle | 7 | 2¾ | 6 |
| | Can | 12 | 2½–2¾ | 4½–5 |
| | Bottle | 12 | 2¼–2¾ | 5–9¾ |
| | | 32 | 2½–3½ | 9¾–11¾ |
| 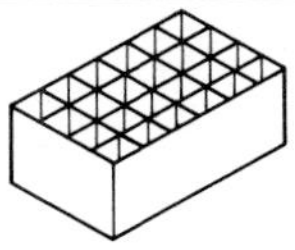 | Case | 12 (24) | 16½ x 10¾ | 9⅝ |
| Beer or wine 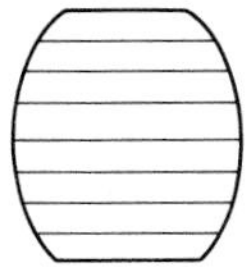 | Keg | ½ barrel (15½ gal) | 16–17½ | 24–25 |
| | | ¼ barrel (7¾ gal) | 16–17½ | 12–16½ |
| Liquor Brandy Gin Rum Whiskey | Bottle | 25.6 | 3½ | 11½ |
| | | 33.8 (1 L) | 3½–5¼ | 11½–14 |
| | | 59.2 | 5½–7 | 11½–14 |
| Cognac | | 25.6 | 3½ | 10½ |
| Wine  | Bottle | 25.6 | 3–3¼ | 12–14½ |
| | | 33.8 (1 L) | 3½–5¼ | 11½–14½ |
| Champagne | Magnum | 57.4 | 6½ | 26½ |
| | Bottle | 25.6 | 3–3¼ | 12–14½ |
| Vermouth | | 25.6 | 3–4 | 12–12¼ |
| Mix and soft drink  | Bottle | 7 | 2¼ | 4½ |
| | Can | 12 | 2¼–2¾ | 4½–5 |
| | Bottle | 12 | 2½ | 9½ |
| | | 16 (1 pt) | 2½ | 11 |
| | | 32 (1 qt) | 2½ | 11¾ |
| | | 33.8 (1 L) | 2½–3 | 11¾–12 |
| | | 67.6 (2 L) | 4 | 12 |

Note: Exact sizes vary widely. Specialty bottles and decanters are common.

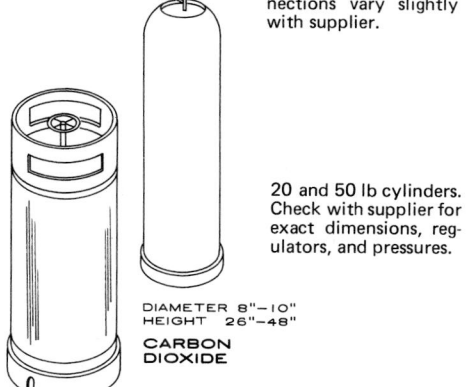

**HANGING GLASS RACKS**

Racks may attach to round or square tubular metal or wood frame. Use hanging rack or attach to soffit or ceiling (use toggles). Check local codes.

Carole Harrison Martinie; Whitefish Bay, Wisconsin

Dimensions and connections vary slightly with supplier.

20 and 50 lb cylinders. Check with supplier for exact dimensions, regulators, and pressures.

DIAMETER 8"–10"
HEIGHT 26"–48"

**CARBON DIOXIDE**

PRESSURIZED 5 GAL (2.5 GAL OR 30 LITER ALSO USED)
DIAMETER 9"
HEIGHT 24"

**PRESSURIZED**

Stainless steel tank for soft drink syrup or wine (in some states).

**PRESSURIZED DISPENSING SYSTEMS**

POSTMIX SODA SYSTEMS: Available in capacities of 2 to 7 6-oz drinks per minute. Dispensing heads may be located a maximum of 250 ft from master unit. Mechanically refrigerated and ice plate systems are available. Both systems require syrup and carbon dioxide tanks, water supply, and electrical hookup. Used in connection with flexible dispensing head or stationary faucets.

BEER AND WINE SYSTEMS: Maximum distance between keg and dispensing head is 150 ft. Kegs to be refrigerated at 35° to 38°F. Allow sufficient space for refrigerated trunk housing lines of 4–6 in. diameter, requiring 24 in. radial turn.

LIQUOR DISPENSING SYSTEMS: Available in mechanical, automatic, and computerized systems. Efficient control of portions, cost, and theft.

NOTE: All dispensing systems should be conveniently located near cocktail station. Consult equipment specialists or factory representatives early in design sequence.

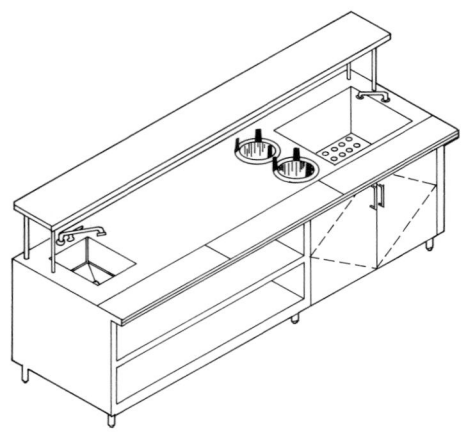

**CHEF TABLE**
DIMENSIONS AS SPECIFIED

**NOTE**

Size depends on individual operation. Illustrated with bain marie, self-leveling dish dispenser, overshelf, cutting board, heat lamp, and undercounter shelving; other options include a heated or refrigerated base. May be equipped as hot food table. For preparation and delivery of food to service personnel.

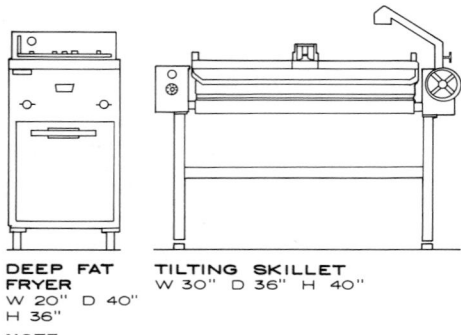

**DEEP FAT FRYER**
W 20" D 40" H 36"

**TILTING SKILLET**
W 30" D 36" H 40"

**NOTE**

Deep fat fryers are available in several, capacities and countertop or floor model types. Fry basket lift may be automatic or manual. For fabricated equipment, drop-in units are available. Fat filter may be self-contained. Gas or electrically operated.

Tilting skillet capacities depend on operational requirements and manufacturer. Types available are countertop, cabinet base, and leg. Operate on gas or electricity.

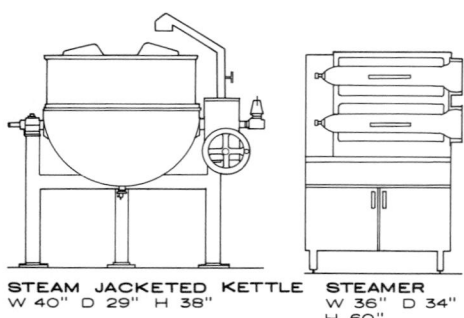

**STEAM JACKETED KETTLE**
W 40" D 29" H 38"

**STEAMER**
W 36" D 34" H 60"

**NOTE**

Steam jacketed kettle capacities are variable, tilting or stationary, tri-leg, pedestal, or wall hung. Wall hung units are expensive to install. Smaller capacity kettles are usually counter top. Units may be gas, electric, or steam.

Steamers are available with one, two, or three compartments. They are self-contained units that use gas, electric, or direct fired steam. Counter or floor models available.

**HOT FOOD EQUIPMENT**

Cini-Grissom Associates, Inc.; Food Service Consultants; Washington, D.C.

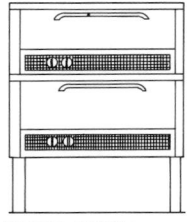

**DECK OVEN**
W 52" D 38" H 60"

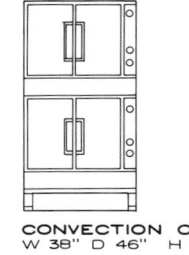

**CONVECTION OVEN**
W 38" D 46" H 60"

**NOTE**

One, two, or three decks, depending on function. Used to bake or roast. Dimensions vary. Equipped with legs or cabinet base.

Convection ovens are available with one or two sections. Single section available with legs or stand, modular or cabinet base. Ovens contain adjustable racks. Gas or electrically operated.

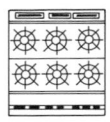

**PLAN**

**GRIDDLE TOP RANGE**

**ELEVATION RANGE**
W 32" D 42" H 40"

**NOTE**

Ranges use gas or electricity and are available with various numbers of burners and cook tops. Fry top is equipped with grease trough, burner top with drip tray, griddle top with spillage channels. Ranges are installed in countertops or mounted on a cabinet or oven base with flue riser and shelves. Install under vented hood and check local codes for fire and sanitary regulations.

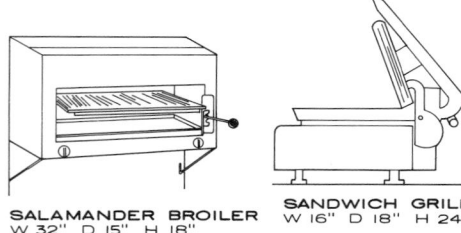

**SALAMANDER BROILER**
W 32" D 15" H 18"

**SANDWICH GRILL**
W 16" D 18" H 24"

**NOTE**

Salamander broiler is installed in the shelf area above the range top. For light broiling and finishing with drip shield to protect range top. Gas or electrically operated.

Sandwich grill is an electric countertop unit. It is available in various capacities.

**TOASTER**
W 11" D 12" H 8"

**NOTE**

Electric pop-up, rotary model available.

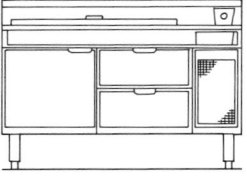

**SANDWICH UNIT**
W 60" D 32" H 42"

**NOTE**

Sandwich unit is used for the preparation of salads and sandwiches. Various capacities and combinations. Refrigerated pans are accessible from top. Base or cabinet is refrigerated. Refrigeration compressor is self-contained or remote.

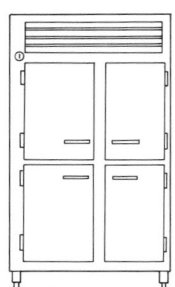

**REFRIGERATOR**
W 52" D 56" H 84"

**NOTE**

Refrigerators are available in many types, such as roll-in, pass through, mobile, and undercounter. They come with sliding or hinged, glass or stainless steel, full or half doors. Units are available with dual temperature control for combination refrigerator/freezer units. Refrigeration compressor may be self-contained or remote.

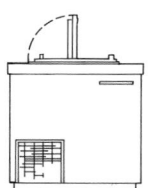

**ICE CREAM CABINET**
W 30" D 17" H 30"

**NOTE**

Electrically operated and available in various types and sizes. Accessories include syrup rail, dipper well, self-leveling dish dispenser, and sink. For door sizes and types consult manufacturer catalogs. Refrigeration compressor is remote or self-contained.

**COLD FOOD EQUIPMENT**

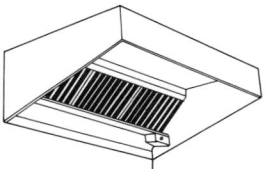

**VIEW**
W VARIES D 46" H 29"

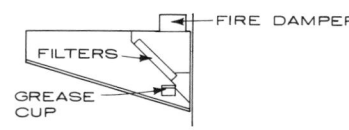

**SECTION**
**NOTE**

Exhaust ventilators are required over equipment producing grease ladened vapors. Hung from wall or ceiling, single depth for one line of equipment or double-sided for use with island equipment. Mesh or baffle washable and removable filters or an internal stationary baffle.

**OVERHEAD VENTILATOR**

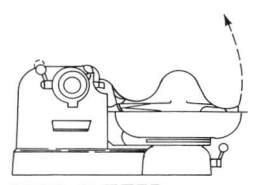

**FOOD CUTTER**
W 32" D 22" H 16"

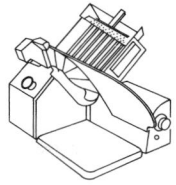

**FOOD SLICER**
W 20" D 24" H 19"

NOTE

Food cutters vary in size and motor capacities. Counter top equipment. Optional attachment equipment available if offered by manufacturer. Safety, sanitary, and electrical codes must be complied with.

Food slicers are counter top equipment of various capacities. Optional feed carriages are available. Check sanitary, safety, and electrical codes.

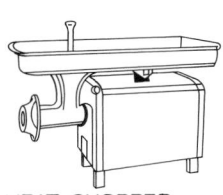

**MEAT CHOPPER**
W 12" D 18" H 24"

**VERTICAL CUTTER MIXER**
W 24" D 22" H 41"

NOTE

Meat choppers are counter top or floor type equipment of various sizes and capacities for chopping fresh and frozen meats. It should be easily accessible for cleaning. Check local electrical, sanitation, and safety codes.

Vertical cutter mixer comes in various sizes, and electrical capacities. For cutting, kneading, mixing, and similar purposes. It is usually a floor unit. Check local safety and sanitation codes.

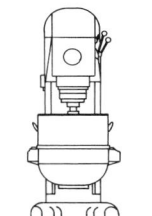

**MIXER**
W 21" D 20" H 45"

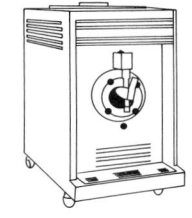

**SOFT SERVE MACHINE**
W 18" D 30" H 32"

NOTE

Mixer is either counter top or floor model and available in many sizes with many types of attachments. Check specifics with manufacturer. Consult local sanitary and electrical codes.

Soft serve machines are either counter or floor model. Accessibility of controls and components is important. Sizes and capacities vary, so consult manufacturer. Check safety and sanitary codes.

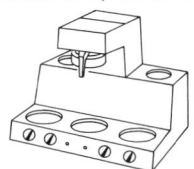

**FIVE STATION COFFEE WARMER**
W 24" D 18" H 24"

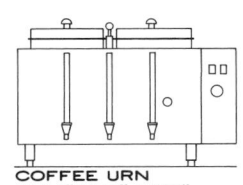

**COFFEE URN**
W 34" D 14" H 36"

NOTE

Coffee warmers are available with various station quantities and electrical capacities. They are used where large capacity is not usually needed. Water line is not required on some models. Warmer may be fully automatic or manually operated.

Coffee urns are usually automatic with twin coffee liners and unlimited water capacity for brewing. Suggested with swivel spray arm and heated coils for incoming water. Other options available. Check local sanitation and plumbing codes.

## PREPARATION EQUIPMENT

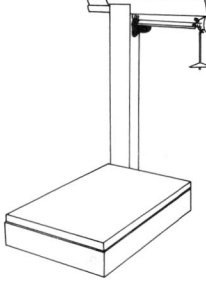

**BEAM SCALE**
W 20" D 36" H 50"

**BENCH SCALE**
W 24" D 30" H 51"

NOTE

Beam scales are accurate and easy to use, generally located at receiving area. Preferably on wheels. Accessories include ratio counting kit with scoops and balance indicator; others available. Capacities are variable.

Bench scales are available in many capacities, with beam and/or dial head. Accessories include platform or cabinet base, wheels, extra pans, and heater in head to protect from moisture and dust.

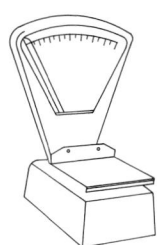

**FAN SCALE**
W 12" D 12" H 20"

NOTE

Fan scales are available in many weighing capacities, generally up to 6 lb. Usually automatic; should have well defined figures and graduations for accurate reading. May be supplied with platter (as shown), scoops, and round pans and equipped with a beam for more accurate and increased weight capacities.

Scales should be of durable, corrosion resistant, and easily cleaned material. Many varieties of scales are available depending on general use. For use in portion control situations, electronic models are very useful.

## SCALES

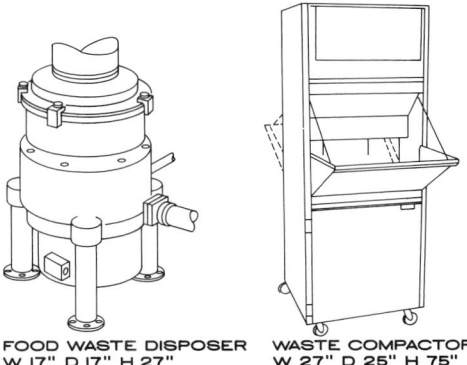

**FOOD WASTE DISPOSER**
W 17" D 17" H 27"

**WASTE COMPACTOR**
W 27" D 25" H 75"

NOTE

Food waste disposers are available in many sizes for specific operational requirements. Options include silver trap, sink stopper, spray rinser, cone with water swirl, sink, and vacuum breaker. Check local plumbing and sanitary codes.

Waste compactors are generally located at point of waste generation or in central accumulation area. Compacted into either bag or box. Reduce labor costs because of less waste handling. An efficient means of reducing volume of waste.

## WASTE HANDLING EQUIPMENT

**CONVEYOR DISHWASHER**
W 64" D 30" H 60"

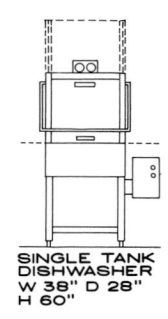

**SINGLE TANK DISHWASHER**
W 38" D 28" H 60"

NOTE

Conveyor dishwashers are available with single tank or two tanks, or with prewash tank, partially or fully automatic rack type. Accessories include inspection door, automatic temperature control with visible thermometers, splash shields, and others. Check local sanitary, safety, and electrical codes.

Single tank dishwashers are generally used in small operations. Manual operation for straight through or corner installations. Available with low temperature for use with sanitizing solution.

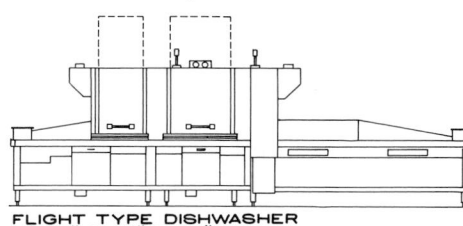

**FLIGHT TYPE DISHWASHER**
W 196" D 30" H 60"

NOTE

Flight type dishwasher is generally automatic with visible water temperature thermometers, inspection doors, and detergent dispensers. Optional equipment includes blow dryers, control sensors, energy saving connections, and other mechanical and electrical equipment. Electrically powered with gas, electrical or steam tank heats. Check electrical, sanitary plumbing, and safety codes.

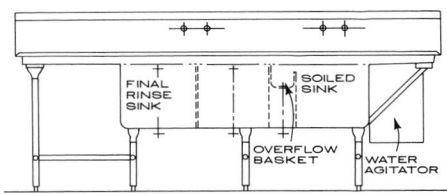

**POT SINK WITH OVERFLOW BASKET.**
**DIMENSIONS AS SPECIFIED**

NOTE

Three compartment pot sink with integral drainboards, overflow compartment, and basket. It is suggested that drainboards shorter than 24 in. long require no legs or braces, drainboards 25 to 30 in. long require brace, and drainboards over 30 in. long require legs and channel framework. Drainboards and sink compartments should have sufficient pitch for complete drainage without pooling. Lever or rotary handle wastes recommended, strainer basket and plug also available. Recirculating water agitator may be installed on soiled compartment for ease in soil removal. Overflow basket may be installed next to soiled compartment with suggested perforated basket. Final rinse sink should be supplied with a sanitizing solution or heater to raise water temperature to required level. Check local codes.

## WARE WASHING EQUIPMENT

Cini-Grissom Associates, Inc.; Food Service Consultants; Washington, D.C.

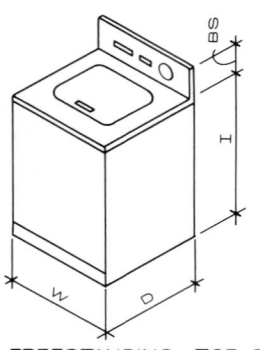
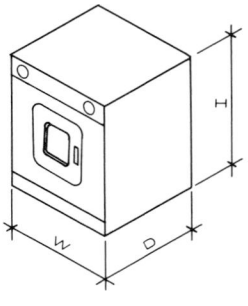

FREESTANDING – TOP OR
FRONT LOADING

UNDER COUNTER

### AUTOMATIC WASHERS (SOME HAVE KICK SPACES, SOME NOT)

|     | MIN. | MAX. | OTHER |
|-----|------|------|-------|
| W   | 25½  | 27   | 25⅝–26¾ |
| D   | 24⅞  | 28²³⁄₃₂ | 25–28⁵⁄₁₆ |
| H   | 36   | 36½  | 36⅛–36¼ |
| BS  | 6³⁄₃₂ | 8¾  | 6½–8½ |

|     | MIN. | MAX. |
|-----|------|------|
| W   | 26¾  | 30¼  |
| D   | 24⅞  | 24⅞  |
| H   | 34½  |      |

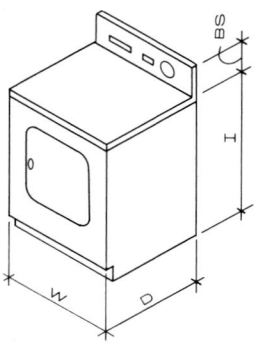
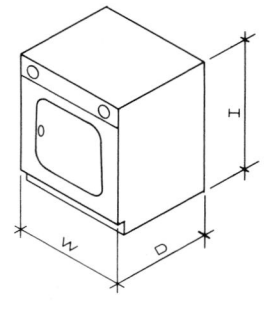

FREESTANDING
FRONT LOADING

UNDER COUNTER

### AUTOMATIC DRYERS (SOME HAVE KICK SPACES, SOME NOT)

|     | MIN. | MAX. | OTHER |
|-----|------|------|-------|
| W   | 26¾  | 31½  | 27–31 |
| D   | 24⅞  | 28²³⁄₃₂ | 25–28⁵⁄₁₆ |
| H   | 36   | 36½  | 36⅛–36¼ |
| BS  | 6³⁄₃₂ | 8¾  | 6½–8½ |

|     | MIN. | MAX. |
|-----|------|------|
| W   | 26¾  |      |
| D   | 24⅞  |      |
| H   | 34½  |      |

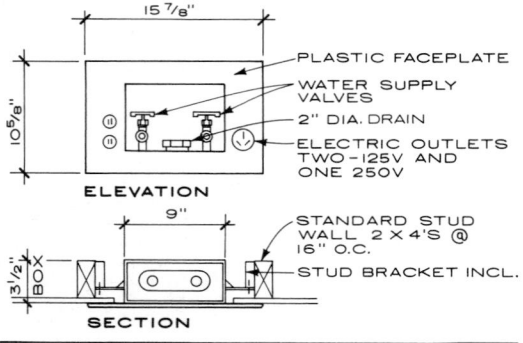

### UTILITY CONNECTION BOX (RECESSED)

ELEVATION

SECTION

- PLASTIC FACEPLATE
- WATER SUPPLY VALVES
- 2" DIA. DRAIN
- ELECTRIC OUTLETS TWO – 125V AND ONE 250V
- STANDARD STUD WALL 2 X 4'S @ 16" O.C.
- STUD BRACKET INCL.

15⅞"
10⅝"
9"
3½" BOX

### GENERAL NOTES

See kitchen & laundry layout pages for locations of washers & dryers and wall chases for pipes & vents and for dishwasher locations.

Where clearances of doors of machines (when open) may be a problem, check manufacturers catalog for "open-door" dimension.

All dimensions given are actual ones but certain variations in body design may affect actual depths of models. Check all units for exact voltage. Some units available with gas.

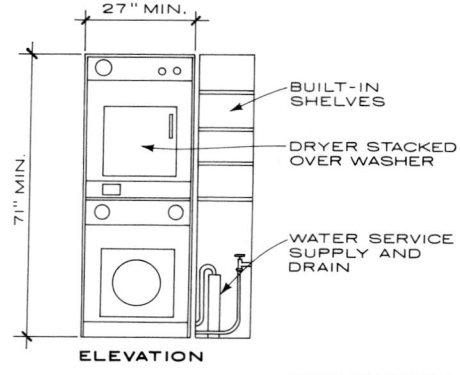
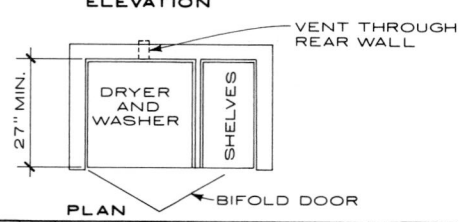

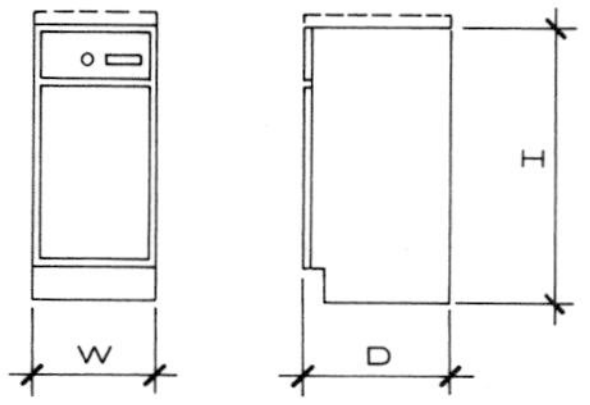

ELEVATION

PLAN

- BUILT-IN SHELVES
- DRYER STACKED OVER WASHER
- WATER SERVICE SUPPLY AND DRAIN
- VENT THROUGH REAR WALL
- BIFOLD DOOR

27" MIN.
71" MIN.
27" MIN.
DRYER AND WASHER
SHELVES

### WASHER AND DRYER STACKED IN CLOSET

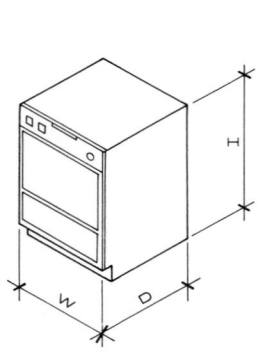
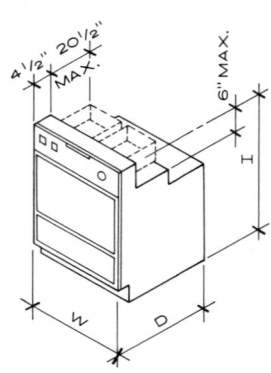
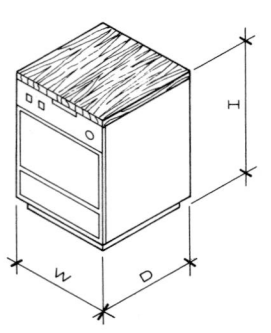

4½"  20½" MAX.
6" MAX.

### AUTOMATIC DISHWASHERS

| UNDER COUNTER | MIN. | MAX. | OTHER |
|---------------|------|------|-------|
| W   | 23    | 24   | 23⅞  |
| D   | 23¹¹⁄₁₆ | 26¼ | 25½  |
| H   | 33½  | 34½  | 34⅛  |

| UNDER SINK | MIN. | MAX. | OTHER |
|------------|------|------|-------|
| W   | 24    | 24¼  | 24   |
| D   | 24    | 25½  | 25   |
| H   | 34½  | 34½  | 34½  |

| MOBILE (WITH COUNTER TOP) | MIN. | MAX. | OTHER |
|---------------------------|------|------|-------|
| W   | 22½  | 27   | 24⅝  |
| D   | 23¹¹⁄₁₆ | 26½ | 25   |
| H   | 34⅛  | 39   | 36   |

### TRASH COMPACTOR: UNDER COUNTER OR FREESTANDING

|     | MIN. | MAX. | OTHER |
|-----|------|------|-------|
| W   | 11⅞  | 17¾  | 14⅞  |
| D   | 18   | 24³⁄₁₆ | 18¼ |
| H   | 33½  | 35   | 34½  |

William G. Miner, AIA, Architect; Washington, D.C.
R. E. Powe, Jr., AIA; Hugh Newell Jacobsen, FAIA; Washington, D.C.

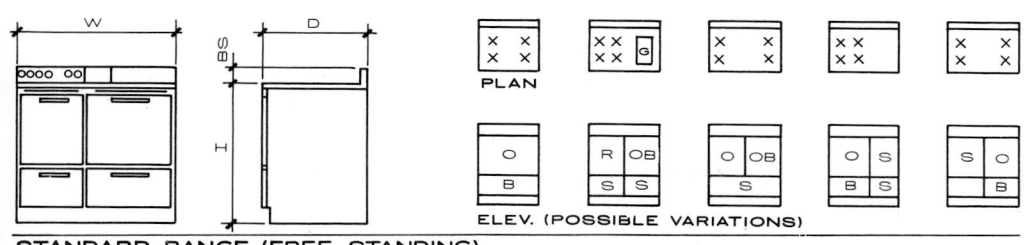

## STANDARD RANGE (FREE STANDING)

**ELEV. (POSSIBLE VARIATIONS)**

**SYMBOLS**
O- OVEN
B- BROILER
G- REVOLVING GRILL
X- BURNER, GAS OR ELECTRIC
W- WARMING OVEN
S- STORAGE
R- ROTISSERIE

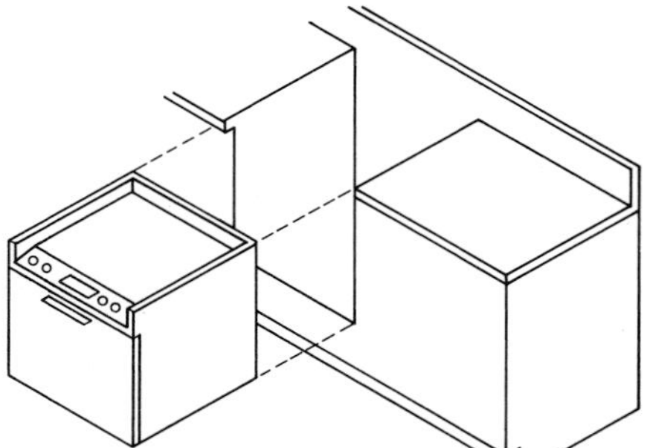

### ONE OVEN—FOUR UNITS

|  | MIN. | MAX. | OTHER |
|---|---|---|---|
| W | 19½ | 40 | 21–30 |
| D | 24¼ | 27½ | 25–26¼ |
| H | 35⅛ | 36⅛ | 35¼–36 |
| BS | 4¹¹⁄₁₆ | 12½ | 8¼–11½ |

### TWO OVENS FOUR UNITS

|  | MIN. | MAX. | OTHER |
|---|---|---|---|
| W | 40 |  |  |
| D | 25 | 27½ | 25½–26¼ |
| H | 35⅛ | 36 | 35¼ |
| BS | 8¼ | 11⅛ | 8⅛–10⅜ |

### DROP-IN RANGE

|  | MIN. | MAX. | OTHER |
|---|---|---|---|
| W | 22⅞ | 30 | 23⅞ |
| D | 22⅛ | 25 | 22½–24 |
| H | 23 | 24¹⁄₁₆ | 23½ |

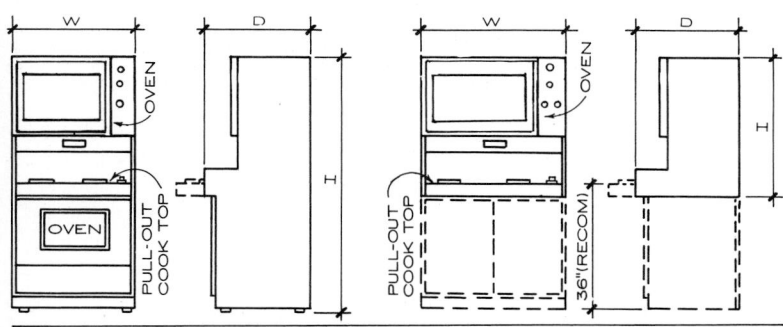

## RANGES WITH EYE LEVEL OVENS

### DOUBLE OVEN—4 units

|  | MIN. | MAX. | OTHER |
|---|---|---|---|
| W | 29⅞ | 30 |  |
| D | 25½ | 27⅝ | 25⅝–27½ |
| H | 61½ | 71¼ | 63¾–67⁷⁄₁₆ |

### SINGLE OVEN TOP ONLY—4 units

|  | MIN. | MAX. | OTHER |
|---|---|---|---|
| W | 29¹³⁄₁₆ | 38⅞ | 29⅞ |
| D | 25½ | 27⅝ | 27¼ |
| H | 33½ | 41¹⁄₁₆ | 36¾ |

### DOUBLE OVEN TOP ONLY—4 units

|  | MIN. | MAX. | OTHER |
|---|---|---|---|
| W | 39 | 40¼ | 40 |
| D | 25½ | 27⅝ | 26¾ |
| H | 34⅞ | 36¾ |  |

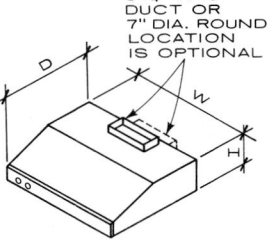

Range hoods are available with vents as shown or without vent. Manufacturers provide accessories such as fans, filters, and lights.

### RANGE HOOD

|  | MIN. | MAX. | OTHER |
|---|---|---|---|
| W | 24 | 72 | 30–66 |
| D | 12 | 27½ | 17–26 |
| H | 5½ | 8⅝ | 5⅝–7½ |

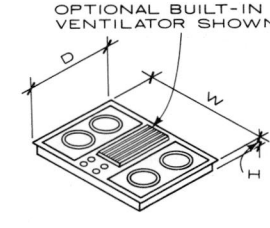

Cook tops are available with two to seven heating elements. Griddles, grills, and built-in ventilators are optional.

### BUILT-IN COOK TOP ELECTRIC OR GAS

|  | MIN. | MAX. |
|---|---|---|
| W | 12 | 48 |
| D | 18 | 22 |
| H | 2 | 3 |

**NOTE**
SELF CLEANING OVENS MUST VENT TO OUTSIDE

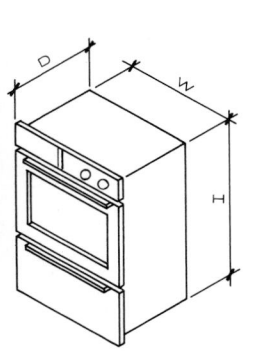

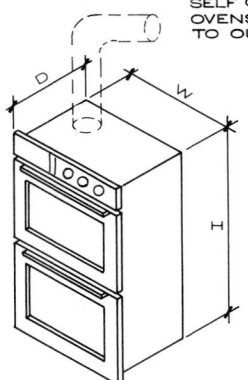

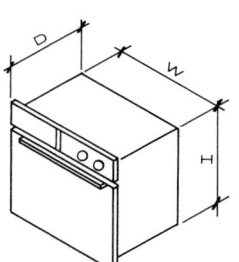

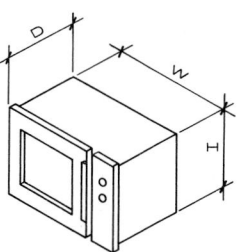

### OVEN AND BROILER

|  | MIN. | MAX. | OTHER |
|---|---|---|---|
| W | 21 | 24¼ | 22½–24 |
| D | 21⅛ | 24 | 22½–22¹¹⁄₁₆ |
| H | 38 | 40⁷⁄₁₆ | 40¾ |

### DOUBLE OVEN

|  | MIN. | MAX. | OTHER |
|---|---|---|---|
| W | 21 | 24¼ | 22½–24 |
| D | 21⅛ | 24 | 22½–22¹¹⁄₁₆ |
| H | 39¼ | 50⅜ | 42–46¹³⁄₁₆ |

### SINGLE OVEN

|  | MIN. | MAX. | OTHER |
|---|---|---|---|
| W | 21 | 24¼ | 22½–24 |
| D | 21⅛ | 24 | 22½–22¹¹⁄₁₆ |
| H | 23½ | 26⅞ | 25 |

### MICROWAVE OVEN

|  | MIN. | MAX. | OTHER |
|---|---|---|---|
| W | 21½ | 24¾ | 22½ |
| D | 14½ | 22 | 18¾ |
| H | 13⅝ | 18 | 17 |

## BUILT-IN WALL OVENS (GAS OR ELECTRIC)

### NOTES

1. Check manufacturers requirements for rough clearances.
2. Dimensions shown are in inches.
3. Optional equipment available for ranges or wall ovens are broilers and rotisseries.

William G. Miner, AIA, Architect; Washington, D.C.
R. E. Powe, Jr., AIA; Hugh Newell Jacobsen, FAIA; Washington, D.C.

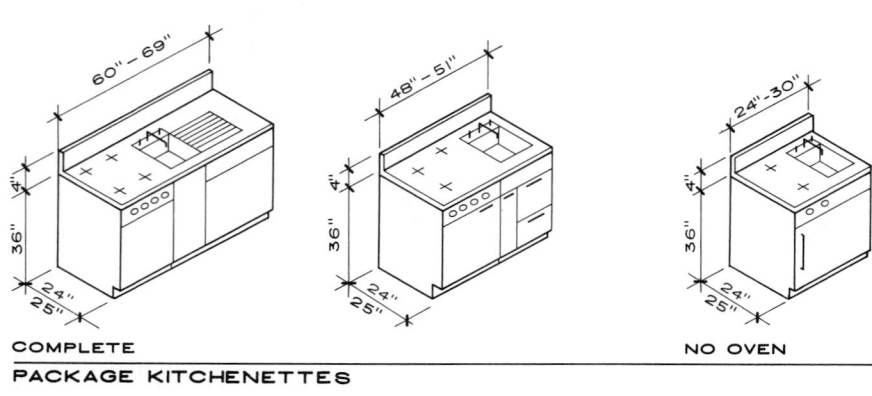

**COMPLETE**          **NO OVEN**

## PACKAGE KITCHENETTES

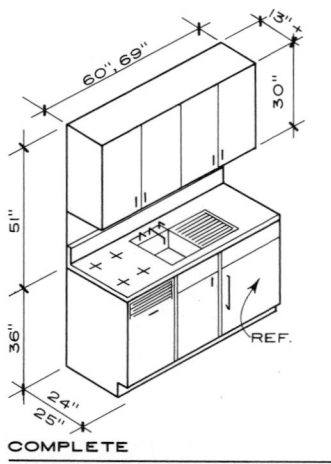
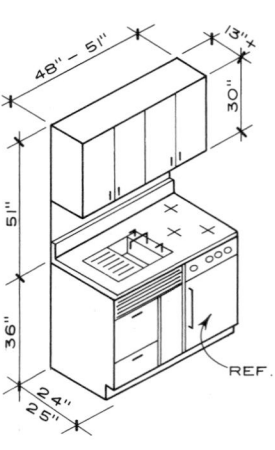
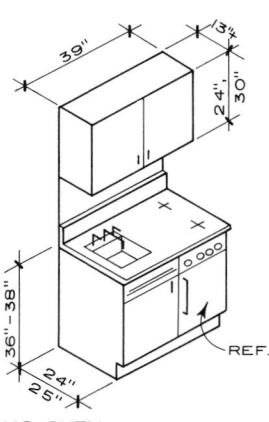

**COMPLETE**          **NO OVEN**

## KITCHENETTE UNITS

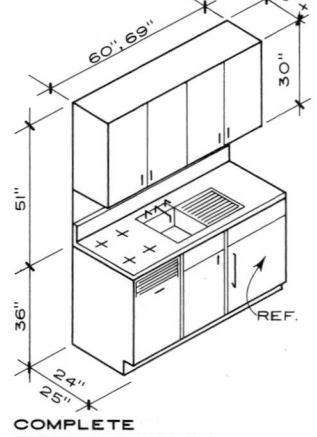
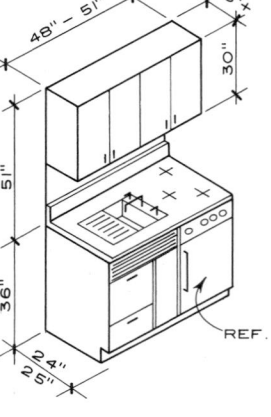
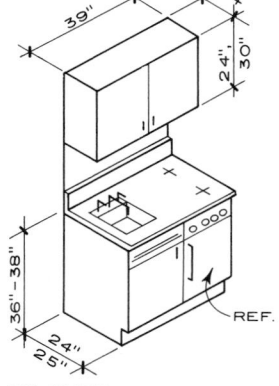

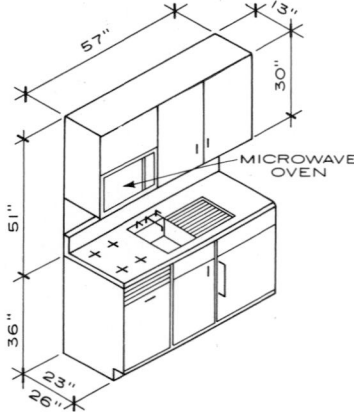
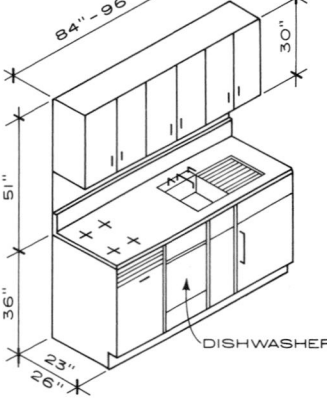

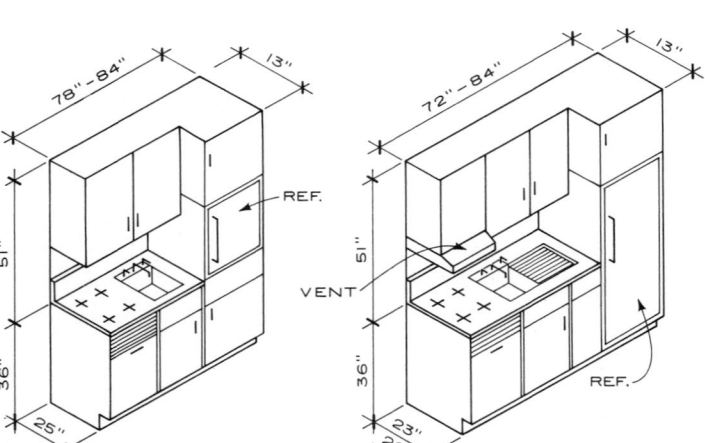

**NOTE**

See manufacturers' catalogues for actual dimensions of specific units which may include: number of burners, size of refrigerator, size of sink, finish materials, and options such as garbage disposer, range hood, microwave oven, ice maker, dishwasher, or freezer.

## SPECIAL KITCHENETTE UNITS

William G. Miner, AIA, Architect; Washington, D.C.

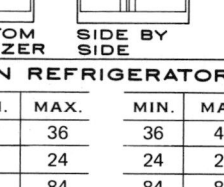

**SINGLE DOOR**    **TOP FREEZER**    **SIDE BY SIDE**

### CONVENTIONAL REFRIGERATORS

|        | MIN.        | MAX.        | MIN.        | MAX.        | MIN.        | MAX.        |
|--------|-------------|-------------|-------------|-------------|-------------|-------------|
| W      | 24          | $32^3/4$    | 28          | $32^3/4$    | $30^1/2$    | $35^3/4$    |
| D      | $26^9/16$   | $31^5/8$    | $28^3/4$    | $31^5/8$    | $29^1/2$    | $32^7/8$    |
| H      | $55^1/2$    | $63^1/2$    |             | 66          | 64          | $68^7/8$    |
| cu ft  | 9.5         | 14.0        | 11.8        | 22.4        | 18.5        | 25.6        |

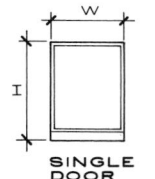
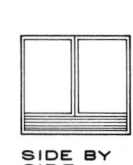
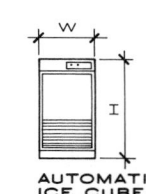

**BOTTOM FREEZER**    **SIDE BY SIDE**    **COMBINATION**

### BUILT-IN REFRIGERATORS

|        | MIN. | MAX.  | MIN. | MAX. | OVERALL |
|--------|------|-------|------|------|---------|
| W      | 30   | 36    | 36   | 48   | 72      |
| D      | 24   | 24    | 24   | 24   | 24      |
| H      | 84   | 84    | 84   | 84   | 73      |
| cu ft  | 19   | 23.6  | 24   | 32   | 42      |

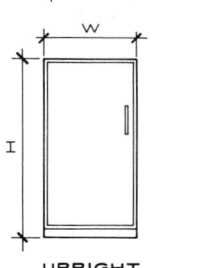

**SINGLE DOOR**    **SIDE BY SIDE**    **AUTOMATIC ICE CUBE MAKER**

### UNDERCOUNTER REFRIGERATORS

|        | OVERALL     | OVERALL     | MIN.        | MAX.         |
|--------|-------------|-------------|-------------|--------------|
| W      | 24          | 36          | 15          | $17^7/8$     |
| D      | $23^3/4$    | $23^3/4$    | $20^3/8$    | $23^{13}/16$ |
| H      | $34^1/2$    | $34^1/2$    | $33^1/8$    | $34^{13}/32$ |
| cu ft  | 5.2         | 6.0         | 35 lb of ice |             |

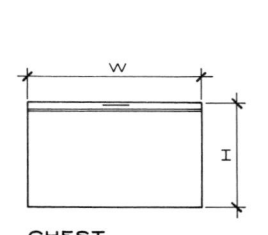

**UPRIGHT**    **CHEST**

### FREEZERS

|        | MIN.        | MAX.         | MIN.        | MAX.        |
|--------|-------------|--------------|-------------|-------------|
| W      | 28          | 32           | 25          | $69^1/2$    |
| D      | $28^7/8$    | $30^{11}/16$ | $23^1/4$    | 31          |
| H      | $59^1/8$    | $70^1/8$     | $34^{11}/16$ | 35         |
| cu ft  | 11.6        | 21.1         |             | 25.3        |

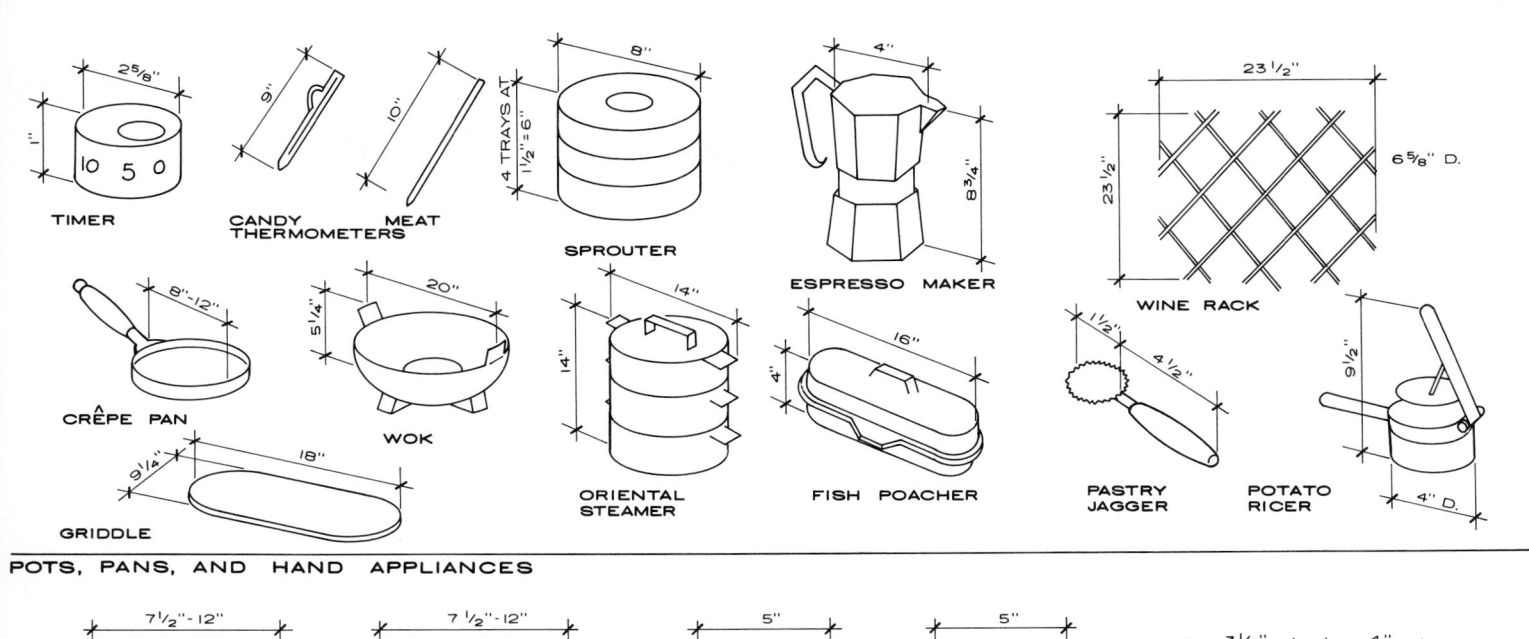

**TIMER** — 2⅝", 1", 10 5 0

**CANDY THERMOMETERS** — 9"

**MEAT** — 10"

**SPROUTER** — 8", 4 TRAYS AT 1½"=6"

**ESPRESSO MAKER** — 4", 8¾"

**WINE RACK** — 23½", 23½", 6⅝" D.

**CRÊPE PAN** — 8"-12"

**WOK** — 20", 5¼"

**ORIENTAL STEAMER** — 14", 14"

**FISH POACHER** — 16", 4"

**PASTRY JAGGER** — 1½", 4½"

**POTATO RICER** — 9½", 4" D.

**GRIDDLE** — 18", 9¼"

## POTS, PANS, AND HAND APPLIANCES

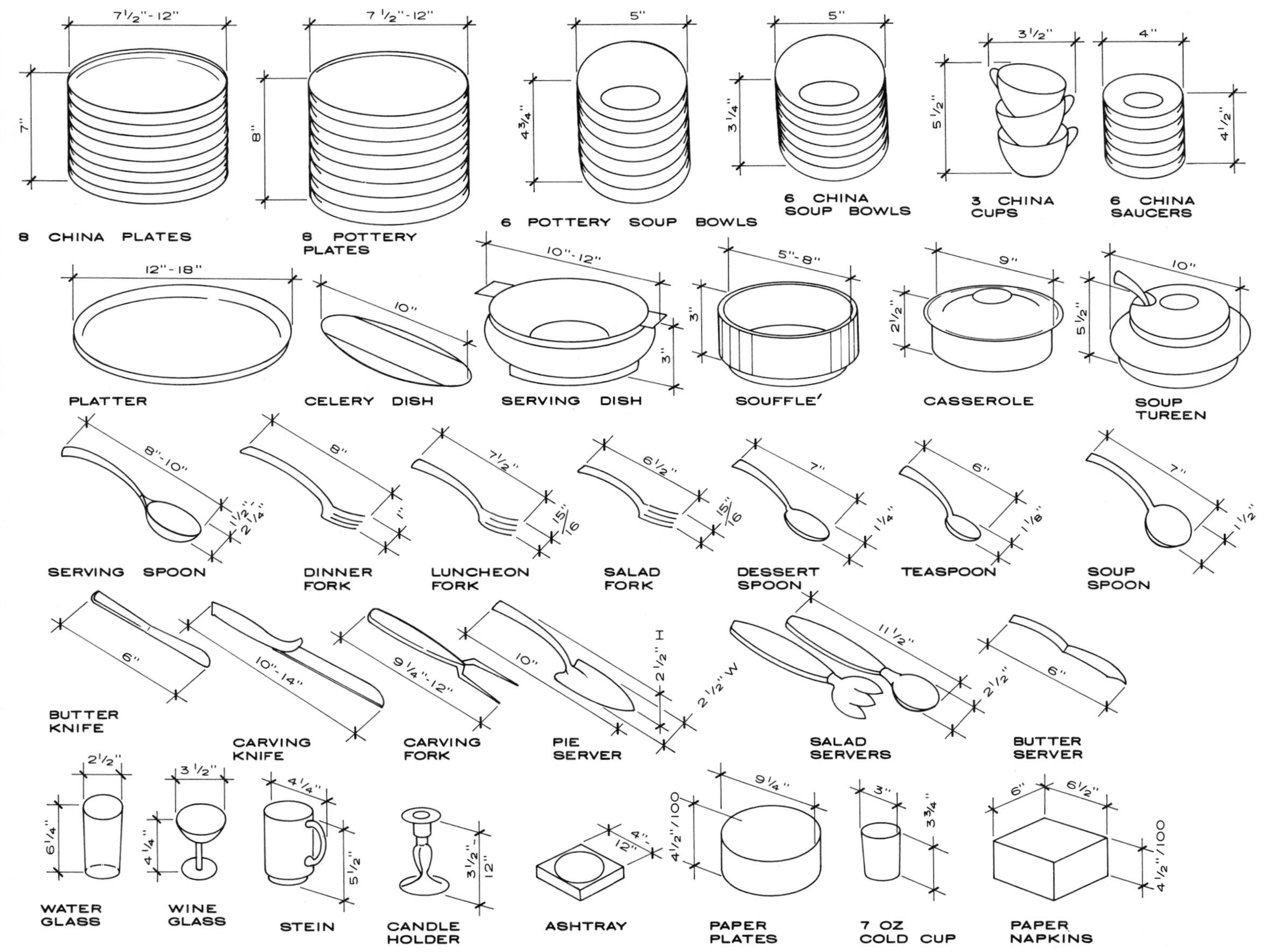

**8 CHINA PLATES** — 7½"-12", 7"

**8 POTTERY PLATES** — 7½"-12", 8"

**6 POTTERY SOUP BOWLS** — 5", 4¾"

**6 CHINA SOUP BOWLS** — 5", 3¼"

**3 CHINA CUPS** — 3½", 5½"

**6 CHINA SAUCERS** — 4", 4½"

**PLATTER** — 12"-18"

**CELERY DISH** — 10"

**SERVING DISH** — 10"-12", 3"

**SOUFFLÉ** — 5"-8", 3"

**CASSEROLE** — 9", 2½"

**SOUP TUREEN** — 10", 5½"

**SERVING SPOON** — 8"-10", 1½", 2¼"

**DINNER FORK** — 8", 1"

**LUNCHEON FORK** — 7½", 15/16"

**SALAD FORK** — 6½", 15/16"

**DESSERT SPOON** — 7"

**TEASPOON** — 6", 1¼"

**SOUP SPOON** — 7", 1⅛"

**BUTTER KNIFE** — 6"

**CARVING KNIFE** — 10"-14"

**CARVING FORK** — 9¼"-12"

**PIE SERVER** — 10", 2½" H, 2½" W

**SALAD SERVERS** — 11½", 2½"

**BUTTER SERVER** — 6"

**WATER GLASS** — 2½", 6¼"

**WINE GLASS** — 3½", 4¼"

**STEIN** — 4¼", 5½"

**CANDLE HOLDER** — 3½", 12"

**ASHTRAY** — 4", 12"

**PAPER PLATES** — 9¼", 4½"/100

**7 OZ COLD CUP** — 3", 3¾"

**PAPER NAPKINS** — 6", 6½", 4½"/100

## DINING ROOM TABLEWARE

E. H. & M. K. Hunter, Architects; Raleigh, North Carolina

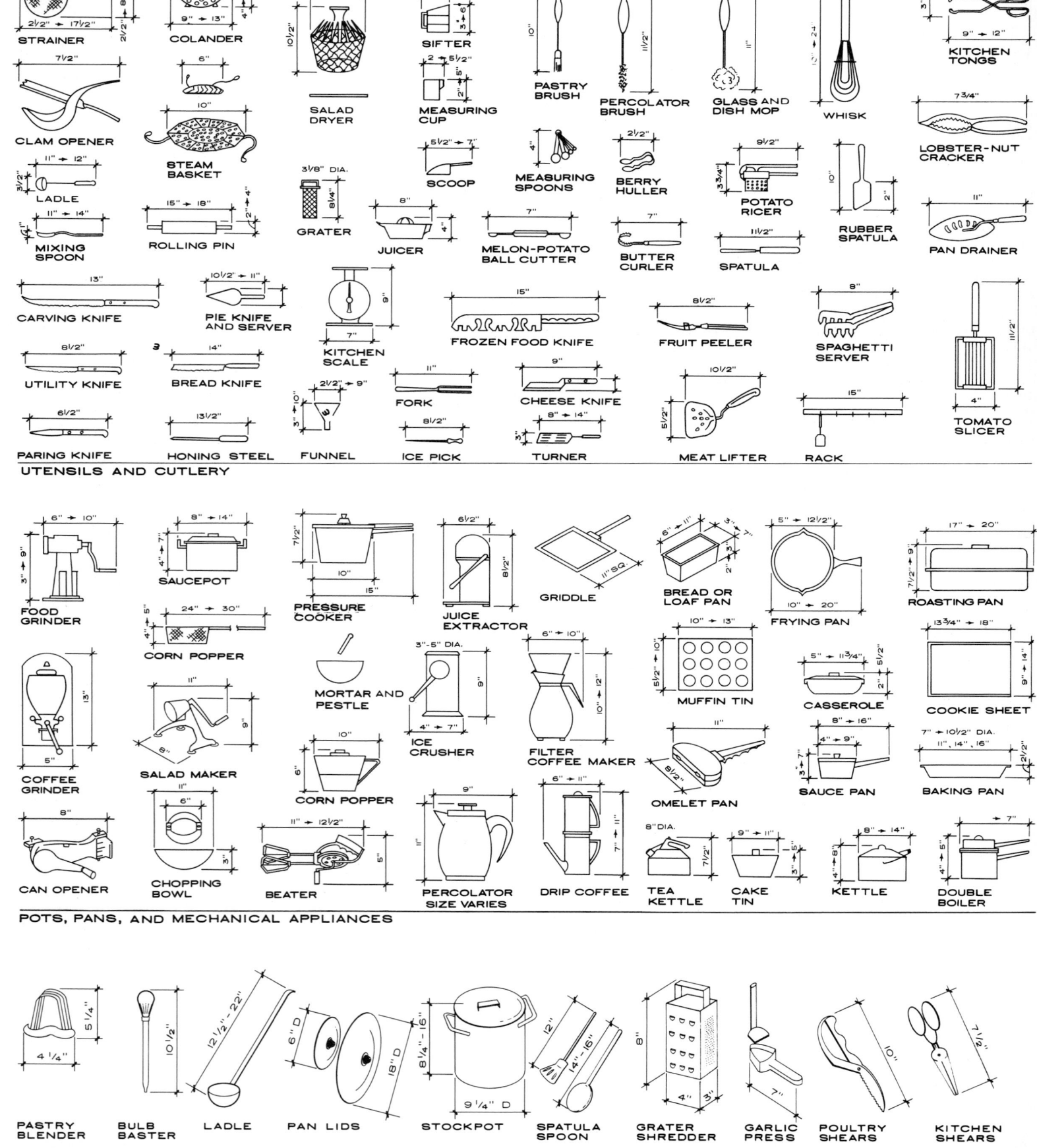

STRAINER COLANDER SIFTER PASTRY BRUSH PERCOLATOR BRUSH GLASS AND DISH MOP WHISK KITCHEN TONGS

CLAM OPENER SALAD DRYER MEASURING CUP LOBSTER-NUT CRACKER

STEAM BASKET SCOOP MEASURING SPOONS BERRY HULLER POTATO RICER RUBBER SPATULA

LADLE GRATER JUICER MELON-POTATO BALL CUTTER BUTTER CURLER SPATULA PAN DRAINER

MIXING SPOON ROLLING PIN

CARVING KNIFE PIE KNIFE AND SERVER KITCHEN SCALE FROZEN FOOD KNIFE FRUIT PEELER SPAGHETTI SERVER

UTILITY KNIFE BREAD KNIFE FORK CHEESE KNIFE TOMATO SLICER

PARING KNIFE HONING STEEL FUNNEL ICE PICK TURNER MEAT LIFTER RACK

**UTENSILS AND CUTLERY**

FOOD GRINDER SAUCEPOT PRESSURE COOKER JUICE EXTRACTOR GRIDDLE BREAD OR LOAF PAN ROASTING PAN

CORN POPPER FRYING PAN

MORTAR AND PESTLE ICE CRUSHER FILTER COFFEE MAKER MUFFIN TIN CASSEROLE COOKIE SHEET

COFFEE GRINDER SALAD MAKER CORN POPPER OMELET PAN SAUCE PAN BAKING PAN

CAN OPENER CHOPPING BOWL BEATER PERCOLATOR SIZE VARIES DRIP COFFEE TEA KETTLE CAKE TIN KETTLE DOUBLE BOILER

**POTS, PANS, AND MECHANICAL APPLIANCES**

PASTRY BLENDER BULB BASTER LADLE PAN LIDS STOCKPOT SPATULA SPOON GRATER SHREDDER GARLIC PRESS POULTRY SHEARS KITCHEN SHEARS

**POTS, PANS, AND HAND APPLIANCES**

E. H. & M. K. Hunter, Architects; Raleigh, North Carolina

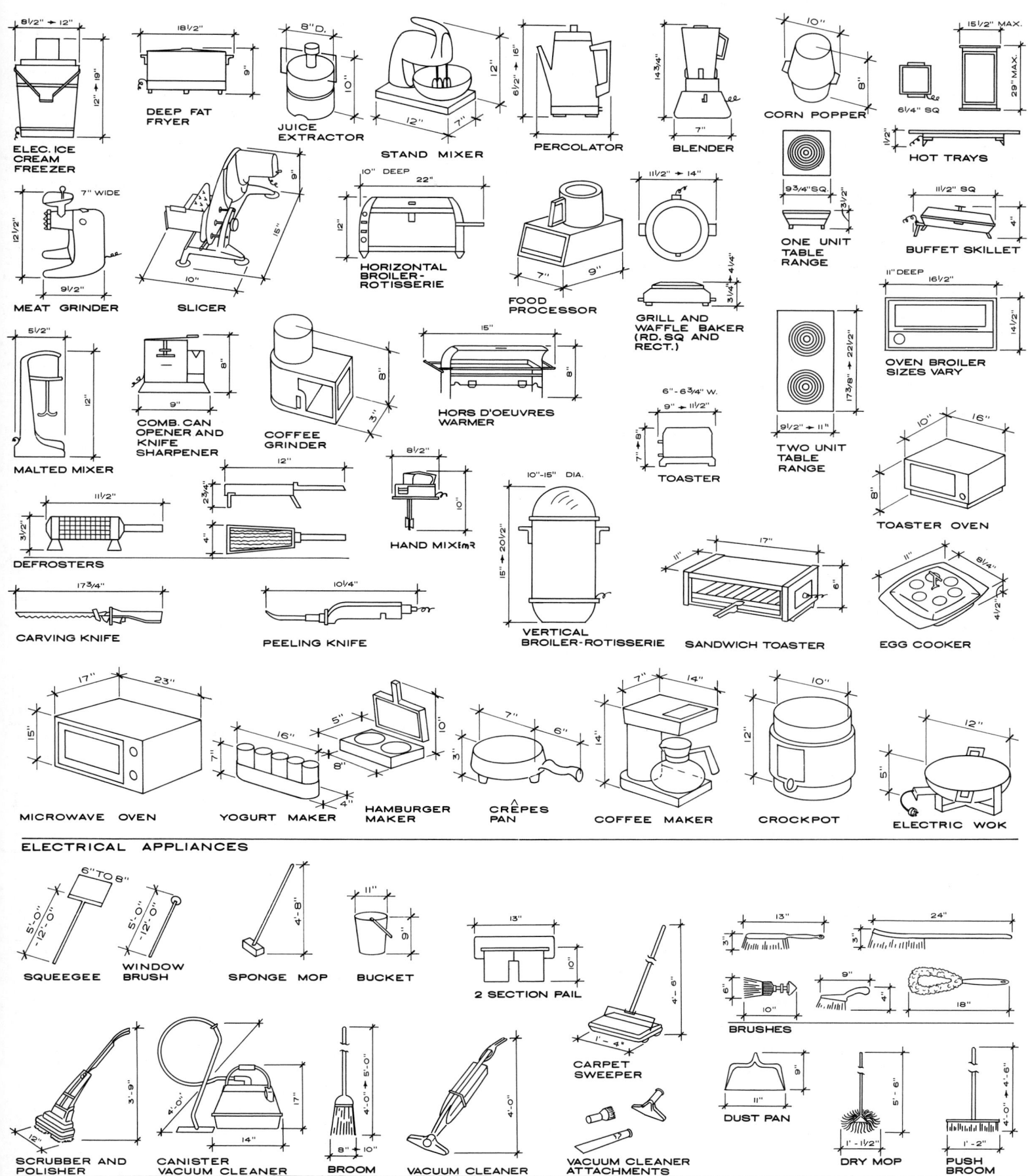

ELEC. ICE CREAM FREEZER

DEEP FAT FRYER

JUICE EXTRACTOR

STAND MIXER

PERCOLATOR

BLENDER

CORN POPPER

HOT TRAYS

MEAT GRINDER

SLICER

HORIZONTAL BROILER-ROTISSERIE

FOOD PROCESSOR

GRILL AND WAFFLE BAKER (RD. SQ AND RECT.)

ONE UNIT TABLE RANGE

BUFFET SKILLET

MALTED MIXER

COMB. CAN OPENER AND KNIFE SHARPENER

COFFEE GRINDER

HORS D'OEUVRES WARMER

TOASTER

TWO UNIT TABLE RANGE

OVEN BROILER SIZES VARY

DEFROSTERS

HAND MIXER

TOASTER OVEN

CARVING KNIFE

PEELING KNIFE

VERTICAL BROILER-ROTISSERIE

SANDWICH TOASTER

EGG COOKER

MICROWAVE OVEN

YOGURT MAKER

HAMBURGER MAKER

CRÊPES PAN

COFFEE MAKER

CROCKPOT

ELECTRIC WOK

## ELECTRICAL APPLIANCES

SQUEEGEE

WINDOW BRUSH

SPONGE MOP

BUCKET

2 SECTION PAIL

CARPET SWEEPER

BRUSHES

SCRUBBER AND POLISHER

CANISTER VACUUM CLEANER

BROOM

VACUUM CLEANER

VACUUM CLEANER ATTACHMENTS

DUST PAN

DRY MOP

PUSH BROOM

## CLEANING EQUIPMENT

E. H. & M. K. Hunter, Architects; Raleigh, North Carolina

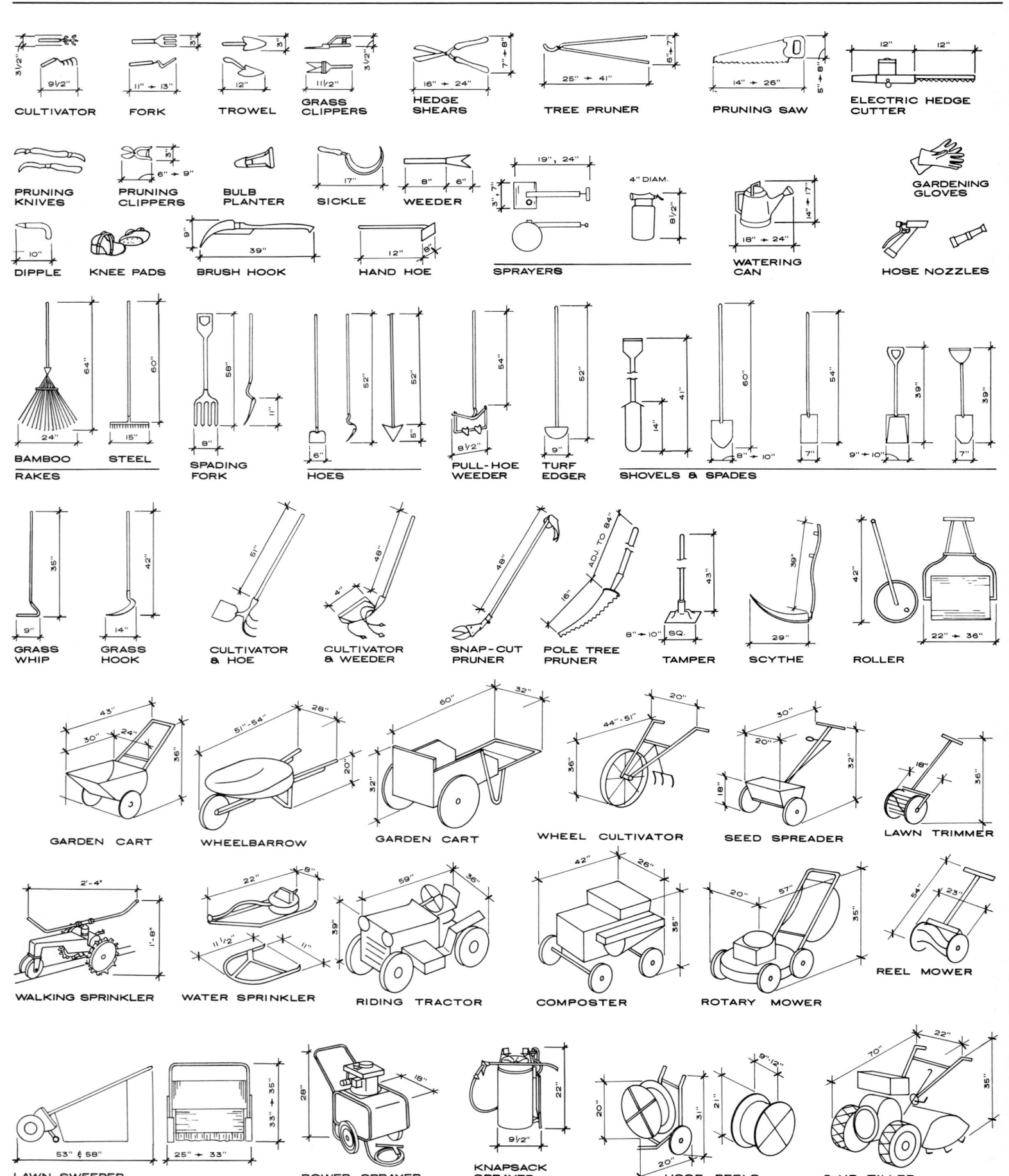

CULTIVATOR

FORK

TROWEL

GRASS CLIPPERS

HEDGE SHEARS

TREE PRUNER

PRUNING SAW

ELECTRIC HEDGE CUTTER

PRUNING KNIVES

PRUNING CLIPPERS

BULB PLANTER

SICKLE

WEEDER

SPRAYERS

WATERING CAN

GARDENING GLOVES

DIPPLE

KNEE PADS

BRUSH HOOK

HAND HOE

HOSE NOZZLES

BAMBOO   STEEL

RAKES

SPADING FORK

HOES

PULL-HOE WEEDER

TURF EDGER

SHOVELS & SPADES

GRASS WHIP

GRASS HOOK

CULTIVATOR & HOE

CULTIVATOR & WEEDER

SNAP-CUT PRUNER

POLE TREE PRUNER

TAMPER

SCYTHE

ROLLER

GARDEN CART

WHEELBARROW

GARDEN CART

WHEEL CULTIVATOR

SEED SPREADER

LAWN TRIMMER

WALKING SPRINKLER

WATER SPRINKLER

RIDING TRACTOR

COMPOSTER

ROTARY MOWER

REEL MOWER

LAWN SWEEPER

POWER SPRAYER

KNAPSACK SPRAYER

HOSE REELS

6 HP TILLER

E. H. & M. K. Hunter, Architects; Raleigh, North Carolina

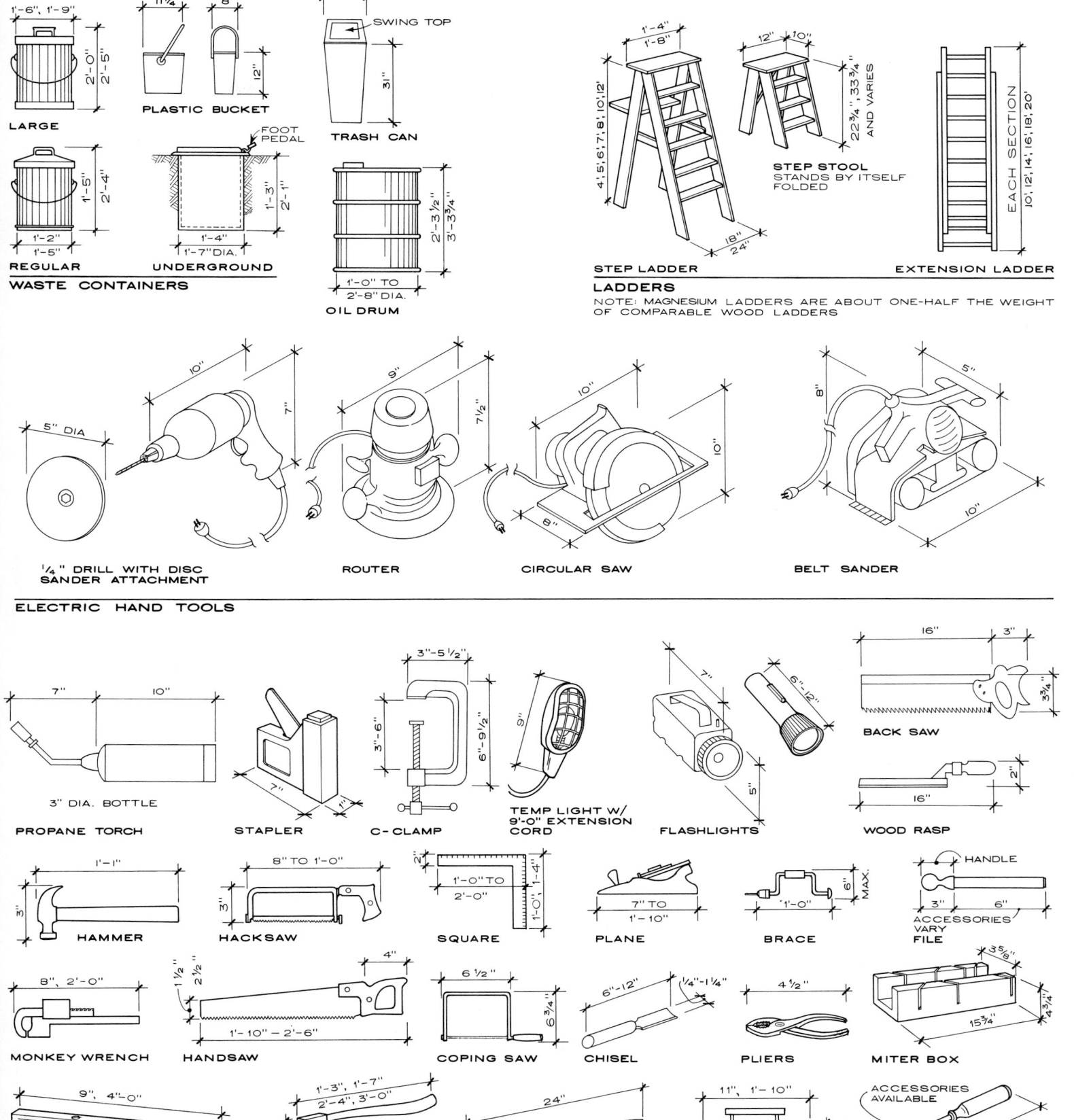

## WASTE CONTAINERS

LARGE

PLASTIC BUCKET

TRASH CAN

SWING TOP

REGULAR

UNDERGROUND

FOOT PEDAL

OIL DRUM

## LADDERS

STEP LADDER

STEP STOOL
STANDS BY ITSELF
FOLDED

EXTENSION LADDER

EACH SECTION

NOTE: MAGNESIUM LADDERS ARE ABOUT ONE-HALF THE WEIGHT
OF COMPARABLE WOOD LADDERS

## ELECTRIC HAND TOOLS

1/4" DRILL WITH DISC
SANDER ATTACHMENT

ROUTER

CIRCULAR SAW

BELT SANDER

## TYPICAL HOUSEHOLD HAND TOOLS

PROPANE TORCH

3" DIA. BOTTLE

STAPLER

C-CLAMP

TEMP LIGHT W/
9'-0" EXTENSION
CORD

FLASHLIGHTS

BACK SAW

WOOD RASP

HAMMER

HACKSAW

SQUARE

PLANE

BRACE

FILE

ACCESSORIES
VARY

HANDLE

MONKEY WRENCH

HANDSAW

COPING SAW

CHISEL

PLIERS

MITER BOX

WOOD LEVEL

HATCHET OR AXE

CROW BAR

3/4" THICK

TOOL BOX

SCREWDRIVER

ACCESSORIES
AVAILABLE

VARIES

E. H. & M. K. Hunter, Architects; Raleigh, North Carolina

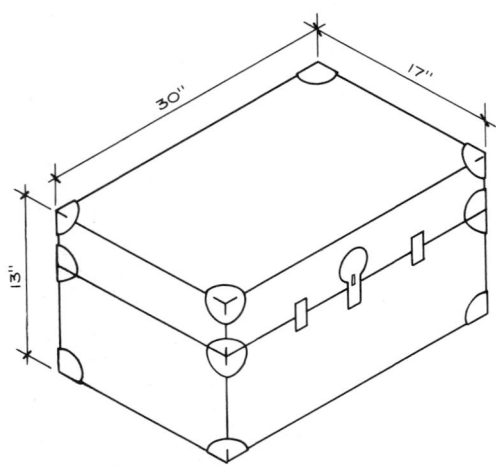

**TRUNK**

| | W | H | D |
|---|---|---|---|
| End table trunk | 18 | 18 | 20 |
| Footlocker | 30¼ | 12½ | 15¾ |
| Car trunk | 30¼ | 16¼ | 15¾ |
| Camp trunk | 33¼ | 21 | 18¾ |
| Packing trunk | 40¼ | 22¼ | 22½ |

**TRUNKS**

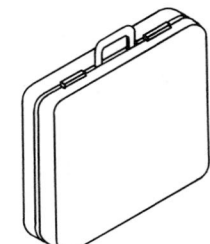

**WOMEN'S LUGGAGE**

| | W | H | D |
|---|---|---|---|
| Carry-on | 20 | 17 | 7 |
| Junior Pullman | 23¾ | 19½ | 8 |
| Pullman | 26¾ | 21½ | 9 |
| Overseas | 32 | 20 | 10 |

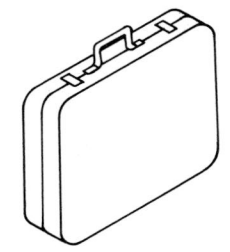

**MEN'S LUGGAGE**

| | W | H | D |
|---|---|---|---|
| Carry-on | 20 | 17 | 7 |
| Two-suiter | 26¾ | 18½ | 8 |
| Three-suiter | 26¾ | 21½ | 9 |
| Overseas | 32 | 20 | 10 |

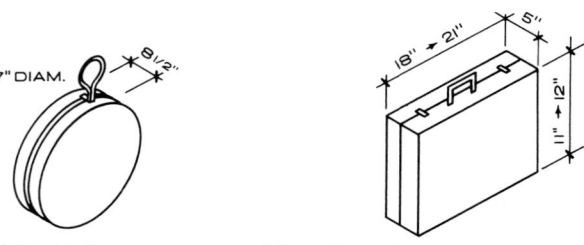

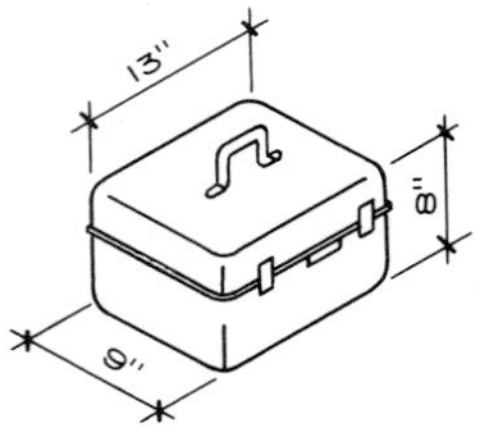

**COSMETIC CASE**          **HAT BOX**          **ATTACHE CASE**

**CASES**

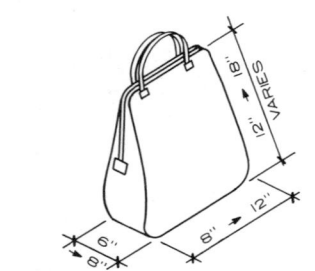

**COSMETIC TOTE**

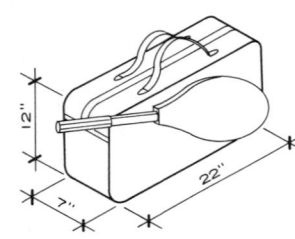

**TENNIS PACK**

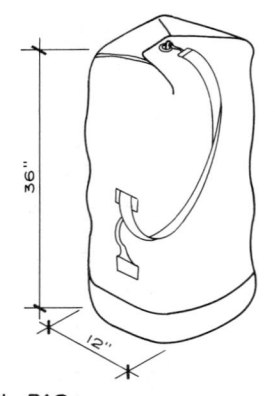

**DUFFEL BAG**

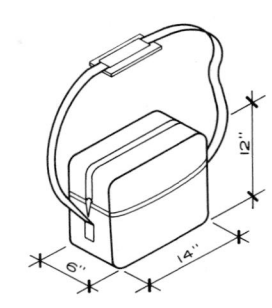

**SHOULDER BAG**

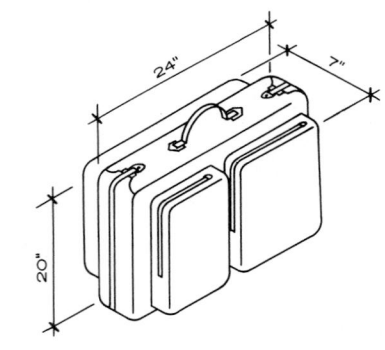

**FLIGHT BAG**

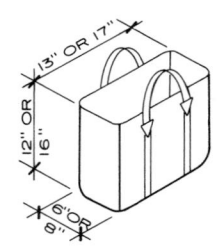

**CARRY-ALL**

**BAGS**

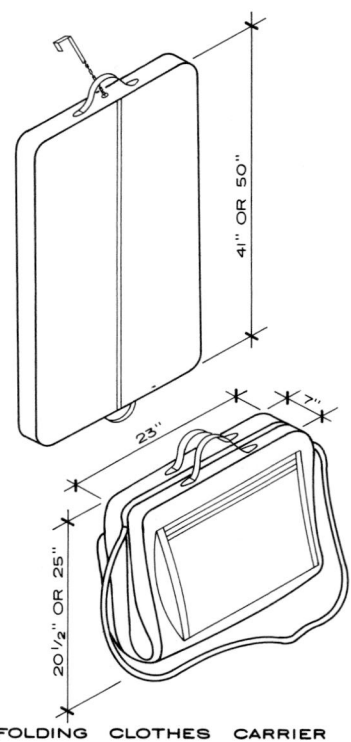

**FOLDING CLOTHES CARRIER**

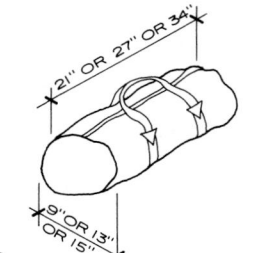

**KIT BAG**

E. H. & M. K. Hunter, Architects; Raleigh, North Carolina

**11**    **RESIDENTIAL EQUIPMENT**

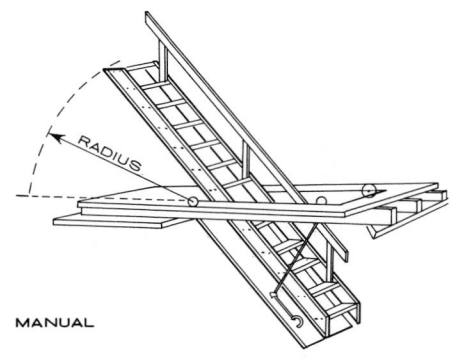

MANUAL

Standard package units are available for floor-to-floor heights from 7 ft up to 13 ft in 1 ft increments. Ladder is inclined at 52° above horizontal. Standard box frame is used for ceiling thickness up to 13 in. Special deep frame is specified for ceiling thicknesses ranging from 13 in. up to 48 in.

Typical rough opening in ceiling = 30 x 72 in.

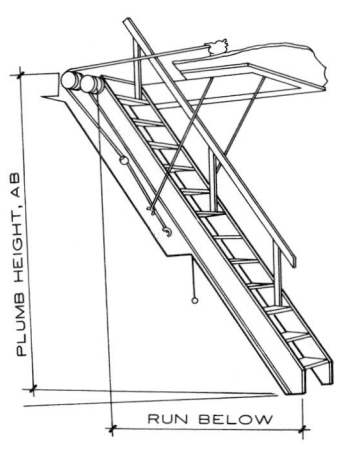

MANUAL

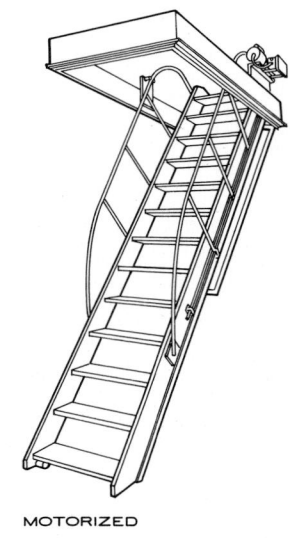

MOTORIZED

## SLIDE UP PIVOT TYPE

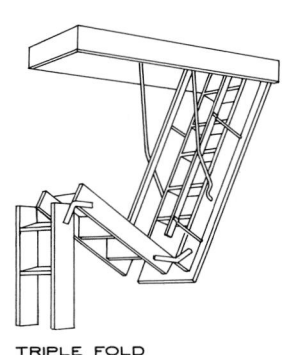

TRIPLE FOLD

### STANDARD SIZES FOR DISAPPEARING STAIRS

| ROUGH OPENING | FLOOR-TO-FLOOR | COIL PROJECTION | LANDING SPACE |
|---|---|---|---|
| 22″ x 48″ | 8′-5″ | 60″ | 58½″ |
| 22″ x 54″ | 8′-9″ | 66″ | 65″ |
| | 10′-0″ | 79″ | 73″ |
| 25½″ x 48″ | 8′-5″ | 60″ | 58½″ |
| 25½″ x 54″ 25½″ x 60″ 30″ x 54″ 30″ x 60″ | 8′-9″ 10′-0″ | 66″ 79″ | 65″ 73″ |

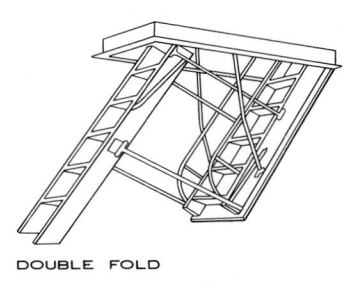

DOUBLE FOLD

## FOLDING TYPE

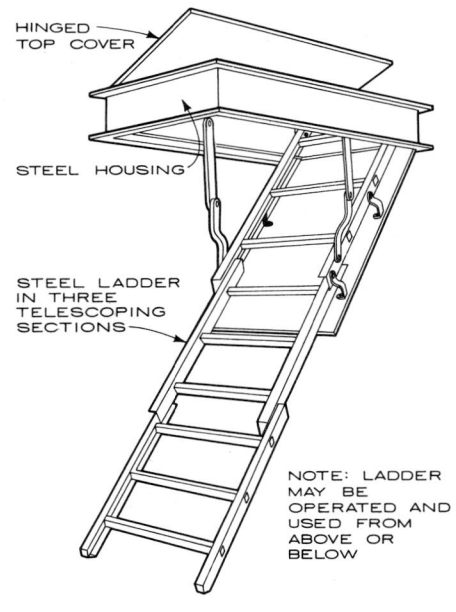

HINGED TOP COVER

STEEL HOUSING

STEEL LADDER IN THREE TELESCOPING SECTIONS

NOTE: LADDER MAY BE OPERATED AND USED FROM ABOVE OR BELOW

Several models are available using three or four telescoping sections.

Floor-to-floor heights ranging from 8 ft up to 13 ft 4 in. can be accommodated as the ladder angle varies from 53° above horizontal up to 74° above horizontal.

### TYPICAL HEIGHTS FOR ONE STANDARD MODEL
(Rough Opening = 24″ x 48″)

| FLOOR-TO-FLOOR | LAND SPACE | ABOVE HORIZONTAL |
|---|---|---|
| 8′-0″ | 72″ | 53° |
| 8′-3″ | 62″ | 61° |
| 8′-6″ | 60″ | 62° |
| 8′-9″ | 73″ | 56° |
| 9′-0″ | 71″ | 57° |
| 9′-3″ | 69″ | 58° |
| 9′-6″ | 59″ | 64° |
| 9′-10″ | 58″ | 65° |
| 10′-2″ | 44″ | 72° |

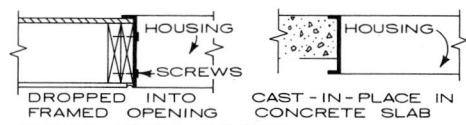

HOUSING

SCREWS

DROPPED INTO FRAMED OPENING

HOUSING

CAST-IN-PLACE IN CONCRETE SLAB

TYPICAL METAL HOUSING INSTALLATION DETAILS

## TELESCOPING ACCESS LADDER

CAUTION SHOULD BE TAKEN IN LOADING ATTIC SPACE WHERE JOIST NOT DESIGNED FOR OCCUPANCY LOADS. IT IS PREFERRED TO INSULATE ENTIRE ROOF.

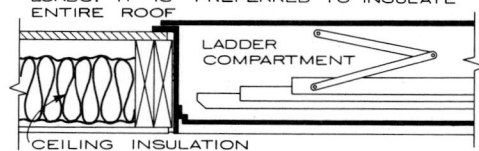

LADDER COMPARTMENT

CEILING INSULATION

**TELESCOPING METAL LADDER**

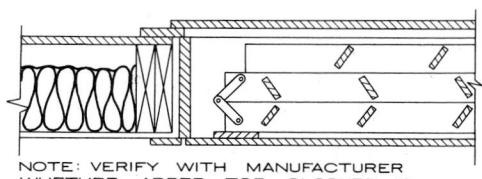

NOTE: VERIFY WITH MANUFACTURER WHETHER ADDED TOP CLOSURE IS COMPATIBLE WITH STAIR PACKAGE

**FOLDING WOODEN STAIR**

WHEN USED FOR ATTIC ACCESS, DISAPPEARING STAIRS MAY COMPROMISE A WELL-INSULATED CEILING. SELECT STAIR PACKAGE WITH TIGHT JOINTS AND DESIGN THAT ALLOWS INSULATION.

## INSULATION CONSIDERATIONS

## NOURISHMENT STATIONS

Nourishment stations are designed to serve patient care units of various sizes and to meet a variety of demands. These units are designed to supplement centralized food service systems and serve special-purpose areas. A nourishment station is typically located within a nurse's station in order to provide facilities for sanitary ice service, serving liquids, prescribed nourishments, supplementary diets, and between-meal food service. The selection of the unit size should be based on the number of patients, the demand for sanitary ice making and storage, and other services required. Units are available with standard ice systems which will serve approximately 50 patients and with extra demand ice systems to serve approximately 70 patients. The construction of these units is generally stainless steel, and they come with various options, including hot plates, microwave oven, undercounter refrigerator, instant hot water dispensing system, and waste disposer. Available options will depend on specific manufacturer.

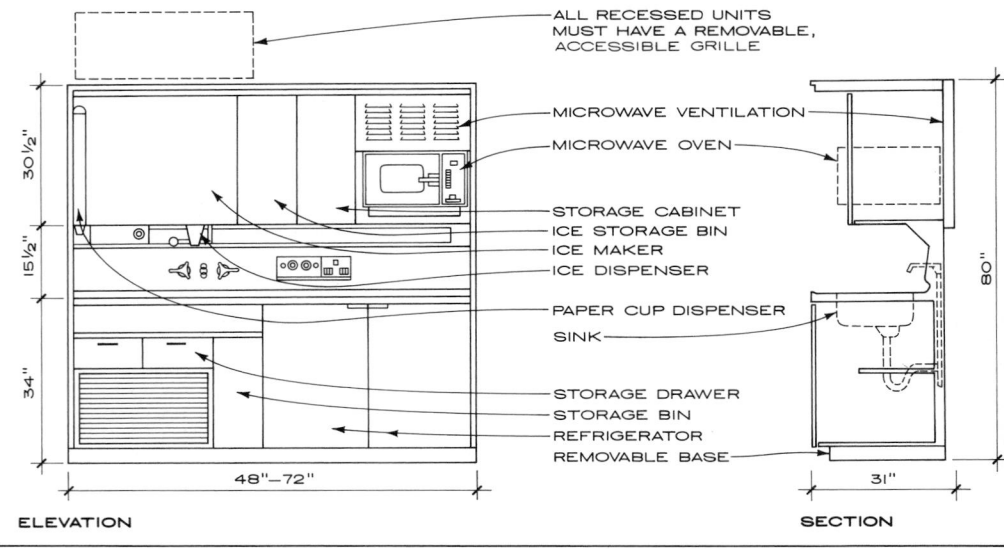

ELEVATION       SECTION

**NOURISHMENT STATION**

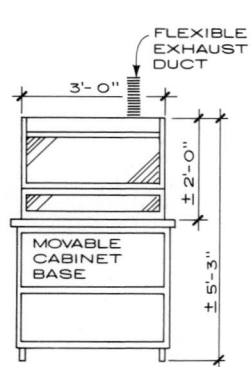

PORTABLE

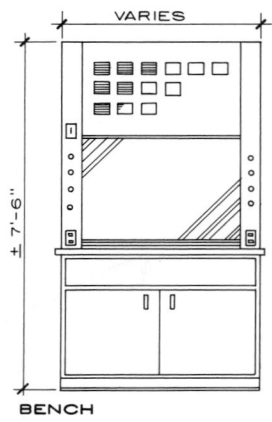

BENCH

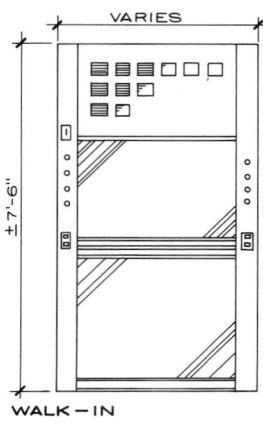

WALK—IN

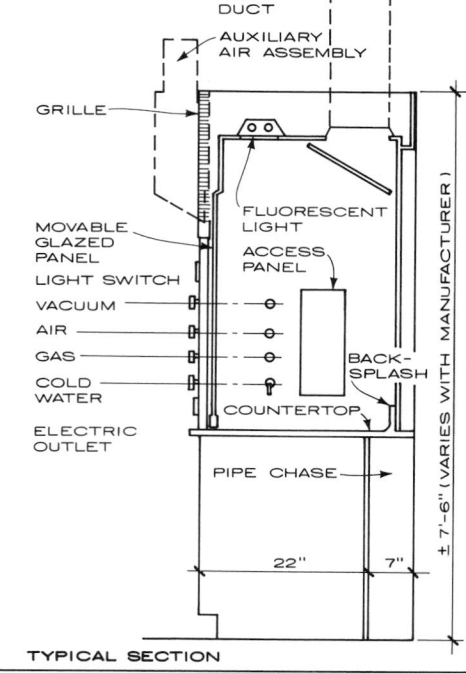

TYPICAL SECTION

## FUME HOODS

### DEFINITION

Fume hoods collect and remove contaminants from the laboratory environment by maintaining a flow of air through the hood and exhausting it to the outside.

### SELECTION

Factors to be considered:

1. Type of laboratory and materials to be handled.
2. Nature of work to be performed.
3. Frequency of usage.
4. Apparatus site.
5. Government codes and regulations.

### CLASSIFICATION

1. CLASS A: Average face velocity 125-150 fpm with minimum at any point of 100-125 fpm.
2. CLASS B: Average face velocity 100 fpm with minimum at any point of 80 fpm.
3. CLASS C: Average face velocity 75-80 fpm with minimums at any point of 50-60 fpm.

Further classification groups these classes A, B, and C within Class I. Class II contains biological safety hoods. Class III includes totally enclosed hoods (with glove holes for performing the work).

These classifications are based on American Industrial Hygiene Association, The American Conference of Governmental Industrial Hygienists, and The National Fire Protection Association (Publication 45).

**FUME HOODS**

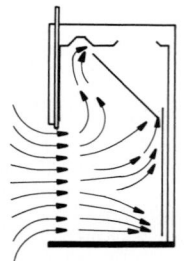
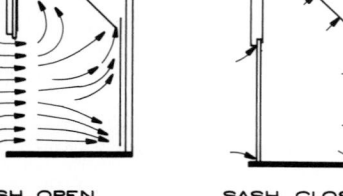

SASH OPEN STANDARD    SASH CLOSED

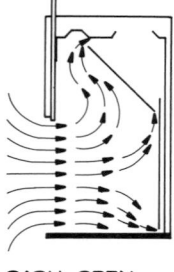

SASH OPEN BYPASS

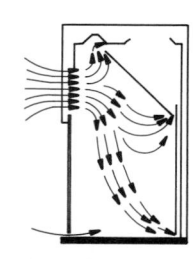

SASH CLOSED

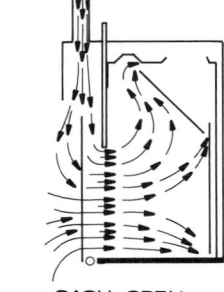

SASH OPEN AUXILIARY AIR

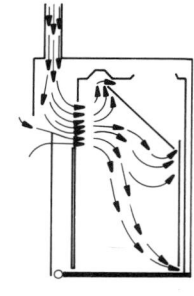

SASH CLOSED

### AIRFLOW PATTERNS

1. STANDARD TYPE: Room air is used to exhaust contaminants.
2. BYPASS TYPE: An additional hood opening is used to maintain a constant volume exhaust from the hood regardless of sash position, limiting high face velocity.
3. AUXILIARY AIR TYPE: Supplemental air is used to reduce room air consumption, either when the quantity of room air is not adequate for hood operation or as an energy saving measure to reduce the quantity of conditioned air removal from the room.

**AIRFLOW PATTERNS**

Blythe + Nazdin Architects, Ltd.; Bethesda, Maryland
Liz Karp; The Architects Collaborative, Inc.; Cambridge, Massachusetts

## 11   LABORATORY EQUIPMENT

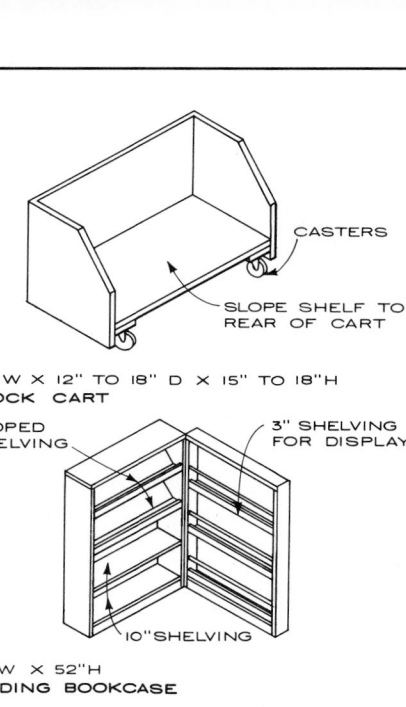

24" W × 12" TO 18" D × 15" TO 18"H
**BLOCK CART**

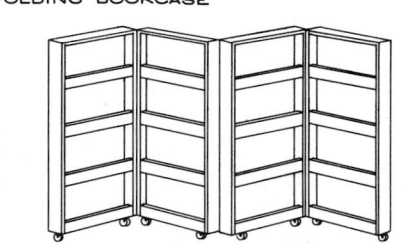

SLOPED SHELVING
3" SHELVING FOR DISPLAY
10" SHELVING

36" W × 52"H
**FOLDING BOOKCASE**

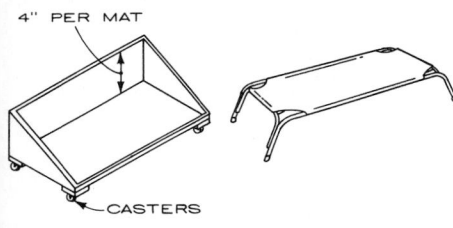

24" W × 3"D × 48"H SECTIONS
**FOLDING BOOKSCREEN**

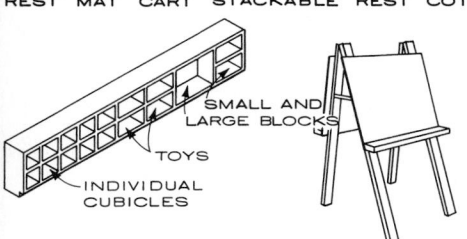

4" PER MAT
CASTERS

26" W × 14"D
**REST MAT CART**

22" TO 27"W × 54" TO 62"D × 12"H
**STACKABLE REST COT**

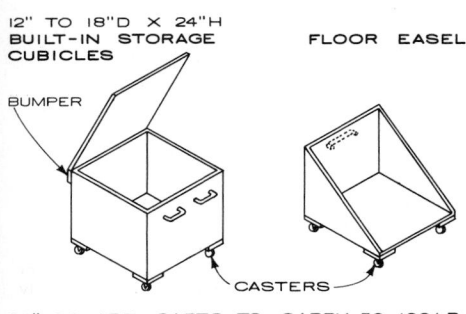

SMALL AND LARGE BLOCKS
TOYS
INDIVIDUAL CUBICLES

12" TO 18"D × 24"H
**BUILT-IN STORAGE CUBICLES**

**FLOOR EASEL**

BUMPER
CASTERS

24" SQUARE CARTS TO CARRY 50-100 LB
**CLAY CART**

**UNDERCOUNTER CLAY CART**

Kent Wong; Hewlett, Jamison, Atkinson & Luey; Portland, Oregon

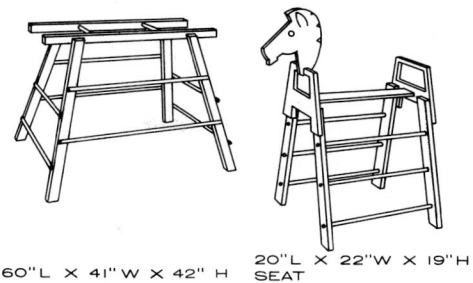

60"L × 41"W × 42" H
**EXERCISE LADDER**

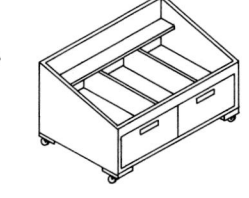

20"L × 22"W × 19"H SEAT
**PLAY HORSE**

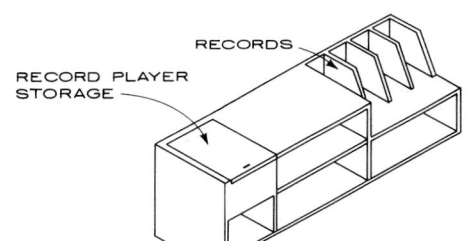

44"L × 20"W × 26"H
**WORKBENCH**

30"W × 24"D × 18" × 24"H
**CARPENTRY TOOL CART**

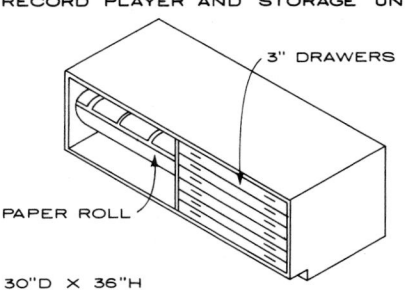

LARGE INSTRUMENT STORAGE
RECORD STORAGE
CASSETTE AND CASSETTE PLAYER STORAGE
RUBBER TIRES
SMALL INSTRUMENT STORAGE

54"W × 18"D × 28"H
**MUSIC CART**

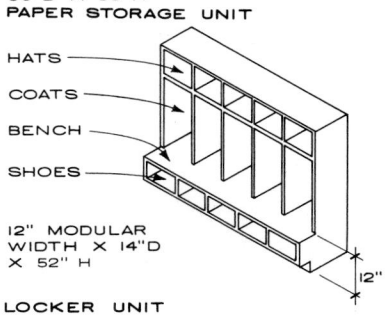

RECORDS
RECORD PLAYER STORAGE

20"D × 24"H
**RECORD PLAYER AND STORAGE UNIT**

3" DRAWERS
PAPER ROLL

30"D × 36"H
**PAPER STORAGE UNIT**

HATS
COATS
BENCH
SHOES

12" MODULAR WIDTH × 14"D × 52" H

12"

**LOCKER UNIT**

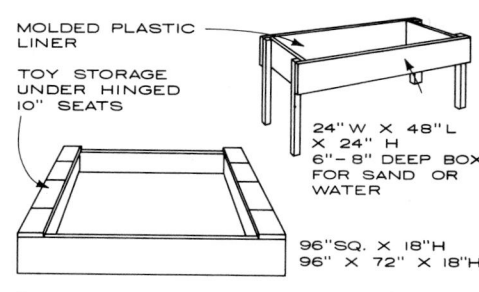

MOLDED PLASTIC LINER
TOY STORAGE UNDER HINGED 10" SEATS
24"W × 48"L × 24" H
6"-8" DEEP BOX FOR SAND OR WATER
96"SQ. × 18"H
96" × 72" × 18"H

**SANDBOXES**

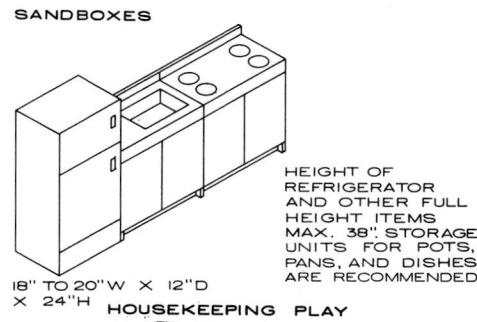

HEIGHT OF REFRIGERATOR AND OTHER FULL HEIGHT ITEMS MAX. 38". STORAGE UNITS FOR POTS, PANS, AND DISHES ARE RECOMMENDED

18" TO 20"W × 12"D × 24"H
**HOUSEKEEPING PLAY**

62"L × 24"W × 36"H
**INDOOR SLIDE**

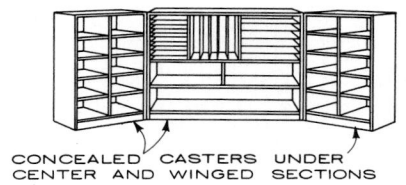

SHELVES MOVABLE IN 2" INTERVALS
CONCEALED CASTERS UNDER CENTER AND WINGED SECTIONS

46"W (CLOSED) × 14"D × 34"H
**FOLDING STORAGE UNIT**

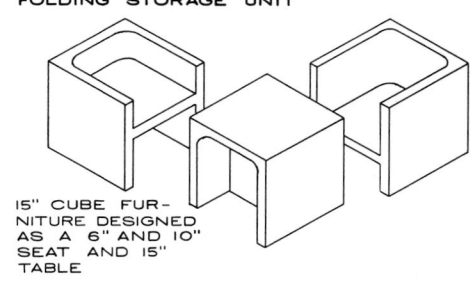

15" CUBE FURNITURE DESIGNED AS A 6" AND 10" SEAT AND 15" TABLE

**PRESCHOOL AND KINDERGARTEN SEATING**

## GENERAL CHAIR AND TABLE REQUIREMENTS

| AGE OF CHILD | CHAIR SEAT HEIGHT | | | | TABLE HEIGHT |
|---|---|---|---|---|---|
| | 8" | 10" | 12" | 14" | |
| 2 years | 80% | 20% | | | — |
| 3 years | 40% | 50% | 10% | | 18" |
| 4 years | | 25% | 75% | | 20" |
| 5 years | | | 75% | 25% | 22" |

## RIGGING SYSTEMS

Manual systems:
1. Hemp (rope and sandbags)
2. Single purchase counterweight
3. Double purchase counterweight
4. Hand-operated winch

Powered winch systems (multiple line drum):
1. Constant speed (AC) electric motor
2. Variable speed—frequency (AC servo) controlled
3. Variable speed (DC) motor
4. Hydraulic motor (variable speed)

Line shaft rigging (series of inline drums):
    Hydraulic and electric motors

Hydraulic cylinder (with compounded lines)

Suspended pipe battens for each line set spaced at 6 or 8 in. on center or more. Length should be sufficient to support masking devices beyond the stage opening.

Lifting lines are commonly 10–12 ft apart using 1½ in. pipe with outside diameter of 1⅞ in. Greater spacing is possible using trussed battens.

Live load design for gridiron floor, exclusive of line sets, is from 50 to 100 lb/sq ft. Refer to local code.

Live load design for loading galleries to support stored counterweight not placed on arbors.

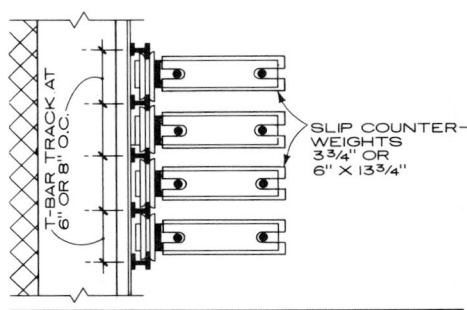

**SECTION A: COUNTERWEIGHTS**

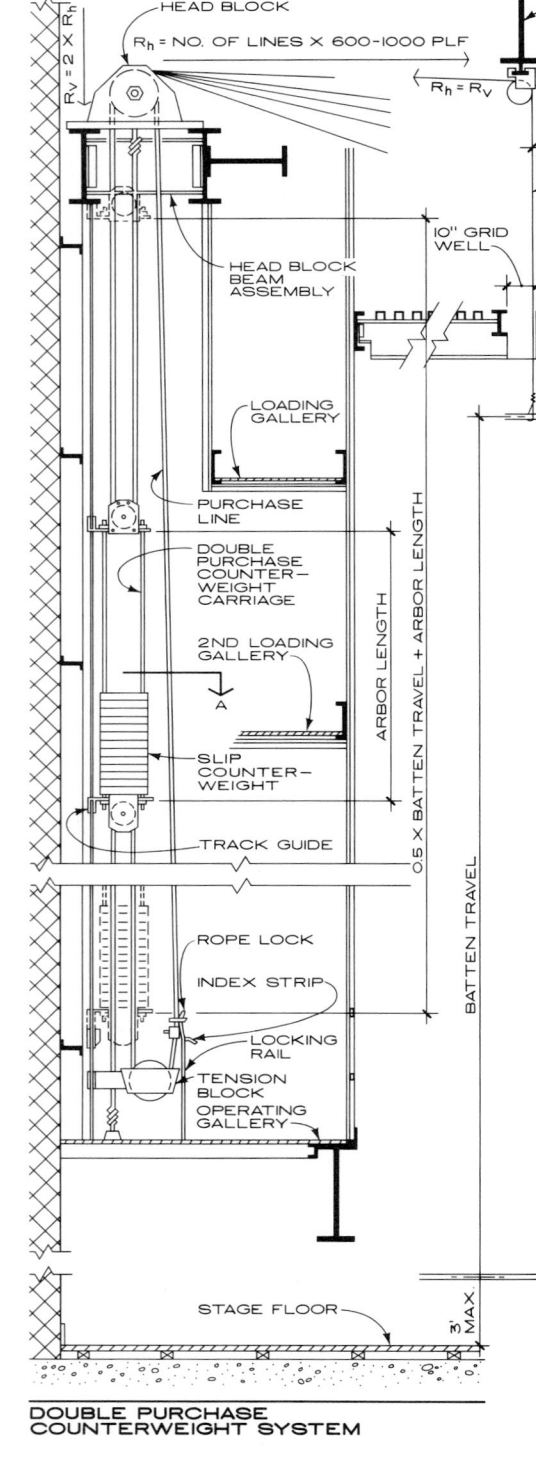

**SINGLE PURCHASE COUNTERWEIGHT SYSTEM**

Travel of arbor carriage is same as batten travel or the full height of the stage wall. Counterweights loaded on arbor carriage should equal weight of scenery and batten.

**DOUBLE PURCHASE COUNTERWEIGHT SYSTEM**

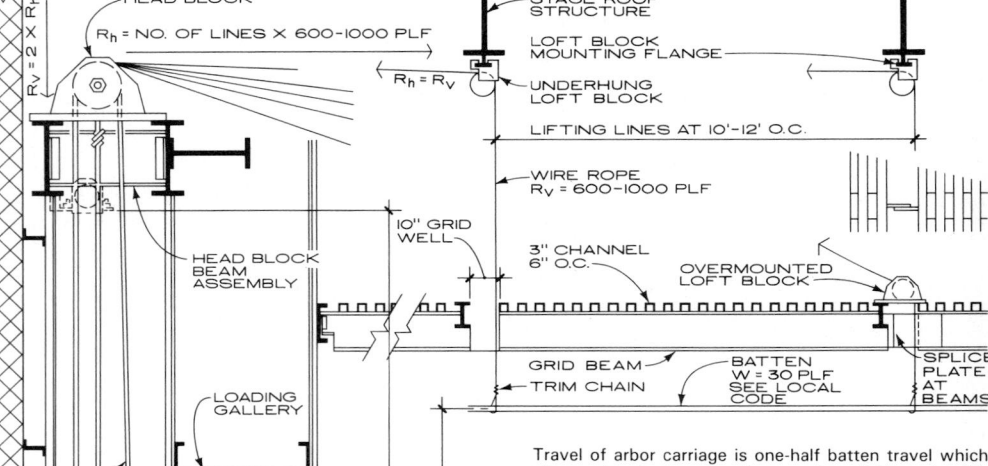

Travel of arbor carriage is one-half batten travel which allows clearance under the counterweight and guide track assembly for stage wing space. Mechanical disadvantage of two requires twice the weight of the scenery and batten to be loaded on the arbor as counterweight for balance.

## STAGE LOFT SPACE ARRANGEMENTS

Permanent or fixed performing area enclosure (lecture hall, recital hall, concert hall):
1. No storage height above permanent ceiling.
2. Spotline rigging through small openings or hinged panels in permanent ceiling sometimes included.

Low loft rigging space—underhung loft blocks from roof or rigging steel:
1. 6 ft 0 in. to 15 ft 0 in. height above stage opening.
2. No vertical storage volume for scenery, etc.
3. Rigging system provides method for hanging, changing and adjusting scenery, and masking curtains and lighting equipment.

Fly loft without grid—underhung loft blocks from roof or rigging steel:
1. Height and volume above a playing stage environment for storing scenery.
2. Rigging of isolated spotlines difficult.
3. Repositioning of loft blocks difficult.
4. Inspection and service of rigging difficult.

Fly loft with grid—overmounted loft blocks at grid wells:
1. Height and volume for storing scenery above the seen stage environment.
2. Spotline rigging from grid convenient.
3. Repositioning of loft blocks convenient.
4. Inspection and service of rigging convenient.
5. Structural resolution of rigging forces at grid wells may result in increased grid weight.
6. Difficult to walk on gridiron through rigging lines.

Fly loft with grid—underhung loft blocks from loft block beams or stage roof beams:
1. Height and volume for storing scenery above the seen stage environment.
2. Spotline rigging from grid convenient.
3. Repositioning of loft blocks convenient.
4. Inspection and service of rigging convenient.
5. Structural resolution of rigging forces at roof structure may result in less grid weight.
6. Convenient to walk on gridiron through rigging lines.

Peter H. Frink, AIA; Assembly Places International; Philadelphia, Pennsylvania

# CHAPTER 12

# *Furnishings*

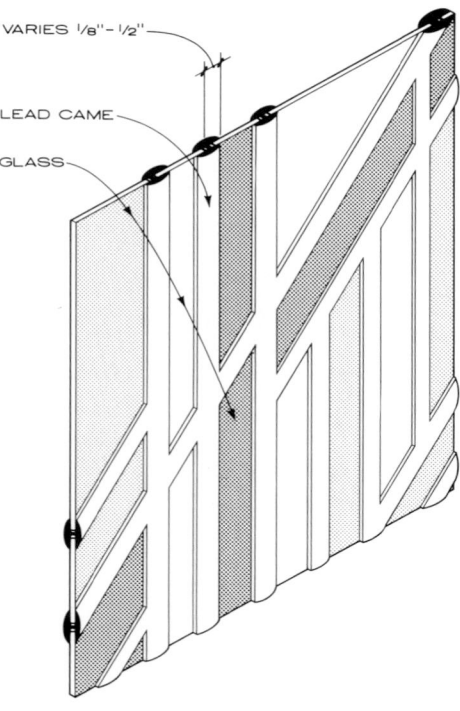

LEADED STAINED GLASS

VARIES 1/8"–1/2"
LEAD CAME
GLASS

## LEADED STAINED GLASS

Leaded stained glass is characterized by pieces of glass joined together with lead cames (H-shaped strips) of various widths. Varying the widths of the cames adds to the window's decorative effect. Lead joints are soldered on both sides of the panel. To prevent leakage a mastic waterproofing material is inserted between the glass and came lead flange.

Bracing bars are fastened to the sash at frequent intervals to strengthen and support the leaded glass. Round bars tied to the leaded glass with twisted copper wires are the most flexible and resilient, allowing for great amounts of thermal movement. Where this system is not suitable, galvanized steel flat bars can be soldered to the surface of the leaded glass.

When the glass requires detail painting, shading, or texturing, it must be done with special mineral pigments and fired at temperatures of 1000°–1200° or higher to assure absolute permanency.

INSTALLATION: It is recommended that leaded glass be installed into specially designed metal frames provided with glazing beads and sealed with a modern flexible glazing material. However, with proper maintenance, high-quality wood frames with suitable division bars are acceptable.

A stained glass studio should be consulted for the location of division bars, mullions, and muntins to best complement the artistic design. Leaded glass weighs approximately 4 lb/sq ft.

OUTSIDE PROTECTION GLASS: Properly made leaded glass does not necessarily need additional glazing to make it waterproof, but it is valuable for insulating purposes and to afford some protection from external damage. Frames should be designed with a 3/4 in. ventilated space between glass and should be arranged for the protection glass to be installed from the exterior and the leaded glass from the interior. Clear glass or textured glass 3/16–1/4 in. thick is most successful.

Depending on geographic location and economics, insulating glass should be considered as the protective outside glazing.

Plexiglas (acrylic) and Lexan (polycarbonate) are two types of plastic protection material that can be employed when protection from vandalism is needed. Outside protection glass should be installed by the stained glass studio whenever possible to ensure an integrated system.

GLAZING SEALANTS: Exterior leaded glass must be pressed into a deep back bed of mastic compound or glazing tape. When outside protection glass is used a watertight seal is not required, and foam tape compressed between the glazing bead and glass may suffice.

SIZE LIMITATIONS: Leaded glass panels should not exceed 12 sq ft, making it necessary to divide larger openings with metal division bars: tee bars for single glazed windows, and special channel bars for windows with outside protection glass.

## FACETED STAINED GLASS

A 20th-century development in the art of stained glass introduced the use of glass dalles 8 x 12 x 1 in., cast in hundreds of different colors that can be cut to any shape and used, in combination with opaque matrix of epoxy resin or reinforced concrete 5/8–1 in. in thickness, to create translucent windows and walls of great beauty.

SIZE LIMITATIONS: No single panel of faceted glass should exceed 16 sq ft. The length to width ratio of each panel should not exceed 4:1. Large openings must have horizontal supports to support the weight of stacked panels. When panels are to be stacked vertically, a minimum matrix thickness of 3/4 in. is recommended. Joints between panels should be sealed with a flexible caulking, as described below.

INSTALLATION: Faceted glass can be installed in frames of masonry, metal, or wood. Frames must be detailed to support the weight of the glass and matrix (approximately 10–13 lb/sq ft) and the thicker edge of epoxy panels. A stained glass studio should be consulted for the location of division bars and mullions to coordinate with the design.

OUTSIDE PROTECTION GLASS: Because of its high resistance to breakage, waterproof construction, and excellent insulating qualities, faceted glass does not usually

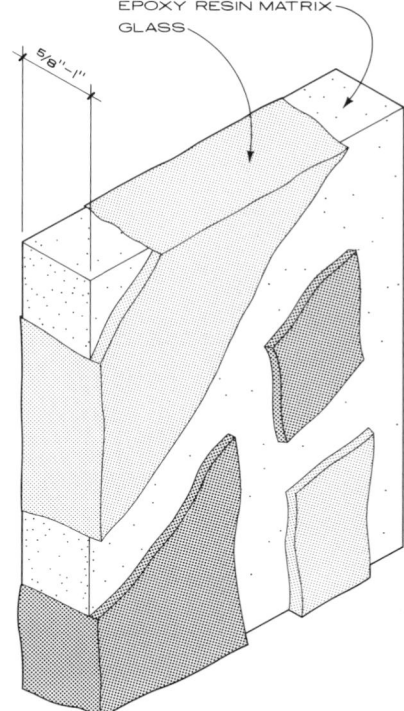

EPOXY RESIN MATRIX
GLASS
5/8"–1"

FACETED STAINED GLASS

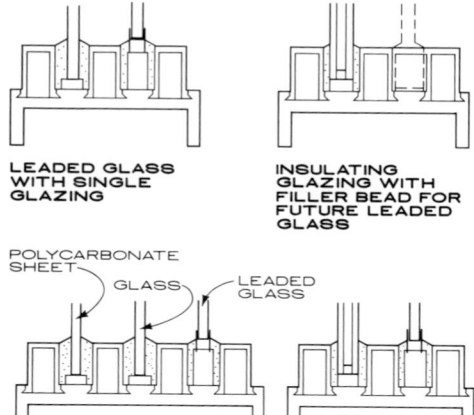

LEADED GLASS WITH SINGLE GLAZING

INSULATING GLAZING WITH FILLER BEAD FOR FUTURE LEADED GLASS

POLYCARBONATE SHEET
GLASS
LEADED GLASS

LEADED GLASS WITH DOUBLE PROTECTIVE GLAZING

LEADED GLASS WITH INSULATING GLAZING

ALUMINUM FRAMES FOR LEADED GLASS

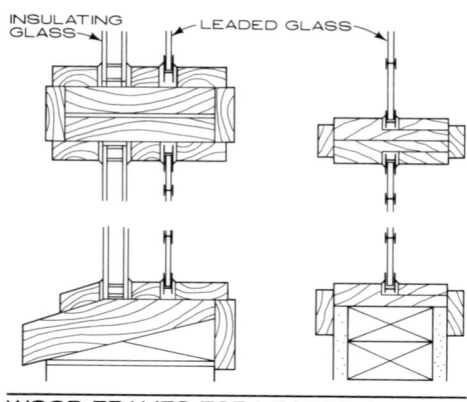

INSULATING GLASS
LEADED GLASS

WOOD FRAMES FOR LEADED GLASS

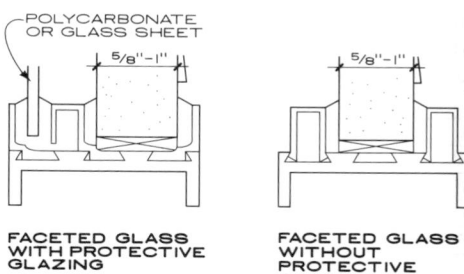

POLYCARBONATE OR GLASS SHEET
5/8"–1"
5/8"–1"

FACETED GLASS WITH PROTECTIVE GLAZING

FACETED GLASS WITHOUT PROTECTIVE GLAZING

ALUMINUM FRAMES FOR FACETED GLASS

need outer glazing. If protection glass is required, 3/4–1 in. ventilated space between the outer surface of the faceted glass and inside surface of the protection glass is recommended. Divisions in the protection glass should be designed by the artist to complement the design.

GLAZING SEALANTS: Faceted glass panels should be set into a nonhardening caulking such as butyl, acrylic, silicone, or polysulfide, used both as bedding and finish bead. For spaces in excess of 1/4 in. between faceted glass and frame, fillers such as ethafoam are recommended under the caulking bead. A clearance of 3/16 in. should be allowed between frame and panel edge for proper expansion and contraction. Neoprene spacers are used to ensure proper clearance.

Further information is available from the Stained Glass Association of America.

Randall S. Lindstrom, AIA; Ware Associates, Inc.; Rockford, Illinois

**12**    **ARTWORK**

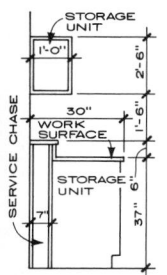

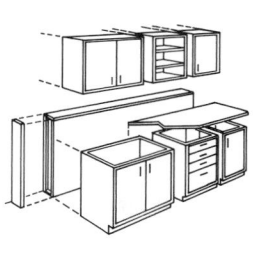

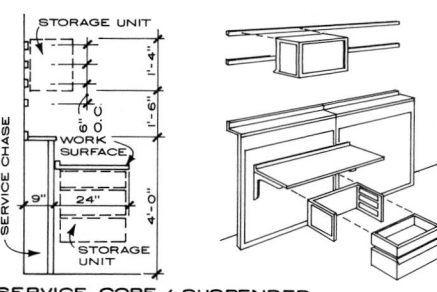

**CONVENTIONAL**

**STRUCTURAL FRAME / SUSPENDED**

**SERVICE CORE / SUSPENDED**

## CASEWORK SYSTEMS

Laboratory casework systems are an assembly of base storage units, work surfaces, and upper storage units. Regardless of the application, mechanical service spaces and waste systems are integral components. Typical systems, in order of increasing flexibility, are the following:

1. THE CONVENTIONAL FIXED SYSTEM: Consists of base cabinet units supporting a work surface and wall mounted upper cabinet units. The cabinets are available in a range of sizes and types. A plumb-

ing chase can be provided as shown or can be within the existing wall cavity. This system is applicable to a high storage situation.

2. THE STRUCTURAL FRAME/SUSPENDED CASE-WORK SYSTEM: Consists of a basic frame designed to support work surfaces, plumbing fixtures, base, and upper storage units. The storage units can be repositioned or removed independently of the countertops. Plumbing space is provided within the basic frame. This system is applicable where work surface space is needed but storage requirements are minimal.

3. THE SERVICE CORE/SUSPENDED CASEWORK SYSTEM: Consists of a basic service core and wall rails designed to support storage components and work surfaces. There is a wide range of sizes and types of storage components available and both the mounting heights and types are readily change-able. In addition, transport components are an interchangeable part of the system. Gas and plumb-ing lines are located within the service core, access-ible through removable panels.

All three types of systems are applicable to wall, peninsula, and island arrangements.

**CASEWORK SYSTEMS**

## CASEWORK UNITS (IN.)

### WALL CABINETS

| | | W | D |
|---|---|---|---|
| A | Single glass hinged door | 12-24 | 13, 18 |
| B | Single metal hinged door | 12-24 | 13, 18 |
| C | Double glass hinged door | 27-48 | 13, 18 |
| D | Sliding glass doors | 27-48 | 13, 18 |
| E | Sliding metal doors | 27-48 | 13, 18 |
| F | Metal hinged doors | 27-48 | 13, 18 |
| G | Open shelves | 15-60 | 13, 18 |

### BASE CABINETS

| | | W | D |
|---|---|---|---|
| H | Single door unit | 12-24 | 18, 22, 25 |
| J | Double door unit | 27-48 | 18, 22, 25 |
| K | Double door sink unit | 27-48 | 18, 22, 25 |
| L | Double door acid storage | 27-48 | 22, 25 |
| M | Drawer unit | 15-48 | 18, 22, 25 |
| N | File unit | 15-48 | 18, 22, 25 |
| O | Pullout single unit | 36-48 | 22, 25 |
| P | Corner storage unit | varies | |

### TALL CABINETS

| | | W | D |
|---|---|---|---|
| Q | Single glass hinged door | 15-24 | 12-22 |
| R | Single metal hinged door | 15-24 | 12-22 |
| S | Double metal hinged door | 30-48 | 12-22 |
| T | Double glass hinged door | 30-48 | 12-22 |
| U | Sliding glass doors | 30-48 | 16-22 |
| V | Open shelves | 24-48 | 12-22 |

Tall cabinets standard height = 84"

NOTE: Consult manufacturer for exact dimensions.

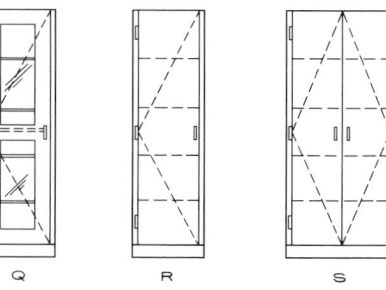

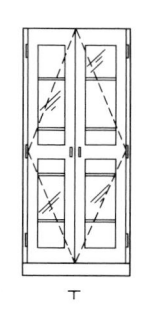

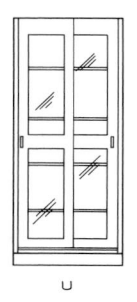

**CONVENTIONAL STEEL CASEWORK**

### LABORATORY TABLE MODULES

Units are available freestanding as island service units or attached to a wall as wall service units. Both systems provide a service chase that runs in the back for the wall service unit and in the center for the island service unit. These modules provide sinks and service fixtures mounted to the counter. The counter tops are fabricated in a variety of stain and acid resistant materials. The storage cabinets below are available in a range of drawer and door arrangements for storage of instruments and equipment, plus sit-down work space when required.

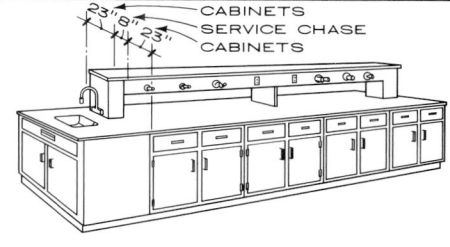

**ISLAND SERVICE UNIT**

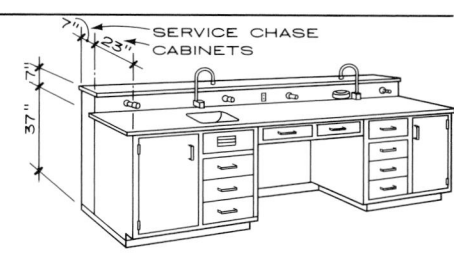

**WALL SERVICE UNIT**

**LABORATORY TABLE MODULES**

Blythe + Nazdin Architects, Ltd.; Bethesda, Maryland
Liz Karp; The Architects Collaborative, Inc.; Cambridge, Massachusetts

**MANUFACTURED CASEWORK**   12

## OVERFILE STORAGE

| TYPE | W | H | D | WEIGHT* |
|---|---|---|---|---|
| Over 2-drawer letter | 30 | 26 or 37 | 29 | 170 |
| Over 2-drawer legal | 36 | | 29 | 308 |
| Over 3-drawer letter | 43 | | 29 | 377 |
| Over 3-drawer legal | 54 | | 29 | 445 |

## VERTICAL FILES

| TYPE | W | H | D | WEIGHT* |
|---|---|---|---|---|
| 5-drawer letter | 15 | 60 | 29 | 405 |
| 5-drawer legal | 18 | 60 | 29 | 430 |
| 4-drawer letter | 15 | 50 | 29 | 324 |
| 4-drawer legal | 18 | 50 | 29 | 344 |
| 3-drawer letter | 15 | 41 | 29 | 258 |
| 3-drawer legal | 18 | 41 | 29 | 162 |
| 2-drawer letter | 15 | 30 | 29 | 162 |
| 2-drawer legal | 18 | 30 | 29 | 172 |

## INSIDE DRAWER DIMENSIONS

| TYPE | W | H | D |
|---|---|---|---|
| Letter | 12¼ | 10½ | 26¾ |
| Legal | 15¼ | 10½ | 26¾ |

*Weights = fully loaded file.

**VERTICAL FILE CABINETS**

## LATERAL FILES

| TYPE | W | H | D | WEIGHT* |
|---|---|---|---|---|
| 5-drawer | 30, 36, 42 | 64 | 18 | 610–843 |
| 4-drawer | 30–36–42 | 52 | 18 | 524–720 |
| 3-drawer | 30, 36, 42 | 40 | 18 | 401–553 |
| 2-drawer | 30, 36, 42 | 32 | 18 | 285–391 |

*Weights = fully loaded file.

**LATERAL FILE CABINETS**

## SPECIAL FILES

| TYPE | W | H | D |
|---|---|---|---|
| A. Custom stack system | 36 | 52 | 18 |
| B. Check file | 15 | 52 | 27 |
| C. Special/double check | 22 | 52 | 27 |
| D. Card record file | 22 | 52 | 27 |
|   6 drawer (3 × 5, 4 × 6 cards) | 22 | 52 | 27 |
|   5 drawer (3 × 5, 4 × 6, 5 × 8) | 22 | 52 | 27 |
| E. Pedestal file | 15 | 28 | 24 |
|   Library card file (see index) | | | |

**SPECIAL FILING CABINETS**

## FIRE INSULATED FILES

| TYPE | W | H | D | WEIGHT* |
|---|---|---|---|---|
| 4-drawer letter | 17 | 52 | 30 | 600 |
| 4-drawer legal | 20 | 52 | 30 | 660 |
| 3-drawer letter | 17 | 51 | 30 | 465 |
| 3-drawer legal | 20 | 41 | 30 | 515 |
| 2-drawer letter | 17 | 28 | 30 | 330 |
| 2-drawer legal | 20 | 28 | 30 | 370 |
| 3-drawer lateral | 39 | 56 | 24 | 1220 |
| 2-drawer lateral | 39 | 39 | 24 | 875 |

*Weight = fully loaded.

**FIRE INSULATED FILE CABINETS**

Associated Space Design, Inc.; Atlanta, Georgia

## PLANNING

1. Users' filing needs should be tabulated in inches and in turn converted into number of cabinets. Consult manufacturer for inches available in specific cabinets.
2. For open space planning, the following square footage allowances should be used:

| TYPES | SPACE ALLOWANCE (FT²) |
|---|---|
| Vertical and 36 in. lateral files | 10 |
| Lateral file for computer printout | 15 |

NOTE: All dimensions shown are approximate. Consult manufacturer for actual dimensions.

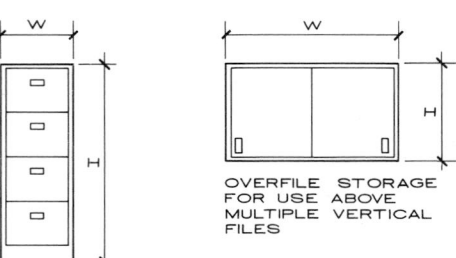

OVERFILE STORAGE FOR USE ABOVE MULTIPLE VERTICAL FILES

STANDARD

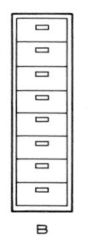
COMPUTER PRINTOUT

VERTICAL LETTER

VERTICAL LEGAL

LATERAL

## FILE CLEARANCES

| | VERTICAL FILES | LATERAL FILES |
|---|---|---|
| A | 106–120 | 82–94 |
| B | 29 | 18 |
| C | 48–62 | 46–58 |
| D | 18–26 | 16–22 |
| E | 30–36 | 30–36 |

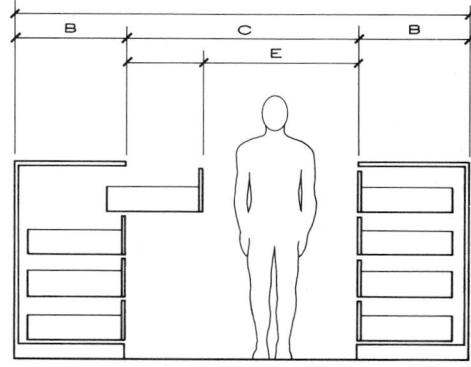

**DIMENSIONS FOR PLANNING**

### NOTES

1. Basic types accommodate multiple configurations of drawers, doors, and shelves.
2. 6 in. drawer accommodates cards and vouchers not exceeding 5 in. in one direction.
3. 12 in. drawer accommodates letter and legal files.
4. 15 in. drawer accommodates computer printouts.
5. Files are available to five-drawer height. Files more than five drawers high are not recommended.
6. Typical overfile storage is 26 or 37 in. high.

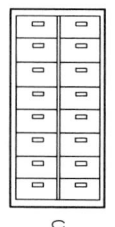 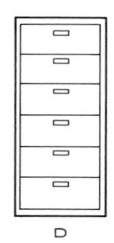 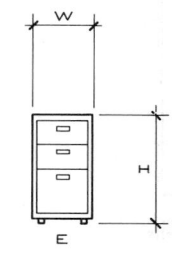

A      B      C      D      E

These units are designed to resist forced entry and are fabricated from heavy gauge steel plate. They are available only in legal size vertical format and are essentially the same size as fire insulated cabinets. They are available with or without fire protection.

## SECURITY FILES

| TYPE | WEIGHT* |
|---|---|
| 5-drawer | 1350 |
| 5-drawer fire insulated | 1650 |
| 4-drawer | 1050 |
| 4-drawer fire insulated | 1400 |
| 2-drawer | 650 |
| 2-drawer fire insulated | 825 |

*Weight = fully loaded

**SECURITY FILE CABINETS**

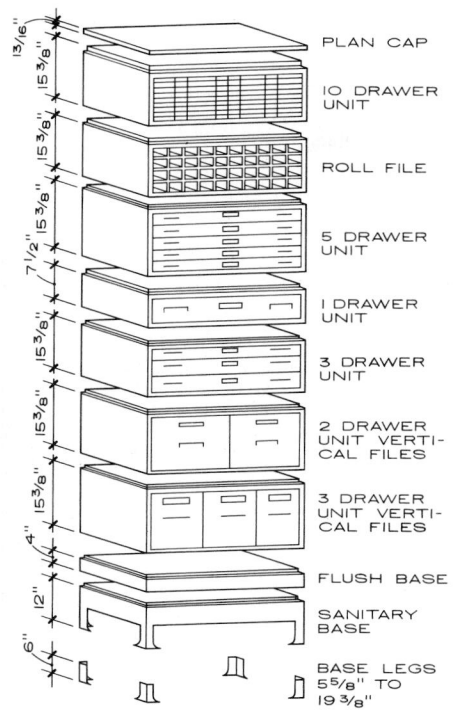

STEEL SHOWN, WOOD SIMILAR; DEPTH 28½" – 50½"; WIDTH 40¾" – 79⁵⁄₁₆"; DRAWER EXTENDS 26" – 42"

**PLAN FILE SYSTEM**

## BIFILE SYSTEM

Units at rear are fixed, while units at front slide from side to side on floor-mounted tracks. Files may be operated either manually or electrically. Sizes of individual units vary by manufacturer.

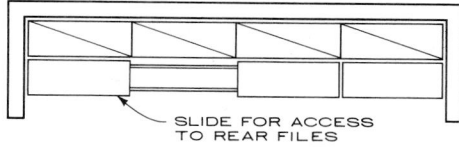

**BIFILE PLAN**

### BIFILE
(2 UNITS DEEP, 12' WIDE, FULLY LOADED)

| TYPE | WEIGHT (LB) |
|---|---|
| 9 Tier, legal | 6200 |
| 9 Tier, letter | 4850 |
| 8 Tier, legal | 5550 |
| 8 Tier, letter | 4350 |
| 7 Tier, legal | 4900 |
| 7 Tier, letter | 3850 |

**CONDENSED FILE SYSTEMS**

## ROTATING FILE SYSTEM

Typically, units at ends of room are single loaded and fixed. Middle units are double loaded and move from side to side on floor-mounted tracks. Files may be operated either manually, mechanically, or electrically. This system permits one aisle to serve many banks of files, resulting in significant square footage savings. This filing system produces concentrated loads and requires close consultation between structural engineer, designer, and manufacturer.

In areas where the designer must consider seismic shock, check with manufacturer for equipping the file units with special seismic anchors.

## NOTE

These units rotate on a ball bearing raceway located in the base. Pushing a foot pedal releases the carriage, which rotates 90° to the next locking position, allowing for access to both banks of files or closure of unit. The system is available in 3- to 8-tier arrangements.

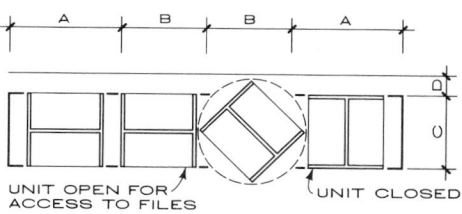

**ROTATING FILE PLAN**

### ROTATING FILES (SINGLE UNIT, FULLY LOADED)

| TYPE | WEIGHT (LB) |
|---|---|
| 8 Tier, legal | 1450 |
| 8 Tier, letter | 900 |
| 7 Tier, legal | 1275 |
| 7 Tier, letter | 825 |
| 5 Tier, legal | 950 |
| 5 Tier, letter | 625 |

### DIMENSIONS FOR PLANNING

| | LETTER (IN.) | LEGAL (IN.) |
|---|---|---|
| A. End unit | 37 | 45 |
| B. Middle unit | 31 | 38 |
| C. Depth of unit | 25 | 31 |
| D. Clearance from wall | 6 | 7 |

### PAPER WEIGHTS

| FILE TYPE | POUNDS PER LINEAL INCH |
|---|---|
| Letter | 1.5 |
| Legal | 2.0 |
| Computer printout, hanging | 1.75 |

**HIGH DENSITY FILE SYSTEM**

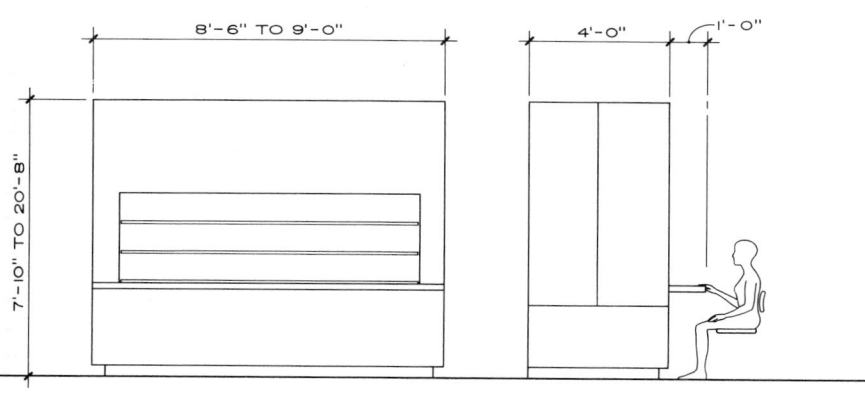

## NOTES

An automated system permits the retrieval of records within seconds. Records are stored in the unit on carriers. Each carrier is individually suspended and equally spaced on a conveyor system. The operator sits or stands at a posting board, and at the touch of a button the proper carrier moves into position so that a record may be pulled or filed.

Records that may be stored in these units include file folders, binders, reference books, ledgers, tape reels, microfilm, and cards.

**AUTOMATED FILE SYSTEM**

Blythe + Nazdin Architects, Ltd.; Bethesda, Maryland
Associated Space Design, Inc.; Atlanta, Tampa, Washington, D.C.
Steven L. Kipples

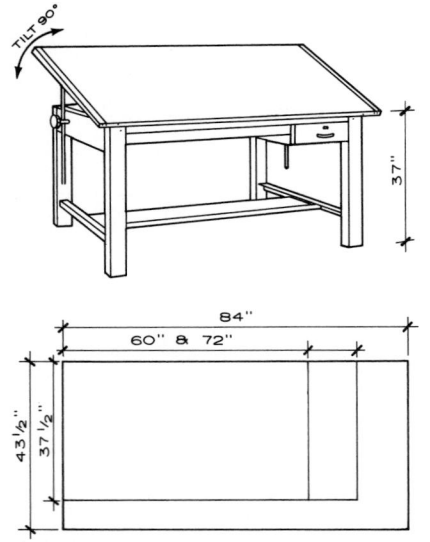

PLAN

Drafting and/or engineering table is available in wood, in steel, or in combination. Various drawer and pedestal arrangements are available.

**DRAFTING TABLE WITH ADJUSTABLE TOP**

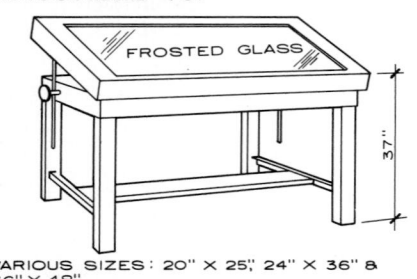

FROSTED GLASS

VARIOUS SIZES: 20" X 25", 24" X 36" & 36" X 48"

**FLUORESCENT TRACING TABLE**

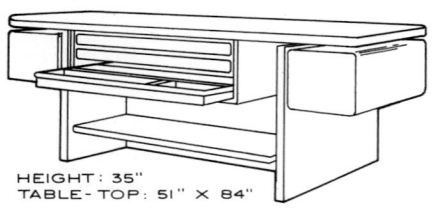

HEIGHT: 35"
TABLE-TOP: 51" X 84"

Service table provides a large worktop and integral storage compartments. Entire offices can be furnished with coordinated units.

**SERVICE TABLE**

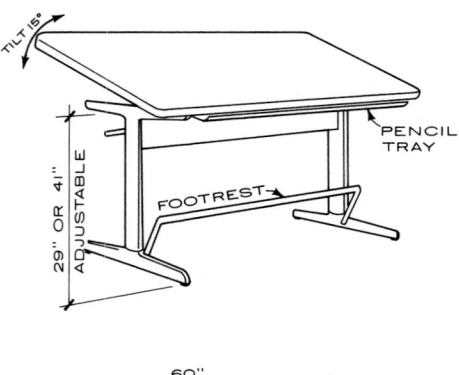

PENCIL TRAY

FOOTREST

PLAN

**ADJUSTABLE WORKING SURFACE**

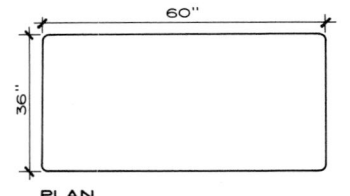

METAL STORAGE TUBE 2½" AND 4" DIAMETER 31" TO 55" LENGTHS

TRANSPARENT PLASTIC STORAGE TUBE 2" DIAMETER 13" TO 55" LENGTHS

**STORAGE TUBES**

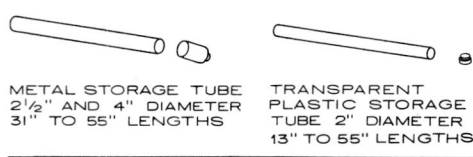

WALL MOUNTED DATA FILES 1¾" X 8" X 11½" SHEET WIDTHS: 12" TO 48"

WALL MOUNTED RACK FILES FOR FRICTION TYPE BINDERS 18" TO 54" AT 6" INTERVALS

12" OR 24"

6 AND 12 BINDERS

FILE VARIATIONS AVAILABLE ON ROLLING STANDS

**WALL RACK**

**PIVOT FILING SYSTEM**

Several manufacturers produce an array of drawing tables with adjustable tops, optional footrests, and pencil drawers.

**COUNTERBALANCED AUTOMATIC DRAFTING TABLE**

BOARD SIZES:
29.5" X 41.3" (75 X 105 CM)
31.5" X 47.3" (80 X 120 CM)
31.5" X 55" (80 X 140 CM)

ROTATES 360°

ADJUSTABLE TILT TO 90°

ADJUSTABLE HEIGHT

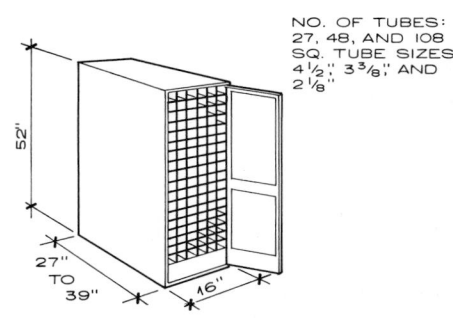

NO. OF TUBES: 27, 48, AND 108
SQ. TUBE SIZES: 4½", 3⅜", AND 2⅛"

**CABINET ROLL FILE**

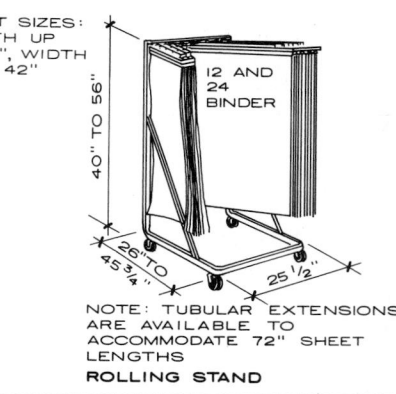

SHEET SIZES: LENGTH UP TO 52", WIDTH 18" TO 42"

12 AND 24 BINDER

NOTE: TUBULAR EXTENSIONS ARE AVAILABLE TO ACCOMMODATE 72" SHEET LENGTHS

**ROLLING STAND**

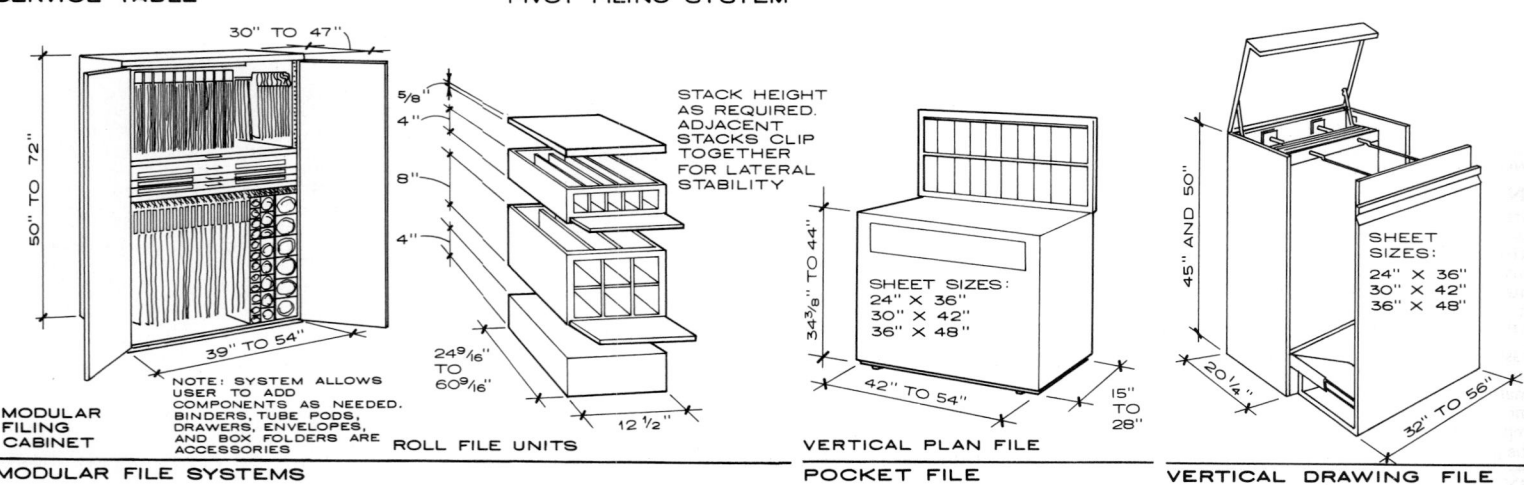

**MODULAR FILING CABINET**

NOTE: SYSTEM ALLOWS USER TO ADD COMPONENTS AS NEEDED. BINDERS, TUBE PODS, DRAWERS, ENVELOPES, AND BOX FOLDERS ARE ACCESSORIES

STACK HEIGHT AS REQUIRED. ADJACENT STACKS CLIP TOGETHER FOR LATERAL STABILITY

**ROLL FILE UNITS**

**MODULAR FILE SYSTEMS**

SHEET SIZES:
24" X 36"
30" X 42"
36" X 48"

**VERTICAL PLAN FILE**

**POCKET FILE**

SHEET SIZES:
24" X 36"
30" X 42"
36" X 48"

**VERTICAL DRAWING FILE**

## DESIGN RATIONALE

Systems furniture is designed primarily for utilization in an open office plan which uses few fixed floor-to-ceiling partitions as compared to conventional office layouts. Open office planning receives its impetus from its ability to respond to requirements for increased flexibility and lower long term expenses. Some of the major areas of response are the following:

1. FLEXIBILITY OF PLANNING: Systems furniture in an open plan maximizes the efficient use of net plannable space. This is the result of the use of more vertical space without fixed floor-to-ceiling partitions, thereby freeing floor area and reducing space planning inefficiencies.

2. FLEXIBILITY OF FUNCTION: Systems furniture allows individual workstation modification so that workstation design can reflect functional requirements of the task performed. In this way, changes in function can be accommodated without total furniture replacement.

3. FLEXIBILITY OF PLAN MODIFICATION: Systems furniture in open office planning allows institutions to respond more easily to organizational changes of size, structure, and function. Open planning allows institutions to respond to change at lower cost by reducing expenses related to partition relocation, HVAC modification, lighting relocation, construction, and moving time.

## NOTES

1. Any open office plan as commonly applied will utilize some enclosed spaces having fixed, floor-to-ceiling partitions.

2. Systems furniture requires careful planning and engineering consultation to achieve the maximum functional advantage.

3. Systems furniture components are not compatible from one manufacturer to another regardless of generic type.

4. The generic types listed below are broad classifications for descriptive purposes only.

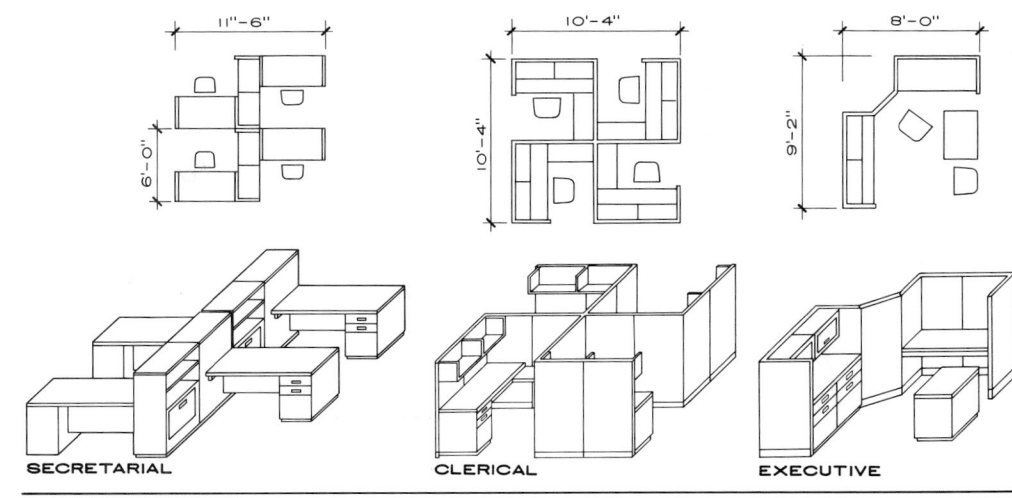

SECRETARIAL   CLERICAL   EXECUTIVE

CONFIGURATIONS

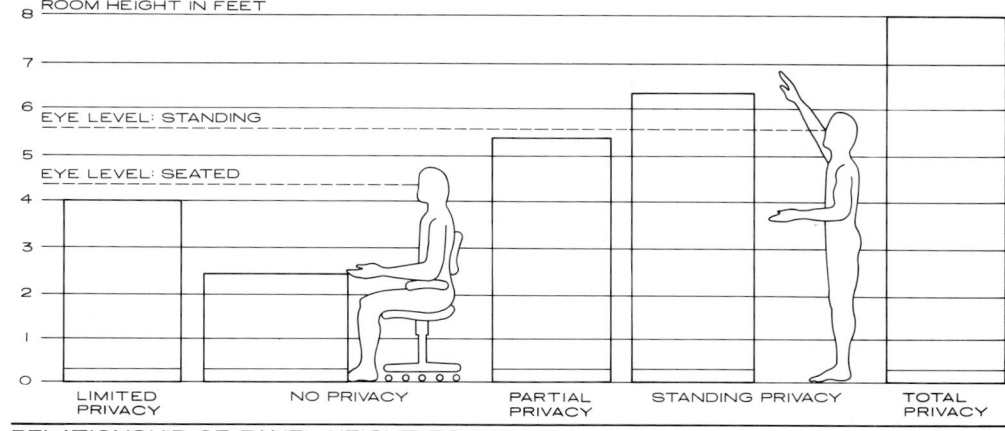

RELATIONSHIP OF PANEL HEIGHT TO PRIVACY

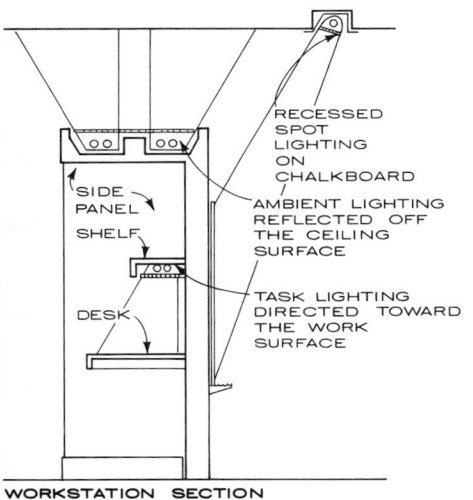

WORKSTATION SECTION

## INTEGRATED LIGHTING

Artificial lighting is integrated into most open office furniture systems. The components consist of task oriented downlights located directly over work surfaces, which provide the user with control of intensity and direction of light. Uplights are mounted in the top of workstations to provide indirect light reflected off the ceiling to the ambient surroundings.

Task/ambient lighting provides more flexibility than do standard ceiling mounted fixtures. It can reduce energy consumption by decreasing general light levels and utilizing more efficient light sources. It can also improve acoustics, since fewer fixtures are installed in the acoustical ceiling.

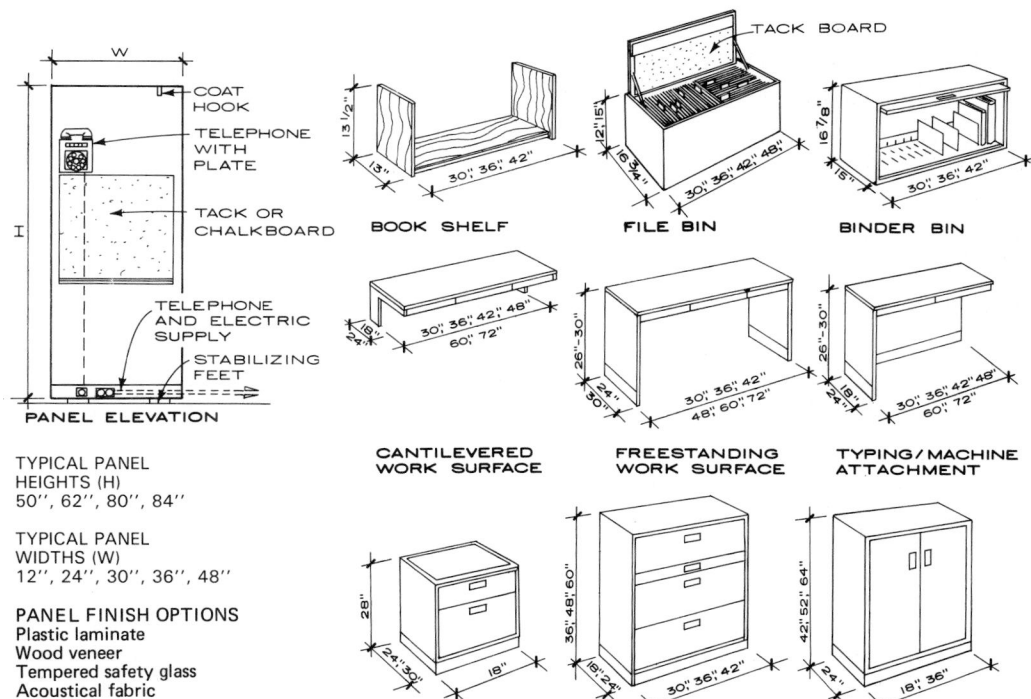

PANEL ELEVATION

TYPICAL PANEL HEIGHTS (H)
50'', 62'', 80'', 84''

TYPICAL PANEL WIDTHS (W)
12'', 24'', 30'', 36'', 48''

PANEL FINISH OPTIONS
Plastic laminate
Wood veneer
Tempered safety glass
Acoustical fabric

NOTE: Consult manufacturer for specific sizes and finishes available.

BOOK SHELF   FILE BIN   BINDER BIN

CANTILEVERED WORK SURFACE   FREESTANDING WORK SURFACE   TYPING/MACHINE ATTACHMENT

DRAWER BASE   FILE CASE   WARDROBE

## SYSTEMS FURNITURE COMPONENTS

Interspace Incorporated; Washington, D.C.

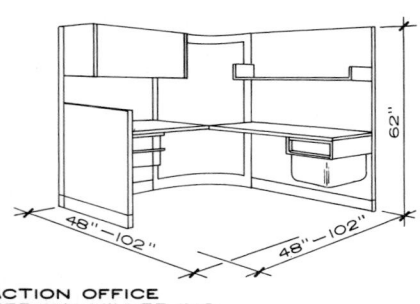

**ACTION OFFICE
HERMAN MILLER, INC.**

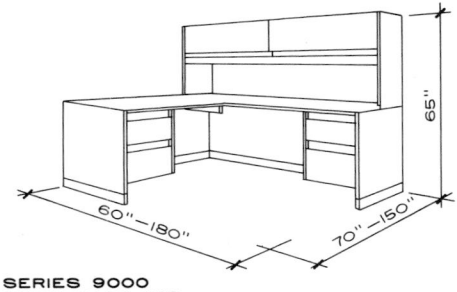

**SERIES 9000
STEELCASE, INC.**

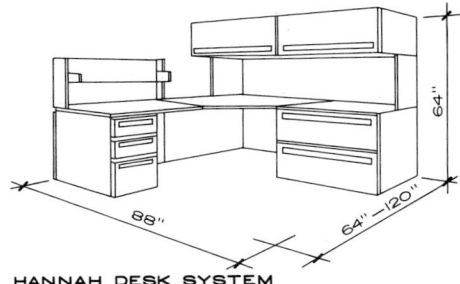

**HANNAH DESK SYSTEM
KNOLL INTERNATIONAL**

## PANEL HUNG TYPE

These systems are based on panels that can be connected at various angles (angle options depend on manufacturer). Panels achieve stability through configuration or by attached stabilizing feet. Components are hung on panels at desired heights (usually on 1 in. increments).

### SYSTEM ADVANTAGES

Panel hung systems usually have a large variety of components. They offer the highest degree of planning flexibility. These systems are easily modified and are relatively light.

### OPTIONS OFFERED (VARY WITH MANUFACTURER)

1. Ability to hang components on fixed, full height partitions.
2. Specialized use components (i.e., hospitals, schools, libraries).
3. Integrated wiring in panels with fast connect or wire manager components for horizontal raceways.
4. Integrated task/ambient lighting components.
5. Multiple standard panel heights (dimensions vary).
6. Fabric covered acoustical panels as structural panel option.
7. Integrated file storage components.

## PANEL ENCLOSURE TYPE

These systems are based on building rectilinear enclosures with panel components. Panels achieve stability through right angle panel-to-panel configuration. Components are hung in panel enclosures (usually at several predetermined mounting heights) and are supported by end panels rather than back panels.

### SYSTEM ADVANTAGES

Assembled systems have a somewhat unitized appearance. They are stable and, when assembled, are not easily moved. They have a relatively high level of flexibility with a more limited number of components and accessories than in most panel hung systems.

### OPTIONS OFFERED (VARY WITH MANUFACTURER)

1. Multiple standard panel heights.
2. Full panel high closed storage units (i.e., wardrobes, shelf).
3. Vertical power poles with lighting outlets, convenience outlets, circuit breakers, telephone raceway.
4. Wire manager components for vertical and horizontal raceways.
5. Integrated task/ambient lighting components and freestanding ambient light units.
6. Fabric covered acoustical panels are structural panel option.
7. Integrated file storage components.

## UNITIZED PANEL TYPE

These systems are based on ganging assembled units and panels to form workstations and workstation groupings. Units are individually stable and panels achieve stability by attachment to units and right angle panel-to-panel configuration. Some of these systems are more componentized than others (similar to panel enclosure type) but are marketed as assembled units. Components within assembled units are usually supported by end panels.

### SYSTEM ADVANTAGES

Assembled systems have a unitized appearance more closely resembling conventional furniture. They are very stable and, when assembled, are not easily moved. They have a relatively high level of flexibility depending on the degree to which they are unitized. These systems simplify purchase, inventory management, and installation because of their unitized character.

### OPTIONS OFFERED (VARY WITH MANUFACTURER)

1. Multiple standard panel heights (dimensions vary).
2. Full panel high closed storage units (i.e., wardrobes, shelf).
3. Wire raceways (horizontal and vertical), convenience outlets, and switches are an integral part of system.
4. Integrated task/ambient light units.
5. Fabric covered acoustical panels usually as hang on or finish panel option.
6. Integrated flexible branch wiring system.
7. Can be used in conventional configurations.

**GENERIC  TYPES  OF  SYSTEM  FURNITURE**

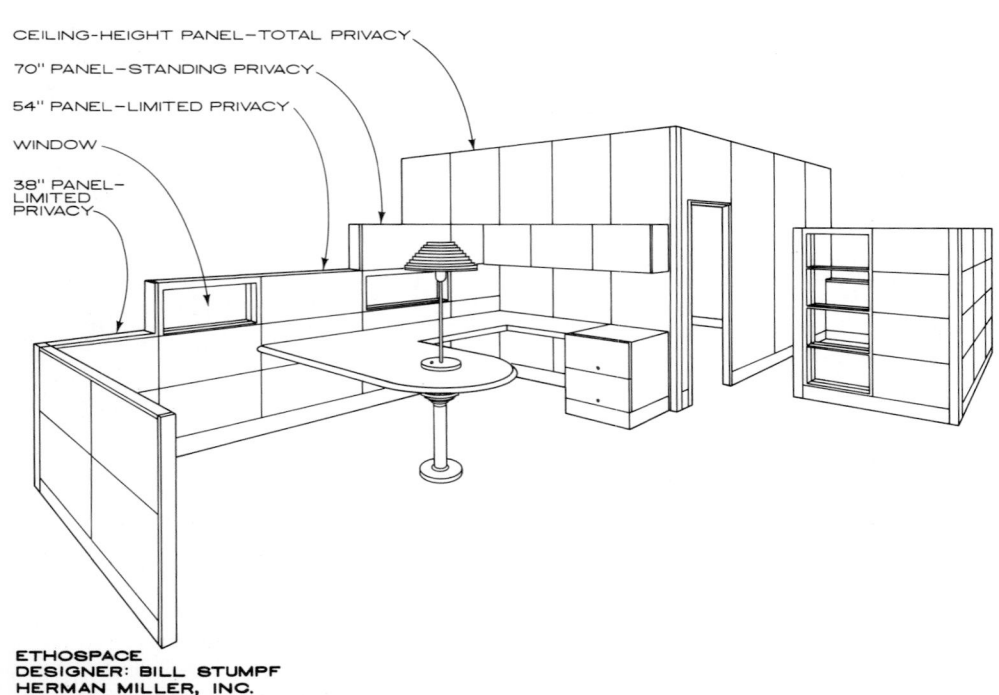

**ETHOSPACE
DESIGNER: BILL STUMPF
HERMAN MILLER, INC.**

**COMPONENT WALL AND PARTITION SYSTEM**

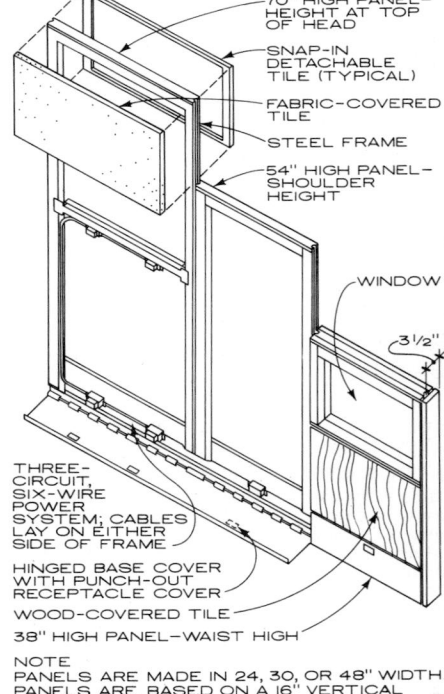

**PANEL COMPONENT**

Interspace Incorporated; Washington, D.C.
Richard J. Vitullo; Washington Grove, Maryland

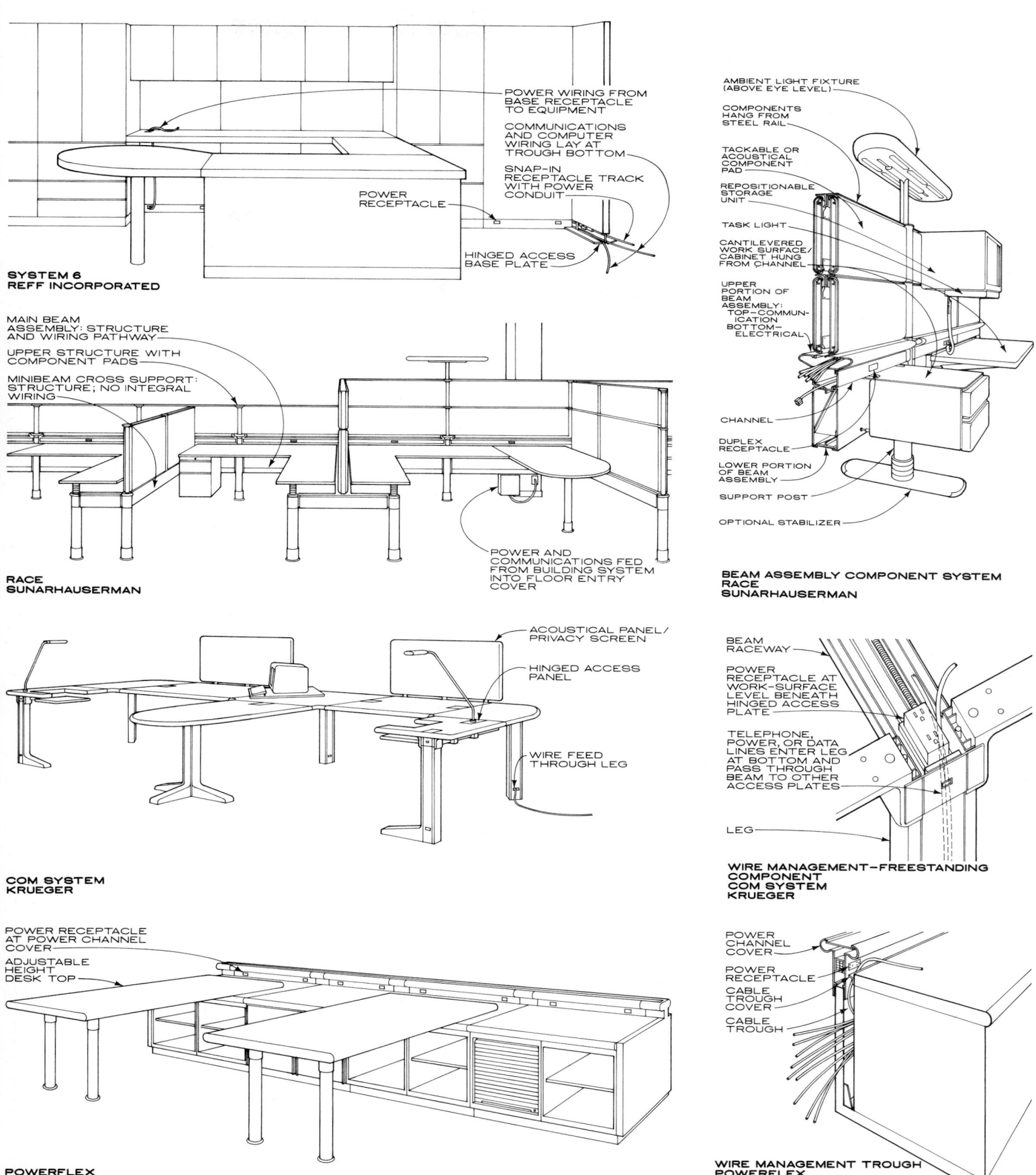

POWER WIRING FROM
BASE RECEPTACLE
TO EQUIPMENT

COMMUNICATIONS
AND COMPUTER
WIRING LAY AT
TROUGH BOTTOM

SNAP-IN
RECEPTACLE TRACK
WITH POWER
CONDUIT

POWER
RECEPTACLE

HINGED ACCESS
BASE PLATE

**SYSTEM 6
REFF INCORPORATED**

MAIN BEAM
ASSEMBLY: STRUCTURE
AND WIRING PATHWAY

UPPER STRUCTURE WITH
COMPONENT PADS

MINIBEAM CROSS SUPPORT:
STRUCTURE; NO INTEGRAL
WIRING

POWER AND
COMMUNICATIONS FED
FROM BUILDING SYSTEM
INTO FLOOR ENTRY
COVER

**RACE
SUNARHAUSERMAN**

ACOUSTICAL PANEL/
PRIVACY SCREEN

HINGED ACCESS
PANEL

WIRE FEED
THROUGH LEG

**COM SYSTEM
KRUEGER**

POWER RECEPTACLE
AT POWER CHANNEL
COVER

ADJUSTABLE
HEIGHT
DESK TOP

**POWERFLEX
JG FURNITURE SYSTEMS, INC.**

**TYPICAL WIRE MANAGEMENT SYSTEMS**

AMBIENT LIGHT FIXTURE
(ABOVE EYE LEVEL)

COMPONENTS
HANG FROM
STEEL RAIL

TACKABLE OR
ACOUSTICAL
COMPONENT
PAD

REPOSITIONABLE
STORAGE
UNIT

TASK LIGHT

CANTILEVERED
WORK SURFACE/
CABINET HUNG
FROM CHANNEL

UPPER
PORTION OF
BEAM
ASSEMBLY:
TOP—COMMUN-
ICATION
BOTTOM—
ELECTRICAL

CHANNEL

DUPLEX
RECEPTACLE

LOWER PORTION
OF BEAM
ASSEMBLY

SUPPORT POST

OPTIONAL STABILIZER

**BEAM ASSEMBLY COMPONENT SYSTEM
RACE
SUNARHAUSERMAN**

BEAM
RACEWAY

POWER
RECEPTACLE AT
WORK-SURFACE
LEVEL BENEATH
HINGED ACCESS
PLATE

TELEPHONE,
POWER, OR DATA
LINES ENTER LEG
AT BOTTOM AND
PASS THROUGH
BEAM TO OTHER
ACCESS PLATES

LEG

**WIRE MANAGEMENT—FREESTANDING
COMPONENT
COM SYSTEM
KRUEGER**

POWER
CHANNEL
COVER

POWER
RECEPTACLE

CABLE
TROUGH
COVER

CABLE
TROUGH

**WIRE MANAGEMENT TROUGH
POWERFLEX
JG FURNITURE SYSTEMS, INC.**

Robert Staples; Staples & Charles Ltd; Washington, D.C.
Richard J. Vitullo; Washington Grove, Maryland

**OFFICE FURNISHINGS** **12**

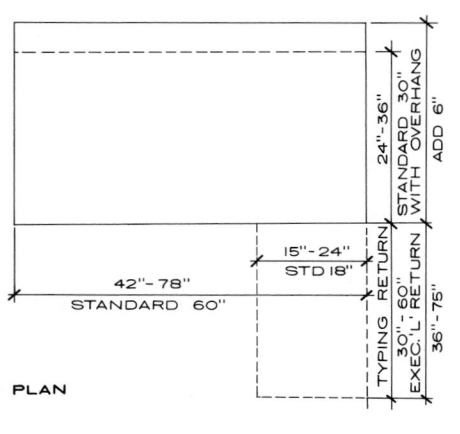

PLAN

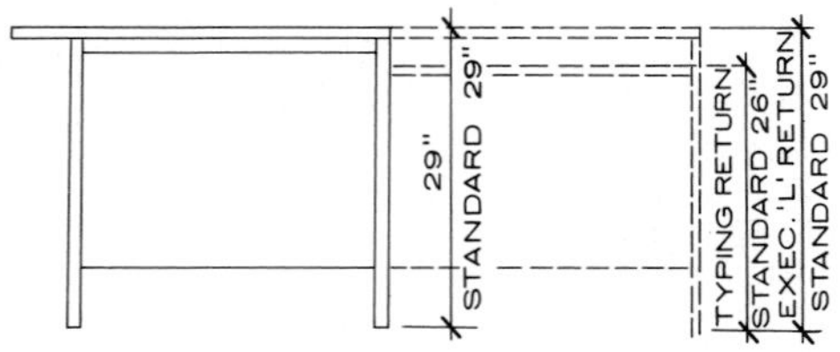

ELEVATION
DESK: SINGLE OR DOUBLE PEDESTAL

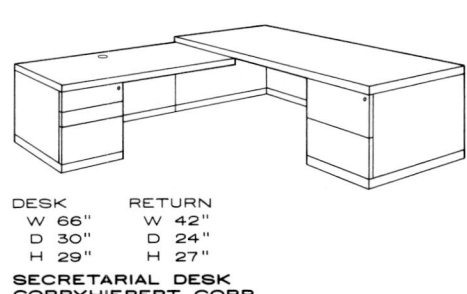

| DESK | RETURN |
|------|--------|
| W 66" | W 42" |
| D 30" | D 24" |
| H 29" | H 27" |

SECRETARIAL DESK
CORRYHIEBERT CORP.

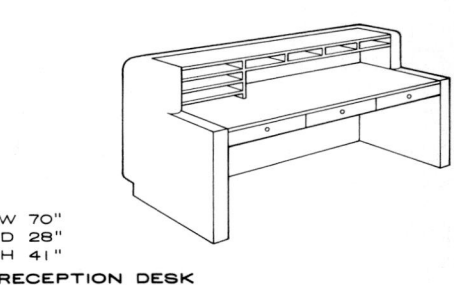

W 70"
D 28"
H 41"

RECEPTION DESK
THE PACE COLLECTION, INC.

W 70"
D 36"
H 29"

DOUBLE PEDESTAL DESK,
SIDE OVERHANG 4200 SERIES
STEELCASE, INC.

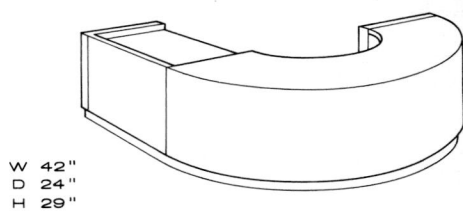

W 42"
D 24"
H 29"

CURVED SEGMENTED DESK
JG FURNITURE SYSTEMS, INC.

BURDICK GROUP
HERMAN MILLER, INC.

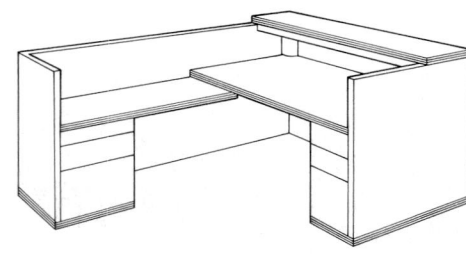

DESK, VARIA CASEGOODS
MUELLER

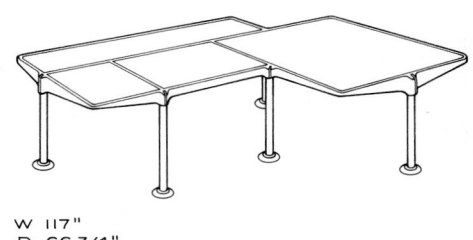

W 117"
D 66 3/4"
H 29"

MENHIR DESK
KRUEGER INTERNATIONAL DIVISION

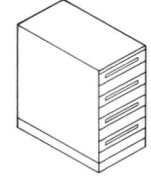

4 BOX DRAWERS

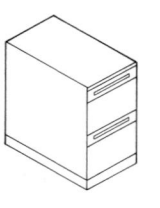

2 FILE DRAWERS

2 BOX DRAWERS
1 FILE DRAWER

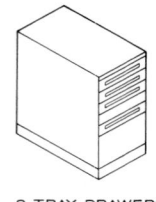

2 TRAY DRAWERS
1 BOX DRAWER
1 FILE DRAWER

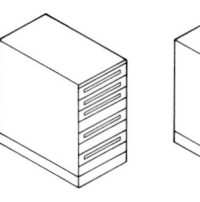

2 TRAY DRAWERS
3 BOX DRAWERS

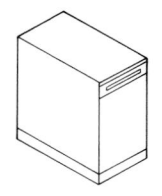

1 HINGED DOOR

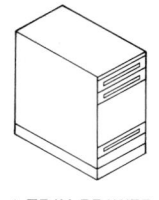

1 TRAY DRAWER
1 DATA PROCESSING
1 BOX DRAWER

NOTE: ALL PEDESTALS – W 15", D 24", H 29"

4600/8600 CREDENZA PEDESTALS
ALL-STEEL, INC.

## TYPICAL CREDENZA DIMENSIONS

| | WIDTH (IN.) | DEPTH (IN.) | HEIGHT (IN.) |
|---|---|---|---|
| One component | 15–30 | 17¾–24 | 25½–29¾ |
| Two component | 30–41½ | 17¾–24 | 25½–29¾ |
| Three component | 45–60½ | 17¾–24 | 25½–29¾ |
| Four component | 60–79¾ | 17¾–24 | 25½–29¾ |
| Five component | 75–98½ | 17¾–24 | 25½–29¾ |

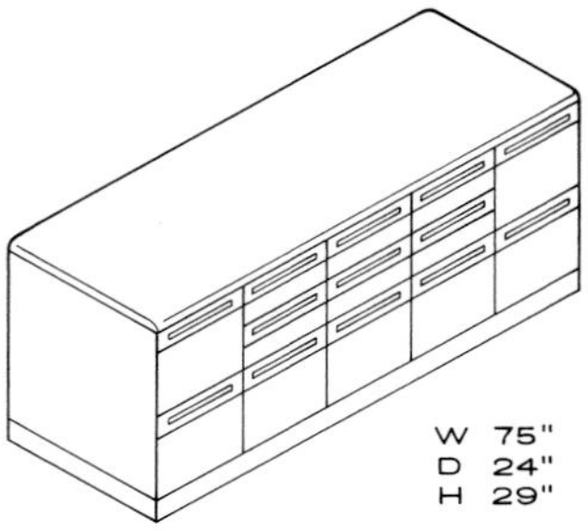

W 75"
D 24"
H 29"

4600/8600 SERIES CREDENZA
ALL-STEEL, INC.

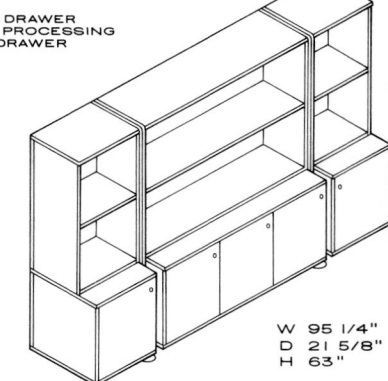

W 95 1/4"
D 21 5/8"
H 63"

MENHIR CABINET
KRUEGER INTERNATIONAL DIV.

Robert Staples; Staples & Charles Ltd; Washington, D.C.
Richard J. Vitullo; Washington Grove, Maryland

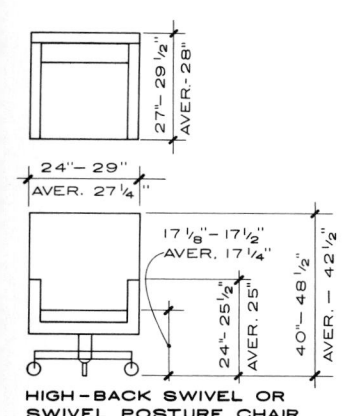

**HIGH-BACK SWIVEL OR SWIVEL POSTURE CHAIR**

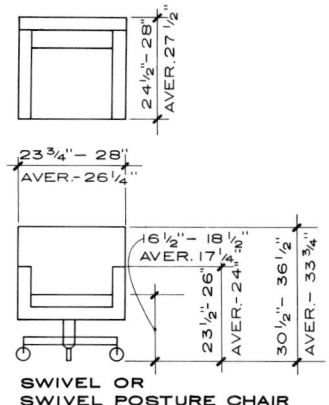

**SWIVEL OR SWIVEL POSTURE CHAIR**

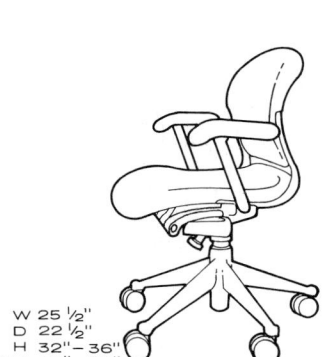

**SECRETARIAL POSTURE CHAIR**

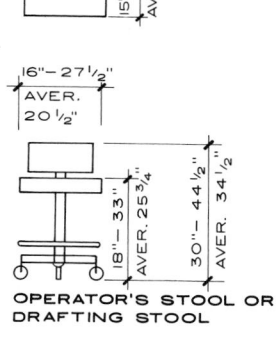

**OPERATOR'S STOOL OR DRAFTING STOOL**

W 22 1/2"
D 23 3/4"
H 40"–42"
SH 18 1/2"–20 1/2"

**HIGH-BACK ALUMINUM GROUP**
**DESIGNER: CHARLES EAMES**
**HERMAN MILLER, INC.**

W 26 1/2"
D 23 1/4"
H 36 1/2"–42"
SH 17"–20"

**ERGON EXECUTIVE WITH ARMS**
**DESIGNER: BILL STUMPF**
**HERMAN MILLER, INC.**

W 25 1/2"
D 22 1/2"
H 32"–36"
SH 16"–20"

**EQUA LOW-BACK WORK CHAIR**
**DESIGNERS:**
**BILL STUMPF / DON CHADWICK**
**HERMAN MILLER, INC.**

W 19"
D 18 1/2"
H 38 1/2"–41 3/4"
SH 25 1/4"–28 1/2"

**DORSAL OPERATIONAL STOOL**
**DESIGNERS:**
**E. AMBASZ / G. PIRETTI**
**KRUEGER, INC.**

W 25 3/4"
D 24 1/4"
H 40"–43 1/2"
SH 18"–21 1/2"

**CONCENTRIX MANAGER CHAIR**
**STEELCASE, INC.**

W 24 3/4"
D 26 1/2"
H 32 1/4"–35"
SH 17 3/4"–20 1/2"

**SAPPER ADVANCED LOW-BACK**
**DESIGNER: RICHARD SAPPER**
**KNOLL INTERNATIONAL**

W 24"
D 24 1/4"
H 31 1/4"–34"
SH 20"–22 1/2"

**MORRISON / HANNAH CHAIR**
**DESIGNERS:**
**A.I. MORRISON / B.R. HANNAH**
**KNOLL INTERNATIONAL**

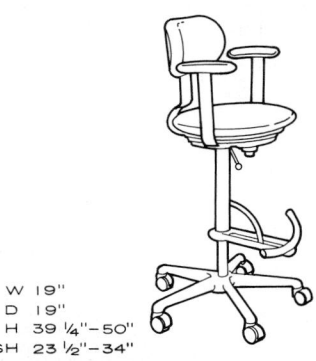

W 25 1/2"
D 21"
H 38"–48 1/2"
SH 21 1/2"–32"

**ADVANCED HIGH TASK CHAIR**
**DESIGNER: NIELS DIFFRIENT**
**KNOLL INTERNATIONAL**

W 27 1/4"
D 27 1/2"
H 43"
SH 18 3/4"–21 1/2"

**BRETON HIGH-BACK CHAIR**
**STOW AND DAVIS**

W 25 1/2"
D 25 1/2"
H 37"–41"
SH 16 1/2"–20 1/2"

**KELLY PNEUMATIC CHAIR**
**DESIGNER: WILLIAM RAFTERY**
**VECTA CONTRACT**

W 23"
D 20"
H 31"–39"
SH 17"–22"

**SERIES 370 OPERATOR**
**ARMCHAIR**
**ELITE / BILRITE**

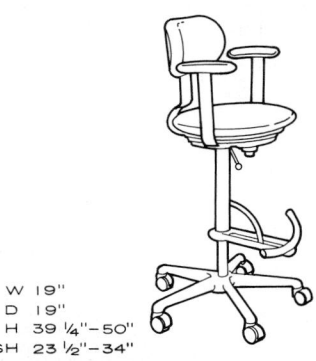

W 19"
D 19"
H 39 1/4"–50"
SH 23 1/2"–34"

**SPRINGBOK TASK STOOL**
**DESIGNER: JOHN BEHRINGER**
**JG FURNITURE SYSTEMS, INC.**

Robert Staples; Staples & Charles Ltd; Washington, D.C.
Richard J. Vitullo; Washington Grove, Maryland

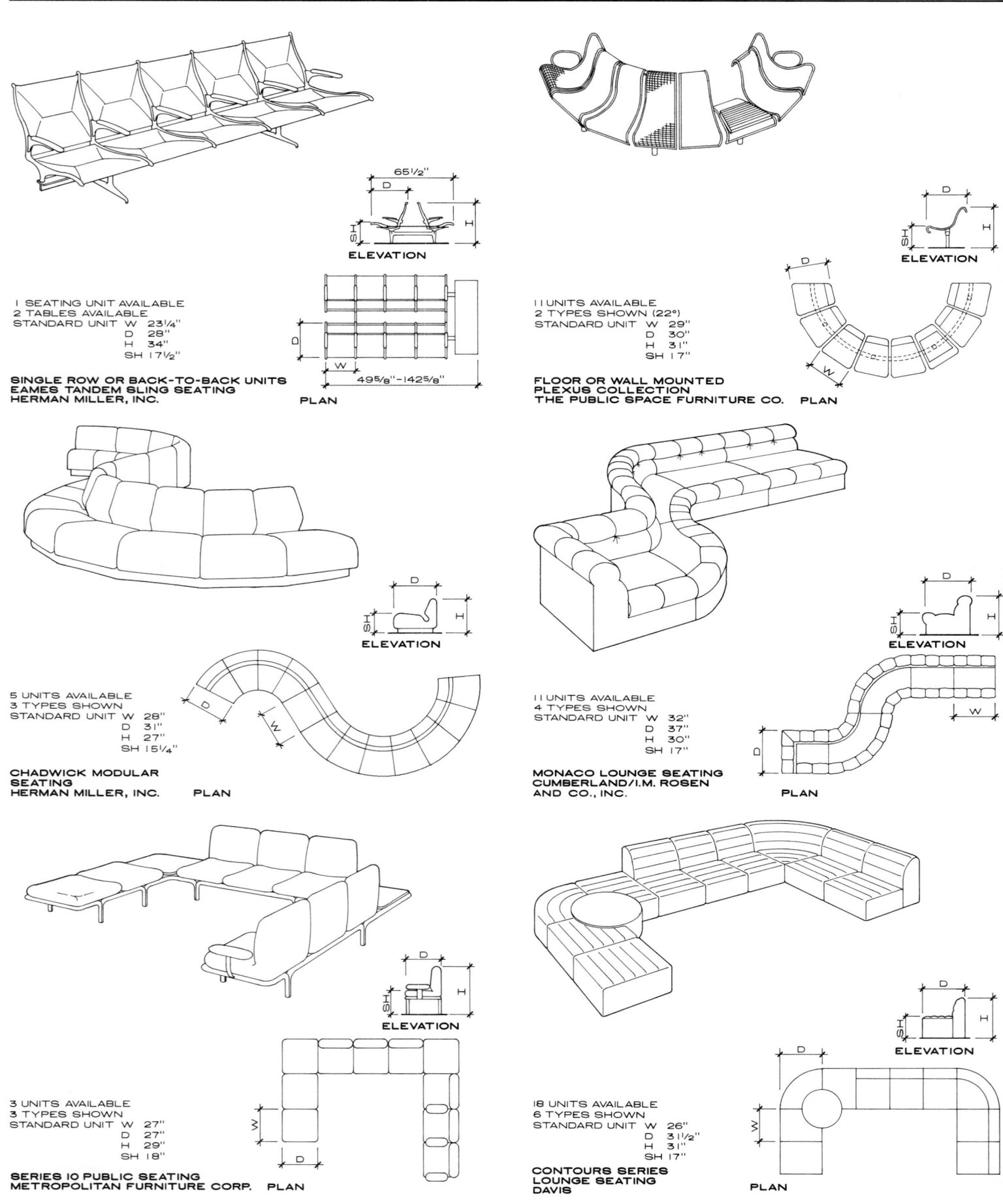

1 SEATING UNIT AVAILABLE
2 TABLES AVAILABLE
STANDARD UNIT W 23¼"
          D   28"
          H   34"
          SH 17½"

**SINGLE ROW OR BACK-TO-BACK UNITS
EAMES TANDEM SLING SEATING
HERMAN MILLER, INC.**

ELEVATION
PLAN
65½"
49⅝"-142⅝"

11 UNITS AVAILABLE
2 TYPES SHOWN (22°)
STANDARD UNIT W 29"
          D   30"
          H   31"
          SH 17"

**FLOOR OR WALL MOUNTED
PLEXUS COLLECTION
THE PUBLIC SPACE FURNITURE CO.    PLAN**

ELEVATION

5 UNITS AVAILABLE
3 TYPES SHOWN
STANDARD UNIT W 28"
          D   31"
          H   27"
          SH 15¼"

**CHADWICK MODULAR
SEATING
HERMAN MILLER, INC.    PLAN**

ELEVATION

11 UNITS AVAILABLE
4 TYPES SHOWN
STANDARD UNIT W 32"
          D   37"
          H   30"
          SH 17"

**MONACO LOUNGE SEATING
CUMBERLAND/I.M. ROSEN
AND CO., INC.    PLAN**

ELEVATION

3 UNITS AVAILABLE
3 TYPES SHOWN
STANDARD UNIT W 27"
          D   27"
          H   29"
          SH 18"

**SERIES 10 PUBLIC SEATING
METROPOLITAN FURNITURE CORP.    PLAN**

ELEVATION

18 UNITS AVAILABLE
6 TYPES SHOWN
STANDARD UNIT W 26"
          D   31½"
          H   31"
          SH 17"

**CONTOURS SERIES
LOUNGE SEATING
DAVIS    PLAN**

ELEVATION

Robert Staples; Staples & Charles Ltd; Washington, D.C.
Richard J. Vitullo; Washington Grove, Maryland

W 19¾"
D 21¼"
H 30"
SH 17¾"

**40/4 CHAIR, 1964
DESIGNER: DAVID ROWLAND
GF FURNITURE SYSTEMS**

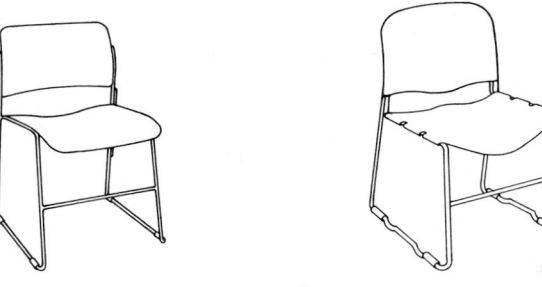

W 21"
D 22"
H 30"
SH 17¼"

**MULTI-CHAIR
STACKS 40 ON A DOLLY
SHAW-WALKER**

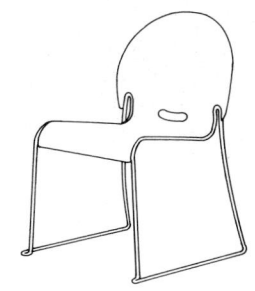

W 20½"
D 24"
H 31½"
SH 18"

**STACKING CHAIR
STACKS 20 ON A DOLLY
NIENKAMPER**

W 20"
D 22"
H 33¾"
SH 18"

**BIBI VADER CHAIR
ACCIAIO, INC.**

W 23⅛"
D 25½"
H 31¾"
SH 18"

**STACKING CHAIR WITH ARM
DESIGNER: CHARLES EAMES
HERMAN MILLER, INC.**

W 18½"
D 17"
H 30"
SH 17½"

**PROPER CHAIR
HERMAN MILLER, INC.**

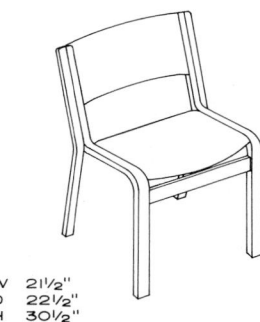

W 23"
D 22"
H 30½"
SH 18½"

**APTA "SMART" CHAIR
DESIGNER: GIANCARLO PIRETTI
CASTELLI/KRUEGER**

W 21½"
D 22½"
H 30½"
SH 18"

**STACKING CHAIR
DESIGNERS: THYGESEN/
SORENSEN
RUDD INTERNATIONAL**

W 18"
D 20½"
H 29½"
SH 17½"

**TABLET ARMCHAIR
TABLET, 23" X 10"
SAMSONITE FURNITURE CO.**

W 18½"
D 19½"
H 29½"
SH 17½"

**PLIA FOLDING CHAIR
DESIGNER: GIANCARLO PIRETTI
CASTELLI/KRUEGER**

W 22"
D 21"
H 32"
SH 18"

**STACKING CHAIR
KINETICS**

W 22"
D 24"
H 30"
SH 17"

**RONDO CHAIR
PERFORATED STEEL
FIXTURES FURNITURE**

DIA. 37½"
H 28½"

**PLANO FOLDING TABLE
DESIGNER: GIANCARLO PIRETTI
CASTELLI/KRUEGER**

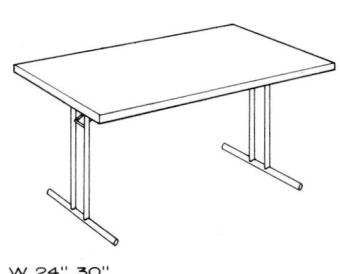

W 24", 30"
D 60", 72"
H 29"

**ENCORE FOLDING TABLE
FIXTURES FURNITURE**

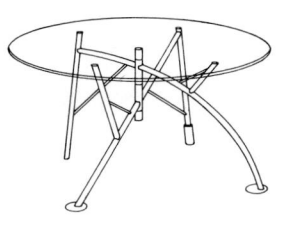

DIA. 48", 54", 60"
H 28¼"

**DOLE MELIPONE FOLDING TABLE
DESIGNER: PHILIPPE STARCK
ICF, INC.**

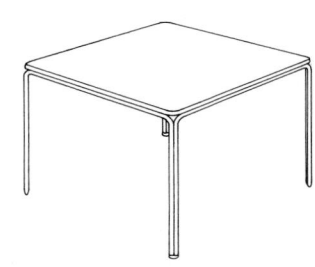

W 24", 30", 34½", 42"
D 24", 30", 34½", 42"
H 29"

**SQUARE STACKING TABLE
FIXTURES FURNITURE**

Robert Staples; Staples & Charles Ltd; Washington, D.C.
Richard J. Vitullo; Washington Grove, Maryland

## TYPICAL END OR SIDE TABLE DIMENSIONS (IN.)

| DESCRIPTION | DEPTH | | WIDTH | | HEIGHT | |
|---|---|---|---|---|---|---|
| | MIN. | MAX. | MIN. | MAX. | MIN. | MAX. |
| RECTANGULAR | 19 | 28 | 21 | 48 | 17 | 28 |
| SQUARE | 15 | 32 | 15 | 32 | 17 | 28 |
| ROUND | 16 | 30 | 16 | 30 | 18 | 22½ |

## TYPICAL LOW TABLE DIMENSIONS (IN.)

| DESCRIPTION | DEPTH | | WIDTH | | HEIGHT | |
|---|---|---|---|---|---|---|
| | MIN. | MAX. | MIN. | MAX. | MIN. | MAX. |
| RECTANGULAR | 15½ | 24 | 21 | 86 | 12 | 18 |
| SQUARE | 36 | 42 | 32 | 42 | 15 | 17 |
| ROUND | 30 | 42 | 20 | 42 | 15 | 16½ |

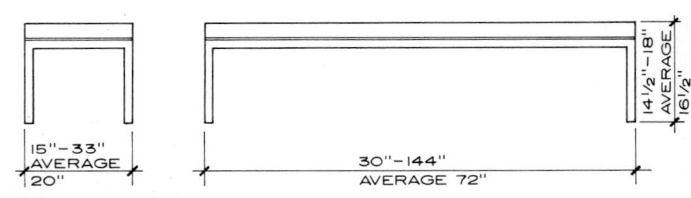

**BENCH DIMENSIONS**

W 54" TO 90"
D 20"
H 18"
**BENCH**
**LEHIGH FURNITURE CORP.**

W 48³⁄₈"
D 21³⁄₈"
H 17¼"
**BENCH**
**ALL-STEEL, INC.**

DIA. 17"
H 22"
**OCCASIONAL TABLE**
**DESIGNER: GEORGE NELSON**
**HERMAN MILLER, INC.**

DIA. 13"
H 15"
**WOODEN SPOOL TABLE**
**DESIGNER: RAY EAMES**
**HERMAN MILLER, INC.**

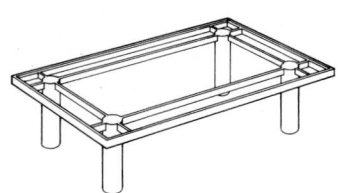

W 45", 60"
D 45", 60"
H 16"
**INTERSECT LOW TABLE**
**BRUETON**

W 63"
D 50"
H 12"
**MERCER TABLE**
**DESIGNER: LUCIA MERCER**
**KNOLL INTERNATIONAL**

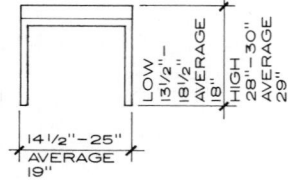
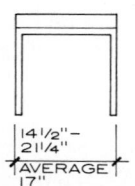

**STOOL DIMENSIONS**

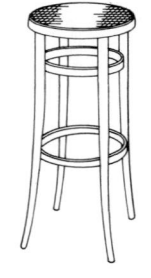

DIA. 17"
H 30"
**WOOD STOOL**
**THONET: DIVISION OF**
**SHELBY WILLIAMS INDUSTRIES,**
**INC.**

W 22½"
D 18"
H 41½"
SH 30"
**FLEDERMAUS BAR CHAIR**
**THONET: DIVISION OF**
**SHELBY WILLIAMS INDUSTRIES,**
**INC.**

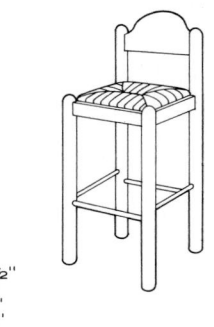

W 16½"
D 19"
H 43"
SH 30"
**PADOVA BAR**
**STOOL. HANK**
**LOEWENSTEIN, INC.**

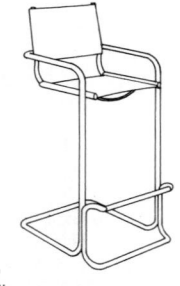

W 18¼"
D 22¼"
H 39½"
SH 27"
**BADEN BAR STOOL**
**LOWENSTEIN/OGGO**

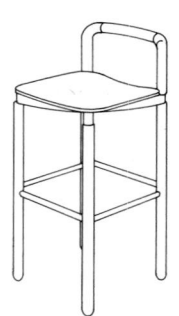

W 18"
D 18"
H 38"
SH 30"
**RUBBER BAR STOOL**
**DESIGNER: BRIAN KANE**
**METROPOLITAN FURNITURE**
**CORP.**

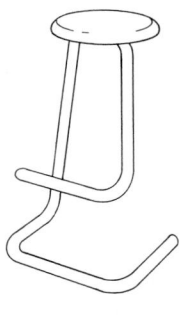

W 16"
D 16"
H 28"
**STOOL**
**KINETICS**

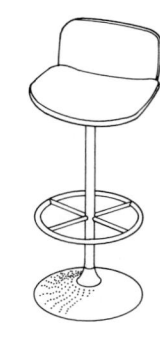

W 19"
D 18"
H 36"
SH 29"
**CARIBE BAR STOOL**
**DESIGNER: ILMARI TAPIOVAARA**
**ICF, INC.**

Robert Staples; Staples & Charles Ltd; Washington, D.C.
Richard J. Vitullo; Washington Grove, Maryland

**12** **FURNITURE ACCESSORIES**

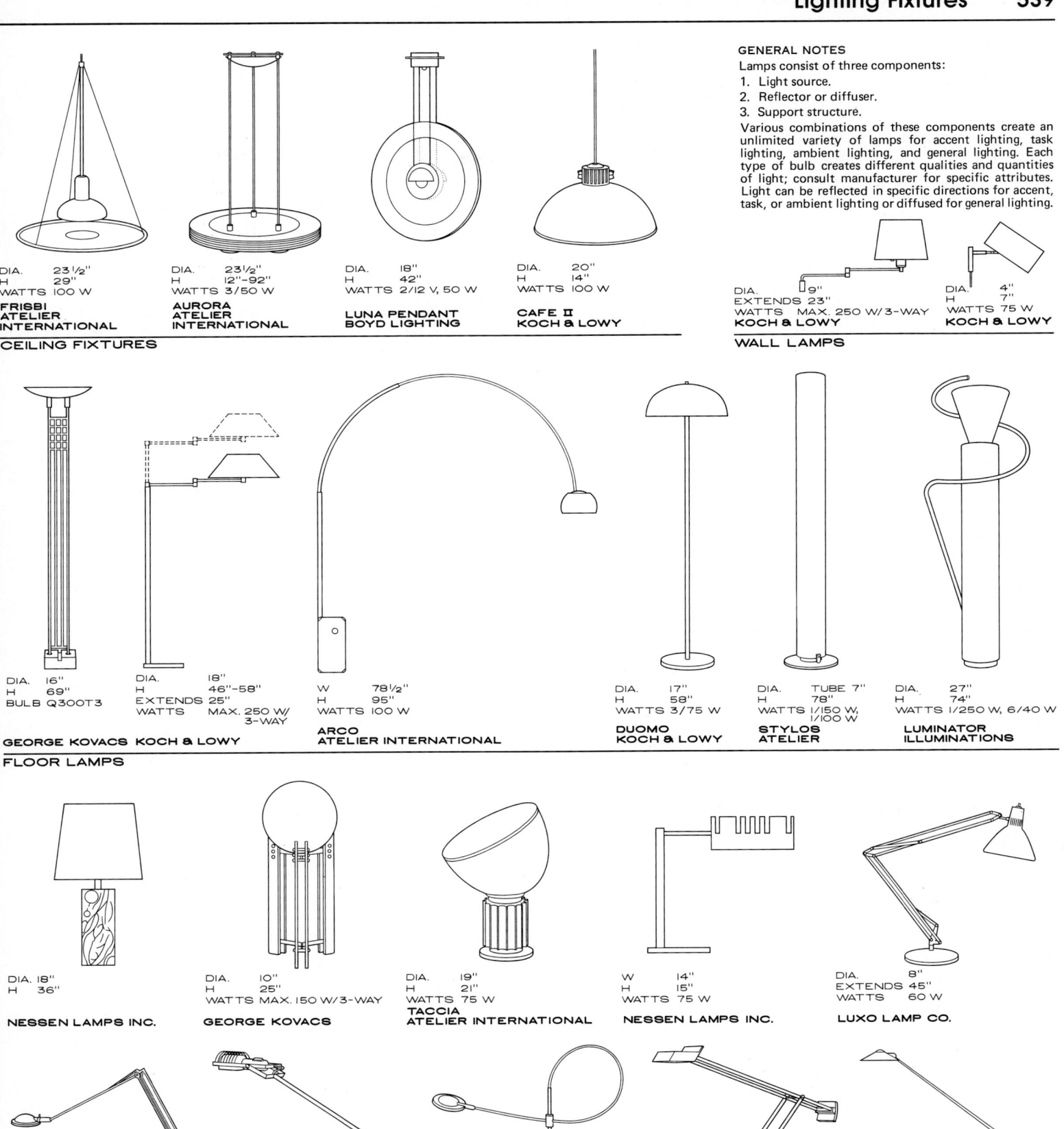

GENERAL NOTES
Lamps consist of three components:
1. Light source.
2. Reflector or diffuser.
3. Support structure.
Various combinations of these components create an unlimited variety of lamps for accent lighting, task lighting, ambient lighting, and general lighting. Each type of bulb creates different qualities and quantities of light; consult manufacturer for specific attributes. Light can be reflected in specific directions for accent, task, or ambient lighting or diffused for general lighting.

DIA.      23½"
H         29"
WATTS 100 W
**FRISBI
ATELIER
INTERNATIONAL**

DIA.      23½"
H         12"–92"
WATTS 3/50 W
**AURORA
ATELIER
INTERNATIONAL**

DIA.      18"
H         42"
WATTS 2/12 V, 50 W
**LUNA PENDANT
BOYD LIGHTING**

DIA.      20"
H         14"
WATTS 100 W
**CAFE II
KOCH & LOWY**

**CEILING FIXTURES**

DIA.           9"
EXTENDS 23"
WATTS   MAX. 250 W/3-WAY
**KOCH & LOWY**

DIA.      4"
H         7"
WATTS 75 W
**KOCH & LOWY**

**WALL LAMPS**

DIA.   16"
H      69"
BULB Q300T3
**GEORGE KOVACS**

DIA.           18"
H         46"–58"
EXTENDS 25"
WATTS    MAX. 250 W/
              3-WAY
**KOCH & LOWY**

W        78½"
H        95"
WATTS 100 W
**ARCO
ATELIER INTERNATIONAL**

DIA.      17"
H         58"
WATTS 3/75 W
**DUOMO
KOCH & LOWY**

DIA.      TUBE 7"
H         78"
WATTS 1/150 W,
           1/100 W
**STYLOS
ATELIER**

DIA.      27"
H         74"
WATTS 1/250 W, 6/40 W
**LUMINATOR
ILLUMINATIONS**

**FLOOR LAMPS**

DIA. 18"
H     36"
**NESSEN LAMPS INC.**

DIA.      10"
H         25"
WATTS MAX. 150 W/3-WAY
**GEORGE KOVACS**

DIA.      19"
H         21"
WATTS 75 W
**TACCIA
ATELIER INTERNATIONAL**

W     14"
H     15"
WATTS 75 W
**NESSEN LAMPS INC.**

DIA.           8"
EXTENDS 45"
WATTS      60 W
**LUXO LAMP CO.**

DIA.           3½"
EXTENDS 37"
WATTS    35 W/12 V
**BERENICE
ARTEMIDE**

W     33" MAX.
H     43" MAX.
WATTS 100 W
**SINTESI
ARTEMIDE**

W     31"
H     29" ADJUSTABLE
WATTS 50 W/12 V
**SIGLA T
IPI**

W     37" MAX.
H     46" MAX.
WATTS 55 W/12 V
**TIZIO
ARTEMIDE**

W     37"
H     23" MAX.
WATTS 50 W/12 V
**FEATHER
GEORGE KOVACS**

**TABLE AND DESK LAMPS**

Robert Staples; Staples & Charles Ltd; Washington, D.C.

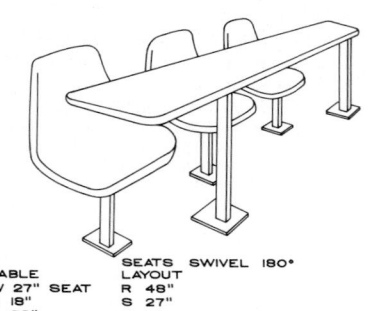

SEMINAR SEATING
KRUEGER

| SEAT | TABLE | SEATS SWIVEL 180° |
|---|---|---|
| W 20" | W 27" SEAT | LAYOUT |
| D 21" | D 18" | R 48" |
| H 31" | H 29" | S 27" |

## NOTES

1. All spacing dimensions are centerline dimensions.
2. Typical seat height is 17 in.
3. Unit dimensions are to farthest extremity.
4. Auditorium seating with tablet arms is used often. See index.
5. Left-handed tablet arms generally are available for fixed arm seating.
6. Ganged seating may be adapted for mounting on level floors, sloped floors and 6 in. to 14 in. risers for tiered seating.

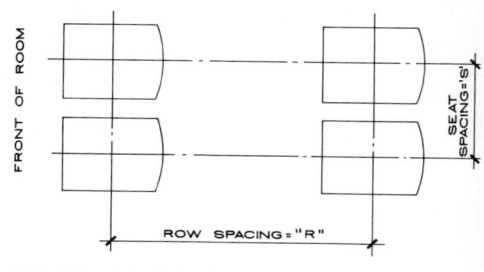

KEY TO LAYOUT DIMENSIONS

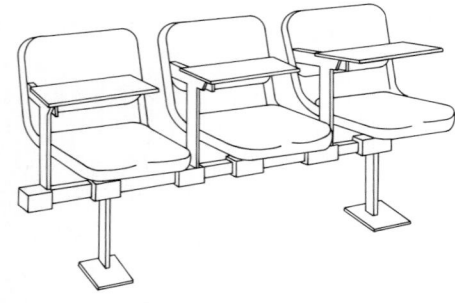

SEQUENCE SEATING
KRUEGER

| UNIT | LAYOUT |
|---|---|
| W 22" SEAT | R 36"-39" |
| D 37" | S 22" |
| H 31" | |

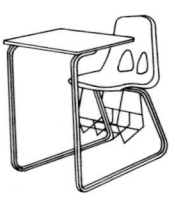

COMBINATION STUDY
TOP DESK
SMITH SYSTEM

| UNIT | LAYOUT |
|---|---|
| W 24" | R 37" |
| D 35" | S 39" |
| H 30" | |

TABLET ARM CHAIR
SMITH SYSTEM

| UNIT | LAYOUT |
|---|---|
| W 19" | R 32" |
| D 30" | S 34" |
| H 30" | |

SEAT HEIGHT
$9\frac{1}{2}$-$17\frac{1}{2}$

OPEN FRONT DESK
AND CHAIR
SMITH SYSTEM

| DESK | CHAIR | LAYOUT |
|---|---|---|
| W 24" | W 18" | R 45" |
| D 18" | D 20" | S 24" |
| H 21"-29" | H 24"-30" | |

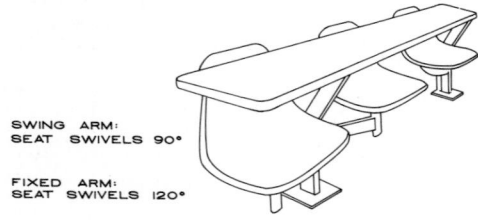

SWING ARM:
SEAT SWIVELS 90°

FIXED ARM:
SEAT SWIVELS 120°

UNIVERSITY SEATING
KRUEGER

| UNIT | SEAT | LAYOUT |
|---|---|---|
| W 27" | | R 41" WITH SWING ARM |
| D 26" | WITH SWING ARM | 48" WITH FIXED ARM |
| 34" | WITH FIXED ARM | S 27" |
| H 31" | | |

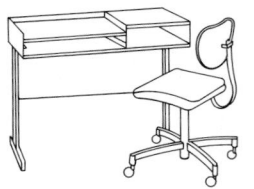

COMBINATION STUDY
TOP DESK
SMITH SYSTEM
"SCHOOL FURNITURE"

| UNIT | LAYOUT |
|---|---|
| W 24" | R 32" |
| D 30" | S 39" |
| H 30" | |

TYPING DESK     CHAIR
SMITH SYSTEM     HON

| DESK | CHAIR | LAYOUT |
|---|---|---|
| W 34" | W 23" | R 45" |
| D 30" | D 23" | S 34" |
| H 29" | H 32" | |

STUDY CARRELL
FLEETWOOD
FURNITURE CO.

| UNIT | AVAILABLE WITH |
|---|---|
| W 31" SEAT | 26" HIGH DESK |
| D 30" | TOP FOR USE |
| H 48" | WITH COMPUTERS |

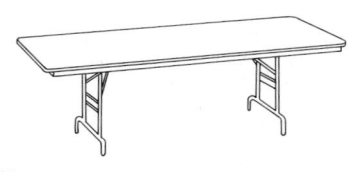
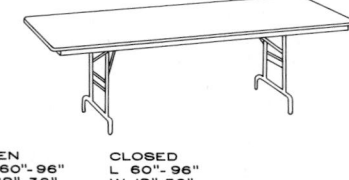

FOLDING TABLE
KRUEGER

| OPEN | CLOSED |
|---|---|
| W 60"-96" | L 60"-96" |
| D 18"-36" | W 18"-36" |
| H 24"-36" | D 4" |

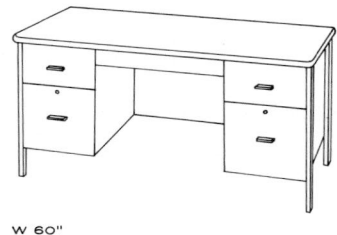

DOUBLE PEDESTAL DESK
SMITH SYSTEM

W 60"
D 30"
H 29"

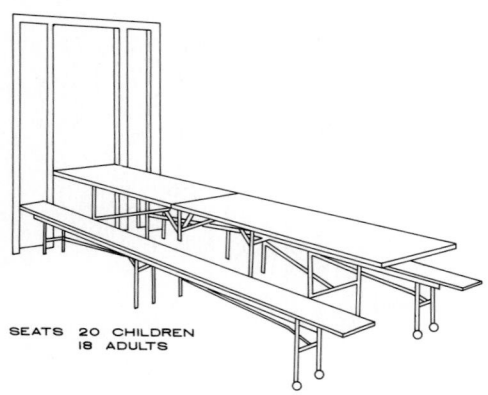

SEATS 20 CHILDREN
18 ADULTS

FOLDING TABLE AND BENCHES
NELSON-ADAMS

| OPEN | CLOSED |
|---|---|
| W 168" | H 86" |
| D 60" | W 60" |
| H 25-30" | D 6" (SURFACE MOUNT) |
| | 1" (RECESSED) |

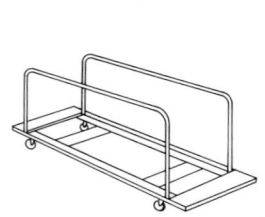

FOLDING TABLE CADDY
KRUEGER

| EMPTY | CAPACITY: UP TO 9 |
|---|---|
| W 78" | TABLES DEPENDING |
| D 27" | ON WIDTH |
| H 28" | |

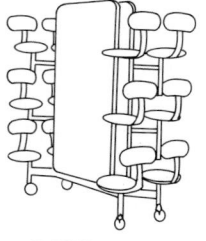

FOLDING TABLE AND CHAIRS
SICO INCORPORATED

| CLOSED |
|---|
| W 60" |
| D 30" |
| H 81"-83" |

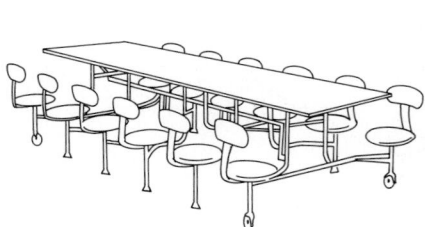

| OPEN | BACKRESTS OPTIONAL |
|---|---|
| W 120" | |
| D 60" | |
| H 26"-29" | |

Jeffrey R. Vandevoort; Talbott Wilson Associates, Inc.; Houston, Texas
ISD Incorporated; Chicago, New York, Boston, Houston

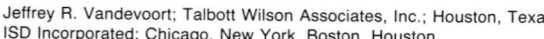

# 12   EDUCATIONAL FURNITURE

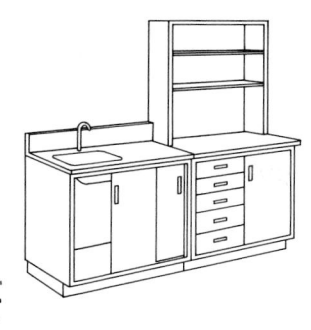

W 48"
D 22"
H 34"

**WORK CENTER**
**FLEETWOOD FURNITURE CO.**

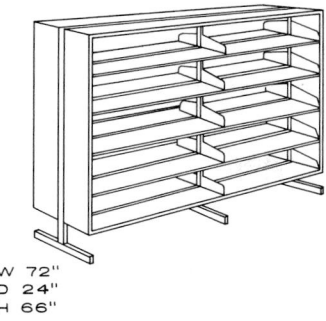

W 72"
D 24"
H 66"

**LIBRARY SHELVING**
**SMITH SYSTEM**

W 24"
D 18"
H 42"

**AUDIO-VISUAL/UTILITY TABLE**
**LUXOR**

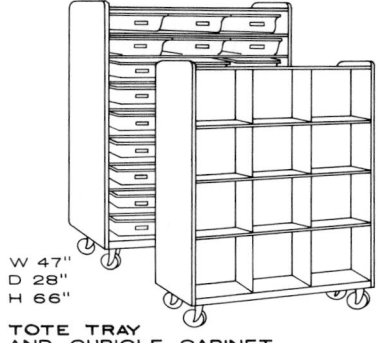

W 47"
D 28"
H 66"

**TOTE TRAY**
**AND CUBICLE CABINET**
**FLEETWOOD FURNITURE CO.**

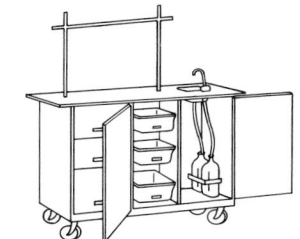

W 60"
D 23"
H 37"

**SCIENCE CABINET**
**FLEETWOOD FURNITURE CO.**

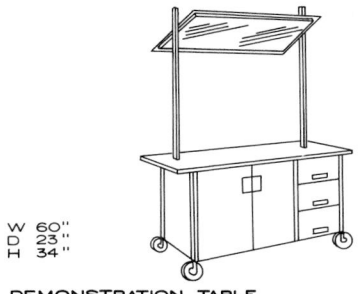

W 60"
D 23"
H 34"

**DEMONSTRATION TABLE**
**FLEETWOOD FURNITURE CO.**

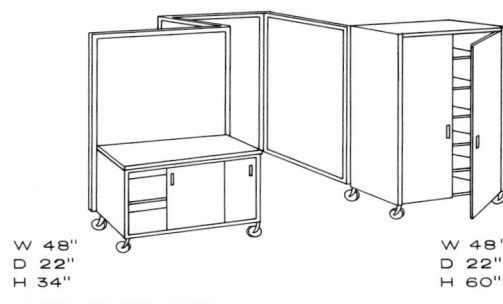

W 48"
D 22"
H 34"

W 48"
D 22"
H 60"

**OPEN PLAN UNIT**
**FLEETWOOD FURNITURE CO.**

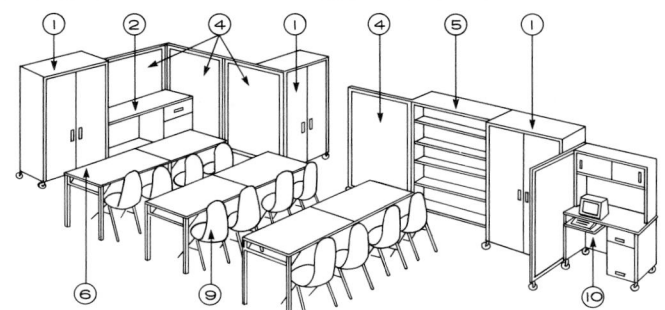

**OPEN PLAN UNITS**
**FLEETWOOD FURNITURE CO.**

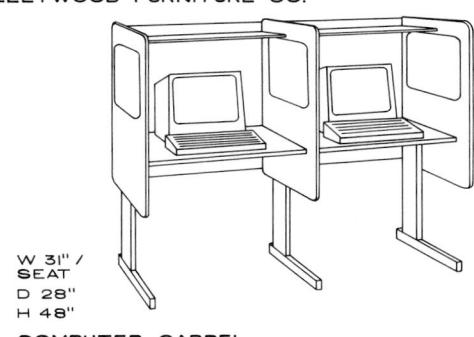

W 31" /
SEAT
D 28"
H 48"

**COMPUTER CARREL**
**FLEETWOOD FURNITURE CO.**

W 48"
D 22"
H 30"

**TOTE TRAY CABINET**
**FLEETWOOD FURNITURE CO.**

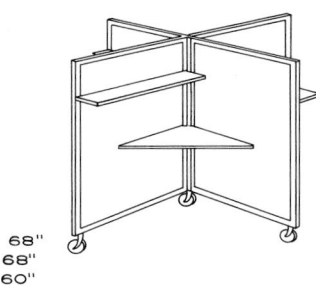

W 68"
D 68"
H 60"

**FOUR PANEL CAROUSEL**
**FLEETWOOD FURNITURE CO.**

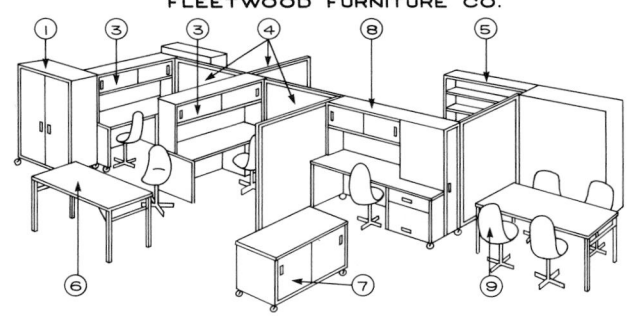

**OPEN PLAN UNITS**
**FLEETWOOD FURNITURE CO.**

## OPEN PLAN UNITS

| KEY | DESCRIPTION | MANUFACTURER | W (IN.) | D (IN.) | H (IN.) | SHELVES | DRAWER |
|---|---|---|---|---|---|---|---|
| 1 | cabinet | Fleetwood Furniture Co. | 48 | 24 | 72 | 8 | 0 |
| 2 | desk | Fleetwood Furniture Co. | 48 | 28 | 29 | 0 | 2 |
| 3 | desk | Fleetwood Furniture Co. | 48 | 28 | 60 | 1 | 2 |
| 4 | partition | Fleetwood Furniture Co. | 48 | | 60 | | |
| 4 | partition | Fleetwood Furniture Co. | 48 | | 72 | | |
| 5 | bookcase | Fleetwood Furniture Co. | 48 | 22 | 60 | 10 | |
| 6 | table | Krueger | 48 | 24 | 29 | | |
| 7 | cabinet | Fleetwood Furniture Co. | 48 | 22 | 34 | 1 | 0 |
| 8 | desk/closet | Fleetwood Furniture Co. | 48 | 28 | 60 | 1 | 2 |
| 9 | chair | Krueger | 21 | 20 | 32 | | |
| 10 | comp. desk | Fleetwood Furniture Co. | 48 | 28 | 60 | 1 | 2 |

NOTES

1. Open classroom layouts are based on modular partition dimensions: 48 in. wide x 60 in. or 72 in. high.
2. Partitions are available with hinges to connect with standard height cabinets, or with casters for freestanding use.
3. Surfaces for partitions are vinyl, porcelain enameled steel, chalkboard, or tackboard.
4. Carrels may be ordered with 31 in. high desktops for use with wheelchairs.
5. Typical seat height is 17 in.
6. Unit dimensions are to farthest extremity.

Jeffrey R. Vandevoort; Talbott Wilson Associates, Inc.; Houston, Texas
ISD Incorporated; Chicago, New York, Boston, Houston

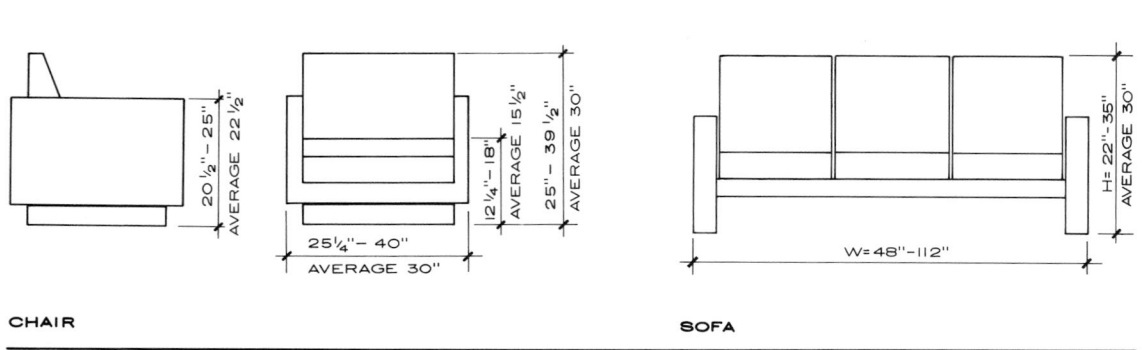

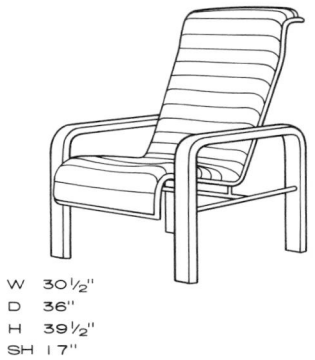

W 30½"
D 36"
H 39½"
SH 17"

CHAIR

SOFA

**HIGH-BACK CHAIR
MUELLER**

**TYPICAL LOUNGE SEATING DIMENSIONS**

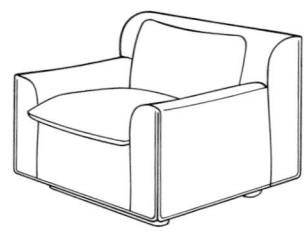

W 36"
D 33"
H 29"

**HELI LOUNGE CHAIR
DESIGNER: OTTO ZAPH
KNOLL INTERNATIONAL**

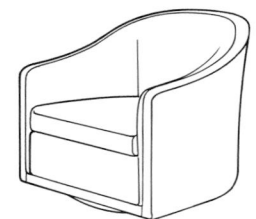

W 32"
D 31"
H 29"
SH 16"

**SWIVEL LOUNGE CHAIR
DESIGNER: BEN BALDWIN
JACK LENOR LARSEN**

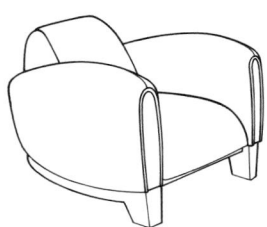

W 35½"
D 39½"
H 26½"
SH 17"

**BUGATTI LOUNGE CHAIR
DESIGNER: FRANZ ROMERO
STENDIG INTERNATIONAL, INC.**

W 36"
D 36"
H 32"
SH 15"

**LOUNGE CHAIR
DESIGNER: GEOFFREY HARCOURT
ARTIFORT / KRUEGER**

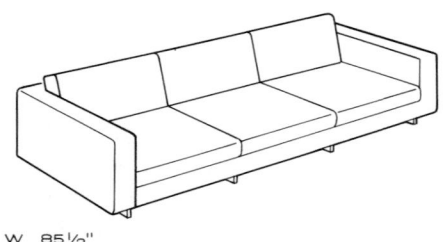

W 85½"
D 36"
H 24¾"
SH 17"

**THREE-PLACE SETTEE
GF**

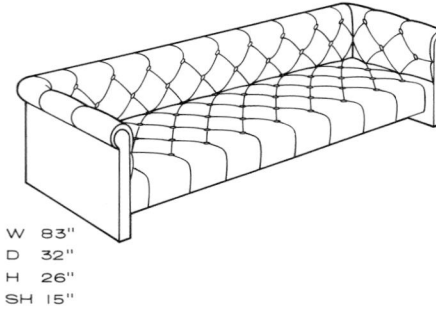

W 83"
D 32"
H 26"
SH 15"

**CLUB SOFA
ZOGRAPHOS DESIGNS, LTD.**

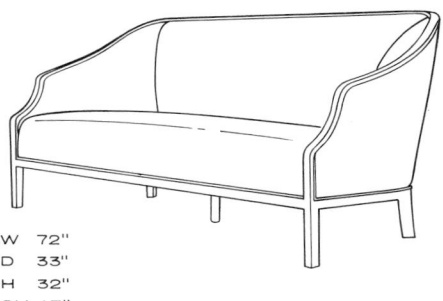

W 72"
D 33"
H 32"
SH 17"

**BANKERS SOFA
DESIGNER: WARD BENNETT
BRICKEL ASSOCIATES, INC.**

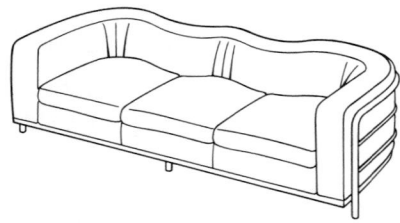

W 76¾"
D 30¾"
H 28½"
SH 17¾"

**ONDA 3-SEAT SOFA
DESIGNERS: DE PAS, D'URBINO, LOMAZZI
ICF, INC.**

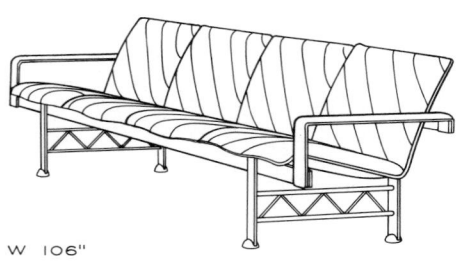

W 106"
D 30"
H 28½"
SH 17"

**SPAN 4-SEAT SOFA
DESIGNER: BURKHARD VOGTHERR
BRAYTON INTERNATIONAL COLLECTION**

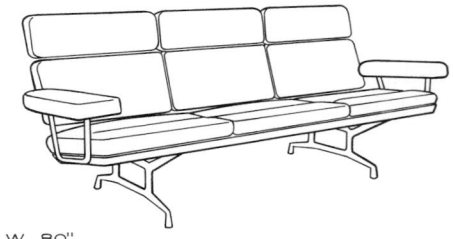

W 80"
D 21"
H 33"
SH 16½"

**3-SEAT SOFA
DESIGNER: CHARLES EAMES
HERMAN MILLER, INC.**

Robert Staples; Staples & Charles Ltd; Washington, D.C.
Richard J. Vitullo; Washington Grove, Maryland

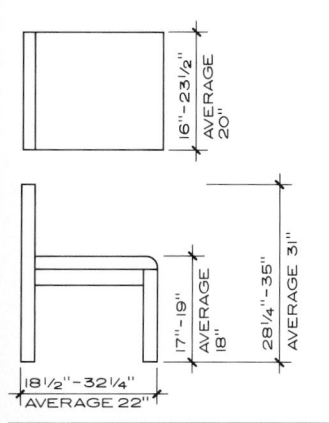

**SIDE CHAIR DIMENSIONS**

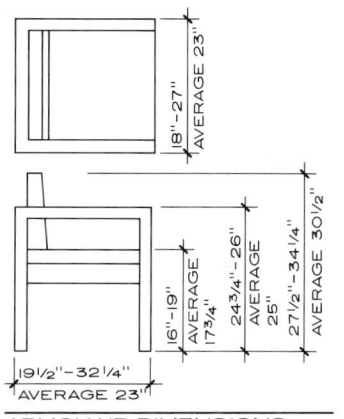

**ARMCHAIR DIMENSIONS**

```
W  16"
D  20"
H  35"
```

**VIENNA CHAIR**
**DESIGNER: MICHAEL THONET**
**THONET INDUSTRIES, INC.**

```
W   17 1/4"
D   18 3/4"
H   34 1/2"
SH  18 1/2"
```

**THALIA SIDE CHAIR**
**DESIGNER: ANNIG SARIAN**
**STENDIG INTERNATIONAL, INC.**

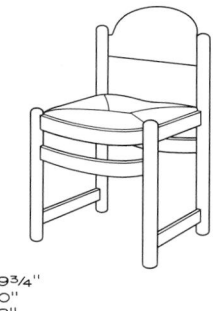

```
W   19 3/4"
D   20"
H   32"
SH  18"
```

**PADOVA II SIDE CHAIR**
**LOWENSTEIN/OGGO**

```
W   21"
D   22 1/2"
H   30"
SH  18"
```

**SIDE CHAIR**
**DESIGNER: HARRY BERTOIA**
**KNOLL INTERNATIONAL**

```
W   20"
D   19"
H   34"
SH  17 1/2"
```

**WINDSOR ARMCHAIR**
**LOWENSTEIN/OGGO**

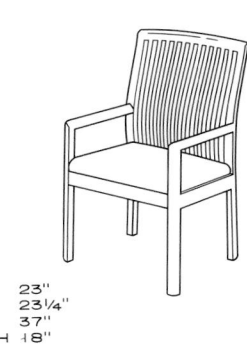

```
W   23"
D   23 1/4"
H   37"
SH  18"
```

**CARRINGTON GUEST CHAIR**
**KIMBALL OFFICE FURNITURE CO.**

```
W   22 1/4"
D   23 1/2"
H   32"
SH  17 3/4"
```

**COURTHOUSE CHAIR**
**GUNLOCKE**

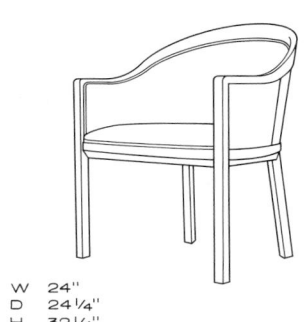

```
W   24"
D   24 1/4"
H   32 1/4"
SH  18"
```

**WOOD FRAME ARMCHAIR**
**DESIGNER: WARD BENNETT**
**BRICKEL ASSOCIATES**

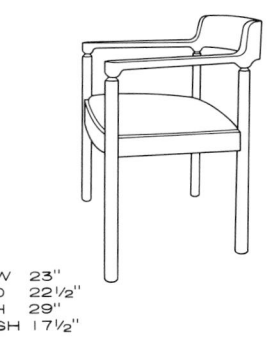

```
W   23"
D   22 1/2"
H   29"
SH  17 1/2"
```

**ARMCHAIR**
**ZOGRAPHOS DESIGNS LTD.**

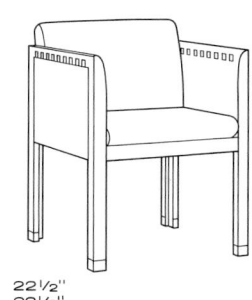

```
W   22 1/2"
D   22 1/2"
H   31"
SH  19"
```

**ARMCHAIR**
**DESIGNER: BRIAN KANE**
**METROPOLITAN FURNITURE**
**CORP.**

```
W   22 3/4"
D   23 1/2"
H   31"
SH  18 1/4"
```

**SNODGRASS OPEN BACK**
**ARMCHAIR**
**STEELCASE**

```
W   23 1/2"
D   22"
H   31"
SH  17 1/2"
```

**VARIX ARMCHAIR**
**SAMSONITE FURNITURE CO.**

```
W   25"
D   31"
H   29"
SH  16 1/2"
```

**VOLKSCHAIR LOUNGE CHAIR**
**RUDD INTERNATIONAL CORP.**

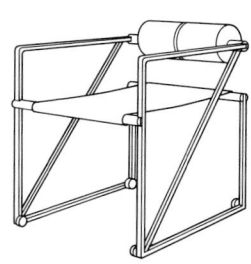

```
W   20 1/2"
D   22 3/4"
H   28 1/4"
SH  18 1/2"
```

**SECONDA ARMCHAIR**
**DESIGNER: MARIO BOTTA**
**ICF, INC.**

Robert Staples; Staples & Charles Ltd; Washington, D.C.
Richard J. Vitullo; Washington Grove, Maryland

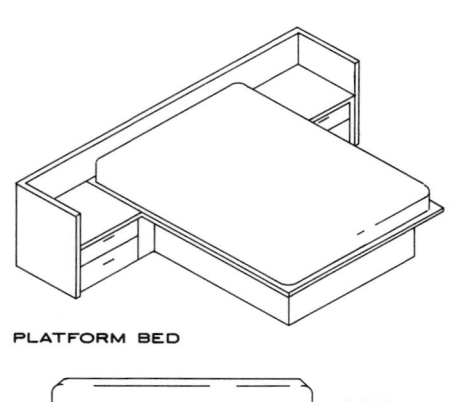

**PLATFORM BED**

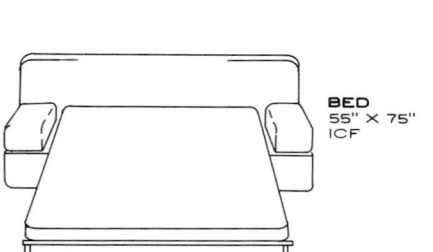

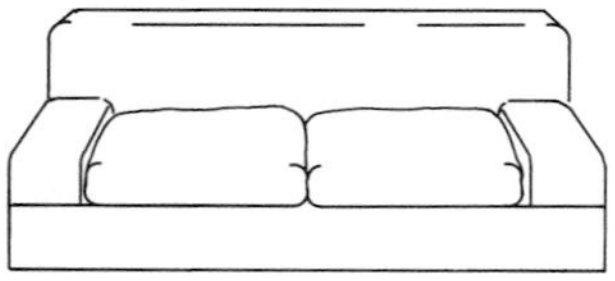

**SOFA**
W 82 ¾"
D 35 ½"
H 28 ¾"

**BED**
55" X 75"
ICF

**SOFA BED ( PULL OUT )**

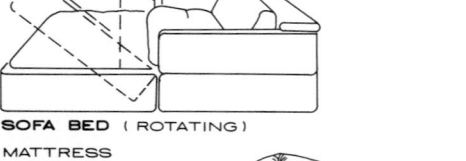

W 71½"
D 43½"
H 29½"
B 8 B AMERICA

**SOFA BED ( ROTATING)**

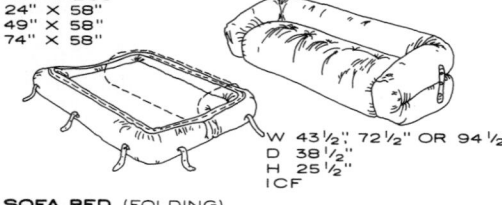

MATTRESS
24" X 58"
49" X 58"
74" X 58"

W 43½", 72½" OR 94½"
D 38½"
H 25½"
ICF

**SOFA BED (FOLDING)**
**BEDS**

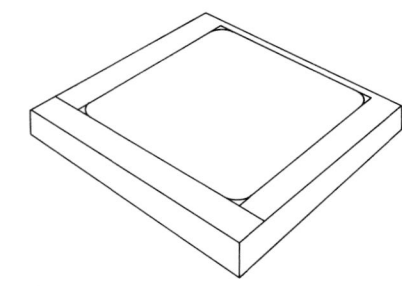

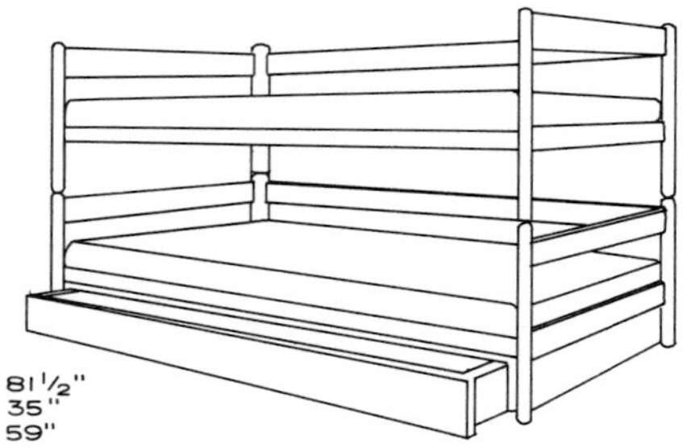

W 81½"
D 35"
H 59"

**ATELIER INTERNATIONAL, LTD.**
**BUNK AND TRUNDLE**

**WATER BED COMPONENTS**

A. Mattress pad
B. Water mattress
C. Safety liner for mattress
D. Heater
E. Base
F. Headboard
G. Side frame

**WATER BED**

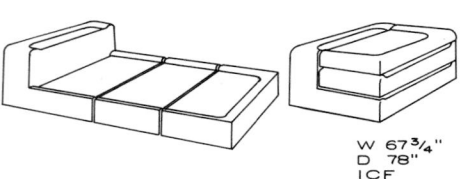

W 67¾"
D 78"
ICF

**SECTIONAL DOUBLE BED**

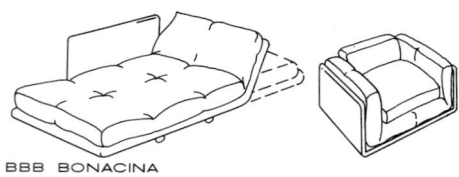

**BBB BONACINA**
**FOLDING ARMCHAIR BED**

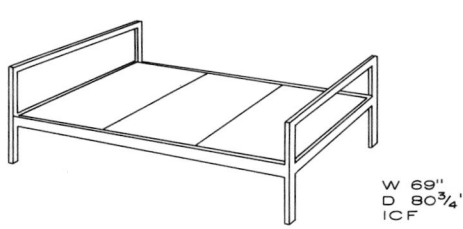

W 69"
D 80¾"
ICF

**BED FRAME**

**STANDARD MATTRESS SIZES**

| | |
|---|---|
| Bunk: | 30" x 75", 33" x 75" |
| Dormitory and hospital: | 36" x 75" & 80" |
| Twin: | 39" x 75", 80" & 84" |
| Double: | 54" x 75" |
| Queen: | 60" x 80" & 84" |
| King: | 76" x 80" & 84" |
| Revolving: | 24"D x 41"W |
| Foldout: | 15"D x 41"W |
| Water bed: | Size varies; Weight of water 62.4 PCF |
| Mattress Innerspring: | 5½"–6½"D |
| Foam: | 4"–7½"D |
| Box spring: | 5½"–9"D (varies with mattress— height to equal average) |

**PILLOW SIZES**

| | |
|---|---|
| Standard: | 26"L x 20"W |
| Queen: | 30"L x 20"W |
| King: | 36"L x 20"W |

W 25½"
L 51"
H 31½"

**THE CHILDREN'S WORKBENCH JUNIOR CRIB**

**STANDARD JUVENILE MATTRESS SIZES (IN.)**

| TYPE | LENGTH | WIDTH |
|---|---|---|
| Bassinet | 36 | 18 |
| Bassinet | 38¾ | 22¼ |
| Junior crib | 46 | 23 |
| Junior crib | 50¾ | 25¼ |
| 6-year crib | 51 | 27 |
| 6-year crib | 56¾ | 31¼ |
| Youth bed | 66 | 33 |
| Youth bed | 76 | 36 |

**FOLDING CHAIR BED**

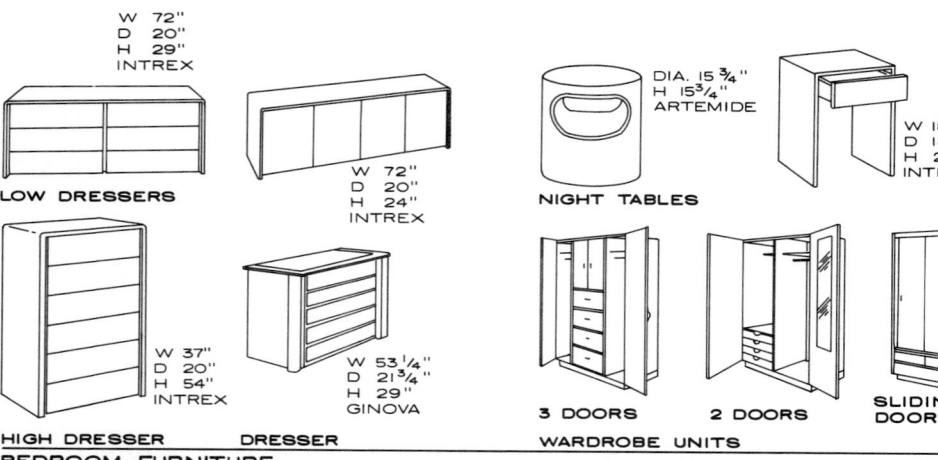

W 72"
D 20"
H 29"
INTREX

**LOW DRESSERS**

W 72"
D 20"
H 24"
INTREX

W 37"
D 20"
H 54"
INTREX

W 53¼"
D 21¾"
H 29"
GINOVA

**HIGH DRESSER**     **DRESSER**
**BEDROOM FURNITURE**

DIA. 15¾"
H 15¾"
ARTEMIDE

W 18"
D 18"
H 24"
INTREX

**NIGHT TABLES**

**3 DOORS**     **2 DOORS**     **SLIDING DOORS**
**WARDROBE UNITS**

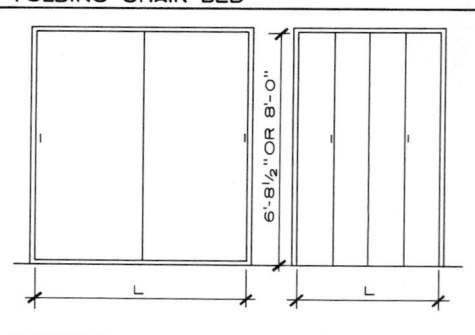

6'-8½" OR 8'-0"

2 PANELS
L 48", 60", 72",
84", 96"

3 PANELS
L 72", 108", 120",
132", 144"

2 PANELS
L 24", 30",
36"

4 PANELS
L 48", 60",
72"

**SLIDING**     **BIFOLD**
**MIRRORED CLOSET DOORS**

Associated Space Design, Inc.; Atlanta, Georgia

## RECTANGULAR

| WIDTH | LENGTH | APPROXIMATE SEATING |
|---|---|---|
| 5'-0" | 20'-0" | 20-22 |
| 4'-6" | 18'-0" | 18-20 |
| 4'-6" | 16'-0" | 16-18 |
| 4'-6" | 14'-0" | 14-16 |
| 4'-0" | 12'-0" | 12-14 |
| 4'-0" | 11'-0" | 10-12 |
| 4'-0" | 10'-0" | 10-12 |
| 4'-0" | 9'-0" | 8-10 |
| 4'-0" | 8'-0" | 8-10 |
| 3'-6" | 9'-0" | 8-10 |
| 3'-6" | 8'-0" | 8-10 |
| 3'-6" | 7'-6" | 6-8 |
| 3'-6" | 7'-0" | 6-8 |
| 3'-0" | 7'-0" | 6-8 |
| 3'-0" | 6'-6" | 6-8 |
| 2'-6" | 5'-6" | 4-6 |
| 2'-6" | 5'-0" | 4-6 |

## SQUARE

| WIDTH | LENGTH | APPROXIMATE SEATING |
|---|---|---|
| 5'-0" | 5'-0" | 8-12 |
| 4'-6" | 4'-6" | 4-8 |
| 4'-0" | 4'-0" | 4-8 |
| 3'-6" | 3'-6" | 4 |
| 3'-0" | 3'-0" | 4 |

## ROUND

| DIAMETER | CIRCUM-FERENCE | APPROXIMATE SEATING |
|---|---|---|
| 8'-0" | 25'-1" | 10-12 |
| 7'-0" | 21'-8" | 8-10 |
| 6'-0" | 18'-9" | 7-8 |
| 5'-0" | 15'-7" | 6-7 |
| 4'-6" | 14'-1" | 5-6 |
| 4'-0" | 12'-6" | 5-6 |
| 3'-6" | 11'-0" | 4-5 |

## BOAT SHAPED

| WIDTH | | LENGTH | APPROXIMATE SEATING |
|---|---|---|---|
| CENTER | END | | |
| 6'-0" | 4'-0" | 20'-0" | 20-24 |
| 5'-6" | 4'-0" | 18'-0" | 18-20 |
| 5'-6" | 4'-0" | 16'-0" | 16-18 |
| 5'-0" | 3'-6" | 14'-0" | 14-16 |
| 4'-6" | 3'-6" | 12'-0" | 12-14 |
| 4'-0" | 3'-2" | 11'-0" | 10-12 |
| 4'-0" | 3'-2" | 10'-0" | 10-12 |
| 3'-6" | 3'-0" | 9'-0" | 8-10 |
| 3'-6" | 3'-0" | 8'-0" | 8-10 |
| 3'-0" | 2'-10" | 7'-0" | 6-8 |
| 3'-0" | 2'-10" | 6'-0" | 6-8 |

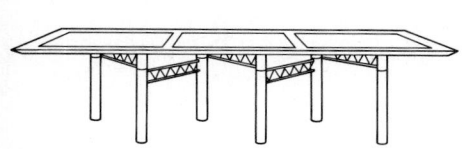

RECTANGLE 48" X 84", 96"
(EXPANDABLE 48" X 48")
MODULAR UNITS TO 280"
H 29"

**ZIPP TABLE**
**DESIGNER: RODNEY KINSMAN**
**DAVIS FURNITURE INDUSTRIES, INC.**

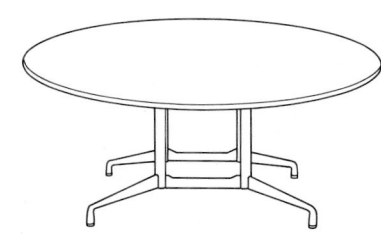

DIA 42"-72"
W 42"-54"
D 72"-144"
H 28½"

**SEGMENTED BASE TABLE**
**DESIGNER: CHARLES EAMES**
**HERMAN MILLER, INC.**

QUARTER CIRCLE: 168" O.D., 48" W
RECTANGULAR: 96" W, 48" D
H 29¼"

**OMEGA MODULAR TABLES**
**STENDIG INTERNATIONAL**

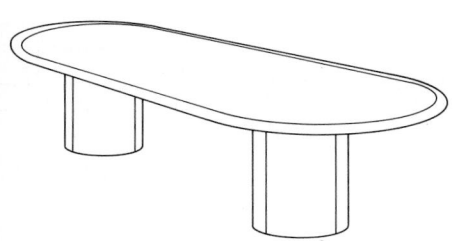

RECTANGULAR OR RADIUS END: 42" X 72" TO
60" X 240"
ROUND OR SQUARE 42"-72"

**CYLINDER BASE TABLES**
**MUELLER**

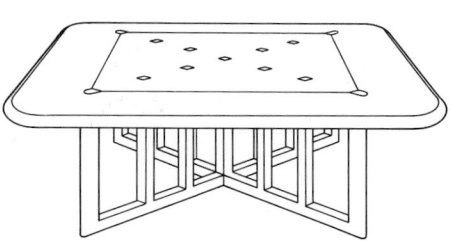

DIA. 36½"-74", SQUARE 31½"-71"
RECTANGULAR 44" X 68", 92", 116"
H 18" OR 28¼"

**DE MENIL TABLES**
**DESIGNER: GWATHMEY SIEGEL**
**ICF, INC.**

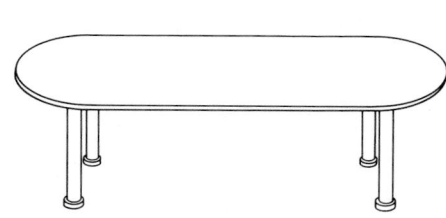

RECTANGULAR OR RADIUS END: 42" X 72" TO
48" X 192"
ROUND OR SQUARE 42", 48", 54"

**THE DONNELLY CONFERENCE TABLE**
**DESIGNER: PHILIP DONNELLY**
**JG FURNITURE SYSTEMS, INC.**

W 78"
D 48"
H 28"

**KNOLL TABLE DESK**
**DESIGNER: FLORENCE KNOLL**
**KNOLL INTERNATIONAL**

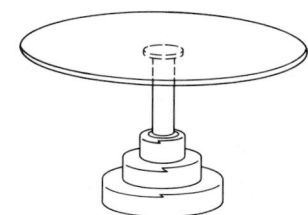

DIA. 24"-57"
SQUARE 39½"-57"
RECTANGLE 16" X 51", 59", 71"

**MENHIR TABLE CONNECTION**
**DESIGNERS: L. AKERBIS,**
**G. STOPPINO**
**ATELIER INTERNATIONAL**

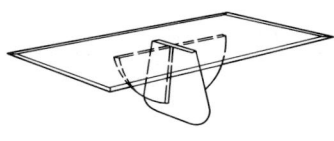

W 42", 48"
D 84", 96"
H 29"

**PINNACLE TABLE**
**DESIGNER: J. WADE BEAM**
**BRUETON**

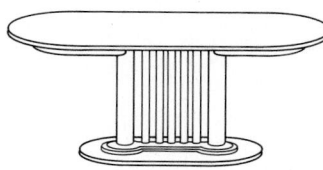

W 55"-75"
D 39½"
H 28½"

**WASHINGTON OVAL**
**EXTENSION TABLE**
**DESIGNER: OTTO BLÜMEL**
**STENDIG INTERNATIONAL, INC.**

Robert Staples; Staples & Charles Ltd; Washington, D.C.

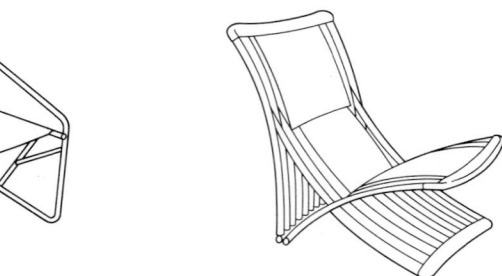

W  22½"
D  22½"
H  34½"
SH 17½"

**NOMAD DINING CHAIR
BROWN JORDAN**

W  24"
D  35"
H  34"
SH 11"

**STEAMER LOUNGE CHAIR
AMBIANT
KNOLL INTERNATIONAL**

W  17½"
D  16"
H  29½"
SH 16"

**STACKING RIO CHAIR
EMU/USA**

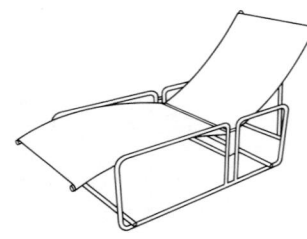

DIA. 8'-0", H 9'-0"
UMBRELLA
DIA. 42", H 28"

**TABLE
TRADEWINDS**

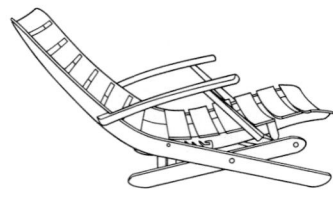

W  25"
D  64"
H  32"
SH 17"

**ADJUSTABLE CHAISE
BROWN JORDAN**

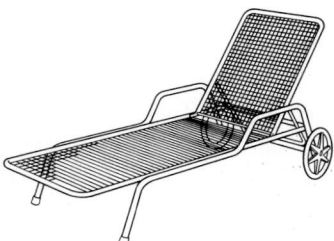

W  25"
D  29"
H  34"
SH 15"

**ADJUSTABLE ARMCHAIR
GROSFILLEX**

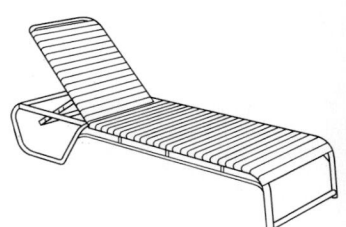

W  24½"
D  75½"
H  37½"
SH 10½"

**POOL BED LOUNGE
EMU/USA**

W  28"
D  82"
H  39"
SH 12"

**STACKABLE SUN LOUNGE
TRADEWINDS**

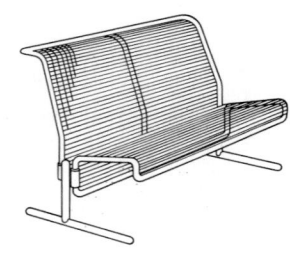

W  26"
D  27½"
H  25½"
SH 13½"

**KANTAN LOUNGE CHAIR
BROWN JORDAN**

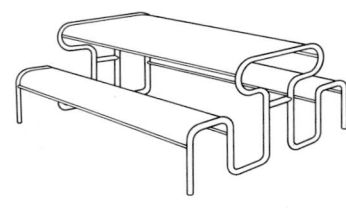

W  48¼"
D  31½"
H  29¾"
SH 17¾"

**TWO-SEAT PARK BENCH
KROIN INC.**

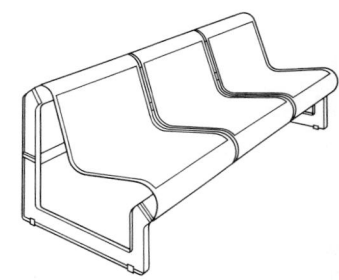

W  72"
D  62"
H  30"
SH 17"

**METAL PICNIC TABLE
FORMS AND SURFACES**

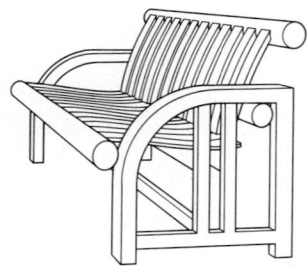

W  70"
D  31½"
H  28"
SH 16"

**LAGOS SEATING
ARTIFORT/KRUEGER**

W  55"
D  29"
H  33"
SH 17"

**GARDEN BENCH
SUMMIT FURNITURE INC.**

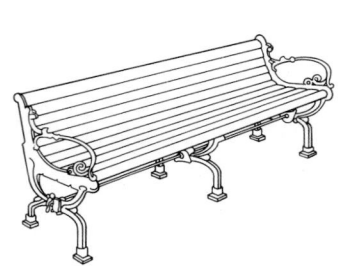

W  60"
D  23½"
H  43½"
SH 15½"

**LIVERPOOL BENCH
INTERNA DESIGNS, LTD.**

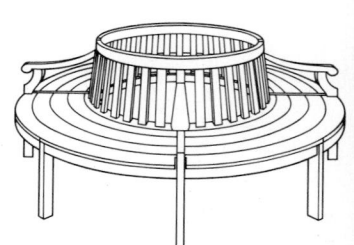

W  72"
D  23"
H  29"
SH 17"

**CHARLESTON BENCH
WOODCRAFTERS OF FLORIDA, INC.**

INSIDE DIA.    38"
OUTSIDE DIA. 76"
H                   36"
SH                 17"

**MONHEGAN TREE BENCH
WEATHEREND/IMAGINEERING, INC.**

Robert Staples; Staples & Charles Ltd; Washington, D.C.
Richard J. Vitullo; Washington Grove, Maryland

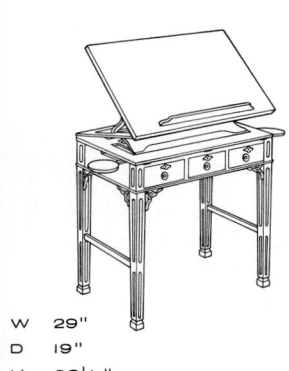

W 29"
D 19"
H 29½"

**ARCHITECT'S TABLE
CHIPPENDALE STYLE 1765
BAKER**

W 58"
D 28⅜"
H 29"

**DOUBLE PEDESTAL DESK
CHIPPENDALE STYLE 1760
BAKER**

W 75¾"
D 14½"
H 94½"

**BREAKFRONT
CHIPPENDALE STYLE
BAKER**

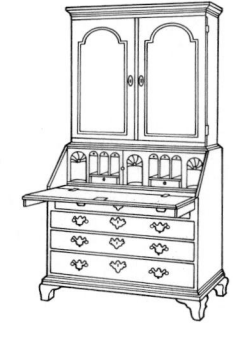

W 40"
D 24½"
H 82½"

**DESK BOOKCASE
HISTORIC NEWPORT STYLE
KITTINGER**

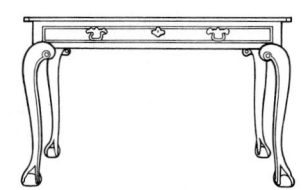

W 46"
D 24"
H 29"

**CENTER TABLE
GEORGE I STYLE 1720
BAKER**

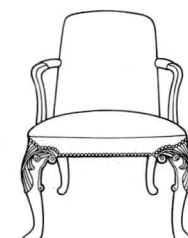

W 25"
D 24"
H 39"
SH 19"

**SHEPHERD'S CROOK ARMCHAIR
GEORGE I STYLE 1718
BAKER**

W 24"
D 22¾"
H 40½"
SH 19"

**OPEN ARMCHAIR
QUEEN ANNE STYLE
KITTINGER**

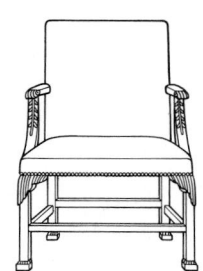

W 26"
D 25¾"
H 39¾"
SH 19"

**WENTWORTH ARMCHAIR
GEORGE II STYLE 1750
BAKER**

W 23¾"
D 22½"
H 45½"
SH 19"

**OPEN ARMCHAIR
CHIPPENDALE STYLE
KITTINGER**

W 26"
D 23½"
H 38⅜"
SH 19¼"

**OPEN ARMCHAIR
CHIPPENDALE STYLE 1750
BAKER**

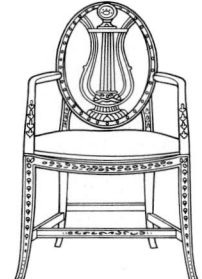

W 22"
D 20⅞"
H 34¼"
SH 19"

**OVAL AND LYRE BACK
ARMCHAIR
SHERATON STYLE 1780
BAKER**

W 21⅞"
D 22⅝"
H 33"
SH 19"

**ARMCHAIR
REGENCY STYLE
KITTINGER**

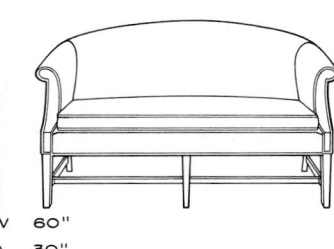

W 60"
D 30"
H 34½"
SH 19"

**LOVE SEAT
SHERIDAN / HEPPLEWHITE
STYLE
KITTINGER**

W 31"
D 28"
H 45½"
SH 19"

**WING CHAIR
CHIPPENDALE STYLE
KITTINGER**

W 33"
D 31½"
H 44"
SH 19"

**WING CHAIR
CHIPPENDALE STYLE
KITTINGER**

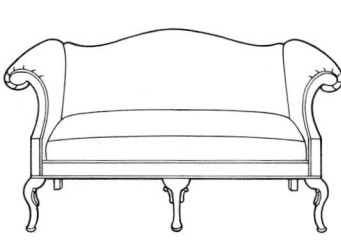

W 66"
D 32"
H 34"   SH 19"

**SETTEE
CHIPPENDALE STYLE
HICKORY BUSINESS
FURNITURE**

Robert Staples; Staples & Charles Ltd; Washington, D.C.
Eric J. Gastier; Darrel Downing Rippeteau Architects, PC; Washington, D.C.

W  18"
D  21"
H  34½"
SH 18"
CAFÉ DAUM CHAIR CIRCA 1849
DESIGNER: MICHAEL THONET
THONET

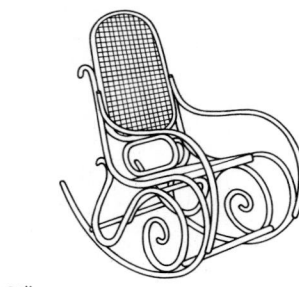

W  21"
D  40"
H  43"
SH 17"
BENTWOOD ROCKER 1860
DESIGNER: MICHAEL THONET
THONET

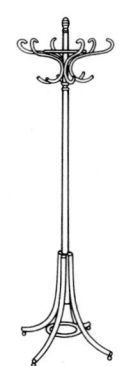
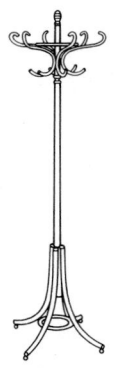

DIA. 23½"
H  76"
BENTWOOD COSTUMER
DESIGNER: MICHAEL THONET
THONET

W  21½"
D  22¼"
H  31"
SH 18½"
CORBUSIER CHAIR 1870
DESIGNER: MICHAEL THONET
THONET

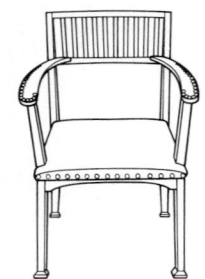

W  27"
D  23"
H  33"
SH 18"
ARMCHAIR CIRCA 1898
DESIGNER: OTTO WAGNER
THONET

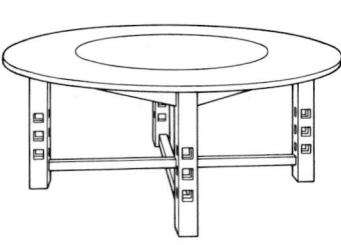

DIA. 75"
H  29"
GSA TABLE 1900
DESIGNER:
CHARLES R. MACKINTOSH
ATELIER INTERNATIONAL

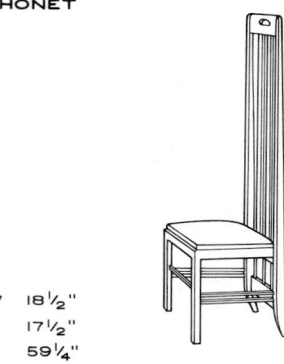
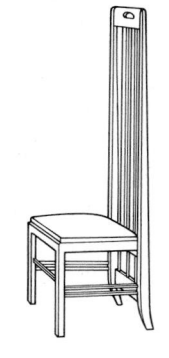

W  18½"
D  17½"
H  59¼"
SH 17½"
INGRAM HIGH CHAIR 1900
DESIGNER:
CHARLES R. MACKINTOSH
ATELIER INTERNATIONAL

W  67"
D  20"
H  63"
SIDEBOARD, 2 1918
DESIGNER:
CHARLES R. MACKINTOSH
ATELIER INTERNATIONAL

W  19½"
D  18"
H  30½"
FLEDERMAUS CHAIR 1905
DESIGNER: JOSEF HOFFMANN
ICF, INC.

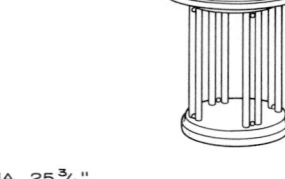

DIA. 25¾"
H  25⅜"
FLEDERMAUS TABLE 1905
DESIGNER: JOSEF HOFFMANN
ICF, INC.

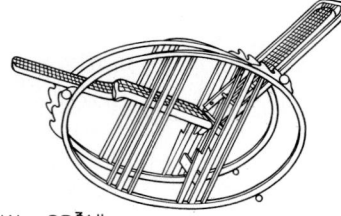

W  28¾"
D  50½"
H  45½"
SH 18"
ROCKING CHAIR 1905
DESIGNER: JOSEF HOFFMANN
ICF, INC.

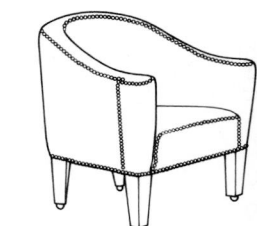

W  31"
D  28½"
H  30¾"
SH 16½"
VILLA GALLIA ARMCHAIR 1913
DESIGNER: JOSEF HOFFMANN
ICF, INC.

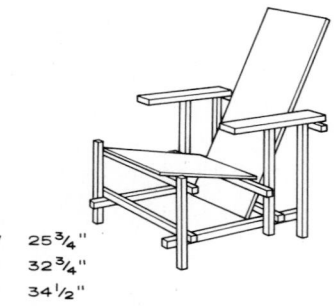

W  25¾"
D  32¾"
H  34½"
SH 13"
RED AND BLUE LOUNGE
CHAIR 1917
DESIGNER: GERRIT RIETVELD
ATELIER INTERNATIONAL

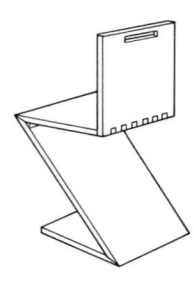

W  14½"
D  17"
H  29"
SH 17"
ZIG ZAG CHAIR 1934
DESIGNER: GERRIT RIETVELD
ATELIER INTERNATIONAL

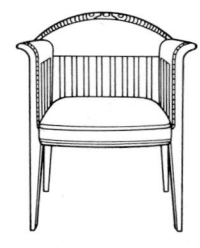

W  26¾"
D  21¼"
H  33"
SH 17¾"
WHITE CHAIR CIRCA 1910
DESIGNER: ELIEL SAARINEN
ICF, INC.

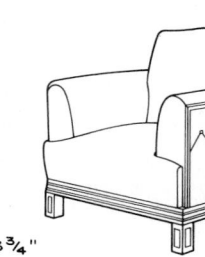

W  33¾"
D  30½"
H  35½"
SH 17¾"
SAARINEN HOUSE LOUNGE
CHAIR 1929/30
DESIGNER: ELIEL SAARINEN
ARKITEKTURA

Robert Staples; Staples & Charles Ltd; Washington, D.C.
Eric J. Gastier; Darrel Downing Rippeteau Architects, PC; Washington, D.C.

**12** **CLASSIC FURNISHINGS**

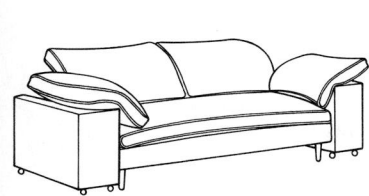

W   94½"
D   35½"
H   34½"
SH  17"
LOTA SOFA 1924
DESIGNER: EILEEN GRAY
PALAZZETTI

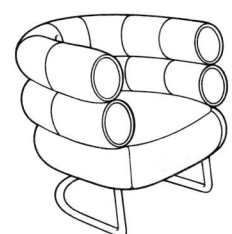

W   35½"
D   32½"
H   29"
SH  16"
POLTRONA ARMCHAIR 1927
DESIGNER: EILEEN GRAY
PALAZZETTI

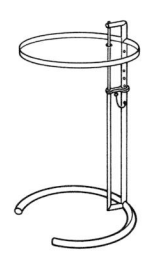

DIA. 20"
H   21" – 36"
ADJUSTABLE HEIGHT TABLE 1927
DESIGNER: EILEEN GRAY
STENDIG INC.

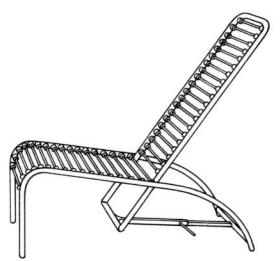

W   21¾"
D   33¾"
H   35¾"
SH  13¼"
LOUNGE CHAIR CIRCA 1920
DESIGNER: RENÉ HERBST
JG FURNITURE SYSTEMS

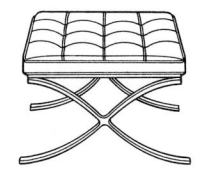

W   23"
D   22"
H   14½"
BARCELONA STOOL 1929
DESIGNER: MIES VAN DER ROHE
KNOLL INTERNATIONAL

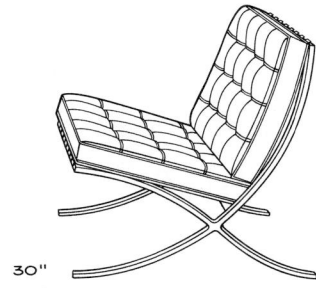

W   30"
D   30"
H   30"
SH  17"
BARCELONA CHAIR 1929
DESIGNER: MIES VAN DER ROHE
KNOLL INTERNATIONAL

W   40"
D   40"
H   17"
BARCELONA TABLE 1929
DESIGNER: MIES VAN DER ROHE
KNOLL INTERNATIONAL

W   18"
D   23"
H   31½"
SH  17"
BRNO ARMCHAIR 1929
DESIGNER: MIES VAN DER ROHE
PALAZZETTI

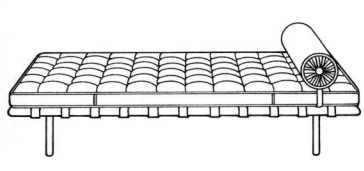

W   78"
D   39"
H   15½"
MIES COUCH
DESIGNER: MIES VAN DER ROHE
KNOLL INTERNATIONAL

W   23⅝"
D   47¼"
H   37½"
CHAISE LOUNGE 1931
DESIGNER: MIES VAN DER ROHE
KNOLL INTERNATIONAL

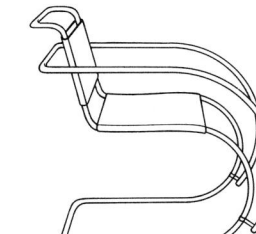

W   21¾"
D   32¼"
H   32¼"
SH  17¼"
MR. CHAIR 1927
DESIGNER: MIES VAN DER ROHE
STENDIG INC.

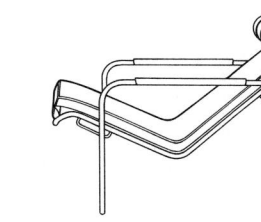

W   21½"
D   43"
H   30"
GENNI LOUNGE CHAIR 1935
DESIGNER: GABRIELE MUCCHI
ICF INC.

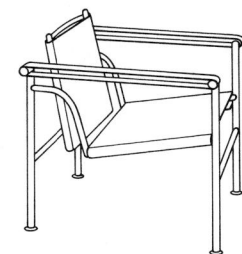

W   23⅝"
D   25⅝"
H   25¼"
SH  15¾"
LC 1 SLING CHAIR 1928
DESIGNER: LE CORBUSIER
ATELIER INTERNATIONAL

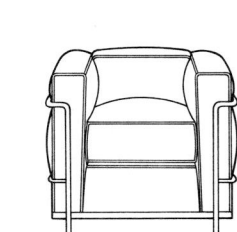

W   30"
D   27½"
H   26½"
SH  17"
LC 2 ARM CHAIR 1929
DESIGNER: LE CORBUSIER
ATELIER INTERNATIONAL

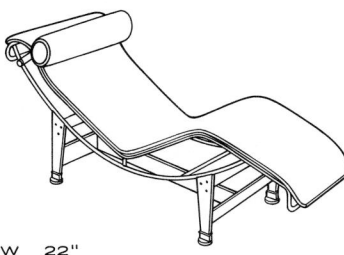

W   22"
D   63"
LC 4 CHAISE LOUNGE 1928
DESIGNER: LE CORBUSIER
ATELIER INTERNATIONAL

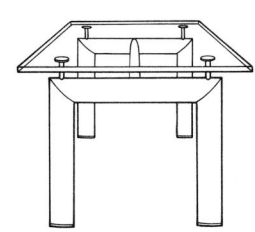

W   90"
D   35½"
H   27" – 29"
LC 6 TABLE 1925 – 28
DESIGNER: LE CORBUSIER
ATELIER INTERNATIONAL

Robert Staples; Staples & Charles Ltd; Washington, D.C.
Eric J. Gastier; Darrel Downing Rippeteau Architects, PC; Washington, D.C.

W 22⅝"
D 21⅝"
H 31¾"
SH 18¼"

CESCA ARM CHAIR 1928
DESIGNER: MARCEL BREUER
KNOLL INTERNATIONAL

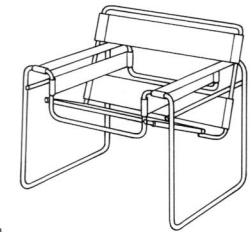

W 30¾"
D 27"
H 28½"
SH 17"

WASSILY CHAIR 1925
DESIGNER: MARCEL BREUER
KNOLL INTERNATIONAL

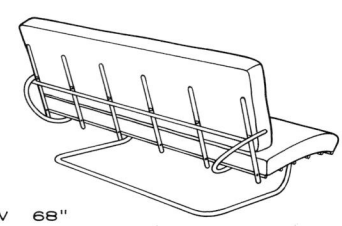

W 68"
D 32"
H 34"
SH 16¾"

SOFA 1931
DESIGNER: MARCEL BREUER
GLOBAL FURNITURE

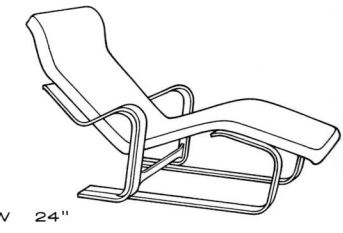

W 24"
D 51"
H 33"

LONG CHAIR 1935/36
DESIGNER: MARCEL BREUER
PALAZZETTI

W 25½"
D 31½"
H 32½"
SH 14½"

BREUER LOUNGE CHAIR 1928
DESIGNER: MARCEL BREUER
ICF, INC.

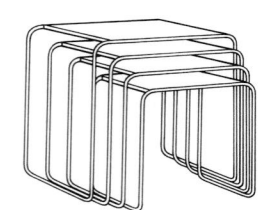

W 26"
D 20"
H 24"

NESTING TABLES 1925
DESIGNER: MARCEL BREUER
THONET

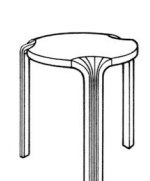

DIA. 15"
H 17¾"

FAN-LEGGED TABLE 1954
DESIGNER: ALVAR AALTO
ICF, INC.

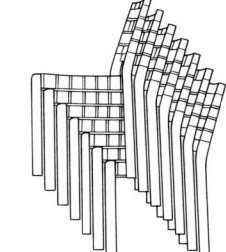

W 19"
D 19¼"
H 31½"
SH 17¾"

STACK CHAIR 1930
DESIGNER: ALVAR AALTO
ICF, INC.

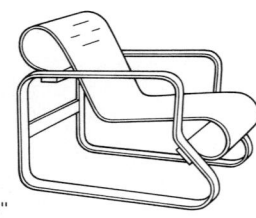

W 23½"
D 31½"
H 25"
SH 13"

"PAIMIO" CHAIR 1930-33
DESIGNER: ALVAR AALTO
PALAZZETTI

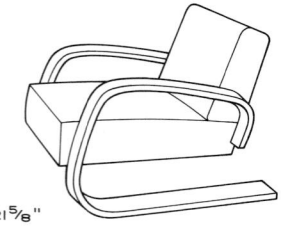

W 21⅝"
D 30¼"
H 25⅝"
SH 14½"

LOUNGE CHAIR 1935
DESIGNER: ALVAR AALTO
ICF, INC.

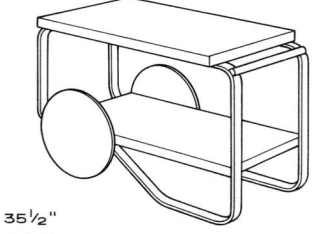

W 35½"
D 19¾"
H 22¼"

TEA TROLLEY 1936/37
DESIGNER: ALVAR AALTO
ICF, INC.

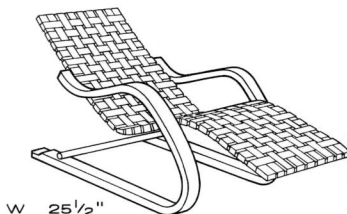

W 25½"
D 63½"
H 26"
SH 10"

CHAISE LOUNGE 1936
DESIGNER: ALVAR AALTO
ICF, INC.

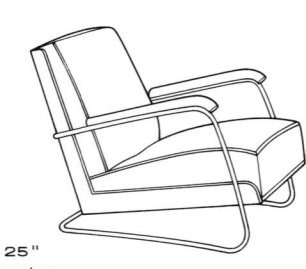

W 25"
D 33¼"
H 31¼"
SH 17¼"

LOUNGE CHAIR 1932-34
DESIGNER: PAULI BLOMSTED
ARKITEKTURA

W 16"
D 18"
H 35"
SH 18"

MIDWAY CHAIR 1914
DESIGNER:
FRANK LLOYD WRIGHT
ATELIER INTERNATIONAL

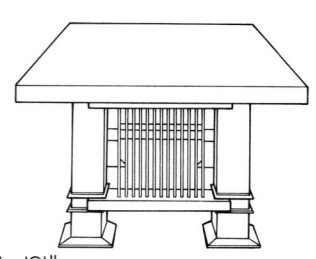

W 101"
D 42"
H 28"

ALLEN TABLE 1917
DESIGNER:
FRANK LLOYD WRIGHT
ATELIER INTERNATIONAL

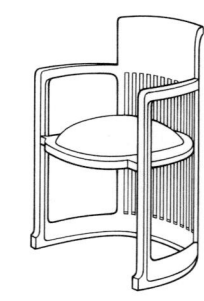

W 21½"
D 22"
H 32"
SH 19½"

BARREL CHAIR 1937
DESIGNER:
FRANK LLOYD WRIGHT
ATELIER INTERNATIONAL

Robert Staples; Staples & Charles Ltd; Washington, D.C.
Eric J. Gastier; Darrel Downing Rippeteau Architects, PC; Washington, D.C.

**12** **CLASSIC FURNISHINGS**

W   25½"
D   20"
H   16"

**OTTOMAN 1948**
**DESIGNER: EERO SAARINEN**
**KNOLL INTERNATIONAL**

W   40"
D   34"
H   35½"
SH  16"

**WOMB CHAIR 1948**
**DESIGNER: EERO SAARINEN**
**KNOLL INTERNATIONAL**

W   26"
D   23½"
H   32"
SH  18½"

**ARMCHAIR 1956**
**DESIGNER: EERO SAARINEN**
**KNOLL INTERNATIONAL**

W   78"
D   48"
H   28½"

**OVAL TABLE 1956**
**DESIGNER: EERO SAARINEN**
**KNOLL INTERNATIONAL**

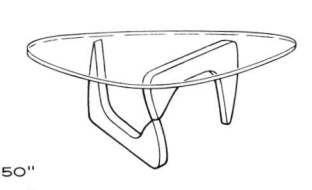

W   50"
D   36"
H   15¾"

**NOGUCHI TABLE 1950**
**DESIGNER: ISAMU NOGUCHI**
**HERMAN MILLER, INC.**

W   33¾"
D   28"
H   30½"
SH  17"

**DIAMOND CHAIR 1952**
**DESIGNER: HARRY BERTOIA**
**KNOLL INTERNATIONAL**

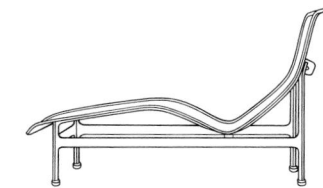

W   24½"
D   58"
H   33¾"
SH  13"

**CONTOUR CHAISE LOUNGE**
**DESIGNER: RICHARD SCHULTZ**
**ICF, INC.**

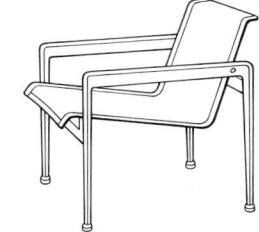

W   26"
D   28¼"
H   26½"
SH  14"

**LOUNGE CHAIR 1966**
**DESIGNER: RICHARD SCHULTZ**
**KNOLL INTERNATIONAL**

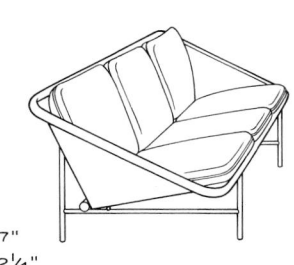

W   87"
D   32¼"
H   29¾"

**SLING SOFA 1964**
**DESIGNER: GEORGE NELSON**
**HERMAN MILLER, INC.**

W   21½"
D   19½"
H   29⅜"
SH  18"

**MOLDED PLYWOOD CHAIR 1946**
**DESIGNER: CHARLES EAMES**
**HERMAN MILLER, INC.**

W   25"
D   25½"
H   31"
SH  17⅝"

**MOLDED FIBERGLASS CHAIR 1949**
**DESIGNER: CHARLES EAMES**
**HERMAN MILLER, INC.**

W   72½"
D   30"
H   35"
SH  16"

**COMPACT SOFA 1952**
**DESIGNER: CHARLES EAMES**
**HERMAN MILLER, INC.**

W   32½"
D   32¾"
H   33½"
SH  15"

**LOUNGE CHAIR 1956**
**DESIGNER: CHARLES EAMES**
**HERMAN MILLER, INC.**

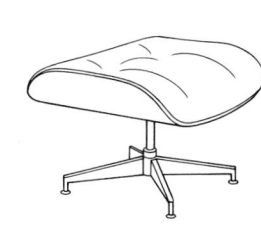

W   26"
D   21"
H   15"

**OTTOMAN 1956**
**DESIGNER: CHARLES EAMES**
**HERMAN MILLER, INC.**

W   28½"
D   24¾"
H   33¾"
SH  17½"

**ALUMINUM GROUP LOUNGE 1958**
**DESIGNER: CHARLES EAMES**
**HERMAN MILLER, INC.**

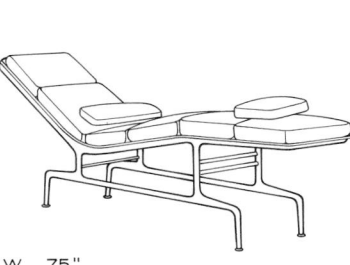

W   75"
D   17½"
H   28¾"
SH  20½"

**CHAISE LOUNGE 1968**
**DESIGNER: CHARLES EAMES**
**HERMAN MILLER, INC.**

Robert Staples; Staples & Charles Ltd; Washington, D.C.
Eric J. Gastier; Darrel Downing Rippeteau Architects, PC; Washington, D.C.

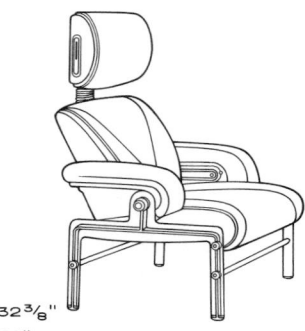

W  32³⁄₈"
D  34"
H  43½"
SH 16³⁄₄"

JEFFERSON CHAIR 1986
DESIGNER: NIELS DIFFRIENT
SUNARHAUSERMAN

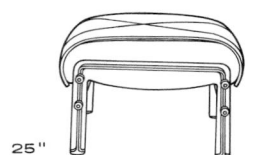

W  25"
D  24"
H  17½"

OTTOMAN 1986
DESIGNER: NIELS DIFFRIENT
SUNARHAUSERMAN

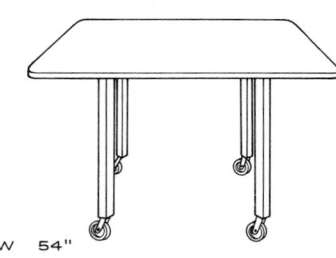

W  54"
D  54"
H  27½"

SQUARE TABLE
DESIGNER: JOSEPH PAUL D'URSO
KNOLL INTERNATIONAL

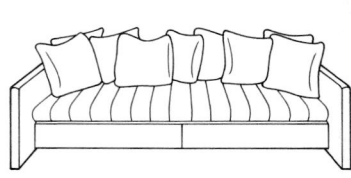

W  96"
D  48"
H  24"
SH 15½"

LARGE SOFA
DESIGNER: JOSEPH PAUL D'URSO
KNOLL INTERNATIONAL

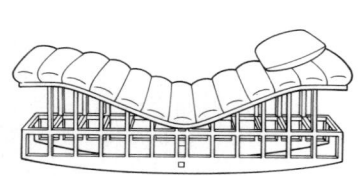

W  72"
D  27½"
H  25⅛"

CHAISE LOUNGE 1982
DESIGNER: RICHARD MEIER
KNOLL INTERNATIONAL

W  21"
D  20"
H  27½"
SH 17½"

CHAIR 1982
DESIGNER: RICHARD MEIER
KNOLL INTERNATIONAL

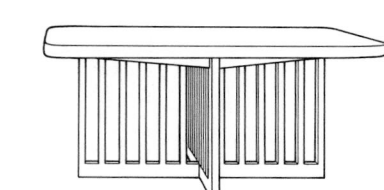

W  60"
D  60"
H  27½"

TABLE 1982
DESIGNER: RICHARD MEIER
KNOLL INTERNATIONAL

W  72"
D  36"
H  32"

CORNELIUS SOFA 1986
DESIGNER: CARLO SANTI
AXIOM DESIGNS

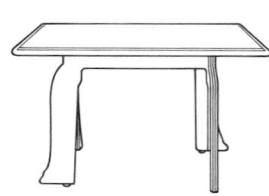

W  48"
D  48"
H  28½"

CABRIOLE LEG TABLE 1984
DESIGNER: ROBERT VENTURI
KNOLL INTERNATIONAL

W  26½"
D  23½"
H  38½"
SH 17½"

QUEEN ANNE CHAIR 1984
DESIGNER: ROBERT VENTURI
KNOLL INTERNATIONAL

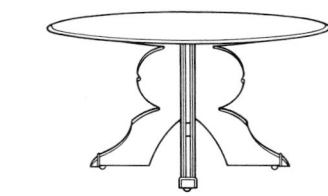

DIA. 60"
H  28½"

URN TABLE 1984
DESIGNER: ROBERT VENTURI
KNOLL INTERNATIONAL

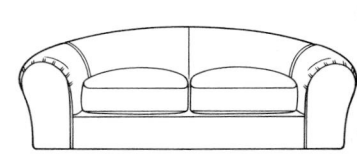

W  87"
D  43½"
H  33³⁄₄"
SH 20"

SOFA 1984
DESIGNER: ROBERT VENTURI
KNOLL INTERNATIONAL

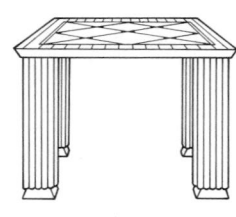

W  40½"
D  40½"
H  29"

TABLE 1982
DESIGNER: MICHAEL GRAVES
SUNARHAUSERMAN

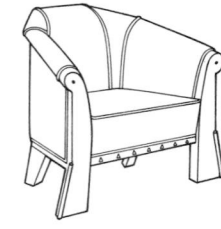

W  32"
D  29"
H  29"

LOUNGE CHAIR 1982
DESIGNER: MICHAEL GRAVES
SUNARHAUSERMAN

DIA. 48"
H  29¼"

TABLE 1986
DESIGNER: MICHAEL McCOY
ARKITEKTURA

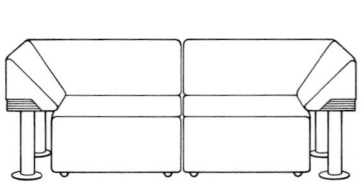

W  74"
D  32"
H  26½"
SH 13½"

QUADRIO SOFA
DESIGNER: MICHAEL McCOY
KRUEGER INTERNATIONAL DIV.

Robert Staples; Staples & Charles Ltd; Washington, D.C.
Eric J. Gastier; Darrel Downing Rippeteau Architects, PC; Washington, D.C.

# CHAPTER 13

## Special Construction

## GENERAL NOTES

The computer-based monitoring and control system (MCS) has many functions: monitoring HVAC and electrical systems, supervisory and intervention control of those systems, energy management and control (EMCS), direct digital control (DDC), fire/security/telecommunications monitoring and control, maintenance scheduling and control, data analysis and report generation, and general building management.

## SYSTEM ELEMENTS

The central console includes the computer, a hard disk for data storage, and the operator–machine interface. Mass storage is typically a 10 megabyte hard disk. The operator–machine interface includes a CRT, a printer, and a keyboard.

The communication link is a coaxial cable or a "twisted pair" of wires. Communication over long distances is usually by telephone lines; modems are used to interface to phone lines. Fiber optics is the newest development in communication; signals are conveyed by light rays rather than electrical impulses.

The field interface device (FID) provides the connection between the MCS and the local loop controls. Intelligent FIDs (IFIDs) can do most of the functions formerly done by the central computer, including intervention control. This cuts down on traffic on the communication link, allowing faster monitoring of error and alarm conditions. If the IFID fails, the local loop devices will continue to function under the "last command" criteria.

A direct digital controller (DDC) takes the place of the controllers in the local loop systems. It can also function as an IFID in interfacing to the MCS. If the DDC fails, the local system will not operate. Local loop controls are those devices contiguous with and used in automatic control of HVAC and electrical systems. This includes DDC, if used. Software includes the programs necessary for correct operation of the computer system.

## ENERGY CONSERVATION

A major factor in economic justification of the MCS is energy conservation. The best available data indicate that the MCS, in itself, may be responsible for a 10% energy savings. Additional savings are realized from upgrading existing systems and controls, improvements in control strategies, and improvements in the operator's understanding of the systems.

## RETROFITTING

Before installing an MCS in an existing building, it is always necessary to retrofit and upgrade the existing systems and controls.

## STAFFING AND TRAINING

A competent, well-trained staff is essential for proper operation of the MCS. Additional skilled personnel or upgrading of existing personnel to a higher skill level will be required to obtain maximum benefit from the MCS. Therefore, personnel costs will be higher, and the owner should be made aware of this.

## SPACE REQUIREMENTS

The central console and operator's station requires a 3 by 6 ft desk, a printer stand with paper storage, a four-drawer file cabinet, and a chair. No special environment is needed beyond that normally required for comfort.

## SECURITY/FIRE/TELECOMMUNICATIONS

For reliability and to meet code requirements, it is preferable that security, fire, and telecommunications systems have their own computers and be separate from the MCS serving the HVAC and electrical systems. The several systems should be linked for communication, to trade data, and carry out such coordinated functions as smoke control.

## ADAPTIVE AND INTELLIGENT CONTROLS

The use of "adaptive" and "intelligent" software systems should increase the energy conservation capability of computerized systems as well as improve overall control and decision making. Adaptive control programs allow the system to continually readjust parameters, especially controller gains, to match changing load conditions.

Roger W. Haines, PE; Laguna Hills, California

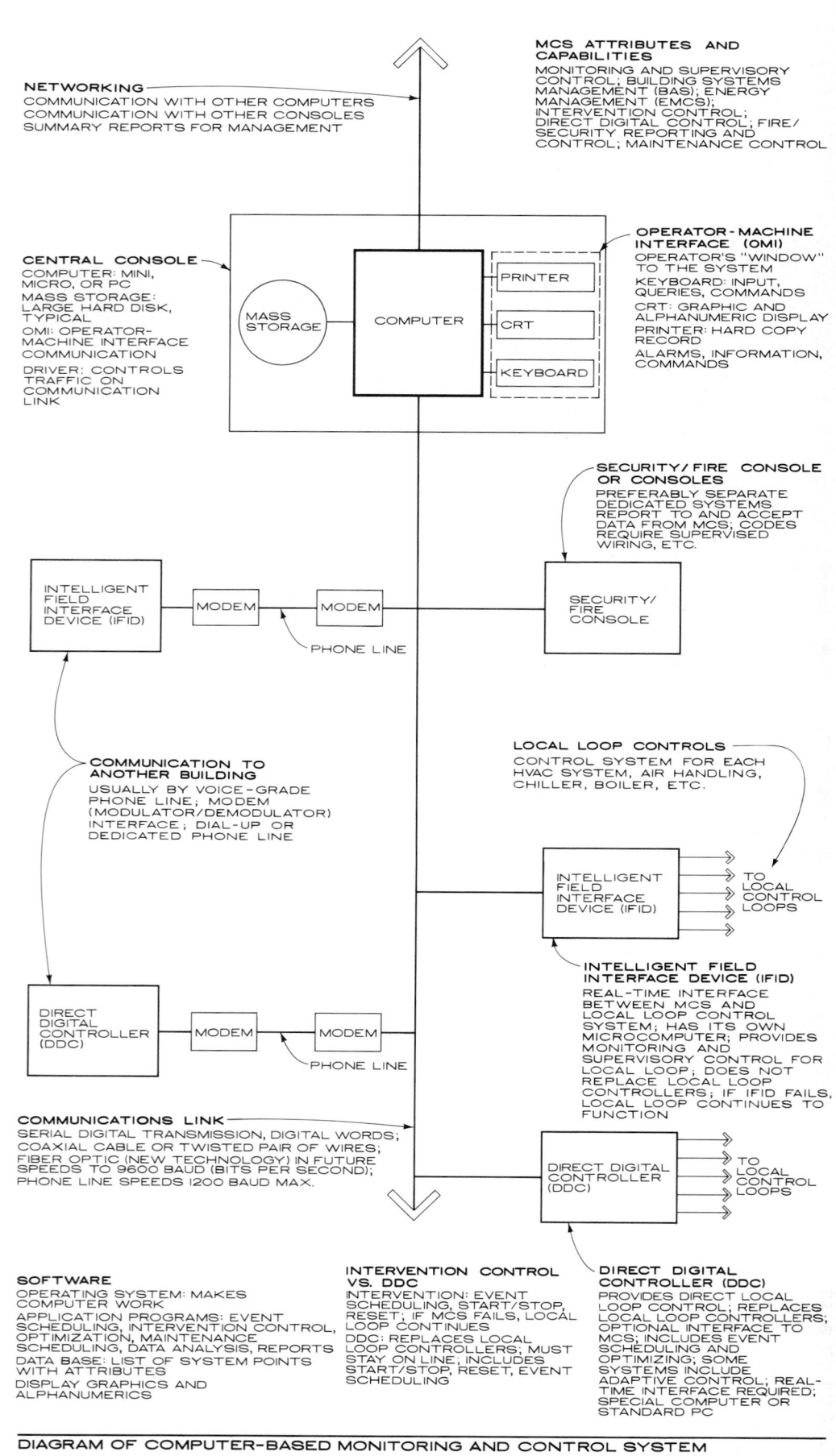

**NETWORKING**
COMMUNICATION WITH OTHER COMPUTERS
COMMUNICATION WITH OTHER CONSOLES
SUMMARY REPORTS FOR MANAGEMENT

**MCS ATTRIBUTES AND CAPABILITIES**
MONITORING AND SUPERVISORY CONTROL; BUILDING SYSTEMS MANAGEMENT (BAS); ENERGY MANAGEMENT (EMCS); INTERVENTION CONTROL; DIRECT DIGITAL CONTROL; FIRE/ SECURITY REPORTING AND CONTROL; MAINTENANCE CONTROL

**CENTRAL CONSOLE**
COMPUTER: MINI, MICRO, OR PC
MASS STORAGE: LARGE HARD DISK, TYPICAL
OMI: OPERATOR-MACHINE INTERFACE COMMUNICATION
DRIVER: CONTROLS TRAFFIC ON COMMUNICATION LINK

MASS STORAGE | COMPUTER | PRINTER | CRT | KEYBOARD

**OPERATOR-MACHINE INTERFACE (OMI)**
OPERATOR'S "WINDOW" TO THE SYSTEM
KEYBOARD: INPUT, QUERIES, COMMANDS
CRT: GRAPHIC AND ALPHANUMERIC DISPLAY
PRINTER: HARD COPY RECORD
ALARMS, INFORMATION, COMMANDS

**SECURITY/ FIRE CONSOLE OR CONSOLES**
PREFERABLY SEPARATE DEDICATED SYSTEMS REPORT TO AND ACCEPT DATA FROM MCS; CODES REQUIRE SUPERVISED WIRING, ETC.

INTELLIGENT FIELD INTERFACE DEVICE (IFID) — MODEM — MODEM — SECURITY/ FIRE CONSOLE
PHONE LINE

**COMMUNICATION TO ANOTHER BUILDING**
USUALLY BY VOICE-GRADE PHONE LINE; MODEM (MODULATOR/DEMODULATOR) INTERFACE; DIAL-UP OR DEDICATED PHONE LINE

**LOCAL LOOP CONTROLS**
CONTROL SYSTEM FOR EACH HVAC SYSTEM, AIR HANDLING, CHILLER, BOILER, ETC.

DIRECT DIGITAL CONTROLLER (DDC) — MODEM — MODEM
PHONE LINE

INTELLIGENT FIELD INTERFACE DEVICE (IFID) — TO LOCAL CONTROL LOOPS

**INTELLIGENT FIELD INTERFACE DEVICE (IFID)**
REAL-TIME INTERFACE BETWEEN MCS AND LOCAL LOOP CONTROL SYSTEM; HAS ITS OWN MICROCOMPUTER; PROVIDES MONITORING AND SUPERVISORY CONTROL FOR LOCAL LOOP; DOES NOT REPLACE LOCAL LOOP CONTROLLERS; IF IFID FAILS, LOCAL LOOP CONTINUES TO FUNCTION

**COMMUNICATIONS LINK**
SERIAL DIGITAL TRANSMISSION, DIGITAL WORDS; COAXIAL CABLE OR TWISTED PAIR OF WIRES; FIBER OPTIC (NEW TECHNOLOGY) IN FUTURE SPEEDS TO 9600 BAUD (BITS PER SECOND); PHONE LINE SPEEDS 1200 BAUD MAX.

DIRECT DIGITAL CONTROLLER (DDC) — TO LOCAL CONTROL LOOPS

**SOFTWARE**
OPERATING SYSTEM: MAKES COMPUTER WORK
APPLICATION PROGRAMS: EVENT SCHEDULING, INTERVENTION CONTROL, OPTIMIZATION, MAINTENANCE SCHEDULING, DATA ANALYSIS, REPORTS
DATA BASE: LIST OF SYSTEM POINTS WITH ATTRIBUTES
DISPLAY GRAPHICS AND ALPHANUMERICS

**INTERVENTION CONTROL VS. DDC**
INTERVENTION: EVENT SCHEDULING, START/STOP, RESET; IF MCS FAILS, LOCAL LOOP CONTINUES
DDC: REPLACES LOCAL LOOP CONTROLLERS; MUST STAY ON LINE; INCLUDES START/STOP, RESET, EVENT SCHEDULING

**DIRECT DIGITAL CONTROLLER (DDC)**
PROVIDES DIRECT LOCAL LOOP CONTROL; REPLACES LOCAL LOOP CONTROLLERS; OPTIONAL INTERFACE TO MCS; INCLUDES EVENT SCHEDULING AND OPTIMIZING; SOME SYSTEMS INCLUDE ADAPTIVE CONTROL; REAL-TIME INTERFACE REQUIRED; SPECIAL COMPUTER OR STANDARD PC

**DIAGRAM OF COMPUTER-BASED MONITORING AND CONTROL SYSTEM**

## GENERAL INFORMATION

Most air structures are primarily designed to resist wind loads. Mechanical blowers must maintain 3 to 5 psf pressure inside the structure at all times. Architectural elements of the building must be detailed to avoid loss of air pressure. Normal entering and exiting should be through revolving doors, while emergency exiting is provided through pressure balanced doors, and vehicles pass through air locks. Avoid using interior furnishings that could possibly puncture the structural membrane. Automatic auxiliary fans should be activated in the event of a pressure drop due to primary power failure.

The structural membrane is usually a nylon, fiberglass, or polyester fabric coated with polyvinyl chloride. Such skins have a life span from 7 to 10 years, and provide fire retardation that passes NFPA 701. A urethane topcoat will reduce dirt adhesion and improve service life. New Teflon coated fiberglass membranes have a life expectancy of more than 25 years. This material is incombustible, passing NFPA 70, with flame spread rating = 10, smoke developed = 50, and fuel contributed = 10. An acoustical liner (NCR = 0.65) is also available.

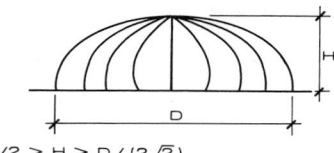

$$D/2 > H > D/(2\sqrt{2})$$

| SPAN LIMITATIONS | VAULT | DOME |
|---|---|---|
| Without cables | D = 120' – 0'' | D = 150' – 0'' |
| With cables | D = 400' – 0'' | D = 600' – 0'' |

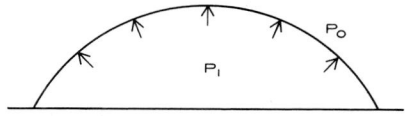

SINGLE MEMBRANE    $P_1 > P_0$

This is the most common type of air structure. The internal pressure ($P_1$) is kept approximately 0.03 psi above the external atmospheric pressure ($P_0$). It is this pressure difference that keeps the dome inflated.

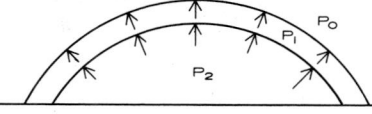

DOUBLE MEMBRANE    $P_2 > P_1 > P_0$

The airspace between the two membranes is used for insulation and security. If the outer skin is punctured the inner skin will remain standing. Both single and double membrane air structures require the constant use of blowers to keep them inflated.

**AIR SUPPORTED**

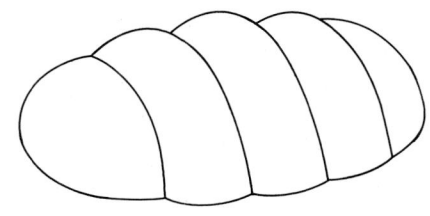

VAULT

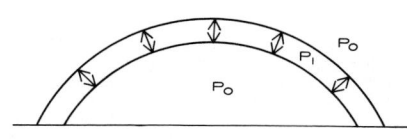

DUAL MEMBRANE    $P_1 > P_0$

Here the internal and external pressures are the same. Only the area between the skins is pressurized. The inflated area of a dual membrane structure can be sealed, thus eliminating the need for constant use of blowers.

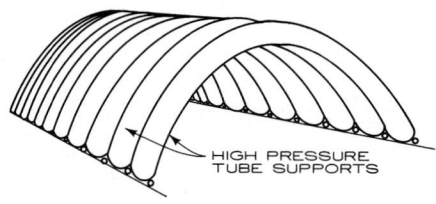

HIGH PRESSURE TUBE SUPPORTS

**AIR INFLATED**

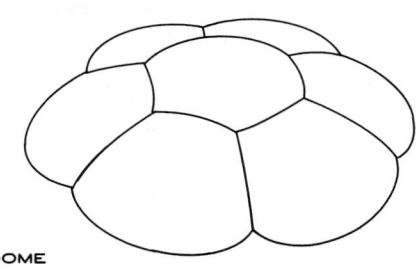

DOME

## BASIC CONFIGURATIONS

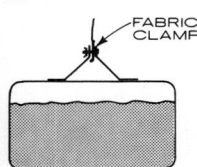

WATER TANK

FABRIC CLAMP

SAND BAGS

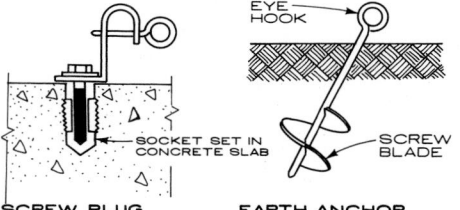

SCREW PLUG

EYE HOOK

SOCKET SET IN CONCRETE SLAB

SCREW BLADE

EARTH ANCHOR

C-PROFILE

MEMBRANE

STRADDLING DOWEL

CABLE

GRADE BEAM

ROD SET IN CONCRETE PIER

ANGLE CLAMP

## ANCHORAGE DETAILS

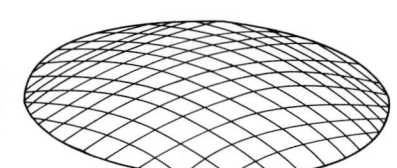

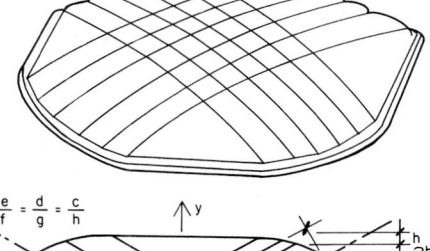

FABRIC CLAMP

COMPRESSION RING

CABLE SOCKET

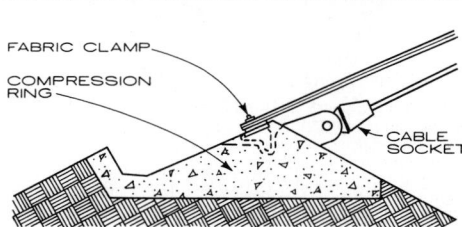

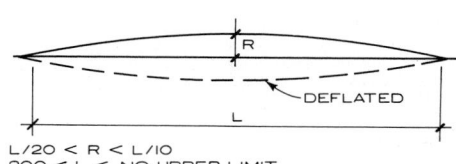

R

DEFLATED

L

L/20 < R < L/10
200 < L < NO UPPER LIMIT

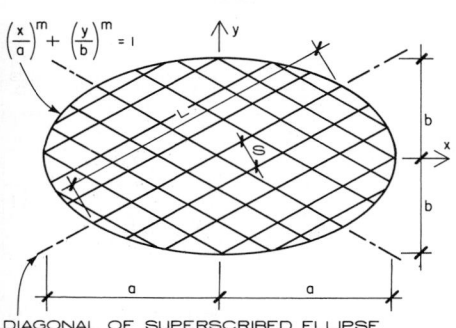

$$\left(\frac{x}{a}\right)^m + \left(\frac{y}{b}\right)^m = 1$$

DIAGONAL OF SUPERSCRIBED ELLIPSE
MAXIMUM CABLE SPACING = 50'-0''

**SUPERELLIPSE PLAN**

**KEY TO NOTATIONS**
a/b—One half of major/minor axes of superellipse.
s—Cable spacing.
L—Length of cable along diagonal of superscribed rectangle of proportions 2a and 2b.
e/f—One half of major/minor axes of superscribed

**LONG SPAN STRUCTURES**

Geiger-Berger Associates, P.C.; New York, New York

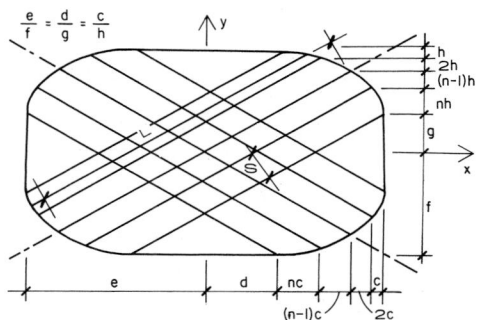

$$\frac{e}{f} = \frac{d}{g} = \frac{c}{h}$$

MAXIMUM STRAIGHT SIDE = 200'-0''
**PROGRESSION PLAN**

rectangle of plan progession.
d/g—One half of straight sides of and parallel to the major/minor axes of the plan progression.
c, 2c, (n-1)c, nc/h, 2h, (n-1)h, nh—The sequences of curve coordinates parallel to the major/minor axes of the plan progression.

## STRUCTURAL CONSIDERATIONS

Membrane strengths up to 1000 lb/in. are available; a safety factor of 4 for short term loading and 8 for long term loading is required. The membrane must be patterned to carry loads without wrinkling. Structural behavior is nonlinear with large displacements. The roof shape shall be established such that the horizontal components of the cable forces result in minimum bending moment in the compression ring under maximum loads. The skewed symmetry indicated permits this condition to be realized. Consult specialist in air structures to integrate structural and architectural requirements.

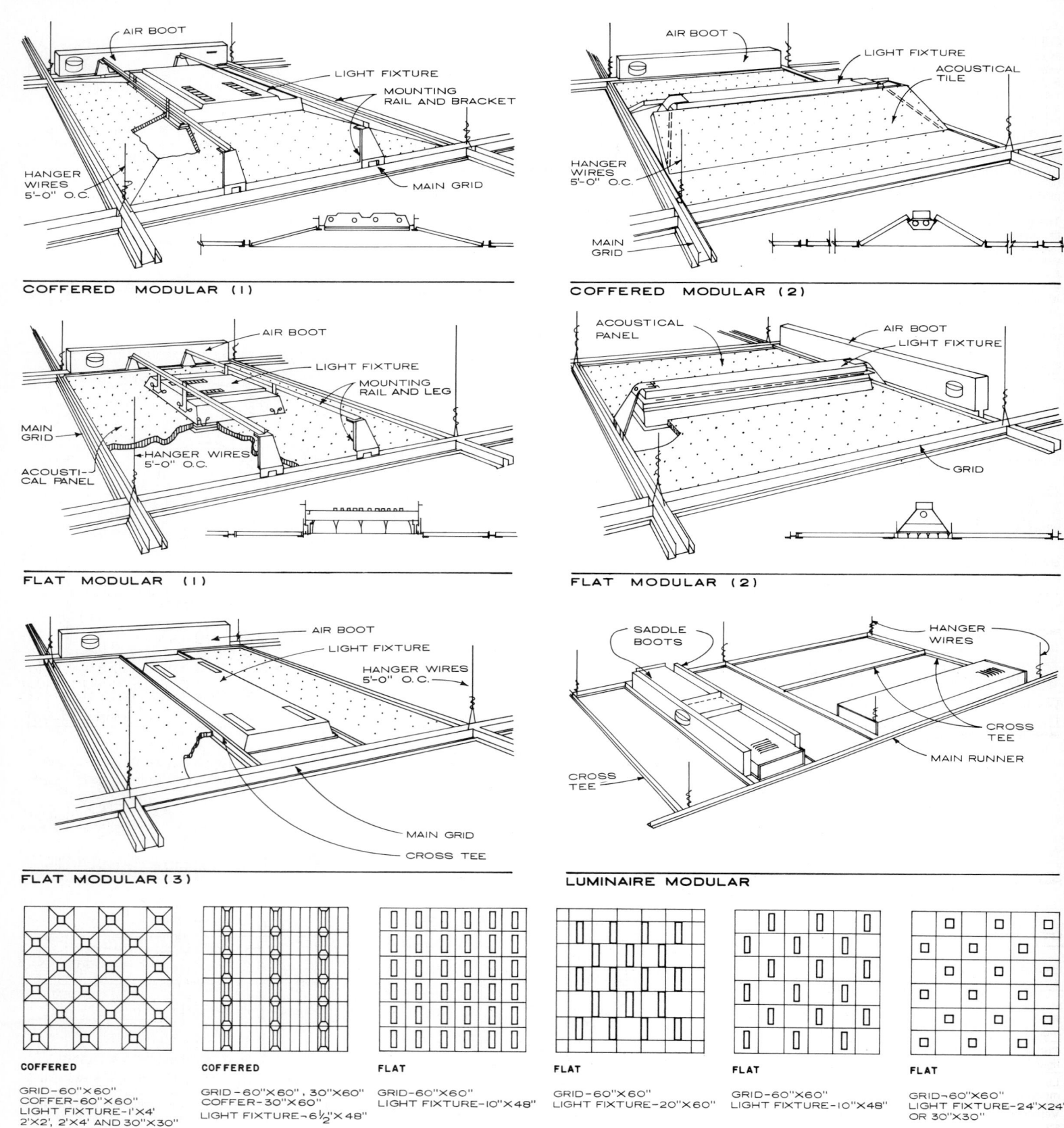

COFFERED   MODULAR   (1)

COFFERED   MODULAR   (2)

FLAT   MODULAR   (1)

FLAT   MODULAR   (2)

FLAT   MODULAR (3)

LUMINAIRE   MODULAR

**COFFERED**

GRID–60"X60"
COFFER–60"X60"
LIGHT FIXTURE–1'X4'
2'X2', 2'X4' AND 30"X30"

**COFFERED**

GRID–60"X60" , 30"X60"
COFFER–30"X60"
LIGHT FIXTURE–6½"X48"

**FLAT**

GRID–60"X60"
LIGHT FIXTURE–10"X48"

**FLAT**

GRID–60"X60"
LIGHT FIXTURE–20"X60"

**FLAT**

GRID–60"X60"
LIGHT FIXTURE–10"X48"

**FLAT**

GRID–60"X60"
LIGHT FIXTURE–24"X24"
OR 30"X30"

REFLECTED   CEILING   PLANS   (INTEGRATED   CEILINGS)

Timothy B. McDonald; Washington, D.C.

# 13   INTEGRATED ASSEMBLIES

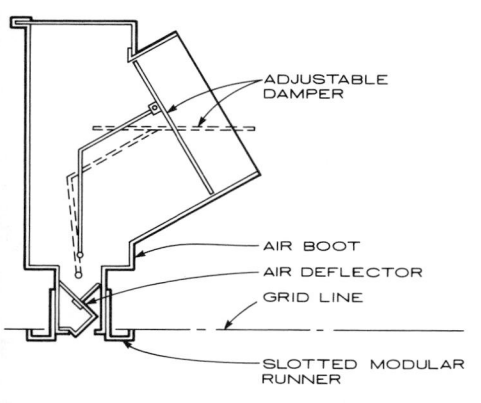

## AIR BOOT SECTION AND DETAIL

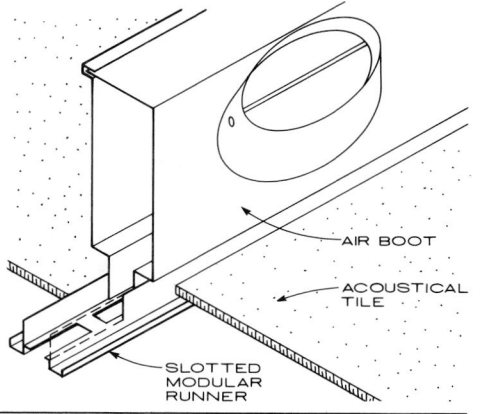

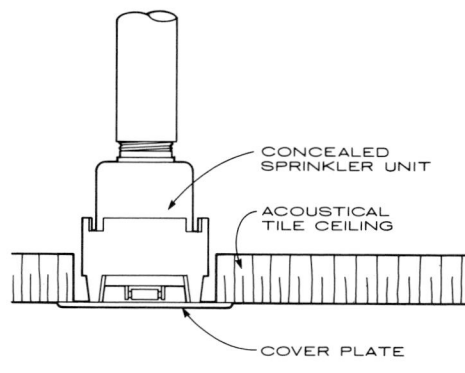

## CONCEALED SPRINKLER

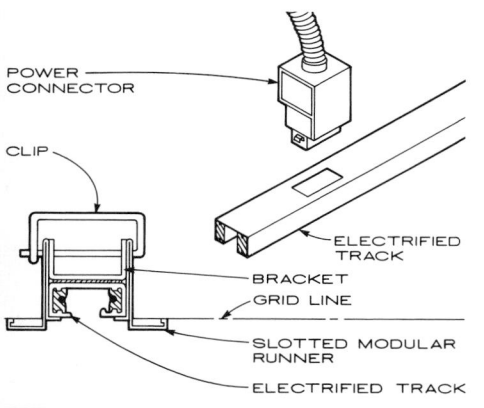

## LIGHT TRACK SECTION AND DETAILS

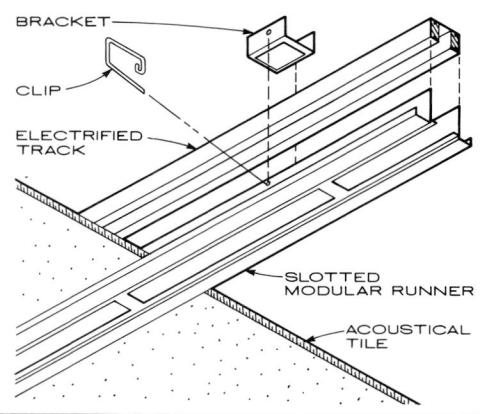

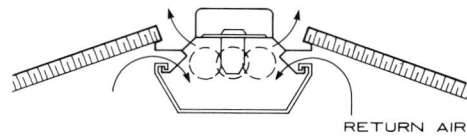

COFFERED FIXTURE

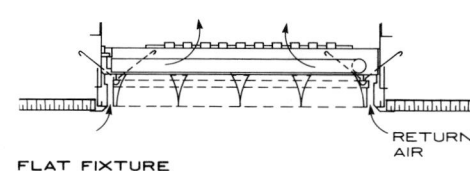

FLAT FIXTURE

## LIGHTING FIXTURES

## INTEGRATED CEILINGS

Integrated ceilings combine lighting, air diffusion, fire protection, and acoustical control into a single, unified unit. Demountable partitions can be accommodated by the use of an adaptor attached on the modular grid lines. A 60 x 60 in. module is basic to most integrated ceiling systems. Custom sized modules are also available.

## LUMINAIRE MODULAR CEILING

The basic configuration is a 60 x 60 in. module divided into four 15 x 60 in. modules.

A recess in the modular defining grid will accommodate demountable partitions, sprinkler heads, and slots for air diffusion.

The basic lighting unit is a $14\frac{1}{2}$ x 48 in. recessed troffer. Air return is by return air light fixtures.

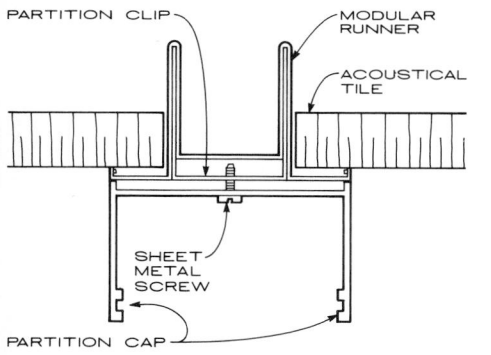

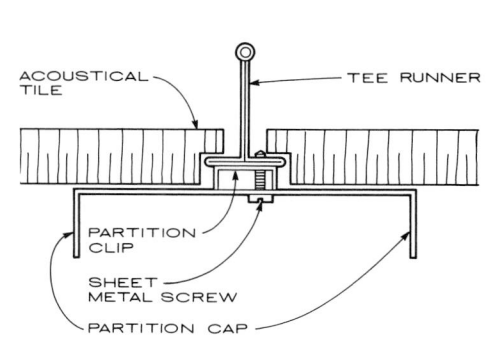

## PARTITION ASSEMBLIES

## COMPONENTS

| CEILING SYSTEMS | HANGER SPACING (o.c.) | WALL MOLDINGS | | | MAIN RUNNERS | | | SPACING | CROSS MEMBERS | | | SPACING (o.c.) | AIR BAR AIR BOOT | | | ACOUSTIC PANELS | | | LIGHT FIXTURES | | |
|---|---|---|---|---|---|---|---|---|---|---|---|---|---|---|---|---|---|---|---|---|---|
| | | L | W | H | L | W | H | | L | W | H | | L | W | H | L | W | H | L | W | H |
| Flat modular | 2'-6'' | 10' | $\frac{3}{4}$'' | $\frac{3}{4}$'' | 10' | $\frac{3}{4}$'' | $1\frac{1}{2}$'' | 5' | 60'' | $\frac{3}{4}$'' | $1\frac{1}{2}$'' | 20'' | 5' | $3\frac{1}{8}$'' | $9\frac{3}{4}$'' | 5' | 20'' | $\frac{5}{8}$'' | – | 1. | – |
| Coffered lighting | 30'' | 60'' | $1\frac{1}{4}$'' | $1\frac{1}{4}$'' | 5' | $2\frac{1}{4}$'' | $1\frac{1}{4}$'' | 5' | 60'' | $2\frac{1}{4}$'' | $1\frac{1}{4}$'' | 5' | 5' | $7\frac{1}{4}$'' | 8'' | 5' | 15'' | $\frac{5}{8}$'' | 48'' | $14\frac{1}{2}$'' | 5'' |
| Luminair modular | 5' | – | – | – | $58\frac{1}{2}$'' | 3'' | $1\frac{1}{2}$'' | 5' | 57'' | $\frac{15}{16}$'' | $1\frac{1}{2}$'' | 5' | 5' | $7\frac{1}{4}$'' | 8'' | 5' | 15'' | $\frac{5}{8}$'' | 48'' | $14\frac{1}{2}$'' | 5'' |
| Vertical screen | 7' Max. | – | – | – | 16' | $1\frac{1}{2}$'' | $1\frac{7}{8}$'' | 7' Max. | 16' Max. | $\frac{5}{8}$'' | 4'' | 2'-6'' | – | 2. | – | – | – | – | – | 2. | – |
| Linear screen | 5' Max. | – | – | – | 16' | $1\frac{27}{32}$'' | $1\frac{1}{4}$'' | 50'' | 3'-16' | 3'' | $\frac{5}{8}$'' | 2'' | – | 3. | – | – | 4. | – | – | 5. | – |

## NOTES

1. Size can vary.
2. No special type necessary.
3. Utilizes slots between panels for delivery and return.

4. Acoustic blanket.
5. Designed to fit panel width.

Timothy B. McDonald; Washington, D.C.

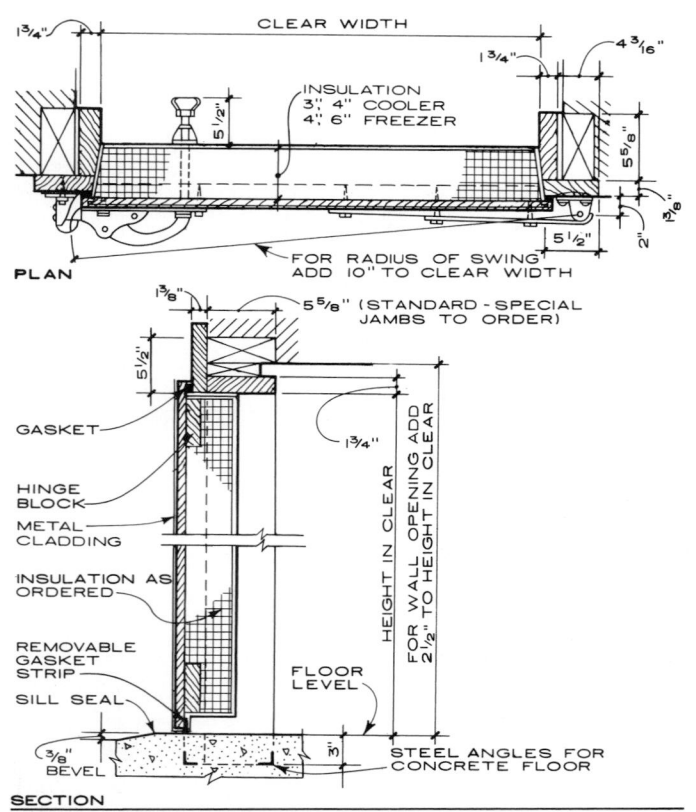

PLAN

SECTION

**TYPICAL DOOR DETAILS**

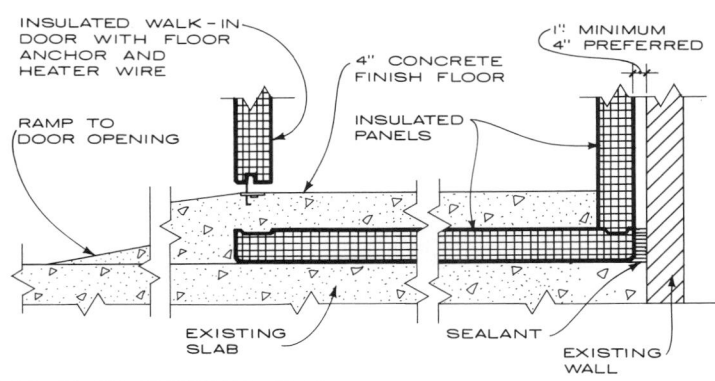

**WALK–IN ON EXISTING SLAB**

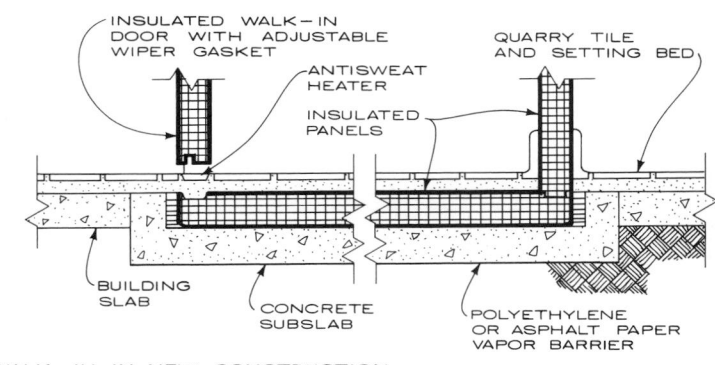

**WALK–IN IN NEW CONSTRUCTION**
**WALK–IN FLOOR DETAILS**

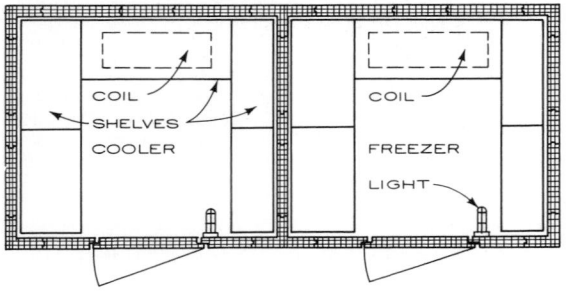

SIDE–BY–SIDE PLAN

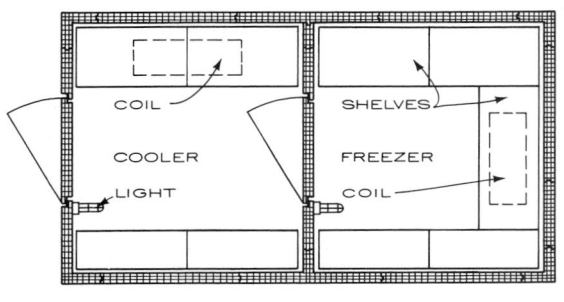

WALK–THROUGH PLAN                SECTION

**WALK–IN TYPICAL PLANS AND SECTION**

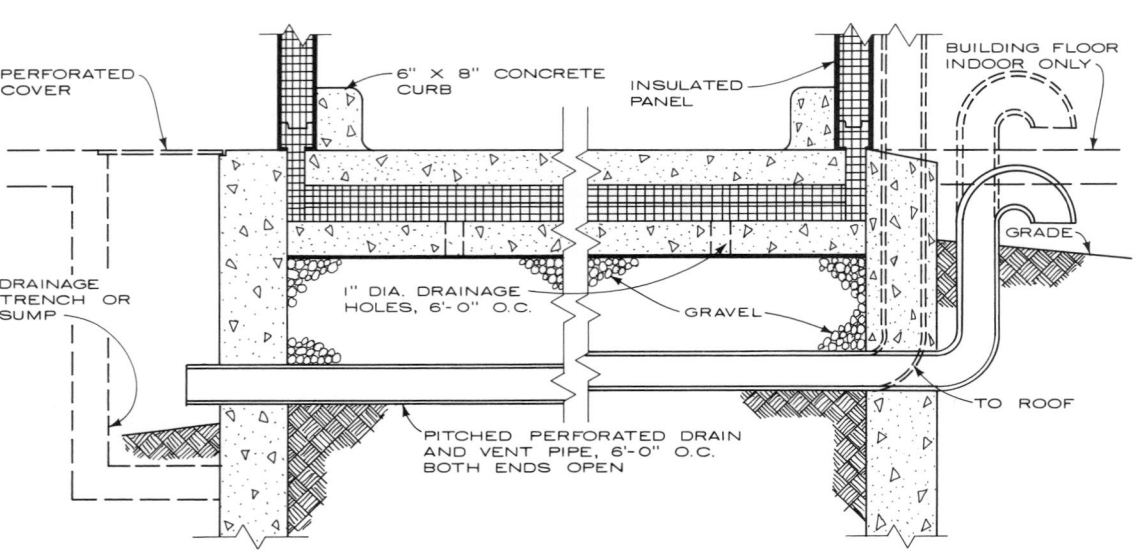

**DRAIN AND VENT DETAIL**

Cini-Grissom Associates, Inc.; Food Service Consultants; Washington, D.C.

## GENERAL NOTES

1. DOORS
   Standard sizes: 2'-6'', 3'-2'', 3'-6'', 4'-0'', 5'-0'' wide x 6'-6'' high; 4'-0'', 5'-0'' wide x 7'-0'' high.
   Sliding, double action, and display doors are available.
   Manual or electrically operated.

2. PREFABRICATED INSULATED PANELS
   Standard sizes: 4'' thick.
   Width: $11\frac{1}{2}$'', 23'', and 46''.
   Height: 7'-6'', 8'-6'', 10'-6'', and 11'-6''.
   Finish material usually aluminum, galvanized steel, or stainless steel.

3. WALK-IN UNIT SIZES
   Widths: 3'-11'', 5'-10'', 7'-9'', 9'-8'', and 11'-7''.
   Lengths: 5'-10'', 7'-9'', 11'-7'', 13'-6'', 15'-5'', 17'-4'', 19'-3''.
   Heights: 7'-6'', 8'-6'', 9'-6'', 10'-6'', 11'-6''.
   Available accessories: stationary or mobile shelf units and adjustable cantilevered shelves, windows, interior partitions, meat rails, floor racks, ramps, and walk-ins.

4. Check local codes for drainage requirements.

# 13    SPECIAL PURPOSE ROOMS

## EXPLOSION PREVENTION

Accidental ignition of flammable solids, liquids, and gases can be prevented best by eliminating potential flammable materials and igniters such as sparks or flames. Hard-finish surfaces of inert, spark-resistant, nonflammable materials should be incorporated, as should sloping horizontal surfaces, coved bases, and coved interior corners (see Fig. 1). Continuous cleanup will minimize the accumulation of dust and debris. Hooded dust-collection systems work well in purging dust from localized areas (see Fig. 2).

Provision should be made for containment of spilled liquids and solids. For flammable gases, ventilation for health safety and prevention of concentrated vapors should be provided.

Explosion-proof electrical devices and grounding systems should be provided in accordance with NEC, NFPA, and insurance underwriters.

## EXPLOSION SUPPRESSION

Explosion suppression is a specialized application in which an extinguishing agent is discharged to snuff out an explosion in its developing stages. Explosion detection systems detect the pressure rise associated with an explosion and immediately discharge extinguishing or suppression agents before damage can occur.

From start to finish, the entire detection/extinguishing process may take only $^{65}/_{1000}$ of a second. This rapid detection and discharge limits application to only very small confined areas. Ideal applications include the interiors of tanks, hoppers, ductwork, or other equipment containing explosive concentrations of vapors, dust, and powders. Refer to NFPA 69.

## SPECIAL EXTINGUISHING SYSTEMS

Automatic fire suppression and extinguishing systems are permanent building installations used to protect the structure, its contents, and its occupants against the hazards of fire and explosion. The nature and magnitude of the hazard will dictate the extinguishing agent and system configuration. Available agents include water (discussed elsewhere), Halon, carbon dioxide, foam, and dry chemicals. Systems may be either total flooding or local application types.

Total flooding systems consist of a fixed supply of extinguishing agent, distribution piping, discharge nozzles, detection devices, alarms, and controls required to achieve a predetermined concentration within an enclosed space or an enclosure around a hazard (see Fig. 3).

Local application systems consist of similar components, as listed above, but are designed to direct extinguishing agents to achieve calculated surface coverages of hazardous areas (see Fig. 4).

HALON SYSTEMS: Halon refers to the family of haloginated hydrocarbon compounds which have very effective fire extinguishing capabilities, but also varying degrees of hazard to human health. Halon 1301 offers the best extinguishing performance with minimum risk to people.

Halon 1301 extinguishes a fire by chemically interrupting the chain reaction of combustion. Halon causes no water damage and leaves no residue, making it ideal for protection of valuable records and electronic equipment. Halon can be discharged in occupied areas, allowing time for orderly shutdown of equipment and evacuation.

The relative high cost of Halon systems mandates that they be used to protect confined areas such as storage vaults, tape libraries or computer rooms, and underfloor spaces.

A typical total-flooding Halon system installation consists of storage cylinders, distribution piping, discharge nozzles, detectors (heat, smoke, UV, etc.), and alarms. Interfaces between the Halon system, HVAC equipment, and electrical equipment are required to ensure adequate shutdown during alarm conditions. Special construction of doors, door closers, partitions, and ceilings is necessary to provide as airtight a space as possible.

Lockwood Greene; New York and Atlanta

Because Halon systems are depleted totally upon discharge, backup or redundant storage cylinders may be required to maintain protection while the system is being serviced and recharged. Local codes or underwriting agencies may require sprinkler backup in areas protected by Halon within sprinklered buildings. Refer to NFPA 12A.

DRY CHEMICAL SYSTEMS: A variety of dry chemical, powderlike products are available for use as extinguishing agents. Although effective against flammable liquid fires and electrical fires, dry chemical systems can result in extensive cleanup problems after discharge and may damage sensitive electronic components or equipment. For these reasons, the most common use of dry chemical systems is for local applications over relatively small areas such as cooking surfaces, dip tanks, and spray booths. Refer to NFPA 17.

CARBON DIOXIDE SYSTEMS: Carbon dioxide ($CO_2$) is a suitable medium for extinguishing flammable liquid fires and fires involving energized electrical equipment. Carbon dioxide systems extinguish fire by reducing the concentrations of oxygen in the air, the vapor phase of the fuel, or both to the point where combustion stops. These systems are generally used in unoccupied areas or where an electrically nonconductive medium is essential. These include electrical equipment rooms, transformers, vaults, or areas containing rotating equipment or flammable liquids. Types of systems include local flooding, local application, hand hose line, and standpipe systems.

Personnel hazards such as suffocation and reduced visibility due to fogging during and after discharge must be considered in the application of total flooding $CO_2$ systems. Such systems must be designed to allow for total evacuation of the area prior to discharge and must also incorporate audible predischarge alarms. Local application systems usually are installed in confined areas such as restaurant range hoods, open top tanks, and printing presses. Activation of $CO_2$ systems may be automatic or manual.

In general, large systems requiring sizable quantities of $CO_2$ use low-pressure storage systems designed for outside installation, while systems requiring small $CO_2$ quantities can use high-pressure storage cylinders designed for placement inside buildings.

Natural leakage occurring around doors, windows, and dampers generally provides sufficient venting of $CO_2$ from rooms, ductwork, and equipment enclosures after discharge; therefore, special venting considerations are required only in gas-tight enclosures. Refer to NFPA 12.

FOAM SYSTEMS: Foaming agents used for fire protection fall into one of three major classes: (1) low-, (2) medium-, and (3) high-expansion foams, as determined by their respective foam-to-solution volume ratios. Foam provides a unique agent for total flooding of confined spaces, transporting water to otherwise inaccessible places, and for volumetric displacement of vapor, heat, and smoke.

Foam is used principally to form a floating blanket on flammable or combustible liquids, preventing or extinguishing fire by excluding air and cooling the fuel. It also prevents reignition by suppressing formation of flammable vapors. Film coating characteristics of fire-fighting foams also provide a measure of protection from adjacent fires.

Foam-type fire suppression systems may consist of portable foam-generating equipment with hand-held nozzles or may involve fixed applications for the protection of entire facilities. Liquid fuel storage and unloading facilities and aircraft hangars and fueling areas often employ foam systems. High-expansion foams also have proved effective in high-rack storage areas. Refer to NFPA, Chapters 11, 11A, and 11B.

## EXPLOSION VENTING

Explosion venting is required in many high-hazard occupancies and is achieved by providing a relief area to the building exterior, thereby controlling the direction of the blast. This requirement depends on the flammability and quantity of the materials within the space and is expressed in square feet of relief area per 100 cubic feet of space.

The relief area may be either brittle material or panels with release fasteners. Brittle relief material such as glass is best placed on the roof and requires a protective screen to limit the size of flying particles. Panel vents normally are placed in walls and require restraining cables. Vents are designed to release at an internal relief pressure, which is a multiple of the design wind load. The remaining walls, roof, and floor are designed to withstand a load that is a multiple of the relief pressure.

Refer to building codes, NFPA, and insurance underwriters for specific requirements and design guidelines.

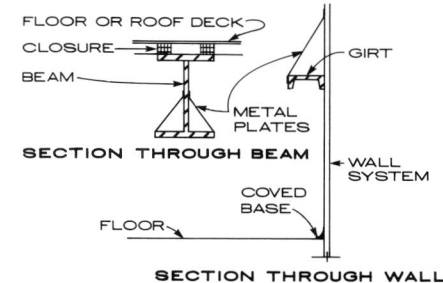

**FIGURE 1**
**MINIMIZING ACCUMULATION OF FLAMMABLE SOLIDS**

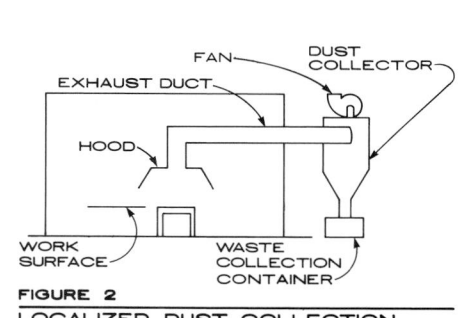

**FIGURE 2**
**LOCALIZED DUST COLLECTION**

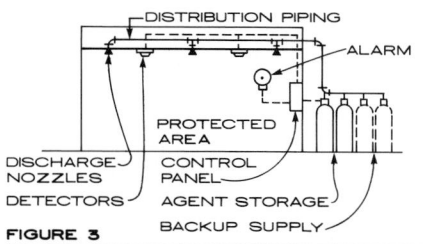

**FIGURE 3**
**TOTAL FLOODING EXTINGUISHING SYSTEM**

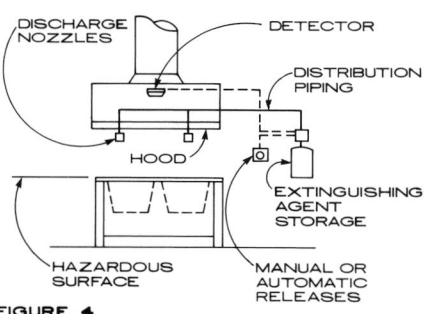

**FIGURE 4**
**LOCAL APPLICATION EXTINGUISHING SYSTEM**

## CLEAN ROOM DESIGN

Clean rooms, enclosed areas with carefully controlled environmental conditions for critical operations in electronics, pharmaceuticals, medicine, food processing, bioscience, aerospace, and manufacturing, are classified by the quantity of particulate matter in the air. Temperature, humidity, pressure, noise, vibration, and airflow patterns also are controlled carefully.

Four air cleanliness classes are defined in Federal Standard No. 209B: Class 100, Class 1000, Class 10,000, and Class 100,000. The numbers refer to particles per cubic foot of air. In a Class 100 clean room the particle count cannot exceed 100 particles/cu ft of a size 0.5 $\mu$m (meter x $10^{-6}$) and larger. For some applications, such as the manufacture of VLSI (very large scale integrated) circuits, an environment cleaner than that defined by Class 100 is required. The unofficial Class 10 clean room based on particles 0.12 $\mu$m has been developed to satisfy this need.

Airborne particles are reduced by HEPA (high efficiency particulate air) filters and controlled air flow. HEPA filters have an efficiency in excess of 99.97% for 0.3 $\mu$m particles. For Class 10 clean rooms, HEPA filters are inadequate. ULPA (ultra low penetration air) filters with an efficiency of 99.9995% for 0.12 $\mu$m particles are used.

Airflow pattern types for clean rooms are conventional and laminar. In a typical conventional flow, air is supplied through HEPA filters in large ceiling outlets, flows generally downward, and is removed near the floor in wall-mounted return registers. This arrangement is satisfactory for Class 100,000, Class 10,000, or Class 1000 clean rooms, but not for Class 100 or Class 10 rooms.

In a laminar flow system, air is supplied through HEPA filters that cover an entire room surface such as the ceiling or a wall. The air travels uniformly across the room and is removed through the entire floor area or opposite wall. The ceiling-to-floor system is a VLF (vertical laminar flow); a wall-to-wall system is a horizontal or crossflow clean room.

In a crossflow room, work stations near the supply air wall are Class 100; the rest of the room meets Class 10,000 requirements. In downflow clean rooms, the entire work area usually meets Class 100 requirements. Laminar flow work stations can be placed in Class 10,000 rooms for localized Class 100 environments.

Typical airflow quantities to filter dust particles sufficiently via the recirculated air path are:

    Class 100,000:  20 air changes/hr—min.
    Class  10,000:  20 air changes/hr—min.
    Class   1000:  50 to 60 air changes/hr—min.
    Class    100:  70 to 90 CFM/sq ft

Thus, in a Class 100 vertical laminar flow clean room, air velocity is maintained at 70 fpm to 90 fpm between the ceiling HEPA filters and the perforated tile floor.

To prevent dust infiltration, clean rooms are kept under positive atmospheric air pressure higher than all adjacent areas. Air locks are provided for entry/exit.

Tiles in clean room raised floors have 23% to 60% free area openings, depending on specific applications. Floor equipment loading characteristics and the degree of constant positive pressure affect floor tile selection.

Ambient temperatures normally are between 65° and 75°F, controlled at 72° ± 2°F. Between 40 and 55% relative humidity with ±5% tolerance is usual. Certain critical applications may require a tolerance of ±0.5°F and ±2% relative humidity. Clean rooms requiring 35% or lower relative humidity may use desiccants or low-temperature brine and chilled water cooling coils for depressing the supply air dew point temperature.

Clean room sound control is important. Double wall ductwork and sound attenuators for axial fans are essential if NC levels of 55 dBA or below are desired. In certain applications vibration control warrants special envelope design and mechanical equipment installation. Construction materials and finishes such as floors, walls, ceilings, and lights are crucial in maintaining particulate levels.

Clean rooms must be tested and certified. See the Institute of Environmental Sciences Recommended Practice No. IES-RP-CC-006-84-T, "Testing Clean Rooms."

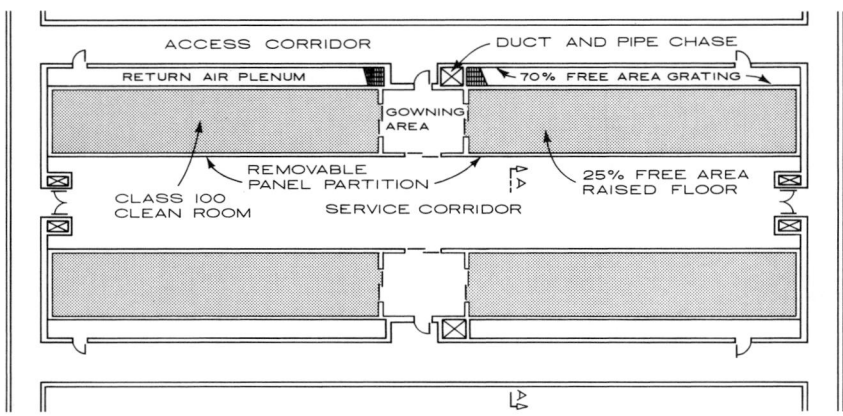

**PLAN VIEW OF CLASS 100 CLEAN ROOM**

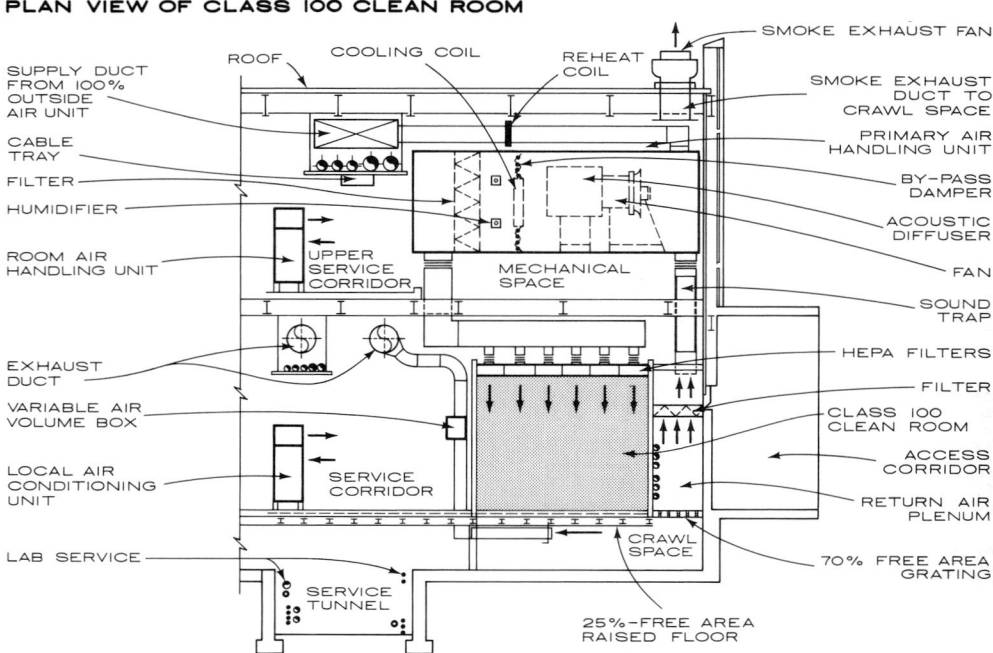

**SECTION A-A THROUGH CLASS 100 CLEAN ROOM**

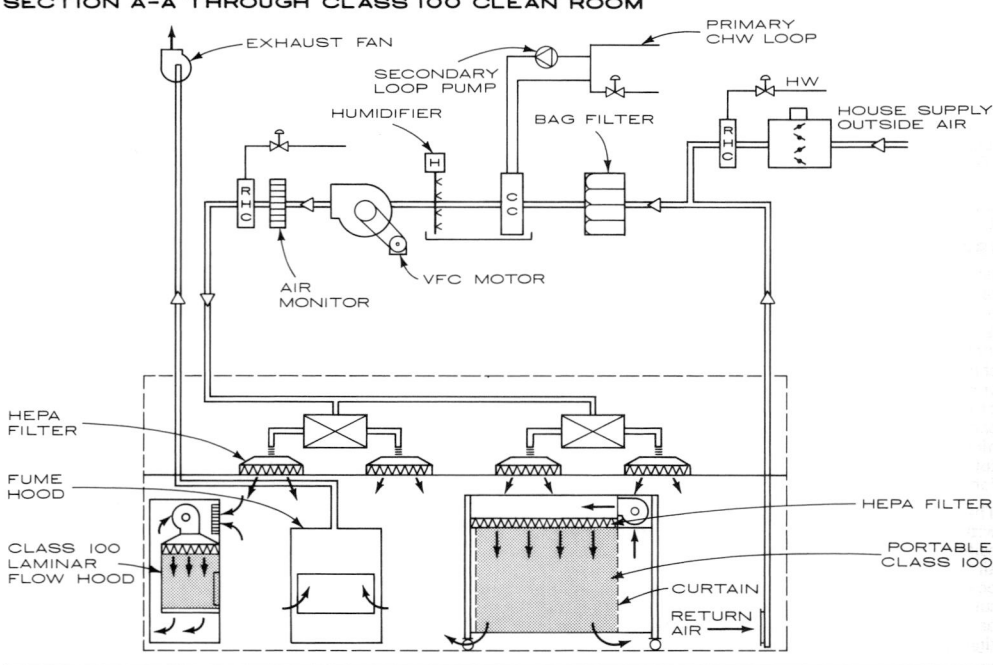

**CLASS 10,000 CLEAN ROOM WITH LOCAL CLASS 100 AREAS**

Joseph R. Loring & Associates, Inc., Consulting Engineers; New York, New York

**13**     **SPECIAL PURPOSE ROOMS**

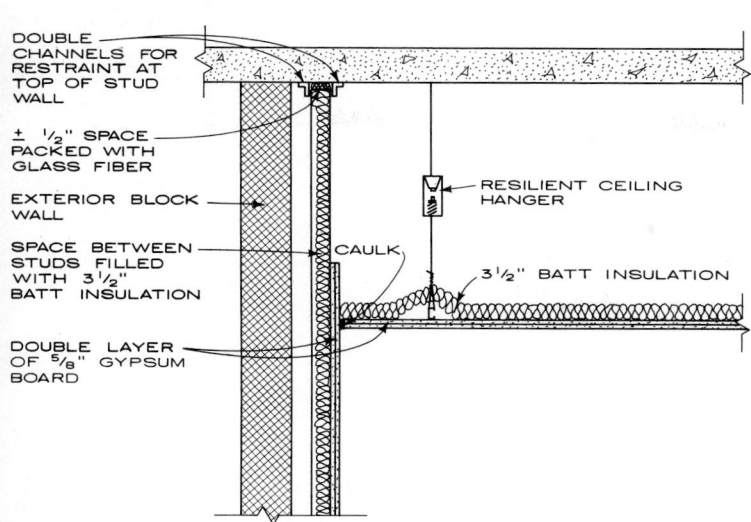

DOUBLE CHANNELS FOR RESTRAINT AT TOP OF STUD WALL

± ½" SPACE PACKED WITH GLASS FIBER

EXTERIOR BLOCK WALL

SPACE BETWEEN STUDS FILLED WITH 3½" BATT INSULATION

DOUBLE LAYER OF ⅝" GYPSUM BOARD

RESILIENT CEILING HANGER

CAULK

3½" BATT INSULATION

UPPER EXTERIOR WALL

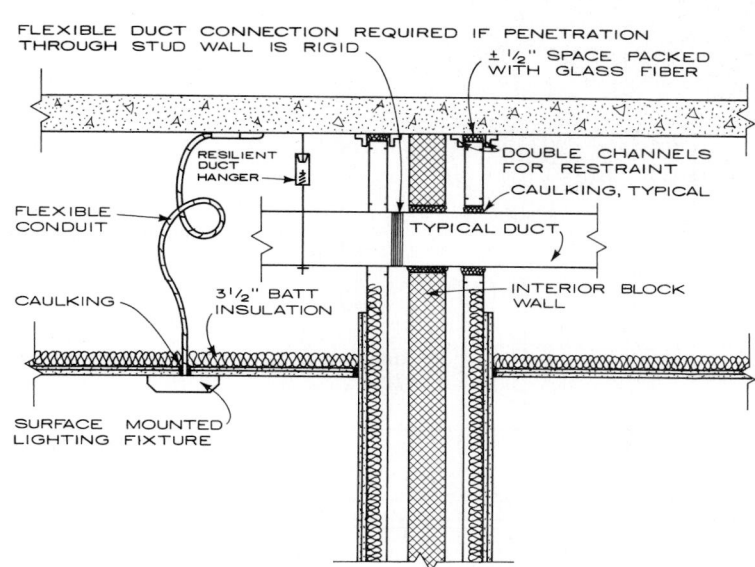

FLEXIBLE DUCT CONNECTION REQUIRED IF PENETRATION THROUGH STUD WALL IS RIGID

± ½" SPACE PACKED WITH GLASS FIBER

RESILIENT DUCT HANGER

FLEXIBLE CONDUIT

CAULKING

3½" BATT INSULATION

SURFACE MOUNTED LIGHTING FIXTURE

DOUBLE CHANNELS FOR RESTRAINT

CAULKING, TYPICAL

TYPICAL DUCT

INTERIOR BLOCK WALL

UPPER INTERIOR WALL WITH HVAC AND ELECTRICAL PENETRATIONS

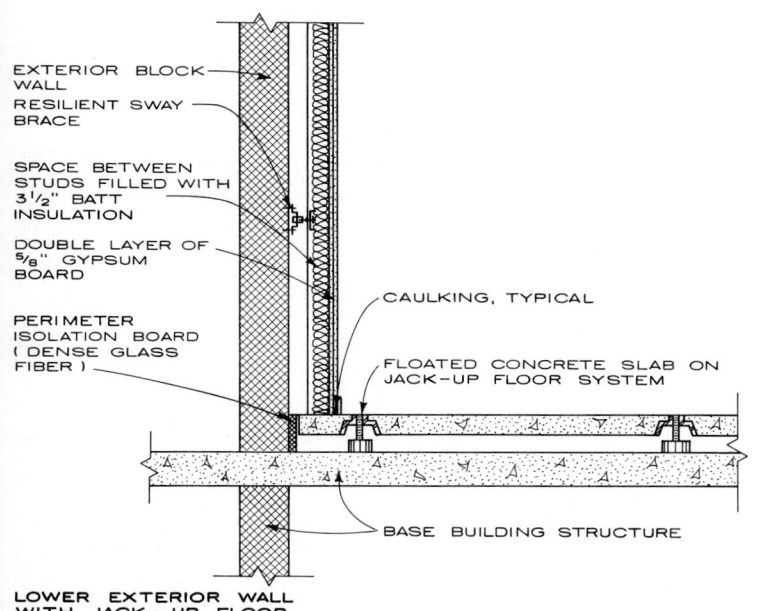

EXTERIOR BLOCK WALL

RESILIENT SWAY BRACE

SPACE BETWEEN STUDS FILLED WITH 3½" BATT INSULATION

DOUBLE LAYER OF ⅝" GYPSUM BOARD

PERIMETER ISOLATION BOARD (DENSE GLASS FIBER)

CAULKING, TYPICAL

FLOATED CONCRETE SLAB ON JACK-UP FLOOR SYSTEM

BASE BUILDING STRUCTURE

LOWER EXTERIOR WALL WITH JACK-UP FLOOR

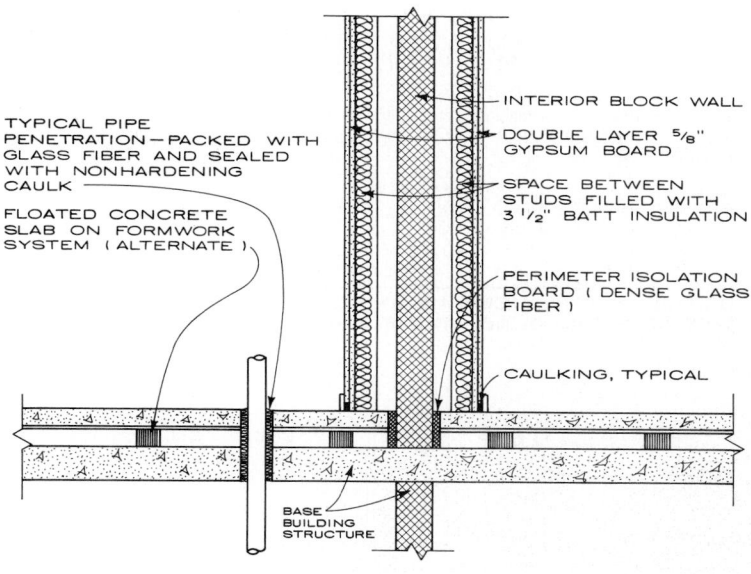

TYPICAL PIPE PENETRATION—PACKED WITH GLASS FIBER AND SEALED WITH NONHARDENING CAULK

FLOATED CONCRETE SLAB ON FORMWORK SYSTEM (ALTERNATE)

INTERIOR BLOCK WALL

DOUBLE LAYER ⅝" GYPSUM BOARD

SPACE BETWEEN STUDS FILLED WITH 3½" BATT INSULATION

PERIMETER ISOLATION BOARD (DENSE GLASS FIBER)

CAULKING, TYPICAL

BASE BUILDING STRUCTURE

LOWER INTERIOR WALL

DETAILS

## ISOLATED ROOMS

Isolated rooms incorporate special constructions to reduce intrusive noise and vibration from outside the room or to contain the sound and impact energy that is generated within the room. Typical applications include music practice rooms, sound studios, testing chambers, mechanical equipment rooms near sensitive areas, spaces exposed to nearby aircraft flyovers, and offices under gymnasiums. Isolated room construction can be very expensive; whenever possible, space planning and layout design should isolate high noise sources from acoustically critical uses so that the need for isolated rooms can be minimized.

The correct design of an isolated room is a "box-within-a-box." The inner box, which is the four walls, ceiling and floor of the isolated room, should be an airtight enclosure of dense impervious materials; this box must be isolated by resilient supports from the surrounding structure. It is also important that the base structure that supports the isolated room be as rigid and massive as possible.

The most effective floor construction is a "floated" concrete pad, which is separated from the base building structure by steel springs, neoprene, or glass fiber isolation mounts. Inner walls can be supported from this slab. Any necessary structural bracing to the base building structure should be with a resilient nonrigid connection. The ceiling of the box can be suspended from resilient hangers, or it can be supported from the walls of the inner box. The diagram shows typical construction details.

It is necessary to avoid all flanking paths between an isolated room and the base building structure. Any penetrations through the walls or connections to outside services must be as well isolated as the room itself. Therefore, there should be flexible connections in ducts and conduit between the inner and outer box, and all piping must be resiliently supported.

Weatherstripped or sound rated doors and double glazed windows should be part of the continuous airtight enclosure that defines the inner box.

The degree of noise reduction that can be attained by an isolated room depends on the type of constructions, their resiliency, the elimination of flanking paths, and the amount of dead airspace that surrounds the inner box. A well-built isolated room can achieve field performance ratings of STC 60 to 70 for airborne sound, and ratings of IIC 80 to 90 for impact noise. However, even minor flanking paths and short circuits can easily degrade these results by 10 points or more. The sound isolation between spaces will be only as great as the weakest sound path.

The advice and assistance of a qualified acoustical consultant should be sought in both the planning and design of isolated rooms and their related special constructions.

In addition to field erected isolated rooms as described above, several manufacturers make prefabricated units. These rooms are sold as self-contained music practice rooms, audiometric booths, and control booths for manufacturing plants. Although the detailing of their constructions is proprietary, one will find the same design approach as outlined here: a separate airtight box kept separate from the building structure. The degree of noise reduction that these prefabricated rooms can attain depends on the parameters used for field erected rooms.

Don Klabin, AIA; Bolt Beranek and Newman, Inc.; Cambridge, Massachusetts

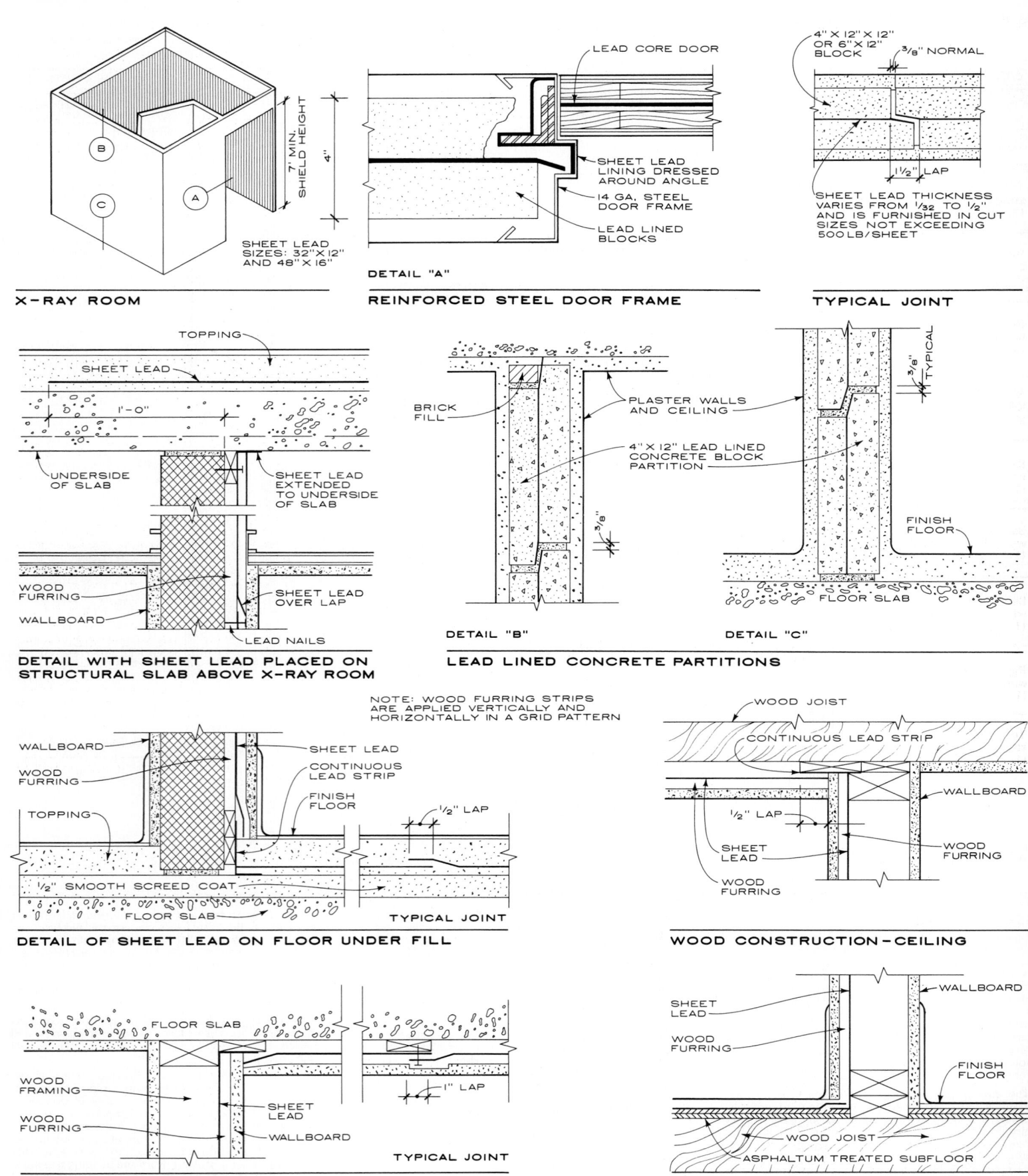

**X-RAY ROOM**

SHEET LEAD SIZES: 32"X12" AND 48"X16"

7' MIN. SHIELD HEIGHT

4"

**REINFORCED STEEL DOOR FRAME**

DETAIL "A"

LEAD CORE DOOR

SHEET LEAD LINING DRESSED AROUND ANGLE

14 GA. STEEL DOOR FRAME

LEAD LINED BLOCKS

**TYPICAL JOINT**

4" X 12" X 12" OR 6" X 12" BLOCK

3/8" NORMAL

1½" LAP

SHEET LEAD THICKNESS VARIES FROM 1/32 TO 1/2" AND IS FURNISHED IN CUT SIZES NOT EXCEEDING 500 LB/SHEET

**DETAIL WITH SHEET LEAD PLACED ON STRUCTURAL SLAB ABOVE X-RAY ROOM**

TOPPING

SHEET LEAD

1'-0"

UNDERSIDE OF SLAB

SHEET LEAD EXTENDED TO UNDERSIDE OF SLAB

WOOD FURRING

WALLBOARD

SHEET LEAD OVER LAP

LEAD NAILS

**LEAD LINED CONCRETE PARTITIONS**

BRICK FILL

PLASTER WALLS AND CEILING

4" X 12" LEAD LINED CONCRETE BLOCK PARTITION

3/8"

DETAIL "B"

3/8" TYPICAL

FINISH FLOOR

FLOOR SLAB

DETAIL "C"

NOTE: WOOD FURRING STRIPS ARE APPLIED VERTICALLY AND HORIZONTALLY IN A GRID PATTERN

**DETAIL OF SHEET LEAD ON FLOOR UNDER FILL**

WALLBOARD

WOOD FURRING

TOPPING

SHEET LEAD

CONTINUOUS LEAD STRIP

FINISH FLOOR

½" LAP

½" SMOOTH SCREED COAT

FLOOR SLAB

TYPICAL JOINT

**WOOD CONSTRUCTION-CEILING**

WOOD JOIST

CONTINUOUS LEAD STRIP

WALLBOARD

½" LAP

SHEET LEAD

WOOD FURRING

WOOD FURRING

**DETAIL OF ATTACHED CEILING**

FLOOR SLAB

WOOD FRAMING

WOOD FURRING

SHEET LEAD

WALLBOARD

1" LAP

TYPICAL JOINT

**WOOD CONSTRUCTION-FLOOR**

SHEET LEAD

WOOD FURRING

WALLBOARD

FINISH FLOOR

WOOD JOIST

ASPHALTUM TREATED SUBFLOOR

John Sava; The Architects Collaborative, Inc.; Cambridge, Massachusetts

**13    RADIATION PROTECTION**

# BUILDING TYPES AND WIDTHS

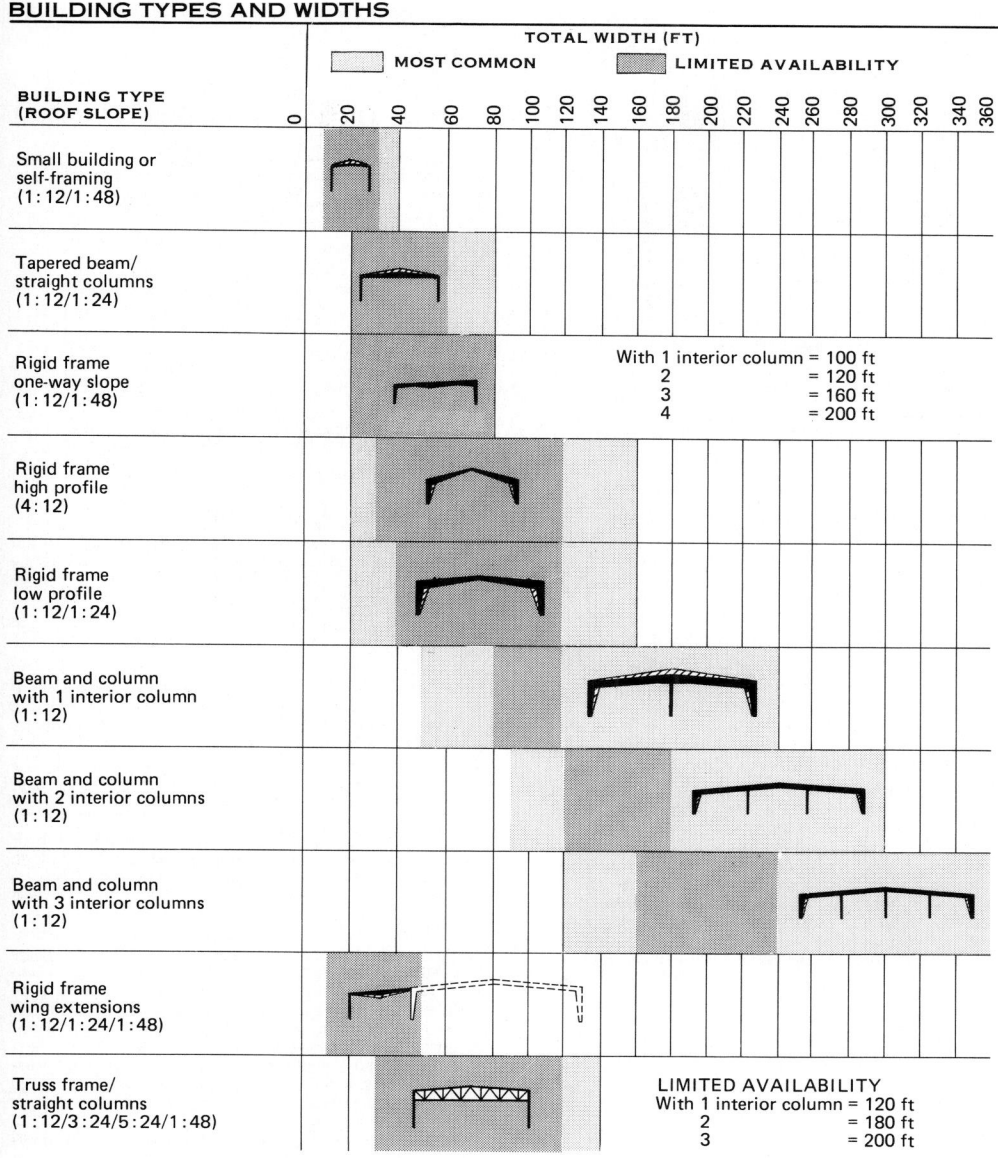

| BUILDING TYPE (ROOF SLOPE) | TOTAL WIDTH (FT) |
|---|---|
| | MOST COMMON   LIMITED AVAILABILITY |
| Small building or self-framing (1:12/1:48) | |
| Tapered beam/ straight columns (1:12/1:24) | |
| Rigid frame one-way slope (1:12/1:48) | With 1 interior column = 100 ft<br>2 = 120 ft<br>3 = 160 ft<br>4 = 200 ft |
| Rigid frame high profile (4:12) | |
| Rigid frame low profile (1:12/1:24) | |
| Beam and column with 1 interior column (1:12) | |
| Beam and column with 2 interior columns (1:12) | |
| Beam and column with 3 interior columns (1:12) | |
| Rigid frame wing extensions (1:12/1:24/1:48) | |
| Truss frame/ straight columns (1:12/3:24/5:24/1:48) | LIMITED AVAILABILITY<br>With 1 interior column = 120 ft<br>2 = 180 ft<br>3 = 200 ft |

## DEFINITIONS, NOTES

Preengineered metal buildings are available in standard framing sizes and types from various manufacturers as proprietary products. The table illustrates the most commonly available systems. The following definitions are used commonly by the metal building industry:

1. BAY: refers to the dimension between centerlines of wall columns along a wall, and the dimension from the outside of an end wall corner column and the centerline of the first side wall column. Spacings range from 18 ft. to 30 ft., with 20 ft. to 25 ft. most common.

2. WIDTH: building dimension measured from outside wall girts surface. Inside clearance varies.

3. EAVE HEIGHT: building dimension measured from bottom of wall column to top of eave strut. Nominal 2 ft. increments varying from 10 ft. to 30 ft.

4. LOADS: loading other than those provided by the manufacturer should be specified at the time of building's structural design. Future additional loads also should be considered.

5. ROOF LIVE LOAD: loads, including snow load, exerted on a roof except dead, wind, and lateral loads. Commonly available in 12, 20, or 40 psf.

6. DEAD LOAD: weight of all permanent roof framing and covering materials only. Varies with manufacturer.

7. LATERAL LOADS: additional dead loads other than the metal building framing such as sprinklers, mechanical and electrical systems, and ceilings. Commonly available in 15, 20, or 25 psf.

8. WIND LOAD: additional loading caused by the wind blowing from any horizontal direction. Commonly available in 15, 20, or 25 psf. Site and atmospheric conditions needing special consideration should be specified.

9. SEISMIC LOAD: specify individual design; required for earthquake zones.

10. AUXILIARY LOADS: additional dynamic live loads other than basic design loads, such as cranes, materials handling systems, and impact loads.

11. The user should verify that individual manufacturer's standard practice and any special design considerations meet or exceed established engineering principles, local practice, and applicable building codes.

12. BRACING: diagonal bracing normally is required in the plane of the columns and beams in one or more bays to prevent racking and to resist lateral loading perpendicular to the span of the frames.

13. GIRTS: members span horizontally and transmit lateral loads (pressure and suction) from the exterior walls to the columns. Sag rods supporting the girts about the weak axis may be necessary to achieve design economy.

14. ANCHOR BOLTS: necessary to resist reactions at column bases. Foundations must be designed for reactions transmitted by the column bases and anchor bolts.

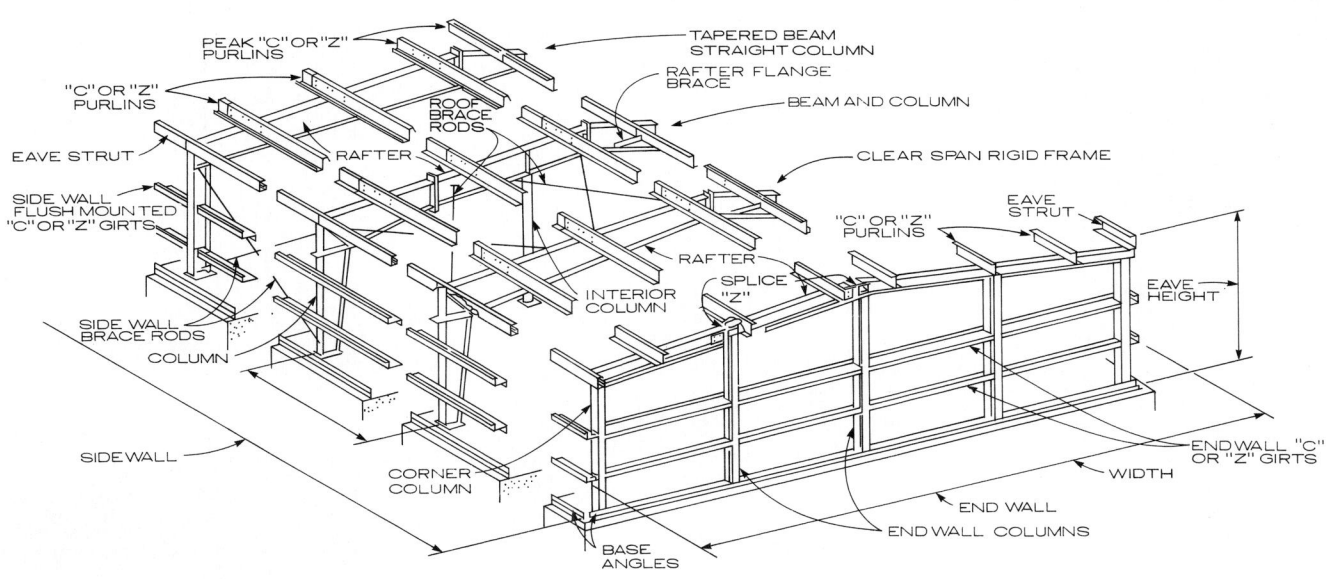

# FRAMING SYSTEMS COMPONENTS

Robert P. Burns, AIA, David Hayes; Robert Burns & Associates; Riverside, Iowa

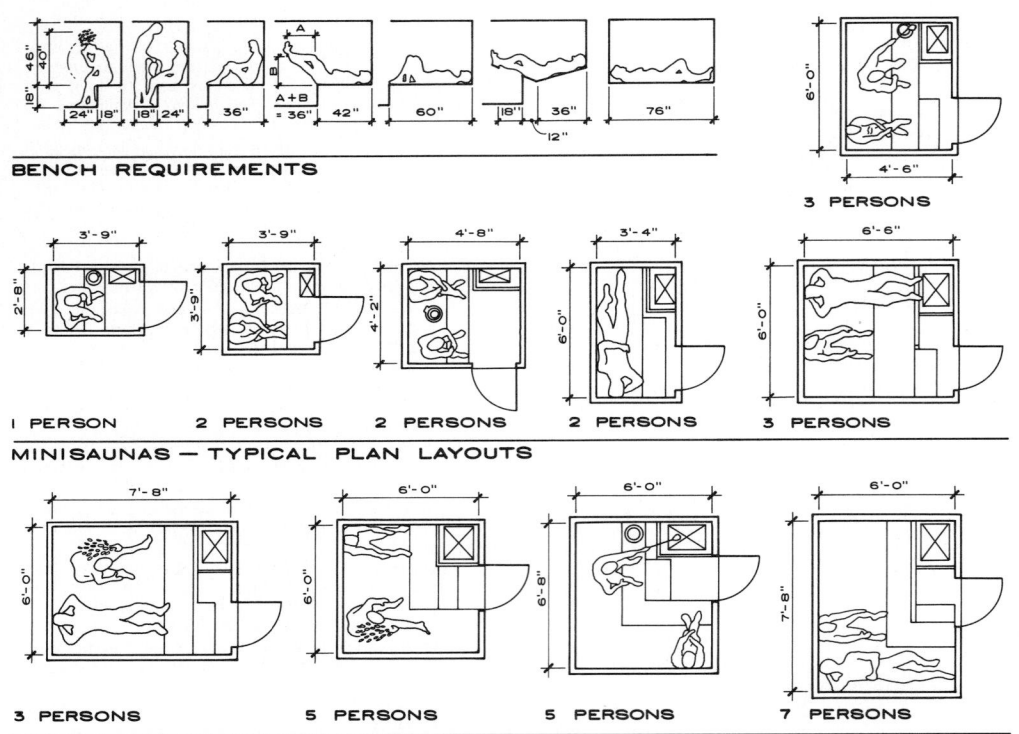

**BENCH REQUIREMENTS**

**MINISAUNAS — TYPICAL PLAN LAYOUTS**

1 PERSON   2 PERSONS   2 PERSONS   2 PERSONS   3 PERSONS

3 PERSONS

**FAMILY SAUNAS — TYPICAL PLAN LAYOUTS**

3 PERSONS   5 PERSONS   5 PERSONS   7 PERSONS

**PLANS**
**PUBLIC SAUNAS**

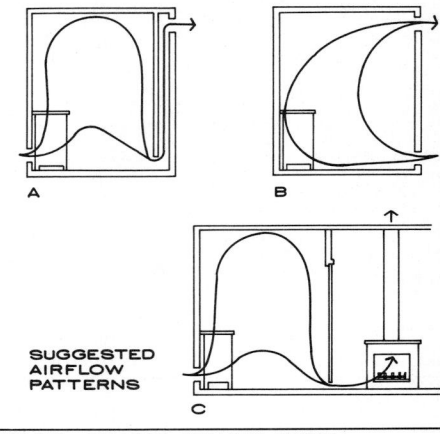

SUGGESTED AIRFLOW PATTERNS

**PANEL SAUNA VENTILATION**

## NATURAL VENTILATION

Air must flow freely into the room—inlet and outlet normally are on opposite walls and at approximately the same level. The inlet situated under the stove creates a strong updraft.

A. A flue or duct provides a chimney action that will pull air off the floor and out.

B. Inlet is low on the wall, with outlet high and directly above it. This ensures ventilation even if wind pressure exists on the wall containing the two ventilators because of the difference in air temperature at the two openings and the effect of normal convection.

C. Suggest fresh air from exterior with outlet through another room, fan, or fireplace.

HEATER: The heater depends on convection for air circulation. It is the preferred method, for the air in a sauna should be as static as possible to heat the sauna in 1 to $1\frac{1}{2}$ hr.

INTERIOR PANELING: Tongue and grooved boards should be at least $\frac{5}{8}$ in. thick, or thicker if possible because of the increased ability to absorb vapor and to retain the timber smell. Boards should not be wider than about six times their thickness. Blind nailing with galvanized or aluminum nails is common. Vapor barrier and insulation under the interior paneling must be completely vaporproof and heat resistant. Most conventional insulating materials are effective; mineral base is preferred; avoid using expanded polystyrene.

DOOR: The opening should be kept as small as possible to minimize loss of heat. Maximum height is 6 ft. Door must open outward as a safety measure. A close fitting rebate on all four sides is usually sufficient insurance against heat loss around the edges. The construction should approach the U value of the walls.

HARDWARE: Because of the weight of the door, a pair of 4 in. brass butt hinges with ball bearings are recommended. A heavy ball or roller catch keeps the door closed. Door handles are made of wood.

LIGHTING: The lighting must be indirect and the fitting unobtrusive. The best position for the light is above and slightly behind the bather's normal field of view. The switch is always outside the hot room.

TYPE OF WOOD: White or western red cedar and redwood are the materials suitable for sauna construction. They should be chosen based on their resistance to splitting and decay, color of the wood, and the thermal capacity of the wood. These woods stain badly by metal.

CEILING HEIGHT: The bigger the volume the more heat required; hence, keep the ceiling as low as possible within the limits imposed by the benches.

The main platform or bench will be about 39 in. above floor in a family sauna or at least 60 in. in a large public sauna. The ceiling is about 43 in. above the highest bench. Average family sauna ceiling height is 82 in., public 110 in.

## DESIGN CONSIDERATIONS

The fundamental purpose of the sauna is to induce perspiration; the higher the temperature, the more quickly perspiration will begin.

The drier the air, the more heat one can stand. Temperatures on the platform can be as high as 212°F, 230°F, and 240°F. A little warm water thrown over the stove stones just before leaving the sauna produces a slightly humid wave of air that suddenly seems hotter and envelops the bather with an invisible glowing cloud, pleasantly stinging the skin. It is usually better to lie than to sit, for the temperature rises roughly 18°F for every 1 ft above the floor level; if one lies, heat is equally dispensed over the entire body. When lying down one may wish to raise one's feet against the wall or ceiling.

The expanded hot air in the sauna contains proportionately less oxygen than the denser atmosphere outside. Bathers sometimes experience faintness unless the air is changed regularly. An amount of fresh air enters each time the door is opened; this is insufficient, however. Normally two adjustable ventilators are built into the walls. One, the air inlet, is usually placed low near the stove. Fresh air should be drawn from outside and not from adjoining rooms where odors can be present.

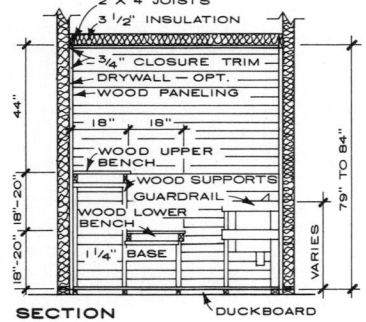

**PLAN**

**SECTION**

**SAUNA ROOM CONSTRUCTION**

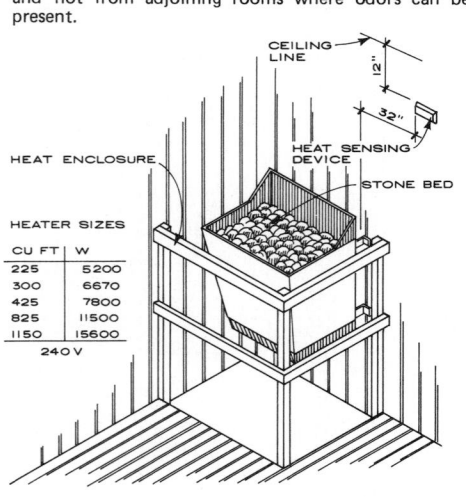

| HEATER SIZES | |
|---|---|
| CU FT | W |
| 225 | 5200 |
| 300 | 6670 |
| 425 | 7800 |
| 825 | 11500 |
| 1150 | 15600 |
| 240 V | |

**STOVE AND THERMOSTAT LOCATION**

Jerry Graham; CTA Architects Engineers; Billings, Montana

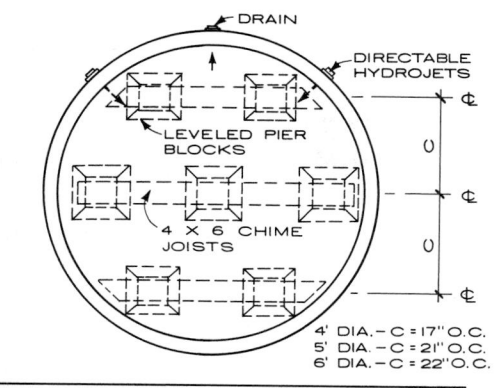

**HOT TUB – PLAN**

4' DIA. – C = 17" O.C.
5' DIA. – C = 21" O.C.
6' DIA. – C = 22" O.C.

DRAIN
DIRECTABLE HYDROJETS
LEVELED PIER BLOCKS
4 X 6 CHIME JOISTS

**HOT TUB – SECTION**

DIRECTABLE HYDROJET
BENCH
DRAIN
GRADE
4 X 6 CHIME JOIST
4" REINFORCED CONCRETE SLAB OR
GRADE
LEVELED CONCRETE PIER BLOCKS

DECK OR PLATFORM
ABOVE GRADE
STEPS
BELOW GRADE
PROVIDE ADEQUATE VENTILATION TO PREVENT WET ROT

**ALTERNATE INSTALLATIONS**

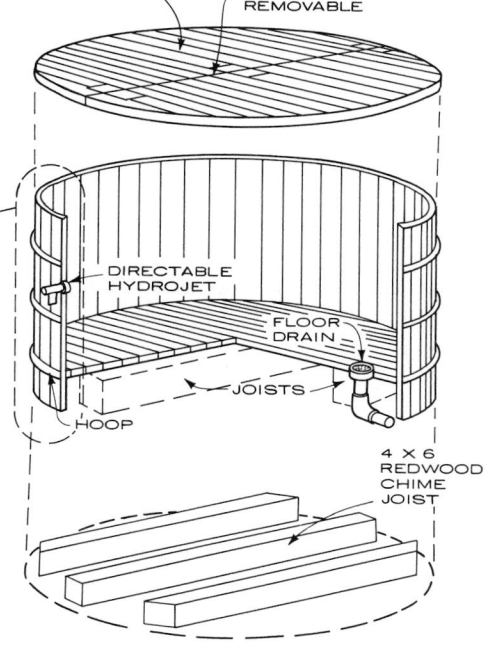

TUB COVER. TO MINIMIZE HEAT LOSS A COVER IS RECOMMENDED. A PRIMARY FOAM BLANKET LIES ON THE SURFACE OF THE WATER. THE SECONDARY 1 X 6 T & G REDWOOD COVER IS FOR SECURITY AND HEAT RETENTION

CENTER HINGE REMOVABLE

DIRECTABLE HYDROJET
FLOOR DRAIN
JOISTS
HOOP
4 X 6 REDWOOD CHIME JOIST

**TYPICAL TUB**

REDWOOD STAVES
DIRECTABLE HYDROJETS
CROZE
FLOOR BOARDS
TUB CHIME

**TYPICAL STAVE DETAIL**

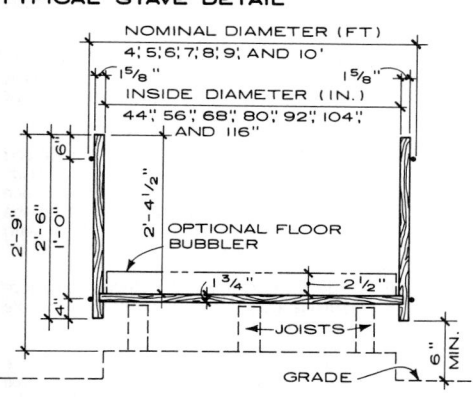

**LOW PROFILE TUB**

NOMINAL DIAMETER (FT)
4, 5, 6, 7, 8, 9, AND 10'
1 5/8"
INSIDE DIAMETER (IN.)
44", 56", 68", 80", 92", 104", AND 116"
2' – 4 1/2"
OPTIONAL FLOOR BUBBLER
1 3/4"    2 1/2"
JOISTS
GRADE
2'-9"  2'-6"  1'-0"  6"  4"
6" MIN.

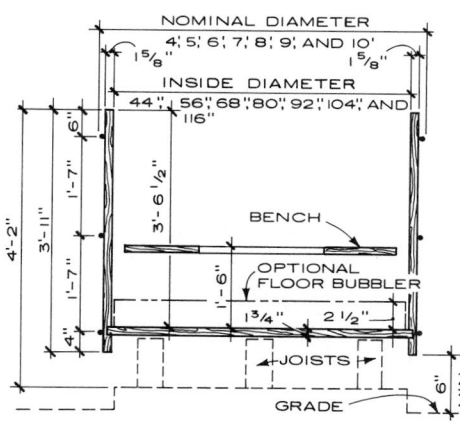

**STANDARD TUB**

NOMINAL DIAMETER
4, 5, 6, 7, 8, 9, AND 10'
1 5/8"
INSIDE DIAMETER
44", 56", 68", 80", 92", 104", AND 116"
3' – 6 1/2"
BENCH
OPTIONAL FLOOR BUBBLER
1 3/4"    2 1/2"
JOISTS
GRADE
4'-2"  3'-11"  1'-7"  1'-7"  6"  1'-6"  4"
6" MIN.
6"

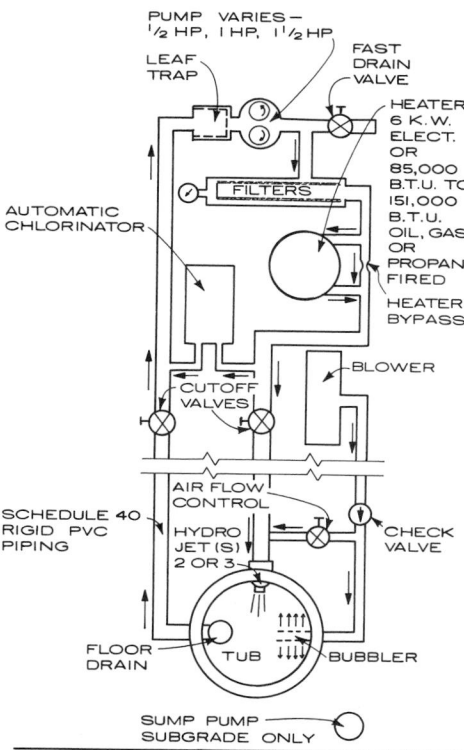

**MECHANICAL SCHEMATIC**

PUMP VARIES – 1/2 HP, 1 HP, 1 1/2 HP
FAST DRAIN VALVE
LEAF TRAP
HEATER – 6 K.W. ELECT. OR 85,000 B.T.U. TO 151,000 B.T.U. OIL, GAS OR PROPANE FIRED
FILTERS
AUTOMATIC CHLORINATOR
HEATER BYPASS
BLOWER
CUTOFF VALVES
AIR FLOW CONTROL
SCHEDULE 40 RIGID PVC PIPING
HYDRO JET(S) 2 OR 3
CHECK VALVE
FLOOR DRAIN
TUB
BUBBLER
SUMP PUMP SUBGRADE ONLY

**NOTES**

Low profile tubs allow the bathers to sit directly on the floor with feet extended. Therapeutically, this style provides direct, close range hydromassage that comes from a floor bubbler. High profile tubs can accommodate more people per diameter foot and allows people to bath standing upright. Tub surfaces are normally left unsealed and will weather naturally to gray. Exterior can be stained or treated with silicone or oil resin to preserve the natural reddish finish. In high altitude, occasional repeated oil treatment is recommended. The size and sophistication of each tub is determined by capacity, budget, and preference for components. The most critical tub support components are the heater, filter system, chlorinator, and automatic cycling and temperature control system. Hydromassage jets are a significant part of every hot tub system. Many types of heaters are available: natural gas, electric, propane, and oil. Their sizes range from 50,000 to 175,000 Btu. All components should be approved and meet local codes and standards. Consult manufacturers for additional information. Tubs made of molded fiberglass with a smooth interior surface are generally referred to as SPAS. Their function and operation is similar to those of the hot tub.

**HOT TUB DIMENSIONS**

| | STANDARD TUB | | | | | | LOW PROFILE TUB | | | | | |
|---|---|---|---|---|---|---|---|---|---|---|---|---|
| NOM. DIA. (FT) | 4 | 5 | 6 | 7 | 8 | 9 10 | 4 | 5 | 6 | 7 | 8 | 9 10 |
| INSIDE DIA. (IN.) | 44 | 56 | 68 | 80 | 92 | 104 116 | 44 | 56 | 68 | 80 | 92 | 104 116 |
| NUMBER OF HOOPS | 3 | 3 | 3 | 3 | 4 | 4 | 2 | 2 | 3 | 3 | 3 | 3 |
| HOOP INTERVAL (IN.) | | | 19 ± 1 IN. | | | | | | 12 ± 1 IN. | | | |
| SEAT SECTIONS | | | 2 3 4 5 | | | | | | SIT ON FLOOR | | | |

**SEATING ARRANGEMENTS:**

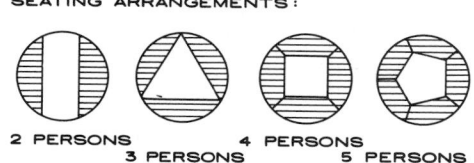

2 PERSONS
3 PERSONS
4 PERSONS
5 PERSONS

Jerry Graham; CTA Architects Engineers; Billings, Montana

## SEISMIC DESIGN

Earthquake forces result from random vertical and horizontal ground vibrations where a structure rests. Frequently vertical forces are neglected in seismic design because of a combination of safety factors in vertical system designs. Some nonstructural elements also require consideration for vertical forces. Earthquake forces may vary in direction, magnitude, and duration, and they are influenced strongly by geological conditions at and around a specific site.

Seismic resistance is achieved by structural elements, including braced frames, moment-resisting frames, shear walls, or a combination of each, connected by horizontal diaphragms. A building's seismic performance is greatly affected by its architectural concept. A building's fundamental period, primarily determined by the building height and proportions, is affected by the nature of the seismic forces. Irregular plan forms can cause torsion and high stress concentrations, reducing the likelihood of torsion. The center of mass and the center of rigidity of horizontal resisting elements should coincide or be close to one another.

In the vertical plane, abrupt changes in strength or stiffness should be avoided because these produce dangerous stress concentration. Horizontal offsets, or "setbacks," should be analyzed with special care for the same reason. All shear walls must be continuous from roof to foundation. Major building form units either should be tied together to respond to earthquake forces as an entity or adequate structural separations must be provided to ensure that pounding-damage does not occur between them.

Most structural materials can be used effectively as elements of a seismic resisting system, although brittle materials, such as concrete, require special detailing when used in highly stressed structures. Because of its ductility, steel is a particularly suitable material. Small conventional wood-framed structures have performed well because they give when subjected to stress.

Seismic building codes emphasize life safety and aim to safeguard against structural collapse. Nonstructural elements, building equipment, and contents also can be life-threatening under seismic conditions. Even if a building structure meets the code intentions, it still can suffer considerable damage and be rendered nonfunctional. This is especially true of essential facilities such as hospitals, fire and police stations, and the like. Equipment and utilities in such buildings need special design attention; some seismic codes specifically mandate it.

### METHODS OF SEISMIC DESIGN

The essential feature of all seismic codes is to provide a standard and simple way to determine seismic forces for design use. The California Uniform Building Code is typical. It states that every structure shall be designed to resist minimum lateral forces that act nonconcurrently in the direction of each main axis. The total lateral force is calculated by applying the formula: $V = ZIKCSW$. V represents dynamic lateral forces as an equivalent shear force applied at the structure's base and distributes to various structure levels on a basis that is described in the code. Coefficient Z defines the seismicity of the site. It is determined by maps provided in the code. I is an importance factor based on the occupancy of the building. K is a coefficient that represents the type of structural system and its ductility (or general ability to absorb energy without collapse). C relates to the period of the building, and S is a coefficient that refers to the nature of the ground. W is the building's total weight.

Dynamic analysis is a more complex form of analysis that yields more precise information about the nature of seismic forces; it is used for buildings of large size, unusual form, or special importance. The process is expensive and time-consuming.

Two general methods exist. The first, and most common, is the response spectrum method. Critical modes of vibration, their period, and size are determined by this technique. The second method is more exact since it reviews the structure with respect to the earthquake time history (divided into small increments of time). This type of analysis results in estimates of building motion, building distortion, building forces, and accelerations for specific locations in the building at defined intervals of the earthquake motion.

Dynamic analysis can be used to determine resonant frequencies, which, coupled with similar ground motion frequencies, may result in dangerous amplification of forces within the building. It also is valuable in establishing seismic characteristics of complex systems such as nuclear power plants where utility systems performance may be critical for continued operation and safety.

### DESIGN JUDGMENT

While analysis can establish design forces, the correct selection and detailing of the structural system remains a matter of engineering judgment in both economy and the ultimate safety of the building. In this, the extent to which the architectural concept assists the engineering design by eliminating potential torsion, stress concentrations, and geometrically induced points of weakness, is of great importance. Recent building damage studies have shown that many apparent structural failures can be traced to architectural decisions.

### LABORATORY TESTING

Full-size structures or details, model structures, and equipment sometimes are tested seismically by laboratory experiment. These involve either shaking tables that realistically can represent ground motions or by various forms of static or pseudodynamic testing. Shaking-table testing is time-consuming and generally is used only for long-term research, although it has been used for critical equipment testing such as computers.

Zone 0—No damage.

Zone 1—Minor damage; distant earthquakes may cause damage to structures with fundamental periods greater than 1.0 second; corresponds to intensities V and VI of the M.M.* Scale.

Zone 2—Moderate damage; corresponds to intensity VII of the M.M.* Scale.

Zone 3—Major damage; corresponds to intensity VIII and higher on the M.M.* Scale.

Zone 4—Those areas within Zone 3 determined by the proximity to certain major fault systems.

*Modified Mercalli Intensity Scale of 1931.

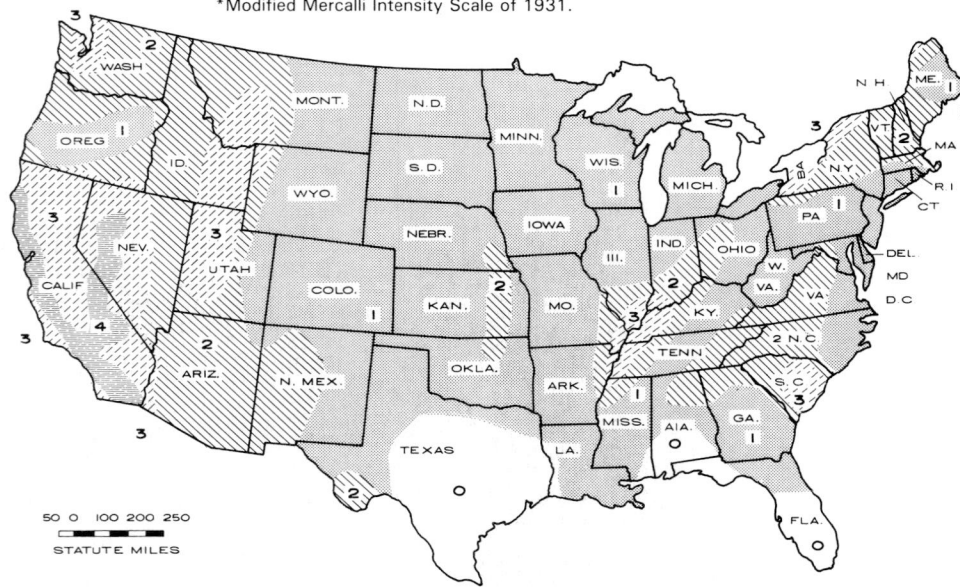

SOURCE SEISMIC RISK MAP OF THE CONTERMINOUS UNITED STATES — AFTER S.T. ALGERMISSEN, "SEISMIC RISK STUDIES IN THE UNITED STATES," PROCEEDINGS OF THE FOURTH WORLD CONFERENCE ON EARTHQUAKE ENGINEERING (VOL. I, PP. 19–27), SANTIAGO, CHILE, 1969.

**SEISMIC ZONES—UNITED STATES**

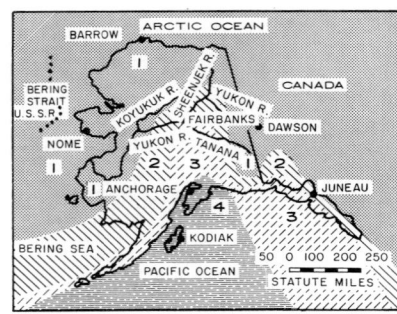

**SEISMIC ZONES—ALASKA**

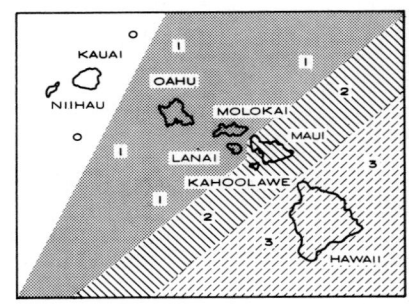

**SEISMIC ZONES—HAWAII**

Attila L. Mocsary, PE; Hope Architects & Engineers; San Diego, California

THE EARTHQUAKE GENERATES
GROUND MOTIONS THAT CAN BE
EXPRESSED IN THREE MUTUALLY
PERPENDICULAR AXES

GROUNDSHAKING, NOT GROUNDRUPTURE,
GENERALLY CAUSES MOST BUILDING DAMAGE

## GROUNDSHAKING

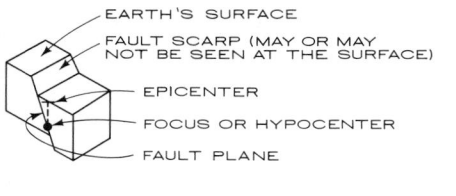

- EARTH'S SURFACE
- FAULT SCARP (MAY OR MAY NOT BE SEEN AT THE SURFACE)
- EPICENTER
- FOCUS OR HYPOCENTER
- FAULT PLANE

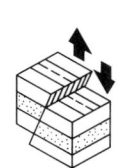

STRIKE SLIP– LEFT LATERAL

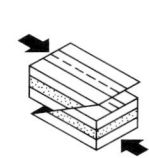

STRIKE SLIP– RIGHT LATERAL

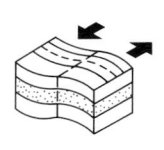

DIP SLIP NORMAL

DIP SLIP REVERSE

THRUST

CONTINUOUS FAULT CREEP

## FAULT TERMINOLOGY AND TYPES

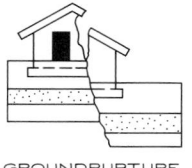
GROUNDRUPTURE

GROUNDSHAKING

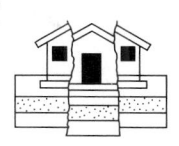
DIFFERENTIAL SUBSIDENCE

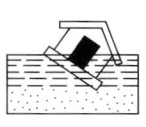
LIQUEFACTION

## FOUNDATION FAILURES - MAIN CAUSES

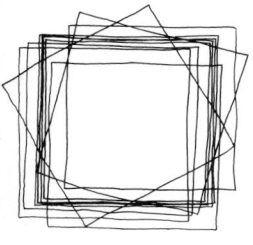

EARTHQUAKE FORCES

THE REALITY

RELEVANT ANALYTICAL AXES:

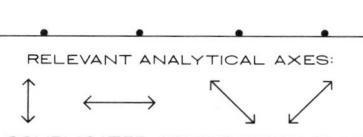

FOR COMPLICATED CONFIGURATIONS, MORE
THAN TWO AXES MAY BE USED FOR ANALYSIS

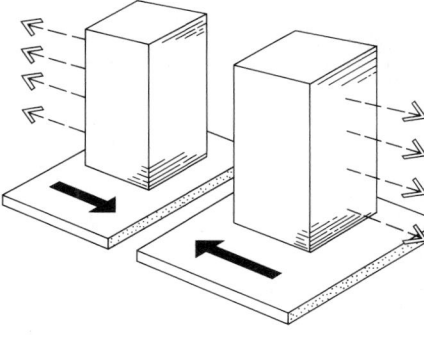

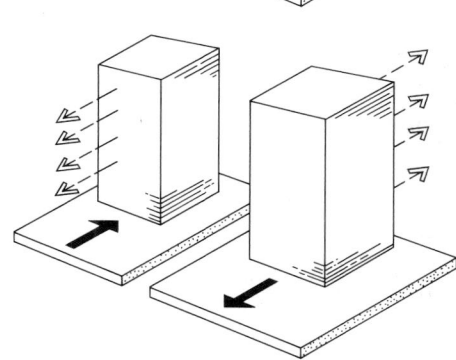

## TYPICAL ANALYTICAL DIAGRAM OF EARTHQUAKE FORCES

## EARTHQUAKE RELATED EVENTS

### SURFACE FAULTING

An earthquake is the result of slippage along a fault plane, sometimes miles below the surface, that creates large earth movement. The fault slippage sometimes, but not always, moves upward through the earth to create visible cracks in the earth's surface known as surface faults. A building located across the surface fault will suffer severe damage. Structures should not be sited over active geologic faults.

### SOIL LIQUEFACTION

A threatening condition and common occurrence in loose sands and silts with high groundwater table (sites located adjoining rivers, lakes, and bays). Earthquake motion can transform the soil into a semi-liquefied state that resembles quicksand.

### TSUNAMI (TIDAL WAVES)

These are earthquake-caused wave movements originating in the ocean. The wave front may move at 400 mph to 500 mph. Pacific Coast sites must be investigated carefully. When a tsunami reaches the coast, its energy is concentrated in a smaller and smaller wave front because the ocean depth decreases.

### SEICHE

A sloshing wave movement in enclosed lakes, bays, or dams created during an earthquake. It can top dams and damage adjacent structures.

### LANDSLIDE

Slope failure, rock fall, avalanche, or earth flow can be triggered by earthquake ground motion. Many landslide-prone areas have been mapped. For projects in these areas, geological evaluation must be conducted before planning.

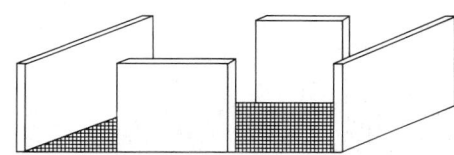

SHEAR WALLS

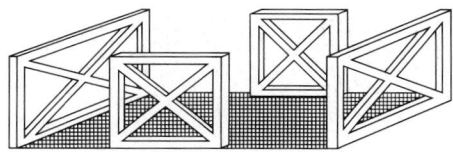

BRACED FRAMES

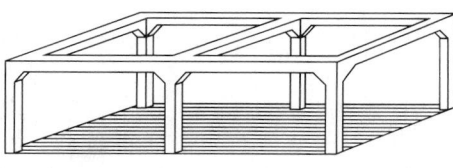

MOMENT-RESISTANT FRAMES

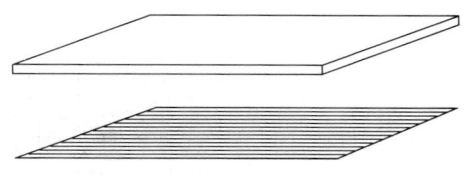

DIAPHRAGMS

## COMPONENTS FOR SEISMIC RESISTANCE

Attila L. Mocsary, PE; Hope Architects & Engineers; San Diego, California
Gary L. McGavin; Wyle Laboratories; El Segundo, California
Alfred M. Kemper, AIA; Kemper & Associates; Los Angeles, California

SEISMIC DESIGN    **13**

CENTER OF RESISTANCE

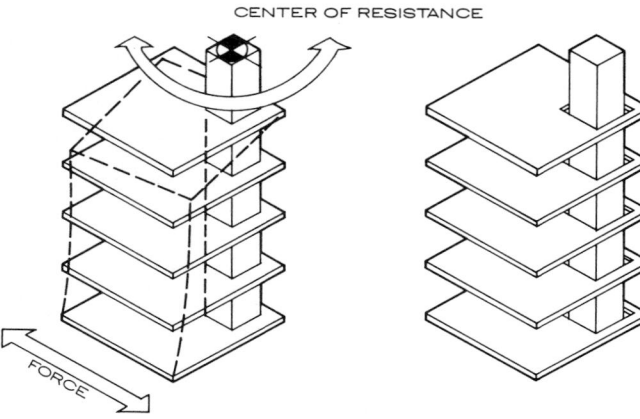

FORCE

PROBLEM: TORSION FROM STIFF ASYMMETRIC CORE

SOLUTION: DISCONNECT CORE (AS SHOWN) OR USE FRAME WITH NON-STRUCTURAL CORE WALLS

**FALSE SYMMETRY**

CENTER OF RESISTANCE

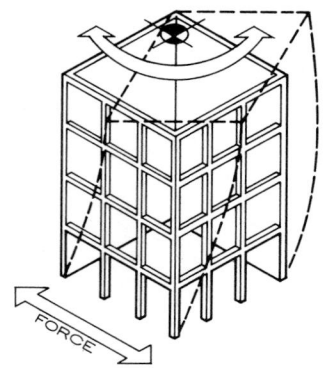
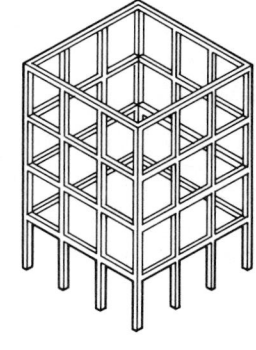

FORCE

PROBLEM: TORSION CAUSED BY EXTREME VARIATION IN STIFFNESS AND STRENGTH

SOLUTION: USE FRAMES AND LIGHTWEIGHT WALLS

**VARIATION IN PERIMETER STRENGTH-STIFFNESS**

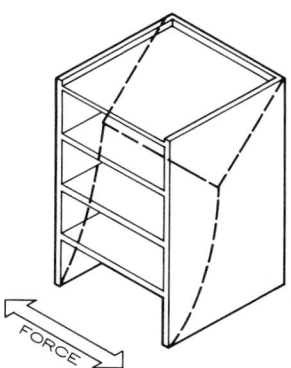
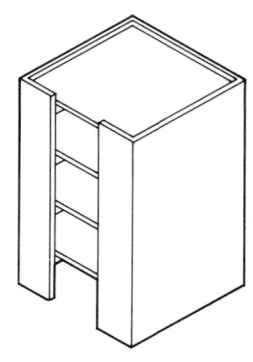

FORCE

PROBLEM: TORSION FROM EXTREME VARIATION IN STRENGTH AND STIFFNESS

SOLUTION: ADD SHEAR WALL OR STIFF FRAME AT OR NEAR OPEN FRONT

**VARIATION IN PERIMETER STRENGTH-STIFFNESS**

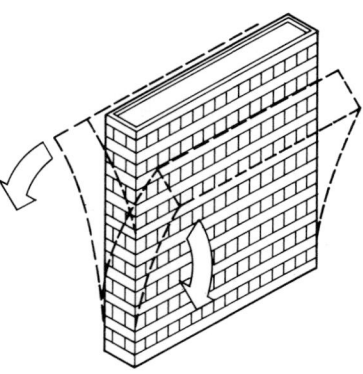

HIGH OVERTURNING FORCES AND LARGE DRIFT

**EXTREME HEIGHT-DEPTH RATIO**

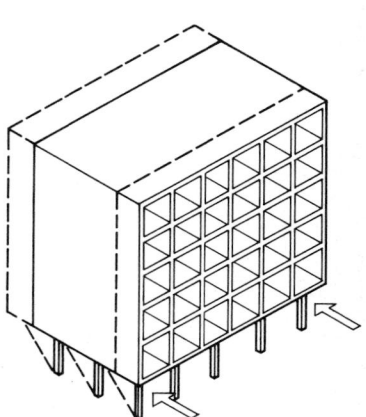

DISCONTINUITIES IN LOAD PATH AND STRESS CONCENTRATION AT HEAVILY LOADED COLUMNS

**DISCONTINUOUS SHEAR WALL**

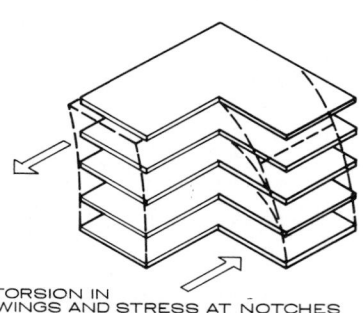
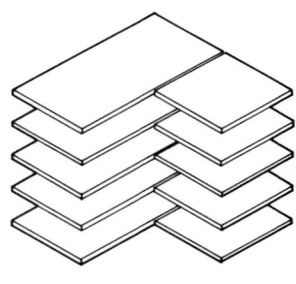

UNIFORM BOX

CENTER BOX

Building configuration has tremendous influence on the performance of structures under seismic loading conditions. Code design forces used for calculation are based on uniform buildings and conditions. If a building is irregular in plan, section, or elevation, the code forces calculated are probably unrealistic. Some examples of structural irregularity are shown here to illustrate seismic responses. Variations in perimeter strength and stiffness, reentrant corner designs, discontinuous shear walls, extreme height–depth or length–depth ratios, and extreme plan area are among the configuration problems which should be studied carefully. In high risk areas, unsuitable building configurations can result in intolerable stresses placed on some specific material or connection causing failure. Those design solutions which perform most successfully are simple, straightforward, symmetrical, continuous and repetitive.

TORSION IN WINGS AND STRESS AT NOTCHES

**RE-ENTRANT CORNER**

ADD SEISMIC JOINT

ARCHITECTURAL RELIEF

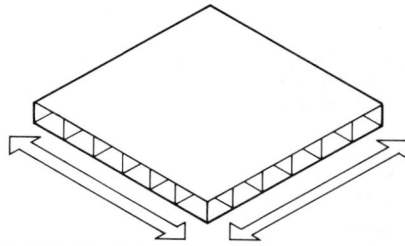
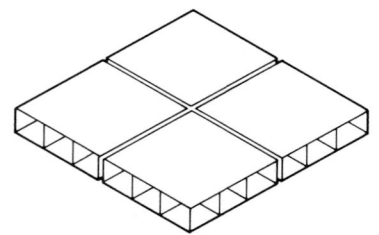

LARGE DIAPHRAGM FORCES
**EXTREME PLAN AREA**

ADD SEISMIC JOINTS

Christine Beall, AIA, CCS; Austin, Texas

**13** **SEISMIC DESIGN**

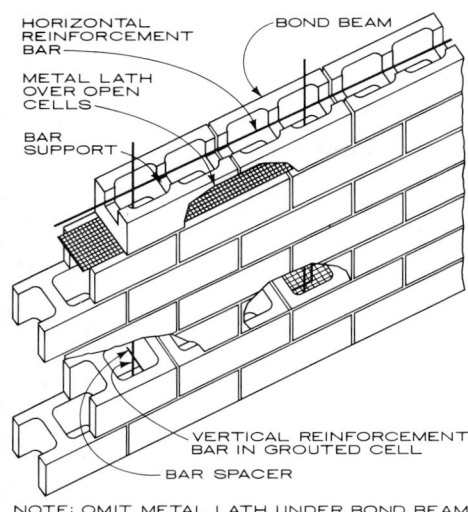

**SECURING OF REINFORCEMENT**

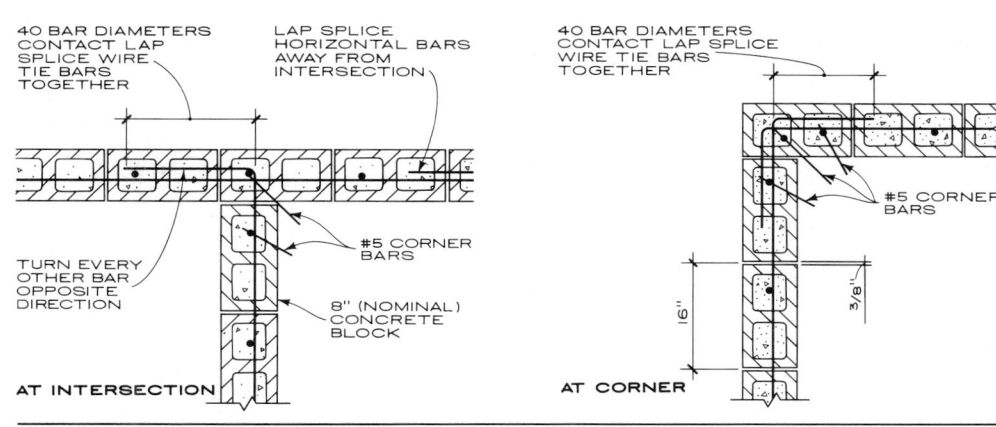

**CONCRETE BLOCK MASONRY**

AT INTERSECTION

AT CORNER

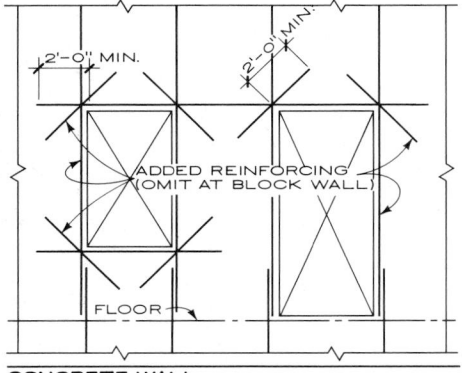

NOTE: SEE APPLICABLE CODE FOR MIN. REINFORCEMENT REQUIRED.

**MASONRY WALL**

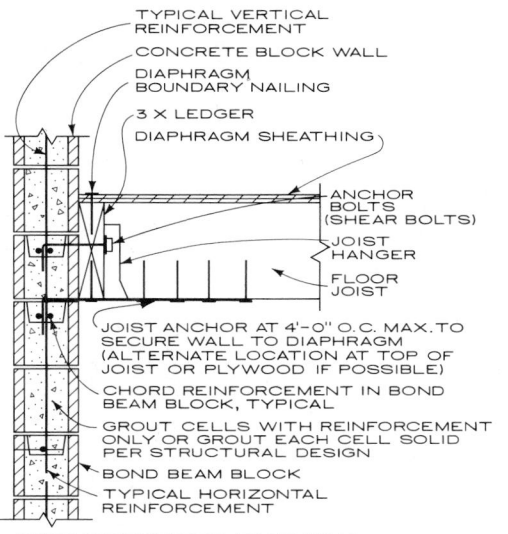

**JOIST PERPENDICULAR TO WALL**

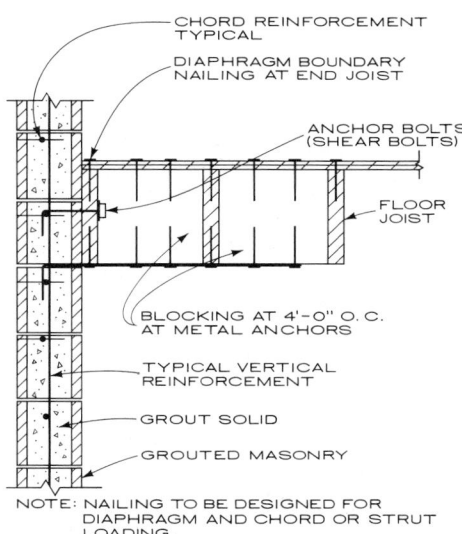

**JOIST PARALLEL TO WALL**

**WOOD DIAPHRAGM WITH MASONRY SHEAR WALL CONNECTIONS**

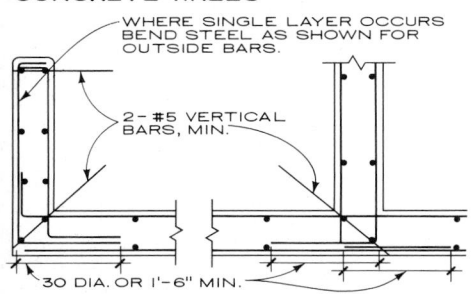

**OPENINGS IN MASONRY AND CONCRETE WALLS**

**CONCRETE WALL**

**INTERSECTION OF CONCRETE OR REINFORCED MASONRY WALLS**

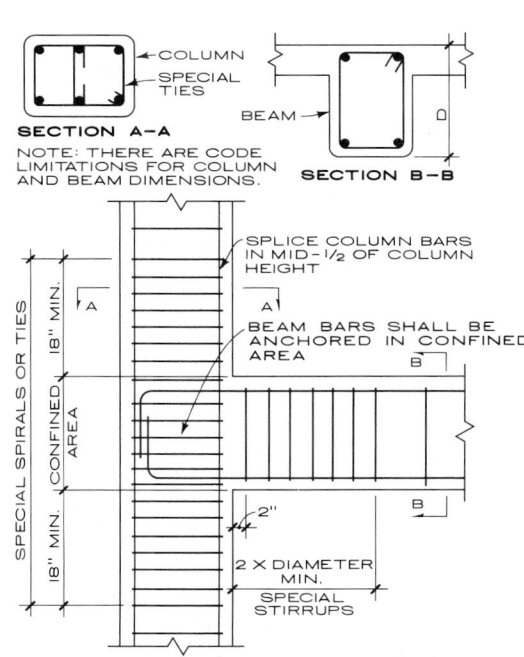

SECTION A–A

NOTE: THERE ARE CODE LIMITATIONS FOR COLUMN AND BEAM DIMENSIONS.

SECTION B–B

**REINFORCING DETAIL FOR DUCTILE MOMENT RESISTING SPACE FRAME CONFINED JOINT**

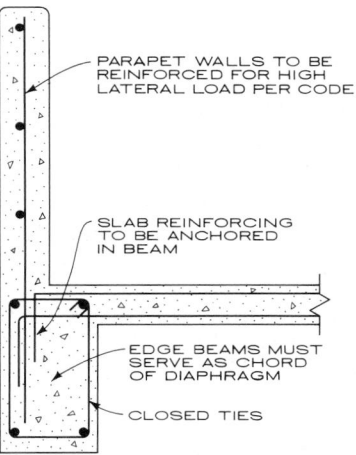

**CONCRETE DIAPHRAGM WITH CONCRETE SPANDREL BEAM AND PARAPET**

NOTE

Details shown are representative of possible construction detailing. In addition to code-defined structural requirements, safety considerations require nonstructural building elements and furnishings to be anchored in areas subjected to seismic movement. These pages show selected details as samples of recommended bracing and anchorage.

Attila L. Mocsary, PE; Hope Architects & Engineers; San Diego, California
Gary L. McGavin; Wyle Laboratories; El Segundo, California
Alfred M. Kemper, AIA; Kemper & Associates; Los Angeles, California

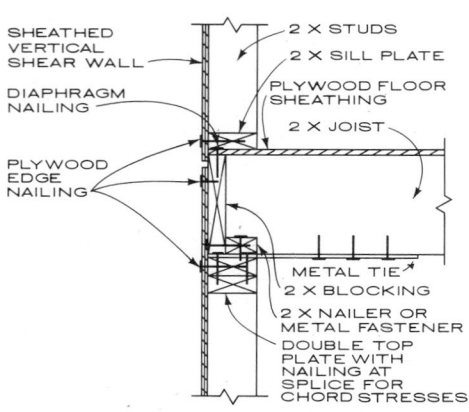

**JOIST PERPENDICULAR TO WALL**

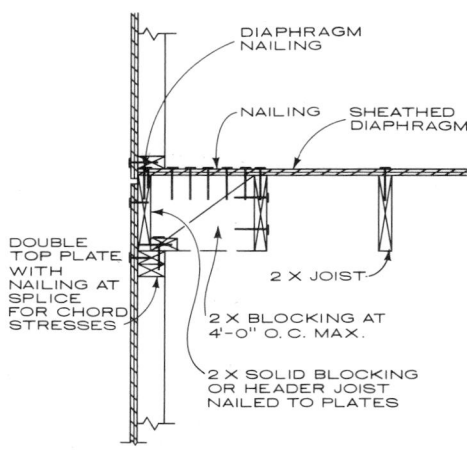

**JOIST PARALLEL TO WALL**

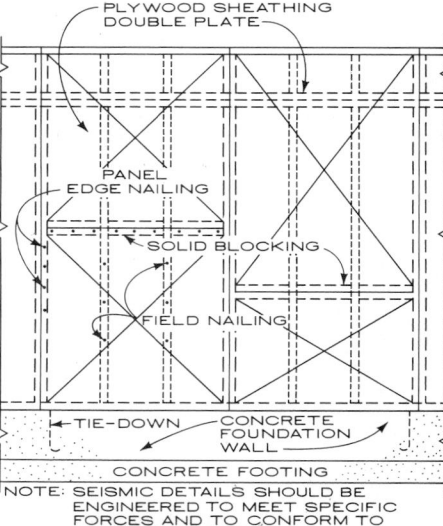

NOTE: SEISMIC DETAILS SHOULD BE ENGINEERED TO MEET SPECIFIC FORCES AND TO CONFORM TO APPLICABLE CODES.

**PLYWOOD SHEATHED SHEAR WALL WITH TIE-DOWNS**

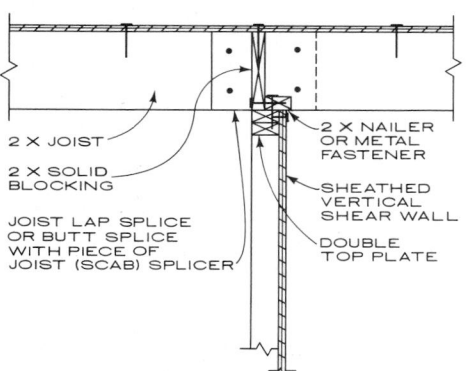

**JOIST PERPENDICULAR TO WALL**

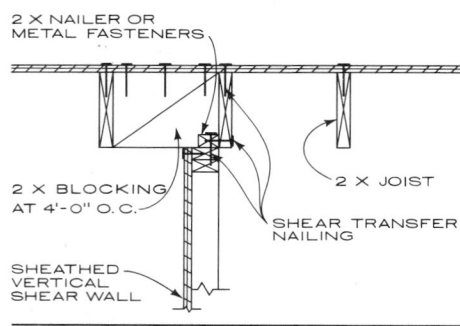

**JOIST PARALLEL TO WALL**

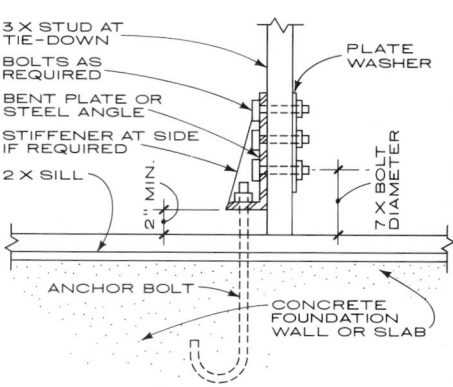

**TIE DOWN**

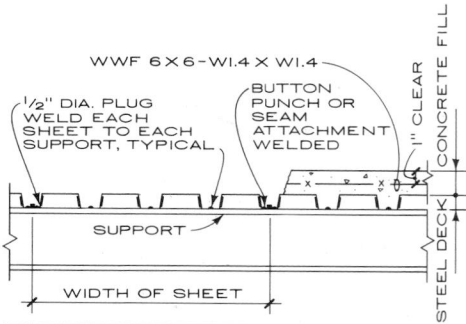

**DECK FLUTES PERPENDICULAR TO SUPPORT**

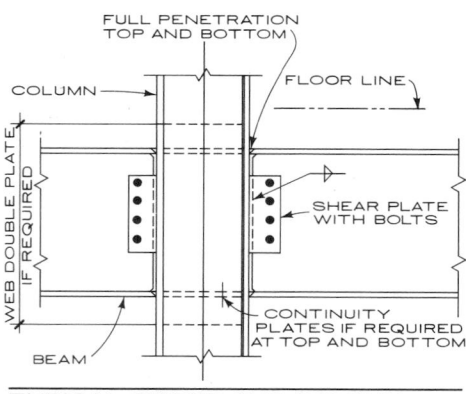

**TYPICAL GIRDER AND COLUMN MOMENT CONNECTION**

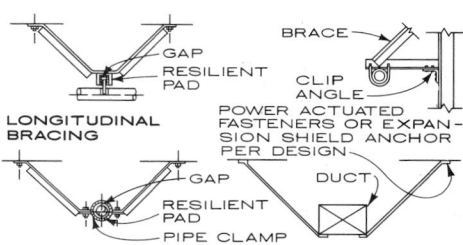

**BRACING FOR PIPES AND DUCTS**

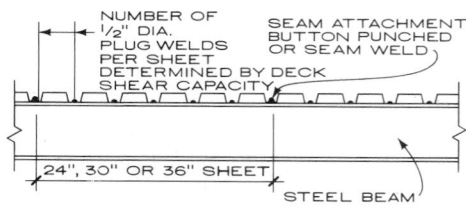

**DECK PERPENDICULAR TO SUPPORT**

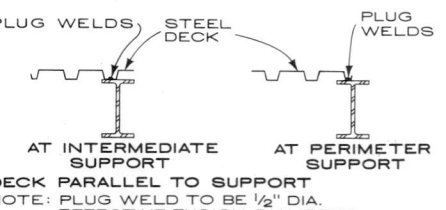

**DECK PARALLEL TO SUPPORT**
NOTE: PLUG WELD TO BE 1/2" DIA. EFFECTIVE FUSION DIAMETER.

**1-1/2" STEEL DECK WELDING PATTERN**

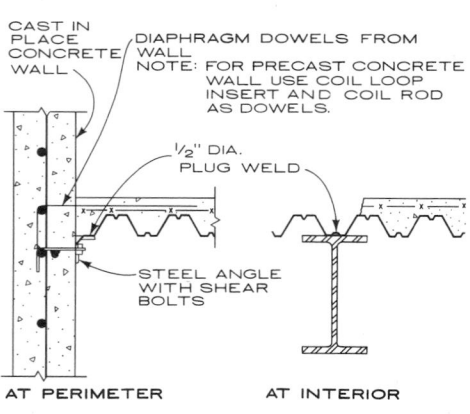

**DECK FLUTES PARALLEL TO SUPPORT**

**STEEL DECK WITH CONCRETE FILL**

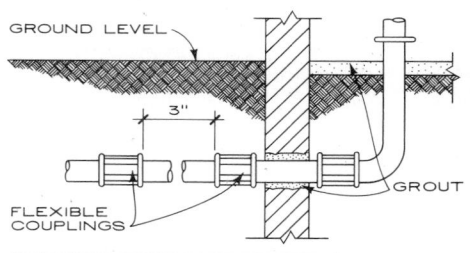

**PIPE ENTERING BUILDING**

**NOTE**
Details shown are representative of possible construction detailing. In addition to code defined structural requirements, safety considerations require nonstructural building elements and furnishings to be anchored in areas subjected to seismic movement. These pages show selected details as samples of recommended bracing and anchorage.

Attila L. Mocsary, PE; Hope Architects & Engineers; San Diego, California
Harold P. King, CEC; King, Benioff, Steinmann, King; Sherman Oaks, California

 **13**     **SEISMIC DESIGN**

# CHAPTER 14

## Conveying Systems

## GENERAL

An elevator system with its hoistway, machine room, and waiting lobbies is a major element in a building and requires special design consideration. Preengineered or custom-made elevator systems can be constructed to meet virtually all vertical transportation needs for passenger, freight, or service.

In all cases, design of an elevator system must be carefully considered throughout all stages of the building design process. During initial stages, the elevator handling capacity and quality of service desired determines the size, number, type, and location of elevator systems. Proper selection depends on type of tenancy, number of occupants, and the building design (number of floors, floor heights, building circulation, etc.). Elevator ARRANGEMENT locates the elevator within the building plan to provide efficient and accessible service. Each elevator system, once selected, requires OPERATIONAL SPACES, hoistway and machine room, and PASSENGER SPACES, lobby, and elevator car.

Proper planning and contact with representatives of the elevator industry and local code officials are essential to each of these design areas.

NOTE: WHERE A HOISTWAY EXTENDS INTO THE TOP FLOOR OF A BUILDING, FIRE RESISTIVE HOISTWAY OR MACHINERY SPACE ENCLOSURES, AS REQUIRED, SHALL BE CARRIED TO THE UNDERSIDE OF THE ROOF IF THE ROOF IS OF FIRE RESISTIVE CONSTRUCTION, AND AT LEAST 3 FT. ABOVE THE TOP SURFACE OF A FIRE NON-RESISTIVE ROOF

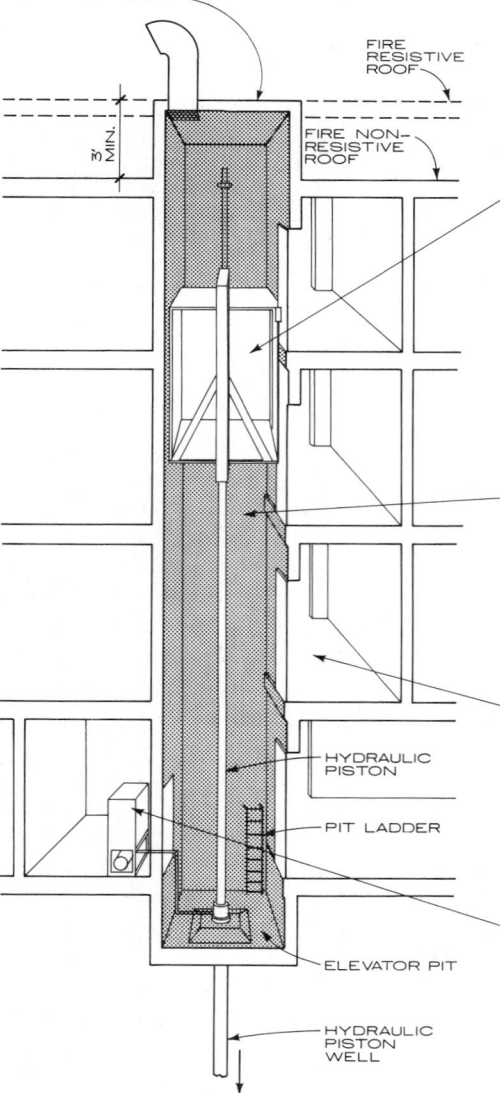

**HYDRAULIC ELEVATOR**

The two most common systems, the HYDRAULIC ELEVATOR and the ELECTRIC ELEVATOR, are shown in the two diagrams on this page. The systems are distinguished mainly by their hoisting mechanisms.

The HYDRAULIC ELEVATOR uses a hydraulic driving machine to raise and lower the elevator car and its load. A hydraulic driving machine is one in which the energy is applied by means of a liquid under pressure in a cylinder equipped with a plunger or piston. The car and driving machine are supported at the pit floor (hoistway base). Lower speeds and the piston length restrict the use of this system to approximately 60 ft. It generally requires the least initial installation expense, but more power is used during operation because of the greater loads imposed on the driving machine.

An ELECTRIC ELEVATOR is a power elevator where the energy is applied by means of an electric driving machine. In the electric driving machine the energy is applied by an electric motor. It includes the motor, brake, and the driving sheave or drum together with its connecting gearing, belt, or chain, if any. High speeds and virtually limitless rise allow this elevator to serve highrise, medium-rise, and lowrise buildings.

## MACHINE ROOM (ELECTRIC ELEVATOR)

Normally located directly over the top of the hoistway—it could also be below at side or rear—the machine room is designed to contain elevator hoisting machine and control equipment. Adequate ventilation, soundproofing, and structural support for the elevator must be considered. Local codes may require that no other electrical or mechanical equipment, not associated with the elevator, be installed in the machine room.

## ELEVATOR CAR

Guided by vertical guide rails, the elevator car conveys passenger or freight between floors. It consists of a car constructed within a supporting platform and frame. Design of the car focuses on the finished ceiling, walls, floor, and doors with lighting, ventilation, and elevator signal equipment.

The car of an hydraulic elevator system is supported by a piston or cylinder.

The car of a hydraulic elevator system is supported by a piston or cylinder.

## HOISTWAY

The hoistway is a shaftway for the travel of one or more elevators. It includes the pit and terminates at the underside of the overhang machinery space floor or grating, or at the underside of the roof where the hoistway does not penetrate the roof. Access to the elevator car and hoistway is normally through hoistway doors located at each floor serviced by the elevator system. Hoistway design is determined by the characteristics of the elevator system selected and by requirements of the applicable code for fire separation, ventilation, soundproofing, or nonstructural elements.

## LOBBY

Elevator waiting areas are designed to allow free circulation of passengers, rapid access to elevator cars, and clear visibility of elevator signals.

## HANDICAP ACCESSIBILITY

Passenger elevators on accessible routes should comply with requirements of ANSI 117.1.

## MACHINE ROOM (HYDRAULIC ELEVATOR)

Normally located near the base of the hoistway, the machine room contains hydraulic equipment and controls. Provisions of adequate ventilation and soundproofing must be considered. Local codes may require that no other electrical or mechanical equipment, not associated with the elevator, be installed in the machine room.

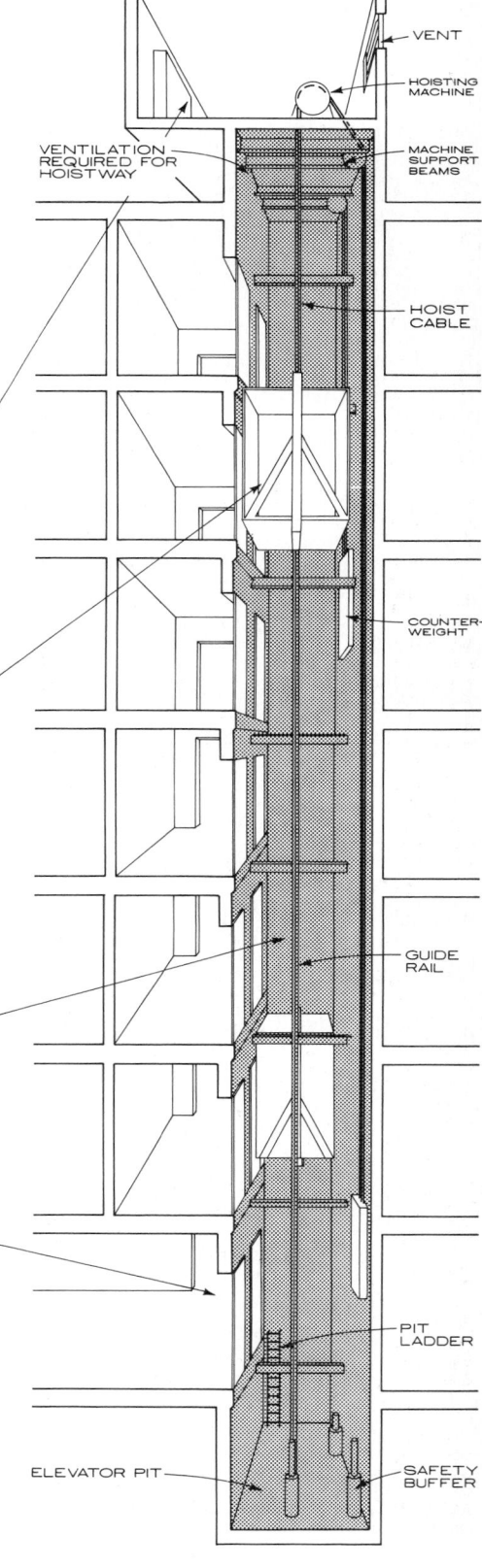

**ELECTRIC ELEVATOR**

Alexander Keyes; Darrel Downing Rippeteau, Architect; Washington, D.C.

**ELEVATORS**

# GENERAL

ELEVATOR SELECTION depends on several factors: the building's physical characteristics, available elevator systems, and code regulations. The functions that relate these selection parameters and indicate the number, size, and type of elevators are, in most cases, complex and are based on the performance of the elevator systems. Representatives of the elevator industry or consulting elevator engineers should be contacted during the selection process to ensure that the most suitable elevator system is chosen.

# PRIVATE RESIDENCES

Elevator selection for private residences can be simplified to a few parameters. By code they are limited in size, capacity, rise, and speed and are installed only in a private residence or a multiple dwelling as a means of access to a single private dwelling.

AVAILABLE ELEVATOR SYSTEMS are outlined on another page. The speed, capacity type, and controls of preengineered systems are generally limited to only a few options.

BUILDING POPULATION analysis involves the identification of the needs of prospective users. Relevant information includes the number of passengers expected to occupy the elevator in one trip and elevator service in a given time period, as well as the number of passengers expected and the possible need for a wheelchair.

BUILDING CHARACTERISTICS affect elevator selection by establishing the building height (distance of elevator travel) and hoistway location. In private residences, the elevator may occupy a tier of closets, an exterior shaft, a room corner, or a stairwell.

# ELEVATOR SELECTION—HOSPITAL

The accompanying diagram illustrates elevator selection parameters in the context of a hospital layout. Actual calculations relating these parameters are complex. Consultation with an elevator industry representative or consulting elevator engineer is recommended.

1. BUILDING HEIGHT: Floor-to-floor height and number of floors.
2. BUILDING POPULATION: Total number of building occupants and expected visitors and their expected distribution throughout the building.
3. BUILDING USE ANALYSIS: Location of offices, patients' rooms, service areas, and ancillary spaces conducive to mass assembly. Primary public circulation areas and primary staff circulation areas should be identified.
4. WAITING AREA: Peak loading and waiting time are two important concepts in providing the quality of elevator service expected by hospital visitors and staff. Different standards are applied according to building use. Consult an elevator engineer.
5. LOCATION OF MAJOR ENTRANCES
6. ELEVATOR SYSTEMS: A large selection of elevator capacities, speed, controls, and type are available. In this case, passenger and service elevators are shown. An elevator with a front and rear entrance serves as a passenger elevator during peak visiting hours. The wide variety of elevator alternatives should be discussed with an elevator engineer to select the system most suitable for each individual situation.

SERVICE REQUIREMENTS: Elevators must have sufficient capacity and speed to meet building service requirements. In this case, the elevator must accommodate a 24 x 76 in. ambulance type stretcher with attendants. Check local requirements.

For patient service in hospitals, to accommodate beds with their attachments, use 5000 lb elevators; platforms 6 ft wide x 9 ft 6 in. deep, doors at least 4 ft wide (4 ft 6 in. width is preferred).

CODE AND REGULATIONS: Recommendations and code restrictions regarding handicapped access, fire safety, elevator controls, and so on, may affect elevator selection. Consult with an elevator industry representative or consulting elevator engineer. As a minimum the ANSI A17.1 for Elevators, Dumbwaiters, Escalators and Moving Walks should be complied with.

NOTE: Elevators should not be considered as emergency exits.

# ELEVATOR SYSTEMS IN BUILDINGS OTHER THAN PRIVATE HOMES

Selection of elevator systems increases in complexity with the size and complexity of the project. Even though the vertical transportation needs of lowrise residential and commercial projects may be simply met, all the parameters listed below should be considered and analyzed with a consulting elevator engineer to ensure proper selection.

# BUILDING POPULATION

The elevator selection process must begin with a thorough analysis of how people will occupy the building.

1. TOTAL POPULATION AND DENSITY: The total number of occupants and visitors and their distribution by floors within a building.
2. PEAK LOADING: Periods when elevators carry the highest traffic loads. For example, peak loading in office buildings coincides with rush hours and/or lunch periods, while peak loading in hospitals may occur during visiting hours.
3. WAITING TIME: The length of time a passenger is expected to wait for the next elevator to arrive. These demands vary according to building use and building occupant expectations. A person willing to wait 50–70 sec in an apartment building may be willing to wait only 20–35 sec in an office building.
4. DEMAND FOR QUALITY: Sophistication of controls and elevator capacity may be varied to cater to the expected taste of passengers. Large elevator cars and the smooth, long life operation of a gearless elevator may convey an image of luxury even if a smaller elevator having a less sophisticated system would be technically sufficient.

# BUILDING CHARACTERISTICS

Physical building characteristics are considered together with population characteristics to determine size, speed, type, and location of elevator systems.

1. HEIGHT: The distance of elevator travel (from lowest terminal to top terminal), number of floors, and floor height.
2. BUILDING USE ANALYSIS: Location of building entrance areas of heavy use such as cafeteria, restaurant, auditorium, and service areas must be identified. Typically, a building should be planned to ensure that no prospective passengers must walk more than 200 ft to reach an elevator.

# ELEVATOR SYSTEMS AND REGULATIONS

The parameters previously described outline the environment in which the elevator operates. Local code regulations and ANSI A17.1 requirements provide further elevator guidelines.

Available elevator systems are analyzed to ensure that suitable speed, capacity, controls, and number of cars are selected.

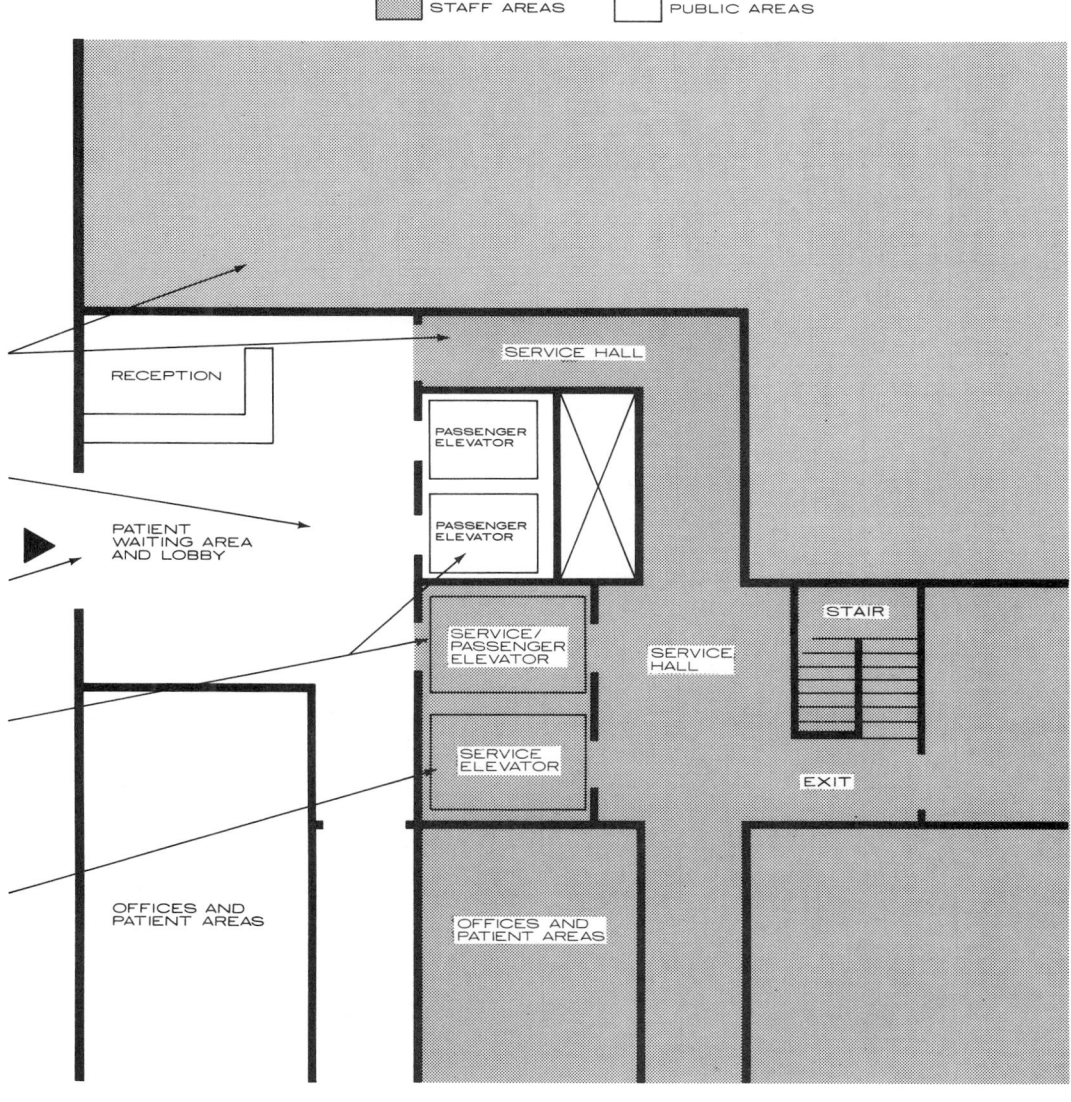

STAFF AREAS    PUBLIC AREAS

RECEPTION

SERVICE HALL

PASSENGER ELEVATOR

PASSENGER ELEVATOR

PATIENT WAITING AREA AND LOBBY

SERVICE/ PASSENGER ELEVATOR

SERVICE HALL

STAIR

SERVICE ELEVATOR

EXIT

OFFICES AND PATIENT AREAS

OFFICES AND PATIENT AREAS

**ELEVATOR SELECTION FACTORS — HOSPITAL**

Alexander Keyes; Darrel Downing Rippeteau, Architect; Washington, D.C.

## GENERAL NOTES

Lowrise buildings may use either the hydraulic or the electric elevator systems. Elevator selection, arrangement, and design of lobby and cars are similar in both cases. The primary differences between the two systems are in their operational requirements. The hydraulic elevator system is described below; the electric elevator system on the next page.

The major architectural considerations of the hydraulic elevator are the machine room, normally located at the base, and the hoistway serving as a fire protected, ventilated passageway for the elevator car. Adequate structure must be provided at the base of the hoistway to bear the load of the elevator car and its supporting piston or cylinder.

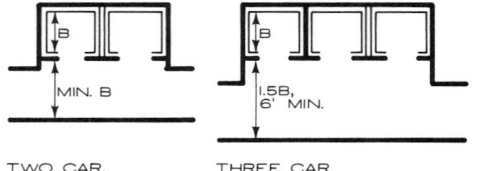

TWO CAR, SIDE BY SIDE  THREE CAR, SIDE BY SIDE

B = DEPTH OF CAR

### NOTES

Certain guidelines lead to effective placement, grouping, and arrangement of elevators within a building. Elevators should be: (a) centrally located, (b) near the main entrance, and (c) easily accessible on all floors. If a building requires more than one elevator, they should be grouped, with possible exception of service elevators.

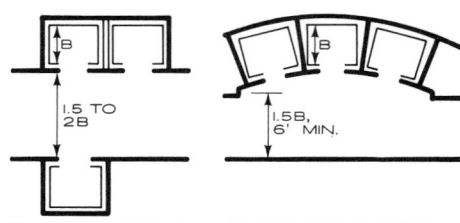

TWO OR THREE CAR, OPPOSITE  THREE CAR, SPECIAL ARRANGEMENT

Within each grouping, elevators should be arranged to minimize walking distance between cars. Sufficient lobby space must be provided to accommodate group movement.

**ELEVATOR ARRANGEMENT, TWO AND THREE CARS** (TYPICAL FOR LOWRISE APPLICATIONS)

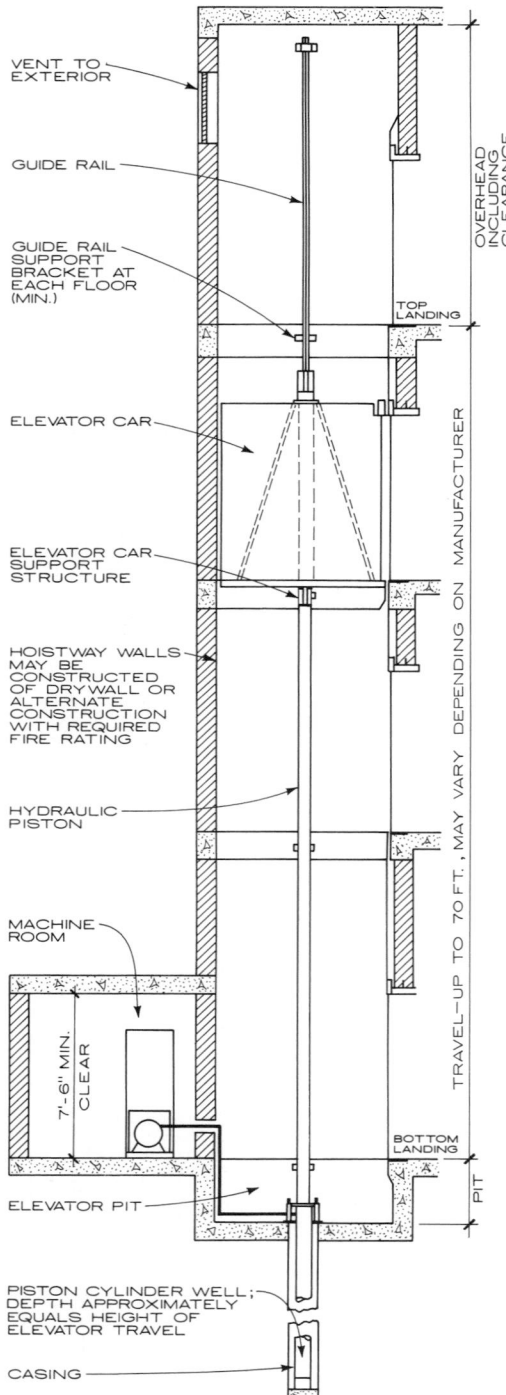

HYDRAULIC ELEVATOR – SECTION

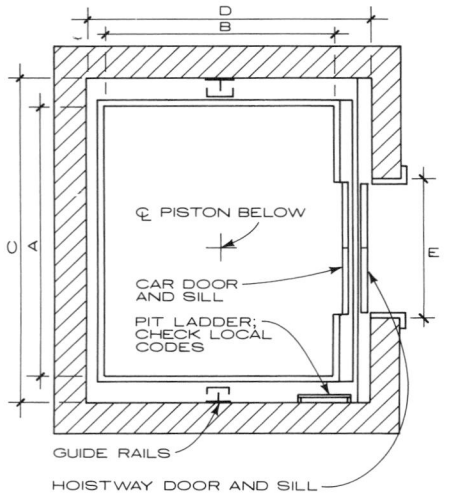

ELEVATOR CAR AND HOISTWAY

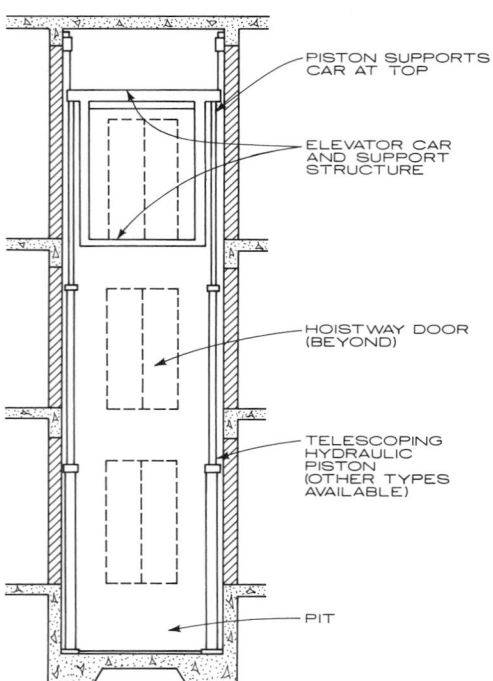

One type of holeless hydraulic elevator uses a telescoping hydraulic piston as the driving machine, eliminating the need for cylinder well excavation. This system is presently limited to a height of three stories or 21 ft 6 in. Other types of holeless hydraulic elevator units are also available using an inverted cylinder attached to the side of the elevator car.

HOLELESS HYDRAULIC ELEVATOR – SECTION

## HYDRAULIC ELEVATOR DIMENSIONS

| RATED LOAD (LB) | DIMENSIONS (FT-IN.) | | | | |
|---|---|---|---|---|---|
| | A | B | C | D | E |
| 1500 | 4-10 | 5-0 | 6-8 | 5-9 | 2-8 |
| 2000 | 6-0 | 5-0 | 7-4 | 5-9 | 3-0 |
| 2500 | 7-0 | 5-0 | 8-4 | 5-9 | 3-6 |
| 3000 | 7-0 | 5-6 | 8-4 | 6-3 | 3-6 |
| 3500 | 7-0 | 6-2 | 8-4 | 6-11 | 3-6 |
| 4000 | 5-8 | 8-9 | 7-4 | 9-8 | 4-0 |

Rated speeds are 75 to 200 fpm.

### NOTES

Elevator car and hoistway dimensions of the preengineered units listed above are for reference purposes only. A broad selection of units is available. Representatives of the elevator industry should be contacted for the dimensions of specific systems.

Hoistway walls normally serve primarily as fireproof enclosures. Check local codes for required fire ratings. Guide rails extend from the pit floor to the underside of the overhead. When excessive floor heights are encountered consult the elevator supplier for special requirements.

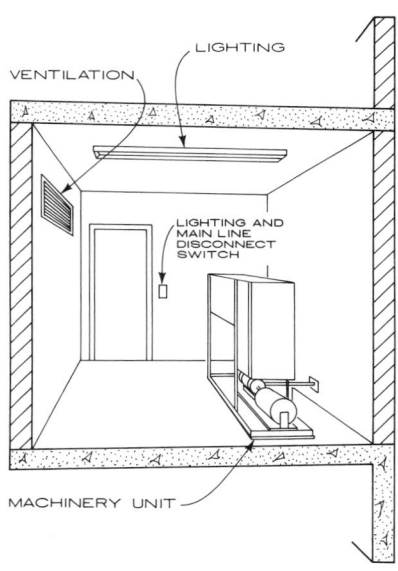

The MACHINE ROOM of a hydraulic elevator system is usually located next to the hoistway at or near the bottom terminal landing. Consult with elevator manufacturers for required dimensions. Refer to local codes.

Machinery consists of a pump and motor drive unit, hydraulic fluid storage tank, and control panel. Adequate ventilation, lighting, and entrance access (usually 3 ft 6 in. x 7 ft) should be provided.

MACHINE ROOM

Alexander Keyes; Darrel Downing Rippeteau, Architect; Washington, D.C.

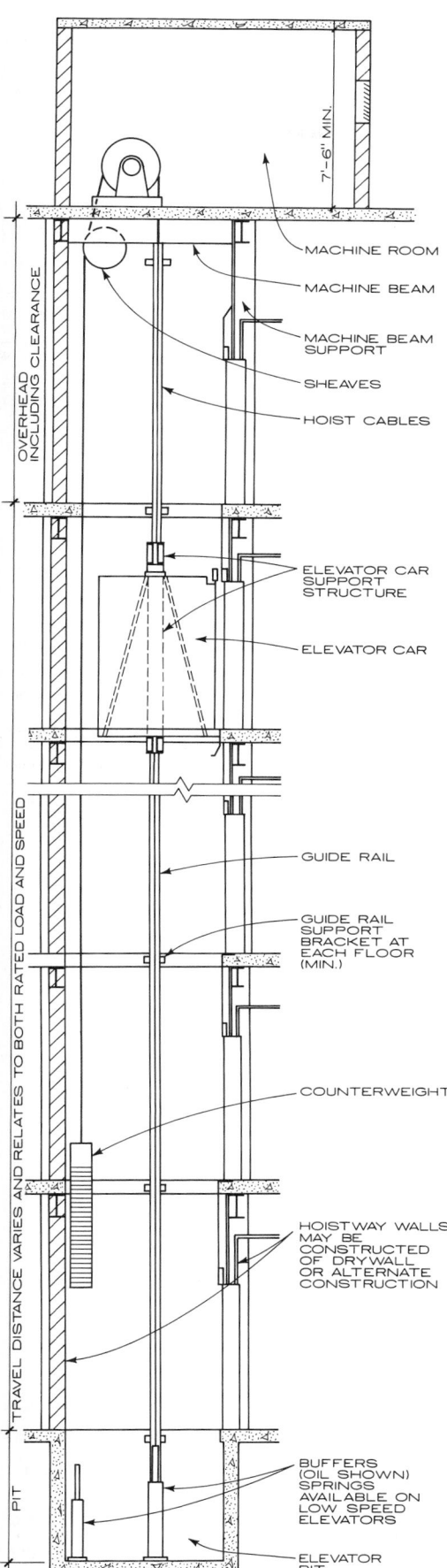

**ELECTRIC ELEVATOR — SECTION**

Labels (top to bottom): MACHINE ROOM; MACHINE BEAM; MACHINE BEAM SUPPORT; SHEAVES; HOIST CABLES; ELEVATOR CAR SUPPORT STRUCTURE; ELEVATOR CAR; GUIDE RAIL; GUIDE RAIL SUPPORT BRACKET AT EACH FLOOR (MIN.); COUNTERWEIGHT; HOISTWAY WALLS; MAY BE CONSTRUCTED OF DRYWALL OR ALTERNATE CONSTRUCTION; BUFFERS (OIL SHOWN) SPRINGS AVAILABLE ON LOW SPEED ELEVATORS; ELEVATOR PIT

Left side labels: OVERHEAD INCLUDING CLEARANCE; 7'-6" MIN.; TRAVEL DISTANCE VARIES AND RELATES TO BOTH RATED LOAD AND SPEED; PIT

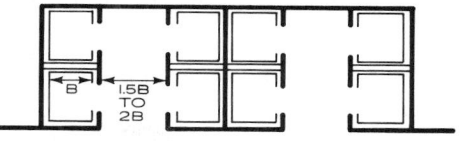

B = DEPTH OF CAR

## NOTES

The largest practical grouping of elevators in a building is eight cars. One row of more than four cars is generally unacceptable. With groupings of four or six cars, waiting lobbies may be alcoved (one end closed) or open at both ends. In case of several elevator groupings, one grouping may serve lower floors, while others are express elevators to upper floors.

(diagram labels) B, 1.5B TO 2B; LOBBY MUST BE OPEN AT BOTH ENDS WITH AN EIGHT CAR GROUPING; B, 1.75B TO 2B, B, 2B

Where 4 or more elevators serve all or the same portion of a building, they shall be located in not less than 2 hoistways, but in no case shall more than 4 elevators be located in any one hoistway.

## ELEVATOR ARRANGEMENTS — FOUR, SIX, AND EIGHT CARS (TYPICAL FOR HIGHRISE APPLICATIONS)

(diagram labels) CONTROLS; MACHINE HOISTING BEAM; GEARLESS HOISTING MACHINE; MOTOR – GENERATOR SET; MACHINE BEAM; HOISTING CABLES; HOISTWAY WALL

### NOTES

The MACHINE ROOM for electric elevators is normally located directly above the hoistway. Space must be provided for the elevator drive, control equipment, and governor with sufficient clearance for equipment installation, repair, or removal. Space requirements vary substantially according to code capacity and speed of the system selected. Adequate lighting and ventilation are required by codes, and sound insulation should be provided.

## MACHINE ROOM (GEARLESS ELEVATOR)

(diagram labels) C, A, D, B, E; COUNTERWEIGHT AND GUIDES; CAR; GUIDES; PIT LADDER; CHECK CODES; STEEL BEAM SUPPORT FOR GUIDE RAIL AT EACH FLOOR (MIN.); HOISTWAY DOOR AND SILL

## ELECTRIC ELEVATOR DIMENSIONS

| RATED LOAD (LB) | DIMENSIONS (FT-IN.) | | | | |
|---|---|---|---|---|---|
| | A | B | C | D | E |
| 2000 | 6-0 | 5-0 | 7-4 | 6-10 | 3-0 |
| 2500 | 7-0 | 5-0 | 8-4 | 6-7 | 3-6 |
| 3000 | 7-0 | 5-6 | 8-4 | 7-1 | 3-6 |
| 3500 | 7-0 | 6-2 | 8-4 | 7-7 | 3-6 |
| 4000 | 5-8 | 8-9 | 7-8 | 9-8 | 4-0 |

### NOTES

Dimensions of preengineered units, listed above, are for reference purposes only. Elevator manufacturers should be consulted for a complete selection.

## ELEVATOR HOISTWAY AND CAR — ELECTRIC ELEVATOR

### NOTES

Medium and highrise buildings utilize ELECTRIC GEARED TRACTION and ELECTRIC GEARLESS TRACTION elevator systems. The main difference between the two systems lies in the hoisting machinery. General design considerations involving hoistway, machine room, and elevator planning are similar.

ELECTRIC GEARLESS TRACTION ELEVATOR systems are available in preengineered units with speeds of 200 to 1200 fpm. Systems with greater speeds are also available. Gearless elevators, when used in conjunction with appropriate controls, offer the advantages of a long life and smoothness of ride.

ELECTRIC GEARED TRACTION ELEVATOR systems are designed to operate within the range of 100 to 350 fpm, which restricts their use to medium rise buildings.

Both geared and gearless drive units are governed by CONTROLS, which coordinate car leveling, passenger calls, collective operation of elevators, door operation, car acceleration and deceleration, and safety applications. A broad range of control systems are available to meet individual building requirements.

STRUCTURAL REQUIREMENTS call for the total weight of the elevator system to be supported by the MACHINE BEAMS and transmitted to the building (or hoistway) structure. Consult with elevator and structural engineers.

If the elevator machine is to be supported solely by the machine room floor slab, the floor slab shall be designed in accordance with the requirements of ANSI A17.1.

Check local codes for required fire enclosures.

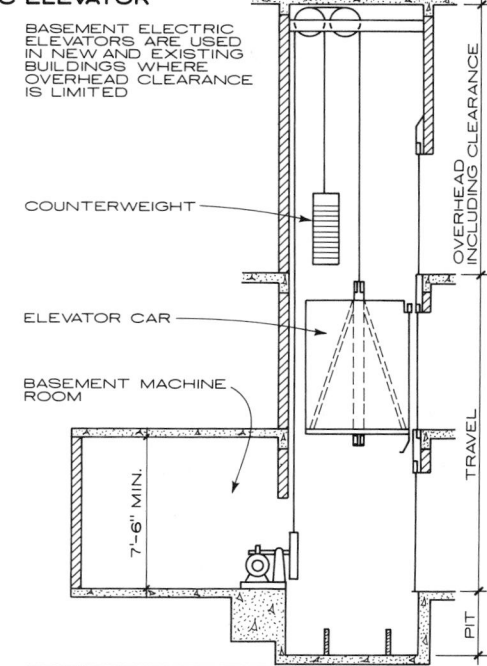

**BASEMENT ELECTRIC ELEVATOR — SECTION**

(diagram labels) BASEMENT ELECTRIC ELEVATORS ARE USED IN NEW AND EXISTING BUILDINGS WHERE OVERHEAD CLEARANCE IS LIMITED; OVERHEAD INCLUDING CLEARANCE; COUNTERWEIGHT; ELEVATOR CAR; BASEMENT MACHINE ROOM; 7'-6" MIN.; TRAVEL; PIT

Alexander Keyes; Darrel Downing Rippeteau, Architect; Washington, D.C.

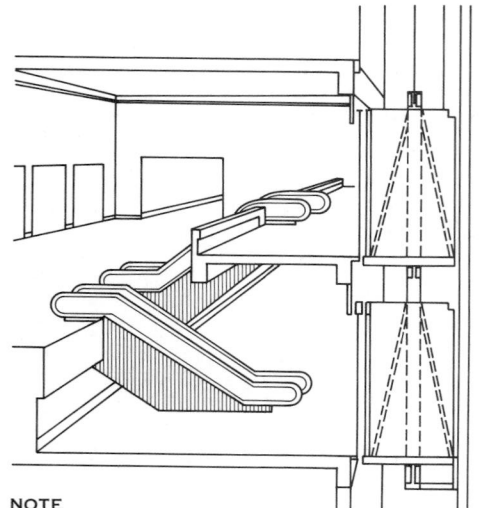

**NOTE**

In buildings with heavy populations double deck elevators permit an increase in handling capacity without increasing the number of elevators. Two cars in tandem operate simultaneously, one serving all floors. Escalators connect the two floors in 2-story lobbies.

**DOUBLE DECK ELEVATOR**

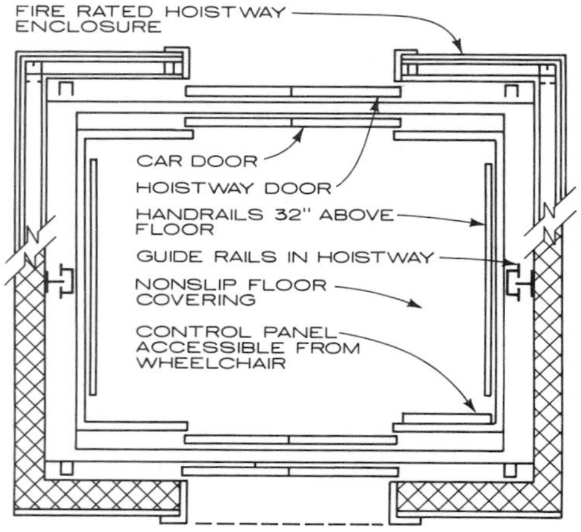

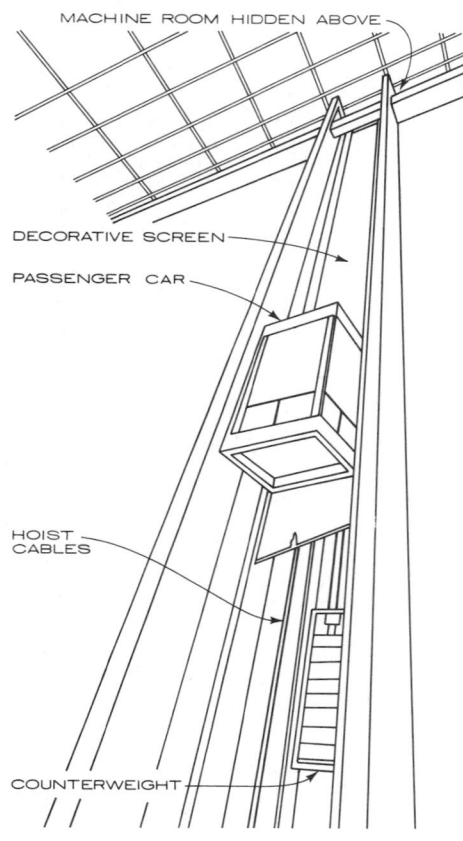

MACHINE ROOM HIDDEN ABOVE

DECORATIVE SCREEN

PASSENGER CAR

HOIST CABLES

COUNTERWEIGHT

**NOTE**

Observation and glassback elevators travel outside of a hoistway or in a hoistway open on one side. Machinery is concealed or designed to be inconspicuous. Elevators may be engineered for hydraulic, geared, or gearless use. Cabs can be custom designed with over 75% of wall area as glass. Glassback cabs provide glass rear panel only. Safety barriers must be provided at floor penetrations and ground floor, completely surrounding that part of elevator not enclosed by hoistway.

**OBSERVATION ELEVATOR**

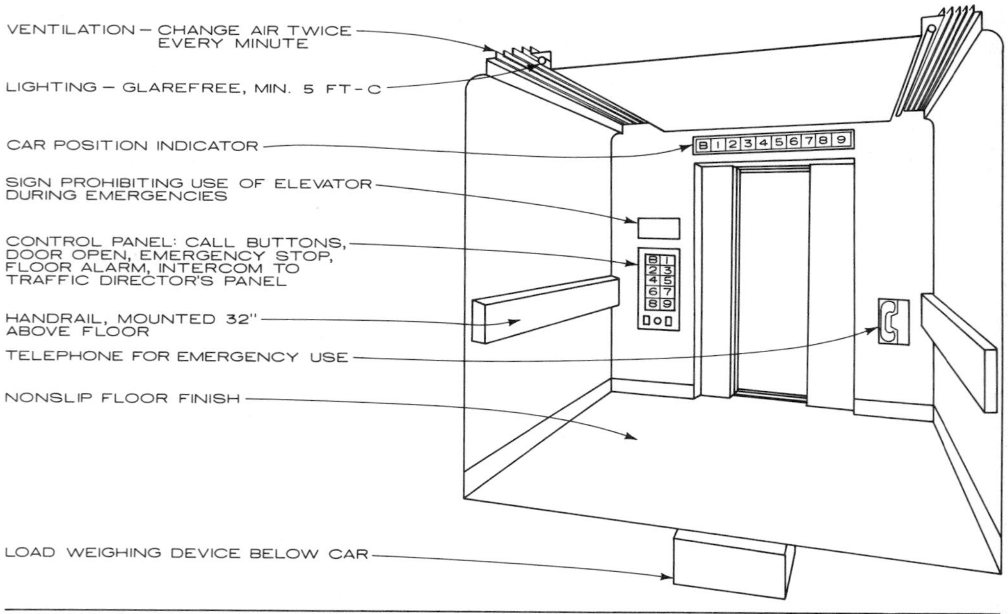

---

FIRE RATED HOISTWAY ENCLOSURE

CAR DOOR

HOISTWAY DOOR

HANDRAILS 32" ABOVE FLOOR

GUIDE RAILS IN HOISTWAY

NONSLIP FLOOR COVERING

CONTROL PANEL ACCESSIBLE FROM WHEELCHAIR

**PLAN OF ELEVATOR CAR WITH REAR DOOR**

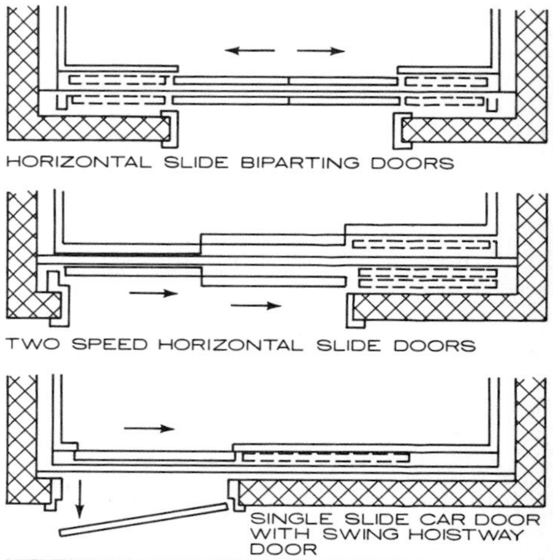

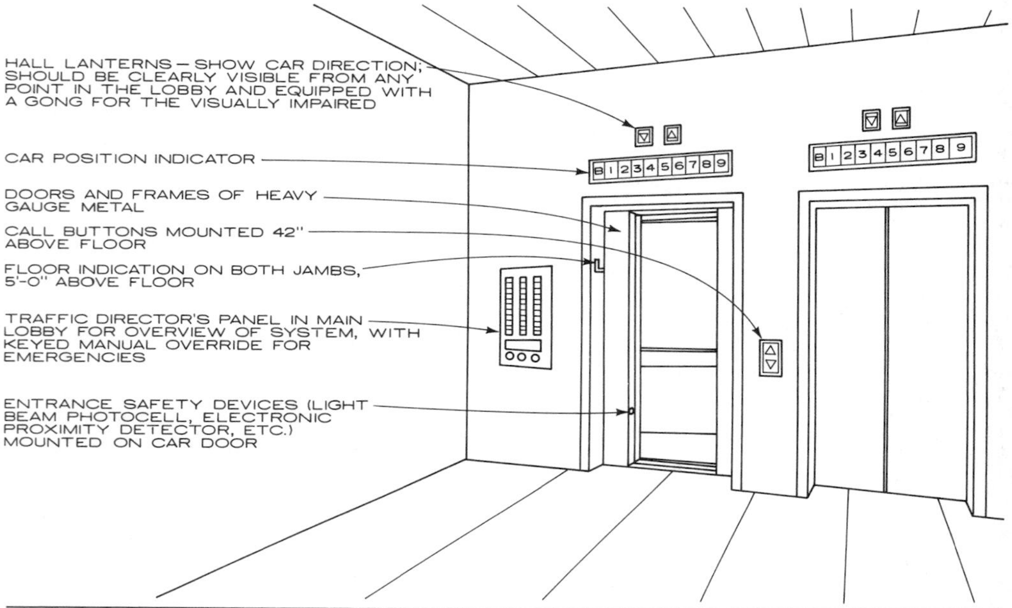

HALL LANTERNS — SHOW CAR DIRECTION; SHOULD BE CLEARLY VISIBLE FROM ANY POINT IN THE LOBBY AND EQUIPPED WITH A GONG FOR THE VISUALLY IMPAIRED

CAR POSITION INDICATOR

DOORS AND FRAMES OF HEAVY GAUGE METAL

CALL BUTTONS MOUNTED 42" ABOVE FLOOR

FLOOR INDICATION ON BOTH JAMBS, 5'-0" ABOVE FLOOR

TRAFFIC DIRECTOR'S PANEL IN MAIN LOBBY FOR OVERVIEW OF SYSTEM, WITH KEYED MANUAL OVERRIDE FOR EMERGENCIES

ENTRANCE SAFETY DEVICES (LIGHT BEAM PHOTOCELL, ELECTRONIC PROXIMITY DETECTOR, ETC.) MOUNTED ON CAR DOOR

**ELEVATOR LOBBY**

---

HORIZONTAL SLIDE BIPARTING DOORS

TWO SPEED HORIZONTAL SLIDE DOORS

SINGLE SLIDE CAR DOOR WITH SWING HOISTWAY DOOR

**ELEVATOR DOOR TYPES**

VENTILATION — CHANGE AIR TWICE EVERY MINUTE

LIGHTING — GLAREFREE, MIN. 5 FT-C

CAR POSITION INDICATOR

SIGN PROHIBITING USE OF ELEVATOR DURING EMERGENCIES

CONTROL PANEL: CALL BUTTONS, DOOR OPEN, EMERGENCY STOP, FLOOR ALARM, INTERCOM TO TRAFFIC DIRECTOR'S PANEL

HANDRAIL, MOUNTED 32" ABOVE FLOOR

TELEPHONE FOR EMERGENCY USE

NONSLIP FLOOR FINISH

LOAD WEIGHING DEVICE BELOW CAR

**INTERIOR OF ELEVATOR CAR**

---

Alexander Keyes; Darrel Downing Rippeteau, Architect; Washington, D.C.

**ELEVATORS**

## NOTES

1. For continuous travel in multistory installations guide rails must be fitted to inside core of turning stairways.
2. Three stories total travel (maximum).
3. Suitable for interior and exterior applications.
4. Speeds: 20–25 fpm. Capacity: 450–500 lb.

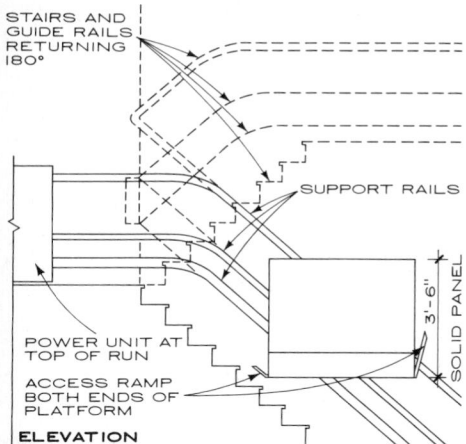

**STAIR LIFT–PLATFORM**

## WHEELCHAIR LIFT REQUIREMENTS

| TYPICAL ANSI A17.1, SEC. 2000.1B | PRIVATE RESIDENCE ANSI A17.1, SEC. 2100.1 |
|---|---|
| 42 in. door: top and bottom landings, mechanical/electrical interlock, solid construction | 36 in. door: top landing, bottom landing can have guard (other requirements similar to 42 in.) |
| Platform sides 42 in. solid construction | Platform 36 in. solid construction |
| Grabrails | Same |
| Enclosure or telescoping toe guard | Obstruction switch on platform |
| Maximum travel 12 ft | Maximum travel 10 ft |
| | Automatic guard 6 in. at bottom landing in lieu of door |
| Key operation | Key operation |

## INCLINED WHEELCHAIR LIFT

| TYPICAL ANSI A17.1, SEC. 2001 | PRIVATE RESIDENCE ANSI A17.1, SEC. 2100 |
|---|---|
| 42 in. self-closing door: solid construction, mechanical/electrical interlock, lower landing | 36 in. self-closing door: solid construction, mechanical/electrical interlock, upper landing |
| 42 in. platform side guard not used as exit, solid construction | 36 in. platform side guard not used as exit, solid construction |
| 6 in. guard permitted in lieu of side guard | 6 in. guard permitted in lieu of side guard |
| 6 in. retractable guard to prevent wheelchair rolling off platform | 6 in. retractable guard to prevent wheelchair rolling off platform |
| Door required at bottom landing | Underside obstruction, switch bottom landing |
| Travel 15 ft | Travel 12 ft |
| Key operation; attendant operation is push button | Key operation; attendant operation is push button and requires door at bottom landing |

**WHEELCHAIR LIFT**

### NOTE

Wheelchair lifts are suitable for retrofits on non-barrier-free buildings. Bridges are available from manufacturers for installation over stairs. Recommended speed: 10–19 fpm. Capacity 500–750 lb.

Lifts operate on standard household current and are suitable for interior and exterior applications.

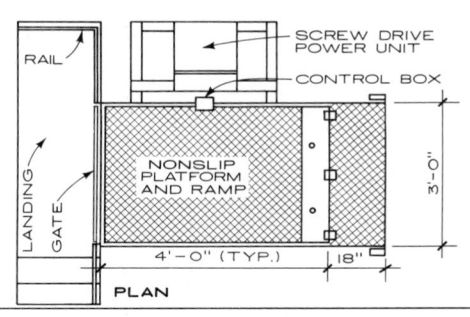

**PLAN**

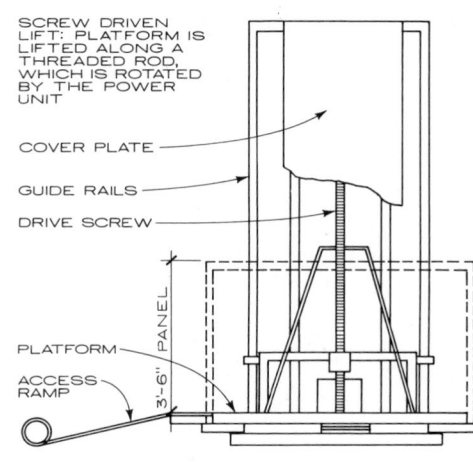

**SIDE VIEW**

### NOTE

Stair lifts can be adapted to straight run and spiral stairs. Standard types run along a track fastened to the steps. Power units, when not contained in a housing under the chair, can be located as shown in section, or in basement or attic. Similar inclined wheelchair lifts are also available for installations down stairs. Recommended speed: 25 fpm. Capacity: 250–350 lb.

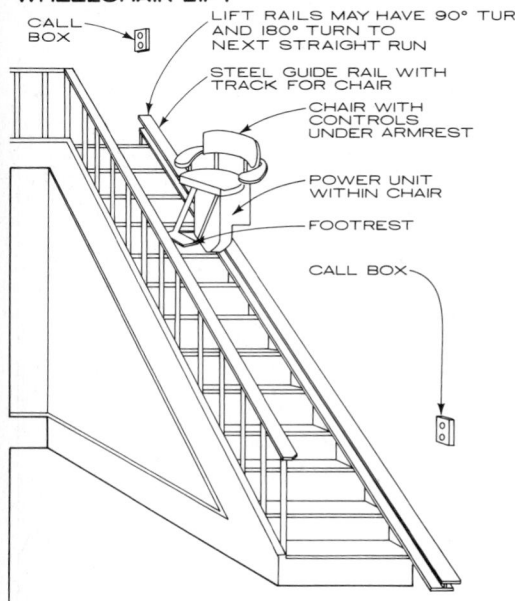

**STAIR LIFT – CHAIR**

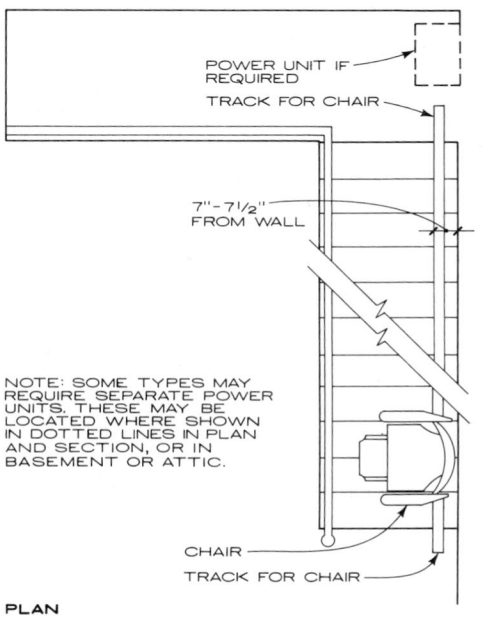

**PLAN**

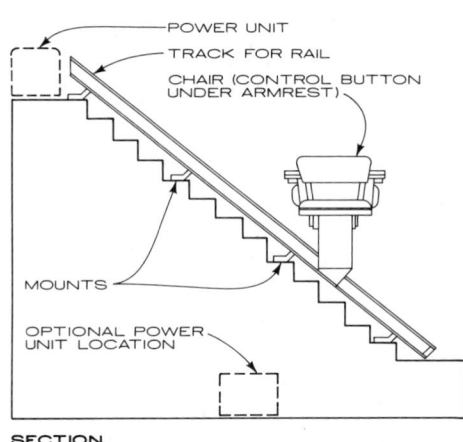

**SECTION**

Beth D. Buffington, AIA; Wilkes, Faulkner, Jenkins, and Bass Architects; Washington, D.C.
Olga Barmine; Darrel Downing Rippeteau, Architect; Washington, D.C.

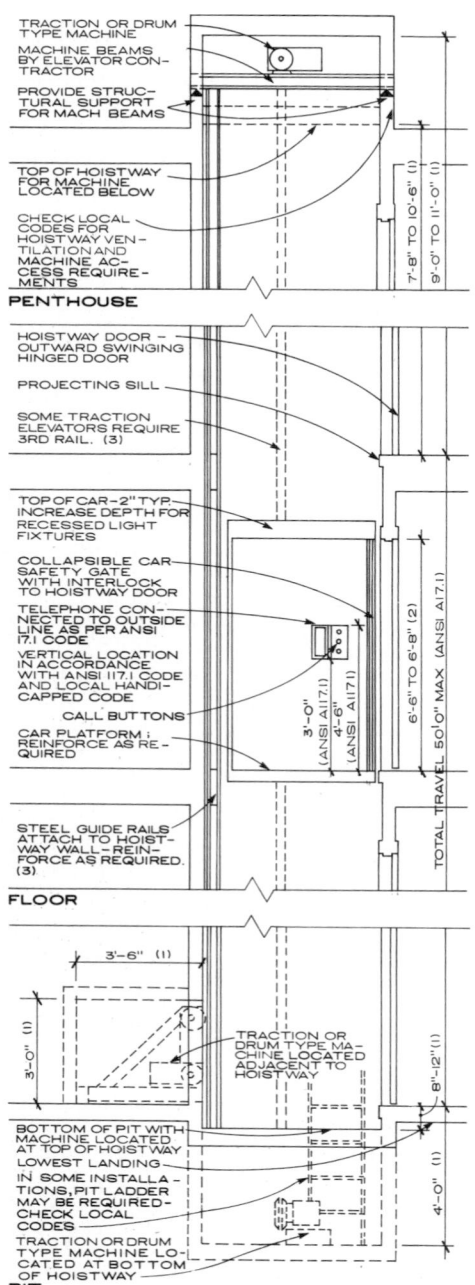

**PENTHOUSE**

**FLOOR**

**PIT**

**ELEVATOR SECTION**

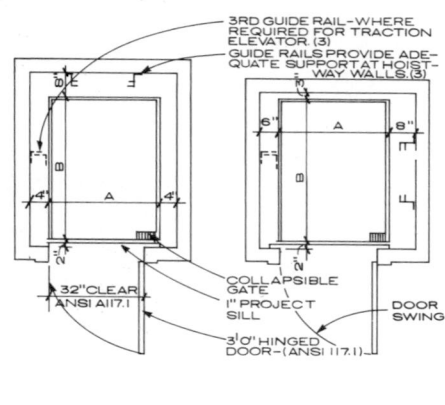

CAR WITH RAILS AT REAR (4,5)    CAR WITH RAILS AT SIDE (4,5)

**RESIDENTIAL ELEVATOR PLANS**

Beth D. Buffington, AIA; Wilkes, Faulkner, Jenkins, and Bass Architects; Washington, D.C.

## RESIDENTIAL ELEVATORS

Typical car sizes, A x B: 36 in. x 36 in., 42 in. x 42 in., 36 in. x 48 in.

12 sq ft platform maximum size allowed by National Elevator Code for residential elevators, ANSI A17.1. This platform size does not meet the National Handicapped Access Code, ANSI A117.1, for use by an unassisted wheelchair-bound person.

Load capacity of drum-type machine is 450 lb. Speed is 30 ft per minute.

Load capacity of traction machine is 700 lb. Speed is 36 ft per minute.

Elevators operate on 220/230 volt, single phase power supply. A disconnect switch must be provided within sight of the machine. A 110V, single phase power supply is required for lighting of machine area of hoistway.

Enclosures are recommended for all hoistways. Fire rating of hoistway enclosure and access doors must be consistent with the fire rating of the building construction. See local codes.

### NOTES

1. Dimensions may vary among manufacturers and according to system selected. Elevators carrying greater loads or operating at higher speeds require more clearance overhead and in pit areas.
2. Elevator cars may have higher interior clearances if desired, which increases overhead clearance required in the hoistway.
3. Guide rails usually are provided by the manufacturer in 5 ft sections. Some manufacturers supply rails that can span from floor structure to floor structure. If the existing structure cannot support the guide rails, manufacturers can provide a self-supporting tower that transmits the load to its base. Increased horizontal clearance in the hoistway is required. If a third guide rail is required, it is supplied in 3 ft 4 in. sections.
4. Dimensions given are appropriate for most applications. For exact dimensions required in specific circumstances, consult manufacturers.
5. Elevator cars can be provided with openings on two sides; guide rails must be located accordingly. Consult manufacturers.

## DUMBWAITERS

Typical car sizes, A x B: 24 in. x 24 in., 30 in. x 30 in., 36 in. x 36 in., 30 in. x 48 in. Smaller sizes are available.

9 sq ft platform maximum size allowed by National Elevator Code for dumbwaiters, ANSI A17.1.

48 in. high car is maximum allowed by National Elevator Code for dumbwaiters, ANSI A17.1.

Load capacity for drum-type machines is 500 lb. Speed is 50 ft per minute.

Drum-type machines are not recommended for installations with total travel of more than 36 ft–40 ft. Maximum total travel 50 ft.

Load capacity of traction machines is 500 lb. Speeds to 500 ft per minute are available.

Dumbwaiters require 3 phase electrical power. For exact voltage consult manufacturer.

### NOTES

1. Dimensions may vary among manufacturers and according to system selected. Dumbwaiters carrying greater loads or operating at higher speeds require more clearance overhead and in pit areas.
2. Guide rails usually are provided by the manufacturer in 5 ft sections. Some manufacturers supply rails that can span from floor structure to floor structure. If existing structure cannot support the guide rails, manufacturers can provide a self-supporting tower that transmits the load to its base. Increased horizontal clearance in the hoistway is required.
3. Vertical dimensions given assume the use of vertical bi-parting doors. The entire door may slide up or down; however, required clearances will vary. Swing hoistway doors also are available. Consult manufacturers.

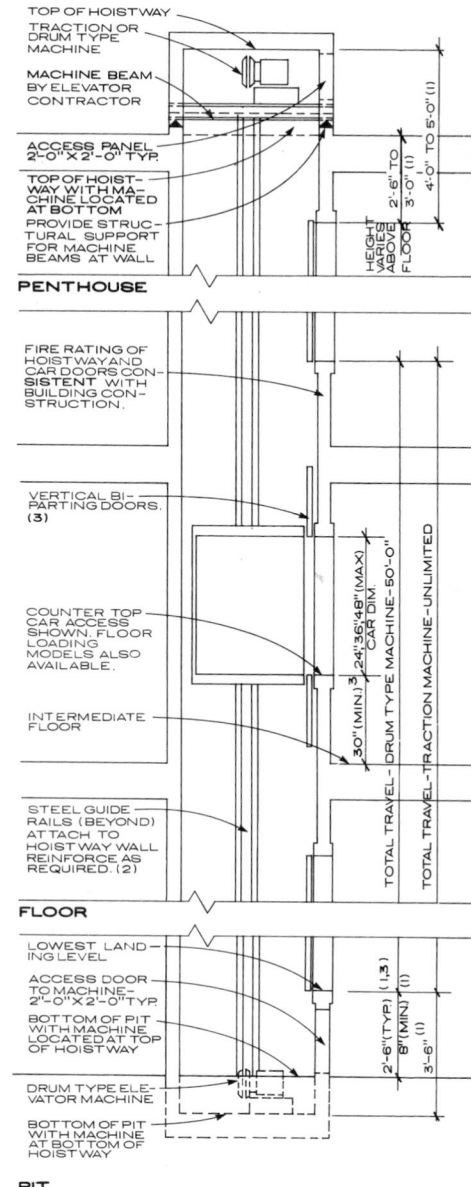

**PENTHOUSE**

**FLOOR**

**PIT**

**DUMBWAITER SECTION**

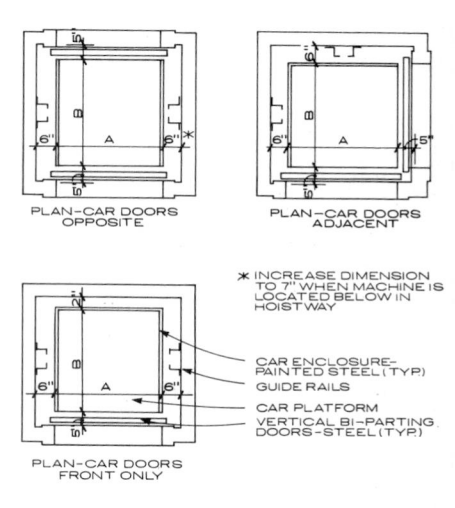

PLAN–CAR DOORS OPPOSITE

PLAN–CAR DOORS ADJACENT

PLAN–CAR DOORS FRONT ONLY

**PLANS OF TYPICAL DUMBWAITERS**

## SERVICE ELEVATORS

Service elevators in industrial, residential, and commercial buildings are often standard passenger elevator packages modified for service use. These modified systems, when compared with custom made freight elevator systems, are generally more economical, are delivered in less time, and have more stringent load ratings related to the platform area. Special provisions include interior cab protection (steel or oak rubbing strips or suitable abuse resistant finish surface) and a door and cab of sufficient size to handle expected loads. Standard horizontal sliding doors can often meet service needs. If the full width of the car platform is needed for loading, vertical biparting doors can be used. If bulky loads are expected only occasionally, a removable car front with swinging hoistway door panels can be provided.

Vertically sliding doors and vertically sliding gates, where permitted by ANSI A17.1, shall conform to the following requirements:

1. At entrances used by passengers they shall be:
   a. Of the balanced counterweighted type which slide in the up direction to open.
   b. Power operated.
2. At entrances used exclusively for freight, they shall be:
   a. Of the balanced counterweighted type or the biparting counterbalanced type.
   b. Manually or power operated.

CAPACITY: Size to largest expected load, with the exception of single one piece loading, which is restricted to 25% of the rated capacity.

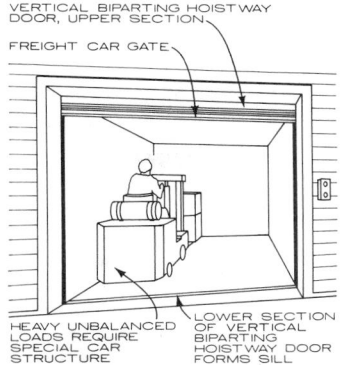

VERTICAL BIPARTING HOISTWAY DOOR, UPPER SECTION

FREIGHT CAR GATE

HEAVY UNBALANCED LOADS REQUIRE SPECIAL CAR STRUCTURE

LOWER SECTION OF VERTICAL BIPARTING HOISTWAY DOOR FORMS SILL

**INTERIOR VIEW**

### FREIGHT ELEVATOR DIMENSIONS

| CAPACITY (LB) | PLATFORM | | HOISTWAY | |
|---|---|---|---|---|
| | WIDTH | DEPTH | WIDTH | DEPTH |
| 2,500 | 5'-4'' | 7'-0'' | 7'-4'' | 8'-2'' |
| 6,000 | 8'-4'' | 10'-0'' | 10'-4'' | 11'-2'' |
| 10,000 | 8'-4'' | 12'-0'' | 11'-4'' | 13'-2'' |
| 16,000 | 10'-4'' | 14'-0'' | 14'-0'' | 15'-2'' |
| 20,000 | 12'-4'' | 20'-4'' | 16'-6'' | 21'-6'' |

**FREIGHT ELEVATOR**

## FREIGHT ELEVATORS

Freight elevators are usually classed as general freight loading, motor vehicle loading, industrial truck or concentrated loading elevators. General freight loading elevators, described below, may be electric drum type or traction or hydraulic elevators.

General freight loading elevators satisfy a variety of material handling requirements with capacities of 2000 to 8000 lb. Industrial truck loading freight elevators require special design considerations to handle truck loads of 10,000 to 20,000 lb or more.

General freight or industrial truck elevators may have either hydraulic or electric drive systems, similar to those described on previous pages. The units are usually custom designed with vertical biparting doors and special structural support to carry increased loads and eccentric loading conditions.

Freight elevators usually operate at slower speeds with simple control systems. Capacity must be sized for the largest expected load.

LIGHT DUTY FREIGHT ELEVATORS with capacities of 1000 to 2500 lb may utilize hydraulic or traction drives. Standard systems are illustrated on other pages of this section. Two special types of light freight elevators, with rises limited according to manufacturer, are the SIDEWALK ELEVATOR and the SELF-SUPPORTING ELEVATOR.

The SIDEWALK ELEVATOR, illustrated on this page with an electric winding drum type machine, rises to a top level through hatch doors. Note that local codes often forbid the raising of an elevator in a public sidewalk; elevators may have to be located within building lines.

The SELF-SUPPORTING FREIGHT ELEVATOR is similar to the sidewalk elevator illustrated and operates within a building up to three stories (rise varies with manufacturer). Weight of the car is transferred through the supporting guide rails to the elevator pit.

With the electric winding drum machine, machinery must lift the full weight of car and its load. The drum must be anchored to the floor to resist uplifting forces. Safety codes forbid use of electric winding drum machines for passenger elevators and restrict their use on freight elevators to a speed not exceeding 50 fpm and a travel not exceeding 40 ft; they shall not be provided with counterweights.

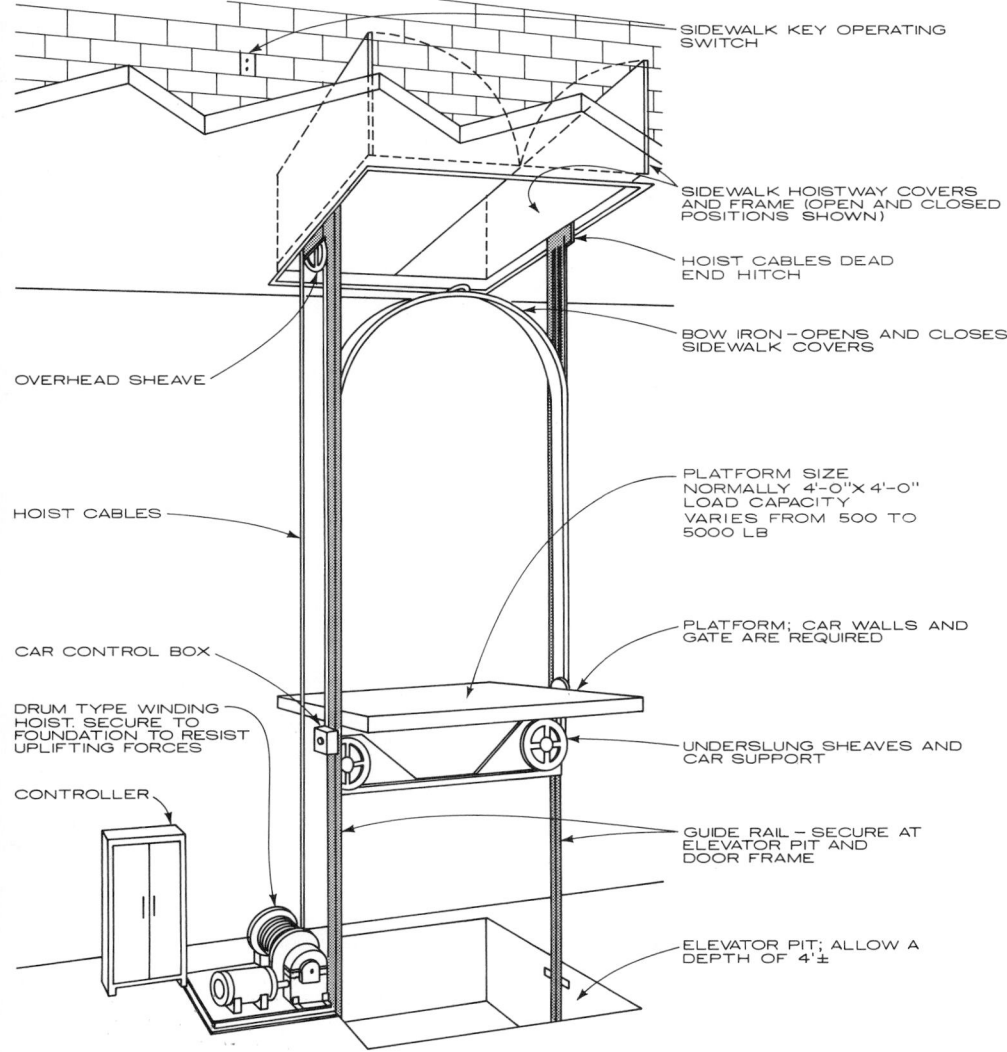

SIDEWALK KEY OPERATING SWITCH

SIDEWALK HOISTWAY COVERS AND FRAME (OPEN AND CLOSED POSITIONS SHOWN)

HOIST CABLES DEAD END HITCH

BOW IRON — OPENS AND CLOSES SIDEWALK COVERS

OVERHEAD SHEAVE

HOIST CABLES

PLATFORM SIZE NORMALLY 4'-0'' X 4'-0'' LOAD CAPACITY VARIES FROM 500 TO 5000 LB

CAR CONTROL BOX

PLATFORM; CAR WALLS AND GATE ARE REQUIRED

DRUM TYPE WINDING HOIST. SECURE TO FOUNDATION TO RESIST UPLIFTING FORCES

UNDERSLUNG SHEAVES AND CAR SUPPORT

CONTROLLER

GUIDE RAIL — SECURE AT ELEVATOR PIT AND DOOR FRAME

ELEVATOR PIT; ALLOW A DEPTH OF 4'±

**SIDEWALK ELEVATOR**

### SELF-SUPPORTING ELEVATOR DIMENSIONS

| CAPACITY (LB) | PLATFORM | | HOISTWAY | |
|---|---|---|---|---|
| | WIDTH | DEPTH | WIDTH | DEPTH |
| 1,500 | 5'-4'' | 6'-1'' | 6'-11'' | 6'-9'' |
| 2,000 | 6'-4'' | 7'-0'' | 7'-11'' | 7'-8'' |
| 2,500 | 6'-4'' | 8'-0'' | 7'-11'' | 8'-8'' |

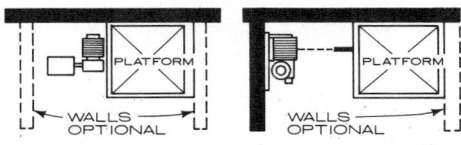

SIDE MOUNTED     WALL MOUNTED

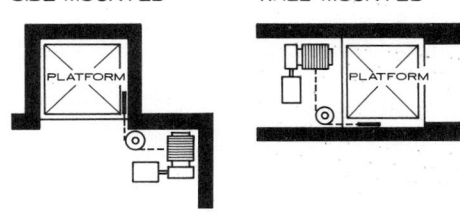

AROUND THE CORNER     MACHINE IN BACK

**MACHINE LAYOUTS — WINDING DRUM TYPE**

Alexander Keyes; Darrel Downing Rippeteau, Architect; Washington, D.C.

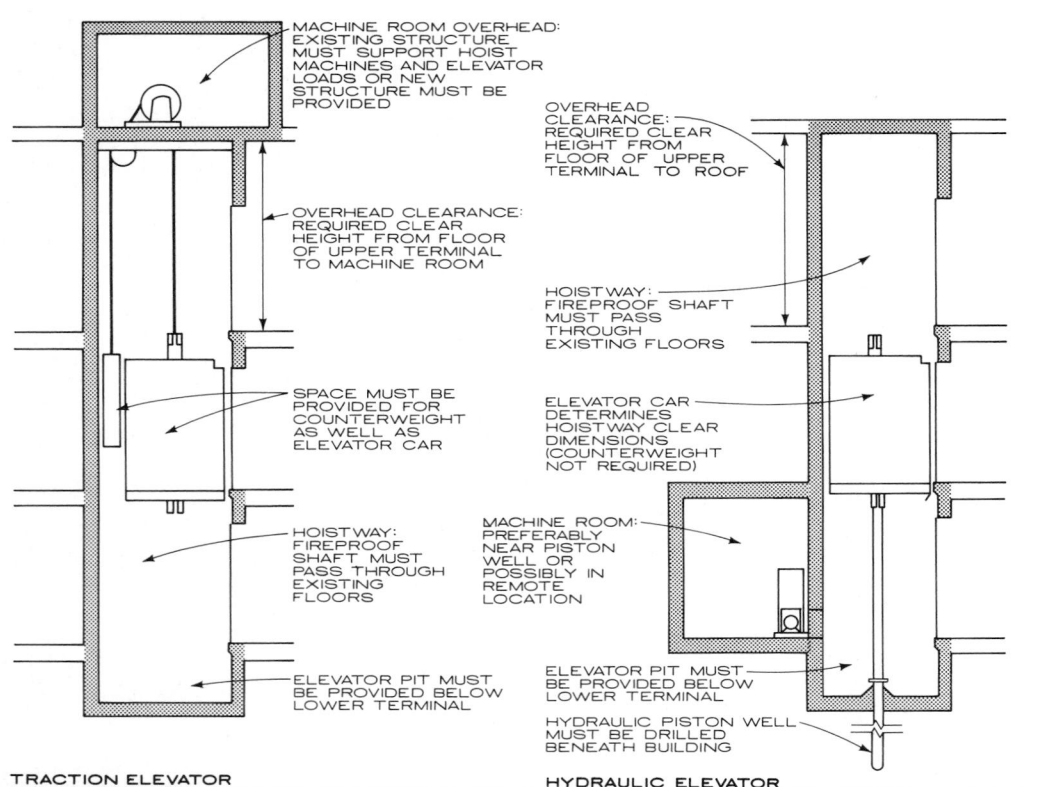

MACHINE ROOM OVERHEAD:
EXISTING STRUCTURE
MUST SUPPORT HOIST
MACHINES AND ELEVATOR
LOADS OR NEW
STRUCTURE MUST BE
PROVIDED

OVERHEAD CLEARANCE:
REQUIRED CLEAR
HEIGHT FROM FLOOR
OF UPPER TERMINAL
TO MACHINE ROOM

SPACE MUST BE
PROVIDED FOR
COUNTERWEIGHT
AS WELL AS
ELEVATOR CAR

HOISTWAY:
FIREPROOF
SHAFT MUST
PASS THROUGH
EXISTING
FLOORS

ELEVATOR PIT MUST
BE PROVIDED BELOW
LOWER TERMINAL

OVERHEAD
CLEARANCE:
REQUIRED CLEAR
HEIGHT FROM
FLOOR OF UPPER
TERMINAL TO ROOF

HOISTWAY:
FIREPROOF SHAFT
MUST PASS
THROUGH
EXISTING FLOORS

ELEVATOR CAR
DETERMINES
HOISTWAY CLEAR
DIMENSIONS
(COUNTERWEIGHT
NOT REQUIRED)

MACHINE ROOM:
PREFERABLY
NEAR PISTON
WELL OR
POSSIBLY IN
REMOTE
LOCATION

ELEVATOR PIT MUST
BE PROVIDED BELOW
LOWER TERMINAL

HYDRAULIC PISTON WELL
MUST BE DRILLED
BENEATH BUILDING

**TRACTION ELEVATOR**

**HYDRAULIC ELEVATOR**

## ELEVATOR RETROFIT

Existing buildings may be retrofitted with the elevator systems previously illustrated. General selection, location, and arrangement guidelines apply. Additional constraints imposed by existing building conditions must also be considered.

HYDRAULIC ELEVATORS generally require the least initial installation expense in buildings of 2 to 6 stories. The hoistway need only be a fireproof shaft, separating the elevator passageway from the rest of the building. Elevator car guide rails are attached from within the hoistway to the existing structural frame at each floor. A machine room is located near the lower terminal, often in an existing basement. The weight of the system bears upon a concrete pad at the base of the hoistway, beneath which a hole must be drilled to accommodate the hydraulic piston, approximately equal in length to the distance of elevator travel. A HOLELESS HYDRAULIC system eliminates the need for this hole but is limited to a rise of 3 stories.

ELECTRIC ELEVATORS can serve buildings of higher rises at greater speeds and generally lower operating costs. Hoisting machines are located above the hoistway and bear the weight of the elevator system. A structural frame must be designed to support these machines within the existing structural system. Sufficient space for a machine room must be provided, often on an existing roof. The hoistway is designed as a fireproof shaft with elevator guide rails attached to the building structure at each floor. An alternate elevator system permits the hoist machines to be located in the basement (see ELECTRIC ELEVATOR SYSTEMS) in situations where low overhead clearance is available. The weight of the system must still be supported at the top of the hoistway.

In all cases, representatives of the elevator industry must be contacted for proper elevator selection and design specifications.

## ELEVATOR RETROFIT

MACHINE ROOM:
HOISTING MACHINES MAY BE OVERHAULED OR MODERNIZED TO PROVIDE GREATER SPEED OR HOISTING CAPACITY. AGE OF MACHINERY AND PRESENT USAGE DEMANDS ARE DETERMINING FACTORS

MODERN CONTROLS ARE OFTEN INSTALLED TO SYNCHRONIZE GROUP ELEVATOR SERVICE AND REDUCE CAR STOPPING AND STARTING TIME

SOUNDPROOFING OR STRUCTURAL REINFORCEMENT MAY BE REQUIRED

ELEVATOR CAR:
EXISTING CAR MAY BE RENOVATED OR REPLACED

IF RENOVATED, CONTROLS AND DOORS MAY BE AUTOMATED TO PROVIDE SELF-SERVICE ELEVATORS, AND REDUCE DOOR OPERATING TIME. CENTER OPENING (HORIZONTAL BIPARTING) DOORS WITH ENTRANCE SAFETY DEVICES (SEE "ELEVATOR CAR DESIGN") REPLACE SINGLE SLIDE DOORS FOR INCREASED EFFICIENCY. THE CAR INTERIOR MAY BE RENOVATED OR RESTORED TO RETAIN ORIGINAL APPEARANCES

IF REPLACED, A FULLY AUTOMATED CAR WITH MODERN CONTROLS MAY BE INSERTED INTO AN EXISTING ELEVATOR HOISTWAY

CONSULT REPRESENTATIVES OF THE ELEVATOR INDUSTRY

HOISTWAY:
ADDITIONAL FIREPROOFING OF HOISTWAY WALLS MAY BE REQUIRED. CHECK LOCAL CODES

HOISTWAY WALLS AND GUIDE RAILS MAY BE SOUNDPROOFED

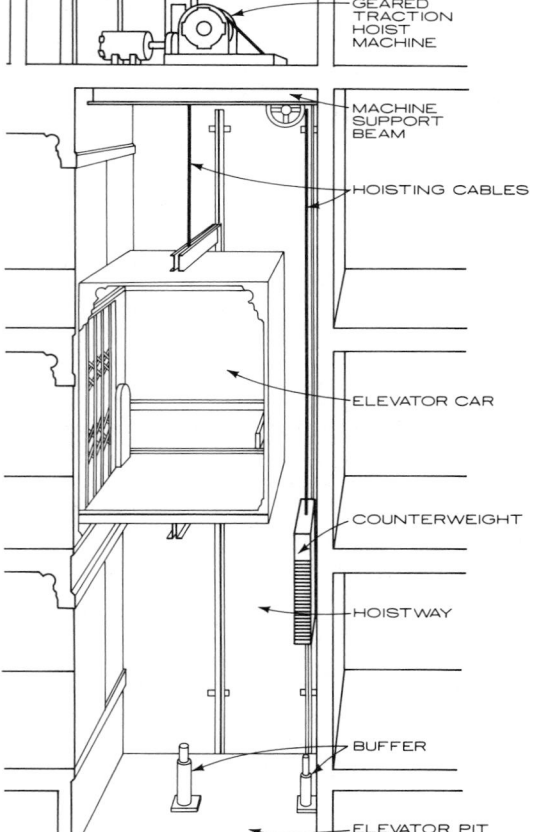

MACHINE ROOM

CONTROLLER

GEARED
TRACTION
HOIST
MACHINE

MACHINE
SUPPORT
BEAM

HOISTING CABLES

ELEVATOR CAR

COUNTERWEIGHT

HOISTWAY

BUFFER

ELEVATOR PIT

## ELEVATOR RENOVATION AND MODERNIZATION

Elevator systems in older buildings may be renovated and modernized to provide improved service. Certain service components (controls, hoist machines, door operators) may be overhauled or modernized, while visual components (elevator car, lobby) may be renovated or restored to original appearance. The extent of modernization will vary in each case; consult representatives of the elevator industry.

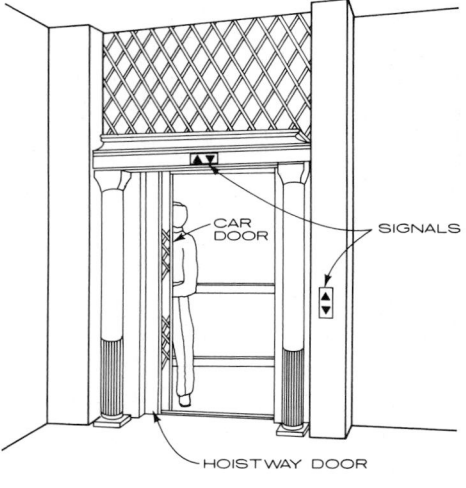

CAR
DOOR

SIGNALS

HOISTWAY DOOR

ELEVATOR LOBBY:
LOBBY MAY BE RESTORED TO RETAIN ORIGINAL APPEARANCES.
NEW SIGNALS AND INDICATORS MAY BE INSERTED INTO AN EXISTING LOBBY WALL (SEE "ELEVATOR LOBBY DESIGN").
HOISTWAY DOORS MAY BE REPLACED FOR INCREASED EFFICIENCY

**ELEVATOR RENOVATION**

Olga Barmine; Darrel Downing Rippeteau, Architect; Washington, D.C.

**14    ELEVATORS**

Escalators are a very efficient form of vertical transportation for very heavy traffic where the number of floors served is limited, normally a maximum of five to six floors. Escalators are not usually accepted as a required exit.

Dimensions shown are general and will vary somewhat with the manufacturer. Consult manufacturers for structural support, electrical supply, and specific dimensional requirements.

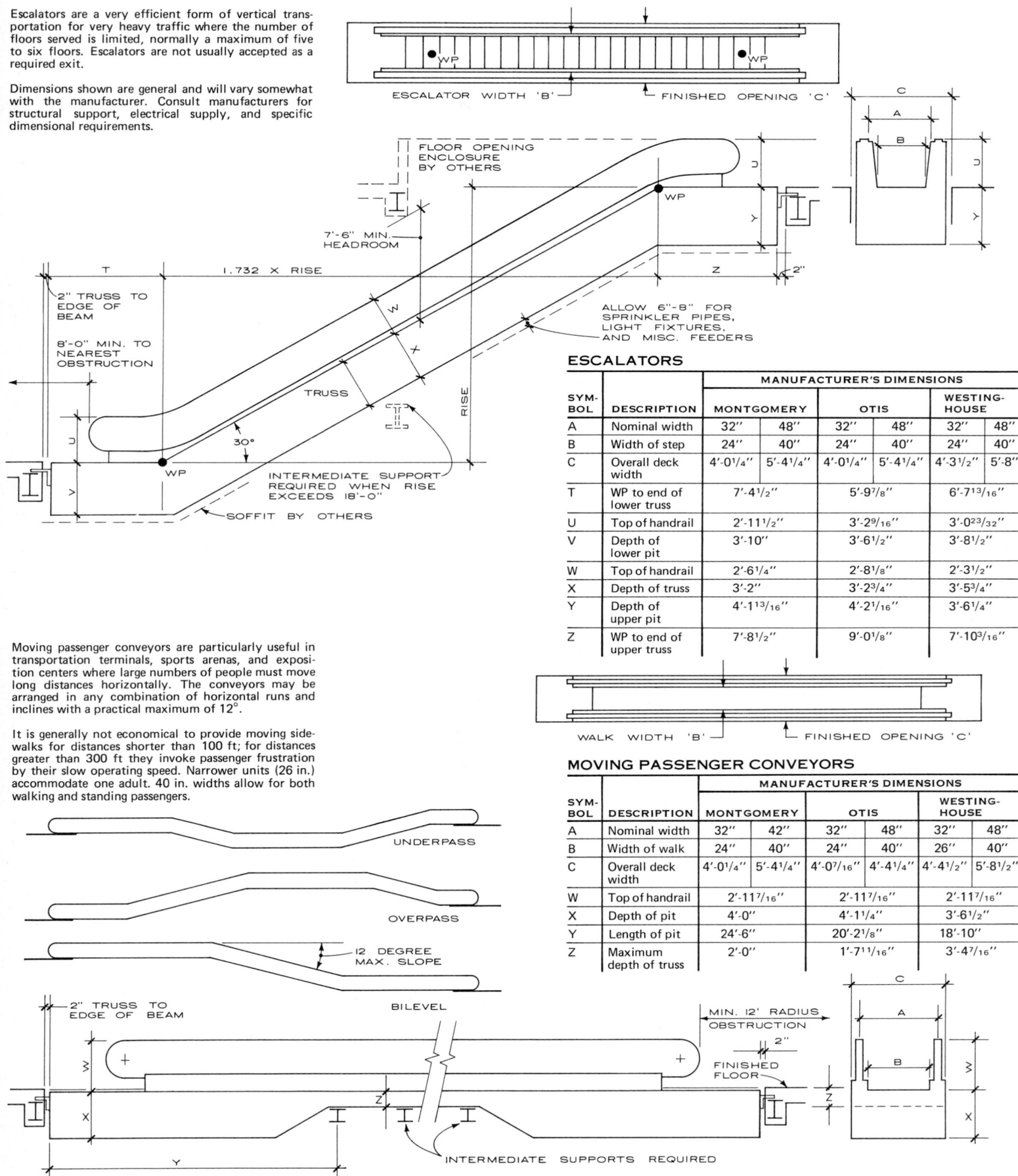

## ESCALATORS

| SYM-BOL | DESCRIPTION | MANUFACTURER'S DIMENSIONS | | | | | |
|---|---|---|---|---|---|---|---|
| | | MONTGOMERY | | OTIS | | WESTING-HOUSE | |
| A | Nominal width | 32″ | 48″ | 32″ | 48″ | 32″ | 48″ |
| B | Width of step | 24″ | 40″ | 24″ | 40″ | 24″ | 40″ |
| C | Overall deck width | 4′-0 1/4″ | 5′-4 1/4″ | 4′-0 1/4″ | 5′-4 1/4″ | 4′-3 1/2″ | 5′-8″ |
| T | WP to end of lower truss | 7′-4 1/2″ | | 5′-9 7/8″ | | 6′-7 13/16″ | |
| U | Top of handrail | 2′-11 1/2″ | | 3′-2 9/16″ | | 3′-0 23/32″ | |
| V | Depth of lower pit | 3′-10″ | | 3′-6 1/2″ | | 3′-8 1/2″ | |
| W | Top of handrail | 2′-6 1/4″ | | 2′-8 1/8″ | | 2′-3 1/2″ | |
| X | Depth of truss | 3′-2″ | | 3′-2 3/4″ | | 3′-5 3/4″ | |
| Y | Depth of upper pit | 4′-1 13/16″ | | 4′-2 1/16″ | | 3′-6 1/4″ | |
| Z | WP to end of upper truss | 7′-8 1/2″ | | 9′-0 1/8″ | | 7′-10 3/16″ | |

Moving passenger conveyors are particularly useful in transportation terminals, sports arenas, and exposition centers where large numbers of people must move long distances horizontally. The conveyors may be arranged in any combination of horizontal runs and inclines with a practical maximum of 12°.

It is generally not economical to provide moving sidewalks for distances shorter than 100 ft; for distances greater than 300 ft they invoke passenger frustration by their slow operating speed. Narrower units (26 in.) accommodate one adult. 40 in. widths allow for both walking and standing passengers.

## MOVING PASSENGER CONVEYORS

| SYM-BOL | DESCRIPTION | MANUFACTURER'S DIMENSIONS | | | | | |
|---|---|---|---|---|---|---|---|
| | | MONTGOMERY | | OTIS | | WESTING-HOUSE | |
| A | Nominal width | 32″ | 42″ | 32″ | 48″ | 32″ | 48″ |
| B | Width of walk | 24″ | 40″ | 24″ | 40″ | 26″ | 40″ |
| C | Overall deck width | 4′-0 1/4″ | 5′-4 1/4″ | 4′-0 7/16″ | 4′-4 1/4″ | 4′-4 1/2″ | 5′-8 1/2″ |
| W | Top of handrail | 2′-11 7/16″ | | 2′-11 7/16″ | | 2′-11 7/16″ | |
| X | Depth of pit | 4′-0″ | | 4′-1 1/4″ | | 3′-6 1/2″ | |
| Y | Length of pit | 24′-6″ | | 20′-2 1/8″ | | 18′-10″ | |
| Z | Maximum depth of truss | 2′-0″ | | 1′-7 11/16″ | | 3′-4 7/16″ | |

Alan H. Rider, AIA; Daniel, Mann, Johnson & Mendenhall; Washington, D.C.

## VERTICAL PALLET LIFT

Used to transport loads from level to level within a conveyor system or for manually loading/unloading at each level. Typically used where basement or second floor serves for storage of reserve or overstock.

Capacity: up to 6000 lb; lift height: up to 20 ft; platform sizes: 13 x 15 to 48 x 72 in.

Lift speed: 20 fpm; installation: floor to floor, with platform either flush with or above floor, depending on loading/unloading technique.

## CIRCULAR CONVEYOR LIFT

Used to transport cartons between operating levels and between work stations within a level. Useful where vertical distance is great while horizontal distance is limited.

Lift height: 45 to 144 in. vertical lift per 360° unit. Lift height is relative to radius of unit. Load sizes: width—6 to 48 in.; length—relative to width and radius of conveyor.

Installation: dependent on height of feed and exit conveyors. System requires shaft through floor of O.D. of conveyor plus 12 in.

## 90° VERTICAL PALLET LIFT

Used to transport unit loads between operating levels in multiple level or multiple floor buildings. Typically used where vertical lift is great and a continuous conveyor system serves in loading/unloading the lift.

Capacity: up to 6000 lb; lift height: up to 80 ft; load sizes: typically 48 x 40 x 72 in.; however, other sizes can be specified; lift speed: 60 fpm; installation: typically installed floor to floor, with shaft through each floor.

## NOTE

Lifts presented show various types with data and nomenclature to illustrate systems and equipment available to move loads vertically. Specific sizes and capacity should be obtained from lift manufacturers.

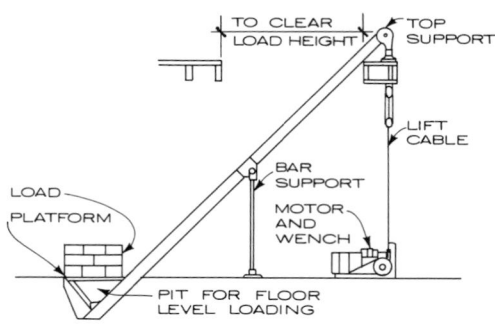

VERTICAL PALLET LIFT

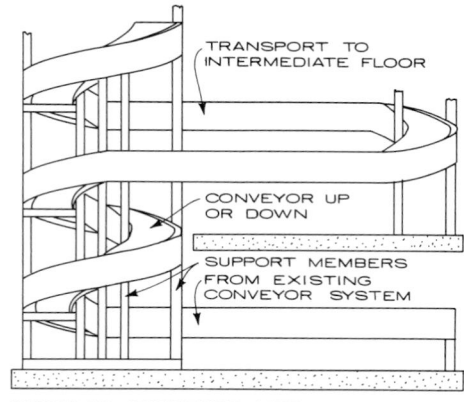

CIRCULAR CONVEYOR LIFT

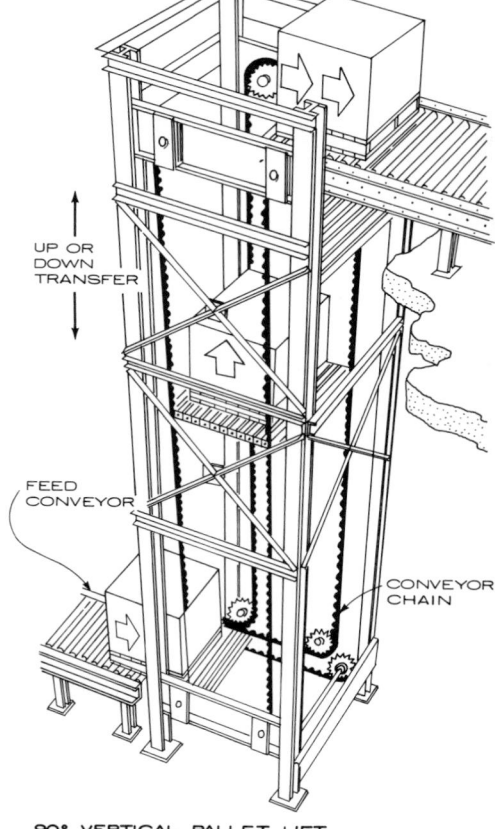

90° VERTICAL PALLET LIFT

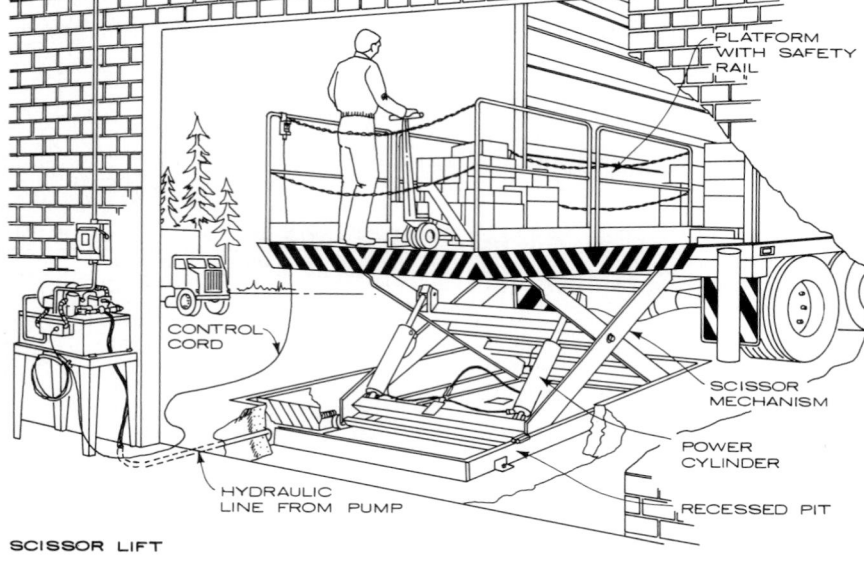

SCISSOR LIFT

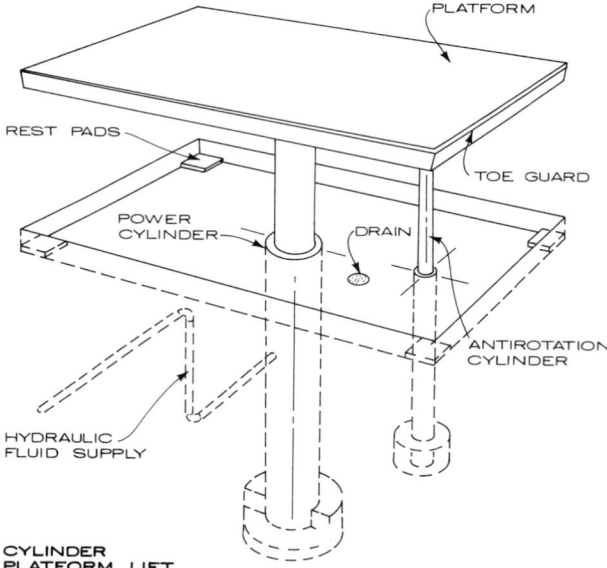

CYLINDER PLATFORM LIFT

**MISCELLANEOUS LIFTS**

## SCISSOR LIFT

Used to raise/lower unit loads to delivery vehicles from ground or floor levels that do not align with vehicles.

Load capacity: 2500 to 30,000 lb; lifting height: up to 12 ft; platform sizes: typically 5 x 7 ft to 8 x 12 ft, but other sizes can be specified; lift rate: cycle rate is manually controlled by loading/unloading rate. Up cycle of lift ranges from 40 to 100 sec depending on lift size.

Installation: lifts available in permanent pit installation or portable aboveground units. Limiting factor on installation is electric power source for hydraulic pump and reservoir.

## CYLINDER PLATFORM LIFT

Used to move unitized loads from floor or ground to delivery vehicle level to facilitate loading/unloading operations. Used also for machine loading/unloading of heavy/bulky materials.

Load capacity: 2000 to 30,000 lb; lifting height: up to 5 ft; platform sizes: typically 5 x 5 ft to 8 x 15 ft, but other sizes can be specified.

Lift rate: cycle rate is manually controlled by loading/unloading rate. Up cycle of lift ranges up to 12 fpm. Installation: pit used to facilitate platform flush with floor or ground for loading/unloading. Cylinder shaft is centered under platform with antirotational shaft at one end. Both shafts recessed into ground.

St. Onge, Ruff & Associates; York, Pennsylvania

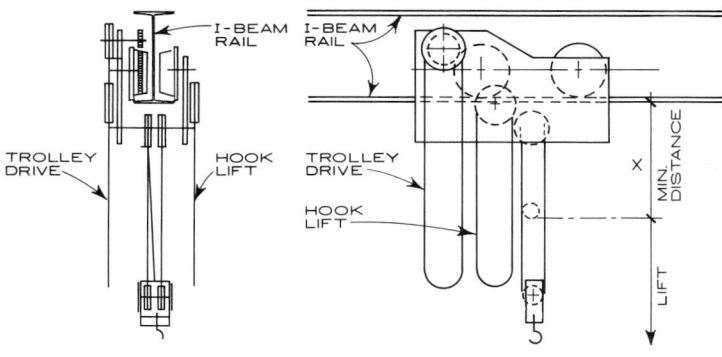

### TROLLEY HOIST DATA

| CAPACITY (TONS) | STANDARD LIFT (FT) | X | STANDARD I-BEAM | MIN. CURVE RADIUS |
|---|---|---|---|---|
| 1/4 | 8 | 8 1/2'' | 5'' | 3'-6'' |
| 1/2 | 8 | 8 1/2'' | 5'' | 3'-6'' |
| 1 | 8 | 11 1/4'' | 6'' | 3'-6'' |
| 1 1/2 | 8 | 13'' | 7'' | 3'-6'' |
| 2 | 9 | 15 1/8'' | 8'' | 4'-6'' |
| 3 | 10 | 18 3/4'' | 10'' | 5'-0'' |
| 4 | 10 | 21 3/4'' | 10'' | 7'-6'' |
| 5 | 12 | 25'' | 12'' | 7'-6'' |
| 6 | 12 | 25'' | 12'' | 7'-6'' |
| 8 | 12 | 31 3/8'' | 15'' | 8'-0'' |
| 10 | 12 | 39'' | 15'' | 8'-0'' |

**TROLLEY HOISTS**

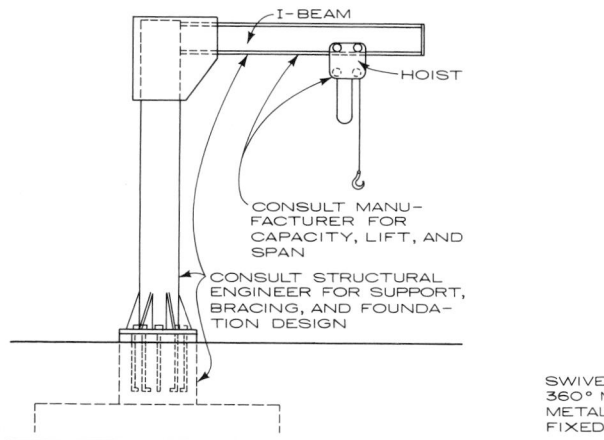

**JIB CRANE**

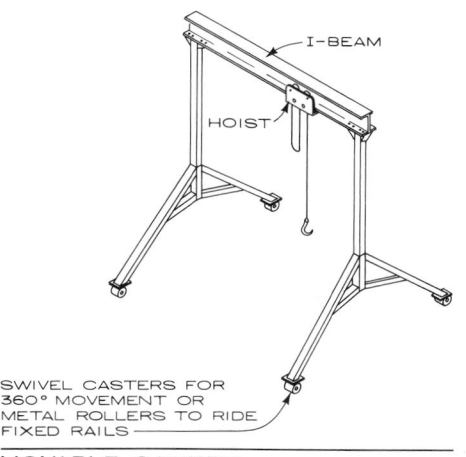

**MOVABLE GANTRY**

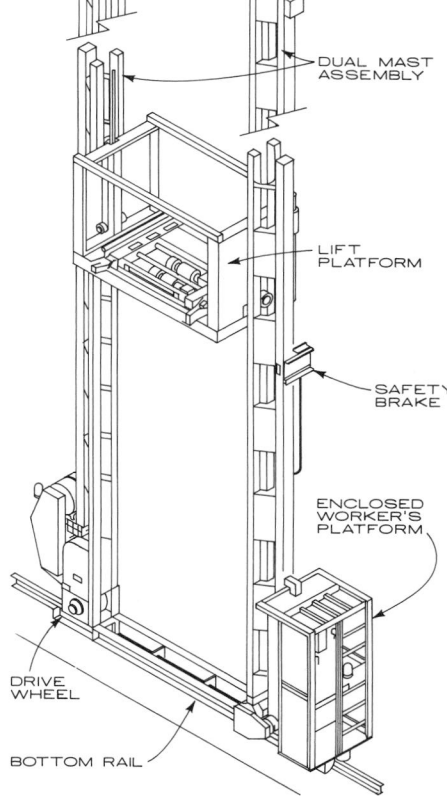

**STACKER CRANE** (CAPACITY 5 TONS)

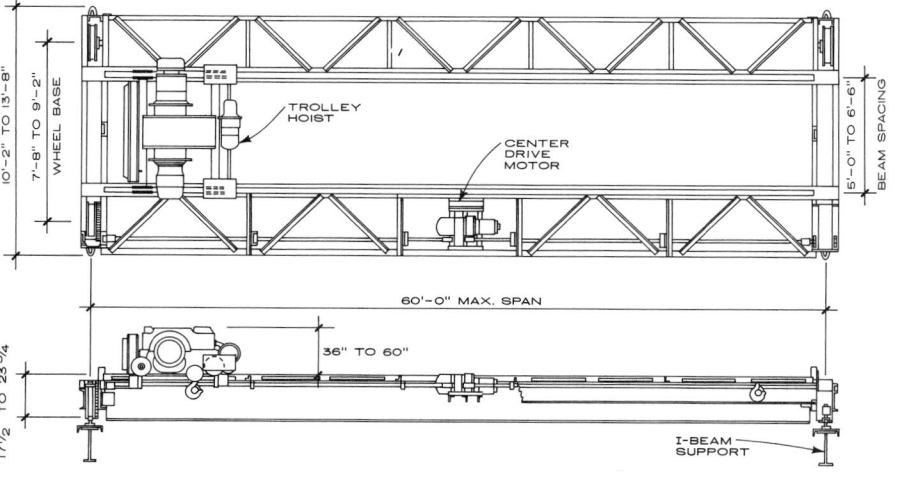

**DOUBLE BEAM CRANE** (CAPACITY 25 TONS)

## CRANES

### JIB CRANE

Typically manufactured to lift loads from 1 to 8 tons, with boom located from 10 to 25 ft above ground. Special care must be taken to design foundation to resist large overturning moment. The jib allows 360° movement around the central support, as well as travel of hoist along the I-beam. Larger sizes usually have motorized hoist as well as motorized rotation of boom.

### MOVABLE GANTRY

Typically manufactured to lift from 1 to 8 tons, with height of 8 to 35 ft. The gantry allows 360° movement if designed with swivel casters, or it can travel along a fixed steel track mounted on the floor. Larger gantries have motorized hoists as well as motorized travel along

a track. The portable gantry is ideal for retrofit applications since often no structural or foundation modifications are required (as long as slab has capacity to support weight of gantry and load).

### DOUBLE BEAM CRANE

Used to handle heavy loads in manufacturing and storage areas where aisle access and load clearances are limited. The beam crane allows two-directional horizontal travel plus vertical lift over the entire area serviced by the crane.

Load capacity: 6000 to 50,000 lb; span: 25 to 60 ft; crane weight: 4500 to 36,000 lb; wheel base: 7 to 13 ft; beam spacing: 5 to 9 ft; working span: 20 to 57 ft; hoist clearance above rail: 37 to 70 in.

### STACKER CRANE

Stacker cranes allow storage/retrieval of loads above conventional fork lift truck heights. Also, multiple loads can be handled by manipulating load platform sizes. Cranes can be computer controlled to reduce manpower demands in S/R operations.

Load capacity: up to 10,000 lb; overall height: 40 to 120 ft; working heights: 2 to 112 ft, depending on load heights; aisle width: 4 to 10 ft, depending on load configuration; aisle overrun: 15 to 20 ft, depending on crane structure; crane weight: up to 34,000 lb, depending on load and crane configuration; travel speeds: horizontal—up to 480 fpm; vertical—up to 120 fpm.

### NOTE

Stacker cranes are typically built to customer specifications. Specific applications and details should be obtained from crane suppliers.

Rodney D. Burrows, AIA, PE; San Francisco, California
St. Onge, Ruff & Associates; York, Pennsylvania

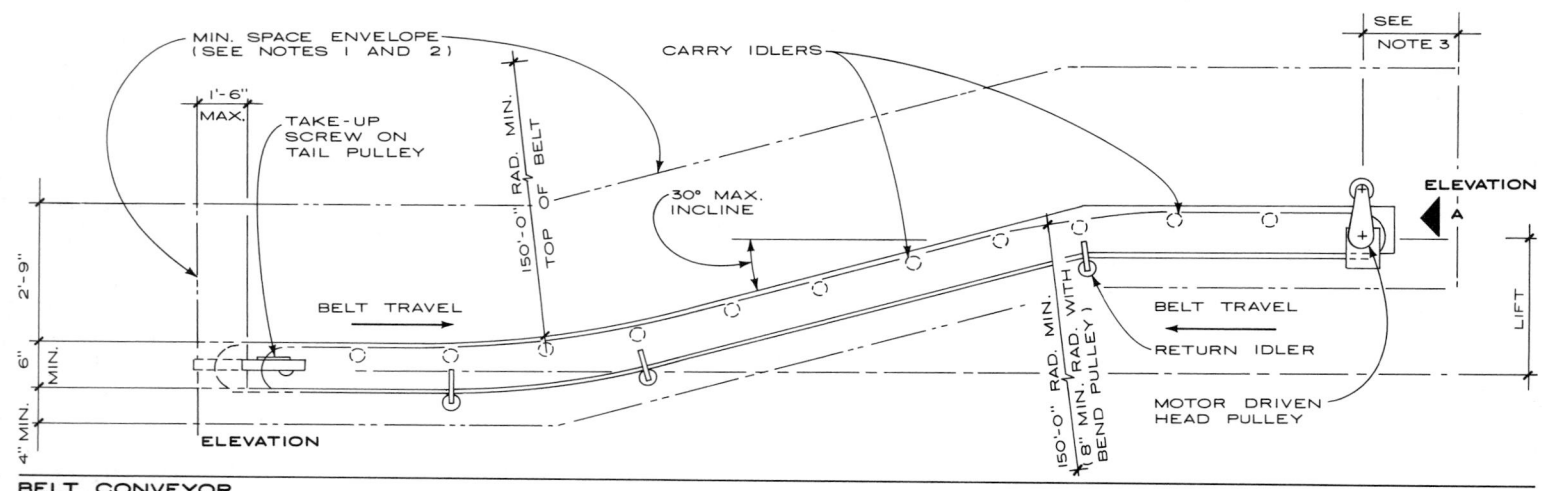

**BELT CONVEYOR**

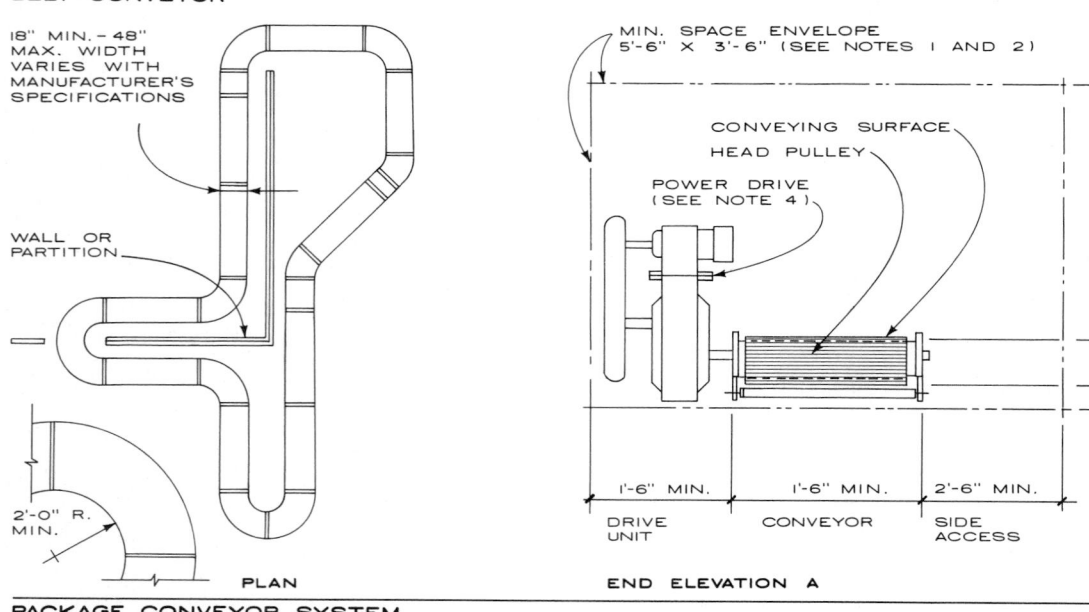

**PACKAGE CONVEYOR SYSTEM**

## COMPARISON OF MATERIAL CONVEYORS

| CONVEYOR | TYPE | APPLICATION | ADVANTAGES | LIMITATIONS |
|---|---|---|---|---|
| Belt | Flat (power drive) | Airport baggage Manufacturing, assembly, and inspection Packaged goods | Very common Many vendors Economical High capacity output Extensive speed range | Frequent maintenance required Friction drive pulley slips Belt replacement and realignment required Will not curve horizontally (powered belt curves are available) |
| | Troughed (power drive) | Bulk handling Dry granular materials Dry solid waste | | |
| Roller | Skate wheel (gravity) | Light duty packages | Mobile units available Can turn in horizontal planes (see typical plan arrangement) Can accumulate loads | Poor for sacked items or resilient outer surfaces Light duty (skate wheel) Limited weight range for rollers Package or unit material Occasional noise problems Regularly inspect wheels or rollers for free rolling |
| | Gravity roller (unpowered) Live roller (power drive) | Medium to heavy duty handling Pallets or other flat bottom containers or items | | |
| Segmented (articulated) moving surface | Pan Apron Slat (All power driven) | Airport baggage Loose waste handling Solid waste handling | Can handle heavy loads Durable carrying surface Can turn in horizontal planes (see typical plan arrangement) Good for steep inclines Handles hot or wet material | Very costly |

**NOTES**

1. Clearance dimensions shown are nominal. Exact dimensions should be determined after specific equipment has been designed.
2. Service access must be provided at tail pulley, drive area, and along at least one side.
3. Trajectory of material leaving the conveyor depends on the material's characteristics and the speed of its travel.
4. Drive unit does not necessarily protrude above belt surface and can be located below the frame and at locations other than at the head pulley.
5. Access safety rails, guards, etc., should comply with applicable codes and with manufacturers' recommendations.

Alpha Engineers, Inc.; Pocatello, Idaho

## GENERAL NOTES

Pneumatic Tube Systems: Use of pneumatic tube systems, under vacuum or pressure, allows transmission of paper, small articles and liquids in "carrier" tubes to and from predetermined stations.

Applicable systems are commercial offices and stores; industrial plants, warehouses and air and rail stations;

banks; hospitals and laboratories. Care should be taken in the latter instances to exclude services in areas where centrifuge action in transmitted liquids is undesirable.

Installation of Systems: Systems can be placed anywhere in or about the area served, exposed or furred in structure, outside or underground. Lines exposed to weather or

through refrigerated spaces must be protected and insulated to prevent condensation in the system. Subsurface installations should be placed in corrugated pipe below the frost line, and tubing should be mill wrapped and joints welded and protected with mill wrap tape and pressure tested.

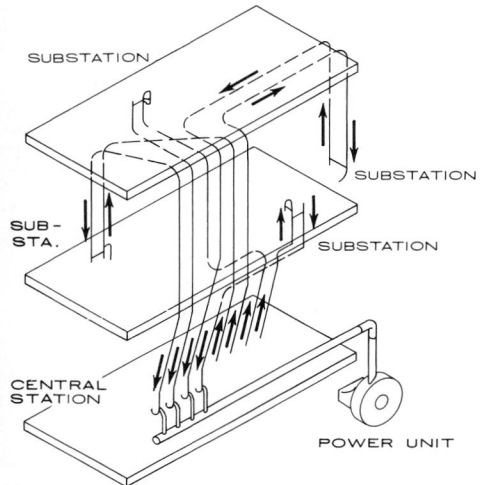

CENTRIFUGAL UNIT

### CENTRIFUGAL EXHAUSTERS AND BLOWERS (This chart shows only extremes for each case.)

| VACUUM | RPM | HP | A | B | C | VACUUM | RPM | HP | A | B | C |
|---|---|---|---|---|---|---|---|---|---|---|---|
| 12 oz | 3500 | 1 min. | 30 | 29 | 20 | 20 oz | 3500 | 1 1/2 min. | 36 | 35 | 20 |
| | | 5 max. | 36 | 35 | 27 | | | 15 max. | 46 | 41 | 42 |
| | 1750 | 7 1/2 min. | 54 | 54 | 34 | | 1750 | 7 1/2 min. | 54 | 54 | 38 |
| | | 50 max. | 93 | 79 | 54 | | | 60 max. | 80 | 67 | 60 |
| 16 oz | 3500 | 1 min. | 30 | 29 | 20 | 24 oz | 3500 | 1 1/2 min. | 36 | 35 | 22 |
| | | 10 max. | 42 | 42 | 31 | | | 25 max. | 59 | 54 | 46 |
| | 1750 | 7 1/2 min. | 54 | 54 | 30 | | 1750 | 7 1/2 min. | 54 | 54 | 36 |
| | | 75 max. | 92 | 80 | 60 | | | 75 max. | 80 | 67 | 60 |

Used indoor or outside, centrifugal types operate on vacuum or vacuum and pressure combinations. Quieter than most types, they are recommended except where

long lines are to be used or where reversible action is required. Sizes vary with horsepower of motor, vacuum and rpm.

## POWER UNITS FOR VACUUM OR PRESSURE

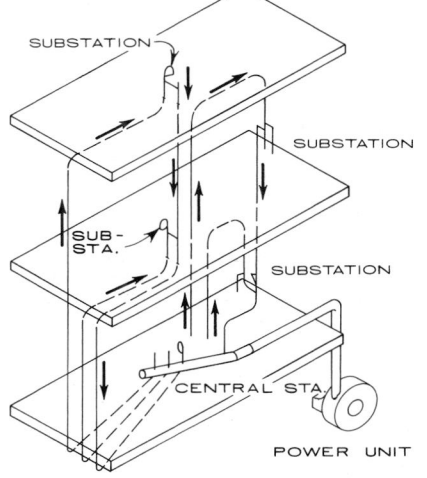

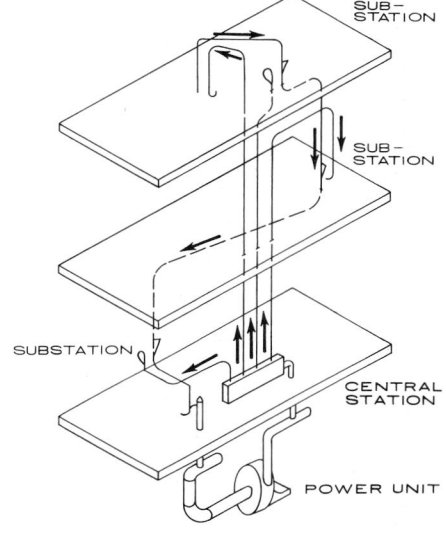

### VACUUM TYPE INDEPENDENT TWIN LINE

This system may dispatch carriers from all stations simultaneously with continuous, nearly unlimited transaction. It may have any number of stations since independent lines run to and from all stations. It is considered to be most efficient, low in maintenance cost, and is the quietest system.

### VACUUM TYPE COMBINATION LINE

This system may dispatch carriers from the central station to all substations via separate lines, but return lines are common. Where intermittent service is satisfactory, such as in mail order houses and industrial plants, this system may be used to advantage.

### VACUUM-PRESSURE TYPE COMBINATION LINE

This system utilizes both vacuum and pressure. It is economical of power and of length of return lines. It is necessary that the number of open ends be the same for the vacuum as for the pressure lines. Provides quick service. Its use is restricted to mercantile houses, drug, grocery and meat packing plants, and similar types of buildings.

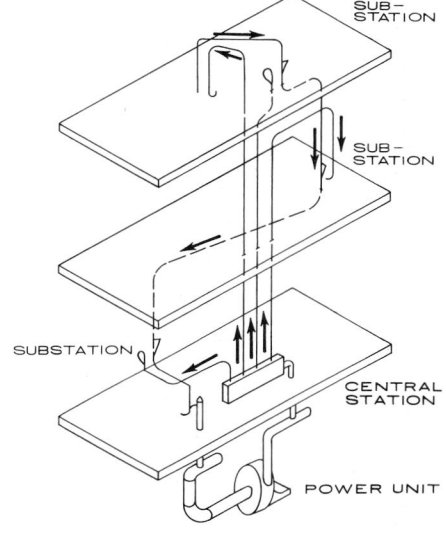

## COMPUTER CONTROLLED SYSTEM

### NOTES

Computer controlled systems consist of control center, stations, transfer units, blowers, transmission piping, and associated wiring. They can be single or multiple zone, utilizing 4-in. or 6-in. diameter carriers. Station attendant inserts carrier in dispatcher, selects station, and presses send button; computer checks address and rejects carrier if station is overloaded or out of service. If station is ready to receive, carrier is accepted as soon as route is clear. Traffic is two-way in all lines using pressure or vacuum. Switching occurs at transfer units, and temporary storage (until route is clear) occurs in interzone storage pipes between zones. Bends are minimum 48-in. radius. Control center is usually located in central area so it can be observed continuously.

Hills Gilbertson Fisher/Centrum Architects, Inc.; Minneapolis, Minnesota
LWH; King and King; Syracuse, New York

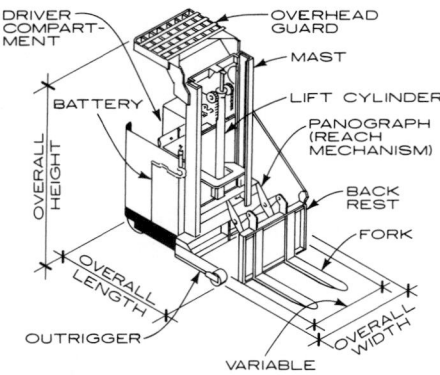

## REACH TRUCK

### APPLICATION

Narrow aisle operations without limiting pallet sizes and rack openings.

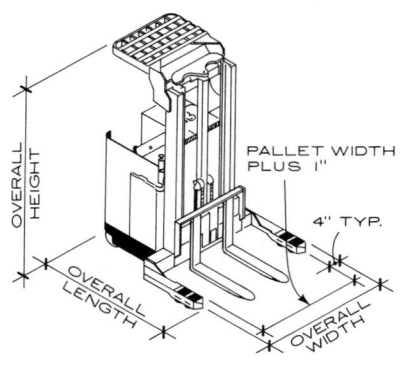

## STRADDLE TRUCK

### APPLICATION

Narrow aisle operations with a fixed pallet width (pallet must fit between outriggers). Clearances must be allowed between pallets and rack uprights for outriggers in rack operations unless a winged pallet is used.

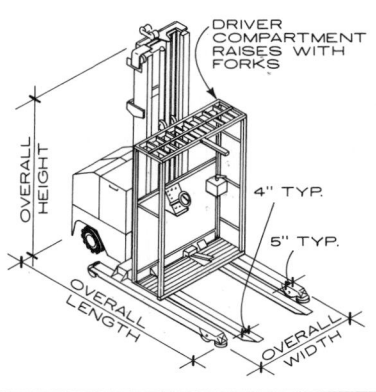

## ORDER PICKER TRUCK

### APPLICATION

Allows access to multiple level pick slots; an efficient technique with a large item base that has limited space for selection line.

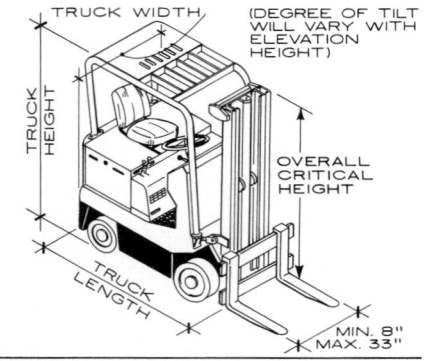

## COUNTERBALANCE TRUCK

### APPLICATION

Ideal for moving large volumes of material where maneuvering area is not limited.

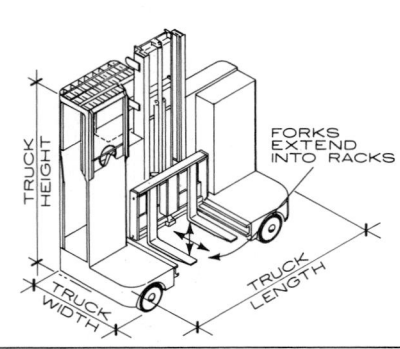

## SIDELOADER TRUCK

### APPLICATION

Allows lift capacity beyond conventional heights with narrow aisle operation plus flexibility to maneuver aisle to aisle.

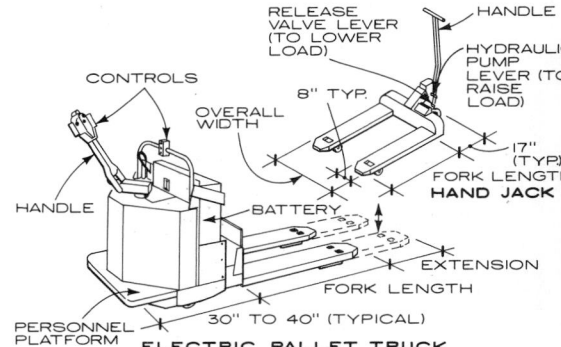

## HAND PALLET TRUCKS

### APPLICATION

Used to transport unitized loads when stacking of loads is not necessary. Ideal for dock work and production areas.

## FORKLIFTS—DIMENSIONS AND CAPACITIES

| | REACH TRUCK | STRADDLE TRUCK | ORDER PICKER TRUCK | COUNTER-BALANCE TRUCK | SIDE-LOADER TRUCK | ELECTRIC PALLET TRUCK | HAND JACK |
|---|---|---|---|---|---|---|---|
| Load capacity (lb) | 2000 to 6000 | 2000 to 6000 | 1500 to 3000 | 2000 to 15,000 | 2000 to 10,000 | 1500 to 6000 | 2000 to 6500 |
| Maximum lift height | 25'-0'' | 25'-0'' | 30'-0'' | 22'-0'' | 30'-0'' | 6'' to 7'' | 4'' to 7³/₄'' |
| Operating aisle width | 6'-4'' to 7'-6'' | 6'-0'' to 8'-2'' | 4'-6'' to 5'-2'' | 10'-3'' to 10'-0'' | Load length plus 20''–30'' | Load or truck length plus 6'' | Load or truck length plus 6'' |
| Intersecting aisle requirement | — | — | 5'-6'' to 17'-0'' | — | 10'-3'' to 12'-8'' | — | 6'-9'' to 10'-5'' |
| Right angle stacking aisle requirement | 6'-0'' to 10'-0'' | 5'-5'' to 9'-6'' | — | 10'-4'' to 14'-2'' | — | Truck length plus 3'-0'' | Truck length plus 3'-0'' |
| Truck weight without load (lb) | 4000 to 8000 | 3000 to 5000 | 5700 to 9500 | 5400 to 22,000 | 9000 to 12,000 | 1000 to 2000 | 250 to 300 |
| Overall truck width | 3'-1'' to 5'-4'' | 3'-0'' to 5'-1'' | 3'-10'' to 5'-10'' | 2'-11'' to 4'-10'' | 4'-0'' to 7'-6'' | 2'-7'' to 3'-2'' | 1'-6'' to 2'-6'' |
| Overall truck height | 6'-0'' to 11'-8'' | 6'-0'' to 11'-8'' | 7'-1'' to 12'-4'' | 5'-8'' to 7'-6'' | 7'-9'' to 12'-9'' | 4'-0'' to 5'-0'' | 4'-0'' |
| Overall truck length without load | 5'-2'' to 6'-0'' | 5'-4'' to 7'-1'' | 7'-4'' to 10'-6'' | 5'-6'' to 9'-7'' | 7'-0'' to 9'-8'' | 5'-7'' to 9'-7'' | 3'-9'' to 7'-5'' |
| Fork length | 2'-6'' to 4'-0'' | 2'-6'' to 4'-0'' | 3'-0'' to 8'-0'' | 2'-6'' to 4'-0'' | 2'-6'' to 4'-6'' | 2'-6'' to 7'-0'' | 2'-0'' to 6'-0'' |
| Travel speeds | Up to 7 mph | Up to 6 mph | Up to 5 mph | Up to 11 mph | Up to 5.5 mph | Up to 5 mph | Manually operated |
| Load speeds (fpm) Lifting Lowering | 27 to 68 67 to 40 | 50 to 104 88 to 61 | 31 to 62 77 to 44 | 30 to 70 110 to 40 | 30 to 70 70 to 40 | 2 to 4 sec 4 to 2 sec | Manually operated |
| Ramp slope | 15 to 23% | 10 to 16% | 3 to 16% | 10 to 37% | Up to 15% | Up to 10% | Manually operated |

### GENERAL NOTES

Data and figures given here represent the ranges of general specification available on forklift trucks. Aisle width is controlled by type of forklift and pallet size used in a warehouse. Specific data and applications should be obtained from material handling engineers. The trucks presented are electrically powered (excluding the hand jack) using industrial batteries as a source of energy. Industrial batteries typically must be charged after each 8-hr shift. Two batteries per truck are typical to allow back-to-back shift operation. The charging operation should take place in an area segregated from the warehouse or production area and must be designed to meet the various OSHA requirements.

St. Onge, Ruff & Associates; York, Pennsylvania

**MATERIAL HANDLING SYSTEMS**

# *Mechanical*

## SEAMLESS STEEL PIPE

| NOMINAL PIPE SIZE | DIMENSION (IN.) O.D. | WALL | CLASS | LB/FT P.E. | LB/FT T&C |
|---|---|---|---|---|---|
| 2" | 2.375 | 0.154 | Std. | 3.65 | 3.68 |
|  | 2.375 | 0.218 | X.S. | 5.02 | 5.07 |
|  | 2.375 | 0.436 | XXS. | 9.03 | — |
| 2½" | 2.875 | 0.203 | Std. | 5.79 | 5.82 |
|  | 2.875 | 0.276 | X.S. | 7.66 | 7.73 |
|  | 2.875 | 0.552 | XXS. | 13.70 | — |
| 3" | 3.500 | 0.216 | Std. | 7.58 | 7.62 |
|  | 3.500 | 0.300 | X.S. | 10.25 | 10.33 |
|  | 3.500 | 0.600 | XXS. | 18.58 | — |
| 3½" | 4.000 | 0.226 | Std. | 9.11 | 9.20 |
|  | 4.000 | 0.318 | X.S. | 12.51 | 12.63 |
|  | 4.000 | 0.634 | XXS. | 22.85 | — |
| 4" | 4.500 | 0.237 | Std. | 10.79 | 10.89 |
|  | 4.500 | 0.337 | X.S. | 14.98 | 15.17 |
|  | 4.500 | 0.674 | XXS. | 27.54 | — |
| 5" | 5.563 | 0.258 | Std. | 14.62 | 14.81 |
|  | 5.563 | 0.375 | X.S. | 20.78 | 21.09 |
|  | 5.563 | 0.750 | XXS. | 38.55 | — |
| 6" | 6.625 | 0.280 | Std. | 18.97 | 19.18 |
|  | 6.625 | 0.432 | X.S. | 28.57 | 28.89 |
|  | 6.625 | 0.864 | XXS. | 53.16 | — |
| 8" | 8.625 | 0.277 | — | 24.70 | 25.55 |
|  | 8.625 | 0.322 | Std. | 28.55 | 29.35 |
|  | 8.625 | 0.500 | X.S. | 43.39 | 43.90 |
|  | 8.625 | 0.875 | XXS. | 72.42 | — |
| 10" | 10.750 | 0.307 | — | 34.34 | 35.75 |
|  | 10.750 | 0.365 | Std. | 40.48 | 41.85 |
|  | 10.750 | 0.500 | X.S. | 54.74 | 55.82 |
| 12" | 12.750 | 0.330 | — | 43.77 | 45.45 |
|  | 12.750 | 0.375 | Std. | 49.56 | 51.15 |
|  | 12.750 | 0.406 | — | 53.53 | — |
|  | 12.750 | 0.500 | X.S. | 65.42 | 66.71 |
|  | 12.750 | 0.687 | — | 88.50 | — |
| 14" | 14.000 | 0.312 | — | 45.68 | — |
|  | 14.000 | 0.375 | Std. | 54.75 | — |
|  | 14.000 | 0.500 | X.S. | 72.09 | — |
| 16" | 16.000 | 0.312 | — | 52.36 | — |
|  | 16.000 | 0.375 | Std. | 62.58 | — |
|  | 16.000 | 0.500 | X.S. | 82.77 | — |
| 18" | 18.000 | 0.312 | — | 59.03 | — |
|  | 18.000 | 0.375 | Std. | 70.59 | — |
|  | 18.000 | 0.500 | X.S. | 93.45 | — |
| 20" | 20.000 | 0.312 | — | 68.71 | — |
|  | 20.000 | 0.375 | Std. | 78.60 | — |
|  | 20.000 | 0.500 | X.S. | 104.13 | — |
| 24" | 24.000 | 0.312 | — | 79.06 | — |
|  | 24.000 | 0.375 | Std. | 94.62 | — |
|  | 24.000 | 0.500 | X.S. | 125.49 | — |

## SEAMLESS STEEL PRESSURE TUBING

| NOMINAL PIPE SIZE | DIMENSION (IN.) O.D. | WALL | CLASS | WEIGHT (LB/FT) |
|---|---|---|---|---|
| ⅛" | 0.405 | 0.068 | Std. | 0.240 |
|  |  | 0.095 | X.S. | 0.310 |
| ¼" | 0.540 | 0.088 | Std. | 0.420 |
|  |  | 0.119 | X.S. | 0.470 |
| ⅜" | 0.675 | 0.091 | Std. | 0.570 |
|  |  | 0.126 | X.S. | 0.740 |
| ½" | 0.840 | 0.109 | Std. | 0.850 |
|  |  | 0.147 | X.S. | 1.087 |
|  |  | 0.187 | — | 1.310 |
|  |  | 0.294 | XXS. | 1.714 |
| ¾" | 1.050 | 0.113 | Std. | 1.130 |
|  |  | 0.154 | X.S. | 1.473 |
|  |  | 0.218 | — | 1.940 |
|  |  | 0.308 | XXS. | 2.440 |
| 1" | 1.315 | 0.133 | Std. | 1.678 |
|  |  | 0.179 | X.S. | 2.171 |
|  |  | 0.250 | — | 2.850 |
|  |  | 0.358 | XXS. | 3.659 |
| 1¼" | 1.660 | 0.140 | Std. | 2.272 |
|  |  | 0.191 | X.S. | 2.996 |
|  |  | 0.250 | — | 3.764 |
|  |  | 0.382 | XXS. | 5.214 |
| 1½" | 1.900 | 0.145 | Std. | 2.717 |
|  |  | 0.200 | X.S. | 3.631 |
|  |  | 0.281 | — | 4.862 |
|  |  | 0.400 | XXS. | 6.408 |

## BUTTWELD STEEL PIPE

| NOMINAL PIPE SIZE | DIMENSION (IN.) O.D. | STANDARD WEIGHT WALL (IN.) | LB/FT P.E. | LB/FT T&C | EXTRA STRONG WALL (IN.) | LB/FT P.E. | LB/FT T&C | DOUBLE EXTRA STRONG WALL (IN.) | LB/FT P.E. | LB/FT T&C |
|---|---|---|---|---|---|---|---|---|---|---|
| ⅛" | 0.405 | 0.068 | 0.24 | 0.24 | 0.095 | 0.31 | 0.32 | — | — | — |
| ¼" | 0.540 | 0.088 | 0.42 | 0.42 | 0.119 | 0.54 | 0.54 | — | — | — |
| ⅜" | 0.675 | 0.091 | 0.57 | 0.57 | 0.126 | 0.74 | 0.74 | — | — | — |
| ½" | 0.840 | 0.109 | 0.85 | 0.85 | 0.147 | 1.09 | 1.09 | — | — | — |
| ¾" | 1.050 | 0.113 | 1.13 | 1.13 | 0.154 | 1.47 | 1.48 | 0.308 | 2.441 | — |
| 1" | 1.315 | 0.133 | 1.68 | 1.68 | 0.179 | 2.17 | 2.18 | 0.358 | 2.659 | — |
| 1¼" | 1.660 | 0.140 | 2.27 | 2.28 | 0.191 | 3.00 | 3.02 | 0.382 | 5.214 | — |
| 1½" | 1.900 | 0.145 | 2.72 | 2.73 | 0.200 | 3.63 | 3.66 | 0.400 | 6.408 | — |
| 2" | 2.375 | 0.154 | 3.65 | 3.68 | 0.218 | 5.02 | 5.07 | — | — | — |
| 2½" | 2.875 | 0.203 | 5.79 | 5.82 | 0.276 | 7.66 | 7.73 | — | — | — |
| 3" | 3.500 | 0.216 | 7.58 | 7.62 | 0.300 | 10.25 | 10.33 | — | — | — |
| 3½" | 4.000 | 0.226 | 9.11 | 9.20 | 0.318 | 12.51 | 12.63 | — | — | — |
| 4" | 4.500 | 0.237 | 10.79 | 10.89 | 0.337 | 14.98 | 15.17 | — | — | — |

## COPPER TUBING

| NOMINAL PIPE SIZE | DIMENSION (IN.) O.D. | TYPE K WALL (IN.) | TYPE K LB/FT | TYPE L AND ACR WALL (IN.) | TYPE L AND ACR LB/FT | TYPE M WALL (IN.) | TYPE M LB/FT | REFRIGERATOR TUBE WALL (IN.) | REFRIGERATOR TUBE LB/COIL |
|---|---|---|---|---|---|---|---|---|---|
|  | ⅛ | — | — | — | — | — | — | 0.030 | 1.74 |
|  | 3/16 | — | — | — | — | — | — | 0.030 | 2.88 |
|  | ¼ | — | — | — | — | — | — | 0.030 | 4.02 |
|  | 5/16 | — | — | — | — | — | — | 0.032 | 5.45 |
| ¼" | ⅜ | 0.035 | 0.145 | 0.030 | 0.126 | 0.025 | 0.106 | 0.032 | 6.70 |
| ⅜" | ½ | 0.049 | 0.269 | 0.035 | 0.198 | 0.025 | 0.145 | 0.032 | 9.10 |
| ½" | ⅝ | 0.049 | 0.344 | 0.040 | 0.285 | 0.028 | 0.204 | 0.035 | 12.55 |
| ⅝" | ¾ | 0.049 | 0.418 | 0.042 | 0.362 | 0.030 | 0.263 | 0.035 | 15.25 |
| ¾" | ⅞ | 0.065 | 0.641 | 0.045 | 0.455 | 0.032 | 0.328 | 0.045 | 22.75 |
| 1" | 1⅛ | 0.065 | 0.839 | 0.050 | 0.655 | 0.035 | 0.465 | 0.050 | 32.75 |
| 1¼" | 1⅜ | 0.065 | 1.040 | 0.055 | 0.884 | 0.042 | 0.682 | 0.055 | 44.20 |
| 1½" | 1⅝ | 0.072 | 1.360 | 0.060 | 1.140 | 0.049 | 0.940 | — | — |
| 2" | 2⅛ | 0.083 | 2.060 | 0.070 | 1.750 | 0.058 | 1.460 | — | — |
| 2½" | 2⅝ | 0.095 | 2.930 | 0.080 | 2.480 | 0.065 | 2.030 | — | — |
| 3" | 3⅛ | 0.109 | 4.000 | 0.090 | 3.330 | 0.072 | 2.680 | — | — |
| 3½" | 3⅝ | 0.120 | 5.120 | 0.100 | 4.290 | 0.083 | 3.580 | — | — |
| 4" | 4⅛ | 0.134 | 6.510 | 0.110 | 5.380 | 0.095 | 4.660 | — | — |
| 5" | 5⅛ | 0.160 | 9.670 | 0.125 | 7.610 | 0.109 | 6.666 | — | — |
| 6" | 6⅛ | 0.192 | 13.900 | 0.140 | 10.200 | 0.122 | 8.920 | — | — |

## RED BRASS PIPE

| NOMINAL PIPE SIZE | DIMENSION (IN.) O.D. | STANDARD WEIGHT WALL (IN.) | STANDARD WEIGHT LB/FT | EXTRA STRONG WALL (IN.) | EXTRA STRONG LB/FT |
|---|---|---|---|---|---|
| ⅛" | 0.405 | 0.062 | 0.253 | 0.100 | 0.363 |
| ¼" | 0.540 | 0.082 | 0.447 | 0.123 | 0.611 |
| ⅜" | 0.675 | 0.090 | 0.627 | 0.127 | 0.829 |
| ½" | 0.840 | 0.107 | 0.934 | 0.149 | 1.230 |
| ¾" | 1.050 | 0.114 | 1.270 | 0.157 | 1.670 |
| 1" | 1.315 | 0.126 | 1.780 | 0.182 | 2.460 |
| 1¼" | 1.660 | 0.146 | 2.630 | 0.194 | 3.390 |
| 1½" | 1.900 | 0.150 | 3.130 | 0.203 | 4.100 |
| 2" | 2.375 | 0.156 | 4.120 | 0.221 | 5.670 |
| 2½" | 2.875 | 0.187 | 5.990 | 0.280 | 8.660 |
| 3" | 3.500 | 0.219 | 8.560 | 0.304 | 11.600 |
| 3½" | 4.000 | 0.250 | 11.200 | 0.321 | 14.100 |
| 4" | 4.500 | 0.250 | 12.700 | 0.341 | 16.900 |
| 5" | 5.562 | 0.250 | 15.800 | 0.375 | 23.200 |
| 6" | 6.625 | 0.250 | 19.000 | 0.437 | 32.200 |

## PVC AND CPVC PIPE DIMENSIONS (IN.)

| NOMINAL PIPE SIZE | SCHEDULE 40 OUTSIDE DIAMETER | SCHEDULE 40 WALL THICKNESS | SCHEDULE 80 OUTSIDE DIAMETER | SCHEDULE 80 WALL THICKNESS |
|---|---|---|---|---|
| ¼ | .540 | .088 | .540 | .119 |
| ⅜ | .675 | .091 | .675 | .126 |
| ½ | .840 | .109 | .840 | .147 |
| ¾ | 1.050 | .113 | 1.050 | .154 |
| 1 | 1.315 | .133 | 1.315 | .179 |
| 1¼ | 1.660 | .140 | 1.660 | .191 |
| 1½ | 1.900 | .145 | 1.900 | .200 |
| 2 | 2.375 | .154 | 2.375 | .218 |
| 2½ | 2.875 | .203 | 2.875 | .276 |
| 3 | 3.500 | .216 | 3.500 | .300 |
| 4 | 4.500 | .237 | 4.500 | .337 |
| 6 | 6.625 | .280 | 6.625 | .432 |
| 8 | 8.625 | .322 | 8.625 | .500 |
| 10 | 10.750 | .365 | 10.750 | .593 |
| 12 | 12.750 | .406 | 12.750 | .687 |
| 14 | 14.000 | .437 |  |  |
| 16 | 16.000 | .500 |  |  |

## PVC (POLYVINYLCHLORIDE) PIPE

| NOMINAL PIPE SIZE | FOR CEMENTING ONLY WALL (IN.) | FOR CEMENTING ONLY PSI AT 73.4°F | FOR CEMENTING OR THREADING WALL (IN.) | PSI AT 73.4°F CEMENT | PSI AT 73.4°F THREAD |
|---|---|---|---|---|---|
| ¼" | — | — | 0.119 | 1130 | 565 |
| ⅜" | 0.031 | 620 | 0.126 | 920 | 460 |
| ½" | 0.109 | 600 | 0.147 | 425 | 425 |
| ¾" | 0.113 | 480 | 0.154 | 690 | 345 |
| 1" | 0.133 | 450 | 0.179 | 630 | 315 |
| 1¼" | 0.140 | 370 | 0.191 | 520 | 260 |
| 1½" | 0.145 | 330 | 0.200 | 470 | 235 |
| 2" | 0.154 | 280 | 0.218 | 400 | 200 |
| 2½" | 0.203 | 300 | 0.276 | 420 | 210 |
| 3" | 0.216 | 260 | 0.300 | 370 | 185 |
| 4" | 0.237 | 220 | 0.337 | 320 | 160 |
| 6" | 0.280 | 180 | 0.432 | 280 | 140 |

## MAXIMUM OPERATING PRESSURE OF CPVC PIPE AT 70°F

| NOMINAL PIPE SIZE (IN.) | MAXIMUM OPERATING PRESSURE, PSI SCHEDULE 40 SOLVENT CEMENTED | SCHEDULE 80 THREADED | SCHEDULE 80 SOLVENT CEMENTED |
|---|---|---|---|
| ¼ | 640 | 450 | 900 |
| ⅜ | 500 | 365 | 730 |
| ½ | 475 | 340 | 680 |
| ¾ | 385 | 275 | 550 |
| 1 | 360 | 250 | 500 |
| 1¼ | 295 | 205 | 415 |
| 1½ | 265 | 185 | 375 |
| 2 | 220 | 160 | 320 |
| 2½ | 240 | 170 | 340 |
| 3 | 210 | 150 | 300 |
| 4 | 175 | 130 | 260 |
| 6 | 140 | 115 | 230 |

Walter H. Sobel, FAIA, & Associates; Chicago, Illinois
Joseph R. Loring & Associates, Inc.; New York, New York

## STAINLESS STEEL PIPE

| NOMINAL PIPE SIZE | DIMENSION O.D. (IN.) | SCHEDULE 5·s | | SCHEDULE 10·s | | SCHEDULE 40·s | |
|---|---|---|---|---|---|---|---|
| | | WALL (IN.) | LB/FT | WALL (IN.) | LB/FT | WALL (IN.) | LB/FT |
| 1/8″ | 0.405 | — | — | 0.049 | 0.186 | 0.068 | 0.245 |
| 1/4″ | 0.540 | — | — | 0.065 | 0.330 | 0.088 | 0.425 |
| 3/8″ | 0.675 | — | — | 0.065 | 0.424 | 0.091 | 0.568 |
| 1/2″ | 0.840 | 0.065 | 0.538 | 0.083 | 0.671 | 0.109 | 0.851 |
| 3/4″ | 1.050 | 0.065 | 0.684 | 0.083 | 0.857 | 0.113 | 1.131 |
| 1″ | 1.315 | 0.065 | 0.868 | 0.109 | 1.404 | 0.133 | 1.679 |
| 1 1/4″ | 1.660 | 0.065 | 1.107 | 0.109 | 1.806 | 0.140 | 2.278 |
| 1 1/2″ | 1.900 | 0.065 | 1.274 | 0.109 | 2.085 | 0.145 | 2.718 |
| 2″ | 2.375 | 0.065 | 1.604 | 0.109 | 2.638 | 0.154 | 3.653 |
| 2 1/2″ | 2.875 | 0.083 | 2.475 | 0.120 | 3.531 | 0.203 | 5.793 |
| 3″ | 3.500 | 0.083 | 3.029 | 0.120 | 4.332 | 0.216 | 7.576 |
| 3 1/2″ | 4.000 | 0.083 | 3.472 | 0.120 | 4.973 | 0.226 | 9.109 |
| 4″ | 4.500 | 0.083 | 3.915 | 0.120 | 5.613 | 0.237 | 10.790 |
| 5″ | 5.563 | 0.109 | 6.350 | 0.134 | 7.770 | 0.258 | 14.620 |
| 6″ | 6.625 | 0.109 | 7.585 | 0.134 | 9.290 | 0.280 | 18.970 |
| 8″ | 8.625 | 0.109 | 9.914 | 0.148 | 13.400 | 0.322 | 28.550 |
| 10″ | 10.750 | 0.134 | 15.190 | 0.165 | 18.700 | 0.365 | 40.480 |
| 12″ | 12.750 | 0.165 | 22.180 | 0.180 | 24.200 | 0.375 | 49.550 |

## ALUMINUM PIPE AND SOFT ALUMINUM TUBING

| NOMINAL PIPE SIZE | ALUMINUM PIPE (PLAIN END) | | | SOFT ALUMINUM TUBING | | |
|---|---|---|---|---|---|---|
| | DIMENSION (IN.) | | WEIGHT (LB/FT) | DIMENSION (IN.) | | LB/50 FT COIL |
| | O.D. | WALL | | O.D. | WALL | |
| 1/2″ | 0.840 | 0.145 | 0.294 | 1/4 | 0.032 | 1.30 |
| 3/4″ | 1.050 | 0.113 | 0.391 | 3/8 | 0.035 | 2.22 |
| 1″ | 1.315 | 0.133 | 0.581 | 1/2 | 0.035 | 3.03 |
| 1 1/4″ | 1.660 | 0.140 | 0.786 | 5/8 | 0.035 | 3.84 |
| 1 1/2″ | 1.900 | 0.145 | 0.940 | — | — | — |
| 2″ | 2.375 | 0.154 | 1.264 | — | — | — |
| 2 1/2″ | 2.875 | 0.203 | 2.004 | — | — | — |
| 3″ | 3.500 | 0.216 | 2.621 | — | — | — |

## COPPER TUBING

1. Type K is a water tube for underground and interior service.
2. Type L is a water tube for interior service only.
3. Type K and type L can be specially cleaned for oxygen service.
4. Type ACR is for air conditioning and refrigeration service.
5. Type M is a nonpressure water tube for aboveground application.

## STAINLESS STEEL PIPE

This is an excellent material to be used whenever corrosion or contamination of process materials is a problem. The corrosion resistance depends greatly on a thin metal oxide layer, which forms a protective film on the surface of the metal. Air forms this film in time. Full or partial destruction of this film will very much affect the corrosion resistance of the alloy. For selection of the proper alloy consult manufacturer.

## ALUMINUM PIPE

This is suitable for water piping and hand railings.

## PLASTIC PIPING

Polyvinyl chloride (PVC) piping ASTM D-1785-83 and chlorinated polyvinyl chloride (CPVC) piping, ASTM specification F441 are accepted by many health authorities for potable water. Schedule 40, 80, and 120 refer to pipe wall thickness.

## SEAMLESS STEEL PIPE

1. ASTM Spec. A-53: This is a general service pipe, suitable for bending, coiling, fusion welding, lapping or flanging. Grade B does not lend itself to close coiling, forge-welding, or cold bends.
2. ASTM Spec. A-106: Manufactured from carbon steel for high temperature, high pressure service. An open hearth steel that comes in Grades A and B. Grade A works well for all forming or welding operations. Grade B has somewhat higher carbon and manganese content, which gives it greater tensile strength but less ductility.

## BUTT WELD STEEL PIPE

This pipe is for ordinary use on steam, water, gas, or air. It is not intended for medium or high pressure or close coiling or bending. Specifications require only hydrostatic testing; there are no chemical requirements.

Walter H. Sobel, FAIA, & Associates; Chicago, Illinois

## CAST IRON, MALLEABLE, AND DUCTILE IRON PIPE FITTING MATERIALS

The material used in the manufacture of cast iron, malleable, and ductile iron pipe fittings should conform to specifications set by ASTM.

## DESIGN: THREADED FITTINGS

Cast iron, malleable, and ductile iron pipe fittings are manufactured according to ANSI standards. Since cast iron has little or no ductility, excessive hammering or shock could cause fitting failure. The use of malleable or ductile fittings is suggested under these conditions.

## DESIGN: DRAINAGE FITTINGS

Drainage fittings should be designed to give unobstructed flow. Fittings with openings at right angles should have pitched threads so that the horizontal line will pitch 1/4 in./ft, assuring positive drainage. Pressure-temperature ratings do not apply to drainage fittings.

## DESIGN: PLUGS, BUSHINGS, AND LOCKNUTS

Common plug designs are square head, countersunk, and bar plug. Face bushings and hexagon head bushings are available in a wide range of sizes, and generally are furnished in cast iron or malleable iron. Some small sizes of plugs, bushings, and locknuts are furnished in steel.

Sprinkler lines, heating and air conditioning systems, and plumbing installations utilize cast iron fittings. There is a wide range of types and sizes of fittings available from various manufacturers. Common types of threaded and flanged fittings:

1. ELBOWS: 90°, 90° reducing, 90° side outlet, 45°–90° long radius, 45°, 11 1/4°, 22 1/2°, three way and drop elbows.
2. TEES: Straight run, reducing outlet, reduced run, other end and outlet equal, reduced on run and outlet, side outlet.

| | |
|---|---|
| Crosses | Laterals |
| Reducers | Couplings |
| Double 45° Y's | Increasers |
| 60° Y's | Unions |
| P traps | Caps |
| Running traps | Plugs |
| Return bends | Locknuts |

## RATED WORKING PRESSURES

## CLASSES 125 AND 250 CAST IRON THREADED FITTINGS
ANSI STANDARD B16.4

| TEMPERATURE (°F) | WORKING PRESSURE, NONSHOCK PSIG | |
|---|---|---|
| | CLASS 125 | CLASS 250 |
| −20 to 150 | 175 | 400 |
| 200 | 165 | 370 |
| 250 | 150 | 340 |
| 300 | 140 | 310 |
| 350 | 125 | 280 |
| 400 | — | 250 |

## CLASSES 125 AND 250 CAST IRON FLANGED FITTINGS
ANSI STANDARD B16.1

| TEMPERATURE (°F) | WORKING PRESSURE, NONSHOCK PSIG | | | | |
|---|---|---|---|---|---|
| | CLASS 125 | | | CLASS 250 | |
| | SIZE 1–12 | SIZE 14–24 | SIZE 30–48 | SIZE 1–12 | SIZE 14–24 |
| −20 to 250 | 200 | 150 | 150 | 500 | 300 |
| 200 | 190 | 135 | 115 | 460 | 280 |
| 225 | 180 | 130 | 100 | 440 | 270 |
| 250 | 175 | 125 | 85 | 415 | 260 |
| 275 | 170 | 120 | 65 | 395 | 250 |
| 300 | 165 | 110 | 50 | 375 | 240 |
| 325 | 155 | 105 | | 355 | 230 |
| 350 | 150 | 100 | | 335 | 220 |
| 375 | 145 | | | 315 | 210 |
| 400 | 140 | | | 290 | 200 |
| 425 | 130 | | | 270 | |
| 450 | 125 | | | 250 | |

## GLASS PIPING

Glass piping is used for acid waste drainlines, and is manufactured to resist fracture from thermal shock between 0° and 100°C.

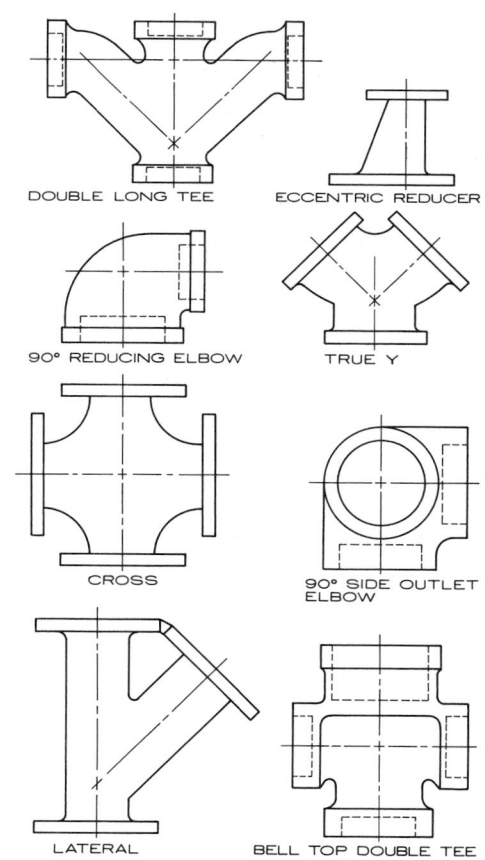

DOUBLE LONG TEE    ECCENTRIC REDUCER

90° REDUCING ELBOW    TRUE Y

CROSS    90° SIDE OUTLET ELBOW

LATERAL    BELL TOP DOUBLE TEE

**VARIOUS PIPE FITTINGS**

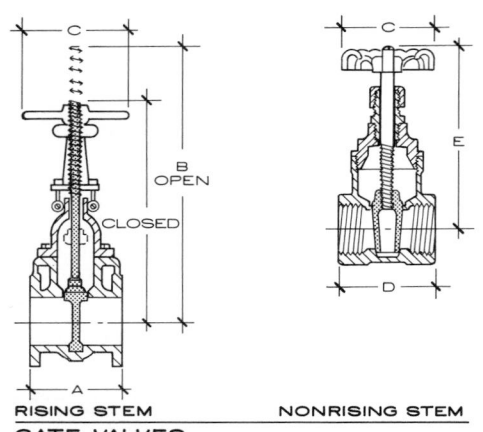

RISING STEM    NONRISING STEM

## GATE VALVES

**NOTE**

Used for on-off service; offers practically no resistance to flow when fully open. Not recommended for throttling or flow modulation. Available in rising and nonrising stems. Suitable for hot and cold water, oil, and gas.

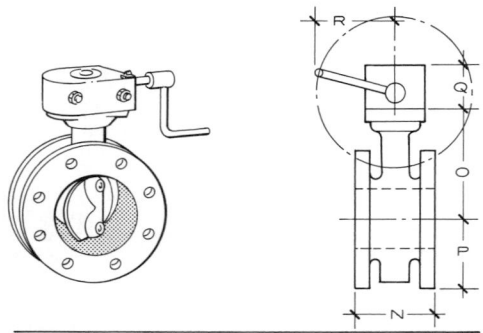

## BUTTERFLY VALVE

**NOTE**

Feature quarter-turn, on-off operation for water, air, gas, or vacuum lines. Recommended for on-off service and some noncritical throttling applications.

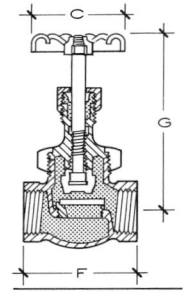

## GLOBE VALVE
**NOTE**

Ideal for throttling service in hot and cold water, oil, and gas piping. Caution must be exercised, however, to avoid extremely close throttling. Vibration may cause valve damage or excessive noise. These valves are seldom used in sizes above 12 in.

**NOTES**

Effectively utilize the globe valves throttling control while providing for a 90° turn in piping. Conditions regarding excessive throttling and size above 12 in., noted for globe valves, also apply to angle valves.

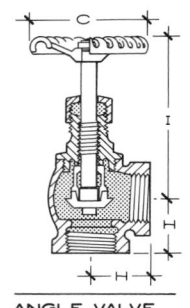

## ANGLE VALVE

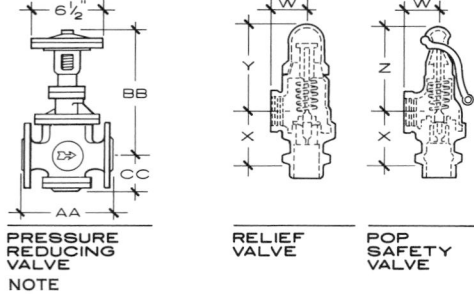

**PRESSURE REDUCING VALVE**    **RELIEF VALVE**    **POP SAFETY VALVE**

**NOTE**

Used in steam, water, air, or gas lines where it is necessary to reduce incoming pressure to the required service pressure. They also maintain it at the point desired.

**NOTE**

Usually spring-loaded valves that open automatically when pressure exceeds limit for which the valve is set. Should always be installed with the stem in a vertical position. Relief valves are usually used for liquids. Safety valves are generally used for steam, air, or other gases.

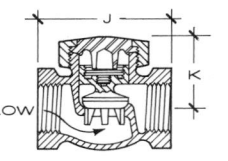 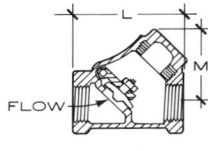

**LIFT CHECK VALVE**    **SWING CHECK VALVE**

**NOTE**

Prevent reversal of flow. For use in horizontal lines only. Generally used in conjunction with globe valves.

**NOTE**

Prevent reversal of flow and are particularly suited to low velocity service. Most swing check valves can be installed in horizontal or vertical upward flow piping. Generally used in conjunction with gate valves.

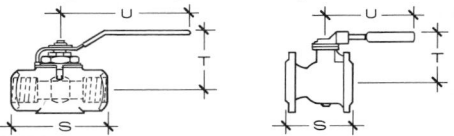

## BALL VALVES
**NOTE**

Feature quarter-turn, on-off operation, straight-through flow, minimum turbulence, low operating torque, tight closure, compact design, and light weight. Available with threaded, solder joint, or flanged ends.

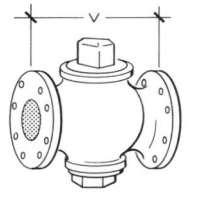 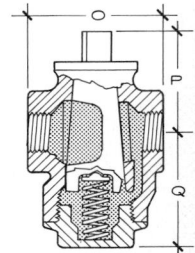

**GAS COCK**    **SPRING—LOADED COCK**

**NOTE**

Available in two-way, three-way, and four-way patterns with threaded or flanged ends. Suitable for cold water, oil, air, or gas.

## VALVE DIMENSIONS
**THREADED UNLESS OTHERWISE NOTED**

| SIZE (IN.) | GATE A | GATE B | GATE C | GATE D | GATE E | GLOBE F | GLOBE G | ANGLE H | ANGLE I | LIFT CHECK J | LIFT CHECK K | SWING CHECK L | SWING CHECK M | SPRING-LOADED COCK O | SPRING-LOADED COCK P | SPRING-LOADED COCK Q | BALL S | BALL T | BALL U | COCK V | RELIEF AND SAFETY W | RELIEF AND SAFETY X | RELIEF AND SAFETY Y | RELIEF AND SAFETY Z | PRESSURE REDUCING AA | PRESSURE REDUCING BB | PRESSURE REDUCING CC |
|---|---|---|---|---|---|---|---|---|---|---|---|---|---|---|---|---|---|---|---|---|---|---|---|---|---|---|---|
| 1/4 | 1³/₄ | 4¹/₂ | 1³/₄ | 1⁷/₈ | 3³/₄ | 1³/₄ | 2³/₄ | ⁷/₈ | 3 | 1⁷/₈ | 1 | 2¹/₈ | 1¹/₂ | | | | 3 | 1¹/₄ | 4 | 1⁵/₈ | | | | | | | |
| 3/8 | 1³/₄ | 4¹/₂ | 1³/₄ | 1⁷/₈ | 3³/₄ | 1⁷/₈ | 2⁷/₈ | 1 | 3¹/₄ | 2 | 1¹/₈ | 2¹/₈ | 1¹/₂ | | | | 3 | 1¹/₄ | 4 | 1³/₄ | 1¹/₈ | 2¹/₄ | 3¹/₈ | 3³/₄ | Flanged | | |
| 1/2 | 2¹/₈ | 5¹/₄ | 2¹/₈ | 2¹/₈ | 3³/₄ | 2¹/₄ | 3¹/₂ | 1¹/₈ | 3³/₄ | 2¹/₂ | 1³/₈ | 2¹/₂ | 1³/₄ | 1¹/₄ | 2¹/₈ | 2³/₈ | 2¹/₂ | 1¹/₄ | 4 | 2¹/₈ | 1¹/₈ | 2¹/₄ | 3¹/₈ | 3³/₄ | 7¹/₂ | 11³/₄ | 3¹/₂ |
| 3/4 | 2¹/₄ | 6¹/₂ | 2⁵/₈ | 2¹/₄ | 4¹/₂ | 2³/₄ | 4 | 1³/₈ | 4¹/₄ | 3 | 1⁷/₈ | 3 | 2¹/₈ | 1⁵/₈ | 2¹/₂ | 2⁷/₈ | 2³/₄ | 1¹/₂ | 4¹/₂ | 2¹/₂ | 1³/₈ | 2³/₄ | 3¹/₄ | 3³/₄ | 7¹/₂ | 11³/₄ | 3¹/₂ |
| 1 | 2³/₄ | 7³/₄ | 2³/₄ | 2⁷/₈ | 5¹/₄ | 3³/₈ | 4¹/₂ | 1⁵/₈ | 5 | 3¹/₂ | 2 | 3³/₄ | 2¹/₂ | 2 | 3¹/₈ | 3¹/₂ | 3¹/₂ | 2¹/₈ | 6 | 3 | 1⁵/₈ | 3¹/₄ | 3⁵/₈ | 4⁵/₈ | 7¹/₂ | 11³/₄ | 3¹/₂ |
| 1¹/₄ | 3 | 9¹/₄ | 3¹/₈ | 3 | 5⁷/₈ | 3⁷/₈ | 4⁷/₈ | 1³/₄ | 5¹/₂ | 4¹/₈ | 2³/₈ | 4¹/₄ | 3 | | | | 4 | 2⁵/₈ | 7 | 3¹/₂ | 2¹/₈ | 3³/₄ | 4¹/₄ | 4³/₈ | 7⁷/₈ | 12 | 3³/₄ |
| 1¹/₂ | 3¹/₄ | 10¹/₂ | 3⁵/₈ | 3¹/₄ | 7¹/₄ | 4¹/₂ | 5¹/₂ | 2¹/₄ | 6¹/₄ | 4⁵/₈ | 2⁵/₈ | 5 | 3¹/₂ | | | | 4¹/₄ | 2³/₄ | 7 | 3³/₄ | 2¹/₂ | 4³/₈ | 5³/₈ | 5¹/₄ | 8³/₈ | 12¹/₂ | 4¹/₄ |
| 2 | 3³/₄ | 12³/₄ | 4³/₄ | 3³/₄ | 8³/₈ | 5¹/₄ | 6 | 2⁵/₈ | 7¹/₂ | 5³/₄ | 3¹/₄ | 6 | 4¹/₄ | | | | 4¹/₂ | 3¹/₈ | 8 | 4⁵/₈ | 2³/₄ | 4¹/₂ | 6⁵/₈ | 6¹/₈ | 10¹/₄ | 12 | 4¹/₂ |

## VALVE DIMENSIONS
**FLANGED UNLESS OTHERWISE NOTED**

| SIZE (IN.) | GATE A | GATE B | GATE C | GATE D | GATE E | GLOBE F | GLOBE G | ANGLE H | ANGLE I | LIFT CHECK J | LIFT CHECK K | SWING CHECK L | SWING CHECK M | BUTTERFLY N | BUTTERFLY O | BUTTERFLY P | BUTTERFLY Q | BUTTERFLY R | BALL S | BALL T | BALL U | COCK V | RELIEF AND SAFETY W | RELIEF AND SAFETY X | RELIEF AND SAFETY Y | RELIEF AND SAFETY Z | PRESSURE REDUCING AA | PRESSURE REDUCING BB | PRESSURE REDUCING CC |
|---|---|---|---|---|---|---|---|---|---|---|---|---|---|---|---|---|---|---|---|---|---|---|---|---|---|---|---|---|---|
| 2 | 8¹/₂ | 18 | 8 | 8¹/₂ | 11 | 8 | 13³/₄ | 4 | 12¹/₂ | Threaded | | 8 | 5 | 1³/₄ | 5¹/₂ | 2¹/₂ | 2⁷/₈ | 5 | | | | | Threaded | | | | | | |
| 2¹/₂ | 9¹/₂ | 19 | 9 | 9¹/₂ | 13¹/₄ | 8¹/₂ | 14¹/₂ | 4¹/₄ | 13 | 6⁷/₈ | 3⁷/₈ | 8¹/₂ | 5¹/₂ | 1⁷/₈ | 6 | 2³/₄ | 2⁷/₈ | 5 | | | | 8⁵/₈ | 3 | 4⁷/₈ | 7⁵/₈ | 7³/₄ | 11⁵/₈ | 13 | 6 |
| 3 | 11¹/₈ | 19⁷/₈ | 10 | 11¹/₈ | 14³/₄ | 9¹/₂ | 16¹/₂ | 4³/₄ | 15 | 8 | 4¹/₂ | 9¹/₂ | 6 | 5 | 6¹/₄ | 3¹/₂ | 2⁷/₈ | 5 | 8 | 7 | 12 | 9⁵/₈ | 3¹/₂ | 5¹/₄ | 8¹/₂ | 9¹/₂ | 12¹/₂ | 13³/₄ | 6³/₄ |
| 4 | 12 | 23³/₄ | 12 | 12 | 17¹/₂ | 11¹/₂ | 19³/₄ | 5³/₄ | 17³/₄ | | | 11¹/₂ | 7 | 5 | 7 | 4¹/₄ | 2⁷/₈ | 5 | 9 | 7¹/₂ | 15 | 12¹/₈ | | | | | 14¹/₄ | 14³/₄ | 7⁵/₈ |
| 6 | 15⁷/₈ | 32¹/₂ | 16 | 15⁷/₈ | 23 | 16 | 24¹/₂ | 8 | 21³/₄ | | | 14 | 9 | 5 | 8 | 5³/₄ | 2⁷/₈ | 5 | 10¹/₂ | 9¹/₄ | 30 | | | | | | 17³/₄ | 19¹/₈ | 10¹/₄ |
| 8 | 16¹/₂ | 40³/₄ | 20 | 16¹/₂ | 30³/₄ | 19¹/₂ | 26¹/₂ | 9³/₄ | 24 | | | 19¹/₂ | 10¹/₄ | 6 | 9¹/₄ | 7¹/₂ | 2⁷/₈ | 5 | 11¹/₂ | 10³/₄ | 37¹/₂ | | | | | | 21¹/₄ | 43¹/₄ | 14¹/₄ |

**NOTES**

1. Sizes are nominal; all dimensions are in inches.
2. Refer to manufacturers' literature for other sizes.
3. Operation of 4 in. size and larger located more than 7 ft. above the floor requires chains, extensions, etc.

Victor J. Saccaro; Hoyem-Basso Associates; Bloomfield Hills, Michigan

**15**    **BASIC MECHANICAL MATERIALS AND METHODS**

## NOTES

The cleanout provides access to horizontal and vertical plumbing lines and stacks and a means to remove obstructions. Generally, cleanouts consist of an iron body and brass plug with neoprene seal. The outlet must be gas tight and watertight and must provide ample space for rodding tools. An adjustable housing will allow for variations in floor fill. Cleanout covers must be designed to support the weight of traffic directed over them. The inside caulk type outlet provides greater ease of installation while the wide flange type assures a waterproof bond between floor covering and cleanout.

Most codes require cleanouts located not more than 50 ft apart in horizontal drainage lines of 4 in. pipe or less and not more than 100 ft apart for larger pipe. Also, install cleanouts at each change of direction greater than 45° and at the base of each vertical waste stack. Access covers should be secured with vandal-proof screws or hinged where these units are likely to be removed.

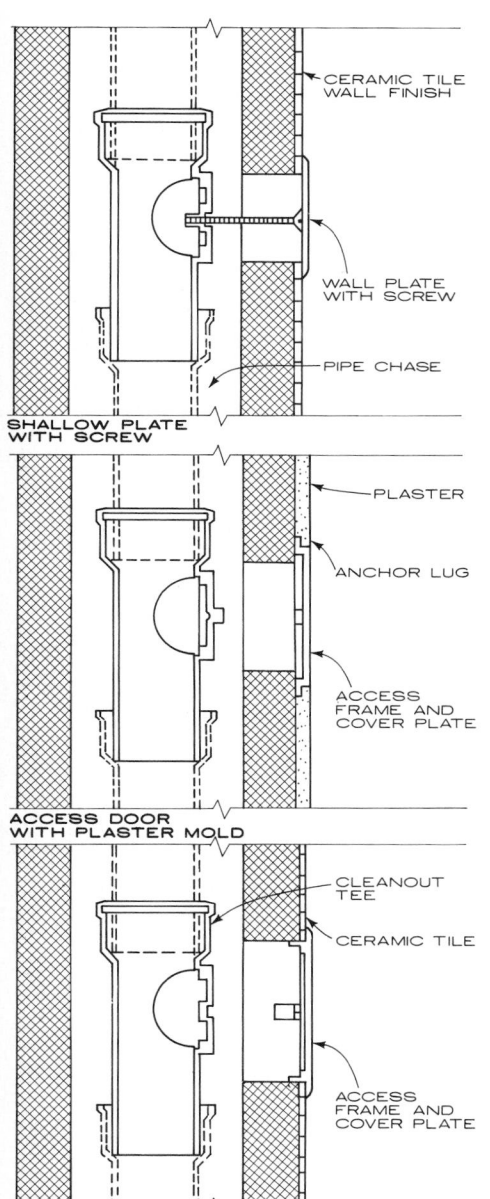

SHALLOW PLATE WITH SCREW

ACCESS DOOR WITH PLASTER MOLD

ACCESS DOOR WITH HINGE

**WALL TYPE CLEANOUTS**

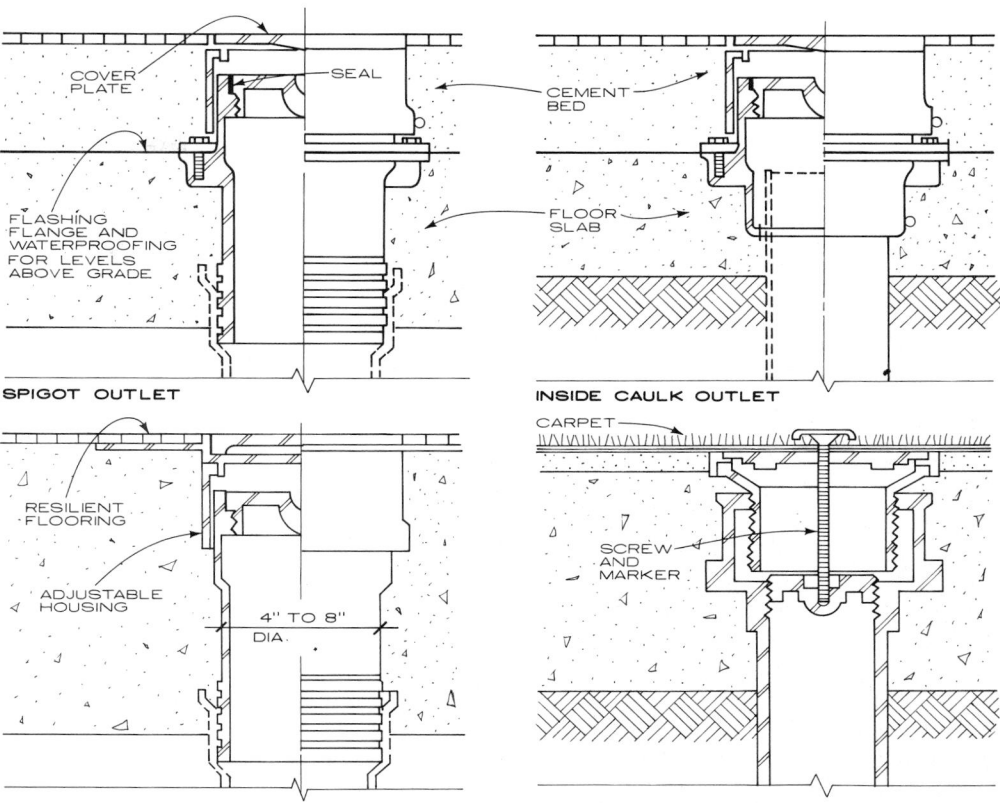

SPIGOT OUTLET

INSIDE CAULK OUTLET

WIDE FLANGE OUTLET

CONCEALED CARPET OUTLET

**FLOOR TYPE CLEANOUTS**

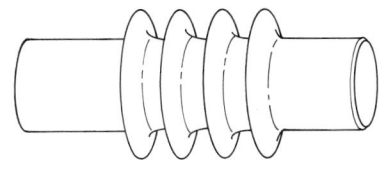

PACKLESS EXPANSION JOINT has stainless steel bellows and carbon steel weld-end nipples (shown) or flanged ends. Sizes 3 in. to 60 in. diameter may have 1 to 10 corrugations. Consult manufacturer for required installation details.

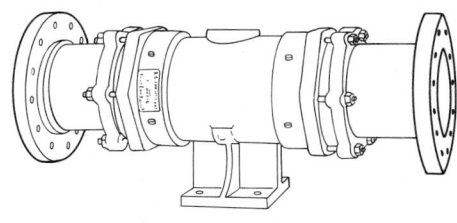

SLIP TYPE EXPANSION JOINT has either internal or external guides. Double joint type is shown with flanged end connections and base. Sizes 1¼ in. to 20 in. are fabricated or cast semi-steel.

**EXPANSION JOINT ASSEMBLIES**

### TOTAL THERMAL EXPANSION OF PIPING MATERIAL (IN.) PER 100 FT ABOVE 32°F

| TEMPERATURE (°F) | CARBON AND CARBON MOLY STEEL | CAST IRON | COPPER | BRASS AND BRONZE | WROUGHT IRON | PLASTIC |
|---|---|---|---|---|---|---|
| 32 | 0 | 0 | 0 | 0 | 0 | 0 |
| 100 | 0.5 | 0.5 | 0.8 | 0.8 | 0.5 | 2.0 |
| 150 | 0.8 | 0.8 | 1.4 | 1.4 | 0.9 | 4.25 |
| 200 | 1.2 | 1.2 | 2.0 | 2.0 | 1.3 | 6.25 |
| 250 | 1.7 | 1.5 | 2.7 | 2.6 | 1.7 | — |
| 300 | 2.0 | 1.9 | 3.3 | 3.2 | 2.2 | — |
| 350 | 2.5 | 2.3 | 4.0 | 3.9 | 2.6 | — |
| 400 | 2.9 | 2.7 | 4.7 | 4.6 | 3.1 | — |
| 450 | 3.4 | 3.1 | 5.3 | 5.2 | 3.6 | — |
| 500 | 3.8 | 3.5 | 6.0 | 5.9 | 4.1 | — |
| 550 | 4.3 | 3.9 | 6.7 | 6.5 | 4.6 | — |
| 600 | 4.8 | 4.0 | 7.4 | 7.2 | 5.2 | — |
| 650 | 5.3 | 4.7 | 8.2 | 7.9 | 5.6 | — |
| 700 | 5.9 | 5.3 | 9.0 | 8.5 | 6.1 | — |
| 750 | 6.4 | 5.8 | — | — | 6.7 | — |
| 800 | 7.0 | 6.3 | — | — | 7.2 | — |
| 850 | 7.4 | — | — | — | — | — |
| 900 | 8.0 | — | — | — | — | — |
| 950 | 8.5 | — | — | — | — | — |
| 1000 | 9.1 | — | — | — | — | — |

Sargent, Webster, Crenshaw & Folley, Architects Engineers Planners; Syracuse, New York

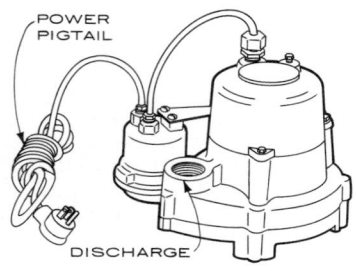

## SUBMERSIBLE

Approximate minimum pit size 24 in. x 24 in. Gpm range to 130 gpm; heads to 50 ft.

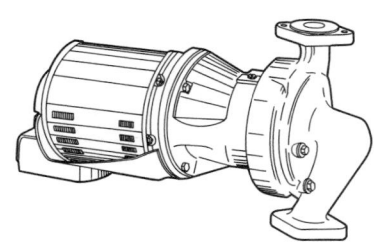

## IN-LINE CENTRIFUGAL

Installed directly in pipeline and supported by pipe and structure. Gpm range to 130 gpm; heads to 50 ft.

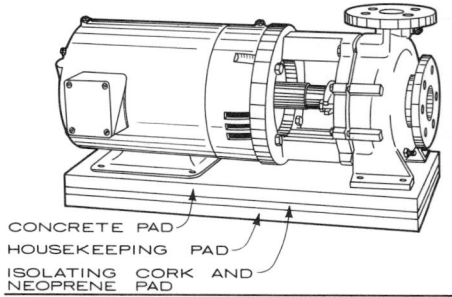

## BASE-MOUNTED CENTRIFUGAL CLOSED COUPLED

Gpm range to 3000 gpm; heads to 360 ft. Required floor space approximately 24 in. x 36 in. to 36 in. x 60 in.

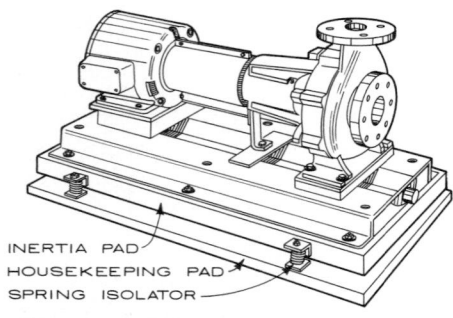

## FRAME-MOUNTED CENTRIFUGAL END SUCTION

Gpm range to 25,000 gpm; head range to 600 ft. Required floor space approximately 24 x 48 in. to 72 x 144 in.

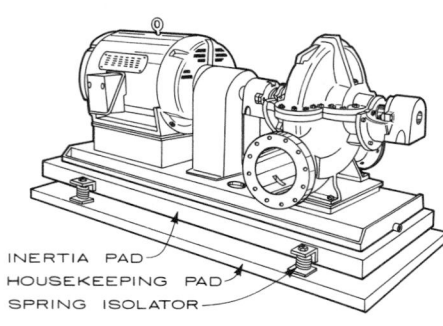

## FRAME-MOUNTED CENTRIFUGAL, DOUBLE SUCTION

Gpm range to 14,000 gpm; head range to 1,200 ft. Available with integral suction sump. Ideal for low net positive suction head application. Less floor space required than for centrifugal pumps.

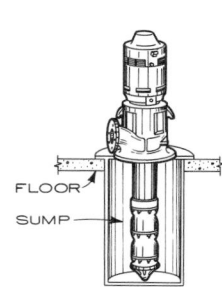

## VERTICAL TURBINE

Sewerage or sump pump for small installations up to 150 gpm to 40 ft. total head. Will operate completely submerged in sump. Suitable for negative suction head.

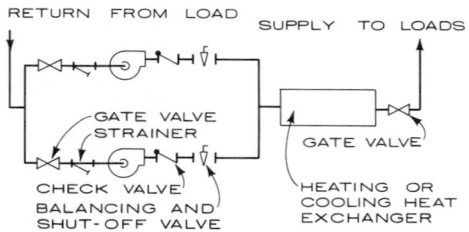

## PARALLEL PUMPING

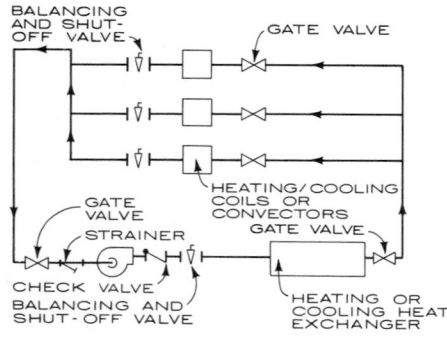

## REVERSE RETURN

### PARALLEL PUMPING

Provides a degree of standby. If one pump fails, approximately 7 percent of flow can be obtained with one pump. It also can be applied to variable flow rate systems where one pump can be shut down under certain operative conditions; also, if flow required is greater than capacity of a single standard pump, parallel pumps can be installed to achieve desired flow rate.

### PRIMARY SECONDARY PUMP

Characteristics of secondary circuit essentially are unaffected by changes in primary circuit or by other secondary circuits. Can be used to provide a different water temperature to each secondary circuit by using mixing valves; also can be used for variable flow primary circuit and constant flow secondary circuits.

### REVERSE RETURN

Provides an approximate equal pressure drop to each secondary heat transfer surface, thereby minimizing balancing requirements. Preferred on extensive piping loops for radiation, fan coil units, etc.

### CONVENTIONAL PUMPING

Least costly and applicable to systems requiring only basic circulation, such as heat exchangers, chillers, and cooling towers. Also can be used for loops to radiation, fan coil units, etc., where runs are short and balancing can be achieved easily.

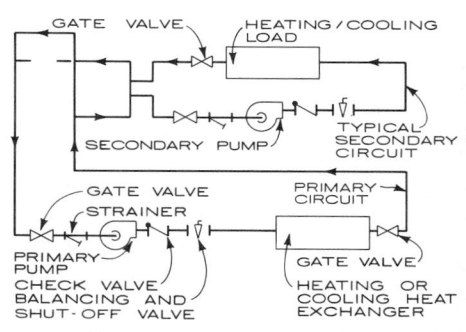

## PRIMARY/SECONDARY CIRCUIT

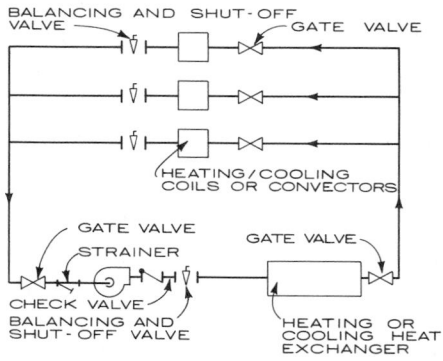

## CONVENTIONAL PUMPING

William Tao & Associates, Inc., Consulting Engineers; St. Louis, Missouri

## GENERAL

Attention must be given to vibration of mechanical equipment to ensure that there is no transmission of objectionable vibration or structureborne noise to the building and occupied spaces. The following general procedure should be followed to avoid problems of vibration and structureborne noise transmission:

1. Evaluate the inherent quietness of the various types of equipment and try to select the types with the lowest sound and vibration levels, consistent with engineering and cost considerations.

2. Locate equipment rooms so they are not directly adjacent to, above, or below areas that are critical from a noise and vibration standpoint. Equipment with inherently large unbalance or vibratory forces should be installed at grade or remote basement locations whenever possible.

3. Locate pipe and duct shafts in utility or service cores near noncritical areas such as elevator shafts, stairwells, and toilets, rather than adjoining critical areas such as bedrooms or private offices.

4. Design supporting structures to be as stiff as possible. Although most equipment room floors are usually 10 or more times stiffer than equipment isolators, they are capable of deflections resulting in floor natural frequencies in the operating speed range of most HVAC equipment. Primary concern is with low speed equipment on long spans that have low natural frequencies and high speed equipment on short span or rigid floors that have high natural frequencies.

5. Specify maximum allowable equipment vibration levels.

6. Provide appropriate vibration isolation for equipment.

Many types of equipment require some support base to maintain alignment of driving and driven components such as fans or where equipment cannot be supported at individual isolator locations. Support bases may be constructed of structural steel members, concrete, or a combination of concrete and structural members, and should always be designed with ample rigidity to resist all starting and operating forces without supplemental hold-down devices. It is common practice to install many types of equipment on inertia blocks as shown below. Inertia blocks or mass of the system have no effect on the efficiency of isolators; however, they do affect the movement of the equipment itself and, as such, can affect the transmission to the building structure through connected piping and ducts.

Inertia blocks should be used for:

1. Equipment that has large unbalance or vibratory forces such as horizontal air compressors, and some reciprocating compressors, and engines. For such equipment, the designer should obtain from the equipment manufacturer the magnitude and frequency of the unbalance forces to permit proper sizing of inertia block.

2. Equipment such as certain large fans, pumps, and compressors, where some type of structural base must be furnished to support driving and driven components and/or maintain alignment.

3. Equipment subject to external forces such as high pressure fans, where use of an inertia block will result in stiffer isolators and thereby limit movement resulting from reaction to pressure thrust.

### NOTE

Within earthquake zones, inertia blocks and other support bases must be designed to resist the horizontal and vertical thrusts that can occur during a seismic event. Heavy equipment mounted on a floating base can easily develop enough motion to fly free of its springs. Excessive lateral movement should be prevented through the use of angle iron stops, spring mounts with integral restraints or all-directional snubbers. All of these devices must be carefully installed so that they do not hinder the normal operation of the isolation system.

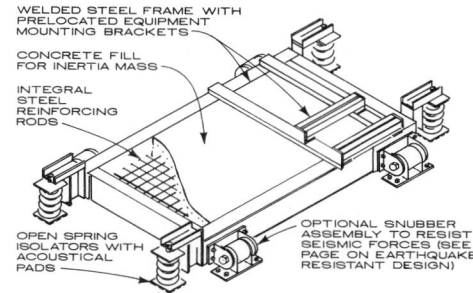

CONCRETE AND STEEL BASE

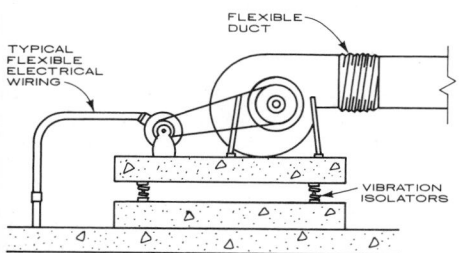

INERTIA BLOCKS

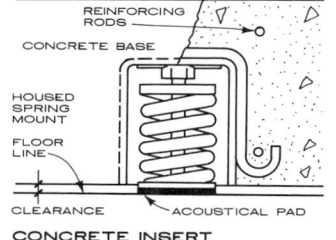

CONCRETE INSERT

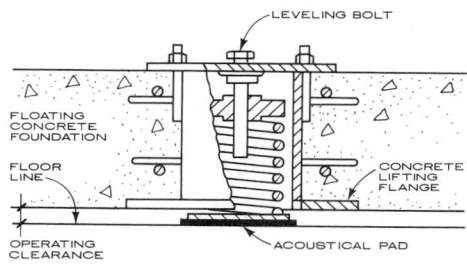

CONCRETE INSERT FOR LARGE BASE

## EQUIPMENT SUPPORT BASES

The choice of isolators for any given application primarily depends on required deflection; however, consideration must also be given to life, cost, and suitability for specific application.

STEEL SPRINGS are the most popular and versatile isolators for HVAC application, since they are available for almost any desired deflection and have virtually unlimited lift. Steel springs, when installed outdoors or in corrosive environments, should be properly protected by the electroplating or other protective coatings. The two basic types of spring isolators are open spring mountings and housed spring mountings.

Open spring mountings consist of a steel spring between a bottom and top plate and usually incorporate an adjustment bolt for leveling. Open spring mounts have become popular, since they avoid the binding and "short circuiting" that can occur with housed mountings. However, misalignment (nonparallel condition of floor and base) should generally be avoided.

It is very important that open springs have proper stiffness in the vertical and horizontal directions so that the springs will be stable and equipment will move sideways.

Housed spring mountings consist of a spring element in a housing incorporating an adjustment bolt for leveling that can be internally located to permit installation of the mount under equipment without legs or holes for an adjustment bolt. The springs in housed mountings are not generally designed to meet stability requirements, since housings limit excessive lateral movement.

It should be noted that all spring mounts must incorporate an elastomeric acoustical and friction pad to prevent the transmission of audible high frequency vibration directly through the spring to the structure.

**VIBRATION ISOLATORS**

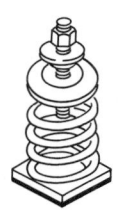

OPEN SPRING

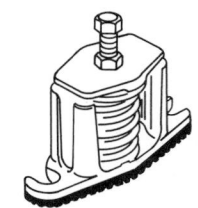

HOUSED SPRING

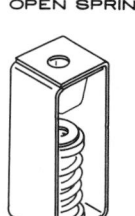

SPRING AND RUBBER

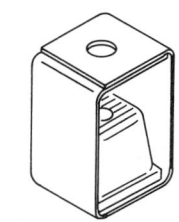

RUBBER HANGER

ISOLATION HANGERS are used for pipe and suspended equipment and usually incorporate rubber, spring, or combination spring and rubber isolator elements. Where spring elements are used, stable springs should be specified. Where isolation hangers are used for suspending piping, provision must be made to accommodate expansion and contraction of pipe due to thermal changes. For pipelines subject to significant thermal movement, this is best accomplished with an eye bolt or swivel arrangement for attachment to structure so that hanger box can swivel to avoid "cocking" of isolation element.

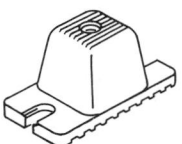

RUBBER MOUNT

NEOPRENE PAD

RUBBER ISOLATORS are available in mount and pad configuration and are generally molded of rubber or neoprene, although other materials such as fiberglass and cork can be used to meet specific service requirements.

Rubber isolators provide a very high resistance to the transmission of noise (high frequency vibration in the acoustical range). In general, their use should be restricted to minor equipment or basement locations.

### COMPARISON TABLE

| RANGE | RPM | SPRINGS | ELAS-TOMERS | CORK |
|---|---|---|---|---|
| Low | Up to 1200 | Required | Unsuitable except for shock | Unsuitable except for shock |
| Medium | 1200–1800 | Excellent | Fair | Not recommended |
| High | Over 1800 | Excellent for critical jobs | Good | Fair to good |

## GENERAL INFORMATION

The insulation and methods described on this page are typical of those used for HVAC work. There are other materials that are equally suitable for use on HVAC and similar systems. The designer should evaluate all available insulating materials and apply what is best suited to the situation with regard to both service and cost. One of the major considerations is the fuel contributed—fire spread—and smoke developed characteristics of various insulating materials. Insulating materials used where air is moved from one area to another such as return and supply air plenums should not exceed a 25/50 fire spread, smoke developed rating.

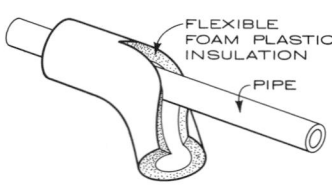

**METHOD PD**

PA GLASS FIBER: Available in both light and heavy density material and with factory applied jacket. Flame spread 25, smoke developed 50; k value 0.25; thickness 1/2 to 2 in. most commonly used. Use multiple layers for greater thickness. Suitable for −60 to +450°F temperature range.

PB PHENOLIC: Molded rigid insulation from neutral phenolic foam, medium density with factory applied jacket. Flame spread 25, smoke developed 50; k value 0.23; suitable for −40 to +250°F temperature range; available in 1, 1½, and 2 in. thickness.

PC POLYURETHANE: Foamed polyurethane, medium density, available with factory applied jacket. Flame spread 25, smoke developed 50 when covered with jacket of 1 mil thick aluminum foil laminated to Kraft paper; available thickness 1 in.; k value 0.16. Polyurethane without proper jacket exceeds 25/50 flame spread/smoke developed rating. Temperature range −100 to +220°F.

PD FOAMED PLASTIC: Flexible foamed plastic insulation, requires no jacket but may be painted with alkyd paint. Fire retardant type available in 3/8 and 1/2 in. thickness with flame spread of 25, smoke developed 200; standard type available in 3/8, 1/2, and 3/4 in. thickness with flame spread and smoke developed exceeding 25/200; k value 0.25; suitable for −40 to +220°F temperature range.

PE CALCIUM SILICATE: Rigid pipe insulation, k value 0.40, with factory jacket, for pipe up to 1200°F.

## PIPE INSULATION

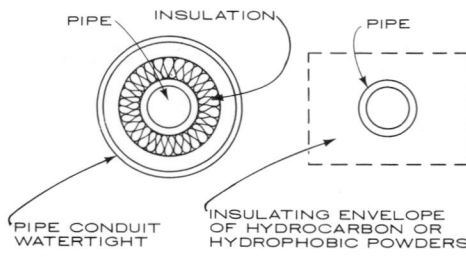

Two of the more common methods of insulating underground piping are shown above. Cathodic protection must be used to prevent corrosion of metallic carrier pipe.

## BELOW-GROUND APPLICATIONS

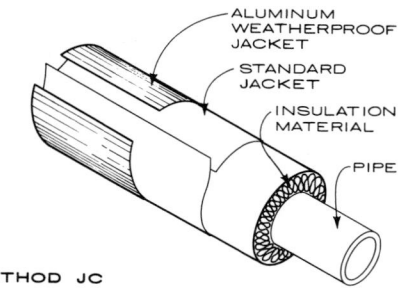

**METHOD JC**

JA HOT OR COLD PIPE: Glass fiber reinforced vinyl coated paper and aluminum foil laminate.

JB HOT PIPE: Presized glass cloth coated with lagging adhesive.

JC WEATHERPROOF: Same as above with additional aluminum jacket or additional roofing felt jacket.

## PIPING JACKETS

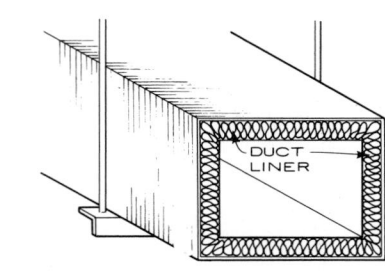

**METHOD DA**

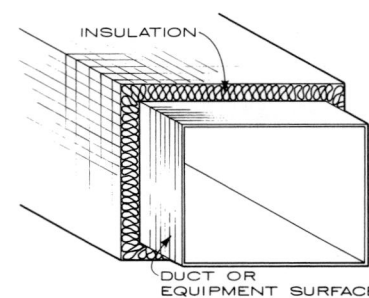

**METHOD DB**

DA DUCT LINER: Glass fiber duct liner, most used densities 3/4, 1½, and 2 lb/cu ft; thickness 1/2, 3/4, and 1 in. most common; coated with neoprene or similar material to limit erosion and reduce coefficient of friction. Serves as insulator and provides sound attenuation of approximately 1 dB/ft. Maximum allowable duct velocity to prevent erosion—4000 fpm or as recommended by manufacturer.

DB EXTERNAL DUCT INSULATION
*Blanket type:* Blanket type light density glass fiber insulation with reinforced aluminum foil vapor barrier facing. This type of duct covering is especially adaptable to round ducts.

*Board type:* Glass fiber board type duct insulation with factory applied vapor barrier jacket. This type of duct covering is especially applicable to rectangular ducts and is available in various densities. Heavy density (6 lb/cu ft) should be used where ducts are subject to potential damage.

DC KITCHEN EXHAUST DUCTS: Calcium silicate block insulation; k = 0.40; wired in place and troweled with insulating cement and finished with canvas jacket. Available in scored block to facilitate forming around large cylindrical shapes.

## DUCT INSULATION

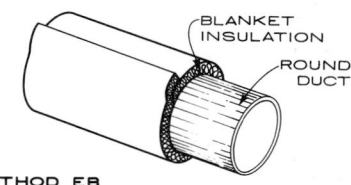

**METHOD EB**

EA EQUIPMENT TO 220°F: Flexible foamed plastic; k = 0.24; available in sheet form.

EB EQUIPMENT TO 450°F: Glass fiber blanket type low density or rigid board type insulation with factory applied vapor barrier jacket; k = 0.25.

EC EQUIPMENT TO 850°F: Glass fiber board with high temperature binder finished with metal mesh, insulating cement and canvas or glass fabric jacket; k = 0.25.

ED EQUIPMENT AND BREECHING TO 1200°F: Calcium silicate block insulation; k = 0.40; wired in place and troweled with insulating cement and finished with aluminum or glass fabric jacket. Available in scored block to facilitate forming around large cylindrical shapes. Mineral wool insulation with wire mesh cover and aluminum or glass fabric jacket also applicable for high temperature applications.

## EQUIPMENT INSULATION

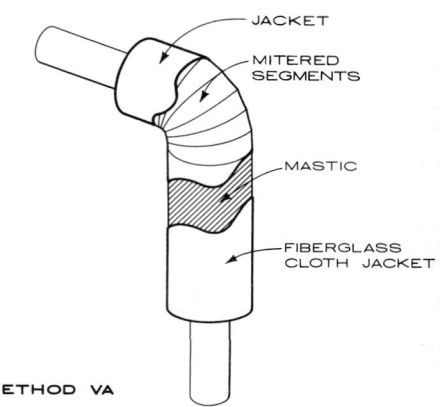

**METHOD VA**

VA Field mitered glass fiber or calcium silicate of same composition as adjacent pipe insulation with jacket of glass fiber reinforced cloth embedded in mastic. As an alternative fittings may be covered with factory fabricated weatherproof PVC or aluminum fitting covers arranged to fit over blanket type insulation inserts, overmitered pipe insulation or overmolded fitting insulators fabricated from calcium silicate, foam glass, urethane, polystyrene, and so on.

## VALVE AND FITTING INSULATION AND JACKETS

## APPLICATIONS
### EQUIPMENT

1. PUMPS (COLD FLUIDS): Use type EA for pumps handling cold fluids. Insulation can be fabricated into a boxlike enclosure and arranged for easy removal to facilitate servicing.

2. PUMPS (HIGH TEMPERATURE HOT WATER, ETC.): Use type EB for pumps handling hot fluids, fabricated same as indicated above for cold fluid pumps.

3. HEAT EXCHANGERS (TO 850°F SURFACE TEMPERATURE): Use type EB or EC depending on surface temperature of vessel.

4. HEAT EXCHANGERS (TO 1200°F SURFACE TEMPERATURES): Use type ED, either calcium silicate or mineral wool.

5. DOMESTIC WATER AND CHILLED WATER TANKS: Use type EA or EB. EB has 25/50 fire spread/smoke developed rating, whereas type EA exceeds these limits.

6. CHILLERS: Use type EA unless restricted by fire spread/smoke developed ratings, in which case use type EB.

David J. McDade; Tomblinson Harburn Associates; Flint, Michigan
William Tao & Associates, Inc., Consulting Engineers; St. Louis, Missouri

 **15** MECHANICAL INSULATION

## HOT PIPING OPERATING ABOVE AMBIENT DEW POINT

### HEAT FLOW

Insulate with enough thickness to satisfy the engineering limits as specified or to maintain the exposed surface temperature below 60°C (140°F) for personnel protection.

### VAPOR FLOW

Install with a permeable jacket to allow moisture and gas flow out of the system. Do not establish a vapor dam at the interface of multiple layer installations.

### WEATHER PROOFING

Install weather resistant jackets with the laps in a rain shield position, sealing only the areas where rain might enter. Weather resistant mastics may be used in place of a jacket. The mastic should be applied in at least two coats, with an open weave glass fabric embedded in the first coat.

### HANGERS

Clevis hangers may be installed directly on pipes operating up to 100°C (212°F). On higher temperature lines the hangers should be external and the pipe should be supported by a saddle and shield.

## COLD PIPING OPERATING BELOW AMBIENT DEW POINT

### HEAT FLOW

Insulate with enough thickness to satisfy the engineering limits as specified or to maintain the exposed surface at a temperature higher than the ambient dew point temperature, whichever is greater. The condensation of atmospheric moisture on the insulation surface must be avoided.

### VAPOR FLOW

Install with a vapor barrier jacket or use insulation of a low permeability, closed cell type. All joints and seams in the vapor barrier must be perfectly sealed and the insulation must be vapor sealed at all terminals, fittings, and valves.

### WEATHER PROOFING

Install weather resistant jacket with the laps in a rain shield position, with all seams, joints, and terminals sealed.

### HANGERS

Clevis hangers or similar devices may be used, but they should be outside the vapor barrier jacket, with a protective shield having enough area to support the load of the pipe and its contents without crushing or indenting the insulation. Some insulations require a load bearing material insert between the shield and the pipe. The load bearing material should be a high density insulation or a poor conductor of heat such as waterproofed wood. Preinsulated hangers are also available for low temperature pipe support.

## INSULATION FOR BOILER BREECHING AND HIGH TEMPERATURE EQUIPMENT

### INSULATION CHOICE

First consideration must be given to the operating temperature of the surfaces to be insulated, as each material has a maximum use temperature. A second consideration concerns the size and shape of the surfaces, as these factors will determine whether it is expedient to use blanket, block, or spray-on insulation.

### HEAT FLOW

Insulate with a great enough thickness to satisfy the engineering limits or to provide personnel protection by limiting the exposed surface temperature to 60°C (140°F).

### VAPOR FLOW

The choice and installation of the insulation and its finish must establish a system that allows free movement of vapor out of the system. Insulation and finishes that contain water or other volatile substances must be exposed to slowly rising temperatures at startup to provide time for vapor escape.

Charles F. Gilbo; Consultant; Lancaster, Pennsylvania

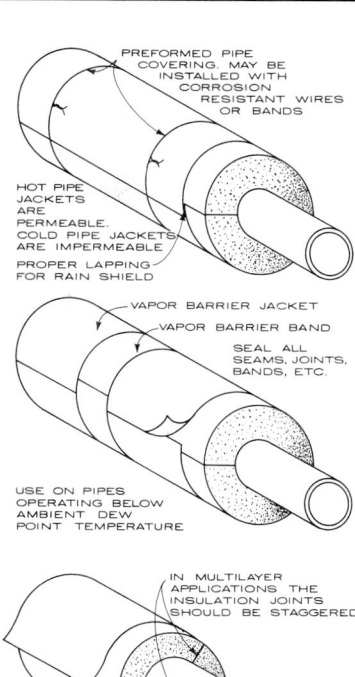

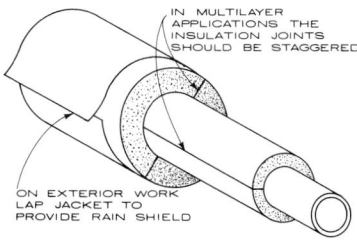

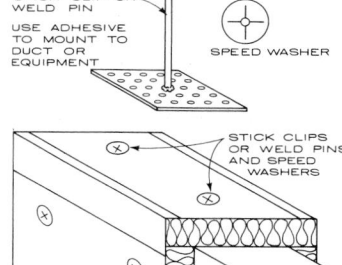

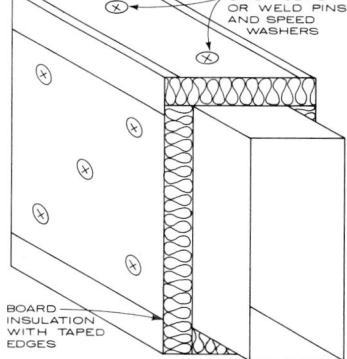

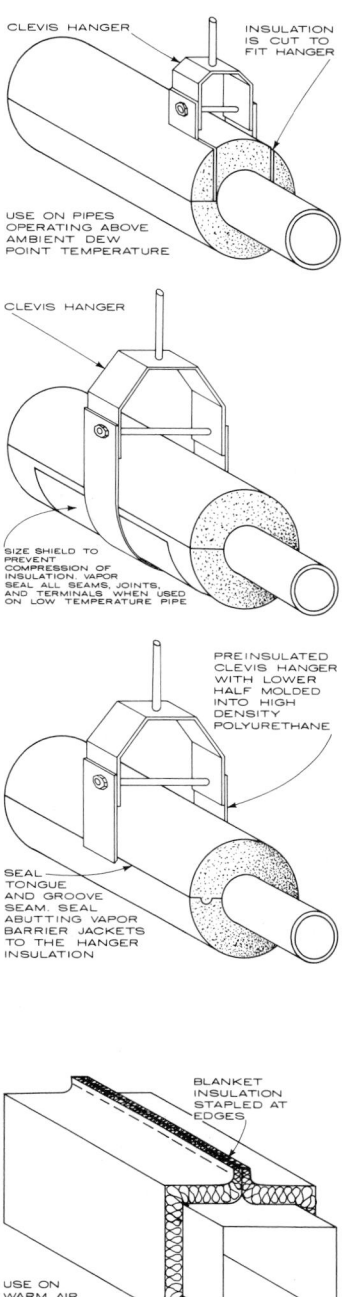

## DUCTS FOR LOW TEMPERATURES

### VAPOR FLOW

Ducts that operate at temperatures below the ambient dew point temperature must be covered with an insulation system that incorporates a near perfect vapor barrier on the warm side of the insulation. Such ducts may also be successfully insulated with flexible, closed celled, low permeability plastic insulation. If stick clips or weld pins are used to hold board type insulation in place, all penetrations of the vapor barrier must be sealed.

### HEAT FLOW

Enough insulation must be used to maintain the temperature of the exposed surface at a level higher than the ambient dew point temperature to prevent the condensation of water. If the engineering specification limits heat flow to the duct, both the limits and condensation control must be considered and the insulation thickness chosen to satisfy the most severe condition.

## DUCTS FOR KITCHEN EXHAUST AND HEATING

### VAPOR FLOW

Ducts that operate at temperatures above ambient dew point temperature may be insulated without vapor sealing; therefore mechanical anchors and fasteners may be used.

### HEAT FLOW

Enough insulation should be used to restrict heat flow to the engineered level. Due consideration must be given to the increased heat flow at the pins, anchors, stick clips, etc.; therefore greater insulation thicknesses are needed when such fasteners are used.

## BUSINESS, MERCANTILE, INDUSTRIAL OTHER THAN FOUNDRY, AND STORAGE

| WATER CLOSETS | EMPLOYEES | LAVATORIES | EMPLOYEES |
|---|---|---|---|
| 1 | 1–15 | 1 | 1–20 |
| 2 | 16–35 | 2 | 21–40 |
| 3 | 36–55 | 3 | 41–60 |
| 4 | 56–80 | 4 | 61–80 |
| 5 | 81–110 | 5 | 81–100 |
| 6 | 111–150 | 6 | 101–125 |
| 7 | 151–190 | 7 | 126–150 |
| | | 8 | 151–175 |
| One additional water closet for each 40 in excess of 190 | | One additional lavatory for each 30 in excess of 175 | |

## INDUSTRIAL, FOUNDRIES, AND STORAGE

| WATER CLOSETS | EMPLOYEES | LAVATORIES | EMPLOYEES |
|---|---|---|---|
| 1 | 1–10 | 1 | 1–8 |
| 2 | 11–25 | 2 | 9–16 |
| 3 | 26–50 | 3 | 17–30 |
| 4 | 51–80 | 4 | 31–45 |
| 5 | 81–125 | 5 | 46–65 |
| One additional water closet for each 45 in excess of 125 | | One additional lavatory for each 25 in excess of 65 | |

## ASSEMBLY, OTHER THAN RELIGIOUS, AND SCHOOLS

| WATER CLOSETS | OCCUPANTS | URINALS | MALE OCCUPANTS | LAVATORIES | OCCUPANTS |
|---|---|---|---|---|---|
| 1 | 1–100 | 1 | 1–100 | 1 | 1–100 |
| 2 | 101–200 | 2 | 101–200 | 2 | 101–200 |
| 3 | 201–400 | 3 | 201–400 | 3 | 201–400 |
| 4 | 401–700 | 4 | 401–700 | 4 | 401–700 |
| 5 | 701–1100 | 5 | 701–1100 | 5 | 701–1100 |
| One additional water closet for each 600 in excess of 1100 | | One additional urinal for each 300 in excess of 1100 | | One additional lavatory for each 1500 in excess of 1100. Such lavatories need not be supplied with hot water | |

### ASSEMBLY, RELIGIOUS

One water closet and one lavatory.

### ASSEMBLY, SCHOOL

For pupils' use:

1. Water closets for pupils; in elementary schools, 1 for each 100 males and 1 for each 35 females; in secondary schools, 1 for each 100 males and 1 for each 45 females.
2. One lavatory for each 50 pupils.
3. One urinal for each 30 male pupils.
4. One drinking fountain for each 150 pupils, but at least one on each floor having classrooms.

Where more than 5 persons are employed, provide fixtures as required for group C1 occupancy.

### INSTITUTIONAL

(Persons whose movements are not limited.) Within each dwelling unit:

1. One kitchen sink.
2. One water closet.
3. One bathtub or shower.
4. One lavatory.

Where sleeping accommodations are arranged as individual rooms, provide the following for each six sleeping rooms:

1. One water closet.
2. One bathtub and shower.
3. One lavatory.

Where sleeping accommodations are arranged as a dormitory, provide the following for each 15 persons (separate rooms for each sex except in dwelling units):

1. One water closet.
2. One bathtub or shower.
3. One lavatory.

### INSTITUTIONAL, OTHER THAN HOSPITALS

(Persons whose movements are limited.) On each story:

1. Water closets: 1 for each 25 males and 1 for each 20 females.
2. One urinal for each 50 male occupants.
3. One lavatory for each 10 occupants.
4. One shower for each 10 occupants.
5. One drinking fountain for each 50 occupants.

Fixtures for employees the same as required for group C1 occupancy, in separate rooms for each sex.

### INSTITUTIONAL, HOSPITALS

For patients' use:

1. One water closet and one lavatory for each 10 patients.
2. One shower or bathtub for each 20 patients.
3. One drinking fountain or equivalent fixture for each 100 patients.

Fixtures for employees the same as required for group C1 occupancy, and separate from those for patients.

### INSTITUTIONAL, MENTAL HOSPITALS

For patients' use:

1. One water closet, one lavatory, and one shower or bathtub, for each 8 patients.
2. One drinking fountain or equivalent fixture for each 50 patients.

Fixtures for employees the same as required for group C1 occupancy, and separate from those for patients.

### INSTITUTIONAL, PENAL INSTITUTIONS

For inmate use:

1. One water closet and one lavatory in each cell.
2. One shower on each floor on which cells are located.
3. One water closet and one lavatory for inmate use available in each exercise area.

Lavatories for inmate use need not be supplied with hot water. Fixtures for employees the same as required for group C1 occupancy, and placed in separate rooms from those used by inmates.

### MISCELLANEOUS

Temporary toilet facilities shall be provided for employees engaged in the construction, alteration, repair, or demolition of buildings on the basis of 1 unit for each 30 persons.

### PUBLIC BATHING OCCUPANCIES

Facilities for bathers at swimming pools shall consist of at least the following:

1. One water closet for each 40 females and 60 males.
2. One urinal for each 60 males.
3. One lavatory for each 60 bathers.
4. One shower for each 40 females and 40 males. In schools such required showers shall equal one third the number of pupils in the largest class.

### BUSINESS (C-1 OCCUPANCY)

Buildings used primarily for the transaction of business, with the handling of merchandise being incidental to the primary use.

### MERCANTILE (C-2 OCCUPANCY)

Buildings used primarily for the display of merchandise and its sale to the public.

### ADDITIONAL REQUIREMENTS

1. One drinking fountain or equivalent fixture for each 75 employees.
2. Urinals may be substituted for not more than one third of the required number of water closets when more than 35 males are employed.

### INDUSTRIAL (C-3 OCCUPANCY)

Buildings used primarily for the manufacture or processing of products.

### STORAGE (C-4 OCCUPANCY)

Buildings used primarily for the storage of or shelter for merchandise, vehicles, or animals.

### ADDITIONAL REQUIREMENTS

1. One drinking fountain or equivalent fixture for each 75 employees.
2. Urinals provided where more than 10 males are employed: 1 for 11–29; 2 for 30–79; one additional urinal for each 80 in excess of 79.

### ASSEMBLY (C-5 OCCUPANCY)

Buildings used primarily for the assembly for athletic, educational, religious, social, or similar purposes.

### ADDITIONAL REQUIREMENT

One drinking fountain for each 1000 occupants, but at least one on each floor.

### MULTIPLE DWELLINGS

Provide plumbing systems and furnish hot and cold water. Provide within each dwelling unit:

1. One kitchen sink.
2. One water closet.
3. One bathtub or shower.
4. One lavatory.

Sleeping accommodations—for each multiple of six sleeping room provide:

1. One water closet.
2. One bathtub or shower.
3. One lavatory.

Sleeping accommodations—dormitories for each multiple of 15 persons provide:

1. One water closet.
2. One bathtub or shower.
3. One lavatory.

Urinals may be substituted for not more than one third of the required number of water closets. Facilities for bathers at swimming pools shall consist of at least the following:

1. One water closet for each 40 females and 60 males.
2. One urinal for each 60 males.
3. One lavatory for each 60 females and 60 males.
4. One shower for each 40 females and 40 males.

### GENERAL NOTES

1. Plumbing fixture requirements shown are based on New York State Uniform Fire Prevention and Building Code and can serve only as a guide. Consult codes in force in area of construction and state and federal agencies (Labor Department, General Services Administration, etc.) and comply with their requirements.
2. Plumbing fixture requirements are to be based on the maximum legal occupancy and not on the actual or anticipated occupancy.
3. Proportioning of toilet facilities between men and women is based on a 50-50 distribution. However, in certain cases conditions of occupancy may warrant additional facilities for men or women above the basic 50-50 distribution.

Sargent, Webster, Crenshaw & Folley, Architects, Engineers, Planners; Syracuse, New York

 **PLUMBING**

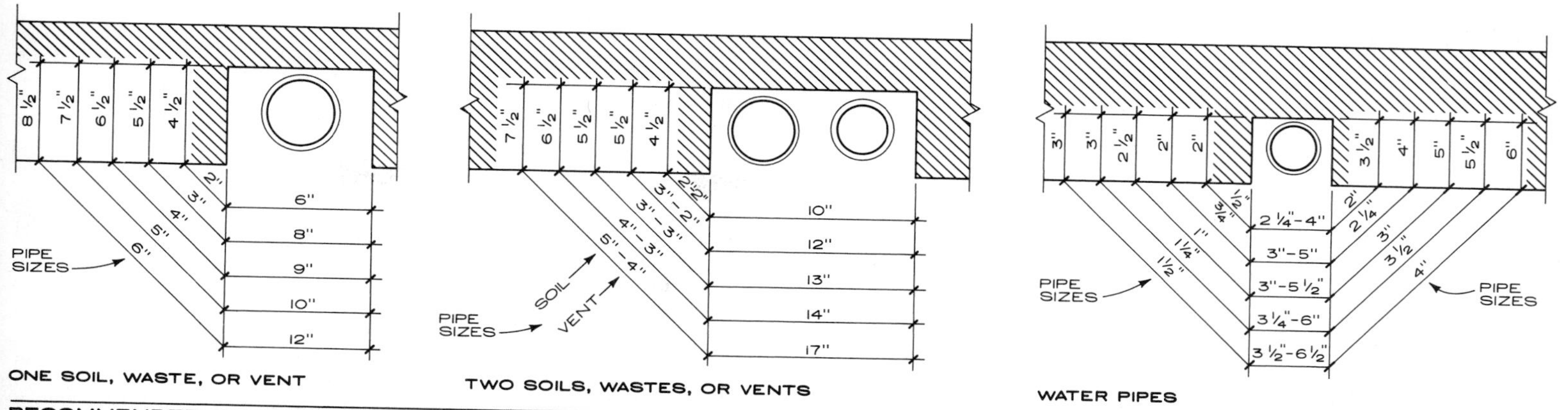

8 1/2"
7 1/2"
6 1/2"
5 1/2"
4 1/2"
2"
3"
4"
5"
6"
6"
8"
9"
10"
12"
PIPE SIZES
ONE SOIL, WASTE, OR VENT
7 1/2"
6 1/2"
5 1/2"
5 1/2"
4 1/2"
2"-2"
3"-2"
3"-3"
4"-3"
5"-4"
10"
12"
13"
14"
17"
SOIL
VENT
PIPE SIZES
TWO SOILS, WASTES, OR VENTS
3"
3"
2 1/2"
2"
2"
3 1/2"
4"
5"
5 1/2"
6"
3/4"
1"
1 1/4"
1 1/2"
2"
2 1/4"
3"
3 1/2"
4"
2 1/4"-4"
3"-5"
3"-5 1/2"
3 1/4"-6"
3 1/2"-6 1/2"
PIPE SIZES
PIPE SIZES
WATER PIPES


RECOMMENDED CHASE SIZES FOR VARIOUS PIPE SIZES WITH HUBS (SEE NOTES 2,3, AND 4 ON THIS PAGE)

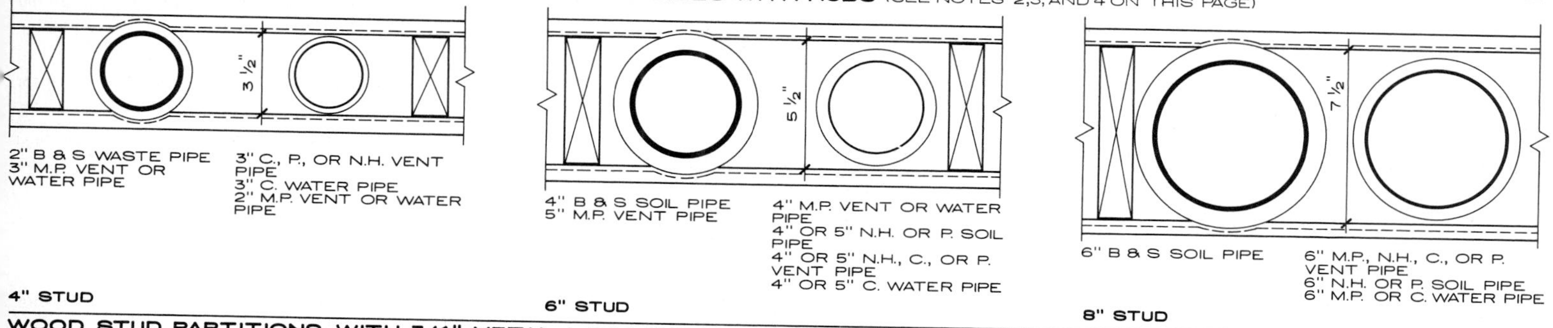

3 1/2"
2" B & S WASTE PIPE
3" M.P. VENT OR WATER PIPE
3" C., P., OR N.H. VENT PIPE
3" C. WATER PIPE
2" M.P. VENT OR WATER PIPE
4" STUD
5 1/2"
4" B & S SOIL PIPE
5" M.P. VENT PIPE
4" M.P. VENT OR WATER PIPE
4" OR 5" N.H. OR P. SOIL PIPE
4" OR 5" N.H., C., OR P. VENT PIPE
4" OR 5" C. WATER PIPE
6" STUD
7 1/2
6" B & S SOIL PIPE
6" M.P., N.H., C., OR P. VENT PIPE
6" N.H. OR P. SOIL PIPE
6" M.P. OR C. WATER PIPE
8" STUD


WOOD STUD PARTITIONS WITH 3/4" METAL LATH AND PLASTER

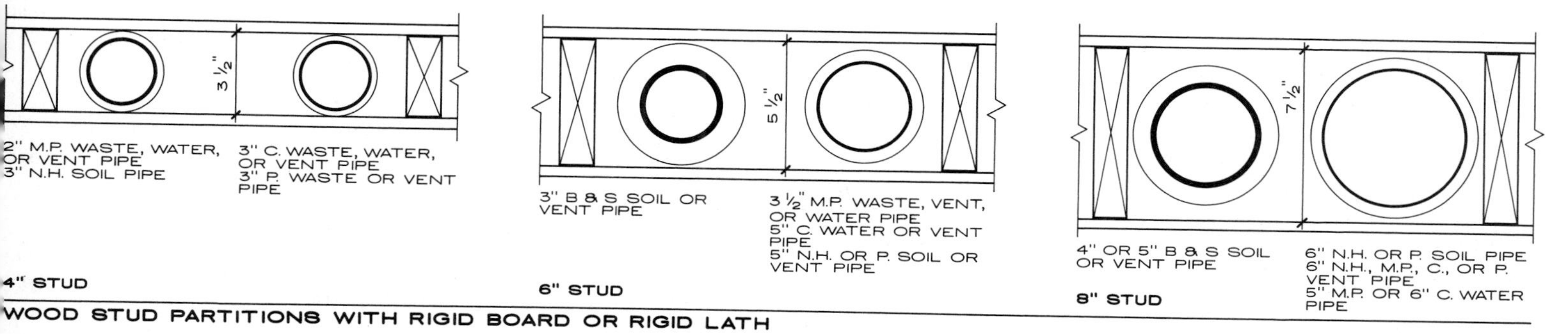

3 1/2"
2" M.P. WASTE, WATER, OR VENT PIPE
3" N.H. SOIL PIPE
3" C. WASTE, WATER, OR VENT PIPE
3" P. WASTE OR VENT PIPE
4" STUD
5 1/2"
3" B & S SOIL OR VENT PIPE
3 1/2" M.P. WASTE, VENT, OR WATER PIPE
5" C. WATER OR VENT PIPE
5" N.H. OR P. SOIL OR VENT PIPE
6" STUD
7 1/2
4" OR 5" B & S SOIL OR VENT PIPE
6" N.H. OR P. SOIL PIPE
6" N.H., M.P., C., OR P. VENT PIPE
5" M.P. OR 6" C. WATER PIPE
8" STUD


WOOD STUD PARTITIONS WITH RIGID BOARD OR RIGID LATH

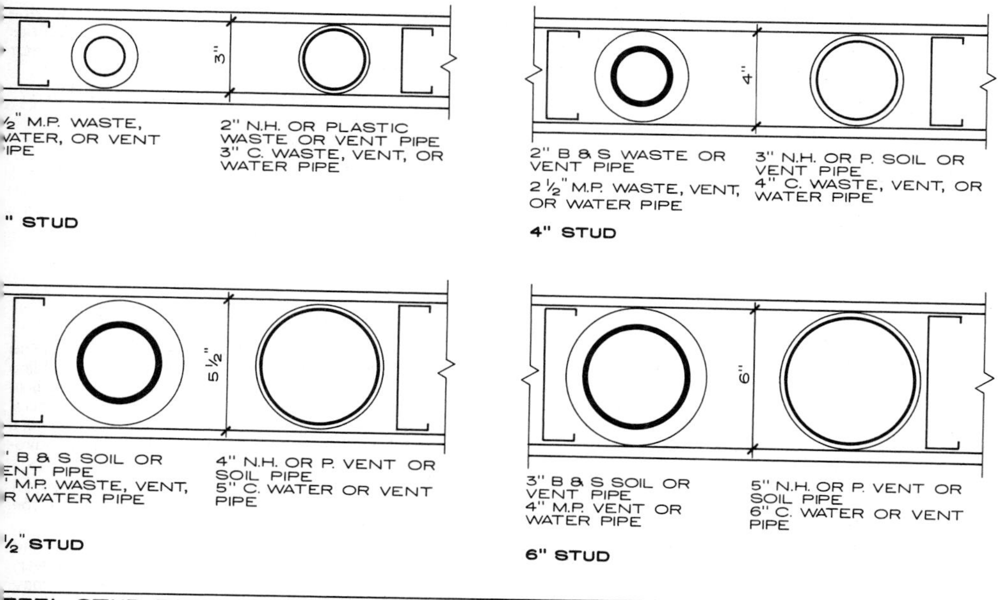

3"
1/2" M.P. WASTE, WATER, OR VENT PIPE
2" N.H. OR PLASTIC WASTE OR VENT PIPE
3" C. WASTE, VENT, OR WATER PIPE
" STUD
4"
2" B & S WASTE OR VENT PIPE
2 1/2" M.P. WASTE, VENT, OR WATER PIPE
3" N.H. OR P. SOIL OR VENT PIPE
4" C. WASTE, VENT, OR WATER PIPE
4" STUD
5 1/2
B & S SOIL OR VENT PIPE
M.P. WASTE, VENT, OR WATER PIPE
4" N.H. OR P. VENT OR SOIL PIPE
5" C. WATER OR VENT PIPE
1/2" STUD
6"
3" B & S SOIL OR VENT PIPE
4" M.P. VENT OR WATER PIPE
5" N.H. OR P. VENT OR SOIL PIPE
6" C. WATER OR VENT PIPE
6" STUD


TEEL STUD PARTITIONS WITH RIGID BOARD

NOTES

1. B&S: extra heavy cast iron bell and spigot (push or caulked joints). C: copper tubing. NH: extra heavy cast iron no-hub pipe. MP: malleable pattern (galvanized or nongalvanized). P: plastic pipe.
2. Recommended chase sizes for various pipes include a 3/4 in. covering. For additional cover subtract 3/4 in. from the amount of cover required; add the result to the desired pipe size dimension.
3. Chases may be provided with or without access. Chases for several pipes, especially those containing main water supply pipes, should be provided with a means of access in case repair is necessary.
4. To size a chase with several pipes, add required widths for each.
5. Partitions with 3/4 in. lath and plaster are shown with certain maximum pipe sizes encroaching on the lath and plaster. Encroaching pipe portions should be coated with asphaltic paint to prevent staining the plaster.
6. When rigid board or lath, such as gypsum board, plaster board, or gypsum lath, is used, the extreme diameter of pipe fitting bead or bell should come within the actual clear dimension of the wall core.
7. Pipe spaces can be enlarged by placing piping between two back-to-back partitions with the required clear space between them.
8. Use steel pipe clearances for hubless pipe installation.

lly Sacher & Associates; Architects Engineers Planners; N. Babylon, Long Island, New York

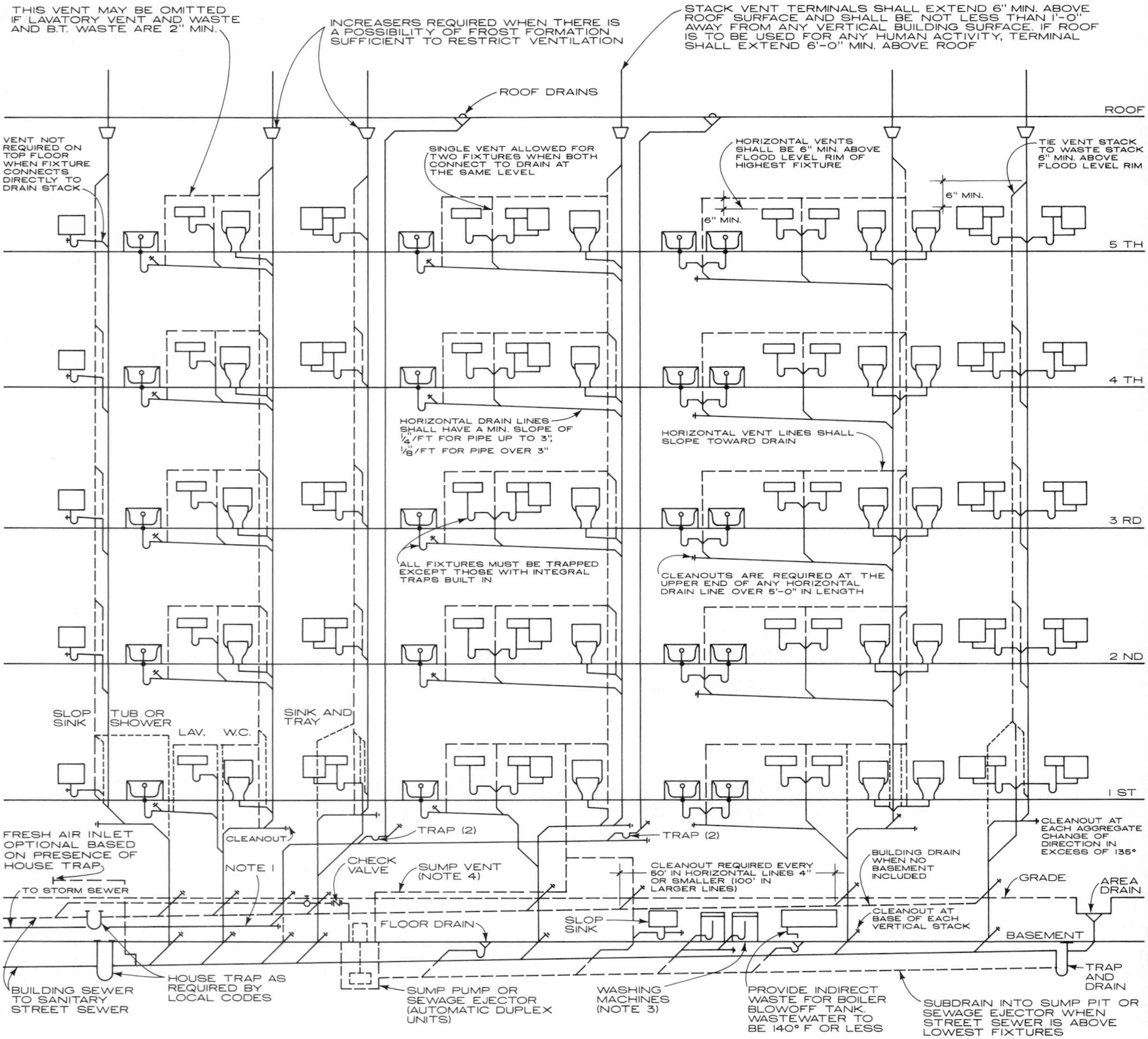

THIS VENT MAY BE OMITTED IF LAVATORY VENT AND WASTE AND B.T. WASTE ARE 2" MIN.

INCREASERS REQUIRED WHEN THERE IS A POSSIBILITY OF FROST FORMATION SUFFICIENT TO RESTRICT VENTILATION

STACK VENT TERMINALS SHALL EXTEND 6" MIN. ABOVE ROOF SURFACE AND SHALL BE NOT LESS THAN 1'-0" AWAY FROM ANY VERTICAL BUILDING SURFACE. IF ROOF IS TO BE USED FOR ANY HUMAN ACTIVITY, TERMINAL SHALL EXTEND 6'-0" MIN. ABOVE ROOF

ROOF DRAINS

ROOF

VENT NOT REQUIRED ON TOP FLOOR WHEN FIXTURE CONNECTS DIRECTLY TO DRAIN STACK

SINGLE VENT ALLOWED FOR TWO FIXTURES WHEN BOTH CONNECT TO DRAIN AT THE SAME LEVEL

HORIZONTAL VENTS SHALL BE 6" MIN. ABOVE FLOOD LEVEL RIM OF HIGHEST FIXTURE

TIE VENT STACK TO WASTE STACK 6" MIN. ABOVE FLOOD LEVEL RIM

6" MIN.

6" MIN.

5 TH

4 TH

HORIZONTAL DRAIN LINES SHALL HAVE A MIN. SLOPE OF $\frac{1}{4}$"/FT FOR PIPE UP TO 3", $\frac{1}{8}$"/FT FOR PIPE OVER 3"

HORIZONTAL VENT LINES SHALL SLOPE TOWARD DRAIN

3 RD

ALL FIXTURES MUST BE TRAPPED EXCEPT THOSE WITH INTEGRAL TRAPS BUILT IN

CLEANOUTS ARE REQUIRED AT THE UPPER END OF ANY HORIZONTAL DRAIN LINE OVER 5'-0" IN LENGTH

2 ND

SLOP SINK

TUB OR SHOWER

LAV.

W.C.

SINK AND TRAY

1 ST

FRESH AIR INLET OPTIONAL BASED ON PRESENCE OF HOUSE TRAP

TO STORM SEWER

CLEANOUT

NOTE 1

CHECK VALVE

TRAP (2)

SUMP VENT (NOTE 4)

TRAP (2)

CLEANOUT REQUIRED EVERY 50' IN HORIZONTAL LINES 4" OR SMALLER (100' IN LARGER LINES)

BUILDING DRAIN WHEN NO BASEMENT INCLUDED

CLEANOUT AT EACH AGGREGATE CHANGE OF DIRECTION IN EXCESS OF 135°

GRADE

AREA DRAIN

CLEANOUT AT BASE OF EACH VERTICAL STACK

BASEMENT

FLOOR DRAIN

SLOP SINK

TRAP AND DRAIN

BUILDING SEWER TO SANITARY STREET SEWER

HOUSE TRAP AS REQUIRED BY LOCAL CODES

SUMP PUMP OR SEWAGE EJECTOR (AUTOMATIC DUPLEX UNITS)

WASHING MACHINES (NOTE 3)

PROVIDE INDIRECT WASTE FOR BOILER BLOWOFF TANK. WASTEWATER TO BE 140° F OR LESS

SUBDRAIN INTO SUMP PIT OR SEWAGE EJECTOR WHEN STREET SEWER IS ABOVE LOWEST FIXTURES

## DIAGRAM NOTES

1. Roof drains and outside area drains must drain into storm drainage sewer where a separate system is available.

2. Traps are required on roof drain and area drain leaders when connected to a combined sanitary and storm sewer system.

3. Provide one washing machine connection for every eight living units (individual connections in each living unit are preferable if space permits). Provide standpipe type indirect waste pipes, 18 in. min. above trap weir. Special consideration must be given to suds pressure zones where washing machines discharge upstream from other fixtures; special venting to nonpressure zones should be provided.

4. Sump vent line shall run independently and unrestricted to the open air when pneumatic type sewage ejectors are used.

### NOTE

The diagram generally indicates plumbing drainage solutions that constitute good plumbing practice. Because of variances between different local codes, some of the items shown may be prohibited in some areas, while other items may far exceed the minimum requirements of local codes. Always consult local codes for exact requirements and for such items as fixture unit allotments, pipe sizing, pipe materials, general regulations, and special conditions.

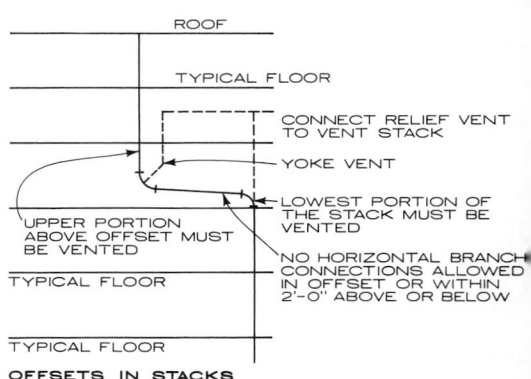

ROOF

TYPICAL FLOOR

CONNECT RELIEF VENT TO VENT STACK

YOKE VENT

LOWEST PORTION OF THE STACK MUST BE VENTED

UPPER PORTION ABOVE OFFSET MUST BE VENTED

TYPICAL FLOOR

NO HORIZONTAL BRANCH CONNECTIONS ALLOWED IN OFFSET OR WITHIN 2'-0" ABOVE OR BELOW

TYPICAL FLOOR

**OFFSETS IN STACKS**

Killebrew/Rucker/Associates, Inc.; Wichita Falls, Texas

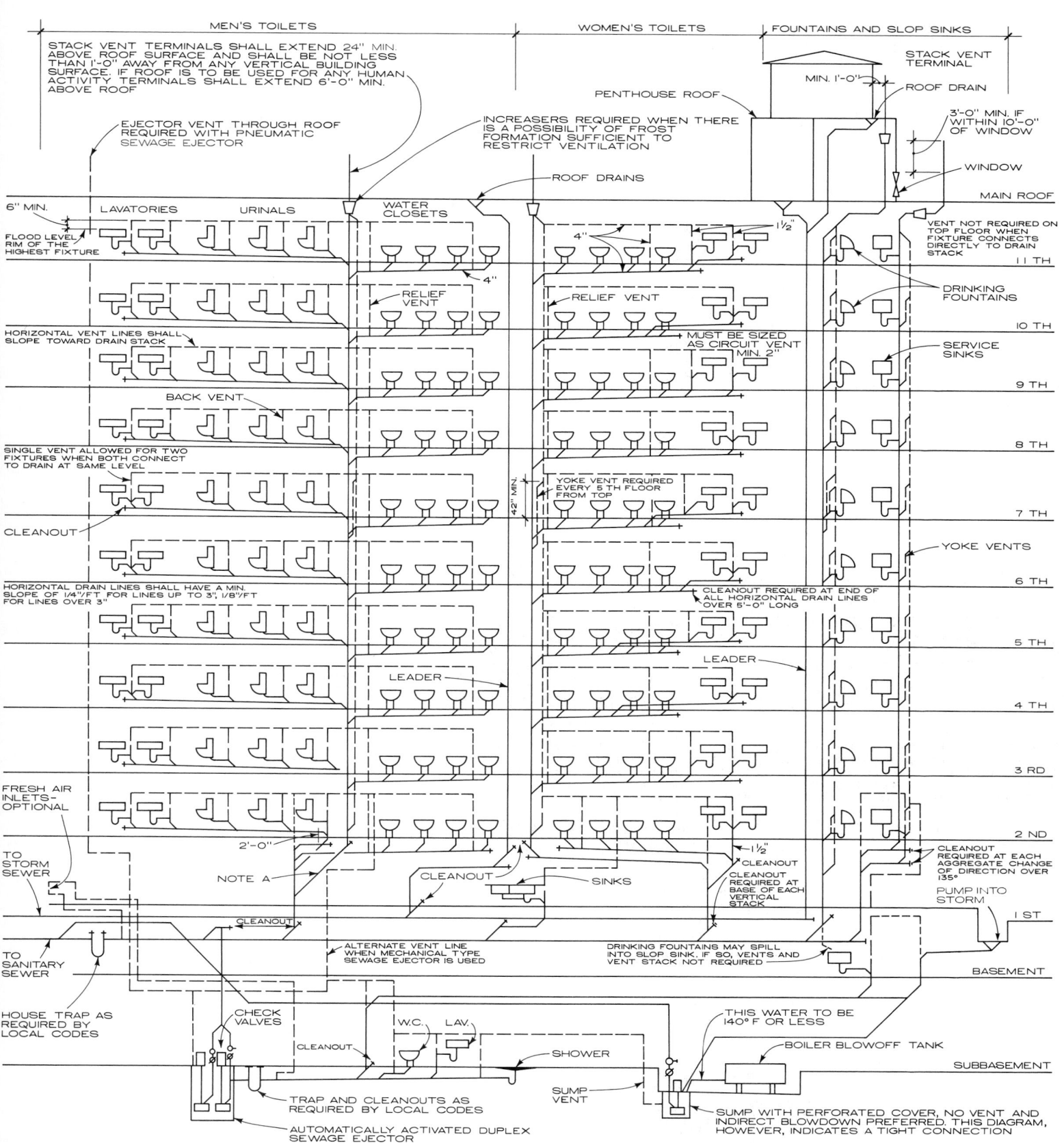

MEN'S TOILETS | WOMEN'S TOILETS | FOUNTAINS AND SLOP SINKS

STACK VENT TERMINALS SHALL EXTEND 24" MIN. ABOVE ROOF SURFACE AND SHALL BE NOT LESS THAN 1'-0" AWAY FROM ANY VERTICAL BUILDING SURFACE. IF ROOF IS TO BE USED FOR ANY HUMAN ACTIVITY TERMINALS SHALL EXTEND 6'-0" MIN. ABOVE ROOF

STACK VENT TERMINAL

MIN. 1'-0"

ROOF DRAIN

PENTHOUSE ROOF

3'-0" MIN. IF WITHIN 10'-0" OF WINDOW

EJECTOR VENT THROUGH ROOF REQUIRED WITH PNEUMATIC SEWAGE EJECTOR

INCREASERS REQUIRED WHEN THERE IS A POSSIBILITY OF FROST FORMATION SUFFICIENT TO RESTRICT VENTILATION

WINDOW

ROOF DRAINS

MAIN ROOF

6" MIN.

LAVATORIES    URINALS

WATER CLOSETS

1½"

VENT NOT REQUIRED ON TOP FLOOR WHEN FIXTURE CONNECTS DIRECTLY TO DRAIN STACK

FLOOD LEVEL RIM OF THE HIGHEST FIXTURE

4"

11 TH

RELIEF VENT

RELIEF VENT

DRINKING FOUNTAINS

4"

10 TH

HORIZONTAL VENT LINES SHALL SLOPE TOWARD DRAIN STACK

MUST BE SIZED AS CIRCUIT VENT MIN. 2"

SERVICE SINKS

9 TH

BACK VENT

8 TH

SINGLE VENT ALLOWED FOR TWO FIXTURES WHEN BOTH CONNECT TO DRAIN AT SAME LEVEL

YOKE VENT REQUIRED EVERY 5 TH FLOOR FROM TOP

42" MIN.

7 TH

CLEANOUT

YOKE VENTS

6 TH

HORIZONTAL DRAIN LINES SHALL HAVE A MIN. SLOPE OF 1/4"/FT FOR LINES UP TO 3", 1/8"/FT FOR LINES OVER 3"

CLEANOUT REQUIRED AT END OF ALL HORIZONTAL DRAIN LINES OVER 5'-0" LONG

5 TH

LEADER

LEADER

4 TH

3 RD

FRESH AIR INLETS- OPTIONAL

1½"

2 ND

TO STORM SEWER

2'-0"

NOTE A

CLEANOUT

SINKS

CLEANOUT

CLEANOUT REQUIRED AT BASE OF EACH VERTICAL STACK

CLEANOUT REQUIRED AT EACH AGGREGATE CHANGE OF DIRECTION OVER 135°

PUMP INTO STORM

1 ST

TO SANITARY SEWER

CLEANOUT

ALTERNATE VENT LINE WHEN MECHANICAL TYPE SEWAGE EJECTOR IS USED

DRINKING FOUNTAINS MAY SPILL INTO SLOP SINK. IF SO, VENTS AND VENT STACK NOT REQUIRED

BASEMENT

HOUSE TRAP AS REQUIRED BY LOCAL CODES

CHECK VALVES

CLEANOUT

W.C.    LAV.

SHOWER

SUMP VENT

THIS WATER TO BE 140° F OR LESS

BOILER BLOWOFF TANK

SUBBASEMENT

TRAP AND CLEANOUTS AS REQUIRED BY LOCAL CODES

AUTOMATICALLY ACTIVATED DUPLEX SEWAGE EJECTOR

SUMP WITH PERFORATED COVER, NO VENT AND INDIRECT BLOWDOWN PREFERRED. THIS DIAGRAM, HOWEVER, INDICATES A TIGHT CONNECTION

## GENERAL NOTES

This diagram generally indicates plumbing drainage solutions that constitute good plumbing practice. Because of variances between different local codes, some of the items shown may be prohibited in some areas, while other items may far exceed the minimum requirements of local codes.

Always consult local codes for exact requirements and for such items as fixture unit allotments, pipe sizing, pipe materials, general regulations, and special conditions.

## NOTE A

45° or less from vertical may be considered as straight stock in sizing, except that no fixtures or branches may be connected within 2 ft of offset.

Killebrew/Rucker/Associates, Inc.; Wichita Falls, Texas

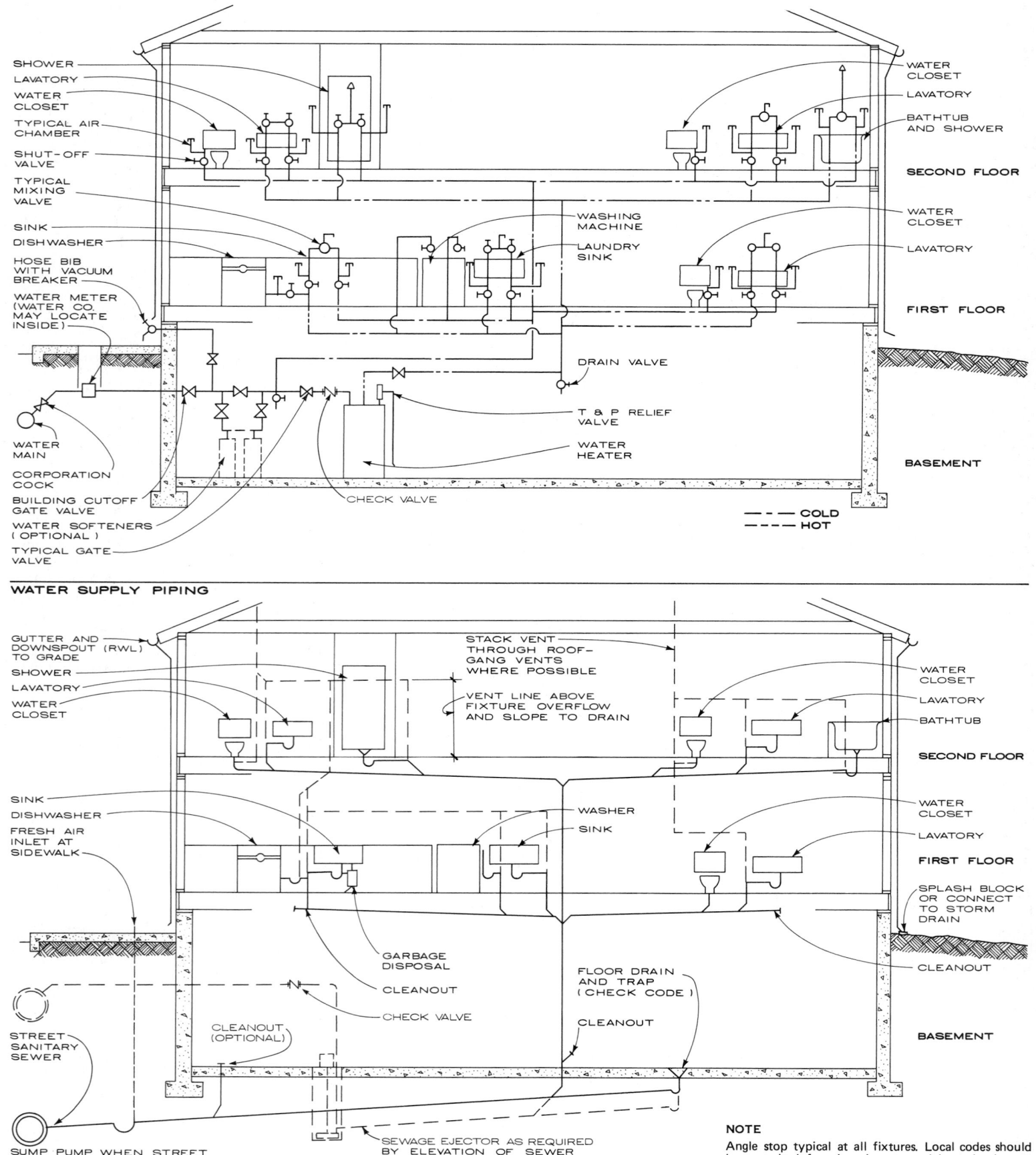

SHOWER
LAVATORY
WATER CLOSET
TYPICAL AIR CHAMBER
SHUT-OFF VALVE
TYPICAL MIXING VALVE
SINK
DISHWASHER
HOSE BIB WITH VACUUM BREAKER
WATER METER (WATER CO. MAY LOCATE INSIDE)
WATER MAIN
CORPORATION COCK
BUILDING CUTOFF GATE VALVE
WATER SOFTENERS (OPTIONAL)
TYPICAL GATE VALVE

WASHING MACHINE
LAUNDRY SINK

WATER CLOSET
LAVATORY
BATHTUB AND SHOWER

SECOND FLOOR

WATER CLOSET
LAVATORY

FIRST FLOOR

DRAIN VALVE
T & P RELIEF VALVE
WATER HEATER
CHECK VALVE

BASEMENT

— · — COLD
— — — HOT

**WATER SUPPLY PIPING**

GUTTER AND DOWNSPOUT (RWL) TO GRADE
SHOWER
LAVATORY
WATER CLOSET
SINK
DISHWASHER
FRESH AIR INLET AT SIDEWALK
STREET SANITARY SEWER
SUMP PUMP WHEN STREET SEWER IS HIGHER THAN LOWEST DRAIN

STACK VENT THROUGH ROOF-GANG VENTS WHERE POSSIBLE
VENT LINE ABOVE FIXTURE OVERFLOW AND SLOPE TO DRAIN
WASHER
SINK
GARBAGE DISPOSAL
CLEANOUT
CHECK VALVE
CLEANOUT (OPTIONAL)
SEWAGE EJECTOR AS REQUIRED BY ELEVATION OF SEWER

WATER CLOSET
LAVATORY
BATHTUB

SECOND FLOOR

WATER CLOSET
LAVATORY

FIRST FLOOR

SPLASH BLOCK OR CONNECT TO STORM DRAIN
CLEANOUT

FLOOR DRAIN AND TRAP (CHECK CODE)
CLEANOUT

BASEMENT

**NOTE**
Angle stop typical at all fixtures. Local codes should be consulted for pipe sizes, materials, and other requirements in plumbing system.

**SOIL, WASTE AND VENT PIPING**

Brent Dickens, AIA, Architect; San Rafael, California

**15** **PLUMBING**

## GENERAL NOTES

Lavatories and work sinks are available in vitreous china (V.C.), enameled cast iron (E.C.I.), enameled steel (E.S.), and stainless steel (S.S.). Typically, floor to rim dimension is 2 ft. 7 in., unless otherwise noted. The most commonly used means of support is the chair or wall carrier with concealed arms. Other methods are detailed below. Consult manufacturer's data for specific fixture design and support recommendations.

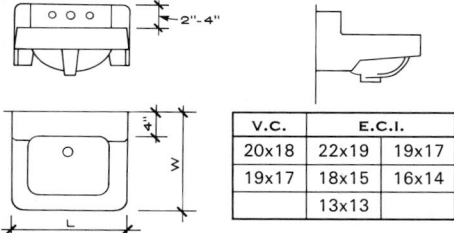

| V.C. | E.C.I. | |
|---|---|---|
| 20x18 | 22x19 | 19x17 |
| 19x17 | 18x15 | 16x14 |
| | 13x13 | |

Shelf-back lavatories generally are rectangular with semi-oval basins. Height of the shelf typically is 4 in.; depth is usually 5 in. Support with metal legs and brackets or concealed carrier.

## SHELF BACK

Corner lavatories are available angled with an oval basin or rectangular with an offset rectangular basin. Support with wall brackets or concealed carrier.

| V.C. |
|---|
| 17x17 |
| 26x20 |

## CORNER

Wash sinks supported with concealed wall brackets for E.C.I. or with angle supports for S.S.

| E.C.I. | | S.S. | | STATIONS |
|---|---|---|---|---|
| 18x36 | 18x48 | 20x48 | | 2 |
| 18x60 | 18x72 | 20x60 | 20x72 | 3 |
| | | 20x96 | | 4 |

## WASH SINKS

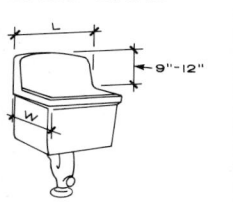

Wall-mounted service sinks are designed for janitorial requirements of hospitals, plants, institutions, office buildings, and schools. Floor to rim dimension is 2 ft. 3 in. to 2 ft. 5 in. Fittings are mounted either on or above the sink back. "H" designates flushing rim design for hospital use specifically.

| V.C. | | E.C.I. | | S.S. | |
|---|---|---|---|---|---|
| 28x22 | 26x20 H | 24x20 | 24x18 | 25x19 | 23x18 |
| 24x22 H | 20x20 H | 22x18 | | | |
| 22x20 | | | | | |

## SERVICE SINKS

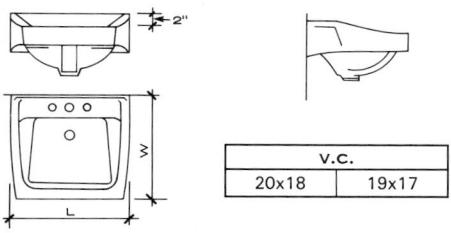

| V.C. | |
|---|---|
| 20x18 | 19x17 |

Ledge-back lavatories generally are rectangular with rectangular basins. Ledge width usually is 4 in. Typically supported with concealed carrier.

## LEDGE BACK

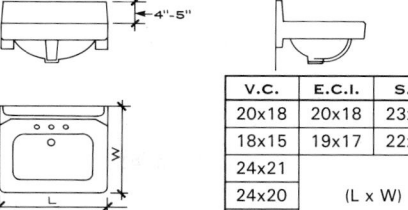

| V.C. | E.C.I. | S.S. |
|---|---|---|
| 20x18 | 20x18 | 23x20 |
| 18x15 | 19x17 | 22x19 |
| 24x21 | | |
| 24x20 | (L x W) | |
| 18x16 | | |

Most flat-back lavatories are rectangular with rectangular or semi-oval basins. Typically, floor to rim dimension is 2 ft. 7 in. Support using metal legs with brackets or with concealed carrier.

## FLAT BACK

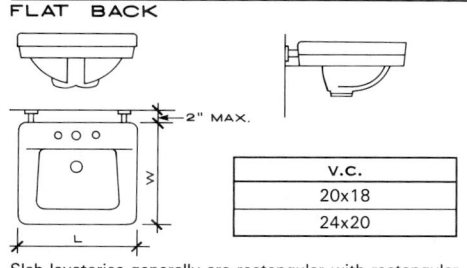

| V.C. |
|---|
| 20x18 |
| 24x20 |

Slab lavatories generally are rectangular with rectangular basins. A 2 in. escutcheon typically spaces lavatory from finish wall. (4 in. and 6 in. also are available.) Vitreous china leg with brackets can be used as alternate means of support.

## SLAB

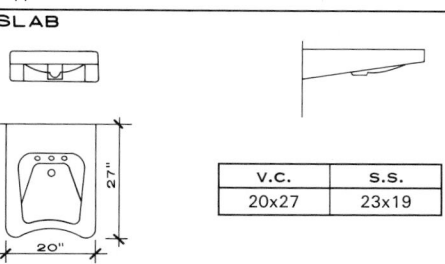

| V.C. | S.S. |
|---|---|
| 20x27 | 23x19 |

Wheelchair lavatories must be supported using a concealed arm carrier. Height from floor to rim is 2 ft. 10 in.

## WHEELCHAIR LAVATORY

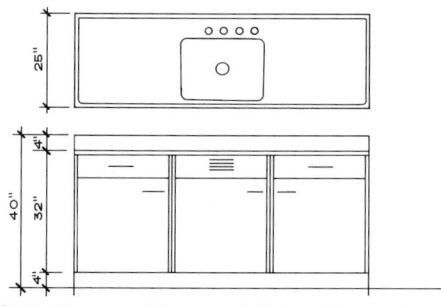

Sink/cabinet assemblies are available in stainless steel with single or double bowls, with or without adjacent drainboards. Lengths of cabinets vary from 42 in. to 96 in., depending on drawer, door, and bowl options.

## CABINET

Built-in lavatories are available oval, rectangular and circular in a variety of basin shapes. Typically, built-ins are now self-rimming but are available with metal rims, or rimless for undercounter installations.

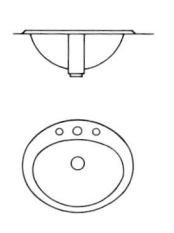

| V.C. | | | E.S. | | E.C.I. | |
|---|---|---|---|---|---|---|
| with Metal Rim | | | | | | |
| 19x16 | 19x15 | 17x14 | 19x16 | 18x18 | 26x18 | 18x18 |
| Self-rimming | | | | | | |
| 28x19 | 26x20 | 24x20 | 20x17 | 19x19 | 33x19 | 28x19 | 21x19 |
| 21x19 | 21x17 | 21x13 | | | 20x17 | 19x19 | 19x16 |
| 19x19 | 19x16 | | | | | |
| Rimless | | | | | | |
| 21x17 | 19x16 | 17x14 | 19x16 | | | |

## BUILT-IN

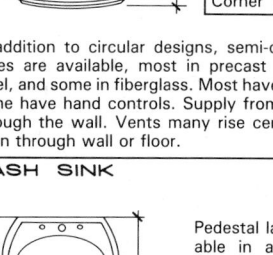

| TYPE | DIAM. (IN.) | NO. USERS |
|---|---|---|
| Circ. | 54 | 8 |
| | 36 | 5 |
| Semi-circ. | 54 | 4 |
| | 36 | 3 |
| Corner | 54 | 3 |

In addition to circular designs, semi-circular and corner types are available, most in precast terrazzo, stainless steel, and some in fiberglass. Most have foot controls, and some have hand controls. Supply from above, below, or through the wall. Vents many rise centrally or come off drain through wall or floor.

## WASH SINK

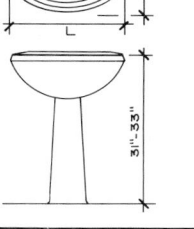

Pedestal lavatories are available in a wide variety of forms, sizes, and basin shapes. See manufacturer for specific designs.

| V.C. | | |
|---|---|---|
| 38x22 | 30x20 | 28x21 |
| 24x19 | 26x22 | 25x21 |
| 22x21 | 20x18 | |

## PEDESTAL LAVATORY

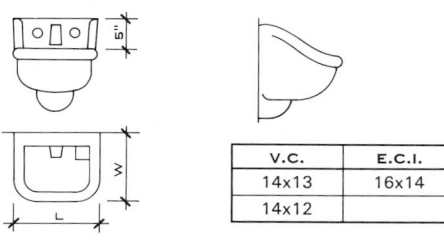

| V.C. | E.C.I. |
|---|---|
| 14x13 | 16x14 |
| 14x12 | |

Institutional lavatories have an integral supply channel to spout and drinking nozzle, strainer, and soap dish. Trap is enclosed in wall. Wall thickness must be specified.

## INSTITUTIONAL LAVATORY

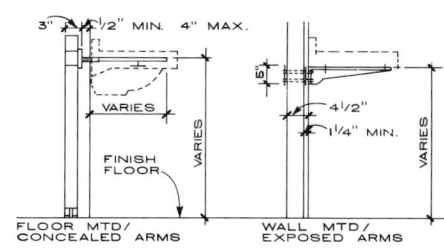

Floor-mounted chair carriers support fixture independent of wall construction. Available with exposed or concealed arms. Wall-mounted carrier with exposed or concealed arms also is available. Additional methods include floor-mounted hanger plate types, floor-mounted bearing plate types, paired metal or single vitreous china leg, in addition to exposed, enameled wall brackets.

## METHODS OF LAVATORY SUPPORT

Robert K. Sherrill; Wilkes, Faulkner, Jenkins & Bass, Washington, D.C.

PLUMBING    15

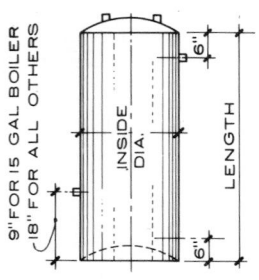

## RANGE BOILER

Galvanized Standard
pressure = 85 psi
Extra heavy pressure = 150 psi
Double extra heavy = 150 psi
2'-0'' dia. tank—tapping is
1½'', others 1''

### RANGE BOILERS

| CAPACITY (GAL) | DIAMETER | LENGTH |
|---|---|---|
| 15 | 1'-0'' | 2'-6'' |
| 30 | 1'-0'' | 5'-0'' |
| 40 | 1'-2'' | 5'-0'' |
| 66 | 1'-6'' | 5'-0'' |
| 82 | 1'-8'' | 5'-0'' |
| 120 | 2'-0'' | 5'-0'' |

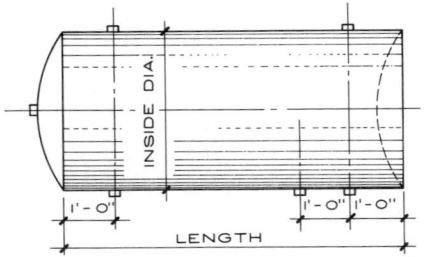

## HOT WATER STORAGE TANK

Manhole 11'' x 15'' in shell or head
Standard pressure = 65 psi
Extra heavy pressure = 100 psi
Tanks used vertically or horizontally.
6 tappings in each tank of diameters listed

**GENERAL WATER TANK DATA**

### PAINTED, ATTIC TYPE

### GALVANIZED EXPANSION TANKS

Galvanized, tapping 1'' Φ
Max. pressure = 30 psi
Max. no. of tappings shown

### EXPANSION TANKS

| CAPACITY (GAL) | DIAMETER | LENGTH |
|---|---|---|
| 10 | 1'-0'' | 1'-8'' |
| 15 | 1'-0'' | 2'-6'' |
| 20 | 1'-2'' | 2'-6'' |
| 30 | 1'-0'' | 5'-0'' |
| 40 | 1'-2'' | 5'-0'' |

### HOT WATER STORAGE TANKS

| CAPACITY (GAL) | DIAMETER | LENGTH |
|---|---|---|
| 82 | 1'-8'' | 5'-0'' |
| 118 | 2'-0'' | 5'-0'' |
| 141 | 2'-0'' | 6'-0'' |
| 220 | 2'-6'' | 6'-0'' |
| 294 | 2'-6'' | 8'-0'' |
| 317 | 3'-0'' | 6'-0'' |
| 428 | 3'-0'' | 8'-0'' |
| 504 | 3'-6'' | 7'-0'' |
| 576 | 3'-6'' | 8'-0'' |
| 720 | 3'-6'' | 10'-0'' |
| 904 | 4'-0'' | 10'-0'' |
| 1008 | 3'-6'' | 14'-0'' |
| 1504 | 4'-0'' | 16'-0'' |
| 1880 | 4'-0'' | 20'-0'' |

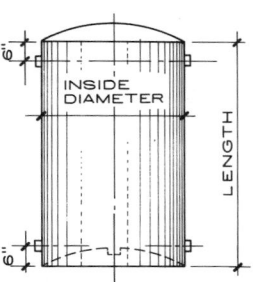

## SOLAR TANK

Galvanized
Double extra heavy = 120 psi
Used vertically only 1'-8''
dia. tank, 1'' tapping, all
others 1½'' tapping

### SOLAR TANKS

| CAPACITY (GAL) | DIAMETER | LENGTH |
|---|---|---|
| 66 | 1'-8'' | 4'-0'' |
| 100 | 2'-0'' | 4'-0'' |
| 150 | 2'-6'' | 4'-0'' |
| 210 | 3'-0'' | 4'-0'' |
| 270 | 3'-0'' | 5'-0'' |

### TAP SIZES

| TANK DIAMETER | TAP DIAMETER |
|---|---|
| 1'-8'' | 1½'' |
| 2'-0'' | 1½'' |
| 2'-6'' | 2'' |
| 3'-0'' | 2'' |
| 3'-6'' | 2'' |
| 4'-0'' | 3'' |

### FORMULAS FOR CAPACITY OF CYLINDRICAL TANKS

$Diameter^2$ x 0.7854 x Length = Volume

Cu. Ft. x 7.4805 =

or

$\dfrac{Cu. In.}{1728}$ x 7.4805 =

} Capacity in Gallons

### WATER DATA

1 gallon = 231 cu. in. 1 cu. ft. weight 62.5 lbs. Tank sizes may vary. See manufacturer's data.

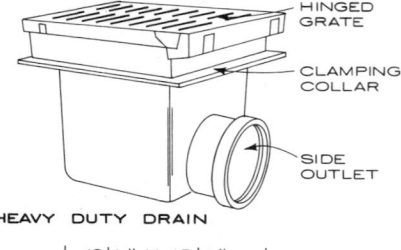

HEAVY DUTY DRAIN

HINGED GRATE
CLAMPING COLLAR
SIDE OUTLET

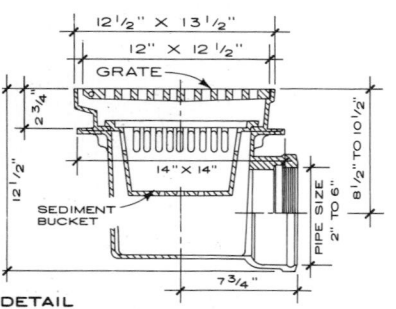

DETAIL

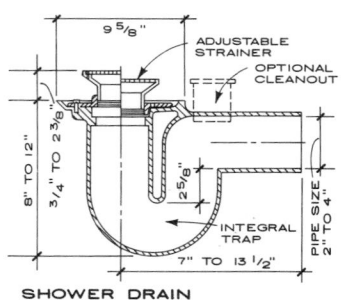

SHOWER DRAIN

STANDARD DRAIN

ADJUSTABLE STRAINER
CLAMPING COLLAR
CAST IRON OUTLET

RECTANGULAR

ANGLE

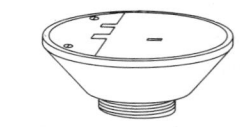

DOME

COVER AND LOCK

### NOTE

Heavy duty strainers are constructed of nickel brass or cast iron. Sediment baskets and backwater valves are optional accessories. Vandalproof covers and locks also are available. In water disposal area, spray nozzles are installed for washdown of drains. Consider baskets in shower drains. Consider heel-proof grates where applicable.

**FLOOR AND SHOWER DRAINS**

William G. Miner, AIA, Architect; Washington, D.C.

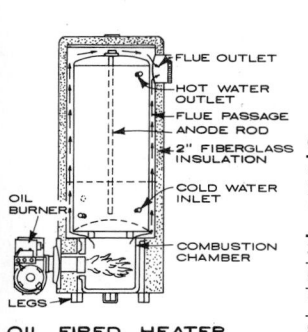

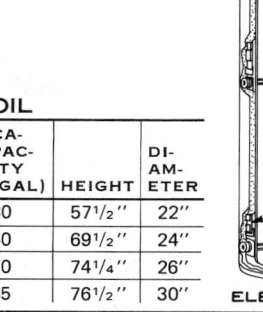

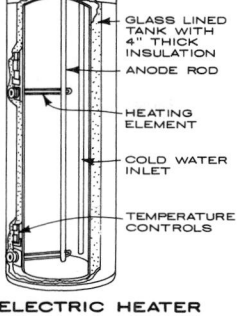

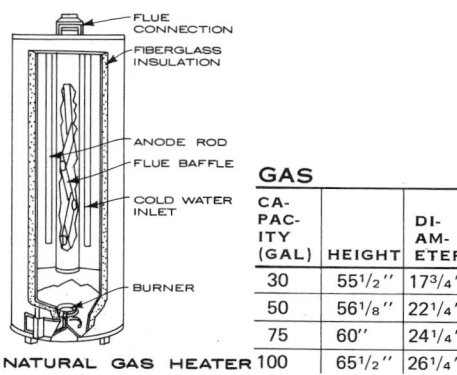

## OIL

| CA-PAC-ITY (GAL) | HEIGHT | DIAMETER |
|---|---|---|
| 30 | 57½" | 22" |
| 50 | 69½" | 24" |
| 70 | 74¼" | 26" |
| 85 | 76½" | 30" |

OIL FIRED HEATER

## ELECTRIC

| CA-PAC-ITY (GAL) | HEIGHT | DIAMETER |
|---|---|---|
| 30 | 45⅝" | 20¼" |
| 52 | 59⅛" | 22¼" |
| 82 | 60¼" | 26¼" |
| 120 | 62¼" | 28¼" |

ELECTRIC HEATER

## GAS

| CA-PAC-ITY (GAL) | HEIGHT | DIAMETER |
|---|---|---|
| 30 | 55½" | 17¾" |
| 50 | 56⅛" | 22¼" |
| 75 | 60" | 24¼" |
| 100 | 65½" | 26¼" |

NATURAL GAS HEATER

## RESIDENTIAL, STORAGE TYPE WATER HEATERS

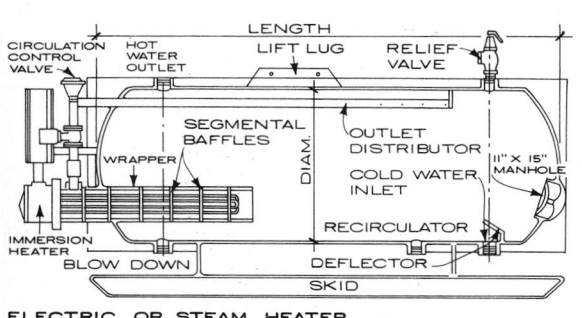

ELECTRIC OR STEAM HEATER

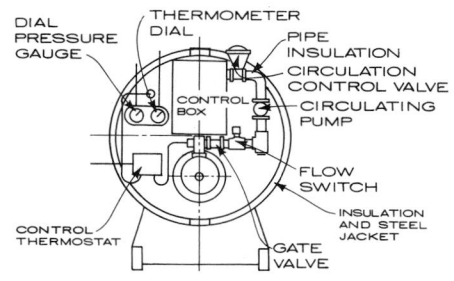

END VIEW

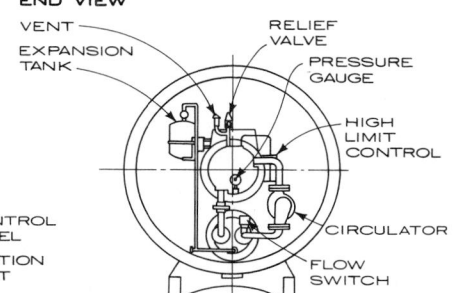

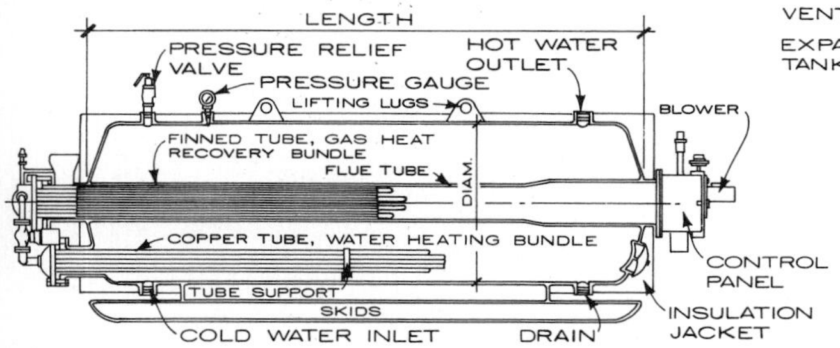

GAS OR OIL FIRED HEATER

END VIEW

## COMMERCIAL, STORAGE TYPE WATER HEATERS

### ELECTRIC/STEAM HEATER DIMENSIONS

| CAPACITY (GAL) | LENGTH | DIAMETER | SPACE TO REMOVE HEATING SECTION | |
|---|---|---|---|---|
| | | | ELECTRIC | STEAM |
| 530 | 96" | 42" | 39" | 12" |
| 1034 | 96" | 60" | 39" | 18" |
| 1300 | 120" | 60" | 39" | 24" |
| 1980 | 120" | 72" | 79" | 29" |
| 2400 | 144" | 72" | 79" | 29" |
| 3150 | 144" | 84" | 79" | 27" |
| 4070 | 144" | 96" | 79" | 27" |

### GAS/OIL HEATER DIMENSIONS

| CAPACITY (GAL) | LENGTH | DIAMETER | SPACE TO REMOVE HEATING SECTION |
|---|---|---|---|
| 560 | 108" | 42" | 85" |
| 820 | 120" | 48" | 87" |
| 1250 | 120" | 60" | 97" |
| 1930 | 120" | 72" | 103" |
| 2340 | 144" | 72" | 103" |
| 3090 | 144" | 84" | 89" |
| 4010 | 144" | 96" | 89" |

**GENERAL NOTE**
These dimensions are for horizontal type heaters only. Space saving, vertical type heaters with same capacities are available from most manufacturers.

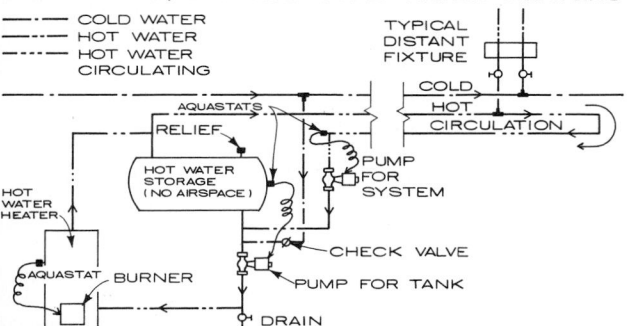

FORCED CIRCULATION SYSTEM

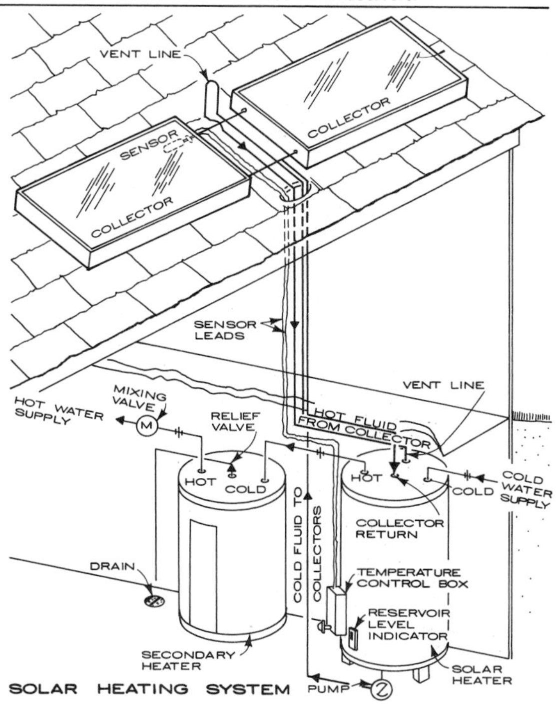

### ESTIMATED HOT WATER DEMAND

| BUILDING TYPE | HOT WATER[1] PER PERSON | HOURLY DEMAND DAY'S USE | DURATION OF PEAK LOAD | STORAGE CAPACITY DAY'S USE | HEATING CAPACITY DAY'S USE |
|---|---|---|---|---|---|
| Residences, apartments, hotels[2] | 20–40 gal/day | ⅐ | 4 hr | ⅕ | ⅐ |
| Office buildings | 2–3 gal/day | ⅕ | 2 hr | ⅕ | ⅙ |
| Factory buildings | 5 gal/day | ⅓ | 1 hr | ⅖ | ⅛ |

1. At 140°F.
2. Allow additional 15 gal per dishwasher and 40 gal per laundry washer.

SOLAR HEATING SYSTEM

Syska & Hennessy, Consulting Engineers; New York, New York

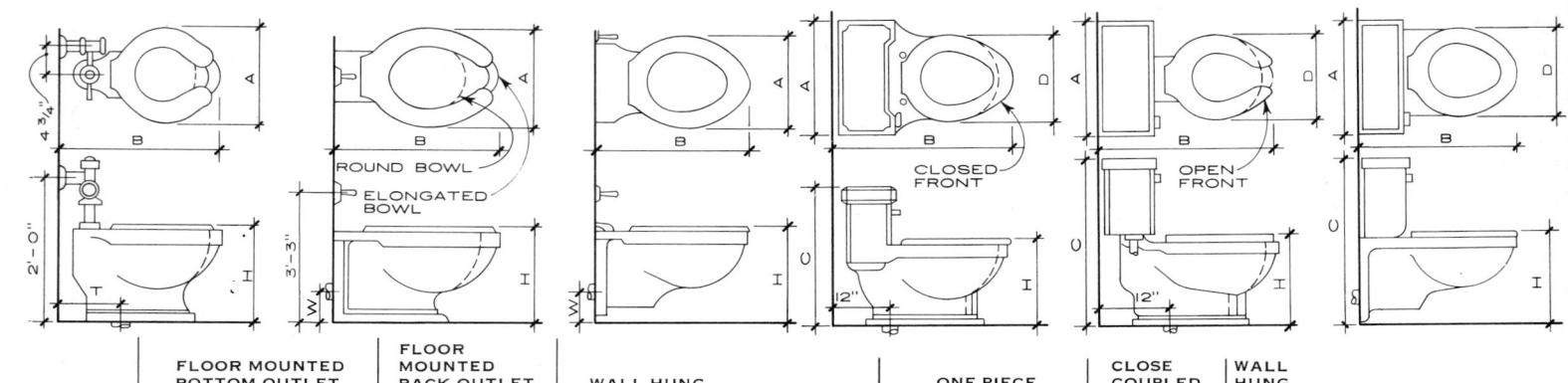

| | FLOOR MOUNTED BOTTOM OUTLET | | | FLOOR MOUNTED BACK OUTLET | | WALL HUNG | |
|---|---|---|---|---|---|---|---|
| | SJ | WD | BO | SJ | BO | SJ | BO |
| A | 14″ | 14″ | 14″ | 14″ | 14″ | 14″ | 14″ |
| Round<br>B<br>Elongated | 24″<br>24½″<br>or<br>26½″ | 27″<br><br>26¼″ | | 20⅛″<br>25½″<br>to<br>26″ | <br>21½″ | <br>21½″<br>to<br>25¾″ | <br>24¼″<br>to<br>26″ |
| H | 14″<br>to<br>14¾″<br>10″*<br>17″†<br>to<br>19″ | 15″ | 15″ | 14½″<br>to<br>15″ | 15″ | 15″ | 15″<br>to<br>15¾″ |
| W | | | | 4¼″<br>or<br>4½″ | 10¼″ | 4″<br>to<br>5½″ | 11½″<br>to<br>12¼″ |
| T | 10″<br>or<br>12″ | 12″<br>to<br>14″ | 9″ | 9″<br>or<br>10″ | 9″<br>or<br>10″ | | |

*For children.
†For handicapped.

| | ONE PIECE | | | CLOSE COUPLED | | WALL HUNG |
|---|---|---|---|---|---|---|
| | SV | SJ | SA | SJ | RT | SJ |
| A | 20¾″<br>to<br>22″ | 20⅝″<br>to<br>23¾″ | 20¾″<br>to<br>21″ | 20⅞″<br>to<br>21½″ | 17″<br>to<br>20⅞″ | 20⅞″<br>to<br>23¾″ |
| Round<br>B | 27¾″ | 24¾″ | 27¾″ | 27½″<br>to<br>29″ | 22″<br>to<br>27⅝″ | 26½″<br>to<br>29¾″ |
| Elongated | 29¼″ | 28½″<br>to<br>29″ | 28½″<br>to<br>29¾″ | 29⅛″<br>to<br>29⅞″ | | 28¼″ |
| C | 20″<br>to<br>23¾″ | 18¾″<br>to<br>20½″ | 18¾″<br>to<br>19½″ | 26⅛″<br>to<br>31⅞″ | 28¼″<br>to<br>31″ | 29″<br>to<br>29½″ |
| D | 14¾″<br>to<br>15½″ | 14¾″<br>to<br>15½″ | 14¾″<br>to<br>15½″ | 14¾″<br>to<br>15½″ | 14¾″<br>to<br>15½″ | 14¾″<br>to<br>15½″ |
| H | 14″<br>to<br>15″ | 14″<br>to<br>15″ | 14½″ | 14″<br>17″†<br>to<br>19″<br>10″* | 14½″<br>to<br>15″ | 15″ |

NOTE: Dimensions include seat. For closed front seats, add 1 in. to B. With seat cover, add ¾ in. to height. All fixtures are of vitreous china except where noted. For concealed carrier wall hung, allow 10½ in. minimum from back of closet to outside edge of soil pipe.

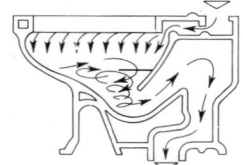 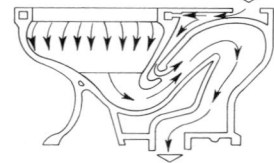 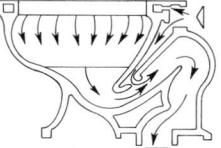 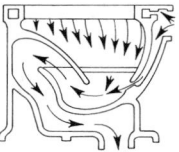 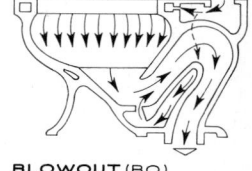

**SIPHON - VORTEX (S-V)**
Quiet, extremely sanitary. Water directed through rim to create vortex. Scours bowl. Folds over into jet; siphon.

**SIPHON - JET (S-J)**
**SIPHON - ACTION (S-A)**
Sanitary, efficient, very quiet. Water enters through rim and siphons in down leg.

**REVERSE - TRAP (R-T)**
Similar to siphon-jet except that trap passageway and water surface area are smaller, moderately noisy.

**WASH - DOWN (W-D)**
Minimum cost. Least efficient, subject to clogging, noisy. Simple washout action through small irregular passageway.

**BLOWOUT (BO)**
Noisy but highly efficient. Strong jet into up leg forces contents out. Use with FV only. Higher pressure required.

## WATER CLOSETS

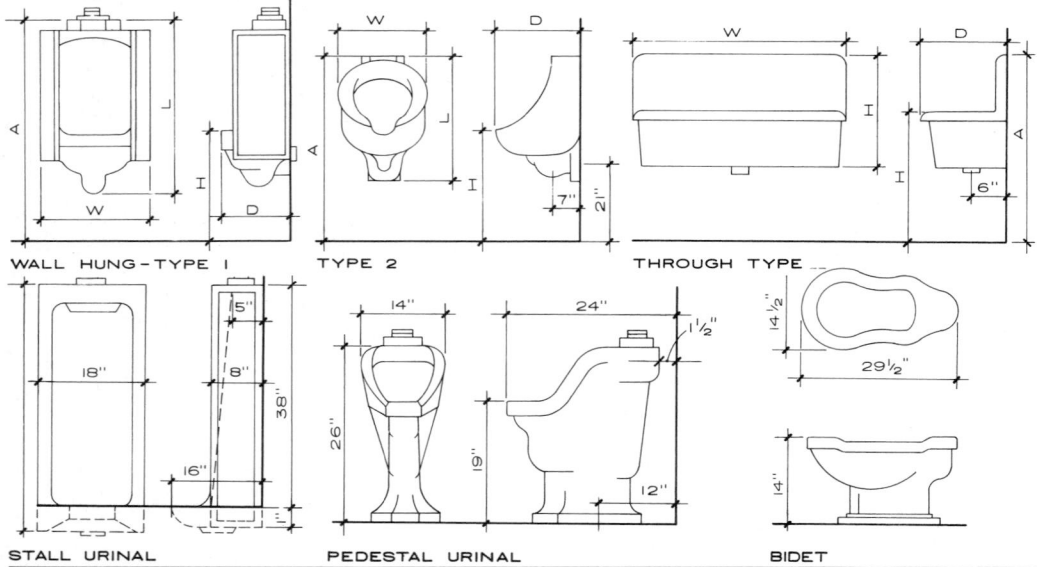

**WALL HUNG - TYPE 1**    **TYPE 2**    **THROUGH TYPE**

**STALL URINAL**    **PEDESTAL URINAL**    **BIDET**

### URINALS AND BIDETS

| | TYPE 1 (SJ, WD, BO) | TYPE 2 | | | THROUGH TYPE |
|---|---|---|---|---|---|
| | | SJ | BO | WD | |
| A | 35″, 42½″ | 35½″<br>to<br>37⅛″ | 26½″<br>to<br>27″ | 34½″<br>to<br>37⅛″ | 32″–34″ |
| W | 13″, 18″ | 13″<br>to<br>14¼″ | 14″ | 12¾″<br>to<br>14¼″ | 36″, 48″, 60″, 72″ |
| L | 18″<br>to<br>30″ | 17″<br>to<br>20″ | 17″<br>to<br>20″ | 17″<br>to<br>20″ | 16″, 17¾″, 18¾″ |
| D | 11¾″<br>to<br>13¼″ | 11¼″<br>to<br>14″ | 11½″<br>to<br>14″ | 12⅞″<br>to<br>14″ | 14″, 18″ |
| H | 24″ | 24″, 17″*, 19″* | | | 24″ |

*For handicapped.

NOTE: Provide minimum 4 in. clear pipe chase for urinal piping and support.

**BATTERY STALLS**
Stall urinals available with seam covers for battery installation on 1′– 9″ or 2′– 0″ centers.

K. Shahid Rab, AIA; Friesen International; Washington, D.C.
B. J. Baldwin; Giffels & Rossetti, Inc.; Detroit, Michigan

## SINGLE BOWL

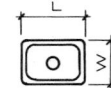

### STAINLESS STEEL

|   | MIN. | MAX. | OTHER |
|---|------|------|-------|
| L | 11½ | 33 | 12½ → 31 |
| W | 13 | 22⅜ | 14 → 22¼ |
| D | 5½ | 12 | 6 → 7½ |

### PORCELAIN ENAMELED STEEL

|   | MIN. | MAX. | OTHER |
|---|------|------|-------|
| L | 24 | 30 | |
| W | 21 | | |
| D | 7⅜ | 8⅛ | |

### ENAMELED CAST IRON

|   | MIN. | MAX. | OTHER |
|---|------|------|-------|
| L | 12 | 30 | |
| W | 12 | 21 | 18→20 |
| D | 6 | 8 | 6½ → 7½ |

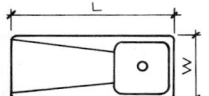

## SINGLE BOWL AND DRAINBOARD (RIGHT OR LEFT)

### STAINLESS STEEL

|   | MIN. | MAX. | OTHER |
|---|------|------|-------|
| L | 33 | 72 | |
| W | 21 | 25 | |
| D | 7 | 7½ | |

### ENAMELED CAST IRON

|   | MIN. | MAX. | OTHER |
|---|------|------|-------|
| L | 42 | 72 | |
| W | 20 | 25 | 24 |
| D | 6 | 8 | 6½ → 7½ |

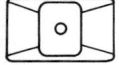

## SINGLE BOWL DOUBLE DRAINBOARD

### STAINLESS STEEL

|   | MIN. | MAX. | OTHER |
|---|------|------|-------|
| L | 54 | 72 | |
| W | 21 | 25 | |
| D | 7 | 7½ | |

### ENAMELED CAST IRON

|   | MIN. | MAX. | OTHER |
|---|------|------|-------|
| L | 54 | 72 | |
| W | 21 | 25 | 24 |
| D | 6 | 8 | 6½ → 7½ |

## DOUBLE BOWL

### STAINLESS STEEL

|   | MIN. | MAX. | OTHER |
|---|------|------|-------|
| L | 28 | 46 | 30 → 42 |
| W | 16 | 22 | 17 → 21¼ |
| D | 5 | 10 | 6½ → 7½ |

### PORCELAIN ENAMELED

|   | MIN. | MAX. | OTHER |
|---|------|------|-------|
| L | 32 | | |
| W | 21 | | |
| D | 7 | 8⅛ | |

### ENAMELED CAST IRON STEEL

|   | MIN. | MAX. | OTHER |
|---|------|------|-------|
| L | 32 | 42 | |
| W | 20 | 25 | |
| D | 6 | 8 | 6½→7½ |

## DOUBLE BOWL AND DRAINBOARD

### STAINLESS STEEL

|   | MIN. | MAX. | OTHER |
|---|------|------|-------|
| L | 60 | 72 | 66 |
| W | 21 | 25 | |
| D | 7 | 7½ | |

### ENAMELED CAST IRON

|   | MIN. | MAX. | OTHER |
|---|------|------|-------|
| L | 54 | 72 | 60 |
| W | 24 | 25 | |
| D | 6 | 8 | 6½ → 7½ |

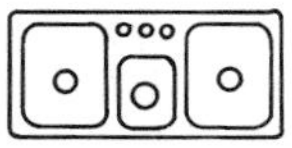

B = TOP OF DISPOSER TO CENTER OF DRAIN

### GARBAGE DISPOSER

|   | MIN. | MAX. | OTHER |
|---|------|------|-------|
| W | 6¼ | 10⅛ | 7⅜ → 9½ |
| B | 6 | 9⅜ | 6⅝ → 8¾ |
| H | 12¾ | 9³⁄₁₆ | 12⅝ → 16 |

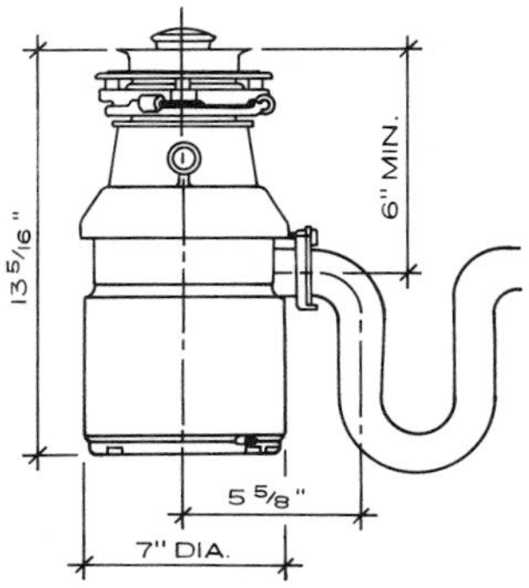

## GARBAGE DISPOSER UNITS

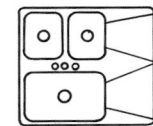

## TRIPLE BOWL

### STAINLESS STEEL

|   | MIN. | MAX. | OTHER |
|---|------|------|-------|
| L | 43 | 54 | 45 |
| W | 22 | | |
| D | 5 | 7½ | |

## TRIPLE BOWL AND DRAINBOARD (ISLAND)

### STAINLESS STEEL

|   | MIN. | MAX. | OTHER |
|---|------|------|-------|
| L | 54½ | 57 | |
| W | 40½ | | |
| D | 4 | 7½ | |

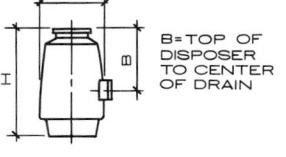

## TRIPLE BOWL AND DOUBLE DRAINBOARD

### STAINLESS STEEL

|   | MIN. | MAX. | OTHER |
|---|------|------|-------|
| L | | 84 | |
| W | | 25 | |
| D | | 7½ | |

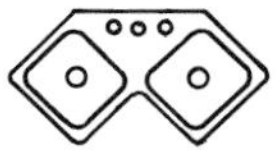

## CORNER BOWL

### STAINLESS STEEL

|   | MIN. | MAX. | OTHER |
|---|------|------|-------|
| L | 31⅞ | 32½ | |
| W | 31⅞ | 32½ | |
| D | 7 | 7½ | |

## BAR SINK

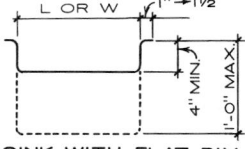

### STAINLESS STEEL

|   | MIN. | MAX. | OTHER |
|---|------|------|-------|
| L | 14 | 16¼ | 15 |
| W | 14 | 20¼ | 15 |
| D | 6 | 7⅜ | 6 |

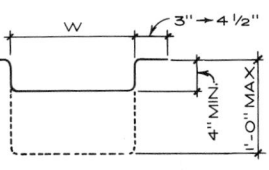

SINK WITH FLAT RIM

SINK WITH BACK LEDGE

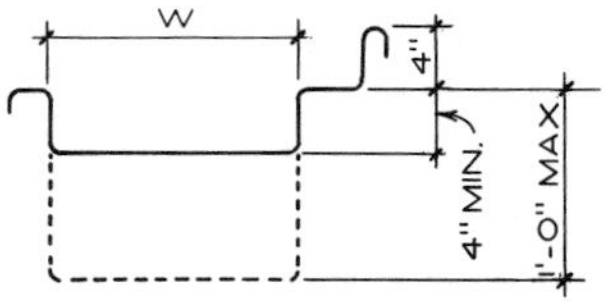

SINK WITH BACK LEDGE AND BACKSPLASH

## NOTES

All dimensions shown on this page are in inches.

Consult manufacturers' literature for variations in bowl finish and available accessories, such as cup strainer, spray head, cutting boards, and trim.

See pages on handicapped accessibility for suggested modifications to mounting height and cabinetry.

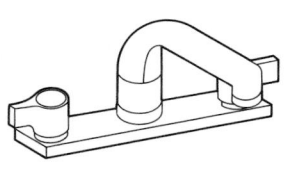

WASHER TYPE          WASHERLESS          GOOSENECK

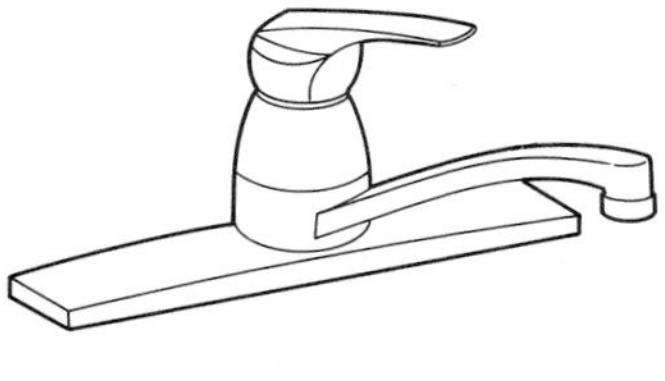

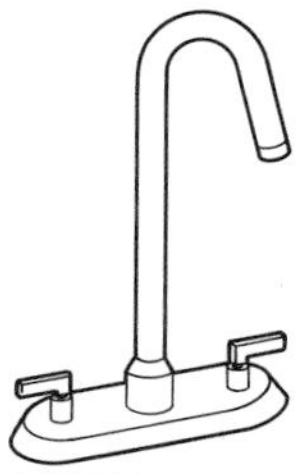

## KITCHEN FAUCETS

Giffels & Rossetti, Inc.; Detroit, Michigan

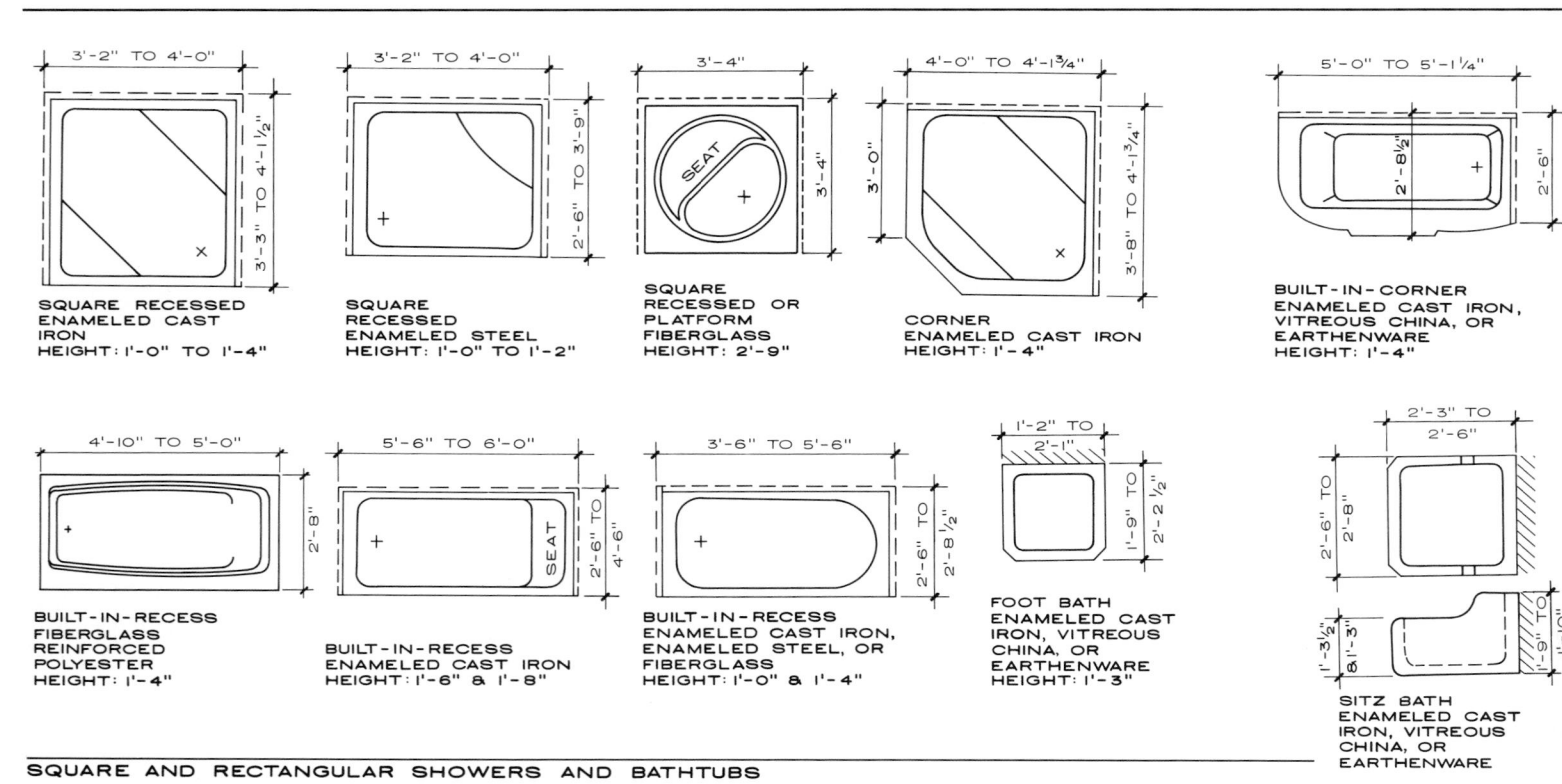

**SQUARE RECESSED ENAMELED CAST IRON**
HEIGHT: 1'-0" TO 1'-4"

**SQUARE RECESSED ENAMELED STEEL**
HEIGHT: 1'-0" TO 1'-2"

**SQUARE RECESSED OR PLATFORM FIBERGLASS**
HEIGHT: 2'-9"

**CORNER ENAMELED CAST IRON**
HEIGHT: 1'-4"

**BUILT-IN-CORNER ENAMELED CAST IRON, VITREOUS CHINA, OR EARTHENWARE**
HEIGHT: 1'-4"

**BUILT-IN-RECESS FIBERGLASS REINFORCED POLYESTER**
HEIGHT: 1'-4"

**BUILT-IN-RECESS ENAMELED CAST IRON**
HEIGHT: 1'-6" & 1'-8"

**BUILT-IN-RECESS ENAMELED CAST IRON, ENAMELED STEEL, OR FIBERGLASS**
HEIGHT: 1'-0" & 1'-4"

**FOOT BATH ENAMELED CAST IRON, VITREOUS CHINA, OR EARTHENWARE**
HEIGHT: 1'-3"

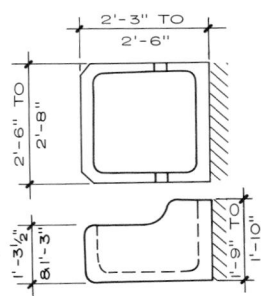

**SITZ BATH ENAMELED CAST IRON, VITREOUS CHINA, OR EARTHENWARE**

**SQUARE AND RECTANGULAR SHOWERS AND BATHTUBS**

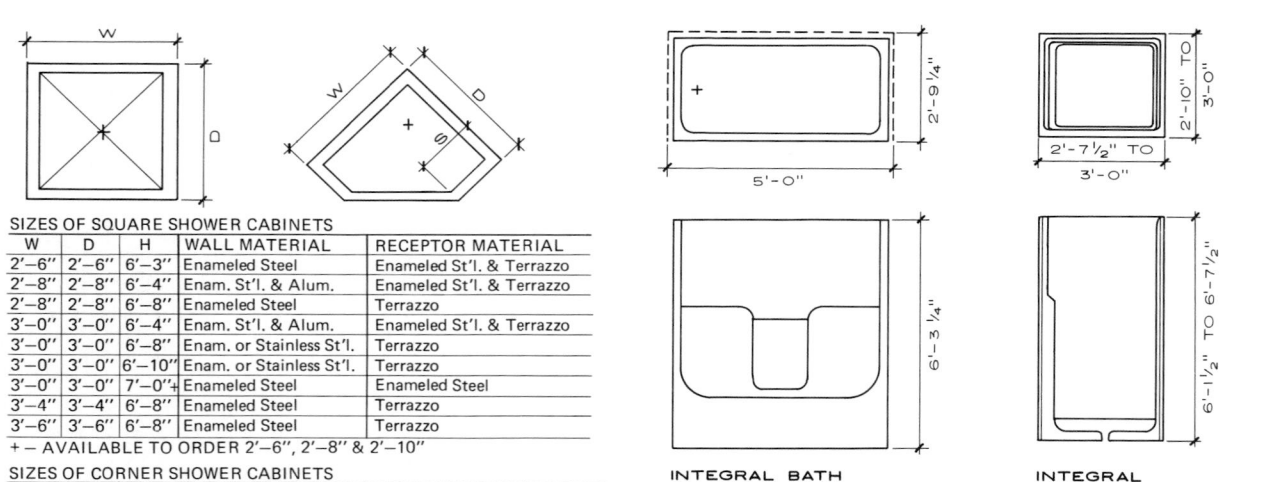

**SIZES OF SQUARE SHOWER CABINETS**

| W | D | H | WALL MATERIAL | RECEPTOR MATERIAL |
|---|---|---|---|---|
| 2'-6" | 2'-6" | 6'-3" | Enameled Steel | Enameled St'l. & Terrazzo |
| 2'-8" | 2'-8" | 6'-4" | Enam. St'l. & Alum. | Enameled St'l. & Terrazzo |
| 2'-8" | 2'-8" | 6'-8" | Enameled Steel | Terrazzo |
| 3'-0" | 3'-0" | 6'-4" | Enam. St'l. & Alum. | Enameled St'l. & Terrazzo |
| 3'-0" | 3'-0" | 6'-8" | Enam. or Stainless St'l. | Terrazzo |
| 3'-0" | 3'-0" | 6'-10" | Enam. or Stainless St'l. | Terrazzo |
| 3'-0" | 3'-0" | 7'-0"+ | Enameled Steel | Enameled Steel |
| 3'-4" | 3'-4" | 6'-8" | Enameled Steel | Terrazzo |
| 3'-6" | 3'-6" | 6'-8" | Enameled Steel | Terrazzo |

+ — AVAILABLE TO ORDER 2'-6", 2'-8" & 2'-10"

**SIZES OF CORNER SHOWER CABINETS**

| W | D | H | S | WALL MAT'L. | PANEL MAT'L. | RECEPTOR |
|---|---|---|---|---|---|---|
| 3'-0" | 3'-0" | 6'-8" | 1'-5" | Enam. St'l. | Enam. St'l. | Terrazzo |
| 3'-4" | 3'-4" | 6'-8" | 1'-7" | Enam. St'l. | Glass | Terrazzo |

**INTEGRAL BATH FIBERGLASS REINFORCED POLYESTER**

**INTEGRAL SHOWER FIBERGLASS REINFORCED POLYESTER**

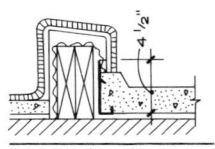

**USED FOR HANDICAPPED**

**SECTION THRU THRESHOLD**

**USED WITH MARBLE**

**EPOXY COATING**

**FREESTANDING SHOWER CABINETS AND BATHTUBS**

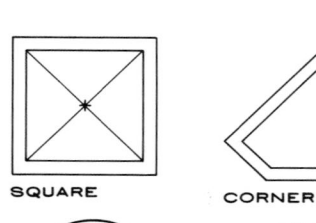

**SQUARE**

**CORNER**

**MULTISTALL**

Wedge Shaped Stalls Grouped in 2's, 3's, 4's, 5's & 6's, with 6'-0" Standard Ht., 5'-6" Intermediate Ht. & 5'-0" Junior Ht.

**SQUARE RECEPTOR — TERRAZZO**

| W | D | REMARKS |
|---|---|---|
| 2'-6" | 2'-6" | Flat for tile, or with threshold |
| 3'-0" | 3'-0" | Flat for tile, or with threshold |
| 3'-4" | 3'-4" | Flat for tile, or with threshold |
| 3'-0" | 3'-0" | Rabbetted for marble wall |
| 6'-0" | 3'-0" | Rabbetted for marble wall |

**CORNER RECEPTOR — TERRAZZO**

| W | D | REMARKS |
|---|---|---|
| 3'-0" | 3'-0" | Flat for tile, or with threshold |
| 3'-4" | 3'-4" | Flat for tile, or with threshold |

**SHOWER RECEPTOR TYPES**

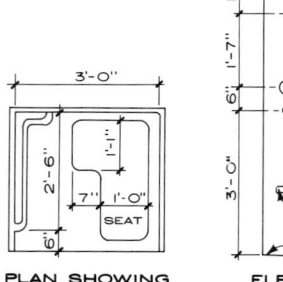
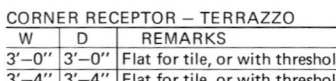

**PLAN SHOWING FOLDING SHOWER SEAT**

**ELEVATION OF PLUMBING WALL**

**SHOWER USED BY HANDICAPPED**

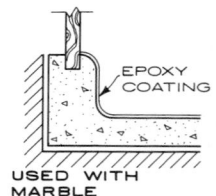

**USED WITH TILE, PLASTER**

**SECTION THRU SIDE**

**NOTE**
Adequate waterproofing should be added to each of the sections.

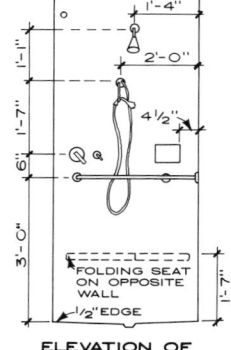

K. Shahid Rab, AIA; Friesen International; Washington, D.C.

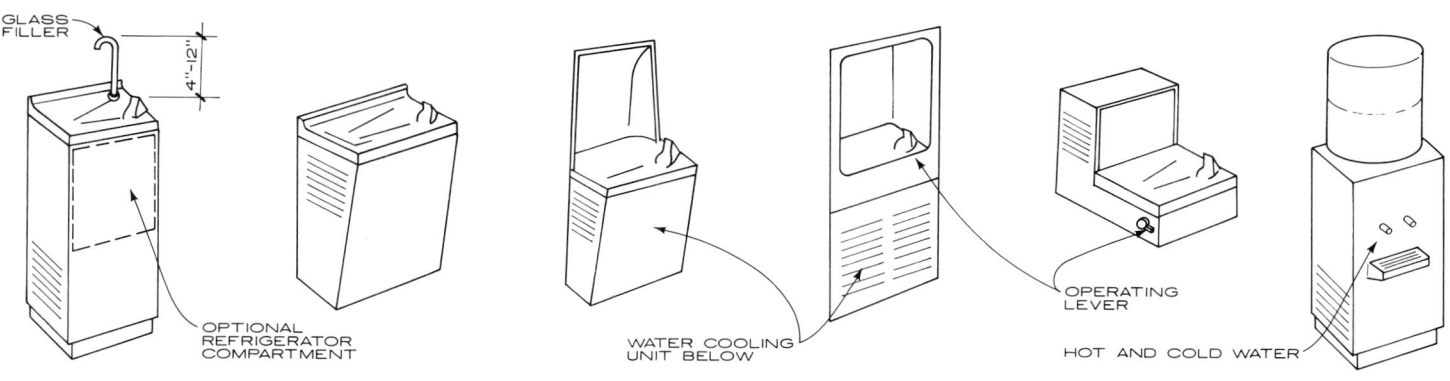

| FLOOR MOUNTED (IN.) FLUSH TO WALL OR FREESTANDING | | | | WALL MOUNTED (IN.) | | | | SEMIRECESSED (IN.) | | | | FULLY RECESSED (IN.) | | | | HANDICAPPED (IN.) | | | | BOTTLE TYPE (IN.) | | | |
|---|---|---|---|---|---|---|---|---|---|---|---|---|---|---|---|---|---|---|---|---|---|---|---|
| H | W | D | GPH | H | W | D | GPH | H | W | D | GPH | H | W | D | GPH | H | W | D | GPH | H | W | D | GPH |
| 30½ | 15 | 15 | 7-12 | 16 | 17 | 13¼ | 2-5 | 35¾ | 17 | 13½ | 11-17 | 50¼ | 18 | 12 | 8-14 | 5 | 14 | 20 | 5-20 | 36 | 12 | 12 | 1 |
| 33½ | 18 | 14½ | 4-20 | 22 | 18 | 14½ | 4-14 | 37½ | 16½ | 14½ | 7-15 | 54¼ | 19 | 12¼ | 7-12 | 7 | 15 | 21 | 20-100 | 40 | 14 | 14 | 2 |
| 40 | 12 | 12 | 3-10 | 26 | 17 | 14 | 5-15 | 39¾ | 18 | 13½ | 7-12 | 55¼ | 21 | 13 | 5-10 | 25 | 18 | 18½ | 7-9 | 44 | 17 | 14 | 1 |
| 41½ | 18 | 14½ | 4-20 | 29½ | 18 | 14½ | 4-20 | 44¼ | 17¼ | 14 | 5-13 | | | | | 28 | 17¼ | 18½ | 7-10 | | | | |

## SELF-CONTAINED WATER COOLERS

Air cooled condensers are used for normal room temperatures; water cooled units for high room temperatures and larger capacities. Many fountain models are available with cold and hot water supply, a glass filler attachment, or refrigerated compartments. There is a wide selection of colors and finishes to choose from.

Floor and wall mounted fountains are made in lower heights for children's use and can be mounted low on the side of regular height models.

Recommended fountain rim heights, above the floor:

1. 40 in.—adults.
2. 30 in.—children.
3. 34-36 max. in.—handicapped.

Special explosionproof fountains are recommended for use in hazardous atmospheres. Corrosion resistant fountains are available as well as a water cooled type for excessively hot and dusty atmospheres.

Power requirements are 110, 115, 230 V; 50 to 60 cycles, single phase AC; otherwise a transformer is used.

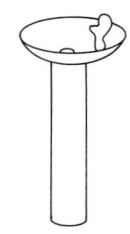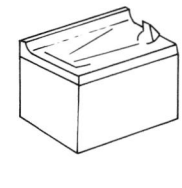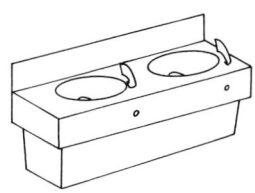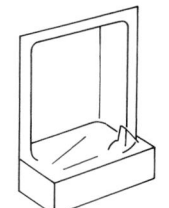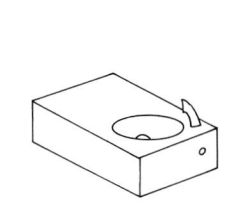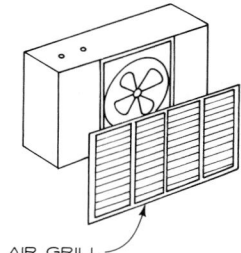

| PEDESTAL DISH (IN.) | | | WALL MOUNTED (IN.) | | | | TWO STATION (IN.) | | | | SEMIRECESSED OR FULLY RECESSED (IN.) | | | | HANDICAPPED (IN.) | | | | REMOTE PACKAGE COOLER (IN.) | | | |
|---|---|---|---|---|---|---|---|---|---|---|---|---|---|---|---|---|---|---|---|---|---|---|
| H | D | SUPPLY/ WASTE | H | W | D | SUPPLY/ WASTE | H | W | D | SUPPLY/ WASTE | H | W | D | SUPPLY/ WASTE | H | W | D | SUPPLY/ WASTE | H | W | D | GPH |
| 38¼ | 4 | ¼, 1½ | 7¾ | 10 | 10 | ⅜, 1¼ | 6 | 39 | 11¼ | ½, 1½ | 27¾ | 17½ | 13 | ⅜, 1¼ | 6 | 12 | 20 | ½, 1¼ | 16¼ | 15¾ | 8 | 5-6 |
| 38¼ | 14¼ | ¼, 1½ | 16 | 17 | 13¼ | ⅜, 1¼ | 15 | 31 | 14 | ½, 1½ | 29 | 21 | 13 | ⅜, 1¼ | 7 | 15 | 21 | ⅜, 1¼ | 22¼ | 30 | 6½ | 6-10 |

**DRINKING FOUNTAINS (FOR USE WITH REMOTE STORAGE COOLERS)**

## DRINKING WATER REQUIREMENTS

| TYPE OF SERVICE | GPH PER PERSON | |
|---|---|---|
| | CUP | BUBBLER |
| Offices, schools, cafeterias, hotels (per room), hospitals (per bed and per attendant) | 0.033 | 0.083 |
| Restaurants | 0.04 | 0.1 |
| Light manufacturing | 0.0573 | 0.143 |
| Heavy manufacturing | 0.08 | 0.20 |
| Hot, heavy manufacturing | 0.10 | 0.25 |
| Theaters per 100 seats | 0.4 gph/ 100 seats | 1.0 gph/ 100 seats |
| Department stores, lobbies, hotel and office buildings | 1.6-2.0 gph/fountain | 4-5 gph/ fountain |

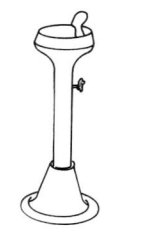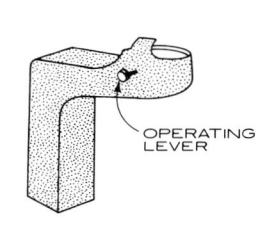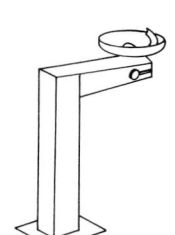

| PEDESTAL (IN.) | | | CONCRETE CYLINDER (IN.) | | | CONCRETE HANDICAPPED (IN.) | | | PROJECTING PEDESTAL (IN.) | | |
|---|---|---|---|---|---|---|---|---|---|---|---|
| H | DIA. | SUPPLY/ WASTE | H | DIA. | SUPPLY/ WASTE | H | L | SUPPLY/ WASTE | H | L | SUPPLY/ WASTE |
| 36 | 12 | ⅜, 1 | 36 | 12 | ½, 1¼ | 33 | 30¾ | ½, 1¼ | 33 | 29¾ | ½, 1¼ |

**OUTDOOR TYPE FOUNTAINS**

William G. Miner, AIA, Architect, Washington, D.C.

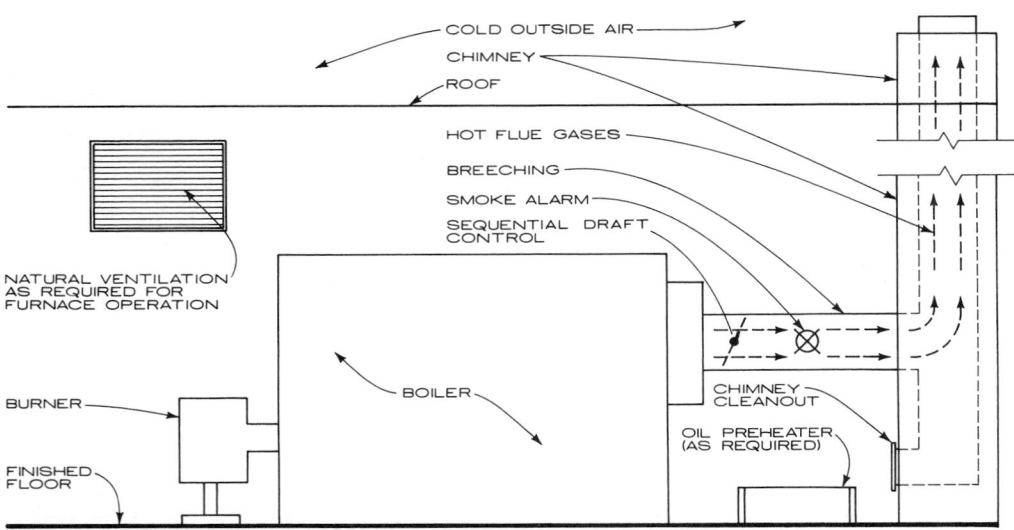

**TYPICAL BOILER EQUIPMENT FOR NATURAL DRAFT INSTALLATION**

## BOILERS AND BURNERS

Two main elements determine overall boiler efficiency: (1) heat transfer surface of boiler and its condition—clean or fouled; (2) burner's ability to convert fuel's calorific (heat) value into useful heat.

Burner efficiency depends on the proper combustion of fuel (air-fuel ratio) and the maintenance (annual tune-up) of the burner. To handle a boiler properly and efficiently, the maintenance staff must be trained to operate the unit and to conduct efficiency tests, which include testing for $CO_2$, stack temperature, smoke, and draft.

NOTE: Air pollution regulations must be obtained from authorities having jurisdiction.

## RATINGS

1. Gross rating = input in Btu/hr.
2. Net rating = output in Btu/hr. = gross rating x efficiency.
3. **FUEL RATINGS**

| FUEL | HEAT VALUE | EFFICIENCY (%) |
|---|---|---|
| Anthracite coal | 14,600 Btu/lb | 65-75 |
| No. 2 oil | 140,000 Btu/gal | 70-80 |
| No. 4 oil | 145,000 Btu/gal | 70-80 |
| No. 6 oil | 150,000 Btu/gal | 70-80 |
| Natural gas | 1052 Btu/cu ft | 70-80 |
| Electricity | 1 W = 3.4 Btuh | 95-100 |

4. Example: If boiler-burner combination is 80% efficient, No. 2 fuel oil is burned, and the total heat load is 168,000 Btu/hr, what is the required firing rate?

$$\text{Firing rate} = \frac{\text{gross rating}}{\text{fuel rating} \times \text{efficiency}}$$

$$\frac{168,000 \text{ (Btu/hr)}}{140,000 \text{ (Btu/gal)} \times 80\% \text{ (.8)}} = 1.5 \text{ gal/hr}$$

NOTE: Gross and net ratings are found on equipment plates.

## CONTROLS

Automatic fuel burning equipment requires a control system that will provide a prescribed sequence of operating events and will take proper corrective action if failure occurs in the equipment or its operation. The basic requirements for oil burners, gas burners, and coal burners (stokers) are the same. The controls can be classified as operating controls, limit controls, and interlocks.

Operating controls initiate the normal starting and stopping of the burner in response to the primary sensor acting through appropriate actuators.

Examples of primary sensors are: a room thermostat for a residential furnace; a pressure actuated switch for a steam boiler; a thermostat for a hot water heater. Since the heat output of a burner may be widely distributed, the location of the primary sensor is important.

An actuator is defined as a device that converts the control system signal into a useful function. Actuators generally consist of valves, dampers, or relays.

Ignition for oil or gas burners is achieved by an electric spark or by a pilot gas flame, all supervised by a flame safeguard system which must meet legal and insurance underwriter's requirements. After ignition is proved, the flame safeguard system then permits the main fuel (gas or oil) to enter the burner for on-line combustion.

Limit controls and interlocks function only when the system exceeds prescribed unsafe operating conditions. They actuate electric switches that will close the fuel valve in the event of an unsafe condition, such as (1) excessive temperature in the combustion chamber or heat exchanger, (2) excessive pressure in a boiler or hot water heater, (3) low water level in a boiler and in larger commercial and industrial burners, (4) high or low gas pressure, (5) low oil pressure, (6) low atomizing media pressure, and (7) low oil temperature when firing residual fuel oil. Separate limit and operating controls are always recommended.

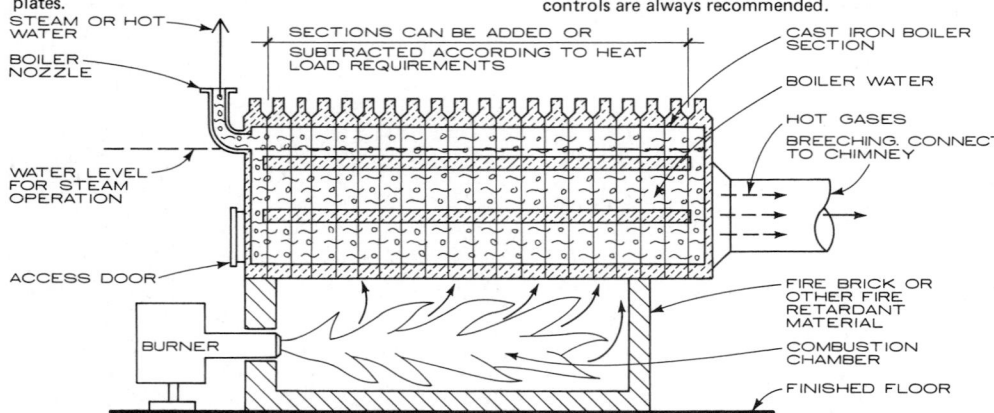

**CAST IRON SECTIONAL TYPE BOILER**

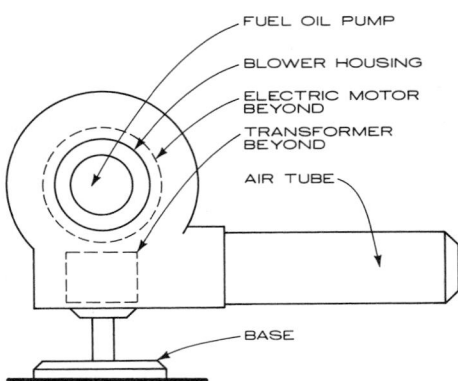

**HIGH PRESSURE GUN TYPE BURNER (NO. 2 FUEL OIL)**
NOTE: FOR DOMESTIC INSTALLATIONS UP TO 10 FAMILIES AND SINGLE STORY COMMERCIAL INSTALLATIONS UP TO 10,000 SQ FT

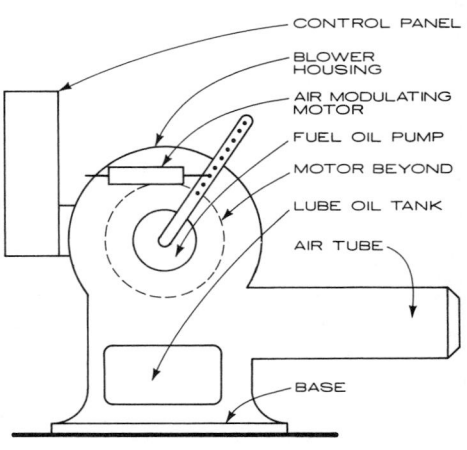

**LOW PRESSURE GUN TYPE BURNER (NO. 4 FUEL OIL AND/OR GAS)**
NOTE: FOR LARGE DOMESTIC, SEMICOMMERCIAL, AND COMMERCIAL INSTALLATIONS

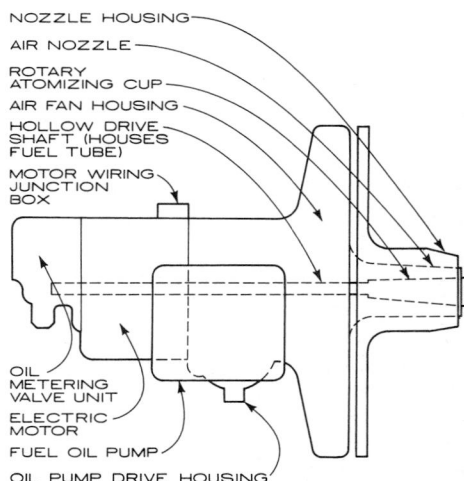

**HORIZONTAL ROTARY TYPE BURNER DIRECT DRIVE (NO. 6 FUEL OIL)**
NOTE: ALSO AVAILABLE WITH BELT DRIVE, USED IN DOMESTIC, SEMICOMMERCIAL, COMMERCIAL, AND HEAVY INDUSTRIAL

**BURNER TYPES**

Kelly Sacher & Associates, Architects Engineers Planners; Seaford, Long Island, New York
Joe H. Shaw; Everett I. Brown Company; Indianapolis, Indiana

**15 HEAT GENERATION**

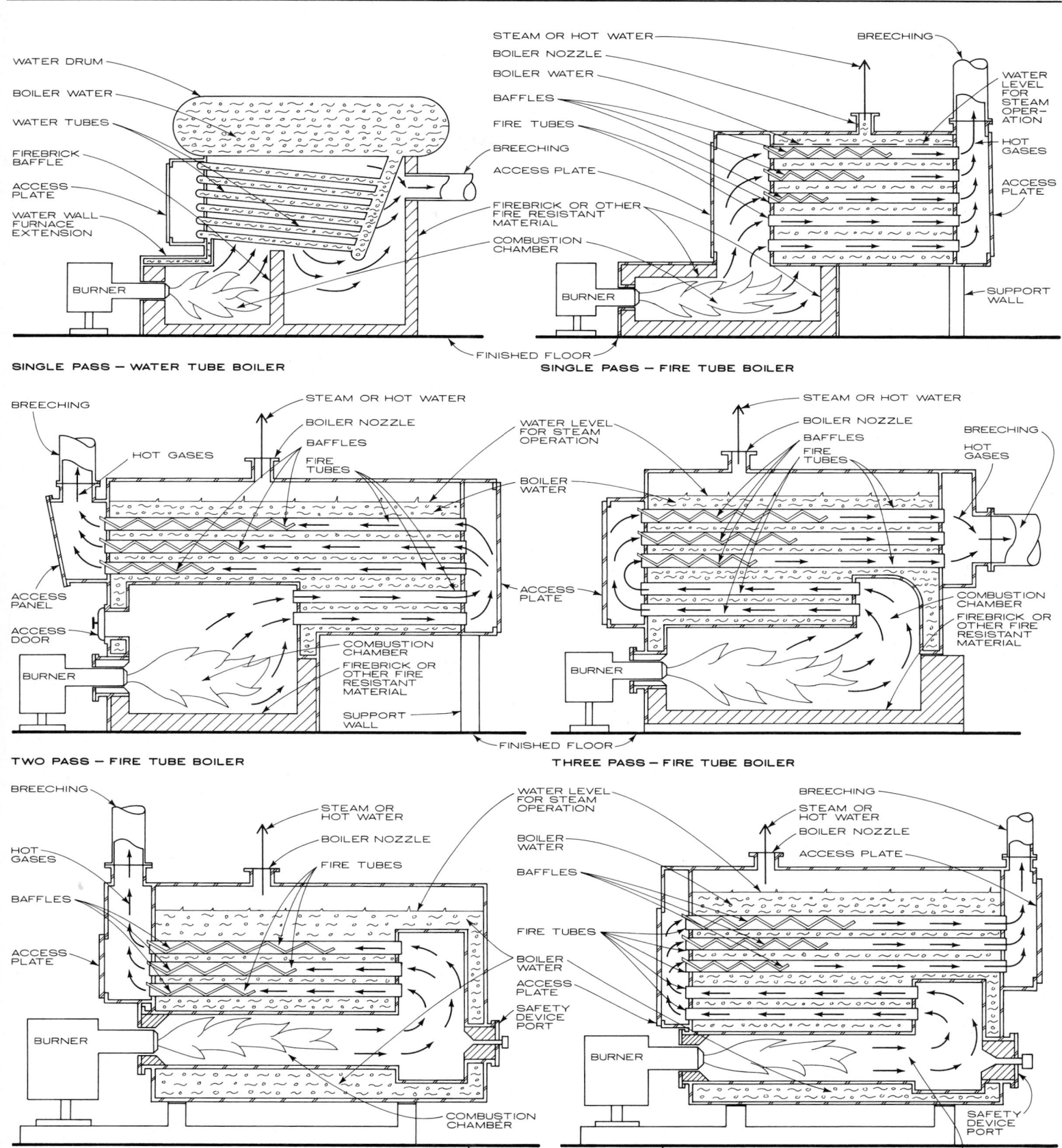

WATER DRUM
BOILER WATER
WATER TUBES
FIREBRICK BAFFLE
ACCESS PLATE
WATER WALL FURNACE EXTENSION
BURNER
BREECHING

**SINGLE PASS — WATER TUBE BOILER**

STEAM OR HOT WATER
BOILER NOZZLE
BOILER WATER
BAFFLES
FIRE TUBES
BREECHING
ACCESS PLATE
FIREBRICK OR OTHER FIRE RESISTANT MATERIAL
COMBUSTION CHAMBER
BURNER
WATER LEVEL FOR STEAM OPERATION
HOT GASES
ACCESS PLATE
SUPPORT WALL
FINISHED FLOOR

**SINGLE PASS — FIRE TUBE BOILER**

BREECHING
HOT GASES
STEAM OR HOT WATER
BOILER NOZZLE
BAFFLES
FIRE TUBES
ACCESS PANEL
ACCESS DOOR
BURNER
WATER LEVEL FOR STEAM OPERATION
BOILER WATER
ACCESS PLATE
COMBUSTION CHAMBER
FIREBRICK OR OTHER FIRE RESISTANT MATERIAL
SUPPORT WALL
FINISHED FLOOR

**TWO PASS — FIRE TUBE BOILER**

STEAM OR HOT WATER
BOILER NOZZLE
BAFFLES
FIRE TUBES
BREECHING
HOT GASES
BURNER
COMBUSTION CHAMBER
FIREBRICK OR OTHER FIRE RESISTANT MATERIAL

**THREE PASS — FIRE TUBE BOILER**

BREECHING
HOT GASES
BAFFLES
ACCESS PLATE
BURNER
STEAM OR HOT WATER
BOILER NOZZLE
FIRE TUBES
WATER LEVEL FOR STEAM OPERATION
BOILER WATER
ACCESS PLATE
SAFETY DEVICE PORT
COMBUSTION CHAMBER
FINISHED FLOOR

**TWO PASS WET — BACK SCOTCH MARINE BOILER**

WATER LEVEL FOR STEAM OPERATION
BOILER WATER
BAFFLES
FIRE TUBES
BOILER WATER
ACCESS PLATE
BURNER
BREECHING
STEAM OR HOT WATER
BOILER NOZZLE
ACCESS PLATE
SAFETY DEVICE PORT
COMBUSTION CHAMBER

**THREE PASS WET — BACK SCOTCH MARINE BOILER**

## TUBE TYPE BOILERS

Kelly Sacher & Associates, Architects Engineers Planners; Seaford, Long Island, New York

## HEAT GENERATION

**15**

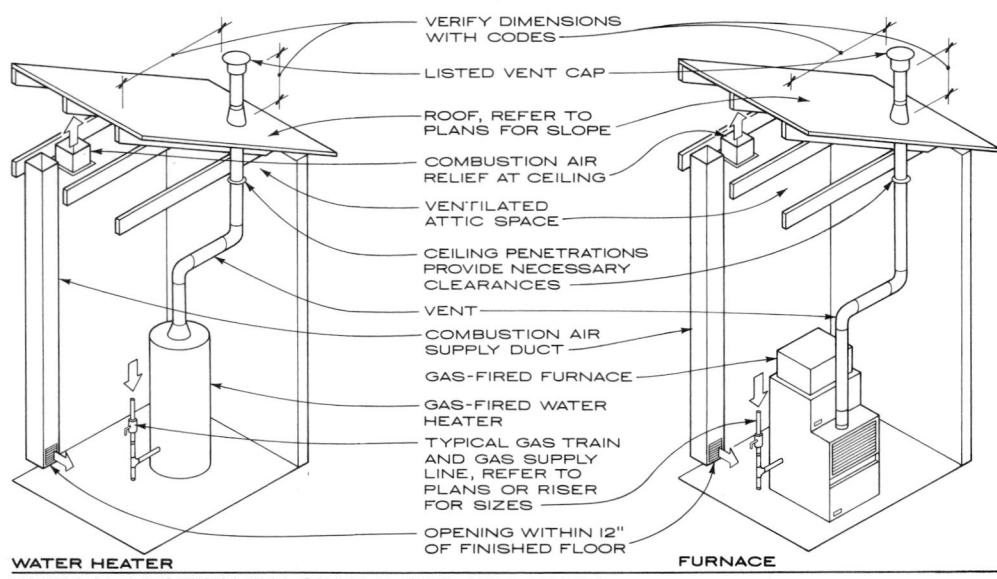

VERIFY DIMENSIONS WITH CODES
LISTED VENT CAP
ROOF, REFER TO PLANS FOR SLOPE
COMBUSTION AIR RELIEF AT CEILING
VENTILATED ATTIC SPACE
CEILING PENETRATIONS PROVIDE NECESSARY CLEARANCES
VENT
COMBUSTION AIR SUPPLY DUCT
GAS-FIRED FURNACE
GAS-FIRED WATER HEATER
TYPICAL GAS TRAIN AND GAS SUPPLY LINE, REFER TO PLANS OR RISER FOR SIZES
OPENING WITHIN 12" OF FINISHED FLOOR

WATER HEATER     FURNACE

**TYPICAL MULTIFAMILY SINGLE GAS APPLIANCE**

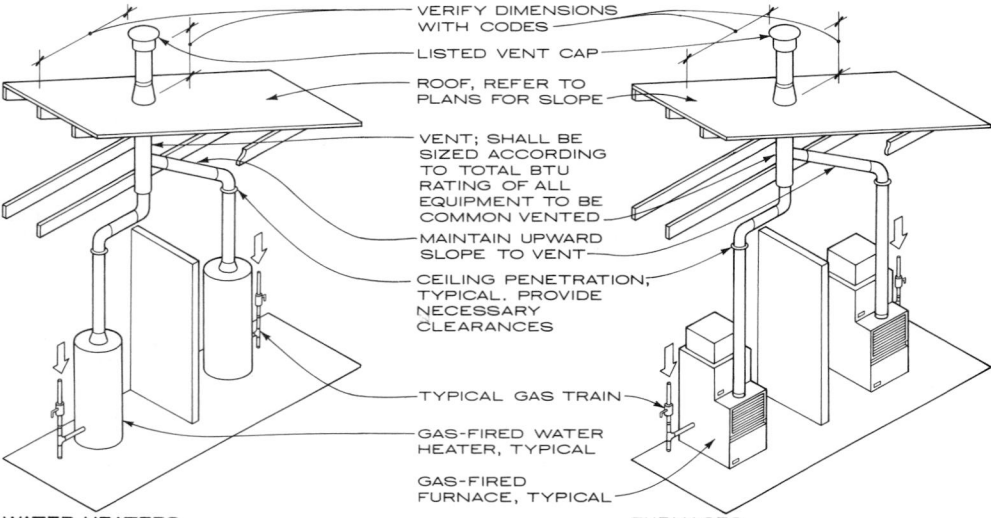

VERIFY DIMENSIONS WITH CODES
LISTED VENT CAP
ROOF, REFER TO PLANS FOR SLOPE
VENT; SHALL BE SIZED ACCORDING TO TOTAL BTU RATING OF ALL EQUIPMENT TO BE COMMON VENTED
MAINTAIN UPWARD SLOPE TO VENT
CEILING PENETRATION; TYPICAL. PROVIDE NECESSARY CLEARANCES
TYPICAL GAS TRAIN
GAS-FIRED WATER HEATER, TYPICAL
GAS-FIRED FURNACE, TYPICAL

WATER HEATERS     FURNACES

**TYPICAL MULTIFAMILY COMMON VENTED GAS APPLIANCES**

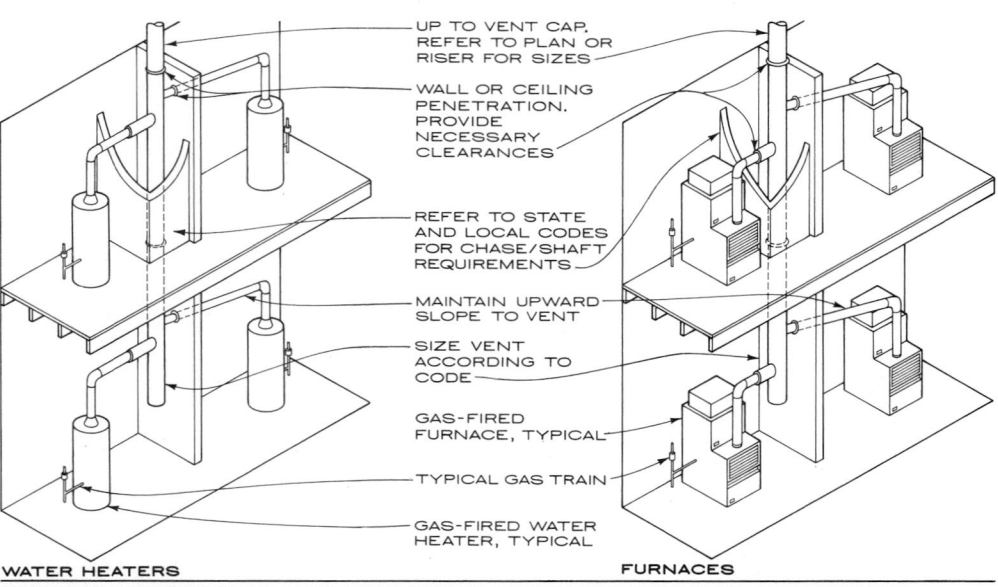

UP TO VENT CAP, REFER TO PLAN OR RISER FOR SIZES
WALL OR CEILING PENETRATION. PROVIDE NECESSARY CLEARANCES
REFER TO STATE AND LOCAL CODES FOR CHASE/SHAFT REQUIREMENTS
MAINTAIN UPWARD SLOPE TO VENT
SIZE VENT ACCORDING TO CODE
GAS-FIRED FURNACE, TYPICAL
TYPICAL GAS TRAIN
GAS-FIRED WATER HEATER, TYPICAL

WATER HEATERS     FURNACES

**TYPICAL MULTISTORY / MULTIFAMILY COMMON VENTED GAS APPLIANCES**

American Gas Association
Richard J. Vitullo; Washington Grove, Maryland

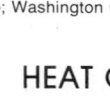 **HEAT GENERATION**

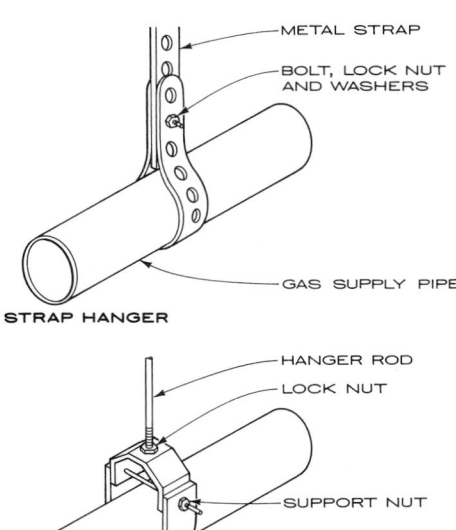

METAL STRAP
BOLT, LOCK NUT AND WASHERS
GAS SUPPLY PIPE

**STRAP HANGER**

HANGER ROD
LOCK NUT
SUPPORT NUT
GAS SUPPLY PIPE

**CLEVIS HANGER**

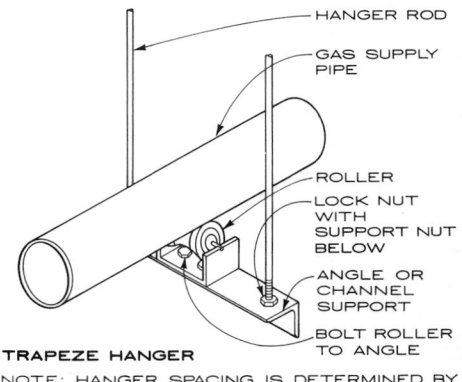

HANGER ROD
GAS SUPPLY PIPE
ROLLER
LOCK NUT WITH SUPPORT NUT BELOW
ANGLE OR CHANNEL SUPPORT
BOLT ROLLER TO ANGLE

**TRAPEZE HANGER**

NOTE: HANGER SPACING IS DETERMINED BY PIPE SIZES AND AT ALL TURNS AND JUNCTIONS

**TYPICAL GAS PIPING HANGERS**

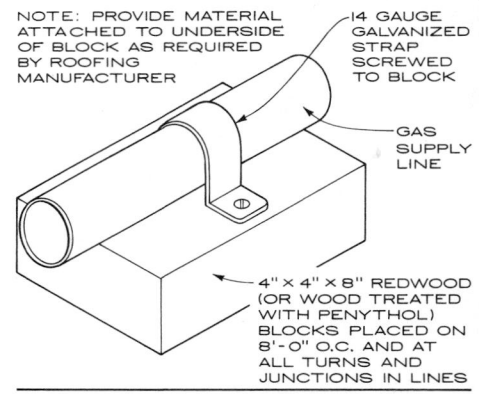

NOTE: PROVIDE MATERIAL ATTACHED TO UNDERSIDE OF BLOCK AS REQUIRED BY ROOFING MANUFACTURER
14 GAUGE GALVANIZED STRAP SCREWED TO BLOCK
GAS SUPPLY LINE
4" X 4" X 8" REDWOOD (OR WOOD TREATED WITH PENYTHOL) BLOCKS PLACED ON 8'-0" O.C. AND AT ALL TURNS AND JUNCTIONS IN LINES

**GAS LINE ROOF SUPPORT BLOCK**

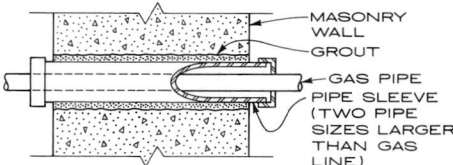

MASONRY WALL
GROUT
GAS PIPE
PIPE SLEEVE (TWO PIPE SIZES LARGER THAN GAS LINE)

NOTE: SLEEVES ENTERING REINFORCED MASONRY WALLS SHALL NOT CONTACT REINFORCING STEEL. SEAL ANNULAR AREA WITH SEALING COMPOUND

**TYPICAL WALL PENETRATION**

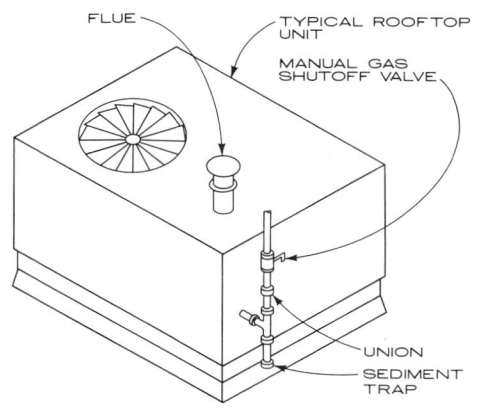

FLUE

TYPICAL ROOFTOP UNIT

MANUAL GAS SHUTOFF VALVE

UNION

SEDIMENT TRAP

**TYPICAL GAS-FIRED ROOFTOP UNIT**

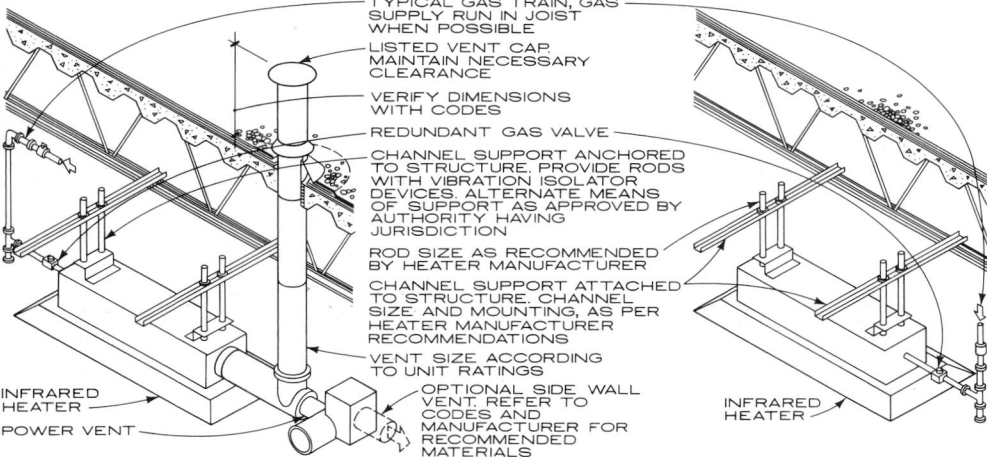

EXTERIOR WALL

WALL FRAMING

GAS-FIRED THROUGH-WALL UNIT

VENT

MAINTAIN MINIMUM DISTANCE BELOW WINDOW

DIRECT VENT FURNACE

GAS TRAIN, REFER TO PLANS FOR SIZES AND LOCATION. PROVIDE UNION, GAS COCK, AND DIRT LEG

A/C CONDENSATE LINE (TRAPPED) TO CONDENSATE DRAIN SYSTEM. REFER TO PLANS FOR SIZES AND LOCATION

**TYPICAL GAS HEATING/ELECTRIC COOLING THROUGH-WALL UNIT**

TYPICAL GAS TRAIN, GAS SUPPLY RUN IN JOIST WHEN POSSIBLE

LISTED VENT CAP, MAINTAIN NECESSARY CLEARANCE

VERIFY DIMENSIONS WITH CODES

REDUNDANT GAS VALVE

CHANNEL SUPPORT ANCHORED TO STRUCTURE. PROVIDE RODS WITH VIBRATION ISOLATOR DEVICES. ALTERNATE MEANS OF SUPPORT AS APPROVED BY AUTHORITY HAVING JURISDICTION

ROD SIZE AS RECOMMENDED BY HEATER MANUFACTURER

CHANNEL SUPPORT ATTACHED TO STRUCTURE. CHANNEL SIZE AND MOUNTING, AS PER HEATER MANUFACTURER RECOMMENDATIONS

VENT SIZE ACCORDING TO UNIT RATINGS

OPTIONAL SIDE WALL VENT. REFER TO CODES AND MANUFACTURER FOR RECOMMENDED MATERIALS

INFRARED HEATER

POWER VENT

INFRARED HEATER

**LOW-INTENSITY POWER VENTED**

**HIGH-INTENSITY UNVENTED**

**TYPICAL GAS-FIRED INFRARED HEATER**

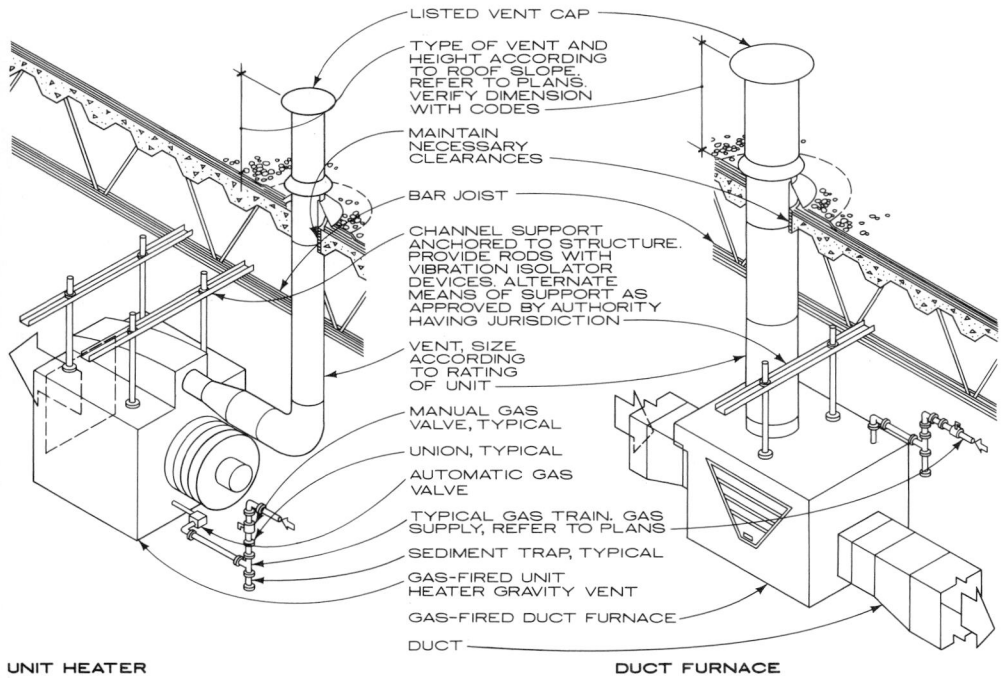

LISTED VENT CAP

TYPE OF VENT AND HEIGHT ACCORDING TO ROOF SLOPE. REFER TO PLANS. VERIFY DIMENSION WITH CODES

MAINTAIN NECESSARY CLEARANCES

BAR JOIST

CHANNEL SUPPORT ANCHORED TO STRUCTURE. PROVIDE RODS WITH VIBRATION ISOLATOR DEVICES. ALTERNATE MEANS OF SUPPORT AS APPROVED BY AUTHORITY HAVING JURISDICTION

VENT, SIZE ACCORDING TO RATING OF UNIT

MANUAL GAS VALVE, TYPICAL

UNION, TYPICAL

AUTOMATIC GAS VALVE

TYPICAL GAS TRAIN. GAS SUPPLY, REFER TO PLANS

SEDIMENT TRAP, TYPICAL

GAS-FIRED UNIT HEATER GRAVITY VENT

GAS-FIRED DUCT FURNACE

DUCT

**UNIT HEATER**

**DUCT FURNACE**

**TYPICAL GAS-FIRED UNITS**

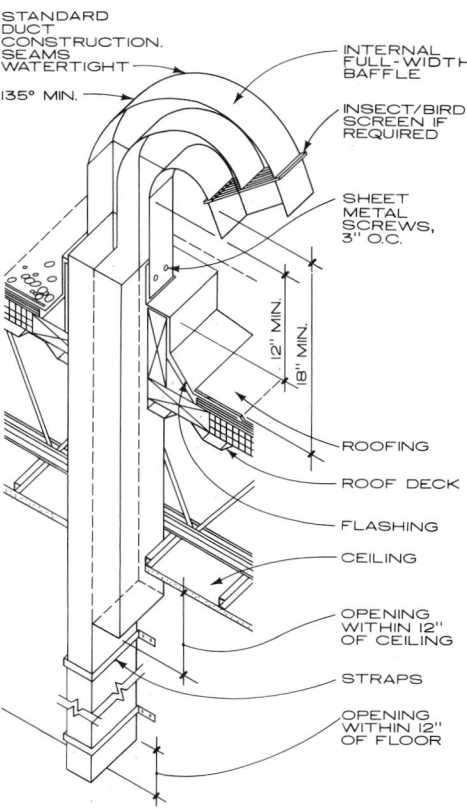

STANDARD DUCT CONSTRUCTION. SEAMS WATERTIGHT

135° MIN.

INTERNAL FULL-WIDTH BAFFLE

INSECT/BIRD SCREEN IF REQUIRED

SHEET METAL SCREWS, 3" O.C.

12" MIN.

8" MIN.

ROOFING

ROOF DECK

FLASHING

CEILING

OPENING WITHIN 12" OF CEILING

STRAPS

OPENING WITHIN 12" OF FLOOR

**TYPICAL GOOSENECK COMBUSTION AIR**

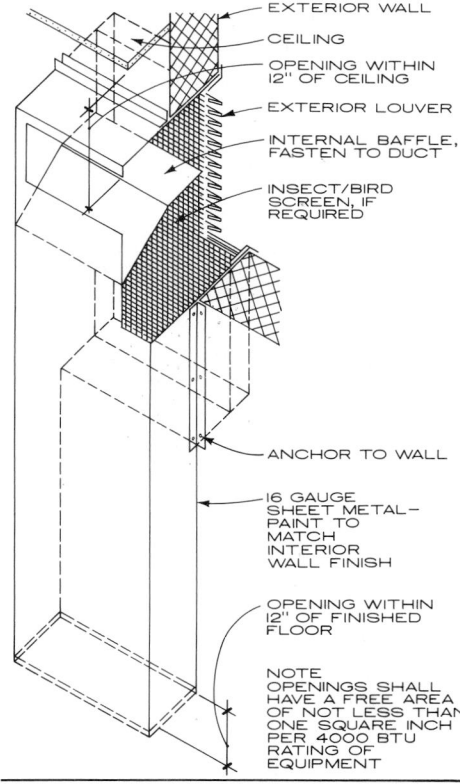

EXTERIOR WALL

CEILING

OPENING WITHIN 12" OF CEILING

EXTERIOR LOUVER

INTERNAL BAFFLE, FASTEN TO DUCT

INSECT/BIRD SCREEN, IF REQUIRED

ANCHOR TO WALL

16 GAUGE SHEET METAL – PAINT TO MATCH INTERIOR WALL FINISH

OPENING WITHIN 12" OF FINISHED FLOOR

NOTE OPENINGS SHALL HAVE A FREE AREA OF NOT LESS THAN ONE SQUARE INCH PER 4000 BTU RATING OF EQUIPMENT

**TYPICAL COMBUSTION AIR LOUVER**

GENERAL NOTE
THESE DRAWINGS ARE FOR REFERENCE ONLY. REFER TO STATE, LOCAL CODES/ ORDINANCES AND MANUFACTURER'S INSTAL- LATION INSTRUCTIONS FOR PARTICULAR REQUIREMENTS GOVERNING MAINTENANCE CLEARANCES, GAS PIPING, COMBUSTION AIR, VENTING, ETC.

American Gas Association
Richard J. Vitullo; Washington Grove, Maryland

**HEAT GENERATION** **15**

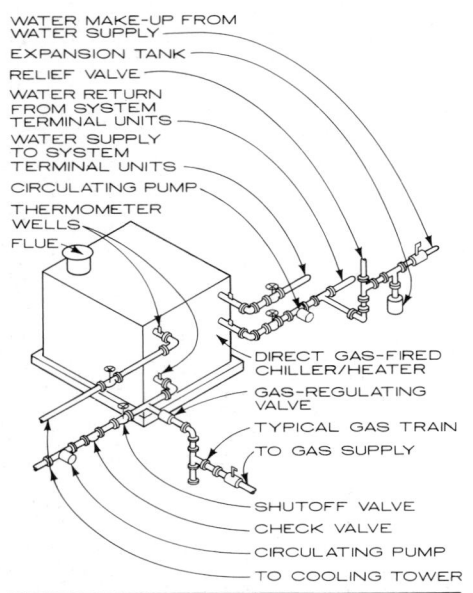

WATER MAKE-UP FROM WATER SUPPLY
EXPANSION TANK
RELIEF VALVE
WATER RETURN FROM SYSTEM TERMINAL UNITS
WATER SUPPLY TO SYSTEM TERMINAL UNITS
CIRCULATING PUMP
THERMOMETER WELLS
FLUE

DIRECT GAS-FIRED CHILLER/HEATER
GAS-REGULATING VALVE
TYPICAL GAS TRAIN
TO GAS SUPPLY

SHUTOFF VALVE
CHECK VALVE
CIRCULATING PUMP
TO COOLING TOWER

**DIRECT GAS-FIRED CHILLER/HEATER**

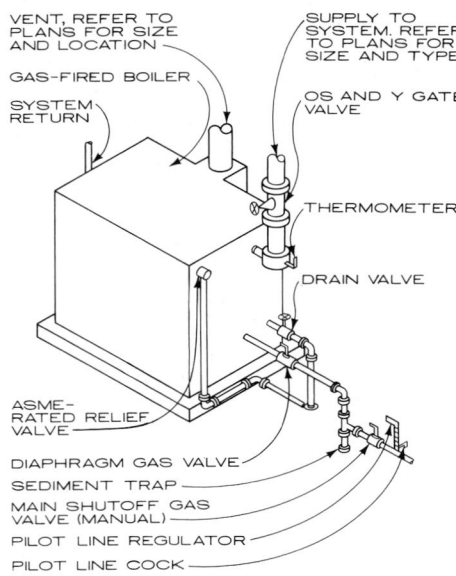

VENT, REFER TO PLANS FOR SIZE AND LOCATION
GAS-FIRED BOILER
SYSTEM RETURN
SUPPLY TO SYSTEM. REFER TO PLANS FOR SIZE AND TYPE
OS AND Y GATE VALVE
THERMOMETER
DRAIN VALVE

ASME-RATED RELIEF VALVE
DIAPHRAGM GAS VALVE
SEDIMENT TRAP
MAIN SHUTOFF GAS VALVE (MANUAL)
PILOT LINE REGULATOR
PILOT LINE COCK

**TYPICAL GAS-FIRED BOILER**

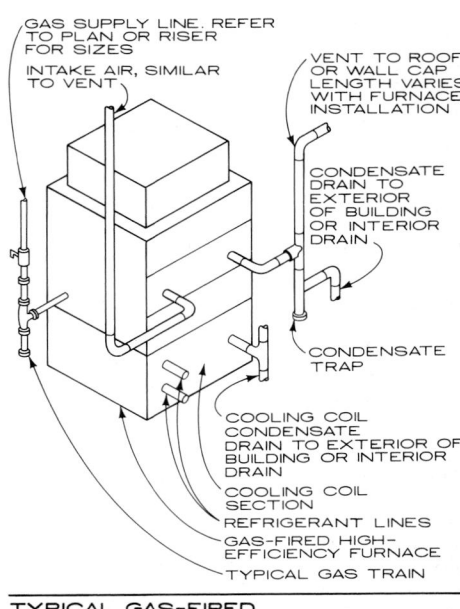

GAS SUPPLY LINE. REFER TO PLAN OR RISER FOR SIZES
INTAKE AIR, SIMILAR TO VENT
VENT TO ROOF OR WALL CAP LENGTH VARIES WITH FURNACE INSTALLATION
CONDENSATE DRAIN TO EXTERIOR OF BUILDING OR INTERIOR DRAIN
CONDENSATE TRAP
COOLING COIL CONDENSATE DRAIN TO EXTERIOR OF BUILDING OR INTERIOR DRAIN
COOLING COIL SECTION
REFRIGERANT LINES
GAS-FIRED HIGH-EFFICIENCY FURNACE
TYPICAL GAS TRAIN

**TYPICAL GAS-FIRED HIGH-EFFICIENCY FURNACE**

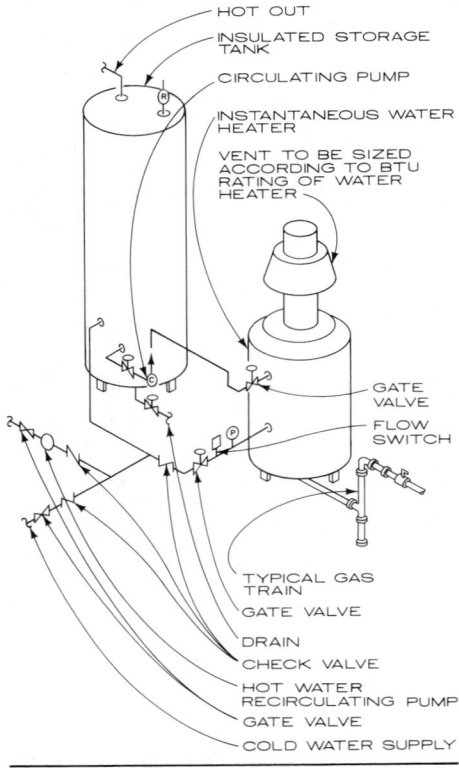

HOT OUT
INSULATED STORAGE TANK
CIRCULATING PUMP
INSTANTANEOUS WATER HEATER
VENT TO BE SIZED ACCORDING TO BTU RATING OF WATER HEATER

GATE VALVE
FLOW SWITCH

TYPICAL GAS TRAIN
GATE VALVE
DRAIN
CHECK VALVE
HOT WATER RECIRCULATING PUMP
GATE VALVE
COLD WATER SUPPLY

**TYPICAL INSTANTANEOUS WATER HEATERS WITH STORAGE TANKS**

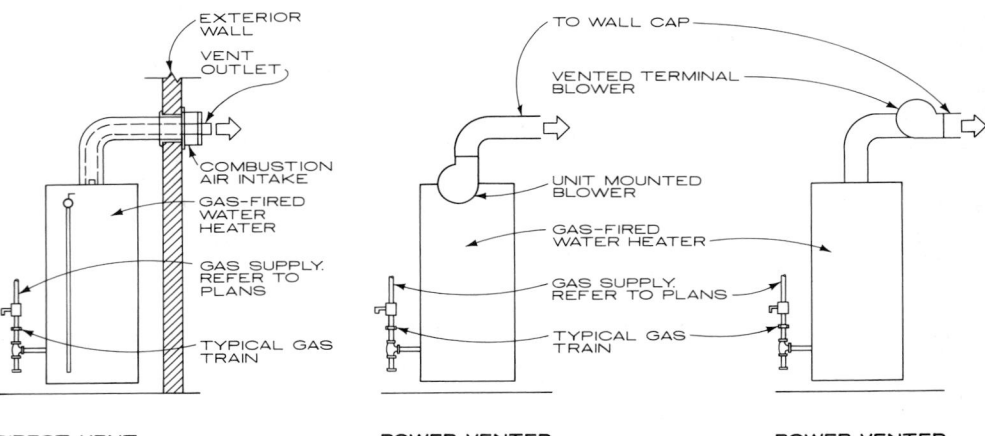

EXTERIOR WALL
VENT OUTLET
COMBUSTION AIR INTAKE
GAS-FIRED WATER HEATER
GAS SUPPLY. REFER TO PLANS
TYPICAL GAS TRAIN

**DIRECT VENT**

TO WALL CAP
VENTED TERMINAL BLOWER
UNIT MOUNTED BLOWER
GAS-FIRED WATER HEATER
GAS SUPPLY, REFER TO PLANS
TYPICAL GAS TRAIN

**POWER VENTED**

**POWER VENTED**

**SIDEWALL VENTED GAS-FIRED WATER HEATERS**

**GENERAL NOTES**

1. For high-efficiency furnace, contractor has option of using combination vent/intake air kit (either wall or roof installation) as allowed by code.

2. Combustion air sizing: Free area of inlet and outlet shall be not less than 1 sq in./4000 Btu/hour or equipment rating for system shown. Alternate methods of combustion air ducting and sizing as approved by authority having jurisdiction.

3. These drawings are for reference only. Refer to state and local codes/ordinances and manufacturer's installation instructions for particular requirements governing maintenance, clearances, gas piping, combustion air, and venting.

American Gas Association
Richard J. Vitullo; Washington Grove, Maryland

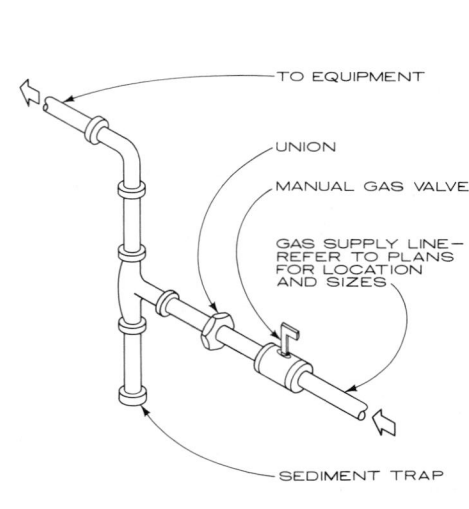

TO EQUIPMENT
UNION
MANUAL GAS VALVE
GAS SUPPLY LINE—REFER TO PLANS FOR LOCATION AND SIZES
SEDIMENT TRAP

**TYPICAL GAS TRAIN**

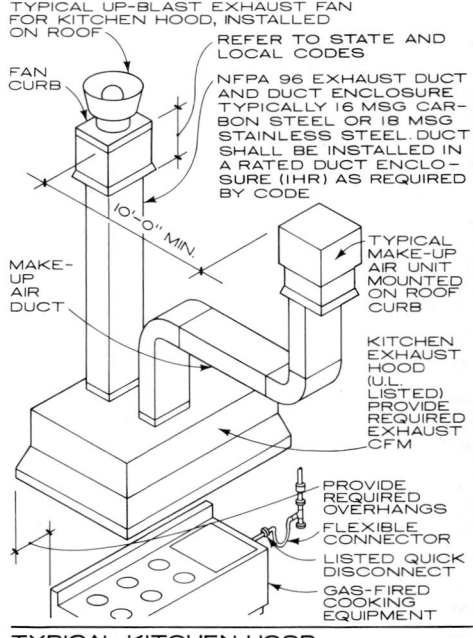

TYPICAL UP-BLAST EXHAUST FAN FOR KITCHEN HOOD, INSTALLED ON ROOF
REFER TO STATE AND LOCAL CODES
FAN CURB
NFPA 96 EXHAUST DUCT AND DUCT ENCLOSURE TYPICALLY 16 MSG CARBON STEEL OR 18 MSG STAINLESS STEEL. DUCT SHALL BE INSTALLED IN A RATED DUCT ENCLOSURE (1HR) AS REQUIRED BY CODE
10'-0" MIN.
MAKE-UP AIR DUCT
TYPICAL MAKE-UP AIR UNIT MOUNTED ON ROOF CURB
KITCHEN EXHAUST HOOD (U.L. LISTED) PROVIDE REQUIRED EXHAUST CFM
PROVIDE REQUIRED OVERHANGS
FLEXIBLE CONNECTOR
LISTED QUICK DISCONNECT
GAS-FIRED COOKING EQUIPMENT

**TYPICAL KITCHEN HOOD INSTALLATION**

15    **HEAT GENERATION**

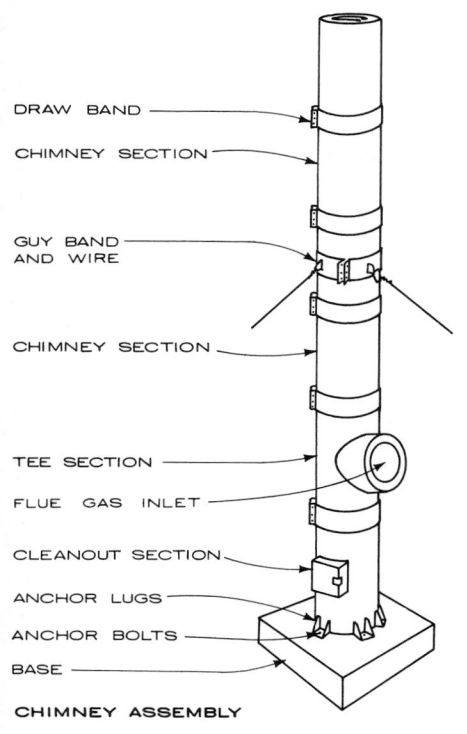

DRAW BAND
CHIMNEY SECTION
GUY BAND AND WIRE
CHIMNEY SECTION
TEE SECTION
FLUE GAS INLET
CLEANOUT SECTION
ANCHOR LUGS
ANCHOR BOLTS
BASE

**CHIMNEY ASSEMBLY**

**MEDIUM HEAT CHIMNEYS**

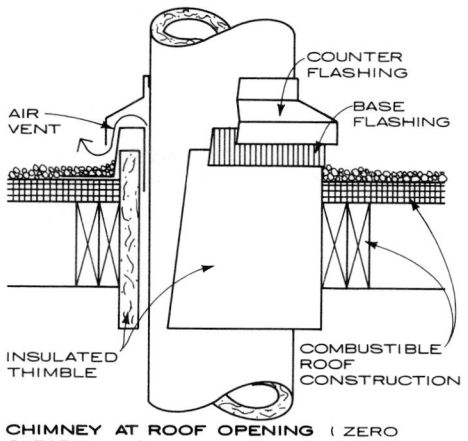

COUNTER FLASHING
BASE FLASHING
AIR VENT
INSULATED THIMBLE
COMBUSTIBLE ROOF CONSTRUCTION

**CHIMNEY AT ROOF OPENING** ( ZERO CLEARANCE )

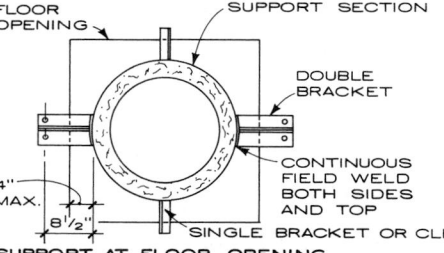

FLOOR OPENING
SUPPORT SECTION
DOUBLE BRACKET
4" MAX.
8 1/2"
CONTINUOUS FIELD WELD BOTH SIDES AND TOP
SINGLE BRACKET OR CLIP

**SUPPORT AT FLOOR OPENING**

## CHIMNEY CONSTRUCTION

The chimney should be supported on a foundation of masonry or reinforced concrete or other noncombustible material having a fire resistance rating of not less than 3 hr. When installed on an appliance, the chimney should be so supported as to not place excessive stress on the appliance. The base of the chimney should be secured to prevent movement of the chimney and anchor lugs should be used for this purpose whenever possible.

A cleanout section may be used in the chimney assembly but must not be used above the chimney inlet.

## CLEARANCES

Chimneys of the medium heat appliance or commercial-industrial incinerator type are not intended to be enclosed in walls of combustible materials. These chimneys should be placed in fire resistive or noncombustible shafts where they extend through any story of a building above that in which the connected appliance is located.

An enclosed chimney may be placed adjacent to walls of combustible material with the following minimum clearances:

    10 to 15 in. I.D. requires 16 in. clearance
    15 to 21 in. I.D. requires 18 in. clearance
    21 to 27 in. I.D. requires 20 in. clearance
    27 to 36 in. I.D. requires 22 in. clearance

Where the chimney passes through a roof of combustible material it shall be installed with an insulated thimble and flashing. This insulated thimble may be installed at zero inch clearance to combustibles.

The chimney should extend at least 3 ft above the highest point where it passes through the roof and 2 ft higher than any ridge within 10 ft.

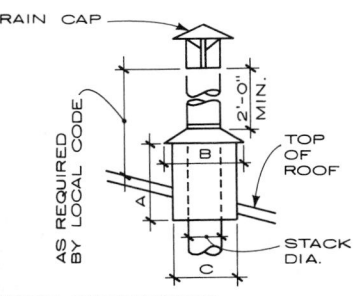

RAIN CAP
2'-0" MIN.
TOP OF ROOF
AS REQUIRED BY LOCAL CODE
STACK DIA.

**ROOF PENETRATION**

### STACK DIAMETER—SINGLE BOILER VENT OR STACK

| BOILER HORSE-POWER | STACK DIAMETER (IN.) | A (IN.) | B (IN.) | C (IN.) |
|---|---|---|---|---|
| 15–20 | 6 | 15 | 15 | 12 |
| 25–40 | 8 | 20 | 20 | 16 |
| 50–60 | 10 | 25 | 25 | 20 |
| 70–100 | 12 | 30 | 30 | 24 |
| 125–200 | 16 | 40 | 40 | 32 |
| 250–350 | 20 | 50 | 50 | 40 |
| 400–800 | 24 | 60 | 60 | 48 |

### STACK DIAMETER— MULTIPLE BOILERS: COMMON BREECHING AND STACK

| BOILER HORSE-POWER | MINIMUM STACK DIAMETER (IN.) | | | | | |
|---|---|---|---|---|---|---|
| | NUMBER OF BOILERS | | | | | |
| | 2 | | 3 | | 4 | |
| | 100 FT | 200 FT | 100 FT | 200 FT | 100 FT | 200 FT |
| 25–40 | 11 | 12 | 13 | 14 | 14 | 16 |
| 50–60 | 13 | 14 | 15 | 16 | 17 | 18 |
| 70–100 | 16 | 17 | 19 | 20 | 21 | 23 |
| 125–200 | 21 | 22 | 24 | 26 | 28 | 30 |
| 250–350 | 26 | 28 | 32 | 34 | 34 | 40 |
| 400–600 | 32 | 34 | 38 | 40 | 42 | 46 |

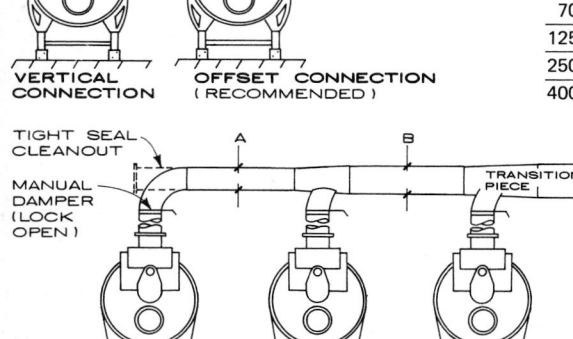

TIGHT SEAL CLEANOUT
STACK
CLEANOUT
DRAIN CONNECTION

**VERTICAL CONNECTION**   **OFFSET CONNECTION** ( RECOMMENDED )

TIGHT SEAL CLEANOUT
MANUAL DAMPER (LOCK OPEN)
A    B    C    D
TRANSITION PIECE
STACK
CLEANOUT
DRAIN CONNECTION

**MULTIPLE BOILERS WITH COMMON BREECHING**

**VENT STACKS**

## VENT STACKS

The purpose of a vent stack is to conduct the products of combustion to a point of safe discharge (atmosphere). Forced draft design eliminates the need for a stack designed to create a draft. An offset type of stack connection to the stub vent on the boiler is preferred. A direct vertical connection can also be made when boiler vent outlets can withstand the direct vertical load of the stack, including the effect of wind and guy wires.

## STACK CONSTRUCTION

The stack can be terminated several feet above the top of the roof. (State and local codes may govern the stack height above the roof.) If down drafts are unavoidable, the stack outlet can be provided with a ventilator. Minimum 12 gauge steel is recommended for stack sections. If the stack will be inaccessible, the use of a noncorrosive material (e.g., glass lining) should be considered.

A rain cap or hood should be used at the top of the stack to minimize the entrance of rain or snow.

### BREECHING DIAMETER— SINGLE AND MULTIPLE BOILERS

| BOILER HORSE-POWER | MINIMUM BREECHING DIAMETER (IN. OD) | | | |
|---|---|---|---|---|
| | A (IN.) 1 BOILER | B (IN.) 2 BOILERS | C (IN.) 3 BOILERS | D (IN.) 4 BOILERS |
| 15–20 | 6 | 8 | 9 | 9 |
| 25–40 | 8 | 10 | 11 | 12 |
| 50–60 | 10 | 12 | 14 | 15 |
| 70–100 | 12 | 15 | 17 | 18 |
| 125–200 | 16 | 20 | 22 | 24 |
| 250–350 | 20 | 25 | 28 | 30 |
| 400–600 | 24 | 30 | 33 | 36 |
| 700–800 | 24 | 34 | 38 | 42 |

Note: Stack diameter should be larger than breeching diameter.

Syska and Hennessy, Consulting Engineers; New York, New York

**HEAT GENERATION**    **15**

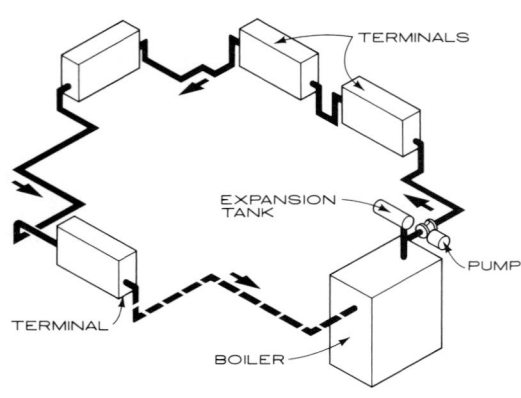

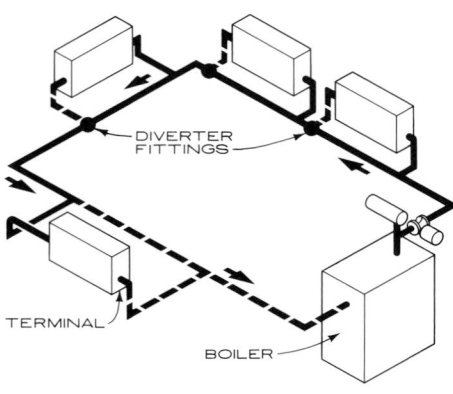

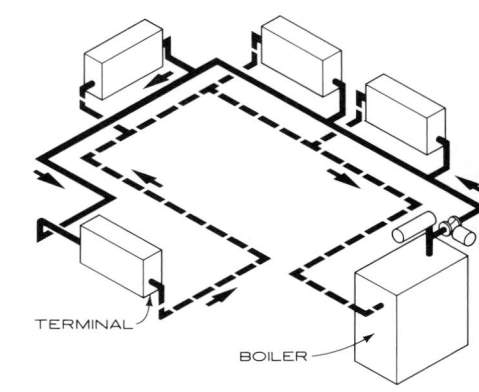

**SERIES SYSTEM**

(+) MINIMAL PIPING
(−) LIMITED INDIVIDUAL UNIT CONTROL

**ONE-PIPE SYSTEM**

(+) LESS PIPING THAN TWO-PIPE SYSTEM
(−) REQUIRED DIVERTER FITTINGS INCREASE RESISTANCE OF SYSTEM, LIMITING SYSTEM SIZE

**TWO-PIPE SYSTEM–DIRECT RETURN**

(+) CAN USE LESS PIPING THAN REVERSE RETURN SYSTEM, ESPECIALLY FOR LINEAR SYSTEM CONFIGURATIONS
(−) REQUIRES BALANCING DEVICES TO REGULATE FLOW THROUGH EACH TERMINAL

**HYDRONIC HEATING SYSTEM TYPES**

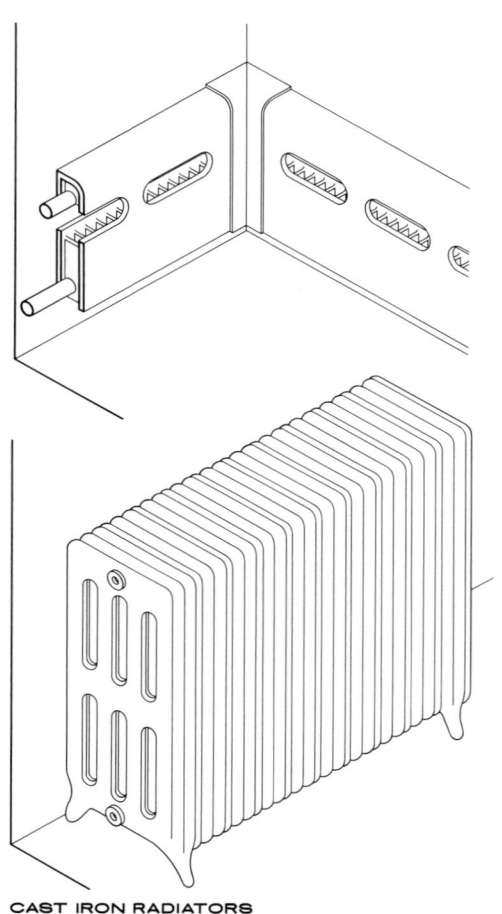

**CAST IRON RADIATORS**

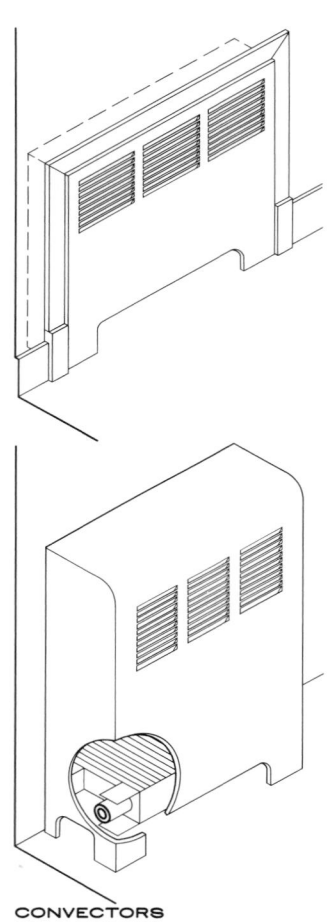

**CONVECTORS**

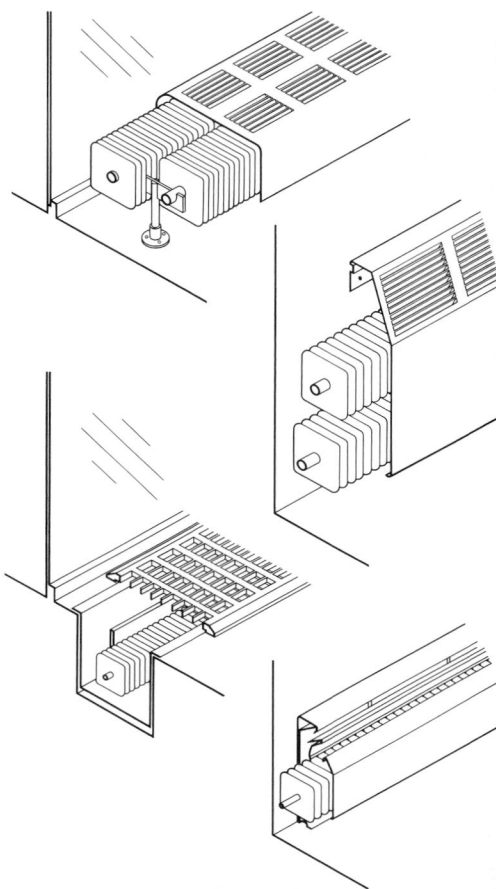

**FIN TUBE APPLICATIONS**

## COMPARATIVE SIZES AND OUTPUT CAPACITIES OF HYDRONIC HEATING TERMINAL UNITS

| UNIT TYPE | CAST IRON RADIATOR | STERLING CONVECTOR | VULCAN FIN TUBE RADIATORS | | RUNTAL STEEL RADIATORS | | | | |
|---|---|---|---|---|---|---|---|---|---|
| | | | FLOORLINE (BASEBOARD) | DURA-VANE | "H" PANEL | "V" PANEL | "R" COLUMN | "C" CONVECTOR | "G" GRILLE (GV AND GV-2) |
| Range of sizes | H 12'' to 3'-9'' L 3'-5'' to 8'-8'' D 4½'' to 1'-1½'' | H 1'-8'' to 5'-8'' L 1'-2'' to 3'-0'' D 4¼'' to 8¼'' | H 8'' to 1'-2'' L As required D 3½'' | H 7'' to 2'-0⁹⁄₁₆'' L As required D 4½'' to 5⁹⁄₁₆'' | H 2'' to 19'-6'' L 2¾'' to 8'-10⅝'' D 1⅝'' to 3⅜'' | H 2¾'' to 2'-5'' L 1'-7¼'' to 19'-6'' D 1⅝'' to 4¾'' | H 1'-3⅝'' to 13' L Up to 19'-6'' D 3¾'' to 6¼'' | H 2¾'' to 1'-4½'' L 1'-7¼'' to 19'-6'' D 1⅞'' to 1'-3¾'' | H 7⅞'' to 3'-11¼'' L 1'-7¾'' to 13'-1'-1½'' D 1¼'' to 2⅜'' |
| Range of output capacities | 110 to 250 Btu/sq ft/ hr per unit | Up to 28,000 Btu/hr per unit | Up to 1790 Btu/hr per linear foot | Up to 3180 Btu/ hr per linear foot | Up to 2943 Btu/ hr per element | Up to 4715 Btu/hr per linear foot | Up to 5354 Btu/ hr per element | Up to 7301 Btu/hr per linear foot | Up to 9473 Btu/hr per linear foot |

Eric J. Gastier; Darrel Downing Rippeteau Architects, PC; Washington, D.C.

**15 HEAT GENERATION**

TERMINAL
BOILER

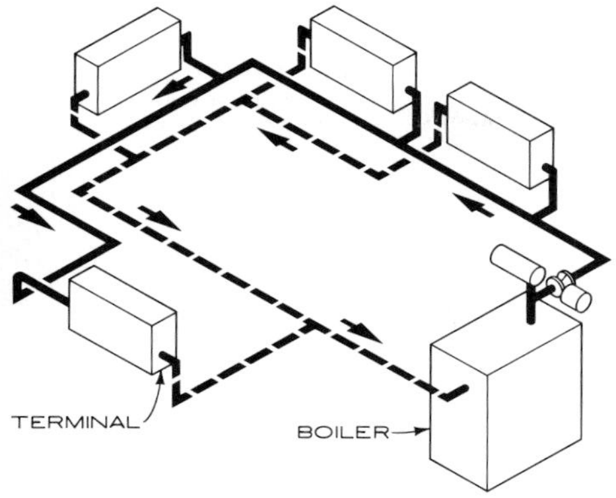

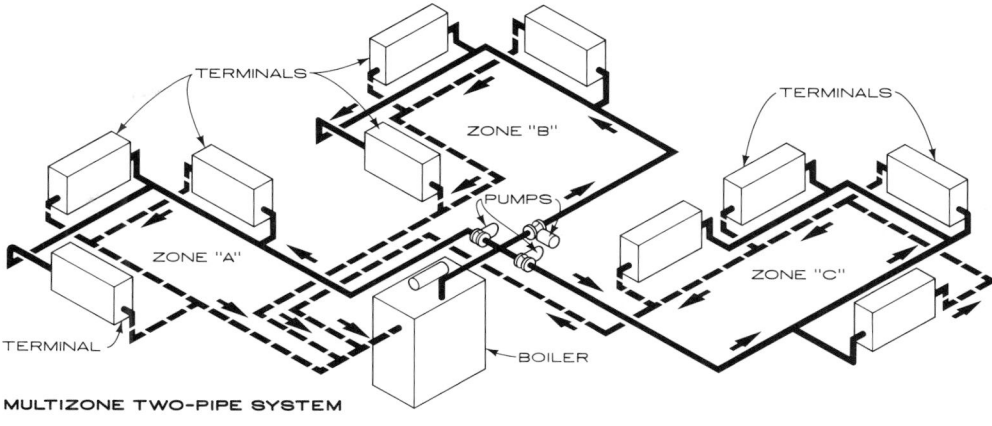

**TWO-PIPE SYSTEM-REVERSE RETURN**

(+) SIMPLIFIED BALANCING OF TERMINAL UNITS
(−) REQUIRES MAXIMUM PIPING FOOTAGE
(MOST BENEFICIAL WITH LARGE SYSTEMS)

TERMINALS
TERMINALS
ZONE "B"
PUMPS
ZONE "A"
ZONE "C"
TERMINAL
BOILER

**MULTIZONE TWO-PIPE SYSTEM**

(+) ALLOWS TEMPERATURES TO VARY BETWEEN ZONES, MAXIMIZING COMFORT AND ENERGY EFFICIENCY
(−) REQUIRES LARGE INITIAL EQUIPMENT COST
(NECESSARY FOR LARGE, MULTIUSE BUILDINGS)

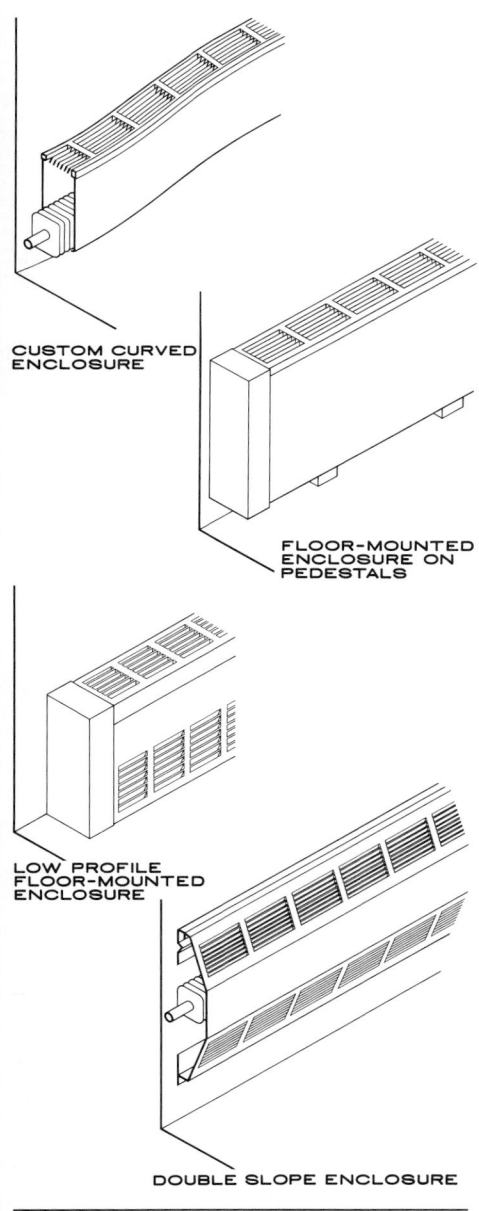

**CUSTOM CURVED ENCLOSURE**

**FLOOR-MOUNTED ENCLOSURE ON PEDESTALS**

**LOW PROFILE FLOOR-MOUNTED ENCLOSURE**

**DOUBLE SLOPE ENCLOSURE**

**VULCAN FIN TUBE RADIATORS**

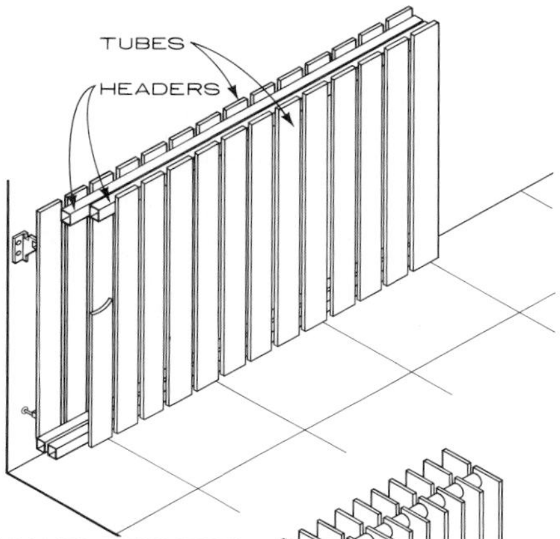

TUBES
HEADERS

**"H" PANEL RADIATOR**

TUBES
HEADER

**"V" PANEL RADIATOR**

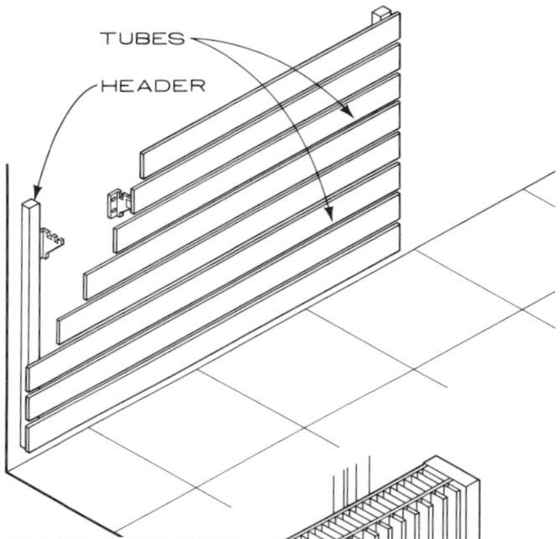

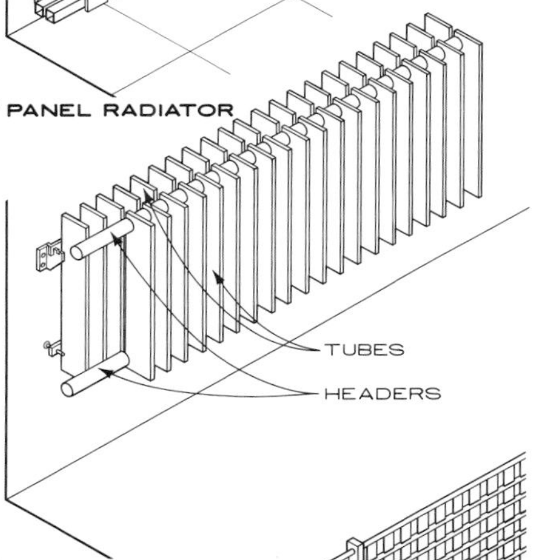

TUBES
HEADERS

**"R" COLUMN RADIATOR**

HEADER
LAMELLAE (OR FINS)
TUBES

**"C" CONVECTOR**

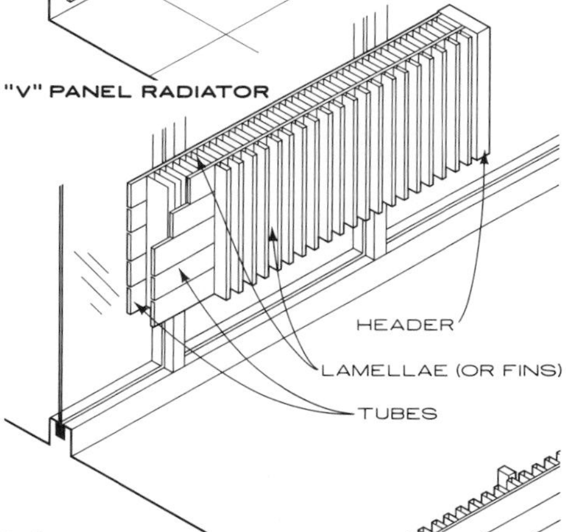

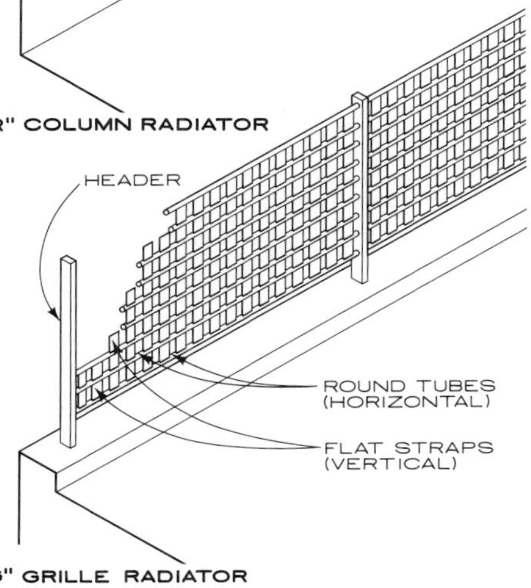

HEADER
ROUND TUBES (HORIZONTAL)
FLAT STRAPS (VERTICAL)

**"G" GRILLE RADIATOR**

LAMELLAE
TUBES

**"C" CONVECTOR**

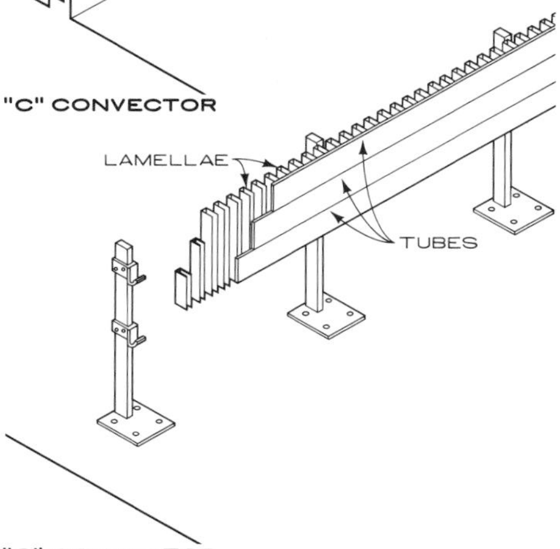

**RUNTAL STEEL RADIATORS**

Eric J. Gastier; Darrel Downing Rippeteau Architects, PC; Washington, D.C.

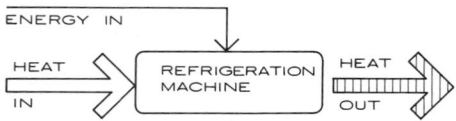

The basic refrigeration cycle performs one simple job; it moves heat from one place to another. Refrigerators move heat from the storage compartment to the surrounding room. Air-conditioners move heat from building rooms to the outside environment. Refrigeration equipment's efficiency is indicated by its Energy Efficiency Rating. EER is an index of the number of BTU's of heat movement accomplished per watt of electrical input energy. The higher the EER, the more efficient, and less costly it will be to operate a given piece of equipment.

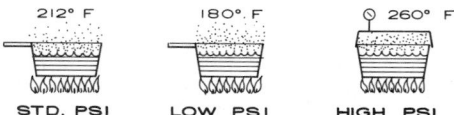

A large quantity of heat is required to boil or evaporate a liquid. This latent or hidden heat is the key to moving large quantities of heat with a small amount of refrigerant.

To move heat from an area of low temperature to an area of high temperature (e.g., a building at 75°F to its environment at 95°F) refrigeration equipment needs to change boiling temperature of the refrigerant. This is accomplished by changing the pressure on the refrigerant.

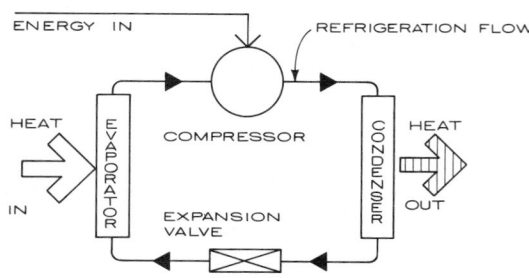

The basic refrigeration cycle includes an evaporator coil which absorbs heat from its surroundings as a refrigerant evaporates internally. The refrigerant vapor is then drawn into a compressor where its pressure and boiling (or condensing) temperature are increased. The refrigerant vapor is then discharged into a condenser coil where it gives up the latent heat absorbed in the evaporator and returns to a liquid state. Finally, liquid refrigerant circulates through an expansion valve where pressure and evaporation temperature are reduced, and the cycle is repeated.

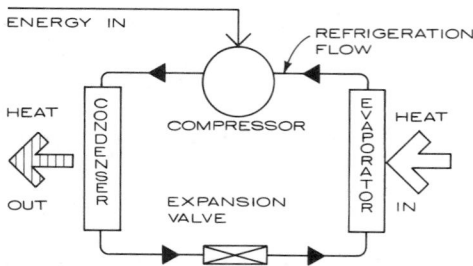

The compressive refrigeration cycle may be reversed to extract heat from a low temperature source (such as outside air) and reject that heat at higher temperature to heat a building. The basic equipment is unchanged with the exception of a four-way reversing valve and controls which permit the condenser and evaporator to exchange functions. The heat pump is more efficient than electrical resistance heat. Its efficiency, of course, is a function of heat source temperature.

F. J. Trost; Texas A & M University; College Station, Texas

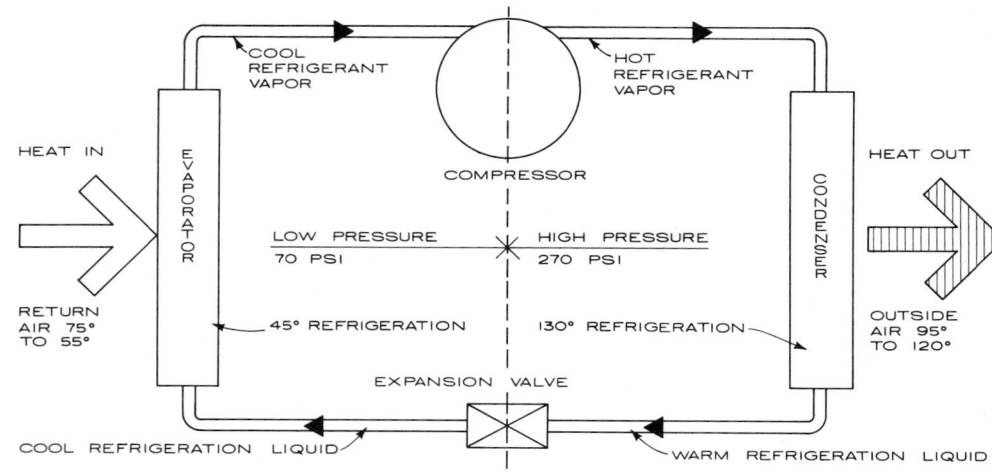

**TYPICAL SYSTEM TEMPERATURES AND PRESSURES**

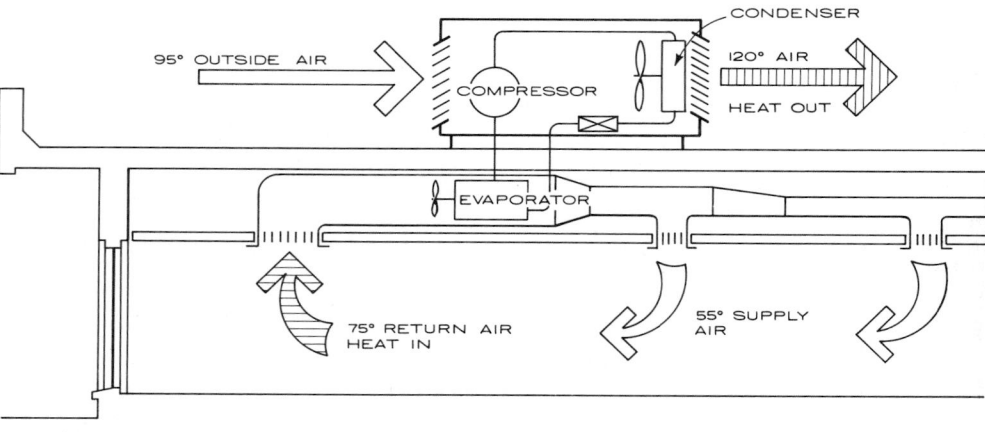

**TYPICAL ROOM APPLICATION**

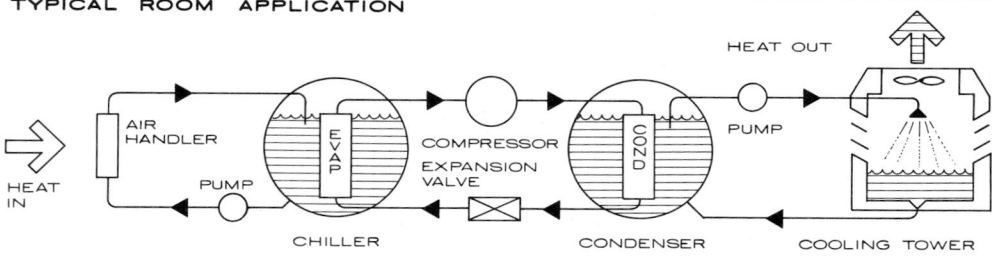

**CHILLER AND COOLING TOWER**

In large buildings it is impractical to move heat with air only, since duct size would be excessive. Therefore, a chiller (water tank) is added to the evaporator, and chilled water is circulated to air handling units throughout the building. Cooling towers are typically installed in such large systems to increase efficiency. Air-conditioning equipment rejecting heat to 85°F cooling tower water will require less input energy than the same equipment rejecting heat to 95°F outside air.

A second refrigeration cycle, the absorption cycle, uses a heat source and an absorbent to move heat. This requires electric energy only for pumps.

The absorber and generator perform the same function as the compressor (see above); and the cycle operates under high vacuum. Generally speaking, absorption systems are less efficient than compressive systems and are a wise choice only when waste heat is available for input energy such as system operation on emergency power during electric power outage.

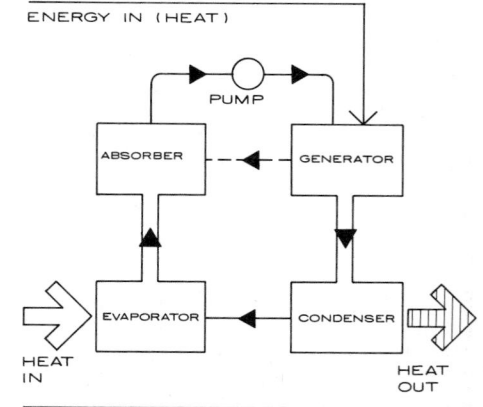

**ABSORPTION CYCLE**

**REFRIGERATION**

### GENERAL NOTES

Chilled water is the most common medium for transferring heat from any type of cooling equipment, such as cooling coils and heat exchangers, to some source of refrigeration.

A chilled water system is a closed circuit system that recirculates water between a mechanical refrigeration water chilling unit and remote cooling equipment, usually operating with water temperatures in the range between 40 and 55°F. There are three types of refrigeration units used in chilled water systems.

1. Centrifugal chiller with electric motor or steam turbine drive.
2. Reciprocating chiller, with electric motor drive.
3. Steam absorption chiller.

When a chilled water piping system also is used to circulate hot water for winter heating, it is called a dual temperature water system. The design water temperature of chilled water systems usually falls in a rather narrow range because of the necessity for dehumidification and to avoid a possible freeze-up in the chiller. Chilled water supply temperatures usually range from 42° to 60° F for normal comfort applications.

Design flow rates depend on the type of terminal apparatus and the supply temperature. In general, a higher temperature rise (or a greater temperature difference between supply and return temperatures) reduces the initial cost and the operating cost of the distribution system and pumps required and increases the efficiency of the chillers. In a given chilled water system, the selection of the design flow rate and the supply temperature, therefore, are closely related.

Although lower chilled water temperatures permit higher rises (or larger temperature difference) lower chiller efficiencies result.

Water treatment may be required in chilled water systems to control corrosion rate, scaling, or algae growth.

Layout of piping systems for chilled water distribution varies greatly depending on system capacity, extent of distribution, type of terminals used, and control scheme to be employed.

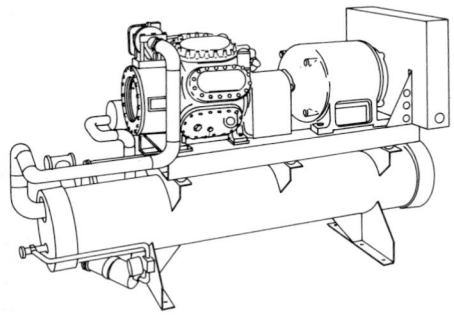

**NOTE**
A typical reciprocating package chiller, ideally suited to smaller jobs requiring less than 200 tons cooling.

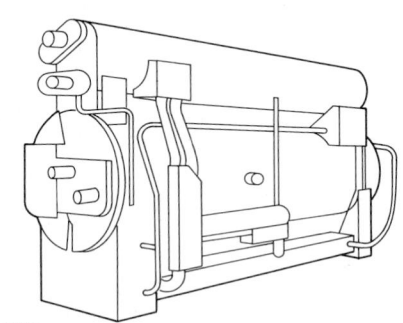

**NOTE**
A two-stage absorption chiller, steam powered for efficient production of 200 to 600 tons of cooling.

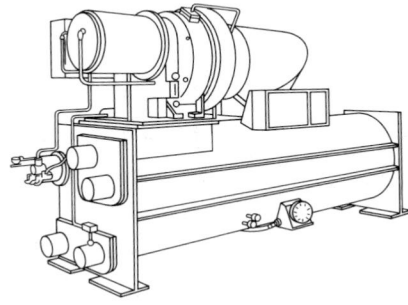

**NOTE**
A centrifugal chiller with a flooded cooler and condenser within a single outer shell. This low pressure unit is typical in ranges of 100 to 400 tons.

### PACKAGE WATER CHILLERS

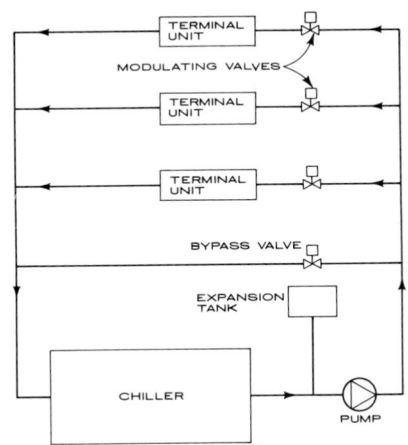

**FIGURE I**
**ELEMENTARY CHILLED WATER SYSTEM**

**NOTE**
A chilled water system basically consists of a refrigeration water chilling unit, a chilled water recirculating pump, terminal cooling equipment, and an expansion tank. A chilled water bypass valve may be required in systems with two-way modulating valve control at the terminal units. As the cooling load on the terminal equipment decreases, the modulating valve closes and reduces the flow through the terminal. When the water flow through the terminal units is significantly throttled, the bypass valve opens gradually to prevent system pressure buildup and to maintain the water flow required for the proper operation of the chiller.

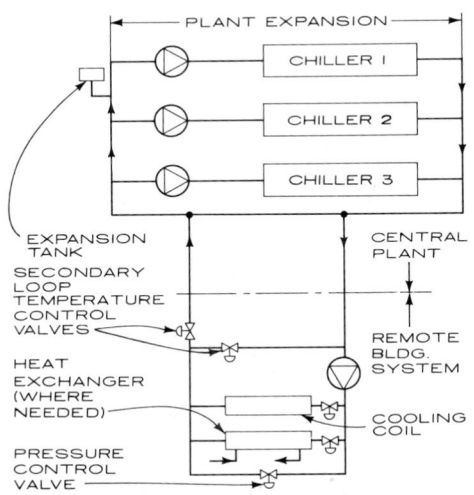

**FIGURE 2**
**PRIMARY/SECONDARY CHILLED WATER PUMPING AND DISTRIBUTION SYSTEM**

**NOTE**
In large campus type applications, the chilled water system consists of multiple chillers and primary and secondary system pumps. The terminal cooling equipment may be chilled water cooling coil of a central air-conditioning unit, closed loop heat exchanger or any other secondary or terminal cooling water system.

The primary loop does not require a pressure control device. The secondary loop pressure control valve operates as described under Elementary Chilled Water System.

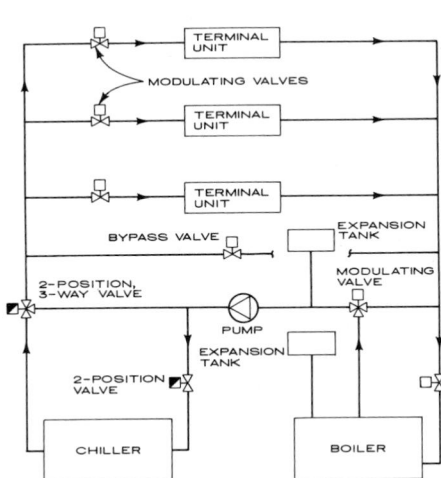

**FIGURE 3**
**TWO-PIPE DUAL TEMPERATURE SYSTEM**

**NOTE**
In a two-pipe dual temperature system hot water is circulated through the terminal units during cold weather and chilled water is circulated during the hot weather. The distribution system may be divided into zones, each of which is capable of changeover from heating to cooling, independent of the other zones.

When the hot and chilled water supply to each terminal unit is in two separate pipes, but the return is in a common pipe, the system is called a three-pipe system. In a four-pipe system, separate supply and return mains for both hot and chilled water are run to each terminal unit.

Joseph R. Loring & Associates, Inc., Consulting Engineers; New York, New York

## GENERAL

The process of removing heat from a refrigerant is called condensing. It is during the condensing process, in a refrigerant cycle, that the refrigerant rejects heat absorbed during the evaporation and compression processes, is reconverted to a liquid state, and becomes ready to repeat the cycle.

To convert the refrigerant from gaseous to liquid state heat exchangers called condensers are used. Air cooled and water cooled condensers are the predominant types used in the building construction industry.

In the less than 50 ton capacity range, water cooled condensers are favored mostly where city water or other water sources such as lake, river, or well are available for once-through use without recirculation of water.

Where water is scarce, as well as in computer rooms and other special air-conditioning applications where year-round temperature and humidity control is required, dry coolers of up to 25 ton capacity are normally used. Where winter ambient is below the water freezing temperature, glycol is added to the condenser water. The heat rejection to the outdoor air is by sensible heat transfer, which is dependent on the dry bulb temperature of the air.

In refrigeration systems larger than 50 ton capacity, water cooled condensers are used to cool the recirculating condenser water. Both the closed circuit evaporative cooler and the cooling tower operate on the principle of evaporative cooling, which is dependent on the wet bulb temperature of the air. The closed circuit evaporative coolers are available in sizes up to 300 tons, and are used when contamination of the condenser water by its direct contact with the outdoor air cannot be tolerated.

Use of cooling tower is generally acceptable in most installations in the building construction industry. Temperature of the water leaving the cooling tower is approximately 7 to 10°F above the wet bulb temperature of the air flowing through the spray deck of the tower.

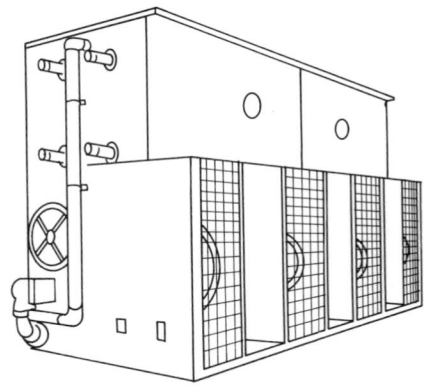

THE EVAPORATIVE CONDENSER combines the functions of a cooling tower and a water cooling condenser. Latent heat transfer is more effective as a means of heat dissipation. This permits a smaller sized unit than an equivalent tonnage air cooled unit, and considerable energy savings in fan horsepower.

Installations can be either indoors in an equipment room with appropriate ducts or outdoors ground mounted or mounted on a roof. When outdoors, adequate protection from freezing must be provided.

For sizing of condensing units, the manufacturers' rating is the only reliable method of determining the unit capacity.

Multiple evaporative condensers may be connected in parallel, or an evaporative condenser may be connected in parallel with a shell and tube condenser. Proper piping and traps must be installed in these cases to prevent unequal loading or overloading.

Two or more independent refrigeration circuits may be incorporated in a single evaporative condenser unit. With the proper circuiting arrangements, each may operate at a different suction and condensing temperature.

Anilkumar V. Patel; Joseph R. Loring & Associates, Inc., Consulting Engineers; New York, New York

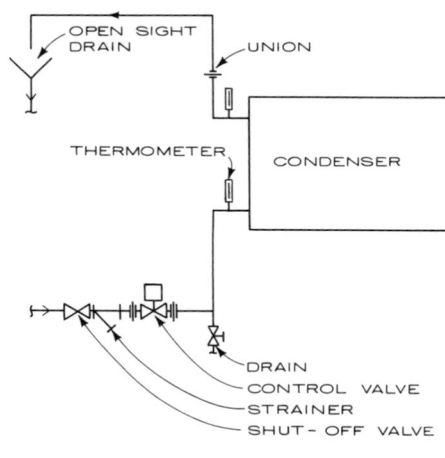

### WATER COOLED CONDENSER

For water cooled condenser using city, well, or river water, the return is run higher than the condenser so that the condenser is always full of water. Water flow through the condenser is regulated by a supply line control valve, which is actuated from condenser head pressure control to maintain a constant condensing temperature with variations in load. City water systems usually require check valves and open sight drains, as shown.

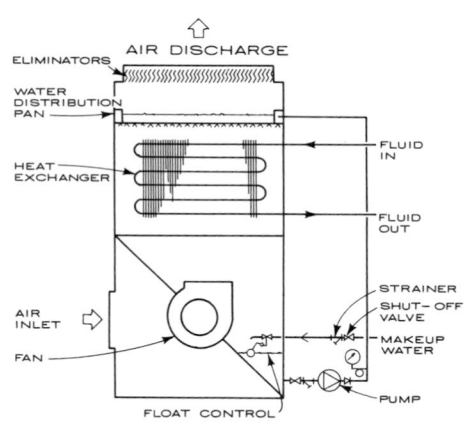

### EVAPORATIVE COOLER

The condenser water is circulated inside the tubes of the unit's heat exchanger. Heat flows from the condenser water through the heat exchanger tubes to the spray water outside, which is cascading downward over the tubes. Air is forced upward through the heat exchanger, evaporating a small percentage of the spray water, absorbing the latent heat of vaporization, and discharging the heat to the atmosphere.

The remaining water falls to the sump to be recirculated by the pump. The water consumed is the amount evaporated plus a small amount that is bled off to limit the concentration of impurities in the pan.

The condenser water circulates through the clean, closed loop of the heat exchanger and is never exposed to the airstream or the spray water outside the heat exchanger tubes.

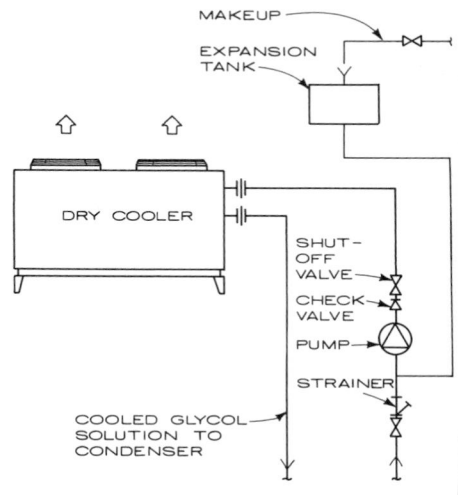

### DRY COOLER

The condenser water-glycol solution is circulated inside the finned tubes of the dry cooler's heat exchanger. Heat flows from the condenser water-glycol solution through the heat exchanger tube walls to the fins. Propeller fans draw air over the fins, which transfer its heat to the air passing over it.

An aquastat sensing the temperature of the solution that leaves the dry cooler cycles the fan(s) to maintain the desired temperature.

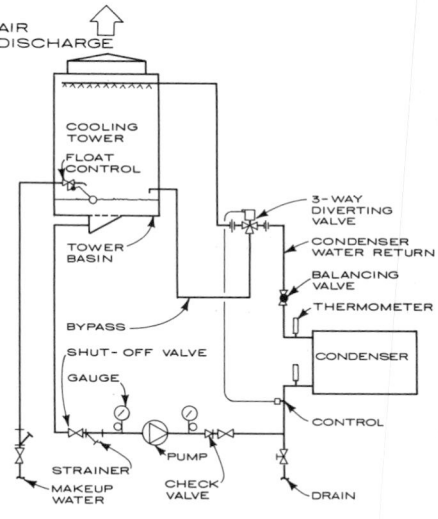

### COOLING TOWER

Water flows to the pump from the tower basin and is discharged under pressure to the condenser and back to the tower where it is cooled through the spray deck. Since it is usually desirable to maintain condenser water temperature above a predetermined minimum, return water is partially bypassed around the tower through a control valve to maintain desired supply water temperature.

In this condenser water system, air is continuously in contact with the water. Special consideration for chemical treatment and allowance for impurities, scale, and corrosion in condenser and piping system designs is then required.

Water flow quantity required depends on the refrigeration system employed and the available temperature of the condenser water. Lower condenser water supply temperature results in increased refrigeration machine efficiency.

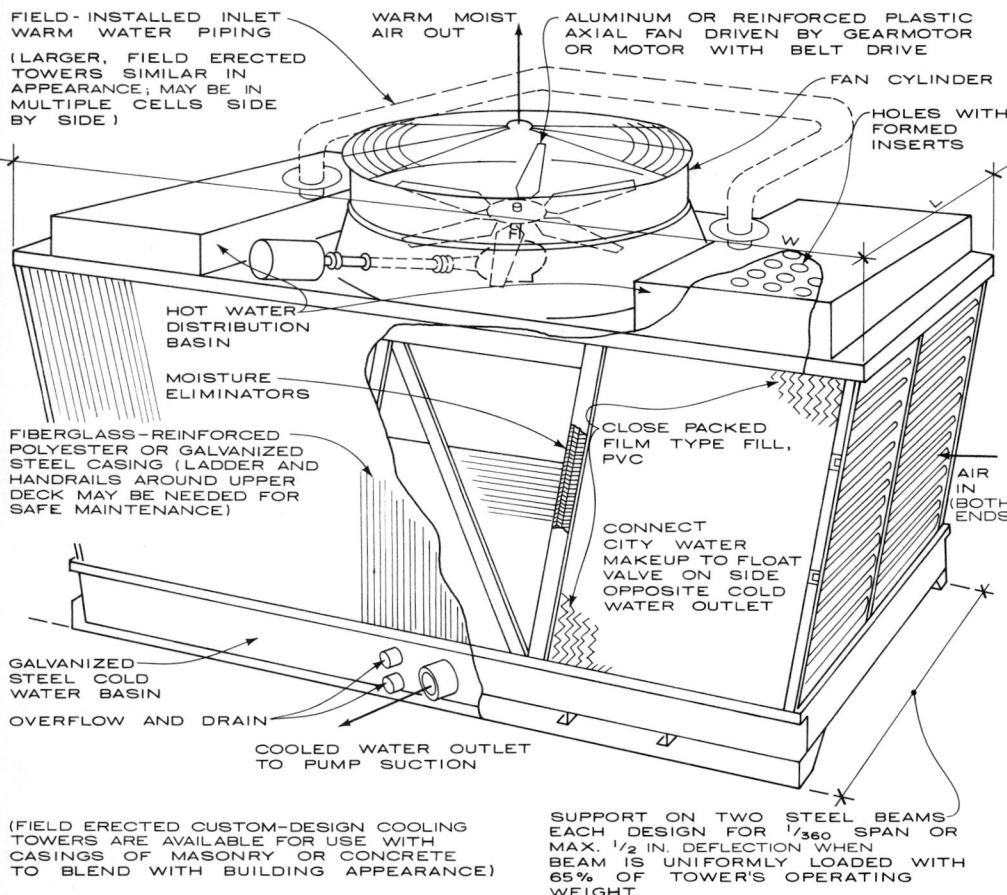

FIELD-INSTALLED INLET WARM WATER PIPING

(LARGER, FIELD ERECTED TOWERS SIMILAR IN APPEARANCE; MAY BE IN MULTIPLE CELLS SIDE BY SIDE)

WARM MOIST AIR OUT

ALUMINUM OR REINFORCED PLASTIC AXIAL FAN DRIVEN BY GEARMOTOR OR MOTOR WITH BELT DRIVE

FAN CYLINDER

HOLES WITH FORMED INSERTS

HOT WATER DISTRIBUTION BASIN

MOISTURE ELIMINATORS

FIBERGLASS-REINFORCED POLYESTER OR GALVANIZED STEEL CASING (LADDER AND HANDRAILS AROUND UPPER DECK MAY BE NEEDED FOR SAFE MAINTENANCE)

CLOSE PACKED FILM TYPE FILL, PVC

CONNECT CITY WATER MAKEUP TO FLOAT VALVE ON SIDE OPPOSITE COLD WATER OUTLET

AIR IN (BOTH ENDS)

GALVANIZED STEEL COLD WATER BASIN

OVERFLOW AND DRAIN

COOLED WATER OUTLET TO PUMP SUCTION

(FIELD ERECTED CUSTOM-DESIGN COOLING TOWERS ARE AVAILABLE FOR USE WITH CASINGS OF MASONRY OR CONCRETE TO BLEND WITH BUILDING APPEARANCE)

SUPPORT ON TWO STEEL BEAMS EACH DESIGN FOR 1/360 SPAN OR MAX. 1/2 IN. DEFLECTION WHEN BEAM IS UNIFORMLY LOADED WITH 65% OF TOWER'S OPERATING WEIGHT

## NOTES

1. Cooling towers cool water for reuse in refrigeration condensers or other heat exchangers. Standard ratings are in tons of refrigeration when cooling 3 gal/min per ton from 95 to 85°F with ambient air at 78°F wet bulb. Selection is based on performance at local outdoor design conditions. Frequently the local outdoor ambient wet bulb temperature used for selection is equal to or exceeded by 1% of summer hours.

2. Fans move air horizontally (crossflow) or up (counterflow) against water falling and wetting the fill or packing, to expose maximum water surface to the air. Reduced air flow reduces tower performance. Architectural enclosures should minimize obstruction to air flow.

3. Warm water is distributed at the top of the cooling tower by spray nozzles or basins with multiple orifices, and cooled water is collected in a basin at the bottom and pumped to condensers. Water is cooled by evaporating a very small portion. Water droplets may also be carried out by the air stream. Minerals and impurities present in all water increase concentration as pure water evaporates, so a little water is "bled" and chemicals are added to minimize scaling, corrosion, or biological fouling of condenser tubes. Towers for critical or large systems should be multicell for maintenance without shutdown.

4. Fan, motor, and water splashing noise may be a nuisance. Fan noise is reduced by two speed motors (about 8 dB at half speed, 15% power, and 60% capacity) and by intake and discharge attenuators (about 12 dB) with 10% power increase. Tower noise is louder in line with fan discharge and intake than in other directions. Each doubling of distance decreases noise about 6 dB. Barriers can reflect some noise from critical directions. Locate towers for free air movement. Avoid hot air recirculation, long piping from pumps and condensers, and inadequate substructures. Cooling towers should be located so that noise and water droplet carryover and fog at air discharge in cold weather will not be a nuisance. Consider seismic and wind load in anchoring tower to supports; towers are usually designed to withstand 30 psf wind load. Basins may be heated for winter use.

## CROSSFLOW INDUCED-DRAFT PACKAGED COOLING TOWER - 200 TO 700 TON CAPACITY PUMPS AVAILABLE IN DUAL CELLS WITH TWICE THE CAPACITY

NOTE
AVAILABLE IN SINGLE MODULES AS SKETCHED, OR END-TO-END OR BACK-TO-BACK DOUBLE INLET

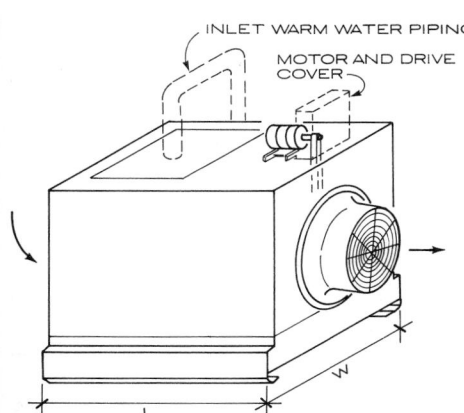

INLET WARM WATER PIPING

MOTOR AND DRIVE COVER

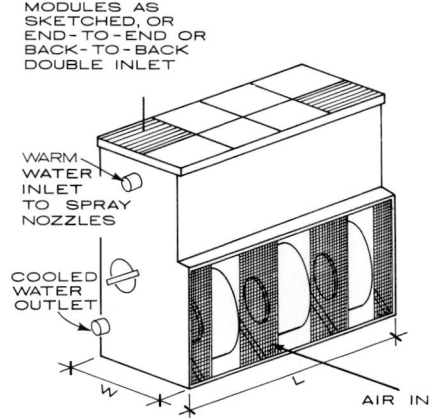

WARM WATER INLET TO SPRAY NOZZLES

COOLED WATER OUTLET

AIR IN

## ENCLOSURE CONSIDERATIONS

Provide liberal wall openings on air inlet sides and mount tower so that air outlet is at top of enclosure. Consider effect of wind on nearby structure and enclosure to minimize hot, moist discharge air from being recirculated into inlet.

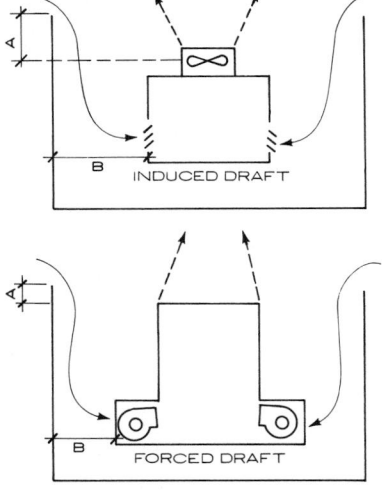

INDUCED DRAFT

FORCED DRAFT

A = Height of enclosure above tower outlet. Minimize or extend shroud up from tower.

B = If enclosure walls have no opening, horizontal distance from tower inlet must increase greatly.

(Power for fan must be increased.)

Consult cooling tower manufacturer for minimum "B" dimension.

### CROSSFLOW INDUCED DRAFT PACKAGE COOLING TOWER

| TONS 3 GPM/TON 95-85-78 | OVERALL DIMENSIONS (IN.) | | | OPERATING WEIGHT (LB.) | MOTOR (HP) |
|---|---|---|---|---|---|
| | L | W | HT. | | |
| 5 | 69 | 33 | 60 | 940 | 1/4 |
| 25 | 75 | 46 | 80 | 1600 | 1 |
| 50 | 84 | 64 | 92 | 2500 | 3 |
| 100 | 93 | 100 | 92 | 4200 | 5 |
| 150 | 100 | 144 | 112 | 8000 | 7½ |

### COUNTERFLOW FORCED DRAFT PACKAGE COOLING TOWER

| TONS 3 GPM/TON 95-85-78 | OVERALL DIMENSIONS (IN.) | | | OPERATING WEIGHT (LB.) | MOTOR (HP) |
|---|---|---|---|---|---|
| | L | W | HT. | | |
| 20 | 36 | 36 | 78 | 950 | 2 |
| 50 | 72 | 36 | 96 | 1700 | 7½ |
| 150 | 144 | 56 | 122 | 4800 | 20 |
| 400 | 140 | 118 | 192 | 14,000 | 50 |

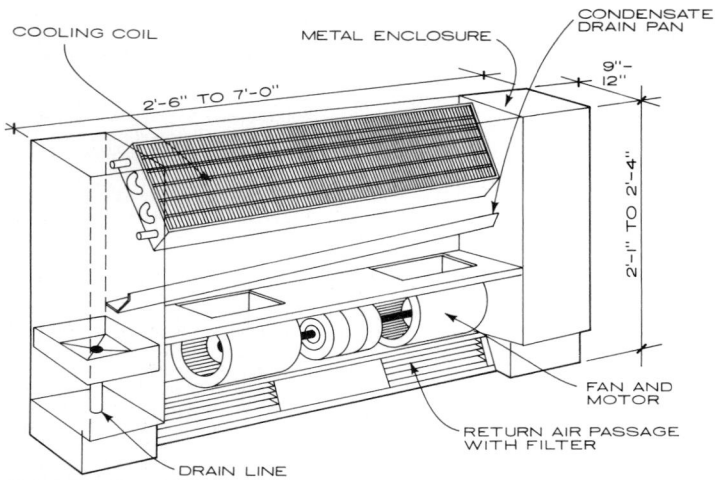

STANDARD FAN COIL UNIT

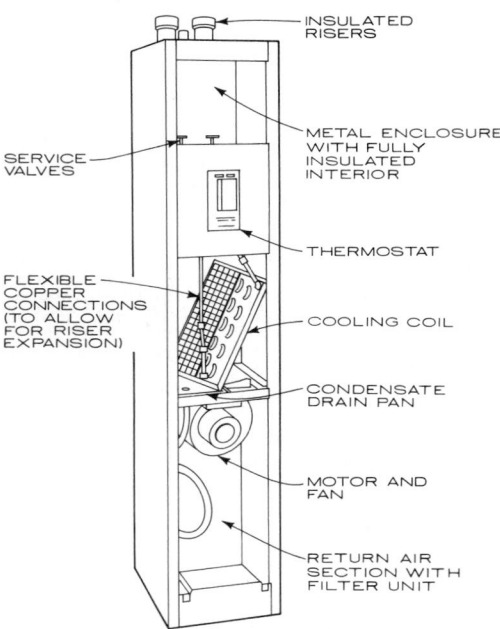

STANDARD HIGHRISE UNIT

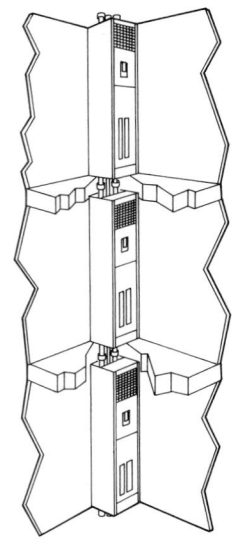

HIGHRISE APPLICATION

**NOTE**

Highrise corner units can be furred into the walls of the room. They minimize the piping from floor to floor since they are stacked and directly connected to the units above and below for water supply, returns, and drains.

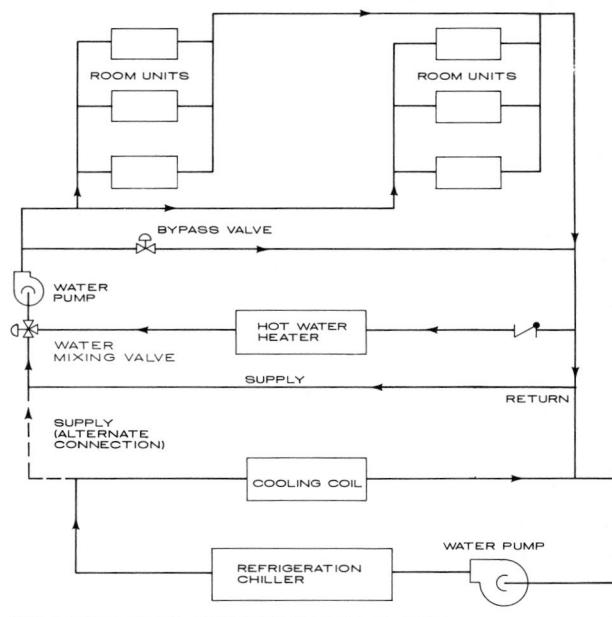

TWO-PIPE (DUAL TEMPERATURE) SYSTEM

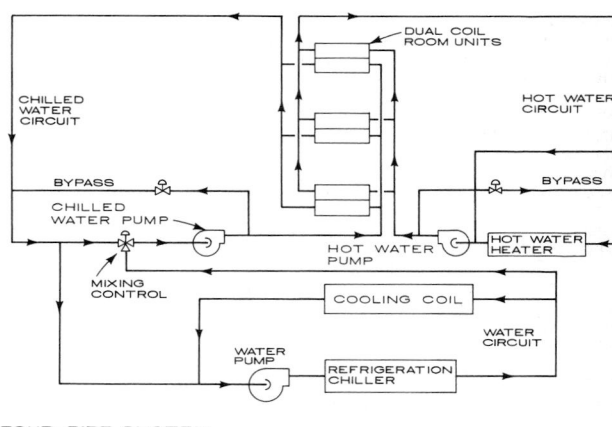

FOUR-PIPE SYSTEM

**PIPING SYSTEMS**

**NOTES**

Chilled water terminals are fan coil units used to dehumidify and cool the airstream injected into the conditioned space.

The typical fan coil unit consists of a finned tube chilled water coil, a fan used to circulate air over the coil and discharge cool air into the conditioned space, a drip pan to collect condensate from the dehumidified air and drain line to transport the condensate away from the fan coil unit.

Fan coil systems are classified into two major groups:

1. A TWO-PIPE SYSTEM uses a single supply pipe (hot or cold depending on the season) and a single return pipe, in a secondary water circuit. Chilled water is introduced into the circuit directly or indirectly from another circuit. If the terminal unit is to provide heat, a hot water, steam, or electric heat exchanger is incorporated into the loop. Direct introduction of hot water from a primary circuit is also employed. The water coil output of each terminal unit is controlled by a local space thermostat.

2. The FOUR-PIPE SYSTEM provides independent sources of heating and cooling to each room unit through separate supply and return chilled water pipes and separate supply and return hot water pipes. The terminal units usually have two separate water coils as well. Local thermostats control the volume of water supplied to each unit.

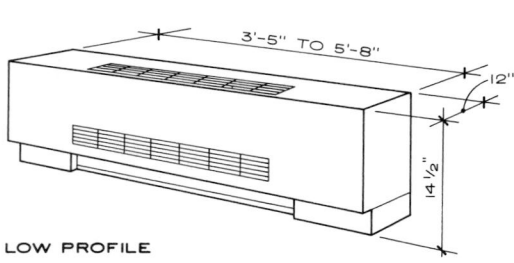

LOW PROFILE

**NOTE**

A low profile fan coil unit is available for installation along window walls, below chalkboards, or in lobbies and hallways where appearance is important. They normally stand free from the wall, with clearance behind the unit for draperies.

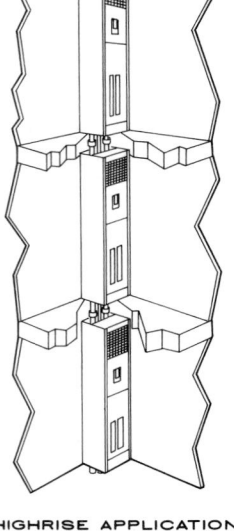

FURRED-IN UNIT

**NOTE**

Furred-in units can be mounted where convenient in the room. They can use ducts to bring in outside air and can be mounted in wall alcoves or ceiling spaces. A removable front panel is needed to conceal the unit and provide complete access to internal components.

## AIR CONDITIONING IN COMPUTER ROOMS

Computers generate great quantities of heat in concentrated areas. To assure proper operation, a precise temperature and humidity environment is required. The range of control may be as narrow as 72° ± 2°F temperature and 50% humidity ±5%.

### TYPES OF SYSTEMS

Spot Coolers: Direct forced air, located at ceiling in return air plenum or on floor. Short ducting can be used. Capacity: 1 to 3½ tons.

Small System Local Units: Forced air can be used as direct spot units, ducted or for pressurized raised floor. Capacity: 3 to 5 tons.

Large System Local Units: Forced air to be used with pressurized raised floor installation. Capacity 6 to 25 tons.

Mainframe Cooling Systems: Independently generated chilled water circulated to computer's Coolant Distribution Unit (CDU) (an intertwined coiled heat exchanger which distributes special coolant directly to the computer in a closed loop system). Capacity: 2½ to 15 tons.

### METHODS OF HEAT REJECTION

Self-Contained Air Cooled: Uses air within building return air plenum, limited to smaller capacity units.

External Air Cooled: Uses outdoor condenser unit and refrigerant lines generally limited to 100 ft above, 30 ft below, or 200 total ft from computer room to outdoor unit.

Water Cooled: Uses closed loop condenser water pumped to external cooling tower to remove heat from condenser within computer room fan coil unit. Cooling tower can be a larger distance from the computer room.

Glycol Cooled: Uses closed loop glycol to carry rejected heat to external dry cooler—allows greater separation of computer room from outside air. With additional coils, the system can provide "free cooling" during colder weather.

Chilled Water: Chilled water pumped from remote chilled water plant to local fan coil unit.

Combination Unit: May use 2 or more means of heat rejection to service the system during different hours of operation or as a backup system in case of primary system failure.

### PLANNING PROCEDURE

1. Determine the location of the computer room within the project building.
2. Evaluate the availability of building services and systems, mechanical chases, and electrical power capacities.
3. Determine the overall heat load and plan size of system with client and engineer.
4. Use qualified engineers to design and engineer the systems, supervise all testing and certifications.
5. Detail the construction of walls, ceiling, and floors to provided a complete "vapor seal."
6. Evaluate energy efficiency ratios of various kinds of equipment proposed.
7. Select the system most appropriate for the conditions and requirements of the project.

### RULES OF THUMB FOR COOLING LOAD ESTIMATES

| | |
|---|---|
| Room design conditions | |
| Temperature | 72° ± 2°/F |
| Relative humidity | 50% ± 5% RH |
| Sensible heat ratio | |
| Sensible heat gain | 0.90–0.98 |
| Total heat gain | |
| Load density (sq ft/ton) | 50–100 |
| Air quantity (CFM/ton) | 550–650 |
| Ventilation rate (CFM/ person) | 10–15 max. |
| Humidification (lb moisture/ 100 CFM of outside air) | 3 |

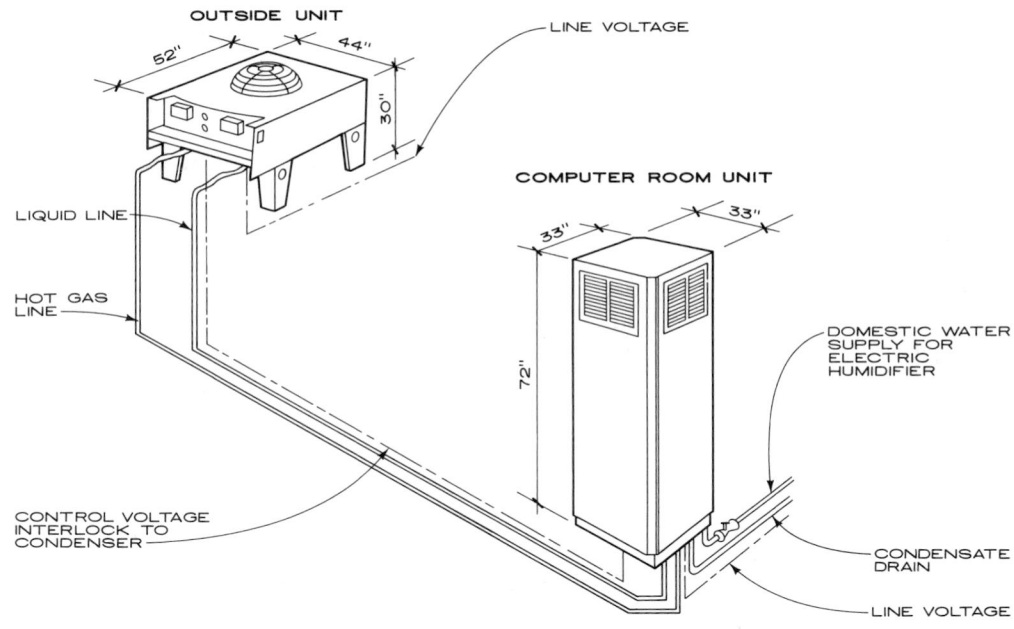

SMALL SYSTEM UNIT WITH OUTSIDE AIR COOLED HEAT REJECTION

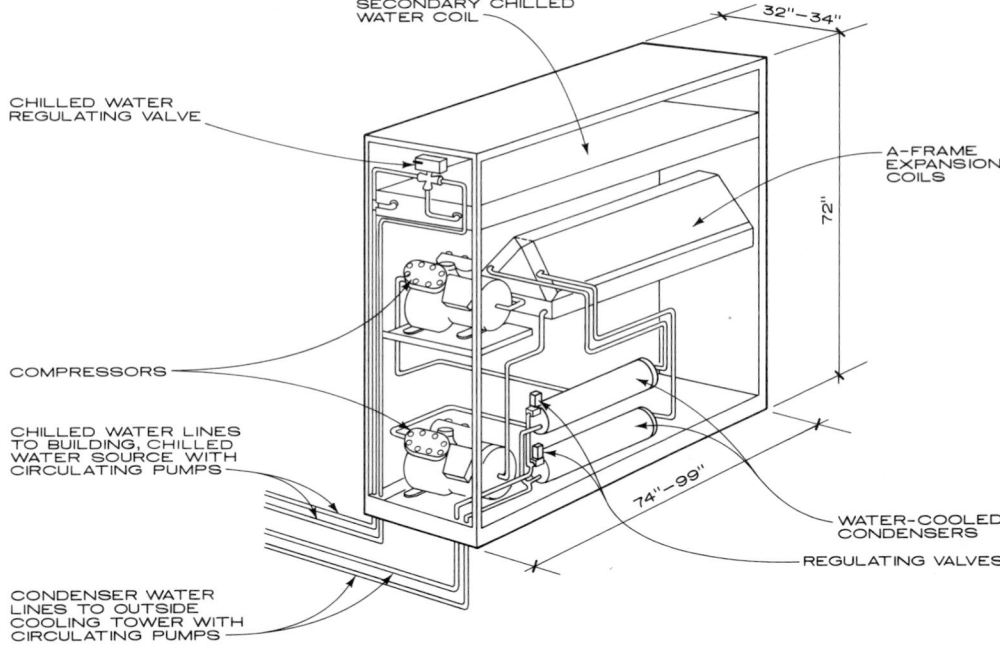

LARGE FORCED AIR SYSTEM WITH COMBINED HEAT REJECTION SYSTEMS

COMPUTER ROOM COOLING UNITS

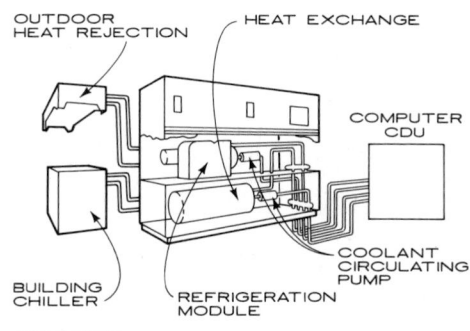

SELF-CONTAINED AIR COOLED HEAT REJECTION

SPOT COOLER

COMBINED HEAT REJECTION

MAINFRAME COOLING SYSTEM

William R. Arnquist, AIA; Donna Vaughan & Associates, Inc.; Dallas, Texas

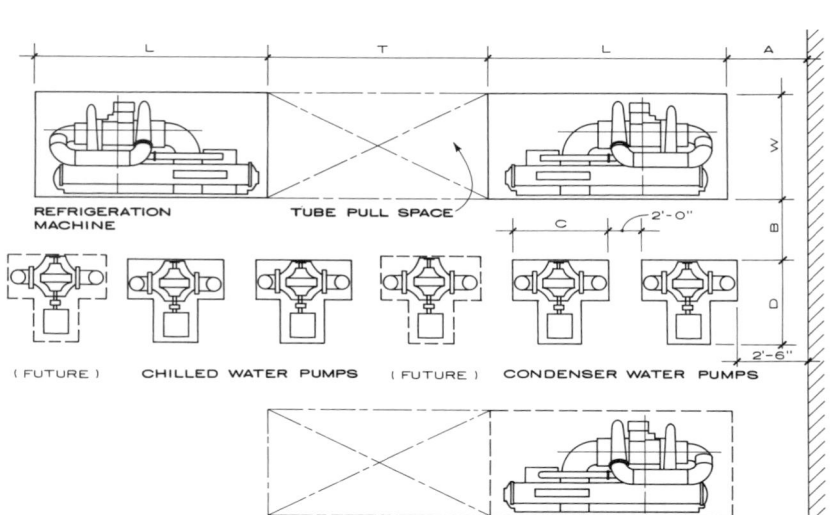

### GENERAL

The capacity of each refrigeration machine is equal to 50% of the peak cooling load.

Each water pump provides the flow requirement of one refrigeration machine. Therefore, one pair of condenser and chilled water pumps is needed for each machine.

The cooling tower may be located on the roof of the refrigeration equipment room or on the ground adjacent to the equipment room. When located on ground, the condenser water outlet(s) on the cooling tower must be not less than 5 ft above the equipment room floor elevation for proper functioning of condenser water pumps.

### EXPANSION OF EQUIPMENT

For operational flexibility of a refrigeration plant, the size of the future refrigeration machine is generally planned to be the same as of the present machines. It may be economically advantageous to oversize some portions of the chilled and condenser waterpipes to handle the future flow rates.

Provision must also be made for expansion of the cooling tower capacity when the future refrigeration machine is installed.

### REFRIGERATION EQUIPMENT ROOM SPACE REQUIREMENTS

| EQUIPMENT (TONS) | DIMENSIONS | | | | | | | | MINIMUM ROOM HEIGHT |
|---|---|---|---|---|---|---|---|---|---|
| | L | W | HEIGHT | T | A | B | C | D | |
| **RECIPROCATING MACHINES** | | | | | | | | | |
| Up to 50 | 10'-0'' | 3'-0'' | 6'-0'' | 8'-6'' | 3'-6'' | 3'-6'' | 4'-0'' | 3'-0'' | 11'-0'' |
| 50 to 100 | 12'-0'' | 3'-0'' | 6'-0'' | 9'-0'' | 3'-6'' | 3'-6'' | 4'-0'' | 3'-6'' | 11'-0'' |
| **CENTRIFUGAL MACHINES** | | | | | | | | | |
| Up to 120 | 17'-0'' | 6'-0'' | 7'-0'' | 16'-6'' | 3'-6'' | 3'-6'' | 4'-6'' | 4'-0'' | 11'-6'' |
| 120 to 225 | 17'-0'' | 6'-0'' | 7'-0'' | 16'-6'' | 3'-6'' | 3'-6'' | 4'-6'' | 4'-0'' | 11'-6'' |
| 225 to 350 | 17'-0'' | 6'-6'' | 7'-6'' | 17'-6'' | 3'-6'' | 3'-6'' | 5'-0'' | 5'-0'' | 11'-6'' |
| 350 to 550 | 17'-0'' | 8'-0'' | 8'-0'' | 16'-6'' | 3'-6'' | 3'-6'' | 6'-0'' | 5'-6'' | 12'-0'' |
| 550 to 750 | 17'-6'' | 9'-0'' | 10'-6'' | 17'-0'' | 3'-6'' | 3'-6'' | 6'-0'' | 5'-6'' | 14'-0'' |
| 750 to 1500 | 21'-0'' | 15'-0'' | 11'-0'' | 20'-0'' | 3'-6'' | 3'-6'' | 7'-6'' | 6'-0'' | 15'-0'' |
| **STEAM ABSORPTION MACHINES** | | | | | | | | | |
| Up to 200 | 18'-6'' | 9'-6'' | 12'-0'' | 18'-0'' | 3'-6'' | 3'-6'' | 4'-6'' | 4'-0'' | 15'-0'' |
| 200 to 450 | 21'-6'' | 9'-6'' | 12'-0'' | 21'-0'' | 3'-6'' | 3'-6'' | 5'-0'' | 5'-0'' | 15'-0'' |
| 450 to 550 | 23'-6'' | 9'-6'' | 12'-0'' | 23'-0'' | 3'-6'' | 3'-6'' | 6'-0'' | 5'-6'' | 15'-0'' |
| 550 to 750 | 26'-0'' | 10'-6'' | 13'-0'' | 25'-6'' | 3'-6'' | 3'-6'' | 6'-0'' | 5'-6'' | 16'-0'' |
| 750 to 1000 | 30'-0'' | 11'-0'' | 14'-0'' | 29'-6'' | 3'-6'' | 3'-6'' | 7'-0'' | 6'-0'' | 17'-6'' |

### REFRIGERATION ROOM LAYOUT

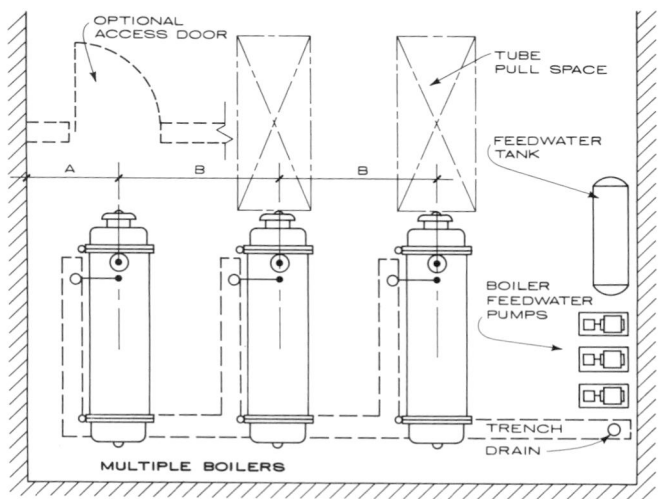

### ROOM DIMENSIONS

Dimension A allows for a minimum 3 ft 6 in. aisle between the water column on the boiler and the wall. Dimension B between boilers allows for a clear aisle of:

3'-6''— 15–200 hp
4'-0''—250–350 hp
5'-0''—400–800 hp

The shortest boiler room length is obtained by allowing for possible future tube replacement (from front or rear of boiler) through a window or doorway. Allowance is only made for minimum door swing at each end of the boiler.

### AIR SUPPLY

Two permanent air supply openings on opposite walls of the boiler room are recommended. These openings should be located below a height of 7 ft with a total clear area of at least 1 sq ft. Air supply openings can be louvered for weather protection.

Size the openings by using the following formula:

$$\text{area (sq ft)} = \frac{CFM}{FPM}$$

Amount of air required (CFM):

Combustion air—max. boiler HP x 2 CMF/BHP

Ventilation air—max. boiler HP x 2 CFM/BHP

NOTE: a total of 10 CFM/BHP applies up to 1000 ft elevation. Add 3% more per 1000 ft of added elevation.

Air velocity required (FPM):

Up to 7 ft height— 250 FPM
Above 7 ft height— 500 FPM
Supply air duct to boiler—1000 FPM

### BOILER ROOM SPACE REQUIREMENTS

| BOILER HP | 15–40 | 50–100 | 125–200 | 250–350 | 400–800 |
|---|---|---|---|---|---|
| Dimension A | 5'-9'' | 6'-6'' | 6'-10'' | 7'-9'' | 8'-6'' |
| Dimension B | 7'-5'' | 8'-9'' | 9'-7'' | 11'-9'' | 14'-3'' |

### BOILER ROOM LAYOUT

Joseph R. Loring & Associates, Inc., Consulting Engineers; New York, New York

**15** **REFRIGERATION**

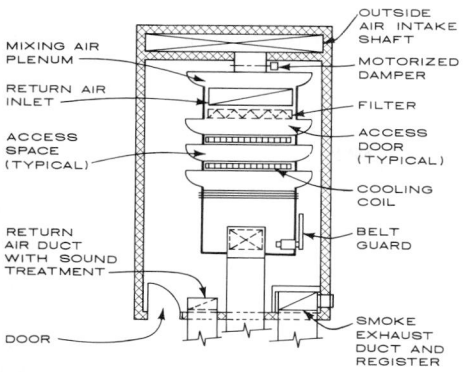

**FIGURE 2
EQUIPMENT ROOM PLAN**

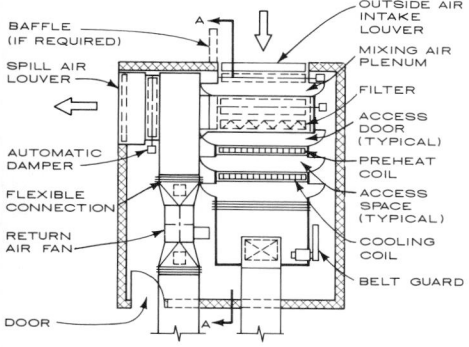

**FIGURE 1
EQUIPMENT ROOM PLAN**

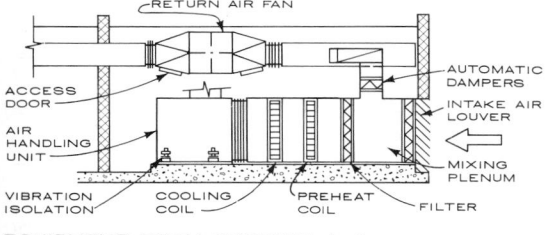

**EQUIPMENT ROOM SECTION A–A**

## NOTES

1. The air-handling equipment room should be located centrally to reduce distances conditioned air must travel from the equipment room to the farthest air-conditioned space. Fan noise transmission to adjacent spaces also must be considered. If the equipment room is located near conference rooms, sleeping quarters, broadcasting studios, or other sound sensitive areas, special treatment of the equipment room area will be required to provide adequate sound and vibration isolation from surrounding areas.

2. Adequate access space must be provided to maintain and replace heating coils, cooling coils, filters, damper motors and linkage, control valves, bearings, fan motors, fans, belts, pulleys, and other parts.

3. Figure 1 shows a typical equipment room plan with one floor-mounted air-conditioning unit and one suspended return air fan. The air-conditioning unit shown is a horizontal draw-through type consisting of fan, cooling coil, preheat coil, filters, return air plenum, outdoor air intake plenum, and access sections on either side of the coils.

4. The outdoor air intake louver and exhaust air louver are located on different walls. Where both intake and exhaust louver must be located on the same wall, they must be as far apart as possible, but not less than 10 ft. in order to reduce the short circuiting between the exhaust and intake air.

5. Figure 2 shows the same system without a return fan, but with exhaust capability via a remote fan.

6. When a horizontal blow-through unit is used, the length of the unit essentially is the same as shown for the draw-through unit.

7. Where higher headroom is available, a vertical unit, which can be only the draw-through type, may be used to reduce the unit's length. Depending on the size of the unit, this reduction in length will range from 2 ft. to 3 ft. 6 in.

8. Figure 1 shows an axial fan for returning air from the conditioned space. The return air fan may not be required where the air-conditioning system is not designed to operate under economizer cycle (cooling by cold outdoor air) mode.

9. A floor-mounted centrifugal single width, single inlet type fan or double width, double inlet type fan, may be used instead of the suspended axial fan shown; however, this generally increases equipment room width.

10. Outside air intake louvers are weatherproof with 50 percent to 60 percent free area. Louver size for conventional intake and exhaust air systems can be determined by allowing 800 ft. to 1,000 ft. per minute velocity through the free area.

11. The quantity of outside air drawn into a system depends on the ventilation criteria of the space being served and the amount of make-up air needed to balance any exhaust air drawn from the same space. The ratio of outside air to the total amount being supplied to a space may be very small. An office may need 10 percent to 20 percent outside air; a laboratory may require 100 percent outside air because of its non-recirculating aspect.

12. The total air quantity supplied to any individual space may vary from 0.5 CFM per sq. ft. for light occupancy (public circulation type office space) to 2 to 3 CFM per sq. ft. for laboratories, restaurants, ballrooms, and similar areas with large internal or external cooling loads.

## EQUIPMENT ROOM SPACE REQUIREMENTS

| | APPROXIMATE OVERALL DIMENSION OF SUPPLY AIR UNITS | | | RECOMMENDED ROOM DIMENSIONS | | |
|---|---|---|---|---|---|---|
| CFM RANGE | W | H | L | W | H | L |
| 1,000– 1,800 | 4'-9'' | 2'-9'' | 14'-9'' | 12'-6'' | 9'-0'' | 18'-9'' |
| 1,801– 3,000 | 5'-0'' | 3'-6'' | 16'-0'' | 13'-9'' | 9'-0'' | 20'-0'' |
| 3,001– 4,000 | 6'-9'' | 4'-6'' | 16'-0'' | 17'-6'' | 9'-0'' | 20'-0'' |
| 4,001– 6,000 | 7'-6'' | 4'-6'' | 16'-9'' | 18'-0'' | 9'-0'' | 20'-9'' |
| 6,001– 7,000 | 7'-6'' | 4'-9'' | 18'-3'' | 18'-6'' | 9'-6'' | 22'-3'' |
| 7,001– 9,000 | 8'-0'' | 5'-0'' | 18'-9'' | 19'-0'' | 10'-0'' | 22'-9'' |
| 9,001–12,000 | 10'-0'' | 5'-6'' | 21'-0'' | 23'-0'' | 11'-0'' | 25'-0'' |
| 12,001–16,000 | 10'-3'' | 6'-0'' | 22'-0'' | 23'-6'' | 12'-6'' | 26'-0'' |
| 16,001–19,000 | 10'-6'' | 6'-6'' | 23'-9'' | 24'-0'' | 13'-0'' | 27'-9'' |
| 19,001–22,000 | 11'-9'' | 7'-3'' | 25'-0'' | 26'-9'' | 15'-0'' | 29'-0'' |
| 22,001–27,000 | 11'-9'' | 8'-6'' | 26'-0'' | 27'-0'' | 16'-0'' | 30'-0'' |
| 27,001–32,000 | 13'-0'' | 9'-9'' | 27'-9'' | 29'-0'' | 18'-0'' | 31'-9'' |

## AIR HANDLING EQUIPMENT ROOM REQUIREMENTS

## AIR FILTRATION AND ODOR REMOVAL

Air filter selection is determined by the degree of cleanliness required. The initial cost, ease of maintenance, improvement of housekeeping, health benefits, and product quality are considerations. Size and quantity of dust and contaminants are also factors.

Filters most often are located at the air inlet of the heating, ventilating, and air-conditioning equipment, providing protection to the equipment and the area served. Filters are located at the equipment discharge and at entry of air into clean rooms, operating rooms, critical health care rooms, and various industrial process areas. Filters located in return air and exhaust air limit the contamination of other areas and the atmosphere.

AIR FILTER types are dry media, viscous (sticky) media, renewable media, and electronic. Filter performance tests and ratings have been established by ASHRAE, NBS, and AFI. The three operating characteristics that distinguish the various types of air cleaners are efficiency, air flow resistance, and dust holding capacity. Efficiency measures the ability of the air cleaner to remove particulate matter from an air stream. Average efficiency over the life of the filter is the most important consideration. Airflow resistance is the static pressure drop across the filter at a given airflow rate. Dust holding capacity defines the amount of a particular type of dust that an air cleaner can hold when operated at a specified airflow rate to some

maximum resistance value, or before its efficiency is seriously reduced as a result of the collected dust. Filter efficiency comparisons should always be based on the same test conditions.

PREFILTERS are required to extend the life of costlier high efficiency filters. High efficiency particulate filters (HEPA), and their integral frames, should be tested and certified in place. Filter pressure

drop gauges are recommended as an aid to economical replacement scheduling for all types of filters.

ODOR REMOVAL is best controlled by limiting the source. Dilution of odors by direct exhaust ventilation is the most common control method. Air washer and carbon filters are usually used for reclaiming odorous air. Ozone treatment and aerosol masking of odors are sometimes used.

## AIR FILTER CHARACTERISTICS

| MEDIA AND TYPE | PERCENT EFFICIENCY RANGE | | DUST HOLDING CAPACITY | AIRFLOW RESISTANCE (IN. WATER) |
|---|---|---|---|---|
| | ATMOSPHERIC DUST | SMALL PARTICLES | | |
| Dry panel throwaway | 15–30 | NA | Excellent | 0.1–0.5 |
| Viscous panel throwaway | 20–35 | NA | Good | 0.1–0.5 |
| Dry panel cleanable | 15–20 | NA | Superior | 0.08–0.5 |
| Viscous panel cleanable | 15–25 | NA | Superior | 0.08–0.5 |
| Mat panel renewable | 10–90 | 0–60 | Good to superior | 0.15–1.0 |
| Roll mat renewable | 10–90 | 0–55 | Good to superior | 0.15–0.65 |
| Roll oil bath | 15–25 | NA | Superior | 0.3 –0.5 |
| Close pleat mat panel | NA | 85–95 | Varies | 0.4–1.0 |
| High efficiency particulate | NA | 95–99.9 | Varies | 1.0–3.0 |
| Membrane | NA | to 100 | NA | NA |
| Electrostatic with mat | 80–98 | NA | Varies | 0.15–1.25 |

John O. Samuel; Joseph R. Loring & Associates, Inc., Consulting Engineers; New York, New York

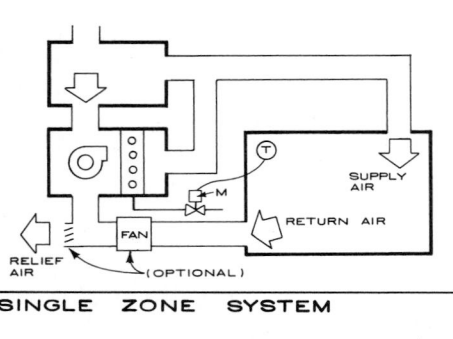
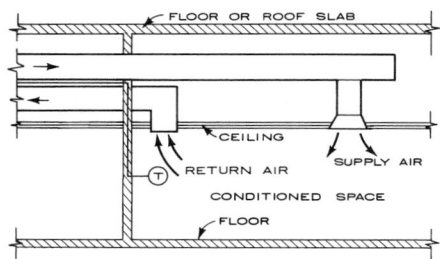

Low pressure system suitable for serving areas requiring only one zone of control. May be used in multiple where more than one zone of control is required. Relatively low first cost. Air handling unit may be blow through or draw through type.

## SINGLE ZONE SYSTEM

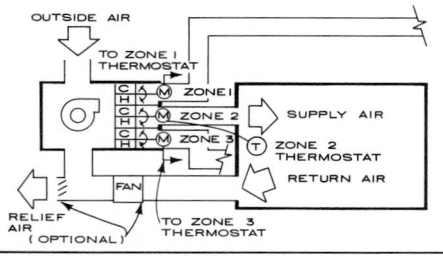
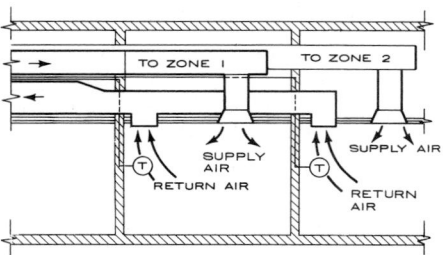

Low pressure system for serving areas requiring more than one zone of control. Practical limit of approximately eight zones per air handling unit. Can be used for simultaneously heating some areas while cooling others; however, control is relatively poor because of leakage at unit dampers and coil wiping. Relatively high first cost and high energy cost. Limited number of manufacturers.

## MULTIZONE SYSTEM

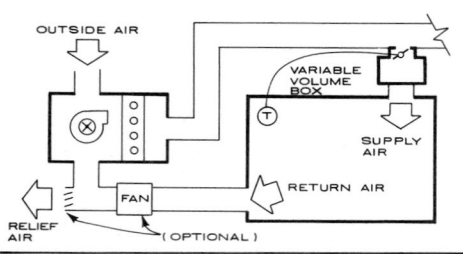
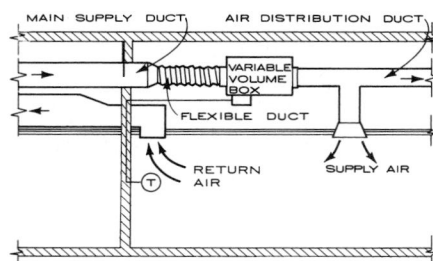

Low, medium, or high pressure system capable of providing a control zone for each box. Can be used for cooling only or for heating and cooling. Changeover from heating to cooling should be zoned by exposure. Provides variable air change rate and not applicable to areas requiring fixed air change rates such as certain hospital and laboratory applications. Relatively low first cost and energy cost. Air handling system may be blow through or draw through type.

## SINGLE DUCT VARIABLE VOLUME SYSTEM

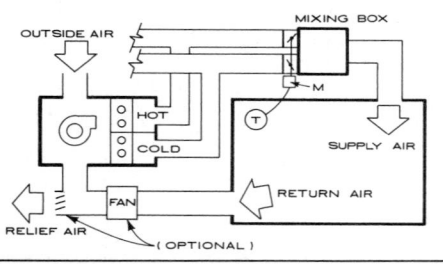
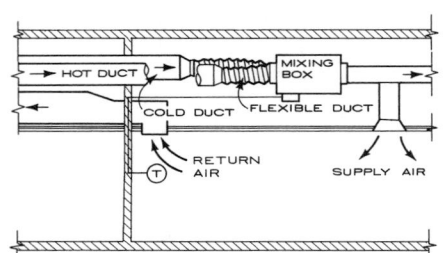

Low, medium, or high pressure system capable of providing a control zone for each box. Provides complete heating and cooling capability with no need for changeover. Available for both constant and variable volume systems (normally does not reduce air flow below 50 percent of maximum). Provides excellent year-round control. Relatively high first cost and energy cost.

## DOUBLE DUCT SYSTEM

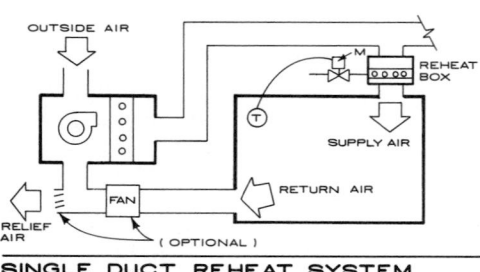
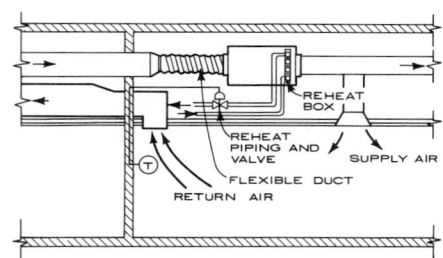

Low, medium, or high pressure system capable of providing a control zone per box. Provides heating and cooling capability (no changeover required). Available for constant and variable volume systems that normally do not reduce airflow below 50% of maximum. Excellent control, high first cost, high energy consumption; use generally limited to laboratory and hospital applications where constant volume and excellent control is required. Air handling system may be blow through or draw through type.

## SINGLE DUCT REHEAT SYSTEM

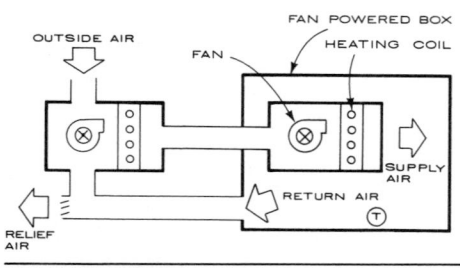
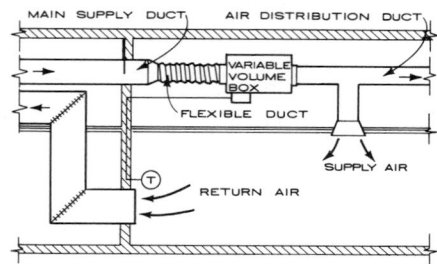

Low, medium, or high pressure system. When heating is required, cooling air damper closes and fan draws air from ceiling void and heats as required. Highly energy efficient control; relatively low first cost. Requires service and maintenance access to fan units at ceiling of occupied areas. Air handling system may be blow through or draw through.

## FAN POWERED VARIABLE AIR VOLUME

William Tao & Associates, Inc., Consulting Engineers; St. Louis, Missouri
Krommenhoek/McKeown & Associates Architects & Engineers; San Diego, California

# AIR DISTRIBUTION

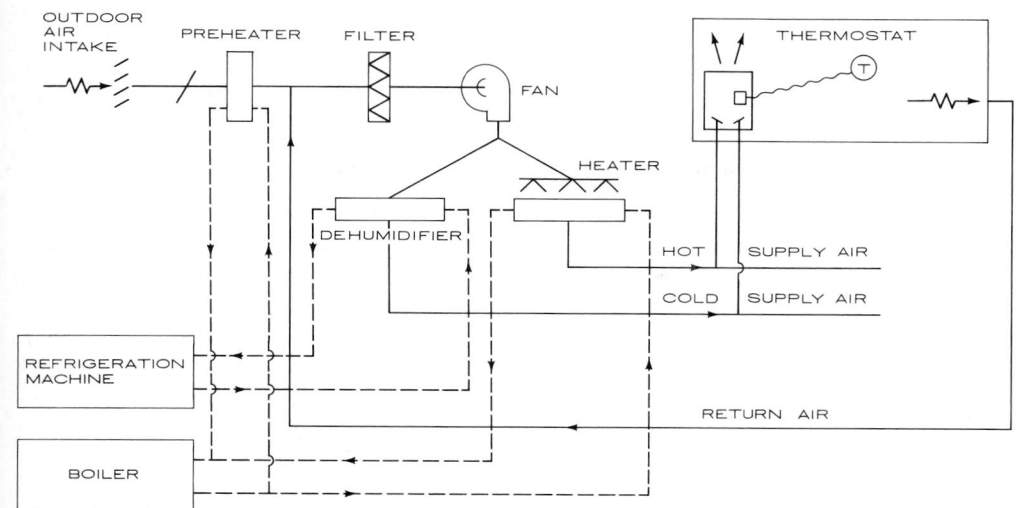

**DOUBLE DUCT, CONSTANT VOLUME**
**ALL-AIR SYSTEMS**

## ALL-AIR SYSTEMS

With all-air systems the heating and refrigeration plants may be located in a central mechanical room some distance from the conditioned space. The air handling station not only cleans the air, but also heats or cools it, humidifies or dehumidifies it. Only the final cooled or heated air is brought through ducts into the conditioned space and distributed through outlets or mixing terminals.

Some common all-air systems are: single duct, variable volume; dual conduit; single duct with reheat or fan-powered terminal; multizone; and double duct.

### SINGLE DUCT, VARIABLE VOLUME

This central station system supplies a single stream of either hot or cold air at normal velocity. Capacity is adjusted to load by automatic volume control. Exterior room systems are zoned by exposure.

Air terminal diffusers are available with self-contained, self-balancing, system-operated controls, which are factory installed and calibrated.

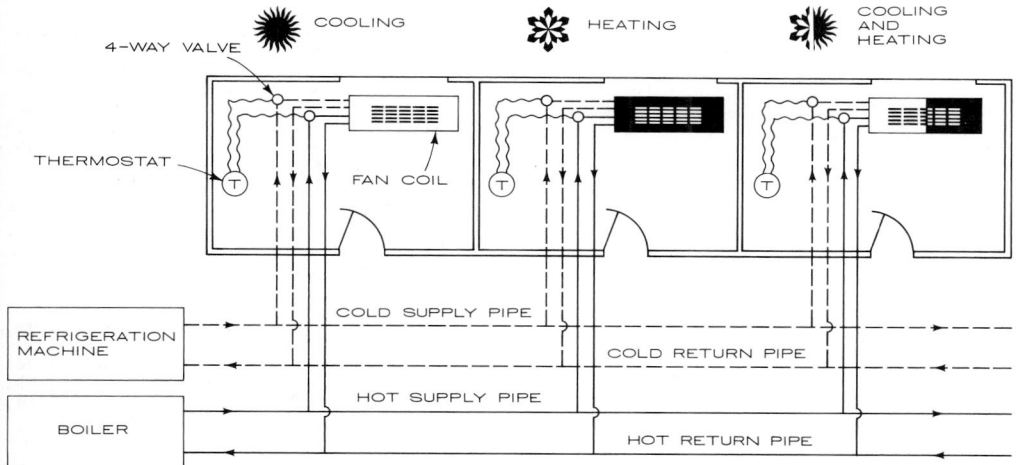

**FOUR-PIPE DISTRIBUTION**
**ALL-WATER SYSTEMS**

## ALL-WATER SYSTEMS

All-water systems have fan coil room terminals with one or two water circuits connected. The cooling medium (such as chilled water or brine) may be supplied from a remote source and circulated through coils in the fan coil terminal located in the conditioned space. These circuits may be either two-pipe or four-pipe distribution. Ventilation comes from a wall opening, from the interior zone system bleed-off, or by infiltration. Another variation uses a separate ventilation unit.

### TWO-PIPE SYSTEMS

Either hot or chilled water is piped throughout the building to a number of fan coil units. One pipe supplies water, the other returns it.

### FOUR-PIPE SYSTEMS

Two separate piping circuits are used—one for hot and one for chilled medium—to provide simultaneous heating and cooling as needed in various building zones.

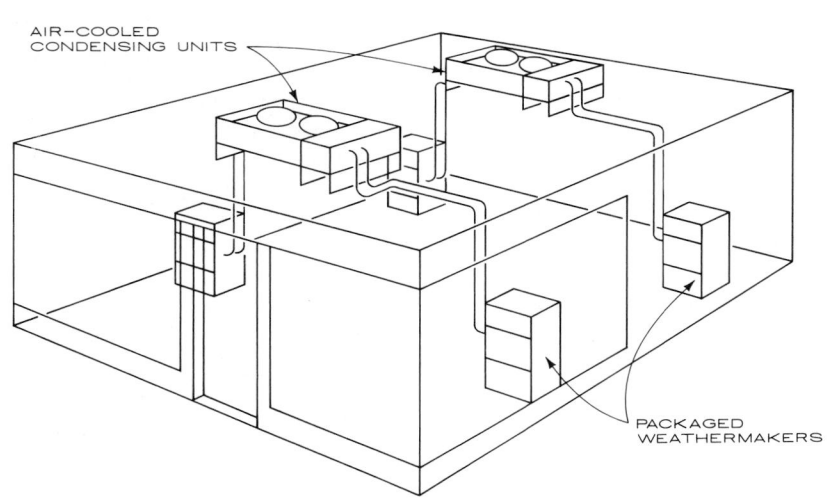

**DIRECT EXPANSION SYSTEMS**

## DIRECT EXPANSION SYSTEMS

Expansion systems use self-contained units in windows, cut into the wall, in the roof, or floor-mounted for extracting or adding heat. Units usually are located in or next to the air-conditioned space and consist only of elements essential to producing cool or heat. Heat can be provided either by reverse cycle type, such as a heat pump, or by supplementary heating elements.

### ROOFTOP SYSTEMS

Rooftop systems use gas or electricity as energy to supply both heating and cooling. The refrigeration component may be remote or roof-mounted type.

### THROUGH-THE-WALL

Cooling normally is achieved in an air-cooled condenser or by centrally circulated water from a cooling tower. Heating is done with gas, electricity, or centrally heated water for year-round air-conditioning.

### PACKAGED SYSTEMS

Systems contain roof-mounted, air-cooled condensing units. A reverse cycle heat pump or supplementary heating is required for year-round operation.

Joseph R. Loring & Associates, Inc., Consulting Engineers; New York, New York
Carrier Corporation; Syracuse, New York

AIR DISTRIBUTION     **15**

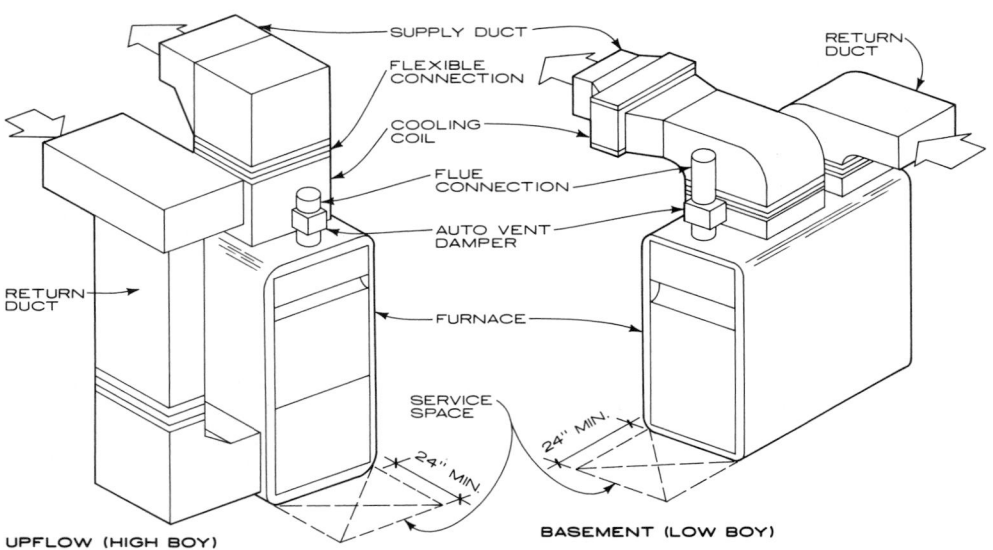

UPFLOW (HIGH BOY)

BASEMENT (LOW BOY)

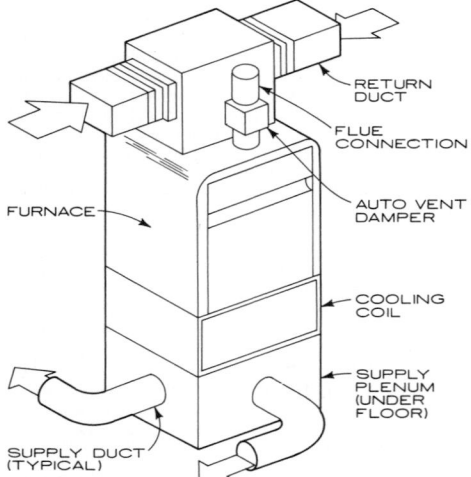

DOWNFLOW (COUNTERFLOW)

**WARM AIR FURNACES**

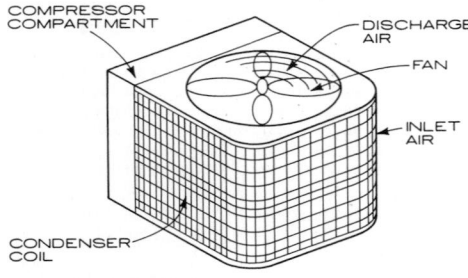

**CONDENSING UNIT**

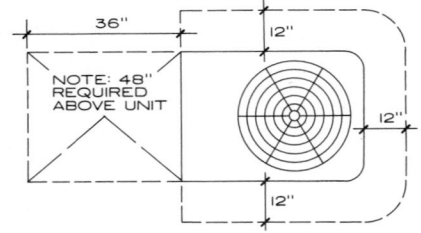

**INSTALLATION CLEARANCES**
**CONDENSING UNIT**

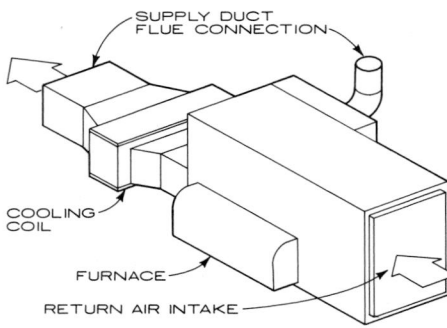

HORIZONTAL

## FLOOR AREA REQUIRED BY WARM AIR FURNACE

| OUTPUT CAPACITY (BTU/HR) | FURNACE FLOOR AREA (SQ FT)* |
|---|---|
| Up to 52,000 | 2.4 |
| 52,000–84,000 | 4.2 |
| 84,000–120,000 | 6.6 |
| 120,000–200,000 | 13.1 |

*Based on net floor area occupied by the upflow or downflow furnace. Low boy unit requires 50% more floor area. Space for combustion air should be added as required by local codes. Adequate space should be provided for service.

## NOTES

1. Warm air furnace units are designed primarily for residential, small commercial, or classroom heating. Cooling can be added to these units by installing a cooling coil downstream from the furnace, with refrigerant compressor and condenser located remotely outside the building.
2. Duct system from the furnace unit can be either above the ceiling or in the floor slab. Above ceiling distribution systems are usually the radial type with high wall registers. Perimeter loop and extended plenum systems in floor slabs provide good air distribution. There are smaller temperature variations across the floor with perimeter loop systems than with radial or extended plenum systems.
3. Duct systems also may be installed below the living spaces, in a crawl space, or in a basement.
4. Two- or three-story buildings using similar warm air furnace and cooling coil combinations are centrally air conditioned via vertical extension of the branch ductwork through walls and partitions. Since all variations of the warm air heating/cooling systems recirculate their air within the building envelope, it is a crucial design requirement to leave return air passage, from each space supplied with air, to the furnace room.

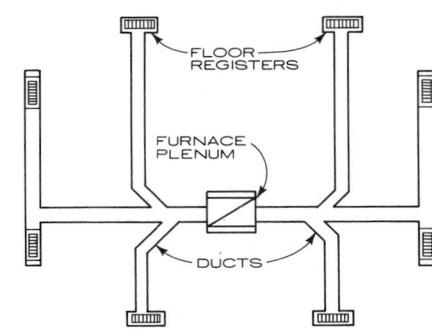

EXTENDED PLENUM SYSTEM

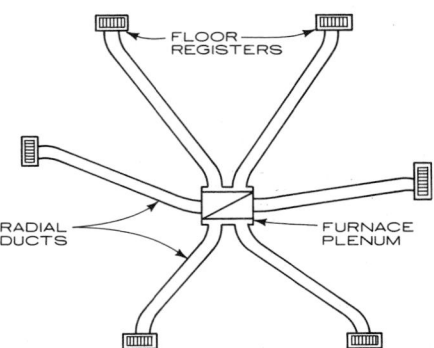

PERIMETER RADIAL SYSTEM

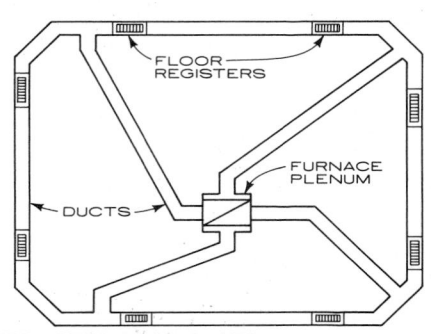

PERIMETER LOOP SYSTEM

**DUCT SYSTEMS**

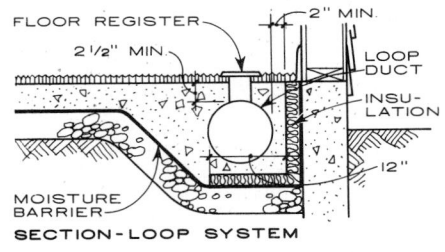

SECTION-LOOP SYSTEM

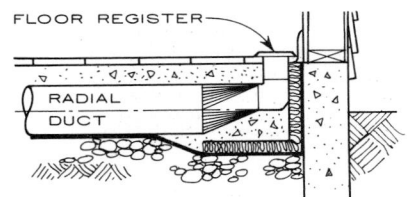

SECTION-RADIAL SYSTEM

**AIR OUTLETS**

DiClemente-Siegel Engineering, Inc.; Southfield, Michigan

**15**    **AIR DISTRIBUTION**

## GUIDELINES: DESIGN AND CONSTRUCTION OF COMMERCIAL DUCTWORK

1. Ductwork for commercial buildings must be able to withstand much higher pressures, both positive for supply air and negative for return or exhaust air, than residential construction. Commercial ductwork must convey air at velocities considerably higher and for longer distances.

2. Design of commercial ductwork is mainly dictated by two parameters, often in conflict: (1) distribution of air throughout the building using least fan energy, and (2) available space in which to locate ductwork, such as shafts and hung ceilings. For this reason, sizing of ductwork has progressed from simplistic methods, particularly the equal friction method, to the total pressure method which can best be done by a computer program. Sizing methods are explained in the ASHRAE "Handbook of Fundamentals" and in the SMACNA publication "HVAC Systems—Duct Design."

3. Air density plays a role in ductwork design. It is air mass that heats or cools a space, not volume. Air at lighter densities, such as in elevated cities (e.g., Denver), requires more air flow in cubic feet per minute (cfm) than cities near sea level. Air density also applies to required cfm for warm air systems, since hot air has a lighter density than cold air.

4. Air delivery to the space must create air movement in the occupied zone (generally 5 ft above the floor to the floor) for optimum thermal comfort. Without good air movement, thermal comfort level will be seriously degraded and excessive air movement will cause drafts. Of six parameters that affect thermal comfort, air movement in the room ranks with ambient temperature as most important. Consult the ASHRAE "Handbook of Fundamentals" for design guidelines on air delivery.

5. Until very recently, construction of ducted air systems for commercial buildings has been divided into three categories: low pressure [positive or negative pressure not exceeding 2 in. water gauge (wg), with air velocities (positive of air supply from 2 to 6 in. wg); high pressure (6–10 in. wg). In 1985, SMACNA published a new standard for construction of commercial ductwork, "HVAC Duct Construction Standards—Metal and Flexible," which bases construction on calculated operating pressure of the system: Positive pressure classes of ½, 1, 2, 3, 4, 6, and 10 in. wg and negative pressure classes of minus ½, 1, 2, and 3 in. wg. This permits designers of commercial duct systems to specify the pressure classification and material required for duct construction; the SMACNA manual "HVAC Duct Construction Standards" specifies options of duct construction to meet the parameters.

6. To preclude noise problems and high-pressure drops due to duct turbulence at fittings, ductwork velocities should be kept, in the main trunk ductwork, below 3000 fpm, and preferably not in excess of 2500 fpm. Ductwork is usually maintained at low velocities, hence low-pressure drops, on discharge of variable air volume (VAV) boxes; a good rule of thumb for sizing ductwork is 0.1 in. wg per 100 ft of duct run.

7. Variable air volume systems are essentially self-balancing; therefore, all VAV ductwork on the high-pressure side, upstream of the VAV boxes, does not require balancing hardware, such as volume dampers. Ductwork on the discharge of VAV boxes can be balanced by trim dampers in the air outlets; however, if downstream duct run has a total pressure drop in excess of 0.25 in. wg, balancing hardware is required to preclude noise in outlets nearest the VAV box.

8. Air systems that are not VAV or equipped with constant volume boxes must be furnished with air balancing hardware.

9. Fire and/or smoke dampers are invariably code requirements and must be shown on the contract drawings; installation is covered in the SMACNA manual.

## TYPES OF DUCTWORK FOR COMMERCIAL BUILDINGS

1. Ductwork construction is dictated by the cross-sectional configuration of the duct and by the material of which it is made.

2. Commercially available ductwork and fittings are usually factory fabricated in round and flat oval cross sections. Square, rectangular, triangular, and other configurations are manufactured in local sheet metal shops to meet specific job requirements. Fittings for other than square and rectangular shapes are customized and generally difficult to make.

3. Round is preferred over rectangular cross-sectional ductwork for the following reasons:
   a. Inherently, round ductwork is structurally stronger than rectangular, particularly when ductwork is under negative pressure (return or exhaust air). This allows duct wall thickness to be lighter for round ducts, performing the same duty (air flow and pressure), hence cheaper in material cost.
   b. Aerodynamics, key to low fan energy, are generally better achieved with properly selected round fittings.
   c. Fabrication (using factory-made round fittings) is considerably facilitated over rectangular, hence lower installation cost for ductwork.
   d. Rectangular ductwork radiates sound by the "drumming" of its sides; round ductwork is stiffer.

4. The greatest disadvantage of round ductwork is its depth, which makes it unsuitable to fit into narrow spaces. Where this occurs, flat-oval ductwork can be used, since it has many of the same advantages. Rectangular ductwork is usually required for trunk ductwork in large sizes carrying substantial air flows.

5. The following duct materials are available:
   a. Galvanized sheet steel: strong, generally resistant to corrosion, durable, easily worked.
   b. Aluminum: light in weight, resistant to water and water vapor corrosion; not as strong as steel, dents easily, and cannot be welded.
   c. Stainless steel: resistant to most types of corrosion and fumes; very strong and can be welded if sheet thickness is at least 18 gauge; good for kitchen exhaust, dishwasher exhaust, and laboratory exhaust. Made in 2 qualities: type 304 and type 316. Type 316 is generally superior in corrosion resistance to the less expensive type 304.
   d. Copper: resistant to water corrosion, can be soldered; structurally weaker than steel and more expensive.
   e. Plastic or plastic-coated steel: used exclusively for corrosion resistance, particularly laboratory exhaust systems.
   f. Carbon steel: subject to rusting, but strong; used for kitchen exhaust and boiler breeching; 16–10 gauge for welding. Check sizes and code requirements.
   g. Fiber glass: limited to rectangular shapes where acoustical attenuation is required; reinforced with metal in larger sizes; no insulation is required. Tape required to secure transverse joints must be type that sticks to the outer surface. Manufacturer's recommendation for tape is critical.

## LABORATORY EXHAUST SYSTEMS

Ductwork design for research laboratory exhausts involves special consideration of unique code requirements for life safety and corrosion prevention:

1. Codes cite NFPA Standard No. 45 to meet criteria for life safety, including duct and fume hood design.

2. Fire dampers are often prohibited on these systems. Greater danger to workers comes from toxic fumes which must be exhausted. If fire dampers are a code requirement, fusible links must be protected from corrosion by chemical fumes.

## ENERGY CONSERVATION: DESIGN OF COMMERCIAL DUCTWORK

1. ASHRAE Standard 90A-1980, "Energy Conservation in New Building Design," has a formula to determine energy-conserving performance of the system, called "air transport factor" (ATF):

ATF = Space-sensible heat removal, Btuh/power input to supply and return fans, Btuh.

If ATF is 5.5 or higher, it meets the energy conservation requirement. Local codes may require higher ATF values. Power input to fans takes into account fan efficiency, fan drive efficiency, and fan motor efficiency. If air is standard (70°F and density at sea level), ATF for supply system reduces to:

ATF = (2.74) × (fan efficiency) × (motor efficiency) × (drive efficiency) × (air temperature difference between supply air and space temperature, °F) (total pressure rise in fan, inches wg)

Since return fan energy is a small fraction of that of supply fan, the equation can be used as a rapid approximation of ATF. However, the complete ATF must be calculated with energy of both supply and return fans to satisfy ASHRAE 90A-1980 or local codes. Units in numerator/denominator of equation can be either Btu/hr or watts, but not both, for dimensional consistency.

2. Air duct fittings should be aerodynamically efficient, selected for the lowest available branch loss coefficient. Round duct systems show loss coefficients that vary for divided flow fittings, from 0.22 to 6.4, while performing the same service. Pressure loss in worst case is 28 times that of the best fitting for divided flow ductwork.

3. Elbows must be carefully chosen. Radius elbows should have a centerline radius equal to 1.5 times duct width or diameter. In square throat elbows, single blades are more efficient than double thickness vanes. The latter should not be used. This has been a recent development in elbow design recommendations.

4. Air face velocities through finned cooling or heating coils with more than two rows should not exceed 500 ft/min for low energy consumption.

5. Variable air volume systems are energy conserving. Design should take into account diversity of air usage on each exposure of building. This permits "looping" of duct system on all 4 building exposures, resulting in economical and efficient duct design.

## DUCT SUPPORTS

Duct supports are specified in the SMACNA manual "HVAC Duct Construction Standards." As a supplement, these guidelines for location of hangers are recommended:

1. Install hangers at right angles to centerline of ducts. Strap hangers should be installed in pairs on exact opposite sides of duct.

2. Hangers are installed adjacent to transverse joints of duct whenever specified spacing intervals of hangers match lengths of duct sections. Base the spacing of hangers on either the duct "cross-sectional area" or "half-perimeter" (SMACNA) method. Hanger intervals derived from these methods are usually combinations of 4, 6, and 8 ft or 5 and 10 ft.

3. Joints of nested fittings, as splits in main duct and joints of direct branch taps into side of main ducts, are considered weak joints in a duct system and require extra hangers.

4. At horizontal changes in duct direction, greater than 20°, one or more sets of hangers (located symmetrically at the center of the elbow) are necessary to prevent overstressing of ordinarily spaced hangers.

5. Locate hangers at both elbows of long vertical offsets close to the centerline of vertical duct. Short offsets need hangers at bottom elbows.

6. Duct risers require support at each floor. Risers passing through building stories more than 15 ft high should be provided with equally spaced intermediate supports. Vertical space between intermediate supports should not exceed 12 ft.

7. Supplementary hangers should be provided for medium or heavyweight equipment installed inside ductwork.

---

H. D. Goodman, PE; Joseph R. Loring & Associates, Inc., Consulting Engineers; New York, New York

AIR DISTRIBUTION 15

## DUCT CONSTRUCTION

Ductwork must be permanent, rigid, nonbuckling, and nonrattling. Joints in ductwork should be airtight. Galvanized iron or aluminum sheets are usually used in the construction of ducts. The ducts may be either round or rectangular in cross section.

In general, supply ducts should be constructed entirely of noncombustible material. Supply ducts serving a single family dwelling need not meet this requirement, except for the first 3 ft from the unit, provided they are used in conjunction with listed heating units, are properly constructed from a base material of metal or mineral, and are properly applied. Warm air ducts passing through cold spaces or located in exposed walls should have 1 to 2 in. of insulation.

Supply ducts must be securely supported by metal hangers, straps, lugs, or brackets. No nails should be driven through duct walls, and no unnecessary holes should be cut in them.

Supply ducts should be equipped with an adjustable locking type damper for air volume control. The damper should be installed in the branch duct as far from the outlet as possible, where it is accessible.

Automatic smoke dampers are required wherever ductwork passes through a rated smoke barrier partition.

Return systems having more than one return intake may be equipped with balancing dampers.

Attention should be given to the elimination of noise. Metal ducts should be connected to the unit by strips of flexible fire resistant fabric. Electrical conduit and piping, if directly connected to the unit, may increase noise transmission. Return air intakes immediately adjacent to the unit may also increase noise transmission. Installation of a fan directly under a return air grille should be avoided.

## DUCT MATERIAL THICKNESS

| ROUND DUCT DIA. OR RECTANGULAR DUCT WIDTH (IN.) | GALVANIZED IRON U.S. GAUGE | ALUMINUM B & S GAUGE |
|---|---|---|
| Ducts enclosed in partitions | | |
| 14 or less | 30 | 24 |
| Over 14 | 28 | 24 |
| Ducts not enclosed in partitions | | |
| 14 or less | 28 | 24 |
| Over 14 | 26 | 23 |

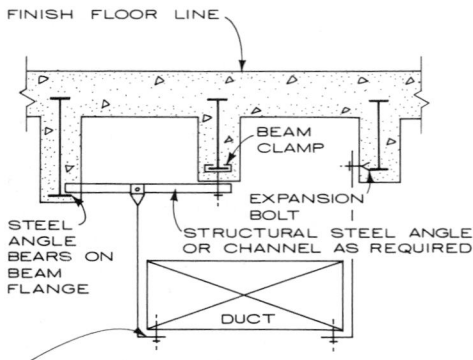

NOTE

On ducts over 48 in. wide hangers shall turn under and fasten to bottom of duct. When cross-sectional area exceeds 8 sq ft duct will be braced by angles on all four sides.

**DUCT SUPPORT DETAIL**

William G. Miner, AIA, Architect, Washington, D.C.

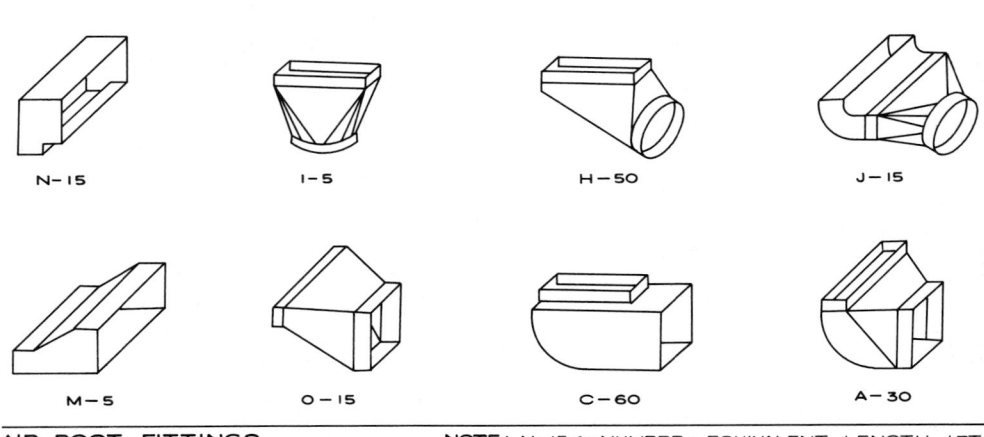

**AIR BOOT FITTINGS**

NOTE: N-15 ← NUMBER = EQUIVALENT LENGTH (FT)
↑ LETTER = SHAPE DESIGNATION

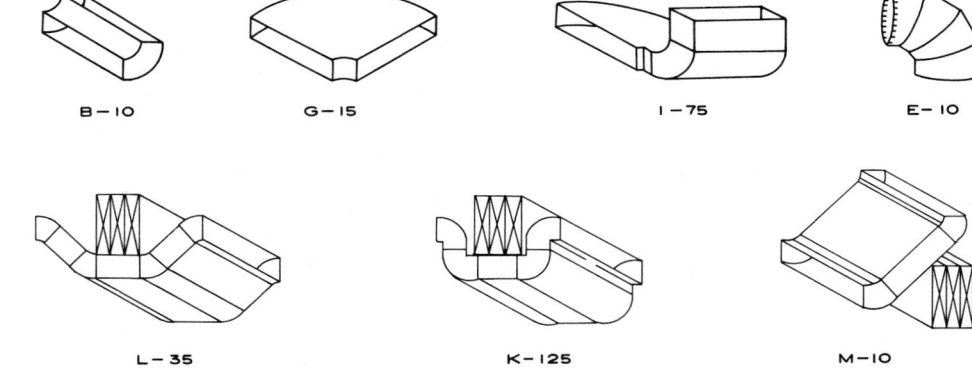

**ANGLES AND ELBOWS FOR BRANCH DUCTS**

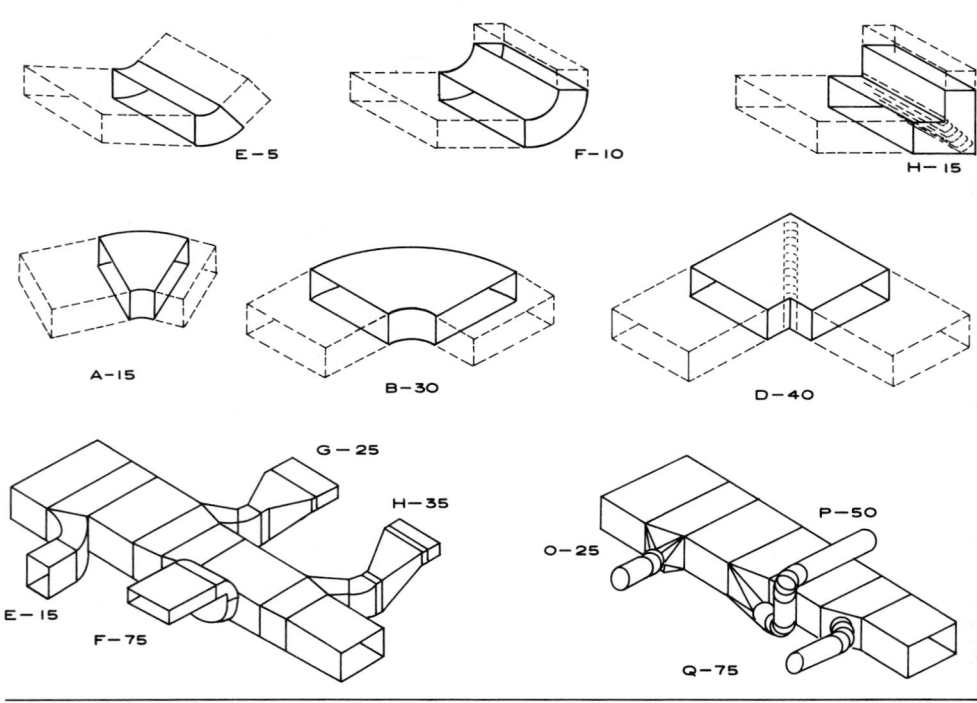

**TRUNK DUCTS AND FITTINGS**

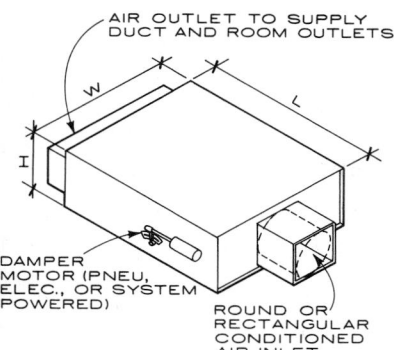

High, medium, or low velocity systems. Inlet pressure required 1/4 to 1 1/2 in. W.C. Capacity range 200 to 3200 cfm per box. Box serves as converter from high to low velocity air system, noise attenuator, and control device by modulating air quantity.

## RANGE OF DIMENSIONS

| CFM | HEIGHT | LENGTH | WIDTH |
|-----|--------|--------|-------|
| 400 | 8"- 9" | 24"-39" | 14"-30" |
| 800 | 10"-11" | 24"-53" | 18"-42" |
| 1600 | 14" | 30"-48" | 22"-44" |
| 2400 | 16" | 42"-60" | 26"-54" |
| 3200 | 18" | 42"-67" | 33"-54" |

**VARIABLE VOLUME PINCH BACK BOX**

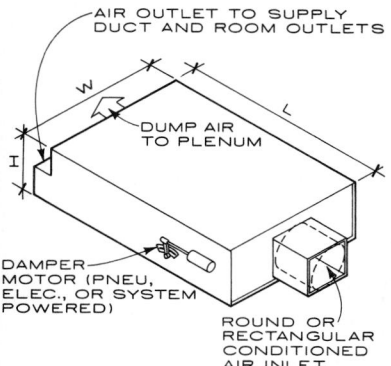

High, medium, or low velocity systems. Inlet pressure required 1/4 to 1 in. W.C. Capacity range 200 to 3200 cfm per box. Available with or without reheat coil. Box serves as converter from high to low velocity air system, noise attenuator, and control device by modulating air quantity to space and/or by reheat.

## RANGE OF DIMENSIONS

| CFM | HEIGHT | LENGTH | WIDTH |
|-----|--------|--------|-------|
| 200 | 8"- 9" | 24"-39" | 12"-19" |
| 400 | 9"-11" | 25"-51" | 12"-24" |
| 800 | 9"-11" | 25"-51" | 22"-31" |
| 1600 | 10"-16" | 25"-51" | 22"-47" |
| 2400 | 10"-16" | 25"-51" | 42"-47" |
| 3200 | 10"-16" | 25"-51" | 42"-47" |

**VARIABLE VOLUME DUMP TYPE BOX**

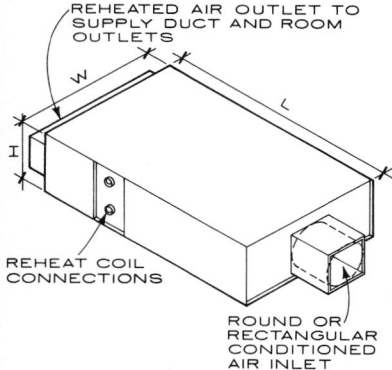

High, medium, or low velocity systems. Inlet pressures 1/2 to 1 1/2 in. W.C. Capacity range 200 to 5000 cfm. Box serves as converter from high to low velocity air system, noise attenuator, and control device by reheat of conditioned air.

## RANGE OF DIMENSIONS

| CFM | HEIGHT | LENGTH | WIDTH |
|-----|--------|--------|-------|
| 200 | 9"-11" | 30"-50" | 16"-22" |
| 400 | 9"-11" | 30"-51" | 18"-30" |
| 800 | 9"-11" | 30"-51" | 22"-42" |
| 1600 | 14"-16" | 48"-55" | 40"-44" |
| 2400 | 16"-18" | 60"-55" | 40"-54" |
| 3200 | 16"-18" | 60"-55" | 16"-66" |
| 5000 | 20"-18" | 60"-55" | 20"-80" |

**REHEAT CONSTANT VOLUME BOX**

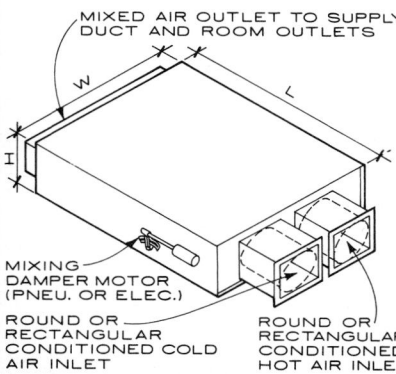

High, medium, or low velocity systems. Inlet pressure 1/4 to 1 1/2 in. W.C. Capacity range from 150 to 2000 cfm per box (low velocity) to 5000 cfm (high velocity). Box serves as converter from high to low velocity air system, noise attenuator, and control device by mixing hot and cold air streams.

## RANGE OF DIMENSIONS

| CFM | HEIGHT | LENGTH | WIDTH |
|-----|--------|--------|-------|
| 400 | 6"-10" | 40"-51" | 30"-19" |
| 800 | 8"-11" | 50"-51" | 42"-24" |
| 1600 | 12"-14" | 48"-51" | 44"-40" |
| 2400 | 14"-18" | 60"-55" | 54"-44" |
| 3200 | 14"-18" | 60"-55" | 54"-44" |
| 5000 | 16"-18" | 60"-55" | 54"-66" |

**DUAL DUCT MIXING BOX**

William Tao & Associates, Inc., Consulting Engineers; St. Louis, Missouri

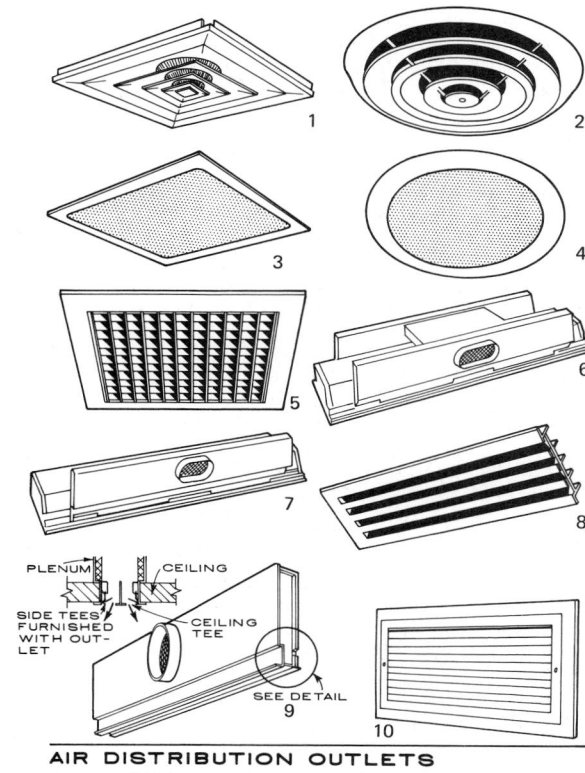

## AIR DISTRIBUTION OUTLETS

### KEY

1 RECTANGULAR LOUVERED FACE DIFFUSER: Available in 1, 2, 3, or 4-way pattern, steel or aluminum. Flanged overlap frame or inserted in 2 X 2 ft or 2 X 4 ft baked enamel steel panel to fit tile modules of lay-in ceilings. Supply or return.

2 ROUND LOUVERED FACE DIFFUSER: Normal 360° air pattern with blank-off plate for other air patterns. Surface mounting for all type ceilings. Normally of steel with baked enamel finish. Supply or return.

3 RECTANGULAR PERFORATED FACE DIFFUSER: Available in 1, 2, 3, or 4-way pattern, steel or aluminum. Flanged overlap frame or 2 X 2 ft and 2 X 4 ft for replacing tile of lay-in ceiling can be used for supply or return air.

4 ROUND PERFORATED FACE DIFFUSER: Normal 360° air pattern with blank-off plate for other air patterns. Steel or aluminum. Flanged overlap frame for all type ceilings. Can be used for supply or return air.

5 LATTICE TYPE RETURN: All aluminum square grid type return grille for ceiling installation with flanged overlap frame or of correct size to replace tile.

6 SADDLE TYPE LUMINAIRE AIR BOOT: Provides air supply from both sides of standard size luminaires. Maximum air delivery (total both sides) approximately 150 to 170 cfm for 4 ft long luminaire.

7 SINGLE SIDE TYPE LUMINAIRE AIR BOOT: Provides air supply from one side of standard size luminaires. Maximum air delivery approximately 75 cfm for 4 ft long luminaire.

8 LINEAR DIFFUSER: Extruded aluminum, anodized, duranodic, or special finishes, one way or opposite direction or vertical down air pattern. Any length with one to eight slots. Can be used for supply or return and for ceiling, sidewall, or cabinet top application.

9 INTEGRATED PLENUM TYPE OUTLET FOR "T" BAR CEILINGS: Slot type outlet, one way or two way opposite direction air pattern. Available in 24, 36, 48, and 60 in. lengths. Replaces or integrates with "T" bar. Approximately 150 to 175 cfm for 4 ft long, two-slot unit.

10 SIDEWALL OR DUCT MOUNTED REGISTER: Steel or aluminum for supply or return. Adjustable horizontal and vertical deflection. Plaster frame available. Suitable for long throw and high air volume.

## WASTE HEAT SOURCES FOR HEAT RECOVERY SYSTEMS

1. Flues of fuel burning heating boilers and furnaces.
2. Refrigeration systems hot gas and condenser water.
3. Exhaust gases from diesel engine and gas turbine driven electric power generating equipment.
4. Cooling water from diesel engine cooling jackets and air compressor aftercoolers.
5. Exhaust steam and condenser water from steam turbine driven electric generators and refrigeration units.
6. Exhaust air from toilet rooms, mechanical equipment rooms, transformer vaults, kitchen range hoods, laundries, laboratory hoods, hospital operating rooms, locker rooms, shower rooms, and swimming pools.
7. Wastewater from washing machines and dishwashers.
8. Internal heat gain from lights, people, and appliances.
9. Heat recovery systems may consist of a direct or indirect heat transfer from airstreams, liquids, refrigerants, water, or gases.

## APPLICATIONS FOR WASTE HEAT RECOVERY SYSTEMS

1. Building space heating.
2. Preheating ventilation outdoor air intake.
3. Air conditioning systems supply air reheat.
4. Preheating domestic hot water and boiler feed water.

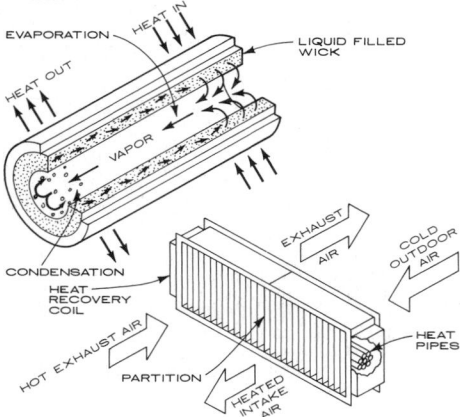

**NOTE**

Counterflow, indirect air-to-air sensible heat transfer. No leakage between airstreams. Alternate evaporation, condensation, and capillary migration of fluid in porous wick lining of tubes. Coil tilting or fact and bypass damper control. Efficiency 50–70%. Modular sizes to 54 in. x 138 in. x 8 rows deep.

**HEAT PIPE**

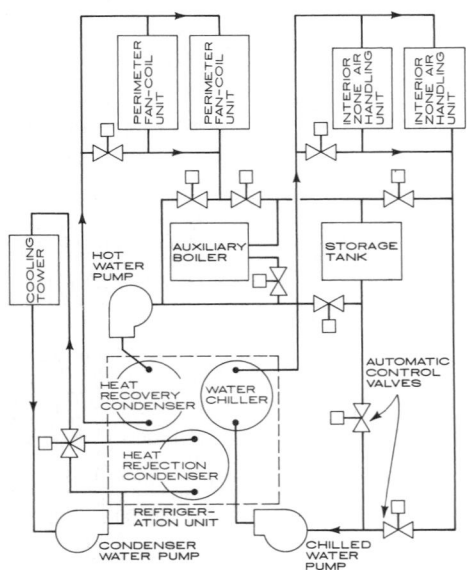

**DUAL CONDENSER WATER CHILLER**

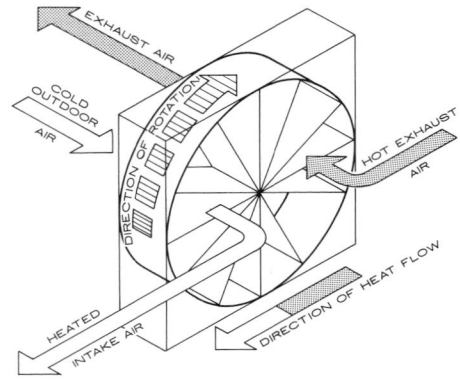

**NOTE**

Sensible heat absorbing aluminum or stainless steel mesh. Dessicant impregnated for latent heat transfer. Leakage 4–8% between opposing airstreams. Added purging section reduces cross-contamination to less than 1%. Speed variations or face and bypass damper capacity control. Efficiency 70–80%. Sizes to 144 in. diameter.

**THERMAL WHEEL**

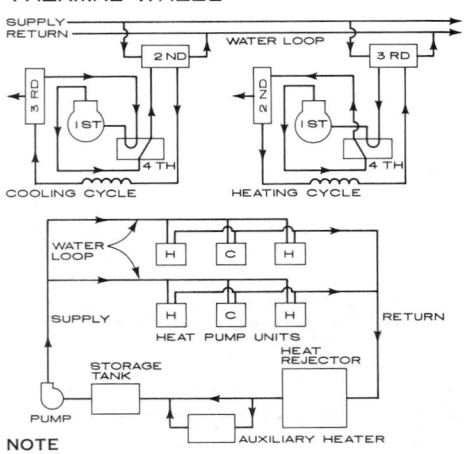

**NOTE**

Heat transfer from cooled to heated areas. Individually controlled heat pump terminal units with air and water coils. Auxiliary heater operation when heat loss exceeds heat gain. Heat rejector operation when heat gain exceeds heat loss. Tank stores excess capacity. Loop water 60–90°F.

**WATER LOOP HEAT PUMPS**

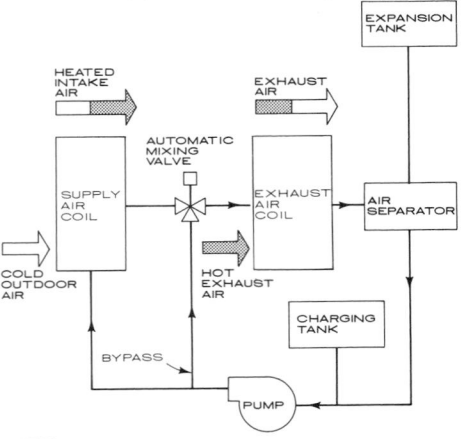

**NOTE**

Indirect sensible heat transfer between remote air streams with no cross-contamination. Exhaust airstream coil construction to suit application. Antifreeze fluid for low air temperatures. Bypass valve temperature control. Computerized equipment selection. Efficiency 50–70%. Modular coils to 20,000 cfm.

**RUNAROUND COILS**

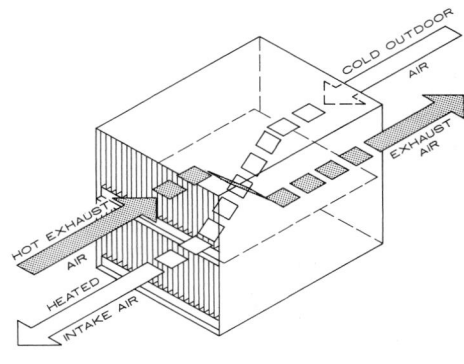

**NOTE**

Counterflow, direct air-to-air type heat exchanger. Sensible heat transfer only. No leakage between airstreams. Corrugated aluminum or stainless steel construction. Washdown spray manifold for dirty exhaust airstreams. Bypass damper temperature control. Modular sizes to 10,000 cfm. Efficiency 60–80%.

**PLATE TYPE HEAT EXCHANGER**

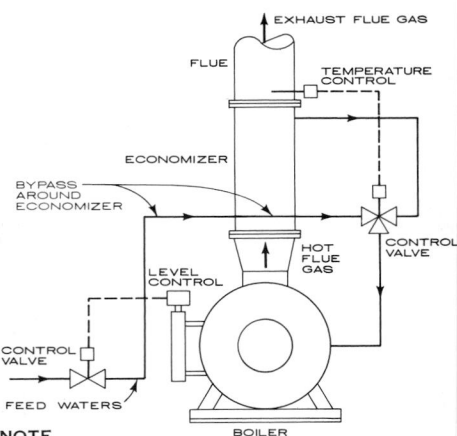

**NOTE**

Direct flue gas to feed water heat transfer for high pressure steam boilers. Boiler flue gas at 500°F leaving economizer at 325°F, heats feed water from 200 to 248°F. Mixing valve maintains minimum stack temperature leaving economizer to prevent moisture condensation in stack.

**BOILER FLUE ECONOMIZER**

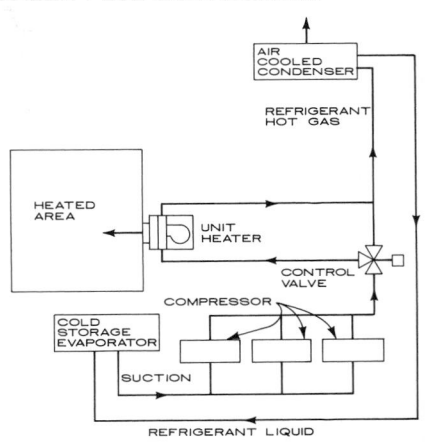

**NOTE**

Rejected heat from cold storage refrigeration system used to heat occupied areas. For heating, hot gas refrigerant from compressor discharge flows through space heating units to extract heat. When heating is not required, hot gas refrigerant flows directly to air cooled condenser for heat rejection to outdoor air.

**REFRIGERANT HOT GAS**

Syska & Hennessy, Consulting Engineers; New York, New York

    **HEAT TRANSFER**

# CHAPTER 16

# *Electrical*

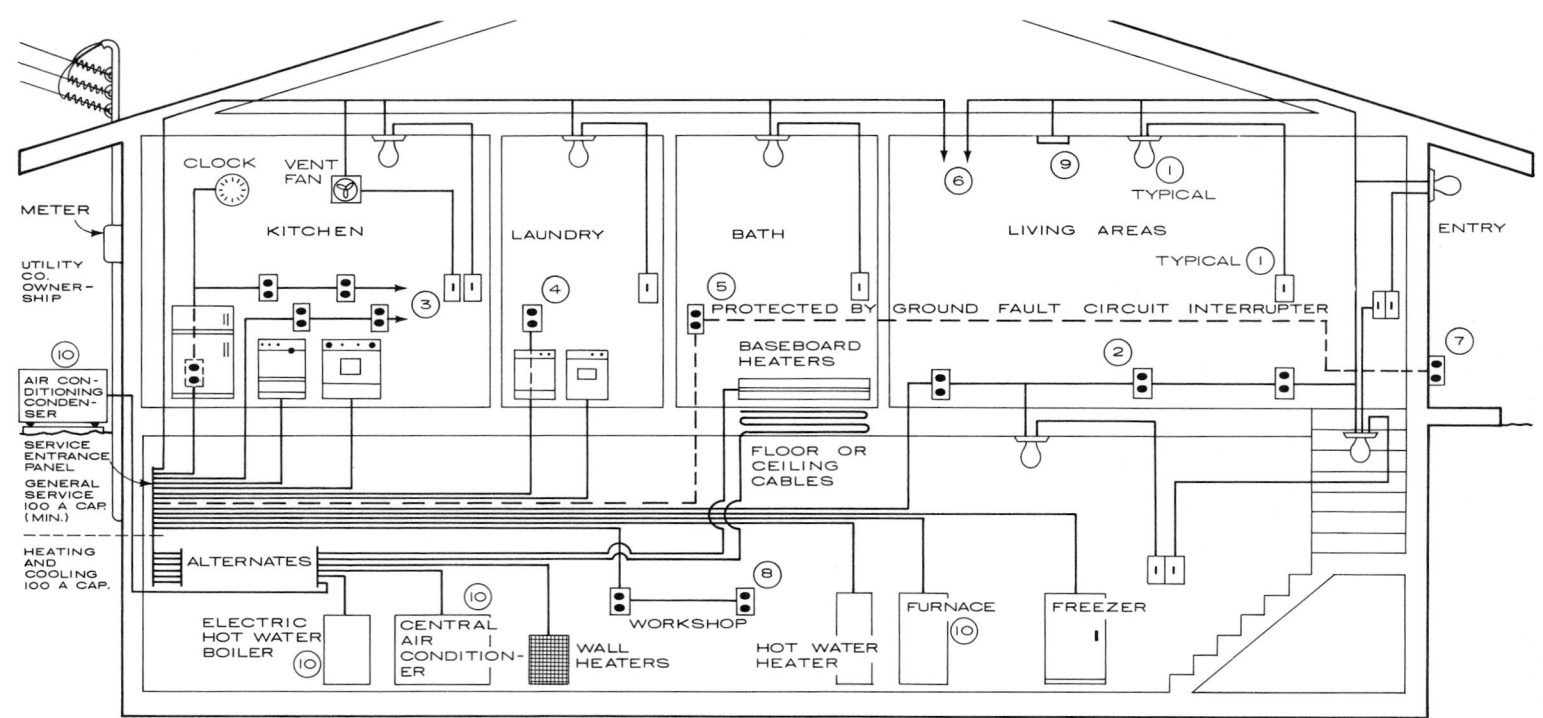

SCHEMATIC  DIAGRAM  OF  TYPICAL  RESIDENTIAL  ELECTRICAL  LAYOUT

## GENERAL REQUIREMENTS

1. A minimum of one wall switch controlled lighting outlet is required in every habitable room, in hallways, stairways, and attached garages, and at outdoor entrances. Exception: in habitable rooms other than kitchens and bathrooms one or more receptacles controlled by a wall switch are permitted in lieu of lighting outlets.
2. In every kitchen, family room, dining room, den, breakfast room, living room, parlor, sunroom, bedroom, recreation room, and similar rooms, receptacle outlets are required such that no point along the floor line in any space is greater than 12 ft, measured horizontally, from an outlet in that space, including any wall space 2 ft or more wide and the wall space occupied by sliding panels in exterior walls.
3. A minimum of two #12 wire 20 A small appliance circuits are required to serve only small appliance

outlets, including refrigeration equipment, in kitchen, pantry, dining room, breakfast room, and family room. Both circuits must extend to kitchen; the other rooms may be served by either one or both of them. No other outlets may be connected to these circuits, other than a receptable installed solely for the supply to and support of an electric clock. In kitchen and dining areas receptacle outlets must be installed at each and every counter space wider than 12 in.
4. A minimum of one #12 wire 20 A circuit must be provided to supply the laundry receptacle(s), and it may have no other outlets.
5. A minimum of one receptacle outlet must be installed in bathroom near the basin and must be provided with ground fault circuit interrupter protection.
6. The code requires sufficient 15 and 20 A circuits to supply 3 W of power for every square foot of floor

space, not including garage and open porch areas. Minimum code suggestion is one circuit per 600 sq ft; one circuit per 500 sq ft is desirable.
7. A minimum of one exterior receptacle outlet is required (two are desirable) and must be provided with ground fault circuit interrupter protection.
8. A minimum of one receptacle outlet is required in basement and garage, in addition to that in the laundry. In attached garages it must be provided with ground fault circuit interrupter protection.
9. Many building codes require a smoke detector in the hallway outside bedrooms or above the stairway leading to upper floor bedrooms.
10. Disconnect switches required.

**NOTE**

Refer to the National Electrical Code (NEC) for further information on residential requirements.

## INDIVIDUAL APPLIANCE CIRCUITS

| TYPE | VOLTS | TYPE | VOLTS |
|------|-------|------|-------|
| Range | 240 | Dishwasher | 120 |
| Separate oven or countertop cooking unit | 240 | Freezer | 120 |
| Water heater | 240 | Oil furnace motor | 120 |
| Automatic washer | 240 | Furnace blower motor | 120 |
| Clothes dryer | 240 | Water pump | 240 |
| Garbage disposal | 240 | Permanently connected appliances > 1000 W | Varies |

## BRANCH CIRCUIT PROTECTION

| | | |
|---|---|---|
| Lighting (general purpose) | #14 wires | 15 A |
| Small appliance | #12 wires | 20 A |
| Individual appliances | #12 wires | 20 A |
| | #10 wires | 30 A |
| | #8 wires | 40 A |
| | #6 wires | 50 A |

## AVERAGE WATTAGES OF COMMON RESIDENTIAL ELECTRICAL DEVICES

| TYPE | WATTS | TYPE | WATTS | TYPE | WATTS |
|------|-------|------|-------|------|-------|
| Air conditioner, central | 2500-6000 | Heating pad | 50-75 | Range oven (separate) | 4000-5000 |
| Air conditioner, room type | 800-2500 | Heat lamp (infrared) | 250 | Razor | 8-12 |
| Blanket, electric | 150-200 | Iron, hand | 600-1200 | Refrigerator | 150-300 |
| Clock | 2-3 | Knife, electric | 100 | Refrigerator, frostless | 400-600 |
| Clothes dryer | 4000-6000 | Lamp, incandescent | 10 upward | Roaster | 1200-1650 |
| Deep fat fryer | 1200-1650 | Lamp, fluorescent | 15-60 | Rotisserie (broiler) | 1200-1650 |
| Dishwasher | 1000-1500 | Lights, Christmas tree | 30-150 | Sewing machine | 60-90 |
| Fan, portable | 50-200 | Microwave oven | 1000-1500 | Stereo (solid state) | 30-100 |
| Food blender | 500-1000 | Mixer | 120-250 | Sunlamp (ultraviolet) | 275-400 |
| Freezer | 300-500 | Percolator | 500-1000 | Television | 50-450 |
| Frying pan, electric | 1000-1200 | Power tools | Up to 1000 | Toaster | 500-1200 |
| Furnace blower | 380-670 | Projector, slide or movie | 300-500 | Vacuum cleaner | 250-1200 |
| Garbage disposal | 500-900 | Radio | 40-150 | Waffle iron | 600-1000 |
| Hair dryer | 350-1200 | Range (all burners and oven "on") | 8000-14000 | Washer, automatic | 500-800 |
| Heater, portable | 1000-1500 | Range top (separate) | 4000-8000 | Water heater | 2000-5000 |

Ed Hesner; Rasmussen & Hobbs Architects, AIA; Tacoma, Washington

**BASIC ELECTRICAL MATERIALS AND METHODS**

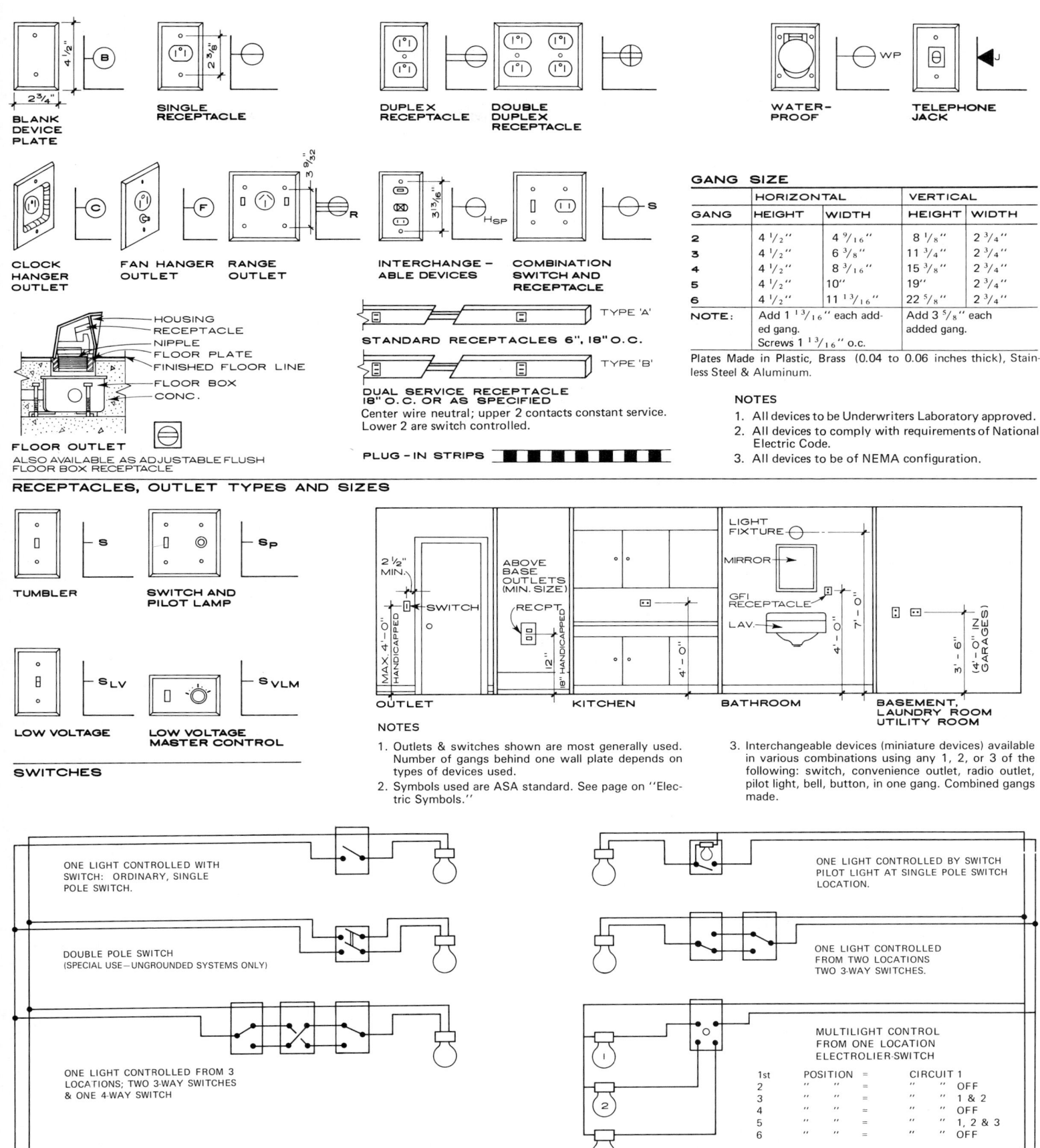

**BLANK DEVICE PLATE**

**SINGLE RECEPTACLE**

**DUPLEX RECEPTACLE**

**DOUBLE DUPLEX RECEPTACLE**

**WATER-PROOF**

**TELEPHONE JACK**

**CLOCK HANGER OUTLET**

**FAN HANGER OUTLET**

**RANGE OUTLET**

**INTERCHANGE-ABLE DEVICES**

**COMBINATION SWITCH AND RECEPTACLE**

**HOUSING**
**RECEPTACLE**
**NIPPLE**
**FLOOR PLATE**
**FINISHED FLOOR LINE**
**FLOOR BOX**
**CONC.**

**FLOOR OUTLET**
ALSO AVAILABLE AS ADJUSTABLE FLUSH FLOOR BOX RECEPTACLE

TYPE 'A'

**STANDARD RECEPTACLES 6", 18" O.C.**

TYPE 'B'

**DUAL SERVICE RECEPTACLE 18" O.C. OR AS SPECIFIED**
Center wire neutral; upper 2 contacts constant service. Lower 2 are switch controlled.

**PLUG–IN STRIPS**

### GANG SIZE

| GANG | HORIZONTAL | | VERTICAL | |
|---|---|---|---|---|
| | HEIGHT | WIDTH | HEIGHT | WIDTH |
| 2 | $4\frac{1}{2}$" | $4\frac{9}{16}$" | $8\frac{1}{8}$" | $2\frac{3}{4}$" |
| 3 | $4\frac{1}{2}$" | $6\frac{3}{8}$" | $11\frac{3}{4}$" | $2\frac{3}{4}$" |
| 4 | $4\frac{1}{2}$" | $8\frac{3}{16}$" | $15\frac{3}{8}$" | $2\frac{3}{4}$" |
| 5 | $4\frac{1}{2}$" | 10" | 19" | $2\frac{3}{4}$" |
| 6 | $4\frac{1}{2}$" | $11\frac{13}{16}$" | $22\frac{5}{8}$" | $2\frac{3}{4}$" |
| NOTE: | Add $1\frac{13}{16}$" each added gang. Screws $1\frac{13}{16}$" o.c. | | Add $3\frac{5}{8}$" each added gang. | |

Plates Made in Plastic, Brass (0.04 to 0.06 inches thick), Stainless Steel & Aluminum.

### NOTES

1. All devices to be Underwriters Laboratory approved.
2. All devices to comply with requirements of National Electric Code.
3. All devices to be of NEMA configuration.

## RECEPTACLES, OUTLET TYPES AND SIZES

**TUMBLER**

**SWITCH AND PILOT LAMP**

**LOW VOLTAGE**

**LOW VOLTAGE MASTER CONTROL**

## SWITCHES

**OUTLET**

**KITCHEN**

**BATHROOM**

**BASEMENT, LAUNDRY ROOM UTILITY ROOM**

### NOTES

1. Outlets & switches shown are most generally used. Number of gangs behind one wall plate depends on types of devices used.
2. Symbols used are ASA standard. See page on "Electric Symbols."
3. Interchangeable devices (miniature devices) available in various combinations using any 1, 2, or 3 of the following: switch, convenience outlet, radio outlet, pilot light, bell, button, in one gang. Combined gangs made.

ONE LIGHT CONTROLLED WITH SWITCH: ORDINARY, SINGLE POLE SWITCH.

DOUBLE POLE SWITCH (SPECIAL USE—UNGROUNDED SYSTEMS ONLY)

ONE LIGHT CONTROLLED FROM 3 LOCATIONS; TWO 3-WAY SWITCHES & ONE 4-WAY SWITCH

ONE LIGHT CONTROLLED BY SWITCH PILOT LIGHT AT SINGLE POLE SWITCH LOCATION.

ONE LIGHT CONTROLLED FROM TWO LOCATIONS TWO 3-WAY SWITCHES.

MULTILIGHT CONTROL FROM ONE LOCATION ELECTROLIER-SWITCH

| 1st | POSITION | = | CIRCUIT 1 |
|---|---|---|---|
| 2 | " " | = | " " OFF |
| 3 | " " | = | " " 1 & 2 |
| 4 | " " | = | " " OFF |
| 5 | " " | = | " " 1, 2 & 3 |
| 6 | " " | = | " " OFF |

NEUTRAL
PHASE

NEUTRAL
PHASE

**SWITCH WIRING DIAGRAMS**

B. J. Baldwin; Giffels & Rossetti, Inc.; Detroit, Michigan

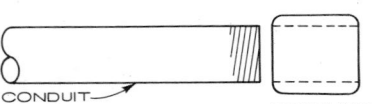 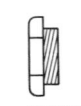

1/2, 3/4, 1, 1 1/4, 1 1/2, 2, 2 1/2, 3, 3 1/2, 4, 4 1/2, 5, 6

CONDUIT — COUPLING — BUSHING — LOCKNUT

### RIGID STEEL CONDUIT (RSC) INTERMEDIATE METALLIC CONDUIT (IMC)
For fireproof construction.
See page on "conduits" for graphic size and weights.

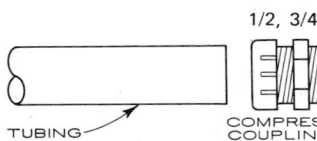 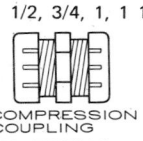  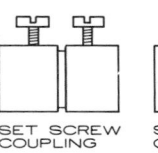 

1/2, 3/4, 1, 1 1/4, 1 1/2, 2

TUBING — COMPRESSION COUPLING — COMPRESSION CONNECTOR — SET SCREW COUPLING — SET SCREW CONNECTOR

### ELECTRICAL METALLIC TUBING
For fireproof construction. Same use as Rigid Conduit above. Walls are thinner, therefore economical.

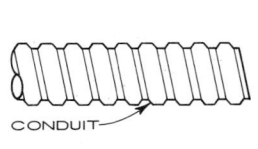 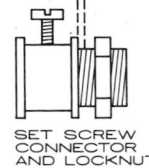 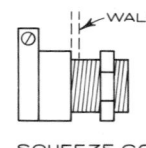 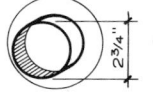

WALL OF JUNCTION BOX

1/2, 3/4, 1, 1 1/4, 1 1/2, 2, 2 1/2, 3.

CONDUIT — SET SCREW CONNECTOR AND LOCKNUT — SQUEEZE CONNECTOR AND LOCKNUT

### FLEXIBLE METALLIC CONDUIT (FMC)
For fireproof construction.

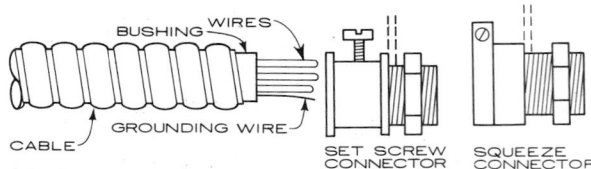

BUSHING — WIRES — GROUNDING WIRE — CABLE — SET SCREW CONNECTOR AND LOCKNUT — SQUEEZE CONNECTOR AND LOCKNUT

2 & 3 Conductor: #14, 12, 10, 8, 6, 4, 2.
4 Conductor: #14, 12, 10, 8, 6, 4.
Lead Covered—
2 cond. in # 14, 12, 10, 8, & 6; 3 cond. in #14, 12, 10, 8, 6, & 4.

### ARMORED CABLE (BX)
For frame construction. Lead covered for wet locations.

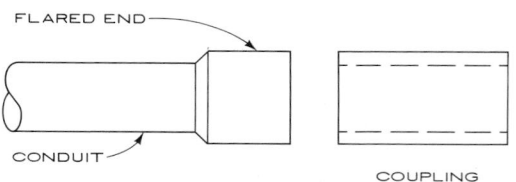

FLARED END — CONDUIT — COUPLING

EPC and EPT same sizes as metallic versions. Available in 3 wall thicknesses (EPT, schedule 40 and 80). Common use underground with or without ·concrete envelope. Ground wire required when used for power cables.

### ELECTRIC PLASTIC CONDUIT AND TUBING (EPC AND EPT)

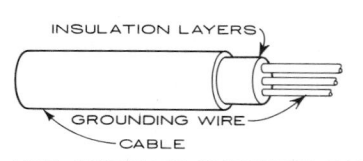 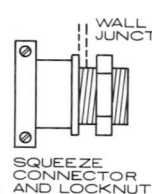

INSULATION LAYERS — GROUNDING WIRE — CABLE — WALL OF JUNCTION BOX — SQUEEZE CONNECTOR AND LOCKNUT

2 and 3 Conductor: #14, 12, 10, 8, 6 & 4

### NON-METALLIC SHEATHED CABLE
For frame construction, where permitted, is cheapest.

### CABLES, CONDUITS AND TUBING
STANDARD NOMINAL SIZES IN INCHES

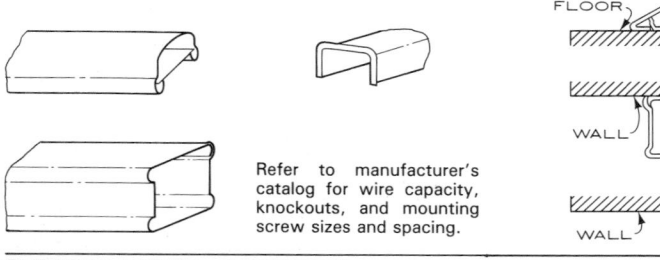

Refer to manufacturer's catalog for wire capacity, knockouts, and mounting screw sizes and spacing.

FLOOR — WALL — WALL

### SURFACE METAL RACEWAYS

Syska & Hennessy; New York, New York
Smith, Hinchman & Grylls Associates, Inc.; Detroit, Michigan
Achla Bahl Madan, AIA, Architect & Interior Designer; Rochester, New York

---

KNOCKOUTS

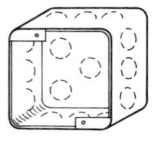 

WIDTH AND DEPTH
3 1/4 x 1 1/2
3 1/2 x 1 1/2
4 x 1 1/2
4 x 2 1/8

BOX — EXTENSION — COVER

### OCTAGONAL
Used in ceilings.

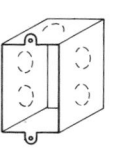 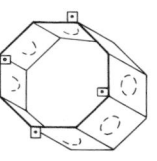 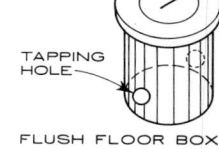

WIDTH AND DEPTH
3 1/4 x 3/4, 1 1/2
3 1/2 x 1/2, 1 1/2
4 x 1/2
*4 x 5/8

* Raised Cover

BOX — RAISED COVER — FLAT COVER

### ROUND
Used in ceilings.

 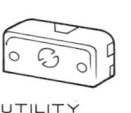

WIDTH AND DEPTH
Square box:
4 x 1 1/2, 2 1/8
4 11/16 x 1 1/2, 2 1/8
2 Gang Box
4 1/2 x 1 3/4 x 6 13/16 long

SQUARE — RECTANGULAR

### RECTANGULAR
Used in walls.

GEM
for switch or receptacle in narrow location 2" wide x 3" long x 2" or 2 1/2" deep
IN MASONRY

4" OCTAGONAL
for concrete 1 1/2, 2, 2 1/2, 3, 3 1/2, 4, 5, 6 deep

TAPPING HOLE

FLUSH FLOOR BOX
for masonry sizes vary

SIZES VARY

ADJUSTABLE JUNCTION BOX — UTILITY BOX — OUTLET AND DEVICE BOX

### EXPOSED-FOR SURFACE RACEWAYS
See manufacturers' catalogs for other fittings.

### OUTLET AND JUNCTION BOXES
SIZES IN INCHES

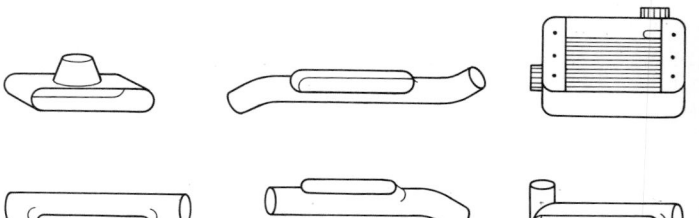

### CONDULETS (FOR EXPOSED WORK)
Condulets made in a great many shapes and sizes; consult manufacturers.

---

**BASIC ELECTRICAL MATERIALS AND METHODS**

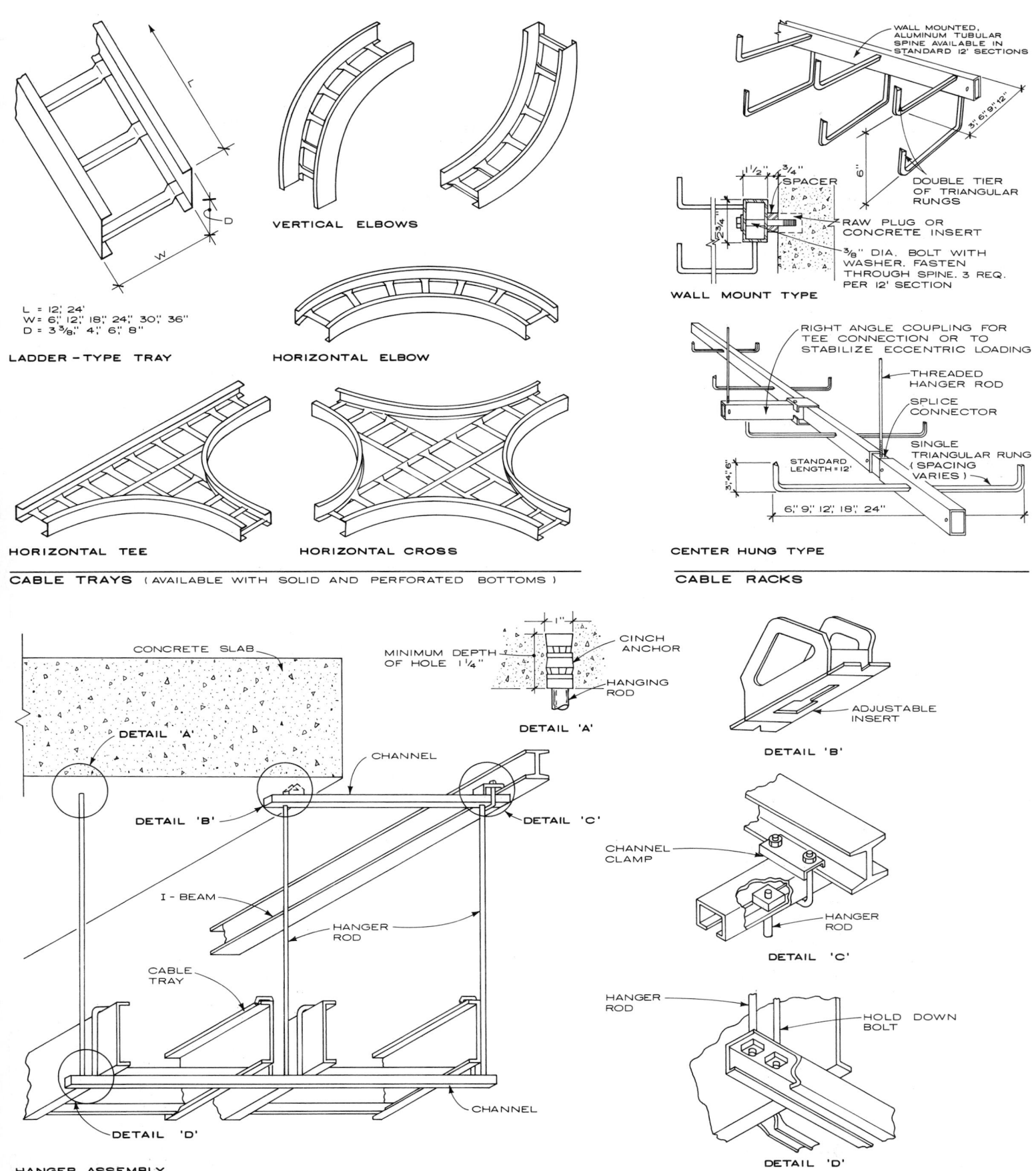

L = 12; 24'
W = 6", 12", 18", 24", 30", 36"
D = 3 3/8", 4", 6", 8"

LADDER – TYPE TRAY

VERTICAL ELBOWS

HORIZONTAL ELBOW

HORIZONTAL TEE

HORIZONTAL CROSS

CABLE TRAYS (AVAILABLE WITH SOLID AND PERFORATED BOTTOMS)

WALL MOUNTED, ALUMINUM TUBULAR SPINE AVAILABLE IN STANDARD 12' SECTIONS

DOUBLE TIER OF TRIANGULAR RUNGS

SPACER

RAW PLUG OR CONCRETE INSERT

3/8" DIA. BOLT WITH WASHER. FASTEN THROUGH SPINE. 3 REQ. PER 12' SECTION

WALL MOUNT TYPE

RIGHT ANGLE COUPLING FOR TEE CONNECTION OR TO STABILIZE ECCENTRIC LOADING

THREADED HANGER ROD

SPLICE CONNECTOR

SINGLE TRIANGULAR RUNG (SPACING VARIES)

STANDARD LENGTH = 12'

6", 9", 12", 18", 24"

CENTER HUNG TYPE

CABLE RACKS

CONCRETE SLAB

DETAIL 'A'

MINIMUM DEPTH OF HOLE 1 1/4"

CINCH ANCHOR

HANGING ROD

DETAIL 'A'

ADJUSTABLE INSERT

DETAIL 'B'

CHANNEL

DETAIL 'B'

DETAIL 'C'

I - BEAM

HANGER ROD

CABLE TRAY

CHANNEL CLAMP

HANGER ROD

DETAIL 'C'

HANGER ROD

HOLD DOWN BOLT

DETAIL 'D'

CHANNEL

DETAIL 'D'

HANGER ASSEMBLY

CABLE TRAY INSTALLATION DETAILS

CH2M Hill, Inc; Corvallis, Oregon

BASIC ELECTRICAL MATERIALS AND METHODS

16

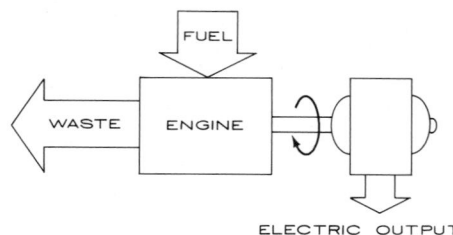

**FIGURE 1**

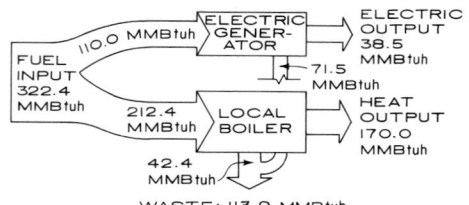

**FIGURE 2**

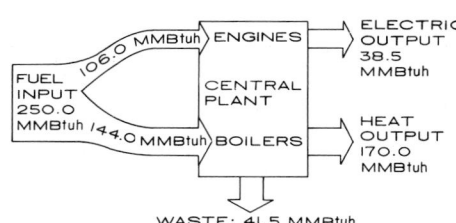

**FIGURE 3**

Co-generation is the integrated production of thermal and electrical (or other mechanical) energy. It usually results from the capture of waste heat from electrical generators.

With conventional utility generator systems, this waste heat is dissipated to the environment through a cooling tower or surrounding bodies of water.

With co-generation systems, the waste heat is usually used to make hot water or steam, which can then be used to heat and cool buildings, make domestic hot water, or be used for process heat.

Conventional electric generation and individual building heating plants will generally have combined peak efficiencies of about 65%.

In the example shown in Fig. 2, 322.4 MMBtuh of fuel is burned to produce 208.5 MMBtuh (65%) of useful heat and electricity. The remaining 113.9 MMBtuh (35+%) is released as waste heat.

Co-generation systems can exceed 80% peak efficiencies. They can be designed for individual buildings or for groups of buildings:

District heating and cooling systems connect a number of buildings together. They offer enhancements to co-

generation systems by increasing the demand for waste heat and, often, by creating a more diversified heating and cooling load to allow the systems to be used for more hours during the year.

In the example shown in Fig. 3 (an actual District Steam/Electric plant in Trenton, NJ), only 250 MMBtuh of fuel is burned to produce the same 208.5 MMBtuh (83+%) of useful heat and electricity as in Fig. 2. Only 41.5 MMBtuh (17%) is released as waste heat.

Burning less fuel not only saves money, but also results in lower levels of thermal and particulate pollution.

## BASIC ELECTRIC CO-GENERATION DISTRICT HEATING SYSTEMS

## BASIC ALTERNATIVES FOR ELECTRIC SERVICE BY CO-GENERATION

| SYSTEM | DESCRIPTION | ADVANTAGES / DISADVANTAGES |
|---|---|---|
| **STAND ALONE** | The co-generation system provides all electricity to the community. There is no connection to the local utility.<br><br>There are several variations to this approach: | Low electric cost to community.<br><br>Systems must be oversized to provide standby capacity for routine maintenance and possible equipment failure. The community must have a good balance between thermal and electric loads. |
| **UTILITY BACKUP** | The simplest possibility: The utility provides only backup power, so the co-generation plant need not be sized with redundant capacity. | Greatest potential flexibility; reduced plant size; lowered first cost.<br><br>Possible high charges by utility for standby capacity; electricity purchased from utility will cost more than self-generated electricity; utility will probably pay a low price for any electricity it buys back. |
| **BUY/SELL** | A more complex arrangement: The utility may provide a portion of the community's electric energy at some times, while at other times co-generated electricity is sold to the utility when the demand for thermal energy results in more electricity being produced than the community can use. | Greatest potential flexibility; reduced plant size; lowered first cost.<br><br>Possible high charges by utility for standby capacity; electricity purchased from utility will cost more than self-generated electricity; utility will probably pay a low price for any electricity it buys back. |
| **SELL ALL ELECTRICITY** | In this arrangement, all of the electricity produced is sold to the local electric utility, resulting in lower cost thermal energy to the community. The community buys all of its electricity from the electric utility, just as it would in a conventional arrangement. | Low-cost thermal energy; simpler relationship with utility company; no thermal/electric balance problems.<br><br>Electricity purchased from utility will cost more than self-generated electricity. |

## NOTES

There are three technologies typically used for the drivers of co-generation systems:

1. DIESEL ENGINES: Similar to car or truck engines; fueled generally by oil or natural gas.

2. COMBUSTION TURBINES: Hot gases from the burning of fuel spin the turbine rotors; fueled generally by oil or natural gas.

3. STEAM TURBINES: Steam produced in a boiler spins the turbine rotors; boilers can be fueled with almost anything that burns (oil, gas, coal, wood, waste, etc.)

Carl Stein, FAIA; New York, New York
Diane Serber, FAIA; New York, New York

## RELATIVE ADVANTAGES/DISADVANTAGES

1. Higher electric efficiency; low maintenance costs for larger sizes. High first cost; most waste heat at low temperature; relatively heavy weight.

2. Low first cost; most waste heat at high temperature; relatively light weight. Low electric generating efficiency; more frequent maintenance required.

3. Waste heat generally at high temperature. Efficient only in larger sizes; requires high-pressure steam.

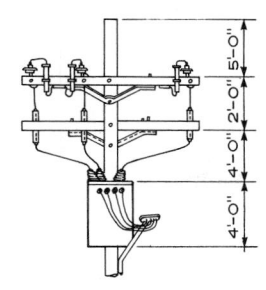

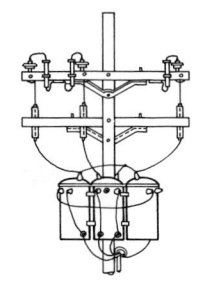

SINGLE OR 3 PHASE      3 PHASE

## OVERHEAD TRANSFORMER

OVERHEAD TRANSFORMER: Three-phase transformers are available up to 500 kVA in a single unit. Three single-phase units can total to 1500 kVA with adequate platform support. Service lateral to building can be either overhead or underground.

Typical dimensions for 13 and 23 kV. See the National Electrical Safety Code (ANSI C2) for required clearances; 6 in. if overhead ground wire is not provided.

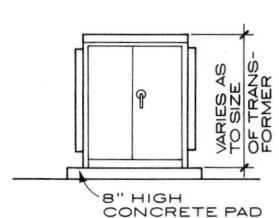

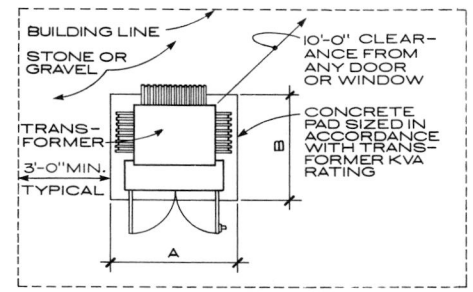

## PAD MOUNTED TRANSFORMER

High voltage compartment requires 10 ft clearance for on-off operation of the insulated stick located on the transformer (known as "hot stick" operation).

| Typical pad sizes: | | A | B |
|---|---|---|---|
| | 75– 500 KVA | 70 in. | 58 in. |
| | 750–2500 KVA | 87 in. | 70 in. |

PAD MOUNTED TRANSFORMER: Pad mounted transformers with weatherproof tamperproof enclosure permit installation at ground level without danger from exposed live parts. Three phase units up to 2500 kVA are available and are normally used with underground primary and secondary feeders.

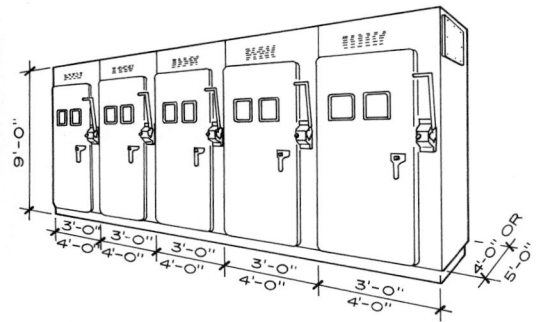

## PRIMARY SWITCHGEAR

PRIMARY SWITCHGEAR: Where the owner's buildings cover a large area such as a college campus or medical center, the application usually requires the use of medium voltages of 5 kV to 34 kV for distribution feeders. Therefore, the utility company will terminate their primary feeders on the owner's metal clad or metal enclosed switchgear. This switchgear may be interior or exterior weatherproof construction. Code clearance in front and back of board must be provided in accordance with the National Electric Code.

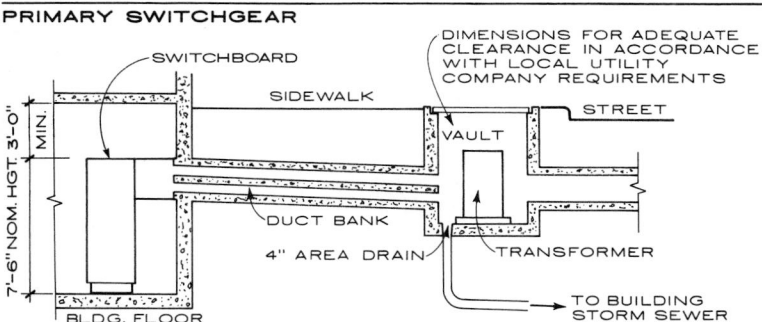

UNDERGROUND VAULT: Underground vaults are generally used for utility company transformers where all distribution feeders are underground. These systems usually constitute a network or spot network. Vaults often are located below the sidewalks and have grating tops.

## UNDERGROUND VAULT

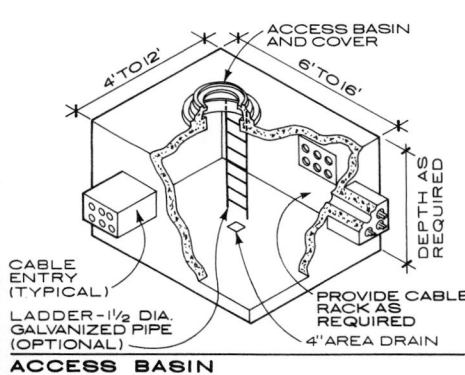

ACCESS BASIN

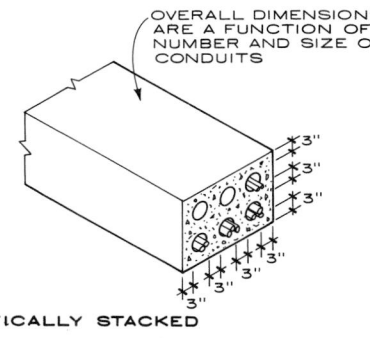

VERTICALLY STACKED

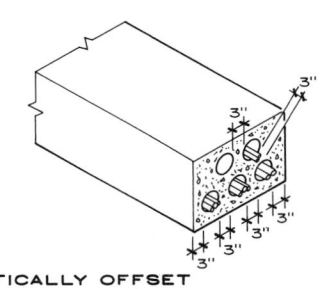

VERTICALLY OFFSET

## UNDERGROUND DUCT BANK

William Tao & Associates, Inc., Consulting Engineers; St. Louis, Missouri
Dennis W. Wolbert; Everett I. Brown Company; Indianapolis, Indiana

**HIGH VOLTAGE DISTRIBUTION**    **16**

## NOTES

Poke-through systems are used in conjunction with overhead branch distribution systems run in accessible suspended ceiling cavities to serve outlets in full height partitions. When services are required at floor locations where adjacent partitions or columns are not available, as in open office planning, they must either be brought down from a wireway assembly (known as a power pole) or up through a floor penetration containing a fire-rated insert fitting and above-floor outlet assembly. To install a poke-through assembly, the floor slab must either be drilled or contain preset sleeves arranged in a modular array. Poke-through assemblies are used in conjunction with cellular deck and underfloor duct systems when precise service location required does not fall directly above its associated system raceway.

With one floor penetration, the single poke-through assembly can serve all the power, communications, and data requirements of a work station. Distribution wiring in the ceiling cavity can be run in raceways. The more cost-effective method is to use armored cable (bx) for power and approved plenum rated cable for communications and data when the ceiling cavity is used for return air. To minimize disturbance to the office space below when a poke-through assembly needs to be relocated or added, a modular system of prewired junction boxes for each service can be provided, although it is more common to elect this option for power only. A different type of wiring system must be selected for a floor slab on grade, above lobby or retail space, above mechanical equipment space, or above space exposed to atmosphere.

Low initial cost of a poke-through system makes it both viable and attractive for investor-owned buildings where tenants are responsible for future changes and for corporate buildings where construction budget is limited. It is effective when office planning includes interconnecting work station panels containing provisions to extend wiring above the floor, reducing the number of floor penetrations needed for services.

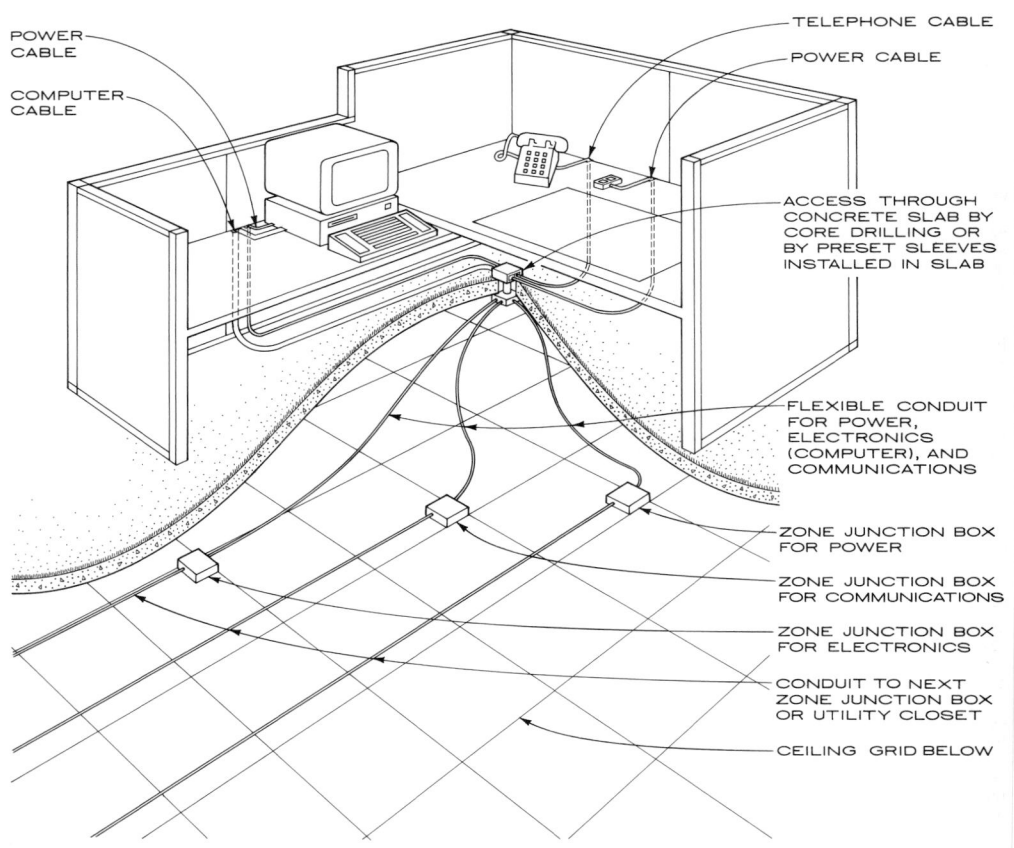

POWER CABLE

COMPUTER CABLE

TELEPHONE CABLE

POWER CABLE

ACCESS THROUGH CONCRETE SLAB BY CORE DRILLING OR BY PRESET SLEEVES INSTALLED IN SLAB

FLEXIBLE CONDUIT FOR POWER, ELECTRONICS (COMPUTER), AND COMMUNICATIONS

ZONE JUNCTION BOX FOR POWER

ZONE JUNCTION BOX FOR COMMUNICATIONS

ZONE JUNCTION BOX FOR ELECTRONICS

CONDUIT TO NEXT ZONE JUNCTION BOX OR UTILITY CLOSET

CEILING GRID BELOW

**POKE-THROUGH HARDWIRE SYSTEM/ZONE JUNCTION BOXES**

## NOTES

Based on projected frequency of future changes in office furniture layouts, a corporate or government organization may elect to preinvest in a permanent raceway system to minimize cost and disturbance to occupants when changes or additions are made. When structural design dictates the use of metal decking, a cellular floor raceway system utilizing trench header ducts becomes the most likely candidate for selection.

Cellular raceways come in a variety of sizes and configurations ranging from 1½ to 3 in. high with cells 8 or 12 in. o.c. and 2 or 3 cells per section. An overall floor deck can be full cellular, where bottom plates are provided throughout, or blended as shown.

Trench header ducts come in various sizes and configurations. Height is adjustable for slab depths above cells of 2½–4 in. and widths vary from 9 to 36 in. Coverplates are ¼ in. thick, with lengths from 6 to 36 in., and can either be secured with spring clips or flush, flathead bolts. Two versions of trench design are available, one consisting of a compartmental bottom tray with a grommeted access hole for each cell it crosses and the other a bottomless trench duct consisting of side rails and a separate wireway in the middle, with grommeted access holes only for the power cells.

When service is needed, floor is core drilled above desired cell, the cell top is drilled into, and an afterset insert with above-floor fitting is attached. If data and communication wiring can occupy the same cell, with power wiring in an adjacent cell, two separate service fittings are required for each work station.

Where it is necessary to eliminate or minimize core drilling, a modular pattern combination of two or three preset service flush outlets can be provided along the cellular sections before the floor is poured, as shown. Upon activation, one flush outlet can serve all the power, communication, and data requirements of a work station.

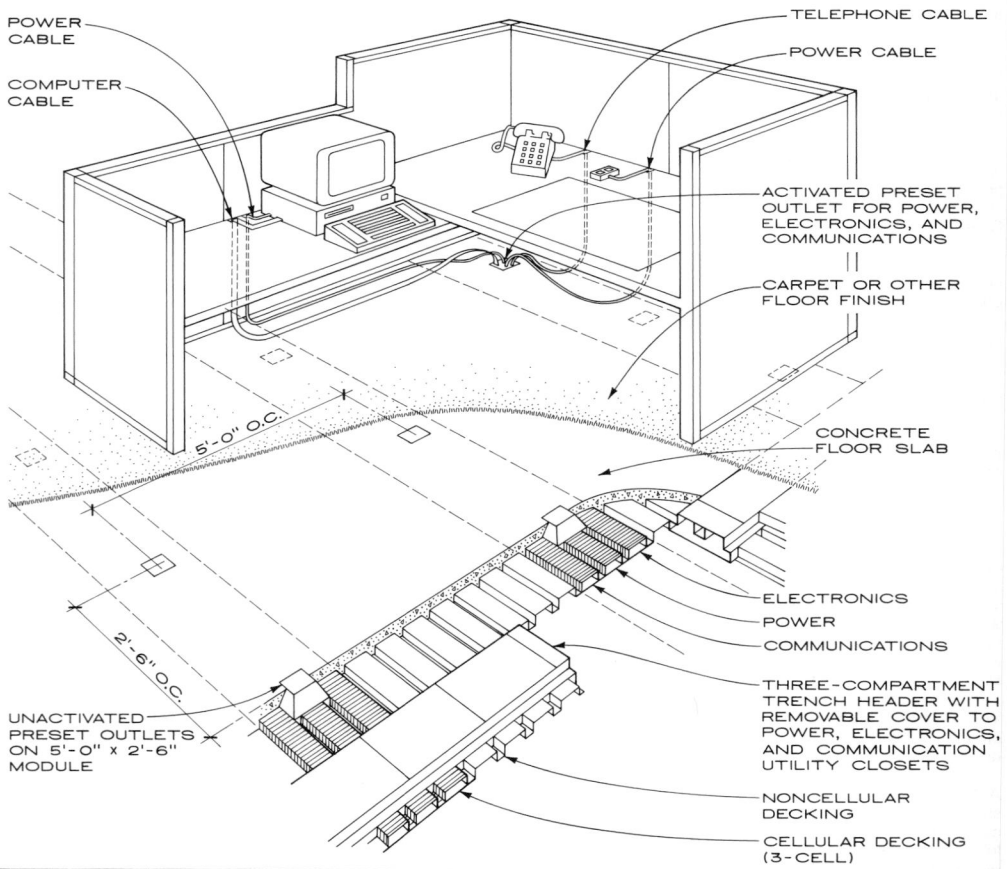

POWER CABLE

COMPUTER CABLE

TELEPHONE CABLE

POWER CABLE

ACTIVATED PRESET OUTLET FOR POWER, ELECTRONICS, AND COMMUNICATIONS

CARPET OR OTHER FLOOR FINISH

CONCRETE FLOOR SLAB

ELECTRONICS

POWER

COMMUNICATIONS

THREE-COMPARTMENT TRENCH HEADER WITH REMOVABLE COVER TO POWER, ELECTRONICS, AND COMMUNICATION UTILITY CLOSETS

NONCELLULAR DECKING

CELLULAR DECKING (3-CELL)

5'-0" O.C.

2'-6" O.C.

UNACTIVATED PRESET OUTLETS ON 5'-0" x 2'-6" MODULE

**ELECTRIFIED CELLULAR DECK SYSTEM/TRENCH HEADER DUCT**

Richard F. Humenn, PE; Joseph R. Loring & Associates, Inc., Consulting Engineers; New York, New York
Gary A. Hall; Hammel Green and Abrahamson; Minneapolis, Minnesota

 **16**    SERVICE AND DISTRIBUTION

**NOTES**

Where projected frequency of future changes is relatively high, a raised access floor system will provide the maximum flexibility and lowest cost to relocate or add services for work stations. When used in conjunction with a modular system of power, communication, and data wiring plug-in receptacles, and cable connector sets, changes can be made without the need of an electrician or wiring technician. Advantages come at a premium, as access floor is the highest in initial cost of all systems described in this section.

Raised access floor is essentially a basic computer floor that is restricted in application to distribute only power, communication, and data services to work stations. The absence of air distribution and high density of cabling associated with computers permits raised floor height to be reduced to nominal 6 in. As the depth of standard 2 ft sq formed steel floor panel is less than 2 in., over 4 in. clear height under the panels provides sufficient clearance to accommodate hardware associated with distributing services. Virtually any variety of above-floor or flush outlets can be mounted on a floor panel and connected to lengths of cable with plug or connector fitting at the other end.

Access floor can be provided with or without stringers, which are used to minimize "creep" effect. Laser beam equipment speeds up accurate leveling of pedestal heights. For a custom installation without ramps or steps, the base floor is structurally designed to be depressed below permanent building elements such as lobbies, stairs, and toilets. Panels can be ordered with factory-installed carpeting or, alternatively, magnetic-backed carpet squares can be added after installation.

The introduction of an access floor does not necessarily require an increase in floor-to-floor height, and if so, the cubage added is at a much lower per unit cost than for the rest of the building. When special attention is given to coordinating lighting with other elements in the suspended ceiling or when lighting is provided below as from the work stations, the cavity can be compressed to compensate for the raised floor.

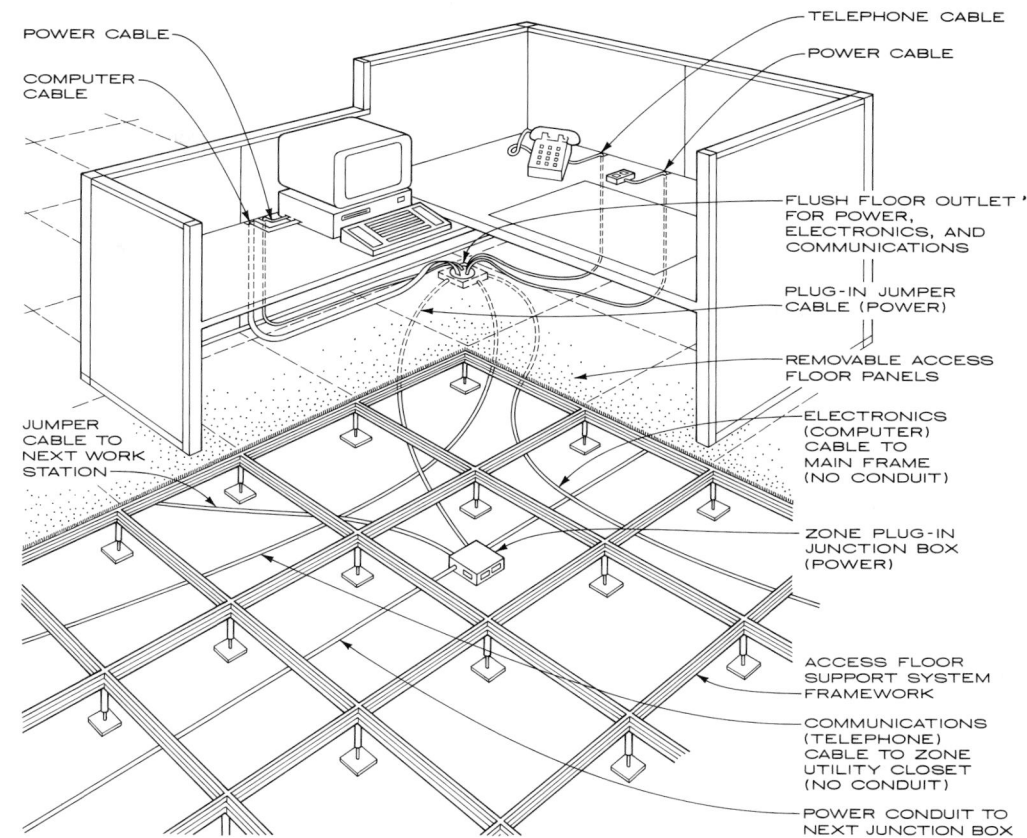

POWER CABLE

COMPUTER CABLE

TELEPHONE CABLE

POWER CABLE

FLUSH FLOOR OUTLET FOR POWER, ELECTRONICS, AND COMMUNICATIONS

PLUG-IN JUMPER CABLE (POWER)

REMOVABLE ACCESS FLOOR PANELS

ELECTRONICS (COMPUTER) CABLE TO MAIN FRAME (NO CONDUIT)

ZONE PLUG-IN JUNCTION BOX (POWER)

ACCESS FLOOR SUPPORT SYSTEM FRAMEWORK

COMMUNICATIONS (TELEPHONE) CABLE TO ZONE UTILITY CLOSET (NO CONDUIT)

POWER CONDUIT TO NEXT JUNCTION BOX

JUMPER CABLE TO NEXT WORK STATION

**RAISED ACCESS FLOOR SYSTEM / MODULAR PLUG-IN DISTRIBUTION**

**NOTES**

Undercarpet flat cable wiring has developed into a viable system to serve work stations. By code, it can only be used with carpet squares to afford an acceptable degree of access. Although there are some limitations in performance for flat communication and data cables, improvements are continually being made. Flat cables are now available for Local Area Network-(LAN) distribution, applicable where communication and data requirements are extensive.

Cables originate at transition boxes located at various intervals along core corridor walls and/or columns that are individually served from distribution centers in utility closets. Boxes can also be cast in the floor or atop a poke-through insert. Cables are not permitted to pass under fixed partitions and must be carefully mapped out to minimize crossovers and clutter.

To install a service fitting, an interface base assembly must first be secured directly to the concrete floor at the flat cable location. The base assembly stabs into conductors of the flat cable and converts them to round wire. When the service fitting is attached, it is activated and ready for use.

Careful consideration must be given to the application of this system based on limitations that may or may not be acceptable under different conditions. For instance, it may be ideal for small areas or renovation of existing buildings where the poke-through or power pole systems are unacceptable or cannot be used. In new buildings where poke-through has been chosen as the base system, the flat cable system is a viable solution in areas where poke-through outlets cannot be installed, such as slab on grade.

Where frequent changes and additions are contemplated, the resulting wear and tear on expensive, glued down carpet tiles may become a distinct disadvantage.

Although this system appears to be simple and inexpensive, it is highly labor intensive and actual installed initial costs and outlet relocation costs are comparable to cellular deck with trench header ducts.

POWER CABLE

COMPUTER CABLE

TELEPHONE CABLE

POWER CABLE

CONDUIT AND WIRE TO POWER CLOSET CONCEALED IN WALL OR CEILING

TRANSITION BOX AT WALL FOR POWER

LOW-PROFILE ELECTRONICS AND COMMUNICATIONS OUTLET

LOW-PROFILE POWER OUTLET

THREE-CIRCUIT FLAT POWER CABLE

POWER CABLE SPLICE

ELECTRONICS (COMPUTER) AND COMMUNICATIONS (TELEPHONE) CABLE TO UTILITY CLOSETS VIA TRANSITION BOXES

ONE-, TWO-, OR THREE-CIRCUIT FLAT POWER CABLE TO ADDITIONAL POWER OUTLETS

CARPET SQUARES (TYPICAL)

**FLAT CABLE WIRING SYSTEM**

Richard F. Humenn, PE; Joseph R. Loring & Associates, Inc., Consulting Engineers; New York, New York
Gary A. Hall; Hammel Green and Abrahamson; Minneapolis, Minnesota

**SERVICE AND DISTRIBUTION    16**

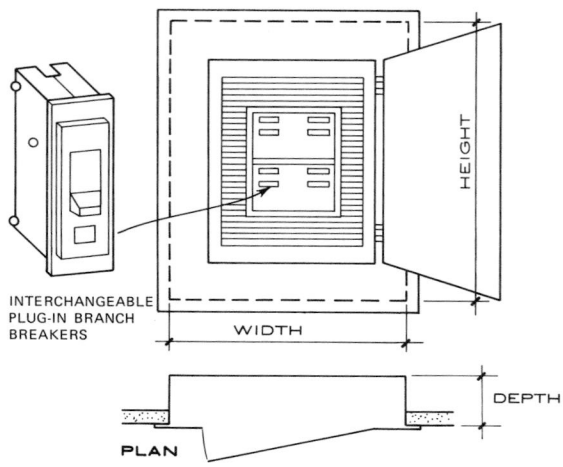

INTERCHANGEABLE
PLUG-IN BRANCH
BREAKERS

HEIGHT

WIDTH

DEPTH

PLAN

PLUG-IN CIRCUIT BREAKER

RESIDENTIAL AND SMALL COMMERCIAL PANEL BOARDS

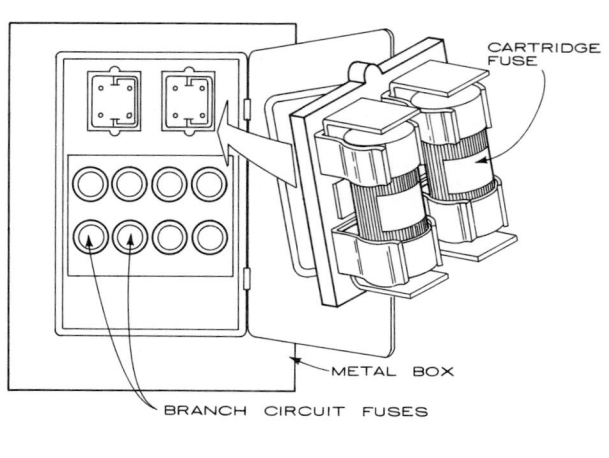

CARTRIDGE
FUSE

METAL BOX

BRANCH CIRCUIT FUSES

FUSE BOX WITH FUSED MAIN DISCONNECTS

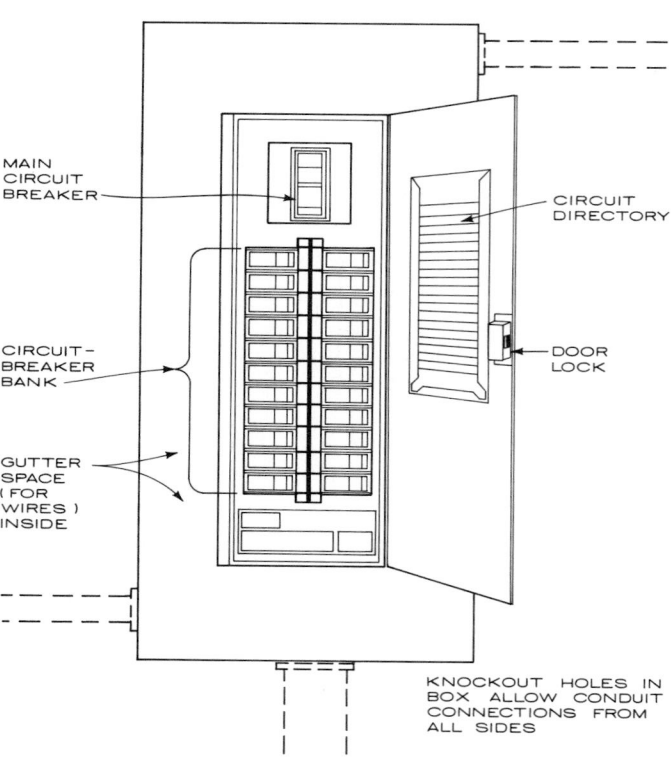

MAIN
CIRCUIT
BREAKER

CIRCUIT
DIRECTORY

CIRCUIT-
BREAKER
BANK

DOOR
LOCK

GUTTER
SPACE
( FOR
WIRES )
INSIDE

KNOCKOUT HOLES IN
BOX ALLOW CONDUIT
CONNECTIONS FROM
ALL SIDES

LARGE RESIDENTIAL PANELBOARD

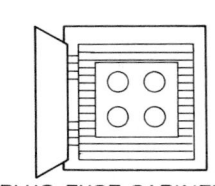

Box dimensions below.
For outside dimension
add 1 1/4" to height &
width.

PLUG FUSE CABINET

PLUG
FUSE

### BOX DIMENSIONS (IN.)

| BRANCHES | HEIGHT | WIDTH | DEPTH |
|---|---|---|---|
| 2 | 6 5/8 | 6 5/8 | 2 3/4 |
| 4 | 6 5/8 | 6 5/8 | 2 3/4 |
| 6 | 11 1/8 | 7 3/8 | 3 1/8 |
| 8 | 14 1/8 | 7 3/8 | 3 1/8 |

Up to 12 branches same as 8 branches

**PLUG FUSE AND PLUG FUSE CABINET**
FOR APARTMENTS AND SMALL HOUSES

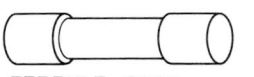

FERRULE TYPE          KNIFE BLADE TYPE

**CARTRIDGE FUSES**

Ferrule contact 1 to 60 amps.
Knife blade contact 70 to 600 amps and larger.
Ferrule type non-renewable.  Knife blade type non-renewable and
renewable link.

### STANDARD FUSE SIZES

Plug Fuse:  1, 3, 5, 6, 8, 10, 15, 20, 25 and 30 amperes.
Cartridge:  1, 3, 6, 10, 15, 20, 25, 30, 35, 40, 50, 60, 70, 80, 90,
100, 110, 125, 150, 175, 200, 225, 250, 275, 300, 325, 350, 400,
450, 500, 600 amperes, and larger.

Standard knife switches are rated at 30, 60, 100, 200, 400 & 600
amps, and take cartridge fuses up to and including their rating.

Circuit breakers at 50 (trip at 15, 20, 30, 40, 50); 100 (trip at 15,
20, 30, 40, 50, 70, 100); 225 (70 — 225, increment 25); 600 (125 —
350, increment 25 & 400, 500, 600 amp.)

### PANELBOARD DIMENSIONS

| MAXIMUM NUMBER OF CIRCUITS | BOX DIMENSIONS (IN.) | | |
|---|---|---|---|
| | WIDTH | HEIGHT | DEPTH |
| 12 | 9–15 | 16–20 | $3^3/_4$–$4^5/_8$ |
| 20 | 9–15 | $20^1/_4$–24 | $3^3/_4$–$4^5/_8$ |
| 30 | 12–15 | 30–33 | $3^3/_4$–$4^5/_8$ |
| 40 | 14–15 | 34–39 | 4–$4^5/_8$ |

Darrel Downing Rippeteau, Architect; Washington, D.C.

**SERVICE AND DISTRIBUTION**

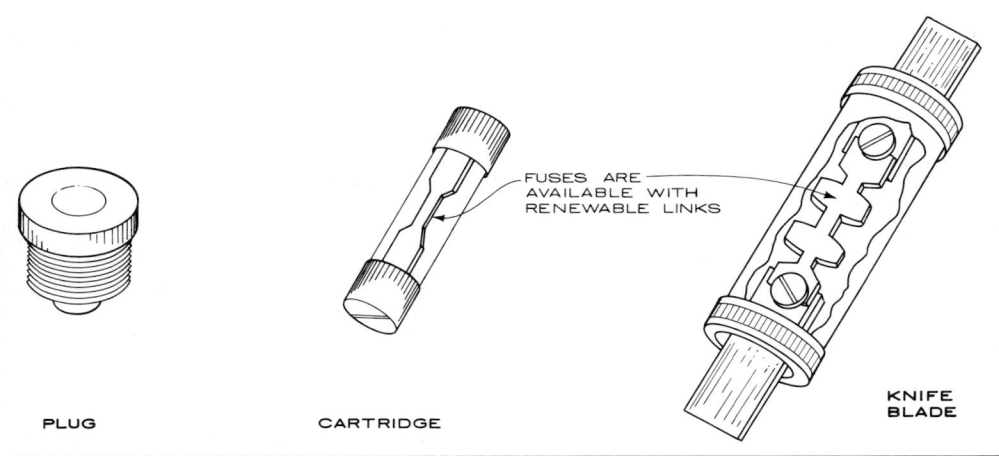

**PLUG FUSES**
1. MAXIMUM VOLTAGE: 125.
2. AMPERE RATING: 1–30 A.
3. FUSE TYPES: S, T

**CARTRIDGE FUSES**
1. MAXIMUM VOLTAGE: 250 and 600.
2. AMPERE RATINGS: $\frac{1}{10}$–60 A.
3. FUSE TYPES: K1, RK1, K5, RK5, J, H, and G.

**KNIFE BLADE FUSES**
1. MAXIMUM VOLTAGE: 250 and 600.
2. AMPERE RATINGS: 70–6000 A.
3. FUSE TYPES: K1, RK1, K5, RK5, J, H, G, and L.

NOTE: Cartridge and knife blade fuses available for short circuit protection up to 200,000 A (Rms).

FUSES ARE AVAILABLE WITH RENEWABLE LINKS

PLUG

CARTRIDGE

KNIFE BLADE

**STANDARD FUSES**

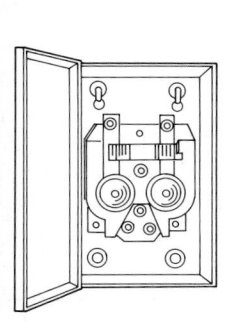

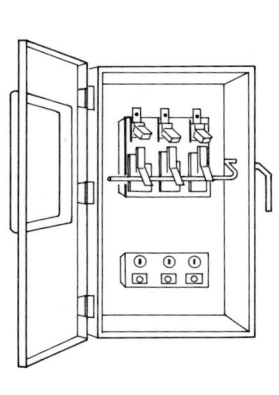

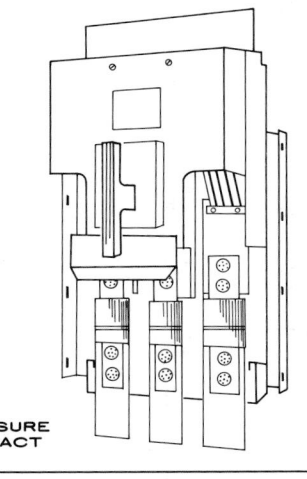

**TOGGLE SWITCHES**
1. MAXIMUM VOLTAGES: 125 VAC/DC, 125 or 250 VAC/DC, or 240 VAC.
2. RATING: 30 A max.

**SAFETY SWITCHES**
1. MAXIMUM VOLTAGES: 240 VAC, 125–250 VDC, 600 VAC.
2. POLES: 2, 3, or 4 plus S/N and/or GRD Lug.
3. TYPES: TG, TH, or TC fusible and no fuse.
4. RATING: 30–1200 A.

**HIGH PRESSURE CONTACT SWITCHES**
1. MAXIMUM VOLTAGES: 240 VAC or 480 VAC.
2. POLES: 3.
3. RATINGS: 800–4000 A.

TOGGLE

KNIFE BLADE

HIGH PRESSURE CONTACT

**DISCONNECT SWITCHES**

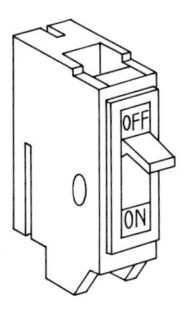

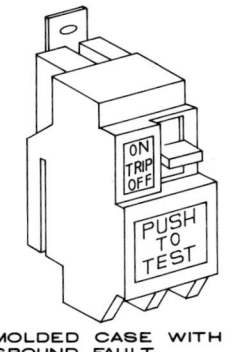

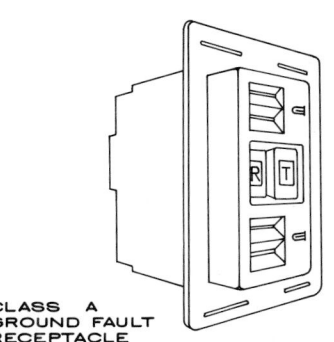

**STANDARD MOLDED CASE CIRCUIT BREAKERS**
1. MAXIMUM VOLTAGES: 120 VAC, 240 VAC, 600 VAC, 125 VDC, and 250 VDC.
2. FRAME SIZES: 100 A, 150 A, 225 A, 400 A, 600 A, 800 A, 1200 A Poles—2 or 3 above 100 A.
3. Current limiting type with fuses.

**MOLDED CASE CIRCUIT BREAKERS INCORPORATING GROUND FAULT CIRCUIT INTERRUPTION**
1. MAXIMUM VOLTAGES: 120 VAC or 120/240 VAC.
2. FRAME SIZE: 100 A ratings, 15–30 A poles—1 or 2.

**CLASS A GROUND FAULT CIRCUIT INTERRUPTION RECEPTACLES**
1. MAXIMUM VOLTAGE: 125 VAC.
2. RATINGS: 15 or 20 A NEMA configuration single outlet.

MOLDED CASE

MOLDED CASE WITH GROUND FAULT

CLASS A GROUND FAULT RECEPTACLE

**CIRCUIT BREAKERS**

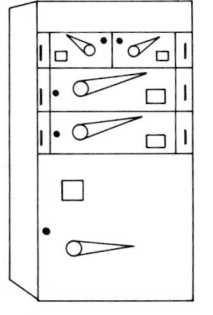

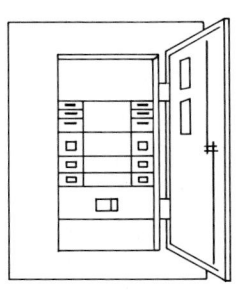

## 3-PHASE CIRCUIT BREAKER PANELS

| MANUFACTURER | MAX. NO. OF POLES | BOX SIZES (IN.) | | |
|---|---|---|---|---|
| | | WIDTH | HEIGHT | DEPTH |
| Square D | 12 | 20 | 20 | 5¾ |
| | 20 | 20 | 23 | 5¾ |
| | 42 | 20 | 35 | 5¾ |
| General Electric Co. | 12 | 20 | 21½ | 5¾ |
| | 20 | 20 | 27½ | 5¾ |
| | 30 | 20 | 33½ | 5¾ |
| | 42 | 20 | 36½ | 5¾ |
| Westinghouse | 12 | 20 | 21 | 5¾ |
| | 18 | 20 | 24 | 5¾ |
| | 30 | 20 | 30 | 5¾ |
| | 42 | 20 | 36 | 5¾ |

SWITCH AND FUSE

CIRCUIT BREAKER

**DISTRIBUTION PANEL BOARDS**

NOTE: Other manufacturers' panels are available in similar sizes.

A. A. Erdman; Sargent, Webster, Crenshaw & Folley; Architects Engineers Planners; Syracuse, New York

**SERVICE AND DISTRIBUTION**

16

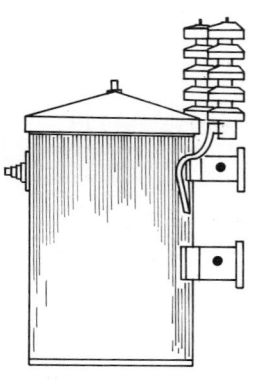 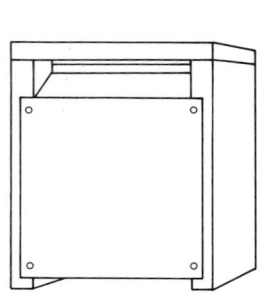 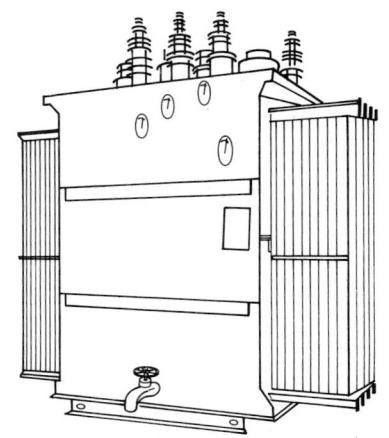 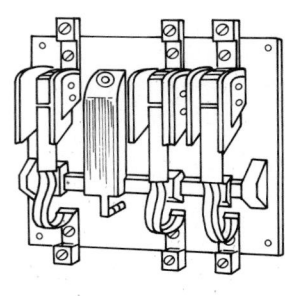

DISTRIBUTION        DRY TYPE            LIQUID FILLED                        LOAD CIRCUITS

DISTRIBUTION: High to low voltage. Immersed in oil. Self-cooled. Primarily mounted on outdoor poles.
DRY: Maximum voltage 600 VAC. Primarily mounted on indoor floors and walls.
LIQUID: Secondary substation transformer with high to low voltage. Primarily a commercial type transformer for the outdoors.

Maximum voltage: 600 VAC. For load circuits that are closed and opened repeatedly various design combinations are allowed. Used for all classes of magnetically held loads, open or closed.

## TRANSFORMERS

## CONTACTOR

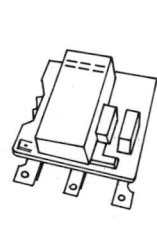 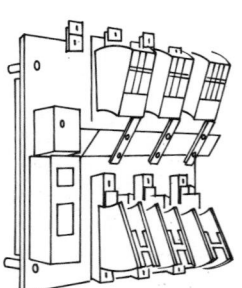 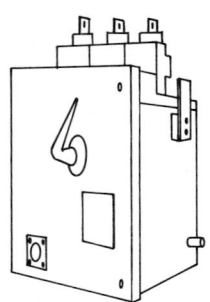

REMOTE CONTROL      AUTOTRANSFER        NETWORK TYPE                        MAIN CIRCUIT BREAKER

REMOTE CONTROL: Provides convenient control of lighting and power circuits from control stations.
AUTOTRANSFER: Automatically transfers loads from a normal source to the emergency source.

Maximum voltage: 125/216 VAC or 277/480 VAC. Interrupting capacity 30,000 and 60,000 A. RMS. SYM. A fault on primary cable or network transformer will open protector to isolate fault from system.

Maximum voltage ratings: 120/240, 3 wire, single phase or 208V/120, 4 wire three phase. Either indoor or outdoor construction. Number of sockets as required by application.

## SWITCHES

## PROTECTOR

## METER BANK

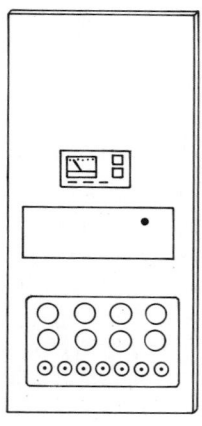 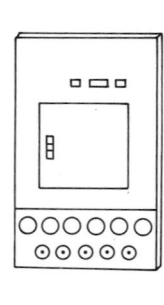 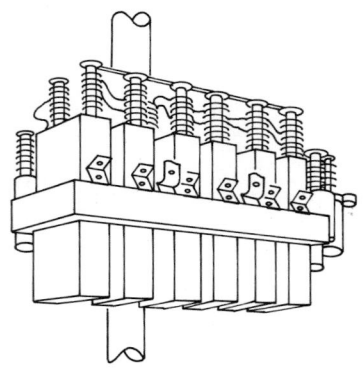 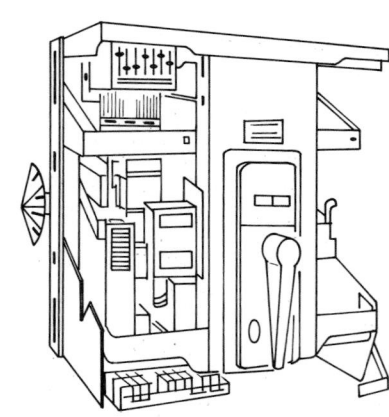

LARGE               SMALL               POLE RACK                           LOW VOLTAGE

PRIMARY VOLTAGES: 120, 208, 240, or 277.
SECONDARY VOLTAGE: 120.
APPLICATION: Power and lighting panels, special panels for hospitals (operating, coronary, and X-ray).

Application: Power factor correction on either low or high voltage systems. Types, indoor or outdoor. Size and voltage as required. Switched or floating.

Maximum voltages: 240 VAC, 480 VAC, 600 VAC, and 250 VDC. Operation is manual or electric. Breaker trip devices: Electromechanical or solid state. Type: stationary or drawout.

## ISOLATED POWER CENTER

## CAPACITOR

## CIRCUIT BREAKER

A. A. Erdman; Sargent, Webster, Crenshaw & Folley; Architects Engineers Planners; Syracuse, New York

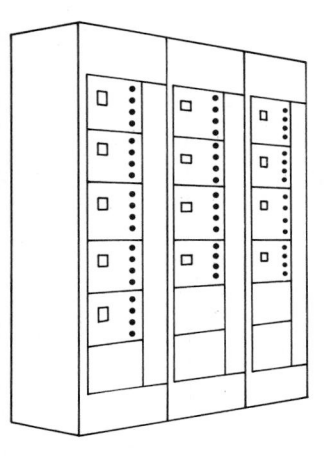

**MOTOR CONTROL CENTER**

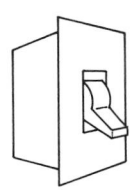

**MANUAL**

**MAGNETIC**

**COMBINATION**

MANUAL: Maximum voltage—240 VAC. Maximum horsepower—1.

MAGNETIC: Maximum voltage—600 VAC. Maximum horsepower—200.

COMBINATION: A magnetic motor starter with a variety of fusible disconnects or circuit breakers.

**MOTOR STARTERS**

UNIT SUBSTATION: Primary entrance cubicle, air interrupter switch, transformer section, and low voltage distribution sections. See manufacturer's literature for type, size, and arrangements. See National Electric Code for required aisle space, ventilation, servicing area, and special building condition requirements.

**UNIT SUBSTATION**

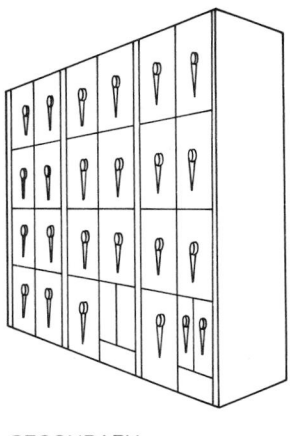

**SECONDARY**

**WITH MAIN**

SWITCHBOARD: Metering compartment, main disconnect, check meters, and low voltage distribution section. See manufacturer's literature for type, size, and arrangements. See National Electric Code for required aisle space, servicing area, and room layout.

**SWITCHBOARDS**

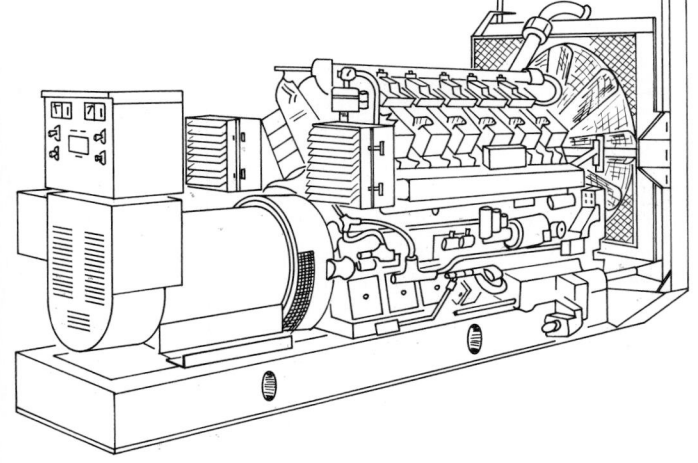

EMERGENCY GENERATOR: Engine driven prime mover, alternator, and controls. Application: to provide emergency power during power outages. See manufacturer's literature for ratings, dimensions, weight, ventilation, and fuel consumption. See National Electric Code for working space requirements and proper application.

**EMERGENCY GENERATOR WITH CONTROL PANEL (800 KW)**

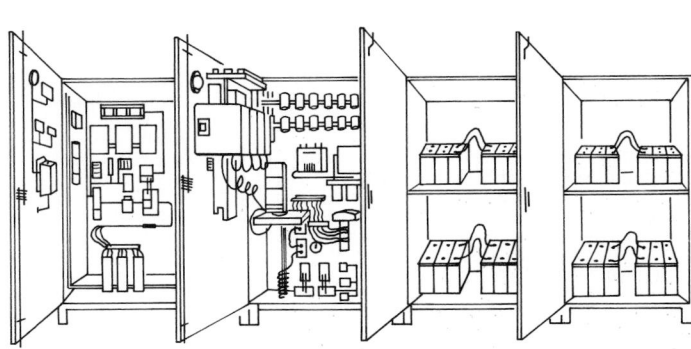

UNINTERRUPTIBLE POWER SUPPLY: D.C. batteries, battery charger, rectifier, and static inverter. Application: to provide continuous power during outage or abnormal transient power conditions. See manufacturer's literature for ratings, dimensions, weight, and ventilation requirements. See National Electric Code for working space requirements.

**UNINTERRUPTIBLE POWER SUPPLY**

A. A. Erdman; Sargent, Webster, Crenshaw & Folley; Architects Engineers Planners; Syracuse, New York

**SERVICE AND DISTRIBUTION**    **16**

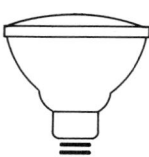

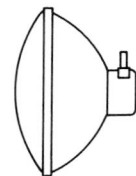

A-19     PS-52     PAR-38     R-40     T-6     PAR-56

## GENERAL SERVICE

| BULB | DIA. (IN.) | LENGTH (IN.) | BASE | WATTS |
|---|---|---|---|---|
| A-15 | $1^{7}/_{8}$ | $3^{1}/_{2}$ | Med. | 15 |
| A-19 | $2^{3}/_{8}$ | $4^{7}/_{16}$ | Med. | 60 |
| A-21 | $2^{5}/_{8}$ | $5^{5}/_{16}$ | Med. | 100 |
| PS-25 | $3^{1}/_{8}$ | $6^{15}/_{16}$ | Med. | 150 |
| PS-30 | $3^{3}/_{4}$ | $8^{1}/_{16}$ | Med. | 300 |
| PS-40 | 5 | $9^{3}/_{4}$ | Mogul | 500 |
| PS-52 | $6^{1}/_{2}$ | $13^{1}/_{16}$ | Mogul | 1000 |

The efficacy of light production by incandescent filament lamps depends on the temperature of the filament—the higher the temperature, the greater the portion of radiated energy that falls in the visible region. Tungsten filaments have a high melting point (3655°K) and low vapor pressure, which permit higher operating temperatures and, as a result, high efficacies. Past improvements in incandescent lamps have involved changes in filament shape. Recent improvements, however, are primarily a result of changes in the atmosphere inside the glass bulb that encloses the filament. The discovery that inert gases retard evaporation of the filament made it possible to design lamps for higher filament temperatures. Today, most incandescent lamps use a fill mixture of argon and nitrogen.

## PARABOLIC REFLECTORS

| BULB | DIA. (IN.) | LENGTH (IN.) | BASE | WATTS |
|---|---|---|---|---|
| R-20 | $2^{1}/_{2}$ | $3^{15}/_{16}$ | Med. | 30 |
| R-30 | $3^{3}/_{4}$ | $5^{3}/_{16}$ | Med. | 75 |
| PAR-38 | $4^{3}/_{4}$ | $5^{5}/_{16}$ | Med. skt. | 150 |
| PAR-38 | $4^{3}/_{4}$ | $5^{5}/_{16}$ | Med. skt. | 150 |
| R-40 | 5 | $6^{1}/_{2}$ | Med. | 150 |
| R-40 | 5 | $6^{1}/_{2}$ | Med. | 300 |
| R-40 | 5 | $7^{1}/_{4}$ | Mogul | 500 |

The most popular incandescent lamps are general service (GS) ones, which range from the 15-W A-15 to the 1500-W PS-52 types and are designed for 120-, 125-, and 130-V circuits. The letter prefix refers to the lamp shape—for example, PS has a pear straight neck; A is of the standard incandescent shape. Other common designations are G for globe and PAR for parabolic aluminizer reflector. The number following the letter prefix is the bulb diameter in eighths of an inch. For the same wattage, GS lamps (750 to 1000 hr of life) are more efficient than extended service (ES) lamps (2500 hr of life). ES lamps—for use where replacement costs are relatively high, such as hard-to-reach locations—achieve long life by use of a filament that is stronger, but less efficacious.

## TUNGSTEN HALOGEN

| BULB | DIA. (IN.) | LENGTH (IN.) | BASE | WATTS |
|---|---|---|---|---|
| T-4 | $1/_{2}$ | $3^{1}/_{8}$ | Minicam | 250 |
| T-4 | $1/_{2}$ | $3^{1}/_{8}$ | Rec. S.C. | 400 |
| PAR-56 | 7 | 5 | End prong | 500 |
| T-3 | $3/_{8}$ | $4^{11}/_{16}$ | Rec. S.C. | 500 |
| T-4 | $1/_{2}$ | $3^{5}/_{8}$ | Minicam | 500 |
| T-6 | $3/_{4}$ | $5^{5}/_{8}$ | Rec. S.C. | 1000 |
| T-3 | $3/_{8}$ | $10^{1}/_{16}$ | Rec. S.C. | 1500 |

TUNGSTEN HALOGEN lamps are a variation of incandescent filament sources. A halogen additive in the bulb reacts chemically with the tungsten, removing deposited tungsten from the bulb and redepositing it on the filament. This results in a lumen maintenance factor of close to 100%. (Lumen maintenance refers to the ability of a lamp to maintain a constant light output.) However, such a lamp does have a definite life, usually a maximum of 3000 hr. The smaller size, good optical control, and high color temperatures of tungsten-halogen lamps, as well as a continuous spectrum, particularly fit theatrical lighting needs.

**INCANDESCENT LAMPS**

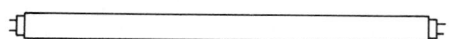

T-12

T-12

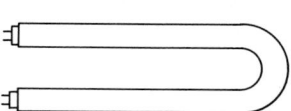

U-BENT

CIRCLINE

## STANDARD TUBE

| BULB | DIA. (IN.) | LENGTH (IN.) | BASE | WATTS |
|---|---|---|---|---|
| T-8 | 1 | 18 | Med. bipin | 15 |
| T-12 | $1^{1}/_{2}$ | 24 | Med. bipin | 20 |
| T-12 | $1^{1}/_{2}$ | 36 | Med. bipin | 30 |
| T-12 | $1^{1}/_{2}$ | 48 | Med. bipin | 40 |
| T-12 | $1^{1}/_{2}$ | 96 | Single pin | 75 |

NOTE: Dimensions are similar for preheat, rapid start, and extended service lamps.

FLUORESCENT lamps offer three to five times the efficacy of incandescent sources and compare favorably with most high intensity discharge sources. Efficacies vary with lamp length, lamp loading, and lamp phosphor coating.

Both geometric design and operating conditions of a fluorescent lamp affect the efficacy with which electrical energy is converted into visible radiation. For example, as lamp diameter increases, efficacy increases, passes through a maximum, then decreases. The length of the lamp also influences its efficacy: the longer it is, the higher the efficacy.

This lamp uses an electric discharge source, in which light is produced predominantly by fluorescent powders activated by ultraviolet energy generated by a mercury arc. The fluorescent lamp cannot be operated directly from the nominal 120-V ac source because the arc discharge would not be established. As a result, it must be operated in series with a ballast that limits the current and provides the starting and operating lamp voltages.

## HIGH OUTPUT (800 MA)

| BULB | DIA. (IN.) | LENGTH (IN.) | BASE | WATTS |
|---|---|---|---|---|
| T-12 | $1^{1}/_{2}$ | 48 | Rec. D.C. | 60 |
| T-12 | $1^{1}/_{2}$ | 72 | Rec. D.C. | 85 |
| T-12 | $1^{1}/_{2}$ | 96 | Rec. D.C. | 110 |
| T-12* | $1^{1}/_{2}$ | 72 | Rec. D.C. | 160 |
| T-12* | $1^{1}/_{2}$ | 96 | Rec. D.C. | 215 |

*Requires 1500 milli amps.

The starting process occurs in two stages. Once a sufficient voltage exists between an electrode and ground, ionization of the gas (mercury plus an inert gas) in the lamp occurs. Then a sufficient voltage must exist across the lamp to extend the ionization throughout the lamp and to develop an arc. Three basic types of ballasts—preheat, instant start, and rapid start—provide means of starting.

For the preheat variety, the electrodes are heated before the application of high voltage across the lamp. Arc initiation in instant start lamps depends entirely on the application of a high voltage (400 to 1000 V) across the lamp, which ejects electrons by field emission. These electrons ionize the gas and initiate arc discharge. The rapid start principle makes use of electrodes that are heated continuously by means of low voltage windings built into the ballast. A power saving feature of rapid start circuits is that the lamps show little change in rated life as a result of frequent on/off/on cycles.

## SPECIAL SHAPES

| BULB | DIA. (IN.) | LENGTH (IN.) | BASE | WATTS |
|---|---|---|---|---|
| U-Bent | $1^{1}/_{2}$ | $22^{1}/_{2}$ | Med. bipin | 40 |
| Circle | $1^{1}/_{8}$ | $8^{1}/_{4}$ dia. | Four pin | 22 |
| Circle | $1^{1}/_{4}$ | 12 dia. | Four pin | 32 |
| Circle | $1^{1}/_{4}$ | 16 dia. | Four pin | 40 |

NOTE: Fluorescent lamps are available in cool white, warm white, and daylight tints.

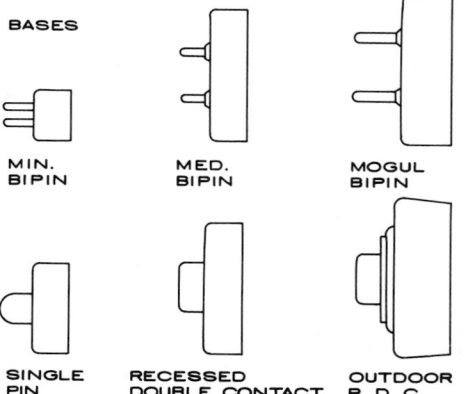

BASES

MIN. BIPIN    MED. BIPIN    MOGUL BIPIN

SINGLE PIN    RECESSED DOUBLE CONTACT    OUTDOOR R.D.C.

**FLUORESCENT LAMPS**

William G. Miner, AIA, Architect; Washington, D.C.

B-21

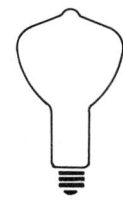
R-60

BT-28

BT-37

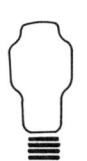
BT-25

E-18

## MERCURY VAPOR

| BULB | DIA. (IN.) | LENGTH (IN.) | BASE | WATTS |
|------|-----------|--------------|------|-------|
| B-17 | 2$\frac{1}{8}$ | 5$\frac{1}{8}$ | Med. | 40 |
| B-21 | 2$\frac{5}{8}$ | 6$\frac{1}{2}$ | Med. | 75 |
| BT-25 | 3$\frac{1}{8}$ | 7$\frac{1}{2}$ | Mogul | 100 |
| BT-28 | 3$\frac{1}{2}$ | 8$\frac{5}{16}$ | Mogul | 250 |
| BT-37 | 4$\frac{5}{8}$ | 11$\frac{1}{2}$ | Mogul | 400 |
| R-60 | 7$\frac{1}{2}$ | 10$\frac{7}{8}$ | Mogul | 400 |
| BT-56 | 7 | 15$\frac{3}{8}$ | Mogul | 1000 |

## METAL-HALIDE

| BULB | DIA. (IN.) | LENGTH (IN.) | BASE | WATTS |
|------|-----------|--------------|------|-------|
| BT-28 | 3$\frac{1}{2}$ | 8$\frac{5}{16}$ | Mogul | 175 |
| BT-37 | 4$\frac{5}{8}$ | 11$\frac{1}{2}$ | Mogul | 400 |
| BT-56 | 7 | 15$\frac{3}{8}$ | Mogul | 1000 |
| BT-56 | 7 | 15$\frac{3}{8}$ | Mogul | 1500 |

## HIGH PRESSURE SODIUM

| BULB | DIA. (IN.) | LENGTH (IN.) | BASE | WATTS |
|------|-----------|--------------|------|-------|
| BT-25 | 3$\frac{1}{8}$ | 7$\frac{5}{8}$ | Mogul | 70 |
| BT-25 | 3$\frac{1}{8}$ | 7$\frac{5}{8}$ | Mogul | 150 |
| BT-28 | 3$\frac{1}{2}$ | 8$\frac{5}{16}$ | Mogul | 150 |
| E-18 | 2$\frac{1}{4}$ | 9$\frac{3}{4}$ | Mogul | 250 |
| E-18 | 2$\frac{1}{4}$ | 9$\frac{3}{4}$ | Mogul | 400 |
| BT-37 | 4$\frac{5}{8}$ | 11$\frac{1}{2}$ | Mogul | 400 |
| E-25 | 3$\frac{1}{8}$ | 15$\frac{1}{16}$ | Mogul | 1000 |

MERCURY lamps, which are now popular for lighting commercial interiors, use argon gas to ease starting because mercury has a low vapor pressure at room temperature. When the lighting circuit is energized, the starting voltage is impressed across the gap between the main electrode and the starting electrode, which creates an argon arc that causes the mercury to vaporize. The lamp warmup process takes 5 to 7 min, depending on ambient temperature conditions. Most mercury lamps are constructed with two envelopes—an inner one that contains the arc and an outer one that shields the arc tube from outside drafts and changes in temperature. The outer envelope usually contains an inert gas.

The mercury spectrum results in greenish-blue light at efficacies of 30 to 65 lm/W, which ranks it between incandescent and fluorescent lamps. Economics favor mercury where burning hours are long, service is difficult, and replacement labor is high. Many mercury lamps lose as much as 50% of their initial output during their rated life of 24,000 hr or more.

METAL-HALIDE lamps are similar in construction to the mercury lamp, except that the arc tube contains various metal halides in addition to mercury. When the halide vapor approaches the high temperature, central core of the discharge, it disassociates into the halogen and the metal, with the metal radiating its appropriate spectrum. As the halogen and metal move near the cooler arc tube wall by diffusion and convection, they recombine, and the cycle repeats itself.

These lamps generate light with more than half the efficacy of the mercury arc, offer a small light source size for optical control, and provide good color rendition as compared with clear mercury. They have been applied in nearly every type of interior and exterior lighting application because they offer an efficient "white," light source. The average rated life of this lamp is 15,000 hr.

In both low pressure and high pressure sodium sources, light is produced by electricity passing through sodium vapor. In the LPS lamp, a starting gas of neon produces

a red glow when the lamp is initially ignited. As heat is generated, the sodium metal vaporizes, and the emitted light turns into the characteristic yellow color.

HIGH PRESSURE SODIUM (HPS) lamps are used for roadway and sidewalk illumination and offer more suitable color rendition characteristics. Sodium is a particularly suitable gas because most of its radiation is concentrated in a wavelength interval where the sensitivity of the human eye is high. It also has a relatively low excitation energy.

The HPS lamp is constructed with two envelopes—the inner being polycrystalline alumina, which is resistant to sodium attack. The arc tube contains xenon as a starting gas and a small amount of sodium-mercury amalgam. The outer glass envelope is evacuated and protects against chemical attack of the arc tube and maintains the arc tube temperature.

HPS sources are compact, yet have high efficacies (up to 140 lm/W) and high lumen maintenance characteristics. They radiate energy across the visible spectrum and produce a golden-white color. They are available in sizes from 70 to 1000 W, with the low wattage sources finding application in residential street lighting and shopping mall illumination.

HPS lamps have five times the efficacy of incandescent sources, more than twice that of mercury, and 50% more than metal-halide.

## HIGH INTENSITY DISCHARGE LAMPS

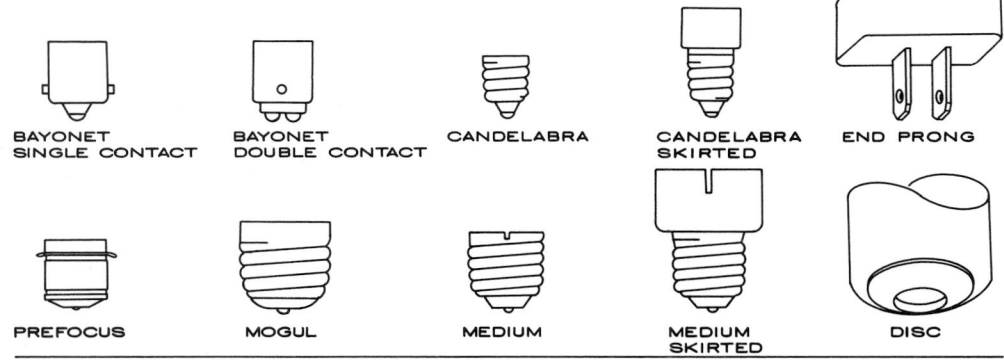

BAYONET SINGLE CONTACT    BAYONET DOUBLE CONTACT    CANDELABRA    CANDELABRA SKIRTED    END PRONG

PREFOCUS    MOGUL    MEDIUM    MEDIUM SKIRTED    DISC

## LAMP BASES

## CHARACTERISTICS OF BASIC LAMP TYPES

| CHARACTERISTICS | INCANDESCENT (INCLUDING TUNGSTEN HALOGEN) | FLUORESCENT | HIGH INTENSITY DISCHARGE (HID) | | |
|-----------------|-------------------------------------------|-------------|------------------|---------------|----------------------|
| | | | MERCURY-VAPOR | METAL-HALIDE | HIGH PRESSURE SODIUM |
| Wattages (lamp only) | 15-1500 | 40-1000 | 40-1000 | 400, 100, 1500 | 75, 150, 250, 400, 1000 |
| Life (hr) | 750-12,000 | 9000-30,000 | 16,000-24,000 | 1500-15,000 | 10,000-20,000 |
| Efficacy (lm/W, lamp only) | 15-25 | 55-88 | 20-63 | 80-100 | 100-130 |
| Color rendition | Very good to excellent | Good to excellent | Poor to very good | Good to very good | Fair |
| Light direction control | Very good to excellent | Fair | Very good | Very good | Very good |
| Source size | Compact | Extended | Compact | Compact | Compact |
| Relight time | Immediate | Immediate | 3-5 min | 10-20 min | Less than 1 min |

William G. Miner, AIA, Architect; Washington, D.C.

## COEFFICIENTS OF UTILIZATION

| TYPICAL LUMINAIRE | MAINT. CAT. | MAXIMUM S/MH GUIDE[4] | RCR[3] | ρcc[1] → 80 ρw[2]=50 | 30 | 10 | 70 ρw=50 | 30 | 10 | 50 ρw=50 | 30 | 10 | 30 ρw=50 | 30 | 10 | 10 ρw=50 | 30 | 10 | 0 |
|---|---|---|---|---|---|---|---|---|---|---|---|---|---|---|---|---|---|---|---|
| | | | | COEFFICIENTS OF UTILIZATION FOR 20% EFFECTIVE FLOOR CAVITY REFLECTANCE (ρFC = 20) | | | | | | | | | | | | | | | |
| Pendant diffusing sphere with incandescent lamp (35½%↑ 45%↓) | V | 1.5 | 0 | .87 | .87 | .87 | .81 | .81 | .81 | .69 | .69 | .69 | .59 | .59 | .59 | .49 | .49 | .49 | .44 |
| | | | 1 | .71 | .67 | .63 | .66 | .62 | .59 | .56 | .53 | .50 | .47 | .45 | .43 | .39 | .37 | .35 | .31 |
| | | | 2 | .61 | .54 | .49 | .56 | .50 | .46 | .47 | .43 | .39 | .39 | .36 | .33 | .32 | .29 | .27 | .23 |
| | | | 3 | .52 | .45 | .39 | .48 | .42 | .37 | .41 | .36 | .31 | .34 | .30 | .26 | .27 | .24 | .22 | .18 |
| | | | 4 | .46 | .38 | .33 | .42 | .36 | .30 | .36 | .30 | .26 | .30 | .26 | .22 | .24 | .21 | .18 | .15 |
| | | | 5 | .40 | .33 | .27 | .37 | .30 | .25 | .32 | .26 | .22 | .26 | .22 | .19 | .21 | .18 | .15 | .12 |
| | | | 6 | .36 | .28 | .23 | .33 | .26 | .21 | .28 | .23 | .19 | .23 | .19 | .16 | .19 | .15 | .13 | .10 |
| | | | 7 | .32 | .25 | .20 | .29 | .23 | .18 | .25 | .20 | .16 | .21 | .16 | .13 | .17 | .13 | .11 | .09 |
| | | | 8 | .29 | .22 | .17 | .27 | .20 | .16 | .23 | .17 | .14 | .19 | .15 | .12 | .15 | .12 | .09 | .07 |
| | | | 9 | .26 | .19 | .15 | .24 | .18 | .14 | .20 | .15 | .12 | .17 | .13 | .10 | .14 | .11 | .08 | .06 |
| | | | 10 | .23 | .17 | .13 | .22 | .16 | .12 | .19 | .14 | .10 | .16 | .12 | .09 | .13 | .09 | .07 | .05 |
| Porcelain enameled ventilated standard dome with incandescent lamp (0%↑ 83½%↓) | IV | 1.3 | 0 | .99 | .99 | .99 | .97 | .97 | .97 | .92 | .92 | .92 | .88 | .88 | .88 | .85 | .85 | .85 | .83 |
| | | | 1 | .88 | .85 | .82 | .86 | .83 | .81 | .83 | .80 | .78 | .79 | .78 | .76 | .77 | .75 | .73 | .72 |
| | | | 2 | .78 | .73 | .68 | .76 | .72 | .67 | .73 | .69 | .66 | .71 | .67 | .64 | .68 | .65 | .63 | .61 |
| | | | 3 | .69 | .62 | .57 | .67 | .61 | .57 | .65 | .60 | .56 | .63 | .58 | .55 | .61 | .57 | .54 | .52 |
| | | | 4 | .61 | .54 | .49 | .60 | .53 | .48 | .58 | .52 | .48 | .56 | .51 | .47 | .54 | .50 | .46 | .45 |
| | | | 5 | .54 | .47 | .41 | .53 | .46 | .41 | .51 | .45 | .41 | .50 | .44 | .40 | .48 | .43 | .40 | .38 |
| | | | 6 | .48 | .41 | .35 | .47 | .40 | .35 | .46 | .39 | .35 | .44 | .39 | .34 | .43 | .38 | .34 | .32 |
| | | | 7 | .43 | .35 | .30 | .42 | .35 | .30 | .41 | .34 | .30 | .39 | .34 | .30 | .38 | .33 | .29 | .28 |
| | | | 8 | .38 | .31 | .26 | .38 | .31 | .26 | .37 | .30 | .26 | .36 | .30 | .26 | .35 | .30 | .26 | .24 |
| | | | 9 | .35 | .28 | .23 | .34 | .27 | .23 | .33 | .27 | .23 | .32 | .27 | .23 | .31 | .26 | .22 | .21 |
| | | | 10 | .31 | .25 | .20 | .31 | .24 | .20 | .30 | .24 | .20 | .29 | .24 | .20 | .29 | .23 | .20 | .18 |
| Prismatic square surface drum (18½%↑ 60½%↓) | V | 1.3 | 0 | .89 | .89 | .89 | .85 | .85 | .85 | .77 | .77 | .77 | .70 | .70 | .70 | .63 | .63 | .63 | .60 |
| | | | 1 | .78 | .75 | .72 | .74 | .72 | .69 | .68 | .66 | .64 | .62 | .60 | .58 | .56 | .55 | .54 | .51 |
| | | | 2 | .69 | .65 | .61 | .66 | .62 | .58 | .61 | .57 | .54 | .56 | .53 | .50 | .51 | .49 | .47 | .44 |
| | | | 3 | .62 | .57 | .52 | .60 | .55 | .50 | .55 | .51 | .47 | .50 | .47 | .44 | .46 | .44 | .41 | .39 |
| | | | 4 | .56 | .50 | .46 | .54 | .49 | .44 | .50 | .45 | .42 | .46 | .42 | .39 | .42 | .39 | .37 | .35 |
| | | | 5 | .51 | .45 | .40 | .49 | .43 | .39 | .45 | .41 | .37 | .42 | .38 | .35 | .39 | .36 | .33 | .31 |
| | | | 6 | .46 | .40 | .36 | .45 | .39 | .35 | .42 | .37 | .33 | .39 | .35 | .31 | .36 | .32 | .30 | .28 |
| | | | 7 | .42 | .36 | .32 | .41 | .35 | .31 | .38 | .33 | .29 | .35 | .31 | .28 | .33 | .29 | .27 | .25 |
| | | | 8 | .39 | .32 | .28 | .37 | .32 | .28 | .35 | .30 | .26 | .32 | .28 | .25 | .30 | .27 | .24 | .22 |
| | | | 9 | .35 | .29 | .25 | .34 | .29 | .25 | .32 | .27 | .24 | .30 | .26 | .23 | .28 | .24 | .22 | .20 |
| | | | 10 | .32 | .27 | .23 | .31 | .26 | .22 | .29 | .25 | .21 | .27 | .23 | .20 | .26 | .22 | .20 | .18 |
| Medium distribution unit with lens plate and inside frost lamp (0%↑ 54½%↓) | V | 1.0 | 0 | .64 | .64 | .64 | .63 | .63 | .63 | .60 | .60 | .60 | .57 | .57 | .57 | .55 | .55 | .55 | .54 |
| | | | 1 | .60 | .58 | .57 | .58 | .57 | .56 | .56 | .55 | .54 | .54 | .53 | .52 | .52 | .52 | .51 | .50 |
| | | | 2 | .55 | .53 | .51 | .54 | .52 | .50 | .52 | .50 | .49 | .51 | .49 | .48 | .49 | .48 | .47 | .46 |
| | | | 3 | .51 | .48 | .46 | .50 | .47 | .45 | .49 | .46 | .44 | .47 | .45 | .44 | .46 | .44 | .43 | .42 |
| | | | 4 | .47 | .44 | .41 | .47 | .44 | .41 | .45 | .43 | .41 | .44 | .42 | .40 | .43 | .41 | .40 | .39 |
| | | | 5 | .44 | .40 | .38 | .43 | .40 | .38 | .42 | .39 | .37 | .41 | .39 | .37 | .40 | .38 | .37 | .36 |
| | | | 6 | .41 | .37 | .35 | .40 | .37 | .35 | .39 | .36 | .34 | .39 | .36 | .34 | .38 | .36 | .34 | .33 |
| | | | 7 | .38 | .34 | .32 | .37 | .34 | .32 | .37 | .34 | .31 | .36 | .33 | .31 | .35 | .33 | .31 | .30 |
| | | | 8 | .35 | .32 | .29 | .35 | .31 | .29 | .34 | .31 | .29 | .34 | .31 | .29 | .33 | .30 | .29 | .28 |
| | | | 9 | .33 | .29 | .27 | .32 | .29 | .27 | .32 | .29 | .26 | .31 | .28 | .26 | .31 | .28 | .26 | .25 |
| | | | 10 | .30 | .27 | .25 | .30 | .27 | .24 | .30 | .27 | .24 | .29 | .26 | .24 | .29 | .26 | .24 | .23 |
| Reflector downlight with baffles and inside frosted lamp (0%↑ 44½%↓) | IV | 0.7 | 0 | .53 | .53 | .53 | .52 | .52 | .52 | .49 | .49 | .49 | .47 | .47 | .47 | .45 | .45 | .45 | .44 |
| | | | 1 | .51 | .50 | .49 | .50 | .49 | .48 | .48 | .47 | .47 | .46 | .46 | .45 | .45 | .44 | .44 | .43 |
| | | | 2 | .48 | .47 | .46 | .48 | .46 | .45 | .46 | .45 | .44 | .45 | .44 | .44 | .44 | .43 | .43 | .42 |
| | | | 3 | .47 | .45 | .44 | .46 | .45 | .43 | .45 | .44 | .43 | .44 | .43 | .42 | .43 | .42 | .41 | .41 |
| | | | 4 | .45 | .43 | .42 | .44 | .43 | .42 | .43 | .42 | .41 | .43 | .41 | .41 | .42 | .41 | .40 | .40 |
| | | | 5 | .43 | .41 | .40 | .43 | .41 | .40 | .42 | .40 | .39 | .41 | .40 | .39 | .41 | .40 | .39 | .38 |
| | | | 6 | .42 | .40 | .39 | .41 | .40 | .38 | .41 | .39 | .38 | .40 | .39 | .38 | .40 | .39 | .38 | .37 |
| | | | 7 | .40 | .38 | .37 | .40 | .38 | .37 | .39 | .38 | .37 | .39 | .38 | .37 | .38 | .37 | .36 | .36 |
| | | | 8 | .39 | .37 | .36 | .38 | .37 | .36 | .38 | .37 | .35 | .38 | .36 | .35 | .37 | .36 | .35 | .35 |
| | | | 9 | .37 | .36 | .34 | .37 | .35 | .34 | .37 | .35 | .34 | .36 | .35 | .34 | .36 | .35 | .34 | .33 |
| | | | 10 | .36 | .34 | .33 | .36 | .34 | .33 | .36 | .34 | .33 | .35 | .34 | .33 | .35 | .34 | .33 | .32 |

### GENERAL NOTES

Luminaire data in this table are based on a composite of generic luminaire types. The polar intensity sketch (candlepower distribution curve) and the corresponding to mounting height guide are representative of many luminaires of each type shown.

### SYMBOLS

1. pcc = percent effective ceiling cavity reflectance.
2. pw = percent wall reflectance.
3. RCR = room cavity ratio.
4. Maximum S/MH guide = ratio of maximum luminaire spacing to mounting or ceiling height above work plane.

Maintenance categories (maint. cat.):

| Cat. I | Bare lamps and strips |
|---|---|
| Cat. II | 15% or more uplight, open or louvered Large louvered, 1 in. or more |
| Cat. III | Less than 15% uplight, open or louvered Small louvered, less than 1 in. |
| Cat. IV | Recessed with closed top only Lighted ceiling with louvers |
| Cat. V | Recessed with total enclosure Surface suspended and enclosed |
| Cat. VI | Totally direct Totally indirect lighting Lighted ceiling with solid diffuser |

Illuminating Engineering Society; New York, New York

## COEFFICIENTS OF UTILIZATION

| TYPICAL LUMINAIRE | MAINT. CAT. | MAXIMUM S/MH GUIDE[4] | RCR[3] ↓ | $\rho cc$[1] → 80 | | | 70 | | | 50 | | | 30 | | | 10 | | | 0 |
|---|---|---|---|---|---|---|---|---|---|---|---|---|---|---|---|---|---|---|---|
| | | | | $\rho w$[2] → 50 | 30 | 10 | 50 | 30 | 10 | 50 | 30 | 10 | 50 | 30 | 10 | 50 | 30 | 10 | 0 |
| R-40 flood without shielding (IV, 0% / 100%) | IV | 0.8 | 0 | 1.18 | 1.18 | 1.18 | 1.16 | 1.16 | 1.16 | 1.11 | 1.11 | 1.11 | 1.06 | 1.06 | 1.06 | 1.01 | 1.01 | 1.01 | .99 |
| | | | 1 | 1.09 | 1.07 | 1.04 | 1.07 | 1.05 | 1.02 | 1.03 | 1.01 | .99 | .99 | .98 | .96 | .96 | .95 | .94 | .92 |
| | | | 2 | 1.01 | .97 | .93 | .99 | .95 | .92 | .96 | .93 | .90 | .93 | .90 | .88 | .90 | .88 | .86 | .84 |
| | | | 3 | .93 | .88 | .84 | .92 | .87 | .83 | .89 | .85 | .81 | .87 | .83 | .80 | .84 | .82 | .79 | .77 |
| | | | 4 | .87 | .81 | .76 | .85 | .80 | .75 | .83 | .78 | .75 | .81 | .77 | .74 | .79 | .76 | .73 | .71 |
| | | | 5 | .80 | .74 | .69 | .79 | .73 | .69 | .77 | .72 | .68 | .76 | .71 | .67 | .74 | .70 | .67 | .65 |
| | | | 6 | .74 | .68 | .63 | .73 | .67 | .63 | .72 | .66 | .62 | .70 | .66 | .62 | .69 | .65 | .61 | .60 |
| | | | 7 | .69 | .62 | .57 | .68 | .62 | .57 | .67 | .61 | .57 | .65 | .60 | .56 | .64 | .60 | .56 | .55 |
| | | | 8 | .64 | .57 | .53 | .63 | .57 | .52 | .62 | .56 | .52 | .61 | .56 | .52 | .60 | .55 | .52 | .50 |
| | | | 9 | .59 | .52 | .48 | .59 | .52 | .48 | .58 | .52 | .48 | .57 | .51 | .48 | .56 | .51 | .47 | .46 |
| | | | 10 | .55 | .49 | .44 | .55 | .48 | .44 | .54 | .48 | .44 | .53 | .48 | .44 | .52 | .47 | .44 | .42 |
| R-40 flood with specular anodized reflector skirt; 45° cutoff (IV, 0% / 85%) | IV | 0.7 | 0 | 1.00 | 1.00 | 1.00 | .98 | .98 | .98 | .94 | .94 | .94 | .90 | .90 | .90 | .86 | .86 | .86 | .84 |
| | | | 1 | .96 | .94 | .92 | .94 | .92 | .91 | .90 | .89 | .88 | .87 | .86 | .85 | .84 | .84 | .83 | .82 |
| | | | 2 | .91 | .88 | .86 | .90 | .87 | .85 | .87 | .85 | .83 | .84 | .83 | .82 | .82 | .81 | .80 | .79 |
| | | | 3 | .87 | .84 | .81 | .86 | .83 | .81 | .84 | .81 | .79 | .82 | .80 | .78 | .80 | .78 | .77 | .76 |
| | | | 4 | .83 | .80 | .77 | .82 | .79 | .77 | .81 | .78 | .76 | .79 | .77 | .75 | .78 | .76 | .74 | .73 |
| | | | 5 | .79 | .76 | .73 | .79 | .75 | .73 | .77 | .74 | .72 | .76 | .73 | .71 | .75 | .73 | .71 | .70 |
| | | | 6 | .76 | .73 | .70 | .76 | .72 | .70 | .75 | .72 | .69 | .74 | .71 | .69 | .73 | .70 | .68 | .67 |
| | | | 7 | .73 | .69 | .66 | .73 | .69 | .66 | .72 | .68 | .66 | .71 | .68 | .66 | .70 | .67 | .65 | .64 |
| | | | 8 | .70 | .66 | .63 | .70 | .66 | .63 | .69 | .65 | .63 | .68 | .65 | .63 | .67 | .65 | .63 | .62 |
| | | | 9 | .67 | .63 | .60 | .67 | .63 | .60 | .66 | .62 | .60 | .65 | .62 | .60 | .65 | .62 | .60 | .59 |
| | | | 10 | .64 | .60 | .58 | .64 | .60 | .58 | .63 | .60 | .58 | .63 | .60 | .57 | .62 | .59 | .57 | .56 |
| Intermediate distribution ventilated reflector with clear HID lamp (III, 1% / 76%) | III | 1.0 | 0 | .91 | .91 | .91 | .89 | .89 | .89 | .84 | .84 | .84 | .81 | .81 | .81 | .77 | .77 | .77 | .75 |
| | | | 1 | .84 | .81 | .79 | .82 | .80 | .78 | .79 | .77 | .76 | .76 | .74 | .73 | .73 | .72 | .71 | .69 |
| | | | 2 | .77 | .73 | .70 | .76 | .72 | .70 | .73 | .70 | .68 | .70 | .68 | .66 | .68 | .66 | .65 | .63 |
| | | | 3 | .71 | .66 | .63 | .69 | .65 | .62 | .67 | .64 | .61 | .65 | .62 | .60 | .63 | .61 | .59 | .57 |
| | | | 4 | .65 | .60 | .56 | .64 | .59 | .56 | .62 | .58 | .55 | .60 | .57 | .54 | .59 | .56 | .54 | .52 |
| | | | 5 | .59 | .54 | .50 | .59 | .54 | .50 | .57 | .53 | .50 | .56 | .52 | .49 | .54 | .51 | .48 | .47 |
| | | | 6 | .54 | .49 | .45 | .54 | .49 | .45 | .52 | .48 | .45 | .51 | .47 | .44 | .50 | .47 | .44 | .42 |
| | | | 7 | .50 | .44 | .40 | .49 | .44 | .40 | .48 | .43 | .40 | .47 | .43 | .39 | .46 | .42 | .39 | .38 |
| | | | 8 | .45 | .40 | .36 | .45 | .40 | .36 | .44 | .39 | .36 | .43 | .39 | .35 | .42 | .38 | .35 | .34 |
| | | | 9 | .41 | .36 | .32 | .41 | .36 | .32 | .40 | .35 | .32 | .39 | .35 | .32 | .38 | .35 | .32 | .30 |
| | | | 10 | .38 | .33 | .29 | .37 | .32 | .29 | .37 | .32 | .29 | .36 | .32 | .29 | .35 | .31 | .28 | .27 |
| Intermediate distribution ventilated reflector with phosphor coated HID lamp (III, 6½% / 75½%) | III | 1.0 | 0 | .96 | .96 | .96 | .93 | .93 | .93 | .87 | .87 | .87 | .82 | .82 | .82 | .77 | .77 | .77 | .75 |
| | | | 1 | .89 | .87 | .84 | .86 | .84 | .83 | .82 | .80 | .79 | .78 | .76 | .75 | .74 | .73 | .72 | .70 |
| | | | 2 | .82 | .79 | .76 | .80 | .77 | .74 | .76 | .74 | .72 | .73 | .71 | .69 | .70 | .68 | .67 | .65 |
| | | | 3 | .76 | .72 | .68 | .74 | .70 | .67 | .71 | .68 | .65 | .68 | .66 | .63 | .66 | .63 | .61 | .60 |
| | | | 4 | .70 | .66 | .62 | .69 | .65 | .61 | .66 | .63 | .60 | .64 | .61 | .58 | .62 | .59 | .57 | .55 |
| | | | 5 | .65 | .60 | .56 | .64 | .59 | .56 | .62 | .58 | .54 | .60 | .56 | .53 | .58 | .55 | .52 | .51 |
| | | | 6 | .60 | .55 | .51 | .59 | .55 | .51 | .57 | .53 | .50 | .56 | .52 | .49 | .54 | .51 | .48 | .47 |
| | | | 7 | .56 | .51 | .47 | .55 | .50 | .46 | .53 | .49 | .46 | .52 | .48 | .45 | .50 | .47 | .44 | .43 |
| | | | 8 | .52 | .47 | .43 | .51 | .46 | .43 | .50 | .45 | .42 | .48 | .44 | .41 | .47 | .43 | .41 | .40 |
| | | | 9 | .48 | .43 | .39 | .47 | .42 | .39 | .46 | .42 | .39 | .45 | .41 | .38 | .44 | .40 | .38 | .36 |
| | | | 10 | .45 | .40 | .36 | .44 | .39 | .36 | .43 | .39 | .36 | .42 | .38 | .35 | .41 | .37 | .35 | .34 |
| Porcelain-enameled reflector with 30°CW x 30°LW shielding (II, 23½% / 57%) | II | 1.0 | 0 | .90 | .90 | .90 | .85 | .85 | .85 | .76 | .76 | .76 | .68 | .68 | .68 | .60 | .60 | .60 | .57 |
| | | | 1 | .81 | .78 | .76 | .77 | .74 | .72 | .69 | .67 | .66 | .62 | .61 | .60 | .56 | .55 | .54 | .57 |
| | | | 2 | .72 | .68 | .64 | .69 | .65 | .62 | .62 | .59 | .57 | .56 | .54 | .52 | .51 | .49 | .47 | .45 |
| | | | 3 | .65 | .59 | .55 | .62 | .57 | .53 | .56 | .52 | .49 | .51 | .48 | .46 | .46 | .44 | .42 | .39 |
| | | | 4 | .58 | .52 | .48 | .56 | .50 | .46 | .51 | .46 | .43 | .46 | .43 | .40 | .42 | .39 | .37 | .35 |
| | | | 5 | .52 | .46 | .41 | .50 | .44 | .40 | .46 | .41 | .38 | .42 | .38 | .35 | .38 | .35 | .33 | .30 |
| | | | 6 | .47 | .41 | .36 | .45 | .39 | .35 | .41 | .37 | .33 | .38 | .34 | .31 | .35 | .31 | .29 | .27 |
| | | | 7 | .43 | .36 | .32 | .41 | .35 | .31 | .38 | .33 | .29 | .34 | .30 | .27 | .32 | .28 | .26 | .24 |
| | | | 8 | .38 | .32 | .28 | .37 | .31 | .27 | .34 | .29 | .26 | .31 | .27 | .24 | .29 | .25 | .23 | .21 |
| | | | 9 | .35 | .29 | .24 | .33 | .28 | .24 | .31 | .26 | .22 | .28 | .24 | .21 | .26 | .22 | .20 | .18 |
| | | | 10 | .32 | .26 | .22 | .30 | .25 | .21 | .28 | .23 | .20 | .26 | .22 | .19 | .24 | .20 | .18 | .16 |
| 2 lamp prismatic wraparound—multiply by 0.95 for 4 lamps (V, 11½% / 58½%) | V | 1.5/1.2 | 0 | .80 | .80 | .80 | .77 | .77 | .77 | .71 | .71 | .71 | .66 | .66 | .66 | .60 | .60 | .60 | .58 |
| | | | 1 | .71 | .69 | .66 | .69 | .66 | .64 | .64 | .62 | .60 | .59 | .58 | .56 | .55 | .54 | .53 | .50 |
| | | | 2 | .64 | .59 | .56 | .61 | .58 | .54 | .57 | .54 | .51 | .53 | .51 | .49 | .49 | .48 | .46 | .44 |
| | | | 3 | .57 | .52 | .48 | .55 | .50 | .47 | .51 | .48 | .45 | .48 | .45 | .42 | .45 | .42 | .40 | .38 |
| | | | 4 | .51 | .46 | .41 | .49 | .44 | .40 | .46 | .42 | .39 | .43 | .40 | .37 | .41 | .38 | .35 | .34 |
| | | | 5 | .46 | .40 | .36 | .44 | .39 | .35 | .41 | .37 | .34 | .39 | .35 | .32 | .37 | .33 | .31 | .29 |
| | | | 6 | .41 | .35 | .31 | .40 | .35 | .31 | .38 | .33 | .30 | .35 | .31 | .28 | .33 | .30 | .27 | .26 |
| | | | 7 | .37 | .31 | .27 | .36 | .31 | .27 | .34 | .29 | .26 | .32 | .28 | .25 | .30 | .27 | .24 | .23 |
| | | | 8 | .33 | .28 | .24 | .32 | .27 | .23 | .30 | .26 | .22 | .29 | .25 | .22 | .27 | .24 | .21 | .19 |
| | | | 9 | .30 | .24 | .20 | .29 | .24 | .20 | .27 | .23 | .19 | .26 | .22 | .19 | .24 | .21 | .18 | .17 |
| | | | 10 | .27 | .22 | .18 | .26 | .21 | .18 | .25 | .20 | .17 | .23 | .19 | .16 | .22 | .18 | .16 | .15 |

COEFFICIENTS OF UTILIZATION FOR 20% EFFECTIVE FLOOR CAVITY REFLECTANCE ($\rho FC = 20$)

Illuminating Engineering Society; New York, New York

## COEFFICIENTS OF UTILIZATION

| TYPICAL LUMINAIRE | MAINT. CAT. | MAXIMUM S/MH GUIDE[4] | RCR[3] ↓ | ρcc[1] → 80 ρw[2] → 50 | 30 | 10 | 70 50 | 30 | 10 | 50 50 | 30 | 10 | 30 50 | 30 | 10 | 10 50 | 30 | 10 | 0 |
|---|---|---|---|---|---|---|---|---|---|---|---|---|---|---|---|---|---|---|---|
| 2 lamp 1 ft wide troffer with 45° plastic louver—multiply by 0.90 for 3 lamps (0% ↑ 46% ↓) | IV | 1.0 | 0 | .54 | .54 | .54 | .53 | .53 | .53 | .51 | .51 | .51 | .48 | .48 | .48 | .46 | .46 | .46 | .45 |
| | | | 1 | .49 | .48 | .46 | .48 | .47 | .46 | .46 | .45 | .44 | .45 | .44 | .43 | .43 | .42 | .42 | .41 |
| | | | 2 | .44 | .42 | .40 | .43 | .41 | .39 | .42 | .40 | .38 | .40 | .39 | .37 | .39 | .38 | .37 | .36 |
| | | | 3 | .40 | .37 | .34 | .39 | .36 | .34 | .38 | .36 | .34 | .37 | .35 | .33 | .36 | .34 | .33 | .32 |
| | | | 4 | .36 | .33 | .30 | .36 | .32 | .30 | .35 | .32 | .30 | .34 | .31 | .29 | .33 | .31 | .29 | .28 |
| | | | 5 | .33 | .29 | .26 | .32 | .29 | .26 | .31 | .28 | .26 | .30 | .28 | .26 | .30 | .27 | .26 | .25 |
| | | | 6 | .30 | .26 | .24 | .29 | .26 | .24 | .29 | .26 | .23 | .28 | .25 | .24 | .27 | .25 | .23 | .22 |
| | | | 7 | .27 | .24 | .21 | .27 | .23 | .21 | .26 | .23 | .21 | .26 | .23 | .21 | .25 | .22 | .21 | .20 |
| | | | 8 | .25 | .21 | .19 | .24 | .21 | .19 | .24 | .21 | .19 | .23 | .21 | .18 | .23 | .20 | .18 | .18 |
| | | | 9 | .22 | .19 | .17 | .22 | .19 | .17 | .22 | .19 | .17 | .21 | .18 | .16 | .21 | .18 | .16 | .16 |
| | | | 10 | .21 | .17 | .15 | .20 | .17 | .15 | .20 | .17 | .15 | .20 | .17 | .15 | .19 | .17 | .15 | .14 |
| Fluorescent unit with flat prismatic lens, 2 lamp 1 ft wide (0% ↑ 56% ↓) | V | 1.4/1.2 | 0 | .66 | .66 | .66 | .65 | .65 | .65 | .62 | .62 | .62 | .59 | .59 | .59 | .57 | .57 | .57 | .56 |
| | | | 1 | .61 | .59 | .57 | .59 | .58 | .56 | .57 | .56 | .54 | .55 | .54 | .53 | .53 | .52 | .51 | .50 |
| | | | 2 | .55 | .52 | .50 | .54 | .51 | .49 | .52 | .50 | .48 | .50 | .48 | .47 | .49 | .47 | .46 | .45 |
| | | | 3 | .50 | .46 | .43 | .49 | .46 | .43 | .47 | .45 | .42 | .46 | .44 | .42 | .45 | .43 | .41 | .40 |
| | | | 4 | .45 | .41 | .38 | .45 | .41 | .38 | .43 | .40 | .38 | .42 | .39 | .37 | .41 | .39 | .37 | .36 |
| | | | 5 | .41 | .37 | .34 | .40 | .36 | .34 | .39 | .36 | .33 | .38 | .35 | .33 | .37 | .35 | .33 | .32 |
| | | | 6 | .37 | .33 | .30 | .37 | .33 | .30 | .36 | .32 | .30 | .35 | .32 | .29 | .34 | .31 | .29 | .28 |
| | | | 7 | .34 | .30 | .27 | .34 | .29 | .27 | .33 | .29 | .26 | .32 | .29 | .26 | .31 | .28 | .26 | .25 |
| | | | 8 | .31 | .26 | .24 | .30 | .26 | .23 | .30 | .26 | .23 | .29 | .26 | .23 | .28 | .25 | .23 | .22 |
| | | | 9 | .28 | .23 | .21 | .27 | .23 | .21 | .27 | .23 | .20 | .26 | .23 | .20 | .26 | .23 | .20 | .19 |
| | | | 10 | .25 | .21 | .18 | .25 | .21 | .18 | .24 | .21 | .18 | .24 | .21 | .18 | .23 | .20 | .18 | .17 |
| 1 ft wide aluminum troffer with 40°CW x 45°LW shielding and single extrahigh-output lamp (0% ↑ 42½% ↓) | IV | 1.1/0.8 | 0 | .50 | .50 | .50 | .49 | .49 | .49 | .47 | .47 | .47 | .45 | .45 | .45 | .43 | .43 | .43 | .42 |
| | | | 1 | .46 | .45 | .44 | .45 | .44 | .43 | .44 | .43 | .42 | .42 | .41 | .41 | .41 | .40 | .40 | .39 |
| | | | 2 | .43 | .41 | .39 | .42 | .40 | .38 | .40 | .39 | .38 | .39 | .38 | .37 | .38 | .37 | .36 | .35 |
| | | | 3 | .39 | .37 | .35 | .39 | .36 | .34 | .37 | .35 | .34 | .36 | .35 | .33 | .35 | .34 | .33 | .32 |
| | | | 4 | .36 | .33 | .31 | .35 | .33 | .31 | .35 | .32 | .31 | .34 | .32 | .30 | .33 | .31 | .30 | .29 |
| | | | 5 | .33 | .30 | .28 | .33 | .30 | .28 | .32 | .29 | .28 | .31 | .29 | .27 | .30 | .29 | .27 | .26 |
| | | | 6 | .31 | .28 | .26 | .30 | .28 | .26 | .30 | .27 | .25 | .29 | .27 | .25 | .28 | .26 | .25 | .24 |
| | | | 7 | .28 | .25 | .23 | .28 | .25 | .23 | .27 | .25 | .23 | .27 | .25 | .23 | .26 | .24 | .23 | .22 |
| | | | 8 | .26 | .23 | .21 | .26 | .23 | .21 | .25 | .23 | .21 | .25 | .23 | .21 | .24 | .22 | .21 | .20 |
| | | | 9 | .24 | .21 | .19 | .24 | .21 | .19 | .23 | .21 | .19 | .23 | .20 | .19 | .22 | .20 | .19 | .18 |
| | | | 10 | .22 | .19 | .17 | .22 | .19 | .17 | .21 | .19 | .17 | .21 | .19 | .17 | .21 | .19 | .17 | .16 |
| Luminous bottom suspended unit with extrahigh-output lamp (66% ↑ 12% ↓) | VI | 1.5 | 0 | .77 | .77 | .77 | .67 | .67 | .67 | .49 | .49 | .49 | .33 | .33 | .33 | .18 | .18 | .18 | .11 |
| | | | 1 | .67 | .64 | .62 | .59 | .57 | .54 | .44 | .42 | .41 | .30 | .29 | .28 | .17 | .16 | .16 | .10 |
| | | | 2 | .59 | .54 | .50 | .51 | .48 | .45 | .38 | .36 | .34 | .26 | .25 | .23 | .15 | .14 | .13 | .09 |
| | | | 3 | .51 | .46 | .42 | .45 | .41 | .37 | .34 | .31 | .28 | .23 | .21 | .20 | .13 | .12 | .12 | .07 |
| | | | 4 | .45 | .40 | .35 | .40 | .35 | .31 | .30 | .27 | .24 | .20 | .18 | .17 | .12 | .11 | .10 | .06 |
| | | | 5 | .40 | .34 | .30 | .35 | .30 | .27 | .26 | .23 | .20 | .18 | .16 | .14 | .10 | .09 | .08 | .05 |
| | | | 6 | .36 | .30 | .26 | .32 | .27 | .23 | .24 | .20 | .18 | .16 | .14 | .12 | .09 | .08 | .07 | .05 |
| | | | 7 | .32 | .26 | .22 | .28 | .23 | .20 | .21 | .18 | .15 | .15 | .12 | .11 | .08 | .07 | .06 | .04 |
| | | | 8 | .29 | .23 | .19 | .25 | .21 | .17 | .19 | .16 | .13 | .13 | .11 | .09 | .08 | .06 | .06 | .03 |
| | | | 9 | .26 | .20 | .17 | .23 | .18 | .15 | .17 | .14 | .12 | .12 | .10 | .08 | .07 | .06 | .05 | .03 |
| | | | 10 | .24 | .18 | .15 | .21 | .16 | .13 | .16 | .12 | .10 | .11 | .09 | .07 | .06 | .05 | .04 | .03 |
| Diffusing plastic or glass — ρcc from below ~65% | | | 1 | | | | .60 | .58 | .56 | .58 | .56 | .54 | | | | | | | |
| | | | 2 | | | | .53 | .49 | .45 | .51 | .47 | .43 | | | | | | | |
| | | | 3 | | | | .47 | .42 | .37 | .45 | .41 | .36 | | | | | | | |
| | | | 4 | | | | .41 | .36 | .32 | .39 | .35 | .31 | | | | | | | |
| | | | 5 | | | | .37 | .31 | .27 | .35 | .30 | .26 | | | | | | | |
| | | | 6 | | | | .33 | .27 | .23 | .31 | .26 | .23 | | | | | | | |
| | | | 7 | | | | .29 | .24 | .20 | .28 | .23 | .20 | | | | | | | |
| | | | 8 | | | | .26 | .21 | .18 | .25 | .20 | .17 | | | | | | | |
| | | | 9 | | | | .23 | .19 | .15 | .23 | .18 | .15 | | | | | | | |
| | | | 10 | | | | .21 | .17 | .13 | .21 | .16 | .13 | | | | | | | |
| Louvered ceiling — ρcc from below ~45% | | | 1 | | | | | | | .51 | .49 | .48 | | | | .47 | .46 | .45 | |
| | | | 2 | | | | | | | .46 | .44 | .42 | | | | .43 | .42 | .40 | |
| | | | 3 | | | | | | | .42 | .39 | .37 | | | | .39 | .38 | .36 | |
| | | | 4 | | | | | | | .38 | .35 | .33 | | | | .36 | .34 | .32 | |
| | | | 5 | | | | | | | .35 | .32 | .29 | | | | .33 | .31 | .29 | |
| | | | 6 | | | | | | | .32 | .29 | .26 | | | | .30 | .28 | .26 | |
| | | | 7 | | | | | | | .29 | .26 | .23 | | | | .28 | .25 | .23 | |
| | | | 8 | | | | | | | .27 | .23 | .21 | | | | .26 | .23 | .21 | |
| | | | 9 | | | | | | | .24 | .21 | .19 | | | | .24 | .21 | .19 | |
| | | | 10 | | | | | | | .22 | .19 | .17 | | | | .22 | .19 | .17 | |

COEFFICIENTS OF UTILIZATION FOR 20% EFFECTIVE FLOOR CAVITY REFLECTANCE (ρFC = 20)

**Diffusing plastic or glass**
1. Ceiling efficiency ~60%; diffuser transmittance ~50%; diffuser reflectance ~40%. Cavity with minimum obstructions and painted with 80% reflectance paint—use ρc = 70
2. For lower reflectance paint or obstructions—use ρc = 50

**Louvered ceiling**
1. Ceiling efficiency ~50%; 45° shielding opaque louvers of 80% reflectance. Cavity with minimum obstructions and painted with 80% reflectance paint—use ρc = 50

Illuminating Engineering Society; New York, New York

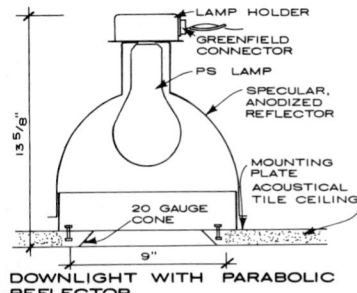

## DOWNLIGHT WITH PARABOLIC REFLECTOR

The open reflector downlight uses general service lamps in a polished parabolic reflector to produce controlled light without a lens. The reflector efficiently redirects the upward component of the light source down through the aperture.

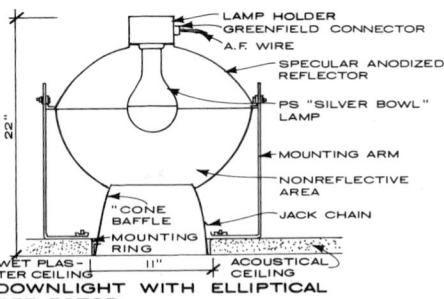

## DOWNLIGHT WITH ELLIPTICAL REFLECTOR

A more sophisticated downlight uses a silver bowl lamp to project light up into an elliptical reflector. When the light source is located at one focal point the output light converges and can be redirected through a constricted aperture at the other focal point.

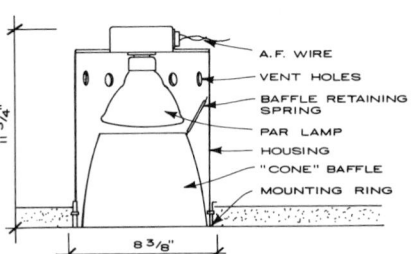

## DOWNLIGHT WITH REFLECTOR LAMP

Downlights without reflectors or lenses are commonly called "cans." They have cylindrical housings and rely on a PAR or R lamp for optical control. Cones, annular rings, or lower type baffles will shield an observer from glare in the normal field of view.

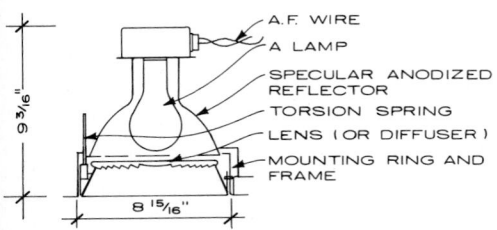

## DOWNLIGHT WITH FRESNEL LENS

One downlight type combines a general service lamp with a reflector housing and a diffusing lens. The lens provides directional control of the light as it leaves the luminaire. The lens covers the ceiling aperture, thus keeping dust from the reflector and providing a heat shield.

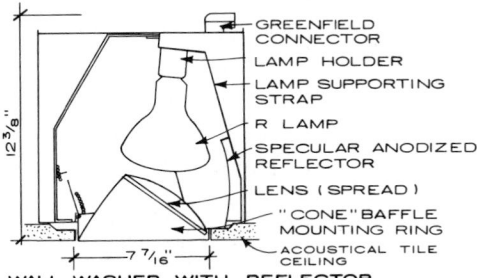

## WALL WASHER WITH REFLECTOR LAMP AND LENS

Wall washers provide shadowless coverage of vertical surfaces with an even "wash" of light. They are used to set a mood within a space, to accent surrounding walls, or to obscure undesirable unevenness of the surface.

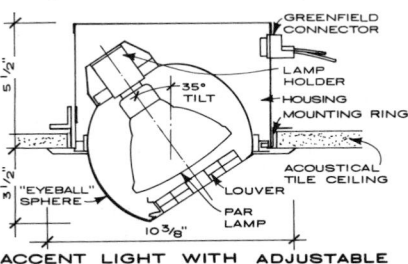

## ACCENT LIGHT WITH ADJUSTABLE REFLECTOR LAMP

The accent light produces an asymmetrical distribution of light and normally allows for adjustments in the lamp position. It is used for gallery lighting to emphasize objects or small wall areas.

## INCANDESCENT FIXTURES

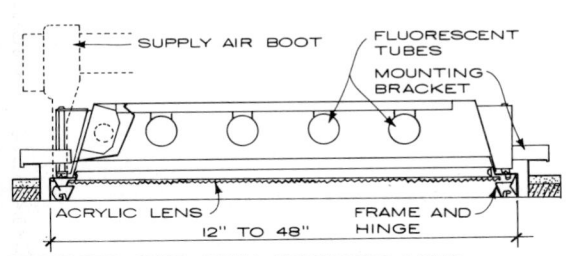

## RECESSED UNIT WITH PRISMATIC LENS

The recessed fluorescent luminaire is usually designed to fit into a standard ceiling grid. A transparent, prismatic lens usually encloses the fixture and directs useful light to the work surface.

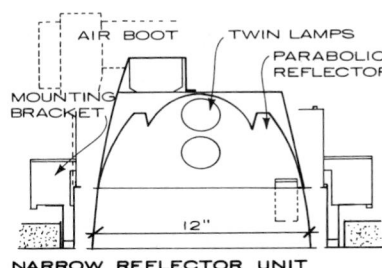

## NARROW REFLECTOR UNIT

Parabolic reflectors are used in narrow profile fixtures to redirect the upward component of the light source down to the task area. The fluorescent lamps are stacked so that one may be switched off without sacrificing the even distribution of light.

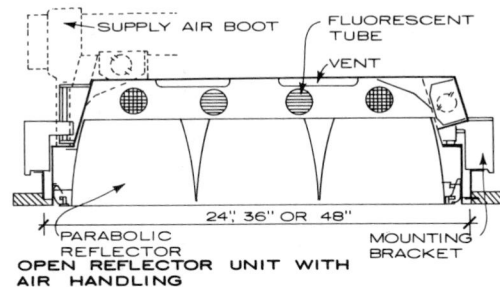

## OPEN REFLECTOR UNIT WITH AIR HANDLING

Some open reflector units are fitted with parabola shaped louver blades to better control glare and veiling reflections. Air fittings are also integrated into the lamp housing for ducted air supply or return.

## FLUORESCENT FIXTURES

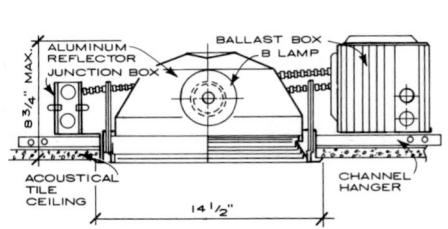

## SQUARE LENS AND REFLECTOR UNIT

HID fixtures are usually preassembled and wired for fast installation. A recessed reflector with a fresnel or prismatic lens will maximize the utilization and control of the high lamp output.

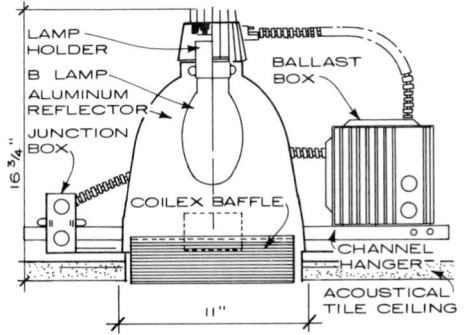

## OPEN REFLECTOR DOWNLIGHT

HID luminaires require a deep ceiling space to fully recess the large lamp housing. Open reflector downlights often use elliptical reflectors that focus the lamp light through a small aperture. Coil or cone baffles help reduce fixture surface brightness.

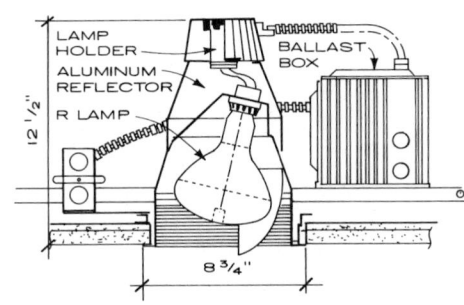

## ADJUSTABLE WALL WASHER

A special scoop insert can be added to a standard downlight fixture to create a HID wall washer unit. The reflector and lamp socket can be rotated for desired positioning of light throw.

## HIGH INTENSITY DISCHARGE FIXTURES

William G. Miner, AIA, Architect; Washington, D.C.

## NOTES

UPS (uninterruptible power supply) is designed to provide continuous power with specific electrical characteristics by conditioning utility company power, battery power, or generator-supplied power.

UPS systems are either on-line, routing power through the UPS system continuously, or off-line systems, which route power through the UPS only when the incoming power is interrupted or departs from the design characteristics. The time required for an off-line, solid state UPS to automatically switch on varies with the type of switch selected. Switching equipment generally increases in cost as the time decreases. The time needs to be matched to the tolerances of the critical equipment being supplied by the UPS to prevent loss of data or other problems.

Battery backup time is selected to allow a controlled shutdown of equipment or to allow a backup generator to be started and stabilize at full power.

Redundant UPS systems may be required if UPS power loss cannot be tolerated for system maintenance or equipment breakdown.

Some equipment can produce electrical disturbances that are fed back into the electrical circuit. This must be prevented through filtering in order to maintain clean power to the other equipment being supplied by the UPS.

The UPS unit and battery should be placed close together. Some UPS cabinets contain sealed batteries; others require separate batteries.

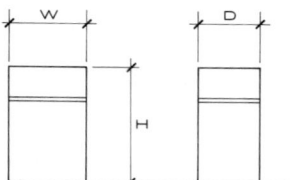

## UPS UNDER 10 KVA SIZES

| WATTS | W (IN.) | D (IN.) | H (IN.) | TIME (MIN.) |
|---|---|---|---|---|
| 200 | 8 | 15 | 6 | 15–20 |
| 800 | 22 | 16 | 9 | 15–20 |
| 1500 | 22 | 16 | 18 | 15–20 |
| KVA | | | | |
| 3.0 | 26 | 19 | 52 | 10 |
| 5.0 | 36 | 19 | 52 | 10 |
| 10.0 | 36 | 19 | 52 | 10 |

A wide variety of UPS systems is available for smaller applications, ranging from desktop models for single microcomputers to floor models that can supply several computers or other equipment.

## UPS UNDER 10 KVA

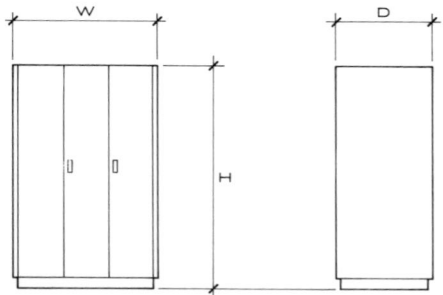

## BATTERY CABINET SIZES

| KVA | TIME (MIN.) | W (IN.) | D (IN.) | H (IN.) | WEIGHT (LB) | NUMBER REQUIRED |
|---|---|---|---|---|---|---|
| 75 | 15 | 40 | 32 | 76 | 2300 | 2 |
| 100 | 15 | 40 | 32 | 76 | 2300 | 3 |
| 200 | 15 | 48 | 32 | 76 | 2300 | 4 |
| 400 | 10 | 40 | 32 | 76 | 2300 | 8 |
| 500 | 7.5 | 40 | 32 | 76 | 2300 | 4 |

## BATTERY CABINET

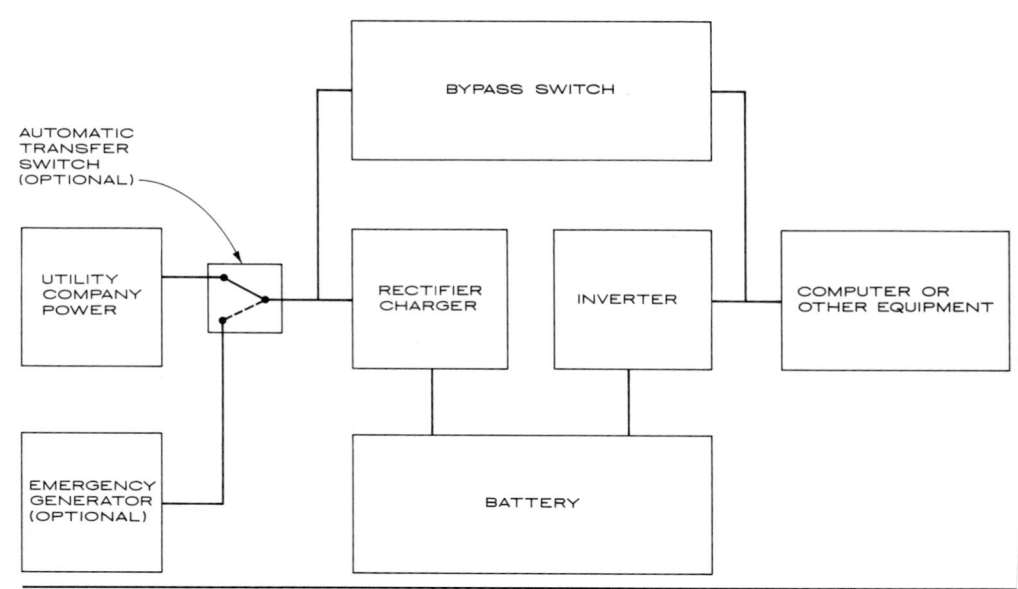

## TYPICAL UPS DIAGRAM

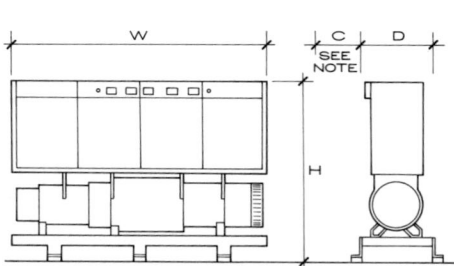

## ROTARY UPS SIZES

| KVA | W (IN.) | D (IN.) | H (IN.) | WEIGHT (LB) |
|---|---|---|---|---|
| 25 | 80 | 24 | 62 | 2,600 |
| 50 | 80 | 24 | 62 | 3,400 |
| 125 | 125 | 32 | 74 | 7,000 |
| 250 | 140 | 32 | 80 | 10,000 |
| 500 | 164 | 60 | 84 | 15,000 |
| 1000 | 173 | 64 | 98 | 32,200 |

Sound level approximately 60 to 80 dB. Heat rejection approximately 400 Btu/hr/KVA at 50 KVA to 250 Btu/hr/KVA at 500 KVA. Maintain room temperature at 70°–80°F. Some units require front and rear clearance for access.

## ROTARY UPS

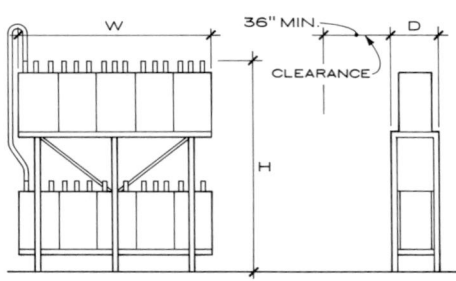

Racks can be placed back to back. Provide shower and eyewash station and ventilation, and maintain approximately 77°F room temperature. Place battery racks close to UPS units. Provide seismic bracing required by code.

## BATTERY RACKS

## SOLID STATE UPS SIZES

| KVA | W (IN.) | D (IN.) | H (IN.) | WEIGHT (LB) |
|---|---|---|---|---|
| 25 | 28 | 32 | 70 | 1,400 |
| 50 | 72 | 36 | 72 | 4,000 |
| 125 | 72 | 36 | 72 | 5,600 |
| 200 | 72 | 36 | 72 | 6,000 |
| 350 | 168 | 32 | 76 | 12,700 |
| 500 | 168 | 40 | 76 | 14,600 |

Sound level approximately 65–70 dB. Heat rejection approximately 450–700 Btu/hr/KVA at 50 KVA to 250 Btu/hr/KVA at 500 KVA. Maintain room temperature at 70°–80°F. Some units require clearance (C) for access.

## SOLID STATE UPS

## BATTERY RACKS
### TWO-TIER RACK SIZES

| KVA | TIME (MIN.) | W (IN.) | D (IN.) | H (IN.) | WEIGHT (LB) | NUMBER REQUIRED |
|---|---|---|---|---|---|---|
| 15 | 30 | 96 | 16 | 54 | 3,100 | 2 |
| 100 | 15 | 168 | 18 | 52 | 10,000 | 4 |
| 250 | 15 | 108 | 18 | 52 | 20,500 | 6 |
| 500 | 15 | 156 | 18 | 52 | 34,600 | 6 |

### THREE-TIER RACK SIZES

| 25 | 15 | 108 | 18 | 79 | 4,300 | 1 |
| 50 | 15 | 108 | 18 | 79 | 5,000 | 1 |
| 100 | 15 | 108 | 18 | 79 | 10,000 | 2 |
| 250 | 15 | 144 | 18 | 79 | 20,500 | 3 |
| 500 | 15 | 108 | 18 | 79 | 34,600 | 6 |

Fred W. Hegel, AIA; Denver, Colorado

## SPECIAL SYSTEMS

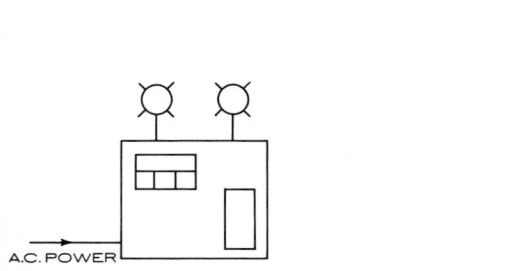

**BATTERY PACK**

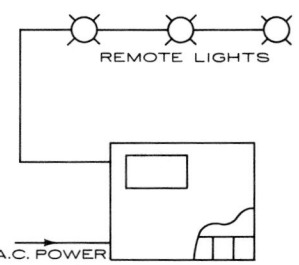

**BATTERIES AND INVERTER**

## BATTERY PACKS AND INVERTERS

Battery powered lighting equipment is utilized to provide minimal emergency illumination required for personnel safety and evacuation purposes in buildings not requiring standby generator power. This equipment is also utilized in buildings requiring standby generator power at central control room, telephone switchboard room, generator room, and electrical switchgear rooms to provide lighting for continuity of critical operations and troubleshooting if the generator fails to start. The batteries require frequent inspection, tests, and maintenance if they are to perform their intended function.

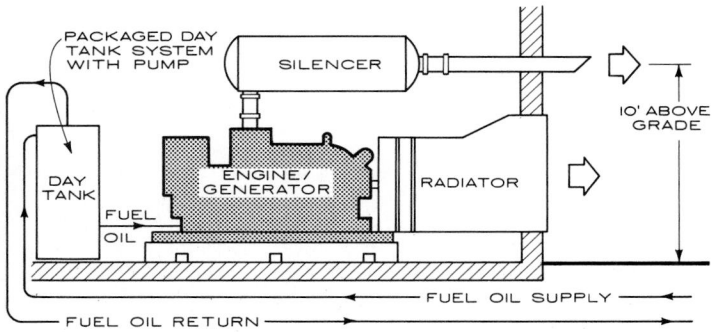

**UNIT MOUNTED RADIATOR**

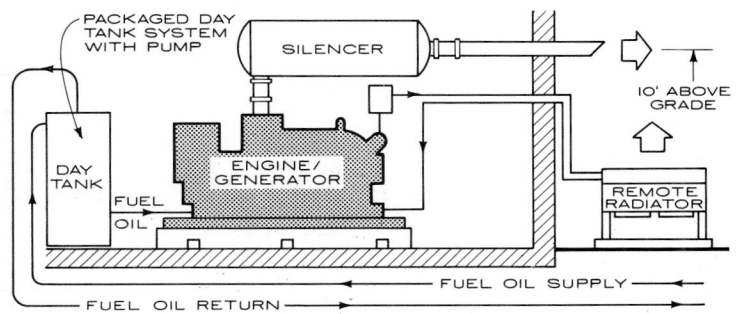

**REMOTE RADIATOR**

## STANDBY GENERATORS

Standby generators are utilized where the life safety lighting requirements and/or the requirements to drive critical equipment are beyond the capacity of battery units. Engines are cooled by methods illustrated, and should be located in rooms separate from main electrical switchgear. Engine rooms must have adequate ventilation for engine and generator radiated heat and must be protected against extreme environments under all conditions of airflow. Room size and space at sides of power generating unit(s) must be adequate for service. Access to room must allow for removal of generation unit. Standby generators require frequent inspections, tests under load conditions, and maintenance if they are to perform their intended function. Vibration isolation provisions are required to prevent vibration transmission to surrounding occupied areas. In addition to the cooling methods illustrated, cooling by heat exchanger, submerged pipe, cooling tower, and evaporative cooler should be considered.

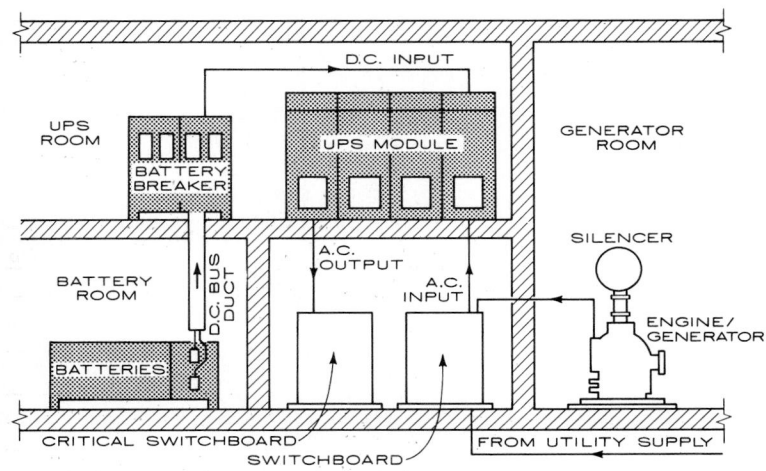

**UNINTERRUPTIBLE POWER SUPPLY SYSTEM**

## UNINTERRUPTIBLE POWER SUPPLY SYSTEM

Uninterruptible power supply (UPS) systems closely control the power supply voltage and frequency to critical equipment such as computers, communications systems, medical instrumentation, and similar sophisticated loads. Such UPS installations often are served from both utility and standby generator sources and provide "buffering" or complete isolation between the service and the critical load. The UPS batteries supply power through the UPS inverter to the critical AC loads until normal or generator power is restored or until the batteries reach end-of-discharge voltage. UPS systems require frequent inspections, tests, and maintenance if they are to perform their intended function.

William Tao & Associates, Inc., Consulting Engineers; St. Louis, Missouri

**SPECIAL SYSTEMS** 16

## GENERAL NOTES

1. Technology is changing constantly, affecting size, cost, and capability of equipment.
2. Generally the same types of detectors and alarms are available for residential and commercial systems.
3. Specific examples are shown for each type of equipment. A wide variety of each type is available, varying in size, shape, and capability. Check with manufacturers for latest information.

## SECURITY SYSTEM DESIGN

Determine if security consultant is required.

1. Identify need for security: prevent loss; reduce loss; internal and external loss; personnel safety; terrorism; trade secrets
2. Determine the level of risk: type of business; geographic location; response time available from police and fire department.
3. Establish budget based on risk, need, and cost including the cost to maintain and operate the system.
4. Determine basic system: local alarm, central station, or proprietary.
5. Begin security system design during initial site planning and schematic building design. Continue to review and develop the system with the building. Consideration of security during design of the building can reduce the cost of the security system and improve its capability.
6. Test all systems thoroughly after installation to avoid false alarms and to ensure complete coverage.

## SYSTEM LAYOUT

1. Systems can range from basic, such as perimeter detectors at exterior doors that trigger an on site alarm, to elaborate systems with access control, fire detection, and environmental systems monitoring and control.
2. Systems are usually built up in layers. An example would be site detection as the first layer, perimeter detection of the exterior building wall openings as the second, space and motion detection third, perimeter of special areas or rooms, fourth, and, finally, specific objects as the fifth layer.

---

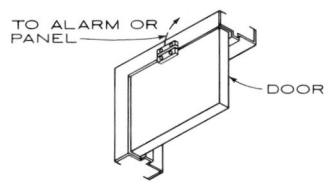

Increasing gap between magnets triggers alarm. Can be used for sliding doors.

**MAGNETIC DETECTOR**

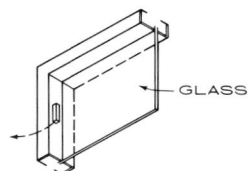

Break in tape opens electrical circuit and sets off alarm.

**METAL FOIL TAPE**

Detects vibration caused by breaking glass or moving window.

**SHOCK DETECTOR**

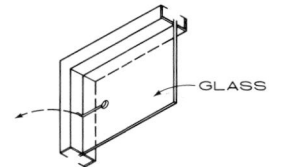

Attached directly to glass. One required on each pane.

**GLASS BREAK DETECTOR**

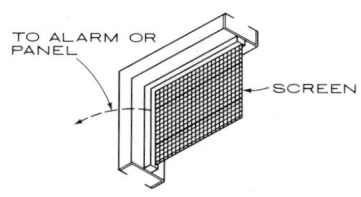

Detects cutting, breaking, or removal of screen.

**SCREEN DETECTOR**

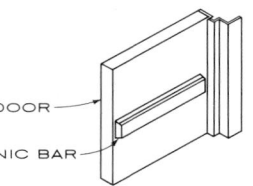

Available with electronic operation to signal use and to allow unlocking from a remote location.

**PANIC BAR**

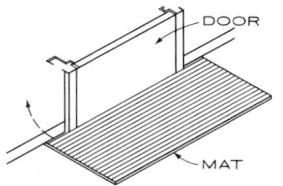

Weight of person on mat triggers alarm.

**PRESSURE DETECTOR**

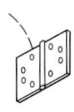

Detects opening of door. Another type conducts power to electric lock.

**ELECTRIC HINGE**

## PERIMETER DETECTORS

---

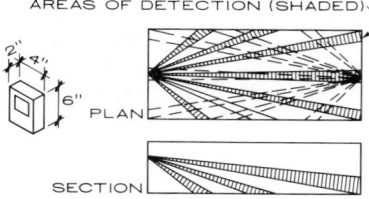

Detects object in heat range of body temperature. Detectors can overlap coverage to eliminate blind spots.

**PASSIVE INFRARED**

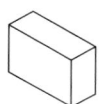

Detects change in sound wave pattern. Not recommended in areas with high acoustical absorption or with equipment emitting high pitched noises.

**ULTRASONIC**

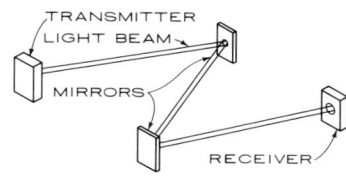

Detects interruption of light beam. Modulated beam is more difficult to bypass. Infrared and photoelectric available.

**LIGHT BEAM**

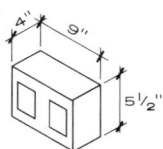

Alarm signal from both detectors is required to trigger alarm. Reduces possibility of false alarms.

**PASSIVE INFRARED WITH ULTRASONIC OR MICROWAVE**

Subject to false alarms from aircraft radar and from movement outside building through windows, wood doors, and the like. Radio waves penetrate glass, wood, and gypsum board and can cover several rooms at once. Must be certified by the FCC and less than 10 milliwatts for safety.

**MICROWAVE**

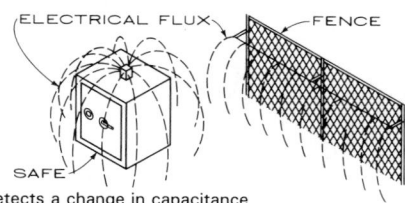

Detects a change in capacitance of the area covered, caused by intrusion. Very versatile and sensitive. Object becomes part of the detector.

**PROXIMITY/CAPACITANCE**

## SPACE AND MOTION DETECTORS

Fred W. Hegel, AIA; Denver, Colorado

## COMMUNICATIONS

CARD READER

NUMERIC KEY PAD

COMBINED CARD READER
AND NUMERIC KEY PAD

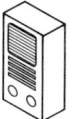

LOCKSET AVAILABLE
IN MORTISE AND
CYLINDRICAL MODELS

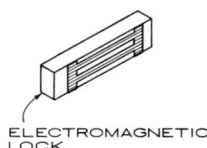
ELECTROMAGNETIC
LOCK

Access control devices can operate a lockset directly with an electronic signal, or through a computer to verify and re-cord access card, code used, time and date, or to notify security personnel to operate the lock.

Available with audio or audio video monitor and remote control to unlock security door.

APARTMENT LOCK

ELECTRIC LOCKS

## ACCESS CONTROL

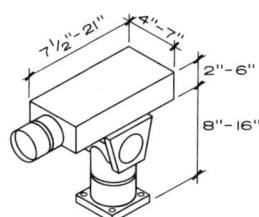

Available with remote controlled base and lens, high resolution, and low light level capability.

VIDEO CAMERA

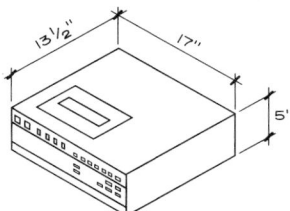

Available with variable speed time lapse or continuous record at alarm signal. Can encode tape with the time and date of event and locate event for playback.

VIDEO RECORDER

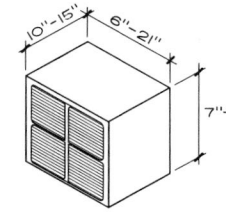

Controls can sequence automatically to view all cameras, or split screen to view four at one time. High resolution screens are available.

VIDEO MONITOR

Alarm sensitivity can be set to reduce false alarms. Can monitor remotely by radio or telephone line.

AUDIO DETECTOR/MICROPHONE

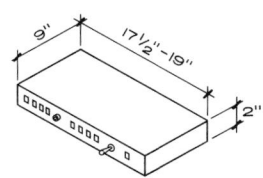
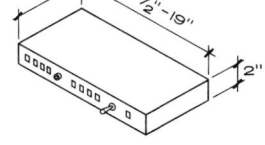

Can control one or multiple cameras and bases adjusting pan, tilt, focus, zoom, and iris from remote location.

VIDEO CAMERA CONTROL

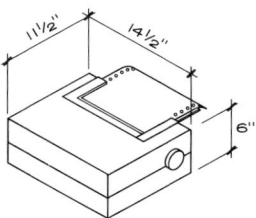

Automatically prints a record of all events with date, time, and alarm location. Can include access card use and instructions for evacuation, etc.

EVENT PRINTER

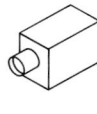

Triggered by alarm signal and preset to take time-lapse pictures at a selected rate.

FILM RECORDER

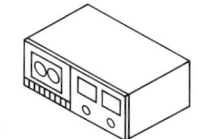

AUDIO RECORDER

## SURVEILLANCE AND RECORDING

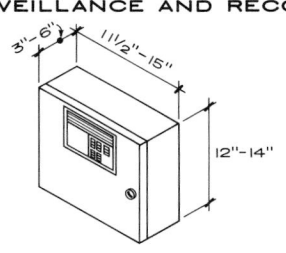

Can monitor security, fire, and environmental systems, and can notify security company of alarm.

MICROPROCESSOR

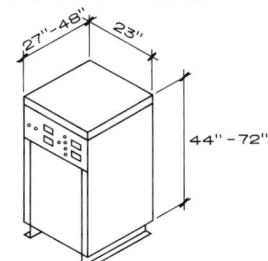

Battery pack with charger to maintain security during power failure.

UNINTERRUPTIBLE POWER

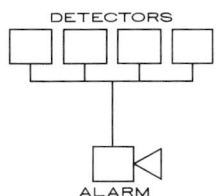

Portable or fixed location alarm button.

WIRELESS ALARM

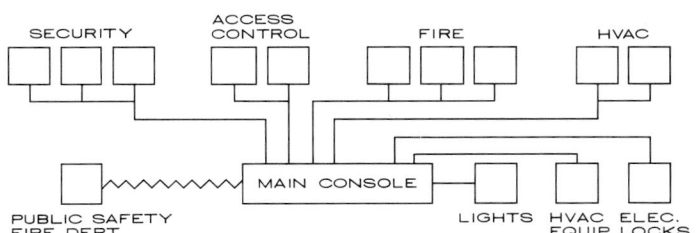

Custom designed for each installation. Can include security, fire, and environmental systems monitoring and control.

MAIN CONTROL CONSOLE

## PANELS AND MISCELLANEOUS

DETECTORS

ALARM

Any detector automatically triggers alarm.

LOCAL ALARM

DETECTORS    ALARM

DEDICATED
PHONE LINE

SECURITY    BUILDING    LIGHTS
COMPANY    MAIN PANEL

Any detector signals off-site security company that notifies public safety, owner, etc.

CENTRAL STATION ALARM

SECURITY    ACCESS
CONTROL    FIRE    HVAC

MAIN CONSOLE

PUBLIC SAFETY
FIRE DEPT.

LIGHTS    HVAC    ELEC.
EQUIP    LOCKS

Owner's on-site personnel monitor alarm signals, and they notify the public safety and fire departments directly. Monitoring and access control, HVAC, etc. also can be included.

PROPRIETARY CONTROL SYSTEM

## ALARM AND NOTIFICATION

Fred W. Hegel, AIA; Denver, Colorado

**COMMUNICATIONS** **16**

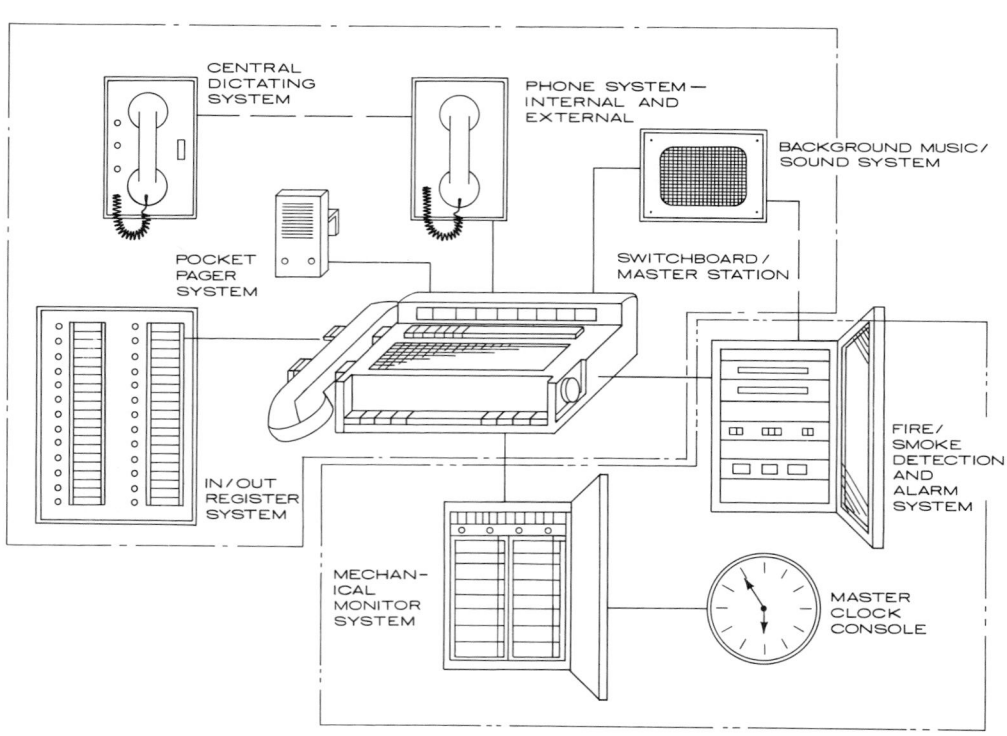

CORRIDOR DOME STATION

PATIENT BEDSIDE STATION

UTILITY/STAFF STATION

MASTER STATION

POCKET PAGE

EMERGENCY (TOILET AND SHOWER) STATION

REMOTE REPLY STATION

CONTROL UNIT

## NURSE CALL SYSTEM

The nurse call system provides immediate two-way communication between patient/staff and staff/staff within a given patient unit through a combination of voice, visual, and audio signals.

1. MASTER STATION: The master station provides the nursing staff with two-way communication to

patient and staff stations, giving audiovisual indications when a call is placed or connecting to a closed loop pocket pager system. In either case, the indicators distinguish between routine and emergency calls.

2. PATIENT BEDSIDE STATION: The basic bedside station includes one calling cord jack, a reset button to clear the call from the bedside, a call-placed indicator that lights when a patient places a call,

and a monitor indicator that lights when the patient's area is being monitored or a call is being answered. Additional features include a pillow speaker with radio/TV control and a privacy indicator when the intercom line is "open."

Types of cordsets: The available cordsets, interchangeable within the same multipurpose receptacle on all patient stations, include the following: pillow speaker units with nurse call buttons and TV/radio controls for general use, explosion-proof pull cord action type for use in an oxygen tent, low pressure geriatric type.

3. EMERGENCY STATIONS: The toilet emergency station consists of a nurse call button and reset button. The shower/bath emergency station is similar but with a cord and ball for call origination. A call from these stations actuates an emergency audio signal and flashing light at the nurse's station and changes the corridor dome light to intermittent flashing.

4. DUTY/STAFF STATIONS: The duty station provides audio and visual indication that a patient is requesting assistance and two-way conversation with the nurse's station. The features include speaker/microphone, combination privacy lamp/cancel button, patient call lamp, nurse call button.

The staff station is similar to the duty station, except that it does not have the patient call lamp. Patient calls are not signaled through staff stations.

5. CORRIDOR DOME STATIONS: Corridor dome lights indicate calls placed from stations within the room and alert all staff members in the corridor that a call has been placed.

6. CONTROL UNIT: The control unit serves as a central system check point during system installation and maintenance. It houses the speech amplifier for the system, a motor flasher for the buzzers and lights, the power system supply, and necessary terminal boards.

7. RESET PROCEDURE: After normal conversations, the patient station can be reset from either the nurse's station or at the patient's station. If the toilet or shower stations originate a call, reset procedure can only be carried out at the emergency station. Any reset procedure will automatically and simultaneously extinguish all call signals in the system corresponding to that call.

**NURSE CALL SYSTEM**

CENTRAL DICTATING SYSTEM

PHONE SYSTEM— INTERNAL AND EXTERNAL

BACKGROUND MUSIC/ SOUND SYSTEM

POCKET PAGER SYSTEM

SWITCHBOARD/ MASTER STATION

FIRE/ SMOKE DETECTION AND ALARM SYSTEM

IN/OUT REGISTER SYSTEM

MECHANICAL MONITOR SYSTEM

MASTER CLOCK CONSOLE

## HOSPITALWIDE CENTRAL SYSTEM

1. Staff and personnel intercommunication is provided by a central phone system and public address/sound system. The phone system consists of an internal network interfaced with the public utility phone company for external calling. The public address/sound system provides background music, in appropriate areas, and voice paging-Code Blue interface and, secondarily, routine paging taking precedence over background music.

2. Monitoring of mechanical services and equipment is coordinated within a central control panel, incorporating also a master clock console. The panel provides instantaneous audiovisual alarms of emergency conditions. The fire alarm system consists of a control panel, manual fire boxes, alarm signals, door holders, and ionization detector units, with monitors at the central switchboard station and the nurse master stations.

All equipment and installation must meet the requirements of the National Electric Code and applicable local codes which frequently stipulate UL approval. With the wide variety of system components and optional features, understanding of the specific facility and administration is essential to satisfy both present and projected future needs.

**HOSPITALWIDE CENTRAL SYSTEM**

Liz Karp; The Architects Collaborative, Inc.; Cambridge, Massachusetts

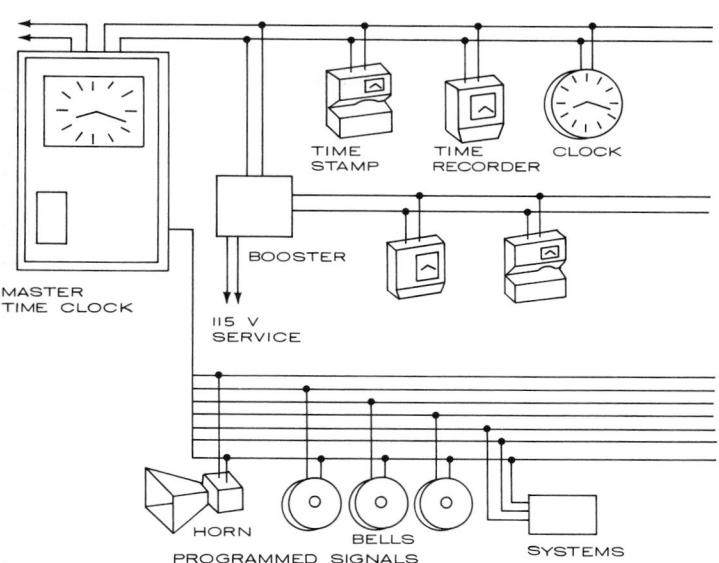

MASTER
TIME CLOCK

TIME
STAMP

TIME
RECORDER

CLOCK

BOOSTER

115 V
SERVICE

HORN

BELLS

SYSTEMS

PROGRAMMED SIGNALS

**SYNCHRONOUS WIRED CLOCK SYSTEM DIAGRAM**

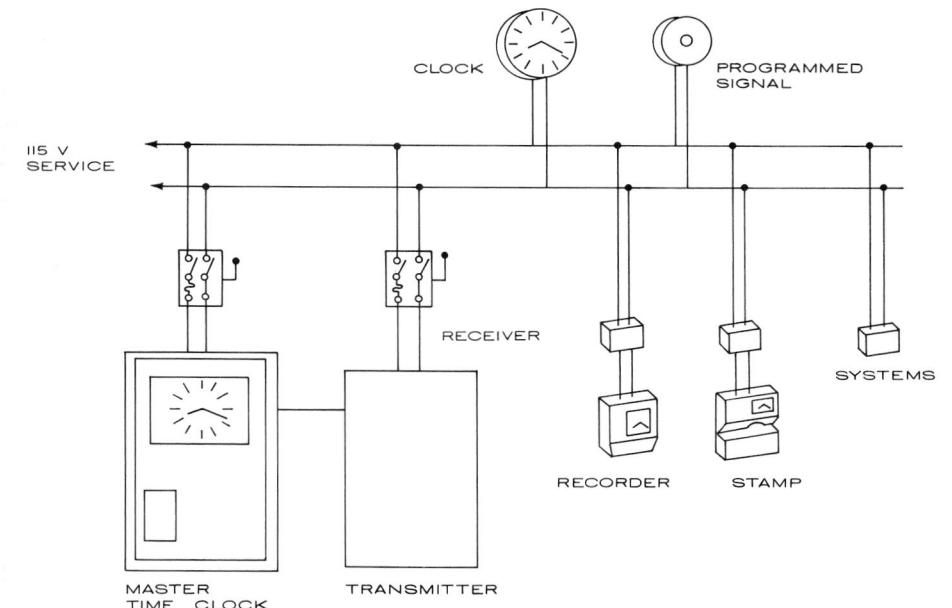

CLOCK

PROGRAMMED
SIGNAL

115 V
SERVICE

RECEIVER

SYSTEMS

MASTER
TIME CLOCK

TRANSMITTER

RECORDER

STAMP

**ELECTRONIC CLOCK SYSTEM DIAGRAM**

## MASTER CLOCK SYSTEMS

Master clock systems, consisting primarily of accurate clock and signaling mechanisms, are used to coordinate separated operations and activities that depend on time. These master systems control the accuracy of indicating clocks, time recorders, and time stamps.

Master clock systems are also used for program and system control, such as daily program activity signaling, day-night heating and air-conditioning, and after-hours lighting control.

The electronic and the synchronous wired systems are the most commonly used ones.

The electronic master clock system transmits high frequency signals over lighting circuits to receivers in the controlled unit. This system is generally used for large numbers of controlled devices because there is no requirement for control wire distribution. Units with their receivers can be added or moved, wherever lighting circuits are available, without regard to control wiring, thus making it particularly useful in renovation work or in multiple building schools.

The synchronous master clock system operates in a similar manner to the electronic system, except the signals are carried over assigned 3-wire clock circuits to the secondary clocks that are driven by synchronous motors. This system can be used for both small and large installations, free from possible circuit interference from other electronic devices.

Booster panels are available to expand either system for highrise buildings or large industrial plants where loads exceed the capacity of the master clock or excessively long runs are required.

The minute impulse system also utilizes master and secondary units, the latter being driven by a DC signal from the master, transmitted at minute intervals, rather than by individual synchronous motors. A correcting signal is also normally transmitted hourly. This system uses a 2-wire connection between units and master.

The dual motor system does not employ a master clock. Instead it utilizes clocks with dual motors; one synchronous for normal drive and one high-speed motor for correction. These clocks depend on their synchronous motors and the constancy of the 60-cycle power supply for accuracy. The high-speed correcting motors merely speed up the clock hands to correct for loss of time because of power interruption. This resetting is centrally controlled, either manually or automatically. The system is separately wired, thus allowing for ease of intentional corrections, such as is required for daylight-saving time.

## GENERAL USES

1. Clock correction.
2. Operations program signaling.
3. After-hours building lighting control.
4. Parking lot lighting control.
5. Day-night utilities control.
6. Sign lighting control.

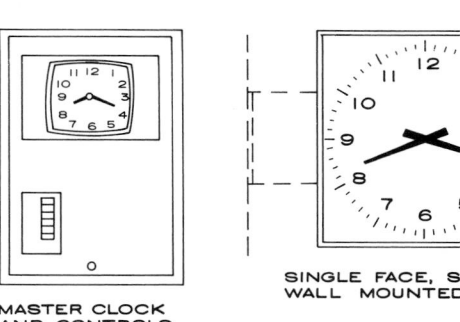

MASTER CLOCK
AND CONTROLS

SINGLE FACE, SQUARE
WALL MOUNTED

DOUBLE FACE ROUND
CEILING MOUNTED

ELAPSED TIME
CLOCK (NON-
CORRECTIVE
SYSTEMS ONLY)

DIGITAL CLOCK
WITH DAY AND
DATE

**TYPICAL CLOCK FACES**

Albert Kahn Associates, Inc., Architects & Engineers; Detroit, Michigan

**COMMUNICATIONS** **16**

## DECENTRALIZED HEATING SYSTEMS

Electric energy is ideally suited to space heating because it is simple to distribute and control. Complete electric heating systems are widely used in residences, schools, and commercial and industrial establishments.

A decentralized electric system applies heating units to individual rooms or spaces. Often the rooms are combined into zones with automatic temperature controls. In terms of heat output, electric in-space heating systems may be classified as natural convection, radiant, or forced air.

```
L    24" to 96"
D     3" to 8"
H    11" to 32"
CAP 1000 W to 4000 W
```

CABINET CONVECTOR (Surface Mounted or Recessed)

### NATURAL CONVECTION UNITS

Heating units for wall mounting, recessed placement or surface placement are made with elements of incandescent bare wire or lower temperature bare wire or sheathed elements. An inner liner or reflector is usually placed between elements so that part of the heat is distributed by convection and part by radiation. Electric convectors should be located so that air movement across the elements is not impeded. Small units with ratings up to 1650 W operate at 120 V. Higher wattage units are made for 208 or higher voltages and require heavy duty receptacles.

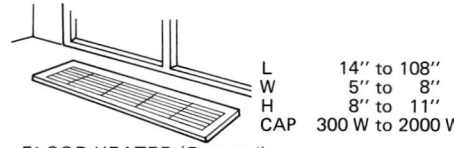

```
L    14" to 108"
W     5" to 8"
H     8" to 11"
CAP 300 W to 2000 W
```

FLOOR HEATER (Recessed)

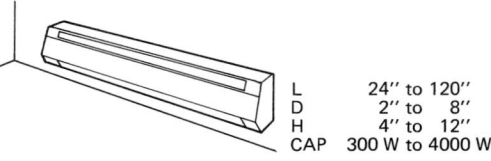

```
L    24" to 120"
D     2" to 8"
H     4" to 12"
CAP 300 W to 4000 W
```

BASEBOARD HEATER (Wall Mounted)

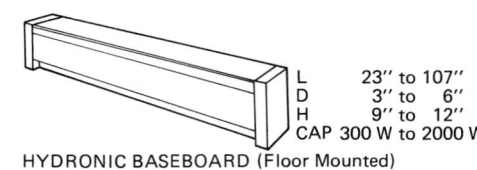

```
L    23" to 107"
D     3" to 6"
H     9" to 12"
CAP 300 W to 2000 W
```

HYDRONIC BASEBOARD (Floor Mounted)

### NATURAL CONVECTION UNITS

```
L    14" to 86"
W     4" to 12"
H     3" to 16"
CAP 500 W to 7000 W
```

INFRARED HEATER (Pendant Mounted) Circular heat lamp is available

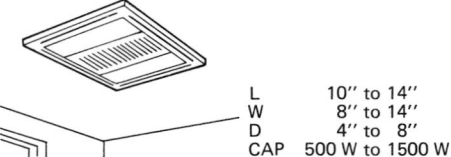

```
L    48" to 144"
W    24" to 48"
D     1"
CAP 500 W to 1000 W
```

RADIANT HEAT PANEL (Surface Mounted or Recessed) Decorative murals are available

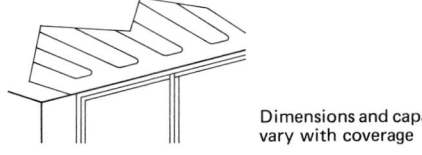

Dimensions and capacity vary with coverage

RADIANT CEILING WITH EMBEDDED CONDUCTORS

### RADIANT HEATING UNITS

#### RADIANT HEATING

Heat is produced by a current that flows in a high resistance wire or ribbon and is then transferred by radiation to a heat absorbing body. Manufacturer's recommendations for clearance between a radiant fixture and combustible materials or occupants should be followed.

#### FORCED AIR UNITS

Unit ventilators and heaters combine common convective heating with controlled natural ventilation.

Unit ventilators are most often mounted on an outside wall for air intake and at windowsills to prevent the down draft of cold air.

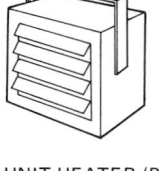

```
L    10" to 14"
W     8" to 14"
D     4" to 8"
CAP 500 W to 1500 W
```

CEILING HEATER (Recessed) Circular unit with light is available

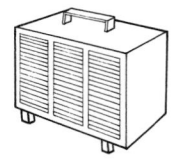

```
W    12" to 52"
D     6" to 22"
H    12" to 26"
CAP 1.5 KW to 50 KW
```

UNIT HEATER (Bracket Mounted)

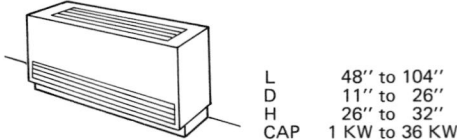

```
L    48" to 104"
D    11" to 26"
H    26" to 32"
CAP 1 KW to 36 KW
```

UNIT VENTILATOR (Surface Mounted or Recessed)

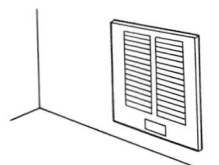

```
W    10" to 18"
D     2" to 6"
H     9" to 24"
CAP 750 W to 4000 W
```

WALL HEATER (Recessed)

```
W    10" to 72"
D     2" to 12"
H     7" to 24"
CAP 500 W to 5000 W
```

PORTABLE HEATER

### FORCED AIR UNITS

## CENTRALIZED HEATING SYSTEMS

A central hot water system with terminal radiators can be operated using an electric hot water boiler that contains immersion heating elements.

An electric furnace, consisting of resistance heating coils and a blower, can supply a ducted warm air system. Electric heating units are also installed in supply ducts to provide final temperatures and relative humidities in central air systems.

Integrated recovery systems make use of heat gains from electrical loads such as lights and motors. The excess heat accumulated from these sources can either be transferred or stored for later use.

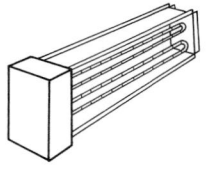

```
L    25"
W    23"
H    35"
CAP 5 KW to 60 KW
```

ELECTRIC FURNACE

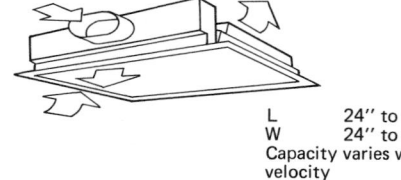

Size varies with duct dimensions
CAP 0.3 KW to 2000 KW

DUCT INSERT HEATER

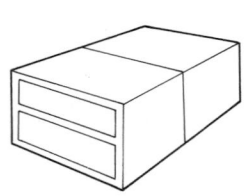

Size varies
CAP 2 KW to 100 KW

HEAT PUMP

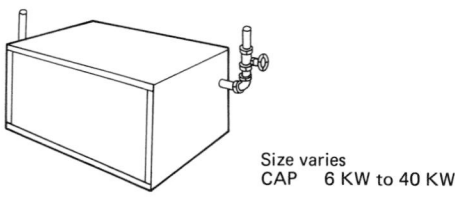

Size varies
CAP 6 KW to 40 KW

ELECTRIC BOILER

```
L    24" to 72"
W    24" to 72"
```
Capacity varies with air velocity

INTEGRATED HEAT RECOVERY Heat is gained from light fixtures

### CENTRALIZED HEATING SYSTEMS

Tseng-Yao Sun, P.E. and Kyoung S. Park, P.E.; Ayres, Cohen and Hayakawa, Consulting Engineers; Los Angeles/San Francisco, California

# 16 ELECTRIC RESISTANCE HEATING

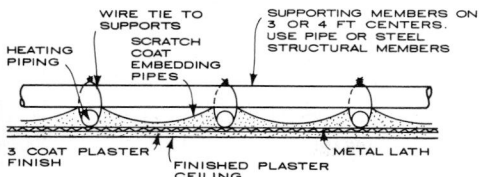

### PIPES IN SUSPENDED PLASTER CEILING

In a suspended plaster ceiling both the lath and the heating coils are securely wired to the support members so that the lath is below but in good contact with the coils. Plaster is then applied to the lath to embed the tubes. Some local codes may prohibit this assembly.

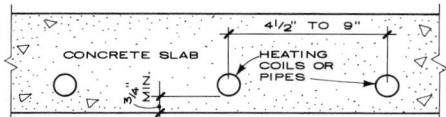

### COILS IN STRUCTURAL CONCRETE SLAB

Heating pipes can be embedded in the lower portion of a concrete slab. If plaster is to be applied to the concrete, the piping may be placed directly on the wood forms. The minimum coverage for an exposed concrete slab is generally ³/₄ in. but may vary with local codes.

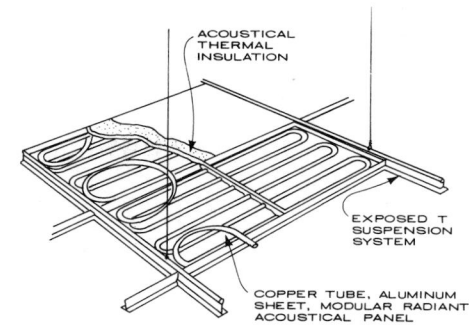

### METAL CEILING PANELS

Metal panel ceiling systems use copper tubing bonded to an aluminum panel which can be mounted into a standard suspended ceiling grid. An insulating blanket is required to reduce the upward flow of heat from the metal panel. The heating pipes can be connected in either a sinuous or parallel flow welded system. A ceiling panel system can also be used for cooling purposes if chilled water is supplied through the tubes.

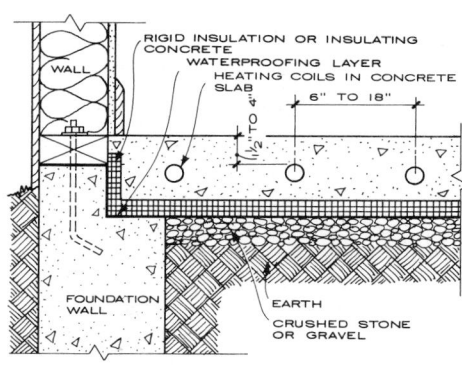

### COILS IN FLOOR SLAB ON GRADE

Plastic, ferrous, or nonferrous heating pipes are used in floor slabs that rest on grade. It is recommended that perimeter insulation be used to reduce thermal losses at the edges. Coils should be embedded completely in the concrete slab and should not rest on an interface. Supports used to position the coils while pouring the slab should be nonabsorbent and inorganic. A layer of waterproofing should be placed above grade to protect insulation and piping.

## LIQUID RADIANT HEATING SYSTEMS

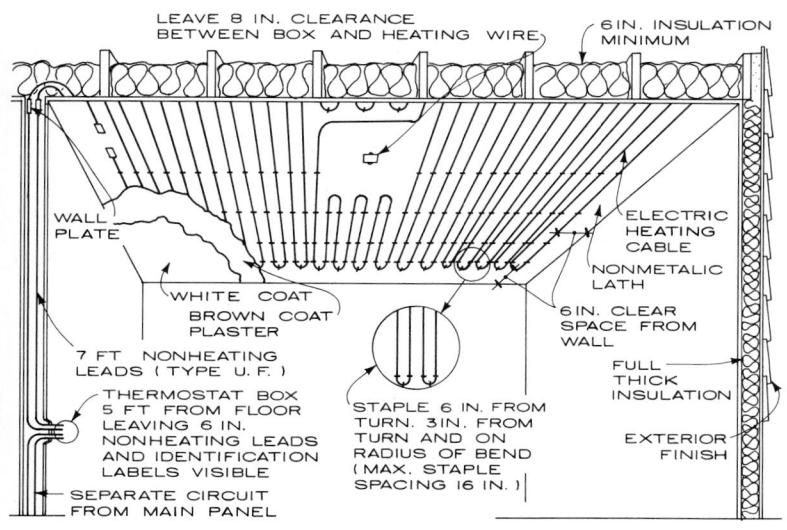

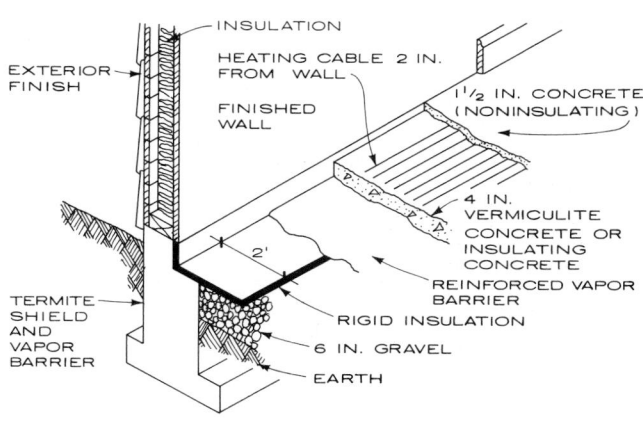

### ELECTRIC HEATING CABLE IN CONCRETE SLAB

Electric heating cables embedded in plaster ceilings or concrete floors or laminated in gypsum board construction are factory-assembled units furnished in standard lengths from 75 to 1800 ft. Standard cable assemblies are normally rated at 2.75 W/linear ft and are available for 120, 208 and 240 V.

## ELECTRIC RADIANT HEATING SYSTEMS

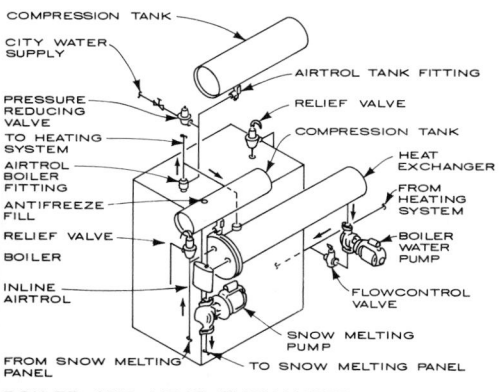

### BOILER AND HEAT EXCHANGER

### DRIVEWAY PIPING PLAN

### HEATING CABLE IN ASPHALT

### EXPANSION JOINT IN CONCRETE WALK OR DRIVEWAY

## SNOW MELTING SYSTEMS

Snow melting systems for driveways and sidewalks can be of the ethylene-glycol type, hot oil or electric cables. The hot liquid types use a central hot water boiler with a heat exchanger that pumps the fluid through tubes embedded in the asphalt pavement.

W. S. Fleming and Associates, Inc.; Fayetteville, New York

Vents, drains, slab pitch, and expansion joints must be provided for in the initial design. A ³/₄ in. pipe or tube on 12 in. centers is used as a standard coil. Header pipes are normally 1¹/₂ in. in diameter. Piping should be supported with a minimum of 2 in. of concrete above and below the pipe.

If piping must pass through a concrete expansion joint, provision should be made to avoid any stresses on the tubing. By dipping the tube below the expansion joint any movement or heaving in the slab can be accommodated. All piping below the level of the concrete slab must be waterproofed and covered with insulation.

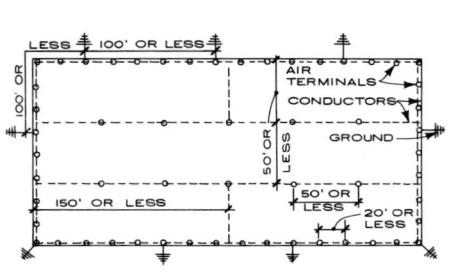

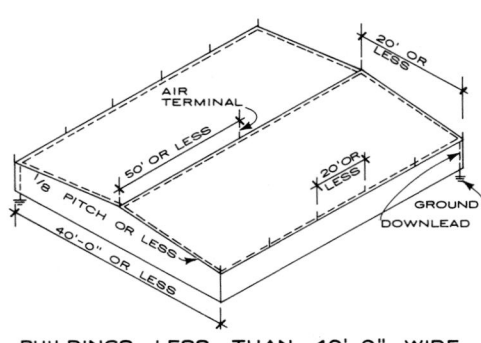

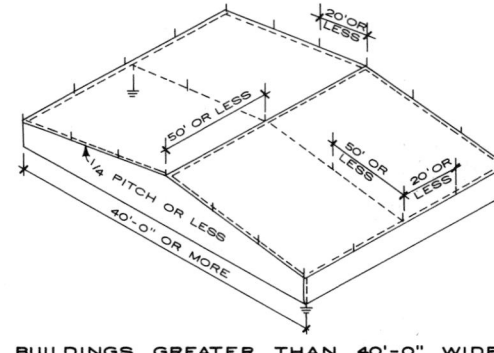

FLAT ROOF PLAN     BUILDINGS LESS THAN 40'-0" WIDE     BUILDINGS GREATER THAN 40'-0" WIDE

**ROOF LAYOUT PLANS**

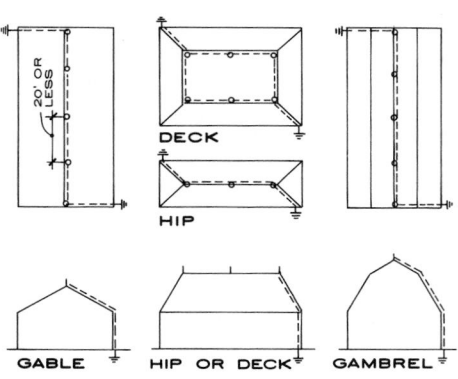

DECK

HIP

GABLE     HIP OR DECK     GAMBREL

**PITCH ROOF TYPES**

## OVERALL SYSTEMS DESIGN

1. Air terminals shall be located around the perimeter of flat roof buildings and along the ridge of pitched roof buildings spaced at 20 ft on center maximum and located not more than 2 ft from ridge ends, outside corners, and edges of building walls.
2. Full size main conductors shall interconnect all air terminals.
3. Additional air terminals shall be located in the center of large open flat roofs at spacings not to exceed 50 ft maximum.
4. Cable runs connecting these center roof air terminals shall not exceed 150 ft in length without a lead back to the perimeter cable.
5. Gently sloping roofs are classed as flat under the rules shown above and are protected in the same fashion as flat roof.
6. Download cables to ground shall be connected to the roof perimeter cable at a maximum spacing of 100 ft on center. Buildings having a perimeter of 250 to 300 ft shall have three downloads. For each additional 100 ft or fraction thereof add one download.
7. No building or structure shall have less than two downloads.

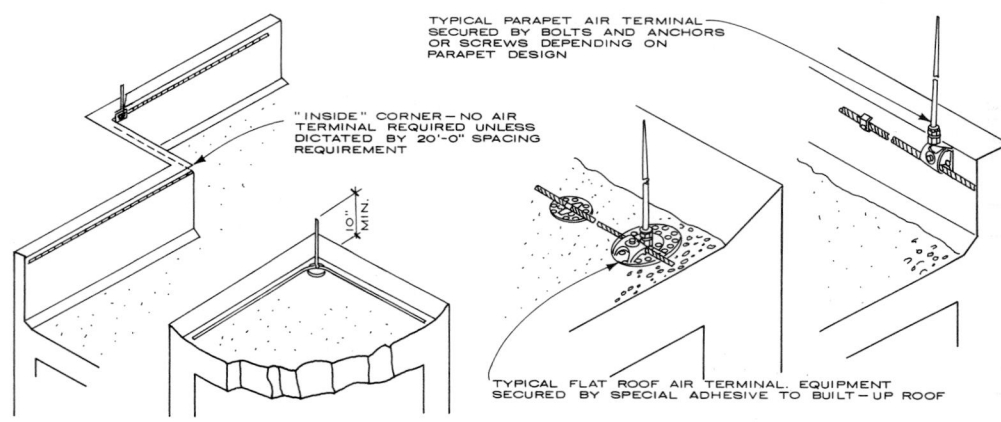

**AIR TERMINALS**

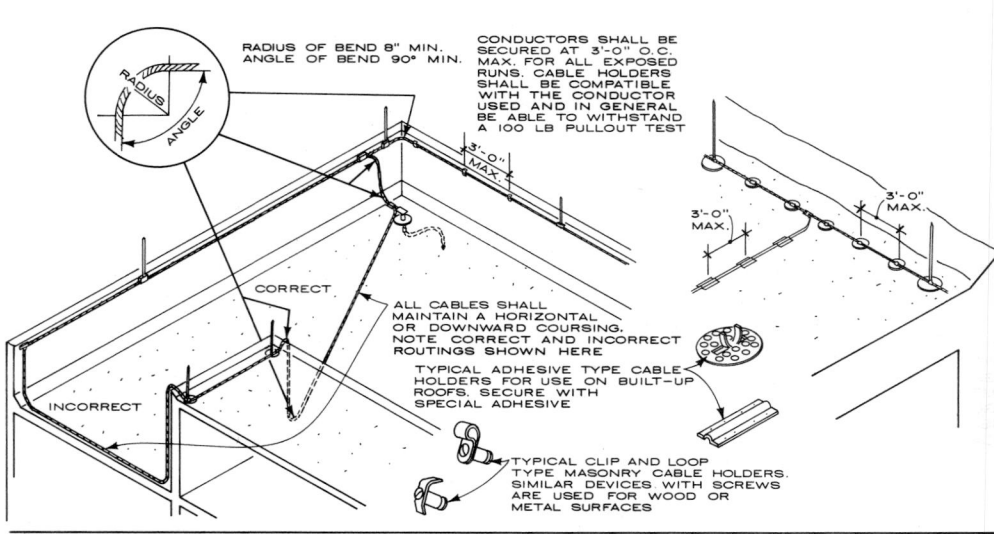

**CONDUCTORS**

## GENERAL NOTES

A lightning protection system is an integrated arrangement of air terminals, bonding connections, arrestors, splicers, and other fittings installed on a structure in order to safely conduct to ground any lightning discharge to the structure.

Lightning protection systems and components are grouped into three categories (U.L. classes) based on building height and intended applications. Class I equipment and systems are for ordinary buildings under 75 ft in height, Class II is for those over 75 ft in height, and Class II Modified is a specialty area covering only large, heavy duty stacks and chimneys similar to those used at power plants, for example. Each of these types of systems consists of five or six major groups of components:

1. Air terminals (lightning rods) located on the roof and building projections.
2. Main conductors that tie the air terminals together and interconnect with the grounding system.
3. Bonds to metal roof structures and equipment.
4. Arrestors to prevent powerline surge damage.
5. Ground terminals, typically rods or plates driven or buried in the earth.
6. Tree protection (usually applicable only to residential work).

Each of these types of equipment and the methods for their installation are covered in the following drawings.

Beyond these material requirements, other factors to be considered relative to lightning protection systems include (a) selection of codes for compliance, (b) inspection criteria (again based on code), (c) criteria to evaluate competency of installing personnel, and (d) requirement for annual inspection and maintenance.

Douglas J. Franklin; Thompson Lightning Protection, Inc.; St. Paul, Minnesota

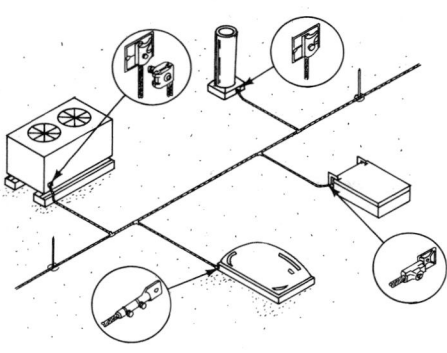

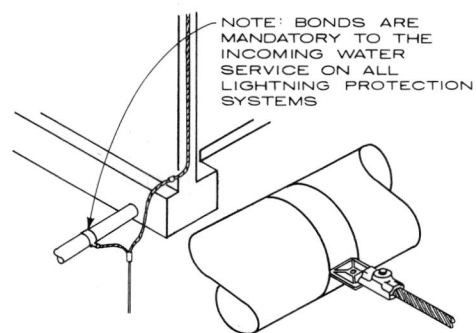

NOTE: BONDS ARE MANDATORY TO THE INCOMING WATER SERVICE ON ALL LIGHTNING PROTECTION SYSTEMS

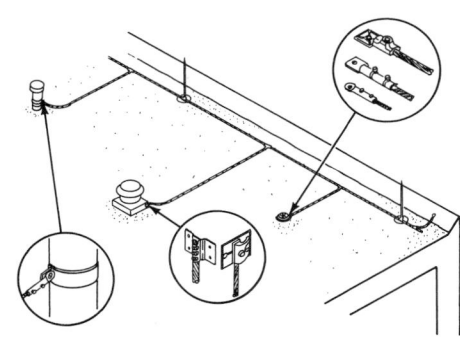

## BONDING

### NOTES

There are two classes of equipment that require bonding to the lightning protection systems.

1. METAL BODIES OF CONDUCTANCE: Larger metal objects located on the roof and subject to direct lightning strike. These objects must be bonded using full size conductor and fittings regardless of their location on the roof. Typical examples as shown include plumbing vents, exhaust fans, air-conditioning units, metal stacks, skylite frames, and roof hatches. Television and radio antennas must also be bonded.

2. METAL BODIES OF INDUCTANCE: Smaller objects such as roof drains, gutters, downspouts, flashings, coping, and expansion joint caps. These require bonding only if within 6 ft of the system.

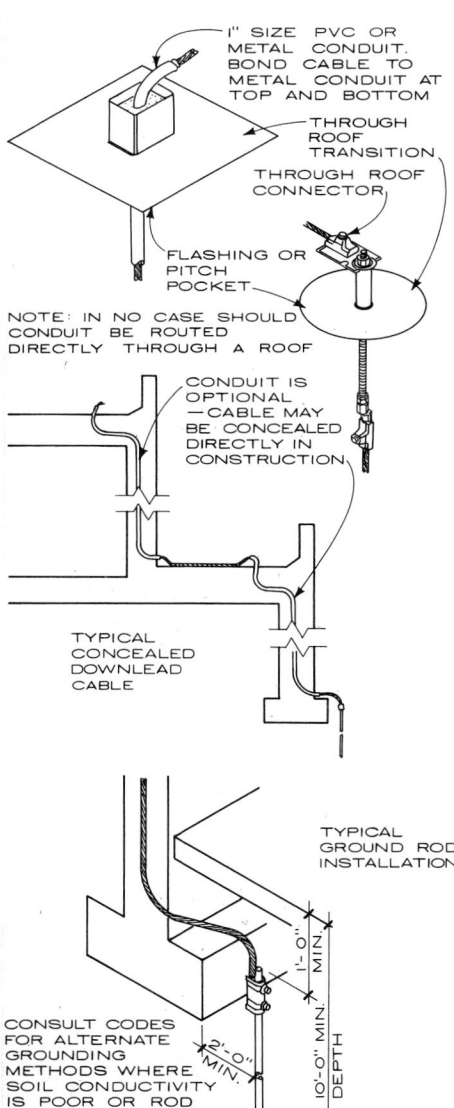

1" SIZE PVC OR METAL CONDUIT. BOND CABLE TO METAL CONDUIT AT TOP AND BOTTOM

THROUGH ROOF TRANSITION

THROUGH ROOF CONNECTOR

FLASHING OR PITCH POCKET

NOTE: IN NO CASE SHOULD CONDUIT BE ROUTED DIRECTLY THROUGH A ROOF

CONDUIT IS OPTIONAL — CABLE MAY BE CONCEALED DIRECTLY IN CONSTRUCTION.

TYPICAL CONCEALED DOWNLEAD CABLE

TYPICAL GROUND ROD INSTALLATION

CONSULT CODES FOR ALTERNATE GROUNDING METHODS WHERE SOIL CONDUCTIVITY IS POOR OR ROD CANNOT BE DRIVEN

1'-0" MIN.

2'-0" MIN.

10'-0" MIN. DEPTH

## DOWNLEADS AND GROUNDS

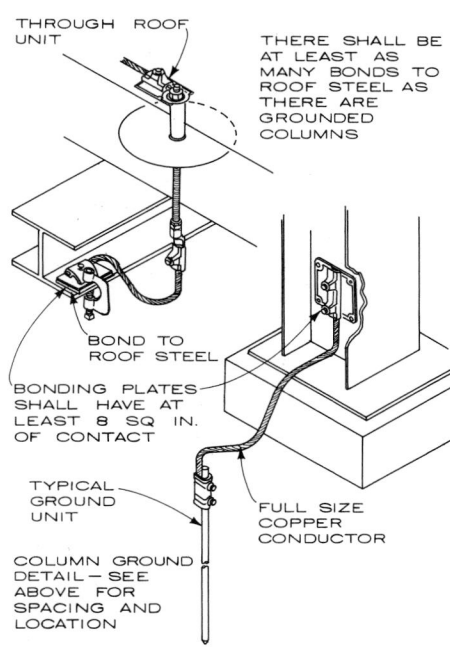

THROUGH ROOF UNIT

THERE SHALL BE AT LEAST AS MANY BONDS TO ROOF STEEL AS THERE ARE GROUNDED COLUMNS

BOND TO ROOF STEEL

BONDING PLATES SHALL HAVE AT LEAST 8 SQ IN. OF CONTACT

TYPICAL GROUND UNIT

FULL SIZE COPPER CONDUCTOR

COLUMN GROUND DETAIL — SEE ABOVE FOR SPACING AND LOCATION

### STEEL FRAME AS CONDUCTOR

### NOTE

In some cases, especially on tall structures, it may be advantageous to substitute the steel frame of a structure for portions of the usual conductor system, normally the downleads. Connections are made to cleaned areas of the building steel, at grade and roof level, and the columns serve to connect the roof and ground systems.

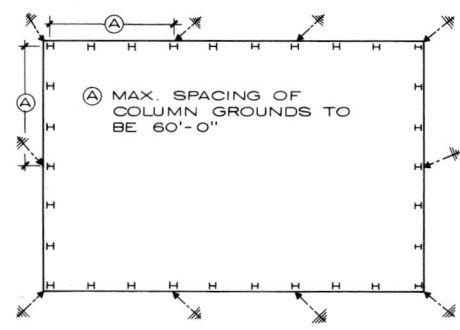

Ⓐ MAX. SPACING OF COLUMN GROUNDS TO BE 60'-0"

## COLUMN GROUND LOCATION

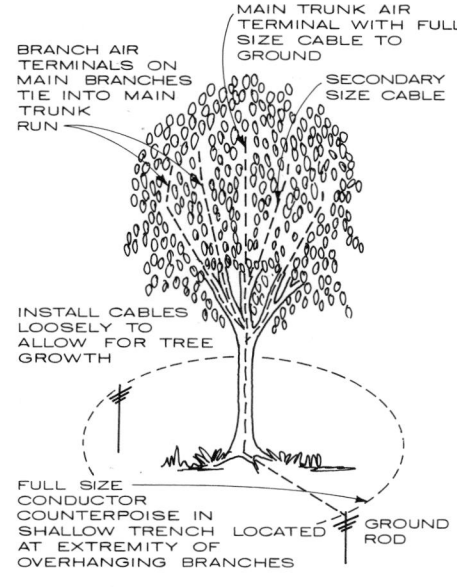

MAIN TRUNK AIR TERMINAL WITH FULL SIZE CABLE TO GROUND

BRANCH AIR TERMINALS ON MAIN BRANCHES TIE INTO MAIN TRUNK RUN

SECONDARY SIZE CABLE

INSTALL CABLES LOOSELY TO ALLOW FOR TREE GROWTH

FULL SIZE CONDUCTOR COUNTERPOISE IN SHALLOW TRENCH LOCATED AT EXTREMITY OF OVERHANGING BRANCHES

GROUND ROD

### TREE INSTALLATION

### OTHER CONSIDERATIONS

1. Arresters should be installed on the electric and telephone services and on all radio and television lead-ins to a structure. Responsibility and jurisdiction for the installation of these devices can vary with locality so that special consideration may have to be given to these items.

2. Trees adjacent to residences pose another special hazard. It is recommended that all trees taller than an adjacent structure that are within 10 ft be fully protected. Consult codes or manufacturer for recommendations on materials and installation requirements.

3. On-site inspections and certification of completed systems, installer competency certification, and guaranteed inspection/maintenance options are all available under existing standards. Consult codes and standards for specifics.

### REFERENCES

The following codes, technical sources, and quality control procedures are standards for lightning protection systems.

1. LIGHTNING PROTECTION INSTITUTE: "Installation Code L.P.I.—175."

2. UNDERWRITERS LABORATORIES: Master Labeled program under "U.L. Installation Requirements 96A."

3. NATIONAL FIRE PROTECTION ASSOCIATION: "Lightning Protection Code N.F.P.A. 78."

Douglas J. Franklin; Thompson Lightning Protection, Inc.; St. Paul, Minnesota

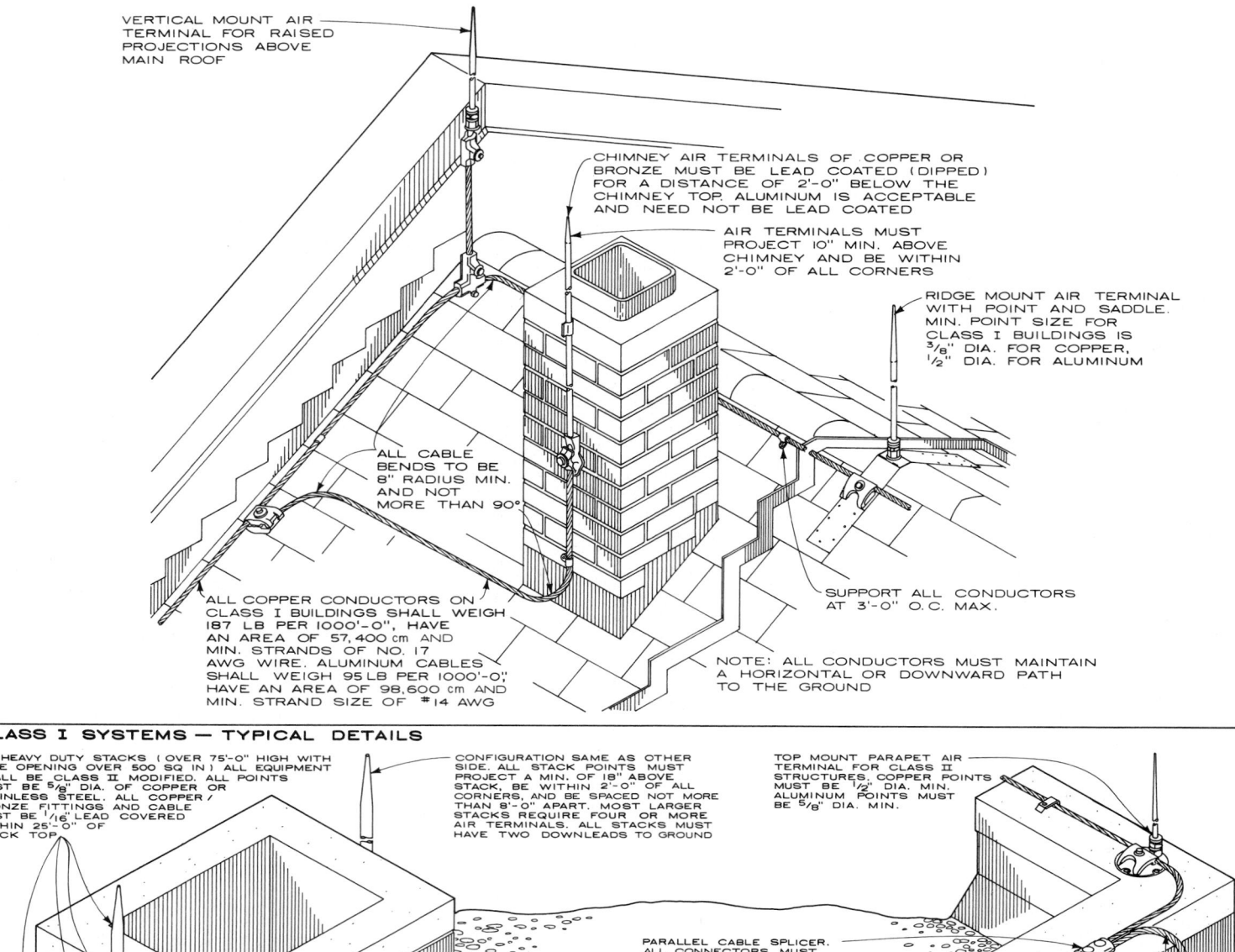

VERTICAL MOUNT AIR TERMINAL FOR RAISED PROJECTIONS ABOVE MAIN ROOF

CHIMNEY AIR TERMINALS OF COPPER OR BRONZE MUST BE LEAD COATED (DIPPED) FOR A DISTANCE OF 2'-0" BELOW THE CHIMNEY TOP. ALUMINUM IS ACCEPTABLE AND NEED NOT BE LEAD COATED

AIR TERMINALS MUST PROJECT 10" MIN. ABOVE CHIMNEY AND BE WITHIN 2'-0" OF ALL CORNERS

RIDGE MOUNT AIR TERMINAL WITH POINT AND SADDLE. MIN. POINT SIZE FOR CLASS I BUILDINGS IS ³⁄₈" DIA. FOR COPPER, ¹⁄₂" DIA. FOR ALUMINUM

ALL CABLE BENDS TO BE 8" RADIUS MIN. AND NOT MORE THAN 90°

ALL COPPER CONDUCTORS ON CLASS I BUILDINGS SHALL WEIGH 187 LB PER 1000'-0", HAVE AN AREA OF 57,400 cm AND MIN. STRANDS OF NO. 17 AWG WIRE. ALUMINUM CABLES SHALL WEIGH 95 LB PER 1000'-0", HAVE AN AREA OF 98,600 cm AND MIN. STRAND SIZE OF #14 AWG

SUPPORT ALL CONDUCTORS AT 3'-0" O.C. MAX.

NOTE: ALL CONDUCTORS MUST MAINTAIN A HORIZONTAL OR DOWNWARD PATH TO THE GROUND

## CLASS I SYSTEMS — TYPICAL DETAILS

ON HEAVY DUTY STACKS (OVER 75'-0" HIGH WITH FLUE OPENING OVER 500 SQ IN) ALL EQUIPMENT SHALL BE CLASS II MODIFIED. ALL POINTS MUST BE ⁵⁄₈" DIA. OF COPPER OR STAINLESS STEEL. ALL COPPER/BRONZE FITTINGS AND CABLE MUST BE ¹⁄₁₆" LEAD COVERED WITHIN 25'-0" OF STACK TOP.

CONFIGURATION SAME AS OTHER SIDE. ALL STACK POINTS MUST PROJECT A MIN. OF 18" ABOVE STACK, BE WITHIN 2'-0" OF ALL CORNERS, AND BE SPACED NOT MORE THAN 8'-0" APART. MOST LARGER STACKS REQUIRE FOUR OR MORE AIR TERMINALS. ALL STACKS MUST HAVE TWO DOWNLEADS TO GROUND

TOP MOUNT PARAPET AIR TERMINAL FOR CLASS II STRUCTURES. COPPER POINTS MUST BE ¹⁄₂" DIA. MIN. ALUMINUM POINTS MUST BE ⁵⁄₈" DIA. MIN.

PARALLEL CABLE SPLICER. ALL CONNECTORS MUST CONTACT CABLE FOR 1 ¹⁄₂" LENGTH

SUPPORT ALL CABLES ON STACKS AT 2'-0" O.C. HORIZONTALLY AND 4'-0" O.C. VERTICALLY

ALL CABLE BENDS TO BE 8" RADIUS MIN. AND NOT MORE THAN 90°

FOR CLASS II STRUCTURES, COPPER CONDUCTORS SHALL WEIGH 375 LB PER 1000'-0", HAVE AN AREA OF 115,000 cm AND STRANDS OF NOT LESS THAN #16 AWG. ALUMINUM CONDUCTORS SHALL WEIGH 190 LB PER 1000'-0", HAVE AN AREA OF 192,000 cm AND STRANDS OF NOT LESS THAN #13 AWG

SUPPORT CABLES ON BUILDING AT 3'-0" O.C. MAX.

CONDUCTOR ON THE TOP 25'-0" OF A STACK OR TO ROOF LEVEL SHALL MEET CLASS II COPPER CRITERIA AND MUST BE COVERED WITH LEAD ¹⁄₁₆" THICK

STRAIGHT SPLICE TRANSITION FROM LEAD COVERED TO BARE CONDUCTOR

FOR EXPOSED DOWNLEADS LOCATED IN SCHOOL YARDS, DRIVEWAYS, WALK AREAS, ETC., WHERE SUBJECT TO DAMAGE OR DISPLACEMENT, PROPER GUARDS SHALL BE PROVIDED. TUBULAR METAL GUARDS MUST BE BONDED TO THE CABLE AT BOTH ENDS

SEE GROUNDING REQUIREMENTS ON OTHER PAGE

## CLASS II SYSTEMS — TYPICAL DETAILS

Douglas J. Franklin; Thompson Lightning Protection, Inc.; St. Paul, Minnesota

# CHAPTER 17

## *Sports*

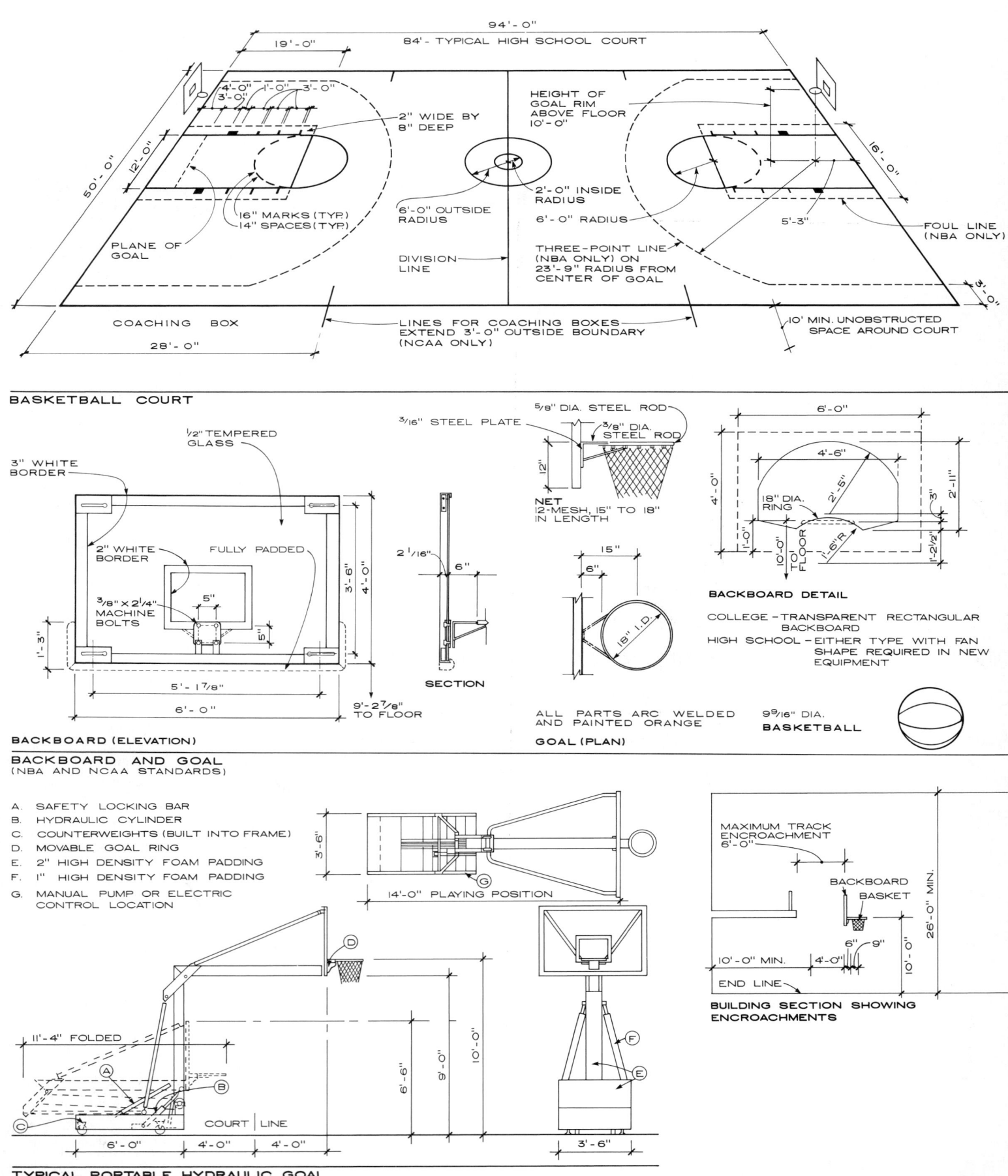

94'-0"
19'-0"
84'- TYPICAL HIGH SCHOOL COURT

4'-0"
3'-0"
1'-0"
3'-0"

2" WIDE BY
8" DEEP

HEIGHT OF
GOAL RIM
ABOVE FLOOR
10'-0"

50'-0"
12'-0"

16" MARKS (TYP.)
14" SPACES (TYP.)

6'-0" OUTSIDE
RADIUS

2'-0" INSIDE
RADIUS

6'-0" RADIUS

16'-0"

5'-3"

FOUL LINE
(NBA ONLY)

PLANE OF
GOAL

DIVISION
LINE

THREE-POINT LINE
(NBA ONLY) ON
23'-9" RADIUS FROM
CENTER OF GOAL

3'-0"

COACHING BOX

LINES FOR COACHING BOXES
EXTEND 3'-0" OUTSIDE BOUNDARY
(NCAA ONLY)

10' MIN. UNOBSTRUCTED
SPACE AROUND COURT

28'-0"

**BASKETBALL COURT**

1/2" TEMPERED
GLASS

5/8" DIA. STEEL ROD

3/16" STEEL PLATE

3/8" DIA.
STEEL ROD

6'-0"

3" WHITE
BORDER

12"

4'-6"

4'-0"

2'-5"

2'-11"

2" WHITE
BORDER

FULLY PADDED

18" DIA.
RING

3"

NET
12-MESH, 15" TO 18"
IN LENGTH

3'-6"
4'-0"

3/8" x 2 1/4"
MACHINE
BOLTS

5"

5"

2 1/16"

6"

1'-0"

10'-0"
TO FLOOR

6'R

1'-2 1/2"

1'-3"

15"

6"

**BACKBOARD DETAIL**

5'- 1 7/8"

SECTION

18" I.D.

COLLEGE - TRANSPARENT RECTANGULAR
BACKBOARD

HIGH SCHOOL - EITHER TYPE WITH FAN
SHAPE REQUIRED IN NEW
EQUIPMENT

6'-0"

9'-2 7/8"
TO FLOOR

ALL PARTS ARC WELDED
AND PAINTED ORANGE

9 9/16" DIA.

**BASKETBALL**

**BACKBOARD (ELEVATION)**

**GOAL (PLAN)**

**BACKBOARD AND GOAL**
(NBA AND NCAA STANDARDS)

A.   SAFETY LOCKING BAR
B.   HYDRAULIC CYLINDER
C.   COUNTERWEIGHTS (BUILT INTO FRAME)
D.   MOVABLE GOAL RING
E.   2" HIGH DENSITY FOAM PADDING
F.   1" HIGH DENSITY FOAM PADDING
G.   MANUAL PUMP OR ELECTRIC
     CONTROL LOCATION

3'-6"

14'-0" PLAYING POSITION

G

MAXIMUM TRACK
ENCROACHMENT
6'-0"

BACKBOARD

BASKET

26'-0" MIN.

D

11'-4" FOLDED

A

B

C

F

E

6'-6"

9'-0"

10'-0"

10'-0" MIN.

6"

9"

4'-0"

10'-0"

END LINE

COURT LINE

6'-0"

4'-0"

4'-0"

3'-6"

**BUILDING SECTION SHOWING
ENCROACHMENTS**

**TYPICAL PORTABLE HYDRAULIC GOAL**

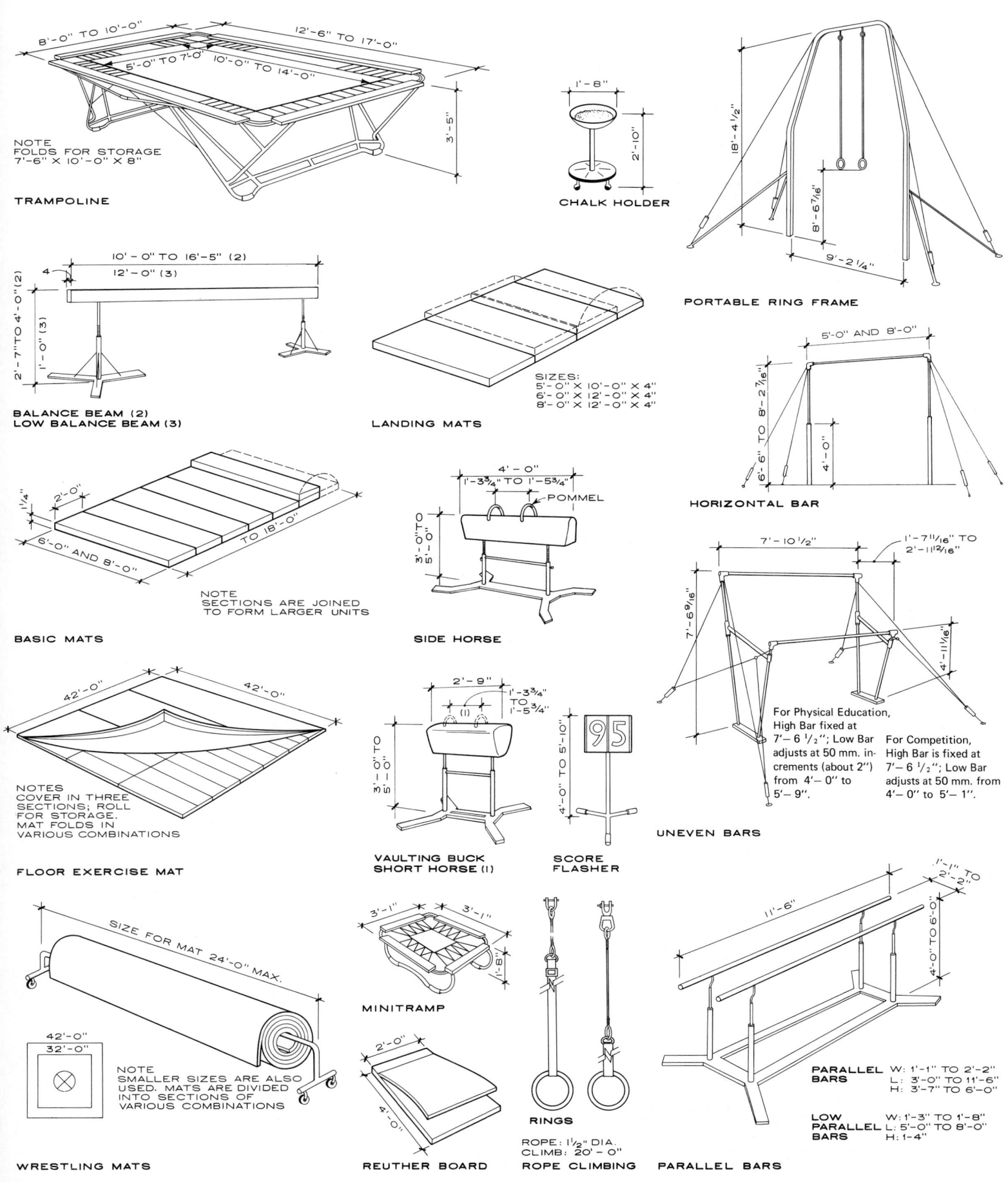

8'-0" TO 10'-0"

12'-6" TO 17'-0"

5'-0" TO 7'-0"    10'-0" TO 14'-0"

3'-5"

**NOTE**
FOLDS FOR STORAGE
7'-6" X 10'-0" X 8"

**TRAMPOLINE**

1'-8"

2'-10"

**CHALK HOLDER**

18'-4 1/2"

8'-6 7/16"

9'-2 1/4"

**PORTABLE RING FRAME**

10'-0" TO 16'-5" (2)

12'-0" (3)

4

2'-7" TO 4'-0" (2)    1'-0" (3)

**BALANCE BEAM (2)**
**LOW BALANCE BEAM (3)**

**SIZES:**
5'-0" X 10'-0" X 4"
6'-0" X 12'-0" X 4"
8'-0" X 12'-0" X 4"

**LANDING MATS**

5'-0" AND 8'-0"

6'- 6" TO 8'-2 1/16"

4'-0"

**HORIZONTAL BAR**

1 1/4"    2'-0"

6'-0" AND 8'-0"    TO 18'-0"

**NOTE**
SECTIONS ARE JOINED
TO FORM LARGER UNITS

**BASIC MATS**

4'-0"
1'-3 3/4" TO 1'-5 3/4"

POMMEL

3'-0" TO 5'-0"

**SIDE HORSE**

7'-10 1/2"    1'-7 11/16" TO 2'-11 12/16"

7'-6 9/16"    4'-11 1/16"

For Physical Education,
High Bar fixed at
7'– 6 1/2''; Low Bar
adjusts at 50 mm. in-
crements (about 2'')
from 4'– 0'' to
5'– 9''.

For Competition,
High Bar is fixed at
7'– 6 1/2''; Low Bar
adjusts at 50 mm. from
4'– 0'' to 5'– 1''.

**UNEVEN BARS**

42'-0"    42'-0"

**NOTES**
COVER IN THREE
SECTIONS; ROLL
FOR STORAGE.
MAT FOLDS IN
VARIOUS COMBINATIONS

**FLOOR EXERCISE MAT**

2'-9"    1'-3 3/4" TO 1'-5 3/4"

(1)

3'-0" TO 5'-0"

**VAULTING BUCK**
**SHORT HORSE (1)**

95

4'-0" TO 5'-10"

**SCORE FLASHER**

1'-1" TO 2'-2"

11'-6"

4'-0" TO 6'-0"

SIZE FOR MAT 24'-0" MAX.

42'-0"
32'-0"

⊗

**NOTE**
SMALLER SIZES ARE ALSO
USED. MATS ARE DIVIDED
INTO SECTIONS OF
VARIOUS COMBINATIONS

**WRESTLING MATS**

3'-1"    3'-1"

1'-8"

**MINITRAMP**

2'-0"

4'-0"

**REUTHER BOARD**

**RINGS**

ROPE: 1 1/2" DIA.
CLIMB: 20'- 0"

**ROPE CLIMBING**

**PARALLEL BARS**

PARALLEL W: 1'-1" TO 2'-2"
BARS       L: 3'-0" TO 11'-6"
           H: 3'-7" TO 6'-0"

LOW
PARALLEL   W: 1'-3" TO 1'-8"
BARS       L: 5'-0" TO 8'-0"
           H: 1-4"

John C. Lunsford, AIA, Varney Sexton Sydnor Associates; Phoenix, Arizona

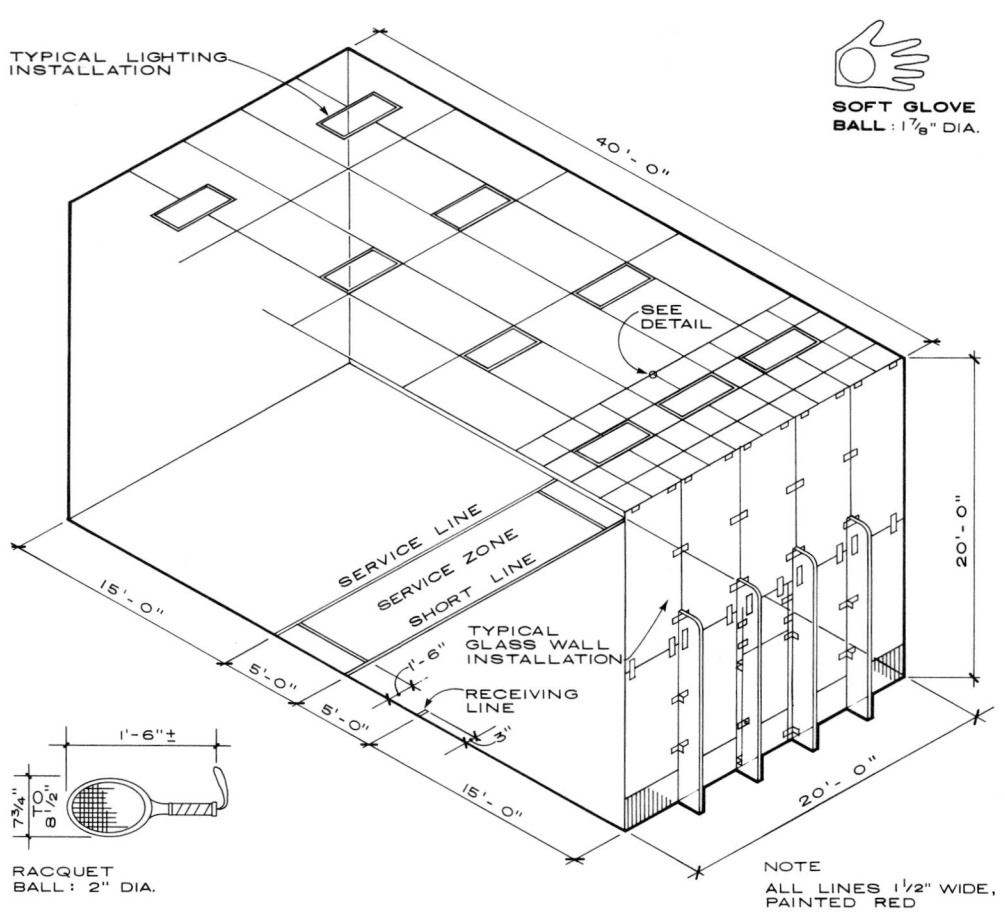

TYPICAL LIGHTING INSTALLATION

40'-0"

20'-0"

SOFT GLOVE
BALL : 1 7/8" DIA.

SERVICE LINE
SERVICE ZONE
SHORT LINE

15'-0"

5'-0"
5'-0"
1'-6"

RECEIVING LINE
3"

TYPICAL GLASS WALL INSTALLATION

15'-0"

20'-0"

RACQUET BALL: 2" DIA.

1'-6"±
7 3/4" TO 8 1/2"

NOTE
ALL LINES 1 1/2" WIDE, PAINTED RED

## HANDBALL / RACQUETBALL / PADDLEBALL COURT

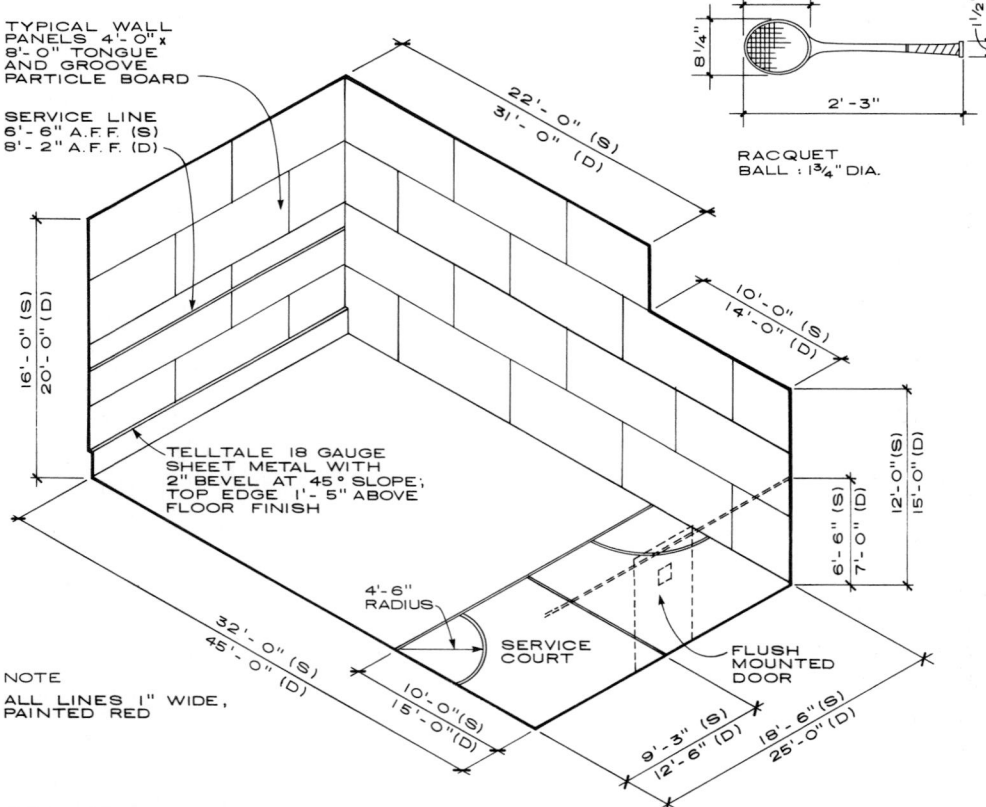

TYPICAL WALL PANELS 4'-0" x 8'-0" TONGUE AND GROOVE PARTICLE BOARD

SERVICE LINE 6'-6" A.F.F. (S) 8'-2" A.F.F. (D)

16'-0" (S) 20'-0" (D)

22'-0" (S)
31'-0" (D)

10'-0" (S)
14'-0" (D)

9"
8 1/4"
1/2"

RACQUET BALL : 1 3/4" DIA.

2'-3"

TELLTALE 18 GAUGE SHEET METAL WITH 2" BEVEL AT 45° SLOPE; TOP EDGE 1'-5" ABOVE FLOOR FINISH

4'-6" RADIUS

SERVICE COURT

FLUSH MOUNTED DOOR

12'-0"(S)
15'-0"(D)

6'-6" (S)
7'-0" (D)

32'-0" (S)
45'-0" (D)

10'-0"(S)
15'-0"(D)

9'-3" (S)
12'-6" (D)

18'-6"(S)
25'-0"(D)

NOTE
ALL LINES 1" WIDE, PAINTED RED

## SQUASH COURT

Timothy B. McDonald; Washington, D.C.

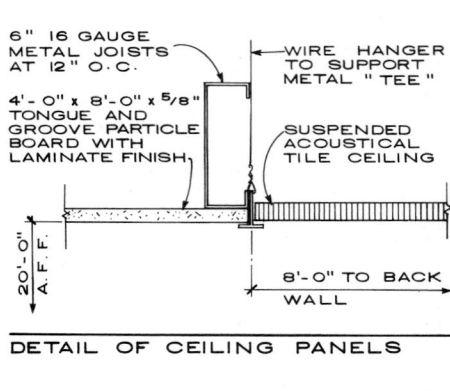

6" 16 GAUGE METAL JOISTS AT 12" O.C.

WIRE HANGER TO SUPPORT METAL "TEE"

4'-0" x 8'-0" x 5/8" TONGUE AND GROOVE PARTICLE BOARD WITH LAMINATE FINISH

SUSPENDED ACOUSTICAL TILE CEILING

20'-0" A.F.F.

8'-0" TO BACK WALL

### DETAIL OF CEILING PANELS

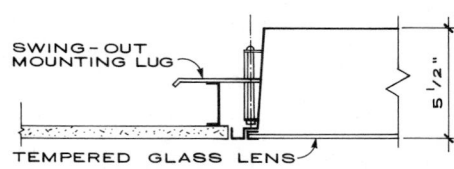

SWING-OUT MOUNTING LUG

5 1/2"

TEMPERED GLASS LENS

### DETAIL OF LIGHT FIXTURE

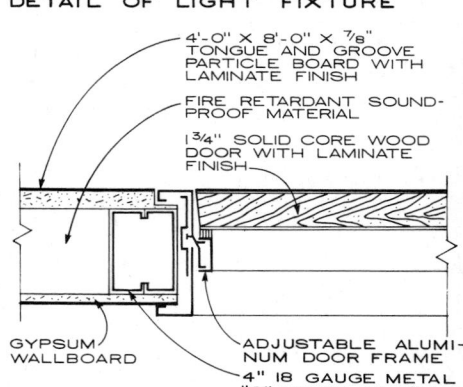

4'-0" X 8'-0" X 7/8" TONGUE AND GROOVE PARTICLE BOARD WITH LAMINATE FINISH

FIRE RETARDANT SOUND-PROOF MATERIAL

1 3/4" SOLID CORE WOOD DOOR WITH LAMINATE FINISH

GYPSUM WALLBOARD

ADJUSTABLE ALUMI-NUM DOOR FRAME

4" 18 GAUGE METAL "C" STUDS AT 16" O.C.

### DETAIL OF FLUSH MOUNTED DOOR AT JAMB

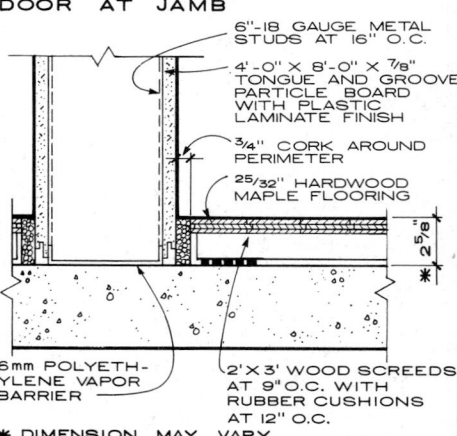

6"-18 GAUGE METAL STUDS AT 16" O.C.

4'-0" X 8'-0" X 7/8" TONGUE AND GROOVE PARTICLE BOARD WITH PLASTIC LAMINATE FINISH

3/4" CORK AROUND PERIMETER

25/32" HARDWOOD MAPLE FLOORING

2 5/8"

6mm POLYETH-YLENE VAPOR BARRIER

2'X3' WOOD SCREEDS AT 9" O.C. WITH RUBBER CUSHIONS AT 12" O.C.

✱ DIMENSION MAY VARY

### SECTION AT COMMON SIDE WALL THROUGH FLOOR

NOTES

1. Materials and installation of glass wall system shall comply with safety and performance criteria for walls established by the standards of the International Squash Racquets Federation, the American Association of Racquetsports Manufacturers and Suppliers, and B.O.C.A.

2. For racquetball courts, temperature and humidity shall be maintained during storage, installation and thereafter as follows: temperature range is 65°-78°F. and humidity to be controlled between 40% and 60% at all times.

3. All dimensions shown are finished court dimensions. D - doubles; S - singles

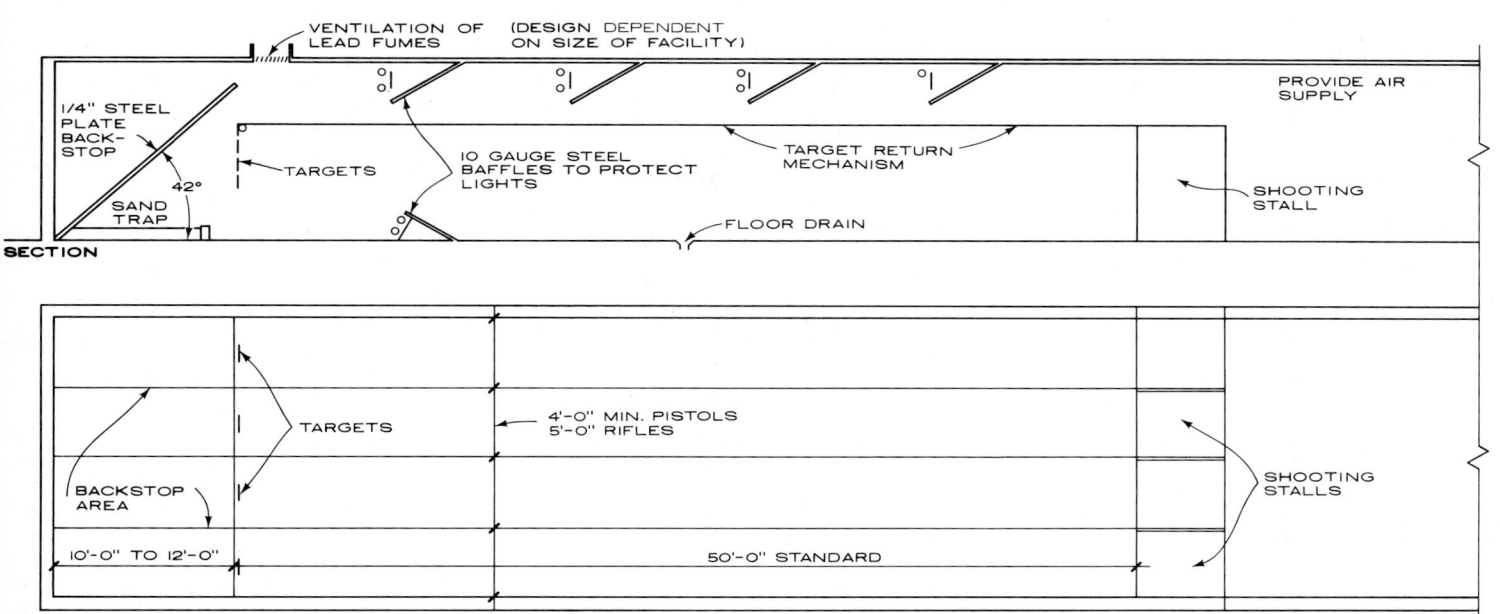

**SECTION**

**PLAN**

## DESIGN PROBLEMS

When planning a firearms range, the following safety considerations must be made:

1. Placement of traps; use of stalls and placement of firing line; provision for space for spectators; protection from ricochet; prevention of spilled powder explosions.
2. Ventilation adequate to dissipate lead fumes.
3. Noise abatement.
4. Lighting.

The use of range design consultants is advisable. Contact the National Rifle Association for information.

## TARGET SHOOTING

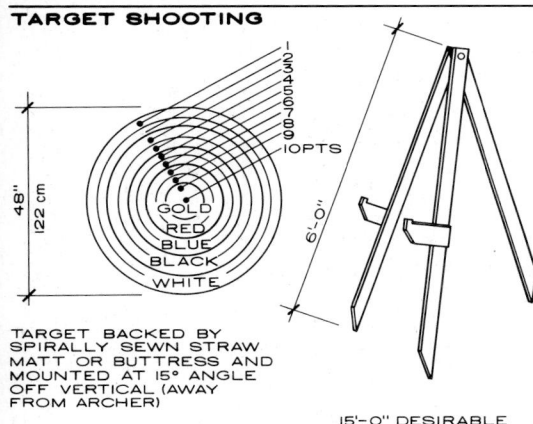

TARGET BACKED BY SPIRALLY SEWN STRAW MATT OR BUTTRESS AND MOUNTED AT 15° ANGLE OFF VERTICAL (AWAY FROM ARCHER)

Archery ranges should be orientated, in the northern hemisphere, so the archer is facing north ±45°. The range surface is to be turf, and free from obstructions or hard objects; likewise, spaces behind and to either side should be clear.

Target backings are made of stitched compressed straw rope called mat or buttress. Targets are made of thick paper with five concentric color zones. Both the mat and target are slanted at a 15° angle off vertical away from the archer.

Modern bows often are wood composites, fiberglass, and graphite. Lengths vary from 72 in. (1.82 M) to 62 in. (1.57 M). Bows are categorized by their draw weight, the amount of energy needed to pull a 28 in. (71 cm) arrow to full draw. Male archers usually use a 50 lb. to 55 lb. bow; female archers usually use 35 lb. to 40 lb. bow.

Arrow shafts are made of wood, graphite, or aluminum tubing. The flecking is made of plastic or feathers.

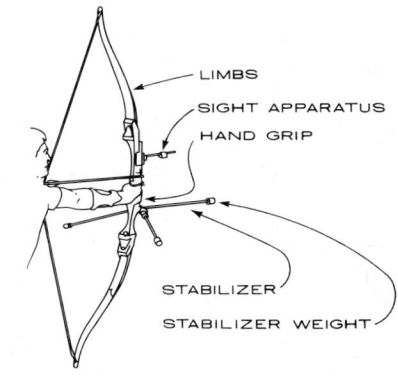

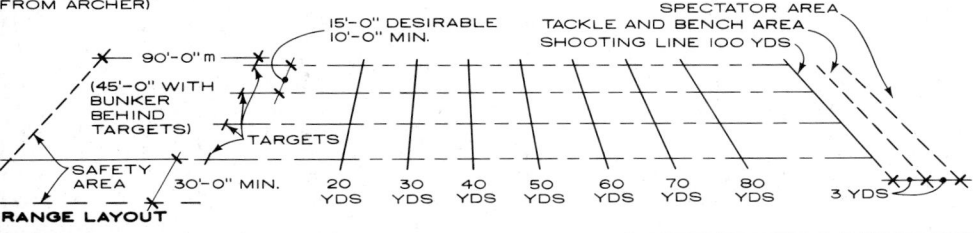

**RANGE LAYOUT**

## ARCHERY

Wooden nonskid flooring is ideal. A rubber piste is used on slippery floors. When a special metallic piste is used, a rubber mat must be placed beneath it to prevent hits on the floor being registered by the electronic scoring device. In competitive fencing, the score is kept by an electronic apparatus, which records each hit, and is linked to the fencers by wires. The wires are kept from trailing the ground by a spring-loaded spool. These spools often are recessed in a pit at each end of the piste.

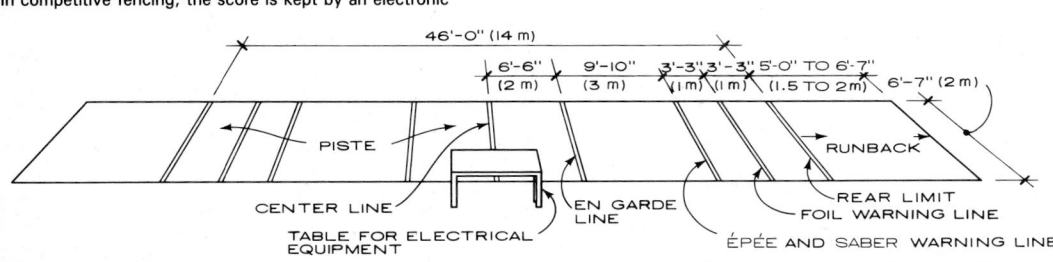

**FENCING**

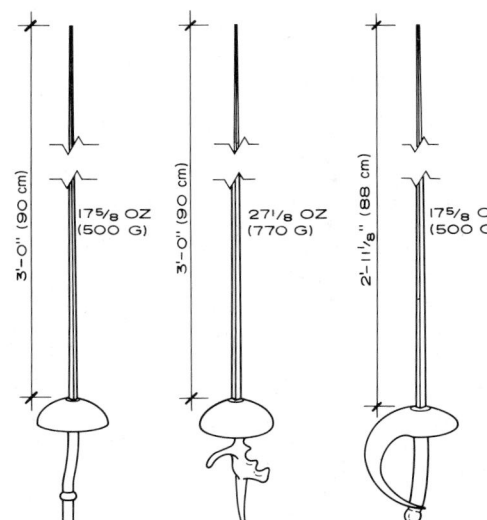

FOIL FRENCH HANDLE    ÉPÉE AMERICAN HANDLE    SABER

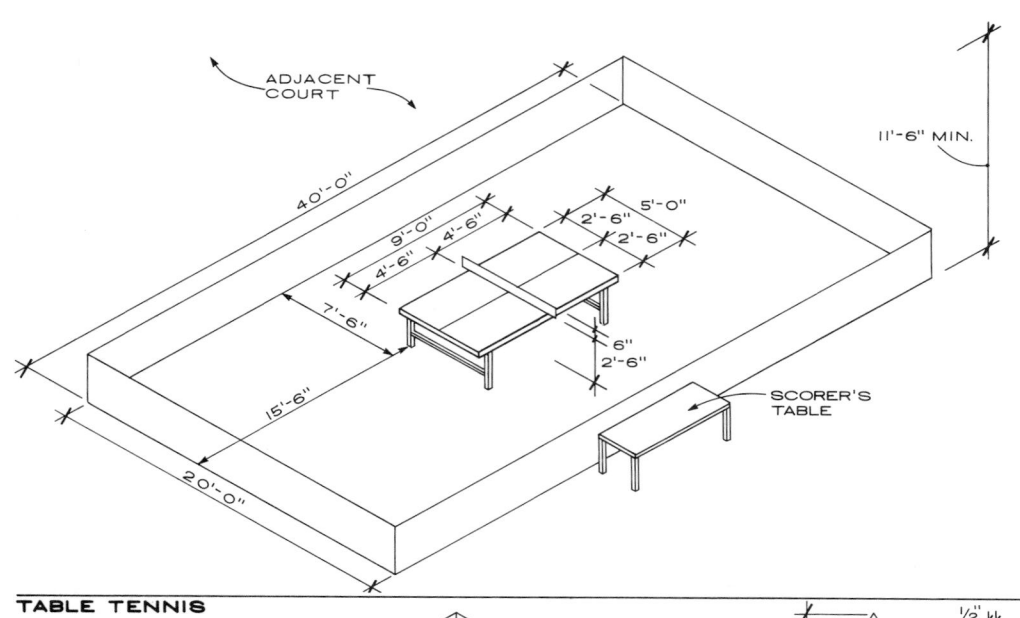

**NOTES**
Flooring should be level, slightly resilient, and not of non-skid material. Walls should be uniformly dark nongloss background to provide enough contrast to help players follow the ball. Lighting often varies for different standards of play, but 150-500 lumens at table height is the acceptable range. This should not be fluorescent or natural lighting, but preferably tungsten halogen. Sectional tables are stored upright when not in use.

**TABLE TENNIS**

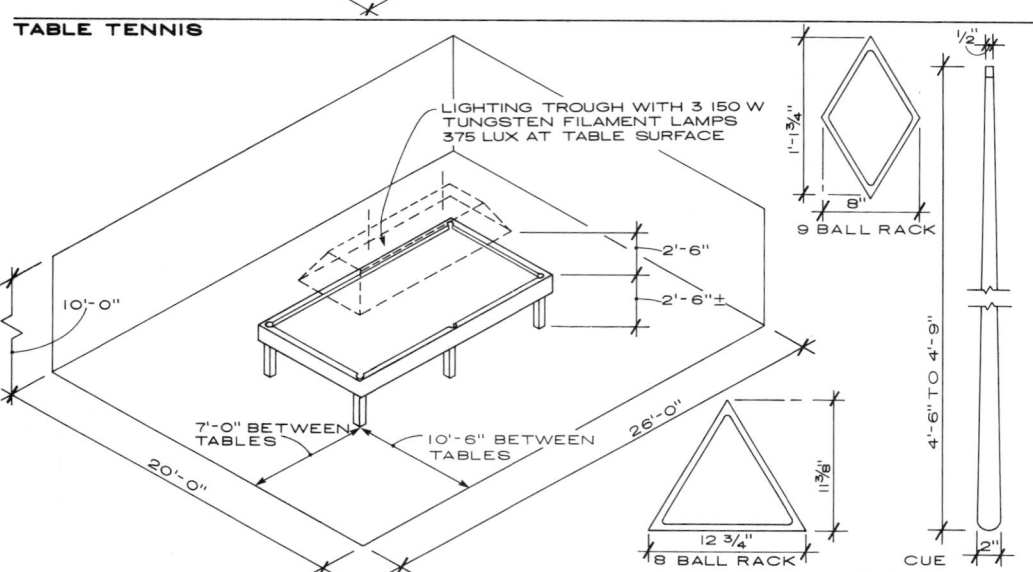

The flooring must be level permanently and be able to withstand point loads. Traditionally designed billiard tables weigh about 1.5 tons spread over eight legs. Lighting must not produce harsh shadows, but some modeling of the balls is desirable. Direct or reflected glare should be avoided, and true color rendering is important in snooker. An overall bright light is needed for each table; natural lighting is not essential. Lighting at the table surface should be approximately 375 lumens, which can be achieved by three 150-watt tungsten filament lamps suspended in a lighting trough. Fluorescent lamps are unacceptable. Some sound insulation is required to prevent distractions from noise outside the playing area.

| TYPE OF TABLE | PLAYING SURFACE | | TABLE SIZE | |
|---|---|---|---|---|
| | W. | L. | W. | L. |
| ENGLISH (SNOOKER) | 5'-9'' | 11'-6'' | 5'-9'' | 12'-9'' |
| STANDARD POOL OR BILL. | 5'-0'' | 10'-0'' | 5'-9'' | 10'-9'' |
| STANDARD POOL OR BILL. | 4'-6'' | 9'-0'' | 5'-3'' | 9'-9'' |
| STANDARD POOL OR BILL. | 4'-0'' | 8'-0'' | 4'-9'' | 8'-9'' |
| JUNIOR POOL | 3'-6'' | 7'-0'' | 4'-3'' | 7'-9'' |
| JUNIOR POOL | 3'-0'' | 6'-0'' | 3'-9'' | 6'-9'' |
| TABLE HEIGHT 2'-6'' ± | | | | |

**BILLIARDS / POCKET BILLIARDS / SNOOKER**

A dart board in a hanging box needs no additional storage. Lighting can be artificial, natural, or both. An adjustable spotlight is advisable. For safety reasons, the playing area should be placed away from doorways and traffic ways. Walls around the board should be surfaced with a material that will not be defaced by the darts.

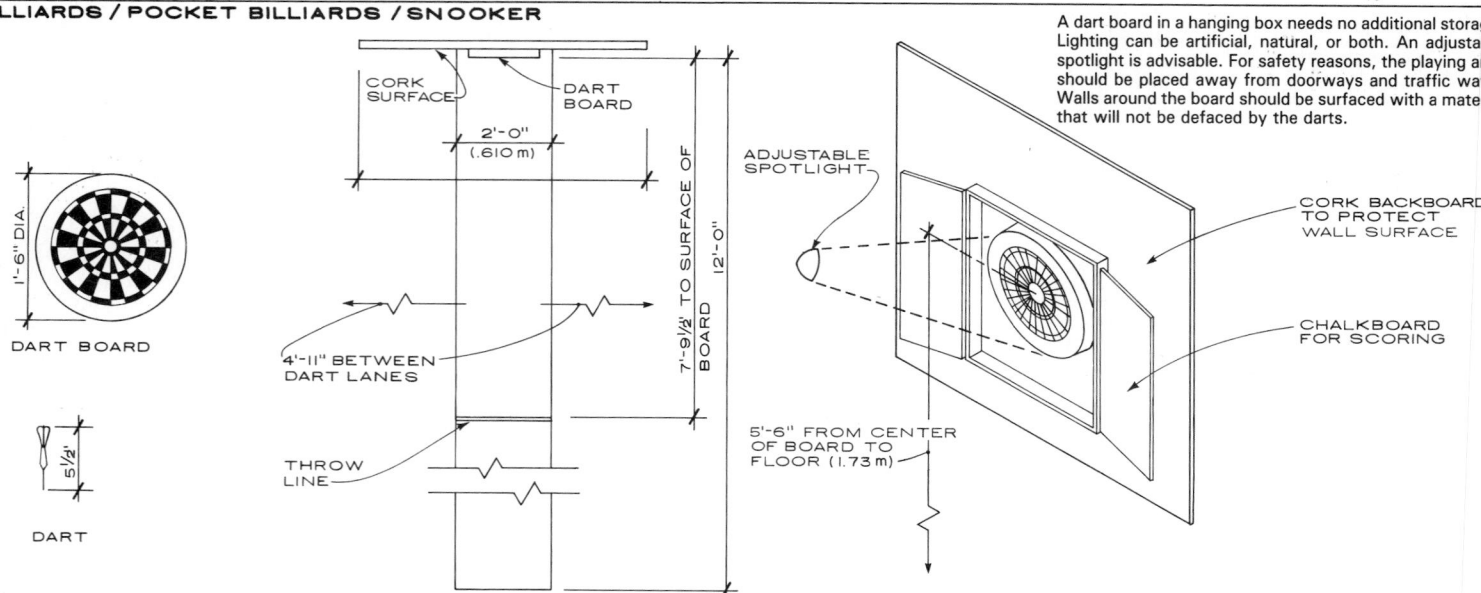

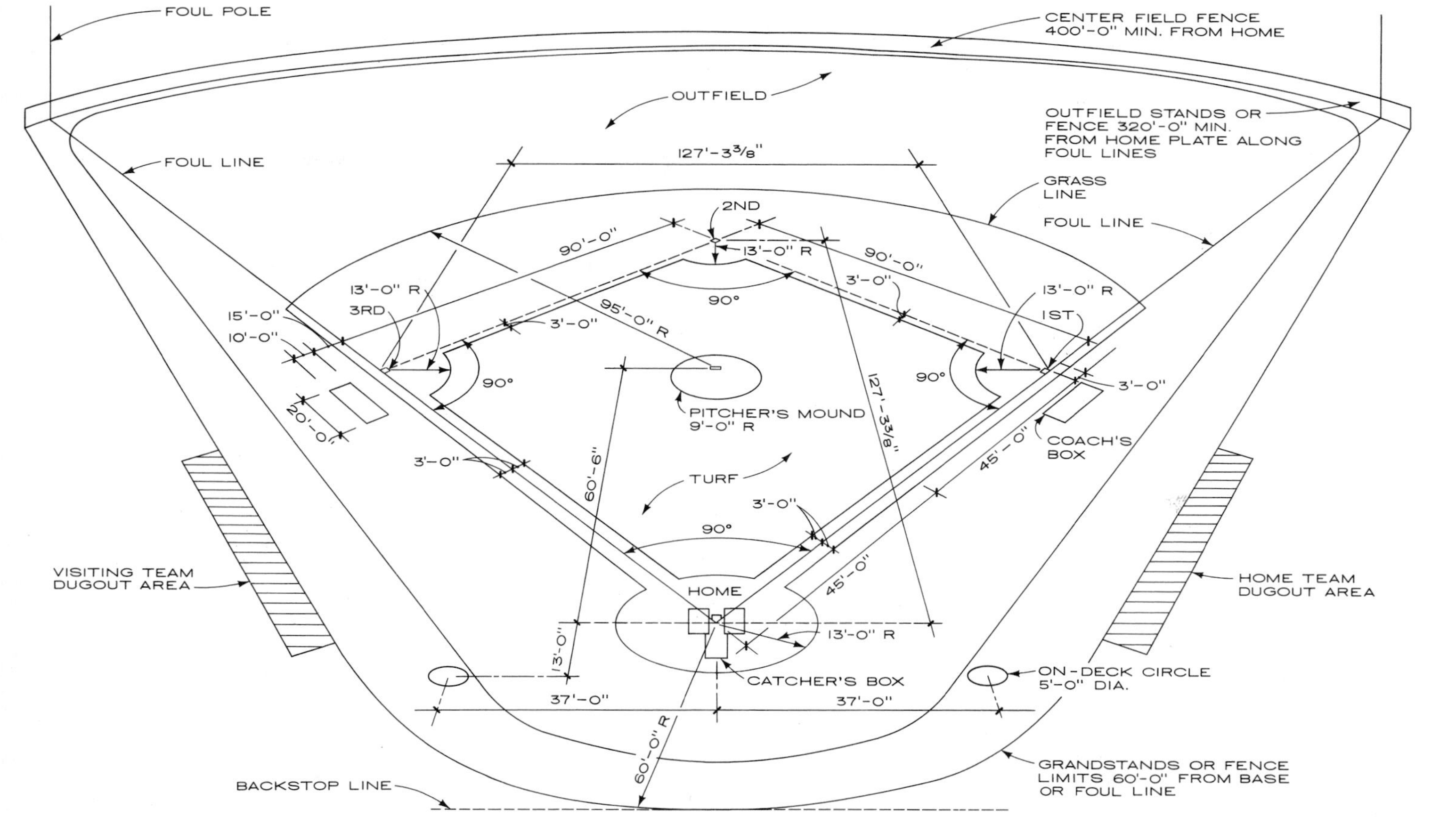

FOUL POLE

CENTER FIELD FENCE
400'-0" MIN. FROM HOME

OUTFIELD

FOUL LINE

OUTFIELD STANDS OR
FENCE 320'-0" MIN.
FROM HOME PLATE ALONG
FOUL LINES

127'-3³⁄₈"

GRASS
LINE

2ND

FOUL LINE

90'-0"

13'-0" R

90'-0"

13'-0" R

3'-0"

3RD

90°

1ST

15'-0"

3'-0"

95'-0" R

90°

10'-0"

3'-0"

PITCHER'S MOUND
9'-0" R

COACH'S
BOX

20'-0"

TURF

VISITING TEAM
DUGOUT AREA

3'-0"

90°

3'-0"

HOME TEAM
DUGOUT AREA

90°

HOME

3'-0"

13'-0" R

CATCHER'S BOX

ON-DECK CIRCLE
5'-0" DIA.

37'-0"

37'-0"

GRANDSTANDS OR FENCE
LIMITS 60'-0" FROM BASE
OR FOUL LINE

BACKSTOP LINE

60'-0" R

**NOTE**
This information is for preliminary planning and design only. For final layouts and design, investigate current rules and regulations of the athletic organization or other authority whose standards will govern.

**ORIENTATION**
No standard—consider time of day for games; months when played; location of field, surrounding buildings and stands. East-northeast recommended by NCAA (home plate to center field).

---

## BASEBALL FIELD

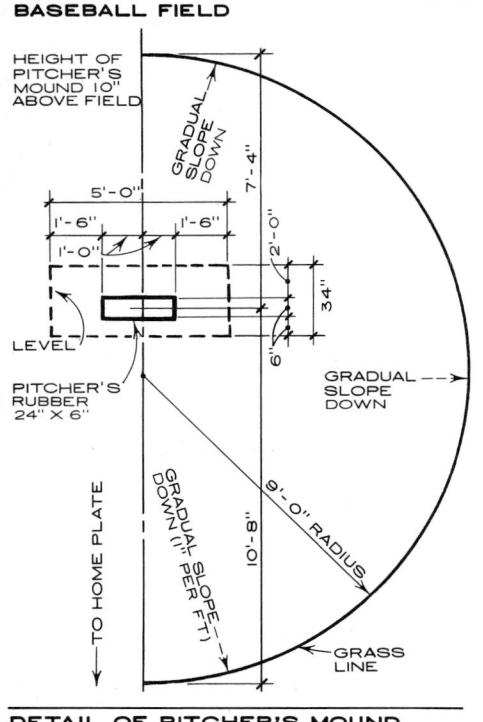

**DETAIL OF PITCHER'S MOUND**

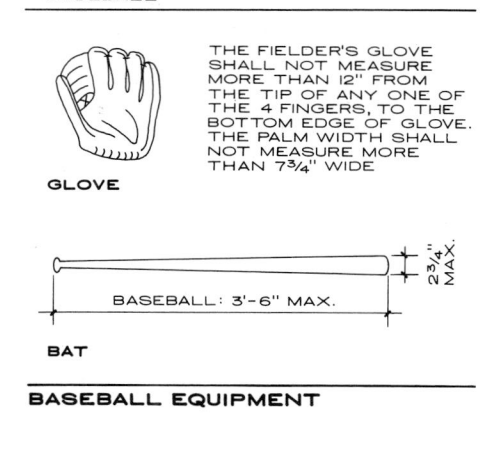

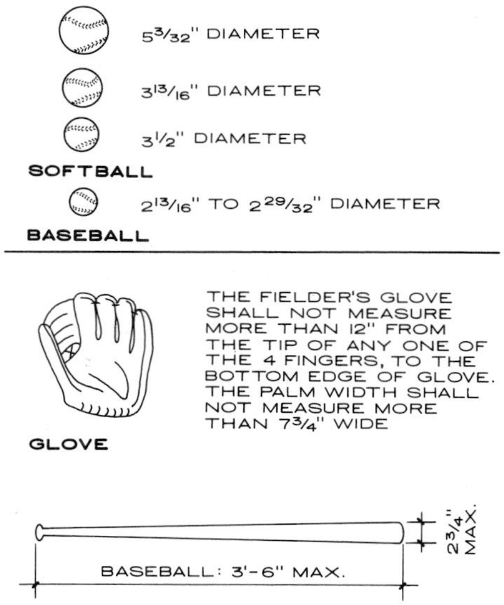

5³⁄₃₂" DIAMETER

3¹³⁄₁₆" DIAMETER

3¹⁄₂" DIAMETER

**SOFTBALL**

2¹³⁄₁₆" TO 2²⁹⁄₃₂" DIAMETER

**BASEBALL**

THE FIELDER'S GLOVE SHALL NOT MEASURE MORE THAN 12" FROM THE TIP OF ANY ONE OF THE 4 FINGERS, TO THE BOTTOM EDGE OF GLOVE. THE PALM WIDTH SHALL NOT MEASURE MORE THAN 7³⁄₄" WIDE

**GLOVE**

BASEBALL: 3'-6" MAX.

2³⁄₄" MAX.

**BAT**

**BASEBALL EQUIPMENT**

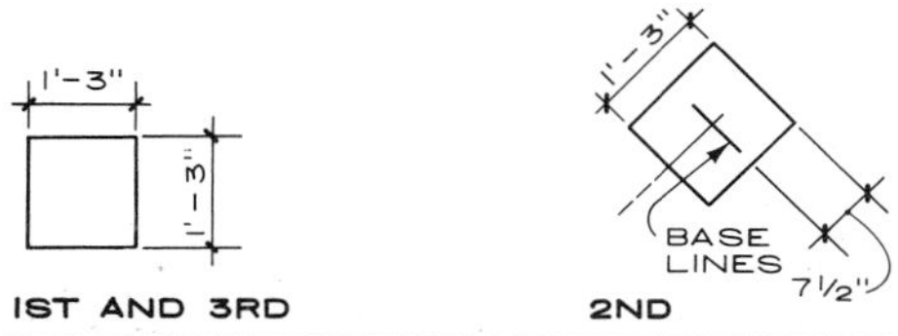

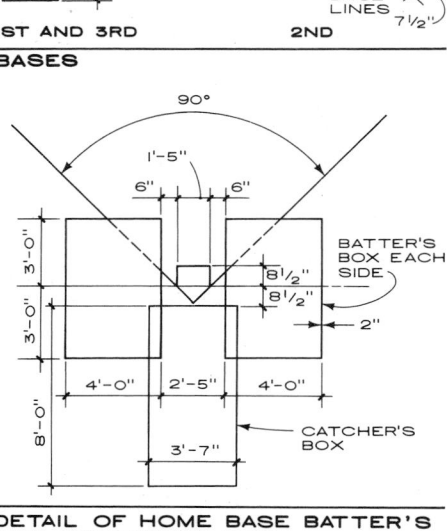

1'-3"

1'-3"

1ST AND 3RD

2ND

BASE LINES
7¹⁄₂"

**BASES**

90°

1'-5"

6"

6"

3'-0"

8¹⁄₂"

8¹⁄₂"

3'-0"

2"

BATTER'S BOX EACH SIDE

4'-0"

2'-5"

4'-0"

8'-0"

3'-7"

CATCHER'S BOX

**DETAIL OF HOME BASE BATTER'S AND CATCHER'S BOX**

Richard J. Vitullo; Washington Grove, Maryland

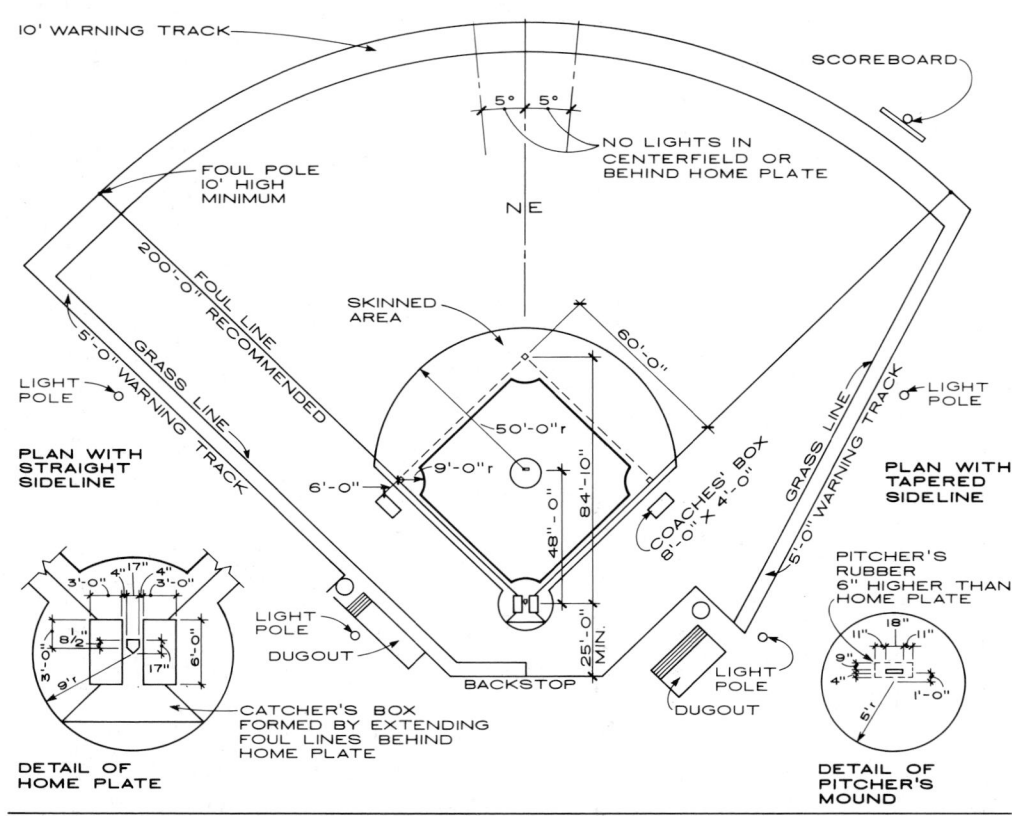

**PLAN OF LITTLE LEAGUE BASEBALL FIELD**

DETAIL OF HOME PLATE

DETAIL OF PITCHER'S MOUND

NOTES

Base lines should be level; if the diamond must pitch, the slope should not be more than 2 percent from third to first base, or vice versa. The minimum slope on turf areas outside the skinned area is 1 percent when there is good subsoil drainage, 2.5 percent when drainage is poor.

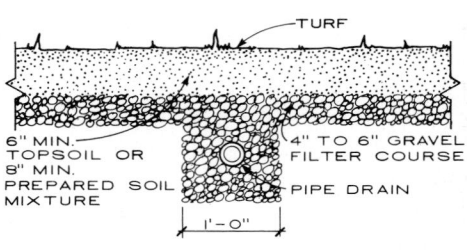

**SECTION OF TURF AND SUBSOIL DRAIN**

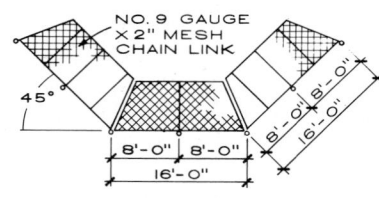

PLAN

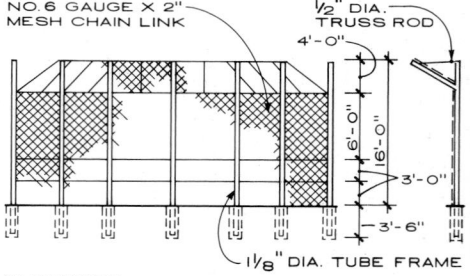

ELEVATION

**SOFTBALL BACKSTOP**

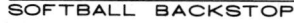

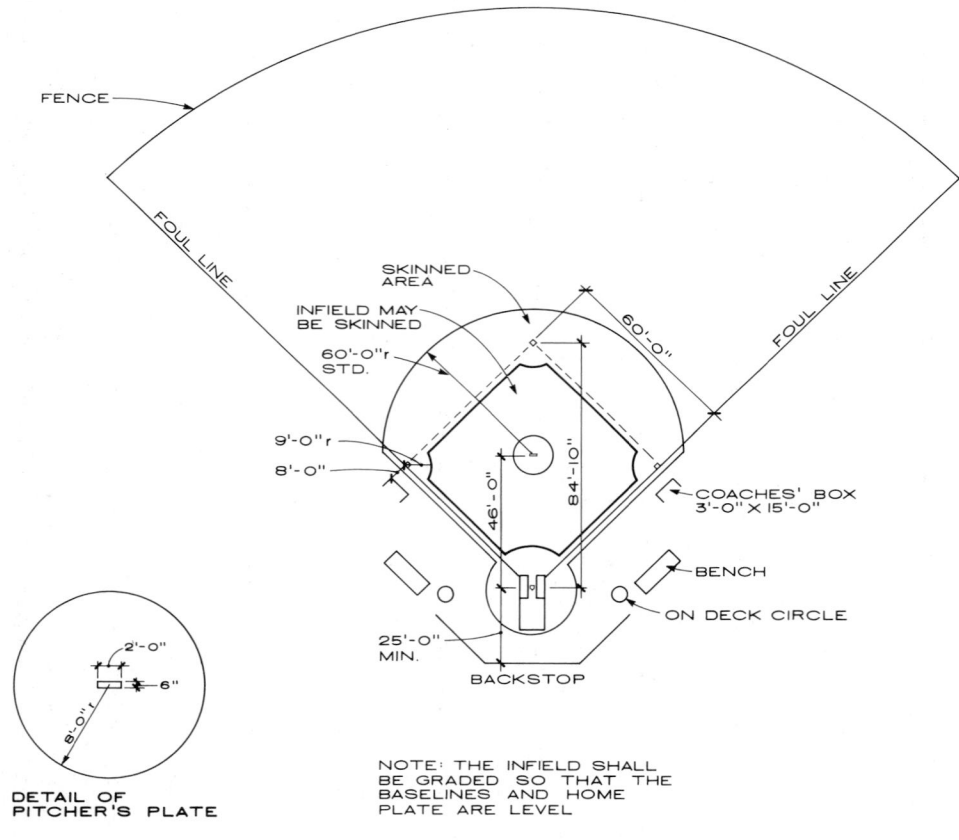

**PLAN OF SOFTBALL FIELD**

DETAIL OF PITCHER'S PLATE

NOTE: THE INFIELD SHALL BE GRADED SO THAT THE BASELINES AND HOME PLATE ARE LEVEL

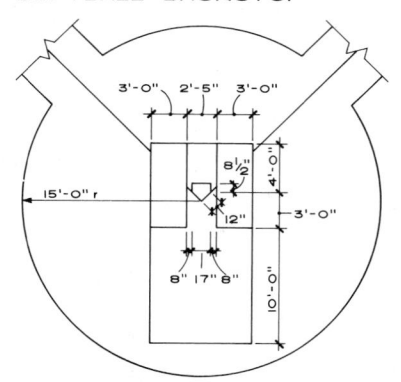

**DETAIL OF HOME PLATE AND CATCHER'S BOX**

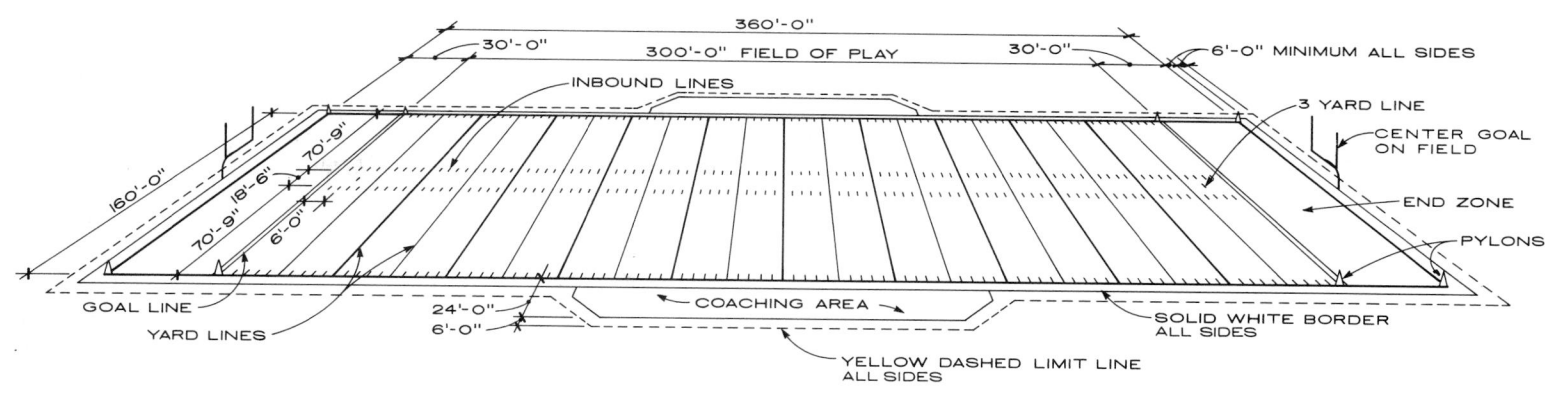

## FOOTBALL - NATIONAL FOOTBALL LEAGUE (NFL)

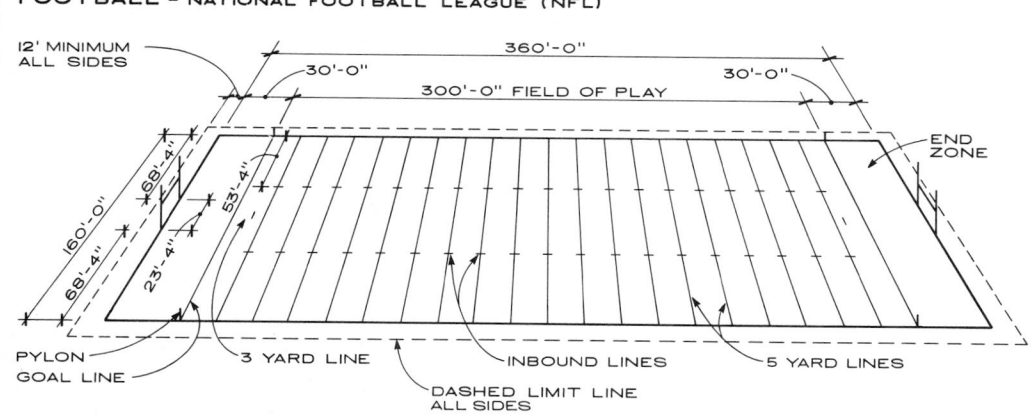

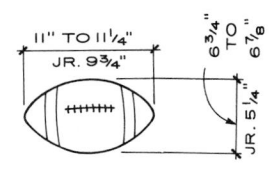

FOOTBALL

## FOOTBALL - NATIONAL COLLEGIATE ATHLETIC ASSOCIATION (NCAA)

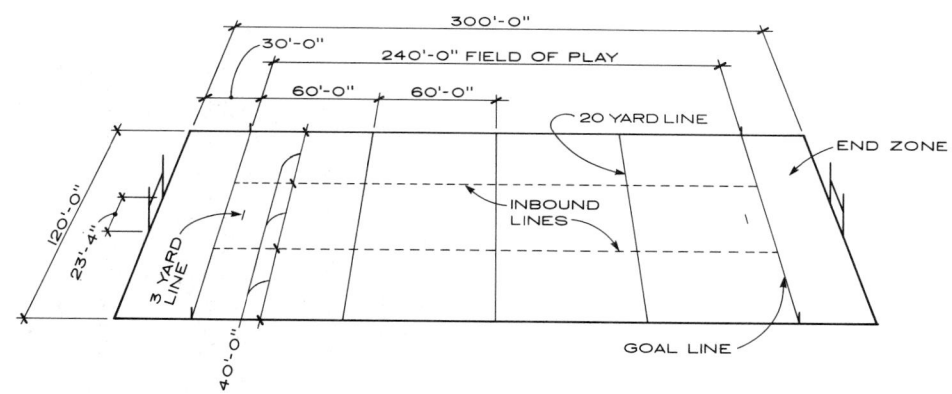

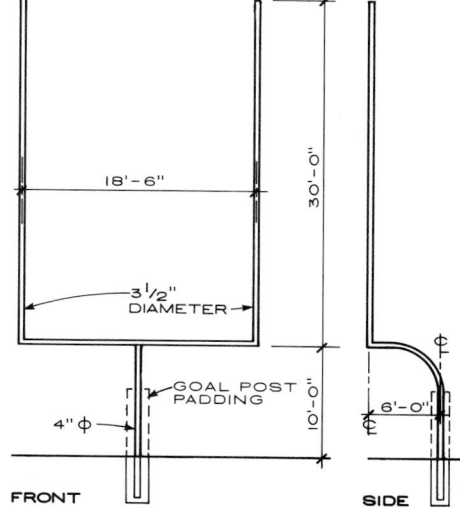

GOAL POSTS MUST BE PADDED IN A MANNER PRESCRIBED BY THE LEAGUE

GOAL POSTS (NFL)

## TOUCH AND FLAG FOOTBALL

**PROFESSIONAL FOOTBALL (NFL)**

The playing field is 360 ft. long by 160 ft. wide. Preferred orientation is with long axis northwest-southeast with no recommended slope. (For further information, contact the NFL.) All lines are 4 in. wide except the goal lines and yellow lines, which are 8 in. wide. All lines are marked with a nontoxic material.

The football, a prolate spheroid with a long axis of 11 in. to 11¼ in., weighs from 14 oz. to 15 oz.

**NCAA FOOTBALL**

The playing field is 300 ft. long by 160 ft. wide with an additional 12 ft. allowed for on all sides. Preferred orientation is with the long axis northwest-southeast. Grading of the field should be from the centerline. Subsoil drainage may be necessary. All field dimension lines are 4 in. wide,

and are marked with a white, nontoxic material. All measurements are from the wide edge of lines marking boundaries. End zone marking should not overlap goal lines, side lines, and end lines. Location of inbound lines is 53 ft. 4 in. for college football. Marks should be 4 in. wide by 2 ft. long.

**TOUCH AND FLAG FOOTBALL**

The playing field is 300 ft. long by 120 ft. wide with an additional 6 ft. allowed for on all sides. Preferred orientation is for the long axis to run northwest-southeast. The recommended slope of 1 percent for proper drainage should run away from each side of the center long axis. All measurements are from the inside edge of the lines, which are 4 in. wide and are marked with a white, nontoxic material.

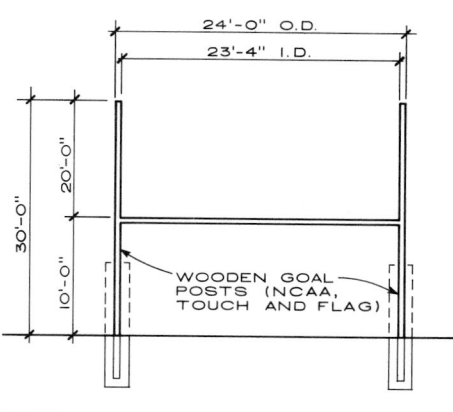

GOAL POSTS

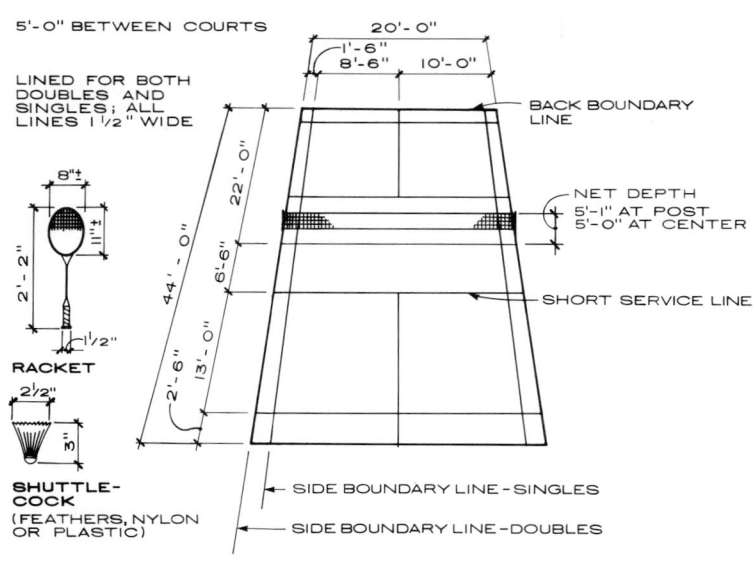

5'-0" BETWEEN COURTS

20'-0"

1'-6"

8'-6"   10'-0"

LINED FOR BOTH
DOUBLES AND
SINGLES; ALL
LINES 1 1/2" WIDE

8"±

11"±

2'-2"

1 1/2"

**RACKET**

2 1/2"

3"

**SHUTTLE-
COCK**
(FEATHERS, NYLON
OR PLASTIC)

44'-0"

22'-0"

6'-6"

13'-0"

2'-6"

BACK BOUNDARY
LINE

NET DEPTH
5'-1" AT POST
5'-0" AT CENTER

SHORT SERVICE LINE

SIDE BOUNDARY LINE – SINGLES

SIDE BOUNDARY LINE – DOUBLES

**BADMINTON**

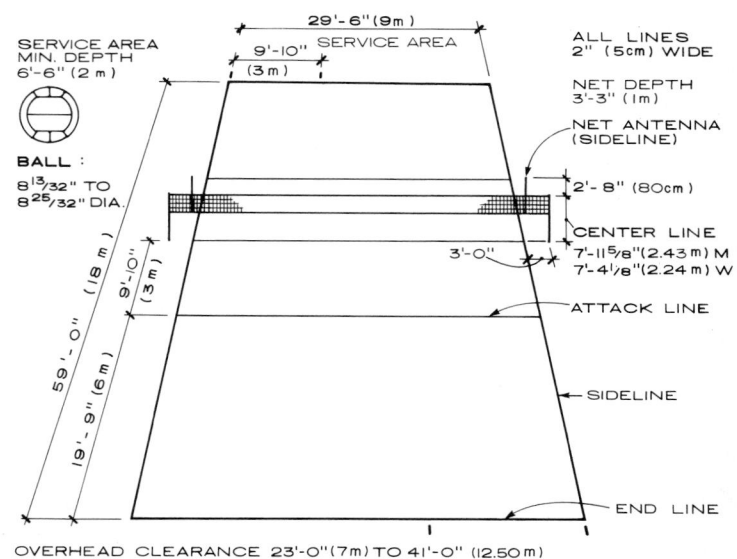

SERVICE AREA
MIN. DEPTH
6'-6" (2 m)

29'-6" (9m)

9'-10"
(3 m)   SERVICE AREA

ALL LINES
2" (5cm) WIDE

**BALL :**
8 13/32" TO
8 25/32" DIA.

59'-0" (18 m)

9'-0" (3m)

19'-9" (6m)

3'-0"

NET DEPTH
3'-3" (1m)

NET ANTENNA
(SIDELINE)

2'-8" (80cm)

CENTER LINE

7'-11 5/8" (2.43 m) M
7'-4 1/8" (2.24 m) W

ATTACK LINE

SIDELINE

END LINE

OVERHEAD CLEARANCE 23'-0" (7m) TO 41'-0" (12.50m)
SPACING BETWEEN COURTS: 6" TO 10'

**VOLLEYBALL**

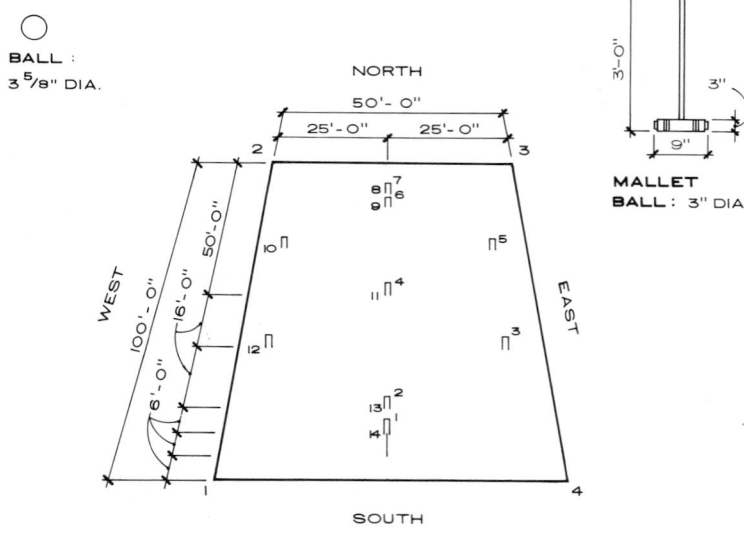

1'-5 1/2"

8 1/2"

9"

**RACKET**
**BALL :** PUNCTURED
TENNIS
BALL

20'-0"

10'-0"

25'-0"

50'-0"

22'-0"

3'-0"

ALL LINES
2" WIDE

NET HEIGHT
2'-7" AT POST
2'-6" AT CENTER

POST 1'-6" AWAY
FROM SIDELINE

SIDELINE

SERVICE LINE

BASELINE

SPACE BEHIND EACH BASELINE TO BACK FENCE : 15'-0" MIN.
SPACE FROM EACH SIDELINE TO SIDE FENCE : 10'-0" MIN.
FENCE SHALL BE 8'-0" HIGH UNLESS OTHERWISE NOTED

**PADDLE   TENNIS**

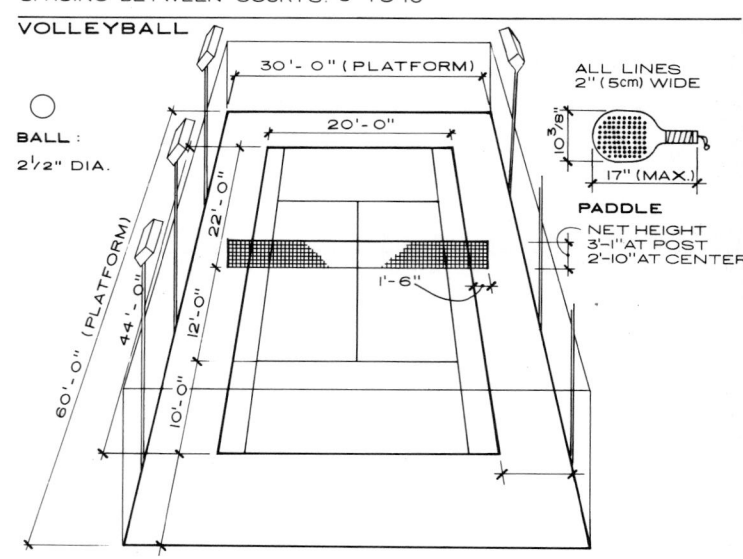

**BALL :**
2 1/2" DIA.

30'-0" (PLATFORM)

20'-0"

22'-0"

44'-0"

12'-0"

10'-0"

60'-0" (PLATFORM)

1'-6"

ALL LINES
2" (5cm) WIDE

10 3/8"

17" (MAX.)

**PADDLE**

NET HEIGHT
3'-1" AT POST
2'-10" AT CENTER

**PLATFORM   TENNIS**

**BALL :**
3 5/8" DIA.

NORTH

50'-0"

25'-0"   25'-0"

2

3

8  7
9  6

10   5

4

12   3

13   2
1

WEST

50'-0"

50'-0"

6'-0"

6'-0"

6'-0"

100'-0"

EAST

1

4

SOUTH

3'-0"

3"

9"

**MALLET**
**BALL :** 3" DIA.

**CROQUET**

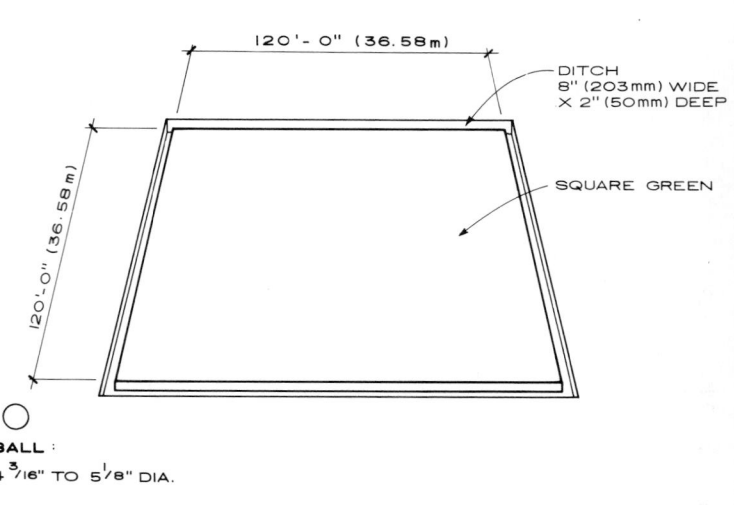

120'-0" (36.58m)

120'-0" (36.58 m)

DITCH
8" (203mm) WIDE
X 2" (50mm) DEEP

SQUARE GREEN

**BALL :**
4 3/16" TO 5 1/8" DIA.

**LAWN   BOWLING**

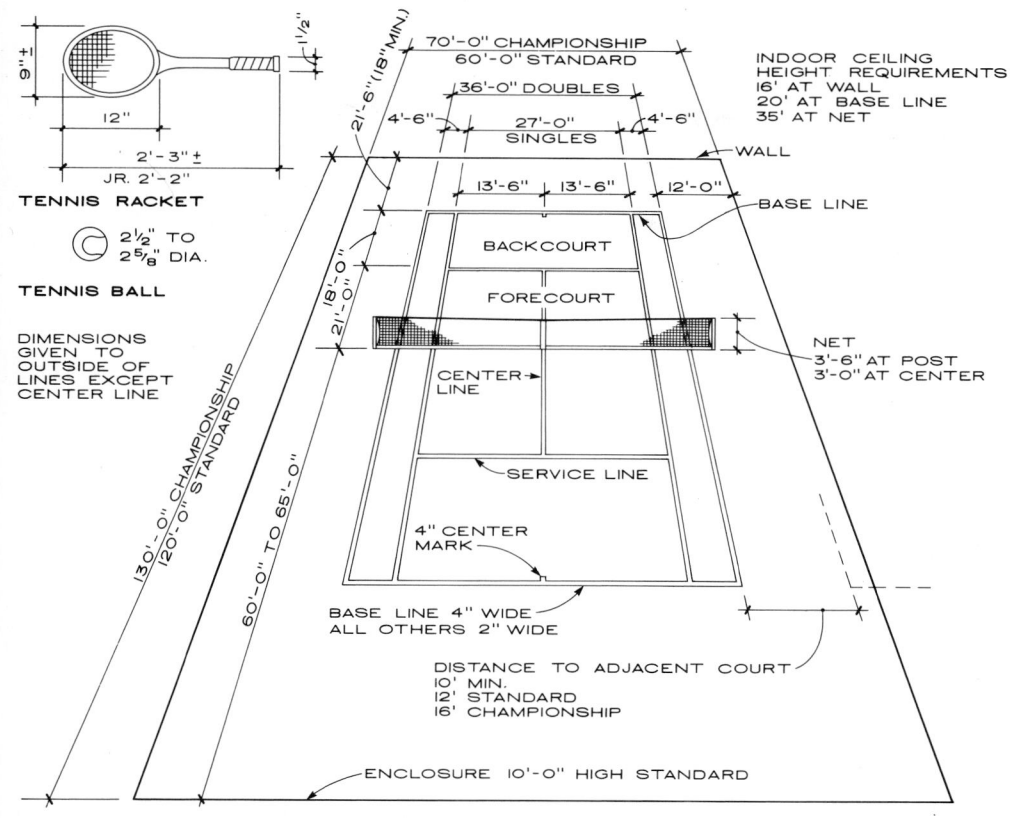

TENNIS RACKET

TENNIS BALL

DIMENSIONS GIVEN TO OUTSIDE OF LINES EXCEPT CENTER LINE

TENNIS COURT

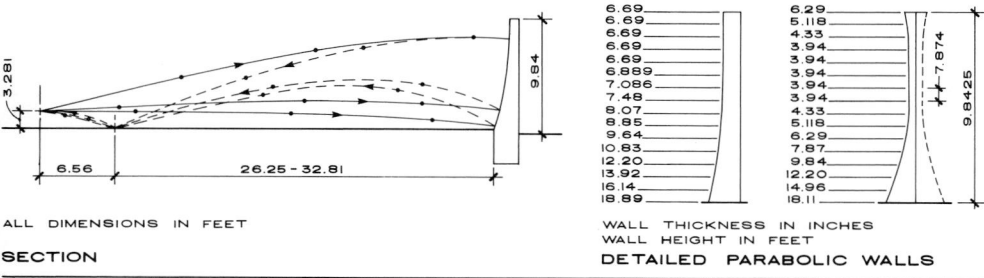

ALL DIMENSIONS IN FEET

SECTION

PRACTICE COURT

WALL THICKNESS IN INCHES
WALL HEIGHT IN FEET

DETAILED PARABOLIC WALLS

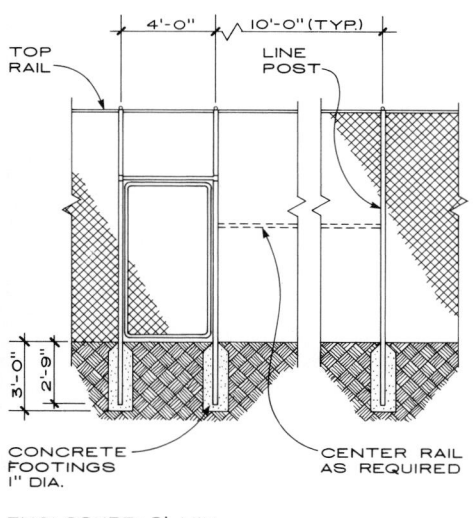

TOP RAIL

LINE POST

CONCRETE FOOTINGS 1" DIA.

CENTER RAIL AS REQUIRED

ENCLOSURE: 8' MIN.
HEIGHTS 10' STANDARD
12' MAX.

ELEVATION OF ENCLOSURE

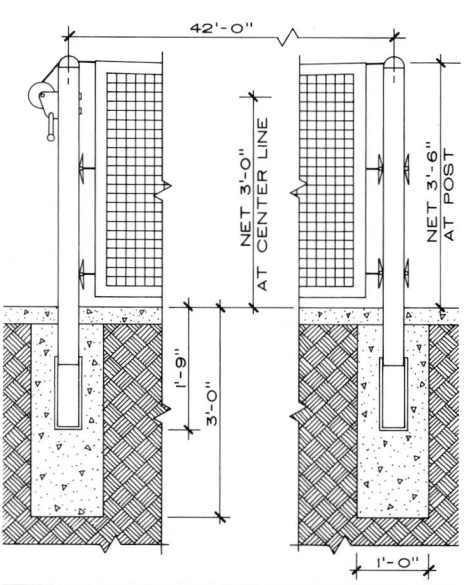

TENNIS POSTS

## ORIENTATION

For the northern states the north-south orientation is recommended. North-northwest by south-southeast at approximately 22° (true north) is recommended for outdoor courts south of the 41st parallel. Particular site characteristics, length of tennis season, and latitude should be taken into consideration when deciding on the most desirable court orientation angle.

## NOTES

1. SURFACE DRAINAGE: Pitch 1 in. per 10 ft for porous and nonporous courts. Each court should be in one plane and pitch side to side; <u>never</u> up or down to middle court.
2. SUBSOIL DRAINAGE: Need for drainage systems depends on soil conditions.

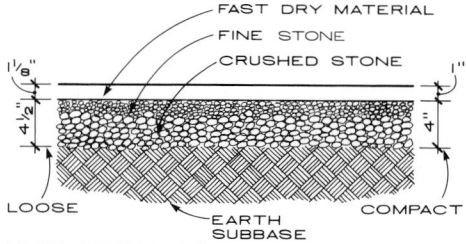

FAST DRY MATERIAL
FINE STONE
CRUSHED STONE
LOOSE
EARTH SUBBASE
COMPACT

**FAST-DRYING SURFACE**

Fast-drying courts are successive layers of crushed green stone or burnt brick and finely ground rock particles mixed with a chemical binder. This surface provides a uniform bounce and allows sliding. A sprinkler system, frequent maintenance, and annual resurfacing are recommended.

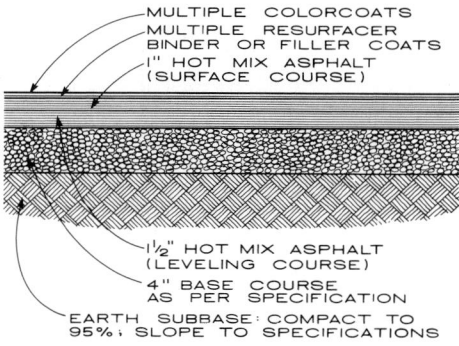

MULTIPLE COLORCOATS
MULTIPLE RESURFACER
BINDER OR FILLER COATS
1" HOT MIX ASPHALT (SURFACE COURSE)
1½" HOT MIX ASPHALT (LEVELING COURSE)
4" BASE COURSE AS PER SPECIFICATION
EARTH SUBBASE: COMPACT TO 95%; SLOPE TO SPECIFICATIONS

**NON-POROUS NON-CUSHIONED SURFACE**

Hot mix asphalt is a mixture of asphalt and aggregate laid in place and compacted before cooling. This surface is laid on a 4 in. base of stone, gravel or perforated macadam, depending on soil conditions.

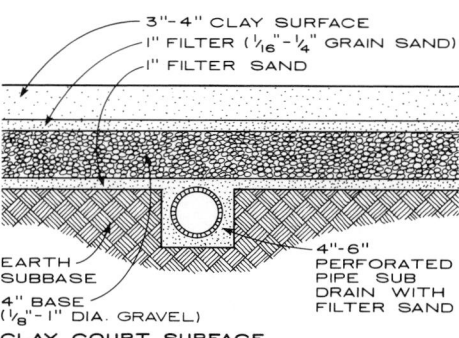

3"-4" CLAY SURFACE
1" FILTER (1/16"-1/4" GRAIN SAND)
1" FILTER SAND
EARTH SUBBASE
4" BASE (1/8"-1" DIA. GRAVEL)
4"-6" PERFORATED PIPE SUB DRAIN WITH FILTER SAND

**CLAY COURT SURFACE**

Clay courts are constructed on a system of open drain tiles overlaid by a bed of gravel sandwiched between two filter layers of sand or fine gravel, and topped by a thick (3 in.- 4 in.) layer of clay. A clay surface also allows sliding and a uniform bounce.

**TENNIS COURT SURFACES**

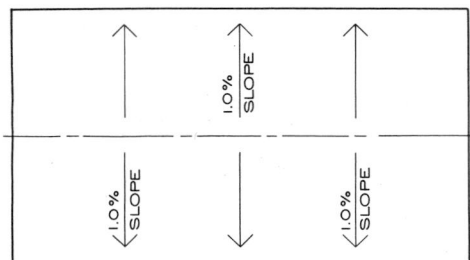

**PREFERRED GRADING**

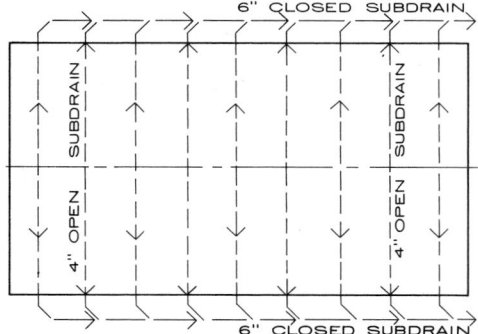

6" CLOSED SUBDRAIN

4" OPEN SUBDRAIN

4" OPEN SUBDRAIN

6" CLOSED SUBDRAIN

**SUBSOIL DRAINAGE**

**RECTANGULAR SPORTS FIELDS**

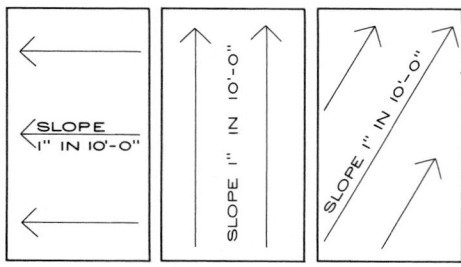

SLOPE 1" IN 10'-0"

SLOPE 1" IN 10'-0"

SLOPE 1" IN 10'-0"

**DRAINAGE DIAGRAMS**

**SPORTS COURTS**

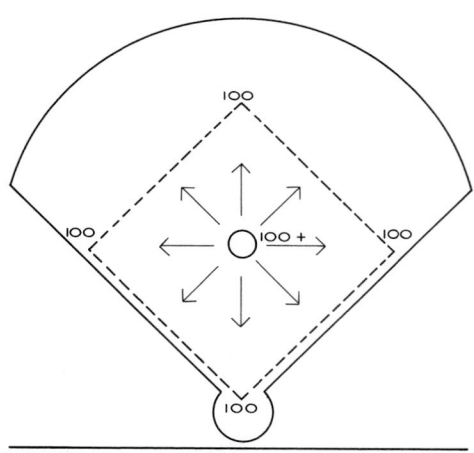

**BASEBALL, SOFTBALL DIAMONDS**

**NOTE**

It is preferable that the base lines be level. If the diamond must pitch, the average slope shall be 2.0% from first base to third base or vice versa.

The minimum slope for drainage on turf areas outside the skinned area is 1.0% when adequate subsoil drainage is provided. The maximum is 2.5%.

Sheryl Maletic; Tomblinson Harburn Associates; Flint, Michigan
J. Paul Raeder; Beckett Raeder Rankin, Inc.; Ann Arbor, Michigan
Lawrence Cook & Associates; Falls Church, Virginia

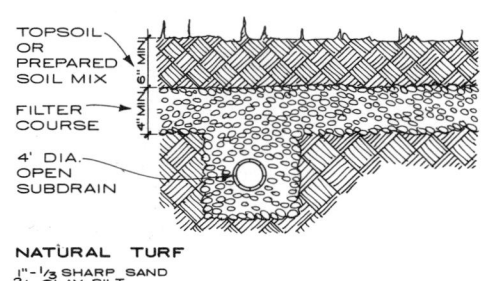

TOPSOIL OR PREPARED SOIL MIX — 4" MIN. 6" MIN.

FILTER COURSE

4' DIA. OPEN SUBDRAIN

**NATURAL TURF**

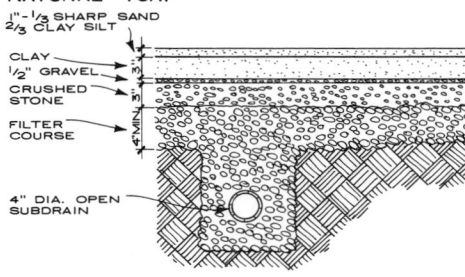

1"-1½ SHARP SAND 2/3 CLAY SILT

CLAY
½" GRAVEL
CRUSHED STONE
FILTER COURSE

4" DIA. OPEN SUBDRAIN

**SAND CLAY**

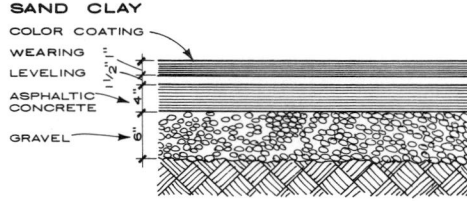

COLOR COATING
WEARING
LEVELING
ASPHALTIC CONCRETE
GRAVEL

**BITUMINOUS CONCRETE**

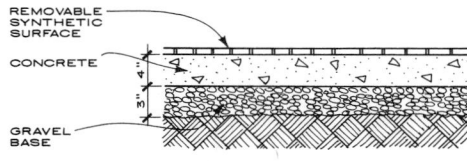

REMOVABLE SYNTHETIC SURFACE
CONCRETE
GRAVEL BASE

**SYNTHETIC SURFACE**

**PLAYING SURFACES**

## TYPICAL GRADING AND DRAINAGE DETAILS

### COURT SURFACES

Paved playing surfaces should be in one plane and pitched from side to side, end to end, or corner to corner diagonally, instead of in two planes pitched to or from the net. Minimum slope should be 1 in. in 10 ft. Subgrade should slope in the same direction as the surface. Perimeter drains may be provided for paved areas. Underdrains are not recommended beneath paved areas.

### PLAYING FIELDS

Preferred grading for rectangular field is a longitudinal crown with 1% slope from center to each side.

Grading may be from side to side or corner to corner diagonally if conditions do not permit the preferred grading.

Subsoil drainage is to slope in the same direction as the surface. Subdrains and filter course are to be used only when subsoil conditions require. Where subsoil drainage is necessary, the spacing of subdrains is dependent on local soil conditions and rainfall.

Subdrains are to have a minimum gradient of 0.15%.

Baseball and softball fields should be graded so that the bases are level.

### LINE PAINTING

All line markings should be acrylic water base paint only. Oil base or traffic paints crack, craze, or peel. Spray painting usually is used. High quality courts should be hand painted. Accuracy of track layouts should be verified by registered land surveyor.

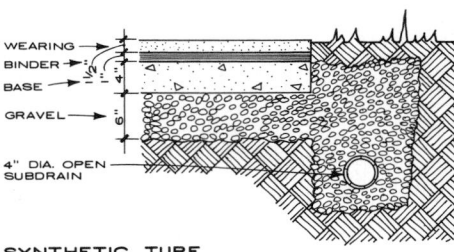

WEARING
BINDER
BASE
GRAVEL

4" DIA. OPEN SUBDRAIN

**SYNTHETIC TURF**

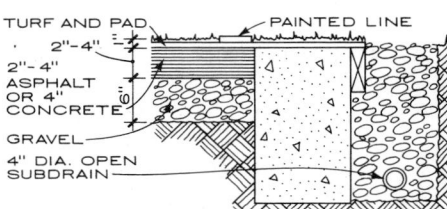

TURF AND PAD
PAINTED LINE
2"-4"
2"-4" ASPHALT OR 4" CONCRETE
GRAVEL
4" DIA. OPEN SUBDRAIN

**FABRIC TYPE ARTIFICIAL TURF WITH ASPHALT OR CONCRETE BASE**

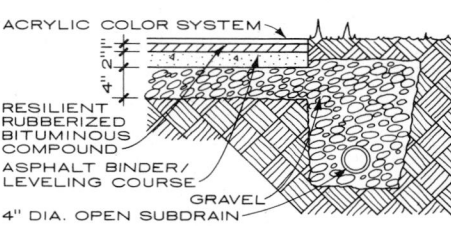

ACRYLIC COLOR SYSTEM
RESILIENT RUBBERIZED BITUMINOUS COMPOUND
ASPHALT BINDER/ LEVELING COURSE
GRAVEL
4" DIA. OPEN SUBDRAIN

**RUBBERIZED ASPHALT SURFACE**

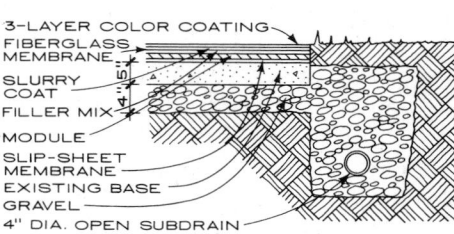

3-LAYER COLOR COATING
FIBERGLASS MEMBRANE
SLURRY COAT
FILLER MIX
MODULE
SLIP-SHEET MEMBRANE
EXISTING BASE
GRAVEL
4" DIA. OPEN SUBDRAIN

**RESURFACING ASPHALT COLOR SYSTEM**

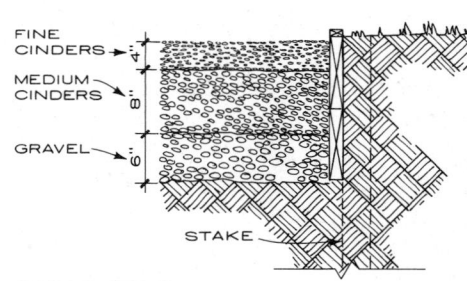

FINE CINDERS
MEDIUM CINDERS
GRAVEL
STAKE

**CINDER TRACK**

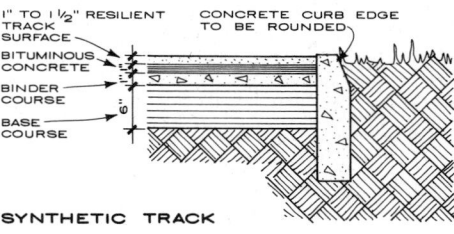

1" TO 1½" RESILIENT TRACK SURFACE
CONCRETE CURB EDGE TO BE ROUNDED
BITUMINOUS CONCRETE
BINDER COURSE
BASE COURSE

**SYNTHETIC TRACK**

**EDGE CONDITIONS**

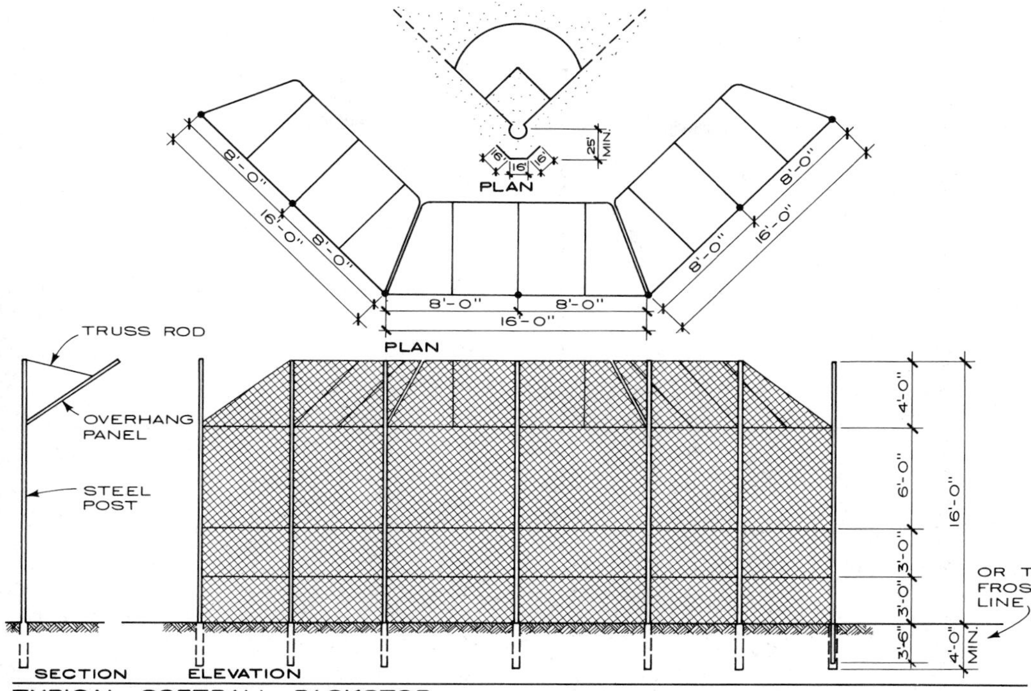

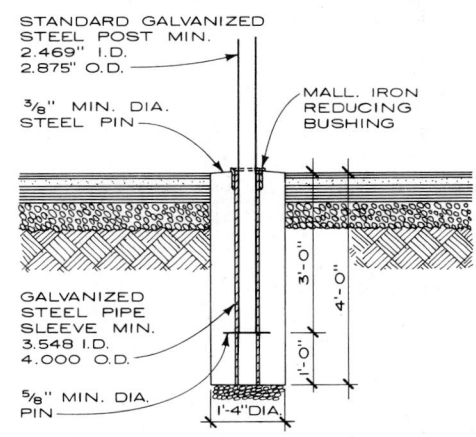

PLAN
25' MIN.
8'-0"
16'-0"
TRUSS ROD
OVERHANG PANEL
STEEL POST
4'-0"
6'-0"
3'-0"
3'-6"
OR TO FROST LINE
4'-0" MIN.
SECTION
ELEVATION

TYPICAL SOFTBALL BACKSTOP

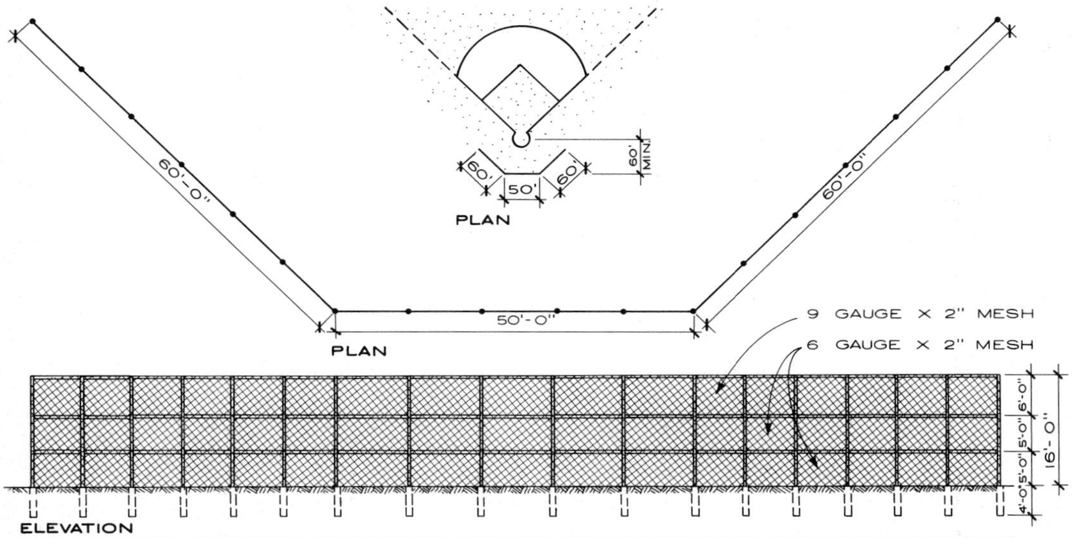

PLAN
60' MIN.
60'-0"
50'-0"
9 GAUGE × 2" MESH
6 GAUGE × 2" MESH
6'-0"
5'-0"
16'-0"
4'-0"
ELEVATION

REGULATION BASEBALL BACKSTOP

4'-0" OVERHANG
6"
1'-6" I.D.
10'-0"
GALVANIZED STEEL PIPE BENT POST 3 ½" MIN. O.D.
TOP OF CONCRETE TO SLOPE AWAY FROM POST
SURFACES VARY
3'-0"
4'-0" OVERHANG 6" 1'-6" I.D.
1¹⁄₁₆" O.D.
2" O.D.
⁵⁄₁₆" × 4" × 6" BOLT PLATE
5 16" × 3" STEEL CLAMP
STANDARD GALVANIZED STEEL PIPE POST 4 ½" O.D. MIN.
TOP OF CONCRETE TO SLOPE AWAY FROM POST
SURFACES VARY
4'-0" MIN.
1'-0"
2'-0" DIA.

BASKETBALL STANDARDS

## BASKETBALL STANDARDS

Backboard support shall have minimum overhang of 4 ft for NCAA with a minimum post diameter of 3½ in. O.D.

Regulation AAU, 5 ft 5 in. overhang, and optional NCAA 4 ft to 6 ft overhang also require a minimum post diameter of 4½ in. O.D.

Footing is to be concrete with a minimum 2 ft diameter and 4 ft depth.

Method of bracing and backboard support varies with manufacturer.

## BACKSTOP SIZE AND DIMENSION

Height and width of baseball backstops are to be determined by sports authorities and local requirements.

## PIPE SIZES

Posts for backstop heights up to 16 ft: use 3 in. O.D.

Posts for backstop heights 18 ft to 24 ft: use 4 in. O.D.

Top, intermediate, and bottom rails: 1⅝ in. O.D.

## WIRE MESH FABRIC

Fabric shall be chain link with galvanized coating or aluminized. (Optional polyvinyl chloride coated steel.)

J. Paul Raeder; Beckett Raeder Rankin, Inc.; Ann Arbor, Michigan
Lawrence Cook & Associates; Falls Church, Virginia

STANDARD GALVANIZED STEEL POST MIN. 2.469" I.D. 2.875" O.D.
⅜" MIN. DIA. STEEL PIN
MALL. IRON REDUCING BUSHING
3'-0"
4'-0"
1'-0"
GALVANIZED STEEL PIPE SLEEVE MIN. 3.548 I.D. 4.000 O.D.
⅝" MIN. DIA. PIN
1'-4" DIA.

REMOVABLE POST

All ferrous metal parts are to be hot dip galvanized after fabrication.

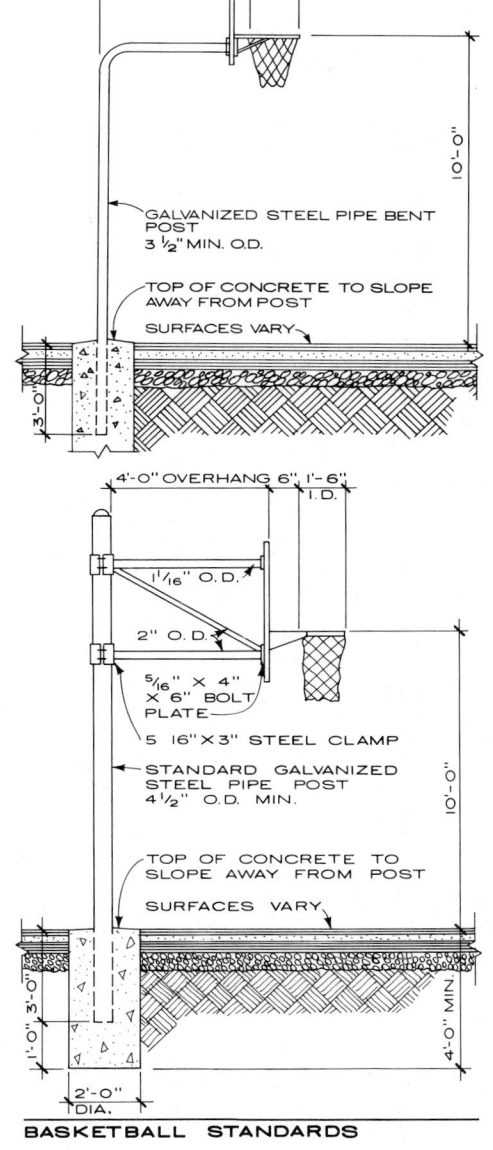

4"
VOLLEYBALL 8'-0¼"
BADMINTON 5'-1"
VOLLEYBALL 3'-0"
BADMINTON 2'-6"
VOLLEYBALL 8'-0"
BADMINTON 5'-0"
½" EYE BOLT
ROPE CLEAT
STANDARD GALVANIZED STEEL POST 3.5" O.D.
SURFACES VARY
CONCRETE
4'-0" MIN.
2"
1'-4" DIA.

VOLLEYBALL AND BADMINTON NET AND POST

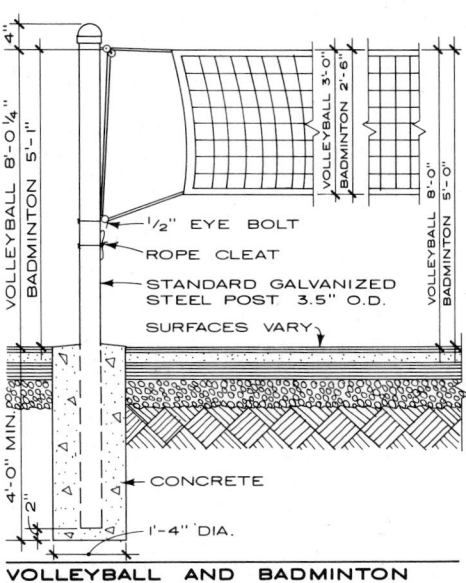

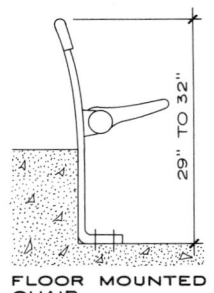

**RISER MOUNTED CHAIR**

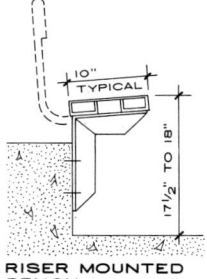

**FLOOR MOUNTED CHAIR**

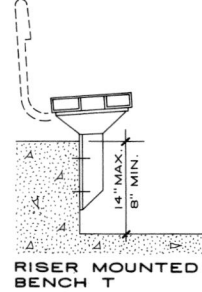

**RISER MOUNTED BENCH L**

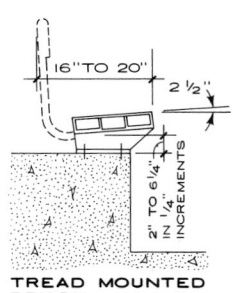

**RISER MOUNTED BENCH T**

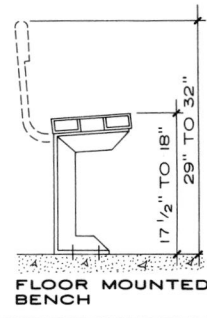

**TREAD MOUNTED BENCH**

**FLOOR MOUNTED BENCH**

## STANDARD SEATS AND SEAT SUPPORTS

### SEATING CAPACITY

Allow 18 in. of bleacher length per person per row. Normal aisle width of 36 in. reduces seating capacity by two seats per row x number of rows x number of aisles. See table below.

### SAFETY AREAS

1. BASEBALL FIELDS: Minimum 60 ft from seating to foul line or baseline at each side of home plate.
2. SOFTBALL FIELDS: Minimum 25 ft from seating to foul line or baseline at each side of home plate.
3. BASKETBALL COURTS: Minimum 6 ft from seating to court sides, 8 in. minimum to court ends.
4. SWIMMING POOLS: Minimum 5 ft from seating to pool decks. Spectator area must be separate from pool area to avoid mixing dry and wet traffic.

### STADIUM SEATING

Concrete risers and treads with seating attached. See typical seats and seat supports above.

### FIXED GRANDSTAND

8 in. rise with 24 in. row spacing typical. Available options include front, end, and back rails, crosswalks, ramps, stairs, aisles, vomitories, closed risers, double foot plates, folding seat backs, and waterproof covers of metal or fiberglass for resurfacing existing wooden bleachers.

### PORTABLE BLEACHERS

3, 4, or 5 row sections typical. Transportable options include wheels and trailer attachments. Bleachers of up to 25 rows may be assembled of portable sections.

### TELESCOPIC BLEACHERS

1. LOWRISE: $9^5/8$ in. normal rise for most uses. 22 in. minimum row spacing gives maximum seating capacity. 24 in. spacing gives greater leg room. 30 or 32 in. spacing provides extra passage and leg room space and space for optional folding back rests.
2. HIGHRISE: Models with $11^5/8$ or 16 in. risers are suggested for pools, balconies, hockey rinks, or similarly difficult viewing situations where seating must be banked more steeply than is normal.

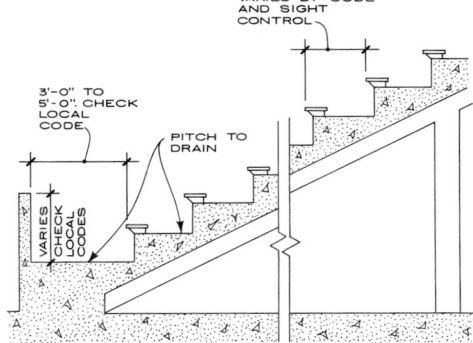

**STADIUM SEATING**

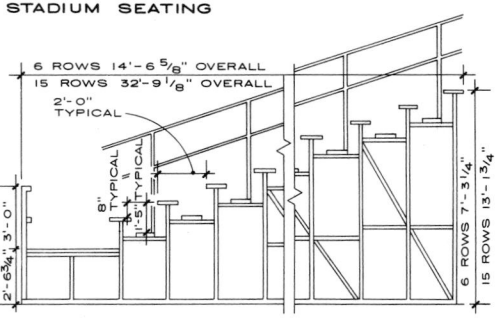

**FIXED GRANDSTAND (ELEVATED)**

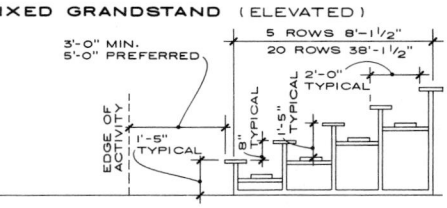

**PORTABLE BLEACHERS**

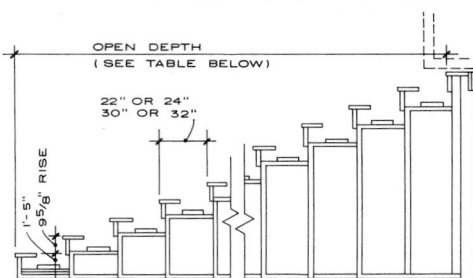

**TELESCOPIC BLEACHERS (HIGHRISE)**

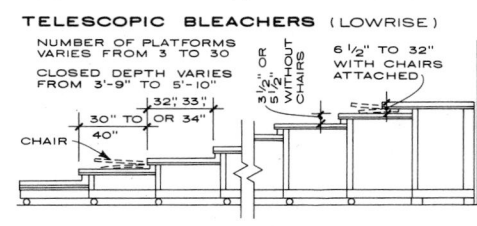

**TELESCOPIC BLEACHERS (LOWRISE)**

**TELESCOPIC PLATFORM**

## SEATING CAPACITY

| ROW | 8 | 12 | 16 | 20 | 24 | 28 | 32 | 36 | 40 |
|---|---|---|---|---|---|---|---|---|---|
| 3 | 16 | 24 | 32 | 40 | 48 | 56 | 64 | 72 | 80 |
| 4 | 21 | 32 | 42 | 53 | 64 | 74 | 85 | 96 | 106 |
| 5 | 26 | 40 | 53 | 66 | 80 | 93 | 106 | 120 | 133 |
| 6 | 32 | 48 | 64 | 80 | 96 | 112 | 128 | 144 | 160 |
| 7 | 37 | 56 | 74 | 93 | 112 | 130 | 149 | 168 | 186 |
| 8 | 42 | 64 | 85 | 106 | 128 | 149 | 170 | 192 | 213 |
| 9 | 48 | 72 | 96 | 120 | 144 | 168 | 192 | 216 | 240 |
| 10 | 53 | 80 | 106 | 133 | 160 | 186 | 213 | 240 | 266 |
| 12 | 64 | 96 | 128 | 160 | 192 | 224 | 256 | 288 | 320 |
| 14 | 74 | 112 | 149 | 186 | 224 | 261 | 298 | 336 | 373 |
| 16 | 85 | 128 | 170 | 213 | 256 | 298 | 341 | 384 | 426 |
| 18 | 96 | 144 | 192 | 240 | 288 | 336 | 384 | 432 | 480 |
| 20 | 106 | 160 | 213 | 266 | 320 | 373 | 426 | 480 | 533 |

LENGTH (FT)

NOTE: Consult manufacturers for additional information.

## GRANDSTANDS AND BLEACHERS DIMENSIONS

| ROW | OPEN DEPTH 22" | 24" | 30" | 32" | $9^5/8$" RISE CLOSED DEPTH 22" OR 24" | 30" OR 32" | $11^5/8$" AND 16" RISE CLOSED DEPTH 22" OR 24" | 30" OR 32" |
|---|---|---|---|---|---|---|---|---|
| 3 | 4'-11$1/2$" | 5'-1$1/2$" | 6'-3$1/2$" | 6'-5$1/2$" | 3'-1$13/16$" | 3'-9$13/16$" | 3'-1$13/16$" | 3'-9$13/16$" |
| 4 | 6'-9$1/2$" | 7'-1$1/2$" | 8'-9$1/2$" | 9'-1$1/2$" | 3'-2$1/8$" | 3'-10$1/8$" | 3'-2$1/8$" | 3'-10$1/8$" |
| 5 | 8'-7$1/2$" | 9'-1$1/2$" | 11'-3$1/2$" | 11'-9$1/2$" | 3'-2$7/16$" | 3'-10$7/16$" | 3'-2$7/16$" | 3'-10$7/16$" |
| 6 | 10'-5$1/2$" | 11'-1$1/2$" | 13'-9$1/2$" | 14'-5$1/2$" | 3'-2$3/4$" | 3'-10$3/4$" | 3'-2$3/4$" | 3'-10$3/4$" |
| 7 | 12'-3$1/2$" | 13'-1$1/2$" | 16'-3$1/2$" | 17'-1$1/2$" | 3'-3$1/16$" | 3'-11$1/16$" | 3'-3$1/16$" | 3'-11$1/16$" |
| 8 | 14'-1$1/2$" | 15'-1$1/2$" | 18'-9$1/2$" | 19'-9$1/2$" | 3'-3$3/8$" | 3'-11$3/8$" | 3'-3$3/8$" | 3'-11$3/8$" |
| 9 | 15'-11$1/2$" | 17'-1$1/2$" | 21'-3$1/2$" | 22'-5$1/2$" | 3'-3$11/16$" | 3'-11$11/16$" | 3'-3$11/16$" | 3'-11$11/16$" |
| 10 | 17'-9$1/2$" | 19'-1$1/2$" | 23'-9$1/2$" | 25'-1$1/2$" | 3'-4" | 4'-0" | 3'-4" | 4'-0" |
| 12 | 21'-5$1/2$" | 23'-1$1/2$" | 28'-9$1/2$" | 30'-5$1/2$" | 3'-4$5/8$" | 4'-0$5/8$" | 3'-4$5/8$" | 4'-0$5/8$" |
| 14 | 25'-1$1/2$" | 27'-1$1/2$" | 33'-9$1/2$" | 35'-9$1/2$" | 3'-5$1/4$" | 4'-1$1/4$" | NOTE: For $11^5/8$" rise of 18 or more rows and 16" rise of 13 or more rows check with manufacturer for modified closed depth dimensions. | |
| 16 | 28'-9$1/2$" | 31'-1$1/2$" | 38'-9$1/2$" | 41'-1$1/2$" | 3'-5$7/8$" | 4'-1$7/8$" | | |
| 18 | 32'-5$1/2$" | 35'-1$1/2$" | 43'-9$1/2$" | 46'-5$1/2$" | 3'-6$1/2$" | 4'-2$1/2$" | | |
| 20 | 36'-1$1/2$" | 39'-1$1/2$" | 48'-9$1/2$" | 51'-9$1/2$" | 3'-7$1/8$" | 4'-3$1/8$" | | |

Erik Johnson; Lawrence Cook & Associates; Falls Church, Virginia
David W. Johnson; Washington, D.C.

**OUTDOOR SPORTS**

## FACTORS INFLUENCING DESIGN

The layout of circulation routes for spectators is affected by the means of egress requirements in leading standards and model building codes. Changes to these standards and codes were based on recommendations developed in 1985 by the Board for Coordination of Model Codes (BCMC) and by committees responsible for National Fire Protection Association (NFPA) standards (particularly NFPA 101-1988 and NFPA 102-1986).

These changes, whether or not reflected in the legal requirements establishing the standards or codes in a particular area, provide a good technical base for using alternative methods of circulation route planning. Incorporating these changes in the planning process requires a firm grasp of underlying principles and would benefit from assistance from a consultant.

Improved design standards for spectator circulation are a result of growing sensitivity to environmental quality and accidents which are sometimes followed by litigation.

## MORE FLEXIBLE EGRESS RULES FOR LARGE BUILDINGS

Changes introduced in NFPA 102-1986 provide flexible egress requirements for open-air or enclosed spectator facilities in larger buildings that qualify as "smoke-protected assembly seating." They address the longer egress time that may be acceptable because of greater control of fire hazards, higher ceilings that keep smoke from blocking egress routes, and similar more flexible rules.

Flexibility in egress requirements also may be applicable in intermediate-sized facilities other than large stadia and arenas. Egress requirements may differ by a factor of five, depending on facility size. Generally, to be treated as smoke-protected assembly seating, all hazards—not only fire—must be addressed. Also, a "life safety evaluation" must be conducted which is acceptable to the authority having jurisdiction. Expert advice on life and fire safety engineering should be retained for a life safety evaluation.

## AISLES

Requirements governing provision of aisles in bleacher seating have, in many cases, been made more stringent. For example, NFPA 102-1986 extended aisle requirements. Some bleacher seating formerly permitted to be without aisles must now be provided with aisles. Missteps and falls, plus normal inconvenience to patrons, are more likely to occur on surfaces serving as seating rather than on designated aisles.

### LOCATION OF AISLES

Liberalized requirements for locating aisles reinterpret such traditional principles as the following.

Path redundancy: Except for travel over short distances, as in a short row of seats served by only one aisle, all spectators must have a choice of at least two egress routes from their seat.

Common path of travel along a row of seats served by a single aisle usually should not exceed 30 ft (9 m) to the point where there are two paths of egress.

Common path of travel or dead end in an aisle often will be compensated for by the path redundancy of the rows of seats served by such aisles at each end of the rows. Blockage of one aisle simply means that spectator movement occurs along rows to the next aisle (and on to the next if necessary). Beyond general limits, noted below, the length and spacing of rows providing such alternative routes may be regulated as follows.

For facilities not providing smoke-protected assembly seating, requirements may call for:

1. Rows to be no longer than 25 seats
2. 12 in. (305 mm) clear width between rows plus 0.6 in. (15 mm) for each additional seat beyond 7 in the row.

For facilities providing smoke-protected assembly seating, requirements may be relaxed to permit:

1. Rows to be no longer than 40 seats
2. 12 in. (305 mm) clear width between rows plus 0.3 in. (8 mm) for each additional seat beyond 14 in the row.

Minimum clear widths: Building upon a principle established with the rules for continental seating, changes in rules for minimum clearances between seat rows and maximum number of seats per row may allow rows to contain up to 100 seats if served by aisles at both ends. Rules on common path of travel (dead ends) limit other aisles to 30–50 ft (9–15 m) lengths. Row length and spacing are interrelated; longer rows require greater clearance between rows:

1. 12 in. (303 mm) plus 0.3 in. (8 mm) for each seat beyond 14 in a row served by two aisles
2. 12 in. (305 mm) plus 0.6 in. (15 mm) for each seat beyond 7 in a row served by only one aisle.

Seat row length limits, beyond which increased spacing is required, may be increased by as much as 50% for larger facilities providing smoke-protected assembly seating.

### AISLE WIDTH

Aisle width also may be subject to newer minimums that take greater account of whether steps are used. Aisle stairs should be:

1. 48 in. (1220 mm) wide at treads and between seats to either side
2. 36 in. (910 mm) wide at treads and clear with seats to one side only
3. If serving five or fewer rows on one side of a handrail, the clear width only is required to be 23 in. (584 mm).

Width for capacity: Changes in the way egress capacity is credited allow more flexibility in aisle width calculation, with small increments in width adding to egress capacity.

1. Level or ramped routes should provide at least 0.2 in. (5 mm) of clear width per person
2. Aisle stairs should provide at least 0.3 in. (8 mm) of clear width per person. Handrails can be within this clear width and should be provided in this case
3. Aisle stairs with risers higher than 7 in. (178 mm) decrease efficiency and safety, requiring the width per person to be increased by 2% for each extra 0.1 in. (3 mm) of height. The maximum height of 9 in. (229 mm), however, is permitted only if sightlines dictate steep seating decks and aisles.

Smoke-protected assembly seating in intermediate-sized and larger buildings may have reduced width requirements for capacity. Depending on the code in use, the incremental widths noted above may be reduced by a factor of five for the largest facilities with intermediate width increments applying, on a sliding scale, to intermediate-sized ones.

### AISLE DETAILS

Handrails are increasingly required on all aisle stairs. Such aisles are subject to all the hazards of stairs in addition to flight lengths, step geometry, use conditions, and profusion of visual distraction. Prudent design calls for functional handrails on all stairs, including aisle stairs and moderately sloped stairs in lower-level seating areas. Ramped aisles also can benefit from handrails and may be a code requirement.

Handrails in the middle of aisles should have gaps every 3 to 5 rows, allowing people to move to the other side of the aisle. Height should be as high as sightlines permit. An intermediate height handrail should be provided for children and to deter people from ducking under the rail. Handrails should be finished with a light or reflective color to reduce heating in full sun.

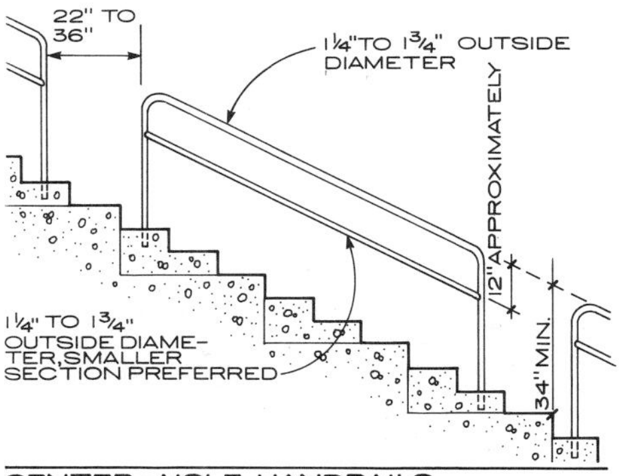
22" TO 36"
1¼"TO 1¾" OUTSIDE DIAMETER
12" APPROXIMATELY
34" MIN.
1¼" TO 1¾" OUTSIDE DIAMETER,SMALLER SECTION PREFERRED

CENTER-AISLE HANDRAILS

## STEP DETAILS

Contrary to much traditional practice, all treads within an aisle stair must be uniform in size. Single or double intermediate steps between seating platforms must not be made smaller so that a larger area is available at the seating platform for entry to and egress from rows. Entry and egress is not compromised by making all steps similar. Safety, as well as comfortable movement along the aisle, is seriously reduced by varying tread size.

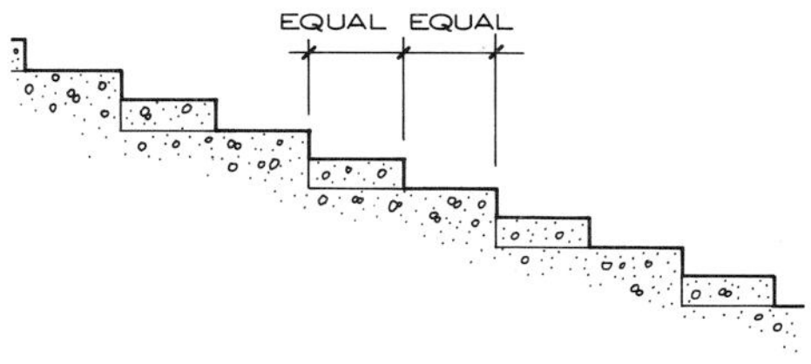
EQUAL EQUAL

AISLE STAIR TREAD UNIFORMITY

Often overlooked during the planning of spectator facilities is the proper design and placement of seating platforms and infill steps forming the aisles. Dimensional nonuniformities between steps should be kept under 3/16 in. (5 mm) between steps. Faulty workmanship and inspection may result in a spectator's fall and subsequent litigation. Step dimensions and all other aspects of aisle design should adhere to general principles of stair safety: a tread (run) of at least 11 in. (279 mm) and riser heights of over 4 in. (100 mm), but not more than 7 in. (178 mm). Tread depth is the most important dimension. Compromises forced by sightlines and resulting steep seating decks are more acceptable in the height of risers. Codes may permit aisle stair risers to be up to 9 in. (229 mm) high.

Tread nosing marking: Stair visibility, particularly for descent, is especially critical in the complex visual settings found in spectator seating facilities. All treads should be marked with a contrasting marking stripe, 1–2 in. (25–51 mm) wide at the nosing. For concrete treads, special durable coatings such as epoxy are available that have a slip-resistant surface. These coatings, similar to concrete, have a good surface for slip resistance when not too highly finished. Chemically treating carpet produces a durable marking stripe. Nosing caps and tapes can be tripping hazards, may work loose, and are not recommended.

Where adjacent riser heights differ by more than 3/16 in. (5 mm) due to changes in seat deck slope, for improving sightlines, distinctive tread nosing marking should be provided to indicate unavoidable differences in step dimensions. Hazard yellow may be the most appropriate color to use where missteps and falls are likely. Spectators have a right to be warned of dangers.

## VOMITORIES VERSUS CROSS AISLES

Cross aisles, unless located with no seating behind them, will invariably cause difficulties with sightlines, spectator circulation, or both. A vomitory, an opening piercing a bank of seats, is a better way of providing access to and egress from an aisle serving seating rows. The key is designing for the minimum number and variety of steps to be negotiated in moving from a seat to a concourse.

Vomitory–aisle configurations are of two common types—symmetrical and nonsymmetrical. The nonsymmetrical type is preferred for minimizing sightline interference for seats located above the vomitory. To optimize spectator flow into the vomitory, the aisle feeding into the vomitory from below should be offset from aisles feeding in from above.

## CONSULTANTS

Expert safety guidance should be sought for the following situations:

1. Smoke protected assembly seating
2. Requirement for a life safety evaluation
3. Local codes not based on a current model code
4. Retrofit of existing spectator facilities
5. Seating decks steeper than 33°
6. Serious unavoidable nonuniformities in stairs.

Jake Pauls, Life Safety Specialist; Hughes Associates, Inc.; Wheaton, Maryland

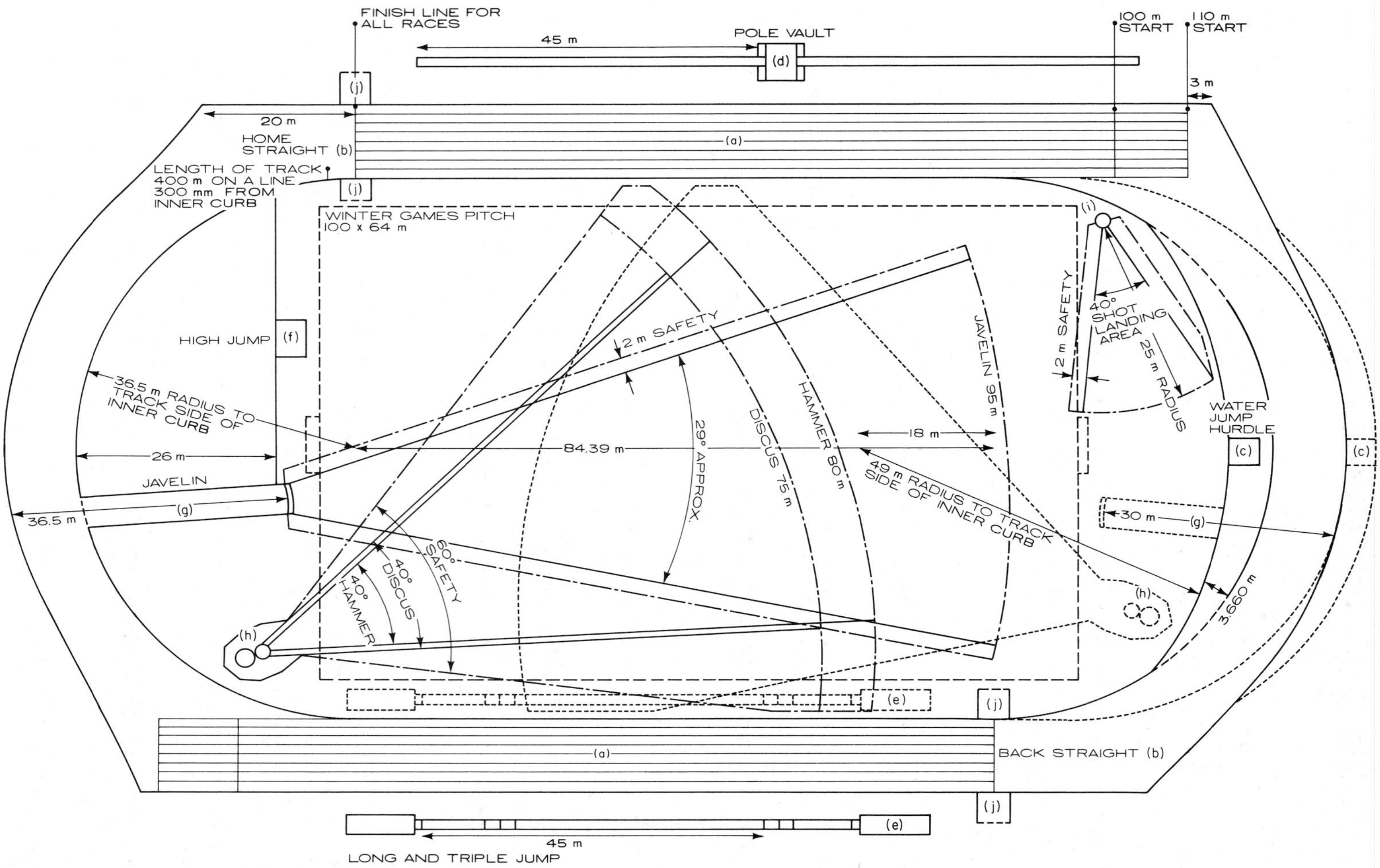

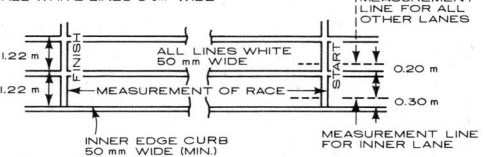

FINISH LINE FOR
ALL RACES

45 m

POLE VAULT
(d)

100 m
START

110 m
START

3 m

20 m

HOME
STRAIGHT (b)

(a)

(j)

LENGTH OF TRACK
400 m ON A LINE
300 mm FROM
INNER CURB

(j)

WINTER GAMES PITCH
100 x 64 m

HIGH JUMP (f)

2 m SAFETY

40°
SHOT
LANDING
AREA

2 m SAFETY

25 m RADIUS

(i)

36.5 m RADIUS TO
TRACK SIDE OF
INNER CURB

JAVELIN 95 m

WATER
JUMP
HURDLE

(c)

(c)

26 m

84.39 m

29° APPROX

DISCUS 75 m

HAMMER 80 m

18 m

49 m RADIUS TO TRACK
SIDE OF INNER CURB

JAVELIN

36.5 m

(g)

60°
SAFETY

40°
DISCUS

30 m

(g)

3.660 m

40°
HAMMER

(h)

(h)

(e)

(j)

BACK STRAIGHT (b)

(a)

(e)

(j)

LONG AND TRIPLE JUMP

45 m

## LAYOUT GUIDE FOR 400 m RUNNING TRACK AND FIELD EVENT LOCATIONS

(a) Number of lanes
(b) Straights
(c) Steeplechase and water jump
(d) Pole vault
(e) Long and triple jumps
(f) High jump
(g) Javelin
(h) Hammer and discus in cage
(i) Putting and shot
(j) Paved areas

ALL WHITE LINES 5 cm WIDE

MEASUREMENT
LINE FOR ALL
OTHER LANES

ALL LINES WHITE
50 mm WIDE

1.22 m

1.22 m

0.20 m

MEASUREMENT OF RACE

0.30 m

INNER EDGE CURB
50 mm WIDE (MIN.)

MEASUREMENT LINE
FOR INNER LANE

### NATIONAL AND INTERNATIONAL COMPETITION

The diagram indicates how a 400 m track with a synthetic surface might be laid out for national and international competition. Different arrangements are possible to suit particular circumstances. For high level competition, however, alternatives for the siting of the throwing circles are of necessity limited if maximum distances are to be safely thrown. For Rules of Competition reference should be made to the Handbook of the International Amateur Athletic Federation.

### TRACK AND LANES

The length of the running track should be not less than 400 m. The track should be not less than 7.32 m in width and should, if possible, be bordered on the inside with concrete or other suitable material, approximately 50 mm high, minimum 50 mm wide. The curb may be raised to permit surface water to drain away, in which case a maximum height of 65 mm must not be exceeded.

Where it is not possible for the inner edge of the running track to have a raised border, the inner edge shall be marked with lines 50 mm wide.

The measurement shall be taken 0.30 m outward from the inner border of the track or, where no border exists, 0.20 m from the line marking the inside of the track.

In all races up to and including 400 m, each competitor shall have a separate lane, with a minimum width

### METHOD OF MARKING LANES
of 1.22 m and a maximum width of 1.25 m to be marked by lines 50 mm in width. The inner lane shall be measured as stated in the preceding text, but the remaining lanes shall be measured 0.20 m from the outer edges of the lines.

In international meetings the track should allow for at least six lanes and, where possible, for eight lanes, particularly for major international events.

The maximum allowance for lateral inclination of tracks shall not exceed 1 : 100, and the inclination in the running direction shall not exceed 1 : 1000.

The lateral inclination of the track should wherever possible be toward the inside lane.

### SURFACE

Synthetic materials provide a consistently good surface capable of continuous and unlimited use in most weather conditions. Maintenance is minimal, consisting of periodic cleaning by hosing down or brushing, the repainting when necessary of the line markings, and an occasional repair.

Cinder surfaces require considerable maintenance by a skilled groundsman every time a track is used. They are not all-weather and seldom provide a consistently good running surface. They are, however, much cheaper to construct and are suitable for club use and training.

On cinder tracks an extra lane is necessary so that

sprint and hurdle events can be run on the six outer lanes to avoid the inner lane, which is subject to heavy use during long distance events.

### ORIENTATION

It is often difficult to reconcile the requirements of wind directions and the need to avoid an approach into the setting sun. For these reasons it is now becoming common practice to provide, where possible, alternative directions for running, jumping, and throwing.

### NUMBER OF LANES

Synthetic all-weather:

| | |
|---|---|
| International competition: | 8 lanes (9.76 m) |
| Area or regional competition: | 6 lanes (7.32 m) |

Cinder:

| | |
|---|---|
| International competition: | 8 lanes (9.76 m) 9 lanes (straights) |
| Area or regional competition: | 7 lanes (8.54 m) |

### THE FINISH

Two white posts shall denote the extremities of the finish line, and shall be placed at least 30 cm from the edge of the track.

The finish posts shall be of rigid construction about 1.4 m high, 80 mm wide, and 20 mm thick.

### FORMULA FOR OTHER TRACK PROPORTIONS

Where a track of wider or narrower proportions or of different length is required, the appropriate dimensions can be calculated from the following formula:

$$L = 2P + 2 \quad (R + 300 \text{ mm})$$

where L = length of track (m)
P = length of parallels or distance apart of centers of curves (m)
R = radius to track side of inner curb (m)
$\pi$ = 3.1416 (not $^{22}/_7$)

It is recommended that the radius of the semicircles should not normally be less than 32 m or more than 42 m for a 400 m circuit.

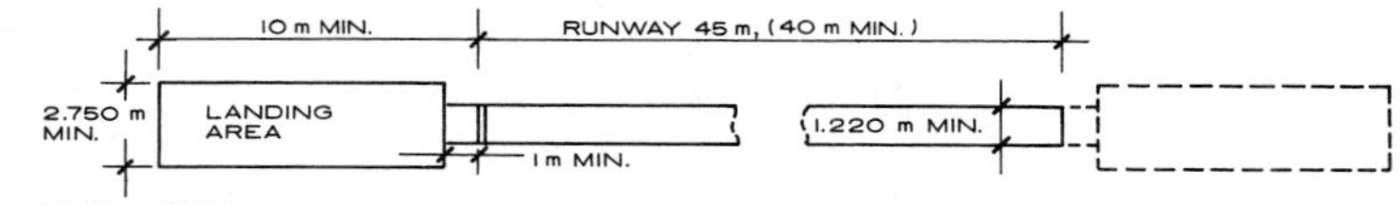

**LONG JUMP**

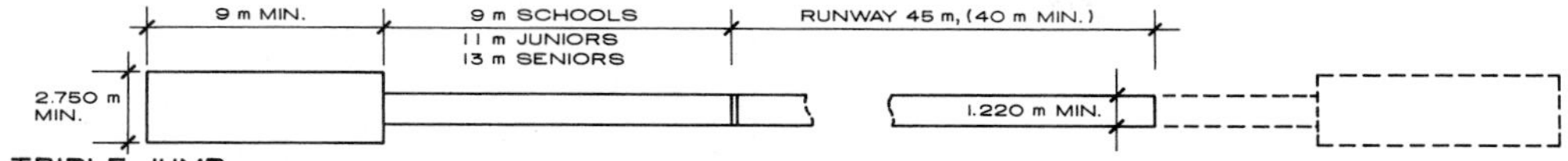

10 m MIN. — RUNWAY 45 m, (40 m MIN.)

2.750 m MIN. — LANDING AREA — 1 m MIN. — 1.220 m MIN.

**TRIPLE JUMP**

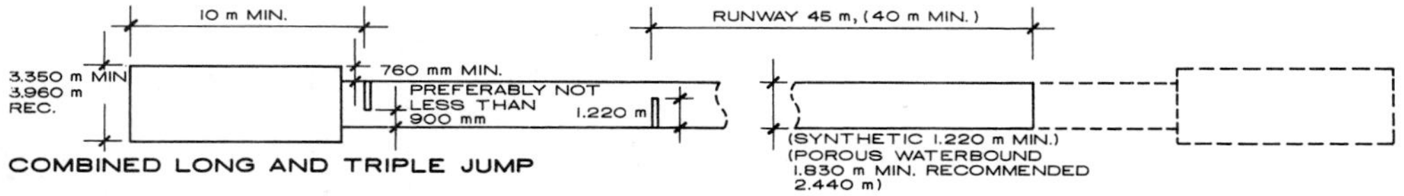

9 m MIN. — 9 m SCHOOLS / 11 m JUNIORS / 13 m SENIORS — RUNWAY 45 m, (40 m MIN.)

2.750 m MIN. — 1.220 m MIN.

**COMBINED LONG AND TRIPLE JUMP**

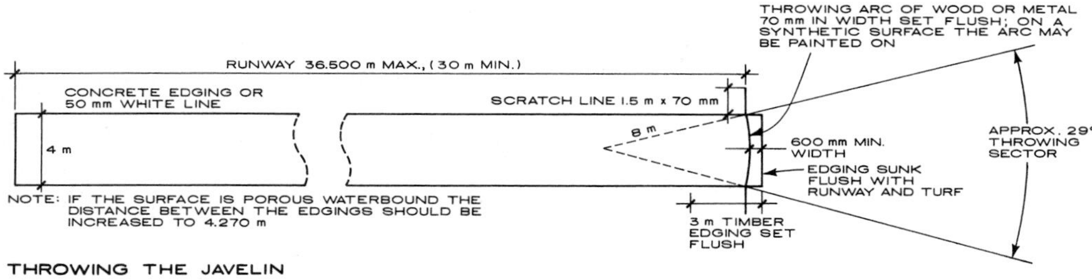

10 m MIN. — RUNWAY 45 m, (40 m MIN.)

3.350 m MIN / 3.960 m REC. — 760 mm MIN. — PREFERABLY NOT LESS THAN 900 mm — 1.220 m

(SYNTHETIC 1.220 m MIN.) (POROUS WATERBOUND 1.830 m MIN. RECOMMENDED 2.440 m)

**THROWING THE JAVELIN**

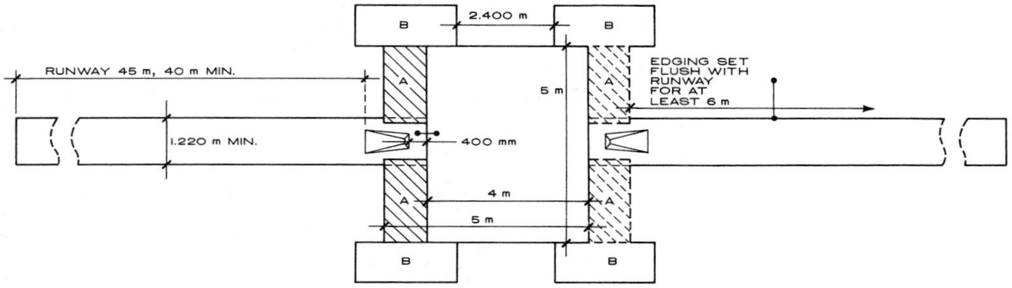

RUNWAY 36.500 m MAX., (30 m MIN.)

CONCRETE EDGING OR 50 mm WHITE LINE — 4 m — SCRATCH LINE 1.5 m x 70 mm

THROWING ARC OF WOOD OR METAL 70 mm IN WIDTH SET FLUSH; ON A SYNTHETIC SURFACE THE ARC MAY BE PAINTED ON

8 m — 600 mm MIN. WIDTH — EDGING SUNK FLUSH WITH RUNWAY AND TURF

APPROX. 29° THROWING SECTOR

3 m TIMBER EDGING SET FLUSH

NOTE: IF THE SURFACE IS POROUS WATERBOUND THE DISTANCE BETWEEN THE EDGINGS SHOULD BE INCREASED TO 4.270 m

**POLE VAULT**

RUNWAY 45 m, 40 m MIN. — 1.220 m MIN.

2.400 m — B — B — 5 m — A — A — 400 mm — 4 m — 5 m — B — B

EDGING SET FLUSH WITH RUNWAY FOR AT LEAST 6 m

**THROWING CIRCLE**

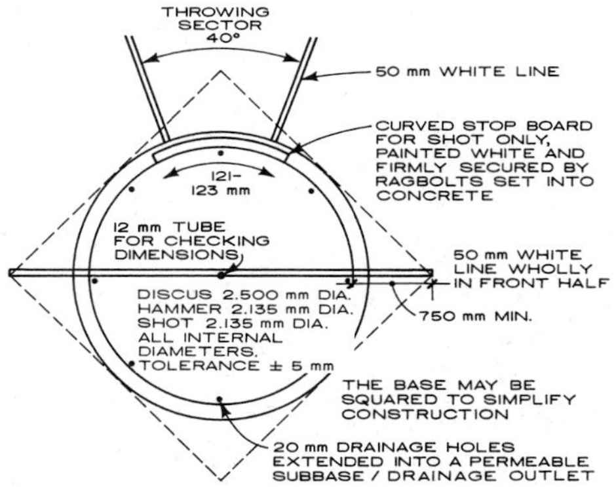

THROWING SECTOR 40°

50 mm WHITE LINE

CURVED STOP BOARD FOR SHOT ONLY, PAINTED WHITE AND FIRMLY SECURED BY RAGBOLTS SET INTO CONCRETE

121–123 mm

12 mm TUBE FOR CHECKING DIMENSIONS

50 mm WHITE LINE WHOLLY IN FRONT HALF

DISCUS 2.500 mm DIA. HAMMER 2.135 mm DIA. SHOT 2.135 mm DIA. ALL INTERNAL DIAMETERS. TOLERANCE ± 5 mm

750 mm MIN.

THE BASE MAY BE SQUARED TO SIMPLIFY CONSTRUCTION

20 mm DRAINAGE HOLES EXTENDED INTO A PERMEABLE SUBBASE / DRAINAGE OUTLET

**HIGH JUMP**

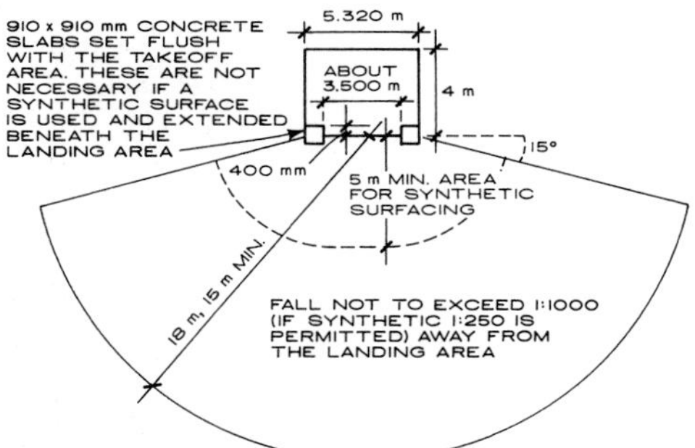

910 x 910 mm CONCRETE SLABS SET FLUSH WITH THE TAKEOFF AREA. THESE ARE NOT NECESSARY IF A SYNTHETIC SURFACE IS USED AND EXTENDED BENEATH THE LANDING AREA

5.320 m — ABOUT 3.500 m — 4 m — 15°

400 mm — 5 m MIN. AREA FOR SYNTHETIC SURFACING

18 m, 15 m MIN.

FALL NOT TO EXCEED 1:1000 (IF SYNTHETIC 1:250 IS PERMITTED) AWAY FROM THE LANDING AREA

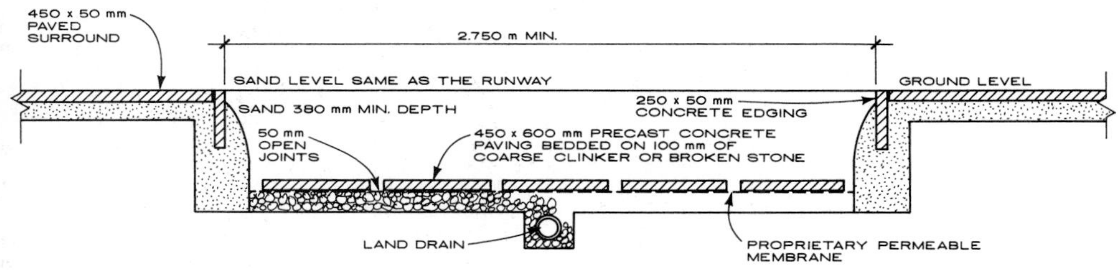

**SECTION OF SAND LANDING AREA**

450 x 50 mm PAVED SURROUND

2.750 m MIN.

SAND LEVEL SAME AS THE RUNWAY — GROUND LEVEL

SAND 380 mm MIN. DEPTH — 250 x 50 mm CONCRETE EDGING

50 mm OPEN JOINTS — 450 x 600 mm PRECAST CONCRETE PAVING BEDDED ON 100 mm OF COARSE CLINKER OR BROKEN STONE

LAND DRAIN — PROPRIETARY PERMEABLE MEMBRANE

---

## 400 m TRACK AND FIELD EVENTS— CONSTRUCTION DETAILS

These details are based on international standards. For additional information consult the IAAF, which is the International Amateur Athletic Federation. These details were provided by the National Playing Fields Association, London, England.

### NOTE

To avoid adverse wind conditions during competition, landing areas for the long and triple jumps are desirable at both ends of the runway. A surround of paving slabs (450 x 600 mm) is an advantage. Takeoff board to be of wood or other suitable rigid material, set level with surface and painted white. See detail.

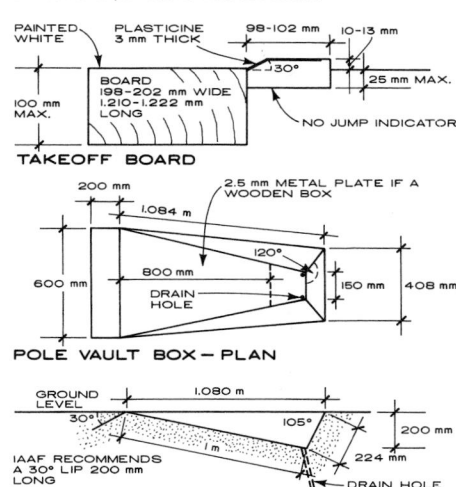

PAINTED WHITE — PLASTICINE 3 mm THICK — 98–102 mm — 10–13 mm

100 mm MAX. — BOARD 198–202 mm WIDE 1.210–1.222 m LONG — 30° — 25 mm MAX.

NO JUMP INDICATOR

**TAKEOFF BOARD**

200 mm — 2.5 mm METAL PLATE IF A WOODEN BOX

1.084 m — 120° — 150 mm — 408 mm

600 mm — 800 mm — DRAIN HOLE

**POLE VAULT BOX – PLAN**

GROUND LEVEL — 1.080 m

30° — 1 m — 105° — 200 mm — 224 mm

IAAF RECOMMENDS A 30° LIP 200 mm LONG — DRAIN HOLE

**POLE VAULT BOX – SECTION**

### POLE VAULT

A = Detachable soft landing units each 1 x 2 m.

B = Concrete platforms each 1 x 2.450 m x 75 mm thick minimum and set level with runway surface.

The soft landing area to be 5 x 5 m minimum. The distance between uprights or extension arms to be 3.660 m minimum/4.370 m maximum. A larger soft landing unit with a 1.300 m extension for the pole vault box cutout giving a total size of 5 x 6.300 m may be provided. The diagram shows a double runway with detachable A units and thus gives a choice of runways according to the wind direction.

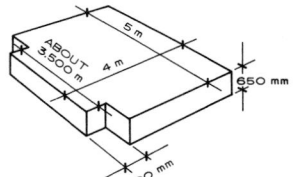

ABOUT 3.500 m — 5 m — 4 m — 650 mm — 400 mm

**HIGH JUMP SOFT LANDING AREA**

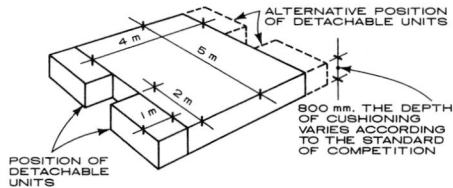

ALTERNATIVE POSITION OF DETACHABLE UNITS

4 m — 5 m — 2 m — 1 m

800 mm. THE DEPTH OF CUSHIONING VARIES ACCORDING TO THE STANDARD OF COMPETITION

POSITION OF DETACHABLE UNITS

### POLE VAULT SOFT LANDING AREA

For outdoor use soft landing units should be laid on duckboards on an ash base or other suitable materials (e.g., precast concrete paving on a porous base with 50 mm open joints).

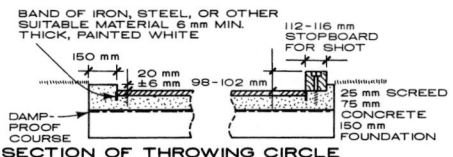

BAND OF IRON, STEEL, OR OTHER SUITABLE MATERIAL 6 mm MIN. THICK, PAINTED WHITE — 112–116 mm STOPBOARD FOR SHOT

150 mm — 20 mm / ± 6 mm — 98–102 mm — 25 mm SCREED / 75 mm CONCRETE / 150 mm FOUNDATION

DAMP-PROOF COURSE

**SECTION OF THROWING CIRCLE**

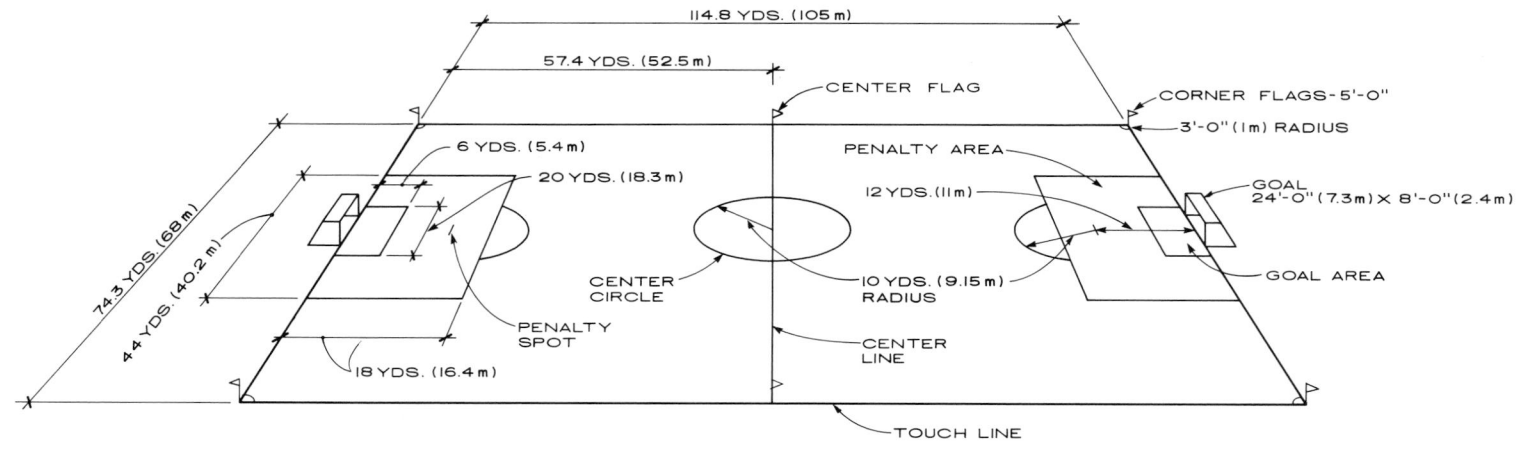

114.8 YDS. (105 m)

57.4 YDS. (52.5 m)

CENTER FLAG

CORNER FLAGS-5'-0"

3'-0"(1m) RADIUS

6 YDS. (5.4 m)

PENALTY AREA

20 YDS. (18.3 m)

12 YDS.(11m)

GOAL
24'-0"(7.3m) X 8'-0"(2.4m)

74.3 YDS.(68 m)

44 YDS. (40.2 m)

CENTER
CIRCLE

GOAL AREA

10 YDS. (9.15 m)
RADIUS

PENALTY
SPOT

18 YDS. (16.4 m)

CENTER
LINE

TOUCH LINE

**SOCCER** – NORTH AMERICAN SOCCER LEAGUE
U.S. SOCCER FEDERATION

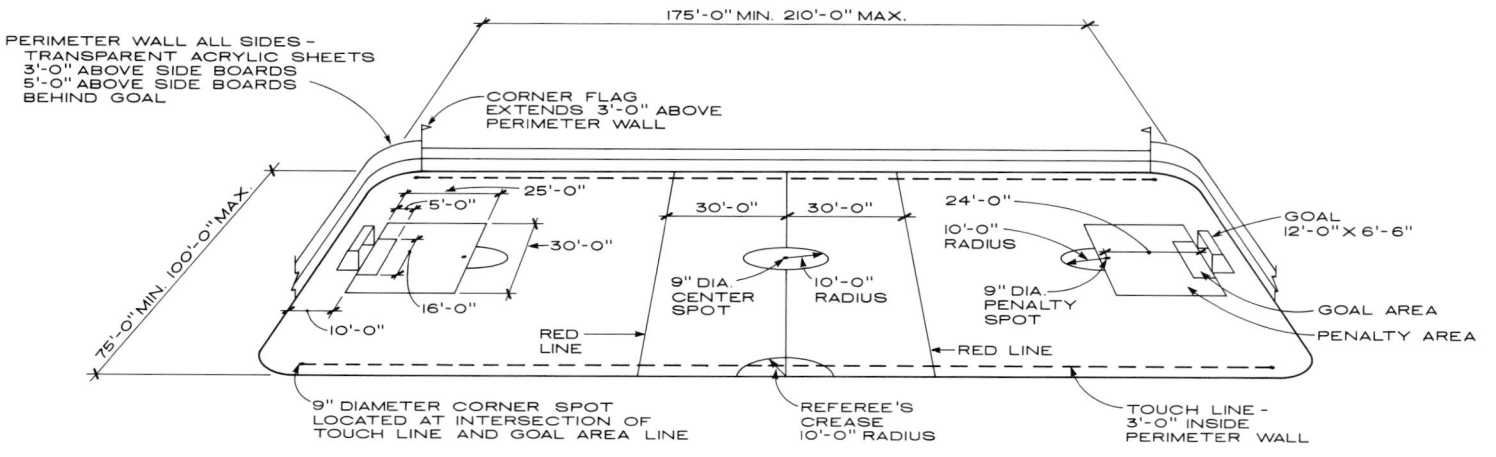

PERIMETER WALL ALL SIDES –
TRANSPARENT ACRYLIC SHEETS
3'-0" ABOVE SIDE BOARDS
5'-0" ABOVE SIDE BOARDS
BEHIND GOAL

175'-0" MIN. 210'-0" MAX.

CORNER FLAG
EXTENDS 3'-0" ABOVE
PERIMETER WALL

25'-0"

5'-0"

30'-0"

30'-0"

30'-0"

24'-0"

10'-0"
RADIUS

GOAL
12'-0" X 6'-6"

75'-0" MIN. 100'-0"MAX.

16'-0"

9" DIA.
CENTER
SPOT

10'-0"
RADIUS

9" DIA.
PENALTY
SPOT

GOAL AREA

10'-0"

RED
LINE

RED LINE

PENALTY AREA

9" DIAMETER CORNER SPOT
LOCATED AT INTERSECTION OF
TOUCH LINE AND GOAL AREA LINE

REFEREE'S
CREASE
10'-0" RADIUS

TOUCH LINE -
3'-0" INSIDE
PERIMETER WALL

NOTE: OVERALL FIELD DIMENSIONS DEPEND ON AVAILABLE PLAYING SURFACE.

**INDOOR SOCCER** – MAJOR INDOOR SOCCER LEAGUE

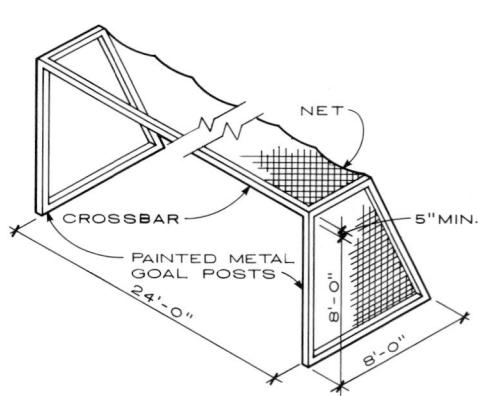

NET

CROSSBAR

5"MIN.

PAINTED METAL
GOAL POSTS

24'-0"

8'-0"

8'-0"

### GOAL

The goal posts and crossbar shall not exceed 5 in. nor be less than 4 in. wide and shall present a flat surface to the playing field. The net must be attached to the ground, goal posts, and crossbar. It must extend back and level with the crossbar for 2 ft. 0 in. (.61 M).

**SOCCER GOAL**

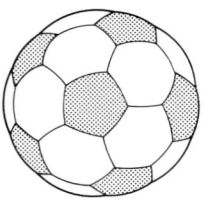

27" (68.58CM) IN
CIRCUMFERENCE
14 TO 16 OZ. (453-897
GRAMS)

### BALL

The ball's surface has thirty-odd black and white panels that enable the players to estimate its direction and speed of spin.

### NOTES AND DEFINITIONS

All dimensions shown are to the inside edge of lines. All lines are to be white and 2 in. wide, except the centerline, which is 5 in. wide.

The long-field orientations in the northern hemisphere should be northwest-southeast for best sun angle during the fall playing season. The preferred drainage is a longitudinal crown with a 1 percent slope from center to each side.

Touchlines are the side boundaries, which are 114 yards (105 M) long.

The centerline is 5 in. (12.7 cm) wide and divides the playing field in half.

The center circle is a 10 yard (9 M) radius from the center of the centerline. At the beginning of each half the ball is kicked off from this circle by one team or the other.

The goal area is the smaller of the two rectangular zones: 20 yards (18.3 M) wide, 6 yards (5.4 M) in front of each goal. Other players can enter the goal area but cannot charge the goalie when he does not have the ball.

The penalty area is the larger of the two rectangular zones: 44 yards (40 M) wide, 18 yards (16.4 M) deep. A major rule infraction in this area allows the other team a penalty kick from the penalty spot.

Refer to rule setting body involved for actual dimensions required. Information shown here is for initial planning only.

Besides all the architectural differences between indoor and outdoor soccer, the natures of the games are deeply contrasted. Refer to the governing bodies, the Major Indoor Soccer League, the U.S. Soccer Federation, the North American Soccer League.

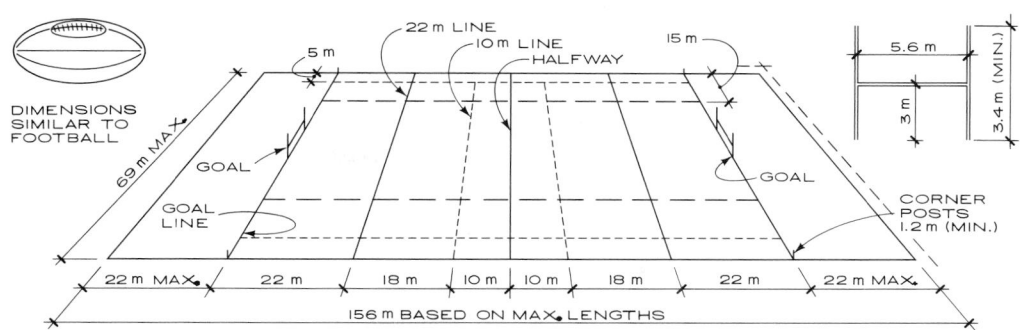

## RUGBY

The playing field is 156 m x 69 m with an additional 3 m safety zone recommended on all sides. The preferred long axis orientation is northwest–southeast; recommended grading is a 1% slope from each side of the axis. All measurements are from the inside line edges, which are marked with a white, nontoxic material.

**RUGBY**

BALL 2½" DIA.

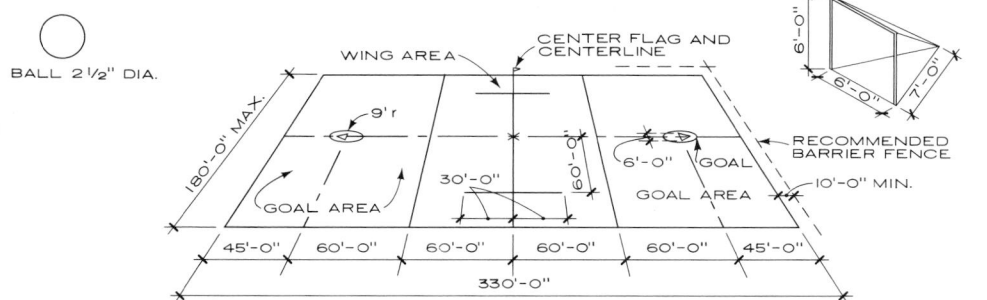

## MEN'S LACROSSE

The playing field is 330 ft (100.58 m) long and from 160 to 180 ft (48–55m) wide, with an additional 20 ft (60.10 m) recommended on all sides. The preferred long axis orientation is northwest–southeast and preferred drainage is a 1% slope away from each side of the longitudinal axis. All dimensions shown are to the inside of the lines except for the centerline. Lines are 2 in. wide and marked with a white, nontoxic material. Flexible flag markers are placed at each corner and on field sidelines at the centerline.

Diameter of the lacrosse ball is 2½ in.; the stick is 3 ft to 6 ft in length.

Further information is available from the National Collegiate Athletic Association.

**LACROSSE (MEN)**

BALL 8⅕" TO 9¼" DIA.

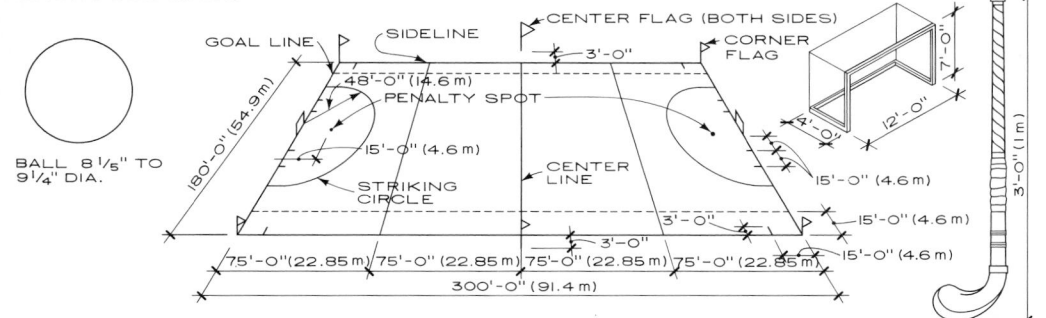

## FIELD HOCKEY

The playing field is 300 ft (91.4 m) x 180 ft (54.9 m) with an additional 10 ft (3.05 m) safety zone recommended on all sides. The preferred long axis orientation is northwest–southeast. Recommended grading is a 1% slope on each side of the longitudinal axis. All measurements shown are from the inside line edges. Lines are 3 in. wide, and marked with a white, nontoxic material.

The field hockey ball is 8⅕ in. to 9¼ in. (20.8–23.5 cm) in circumference and weighs 5½ oz. (156 g). The stick is 3 ft (1 m) long with a wooden head and cane handle with a cork or rubber insert.

Further information is available from the United States Field Hockey Association.

**FIELD HOCKEY**

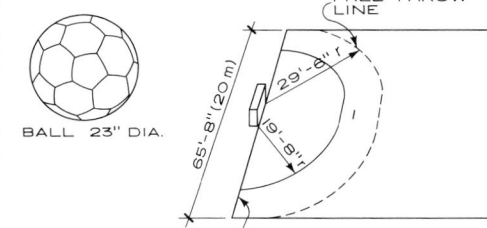

BALL 23" DIA.

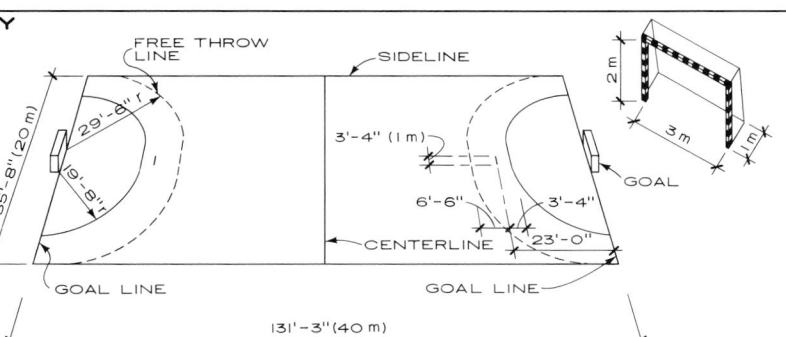

## INDOOR TEAM HANDBALL

The playing field is 131 ft 4 in. (40 m) x 65 ft 8 in. (20 m) with an additional 6 ft (2 m) unobstructed space on all sides. Preferred orientation is northwest–southeast along the longitudinal axis with a 1% slope away from each side of that axis. All dimensions shown are from the inside line edges except the centerline. All lines are 2 in. wide and marked with a white, nontoxic material.

The men's handball is 23 in. (58.4 cm) in circumference and weighs 16 oz. (453.6 g).

**TEAM HANDBALL**

BALL 4½" DIA.

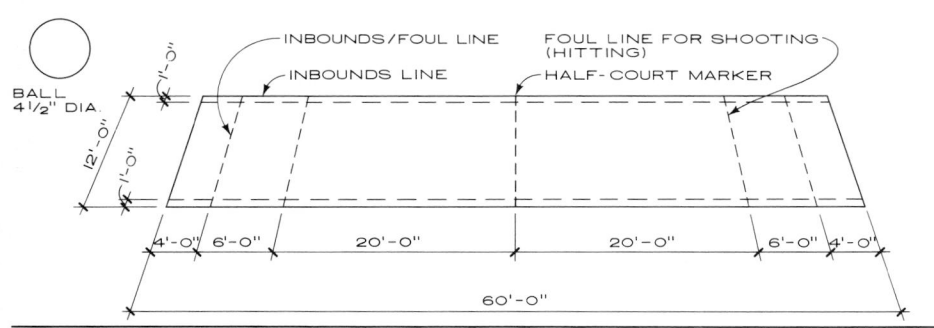

## BOCCE

The court is 60 ft (18.28 m) x 12 ft (3.65 m). Although orientation is of minor importance, it is preferred that the long axis run north–south. The surface should be flat without slope when it is stone, dust, or clay with adequate underdrainage and 1 percent slope in any direction when turf.

The ball is 4½ in. in diameter and weighs 32 oz.

Further information is available from the International Bocce Association, Inc.

**BOCCE BALL (BOCCIE)**

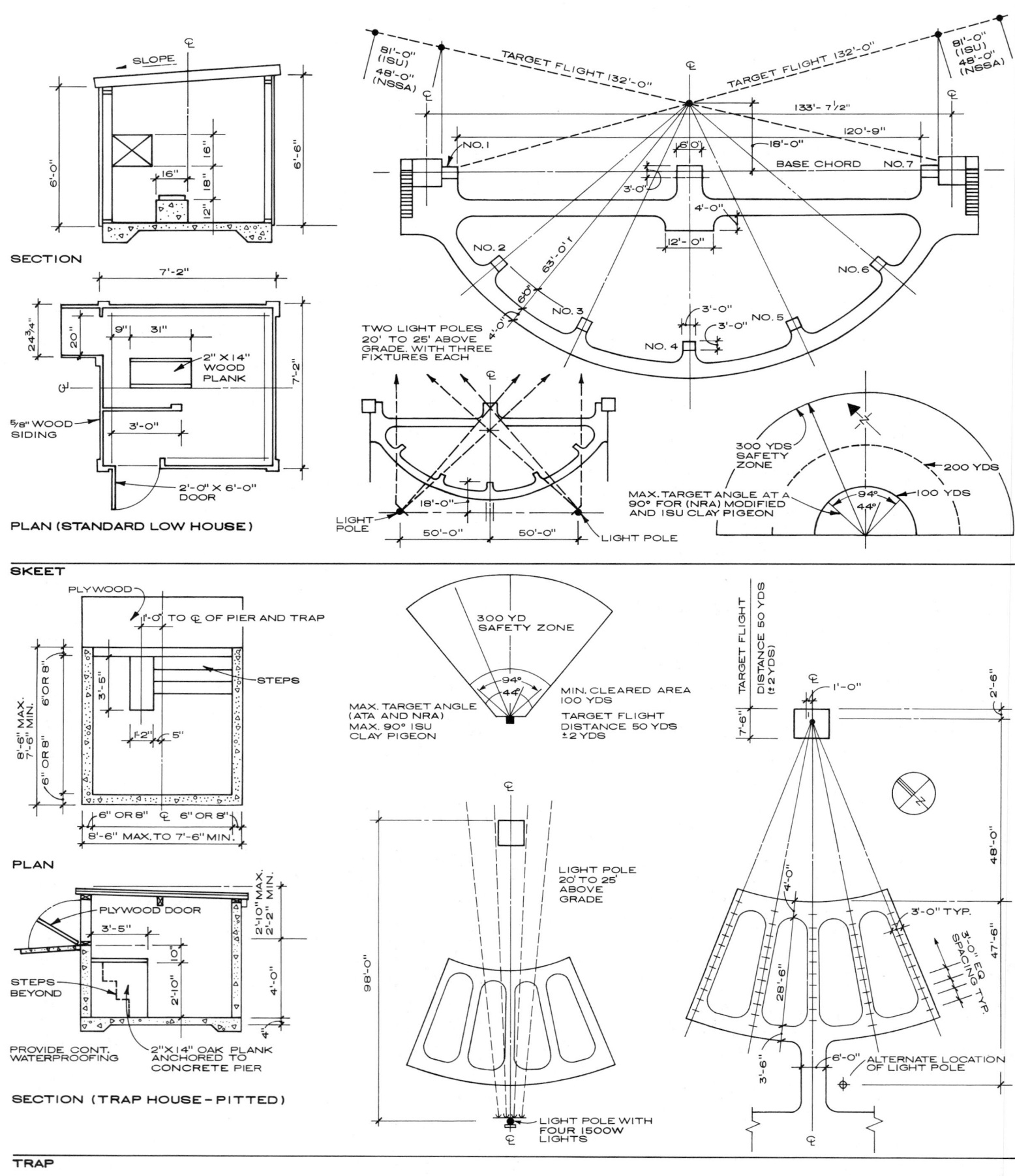

SECTION

PLAN (STANDARD LOW HOUSE)

SKEET

PLAN

SECTION (TRAP HOUSE – PITTED)

TRAP

**NOTES**

1. The drawings below illustrate the use of a 7-point dimension grid that expresses the minimum desirable dimensions to be used when either specifying or designing a rectangular shaped pool for residential use.
2. Width, length, and depth dimensions may apply to residential pools of any shape.
3. The minimum length with diving board and wading area is 28 ft. The average length of a residential pool is 28 to 40 ft.
4. Standards for residential swimming pools have been published by the National Spa and Pool Institute (1974).

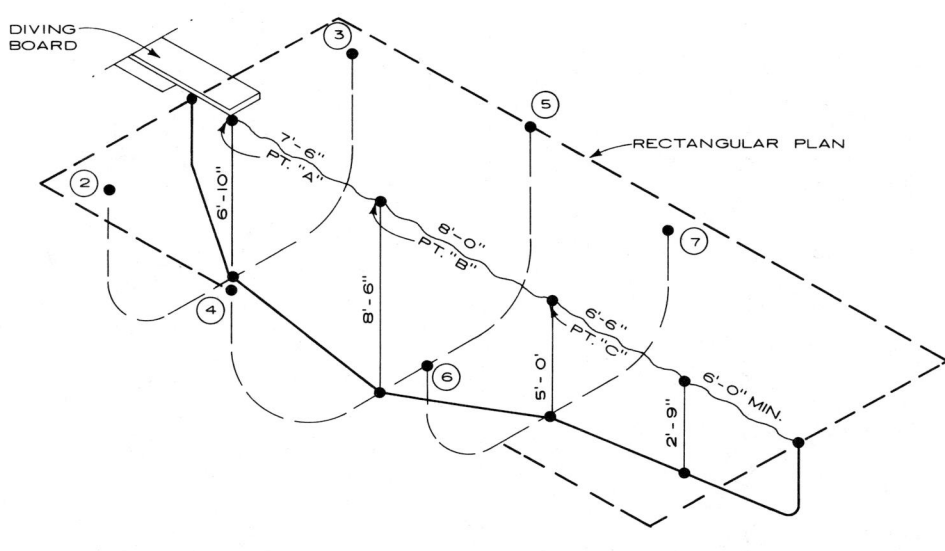

ISOMETRIC OVERLAY VIEW

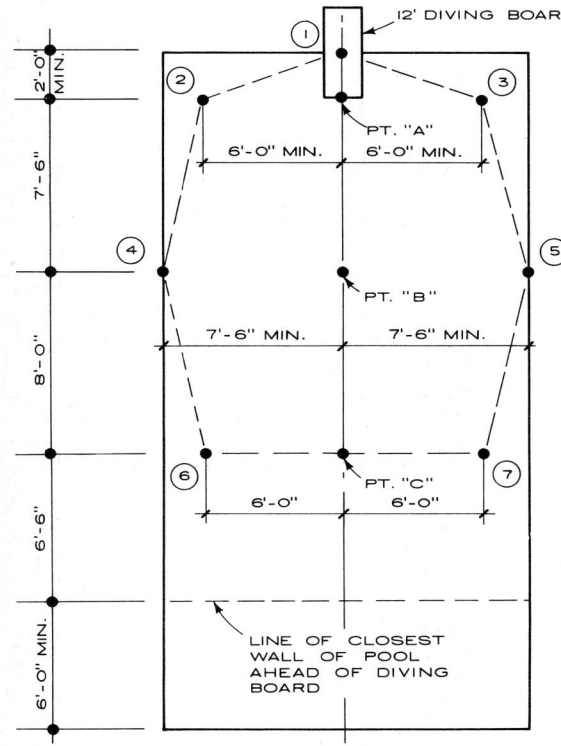

7-POINT GRID DIMENSION PLAN

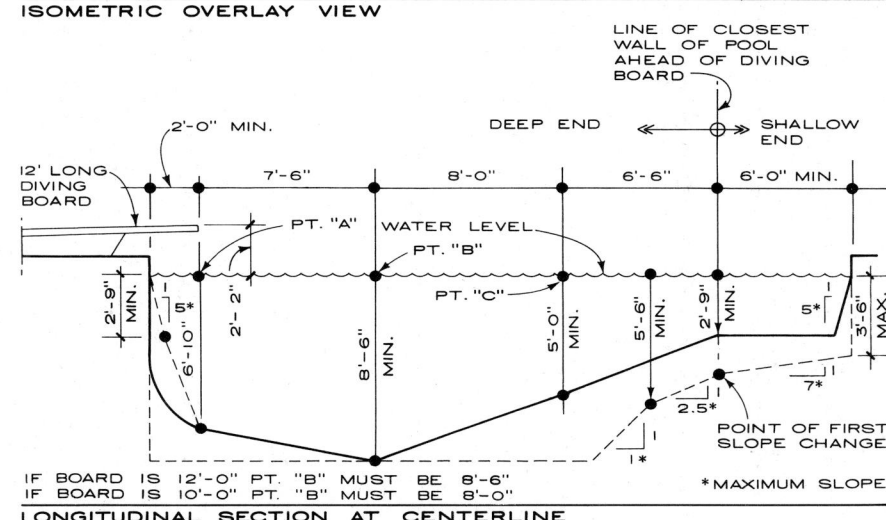

IF BOARD IS 12'-0" PT. "B" MUST BE 8'-6"
IF BOARD IS 10'-0" PT. "B" MUST BE 8'-0"

LONGITUDINAL SECTION AT CENTERLINE

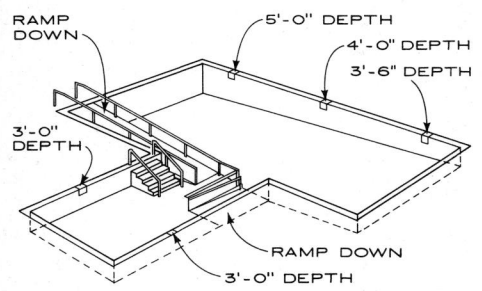

HANDICAPPED POOL ACCESS

Haver, Nunn and Collamer; Phoenix, Arizona

## PERMITS AND RESTRICTIONS

Required in most areas from building, health, plumbing, and electrical departments and zoning boards. Check for setback restrictions and easements covering power and telephone lines, sewers, and storm drains.

## SITE CONSIDERATIONS

Check the site for the following conditions, each of which will considerably increase the cost.

1. Fill that is more than 3 ft below pool deck.
2. Hard rock that requires drilling and blasting.
3. Underground water or springs that necessitate pumping or drains.
4. Accessibility of the site for mechanical equipment, minimum entry 8 ft wide by 7 ft 8 in. high, with a grade easy enough for a truck to reach the site.
5. Place the pool where it will get the most sun during swimming season. If possible, place deep end so a diver dives away from, not into, the afternoon sun. Avoid overhanging tree branches near the pool.
6. The slope of the site should be as level as possible; a steep slope requires retaining walls for the pool.
7. The surface deck around the pool should be of a slip-resistant surface.
8. A surrounding fence is recommended to protect pool area from unwanted visitors and to prevent accidents.

## CONSTRUCTION AND SHAPES

Pools may be made of reinforced concrete (poured on the job, precast, or gunite sprayed), concrete block, steel, aluminum, or plastic with or without block backup. Concrete, aluminum, fiberglass, and steel pools are available in any shape—rectangular, square, kidney, oval or free form. Complete plastic installations and plastic pool liners with various backups are available only in manufacturers' standard shapes and sizes.

A rectangular pool is the most practical if site permits, since it gives the longest swimming distance.

## POOL CAPACITY

Rule of thumb: 36 sq ft for each swimmer, 100 sq ft for each diver. A pool of 20 x 40 ft accommodates 14 persons at a time, but since not everyone is in the pool at once, pool and surroundings are adequate for 30 to 40 people.

## FILTER REQUIREMENTS

Filter, motor, and electrical equipment shall be sheltered and waterproofed.

## GENERAL

Public pools are generally considered to be those that belong to municipalities, schools, country clubs, hotels, motels, apartments, and resorts. Permits for their construction are required in most areas from local and state boards of health as well as the departments of building, plumbing, and electricity.

Community pools should be integrated with existing and projected recreational facilities, such as picnic areas and parks, for maximum usage. Transportation access should be good, and there should be ample parking space. In a hot climate, enough shade should be provided, particularly in the lounging areas, and be so located that it can be easily converted to spectator space by erecting bleachers.

## POOL DESIGN

Formerly most public pools were designed to meet competitive swimming requirements. The trend today is to provide for all-around use. The following should be considered:

1. Ratio of shallow water to deep water. Formerly 60% of pool area 5 ft deep and less was considered to be adequate. Now 80% is considered more realistic.
2. Ratio of loungers to bathers. Generally, no more than one-third of people attending a public pool are in the water at one time. Consequently the 6 to 8 ft walks formerly surrounding pools and used for lounging have been enlarged so that lounging area now approximates pool size.
3. For capacity formula see "Public Swimming Pool Capacity" diagram on another page.

## RECOMMENDED DIMENSIONS

| RELATED DIVING EQUIPMENT | | MINIMUM DIMENSIONS | | | | | | | | MINIMUM WIDTH OF POOL AT: | | |
|---|---|---|---|---|---|---|---|---|---|---|---|---|
| MAX. BOARD LENGTH | MAX. HEIGHT OVER WATER | $D_1$ | $D_2$ | R | $L_1$ | $L_2$ | $L_3$ | $L_4$ | $L_5$ | PT. A | PT. B | PT. C |
| 10' | 2/3 m 26'' | 2.13 m 7'-0'' | 2.59 m 8'-6'' | 1.68 m 5'-6'' | 0.76 m 2'-6'' | 2.44 m 8'-0'' | 3.20 m 10'-6'' | 2.13 m 7'-0'' | 8.53 m 28'-0'' | 4.88 m 16'-0'' | 5.49 m 18'-0'' | 5.49 m 18'-0'' |
| 12' | 3/4 m 30'' | 2.29 m 7'-6'' | 2.74 m 9'-0'' | 1.83 m 6'-0'' | 0.91 m 3'-0'' | 2.74 m 9'-0'' | 3.66 m 12'-0'' | 1.22 m 4'-0'' | 8.53 m 28'-0'' | 5.49 m 18'-0'' | 6.10 m 20'-0'' | 6.10 m 20'-0'' |
| 16' | 1 m | 2.59 m 8'-6'' | 3.05 m 10'-0'' | 2.13 m 7'-0'' | 1.22 m 4'-0'' | 3.05 m 10'-0'' | 4.57 m 15'-0'' | 0.61 m 2'-0'' | 9.45 m 31'-0'' | 6.10 m 20'-0'' | 6.71 m 22'-0'' | 6.71 m 22'-0'' |
| 16' | 3 m | 3.35 m 11'-0'' | 3.66 m 12'-0'' | 2.59 m 8'-6'' | 1.83 m 6'-0'' | 3.20 m 10'-6'' | 6.40 m 21'-0'' | 0 | 11.43 m 37'-6'' | 6.70 m 22'-0'' | 7.32 m 24'-0'' | 7.32 m 24'-0'' |

Data source: National SPA and Swimming Pool Institute.

$L_2$, $L_3$, and $L_4$ combined represent the minimum distance from the tip of board to pool wall opposite diving equipment.

For board heights exceeding 3 m or for platform diving facilities; comply with dimensional requirements of FINA, USS, NCAA, N.F., etc.

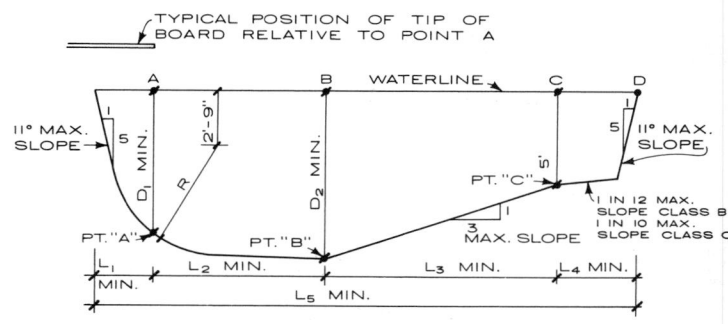

NOTE: Placement of boards shall observe the following minimum dimensions. With multiple board installations minimum pool widths must be increased accordingly.

| | |
|---|---|
| 1 m or deck level board to pool side | 9' (2.74 m) |
| 3 m board to pool side | 11' (3.35 m) |
| 1 m or deck level board to 3 m board | 10' (3.05 m) |
| 1 m or deck level to another 1 m or deck level board | 8' (2.44 m) |
| 3 m to another 3 m board | 10' (3.05 m) |

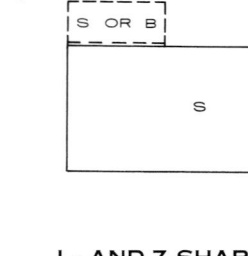

### T-SHAPED POOL

Provides large shallow area(s). Diving area off to one side. Water in large part of pool from 3 ft 6 in. to 5 ft deep, adequate for regular competitive events.

### L- AND Z-SHAPED POOL

These two shapes generally desired for large 50 m pools.

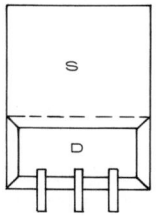

### RECTANGULAR POOL

Standard design. Good for competitive swimming and indoor pool design. Shallow area often inadequate.

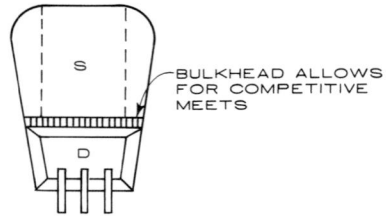

### FAN SHAPED POOL

Successful where there is a high percentage of children. Largest area for shallow depth. Deep area can be roped off or separated by bulkhead.

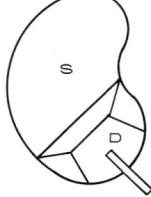

### FREE FORM POOL

Kidney and oval shapes are the most common free forms. Use only where competitive meets are not a consideration.

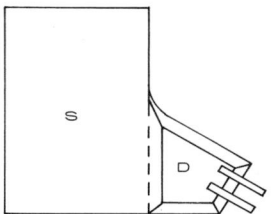

### MODIFIED L POOL

Provides for separate diving area. Shallow area with 4 ft min. depth may be roped off for competitive meets.

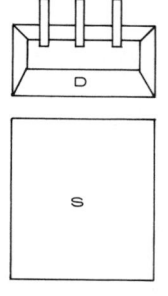
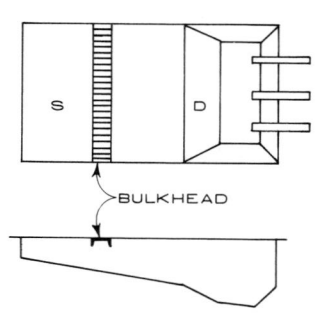

### MULTIPLE POOLS

Separate pools for beginners, divers, and swimmers. Ultimate in desirability especially if pool is intended for large numbers of people. Variation at left shows single pool and bulkhead over it with advantage that swimmers are kept out of area reserved for beginners. Both designs may use common filtration system.

### WADING POOLS

Generally provided in connection with community and family club pools. Placed away from swimming area to avoid congestion. If near swimming pool, wading area should be fenced off for children's protection. To add play appeal provide spray fittings and small fountains in pool. Also provide seats and benches for adults who accompany children to pool.

## PUBLIC POOL SHAPES

NOTE: S = swimming pool, D = diving pool, B = beginners' pool.

R. Jackson Smith, AIA; Designed Environments, Inc.; Stamford, Connecticut
National Swimming Pool Institute; Washington, D.C.

## AQUATICS

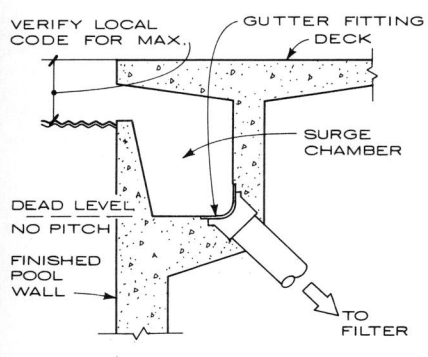

**FULLY RECESSED OVERFLOW GUTTER**

**RIMFLOW SYSTEM**

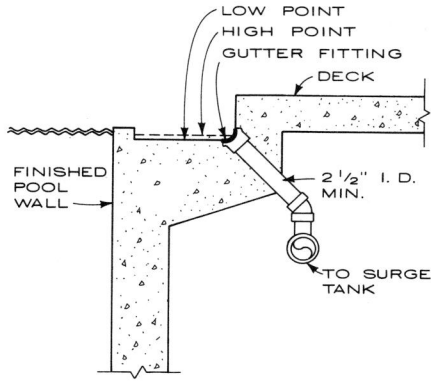

**ROLL-OUT OVERFLOW GUTTER**

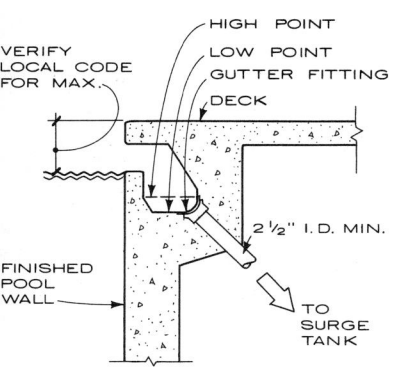

**FULLY RECESSED GUTTER**

**STAINLESS STEEL RECESSED SKIMMER**

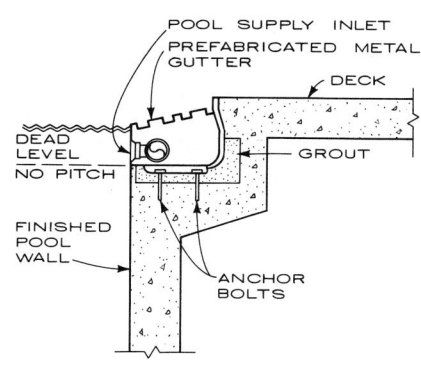

**PREFABRICATED OVERFLOW GUTTER**

## PERIMETER OVERFLOW SYSTEMS

**NOTES**

1. A perimeter overflow system must be provided on all public swimming pools. It must be designed and constructed so that the water level of the pool is maintained at the operating level of the overflow rim or weir device. Dimension from the deck to the water level is determined by applicable codes.
2. Perimeter type overflow systems, when used as the only overflow system on the pool, must extend around a minimum 50% of the swimming pool perimeter. Perimeter overflow systems must be connected to the circulation system with a system surge capacity of not less than 1 gal/sq ft of pool surface.
3. The perimeter overflow system in combination with the upper rim of the pool must constitute a handhold. It must be designed to prevent the entrapment of swimmer's arms, legs, or feet and to permit inspection and cleaning.
4. The hydraulic capacity of the overflow system must be sufficient to handle 100% of the circulation flow.
5. When roll-out or flush deck type of perimeter overflows are used on competitive pools, the ends of the pool must be provided with a visual barrier that can be seen by swimmers.
6. Perimeter overflows are commonly used on public swimming pools. Some state health departments do not approve skimmers on public swimming pools that exceed a certain surface area. Current state codes or swimming pool regulations must be checked to determine limits of use, minimum dimensions, and other factors dealing with overflow design.
7. Metal swimming pool systems are available that have a built-in perimeter overflow. In addition to the overflow channel, the metal liner may also contain the return waterline from the filtration system. A metal liner that incorporates a cove between wall and floor is desirable to facilitate cleaning.
8. Deck areas adjoining the overflow system are generally required to slope away from it to separate drains. When deck is sloped to pool overflow, provide for diverting pool overflow to waste during deck cleaning.

National Swimming Pool Institute; Washington, D.C.

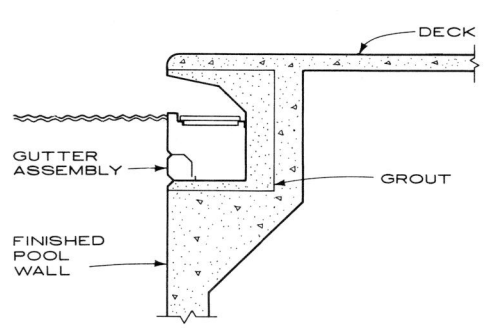

**PLAN**    **SECTION**
**FLAT TYPE GUTTER FITTINGS**

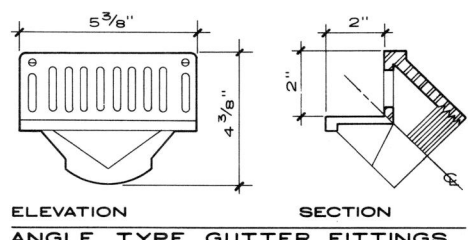

**ELEVATION**    **SECTION**
**ANGLE TYPE GUTTER FITTINGS**

9. Perimeter type overflows may be custom built to conform to the design selected. Ceramic tile is the preferred material for the top 6 in. of the pool wall, the pool rim, the gutter, and the deck for indoor swimming pools. Gratings for deep overflow gutters may be of precast concrete, plastic, or metal.
10. Proprietary overflow systems are available that have the characteristics of many of the perimeter overflow types shown. Stainless steel is commonly used because of its corrosion resistance. Aluminum overflow systems have a coating or enamel finish. Slotted precast concrete units are also available.
11. Surfaces subject to traffic must be nonslip.

## SURFACE SKIMMERS

When surface skimmers are used, one must be provided for each 500 sq ft, or fraction thereof, of the pool surface. When two or more skimmers are used, they must be located so as to maintain effective skimming action over the entire surface of the swimming pool. Skimmers may not be permitted on larger pools. See local health department codes for limitation on public pools. Skimmers are not recommended for competitive pools.

Surface skimmers are available from many swimming pool suppliers. Metal or plastic units are available in various capacities. An access cover in the deck permits removal and cleaning of the strainer. Surface skimmers should comply with the joint National Swimming Pool Institute—National Sanitation Foundation performance standards.

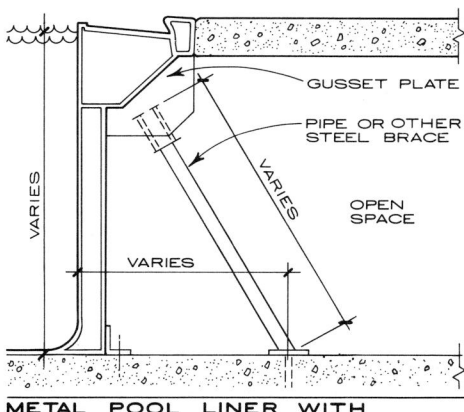

**METAL POOL LINER WITH OVERFLOW**

Often used in rooftop or other above grade installations where weight is a primary factor in design.

## LENGTH OF POOLS

25 yards is the minimum length for American records, and meets interscholastic and intercollegiate requirements. (Pool should be 75 ft-1½ in. long to allow for electronic timing panels at one end.)

Standards for international competition are shown on 50 meter pool page.

## WIDTH OF POOLS

Drawing below shows 7 ft lanes with pool width of 45 ft (6 lanes). Strictly competitive pools should have 8 ft lanes, with pool width of 83 ft (10 lanes). Minimum widths include additional 18 in. width outside lanes on both sides of pool.

## NOTES

Gutters at sides of pool are desirable to reduce wave action in swimming meets or water polo. See lighting standards and diving board standards on other pages of this series for additional requirements for competitive pools.

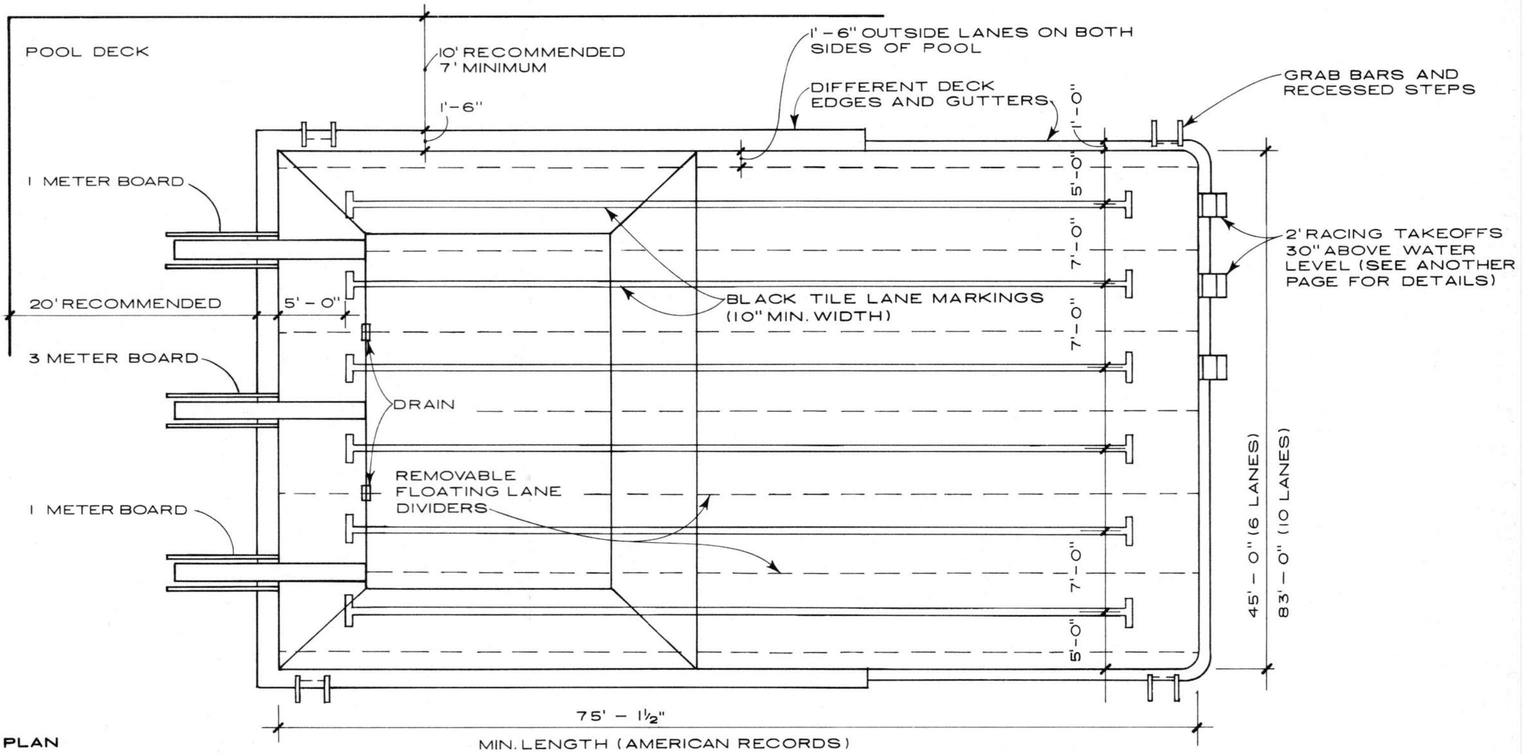

POOL DECK

10' RECOMMENDED
7' MINIMUM

1'-6"

1'-6" OUTSIDE LANES ON BOTH SIDES OF POOL

DIFFERENT DECK EDGES AND GUTTERS

GRAB BARS AND RECESSED STEPS

1 METER BOARD

20' RECOMMENDED

5'-0"

3 METER BOARD

DRAIN

1 METER BOARD

REMOVABLE FLOATING LANE DIVIDERS

BLACK TILE LANE MARKINGS (10" MIN. WIDTH)

2' RACING TAKEOFFS 30" ABOVE WATER LEVEL (SEE ANOTHER PAGE FOR DETAILS)

45'-0" (6 LANES)
83'-0" (10 LANES)

75'-1½"
MIN. LENGTH (AMERICAN RECORDS)

**PLAN**

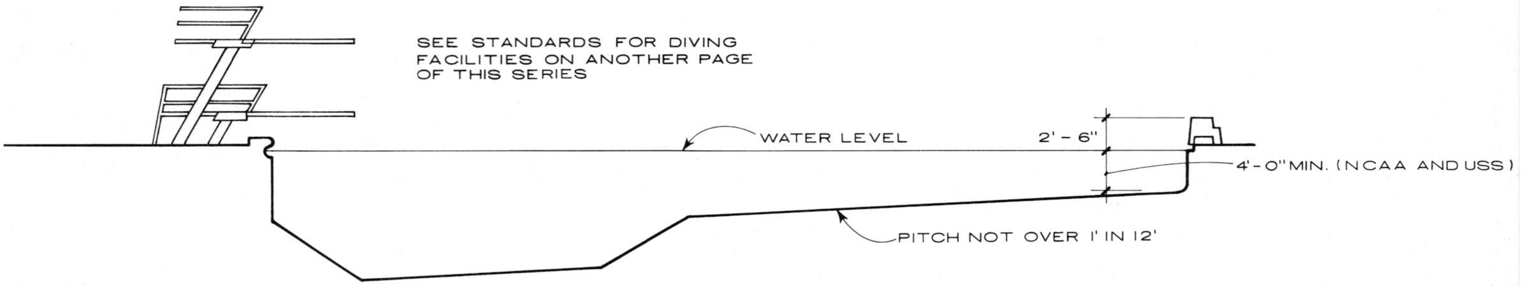

SEE STANDARDS FOR DIVING FACILITIES ON ANOTHER PAGE OF THIS SERIES

WATER LEVEL

2'-6"

4'-0" MIN. (NCAA AND USS)

PITCH NOT OVER 1' IN 12'

**LONGITUDINAL SECTION**
**25 YARD POOL**

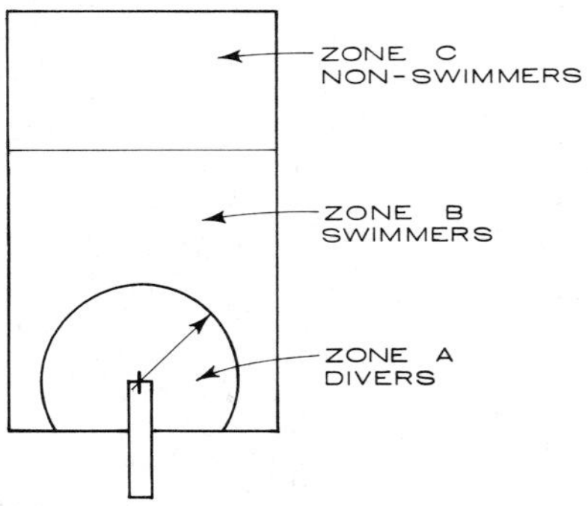

ZONE C
NON-SWIMMERS

ZONE B
SWIMMERS

ZONE A
DIVERS

Swimming pool capacity requirements vary from one locality to another: check local regulations. The following is suggested by the American Public Health Association.

| | | |
|---|---|---|
| **FORMULA DERIVATION:** | **ZONE A** | Diving area defined by 10 ft radius from diving board or platform.<br>12 divers per board; 2–3 in water, the rest on shore.<br>Or allow 300 sq ft of pool water surface per board. |
| | **ZONE B** | Swimming area; 24 sq ft per swimmer. Based on volume displaced by each swimmer (⅘ square of average ht) and adjusted by the number of swimmers using pool at one time (⅔ total swimmers). |
| | **ZONE C** | Nonswimmer area. 10 sq ft per person. Based on volume displaced by person (½ area allowed per swimmer) and adjusted by number not using water—50% (in some pools with large number of nonswimmers, figure may be as high as 75%). |

**FORMULA:**

$$\text{Max. pool capacity} = 12 \times \frac{\text{No. diving boards}}{\text{or platforms}} + \frac{\text{Area Zone B}}{24} + \frac{\text{Area Zone C}}{10}$$

**PUBLIC SWIMMING POOL CAPACITY**

R. Jackson Smith, AIA; Designed Environments, Inc.; Stamford, Connecticut

**AQUATICS**

**GENERAL NOTES**

For judging competitive meets, FINA officials recommend the springboard and diving platform arrangement indicated below in plan. Diving dimensions meet minimum FINA standards. Fifty meters is minimum length for world records.

**NOTE**

*Length should be 50.03 m allowing an extra .03 m to compensate for possible future tile facing, structural defects and electrical timing panels.

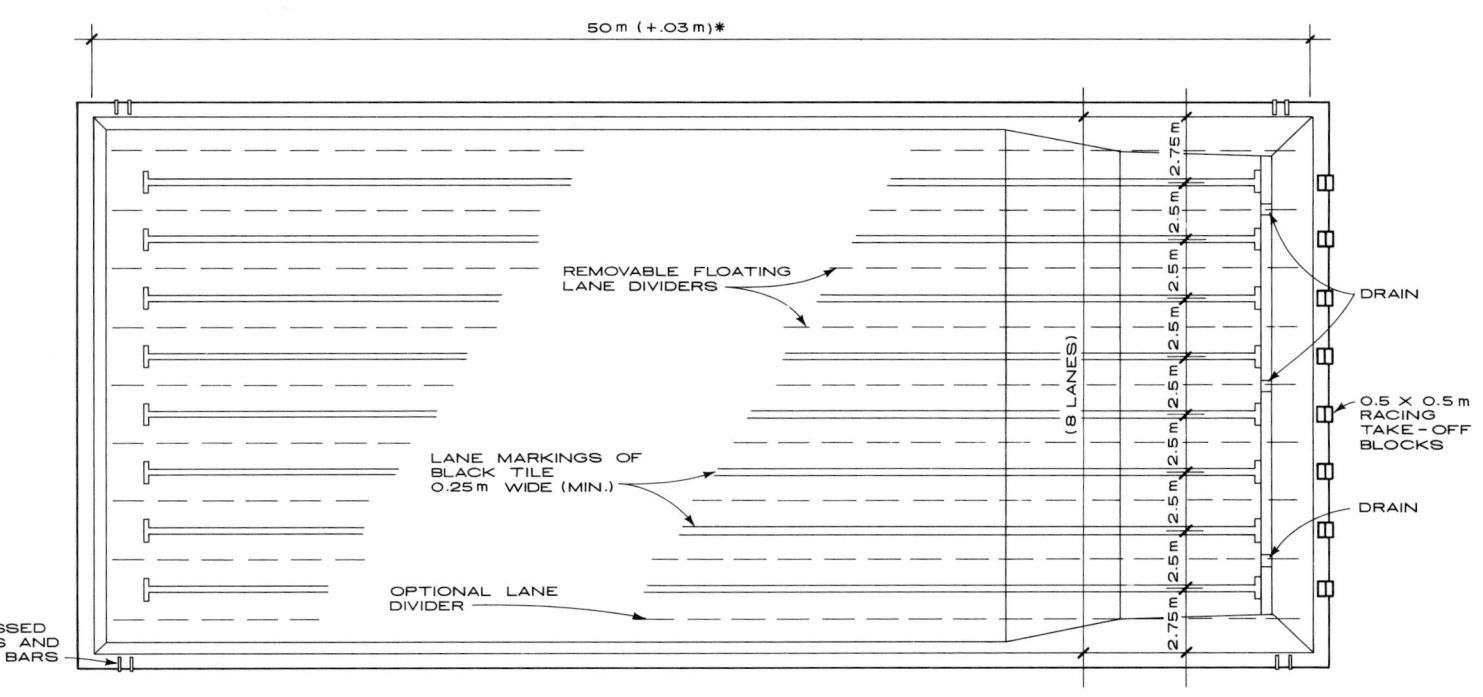

**PLAN**

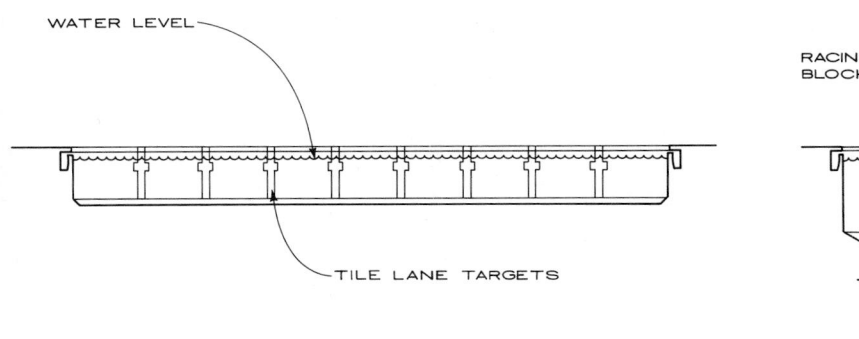

**CROSS SECTION**

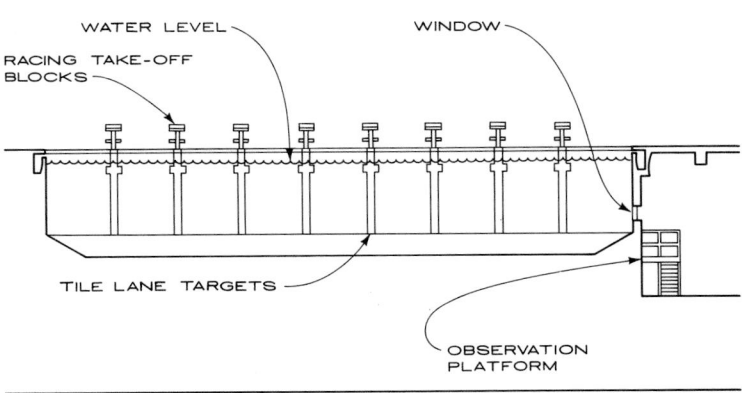

**CROSS SECTION**

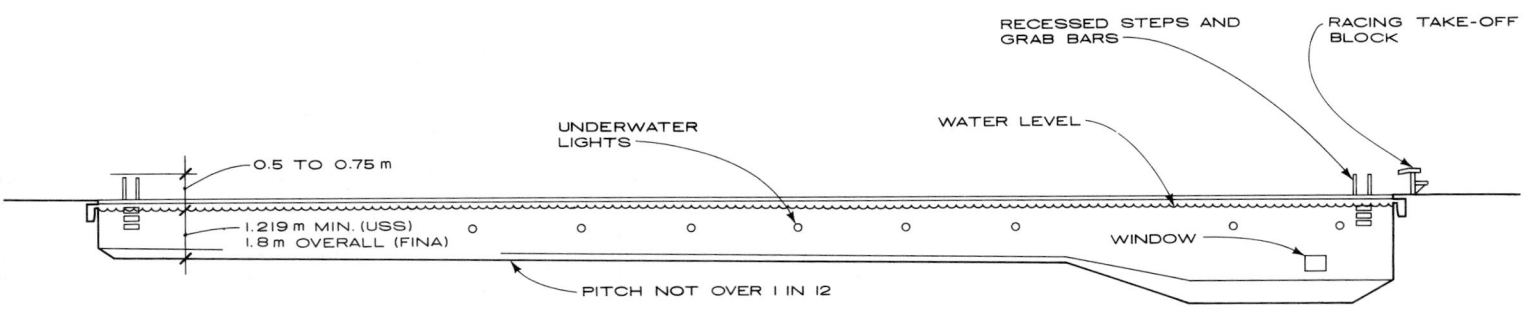

**LONGITUDINAL SECTION**

Flewelling & Moody; Los Angeles, California
Richard J. Vitullo; Washington Grove, Maryland

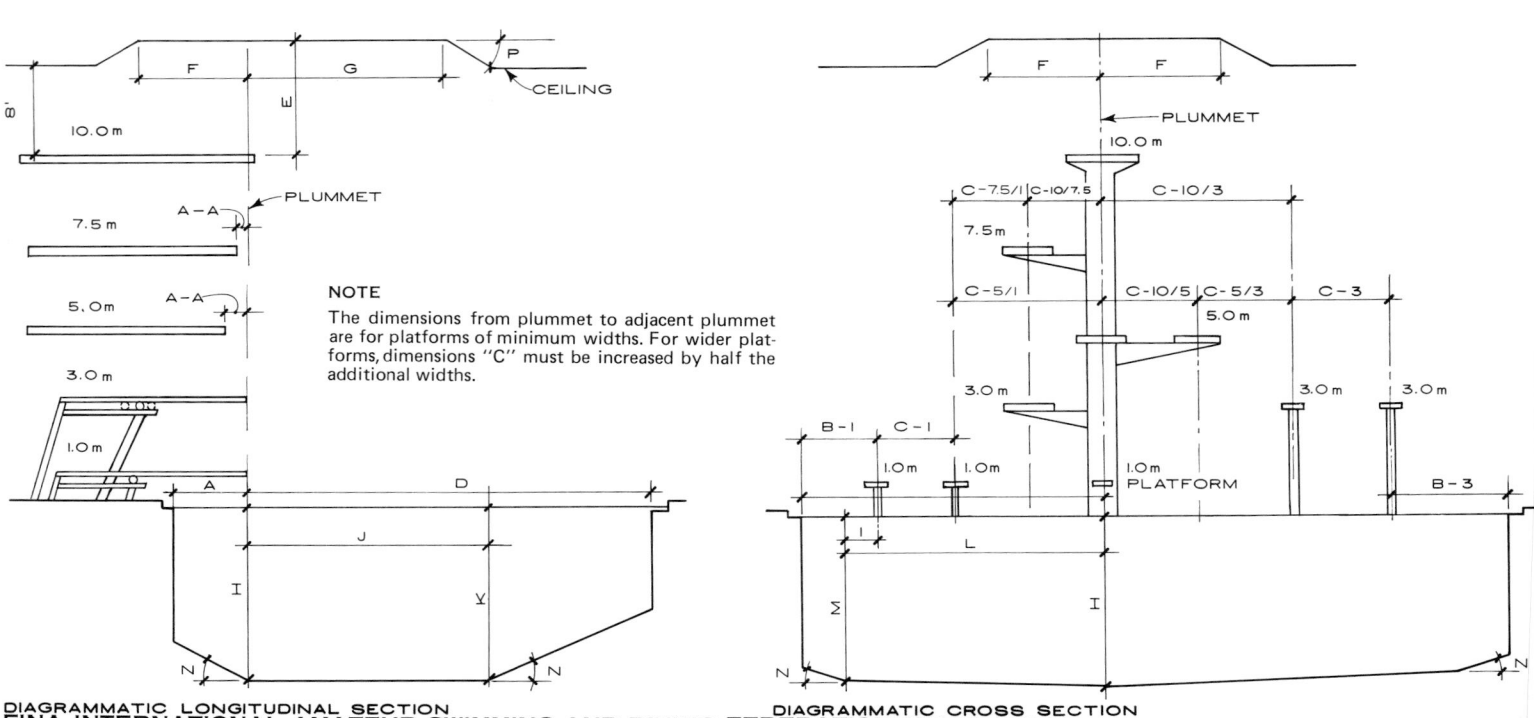

**NOTE**

The dimensions from plummet to adjacent plummet are for platforms of minimum widths. For wider platforms, dimensions "C" must be increased by half the additional widths.

DIAGRAMMATIC LONGITUDINAL SECTION    DIAGRAMMATIC CROSS SECTION

## FINA INTERNATIONAL AMATEUR SWIMMING AND DIVING FEDERATION STANDARDS

| DIMENSIONS FOR DIVING FACILITIES | | | SPRINGBOARDS | | | | PLATFORMS | | | | | | | |
|---|---|---|---|---|---|---|---|---|---|---|---|---|---|---|
| | | | 1 METER | 3 METER | 1 METER | 3 METER | 5 METER | | 7.5 METER | | 10 METER | | | |
| | | LENGTH | 5.0 | 5.0 | 4.5 | 5.0 | 6.0 | | 6.0 | | 6.0 | | | |
| | | WIDTH | 0.5 | 0.5 | 0.6 | 0.8 | 1.5 | | 1.5 | | 2.0 | | | |
| | | HEIGHT | 1.0 | 3.0 | 1.0 | 0.8 | 5.0 | | 7.5 | | 10.0 | | | |
| A | FROM PLUMMET: BACK TO POOL WALL | DESIG. | A-1 | A-3 | A-1 (PL) | A-3 (PL) | A-5 | | A-7.5 | | A-10 | | | |
| | | MIN. | 1.50 | 1.50 | 0.75 | 1.25 | 1.25 | | 1.50 | | 1.50 | | | |
| | | PREF. | 1.80 | 1.80 | | | 1.50 | | | | | | | |
| A-A | FROM PLUMMET: BACK TO PLATFORM DIRECTLY BELOW | DESIG. | | | | | AA-5/1 | | A-7.5/3 | | AA-10/5 | | | |
| | | MIN. | | | | | 0.75 | | 0.75 | | 0.75 | | | |
| | | PREF. | | | | | | | 1.50 | | 1.50 | | | |
| B | FROM PLUMMET: TO POOL WALL AT SIDE | DESIG. | B-1 | B-3 | B-1 (PL) | B-3 (PL) | B-5 | | B-7.5 | | B-10 | | | |
| | | MIN. | 2.50 | 3.50 | 2.30 | 2.90 | 4.25 | | 4.50 | | 5.25 | | | |
| | | PREF. | 3.00 | | | | | | | | | | | |
| C | FROM PLUMMET TO ADJACENT PLUMMET | DESIG. | C-1 | C-3 | C-3/1 | C-1/1 (PL) | C-3/1 (PL) | C-5/3 (PL) | C-5/1 | C-7.5/3/1 | C-10/7.5 | C-10/7.5/3 | C-10/3/1 |
| | | MIN. | 2.40 | 2.60 | 2.60 | 1.65 | 2.10 | 2.10 | 2.10 | 2.10 | 2.50 | 2.75 | 2.75 |
| | | PREF. | 2.40 | 2.40 | 1.4/3.0 | | | | | | | | |
| D | FROM PLUMMET TO POOL WALL AHEAD | DESIG. | D-1 | D-3 | D-1 (PL) | D-3 (PL) | D-5 | | D-7.5 | | D-10 | | | |
| | | MIN. | 9.00 | 10.25 | 8.00 | 9.50 | 10.25 | | 11.00 | | 13.50 | | | |
| | | PREF. | | | | | | | | | | | | |
| E | PLUMMET, FROM BOARD TO CEILING OVERHEAD | DESIG. | | E-1 | E-3 | E-1 (PL) | E-3 (PL) | | E-5 | | E-7.5 | | E-10 | |
| | | MIN. | | 5.00 | 5.00 | 3.00 | 3.00 | | 3.00 | | 3.20 | | 3.40 | |
| | | PREF. | | | | | | | 3.40 | | 3.40 | | 5 00 | |
| F | CLEAR OVERHEAD, BEHIND AND EACH SIDE OF PLUMMET | DESIG. | F-1 | E-1 | F-3 | E-3 | F-1 (PL) | F-3 (PL) | F-5 | E-5 | F-7.5 | E-7.5 | F-10 | E-10 |
| | | MIN. | 2.50 | 5.00 | 2.50 | 5.00 | 2.75 | 2.75 | 2.75 | 3.00 | 2.75 | 3.20 | 2.75 | 3.40 |
| | | PREF. | | | | | | | 3.40 | | 3.40 | | 5.00 | |
| G | CLEAR OVERHEAD, AHEAD OF PLUMMET | DESIG. | G-1 | E-1 | G-3 | E-3 | G-1 (PL) | G-3 (PL) | G-5 | E-5 | G-7.5 | E-7.5 | G-10 | E-10 |
| | | MIN. | 5.00 | 5.00 | 5.00 | 5.00 | 5.00 | 5.00 | 5.00 | 3.00 | 5.00 | 3.20 | 6.00 | 3.40 |
| | | PREF. | | | | | | | 3.40 | | 3.40 | | 5.00 | |
| H | DEPTH OF WATER AT PLUMMET | DESIG. | | H-1 | | H-3 | H-1 (PL) | H-3 (PL) | | H-5 | | H-7.5 | | H-10 |
| | | MIN. | | 3.40 | | 3.80 | 3.40 | 3.60 | 3.40 | 3.80 | | 4.10 | | 4.50 |
| | | PREF. | | 3.80 | | 4.00 | | 3.80 | | 4.00 | | 4.50 | | 5.00 |
| J-K | DISTANCE, DEPTH OF WATER, AHEAD OF PLUMMET | DESIG. | J-1 | K-1 | J-3 | K-3 | J/K-1 (PL) | J/K-3 (PL) | J-5 | K-5 | J-7.5 | K-7.5 | J-10 | K-10 |
| | | MIN. | 5.00 | 3.30 | 6.00 | 3.70 | 5.0/3.3 | 6.0/3.3 | 6.00 | 3.70 | 8.00 | 4.00 | 11.00 | 4.25 |
| | | PREF. | | 3.70 | | 3.90 | | 3.70 | | 3.90 | | 4.40 | | 4.75 |
| L-M | DISTANCE, DEPTH OF WATER, EACH SIDE OF PLUMMET | DESIG. | L-1 | M-1 | L-3 | M-3 | L/M-1 (PL) | L/M-3 (PL) | L-5 | M-5 | L-7.5 | M-7.5 | L-10 | M-10 |
| | | MIN. | 2.50 | 3.30 | 3.25 | 3.70 | 2.05/3.3 | 2.65/3.5 | 4.25 | 3.70 | 4.50 | 4.00 | 5.25 | 4.25 |
| | | PREF. | | 3.70 | | 3.90 | | | | 3.90 | | 4.40 | | 4.75 |
| N P | MAXIMUM ANGLE OF SLOPE TO REDUCE DIMENSIONS BEYOND FULL REQUIREMENTS | POOL BOTTOM | = 30 Degrees (Approximately 1 ft vertical to 2 ft horizontal) | | | | | | | | | | | |
| | | CEILING HEIGHT | = 30 Degrees | | | | | | | | | | | |

R. Jackson Smith, AIA; Designed Environments, Inc.; Stamford, Connecticut

**AQUATICS**

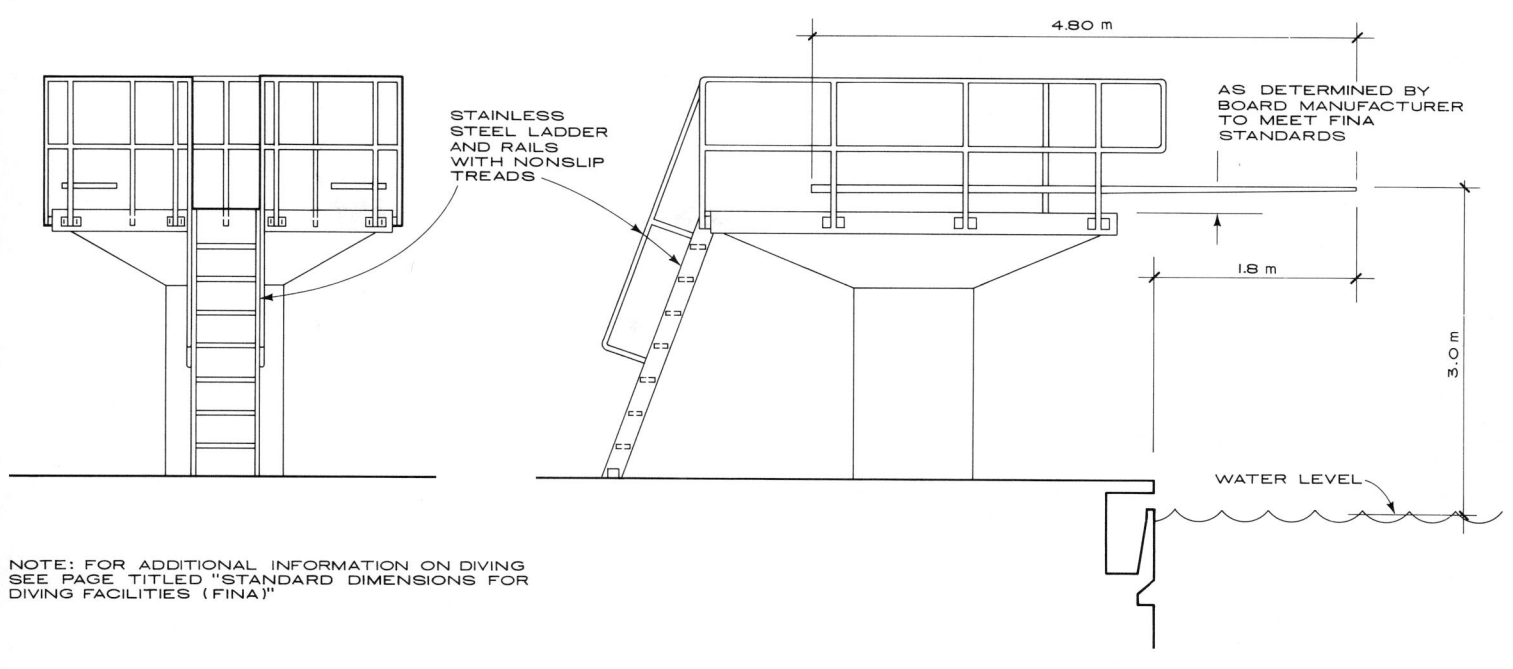

STAINLESS STEEL LADDER AND RAILS WITH NONSLIP TREADS

4.80 m

AS DETERMINED BY BOARD MANUFACTURER TO MEET FINA STANDARDS

1.8 m

3.0 m

WATER LEVEL

NOTE: FOR ADDITIONAL INFORMATION ON DIVING SEE PAGE TITLED "STANDARD DIMENSIONS FOR DIVING FACILITIES (FINA)"

REAR ELEVATION          SIDE ELEVATION

**3 METER DIVING BOARD**

## GENERAL NOTES

Both 1 m and 3 m boards are required for amateur, collegiate, and international meets. All boards shall have a nonslip surface. Consult FINA Handbook. FINA is the Fédération Internationale de Natation Amateur.

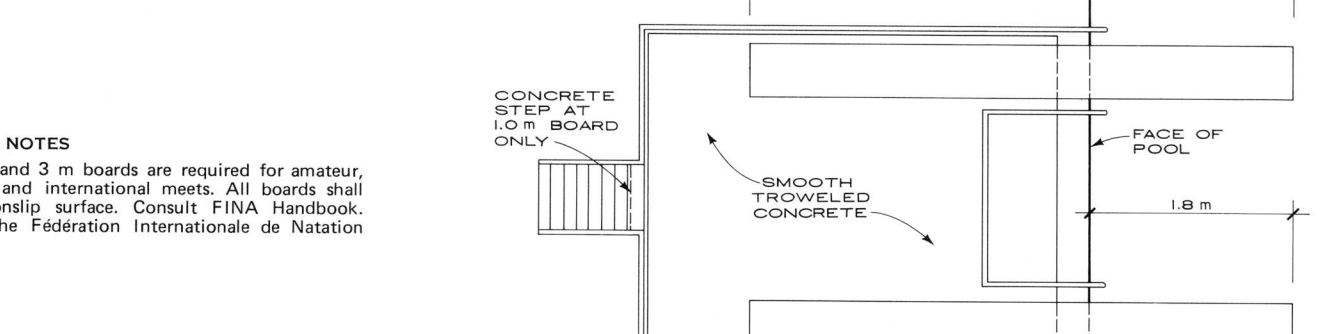

CONCRETE STEP AT 1.0 m BOARD ONLY

4.80 m

SMOOTH TROWELED CONCRETE

FACE OF POOL

1.8 m

STAINLESS STEEL RAIL

PLAN

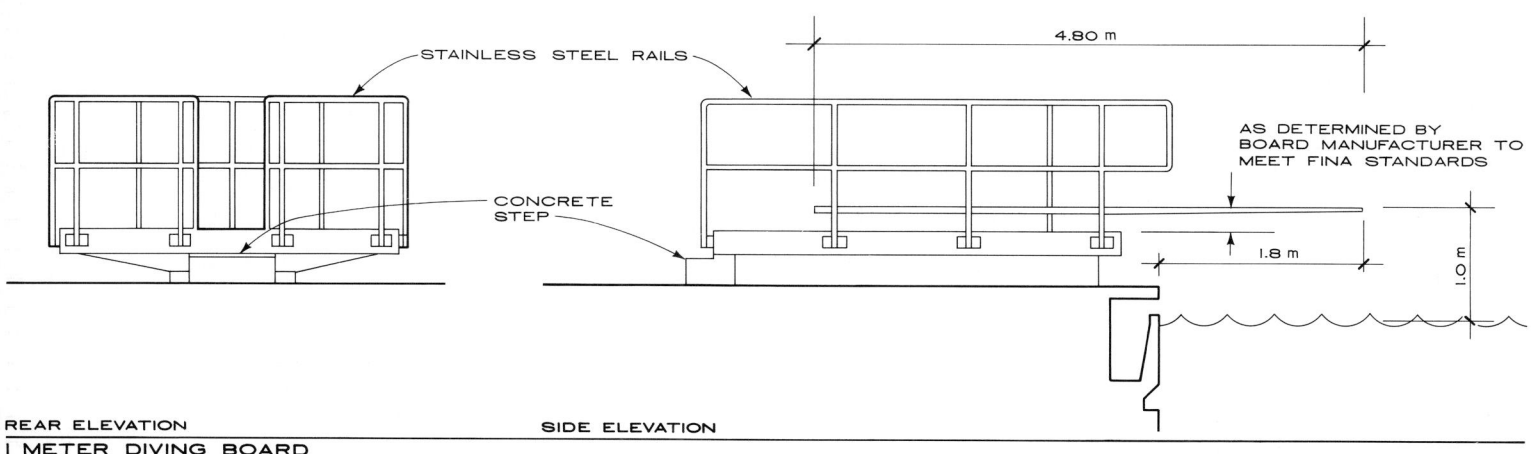

STAINLESS STEEL RAILS

4.80 m

AS DETERMINED BY BOARD MANUFACTURER TO MEET FINA STANDARDS

CONCRETE STEP

1.8 m

1.0 m

REAR ELEVATION          SIDE ELEVATION

**1 METER DIVING BOARD**

Flewelling & Moody; Los Angeles, California
Richard J. Vitullo; Washington Grove, Maryland

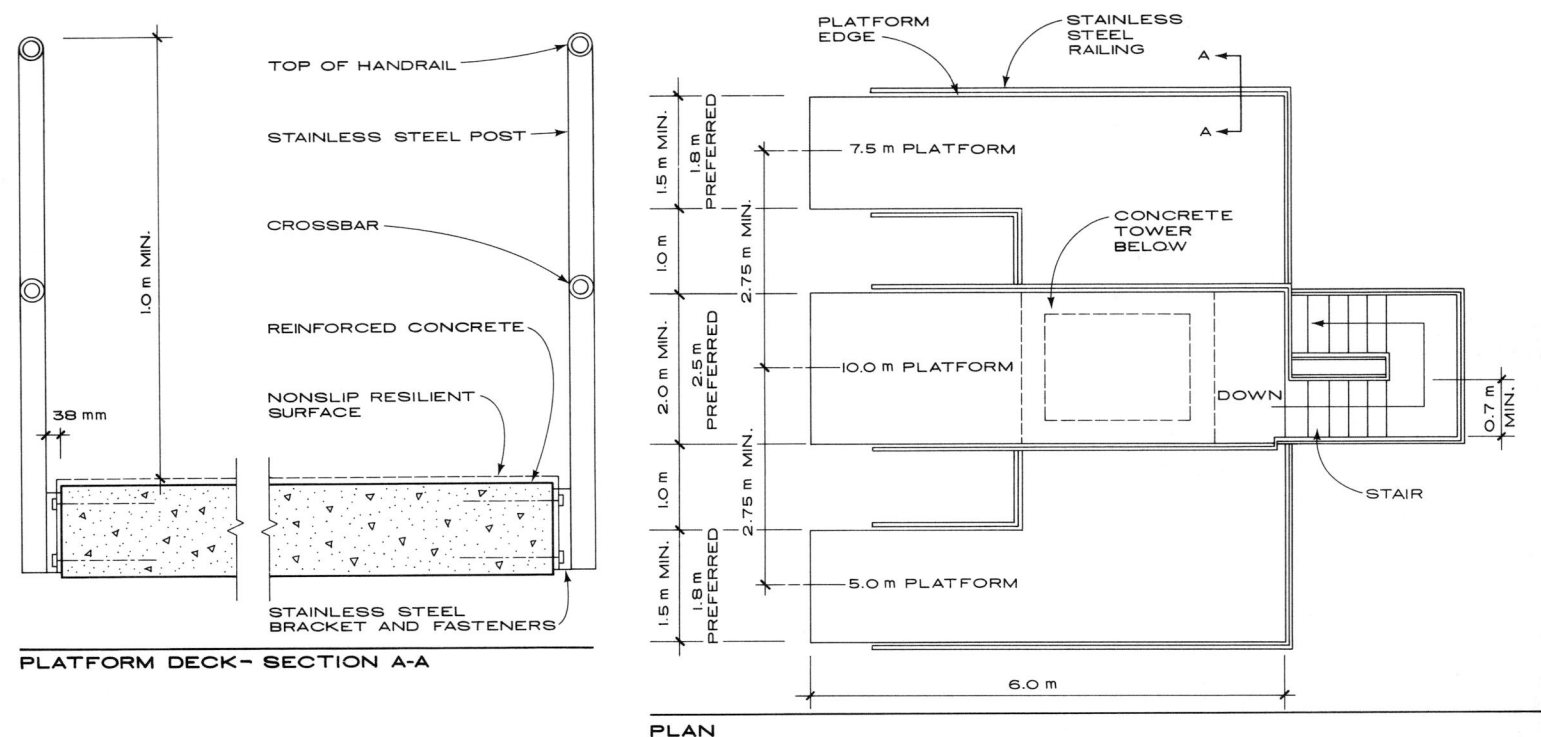

TOP OF HANDRAIL

STAINLESS STEEL POST

CROSSBAR

REINFORCED CONCRETE

NONSLIP RESILIENT SURFACE

1.0 m MIN.

38 mm

STAINLESS STEEL BRACKET AND FASTENERS

**PLATFORM DECK- SECTION A-A**

PLATFORM EDGE

STAINLESS STEEL RAILING

A

7.5 m PLATFORM

1.5 m MIN.
1.8 m PREFERRED

1.0 m
2.75 m MIN.

CONCRETE TOWER BELOW

10.0 m PLATFORM

2.0 m MIN.
2.5 m PREFERRED

DOWN

0.7 m MIN.

1.0 m
2.75 m MIN.

STAIR

5.0 m PLATFORM

1.5 m MIN.
1.8 m PREFERRED
2.75 m

6.0 m

**PLAN**

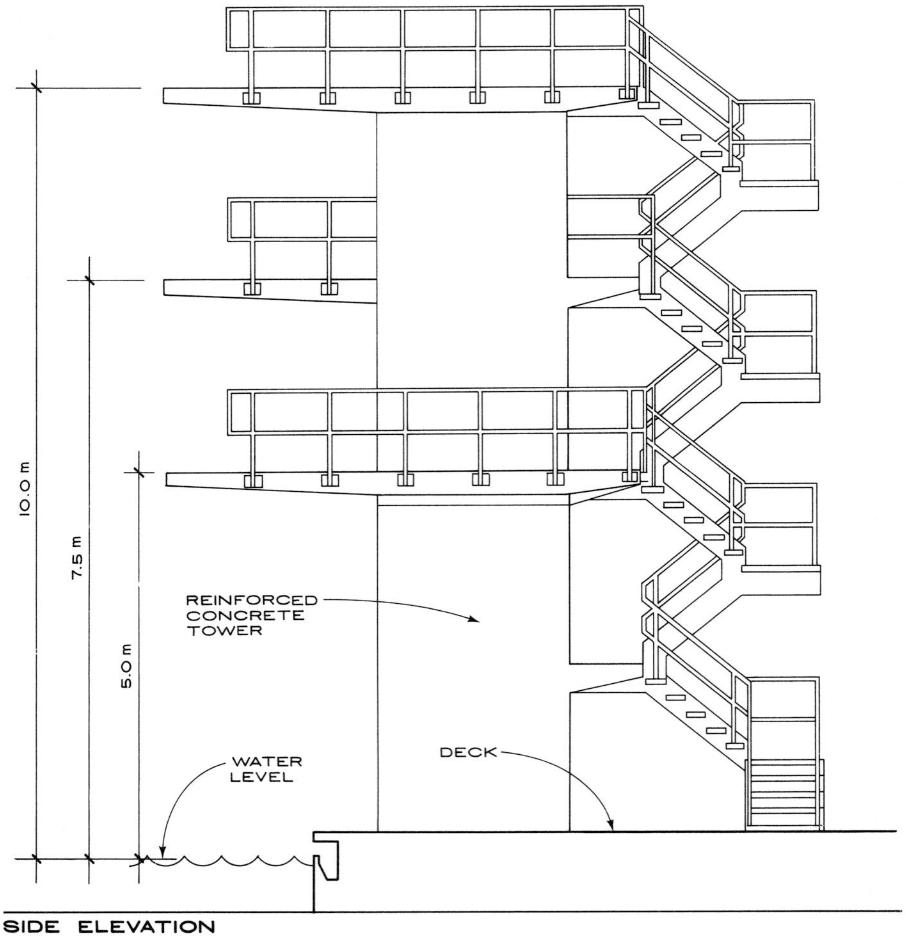

10.0 m

7.5 m

5.0 m

REINFORCED CONCRETE TOWER

WATER LEVEL

DECK

**SIDE ELEVATION**

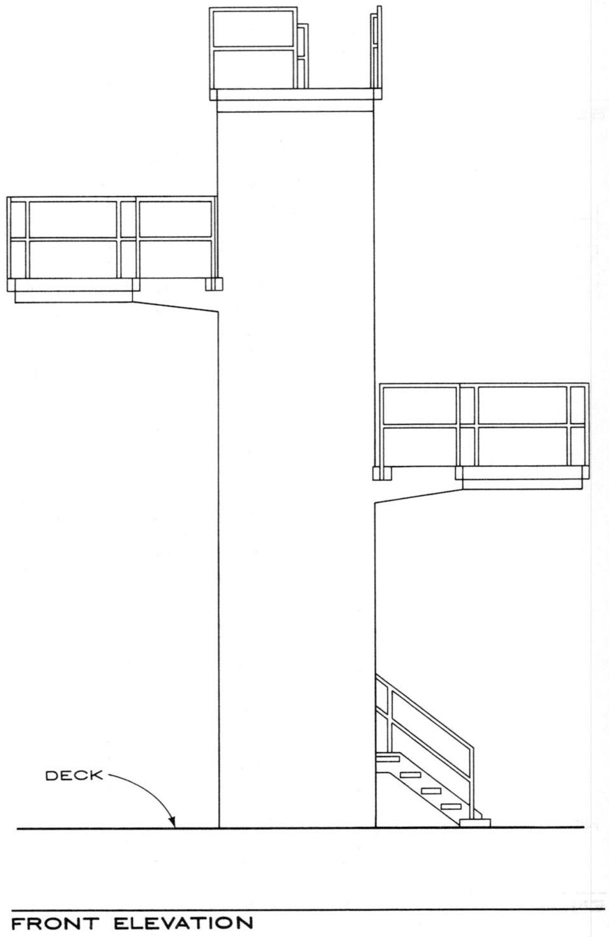

DECK

**FRONT ELEVATION**

Flewelling & Moody; Los Angeles, California
Richard J. Vitullo; Washington Grove, Maryland

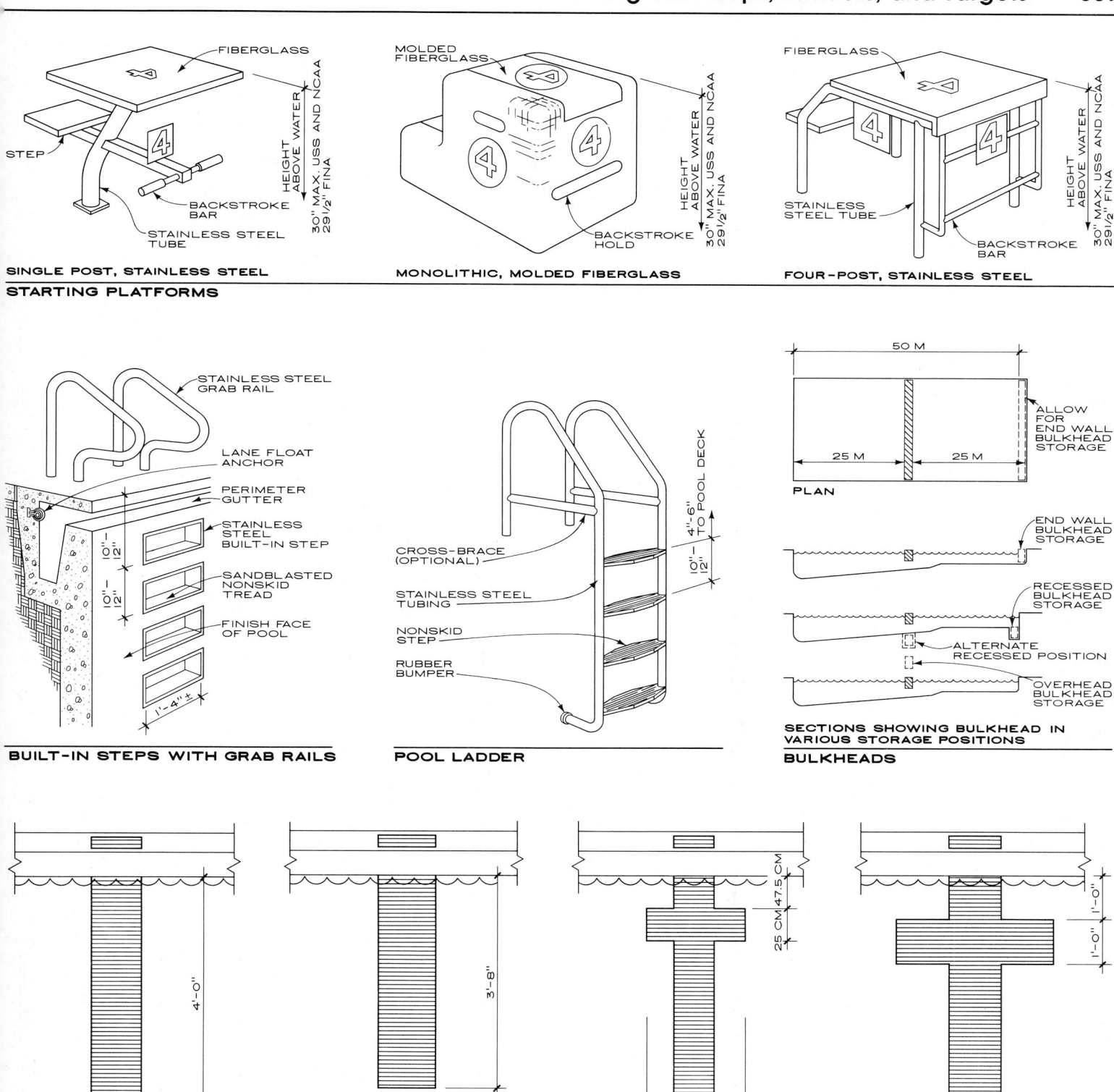

**SINGLE POST, STAINLESS STEEL**

**MONOLITHIC, MOLDED FIBERGLASS**

**FOUR-POST, STAINLESS STEEL**

**STARTING PLATFORMS**

**BUILT-IN STEPS WITH GRAB RAILS**

**POOL LADDER**

**SECTIONS SHOWING BULKHEAD IN VARIOUS STORAGE POSITIONS**

**BULKHEADS**

**USS**

**NFHS**

**FINA**

**NCAA**

NOTE: COLOR OF END WALL TARGETS SHOULD BE DARK AND CONTRASTING TO THE GENERAL COLOR OF THE POOL (BLACK PREFERABLE)

**END WALL TARGETS**

Richard J. Vitullo; Washington Grove, Maryland

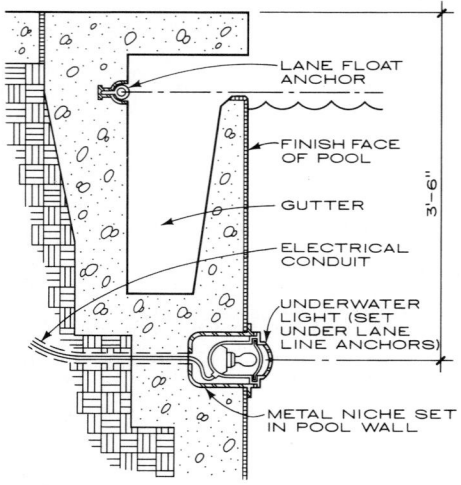

**SECTION**
**GUTTER DETAIL SHOWING UNDERWATER LIGHTING**

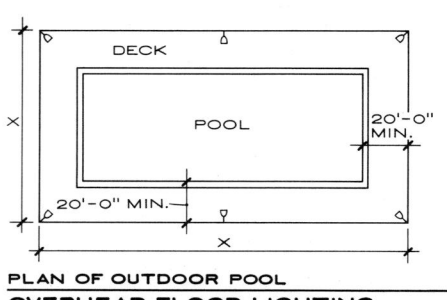

**PLAN OF OUTDOOR POOL**
**OVERHEAD FLOOD LIGHTING**

**NOTE**

Distance "x" for spacing of lights not to exceed four times the actual mounting height of lamp in light fixture. For outdoor above-water lighting, flood lights should be mounted at least 20 ft above the water. Select lamps to allow 1.0 W/sq ft minimum for flood lights. Consult USS or NCAA for specific requirements for championship meets. USS rules for championship meets require a minimum of 40 fc 3 ft above the water surface. For interior above-water lighting, concentration of 100 fc is recommended and should be directly over turning end and finish line. (This is a specific requirement for national championship meets.) A power source for additional lighting should be available for use with television, movies, and special events. Buildings housing indoor pools should not have deck-level windows in walls facing pool ends to prevent glare. Deck-level windows at side should be tinted.

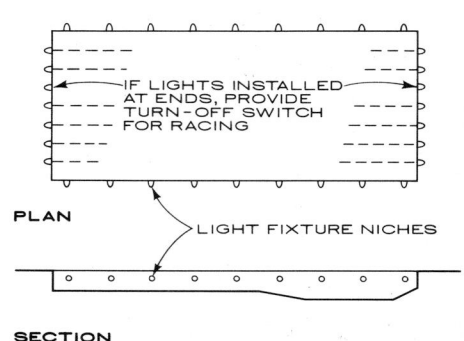

**PLAN**

**SECTION**
**UNDERWATER POOL LIGHTING**

**NOTES FOR WET AND DRY NICHE UNDERWATER LIGHTS**

Underwater lighting type and dimensions should be in accordance with NEC (article 680) regulations.

Underwater lights will require 0.5 to 2.0 W/sq ft of water area and should be sized accordingly.

Box connections for dry or wet niches should be a minimum of 4 ft 0 in. away from the side wall of the pool and 8 in. above the deck. Low voltage wiring should be used for all dry or wet niche lighting fixtures. This requires a transformer located, by code, a specific distance away from pool wall and above deck.

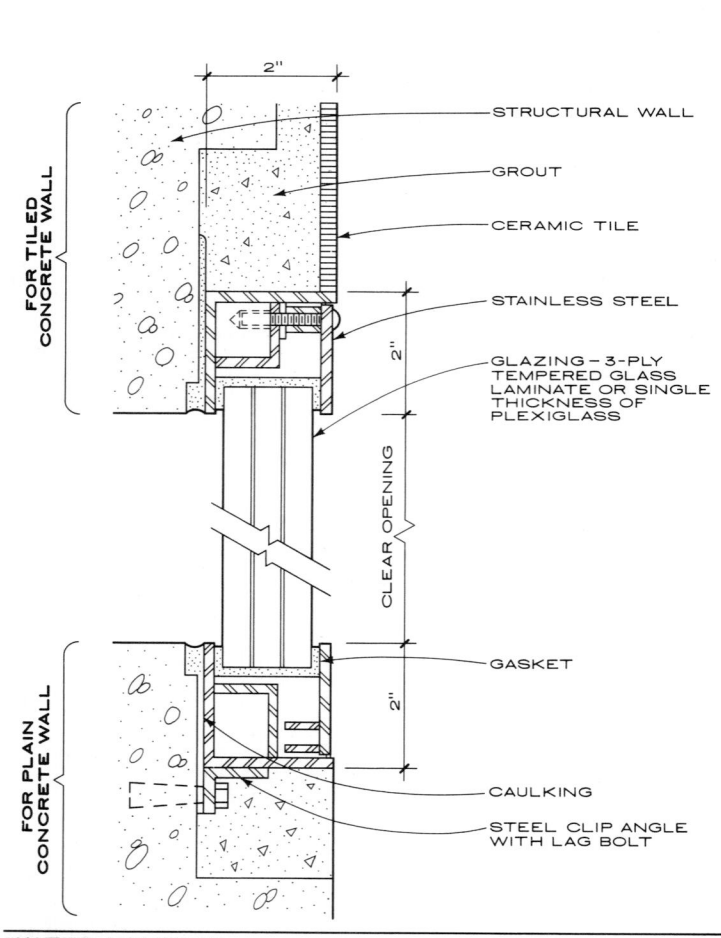

**WATER WINDOW**

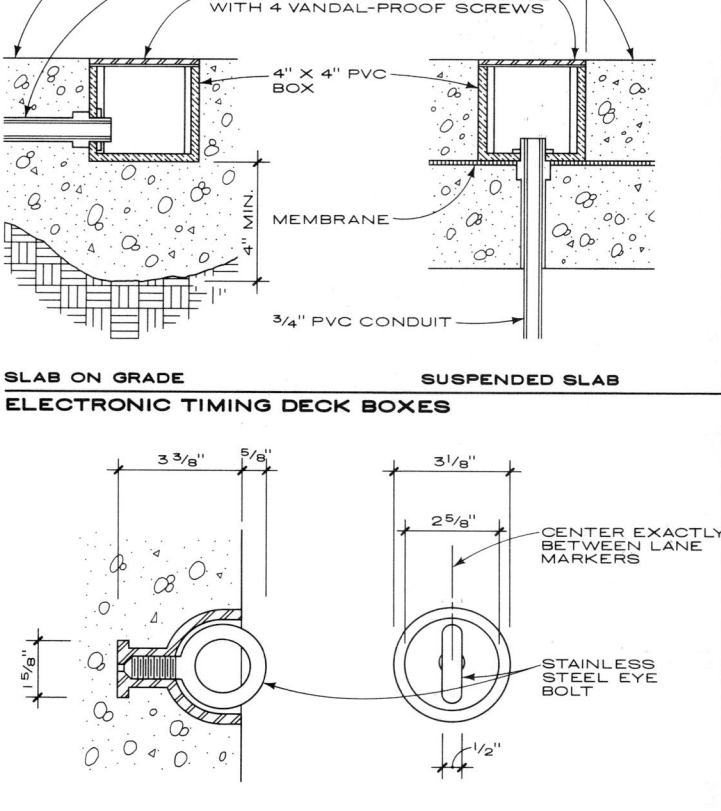

**SLAB ON GRADE**          **SUSPENDED SLAB**
**ELECTRONIC TIMING DECK BOXES**

**SECTION**          **ELEVATION**
**LANE FLOAT ANCHOR**

Flewelling & Moody; Los Angeles, California
Richard J. Vitullo; Washington Grove, Maryland

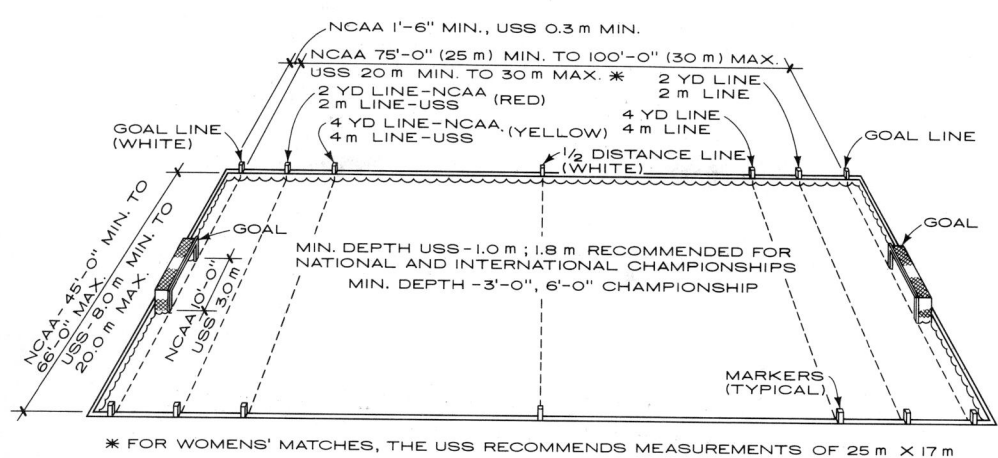

NOTES

Distinctive marks must be provided on both sides of field of play indicating goal lines, 2 and 4 yd (or meter) lines, and ½ distance between goal lines. These must be clearly visible from any position within the field of play. Allow sufficient space on walkways so referees may move freely from end to end of field of play. Provide space at goal lines for goal judges.

GOAL REQUIREMENTS

Posts and crossbar, rigid and perpendicular. USS, wood or metal, 3 in. sq, painted white; NCAA, metal 1½ in. diameter, painted yellow or orange. Nets to hang loosely on frame. For USS, the underside of the crossbar must be 0.90 m above water surface when water is 1.50 m or more in depth, and 2.40 m from the bottom of the bath when the depth of the water is less than 1.50 m.

Frames are custom made, with bracing placed where necessary. It is recommended that they be collapsible for easy storage. Anchorage methods depend on pool design, with those above commonly used, or brass couplings may be placed in pool walls to which frame is attached. If pool is longer than required length, one of the goals may be floated and anchored with guy wires.

✱ FOR WOMENS' MATCHES, THE USS RECOMMENDS MEASUREMENTS OF 25 m X 17 m

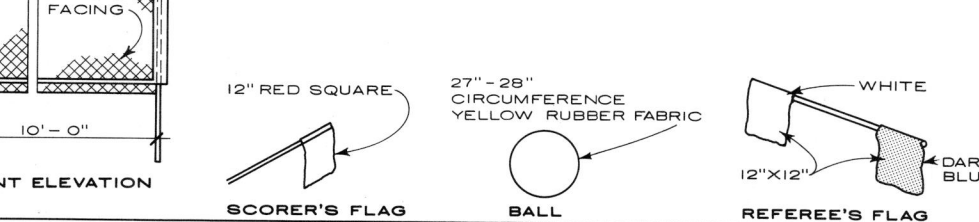

**WATER POLO**

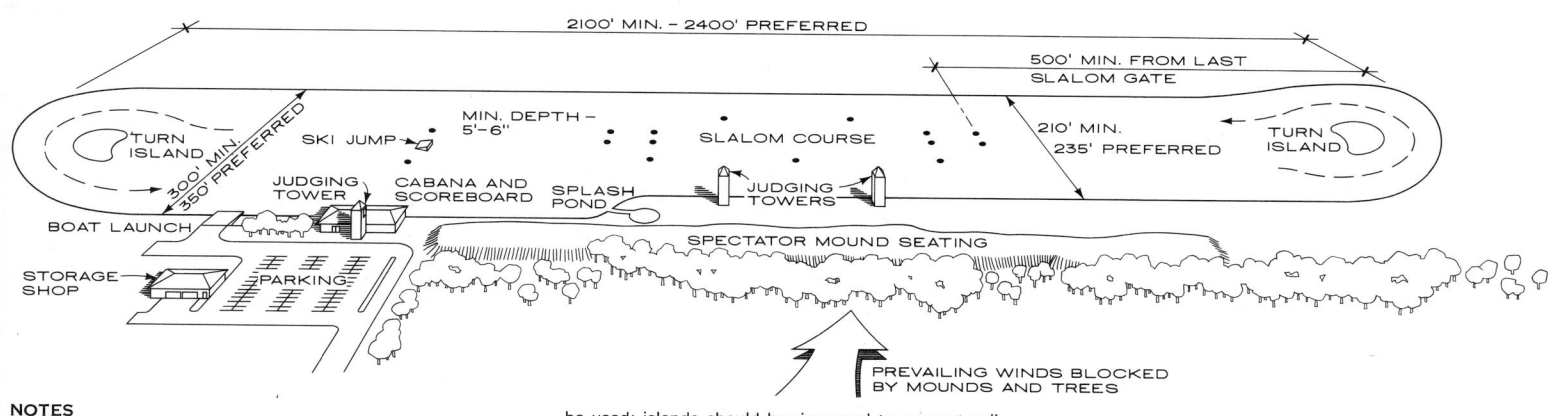

NOTES

1. To decrease turbidity caused by boat wake, an island running down the center of the lake may be built in addition to turn islands. Floating breakwaters may also be used; islands should be riprapped to prevent soil erosion.

2. A gradual (ratio 6:1) sandy slope along shorelines lets wave action die without rolling back.

**WATER SKI LAKE**

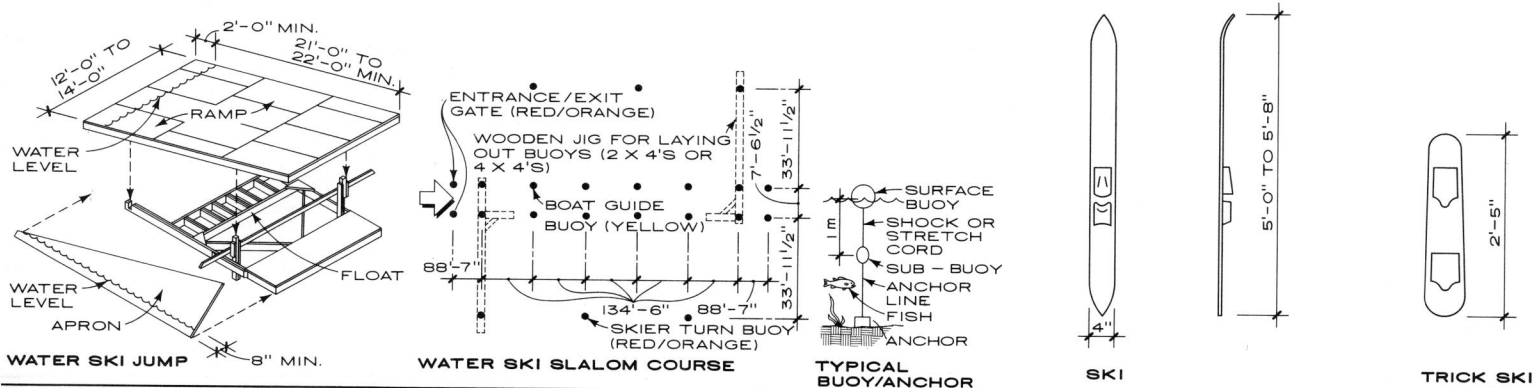

**WATER SKIING AND JUMPING**

Richard J. Vitullo; Washington Grove, Maryland

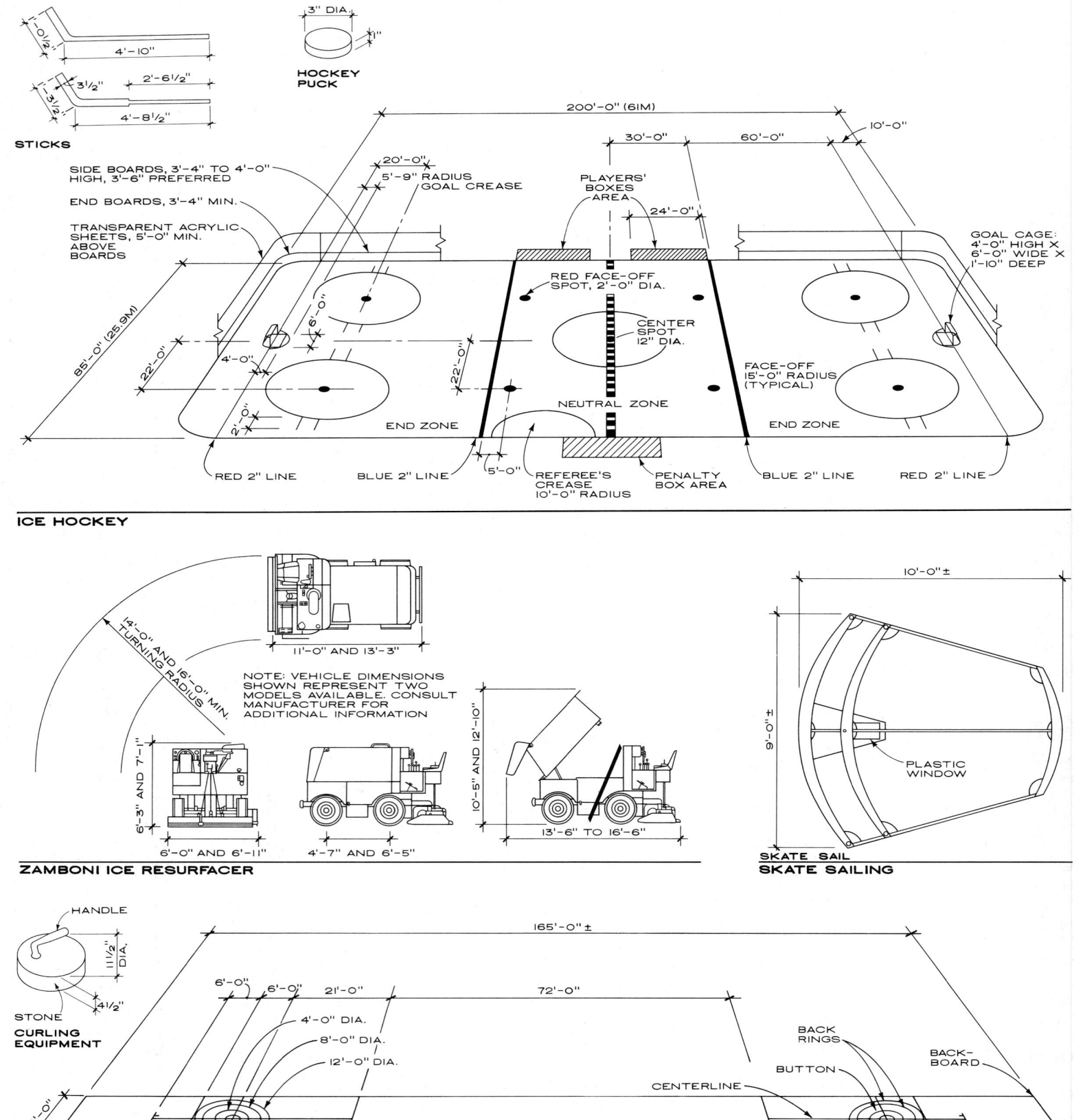

**STICKS**

3" DIA.

**HOCKEY PUCK**

**ICE HOCKEY**

SIDE BOARDS, 3'-4" TO 4'-0" HIGH, 3'-6" PREFERRED

END BOARDS, 3'-4" MIN.

TRANSPARENT ACRYLIC SHEETS, 5'-0" MIN. ABOVE BOARDS

5'-9" RADIUS GOAL CREASE

PLAYERS' BOXES AREA

200'-0" (61M)

GOAL CAGE: 4'-0" HIGH X 6'-0" WIDE X 1'-10" DEEP

RED FACE-OFF SPOT, 2'-0" DIA.

CENTER SPOT 12" DIA.

FACE-OFF 15'-0" RADIUS (TYPICAL)

85'-0" (25.9M)

END ZONE    NEUTRAL ZONE    END ZONE

RED 2" LINE    BLUE 2" LINE    REFEREE'S CREASE 10'-0" RADIUS    PENALTY BOX AREA    BLUE 2" LINE    RED 2" LINE

**ZAMBONI ICE RESURFACER**

NOTE: VEHICLE DIMENSIONS SHOWN REPRESENT TWO MODELS AVAILABLE. CONSULT MANUFACTURER FOR ADDITIONAL INFORMATION

14'-0" AND 16'-0" MIN. TURNING RADIUS

11'-0" AND 13'-3"

6'-3" AND 7'-1"

6'-0" AND 6'-11"

4'-7" AND 6'-5"

10'-5" AND 12'-10"

13'-6" TO 16'-6"

**SKATE SAILING**

SKATE SAIL

PLASTIC WINDOW

10'-0" ±

9'-0" ±

**CURLING**

CURLING EQUIPMENT

HANDLE

STONE

11 1/2" DIA.

4 1/2"

165'-0" ±

HACK    HOG LINE    HOUSE    BACK LINE

6'-0"    6'-0"    21'-0"    72'-0"

4'-0" DIA.
8'-0" DIA.
12'-0" DIA.

14'-0"

BACK RINGS    BUTTON    BACK-BOARD    CENTERLINE    FRONT RINGS    SWEEPING SCORE OR TEE LINE

Richard J. Vitullo; Washington Grove, Maryland

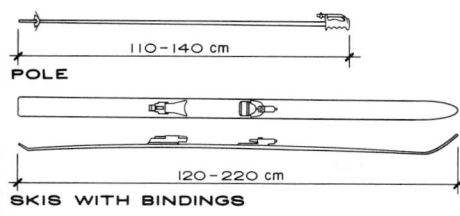

**POLE**          110-140 cm

**SKIS WITH BINDINGS**          120-220 cm

**BOOT**

## BASIC EQUIPMENT

## VERTICAL DROP AND GATE SPECIFICATIONS FOR FIS AND USSA COURSES

| EVENT | FIS DROP (M) MIN. | FIS DROP (M) MAX. | NO. OF GATES MIN. | NO. OF GATES MAX. | USSA DROP (M) MIN. | NO. OF GATES MIN. |
|---|---|---|---|---|---|---|
| DOWNHILL | | | | | | |
| One-run: men | 500 | 1000 | | | 400 | |
| women | 500 | 700 | | | 400 | |
| Two-run (each) | 450 | | | | | |
| SLALOM | | | | | | |
| Men | 140 | 220 | 52 | 78 | 120 | 42 |
| Women | 120 | 180 | 42 | 63 | 120 | 42 |
| GIANT SLALOM | | | | | | |
| Men | 250 | 400 | 30 | 60 | 250 | 33 |
| Women | 250 | 350 | 30 | 53 | 250 | 33 |
| SUPER GIANT SLALOM | | | | | | |
| Men | 500 | 650 | 35 | 65 | 350 | 30 |
| Women | 350 | 500 | 30 | 50 | 350 | 30 |

FIS = Federation Internationale de Ski

USSA = United States Ski Association

## ACCEPTABLE TERRAIN GRADIENTS FOR SLOPES AND TRAILS

| SKILL LEVEL | TERRAIN GRADIENTS LOW | TERRAIN GRADIENTS HIGH |
|---|---|---|
| Beginner/novice | 8% | 25% |
| Intermediate | 15% | 40% |
| Advanced intermediate/expert | 25% | 70% |
| Average Olympic downhill | 23% | 30% |

## BASE LODGE

Base lodge size in sq ft = (mountain capacity/seat turn-over rate x sq ft/person.

Seat turnover rate—number of persons served per seat per day depends upon weather and temperature.

Typically:  3 (cold/overcast)
            5 (warm/clear)

Typical sq ft/person at ski lodge:
    30 (local ski area)
    35 (destination ski area)

Edge of lodge to be:  minimum 100 ft
                      optimal 150 ft
                      suitable 100–300 ft
from lift terminals.

Stairs with long treads (14–16 in.) and low risers (6 in.) to accommodate ski boots.

Protect entry/doorways from snowfall/dripping.

Locate windows above snow level.

Ski rental space = 3 sq ft per rental setup (skis, boots, poles).

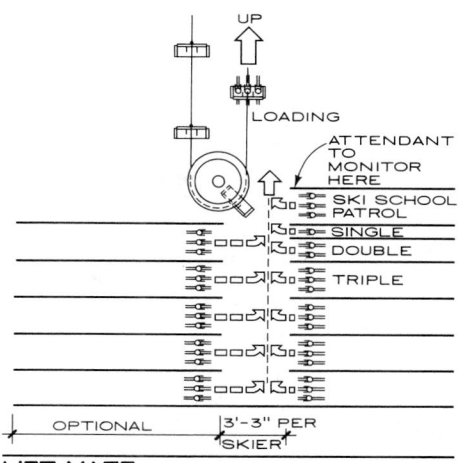

**LIFT MAZE**

## LIFT MAZE AREA REQUIRED FOR 10-MINUTE LIFT LINE

| LIFT TYPE | WIDTH (EACH ROW) | AREA (SQ FT) |
|---|---|---|
| Double | 5 ft 0 in. | 2500 |
| Triple | 7 ft 6 in. | 3750 |
| Quad | 10 ft 0 in. | 5000 |

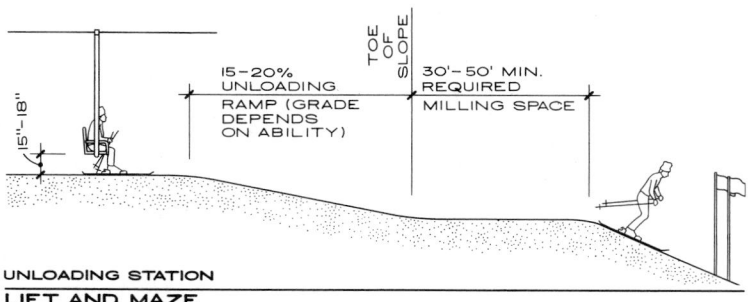

**UNLOADING STATION**

**LIFT AND MAZE**

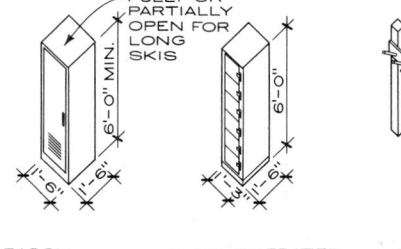

**SEASON LOCKER**          **COIN-OPERATED LOCKER**          **REGULAR TYPE**          **COIN-OPERATED TYPE**

**LOCKERS**          **SKI RACKS**

**LOCKERS AND SKI RACKS**

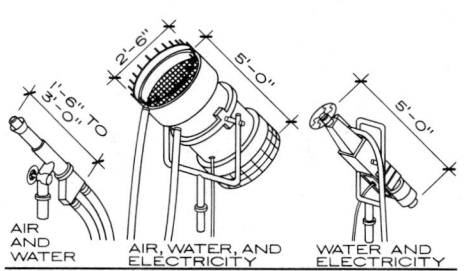

**AIR AND WATER**          **AIR, WATER, AND ELECTRICITY**          **WATER AND ELECTRICITY**

**SNOWMAKING MACHINES**

**SNOWMAKING MACHINE MOUNT**          **SNOWMAKING MACHINE MOUNT**

**SNOWMAKING MACHINE CARRIAGE**          **SNOWMAKING MACHINE SLED**

**MAINTENANCE AND SNOWMAKING EQUIPMENT**

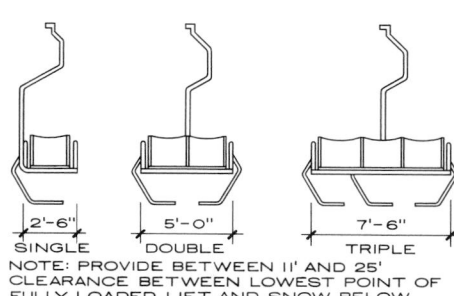

**SINGLE**  2'-6"          **DOUBLE**  5'-0"          **TRIPLE**  7'-6"

NOTE: PROVIDE BETWEEN 11' AND 25' CLEARANCE BETWEEN LOWEST POINT OF FULLY LOADED LIFT AND SNOW BELOW

**LIFT CHAIRS**

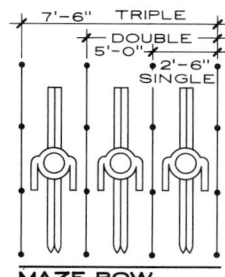

7'-6" TRIPLE — 5'-0" DOUBLE — 2'-6" SINGLE

**MAZE ROW**

**NOTE**

Lift mazes to be located downhill of or to the side of loading point.

Mazes to be graded as flat as possible.

Approach to loading point to be graded at 3% downhill for distance of 50 ft minimum.

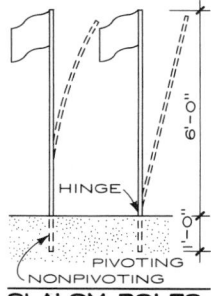

**HINGE**

**PIVOTING**          **NONPIVOTING**

**SLALOM POLES**

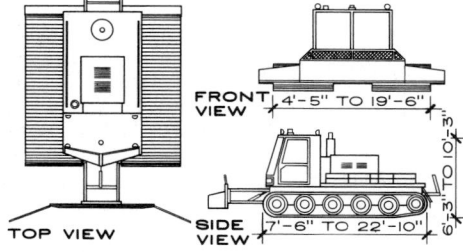

**FRONT VIEW**  4'-5" TO 19'-6"

**TOP VIEW**          **SIDE VIEW**  7'-6" TO 22'-10"

**OVERSNOW VEHICLES**

## MAINTENANCE BUILDING

Area required: 100 sq ft per oversnow vehicle includes vehicle storage, parts and general storage, office, toilets. Does not include snowmaking system.

Doors: 16–20 ft wide, 14–16 ft high for main vehicle entry doors.

Eliot W. Goldstein, AIA, and Chan Li Lin; James Goldstein & Partners; Millburn, New Jersey

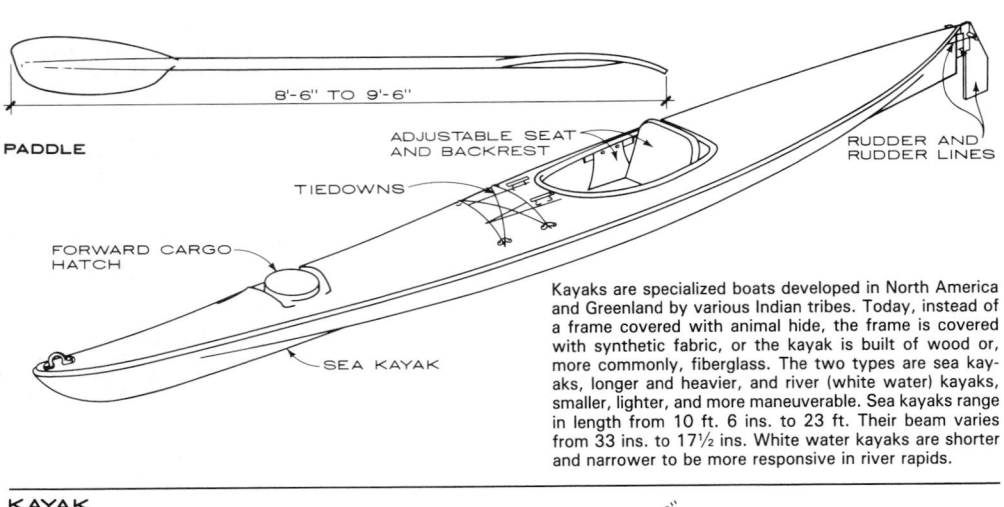

PADDLE

8'-6" TO 9'-6"

ADJUSTABLE SEAT AND BACKREST

TIEDOWNS

FORWARD CARGO HATCH

RUDDER AND RUDDER LINES

SEA KAYAK

Kayaks are specialized boats developed in North America and Greenland by various Indian tribes. Today, instead of a frame covered with animal hide, the frame is covered with synthetic fabric, or the kayak is built of wood or, more commonly, fiberglass. The two types are sea kayaks, longer and heavier, and river (white water) kayaks, smaller, lighter, and more maneuverable. Sea kayaks range in length from 10 ft. 6 ins. to 23 ft. Their beam varies from 33 ins. to 17½ ins. White water kayaks are shorter and narrower to be more responsive in river rapids.

## KAYAK

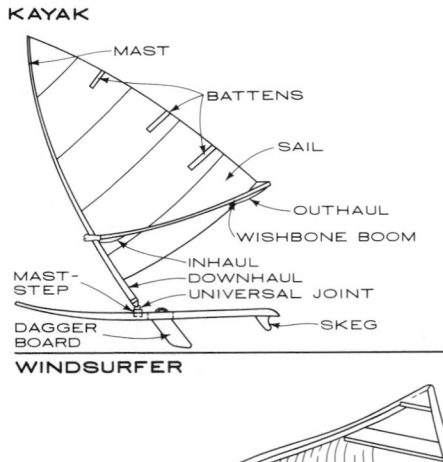

MAST

BATTENS

SAIL

OUTHAUL

WISHBONE BOOM

INHAUL

MAST-STEP

DOWNHAUL

UNIVERSAL JOINT

DAGGER BOARD

SKEG

## WINDSURFER

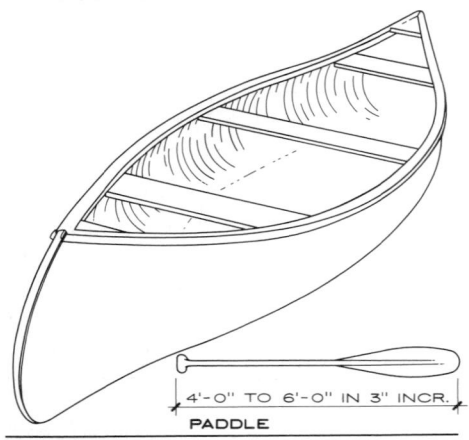

4'-0" TO 6'-0" IN 3" INCR.

PADDLE

## CANOE

Canoes have shallow draft, and they range in length from 12 ft. to 35 ft. They can be paddled, sailed, or motored, and they can be loaded with equipment. They are constructed of wood, fiberglass, or aluminum.

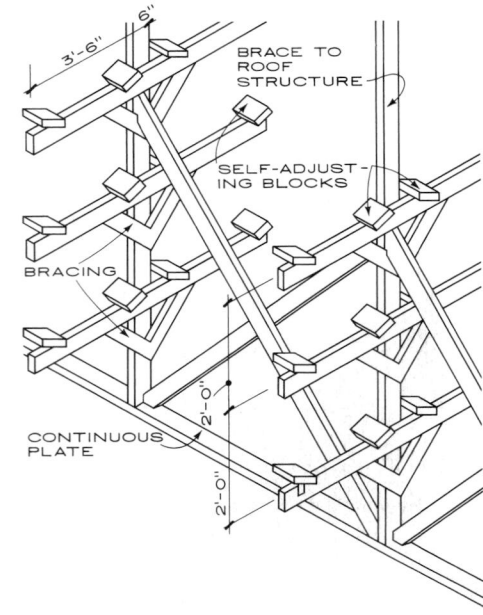

3'-6"    6"

BRACE TO ROOF STRUCTURE

SELF-ADJUSTING BLOCKS

BRACING

2'-0"    2'-0"

CONTINUOUS PLATE

## ROWING SHELL STORAGE RACK

Storage for rowing shells requires: two racks 8 feet apart for single and double; three racks 8 feet apart for eight-oared. Shells used daily should not be stored higher than 6 ft. Storage racks can be adapted easily to hold kayaks or canoes by adjusting the spacing between racks and the height between horizontal members.

Racing shells, built primarily of carbon fiber or plastic, are narrow and unstable in the water. There are two rowing styles: sweep rowing, where oarsmen work one oar with both hands; and sculling, where each oarsman works two oars, one in each hand. Sweeps are 12 ft. to 13 ft. long; sculling oars are 9 ft. 6 ins. to 10 ft. long.

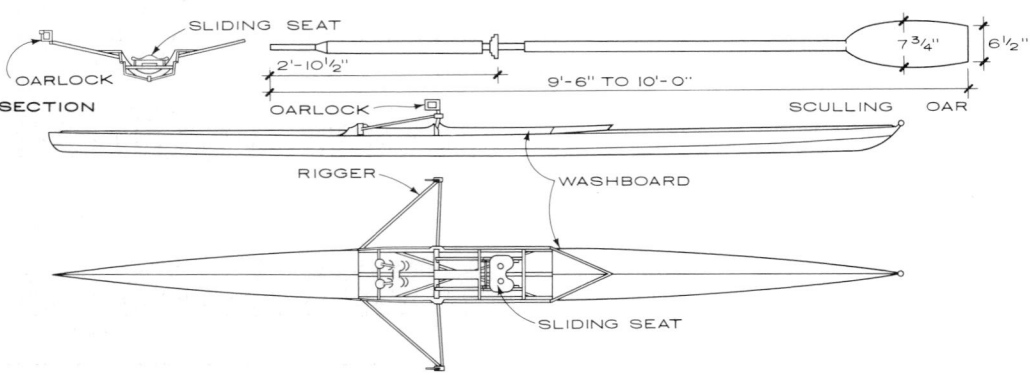

SLIDING SEAT

OARLOCK

SECTION

OARLOCK

RIGGER

WASHBOARD

SLIDING SEAT

2'-10½"    9'-6" TO 10'-0"    7¾"    6½"

SCULLING    OAR

## ROWING SHELL

Timothy B. McDonald; Washington, D.C.

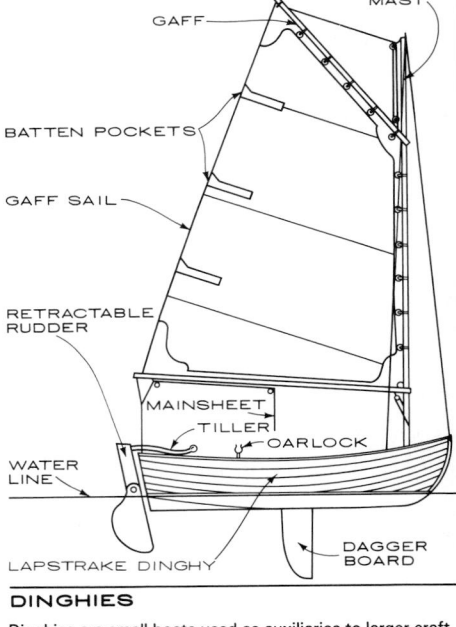

MAST

GAFF

BATTEN POCKETS

GAFF SAIL

RETRACTABLE RUDDER

MAINSHEET

TILLER

OARLOCK

WATER LINE

LAPSTRAKE DINGHY

DAGGER BOARD

## DINGHIES

Dinghies are small boats used as auxiliaries to larger craft. They also can be sailed and raced on their own. They vary in length from 6 ft. to 16 ft., and they are 2 ft. 10 ins. to 5 ft. 6 ins. in beam. They are constructed of wood or fiberglass, and they can be rigged for sail, rowing, or motoring.

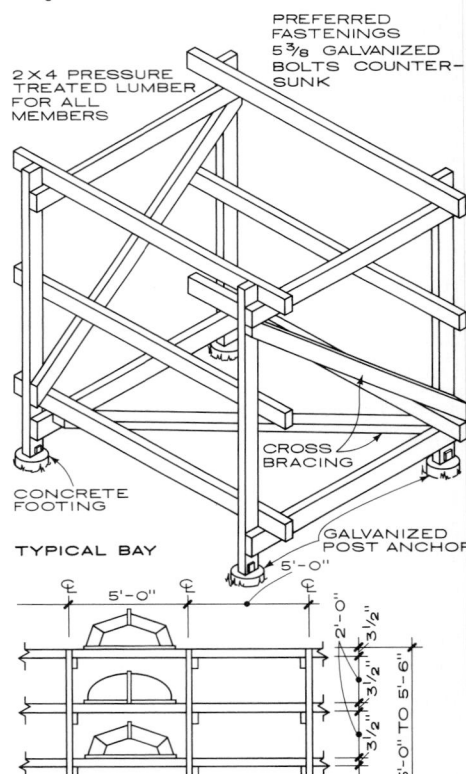

PREFERRED FASTENINGS 5⅜ GALVANIZED BOLTS COUNTERSUNK

2 X 4 PRESSURE TREATED LUMBER FOR ALL MEMBERS

CROSS BRACING

CONCRETE FOOTING

GALVANIZED POST ANCHOR

TYPICAL BAY

5'-0"

ELEVATION

5'-0"    5'-0"    2'-0"    3½    3½    3½    5'-0" TO 5'-6"

## DINGHY STORAGE RACK

Dinghy racks store the small boats year round, and should be weather-treated. The rack members are fastened with countersunk bolts to avoid damaging dinghies. Racks must be able to support the weight of the boats and anyone climbing on the racks.

17    BOATING

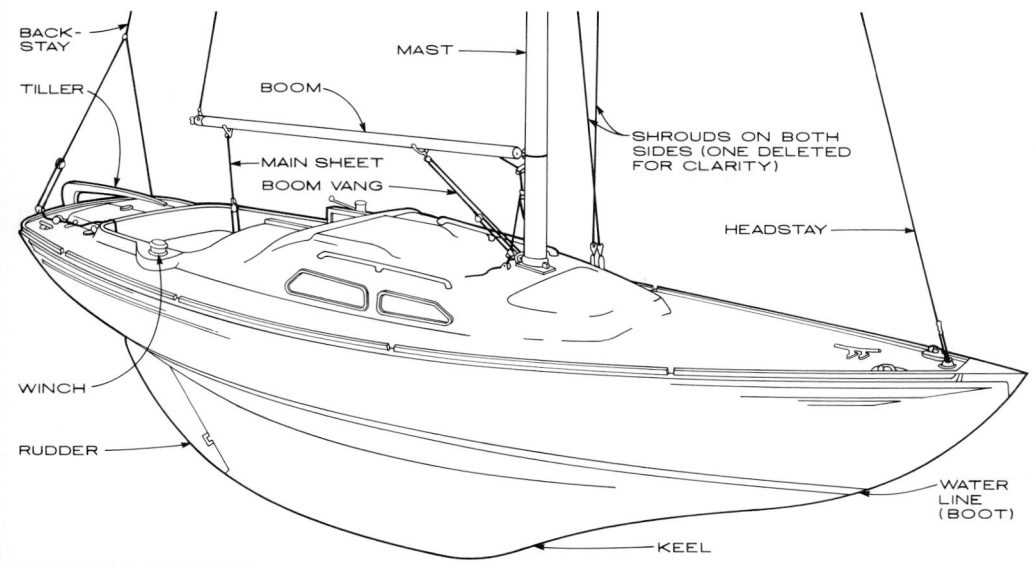

BACK-STAY
TILLER
BOOM
MAST
MAIN SHEET
BOOM VANG
SHROUDS ON BOTH SIDES (ONE DELETED FOR CLARITY)
HEADSTAY
WINCH
RUDDER
WATER LINE (BOOT)
KEEL

**MONOHULL SAILBOAT**

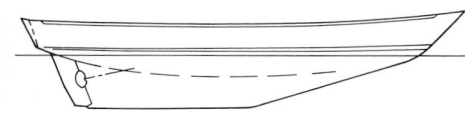

**FULL KEEL**

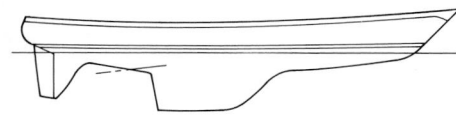

**FIN KEEL**

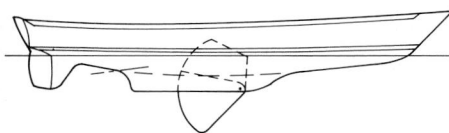

**FIN KEEL / CENTER BOARD**

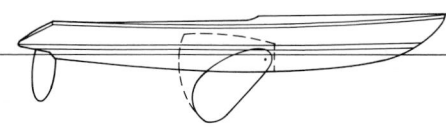

**CENTER BOARD**

**MONOHULL - BASIC UNDERWATER HULL SHAPES**

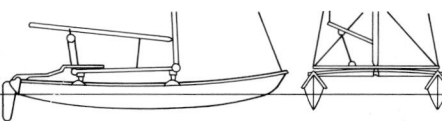

**MULTIHULL**

## DEFINITIONS

1. Length overall—LOA—boat's greatest length excluding bowsprits rudder or other extensions.
2. Length of water line—LWL—boat's greatest length at the water level excluding extensions such as rudders.
3. Beam—boat's maximum breadth.
4. Draft—distance from the waterline to the bottom of the boat's keel determining the least depth of water the boat can operate in: i.e., the amount it draws.
5. Displacement—weight of the water that the boat displaces.

## NOTES FOR BASIC RIGS

### LATEEN

Ancestor of the fore and aft rigs shown here. It dates back thousands of years and is still used in many parts of the world.

## CATBOAT RIG

Traditionally puts a lot of sail area on one short mast, as shown here, which is stepped far forward in the boat.

### SLOOP

Design with two basic sails, mainsail and headsail; the latter, called a "fractional rig," is set either to the masthead or some distance below the masthead.

### CUTTER

Like the sloop, a cutter rig has one mast carrying two headsails instead of one. The inner sail is the forestay sail and the outer sail is the jib.

### YAWL

Unlike the sloop or cutter, the yawl is a two masted rig consisting of a mainmast and a mizzen mast that is stepped abaft (behind) the rudder post. The mizzen sail is much smaller than the main sail.

### KETCH

Like the yawl, the ketch is also a two-masted rig; however, the mizzen mast is stepped forward of the rudder post and is larger than the yawl's mizzen. This placement dictates a smaller mainsail.

### SCHOONER

Usually two-masted but can be three-masted. Commonly the foremast is the shorter of the two, and may be gaff or marconi rigged or at times a combination of both.

A combination of mast and rigging placement (where the mast is stepped), along with size, type and number of sails, make up the main differences in sailboat rigs. Today the most common is the marconi rig distinguished by a triangular mainsail, but it is not unusual for boats to be rigged with a traditional gaff, which is a four-sided sail that hangs from a spar called a gaff. In some instances marconi and gaff rigs are used together as shown on the schooner below.

Headsails are triangular sails set ahead of the mast. Basic headsails are the jib, working jib, staysail, and genoa. The working jib, unlike other jibs, does not overlap the mast and is often attached to a boom for easier control. Jibs and genoas do overlap the mast and mainsail. The forestaysail is combined with the jib to create a double-headsail and is used primarily on cutters and schooners.

Spinnakers, usually the largest sail set before the mast, come in several different shapes and sizes according to use.

## EXAMPLES

| | LOA | LWL | BEAM | | DRAFT | |
|---|---|---|---|---|---|---|
| **FULL KEEL BOATS** | | | | | | |
| Folkboat | 25'-10" | 19'-10" | 7'-4" | | 3'-11" | |
| Cape Dory 45 | 45'-3" | 33'-6" | 13'-0" | | 6'-3" | |
| **FIN KEEL BOATS** | | | | | | |
| Tartan 28 | 28'-3" | 23'-3" | 9'-10" | | 4'-11" | |
| O'Day 35 | 35'-0" | 28'-9" | 11'-3" | | 5'-7" | |
| **FIN/CENTERBOARD** | | | | UP | | DOWN |
| Cape Dory (270) | 27'-3" | 20'-9" | 9'-5" | 3'-0" | | 7'-0" |
| Tartan 37 | 37'-3" | 28'-6" | 11'-9" | 4'-2" | | 7'-9" |
| **CENTERBOARD** | | | | UP | | DOWN |
| Sunfish | 13'-10" | 13'-10" | 4'-1/2" | 3" | | 2'-8" |
| Laser | 13'-10" | 12'-6" | 4'-6" | 6" | | 2'-8" |
| El Toro | 8'-0" | 7'-0" | 3'-10" | 3" | | 1'-10" |
| **MULTIHULLS** | | | | | | |
| Hobie 16 | 16'-7" | 15'-9" | 7'-11" | | 10" | |

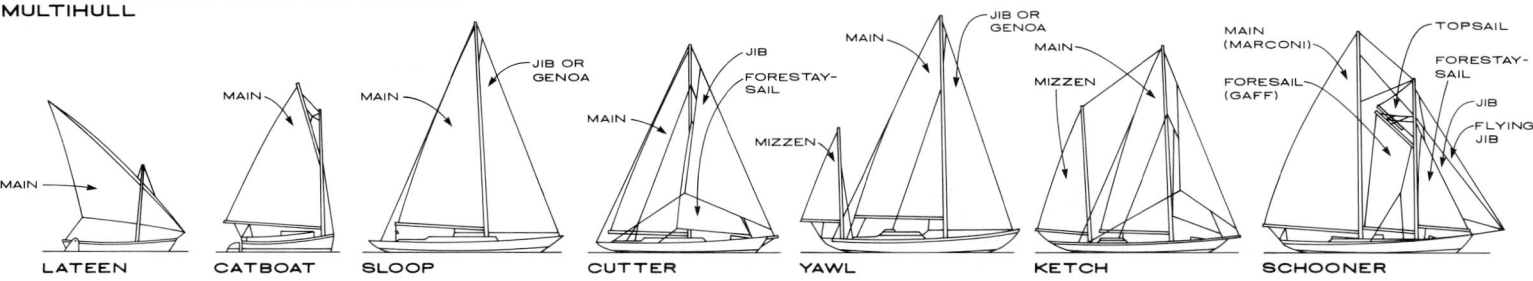

LATEEN — MAIN

CATBOAT — MAIN

SLOOP — JIB OR GENOA, MAIN

CUTTER — JIB, FORESTAY-SAIL, MAIN

YAWL — JIB OR GENOA, MAIN, MIZZEN

KETCH — MAIN, MIZZEN

SCHOONER — MAIN (MARCONI), FORESAIL (GAFF), TOPSAIL, FORESTAY-SAIL, JIB, FLYING JIB

**BASIC BOAT RIGS**

Timothy B. McDonald; Washington, D.C.

## HOT-AIR AND GAS BALLOONS

| CLASS | VOLUME cFx1000 | DIAMETER (FT) | HEIGHT (FT) | CREW |
|---|---|---|---|---|
| AX–1 | 8.5 | 25 | 28 | 1 |
| AX–2 | 12.2–14 | 28–32 | 28–37 | 1 |
| AA/AX–3 | 17–22 | 30–34 | 30–45 | 1–3 |
| AA/AX–4 | 27.5–33.4 | 34–41 | 34–67 | 1–6 |
| AA/AX–5 | 37.1–45 | 39–46 | 46–73 | 1–6 |
| AA/AX–6 | 55–59.3 | 47–50 | 51–80 | 1–6 |
| AX–7 | 60–77.7 | 50–56 | 53–64 | 1–4 |
| AX–8 | 80–106 | 54–62 | 57–72 | 3–6 |
| AX–9 | 139–160 | N/A | N/A | 4–12 |

NOTE: Deflated balloon including burner can be stored in the crew basket for transporting in a small pickup truck.

**BALLOONS**

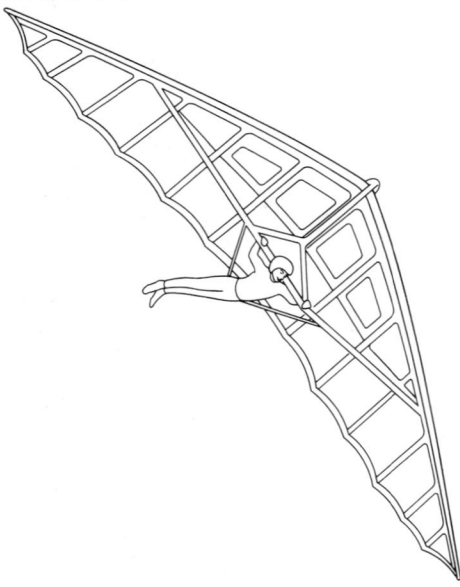

## FLEXIBLE WING HANG GLIDER

| SPAN | LEADING EDGE | KEEL | WEIGHT (LB) |
|---|---|---|---|
| 24 ft 9 in. to 38 ft 2 in. | 16 ft 0 in. to 21 ft 0 in. | 7 ft 2 in. to 13 ft 5 in. | 41 to 78 |

**HANG GLIDERS**

Marr Knapp Crawfis Associates, Inc.; Mansfield, Ohio
Jane's All the World's Aircraft, 82–83

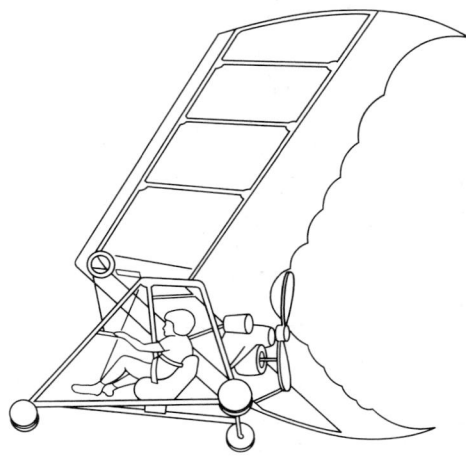

## LIGHT PLANES (MICROLIGHTS) USUALLY DRIVEN BY LIGHT, LOW-POWERED ENGINES

| WING SPAN | LENGTH | HEIGHT | PROPELLER | WEIGHT EMPTY (LB) |
|---|---|---|---|---|
| 30 ft to 37 ft | 10 ft 6 in. to 19 ft 6 in. | 5 ft 6 in. to 10 ft 0 in. | 3 ft 6 in. to 4 ft 6 in. | 120 to 245 |

NOTE: Physical sizes for models with solar-powered electrical motors exceed the data given above.

### LIGHT/MICRO PLANES

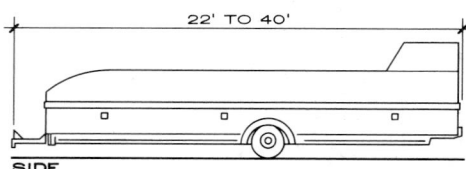

SIDE

22' TO 40'

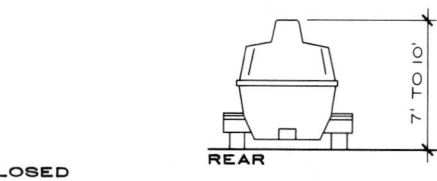

CLOSED

REAR    7' TO 10'

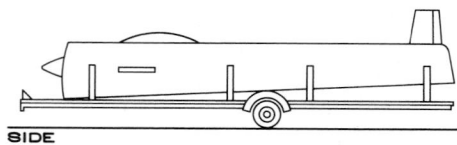

SIDE

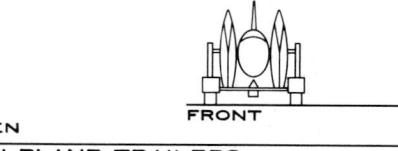

OPEN    FRONT

**SAILPLANE TRAILERS**

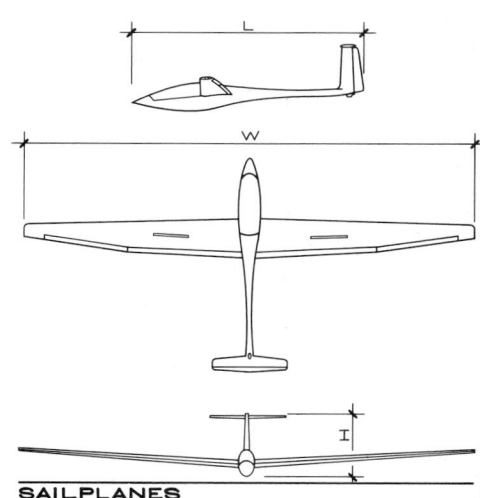

**SAILPLANES**

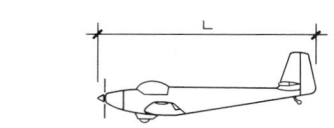

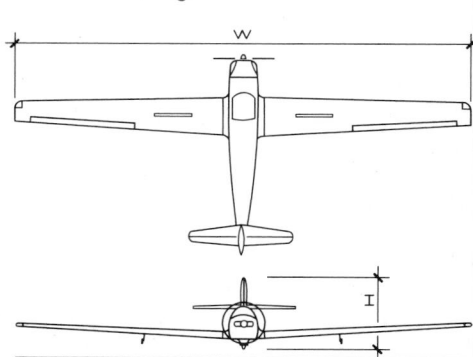

**MOTOR GLIDERS**

### SOARING

1. Sailplanes with winch or auto-tow launch: constructed of aluminum, fiberglass, carbon composites, wood, specially treated fabric stretched over metal tubing, or any combination of these materials.

Size ranges:
Wingspan (W) from under 40 to over 72 ft.
Fuselage (L) from 20 to 30 ft.
Height (H) from 3 to 9.3 ft.
Empty weight from 250 (one seat) to 1,000 lb (three-seat models).

Major design classes for national competitions:
Open class: Wingspan over 72 ft (22 m).
15-m class: Wingspan up to 49.2 ft (15 m) with modifications to increase performance.
Standard class: Similar to 15-m class, no flaps.
Sports class: For older, lower performance models, including home-builts and sailplanes not qualifying for other classes.

2. Motor gliders, self-launching or with auxiliary power engines for use after auto-tow launch: various designs available fully manufacturer assembled or in kit.

Manufacturer-assembled motor gliders are similar in size to sailplanes. Wingspans range from 40 to 68 ft. Landing runs range from 300 to under 1,000 ft.

Kit-built motor gliders offer wingspans from as little as 15 ft 8 in. to approximately 42 ft, with a wide range of specifications.

Source: Soaring Society of America, P.O. Box 66071, Los Angeles, CA 90066.

**SOARING**

RECOMMENDED READING

Jane's All the World's Aircraft, Jane's Publishing Company Limited, 238 City Road, London EC1V 2PU, England.

**AIR SPORTS**

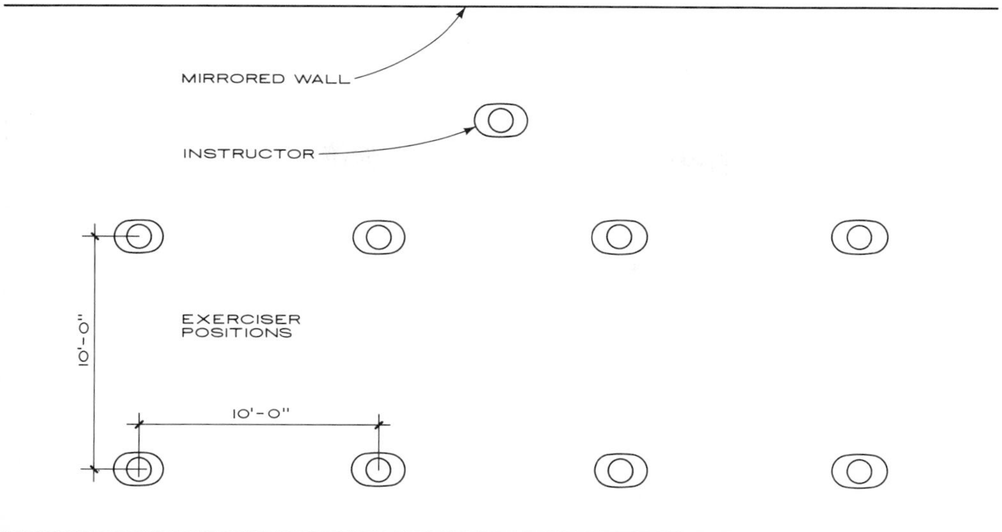

MIRRORED WALL

INSTRUCTOR

EXERCISER
POSITIONS

10'-0"

10'-0"

## AEROBICS TRAINING AREA

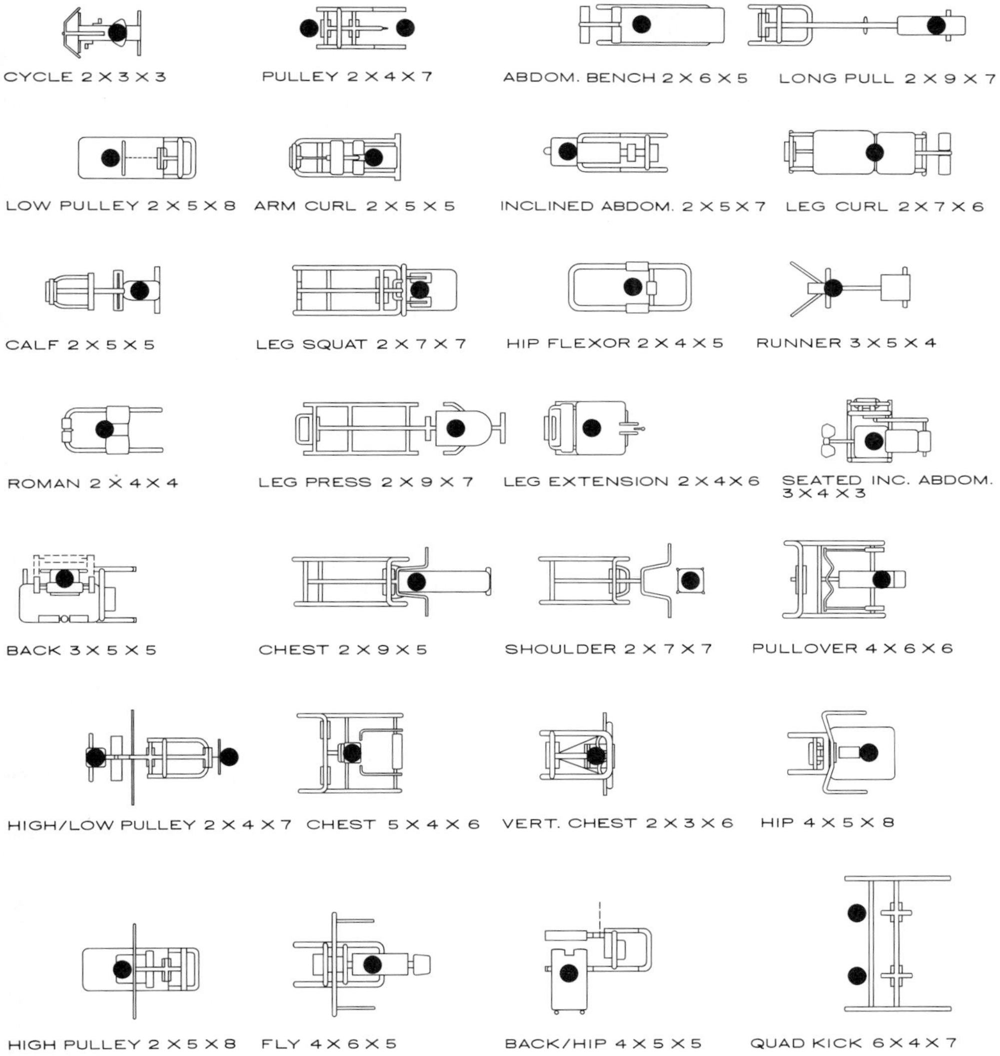

CYCLE 2 X 3 X 3

PULLEY 2 X 4 X 7

ABDOM. BENCH 2 X 6 X 5

LONG PULL 2 X 9 X 7

LOW PULLEY 2 X 5 X 8

ARM CURL 2 X 5 X 5

INCLINED ABDOM. 2 X 5 X 7

LEG CURL 2 X 7 X 6

CALF 2 X 5 X 5

LEG SQUAT 2 X 7 X 7

HIP FLEXOR 2 X 4 X 5

RUNNER 3 X 5 X 4

ROMAN 2 X 4 X 4

LEG PRESS 2 X 9 X 7

LEG EXTENSION 2 X 4 X 6

SEATED INC. ABDOM.
3 X 4 X 3

BACK 3 X 5 X 5

CHEST 2 X 9 X 5

SHOULDER 2 X 7 X 7

PULLOVER 4 X 6 X 6

HIGH/LOW PULLEY 2 X 4 X 7

CHEST 5 X 4 X 6

VERT. CHEST 2 X 3 X 6

HIP 4 X 5 X 8

HIGH PULLEY 2 X 5 X 8

FLY 4 X 6 X 5

BACK/HIP 4 X 5 X 5

QUAD KICK 6 X 4 X 7

● INDICATES APPROXIMATE USER POSITION. PROXIMITY TO WALL
AND OTHER MACHINES VARIES. DIMENSIONS TO NEAREST
FOOT W X D X H

## WEIGHT TRAINING MACHINES

Frederick C. Krenson, AIA; Rosser Fabrap International; Atlanta, Georgia

## AEROBICS

Aerobics is taught in a classroom setting. Space requirements are 100 sq ft per person plus an instructor. Flooring should be firm but resilient, such as a court floor. Ceilings should be acoustically absorptive. One or two walls should be mirrored, and stretching bars should be provided. The instructor's area at the front of the room may include voice amplification and a control or sound system. Use of videotape for teaching purposes should be considered.

## TRAINING EQUIPMENT

Exercise and weight training equipment is available from a variety of manufacturers. Combinations of equipment, or circuits, can be arranged to develop particular muscle groups or endurance. Equipment manufacturers can assist with proper spacing and clearances. Overall supervision of training areas is recommended, both for equipment safety and proper conditioning use. Ceiling height should be as required by equipment, but should not be less than 10 ft high. Training room arrangement may include mirrors on one or two walls, computerization of certain pieces of equipment, a record-keeping area for users, soft flooring to reduce impact noise, as well as other acoustical treatment. The weight of the machinery and proper ventilation should be considered. Other pieces of equipment such as treadmills and exercycles may be research related and require ancillary monitoring and data-keeping equipment. Loose equipment, such as dumbbells and barbells, complements power racks and may be preferred by some users or programs. Olympic weights and an Olympic lifting platform may be coordinated with a videotaping system.

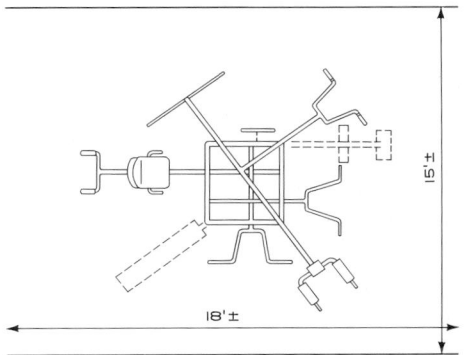

15'±

18'±

## NOTE

The multiple station machine combines the functions of a variety of individual training devices into one machine. It is less costly than multiple machines and requires less space.

## MULTIPLE STATION

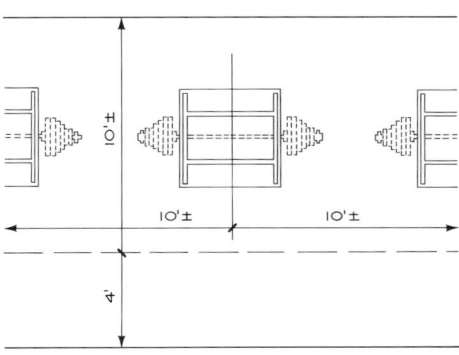

10'±

10'±

10'±

4'

## NOTE

The power rack is designed for confined free weights. It often involves a user, spotters, coaches, and observers and may be placed in front of mirrors. This machine should be on soft flooring such as rubber. Benches and other accessories may be used with the power rack.

## POWER RACK

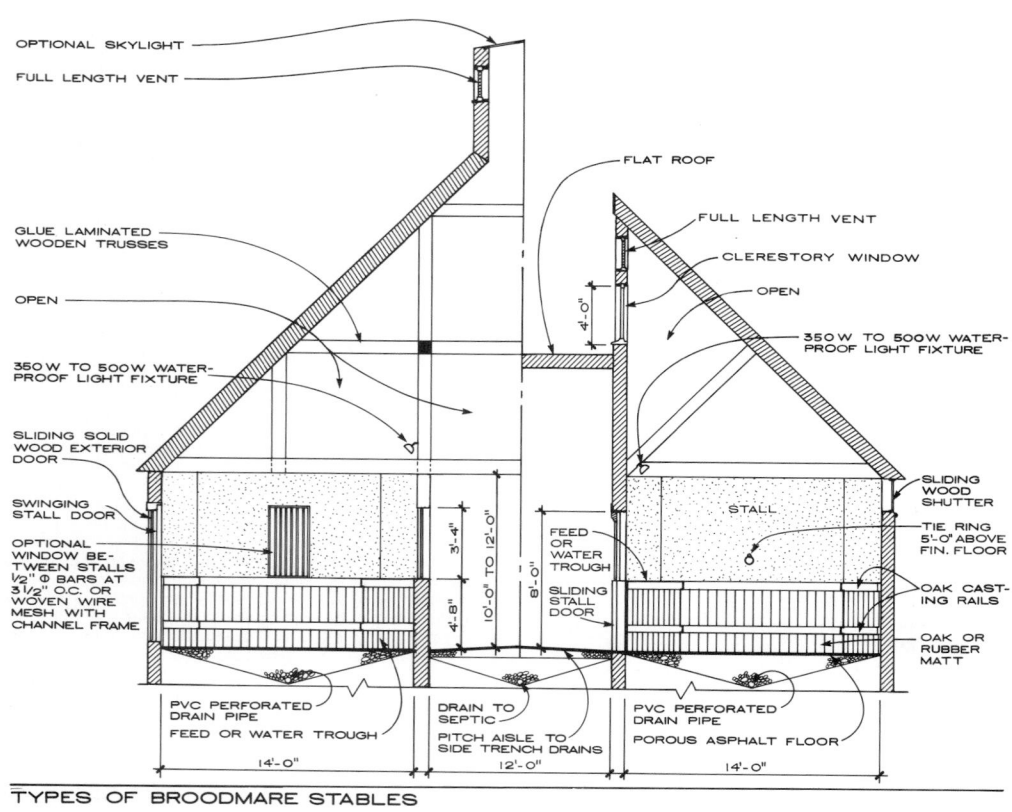

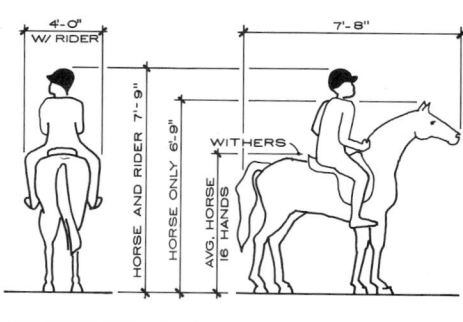

ONE HAND EQUALS 4"

**CLEARANCES FOR HORSE AND RIDER**

**TYPES OF BROODMARE STABLES**

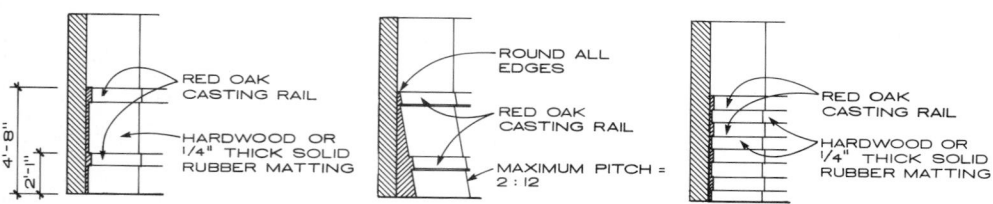

**TYPICAL STALL TREATMENT FOR CASTING PREVENTION**

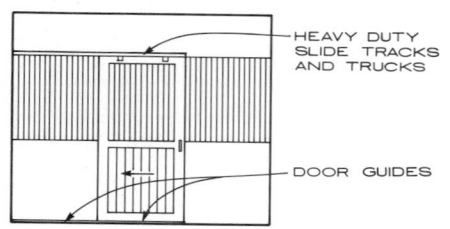

**TYPICAL SLIDING AISLE DOOR**

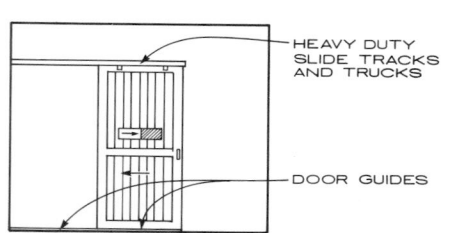

**SOLID WOOD FOALING STALL WITH VIEW THROUGH**

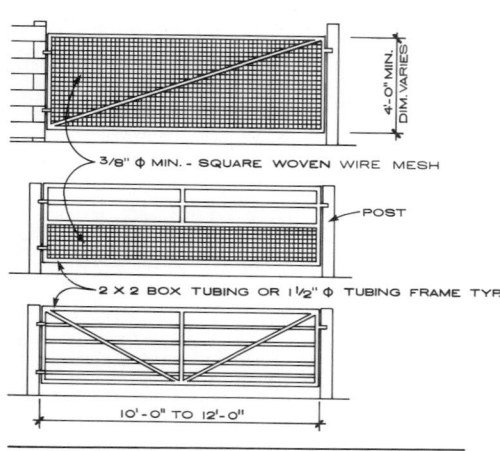

**STANDARD GATES**

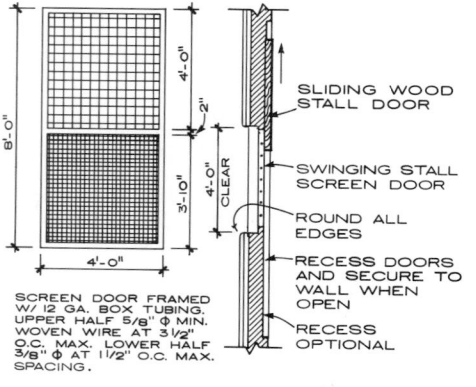

**BROODMARE STALL SCREEN**

**BROODMARE EXTERIOR STALL DOOR PLAN**

Theodore M. Ceraldi & Associates, Architects; Nyack, New York

**NOTES**

Barns: masonry and glue-laminated construction for fire-resistance. Stalls: furred out, finished with red oak, hardwood, or ¼ in. rubber matting. Casting rails: 2 in. x 6 in. red oak, edges rounded, sealed with boiled linseed oil. Countersink fastener heads, plug. Stall corners: rounded or 45° walls to casting rail. Ventilation: high open slots with optional sliding wood shutter. Windows: safety glass only, minimum of 8 ft. above floor. Floor: 3 in. porous asphalt (percolation of one gallon in ten seconds) over 18 in. crushed stone with a porous drain pipe pitched to take effluent away from barn areas. Check local codes on septic requirements. Floors: rough concrete or skid-resistant brick pavers with a central floor drain to catch basin. Grates: cast iron or pre-cast concrete centered in stall with perforations no larger than 1 in. diameter or 1 in. sq. Floor: sloped to center drain. Provide optional infrared heaters in all horse wash areas at maximum 10 ft. above floor. Aisle floors: porous asphalt, paving bricks set in 2 in. sand, or diamond scored concrete with trench drains to each side.

Tack room area varies with the type of stable. Riding stables have at least one bridle and saddle per horse or pony. Saddle and bridle racks can be fastened in rows, one over another. Additional space is needed for groom equipment, sometimes stored in tack trunks. In broodmare stables, tack is mainly halters and grooming supplies. Tack room and foaling stall must be heated. Foaling stall heat: controllable to raise it as quickly as possible to 75° minimum and to maintain it. Foaling stall floor: seamless, rubberized material, minimum 1 in. thick, texturized, and pitched to a separate drain and catch basin (not connected to main barn drainage). Rubberized flooring turned up the walls, minimum of 24 in. Foaling stall adjoined by the situp room (also heated) with a one-way unbreakable glass panel and/or slide shutter for the groom to observe.

All feed and grain storage bins are lined with galvanized steel for vermin control. Feed amounts vary widely. As a guideline, a horse under medium to heavy workload is fed 15 lbs. of grain plus hay per day. All hay and bedding must be stored in a separate dry barn due to fire risk. As horses are grazing animals, hay mangers are not recommended; place hay in a corner on the stall floor. All roofs should have a minimum 7/12 pitch and continuous full length vents under the eaves and at ridges. Sliding doors are preferable. All swinging dutch doors or full doors should have a 180° swing to wall and fasten. Stalls should have heavy duty slide bolts, kick over bolts, and/or locking pins. All hardware should be smooth with no sharp protrusions and inaccessible to horses at the stalls. All light fixtures should be guarded and/or waterproofed. Light switches: located in a central panel away from wet areas. Lighting levels vary. Depending on the program, stalls are lighted with a single floodlight over the inside stall door at the ceiling or 10 ft. to 12 ft. above finished floor. Aisles can be lighted by incandescent or fluorescent lamps. Broodmares and stallions require brighter light and lighting programs to keep fertility levels maximized (approximately 100 foot candles should be achieved at 5 ft. 0 in. above finished floor per stall). Aisles may have lower light levels of 40 foot candles, except examination or display areas, which must have additional light available on demand.

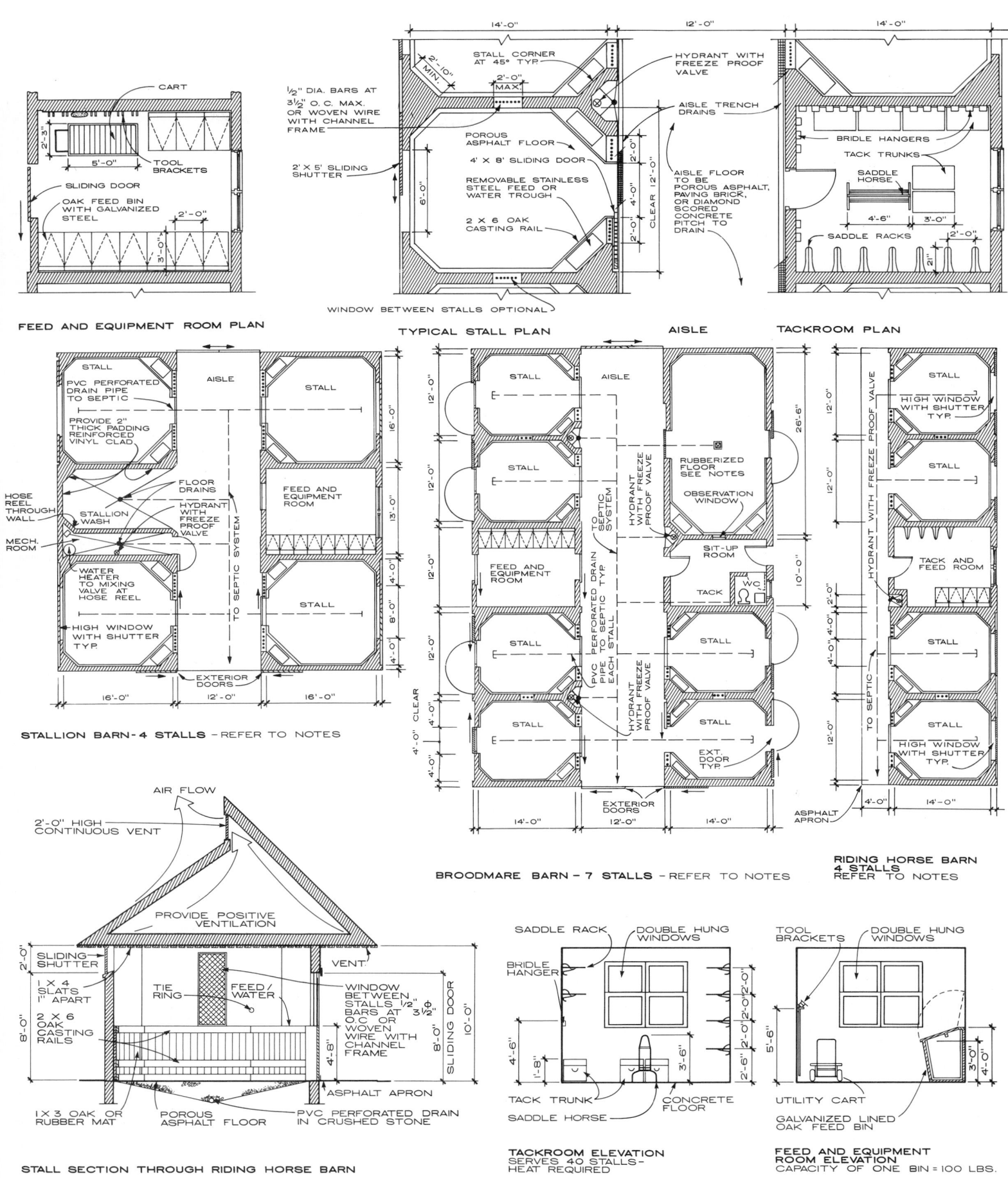

FEED AND EQUIPMENT ROOM PLAN

TYPICAL STALL PLAN

AISLE

TACKROOM PLAN

STALLION BARN-4 STALLS - REFER TO NOTES

BROODMARE BARN - 7 STALLS - REFER TO NOTES

RIDING HORSE BARN 4 STALLS REFER TO NOTES

STALL SECTION THROUGH RIDING HORSE BARN

TACKROOM ELEVATION
SERVES 40 STALLS-
HEAT REQUIRED

FEED AND EQUIPMENT
ROOM ELEVATION
CAPACITY OF ONE BIN = 100 LBS.

Theodore M. Ceraldi & Associates, Architects; Nyack, New York

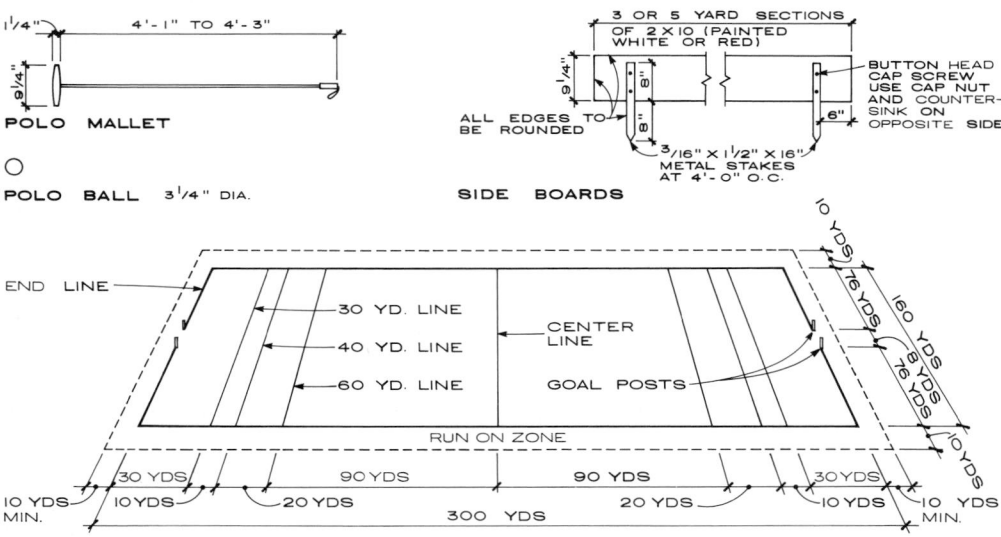

POLO MALLET

POLO BALL 3¼" DIA.

SIDE BOARDS

OUTDOOR POLO FIELD

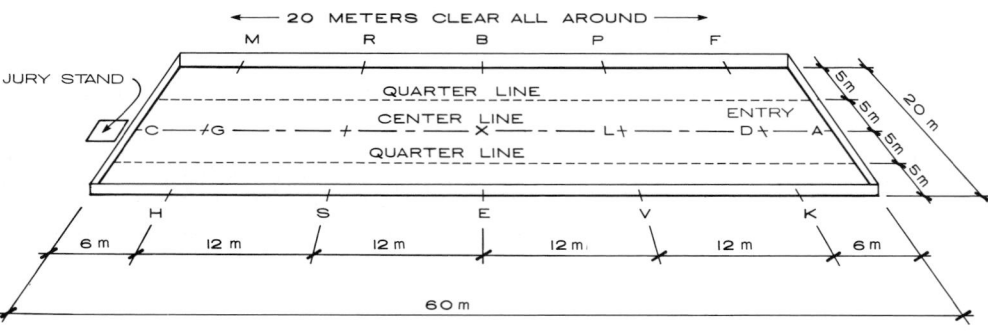

STANDARD DRESSAGE ARENA

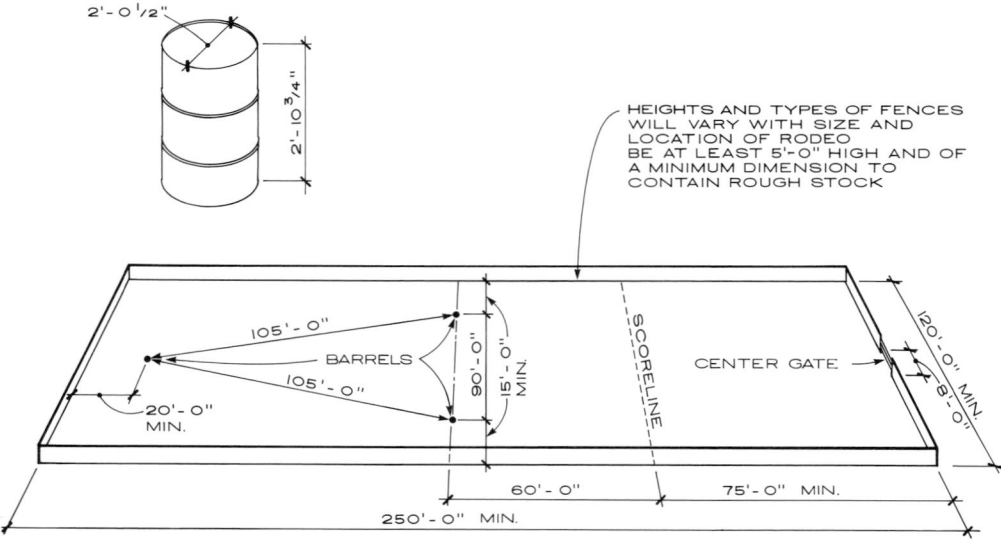

STANDARD BARREL COURSE

Theodore M. Ceraldi & Associates, Architects; Nyack, New York

## POLO

Outdoor or high goal polo is played with two teams of four players each. There can be as many as forty horses per team, and stabling and picket areas are needed for the horses. Spectator stands to accommodate three to six thousand people are needed, depending on the level of play.

The field surface should be grass cut smooth and short enough for the ball to roll straight and easily. The field side boundaries are 10 in. high side boards with a minimum of 10 yards run on, known as the safety zone, beyond. Goal posts must be vertical and light enough to break upon collision. Goal posts are 10 ft. high, and 8 yds. apart. About twenty balls are used in a game.

Arena polo is played at smaller clubs or indoors where less space is available. A playing area of 300 ft. by 150 ft. is considered ideal. Goals, at opposite ends of the field, are 10 ft. in width by 12 ft. in height, inside measurement. In smaller arenas the goal size may be reduced, but to not less than 8 ft. in width by 10 ft.in height. The arena shall be clearly marked at the center and at points 15 yds. and 25 yds. perpendicular to each goal. The inflated arena polo ball shall be not less than 4¼ in. nor more than 4½ in. in diameter.

Further information: United States Polo Association, Oak Brook, Ill.

## DRESSAGE

The arena should be on as level ground as possible. The standard arena is 60 meters x 20 meters. The small arena is 40 meters x 20 meters. The enclosure itself should con- sist of a low fence about 0.30 meters high. The part of the fence at letter A should be easily removable to let competitors in and out of the arena. Arenas must be sep- arated from the public by a distance of not less than 20 meters.

The letters, clearly marked, should be placed outside the enclosure about 0.50 meters from the fence. A red line painted on the fence 20 cm. high locates the exact point of the letters on the track. The center line, throughout its length, and the three points D, X, and G should be as clearly marked as possible, without frightening the horses. It is recommended, on grass arenas, to mow the grass on the center line shorter than other parts of the arena, and on a sand arena, to roll or rake the center line.

An exercise area must be provided far enough away from the arena so as not to disturb the competitors.

## SHOW

Horse show rings vary in size according to type of activity performed. A basic outdoor ring size for hunters and jump- ers is 150 ft.x 300 ft. Combined training requires a stad- ium show ring of 80 meters x 80 meters, as well as a dressage ring. The appropriate breed or show association should be contacted for current and specific regulations.

Flat classes need a level arena with solid footing. There should be one definite opening for an 'in' gate; preferable are separate openings for in and out gates. Rings for flat classes should be large enough to accommodate comfort- ably the number of horses.

Show management must provide sufficient area for schooling horses. It is recommended that separate school- ing areas be provided for hunters and jumpers since dif- ferent types of jumps are used for each. Jumps may vary from a single jump consisting of a single bar 4 in. in di- ameter and 6 ft. long, hung in cups from two uprights, to various combinations of two and three fences, water jumps, banks, and ditches—depending on the skill level of the class.

Further information: American Horse Show Association, New York, N.Y.

## RODEO

Rodeo consists of several events involving timed contests such as calf roping and barrel riding, and rough stock events such as steer wrestling and bull riding. Arenas may vary in size but must be enclosed with fencing to control the various livestock. Barriers and chutes for timed events should be at the opposite end of arena from chutes for rough stock events. Stables, pens, and corrals for holding stock must be provided, as well as area for contestants to exercise their animals. Grandstand seating is standard; the number of spectators varies with the number and com- petition level of rodeo participants.

Barrels must be regulation 55 gal. size metal or rubber and enclosed on both ends.

Further information: International Professional Rodeo As- sociation, Pauls Valley, Okla.

# CHAPTER 18

# Energy Design

## INTRODUCTION

Energy design analyses should be directed toward understanding the inherent energy characteristics of each particular building type. Each type has peculiar attributes, including occupancy, layout, lighting, envelope, glazing, equipment, and zoning characteristics. These attributes and their effect on total energy use should be understood. This gives the designer a clearer picture of the overall goal, as well as opportunities and constraints, faced in providing an energy-conscious building.

These energy performance targets are presented to assist the designer in recognizing appropriate ranges of energy use for specific building types and identifying the elements of energy end use for these building types.

The targets are by necessity ranges of BTUs per square foot per year and depend on several factors, including the amount of multiuse space in the building. Three climate conditions are shown for each building type, although these conditions are not as influential in commercial buildings as in residential because of the high internal cooling loads found in these building types.

The following are primary design concerns for each building type:

Office buildings: Control of heat gain, especially from artificial lighting and solar; conduction heat gains/losses through the envelope; and reduction of power requirements for lighting.

Educational facilities: HVAC systems, lighting systems, and other design strategies that can handle both large and small loads efficiently between diverse functional areas and occupancies during variable time periods.

Retail stores: Reduction of high and "steady state" internal heat loads, primarily due to high uniform lighting loads and high occupant densities.

Multifamily buildings: Control of "skin-load dominated" conditions, especially through conduction and infiltration; and power requirements from domestic hot water heating.

Hotels: A complex mix of functions, usage patterns, and occupancy levels results in high domestic hot water consumption, high ventilation requirements, and large conduction and infiltration gains/losses.

Hospitals: Selection and zoning of HVAC systems to serve diverse functional areas, varying operational and use profiles, high internal loads, and 24-hr occupancies.

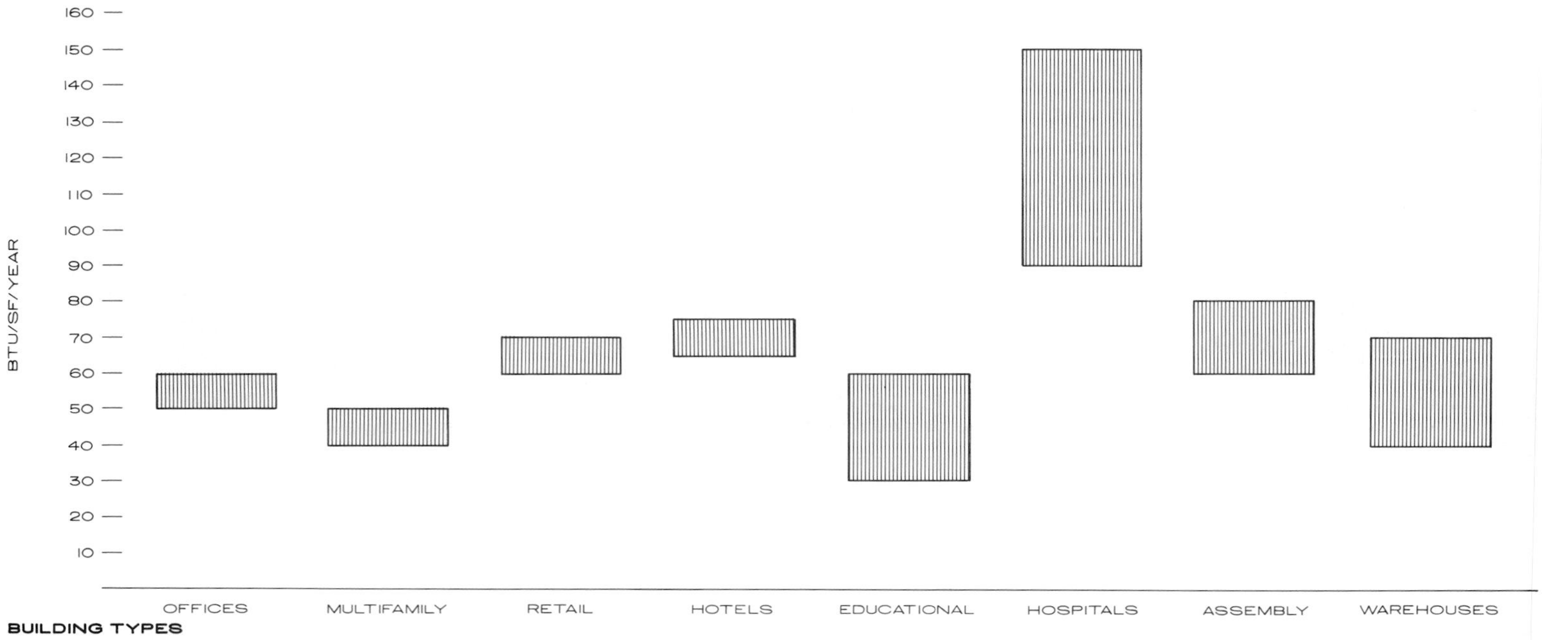

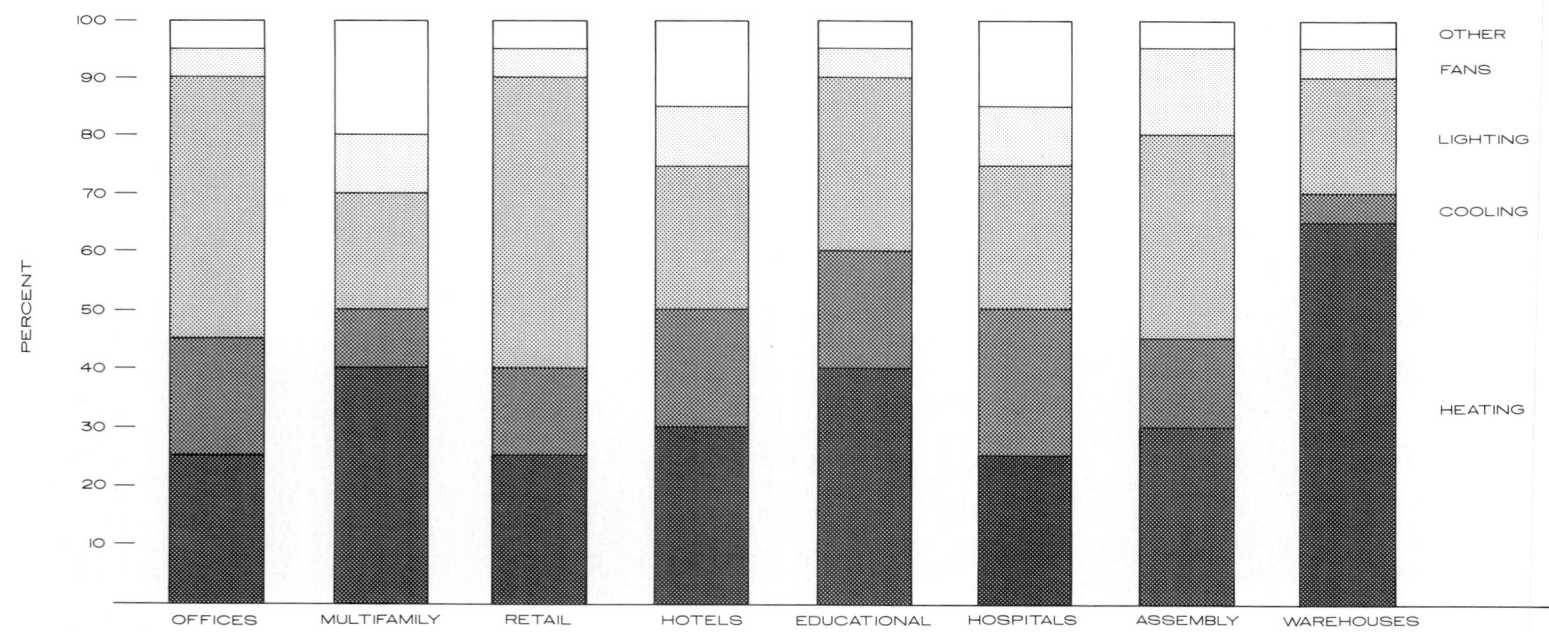

**TOTAL ENERGY USE**

**ENERGY END USE**

Earle Kennett; Nanita/Kennett Associates; Gaithersburg, Maryland

**BUILDING ENERGY TARGETS**

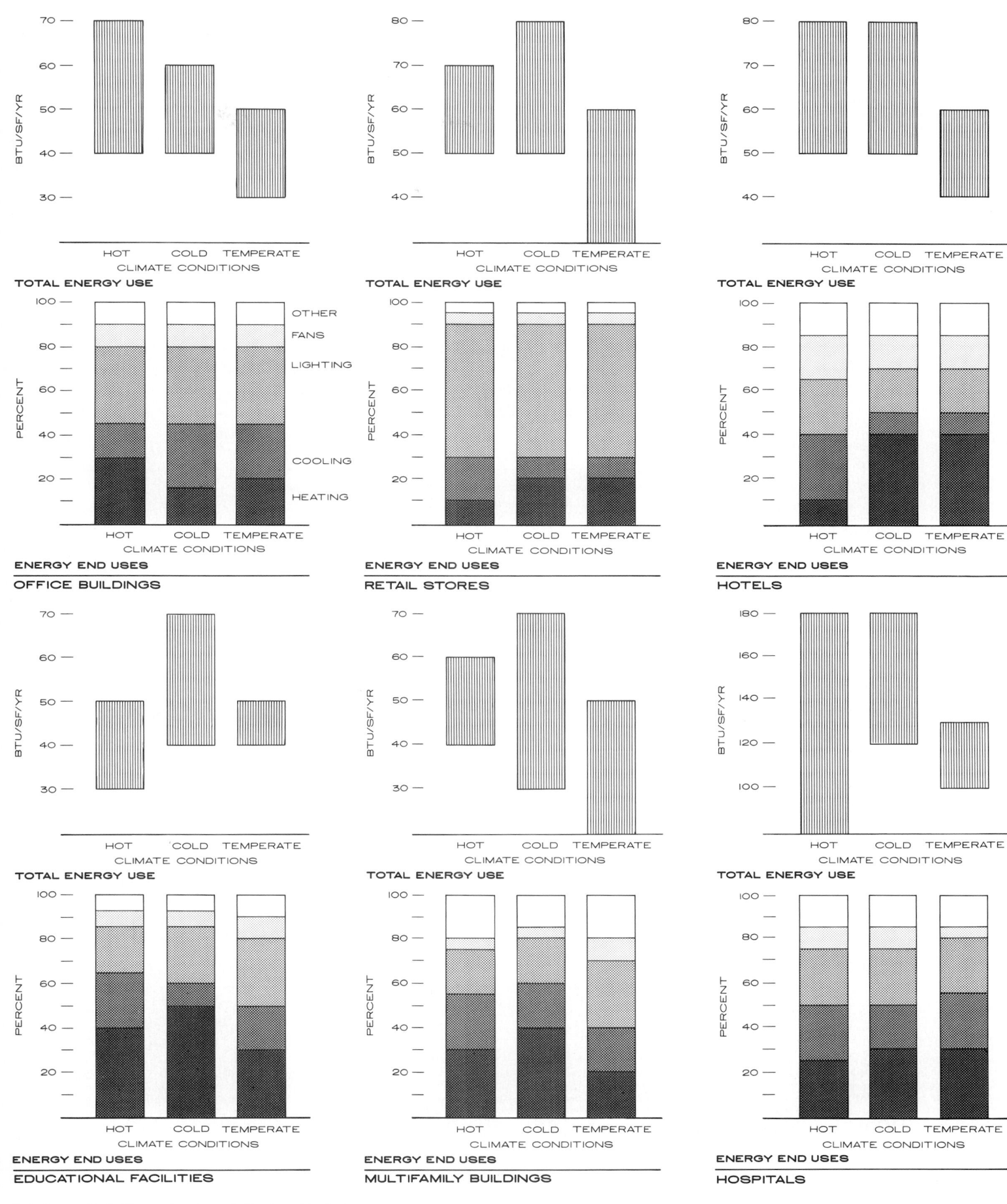

TOTAL ENERGY USE

ENERGY END USES
OFFICE BUILDINGS

TOTAL ENERGY USE

ENERGY END USES
RETAIL STORES

TOTAL ENERGY USE

ENERGY END USES
HOTELS

TOTAL ENERGY USE

ENERGY END USES
EDUCATIONAL FACILITIES

TOTAL ENERGY USE

ENERGY END USES
MULTIFAMILY BUILDINGS

TOTAL ENERGY USE

ENERGY END USES
HOSPITALS

Earle Kennett; Nanita/Kennett Associates; Gaithersburg, Maryland

## STRATEGIES OF CLIMATE CONTROL

The bioclimatic chart (Olgyay, *Design with Climate*, updated by Givoni and Arens) is presented here in standard psychrometric format. Plotting temperature and humidity data on the chart identifies cooling strategies for buildings dominated by envelope loads. The heavy lines in Figure 1 delineate limits within which ventilation, massive construction, evaporative space cooling, and clothing can maintain thermal comfort indoors.

## VENTILATION

Whole-house (exhaust) fans provide up to 60 air changes per hour and, like continuous cross ventilation, maintain indoor temperatures close to the outdoors. As long as outdoor conditions are within the comfort zone, "air-exchange ventilation" maintains indoor comfort. "Body ventilation" is best provided by ceiling (paddle) fans. They are effective up to 70% relative humidity and 85°F ET*, with a maximum air speed of 3 fps and light clothing (0.4–0.6 clo).

## THERMAL MASS

A very massive building envelope can maintain indoor comfort if outdoor air temperature does not exceed the thermal mass limit on the chart (roughly equal to 89°F ET*). This requires that (1) the envelope is shaded or reflective enough that its average daily outside surface temperature is no higher than the daily mean air temperature; (2) the envelope is massive enough to average daily temperature fluctuations; and (3) there is no daytime ventilation of the indoors. Nighttime ventilation extends the upper limit by cooling the envelope from both sides.

## EVAPORATIVE SPACE COOLING

Intake ventilation air is evaporatively cooled by drawing it through wetted mats or filters. The technique is suited to arid and semiarid regions and requires a fan-powered ventilation system. The limits are 71.5°F wet-bulb temperature and in excess of 105°F dry bulb, which is a conservative upper bound.

## OTHER CLIMATIC ELEMENTS

Wind speeds and direction are important for site analysis and for orienting the building for shelter from winter winds and to capture cooling breezes. Solar radiation data ("irradiation" or "insolation") is necessary for solar heating and daylighting design. Insolation, measured in BTU/sq ft/day or per hour, is a function of latitude, sky conditions, and angle of incidence to the receiving surface (see Kasuda and Ishii, 1977). Ground temperatures at various depths can be estimated from well-water temperatures (see Labs, 1981).

### REFERENCES

1. *Local Climatic Summaries*, National Climatic Center, Environmental Data Service, Asheville, NC 28801.
2. T. Kusuda and K. Ishii, *Hourly Solar Radiation Data for Vertical and Horizontal Surfaces on Average Days in the U.S. and Canada*, NBS BSS 96, 1977, U.S. Govt. Printing Office No. C13.29/2:96.
3. *Engineering Weather Data*, Air Force Design Manual 88-29 (Army TM 5-785, Navy NAVFAC P-89), 1978.
4. K. Labs, *Regional Analysis of Ground and Above-Ground Climate*, Oak Ridge National Laboratory (NTIS No. ORNL/Sub-81/40451/1), 1981.
5. D. Watson and K. Labs, *Climatic Design*, McGraw-Hill, New York, 1983.
6. E. Arens et al., "Thermal Comfort under an Extended Range of Environmental Conditions," ASHRAE *Transactions*, vol. 92, part 1B, 1986, pp. 18–26.

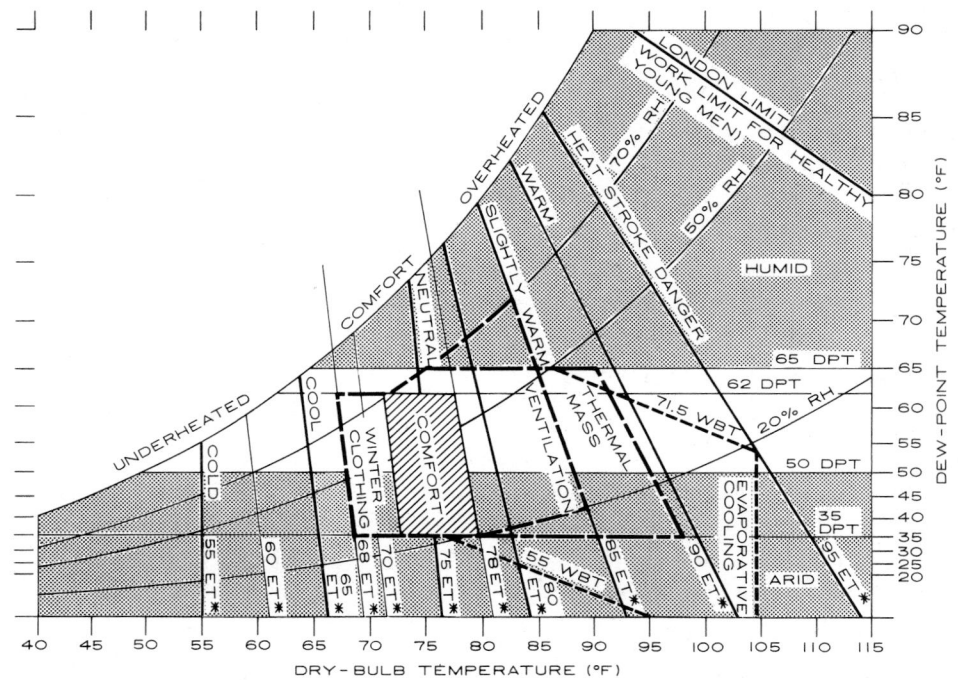

**FIGURE 1**
**BUILDING BIOCLIMATIC CHART (AFTER GIVONI)**

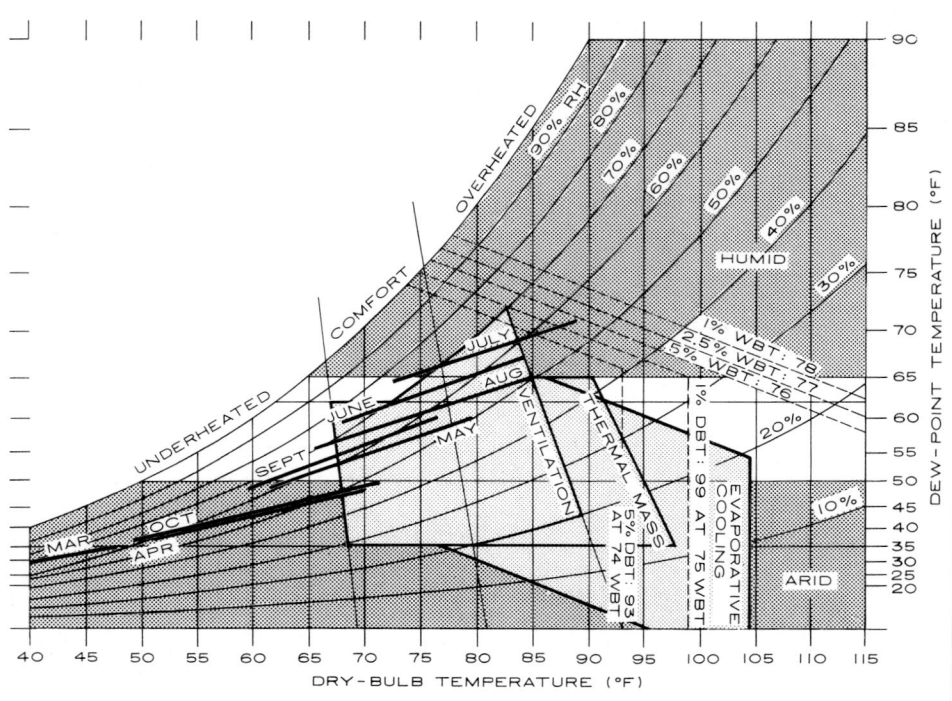

**FIGURE 2**
**EXAMPLE ANALYSIS: KANSAS CITY (WATSON AND LABS)**

## TERMINOLOGY

The effective temperature, ET*, refers to any set of temperature and humidity conditions that gives the same sensation of comfort as the stated temperature at 50% relative humidity (RH). ET* plotted here assumes light office clothing (0.6 clo) and very little air movement. One can feel as comfortable at 80°F with 20% RH as at 76°F at 80% RH; both are 78°F ET*. The ASHRAE comfort zone is bounded by an upper humidity limit of about 62°F dew point; 65°F is a conservative limit. A mean daily dew-point temperature of 50°F produces diurnal air temperature swings in excess of 30°F.

Donald Watson, FAIA; Trumbull, Connecticut

## PLOTTING DATA ON THE CHART

Combined temperature and humidity conditions at any moment can be plotted as a point on the chart. Graphing hourly data tracks the daily pattern, but daily maximum and minimum temperatures with their coincident humidities are usually adequate. Plotting a single day for each month summarizes the year at a glance (see Watson and Labs, 1983).

Example: Figure 2 plots 7 months of the year in Kansas City and shows ASHRAE summer air-conditioning design temperatures. The daily minimum dry-bulb temperature is coupled with the daily minimum dew point, while the daily maximum dry bulb is coupled with the daily maximum wet bulb. Much of the year falls below the lower comfort limit of 68°F ET* and is "underheated." Conditions exceeding 78°F ET* are "overheated." Ventilation satisfies most cooling needs, but the fact that design temperatures exceed the ventilation limit shows that some air conditioning is necessary.

## DESIGN FOR ENERGY CONSERVATION

Regional design for energy conservation aims to minimize use of conventionally powered heating, cooling, and lighting by using natural energy available at the building site. Site planning and building orientation, massing, and envelope design are the principal means for managing climate-driven conduction, convection, radiation, and vapor transfer. Climatic design strategies are selected in response to outdoor microclimatic conditions, defined as "underheated" or "overheated" with respect to indoor human comfort parameters.

## CLIMATIC REGIONS (MAP 1)

Map 1 delineates regions according to climatic control strategies. Regions exceeding 800 annual heating degree days (HDD) are predominantly "underheated," in which cooling is subordinate to solar heating and heat conservation strategies. Regions with fewer than 200 annual HDD require little heating in comparison to cooling and are predominantly "overheated" for design purposes. The large temperate region between 2000 and 8000 HDD has both heating and cooling requirements that must be balanced so that design features favoring heating do not add to the cooling load, and vice versa.

Suitability of ventilation and evaporative cooling are related to atmospheric humidity during summer months. Regions having a combined July and August average dew point temperature greater than 65°F may be considered "humid," and those averaging less than 50°F dew point may be considered "arid." The entire southeast quadrant of the U.S. has mean daily humidities exceeding comfort limits under still air conditions. The main control problem in this region is to balance ventilation with dehumidification and mechanical cooling.

The 50°F dew point temperature is an arbitrary way of defining atmospheric aridity, but it is convenient since it produces an outdoor daily temperature range of roughly 30°F dry-bulb. Arid and semiarid conditions favor evaporative and radiative cooling and generally disfavor summer daytime ventilation. While massive building envelopes can be advantageous in any region with a significant number of days having average daily temperatures in the upper 70s, mass is especially valuable in arid regions with extremely high daily maxima.

## SOLAR HEATING POTENTIAL (MAP 2)

Map 2 depicts solar heating capability in relation to heating load for envelope-dominated buildings. The lines plot the average daily solar gain transmitted through vertical south-facing double glazing, coincident with the need for heat on days when the average daily temperature is less than 65°F. It is calculated by the relation

$$\text{Average solar gain} = \frac{\text{sum(solar gain} \times \text{HDD)}}{\text{sum(HDD)}}$$

The units are Btu/day/sq ft of glazing. Values assume a ground reflection of 30%. The map indicates that, for instance, solar energy can satisfy the same percentage of the envelope heating load in Philadelphia, PA; Huntsville, AL; Oshkosh, WI; and Eugene, OR.

## UNDISTURBED GROUND TEMPERATURE (MAP 3)

At "steady state" depth (20–30 ft), ground temperature is the same as well water temperature, as plotted on Map 3. Ground temperatures vary considerably throughout the first 10 ft of earth and are elevated by heat losses from buildings. Heated buildings lose some heat to the deep ground throughout most of the U.S., but the earth is not an effective heat sink in the regions where cooling is most needed. Earth-tempered design requires special analysis of thermal soil–structure interaction.

Donald Watson, FAIA; Trumbull, Connecticut
Kenneth Labs; New Haven, Connecticut

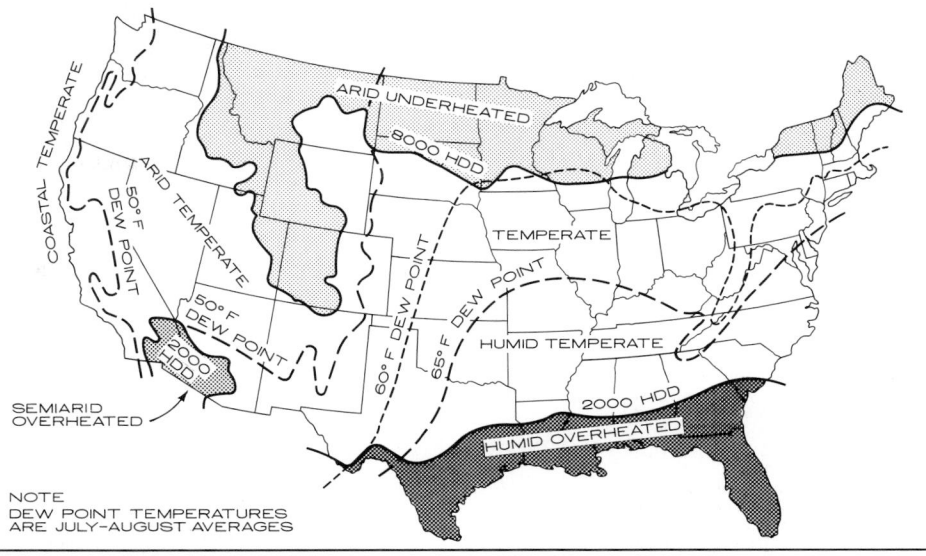

MAP 1: U.S. REGIONS BASED UPON CLIMATIC DESIGN CONDITIONS

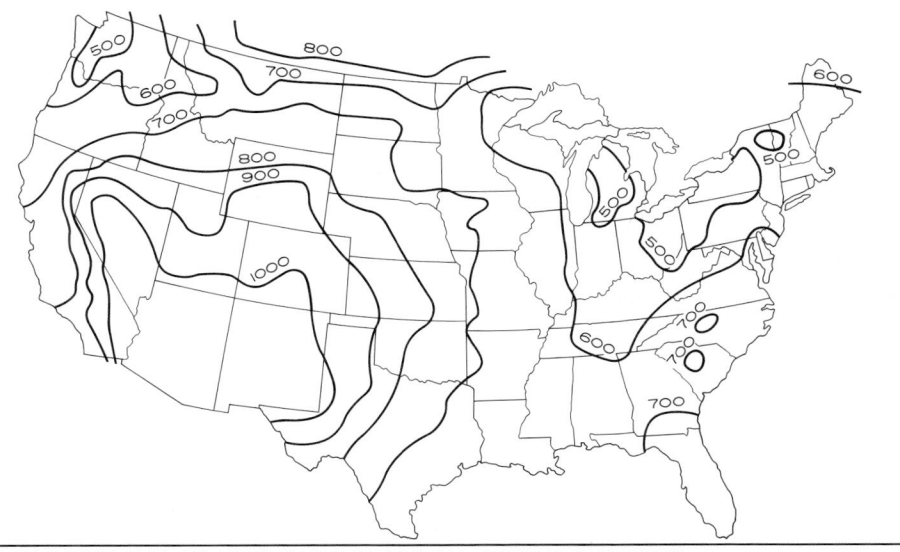

MAP 2: PASSIVE SOLAR HEATING POTENTIAL (BTU/SQ FT/DD)
DATA SOURCE: DOUG BALCOMB, U.S. DEPT. OF ENERGY

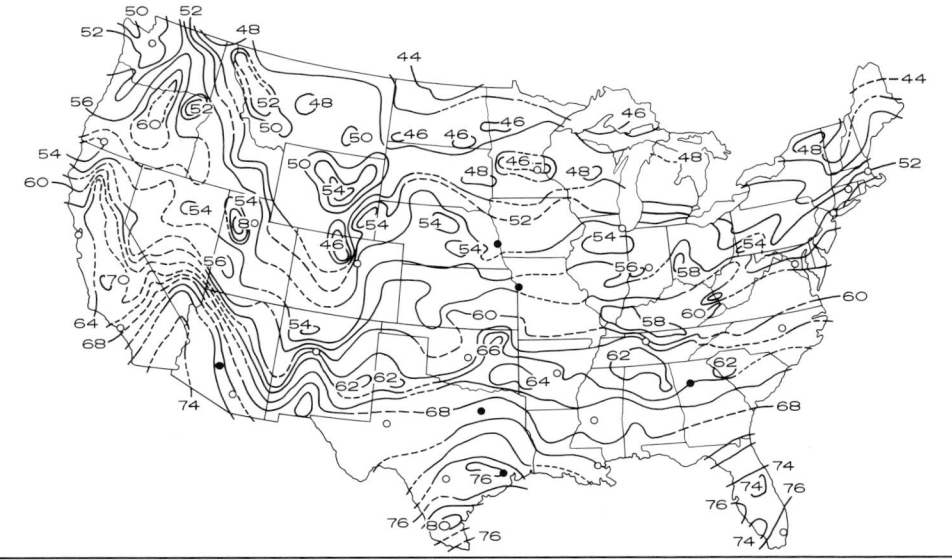

MAP 3: DEEP-GROUND TEMPERATURES (°F)
DATA SOURCE: NATIONAL WELL WATER ASSOCIATION

## WINTER WEATHER DATA AND DESIGN CONDITIONS FOR THE UNITED STATES AND CANADA

| STATE OR PROVINCE | CITY | LATITUDE (° ') | LONGITUDE (° ') | ELEVATION (FT) | WINTER DESIGN TEMP.* | AVE. WINTER TEMP.† | SEPT | OCT | NOV | DEC | JAN | FEB | MAR | APR | MAY | TOTAL |
|---|---|---|---|---|---|---|---|---|---|---|---|---|---|---|---|---|
| Ala. | Birmingham | 33 3 | 86 5 | 61 | 21 | 54.2 | 6 | 93 | 363 | 555 | 592 | 462 | 363 | 108 | 9 | 2551 |
| | Mobile | 30 4 | 88 1 | 119 | 29 | 59.9 | 0 | 22 | 213 | 357 | 415 | 300 | 211 | 42 | 0 | 1560 |
| Alaska | Fairbanks | 64 5 | 147 5 | 436 | -47 | 6.7 | 642 | 1203 | 1833 | 2254 | 2359 | 1901 | 1739 | 1068 | 555 | 14,279 |
| | Juneau | 58 2 | 134 4 | 17 | 1 | 32.1 | 483 | 725 | 921 | 1135 | 1237 | 1070 | 1073 | 810 | 601 | 9075 |
| Ariz. | Flagstaff | 35 1 | 111 4 | 6973 | 4 | 35.6 | 201 | 558 | 867 | 1073 | 1169 | 991 | 911 | 651 | 437 | 7152 |
| | Tucson | 32 1 | 111 0 | 2584 | 32 | 58.1 | 0 | 25 | 231 | 406 | 471 | 344 | 242 | 75 | 6 | 1800 |
| Ark. | Little Rock | 34 4 | 92 1 | 257 | 20 | 50.5 | 9 | 127 | 465 | 716 | 756 | 577 | 434 | 126 | 9 | 3219 |
| Calif. | Bakersfield | 35 2 | 119 0 | 495 | 32 | 55.4 | 0 | 37 | 282 | 502 | 546 | 364 | 267 | 105 | 19 | 2122 |
| | Sacramento | 38 3 | 121 3 | 17 | 32 | 54.4 | 0 | 62 | 312 | 533 | 561 | 392 | 310 | 173 | 76 | 2419 |
| | San Diego | 32 4 | 117 1 | 19 | 44 | 59.5 | 21 | 43 | 135 | 236 | 298 | 253 | 214 | 135 | 90 | 1458 |
| | San Francisco | 37 5 | 122 3 | 52 | 40 | 55.1 | 102 | 118 | 231 | 388 | 443 | 336 | 319 | 279 | 239 | 3001 |
| Colo. | Alamosa | 37 3 | 105 5 | 7536 | -6 | 29.7 | 279 | 639 | 1065 | 1420 | 1476 | 1162 | 1020 | 696 | 440 | 8529 |
| | Denver | 39 5 | 104 5 | 5283 | 1 | 37.6 | 117 | 428 | 819 | 1035 | 1132 | 938 | 887 | 558 | 288 | 6283 |
| Conn. | Hartford | 41 1 | 73 1 | 7 | 9 | 37.3 | 117 | 394 | 714 | 1101 | 1190 | 1042 | 908 | 519 | 205 | 6235 |
| Del. | Wilmington | 39 4 | 75 3 | 78 | 14 | 42.5 | 51 | 270 | 588 | 927 | 980 | 874 | 735 | 387 | 112 | 4930 |
| D.C. | Washington | 38 5 | 77 0 | 14 | 17 | 45.7 | 33 | 217 | 519 | 834 | 871 | 762 | 626 | 288 | 74 | 4224 |
| Fla. | Miami | 25 5 | 80 2 | 7 | 47 | 71.1 | 0 | 0 | 0 | 65 | 74 | 56 | 19 | 0 | 0 | 214 |
| | Tallahassee | 30 2 | 84 2 | 58 | 30 | 60.1 | 0 | 28 | 198 | 360 | 375 | 286 | 202 | 36 | 0 | 1485 |
| Ga. | Atlanta | 33 4 | 84 3 | 1005 | 22 | 51.7 | 18 | 124 | 417 | 648 | 636 | 518 | 428 | 147 | 25 | 2961 |
| | Savannah | 32 1 | 81 1 | 52 | 27 | 57.8 | 0 | 47 | 246 | 437 | 437 | 353 | 254 | 45 | 0 | 1819 |
| Hawaii | Honolulu | 21 2 | 158 0 | 7 | 63 | 74.2 | 0 | 0 | 0 | 0 | 0 | 0 | 0 | 0 | 0 | 0 |
| Idaho | Boise | 43 3 | 116 1 | 2842 | 10 | 39.7 | 132 | 415 | 792 | 1017 | 1113 | 854 | 722 | 438 | 245 | 5809 |
| Ill. | Chicago | 42 0 | 87 5 | 658 | -4 | 35.8 | 117 | 381 | 807 | 1166 | 1265 | 1086 | 939 | 534 | 260 | 6639 |
| | Springfield | 39 5 | 89 4 | 587 | 2 | 40.6 | 72 | 291 | 696 | 1023 | 1135 | 935 | 769 | 354 | 136 | 5429 |
| Ind. | Indianapolis | 39 4 | 86 2 | 793 | 2 | 39.6 | 90 | 316 | 723 | 1051 | 1113 | 949 | 809 | 432 | 177 | 5699 |
| Iowa | Des Moines | 41 3 | 93 4 | 948 | -5 | 35.5 | 96 | 363 | 828 | 1225 | 1370 | 1187 | 915 | 438 | 180 | 6588 |
| Kan. | Goodland | 39 2 | 101 4 | 3645 | 0 | 37.8 | 81 | 381 | 810 | 1073 | 1166 | 955 | 884 | 507 | 236 | 6141 |
| | Topeka | 39 0 | 95 4 | 877 | 4 | 41.7 | 57 | 270 | 672 | 980 | 1122 | 893 | 722 | 330 | 124 | 5182 |
| Ky. | Lexington | 38 0 | 84 4 | 979 | 8 | 43.8 | 54 | 239 | 609 | 902 | 946 | 818 | 685 | 325 | 105 | 4683 |
| La. | New Orleans | 30 0 | 90 2 | 3 | 33 | 61.8 | 0 | 12 | 165 | 291 | 344 | 241 | 177 | 24 | 0 | 1254 |
| | Shreveport | 32 3 | 93 5 | 252 | 25 | 56.2 | 0 | 47 | 297 | 477 | 552 | 426 | 304 | 81 | 0 | 2184 |
| Me. | Portland | 43 4 | 70 2 | 61 | -1 | 33.0 | 195 | 508 | 807 | 1215 | 1339 | 1182 | 1042 | 675 | 372 | 7511 |
| Md. | Baltimore | 39 1 | 76 4 | 146 | 13 | 43.7 | 48 | 264 | 585 | 905 | 936 | 820 | 679 | 327 | 90 | 4654 |
| Mass. | Boston | 42 2 | 71 0 | 15 | 9 | 40.0 | 60 | 316 | 603 | 983 | 1088 | 972 | 846 | 513 | 208 | 5634 |
| Mich. | Detroit | 42 2 | 83 0 | 633 | 6 | 37.2 | 87 | 360 | 738 | 1088 | 1181 | 1058 | 936 | 522 | 220 | 6232 |
| | Escanaba | 45 4 | 87 0 | 594 | -7 | 29.6 | 243 | 539 | 924 | 1293 | 1445 | 1296 | 1203 | 777 | 456 | 8481 |
| Minn. | Duluth | 46 5 | 92 1 | 1426 | -16 | 23.4 | 330 | 632 | 1131 | 1581 | 1745 | 1518 | 1355 | 840 | 490 | 10,000 |
| | Minneapolis | 44 5 | 93 1 | 822 | -12 | 28.3 | 189 | 505 | 1014 | 1454 | 1631 | 1380 | 1166 | 621 | 288 | 8322 |
| Miss. | Jackson | 32 2 | 90 1 | 330 | 25 | 55.7 | 0 | 65 | 315 | 502 | 546 | 414 | 310 | 87 | 0 | 2239 |
| Mo. | Columbia | 39 0 | 92 2 | 778 | 4 | 42.3 | 54 | 251 | 651 | 967 | 1076 | 875 | 716 | 324 | 121 | 5046 |
| Mont. | Billings | 45 5 | 108 3 | 3367 | -10 | 34.5 | 186 | 487 | 897 | 1135 | 1296 | 1100 | 970 | 570 | 285 | 7049 |
| | Missoula | 46 5 | 114 1 | 3200 | -6 | 31.5 | 303 | 651 | 1035 | 1287 | 1420 | 1120 | 970 | 621 | 391 | 8125 |
| Neb. | North Platte | 41 1 | 100 4 | 2779 | -4 | 35.5 | 123 | 440 | 885 | 1166 | 1271 | 1039 | 930 | 519 | 248 | 6684 |
| | Omaha | 41 2 | 95 5 | 978 | -3 | 35.6 | 105 | 357 | 828 | 1175 | 1355 | 1126 | 939 | 465 | 208 | 6612 |
| Nev. | Las Vegas | 36 1 | 115 1 | 2162 | 28 | 53.5 | 0 | 78 | 387 | 617 | 688 | 487 | 335 | 111 | 6 | 2709 |
| | Reno | 39 3 | 119 5 | 4404 | 10 | 39.3 | 204 | 490 | 801 | 1026 | 1073 | 823 | 729 | 510 | 357 | 6332 |
| N.H. | Concord | 43 1 | 71 3 | 339 | -3 | 33.0 | 177 | 505 | 822 | 1240 | 1358 | 1184 | 1032 | 636 | 298 | 7383 |
| N.J. | Trenton | 40 1 | 74 5 | 144 | 14 | 42.4 | 57 | 264 | 576 | 924 | 989 | 885 | 753 | 399 | 121 | 4980 |
| N.M. | Albuquerque | 35 0 | 106 4 | 5310 | 16 | 12.0 | 12 | 229 | 642 | 868 | 930 | 703 | 595 | 288 | 81 | 4348 |
| N.Y. | Buffalo | 43 0 | 78 4 | 705 | 6 | 34.5 | 141 | 440 | 777 | 1156 | 1256 | 1145 | 1039 | 645 | 329 | 7062 |
| | New York | 40 5 | 74 0 | 132 | 15 | 42.8 | 30 | 233 | 540 | 902 | 986 | 885 | 760 | 408 | 118 | 4871 |
| N.C. | Charlotte | 35 0 | 81 0 | 735 | 22 | 50.4 | 6 | 124 | 438 | 691 | 691 | 582 | 481 | 156 | 22 | 3191 |
| | Wilmington | 34 2 | 78 0 | 30 | 26 | 54.6 | 0 | 74 | 291 | 521 | 546 | 462 | 357 | 96 | 0 | 2347 |
| N.D. | Bismarck | 46 5 | 100 5 | 1647 | -19 | 26.6 | 222 | 577 | 1088 | 1463 | 1708 | 1442 | 1203 | 645 | 329 | 8851 |
| Ohio | Cleveland | 41 2 | 81 5 | 777 | 5 | 37.2 | 105 | 384 | 738 | 1088 | 1159 | 1047 | 918 | 552 | 260 | 6351 |
| | Columbus | 40 0 | 82 5 | 812 | 5 | 39.7 | 84 | 347 | 714 | 1039 | 1088 | 949 | 809 | 426 | 171 | 5660 |
| Okla. | Oklahoma City | 35 2 | 97 4 | 1280 | 13 | 48.3 | 15 | 164 | 498 | 766 | 868 | 664 | 527 | 189 | 34 | 3725 |
| | Tulsa | 36 1 | 95 5 | 650 | 13 | 47.7 | 18 | 158 | 522 | 787 | 893 | 683 | 539 | 213 | 47 | 3860 |
| Ore. | Salem | 45 0 | 123 0 | 195 | 23 | 45.4 | 111 | 338 | 594 | 729 | 822 | 647 | 611 | 417 | 273 | 4754 |
| Pa. | Pittsburgh | 40 3 | 80 1 | 1137 | 5 | 38.4 | 105 | 375 | 726 | 1063 | 1119 | 1002 | 874 | 480 | 195 | 5987 |
| | Williamsport | 41 1 | 77 0 | 527 | 7 | 38.5 | 111 | 375 | 717 | 1073 | 1122 | 1002 | 856 | 468 | 177 | 5934 |
| R.I. | Providence | 41 4 | 71 3 | 55 | 9 | 38.8 | 96 | 372 | 660 | 1023 | 1110 | 988 | 868 | 534 | 236 | 5954 |
| S.C. | Columbia | 34 0 | 81 1 | 217 | 24 | 54.0 | 0 | 84 | 345 | 577 | 570 | 470 | 357 | 81 | 0 | 2484 |
| S.D. | Rapid City | 44 0 | 103 0 | 3165 | -7 | 33.4 | 165 | 481 | 897 | 1172 | 1333 | 1145 | 1051 | 615 | 326 | 7345 |
| Tenn. | Nashville | 36 1 | 86 4 | 577 | 14 | 48.9 | 30 | 158 | 495 | 732 | 778 | 644 | 512 | 189 | 40 | 3578 |
| Texas | Brownsville | 25 5 | 97 3 | 16 | 39 | 67.6 | 0 | 0 | 66 | 149 | 205 | 106 | 74 | 0 | 0 | 600 |
| | Dallas | 32 5 | 96 5 | 481 | 22 | 55.3 | 0 | 62 | 321 | 524 | 601 | 440 | 319 | 90 | 6 | 2363 |
| | El Paso | 31 5 | 106 2 | 3918 | 24 | 52.9 | 0 | 84 | 414 | 648 | 685 | 445 | 319 | 105 | 0 | 2700 |
| | Houston | 29 4 | 95 2 | 50 | 32 | 61.0 | 0 | 6 | 183 | 307 | 384 | 288 | 192 | 36 | 0 | 1396 |
| Utah | Salt Lake City | 40 5 | 112 0 | 4220 | 8 | 38.4 | 81 | 419 | 849 | 1082 | 1172 | 910 | 763 | 459 | 233 | 6052 |
| Vt. | Burlington | 44 3 | 73 1 | 331 | 7 | 29.4 | 207 | 539 | 891 | 1349 | 1513 | 1333 | 1187 | 714 | 353 | 8269 |
| Va. | Lynchburg | 37 2 | 79 1 | 947 | 16 | 46.0 | 51 | 223 | 540 | 822 | 849 | 731 | 605 | 267 | 78 | 4166 |
| Wash. | Seattle | 47 4 | 122 2 | 14 | 27 | 46.9 | 129 | 329 | 543 | 657 | 738 | 599 | 577 | 396 | 242 | 4424 |
| W. Va. | Charleston | 38 2 | 81 4 | 939 | 11 | 44.8 | 63 | 254 | 591 | 865 | 880 | 770 | 648 | 300 | 96 | 4476 |
| Wisc. | Green Bay | 44 3 | 88 1 | 683 | -9 | 30.3 | 174 | 484 | 924 | 1333 | 1494 | 1313 | 1141 | 654 | 305 | 8029 |
| Wyo. | Casper | 42 5 | 106 3 | 5319 | -5 | 33.4 | 192 | 524 | 942 | 1169 | 1290 | 1084 | 1020 | 651 | 381 | 7410 |
| **CANADA** | | | | | | | | | | | | | | | | |
| Alta. | Edmonton | 53 34 | 113 31 | 2219 | -25 | — | 411 | 738 | 1215 | 1603 | 1810 | 1520 | 1330 | 765 | 400 | 10,268 |
| B.C. | Vancouver | 49 11 | 123 10 | 16 | 19 | — | 219 | 456 | 657 | 787 | 862 | 723 | 676 | 501 | 310 | 5515 |
| Man. | Winnipeg | 49 54 | 97 14 | 786 | -27 | — | 322 | 683 | 1251 | 1757 | 2008 | 1719 | 1465 | 813 | 405 | 10,679 |
| N.S. | Halifax | 44 39 | 63 34 | 83 | 5 | — | 180 | 457 | 710 | 1074 | 1213 | 1122 | 1030 | 742 | 487 | 7361 |
| Ont. | Toronto | 43 41 | 79 38 | 578 | -1 | — | 151 | 439 | 760 | 1111 | 1233 | 1119 | 1013 | 616 | 298 | 6827 |
| Que. | Montreal | 45 28 | 73 45 | 98 | -10 | — | 165 | 521 | 882 | 1392 | 1566 | 1381 | 1175 | 684 | 316 | 8203 |

*Based on 97.5% Design Dry-Bulb values found in ASHRAE Handbook of Fundamentals, 1977.
†October–April, inclusive. ASHRAE Systems Handbook, 1976.
‡Based on the period 1931–1960, inclusive. ASHRAE Systems Handbook, 1976.

CLIMATE

# THERMAL COMFORT

Human thermal comfort is determined by the body's ability to dissipate the heat and moisture that are produced continuously by metabolic action. The rate of heat production varies with the size, age, sex, and degree of activity of the individuals whose comfort is under consideration. For men of average size, seated and doing light work, the metabolic rate is about 450 Btu/hr; for women under similar circumstances the comparable rate is about 385 Btu/hr. For a 155 lb man seated and doing moderate to heavy work, the rate ranges from 650 to 800 Btu/hr; standing and walking about while doing moderately heavy work will raise the rate to 1000 Btu/hr while the hardest sustained work will result in a metabolic rate of 2000 to 2400 Btu/hr. For an office with the usual complement of men and women, an average metabolic rate will range from 400 to 450 Btu/hr per person.

Thermal comfort is attained when the environment surrounding the individual can remove the bodily heat and moisture at the rate at which they are being produced. The removal, accomplished by convection, evaporation, and radiation, is regulated by the dry bulb temperature, the vapor pressure, and rate of movement of the air and the mean radiant temperature (MRT) of the surrounding surfaces. MRT is defined by ASHRAE as the temperature of an imaginary black enclosure in which the individual experiences the same rate of radiant heat exchange as in the actual environment. (See 1985 ASHRAE Handbook of Fundamentals, Chapter 8, for more information on MRT and human comfort.)

Heat and moisture removal are also strongly affected by the nature and amount of clothing being worn and by its insulating value. This quality can be evaluated in terms of a thermal resistance unit designated by clo, where 1 clo = 0.88°F/(Btu/hr · sq ft). Typical masculine office attire, complete with warm jacket and light trousers, has an insulating value of 1.12 clo while a woman's office dress is rated at 0.73 clo. Values for other combinations are given in the ASHRAE reference cited above, page 8.6, Table 1-D. Uncomfortably low ambient air temperatures can be made tolerable by putting on more and heavier clothing, thus increasing the clo value; the converse, unfortunately, is not true.

The properties of atmospheric air-water vapor mixtures in the temperature range normally experienced by the human body can be shown effectively on psychrometric charts, which can take many different forms. The most familiar is that put forth by Willis H. Carrier, who is generally regarded as the originator of the air-conditioning industry in the U.S.A. On the Carrier-type chart, shown in modified form in Fig. 1, the humidity ratio of moist air, in pounds or grains (1 lb = 7000 grains) of water vapor per pound of dry air, is plotted against the dry bulb temperature of the air. Significant psychrometric data are given in the table at temperature intervals of 5°F from 50 to 90°F.

The relative humidity of moist air is the ratio, expressed as a percentage, of the amount of water vapor actually present in a given quantity of that air to the amount that the same quantity of air could contain if it were completely saturated at the same temperature and pressure. The uppermost curved line on the chart, called the saturation line, denotes 100% relative humidity. The wet bulb temperature, measured by a thermometer with a water wetted sensor over which the air-vapor mixture is flowing rapidly (800 to 900 fpm) is used in combination with the dry bulb temperature to find the % RH at conditions other than saturation. For example, at 75°F dry bulb and 60°F wet bulb the relative humidity is seen to be 40%.

The humidity ratio at this condition is 53 grains/lb of dry air while the dew point temperature, found by following the horizontal line of constant humidity ratio to its intersection with the saturation line, is 50°F.

The relatively restricted range of conditions within which most lightly clothed sedentary adults in the U.S.A. will experience thermal comfort is shown by the cross-hatched area on Fig. 1. Known as the ASHRAE comfort zone (also called "comfort envelope"), this area on the psychrometric chart represents the combinations of dry bulb temperature and relative humidity, which, when combined with an air movement of 45 fpm or less, will meet the thermal needs of most adults. For this chart, MRT = dry bulb temperature.

The effective temperature lines shown on Fig. 1 represent combinations of dry bulb temperature and relative humidity that will produce the same rate of heat and moisture dissipation by radiation, convection, and evaporation as an individual would experience in a black enclosure at the specified temperature and 50% relative humidity. As the % RH rises, the dry bulb temperature must be slightly reduced to produce the same feeling of comfort; as the % RH falls toward the 10 to 20% level experienced in desert climates, the dry bulb temperature may rise slightly without inducing discomfort.

An indoor temperature between 70°F and 80°F will be tolerable for most lightly clothed adults. Additional clothing (higher clo values) may help offset the discomfort of most building occupants at the lower end of the comfort range regardless of the % RH, but extremities will be uncomfortably cold.

Thermal comfort is directly related to the manner in which heat flows through or about building materials, whether by means of convection, radiation, or conduction.

Convection takes place when a fluid, such as gas, or a liquid is heated and moved from one place to another. When warm air in a room rises and forces the cooler air down, convection is taking place.

Radiation is the transfer of heat by electromagnetic waves from a warmer surface to a cooler one. A person sitting in the sun by a window absorbs radiant heat.

Conduction is heat transfer between adjacent molecules within a single or two separate bodies in direct contact. This occurs when a person touches a sun-warmed window or when the handle of a poker gets warm after a few minutes when the other end is placed in a fire.

The upper range of the comfort zone for summer operation of public buildings will be tolerable for most lightly clothed adults until the relative humidity rises above 60 to 65%. At that condition, discomfort will be experienced by many building occupants because of their inability to dissipate metabolic moisture. Increases in air velocity are beneficial under these conditions, but velocities above about 70 fpm will generally result in unpleasant working conditions because of drafts, blowing papers, and so on.

Figure 2 shows another version of the psychrometric chart in which wet bulb temperatures are plotted against dry bulb temperatures, with straight lines of constant % RH running upward from lower left to upper right. The effect of air velocity and clothing thermal resistance (expressed as clo units) is shown by the curved lines near the center of each diagram.

For these conditions, in which the mean radiant temperature equals the dry bulb temperature, relative humidity has only a small effect. As the activity level of the room occupants is lowered, reducing the metabolic rate, the comfortable air temperature range moves upward; as the activity level is increased, cooler air is required.

The effects of radiant energy transfer between individuals and the surfaces surrounding them can have significant influence on sensations of comfort or discomfort. An increase of 1°F in MRT is approximately equivalent to a 1.5°F increase in ambient air temperature. The use of radiant heating from moderately warm surfaces can help to offset the discomfort caused by air temperatures that are significantly below the ASHRAE comfort zone. Conversely, discomfort can be caused by large heated areas, such as sun warmed windows. An excessively high MRT can require a significant reduction in air temperature to create comfort. For an individual exposed to direct sunshine entering through an unshaded window, discomfort is almost certain to result.

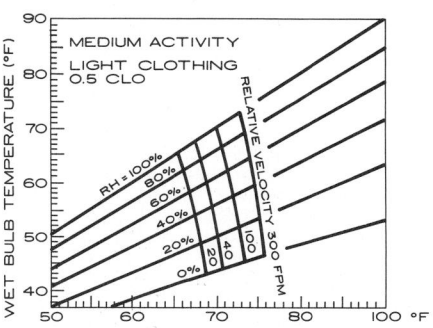

AIR TEMPERATURE = MEAN RADIANT TEMPERATURE

**FIGURE 2**

NOTE: Modified comfort chart for men, medium activity = 750 Btu/hr, thermal resistance of "light-clothing" = 0.5 clo.

**MODIFIED COMFORT CHART**

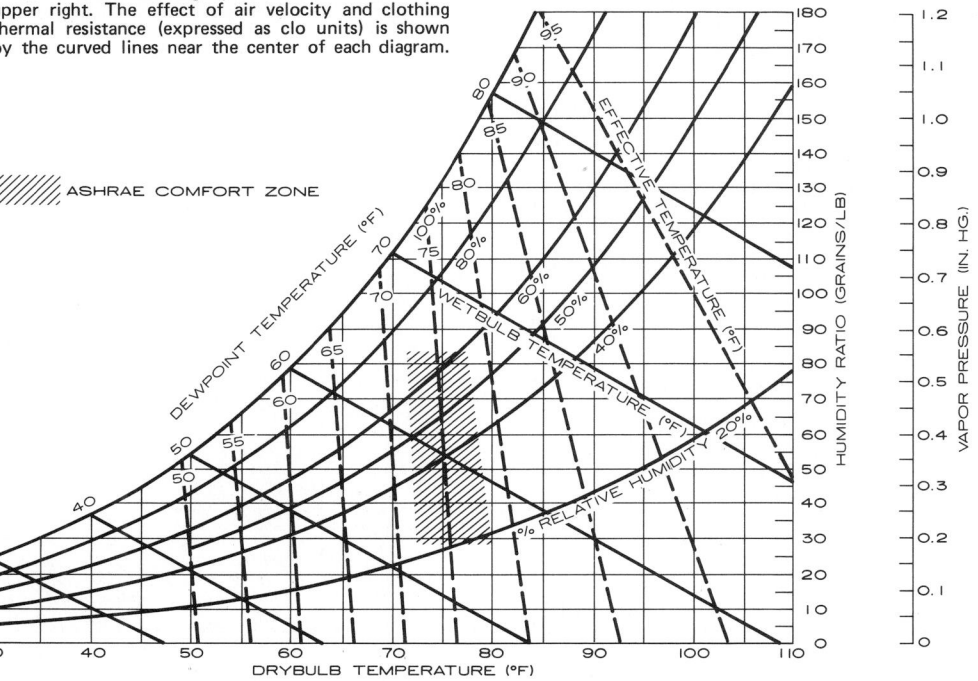

**FIGURE 1**

**PSYCHROMETRIC CHART**

John I. Yellott, P.E., Professor Emeritus, College of Architecture, Arizona State University; Tempe, Arizona

## CLIMATE

Cold climates in North America are generally north of the 40th parallel. Very cold is identified by the southern boundary of the 32°F mean annual temperature and includes most of Canada and Alaska except along the Pacific coast. Permafrost extends from below Hudson Bay and just north of the southern coast of Alaska to the Arctic Ocean. The Arctic Circle designates the southernmost point where continuous daylight in summer and continuous darkness in winter exist.

## PLANNING DETERMINANTS

Cold climates generally require multidisciplined considerations for extremes of physical, economic, sociological, and environmental conditions. These include very cold temperatures, high winds, drifting snow, continuous darkness and low sun angles, permafrost, minimal and costly transportation and communication, and subsequent isolation.

## DESIGN

Responses to planning determinants suggest aerodynamic design, isolation from permafrost, maximum insulation, self-sufficient utilities, backup systems for emergency, privacy without isolation, variety, and color. Labor is costly, suggesting maximum prefabrication. (Modular components can be used where barges can navigate.)

## THERMOPILES AND PROBES

Self-contained passive two-phase liquid or vapor convection systems are widely used for new construction and stabilization, either directly as a pipe pile or in smaller pipes (probes) that can be placed alongside a pile or under slab or foundation. Systems rely on temperature differences and natural convection for drawing heat from the ground to keep it frozen or refrozen, and radiating heat to the air.

## UTILITIES

Utilidors or utiliducts are the most common way to provide protection, easy access, and insulation of utility lines to avoid disturbance to the permafrost. Human waste at isolated facilities may be handled by compost privies (waterless toilets) and chemical toilets or self-contained treatment systems. Disposal systems include incineration and sewage lagoons.

## PERMAFROST, ICE WEDGES AND LENSES, AND FROST HEAVE

DEFINITION OF PERMAFROST: Ground of any kind that stays colder than the freezing temperature of water throughout several years. Depth can extend to 2,000 ft below active layer.

## TERMS

ACTIVE LAYER: Top layer of ground subject to annual freezing and thawing. Up to 10 ft or only 18 in. over some permafrost.

FROST HEAVING: Lifting or heaving of soil surface created by the freezing of subsurface frost-susceptible material.

FROST-SUSCEPTIBLE SOIL: Soil that has enough permeability and capillary action (wickability) to expand upon freezing.

ICE LENSE (TABER ICE): Subsurface pocket of ice in soil.

ICE WEDGE: Wedge-shaped mass of ice within thaw zone. Wedges range up to 3 or 4 ft wide and 10 ft deep.

PERELETOK: Frozen layer at the base of the active layer that remains unthawed during some cold summers.

RESIDUAL THAW ZONE: Layer of unfrozen ground between the permafrost and active layer. This layer does not exist when annual frost extends to the permafrost, but is present during some warm winters.

## SITE PLANNING

Blowing snow with high winds, low sun angles, and long periods of darkness are the dominant design factors. Minimizing obstructions that cause snow drifting and placing the long axis of a structure parallel to the prevailing wind help. Buildings can be spaced to avoid the long shadows cast by low winter sun angles. Darkness is a physical and psychological problem that suggests adequate lighting and signage.

Edwin B. Crittenden, FAIA, and John N. Crittenden, AIA; Anchorage, Alaska

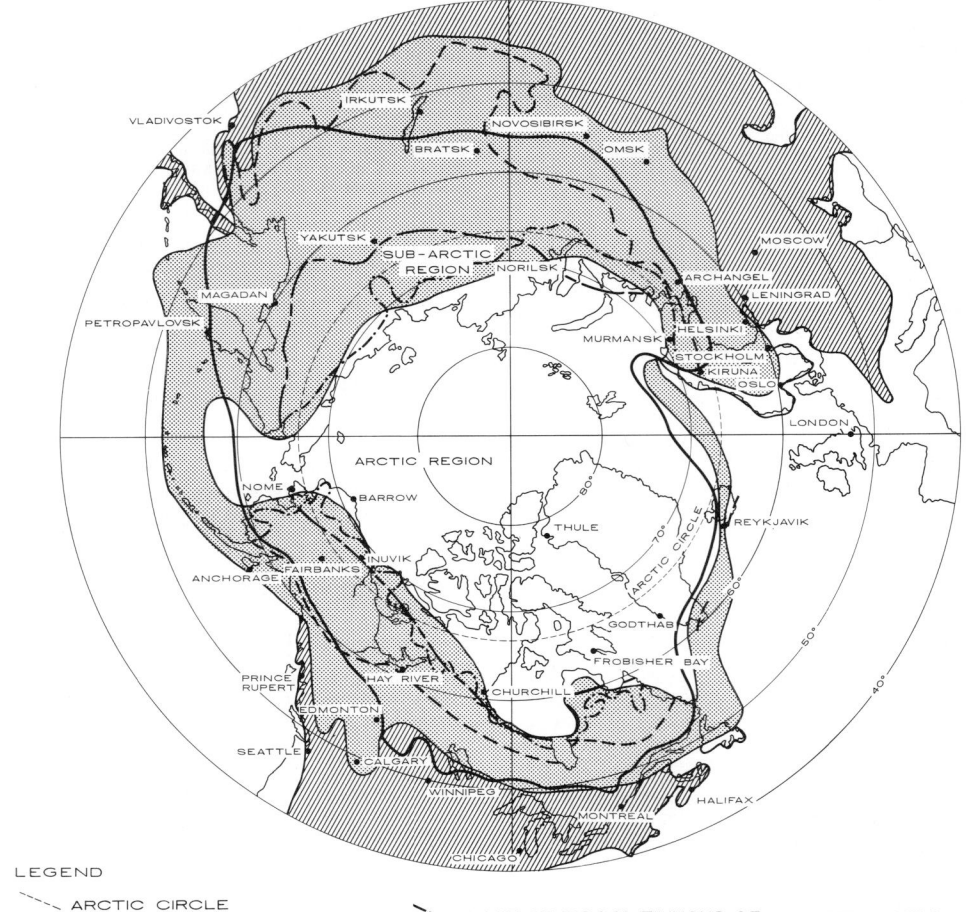

LEGEND

- – ·· – ARCTIC CIRCLE
- ▬▬▬ 32° F MEAN ANNUAL TEMPERATURE
- – – – LIMIT OF CONTINUOUS PERMAFROST
- – – – LIMIT OF DISCONTINUOUS OR SPORADIC PERMAFROST
- – ·· – NORTHERN BOUNDARY OF TREES
- ☐ ARCTIC | COLD DRY
- ▤ SUB-ARCTIC | 
- ▨ COLD WET

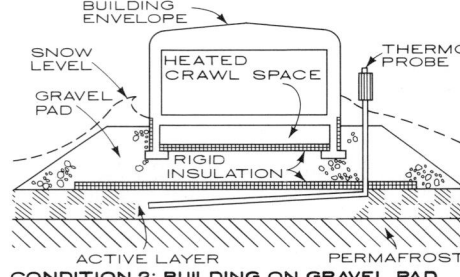

CONDITION 1: ELEVATED BUILDING ON PILES

CONDITION 2: BUILDING ON GRAVEL PAD

## CONDITION OF BUILDINGS ON PERMAFROST

CONDITION 1: Building elevated on piles allows the dissipation of building heat to prevent ground thaw, the refreezing of ground by the cold winter air, and the prevention of snow buildup. Piles may be wooden, requiring anchoring to avoid uplift or thermopiles to refreeze or keep the ground frozen.

CONDITION 2: Building elevated on non-frost-susceptible gravel pad to provide insulation in addition to existing ground cover. Rigid insulation adds to the protection from thaw of the permafrost. Thermoprobes are used to refreeze fill and keep permafrost frozen.

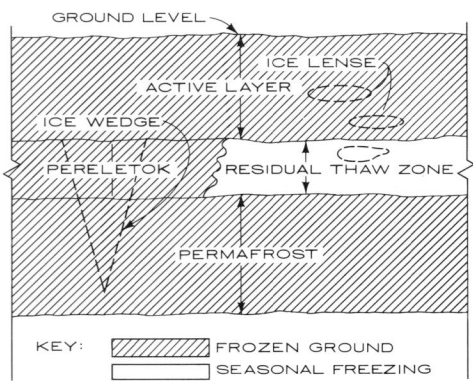

KEY:
▨ FROZEN GROUND
☐ SEASONAL FREEZING

## REFERENCES

Johnston, G. H., Permafrost Engineering, Design and Construction, National Research Council of Canada, John Wiley & Sons, New York, 1981.

Phukan, Arvind, Frozen Ground Engineering, Prentice Hall, Englewood, NJ, 1985.

Rice, Eb, Building in the North, Geophysical Institute, University of Alaska, Fairbanks, AK, 1975.

Zrudlo, Leo R., Psychological Problems and Environmental Design in the North, Collection Nordicana, Université Laval, Montreal, Canada, 1972.

## 18  ENERGY DESIGN

## STRATEGIES OF CLIMATE CONTROL

Underheated conditions occur in both humid and arid regions and dominate much of the U.S. The strategies are to minimize conduction and infiltration losses and to take advantage of winter solar gain. Humidity affects sky clearness and availability of solar radiation, making optimization of solar glazing area one of the main opportunities of regional design. Moisture movement through the building shell must be controlled. It is driven by air leakage (exfiltration) and by vapor diffusion, which is related to temperature differences.

## MINIMIZE CONDUCTION LOSSES

Minimize ratio of envelope to heated floor area. Minimize foundation perimeter length. Insulate envelope components in proportion to indoor–outdoor temperature difference. Minimize areas of windows, doors, and other envelope components of inherently low R value. Detail to avoid thermal bridging. Provide movable insulation for glazed areas.

## MINIMIZE INFILTRATION LOSSES

Plant vegetation to create wind-sheltered building sites. Shape building to minimize exposure to winter wind. Orient doors and windows away from winter wind. Specify weatherstripping and infiltration barrier.

## CAPTURE SOLAR GAIN

Provide high-transmittance south-facing glazing. Provide thermal mass indoors to store solar gains.

## INSULATION

Insulation requirements are proportional to heating loads. The foundation is often underinsulated and can be a major source of heat loss. The desirable insulation level depends on basement temperature and insulation levels in the rest of the building. An approximate thermal optimum is:

$$R_{ins} = \frac{T_{bsmt} - T_0}{T_1 - T_0} R_{ref} - R_{wall}$$

$R_{ins}$ = R value to be added to basement wall above grade

$R_{ref}$ = R value of superstructure wall

$R_{wall}$ = R value of uninsulated basement foundation wall

$T_{bsmt}$ = average seasonal temperature of basement

$T_1$ = average seasonal temperature of living space

$T_0$ = average seasonal outdoor temperature

The added foundation insulation above grade is $R_{ins}$. It should decrease with depth by R − 2 per foot in ordinary soils and R − 1.5 in wet soils. A horizontal skirt can be used to reduce floor perimeter losses. Exterior insulation keeps the wall warm and eliminates condensation and thermal bridges. As seasonal basement temperature decreases, losses to it from the superstructure increase, and basement ceiling R value should increase. As a very rough rule, the basement ceiling R value should be greater than $(R_{ref} - R_{ins})$.

## SOLAR DESIGN AND DAYLIGHTING

The most advantageous south glazing area depends on thermal and climatic factors. Rules of thumb have been prepared (Los Alamos National Laboratory) and more sophisticated methods are available for desktop computers.

The advantage of glazing for daylighting has to be weighed against the penalty of winter heat loss. In predominantly cloudy climates, skylighting can be designed without significant shading, but not without concern for glare. In clear, sunny climates and in warmer regions, daylight glazing may require shading to reduce undesired heat gain. South glazing has the combined advantages of daylighting, winter heat gain, and economical summer shading.

### REFERENCES

1. Los Alamos National Laboratory, *Passive Solar Heating Analysis*, ASHRAE, Atlanta, 1984.
2. National Research Council, Canada, Ottawa, Ontario, K1A OR6: *Construction Details for Air Tightness* (nonresidential), NRCC 18291, 1980; *Exterior Walls: Understanding the Problems*, NRCC 21203, 1983; *Humidity, Condensation and Ventilation in Houses*, NRCC 23293, 1984; J. Latta, *The Principles and Dilemmas of Designing Durable House Envelopes for the North*, Building Practice Note 52, 1985.

Donald Watson, FAIA; Trumbull, Connecticut
Kenneth Labs; New Haven, Connecticut

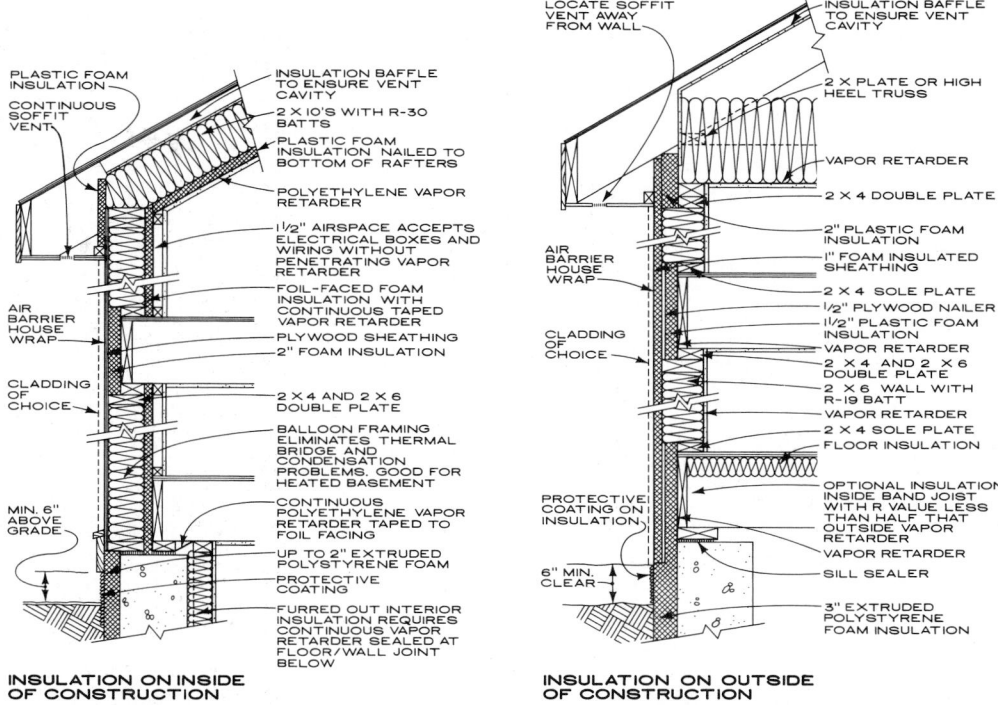

INSULATION ON INSIDE OF CONSTRUCTION

INSULATION ON OUTSIDE OF CONSTRUCTION

**ENERGY-EFFICIENT WALL SECTIONS**

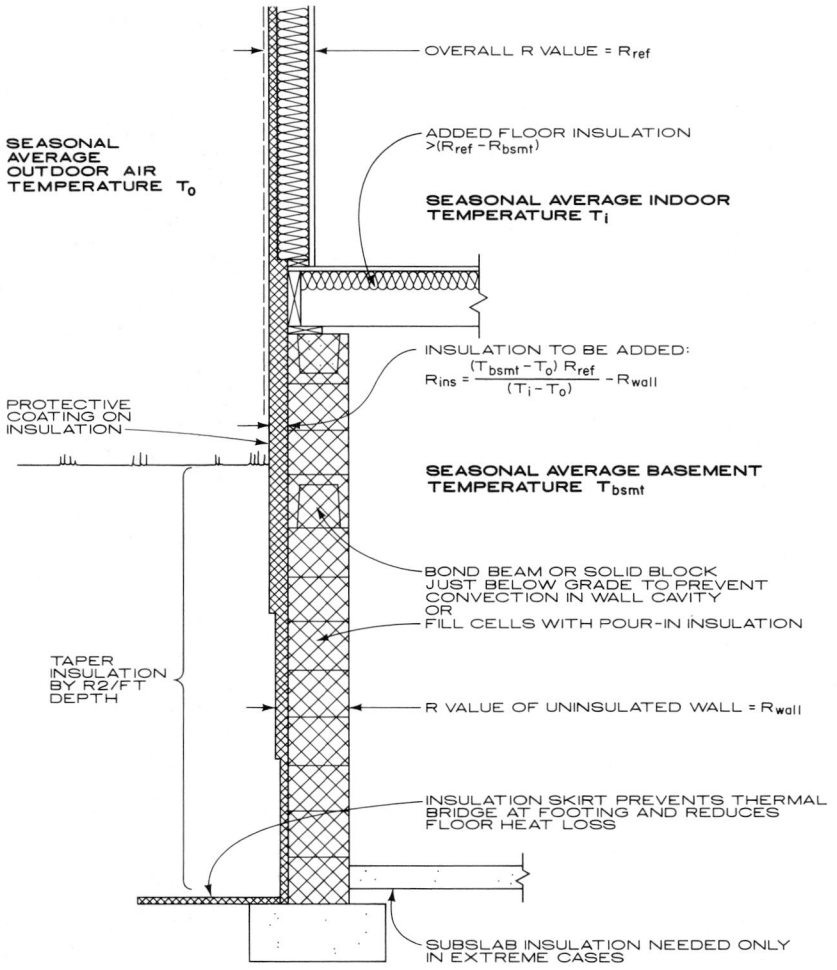

**BASEMENT FOUNDATION AND FLOOR INSULATION**

## STRATEGIES OF CLIMATE CONTROL

Dry, clear atmospheres lead to high insolation levels, high daytime sol-air temperatures, very high sol-air temperatures, and large thermal radiation losses. These factors produce daily temperature ranges in excess of 30°F. Although daytime air temperatures may be too high for ventilation, nighttime temperatures often fall below comfort limits and are useful for cooling. Arid regions in the U.S. have winter heating requirements, especially at night. Clear skies greatly favor passive solar heating.

High daytime temperatures and solar loads require measures that reduce heat gain. Evaporative roof spray systems dissipate absorbed solar heat, but consume large quantities of water and decrease in value with increases in roof insulation. Evaporative space cooling systems are often effective substitutes for refrigerant air conditioning. Deep ground temperatures are too high and soil thermal conductivity too low in hot, arid regions for the earth to be a useful cooling sink in conventional construction. Low conductivity makes the soil a good buffer against surface conditions, and earth-integrated design can take advantage of seasonal cold storage, so earth coupling does offer opportunities.

### MINIMIZE SOLAR GAINS

Plant trees to shade roof and east and west walls. Shape building to minimize solar load on envelope. Cluster buildings to shade one another. Provide shading for outdoor pedestrian and living areas (ramadas and pergolas), and shade all glazing during overheated period. Use carport or garage as buffer on west side. Use light-colored surfacing on walls and roof.

### MINIMIZE CONDUCTIVE GAINS

Insulate envelope components in proportion to (sol-air–indoor) temperature difference. Use radiant barrier in attic or cathedral ceiling. Use thermally massive envelope materials. Insulate perimeter of slab-on-grade floors.

### PROMOTE VENTILATION LOSSES

Site building to exploit nighttime breezes. Arrange floor plan for internal air movement, especially to cool thermal mass. Consider a whole-house fan for night cooling. Ventilate building envelope (attic or roof, walls).

## THERMAL MASS AND INSULATION CONCEPTS

Massive walls of sufficient thickness can average daily outdoor temperatures and maintain nearly constant indoor surface temperatures. This thickness (in feet) for an uninsulated homogeneous wall must be greater than 6.4 $(k/wc)^{1/2}$, where k is thermal conductivity in Btu/ft(hr)F, w is density in lb/cu ft, and c is specific heat in Btu/(lb)F. The minimum thickness is 14 in. for poured concrete, 12 in. for brick, 9 in. for adobe, and 6 in. for pine log. Less thick walls reduce, but do not eliminate, the temperature swing. The ratio of interior to exterior fluctuation is termed the "decrement factor." Values for some composite walls are given in the table.

A completely shaded, uninsulated massive wall can do no better than maintain a temperature near the outdoor daily average at the interior, unless the space is ventilated at night. Uninsulated mass walls have low R values and are not economically suitable for heated and air-conditioned buildings. Insulating outside the mass has the greatest benefit: It reduces heat gain while allowing the wall to store "coolth" from nighttime ventilation. Insulation also allows less mass to be used. The thermally optimal storage thickness (in feet) of mass that is well insulated on the outside is 3.3 $(k/wc)^{1/2}$. Less thickness is still beneficial.

Insulating inside the mass or adding mass outside an insulated frame wall (brick veneer) improves performance over either case alone. Both are inferior to outside insulation and slightly less effective than walls with integral insulation (masonry with core insulation). The optimal insulation and mass combinations vary with climate and conditioning hours of the building.

### THERMAL MASS TIME DELAY

Mass delays the transfer of heat to the interior. Its usefulness depends on occupancy and air-conditioning schedules. While a masonry west wall can relieve an office building of peak loads during business hours, for example, it would be inappropriate for a west-facing bedroom. The delay rate in hours per foot for a homogeneous wall is about 1.4$(wc/k)^{1/2}$ in thickness.

## INTERIOR ZONING AND DAYLIGHTING

Vernacular house design in hot, arid regions uses low mass construction for sleeping areas and high mass for daytime activity areas. The low mass zone is ventilated and cools off quickly at night, while the massive zone has little window area. Evaporative space coolers can provide comfort more than 90% of the time at elevations above 1500 ft and more than 50% at elevations below 1500 ft throughout the Southwest. Ducts should be sized for 1200 fpm (for silence and efficiency) to 1600 fpm.

Clear, sunny skies make daylighting dependable and predictable for design. Small window and skylight areas are effective. Apertures should be shaded at the exterior. Reflected light from the ground and from light shelves is useful, but glare from uncontrolled reflecting surfaces must be kept from view.

### REFERENCES


1. K. Clark and P. Paylore, *Desert Housing: Balancing Experience and Technology for Dwelling in Hot Arid Zones*, Office of Arid Land Studies, University of Arizona, Tucson.
2. J. Cook, *Cool Houses for Desert Suburbs*, Arizona Solar Energy Commission, Phoenix, 1984.
3. H. Kessler, *Passive Solar Design for Arizona*, Arizona Solar Energy Commission, Phoenix, 1983.
4. A. Olgyay and V. Olgyay, *Solar Control and Shading Devices*, Princeton University Press, Princeton, 1957.
5. S. Byrne and R. Ritschard, "A Parametric Analysis of Thermal Mass in Residential Buildings," LBL-20288, Lawrence Berkeley Laboratory, Berkeley, CA 94720, 1985.


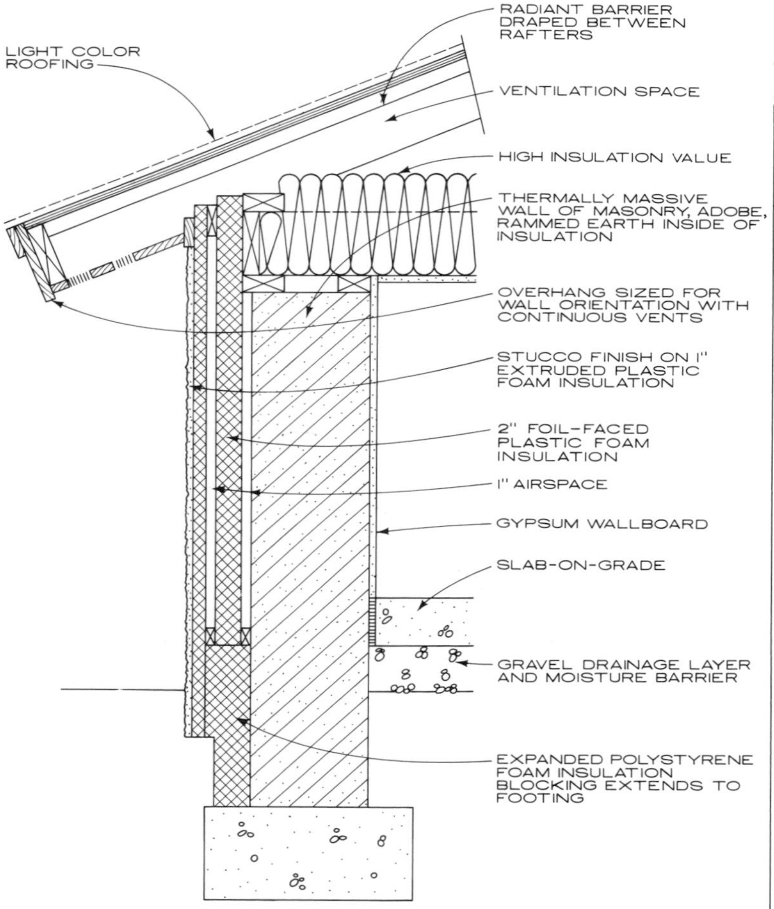

LIGHT COLOR ROOFING
RADIANT BARRIER DRAPED BETWEEN RAFTERS
VENTILATION SPACE
HIGH INSULATION VALUE
THERMALLY MASSIVE WALL OF MASONRY, ADOBE, RAMMED EARTH INSIDE OF INSULATION
OVERHANG SIZED FOR WALL ORIENTATION WITH CONTINUOUS VENTS
STUCCO FINISH ON 1" EXTRUDED PLASTIC FOAM INSULATION
2" FOIL-FACED PLASTIC FOAM INSULATION
1" AIRSPACE
GYPSUM WALLBOARD
SLAB-ON-GRADE
GRAVEL DRAINAGE LAYER AND MOISTURE BARRIER
EXPANDED POLYSTYRENE FOAM INSULATION BLOCKING EXTENDS TO FOOTING


ENERGY-EFFICIENT WALL SECTION
INTERIOR MASS WITH OUTSIDE INSULATION

### THERMAL PERFORMANCE (TIME LAG) OF VARIOUS WALL SECTIONS

| WALL DESCRIPTION | U VALUE (WINTER) | HEAT GAIN BTU/HR/SQ FT (DARK COLOR) AVERAGE ORIENTATION | WEST ORIENTATION | TIME LAG (HR) | AMPLITUDE DECREMENT FACTOR |
|---|---|---|---|---|---|
| 8″ brick and lightweight concrete (100 lb density) block 2″ polystyrene insulation board ½″ gypsum wallboard | 0.073 | 2.06 | 1.75 | 4 | 0.40 |
| 6″ precast concrete (140 lb density) sandwich panel 2″ polyurethane core | 0.065 | 1.82 | 1.55 | 4 | 0.40 |
| ½″ plywood siding ½″ insulation board sheathing, wood studs. Full batt (R-11) insulation ½″ gypsum wallboard | 0.076 | 3.05 | 4.60 | 2 | 0.75 |
| 4″ brick veneer ½″ insulation board sheathing. Wood studs full batt (R-11) insulation ½″ gypsum wallboard | 0.077 | 2.18 | 1.95 | 4 | 0.62 |
| 8″ brick wall (hollow units) 1″ x 2″ furring. ½″ gypsum wallboard | 0.316 | 7.37 | 5.90 | 6 | 0.25 |

Donald Watson, FAIA; Trumbull, Connecticut
Kenneth Labs; New Haven, Connecticut

## STRATEGIES OF CLIMATE CONTROL

Humid overheated conditions are most severe along the Gulf Coast, but occur across the entire southeastern U.S. Atmospheric moisture limits radiation exchange, resulting in daily temperature ranges less than 20°F. High insolation gives first priority to shading. Much of the overheated period is only a few degrees above comfort limits, so air movement can cool the body. Ground temperatures are generally too high for the earth to be useful as a heat sink, although slab-on-grade floor mass is useful. The strategies are to resist solar and conductive heat gains and to take best advantage of ventilation.

### MINIMIZE SOLAR GAINS

1. Plant trees to shade roof and east and west walls.
2. Shape building to minimize solar load on envelope.
3. Shade all glazing during overheated period.
4. Shade north elevation in subtropical latitudes.
5. Use light-colored surfacing on walls and roof.

### MINIMIZE CONDUCTIVE GAINS

1. Insulate envelope components in proportion to sol-air–indoor temperature difference.
2. Use radiant barrier in attic space.
3. Consider thermally massive envelope materials to reduce peak air-conditioning loads.
4. Use slab-on-grade instead of crawl space and insulate only at perimeter.

### PROMOTE VENTILATION LOSSES

1. Orient building to benefit from breezes.
2. Use plantings to funnel breezes into building, but be careful not to obstruct vent openings.
3. Use wing walls and overhangs to direct breezes into building.
4. Locate openings and arrange floor plan to promote cross ventilation.
5. Plan interior for effective use of whole-house fan.
6. Ventilate building envelope (attic or roof, walls).

## SPACE VENTILATION

"Air-change ventilation" brings outdoor temperatures indoors by breezes or whole-house exhaust fans. Whole-house fans yield about 60 air changes per hour (ACH) and are useful only as long as outdoor conditions are within comfort limits (72°–82°F). They may offer 30–50% savings in electricity costs over air conditioning. Whole-house fans do not provide high enough airflow rates for body ventilation. Ceiling (paddle) fans are recommended for air movement and can maintain comfort with indoor temperatures up to 85°F ET*. Air conditioning is necessary above 85°F ET*. The issue of when to ventilate and when to air condition is a function of building type, occupancy hours, heat and moisture capacity of the structure, and climatic subregion. Humidity is a factor, as night air may be cool but excessively humid.

## ROOFS AND ATTICS

The attic should be designed to ventilate naturally. Most of the heat gain to the attic floor is by radiation from the underside of the roof. While ventilation is unable to interrupt this transfer, most of it can be stopped by an aluminum foil radiant barrier. Foil facings on rigid insulation and sheathing can be used as radiant barriers when installed facing an airspace.

Roof spray systems can dissipate most of the solar load, leaving the roof temperature near the ambient dry-bulb instead of the sol-air temperature. The theoretical lowest temperature that the roof can be cooled to by evaporation is the wet-bulb, but is not attainable under real daytime conditions. The cost-effectiveness of spray systems depends on the roof section, R value, building type, climatic region, and other factors. Spray systems are most advantageous for poorly insulated flat roofs.

## WALLS

Radiant barriers enhance the performance of walls by reducing solar gain. They are most effective on east and west walls and are recommended for predominantly overheated regions [<2000 heating degree days (HDD), >2500 cooling degree days (CDD)]. They are not recommended on south walls except where CDD exceed 3500. Radiant barriers must face an airspace and can be located on either side of the wall structure. Outside placement allows the cavity to be vented. This enhances summer wall performance, but admitting cold air degrades it during winter. Venting is recommended for regions having more than 3500 CDD. Discharging the cavity into the attic ensures best vent action. Thermal mass in walls reduces peak air-conditioning loads and delays peak heat gain. By damping off some of the peak load, massive walls help keep indoor temperatures in the range where ceiling (paddle) fans and airflow from cross ventilation provide comfort.

## DAYLIGHTING

Windows and skylights should be shaded to prevent undesired heat gain. North- and south-facing glazing is shaded most easily for predictable daylighting. Light-colored reflective sunshades and ground surfaces will bounce the light and minimize direct gain. Cloudy or hazy sky conditions are a source of brightness and glare.

### REFERENCES

1. S. Chandra et al. *Cooling with Ventilation*, Solar Energy Research Institute, Golden, CO, 1982.
2. P. Fairey, "Radiant Barrier Systems," Design Notes 6 and 7, Florida Solar Energy Center, Cape Canaveral, 1984.
3. P. Fairey, S. Chandra, A. Kerestecioglu, "Ventilative Cooling in Southern Residences: A Parametric Analysis," PF-108-86, Florida Solar Energy Center, Cape Canaveral, 1986.

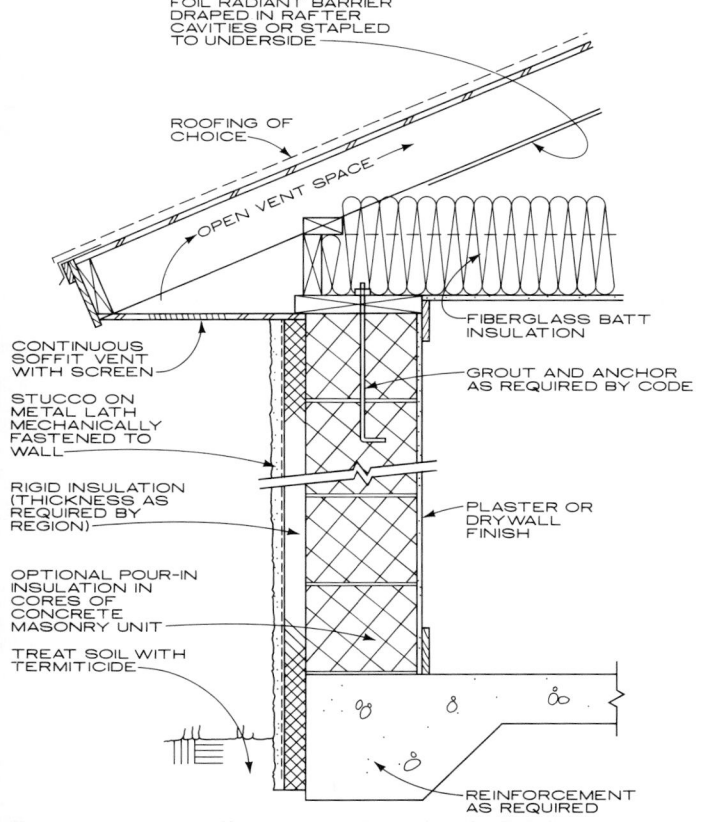

**ENERGY-EFFICIENT WALL SECTION: VENTED SKIN MASONRY WALL WITH INSIDE INSULATION**

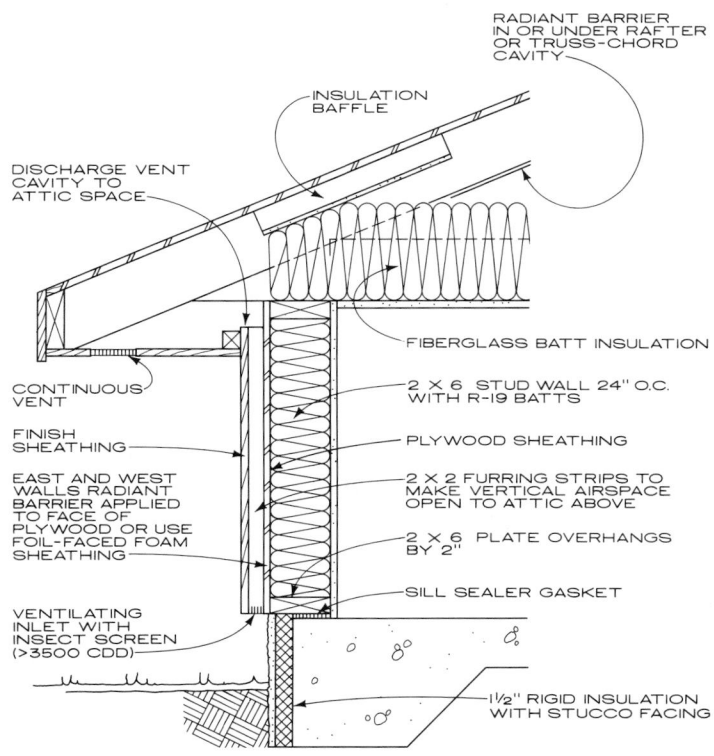

**ENERGY-EFFICIENT WALL SECTION: VENTED SKIN WALL WITH RADIANT BARRIER**

Donald Watson, FAIA; Trumbull, Connecticut
Kenneth Labs; New Haven, Connecticut

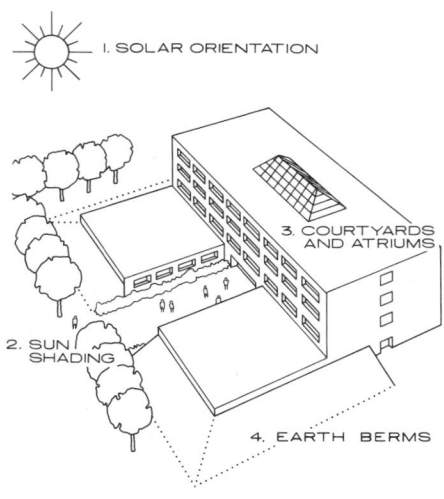

SITE PLANNING AND ORIENTATION

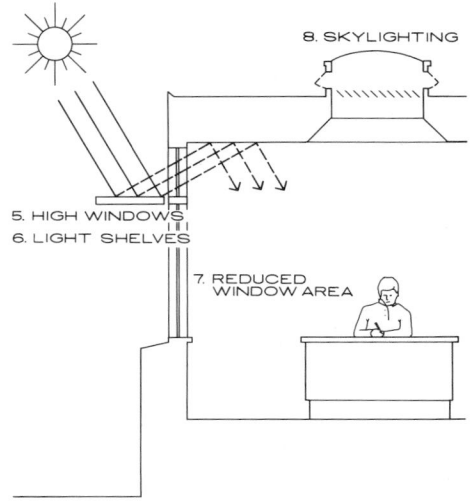

DAYLIGHTING

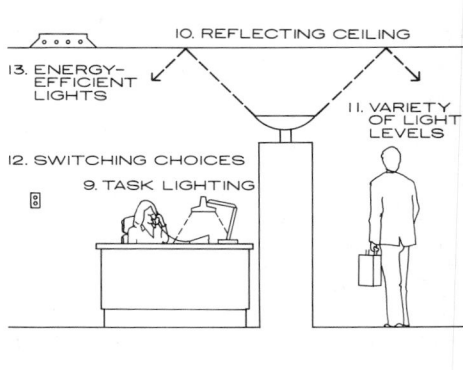

ENERGY-EFFICIENT LIGHTING

## ENERGY-CONSERVING DESIGN: NONRESIDENTIAL BUILDINGS

Energy-conserving design for nonresidential buildings is justified by savings in operating costs which result in a lower "life-cycle" investment. For large buildings of all types, the best opportunities are most likely to be found in electricity costs; depending upon the demand charges of the local utility, "peak load" reduction and/or "shifting" (diurnal or seasonal) measures may prove to be cost-effective. Concurrently, lower electric use by effective daylighting and by cooling load reduction (window orientation and solar controls) will be cost-effective, since these loads are typically interrelated and use expensive forms of energy. When these loads and costs are reduced, heating cost reduction by solar and energy-conserving techniques also applies to larger buildings. Energy-conserving opportunities are best addressed by a whole-systems team approach of architecture, HVAC, lighting, and controls engineering. For example, high levels of insulation or of thermal mass may be cost justified when these also result in substantially reduced mechanical system sizes and power requirements.

The architect should consider the following items in designing an energy-efficient nonresidential building, regardless of size and building type.

## SITE PLANNING AND ORIENTATION

1. ORIENT THE LONGER WALLS OF A BUILDING TO FACE NORTH–SOUTH

Walls that face the equator (e.g., the noonday sun) are ideal for windows oriented to admit daylighting with minimum cost for shading or sun control (i.e., relatively small horizontal overhangs create effective shading). Walls and windows facing east and west, on the other hand, are sources of undesirable overheating and are difficult to shade effectively. In a cool climate, windows facing the equator can gain useful wintertime heating from the sun. (See also "Daylighting" criteria.)

2. PROVIDE SUN SHADING TO SUIT CLIMATE AND USE VARIATIONS

Buildings can be located in groups to shade one another. Landscaping and sun shading can be used to shade building surfaces, especially windows, during overheated hours. Functions can be located within a building to coincide with solar gain benefit or liability. For example, cafeterias are ideally exposed to noontime winter sun in cool and temperate climates or placed in the midday shade in warm climates; low-use areas (storage areas) can be used as climatic buffers placed on the east or west in hot climates or on the north in cool climates.

3. CREATE COURTYARDS AND ENCLOSED ATRIUMS

Semienclosed courtyards (in warm climates) and enclosed atriums (in temperate and cool climates) can be formed by groups of buildings to provide areas for planting, shading, water fountains, and other microclimatic benefits. Atriums can also be used as light courts and

Donald Watson, FAIA; Trumbull, Connecticut

ventilating shafts. Indoor or outdoor planted areas provide evaporative cooling for local breezes when located near buildings.

4. USE EARTH BERMS FOR CLIMATIC BUFFERING

Earth berms (sloped or terraced, formed simply by grading earth against the wall of a building) help to buffer the building against temperature extremes of both heat and cold. The planting on earth berms also provides evaporative cooling near the building. Earth berms can be construction cost savers because the foundation does not have to be as deep (in single-storied construction); the earth and ground cover is often less costly than other wall finishing materials. Its long-term maintenance can also be lower than conventional materials.

## DAYLIGHTING

5. PLACE WINDOWS HIGH IN THE WALL OF EACH FLOOR

Windows placed high in the wall near the ceiling provide the most daylight for any given window area, permitting daylight to penetrate more deeply into the interior.

6. USE LIGHT SHELVES

Light shelves are horizontal projections placed on the outside and below a window to reflect sunlight into the interior. Typically placed just above eye level, the light shelf reflects daylight onto the interior ceiling, making it a light-reflecting surface (instead of a dark, shaded surface typical of a conventional interior ceiling). At the same time, the light shelf shades the lower portion of the window, reducing the amount of light near the window, which is typically overlit. The result is more balanced daylighting with less glare and contrast between light levels in the interior.

7. SIZE WINDOWS ACCORDING TO USE AND ORIENTATION

Because window glass has little or no resistance to heat flow, it is one of the primary sources of energy waste and discomfort. Window areas should be shaded against direct solar gain during overheated hours. Even when shaded, windows gain undesired heat when the outdoor temperature exceeds the human comfort limit. Window areas should therefore be kept to a reasonable minimum, justified by clearly defined needs for view, visual relief, ventilation, and/or daylighting. Double glazing should be considered for all windows for energy efficiency and comfort in cool and temperate climates. In warm climates, double, tinted, or reflective glass should be considered, depending upon building size and use.

8. USE SKYLIGHTING FOR DAYLIGHTING, WITH PROPER SOLAR CONTROLS

Skylighting that is properly sized and oriented is an efficient and cost-effective source of lighting. Consider that for most office buildings, sunlight is available for nearly the entire period of occupancy and that the lighting re-

quirement for interior lighting is only about 1% of the amount of light available outside. Electric lighting costs, peak demand charges, and work interruptions during power brownouts can be greatly reduced by using daylight. Cost-effective, energy-efficient skylights can be small, spaced widely, with "splayed" interior light wells that help reflect and diffuse the light. White-painted ceilings and walls further improve the efficiency of daylighting (by as much as 300% if compared with dark interior finishes). Skylights should include some means to control undesired solar gain by one or more of the following means: (a) Face the skylight to the polar orientation; (b) provide exterior light-reflecting shading; (c) provide movable sunshades on the inside, with a means to vent the heat above the shade.

## ENERGY-EFFICIENT LIGHTING

9. USE TASK LIGHTING, WITH INDIVIDUAL CONTROLS

Lamps for task lighting are ideally located near the work surface and are adjustable to eliminate reflective glare. The energy-efficient advantages are that less light output is required (reduced geometrically as a function of its closer distance to the task) and the lamp can be switched off when not needed.

Note: General light levels should be reduced below conventional standards and sources of reflective glare from ceiling lights and windows eliminated in areas where cathode ray tubes (CRTs) are used.

10. USE THE CEILING AS A LIGHT-REFLECTIVE SURFACE

By using "uplights," either ceiling pendants or lamps mounted on partitions and/or cabinets, the ceiling surface can be used as a light reflector. This has several advantages: (a) fewer fixtures are required for general area ("ambient") lighting; (b) the light is indirect, eliminating the sources of visual discomfort due to glare and reflection, (c) if light shelves are used, the ceiling is the light reflector for both natural and artificial light, an advantage for the occupant's sense of visual order.

11. EMPLOY A VARIETY OF LIGHT LEVELS

In any given interior, a variety of light levels improves visual comfort. Light levels can be reduced in low-use areas, storage, circulation, and lounge areas. Daylighting can also be used to provide variety of lighting, thereby reducing monotone interiors.

12. PROVIDE SWITCHING CHOICES, TO ACCOMMODATE SCHEDULE AND DAYLIGHT AVAILABILITY

Areas near windows that can be naturally lit should have continuous dimming controls to dim lights that are not needed. Other areas should have separate switching to coincide with different schedules and uses. Consider occupant-sensing light switches in areas of occasional use, such as washrooms, storage, and warehouse areas.

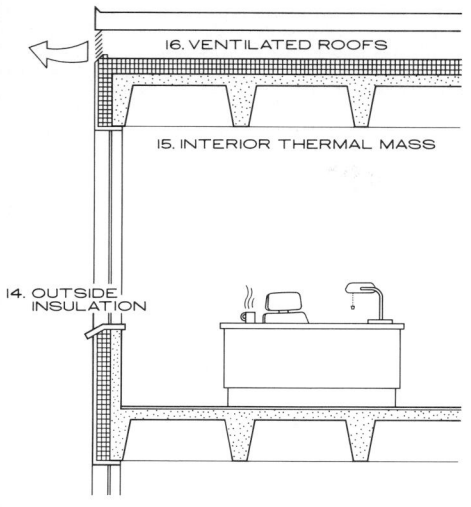

**THERMAL CONSTRUCTION**

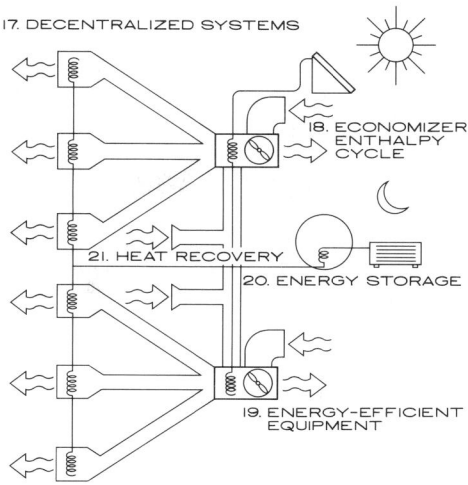

**ENERGY-EFFICIENT MECHANICAL SYSTEMS**

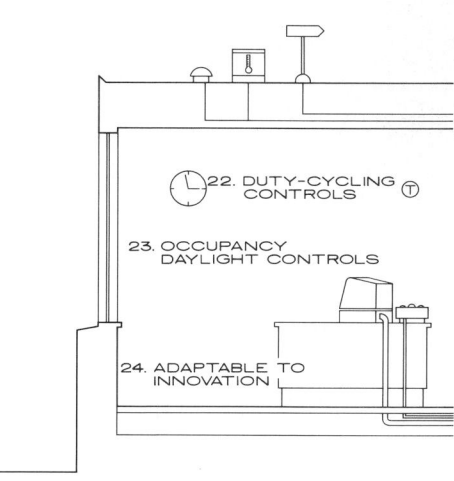

**SMART BUILDING CONTROLS**

### 13. USE ENERGY-EFFICIENT LIGHTS AND LUMINAIRES

Use the most efficient light source for the requirement: these might be fluorescent bulbs, high-intensity discharge lamps, or high-voltage/high-frequency lights. Compact fluorescent lights with high-efficiency ballasts have advantages of low wattage, low waste heat, long life, and good color rendering. Incandescent lights use less energy when switched on, so these are appropriate for occasional use and short-term lighting. Luminaires should also be evaluated for how efficiently they diffuse, direct, or reflect the available light.

## THERMAL CONSTRUCTION
### 14. PLACE INSULATION ON THE OUTSIDE OF THE STRUCTURE

Insulation is one of the most cost-effective means of energy conservation. Insulation placed on the outer face of a wall or roof protects the structure from the extremes of the outside temperature (with the added benefit of lengthening the life of the roof waterproofing membrane) and adds the massiveness of the structure to the thermal response of the interior (see Criteria 15). In localities where "resistance insulation" is not available, the combination of airspaces and high capacitance materials (such as masonry and/or earth berms) should be designed for effective thermal dampening or time lag (the delay and diffusion of outside temperature extremes that are transmitted to the interior). As an alternative to insulating roof structures in hot climates, a "radiant barrier" consisting of a continuous sheet of reflective foil with a low emissivity coating and an airspace around it serves as an effective shield against undesired heat gain.

### 15. UTILIZE THERMAL MASS ON BUILDING INTERIOR

In office buildings, thermally massive construction (such as masonry and concrete which have good heat storage capacity) benefits the energy-efficient operation of heating and cooling equipment as follows:

(a) Cooling benefits: Thermal mass absorbs the "overheating" that is inevitable in an office space due to the buildup of heat from people, equipment, lighting, rising afternoon temperature, and solar gain. The more thermal mass that is effectively exposed to an interior space (ceiling and walls), the greater is the saving on air conditioning in the afternoon, with the potential to delay the overheating until early evening when electric rates may be lower and/or outdoor air may be low enough to cool the mass by night ventilation. (The "night cooling" option is especially favorable in warm, dry climates due to predictably cooler nighttime temperatures.)

(b) Heating benefits: In temperate and cool climates, thermal mass helps absorb and store wintertime passive solar heat. This is especially effective if the thermal mass is on the building interior and directly heated by the sun (made possible by design of various corridor, stairway, and half-height partition arrangements).

Donald Watson, FAIA; Trumbull, Connecticut

### 16. USE LIGHT-CONSTRUCTED VENTILATED ROOFS IN HOT CLIMATES

In hot climates, the roof is the primary source of undesired heat gain. Energy-efficient roof designs should be considered. One of the best for hot climates is a ventilated double roof wherein the outside layer is a light-colored and lightweight material which shades the solar heat from the inner roof, which should be well insulated. As described in Strategy 14, a "radiant barrier" can be considered as an alternative to resistance insulation to serve as a shield against thermal transfer through the ceiling portion of the roof structure.

## ENERGY-EFFICIENT MECHANICAL SYSTEMS
### 17. USE DECENTRALIZED AND MODULAR SYSTEMS

Heating and cooling equipment is most efficient when sized to the average load condition, not the "peak" or extreme condition. Use modular unit boilers, chillers, pumps, and fans in series so that the average operating load can be met by a few modules operating at peak efficiency rather than a single unit that is oversized for normal conditions. Zone the distribution systems to meet different loads due to orientation, use, and schedule. Use variable-air-volume (VAV) systems to reduce fan energy requirements and to lower duct sizes and costs (the system can be designed for the predominant load, not the sum of the peak loads). Decentralized air-handling systems have smaller trunk lines and duct losses. Dispersed air handlers, located close to their end use, can be reduced in size from conventional system sizes if hot and chilled water is piped to them (a decentralized air-handling system with a centralized plant).

### 18. USE ECONOMIZER/ENTHALPY CYCLE COOLING

Economizer/enthalpy cycle cooling uses outdoor air when it is cool enough for direct ventilation and/or when the outdoor air has a lower heat content than indoor air (so that it can be cooled evaporatively without raising indoor humidity). Although useful in all climates, direct or indirect evaporative cooling systems are especially effective in hot, dry climates.

### 19. USE ENERGY-EFFICIENT EQUIPMENT

The energy efficiency of mechanical equipment varies greatly. Consider heat pumps for cooling and for heating to replace separate chiller and boiler units. Heat pumps can also use local water sources or water storage (see Criteria 20 below). Newly developed mechanical heating equipment, such as gas-fired pulse combustion boilers, is achieving very high (up to 85%) annual operating efficiencies.

### 20. USE ENERGY STORAGE FOR COOLING

Chilled water storage has several advantages: It permits water chilling or ice-making at night under more favorable ambient conditions and possible lower electric rates;

perhaps more important, it reduces or eliminates peak-hour energy consumption, thereby reducing demand charges.

### 21. USE HEAT RECOVERY FOR HEATING

In cool and temperate climates, heat can be recovered from warm zones of a building and recirculated to underheated areas. Recoverable heat sources include equipment, process heat, and passive solar gain. Heat recovery wheels or coils can be used where indoor air needs to be ventilated, transferring heat into the incoming fresh airstream. In all climates, process heat or active solar heat (e.g., from solar collectors) can be used for domestic hot water or for tempering incoming fresh air.

## "SMART BUILDING" CONTROLS
### 22. USE SMART THERMOSTATS

"Duty-cycling" temperature controls can be programmed for different time schedules and thermal conditions, the simplest being the day–night setback. Newer controls are "predictive," sensing outdoor temperature trends and then selecting the system operation most appropriate to the condition.

### 23. USE OCCUPANCY- AND DAYLIGHT-SENSING LIGHTING CONTROLS

Automatic switching of lights according to the building occupant schedule and the daylight condition is recommended, with manual override for nighttime occupancy. Photosensors should be placed in areas that can be predictably lit by natural light.

### 24. BE PREPARED FOR RAPID INNOVATION IN BUILDING CONTROL SYSTEMS

Newly developing "smart" building systems include microprocessing for thermal and light control, fire and air-quality precautions, equipment failure, and operations/maintenance requirements (along with new communication and office management systems). These innovations require that electric wiring be easily changed, such as through "double-floor" construction.

### REFERENCES

Burt Hill Kosar Rittelmann Associates: *Small Office Building Handbook*, New York: Van Nostrand Reinhold, 1985.

Burt Hill Kosar Rittelmann Associates: *Commercial Building Design*, New York: Van Nostrand Reinhold, 1987.

McGuiness, Stein, and Reynolds: *Mechanical and Electric Equipment for Buildings*, New York: John Wiley & Sons, 7th Edition, 1988.

Solar Energy Research Institute: *Design of Energy-Responsive Commercial Buildings*, New York: John Wiley Interscience, 1985.

Watson, Donald, editor: *Energy Conservation through Building Design*, New York: McGraw-Hill Book Company, 1979.

## ENERGY-EFFICIENT ATRIUM DESIGN

In its original meaning, an atrium was the open courtyard of a Roman house. Today an atrium is a glazed courtyard on the side of or within a building. If issues of heating, cooling, and lighting are ignored, atrium designs can add significantly to the energy cost of the building as well as require above-average energy to maintain comfort within them. On the other hand, energy-efficient atrium spaces can contribute savings through natural lighting, passive heating, and natural cooling strategies. (Any multistoried space raises concerns for fire safety and requires special attention.)

Atrium spaces are more responsive to the influence of the outside climate than conventional buildings, and their design therefore will follow local climate requirements. Design also will depend on the specific function and goals of the atrium: to supply daylighting for itself or to adjacent spaces; to provide comfort for sedentary human occupancy or plants; or to serve only as a semiconditioned space for circulation. The challenge of energy-efficient atrium design is to combine various and perhaps conflicting requirements for passive heating, natural cooling, and daylighting using the geometry of the atrium, its orientation, and solar and insulation controls at the glazing surfaces. These architectural choices need to be integrated with the mechanical engineering to assure that the passive energy opportunities will in fact effectively reduce building energy use.

## PASSIVE SOLAR HEATING OPPORTUNITIES

Atriums designed with large glass areas overheat during the day, providing potentially recoverable heat to parts of the adjacent building, such as its outer perimeter, which can be transferred by air or by an air-to-water heat pump. In cool climates and in buildings with a predominant heat load (such as a residential or hotel structure), using this solar heat gain can be cost-effective. In such a case, vertical glass facing the south captures winter sun while incurring minimum summer heat gain liability. If the atrium space requires sedentary occupant comfort, heat storage within the space and energy-efficient glazing also is beneficial.

## NATURAL COOLING OPPORTUNITIES

To reduce required cooling in an atrium, protection from the summer sun is essential. It can be accomplished by glass orientation, protective coatings as part of the glazing, and shading devices, which may or may not be movable. In hot, sunny climates, relatively small amounts of glass can meet daylighting objectives while reducing the solar gain liability. In warm, humid climates with predominantly cloudy skies (the sky is nonetheless a source of undesirable heat gain), the north-facing orientation should be favored for large glazed areas. Mechanical ventilation should facilitate the upward flow of natural ventilation. Spot cooling by air-conditioning lower atrium areas is a relatively efficient means of keeping some areas comfortable for occupancy without fully conditioning the entire volume of air.

## DAYLIGHTING OPPORTUNITIES

An atrium with the predominant function to provide natural lighting takes its shape from the predominant sky condition. In cool, cloudy climates, the atrium cross section ideally would be stepped outward as it gets higher in order to increase overhead lighting. In hot, sunny locations with clear sunny skies, the cross section is like a large lighting fixture designed to reflect, diffuse, and make usable the light from above. This purpose is complicated by the light source—the sun—as it changes position with respect to the building throughout the day and the year.

## WINTERGARDEN ATRIUM DESIGN

Healthy greenery can be incorporated in atrium design. The designer needs to know the unique horticultural requirements for the plant species for lighting, heating, and cooling, which could be quite different from those for human occupancy. Generally, plants need higher light levels and cooler temperatures than might be comfortable for humans. The most efficient manner to keep plants heated is with plant bed or root heating, as with water tubes or air tubes in gravel or earth. Plants also benefit from gentle air movement, which reduces excessive moisture that might rot the plants and circulates $CO_2$ needed for growth.

Donald Watson, FAIA; Trumbull, Connecticut

## RELATIVE IMPORTANCE OF DESIGN PRINCIPLES IN VARIOUS CLIMATES

| ATRIUM ENERGY-DESIGN PRINCIPLE | COLD/CLOUDY SEATTLE CHICAGO MINNEAPOLIS | COOL/SUNNY DENVER ST. LOUIS BOSTON | WARM/DRY LOS ANGELES PHOENIX MIDLAND, TX | HOT/WET HOUSTON NEW ORLEANS MIAMI |
|---|:---:|:---:|:---:|:---:|
| **HEATING** | | | | |
| H1 To maximize winter solar heat gain, orient the atrium aperture to the south. | ● | □ | ▼ | |
| H2 For radiant heat storage and distribution, place interior masonry directly in the path of the winter sun. | ▼ | □ | ● | |
| H3 To prevent excessive nighttime heat loss, consider an insulating system for the glazing. | ● | □ | | |
| H4 To recover heat, place a return air duct high in the space, directly in the sun. | □ | ● | ▼ | |
| **COOLING** | | | | |
| C1 To minimize solar gain, provide shade from the summer sun. | | □ | □ | ● |
| C2 Use the atrium as an air plenum in the mechanical system of the building. | □ | □ | □ | □ |
| C3 To facilitate natural ventilation, create a vertical "chimney" effect with high outlets and low inlets. | □ | □ | □ | ● |
| **LIGHTING** | | | | |
| L1 To maximize daylight, use a stepped section (in predominantly cloudy areas). | □ | ▼ | | |
| L2 To maximize daylight, select skylight glazing for predominant sky condition (clear and horizontal in predominantly cloudy areas). | □ | □ | | □ |
| L3 Provide sun and glare control. | □ | □ | ● | □ |

Key: ● = Very important; □ = positive benefit; ▼ = discretionary use.

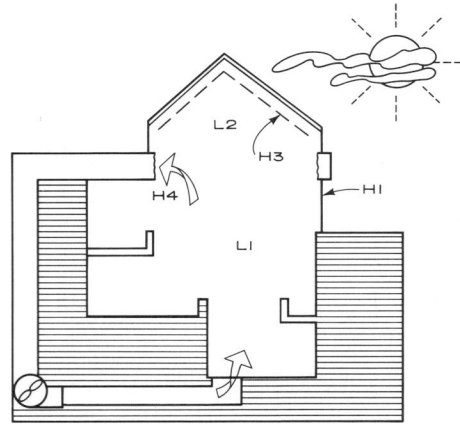

COLD/CLOUDY

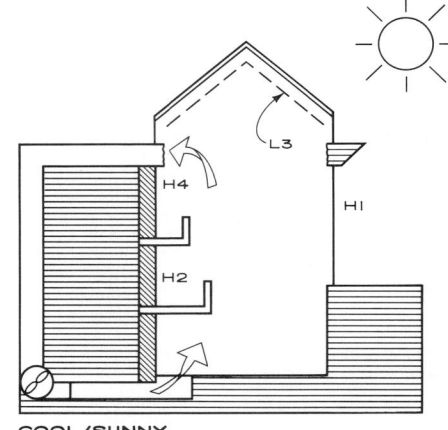

COOL/SUNNY

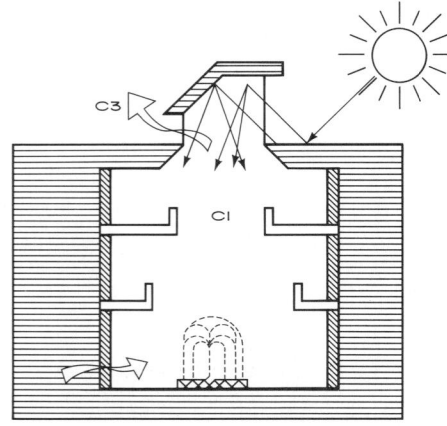

WARM/DRY

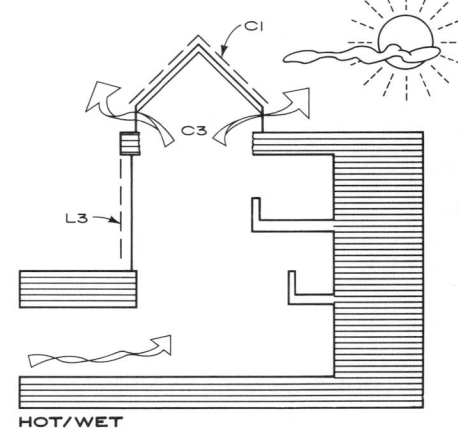

HOT/WET

The term "alternate energy systems" describes uses of climatic resources—sun, wind, precipitation/humidity, and temperature—to provide all or part of the energy requirements of a building. Their development has paralleled the uncertain cost and availability of conventional energy supplies. New design concepts—passive solar and cooling and daylighting designs—have become part of recommended building practice. More advanced technologies have been developed, but their widespread use awaits either more experience with them or more penalizing energy prices. Some can be easily incorporated into a building design, requiring only careful design integration of architectural and heating, cooling, and lighting systems. A number of factors can change the economic constraints upon what is and is not cost-justified: the need for emergency preparedness, the prospect of interruptible or increasingly costly conventional fuel supplies, environmental pollution from fossil fuel combustion, and limited capacity of existing power plants. These concerns suggest that they be given full consideration together with energy conservation/load reduction techniques so that our long-term reliance upon conventional and nonrenewable energy sources can be minimized.

The practical approach to alternate energy system design begins with analysis of the energy requirement of the building "end use": the temperature, humidity, air flow, and lighting levels required for human comfort, and the related power demands for productive activity. The various sources for supplying heating, cooling, lighting, and electric power can then be matched to the end use in terms of "thermodynamic" efficiency, comfort, operational cost, and reliability. High levels of energy conservation and renewable energy use can make life-cycle economic gains possible, such as by downsizing mechanical system sizes or through "off-peak" loading of the building's energy requirement to reduce or eliminate "demand charges," as is possible when a building has a large energy storage system.

The figure diagrams the various alternate energy system components. The building itself is shown as an energy collection, storage, and distribution system. Choices include system components that are separate from the building (though presumably nearby) and those that must be integrated with it.

## REMOTE ENERGY COLLECTORS
(ELECTRICAL)

Three contenders for alternate electric power are windmills, microhydro dams, and photovoltaic panels. Photovoltaic systems use the photons of sunlight to generate electricity across a grid of cells in a solar collector. These can be mounted on the roof of a building or can be "remote," since electricity is easily distributed from its point of collection. Site engineering concerns are major, but building design criteria are minor, limited only to storage battery location and the electric distribution system within the building. The economic viability of these choices is greatly improved by reduction of the electric load requirement achievable by energy-efficient lighting and equipment.

## REMOTE ENERGY STORAGE
(THERMAL)

Energy storage near a building site has proved to be viable when the site is large enough, made part of seasonal (6-month) storage, and serves groups of buildings (district heating/cooling). These include:

Underground thermal storage: Heat generated by solar collectors (either air type or liquid type) can be stored within a large mass of earth, in existing caverns, or in newly dug clay or soil beds. In Kerava Solar Village near Helsinki, Finland, solar collectors mounted on the south-facing roofs of 44 apartments supply solar-heated water to a 400,000 gal water tank which in turn heats 338,500 cu ft of rock surrounding the tank embedded 66 ft in the earth.

Acquifier systems: A variation of thermal storage that is "charged" by solar collectors are systems using natural or man-made acquifiers for seasonal storage, thus utilizing groundwater temperature for heating and cooling, generally relying upon a water-to-water heat pump to change the groundwater temperature to the end-use requirement for heating and cooling.

Ice storage systems: Ice storage systems use ice-making, either "seasonal" for 6-month storage or "diurnal," at night for next-day use, to provide building cooling. The advantage of making ice in winter is obvious, imposing

only the cost of a large storage area logically located within the subgrade basement of a building, but which can also be separate. Diurnal systems are cost-effective when there are advantages of "off-peak" utility rates and/or significantly cooler nighttime temperatures.

Solar ponds: Solar ponds are salt ponds that exploit the temperature gradient effect of salt water. First documented by Russian scientist von Kaleczinsky in 1902, water a few feet below a confined body of salt water reaches temperatures up to 185°F due to the varying salinity of the water: The bottom of the pond is a bed of salt in which heat is efficiently stored because heated salt-rich water does not rise, while the surface of relatively fresh water above is clear, allowing solar heat to be transmitted through it and at the same time insulating the denser layers below. In Israel and Australia, such solar ponds have been used as a source of thermal energy and to drive engines for electric generation. While only half as efficient as a solar collector, the relatively low cost of solar ponds (reportedly ten times less costly per unit of collector surface) indicates their potential.

## INTEGRATED BUILDING SYSTEMS

A building designed to efficiently use climatic resources for heating, cooling, lighting, and electric power generation is properly considered an alternate energy system. Means for doing so are tabulated in the table and summarized below as a checklist for designers.

South wall: The south-facing wall of a building (in the Northern hemisphere) is an efficient energy resource. The low-angled winter sun can bring into a building interior the benefits of winter heat and light. Shading the south facade in summer can be efficiently accomplished with relatively short overhangs. Because of this, passive solar heating, summer shading, and year-round daylighting can

and ought to be made part of south-wall design. Solar heat can be stored in thermal storage placed in the sun behind glass or ducted/piped to the building interior.

Roof: The roof of a building can be used for mounting "active" solar collectors for heating, photovoltaic collectors for generating electricity, or skylights for daylighting. In hot climates, the roof is also an alternate energy resource if used for evaporative or radiant cooling.

Atrium: Atria design can be integrated into a "whole building" daylighting system and combined with the mechanical air movement system wherein it can economically replace ducting in ventilative cooling and heat recovery systems. Skylights, enhanced with light and heat reflectors, can be designed to reflect sunlight deep within a building.

Below-ground/basement: The below-ground construction of a building can be used for thermal storage, as described above. In single-storied or low-rise buildings, "ground coupling" utilizes the relatively stable temperatures of the surrounding earth to provide an economical heating/cooling flywheel effect.

## OTHER ENERGY FLOWS WITHIN A BUILDING

Alternate energy design addresses all energy and resource requirements involved in building construction and use, including plant growth in interior and exterior gardens; water collection, purification, and reuse; and resource recycling and organic waste treatment/nutrient recovery. These energy flows, together with the ecological role of the surrounding landscape, are properly considered as biological system requirements of living efficiently within the limits of climate and environment.

SITE AND BUILDING AS ENERGY COLLECTION, STORAGE, AND DISTRIBUTION SYSTEM

## EXAMPLES OF ENERGY-EFFICIENT ARCHITECTURAL ELEMENTS

| ELEMENTS | HEATING | COOLING | LIGHTING |
|---|---|---|---|
| South wall | South-facing glass<br>Trombe wall<br>Sunspace | Reflective glass<br>Sunshades | Venetian blinds<br>Light shelf |
| Roof | Active solar collectors<br>South-facing clerestories | Evaporative cooling<br>Skytherm (radiant cooling) | Skylighting<br>Photovoltaic collectors |
| Atrium | South-oriented glazing<br>Storage mass in sun | Shaded courtyard<br>Ventilating chimney | Light shaft<br>Light reflectors |
| Ground/basement | Thermal storage | "Coolth" storage | |

Donald Watson, FAIA; Trumbull, Connecticut

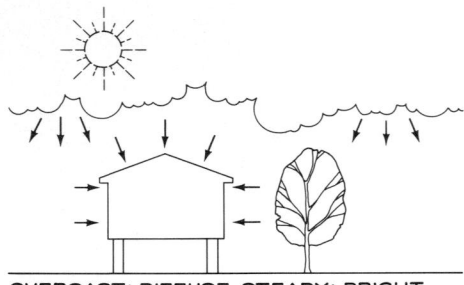

OVERCAST: DIFFUSE, STEADY; BRIGHT OR DARK

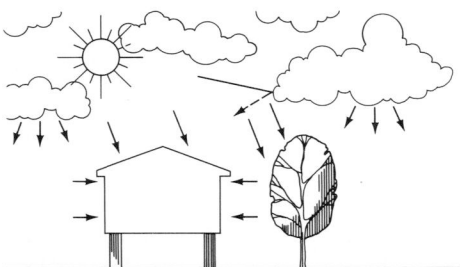

PARTLY CLOUDY: INTENSE/DIFFUSE; DIRECT BRIGHT

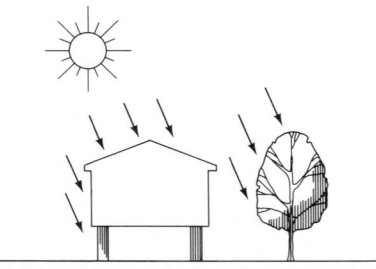

CLEAR: INTENSE, DIRECT BRIGHT, BLUE

**DAYLIGHT**

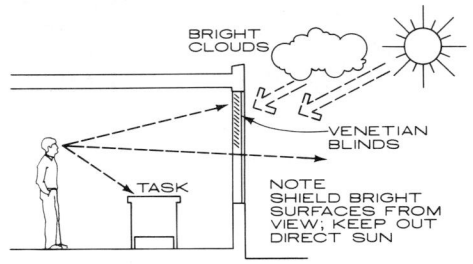

QUALITY DAYLIGHTING

SOLAR GAIN OPTIMIZATION

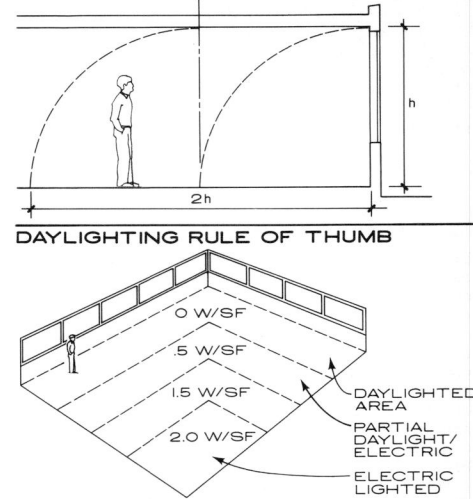

DAYLIGHTING RULE OF THUMB

DAYLIGHTING BY ZONE/ THREE-STEP SWITCHING

## INTRODUCTION

Ample daylight is available throughout most of North America for lighting interior spaces during a large portion of the working day. This daylight may be used for critical visual tasks or for ambient lighting, to be supplemented with electric task lights. Daylight is thought by most to be psychologically desirable and there is much evidence that it is biologically beneficial. The variability of daylight from one moment to the next produces visual stimulus and provides a psychological contact with the outdoors which most people find extremely satisfying. Its use in place of, or in conjunction with, other lighting sources can conserve energy, but energy is conserved only if electric light sources are adequately controlled through on–off switching and/or dimming.

## SOURCE

Daylight comes from the sun, bright and direct; it often comes filtered, diffused, and scattered by clouds, and it is reflected by the ground and other surfaces. The availability of daylight for a particular location can be determined from charts published by the Illuminating Engineering Society (IES), "Recommended Practice of Daylighting"; from the Solar Energy Research Institute (SERI), "Daylight Availability Data for Selected Cities in the U.S."; and from "Daylight in Architecture," by Benjamin Evans, McGraw-Hill, 1981.

It has been traditional, particularly in Europe, to consider the overcast sky as the minimum daylighting condition and to design buildings accordingly, but in North America the clear sky with sun and the partly cloudy sky are more common and generally more critical to building design for good daylighting.

Direct sun contains the maximum quantity of all wavelengths of radiation, including infrared which causes the sensation of heat. Smaller quantities of infrared as well as ultraviolet, which can cause material deterioration, come from the diffuse light of the sky and clouds.

Benjamin Evans, FAIA; Blacksburg, Virginia

## QUALITY IN DAYLIGHTING

The principles of good lighting apply equally to daylight and electric light. Of principal concern in daylighting is the glare that may result when building occupants peripherally see bright clouds or sunlighted surfaces while trying to perform visual tasks.

Direct sun in interiors where critical visual tasks are performed is generally to be avoided. Thus, apertures that allow vision to the exterior must provide for shielding (or filtering) of exterior excessive brightnesses, or work stations must be oriented away from the apertures. Partly cloudy skies may contribute major quantities of daylight but also can be excessively bright and, therefore, should be shielded from view. Energy savings from switching or dimming of electric lights depend on daylight intensity and on the percentage of the year that daylight is available.

## SOLAR-THERMAL GAINS/LOSSES

Daylight includes a significant amount of radiation that produces heat. This may be beneficial during the heating season, allowing for a reduction in other interior heating, or it may be detrimental during the cooling season, requiring additional air conditioning. Shading can be configured to reduce direct sun heating during warm weather while allowing some sun penetration in winter.

The quantity of radiant heat gain from the direct sun through glazing can be determined using the following formula:

Solar heat gain (Btu/hr) = insolation* x exposed area of glazing x transmissivity of glazing x hours of exposure

(* in Btu/hr/sq ft)

Glazing also allows for transmission of heat between outdoors and indoors via conductivity and convection. These heat losses or gains can be determined with the following formula:

Thermal gains/losses (Btu/hr) = exposed area of glazing x outdoor temperature x maintained indoor temperature x U factor of glazing x hours of exposure

## ENERGY USE CONTROLS

Energy-efficient lighting design requires that electric lights remain off when daylighting levels are sufficient. The two principal types of lighting controls are selective switching (on/off) and dimming. These controls can eliminate or reduce work plane footcandles from electric lights by task, area, or zone. The simplest version of this is switching off the luminaires near the windows or at other points when and where the daylight is sufficient. Automatic dimming of luminaires can ensure that the total quantity of illumination on the work plane is maintained even as the daylight disappears or is reduced by clouds.

Switches can be controlled manually or by photosensors that switch luminaires off or on depending on the levels of daylight available; by timers that switch lights according to some preselected times (e.g., off at 8:00 am and on at 6:00 pm); by a sensor that responds to the presence of occupants.

Switching can be categorized as two, three, four, or five step. The two step is a simple on/off of all lamps on the circuit. The three-step mode requires a luminaire with two lamps or multiples of two. The three steps are all on, all off, or half on. Similar switching can be with luminaires with multiples of three or four lamps. Multilevel switching can maintain illumination levels more evenly and increase energy savings over two-step systems.

Most incandescent lamps can be dimmed, and lamps that require ballasts (e.g., fluorescent) can be dimmed if equipped with an appropriate ballast. Automatic switching and dimming controls combined with thoughtfully selected control zones allow electric lighting levels to reliably and economically respond to available daylight levels.

Energy-efficient design is a function of not only the energy used by electric lights, but also of the effect of heat given off by lights on cooling and heating systems. The approximate heat gain from an average electric lighting system can be calculated as follows:

Heat gain (Btu/hr) = footcandles/sq ft x area x .06 watt/footcandle x 3.41 Btu/hr/watt

Calculation of the electric energy used in the operation of a lighting system can be determined by the following equation:

Energy (watts/hr) = watts per luminaire* x number of luminaires x hours of operation

(* including watts for ballast)

Determining the amount of daylight that any interior space will receive during the course of the day or year is a complex process involving the determination of (1) the amount of daylight available on any aperture at appropriate times, (2) the amount of daylight that will reach interior areas, through calculations or by studies using scale models, (3) the results of step two modified by local weather data according to the percentage of cloud cover expected, and (4) the percentage of electric lighting that can be reduced or eliminated. (For scale model studies see "Daylight in Architecture," by Benjamin Evans, McGraw-Hill, 1981; see also "A Method for Predicting Energy Savings Attributed to Daylighting," by Claude L. Robbins and Kerry C. Hunter, Solar Energy Research Institute, 1982.)

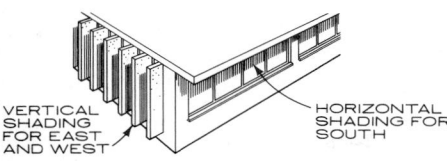

**SHADING DEVICES BY ORIENTATION**

VERTICAL SHADING FOR EAST AND WEST — HORIZONTAL SHADING FOR SOUTH

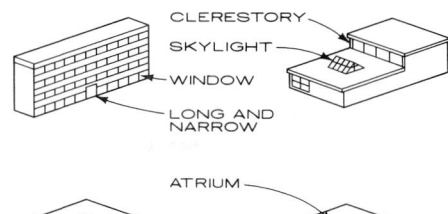

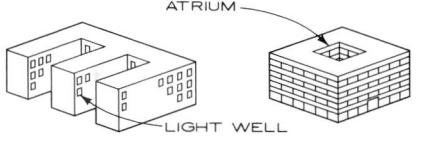

**BUILDING CONFIGURATIONS**

CLERESTORY — SKYLIGHT — WINDOW — LONG AND NARROW — ATRIUM — LIGHT WELL

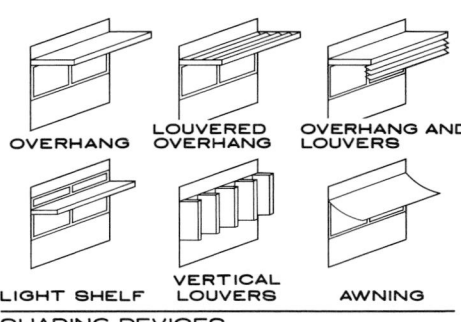

OVERHANG — LOUVERED OVERHANG — OVERHANG AND LOUVERS — LIGHT SHELF — VERTICAL LOUVERS — AWNING

**SHADING DEVICES**

SUNLIGHT BOUNCED OFF ROOF — SOLAR CONTROL — VISUAL SHADING

**CLERESTORY**

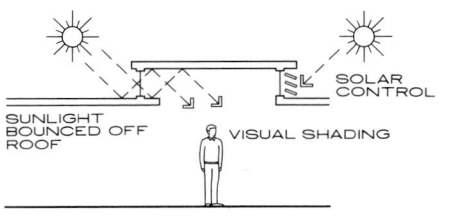

EGGCRATE LOUVERS FOR VISUAL SHIELDING — MOVABLE PANELS FOR SOLAR CONTROL AND NIGHT INSULATION — SUSPENDED BAFFLES BOUNCE LIGHT ONTO CEILING

**SKYLIGHT CONTROLS**

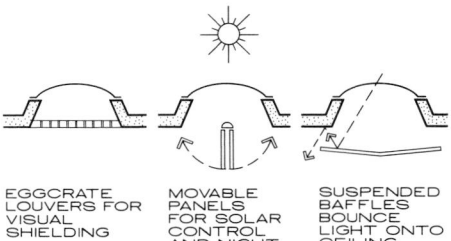

SKYLIGHT — HATCH — LIGHT CELL — PHOTO-METER — HORIZONTAL REFERENCE MEASUREMENT

**DAYLIGHTING SCALE MODELS**

## ORIENTATION

Usable daylight is available to apertures oriented in any direction, although the amount will differ with each orientation. Of principal concern is the location of the sun relative to a building fenestration. Apertures to the north receive only sky-contributed illumination and so will require larger areas of glazing than orientations with exposure to direct sun. Advantages of north apertures include the resulting soft, diffuse north sky light and lack of need for sun controls. However, sky glare controls still need to be considered.

East and west facades require treatment to avoid the bright early and late direct sun. This is usually best accomplished with vertical louvers or a mix of vertical and horizontal (eggcrate) louvers. The location of the sun at any time relative to any aperture can be determined using the charts on the Solar Angles pages.

South facades provide the best opportunity for daylighting. Horizontal controls (e.g., overhangs, light shelves, louvers, venetian blinds) respond best to the sun in the southern sky quadrant. Apertures can be designed such that when the sun is high in the sky during the summer there is no sun penetration, but in the winter some low-altitude sun can be admitted.

## CONFIGURATION

Building configuration is also important in daylighting. Multistory buildings will be most effective if they are long and narrow, allowing maximum vertical glazing per square foot of floor space. A rule of thumb is that daylighting (allowing electric lights to be turned off) can be achieved to a depth of about 2.5 times the height of the windows, or about 15–20 ft from the windows.

Buildings wrapped around courtyards, light wells, and atria can be effectively daylighted if properly designed. Open spaces must be large enough so as not to block light from the sky from reaching interior spaces. The effectiveness of such light wells can be improved by using high-reflecting, diffuse exterior finishes such as white paint, light-colored tile, or concrete. Direct sun illuminating these surfaces, however, may make them very bright when viewed from the building interior.

In single-story buildings the configuration is not so important, since roof apertures (e.g., skylights, clerestories) can be used to illuminate interior spaces, with or without peripheral windows.

## ARCHITECTURAL CONTROLS

Shading/Reflecting Devices: Shading devices can be used to prevent penetration of direct sun and to shield view of the sky. Some shading devices also reflect daylight toward the interior (e.g., light shelves). Light shelves, however, are not very effective in reflecting diffuse light from the sky and are cost-effective only when necessary to shade direct sun. Venetian blinds are very effective for shading direct sun, and they can be adjusted for total blackout and raised and lowered as needed. Sun screen consisting of tiny horizontal louvers can also be effective in shading.

Glazing: Tinted glazing (glass or plastic) reduces the apparent brightness of exterior objects from the interior, but it also reduces the amount of transmitted daylight, which must be supplemented by electric light. Heat-reflecting and other variable spectrum transmission glazing is available that tends to reduce the transmission of heat more than light, but may produce only a small advantage (check manufacturer's data). Directional glass block is useful in directing incoming light toward the ceiling, providing a low brightness image from the interior. Translucent materials exposed to direct sun diffuse incoming light and can be excessively bright when viewed from the interior.

Benjamin Evans, FAIA; Blacksburg, Virginia

Finishes/Surfaces: All surfaces absorb and reflect light to varying degrees. Light-colored surfaces, particularly the ceiling, generally increase the light available on the interior. Floors are usually the least effective surface in reflecting light to the work plane. Avoid highly reflective or slick finishes on large areas.

Apertures: Windows, clerestories, and skylights can be used for effective daylighting, provided they are equipped with proper shading devices. Glazing located above the work plane (e.g., high windows) is more effective in producing work plane illumination than glazing close to the floor. Clerestories and skylights are valuable in single-story buildings. The effect of clerestories can be improved by using light-colored roof surfaces to reflect exterior daylight into the aperture, but direct sun penetration may still be a concern. Clerestories and skylights both may produce glare if the sky is not properly shielded from interior view.

Geometry: The geometry or shape of interior spaces is generally not significant in achieving good daylighting. Interior walls and partitions, of course, can prevent or reduce daylight penetration into other areas, but this can often be offset by using glass in the upper portions of interior partitions. The shape and slope of the ceiling can increase interior daylight by very small amounts, but usually not enough to be cost-effective.

Spectral Transmission: The amount of light radiation received on earth depends on the amount and content of atmosphere through which the light must pass. Therefore, the color of the daylight received in buildings varies by time of day and quantity of air pollution. Generally, daylight tends to be warm (i.e., more light from the red/orange end of the spectrum) early and late in the day and cooler (i.e., blue/violet) toward midday.

Coordination of daylighting with electric lighting requires selection of interior lamps that will produce colors compatible with that of daylight. Some fluorescent lamps, particularly the new triphosphorus lamps, and metal halides are similar to daylight in color.

Ultraviolet radiation is considered to cause damage to materials such as paintings, drapes, carpets, and furniture coverings. While regular glass eliminates much of the ultraviolet energy, additional protection can be achieved by using ultraviolet filters. This is especially useful in museums.

## ANALYSIS

Physical Scale Models: Daylight in a scale model will behave exactly as in the full-scale building provided that all details are identical and the model is tested under an identical sky. Relatively simple models can be used to compare design alternatives (e.g., horizontal vs. vertical window) and to determine approximate footcandle levels. Certain details and surface finishes, however, are critical for meaningful model studies, and proper instruments must be used.

Computers: Several computer programs have been developed for analyzing building designs. Each program is designed to produce a particular sophistication of analysis using a limited variety of parameters.

For further discussion of these issues, see Benjamin Evans, "Daylight in Architecture" (McGraw-Hill, 1981) and Fuller Moore, "Concepts and Practice of Architectural Daylighting" (Van Nostrand Reinhold, 1985).

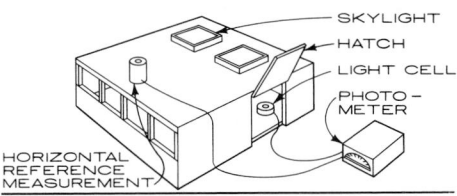

## REFLECTION FACTORS OF TYPICAL SURFACES

| SURFACE TYPE | PERCENT |
| --- | --- |
| Concrete | 20–40 |
| Red brick | 10–25 |
| Dark stone | 10–30 |
| Light stone | 20–50 |
| Grass | 5–10 |
| Dirt | 10–20 |
| Snow | 70–80 |
| White ceiling | 75–80 |
| Wood floor | 20–30 |
| Tile floor | 15–20 |

## TRANSMISSIVITY OF TYPICAL GLAZING 1/8" THICK

| GLAZING MATERIAL | PERCENT |
| --- | --- |
| Clear glass | 85–90 |
| Tinted glass | 30–60 |
| Bronze glass | 65–75 |
| Reflective glass | 8–50 |
| Heat-absorbing glass | 70–80 |
| Glass block | 60–80 |
| Clear plastic | 80–92 |
| Translucent plastic | 10–80 |

## BASIC PRINCIPLES

The diagrams presented in this discussion are based on an isolated building. Neighboring buildings and landscaping can substantially affect airflow and should be taken into account when evaluating ventilation strategies.

As wind approaches the face of a building the airflow is slowed, creating positive pressure and a cushion of air on the building's windward face. This cushion of air, in turn, diverts the wind toward the building sides. Airflow as it passes along the sidewalls separates from building wall surfaces and, coupled with high-speed airflow, creates suction (negative pressure) along these wall surfaces. On the building leeward side a big slow-moving eddy is created. Suction on the leeward side of the building is less than on the sidewalls (see Figure 1).

If windows are placed in both windward and leeward faces, the building would be cross ventilated and eddies will develop against the main airflow direction (see Figure 2). Ventilation can be enhanced by placing windows in sidewalls due to the increased suction at this location; also, greater air recirculation within the building will occur due to air inertia (see Figure 3). Winds often shift direction, and for oblique winds, ventilation is best for rooms with windows on three adjacent walls (see Figure 4) than on two opposite walls (see Figure 5). However, if wind is from the one windowless side, then ventilation is poor, since all openings are in suction (see Figure 6).

If the building configuration only allows for windows in one wall, then negligible ventilation will occur with the use of a single window, because there is not a distinct inlet and outlet. Ventilation can be improved slightly with two widely spaced windows. Airflow can be enhanced in these situations by creating positive and negative pressure zones by use of architectural features such as wing walls (see Figure 7). Care must be exercised in developing these features to avoid counteracting the natural airflow, thereby weakening ventilation (see Figure 8).

## AIR JETS

As airflow passes through a well-ventilated room, it forms an "air jet." If the windows are centered in a room, it forms a free jet (see Figure 9). If, however, the openings are near the room walls, ceiling, or floor, the airstream attaches itself to the surface, forming a wall jet (see Figure 10). Since heat removal from building surfaces is enhanced with increased airflow, the formation of wall jets is important in effecting rapid structure cooling. To improve the overall airflow within a room, offsetting the inlet and outlet will promote greater mixing of room air (see Figure 11).

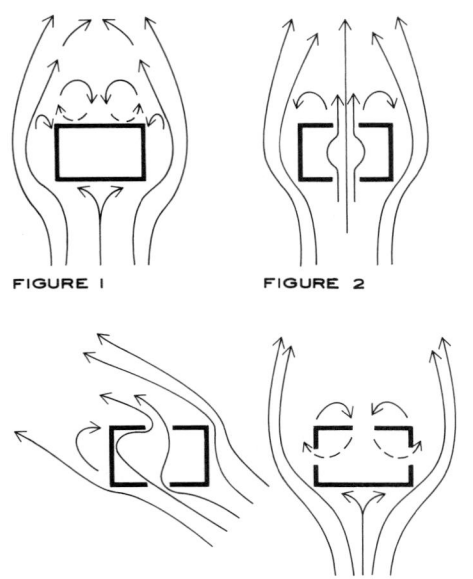

FIGURE I    FIGURE 2    FIGURE 3    FIGURE 4

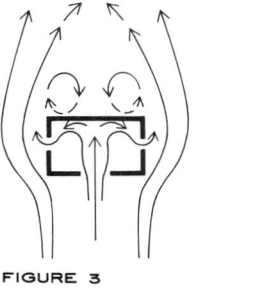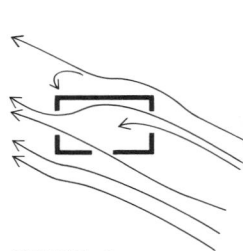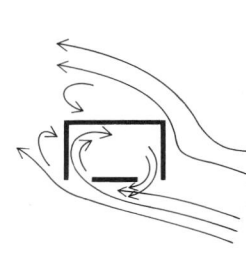

FIGURE 5    FIGURE 6    FIGURE 7    FIGURE 8

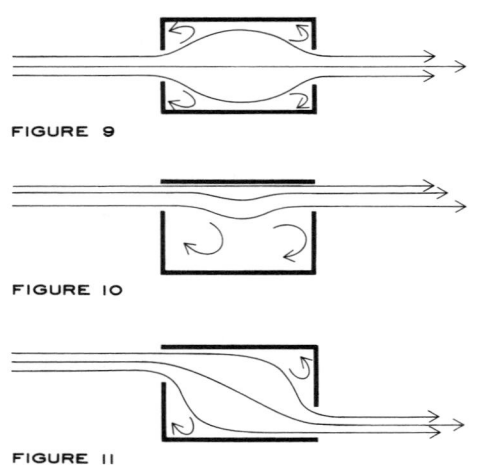

FIGURE 9

FIGURE 10

FIGURE 11

## WINDOW SIZE

Airflow within a given room increases as window size increases, and to maximize airflow, the inlet and outlet opening should be the same size. Reducing the inlet size relative to the outlet increases inlet velocities. Making the outlet smaller than the inlet creates low but more uniform airspeed.

W. Fred Roberts Jr., AIA; Roberts & Kirchner Architects; Lexington, Virginia

## VENTILATION AIR CHANGE RATE

The natural air change rate within a building depends on several factors: speed and direction of winds at building site; the external geometry of building and adjacent surroundings; window type, size, location, and geometry; and the building's internal partition layout. Each of these factors may have an overriding influence on the air change rate of a given building.

Natural ventilation can be accomplished by wind-driven methods or by solar chimneys (stack effect). However, the stack effect is weak and works best during hours when air temperatures are highest and ventilation may not be desirable. In many areas ventilation is best accomplished during the night hours when temperatures are lowest. The night average wind speed is generally about 75% of the 24-hr average wind speed reported by weather bureaus. Often wind speeds are insufficient to accomplish effective people cooling; therefore, ventilating for structure cooling rather than people cooling should be the first design goal. As a rule of thumb, an average of 30 air changes per hour should provide adequate structure cooling, maintaining air temperatures most of the time within 1.5°F of outdoor temperatures.

## EXTERNAL EFFECTS

The leeward wake of typical residential buildings extends roughly four and one-half times the ground-to-eave height. For buildings spaced greater than this distance, the general wind direction will remain unchanged. For design purposes, vegetation should be considered for its effect on wind speed, which can be as great as 30–40% in the vegetation's immediate vicinity. Its effect on wind direction is not well established and should not be relied upon in establishing ventilation strategies.

## RULE OF THUMB EXAMPLE

Determine inlet window opening area to achieve 30 air changes per hour in a house of 1200 sq ft with a ceiling height of 8 ft and awning windows with insect screens.

Required airflow (CFM)
= House volume x air changes per hr/60

Required airflow = (1200 x 8) x 30/60 = 4800 CFM

From local National Oceanic and Atmospheric Administration (NOAA) weather data, determine site wind conditions for design month. For the example above, average wind speed at 10 m above ground level = 7 mph or 616 ft/min at 30° incidence angle to the house face. Note that site wind speeds are generally less than NOAA data, usually collected at airports.

To determine the required inlet area, divide the house airflow by the wind speed passing through openings in the windward building face. To establish this wind speed,

the site wind speed must be modified by the effects of building angle relative to wind direction and porosity of the window opening.

Figure 12 charts the effect of wind incidence angle on airflow rates (based on wind tunnel tests on model buildings with equal inlet and outlet areas equaling 12% of inlet wall areas). Table 1 establishes porosity factors for typical window arrangements. By multiplying the site wind speed by the window air speed factor (WAF) and window porosity factor (WPF), the effective wind speed can be determined. Therefore:

$$\text{Inlet window area} = \frac{\text{Airflow}}{\text{Wind speed x WAF x WPF}}$$

$$\text{Inlet window area} = \frac{4800}{616 \times 0.35 \times 0.75} = 29.7 \text{ sq ft}$$

In the example above, therefore, providing a total of 60 sq ft of insect screened awning windows will provide the required ventilation of 30 air changes per hour.

For best results, the 60 sq ft of windows should be split equally between inlets and outlets. However, adequate airflows can be maintained for anywhere from 40/60 to 60/40 split between inlets and outlets.

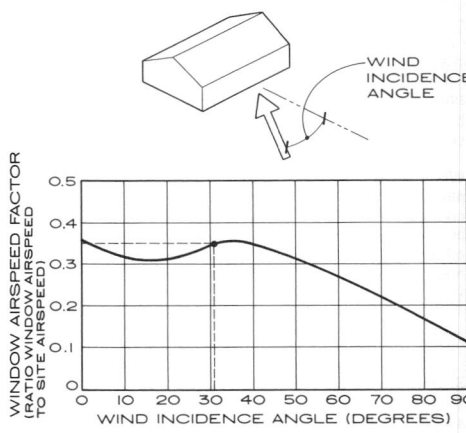

FIGURE 12

## TABLE 1 POROSITY FACTORS

| WINDOW TYPE | FACTOR |
|---|---|
| Fully open awning or projecting window | 0.75 |
| Awning window with 60% porosity insect screen | 0.65 |
| 60% porosity insect screen only | 0.85 |

## PASSIVE SOLAR DESIGN

Passive solar heating and cooling systems, which rely on natural energy flow through and around a building, are divided into three generic categories, including:

1. DIRECT GAIN/LOSS: Heat is collected directly within the space or, for cooling, lost or dissipated directly from the space.
2. INDIRECT GAIN/LOSS: Heat gain or loss occurs at the weatherskin.
3. ISOLATED GAIN/LOSS: Heat gain or loss occurs away from the weatherskin. Cooling, for example, can include induced air precooled from the earth's mass ("coolth" tubes) or cooling ponds.

Systems can be combined depending on thermal needs.

## SPACE HEATING CONCEPTS

As part of any passive system's development, energy conservation elements should be considered. With passive solar heating, preventing heat loss or keeping it at a minimum is fundamental to ensure that the heating system is most effective. These elements include adequate insulation, building orientation, surface-to-volume ratios, and appropriate materials, texture, and finish choices. The space heating success depends on adequate solar energy collection, storage, distribution, and control, all of which occur by natural, nonmechanical means using the three basic heat transfer processes: conduction, convection, and radiation. Efficient passive system operation often involves some user control to alter or override energy flows within a building or at its weatherskin.

1. Solar collection surfaces generally are transparent or translucent plastics, fiberglass, or glass oriented in a southerly direction. Material degradation can be caused by solar exposure and other weather elements. Insulating these collection areas to control nighttime loss is especially important in extreme climates.
2. Thermal storage materials include concrete, brick, sand, tile, stone, and water or other liquids. Phase change materials such as eutetic salts and paraffins also are feasible. Storage should be placed to receive maximum solar exposure, either directly or indirectly. Adequate thermal storage capacity allows the sun's heat to be absorbed and retained until it is needed, and it helps to reduce internal temperature fluctuations.
3. Heat distribution occurs naturally by conduction, convection, and radiation. Generally fans and other mechanical energy distribution equipment are avoided; however, sometimes they are required for fine-tuned operations.
4. Control mechanisms such as vents, dampers, movable insulation, and shading devices can assist in balanced heat distribution.

## SPACE COOLING CONCEPTS

Passive solar cooling, like passive heating, tempers interior space temperatures using natural thermal phenomena. A structure designed for natural cooling should incorporate features that reduce external heat gains and dissipate internal heat gains, including adequate insulation, overhangs, shading, orientation, surface color and texture, and similar factors. When possible, external heat gain should be controlled before it reaches or penetrates the weatherskin.

When cooling is necessary, heat dissipation is accomplished by cooling interior thermal mass, air, or both with conduction, convection, and radiation. Evaporation in hot arid regions and dehumidification in hot humid regions are primary cooling design concerns. Many passive cooling methods exist:

1. Site cooling—through vegetative control, water bodies, and adjacent land forms and materials.
2. Earth cooling—by using groundwater or the earth's mass with earth sheltering or "coolth" tubes.
3. Radiative cooling—heat loss to the sky or cooler objects.
4. Ventilative cooling—cross ventilation through spaces, double roofs, attics, or walls, induced or forced ventilation by pressure or temperature differences.
5. Vapor cooling—evaporative cooling to remove sensible heat, dehumidification to remove latent heat.
6. Flywheel cooling—cooling by internal thermal mass or rockbeds.

| TYPES | HEATING | COOLING |
|---|---|---|
| | | |

### DIRECT GAIN/LOSS

Direct gain is the most common passive solar building approach; most structures use it to some degree. Collection and storage are integral with the space. Southerly oriented glazing (collector) admits winter solar radiation to the space beyond. Thermal storage, incorporated within the building structure, absorbs solar energy. During the cooling season windows, walls, and roofs can be operable or openable for natural or induced ventilation, cooling both the mass and space.

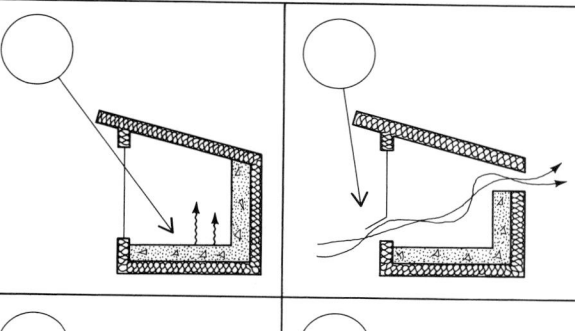

### THERMAL STORAGE WALL—MASS WALL

Thermal storage walls are based on a "sun to mass to space" concept. Collection and storage are separated from the space, but linked thermally. Energy is transferred by conduction through the wall, then by radiation to the space. A mass wall can be vented during the day, if warranted, to the interior by a convective heat flow. In the mass wall system, storage usually is in masonary or concrete directly behind the south glazing. Mass walls should be vented to the exterior and shaded during summer months.

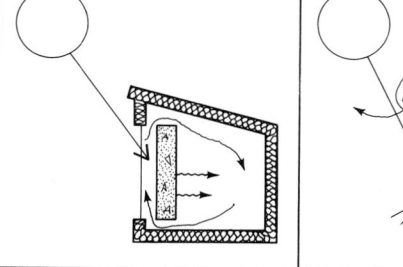

### THERMAL STORAGE WALL—WATER WALL

In a water wall system a liquid, often held in barrels or tubes directly behind south-facing glass, acts as the thermal storage medium. Potential water problems are corrosion and bacteria and algae growth. Solar radiation is absorbed by the contained water. This energy is released gradually as needed to the interior. A water wall should be shaded or vented to the exterior during cooling periods. Provide freeze protection where required.

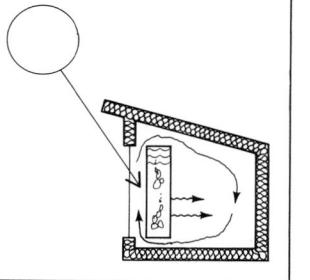
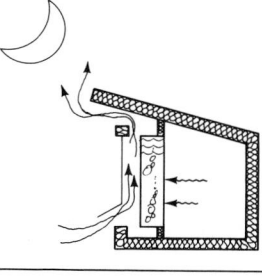

### ROOF POND

In a roof pond system the liquid storage mass is in the ceiling or roof. In heating seasons, insulation panels are moved to expose the storage mass to the sun in the day. Energy is absorbed by the roof pond. At night the panels are replaced over the storage, allowing stored heat to radiate to the building's interior. The process is reversed in summer. The roof pond, insulated from the high summer sun during the day, absorbs the building's internal heat. At night the insulation is opened to allow stored heat to radiate to the sky. Roof ponds are not recommended for private clients.

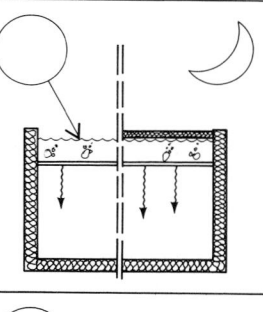
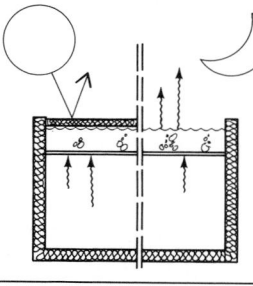

### SUNSPACE

In sunspace designs, solar collection and primary thermal storage often are isolated from living spaces, although variations are possible. This allows the solar system to function independently of the building interior, although heat can be drawn from the sunspace as needed. Thermal storage in the living area is classed as an indirect system. Even on clear winter days sunspaces may overheat sometimes because of large glazed areas. For cooling, the sunspace can be used to induce a convective flow from the exterior, and should be shaded, preferably on the exterior.

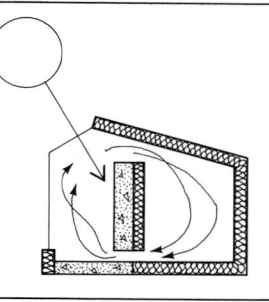
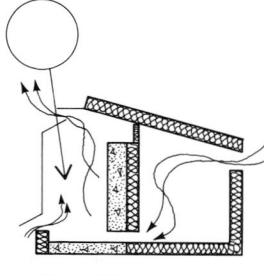

### THERMOSIPHON

Thermosiphon, natural convection systems, rely on the rise and fall of heated and cooled elements such as air. As temperatures change, air moves without mechanical assistance. When the sun warms a collector surface, warm air rises. Simultaneously cooler air is pulled from the storage bottom, causing a natural convection loop. Heat is convected into the space or stored in the thermal mass until needed. In cooling seasons, collectors may be used as a thermal chimney. Warm air rises, inducing precooled air from the ground or other source up through the storage mass to cool it.

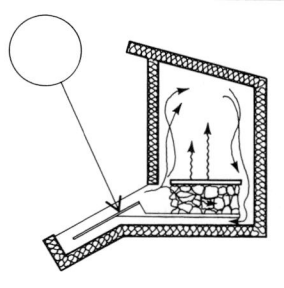
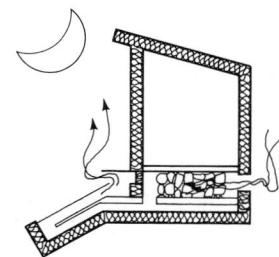

Dennis A. Andrejko, AIA; Andrejko & Associates; Williamsville, New York

## PASSIVE SOLAR HEATING—DESIGN PROCEDURE

The focus of this section is on winter heating between U.S. latitudes 32°N and 48°N. The following design and calculation procedure is applicable to

1. Building types that have space heating requirements dominated by heat loss through the exterior skin of the building.
2. Buildings with a small internal heat contribution from lights, people, and equipment such as residences, small commercial, industrial, and institutional buildings, and large daylit buildings whose internal heat gain is only a small portion of their total heating requirement.

Passive solar heating systems are integral to building design. The concepts relating to system operation must be applied at the earliest stages of design decision making.

Passive systems demand a skillful integration of all the architectural elements within each space—glazing, walls, floor, roof, and in some cases even interior surface colors. The way in which the glazing and thermal mass (heat storage materials, i.e., masonry, water) are designed generally determines the efficiency and level of thermal comfort provided by the system. Two concepts are critical to understanding the thermal performance of passively heated space. They are

1. That the quantity of south glazing, insulating properties of the space, and the outdoor climatic conditions will determine the number of degrees the average indoor temperature in a space is above the average outdoor temperature on any given day (ΔT).
2. That the size, distribution, material, and in some cases (direct gain systems) surface color of thermal mass in the space will determine the daily fluctuation above and below the average indoor temperature (see Figure 1).

Calculating heat gain and loss is a relatively straightforward procedure. The storage and control of heat in a passively heated space, however, is the major problem confronting most designers. In the process of storing and releasing heat, thermal mass in a space will fluctuate in temperature, yet the object of the heating system is to maintain a relatively constant interior temperature. For each system, the integration of thermal mass in a space will determine the fluctuation of indoor temperature over the day.

### EXAMPLE

In a direct gain system, with masonry thermal mass, the major determinant of fluctuations of indoor air temperature is the amount of exposed surface area of masonry in the space; in a thermal storage wall system, it is the thickness of the material used to construct the wall. The following is a procedure for sizing both direct gain and thermal storage wall systems.

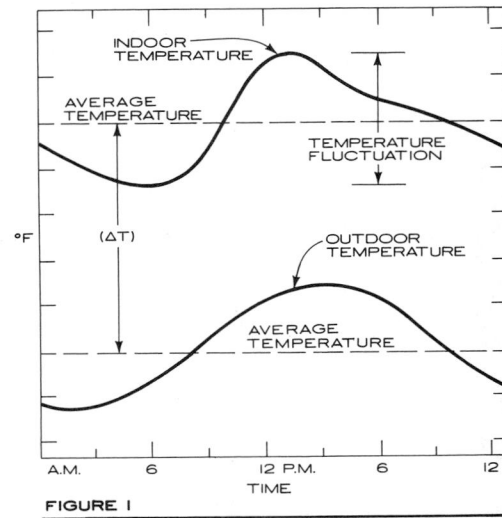

**FIGURE I**

**DAILY TEMPERATURE FLUCTUATION**

## DIRECT GAIN

Direct gain systems are characterized by daily fluctuations of indoor temperatures, which range from only 10°F to as much as 30°F. The heating system cannot be turned on or off, since there is little control of natural heat flows in the space. To prevent overheating, shading devices are used to reduce solar gain, or excess heat is vented by opening windows or activating an exhaust fan.

The major glass areas (collector) of each space must be oriented to the south (±30°) for maximum solar heat gain in winter. These windows can serve other functions as well, such as openings for light and for views.

Each space must also contain enough mass for the storage of solar heat gain. This implies masonry in the building, but the masonry can be as thin as 4 in. in cold climates and 1½–2 in. in very mild climates.

SOUTH GLAZING: One criterion for a well-designed space is that it gains enough solar energy, on an average sunny day in winter, to maintain an average space temperature of ±68°F over the 24-hr period. By establishing this criterion, it is possible to develop ratios for the preliminary sizing of south glazing. Table 1 (see next page) lists ratios for various climates and locations.

In a direct gain system, sunlight can also be admitted into a space through clerestories and skylights as well as vertical south-facing windows. This approach may be taken (1) for privacy, (2) because of shading on the south facades, (3) because spaces are located along facades other than south, and (4) to avoid direct sunlight on people and furniture. Use the following guidelines when designing clerestories and skylights:

1. CLERESTORY: Locate the clerestory at a distance in front of interior mass wall of roughly 1 to 1.5 times the height of the clerestory above the finished floor. Make the ceiling of the clerestory a light color to reflect and diffuse sunlight down into the space. In regions with heavy snowfall, locate the sill of the clerestory glazing 18 in. or more above the roof surface (see Figure 2, next page).
2. SAWTOOTH CLERESTORIES: Make the angle (as measured from horizontal) equal to or smaller than the altitude of the sun at noon on December 21, the winter solstice. Make the underside of the clerestories a light color (see Figure 3, next page).
3. SKYLIGHT: Use a south-facing or horizontal skylight with a reflector to increase solar gain in winter, and shade both horizontal and south-facing skylights in summer to prevent excessive solar gain (see Figure 4, next page).

THERMAL STORAGE MASS: The two most common materials used for storing heat are masonry and water. Masonry materials transfer heat from their surface to the interior at a slow rate. If direct sunlight is applied to the surface of a dark masonry material for an extended period of time, it will become uncomfortably hot, thereby giving much of its heat to the air in the space rather than heat conducting it away from the surface for storage. This results in daytime overheating and large daily temperature fluctuations in the space. To reduce fluctuations, direct sunlight should be spread over a large surface area of masonry. To accomplish this:

1. Construct interior walls and floors of masonry at least 4 in. in thickness.
2. Diffuse direct sunlight over the surface area of the masonry either by using a translucent glazing material—placing a number of small windows so that they admit sunlight in patches—or by reflecting direct sunlight off a light-colored interior surface first (see Figure 5, next page).
3. Use the following guidelines for selecting interior surface color and finishes:
   a. Masonry floors of a medium to dark color.
   b. Masonry walls of any color.
   c. Lightweight construction (little thermal mass) of a light color to reflect sunlight onto masonry surfaces.
   d. No wall-to-wall carpeting over masonry floors.

By following these recommendations, one can control temperature fluctuations in the space on clear winter days to approximately 10°–15°F. These temperature fluctuations are for clear winter days and for at least 6 sq ft of exposed masonry surface area for each square foot of south glazing.

## THERMAL STORAGE WALLS

The predominant architectural expression of a thermal storage wall building is south-facing glass. The glass functions as a collecting surface only and admits no natural light into the space. However, windows can be included in the wall to admit natural light and direct heat and to permit a view.

Either water or masonry can be used for a thermal storage wall (a masonry thermal storage wall with thermocirculation vents is often referred to as a Trombe wall). Since the mass is concentrated along the south face of the building, there is no limit to the choice of construction materials and interior finishes in the remainder of the building.

SOUTH GLAZING: The criterion for a double-glazed thermal storage wall is the same as for a direct gain system—that it transmit enough heat on an average sunny winter day to supply a space with all its heating needs for that day. Tables 1 and 2 (see next page) list guidelines for sizing the glazing of masonry or water walls, respectively.

WALL DETAILS: While the procedure above gives guidelines for the overall size (surface area) of a thermal storage wall, the efficiency of the wall as a heating system depends mainly on its thickness, material, and surface color. (See Table 3, next page.) If the wall is too thin, the space will overheat during the day and be too cool in the evening; if it is too thick, it becomes inefficient as a heating source, since little energy is transmitted through it.

The choice of wall thickness, within the range given for each material in Table 3 (see next page), will determine the air temperature fluctuation in the space over the day. As a general rule, the greater the wall thickness, the smaller the indoor fluctuation. Table 4 (see next page) can be used to select a wall thickness.

The greater the absorption of solar energy at the exterior face of a thermal wall, the greater the quantity of incident energy transferred through the wall in the building. Therefore, make the outside face of the wall dark (preferably black) with a solar absorption of at least 85%.

Edward Mazria, AIA, Architect; Edward Mazria & Associates; Albuquerque, New Mexico

**PASSIVE SOLAR**

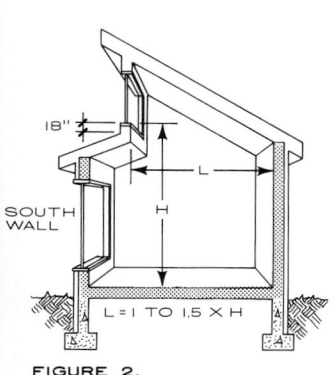

FIGURE 2.
CLERESTORY

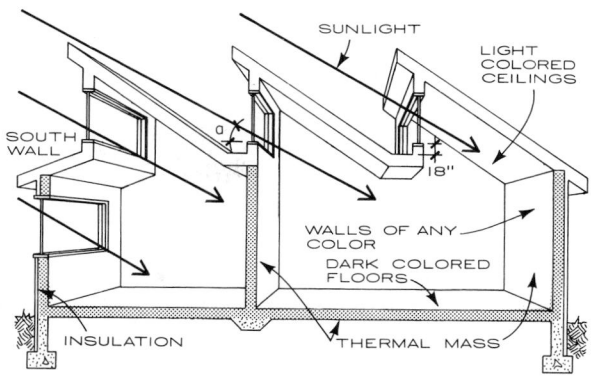

FIGURE 3. SAWTOOTH CLERESTORIES

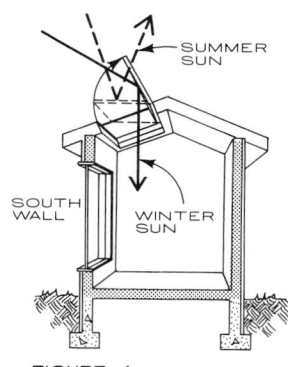

FIGURE 4.
SKYLIGHT

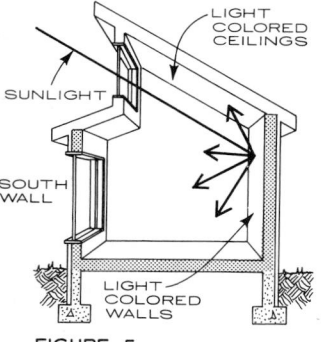

FIGURE 5.
REFLECTING DIRECT
SUNLIGHT

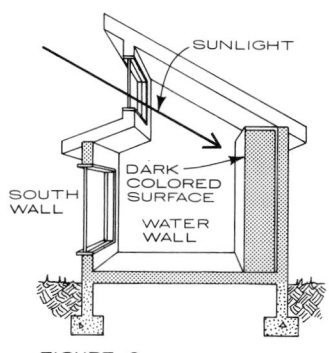

FIGURE 6.
WATER WALL

## DIRECT GAIN SYSTEMS

### TABLE 1. SIZING SOLAR GLAZING FOR DIRECT GAIN, VENTED TROMBE WALL, AND WATER WALL SYSTEMS

| | SQUARE FEET OF GLAZING NEEDED FOR EACH SQUARE FOOT OF FLOOR AREA | | | |
| | 36°F NL | | 44°F NL | |
| AVERAGE WINTER TEMPERATURE (CLEAR DAY) | LOW HEAT LOSS | HIGH HEAT LOSS | LOW HEAT LOSS | HIGH HEAT LOSS |
|---|---|---|---|---|
| **Cold climates** | | | | |
| 20°F | 0.23 | 0.46 | 0.30 | 0.60 |
| 25°F | 0.18 | 0.37 | 0.23 | 0.46 |
| 30°F | 0.15 | 0.30 | 0.17 | 0.34 |
| **Temperate climates** | | | | |
| 35°F | 0.12 | 0.23 | 0.13 | 0.26 |
| 40°F | 0.09 | 0.18 | 0.10 | 0.20 |
| 45°F | 0.06 | 0.13 | 0.08 | 0.15 |

**NOTES**

1. Convective connections to building.
2. Temperatures listed are for December and January (usually the coldest months) and are monthly averages.
3. Low heat loss: Space with a net load coefficient (NLC)

= 3 Btu/day/sq ft/°F. A space with little exposed external surface area.
4. High heat loss: Space with an NLC = 6 Btu/day/sq ft/°F. A space with a large amount of exposed external surface area.
5. The NLC is the total building heat loss less the loss through the solar aperture.

### TABLE 2. SIZING SOLAR GLAZING FOR UNVENTED MASONRY THERMAL STORAGE WALL SYSTEMS

| | SQUARE FEET OF GLAZING NEEDED FOR EACH SQUARE FOOT OF FLOOR AREA | | | |
| | 36°F NL | | 44°F NL | |
| AVERAGE WINTER TEMPERATURE (CLEAR DAY) | LOW HEAT LOSS | HIGH HEAT LOSS | LOW HEAT LOSS | HIGH HEAT LOSS |
|---|---|---|---|---|
| **Cold climates** | | | | |
| 20°F | 0.33 | 0.66 | 0.43 | 0.85 |
| 25°F | 0.30 | 0.60 | 0.35 | 0.70 |
| 30°F | 0.26 | 0.52 | 0.30 | 0.60 |
| **Temperate climates** | | | | |
| 35°F | 0.20 | 0.40 | 0.23 | 0.46 |
| 40°F | 0.15 | 0.30 | 0.17 | 0.34 |
| 45°F | 0.12 | 0.23 | 0.13 | 0.26 |

**NOTES**

1. No convective connections to building.
2. Temperatures listed are for December and January (usually the coldest months) and are monthly averages.
3. Low heat loss: Space with a net load coefficient (NLC)

= 3 Btu/day/sq ft/°F. A space with little exposed external surface area.
4. High heat loss: Space with an NLC = 6 Btu/day/sq ft/°F. A space with a large amount of exposed external surface area.
5. The NLC is the total building heat loss less the loss through the solar aperture.

Edward Mazria, AIA, Architect; Edward Mazria & Associates; Albuquerque, New Mexico

### TABLE 3. SUGGESTED MATERIAL THICKNESS FOR INDIRECT GAIN THERMAL STORAGE WALLS

| MATERIAL | RECOMMENDED THICKNESS |
|---|---|
| Brick (common) | 10 to 14 in. |
| Concrete (dense) | 12 to 18 in. |
| Water | 6 in. or more |

NOTE: When using water in tubes, cylinders, or other types of circular containers, have a container of at least a 9½ in. diameter or holding ½ cu ft (31 lb, 3.7 gal) of water for each one square foot of glazing.

### TABLE 4. APPROXIMATE SPACE TEMPERATURE FLUCTUATIONS AS A FUNCTION OF INDIRECT GAIN THERMAL STORAGE WALL MATERIAL AND THICKNESS

| | THICKNESS (IN.) | | | | | |
| MATERIALS | 4 | 8 | 12 | 16 | 20 | 24 |
|---|---|---|---|---|---|---|
| Brick (common) | — | 24° | 11° | 7° | — | — |
| Concrete (dense) | — | 28° | 16° | 10° | 6° | 5° |
| Water (31°F) | — | 18° | 13° | 11° | 10° | 9° |

NOTE: Assumes a double glazed thermal wall. If additional mass is located in the space, such as masonry walls and/or floors, then temperature fluctuations will be less than those listed. Values are given for clear winter days.

## PRINCIPLES

Thermal storage wall systems are solar space heating devices that can also be used for space cooling in some climates. They consist generally of south-facing massive walls, an airspace, and are then sealed to the exterior by a glass or plastic glazing system. As solar radiation is transmitted through the glazing material, the wall is heated during sunlit hours; in turn the heated wall then radiates warmth to the interior space during the night. Additional components can be added to enhance cold climate performance, such as selective surface foils, night insulation systems, reflectors, and exterior vents to control overheating in mild climates.

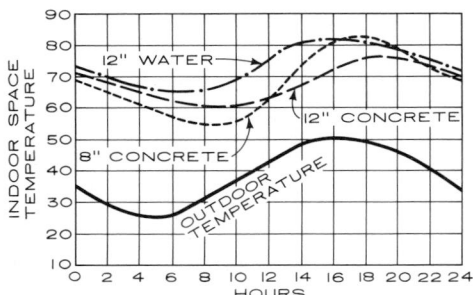

FIGURE 1

## WALL PERFORMANCE

Figure 1 illustrates the characteristic performance of three thermal storage walls during one clear January day 24-hr cycle in a well-insulated house with ½ sq ft of wall for each square foot of room area, located in the U.S. Pacific Northwest. The two thicknesses of concrete wall shown in the graph demonstrate that by adding wall depth the resulting fluctuation in interior space temperature is reduced, and wall peak temperature is shifted toward the night hours when heat is most needed. Also it can be seen that by using a water wall with the same volume as the 12 in. concrete wall, the response of the wall to solar heating is enhanced; however, maximum heat transmission to the building interior occurs earlier in the evening when less heat is needed.

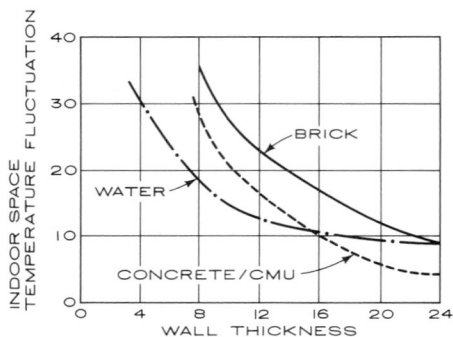

FIGURE 2

## TEMPERATURE FLUCTUATION

Figure 2 illustrates space temperature fluctuations that can be expected for a one-day cycle using three different wall materials of varying thicknesses and the same design conditions as depicted in Figure 1. The wall types shown are solid brick, concrete or concrete masonry units grouted solid, and water.

## WALL AREA VS. FLOOR AREA

Figure 3 gives rule of thumb guidelines for surface area of storage wall, using a wall thickness of between 8 and 18 in., compared to square feet of floor area to be heated for four latitudes. Example: Find the required wall area for a 250 sq ft room located at 40° north latitude with an average outdoor temperature of 34°F during the coldest winter month. On the "Y" axis find 34°, move right on the graph to the 40° latitude line, and then down the graph to the "X" axis, finding the wall vs. floor ratio of 0.45. Multiply 0.45 times the floor area of 250 sq ft, for a suggested wall area of 112.5 sq ft.

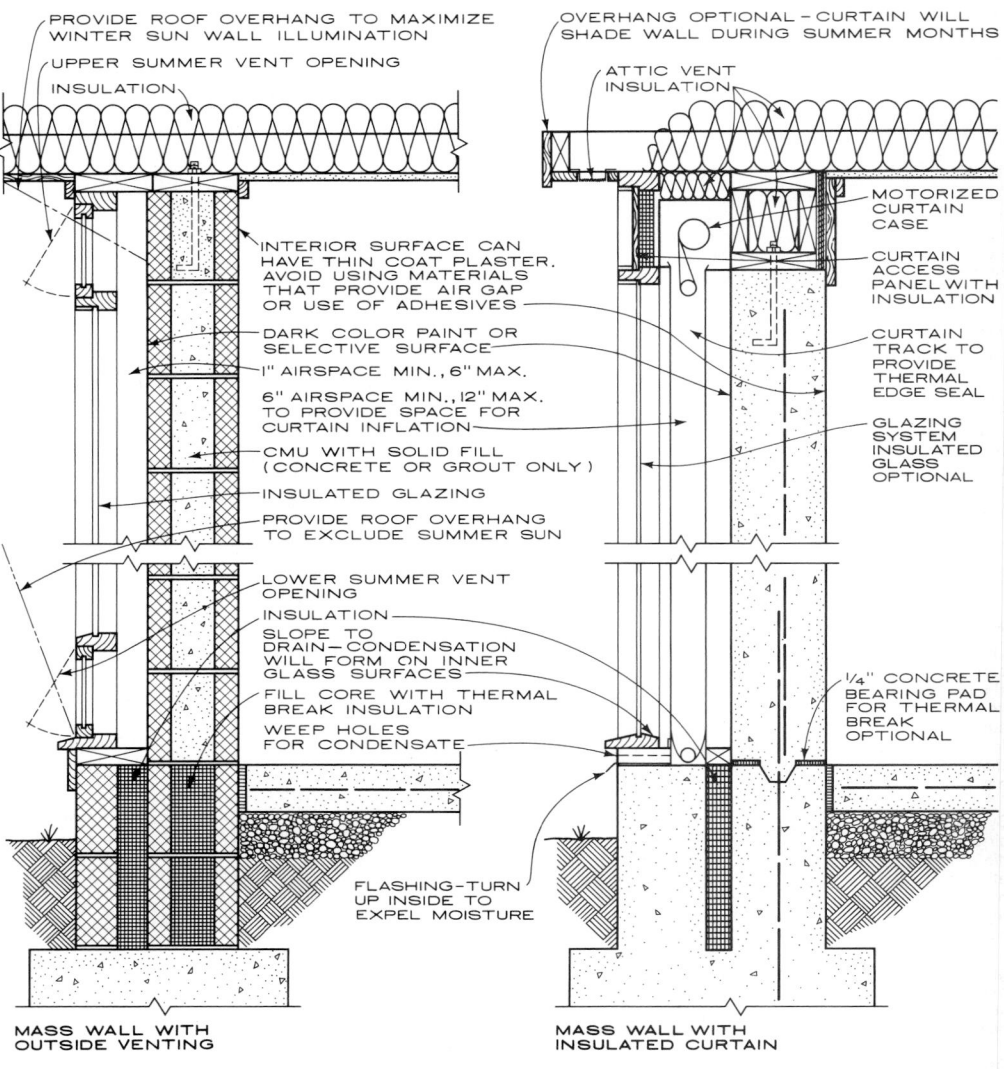

MASS WALL WITH OUTSIDE VENTING

MASS WALL WITH INSULATED CURTAIN

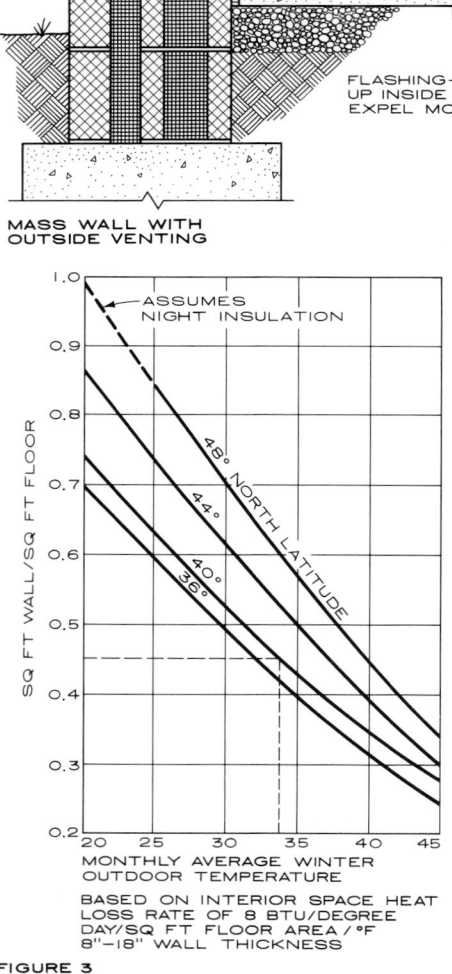

FIGURE 3

BASED ON INTERIOR SPACE HEAT LOSS RATE OF 8 BTU/DEGREE DAY/SQ FT FLOOR AREA / °F 8"–18" WALL THICKNESS

## WATER WALLS

Thermal storage walls of the water container type are generally designed as an integral part of the heated space. Fiberglass, plastic, glass, or metal containers can be used; however, if steel is used, a rust inhibitor should be added to the water, and in all cases algicide should be added to prevent algae growth. Water containers are also manufactured that fit within wood-framed walls and appear as translucent windows from the interior or that can be covered with dry wall.

## INTERNAL MASS

Mass thermal walls can also be used within rooms that are directly heated by solar radiation entering through windows (direct gain system), but where the wall is not directly illuminated by the sun. In this application the wall acts as a heat sink, absorbing excess spacial heat during sunlit hours and giving back heat during the night, reducing spacial temperature swings. As a rule of thumb, provide internal mass wall area at the rate of six times the direct gain window area.

## COOLING

The use of thermal storage walls for cooling involves the isolation of the wall from the exterior and, in particular, solar radiation during the sunlit hours, then exposing the wall surfaces to air jets of cool night air either by forced or natural ventilation to reduce the wall's internal temperature. The wall then functions as a heat sink during the warm hours the following day, to absorb internal spacial heat, thereby maintaining comfortable indoor temperatures.

W. Fred Roberts Jr., AIA; Roberts & Kirchner Architects; Lexington, Virginia

**PASSIVE SOLAR**

## INTRODUCTION

This page concerns thermal storage applications for heating and cooling buildings and heating domestic or service water. Nearly 80% of the energy used in buildings is for these purposes. The discussion here focuses on thermal storage in materials that are not an integral part of the building structure.

### LIMITED CAPACITY HEATING/COOLING DEVICE

This includes applications where the momentary demand for heating/cooling exceeds the capacity of the heating/cooling device. In such cases thermal storage is used in conjunction with limited capacity heating/cooling equipment to meet peak demand.

### LOW-COST ENERGY

The availability of low-cost energy often does not coincide with the need. Thermal storage can be charged with low-cost energy when it is available and discharged when the stored energy is needed later. A conventional heating or cooling appliance may be used to augment stored energy. Waste heat from refrigeration equipment may be useful for heating service water. Because the demand for hot water may not coincide with the availability of waste heat, waste heat storage is required.

## APPLICATIONS

Limited capacity appliance: The most widespread application of thermal storage is probably that of storage-type electric resistance water heaters. A tank of water is heated by an electric resistance element that is not of sufficient capacity to heat the water during peak demand for hot water. However, enough hot water is stored so that when the peak demand occurs, there is sufficient hot water stored to satisfy demand.

By using thermal storage in conjunction with a smaller air-conditioning unit than would normally be used to handle a given cooling load, a substantial savings in operating costs can often be realized. The savings comes primarily from operating the unit at night. The lower heat rejection temperature at night means that the compressor does less work even though it accomplishes the same amount of cooling. Since the need for cooling is usually greatest during the day, the coolness generated at night must be stored for use during the day. Chilled water storage, ice reservoirs, and phase change materials are being used increasingly in buildings for coolness storage.

Off-peak power: Storage of warmth generated by off-peak power can effectively reduce operating costs. Off-peak power is often available from electric utility companies at a significantly lower cost than normal electric power. Energy storage is essential for the customer to satisfy their needs throughout the day when off-peak power is not available and yet realize the savings resulting from use of off-peak power. Off-peak rates are widely available for domestic water heating and to a lesser degree for space heating and air conditioning.

Waste heat: Without thermal storage, use of waste heat may not be feasible because waste heat is often not available when heating is needed. Heat that is normally dumped to the atmosphere from refrigeration condensers can be used to heat buildings and service water. A rapidly growing approach to waste heat recovery is the use of a heat exchanger in the refrigerant line leaving the compressor of an air conditioner.

The envelope and structure of many buildings are of sufficiently low mass that the amount of heat that can be stored in those components is so small as to be not worth the trouble. A wood-frame building is an example of a low-mass structure. A thermal storage chamber could be installed in the building to store coolness during the summer and to store heat during the winter. The chamber could be cooled during the summer by nighttime ventilation, by evaporative cooling, or by the nighttime operation of mechanical cooling equipment. During the winter the storage chamber could be heated by passive gain to the building.

Active solar heat storage: Thermal storage is usually an essential part of solar water and space heating systems. Solar heat is collected and stored during the day and released at night as needed. Commercial applications are similar.

Everett M. Barber Jr.; Guilford, Connecticut

## PRINCIPAL DESIGN CONCERNS

Quality of thermal energy to be stored: Energy to be stored must be available at a temperature level sufficient for it to be useful when needed.

Suitability of storage media: Certain thermal storage materials are more appropriate than others for a given thermal storage task. For example, a phase change material (PCM) with a phase change temperature of 150°F would be inappropriate for passive solar heating/cooling because the temperatures available for storage are not that high.

Encouraging thermal gradients in the storage media: A heat source that has a much higher temperature than the heat storage media will give up its heat to that storage much more readily than will a heat source that is close to the temperature of the storage media. A similar effect occurs with storage of coolness. The greater the temperature difference between the stored energy and that needed to satisfy the load, the less energy must be expended to satisfy the load.

Interface with auxiliary heating/cooling system: It is usually not cost-effective to size a thermal storage system to handle the entire load under all conditions. Some type of auxiliary system is therefore necessary to supplement the storage system. The two systems should be configured so that the thermal storage can be drawn upon first to satisfy the entire load. Once the quality of energy in the thermal storage has been depleted to the point that it is no longer practical to use alone, then the auxiliary system can be used to augment the flow of heat from the storage media. If the thermal storage is entirely depleted, then the auxiliary system can assume the entire load.

When both thermal energy generated at off-peak rates and heat such as solar energy are to be stored, the solar heat storage should be separated from heat produced by off-peak power. If they are not separated, the electric heaters, commonly used for off-peak storage, can heat the stored energy to a temperature level above which the solar collectors would collect little useful heat.

In instances where the cost of conventional energy does not vary with the time of day, the storage and auxiliary systems should be controlled so that the relatively inexpensive stored energy is consumed before the more expensive conventional fuel. This may not be the best practice where the cost of the conventional fuel varies with the time of day.

Duration of thermal storage: The duration over which warmth or coolness is stored is an important factor. At present, thermal storage is most often used in applications of several hours' to several days' duration.

Choice of heat transfer fluid: All other factors being equal, less energy is needed to transport the same amount of heat in a system using a liquid such as water than in a system using air; that is, the pumping energy used to move water is a fraction of the fan energy needed to move the same amount of heat with air. Often factors other than pumping costs will determine the fluid to be used.

## CHARACTERISTICS OF HEAT STORAGE MATERIALS

Thermal storage materials may be separated into sensible heat storage materials and phase change materials. Sensible heat storage materials such as water and rock change temperature as heat is added or removed, but they do not change in physical state. Phase change materials also change in temperature as heat is added or removed over a portion of their heating/cooling cycle, but at the temperature at which they change phase, heat can be added or removed without a change in temperature.

### SENSIBLE HEAT STORAGE MATERIALS

Both water and rock are commonly used sensible heat storage materials. Water may be contained by a tank, an aquifer, a cavern or mine, or a pond. Rock is most frequently used in pebble form. Heat is added to or removed from the water while it is in liquid form and added to or removed from rock in solid form. In some types of systems the same water used to store heat can also be used as the heat transfer fluid. This precludes the cost and inefficiency inherent with heat exchangers. Where water is used for thermal storage, thermal gradients can be encouraged by the choice and location of supply and return openings to the tank, by use of a diffuser to minimize mixing of fluid entering the tank, and by use of diaphragms, baffles, segmented tanks, or multiple tanks. Containers having a high ratio of height to diameter are also useful for encouraging stratification.

Water has a higher heat capacity than pebbles; thus the volume of water needed to store a given quantity of heat is about one-third of the volume of pebbles needed.

When air is the heat transfer fluid used to charge and discharge a pebble bed, no heat exchanger is required.

Where pebbles are used for thermal storage, temperature gradients can be developed easily and preserved by charging the bed with air moving through in one direction and discharging it with air moving through in the opposite direction. An alternative approach involves charging and discharging the bed with flow in one direction only. One-way flow significantly lessens the quality of heat available from the pebble bed and results in a considerable lag before recently added heat is available from the bed.

### PHASE CHANGE MATERIALS

Water is often used as a thermal storage medium for cooling buildings. If water is cooled to the freezing point, it changes phase and becomes ice. Once the water reaches its freezing point, then heat must be removed from the water until it has solidified before it can drop further in temperature.

Materials other than water exist which change phase at temperatures suitable for a variety of thermal storage applications. A given PCM can be selected because it has a phase change temperature that is suited for the temperature of the heat available to be stored and for the load.

As a PCM passes through its phase change point, it can absorb a great deal of heat. A PCM continues to absorb heat at a constant temperature until it has completely changed phase. Primarily due to their high heat capacity at the phase change temperature, PCMs store much more heat than can water or pebbles in the same volume. Thus, a phase change system takes up far less space in a building than does a sensible heat storage container to store the same quantity of useful heat.

The efficiency of a solar collector depends on the temperature difference between the collector and the surrounding air. The lower the temperature at which the collector must operate, the higher its efficiency. If a sensible heat storage medium is uniform in temperature because efforts were not made to encourage stratification, then the collectors will not operate as efficiently as they would if they were connected to a stratified storage. Since a PCM can absorb heat for a long time at the phase change point, a solar collector delivering heat to a PCM can often operate more efficiently than it would if it were delivering heat to a sensible heat storage container at a uniform temperature.

## SYSTEM SIZING

The variation of the load over time must be known or estimated. The temperature level of the energy needed to satisfy the load must be known. An estimate must be made of the amount of heat available for storage and of the temperature level of that heat.

A number of computer programs exist that can be used to estimate the heating and cooling load of residential and small commercial buildings. Several such programs are EEDO, CALPASS, SLR, and FLOAD. For large buildings the most well-documented, verified, and maintained computer program for building energy requirement estimating is DOE2.1c. The program has a separate thermal storage module that can be used for thermal storage studies.

### REFERENCE

For detailed information on thermal storage design, see R. L. Cole et al.: "Design and Installation Manual for Thermal Energy Storage," Argonne National Laboratory Report No. ANL-79-15, second edition, 1980.

## INTRODUCTION

Solar energy can be used to heat water for many applications, including domestic water for residential use, pool water, service water for commercial use, a variety of industrial applications, and agricultural uses. This section is limited to domestic water heating for residential use.

A solar water heating system can be an attractive investment for consumers as well as suppliers of energy. Studies by electric utility companies have shown that residential solar water heating systems have a significant potential for peak load reduction. Since the primary reason for increasing electrical generating capacity is to meet peak loads, the increased use of solar water heating can help to postpone the day when new generating facilities will be needed.

Most solar equipment is more expensive than conventional water heating equipment. Therefore, the savings that result from using solar energy instead of conventional fuel must be sufficient to provide an acceptable return on investment in the added cost of the solar equipment. The savings can be maximized by increasing the portion of the year that available solar energy is used, displacing expensive fuels, and using solar energy in regions where there is abundant sunshine.

## SYSTEM SELECTION CRITERIA

### CLIMATE

If freezing weather is of little or no concern, then systems without automatic freeze protection can be used. These systems are preferred because they are usually more efficient and reliable than those with automatic freeze protection. Unfortunately, in the United States there are few places where there is zero risk of freezing, hence some type of automatic freeze protection is usually desirable.

### QUALITY OF WATER TO BE HEATED

Water quality may dictate the type of solar system that should be used. If the water is "hard" (i.e., it contains a higher than normal percentage of dissolved carbonates) or if the water tends to be acidic (pH much below 7), then a type of system that isolates the solar collectors from the potable water is preferred. Isolation, usually achieved by the use of a heat exchanger, protects the solar equipment from the harmful water.

### HOT WATER DEMAND

In the United States the average person uses 20 gal of hot water per day. Thus, the solar collector area and storage tank must be sized to provide the anticipated demand.

### MOUNTING OF COLLECTORS

Roof structure: The strength of the roof may be a factor in determining the type of solar water heating system as well as the type of system support hardware that should be used. (See pages on structural support of collectors for further information.) Ground mounting can be an attractive alternative to roof mounting.

Tilt/orientation: These factors have a bearing on system performance, but they usually have little bearing on the type of system to be used. A rule of thumb is to mount collectors used for domestic water heating at a tilt equal to the local latitude, the tilt angle measured from the horizontal. (See pages on active solar collection for further information on collector tilt and orientation.)

Shade: The location of the collectors and their relationship to anticipated shade should be considered before installing the equipment. The performance of solar collectors can be severely diminished by shading.

### COLLECTOR ELEVATION WITH RESPECT TO HEAT STORAGE

Collectors below storage: Any one of the system types that rely on natural circulation can be used. These systems should be used where climate permits because they are more reliable and have a higher efficiency than other solar water heating systems.

Collectors above storage: This relationship between collectors and storage, although somewhat less desirable than placing collectors below storage, is frequently used where architectural constraints dictate.

Collectors and storage combined: Some water heater designs include the collectors and storage combined in the same enclosure. This configuration is used to reduce the installation cost of the system. It is somewhat less efficient than the two choices above.

### COLLECTOR AREA VS. STORAGE CAPACITY

The typical relationship between collector area and storage volume is 1.30 to 1.70 gal of water per square foot of collector.

### AIR COOLED VS. LIQUID COOLED

Air-cooled solar systems used exclusively for water heating are much less efficient than liquid-cooled systems used for the same purpose. Only where the air-cooled systems are used primarily for space heating and secondarily for water heating can their use be justified.

## COLLECTOR/STORAGE RELATIONSHIPS

### COLLECTORS BELOW STORAGE

Natural circulation, all liquid: Circulation occurs between the collectors and storage tank due to the density difference between the fluid that is warmed by the sun in the collectors and the cooler fluid in the storage tank. Gravity provides the driving force for circulation. This type of system is ideally suited for climates where there is minimal risk of freeze damage to the collectors. This is the most efficient and reliable of all solar water heating systems.

Variations of the above system have been developed for cold climates. Their main disadvantage is that they usually require antifreeze to transport heat from the collector to the storage tank. The antifreeze necessitates the use of a heat exchanger. Under the low driving force of natural circulation the heat exchanger effectiveness is poor.

Automatic valves can be used to drain the collectors at night, thereby avoiding the heat exchanger. However, the long-term reliability of the automatic draining systems in cold climates has been found to be poor in comparison to that of the antifreeze systems.

Natural circulation, liquid–vapor: These systems also rely on circulation due to density difference. They use a low boiling point fluid such as a refrigerant in the collector. Above the collector is a heat exchanger containing the water to be heated. The refrigerant boils in the collector, and the vapor rises to the heat exchanger where it is cooled by the water to be heated. The refrigerant condenses, then the condensate returns to the collector. The low boiling point fluid does not freeze, hence the systems can be used in cold climates. A benefit of this type of system over the all liquid system is the absence of reverse circulation at night which can result in the loss of heat from the storage tank.

### COLLECTORS ABOVE STORAGE

Often architectural factors dictate that the collector be located above the storage tank. With the heated fluid above the cooler fluid gravity can no longer be used as the driving force for circulation. A motor-driven circulator is used to force the circulation of a heat transport fluid between collectors and storage. A differential temperature controller is used to turn the circulator on and off. When the temperature of the collectors exceeds the temperature of the storage tank by some preset temperature difference, then the controller starts the circulator. When the temperature of the collectors falls to within a few degrees of the temperature of storage tank, then the controller shuts off the circulator. An alternative to using the temperature control is to power the circulator directly from the output of a small photovoltaic array.

Several types of widely used forced circulation solar water heating systems are the following:

Open loop, recirculation: The most widely used in climates where freezing is of little concern. The domestic water is heated directly in the collectors. When the temperature of the water in the collectors approaches freezing, the controller circulates heated water from storage to warm the collectors.

Manufacturers of solar systems generally have recommended that these systems be used in climates where the freezing conditions occur no more than about 30 days per year. In colder regions the energy needed to keep the collectors from freezing can detract considerably from the system performance.

Open loop, drain down: This type of system functions as the one above to collect heat; however, it includes a valving arrangement that permits the water to be drained from the collectors and piping when the water temperature in the collectors approaches freezing.

While the efficiency of these systems is superior to that of the systems using heat exchangers, experience has shown the reliability of these systems in cold climates to be poor in comparison to that of antifreeze systems. These systems are particularly prone to freeze damage.

Closed loop, drain back: This type of system includes the use of a separate fluid, such as water, which is circulated through the collectors where it is heated and then through a heat exchanger where it gives up its heat to the domestic water. When the circulating pump shuts off, the water in the collectors and collector supply and return piping drains back into a reservoir. Freeze protection of this system occurs when the water drains back into the reservoir located in a heated space. This system has the added benefit that the water can be drained from the collectors to prevent the system from overheating.

Closed loop, antifreeze: The most widely used of the forced circulation type solar water heating systems employed in cold climates. Experience has shown this to be the most reliable of the forced circulation systems. A circulator moves the antifreeze between the collectors and a heat exchanger in or near the storage tank where the heat is transferred to the domestic water. A variety of antifreeze liquids is used such as propylene glycol, silicon oil, and ethylene glycol. The first two are nontoxic. A single wall heat exchanger is adequate when nontoxic fluids are used. When the heat transfer fluid is toxic, then a double wall heat exchanger with a vent should be used to separate the antifreeze from the fluid to be heated.

As noted, some means is needed to prevent a system from overheating during prolonged periods of little or no demand. The drain back and drain down systems can be turned off during periods of no demand. The antifreeze systems can be set to run continually so that heat collected during the day is dumped at night.

### COLLECTOR AND STORAGE COMBINED

These systems are known by a variety of names: breadbox, batch heater, integral storage collector. Their appeal is their "appliance-like" nature. They can be installed simply and quickly, needing only connection to a water supply and return line. The majority of these systems are used in nonfreezing regions. Several configurations have been devised for use in climates where freezing occurs. While these systems are usually less expensive to install than other types of solar water heating systems, they are not as efficient as the other systems because of the larger heat losses from the heat storage container at night. The storage container is more difficult to insulate than those in systems where collector and storage are separated. Another disadvantage of this type of system is that it is much heavier than collectors alone. Roof reinforcement may be required. Generally they do not have the heat storage capacity of the systems in which collectors and storage are separated.

## SYSTEM SIZING

The optimum collector area and storage capacity are determined by the hot water demand; the time of day of the hot water demand; the climate, primarily the amount of sunlight; the economics of the system; and the efficiency of the equipment. For rough estimations, a system having about 60 sq ft of collector and an 80 gal tank in the northeastern U.S. will provide between 55 and 75% of the annual hot water requirement of a family of 4. In the southwestern U.S., a collector area of 40 sq ft and storage tank of 80 gal will provide about the same percentage range of the annual water heating requirement.

A number of computer programs have been developed that will give a more careful estimate of the size of solar water heating system components. Three of the better known programs are FCHART, SOLCOST, and RSVP.

## AUXILIARY HEATING SOURCE

A solar heating system is usually used with some type of auxiliary heating equipment. The auxiliary heater may be located in the solar heat storage tank or it may be a separate appliance. Many solar water heating systems are of the single tank type. In this case, the auxiliary heater is usually an electric element positioned in the upper portion of the solar tank. Regardless of the availability of sunlight the electric element maintains a reservoir of heated water in the upper part of the tank. The water below the element is heated only by the solar system until the solar heated water exceeds the temperature setting of the thermostat controlling the electric element.

If a separate auxiliary heater is used, then the solar heating system is placed in a preheat relationship to the auxiliary heater. An auxiliary heater should never be used to heat water before it goes to the collectors. Doing so will cause the collectors to operate at a higher temperature than if the water had not been heated. Since the efficiency of a collector varies inversely with the temperature difference between absorber and ambient temperature, using conventional fuel to heat the solar storage would only decrease the efficiency of the collectors.

Everett M. Barber Jr.; Guilford, Connecticut

## SOLAR RADIANT ENERGY

Solar energy reaches the earth's surface in the form of electromagnetic radiation in the wavelength band between 0.3 and 3.0 micrometers (μm). Beyond the earth's atmosphere, at the average earth-sun distance (about 93 million miles) the radiant flux density on a surface normal to the solar rays is now thought to be 1377 W/sq m or 437 Btu/hr · sq ft. This quantity, known as the solar constant, is apparently subject to minor fluctuations caused by small changes in the sun's output of shortwave (ultraviolet) radiation. An earlier value, 1353 W/sq m or 429.2 Btu/hr · sq ft continues to be widely used pending further measurements from outer space.

At the surface of the earth, solar irradiance falling on horizontal surfaces varies from zero at sunrise to a maximum that, at sea level, may be as high as 325 Btu/hr · sq ft (945 W/sq m) at noon on a clear day. The intensity falls to zero again at sunset. Clear day irradiance values for horizontal and tilted surfaces with varying orientations are given in ASHRAE Publication GRP 170. Values for average day conditions can be found in "Hourly Solar Radiation Data for Vertical and Horizontal Surfaces on Average Days in the United States and Canada" published by the National Bureau of Standards in their Building Science Series 96. A wealth of data on horizontal irradiance is to be found in the "Climatic Atlas of the U.S." and in the publications of the National Weather Service, Asheville, NC. Methods of estimating direct, diffuse, and reflected radiation are given in Chapter 26, 1977 ASHRAE Handbook of Fundamentals.

## SOLAR COLLECTION AND UTILIZATION

Solar radiant energy can be put to use at low and moderate temperatures by flat plate collectors, Figure 1, in which a blackened sheet of metal is used to absorb the incoming radiation and covert it to heat. This heat is then conducted to a fluid that passes through tubes or passages integral with or attached to the plate. To minimize loss of heat from the absorber plate, glazing (single or double, with glass or a heat resistant plastic) is used to reduce convection and to suppress longwave radiation exchange with the sky. The rear surface of the collector plate is insulated carefully, preferably with glass fiber that can withstand the relatively high temperatures (300 to 400°F) that can exist under "stagnation" conditions. This occurs when the collector is exposed to full sunshine with no heat transfer fluid flowing through it. The entire unit is contained within a weatherproof box, and connecting pipes or ducts are provided to bring the fluid to the collector and to carry it away after it has been heated. Details of many types of flat plate collectors are given in Chapter 58, 1978 ASHRAE Handbook of Applications. Performance calculations and test data are given in ASHRAE Publication GRP 170.

When high temperatures are required for industrial or power generation applications, concentrating collectors must be used. These reflect or refract a large amount to solar energy onto a relatively small absorber area, thus reducing the surface available for heat loss and enabling the fluid to attain temperatures that can exceed 1000°F. Such collectors must "track the sun" because they can use only the direct beam radiation from the solar disk. Some concentrating collectors remain essentially fixed, but these are limited to concentration ratios of less than 3 : 1.

## SOLAR ENERGY UTILIZATION SYSTEMS

A system for using solar energy consists of an array of collectors, a storage subsystem, and another subsystem, which is generally quite conventional, for distributing the heated fluid and returning it to storage. Pumps or fans are used to circulate the heat transfer fluid, and control devices are used to start and stop the circulators. Auxiliary or standby heat sources are generally needed to carry part of the load when demand is exceptionally heavy and the thermal storage is depleted due to long periods of unfavorable weather.

Figure 2 shows a simple system for providing space heating and domestic hot water, using a drain-down procedure in which the collectors are emptied whenever the pump P1 stops. A differential controller senses the temperatures of the collector plate and the water and starts the circulating pump P1 when the sun has heated the plate above the water temperature. The pump is stopped when the plate temperature drops to

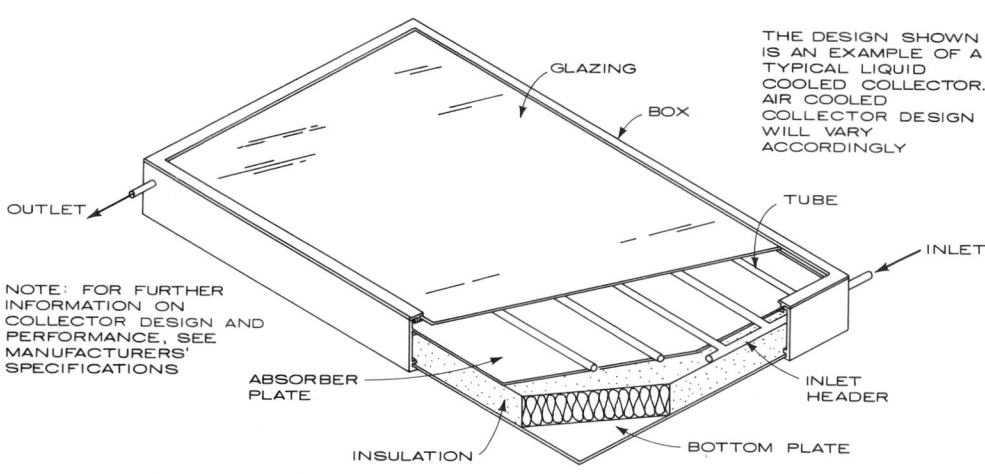

FIGURE 1. TYPICAL FLAT PLATE COLLECTOR

THE DESIGN SHOWN IS AN EXAMPLE OF A TYPICAL LIQUID COOLED COLLECTOR. AIR COOLED COLLECTOR DESIGN WILL VARY ACCORDINGLY

NOTE: FOR FURTHER INFORMATION ON COLLECTOR DESIGN AND PERFORMANCE, SEE MANUFACTURERS' SPECIFICATIONS

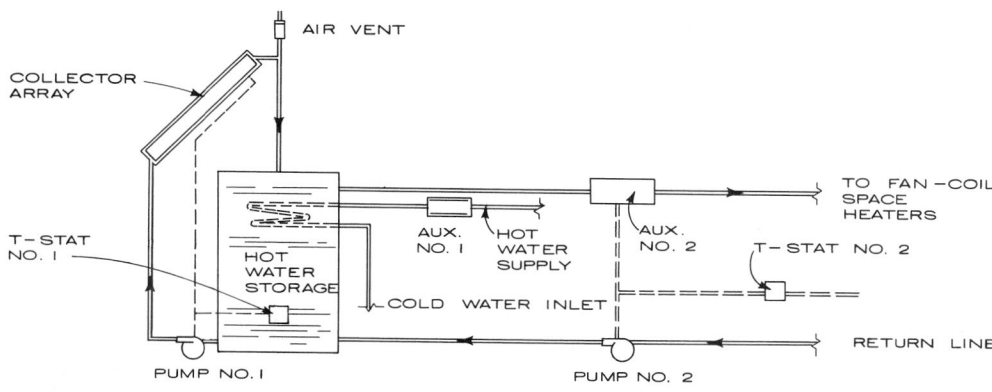

FIGURE 2. DRAIN – BACK SOLAR WATER SYSTEM

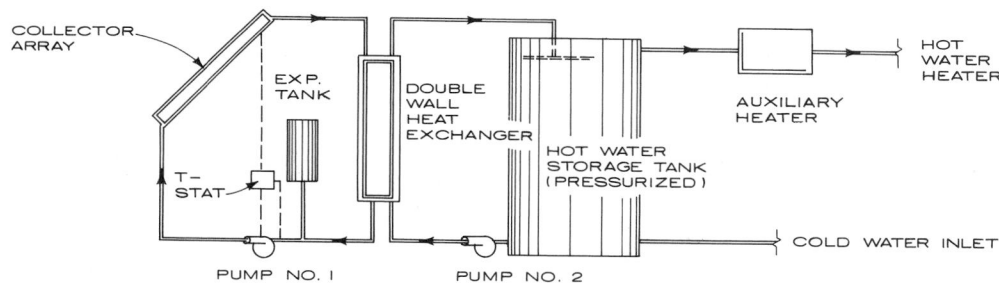

FIGURE 3. SOLAR WATER HEATING SYSTEM

the point where collection of heat is no longer possible.

Domestic hot water is provided by a pipe coil or a small tank located near the top of the main storage tank. The domestic hot water system operates under full line pressure whereas the main tank is at essentially atmospheric pressure, so any leakage would normally be into the main tank. Because of the very remote possibility of a back flow from the main tank into the city water supply, some plumbing codes require a double wall heat exchanger for this service. An auxiliary heater is provided to ensure an adequate supply of hot water at all times.

Since solar heat collection systems work more efficiently when the temperature difference between the collector and the ambient air is relatively low, fancoil units with large areas of finned tube heat transfer surface are generally selected for the space heating assignment. These can be used with water temperatures as low as 100°F. The auxiliary heat source in many solar installations will be electricity, and the heater may use simple direct resistance elements. When cooling is required as well as heating, a heat pump may

prove to be a wise choice, particularly when large amounts of auxiliary energy are likely to be needed.

## FREEZE PROTECTION FOR LIQUID SYSTEMS

When water is used as the heat transfer fluid, freeze protection must always be provided, since there is no location within the continental United States where freezing has never been known to occur. The drain-down system shown in Figure 2 is a fail-safe method to provide such protection but it has certain disadvantages that, in many applications, make the use of a freezing point depressant advisable. Figure 3 shows a widely used system in which water plus ethylene glycol or propylene glycol, or some similar antifreeze fluid, is circulated through the collector array by pump P1. A double wall heat exchanger is used to transfer the collected heat to the service hot water which is under full line pressure, and a standby heater is provided to raise the temperature of the sun heated water to the conventional 140°F. Since domestic hot water is rarely actually used at 140°F, it is beneficial to use a lower thermostat setting for the hot water and to use less cold water for dilution.

John I. Yellott, P.E. and Gary Yabumoto; College of Architecture, Arizona State University; Tempe, Arizona

## AIR SYSTEMS

Air collectors carry serious limitations, primarily because the temperatures that they deliver are low and the space requirements for air ducts are high. Air collectors can be appropriate, however, for applications requiring low process heat or involving the regeneration of desiccant material for dehumidification.

The key issue in air system design is to minimize air leakage in areas where cold outside air is present—between collectors, for example, or in uninsulated chases. One effective installation approach entails mounting the collectors integrally with the roof and keeping all duct connections below the roof. Air collectors have also been mounted on flat roofs, at an angle, with housings erected to protect the back of the collector enclosures and their ductwork. Steps should always be taken to prevent exposure of collector connections and ductwork to the weather.

An air system's heat storage container should allow air moving to and from the container to circulate through the entire storage mass, without "short-circuiting." The container should be adequately insulated, and all joints—especially around the top—should be tightly sealed. Do not install a drain at the bottom of the container; it might provide access for animals, insects, or odors.

The system's fan and duct configuration must allow for the delivery of heated air directly from collectors to load, from collectors to storage, and, indirectly, from storage to load. This requires two pairs of interconnected dampers. Solar fan components that provide integral fan dampers and controllers are available. If a coil is to be used to heat water, it should be located beyond the fan to minimize any chance of its freezing.

These issues, reviewed here as a checklist for architects, have been thoroughly documented. Correction measures can be incorporated into the specification, manufacture, and installation of active solar collection systems.

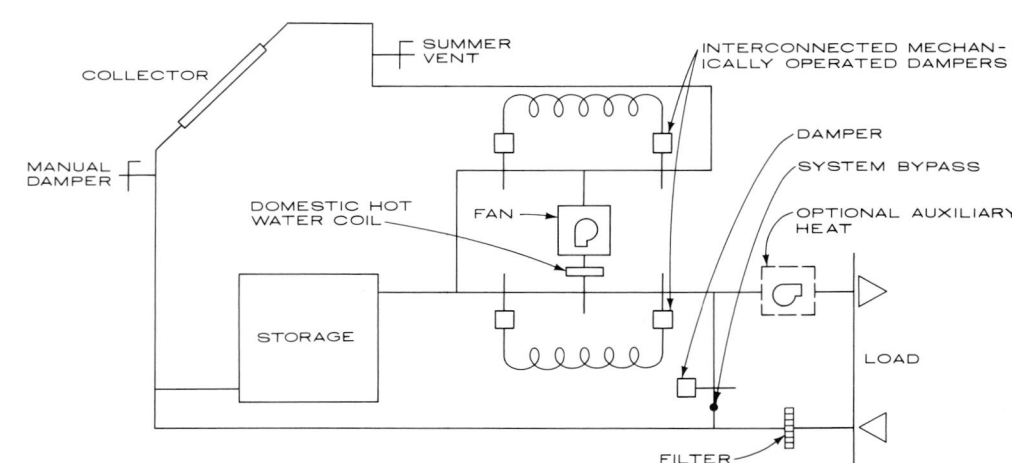

**AIR SYSTEM**

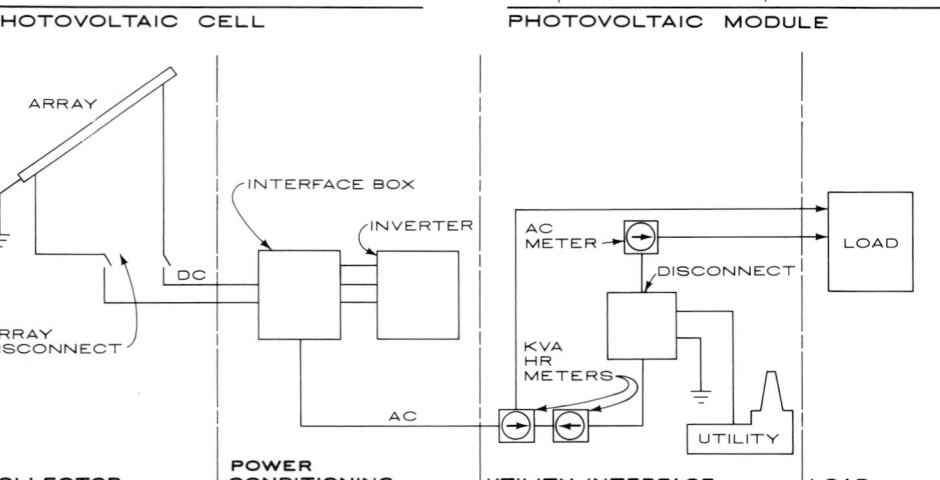

**COLLECTOR TO LOAD**    **COLLECTOR TO STORAGE**    **STORAGE TO LOAD**

**AIR SYSTEM MODES**

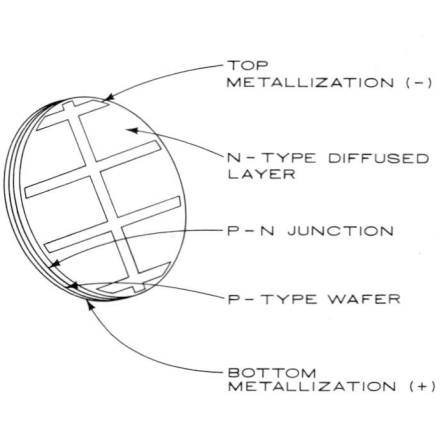

**PHOTOVOLTAIC CELL**

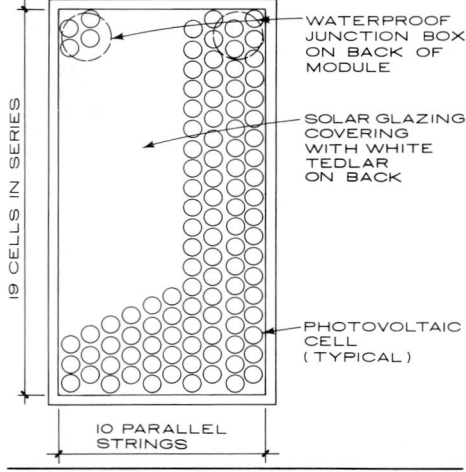

**PHOTOVOLTAIC MODULE**

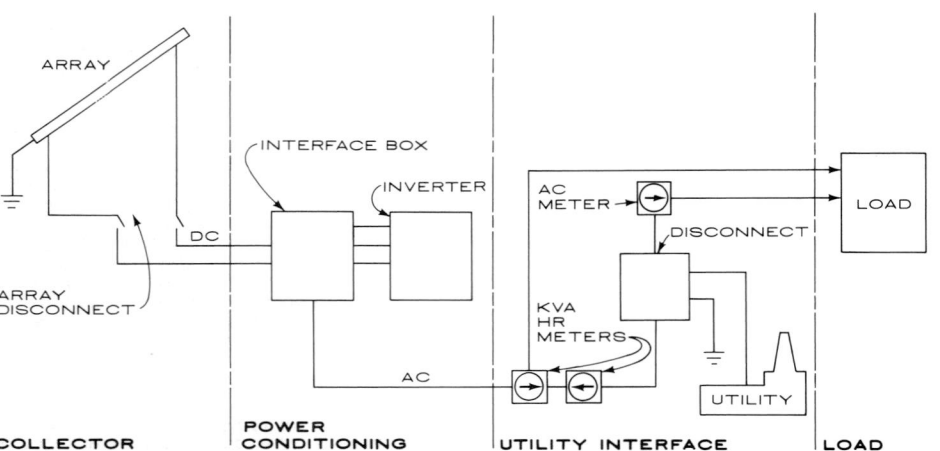

**PHOTOVOLTAIC SYSTEM**

## PHOTOVOLTAIC SYSTEMS

Photovoltaic (PV) solar systems convert sunlight into direct current. Their rapidly decreasing cost may well make them competitive within the next decade with some sources of electricity. At present, however, the lack of cost-effective battery storage limits common PV system applications to the public utilities, which are uniquely capable of both supplying additional energy and purchasing excess energy.

The basic collection component of a PV system is the photovoltaic cell, a layered semiconductor that is generally fashioned from crystalline silicon. A group of cells, usually interconnected both in series and parallel, is encapsulated to form a module. An array is an assembly of modules.

The major factors considered in the sizing of a PV array are its anticipated loads and its power conditioning system (PCS) capacities. The design of an array depends on the module to be installed. Since no single module provides the commonly required voltage, several modules must be installed in series to achieve the proper voltage; groups of similar modules are then connected in parallel to provide the required amperage. The design of an array must facilitate this grouping of modules in series and parallel.

Modules can be installed in three ways: integrally (replacing the sheathing and roofing); applied (set directly on the sheathing, as roofing, or directly on the roofing itself); and standoff, or rack mounted (above the roof and either parallel or at an angle to it). The primary installation considerations are the tilt and orientation of the roof and the vent requirements of the module. The latter consideration can seriously affect system efficiency. Modules are adversely affected by heat, losing approximately ±0.003% efficiency for each degree Farenheit rise in temperature. Applied installations, therefore, are less efficient, because the modules are unable to discharge heat. Rack mounting, which allows air to circulate freely behind the modules, is often the most efficient installation technique. Some PV systems capture the heat discharged by the modules and supply it directly to interior spaces as heated air or exhaust it directly to the exterior; in these installations, the collectors are attached and ducted as they would be in an air collector system.

The major component of the PCS is the inverter, which converts the DC power generated by the array into AC power used by the load. The PCS also synchronizes the PV array's power output to make it compatible with the local utility company's output. The number of available PCS capacities is limited and is thus a controlling factor in the sizing of PV systems.

Stephen Weinstein, AIA; The Ehrenkrantz Group; New York, New York

**18**    **ACTIVE SOLAR**

The design of a solar collector array and its support structure can have an important influence on overall building appearance and be a key determinant of the total cost of the solar heating system. It is also the aspect of the system that the architect can most easily control.

Because there are no industry standards for collector size, piping, or mounting hardware, it is essential that the architect know which collector system will be installed before he or she begins final detailing and design. If the collector array is to be selected as part of a total bid package, for example, sizing and coordination problems may result, and the architect may lose control of the array's structural underpinnings and the building's overall appearance.

## ANCHORING THE SUPPORT STRUCTURE

Rooftop collector supports should be anchored directly to structural members, not to wood or metal decking; otherwise, wind-induced uplift forces and point loading may cause roofing—and possibly structural—failure. In steel buildings, vertical supports must be secured directly to joists or beams. In wood buildings, securing the collector supports directly to structural members will normally require the installation of some form of blocking, under the decking and between rafters, to transfer the load.

## DESIGNING THE ARRAY

When a collector array is to be placed on a light steel-framed roof, the direction of the joints in the array's support structure becomes a critical design issue. It is often necessary to stagger the array's vertical supports to ensure an even distribution of the load. Some roofs cannot support such a load and thus must be clear-spanned. The array support structure in such cases is likely to be particularly expensive; intricate long-span space-frame structures are invariably costly and cost-ineffective.

## AVOIDING ROOFING PROBLEMS

Leaky roofs are a persistent problem in solar installations. Problems can be anticipated and minimized by following these guidelines:

- Minimize roof penetrations. Collector supports constructed of pipe, if used in a large array as shown, require one roof penetration for every 60 sq ft of roof area, approximately; long-span design, by comparison, calls for one roof penetration roughly every 225 sq ft. Roof penetrations can also be avoided by using solar piping supports that rest directly on the roof, as shown; these prevent undue roof stress caused by pipe movement.
- Properly detail the flashing of vertical supports at the roofline. Except on pitched roofs (and often even then), wood-blocking bolted directly through the roof will ultimately generate leaks, regardless of the amount of roofing cement applied. The best approach is to use a neoprene roofing sleeve. The next best is base flashing and canopy detail. Less preferable is a pitch pocket, properly constructed. Other approaches—those using site-fabricated curbs and other techniques—tend to fail. If blocking is to be secured directly to a sloped roof, then roofing cement should be applied between each layer of shingles, between shingles and deck, and between shingles and blocking.

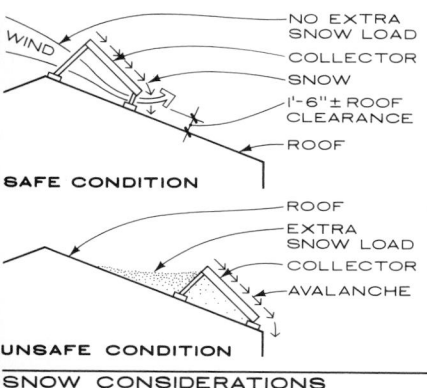

**SAFE CONDITION**

NO EXTRA SNOW LOAD
COLLECTOR
SNOW
1'-6"± ROOF CLEARANCE
ROOF
WIND

**UNSAFE CONDITION**

ROOF
EXTRA SNOW LOAD
COLLECTOR
AVALANCHE

**SNOW CONSIDERATIONS**

Stephen Weinstein, AIA; The Ehrenkrantz Group; New York, New York

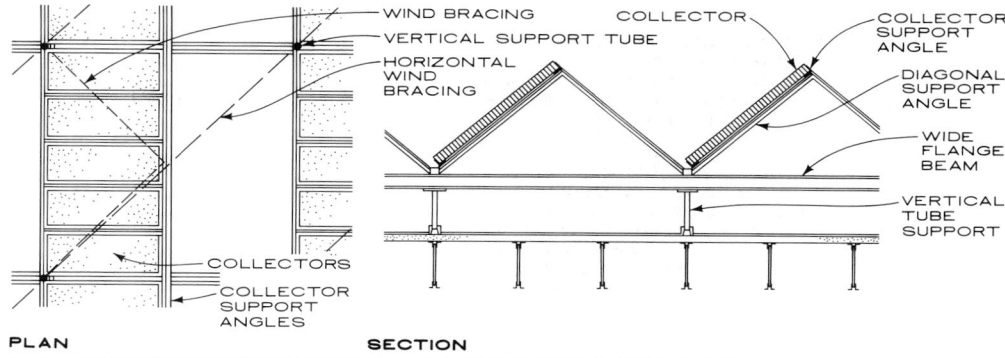

WIND BRACING
VERTICAL SUPPORT TUBE
HORIZONTAL WIND BRACING
COLLECTOR
COLLECTOR SUPPORT ANGLE
DIAGONAL SUPPORT ANGLE
WIDE FLANGE BEAM
VERTICAL TUBE SUPPORT
COLLECTORS
COLLECTOR SUPPORT ANGLES

**PLAN**     **SECTION**

**COLLECTOR SUPPORT**

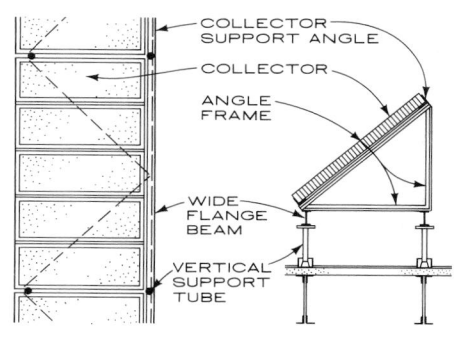

COLLECTOR SUPPORT ANGLE
COLLECTOR
ANGLE FRAME
WIDE FLANGE BEAM
VERTICAL SUPPORT TUBE

**PLAN**     **SECTION**

**COLLECTOR SUPPORT**

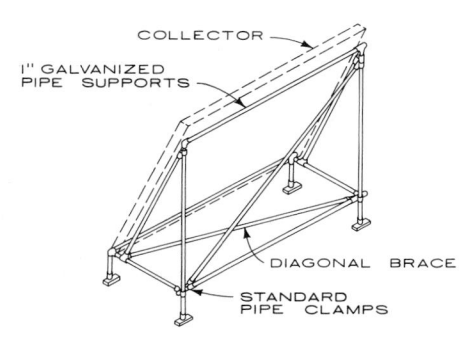

COLLECTOR
1" GALVANIZED PIPE SUPPORTS
DIAGONAL BRACE
STANDARD PIPE CLAMPS

**PIPE RACK MOUNTING**

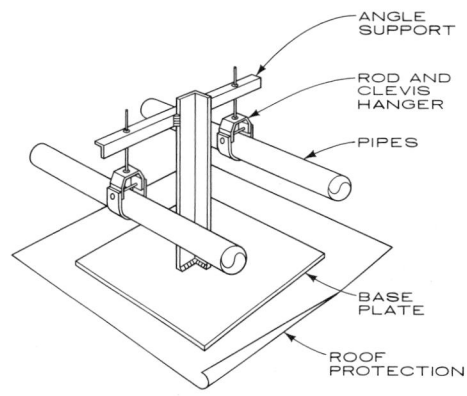

ANGLE SUPPORT
ROD AND CLEVIS HANGER
PIPES
BASE PLATE
ROOF PROTECTION

**PIPE SUPPORT**

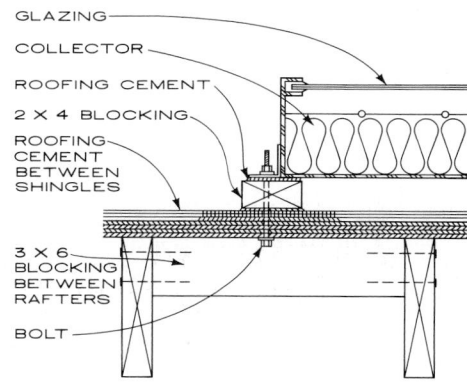

GLAZING
COLLECTOR
ROOFING CEMENT
2 X 4 BLOCKING
ROOFING CEMENT BETWEEN SHINGLES
3 X 6 BLOCKING BETWEEN RAFTERS
BOLT

**SLOPED ROOF**

- Do not create dams. Any form of continuous blocking or curb will—unless installed at a right angle to the slope of a pitched roof—invariably dam a portion of the roof and ultimately cause built-up roofing to fail.
- Specify that all work be performed by the appropriate trade. Support flashing, for instance, is often installed by the steel erector or the plumbing contractor rather than by the roofing contractor.
- Protect the roof. Specify that the roof in general be protected during construction and that permanent walkways be installed to provide access to the system once it is in use.
- Mount collectors on a sloped roof unless the pitch is so flat that the loss of year-round efficiency in performance will be too great. When collectors and sloped roof are parallel, allow a 1½ in. airspace between them to prevent deterioration of the roofing material and the collector enclosures. Do not mount collectors integrally with the roofing unless the collectors are specifically designed for integral mounting; as a rule, only air collectors are so designed. In cold regions, mount collectors as near the roof peak as possible to minimize damming and snow buildup and to lessen the chance of a dangerous snow slide—a particular threat when an array is located above an entry.
- On a flat roof, mount collectors between 2 ft 6 in. and 3 ft above the roof rather than directly on the roof. This prevents snow buildup, permits adequately sloped pipe runs, and—most important—allows for the installation of proper roof penetrations and for future roof repair and replacement.

## INTRODUCTION

Passive solar optics (PSO) is a means of directing sunlight to surfaces within a building that would not normally receive the direct beam component of sunlight.

A PSO system has three major passive elements: collector array, clerestory window, and reflector array (see Figure 1). All three elements are arranged so that their lengths are parallel and generally run east-west. The collector array faces south and contains several independent fresnel reflective panels 1 to 2 ft high and 4 to 8 ft long. The topmost panel is aimed at a low horizon (typically 15°–25° off horizontal). Each successively abutting collector panel is aimed higher until all the desired annual solar horizons are within one or more regions of the collector array. Collector panels have overlapping fields of view, which enable uniform, continuous coverage of the atrium floor.

## AESTHETICS AND ECONOMIC ADVANTAGES

PSO illumination will usually appear as softened equatorial light, bright but not harsh, and mostly vertical. The economic implications of the PSO system allow for the reduction of the size of atria, light wells, and roof apertures.

By targeting sunlight, PSO generally puts more light at the bottom of atria than conventional skylights, particularly as atria height increases. Energy savings are achieved by reduced hours of electrical light operation. The PSO also reduces insolation loads in atria.

Since the qualities of sunlight vary regionally and seasonally, a PSO can be designed to respond to such variations by dedicating more collector panels to either low winter solar horizons or high summer horizons. A comparison of a horizontal skylight with a PSO system that is not optimized for either summer or winter performance reveals that the PSO system and skylight would deliver about the same amount of solar energy to an interior space on the equinox days. At summer solstice a PSO system would deliver less total energy than the skylight, although that of the PSO would be more uniform and have greater intensity at the atrium floor. In the case of a tall atrium (7 stories), the floor of the atrium could be 5 times brighter on average than a conventional solution. During winter solstice, the PSO system would generally admit more solar energy than a horizontal skylight.

## SYSTEM DESIGN

The tables below require the building's latitude; orientation of the collectors is assumed to be due south. Table 1 gives the angles of the collectors (C) and reflectors (R) to be used for a given latitude. Table 2 gives the lengths of the collectors and reflectors based on the width of the horizontal opening (W). Table 3 estimates schematic design illumination values for selected latitudes and various ranges of the width of the horizontal opening and height from the bottom of the glazing to the floor (H). The basis of the table is the sun's angle at solar noon for various latitudes during the summer solstice (SS), spring/fall equinox (E), and winter solstice (WS). The sun's illuminance is 7500 footcandles. The values listed in Table 3 approximate the average illuminance on the floor for the minimum target width (see Figure 1). The collector and reflector design angles are averaged for an ideal design for each particular width, height, and latitude. Actual angles may vary as much as 5°. The system design and estimated illuminances should therefore only be used for schematic design purposes.

After determining the appropriate PSO system, Tables 1 and 2 can be used to draw the system:

1. Estimate location of clerestory window and draw horizontal and vertical reference lines through a point at its base.
2. Locate midpoint of collector 3 (C3). Distance from the vertical reference line to midpoint of C3 is W ft. Distance from the horizontal reference line to C3 is (13 x W)/24 ft.
3. Locate midpoint of reflector 2 (R2). Distance from vertical reference line to midpoint of R2 is W/2 ft. Distance from horizontal reference line to R2 is (23 x W)/48 ft.
4. Using the angles in Table 1 and lengths in Table 2, draw the PSO system using midpoints of C3 and R2 as starting points.
5. Adjust collector–reflector arrangement to north or south to best fit the structural system. Finalize location of clerestory window by shifting it just north of R3.
6. The target point will be directly below midpoint of R2 and on the floor. Minimum target width should be calculated and is equal to W + (H x 0.174).

### TABLE 1. PSO STANDARD SYSTEM DESIGN ANGLES (DEGREES)

| ZONE | COLLECTORS | | | | | REFLECTORS | | |
|---|---|---|---|---|---|---|---|---|
| | c1 | c2 | c3 | c4 | c5 | R1 | R2 | R3 |
| 46 N. LAT | 84.0 | −85.0 | −71.5 | −55.5 | −38.0 | −61.0 | −47.5 | −28.0 |
| 40 N. LAT | 87.0 | −82.0 | −68.5 | −52.5 | −35.0 | −61.0 | −47.5 | −28.0 |
| 34 N. LAT | 90.0 | −79.0 | −65.5 | −49.5 | −32.0 | −61.0 | −47.5 | −28.0 |
| 28 N. LAT | −87.0 | −76.0 | −62.5 | −46.5 | −29.0 | −61.0 | −47.5 | −28.0 |

NOTES: 1. See diagram 1 for sign convention.
2. Angles for each zone are for all heights (H) and widths (W).

### TABLE 2. PSO STANDARD COMPONENT LENGTHS (FT)

| WIDTH (W) | COLLECTORS | | | | | REFLECTORS | | |
|---|---|---|---|---|---|---|---|---|
| | c1 | c2 | c3 | c4 | c5 | R1 | R2 | R3 |
| 4' | 1'-0" | 1'-0" | 1'-0" | 1'-0" | 1'-0" | 3'-0" | 2'-0" | 2'-0" |
| 8' | 2'-0" | 2'-0" | 2'-0" | 2'-0" | 2'-0" | 6'-0" | 4'-0" | 4'-0" |
| 12' | 3'-0" | 3'-0" | 3'-0" | 3'-0" | 3'-0" | 9'-0" | 6'-0" | 6'-0" |
| 16' | 4'-0" | 4'-0" | 4'-0" | 4'-0" | 4'-0" | 12'-0" | 8'-0" | 8'-0" |
| 20' | 5'-0" | 5'-0" | 5'-0" | 5'-0" | 5'-0" | 15'-0" | 10'-0" | 10'-0" |

NOTE: Lengths given are for all zones and all heights (H) for the given width (W).

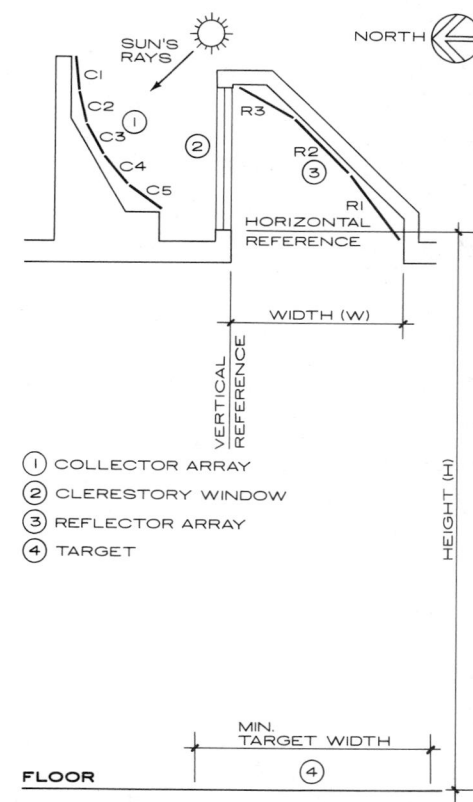

SIGN CONVENTION

① COLLECTOR ARRAY
② CLERESTORY WINDOW
③ REFLECTOR ARRAY
④ TARGET

**FIGURE I. PASSIVE SOLAR OPTICS SYSTEM DIAGRAM**

### TABLE 3. SCHEMATIC DESIGN ILLUMINATION VALUES*

| | ZONE 1: 46° NORTH LATITUDE | | | | | | | | | | | | | | |
|---|---|---|---|---|---|---|---|---|---|---|---|---|---|---|
| | w = 4' | | | w = 8' | | | w = 12' | | | w = 16' | | | w = 20' | | |
| HEIGHT (H) | SS | E | WS | SS | E | WS | SS | E | WS | SS | E | WS | SS | E | WS |
| 12' | 809 | 984 | 772 | 1177 | 1244 | 1191 | 1350 | 1357 | 1331 | 1456 | 1436 | 1397 | 1543 | 1484 | 1401 |
| 24' | 456 | 643 | 458 | 820 | 976 | 766 | 1033 | 1132 | 1021 | 1174 | 1234 | 1183 | 1272 | 1302 | 1275 |
| 36' | 316 | 469 | 330 | 600 | 782 | 589 | 824 | 980 | 769 | 980 | 1089 | 928 | 1092 | 1171 | 1079 |
| 48' | 239 | 358 | 257 | 474 | 641 | 476 | 664 | 846 | 642 | 822 | 980 | 770 | 945 | 1073 | 878 |
| 60' | 186 | 296 | 211 | 381 | 536 | 403 | 555 | 732 | 548 | 700 | 881 | 672 | 826 | 979 | 764 |
| 72' | 160 | 244 | 178 | 324 | 472 | 341 | 477 | 645 | 482 | 604 | 782 | 594 | 719 | 899 | 690 |

| | ZONE 2: 40° NORTH LATITUDE | | | | | | | | | | | | | | |
|---|---|---|---|---|---|---|---|---|---|---|---|---|---|---|---|
| | w = 4' | | | w = 8' | | | w = 12' | | | w = 16' | | | w = 20' | | |
| HEIGHT (H) | SS | E | WS | SS | E | WS | SS | E | WS | SS | E | WS | SS | E | WS |
| 12' | 817 | 967 | 804 | 1183 | 1225 | 1267 | 1348 | 1339 | 1432 | 1460 | 1416 | 1487 | 1543 | 1473 | 1482 |
| 24' | 452 | 629 | 478 | 840 | 967 | 806 | 1056 | 1127 | 1083 | 1184 | 1221 | 1268 | 1282 | 1285 | 1367 |
| 36' | 308 | 456 | 343 | 607 | 780 | 610 | 835 | 971 | 804 | 1001 | 1082 | 979 | 1110 | 1156 | 1160 |
| 48' | 233 | 349 | 268 | 470 | 638 | 478 | 667 | 829 | 672 | 843 | 965 | 810 | 970 | 1055 | 935 |
| 60' | 185 | 286 | 213 | 380 | 524 | 398 | 560 | 718 | 560 | 708 | 869 | 699 | 843 | 967 | 806 |
| 72' | 157 | 244 | 176 | 323 | 457 | 340 | 476 | 632 | 481 | 608 | 780 | 611 | 731 | 887 | 716 |

| | ZONE 3: 34° NORTH LATITUDE | | | | | | | | | | | | | | |
|---|---|---|---|---|---|---|---|---|---|---|---|---|---|---|---|
| | w = 4' | | | w = 8' | | | w = 12' | | | w = 16' | | | w = 20' | | |
| HEIGHT (H) | SS | E | WS | SS | E | WS | SS | E | WS | SS | E | WS | SS | E | WS |
| 12' | 735 | 822 | 923 | 1099 | 1275 | 1192 | 1280 | 1426 | 1315 | 1391 | 1480 | 1384 | 1456 | 1470 | 1426 |
| 24' | 412 | 616 | 616 | 751 | 822 | 938 | 964 | 1089 | 1088 | 1106 | 1273 | 1194 | 1213 | 1381 | 1258 |
| 36' | 289 | 353 | 453 | 547 | 633 | 751 | 752 | 826 | 940 | 905 | 987 | 1061 | 1024 | 1173 | 1131 |
| 48' | 224 | 259 | 347 | 428 | 498 | 618 | 603 | 688 | 812 | 754 | 825 | 943 | 873 | 1034 | 950 |
| 60' | 174 | 217 | 279 | 348 | 410 | 513 | 505 | 582 | 701 | 639 | 725 | 842 | 754 | 826 | 945 |
| 72' | 143 | 173 | 241 | 300 | 348 | 451 | 431 | 499 | 620 | 553 | 632 | 752 | 658 | 742 | 866 |

| | ZONE 4: 28° NORTH LATITUDE | | | | | | | | | | | | | | |
|---|---|---|---|---|---|---|---|---|---|---|---|---|---|---|---|
| | w = 4' | | | w = 8' | | | w = 12' | | | w = 16' | | | w = 20' | | |
| HEIGHT (H) | SS | E | WS | SS | E | WS | SS | E | WS | SS | E | WS | SS | E | WS |
| 12' | 407 | 932 | 804 | 656 | 1168 | 1252 | 774 | 1277 | 1405 | 838 | 1343 | 1446 | 885 | 1384 | 1438 |
| 24' | 202 | 603 | 471 | 422 | 921 | 811 | 572 | 1066 | 1055 | 661 | 1164 | 1255 | 724 | 1227 | 1344 |
| 36' | 120 | 435 | 322 | 286 | 727 | 621 | 427 | 918 | 804 | 528 | 1032 | 962 | 603 | 1104 | 1142 |
| 48' | 83 | 332 | 255 | 215 | 597 | 488 | 329 | 787 | 684 | 432 | 921 | 803 | 507 | 1012 | 920 |
| 60' | 60 | 269 | 217 | 162 | 497 | 409 | 265 | 675 | 578 | 356 | 821 | 711 | 437 | 920 | 807 |
| 72' | 39 | 232 | 180 | 132 | 431 | 336 | 218 | 595 | 491 | 296 | 730 | 625 | 370 | 840 | 728 |

*W = width, SS = summer solstice, E = spring/fall equinox, WS = winter solstice

David Eijadi, AIA, and Kyle Williams; BRW, Inc.; Minneapolis, Minnesota

**ACTIVE SOLAR**

## CONSTRUCTION ASSEMBLIES

The construction of the system can be divided into three parts: superstructure, framework, and reflective panels. The function of the exterior collector superstructure is to provide support for an adjustable framework which in turn supports the lens panels. The superstructure and the framework should be of the same material. The superstructure of the exterior collector can be constructed of many different materials. Steel, aluminum, and wood are the best among the choices. Each must be protected against the climate. Steel in particular should be treated to minimize rusting and rust water runoff onto the lenses. Vertical supports of the superstructure can be up to 10 ft apart.

The exterior framework element is basically a picture frame for the lens panel. The frames will be approximately 1 ft 0 in. to 2 ft 0 in. in vertical height and 4 ft 0 in. to 10 ft 0 in. in horizontal length. Each frame should be slightly larger than the lens panel it is to contain to permit expansion. Each frame should be designed to permit angular adjustment during installation through the use of oversized and slotted holes.

The reflective panel is comprised of three basic elements: the thin lens film, an acrylic substrate, and a structural backer panel. It is possible to create a structural backer panel of acrylic, thus making this a two-element assembly, as illustrated. The self-adhesive lens material is adhered to the acrylic substrate, with the lenticular grooves running horizontally. The edges of the lens and substrate are then sealed with a waterproof tape.

The superstructure for the interior reflector can be made of wood or steel framing with an exterior cladding of metal, wood, or roofing as is appropriate to the building, climate, and budget. The window in this assembly should be of clear glass. Insulated glazing is not required but may be desirable. (See roofing, glazing, and flashing sections.)

The interior framework to support the lens panels should be made of "T"-shaped cross sections of aluminum, wood, or steel. Lens panels, constructed in the same manner as the exterior panels, can then be dropped into place as is done with acoustical ceilings.

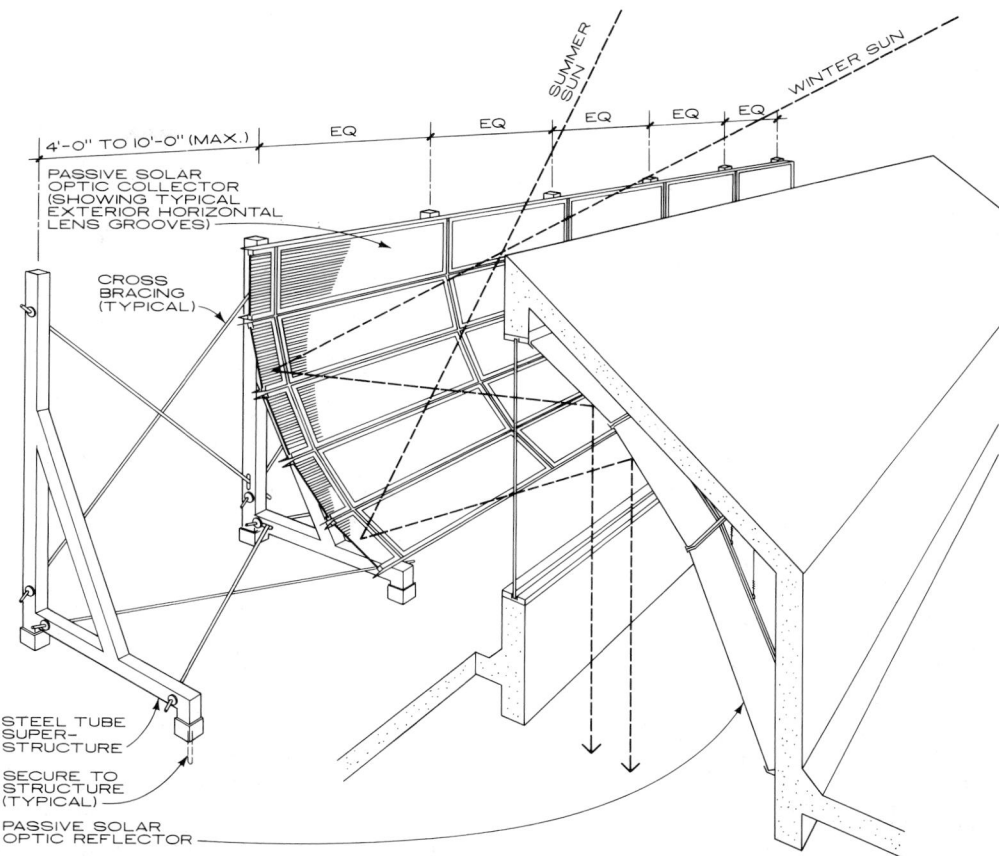

PASSIVE SOLAR OPTIC SYSTEM

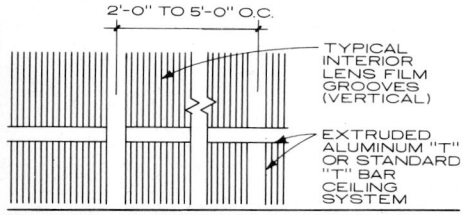

### PARTIAL ELEVATION OF INTERIOR REFLECTOR PANELS

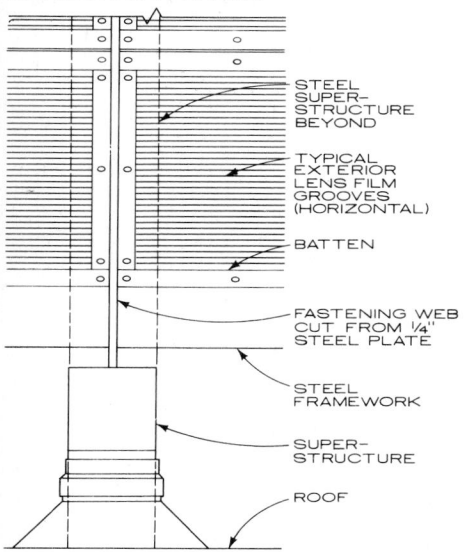

### PARTIAL ELEVATION OF EXTERIOR COLLECTOR PANELS

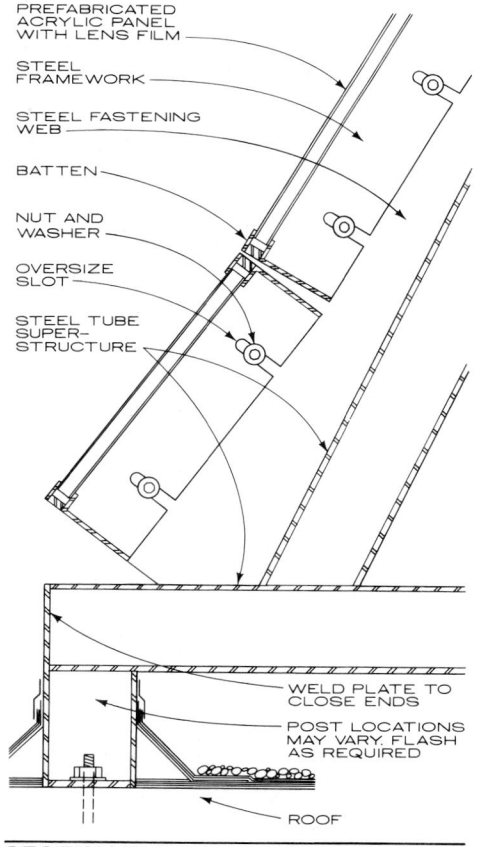

### SECTION THROUGH EXTERIOR COLLECTOR FRAME

### DETAIL OF EXTERIOR COLLECTOR FRAME

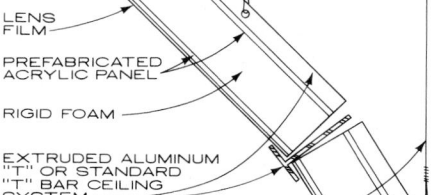

### DETAIL OF INTERIOR REFLECTOR FRAME

David Eijadi, AIA, and Kyle Williams; BRW, Inc.; Minneapolis, Minnesota

ACTIVE SOLAR     18

## CALCULATION OF SOLAR POSITION

The sun's altitude above the horizontal plane, A, and the solar azimuth, B, as measured toward the north from the south-north line in the horizontal plane, can be calculated accurately for any location, date, and time of day by using the following formulas:

$$\sin A = \cos L \cos d \cos H + \sin L \sin d$$

$$\cos B = \frac{\sin A \sin L - \sin d}{\cos A \cos L}$$

where

d = solar declination (angle between earth-sun line and equatorial plane)

H = hour angle of the sun = 15° x number of hours from local solar noon

**Example:** find solar altitude and azimuth for L = 40° north; local solar time = 2:00 P.M., H = 30°; date = March 21, d = 0.0°

$$\sin A = 0.766 \times 1.00 \times 0.866 + 0.643 \times 0.00$$

$$= 0.663$$

$$A = \text{arc sin } 0.663 = 41.53°$$

$$\cos B = \frac{0.663 \times 0.643 - 0.00}{0.749 \times 0.766} = 0.743$$

$$B = \text{arc cos } 0.743 = 41.98°$$

## SOLAR-SURFACE ANGLES

The direction of the earth-sun line OQ is defined by the solar altitude A (angle HOQ) and the solar azimuth B (angle HOS). These can be calculated when the location (latitude), date (declination), and time of day (hour angle) are known. The surface azimuth S is the angle SOP between the south-north line SON and the normal to the surface OP. The surface-solar azimuth G is the angle HOP.

The angle of incidence $\theta$ depends on the orientation and tilt of the irradiated surface. For a horizontal surface, $\theta_H$ is the angle QOV between the earth-sun line OQ and the vertical line OV. For the vertical surface shown above as facing SSE, the angle of incidence $\theta_V$ is the angle QOP between the earth-sun line OQ and the normal to the surface, OP. For surfaces such as solar collectors, which are generally tilted at some angle T upward from the horizontal, the incident angle $\theta_T$ may be found from the equation:

$$\text{cosine } \theta_T = \text{cosine A cosine S sine T} + \text{sine A cosine T}$$

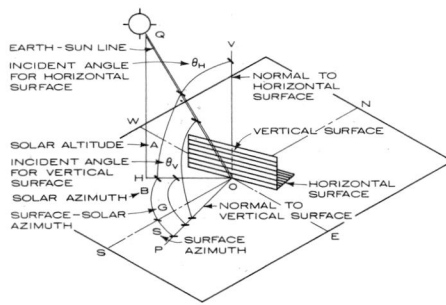

## DIRECT NORMAL SOLAR INTENSITY

At the earth's surface on a clear day, $I_{DN}$ is represented by:

$$I_{DN} = \frac{A}{\exp(B/\sin)}$$

where

A = apparent solar irradiation at air mass = 0

B = atmospheric extinction coefficent

Values of $I_{DN}$ based on these data are given in the following tables for the daylight hours of the 21st day of each month, for latitudes 24° to 64° North.

Values of A and B vary during the year because of seasonal changes in the dust and water vapor content of the atmosphere, and because of the changing earth-sun distance. For very clear atmospheres, the value of $I_{DN}$ can be 15 percent higher than indicated by the equation above.

For locations where clear, dry skies predominate, and at high elevations, values found by using the equation should be multiplied by a clearness factor. Refer to ASHRAE 1985 Fundamentals Handbook for additional data.

The tabulated figures are based on total solar heat gains for DSA glass, and a ground reflectance of 0.20.

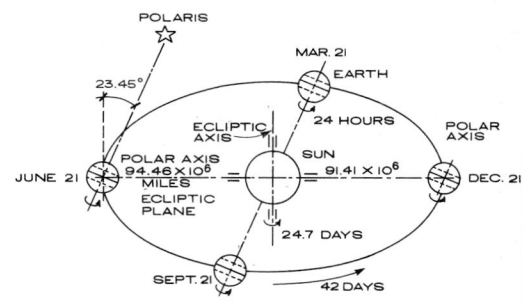

SOLAR ANGLE DIAGRAM

### 24°N LATITUDE    SOLAR HEAT GAIN FACTORS

**JUNE 21**

| AM | | ALT | AZM | BTU/SQ FT. HR | | | | | | |
|----|----|-----|-----|---|----|---|----|---|----|-----|
| | | | | S | SE | E | NE | N | SW | HOR |
| 6 | 6 | 9 | 112 | 7 | 39 | 94 | 93 | 36 | 39 | 17 |
| 7 | 5 | 22 | 107 | 18 | 94 | 192 | 177 | 55 | 94 | 77 |
| 8 | 4 | 36 | 103 | 27 | 117 | 212 | 184 | 50 | 117 | 145 |
| 9 | 3 | 49 | 99 | 34 | 116 | 192 | 158 | 43 | 116 | 201 |
| 10 | 2 | 63 | 95 | 39 | 96 | 146 | 113 | 41 | 96 | 245 |
| 11 | 1 | 76 | 91 | 42 | 64 | 82 | 65 | 42 | 64 | 271 |
| 12 | | 89 | 0 | 43 | 43 | 43 | 43 | 43 | 43 | 279 |
| | PM | | | S | SW | W | NW | N | SE | HOR |

**MARCH 21 (SEPTEMBER 21 SIMILAR BUT VARIES)**

| AM | | ALT | AZM | S | SE | E | NE | N | SW | HOR |
|----|----|-----|-----|---|----|---|----|---|----|-----|
| 7 | 5 | 14 | 84 | 17 | 145 | 186 | 115 | 11 | 10 | 36 |
| 8 | 4 | 27 | 77 | 48 | 204 | 234 | 124 | 18 | 18 | 112 |
| 9 | 3 | 40 | 68 | 82 | 214 | 215 | 85 | 25 | 25 | 180 |
| 10 | 2 | 52 | 55 | 112 | 195 | 162 | 41 | 30 | 31 | 232 |
| 11 | 1 | 62 | 33 | 139 | 154 | 85 | 34 | 33 | 43 | 264 |
| 12 | | 66 | 0 | 137 | 96 | 35 | 34 | 34 | 95 | 275 |
| | PM | | | S | SW | W | NW | N | SE | HOR |

**DECEMBER 21**

| AM | | ALT | AZM | S | SE | E | NE | N | SW | HOR |
|----|----|-----|-----|---|----|---|----|---|----|-----|
| 7 | 5 | 3 | 63 | 12 | 27 | 25 | 7 | 1 | 1 | 2 |
| 8 | 4 | 15 | 55 | 118 | 209 | 174 | 29 | 10 | 11 | 44 |
| 9 | 3 | 26 | 46 | 174 | 252 | 180 | 19 | 17 | 18 | 107 |
| 10 | 2 | 34 | 34 | 209 | 247 | 137 | 22 | 22 | 44 | 157 |
| 11 | 1 | 40 | 18 | 230 | 216 | 69 | 25 | 25 | 104 | 188 |
| 12 | | 43 | 0 | 237 | 167 | 27 | 26 | 26 | 164 | 199 |
| | PM | | | S | SW | W | NW | N | SE | HOR |

### 32°N LATITUDE    SOLAR HEAT GAIN FACTORS

**JUNE 21**

| AM | | ALT | AZM | BTU/SQ FT. HR | | | | | | |
|----|----|-----|-----|---|----|---|----|---|----|-----|
| | | | | S | SE | E | NE | N | SW | HOR |
| 5 | 7 | 1 | 118 | | | | | | | |
| 6 | 6 | 12 | 110 | 10 | 55 | 127 | 123 | 44 | 10 | 28 |
| 7 | 5 | 24 | 103 | 20 | 108 | 201 | 176 | 47 | 20 | 88 |
| 8 | 4 | 37 | 97 | 27 | 135 | 214 | 171 | 36 | 27 | 151 |
| 9 | 3 | 50 | 89 | 32 | 139 | 193 | 137 | 35 | 32 | 204 |
| 10 | 2 | 62 | 80 | 38 | 123 | 146 | 86 | 38 | 36 | 244 |
| 11 | 1 | 74 | 61 | 43 | 89 | 82 | 47 | 40 | 41 | 269 |
| 12 | | 81 | 0 | 58 | 52 | 42 | 41 | 41 | 52 | 276 |
| | PM | | | S | SW | W | NW | N | SE | HOR |

**MARCH 21 (SEPTEMBER 21 SIMILAR BUT VARIES)**

| AM | | ALT | AZM | S | SE | E | NE | N | SW | HOR |
|----|----|-----|-----|---|----|---|----|---|----|-----|
| 7 | 5 | 13 | 82 | 17 | 145 | 186 | 115 | 11 | 10 | 36 |
| 8 | 4 | 25 | 73 | 48 | 204 | 234 | 124 | 18 | 18 | 112 |
| 9 | 3 | 37 | 62 | 82 | 214 | 215 | 85 | 25 | 25 | 180 |
| 10 | 2 | 47 | 47 | 112 | 195 | 162 | 41 | 30 | 31 | 232 |
| 11 | 1 | 55 | 27 | 139 | 154 | 85 | 34 | 33 | 43 | 264 |
| 12 | | 58 | 0 | 137 | 96 | 35 | 34 | 34 | 95 | 275 |
| | PM | | | S | SW | W | NW | N | SE | HOR |

**DECEMBER 21**

| AM | | ALT | AZM | S | SE | E | NE | N | SW | HOR |
|----|----|-----|-----|---|----|---|----|---|----|-----|
| 8 | 4 | 10 | 54 | 97 | 166 | 135 | 19 | 7 | 7 | 22 |
| 9 | 3 | 20 | 44 | 171 | 238 | 162 | 15 | 14 | 15 | 72 |
| 10 | 2 | 28 | 31 | 216 | 246 | 127 | 18 | 18 | 52 | 119 |
| 11 | 1 | 33 | 16 | 243 | 222 | 63 | 21 | 21 | 116 | 148 |
| 12 | | 35 | 0 | 252 | 177 | 23 | 22 | 22 | 177 | 158 |
| | PM | | | S | SW | W | NW | N | SE | HOR |

## NOTES

1. Time is solar time.
2. Dates vary year to year within plus or minus two days of the 21st day of the month.

Gary L. Powell; College of Architecture, Arizona State University; Tempe, Arizona

18 **ENERGY ANALYSIS**

## 40°N LATITUDE — SOLAR HEAT GAIN FACTORS

### JUNE 21

| AM | | ALT | AZM | S | SE | E | NE | N | SW | HOR |
|---|---|---|---|---|---|---|---|---|---|---|
|  |  |  |  |  |  | BTU/SQ FT. HR |  |  |  |  |
| 5 | 7 | 4 | 117 | 1 | 6 | 20 | 21 | 10 | 1 | 3 |
| 6 | 6 | 15 | 108 | 13 | 70 | 151 | 143 | 48 | 13 | 40 |
| 7 | 5 | 26 | 100 | 22 | 122 | 207 | 173 | 37 | 21 | 97 |
| 8 | 4 | 37 | 91 | 29 | 152 | 216 | 156 | 30 | 27 | 153 |
| 9 | 3 | 49 | 80 | 45 | 161 | 192 | 114 | 33 | 32 | 201 |
| 10 | 2 | 60 | 66 | 69 | 148 | 145 | 63 | 35 | 36 | 238 |
| 11 | 1 | 69 | 42 | 88 | 116 | 81 | 40 | 38 | 41 | 260 |
| 12 |  | 73 | 0 | 95 | 72 | 41 | 38 | 38 | 72 | 267 |
| PM |  |  |  | S | SW | W | NW | N | SE | HOR |

### MARCH 21 (SEPTEMBER 21 SIMILAR BUT VARIES)

| AM | | ALT | AZM | S | SE | E | NE | N | SW | HOR |
|---|---|---|---|---|---|---|---|---|---|---|
| 7 | 5 | 11 | 80 | 22 | 135 | 163 | 93 | 9 | 8 | 26 |
| 8 | 4 | 23 | 70 | 74 | 211 | 218 | 91 | 16 | 16 | 85 |
| 9 | 3 | 33 | 57 | 128 | 236 | 203 | 47 | 21 | 22 | 143 |
| 10 | 2 | 42 | 42 | 171 | 229 | 153 | 27 | 25 | 29 | 186 |
| 11 | 1 | 48 | 23 | 197 | 198 | 78 | 28 | 28 | 77 | 213 |
| 12 |  | 50 | 0 | 206 | 145 | 31 | 29 | 29 | 145 | 223 |
| PM |  |  |  | S | SW | W | NW | N | SE | HOR |

### DECEMBER 21

| AM | | ALT | AZM | S | SE | E | NE | N | SW | HOR |
|---|---|---|---|---|---|---|---|---|---|---|
| 8 | 4 | 5 | 53 | 50 | 84 | 67 | 8 | 3 | 3 | 6 |
| 9 | 3 | 14 | 42 | 151 | 205 | 135 | 11 | 10 | 13 | 39 |
| 10 | 2 | 21 | 29 | 210 | 232 | 113 | 14 | 14 | 55 | 77 |
| 11 | 1 | 25 | 15 | 242 | 217 | 56 | 17 | 17 | 120 | 104 |
| 12 |  | 27 | 0 | 253 | 178 | 19 | 18 | 18 | 178 | 113 |
| PM |  |  |  | S | SW | W | NW | N | SE | HOR |

## 48°N LATITUDE — SOLAR HEAT GAIN FACTORS

### JUNE 21

| AM | | ALT | AZM | S | SE | E | NE | N | SW | HOR |
|---|---|---|---|---|---|---|---|---|---|---|
|  |  |  |  |  |  | BTU/SQ FT. HR |  |  |  |  |
| 5 | 7 | 8 | 117 | 5 | 24 | 72 | 76 | 35 | 5 | 12 |
| 6 | 6 | 17 | 106 | 14 | 84 | 169 | 155 | 46 | 14 | 51 |
| 7 | 5 | 27 | 96 | 23 | 135 | 211 | 165 | 29 | 21 | 103 |
| 8 | 4 | 37 | 85 | 34 | 168 | 215 | 139 | 29 | 27 | 152 |
| 9 | 3 | 47 | 72 | 66 | 180 | 190 | 91 | 31 | 31 | 193 |
| 10 | 2 | 56 | 55 | 101 | 171 | 143 | 45 | 34 | 36 | 225 |
| 11 | 1 | 63 | 31 | 126 | 142 | 79 | 38 | 36 | 49 | 246 |
| 12 |  | 65 | 0 | 134 | 96 | 40 | 37 | 37 | 96 | 252 |
| PM |  |  |  | S | SW | W | NW | N | SE | HOR |

### MARCH 21 (SEPTEMBER 21 SIMILAR BUT VARIES)

| AM | | ALT | AZM | S | SE | E | NE | N | SW | HOR |
|---|---|---|---|---|---|---|---|---|---|---|
| 7 | 5 | 10 | 79 | 23 | 123 | 145 | 80 | 7 | 7 | 20 |
| 8 | 4 | 20 | 67 | 82 | 206 | 204 | 76 | 14 | 14 | 68 |
| 9 | 3 | 28 | 53 | 142 | 239 | 193 | 3 | 19 | 20 | 118 |
| 10 | 2 | 35 | 38 | 189 | 237 | 146 | 24 | 23 | 33 | 156 |
| 11 | 1 | 40 | 20 | 218 | 210 | 74 | 25 | 25 | 94 | 180 |
| 12 |  | 42 | 0 | 228 | 161 | 27 | 26 | 26 | 161 | 188 |
| PM |  |  |  | S | SW | W | NW | N | SE | HOR |

### DECEMBER 21

| AM | | ALT | AZM | S | SE | E | NE | N | SW | HOR |
|---|---|---|---|---|---|---|---|---|---|---|
| 8 | 4 | 1 | 53 |  |  |  |  |  |  |  |
| 9 | 3 | 8 | 41 | 100 | 133 | 86 | 6 | 5 | 8 | 13 |
| 10 | 2 | 14 | 28 | 179 | 194 | 91 | 10 | 10 | 49 | 38 |
| 11 | 1 | 17 | 14 | 220 | 195 | 46 | 12 | 12 | 111 | 57 |
| 12 |  | 19 | 20 | 233 | 163 | 14 | 13 | 13 | 168 | 65 |
| PM |  |  |  | S | SW | W | NW | N | SE | HOR |

## 56°N LATITUDE — SOLAR HEAT GAIN FACTORS

### JUNE 21

| AM | | ALT | AZM | S | SE | E | NE | N | SW | HOR |
|---|---|---|---|---|---|---|---|---|---|---|
|  |  |  |  |  |  | BTU/SQ FT. HR |  |  |  |  |
| 4 | 8 | 4 | 127 | 1 | 3 | 18 | 22 | 13 | 1 | 3 |
| 5 | 7 | 11 | 115 | 9 | 40 | 115 | 119 | 53 | 9 | 25 |
| 6 | 6 | 28 | 92 | 16 | 97 | 182 | 160 | 42 | 16 | 62 |
| 7 | 5 | 28 | 92 | 24 | 147 | 213 | 156 | 25 | 22 | 105 |
| 8 | 4 | 36 | 79 | 46 | 181 | 213 | 122 | 27 | 26 | 146 |
| 9 | 3 | 44 | 64 | 91 | 196 | 187 | 69 | 30 | 30 | 181 |
| 10 | 2 | 51 | 46 | 132 | 190 | 139 | 36 | 33 | 35 | 208 |
| 11 | 1 | 56 | 25 | 159 | 164 | 76 | 35 | 34 | 65 | 225 |
| 12 |  | 57 | 0 | 168 | 119 | 38 | 35 | 35 | 119 | 231 |
| PM |  |  |  | S | SW | W | NW | N | SE | HOR |

### MARCH 21 (SEPTEMBER 21 SIMILAR BUT VARIES)

| AM | | ALT | AZM | S | SE | E | NE | N | SW | HOR |
|---|---|---|---|---|---|---|---|---|---|---|
| 7 | 5 | 8 | 77 | 21 | 105 | 121 | 65 | 6 | 6 | 14 |
| 8 | 4 | 16 | 64 | 84 | 194 | 185 | 61 | 12 | 12 | 49 |
| 9 | 3 | 23 | 50 | 148 | 233 | 179 | 23 | 16 | 17 | 89 |
| 10 | 2 | 29 | 35 | 198 | 238 | 136 | 20 | 19 | 39 | 122 |
| 11 | 1 | 33 | 18 | 230 | 215 | 68 | 21 | 21 | 106 | 142 |
| 12 |  | 34 | 0 | 241 | 170 | 24 | 22 | 22 | 170 | 149 |
| PM |  |  |  | S | SW | W | NW | N | SE | HOR |

### DECEMBER 21

| AM | | ALT | AZM | S | SE | E | NE | N | SW | HOR |
|---|---|---|---|---|---|---|---|---|---|---|
| 9 | 3 | 2 | 40 | 4 | 5 | 3 | 0 | 0 | 0 | 0 |
| 10 | 2 | 7 | 27 | 96 | 103 | 47 | 4 | 4 | 27 | 9 |
| 11 | 1 | 10 | 14 | 154 | 135 | 30 | 6 | 6 | 78 | 19 |
| 12 |  | 11 | 0 | 171 | 120 | 8 | 7 | 7 | 120 | 23 |
| PM |  |  |  | S | SW | W | NW | N | SE | HOR |

## 64°N LATITUDE — SOLAR HEAT GAIN FACTORS

### JUNE 21

| AM | | ALT | AZM | S | SE | E | NE | N | SW | HOR |
|---|---|---|---|---|---|---|---|---|---|---|
|  |  |  |  |  |  | BTU/SQ FT. HR |  |  |  |  |
| 4 | 8 | 9 | 126 | 7 | 14 | 78 | 96 | 53 | 7 | 16 |
| 5 | 7 | 15 | 114 | 12 | 55 | 145 | 148 | 62 | 12 | 39 |
| 6 | 6 | 21 | 101 | 18 | 110 | 192 | 162 | 36 | 17 | 71 |
| 7 | 5 | 28 | 87 | 25 | 158 | 213 | 145 | 24 | 22 | 105 |
| 8 | 4 | 34 | 73 | 62 | 192 | 208 | 104 | 25 | 25 | 137 |
| 9 | 3 | 40 | 58 | 115 | 208 | 181 | 51 | 28 | 29 | 165 |
| 10 | 2 | 45 | 40 | 157 | 204 | 134 | 32 | 30 | 36 | 186 |
| 11 | 1 | 48 | 21 | 184 | 180 | 72 | 32 | 32 | 82 | 199 |
| 12 |  | 49 | 0 | 193 | 138 | 35 | 32 | 32 | 138 | 203 |
| PM |  |  |  | S | SW | W | NW | N | SE | HOR |

### MARCH 21 (SEPTEMBER 21 SIMILAR BUT VARIES)

| AM | | ALT | AZM | S | SE | E | NE | N | SW | HOR |
|---|---|---|---|---|---|---|---|---|---|---|
| 7 | 5 | 7 | 76 | 17 | 79 | 90 | 47 | 4 | 4 | 9 |
| 8 | 4 | 13 | 63 | 78 | 170 | 158 | 46 | 9 | 9 | 32 |
| 9 | 3 | 18 | 48 | 143 | 215 | 159 | 16 | 13 | 14 | 59 |
| 10 | 2 | 22 | 33 | 194 | 226 | 122 | 16 | 16 | 42 | 84 |
| 11 | 1 | 25 | 17 | 228 | 209 | 60 | 17 | 17 | 109 | 99 |
| 12 |  | 26 | 0 | 239 | 168 | 19 | 18 | 18 | 168 | 105 |
| PM |  |  |  | S | SW | W | NW | N | SE | HOR |

### DECEMBER 21

| AM | | ALT | AZM | S | SE | E | NE | N | SW | HOR |
|---|---|---|---|---|---|---|---|---|---|---|
| 11 | 1 | 2 | 14 | 4 | 3 | 1 | 0 | 0 | 2 | 0 |
| 12 |  | 3 | 0 | 15 | 11 | 1 | 0 | 0 | 11 | 1 |
| PM |  |  |  | S | SW | W | NW | N | SE | HOR |

## NOTES

1. Time is solar time.
2. Dates vary year to year within plus or minus two days of the 21st day of the month.
3. For additional data refer to ASHRAE Handbook, 1985 Fundamentals.

Gary L. Powell; Arizona State University; Tempe, Arizona

## SOLAR ANGLES

The position of the sun in relation to specific geographic locations, seasons, and times of day can be determined by several methods. Model measurements, by means of solar machines or shade dials, have the advantage of direct visual observations. Tabulative and calculative methods have the advantage of exactness. However, graphic projection methods are usually preferred by architects, as they are easily understood and can be correlated to both radiant energy and shading calculations.

## SOLAR PATH DIAGRAMS

A practical graphic projection is the solar path diagram method. Such diagrams depict the path of the sun within the sky vault as projected onto a horizontal plane. The horizon is represented as a circle with the observation point in the center. The sun's position at any date and hour can be determined from the diagram in terms of its altitude ($\beta$) and azimuth ($\phi$). (See figure on right.) The graphs are constructed in equidistant projection. The altitude angles are represented at 10° intervals by equally spaced concentric circles; they range from 0° at the outer circle (horizon) to 90° at the center point. These intervals are graduated along the south meridian. Azimuth is represented at 10° intervals by equally spaced radii; they range from 0° at the south meridian to 180° at the north meridian. These intervals are graduated along the periphery. The solar bearing will be to the east during morning hours, and to the west during afternoon hours.

(CONTINUED NEXT PAGE)

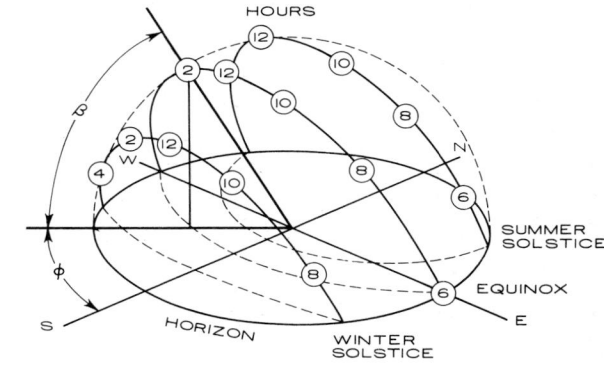

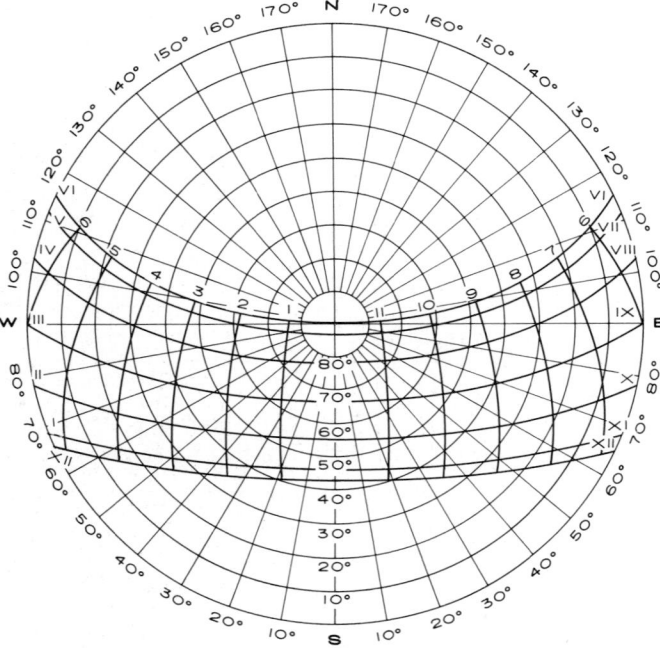

**24°N LATITUDE**

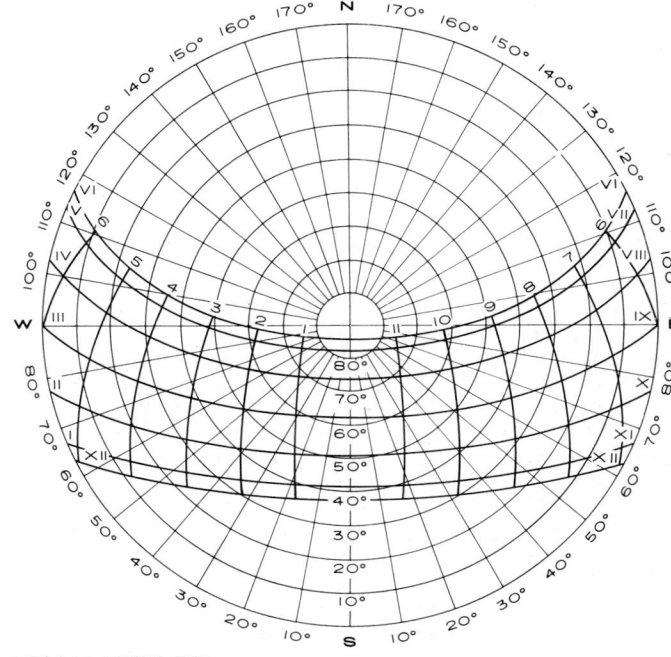

**28°N LATITUDE**

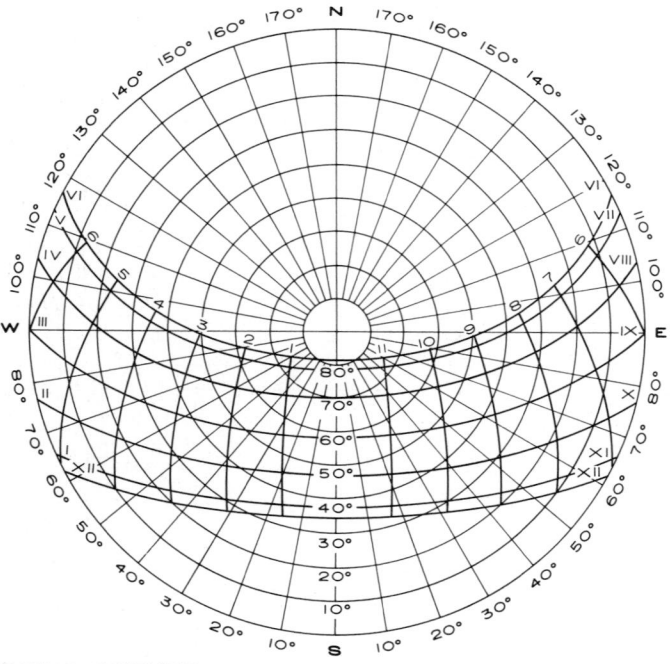

**32°N LATITUDE**

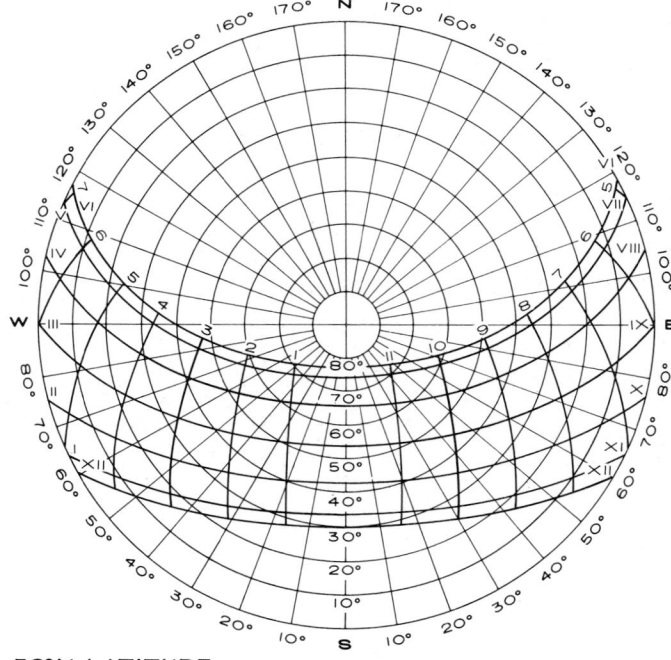

**36°N LATITUDE**

Victor Olgyay, AIA; Associate Professor; School of Architecture, Princeton University; Princeton, New Jersey

**18** **SOLAR ANGLES**

## SOLAR PATH DIAGRAMS (CONTINUED)

The earth's axis is inclined 23°27' to its orbit around the sun and rotates 15° hourly. Thus, from all points on the earth, the sun appears to move across the sky vault on various parallel circular paths with maximum declinations of ±23°27'. The declination of the sun's path changes in a cycle between the extremes of the summer solstice and winter solstice. Thus the sun follows the same path on two corresponding dates each year. Due to irregularities between the calendar year and the astronomical data, here a unified calibration is adapted. The differences, as they do not exceed 41', are negligible for architectural purposes.

## DECLINATION OF THE SUN

| DATE | DECLINATION | CORRESP. DATE | DECLINATION | UNIFIED CALIBR. |
|------|-------------|---------------|-------------|-----------------|
| June 21 | +23°27' | | | +23°27' |
| May 21 | +20°09' | July 21 | +20°31' | +20°20' |
| Apr. 21 | +11°48' | Aug. 21 | +12°12' | +12°00' |
| Mar. 21 | +0°10' | Sep. 21 | +0°47' | +0°28' |
| Feb. 21 | −10°37' | Oct. 21 | −10°38' | −10°38' |
| Jan. 21 | −19°57' | Nov. 21 | −19°53' | −19°55' |
| Dec. 21 | −23°27' | | | −23°27' |

The elliptical curves in the diagrams represent the horizontal projections of the sun's path. They are given on the 21st day of each month. Roman numerals designate the months. A cross grid of curves graduate the hours indicated in arabic numerals. Eight solar path diagrams are shown at 4° intervals from 24°N to 52°N latitude.

## EXAMPLE

Find the sun's position in Columbus, Ohio, on February 21, 2 P.M.:

STEP 1. Locate Columbus on the map. The latitude is 40°N.

STEP 2. In the 40° sun path diagram select the February path (marked with II), and locate the 2 hr line. Where the two lines cross is the position of the sun.

STEP 3. Read the altitude on the concentric circles (32°) and the azimuth along the outer circle (35°30'W).

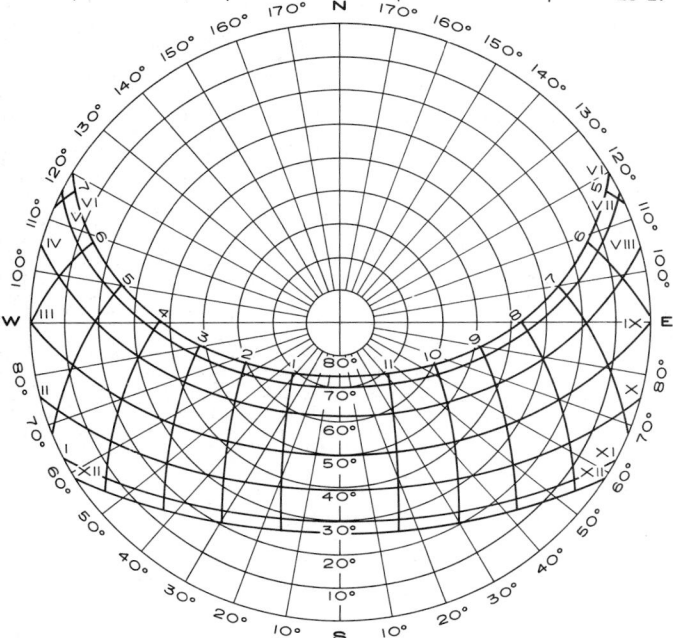

**40°N LATITUDE**

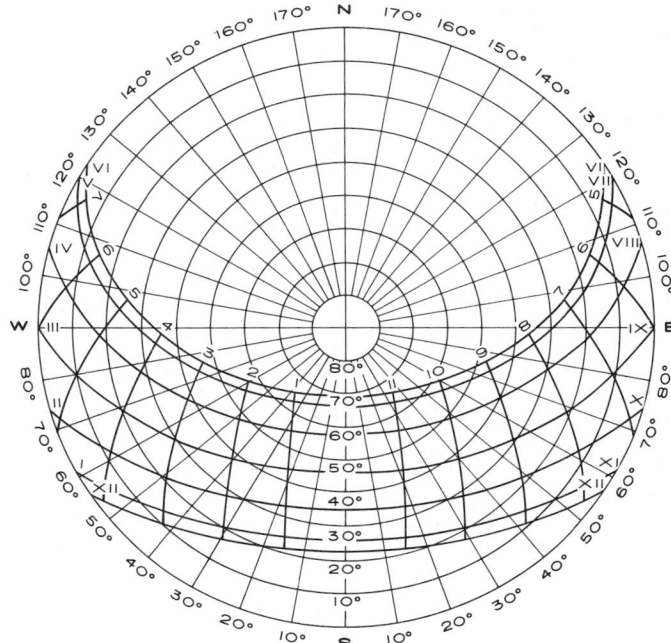

**44°N LATITUDE**

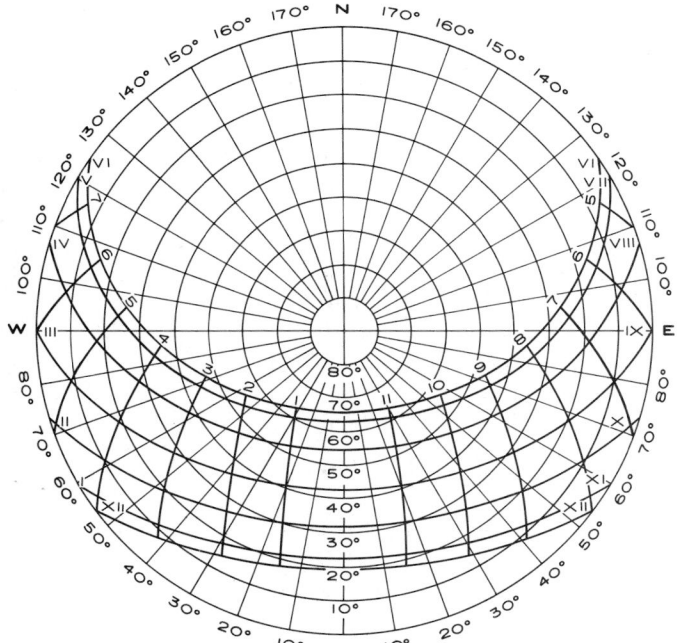

**48°N LATITUDE**

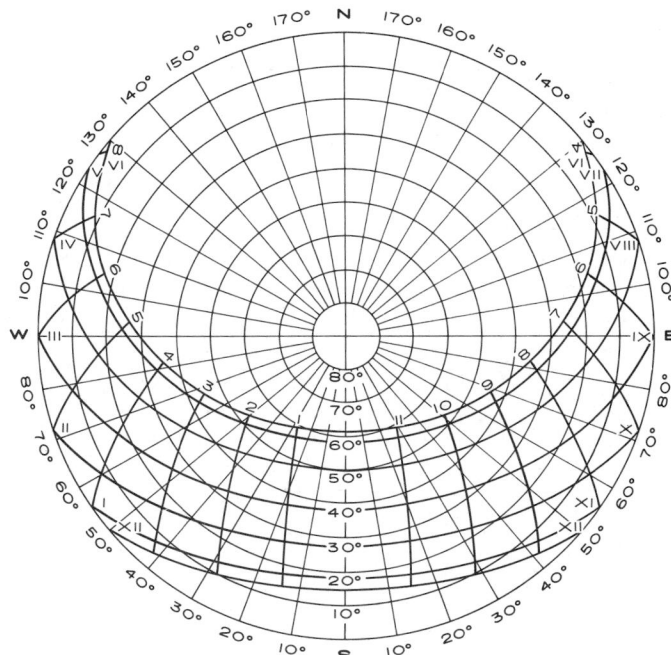

**52°N LATITUDE**

Victor Olgyay, AIA; Associate Professor; School of Architecture, Princeton University; Princeton, New Jersey

**SOLAR ANGLES** **18**

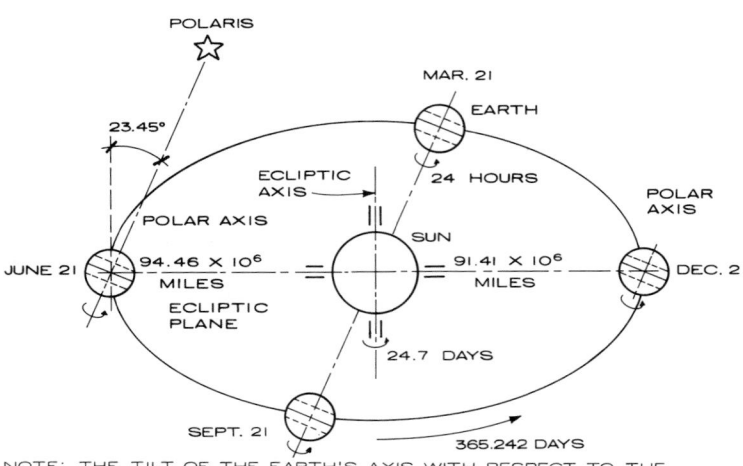

NOTE: THE TILT OF THE EARTH'S AXIS WITH RESPECT TO THE ECLIPTIC AXIS CAUSES THE CHANGING SEASONS AND THE ANNUAL VARIATIONS IN NUMBER OF HOURS OF DAYLIGHT AND DARKNESS

**ANNUAL MOTION OF THE EARTH ABOUT THE SUN**

NOTE: Q DESIGNATES THE SUN'S POSITION SO OQ IS THE EARTH – SUN LINE WHILE OP' IS THE NORMAL TO THE TILTED SURFACE AND OP IS PERPENDICULAR TO THE INTERSECTION, OM, BETWEEN THE TILTED SURFACE AND THE HORIZONTAL PLANE

**SOLAR ANGLES WITH RESPECT TO A TILTED SURFACE**

## SOLAR CONSTANT

The sun is located at one focus of the earth's orbit, and we are only 147.2 million km (91.4 million miles) away from the sun in late December and early January, while the earth-sun distance on July 1 is about 152.0 million km (94.4 million miles).

Solar energy approaches the earth as electromagnetic radiation at wavelengths between 0.25 and 5.0 μm. The intensity of the incoming solar irradiance on a surface normal to the sun's rays beyond the earth's atmosphere, at the average earth-sun distance, is designated as the solar constant, $I_{sc}$. Although the value of $I_{sc}$ has not yet been precisely determined by verified measurements made in outer space, the most widely used value is 429.2 Btu/sq ft · hr (1353 W/sq m) and the current ASHRAE values are based on this estimate. More recent measurements made at extremely high altitudes indicate that $I_{sc}$ is probably close to 433.6 Btu/sq ft · hr (1367 W/sq m). The unit of radiation that is widely used by meteorologists is the langley, equivalent to one kilogram calorie/square centimeter. To convert from langleys/day to Btu/sq ft · day, multiply Ly/day by 3.67. To convert from W/sq m to Btu/sq ft · hr, multiply the electrical unit by 0.3172.

## SOLAR ANGLES

At the earth's surface the amount of solar radiation received and the resulting atmospheric temperature vary widely, primarily because of the daily rotation of the earth and the fact that the rotational axis is tilted at an angle of 23.45° with respect to the orbital plane. This tilt causes the changing seasons with their varying lengths of daylight and darkness. The angle between the earth-sun line and the orbital plane, called the solar declination, d, varies throughout the year, as shown in the following table for the 21st day of each month.

| | | | |
|---|---|---|---|
| JAN −19.9° | APR +11.9° | JUL +20.5° | OCT −10.7° |
| FEB −10.6° | MAY +20.3° | AUG +12.1° | NOV −19.9° |
| MAR 0.0° | JUN +23.5° | SEP 0.0° | DEC −23.5° |

Very minor changes in the declination occur from year to year, and when more precise values are needed the almanac for the year in question should be consulted.

The earth's annual orbit about the sun is slightly elliptical, and so the earth-sun distance is slightly greater in summer than in winter. The time required for each annual orbit is actually 365.242 days rather than the 365 days shown by the calendar, and this is corrected by adding a 29th day to February for each year (except century years) that is evenly divisible by 4.

To an observer standing on a particular spot on the earth's surface, with a specified longitude, LON, and latitude, L, it is the sun that appears to move around the earth in a regular daily pattern. Actually it is the earth's rotation that causes the sun's apparent motion. The position of the sun can be defined in terms of its altitude β above the horizon (angle HOQ) and its azimuth φ, measured as angle HOS in the horizontal plane.

At solar noon, the sun is, by definition, exactly on the meridian that contains the south-north line, and consequently the solar azimuth φ is 0.0°. The noon altitude β is:

$$= 90° - L + \delta$$

Because the earth's daily rotation and its annual orbit around the sun are regular and predictable, the solar altitude and azimuth may be readily calculated for any desired time of day as soon as the latitude, longitude, and date (declination) are specified.

## SHADOW CONSTRUCTION WITH TRUE SUN ANGLES

Required information: angle of orientation in relation to north-south axis (C), azimuth φ, and altitude angle β of the sun at the desired time (Figure 1).

STEP 1. Lay out building axis, true south and azimuth φ of sun in plan (Figure 2).

STEP 2. Lay out altitude β upon azimuth φ. Construct any perpendicular to φ. From the intersection of this perpendicular and φ project a line perpendicular to elevation plane (building orientation). Measure distance x along this line from elevation plane. Connect the point at distance x from elevation plane to center to construct sun elevation β (Figure 2).

STEP 3. Use sun plan φ + C and sun elevation β to construct shadows in plan and elevation in conventional way (Figure 3).

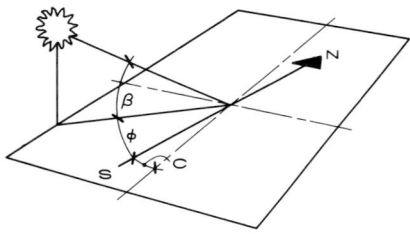

**FIGURE I**

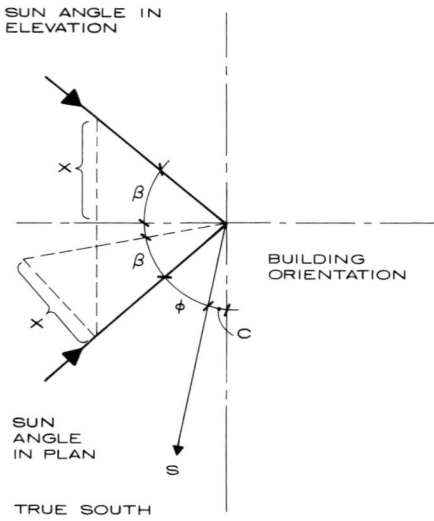

SUN ANGLE IN ELEVATION

BUILDING ORIENTATION

SUN ANGLE IN PLAN

TRUE SOUTH

**FIGURE 2**

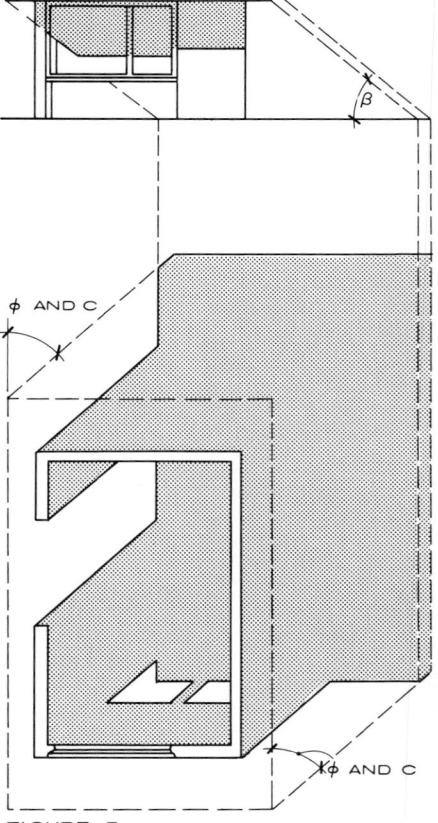

**FIGURE 3**

John I. Yellott, P.E.; College of Architecture, Arizona State University; Tempe, Arizona

## NOTES

To visualize the thermal impacts on differently exposed surfaces four locations are shown approximately at the 24°, 32°, 40° and 44° latitudes. The forces are indicated on average clear winter and summer days. The air temperature variation is indicated by the outside concentric circles. Each additional line represents a 2°F difference from the lowest daily temperature. The direction of the impact is indicated according to the sun's direction as temperatures occur. (Note the low temperatures at the east side, and the high ones in westerly directions.)

The total (direct and diffuse) radiation impact on the various sides of the building is indicated with arrows. Each arrow represents 250 Btu/sq ft · day radiation. At the bottom of the page the radiations are expressed in numerical values.

The values show that in the upper latitudes the south side of a building receives nearly twice as much radiation in winter as in summer. This effect is even more pronounced at the lower latitudes, where the ratio is about one to four. Also, in the upper latitudes, the east and west sides receive about 2½ times more radiation in summer than in winter. This ratio is not as large in the lower latitudes; but it is noteworthy that in summer these sides receive two to three times as much radiation as the south elevation. In the summer the west exposure is more disadvantageous than the east exposure, as the afternoon high temperatures combine with the radiation effects. In all latitudes the north side receives only a small amount of radiation, and this comes mainly in the summer. In the low latitudes, in the summer, the north side receives nearly twice the impact of the south side. The amount of radiation received on a horizontal roof surface exceeds all other sides.

Experimental observations were conducted on the thermal behavior of building orientation at Princeton University's Architectural Laboratory. Below are shown the summer results of structures exposed to the cardinal directions. Note the unequal heat distribution and high heat impact of the west exposure compared to the east orientation. The southern direction gives a pleasantly low heat volume, slightly higher, however, than the north exposure.

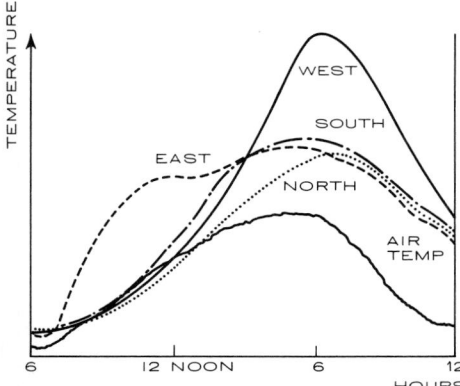

ROOM TEMPERATURE IN
DIFFERENTLY ORIENTED HOUSES

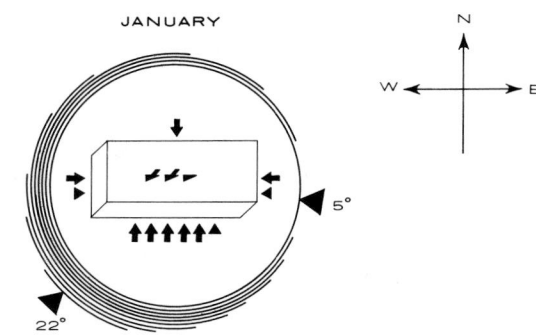

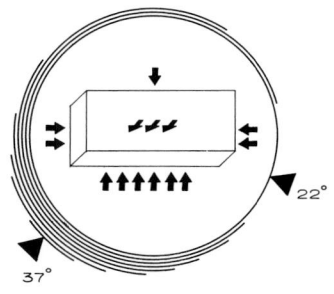

MINNEAPOLIS, MINN.

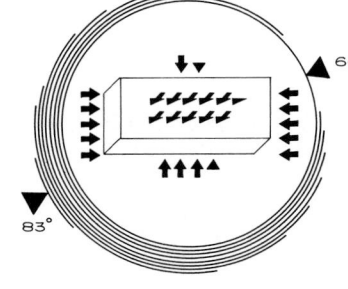

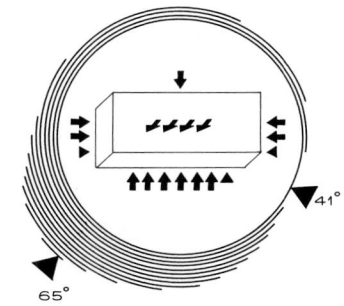

NEW YORK AREA

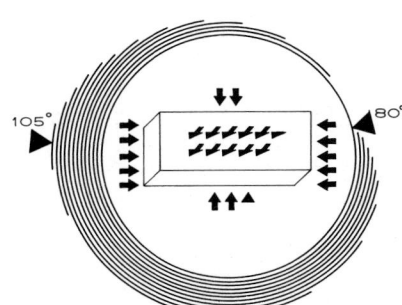

PHOENIX, ARIZ.

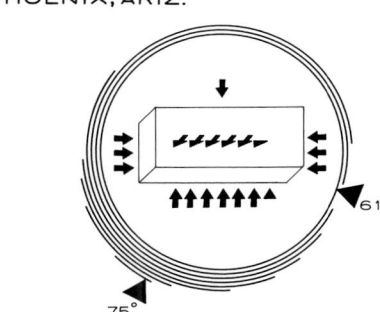

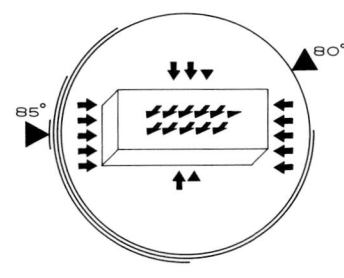

MIAMI, FLA.

## ORIENTATION: CONCLUSIONS

1. The optimum orientation will lie near the south; however, will differ in the various regions, and will depend on the daily temperature distribution.
2. In all regions an orientation eastward from south gives a better yearly performance and a more equal daily heat distribution. Westerly directions perform more poorly with unbalanced heat impacts.
3. The thermal orientation exposure has to be correlated with the local wind directions.

Victor Olgyay, AIA; Associate Professor; School of Architecture, Princeton University; Princeton, New Jersey

### TOTAL DIRECT AND DIFFUSED RADIATION (BTU/SQ FT · DAY)

| LATITUDE | SEASON | EAST | SOUTH | WEST | NORTH | HORIZONTAL |
|---|---|---|---|---|---|---|
| 44° LATITUDE | WINTER | 416 | 1374 | 416 | 83 | 654 |
| | SUMMER | 1314 | 979 | 1314 | 432 | 2536 |
| 40° LATITUDE | WINTER | 517 | 1489 | 517 | 119 | 787 |
| | SUMMER | 1277 | 839 | 1277 | 430 | 2619 |
| 32° LATITUDE | WINTER | 620 | 1606 | 620 | 140 | 954 |
| | SUMMER | 1207 | 563 | 1207 | 452 | 2596 |
| 24° LATITUDE | WINTER | 734 | 1620 | 734 | 152 | 1414 |
| | SUMMER | 1193 | 344 | 1193 | 616 | 2568 |

## SHADING DEVICES

The effect of shading devices can be plotted in the same manner as the solar path was projected. The diagrams show which part of the sky vault will be obstructed by the devices and are projections of the surface covered on the sky vault as seen from an observation point at the center of the diagram. These projections also represent those parts of the sky vault from which no sunlight will reach the observation point; if the sun passes through such an area the observation point will be shaded.

## SHADING MASKS

Any building element will define a characteristic form in these projection diagrams, known as "shading masks." Masks of horizontal devices (overhangs) will create a segmental pattern; vertical intercepting elements (fins) produce a radial pattern; shading devices with horizontal and vertical members (eggcrate type) will make a combinative pattern. A shading mask can be drawn for any shading device, even for very complex ones, by geometric plotting. As the shading masks are geometric projections they are independent of latitude and exposed directions, therefore they can be used in any location and at any orientation. By overlaying a shading mask in the proper orientation on the sun-path diagram, one can read off the times when the sun rays will be intercepted. Masks can be drawn for full shade (100% mask) when the observation point is at the lowest point of the surface needing shading; or for 50% shading when the observation point is placed at the halfway mark on the surface. It is customary to design a shading device in such a way that as soon as shading is needed on a surface the masking angle should exceed 50%. Solar calculations should be used to check the specific loads. Basic shading devices are shown below, with their obstruction effect on the sky vault and with their projected shading masks.

## SHADING MASK PROTRACTOR

The half of the protractor showing segmental lines is used to plot lines parallel and normal to the observed vertical surface. The half showing bearing and altitude lines is used to plot shading masks of vertical fins or any other obstruction objects. The protractor is in the same projection and scale as the sun-path diagrams (see pages on solar angles); therefore it is useful to transfer the protractor to a transparent overlay to read the obstruction effect.

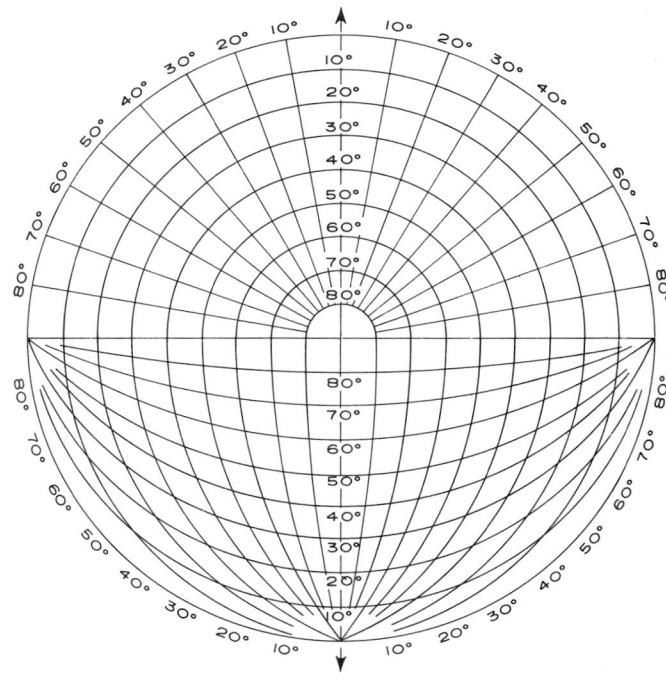

**SHADING MASK PROTRACTOR**

**HORIZONTAL**      **VERTICAL**      **EGGCRATE**

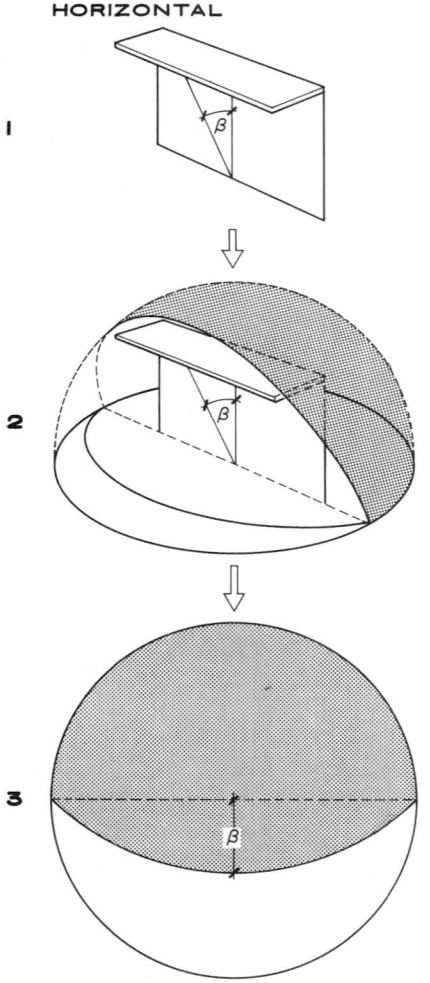

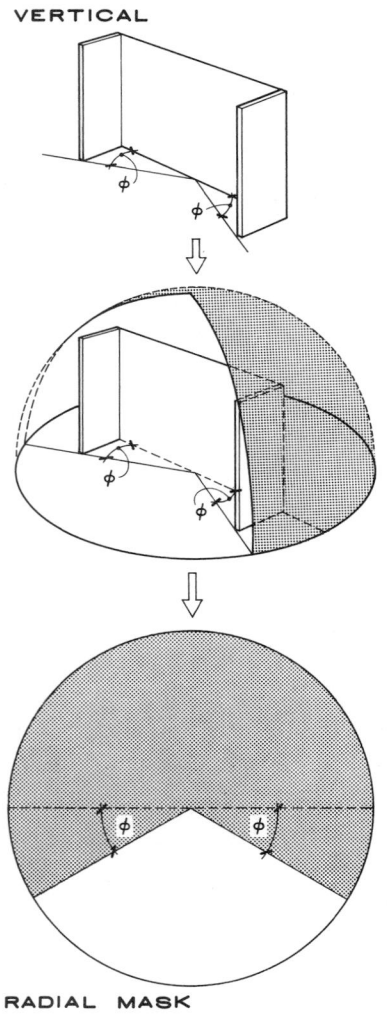

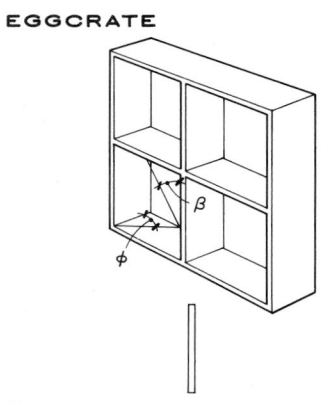

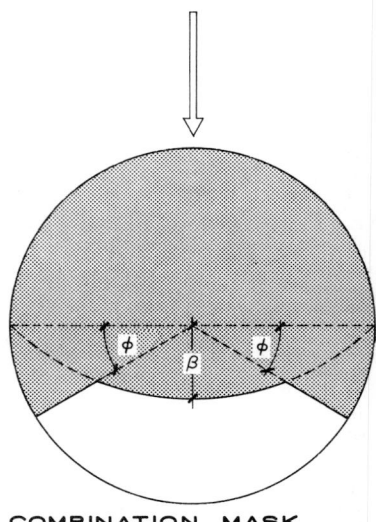

Horizontal devices produce segmental obstruction patterns, vertical fins produce radial patterns, and eggcrate devices produce combination patterns.

**SEGMENTAL MASK**      **RADIAL MASK**      **COMBINATION MASK**

Victor Olgyay, AIA; Associate Professor; School of Architecture, Princeton University; Princeton, New Jersey

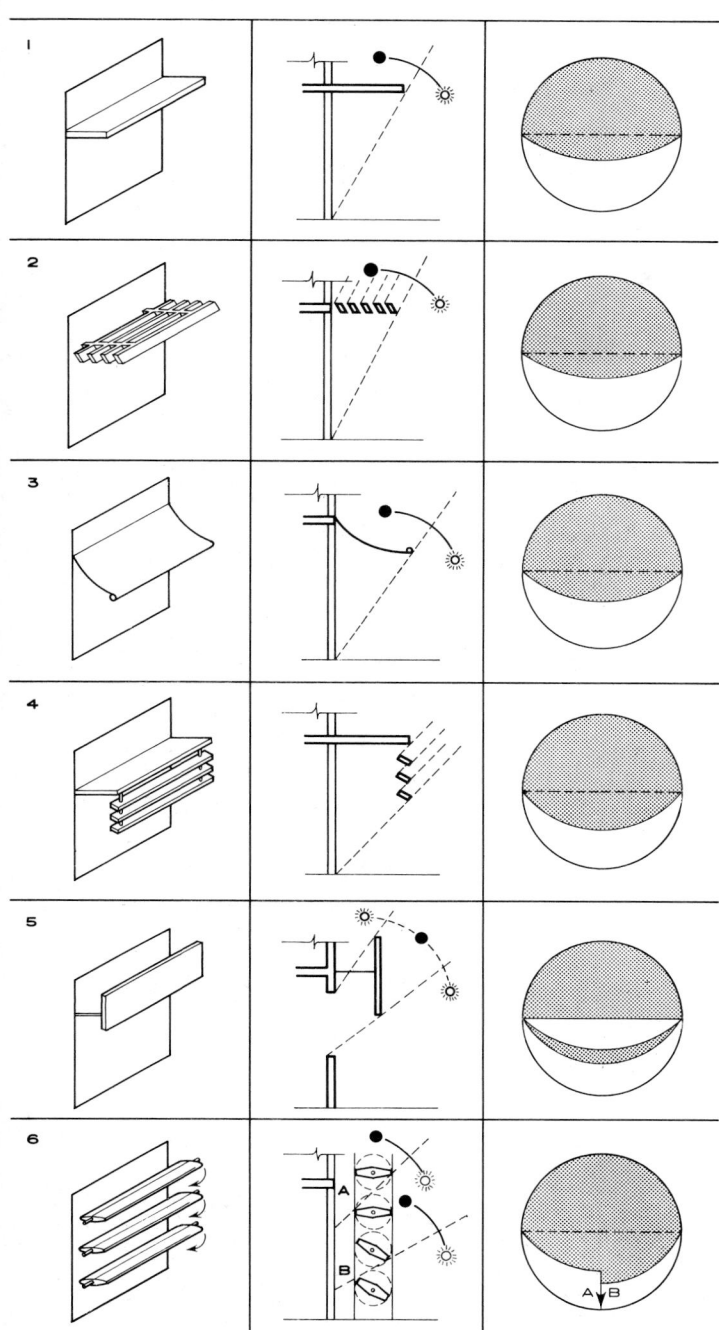

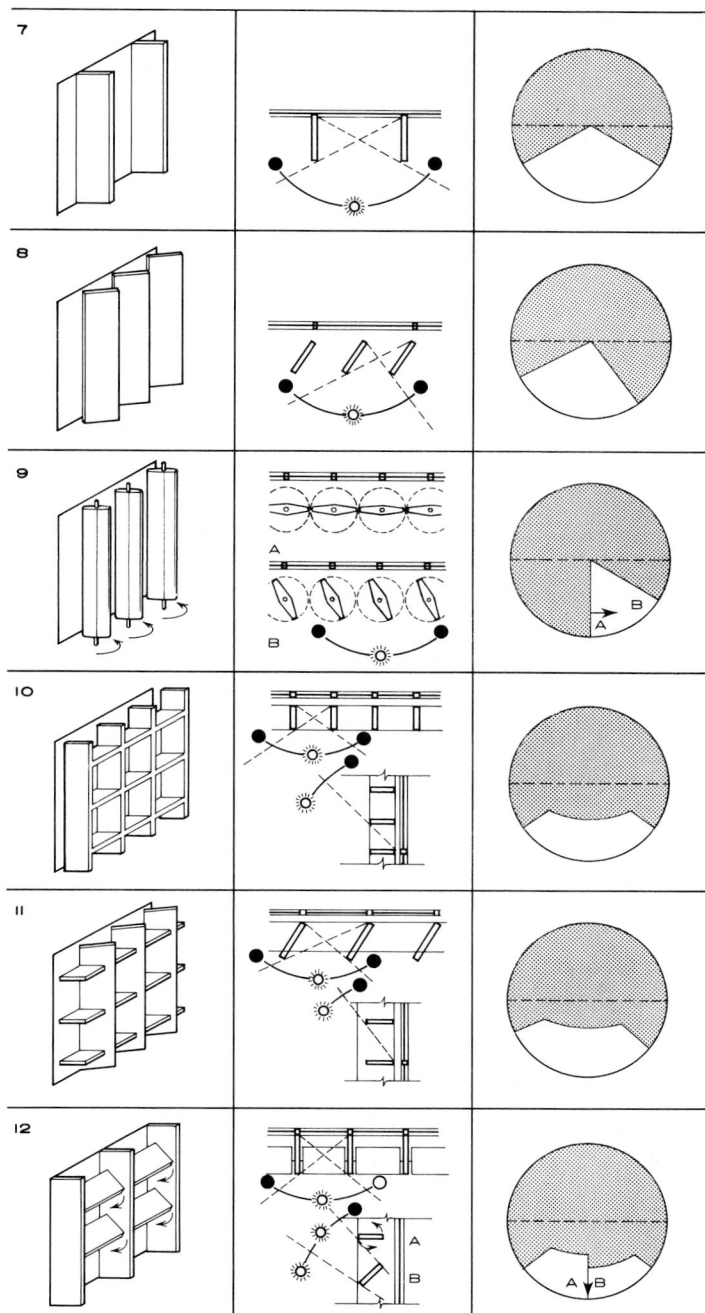

**EXAMPLES OF VARIOUS TYPES OF SHADING DEVICES**

The illustrations show a number of basic types of devices, classified as horizontal, vertical, and eggcrate types. The dash lines shown in the section diagram in each case indicate the sun angle at the time of 100% shading. The shading mask for each device is also shown, the extent of 100% shading being indicated by the gray area.

General rules can be deduced for the types of shading devices to be used for different orientations. Southerly orientations call for shading devices with segmental mask characteristics, and horizontal devices work in these directions efficiently. For easterly and westerly orientations vertical devices serve well, having radial shading masks. If slanted, they should incline toward the north, to give more protection from the southern positions of the sun. The eggcrate type of shading device works well on walls facing southeast, and is particularly effective for southwest orientations. Because of this type's high shading ratio and low winter head admission; its best use is in hot climate regions. For north walls, fixed vertical devices are recommended; however, their use is needed only for large glass surfaces, or in hot regions. At low latitudes on both south and north exposures eggcrate devices work efficiently.

Whether the shading devices be fixed or movable, the same recommendations apply in respect to the different orientations. The movable types can be most efficiently utilized where the sun's altitude and bearing angles change rapidly: on the east, southeast, and especially, because of the afternoon heat, on the southwest and west.

Victor Olgyay, AIA; Associate Professor; School of Architecture, Princeton University; Princeton, New Jersey

**HORIZONTAL TYPES** 1. Horizontal overhangs are most efficient toward south, or around southern orientations. Their mask characteristics are segmental. 2. Louvers parallel to wall will have the advantage of permitting air circulation near the elevation. Slanted louvers will have the same characteristics as solid overhangs, and can be made retractable. 4. When protection is needed for low sun angles, louvers hung from solid horizontal overhangs are efficient. 5. A solid, or perforated screen strip parallel to wall cuts out the lower rays of the sun. 6. Movable horizontal louvers change their segmental mask characteristics according to their positioning.

**VERTICAL TYPES** 7. Vertical fins serve well toward the near east and near west orientations. Their mask characteristics are radial. 8. Vertical fins oblique to wall will result in asymmetrical mask. Separation from wall will prevent heat transmission. 9. Movable fins can shade the whole wall, or open up in different directions according to the sun's position.

**EGGCRATE TYPES** 10. Eggcrate types are combinations of horizontal and vertical types, and their masks are superimposed diagrams of the two masks. 11. Solid eggcrate with slanting vertical fins results in asymmetrical mask. 12. Eggcrate device with movable horizontal elements shows flexible mask characteristics. Because of their high shading ratio, eggcrates are efficient in hot climates.

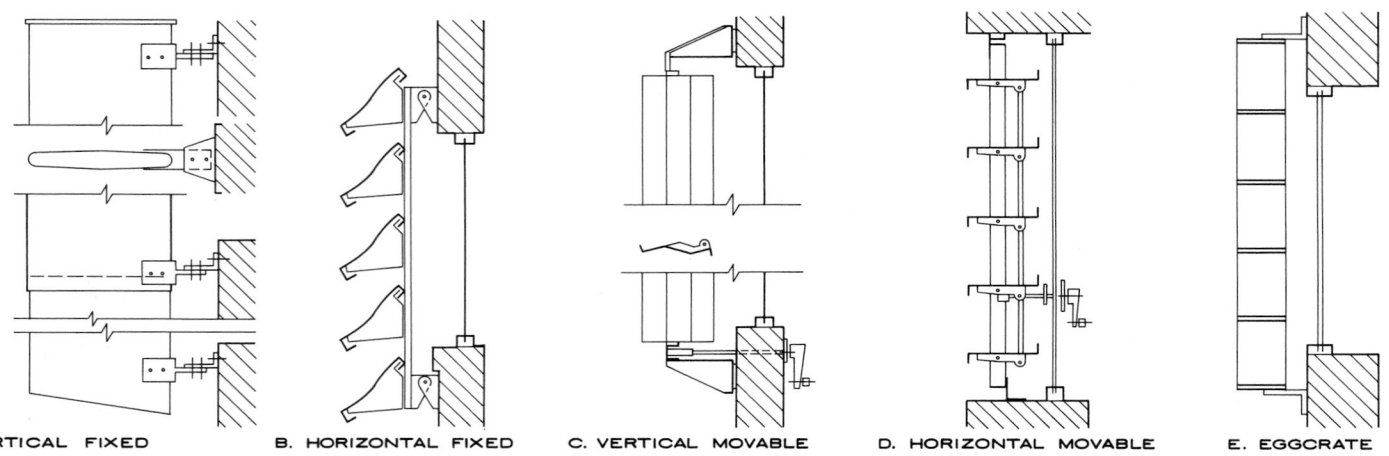

| A. VERTICAL FIXED | B. HORIZONTAL FIXED | C. VERTICAL MOVABLE | D. HORIZONTAL MOVABLE | E. EGGCRATE |

## TYPICAL SUN SHADES AND CONTROLS

A. This device is effective on an east or west wall and can be attached at any degree of angle to facade. If slanted, it should incline to north. Fins are made in floor-to-floor lengths, capped at top and bottom, and telescoped top into bottom at intermediate levels.

B. This device is effective on any side of a building. Blades have a maximum length of 20 ft with supports of 6 ft on center.

C. Used on east or west side of building. This type may interfere with view. Many models are available up to 27 in. wide and 12 ft high.

D. Although this is effective on any side of a building, it is the least restrictive to view when used on the south side. It is usually hinged at the head for emergency exit and window washing. Blades are 9 in. deep; maximum width is 6 ft.

E. This type is very effective on southeast and southwest orientations. It is efficient in hot climates especially if bars can be tilted to more effective angles. All dimensions are variable according to desired function.

## EXTERIOR SUN CONTROLS

The incidence of the sun's rays on a building transmits solar energy to the interior of the building. Since the heat gain through glass is particularly high, various forms of solar control for fenestration have been developed to reduce the use of mechanical equipment for cooling.

The most efficient of these is exterior shading, that is, avoiding the penetration of solar heat through the skin of the building. Exterior shading devices vary according to climate, orientation, and building function and are manufactured to suit specific conditions. They are strong design elements.

Sunshades (fixed horizontal or vertical fins, outriggers, and grills) shade glass completely or partially at critical times. Sun controls (movable horizontal or vertical fins) regulate the quantity of solar heat and light admitted through the glass, which is clear. Adjusting mechanisms can be manual or electric and can be automatically operated with time or photoelectric controls.

Aluminum, either sheet or extruded, is the standard material. Anodic and baked enamel coatings are available as finishes.

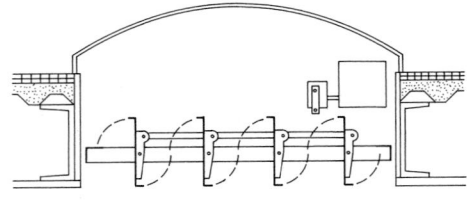

**F. OUTRIGGER**

F. Overhangs are most effectively used on the south side of a building. Wall brackets are made of cast aluminum. Projections greater than 6 ft require structural support or hangers.

**G. SKYLIGHT SHUTTER**

G. Perimeter framing should be designed to suit mounting conditions. Electrically operated shutters are available. Maximum width is 10 ft; length is unlimited.

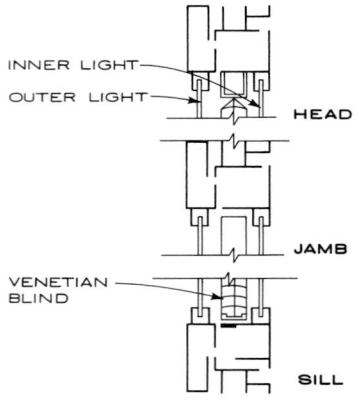

**H. SHUTTER PANELS**

**I. INTEGRAL VENETIAN BLINDS**

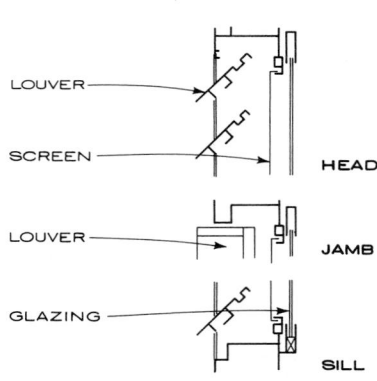

**J. INTEGRAL HORIZONTAL SHADES**

## SPECIAL WINDOW TREATMENT

H. These panels are effective solar screens. The aluminum louvers are spaced to preserve the outside view and admit soft, diffused light while eliminating heat and glare. Horizontal slats snap onto stringer supports which can be easily attached to most structures.

I. This window type combines the thermal insulating values of dual glazing with the advantage of semi-external shading. An aluminum blind is provided between two pieces of glass, each in its own frame and each frame pivoted horizontally or vertically to make cleaning possible. The cavity between the two pieces of glass is ventilated to avoid condensation and to equalize air pressure.

The venetian blind can be tilted and, in some models, raised with controls on the interior window frame.

Window frames are constructed of aluminum, teak or pine.

J. A combination of exterior adjustable horizontal louvers and window frame, this window can be double hung, sliding, jalousie, or fixed. Louvers can be aluminum alloy extrusions, redwood, or glass.

Graham Davidson, Architect; Washington, D.C.

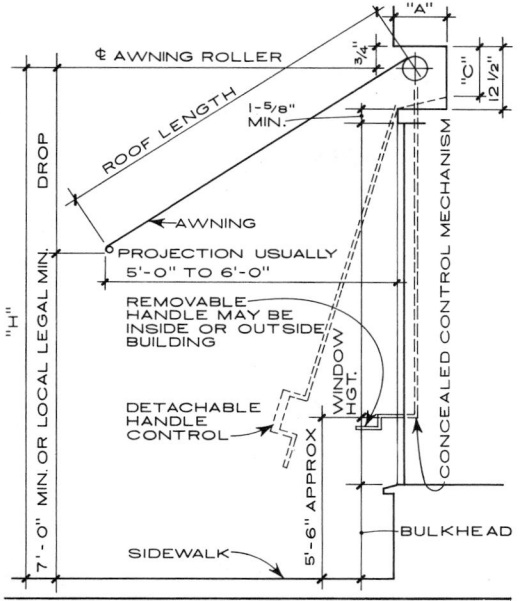

## DIAGRAMMATIC SECTION
## RECESSED BOX INSTALLATION

**AWNING MATERIALS:**
1. Canvas
2. Interlocking metal slats
   a. aluminum
   b. bronze
   c. stainless steel
3. Fiberglass

**AWNING OPERATORS:**
1. Detachable handle control
2. Gear box & shaft (concealed or exposed) with removable handle inside or outside of building
3. Electric control

### AWNING BOX CLEARANCES:

| Recessed box sizes | | "H" | "A" | "B" | "C" |
|---|---|---|---|---|---|
| A. lateral arm type | 9'-6" to 11'-0" | 10" | 10 1/2" | 10" |
| | 9'-6" to 12'-0" | 10 1/2" | 12" | 10" |
| | 9'-6" to 14'-0" | 11" | 13 1/2" | 10" |
| B. outrigger arm type | varies | 6'-2" | 6'-2" | 6'-2" |

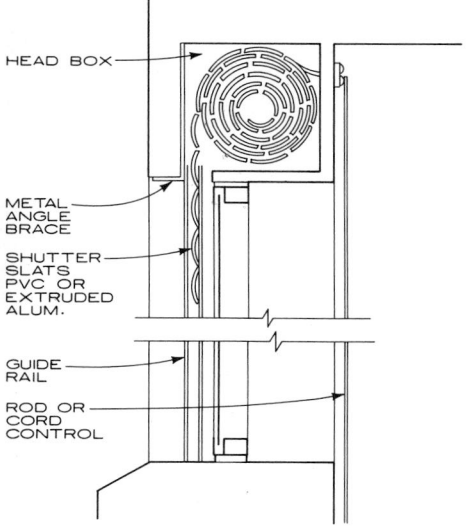

**NOTE**

Rolling shutters provide sun control not only by shading windows from direct sun rays but also by way of two dead airspaces—one between shutter and window, the other within the shutter extrusions to serve as insulation. The dead airspaces work as well in winter to prevent the escape of heat from the interior. In addition, shutters are useful as privacy and security measures. They can be installed in new or existing construction and are manufactured in standard window sizes.

## ROLLING SHUTTERS

Graham Davidson, Architect; Washington, D.C.

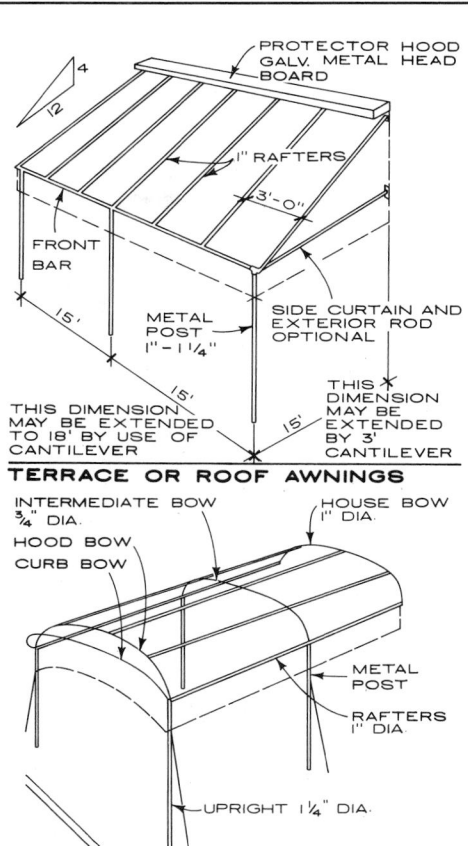

## TERRACE OR ROOF AWNINGS

## CANOPIES - LOW CURVED BOW SHOWN

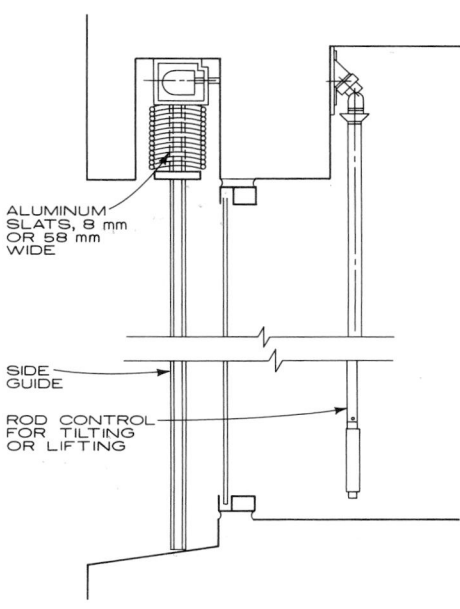

**NOTE**

External blinds protect the building interior from solar gain and glare, but can be raised partially or fully to the head when not needed. Manual or electric control is from inside the building.

## EXTERNAL VENETIAN BLINDS

## TERRACE OR ROOF AWNINGS

To provide complete sun protection and shade, the overall length of the awning bar should extend 3 in. past the glass line on both sides. For proper sunshade protection, awnings should project at least as far forward from the face of the window as the bottom of the window is below the front bar of the awning.

The wall measurement of an awning is the distance down the face of the building from the point where the awning attaches to the face of the building (or from the center of the roller in the case of the roller type awning).

The projection of an awning is the distance from the face of the building to the front bar of the awning in its correct projected position.

Right and left of an awning are your right and left as you are facing the awning looking into the building.

Framework consists of galvanized steel pipe, with non-rattling fittings. Awning is lace-on type canvas with rope reinforced eave. Protector hood is galvanized sheet metal or either bronze, copper, or aluminum.

Sizes of members should be checked by calculation for conditions not similar to those shown on this page.

Consult local building code for limitations on height and setback.

## COVERED WALKWAYS

Covered walkways are available with aluminum fascia and soffit panels in a number of profiles. The fascia panels are supported with pipe columns and steel or aluminum structural members if necessary. Panels can cantilever up to 30% of span. Canopy designs can be supported from above.

Another method of providing covered exterior space is with stressed membrane structures. Using highly tensile synthetic fabric and cable in collaboration with compression members, usually metal, dynamic and versatile tentlike coverings can be created. Membrane structures are especially suited to temporary installations.

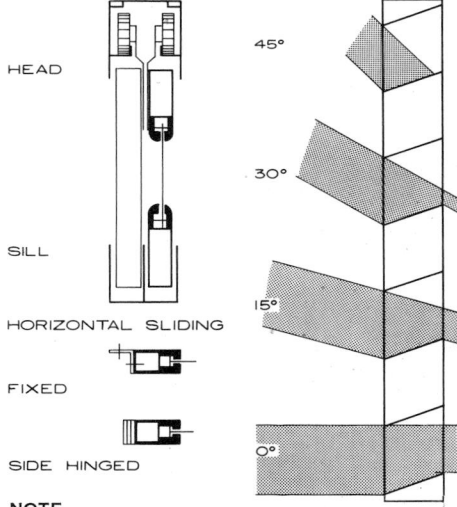

**NOTE**

These miniature external louvers shade windows from direct sunlight and glare while allowing a high degree of visibility, light, ventilation, insect protection, and daytime privacy. Much like a woven metal fabric, they are not strong architectural elements but present a uniform appearance in the areas covered. The solar screen is installed in aluminum frames and can be adapted to suit most applications.

## SOLAR SCREEN SIZES

| MATERIAL | LOUVERS | TILT | VERTICAL SPACING | SIZE (WIDTHS) |
|---|---|---|---|---|
| Aluminum | 17" | 17° | 1" o.c. | 18"-48" |
| Bronze | 17", 23" | 20° | 1/2" o.c. | Up to 72 1/2" |

Aluminum screens are available in black or light green. Bronze screens come in black only.

## SOLAR SCREENS

## STRUCTURAL CONSIDERATIONS

Earth sheltered structures are usually deeper and the loads greater than for basements. Hydrostatic and compaction loads add to the triangular soil loading on walls (Figure 1). Floors below water level are subjected to uplift of 62.4 psf per foot depth below water level and may require special design (Figure 2) to resist the load and to provide a uniform support plane for the waterproof membrane. Roof live loads in urban areas may include public assembly at 100 psf, in addition to soil, plants, and furnishings. Saturated soils and gravel are usually taken at 120 pcf. Tree loads are related to species and size. Tree weights can be estimated for preliminary design by the logarithmic relation

$$\log(wt) = x + 2.223 \log(dia.) + 0.339 \log(ht)$$

where (wt) is in pounds, (dia.) is trunk diameter in inches at breast height, and (ht) is in feet. Forest trees range in x from 0.6 for fir to 0.8 for birch, with spruce and maple at about 0.7. The equation has not been tested for lawn trees, so it must be used with caution. Site investigation is important to determine soil bearing and drainage capacity, shearing strength, and water level. Hillside designs produce unbalanced lateral loads that may recommend interior wall buttressing.

## LANDSCAPE CONSIDERATIONS

Rooftop plantings require adequate soil depth (Figure 3), underdrainage, and irrigation. Lightweight soil mixes reduce roof loads, but are not suitable under foot. Highly trafficked roofs may require special sandy soil mixes used for golf greens and athletic fields to resist compaction and root damage. Plant materials should be drought-resistant and hardier than normal, since roof soil may be colder than lawn soil.

## DRAINAGE AND MOISTURE CONSIDERATIONS

Footing drains draw down the water table and prevent ponding in the backfill. Exterior location is more effective, but is subject to abuse during backfilling and to subsequent settlement. Underslab drains are easier to install correctly and are less likely to fail. Unless both are used, weep holes should be installed through the footing to connect underfloor and perimeter systems. A polyethylene sheet keeps water vapor from entering the slab, and through-joint flashing prevents capillary transfer of soil moisture through the footing to the slab. The waterproofing system must be suited to the structural system and the surface condition of the substrate. Plastic waterstops complicate joint forming and may conceal the source of leaks, disadvantages that usually outweigh whatever benefit they may provide. Chemical (e.g., bentonite base) waterstops do not have these disadvantages.

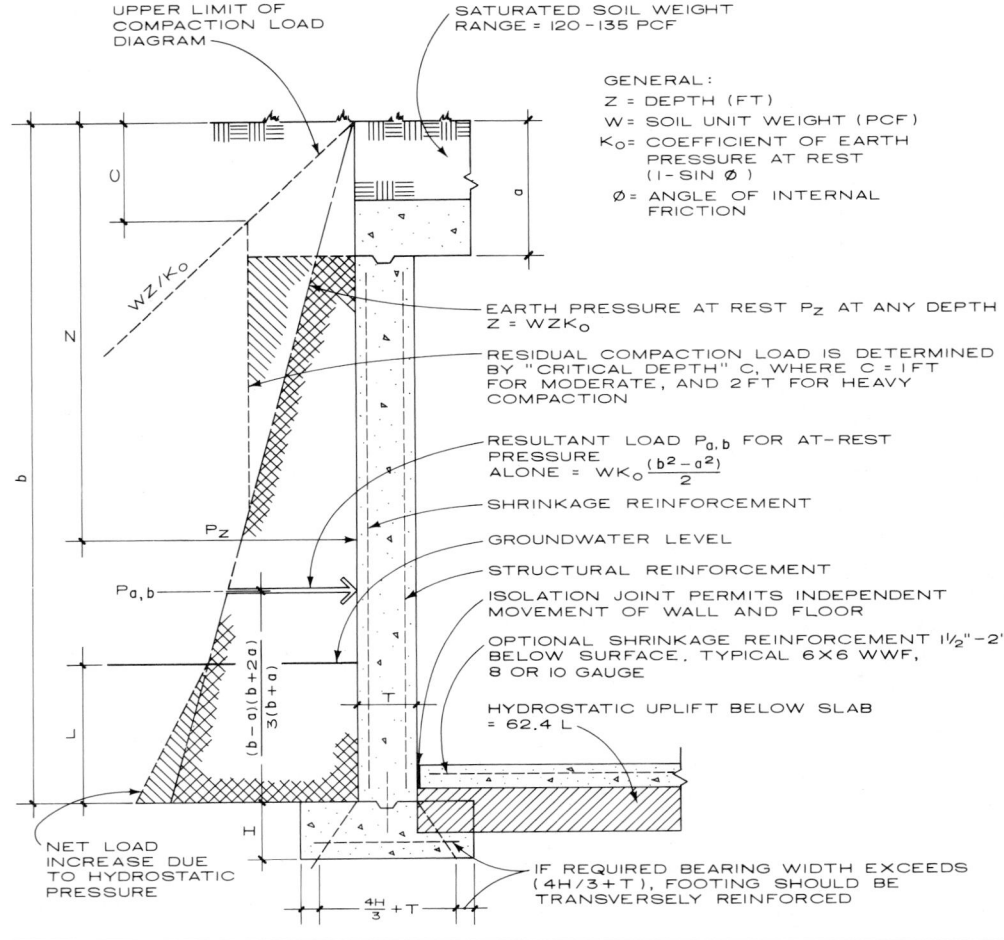

GENERAL:
Z = DEPTH (FT)
W = SOIL UNIT WEIGHT (PCF)
$K_o$ = COEFFICIENT OF EARTH PRESSURE AT REST (1 - SIN $\emptyset$)
$\emptyset$ = ANGLE OF INTERNAL FRICTION

SATURATED SOIL WEIGHT RANGE = 120 - 135 PCF

EARTH PRESSURE AT REST $P_z$ AT ANY DEPTH Z = $WZK_o$

RESIDUAL COMPACTION LOAD IS DETERMINED BY "CRITICAL DEPTH" C, WHERE C = 1 FT FOR MODERATE, AND 2 FT FOR HEAVY COMPACTION

RESULTANT LOAD $P_{a,b}$ FOR AT-REST PRESSURE ALONE = $WK_o \frac{(b^2 - a^2)}{2}$

SHRINKAGE REINFORCEMENT

GROUNDWATER LEVEL

STRUCTURAL REINFORCEMENT

ISOLATION JOINT PERMITS INDEPENDENT MOVEMENT OF WALL AND FLOOR

OPTIONAL SHRINKAGE REINFORCEMENT 1½"-2" BELOW SURFACE. TYPICAL 6×6 WWF, 8 OR 10 GAUGE

HYDROSTATIC UPLIFT BELOW SLAB = 62.4 L

IF REQUIRED BEARING WIDTH EXCEEDS (4H/3 + T), FOOTING SHOULD BE TRANSVERSELY REINFORCED

NET LOAD INCREASE DUE TO HYDROSTATIC PRESSURE

**FIGURE 1 COMPOSITE LOAD DIAGRAM**

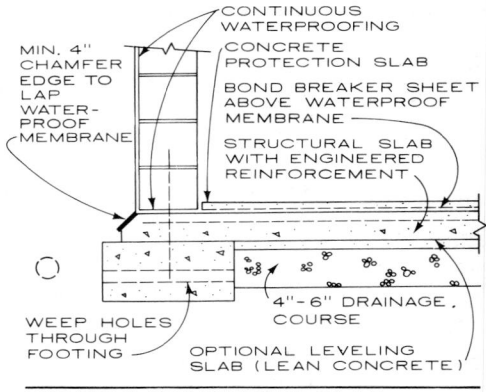

CONTINUOUS WATERPROOFING

CONCRETE PROTECTION SLAB

BOND BREAKER SHEET ABOVE WATERPROOF MEMBRANE

STRUCTURAL SLAB WITH ENGINEERED REINFORCEMENT

MIN. 4" CHAMFER EDGE TO LAP WATER-PROOF MEMBRANE

4"-6" DRAINAGE COURSE

WEEP HOLES THROUGH FOOTING

OPTIONAL LEVELING SLAB (LEAN CONCRETE)

**FIGURE 2 REINFORCED SLAB (GERMAN APPROACH)**

### RECOMMENDED REFERENCES

1. B. Anderson, "Waterproofing and the Design Professional," *The Construction Specifier*, March 1986, pp. 84–97.
2. J. Carmody and R. Sterling, *Earth Sheltered Housing Design*, 2nd Ed., Van Nostrand Reinhold, New York, 1985, 350 pp.
3. R. Sterling, W. Farnan, J. Carmody, *Earth Sheltered Residential Design Manual*, Van Nostrand Reinhold, New York, 1982, 252 pp.
4. U.S. Navy, *Earth Sheltered Buildings*, NAVFAC Design Manual 1.4, U.S. Government Printing Office, 1983.
5. Moreland Associates, *Earth Covered Buildings: An Exploratory Analysis for Hazard and Energy Performance*, Federal Emergency Management Agency, 1981.

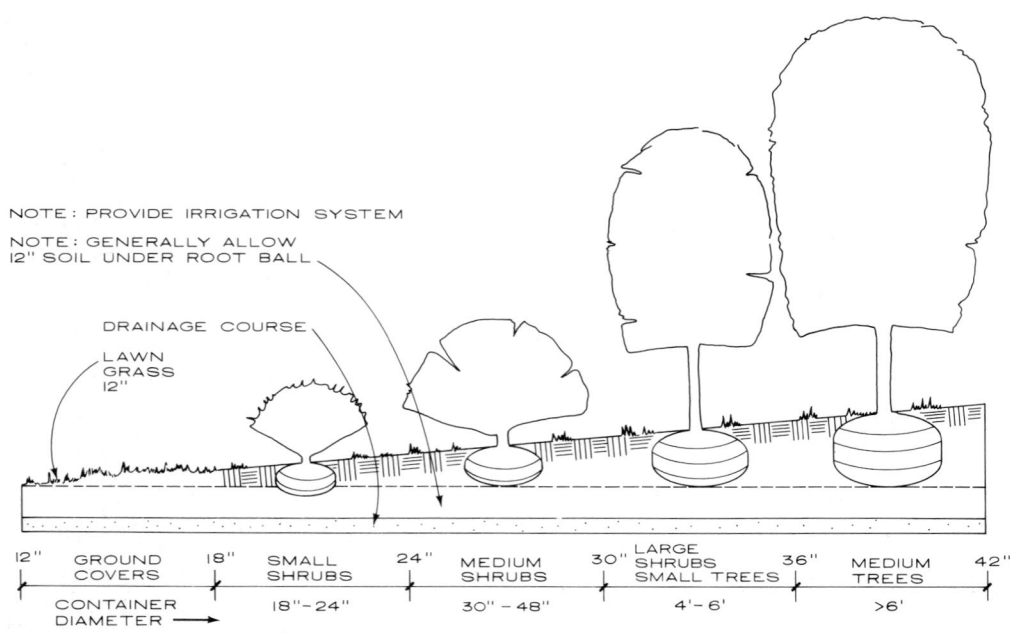

NOTE: PROVIDE IRRIGATION SYSTEM

NOTE: GENERALLY ALLOW 12" SOIL UNDER ROOT BALL

DRAINAGE COURSE

LAWN GRASS 12"

| 12" | GROUND COVERS | 18" | SMALL SHRUBS | 24" | MEDIUM SHRUBS | 30" | LARGE SHRUBS SMALL TREES | 36" | MEDIUM TREES | 42" |
|---|---|---|---|---|---|---|---|---|---|---|
| CONTAINER DIAMETER → | | | 18"-24" | | 30"-48" | | 4'-6' | | >6' | |

**FIGURE 3 PLANT SOIL COVER REQUIREMENTS**

Kenneth Labs; New Haven, Connecticut

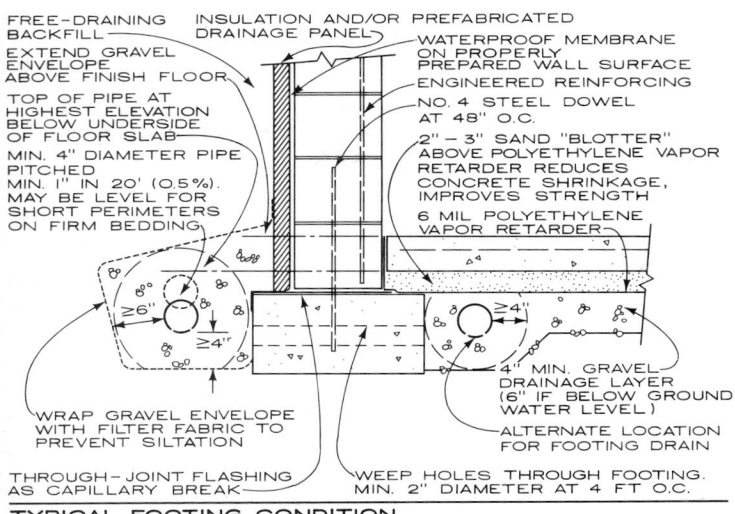

**TYPICAL FOOTING CONDITION**

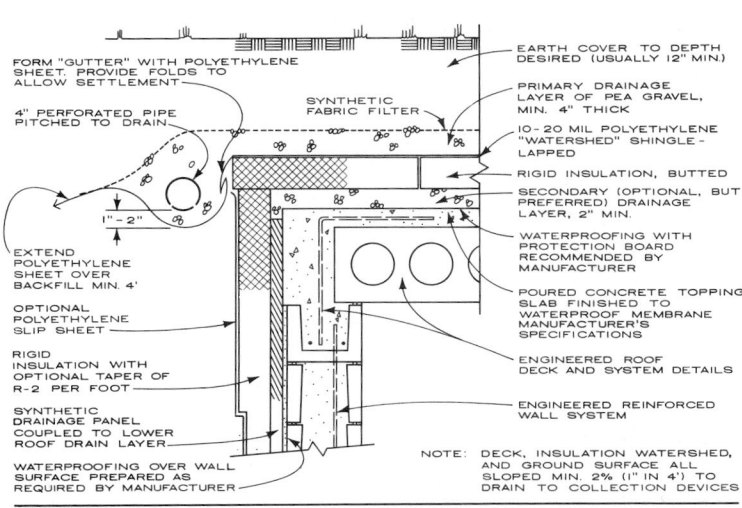

**ROOF EDGE DETAIL**

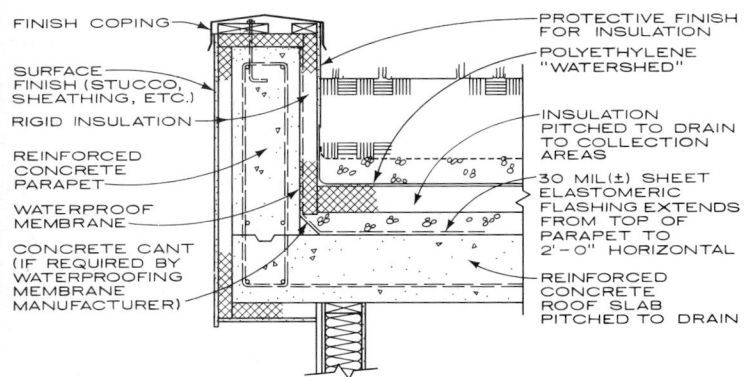

**CONCRETE PERIMETER PARAPET**

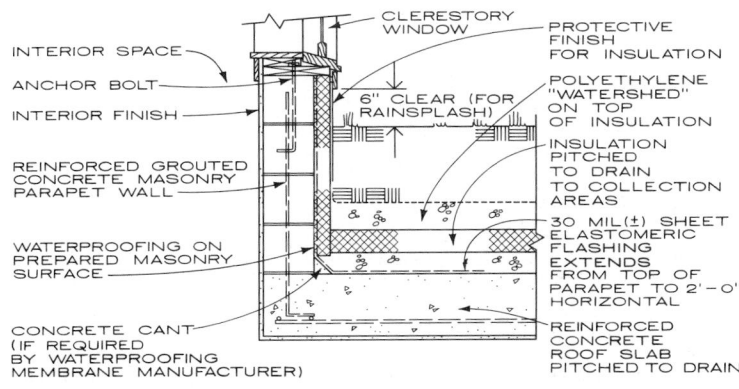

**MASONRY INTERIOR PARAPET**

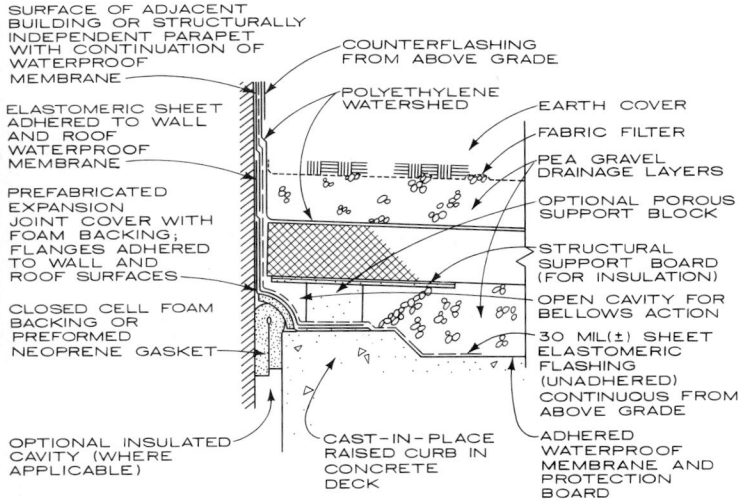

**FLEXIBLE JOINT AT ROOF EDGE**

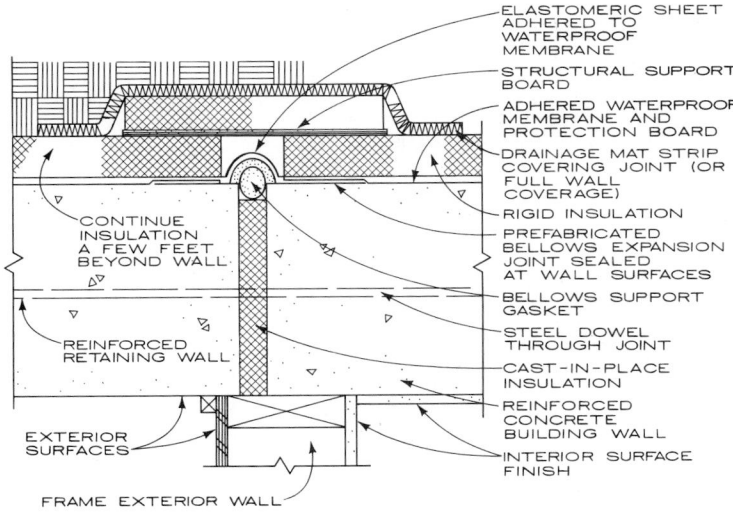

**THERMAL BREAK AT RETAINING WING WALL (PLAN)**

## THERMAL CONSIDERATIONS

Exterior insulation keeps walls and roofs warm and at a stable temperature. This minimizes dimensional change and indoor surface condensation and keeps elastomeric waterproofing pliable. Exterior insulation consumes no indoor space, but it is sometimes attacked by rodents and insects. Extruded polystyrene is usually preferred for its resistance to water absorption. Roof insulation should be placed within the drainage layer so that it does not sit in water or impede drainage. Gravel is not always needed under the insulation, especially if the insulation is pitched to drain and is covered with polyethylene sheets. All seepage planes should be sloped a minimum of 1 in. in 4 ft.

Soil has little thermal resistance, so roof winter thermal performance depends largely on added insulation. Heat loss from earth-covered roofs is nearly constant at

$$Q = (T_1 - T_0)/R$$

where Q is heat loss in Btu/ft²[hr]°F, $T_1$ and $T_0$ are indoor and outdoor air temperatures (°F) averaged over the preceding few days, and R is the thermal resistance of the overall roof assembly. Wet soil has an R value of slightly less than 1.0 per foot thickness.

Kenneth Labs; New Haven, Connecticut

## TYPES OF UNDERGROUND SPACE

Commercial underground buildings can be classified in a number of ways:

1. Cut-and-cover buildings: Buildings relatively near the surface. The structure supports earth loads from above and on the sides. The term "earth-sheltered" usually refers to cut-and-cover buildings. Also, distinctions can be made between buildings that are fully beneath existing grade and those that are bermed.
2. Mined space: Building area is created by excavating in self-supporting soil or rock.

Underground building type is determined primarily by the site, topography, and program requirements. The ability to create mined space is determined by local soils and geology. Further classification of underground buildings often is based on the surface opening. Categories include windowless chambers, atrium designs, and elevational designs (windows along a single wall).

### GENERAL ADVANTAGES

Some of the many advantages associated with underground buildings are:

1. Limited visual impact of the building in natural or historical settings.
2. Preservation of surface open space above the building in dense urban or campus settings.
3. Efficient land use by extending buildings beyond normal setbacks or by building into otherwise unbuildable slopes.
4. Environmental benefits such as reducing water runoff and preserving or increasing plant and animal habitat.
5. Protection from tornadoes, storms, and fire.
6. Provision of civil defense shelters.
7. Increased security against vandalism and theft.
8. Insulation from noise and vibration, permitting some incompatible uses to be located in closer proximity.
9. Reduced exterior maintenance.
10. Reduced construction costs for exterior finishing materials and mechanical equipment.
11. Reduced life-cycle costs of the building based on reduced heating, cooling, maintenance, and insurance costs.

### ENERGY-RELATED ADVANTAGES AND LIMITATIONS

In most climates underground buildings have characteristics that reduce heating and cooling loads when compared with above-ground structures. Advantages from improved energy efficiency include:

1. Reduced winter heat loss because of moderate below-grade temperatures and reduced cold infiltration.
2. Reduced summer heat gain especially when earth-bermed walls are planted with grass or ground cover. Peak cooling loads are reduced.
3. Direct cooling from earth in summer.
4. Daily and seasonal temperature fluctuations are reduced, resulting in smaller HVAC equipment sizes.
5. Large mass below-grade concrete buildings can store sun heat and off-peak electric power.

The U.S. deep-ground temperature map illustrates variations in the below-grade environment. At about 25 ft. and deeper, temperatures of undisturbed ground remain approximately constant. Ground temperatures around an in-ground building rise. Buildings nearer to the surface initially experience some temperature variations that stabilize in time.

Energy-conserving benefits are affected by climate, ground temperatures, degree of exposure, building depth, mechanical system design, and building use. Buildings requiring high levels of mechanical ventilation are less likely to benefit from below-grade placement than buildings with low to moderate ventilation requirements. Maximum energy benefits are derived from building uses such as cold storage, or precision temperature and humidity conditions control (i.e., laboratories, libraries, and special materials storage).

### DISADVANTAGES

Underground building limitations present a number of disadvantages over conventional construction. Most of these can be overcome by design. Among the limitations are:

1. Limited opportunities for natural light and exterior views;
2. Limited entrance and service access;
3. Limited view of the building and its entrance;
4. Increased costs on sites that have water tables, bedrock near the surface, or adjacent buildings with shallow foundations;
5. Increased construction costs for heavier structures (especially if earth is placed on the roof), and high-quality waterproofing systems.

### SPECIAL DESIGN CONCERNS

Entrance design: Entrances should be visible and clear from the exterior. Descending may occur inside or outside the building. If possible, large spaces and natural light should be provided in the entrance area. Various underground building entrance approaches are shown in drawings at the right.

Natural light and view: A primary concern in designing underground buildings is offsetting the possible negative psychological and physiological effects of windowless environments. In addition to admitting sunlight, windows provide orientation, variety, and a similarity to above-ground space. As shown in drawings at the right conventional windows, skylights, and courtyards are effective means of providing light and view in near-surface underground buildings. Where these techniques are inadequate, beamed or reflected daylighting systems may be explored.

Interior design: In underground spaces with limited opportunities for natural light and view, building interior should be organized to provide maximum exposure to light and view for the greatest number of users at each opportunity. Design techniques include large interior courtyards, high ceilings, glass walls, plants, warm colors, variety in design and lighting, and full spectrum artificial lights.

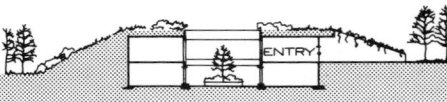

ENTRANCE INTO A BERMED STRUCTURE

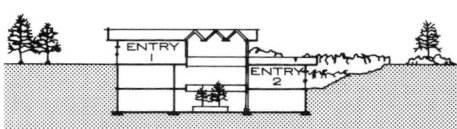

ENTRANCES AT GRADE AND SUBGRADE LEVELS

**BUILDING ENTRANCE DESIGN**

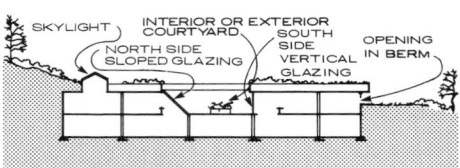

BUILDING SET INTO A SLOPING SITE

**NATURAL LIGHT AND VIEW**

### INSULATION AND WATERPROOFING

Generally, waterproofing should be applied to all below-grade roofs and walls. When a building floor is below the water table level, waterproofing must be placed beneath the floor as well. On below-grade roofs and walls, waterproofing applied directly on the substrate (concrete, wood) is recommended. Insulation and drainage layers then can be placed over the waterproofing (see roof detail below).

When insulation is used in a below-grade application outside of the waterproofing, two characteristics are crucial:

1. Ability to resist structural loads from the earth (this limits selection to rigid board products).
2. Ability to maintain R-value and to resist degradation during constant and severe exposure to water and moisture.

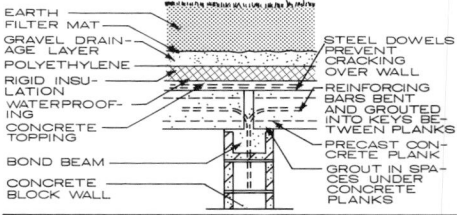

**ROOF DETAIL**

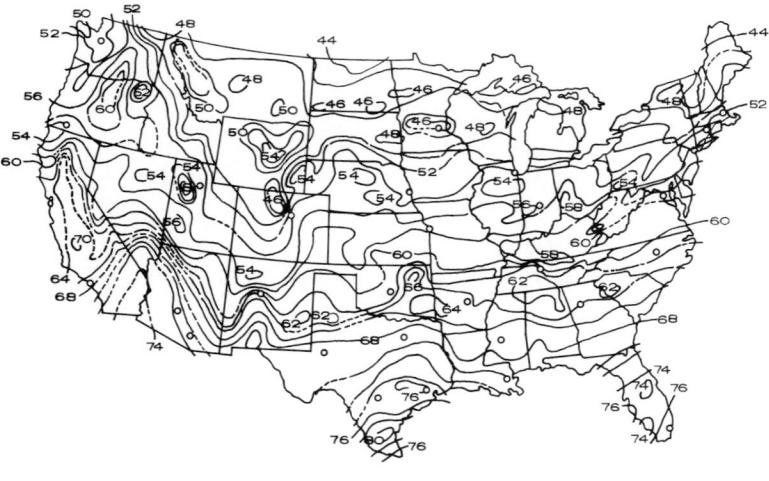

U.S. DEEP-GROUND TEMPERATURE MAP

## SUGGESTED AMOUNTS OF BELOW-GRADE INSULATION

| HEATING/COOLING DEGREE DAYS (BASE; 65°F) | SUGGESTED RANGE OF BELOW-GRADE INSULATION[1] | | |
|---|---|---|---|
| | ROOFS AND[2] UPPER WALL | LOWER WALL[3] | REMOTE FLOOR[4] AREAS |
| 8,000–11,000/0–500 | R-20–R-40 | R-5–R-20 | 0–R-5 |
| 5,000–8,000/500–1,500 | R-20–R-30 | R-5–R-10 | 0–R-5 |
| 2,000–5,000/1,500–2,500 | R-10–R-20 | 0–R-5 | 0 |
| over 2,000/under 2,000 | R-10–R-20 | 0 | 0 |

### NOTES

1. This table is a general guide only and assumes an earth cover thickness in the range of 12 in. to 30 in. for the earth-covered roof.
2. Earth-covered roof with 12 in. to 30 in. of cover and walls within 8 ft of the ground surface.
3. Earth-covered wall surfaces farther than 8 ft from the ground surface.
4. Floor areas remote (i.e., more than 10 ft from the ground surface) not used as a solar storage area or for heat distribution.

David Eijadi, AIA, and Kyle Williams; BRW, Inc.; Minneapolis, Minnesota

# 18   EARTH SHELTERS

## GENERAL NOTES

Building attics, crawl spaces, and basements must be ventilated to remove moisture and water vapor resulting from human activity within the building. Moisture in basements and crawl spaces can occur, in addition, from water in the surrounding soil. The quantity of water vapor depends on building type (e.g., residence, school, hospital), activity (e.g., kitchen, bathroom, laundry), and air temperature and relative humidity. Proper ventilation and insulation must be combined so that the temperature of the ventilated space does not fall below the dew point; this is especially critical with low outdoor temperatures and high inside humidity. Inadequate ventilation will cause condensation and eventual deterioration of framing, insulation, and interior finishes.

The vent types shown allow natural ventilation of roofs and crawl spaces. Mechanical methods (e.g., power attic ventilators, whole house fans) can combine living space and attic ventilation, but openings for natural roof ventilation must still be provided. Protect all vents against insects and vermin with metal or fiberglass screen cloth. Increase net vent areas as noted in table.

## VENTILATION REQUIREMENTS TO PREVENT CONDENSATION

| SPACE | ROOF TYPE | TOTAL NET AREA OF VENTILATION | REMARKS |
|---|---|---|---|
| Joist (ceiling on underside of joists) | Flat | 1/300. Uniformly distributed at eaves | Vent each joist space at both ends. Provide at least 1 1/2" free space above insulation for ventilation |
| | Sloped | Ditto | Ditto. On gable roofs, drill 1" diameter holes through ridge beam in each joist space to provide through-ventilation to both sides of roof |
| Attic (unheated) | Gable | 1/300. At least two louvers on opposite sides near ridge | |
| | Hip | 1/300. Uniformly distributed at eaves. Provide additional 1/600 at ridge, with all vents interconnected | Ridge vents create stack effect from eaves; both are recommended over eaves vents alone |

Total net vent area = 1/300 of building area at eaves line. With screens increase net area by: 1/4" screen, 1.0; #8 screen, 1.25; #16 screen, 2.00.

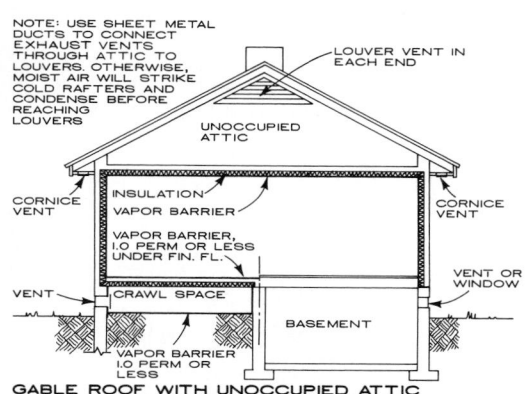

**GABLE ROOF WITH UNOCCUPIED ATTIC**
CORNICE VENTS NOT REQUIRED IF AREA IS SMALL

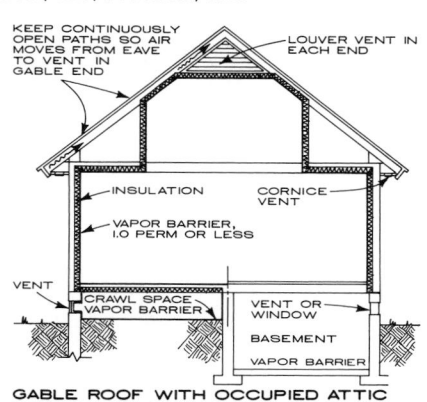

**GABLE ROOF WITH OCCUPIED ATTIC**
CORNICE VENTS REQUIRED TO CREATE "STACK EFFECT" TO RIDGE

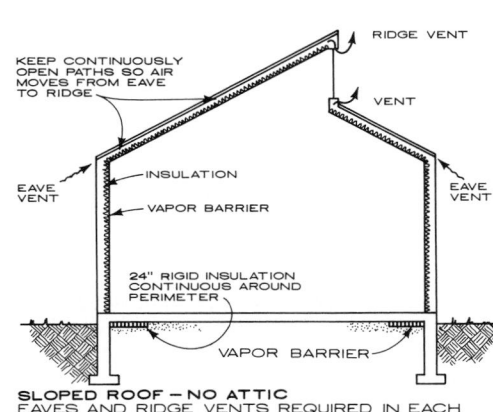

**SLOPED ROOF – NO ATTIC**
EAVES AND RIDGE VENTS REQUIRED IN EACH JOIST SPACE

## TYPICAL ATTIC AND CRAWL SPACE VENTILATION APPLICATIONS

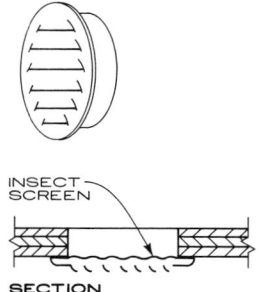

**SECTION**
**ALUMINUM CIRCULAR LOUVERS**
1"–3" DIA.

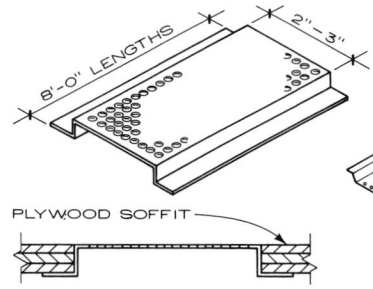

**SECTION**
**STAMPED OR EXTRUDED VENT STRIP**

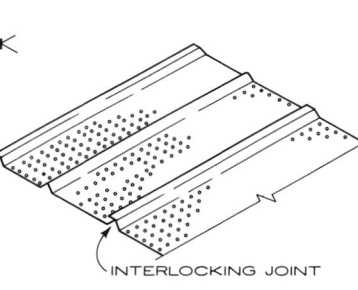

**PERFORATED – PREFINISHED ALUMINUM SOFFIT PANELS**
10" X 10' – 0" LONG. ALSO IN ROLLS

## EAVES VENTILATING MATERIALS

### NOTE

Vapor barriers minimize moisture migration to attics and crawl spaces; their use is required for all conditions. Always locate vapor barriers on the warm (room) side of insulation. Provide ventilation on the cold side; this permits cold/hot weather ventilation while minimizing heat gain/loss.

### CRAWL SPACES VENTILATION

Crawl spaces under dwellings where earth is damp and uncovered require a high rate of ventilation. Provide at least one opening per side, as high as possible. Calculate total net area by the formula:

$$a = \frac{2L}{100} + \frac{A}{300}$$

where

L = crawl space perimeter (linear ft)
A = crawl space area (sq ft)
a = total net vent area (sq ft)

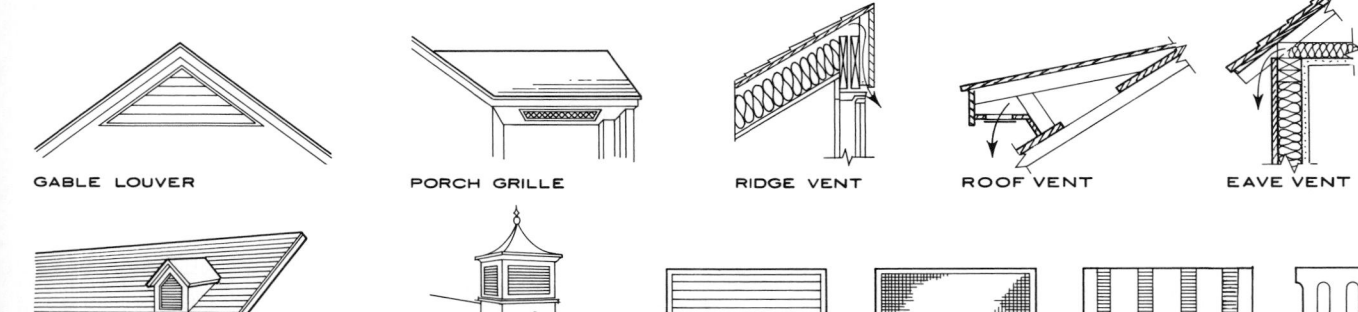

GABLE LOUVER    PORCH GRILLE    RIDGE VENT    ROOF VENT    EAVE VENT    CORNICE VENT

DORMER LOUVER    CUPOLA    LOUVER    WIRE SCREEN    BRICK SCREEN    CONCRETE BLOCK    HOLLOW TILE

## TYPICAL ATTIC AND CRAWL SPACE VENT OPENINGS

David Metzger, Architect, CSI; Wilkes and Faulkner Associates; Washington, D.C.

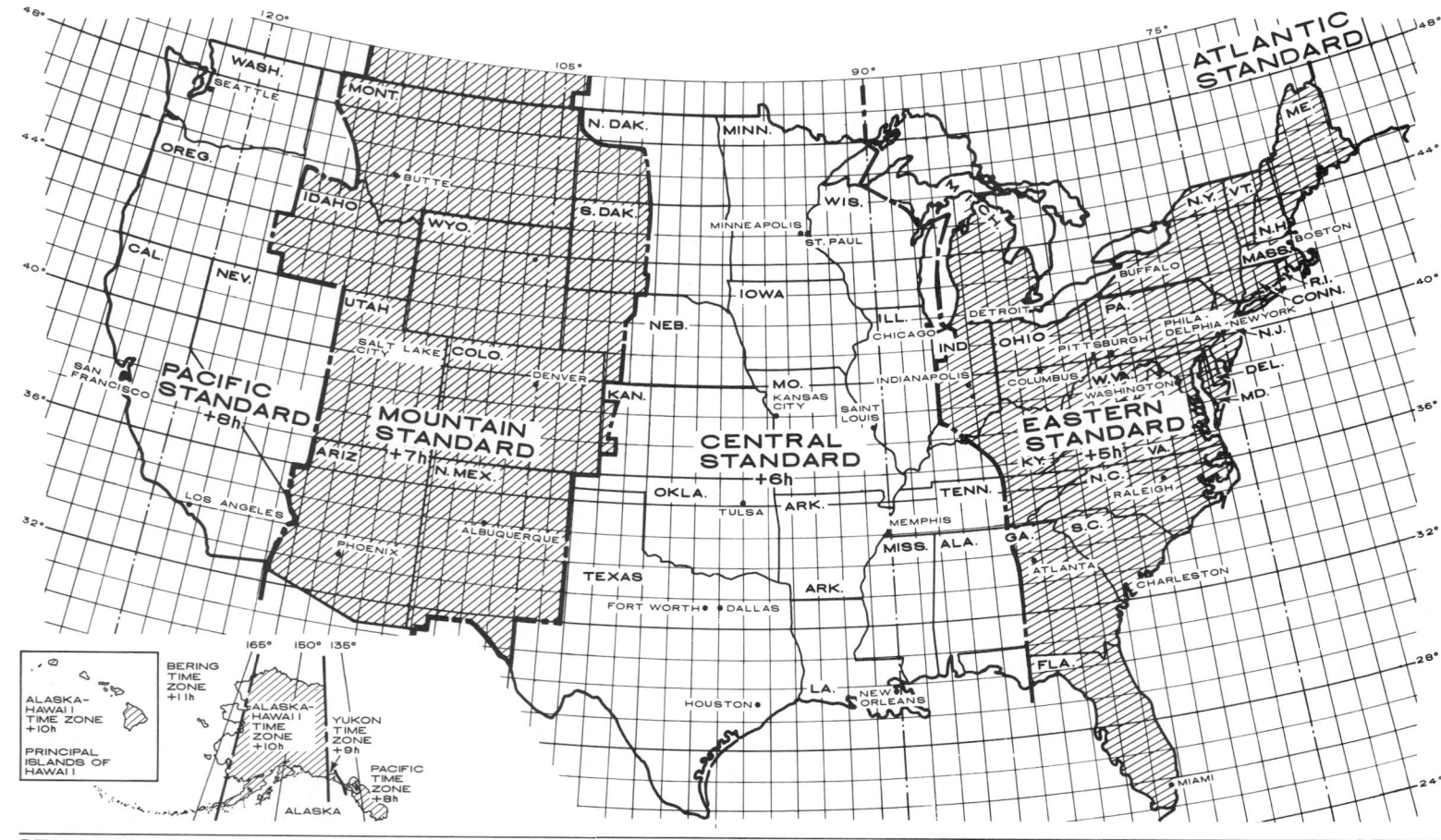

**STANDARD TIME ZONES OF THE UNITED STATES**
NOTE: Greenwich Standard Time is 0 h.

## SOLAR TIME

Solar time generally differs from local standard or daylight saving time, and the difference can be significant, particularly when DST is in effect.

Because the sun appears to move at the rate of 360°/24 hr, its apparent motion is 4 min/1° of longitude. The procedure for finding AST (apparent solar time), explained in detail in the references cited previously, is

$$AST = LST + ET + 4(LSM - LON)$$

where ET = equation of time (min)
  LSM = local standard time meridian (degrees of arc)
  LON = local longitude, degrees of arc
  4 = minutes of time required for 1.0° rotation of earth

The longitudes of the six standard time meridians that affect the United States are: eastern ST, 75°; central ST, 90°; mountain ST, 105°; Pacific ST, 120°; Yukon ST, 135°; Alaska-Hawaii ST, 150°.

The equation of time is the measure, in minutes, of the extent by which solar time, as told by a sundial, runs faster or slower than civil or mean time, as determined by a clock running at a uniform rate. The table below gives values of the declination and the equation of time for the 21st day of each month of a typical year (other than a leap year). This date is chosen because of its significance on four particular days: (a) the winter solstice, December 21, the year's shortest day, $\delta = -23°$ 27 min; (b) the vernal and autumnal equinoxes, March 21 and September 21, when the declination is zero and the day and night are equal in length; and (c) the summer solstice, June 21, the year's longest day, $\delta = +23°$ 27 min.

### EXAMPLES

Find AST at noon, local summer time, on July 21 for Washington, D.C., longitude = 77°; and for Chicago, longitude = 87.6°.

### SOLUTIONS

In summer, both Washington and Chicago use daylight saving time, and noon, local summer time, is actually 11:00 a.m., local standard time. For Washington, in the eastern time zone, the local standard time meridian is 75° east of Greenwich, and for July 21, the equation of time is -6.2 min. Thus noon, Washington summer time, is actually

$$11:00 - 6.2 \text{ min} + 4 \times (75 - 77) = 10:46 \text{ a.m.}$$

For Chicago, in the central time zone, the local standard time meridian is 90°. Chicago lies 2.4° east of that line, and noon, Chicago summer time, is

$$11:00 - 6.2 \text{ min} + 4 \times 2.4 = 11:03 \text{ a.m.}$$

The hour angle, H, for these two examples would be

for Washington: $H = 0.25 \times (12:00 - 10:46)$
$= 0.25 \times 74 = 18.8°$ east

for Chicago: $H = 0.25 \times (12:00 - 11:03)$
$= 14.25°$ east

## YEAR DATE, DECLINATION, AND EQUATION OF TIME FOR THE 21ST DAY OF EACH MONTH; WITH DATA* (A, B, C) USED TO CALCULATE DIRECT NORMAL RADIATION INTENSITY AT THE EARTH'S SURFACE

| MONTH | JAN. | FEB. | MAR. | APR. | MAY | JUNE | JULY | AUG. | SEPT. | OCT. | NOV. | DEC. |
|---|---|---|---|---|---|---|---|---|---|---|---|---|
| Day of the year† | 21 | 52 | 80 | 111 | 141 | 173 | 202 | 233 | 265 | 294 | 325 | 355 |
| Declination, ($\delta$) degrees | -19.9 | -10.6 | 0.0 | +11.9 | +20.3 | +23.45 | +20.5 | +12.1 | 0.0 | -10.7 | -19.9 | -23.45 |
| Equation of time (min) | -11.2 | -13.9 | -7.5 | +1.1 | +3.3 | -1.4 | -6.2 | -2.4 | +7.5 | +15.4 | +13.8 | +1.6 |
| Solar noon | Late | | | Early | | | Late | | | Early | | |
| A: Btuh/sq ft | 390 | 385 | 376 | 360 | 350 | 345 | 344 | 351 | 365 | 378 | 387 | 391 |
| B: 1/m | 0.142 | 0.144 | 0.156 | 0.180 | 0.196 | 0.205 | 0.207 | 0.201 | 0.177 | 0.160 | 0.149 | 0.142 |
| C: dimensionless | 0.058 | 0.060 | 0.071 | 0.097 | 0.121 | 0.134 | 0.136 | 0.122 | 0.092 | 0.073 | 0.063 | 0.057 |

*A is the apparent solar irradiation at air mass zero for each month; B is the atmospheric extinction coefficient; C is the ratio of the diffuse radiation on a horizontal surface to the direct normal irradiation.
†Declinations are for the year 1964.

John I. Yellott, P.E.; College of Architecture, Arizona State University; Tempe, Arizona

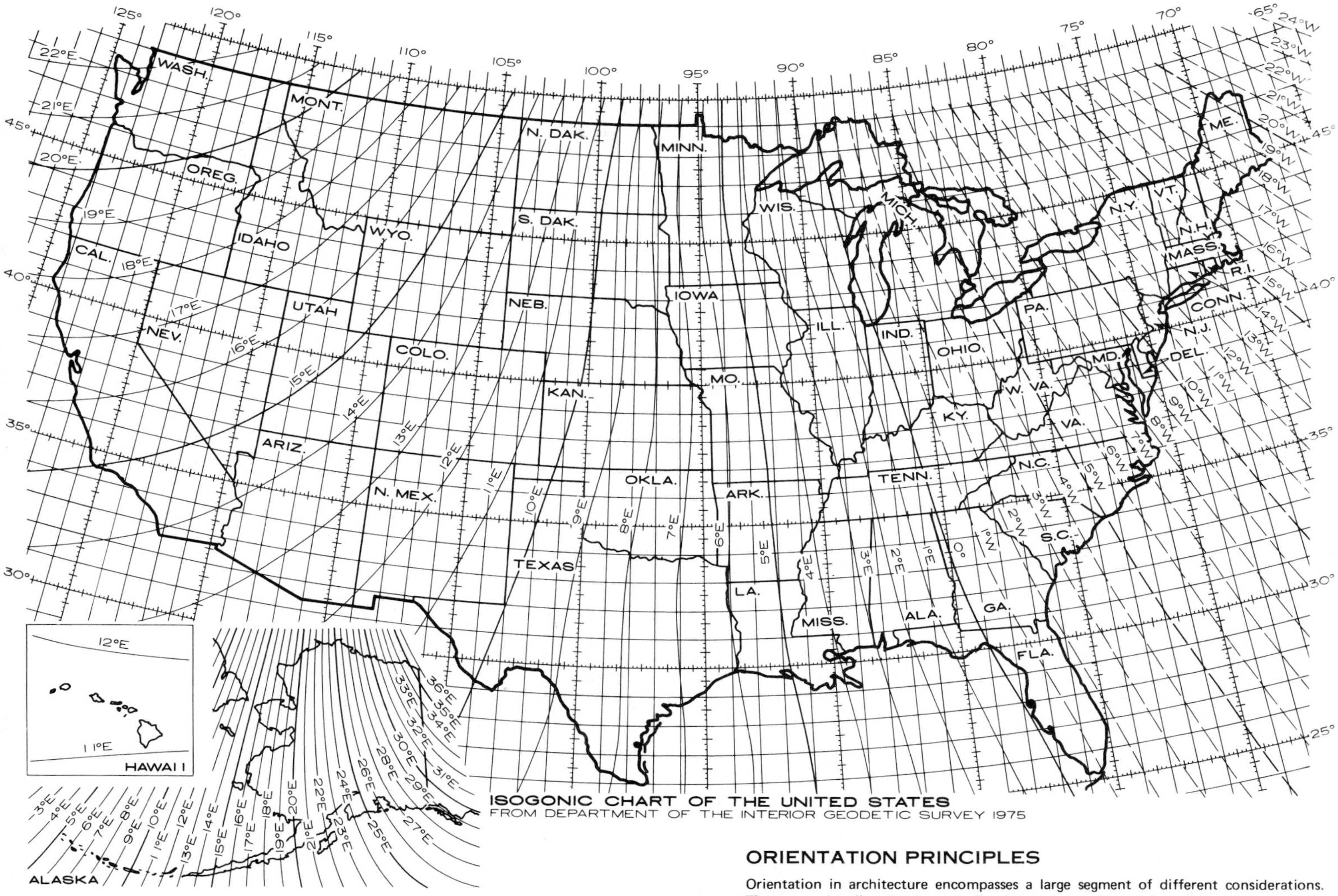

ISOGONIC CHART OF THE UNITED STATES
FROM DEPARTMENT OF THE INTERIOR GEODETIC SURVEY 1975

## ORIENTATION PRINCIPLES

Orientation in architecture encompasses a large segment of different considerations. The expression "total orientation" refers both to the physiological and psychological aspects of the problem.

At the physiological side the factors which affect our senses and have to be taken into consideration are: the thermal impacts—the sun, wind, and temperature effects acting through our skin envelope; the visible impacts—the different illumination and brightness levels affecting our visual senses; the sonic aspects—the noise impacts and noise levels of the surroundings influencing our hearing organs. In addition, our respiratory organs are affected by the smoke, smell, and dust of the environs.

On the psychological side, the view and the privacy are aspects in orientation which quite often override the physical considerations.

Above all, as a building is only a mosaic unit in the pattern of a town organization, the spatial effects, the social intimacy, and its relation to the urban representative directions—aesthetic, political, or social—all play a part in positioning a building.

## THERMAL FORCES INFLUENCING ORIENTATION

The climatic factors such as wind, solar radiation, and air temperature play the most eminent role in orientation. The position of a structure in northern latitudes, where the air temperature is generally cool, should be oriented to receive the maximum amount of sunshine without wind exposure. In southerly latitudes, however, the opposite will be desirable; the building should be turned on its axis to avoid the sun's unwanted radiation and to face the cooling breezes instead.

At right the figure shows these regional requirements diagrammatically.

Adaptation for wind orientation is not of great importance in low buildings, where the use of windbreaks and the arrangement of openings in the high and low pressure areas can help to ameliorate the airflow situation. However, for high buildings, where the surrounding terrain has little effect on the upper stories, careful consideration has to be given to wind orientation.

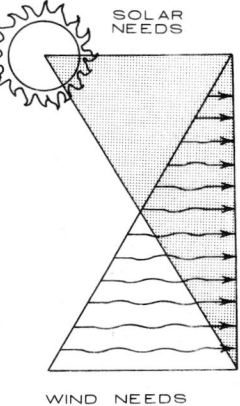

SOLAR NEEDS

WIND NEEDS

## COMPASS ORIENTATION

The above map is the isogonic chart of the United States. The wavy lines from top to bottom show the compass variations from the true north. At the lines marked E the compass will point east of true north; at those marked W the compass will point west of true north. According to the location, correction should be done from the compass north to find the true north.

EXAMPLE:    On a site in Wichita, Kansas, find the true north.

STEP 1.    Find the compass orientation on the site.

STEP 2.    Locate Wichita on the map. The nearest compass variation is the 10°E line.

STEP 3.    Adjust the orientation correction to true north.
The graphical example illustrates a building which lies 25° east with its axis from the compass orientation.

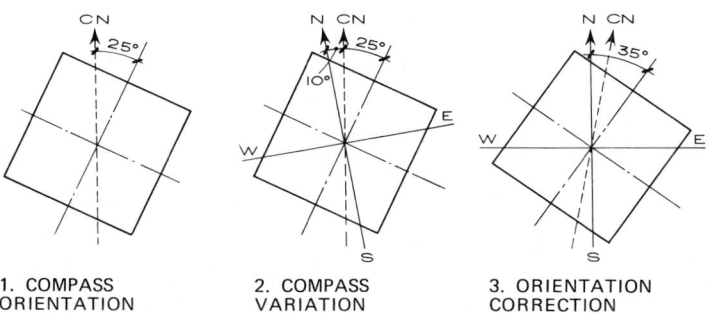

1. COMPASS
ORIENTATION

2. COMPASS
VARIATION

3. ORIENTATION
CORRECTION

Victor Olgyay, AIA; Associate Professor; School of Architecture, Princeton University; Princeton, New Jersey

## DEFINITIONS AND SYMBOLS

BRITISH THERMAL UNIT (Btu): The quantity of heat required to raise the temperature of one pound of water one degree Fahrenheit (specifically, from 59°F to 60°F).

DEGREE DAYS (DD): A temperature-time unit used in estimating building heating requirements. For any given day, the number of DD equals the difference between the reference temperature, usually 65°F, and the mean temperature of the outdoor air for that day. DD per month or per year are the sum of the daily DD for that period. (Check locality for reference temperatures.)

DEWPOINT TEMPERATURE: The temperature corresponding to 100% relative humidity for an air-vapor mixture at constant pressure.

EMITTANCE (e): The ratio of the radiant energy emitted by a surface to that emitted by a perfect radiator (a black body) at the same temperature.

HUMIDITY, ABSOLUTE: The weight of water vapor contained in a unit volume of an air-vapor mixture.

HUMIDITY RATIO: The ratio of the mass of water vapor to the mass of dry air in a given air-vapor mixture.

HUMIDITY, RELATIVE (RH): The ratio of the partial pressure of the water vapor in a given air-vapor mixture to the saturation pressure of water at the existing temperature.

ISOTHERM: A line on a graph or map joining points of equal temperature.

OVERALL HEAT TRANSFER COEFFICIENT (U or $1/R_T$): The rate of heat transfer under steady state conditions through a unit area of a building component caused by a difference of one degree between the air temperatures on the two sides of the component. In U.S. practice, the units are Btu/sq ft · hr · °F.

PERM: Unit of water vapor transmission through a material, expressed in grains of vapor per hour per inch of mercury pressure difference (7000 grains = 1 lb).

REFLECTANCE: The ratio of the radiant energy reflected by a surface to the energy incident upon the surface.

SURFACE HEAT TRANSFER COEFFICIENT (h): The rate of heat transfer from a unit area of a surface to the adjacent air and environment caused by a temperature difference of one degree between the surface and the air. In U.S. practice, the units are Btu/sq ft · hr · °F.

THERM: A unit of thermal energy equal to 100,000 Btu.

THERMAL CONDUCTANCE (C or 1/R): Time rate of heat flow through unit area of a material when a temperature difference of one degree is maintained across a specified thickness of the material. In U.S. practice, the units are Btu/hr · sq ft · °F.

THERMAL CONDUCTIVITY (k): Time rate of heat flow through unit area and unit thickness of a homogeneous material when a temperature of gradient of one degree is maintained in the direction of heat flow. In U.S. practice, the units are: Btu/hr · sq ft · (F/in.) or, when thickness is measured in feet, Btu/hr · ft · °F.

THERMAL RESISTANCE (R): Unit of resistance to heat flow, expressed as temperature difference required to cause heat to flow through a unit area of a building component or material at the rate of one heat unit per hour. In U.S. practice, the units are F/Btu/hr · ft²).

TOTAL THERMAL RESISTANCE ($R_t$): The total resistance to heat flow through a complete building section or construction assembly, generally expressed as the temperature difference in °F needed to cause heat to flow at the rate of 1 Btu per hour per sq ft of area.

VAPOR RETARDANT LOW PERMEABILITY: A layer applied to surfaces enclosing a humid space to prevent moisture migration to a point where it may condense because of reduced temperature.

VAPOR PERMEABILITY: The property of a material that permits migration of water vapor under the influence of a difference in vapor pressure across the material.

VAPOR PERMEANCE: The ratio of the water vapor flow rate, in grains per hour, through a material of any specified thickness to the vapor pressure difference between the two surfaces of the material, expressed in inches of mercury. The unit is the perm.

VAPOR PRESSURE ($P_v$): The partial pressure of the water vapor in an air-vapor mixture. It is determined by the dewpoint temperature or by the drybulb temperature and the relative humidity of the mixture. The units are psi or inches of mercury.

## THERMAL TRANSMISSION

Problems in the performance of building construction materials and assemblies are frequently associated with undesirable flow of heat, moisture, or both. The heat transfer characteristics of most building materials are published in standard references such as the ASHRAE Handbook of Fundamentals. While the published data are subject to manufacturing and testing tolerances and judgment must be used in applying them, they may generally be used with confidence for design purposes.

Heat transmission coefficients are generally expressed as conductivities, k, for which the thickness unit is 1 in., or in conductances, C, for a specified thickness. The resistance to heat flow through a material, R, is the reciprocal of the conductance. For a homogeneous material of thickness L in., the thermal resistance R = L/k.

For a surface or an airspace, where the heat flows by both radiation and convection, combined coefficients are used, symbolized by h with a subscript to designate which particular surface or airspace is being considered. Thermal resistances at surfaces and across airspaces are again designated by R with an appropriate subscript, where R = 1/h. Such R values are strongly influenced by the nature and orientation of the surfaces.

To estimate the rate of heat flow through a building section, the total resistance ($R_t$) of that section is found by reference to published standard value or by adding the resistances of the individual components of the section. The overall coefficient U is then found as the reciprocal of the total resistance: $U = 1/R_t$. The rate of heat flow Q (Btu/hr) through a wall section of exposed area A sq ft is the product of the overall coefficient U, the area A and the temperature difference ($t_i - t_o$): $Q = U \times A \times (t_i - t_o)$. This heat flow may be inward or outward, depending on $t_i$ and $t_o$. The general procedure for finding the total thermal resistance and the U value for a given building section on which the sun is not shining is as follows:

1. Select the design outdoor conditions of air temperature (dry bulb), wind speed, and wind direction from local Weather Service records or ASHRAE recommendations. From this information select an outer surface coefficient $h_o$ which will generally be 4.0 Btu/sq ft · hr · °F for summer and 6.0 for winter. Determine the indoor surface coefficient $h_i$ which will be 1.46 Btu/sq ft · hr · °F under most conditions unless forced airflow exists along the wall of the window. Convert these to resistances with $R_o = 1/h_o$ and $R_i = 1/h_i$.
2. List all of the component elements of the section and determine the thermal resistance of each element by dividing the actual (not the nominal) thickness by its thermal conductivity k, except for airspaces. For airspaces, the thickness is taken into account in the conductance $h_{as}$ and the thermal resistance $R_{as}$ is the reciprocal of the conductance.
3. The total resistance of the building section is simply the sum of the individual resistances (make sure that every component is included properly). The U value of the section is then found from: $U = 1/R_t$. The U x A product is often needed to simplify the calculation of the total heat flow into or out of the building's envelope, as well as for the computations used to determine compliance with building energy performance standards.
4. For such building components as windows, skylights, and doors, U values may be found in standard references, for example, the ASHRAE Handbook of Fundamentals. Thermal resistances for a wide variety of common building materials are given in the table presented later in this section.

### GENERAL NOTES

The foregoing does not include consideration of heat losses or gains due to ventilation air in large buildings or to infiltration of outdoor air through openings, cracks around windows and doors, construction imperfections, and so on. The energy required to heat this air in winter or to cool and dehumidify it in summer must be carefully estimated by methods given in the ASHRAE Handbook of Fundamentals. During both summer and winter, effects of the sun on both walls and windows must be taken into account.

The solution to the basic problem of attaining acceptable heat flow rates involves the selection of materials that are appropriate for the intended service and the incorporation of enough insulation within the building section to reduce the inward or outward heat flow to the desired rate. Since the indoor-outdoor temperature difference is one of the essential factors in the heat flow equation, the indoor temperature must be selected to comply with the pertinent code or other restriction. Temperatures from 65 to 72°F are generally used in winter while 75 to 78°F are typical summer values.

Selection of the outdoor design values involves careful consideration of the number of hours per year during which exceptionally low or high temperatures are encountered. National Weather Service temperature data are available for most locations in the United States and similar data exist for principal cities throughout the world. For winter design purposes, dry bulb temperatures are usually listed, which are exceeded by 99 and 97.5% of the total hours (2160) in December, January, and February. The 97.5% value is generally used for designing. Since the 54 hr (approximately) during which the outdoor air temperature will be lower than the stated value are experienced at intervals throughout the winter months. These temperatures are usually encountered in the early morning hours before sunrise, so that winter design heating loads tend to ignore solar effects. In summer, solar loads tend to dominate the air-conditioning picture.

Thermal conductances for walls, roofs, doors, and windows are combined in many of the energy conservation building standards to give a weighted average U value, designated as $U_o$. Allowable values for $U_o$ depend on the building type and size and the number of heating degree days experienced at the building's location.

$$U_o = \frac{U_{xw} \times A_w + U_f \times A_f + U_d \times A_d}{A_w + A_f + A_d}$$

where the subscripts w, f, and d designate walls, fenestration, and door, respectively.

In many locations, allowable $U_0$ values may be specified in the applicable building code directly or by reference to an accepted standard, such as ASHRAE Standard 90. Estimation of summer cooling loads is also accomplished by using the U x A products as determined above, to which solar loads from fenestration must be added. Thermal resistances may be slightly higher in summer than in winter for the same building section. By far the largest factor in most building heat gain is the load imposed by solar radiation entering through fenestration. Cooling load is also increased by internal heat sources within the structure, including lighting, miscellaneous electrical loads, and the people in the building. Latent heat loads from moisture removal must also be considered. Properly qualified consultants should be called in to give advice in this field even before the orientation and fenestration of a proposed new building are fixed.

The energy conservation standards mentioned above also include provisions dealing with summer cooling requirements, which are set primarily by the latitude of the city in which the structure will be erected. The mass of the proposed building in terms of weight per square foot of wall area is also introduced to compensate in part for time lags caused by the thermal capacity of building components. It should be noted that cooling, a year-round requirement in many large buildings with high internal loads, is more costly in terms of energy consumption and cost than is heating. The internal heat gains that are helpful in winter are harmful in summer, since they can add greatly to the building's cooling load.

John I. Yellott, P.E.; College of Architecture, Arizona State University; Tempe, Arizona

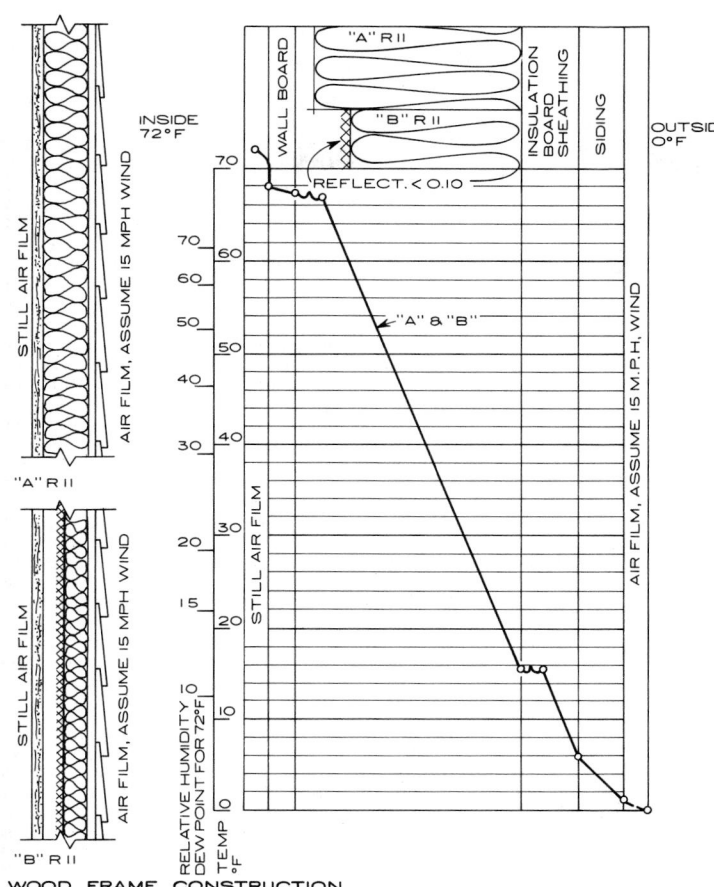

WOOD FRAME CONSTRUCTION

| | WALL "A" | | | WALL "B" | | |
|---|---|---|---|---|---|---|
| | R F/Btu* | °F Diff. Due to R* | Temp °F* | R F/Btu* | °F Diff Due to R* | Temp °F* |
| Indoor room air | | | 72.0 | | | 72.0 |
| Still air film (indoor) | 0.68 | 3.2 | | 0.68 | 3.2 | |
| Indoor face of wall board | | | 68.8 | | | 68.8 |
| Gypsum or plaster board (1/2 in.) | 0.45 | 2.1 | | 0.45 | 2.1 | |
| Back face of wall board | | | 66.7 | | | 66.7 |
| Stud air space remaining | negl. | — | | | | |
| Inner face of insulation | | | 66.7 | | | 66.7 |
| Thermal insulation, R11-wo/refl. | 11.00 | 51.37 | | | | |
| -w/refl. | | | | 11.00 | 51.37 | |
| Outer face of insulation | | | 15.3 | | | 15.3 |
| Inner face of sheathing | | | 15.3 | | | 15.3 |
| Sheathing, 25/32 in., 20 lb. | 2.06 | 9.6 | | 2.06 | 9.6 | |
| Outer face of sheathing | | | 5.7 | | | 5.7 |
| Inner face of siding | | | 5.7 | | | 5.7 |
| Siding, wood, 3/4 x 10, lapped | 1.05 | 4.9 | | 1.05 | 4.95 | |
| Outer face of siding | | | 0.8 | | | 0.8 |
| Outdoor air film (15 mph wind) | 0.17 | 0.80 | | 0.17 | 0.80 | |
| Outdoor air | | | 0 | | | 0 |
| **TOTALS** | 15.41 | 72.0 | | 15.41 | 72.0 | |

$$\text{Heat Loss/sf} = \frac{\text{Temp. Diff., Room to Outdoors}}{\text{Total Resistance, R}} = \frac{72-0}{15.41} = 4.7 \text{ Btu/hr.}$$ applies to insulated areas only; studs and other materials are heat paths which increase heat loss.

Wall "A"—Full thick fibrous insulation R11, non-reflective faces, air spaces insufficient to provide any significant resistance.

Wall "B"—Reflective faced fibrous insulation, R11 with the facing; air space 3/4 in. or more in width required with the facing to provide R11; that space must not be counted a second time.

Insulation thicknesses are not specified but only the R value of the material as manufactured; proper installation is implied.

*Decimals are used to check calculations only — fractional Btu's are usually of no consequence.

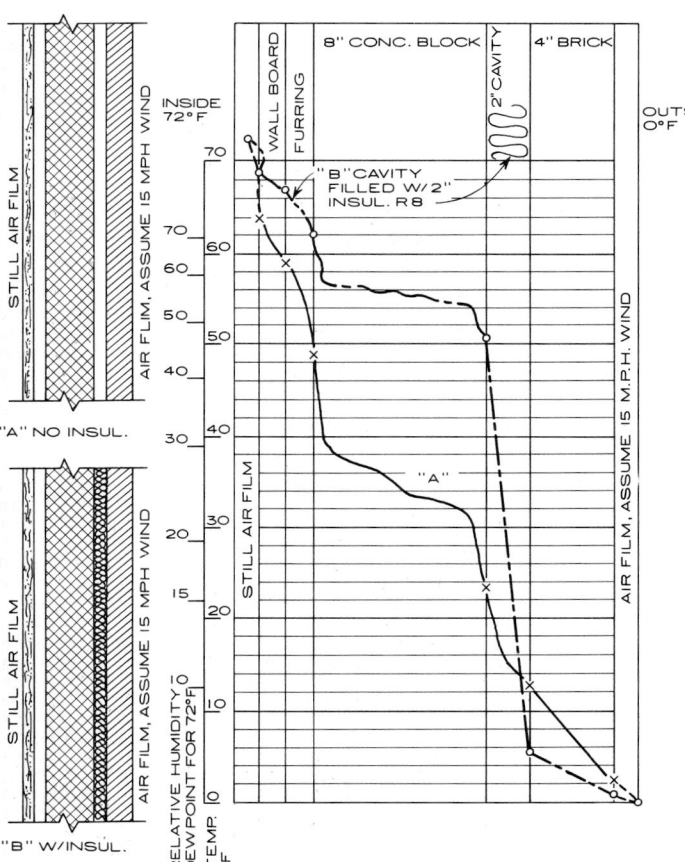

MASONRY CAVITY WALL CONSTRUCTION

| | WALL "A" | | | WALL "B" | | |
|---|---|---|---|---|---|---|
| | R F/Btu* | °F Diff. Due to R* | Temp °F* | R F/Btu* | °F Diff. Due to R* | Temp °F* |
| Indoor room air | | | 72.0 | | | 72.0 |
| Still air film (indoor) | 0.68 | 10.55 | | 0.68 | 4.16 | |
| Indoor face of wall board | | | 61.45 | | | 67.84 |
| Gypsum or plaster board (1/2 in.) | 0.45 | 6.98 | | 0.45 | 2.76 | |
| Back face of wall board | | | 54.47 | | | 65.08 |
| Furring air space (3/4 in.) | 0.90 | 13.95 | | 0.90 | 5.52 | |
| Inner face of concrete block | | | 40.52 | | | 59.56 |
| Concrete block, 8 in., 3 oval core sand & gravel | 1.11 | 17.10 | | 1.11 | 6.80 | |
| Outer face of concrete block | | | 23.42 | | | 52.76 |
| "A" cavity, 2 in. air space | 0.90 | 13.95 | | — | — | |
| "B" cavity, filled w/insulation R8 | — | — | | 8.0 | 49.04 | |
| Inner face of face brick | | | 9.47 | | | 3.72 |
| Face brick, nom. 4 in. | 0.44 | 6.83 | | 0.44 | 2.70 | |
| Outer face of face brick | | | 2.64 | | | 1.02 |
| Outdoor air film (15 mph wind) | 0.17 | 2.63 | | 0.17 | 1.04 | |
| Outdoor air | | | 0 | | | 0 |
| **TOTALS** | 4.65 | 72.01 | | 11.75 | 72.02 | |

$$\text{Heat Loss/sf} = \frac{\text{Temp. Diff., Room to Outdoors}}{\text{Total Resistance, R}} = \frac{72-0}{4.65} = 15.5 \text{ Btu/hr.} \quad \frac{72-0}{11.75} = 6.13 \text{ Btu/hr.}$$

Wall "A"—2 in. open cavity

Wall "B"—2 in. cavity filled with insulation R8. (Verify if water-repellent type is required) R value is for material as manufactured; proper installation is implied.

*Decimals are used to check calculations only—fractional Btu's are usually of no consequence.

NOTE: In tabulation the considerable difference between the temperatures of inside surfaces of the two walls. Occupants of conventional rooms with Wall "A" will be less comfortable than with Wall "B" because of colder inside surface temperature; 61°F vs. 68°F.

Owen L. Delevante, AIA; Glen Rock, New Jersey
E. C. Shuman, P.E.; Consulting Engineer; State College, Pennsylvania

## THERMAL VALUES OF MATERIALS

| MATERIAL & DESCRIPTION | DENSITY (lb per cu ft) | RESISTANCE (R)[a] Per inch thickness (1/k) | RESISTANCE (R)[a] For thickness listed (1/C) |
|---|---|---|---|
| BUILDING BOARDS, PANELS, FLOORING, ETC. | | | |
| Gypsum or plaster board　　　3/8 in. | 50 | — | 0.32 |
| Gypsum or plaster board　　　1/2 in. | 50 | — | 0.45 |
| Plywood | 34 | 0.04 | — |
| Sheathing, fiberboard　　　　1/2 in. | 18 | — | 1.32 |
| 　　　　　　　　　　　　　25/32 in. | 18 | — | 2.06 |
| | 22 | 2.44 | — |
| | 25 | 2.28 | — |
| Wood fiberboard, lam. or homogeneous | 30 | 2.00 | — |
| | 50 | 1.37 | — |
| Particleboard　　　　　　　　5/8 in. | 40 | — | 0.82 |
| Wood subfloor　　　　　　　　3/4 in. | — | — | 0.44 |
| BUILDING PAPER | | | |
| Vapor-permeable felt | — | — | 0.06 |
| Vapor-seal, 2 layers of mopped 15 lb felt | — | — | 0.12 |
| Vapor-seal, plastic film | — | — | Negl. |
| FINISH FLOORING MATERIALS | | | |
| Carpet and fibrous pad | — | — | 2.08 |
| Carpet and rubber pad | — | — | 1.23 |
| Hardwood　　　　　　　　　　25/32 in. | — | — | 0.71 |
| Terrazzo　　　　　　　　　　　1 in. | — | — | 0.08 |
| Tile-asphalt, linoleum, vinyl, rubber | — | — | 0.05 |
| INSULATING MATERIALS | | | |
| *Blanket and Batt*[b] | | | |
| Mineral wool, fibrous form | | | |
| processed from rock, slag, or glass | | | |
| 　　　　　　　　　　　　　1–3 in. | 0.3–2.0 | 4.16 | — |
| 　　　　　　　　　　　　　3–4 in. | | — | 11.0 |
| 　　　　　　　　　　　5 1/2–6 1/2 in. | | — | 19.0 |
| 　　　　　　　　　　　　　9–10 in. | | — | 30.0 |
| Wood fiber | | | |
| *Boards and slabs* | | | |
| Cellular glass | 8.5 | 2.86 | — |
| Glass fiber | 4–9 | 4.00 | — |
| Expanded rubber (rigid) | 4.5 | 4.55 | — |
| Expanded polyurethane (R-11 blown) | | | |
| (Thickness 1 in. & greater) | 1.5 | 6.25 | — |
| Expanded polystyrene, extruded | | | |
| Cut cell surface | 1.8 | 4.00 | — |
| Smooth skin surface | 1.8–3.5 | 5.00 | — |
| Expanded polystyrene, molded beads | 1.0 | 3.85 | — |
| | | | — |
| Mineral fiber with resin binder | 15 | 3.45 | — |
| Mineral fiberboard, wet felted | | | |
| Core or roof insulation | 16–17 | 2.94 | — |
| Acoustical tile | 18 | 2.86 | — |
| Acoustical tile | 21 | 2.70 | — |
| Mineral fiberboard, wet molded | | | |
| Acoustical tile[c] | 23 | 2.38 | — |
| Wood or cane fiberboard | | | |
| Acoustical tile[c]　　　　　　1/2 in. | — | — | 1.19 |
| Acoustical tile[c]　　　　　　3/4 in. | — | — | 1.78 |
| Interior finish (plank, tile) | 15 | 2.86 | — |
| Cement fiber slabs (shredded with portland | | | |
| cement boards) | 25.0–27.0 | 2.00 | — |
| *Loose Fill* | | | |
| Mineral fiber | | | |
| (glass, slag, or rock) | | | |
| 　　　　　　　　　　　　　5 in. | 0.6–2.0 | — | 11.00 |
| 　　　　　　　　　　6 1/2–8 3/4 in. | 0.6–2.0 | — | 19.00 |
| 　　　　　　　　10 1/4–13 3/4 in. | 0.6–2.0 | — | 30.00 |
| Vermiculite (exfoliated) | 4.0–6.0 | 2.27 | — |
| | 7.0–8.2 | 2.13 | — |
| Perlite (expanded) | 2.0–4.1 | 3.50 | — |
| | 4.1–7.4 | 3.00 | — |
| | 7.4–11.0 | 2.60 | — |
| Wood fiber, softwoods | 2.0–3.5 | 3.33 | — |
| MASONRY MATERIALS—CONCRETES | | | |
| Cement mortar | 116 | 0.20 | — |
| Gypsum-fiber concrete, | | | |
| 87 1/2% gypsum, 12 1/2% wood chips | 51 | 0.60 | — |
| Lightweight aggregates including | 120 | 0.19 | — |
| expanded shale, clay or slate; | 100 | 0.28 | — |
| expanded slags; cinders; pumice; | 80 | 0.40 | — |
| perlite; vermiculite; also | 60 | 0.59 | — |
| cellular concretes | 40 | 0.86 | — |
| | 30 | 1.11 | — |
| | 20 | 1.43 | — |
| Sand & gravel or stone aggregate | 140 | 0.11 | — |
| (oven dried) | | | |
| Sand & gravel or stone aggregate | 140 | 0.08 | — |
| (not dried) | | | |
| Stucco | 116 | 0.20 | — |

## THERMAL VALUES OF MATERIALS

| MATERIAL & DESCRIPTION | DENSITY (lb per cu ft) | RESISTANCE (R)[a] Per inch thickness (1/k) | RESISTANCE (R)[a] For thickness listed (1/C) |
|---|---|---|---|
| MASONRY UNITS | | | |
| Brick, common[d] | 120 | 0.20 | — |
| Brick, face[e] | 130 | 0.11 | — |
| Clay tile, hollow: | — | — | 0.80 |
| 1 cell deep　　　　　　　　3 in. | — | — | 1.11 |
| 1 cell deep　　　　　　　　4 in. | — | — | 1.52 |
| 2 cells deep　　　　　　　6 in. | — | — | 1.85 |
| 2 cells deep　　　　　　　8 in. | | | |
| Concrete blocks, three oval core: | | | |
| Sand & gravel aggregate　4 in. | — | — | 0.71 |
| 　　　　　　　　　　　　8 in. | — | — | 1.11 |
| 　　　　　　　　　　　12 in. | — | — | 1.28 |
| Cinder aggregate　　　　3 in. | — | — | 0.86 |
| 　　　　　　　　　　　　4 in. | — | — | 1.11 |
| 　　　　　　　　　　　　8 in. | — | — | 1.72 |
| 　　　　　　　　　　　12 in. | — | — | 1.89 |
| Lightweight aggregate　　3 in. | — | — | 1.27 |
| (expanded shale, clay, slate　4 in. | — | — | 1.50 |
| or slag; pumice)　　　　8 in. | — | — | 2.00 |
| 　　　　　　　　　　　12 in. | — | — | 2.27 |
| Concrete blocks, rectangular core: | | | |
| Sand & gravel aggregate | | | |
| 2 core, 8 in. 36 lb. | — | — | 1.04 |
| Lightweight aggregate (expanded | | | |
| shale, clay, slate or slag; pumice) | | | |
| 3 core, 6 in. 19 lb. | — | — | 1.65 |
| 2 core, 8 in. 24 lb. | — | — | 2.18 |
| 3 core, 12 in. 38 lb. | — | — | 2.48 |
| Granite, marble | 150–175 | 0.05 | — |
| Stone, lime or sand | — | 0.08 | — |
| METALS | | | |
| Aluminum | 171 | 0.0007 | — |
| Brass, red | 524–542 | 0.0010 | — |
| Brass, yellow | 524–542 | 0.0012 | — |
| Copper, cast rolled | 550–555 | 0.0004 | — |
| Iron, gray cast | 438–445 | 0.0030 | — |
| Iron, pure | 474–493 | 0.0023 | — |
| Lead | 704 | 0.0041 | — |
| Steel, cold drawn | 490 | 0.0032 | — |
| Steel, | | | |
| stainless, type 304 | | 0.0055 | — |
| Zinc, cast | | 0.0013 | — |
| PLASTERING MATERIALS | | | |
| Cement plaster, | | | |
| sand aggregate | 116 | 0.20 | — |
| Sand aggregate　　　　　　1/2 in. | — | — | 0.10 |
| Sand aggregate　　　　　　3/4 in. | — | — | 0.15 |
| Gypsum plaster: | | | |
| Lightweight aggregate　　1/2 in. | 45 | — | 0.32 |
| Lightweight aggregate　　5/8 in. | 45 | — | 0.39 |
| Lightweight aggregate, | | | |
| on metal lath　　　　　3/4 in. | — | — | 0.47 |
| Perlite aggregate | 45 | 0.67 | — |
| Sand aggregate | 105 | 0.18 | — |
| Sand aggregate　　　　　　1/2 in. | 105 | — | 0.09 |
| Sand aggregate　　　　　　5/8 in. | 105 | — | 0.11 |
| Sand aggregate, | | | |
| on metal lath　　　　　3/4 in. | — | — | 0.13 |
| Vermiculite aggregate | 45 | 0.59 | — |
| ROOFING | | | |
| 1-ply membrane　　　　0.048 in. | 83 | — | 0.50 |
| Asphalt roll roofing | 70 | — | 0.15 |
| Asphalt shingles | 70 | — | 0.44 |
| Built-up roofing　　　　　　3/8 in. | 70 | — | 0.33 |
| Slate　　　　　　　　　　　1/2 in. | — | — | 0.05 |
| SIDING MATERIALS | | | |
| (On Flat Surface) | | | |
| Shingles: | | | |
| Wood, 16 in., 7 1/2 in. exposure | — | — | 0.87 |
| Wood, double, 16 in., | | | |
| 12 in. exposure | — | — | 1.19 |
| Wood, plus insul. backer board, 5/16 in. | — | — | 1.40 |
| Siding: | | | |
| Aluminum (hollow backed | | | |
| over sheathing) | — | — | 0.61 |
| Vinyl (hollow backed | | | |
| over sheathing)　　　0.04 in. | — | — | 1.00 |
| Cedar shakes　　　　　　1/2 in. | — | — | 0.94 |
| 　　　　　　　　　　　　3/4 in. | — | — | 1.69 |
| Wood, drop, 1 x 8 in. | — | — | 0.79 |
| Wood, bevel, 1/2 x 8 in., lapped | — | — | 0.81 |
| Wood, bevel, 3/4 x 10 in., lapped | — | — | 1.05 |
| Architectural glass | — | — | 0.10 |

D. Richard Stroup, AIA; Craig, Gaulden & Davis, Architects; Greenville, South Carolina

## THERMAL VALUES OF MATERIALS

| MATERIAL & DESCRIPTION | | DENSITY (lb per cu ft) | RESISTANCE (R)[a] | |
|---|---|---|---|---|
| | | | Per inch thickness (1/k) | For thickness listed (1/C) |
| **WOODS** | | | | |
| Maple, oak, and similar hardwoods | | 45 | 0.91 | — |
| Fir, pine, and similar softwoods | | 32 | 1.25 | |
| Fir, pine, and similar softwoods | | | | |
| | $^{25}/_{32}$ in. | 32 | — | 0.98 |
| | 1½ in. | 32 | — | 1.89 |
| | 2½ in. | 32 | — | 3.12 |
| | 3½ in. | 32 | — | 4.35 |
| Door, 1-¾ in. thick solid wood core | | | | 3.13 |
| 1⅜ in. hollow core | | | | 2.22 |

## STEEL DOORS (NOMINAL THICKNESS 1¾ IN.)

| | | | |
|---|---|---|---|
| Mineral fiber core | — | — | 1.69 |
| Solid urethane foam core* | — | — | 5.56 |
| Solid polystyrene core* | — | — | 2.13 |

*With thermal break.

## AIR SURFACES

| Position of Surface | Direction of Heat Flow | Type of Surface | | |
|---|---|---|---|---|
| | | Non-Reflective Materials | Reflective Aluminum Coated Paper | Highly Reflective Foil |
| | | Resistance (R) | Resistance (R) | Resistance (R) |
| **STILL AIR** | | | | |
| Horizontal | Upward | 0.61 | 1.10 | 1.32 |
| 45° slope | Upward | 0.62 | 1.14 | 1.37 |
| Vertical | Horizontal | 0.68 | 1.35 | 1.70 |
| 45° slope | Down | 0.76 | 1.67 | 2.22 |
| Horizontal | Down | 0.92 | 2.70 | 4.55 |
| **MOVING AIR** (any position) | | | | |
| 15 mph wind | Any | 0.17 (winter) | — | — |
| 7½ mph wind | Any | 0.25 (summer) | — | — |

## AIR SPACES

| Position of Air Space and Thickness (inches) | | Heat Flow Dir. | Season | Types of Surfaces on Opposite Sides | | |
|---|---|---|---|---|---|---|
| | | | | Both Surfaces Non-Reflective Materials | Aluminum Coated Paper/ Non-Reflective Materials | Foil/ Non-Reflective Materials |
| | | | | Resistance (R) | Resistance (R) | Resistance (R) |
| Horizontal | ¾ | Up | W | 0.87 | 1.71 | 2.23 |
| | ¾ | | S | 0.76 | 1.63 | 2.26 |
| | 4 | | W | 0.94 | 1.99 | 2.73 |
| | 4 | | S | 0.80 | 1.87 | 2.75 |
| 45° slope | ¾ | Up | W | 0.94 | 2.02 | 2.78 |
| | ¾ | | S | 0.81 | 1.90 | 2.81 |
| | 4 | | W | 0.96 | 2.13 | 3.00 |
| | 4 | | S | 0.82 | 1.98 | 3.00 |
| Vertical | ¾ | Down | W | 1.01 | 2.36 | 3.48 |
| | ¾ | | S | 0.84 | 2.10 | 3.28 |
| | 4 | | W | 1.01 | 2.34 | 3.45 |
| | 4 | | S | 0.91 | 2.16 | 3.44 |
| 45° slope | ¾ | Down | W | 1.02 | 2.40 | 3.57 |
| | ¾ | | S | 0.84 | 2.09 | 3.24 |
| | 4 | | W | 1.08 | 2.75 | 4.41 |
| | 4 | | S | 0.90 | 2.50 | 4.36 |
| Horizontal | ¾ | Down | W | 1.02 | 2.39 | 3.55 |
| | 1½ | | W | 1.14 | 3.21 | 5.74 |
| | 4 | | W | 1.23 | 4.02 | 8.94 |
| | ¾ | | S | 0.84 | 2.08 | 3.25 |
| | 1½ | | S | 0.93 | 2.76 | 5.24 |
| | 4 | | S | 0.99 | 3.38 | 8.08 |

D. Richard Stroup, AIA; Craig, Gaulden & Davis, Architects; Greenville, South Carolina

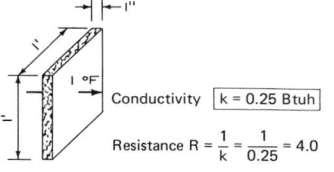

Conductivity  k = 0.25 Btuh

Resistance $R = \frac{1}{k} = \frac{1}{0.25} = 4.0$

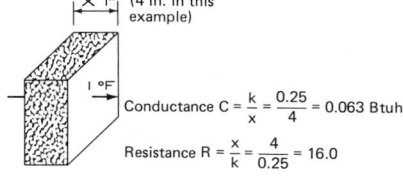

X 1" (4 in. in this example)

Conductance $C = \frac{k}{x} = \frac{0.25}{4} = 0.063$ Btuh

Resistance $R = \frac{x}{k} = \frac{4}{0.25} = 16.0$

GLASS FIBER INSULATION BOARD

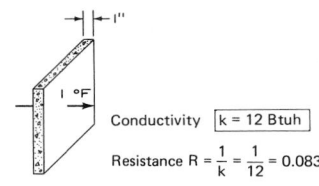

Conductivity  k = 12 Btuh

Resistance $R = \frac{1}{k} = \frac{1}{12} = 0.083$

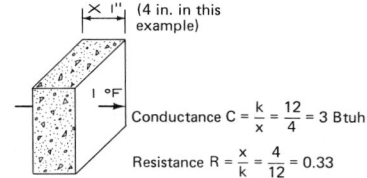

X 1" (4 in. in this example)

Conductance $C = \frac{k}{x} = \frac{12}{4} = 3$ Btuh

Resistance $R = \frac{x}{k} = \frac{4}{12} = 0.33$

SAND AND GRAVEL CONCRETE

NOTES: Standard unit of area 1 sq ft.
Standard unit temperature differential 1°F.

### HEAT FLOW RATE

**FOOTNOTES**

a. Resistances are representative values for dry materials and are intended as design (not specification) values for materials in normal use. Unless shown otherwise in descriptions of materials, all values are for 75°C mean temperature.

b. Includes paper backing and facing if any. In cases where insulation forms a boundary (highly reflective or otherwise) of an airspace, refer to appropriate table for the insulating value of the airspace. Some manufacturers of batt and blanket insulation mark their products with R value, but they can ensure only the quality of the material as shipped.

c. Average values only are given, since variations depend on density of the board and on the type, size, and depth of perforations.

d. Thicknesses supplied by different manufacturers may vary depending on the particular material.

e. Values will vary if density varies from that listed.

f. Data on rectangular core concrete blocks differ from the data for oval core blocks because of core configuration, different mean temperature, and different unit weight. Weight data on oval core blocks not available.

g. Weight of units approx. 7⅝ high by 15⅝ long are given to describe blocks tested. Values are for 1 sq ft area.

h. Thermal resistance of metals is so low that in building constructions it is usually ignored. Values shown emphasize relatively easy flow of heat along or through metals so that they are usually heat leaks, inward or outward.

i. Spaces of uniform thickness bounded by moderately smooth surfaces.

j. Values shown not applicable to interior installations of materials listed.

k. Winter is heat flow up; summer is heat flow down.

l. Based on area of opening, not on total surface area.

Based on data from ASHRAE Handbook of Fundamentals, 1977, Chapter 22.

## ENERGY ANALYSIS

An energy analysis can be accomplished by a variety of techniques: manual, graphic, calculator, microcomputer, and mainframe computer. The purpose of energy analysis is to evaluate mathematically the energy required to maintain the interior environment of proposed or existing buildings and their support systems. When estimating energy needs of a proposed or existing building, it is necessary to account for the energy use in each of the following categories:

1. Offsetting heat losses through the building envelope (heating).
2. Offsetting heat gains through the building envelope (cooling).
3. Heating or cooling ventilation air.
4. Offsetting or using heat gain from occupants, lights, and process loads.
5. Offsetting or using solar gain.
6. Energy required for lights and miscellaneous use.
7. Motor loads for air movement and energy transfer.
8. Heating domestic hot water.
9. Energy used to reheat and recool.
10. Energy for humidification and dehumidification.
11. Energy for vertical, horizontal movement of people.
12. Miscellaneous—convenience outlets, etc.
13. Food service.

With the wide range of energy analysis tools available, it is important to select the appropriate tool for each design stage. Less sophistication is needed in the early design stages than in the final stages. To obtain maximum benefit from energy analysis, the process should start in the early schematic design stages. Following is a possible energy analysis sequence.

### SCHEMATIC DESIGN PHASE

Calculated manually, graphically, or with simple computer programs, analysis in the schematic design phase should take into consideration building orientation and solar and daylighting impact on the energy required for heating, cooling, and lighting. The ideal analysis tool is a microcomputer program that permits the designer to incorporate more and more data about the building as the design progresses, without reentering previous data. Results of the schematic analysis should guide the designer in deciding on orientation, massing, and building configuration. The decision made in these early studies will have a major impact on optimum energy use in the final design.

### DESIGN DEVELOPMENT PHASE

As design decisions become final and construction materials are selected, the energy analysis should be upgraded. The analysis procedure should allow adjustments for daylighting and building mass. Operating, occupancy, lighting, and motor profiles should be accommodated. Also to be considered are mechanical equipment responses and ventilation loads. As a minimum, the analysis procedure should include a variable base degree hour or bin factor for weather data.

### CONSTRUCTION DOCUMENT PHASE

As the construction documents near completion, a more sophisticated analysis can be made. An hour-by-hour analysis can be made by a mainframe computer. The mechanical equipment can be modeled as it would respond to the hourly heating and cooling loads. Thus, energy wasted by mechanical systems is accounted for. Profiles of building operation, occupancy, lighting, etc. are adjusted to the final design, and the energy needs projection is close to that of the final building.

Energy analysis for existing buildings being modified or recycled can be done by any of the above procedures that track building operation, occupancy, lighting, ventilation, and motor profiles. This can be done by mainframe computers on an hour-by-hour analysis or by microcomputers using programs with a variable base degree hour or bin method of processing weather data. Existing buildings are easier to analyze than new buildings because operational profiles are known.

For an energy analysis to provide maximum benefit to the designer, the building's annual energy use should be broken down as in the example at right. As modifications are made, projected increase or decrease percentages should be shown.

| EXAMPLE OF TOTAL ANNUAL ENERGY USE BY FUEL TYPE | ENERGY USE PER YEAR | PERCENT OF TOTAL | REDUCTION IN ENERGY USE | PERCENT OF REDUCTION |
|---|---|---|---|---|
| **ELECTRICITY (In kilowatt hours)** | | | | |
| Cooling | 42,424 KWH | (16.3%) | −16,753 KWH | (28.3%) |
| Lighting | 150,573 KWH | (58.0%) | | |
| Motor operation | 58,829 KWH | (22.7%) | −21,598 KWH | (26.9%) |
| Miscellaneous power | 7,781 KWH | (3.0%) | | |
| TOTAL ELECTRICAL USE | 259,607 KWH | | −38,351 KWH | (12.9%) |
| | | | | |
| **NATURAL GAS (In thousands of square feet)** | | | | |
| Heating | 1,397 MCF | (84.8%) | −1,863 MCF | (57.1%) |
| Domestic water heating | 58 MCF | (3.5%) | | |
| Food service | 193 MCF | (11.7%) | | |
| TOTAL NATURAL GAS USE | 1,648 MCF | | −1,863 MCF | (53.1%) |
| **BREAKDOWN OF TOTAL ANNUAL ENERGY USE** | | | | |
| **HEATING (In millions of BTU)** | | | | |
| Roof loss | 877.8 MMBTU | (34.0%) | −719.0 MMBTU | (45.0%) |
| Wall loss | 127.1 MMBTU | (4.9%) | −104.1 MMBTU | (45.0%) |
| Window loss | 26.2 MMBTU | (1.0%) | −21.5 MMBTU | (45.0%) |
| Door loss | 115.2 MMBTU | (4.5%) | −94.3 MMBTU | (45.0%) |
| Slab Edge loss | 77.3 MMBTU | (3.0%) | −63.3 MMBTU | (45.0%) |
| Infiltration loss—doors | 166.2 MMBTU | (6.4%) | −136.2 MMBTU | (45.0%) |
| Ventilation loss | 0.1 MMBTU | (0.0%) | −812.9 MMBTU | (100.0%) |
| Morning warm-up | 49.1 MMBTU | (1.9%) | +32.7 MMBTU | (200.0%) |
| TOTAL | 1,439.1 MMBTU | (55.7%) | −1,918.4 MMBTU | (57.1%) |
| | | | | |
| **COOLING (In millions of BTU)** | | | | |
| Conduction solid surfaces | 13.9 MMBTU | (0.5%) | −1.4 MMBTU | (9.0%) |
| Conduction glazed surfaces | 2.9 MMBTU | (0.1%) | −0.3 MMBTU | (9.0%) |
| Solar gain | 27.8 MMBTU | (1.1%) | +0.3 MMBTU | (1.1%) |
| Ventilation gain | 0.1 MMBTU | (0.0%) | −55.8 MMBTU | (99.9%) |
| Lighting gain | 39.0 MMBTU | (1.5%) | +1.3 MMBTU | (3.4%) |
| Equipment gain | 4.1 MMBTU | (0.2%) | | |
| Occupant gain | 35.7 MMBTU | (1.4%) | +1.6 MMBTU | (4.7%) |
| Air handler gain | 21.4 MMBTU | (0.8%) | −2.8 MMBTU | (11.5%) |
| TOTAL | 144.8 MMBTU | (5.6%) | −57.2 MMBTU | (28.3%) |
| | | | | |
| **LIGHTING (In millions of BTU)** | 513.9 MMBTU | (19.9%) | | |
| | | | | |
| **MOTOR OPERATION (In millions of BTU)** | 200.8 MMBTU | (7.8%) | −73.7 MMBTU | (26.9%) |
| | | | | |
| **DOMESTIC WATER HEATING (In millions of BTU)** | 60.0 MMBTU | (2.3%) | | |
| | | | | |
| **MISCELLANEOUS USE (In millions of BTU)** | | | | |
| Convenience electric power | 26.6 MMBTU | (1.0%) | | |
| Food Service | 198.3 MMBTU | (7.7%) | | |
| TOTAL | 224.8 MMBTU | (8.7%) | | |
| | | | | |
| **TOTAL ANNUAL ENERGY USE (In millions of BTU)** | | | | |
| 70,147 BTU/per sq. ft. | 2,583.4 MMBTU | TOTAL | −2,049.3 MMBTU | (44.2%) |

## ANALYSIS PROCEDURE CAPABILITY AT VARIOUS DESIGN STAGES

| | | DESIGN STAGE | | |
|---|---|---|---|---|
| CONCEPT | ANALY-SIS MODE | SCHE-MATIC | DE-SIGN | CON-STRUC-TION |
| Orientation | M,G,MC | X | X | X |
| Solar | M,G,MC | X | X | X |
| Daylighting | M,G,MC | X | X | X |
| Configuration | G | X | X | X |
| Mass | MC | | X | X |
| Oper. profiles | M,MC | | X | X |
| Occup. profiles | M,MC | | X | X |
| Light. profiles | M,MC | | X | X |
| Motor profiles | M,MC | | X | X |
| Mech. response | MC,MF | | | X |
| Hourly analysis | MF | | | |

M = Manual       MC = Microcomputer
G = Graph        MF = Mainframe

## COMPONENTS OF ENERGY USE IN BUILDING

| | ENERGY LOADS | | | |
|---|---|---|---|---|
| COMPONENT | HEAT-ING ENERGY | COOL-ING ENERGY | OTHER ENERGY | IM-PACT TOTAL |
| Building envelope | + | + | | + |
| Solar gain | − | + | | + or − |
| Ventilation | + | + | | + |
| Occupants | − | + | | + or − |
| Lights | − | + | + | + |
| Motors | − | + | + | |
| Domestic hot water | 0 | 0 | + | + |
| Reheat | + | 0 | | + |
| Recool | 0 | + | | + |
| Humidification | + | 0 | | + |
| Dehumidification | | + | | + |
| Vertical and horizontal movement of people | 0 | 0 | + | + |

+   Add to load
−   Reduces load
0   Has no impact

Huber H. Buehrer, AIA, PE; Buehrer Group; Maumee, Ohio

# WINDOW DETAILING

Energy characteristics of building glazing primarily are transmission of solar heat and light and thermal resistance. Solar heat gain through glass is calculated by adding solar heat gains to conductive heat gains or losses, and multiplied by the glazing area, expressed as:

$Q = A(SC \times SHGF + U(t_o - t_i)$

$Q$ = Glazing heat gain

$A$ = Area of glazing

$SC$ = Shading Coefficient

$SHGF$ = Solar Heat Gain Factors

$U$ = Inverse of the thermal resistance (R-Value)

$T_o$ = Temperature outside

$T_i$ = Temperature inside

The shading coefficient and U-values of fenestration types vary significantly. Solar heat gain is dependent on geographic orientation, latitude, date, and time of day. Values for solar heat gain factors are in the ASHRAE Handbook of Fundamentals. Climate and building type are important, especially the shading coefficient and the U-value, in selecting the glazing. In cold climates where there is little internal heat gain, high shading coefficients and low winter U-values provide solar heating variables. In hot climates, buildings that have high internal loads, low shading coefficients, and low summer U-values help provide cooling solutions. Selecting the proper glazing can be extremely complex when evaluating all variables that affect annual energy performance (use and peak loads).

In addition to thermal considerations, glazing can reduce internal loads by using daylight to reduce electric light loads, providing significant savings in buildings with high lighting loads. At the same time, glazing can reduce cooling loads caused by internal heat gain of electric lights.

Choosing glazing for specific climates, building types, occupancy uses, orientations, and applications can provide many options for designers. The following table summarizes glazing performance characteristics of daylight transmittance, U-values (summer and winter), shading coefficients, and relative heat gains. Refer to manufacturers' literature for further information.

## GLAZING PERFORMANCE CHARACTERISTICS

| GLASS TYPE | GLASS THICKNESS (INCHES) | UNIT THICKNESS | DAYLIGHT TRANSMITTANCE (%) | WINTER NIGHTTIME U-VALUE/R-VALUE | SUMMER DAYTIME U-VALUE/R-VALUE | SHADING COEFFICIENT | RELATIVE HEAT GAIN |
|---|---|---|---|---|---|---|---|
| **CLEAR** | | | | | | | |
| Clear Single Glass | 1/8 | | | | | | |
| Clear Single Glass | 1/4 | | 89 | 1.3/0.88 | 1.04/0.96 | .95 | 204 |
| Clear Single Glass | 1/2 | | 86 | 1.09/0.92 | 1.03/0.97 | .86 | 186 |
| Clear Double Glass | 1/8 | 1 | 82 | .49/ | .52/ | .89 | 186 |
| Clear Double Glass | 1/4 | 1 | 80 | .49/2.04 | .56/1.79 | .82 | 171 |
| Clear Double Glass with Low-e Film | 1/4 | | 72 | .31/3.23 | .32-.33/3.03-3.13 | .66-.73 | 138-150 |
| Clear Triple Glass | 1/8 | 1 | 74 | .36/ | .42/ | .81 | 167 |
| Clear Triple Glass | 1/4 | 1-1/4 | 72 | .39 | .45/ | .72 | 151 |
| Clear Insulating Glass with Suspended Low-e Film | 1/4 | opt. | 69 | .23/4.3 | .37/2.7 | .66 | 137 |
| Clear Insulating Glass with Suspended Low-e Film | 1/4 | opt. | 54 | .22/4.5 | .36/2.8 | .48 | 101 |
| Clear Insulating Glass with Suspended Low-e Film | 1/4 | opt. | 37 | .21/4.8 | .35/2.8 | .34 | 73 |
| **BROWN** | | | | | | | |
| Light Brown Single Glass | 1/4 | | 52 | 1.13/0.88 | 1.10/0.91 | .71 | 157 |
| Dark Brown Single Glass | 1/4 | | 5-21 | .89-1.13/.88-1.12 | .89-1.13/.88-1.12 | .27-.51 | 66-119 |
| Double Glass Light Brown/Clear | 1/4 | | 42-47 | .31-.48/2.04-3.23 | .33-.57/1.75-3.23 | .49-.57 | 102-122 |
| Double Glass Dark Brown/Clear | 1/4 | | 5-19 | .41-.49/2.04-2.44 | .47-.58/1.72-2.13 | .16-.38 | 38-85 |
| Double Glass Light Brown/Clear with Low-e Film | 1/4 | | 42 | .31/3.23 | .33/3.23 | .49 | 102 |
| Insulating Glass Light Brown/Clear | 1/4 | | 54 | .23/4.3 | .31/3.2 | .57 | 118 |
| Insulating Glass Dark Brown/Clear | 1/4 | | 31 | .22/4.5 | .36/2.8 | .33 | 71 |
| Insulating Glass Light Brown/Clear with Suspended Low-e Film | 1/4 | | 22 | .21/4.8 | .35/2.8 | .25 | 55 |
| **GREEN** | | | | | | | |
| Light Green Single Glass | 1/4 | | 75 | 1.13/0.88 | 1.10/0.91 | .69 | 154 |
| Blue Green Single Glass | 1/4 | | 18-27 | 0.96-0.99/1.01-1.04 | 0.99-1.02/0.98-1.01 | .35-.41 | 84-96 |
| Dark Green Single Glass | 1/4 | | 7-16 | 0.88-0.95/1.05-1.14 | 0.89-0.98/1.02-1.12 | .26-.35 | 64-83 |
| Double Glass Light Green/Clear | 1/4 | | 67 | 0.49-0.50/2.0-2.04 | 0.57-0.59/1.70-1.75 | .55-.57 | 118-122 |
| Double Glass Blue Green/Clear | 1/4 | | 17-24 | 0.44-0.45/2.22-2.27 | 0.52-0.54/1.85-1.92 | .22-.28 | 53-64 |
| Double Glass Dark Green/Clear | 1/4 | | 6-10 | 0.40-0.42/2.38-2.50 | 0.47-0.50/2.00-2.13 | .15-.19 | 38-45 |
| Double Glass Light Green/Clear with Low-e Film | 1/4 | | 61 | 0.31/3.23 | 0.33/3.03 | .34 | 92 |
| Insulating Glass Light Green with Suspended Low-e Film | 1/4 | | 58 | 0.23/4.3 | 0.37/2.7 | .47 | 99 |
| Insulating Glass Dark Green with Suspended Low-e Film | 1/4 | | 45 | 0.22/4.5 | 0.36/2.8 | .39 | 83 |
| **BLUE** | | | | | | | |
| Blue Single Glass | 1/4 | | | | | | |
| Dark Blue Single Glass | 1/4 | | 21-30 | 0.97-0.99/1.01-1.03 | 0.97-0.99/1.01-1.03 | .36-.46 | 87-105 |
| Double Glass Blue/Clear | 1/4 | | 51 | 0.50/2.0 | 0.59/1.7 | .58 | 124 |
| Double Glass Dark Blue/Clear | 1/4 | | 19-27 | 0.44-0.45/2.22-2.27 | 0.51-0.53/1.89-1.96 | .26-.34 | 59-76 |
| Double Glass Blue Clear with Low-e Film | 1/4 | | | | | | |
| Insulating Glass Blue with Suspended Low-e Film | 1/4 | | 44 | .23/4.3 | .37/2.7 | .46 | 97 |
| Insulating Glass Blue with Suspended Low-e Film | 1/4 | | 34 | .22/4.5 | .36/2.8 | .35 | 75 |
| Insulating Glass Blue with Suspended Low-e Film | 1/4 | | 24 | .21/4.8 | .35/2.8 | .27 | 59 |
| **GRAY** | | | | | | | |
| Light Gray Single Glass | 1/4 | | 41 | 1.13/0.88 | 1.10/0.91 | .69 | 154 |
| Dark Gray Single Glass | 1/4 | | 4-10 | 0.88-0.96/1.04-1.14 | 0.09-.99/1.01-1.71 | .27-.35 | 66-84 |
| Double Glass Light Gray/Clear | 1/4 | | 37 | 0.49-0.50/2.0-2.04 | 0.57-0.59/1.70-1.75 | .55-.56 | 118-120 |
| Double Glass Dark Gray/Clear | 1/4 | | 4-9 | 0.41-0.44/2.27-2.44 | 0.48-0.52/1.92-2.13 | .16-.23 | 38-52 |
| Double Glass Light Gray/Clear with Low-e Film | 1/4 | | 33 | 0.31/3.23 | 0.33/3.03 | .44 | 92 |
| Insulating Glass Light Gray with Suspended Low-e Film | 1/4 | | 32 | 0.23/4.3 | 0.37/2.7 | .42 | 89 |
| Insulating Glass Dark Gray with Suspended Low-e Film | 1/4 | | 25 | 0.22/4.5 | 0.36/2.8 | .30 | 65 |
| Insulating Glass with Suspended Low-e | 1/4 | | 17 | 0.21/4.8 | 0.35/2.8 | .23 | 51 |
| **BLACK** | | | | | | | |
| Black Single Glass | 1/4 | | 14 | 1.13/0.88 | 1.11/0.90 | .65 | 146 |
| Double Glass Black/Clear | 1/4 | | 13 | 0.49/2.04 | 0.58/1.72 | .51 | 110 |
| Insulating Glass Black with Suspended Low-e | 1/4 | | 6-8 | .21-.22/4.5-4.8 | .35-.36/2.8 | .16-.22 | 37-49 |

Gregory Franta, AIA; Denver, Colorado

## SOLAR GAINS THROUGH SUNLIT FENESTRATION

Heat gains through sunlit fenestration constitute major sources of cooling load in summer. In winter, discomfort is often caused by excessive amounts of solar radiation entering through south facing windows. By contrast, passive solar design depends largely on admission and storage of the radiant energy falling on south facing and horizontal surfaces. Admission takes place both by transmission through glazing and by inward flow of absorbed energy. With or without the sun, heat flows through glazing, either inwardly or outwardly, whenever there is a temperature difference between the indoor and outdoor air. These heat flows may be calculated in the following manner.

The solar heat gain is estimated by a two-step process. The first step is to find, either from tabulated data or by calculation, the rate at which solar heat would be admitted under the designated conditions through a single square foot of double strength ($1/8$ in.) clear sheet glass. This quantity, called the solar heat gain factor (SHGF), is set by (a) the local latitude; (b) the date, hence the declination; (c) the time of day (solar time should be used); (d) the orientation of the window.

Tabulated values of SHGF are given in the 1981 ASHRAE Handbook of Fundamentals, Chapter 27, for latitudes from $0°$ (the equator) to $64°$ N by $8°$ increments and for orientations around the compass from N to NNW, by $22.5°$ increments. Selected values from the $40°$ table are given in an adjacent column.

Each individual fenestration system, consisting of glazing and shading devices, has a unique ability to admit solar heat. This property is evaluated in terms of its shading coefficient (SC), which is the ratio of the amount of solar heat admitted by the system under consideration to the solar heat gain factor for the same conditions. In equation form, this becomes:

$$\text{solar heat gain (Btu/sq ft} \cdot \text{hr)} = SC \times SHGF$$

Values of the shading coefficient are given in Chapter 27 of the 1981 ASHRAE Handbook of Fundamentals for the most widely used glazing materials alone and in combination with internal and external shading devices. Selected values for single and double glazing are given below:

## SHADING COEFFICIENT FOR SELECTED GLAZING SYSTEMS

| TYPE OF GLASS | SOLAR TRANS-MISSION | SHADING COEFFICIENT, SC |
|---|---|---|
| Clear | | |
| $1/8$ in. | 0.86 | 1.00 |
| $1/4$ in. | 0.78 | 0.94 |
| Heat absorbing | | |
| $1/8$ in. | 0.64 | 0.83 |
| $1/4$ in. | 0.46 | 0.69 |
| Insulating glass, clear both lights | | |
| $1/8 + 1/8$ in. | 0.71 | 0.88 |
| $1/4 + 1/4$ in. | 0.61 | 0.81 |
| Heat absorbing out Clear in, $1/4$ in. | 0.36 | 0.55 |

For combinations of glazing and shading devices, see the ASHRAE chapter cited above.

The heat flow due to temperature difference is found by multiplying the U-value for the specified fenestration system by the area involved and by the applicable temperature difference:

$$Q = A \times [SC \times SHGF + U \times (t_o - t_i)]$$

The same equation is used for both summer and winter, with appropriate U-values, but in winter the conduction heat flow is usually outward because the outdoor air is colder than the indoor air.

**Example:** find the total heat gain, in Btu/sq ft · hr, for 1000 sq ft of unshaded $1/4$ in. heat absorbing single glass, facing west, in Denver ($40°$N latitude) at 4:00 P.M. solar time on October 21. Indoor air temperature is $70°$F; outdoor air temperature is $40°$F.

**Solution:** from the accompanying table, for 4:00 P.M. on October 21 find the SHGF for west facing fenestration on October 21 to be 173 Btu/sq ft · hr. For $1/4$ in. heat absorbing glass, SC = 0.69 and U for winter conditions is 1.10 Btu/sq ft · hr · °F.

$$Q = 1000 \times [0.69 \times 173 + 1.10 \times (40 - 70)]$$
$$= 1000 \times (119.4 - 33.0) = 86,400 \text{ Btu/hr}$$

Even though the outdoor air is $30°$ cooler than the indoor air, the net heat gain through the window in question would be equivalent to 7.2 tons of refrigeration.

For the same window area in summer, on August 21 at 4:00 P.M. solar time, SHGF = 216, and the air temperatures may be taken as $95°$F outdoors and $78°$F indoors. The total heat gain will be:

$$Q = 1000 \times [0.69 \times 216 + 1.04 \times (95 - 78)]$$
$$= 1000 \times (149.0 + 17.7) = 166,700 \text{ Btu/hr}$$
$$= 13.9 \text{ tons of refrigeration}$$

The cooling load can be reduced by selecting a fenestration system with lower shading coefficient and U-value. Under the same conditions, a double glazed window with two lights of $1/4$ in. clear glass and a highly reflective translucent inner shading device would have U = 0.52 and SC = 0.37. The cooling load would then be reduced to 88,760 Btu/hr or 7.4 tons of refrigeration.

## SOL-AIR TEMPERATURE

When the opaque surfaces of a structure are struck by solar radiation, much of the energy is absorbed by the irradiated surface, raising its temperature and increasing the rate of heat flow into the roof or wall. The time lag between the onset of irradiation and the resulting rise in the indoor surface temperature depends on the thickness and mass per unit area of the building element and on the thermal conductivity, specific heat, and density of the materials. The time lag is negligible for an uninsulated metal roof, but it can be a matter of hours for a massive concrete or masonry wall.

Heat flow through sunlit opaque building elements is estimated by using the sol-air temperature, $t_{sa}$, defined as an imaginary outdoor temperature that, in the absence of sunshine, would give the same rate of heat flow as actually exists at the specified time under the combined influence of the incident solar radiation and the ambient air temperature.

$$t_{sa} = I \times \text{Abs.}/h_o$$

where I = solar irradiance (Btu/sq ft · hr)

Abs. = surface absorptance, dimensionless

$h_o$ = outer surface coefficient (Btu/sq ft · hr · °F)

Surface absorptances range from as low as 0.30 for a white surface to 0.95 for a black built-up roof. Values of $h_o$ range from the conventional 4.0 for summer with an assumed wind speed of 7.5 mph to a still air value of 3.0.

**Example:** find the rate of heat flow through a 1000 sq ft uninsulated black built-up roof, U = 0.3, under strong summer sunshine, I = 300 Btu/sq ft · hr, still air with $100°$F outdoors, $78°$F indoors.

**Solution:** the sol-air temperature is found from

$$t_{sa} = 300 \times \frac{0.95}{3.0} + 100 = 195°F$$

The rate of heat flow, neglecting the time lag, is

$$Q = 1000 \times 0.3 \times (195 - 78) = 35,100 \text{ Btu/hr}$$

With no sunshine on the roof, the heat flow is

$$\text{heat flow} = 1000 \times 0.3 \times (100 - 78) = 6600 \text{ Btu/hr}$$

The effect of the solar radiation is thus to increase the heat flow rate by 88%. A more massive roof with a lower U-value would show considerably less effect of the incoming solar radiation.

## SOLAR INTENSITY AND SOLAR HEAT GAIN FACTORS FOR 40°N LATITUDE

| DATE | SOLAR TIME (A.M.) | DIRECT NORMAL (BTUH/SQ FT) | SOLAR HEAT GAIN FACTORS (BTUH/SQ FT) | | | | | SOLAR TIME (P.M.) |
|---|---|---|---|---|---|---|---|---|
| | | | N | E | S | W | HOR | |
| Jan 21 | 8 | 142 | 5 | 111 | 75 | 5 | 14 | 4 |
| | 10 | 274 | 16 | 124 | 213 | 16 | 96 | 2 |
| | 12 | 294 | 20 | 21 | 254 | 21 | 133 | 12 |
| Feb 21 | 8 | 219 | 10 | 183 | 94 | 10 | 43 | 4 |
| | 10 | 294 | 21 | 143 | 203 | 21 | 143 | 2 |
| | 12 | 307 | 24 | 25 | 241 | 25 | 180 | 12 |
| Mar 21 | 8 | 250 | 16 | 218 | 74 | 16 | 85 | 4 |
| | 10 | 297 | 25 | 153 | 171 | 25 | 186 | 2 |
| | 12 | 307 | 29 | 31 | 206 | 31 | 223 | 12 |
| Apr 21 | 6 | 89 | 11 | 88 | 5 | 5 | 11 | 6 |
| | 8 | 252 | 22 | 224 | 41 | 21 | 123 | 4 |
| | 10 | 286 | 31 | 152 | 121 | 31 | 217 | 2 |
| | 12 | 293 | 34 | 36 | 154 | 36 | 252 | 12 |
| May 21 | 6 | 144 | 36 | 141 | 10 | 10 | 31 | 6 |
| | 8 | 250 | 27 | 220 | 29 | 25 | 146 | 4 |
| | 10 | 277 | 34 | 148 | 83 | 34 | 234 | 2 |
| | 12 | 284 | 37 | 40 | 113 | 40 | 265 | 12 |
| June 21 | 6 | 155 | 48 | 151 | 13 | 13 | 40 | 6 |
| | 8 | 246 | 30 | 216 | 29 | 27 | 153 | 4 |
| | 10 | 272 | 35 | 145 | 69 | 35 | 238 | 2 |
| | 12 | 279 | 38 | 41 | 95 | 41 | 267 | 12 |
| Jul 21 | 6 | 138 | 37 | 137 | 11 | 11 | 32 | 6 |
| | 8 | 241 | 28 | 216 | 30 | 26 | 145 | 4 |
| | 10 | 269 | 35 | 146 | 81 | 35 | 231 | 2 |
| | 12 | 276 | 38 | 41 | 109 | 41 | 262 | 12 |
| Aug 21 | 6 | 81 | 12 | 82 | 6 | 5 | 12 | 6 |
| | 8 | 237 | 24 | 216 | 41 | 23 | 122 | 4 |
| | 10 | 272 | 32 | 150 | 116 | 32 | 214 | 2 |
| | 12 | 280 | 35 | 38 | 149 | 38 | 247 | 12 |
| Sep 21 | 8 | 230 | 17 | 205 | 71 | 17 | 82 | 4 |
| | 10 | 280 | 27 | 148 | 165 | 27 | 180 | 2 |
| | 12 | 290 | 30 | 32 | 200 | 32 | 215 | 12 |
| Oct 21 | 8 | 204 | 11 | 173 | 89 | 11 | 43 | 4 |
| | 10 | 280 | 21 | 139 | 196 | 21 | 140 | 2 |
| | 12 | 294 | 25 | 27 | 234 | 27 | 177 | 12 |
| Nov 21 | 8 | 136 | 5 | 108 | 72 | 5 | 14 | 4 |
| | 10 | 268 | 16 | 122 | 209 | 16 | 96 | 2 |
| | 12 | 288 | 20 | 21 | 250 | 21 | 132 | 12 |
| Dec 21 | 8 | 89 | 3 | 67 | 50 | 3 | 6 | 4 |
| | 10 | 261 | 14 | 113 | 146 | 14 | 77 | 2 |
| | 12 | 285 | 18 | 19 | 253 | 19 | 113 | 12 |
| | | | N | W | S | E | HOR | PM |

John I. Yellott, P.E., Professor Emeritus; College of Architecture, Arizona State University; Tempe, Arizona

# 18 THERMAL TRANSMISSION

## GLASS, GLASS BLOCK AND PLASTIC SHEET

| MATERIAL AND DESCRIPTION | OVERALL HEAT TRANSMISSION COEFFICIENT (U) | SEASONS | RESISTANCE (R) |
|---|---|---|---|
| **VERTICAL PANELS—EXTERIOR** | | | |
| Flat Glass | | | |
| Single glass | 1.10 | Winter | 0.91 |
| | 1.04 | Summer | 0.96 |
| Insulating glass, two lights of glass | | | |
| 3/16 in. airspace | 0.62 | Winter | 1.61 |
| | 0.65 | Summer | 1.54 |
| 1/4 in. airspace | 0.58 | Winter | 1.72 |
| | 0.61 | Summer | 1.64 |
| 1/2 in. airspace | 0.49 | Winter | 2.04 |
| | 0.56 | Summer | 1.79 |
| Insulating glass, three lights of glass | | | |
| 1/4 in. airspaces | 0.39 | Winter | 2.56 |
| | 0.44 | Summer | 2.22 |
| 1/2 in. airspaces | 0.31 | Winter | 3.23 |
| | 0.39 | Summer | 2.56 |
| 1/2 in. airspaces, low emittance coating | | | |
| e = 0.20 | 0.32 | Winter | 3.13 |
| | 0.38 | Summer | 2.63 |
| e = 0.40 | 0.38 | Winter | 2.63 |
| | 0.45 | Summer | 2.22 |
| e = 0.60 | 0.43 | Winter | 2.33 |
| | 0.51 | Summer | 1.96 |
| Storm windows | | | |
| 1–4 in. airspace | 0.50 | Winter | 2.00 |
| | 0.50 | Summer | 2.00 |
| Glass Block | | | |
| 6 x 6 x 4 in. thick (nom.) | 0.60 | Winter | 1.67 |
| | 0.57 | Summer | 1.76 |
| 8 x 8 x 4 in. thick (nom.) | 0.56 | Winter | 1.79 |
| | 0.54 | Summer | 1.85 |
| With cavity divider | 0.48 | Winter | 2.08 |
| | 0.46 | Summer | 2.17 |
| 12 x 12 x 4 in. thick (nom.) | 0.52 | Winter | 1.92 |
| | 0.50 | Summer | 2.00 |
| With cavity divider | 0.44 | Winter | 2.27 |
| | 0.42 | Summer | 2.38 |
| 12 x 12 x 2 in. thick (nom.) | 0.60 | Winter | 1.67 |
| | 0.57 | Summer | 1.76 |
| Single Plastic Sheet | | | |
| 1/8 in. thick (nom.) | 1.06 | Winter | 0.94 |
| | 0.98 | Summer | 1.02 |
| 1/4 in. thick (nom.) | 0.96 | Winter | 1.04 |
| | 0.89 | Summer | 1.12 |
| **HORIZONTAL PANELS—EXTERIOR** | | | |
| Flat Glass | | | |
| Single glass | 1.23 | Winter | 0.81 |
| | 0.83 | Summer | 1.20 |
| Insulating glass, two lights of glass | | | |
| 3/16 in. airspace | 0.70 | Winter | 1.43 |
| | 0.57 | Summer | 1.75 |
| 1/4 in. airspace | 0.65 | Winter | 1.54 |
| | 0.54 | Summer | 1.85 |
| 1/2 in. airspace | 0.59 | Winter | 1.69 |
| | 0.49 | Summer | 2.04 |
| Glass Block | | | |
| 11 x 11 x 3 in. thick with cavity divider | 0.53 | Winter | 1.89 |
| | 0.35 | Summer | 2.86 |
| 12 x 12 x 4 in. thick with cavity divider | 0.51 | Winter | 1.96 |
| | 0.34 | Summer | 2.94 |
| Plastic Bubbles[k] | | | |
| Single walled | 1.15 | Winter | 0.87 |
| | 0.80 | Summer | 1.25 |
| Double walled | 0.70 | Winter | 1.43 |
| | 0.46 | Summer | 2.17 |

John I. Yellott, P.E.; College of Architecture, Arizona State University; Tempe, Arizona

## NOTES

The thermal conductivity of glass is relatively high (k = 7.5), and, for single glazing, most of the thermal resistance is imposed at the indoor and outdoor surfaces. Indoors, approximately two-thirds of the heat flows by radiation to the room surfaces and only one-third flows by convection. This can be materially affected by the use of forced airflow from induction units, for example. The inner surface coefficient of heat transfer, $h_i$, can be substantially reduced by applying a low emittance metallic film to the glass.

For glazing with airspaces, the U value can be reduced to a marked degree by the use of low emittance films. This process imparts a variable degree of reflectance to the glass, thereby reducing its Shading Coefficient. Manufacturers' literature should be consulted for more details on this important subject. Also consult Chapter 27 of the 1981 ASHRAE Handbook of Fundamentals.

## FOOTNOTES

a. Resistances are representative values for dry materials and are intended as design (not specification) values for materials in normal use. Unless shown otherwise in descriptions of materials, all values are for 75°C mean temperature.

b. Includes paper backing and facing if any. In cases where insulation forms a boundary (highly reflective or otherwise) of an airspace, refer to appropriate table for the insulating value of the airspace. Some manufacturers of batt and blanket insulation mark their products with R value, but they can ensure only the quality of the material as shipped.

c. Average values only are given, since variations depend on density of the board and on the type, size, and depth of perforations.

d. Thicknesses supplied by different manufacturers may vary depending on the particular material.

e. Values will vary if density varies from that listed.

f. Data on rectangular core concrete blocks differ from the data for oval core blocks because of core configuration, different mean temperature, and different unit weight. Weight data on oval core blocks not available.

g. Weight of units approx. 7⅝ high by 15⅝ long are given to describe blocks tested. Values are for 1 sq ft area.

h. Thermal resistance of metals is so low that in building constructions it is usually ignored. Values shown emphasize relatively easy flow of heat along or through metals so that they are usually heat leaks, inward or outward.

i. Spaces of uniform thickness bounded by moderately smooth surfaces.

j. Values shown not applicable to interior installations of materials listed.

k. Winter is heat flow up; summer is heat flow down.

l. Based on area of opening, not on total surface area.

Based on data from ASHRAE Handbook of Fundamentals, 1977, Chapter 22.

## COEFFICIENT OF HEAT TRANSMISSION

Calculations of heating and cooling loads are based on the rate of heat flow through building sections along with ventilation and moisture requirements. The symbol U designates the overall coefficient of heat transmission for any section of building shell. The units for U are Btu's per square foot of building section per hour per °F temperature difference between inside and outside air (Btu/sq ft · hr · °F).

U-values of composite building sections are calculated by first determining the individual conductivities (k) or conductances (C) of each material comprising the section. The conductivity of a homogeneous material is measured as Btu's per square foot per hour per °F temperature difference per inch thickness of the material. The reciprocal, R, is the thermal resistivity. The resistance of any thickness of a material is its resistivity per inch times its total thickness. Nonhomogeneous materials such as concrete masonry units are given conductance and resistance values for their standard thicknesses. In calculating the overall U-coefficients only the resistances are used. The sum is taken of the resistance values of all the materials in the section plus the resistance values of the inside and outside surface films to yield an overall R-value. The reciprocal, 1/R equals the U-coefficient.

## FACTORS AFFECTING INSULATION PERFORMANCE

The most serious factor affecting the performance of building insulation is the presence of water. While the effect of moisture is not too serious when moisture exists in the vapor phase, the conductivity is greatly increased by the presence of condensed moisture. Water or ice in insulation will impair or destroy the insulating value; it may cause deterioration of the insulation or eventual structural damage by rot, corrosion, or the expansion action of freezing water. Whether or not moisture accumulates within the insulation depends on the operating temperatures, ambient conditions, and the effectiveness of water vapor barriers in relation to other vapor resistances within the composite structure.

The moisture resistance depends on the basic material of the insulation and the type of physical structure. Most insulations are hygroscopic and will gain or lose moisture in proportion to the relative humidity of the air in contact with the insulation. Fibrous and granular insulations permit transmission of water vapor to the colder side of the structure. A vapor barrier should, therefore, be used with the materials and installed on the warm side where moisture transmission is a factor. Certain insulations with a closed cellular structure are relatively impervious to water and water vapor. Often, these materials are marketed as rigid boards and installed on the outside of stud work as sheathing. To avoid moisture accumulation, in this application their vapor permeance should be at least five times that of the interior vapor barrier, or they should be modified by perforations or venting along their joints to allow water vapor to escape.

Conductivity also varies with density. A change in density due to the degree of compaction of fibrous or granular types of insulation increases conductivity. For fibrous types, minimum conductivity is ideally obtained when fibers are uniformly spaced and are perpendicular to the direction of heat flow. Other factors such as the diameter of the fiber or the amount of binder that influence the bond or contact of the fiber may also affect conductivity.

For cellular insulation a specific combination of cell size and density will produce an optimum thermal conductivity. The type of gas trapped in the cells also affects conductivity. Flourocarbon gas, having a lower conductivity than air, is used to expand rigid urethane to maximize its thermal resistance. Unless encased in a gas impermeable membrane, urethane conductivities usually increase over time as oxygen and nitrogen seep into the cell structure and the flourocarbon gas diffuses out.

## THE IMPORTANCE OF PROPER DESIGN AND INSTALLATION

To perform at maximum efficiency, insulation systems must be properly designed and their installation closely supervised. Vapor barriers must be properly located in the wall section and carefully placed to fully cover all areas. Edges should be sealed and joints overlapped. Attachment by glueing instead of stapling should be practiced if possible because the effectiveness of vapor barriers may be greatly reduced if openings, even very small ones, exist in the barrier.

Low density fibrous and loose fill insulations, though widely used, are most susceptible to increased heat transfer by improper installation. If batts or granular materials are compacted, conductivities increase because of higher densities. These types of insulations should also completely fill the space between studs or rafters to prevent convective air currents and infiltration. The performance of fibrous batts installed vertically with airspaces on either side is seriously impaired because of the air interchange between the two voids. Special attention should also be given to the sources of greatest heat loss. Insulating and sealing window frames, wall plates at foundations, and electrical outlets along perimeter walls is crucial for reducing air infiltration. The perimeter of the floor joist system in frame construction, ordinarily overlooked, should be detailed to allow space for application of insulation along its length.

## ECONOMIC THICKNESS

The cost of lost energy is directly related to the rate of heat transfer through the insulation and the dollar value of that energy. As shown in the figure, the cost of lost energy decreases as insulation thickness increases. Since the optimal economic thickness is the lowest total cost of lost energy plus the installed insulation over the life of the insulation, these two costs must be compared on similar terms. Either the cost of insulation must be annualized and compared to the average annual cost of the lost energy, or the cost of the energy lost each year must be expressed in present dollars and compared to the annual cost of the insulation investment.

The economic thickness will be affected by the length of time over which the insulation cost is annualized. With the life cycle-cost method the economic thickness is usually greatest because the fuel savings that would accrue over the many years the insulation is in service can be used to pay for the most insulation (i.e., the payback period = the life cycle). If a shorter payback is required for the insulation, this maximum life cycle economic thickness becomes thinner because there are fewer years of energy savings allotted to pay for the insulation.

The annualized cost of installed insulation must be adjusted for the cost of money that can be a discount rate including the desired rate of return on the insulation investment. Cost of maintenance should also be included in the annual costs.

The cost of fuel including efficiency conversion plus the expected yearly price escalation above the inflation rate or the average cost of fuel over the life cycle or payback period should be forecast as accurately as possible before calculating economic thickness.

## MATERIAL PROPERTIES OF COMMON BUILDING INSULATION

| BUILDING INSULATIONS | DENSITY (LB/CU FT) | RESISTANCE (R) (HR/SQ FT · °F · BTU PER 1 IN. THICKNESS) | WATER VAPOR PERMEABILITY (PERM-IN.) | WATER ABSORPTION (% BY WEIGHT) | SURFACE BURNING CHARACTERISTICS — FLAME SPREAD | SURFACE BURNING CHARACTERISTICS — SMOKE DEVELOPED | TOXICITY | EFFECTS OF AGING — DIMENSIONAL STABILITY | DEGRADATION DUE TO — TEMPERATURE | DEGRADATION DUE TO — MOISTURE | DEGRADATION DUE TO — FUNGAL OR BACTERIAL GROWTH | DEGRADATION DUE TO — WEATHERING | CORROSIVENESS |
|---|---|---|---|---|---|---|---|---|---|---|---|---|---|
| Fiberglass (batts and blankets) | 0.6–1.0 | 3.14 to 3.5 | 100 | 1% | 5–20 | 0–50 | Some fumes if burned | None | OK below 450°F | None | None | None | None |
| Rock or slag wool | 1.5–2.5 | 3.2–3.7 | 100 | 2% | 5–20 | 0–20 | None | None | None | Transient | None | None | None |
| Cellulose | 2.2–3.0 | 3.2–3.7 | High | 5–20% | 15–40 | 0–45 | CO if burned | Settles 0–20% | None | ? | Maybe | ? | Steel Aluminum Copper |
| Molded polystyrene | 0.8–2.0 | 3.8–4.4 | 1.2–3.0 | 4%[1] | 5–25 | 10–400 | CO if burned | None | If above 165°F | None | None | UV degrades | None |
| Extruded polystyrene | 0.8–2.0 | 3.8–4.4 | 1.2–3.0 | 0.7% | 5–25 | 10–400 | CO if burned | None | If above 165°F | None | None | UV degrades | None |
| Polyurethane | 2.0 | 5.8–6.2[2] | 2–3 | Negligible | 30–50 | 155–200 | CO if burned | 0–12% change | If above 250°F | ? | None | None | None |
| Polyisocyanurate | 2.0 | 5.8–6.2[2] | 2–3 | Negligible | 25 | 55–200 | CO if burned | 0–12% change | If above 250°F | ? | None | None | None |
| Perlite (loose fill) | 2–11 | 2.5–3.7 | High | Low | 0 | 0 | None | None | If above 1200°F | None | None | None | None |
| Vermiculite (loose fill) | 4–10 | 2.4–3.0 | High | None | 0 | 0 | None | None | If above 1000°F | None | None | None | None |
| Insulating concrete | 12–88 | 0.85[4]/1.2[5] | Varies with density | ? | 0 | 0 | None | None | If above 1000°C | None | None | Below 30#/ft[3] | None |

NOTES
1. By volume.
2. Aged unfaced or spray applied.
3. At 60% rh, 65°F.
4. At 40 lb/cu ft.
5. At 25 lb/cu ft.

David F. Hill; Burt Hill Kosar Rittelmann Associates; Butler, Pennsylvania

## THERMAL INSULATION

Thermal insulation controls heat flow under temperatures ranging from absolute zero to 3000°F. This broad range can be subdivided into four general temperature regimes that classify applications for various types of insulation:

1. LOW TEMPERATURES: Insulation for vessels containing cryogenic materials, such as liquefied natural gas.
2. AMBIENT TEMPERATURES: Insulation for building structures.
3. MEDIUM TEMPERATURES: Insulation for tanks, pipes, and equipment in industrial process heat applications.
4. HIGH TEMPERATURES: Refractory or other specialized insulation materials used in foundry work, nuclear power facilities, the aerospace industry, and so on.

Architects and builders are generally concerned with the design and material performance of building insulations that operate within ambient temperature limits. As temperatures range much above or below ambient conditions, design and performance requirements change and must be matched with insulation materials that withstand the stress introduced by extreme temperatures, large temperature differentials, and thermal cycling.

## BUILDING INSULATION—THERMAL FUNCTIONS

The two major functions of building insulations are to (1) control temperatures of inside surfaces that affect the comfort of occupants and aid or deter condensation and (2) conserve energy by reducing heat transmission through building sections that determine the energy requirements for both heating and cooling. Economics in fuel consumption can be calculated with reasonable accuracy and balanced against initial costs of insulation and the costs for heating and cooling with equipment (see figure).

## ADDITIONAL FUNCTIONS

Thermal insulations may also perform several other functions:

1. Add structural strength to a wall, ceiling, or floor section.
2. Provide support for a surface finish.
3. Impede water vapor transmission.
4. Prevent or reduce damage to equipment and structure from exposure to fire and freezing conditions.
5. Reduce noise and vibration.

## BASIC MATERIALS

Thermal insulation is made from the following basic materials:

1. MINERAL FIBROUS: Material such as glass, rock, slag, or asbestos that is melted and spun into thin fibers.
2. MINERAL CELLULAR: Material such as foamed glass, calcium silicate, perlite, vermiculite, foamed concrete, or ceramic.
3. ORGANIC FIBROUS: Material such as wood, cane, cotton, hair, cellulose, or synthetic fibers.
4. ORGANIC CELLULAR: Material such as cork, foamed rubber, polystyrene, or polyurethane.
5. METALLIC: Aluminum or other foils, or metallized organic reflective membranes that must face air, gas filled, or evacuated spaces.

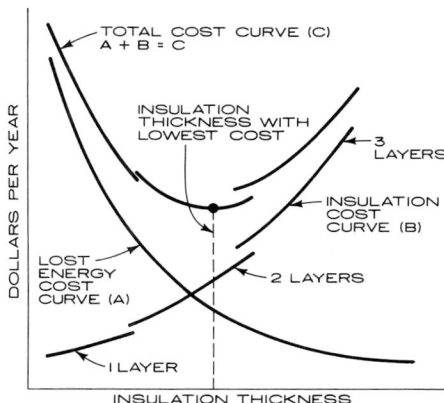

**DETERMINATION OF ECONOMIC THICKNESS OF INSULATION**

## PHYSICAL STRUCTURE AND FORM

Thermal insulation is available in the following physical forms:

1. LOOSE FILL: Dry granules, nodules, or fibers poured or blown into place.
2. FLEXIBLE OR SEMIRIGID: Blankets and batts of wool-like material.
3. RIGID: Boards and blocks.
4. MEMBRANE: Reflective insulation.
5. SPRAY APPLIED: Mineral fiber or insulating concrete.
6. POURED-IN-PLACE: Insulating concrete.
7. FOAMED-IN-PLACE: Polyurethane, urea formaldehyde.

## MECHANISMS OF HEAT TRANSFER

Heat flows through materials and space by conduction, convection, and radiation. Convection and conduction are functions of the roughness of surfaces, air movement, and the temperature difference between the air and surface. Mass insulations, by their low densities, are designed to suppress conduction and convection across their sections by the entrapment of air molecules within their structure. Convective air currents are stilled by the surrounding matrix of fibers or cells, and the chances of heat transfer by the collision of air molecules is reduced. Radiant heat transfer between objects operates independently of air currents and is controlled by the character of the surfaces (emissivity) and the temperature difference between warm objects emitting radiation and cooler objects absorbing radiation.

The resistance of these modes of heat transfer may be retarded by the elements of a building wall section.

1. OUTSIDE SURFACE FILMS: The outside surface traps a thin film of air, which resists heat flow. This film varies with wind velocity and surface roughness.
2. MATERIAL LAYERS: Each layer of material contributes to the resistance of heat flow, usually according to its density. A layer of suitable insulation is normally many times more effective in resisting heat transfer than the combination of all other materials in the section.
3. AIRSPACE: Each measurable airspace also adds to the overall resistance. Foil faced surfaces of low emissivities that form the boundaries of the airspace can further reduce the rate of radiant transfer across the space.
4. INSIDE SURFACE FILM: The inside surface of the building section also traps a thin film of air. The air film thus formed is usually thicker because of much lower air velocities.

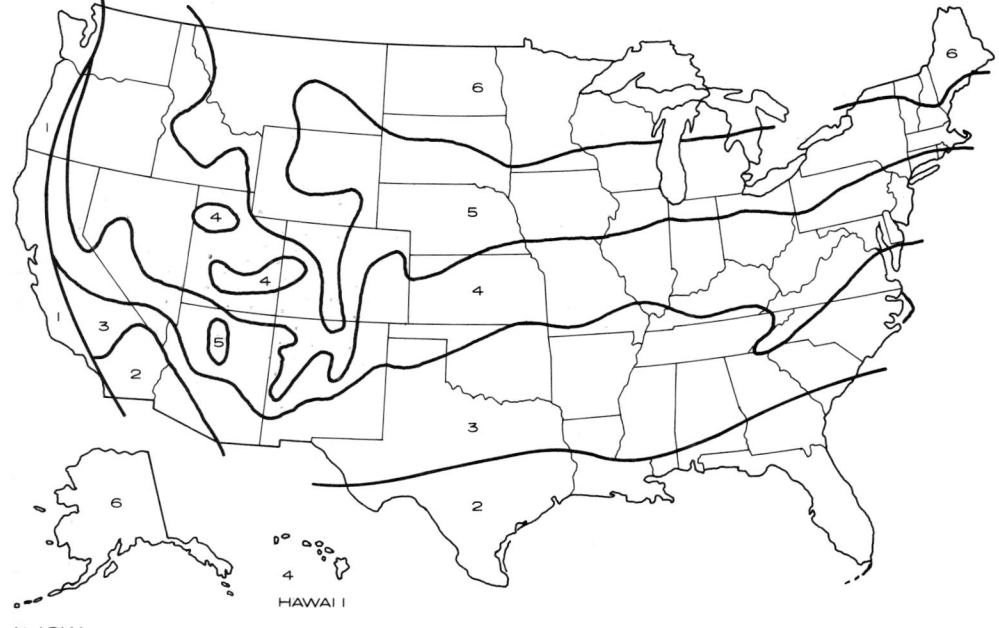

ALASKA

HAWAII

NOTE: RECOMMENDED INSULATION ZONES FOR HEATING AND COOLING

## INSULATION ZONES

## RECOMMENDED MINIMUM THERMAL RESISTANCES (R) OF INSULATION

| ZONE | CEILING | WALL | FLOOR |
|---|---|---|---|
| 1 | 19 | 11 | 11 |
| 2 | 26 | 13 | 11 |
| 3 | 26 | 19 | 13 |
| 4 | 30 | 19 | 19 |
| 5 | 33 | 19 | 22 |
| 6 | 38 | 19 | 22 |

NOTE: The minimum insulation R values recommended for various parts of the United States as delineated on the map of insulation zones.

David F. Hill; Burt Hill Kosar Rittelmann Associates; Butler, Pennsylvania
Donald Bosserman, AIA; Saunders, Cheng & Appleton; Alexandria, Virginia

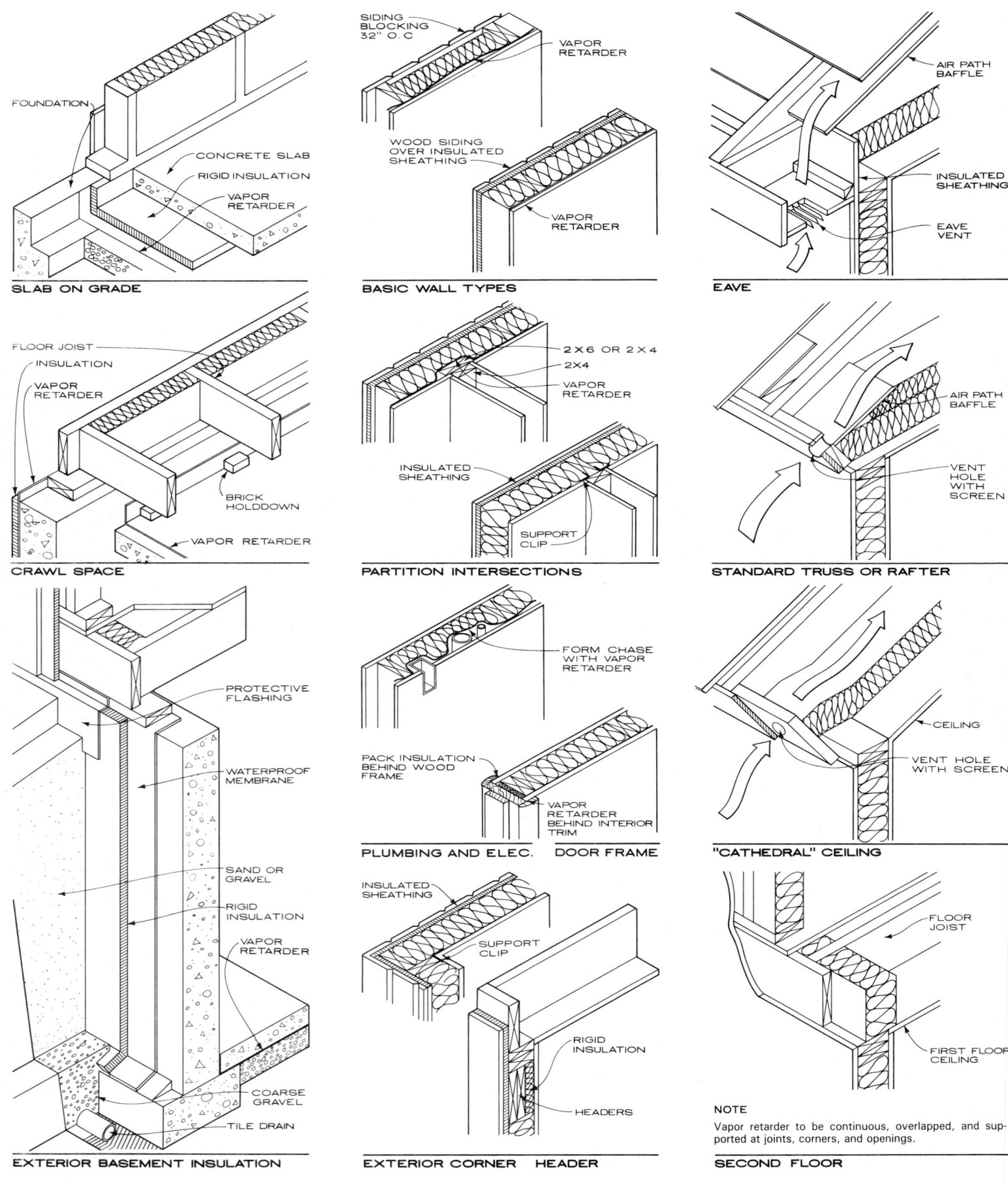

FOUNDATION

CONCRETE SLAB

RIGID INSULATION

VAPOR RETARDER

**SLAB ON GRADE**

SIDING
BLOCKING
32" O.C

VAPOR
RETARDER

WOOD SIDING
OVER INSULATED
SHEATHING

VAPOR
RETARDER

**BASIC WALL TYPES**

AIR PATH
BAFFLE

INSULATED
SHEATHING

EAVE
VENT

**EAVE**

FLOOR JOIST

INSULATION

VAPOR
RETARDER

BRICK
HOLDDOWN

VAPOR RETARDER

**CRAWL SPACE**

2X6 OR 2X4

2X4

VAPOR
RETARDER

INSULATED
SHEATHING

SUPPORT
CLIP

**PARTITION INTERSECTIONS**

AIR PATH
BAFFLE

VENT
HOLE
WITH
SCREEN

**STANDARD TRUSS OR RAFTER**

PROTECTIVE
FLASHING

WATERPROOF
MEMBRANE

SAND OR
GRAVEL

RIGID
INSULATION

VAPOR
RETARDER

COARSE
GRAVEL

TILE DRAIN

**EXTERIOR BASEMENT INSULATION**

FORM CHASE
WITH VAPOR
RETARDER

PACK INSULATION
BEHIND WOOD
FRAME

VAPOR
RETARDER
BEHIND INTERIOR
TRIM

**PLUMBING AND ELEC.**   **DOOR FRAME**

INSULATED
SHEATHING

SUPPORT
CLIP

RIGID
INSULATION

HEADERS

**EXTERIOR CORNER**   **HEADER**

CEILING

VENT HOLE
WITH SCREEN

**"CATHEDRAL" CEILING**

FLOOR
JOIST

FIRST FLOOR
CEILING

**NOTE**
Vapor retarder to be continuous, overlapped, and supported at joints, corners, and openings.

**SECOND FLOOR**

Timothy B. McDonald; Washington, D.C.

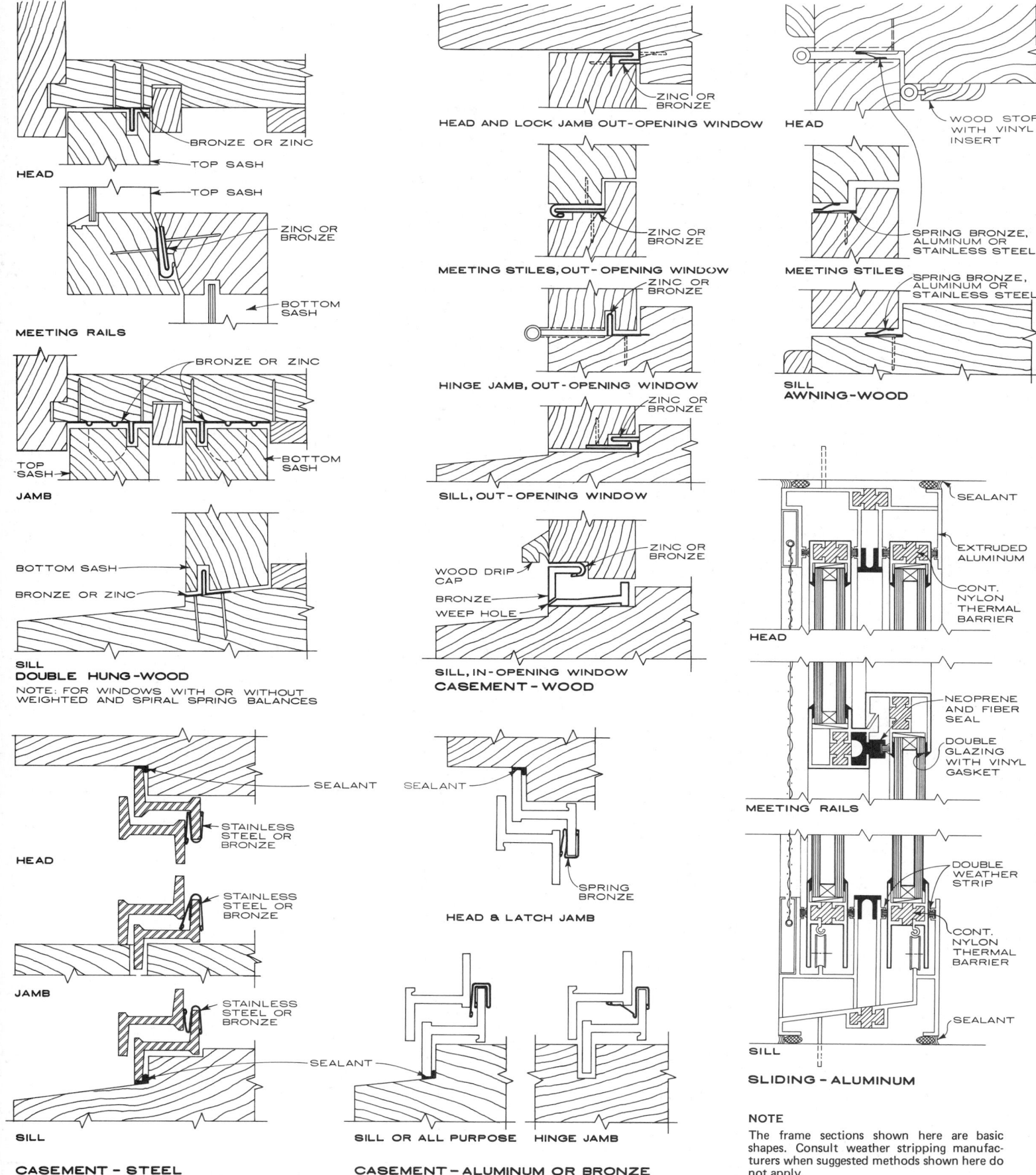

HEAD

BRONZE OR ZINC

TOP SASH

MEETING RAILS

TOP SASH

ZINC OR BRONZE

BOTTOM SASH

BRONZE OR ZINC

TOP SASH

BOTTOM SASH

JAMB

BOTTOM SASH

BRONZE OR ZINC

SILL
**DOUBLE HUNG-WOOD**
NOTE: FOR WINDOWS WITH OR WITHOUT WEIGHTED AND SPIRAL SPRING BALANCES

ZINC OR BRONZE

HEAD AND LOCK JAMB OUT-OPENING WINDOW

ZINC OR BRONZE

MEETING STILES, OUT-OPENING WINDOW

ZINC OR BRONZE

HINGE JAMB, OUT-OPENING WINDOW

ZINC OR BRONZE

SILL, OUT-OPENING WINDOW

WOOD DRIP CAP

BRONZE
WEEP HOLE

ZINC OR BRONZE

SILL, IN-OPENING WINDOW
**CASEMENT-WOOD**

HEAD

WOOD STOP WITH VINYL INSERT

SPRING BRONZE, ALUMINUM OR STAINLESS STEEL

MEETING STILES

SPRING BRONZE, ALUMINUM OR STAINLESS STEEL

SILL
**AWNING-WOOD**

SEALANT

EXTRUDED ALUMINUM

CONT. NYLON THERMAL BARRIER

HEAD

NEOPRENE AND FIBER SEAL

DOUBLE GLAZING WITH VINYL GASKET

MEETING RAILS

DOUBLE WEATHER STRIP

CONT. NYLON THERMAL BARRIER

SEALANT

SILL
**SLIDING - ALUMINUM**

HEAD

SEALANT

STAINLESS STEEL OR BRONZE

JAMB

STAINLESS STEEL OR BRONZE

STAINLESS STEEL OR BRONZE

SEALANT

SILL

**CASEMENT - STEEL**

SEALANT

SPRING BRONZE

HEAD & LATCH JAMB

SILL OR ALL PURPOSE     HINGE JAMB

**CASEMENT - ALUMINUM OR BRONZE**

**NOTE**
The frame sections shown here are basic shapes. Consult weather stripping manufacturers when suggested methods shown here do not apply.

Dan Cowling & Associates, Inc.; Little Rock, Arkansas

**WEATHER STRIPPING**     18

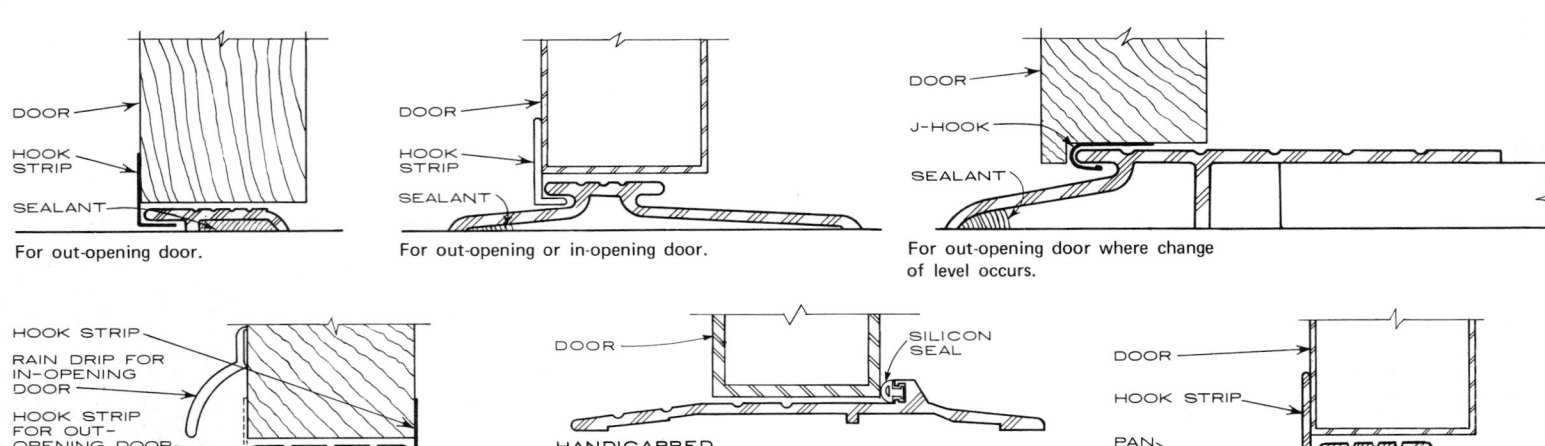

For out-opening door.

For out-opening or in-opening door.

For out-opening door where change of level occurs.

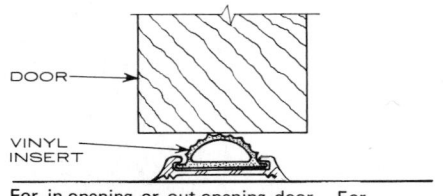

For in-opening door (as shown) and out-opening door where change of level occurs.

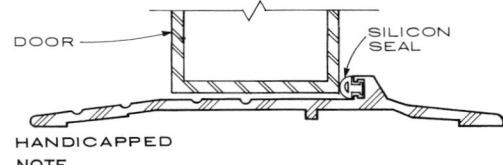

**HANDICAPPED**

**NOTE**
To meet accessibility standards, thresholds should not be higher than ¾ in. for sliding doors or ½ in. high for other door types. Raised thresholds and floor level changes at doorways should be beveled at a slope no greater than 1 in 2.

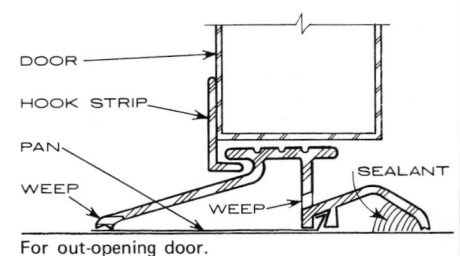

For out-opening door.

**INTERLOCKING THRESHOLDS**

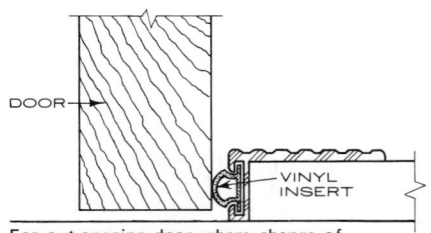

For in-opening or out-opening door. For mounting on floor or bottom of door.

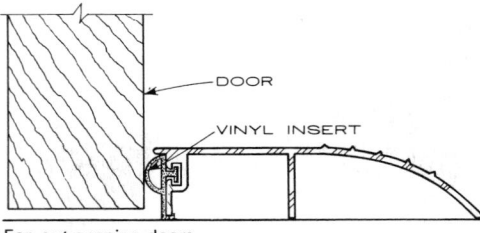

For out-opening door. A similar threshold is available with weeps and drain pan.

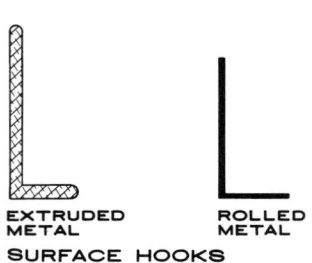

**EXTRUDED METAL**     **ROLLED METAL**

**SURFACE HOOKS**

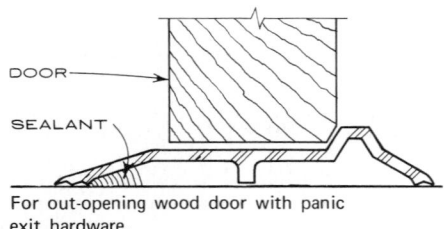

For out-opening door where change of level occurs.

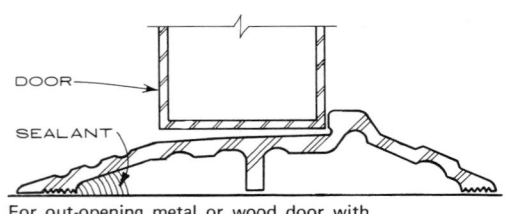

For out-opening doors.

**VINYL INSERT THRESHOLDS**

**EXTRUDED METAL**

**ROLLED METAL**

**CONCEALED HOOKS**

**INTERLOCKING HOOK STRIPS**

**NOTE**
Hook strips are available in aluminum, brass, bronze, and zinc, and vary in thickness and dimensions. Consult manufacturers' catalogs.

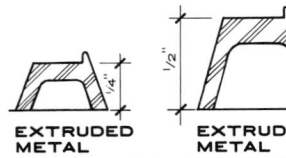

**EXTRUDED METAL**     **EXTRUDED METAL**

**THRESHOLD ELEVATORS**

**NOTE**
Available in alum. and bronze. Consult manufacturers' catalogs.

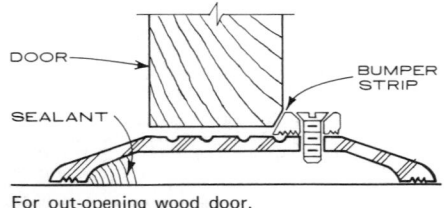

For out-opening wood door with panic exit hardware.

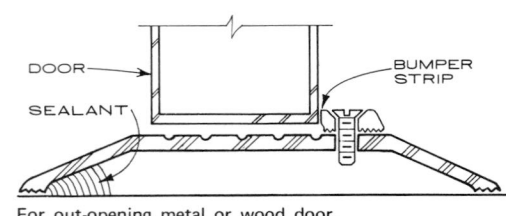

For out-opening metal or wood door with panic hardware.

**LATCH TRACK THRESHOLDS**

**GENERAL NOTE**

Thresholds are available in bronze and aluminum with a wide selection of shapes and dimensions.

For out-opening wood door.

For out-opening metal or wood door.

**FLAT SADDLE THRESHOLDS**

Dan Cowling & Associates, Inc.; Little Rock, Arkansas

**18**     **WEATHER STRIPPING**

# CHAPTER 19

# Historic Preservation

## INTRODUCTION

Historic buildings represent the most tangible evidence of the nation's history and culture. They add interest, identity, and variety to our streets and neighborhoods. At the same time, because of their age, methods of construction, materials, and finishes, they present special challenges to architects. Historic buildings frequently involve materials and systems that are difficult to evaluate in terms of their physical behavior, especially when trying to evaluate them against modern standards and codes. Because historic buildings are essentially different from new buildings in these respects, it is important to remember that the approaches that would be taken in designing a new building generally do not apply to the rehabilitation of a historic building.

## UNDERSTANDING PRESERVATION OBJECTIVES

Almost any preservation or adaptive use project will involve a variety of approaches which may include partial restoration, rehabilitation, and limited reconstruction. These ''preservation objectives'' must be balanced against the client's needs, life safety, or seismic requirements, and a host of other pressures on the building program. When undertaking work on a historic building, there are two basic objectives: to preserve *historic materials* and to preserve the *historic character*. If a building's materials and historic character are preserved, then it will continue to convey its sense of history.

Historic materials are those materials used in construction (the wooden siding, the slate roof, or the terra-cotta cornice) that comprise the building. Although every building has undergone repair, replacement, and alteration over the years, the purpose of any preservation project should be to retain as much as possible of the surviving historic materials in the course of treatment. By historic character we mean those tangible features of the building that help to distinguish it from another. Aspects that give a historic building its individuality may include its form, the relationship between solids to voids, the materials, craftsmanship details, physical features such as porches and the roof, and decorative details. The historic character can be seriously impacted by small changes; for example, applying a thin layer of paint to a historically unpainted building, replacing windows with new ones of different size and shape, or introducing a suspended ceiling within a tall room.

Each historic building is unique in its evolution, use, performance, and maintenance. Part of this uniqueness involves the changes to the building in its past, to its finishes, form, or floor plan. The architect should remember that changes that may have occurred in the past frequently have acquired historic value or possess architectural significance in their own right, just as the new work on historic buildings may acquire some historic significance in the future. A building is not fixed in time at the date of its construction, but represents the flow of continuity of history through the years.

Many historic buildings are renovated for new uses. If the primary objective is to preserve the historic building while accommodating new needs, the architect first must understand the building and the character of its features and spaces. The challenge is to make both the historic building and the new uses work together.

The federal government's *Secretary of the Interior's Standards for Rehabilitation* provides the overall philosophy to guide work undertaken on historic buildings. While these ten standards are general in nature, they help the architect sort out preservation objectives from the host of other program objectives for the building. The architect is urged to refer to the Standards and the accompanying *Guidelines for Rehabilitating Historic Buildings*—these guidelines are periodically updated and are organized by architectural components in broad categories such as building exterior materials, roofs, windows, storefronts, structural systems, interior features, and finishes. The Standards and Guidelines form the basis for the following historic preservation section of *Architectural Graphic Standards*. The guidance recommends the identification of character-defining spaces, features, materials, and finishes as a first step in the rehabilitation process and suggests a hierarchy in selecting appropriate preservation treatments, from those requiring the least disturbance of historic materials to those requiring greater intervention. Considering the unknown conditions that will be encountered during the progress of the work, frequent reference to the Standards and Guidelines is integral to both planning and executing a project.

## UNDERSTANDING THE HISTORIC BUILDING AS A SYSTEM

The architect should remember that building materials are not inert and that they have many other properties than their compressive or tensile strength. The architect should never look at the materials in isolation, but as part of the historic building *system*. Such systems will react to changes in the environment, and the materials are frequently chemically active. Both the systems and the materials will react to almost any human intervention. For example, applying a chemical coating to the exterior walls of a building is a treatment that could affect the transmission of moisture and vapor through the walls.

## COMMON PRESERVATION PROJECT PROBLEMS

The following is a list of problem areas that frequently arise in rehabilitation projects which should be investigated and considered in advance. A historic preservation specialist may be required to address some of these problem areas.

1. Moisture Problems: Perhaps the single most pervasive problem of existing buildings is the penetration of moisture from both within and without. Without understanding the causes (rather than the symptoms) of this problem, it is difficult to select a remedial solution. Many high-tech products (coatings, water repellents) may cause more harm than good. To reduce moisture problems, buildings should be made weathertight (e.g., install proper gutters and downspouts, repair roof, repoint cracks, proper surface grading).

2. Hard to Find Replacement Materials: Careful planning may be required to deal with the logistics of getting special materials and specially fabricated components. Materials that may be difficult and/or time-consuming to obtain can range from decorative terracotta, certain brownstones, sandstones, and marbles. Some metal components may be difficult to repair or fabricate, especially deteriorated ornamental sheet metal cornices, window hoods, roof cresting, and certain ornamental metal shingles.

3. Hard to Find Crafts: Stonecutters, wood-carvers, slaters, stencilers, wood turners, parquet floor layers, plasterers, gilders, grainers, and marblers are all craftspeople that may be difficult to specify their services and get the desired craft effect if the architect cannot demonstrate either by example or prototype what is expected of them. The architect may have to identify a ''sample'' of craftsmanship to ascertain that certain preservation objectives can be met. That sample may be an isolated artifact, may be in place on the historic building, or may even be on another building.

4. Energy Conservation: Improving the energy performance of historic buildings is a generally desirable goal, but some energy-conserving features such as tinted glazing can alter the historic appearance of the building. Any energy conservation treatments that will have a negative impact on the building's historic features should be carefully evaluated. Furring out the inside surface of exterior walls for insulation will require that paneling and trim be carefully removed and reapplied, otherwise the extra thickness of the insulation and wall finish will change the architectural relationships between openings, wall surfaces, and trim.

5. The Unintended Impact of New Technology: Other problems can result from the application of modern architectural practices to historic buildings so that the introduction of high-strength portland cements, elastomeric compounds, water repellents, or epoxy coatings may create a host of secondary problems not anticipated by the architect and which may result from using standardized specifications.

## FOR THE RECORD

Dealing with a historic building is both a challenge and an opportunity. If the building is significant, the architect has a responsibility not only to preserve, but to leave a record for the future. Such a record should at least include a summary of the research, measured drawings to the Standards of the Historic American Buildings Survey, a record of the information uncovered during work on the building, and information about the treatments as planned and as carried out.

## STANDARDS FOR REHABILITATION

1. Every reasonable effort shall be made to provide a compatible use for a property which requires minimal alteration of the building, structure, or site and its environment, or to use a property for its originally intended purpose.

2. The distinguishing original qualities or character of a building, structure, or site and its environment shall not be destroyed. The removal or alteration of any historic material or distinctive architectural features should be avoided when possible.

3. All buildings, structures, and sites shall be recognized as products of their own time. Alterations that have no historic basis and that seek to create an earlier appearance shall be discouraged.

4. Changes that may have taken place in the course of time are evidence of the history and development of a building, structure, or site and its environment. These changes may have acquired significance in their own right, and this significance shall be recognized and respected.

5. Distinctive stylistic features or examples of skilled craftsmanship which characterize a building, structure, or site shall be treated with sensitivity.

6. Deteriorated architectural features shall be repaired rather than replaced, wherever possible. In the event replacement is necessary, the new material should match the material being replaced in composition, design, color, texture, and other visual qualities. Repair or replacement of missing architectural features should be based on accurate duplications of features, substantiated by historic, physical, or pictorial evidence rather than on conjectural designs or the availability of different architectural elements from other buildings or structures.

7. The surface cleaning of structures shall be undertaken with the gentlest means possible. Sandblasting and other cleaning methods that will damage the historic building materials shall not be undertaken.

8. Every reasonable effort shall be made to protect and preserve archeological resources affected by, or adjacent to, any project.

9. Contemporary design for alterations and additions to existing properties shall not be discouraged when such alterations and additions do not destroy significant historical, architectural, or cultural material, and such design is compatible with the size, scale, color, material, and character of the property, neighborhood, or environment.

10. Wherever possible, new additions or alterations to structures shall be done in such a manner that if such additions or alterations were to be removed in the future, the essential form and integrity of the structure would be unimpaired.

Lee H. Nelson, FAIA; Preservation Assistance Division, National Park Service; Washington, D.C.
Eric J. Gastier; Darrel Downing Rippeteau Architects, PC; Washington, D.C.

 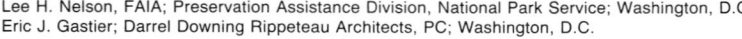

**INTRODUCTION**

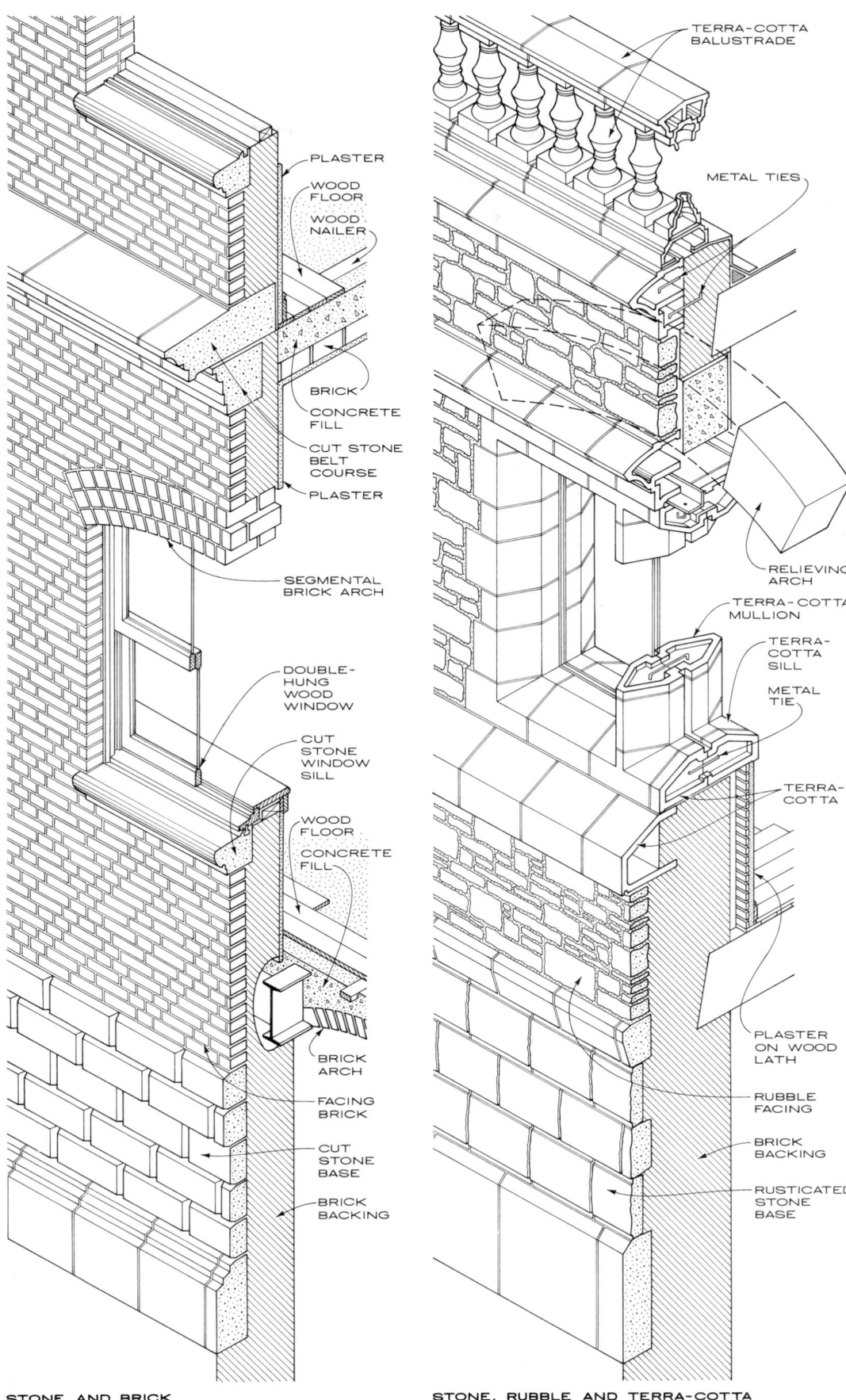

PLASTER

WOOD FLOOR

WOOD NAILER

BRICK

CONCRETE FILL

CUT STONE BELT COURSE

PLASTER

SEGMENTAL BRICK ARCH

DOUBLE-HUNG WOOD WINDOW

CUT STONE WINDOW SILL

WOOD FLOOR

CONCRETE FILL

BRICK ARCH

FACING BRICK

CUT STONE BASE

BRICK BACKING

TERRA-COTTA BALUSTRADE

METAL TIES

RELIEVING ARCH

TERRA-COTTA MULLION

TERRA-COTTA SILL

METAL TIE

TERRA-COTTA

PLASTER ON WOOD LATH

RUBBLE FACING

BRICK BACKING

RUSTICATED STONE BASE

STONE AND BRICK

STONE, RUBBLE AND TERRA-COTTA

## MASONRY – TYPICAL WALL SECTIONS

Lee H. Nelson, FAIA, H. Ward Jandl, Anne Grimmer, Kay D. Weeks; Preservation Assistance Division, National Park Service; Washington, D.C.
Eric J. Gastier; Darrel Downing Rippeteau Architects, PC; Washington, D.C.

## INTRODUCTION

The function of masonry units such as brick or stone is related to the thickness of a wall, the mortar, the bond, and the quality of workmanship. The relationship of all these materials determines the historic building's structural soundness as well as its appearance. While masonry is among the most durable of historic building materials, it is also the most susceptible to damage by improper maintenance or repair techniques and harsh or abrasive cleaning methods.

Stone is one of the more lasting of masonry building materials and has been used throughout the history of American building construction. In the 17th and 18th centuries, stone was primarily used for decorative details and trim work on brick buildings. Where stone was plentiful, even simple buildings had stone foundations and chimneys. Stonework on most buildings was roughly finished, but more elaborate stone structures often featured finely tooled or carved decorative surfaces. The kinds of stone most commonly encountered on historic buildings in the U.S. include various types of sandstone (brownstone), limestone, marble, granite, slate, and fieldstones.

Brick varied considerably in size and quality. Before 1870, brick clays were pressed into molds and were often unevenly fired. The quality of brick depended on the type of clay available and the brick-making techniques; by the 1870s—with the perfection of an extrusion process—bricks became more uniform and durable.

Terra-cotta is also a kiln-dried clay product popular from the late 19th century until the 1930s. Brownstone terra-cotta was the earliest type used throughout the last half of the 19th century. It was hollow cast, glazed or unglazed, and was generally used in conjunction with brick to imitate brownstone. Fireproof terra-cotta was developed for use in high-rise buildings. Inexpensive, lightweight, and fireproof, these rough-finished hollow building blocks were well suited to span I-beams in floor, wall, and ceiling construction. Glazed architectural terra-cotta consists of hollow units hand cast in molds or carved in clay and heavily glazed and fired. The development of the steel-frame office building in the early 20th century and the eclectic taste of the time contributed to its widespread use.

Adobe, which consists of sun-dried earthen bricks, was one of the earliest permanent building materials used in the U.S., primarily in the Southwest where it is still a popular building material.

Mortar is used to bond together masonry units. Historic mortar was generally quite soft and consisted primarily of lime, sand, and other additives such as crushed oyster shells, partially burned lime, animal hair, particles of clay, or pigments to color the mortar to match or contrast with the masonry units. While natural cement was included in some mortars beginning in the early 19th century, most historic mortar did not contain portland cement until after 1880 when it was used in combination with the newly available, harder extruded bricks, which required a more rigid and nonabsorbing mortar.

Traditional stucco, sometimes referred to as plaster, was also heavily lime based and had much the same composition as historic mortar, with regional variations that reflected the availability of certain materials. Like mortar, the composition of stucco increased in hardness with the addition of portland cement toward the end of the 19th century. In the 18th and 19th centuries, stucco was often scored to resemble cut stone and was used as a finish coat directly over stone, brick, or log construction. In the early 20th century, stucco took on significance as a building material in its own right and was applied (often with a decorative textured finish) directly over wood or metal lath attached to the building's structural framework.

Concrete has a long history, being variously made of tabby, volcanic ash, and later of natural hydraulic cements; the latter was first given limited use in the early 19th century in some mortars before the introduction of portland cement in the 1870s. From that time on, concrete has been used in its precast form for structural blocks or ''cast stone'' to simulate entire stone facades or smaller architectural details. In the 20th century, this has further evolved into precast structural elements.

## PRESERVATION APPROACHES

Masonry features that are important in defining the overall historic character of the building include walls, brackets, railings, cornices, window architraves, door pediments, steps, and columns, with tooling and bonding patterns, coatings, color, and joint details.

Making inappropriate visual changes to historic masonry surfaces in the process of rehabilitation, such as applying paint or other coatings to masonry that has been historically unpainted, can easily change the entire character of the building. Similarly, paint should not be removed from historically painted masonry.

The various causes of mortar joint deterioration (such as leaking roofs or gutters, differential settlement of the building, capillary action, or extreme weather exposure) should be identified before selecting an appropriate remedial treatment.

Masonry should only be cleaned in order to halt deterioration or to remove heavy soiling. Cleaning masonry surfaces when they are not heavily soiled in order to create a new appearance can needlessly introduce chemicals or moisture into historic materials. If it is determined that cleaning is necessary, tests should be conducted prior to cleaning and observed over a sufficient period of time so that both the immediate effects and the long-range effects are known.

Brick or stone surfaces should be cleaned with the gentlest method possible, such as water and detergents, using natural bristle brushes. They should never be sandblasted using dry or wet grit or other abrasives. These methods of cleaning permanently erode the surface of the material. Cleaning methods involving water or liquid chemical solutions should not be used when there is any possibility of freezing temperatures, and chemical products should never be used that will damage masonry, such as using acid on limestone or marble.

If repainting of historically painted masonry is necessary, the damaged paint should be removed to the next sound layer using the gentlest method possible prior to repainting. Colors should be used that are historically appropriate to the building and district.

Masonry walls and other masonry features should be repaired whenever there is evidence of deterioration. This may include disintegrating mortar, loose bricks, damp walls, or damaged plasterwork.

In preparation for repointing, deteriorated mortar should be removed by carefully hand-raking the joints to avoid damaging the masonry. Electric saws should never be used.

Old mortar should be duplicated in strength, composition, color, and texture. Repointing with mortar of high portland cement content can create a bond that is stronger than the historic material, damaging historic masonry as a result of the differing coefficient of expansion and the differing porosity of the material and the mortar.

When repointing, the use of traditional materials and methods is strongly recommended rather than synthetic caulking compounds and ''scrub'' coating techniques. Old mortar joints should be duplicated in width and in joint profile.

Stucco should be repaired by removing only the damaged material and patching with new stucco that duplicates the old in strength, composition, color, and texture. Mud plaster should be used as a surface coating over unfired, unstabilized adobe, in order to bond to the adobe. Cement stucco, on the other hand, will not bond properly, enabling moisture to become entrapped between materials. Concrete may be repaired by cutting the deteriorated portion back to a sound surface, then removing the source of deterioration—often corrosion on metal reinforcement bars—by sandblasting or chemical cleaning of the re-bars. The new concrete patch must be applied carefully so it will bond satisfactorily with, and match, the historic concrete.

Masonry features may be repaired by patching, piecing in, or consolidating the masonry using recognized preservation methods. Repair may also include the limited replacement in kind of those extensively deteriorated or missing parts of masonry features such as terra-cotta brackets or stone balusters when there are surviving prototypes.

A masonry feature that is too deteriorated or damaged to repair should be replaced in kind. If the historic form and detailing are still evident, they should be used to restore the feature.

If a masonry feature is completely missing and there is sufficient historical, pictorial, and physical documentation, the missing feature should be accurately restored. In the absence of documentation, the replacement masonry feature may be a new design that is compatible with the size, scale, and color of the historic building.

Finally, for both repair and replacement treatments, using the same kind of material is always preferred; however, if this is not technically or economically feasible, a compatible substitute material with the same visual and physical qualities may be considered.

### EFFECTS OF TEMPERATURE CHANGE ON MASONRY

A. FLEXIBLE MORTAR (LIME)    B. INFLEXIBLE MORTAR (CEMENT)

NORMAL

HOT (BRICKS EXPAND)

MORTAR COMPRESSES    SPALLING

COLD (BRICKS CONTRACT)

MORTAR FLEXES    CRACKS OPEN UP

FLEXIBLE MORTAR (A) EXPANDS AND CONTRACTS WITH TEMPERATURE CHANGES. BRICKS BONDED BY INFLEXIBLE MORTAR (B) TEND TO SPALL AT THE EDGES (THE AREA OF GREATEST STRESS) IN HOT WEATHER AND SEPARATE FROM THE MORTAR IN COLD WEATHER

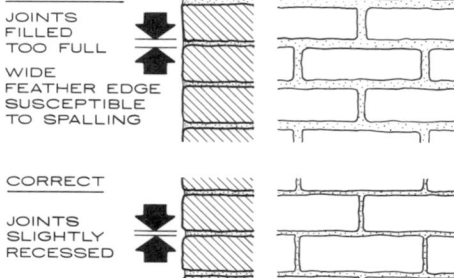

### PREPARATION OF MORTAR JOINTS FOR REPOINTING

INCORRECT
MORTAR NOT CLEANED OUT TO A SUFFICIENT UNIFORM DEPTH

EDGES OF BRICKS DAMAGED BY TOOL OR GRINDER, CREATES WIDER JOINT

CORRECT
MORTAR CLEANED OUT TO A UNIFORM DEPTH OF ABOUT 1"

UNDAMAGED EDGES OF BRICK

INCORRECT
JOINTS FILLED TOO FULL

WIDE FEATHER EDGE SUSCEPTIBLE TO SPALLING

CORRECT
JOINTS SLIGHTLY RECESSED

### PROPER REPOINTING OF MASONRY JOINTS

A. COLONIAL GRAPEVINE JOINT, FLEMISH BOND
CIRCA 1720

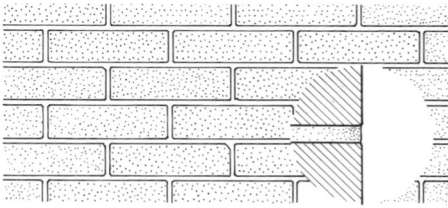

B. BEADED JOINT, FLEMISH BOND
CIRCA 1809

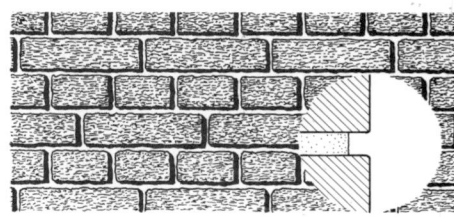

C. FLUSH JOINT, COMMON BOND
MID-19TH CENTURY

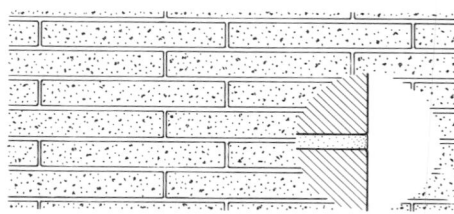

D. RAKED JOINT, ENGLISH BOND
EARLY 20TH CENTURY

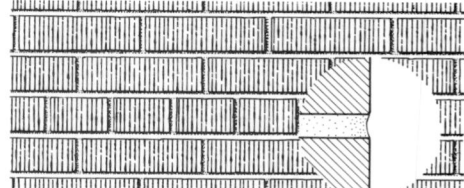

E. FLUSH JOINT, ONE-THIRD RUNNING BOND
EARLY 20TH CENTURY

F. CONCAVE JOINT, COMMON BOND
EARLY 20TH CENTURY

NOTE THE DIFFERENCE IN UNIFORMITY OF HANDMADE (A AND B) AND MACHINE-MADE (C–F) BRICKS. IN A, B AND F, THE VERTICAL JOINTS WERE STRUCK BEFORE THE HORIZONTALS. IN B AND E, THE VERTICAL JOINTS ARE NARROWER THAN THE HORIZONTALS

### JOINT TYPES AND BRICK BONDING PATTERNS

Lee H. Nelson, FAIA, H. Ward Jandl, Anne Grimmer, Kay D. Weeks; Preservation Assistance Division, National Park Service; Washington, D.C.
Eric J. Gastier; Darrel Downing Rippeteau Architects, PC; Washington, D.C.

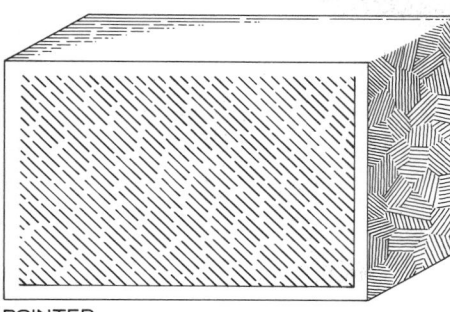

**POINTED**

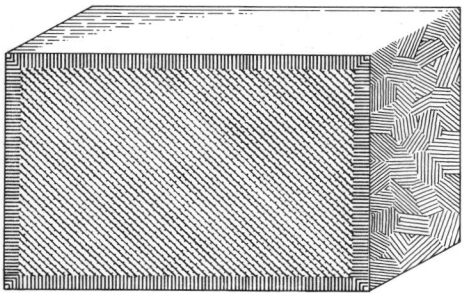

**BROACHED**

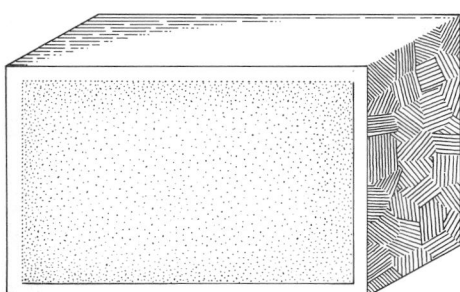

**BUSH-HAMMERED**

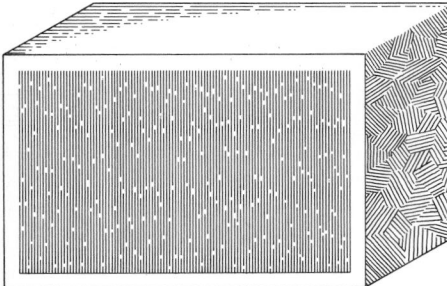

**PATENT-HAMMERED**

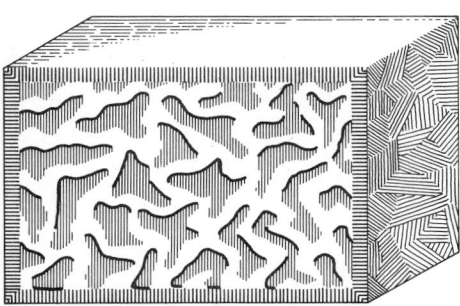

**VERMICULATED**

**STONEWORK FINISHES**

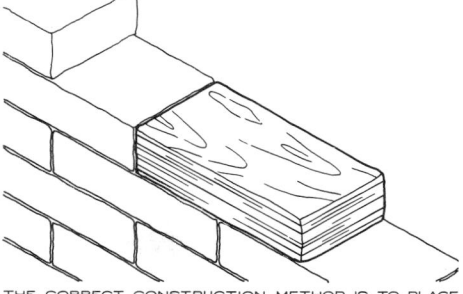

THE CORRECT CONSTRUCTION METHOD IS TO PLACE STONE ON ITS NATURAL BED AS IT ORIGINALLY LAY IN THE QUARRY

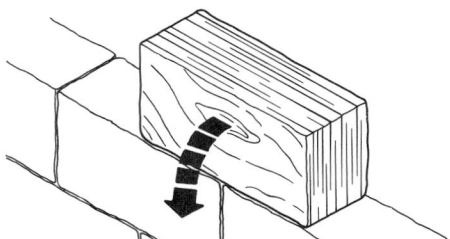

A FACE-BEDDED STONE SCALES IN LAYERS BECAUSE IT WAS PLACED ON END WITH ITS BEDDING PLANES PARALLEL TO THE FACE OF THE WALL. FACE BEDDING ACCOUNTS FOR THE POOR CONDITION OF MANY MID-19TH CENTURY BROWNSTONE BUILDINGS (ARROW INDICATES SCALING)

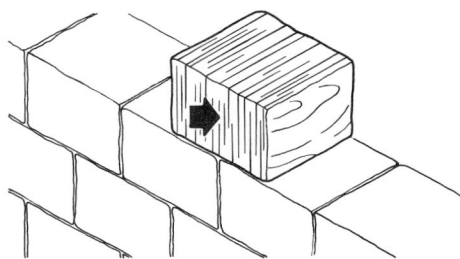

AN EDGE-BEDDED STONE HAS ITS BEDDING PLANES PERPENDICULAR TO THE FACE OF THE WALL. SEAMS ON THE EXPOSED SURFACE (INDICATED BY THE ARROW) WILL WASH OUT IN TIME

**STONE BEDDING METHODS**

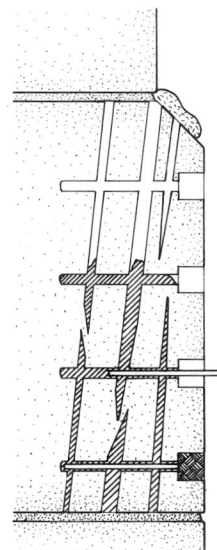

PROCEDURE

1. SEAL CRACKS WITH NON-OILY CLAY

2. DRILL STAGGERED ROWS OF HOLES (MAX. DIAMETER 1/4") THROUGH FACE OF STONE

3. FILL HOLES WITH ADHESIVE GROUT

4. INSERT AND COUNTERSINK PINS. DIAMETER SHOULD BE 1/8" SMALLER THAN HOLES

5. PATCH HOLES WITH COMPOSITE PATCHING MATERIAL

**THROUGH-SURFACE STONE REPAIR**

PROCEDURE

1. CLEAN SURFACES TO BE JOINED

2. PROTECT ADJACENT SURFACES WITH RUBBER CEMENT

3. DRILL STAGGERED ROWS OF HOLES: DEPTH = 4 X PIN DIAMETER DIAMETER = PIN DIAMETER + 1/8"

4. FILL HOLES WITH RIGID (HIGH MODULUS) EPOXY ADHESIVE

5. SET PINS

6. COAT STONE SURFACES TO BE JOINED WITH FLEXIBLE (LOW MODULUS) EPOXY ADHESIVE

7. SET DETACHED PIECE IN PLACE. GENTLY TAP WITH RUBBER MALLET TO SEAT STONE

8. CLEAN OFF RUBBER CEMENT

**CONCEALED REPAIR FOR STONE**

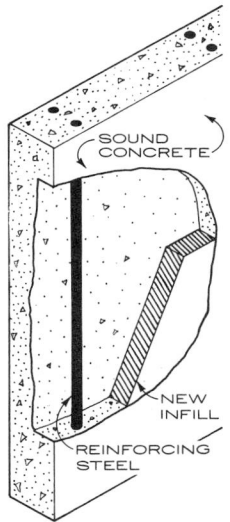

PROCEDURE

1. REMOVE LOOSE DETERIORATED CONCRETE TO SOUND CONCRETE. CUT SQUARE SHOULDERS AT EDGE OF REPAIR AREA. EXPOSE ALL SIDES OF REINFORCING STEEL

2. SANDBLAST CONCRETE AND REINFORCING STEEL CLEAN

3. IMMEDIATELY APPLY PROTECTIVE COATING SYSTEM TO REINFORCEMENT

4. MOISTEN CONCRETE SURFACE AND ALLOW TO DRY UNTIL DAMP

5. INSTALL MORTAR, EPOXY-MODIFIED BOND COAT AND CONCRETE, OR EPOXY-MODIFIED BOND COAT AND PORTLAND CEMENT CONCRETE, DEPENDING ON REPAIR DEPTH

6. CURE AS NECESSARY

SOUND CONCRETE

NEW INFILL

REINFORCING STEEL

**SPALLED CONCRETE REPAIR (EXTERIOR WALLS)**

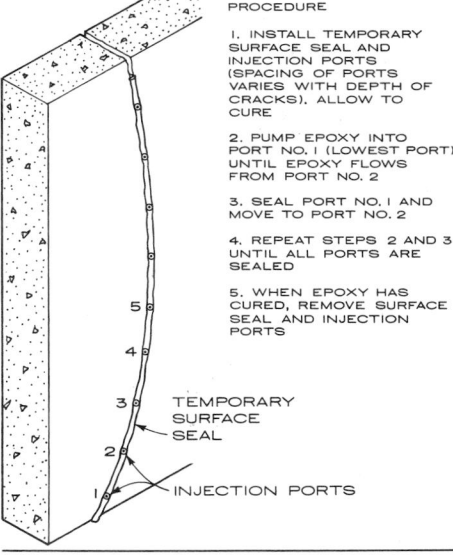

PROCEDURE

1. INSTALL TEMPORARY SURFACE SEAL AND INJECTION PORTS (SPACING OF PORTS VARIES WITH DEPTH OF CRACKS). ALLOW TO CURE

2. PUMP EPOXY INTO PORT NO. 1 (LOWEST PORT) UNTIL EPOXY FLOWS FROM PORT NO. 2

3. SEAL PORT NO. 1 AND MOVE TO PORT NO. 2

4. REPEAT STEPS 2 AND 3 UNTIL ALL PORTS ARE SEALED

5. WHEN EPOXY HAS CURED, REMOVE SURFACE SEAL AND INJECTION PORTS

TEMPORARY SURFACE SEAL

INJECTION PORTS

**FRACTURED CONCRETE REPAIR (WALLS AND SLABS)**

Lee H. Nelson, FAIA, H. Ward Jandl, Anne Grimmer, Kay D. Weeks; Preservation Assistance Division, National Park Service; Washington, D.C.
Eric J. Gastier; Darrel Downing Rippeteau Architects, PC; Washington, D.C.

# INTRODUCTION

Because it can be easily shaped by sawing, planing, carving, and gouging, wood is used for architectural features such as clapboards, cornices, brackets, entablatures, shutters, columns, and balustrades. These wooden features, both functional and decorative, may be important in defining the historic character of the building and thus their retention, protection, and repair are important in rehabilitation projects.

Wood has played a central role in American building during every period and in every style. Whether as structural membering, exterior cladding, roofing, interior finishes, or decorative features, wood is frequently an essential component of historic and older buildings.

## PRESERVATION APPROACHES

While loss of some exterior wood to weathering is inevitable, taking steps to maximize its retention should be an integral part of any work on a historic building.

Radical changes to the historic appearance of wood surfaces should be avoided, such as changing the type of finish or its color, or stripping historically painted surfaces to bare wood, then applying clear finishes or stains in order to create a ''natural'' look. Special finishes, such as marbling or graining, are evidence of individual craftsmanship and should be retained and preserved.

The causes of wood deterioration should be identified and corrected, such as faulty flashing, leaking gutters, cracks and holes in siding, deteriorated caulking, plants growing too close to wood surfaces, or insect or fungus infestation.

Painted wood surfaces should be inspected to determine whether repainting is necessary or if cleaning is all that is required. Paint should not be removed that is firmly adhering to, and thus, protecting wood surfaces. If surfaces need painting, the damaged or deteriorated paint should only be removed to the next sound layer, using the gentlest method possible (hand scraping and hand sanding).

It is never appropriate to use destructive paint removal methods such as propane or butane torches, sandblasting, or waterblasting. These methods can irreversibly damage woodwork and could penetrate through to damage interior fabric.

Electric hot-air guns may be used effectively on decorative wood features and electric heat plates on flat wood surfaces when paint is so deteriorated that total removal is necessary prior to repainting.

Wood features can be repaired by patching, consolidating, or otherwise reinforcing the wood using recognized preservation methods. More often, however, repair will involve the replacement in kind of extensively deteriorated or missing parts of wood features where there are surviving prototypes. Examples include brackets, moldings, balusters, or sections of siding.

A wood feature too deteriorated to repair should be replaced in kind. If the historic form and detailing are still evident, they should be used to restore the feature. If a wood feature is missing and there is sufficient historical, pictorial, and physical documentation, the missing feature should be restored. Replacing a deteriorated or missing wood feature based on insufficient documentation can create a false historic appearance and can have a more significant negative impact on the historic character than not replacing the feature at all.

For both repair and replacement, using the same kind of material is always preferred. If this is not feasible, a compatible substitute material may be used if it conveys the same historic appearance as wood and is physically and chemically compatible.

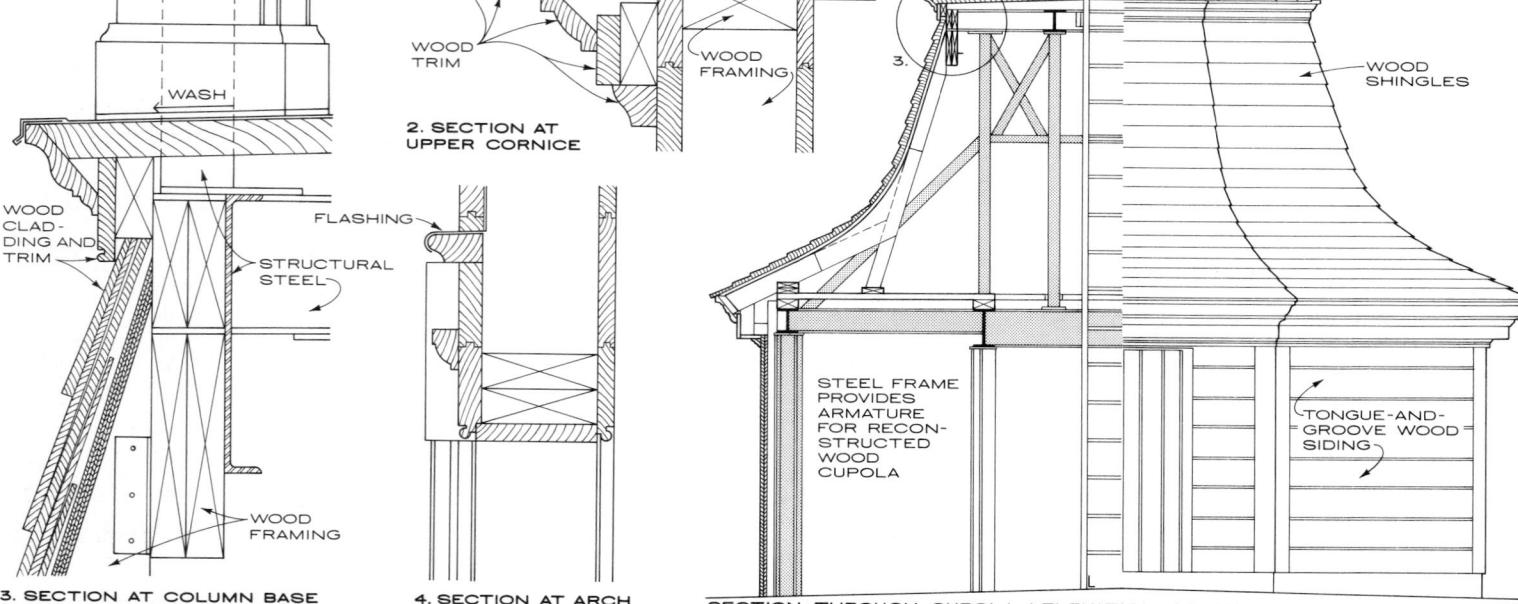

WEST ELEVATION

COPPER-COVERED WOOD BALL

TURNED WOOD CONE

WOOD SHINGLES

WOOD CORNICE

APPLIED WOOD CARVINGS

TONGUE-AND-GROOVE WOOD SIDING

WOOD COLUMN COVER AND BASE

WOOD SHINGLES

TONGUE-AND-GROOVE WOOD SIDING

STEEL FRAME PROVIDES ARMATURE FOR RECONSTRUCTED WOOD CUPOLA

STEEL COLUMN

WOOD BLOCKING

WOOD CLADDING

I. PLAN OF COLUMN

WASH

WOOD CLADDING AND TRIM

STRUCTURAL STEEL

WOOD FRAMING

3. SECTION AT COLUMN BASE

STRUCTURAL STEEL

STRUCTURAL STEEL

WOOD TRIM

WOOD FRAMING

2. SECTION AT UPPER CORNICE

FLASHING

4. SECTION AT ARCH

SECTION THROUGH CUPOLA / ELEVATION OF CUPOLA

**OLD STATE HOUSE, DOVER, DE (McCUNE ASSOCIATES, RESTORATION ARCHITECTS, 1977)**
Lee H. Nelson, FAIA, H. Ward Jandl, Sharon C. Park, AIA, Michael J. Auer; Preservation Assistance Division, National Park Service; Washington, D.C.
Eric J. Gastier; Darrel Downing Rippeteau Architects, PC; Washington, D.C.

**WOOD**

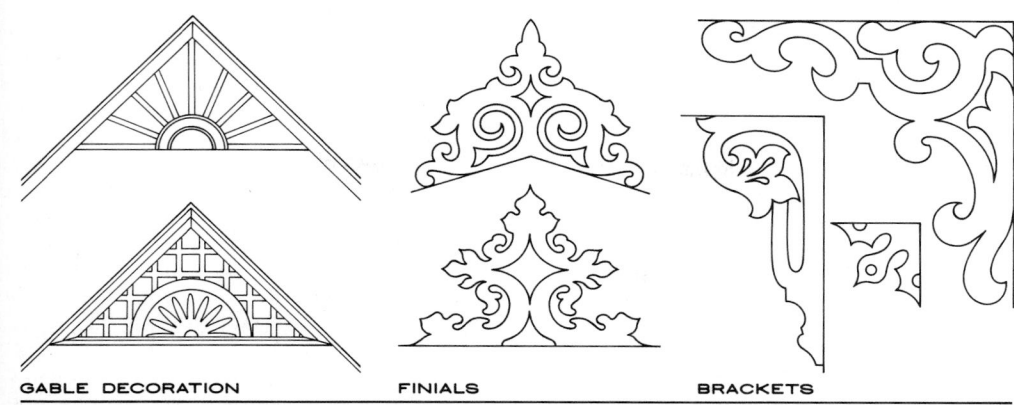

GABLE DECORATION          FINIALS                    BRACKETS

## DECORATIVE WOOD ELEMENTS

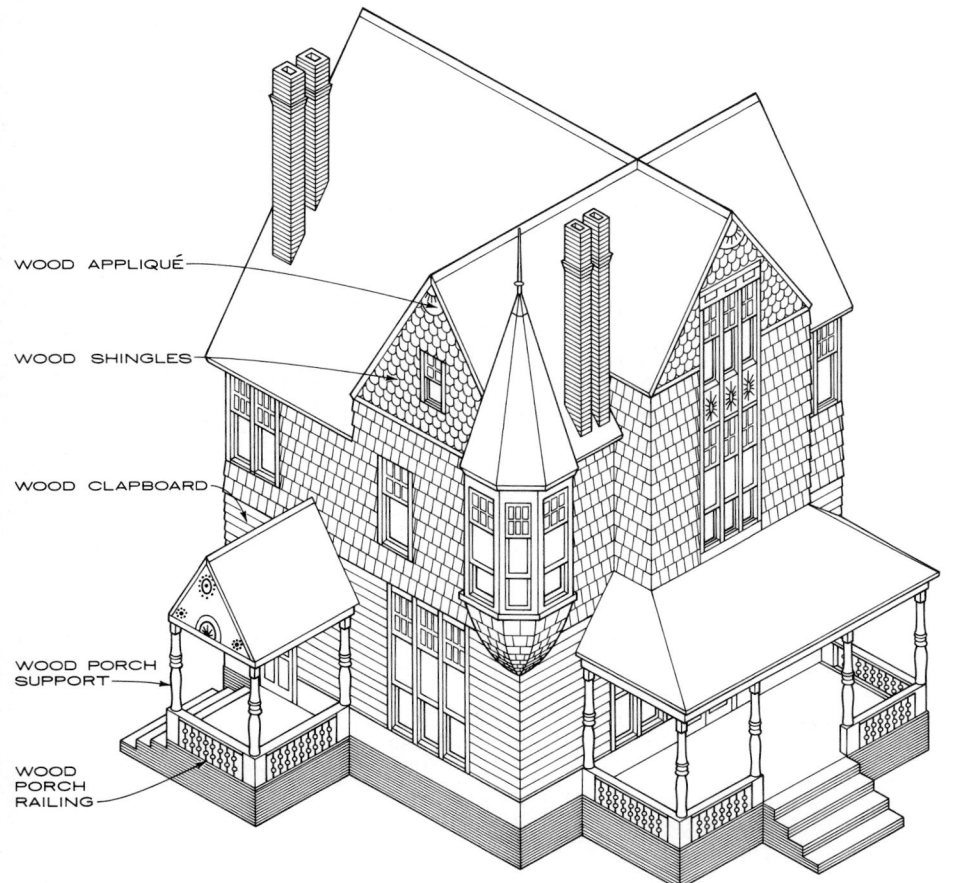

WOOD APPLIQUÉ

WOOD SHINGLES

WOOD CLAPBOARD

WOOD PORCH SUPPORT

WOOD PORCH RAILING

**TYPICAL QUEEN ANNE HOUSE, CIRCA 1880 (BASED ON A DESIGN OF LAMB AND WHEELER, ARCHITECTS)**

**WOOD PORCH RAILING PATTERNS (CUT BY SCROLL SAW FROM THIN WOOD STOCK)**

Lee H. Nelson, FAIA, H. Ward Jandl, Sharon C. Park, AIA, Michael J. Auer; Preservation Assistance Division, National Park Service; Washington, D.C.
Eric J. Gastier; Darrel Downing Rippeteau Architects, PC; Washington, D.C.

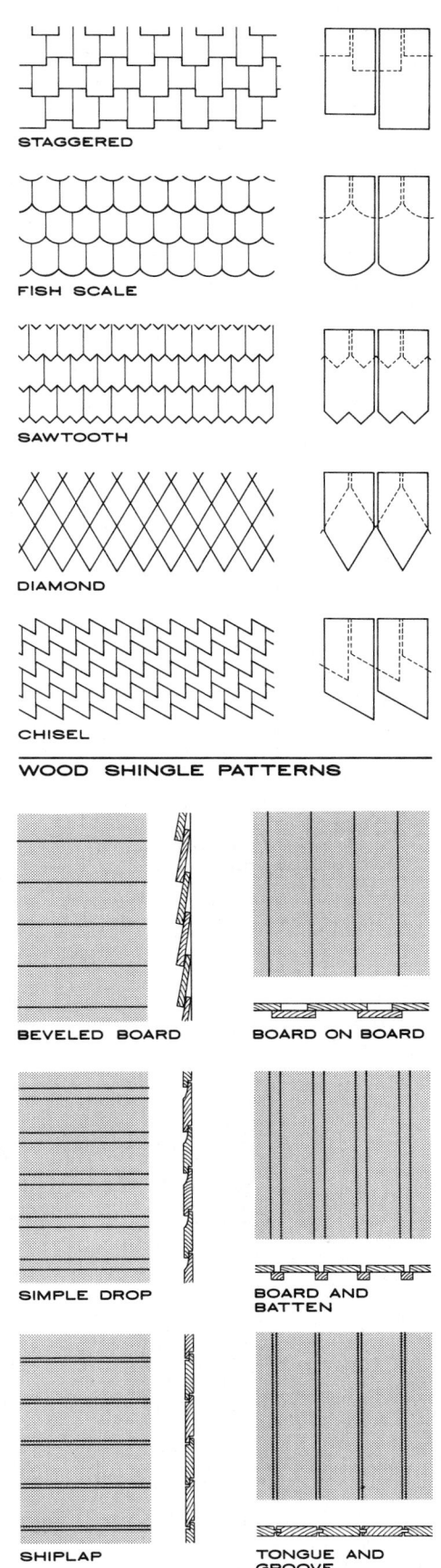

STAGGERED

FISH SCALE

SAWTOOTH

DIAMOND

CHISEL

## WOOD SHINGLE PATTERNS

BEVELED BOARD          BOARD ON BOARD

SIMPLE DROP            BOARD AND BATTEN

SHIPLAP                TONGUE AND GROOVE

## WOOD SIDING - PROFILES AND PATTERNS

# INTRODUCTION

Architectural metal features—such as cast-iron facades, porches, and steps; sheet metal cornices, siding, roofs, roof cresting, and storefronts; and cast or rolled metal doors, window sash, entablatures, and hardware—are often highly decorative and may be important in defining the overall historic character of the building.

Metals commonly used in historic American building construction include lead, tin, zinc, copper, bronze, brass, iron, steel, and, to a lesser extent, nickel alloys, stainless steel, and aluminum. A high degree of craftsmanship went into fabrication of the metals in older American buildings. Often it was local artisans who designed and built fine staircases, exterior light standards, railings, or metal sculptures.

# PRESERVATION APPROACHES

Before beginning any preservation work on metal features, it is critical that the metal be correctly identified; different metals have unique properties and thus require distinct preservation treatments. Inappropriate treatments to metal features can inadvertently result in their damage or loss.

Changes to architectural metal finishes can result in changing the historic character of a building.

Protecting architectural metals from corrosion should be the focus of a cyclical maintenance program. Proper drainage should be provided so that water does not stand on flat, horizontal surfaces or accumulate in curved, decorative features.

Incompatible metals should never be placed together without a reliable separation material or galvanic corrosion of the less noble metal will occur; e.g., copper corrodes cast iron, steel, tin, and aluminum.

Architectural metals should be carefully cleaned with the gentlest method possible to remove corrosion prior to repainting or applying other appropriate protective coatings. Local codes should also be checked to ensure compliance with environmental safety requirements. For some metals, such as bronze or copper, the surface coating or patina may serve as a protective coating and should not be removed. Soft metals such as lead, tin, copper, terneplate, and zinc should be cleaned with appropriate chemical methods because their finishes can be abraded by blasting methods, such as grit blasting.

Harder metals, such as cast iron, wrought iron, and steel, may be hand scraped and wire-brushed to remove paint buildup and corrosion. If these methods prove ineffective, low-pressure dry grit blasting may be appropriate if the surface is not damaged or abraded. Adjacent wood or masonry should be protected from all cleaning efforts.

Applying appropriate paint or other coating systems immediately after cleaning decreases the corrosion rate of metals or alloys. If an architectural metal is being repainted, the colors should be appropriate to the historic building or district.

Architectural metal features can often be repaired by patching, splicing, or otherwise reinforcing the metal following recognized preservation methods. Repairs also involve the limited replacement in kind of those extensively deteriorated or missing parts of features when there are surviving prototypes. Examples are porch railings or roof cresting. An architectural metal feature that is too deteriorated to repair should be replaced in kind. If the historic form and detailing are still evident, they can be used to guide the new work.

If an architectural metal feature is completely missing and there is sufficient historical, pictorial, and physical documentation, the missing features should be accurately restored. In the absence of sufficient documentation, the replacement metal feature may be a new design that is compatible with the size, scale, material, and color of the historic building.

Finally, for both repair and replacement treatments, using the same kind of metal is always preferred. If this is not feasible, a compatible substitute material may be used if it conveys the same visual appearance as the historic material and is chemically and physically compatible.

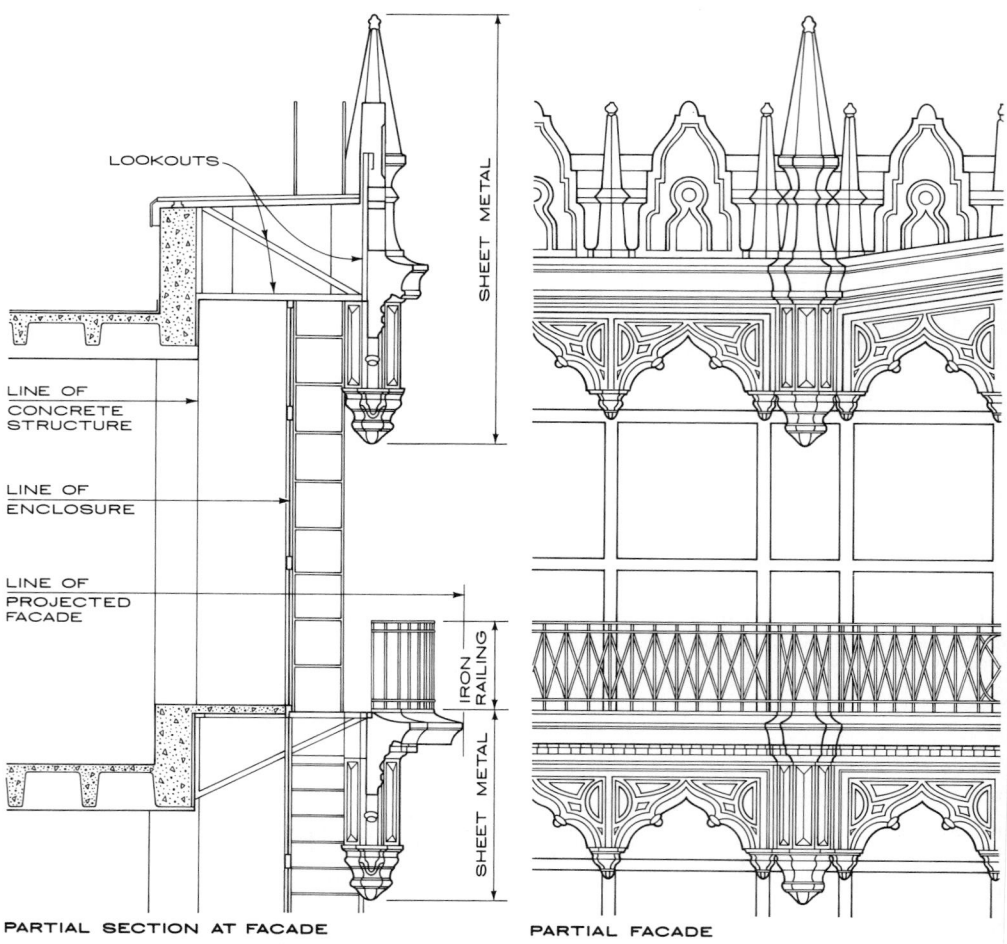

HALLIDIE BUILDING, SAN FRANCISCO, CA, 1918 (WILLIS POLK – ARCHITECT)

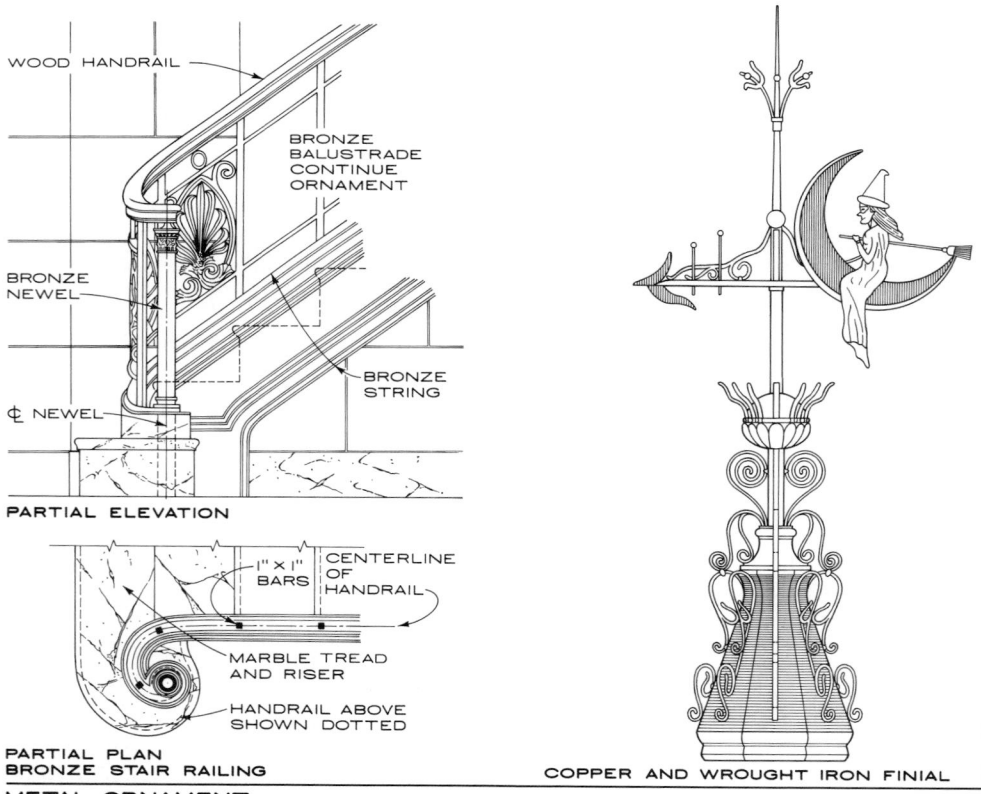

METAL ORNAMENT

Lee H. Nelson, FAIA, H. Ward Jandl, Camille Martone, Kay D. Weeks; Preservation Assistance Division, National Park Service; Washington, D.C.
Eric J. Gastier; Darrel Downing Rippeteau Architects, PC; Washington, D.C.

# ARCHITECTURAL METALS

# INTRODUCTION

The roof—with its shape; features such as cresting, dormers, cupolas, and chimneys; and the size, color, and patterning of the roofing material—is an important design element of many historic buildings. In addition a weathertight roof is essential to the long-term preservation of the entire structure.

Historic roofing is in large measure a reflection of available materials, levels of construction technology, the weather, and cost. For example, throughout the country in all periods of history, wood shingles have been used—their size, shape, and detailing differing according to regional craft practices. European settlers used clay tile for roofing as early as the mid-17th century. In some cities, such as New York and Boston, clay was popularly used as a precaution against fire. The Spanish influence in the use of clay tiles is found in the southern, southwestern, and western states. In the mid-19th century, tile roofs were often replaced by sheet-metal roofs, which were lighter and easier to install and maintain. Another practice settlers brought to the New World was slate roofing, and evidence of its use dates from the mid-17th century. Slate has been popular for its durability, fireproof qualities, and its decorative applications. The use of metals for roofing and roof features dates from the 18th century and includes the use of sheet iron, corrugated iron, galvanized metal, tinplate, and zinc. Awareness of these and other traditions of roofing materials and their detailing will contribute to more sensitive treatments.

# PRESERVATION APPROACHES

The configuration of a historic building can be radically changed by adding new features to the roof, such as dormer windows, vents, skylights, or mechanical and service equipment. Adding an additional floor or floors at the roofline is possibly the most difficult rehabilitation change to accomplish without dramatically changing the historic character of the building. For this reason, the roof's shape, size, color, and patterning should be retained in any preservation project.

Routine maintenance of the building includes cleaning of gutters and downspouts and replacing deteriorated flashing. Roof sheathing should also be checked for proper venting to prevent moisture condensation and water penetration and to ensure that materials are free from insect infestation. When water and debris are permitted to collect, damage may occur to roof fasteners, sheathing, and the underlying structure.

In certain cases, such as storm or fire damage, only portions of a roof or a damaged roofing feature will need repair. The repaired area should match the visual qualities of the historic roof. Some repairs involve less difficulty than others. Normally, individual slates can be replaced without major disruption to the rest of the roof; replacing flashing, on the other hand, can require substantial removal of surrounding materials. If it is the substrate or a support material that has deteriorated, many of the more durable surface materials such as slate or tile can be reused if handled carefully during the repair.

A roof feature that is too deteriorated to repair should be replaced in kind. With some exceptions, most historic roofing materials are available today. Special roofing materials, such as tile or embossed metal shingles, can be produced by manufacturers of related products that are commonly used elsewhere, either on the exterior or interior of a structure. With some creative thinking and research, the historic materials usually can be found. Examples include a large section of roofing, a dormer, decorative roof cresting, or a chimney.

For both repair and replacement of historic roofing, compatible substitute materials may be considered if the same kind of material is technically or economically infeasible; however, the substitute material needs to convey the same visual appearance and be physically and chemically compatible with the surrounding materials.

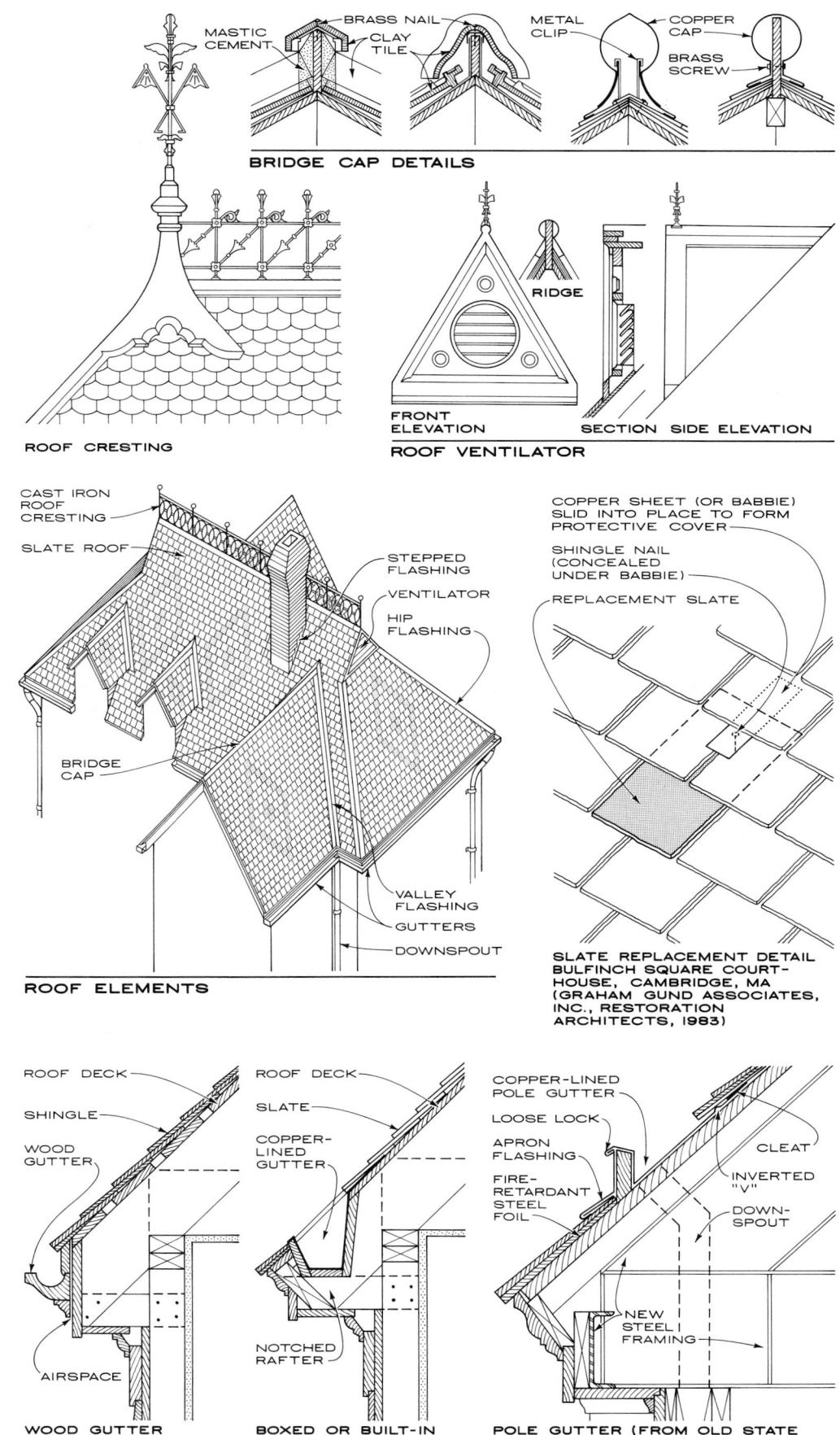

BRIDGE CAP DETAILS

ROOF CRESTING

ROOF VENTILATOR

ROOF ELEMENTS

SLATE REPLACEMENT DETAIL BULFINCH SQUARE COURT-HOUSE, CAMBRIDGE, MA (GRAHAM GUND ASSOCIATES, INC., RESTORATION ARCHITECTS, 1983)

GUTTER DETAILS

WOOD GUTTER

BOXED OR BUILT-IN GUTTER

POLE GUTTER (FROM OLD STATE HOUSE, DOVER, DE)

Lee H. Nelson, FAIA, H. Ward Jandl, Sharon C. Park, AIA; Preservation Assistance Division, National Park Service; Washington, D.C.
Eric J. Gastier; Darrel Downing Rippeteau Architects, PC; Washington, D.C.

## INTRODUCTION

As one of the few parts of a building serving both as an interior and exterior feature, windows are nearly always an important part of the historic character of a building. In most buildings, windows also comprise a considerable amount of the historic fabric of the wall plane and thus are deserving of special consideration. It is essential that the historic character of the windows be assessed together with their physical condition before specific repair or replacement work is undertaken. Emphasis should be placed on repairing existing windows, where possible, and improving their performance, such as with retrofitting weatherstripping to reduce air infiltration. Replacement windows should closely match the historic ones.

## PRESERVATION APPROACHES

Technology and prevailing architectural styles have shaped the history of windows in the United States, starting in the 17th century with wooden casement windows with tiny glass panes seated in lead cames. From the transitional single-hung sash in the early 1700s to the true double-hung sash later in the same century,

VENETIAN WINDOW FROM THE OLD STATE HOUSE
DOVER, DE (McCUNE ASSOCIATES, RESTORATION ARCHITECTS)

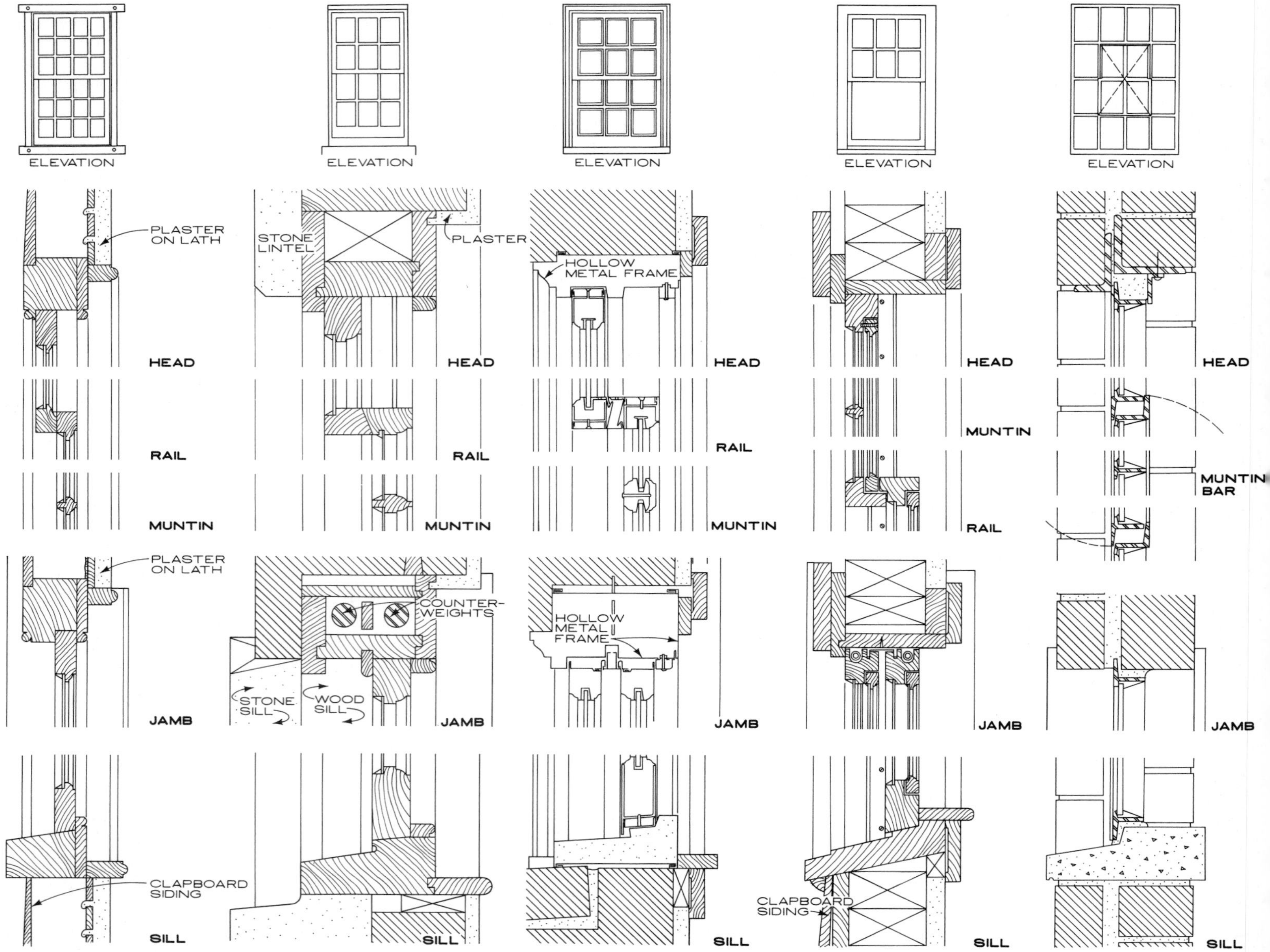

these early wooden windows were characterized by small panes, wide muntins, and the way in which decorative trim was used on both the exterior and interior of the window. As the sash thickness increased by the turn of the 19th century, muntins narrowed in width but increased in thickness according to the size of the window and design practices. Regional traditions continued to have an impact on window design, such as with the long-term use of ''French windows'' in the deep South. By the mid-19th century, two-over-two lights were common; the manufacturing of plate glass in the United States by the late 19th century allowed for dramatic use of large sheets of glass in commercial and office buildings. With mass-produced windows, mail order distribution, and changing architectural styles, it was possible to obtain a wide range of window designs and light patterns in sash. Popular versions of Arts and Crafts houses constructed in the early 20th century frequently utilized smaller lights in the upper sash set in groups or pairs and saw the reemergence of casement windows. In the early 20th century, the desire for fireproof building construction in dense urban areas contributed to the growth of a thriving steel window industry along with a market for hollow metal and metal clad wooden windows.

ELEVATION     ELEVATION     ELEVATION     ELEVATION     ELEVATION

PLASTER ON LATH — STONE LINTEL — PLASTER — HOLLOW METAL FRAME

HEAD     HEAD     HEAD     HEAD     HEAD

RAIL     RAIL     RAIL     MUNTIN     MUNTIN

MUNTIN     MUNTIN     MUNTIN     RAIL     MUNTIN BAR

PLASTER ON LATH — COUNTER-WEIGHTS — HOLLOW METAL FRAME

STONE SILL — WOOD SILL

JAMB     JAMB     JAMB     JAMB     JAMB

CLAPBOARD SIDING — CLAPBOARD SIDING

SILL     SILL     SILL     SILL     SILL

SINGLE-HUNG WOODEN WINDOW SOLID MORTISE AND TENON FRAME EARLY 18TH CENTURY

DOUBLE-HUNG WOODEN WINDOW MID-19TH CENTURY

STANDARD HOLLOW GALVANIZED IRON DOUBLE-HUNG WINDOW CIRCA 1910

DOUBLE-GLAZED DOUBLE-HUNG WOODEN WINDOW 1930S

HORIZONTAL PIVOTED STEEL WINDOW EARLY 20TH CENTURY

Lee H. Nelson, FAIA, H. Ward Jandl, Charles Fisher; Preservation Assistance Division, National Park Service; Washington, D.C.
Eric J. Gastier; Darrel Downing Rippeteau Architects, PC; Washington, D.C.

WINDOWS

## PRESERVATION APPROACHES

An in-depth survey of the condition of existing windows should be undertaken early in the planning of a rehabilitation to allow time to fully explore repair and upgrading methods and possible replacement options, if merited. Peeling paint, broken glass, stuck sash, and high air infiltration are no indication that existing windows are beyond repair and that their performance cannot be enhanced.

The wood and architectural metal which comprise the window frame, sash, muntins, and surrounds should be maintained through appropriate surface treatments such as cleaning, rust removal, limited paint removal, reapplication of protective coating systems, and reglazing where necessary.

Windows should be made weathertight by recaulking and replacing or installing weatherstripping. These actions also improve thermal efficiency. Retrofitting or replacing windows should never be a substitute for proper maintenance of the sash, frame, and glazing.

Window frames and sash can be repaired by patching, splicing, consolidating, or otherwise reinforcing historic materials.

Window repair can include replacement of deteriorated components such as sash cords, muntins, and sills.

Serviceable window hardware such as brass lifts and sash locks can be reused in the course of repairs and should not be discarded in favor of new hardware.

Thermal efficiency can be improved with weatherstripping, storm windows, caulking, interior shades, and, if historically appropriate, blinds and awnings. Replacing historic multipaned sash with new thermal sash is inappropriate when the historic sash are in repairable condition.

Interior storm windows should have airtight gaskets, ventilating holes, and/or removable clips or operability features to ensure proper maintenance and to avoid potential condensation damage to historic windows.

Exterior storm windows should be selected that do not damage or obscure the windows and frames. It is not appropriate to install new exterior storm windows that are inappropriate in size and are not painted the same color as the sash trim.

Tinted or reflective glazing should never be used on character-defining or other conspicuous elevations. Lightly tinted glazing could be used on non-character-defining elevations if other energy retrofitting alternatives are not possible and after conclusively establishing a need for such a treatment.

A historic window that is too deteriorated to repair should in most cases be replaced in kind, that is, using the same kind of material (wood for wood; steel for steel) and using the same sash and pane configuration and other design details.

In some cases, the historic windows (frame, sash, and glazing) may be completely missing. The preferred option for replacement is always an accurate restoration using historical, pictorial, and physical documentation.

Where fixed windows are being installed, the glass and frames should be set in the same planes as the historic sash, with all detailing duplicated.

When replacing historic multipaned sash with new sash, true integral muntins should be utilized, particularly on smaller buildings, windows on large buildings close to the pedestrianway, on ornate windows, where windows are part of a significant interior space, and where a building has high historic merit.

On certain types of large buildings, particularly high-rises, aluminum windows may be a suitable replacement for historic wooden sash provided wooden replacements are not practical and the design detail of the historic windows can be matched. Historic color duplication, custom contour panning, incorporation of ⅝ in. deep trapezoidal exterior muntin grids where applicable, retention of the same glass-to-frame ratio, matching of the historic reveal, and duplication of the frame width, depth, and such existing decorative details as arched tops should all be components in aluminum replacement windows selected for use on historic buildings.

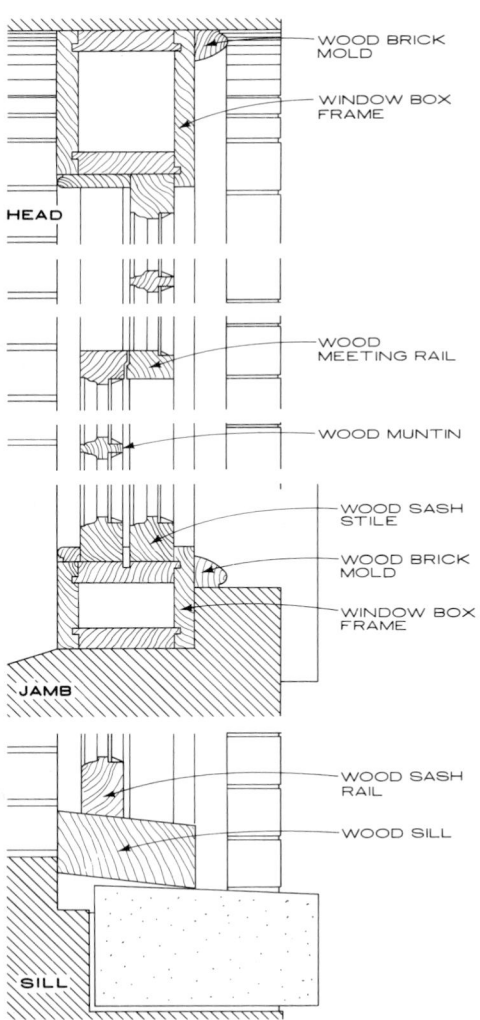

**LATE 19TH CENTURY MILL WINDOW**

REPAIR WHENEVER POSSIBLE.
IN SOME CASES, REPLACEMENT OF SASH AND REUSE OF FRAMES AND HARDWARE MAY BE POSSIBLE

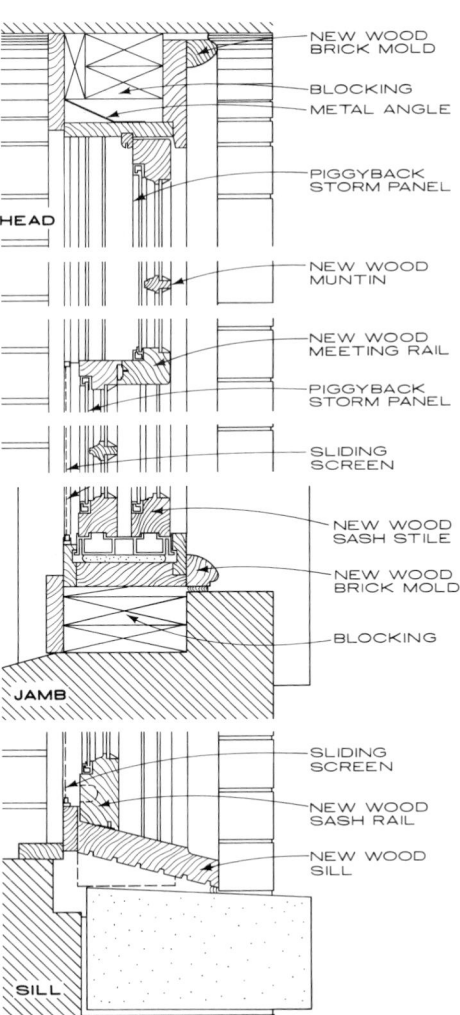

**WOOD REPLACEMENT WINDOW**

APPROPRIATE WHEN HISTORIC WINDOW IS BEYOND REPAIR. IN MANY CASES, PIGGYBACK INTERIOR STORM PANELS ATTACHED TO NEW SASH AND/OR INTERIOR MOUNTED INSECT SCREENS ARE SUITABLE UPGRADED FEATURES. EXTERIOR APPEARANCE OF HISTORIC WINDOW SHOULD BE RETAINED

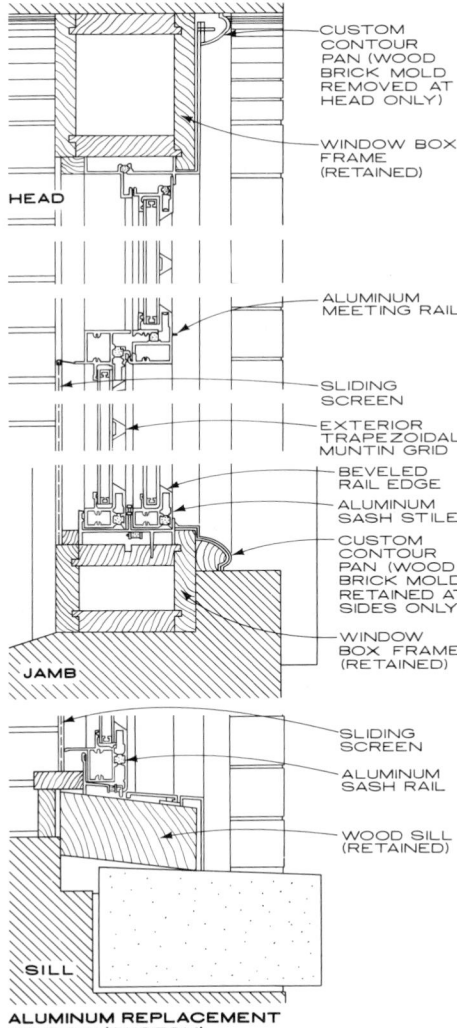

**ALUMINUM REPLACEMENT WINDOW (CUSTOM)**

APPROPRIATE IN SOME CASES, PARTICULARLY IN EARLY 20TH CENTURY HIGH-RISES. SPECIAL FEATURES TO BE SPECIFIED: BEVELED RAIL AND STILE EDGES, CUSTOM CONTOUR PANNING, CUSTOM COLOR, TRAPEZOIDAL EXTERIOR MUNTIN GRID, AND CLOSELY MATCHED SIGHT LINES

**REPAIR/REPLACEMENT STRATEGIES FOR HISTORIC WOOD WINDOWS**

Lee H. Nelson, FAIA, H. Ward Jandl, Charles Fisher; Preservation Assistance Division, National Park Service; Washington, D.C.
Eric J. Gastier; Darrel Downing Rippeteau Architects, PC; Washington, D.C.

## INTRODUCTION

Entrances and porches are quite often the focus of historic buildings, particularly when they occur on primary elevations. Together with their functional and decorative features such as doors, steps, balustrades, pilasters, and entablatures, they can be extremely important in defining the overall character of a building.

Usually entrances and porches were integral components of a historic building's design; for example, porches on Greek Revival houses, with Doric or Ionic columns and pediments, echoed the architectural elements and features of the larger building. Central one-bay porches or arcaded porches are evident in Italianate style buildings of the 1860s. Doors of Renaissance Revival style buildings frequently supported entablatures or pediments. Porches were particularly prominent features of Eastlake and Stick Style houses; porch posts, railings, and balusters were characterized by a massive and robust quality, with members turned on a lathe. Porches of bungalows of the early 20th century were characterized by tapered porch posts, exposed post and beams, and low-pitched roofs with wide overhangs. Art Deco commercial buildings were entered through stylized glass and stainless steel doors.

## PRESERVATION APPROACHES

The materials that comprise entrances and porches—masonry, wood, and architectural metal—should be protected and maintained through appropriate surface treatments such as cleaning, rust removal, limited paint removal, and reapplication of protective coating systems. The overall condition of materials should be evaluated to determine whether more than protection and maintenance are required.

Removing or radically changing primary entrances will in most cases change the overall appearance of the build-

ing. Entrances and porches should never be removed because the building has been reoriented to accommodate a new use.

If barrier-free access is required to a historic building, it should be introduced in such a manner that does not destroy significant material or that does not interfere with the historic design.

Entrances and porches can be repaired by reinforcing deteriorated historic materials—patching, splicing, and reinforcing with epoxies are examples. Limited replacement in kind of those extensively deteriorated or missing parts of repeated features may be undertaken where there are surviving prototypes. Examples include balustrades, cornices, entablatures, columns, sidelights, and stairs.

Only when an entire entrance or porch is too deteriorated to repair—or is missing—should total replacement be considered. If the historic form and detailing are still evident, this evidence should be used to restore the entrance or porch.

If the entrance or porch is missing, restoration should be based on historical, pictorial, and physical evidence rather than on conjectural designs or the availability of elements from neighboring buildings.

When insufficient documentation exists for an accurate restoration, the replacement entrance or porch may be a new design that is consistent with the size, scale, material, and color of the historic building. Care must be taken not to create a false historic appearance in the new work.

Compatible substitute material may be considered if replicating with the historic material is technically or economically infeasible; the substitute material needs to convey the same visual appearance and be physically and chemically compatible.

PORCH AND ENTRY

**655 HUGHES STREET, CAPE MAY, NJ**

PORCH AND ENTRY

**FENDALL HALL, EUFAULA, AL (NICHOLAS H. HOLMES, RESTORATION ARCHITECT, 1975)**

PORCH AND ENTRY

**GUNSTON HALL, FAIRFAX COUNTY, VA**

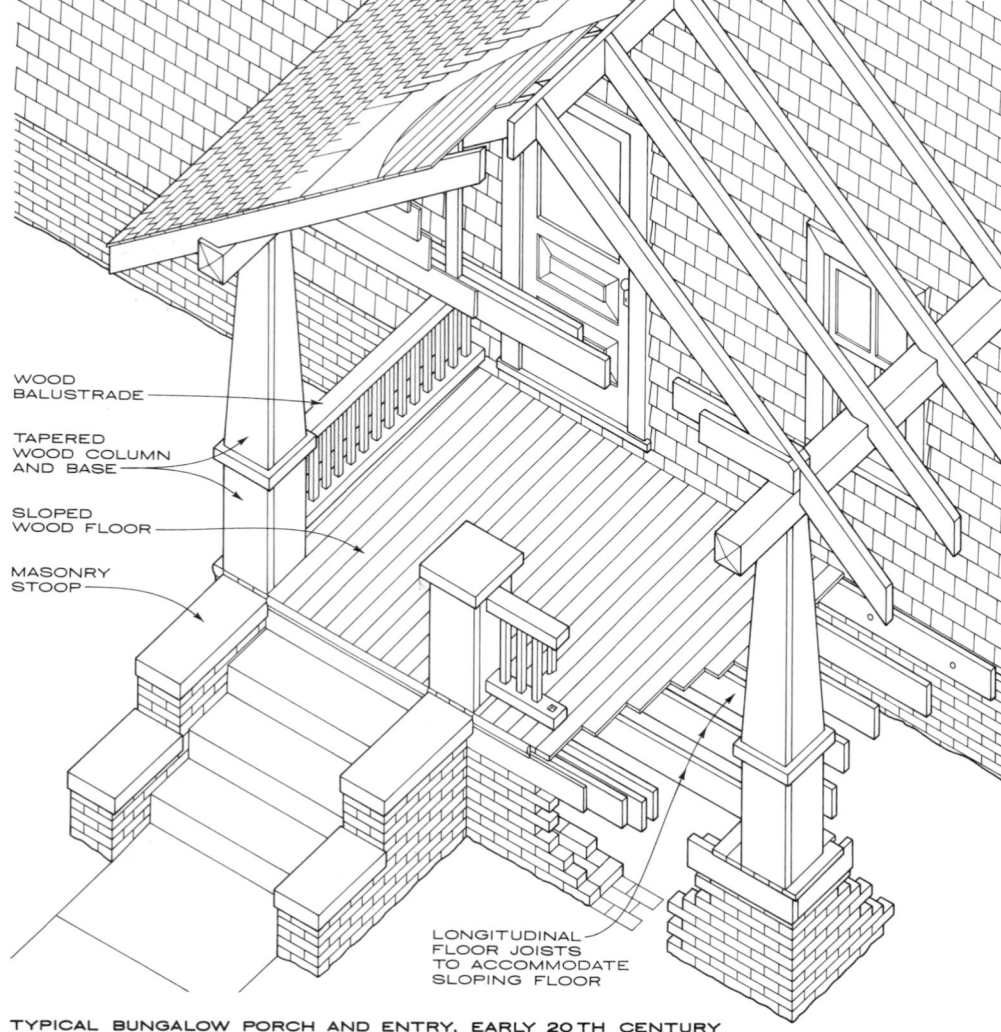

WOOD BALUSTRADE

TAPERED WOOD COLUMN AND BASE

SLOPED WOOD FLOOR

MASONRY STOOP

LONGITUDINAL FLOOR JOISTS TO ACCOMMODATE SLOPING FLOOR

**TYPICAL BUNGALOW PORCH AND ENTRY, EARLY 20TH CENTURY**

Lee H. Nelson, FAIA, H. Ward Jandl, Camille Martone, Kay D. Weeks; Preservation Assistance Division, National Park Service; Washington, D.C.
Eric J. Gastier; Darrel Downing Rippeteau Architects, PC; Washington, D.C.

 **19** **ENTRANCES AND PORCHES**

## INTRODUCTION

The storefront is usually the most prominent feature of a historic commercial building, playing a crucial role in a store's advertising and merchandising strategy. Although a storefront normally does not extend beyond the first story, the rest of the building is often related to it visually through a unity of form and detail. Planning should always consider the entire building; window patterns on the upper floors, cornice elements, and other decorative features should be carefully retained, in addition to the storefront itself.

The earliest extant storefronts in the United States, dating from the late 18th and early 19th centuries, had bay or oriel windows and provided limited display space. The 19th century witnessed the progressive enlargement of display windows as plate glass became available in increasingly larger units. The use of cast iron columns and lintels at ground floor level permitted structural members to be reduced in size. Recessed entrances provided shelter for sidewalk patrons and further enlarged display areas. In the 1920s and 1930s, aluminum, colored structural glass, stainless steel, glass block, neon, and other new materials were introduced to create Art Deco

storefronts. The growing appreciation of historic buildings in recent years has prompted many owners to remove inappropriate changes and restore the historic appearance.

## PRESERVATION APPROACHES

Functional and decorative features that make up the historic storefront include display windows, lower window panels, transoms, business signs, entrance doors, and entablatures. Materials that make up a storefront—cast iron, bronze, wood, pressed metal, structural glass—should be identified before undertaking any preservation work.

Removal of inappropriate, nonhistoric cladding as well as later alterations such as oversized awnings and signs can enhance a historic storefront.

The historic storefront should be secured by boarding up windows and installing alarm systems prior to and during rehabilitation. Unsecured doors and broken windows permit interior features and finishes to be subjected to damage by weather or vandalism.

Historic features such as cracked display windows, deteriorated wooden lower window panels, and rusted metal structural members should be repaired wherever possible rather than replaced.

Repairs are best made using historic materials; however, substitute materials may be appropriate if they convey the same visual appearance as the surviving components of the storefront.

Only if an entire storefront is missing or is too deteriorated to repair should total replacement be considered. The historic form and detailing should be used to restore the storefront.

Restoration should be based on historical and pictorial evidence rather than on conjectural designs or the availability of elements from neighboring buildings. When insufficient documentation exists for an accurate restoration, the replacement storefront may be a new design that is consistent with the size, scale, material, and color of the historic building.

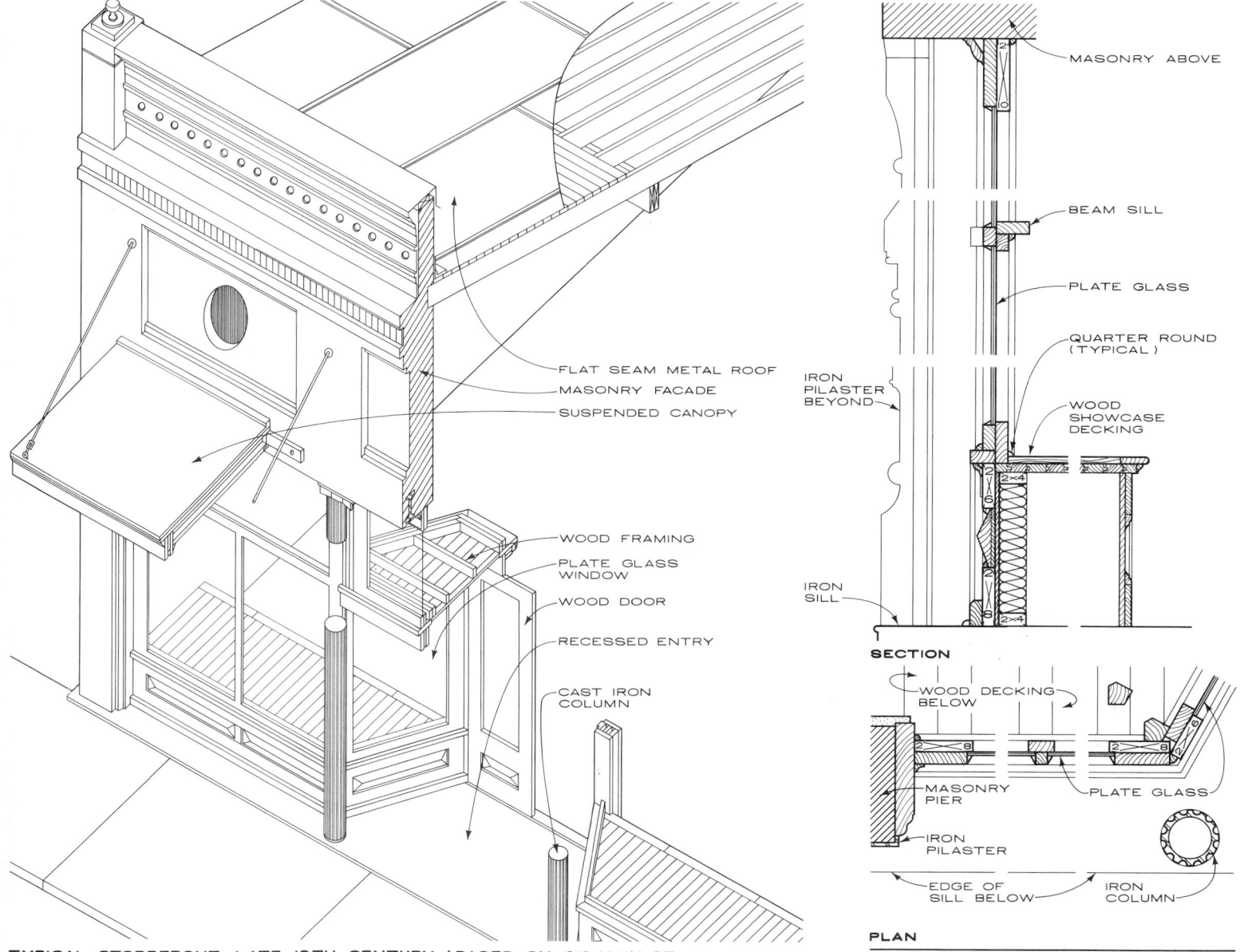

**TYPICAL STOREFRONT, LATE 19TH CENTURY (BASED ON 610 MAIN ST., VAN BUREN, AR, DAVID FITTS – ARCHITECT)**

**STOREFRONT DETAILS**

Lee H. Nelson, FAIA, H. Ward Jandl, Michael J. Auer; Preservation Assistance Division, National Park Service; Washington, D.C.
Eric J. Gastier; Darrel Downing Rippeteau Architects, PC; Washington, D.C.

## INTRODUCTION

If features of the structural system are exposed, such as load-bearing brick walls, cast iron columns, roof trusses, posts and beams, vigas, or stone foundation walls, they may be important in defining the building's overall historic character.

Structural systems in architecture are composed of structural elements (such as beams, piers, and trusses) and building materials (wood, steel, and masonry) that together form the walls, floors, and roofing of buildings.

The types of structural systems found in America include, but certainly are not limited to, the following: wooden frame construction (17th century), balloon frame construction (19th century), load-bearing masonry construction (18th century), brick cavity wall construction (19th century), heavy timber post and beam industrial construction (19th century), fireproof iron construction (19th century), heavy masonry and steel construction (19th century), skeletal steel construction (19th century), and concrete slab and post construction (20th century).

## PRESERVATION APPROACHES

A significant structural system or distinctive structural features should be identified prior to any work. To accommodate new uses within a historic building, structural upgrading should be done in a sensitive manner. Installing equipment or mechanical systems that result in numerous cuts, splices, or alterations to historic structural members should always be avoided.

If excavations or regrading—either adjacent to or within a historic building—are being planned, studies should be

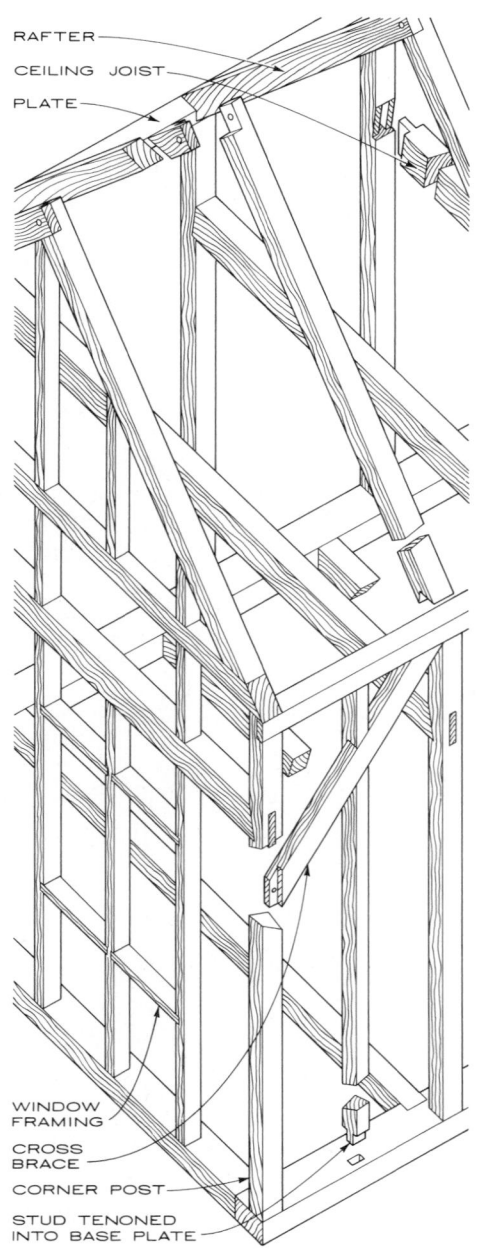

RAFTER
CEILING JOIST
PLATE
WINDOW FRAMING
CROSS BRACE
CORNER POST
STUD TENONED INTO BASE PLATE

**TYPICAL 18TH CENTURY MORTISE AND TENON WOOD FRAMING**

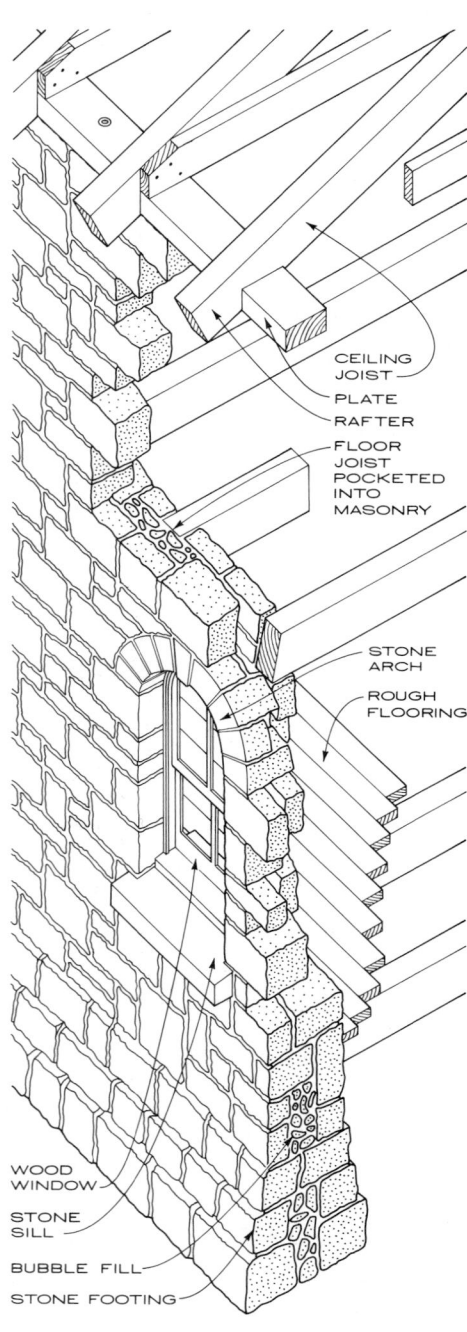

CEILING JOIST
PLATE
RAFTER
FLOOR JOIST POCKETED INTO MASONRY
STONE ARCH
ROUGH FLOORING
WOOD WINDOW
STONE SILL
BUBBLE FILL
STONE FOOTING

**18TH AND 19TH CENTURIES LOAD-BEARING MASONRY**

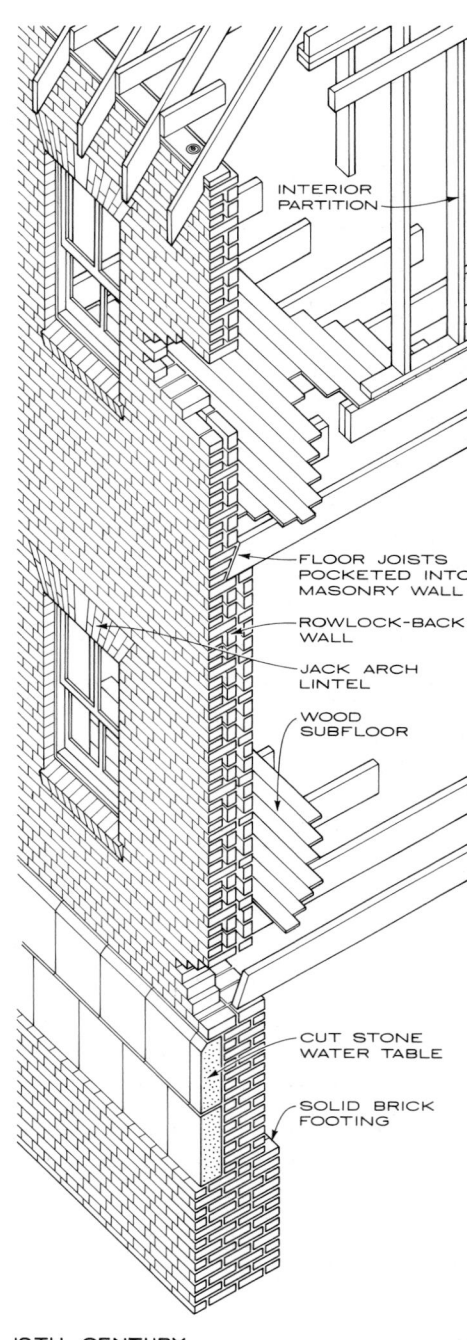

INTERIOR PARTITION
FLOOR JOISTS POCKETED INTO MASONRY WALL
ROWLOCK-BACK WALL
JACK ARCH LINTEL
WOOD SUBFLOOR
CUT STONE WATER TABLE
SOLID BRICK FOOTING

**19TH CENTURY BRICK CAVITY WALL**

## STRUCTURAL SYSTEMS

Lee H. Nelson, FAIA, H. Ward Jandl, Sharon C. Park, AIA, Kay D. Weeks; Preservation Assistance Division, National Park Service; Washington, D.C.
Eric J. Gastier; Darrel Downing Rippeteau Architects, PC; Washington, D.C.

**19** **STRUCTURAL SYSTEMS**

done first to ascertain potential damage. Inappropriate excavations can cause the historic foundation to settle, shift, or fail.

Structural problems, such as deflection of beams, racking of structural members, or cracking and bowing of walls, should be treated—not cosmetically covered over. A deteriorated load-bearing masonry wall should be reinforced and retained wherever possible, not replaced with a new wall that is veneered using old brick.

Structural systems may be protected by cyclical cleaning of roof gutters and downspouts; replacing roof flashing;

keeping masonry, wood, and architectural metals in a sound condition; and assuring that structural members are free from insect infestation.

The structural system should be repaired by augmenting or upgrading individual parts or features. For example, weakened structural members such as floor framing can be paired with a new member, braced, or otherwise supplemented and reinforced.

Structural upgrading should never be undertaken in a manner that diminishes the historic character of the building, such as installing exterior strapping channels.

In instances where seismic upgrading is necessary, it is best to use grouted bolts as opposed to exposed plates and to locate diaphragms on unornamented surfaces or to consider other options that reduce the visual and physical impact of the code-required change.

If exposed elements of the structural system are beyond repair, the replacements need to convey the same form, design, and overall visual appearance as the historic feature, to equal the load-bearing capabilities of the historic material, and to be physically and chemically compatible.

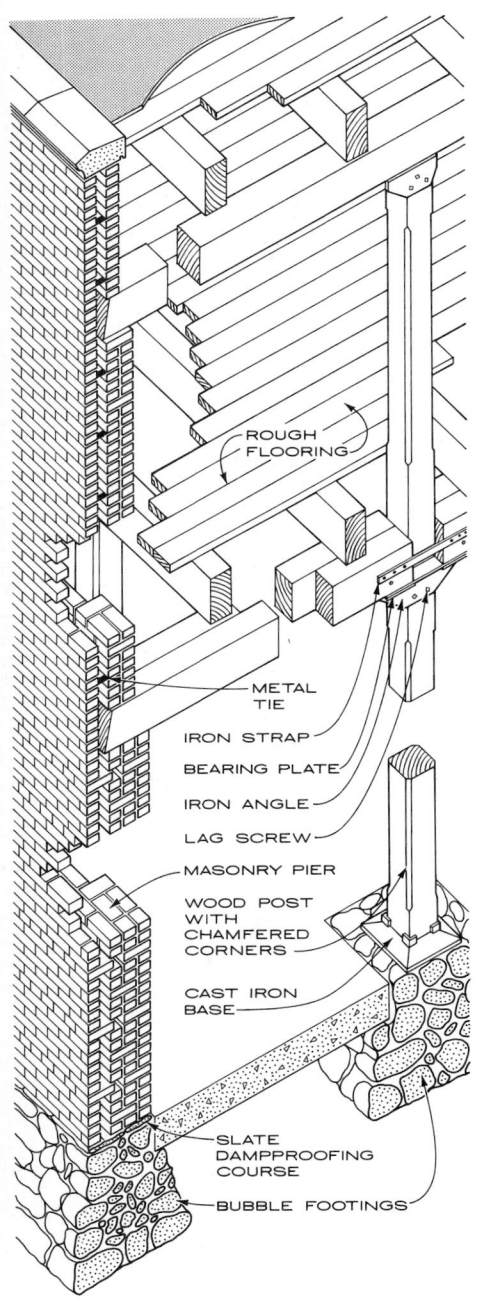

ROUGH FLOORING

METAL TIE
IRON STRAP
BEARING PLATE
IRON ANGLE
LAG SCREW
MASONRY PIER
WOOD POST WITH CHAMFERED CORNERS
CAST IRON BASE
SLATE DAMPPROOFING COURSE
BUBBLE FOOTINGS

**19TH AND EARLY 20TH CENTURIES HEAVY TIMBER POST AND BEAM**

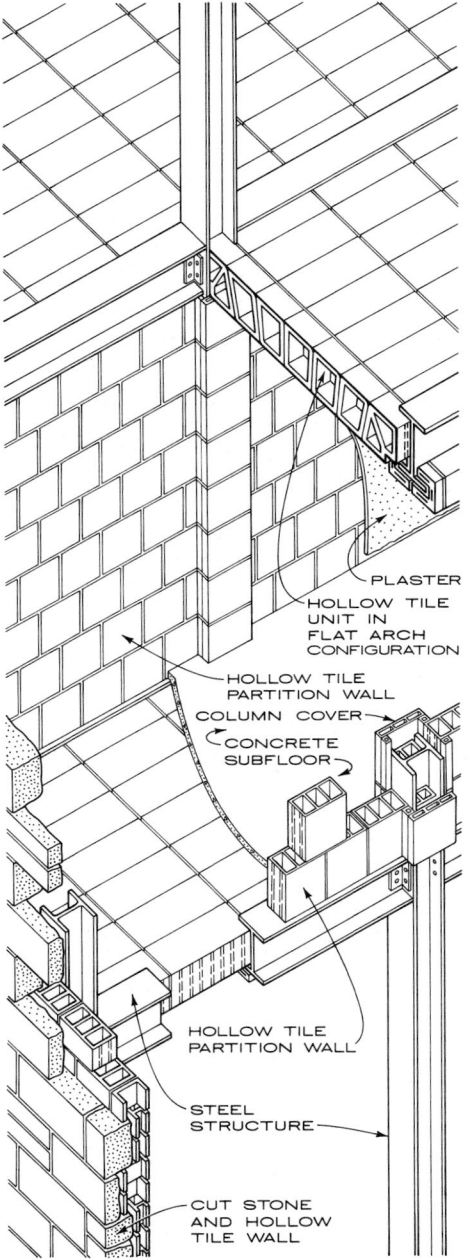

PLASTER
HOLLOW TILE UNIT IN FLAT ARCH CONFIGURATION
HOLLOW TILE PARTITION WALL
COLUMN COVER
CONCRETE SUBFLOOR
HOLLOW TILE PARTITION WALL
STEEL STRUCTURE
CUT STONE AND HOLLOW TILE WALL

**LATE 19TH AND EARLY 20TH CENTURIES FIREPROOF CONSTRUCTION**

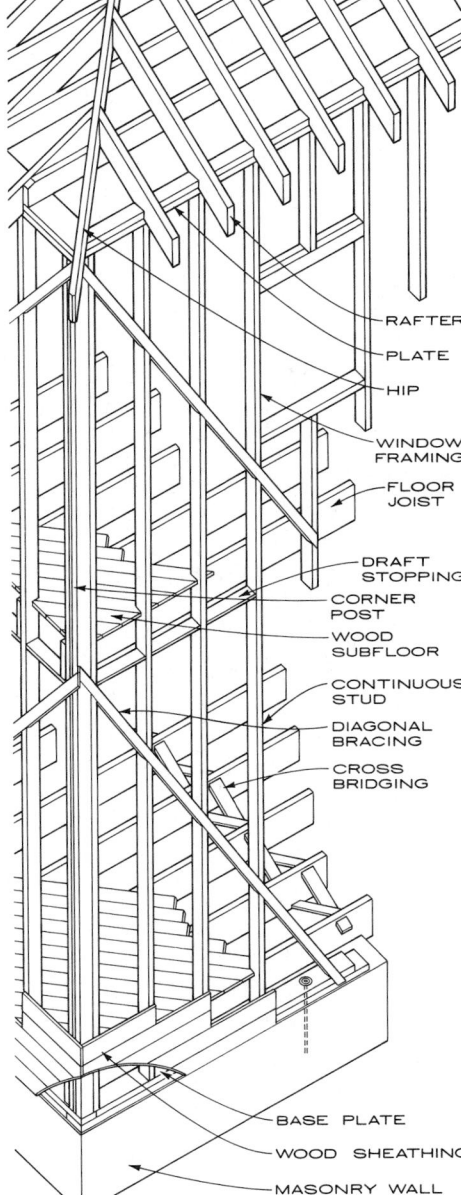

RAFTER
PLATE
HIP
WINDOW FRAMING
FLOOR JOIST
DRAFT STOPPING
CORNER POST
WOOD SUBFLOOR
CONTINUOUS STUD
DIAGONAL BRACING
CROSS BRIDGING
BASE PLATE
WOOD SHEATHING
MASONRY WALL

**20TH CENTURY BALLOON FRAMING**

**STRUCTURAL SYSTEMS**

Lee H. Nelson, FAIA, H. Ward Jandl, Sharon C. Park, AIA, Kay D. Weeks; Preservation Assistance Division, National Park Service; Washington, D.C.
Eric J. Gastier; Darrel Downing Rippeteau Architects, PC; Washington, D.C.

STRUCTURAL SYSTEMS　19

## INTRODUCTION

An interior floor plan, the arrangement and sequence of spaces, and built-in features and applied finishes are individually and collectively important in defining the historic character of the building. Their identification, retention, protection, and repair should be given prime consideration in every rehabilitation project.

In evaluating historic interiors prior to rehabilitation, it should be kept in mind that interiors are comprised of a series of primary and secondary spaces. This is applicable to all buildings, from courthouses to cathedrals to cottages and office buildings. Primary spaces, including entrance halls, parlors, living rooms, assembly rooms, and lobbies, are defined not only by their features and finishes, but by the size and proportion of the rooms themselves—purposely created to be the visual attraction or functioning ''core'' of the building. Care should be taken to retain the essential proportions of primary interior spaces and not to damage, obscure, or destroy distinctive features and finishes.

Secondary spaces include areas and rooms that ''service'' the primary spaces and may include kitchens, bathrooms, mail rooms, utility spaces, secondary hallways, firestairs, and office cubicles in a commercial or office space. Extensive changes can often be made in these less important areas without having a detrimental effect on the overall historic character.

## PRESERVATION APPROACHES

Distinctive interior spaces, features, and finishes should be identified, then carefully retained and preserved in any work project. Examples include columns, cornices, baseboards, fireplaces and mantels, paneling, light fixtures, hardware, flooring, and wallpaper, plaster, paint, and finishes such as stenciling, marbling, and graining.

Distinctive interior spaces should not be altered by inserting a floor, cutting through the floor, lowering ceilings, or adding or removing walls.

Historically finished surfaces such as paint, plaster, or other finishes should not be stripped (e.g., removing plaster to expose masonry surfaces such as brick walls or a chimney piece). It is also inappropriate to strip painted wood to a bare wood surface, then apply a clear finish or stain to create a ''natural, new look.'' Distinctive finishes such as marbling or graining on doors or paneling should be repaired, not covered over or removed. Conversely, paint, plaster, or other finishes should not be applied to surfaces that have been historically unfinished to create a new appearance.

Code-required fire suppression systems (such as a sprinkler system for a wood-frame mill building) should be sensitively designed so that character-defining features are not covered.

Interior features should be protected against gouging, scratching, and denting during project work by covering them with heavy canvas or plastic sheets. Destructive methods of paint removal such as propane or butane torches or sandblasting should never be used because they can irreversibly damage the historic materials that comprise interior features.

Interior features and finishes can often be repaired and preserved by reinforcing the historic materials. Repair may involve the limited replacement in kind of those extensively deteriorated or missing parts of repeated fea-

tures when there are surviving prototypes such as stairs. Examples include balustrades, wood paneling, columns, or decorative wall coverings or ornamental tin or plaster ceilings. If an interior feature or finish is too deteriorated to repair or is missing, its replacement should be based on historical and pictorial evidence rather than on conjectural designs or the availability of elements from neighboring buildings.

In cases where insufficient documentation exists for an accurate restoration of an interior feature or finish, the replacement should be compatible in scale, design, materials, color, and texture with the surviving interior features and finishes. A new design element should be distinguishable from the old and not create a false historic appearance.

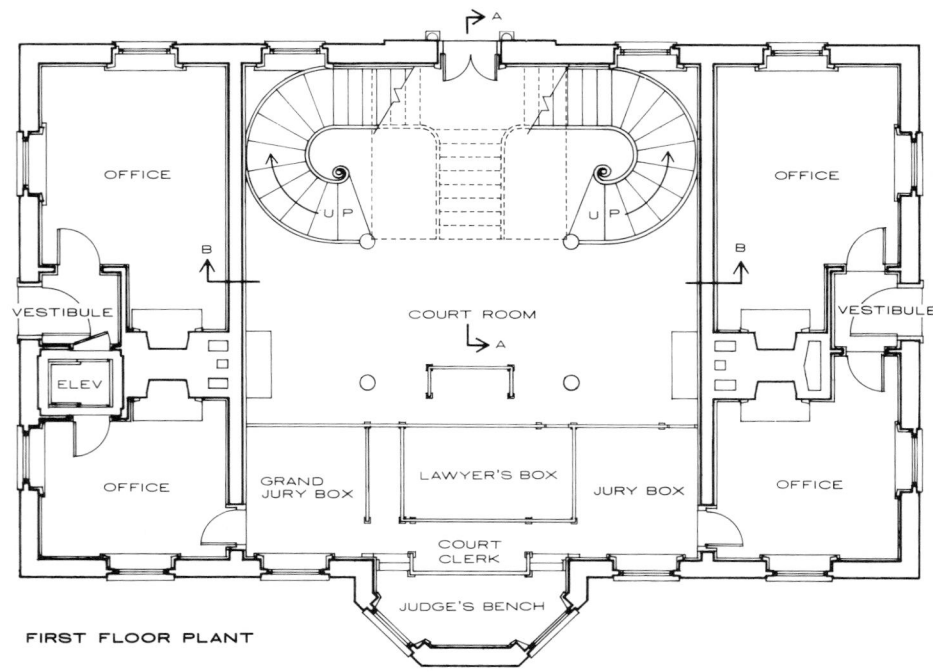

FIRST FLOOR PLAN

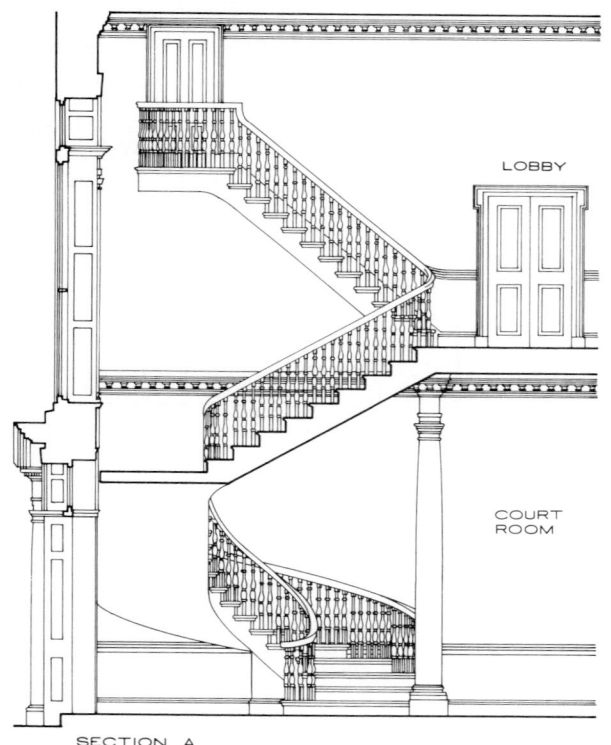

SECTION A

**PARTIAL TRANSVERSE SECTION**

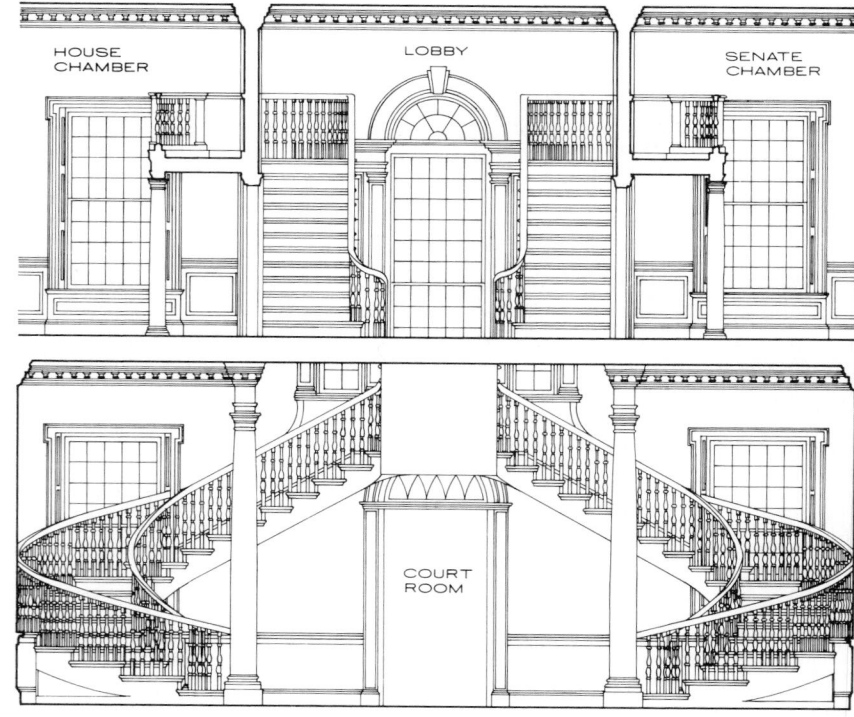

SECTION B

**PARTIAL LONGITUDINAL SECTION**

**OLD STATE HOUSE, DOVER, DE (McCUNE ASSOCIATES, RESTORATION ARCHITECTS, 1977)**

Lee H. Nelson, FAIA, H. Ward Jandl, Camille Martone, Kay D. Weeks; Preservation Assistance Division, National Park Service; Washington, D.C.
Eric J. Gastier; Darrel Downing Rippeteau Architects, PC; Washington, D.C.

**INTERIORS**

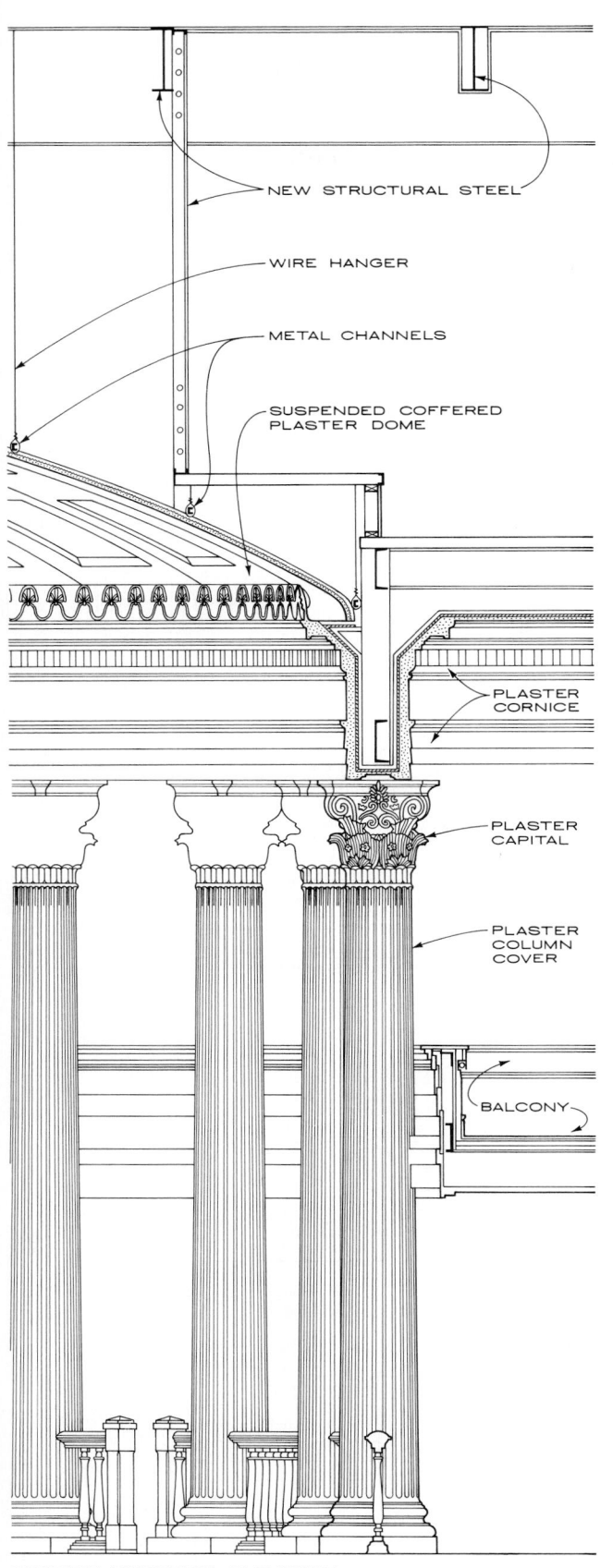

NEW STRUCTURAL STEEL

WIRE HANGER

METAL CHANNELS

SUSPENDED COFFERED PLASTER DOME

PLASTER CORNICE

PLASTER CAPITAL

PLASTER COLUMN COVER

BALCONY

**SECTION / INTERIOR ELEVATION**
**OLD CAPITOL BUILDING, SPRINGFIELD, IL**
**(FERRY AND HENDERSON - ARCHITECTS FOR**
**RESTORATION, 1967)**

STEEL HANGER

4 × 4 METAL CHANNEL

GLASS DOME

HEAVY WIRE SUSPENDER

¾" METAL CHANNEL

PLASTER

EGG AND DART ORNAMENT

PLASTER PANEL

WOOD PLASTER AND CAPITAL

EGG AND DART ORNAMENT

SUNK CHANNEL

**SECTION / INTERIOR ELEVATION**
**VENTURA COUNTY COURTHOUSE, SAN BUENA, VENTURA, CA,**
**1911 (ALBERT C. MARTIN - ARCHITECT)**

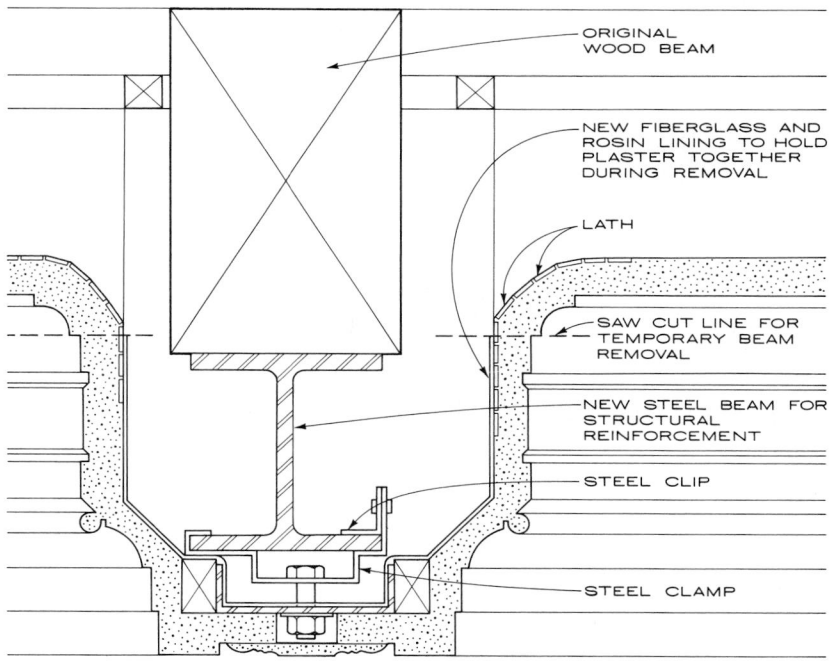

ORIGINAL WOOD BEAM

NEW FIBERGLASS AND ROSIN LINING TO HOLD PLASTER TOGETHER DURING REMOVAL

LATH

SAW CUT LINE FOR TEMPORARY BEAM REMOVAL

NEW STEEL BEAM FOR STRUCTURAL REINFORCEMENT

STEEL CLIP

STEEL CLAMP

**ORNAMENTAL PLASTER BEAM REMOVAL AND REPLACEMENT DETAIL**
**CROCKER ART GALLERY, SACRAMENTO, CA**
**(ROSEKRANS AND BRODER, INC. - ARCHITECTS FOR RESTORATION,**
**1978)**

**ORNAMENTAL PLASTER**

Lee H. Nelson, FAIA, H. Ward Jandl, Camille Martone, Kay D. Weeks; Preservation Assistance Division, National Park Service;
Washington, D.C.
Eric J. Gastier; Darrel Downing Rippeteau Architects, PC; Washington, D.C.

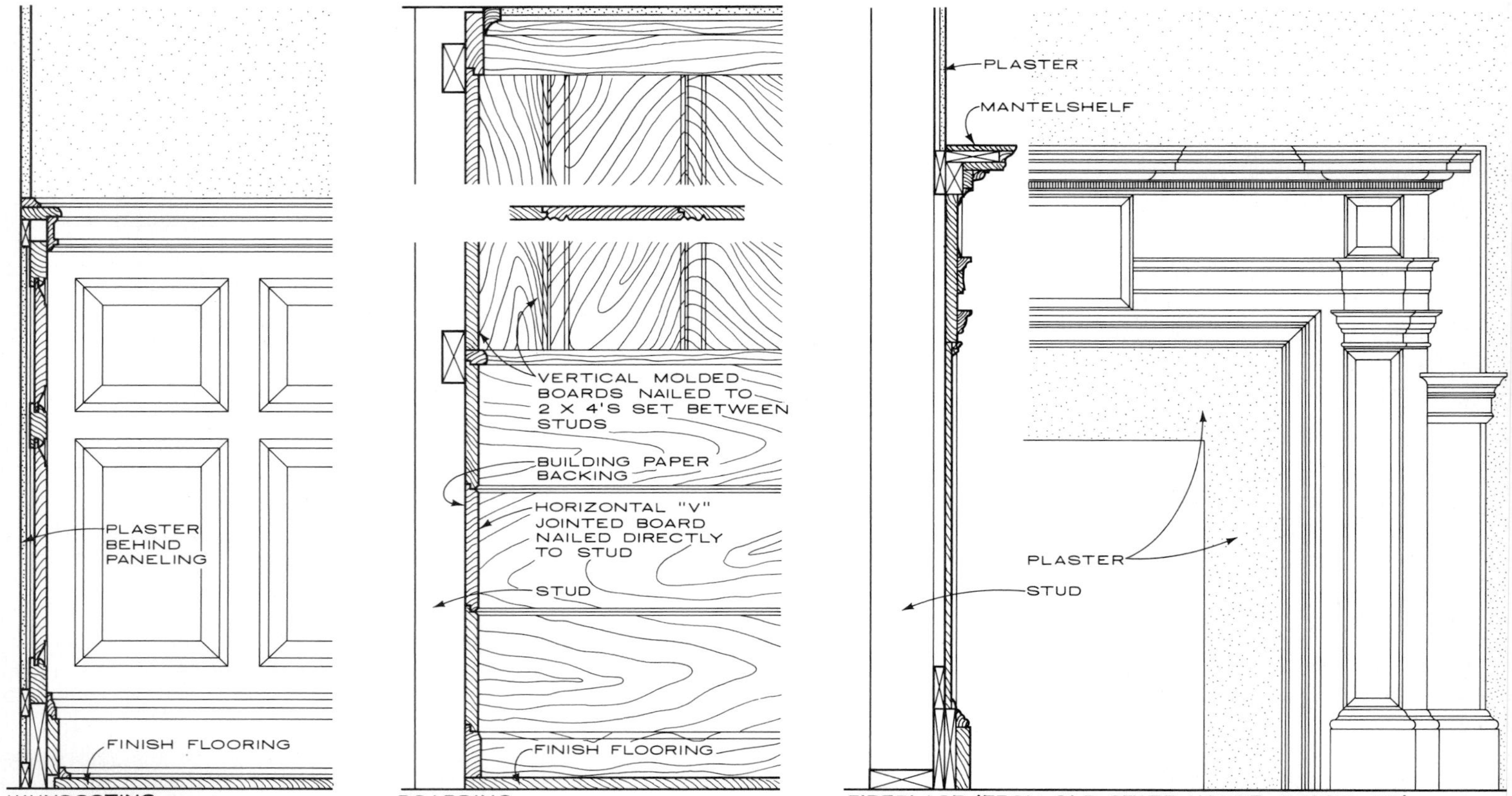

PLASTER

MANTELSHELF

VERTICAL MOLDED
BOARDS NAILED TO
2 X 4'S SET BETWEEN
STUDS

BUILDING PAPER
BACKING

HORIZONTAL "V"
JOINTED BOARD
NAILED DIRECTLY
TO STUD

STUD

PLASTER

STUD

PLASTER
BEHIND
PANELING

FINISH FLOORING

FINISH FLOORING

WAINSCOTING

BOARDING

FIREPLACE (FROM OLD STATE HOUSE, DOVER, DE)

**WOOD PANELING AND CABINETRY WORK**

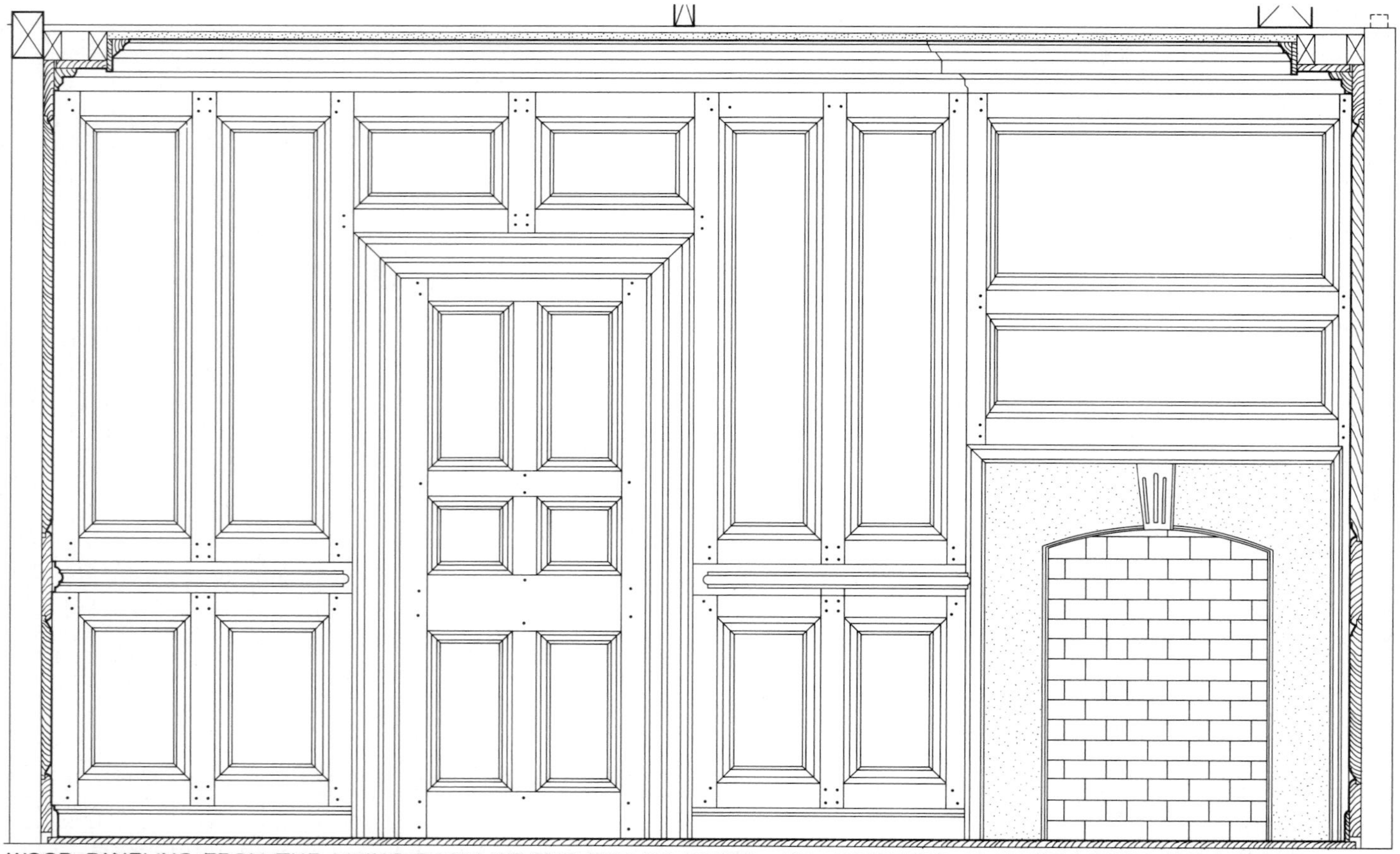

**WOOD PANELING FROM THE LIVING ROOM OF THE TAYLOE HOUSE, WILLIAMSBURG, VA (PERRY, SHAW AND HEPBURN, CONSULTING ARCHITECTS FOR RESTORATION, 1949)**

Lee H. Nelson, FAIA, H. Ward Jandl, Camille Martone, Kay D. Weeks; Preservation Assistance Division, National Park Service; Washington, D.C.
Eric J. Gastier; Darrel Downing Rippeteau Architects, PC; Washington, D.C.

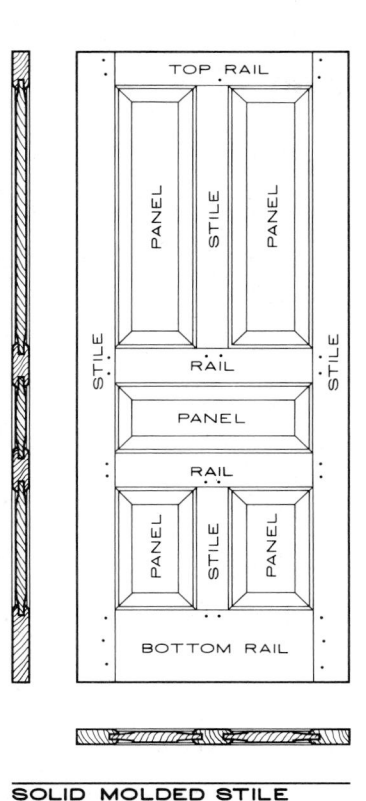

**SOLID MOLDED STILE
WOOD DOOR**

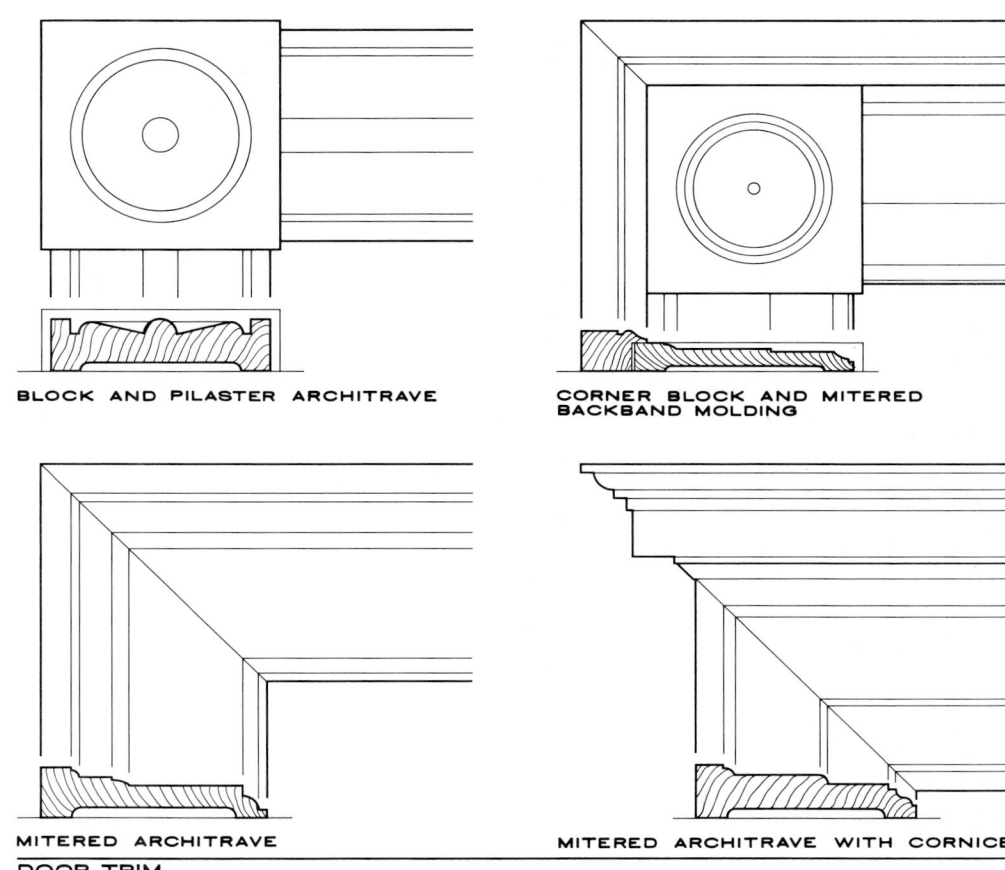

**BLOCK AND PILASTER ARCHITRAVE**

**CORNER BLOCK AND MITERED
BACKBAND MOLDING**

**MITERED ARCHITRAVE**

**DOOR TRIM**

**MITERED ARCHITRAVE WITH CORNICE**

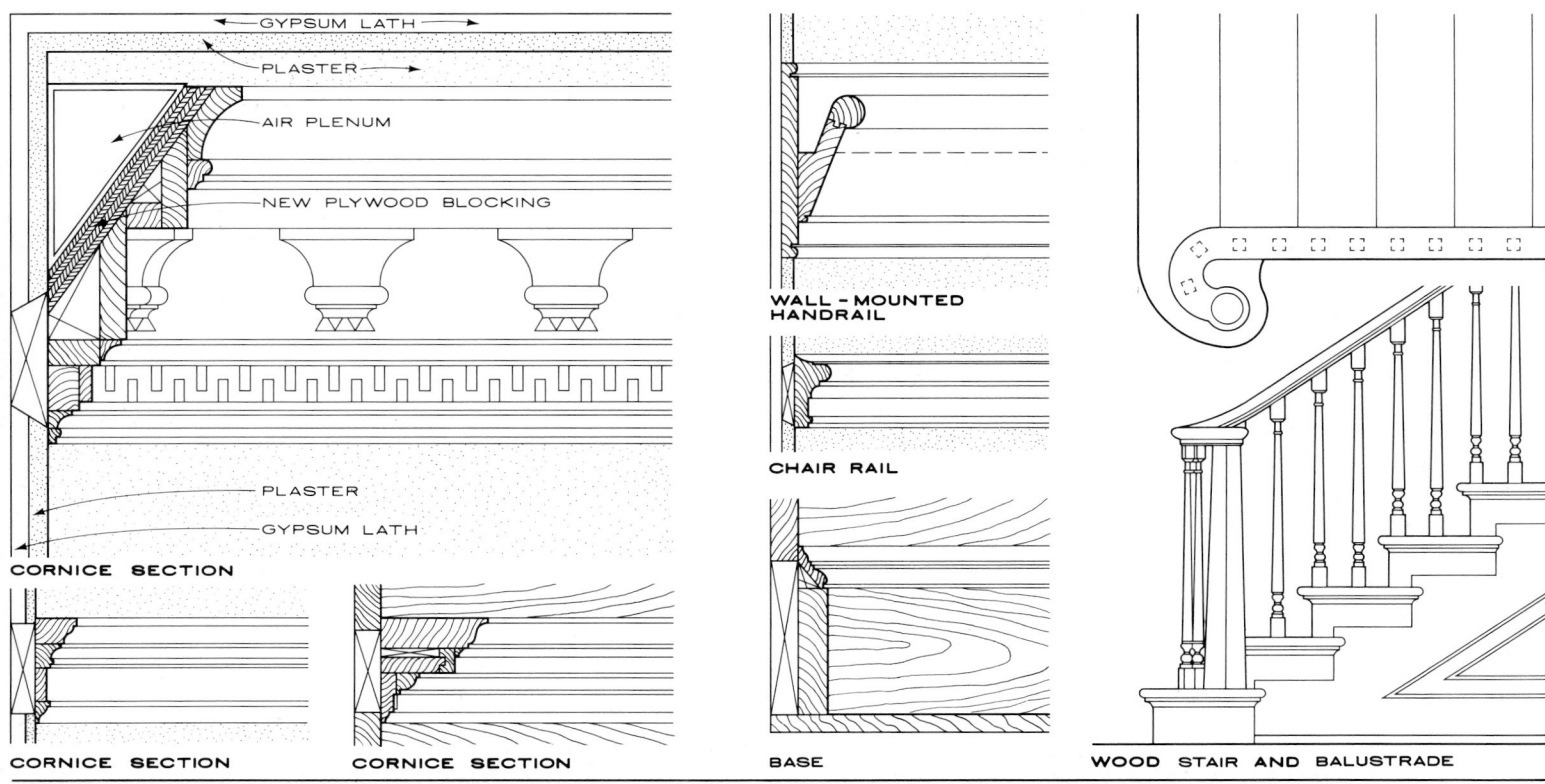

**CORNICE SECTION**

**CORNICE SECTION**

**CORNICE SECTION**

**WALL-MOUNTED
HANDRAIL**

**CHAIR RAIL**

**BASE**

**WOOD STAIR AND BALUSTRADE**

**INTERIOR WOOD DETAILS FROM THE OLD STATE HOUSE, DOVER, DE (McCUNE ASSOCIATES, RESTORATION
ARCHITECTS, 1977)**

Lee H. Nelson, FAIA, H. Ward Jandl, Camille Martone, Kay D. Weeks; Preservation Assistance Division, National Park Service;
Washington, D.C.
Eric J. Gastier; Darrel Downing Rippeteau Architects, PC; Washington, D.C.

## INTRODUCTION

The visible features of historic heating, lighting, ventilating, and plumbing systems may sometimes help define the overall historic character of the building and should thus be retained and repaired whenever possible. Realistically, the systems themselves (the compressors, boilers, generators, and their ductwork, wiring, and pipes) will generally need to be upgraded or entirely replaced in order to accommodate the new use and to meet code requirements. However, the visible portions of a system, the grilles, registers, lighting fixtures, and ornamental switchplates may be important in helping to define the interior historic character of a building. Therefore, the identification of such character-defining features should take place together with an evaluation of their physical condition early in project planning. The significant visual features of a building's mechanical, plumbing, and electrical system should be retained as part of historic preservation.

Mechanical, lighting, and plumbing systems were largely a product of the industrial age. The 19th century interest in hygiene, personal comfort, and the reduction of the spread of disease were met with the development of central heating, piped water, piped gas, and a network of underground cast iron sewers. Vitreous tiles in kitchens, baths, and hospitals could be cleaned easily and regularly. The mass production of cast iron radiators made central heating affordable to many; some radiators were elaborate and included special warming chambers for plates or linens. Ornamental grilles and brass registers created decorative covers for functional heaters in public spaces. By the turn of the 20th century, it was common to have all these modern amenities as an integral part of the building.

The greatest impact of the 20th century was the use of electricity for interior lighting, forced air ventilation, elevators for tall buildings, exterior lighting, and electric heat. The new age of technology brought an increasingly high level of design and decorative art to the functional elements of mechanical, electrical, and plumbing systems.

## PRESERVATION APPROACHES

Mechanical, plumbing, and electrical systems and their features should be maintained through cyclical cleaning and other appropriate measures. Adequate ventilation of attics, crawl spaces, and cellars should be provided to prevent accelerated deterioration of mechanical systems due to moisture problems.

New systems should be installed in a manner that does not destroy or damage significant architectural material and that make use of decorative elements of older systems—switchplates, ventilator grilles, lighting fixtures, etc.

Before total replacement of historic mechanical systems is considered, efforts should be made to evaluate the upgrading of the present system. Any ornamental features, such as significant lighting fixtures, should be retained after rewiring.

Often, to accommodate a continuing or new use, the historic mechanical system needs to be totally replaced with a new system. This new system needs to be installed in a manner that minimizes alterations to the building's floor plan and exterior elevations and causes the least damage to the historic building materials.

If a new mechanical system needs to be installed in a historic building, the vertical runs of ducts, pipes, and cables should be placed in closets, service rooms, and wall cavities rather than in architecturally significant spaces. Mechanical equipment should not be concealed in walls or ceilings in a manner that requires the removal of significant historic building materials.

New "dropped" acoustical ceilings that hide mechanical equipment should not be installed when this destroys the proportions of character-defining interior spaces, obscures window openings, or covers over decorative ceilings.

Cutting through features such as masonry walls in order to install heating/air-conditioning units should always be avoided. If new air-conditioning units are installed in window frames, the sash and frames should be protected from moisture condensation. Window installations should be considered only when all other viable heating/cooling systems would result in significant damage to historic materials.

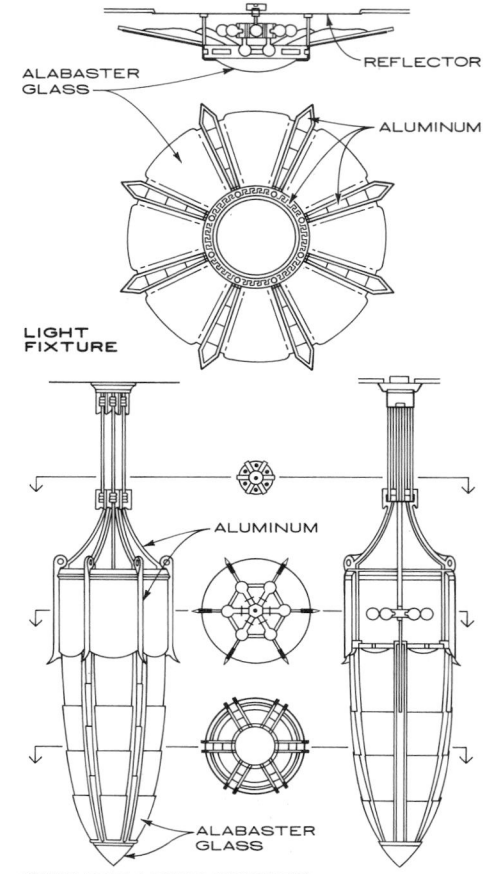

LIGHT FIXTURE

ALABASTER GLASS
REFLECTOR
ALUMINUM

PENDANT LIGHT FIXTURE

ALUMINUM
ALABASTER GLASS

**DETAILS FROM THE DEPARTMENT OF JUSTICE BUILDING, WASHINGTON, DC, 1933 (ZANTZINGER, BORIE AND MEDARY)**

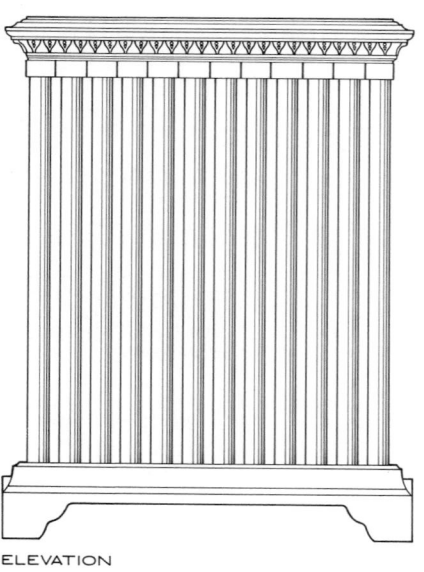

ELEVATION

PLAN

STEAM RADIATOR

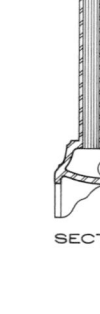

SECTION

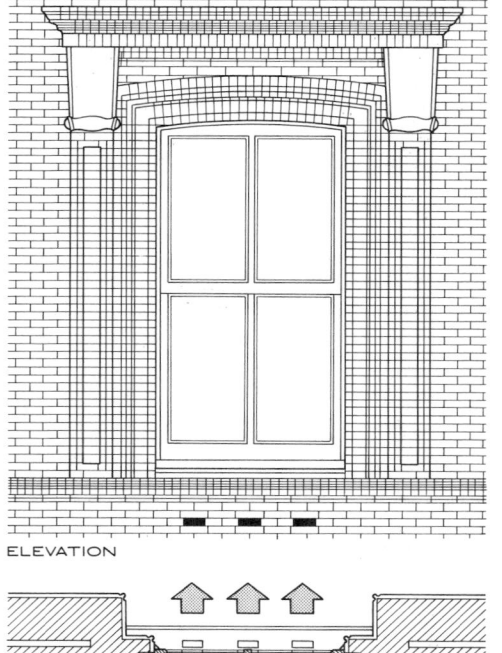

ELEVATION

PLAN

AIR FLOW

NATURAL VENTILATION SYSTEM (AT FIRST STORY WINDOW)

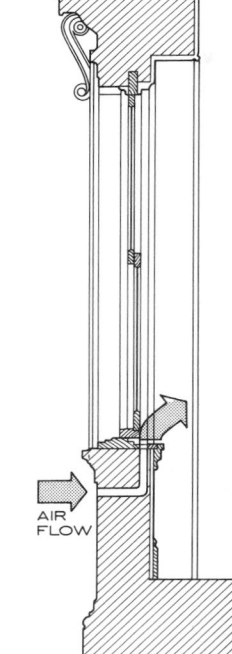

AIR FLOW

SECTION

**DETAILS FROM THE PENSION BUILDING, WASHINGTON, DC, 1882 (MONTGOMERY C. MEIGS - ARCHITECT)**

Lee H. Nelson, FAIA, H. Ward Jandl, Sharon C. Park, AIA, Kay D. Weeks; Preservation Assistance Division, National Park Service; Washington, D.C.
Eric J. Gastier; Darrel Downing Rippeteau Architects, PC; Washington, D.C.

# 19  MECHANICAL SYSTEMS

## INTRODUCTION

The following checklist is intended to suggest the range of preservation factors an architect should consider during the course of rehabilitating historic buildings. It is not exhaustive, and some factors will not apply to all structures or preservation projects.

## CHECK HISTORIC DESIGNATION AND AVAILABLE DOCUMENTATION

Is the building a local landmark or located in a locally designated historic district?

Is it in a historic district that is listed in the National Register of Historic Places? Does it contribute to the historic significance of that district?

Is it individually listed in the National Register of Historic Places?

What historical or architectural documentation is available about the building(s) or site? For example:

- National Register nominations
- recorded by Historic American Buildings Survey/Historic American Engineering Record
- state or local historical survey or inventory
- local documents, views, photographs in libraries, archives, historical societies

## CHECK LEGAL REQUIREMENTS

Are there already easements or local ordinances governing alterations to property (deed records, zoning offices)?

How do the state and local building codes apply to your historic structure? What impact will they have upon the character and integrity of the building? Are code variances available? Are there code equivalency possibilities for your particular building?

Will there be federal funds involved in the project which will require review by the State Historic Preservation Office and consultation with the Advisory Council on Historic Preservation? Will federal investment tax credits be used? If so, are you familiar with the *Secretary of the Interior's Standards for Rehabilitation and Guidelines for Rehabilitating Historic Buildings* as well as the National Park Service certification procedures Chapter 1, Title 36 of the Code of Federal Regulations, Part 67? Have you obtained a copy of the Historic Preservation Certification Application form from the State Historic Preservation Officer?

- Note that for federal investment tax credits, the Secretary's Standards take precedence over local requirements.

## EVALUATE HISTORIC CHARACTER/ SIGNIFICANCE OF STRUCTURE

Have you identified, listed, and prioritized the character-defining aspects of the building? These may include its form, materials, workmanship, features, color, relationship of solids to voids, and interior spaces—all those physical features or tangible aspects of the building that define its historic character.

Some original features may not be important contributors to the historic character and some will be all important. For example, a brick building may have been painted at an early date and its painted appearance may be an important aspect of its historic character.

What have been the architectural changes over time? These may include:

- new additions
- changes to surfaces and finishes (slates to asphalt, polychrome to monochrome)
- blocking of windows
- changes to grade
- loss of cornice
- false fronts
- changes to basic plan (single family to multiple family).

Are any of the changes significant and worth preserving or do they detract from the building?

Has the architectural integrity of the building and its setting been assessed? Architectural integrity means the intactness of the building as an architectural system (its plan, features, materials, finishes, structural system, and the presence of architectural features).

## ASSESS PHYSICAL CONDITION

Are there gross physical problems that threaten the building's architectural and structural integrity?

Has a structural survey been performed to determine deficiencies due to settlement, deflection of beams, seismic inadequacy, and cuts through structural members for mechanical pipes and ducts?

Are there inherent materials damage, such as materials failure due to poor original design, poor original materials, severe environmental or moisture problems, neglect, improper maintenance, etc.?

Is there man-inflicted damage, such as ornamentation removed, inappropriate coatings, bad repointing or cleaning, insensitive additions, or partitioning of significant interior spaces?

Are historic features hidden behind later alterations? These may include ornamental ceilings or cornices hidden above dropped ceilings.

## DEVELOP PRESERVATION PROJECT PLANS

Will it be necessary to write unique specifications rather than use standard specifications to apply to work performed on a historic building?

Will testing be needed to determine the performance of the materials or the systems? Note that it may be necessary to review test results with consultants or laboratories.

Will the project involve hard-to-find replacement materials such as terra-cotta or ornamental metals that may require critical path logistical planning?

Will the project involve hard-to-find crafts such as stone carving or ornamental plastering, and if so, can the necessary expertise be found?

Can samples or models be made available to establish the standard of craftsmanship for the project?

Will the project involve energy conservation measures? Have measures been chosen that retain historic materials and finishes to the maximum extent possible?

Will new uses require upgrading the live loading capacity of wooden floor joists? How do the preservation objectives affect the decision making? For instance, it is better to double up existing joists with a parallel member than

Will new uses require upgrading the live loading capacity of wooden floor joists? How do the preservation objectives affect the decision making? For instance, it is better to double up existing joists with a parallel member than to remove historic materials, and if an ornamental ceiling would be damaged by this approach, a structural engineer should investigate other alternatives.

Has the impact of new additions and adjacent new construction been minimized by keeping the size, shape, materials, and detailing in scale with the surrounding environment?

What protective measures will be taken to preserve important character-defining features and finishes during the construction work?

On the exterior, will the rehabilitation work cause loss of significant historic fabric or seriously damage the historic character? Loss of historic fabric or change of historic character often occur when:

- storefronts are altered
- visible skylights are added to a roof
- new dormers are added on prominent roofs
- whole new floors are added on top of an existing building
- porches are enclosed
- new window openings are created
- tinted films or reflective coatings are added to windows
- new window sash are historically inappropriate as to configuration and detailing.

On the interior, will the rehabilitation cause loss of significant historic fabric or seriously damage the historic character? Loss of fabric or change of character often occur when:

- interiors are partitioned and there is a loss of significant sequence of spaces
- interior plaster is removed to expose brickwork
- interiors are gutted, as might occur to introduce new atriums, new floor levels, or to reconfigure spaces
- significant stairs are removed or altered.

Will there be a professional on site during construction to ensure that work is carried out according to established preservation principles?

Have construction personnel received adequate training in undertaking historic preservation work?

## CREDITS FOR PRESERVATION SECTION

This section was prepared by the following staff of the Preservation Assistance Division, National Park Service: Lee H. Nelson, FAIA; H. Ward Jandl, Michael J. Auer; Charles E. Fisher; Anne Grimmer; Camille Martone; Sharon C. Park, AIA; and Kay D. Weeks.

## OTHER SOURCES OF TECHNICAL PRESERVATION INFORMATION

### PRESERVATION ASSISTANCE DIVISION

National Park Service
P.O. Box 37127
Washington, DC 20013-7127

The Preservation Assistance Division has developed numerous technical publications on preserving and rehabilitating historic buildings. These publications are available from the Superintendent of Documents, Government Printing Office, Washington, DC 20402.

### NATIONAL PARK SERVICE REGIONAL OFFICES WITH NATIONAL REGISTER PROGRAMS

Cultural Resources Division
Alaska Regional Office, National Park Service
2525 Gambell Street, Room 107
Anchorage, AL 99503

Preservation Services Division
Mid-Atlantic Regional Office, National Park Service
600 Arch Street, Room 9414
Philadelphia, PA 19106

Division of Cultural Resources
Rocky Mountain Regional Office, National Park Service
12795 West Alameda Parkway
P.O. Box 25287
Lakewood, CO 80225

Preservation Services Division
Southeast Regional Office, National Park Service
75 Spring Street, SW
Atlanta, GA 30303

National Register Programs
Western Regional Office, National Park Service
450 Golden Gate Avenue
P.O. Box 36063
San Francisco, CA 94102

### STATE HISTORIC PRESERVATION OFFICERS

For the name and address of the state historic preservation officer in your state, contact:

National Conference of State Historic Preservation Officers
Hall of the States
444 N. Capitol Street, NW, Suite 332
Washington, DC 20001

AIA State Preservation Coordinators
Call the Historic Resources Committee Staff Director at the AIA Headquarters to make contact with the AIA state preservation coordinator.

The Association for Preservation Technology
P.O. Box 2487, Station D
Ottawa, Ontario
Canada K1P 5W6

National Trust for Historic Preservation
1785 Massachusetts Avenue, NW
Washington, DC 20036

The Old-House Journal
69A Seventh Avenue
Brooklyn, NY 11217

Lee H. Nelson, FAIA; Preservation Assistance Division, National Park Service; Washington, D.C.
Eric J. Gastier; Darrel Downing Rippeteau Architects, PC; Washington, D.C.

## MEASURED DRAWINGS OF HISTORIC STRUCTURES

Measured drawings are similar to as-built architectural drawings except that they are generally produced years after a structure is built, not immediately after construction. They are used as base drawings for projects involving existing structures, but also record the architect's careful examination and study of both older and newer building components. Measured drawings portray conditions at the time of documentation, including the accretions, alterations, and deletions that have occurred from the original. Their content will vary depending upon the nature of the project.

A preliminary step in producing measured drawings should be to make an on-site reconnaissance of the site. Take notes on a systematic basis, recording the overall dimensions, design, materials, structural and decorative details, and present condition. Making sketched floor plans will help to organize the information. From the gathered observations, determine the number, type, and scale of the required measured drawings.

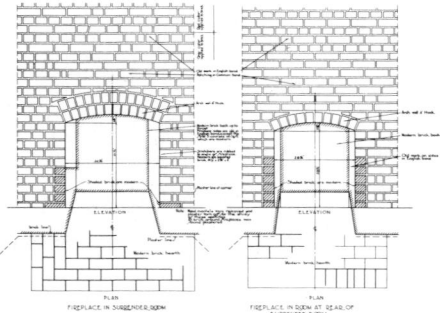

Moore House, Yorktown, VA (by F. Nichols)

Measured drawings of existing conditions at the site of the British surrender at Yorktown were part of the first historic structures report prepared by the National Park Service in 1935. The architect has annotated conditions and apparent periods of various elements. Plaster was removed from the chimney, revealing its brick construction, which was recorded before being replastered.

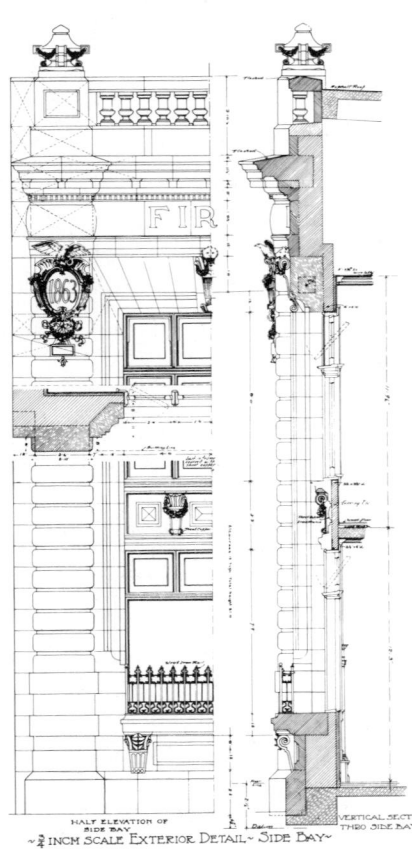

First National Bank, Toledo, OH (George S. Mills, Architect)

When existing condition measured drawings are needed:

1. Do any drawings or measurements exist or must they be produced?
2. If drawings or measurements exist, are they accurate and useful to the current need?
3. If measurements must be taken, what tools and expertise are required and available to produce them?
4. Does the structure itself, its size, condition, use, and accessibility dictate the manner in which it can be measured?

Structural members were located and sized in this axonometric drawing that both explains and interprets historic building techniques.

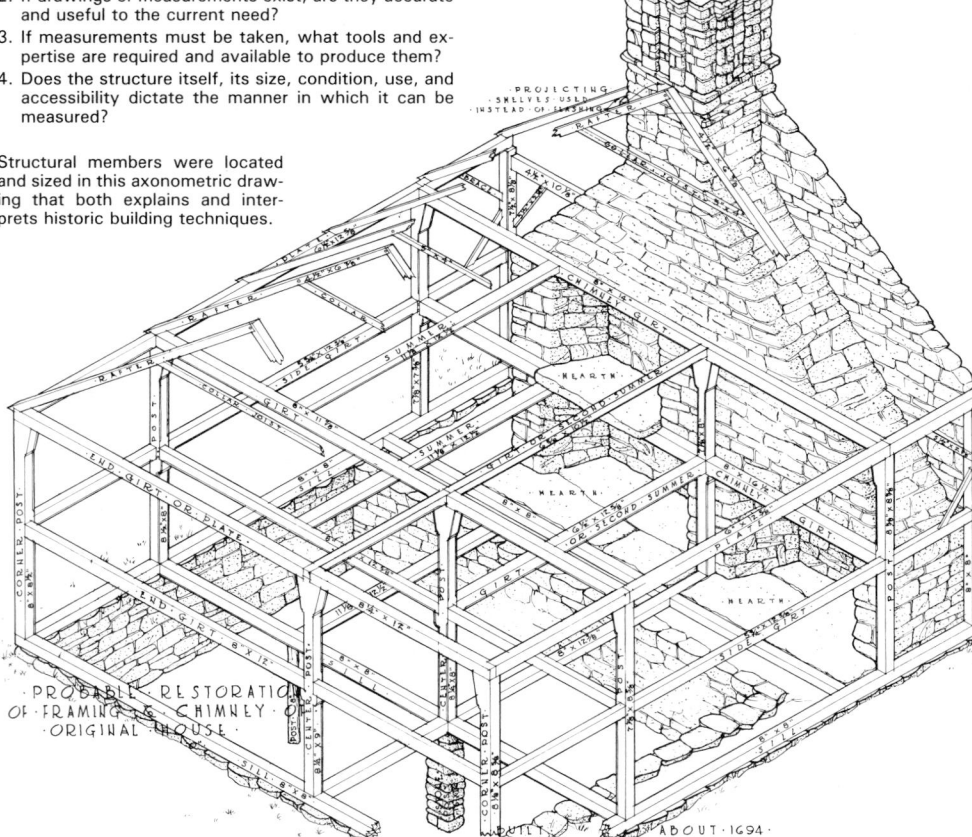

Valentine Whitman, Jr., House, Limerock, RI (by W.R. Colvin)

## HISTORICAL RESEARCH

A basic assumption in producing measured drawings is that other sources for drawings do not meet the needs of the project being undertaken. Measured drawings are based primarily on physical evidence, but may rely on other sources for information. Documentary sources can provide evidence of former conditions and help to interpret physical fabric. Historic views, whether drawn or photographed, can be invaluable. A key factor in any measured drawing is understanding the accuracy and limitations of the sources for the measurements.

Original architectural drawings are most likely found in the possession of the original architectural firm or its successor firm. They may also be found in the building, in the company archives, or in the owner's papers. The National Union Index to Architectural Records, which tracks the location of architectural records throughout the United States, can be searched by contacting the Prints and Photographs Division, Library of Congress, Washington, DC 20540. Regional and local repositories of historical records may have architectural records. Another source for locating graphic records are finding aids such as the *Avery Index to Architectural Periodicals* (Boston: G.K. Hall & Co., 1973). Because of the expense of producing measured drawings, it is worth the effort to attempt to locate original drawings, specifications, and photographs.

The original 1904 drawings for this bank (left) were located in the files of another firm and photographically copied. They provide both dimensional information and construction details that would have required destructive investigation to determine.

The historic evolution of a house (right) explained in graphics and words. The drawings alone would not give historical data; description alone would not convey how the various alterations appeared.

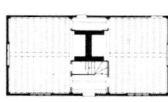

**FIRST PERIOD 1680**

The structure's original center chimney plan contained two principal rooms on each floor. The interior was lit by groups of three casement windows with transom lights above. Two large facade gables were arranged symmetrically on the south slope of the roof.

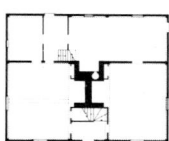 

**SECOND PERIOD 1720**

For an unknown reason the east end of the house was taken down about 1720 and replaced by a one-story lean-to. A lean-to against the north wall was also added at this time. In addition to these changes in plan, the remaining facade gable was removed.

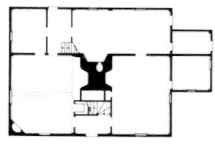 

**THIRD PERIOD 1750**

The major alterations of the house about 1750 were the rebuilding of the east end to two full stories and the addition of a small one-story structure to the east wall. The west end was left substantially unaltered.

Mulford House, East Hampton, NY (by Anne E. Weber)

John A. Burns, AIA; HABS/HAER, National Park Service; Washington, D.C.

## DEGREE OF COMPLETENESS

The significance of the building and its individual features and the type of information essential in the finished drawings determine the degree of completeness of the drawings. A large and elaborate historic building will require more drawings than a more modest structure.

1. Decide what drawings will best explain and illustrate the various features of the structure. Then determine what measurements are needed to produce the drawings.
2. Decide on the level of detail required in the finished

## MEASUREMENT TECHNIQUES

1. DOCUMENTARY. Locating and duplicating copies of original drawings is the simplest way to produce measured drawings. The copies must be checked against the actual structure to determine their accuracy, whether the building was constructed as drawn, and how closely the drawings portray current conditions.
2. HAND MEASURING. When hand measuring, all dimensions are assumed to be either horizontal or vertical. Inclined dimensions can be converted by using trigonometry. The most accurate way to hand measure a string of dimensions is by measuring from a common point so that the dimensions are cumulative. Consecutive measurements made individually are less accurate because any errors are compounded when strings of dimensions are added.

Time can be saved if certain assumptions can be made, such as using the floor as a level datum plane and assuming the rooms are square and the walls are plumb. Whatever assumptions are made when taking the measurements will govern the accuracy of the measured drawings. Inaccessible features can be measured by counting repetitive materials of known dimension such as brick courses in a chimney.

There are two basic hand measuring techniques. One system is to directly measure the architectural features to locate them in relation to each other. Control points can be established by measuring a network of triangles that can be drawn as rigid figures. Room shapes can be determined by measuring the diagonals of a room. This technique works well on structures that are reasonably regular.

The second method establishes a grid from which the structure is measured. Features are located in relation to the grid rather than to each other. This technique is especially useful for irregular or distorted buildings.

3. SURVEYING. It may be necessary to survey a traverse to establish accurate control points from which to measure a structure or to locate site features that cannot be measured directly.
4. PHOTOGRAPHIC. The science of measuring from photographs is photogrammetry. The simplest form of photogrammetry of interest to architects is rectified photography. Rectified photography manipulates and enlarges a photograph so that an architectural feature with a few known dimensions is reproduced at a given scale. It is best used to record features in a single plane, such as room elevations or flat facades. It is not accurate for measuring objects either in front of or behind the plane of the subject that has been enlarged to scale. Positioning targets at known locations on the subject and placing a measuring stick in the field of view can increase accuracy.

Stereophotogrammetry uses two photographs taken from known positions in relation to the building. After taking some dimensions in the field of view and determining the specifications of the camera, accurate plottings can be made at any desired scale. Because this technique uses photographs, conditional information is recorded. Also, photographs record in a generalized way all that the camera "sees," so that many different measurements can be made. Hand measuring, by contrast, only records measurements that are consciously taken and written down.

Analytical photogrammetry can produce measurements of missing or deteriorated features from historic photographs if some dimensions can be determined in the photographs. Accuracy is dependent on the quantity and quality of the historic photographs. The technique is more accurate if the historic photographs can be combined with contemporary photogrammetry.

Photogrammetry records large structures without scaffolding and in much less time than by hand measuring or surveying. Other benefits are that photogrammetric images record conditional information and that the plates can be stored and plotted when necessary.

John A. Burns, AIA; HABS/HAER, National Park Service; Washington, D.C.

drawings. This will determine both the scales of the drawings and the precision of the measurements needed to make the drawings. For instance, at the common scale of $\frac{1}{4}'' = 1'\text{-}0''$, the smallest distance that can be accurately drawn is approximately 1 in.

3. Determine what level of accuracy is needed in the measurements. Dimensions to the nearest inch may be adequate for plans but inadequate for details, where measurements to the nearest $\frac{1}{16}$ in. or $\frac{1}{8}$ in. would be required.

Measured drawings will require differing levels of detail and annotation depending on the ultimate use of the

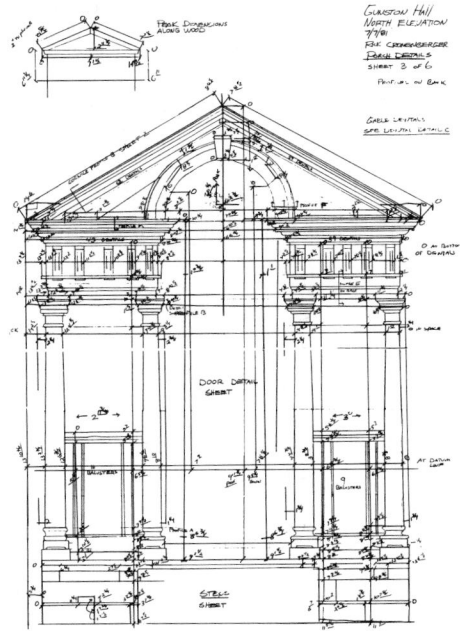

Gunston Hall, Lorton vic., VA (by Richard J. Cronenberger)

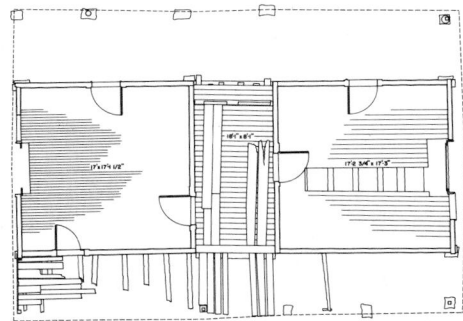

Butler Dogtrot, Tishomingo vic., MS (by Peter Darlow)

Buildings too irregular to measure directly are measured from a grid established in and around the structure. The dimension strings give only the overall measurements necessary to describe the basic configuration. More precise information on the shape and distortions of the house is accessible in the field records.

drawings. Measured drawings intended to provide the basis for restoration will require extensive dimensions and annotations to record all the historical and conditional information. Measured drawings intended for maintenance purposes may need little more than material indications and basic dimensions in order to be able to calculate gross areas needing treatment. Measured drawings produced as mitigation are the "last rites" for a structure planned to be demolished, recording for future generations all its salient features. Measured drawings intended to serve as protection from catastrophic loss must be detailed enough to allow the exact replication of a highly significant building should it be destroyed.

Comparison of direct field measurements of a porch and the finished detail drawing. Field notes are the primary source; the drawings cannot be more accurate than the field measurements. Many more dimensions are recorded in the field notes than are actually written on the final drawing, so it is important to save and organize the field notes for future reference.

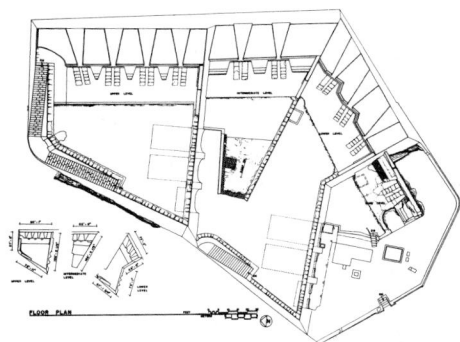

La Trinidad Counterguard, San Juan, PR (by Todd Wambach)

A large and irregular structure such as a fort can be measured accurately using an electronic distance measuring theodolite to produce angle and distance measurements.

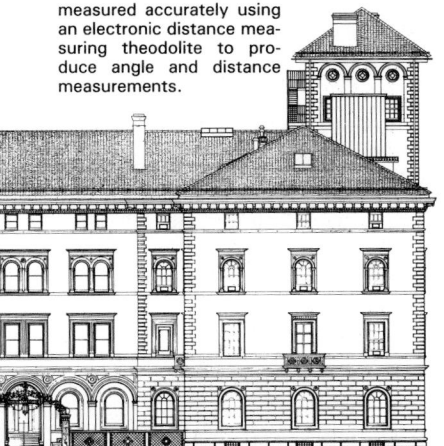

Villard Houses, New York, NY (by Perry Borchers, Soottipong Winyoopradist, and Varathorn Bookman)

## THE HISTORIC AMERICAN BUILDINGS SURVEY

The Historic American Buildings Survey (HABS) is a collection of graphic and written documentation on more than 20,000 historic buildings throughout the United States. The graphic records consist of 44,000 architectural measured drawings and 120,000 large format photographs, supported by 48,000 pages of written data. Administered by the National Park Service, with technical assistance from the American Institute of Architects, the completed records are reproducible and are accessible through the Prints and Photographs Division of the Library of Congress.

HABS measured drawings show conditions at the time a structure was recorded, including alterations and additions to the original since it was built. While measured drawings are utilitarian, HABS measured drawings must additionally meet all HABS standards for content, accuracy, verifiability, archival stability, and reproducibility. HABS measured drawings are prepared for historic structures:

1. When restoration or rehabilitation work is planned, to establish existing conditions prior to beginning treatment.
2. As part of normal conservation and maintenance of a structure.
3. As insurance against catastrophic loss, should something happen to the structure.
4. As easement documentation.
5. When demolition is planned, to keep a permanent record for future generations.
6. For public information or interpretation.
7. As scholarship.

HABS measured drawings are produced for any or several of the above reasons. HABS drawings include site plans, landscape plans, floor plans, elevations, sections, details, and interpretive drawings. Field records and measurements are retained for future use and reference.

Independence Hall (north elevation), Philadelphia, PA (by Dennett, Muessig, Ryan & Associates)

### TALL CASE CLOCK

Glass plate photogrammetric stereopairs of Independence Hall were produced so that the entire exterior and significant portions of the interior could be plotted. Objects as small as ⅛ in. are discernible in the plates. The original of the HABS drawing of the north elevation was produced for public information and maintenance purposes at ³⁄₁₆″ = 1′-0″ and thus cannot portray all the detail recorded in the plates. Even so, the differences between the basement window arches on either side of the door and the fact that the tower is off-center are easily visible. The larger scale drawing of the clock was plotted from plates made at the same distance from the building.

### PRODUCING HABS MEASURED DRAWINGS

Architects interested in producing HABS measured drawings as part of a rehabilitation or restoration project, as mitigation, or as part of their professional practice should consult *Recording Historic Structures* (Washington, DC: AIA Press, 1988). Additional information and mylar drawing sheets preprinted with the HABS title blocks are available from the HABS office (Historic American Buildings Survey, National Park Service, P.O. Box 37127, Washington, DC 20013-7127).

The standards for documentation to be included in the HABS collection are as follows:

1. Content. Documentation shall adequately explicate and illustrate what is significant or valuable about the historic building, site, structure, or object being documented.

2. Quality. Documentation shall be prepared accurately from reliable sources with limitations clearly stated to permit independent verification of the information.
3. Materials. Documentation shall be prepared on materials that are readily reproducible, durable, and in standard sizes.
4. Presentation. Documentation shall be clearly and concisely produced.

Completed HABS measured drawings are a secure, permanent record of a historic structure prepared on archival materials and stored under controlled archival conditions. They make information on historic buildings available to the public and serve as a form of insurance against catastrophic loss.

HABS relies on the generosity of architects and organizations as a major source for architectural documentation. Donated records have been and continue to be a significant part of the HABS collection.

John A. Burns, AIA; HABS/HAER, National Park Service; Washington, D.C.

**RECORDING HISTORIC BUILDINGS**

A longitudinal section of Adler and Sullivan's Auditorium Building reveals the overall configuration of the structure and the major interior spaces. The hotel portion is on the left with a dining hall on the top floor, stage house and theater in the center, banquet hall above the sloping roof of the theater, rehearsal hall above the rear of the theater, and office space on the right. HABS recorded the structural and mechanical systems of the building as part of a master plan for renovation and restoration work. This drawing was produced from historic drawings, photographs and specifications, and contemporary field measurements, and illustrates the building as it was completed in 1890. Large structures such as this must be composed on several HABS sheets to be drawn at a reasonable scale.

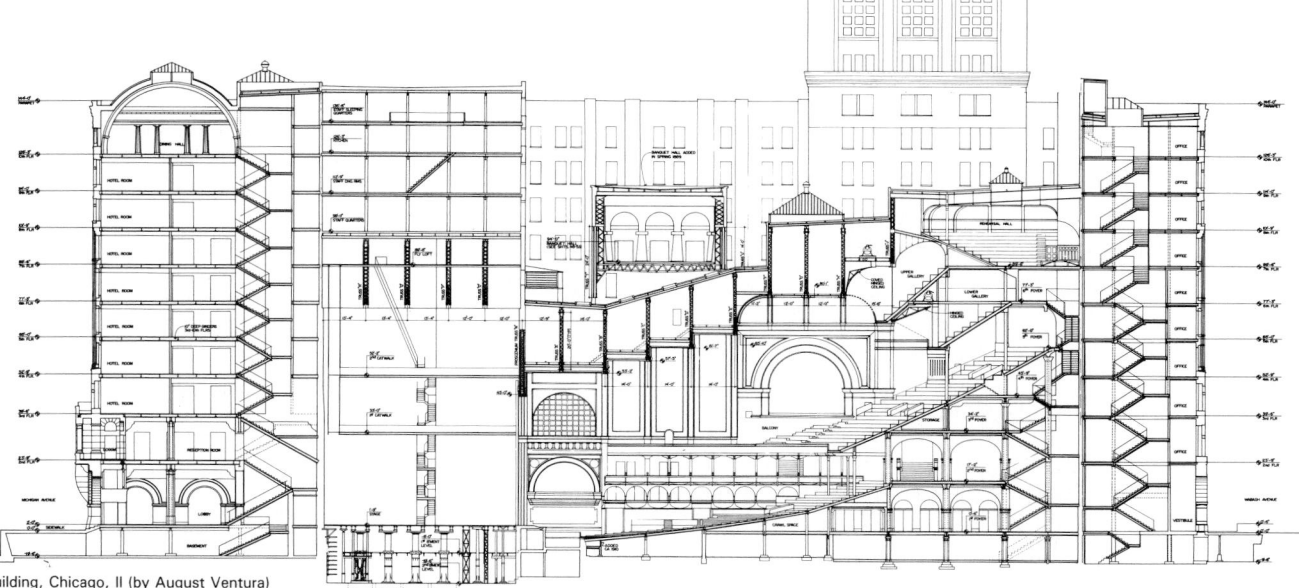

Auditorium Building, Chicago, Il (by August Ventura)

Villard Houses Dining Room, New York, NY (by Perry Borchers, Soottipong Winyoopradist, and Kun-Hyuck Ahn)

Decorative and sculptural details are difficult to measure and delineate because there are few hard edges. Photogrammetry offers the capability of making precise contour maps of sculptural surfaces.

## REPRODUCTIONS OF HABS DOCUMENTATION

All Historic American Buildings Survey documentation is in the public domain and may be reproduced for the cost of the reproductions. For each measured drawing there is a reproducible copy; for each photograph there is a large format negative; data pages can be photocopied. The HABS collection is accessible to the public in the Prints and Photographs Division of the Library of Congress in Washington, DC, either in person or by mail inquiry. Questions concerning documentation in the HABS collection should be sent to the Prints and Photographs Division, Library of Congress, Washington, DC 20540. Reproductions can be ordered through the Library of Congress Photoduplication Service at the same address. If used in a publication, HABS requests that the program and the individual responsible (delineator, photographer, historian) be appropriately credited.

John A. Burns, AIA; HABS/HAER, National Park Service; Washington, D.C.

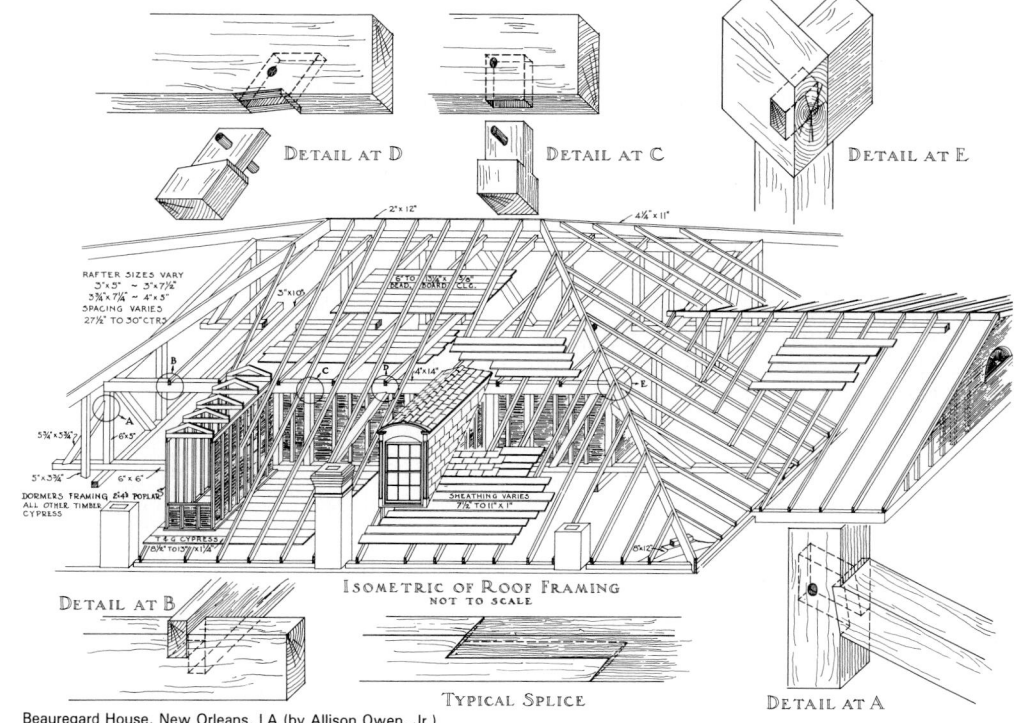

Beauregard House, New Orleans, LA (by Allison Owen, Jr.)

Cutaway isometric drawings depict complex shapes such as roof framing in an effective manner. HABS records structural and mechanical systems when they are accessible. Buildings undergoing restoration offer the opportunity to record historic structural and mechanical systems while they are exposed.

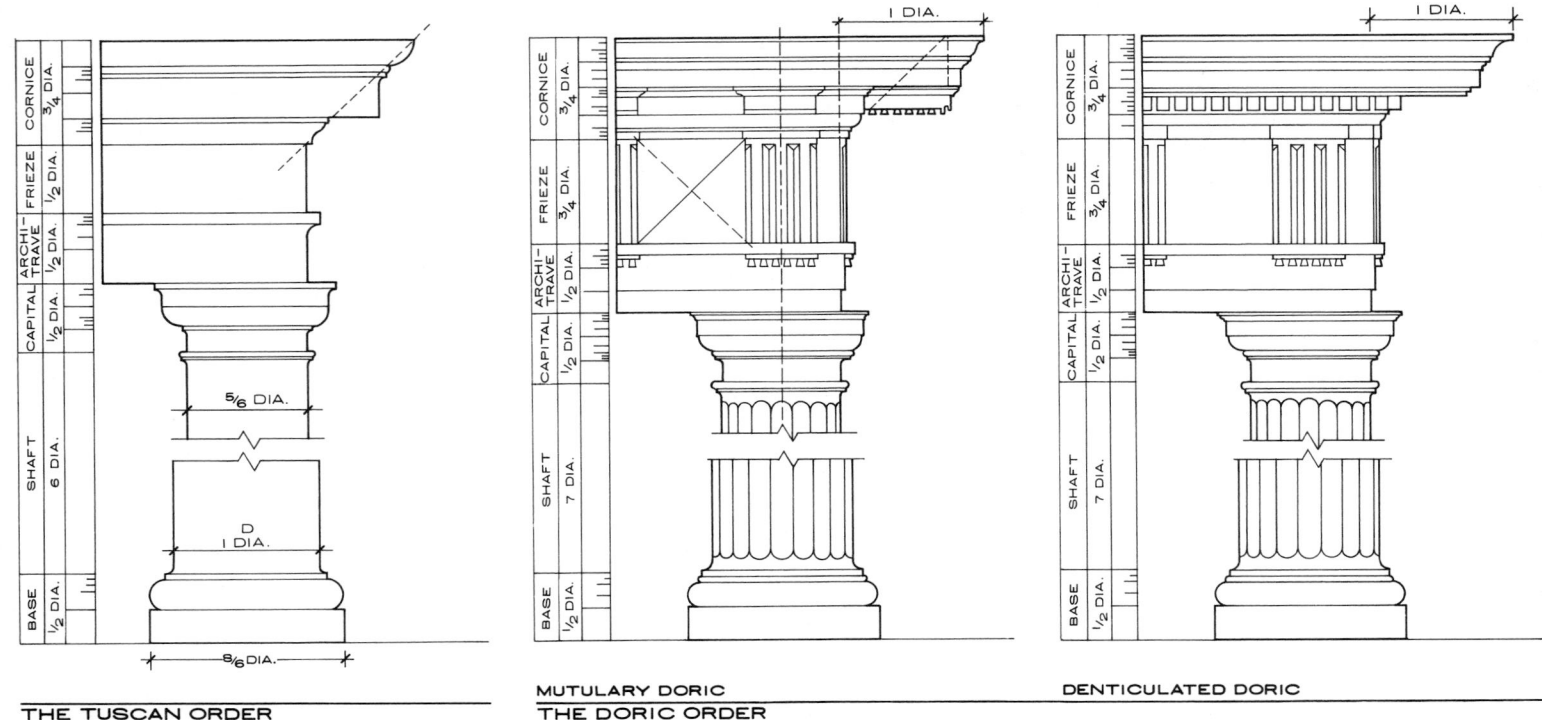

CORNICE
3/4 DIA.
FRIEZE
1/2 DIA.
ARCHI-TRAVE
1/2 DIA.
CAPITAL
1/2 DIA.
SHAFT
6 DIA.
BASE
1/2 DIA.
5/6 DIA.
D
1 DIA.
8/6 DIA.

THE TUSCAN ORDER

1 DIA.
CORNICE
3/4 DIA.
FRIEZE
3/4 DIA.
ARCHI-TRAVE
1/2 DIA.
CAPITAL
1/2 DIA.
SHAFT
7 DIA.
BASE
1/2 DIA.
1 DIA.
CORNICE
3/4 DIA.
FRIEZE
3/4 DIA.
ARCHI-TRAVE
1/2 DIA.
CAPITAL
1/2 DIA.
SHAFT
7 DIA.
BASE
1/2 DIA.

MUTULARY DORIC

DENTICULATED DORIC

THE DORIC ORDER

A PARALLEL COMPARISON BASED ON VIGNOLA PROPORTIONS IN TERMS OF A CONSTANT LOWER DIAMETER

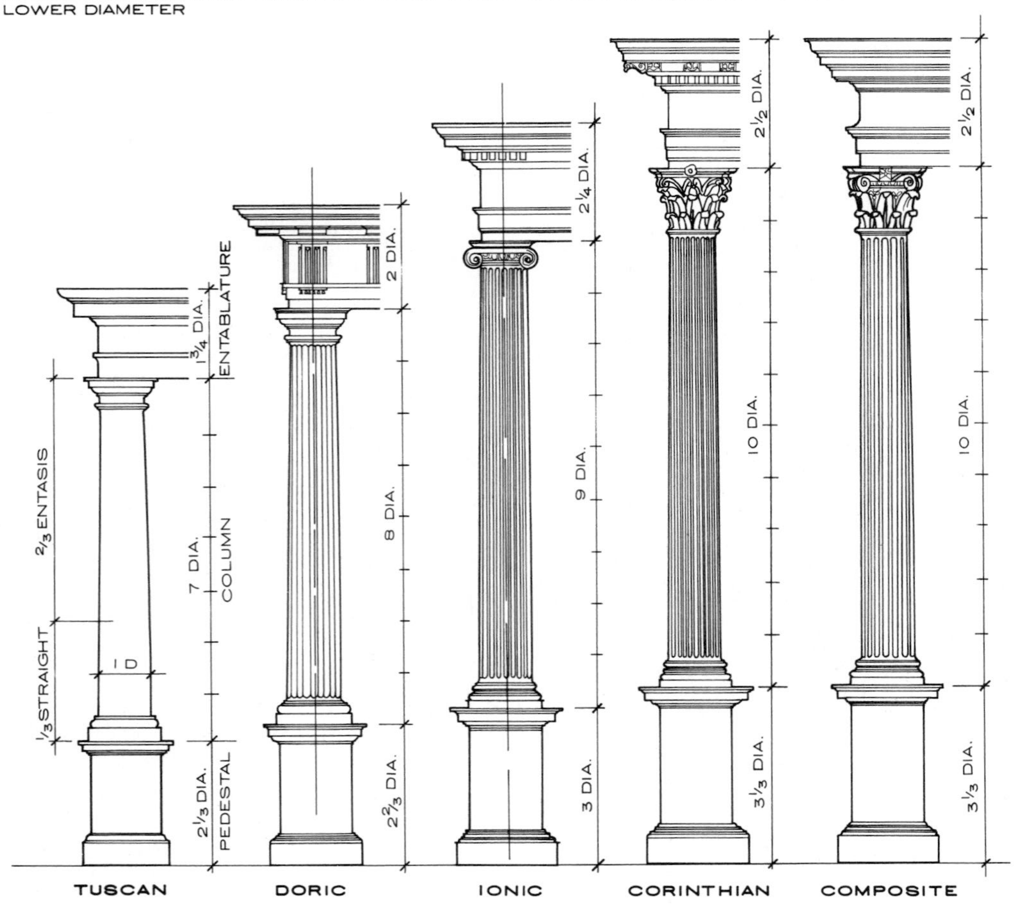

2/3 ENTASIS
1/3 STRAIGHT
1 D
3/4 DIA.
ENTABLATURE
7 DIA.
COLUMN
2 1/3 DIA.
PEDESTAL
2 DIA.
8 DIA.
2 2/3 DIA.
2 1/4 DIA.
9 DIA.
3 DIA.
2 1/2 DIA.
10 DIA.
3 1/3 DIA.
2 1/2 DIA.
10 DIA.
3 1/3 DIA.
TUSCAN
DORIC
IONIC
CORINTHIAN
COMPOSITE

THE FIVE CLASSICAL ORDERS

CYMA RECTA WITH ACANTHUS
OVOLO WITH EGG AND DART
ASTRAGAL WITH BEAD AND REEL
CYMA REVERSA WITH WATER LEAF AND TONGUE
CYMA REVERSA WITH ACANTHUS
TORUS WITH BAY LEAF AND GAR-LAND
CYMA RECTA
FILLET
CYMA REVERSA
FASCIA
OVOLO
BEAD
DENTILS
FILLET
CYMA REVERSA
FILLET - RAISED AND SUNK
CAVETTO
SCOTIA
3/4 HOLLOW
OVOLO
TORUS IF LARGE BEAD OR ASTRAGAL IF SMALL
3/4 ROUND
CYMA RECTA
CYMA REVERSA
BEAK
THUMB
FASCIA OR FACE

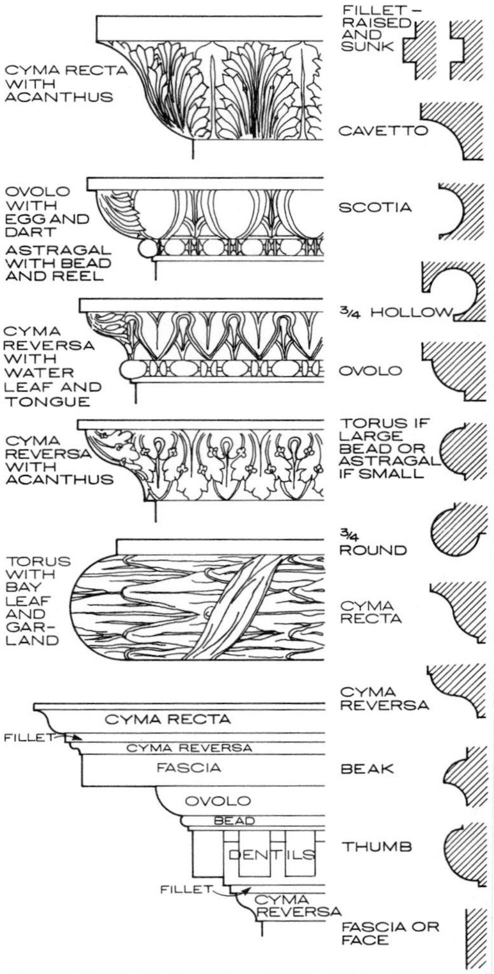

TYPES OF MOLDING AND ORNAMENTS

David Kulick and Roy W. Lewis, Jr.; Alvin Holm AIA, Architects; Philadelphia, Pennsylvania

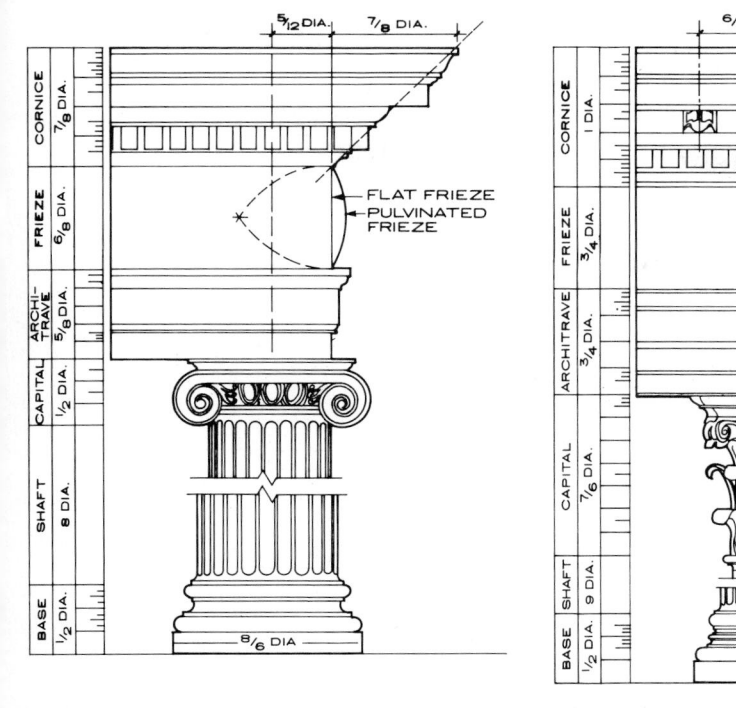

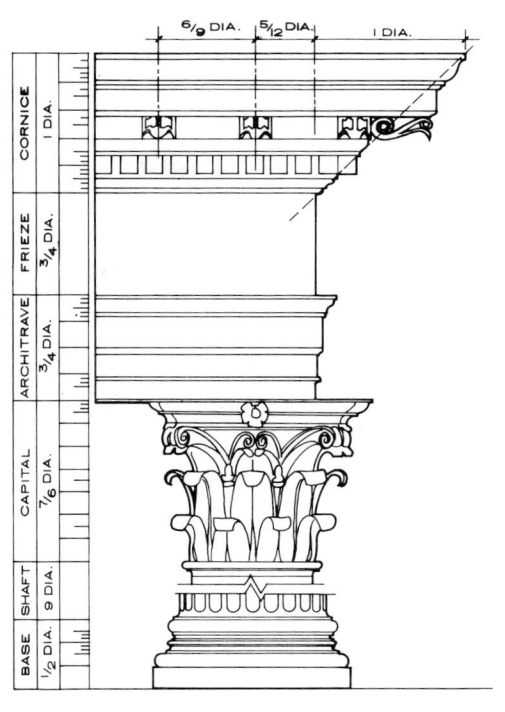

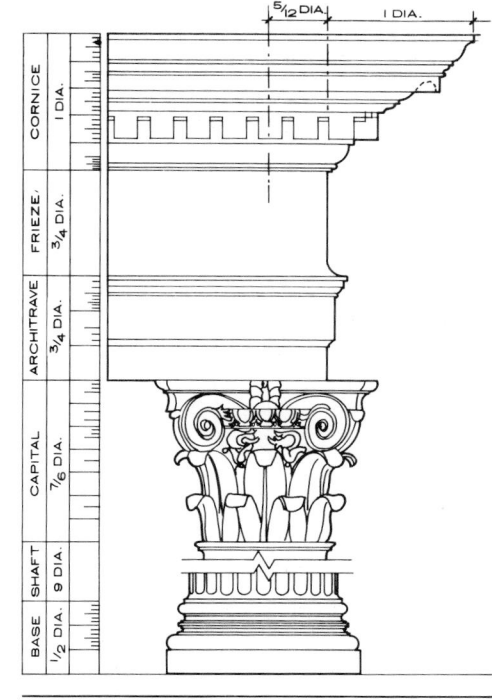

THE IONIC ORDER

THE CORINTHIAN ORDER

THE COMPOSITE ORDER

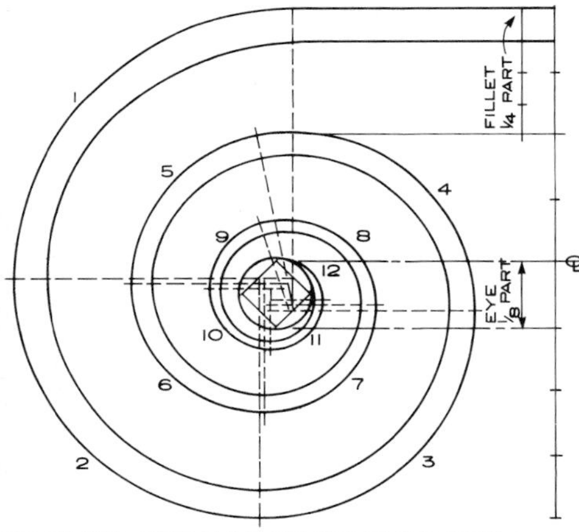

BELOW THE CENTERLINE OF THE VOLUTE, DRAW A CIRCLE WITH A DIAMETER OF 1/8 THE HEIGHT OF THE VOLUTE. INSCRIBE A ROTATED, QUARTERED SQUARE WITHIN THIS CIRCLE OR "EYE." THE SIXTH POINTS OF THE CENTERLINES OF THIS SQUARE GIVE THE CENTERS FOR A SERIES OF DIMINISHING ARCS. FROM CENTER 1 DRAW ARC 1, FROM CENTER 2, ARC 2, ETC. SUCCESSIVE ARCS MEET AT A LINE DEFINED BY THEIR CENTERS. THE INNER LINE OF THE FILLET IS GAINED BY REPEATING THE PROCESS SHOWN BELOW USING THE SECONDARY CENTERS SHOWN BELOW

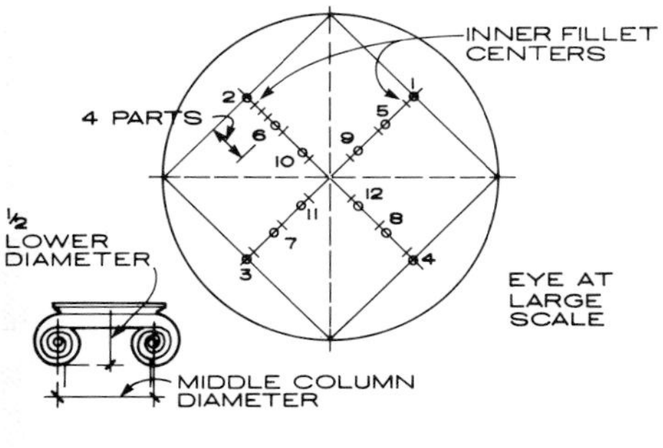

INNER FILLET CENTERS

4 PARTS

1/2 LOWER DIAMETER

EYE AT LARGE SCALE

MIDDLE COLUMN DIAMETER

CONSTRUCTION OF VOLUTE

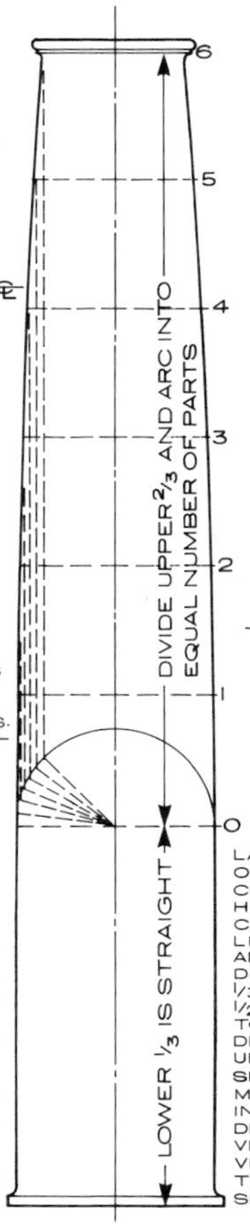

LAY OUT COLUMN HEIGHT, CENTERLINE, UPPER AND LOWER DIAMETERS AT 1/3 POINT, DRAW 1/2 CIRCLE EQUAL TO BASE DIAMETER. DROP A LINE FROM THE UPPER DIAMETER TO THE SEMICIRCLE, DIVIDE THE RESULTING MINOR ARC AND UPPER 2/3 OF SHAFT INTO AN EQUAL NUMBER OF EQUAL PARTS. DRAW VERTICAL LINES FROM THE ARC DIVISIONS TO THE HORIZONTAL SHAFT DIVISIONS. THE RESULTING POINTS DEFINE THE CURVED PROFILE OF THE COLUMN SHAFT

ENTASIS

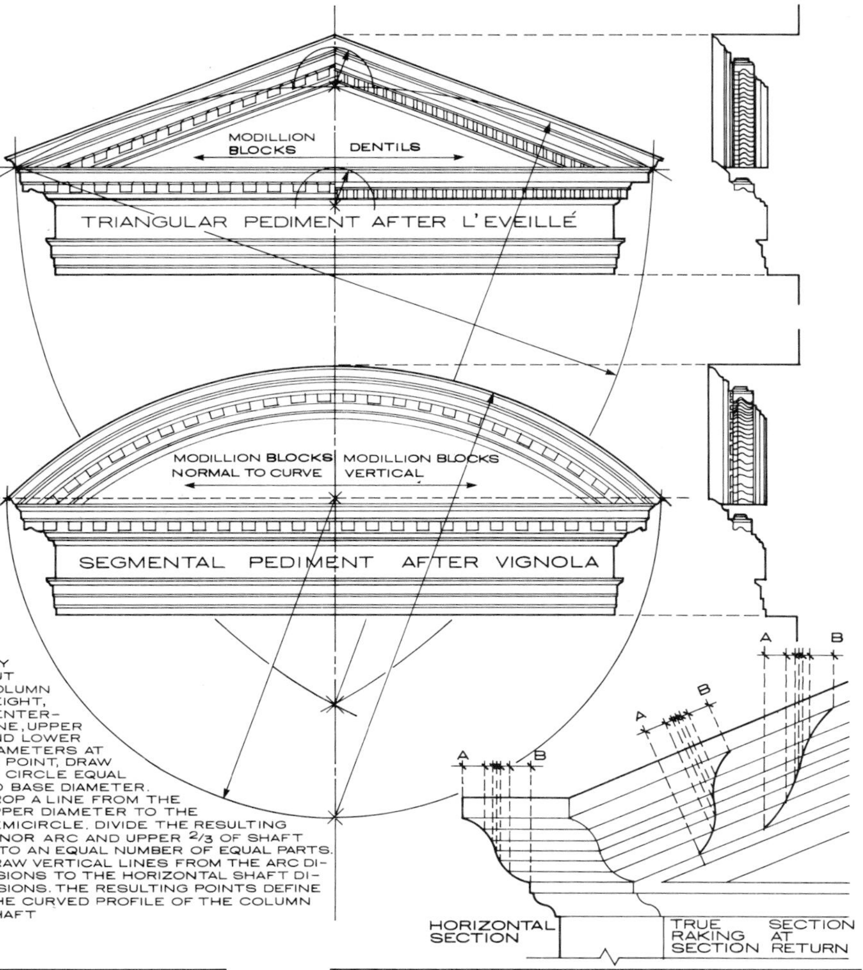

TRIANGULAR PEDIMENT AFTER L'EVEILLÉ

MODILLION BLOCKS    DENTILS

SEGMENTAL PEDIMENT AFTER VIGNOLA

MODILLION BLOCKS NORMAL TO CURVE    MODILLION BLOCKS VERTICAL

HORIZONTAL SECTION    TRUE RAKING SECTION    SECTION AT RETURN

PEDIMENT

David Kulick and Roy W. Lewis, Jr.; Alvin Holm AIA, Architects; Philadelphia, Pennsylvania

# Appendixes

## PLUMBING PIPING

| | |
|---|---|
| SOIL, WASTE OR LEADER (ABOVE GRADE) | —————— |
| SOIL, WASTE OR LEADER (BELOW GRADE) | — — — — |
| VENT | - - - - - - |
| COMBINATION WASTE AND VENT | ——SV—— |
| ACID WASTE | ——AW—— |
| ACID VENT | — — —AV — — — |
| INDIRECT DRAIN | ——IW—— |
| STORM DRAIN | ——S—— |
| COLD WATER | — - — - — - |
| SOFT COLD WATER | —— SW —— |
| INDUSTRIALIZED COLD WATER | ——ICW—— |
| CHILLED DRINKING WATER SUPPLY | ——DWS—— |
| CHILLED DRINKING WATER RETURN | ——DWR—— |
| HOT WATER | — -- — -- — |
| HOT WATER RETURN | — --- — --- — |
| SANITIZING HOT WATER SUPPLY (180° F.) | ─/─ - - ─/─ - - ─/ |
| SANITIZING HOT WATER RETURN (180° F.) | ─/─ - - - ─/─ - - |
| INDUSTRIALIZED HOT WATER SUPPLY | ——IHW—— |
| INDUSTRIALIZED HOT WATER RETURN | ——IHR—— |
| TEMPERED WATER SUPPLY | ——TWS—— |
| TEMPERED WATER RETURN | ——TWR—— |
| FIRE LINE | —— F —— F —— |
| WET STANDPIPE | ——WSP—— |

| | |
|---|---|
| DRY STANDPIPE | ——DSP—— |
| COMBINATION STANDPIPE | —— CSP —— |
| MAIN SUPPLIES SPRINKLER | —— S —— |
| BRANCH AND HEAD SPRINKLER | —o——o— |
| GAS - LOW PRESSURE | ——G——G—— |
| GAS - MEDIUM PRESSURE | ——MG—— |
| GAS- HIGH PRESSURE | ——HG—— |
| COMPRESSED AIR | ——A—— |
| VACUUM | ——V—— |
| VACUUM CLEANING | ——VC—— |
| OXYGEN | ——O—— |
| LIQUID OXYGEN | ——LOX—— |
| NITROGEN | ——N—— |
| LIQUID NITROGEN | ——LN—— |
| NITROUS OXIDE | ——NO—— |
| HYDROGEN | ——H—— |
| HELIUM | ——HE—— |
| ARGON | ——AR—— |
| LIQUID PETROLEUM GAS | ——LPG—— |
| INDUSTRIAL WASTE | ——INW—— |
| PNEUMATIC TUBES TUBE RUNS | ——PN—— |
| CAST IRON | ——CI—— |
| CULVERT PIPE | ——CP—— |
| CLAY TILE | ——CT—— |
| DUCTILE IRON | ——DI—— |
| REINFORCED CONCRETE | ——RCP—— |
| DRAIN - OPEN TILE OR AGRICULTURAL TILE | ═══ |

## HEATING PIPING

| | |
|---|---|
| HIGH PRESSURE STEAM | ——HPS—— |
| MEDIUM PRESSURE STEAM | ——MPS—— |
| LOW PRESSURE STEAM | ——LPS—— |
| HIGH PRESSURE RETURN | ——HPR—— |
| MEDIUM PRESSURE RETURN | ——MPR—— |
| LOW PRESSURE RETURN | ——LPR—— |
| BOILER BLOW OFF | ——BD—— |
| CONDENSATE OR VACUUM PUMP DISCHARGE | ——VPD—— |
| FEEDWATER PUMP DISCHARGE | ——PPD—— |
| MAKE UP WATER | ——MU—— |
| AIR RELIEF LINE | ——V—— |
| FUEL OIL SUCTION | ——FOS—— |
| FUEL OIL RETURN | ——FOR—— |
| FUEL OIL VENT | ——FOV—— |
| COMPRESSED AIR | ——A—— |
| HOT WATER HEATING SUPPLY | ——HW—— |
| HOT WATER HEATING RETURN | ——HWR—— |

## AIR CONDITIONING PIPING

| | |
|---|---|
| REFRIGERANT LIQUID | ——RL—— |
| REFRIGERANT DISCHARGE | ——RD—— |
| REFRIGERANT SUCTION | ——RS—— |
| CONDENSER WATER SUPPLY | ——CWS—— |
| CONDENSER WATER RETURN | ——CWR—— |
| CHILLED WATER SUPPLY | ——CHWS—— |
| CHILLED WATER RETURN | ——CHWR—— |
| MAKE UP WATER | ——MU—— |
| HUMIDIFICATION LINE | ——H—— |
| DRAIN | ——D—— |
| BRINE SUPPLY | ——B—— |
| BRINE RETURN | ——BR—— |

Amor Halperin, PE; Ayres, Cohen, and Hayakawa; Consulting Engineers; Los Angeles/San Francisco, California
Joseph R. Loring & Associates, Inc., Consulting Engineers; New York, New York

GRAPHIC STANDARDS

| FITTINGS | VALVES | MISCELLANEOUS |
|---|---|---|
| ELBOW – 90° | GATE | FLANGED CONNECTION |
| ELBOW – 45° | GLOBE | SCREWED CONNECTION |
| ELBOW – TURNED UP | HOSE GATE | BELL AND SPIGOT JOINT |
| ELBOW – TURNED DOWN | HOSE GLOBE | WELD CONNECTION |
| ELBOW – LONG RAD. | ANGLE GATE – ELEV. | SOLDER CONNECTION |
| ELBOW – SIDE OUTLET DOWN | ANGLE GATE – PLAN | EXPANSION JOINT |
| ELBOW – SIDE OUTLET UP | ANGLE GLOBE – ELEV. | UNION |
| BASE ELBOW | ANGLE GLOBE – PLAN | ALIGNMENT GUIDE |
| DOUBLE BRANCH ELBOW | SWING CHECK | REDUCER |
| REDUCING ELBOW | ANGLE CHECK | BALL JOINT |
| SINGLE SWEEP TEE | SAFETY | PIPE ANCHOR |
| DOUBLE SWEEP TEE | COCK | EXPANSION LOOP |
| STRAIGHT TEE | QUICK OPEN | REDUCING FLANGE |
| TEE OUTLET UP | FLOAT | AIR VENT, AUTOMATIC |
| TEE OUTLET DOWN | MOTOR OPERATION GATE | AIR VENT, MANUAL |
| TEE – SIDE OUTLET UP | MOTOR OPERATION GLOBE | CAPS |
| TEE – SIDE OUTLET DOWN | DIAPHRAGM | CROSSOVER |
| STRAIGHT CROSS | AUTO BYPASS | CONCENTRIC REDUCER |
| LATERAL | AUTO GOVERNOR OPERATION | ECCENTRIC REDUCER |

NOTE: FITTINGS AND VALVES ARE SHOWN WITH FLANGED CONNECTIONS

Sargent, Webster, Crenshaw & Folley, Architects Engineers Planners; Syracuse, New York
Harrison D. Goodman, PE; Joseph R. Loring & Associates, Inc., Consulting Engineers; New York, New York

 **GRAPHIC STANDARDS**

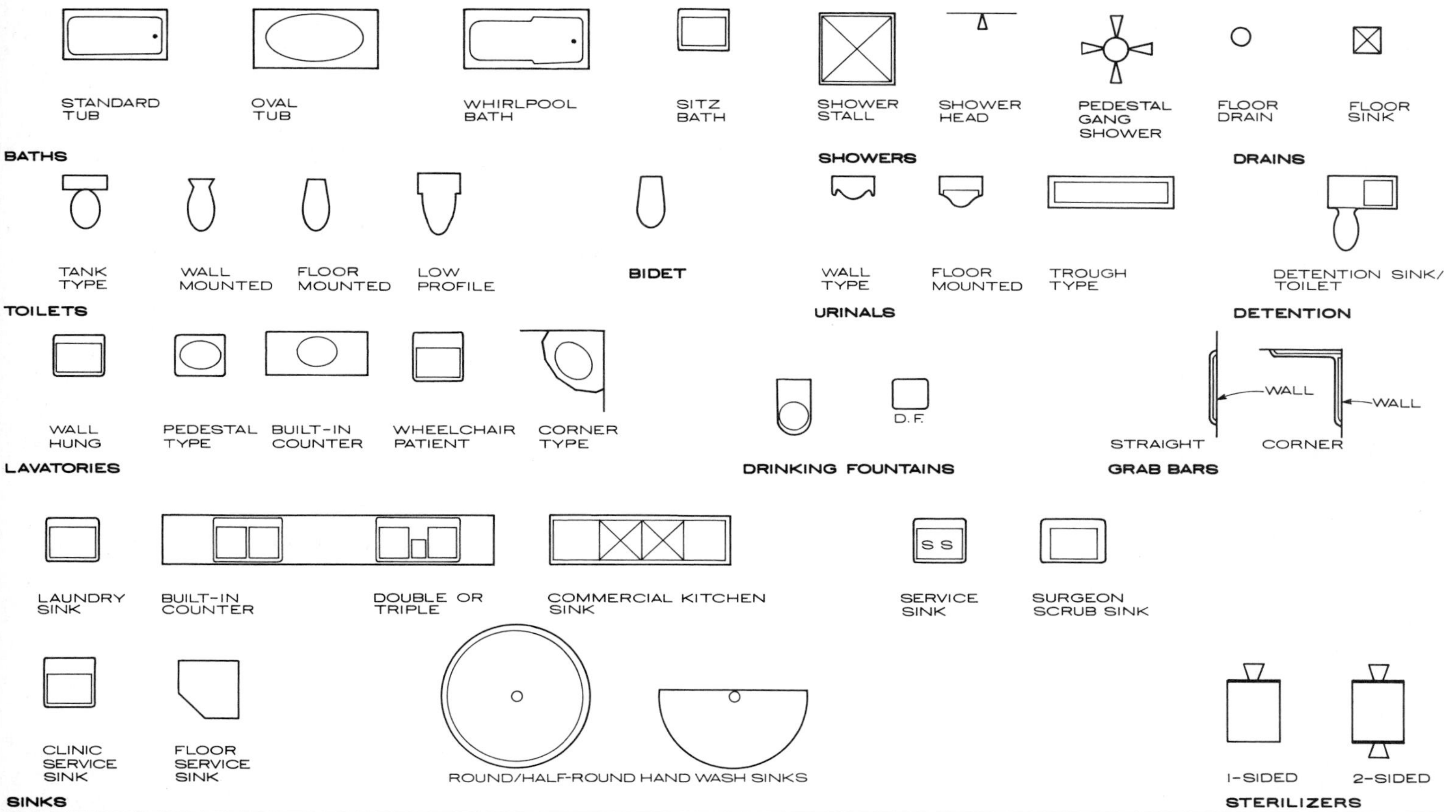

**STANDARD TUB**  **OVAL TUB**  **WHIRLPOOL BATH**  **SITZ BATH**  **SHOWER STALL**  **SHOWER HEAD**  **PEDESTAL GANG SHOWER**  **FLOOR DRAIN**  **FLOOR SINK**

**BATHS**  **SHOWERS**  **DRAINS**

**TANK TYPE**  **WALL MOUNTED**  **FLOOR MOUNTED**  **LOW PROFILE**  **BIDET**  **WALL TYPE**  **FLOOR MOUNTED**  **TROUGH TYPE**  **DETENTION SINK/TOILET**

**TOILETS**  **URINALS**  **DETENTION**

**WALL HUNG**  **PEDESTAL TYPE**  **BUILT-IN COUNTER**  **WHEELCHAIR PATIENT**  **CORNER TYPE**

**LAVATORIES**  **DRINKING FOUNTAINS**  D.F.  **GRAB BARS**  WALL  WALL  **STRAIGHT**  **CORNER**

**LAUNDRY SINK**  **BUILT-IN COUNTER**  **DOUBLE OR TRIPLE**  **COMMERCIAL KITCHEN SINK**  **SERVICE SINK**  S S  **SURGEON SCRUB SINK**

**CLINIC SERVICE SINK**  **FLOOR SERVICE SINK**  **ROUND/HALF-ROUND HAND WASH SINKS**  **1-SIDED**  **2-SIDED**

**SINKS**  **STERILIZERS**

## PLAN SYMBOLS

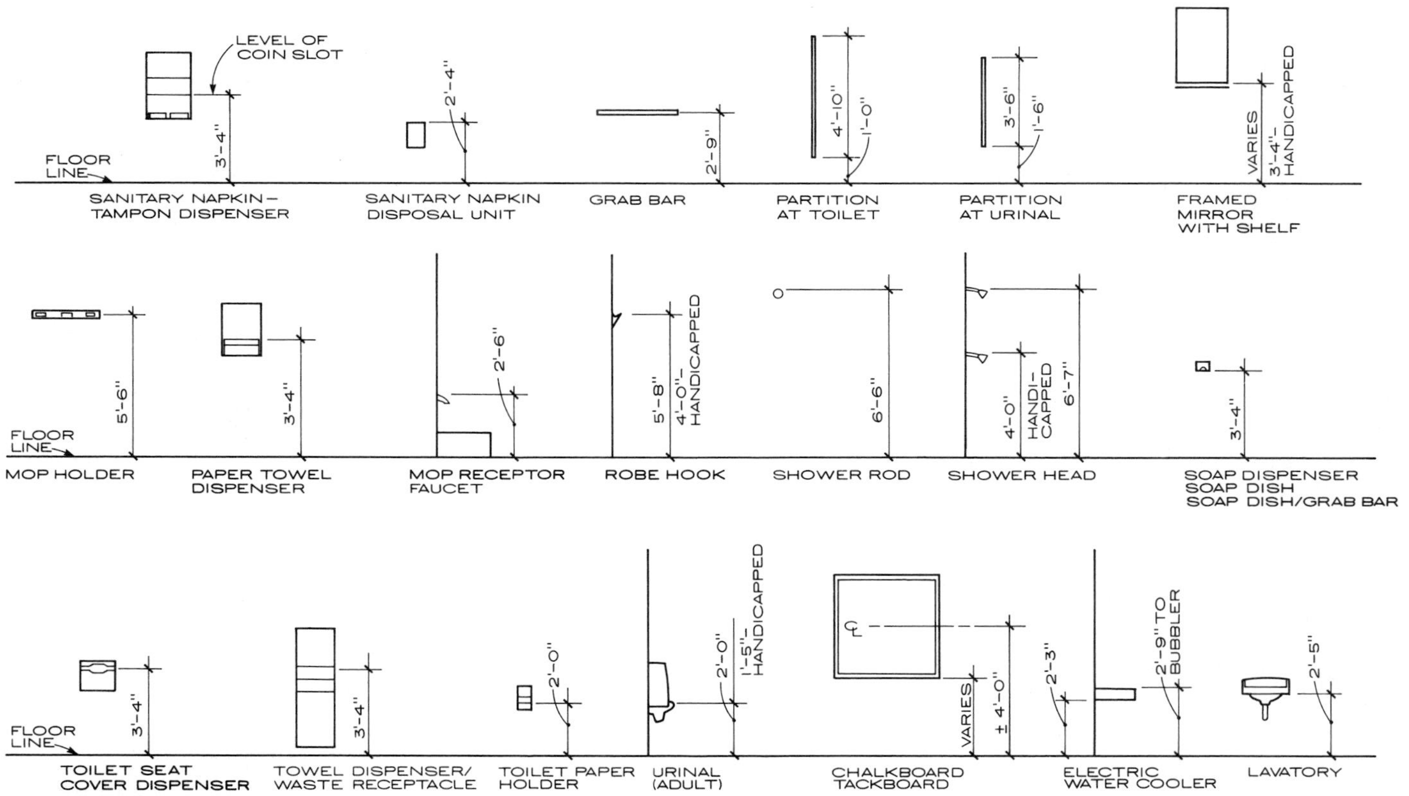

LEVEL OF COIN SLOT

FLOOR LINE

3'-4"   2'-4"   2'-9"   4'-10"   1'-0"   3'-6"   1'-6"   VARIES 3'-4" HANDICAPPED

**SANITARY NAPKIN– TAMPON DISPENSER**  **SANITARY NAPKIN DISPOSAL UNIT**  **GRAB BAR**  **PARTITION AT TOILET**  **PARTITION AT URINAL**  **FRAMED MIRROR WITH SHELF**

FLOOR LINE

5'-6"   3'-4"   2'-6"   5'-8" 4'-0" HANDICAPPED   6'-6"   4'-0" HANDI-CAPPED   6'-7"   3'-4"

**MOP HOLDER**  **PAPER TOWEL DISPENSER**  **MOP RECEPTOR FAUCET**  **ROBE HOOK**  **SHOWER ROD**  **SHOWER HEAD**  **SOAP DISPENSER SOAP DISH SOAP DISH/GRAB BAR**

FLOOR LINE

3'-4"   3'-4"   2'-0"   2'-0"   1'-5" HANDICAPPED   VARIES ± 4'-0"   2'-3"   2'-9" TO BUBBLER   2'-5"

**TOILET SEAT COVER DISPENSER**  **TOWEL DISPENSER/ WASTE RECEPTACLE**  **TOILET PAPER HOLDER**  **URINAL (ADULT)**  **CHALKBOARD TACKBOARD**  **ELECTRIC WATER COOLER**  **LAVATORY**

## MOUNTING HEIGHTS

Dale Switzer, AIA; Hope Architects & Engineers; San Diego, California

**GRAPHIC STANDARDS**

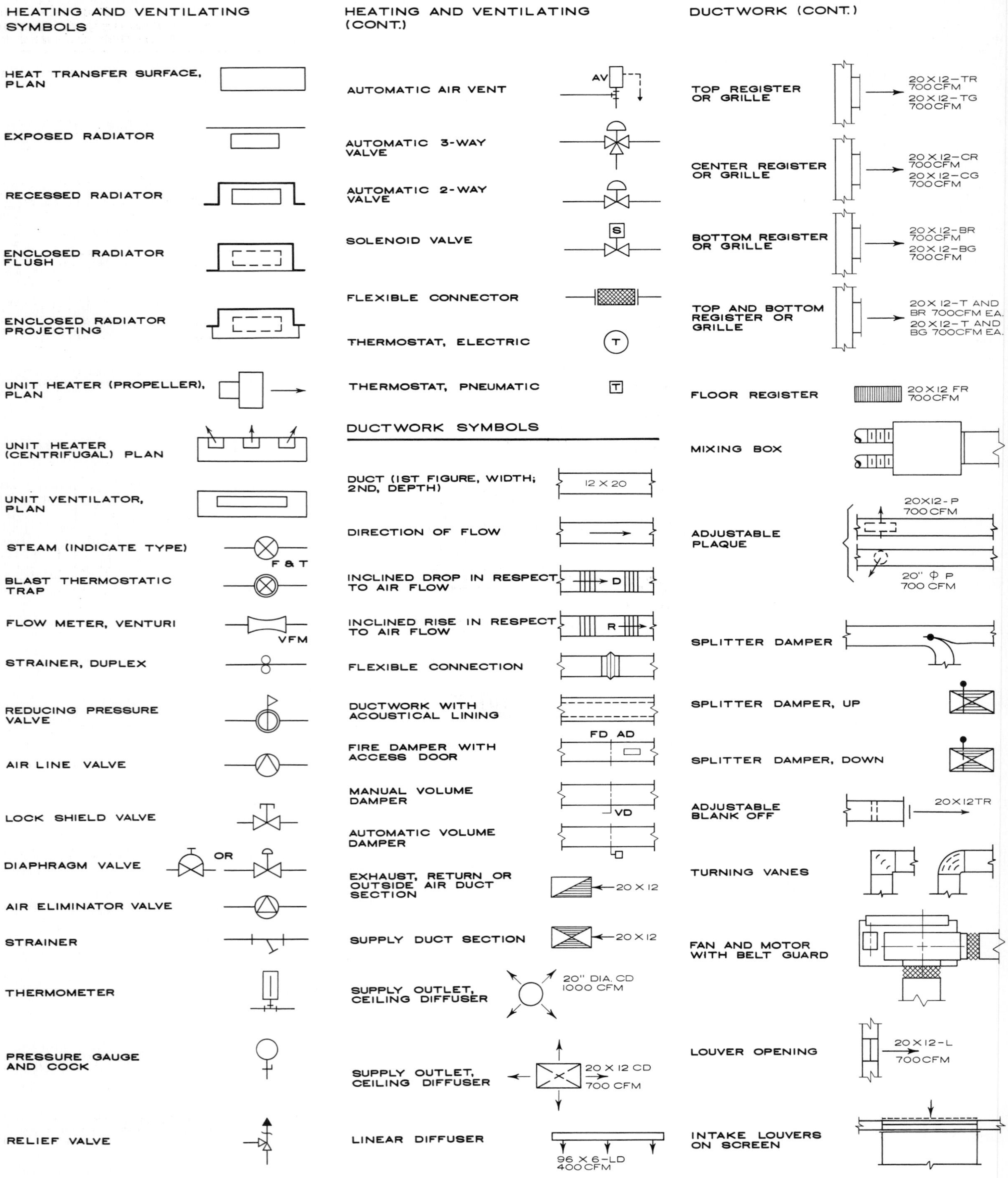
HEATING AND VENTILATING SYMBOLS
HEAT TRANSFER SURFACE, PLAN
EXPOSED RADIATOR
RECESSED RADIATOR
ENCLOSED RADIATOR FLUSH
ENCLOSED RADIATOR PROJECTING
UNIT HEATER (PROPELLER), PLAN
UNIT HEATER (CENTRIFUGAL) PLAN
UNIT VENTILATOR, PLAN
STEAM (INDICATE TYPE)
F & T
BLAST THERMOSTATIC TRAP
FLOW METER, VENTURI
VFM
STRAINER, DUPLEX
REDUCING PRESSURE VALVE
AIR LINE VALVE
LOCK SHIELD VALVE
DIAPHRAGM VALVE
OR
AIR ELIMINATOR VALVE
STRAINER
THERMOMETER
PRESSURE GAUGE AND COCK
RELIEF VALVE
HEATING AND VENTILATING (CONT.)
AUTOMATIC AIR VENT
AV
AUTOMATIC 3-WAY VALVE
AUTOMATIC 2-WAY VALVE
SOLENOID VALVE
S
FLEXIBLE CONNECTOR
THERMOSTAT, ELECTRIC
T
THERMOSTAT, PNEUMATIC
T
DUCTWORK SYMBOLS
DUCT (1ST FIGURE, WIDTH; 2ND, DEPTH)
12 X 20
DIRECTION OF FLOW
INCLINED DROP IN RESPECT TO AIR FLOW
D
INCLINED RISE IN RESPECT TO AIR FLOW
R
FLEXIBLE CONNECTION
DUCTWORK WITH ACOUSTICAL LINING
FIRE DAMPER WITH ACCESS DOOR
FD AD
MANUAL VOLUME DAMPER
VD
AUTOMATIC VOLUME DAMPER
EXHAUST, RETURN OR OUTSIDE AIR DUCT SECTION
20 X 12
SUPPLY DUCT SECTION
20 X 12
SUPPLY OUTLET, CEILING DIFFUSER
20" DIA. CD
1000 CFM
SUPPLY OUTLET, CEILING DIFFUSER
20 X 12 CD
700 CFM
LINEAR DIFFUSER
96 X 6–LD
400 CFM
DUCTWORK (CONT.)
TOP REGISTER OR GRILLE
20 X 12–TR
700 CFM
20 X 12–TG
700 CFM
CENTER REGISTER OR GRILLE
20 X 12–CR
700 CFM
20 X 12–CG
700 CFM
BOTTOM REGISTER OR GRILLE
20 X 12–BR
700 CFM
20 X 12–BG
700 CFM
TOP AND BOTTOM REGISTER OR GRILLE
20 X 12–T AND BR 700 CFM EA.
20 X 12–T AND BG 700 CFM EA.
FLOOR REGISTER
20 X 12 FR
700 CFM
MIXING BOX
ADJUSTABLE PLAQUE
20 X 12 - P
700 CFM
20" Φ P
700 CFM
SPLITTER DAMPER
SPLITTER DAMPER, UP
SPLITTER DAMPER, DOWN
ADJUSTABLE BLANK OFF
20 X 12 TR
TURNING VANES
FAN AND MOTOR WITH BELT GUARD
LOUVER OPENING
20 X 12–L
700 CFM
INTAKE LOUVERS ON SCREEN

Amor Halperin, PE; Ayres, Cohen and Hayakawa; Consulting Engineers; Los Angeles/San Francisco, California
Joseph R. Loring & Associates, Inc., Consulting Engineers; New York, New York

## INSTITUTIONAL COMMERCIAL AND INDUSTRIAL OCCUPANCIES

NURSES CALL SYSTEM DEVICES. (ANY TYPE)

PAGING SYSTEM DEVICES (ANY TYPE)

FIRE ALARM SYSTEM DEVICES (ANY TYPE)

STAFF REGISTER SYSTEM (ANY TYPE)

ELECTRICAL CLOCK SYSTEM DEVICES (ANY TYPE)

COMPUTER DATA SYSTEM DEVICES

PRIVATE TELEPHONE SYSTEM DEVICES

WATCHMAN SYSTEM DEVICES

SOUND SYSTEM

FACP — FIRE ALARM CONTROL PANEL

SC — SIGNAL CENTRAL STATION

CR — CARD READER

AUXILIARY SYSTEM CIRCUITS

Any line without further designation indicates two-wire system. For a greater number of wires, designate with numerals in manner similar to: 12- no. 18W - ¾" C. Designate by numbers corresponding to listing in schedule.

A, B, C, ETC. SPECIAL AUXILIARY OUTLETS

Subscript lettering refers to notes on drawings or detailed description in specifications.

## PANELBOARDS

FLUSH MOUNTED PANELBOARD AND CABINET

SURFACE - MOUNTED PANELBOARD AND CABINET

## BUSDUCTS AND WIREWAYS

T T T TROLLEY DUCT

B B B BUSWAY (SERVICE, FEEDER OR PLUG-IN)

C C C CABLE THROUGH LADDER OR CHANNEL

W W W WIREWAY

## SIGNALING SYSTEM OUTLETS RESIDENTIAL OCCUPANCIES

PUSH BUTTON

BUZZER

BELL

BELL AND BUZZER COMBINATION

ANNUNCIATOR

COMPUTER DATA OUTLET

INTERCONNECTING TELEPHONE

TELEPHONE SWITCHBOARD

BT BELL RINGING TRANSFORMER

D ELECTRIC DOOR OPENER

CH CHIME

TV TELEVISION OUTLET

T THERMOSTAT

## UNDERGROUND ELECTRICAL DISTRIBUTION OR LIGHTING SYSTEM

M MANHOLE

H HANDHOLE

TM TRANSFORMER- MANHOLE OR VAULT

TP TRANSFORMER PAD

UNDERGROUND DIRECT BURIAL CABLE

UNDERGROUND DUCT LINE

STREET LIGHT STANDARD FED FROM UNDERGROUND CIRCUIT

## ELECTRICAL DISTRIBUTION OR LIGHTING SYSTEM, AERIAL

POLE

STREET LIGHT AND BRACKET

TRANSFORMER

PRIMARY CIRCUIT

SECONDARY CIRCUIT

DOWN GUY

HEAD GUY

SIDEWALK GUY

SERVICE WEATHER

## PANELS CIRCUITS AND MISCELLANEOUS

LIGHTING PANEL

POWER PANEL

WIRING, CONCEALED IN CEILING OR WALL

WIRING, CONCEALED IN FLOOR

WIRING EXPOSED

HOME RUN TO PANEL BOARD.
Indicate number of circuits by number of arrows. Any circuit without such designation indicates a two-wire circuit. For a greater number of wires indicate as follows: —/// (3 wires) —//// (4 wires), etc.

FEEDERS
Use heavy lines and designate by number corresponding to listing in feeder schedule.

WIRING TURNED UP

WIRING TURNED DOWN

G GENERATOR

M MOTOR

I INSTRUMENT (SPECIFY)

T TRANSFORMER (OR DRAW TO SCALE)

CONTROLLER

EXTERNALLY OPERATED DISCONNECT SWITCH

PULL BOX

Frederick R. Brown, PE; Ayres, Cohen and Hayakawa; Consulting Engineers; Los Angeles/San Francisco, California
Richard F. Humenn, PE; Joseph R. Loring & Associates, Inc., Consulting Engineers; New York, New York

GRAPHIC STANDARDS

## LIGHTING OUTLETS

CEILING, WALL

OUTLET BOX AND INCANDESCENT LIGHTING FIXTURE. SLASH INDICATES FIXTURE ON EMERGENCY SERVICE

INCANDESCENT LIGHTING TRACK

BLANKED OUTLET

DROP CORD

EXIT LIGHT AND OUTLET BOX, DIRECTIONAL ARROWS AS INDICATED. SHADED AREAS DENOTE FACES

OUTDOOR POLE ARM MOUNTED FIXTURES

JUNCTION BOX

LAMP HOLDER WITH PULL SWITCH

MULTIPLE FLOODLIGHT ASSEMBLY

EMERGENCY BATTERY PACK WITH CHARGER AND SEALED BEAM HEADS

REMOTE EMERGENCY SEALED BEAM HEAD WITH OUTLET BOX

OUTLET CONTROLLED BY LOW VOLTAGE SWITCHING WHEN RELAY IS INSTALLED IN OUTLET BOX

INDIVIDUAL FLUORESCENT FIXTURE. SLASH INDICATES FIXTURE ON EMERGENCY SERVICE

OUTLET BOX AND FLUORESCENT LIGHTING STRIP FIXTURE

CONTINUOUS ROW FLUORESCENT FIXTURE

SURFACE-MOUNTED FLUORESCENT

## RECEPTACLE OUTLETS

SINGLE RECEPTACLE OUTLET

DUPLEX RECEPTACLE OUTLET

TRIPLEX RECEPTACLE OUTLET

QUADRUPLEX RECEPTACLE OUTLET

DUPLEX RECEPTACLE OUTLET-SPLIT WIRED

TRIPLEX RECEPTACLE OUTLET-SPLIT WIRED

SINGLE SPECIAL PURPOSE RECEPTACLE OUTLET

DUPLEX SPECIAL PURPOSE RECEPTACLE OUTLET

R    RANGE OUTLET

DW   SPECIAL PURPOSE CONNECTION

CLOSED CIRCUIT TELEVISION CAMERA

C    CLOCK HANGER RECEPTACLE

F    FAN HANGER RECEPTACLE

FLOOR SINGLE RECEPTACLE OUTLET

FLOOR DUPLEX RECEPTACLE OUTLET

FLOOR SPECIAL PURPOSE OUTLET

DATA OUTLET IN FLOOR

FLOOR TELEPHONE OUTLET-PRIVATE

UNDERFLOOR DUCT AND JUNCTION BOX FOR TRIPLE, DOUBLE, OR SINGLE DUCT SYSTEM AS INDICATED BY NUMBER OF PARALLEL LINES

CELLULAR FLOOR HEADER DUCT

## SWITCH OUTLETS

| | |
|---|---|
| S | SINGLE POLE SWITCH |
| $S_2$ | DOUBLE POLE SWITCH |
| $S_3$ | THREE-WAY SWITCH |
| $S_4$ | FOUR-WAY SWITCH |
| $S_D$ | AUTOMATIC DOOR SWITCH |
| $S_K$ | KEY OPERATED SWITCH |
| $S_P$ | SWITCH AND PILOT LAMP |
| $S_{CB}$ | CIRCUIT BREAKER |
| $S_{WCB}$ | WEATHERPROOF CIRCUIT BREAKER |
| $S_{DM}$ | DIMMER |
| $S_{RC}$ | REMOTE CONTROL SWITCH |
| $S_{WP}$ | WEATHERPROOF SWITCH |
| $S_F$ | FUSED SWITCH |
| $S_{WF}$ | WEATHERPROOF FUSED SWITCH |
| $S_L$ | SWITCH FOR LOW VOLTAGE SWITCHING SYSTEM |
| $S_{LM}$ | MASTER SWITCH FOR LOW VOLTAGE SWITCHING SYSTEM |
| $S_T$ | TIME SWITCH |
| Ⓢ | CEILING PULL SWITCH |

SWITCH AND SINGLE RECEPTACLE

SWITCH AND DOUBLE RECEPTACLE

A,B,C ETC. ⎫
A,B,C ETC. ⎬ SPECIAL OUTLETS
S A,B,C ETC. ⎭

Any standard symbol given above with the addition of lowercase subscript lettering may be used to designate some special variation of standard equipment of particular interest in a specific set of architectural plans.

When used they must be listed in the schedule of symbols on each drawing and if necessary further described in the specifications.

Frederick R. Brown, PE; Ayres, Cohen and Hayakawa; Consulting Engineers; Los Angeles/San Francisco, California
Richard F. Humenn, PE; Joseph R. Loring & Associates, Inc., Consulting Engineers; New York. New York

GRAPHIC STANDARDS

## HEAT-POWER APPARATUS

STEAM GENERATOR (BOILER) .....

FLUE GAS REHEATER
(INTERMEDIATE SUPERHEATER)..

LIVE STEAM SUPERHEATER ......
OR REHEATER

FEED HEATER WITH
AIR OUTLET .....................

CONDENSER, SURFACE··········

STEAM TURBINE .................

CONDENSING TURBINE ..........

OPEN TANK .....................

CLOSED TANK ...................

AUTOMATIC REDUCING VALVE ....

AUTOMATIC BYPASS VALVE .....

AUTOMATIC VALVE
OPERATED BY GOVERNOR ......

BOILER FEED PUMP.............

SERVICE PUMP .................

CONDENSATE PUMP ...........

CIRCULATING WATER PUMP .....

AIR PUMP .....................

OIL PUMP .....................

RECIPROCATING PUMP ..........

AIR EJECTOR
(DYNAMIC PUMP)

VACUUM TRAP .................

## REFRIGERATION

THERMOSTAT, SELF-CONTAINED

THERMOSTAT, REMOTE BULB ...

PRESSURE SWITCH ............

EXPANSION VALVE, HAND.......

EXPANSION VALVE, AUTOMATIC.

EXPANSION VALVE,
THERMOSTATIC ................

EVAPORATOR PRESSURE
REGULATING VALVE,
THROTTLING TYPE
(EVAPORATOR SIDE)

EVAPORATOR PRESSURE
REGULATING VALVE,
THERMOSTATIC, THROTTLING
TYPE

EVAPORATOR PRESSURE
REGULATING VALVE
SNAP-ACTION

COMPRESSOR SUCTION VALVE,
PRESSURE LIMITING,
THROTTLING TYPE
(COMPRESSOR SIDE)

CONSTANT PRESSURE VALVE,
SUCTION

THERMAL BULB .................

SCALE TRAP ..................

DRYER .......................

FILTER AND STRAINER    ....

COMBINATION STRAINER
AND DRYER

SIGHT GLASS .................

FLOAT VALVE
HIGH SIDE

FLOAT VALVE
LOW SIDE

GAUGE ......................

COOLING TOWER .............

EVAPORATOR,
FINNED TYPE, NATURAL
CONVECTION

EVAPORATOR,
FORCED CONVECTION ........

IMMERSION COOLING UNIT ....

CONDENSER,
AIR-COOLED,
FINNED, FORCED AIR

CONDENSER,
WATER-COOLED,
SHELL AND TUBE

CONDENSER
EVAPORATIVE

HEAT EXCHANGER

CONDENSING UNIT
AIR COOLED

CONDENSING UNIT
WATER COOLED

PRESSURE SWITCH WITH
HIGH PRESSURE CUT-OUT

COMPRESSOR

COMPRESSOR
OPEN CRANKCASE
RECIPROCATING, DIRECT
DRIVE

COMPRESSOR
OPEN CRANKCASE
RECIPROCATING BELTED

COMPRESSOR
ENCLOSED CRANKCASE,
ROTARY, BELTED

Amor Halperin, PE; Ayres, Cohen and Hayakawa; Consulting Engineers; Los Angeles/San Francisco, California

GRAPHIC STANDARDS

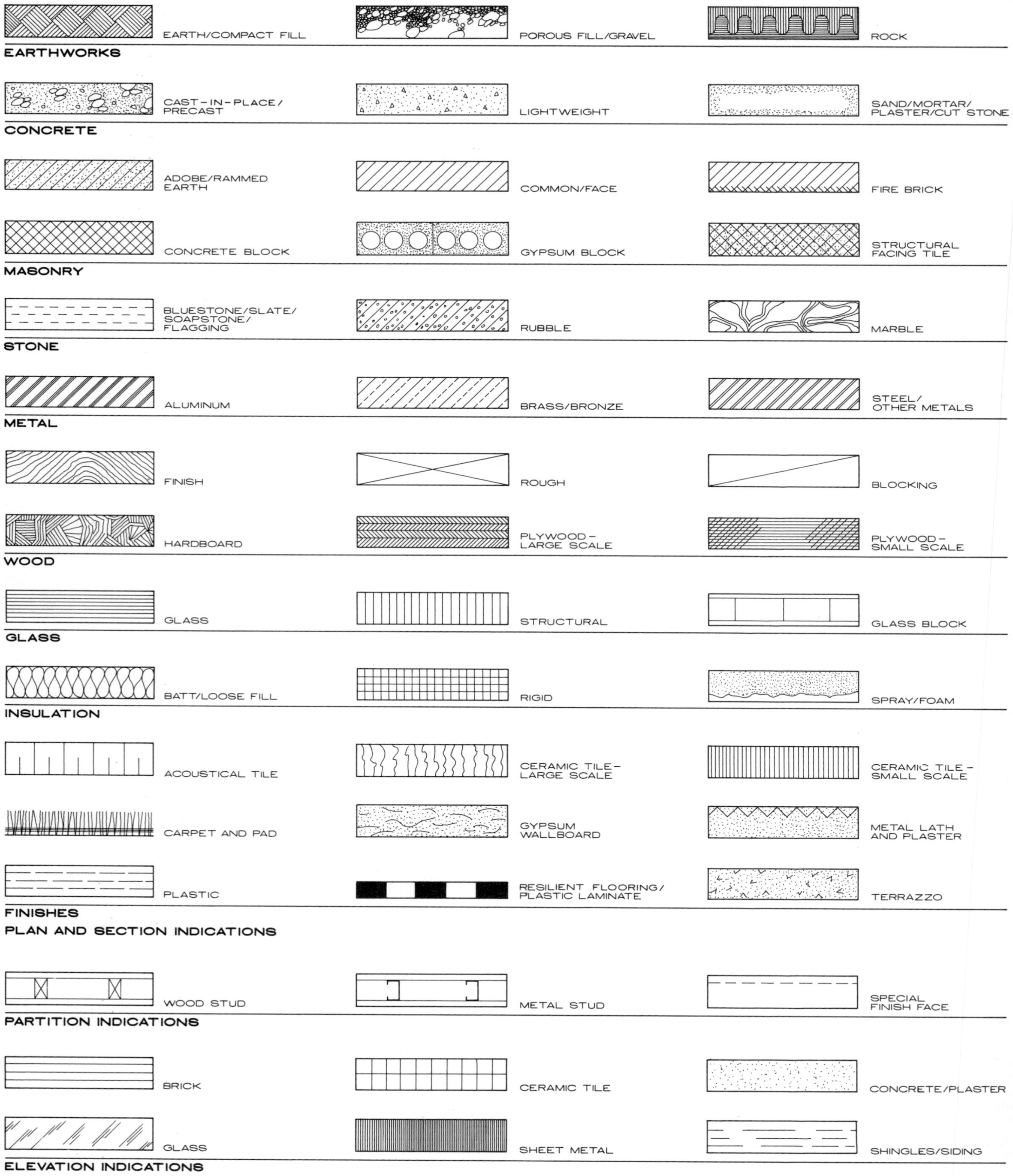

| | | |
|---|---|---|
| EARTH/COMPACT FILL | POROUS FILL/GRAVEL | ROCK |

**EARTHWORKS**

| | | |
|---|---|---|
| CAST-IN-PLACE/ PRECAST | LIGHTWEIGHT | SAND/MORTAR/ PLASTER/CUT STONE |

**CONCRETE**

| | | |
|---|---|---|
| ADOBE/RAMMED EARTH | COMMON/FACE | FIRE BRICK |
| CONCRETE BLOCK | GYPSUM BLOCK | STRUCTURAL FACING TILE |

**MASONRY**

| | | |
|---|---|---|
| BLUESTONE/SLATE/ SOAPSTONE/ FLAGGING | RUBBLE | MARBLE |

**STONE**

| | | |
|---|---|---|
| ALUMINUM | BRASS/BRONZE | STEEL/ OTHER METALS |

**METAL**

| | | |
|---|---|---|
| FINISH | ROUGH | BLOCKING |
| HARDBOARD | PLYWOOD – LARGE SCALE | PLYWOOD – SMALL SCALE |

**WOOD**

| | | |
|---|---|---|
| GLASS | STRUCTURAL | GLASS BLOCK |

**GLASS**

| | | |
|---|---|---|
| BATT/LOOSE FILL | RIGID | SPRAY/FOAM |

**INSULATION**

| | | |
|---|---|---|
| ACOUSTICAL TILE | CERAMIC TILE – LARGE SCALE | CERAMIC TILE – SMALL SCALE |
| CARPET AND PAD | GYPSUM WALLBOARD | METAL LATH AND PLASTER |
| PLASTIC | RESILIENT FLOORING/ PLASTIC LAMINATE | TERRAZZO |

**FINISHES**

**PLAN AND SECTION INDICATIONS**

| | | |
|---|---|---|
| WOOD STUD | METAL STUD | SPECIAL FINISH FACE |

**PARTITION INDICATIONS**

| | | |
|---|---|---|
| BRICK | CERAMIC TILE | CONCRETE/PLASTER |
| GLASS | SHEET METAL | SHINGLES/SIDING |

**ELEVATION ANDICATIONS**

John Ray Hoke, Jr., AIA; Washington, D.C.

 **GRAPHIC STANDARDS**

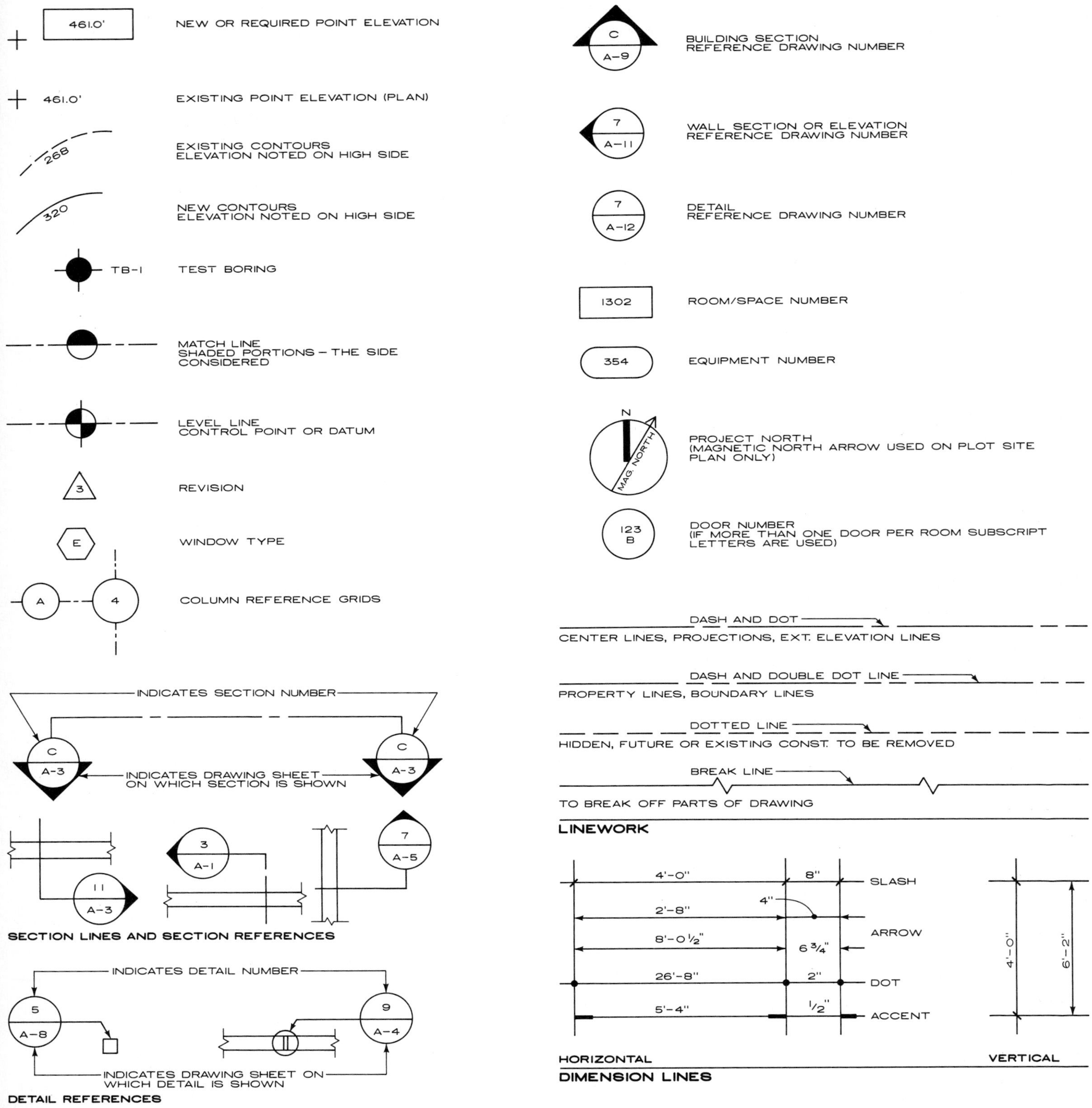

461.0'    NEW OR REQUIRED POINT ELEVATION

461.0'    EXISTING POINT ELEVATION (PLAN)

268    EXISTING CONTOURS
ELEVATION NOTED ON HIGH SIDE

320    NEW CONTOURS
ELEVATION NOTED ON HIGH SIDE

TB-1    TEST BORING

MATCH LINE
SHADED PORTIONS — THE SIDE
CONSIDERED

LEVEL LINE
CONTROL POINT OR DATUM

3    REVISION

E    WINDOW TYPE

A    4    COLUMN REFERENCE GRIDS

INDICATES SECTION NUMBER

C / A-3    INDICATES DRAWING SHEET
ON WHICH SECTION IS SHOWN

C / A-3

11 / A-3    3 / A-1    7 / A-5

**SECTION LINES AND SECTION REFERENCES**

INDICATES DETAIL NUMBER

5 / A-8    11    9 / A-4

INDICATES DRAWING SHEET ON
WHICH DETAIL IS SHOWN

**DETAIL REFERENCES**

## GRAPHIC SYMBOLS

The symbols shown are those that seem to be the most common and acceptable, judged by the frequency of use by the architectural offices surveyed. This list can and should be expanded by each office to include symbols generally used by it, but not indicated here. Adoption of these symbols as standard practice is desirable to improve communication in the industry.

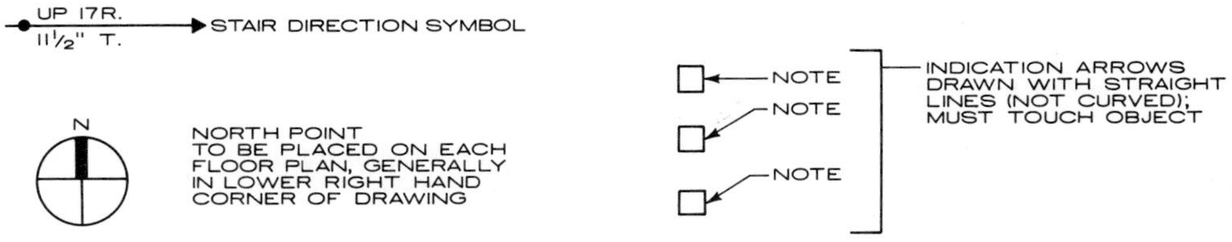

John Ray Hoke, Jr., AIA; Washington, D.C.

C / A-9    BUILDING SECTION
REFERENCE DRAWING NUMBER

7 / A-11    WALL SECTION OR ELEVATION
REFERENCE DRAWING NUMBER

7 / A-12    DETAIL
REFERENCE DRAWING NUMBER

1302    ROOM/SPACE NUMBER

354    EQUIPMENT NUMBER

N / MAG NORTH    PROJECT NORTH
(MAGNETIC NORTH ARROW USED ON PLOT SITE
PLAN ONLY)

123 / B    DOOR NUMBER
(IF MORE THAN ONE DOOR PER ROOM SUBSCRIPT
LETTERS ARE USED)

DASH AND DOT
CENTER LINES, PROJECTIONS, EXT. ELEVATION LINES

DASH AND DOUBLE DOT LINE
PROPERTY LINES, BOUNDARY LINES

DOTTED LINE
HIDDEN, FUTURE OR EXISTING CONST. TO BE REMOVED

BREAK LINE
TO BREAK OFF PARTS OF DRAWING

**LINEWORK**

4'-0"    8"    SLASH
2'-8"    4"    ARROW
8'-0½"    6¾"    
26'-8"    2"    DOT
5'-4"    ½"    ACCENT

4'-0"    6'-2"

**HORIZONTAL**    **VERTICAL**
**DIMENSION LINES**

UP 17R.
11½" T.    STAIR DIRECTION SYMBOL

N    NORTH POINT
TO BE PLACED ON EACH
FLOOR PLAN, GENERALLY
IN LOWER RIGHT HAND
CORNER OF DRAWING

NOTE
NOTE
NOTE    INDICATION ARROWS
DRAWN WITH STRAIGHT
LINES (NOT CURVED);
MUST TOUCH OBJECT

**GRAPHIC STANDARDS**

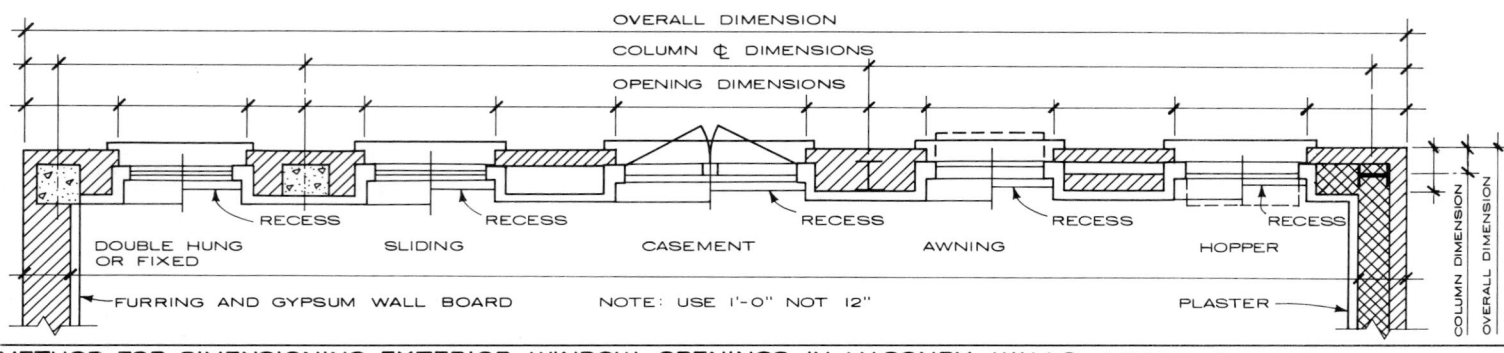

**METHOD FOR DIMENSIONING EXTERIOR WINDOW OPENINGS IN MASONRY WALLS** ( DOORS SIMILAR )

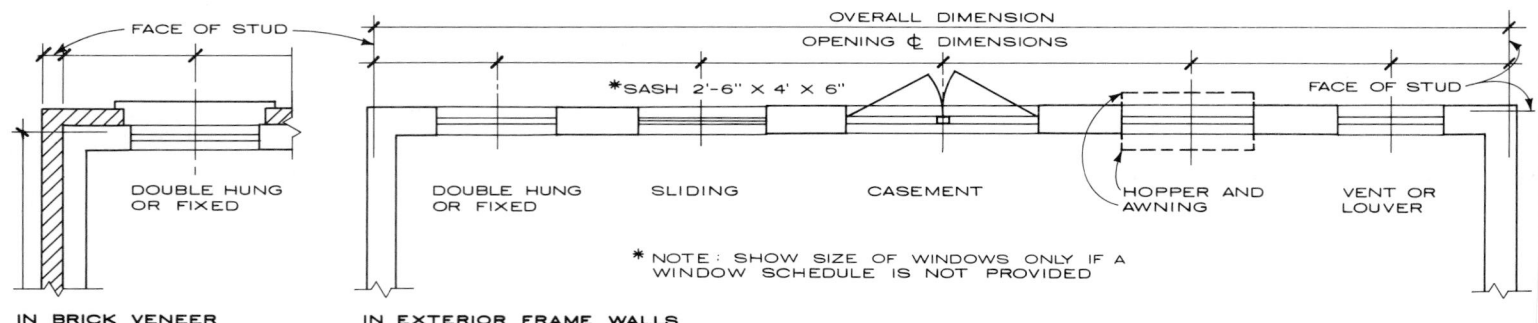

**METHOD FOR DIMENSIONING EXTERIOR WINDOW OPENINGS IN FRAME WALLS** ( DOORS SIMILAR )

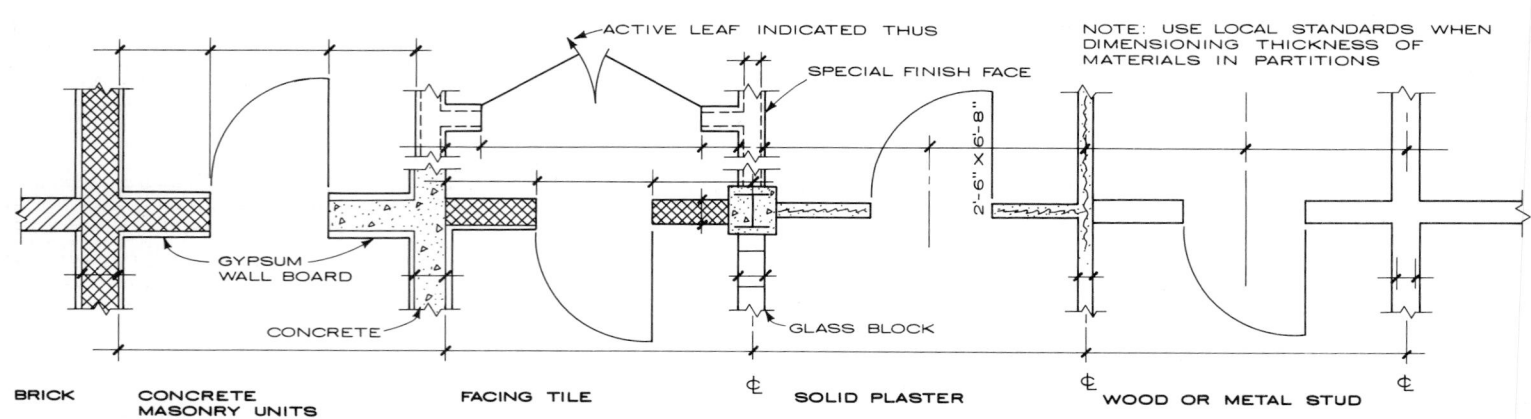

**METHOD FOR DIMENSIONING AND INDICATIONS OF INTERIOR PARTITIONS AND DOORS**

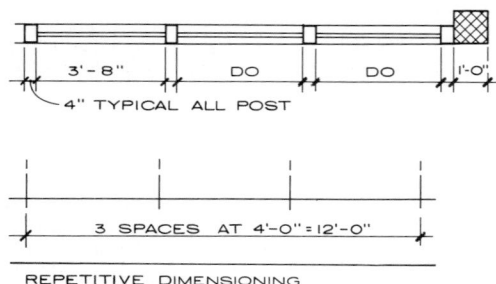

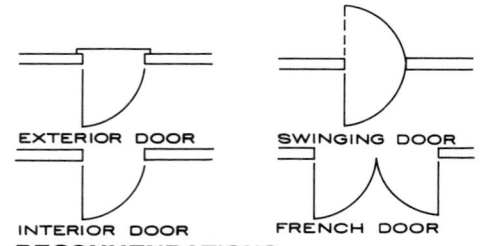

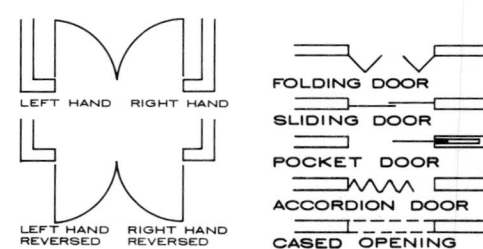

## GENERAL NOTES

Dimensioning should start with critical dimensions and should be kept to a minimum. Consideration must be given to the trades using them and the sequencing adjusted to their respective work. It is also necessary to bear in mind that tolerances in actual construction will be varied. This means that as-built dimensions do not always coincide with design dimensions. Dimensioning from established grids or structural elements, such as columns and structural walls, assists the trades that must locate their work prior to that of others.

John Ray Hoke, Jr., AIA; Washington, D.C.

## RECOMMENDATIONS

1. Dimensions under 1 ft shall be noted in inches. Dimensions 1 ft and over shall be expressed in feet.
2. Fractions under 1 in. shall NOT be preceded by a zero. Fractions must have a diagonal dividing line between numerator and denominator.
3. Dimension points to be noted with a short blunt 45° line. Dash to be oriented differently for vertical (*) and horizontal (*) runs of dimensions. Modular dimension points may be designated with an arrow or a dot.
4. Dimension all items from an established grid or reference point and do not close the string of dimensions to the next grid or reference point.
5. Dimension: to face of concrete or masonry work; to centerlines of columns or other grid points; to centerlines of partitions. In nonmodular wood construction dimension to critical face of studs. When a clear dimension is required, dimension to the finish faces and note as such. Do not use the word "clear."
6. Dimension as much as possible from structural elements.
7. Overall readability, conciseness, completeness, and accuracy must be foremost in any dimensional system. It takes experience to determine how to use dimensions to the best advantage.

**GRAPHIC STANDARDS**

## PARALINE DRAWINGS

Paraline drawings are sometimes referred to as AXONOMETRIC (Greek) or AXIOMETRIC (English) drawings. These drawings are projected pictorial representations of an object which give a three-dimensional quality. They can be classified as orthographic projections inasmuch as the plan view is rotated and the side view is tilted. The resulting "front" view is projected at a 90° angle to the picture plane (as illustrated in the projected method). These drawings differ from perspective drawings, since the projection lines remain parallel instead of converging to a point on the horizon.

Drawings prepared by using the projection method require three views of the object, which tends to be more time-consuming and complex than drawing by the direct measuring method. The following drawings utilize this method; they are simple to draw and represent reasonably accurate proportions.

## OBLIQUE

In an oblique drawing one face (either plan or elevation) of the object is drawn directly on the picture plane. Projected lines are drawn at a 30 or 45° angle to the picture plane. The length of the projecting lines is determined as illustrated and varies according to the angle chosen.

## DIMETRIC

A dimetric drawing is similar to oblique, with one exception—the object is rotated so that only one of its corners touches the picture plane. The most frequently used angle for the projecting lines is an equal division of 45° on either side of the leading edge. A 15° angle is sometimes used when it is less important to show the "roof view" of the object.

## ISOMETRIC

The isometric, a special type of dimetric drawing, is the easiest and most popular paraline drawing. All axes of the object are simultaneously rotated away from the picture plane and kept at the same angle of projection (30° from the picture plane). All legs are equally distorted in length at a given scale and therefore maintain an exact proportion of 1:1:1.

## TRIMETRIC

The trimetric drawing is similar to the dimetric, except that the plan of the object is rotated so that the two exposed sides of the object are not at equal angles to the picture plane. The plan is usually positioned at 30/60° angle to the ground plane. The height of the object is reduced proportionately as illustrated (similar to the 45° dimetric).

## SHADES AND SHADOWS

Shades and shadows are easily constructed and can be very effective in paraline drawings. The location of the light source will determine the direction of the shadows cast by the object. The shade line is the line (or the edge) that separates the light area from the shaded areas of the object. Shadows are constructed by drawing a line, representing a light ray, from a corner of the lighted surface at a 45° angle to the ground plane. Shadows cast by a vertical edge of the object will be drawn midway in the angle created by the intersection of the projected line of the object and the ground, or baseline (the baseline represents the intersection of the picture plane). The 45° light ray is extended until it meets the shadow line (as illustrated), and this point determines the length of the shadow for any given vertical height of the object. Shadow lines of all vertical edges of the object are drawn parallel to one another.

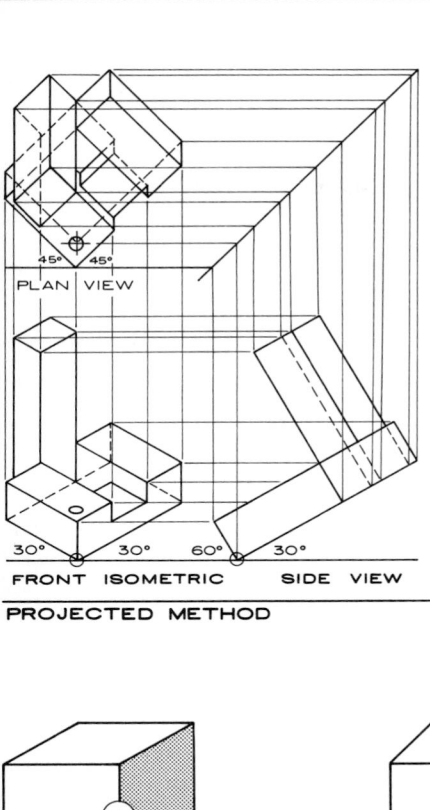

PLAN VIEW
45° 45°

FRONT ISOMETRIC    SIDE VIEW
30° 30° 60° 30°

**PROJECTED METHOD**

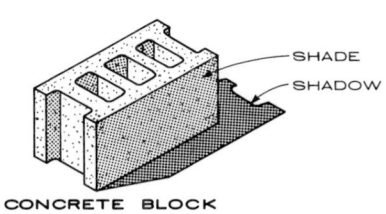

SHADE
SHADOW

CONCRETE BLOCK

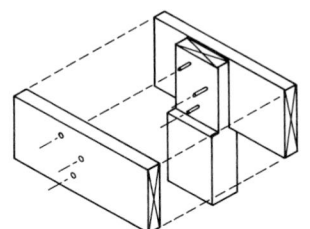

EXPLODED VIEW OF DETAIL

**ISOMETRIC**

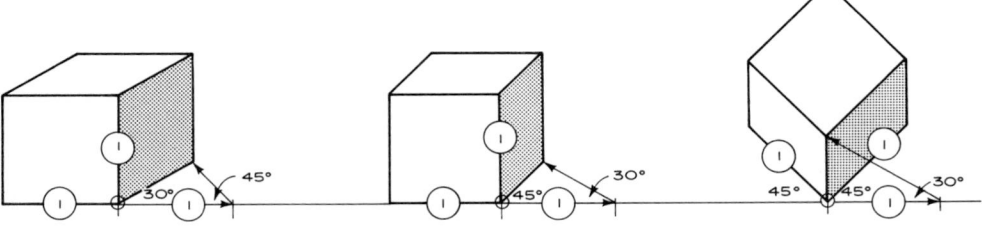

30° OBLIQUE       45° OBLIQUE       45° DIMETRIC
  30°   45°         45°   30°        45° 45°   30°
                                     ( ROTATED PLAN )

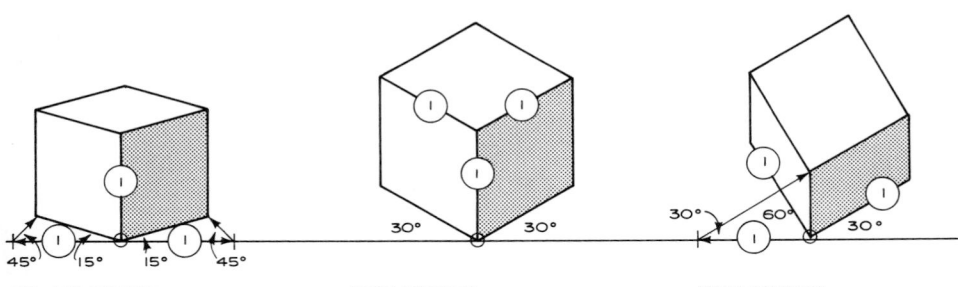

15° DIMETRIC       ISOMETRIC        TRIMETRIC
45° 15° 15° 45°   ( 30° DIMETRIC )  ( ROTATED PLAN )
                  30°   30°         30° 60° 30°

**AXIOMETRIC — MEASURED METHOD**

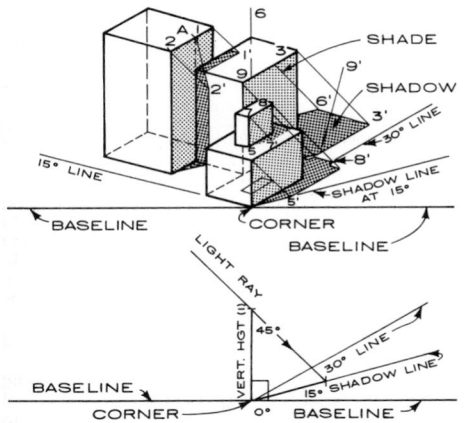

SHADE
SHADOW
30° LINE
15° LINE
SHADOW LINE AT 15°
BASELINE    CORNER
BASELINE

LIGHT RAY
VERT. HGT (1)
45°
30° LINE
15° SHADOW LINE
BASELINE
CORNER    0°    BASELINE

**15 / 30° TRIMETRIC SHADOW**

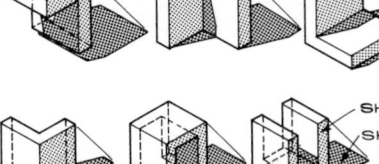

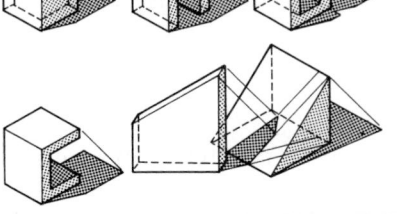

SHADE
SHADOW

**SHADES AND SHADOWS**

Jim Maeda; Samuel J. De Santo and Associates; New York, New York

## GRAPHIC METHODS

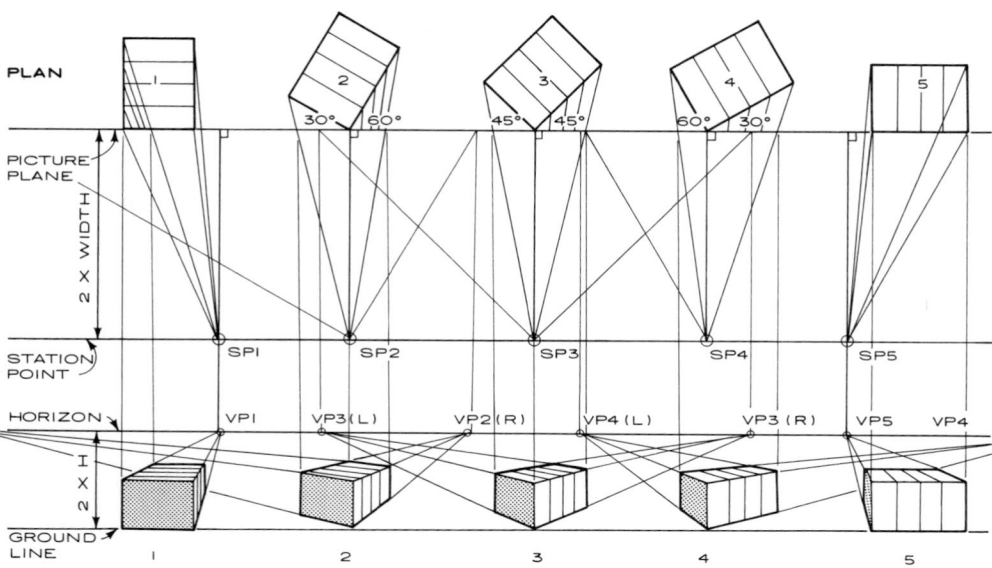

PERSPECTIVE — PROJECTION METHOD

### GENERAL NOTES

Before the drawing can be laid out, the following information must be obtained:

1. An approximation of the overall dimensions of the building.
2. The location of the building in relation to the picture plane.
3. The orientation of the building, either in front of or behind the picture plane.

While the building can be located anywhere in the drawing—in front of, behind, or at any angle to the picture plane—the simplest approach is to place the building at the picture plane. The horizontal lines of the building would be parallel to the picture plane in a one-point perspective or placed at an angle to the picture plane. Usually this will be a 30/60 or 45° angle in a two-point perspective.

### TERMS AND CONCEPTS

1. THE OBJECT: Called a building in this example.
2. THE PICTURE PLANE: An imaginary, transparent plane, onto or through which the object is perceived in a perspective rendering. It is:
   a. Parallel to one face of the drawing paper, if it is a one-point perspective.
   b. Perpendicular to the ground line and at any angle to the building if it is a two-point perspective.
   c. Tilted and placed at any angle to the building if it is a three-point perspective.
   d. A curved plane if it is a wide angle perspective view.
3. HORIZON LINE: A line drawn on the picture plane to represent the horizon. It is usually located at the point where all parallel lines recede away from the viewer and finally converge. This point is aptly designated as the vanishing point. Note that although the horizon is generally thought of as a horizontal line, in certain applications it could be vertical, or even at an angle, to the picture plane. For example, in drawing shades and shadows it appears to be at a 90° angle and in a three-point perspective it appears to be slanted.
4. STATION POINT: The point from which the object is being viewed or, in other words the point from which the viewer is seeing the building. The location of this point will be the factor that determines the width of the drawing. A 30° cone of vision is drawn from the station point; as the viewer moves away from the object, the cone widens, the object becomes smaller, and more material is included in the area surrounding the object. A common way of determining the distance between the station point and the picture plane is by referring to the following parameters:

   Minimum—1.73 times the width of the drawing.
   Average—2.00 times the width of the drawing.
   Maximum—2.50 times the width of the drawing.

5. VANISHING POINT(S): A specific point or points located on the horizon line, where all parallel lines, drawn in perspective, converge or terminate. The location of the vanishing point varies with the type of perspective drawing. In a two-point perspective, the distance between the vanishing point left and the vanishing point right is estimated as being approximately four times the overall size of the building.
6. VISUAL RAY: An imaginary line drawn from the station point to any specific point lying within the designated scope of the plan layout of the object. The point at which this projected line passes through the picture plane will determine the location of that point in the perspective drawing.
7. GROUND PLANE: The ground on which the viewer is standing. In plan, this is determined at the station point. In perspective, it is the primary plane on which the building is sited. When the lines of this plane are extended to infinity, it becomes the horizon line. The intersection formed when the picture plane and the ground plane come together is called the ground line. In this way the horizontal dimension of the drawing is determined. The vertical dimension is determined by the vertical distance from the ground line to the horizon line. This should be approximately twice the height of object, in perspective, or a 30° cone in elevation.
8. ONE-POINT INTERIOR PERSPECTIVE: The most frequently used application of a one-point perspective. This is the same method as that used in setting up a one-point exterior perspective, except for the limitations that the confinement of space places on the location of the vanishing points. The vanishing point is usually located at the sitting or standing height of an average person within the space (eye level can be considered to be at 5 ft 4 in. from the floor. In most cases, the vanishing point is located within the confines of the enclosed space being represented in the drawing.
9. TWO-POINT PERSPECTIVE USING THE MEASURING POINT METHOD: This is a simplified alternative to the conventional method of laying out the plan picture plane and projecting the vanishing lines. The measuring point method of drawing a two-point perspective eliminates the necessity of the preliminary layout of the plan. One of the obvious advantages of this method is the ease with which the size of the drawing can be adjusted. A perspective can be made larger by simply increasing the scale of the drawing.

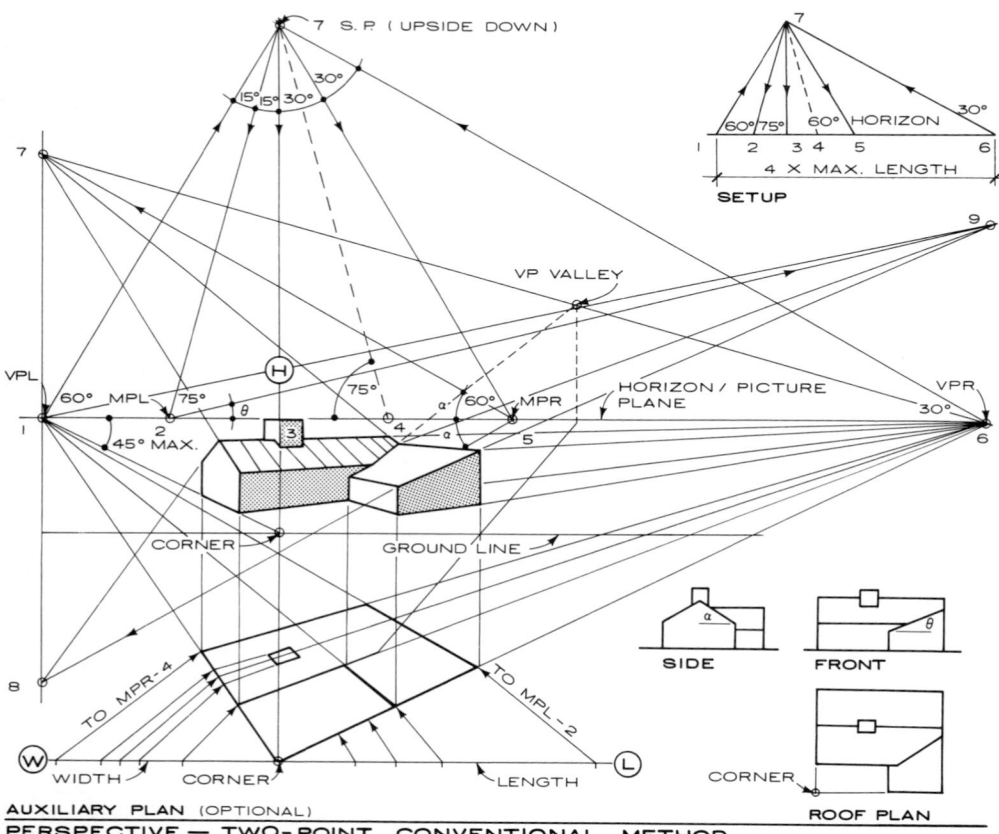

PERSPECTIVE — TWO-POINT CONVENTIONAL METHOD

Jim Maeda; Samuel J. De Santo and Associates; New York, New York

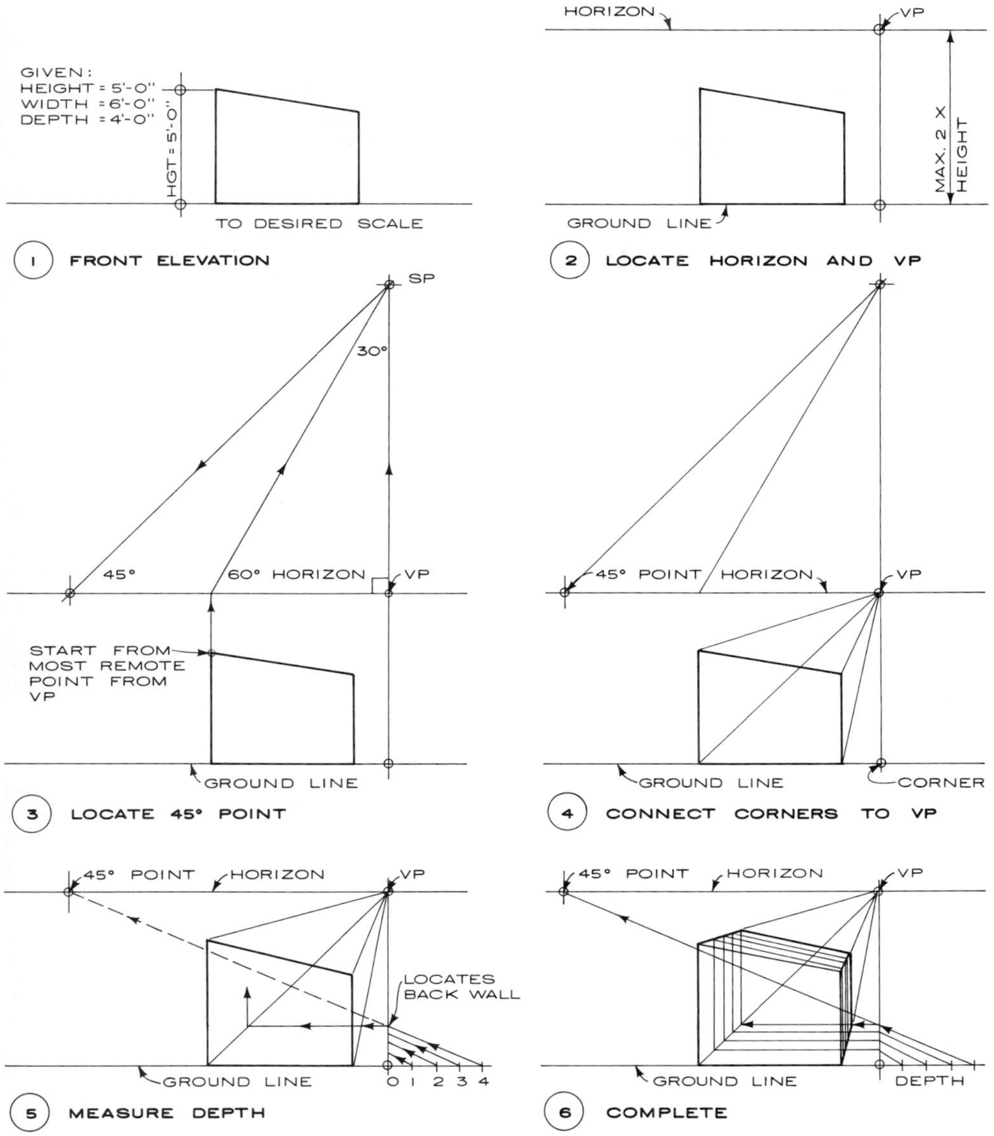

## ONE-POINT PERSPECTIVE BY 45° MEASURING POINT

GIVEN:
HEIGHT = 5'-0"
WIDTH = 6'-0"
DEPTH = 4'-0"

HGT = 5'-0"

TO DESIRED SCALE

① FRONT ELEVATION

---

HORIZON    VP

MAX 2 X HEIGHT

GROUND LINE

② LOCATE HORIZON AND VP

---

SP

30°

45°    60° HORIZON    VP

START FROM MOST REMOTE POINT FROM VP

GROUND LINE

③ LOCATE 45° POINT

---

45° POINT    HORIZON    VP

GROUND LINE    CORNER

④ CONNECT CORNERS TO VP

---

45° POINT    HORIZON    VP

LOCATES BACK WALL

GROUND LINE    0 1 2 3 4

⑤ MEASURE DEPTH

---

45° POINT    HORIZON    VP

GROUND LINE    DEPTH

⑥ COMPLETE

---

**ONE-POINT PERSPECTIVE BY 45° MEASURING POINT**

## ONE-POINT MEASURED INTERIOR PERSPECTIVE

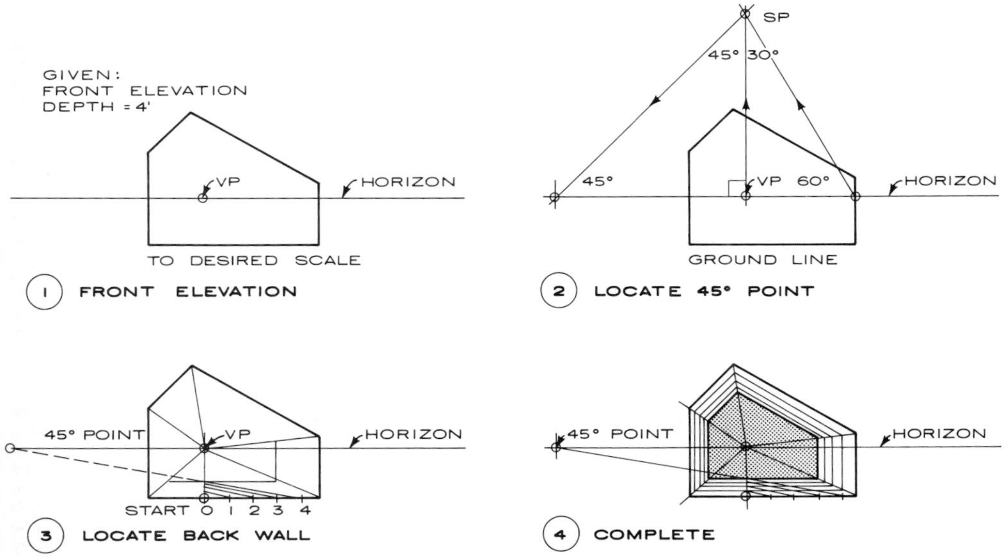

GIVEN:
FRONT ELEVATION
DEPTH = 4'

VP    HORIZON

TO DESIRED SCALE

① FRONT ELEVATION

---

SP

45° 30°

45°    VP 60°    HORIZON

GROUND LINE

② LOCATE 45° POINT

---

45° POINT    VP    HORIZON

START 0 1 2 3 4

③ LOCATE BACK WALL

---

45° POINT    HORIZON

④ COMPLETE

---

**ONE-POINT MEASURED INTERIOR PERSPECTIVE**

Jim Maeda; Samuel J. De Santo and Associates; New York, New York

---

## ONE-POINT PERSPECTIVE

The one-point perspective is probably the least complicated of the projected perspective methods. The primary face of the building or object is placed directly on the picture plane. The adjacent planes, generally connected to the primary plane at right angles, converge to the vanishing point—which can be either in front of or behind the picture plane. The vanishing point, located on the horizon line, also determines the height from which the building is viewed.

The conventional method of laying out a one-point exterior perspective is illustrated on the preceding page. A plan view, roof view, and elevation are required for the layout. The size of the object, and therefore the drawing, can be increased or decreased by moving the plan further in front of or behind the picture plane. This method is more flexible but much more complicated and time-consuming than the method that follows.

### EXTERIOR ONE-POINT PERSPECTIVE

① Draw the primary elevation of the building to scale.

② Locate the horizon above the ground line at the desired level (eye level is at approximately 5 ft 4 in.). To ensure that the final perspective will fall within the 60° cone vision, the height should not exceed 2X the height of the building. The VP is located left or right arbitrarily depending on the view desired.

③ A 45° vanishing point can be graphically located by starting at the most remote point of the roof and extending a vertical line to the horizon line. From this point, draw a line upward, at a 60° angle. Another line should be drawn vertically upward from the vanishing point. The station point (upside down) is located at the point where these two lines intersect. From the station point, draw a line at a 45° angle to meet the horizon line. This point will be the vanishing point for all lines that are positioned at 45° angle and parallel to the picture plane.

④ From each corner of the primary elevation, draw a line to the vanishing point.

⑤ The correct building depth (drawn at 6 ft in the illustration) is measured along the ground line—on the picture plane—starting at point 0. Draw a line connecting this point to the 45° point on the horizon line. The point at which this line intersects the line extended between the lower corner of the elevation to the vanishing point will determine the location of the back wall of the building.

⑥ The perspective is completed by constructing the back wall at the location established in step 5 and connecting it to the front wall. Note that the lines that are drawn at a 45° angle in the drawing remain parallel to each other as they are extended in perspective.

### ONE-POINT INTERIOR AND SECTIONAL PERSPECTIVE

① Draw the primary elevation, or section, to scale. Locate the horizon line and vanishing point within the confines of the interior space.

② A 45° point is located in a similar manner to the one-point exterior perspective. The station point is established by drawing a line, at a 60° angle, from the most remote point in the elevation to intersect another line extended upward at a perpendicular from the vanishing point.

③ The room depth is determined by starting at point 0 on the ground line and measuring the appropriate distance to the 45° point on the horizon line. The back wall is located where these two lines come together.

④ Complete the back wall as illustrated. Note that all lines occurring at a 45° angle in the elevation remain parallel in perspective. All surfaces that are parallel to the picture plane will remain parallel in perspective.

## GRAPHIC METHODS

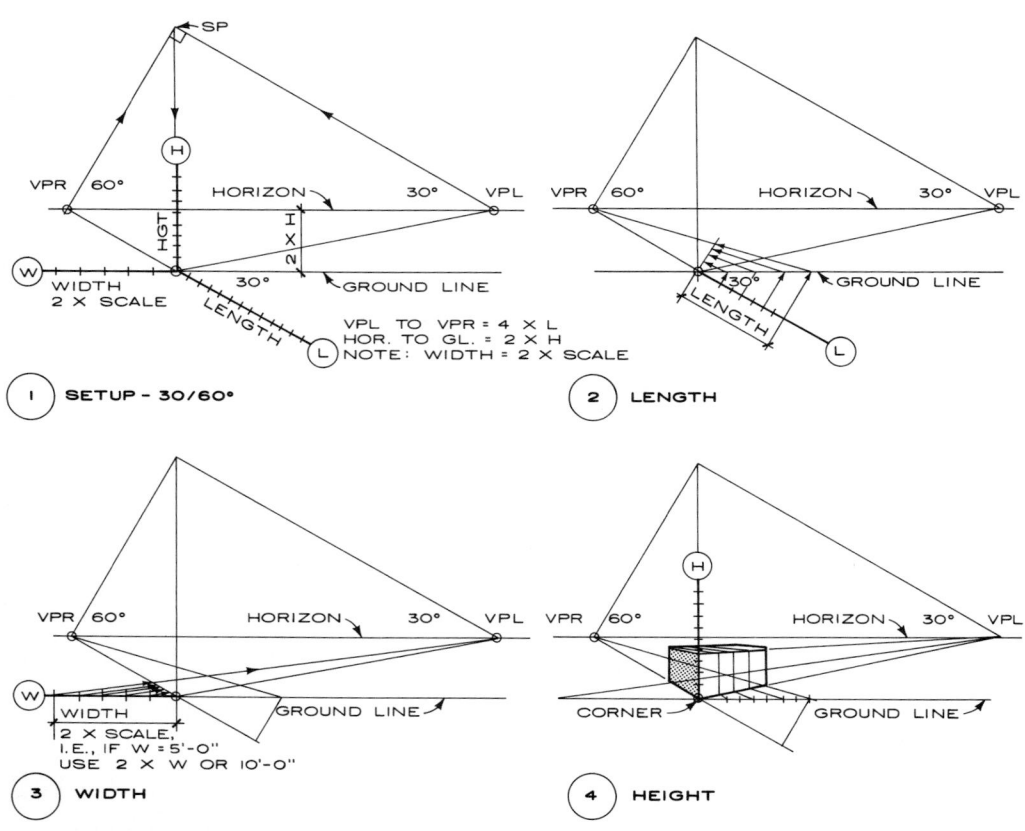

① **SETUP – 30/60°**

② **LENGTH**

VPL TO VPR = 4 × L
HOR. TO GL. = 2 × H
NOTE: WIDTH = 2 × SCALE

③ **WIDTH**

WIDTH
2 X SCALE,
I.E., IF W = 5'-0"
USE 2 X W OR 10'-0"

④ **HEIGHT**

**TWO-POINT PERSPECTIVE — 30/60° MEASURED SYSTEM**

## TWO-POINT PERSPECTIVE

The projection method of constructing a two-point perspective is illustrated on the preceding page. This is the most widely used and most flexible method of drawing a two-point perspective. It can be taken from any viewpoint by simply turning the plan to the desired position in the preliminary layout. The size of the perspective can also be adjusted by moving the plan in front of the picture plane for a larger drawing and behind the picture plane for a smaller drawing. As in all projected methods, an inordinate amount of time and energy is devoted to the layout. The measured method is equally accurate, less time-consuming, and much easier to construct, since it eliminates the need to lay out the drawing in plan. The desired size of the drawing is determined by drawing the primary elevation at the desired scale.

### 30/60° MEASURED SYSTEM

① SET-UP: Draw a horizon line and locate VPR and VPL separated at a distance that is approximately 4 to 4.5 × the maximum width of the building. Follow the illustration to locate the station point and leading corner of the building.

② LENGTH: Measure, to scale, the length of the building along length line L. A perpendicular line is drawn from these designated points to the ground line. The vanishing perspective lines are then drawn directly from these points to the appropriate vanishing point (VPL). In this way the correct length of the line can be determined. Note what happens when equally spaced points are projected from the ground line to the vanishing point. The visual distance (length) between them, as they get closer to the vanishing point, is progressively foreshortened.

③ WIDTH: The width is measured along the width line (see illustration) at double the scale. That is, if the perspective is drawn at a scale of ⅛ in. = 1 ft and a particular line is to be drawn at 5 ft, measure 5 ft at ¼-in. scale starting at the corner and measure to the left of the corner horizontally. A line is drawn from each point on the width line to the appropriate vanishing point (VPR). The intersections of the length and width vanishing lines will define the "plan" in perspective.

④ HEIGHT: Since the leading corner of the building is placed directly on the picture plane, the height is measured, to scale, directly on the H line. It is then carried to VPL and VPR as illustrated.

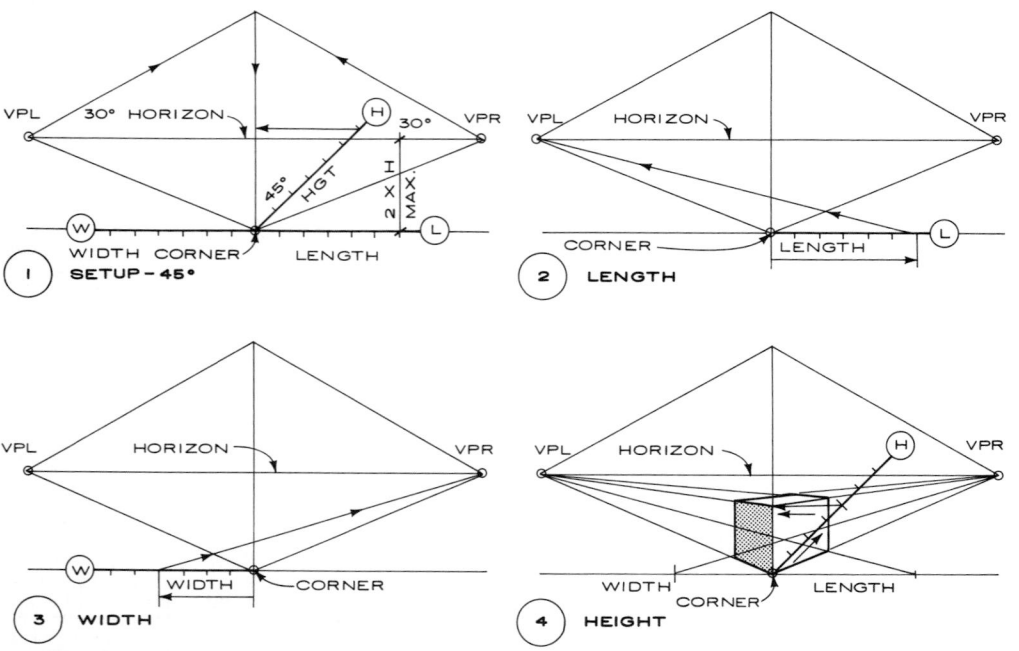

① **SETUP – 45°**

② **LENGTH**

③ **WIDTH**

④ **HEIGHT**

**TWO-POINT PERSPECTIVE — 45° MEASURED SYSTEM**

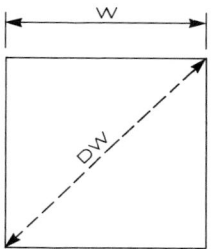

### 45° METHOD SYSTEM

① SET-UP: Similar to the method used in the 30/60° set-up, the vanishing points are placed on the horizon line and separated by 2.5 × the diagonal width plus the maximum width of the building. Complete the set-up as illustrated.

② LENGTH: Measure, to scale, the length of the building along the length line L. Connect the points directly to VPL.

③ WIDTH: In this set-up, the width is the same as the length scale. Measure the width of the building along the width line W. The length and width lines will form an outline of the "plan" in perspective.

④ HEIGHT: The height line is positioned at a 45° angle and marked off to scale. A line representing the leading corner of the building is drawn perpendicular to the ground line. Connect or draw a line from the measurement points along the height line to the vertical corner line. As in the 30/60° setup, these points are then carried to VPR and VPL.

Jim Maeda; Samuel J. De Santo and Associates; New York, New York

 **GRAPHIC METHODS**

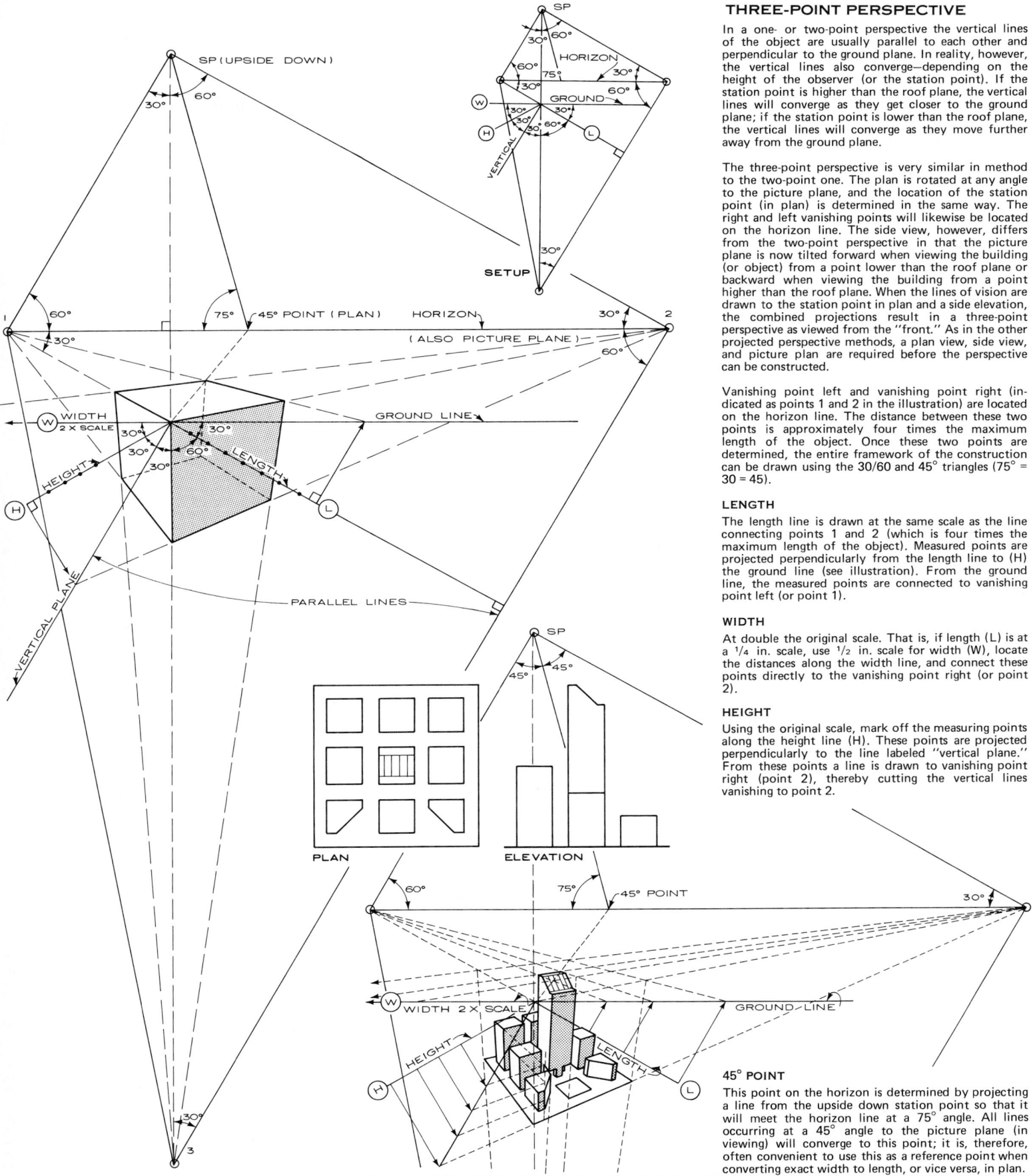

PROJECTING THE PERSPECTIVE

Jim Maeda; Samuel J. De Santo and Associates; New York, New York

## THREE-POINT PERSPECTIVE

In a one- or two-point perspective the vertical lines of the object are usually parallel to each other and perpendicular to the ground plane. In reality, however, the vertical lines also converge—depending on the height of the observer (or the station point). If the station point is higher than the roof plane, the vertical lines will converge as they get closer to the ground plane; if the station point is lower than the roof plane, the vertical lines will converge as they move further away from the ground plane.

The three-point perspective is very similar in method to the two-point one. The plan is rotated at any angle to the picture plane, and the location of the station point (in plan) is determined in the same way. The right and left vanishing points will likewise be located on the horizon line. The side view, however, differs from the two-point perspective in that the picture plane is now tilted forward when viewing the building (or object) from a point lower than the roof plane or backward when viewing the building from a point higher than the roof plane. When the lines of vision are drawn to the station point in plan and a side elevation, the combined projections result in a three-point perspective as viewed from the "front." As in the other projected perspective methods, a plan view, side view, and picture plan are required before the perspective can be constructed.

Vanishing point left and vanishing point right (indicated as points 1 and 2 in the illustration) are located on the horizon line. The distance between these two points is approximately four times the maximum length of the object. Once these two points are determined, the entire framework of the construction can be drawn using the 30/60 and 45° triangles (75° = 30 = 45).

### LENGTH

The length line is drawn at the same scale as the line connecting points 1 and 2 (which is four times the maximum length of the object). Measured points are projected perpendicularly from the length line to (H) the ground line (see illustration). From the ground line, the measured points are connected to vanishing point left (or point 1).

### WIDTH

At double the original scale. That is, if length (L) is at a $1/4$ in. scale, use $1/2$ in. scale for width (W), locate the distances along the width line, and connect these points directly to the vanishing point right (or point 2).

### HEIGHT

Using the original scale, mark off the measuring points along the height line (H). These points are projected perpendicularly to the line labeled "vertical plane." From these points a line is drawn to vanishing point right (point 2), thereby cutting the vertical lines vanishing to point 2.

### 45° POINT

This point on the horizon is determined by projecting a line from the upside down station point so that it will meet the horizon line at a 75° angle. All lines occurring at a 45° angle to the picture plane (in viewing) will converge to this point; it is, therefore, often convenient to use this as a reference point when converting exact width to length, or vice versa, in plan.

GRAPHIC METHODS

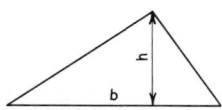

**TRIANGLE**
AREA = 1/2 ANY ALTITUDE
X ITS BASE (ALTITUDE
IS PERPENDICULAR
DISTANCE TO OPPOSITE
VERTEX OR CORNER.)
$A = \frac{1}{2} b \times h$

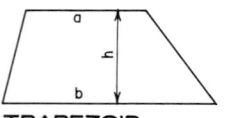

**TRAPEZOID**
AREA = 1/2 SUM OF PARALLEL
SIDES X ALTITUDE
$A = \frac{h(a+b)}{2}$

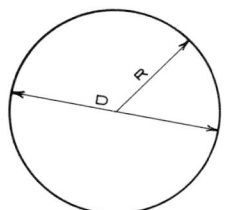

**CIRCLE**
AREA = $\frac{\pi D^2}{4}$ = $\pi R^2$
CIRCUMFERENCE = $2\pi R = \pi D$
($\pi$ = 3.14159265359)

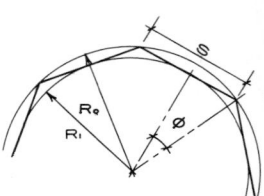

**REGULAR POLYGON**
AREA = $\frac{n S R_i}{2}$
(n = NUMBER OF SIDES)
ANY SIDE $S = 2\sqrt{R_o^2 - R_i^2}$
$R_i = \frac{S}{2 \tan \phi}$    $R_o = \frac{S}{2 \sin \phi}$

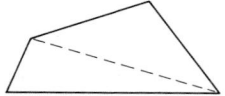

**TRAPEZUM**
(IRREGULAR
QUADRILATERAL)
AREA = DIVIDE FIGURE
INTO TWO TRIANGLES
AND FIND AREAS AS
ABOVE

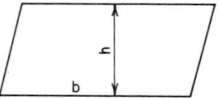

**PARALLELOGRAM**
AREA = EITHER SIDE
X ALTITUDE

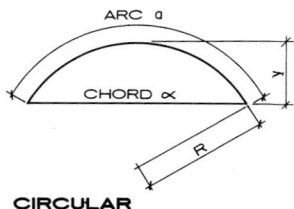

**CIRCULAR
SEGMENT**
AREA = (LENGTH OF ARC a X R − α(R−y)
CHORD α = $2\sqrt{2yR - y^2}$
= $2R \sin \frac{A°}{2}$

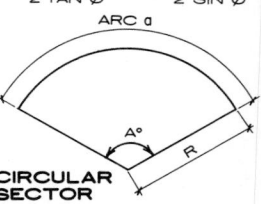

**CIRCULAR
SECTOR**
AREA = 1/2 LENGTH OF
ARC a X R
= AREA OF CIRCLE X $\frac{A°}{360}$
= $0.0087 R^2 A°$
ARC a = $\frac{\pi R A°}{180°}$ = $0.0175 R A°$

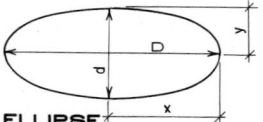

**ELLIPSE**
AREA = .7854 Dd
APPROX. PERIMETER
= $\pi \sqrt{2(x^2 + y^2)}$

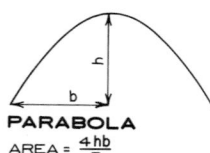

**PARABOLA**
AREA = $\frac{4hb}{3}$

---

## GEOMETRIC PROPERTIES OF PLANE FIGURES

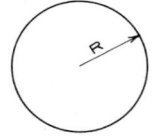

**SPHERE**
VOLUME = $\frac{4\pi R^3}{3}$
= $0.5236 D^3$
SURFACE = $4\pi R^2$
= $\pi D^2$

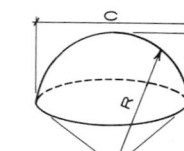

**SEGMENT OF
SPHERE**
VOLUME = $\frac{1\pi b^2 (3R-b)}{3}$
(OR SECTOR − CONE)
SURFACE = $2\pi R b$
(NOT INCLUDING
SURFACE OF
CIRCULAR BASE)

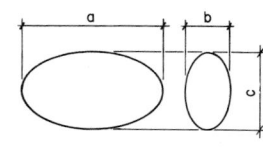

**SECTOR OF
SPHERE**
VOLUME = $\frac{2\pi R^2 b}{3}$
SURFACE = $\frac{\pi R (4b+c)}{2}$
( OR: SEGMENT +
CONE )

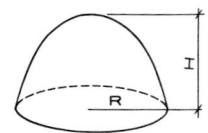

**ELLIPSOID**
VOLUME = $\frac{\pi abc}{6}$
SURFACE: NO SIMPLE
RULE

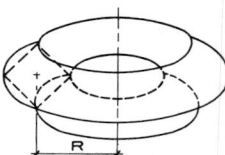

**PARABOLOID OF
REVOLUTION**
VOLUME = AREA OF
CIRCULAR BASE X
1/2 ALTITUDE.
SURFACE: NO
SIMPLE RULE

**CIRCULAR RING
OF ANY SECTION**
R = DISTANCE FROM
AXIS OF RING TO TRUE
CENTER OF SECTION
VOLUME = AREA OF
SECTION X $2\pi R$
SURFACE = PERIMETER
OF SECTION X $2\pi R$
(CONSIDER THE
SECTION ON ONE SIDE
OF AXIS ONLY )

---

## VOLUMES AND SURFACES OF DOUBLE - CURVED SOLIDS

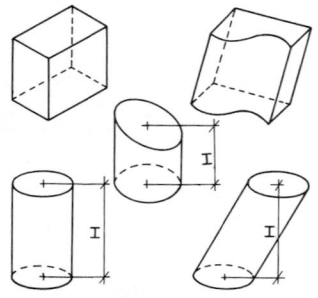

**ANY PRISM OR CYLINDER,
RIGHT OR OBLIQUE,
REGULAR OR IRREGULAR.**
Volume = area of base x altitude

Altitude = distance between parallel bases, measured perpendicular to the bases. When bases are not parallel, then Altitude = perpendicular distance from one base to the center of the other.

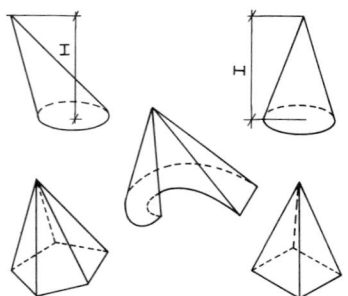

**ANY PYRAMID OR CONE,
RIGHT OR OBLIQUE,
REGULAR OR IRREGULAR.**
Volume = area of base x 1/3 altitude

Altitude = distance from base to apex, measured perpendicular to base.

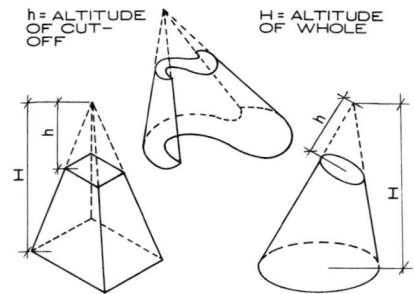

h = ALTITUDE OF CUT-OFF    H = ALTITUDE OF WHOLE

**ANY FRUSTUM OR TRUNCATED
PORTION OF THE SOLIDS
SHOWN**
Volume: From the volume of the whole solid, if complete, subtract the volume of the portion cut off.

The altitude of the cut-off part must be measured perpendicular to its own base.

**SURFACES OF SOLIDS**

The area of the surface is best found by adding together the areas of all the faces.

The area of a right cylindrical surface = perimeter of base x length of elements (average length if other base is oblique).

The area of a right conical surface = perimeter of base x 1/2 length of elements.

There is no simple rule for the area of an oblique conical surface, or for a cylindrical one where neither base is perpendicular to the elments. The best method is to construct a development, as if making a paper model, and measure its area by one of the methods given on the next page.

---

## VOLUMES AND SURFACES OF TYPICAL SOLIDS

 **GRAPHIC METHODS**

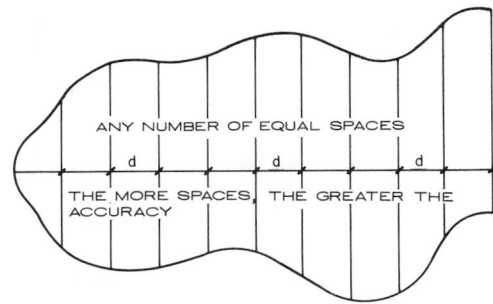

## TO FIND THE AREA OF AN IRREGULAR PLANE FIGURE

1. Divide the figure into parallel strips by equally spaced parallel lines.

2. Measure the length of each of the parallel lines.

3. Obtain a summation of the unit areas by one of these 3 "rules".

### TRAPEZOID RULE

Add together the length of the parallels, taking the first and last at $1/2$ value, and multiply by the width of the internal "d". This rule is sufficiently accurate for estimating and other ordinary purposes.

### SIMPSON'S RULE

Add the parallels, taking the first and last at full value, second, the fourth, sixth, etc. from each end at 4 times full value, and the third, fifth, seventh, etc. from each end at 2 times the value, then multiply by $1/3$ d. This rule works only for an even number of spaces and is accurate for areas bounded by smooth curves.

### DURAND'S RULE

Add the parallels taking the first and last at $5/12$ value, the second from each end at $13/12$ value, and all others at full value, then multiply by d. This rule is the most accurate for very irregular shapes.

### NOTE

Irregular areas may be directly read off by means of a simple instrument called a Planimeter.

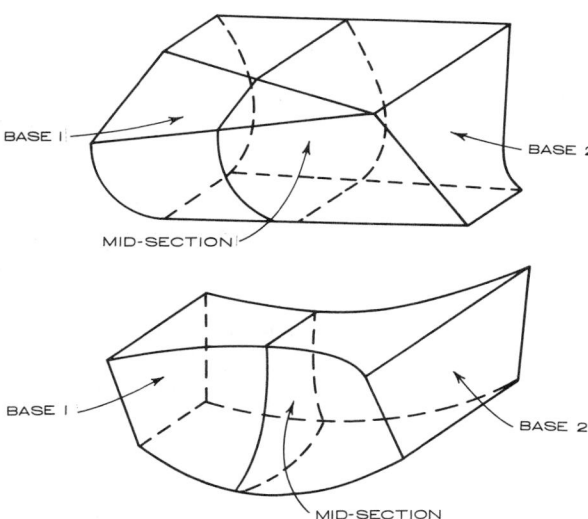

## TO FIND THE VOLUME OF AN IRREGULAR FIGURE BY THE PRISMATOID FORMULA

Construct a section midway between the bases. Add 4 to the sum of the areas of the 2 bases and multiply the quantity by the area of the mid-section. Then multiply the total by $1/6$ the perpendicular distance between the bases.

$V = [($area of base$_1$ + area of base$_2$ + 4$)$ (area of midsection) $\times\ 1/6$ perpendicular distance between bases.

This formula is quite accurate for any solid with two parallel bases connected by a surface of straight line elements (upper figure), or smooth simple curves (lower figure).

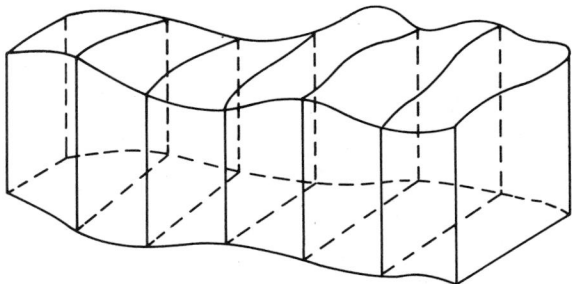

## TO FIND THE VOLUME OF A VERY IRREGULAR FIGURE BY THE SECTIONING METHOD

1. Construct a series of equally spaced sections or profiles.

2. Determine the area of each section by any of the methods shown at left (preferably with a Planimeter).

3. Apply any one of the 3 summation "rules" given at left, to determine the total volume.

This method is in general use for estimating quantities of earthwork, etc.

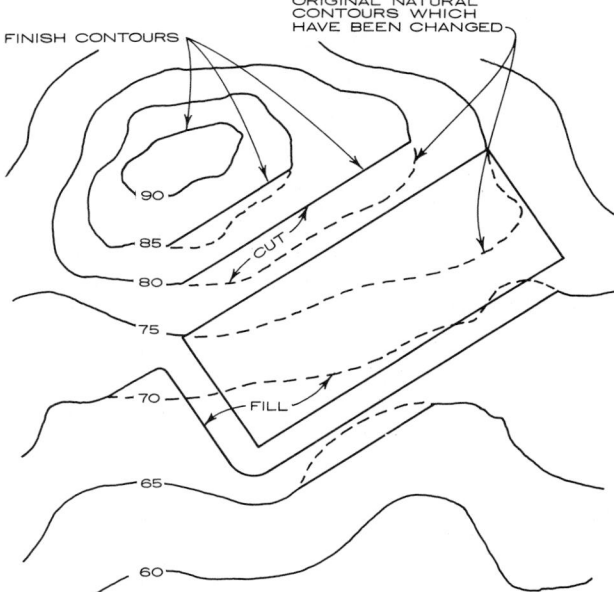

## TO FIND THE VOLUME OF CUT AND FILL DIRECTLY FROM THE CONTOUR PLAN

1. Draw "finish" and "original" contours on same contour map.

2. Measure the differential areas between new and old contours of each contour and enter in columns according to whether cut or fill.

3. Add up each column and multiply by the contour interval to determine the volume in cubic feet.

### EXAMPLE

| CONTOUR | CUT | | FILL | |
|---|---|---|---|---|
| 85 | | 300 | | |
| 80 | | 960 | | |
| 75 | 2,460 − 2 = | 1,230 | 3,800 − 2 = | 1,900 |
| 70 | | 20 | | 2,200 |
| | | 9,200 | | 6,800 |
| | | ×5 | | ×5 |
| TOTALS | | 46,000 cu. ft. | | 34,000 cu. ft. |

### NOTE

1. Where a cut or fill ends directly on a contour level use $1/2$ value.

2. The closer the contour interval, the greater the accuracy.

This method is more rapid than the sectioning method, and is sufficiently accurate for simple estimating purposes and for balancing of cut and fill.

GRAPHIC METHODS

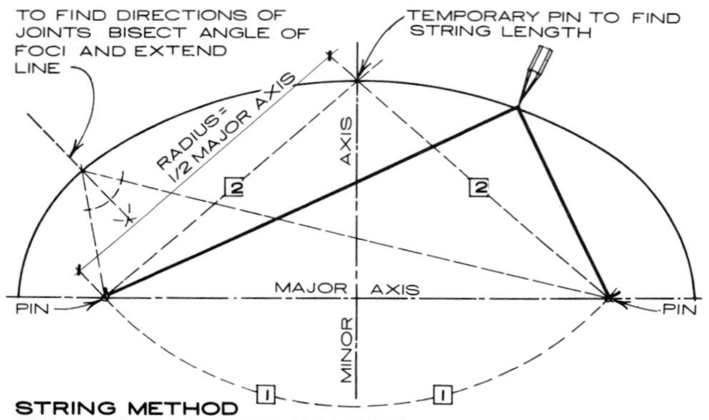

## STRING METHOD
(FOR LARGE SCALE AND FULL SIZE.)

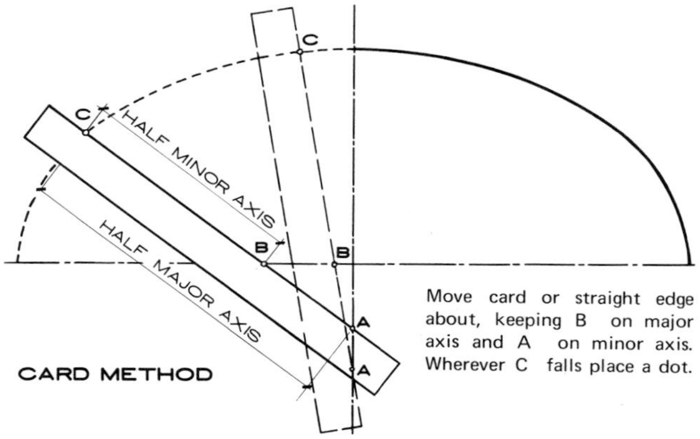

TO FIND DIRECTIONS OF JOINTS BISECT ANGLE OF FOCI AND EXTEND LINE

TEMPORARY PIN TO FIND STRING LENGTH

RADIUS = 1/2 MAJOR AXIS

AXIS

MAJOR AXIS

MINOR

PIN   PIN

## CARD METHOD

HALF MINOR AXIS

HALF MAJOR AXIS

Move card or straight edge about, keeping B on major axis and A on minor axis. Wherever C falls place a dot.

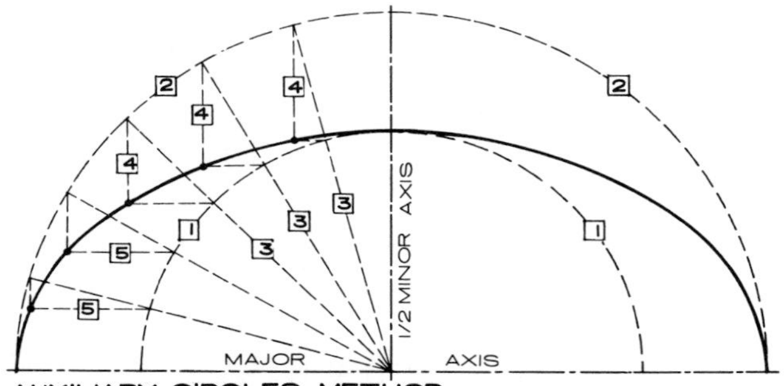

## AUXILIARY CIRCLES METHOD

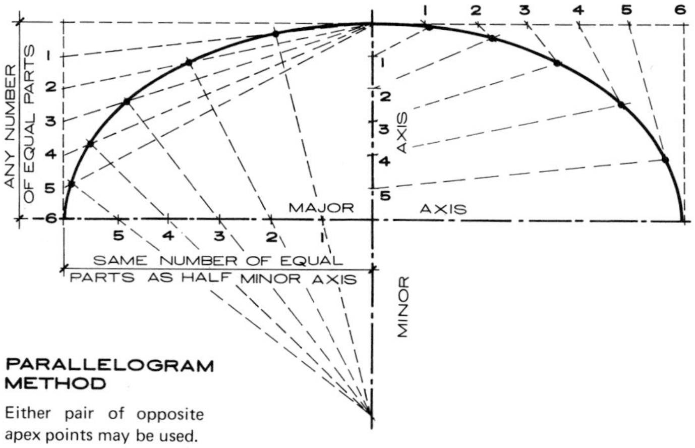

1/2 MINOR AXIS

MAJOR   AXIS

## PARALLELOGRAM METHOD

ANY NUMBER OF EQUAL PARTS

AXIS

MAJOR   AXIS

MINOR

SAME NUMBER OF EQUAL PARTS AS HALF MINOR AXIS

Either pair of opposite apex points may be used.

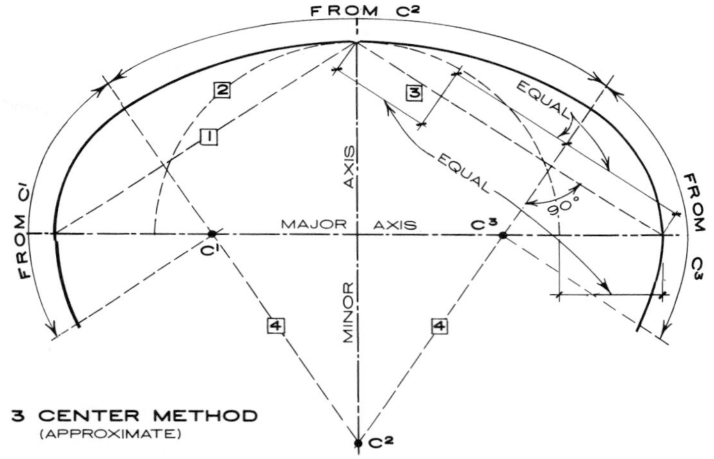

## 3 CENTER METHOD
(APPROXIMATE)

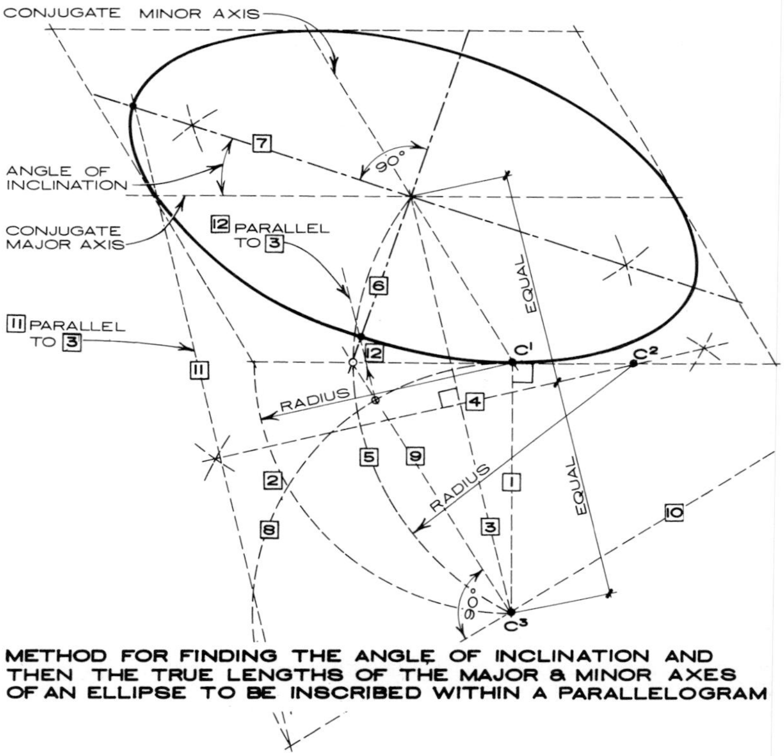

FROM $C^2$

EQUAL

EQUAL

90°

MAJOR   AXIS

AXIS

MINOR

$C^1$

$C^3$

FROM $C^1$

FROM $C^3$

$C^2$

## METHOD FOR FINDING THE ANGLE OF INCLINATION AND THEN THE TRUE LENGTHS OF THE MAJOR & MINOR AXES OF AN ELLIPSE TO BE INSCRIBED WITHIN A PARALLELOGRAM

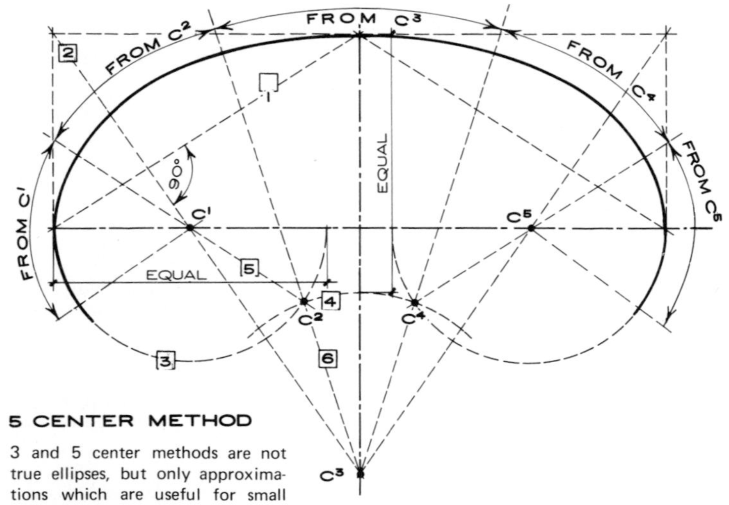

CONJUGATE MINOR AXIS

ANGLE OF INCLINATION

CONJUGATE MAJOR AXIS

90°

PARALLEL TO 3

PARALLEL TO 3

RADIUS

RADIUS

EQUAL

EQUAL

$C^1$

$C^2$

$C^3$

90°

## 5 CENTER METHOD

FROM $C^2$

FROM $C^3$

FROM $C^1$

FROM $C^4$

FROM $C^5$

90°

EQUAL

EQUAL

$C^1$

$C^5$

$C^2$

$C^4$

$C^3$

3 and 5 center methods are not true ellipses, but only approximations which are useful for small scale drawings.

### NOTE

1. Using the conjugate axes, the ellipse can be drawn directly by using the parallelogram method.

2. Using the true lengths of the axes, the ellipse may be drawn with any one of the methods illustrated on this page.

 **GRAPHIC METHODS**

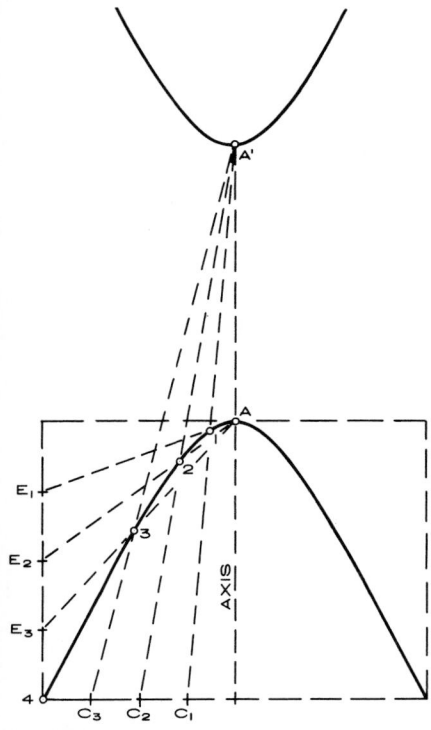

## HYPERBOLA
### PARALLELOGRAM METHOD
GIVEN:

Axis, two apexes (A and A') and a chord.

1. Draw surrounding parallelogram.
2. Divide chord in whole number of equal spaces ($C_1$, $C_2$, $C_3$, etc.).
3. Divide edge of parallelogram into same integral number of equal spaces ($E_1$, $E_2$, $E_3$, etc.).
4. Join A to points E on edge; join A' to points C on chord. Intersection of these rays are points on curve.

This method can be used equally well for any type of orthogonal or perspective projection, as shown by example of ellipse.

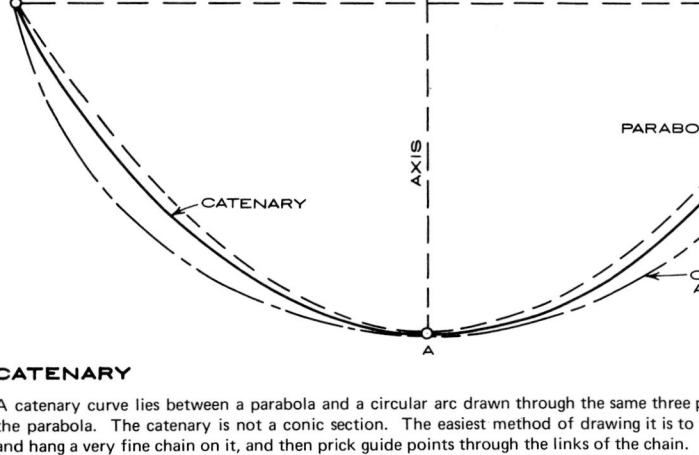

## CATENARY

A catenary curve lies between a parabola and a circular arc drawn through the same three points, but is closer to the parabola. The catenary is not a conic section. The easiest method of drawing it is to tilt the drafting board and hang a very fine chain on it, and then prick guide points through the links of the chain.

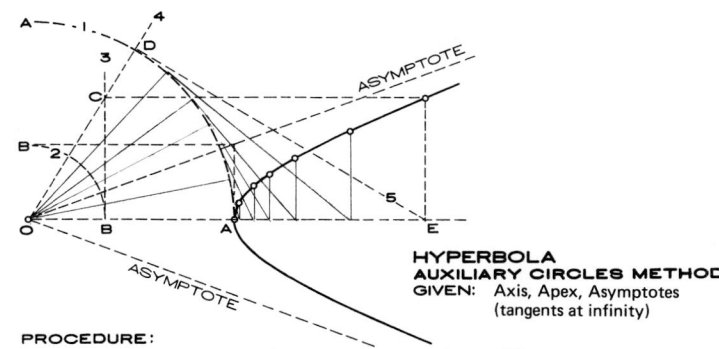

## HYPERBOLA
### AUXILIARY CIRCLES METHOD
GIVEN: Axis, Apex, Asymptotes
(tangents at infinity)

PROCEDURE:

1. Draw auxiliary circles with OB and OA as radii:  note $\dfrac{OB}{OA}$ = slope of asymptote.
2. Erect perpendicular 3 where circle 2 intersects axis.
3. Draw any line 4 through 0, intersecting circle 1 at B and line 3 at C.
4. Draw line 5 through C parallel to axis.
5. Draw tangent 6 at D, intersecting axis at E.
6. Erect perpendicular 7 at E, intersecting 5 at P, a point on hyperbola.

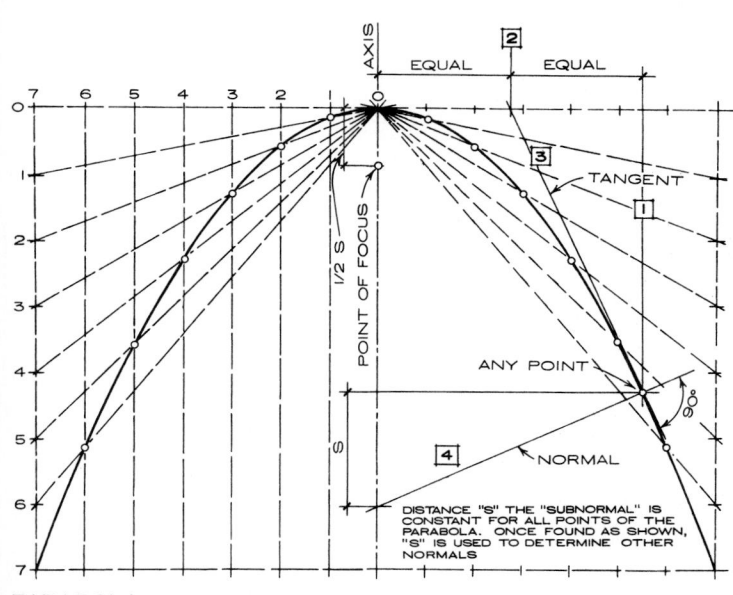

## PARABOLA
### PARALLELOGRAM METHOD

This method is comparable to the "Parallelogram Method" shown for the hyperbola above and the ellipse on previous page. The other apex 'A' is at infinity.

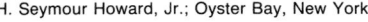
H. Seymour Howard, Jr.; Oyster Bay, New York

## PARABOLA
### ENVELOPE OF TANGENTS

This method does not give points on the curve, but a series of tangents within which the parabola can be drawn.

## GRAPHIC METHODS

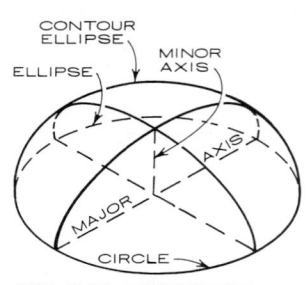

## OBLATE SPHEROID

An ellipse rotated about its minor axis.

**NOTES**

1. The dome shapes shown above are SURFACES OF POSITIVE CUR-VATURE, that is, the centers of both principal radii of curvature are on the same side of the surface.

2. SURFACES OF NEGATIVE CURVATURE (saddle shapes) such as those shown below, are surfaces in which the centers of the two principal radii of curvature are on opposite sides of the surface.

## PROLATE SPHEROID

An ellipse rotated about its major axis.

## PARABOLOID OF REVOLUTION

A parabola rotated about its axis.

The elliptic paraboloid is similar, but its plan is an ellipse instead of circle, and vertical sections are varying parabolas.

## GENERAL ELLIPSOID

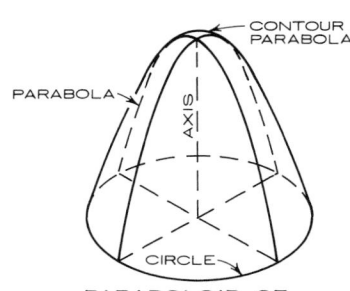

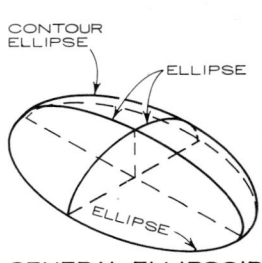

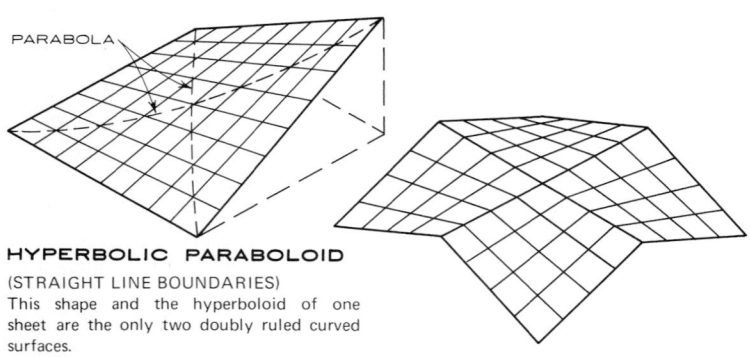

## HYPERBOLIC PARABOLOID

**(STRAIGHT LINE BOUNDARIES)**

This shape and the hyperboloid of one sheet are the only two doubly ruled curved surfaces.

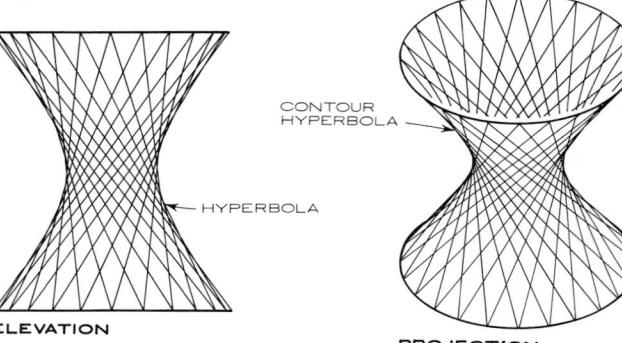

**ELEVATION**

**PROJECTION**

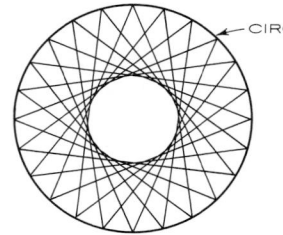

**PLAN**
## HYPERBOLOID OF REVOLUTION
(OR HYPERBOLOID OF ONE SHEET)

**NOTE**

This shape is a doubly ruled surface, which can also be drawn with ellipses as plan sections instead of the circles shown.

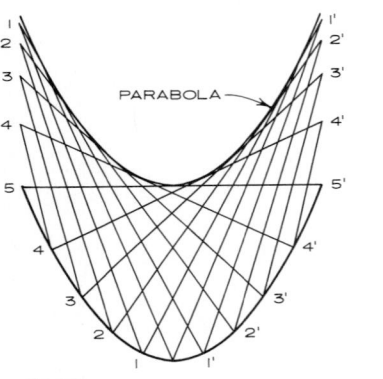

**SECTION A–A**

**SECTION B–B**

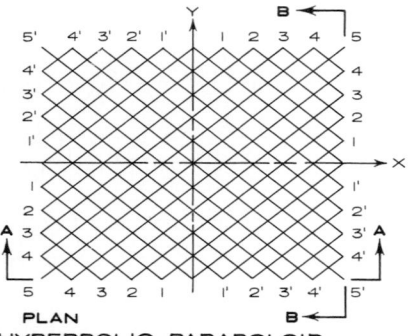

**PLAN**
## HYPERBOLIC PARABOLOID
(PARABOLA BOUNDARIES)

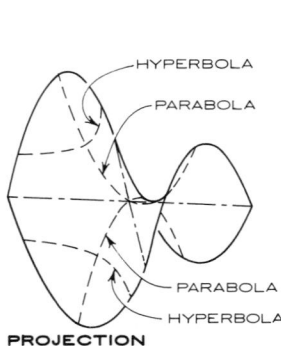

**PROJECTION**

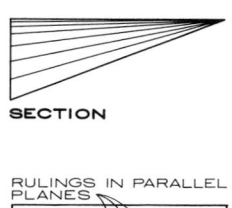

**SECTION**

**PLAN**
## CONOID
(SINGLY RULED SURFACE)

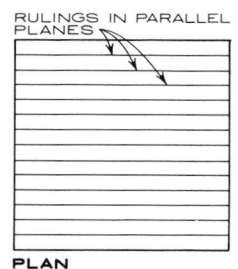

**ELEVATION**

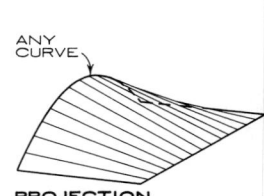

**PROJECTION**

# GRAPHIC METHODS

## DECIMALS OF A FOOT

| FRACTION | DECIMAL | FRACTION | DECIMAL | FRACTION | DECIMAL |
|---|---|---|---|---|---|
| $1/16$ | 0.0052 | $4\text{-}1/16$ | 0.3385 | $8\text{-}1/16$ | 0.6719 |
| $1/8$ | 0.0104 | $4\text{-}1/8$ | 0.3438 | $8\text{-}1/8$ | 0.6771 |
| $3/16$ | 0.0156 | $4\text{-}3/16$ | 0.3490 | $8\text{-}3/16$ | 0.6823 |
| $1/4$ | 0.0208 | $4\text{-}1/4$ | 0.3542 | $8\text{-}1/4$ | 0.6875 |
| $5/16$ | 0.0260 | $4\text{-}5/16$ | 0.3594 | $8\text{-}5/16$ | 0.6927 |
| $3/8$ | 0.0313 | $4\text{-}3/8$ | 0.3646 | $8\text{-}3/8$ | 0.6979 |
| $7/16$ | 0.0365 | $4\text{-}7/16$ | 0.3698 | $8\text{-}7/16$ | 0.7031 |
| $1/2$ | 0.0417 | $4\text{-}1/2$ | 0.3750 | $8\text{-}1/2$ | 0.7083 |
| $9/16$ | 0.0469 | $4\text{-}9/16$ | 0.3802 | $8\text{-}9/16$ | 0.7135 |
| $5/8$ | 0.0521 | $4\text{-}5/8$ | 0.3854 | $8\text{-}5/8$ | 0.7188 |
| $11/16$ | 0.0573 | $4\text{-}11/16$ | 0.3906 | $8\text{-}11/16$ | 0.7240 |
| $3/4$ | 0.0625 | $4\text{-}3/4$ | 0.3958 | $8\text{-}3/4$ | 0.7292 |
| $13/16$ | 0.0677 | $4\text{-}13/16$ | 0.4010 | $8\text{-}13/16$ | 0.7344 |
| $7/8$ | 0.0729 | $4\text{-}7/8$ | 0.4063 | $8\text{-}7/8$ | 0.7396 |
| $15/16$ | 0.0781 | $4\text{-}15/16$ | 0.4115 | $8\text{-}15/16$ | 0.7448 |
| $1\text{-}$ | 0.0833 | $5\text{-}$ | 0.4167 | $9\text{-}$ | 0.7500 |
| $1\text{-}1/16$ | 0.0885 | $5\text{-}1/16$ | 0.4219 | $9\text{-}1/16$ | 0.7552 |
| $1\text{-}1/8$ | 0.0938 | $5\text{-}1/8$ | 0.4271 | $9\text{-}1/8$ | 0.7604 |
| $1\text{-}3/16$ | 0.0990 | $5\text{-}3/16$ | 0.4323 | $9\text{-}3/16$ | 0.7656 |
| $1\text{-}1/4$ | 0.1042 | $5\text{-}1/4$ | 0.4375 | $9\text{-}1/4$ | 0.7708 |
| $1\text{-}5/16$ | 0.1094 | $5\text{-}5/16$ | 0.4427 | $9\text{-}5/16$ | 0.7760 |
| $1\text{-}3/8$ | 0.1146 | $5\text{-}3/8$ | 0.4479 | $9\text{-}3/8$ | 0.7813 |
| $1\text{-}7/16$ | 0.1198 | $5\text{-}7/16$ | 0.4531 | $9\text{-}7/16$ | 0.7865 |
| $1\text{-}1/2$ | 0.1250 | $5\text{-}1/2$ | 0.4583 | $9\text{-}1/2$ | 0.7917 |
| $1\text{-}9/16$ | 0.1302 | $5\text{-}9/16$ | 0.4635 | $9\text{-}9/16$ | 0.7969 |
| $1\text{-}5/8$ | 0.1354 | $5\text{-}5/8$ | 0.4688 | $9\text{-}5/8$ | 0.8021 |
| $1\text{-}11/16$ | 0.1406 | $5\text{-}11/16$ | 0.4740 | $9\text{-}11/16$ | 0.8073 |
| $1\text{-}3/4$ | 0.1458 | $5\text{-}3/4$ | 0.4792 | $9\text{-}3/4$ | 0.8125 |
| $1\text{-}13/16$ | 0.1510 | $5\text{-}13/16$ | 0.4844 | $9\text{-}13/16$ | 0.8177 |
| $1\text{-}7/8$ | 0.1563 | $5\text{-}7/8$ | 0.4896 | $9\text{-}7/8$ | 0.8229 |
| $1\text{-}15/16$ | 0.1615 | $5\text{-}15/16$ | 0.4948 | $9\text{-}15/16$ | 0.8281 |
| $2\text{-}$ | 0.1667 | $6\text{-}$ | 0.5000 | $10\text{-}$ | 0.8333 |
| $2\text{-}1/16$ | 0.1719 | $6\text{-}1/16$ | 0.5052 | $10\text{-}1/16$ | 0.8385 |
| $2\text{-}1/8$ | 0.1771 | $6\text{-}1/8$ | 0.5104 | $10\text{-}1/8$ | 0.8438 |
| $2\text{-}3/16$ | 0.1823 | $6\text{-}3/16$ | 0.5156 | $10\text{-}3/16$ | 0.8490 |
| $2\text{-}1/4$ | 0.1875 | $6\text{-}1/4$ | 0.5208 | $10\text{-}1/4$ | 0.8542 |
| $2\text{-}5/16$ | 0.1927 | $6\text{-}5/16$ | 0.5260 | $10\text{-}5/16$ | 0.8594 |
| $2\text{-}3/8$ | 0.1979 | $6\text{-}3/8$ | 0.5313 | $10\text{-}3/8$ | 0.8646 |
| $2\text{-}7/16$ | 0.2031 | $6\text{-}7/16$ | 0.5365 | $10\text{-}7/16$ | 0.8698 |
| $2\text{-}1/2$ | 0.2083 | $6\text{-}1/2$ | 0.5417 | $10\text{-}1/2$ | 0.8750 |
| $2\text{-}9/16$ | 0.2135 | $6\text{-}9/16$ | 0.5469 | $10\text{-}9/16$ | 0.8802 |
| $2\text{-}5/8$ | 0.2188 | $6\text{-}5/8$ | 0.5521 | $10\text{-}5/8$ | 0.8854 |
| $2\text{-}11/16$ | 0.2240 | $6\text{-}11/16$ | 0.5573 | $10\text{-}11/16$ | 0.8906 |
| $2\text{-}3/4$ | 0.2292 | $6\text{-}3/4$ | 0.5625 | $10\text{-}3/4$ | 0.8958 |
| $2\text{-}13/16$ | 0.2344 | $6\text{-}13/16$ | 0.5677 | $10\text{-}13/16$ | 0.9010 |
| $2\text{-}7/8$ | 0.2396 | $6\text{-}7/8$ | 0.5729 | $10\text{-}7/8$ | 0.9063 |
| $2\text{-}15/16$ | 0.2448 | $6\text{-}15/16$ | 0.5781 | $10\text{-}15/16$ | 0.9115 |
| $3\text{-}$ | 0.2500 | $7\text{-}$ | 0.5833 | $11\text{-}$ | 0.9167 |
| $3\text{-}1/16$ | 0.2552 | $7\text{-}1/16$ | 0.5885 | $11\text{-}1/16$ | 0.9219 |
| $3\text{-}1/8$ | 0.2604 | $7\text{-}1/8$ | 0.5938 | $11\text{-}1/8$ | 0.9271 |
| $3\text{-}3/16$ | 0.2656 | $7\text{-}3/16$ | 0.5990 | $11\text{-}3/16$ | 0.9323 |
| $3\text{-}1/4$ | 0.2708 | $7\text{-}1/4$ | 0.6042 | $11\text{-}1/4$ | 0.9375 |
| $3\text{-}5/16$ | 0.2760 | $7\text{-}5/16$ | 0.6094 | $11\text{-}5/16$ | 0.9427 |
| $3\text{-}3/8$ | 0.2813 | $7\text{-}3/8$ | 0.6146 | $11\text{-}3/8$ | 0.9479 |
| $3\text{-}7/16$ | 0.2865 | $7\text{-}7/16$ | 0.6198 | $11\text{-}7/16$ | 0.9531 |
| $3\text{-}1/2$ | 0.2917 | $7\text{-}1/2$ | 0.6250 | $11\text{-}1/2$ | 0.9583 |
| $3\text{-}9/16$ | 0.2969 | $7\text{-}9/16$ | 0.6302 | $11\text{-}9/16$ | 0.9635 |
| $3\text{-}5/8$ | 0.3021 | $7\text{-}5/8$ | 0.6354 | $11\text{-}5/8$ | 0.9688 |
| $3\text{-}11/16$ | 0.3073 | $7\text{-}11/16$ | 0.6406 | $11\text{-}11/16$ | 0.9740 |
| $3\text{-}3/4$ | 0.3125 | $7\text{-}3/4$ | 0.6458 | $11\text{-}3/4$ | 0.9792 |
| $3\text{-}13/16$ | 0.3177 | $7\text{-}13/16$ | 0.6510 | $11\text{-}13/16$ | 0.9844 |
| $3\text{-}7/8$ | 0.3229 | $7\text{-}7/8$ | 0.6563 | $11\text{-}7/8$ | 0.9896 |
| $3\text{-}15/16$ | 0.3281 | $7\text{-}15/16$ | 0.6615 | $11\text{-}15/16$ | 0.9948 |
| $4\text{-}$ | 0.3333 | $8\text{-}$ | 0.6667 | $12\text{-}$ | 1.0000 |

## DECIMALS OF AN INCH

| FRACTION | DECIMAL |
|---|---|
| $1/64$ | 0.015625 |
| $1/32$ | 0.03125 |
| $3/64$ | 0.046875 |
| $1/16$ | 0.0625 |
| $5/64$ | 0.078125 |
| $3/32$ | 0.09375 |
| $7/64$ | 0.109375 |
| $1/8$ | 0.125 |
| $9/64$ | 0.140625 |
| $5/32$ | 0.15625 |
| $11/64$ | 0.171875 |
| $3/16$ | 0.1875 |
| $13/64$ | 0.203125 |
| $7/32$ | 0.21875 |
| $15/64$ | 0.234375 |
| $1/4$ | 0.250 |
| $17/64$ | 0.265625 |
| $9/32$ | 0.28125 |
| $19/64$ | 0.296875 |
| $5/16$ | 0.3125 |
| $21/64$ | 0.328125 |
| $11/32$ | 0.34375 |
| $23/64$ | 0.359375 |
| $3/8$ | 0.375 |
| $25/64$ | 0.390625 |
| $13/32$ | 0.40625 |
| $27/64$ | 0.421875 |
| $7/16$ | 0.4375 |
| $29/64$ | 0.453125 |
| $15/32$ | 0.46875 |
| $31/64$ | 0.484375 |
| $1/2$ | 0.500 |
| $33/64$ | 0.515625 |
| $17/32$ | 0.53125 |
| $35/64$ | 0.546875 |
| $9/16$ | 0.5625 |
| $37/64$ | 0.578125 |
| $19/32$ | 0.59375 |
| $39/64$ | 0.609375 |
| $5/8$ | 0.625 |
| $41/64$ | 0.640625 |
| $21/32$ | 0.65625 |
| $43/64$ | 0.671875 |
| $11/16$ | 0.6875 |
| $45/64$ | 0.703125 |
| $23/32$ | 0.71875 |
| $47/64$ | 0.734375 |
| $3/4$ | 0.750 |
| $49/64$ | 0.765625 |
| $25/32$ | 0.78125 |
| $51/64$ | 0.796875 |
| $13/16$ | 0.8125 |
| $53/64$ | 0.828125 |
| $27/32$ | 0.84375 |
| $55/64$ | 0.859375 |
| $7/8$ | 0.875 |
| $57/64$ | 0.890625 |
| $29/32$ | 0.90625 |
| $59/64$ | 0.921875 |
| $15/16$ | 0.9375 |
| $61/64$ | 0.953125 |
| $31/32$ | 0.96875 |
| $63/64$ | 0.984375 |
| $1''$ | 1.000 |

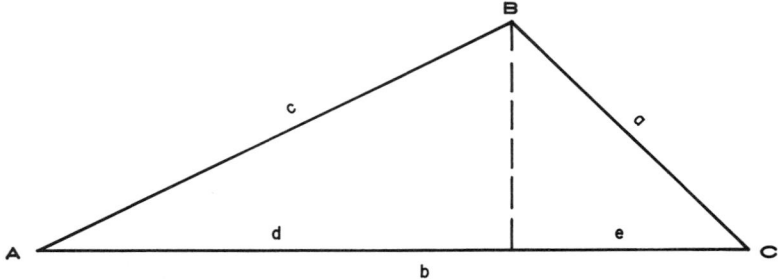

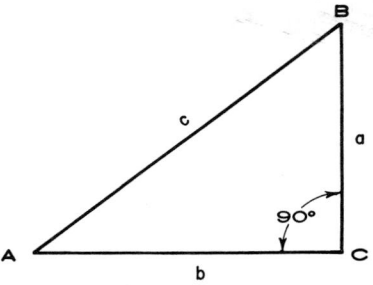

## OBLIQUE TRIANGLES

| FIND | GIVEN | SOLUTION |
|---|---|---|
| | A B b | $b \sin A \div \sin B$ |
| | A B c | $c \sin A \div \sin (A+B)$ |
| | A C b | $b \sin A \div \sin (A+C)$ |
| a | A C c | $c \sin A \div \sin C$ |
| | B C b | $b \sin (B+C) \div \sin B$ |
| | B C c | $c \sin (B+C) \div \sin C$ |
| | A b c | $\sqrt{b^2 + c^2 - 2bc \cdot \cos A}$ |
| | A B a | $a \sin B \div \sin A$ |
| | A B c | $c \sin B \div \sin (A+B)$ |
| | A C a | $a \sin (A+C) \div \sin A$ |
| b | A C c | $c \sin (A+C) \div \sin C$ |
| | B C a | $a \sin B \div \sin (B+C)$ |
| | B C c | $c \sin B \div \sin C$ |
| | B a c | $\sqrt{a^2 + c^2 - 2ac \cdot \cos B}$ |
| | A B a | $a \sin (A+B) \div \sin A$ |
| | A B b | $b \sin (A+B) \div \sin B$ |
| | A C a | $a \sin C \div \sin A$ |
| c | A C b | $b \sin C \div \sin (A+C)$ |
| | B C a | $a \sin C \div \sin (B+C)$ |
| | B C b | $b \sin C \div \sin B$ |
| | C a b | $\sqrt{a^2 + b^2 - 2ab \cdot \cos C}$ |
| ½ (B+C) | A b c | $90° - ½ A$ |
| ½ (B−C) | | $\tan = [(b-c) \tan (90° - ½ A)] \div (b+c)$ |
| ½ (A+C) | B a c | $90° - ½ B$ |
| ½ (A−C) | | $\tan = [(a-c) \tan (90° - ½ B)] \div (a+c)$ |
| ½ (A+B) | C a b | $90° - ½ C$ |
| ½ (A−B) | | $\tan = [(a-b) \tan (90° - ½ C)] \div (a+b)$ |

| FIND | GIVEN | SOLUTION |
|---|---|---|
| | a b c s | $\sin ½ A = \sqrt{(s-b)(s-c) \div bc}$ |
| | a b c s | $\cos ½ A = \sqrt{s(s-a) \div bc}$ |
| | a b c s | $\tan ½ A = \sqrt{(s-b)(s-c) \div s(s-a)}$ |
| A | B a b | $\sin A = a \sin B \div b$ |
| | B a c | $½ (A+C) + ½ (A-C)$ |
| | C a b | $½ (A+B) + ½ (A-B)$ |
| | C a c | $\sin A = a \sin C \div c$ |
| | a b c s | $\sin ½ B = \sqrt{(s-a)(s-c) \div ac}$ |
| | a b c s | $\cos ½ B = \sqrt{s(s-b) \div ac}$ |
| | a b c s | $\tan ½ B = \sqrt{(s-a)(s-c) \div s(s-b)}$ |
| B | A a b | $\sin B = b \sin A \div a$ |
| | A b c | $½ (B+C) + ½ (B-C)$ |
| | C a b | $½ (A+B) - ½ (A-B)$ |
| | C a c | $\sin B = b \sin C \div c$ |
| | a b c s | $\sin ½ C = \sqrt{(s-a)(s-b) \div ab}$ |
| | a b c s | $\cos ½ C = \sqrt{s(s-c) \div ab}$ |
| | a b c s | $\tan ½ C = \sqrt{(s-a)(s-b) \div s(s-c)}$ |
| C | A a c | $\sin C = c \sin A \div a$ |
| | A b c | $½ (B+C) - ½ (B-C)$ |
| | B a c | $½ (A+C) - ½ (A-C)$ |
| | B b c | $\sin C = c \sin B \div b$ |
| | a b c | $\sqrt{s(s-a)(s-b)(s-c)}$ |
| AREA | C a b | $½ ab \sin C$ |
| s | a b c | $(a + b + c) \div 2$ |
| d | a b c s | $(b^2 + c^2 - a^2) \div 2b$ |
| e | a b c s | $(a^2 + b^2 - c^2) \div 2b$ |

## RIGHT TRIANGLES

| FIND | GIVEN | SOLUTION |
|---|---|---|
| | a b | $\tan A = a \div b$ |
| A | a c | $\sin A = a \div c$ |
| | b c | $\cos A = b \div c$ |
| | a b | $\tan B = b \div a$ |
| B | a c | $\cos B = a \div c$ |
| | b c | $\sin B = b \div c$ |
| a | A b | $b \tan A$ |
| | A c | $c \sin A$ |
| b | A a | $a \div \tan A$ |
| | A c | $c \cos A$ |
| c | A a | $a \div \sin A$ |
| | A b | $b \div \cos A$ |
| AREA | a b | $ab \div 2$ |

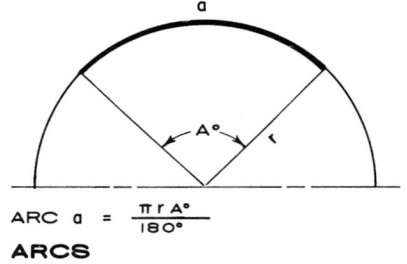

$$\text{ARC } a = \frac{\pi r A°}{180°}$$

**ARCS**

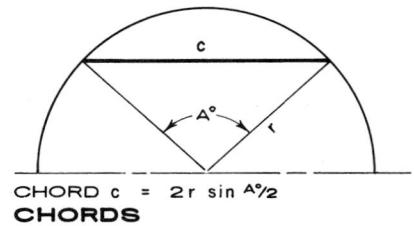

$$\text{CHORD } c = 2r \sin \tfrac{A°}{2}$$

**CHORDS**

MATHEMATICAL DATA

# TRUCKING - CLEARANCES and DETAILS

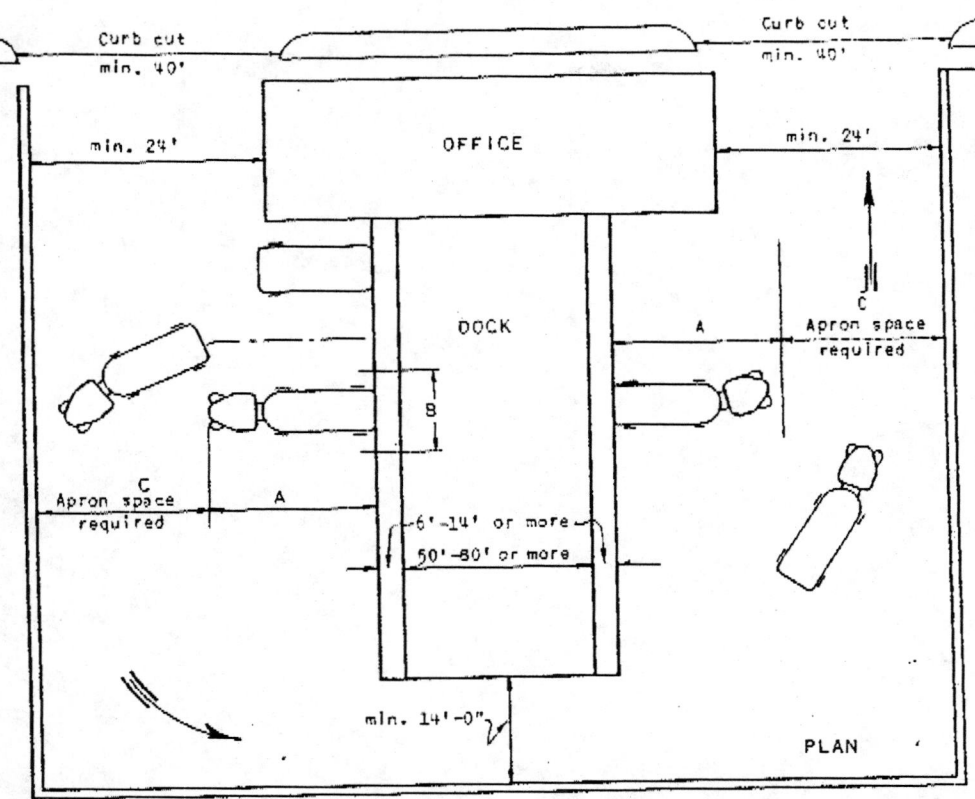

Curb cut min. 40'

Curb cut min. 40'

min. 24'      OFFICE      min. 24'

DOCK

Apron space required

A

C

Apron space required

A

6'-14' or more

50'-80' or more

min. 14'-0"

PLAN

Curb cut: used to prevent accident on swing into yard or gate.

Traffic flow #1
Counter clockwise around dock, preferred since it permits backing from left (driver's side)

APRON SPACE required for maneuver into or out of position for tractor trailer

| A | B | C |
|---|---|---|
| Tractor trailer length | Width of position | Apron space required |
| 35' | 10' | 46' |
|  | 12' | 43' |
|  | 14' | 39' |
| 40' | 10' | 48' |
|  | 12' | 44' |
|  | 14' | 42' |
| 45' | 10' | 57' |
|  | 12' | 49' |
|  | 14' | 48' |

## LOADING OF MOTOR VEHICLES

DATA SUPPLIED BY OPERATIONS COUNCIL, AMERICAN TRUCKING ASSOCIATIONS INC.

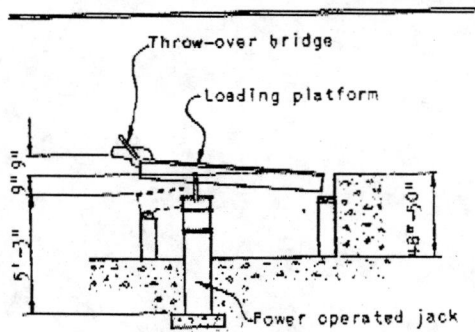
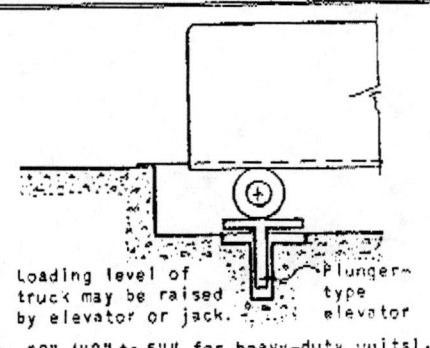
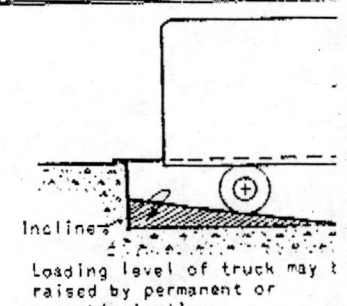

Throw-over bridge — Loading platform — Power operated jack

Loading level of truck may be raised by elevator or jack. Plunger-type elevator

Incline. Loading level of truck may be raised by permanent or moveable incline

Loading levels of trailer ("L") variable from 44" to 50" (48" to 54" for heavy-duty units). For van-type trucks 42" to 46" (44" 46" average). For delivery trucks 25" to 31".

## LOADING DOCK LEVELING DEVICES    SECTIONS

DATA CHECKED BY OPERATIONS COUNCIL AMERICAN TRUCKING ASSOCIATIONS INC.

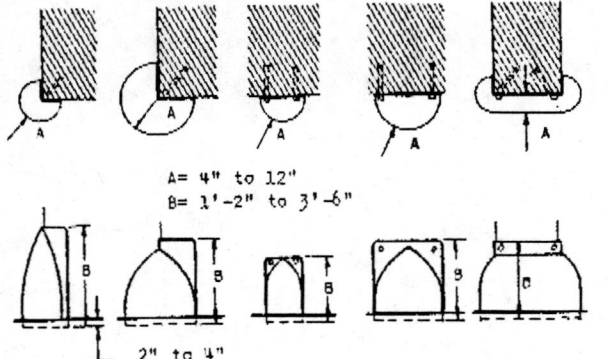
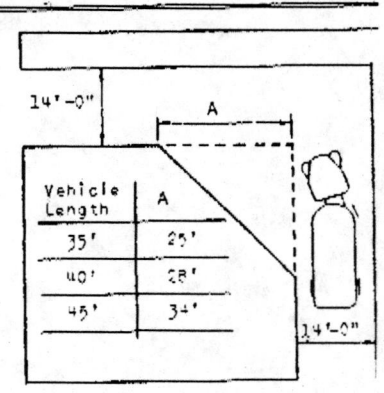

Used for protection of door jams, walls, and corners. May be combined with corners & col. guards.
Usually made of cast iron, ½" min. thickness. For heavy traffic, thicker metal is required.
Other patterns available. Sizes given are made by most manufacturers, though given pattern may vary.

A= 4" to 12"
B= 1'-2" to 3'-6"

2" to 4"

## WHEEL GUARDS

14'-0"

A

| Vehicle Length | A |
|---|---|
| 35' | 25' |
| 40' | 28' |
| 45' | 34' |

14'-0"

## TURNING CLEARANCE FOR INSIDE DRIVEWAY

DATA FROM "ARCHITECTURAL METAL HANDBOOK" BY PERMISSION OF THE NATIONAL ASSOCIATION ARCHITECTURAL METAL MFRS.

# TRUCK and TRAILER SIZES

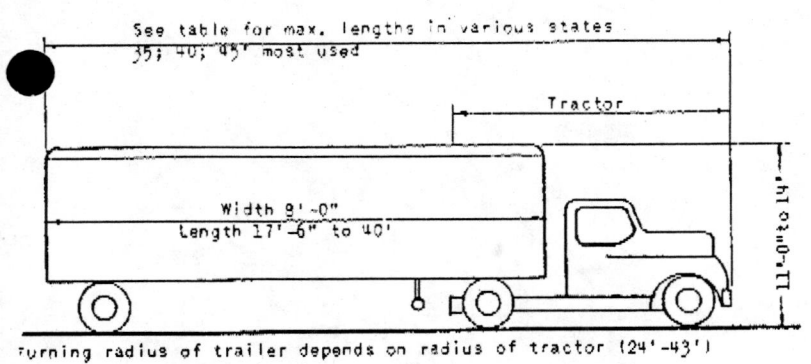

See table for max. lengths in various states
35; 40; 45' most used

Tractor

Width 8'-0"
Length 17'-6" to 40'

11'-0" to 14'

Turning radius of trailer depends on radius of tractor (24'-43')

| Max. Length | States |
|---|---|
| 45' | Ala. Conn. Ga. Ill. Iowa. Ky. Me. Mass. Minn. Miss. Mo. N.D. N.H. N.J. Ohio Tenn. Tex. Va. W.Va. |
| 48' | N.C. |
| 50' | Ark.D.C. Del.Fla.Ind.Kans.La.Nebr. N.Y. Okla. Ore. R.I. S.C. S.D. Vt. Wisc. |
| 55' | Md. Mich. |
| 60' | Calif.Colo. Idaho Mont.Utah.Wash.Wyo. |
| 65' | Ariz. N.M. Nevada (no restriction) |

## SEMI-TRAILER & TRUCK TRACTOR

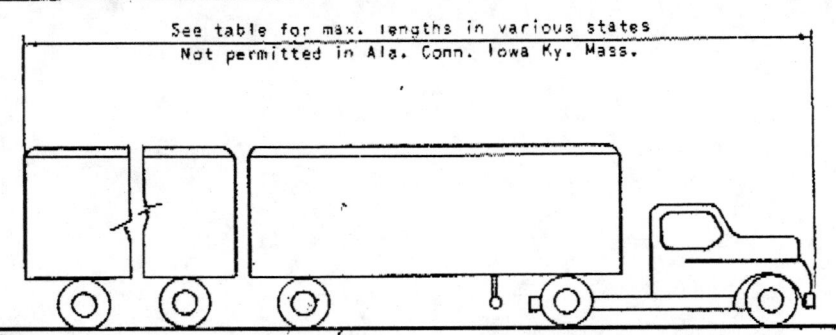

See table for max. lengths in various states
Not permitted in Ala. Conn. Iowa Ky. Mass.

In many western states combinations of truck & full trailer and tractor semi-trailer & full trailer are used to full legal length.

| Max. Length | States |
|---|---|
| 45' | Ga.Ill.Me.Minn.Miss.Mo.N.D. N.H. Tenn. Tex. Va. W.Va. |
| 48' | N.C. |
| 50' | Ark.D.C. Fla.Ind.Kans.Nebr. N.J. N.Y. Okla.Pa.R.I. S.C. S.D. Oreg.Vt.Wisc. |
| 55' | Md. Mich. |
| 60' | Calif. Colo. Del. La. Mont. Ohio. Wash. Wyo. Utah. |
| 65' | Ariz.Idaho N.M. Nevada (no restriction) |

## FULL TRAILER SEMI-TRAILER & TRUCK TRACTOR

DATA CHECKED BY OPERATIONS COUNCIL. AMERICAN TRUCKING ASSOCIATIONS INC.

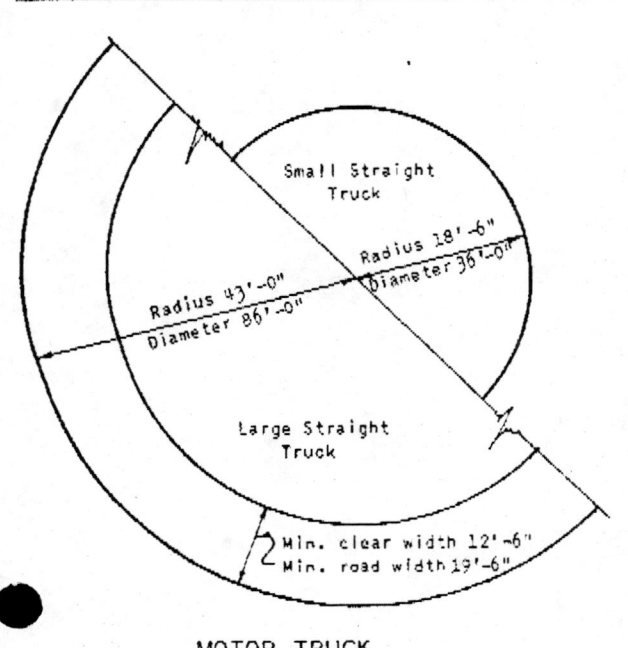

Small Straight Truck
Radius 18'-6"
Diameter 36'-0"
Radius 43'-0"
Diameter 86'-0"
Large Straight Truck
Min. clear width 12'-6"
Min. road width 19'-6"

MOTOR TRUCK
TURNING RADII

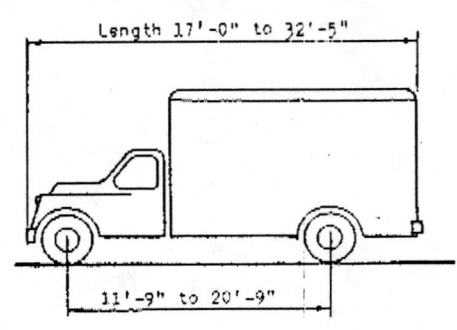

Length 17'-0" to 32'-5"

11'-9" to 20'-9"

Width 8'-0"±
variable usually appr.8'-0"
front 4'-10" to 6'-8-3/8"
rear 5'-0" to 6'-0 1/8"

VAN TYPE TRUCK

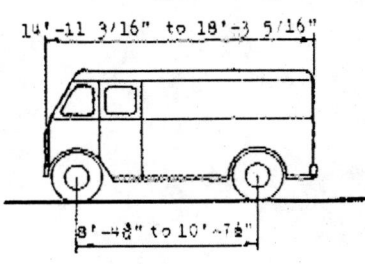

14'-11 3/16" to 18'-3 5/16"

8'-4⅜" to 10'-7⅜"

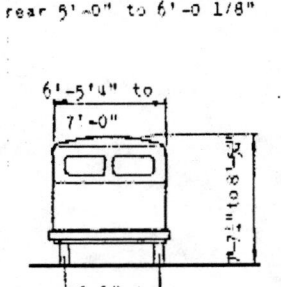

6'-5'4" to 7'-0"

5'-1" to 5'-4⅜"

DELIVERY TRUCK

# DIMENSIONS OF MOTOR VEHICLES

## NATURAL SINES

| ANGLE | 0′ | 10′ | 20′ | 30′ | 40′ | 50′ | 60′ | |
|---|---|---|---|---|---|---|---|---|
| 0° | 0.00000 | 0.00291 | 0.00582 | 0.00873 | 0.01164 | 0.01454 | 0.01745 | 89° |
| 1 | 0.01745 | 0.02036 | 0.02327 | 0.02618 | 0.02908 | 0.03199 | 0.03490 | 88 |
| 2 | 0.03490 | 0.03781 | 0.04071 | 0.04362 | 0.04653 | 0.04943 | 0.05234 | 87 |
| 3 | 0.05234 | 0.05524 | 0.05814 | 0.06105 | 0.06395 | 0.06685 | 0.06976 | 86 |
| 4 | 0.06976 | 0.07266 | 0.07556 | 0.07846 | 0.08136 | 0.08426 | 0.08716 | 85 |
| 5 | 0.08716 | 0.09005 | 0.09295 | 0.09585 | 0.09874 | 0.10164 | 0.10453 | 84 |
| 6 | 0.10453 | 0.10742 | 0.11031 | 0.11320 | 0.11609 | 0.11898 | 0.12187 | 83 |
| 7 | 0.12187 | 0.12476 | 0.12764 | 0.13053 | 0.13341 | 0.13629 | 0.13917 | 82 |
| 8 | 0.13917 | 0.14205 | 0.14493 | 0.14781 | 0.15069 | 0.15356 | 0.15643 | 81 |
| 9 | 0.15643 | 0.15931 | 0.16218 | 0.16505 | 0.16792 | 0.17078 | 0.17365 | 80 |
| 10 | 0.17365 | 0.17651 | 0.17937 | 0.18224 | 0.18509 | 0.18795 | 0.19081 | 79 |
| 11 | 0.19081 | 0.19366 | 0.19652 | 0.19937 | 0.20222 | 0.20507 | 0.20791 | 78 |
| 12 | 0.20791 | 0.21076 | 0.21360 | 0.21644 | 0.21928 | 0.22212 | 0.22495 | 77 |
| 13 | 0.22495 | 0.22778 | 0.23062 | 0.23345 | 0.23627 | 0.23910 | 0.24192 | 76 |
| 14 | 0.24192 | 0.24474 | 0.24756 | 0.25038 | 0.25320 | 0.25601 | 0.25882 | 75 |
| 15 | 0.25882 | 0.26163 | 0.26443 | 0.26724 | 0.27004 | 0.27284 | 0.27564 | 74 |
| 16 | 0.27564 | 0.27843 | 0.28123 | 0.28402 | 0.28680 | 0.28959 | 0.29237 | 73 |
| 17 | 0.29237 | 0.29515 | 0.29793 | 0.30071 | 0.30348 | 0.30625 | 0.30902 | 72 |
| 18 | 0.30902 | 0.31178 | 0.31454 | 0.31730 | 0.32006 | 0.32282 | 0.32557 | 71 |
| 19 | 0.32557 | 0.32832 | 0.33106 | 0.33381 | 0.33655 | 0.33929 | 0.34202 | 70 |
| 20 | 0.34202 | 0.34475 | 0.34748 | 0.35021 | 0.35293 | 0.35565 | 0.35837 | 69 |
| 21 | 0.35837 | 0.36108 | 0.36379 | 0.36650 | 0.36921 | 0.37191 | 0.37461 | 68 |
| 22 | 0.37461 | 0.37730 | 0.37999 | 0.38268 | 0.38537 | 0.38805 | 0.39073 | 67 |
| 23 | 0.39073 | 0.39341 | 0.39608 | 0.39875 | 0.40141 | 0.40408 | 0.40674 | 66 |
| 24 | 0.40674 | 0.40939 | 0.41204 | 0.41469 | 0.41734 | 0.41998 | 0.42262 | 65 |
| 25 | 0.42262 | 0.42525 | 0.42788 | 0.43051 | 0.43313 | 0.43575 | 0.43837 | 64 |
| 26 | 0.43837 | 0.44098 | 0.44359 | 0.44620 | 0.44880 | 0.45140 | 0.45399 | 63 |
| 27 | 0.45399 | 0.45658 | 0.45917 | 0.46175 | 0.46433 | 0.46690 | 0.46947 | 62 |
| 28 | 0.46947 | 0.47204 | 0.47460 | 0.47716 | 0.47971 | 0.48226 | 0.48481 | 61 |
| 29 | 0.48481 | 0.48735 | 0.48989 | 0.49242 | 0.49495 | 0.49748 | 0.50000 | 60 |
| 30 | 0.50000 | 0.50252 | 0.50503 | 0.50754 | 0.51004 | 0.51254 | 0.51504 | 59 |
| 31 | 0.51504 | 0.51753 | 0.52002 | 0.52250 | 0.52498 | 0.52745 | 0.52992 | 58 |
| 32 | 0.52992 | 0.53238 | 0.53484 | 0.53730 | 0.53975 | 0.54220 | 0.54464 | 57 |
| 33 | 0.54464 | 0.54708 | 0.54951 | 0.55194 | 0.55436 | 0.55678 | 0.55919 | 56 |
| 34 | 0.55919 | 0.56160 | 0.56401 | 0.56641 | 0.56880 | 0.57119 | 0.57358 | 55 |
| 35 | 0.57358 | 0.57596 | 0.57833 | 0.58070 | 0.58307 | 0.58543 | 0.58779 | 54 |
| 36 | 0.58779 | 0.59014 | 0.59248 | 0.59482 | 0.59716 | 0.59949 | 0.60182 | 53 |
| 37 | 0.60182 | 0.60414 | 0.60645 | 0.60876 | 0.61107 | 0.61337 | 0.61566 | 52 |
| 38 | 0.61566 | 0.61795 | 0.62024 | 0.62251 | 0.62479 | 0.62706 | 0.62932 | 51 |
| 39 | 0.62932 | 0.63158 | 0.63383 | 0.63608 | 0.63832 | 0.64056 | 0.64279 | 50 |
| 40 | 0.64279 | 0.64501 | 0.64723 | 0.64945 | 0.65166 | 0.65386 | 0.65606 | 49 |
| 41 | 0.65606 | 0.65825 | 0.66044 | 0.66262 | 0.66480 | 0.66697 | 0.66913 | 48 |
| 42 | 0.66913 | 0.67129 | 0.67344 | 0.67559 | 0.67773 | 0.67987 | 0.68200 | 47 |
| 43 | 0.68200 | 0.68412 | 0.68624 | 0.68835 | 0.69046 | 0.69256 | 0.69466 | 46 |
| 44° | 0.69466 | 0.69675 | 0.69883 | 0.70091 | 0.70298 | 0.70505 | 0.70711 | 45° |
| | 60′ | 50′ | 40′ | 30′ | 20′ | 10′ | 0′ | ANGLE |

NATURAL COSINES

## NATURAL SINES

| ANGLE | 0′ | 10′ | 20′ | 30′ | 40′ | 50′ | 60′ | |
|---|---|---|---|---|---|---|---|---|
| 45° | 0.70711 | 0.70916 | 0.71121 | 0.71325 | 0.71529 | 0.71732 | 0.71934 | 44° |
| 46 | 0.71934 | 0.72136 | 0.72337 | 0.72537 | 0.72737 | 0.72937 | 0.73135 | 43 |
| 47 | 0.73135 | 0.73333 | 0.73531 | 0.73728 | 0.73924 | 0.74120 | 0.74314 | 42 |
| 48 | 0.74314 | 0.74509 | 0.74703 | 0.74896 | 0.75088 | 0.75280 | 0.75471 | 41 |
| 49 | 0.75471 | 0.75661 | 0.75851 | 0.76041 | 0.76229 | 0.76417 | 0.76604 | 40 |
| 50 | 0.76604 | 0.76791 | 0.76977 | 0.77162 | 0.77347 | 0.77531 | 0.77715 | 39 |
| 51 | 0.77715 | 0.77897 | 0.78079 | 0.78261 | 0.78442 | 0.78622 | 0.78801 | 38 |
| 52 | 0.78801 | 0.78980 | 0.79158 | 0.79335 | 0.79512 | 0.79688 | 0.79864 | 37 |
| 53 | 0.79864 | 0.80038 | 0.80212 | 0.80386 | 0.80558 | 0.80730 | 0.80902 | 36 |
| 54 | 0.80902 | 0.81072 | 0.81242 | 0.81412 | 0.81580 | 0.81748 | 0.81915 | 35 |
| 55 | 0.81915 | 0.82082 | 0.82248 | 0.82413 | 0.82577 | 0.82741 | 0.82904 | 34 |
| 56 | 0.82904 | 0.83066 | 0.83228 | 0.83389 | 0.83549 | 0.83708 | 0.83867 | 33 |
| 57 | 0.83867 | 0.84025 | 0.84182 | 0.84339 | 0.84495 | 0.84650 | 0.84805 | 32 |
| 58 | 0.84805 | 0.84959 | 0.85112 | 0.85264 | 0.85416 | 0.85567 | 0.85717 | 31 |
| 59 | 0.85717 | 0.85866 | 0.86015 | 0.86163 | 0.86310 | 0.86457 | 0.86603 | 30 |
| 60 | 0.86603 | 0.86748 | 0.86892 | 0.87036 | 0.87178 | 0.87321 | 0.87462 | 29 |
| 61 | 0.87462 | 0.87603 | 0.87743 | 0.87882 | 0.88020 | 0.88158 | 0.88295 | 28 |
| 62 | 0.88295 | 0.88431 | 0.88566 | 0.88701 | 0.88835 | 0.88968 | 0.89101 | 27 |
| 63 | 0.89101 | 0.89232 | 0.89363 | 0.89493 | 0.89623 | 0.89752 | 0.89879 | 26 |
| 64 | 0.89879 | 0.90007 | 0.90133 | 0.90259 | 0.90383 | 0.90507 | 0.90631 | 25 |
| 65 | 0.90631 | 0.90753 | 0.90875 | 0.90996 | 0.91116 | 0.91236 | 0.91355 | 24 |
| 66 | 0.91355 | 0.91472 | 0.91590 | 0.91706 | 0.91822 | 0.91936 | 0.92050 | 23 |
| 67 | 0.92050 | 0.92164 | 0.92276 | 0.92388 | 0.92499 | 0.92609 | 0.92718 | 22 |
| 68 | 0.92718 | 0.92827 | 0.92935 | 0.93042 | 0.93148 | 0.93253 | 0.93358 | 21 |
| 69 | 0.93358 | 0.93462 | 0.93565 | 0.93667 | 0.93769 | 0.93869 | 0.93969 | 20 |
| 70 | 0.93969 | 0.94068 | 0.94167 | 0.94264 | 0.94361 | 0.94457 | 0.94552 | 19 |
| 71 | 0.94552 | 0.94646 | 0.94740 | 0.94832 | 0.94924 | 0.95015 | 0.95106 | 18 |
| 72 | 0.95106 | 0.95195 | 0.95284 | 0.95372 | 0.95459 | 0.95545 | 0.95630 | 17 |
| 73 | 0.95630 | 0.95715 | 0.95799 | 0.95882 | 0.95964 | 0.96046 | 0.96126 | 16 |
| 74 | 0.96126 | 0.96206 | 0.96285 | 0.96363 | 0.96440 | 0.96517 | 0.96593 | 15 |
| 75 | 0.96593 | 0.96667 | 0.96742 | 0.96815 | 0.96887 | 0.96959 | 0.97030 | 14 |
| 76 | 0.97030 | 0.97100 | 0.97169 | 0.97237 | 0.97304 | 0.97371 | 0.97437 | 13 |
| 77 | 0.97437 | 0.97502 | 0.97566 | 0.97630 | 0.97692 | 0.97754 | 0.97815 | 12 |
| 78 | 0.97815 | 0.97875 | 0.97934 | 0.97992 | 0.98050 | 0.98107 | 0.98163 | 11 |
| 79 | 0.98163 | 0.98218 | 0.98272 | 0.98325 | 0.98378 | 0.98430 | 0.98481 | 10 |
| 80 | 0.98481 | 0.98531 | 0.98580 | 0.98629 | 0.98676 | 0.98723 | 0.98769 | 9 |
| 81 | 0.98769 | 0.98814 | 0.98858 | 0.98902 | 0.98944 | 0.98986 | 0.99027 | 8 |
| 82 | 0.99027 | 0.99067 | 0.99106 | 0.99144 | 0.99182 | 0.99219 | 0.99255 | 7 |
| 83 | 0.99255 | 0.99290 | 0.99324 | 0.99357 | 0.99390 | 0.99421 | 0.99452 | 6 |
| 84 | 0.99452 | 0.99482 | 0.99511 | 0.99540 | 0.99567 | 0.99594 | 0.99619 | 5 |
| 85 | 0.99619 | 0.99644 | 0.99668 | 0.99692 | 0.99714 | 0.99736 | 0.99756 | 4 |
| 86 | 0.99756 | 0.99776 | 0.99795 | 0.99813 | 0.99831 | 0.99847 | 0.99863 | 3 |
| 87 | 0.99863 | 0.99878 | 0.99892 | 0.99905 | 0.99917 | 0.99929 | 0.99939 | 2 |
| 88 | 0.99939 | 0.99949 | 0.99958 | 0.99966 | 0.99973 | 0.99979 | 0.99985 | 1 |
| 89° | 0.99985 | 0.99989 | 0.99993 | 0.99996 | 0.99998 | 1.00000 | 1.00000 | 0° |
| | 60′ | 50′ | 40′ | 30′ | 20′ | 10′ | 0′ | ANGLE |

NATURAL COSINES

## NATURAL TANGENTS

| ANGLE | 0′ | 10′ | 20′ | 30′ | 40′ | 50′ | 60′ | |
|---|---|---|---|---|---|---|---|---|
| 0° | 0.00000 | 0.00291 | 0.00582 | 0.00873 | 0.01164 | 0.01455 | 0.01746 | 89° |
| 1 | 0.01746 | 0.02036 | 0.02328 | 0.02619 | 0.02910 | 0.03201 | 0.03492 | 88 |
| 2 | 0.03492 | 0.03783 | 0.04075 | 0.04366 | 0.04658 | 0.04949 | 0.05241 | 87 |
| 3 | 0.05241 | 0.05533 | 0.05824 | 0.06116 | 0.06408 | 0.06700 | 0.06993 | 86 |
| 4 | 0.06993 | 0.07285 | 0.07578 | 0.07870 | 0.08163 | 0.08456 | 0.08749 | 85 |
| 5 | 0.08749 | 0.09042 | 0.09335 | 0.09629 | 0.09923 | 0.10216 | 0.10510 | 84 |
| 6 | 0.10510 | 0.10805 | 0.11099 | 0.11394 | 0.11688 | 0.11983 | 0.12278 | 83 |
| 7 | 0.12278 | 0.12574 | 0.12869 | 0.13165 | 0.13461 | 0.13758 | 0.14054 | 82 |
| 8 | 0.14054 | 0.14351 | 0.14648 | 0.14945 | 0.15243 | 0.15540 | 0.15838 | 81 |
| 9 | 0.15838 | 0.16137 | 0.16435 | 0.16734 | 0.17033 | 0.17333 | 0.17633 | 80 |
| 10 | 0.17633 | 0.17933 | 0.18233 | 0.18534 | 0.18835 | 0.19136 | 0.19438 | 79 |
| 11 | 0.19438 | 0.19740 | 0.20042 | 0.20345 | 0.20648 | 0.20952 | 0.21256 | 78 |
| 12 | 0.21256 | 0.21560 | 0.21864 | 0.22169 | 0.22475 | 0.22781 | 0.23087 | 77 |
| 13 | 0.23087 | 0.23393 | 0.23700 | 0.24008 | 0.24316 | 0.24624 | 0.24933 | 76 |
| 14 | 0.24933 | 0.25242 | 0.25552 | 0.25862 | 0.26172 | 0.26483 | 0.26795 | 75 |
| 15 | 0.26795 | 0.27107 | 0.27419 | 0.27732 | 0.28046 | 0.28360 | 0.28675 | 74 |
| 16 | 0.28675 | 0.28990 | 0.29305 | 0.29621 | 0.29938 | 0.30255 | 0.30573 | 73 |
| 17 | 0.30573 | 0.30891 | 0.31210 | 0.31530 | 0.31850 | 0.32171 | 0.32492 | 72 |
| 18 | 0.32492 | 0.32814 | 0.33136 | 0.33460 | 0.33783 | 0.34108 | 0.34433 | 71 |
| 19 | 0.34433 | 0.34758 | 0.35085 | 0.35412 | 0.35740 | 0.36068 | 0.36397 | 70 |
| 20 | 0.36397 | 0.36727 | 0.37057 | 0.37388 | 0.37720 | 0.38053 | 0.38386 | 69 |
| 21 | 0.38386 | 0.38721 | 0.39055 | 0.39391 | 0.39727 | 0.40065 | 0.40403 | 68 |
| 22 | 0.40403 | 0.40741 | 0.41081 | 0.41421 | 0.41763 | 0.42105 | 0.42447 | 67 |
| 23 | 0.42447 | 0.42791 | 0.43136 | 0.43481 | 0.43828 | 0.44175 | 0.44523 | 66 |
| 24 | 0.44523 | 0.44872 | 0.45222 | 0.45573 | 0.45924 | 0.46277 | 0.46631 | 65 |
| 25 | 0.46631 | 0.46985 | 0.47341 | 0.47698 | 0.48055 | 0.48414 | 0.48773 | 64 |
| 26 | 0.48773 | 0.49134 | 0.49495 | 0.49858 | 0.50222 | 0.50587 | 0.50953 | 63 |
| 27 | 0.50953 | 0.51320 | 0.51688 | 0.52057 | 0.52427 | 0.52798 | 0.53171 | 62 |
| 28 | 0.53171 | 0.53545 | 0.53920 | 0.54296 | 0.54673 | 0.55051 | 0.55431 | 61 |
| 29 | 0.55431 | 0.55812 | 0.56194 | 0.56577 | 0.56962 | 0.57348 | 0.57735 | 60 |
| 30 | 0.57735 | 0.58124 | 0.58513 | 0.58905 | 0.59297 | 0.59691 | 0.60086 | 59 |
| 31 | 0.60086 | 0.60483 | 0.60881 | 0.61280 | 0.61681 | 0.62083 | 0.62487 | 58 |
| 32 | 0.62487 | 0.62892 | 0.63299 | 0.63707 | 0.64117 | 0.64528 | 0.64941 | 57 |
| 33 | 0.64941 | 0.65355 | 0.65771 | 0.66189 | 0.66608 | 0.67028 | 0.67451 | 56 |
| 34 | 0.67451 | 0.67875 | 0.68301 | 0.68728 | 0.69157 | 0.69588 | 0.70021 | 55 |
| 35 | 0.70021 | 0.70455 | 0.70891 | 0.71329 | 0.71769 | 0.72211 | 0.72654 | 54 |
| 36 | 0.72654 | 0.73100 | 0.73547 | 0.73996 | 0.74447 | 0.74900 | 0.75355 | 53 |
| 37 | 0.75355 | 0.75812 | 0.76272 | 0.76733 | 0.77196 | 0.77661 | 0.78129 | 52 |
| 38 | 0.78129 | 0.78598 | 0.79070 | 0.79544 | 0.80020 | 0.80498 | 0.80978 | 51 |
| 39 | 0.80978 | 0.81461 | 0.81946 | 0.82434 | 0.82923 | 0.83415 | 0.83910 | 50 |
| 40 | 0.83910 | 0.84407 | 0.84906 | 0.85408 | 0.85912 | 0.86419 | 0.86929 | 49 |
| 41 | 0.96929 | 0.87441 | 0.87955 | 0.88473 | 0.88992 | 0.89515 | 0.90040 | 48 |
| 42 | 0.90040 | 0.90569 | 0.91099 | 0.91633 | 0.92170 | 0.92709 | 0.93252 | 47 |
| 43 | 0.93252 | 0.93797 | 0.94345 | 0.94896 | 0.95451 | 0.96008 | 0.96569 | 46 |
| 44° | 0.96569 | 0.97133 | 0.97700 | 0.98270 | 0.98843 | 0.99420 | 1.00000 | 45° |
| | 60′ | 50′ | 40′ | 30′ | 20′ | 10′ | 0′ | ANGLE |

NATURAL COTANGENTS

## NATURAL TANGENTS

| ANGLE | 0′ | 10′ | 20′ | 30′ | 40′ | 50′ | 60′ | |
|---|---|---|---|---|---|---|---|---|
| 45° | 1.00000 | 1.00583 | 1.01170 | 1.01761 | 1.02355 | 1.02952 | 1.03553 | 44° |
| 46 | 1.03553 | 1.04158 | 1.04766 | 1.05378 | 1.05994 | 1.06613 | 1.07237 | 43 |
| 47 | 1.07237 | 1.07864 | 1.08496 | 1.09131 | 1.09770 | 1.10414 | 1.11061 | 42 |
| 48 | 1.11061 | 1.11713 | 1.12369 | 1.13029 | 1.13694 | 1.14363 | 1.15037 | 41 |
| 49 | 1.15037 | 1.15715 | 1.16398 | 1.17085 | 1.17777 | 1.18474 | 1.19175 | 40 |
| 50 | 1.19175 | 1.19882 | 1.20593 | 1.21310 | 1.22031 | 1.22758 | 1.23490 | 39 |
| 51 | 1.23490 | 1.24227 | 1.24969 | 1.25717 | 1.26471 | 1.27230 | 1.27994 | 38 |
| 52 | 1.27994 | 1.28764 | 1.29541 | 1.30323 | 1.31110 | 1.31904 | 1.32704 | 37 |
| 53 | 1.32704 | 1.33511 | 1.34323 | 1.35142 | 1.35968 | 1.36800 | 1.37638 | 36 |
| 54 | 1.37638 | 1.38484 | 1.39336 | 1.40195 | 1.41061 | 1.41934 | 1.42815 | 35 |
| 55 | 1.42815 | 1.43703 | 1.44598 | 1.45501 | 1.46411 | 1.47330 | 1.48256 | 34 |
| 56 | 1.48256 | 1.49190 | 1.50133 | 1.51084 | 1.52043 | 1.53010 | 1.53987 | 33 |
| 57 | 1.53987 | 1.54972 | 1.55966 | 1.56969 | 1.57981 | 1.59002 | 1.60033 | 32 |
| 58 | 1.60033 | 1.61074 | 1.62125 | 1.63185 | 1.64256 | 1.65337 | 1.66428 | 31 |
| 59 | 1.66428 | 1.67530 | 1.68643 | 1.69766 | 1.70901 | 1.72047 | 1.73205 | 30 |
| 60 | 1.73205 | 1.74375 | 1.75556 | 1.76749 | 1.77955 | 1.79174 | 1.80405 | 29 |
| 61 | 1.80405 | 1.81649 | 1.82906 | 1.84177 | 1.85462 | 1.86760 | 1.88073 | 28 |
| 62 | 1.88073 | 1.89400 | 1.90741 | 1.92098 | 1.93470 | 1.94858 | 1.96261 | 27 |
| 63 | 1.96261 | 1.97681 | 1.99116 | 2.00569 | 2.02039 | 2.03526 | 2.05030 | 26 |
| 64 | 2.05030 | 2.06553 | 2.08094 | 2.09654 | 2.11233 | 2.12832 | 2.14451 | 25 |
| 65 | 2.14451 | 2.16090 | 2.17749 | 2.19430 | 2.21132 | 2.22857 | 2.24604 | 24 |
| 66 | 2.24604 | 2.26374 | 2.28167 | 2.29984 | 2.31826 | 2.33693 | 2.35585 | 23 |
| 67 | 2.35585 | 2.37504 | 2.39449 | 2.41421 | 2.43422 | 2.45451 | 2.47509 | 22 |
| 68 | 2.47509 | 2.49597 | 2.51715 | 2.53865 | 2.56046 | 2.58261 | 2.60509 | 21 |
| 69 | 2.60509 | 2.62791 | 2.65109 | 2.67462 | 2.69853 | 2.72281 | 2.74748 | 20 |
| 70 | 2.74748 | 2.77254 | 2.79802 | 2.82391 | 2.85023 | 2.87700 | 2.90421 | 19 |
| 71 | 2.90421 | 2.93189 | 2.96004 | 2.98869 | 3.01783 | 3.04749 | 3.07768 | 18 |
| 72 | 3.07768 | 3.10842 | 3.13972 | 3.17159 | 3.20406 | 3.23714 | 3.27085 | 17 |
| 73 | 3.27085 | 3.30521 | 3.34023 | 3.37594 | 3.41236 | 3.44951 | 3.48741 | 16 |
| 74 | 3.48741 | 3.52609 | 3.56557 | 3.60588 | 3.64705 | 3.68909 | 3.73205 | 15 |
| 75 | 3.73205 | 3.77595 | 3.82083 | 3.86671 | 3.91364 | 3.96165 | 4.01078 | 14 |
| 76 | 4.01078 | 4.06107 | 4.11256 | 4.16530 | 4.21933 | 4.27471 | 4.33148 | 13 |
| 77 | 4.33148 | 4.38969 | 4.44942 | 4.51071 | 4.57363 | 4.63825 | 4.70463 | 12 |
| 78 | 4.70463 | 4.77286 | 4.84300 | 4.91516 | 4.98940 | 5.06584 | 5.14455 | 11 |
| 79 | 5.14455 | 5.22566 | 5.30928 | 5.39552 | 5.48451 | 5.57638 | 5.67128 | 10 |
| 80 | 5.67128 | 5.76937 | 5.87080 | 5.97576 | 6.08444 | 6.19703 | 6.31375 | 9 |
| 81 | 6.31375 | 6.43484 | 6.56055 | 6.69116 | 6.82694 | 6.96823 | 7.11537 | 8 |
| 82 | 7.11537 | 7.26873 | 7.42871 | 7.59575 | 7.77035 | 7.95302 | 8.14435 | 7 |
| 83 | 8.14435 | 8.34496 | 8.55555 | 8.77689 | 9.00983 | 9.25530 | 9.51436 | 6 |
| 84 | 9.51436 | 9.78817 | 10.07803 | 10.38540 | 10.71191 | 11.05943 | 11.43005 | 5 |
| 85 | 11.43005 | 11.82617 | 12.25051 | 12.70621 | 13.19688 | 13.72674 | 14.30067 | 4 |
| 86 | 14.30067 | 14.92442 | 15.60478 | 16.34986 | 17.16934 | 18.07498 | 19.08114 | 3 |
| 87 | 19.08114 | 20.20555 | 21.47040 | 22.90377 | 24.54176 | 26.43160 | 28.63625 | 2 |
| 88 | 28.63625 | 31.24158 | 34.36777 | 38.18846 | 42.96408 | 49.10388 | 57.28996 | 1 |
| 89° | 57.28996 | 68.75009 | 85.93979 | 114.58865 | 171.88540 | 343.77371 | Infinite | 0° |
| | 60′ | 50′ | 40′ | 30′ | 20′ | 10′ | 0′ | ANGLE |

NATURAL COTANGENTS

MATHEMATICAL DATA A

## NATURAL SECANTS

| ANGLE | 0′ | 10′ | 20′ | 30′ | 40′ | 50′ | 60′ | |
|---|---|---|---|---|---|---|---|---|
| 0° | 1.00000 | 1.00001 | 1.00002 | 1.00004 | 1.00007 | 1.00011 | 1.00015 | 89° |
| 1 | 1.00015 | 1.00021 | 1.00027 | 1.00034 | 1.00042 | 1.00051 | 1.00061 | 88 |
| 2 | 1.00061 | 1.00072 | 1.00083 | 1.00095 | 1.00108 | 1.00122 | 1.00137 | 87 |
| 3 | 1.00137 | 1.00153 | 1.00169 | 1.00187 | 1.00205 | 1.00224 | 1.00244 | 86 |
| 4 | 1.00244 | 1.00265 | 1.00287 | 1.00309 | 1.00333 | 1.00357 | 1.00382 | 85 |
| 5 | 1.00382 | 1.00408 | 1.00435 | 1.00463 | 1.00491 | 1.00521 | 1.00551 | 84 |
| 6 | 1.00551 | 1.00582 | 1.00614 | 1.00647 | 1.00681 | 1.00715 | 1.00751 | 83 |
| 7 | 1.00751 | 1.00787 | 1.00825 | 1.00863 | 1.00902 | 1.00942 | 1.00983 | 82 |
| 8 | 1.00983 | 1.01024 | 1.01067 | 1.01111 | 1.01155 | 1.01200 | 1.01247 | 81 |
| 9 | 1.01247 | 1.01294 | 1.01342 | 1.01391 | 1.01440 | 1.10491 | 1.01543 | 80 |
| 10 | 1.01543 | 1.01595 | 1.01649 | 1.01703 | 1.01758 | 1.01815 | 1.01872 | 79 |
| 11 | 1.01872 | 1.01930 | 1.01989 | 1.02049 | 1.02110 | 1.02171 | 1.02234 | 78 |
| 12 | 1.02234 | 1.02298 | 1.02362 | 1.02428 | 1.02494 | 1.02562 | 1.02630 | 77 |
| 13 | 1.02630 | 1.02700 | 1.02770 | 1.02842 | 1.02914 | 1.02987 | 1.03061 | 76 |
| 14 | 1.03061 | 1.03137 | 1.03213 | 1.03290 | 1.03368 | 1.03447 | 1.03528 | 75 |
| 15 | 1.03528 | 1.03609 | 1.03691 | 1.03774 | 1.03858 | 1.03944 | 1.04030 | 74 |
| 16 | 1.04030 | 1.04117 | 1.04206 | 1.04295 | 1.04385 | 1.04477 | 1.04569 | 73 |
| 17 | 1.04569 | 1.04663 | 1.04757 | 1.04853 | 1.04950 | 1.05047 | 1.05146 | 72 |
| 18 | 1.05146 | 1.05246 | 1.05347 | 1.05449 | 1.05552 | 1.05657 | 1.05762 | 71 |
| 19 | 1.05762 | 1.05869 | 1.05976 | 1.06085 | 1.06195 | 1.06306 | 1.06418 | 70 |
| 20 | 1.06418 | 1.06531 | 1.06645 | 1.06761 | 1.06878 | 1.06995 | 1.07115 | 69 |
| 21 | 1.07115 | 1.07235 | 1.07356 | 1.07479 | 1.07602 | 1.07727 | 1.07853 | 68 |
| 22 | 1.07853 | 1.07981 | 1.08109 | 1.08239 | 1.08370 | 1.08503 | 1.08636 | 67 |
| 23 | 1.08636 | 1.08771 | 1.08907 | 1.09044 | 1.09183 | 1.09323 | 1.09464 | 66 |
| 24 | 1.09464 | 1.09606 | 1.09750 | 1.09895 | 1.10041 | 1.10189 | 1.10338 | 65 |
| 25 | 1.10338 | 1.10488 | 1.10640 | 1.10793 | 1.10947 | 1.11103 | 1.11260 | 64 |
| 26 | 1.11260 | 1.11419 | 1.11579 | 1.11740 | 1.11903 | 1.12067 | 1.12233 | 63 |
| 27 | 1.12233 | 1.12400 | 1.12568 | 1.12738 | 1.12910 | 1.13083 | 1.13257 | 62 |
| 28 | 1.13257 | 1.13433 | 1.13610 | 1.13789 | 1.13970 | 1.14152 | 1.14335 | 61 |
| 29 | 1.14335 | 1.14521 | 1.14707 | 1.14896 | 1.15085 | 1.15277 | 1.15470 | 60 |
| 30 | 1.15470 | 1.15665 | 1.15861 | 1.16059 | 1.16259 | 1.16460 | 1.16663 | 59 |
| 31 | 1.16663 | 1.16868 | 1.17075 | 1.17283 | 1.17493 | 1.17704 | 1.17918 | 58 |
| 32 | 1.17918 | 1.18133 | 1.18350 | 1.18569 | 1.18790 | 1.19012 | 1.19236 | 57 |
| 33 | 1.19236 | 1.19463 | 1.19691 | 1.19920 | 1.20152 | 1.20386 | 1.20622 | 56 |
| 34 | 1.20622 | 1.20859 | 1.21099 | 1.21341 | 1.21584 | 1.21830 | 1.22077 | 55 |
| 35 | 1.22077 | 1.22327 | 1.22579 | 1.22833 | 1.23089 | 1.23347 | 1.23607 | 54 |
| 36 | 1.23607 | 1.23869 | 1.24134 | 1.24400 | 1.24669 | 1.24940 | 1.25214 | 53 |
| 37 | 1.25214 | 1.25489 | 1.25767 | 1.26047 | 1.26330 | 1.26615 | 1.26902 | 52 |
| 38 | 1.26902 | 1.27191 | 1.27483 | 1.27778 | 1.28075 | 1.28374 | 1.28676 | 51 |
| 39 | 1.28676 | 1.28980 | 1.29287 | 1.29597 | 1.29909 | 1.30223 | 1.30541 | 50 |
| 40 | 1.30541 | 1.30861 | 1.31183 | 1.31509 | 1.31837 | 1.32168 | 1.32501 | 49 |
| 41 | 1.32501 | 1.32838 | 1.33177 | 1.33519 | 1.33864 | 1.34212 | 1.34563 | 48 |
| 42 | 1.34563 | 1.34917 | 1.35274 | 1.35634 | 1.35997 | 1.36363 | 1.36733 | 47 |
| 43 | 1.36733 | 1.37105 | 1.37481 | 1.37860 | 1.38242 | 1.38628 | 1.39016 | 46 |
| 44° | 1.39016 | 1.39409 | 1.39804 | 1.40203 | 1.40606 | 1.41012 | 1.41421 | 45° |
| | 60′ | 50′ | 40′ | 30′ | 20′ | 10′ | 0′ | ANGLE |

NATURAL COSECANTS

## NATURAL SECANTS

| ANGLE | 0′ | 10′ | 20′ | 30′ | 40′ | 50′ | 60′ | |
|---|---|---|---|---|---|---|---|---|
| 45° | 1.41421 | 1.41835 | 1.42251 | 1.42672 | 1.43096 | 1.43524 | 1.43956 | 44° |
| 46 | 1.43956 | 1.44391 | 1.44831 | 1.45274 | 1.45721 | 1.46173 | 1.46628 | 43 |
| 47 | 1.46628 | 1.47087 | 1.47551 | 1.48019 | 1.48491 | 1.48967 | 1.49448 | 42 |
| 48 | 1.49448 | 1.49933 | 1.50422 | 1.50916 | 1.51415 | 1.51918 | 1.52425 | 41 |
| 49 | 1.52425 | 1.52938 | 1.53455 | 1.53977 | 1.54504 | 1.55036 | 1.55572 | 40 |
| 50 | 1.55572 | 1.56114 | 1.56661 | 1.57213 | 1.57771 | 1.58333 | 1.58902 | 39 |
| 51 | 1.58902 | 1.59475 | 1.60054 | 1.60639 | 1.61229 | 1.61825 | 1.62427 | 38 |
| 52 | 1.62427 | 1.63035 | 1.63648 | 1.64268 | 1.64894 | 1.65526 | 1.66164 | 37 |
| 53 | 1.66164 | 1.66809 | 1.67460 | 1.68117 | 1.68782 | 1.69452 | 1.70130 | 36 |
| 54 | 1.70130 | 1.70815 | 1.71506 | 1.72205 | 1.72911 | 1.73624 | 1.74345 | 35 |
| 55 | 1.74345 | 1.75073 | 1.75808 | 1.76552 | 1.77303 | 1.78062 | 1.78829 | 34 |
| 56 | 1.78829 | 1.79604 | 1.80388 | 1.81180 | 1.81981 | 1.82790 | 1.83608 | 33 |
| 57 | 1.83608 | 1.84435 | 1.85271 | 1.86116 | 1.86970 | 1.87834 | 1.88708 | 32 |
| 58 | 1.88708 | 1.89591 | 1.90485 | 1.91388 | 1.92302 | 1.93226 | 1.94160 | 31 |
| 59 | 1.94160 | 1.95106 | 1.96062 | 1.97029 | 1.98008 | 1.98998 | 2.00000 | 30 |
| 60 | 2.00000 | 2.01014 | 2.02039 | 2.03077 | 2.04128 | 2.05191 | 2.06267 | 29 |
| 61 | 2.06267 | 2.07356 | 2.08458 | 2.09574 | 2.10704 | 2.11847 | 2.13005 | 28 |
| 62 | 2.13005 | 2.14178 | 2.15366 | 2.16568 | 2.17786 | 2.19019 | 2.20269 | 27 |
| 63 | 2.20269 | 2.21535 | 2.22817 | 2.24116 | 2.25432 | 2.26766 | 2.28117 | 26 |
| 64 | 2.28117 | 2.29487 | 2.30875 | 2.32282 | 2.33708 | 2.35154 | 2.36620 | 25 |
| 65 | 2.36620 | 2.38107 | 2.39614 | 2.41142 | 2.42692 | 2.44264 | 2.45859 | 24 |
| 66 | 2.45859 | 2.47477 | 2.49119 | 2.50784 | 2.52474 | 2.54190 | 2.55930 | 23 |
| 67 | 2.55930 | 2.57698 | 2.59491 | 2.61313 | 2.63162 | 2.65040 | 2.66947 | 22 |
| 68 | 2.66947 | 2.68884 | 2.70851 | 2.72850 | 2.74881 | 2.76945 | 2.79043 | 21 |
| 69 | 2.79043 | 2.81175 | 2.83342 | 2.85545 | 2.87785 | 2.90063 | 2.92380 | 20 |
| 70 | 2.92380 | 2.94737 | 2.97135 | 2.99574 | 3.02057 | 3.04584 | 3.07155 | 19 |
| 71 | 3.07155 | 3.09774 | 3.12440 | 3.15155 | 3.17920 | 3.20737 | 3.23607 | 18 |
| 72 | 3.23607 | 3.26531 | 3.29512 | 3.32551 | 3.35649 | 3.38808 | 3.42030 | 17 |
| 73 | 3.42030 | 3.45317 | 3.48671 | 3.52094 | 3.55587 | 3.59154 | 3.62796 | 16 |
| 74 | 3.62796 | 3.66515 | 3.70315 | 3.74198 | 3.78166 | 3.82223 | 3.86370 | 15 |
| 75 | 3.86370 | 3.90613 | 3.94952 | 3.99393 | 4.03938 | 4.08591 | 4.13357 | 14 |
| 76 | 4.13357 | 4.18238 | 4.23239 | 4.28366 | 4.33622 | 4.39012 | 4.44541 | 13 |
| 77 | 4.44541 | 4.50216 | 4.56041 | 4.62023 | 4.68167 | 4.74482 | 4.80973 | 12 |
| 78 | 4.80973 | 4.87649 | 4.94517 | 5.01585 | 5.08863 | 5.16359 | 5.24084 | 11 |
| 79 | 5.24084 | 5.32049 | 5.40263 | 5.48740 | 5.57493 | 5.66533 | 5.75877 | 10 |
| 80 | 5.75877 | 5.85539 | 5.95536 | 6.05886 | 6.16607 | 6.27719 | 6.39245 | 9 |
| 81 | 6.39245 | 6.51208 | 6.63633 | 6.76547 | 6.89979 | 7.03962 | 7.18530 | 8 |
| 82 | 7.18530 | 7.33719 | 7.49571 | 7.66130 | 7.83443 | 8.01565 | 8.20551 | 7 |
| 83 | 8.20551 | 8.40466 | 8.61379 | 8.83367 | 9.06515 | 9.30917 | 9.56677 | 6 |
| 84 | 9.56677 | 9.83912 | 10.12752 | 10.43343 | 10.75849 | 11.10455 | 11.47371 | 5 |
| 85 | 11.47371 | 11.86837 | 12.29125 | 12.74550 | 13.23472 | 13.76312 | 14.33559 | 4 |
| 86 | 14.33559 | 14.95788 | 15.63679 | 16.38041 | 17.19843 | 18.10262 | 19.10732 | 3 |
| 87 | 19.10732 | 20.23028 | 21.49368 | 22.92559 | 24.56212 | 26.45051 | 28.65371 | 2 |
| 88 | 28.65371 | 31.25758 | 34.38232 | 38.20155 | 42.97571 | 49.11406 | 57.29869 | 1 |
| 89° | 57.29869 | 68.75736 | 85.94561 | 114.59301 | 171.88831 | 343.77516 | Infinite | 0° |
| | 60′ | 50′ | 40′ | 30′ | 20′ | 10′ | 0′ | ANGLE |

NATURAL COSECANTS

## FUNCTIONS OF NUMBERS

| NO. | SQUARE | CUBE | SQUARE ROOT | CUBE ROOT | LOGARITHM | 1000 x RECIPROCAL | NO. = DIAMETER CIRCUM. | AREA |
|---|---|---|---|---|---|---|---|---|
| 1 | 1 | 1 | 1.0000 | 1.0000 | 0.00000 | 1000.000 | 3.142 | 0.7854 |
| 2 | 4 | 8 | 1.4142 | 1.2599 | 0.30103 | 500.000 | 6.283 | 3.1416 |
| 3 | 9 | 27 | 1.7321 | 1.4422 | 0.47712 | 333.333 | 9.425 | 7.0686 |
| 4 | 16 | 64 | 2.0000 | 1.5874 | 0.60206 | 250.000 | 12.566 | 12.5664 |
| 5 | 25 | 125 | 2.2361 | 1.7100 | 0.69897 | 200.000 | 15.708 | 19.6350 |
| 6 | 36 | 216 | 2.4495 | 1.8171 | 0.77815 | 166.667 | 18.850 | 28.2743 |
| 7 | 49 | 343 | 2.6458 | 1.9129 | 0.84510 | 142.857 | 21.991 | 38.4845 |
| 8 | 64 | 512 | 2.8284 | 2.0000 | 0.90309 | 125.000 | 25.133 | 50.2655 |
| 9 | 81 | 729 | 3.0000 | 2.0801 | 0.95424 | 111.111 | 28.274 | 63.6173 |
| 10 | 100 | 1000 | 3.1623 | 2.1544 | 1.00000 | 100.000 | 31.416 | 78.5398 |
| 11 | 121 | 1331 | 3.3166 | 2.2240 | 1.04139 | 90.9091 | 34.558 | 95.0332 |
| 12 | 144 | 1728 | 3.4641 | 2.2894 | 1.07918 | 83.3333 | 37.699 | 113.097 |
| 13 | 169 | 2197 | 3.6056 | 2.3513 | 1.11394 | 76.9231 | 40.841 | 132.732 |
| 14 | 196 | 2744 | 3.7417 | 2.4101 | 1.14613 | 71.4286 | 43.982 | 153.938 |
| 15 | 225 | 3375 | 3.8730 | 2.4662 | 1.17609 | 66.6667 | 47.124 | 176.715 |
| 16 | 256 | 4096 | 4.0000 | 2.5198 | 1.20412 | 62.5000 | 50.265 | 201.062 |
| 17 | 289 | 4913 | 4.1231 | 2.5713 | 1.23045 | 58.8235 | 53.407 | 226.980 |
| 18 | 324 | 5832 | 4.2426 | 2.6207 | 1.25527 | 55.5556 | 56.549 | 254.469 |
| 19 | 361 | 6859 | 4.3589 | 2.6684 | 1.27875 | 52.6316 | 59.690 | 283.529 |
| 20 | 400 | 8000 | 4.4721 | 2.7144 | 1.30103 | 50.0000 | 62.832 | 314.159 |
| 21 | 441 | 9261 | 4.5826 | 2.7589 | 1.32222 | 47.6190 | 65.973 | 346.361 |
| 22 | 484 | 10648 | 4.6904 | 2.8020 | 1.34242 | 45.4545 | 69.115 | 380.133 |
| 23 | 529 | 12167 | 4.7958 | 2.8439 | 1.36173 | 43.4783 | 72.257 | 415.476 |
| 24 | 576 | 13824 | 4.8990 | 2.8845 | 1.38021 | 41.6667 | 75.398 | 452.389 |
| 25 | 625 | 15625 | 5.0000 | 2.9240 | 1.39794 | 40.0000 | 78.540 | 490.874 |
| 26 | 676 | 17576 | 5.0990 | 2.9625 | 1.41497 | 38.4615 | 81.681 | 530.929 |
| 27 | 729 | 19683 | 5.1962 | 3.0000 | 1.43136 | 37.0370 | 84.823 | 572.555 |
| 28 | 784 | 21952 | 5.2915 | 3.0366 | 1.44716 | 35.7143 | 87.965 | 615.752 |
| 29 | 841 | 24389 | 5.3852 | 3.0723 | 1.46240 | 34.4828 | 91.106 | 660.520 |
| 30 | 900 | 27000 | 5.4772 | 3.1072 | 1.47712 | 33.3333 | 94.248 | 706.858 |
| 31 | 961 | 29791 | 5.5678 | 3.1414 | 1.49136 | 32.2581 | 97.389 | 754.768 |
| 32 | 1024 | 32768 | 5.6569 | 3.1748 | 1.50515 | 31.2500 | 100.531 | 804.248 |
| 33 | 1089 | 35937 | 5.7446 | 3.2075 | 1.51851 | 30.3030 | 103.673 | 855.299 |
| 34 | 1156 | 39304 | 5.8310 | 3.2396 | 1.53148 | 29.4118 | 106.814 | 907.920 |
| 35 | 1225 | 42875 | 5.9161 | 3.2711 | 1.54407 | 28.5714 | 109.956 | 962.113 |
| 36 | 1296 | 46656 | 6.0000 | 3.3019 | 1.55630 | 27.7778 | 113.097 | 1017.88 |
| 37 | 1369 | 50653 | 6.0828 | 3.3322 | 1.56820 | 27.0270 | 116.239 | 1075.21 |
| 38 | 1444 | 54872 | 6.1644 | 3.3620 | 1.57978 | 26.3158 | 119.381 | 1134.11 |
| 39 | 1521 | 59319 | 6.2450 | 3.3912 | 1.59106 | 25.6410 | 122.522 | 1194.59 |
| 40 | 1600 | 64000 | 6.3246 | 3.4200 | 1.60206 | 25.0000 | 125.66 | 1256.64 |
| 41 | 1681 | 68921 | 6.4031 | 3.4482 | 1.61278 | 24.3902 | 128.81 | 1320.25 |
| 42 | 1764 | 74088 | 6.4807 | 3.4760 | 1.62325 | 23.8095 | 131.95 | 1385.44 |
| 43 | 1849 | 79507 | 6.5574 | 3.5034 | 1.63347 | 23.2558 | 135.09 | 1452.20 |
| 44 | 1936 | 85184 | 6.6332 | 3.5303 | 1.64345 | 22.7273 | 138.23 | 1520.53 |
| 45 | 2025 | 91125 | 6.7082 | 3.5569 | 1.65321 | 22.2222 | 141.37 | 1590.43 |

## FUNCTIONS OF NUMBERS

| NO. | SQUARE | CUBE | SQUARE ROOT | CUBE ROOT | LOGARITHM | 1000 x RECIPROCAL | NO. = DIAMETER CIRCUM. | AREA |
|---|---|---|---|---|---|---|---|---|
| 46 | 2116 | 97336 | 6.7823 | 3.5830 | 1.66276 | 21.7391 | 144.51 | 1661.90 |
| 47 | 2209 | 103823 | 6.8557 | 3.6088 | 1.67210 | 21.2766 | 147.65 | 1734.94 |
| 48 | 2304 | 110592 | 6.9282 | 3.6342 | 1.68124 | 20.8333 | 150.80 | 1809.56 |
| 49 | 2401 | 117649 | 7.0000 | 3.6593 | 1.69020 | 20.4082 | 153.94 | 1885.74 |
| 50 | 2500 | 125000 | 7.0711 | 3.6840 | 1.69897 | 20.0000 | 157.08 | 1963.50 |
| 51 | 2601 | 132651 | 7.1414 | 3.7084 | 1.70757 | 19.6078 | 160.22 | 2042.82 |
| 52 | 2704 | 140608 | 7.2111 | 3.7325 | 1.71600 | 19.2308 | 163.36 | 2123.72 |
| 53 | 2809 | 148877 | 7.2801 | 3.7563 | 1.72428 | 18.8679 | 166.50 | 2206.18 |
| 54 | 2916 | 157464 | 7.3485 | 3.7798 | 1.73239 | 18.5185 | 169.65 | 2290.22 |
| 55 | 3025 | 166375 | 7.4162 | 3.8030 | 1.74036 | 18.1818 | 172.79 | 2375.83 |
| 56 | 3136 | 175616 | 7.4833 | 3.8259 | 1.74819 | 17.8571 | 175.93 | 2463.01 |
| 57 | 3249 | 185193 | 7.5498 | 3.8485 | 1.75587 | 17.5439 | 179.07 | 2551.76 |
| 58 | 3364 | 195112 | 7.6158 | 3.8709 | 1.76343 | 17.2414 | 182.21 | 2642.08 |
| 59 | 3481 | 205379 | 7.6811 | 3.8930 | 1.77085 | 16.9492 | 185.35 | 2733.97 |
| 60 | 3600 | 216000 | 7.7460 | 3.9149 | 1.77815 | 16.6667 | 188.50 | 2827.43 |
| 61 | 3721 | 226981 | 7.8102 | 3.9365 | 1.78533 | 16.3934 | 191.64 | 2922.47 |
| 62 | 3844 | 238328 | 7.8740 | 3.9579 | 1.79239 | 16.1290 | 194.78 | 3019.07 |
| 63 | 3969 | 250047 | 7.9373 | 3.9791 | 1.79934 | 15.8730 | 197.92 | 3117.25 |
| 64 | 4096 | 262144 | 8.0000 | 4.0000 | 1.80618 | 15.6250 | 201.06 | 3216.99 |
| 65 | 4225 | 274625 | 8.0623 | 4.0207 | 1.81291 | 15.3846 | 204.20 | 3318.31 |
| 66 | 4356 | 287496 | 8.1240 | 4.0412 | 1.81954 | 15.1515 | 207.35 | 3421.19 |
| 67 | 4489 | 300763 | 8.1854 | 4.0615 | 1.82607 | 14.9254 | 210.49 | 3525.65 |
| 68 | 4624 | 314432 | 8.2462 | 4.0817 | 1.83251 | 14.7059 | 213.63 | 3631.68 |
| 69 | 4761 | 328509 | 8.3066 | 4.1016 | 1.83885 | 14.4928 | 216.77 | 3739.28 |
| 70 | 4900 | 343000 | 8.3666 | 4.1213 | 1.84510 | 14.2857 | 219.91 | 3848.45 |
| 71 | 5041 | 357911 | 8.4261 | 4.1408 | 1.85126 | 14.0845 | 223.05 | 3959.19 |
| 72 | 5184 | 373248 | 8.4853 | 4.1602 | 1.85733 | 13.8889 | 226.19 | 4071.50 |
| 73 | 5329 | 389017 | 8.5440 | 4.1793 | 1.86332 | 13.6986 | 229.34 | 4185.39 |
| 74 | 5476 | 405224 | 8.6023 | 4.1983 | 1.86923 | 13.5135 | 232.48 | 4300.84 |
| 75 | 5625 | 421875 | 8.6603 | 4.2172 | 1.87506 | 13.3333 | 235.62 | 4417.86 |
| 76 | 5776 | 438976 | 8.7178 | 4.2358 | 1.88081 | 13.1579 | 238.76 | 4536.46 |
| 77 | 5929 | 456533 | 8.7750 | 4.2543 | 1.88649 | 12.9870 | 241.90 | 4656.63 |
| 78 | 6084 | 474552 | 8.8318 | 4.2727 | 1.89209 | 12.8205 | 245.04 | 4778.36 |
| 79 | 6241 | 493039 | 8.8882 | 4.2908 | 1.89763 | 12.6582 | 248.19 | 4901.67 |
| 80 | 6400 | 512000 | 8.9443 | 4.3089 | 1.90309 | 12.5000 | 251.33 | 5026.55 |
| 81 | 6561 | 531441 | 9.0000 | 4.3267 | 1.90849 | 12.3457 | 254.47 | 5153.00 |
| 82 | 6724 | 551368 | 9.0554 | 4.3445 | 1.91381 | 12.1951 | 257.61 | 5281.02 |
| 83 | 6889 | 571787 | 9.1104 | 4.3621 | 1.91908 | 12.0482 | 260.75 | 5410.61 |
| 84 | 7056 | 592704 | 9.1652 | 4.3795 | 1.92428 | 11.9048 | 263.89 | 5541.77 |
| 85 | 7225 | 614125 | 9.2195 | 4.3968 | 1.92942 | 11.7647 | 267.04 | 5674.50 |
| 86 | 7396 | 636056 | 9.2736 | 4.4140 | 1.93450 | 11.6279 | 270.18 | 5808.80 |
| 87 | 7569 | 658503 | 9.3274 | 4.4310 | 1.93952 | 11.4943 | 273.32 | 5944.68 |
| 88 | 7744 | 681472 | 9.3808 | 4.4480 | 1.94448 | 11.3636 | 276.46 | 6082.12 |
| 89 | 7921 | 704969 | 9.4340 | 4.4647 | 1.94939 | 11.2360 | 279.60 | 6221.14 |
| 90 | 8100 | 729000 | 9.4868 | 4.4814 | 1.95424 | 11.1111 | 282.74 | 6361.73 |

A MATHEMATICAL DATA

## GENERAL

Solid waste handling and disposal is a basic building service and requires careful planning. Environmental concerns for waste generation, collection, storage, and disposal are essential design considerations. In order to establish the appropriate size and arrangement of waste storage areas and to determine the need for waste handling equipment, it is necessary to estimate the quantity and types of solid waste to be generated at the project site. Consideration must be given to the type of project, building mass and height, the number of occupants, duration of occupancy, and possibilities for special wastes (such as flammable materials, toxic materials, liquids, and bulk items).

## DESIGN REQUIREMENTS

The project design should address the need for special rooms and/or containers within individual building spaces (e.g., offices, apartments, laboratories, work bays); the means for solid waste collection within the various parts of a building, frequency of collection, and method for transporting the material; the possible use of chutes in multistory buildings (and involvement of related fire prevention devices); and the frequency and means for removing refuse from the project site. Design consideration should be given to the types of collection containers, holding bins, possible use of compactors, and size, location, and access requirements for equipment.

## SOLID WASTE ESTIMATING

The following tables provide some basic data regarding solid waste generation to assist in determining approximate quantities and types of solid waste materials generated in various building types and at tourist facilities. Make adjustments for special project types resulting in quantities or types of waste materials that vary from normal conditions. Use of compactors reduces space needs for solid waste storage and may be essential for some projects. Determination of size, type, location, and means for loading and operating (i.e., manual or automatic) should be worked out with the project's management. Use of disinfectants, insecticides, and deodorizing agents should be considered.

## ANNUAL VOLUME OF SOLID WASTE FLOWS, 1981

| | |
|---|---|
| Residential | 110 million tons/year |
| Commercial* | 40 million tons/year |
| Industrial[†] | 50–350 million tons/year |

*Includes apartment houses, offices, hospitals, schools, commercial establishments.
[†]Waste generated by manufacturing—estimates vary because much is disposed of on company property, never showing up as material handled by the waste collection and disposal industry.

## DISPOSITION OF MUNICIPAL SOLID WASTE 1984

| DISPOSAL METHOD | FACILITIES | % DISPOSAL |
|---|---|---|
| *Landfills (Total)*[1] | 10,467 | 90 |
| Publicly owned/operated | 6,595 | — |
| Publicly owned/privately operated | 449 | — |
| Privately owned/operated | 1,360 | — |
| Other (industrial on-site or not specified) | 2,133 | — |
| *Resource Recovery* | | |
| Waste-to-energy incineration | | 4 |
| —Operating | 62 | — |
| —Under construction/ advanced planning | 53 | — |
| —Conceptual[2] | 124 | 6 |
| *Recycling* | N/A | 6 |

[1]Forty-four states surveyed.
[2]Includes projects examined in feasibility studies and for which requests for qualifications (RFQ's) or requests for proposals (RFP's) have been issued.

## DENSITIES OF PURE REFUSE COMPONENTS

| COMPONENT | SPECIFIC GRAVITY | DENSITY (LB./CU. FT.) |
|---|---|---|
| Aluminum | 2.70 | 168 |
| Cardboard | 0.69 | 43 |
| Glass | 2.50 | 156 |
| Paper | 0.7–1.15 | 44–72 |
| Steel | 7.70 | 480 |
| Wood | 0.60 | 37 |
| Plastics | | |
| Acrylic | 1.18 | — |
| ABS | 1.03 | 64 |
| Polyethylene | 0.94 | 59 |
| Polypropylene | 0.90 | 56 |
| Polystyrene | 1.05 | 65 |
| PVC | 1.25 | 78 |

## QUANTITIES OF WASTE GENERATED BY CATEGORY OF TOURISTS

| CATEGORY | GENERATION RATE (LB/VISITOR/DAY) |
|---|---|
| Campers | 5 |
| Motels | 5 |
| Visiting relatives/friends | 3 |
| Renting cottages | 5 |
| Day through trip | 3 |
| Skiers | 8 |
| Vacation home owners | 4 |

## CONVERSION TABLE

| | |
|---|---|
| One cubic yard | = 27 cubic feet or 46.656 cubic inches |
| One gallon | = 231 cubic inches |
| One 20-gallon can | = 0.1 cubic yards |
| One 30-gallon can | = 0.15 cubic yards |
| One 55-gallon can | = 0.27 cubic yards |

## SOLID WASTE GENERATION RATES

| BUILDING TYPE | POUNDS/DAY | APPROXIMATE EQUIVALENT IN LOOSE CUBIC YARDS |
|---|---|---|
| Apartment | 2.5/person | .025 |
| | 4/bedroom | .040 |
| | 8/unit | .080 |
| Cafeteria | 1/meal served | .005 |
| Department store | 75 corrugated/$1000 sales | 1.500 |
| | 15 other waste/$1000 sales | .060 |
| Discount store | 60 other waste/$1000 sales | 1.200 |
| | 10 other waste/$1000 sales | .040 |
| Fast food | 200/$1000 sales | 2.500 |
| Hospital | 16/occupied bed | .100 |
| Hotel | | |
| First class | 3.2/room/ + 2/meal served | .030 + .010 |
| Medium class | 1.7/room + 1.2/meal served | .020 + .006 |
| Manufacturing | | |
| 100–400 employees | 3/person—survey should be made | .020 |
| 400–3000 employees | 7/person—this information for screening only | .047 |
| Motel | 2/room | .020 |
| Nursing and retirement home | 5/person | .030 |
| Office | 1/100 sq ft | .009 |
| Restaurant | 1.5/meal served | .008 |
| School | 0.5/person without cafeteria | .005 |
| | 1/person with cafeteria | .010 |
| Shopping mall | 2.5/100 sq ft | .018 |
| Supermarket | 100 corrugated/$1000 sales | 2.000 |
| | 65 other waste/$1000 sales | .260 |
| Warehouse | 1/100 sq ft | .020 |
| Community wide | | |
| Residential* | 2.5–3.5/person | — |
| Commercial[†] | 0.9–1.6/person | — |

*Solid waste collected by residential collection system only. Usually includes buildings with 1–4 dwelling units.
[†]Generally includes apartments and condominiums of more than 4 units collected under a commercial system.

National Solid Wastes Management Association; Washington, D.C.

## NATIONAL AVERAGE COMPOSITION OF MUNICIPAL SOLID WASTE (PERCENT AS-DISPOSED WEIGHT)*

| MATERIAL | RANGE | AVERAGE |
|---|---|---|
| Paper | 36.6–43.9 | 40 |
| Glass | 8.4–10.3 | 9 |
| Metals | 8.4–10.1 | 9 |
| Plastics | 1.1–4.1 | 2 |
| Rubber and leather | 1.2–2.7 | 2 |
| Textiles | 1.6–2.7 | 2 |
| Wood | 2.5–3.7 | 3 |
| Food waste | 13.3–20.2 | 17 |
| Yard waste | 7.9–17.4 | 13 |
| Miscellaneous inorganics | 1.5–4.5 | 3 |

*Includes residential, commercial, and institutional sources.

## DENSITIES OF MUNICIPAL SOLID WASTES

| MATERIAL | LB/CU YD |
|---|---|
| Loose refuse ("as placed") | 100–200 |
| Refuse from a compactor truck (after dumping) | 350–400 |
| Refuse in a compactor truck | 500–1000 |
| Refuse baled in a paper baler | 800–1200 |
| Refuse in a landfill | 1200–1300 |
| (after degradation and settling) | 1700–1900 |
| Flattened aluminum cans | 250 |
| Flattened ferrous cans | 800–900 |

# WEIGHTS OF MATERIALS  A

| BRICK AND BLOCK MASONRY | PSF |
|---|---|
| 4" brickwork | 40 |
| 4" concrete block, stone or gravel | 34 |
| 4" concrete block, lightweight | 22 |
| 4" concrete brick, stone or gravel | 46 |
| 4" concrete brick, lightweight | 33 |
| 6" concrete block, stone or gravel | 50 |
| 6" concrete block, lightweight | 31 |
| 8" concrete block, stone or gravel | 55 |
| 8" concrete block, lightweight | 35 |
| 12" concrete block, stone or gravel | 85 |
| 12" concrete block, lightweight | 55 |

| CONCRETE | | PCF |
|---|---|---|
| Plain | Cinder | 108 |
| | Expanded slag aggregate | 100 |
| | Expanded clay | 90 |
| | Slag | 132 |
| | Stone and cast stone | 144 |
| Reinforced | Cinder | 111 |
| | Slag | 138 |
| | Stone | 150 |

| FINISH MATERIALS | PSF |
|---|---|
| Acoustical tile unsupported per 1/2" | 0.8 |
| Building board, 1/2" | 0.8 |
| Cement finish, 1" | 12 |
| Fiberboard, 1/2" | 0.75 |
| Gypsum wallboard, 1/2" | 2 |
| Marble and setting bed | 25-30 |
| Plaster, 1/2" | 4.5 |
| Plaster on wood lath | 8 |
| Plaster suspended with lath | 10 |
| Plywood, 1/2" | 1.5 |
| Tile, glazed wall 3/8" | 3 |
| Tile, ceramic mosaic, 1/4" | 2.5 |
| Quarry tile, 1/2" | 5.8 |
| Quarry tile, 3/4" | 8.6 |
| Terrazzo 1", 2" in stone concrete | 25 |
| Vinyl tile, 1/8" | 1.33 |
| Hardwood flooring, 25/32" | 4 |
| Wood block flooring, 3" on mastic | 15 |

| FLOOR AND ROOF (CONCRETE) | | PSF |
|---|---|---|
| Flexicore, 6" precast lightweight concrete | | 30 |
| Flexicore, 6" precast stone concrete | | 40 |
| Plank, cinder concrete, 2" | | 15 |
| Plank, gypsum, 2" | | 12 |
| Concrete, reinforced, 1" | Stone | 12.5 |
| | Slag | 11.5 |
| | Lightweight | 6-10 |
| Concrete, plain, 1" | Stone | 12 |
| | Slag | 11 |
| | Lightweight | 3-9 |

| FUELS AND LIQUIDS | PCF |
|---|---|
| Coal, piled anthracite | 47-58 |
| Coal, piled bituminous | 40-54 |
| Ice | 57.2 |
| Gasoline | 75 |
| Snow | 8 |
| Water, fresh | 62.4 |
| Water, sea | 64 |

| GLASS | PSF |
|---|---|
| Polished plate, 1/4" | 3.28 |
| Polished plate, 1/2" | 6.56 |
| Double strength, 1/8" | 26 oz |
| Sheet A, B, 1/32" | 45 oz |
| Sheet A, B, 1/4" | 52 oz |

| Insulating glass 5/8" plate with airspace | 3.25 |
|---|---|
| 1/4" wire glass | 3.5 |
| Glass block | 18 |

| INSULATION AND WATERPROOFING | PSF |
|---|---|
| Batt, blankets per 1" thickness | 0.1-0.4 |
| Corkboard per 1" thickness | 0.58 |
| Foamed board insulation per 1" thickness | 2.6 oz |
| Five-ply membrane | 5 |
| Rigid insulation | 0.75 |

| LIGHTWEIGHT CONCRETE | PSF |
|---|---|
| Concrete, aerocrete | 50-80 |
| Concrete, cinder fill | 60 |
| Concrete, expanded clay | 85-100 |
| Concrete, expanded shale-sand | 105-120 |
| Concrete, perlite | 35-50 |
| Concrete, pumice | 60-90 |

| METALS | PCF |
|---|---|
| Aluminum, cast | 165 |
| Brass, cast, rolled | 534 |
| Bronze, commercial | 552 |
| Bronze, statuary | 509 |
| Copper, cast or rolled | 556 |
| Gold, cast, solid | 1205 |
| Gold coin in bags | 509 |
| Iron, cast gray, pig | 450 |
| Iron, wrought | 480 |
| Lead | 710 |
| Nickel | 565 |
| Silver, cast, solid | 656 |
| Silver coin in bags | 590 |
| Tin | 459 |
| Stainless steel, rolled | 492-510 |
| Steel, rolled, cold drawn | 490 |
| Zinc, rolled, cast or sheet | 449 |

| MORTAR AND PLASTER | PCF |
|---|---|
| Mortar, masonry | 116 |
| Plaster, gypsum, sand | 104-120 |

| PARTITIONS | PSF |
|---|---|
| 2 x 4 wood stud, GWB, two sides | 8 |
| 4" metal stud, GWB, two sides | 6 |
| 4" concrete block, lightweight, GWB | 26 |
| 6" concrete block, lightweight, GWB | 35 |
| 2" solid plaster | 20 |
| 4" solid plaster | 32 |

| ROOFING MATERIALS | PSF |
|---|---|
| Built up | 6.5 |
| Concrete roof tile | 9.5 |
| Copper | 1.5-2.5 |
| Corrugated iron | 2 |
| Deck, steel without roofing or insulation | 2.2-3.6 |
| Fiberglass panels (2 1/2" corrugated) | 5-8 oz |
| Galvanized iron | 1.2-1.7 |
| Lead, 1/8" | 6-8 |
| Plastic sandwich panel, 2 1/2" thick | 2.6 |
| Shingles, asphalt | 1.7-2.8 |
| Shingles, wood | 2-3 |
| Slate, 3/16" to 1/4" | 7-9.5 |
| Slate, 3/8" to 1/2" | 14-18 |
| Stainless steel | 2.5 |
| Tile, cement flat | 13 |
| Tile, cement ribbed | 16 |
| Tile, clay shingle type | 8-16 |
| Tile, clay flat with setting bed | 15-20 |

| Wood sheathing per inch | 3 |
|---|---|

| SOIL, SAND, AND GRAVEL | PCF |
|---|---|
| Ashes or cinder | 40-50 |
| Clay, damp and plastic | 110 |
| Clay, dry | 63 |
| Clay and gravel, dry | 100 |
| Earth, dry and loose | 76 |
| Earth, dry and packed | 95 |
| Earth, moist and loose | 78 |
| Earth, moist and packed | 96 |
| Earth, mud, packed | 115 |
| Sand or gravel, dry and loose | 90-105 |
| Sand or gravel, dry and packed | 100-120 |
| Sand or gravel, dry and wet | 118-120 |
| Silt, moist, loose | 78 |
| Silt, moist, packed | 96 |

| STONE (ASHLAR) | PCF |
|---|---|
| Granite, limestone, crystalline | 165 |
| Limestone, oolitic | 135 |
| Marble | 173 |
| Sandstone, bluestone | 144 |
| Slate | 172 |

| STONE VENEER | PSF |
|---|---|
| 2" granite, 1/2" parging | 30 |
| 4" granite, 1/2" parging | 59 |
| 6" limestone facing, 1/2" parging | 55 |
| 4" sandstone or bluestone, 1/2" parging | 49 |
| 1" marble | 13 |
| 1" slate | 14 |

| STRUCTURAL CLAY TILE | PSF |
|---|---|
| 4" hollow | 23 |
| 6" hollow | 38 |
| 8" hollow | 45 |

| STRUCTURAL FACING TILE | PSF |
|---|---|
| 2" facing tile | 14 |
| 4" facing tile | 24 |
| 6" facing tile | 34 |
| 8" facing tile | 44 |

| SUSPENDED CEILINGS | PSF |
|---|---|
| Mineral fiber tile 3/4", 12" x 12" | 1.2-1.57 |
| Mineral fiberboard 5/8", 24" x 24" | 1.4 |
| Acoustic plaster on gypsum lath base | 10-11 |

| WOOD | PCF |
|---|---|
| Ash, commercial white | 40.5 |
| Birch, red oak, sweet and yellow | 44 |
| Cedar, northern white | 22.2 |
| Cedar, western red | 24.2 |
| Cypress, southern | 33.5 |
| Douglas fir (coast region) | 32.7 |
| Fir, commercial white; Idaho white pine | 27 |
| Hemlock | 28-29 |
| Maple, hard (black and sugar) | 44.5 |
| Oak, white and red | 47.3 |
| Pine, northern white sugar | 25 |
| Pine, southern yellow | 37.3 |
| Pine, ponderosa, spruce: eastern and sitka | 28.6 |
| Poplar, yellow | 29.4 |
| Redwood | 26 |
| Walnut, black | 38 |

**NOTE**

To establish uniform practice among designers, it is desirable to present a list of materials generally used in building construction, together with their proper weights. Many building codes prescribe the minimum weights of only a few building materials. It should be noted that there is a difference of more than 25% in some cases.

**WEIGHTS OF MATERIALS**

## SI METRIC BACKGROUND DATA

The metric system originated in France as a product of the French Revolution, and gained gradual acceptance in Europe and in the French and Spanish colonies. In 1875 the United States joined 16 other countries in signing the Treaty of the Meter. The work of the General Conference of Weights and Measures resulted in a revised metric system in 1960, named Système International d'Unités (SI). It is this SI metric system that is referenced in the US Metric Act of 1975, and is presented in this chapter.

The Metric Conversion Act, Public Law 94-168, calls for a voluntary conversion process, and established the US Metric Board. In 1972 the American National Metric Council (ANMC) was formed under the sponsorship of the American National Standards Institute (ANSI). Involving more than 300 trade, professional, labor, consumer, and government organizations and more than 400 major corporations, the American National Metric Council has organized the voluntary conversion process. The ANMC Construction Industries Coordinating Committee (CICC) has prepared a conversion plan for adoption by the industry.

ANSI/ASTM Metric Standards are developed under the jurisdiction of ASTM Committee E-6 on Performance of Building Constructions. Subcommittee E 06.62 on Coordination of Dimensions for Building Materials and Systems has responsibility for such ANSI/ASTM Standards as E621-78 "Metric (SI) Units in Building Design and Construction." In addition, the Center for Building Technology of the National Bureau of Standards has published a number of Technical Notes and other special publications concerning metric conversion and dimensional coordination. The American Institute of Architects, with the cooperation of the ANMC, and the Center for Building Technology, has produced the "AIA Metric Building and Construction Guide." This chapter is based on information contained in that publication.

## THE SI SYSTEM

Although the metric (SI) system applies to all measurement related systems, this chapter concerns the application of the SI System to construction. Concepts of dimensional coordination, although not restricted to the metric system, are seen as an essential part of a smooth transition of the construction industry to the use of the metric (SI) system.

## MATERIALS AND COMPONENTS FOR METRIC BUILDING IN THE TRANSITIONAL PERIOD—SUGGESTED ADAPTATION IN DESIGN AND CONSTRUCTION FOR VARIOUS PRODUCT CATEGORIES*

| CATEGORY | COMPLEXITY OF ADAPTATION | TYPICAL EXAMPLES OF MATERIALS AND COMPONENTS | ADAPTIVE ACTION IN DESIGN | ADAPTIVE ACTION IN CONSTRUCTION |
|---|---|---|---|---|
| **A. DIMENSIONAL COORDINATION NOT REQUIRED** | | | | |
| A.1 | No change in materials—no problems foreseen | Formless or plastic materials: water, paint, mastics, tar; sand, cement, lime, dry mortar mix, loose-fill insulation; ready-mixed concrete, pre-mixed masonry mortar | Specify in metric units. Develop necessary site guidelines | Weigh or measure in metric quantities. Use metric data on coverage, mix ratios, etc. |
| A.2 | Customary sizes usable—interim "soft conversion" | Structural steel sections, reinforcing bars, pipes, tubes, hardware, fixtures, fittings | Specify metric equivalents or show permissible substitutions. Select preferred "free" dimensions such as length or center-lines | Order or cut to metric length; set out to coordinated center-lines |
| **B. MINOR SITE ADJUSTMENTS TO COORDINATE WITH PREFERRED DIMENSIONS** | | | | |
| B.1 | Modification in one direction to fit in with preferred dimensions | a. Adjustment by trimming: lumber studs and joists, laminates, roofing, gutters<br>b. Adjustment by lapping: shingles, tar felt, underlay, sheathing, waterproof membranes<br>c. Adjustment by change in joint width: bricks, blocks, ceramic tiles | Specify preferred metric dimensions to expedite the transition. Indicate construction adjustments in drawings or instructions | Set out project in preferred building dimensions and adjust products accordingly |
| **C. DIMENSIONAL COORDINATION REQUIRED** | | | | |
| C.1 | Purpose-made items—no difficulties foreseen | Precast panels and slabs, door assemblies, window assemblies, fabricated metalwork, built-in units | Specify rationalized metric sizes | Order or fabricate components in rationalized metric sizes |
| C.2 | Reshaping of customary dimensions possible | Glazing, plywood, gypsum wallboard, sheathing, lath, rigid insulation materials | Investigate supply in rationalized metric sizes and specify | Order rationalized metric sizes. Cut off site or on site |
| C.3 | Reshaping of customary dimensions difficult, costly, or impossible | Windows, doors, metal partitions, metal roof decking, fluorescent fixture, metal cladding panels, stainless steel sections and sinks, large ceramic panels, distribution boards and panels, fixed appliances and cabinets, lockers | Preorder preferred sizes before job commencement. Discuss trial batches with manufacturers. Use adaptive design and detailing | Adapt during the interim period until preferred metric sizes emerge. Construct suitable openings or spaces for non-coordinated components and assemblies |

*The list may be expanded or modified to suit particular market conditions.

## LINEAR MEASURE—EQUIVALENTS

| MILLIMETERS | CENTIMETERS | DECIMETERS | METERS | DECAMETERS | HECTOMETERS | KILOMETERS | YARDS |
|---|---|---|---|---|---|---|---|
| 1 | 0.1 | 0.01 | 0.001 | 0.0001 | 0.00001 | 0.000001 | |
| 10 | 1 | 0.1 | 0.01 | 0.001 | 0.0001 | 0.00001 | |
| 100 | 10 | 1 | 0.1 | 0.01 | 0.001 | 0.0001 | |
| 1,000 | 100 | 10 | 1 | 0.1 | 0.01 | 0.001 | 1.0936 |
| 10,000 | 1,000 | 100 | 10 | 1 | 0.1 | 0.01 | |
| 100,000 | 10,000 | 1,000 | 100 | 10 | 1 | 0.1 | |
| 1,000,000 | 100,000 | 10,000 | 1,000 | 100 | 10 | 1 | |
| | | | .9144 | | | | 1 |

## AREA MEASURE—EQUIVALENTS

| SQUARE MILLIMETERS | SQUARE CENTIMETERS | SQUARE DECIMETERS | SQUARE METERS | ARES | HECTARES | SQUARE KILOMETERS | ACRES |
|---|---|---|---|---|---|---|---|
| 1 | 0.01 | 0.0001 | 0.000001 | | | | |
| 100 | 1 | 0.01 | 0.0001 | 0.000001 | | | |
| 10,000 | 100 | 1 | 0.01 | 0.0001 | 0.000001 | | |
| 1,000,000 | 10,000 | 100 | 1 | 0.01 | 0.0001 | 0.000001 | |
| | 1,000,000 | 10,000 | 100 | 1 | 0.01 | 0.0001 | |
| | | 1,000,000 | 10,000 | 100 | 1 | 0.01 | 2.471 |
| | | | 1,000,000 | 10,000 | 100 | 1 | 247.1 |
| | | | | 40.47 | .4047 | | 1 |

METRIC

# SI UNITS AND RULES FOR USE

Specific rules for use, type style, and punctuation have been established by the General Conference on Weights and Measures (CGPM); the National Bureau of Standards (NBS) is responsible for determining preferred usage in the United States.

Standard, lowercase type is used for unit names and symbols, except when the symbols are derived from proper names, such as newton (N) or pascal (Pa). There is one exception to this in the use of the capital letter L as the symbol for liter. This is because the lowercase "l" was thought by the U.S. Department of Commerce to be easily confused with the numeral "1." Symbols are not followed by a period or a full stop, except at the end of a sentence. The symbols for all quantities, such as length, mass, and time, are printed in italic ($l$, $k$, $s$, . . . ). In typewriting and longhand, underlining is an acceptable substitute for italic letters. Unit names are used in the plural to express numerical values greater than 1, equal to 0, or less than −1. All other values take the singular form of the unit name, thus 100 meters, 1.1 meters, 0 degrees Celsius, −4 degrees Celsius, 0.5 meter, 1/2 liter, −0.2 degree Celsius, −1 degree Celsius. The plural of unit names is formed by adding an "s." Exceptions are hertz, lux, and siemens, which remain unchanged, and henry, which becomes henries. Symbols are the same in both singular and plural.

Prefixes denoting decimal multiples and submultiples (allowing SI units to express magnitudes from the subatomic to the astronomic) are governed by the same rules concerning capitalization and punctuation.

It is important to note that mega, giga, and tera (M, G, T) are capitalized in symbol form to avoid confusion with established unit symbols, but they maintain the lowercase form when spelled out in full. No space is left between the prefix and the letter for the unit name, thus mL (milliliter), mm (millimeter), kA (kiloampere).

Preference is given to the use of decimal multiples that are related to the basic units by multiples of 1000. As far as possible, prefixes denoting magnitudes of 100, 10, 0.1, and 0.01 should be limited. Certain multiples of SI units, not likely to be extensively used, have been given special names (Table 4).

The prefix symbol is considered to be part of the unit symbol and is attached to it without a space or dot, thus km not k m, k-m, or k.m.

A space is left between a numeral and the unit name or symbol to which it refers, thus 20 mm, $10^6$ N. In angle measure no space is left between the numeral and the degree symbol, thus 27°. The symbol for degree Celsius °C is an inseparable symbol with no space between the two parts; it is also preferable to leave no space between the numeral and the unit, thus 20°C.

When a quantity is used as an adjective, it is preferable to use a hyphen instead of a space between the number and the unit name or between the number and the symbol; thus a 3-meter pole, a 35-mm film.

In the United States and Canada, the decimal point is a dot on the line, but in some other countries a comma or a raised dot is used.

Decimal notation is preferred with metric measurements, but simple fractions are acceptable (except on engineering drawings), such as those where the denominator is 2, 3, 4, 5, 8, and 10.

**Examples:** 0.5 g, 1.75 kg, and 0.7 L are preferred; 1/2 g, 1 3/4 kg, and 7/10 L are acceptable (except on engineering drawings).

A zero before the decimal point should be used in numbers between 1 and −1 to prevent the possibility that a faint decimal point will be overlooked.

**Example:** The oral expression "point seven five" is written 0.75.

Since the comma is used as the decimal marker in many countries, a comma should not be used to separate groups of digits. Instead, the digits should be separated into groups of three, counting both to the left and to the right from the decimal point, and a space used to separate the groups of three digits. The space should be of fixed width, equal to that formerly occupied by the comma.

**Examples:** 4 720 525     0. 528 75

If there are only four digits to the left or right of the decimal point, the space is acceptable but is not preferred.

**Examples:** 6875 or 6 875
0.1234 or 0.123 4

However, in a column with other numbers that show the space and are aligned on the decimal point, the space is necessary.

**Example:**
```
        14.8
     3 780
  +12 100
   15 894.8
```

Compound units are those formed by combining simple units by means of the mathematical signs for multiplication and division and by the use of exponents.

When writing symbols for units such as square centimeter or cubic meter, the symbol for the unit should be written followed by the superscript 2 or 3, respectively, thus 26 $cm^2$ and 14 $m^3$.

For a compound unit that is a quotient, "per" should be used to form the name (kilometer per hour) and a slash (/) to form the symbol (km/h). There is no space before or after the slash. Compound units that are quotients may also be written by using negative exponents ($km \cdot h^{-1}$).

For everyday rounding of metric values obtained by converting untoleranced customary values, the following simplified rules are suggested:

1. If the customary value is expressed by a combination of units such as feet and inches, or pounds and ounces, first express it in terms of the smaller unit.
   **Example:** 14 ft 5 in. = 173 in.
2. When the digits to be discarded begin with a 5 or more, increase by one unit the last digit retained.
   **Example:** 8.3745, if rounded to three digits, would be 8.37; if rounded to four digits, be 8.375.
3. Multiply the customary value by the conversion factor. If the first significant digit of the metric value is equal to or larger than the first significant digit of the customary value, round the metric value to the same number of significant digits as there are in the customary value.
   **Examples:** 11 mi x 1.609 km/mi = 17.699 km, which rounds to 18 km

   61 mi x 1.609 km/mi = 98.149 km, which rounds to 98 km
4. If smaller, round to one more significant digit.
   **Examples:** 66 mi x 1.609 km/mi = 106.194 km, which rounds to 106 km

   8 ft x 0.3048 m/ft = 2.4384 m, which rounds to 2.4 m
   **Exceptions:** It is sometimes better to round to one less digit than specified above. For example, according to the foregoing, 26 pounds per square inch air pressure in an automobile tire would be converted as follows:

   26 psi* x 6.895 kPa/psi = 179.27 kPa

   which rounds to 179 kPa

   but kPa, where the zero is not a significant digit, would usually be better because tire pressures are not expected to be very precise. The rules do not apply to conversion of °F to °C.
5. Where a customary value represents a maximum or minimum limit that must be respected, the rounding must be in the direction that does not violate the original limit.

## TABLE 1. SI BASE UNITS

| PHYSICAL QUANTITY | UNIT | SYMBOL |
|---|---|---|
| Length | Meter | m |
| Mass | Kilogram | k |
| Time | Second | s |
| Electric current | Ampere | A |
| Thermodynamic temperature | Kelvin | K |
| Luminous intensity | Candela | cd |
| Amount of substance | Mole | mol |

## TABLE 2. SI SUPPLEMENTARY UNITS

| PHYSICAL QUANTITY | UNIT | SYMBOL |
|---|---|---|
| Plane angle | Radian | rad |
| Solid angle | Steradian | sr |

## TABLE 3. DERIVED UNITS WITH COMPOUND NAMES

| PHYSICAL QUANTITY | UNIT | SYMBOL |
|---|---|---|
| Area | Square meter | $m^2$ |
| Volume | Cubic meter | $m^3$ |
| Density | Kilogram per cubic meter | $kg/m^3$ |
| Velocity | Meter per second | m/s |
| Angular velocity | Radian per second | rad/s |
| Acceleration | Meter per second squared | $m/s^2$ |
| Angular acceleration | Radian per second squared | $rad/s^2$ |
| Volume rate of flow | Cubic meter per second | $m^3/s$ |
| Moment of inertia | Kilogram meter squared | $kg \cdot m^2$ |
| Moment of force | Newton meter | $N \cdot m$ |
| Intensity of heat flow | Watt per square meter | $W/m^2$ |
| Thermal conductivity | Watt per meter Kelvin | $W/m \cdot K$ |
| Luminance | Candela per square meter | $cd/m^2$ |

## TABLE 4. MULTIPLES OF SI UNITS WITH SPECIAL NAMES

| PHYSICAL QUANTITY | NAME | SYMBOL | MAGNITUDE |
|---|---|---|---|
| Volume | Liter | L | $10^{-3}$ $m^3$ = 0.0001 $m^3$ |
| Mass | Megagram (metric ton) | Mg(t) | $10^3$ kg = 1000 kg |
| Area | Hectare | ha | $10^4$ $m^2$ = 10 000 $m^2$ |
| Pressure | Millibar* | mbar* | $10^2$ Pa = 100 Pa |

*Used for meteorological purposes only.

METRIC

## MEASUREMENT OF LENGTH

The basic SI unit of length is the meter. Fractions or multiples of the base unit are expressed with prefixes, only some of which are recommended for construction. In order to be clear, avoid those prefixes that are not specifically recommended for construction.

Common SI units for length as used in construction are:

| UNIT NAME | SYMBOL | COMMENT | COMPUTER SYMBOL |
|---|---|---|---|
| Meter | m | Also spelled metre | M |
| Millimeter | mm | 0.001 meter | MM |
| Kilometer | km | 1000 meters | KM |
| Micrometer | um | 0.000 001 meter | UM |

Note: Centimeter is not recommended for construction.

The recommended unit for dimensioning buildings is the millimeter. The use of the meter would be limited to large dimensions, such as levels, overall dimensions, and engineering computations. Meters are also used for estimating and land surveying. On architectural drawings, dimensions require no symbol if millimeters are consistently used.

Kilometers are used for transportation and surveying. Micrometers would be used for thicknesses of materials, such as coatings.

Conversion factors for length are shown below:

| METRIC | CUSTOMARY |
|---|---|
| 1 meter | 3.280 84 feet or 1.093 61 yards |
| 1 millimeter | 0.039 370 1 inch |
| 1 kilometer | 0.621 371 mile or 49.709 6 chains |
| 1 micrometer | 0.000 393 7 inch or 0.3937 mils |

| CUSTOMARY | METRIC |
|---|---|
| 1 mile | 1.609 344 km |
| 1 chain | 20.1168 m |
| 1 yard | 0.9144 m |
| 1 foot | 0.3048 m / 304.8 mm |
| 1 inch | 25.4 mm |

(1 U.S. survey foot = 0.304 800 6 m.)

The recommended linear basic module for construction is 100 mm in the United States. See page on dimensional coordination for application of this basic module. This is very close to the 4 in. module in general use for light construction. Scales of drawing relate to units of length. Use meters on all drawings with scale ratios between 1:200 and 1:2000. Use millimeters on drawings with scale ratios between 1:1 and 1:200.

## MEASUREMENT OF AREA

There are no basic SI metric units for area. Rather, area units are derived from units for length, as follows:

| UNIT NAME | SYMBOL | COMMENT |
|---|---|---|
| Square meter | m² | 1 m² = 10⁶ mm² |
| Square millimeter | mm² | |
| Square kilometer | km² | Land area |
| Hectare | ha | 1 ha = 10 000 m² |

Note that the hectare, although not an SI unit, is acceptable as a supplemental unit. It is used for surface measurement of land and water only.

At times, area is expressed by linear dimensions such as 40 mm x 90 mm; 300 x 600. Normally the width is written first and depth or height second.

The square centimeter is not recommended for construction. Such measurements may be converted to millimeters (1 cm² = 100 mm²) or to meters (1 cm² = 10⁻⁴ m² = 0.0001 m²).

Conversion factors for area are shown below.

| METRIC | CUSTOMARY |
|---|---|
| 1 km² | 0.386 101 mile² (U.S. Survey) |
| 1 ha | 2.471 04 acre (U.S. Survey) |
| 1 m² | 10.7639 ft² / 1.195 99 yd² |
| 1 mm² | 0.001 550 in.² |

| CUSTOMARY | METRIC |
|---|---|
| 1 mile² (U.S. Survey) | 2.590 00 km² |
| 1 acre (U.S. Survey) | 0.404 687 ha / 4046.87 m² |
| 1 yd² | 0.836 127 m² |
| 1 ft² | 0.092 903 m² |
| 1 in.² | 645.16 mm² |

## MEASUREMENT OF VOLUME AND SECTION MODULUS

There are no basic SI metric units for volume, but these are derived from units for length as well as non-SI units that are acceptable for use.

| UNIT NAME | SYMBOL | COMMENT |
|---|---|---|
| Cubic meter | m³ | 1 m³ = 1000 L |
| Cubic millimeter | mm³ | |
| Liter | L | Volume of fluids |
| Milliliter | mL | 1 mL = 1 cm³ |
| Cubic centimeter | cm³ | 1 cm³ = 1000 mm³ |

In construction, the cubic meter is used for volume and capacity of large quantities of earth, concrete, sand, and so on. It is preferred for all engineering purposes.

The section modulus is also expressed as unit of length to the third power (m³ and mm³).

Conversion factors are listed below.

## VOLUME, MODULUS OF SECTION

| METRIC | CUSTOMARY |
|---|---|
| 1 m³ | 0.810 709 x 10³ acre ft / 1.307 95 yd³ / 35.3147 ft³ / 423.776 board ft |
| 1 mm³ | 61.0237 x 10⁻⁶ in.³ |

| CUSTOMARY | METRIC |
|---|---|
| 1 acre ft | 1233.49 m³ |
| 1 yd³ | 0.764 555 m³ |
| 100 board ft | 0.028 316 8 m³ |
| 1 ft³ | 16.387 1 mm³ / 28 3168 1 (cm³) |
| 1 in.³ | 16.3871 mL(cm³) |

## LIQUID, CAPACITY

| METRIC | CUSTOMARY |
|---|---|
| 1 L | 0.035 3147 ft³ / 0.264 172 gal (U.S.) / 1.056 69 qt (U.S.) |
| 1 mL | 0.061 023 7 in.³ |

| CUSTOMARY | METRIC |
|---|---|
| 1 gal (U.S. liquid) | 3.785 41 L |
| 1 qt (U.S. liquid) | 946.353 mL |
| 1 pt (U.S. liquid) | 473.177 mL |
| 1 fl oz (U.S.) | 29.5735 mL |

NOTE: 1 gal (U.K.) = approximately 1.2 gal (U.S.).

## MEASUREMENT OF MASS

The SI metric system recommends the use of the word mass in place of the more common word weight, because weight refers specifically to the pull of gravity, which can vary in different locations. The SI system also separates the concept of mass from that of force.

SI metric units and other acceptable units for mass are:

| UNIT NAME | SYMBOL | COMMENT |
|---|---|---|
| Kilogram | kg | Most used |
| Gram | g | |
| Metric ton | t | 1 t = 1000 kg |

The kilogram is based on a prototype, and unlike other SI units cannot be derived without reference to the international prototype kilogram maintained under specified conditions at the International Bureau of Weights and Measures (BIPM) near Paris, France.

Conversion factors are listed below.

| METRIC | CUSTOMARY |
|---|---|
| 1 kg | 2.204 62 lb (avoirdupois) / 35.2740 02 oz (avoirdupois) |
| 1 metric ton | 1.102 31 ton (short, 2000 lb) / 2204.62 lb |
| 1 g | 0.035 274 oz / 0.643 015 pennyweight |

| CUSTOMARY | METRIC |
|---|---|
| 1 ton (short) | 0.907 185 metric ton (megagram) / 907.185 kg |
| 1 lb | 0.453 592 kg |
| 1 oz | 28.3495 9 g |
| 1 pennyweight | 1.555 17 g |

NOTE: A long ton (2240 lb) = 1016.05 kg or 1.016 05 metric ton.

## TIME

The SI unit for time is the second, from which other units of time are derived. In construction measurements, such as flow rates, the use of minutes is not recommended, so that cubic meters per second, liters per second, or cubic meters per hour would be normally used. Time symbols are as follows:

| Second | s |
|---|---|
| Minute | min |
| Hour | h |
| Day | d |
| Month | — |
| Year | a (365 days or 31 536 000 seconds) |

For clarity, international recommendations for writing time and dates are as follows:

| Time | Express by hour/minute/second on a 24 hour day: |
|---|---|
| | 03:20:30 |
| | 16:45 |
| Dates | Express by year/month/day: |
| | 1978-06-30 |
| | 1978 06 30 (second preference) |
| | 19780630 (computer entry) |

## MEASUREMENT OF TEMPERATURE

The SI base unit of temperature is the Kelvin, which is a scale based on absolute zero. The allowable unit Celsius is equal to the Kelvin unit except that 0° Celsius is the freezing point of water. Thus a temperature listed in degrees Celsius plus 275.15 degrees is the temperature in degrees Kelvin. Celsius is in common use for construction, not Kelvin.

| CUSTOMARY | METRIC |
|---|---|
| 1°F | 0.555 556°C / ⁵/₉° C or ⁵/₉ K |

| METRIC | CUSTOMARY |
|---|---|
| 1°C | 1 K / 1.8°F |

NOTE: Centigrade is not recognized as part of the SI system.

## PLANE ANGLE

While the SI unit for plane angle is the radian, the customary units degree (°), minute ('), and second (") of arc will be retained in most applications in construction, engineering, and land surveying.

| CUSTOMARY | METRIC |
|---|---|
| 1° | (π/180) rad |

METRIC

## ENERGY RELATIONSHIP

SI metric units provide a direct, coherent relationship between mechanical, thermal, and electrical energy.

The ampere (A) (SI base unit) is that constant current which, if maintained in two straight, parallel conductors of infinite length and of negligible cross section, placed 1 meter apart in a vacuum, would produce between these conductors a force equal to $2 \times 10^{-7}$ newton per meter of length.

One newton (N) is that force which gives to a mass of 1 kilogram (kg) an acceleration of 1 meter per second squared ($m/s^2$). Hence $1.0 \text{ N} = 1.0 \text{ kg} \cdot m/s^2$.

One joule (J) is the work done when the point of application of a force of 1 newton moves a distance of 1 meter along the line of action of the force. Hence $1.0 \text{ J} = 1.0 \text{ N} \cdot m$.

A watt (W) is the power which in 1 second gives rise to the energy of 1 joule. Conversely, a joule is a watt-second.

Since the customary coherent relationships with other electrical quantities will still prevail, the observations made above in respect to work, energy, quantity of heat, and power may be summarized, from a "units" point of view as follows:

$$N \cdot m = J \quad J/s = W \quad J = W \cdot s \quad W = A \cdot V \quad J = A \cdot V \cdot s$$

## MASS

The preferred unit multiples of mass are milligram, gram, kilogram, and megagram (or metric ton), which are written respectively as:

$$mg \quad g \quad kg \quad Mg \quad (or \ t)$$

Weight is predominantly a concept of the customary "gravitational" (kg) an acceleration of 1 meter per second dealing with mass and with the forces related to the acceleration of a mass, there is no special name for a unit of weight in SI.

Weight is a particular force due solely to gravitational attraction on a mass.

## FORCE

Since SI is a coherent system and since the fundamental law of physics (F $\alpha$ ma) states that force is dependent solely on mass and on acceleration,

1.0 kg accelerated at 1.0 $m/s^2$

$$\longrightarrow 1.0 \text{ force unit}$$
$$\longrightarrow 1.0 \text{ newton } (1.0 \text{ N})$$

The use of the name "newton" for the unit of force should fix in the mind the full significance of the distinctions between mass and force.

Normally a mass to be supported or moved will be specified or labeled in terms of kilograms (kg), but all forces acting on structure, either gravitationally or laterally (including wind, sway, and impact), should be specified or determined ultimately in terms of newtons (N).

Based on customary gravitational usage:

Mass: 1.0 slug    32.17 lb    14.59 kg
          1.488 kgf/(m/s²)

Force: 1.0 lbf    32.17 pdl    4.448 N
          0.4536 kgf

Based on SI usage:

Mass: 1.0 kg    2.205 lb    0.068 52 slug
          0.1020 kgf/(m/s²)

Force: 1.0 N    7.233 pdl    0.2248 lbf
          0.1020 kgf

The force definitions are as follows:

The "newton" is the force required to accelerate 1 kilogram mass at the rate of 1.0 $m/s^2$.

The "poundal" is the force required to accelerate 1 pound of mass at the rate of 1.0 $ft/s^2$.

The "pound force" is the force required to accelerate 1 pound of mass at the rate of 32.1740 $ft/s^2$.

The related definitions for the derived mass units are:

The "slug" is that mass which, when acted upon by 1 pound-force, will be accelerated at the rate of 1.0 $ft/s^2$.

The gravitational metric unit of mass is that unit of mass which, when acted upon by 1 kilogram-force, will be accelerated at 1.0 $m/s^2$. There seems to be no generally accepted name or symbol for this gravitational unit of mass, except the inference to the kilogram.

The "kilogram" and the "pound" are base units, not derived units as are the slug and the gravitational metric unit of mass. The kilogram and the pound relate directly to an artifact of mass which, by convention, is regarded as dimensionally independent—thus the name "base unit."

## DERIVED UNITS WITH SPECIAL NAMES

| PHYSICAL QUANTITY | UNIT | SYMBOL | DERIVATION |
|---|---|---|---|
| Frequency | Hertz | Hz | $s^{-1}$ |
| Force | Newton | N | $kg \cdot m/s^2$ |
| Pressure, stress | Pascal | Pa | $N/m^2$ |
| Work, energy, quantity of heat | Joule | J | $N \cdot m$ |
| Power | Watt | W | J/s |
| Electric charge | Coulomb | C | $A \cdot s$ |
| Electric potential | Volt | V | W/A |
| Electric capacitance | Farad | F | C/V |
| Electric resistance | Ohm | O | V/A |
| Electric conductance | Siemens | S | $\Omega^{-1}$ |
| Magnetic flux | Weber | Wb | $V \cdot s$ |
| Magnetic flux density | Tesla | T | $Wb/m^2$ |
| Inductance | Henry | H | Wb/A |
| Celsius temperature | Degree Celsius | °C | K |
| Luminous flux | Lumen | lm | $cd \cdot sr$ |
| Illumination | Lux | lx | $lm/m^2$ |
| Activity | Becquerel | Bq | $s^{-1}$ |
| Absorbed dose | Gray | Gy | J/kg |

## COMPARISON OF UNIT SYSTEMS

| QUANTITY | MASS LENGTH, TIME (ABSOLUTE) | | FORCE, LENGTH, TIME (GRAVITATIONAL) | | CUSTOMARY COMBINED SYSTEM |
|---|---|---|---|---|---|
| | SI | ENGLISH | METRIC | ENGLISH | |
| Mass | kg | lb | kgf/(m/s²) | lbf/(ft/s²) (slug) | lb (alt: lbm) |
| Force | kg m/s² N (newton) | lb ft/s² 1 dp (poundal) | kgf (alt:kp) | lbf | lbf |
| Coherence factor | 1.0 | 1.0 | 1.0 | 1.0 | 1/32.17 |

## COMPARATIVE ANALYSIS OF SOME APPROXIMATE PHYSICAL PROPERTIES[a] FOR REPRESENTATIVE ENGINEERING MATERIALS

| COEFFICIENT OF LINEAR EXPANSION $\alpha$ ($10^6$ IN./IN °F) | ALLOWABLE STRESSES (LBF/IN.² x 10³) | | | ELASTIC MODULUS (LBF/IN.² x 10⁶) | | WEIGHT DENSITY W (LB/FT³) | MATERIAL | MASS DENSITY $\rho$ (KG/M³) | ELASTIC MODULUS (GPA = GN/M²) | | ALLOWABLE STRESSES (MPA = MN/M²) | | | COEFFICIENT OF LINEAR EXPANSION $\alpha \, \mu M/(M \cdot K)$ |
|---|---|---|---|---|---|---|---|---|---|---|---|---|---|---|
| | $\sigma_f^b$ | $\sigma_c^c$ | $\tau_s$ | E | G | | | | E | G | $\sigma_f^b$ | $\sigma_c^c$ | $\tau_s$ | |
| 6.5 | 20 | 20 | 10 | 30 | 12 | 490 | Mild steel | 7850 | 200 | 80 | 140 | 140 | 70 | 11.7 |
| 6.9 | 24 | 24 | 15 | 30 | 12 | 490 | High-strength steel | 7850 | 200 | 80 | 165 | 165 | 100 | 12.4 |
| 6.0 | 3 | 10 | 2 | 15 | 6 | 450 | Cast iron | 7200 | 100 | 40 | 20 | 70 | 15 | 10.8 |
| 9.3 | 8 | 8 | 5 | 17 | 6.4 | 560 | Copper | 8960 | 120 | 45 | 55 | 55 | 35 | 16.7 |
| 10.4 | 12 | 8 | 6 | 13 | 5 | 520 | Brass | 8300 | 90 | 35 | 80 | 55 | 40 | 18.7 |
| 13.0 | 16 | 15 | 8 | 10.3 | 4 | 170 | Aluminum | 2700 | 70 | 27 | 110 | 100 | 55 | 23.4 |
| | | | | | | | Timber | | | | | | | |
| 1.7 | 1.3 | 0.8 | 0.05 | 1.2 | — | 27 | Softwood | 430 | 9 | — | 9.6 | 5.5 | 0.3 | 3.1 |
| 2.5 | 1.8 | 1.2 | 0.10 | 1.6 | — | 48 | Hardwood | 770 | 12 | — | 12.4 | 8.3 | 0.7 | 4.5 |
| 6.2 | 1.2 | 1.0 | 0.15 | 2.5 | — | 150 | Concrete (reinf.) | 2400 | 17 | — | 8.3 | 6.9 | 1.0 | 11.2 |
| — | — | 0.03 | — | — | — | 105 | Soil | 1680 | — | — | — | 0.2 | — | — |
| 4.4 | — | 0.3 | — | — | — | 165 | Rock | 2640 | — | — | — | 2.0 | — | 7.9 |
| | — | — | — | — | — | 62.4 | Water | 1000 | — | — | — | — | — | |

NOTE: Values given are rounded in each system and are not direct conversions.
[a] For use only for comparing representative values in the respective unit systems; not intended for design. For design purposes see other standard references such as ANSI, AISC, ACI, and IFI.
[b] Extreme fiber bending.
[c] Short compression block; in timber, parallel to grain.

METRIC

## UNITS FOR USE IN HEAT TRANSFER CALCULATIONS

| QUANTITY NAME | SI UNIT | UNIT NAME | CONVERSION FACTOR | |
|---|---|---|---|---|
| Energy, quantity of heat (E, Q) | J(W · s) | joule | 1 Btu (int.) | = 1.055 056 kJ |
| | | | 1 kWh | = 3.6 MJ |
| | | | 1 therm | = 105.5056 MJ |
| Heat flow rate (P, q) | W(J/s) | watt | 1 Btu/h | = 0.293 071 W |
| | | | 1 Btu/s | = 1.055 056 kW |
| | | | 1 ton (refrig.) | = 3.516 800 kW |
| Specific energy, calorific value (mass basis) | J/kg | joule per kilogram | 1 Btu/lb | = 2.326 kJ/kg |
| Irradiation, intensity of heat flow, heat loss from surfaces | W/m² | watt per square meter | 1 Btu/ft² · h | = 3.152 481 W/m² |
| | | | 1 W/ft² | = 10.763 91 W/m² |
| | | | 1 Btu/ft² · s | = 11.348 93 kW/m² |
| Specific heat capacity (mass basis) | J/(kg · K) | joule per kilogram kelvin | 1 Btu/lb · °F | = 4.1868 kJ/(kg · K) |
| Thermal conductivity (k-value) | W/(m · K) | watt per meter kelvin | 1 Btu · in/h · ft² · °F | = 0.144 228 W/(m · K) |
| | | | 1 Btu · in/s · ft² · °F | = 519.2204 W/(m · K) |
| | | | 1 Btu/h · ft · °F | = 1.730 73 W/(m · K) |
| Thermal conductance, coefficient of heat transfer (c, U-value) | W/(m² · K) | watt per square meter kelvin | 1 Btu/h · ft² · °F | = 5.678 26 W/(m² · K) |
| Thermal resistance, thermal insulance (R) | m² · K/W | square meter kelvin per watt | 1 °F · h · ft²/Btu | = 0.176 110 m² · K/W |

## HEAT TRANSFER IN BUILDINGS

Heat transfer calculations, involving heat loss, heat gain, or thermal insulating properties of materials, will be simplified in SI because of the coherent relationships between units used. Heat transfer units are generally derived from the unit for temperature (kelvin or degree Celsius), the unit for energy and quantity of heat (joule), the unit for heat transfer rate (watt), and the units for time (second), length (meter), areas (square meter), and mass (kilogram).

## TEMPERATURE

The Celsius temperature scale, for which the zero reference is the freezing point of water, will also be used for ambient temperatures.

## TIME

Use of the hour (h), as in 5 km/h, and the day (d), as in m³/d, will occur in special cases, but the use of the minute (min) will be deemphasized in favor of the second (s).

## HEATING DEGREE-DAYS

For heating design purposes and the determination of suitable insulation, the concept of heating degree-days, founded on a base temperature of 65°F (18.33°C), will possibly be revised to use a base temperature of 18°C (64.4°F).

In heat transfer through a composite element, such as a building wall, a sequence of conduction and convection coefficients may be involved. As in other "series type" problems the approach to determining the combined or "overall" coefficient U is based on the sum of the resistances, which is the sum of the reciprocals of the conductances in the path of the heat transfer.

The following definitions can be used to identify the coefficients:

K = thermal conductance;

$$K = \frac{kA}{L} \cdot \frac{W}{m \cdot K} \times \frac{m^2}{m} = W/K$$

R = thermal resistance;

$$R = \frac{L}{kA} \cdot \frac{m \cdot K}{W} \times \frac{m}{m^2} = K/W$$

Frequently, these factors may be stated in terms of unit areas. Any data taken from reference tables should be checked carefully.

The overall heat transfer relationship can be stated as:

$$q = U \cdot A \cdot \Delta T$$

where q = heat transfer rate
A = cross-sectional area of heat, W(=J/s) transfer path, m²
ΔT = overall temperature differential, K
U = overall heat transfer coefficient, W/(m · K)

To determine U is often necessary to use the relationship:

$$\frac{1}{U} = R_1 + R_2 + R_3, \text{ etc.}; \qquad \frac{1}{U} = R_1$$

Alternatively, this may be stated as:

$$R_1 = \frac{1}{h_i} + \frac{L_2}{k_2} + \frac{L_3}{k_3} + \frac{1}{h_c}$$

## EXAMPLE CALCULATION OF HEAT LOSS THROUGH A WALL

An exterior building wall consists of 100 mm of brick, 200 mm of dense concrete, and 20 mm of gypsum plaster, for which the thermal conductivities are, respectively, k = 0.50, 1.50, and 1.20 W/(m · K). The surface heat transfer (film) coefficients are as follows: (interior) $h_i$ = 8.1 and (exterior) $h_c$ = 19.0 W/(m² · K). What is the heat loss through a 2400 mm (2.4 m) by 6000 mm (6.0 m) panel of this wall when there is a temperature difference of 30°C (30°K)?

## THERMAL CONDUCTIVITY

The thermal conductivity, or k-value, of a material is defined as the amount of heat energy conducted through a unit area of unit thickness in unit time with unit temperature difference between the two faces. In SI the unit W/(m · K) replaces Btu · in/h · ft² · °F, but if unit time is considered useful, the alternative expression is J/(s · m · K), because 1 W = 1 J/s. Unit thickness has been canceled out against unit area; otherwise the expression should be J · m/(s · m² · K), which directly resembles the customary expression in terms of constituent units.

## OVERALL HEAT TRANSFER

Conductivity generally increases with the level of absolute temperature. Some typical thermal conductivities (k-values) at 300 K are:

| MATERIAL OR SUBSTANCE | K = W/m · K |
|---|---|
| Copper | 386 |
| Aluminum | 202 |
| Steel | 55 |
| Concrete | 0.9-1.4 |
| Glass | 0.8-1.1 |
| Brick | 0.4-0.7 |
| Water | 0.614 |
| Mineral wool | 0.04 |
| Air | 0.0262 |

Computation of thermal resistance:

$$R_T = \frac{1}{8.1} + \frac{0.100}{0.50} + \frac{0.200}{1.50} + \frac{0.020}{1.20} + \frac{1}{19.0}$$

$$= 0.5261 \text{ m}^2 \cdot K/W$$

$$U = \frac{1}{R_T}; \qquad U = 1.901 \text{ W}/(m^2 \cdot K)$$

$$q = U \cdot A \cdot \Delta T$$

$$q = 1.901(2.4 \times 6.0)30$$

$$= 821 \text{ W} = 821 \text{ J/s}$$

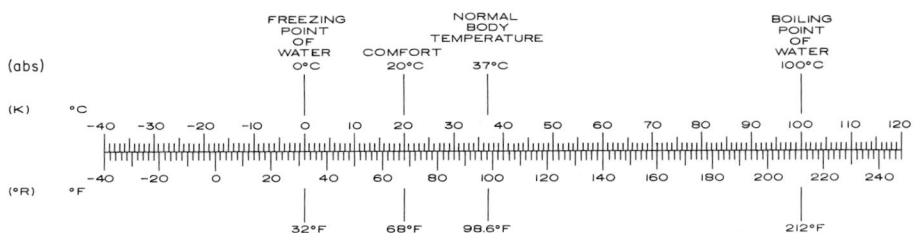

TEMPERATURE CONVERSION

## ENERGY VALUES FOR ALTERNATIVE ENERGY SOURCES

| ENERGY SOURCE AND QUANTITY | VALUE (MEGAJOULES, MJ) |
|---|---|
| 1 kg of dry wood (8600 Btu/lb) | 20 |
| 1 kg of bituminous coal (25 800 000 Btu/ton) | 30 |
| 1 L of kerosene (135 000 Btu/gal) | 37.6 |
| 1 L of crude oil (5 800 000 Btu/barrel) | 38.5 |
| 1 m³ of natural gas (1050 Btu/ft³) | 39 |
| 1 kWh of electricity | 3.6 |
| 1 therm (100,000 Btu) | 105.5 |

METRIC

## MOMENT BENDING, TORSIONAL

Bending moment and torsional moment are concepts of statics. Both involve the production of a force and a perpendicular distance, the latter being termed the moment arm. Thus the primary SI unit is the newton-meter, which may be symbolized as $N \cdot m$, $kN \cdot m$, and so on.

## TORQUE

When rotation occurs as a result of an applied moment the condition is one requiring the application of the principles of dynamics. In such cases the key factor is torque, which is based on a product of force and distance moved along the line of action of the force. This product is expressed in newton-meters per radian ($N \cdot m/rad$), which is equal to joules per radian ($J/rad$). The radian may be omitted where only complete revolutions are of concern or where dynamic conditions are equated instantaneously with static conditions.

## PRESSURE, STRESS, ELASTIC MODULUS

These may be stated directly either in pascals (Pa) or in newtons per square meter ($N/m^2$). Common multiples are kPa, MPa, GPa or $kN/m^2$, $MN/m^2$, $GN/m^2$. Occasionally stress is expressed in newtons per square millimeter ($N/mm^2$).

## MOMENT OF INERTIA

The mass moment of inertia of any body relating to rotation about a given axis is the second moment of the particles of that mass about the given axis and as such is given generally in kilogram-square meters per radian squared ($kg \cdot m^2/rad^2$). The radius of gyration is normally given in meters per radian ($m/rad$). The radian may be omitted where only complete revolutions are of concern or where dynamic conditions are equated instantaneously with static conditions.

Second moment of area (1) and section modulus (S) of the cross-section of structural sections or machine parts are usually preferred in terms of $10^6$ $mm^4$ and $10^3$ $mm^3$, respectively, for consistency with other dimensions of sections, which usually will be given in millimeters.

## ANGULAR MEASURE

The "radian" (rad), although not a base unit, is specifically identified as a "supplementary unit" and as such is the preferred unit for measurement of plane angles. The customary units of degrees, minutes, and seconds of angular measure are considered to be outside SI, but are acceptable where there is a specific practical reason to use them, as in cartography. If degrees are to be used, a statement of parts of degrees in decimals is preferred. The SI unit of solid angle is the "steradian" (sr).

## FLUID MECHANICS

Fluid mechanics utilizes the physical concepts of density (mass per unit volume), dynamic viscosity, kinematic viscosity, surface tension, potential energy, and pressure in dealing with the flow of relatively incompressible fluids at constant temperatures. There is a proper SI expression for each of these quantities, derived from base units in accordance with applicable physical relationships. Metric considerations in fluid mechanics are discussed in other engineering metric reference sources.

## UNITS OUTSIDE SI NOT RECOMMENDED FOR USE

| UNIT NAME | SYMBOL | VALUE IN SI UNITS | |
|---|---|---|---|
| dyne | dyn | $10^{-5}$ N | (or 10 uN) |
| bar | bar | $10^5$ Pa | (or 100 kPa) |
| erg | erg | $10^{-7}$ J | (or 100 nJ) |
| poise | P | $10^{-1}$ Pa $\cdot$ s | (or 100 mPa $\cdot$ s) |
| stokes | St | $10^{-4}$ $m^2/s$ | (or 100 $mm^2/s$) |
| gauss | Gs, (G) | $10^{-4}$ T | (or 100 uT) |
| maxwell | Mx | $10^{-8}$ Wb | (or 10 nWb) |
| stilb | sb | $10^4$ $cd/m^2$ | (or 10 $kcd/m^2$) |
| phot | ph | $10^4$ lx | (or 10 klx) |
| kilogram-force | kgf | 9.806 65 N | |
| calorie (int.) | cal | 4.1868 J | |
| kilocalorie (int.) | kcal | 4.1868 kJ | |
| torr | torr | 133.322 Pa | |
| oersted | Oe | 79.5775 A/m | |

## ROUNDING OF NUMBERS

Conversion from one measuring system to another requires rounding of numbers. For example, a quantity rounded to the nearest meter has an implied precision of ±0.5 m, while a quantity rounded to the nearest foot has an implied precision of ±0.5 ft. The two are quite different. If a quantity in feet (to the nearest foot) is to be converted to meters, any rounding should be to the nearest 0.3 m.

In making the changeover to SI, critical decisions about new rounded values will be required for many factors widely used in technical work.

## SIGNIFICANT DIGITS

In general, the result of any multiplication, division, addition, or subtraction cannot be given in more significant digits than are present in any one component of the original data. This condition pertains regardless of the number of decimal places in which a conversion factor is given.

In reference tables conversion factors should be stated to a substantial number of decimal places to cover a wide range of uses. It is the responsibility of the user to interpret the resultant decimal number to the extent applicable.

Example: What is the equivalent of 3 miles in terms of kilometers?

| CONVERSION FACTOR | DIRECT MULTIPLICATION | | SIGNIFICANT EQUIVALENT | |
|---|---|---|---|---|
| miles to kilometers = 1.609 | 3 mi = 4.827 km | | 3 mi | 5 km |
| Or, in reverse form: kilometers to miles = 0.6214 | 5 km = 3.107 mi | | 5 km | 3 mi |

## ABANDONED UNITS

For various reasons many derived and specialized units will fall into disuse as the changeover to SI progresses. Some, like British thermal unit (Btu) and horsepower (hp), will be dropped because they are based on the inch-pound (English) system.

Former metric units, of the c.g.s. variety, are no longer recommended. In addition a number of traditional metric units are outside SI, and their use is to be avoided.

## SINGLE LINE, DUAL SCALE CHARTS

Conversions also can be interpreted on a single line, dual scale, graphical representation.

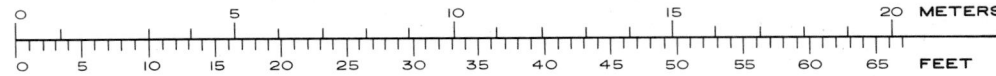

**METERS TO FEET**   (CONVERSION FACTORS   1 M = 3.281 FT,   1 FT = 0.3048 M)

## ACOUSTICS

SI units have been applied in acoustics to define frequency (hertz), sound power (watt), sound intensity (watt per square meter), and sound pressure level (pascal).

The reference quantities for the dimensionless logarithmic unit decibel (dB) are also expressed in SI units.

1. Sound power reference quantity: $1\ pW = 10^{-12}\ W$; therefore

$$\text{sound power level (dB)} = 10\ \log_{10} \frac{\text{actual power (W)}}{10^{-12}}$$

2. Sound intensity reference quantity: $1\ pW/m^2 = 10^{-12}\ W/m2$; therefore

$$\text{sound intensity level (dB)} = 10\ \log_{10} \frac{\text{actual intensity (W/m}^2)}{10^{-12}}$$

3. Sound pressure reference quantity: $20\ Pa = 2 \times 20 \times 10^6\ Pa$; therefore

$$\text{sound pressure level (dB)} = 20\ \log_{10} \frac{\text{actual pressure (Pa)}}{20 \times 10^6}$$

## ELECTRICITY AND MAGNETISM

Electrical engineering, for many years, has used metric (SI) units as practical electrical units. These units are all coherent in that they are formed directly from SI base and derived units on a unity (one-to-one) basis.

The only changes involved the use of the term "siemens" (S) for electrical conductance, instead of the previous name "mho," and the replacement of the cycle per second with the SI unit hertz (Hz).

The kilowatt-hour (kWh) is not an SI unit but will probably be retained for the measurement of electrical energy consumption because of its long history and extensive use. The recalibration of existing electricity meters from kilowatt-hours to megajoules (MJ), on the basis of 1 kWh = 3.6 MJ, hardly seems justified at this time. However, the kilowatt-hour should not be introduced into new areas.

## ILLUMINATION ENGINEERING

The SI units for luminous intensity, the candela (cd), and for luminous flux, the lumen (lm), are already in general use in the United States.

Illuminance (luminous flux per unit area) will be expressed in the derived SI unit lux (lx), which is a special name for the lumen per square meter ($lm/m^2$). The lux (lx) and kilolux (klx) replace the footcandle, which is also known as the lumen per square foot.

Similarly, the SI unit of luminance, the candela per square meter ($cd/m^2$), replaces the candela per square foot, the lambert, and the footlambert.

Conversion factors are:

```
        1 lx =  0.092 footcandle
1 footcandle = 10.7639 lx
       1 klx = 92.903 footcandles
    1 cd/m² =  0.092 903 cd/ft²
             =  0.291 964 footlambert
    1 cd/ft² = 10.7639 cd/m²
1 footlambert =  3.426 259 cd/m²
```

## UNITS FOR ELECTRICITY AND MAGNETISM

| QUANTITY | UNIT NAME | SYMBOL | DERIVATION | REMARKS |
|---|---|---|---|---|
| Electric current | ampere | A | | SI base unit |
| Current density | ampere per square meter | $A/m^2$ | | |
| Magnetic field strength | ampere per meter | A/m | | |
| Electric charge quantity of electricity | coulomb | C | $(A \cdot s)$ | |
| Electric charge density | coulomb per cubic meter | $C/m^3$ | | |
| Electric potential, electromotive force | volt | V | (W/A) | |
| Electric field strength | volt per meter | V/m | | 1 V/m = 1 N/C |
| Electric capacitance | farad | F | (C/V) | |
| Permittivity | farad per meter | F/m | | |
| Electric resistance | ohm | $\Omega$ | (V/A) | |
| Electric conductance | siemens | S | (A/V) | Replaces "mho"; also equals $1/\Omega$ |
| Electric power | watt | W | $(V \cdot A)$ | Also equals J/s |
| Magnetic flux | weber | Wb | $(V \cdot s)$ | |
| Magnetic flux density | tesla | T | $(Wb/m^2)$ | 1 T = 1 V $\cdot$ $s/m^2$ |
| Inductance | henry | H | (Wb/A) | 1 H = 1 V $\cdot$ s/A |
| Permeability | henry per meter | H/m | | |

 METRIC

## METRIC DRAWINGS

Metric drawing sizes are those set by the International Standards Organization (ISO), "A" Series, with a $1 : \sqrt{2}$ aspect ratio. These sizes are suitable for reduction using a 35 mm microfilm frame. Metric drawing scales are comparable to U.S. customary scales, as shown in the table. The metric system favors the use of ratios to define slopes, and a table comparing this with pitches and percentages is shown. Other recommended metric drawing practices are similar to customary standard drawing practices.

## DRAWING SHEET DIMENSIONS (MM)

| SIZE | SHEET SIZE | TOP AND BOT-TOM | BIND-ING MAR-GIN | RIGHT BOR-DER | NET SIZE |
|---|---|---|---|---|---|
| A0 | 1189 x 841 | 20 | 40 | 16 | 1133 x 801 |
| A1 | 841 x 594 | 14 | 28 | 12 | 801 x 566 |
| A2 | 594 x 420 | 10 | 20 | 8 | 566 x 400 |
| A3 | 420 x 297 | 7 | 20 | 6 | 394 x 283 |
| A4* | 210 x 297 | 7 | 20 | 6 | 184 x 283 |
| B1 | 1000 x 707 | 14 | 28 | 12 | 960 x 679 |

*The filing edge of A4 size sheets is the long edge.

## COMPARISON OF DRAWING SCALES

| METRIC SCALES | CUSTOMARY RATIO | CUSTOMARY SCALES |
|---|---|---|
| 1:5 | 1:4 | 3″ = 1′0″ |
| 1:10 | 1:18 | 1 1/2″ = 1′0″ |
|  | 1:12 | 1″ = 1′0″ |
| 1:20 | 1:16 | 3/4″ = 1′0″ |
|  | 1:24 | 1/2″ = 1′0″ |
| 1:50 | 1:48 | 1/4″ = 1′0″ |
| 1:100 | 1:96 | 1/8″ = 1′0″ |
| 1:200 | 1:92 | 1/16″ = 1′0″ |
| 1:500 | 1:384 | 1/32″ = 1′0″ |
|  | 1:480 | 1″ = 40′0″ |
|  | 1:600 | 1″ = 50′0″ |
| 1:1000 | 1:960 | 1″ = 80′0″ |
|  | 1:1200 | 1″ = 100′0″ |
| 1:2000 | 1:2400 | 1″ = 200′0″ |
| 1:5000 | 1:4800 | 1″ = 400′0″ |
|  | 1:6000 | 1″ = 500′0″ |
| 1:10 000 | 1:10 560 | 6″ = 1 mi |
|  | 1:12 000 | 1″ = 1000′0″ |
| 1:25 000 | 1:21 120 | 3″ = 1 mi |
|  | 1:24 000 | 1″ = 2000′0″ |
| 1:50 000 | 1:63 360 | 1″ = 1 mi |
| 1:100 000 | 1:126 720 | 1/2″ = 1 mi |

## EXPRESSION OF SLOPE

| RATIO Y/X | ANGLE | ANGLE (RAD) | PERCENTAGE (%) |
|---|---|---|---|
| **Shallow slopes** | | | |
| 1:100 | 0°34′ | 0.0100 | 1 |
| 1:67 | 0°52′ | 0.0150 | 1.5 |
| 1:57 | 1° | 0.0175 | 1.75 |
| 1:50 | 1°09′ | 0.0200 | 2 |
| 1:40 | 1°26′ | 0.0250 | 2.5 |
| 1:33 | 1°43′ | 0.0300 | 3 |
| 1:29 | 2° | 0.0349 | 3.5 |
| 1:25 | 2°17′ | 0.0399 | 4 |
| 1:20 | 2°52′ | 0.0499 | 5 |
| 1:19 | 3° | 0.0524 | 5.25 |
| **Slight slopes** | | | |
| 1:17 | 3°26′ | 0.0599 | 6 |
| 1:15 | 3°48′ | 0.0664 | 6.7 |
| 1:14.3 | 4° | 0.0698 | 7 |
| 1:12 | 4°46′ | 0.0832 | 8.3 |
| 1:11.4 | 5° | 0.0873 | 8.75 |
| 1:10 | 5°43′ | 0.0998 | 10 |
| 1:9.5 | 6° | 0.1047 | 10.5 |
| 1:8 | 7°07′ | 0.1245 | 12.5 |
| 1:7.1 | 8° | 0.1396 | 14 |
| 1:6.7 | 8°32′ | 0.1490 | 15 |
| 1:6 | 9°28′ | 0.1652 | 16.7 |
| 1:5.7 | 10° | 0.1745 | 17.6 |
| 1:5 | 11°19′ | 0.1975 | 20 |
| 1:4.5 | 12°30′ | 0.2182 | 22.2 |
| 1:4 | 14°02′ | 0.2450 | 25 |
| **Medium slopes** | | | |
| 1:3.7 | 15° | 0.2618 | 25.8 |
| 1:3.3 | 16°42′ | 0.2915 | 30 |
| 1:3 | 18°26′ | 0.3217 | 33.3 |
| 1:2.75 | 20° | 0.3491 | 36.4 |
| 1:2.5 | 21°48′ | 0.3805 | 40 |
| 1:2.4 | 22°30′ | 0.3927 | 41.4 |
| 1:2.15 | 25° | 0.4363 | 46.6 |
| 1:2 | 26°34′ | 0.4537 | 50 |
| 1:1.73 | 30° | 0.5326 | 57.5 |
| 1:1.67 | 30°58′ | 0.5405 | 60 |
| 1:1.5 | 33°42′ | 0.5880 | 67 |
| 1:1.33 | 36°52′ | 0.6434 | 75 |
| 1:1.2 | 40° | 0.6981 | 84 |
| 1:1 | 45° | 0.7854 | 100 |
| **Steep slopes** | | | |
| 1.19:1 | 50° | 0.8727 | 119 |
| 1.43:1 | 55° | 0.9599 | 143 |
| 1.5:1 | 56°19′ | 0.9827 | 150 |
| 1.73:1 | 60° | 1.0472 | 173 |
| 2:1 | 63°26′ | 1.1071 | 200 |
| 2.15:1 | 65° | 1.1345 | 215 |
| 2.5:1 | 68°12′ | 1.1903 | 250 |
| 2.75:1 | 70° | 1.2217 | 275 |
| 3:1 | 71°34′ | 1.2491 | 300 |
| 3.73:1 | 75° | 1.3090 | 373 |
| 4:1 | 75°58′ | 1.3253 | 400 |
| 5:1 | 78°42′ | 1.3735 | 500 |
| 5.67:1 | 80° | 1.3963 | 567 |
| 6:1 | 80°32′ | 1.4056 | 600 |
| 11.43:1 | 85° | 1.4835 | 1143 |
| ∞ | 90° | 1.5708 | ∞ |

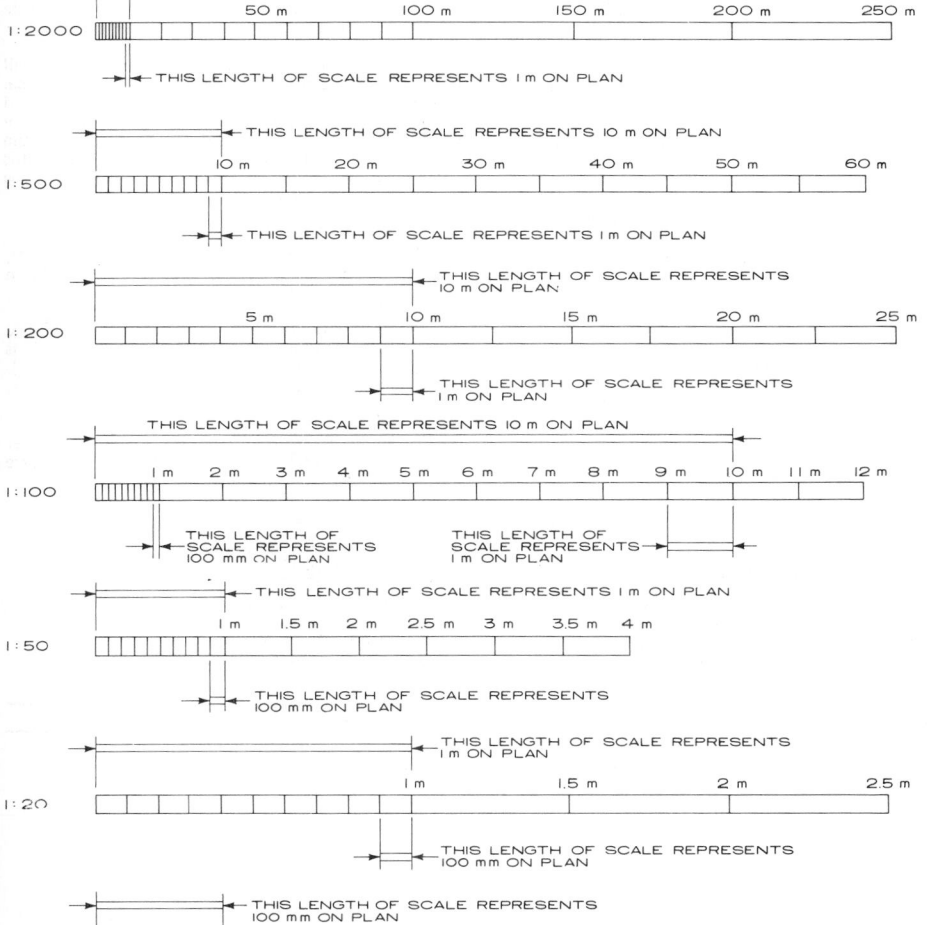

**METRIC LENGTHS TO SCALE**

METRIC ⟨A⟩

## HORIZONTAL CONTROLLING DIMENSIONS (mm)

| DIMENSIONS | MULTIPLES OF MULTIMODULES | | | | | MOST PRE-FERRED VALUES |
|---|---|---|---|---|---|---|
| | 300 | 600 | 1200 | 3000 | 6000 | |
| 300 | x | | | | | |
| 600 | x | x | | | | x |
| 900 | x | | | | | |
| 1 200 | x | x | x | | | x |
| 1 500 | x | | | | | |
| 1 800 | x | x | | | | x |
| 2 100 | x | | | | | |
| 2 400 | x | x | x | | | x |
| 2 700 | x | | | | | |
| 3 000 | x | x | | x | | x |
| 3 300 | x | | | | | |
| 3 600 | x | x | x | | | x |
| 4 200 | | x | | | | |
| 4 800 | | x | x | | | x |
| 5 400 | | x | | | | |
| 6 000 | | x | x | x | x | x |
| 6 600 | | x | | | | |
| 7 200 | | x | x | | | x |
| 7 800 | | x | | | | |
| 8 400 | | x | x | | | x |
| 9 000 | | x | | x | | x |
| 9 600 | | x | x | | | x |
| 10 800 | | x | | | | |
| 12 000 | | x | x | x | x | x |
| 13 200 | | x | | | | |
| 14 000 | | x | | | | |
| 15 000 | | | x | x | | |
| 15 600 | | x | | | | |
| 16 800 | | x | | | | |
| 18 000 | | x | x | x | x | x |
| 19 200 | | x | | | | |
| 20 400 | | x | | | | |
| 21 000 | | | x | x | | |
| 21 600 | | x | | | | |
| 22 800 | | x | | | | |
| 24 000 | | x | x | x | x | x |
| 25 200 | | x | | | | |
| 26 400 | | x | | | | |
| 27 000 | | | x | x | | |
| 27 600 | | x | | | | |
| 30 000 | | | x | x | x | x |

## NOMINAL AND COORDINATING DIMENSIONS FOR CLAY MASONRY: FULL SIZE UNITS

| NOMINAL HEIGHT (mm) | COORDINATING HEIGHT (mm) | COORDINATING LENGTH (mm) |
|---|---|---|
| 50 | 2 courses to 100 | 300 |
| 67 | 3 courses to 200 | 200 / 300 |
| 75 | 4 courses to 300 | 200 / 300 |
| 80 | 5 courses to 400 | 200 / 300 |
| 100 | 100 | 200 / 300 / 400 |
| 133 | 3 courses to 400 | 200 / 300 / 400 |
| 150 | 2 courses to 300 | 300 / 400 |
| 200 | 200 | 200 / 300 / 400 |
| 300 | 300 | 300 |

Note: For horizontal flexibility and/or to maintain bond patterns, the following supplementary lengths may be required:

| NOMINAL LENGTH (mm) | SUPPLEMENTARY LENGTHS (mm) |
|---|---|
| 200 | 100 |
| 300 | 100, 150, 200, 250 |
| 400 | 100, 200, 300 |

## PREFERRED SIZES FOR BUILDING COMPONENTS AND ASSEMBLIES

| CATE-GORY | EXAM-PLES | PREFERRED SIZES (mm) | | |
|---|---|---|---|---|
| | | 1ST | 2ND | |
| Small (under 500 mm) | Brick block, tile, paving units | 100 / 200 / 300 / 400 | 25 / 50 / 75 / 150 / 250 | |
| Medium (under 1 500 mm) | Panels, parti-tions, doorsets, windows, slabs | 600 / 800 / 900 / 1 200 | 500 / 700 / 1 000 / 1 400 See Note 1 | |
| Large (under 3 600 mm) | Precast floor and wall units, panels, doors, windows, stairs | 1 800 / 2 400 / 3 000 / 3 600 | (n x 300) 1 500 / 2 100 / 2 700 / 3 300 | (n x 200) 1 600 / 2 000 / 2 200 / 2 600 / 2 800 / 3 200 / 3 400 |
| | | | See Note 2 | |
| Very Large (over 3 600 mm) | Prefabri-cated building elements, precast floor and roof sections | 4 800 / 6 000 / 7 200 / 8 400 / 9 500 / 10 800 / 12 000 | (n x 600) 4 200 / 6 600 / 7 800 / 9 000 / 10 200 / 11 400 | (n x 1 500) 4 500 / 7 500 / 10 500 |
| | | | See Note 3 | |

### NOTES

1. For the purposes of rationalization, those multiples of 100 mm, above 1 000 mm, that are prime numbers (e.g., 1 100, 1 300) constitute a lower order of preferences when special requirements exist.
2. Alternative second preferences are shown; for vertical dimensions the use of multiples of 200 mm may sometimes be more appropriate than the use of multiples of 300 mm, as with masonry materials.
3. Alternative second preferences are shown; for some projects it will be more appropriate to size large components or assemblies in multiples of 1 500 mm.

## PRODUCTS FOR USE IN THE VERTICAL PLANE: MASONRY PANELS

| VERTICAL (mm) | HORIZONTAL (mm) | | |
|---|---|---|---|
| | 600 x n | 300 x n | 200 x n |
| 600 x n | 1 | 2 | 3 |
| 220 x n | 2 | 3 | 3 |
| 100 x n | 3 | 3 | |

## GENERAL NOTES

Preferred sizes and dimensions allow better coordination between manufactured components, design, and construction operations. The tables are presented to allow an open system of selection compatible with dimensional coordination concepts presented on the preceding pages. Preferred dimensions in building are selected multimodules for horizontal and vertical applications derived from the basic 100 mm module.

The preferred dimension concept is similar to the customary 4 in. module concept presently in use in the construction industry. As an example, preferred horizontal controlling dimensions similar to the customary 1, 2, or 4 ft multimodule in metric terms may be stated this way:

up to 3600 mm : 300 mm

up to 9600 mm : 600 mm

above 9600 mm : 1200 mm

For large dimensions, 6000 mm may be more useful or, as a second preference, 3000 mm.

Certain numbers are preferred because they are divisible by 2 or 3. Such numbers are 600, 1200, 1800, 2400 mm, as indicated in the table. The long history of using such multimodules is incorporated in the conversion plans to SI metric.

Refer to standards and manufacturer's data for application of the preferred SI metric sizes and dimensions.

## PREFERRED DIMENSIONS FOR PANELS AND PLANKS

| TYPE | PREFERENCE | WIDTH (mm) | LENGTH (mm) |
|---|---|---|---|
| Panels | First | 1 200 | 2 400 |
| | Second | 600 | 2 400 / 3 000 |
| | | 1 200 | 1 200 / 1 800 / 3 000 / 3 600 |
| | Third | 1 200 | 2 100 / 2 700 |
| Planks | First | 400 | 2 400 |
| | Second | 400 | 3 000 / 3 600 |

## PREFERRED DOOR SIZES

| HEIGHT (mm) | SINGLE WIDTH | | | | DOUBLE WIDTH | | |
|---|---|---|---|---|---|---|---|
| | 700* | 800 | 900 | 1 000 | 1 200 | 1 500 | 1 800 |
| 2 100 | 2 | 2 | 1 | 2 | 1 | 1 | 1 |
| 2 200 | 2 | 2 | 2 | 1 | 2 | 2 | 1 |
| 2 400 | 2 | 1 | 1 | 1 | 2 | 2 | 1 |

*Too narrow for wheelchair use.

## PREFERRED SIZES FOR WINDOWS

| HEIGHT (mm) | WIDTH (mm) | | | | | | | | |
|---|---|---|---|---|---|---|---|---|---|
| 1ST PREFER-ENCE | 600 | | 1200 | | 1800 | | 2400 | | 3000 |
| 1ST 2ND | | 900 | | 1500 | | 2100 | | 2700 | |
| 600 | 1 | 2 | 1 | 2 | 1 | 2 | 1 | 2 | 1 |
| 800 | 2 | 3 | 2 | 3 | 2 | 3 | 2 | 3 | 2 |
| 900 | 2 | 3 | 2 | 3 | 2 | 3 | 2 | 3 | 2 |
| 1000 | 2 | 3 | 2 | 3 | 2 | 3 | 2 | 3 | 2 |
| 1200 | 1 | 2 | 1 | 2 | 1 | 2 | 1 | 2 | 1 |
| 1400 | 2 | 3 | 2 | 3 | 2 | 3 | 2 | 3 | 2 |
| 1500 | 2 | 3 | 2 | 3 | 2 | 3 | 2 | 3 | 2 |
| 1600 | 2 | 3 | 2 | 3 | 2 | 3 | 2 | 3 | 2 |
| 1800 | 1 | 2 | 1 | 2 | 1 | 2 | 1 | 2 | 1 |
| 2000 | 2 | 3 | 2 | 3 | 2 | 3 | 2 | 3 | 2 |
| 2100 | 2 | 3 | 2 | 3 | 2 | 3 | 2 | 3 | 2 |
| 2400 | 1 | 2 | 1 | 2 | 1 | 2 | 1 | 2 | 1 |
| 2700 | 2 | 3 | 2 | 3 | 2 | 3 | 2 | 3 | 2 |
| 3000 | 1 | 2 | 1 | 2 | 1 | 2 | 1 | 2 | 1 |

Note: In some construction, widths of 1000, 1400, 1600, and 2000 mm may be required for brick or block sizes and, combined with first preference heights, may be substituted as a third preference series of sizes.

METRIC

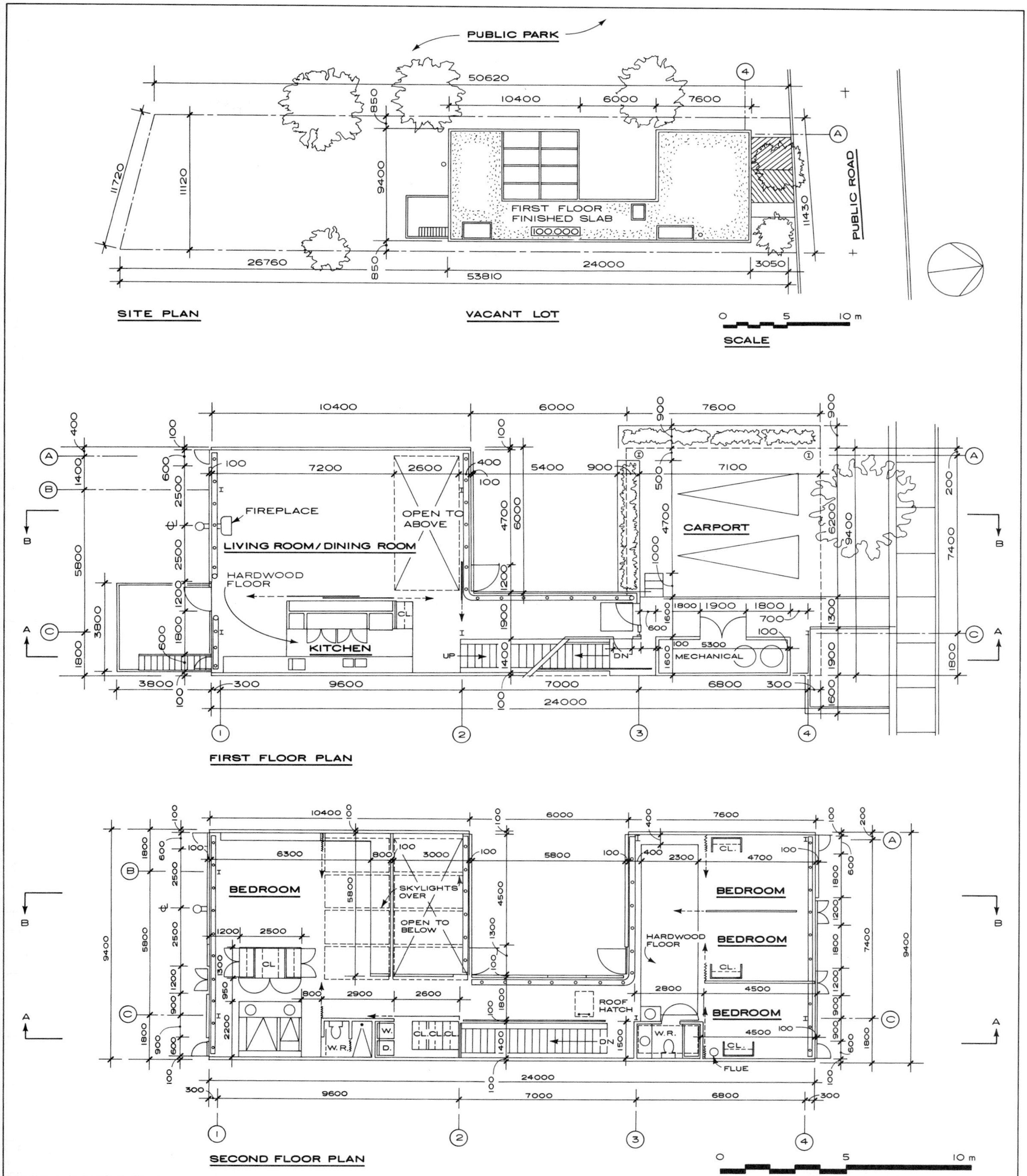

SITE PLAN

PUBLIC PARK

50620
10400  6000  7600

850
9400
11720
11120
11430

FIRST FLOOR
FINISHED SLAB
100000

PUBLIC ROAD

26760  850  53810  24000  3050

VACANT LOT

SCALE
0  5  10 m

**FIRST FLOOR PLAN**

10400  6000  900  7600  900

400  100  100  400  500  200
7200  2600  5400  900  7100
1400  600  100  4700  4700  6200  9400  7400
2500  6000

FIREPLACE

OPEN TO ABOVE

CARPORT

LIVING ROOM / DINING ROOM

HARDWOOD FLOOR

5800  2500  1200  1900  1000  1800  1900  1800  700  100

KITCHEN  CL

3800  600  1800  UP  DN  1800
1800  1400  1600  600  5300  MECHANICAL  1900

3800  300  9600  7000  6800  300
24000

1  2  3  4

**SECOND FLOOR PLAN**

10400  6000  400  7600  200

1800  600  100  800  100  3000  100  5800  100  400  2300  CL  4700  100  1800
2500  5800  4500  2500
6300

BEDROOM

SKYLIGHTS OVER

OPEN TO BELOW

BEDROOM

HARDWOOD FLOOR

BEDROOM

9400  5800  2500  1300  1800  7400  9400
1200  2500  1300  2800  4500

CL  800  2900  2600  ROOF HATCH  BEDROOM
900  1200  950  2200  W.R.  W. D.  CL.CL.CL  DN  W.R.  4500  100  900  900  600
1800  600  1400  1500  CL
FLUE

300  9600  7000  6800  300
24000

1  2  3  4

0  5  10 m

THE WOLF RESIDENCE, TORONTO, CANADA, COMPLETED 1974. ARCHITECTS: A.J. DIAMOND AND BARTON MYERS. DESIGNED BY BARTON MYERS

Robert Hill, Barton Myers Associates; Toronto, Canada

METRIC

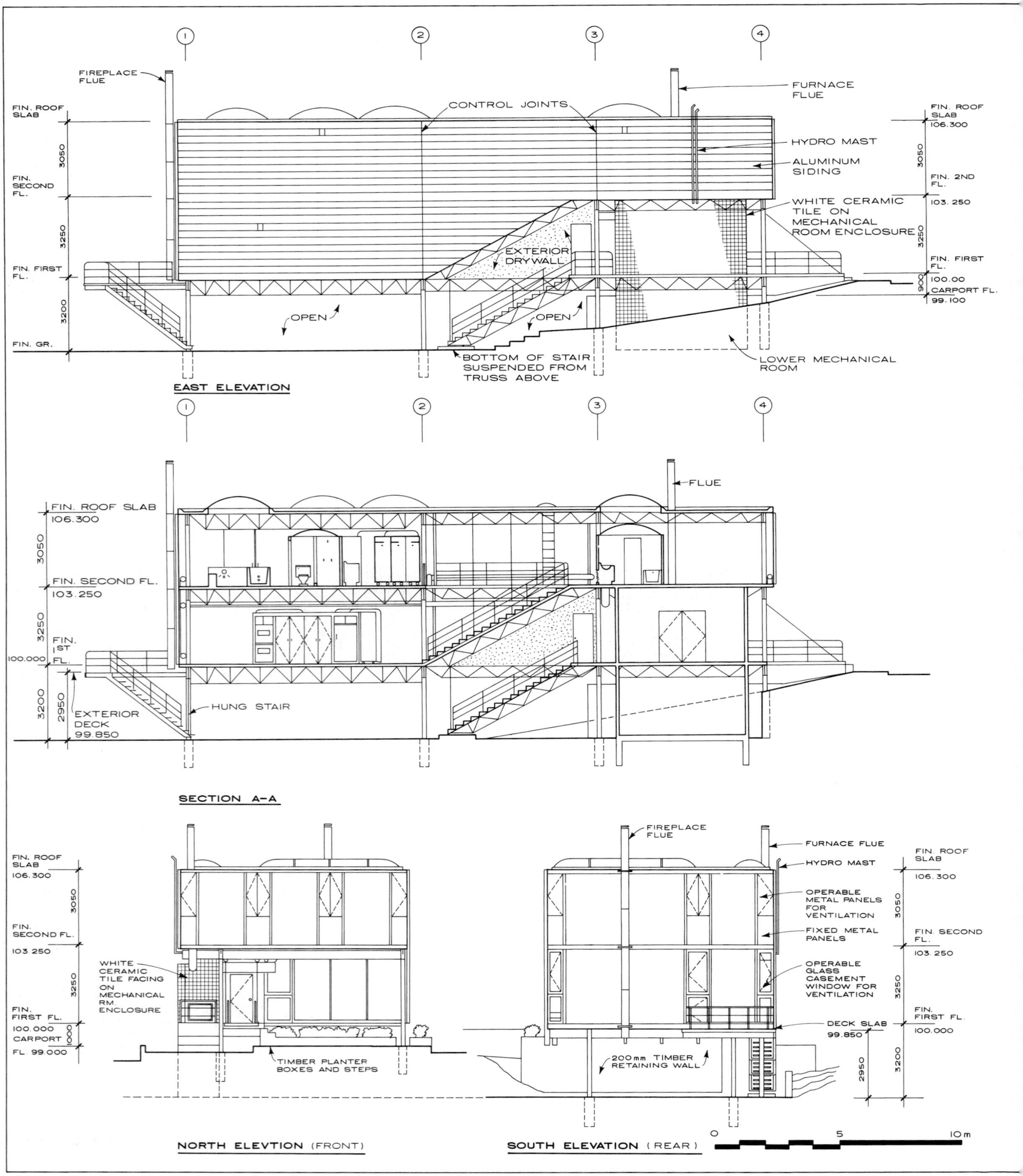

FIREPLACE
FLUE

FIN. ROOF
SLAB

3050

FIN.
SECOND
FL.

3250

FIN. FIRST
FL.

3200

FIN. GR.

CONTROL JOINTS

FURNACE
FLUE

FIN. ROOF
SLAB
106.300

HYDRO MAST

ALUMINUM
SIDING

3050

FIN. 2ND
FL.
103.250

EXTERIOR
DRYWALL

WHITE CERAMIC
TILE ON
MECHANICAL
ROOM ENCLOSURE

3250

FIN. FIRST
FL.

900

100.00
CARPORT FL.
99.100

OPEN

OPEN

BOTTOM OF STAIR
SUSPENDED FROM
TRUSS ABOVE

LOWER MECHANICAL
ROOM

**EAST ELEVATION**

FLUE

FIN. ROOF SLAB
106.300

3050

FIN. SECOND FL.
103.250

3250

FIN.
1ST
FL.
100.000

3200    2950

EXTERIOR
DECK
99.850

HUNG STAIR

**SECTION A-A**

FIREPLACE
FLUE

FURNACE FLUE

FIN. ROOF
SLAB
106.300

FIN. ROOF
SLAB
106.300

3050

HYDRO MAST

OPERABLE
METAL PANELS
FOR
VENTILATION

3050

FIN. SECOND
FL.

FIN.
SECOND FL.

103.250

FIXED METAL
PANELS

103.250

WHITE
CERAMIC
TILE
FACING
ON
MECHANICAL
RM.
ENCLOSURE

3250

OPERABLE
GLASS
CASEMENT
WINDOW FOR
VENTILATION

3250

FIN.
FIRST FL.
100.000
CARPORT
FL. 99.000

DECK SLAB
99.850

FIN.
FIRST FL.
100.000

3200

2950

TIMBER PLANTER
BOXES AND STEPS

200 mm TIMBER
RETAINING WALL

**NORTH ELEVTION** (FRONT)

**SOUTH ELEVATION** (REAR)

0          5          10 m

Robert Hill, Barton Myers Associates; Toronto, Canada

  **METRIC**

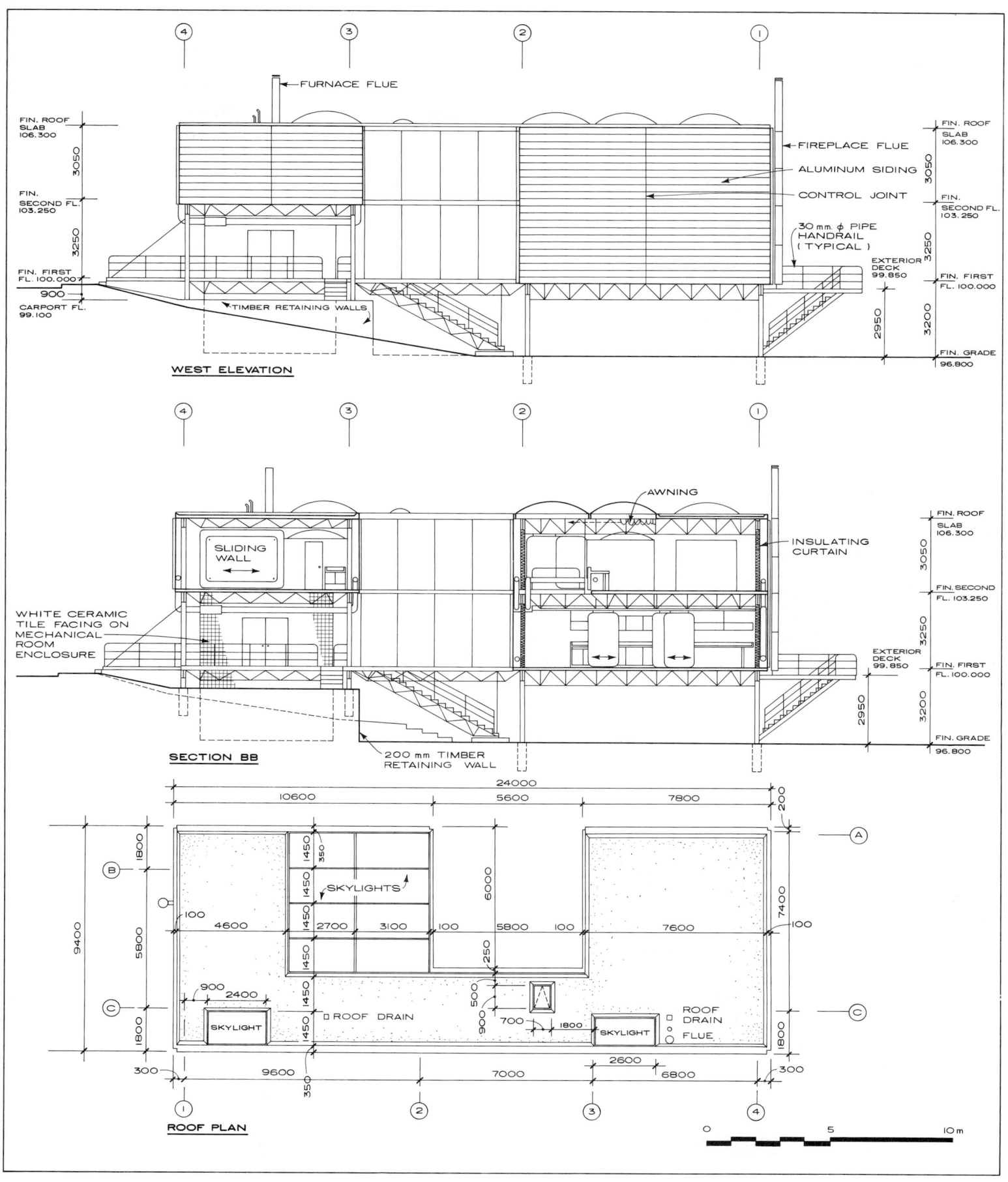

WEST ELEVATION

FURNACE FLUE

FIN. ROOF SLAB 106.300
3050
FIN. SECOND FL. 103.250
3250
FIN. FIRST FL. 100.000
900
CARPORT FL. 99.100

TIMBER RETAINING WALLS

FIREPLACE FLUE
ALUMINUM SIDING
CONTROL JOINT
30 mm. φ PIPE HANDRAIL (TYPICAL)

FIN. ROOF SLAB 106.300
3050
FIN. SECOND FL. 103.250
3250
EXTERIOR DECK 99.850
FIN. FIRST FL. 100.000
2950
3200
FIN. GRADE 96.800

SECTION BB

SLIDING WALL

WHITE CERAMIC TILE FACING ON MECHANICAL ROOM ENCLOSURE

200 mm TIMBER RETAINING WALL

AWNING
INSULATING CURTAIN

FIN. ROOF SLAB 106.300
3050
FIN. SECOND FL. 103.250
3250
EXTERIOR DECK 99.850
FIN. FIRST FL. 100.000
2950
3200
FIN. GRADE 96.800

ROOF PLAN

24000
10600   5600   7800   200
1800
100   4600   2700   3100   100   5800   100   7600   100
9400   5800   6000   7400
1450   1450   1450   350   250   500
900   2400   900   700   1800
SKYLIGHT   ROOF DRAIN   SKYLIGHT   ROOF DRAIN   FLUE
300   9600   350   7000   2600   6800   300
SKYLIGHTS

A   B   C

0   5   10 m

Robert Hill, Barton Myers Associates; Toronto, Canada

METRIC   A

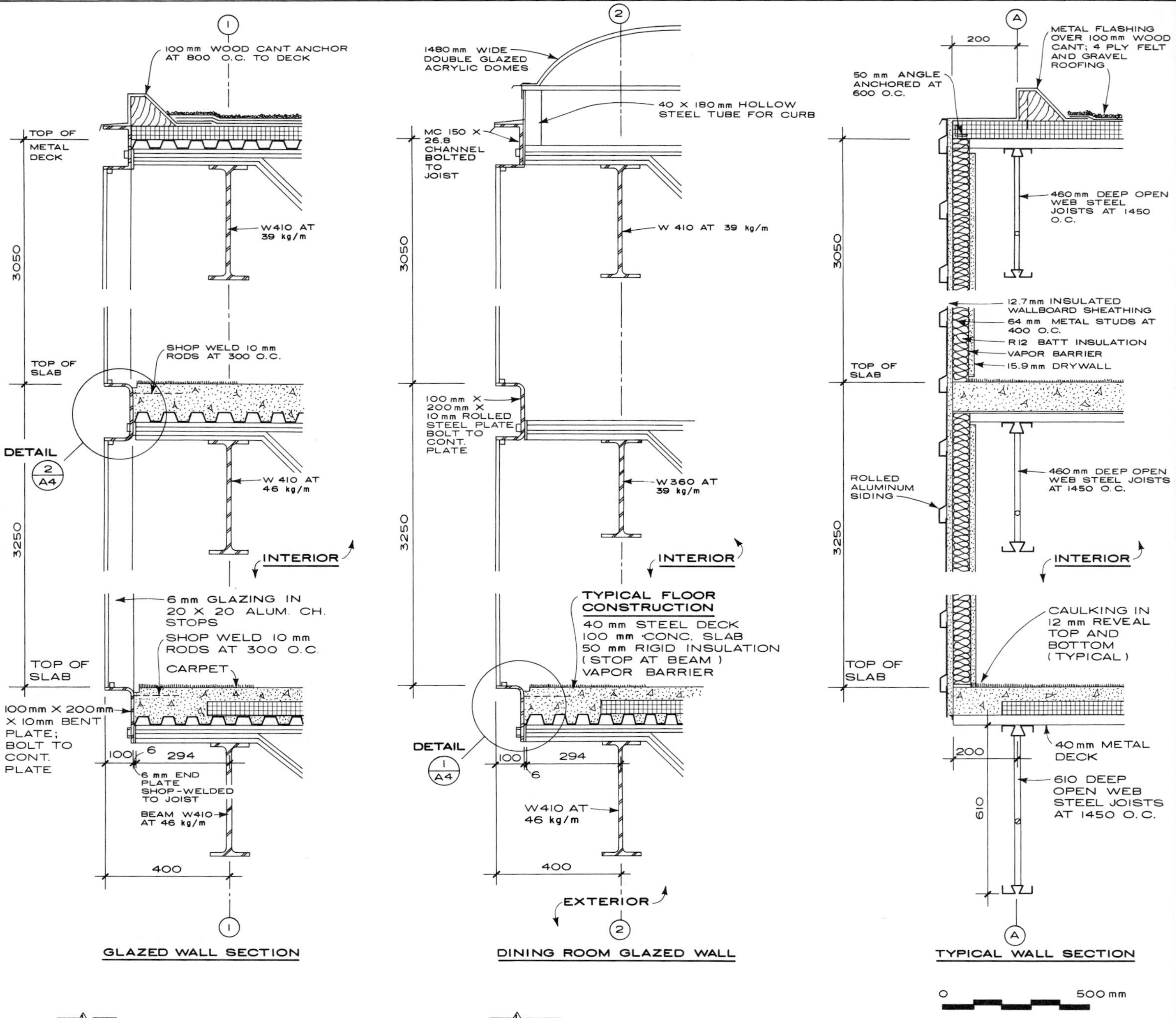

①    100 mm WOOD CANT ANCHOR AT 800 O.C. TO DECK

TOP OF METAL DECK

3050

W410 AT 39 kg/m

TOP OF SLAB

SHOP WELD 10 mm RODS AT 300 O.C.

DETAIL ② A4

3250

W 410 AT 46 kg/m

INTERIOR

6 mm GLAZING IN 20 X 20 ALUM. CH. STOPS

SHOP WELD 10 mm RODS AT 300 O.C.

CARPET

TOP OF SLAB

100mm X 200mm X 10mm BENT PLATE; BOLT TO CONT. PLATE

100 | 6 | 294

6 mm END PLATE SHOP-WELDED TO JOIST

BEAM W410 AT 46 kg/m

400

①

**GLAZED WALL SECTION**

---

②

1480 mm WIDE DOUBLE GLAZED ACRYLIC DOMES

40 X 180 mm HOLLOW STEEL TUBE FOR CURB

MC 150 X 26.8 CHANNEL BOLTED TO JOIST

3050

W 410 AT 39 kg/m

100 mm X 200 mm X 10 mm ROLLED STEEL PLATE BOLT TO CONT. PLATE

W 360 AT 39 kg/m

INTERIOR

**TYPICAL FLOOR CONSTRUCTION**
40 mm STEEL DECK
100 mm CONC. SLAB
50 mm RIGID INSULATION (STOP AT BEAM)
VAPOR BARRIER

DETAIL ① A4

100 | 294 | 6

W410 AT 46 kg/m

400

EXTERIOR

②

**DINING ROOM GLAZED WALL**

---

Ⓐ

200

METAL FLASHING OVER 100 mm WOOD CANT; 4 PLY FELT AND GRAVEL ROOFING

50 mm ANGLE ANCHORED AT 600 O.C.

3050

460 mm DEEP OPEN WEB STEEL JOISTS AT 1450 O.C.

12.7 mm INSULATED WALLBOARD SHEATHING
64 mm METAL STUDS AT 400 O.C.
R12 BATT INSULATION
VAPOR BARRIER
15.9 mm DRYWALL

TOP OF SLAB

3250

ROLLED ALUMINUM SIDING

460 mm DEEP OPEN WEB STEEL JOISTS AT 1450 O.C.

INTERIOR

CAULKING IN 12 mm REVEAL TOP AND BOTTOM (TYPICAL)

TOP OF SLAB

200

40 mm METAL DECK

610

610 DEEP OPEN WEB STEEL JOISTS AT 1450 O.C.

Ⓐ

**TYPICAL WALL SECTION**

0      500 mm

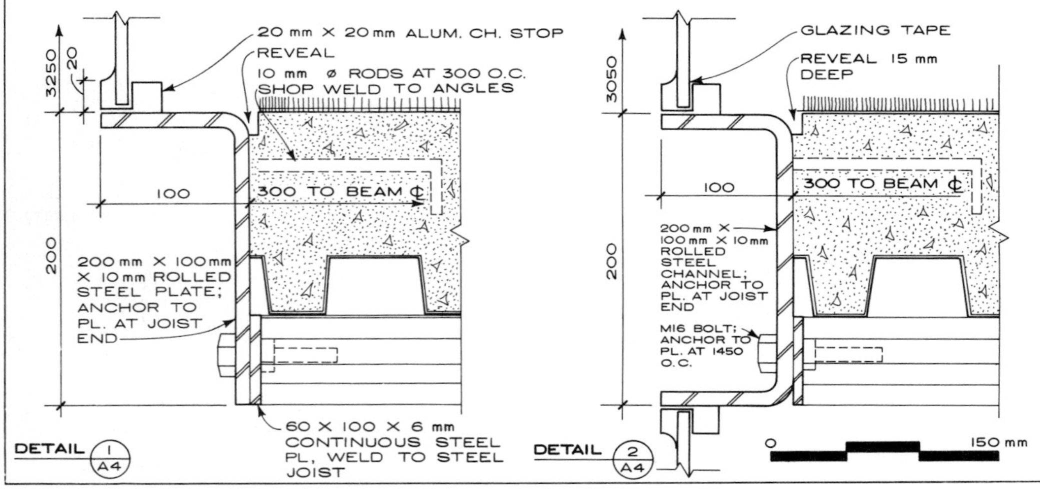

---

3250 | 20

20 mm X 20 mm ALUM. CH. STOP

REVEAL

10 mm Ø RODS AT 300 O.C. SHOP WELD TO ANGLES

100

300 TO BEAM ℄

200

200 mm X 100mm X 10mm ROLLED STEEL PLATE; ANCHOR TO PL. AT JOIST END

60 X 100 X 6 mm CONTINUOUS STEEL PL. WELD TO STEEL JOIST

DETAIL ① A4

---

3050

GLAZING TAPE

REVEAL 15 mm DEEP

100

300 TO BEAM ℄

200 mm X 100mm X 10mm ROLLED STEEL CHANNEL; ANCHOR TO PL. AT JOIST END

200

M16 BOLT; ANCHOR TO PL. AT 1450 O.C.

DETAIL ② A4

0      150 mm

---

**NOTES**

1. All dimensions shown are in millimetres, using the axial technique of measurement and a grid plan based on a 100 mm plan module.
2. On site plan, sections, and elevations, note that all floor elevations are in metres.
3. All steel sections are dimensioned in millimetres, with weights of lengths in kilograms per metre.
4. Stock lumber dimensions have been "soft converted" to metric equivalents, since lumber will continue to be produced in imperial sizes to meet American Lumber Standards (ALS) requirements.
5. New metric stock door sizes for interior and exterior doors are employed throughout.

Robert Hill, Barton Myers Associates; Toronto, Canada

 **METRIC**

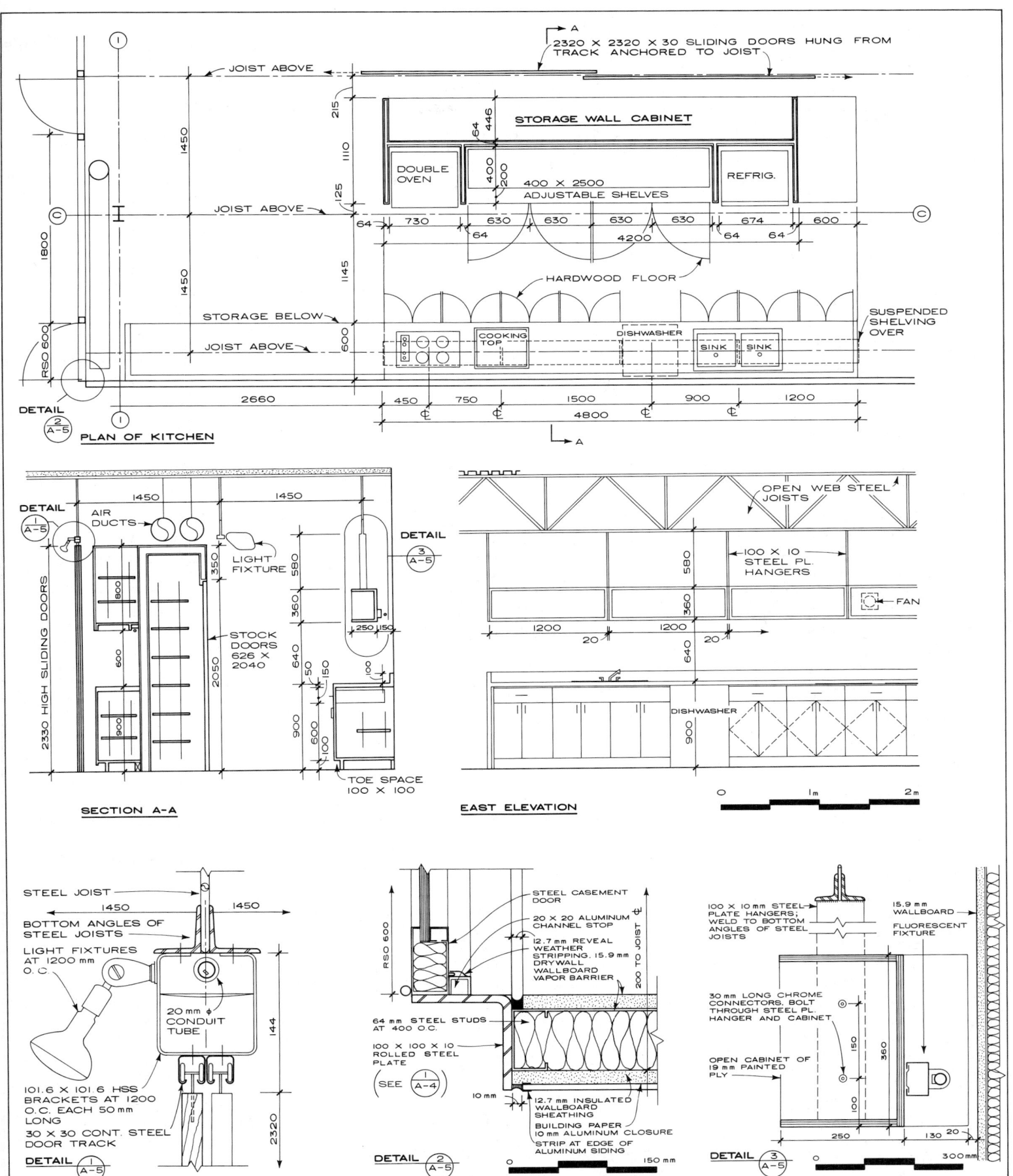

**PLAN OF KITCHEN**

**SECTION A-A**

**EAST ELEVATION**

**DETAIL** 1/A-5

**DETAIL** 2/A-5

**DETAIL** 3/A-5

Robert Hill, Barton Myers Associates; Toronto, Canada

**METRIC** A

## INCHES AND FRACTIONS TO MILLIMETERS (1 IN. = 25.4 mm)

| INCHES | 0 | 1 | 2 | 3 | 4 | 5 | 6 | 7 | 8 | 9 | 10 | 11 |
|---|---|---|---|---|---|---|---|---|---|---|---|---|
| | | | | | | MILLIMETERS (mm) | | | | | | |
| 0 | . . . | 25.40 | 50.80 | 76.20 | 101.60 | 127.00 | 152.40 | 177.80 | 203.20 | 228.60 | 254.00 | 279.40 |
| 1/16 | 1.59 | 26.99 | 52.39 | 77.79 | 103.19 | 128.59 | 153.99 | 179.39 | 204.79 | 230.19 | 255.59 | 280.99 |
| 1/8 | 3.18 | 28.58 | 53.98 | 79.38 | 104.78 | 130.18 | 155.58 | 180.98 | 206.38 | 231.78 | 257.18 | 282.58 |
| 3/16 | 4.76 | 30.16 | 55.56 | 80.96 | 106.36 | 131.76 | 157.16 | 182.56 | 207.96 | 233.36 | 258.76 | 284.16 |
| 1/4 | 6.35 | 31.75 | 57.15 | 82.55 | 107.95 | 133.35 | 158.75 | 184.15 | 209.55 | 234.95 | 260.35 | 285.75 |
| 5/16 | 7.94 | 33.34 | 58.74 | 84.14 | 109.54 | 134.94 | 160.34 | 185.74 | 211.14 | 236.54 | 261.94 | 287.34 |
| 3/8 | 9.53 | 34.93 | 60.33 | 85.73 | 111.13 | 136.53 | 161.93 | 187.33 | 212.73 | 238.13 | 263.53 | 288.93 |
| 7/16 | 11.11 | 36.51 | 61.91 | 87.31 | 112.71 | 138.11 | 163.51 | 188.91 | 214.31 | 239.71 | 265.11 | 290.51 |
| 1/2 | 12.70 | 38.10 | 63.50 | 88.90 | 114.30 | 139.70 | 165.10 | 190.50 | 215.90 | 241.30 | 266.70 | 292.10 |
| 9/16 | 14.29 | 39.69 | 65.09 | 90.49 | 115.89 | 141.29 | 166.69 | 192.09 | 217.49 | 242.89 | 268.29 | 293.69 |
| 5/8 | 15.88 | 41.28 | 66.68 | 92.08 | 117.48 | 142.88 | 168.28 | 193.68 | 219.08 | 244.48 | 269.88 | 295.28 |
| 11/16 | 17.46 | 42.86 | 68.26 | 93.66 | 119.06 | 144.46 | 169.86 | 195.26 | 220.66 | 246.06 | 271.46 | 296.86 |
| 3/4 | 19.05 | 44.45 | 69.85 | 95.25 | 120.65 | 146.05 | 171.45 | 196.85 | 222.25 | 247.65 | 273.05 | 298.45 |
| 13/16 | 20.64 | 46.04 | 71.44 | 96.84 | 122.24 | 147.64 | 173.04 | 198.44 | 223.84 | 249.24 | 274.64 | 300.04 |
| 7/8 | 22.23 | 47.63 | 73.03 | 98.43 | 123.83 | 149.23 | 174.63 | 200.03 | 225.43 | 250.83 | 276.23 | 301.63 |
| 15/16 | 23.81 | 49.21 | 74.61 | 100.01 | 125.41 | 150.81 | 176.21 | 201.61 | 227.01 | 252.41 | 277.81 | 303.21 |

## FEET AND INCHES TO MILLIMETERS (1 FT = 304.8 mm; 1 IN. = 25.4 mm)

| INCHES | 0 | 1 | 2 | 3 | 4 | 5 | 6 | 7 | 8 | 9 | 10 | 11 |
|---|---|---|---|---|---|---|---|---|---|---|---|---|
| MILLIMETERS | . . . | 25 | 51 | 76 | 102 | 127 | 152 | 178 | 203 | 229 | 254 | 279 |
| | 0 | 1 | 2 | 3 | 4 | 5 | 6 | 7 | 8 | 9 | |
| FEET | | | | | | MILLIMETERS (mm) | | | | | |
| 0 | . . . | 305 | 610 | 914 | 1 219 | 1 524 | 1 829 | 2 134 | 2 438 | 2 743 | |
| 10 | 3 048 | 3 353 | 3 658 | 3 962 | 4 267 | 4 572 | 4 877 | 5 182 | 5 486 | 5 791 | |
| 20 | 6 096 | 6 401 | 6 706 | 7 010 | 7 315 | 7 620 | 7 925 | 8 230 | 8 534 | 8 839 | |
| 30 | 9 144 | 9 449 | 9 754 | 10 058 | 10 363 | 10 668 | 10 973 | 11 278 | 11 582 | 11 887 | |
| 40 | 12 192 | 12 497 | 12 802 | 13 106 | 13 411 | 13 716 | 14 021 | 14 326 | 14 630 | 14 935 | |
| 50 | 15 240 | 15 545 | 15 850 | 16 154 | 16 459 | 16 764 | 17 069 | 17 374 | 17 678 | 17 983 | |
| 60 | 18 288 | 18 593 | 18 898 | 19 202 | 19 507 | 19 812 | 20 117 | 20 422 | 20 726 | 21 031 | |
| 70 | 21 336 | 21 641 | 21 946 | 22 250 | 22 555 | 22 860 | 23 165 | 23 470 | 23 774 | 24 079 | |
| 80 | 24 384 | 24 689 | 24 994 | 25 298 | 25 603 | 25 908 | 26 213 | 26 518 | 26 882 | 27 127 | |
| 90 | 27 432 | 27 737 | 28 042 | 28 346 | 28 651 | 28 956 | 29 261 | 29 566 | 29 870 | 30 175 | |
| 100 | 30 480 | 30 785 | 31 090 | 31 394 | 31 699 | 32 004 | 32 309 | 32 614 | 32 918 | 33 223 | |
| 110 | 33 528 | 33 833 | 34 138 | 34 442 | 34 747 | 35 052 | 35 357 | 35 662 | 35 966 | 36 271 | |
| 120 | 36 576 | 36 881 | 37 186 | 37 490 | 37 795 | 38 100 | 38 405 | 38 710 | 39 014 | 39 319 | |
| 130 | 39 624 | 39 929 | 40 234 | 40 538 | 40 843 | 41 148 | 41 453 | 41 758 | 42 062 | 42 367 | |
| 140 | 42 672 | 42 977 | 43 282 | 43 586 | 43 891 | 44 196 | 44 501 | 44 806 | 45 110 | 45 415 | |
| 150 | 45 720 | | | | | | | | | | |

## FEET TO METERS (1 FT = 0.304 8 m)

| FEET | 0 | 1 | 2 | 3 | 4 | 5 | 6 | 7 | 8 | 9 |
|---|---|---|---|---|---|---|---|---|---|---|
| | | | | | | METERS (m) | | | | |
| 0 | . . . | 0.305 | 0.610 | 0.914 | 1.219 | 1.524 | 1.829 | 2.134 | 2.438 | 2.743 |
| 10 | 3.048 | 3.353 | 3.658 | 3.962 | 4.267 | 4.572 | 4.877 | 5.182 | 5.486 | 5.791 |
| 20 | 6.096 | 6.401 | 6.706 | 7.010 | 7.315 | 7.620 | 7.925 | 8.230 | 8.534 | 8.839 |
| 30 | 9.144 | 9.449 | 9.754 | 10.058 | 10.363 | 10.668 | 10.973 | 11.278 | 11.582 | 11.887 |
| 40 | 12.192 | 12.497 | 12.802 | 13.106 | 13.411 | 13.716 | 14.021 | 14.326 | 14.630 | 14.935 |
| 50 | 15.240 | 15.545 | 15.850 | 16.154 | 15.459 | 16.764 | 17.069 | 17.374 | 17.678 | 17.983 |
| 60 | 18.288 | 18.593 | 18.898 | 19.202 | 19.507 | 19.812 | 20.117 | 20.422 | 20.726 | 21.031 |
| 70 | 21.336 | 21.641 | 21.946 | 22.250 | 22.555 | 22.860 | 23.165 | 23.470 | 23.774 | 24.079 |
| 80 | 24.384 | 24.689 | 24.994 | 25.298 | 25.603 | 25.908 | 26.213 | 26.518 | 26.822 | 27.127 |
| 90 | 27.432 | 27.737 | 28.042 | 28.346 | 28.651 | 28.956 | 29.261 | 29.566 | 29.870 | 30.175 |
| 100 | 30.480 | 30.785 | 31.090 | 31.394 | 31.699 | 32.004 | 32.309 | 32.614 | 32.918 | 33.223 |
| 110 | 33.528 | 33.833 | 34.138 | 34.442 | 34.747 | 35.052 | 35.357 | 35.662 | 35.966 | 36.271 |
| 120 | 36.576 | 36.881 | 37.186 | 37.490 | 37.795 | 38.100 | 38.405 | 38.710 | 39.014 | 39.319 |
| 130 | 39.624 | 39.929 | 40.234 | 40.538 | 40.843 | 41.148 | 41.453 | 41.758 | 42.062 | 42.367 |
| 140 | 42.672 | 42.977 | 43.282 | 43.586 | 43.891 | 44.196 | 44.501 | 44.806 | 45.110 | 45.415 |
| 150 | 45.720 | 46.025 | 46.330 | 46.634 | 46.939 | 47.244 | 47.549 | 47.854 | 48.158 | 48.463 |
| 160 | 48.768 | 49.073 | 49.378 | 49.682 | 49.987 | 50.292 | 50.597 | 50.902 | 51.206 | 51.511 |
| 170 | 51.816 | 52.121 | 52.426 | 52.730 | 53.035 | 53.340 | 53.645 | 53.950 | 54.254 | 54.559 |
| 180 | 54.864 | 55.169 | 55.474 | 55.778 | 56.083 | 56.388 | 56.693 | 56.998 | 57.302 | 57.607 |
| 190 | 57.912 | 58.217 | 58.522 | 58.826 | 59.131 | 59.436 | 59.741 | 60.046 | 60.350 | 60.655 |
| 200 | 60.960 | | | | | | | | | |

METRIC

## MILES TO KILOMETERS (1 MI = 1.609 344 km)

| MILES | 0 | 1 | 2 | 3 | 4 | 5 | 6 | 7 | 8 | 9 |
|---|---|---|---|---|---|---|---|---|---|---|
| | | | | | KILOMETERS (km) | | | | | |
| 0 | . . . | 1.609 | 3.219 | 4.828 | 6.437 | 8.047 | 9.656 | 11.265 | 12.875 | 14.484 |
| 10 | 16.093 | 17.703 | 19.312 | 20.921 | 22.531 | 24.140 | 25.750 | 27.359 | 28.968 | 30.578 |
| 20 | 32.187 | 33.796 | 35.406 | 37.015 | 38.624 | 40.234 | 41.843 | 43.452 | 45.062 | 46.671 |
| 30 | 48.280 | 49.890 | 51.499 | 53.108 | 54.718 | 56.327 | 57.936 | 59.546 | 61.155 | 62.764 |
| 40 | 64.374 | 65.983 | 67.592 | 69.202 | 70.811 | 72.420 | 74.030 | 75.639 | 77.249 | 78.858 |
| 50 | 80.467 | 82.077 | 83.686 | 85.295 | 86.905 | 88.514 | 90.123 | 91.733 | 93.342 | 94.951 |
| 60 | 96.561 | 98.170 | 99.779 | 101.389 | 102.998 | 104.607 | 106.217 | 107.826 | 109.435 | 111.045 |
| 70 | 112.654 | 114.263 | 115.873 | 117.482 | 119.091 | 120.701 | 122.310 | 123.919 | 125.529 | 127.138 |
| 80 | 128.748 | 130.357 | 131.966 | 133.576 | 135.185 | 136.794 | 138.404 | 140.013 | 141.622 | 143.232 |
| 90 | 144.841 | 146.450 | 148.060 | 149.669 | 151.278 | 152.888 | 154.497 | 156.106 | 157.716 | 159.325 |
| 100 | 160.934 | 162.544 | 164.153 | 165.762 | 167.372 | 168.981 | 170.590 | 172.200 | 173.809 | 175.418 |
| 110 | 177.028 | 178.637 | 180.247 | 181.856 | 183.465 | 185.075 | 186.684 | 188.293 | 189.903 | 191.512 |
| 120 | 193.121 | 194.731 | 196.340 | 197.949 | 199.559 | 201.168 | 202.777 | 204.387 | 205.996 | 207.605 |
| 130 | 209.215 | 210.824 | 212.433 | 214.043 | 215.652 | 217.261 | 218.871 | 220.480 | 222.089 | 223.699 |
| 140 | 225.308 | 226.918 | 228.527 | 230.136 | 231.746 | 233.355 | 234.964 | 236.574 | 238.183 | 239.792 |
| 150 | 241.402 | 243.011 | 244.620 | 246.230 | 247.839 | 249.448 | 251.058 | 252.667 | 254.276 | 255.866 |
| 160 | 257.495 | 259.104 | 260.714 | 262.323 | 263.932 | 265.542 | 267.151 | 268.760 | 270.370 | 271.979 |
| 170 | 273.588 | 275.198 | 276.807 | 278.417 | 280.026 | 281.635 | 283.245 | 284.854 | 286.463 | 288.073 |
| 180 | 289.682 | 291.291 | 292.901 | 294.510 | 296.119 | 297.729 | 299.338 | 300.947 | 302.557 | 304.166 |
| 190 | 305.775 | 307.385 | 308.994 | 310.603 | 312.213 | 313.822 | 315.431 | 317.041 | 318.650 | 320.259 |
| 200 | 321.869 | | | | | | | | | |

## SQUARE INCHES TO SQUARE MILLIMETERS (1 IN.² = 645.16 mm²)

| SQUARE INCHES | 0 | 1 | 2 | 3 | 4 | 5 | 6 | 7 | 8 | 9 |
|---|---|---|---|---|---|---|---|---|---|---|
| | | | | | SQUARE MILLIMETERS (mm²) | | | | | |
| 0 | . . . | 0.645 | 1.290 | 1.935 | 2.581 | 3.226 | 3.781 | 4.516 | 5.161 | 5.806 |
| 10 | 6.452 | 7.097 | 7.742 | 8.387 | 9.032 | 9.677 | 10.323 | 10.968 | 11.613 | 12.258 |
| 20 | 12.903 | 13.548 | 14.194 | 14.839 | 15.484 | 16.129 | 16.774 | 17.419 | 18.064 | 18.710 |
| 30 | 19.355 | 20.000 | 20.645 | 21.290 | 21.935 | 22.581 | 23.226 | 23.871 | 24.516 | 25.161 |
| 40 | 25.806 | 26.452 | 27.097 | 27.742 | 28.387 | 29.032 | 29.677 | 30.323 | 30.968 | 31.613 |
| 50 | 32.258 | 32.903 | 33.548 | 34.193 | 34.839 | 35.484 | 36.129 | 36.774 | 37.419 | 38.064 |
| 60 | 38.710 | 39.355 | 40.000 | 40.645 | 41.290 | 41.935 | 42.581 | 43.226 | 43.871 | 44.516 |
| 70 | 45.161 | 45.806 | 46.452 | 47.097 | 47.742 | 48.387 | 49.032 | 49.677 | 50.322 | 50.968 |
| 80 | 51.613 | 52.258 | 52.903 | 53.548 | 54.193 | 54.839 | 55.484 | 56.129 | 56.774 | 57.419 |
| 90 | 58.064 | 58.710 | 59.355 | 60.000 | 60.645 | 61.290 | 61.935 | 62.581 | 63.226 | 63.871 |
| 100 | 64.516 | 65.161 | 65.806 | 66.451 | 67.097 | 67.742 | 68.387 | 69.032 | 69.677 | 70.322 |
| 110 | 70.968 | 71.613 | 72.258 | 72.903 | 73.548 | 74.193 | 74.839 | 75.484 | 76.129 | 76.774 |
| 120 | 77.419 | 78.064 | 78.710 | 79.355 | 80.000 | 80.645 | 81.290 | 81.935 | 82.580 | 83.226 |
| 130 | 83.871 | 84.516 | 85.161 | 85.806 | 86.451 | 87.097 | 87.742 | 88.387 | 89.032 | 89.677 |
| 140 | 90.322 | 90.968 | 91.613 | 92.258 | 92.903 | | | | | |

## SQUARE FEET TO SQUARE METERS (1 FT² = 0.0929 m²)

| SQUARE FEET | 0 | 1 | 2 | 3 | 4 | 5 | 6 | 7 | 8 | 9 |
|---|---|---|---|---|---|---|---|---|---|---|
| SQUARE METER | . . . | 0.09 | 0.19 | 0.28 | 0.37 | 0.46 | 0.56 | 0.65 | 0.74 | 0.84 |

| SQUARE FEET | 0 | 10 | 20 | 30 | 40 | 50 | 60 | 70 | 80 | 90 |
|---|---|---|---|---|---|---|---|---|---|---|
| | | | | | SQUARE METERS (m²) | | | | | |
| 0 | . . . | 0.93 | 1.86 | 2.79 | 3.72 | 4.65 | 5.57 | 6.50 | 7.43 | 8.36 |
| 100 | 9.29 | 10.22 | 11.15 | 12.08 | 13.01 | 13.94 | 14.86 | 15.79 | 16.72 | 17.65 |
| 200 | 18.58 | 19.51 | 20.44 | 21.37 | 22.30 | 23.23 | 24.15 | 25.08 | 26.01 | 26.94 |
| 300 | 27.87 | 28.80 | 29.73 | 30.66 | 31.59 | 32.52 | 33.45 | 34.37 | 35.30 | 36.23 |
| 400 | 37.16 | 38.09 | 39.02 | 39.95 | 40.88 | 41.81 | 42.74 | 43.66 | 44.59 | 45.52 |
| 500 | 46.45 | 47.38 | 48.31 | 49.24 | 50.17 | 51.10 | 52.03 | 52.95 | 53.88 | 54.81 |
| 600 | 55.74 | 56.67 | 57.60 | 58.53 | 59.46 | 60.39 | 61.32 | 62.25 | 63.17 | 64.10 |
| 700 | 65.03 | 65.96 | 66.89 | 67.82 | 68.75 | 69.68 | 70.61 | 71.54 | 72.46 | 73.39 |
| 800 | 74.32 | 75.25 | 76.18 | 77.11 | 78.04 | 78.97 | 79.90 | 80.83 | 81.75 | 82.68 |
| 900 | 83.61 | 84.54 | 85.47 | 86.40 | 87.33 | 88.26 | 89.19 | 90.12 | 91.04 | 91.97 |
| 1000 | 92.90 | 93.83 | 94.76 | 95.69 | 96.62 | 97.55 | 98.48 | 99.41 | 100.34 | 101.26 |
| 1100 | 102.19 | 103.12 | 104.05 | 104.98 | 105.91 | 106.84 | 107.77 | 108.70 | 109.63 | 110.55 |
| 1200 | 111.48 | 112.41 | 113.34 | 114.27 | 115.20 | 116.13 | 117.06 | 117.99 | 118.92 | 119.84 |
| 1300 | 120.77 | 121.70 | 122.63 | 123.56 | 124.49 | 125.42 | 126.35 | 127.28 | 128.21 | 129.14 |
| 1400 | 130.06 | 130.99 | 131.92 | 132.85 | 133.78 | 134.71 | 135.64 | 136.57 | 137.50 | 138.43 |
| 1500 | 139.35 | | | | | | | | | |

METRIC   A

## ACRES TO HECTARES (1 ACRE = 0.404 685 6 ha)

| ACRES | 0 | 1 | 2 | 3 | 4 | 5 | 6 | 7 | 8 | 9 |
|---|---|---|---|---|---|---|---|---|---|---|
| HECTARES | ... | 0.40 | 0.81 | 1.21 | 1.62 | 2.02 | 2.43 | 2.83 | 3.24 | 3.64 |

| ACRES | 0 | 10 | 20 | 30 | 40 | 50 | 60 | 70 | 80 | 90 |
|---|---|---|---|---|---|---|---|---|---|---|
| | | | | | HECTARES (ha) | | | | | |
| 0 | ... | 4.05 | 8.09 | 12.14 | 16.19 | 20.23 | 24.28 | 28.33 | 32.37 | 36.42 |
| 100 | 40.47 | 44.52 | 48.56 | 52.61 | 56.66 | 60.70 | 64.75 | 68.80 | 72.84 | 76.89 |
| 200 | 80.94 | 84.98 | 89.03 | 93.08 | 97.12 | 101.17 | 105.22 | 109.27 | 113.31 | 117.36 |
| 300 | 121.41 | 125.45 | 129.50 | 133.55 | 137.59 | 141.64 | 145.69 | 149.73 | 153.78 | 157.83 |
| 400 | 161.87 | 165.92 | 169.97 | 174.01 | 178.06 | 182.11 | 186.16 | 190.20 | 194.25 | 198.30 |
| 500 | 202.34 | 206.39 | 210.44 | 214.48 | 218.53 | 222.58 | 226.62 | 230.67 | 234.72 | 238.76 |
| 600 | 242.81 | 246.86 | 250.91 | 254.95 | 259.00 | 263.05 | 267.09 | 271.14 | 275.19 | 279.23 |
| 700 | 283.28 | 287.33 | 291.37 | 295.42 | 299.47 | 303.51 | 307.56 | 311.61 | 315.65 | 319.70 |
| 800 | 323.75 | 327.80 | 331.84 | 335.89 | 339.94 | 343.98 | 348.03 | 352.08 | 356.12 | 360.17 |
| 900 | 364.22 | 368.26 | 372.31 | 376.36 | 380.40 | 384.45 | 388.50 | 392.55 | 396.59 | 400.64 |
| 1000 | 404.69 | | | | | | | | | |

## CUBIC FEET TO CUBIC METERS (1 FT$^3$ = 0.0283 m$^3$)

| CUBIC FEET | 0 | 1 | 2 | 3 | 4 | 5 | 6 | 7 | 8 | 9 |
|---|---|---|---|---|---|---|---|---|---|---|
| | | | | | CUBIC METERS (m$^3$) | | | | | |
| 0 | ... | 0.028 | 0.057 | 0.085 | 0.113 | 0.142 | 0.170 | 0.198 | 0.227 | 0.255 |
| 10 | 0.283 | 0.311 | 0.340 | 0.368 | 0.396 | 0.425 | 0.453 | 0.481 | 0.510 | 0.538 |
| 20 | 0.566 | 0.595 | 0.623 | 0.651 | 0.680 | 0.708 | 0.736 | 0.765 | 0.793 | 0.821 |
| 30 | 0.850 | 0.878 | 0.906 | 0.934 | 0.963 | 0.991 | 0.019 | 1.048 | 1.076 | 1.104 |
| 40 | 1.133 | 1.161 | 1.189 | 1.218 | 1.246 | 1.274 | 1.303 | 1.331 | 1.359 | 1.386 |
| 50 | 1.416 | 1.444 | 1.472 | 1.501 | 1.529 | 1.557 | 1.586 | 1.614 | 1.642 | 1.671 |
| 60 | 1.699 | 1.727 | 1.756 | 1.784 | 1.812 | 1.841 | 1.869 | 1.897 | 1.926 | 1.954 |
| 70 | 1.982 | 2.010 | 2.034 | 2.067 | 2.095 | 2.124 | 2.152 | 2.180 | 2.209 | 2.237 |
| 80 | 2.265 | 2.293 | 2.322 | 2.350 | 2.379 | 2.407 | 2.435 | 2.464 | 2.492 | 2.520 |
| 90 | 2.549 | 2.577 | 2.605 | 2.633 | 2.662 | 2.690 | 2.718 | 2.747 | 2.775 | 2.803 |
| 100 | 2.832 | 2.860 | 2.888 | 2.917 | 2.945 | 2.973 | 3.002 | 3.030 | 3.058 | 3.087 |
| 110 | 3.115 | 3.143 | 3.171 | 3.200 | 3.228 | 3.256 | 3.285 | 3.313 | 3.341 | 3.370 |
| 120 | 3.398 | 3.426 | 3.455 | 3.483 | 3.511 | 3.540 | 3.568 | 3.596 | 3.625 | 3.653 |
| 130 | 3.681 | 3.710 | 3.738 | 3.766 | 3.794 | 3.823 | 3.851 | 3.879 | 3.908 | 3.936 |
| 140 | 3.964 | 3.993 | 4.021 | 4.049 | 4.078 | 4.106 | 4.134 | 4.163 | 4.191 | 4.219 |
| 150 | 4.248 | 4.276 | 4.304 | 4.332 | 4.361 | 4.389 | 4.417 | 4.446 | 4.474 | 4.502 |
| 160 | 4.531 | 4.559 | 4.587 | 4.616 | 4.644 | 4.672 | 4.701 | 4.729 | 4.757 | 4.786 |
| 170 | 4.814 | 4.482 | 4.870 | 4.899 | 4.927 | 4.955 | 4.984 | 5.012 | 5.040 | 5.069 |
| 180 | 5.097 | 5.125 | 5.154 | 5.182 | 5.210 | 5.239 | 5.267 | 5.295 | 5.234 | 5.352 |
| 190 | 5.380 | 5.409 | 5.437 | 5.465 | 5.493 | 5.522 | 5.550 | 5.578 | 5.606 | 5.635 |
| 200 | 5.663 | | | | | | | | | |

NOTE: 1 cubic meter (m$^3$) equals 1000 liters (L). Cubic feet can be converted to liters by shifting the decimal point three places to the right; for example, 125 cubic feet = 3.540 m$^3$ = 3540 L.

## GALLONS TO LITERS (1 GAL [U.S.] = 3.785 41 L)

| GALLONS | 0 | 1 | 2 | 3 | 4 | 5 | 6 | 7 | 8 | 9 |
|---|---|---|---|---|---|---|---|---|---|---|
| | | | | | LITERS (L) | | | | | |
| 0 | ... | 3.79 | 7.57 | 11.36 | 15.14 | 18.93 | 22.71 | 26.50 | 30.28 | 34.07 |
| 10 | 37.85 | 41.64 | 45.42 | 49.21 | 53.00 | 56.78 | 60.57 | 64.35 | 68.14 | 71.92 |
| 20 | 75.71 | 79.49 | 83.28 | 87.06 | 90.85 | 94.64 | 98.42 | 102.21 | 105.99 | 109.78 |
| 30 | 113.56 | 117.35 | 121.13 | 124.92 | 128.70 | 132.49 | 136.27 | 140.06 | 143.85 | 147.63 |
| 40 | 151.42 | 155.20 | 158.99 | 162.77 | 166.56 | 170.34 | 174.13 | 177.91 | 181.70 | 185.49 |
| 50 | 189.27 | 193.06 | 196.84 | 200.63 | 204.41 | 208.20 | 211.98 | 215.77 | 219.55 | 223.34 |
| 60 | 227.12 | 230.91 | 234.70 | 238.48 | 242.27 | 246.05 | 249.84 | 253.62 | 257.41 | 261.19 |
| 70 | 264.98 | 268.76 | 272.55 | 276.34 | 280.12 | 283.91 | 287.69 | 291.48 | 295.26 | 299.05 |
| 80 | 302.83 | 306.62 | 310.40 | 314.19 | 317.97 | 321.76 | 325.55 | 329.33 | 333.12 | 336.90 |
| 90 | 340.69 | 344.47 | 348.26 | 352.04 | 355.83 | 359.61 | 363.40 | 367.18 | 370.97 | 374.76 |

| GALLONS | 0 | 10 | 20 | 30 | 40 | 50 | 60 | 70 | 80 | 90 |
|---|---|---|---|---|---|---|---|---|---|---|
| 100 | 378.5 | 416.4 | 454.2 | 492.1 | 530.0 | 567.8 | 605.7 | 643.5 | 681.4 | 719.2 |
| 200 | 757.1 | 794.9 | 832.8 | 870.6 | 908.5 | 946.4 | 984.2 | 1022.1 | 1059.9 | 1097.8 |
| 300 | 1135.6 | 1173.5 | 1211.3 | 1249.2 | 1287.0 | 1324.9 | 1362.7 | 1400.6 | 1438.5 | 1476.3 |
| 400 | 1514.2 | 1552.0 | 1589.9 | 1627.7 | 1665.6 | 1703.4 | 1741.3 | 1779.1 | 1817.0 | 1854.9 |
| 500 | 1892.7 | 1930.6 | 1968.4 | 2006.3 | 2044.1 | 2082.0 | 2119.8 | 2157.7 | 2195.5 | 2233.4 |
| 600 | 2271.2 | 2309.1 | 2347.0 | 2384.8 | 2422.7 | 2460.5 | 2498.4 | 2536.2 | 2574.1 | 2611.9 |
| 700 | 2649.8 | 2687.6 | 2725.5 | 2763.4 | 2801.2 | 2839.1 | 2876.9 | 2914.8 | 2952.6 | 2990.5 |
| 800 | 3028.3 | 3066.3 | 3104.0 | 3141.9 | 3179.7 | 3217.6 | 3255.5 | 3293.3 | 3331.2 | 3369.0 |
| 900 | 3406.9 | 3444.7 | 3482.6 | 3520.4 | 3558.3 | 3596.1 | 3634.0 | 3671.8 | 3709.7 | 3747.6 |
| 1000 | 3785.4 | | | | | | | | | |

METRIC

## POUNDS TO KILOGRAMS (1 LB = 0.453 592 kg)

| POUNDS | 0 | 1 | 2 | 3 | 4 | 5 | 6 | 7 | 8 | 9 |
|---|---|---|---|---|---|---|---|---|---|---|
| | | | | | KILOGRAMS (kg) | | | | | |
| 0 | . . . | 0.45 | 0.91 | 1.36 | 1.81 | 2.27 | 2.72 | 3.18 | 3.63 | 4.08 |
| 10 | 4.54 | 4.99 | 5.44 | 5.90 | 6.35 | 6.80 | 7.26 | 7.71 | 8.16 | 8.62 |
| 20 | 9.07 | 9.53 | 9.98 | 10.43 | 10.89 | 11.34 | 11.79 | 12.25 | 12.70 | 13.15 |
| 30 | 13.61 | 14.06 | 14.52 | 14.97 | 15.42 | 15.88 | 16.33 | 16.78 | 17.24 | 17.69 |
| 40 | 18.14 | 18.60 | 19.05 | 19.50 | 19.96 | 20.41 | 20.87 | 21.32 | 21.77 | 22.23 |
| 50 | 22.68 | 23.13 | 23.59 | 24.04 | 24.49 | 24.95 | 25.40 | 25.85 | 26.31 | 26.76 |
| 60 | 27.22 | 27.67 | 28.12 | 28.58 | 29.03 | 29.48 | 29.94 | 30.39 | 30.84 | 31.30 |
| 70 | 31.75 | 32.21 | 32.66 | 33.11 | 33.57 | 34.02 | 34.47 | 34.93 | 35.38 | 35.83 |
| 80 | 36.29 | 36.74 | 37.19 | 37.65 | 38.10 | 38.56 | 39.01 | 39.46 | 39.92 | 40.37 |
| 90 | 40.82 | 41.28 | 41.73 | 42.18 | 42.64 | 43.09 | 43.54 | 44.00 | 44.45 | 44.91 |
| 100 | 45.36 | 45.81 | 46.27 | 46.72 | 47.17 | 47.63 | 48.08 | 48.53 | 48.99 | 49.44 |
| 110 | 49.90 | 50.35 | 50.80 | 51.26 | 51.71 | 52.16 | 52.62 | 53.07 | 53.52 | 53.98 |
| 120 | 54.43 | 54.88 | 55.34 | 55.79 | 56.25 | 56.70 | 57.15 | 57.61 | 58.06 | 58.51 |
| 130 | 58.97 | 59.42 | 59.87 | 60.33 | 60.78 | 61.24 | 61.69 | 62.14 | 62.60 | 63.05 |
| 140 | 63.50 | 63.96 | 64.41 | 64.86 | 65.32 | 65.77 | 66.22 | 66.68 | 67.13 | 67.59 |
| 150 | 68.04 | 68.49 | 68.95 | 69.40 | 69.85 | 70.31 | 70.76 | 71.21 | 71.67 | 72.12 |
| 160 | 72.57 | 73.03 | 73.48 | 73.94 | 74.39 | 74.84 | 75.30 | 75.75 | 76.20 | 76.66 |
| 170 | 77.11 | 77.56 | 78.02 | 78.47 | 78.93 | 79.38 | 79.83 | 80.29 | 80.74 | 81.19 |
| 180 | 81.65 | 82.10 | 82.55 | 83.01 | 83.46 | 83.91 | 84.37 | 84.82 | 85.28 | 85.73 |
| 190 | 86.18 | 86.64 | 87.09 | 87.54 | 88.00 | 88.45 | 88.90 | 89.36 | 89.81 | 90.26 |
| 200 | 90.72 | | | | | | | | | |

## U.S. SHORT TONS (2000 LB) TO METRIC TONS (1 TON = 0.907 185 t)

| SHORT TONS | 0 | 1 | 2 | 3 | 4 | 5 | 6 | 7 | 8 | 9 |
|---|---|---|---|---|---|---|---|---|---|---|
| | | | | | METRIC TONS (t) | | | | | |
| 0 | . . . | 0.907 | 1.814 | 2.722 | 3.629 | 4.536 | 5.443 | 6.350 | 7.257 | 8.165 |
| 10 | 9.072 | 9.979 | 10.886 | 11.793 | 12.701 | 13.608 | 14.515 | 15.422 | 16.329 | 17.237 |
| 20 | 18.144 | 19.051 | 19.958 | 20.865 | 21.772 | 22.680 | 23.587 | 24.494 | 25.401 | 26.308 |
| 30 | 27.216 | 28.123 | 29.030 | 29.937 | 30.844 | 31.751 | 32.659 | 33.566 | 34.473 | 35.380 |
| 40 | 36.287 | 37.195 | 38.102 | 39.009 | 39.916 | 40.823 | 41.731 | 42.638 | 43.545 | 44.452 |
| 50 | 45.359 | 46.266 | 47.174 | 48.081 | 48.988 | 49.895 | 50.802 | 51.710 | 52.617 | 53.524 |
| 60 | 54.431 | 55.338 | 56.245 | 57.153 | 58.060 | 58.967 | 59.874 | 60.781 | 61.689 | 62.596 |
| 70 | 63.503 | 64.410 | 65.317 | 66.225 | 67.132 | 68.039 | 68.946 | 69.853 | 70.760 | 71.668 |
| 80 | 72.575 | 73.482 | 74.389 | 75.296 | 76.204 | 77.111 | 78.018 | 78.925 | 79.832 | 80.739 |
| 90 | 81.647 | 82.554 | 83.461 | 84.368 | 85.275 | 86.183 | 87.090 | 87.997 | 88.904 | 89.811 |
| 100 | 90.718 | | | | | | | | | |

NOTE: 1 metric ton (t) equals 1000 kilograms (kg). U.S. short tons can be converted to kilograms by shifting the decimal point three places to the right; for example, 48 short tons = 43.545 t = 43.545 kg (rounded to the nearest kilogram).

## POUNDS PER CUBIC FOOT TO KILOGRAMS PER CUBIC METER (1 LB/FT$^3$ = 16.018 46 kg/m$^3$)

| POUNDS PER CUBIC FOOT | 0 | 1 | 2 | 3 | 4 | 5 | 6 | 7 | 8 | 9 |
|---|---|---|---|---|---|---|---|---|---|---|
| | | | | | KILOGRAMS PER CUBIC METER (kg/m$^3$) | | | | | |
| 0 | . . . | 16.0 | 32.0 | 48.1 | 64.1 | 80.1 | 96.1 | 112.1 | 128.1 | 144.2 |
| 10 | 160.2 | 176.2 | 192.2 | 208.2 | 224.3 | 240.3 | 256.3 | 272.3 | 288.3 | 304.4 |
| 20 | 320.4 | 336.4 | 352.4 | 368.4 | 384.4 | 400.5 | 416.5 | 432.5 | 448.5 | 464.5 |
| 30 | 480.6 | 496.6 | 512.6 | 528.6 | 544.6 | 560.6 | 576.7 | 592.7 | 608.7 | 624.7 |
| 40 | 640.7 | 656.8 | 672.8 | 688.8 | 704.8 | 720.8 | 736.8 | 752.9 | 768.9 | 784.9 |
| 50 | 800.9 | 816.9 | 833.0 | 849.0 | 865.0 | 881.0 | 897.0 | 913.1 | 929.1 | 945.1 |
| 60 | 961.1 | 977.1 | 993.1 | 1009.2 | 1025.2 | 1041.2 | 1057.2 | 1073.2 | 1089.3 | 1105.3 |
| 70 | 1121.3 | 1137.3 | 1153.3 | 1169.3 | 1185.4 | 1201.4 | 1217.4 | 1233.4 | 1249.4 | 1265.5 |
| 80 | 1281.5 | 1297.5 | 1313.5 | 1329.5 | 1345.6 | 1361.6 | 1377.6 | 1393.6 | 1409.6 | 1425.6 |
| 90 | 1441.7 | 1457.7 | 1473.7 | 1489.7 | 1505.7 | 1521.8 | 1537.8 | 1553.8 | 1569.8 | 1585.8 |
| 100 | 1601.8 | 1617.9 | 1633.9 | 1649.9 | 1665.9 | 1681.9 | 1698.0 | 1714.0 | 1730.0 | 1746.0 |
| 110 | 1762.0 | 1778.0 | 1794.1 | 1810.1 | 1826.1 | 1842.1 | 1858.1 | 1874.2 | 1890.2 | 1906.2 |
| 120 | 1922.2 | 1938.2 | 1954.3 | 1970.3 | 1986.3 | 2002.3 | 2018.3 | 2034.3 | 2050.4 | 2066.4 |
| 130 | 2082.4 | 2098.4 | 2114.4 | 2130.5 | 2146.5 | 2162.5 | 2178.5 | 2194.5 | 2210.5 | 2226.6 |
| 140 | 2242.6 | 2258.6 | 2274.6 | 2290.6 | 2306.7 | 2322.7 | 2338.7 | 2354.7 | 2370.7 | 2386.8 |
| 150 | 2402.8 | 2418.8 | 2434.8 | 2450.8 | 2466.8 | 2482.9 | 2498.9 | 2514.9 | 2590.9 | 2546.9 |
| 160 | 2563.0 | 2579.0 | 2595.0 | 2611.0 | 2627.0 | 2643.0 | 2659.1 | 2675.1 | 2691.1 | 2707.1 |
| 170 | 2723.1 | 2739.2 | 2755.2 | 2771.2 | 2787.2 | 2803.2 | 2819.2 | 2835.3 | 2851.3 | 2867.3 |
| 180 | 2883.3 | 2899.3 | 2915.4 | 2931.4 | 2947.4 | 2963.4 | 2979.4 | 2995.4 | 3011.5 | 3027.5 |
| 190 | 3043.5 | 3059.5 | 3075.5 | 3091.6 | 3107.6 | 3123.6 | 3139.6 | 3155.6 | 3171.7 | 3187.7 |
| 200 | 3203.7 | | | | | | | | | |

METRIC

## POUNDS-FORCE PER SQUARE INCH (PSI) TO MEGAPASCALS (MPa) (1 PSI = 0.006 895 MPa)

| POUNDS-FORCE PER SQUARE INCH | 0 | 10 | 20 | 30 | 40 | 50 | 60 | 70 | 80 | 90 |
|---|---|---|---|---|---|---|---|---|---|---|
| | | | | | MEGAPASCALS (MPa) | | | | | |
| 0 | ... | 0.069 | 0.138 | 0.207 | 0.276 | 0.345 | 0.414 | 0.483 | 0.552 | 0.621 |
| 100 | 0.689 | 0.758 | 0.827 | 0.896 | 0.965 | 1.034 | 1.103 | 1.172 | 1.241 | 1.310 |
| 200 | 1.379 | 1.448 | 1.517 | 1.586 | 1.655 | 1.724 | 1.793 | 1.862 | 1.931 | 1.999 |
| 300 | 2.068 | 2.137 | 2.206 | 2.275 | 2.344 | 2.413 | 2.482 | 2.551 | 2.620 | 2.689 |
| 400 | 2.758 | 2.827 | 2.896 | 2.965 | 3.034 | 3.103 | 3.172 | 3.241 | 3.309 | 3.378 |
| 500 | 3.447 | 3.516 | 3.585 | 3.654 | 3.723 | 3.792 | 3.861 | 3.903 | 3.999 | 4.068 |
| 600 | 4.137 | 4.206 | 4.275 | 4.344 | 4.413 | 4.482 | 4.551 | 4.619 | 4.688 | 4.757 |
| 700 | 4.826 | 4.895 | 4.964 | 5.033 | 5.102 | 5.171 | 5.240 | 5.309 | 5.378 | 5.447 |
| 800 | 5.516 | 5.585 | 5.654 | 5.723 | 5.792 | 5.861 | 5.929 | 5.998 | 6.067 | 6.136 |
| 900 | 6.205 | 6.274 | 6.343 | 6.412 | 6.481 | 6.550 | 6.619 | 6.688 | 6.757 | 6.826 |
| | 0 | 100 | 200 | 300 | 400 | 500 | 600 | 700 | 800 | 900 |
| 1000 | 6.895 | 7.584 | 8.274 | 8.963 | 9.653 | 10.342 | 11.032 | 11.721 | 12.411 | 13.100 |
| 2000 | 13.790 | 14.479 | 15.168 | 15.858 | 16.547 | 17.237 | 17.926 | 18.616 | 19.305 | 19.995 |
| 3000 | 20.684 | 21.374 | 22.063 | 22.753 | 23.442 | 24.132 | 24.821 | 25.511 | 26.200 | 26.890 |
| 4000 | 27.579 | 28.269 | 28.958 | 29.647 | 30.337 | 31.026 | 31.716 | 32.405 | 33.095 | 33.784 |
| 5000 | 34.474 | 35.163 | 35.853 | 36.542 | 37.232 | 37.921 | 38.611 | 39.300 | 39.990 | 40.679 |
| 6000 | 41.369 | 42.058 | 42.747 | 43.437 | 44.126 | 44.816 | 45.505 | 46.195 | 46.884 | 47.574 |
| 7000 | 48.263 | 48.953 | 49.642 | 50.332 | 51.021 | 51.711 | 52.400 | 53.090 | 53.779 | 54.469 |
| 8000 | 55.158 | 55.848 | 56.537 | 57.226 | 57.916 | 58.605 | 59.295 | 59.984 | 60.674 | 61.363 |
| 9000 | 62.053 | 64.742 | 63.432 | 64.121 | 64.811 | 65.500 | 66.190 | 66.879 | 67.569 | 68.258 |
| 10 000 | 68.948 | | | | | | | | | |

NOTE: 1 megapascal (MPa) is equal to 1 meganewton per square meter ($MN/m^2$) and to 1 newton per square millimeter ($N/mm^2$).

## POUNDS-FORCE PER SQUARE FOOT TO KILOPASCALS (kPa) = 0.047 88 kN/m²

| POUNDS-FORCE PER SQUARE FOOT | 0 | 10 | 20 | 30 | 40 | 50 | 60 | 70 | 80 | 90 |
|---|---|---|---|---|---|---|---|---|---|---|
| | | | | | KILOPASCALS ($kPa = kN/m^2$) | | | | | |
| 0 | — | 0.479 | 0.958 | 1.436 | 1.915 | 2.394 | 2.873 | 3.352 | 3.830 | 4.309 |
| 100 | 4.788 | 5.267 | 5.746 | 6.224 | 6.703 | 7.182 | 7.661 | 8.140 | 8.618 | 9.097 |
| 200 | 9.576 | 10.055 | 10.534 | 11.013 | 11.491 | 11.970 | 12.449 | 12.928 | 13.406 | 13.886 |
| 300 | 14.364 | 14.843 | 15.322 | 15.800 | 16.279 | 16.758 | 17.237 | 17.716 | 18.195 | 18.673 |
| 400 | 19.152 | 19.631 | 20.110 | 20.589 | 21.067 | 21.546 | 22.025 | 22.504 | 22.983 | 23.461 |
| 500 | 23.910 | 24.419 | 24.898 | 25.377 | 25.855 | 26.334 | 26.813 | 27.292 | 27.771 | 28.249 |
| 600 | 28.728 | 29.207 | 29.686 | 31.165 | 30.643 | 31.122 | 31.601 | 32.080 | 32.559 | 33.037 |
| 700 | 33.516 | 33.995 | 34.474 | 34.953 | 35.431 | 35.910 | 36.389 | 36.868 | 37.347 | 37.825 |
| 800 | 38.304 | 38.783 | 39.262 | 39.741 | 40.219 | 40.698 | 41.177 | 41.656 | 42.135 | 42.613 |
| 900 | 43.092 | 43.571 | 44.050 | 44.529 | 45.007 | 45.486 | 45.965 | 46.444 | 46.923 | 47.401 |
| 1000 | 47.880 | | | | | | | | | |

NOTE: 1 kilopascal (kPa) is equal to 1 kilonewton per square meter ($kN/m^2$).

## LUMENS PER SQUARE FOOT TO LUX (lm/m²) AND KILOLUX (1 lm/FT² = 10.7639 lx)

| LUMENS PER SQUARE FOOT | 0 | 1 | 2 | 3 | 4 | 5 | 6 | 7 | 8 | 9 |
|---|---|---|---|---|---|---|---|---|---|---|
| | | | | | LUX ($lm/m^2$) | | | | | |
| 0 | ... | 10.8 | 21.5 | 32.3 | 43.1 | 53.8 | 64.6 | 75.3 | 86.1 | 96.9 |
| 10 | 107.6 | 118.4 | 129.2 | 139.9 | 150.7 | 161.5 | 172.2 | 183.0 | 193.8 | 204.5 |
| 20 | 215.3 | 226.0 | 236.8 | 247.6 | 258.3 | 269.1 | 279.9 | 290.6 | 301.4 | 312.2 |
| 30 | 322.9 | 333.7 | 344.4 | 355.2 | 366.0 | 376.7 | 387.5 | 398.3 | 409.0 | 419.8 |
| 40 | 430.6 | 441.3 | 452.1 | 462.8 | 473.6 | 484.4 | 495.1 | 505.9 | 516.7 | 527.4 |
| 50 | 538.2 | 549.0 | 559.7 | 570.5 | 581.3 | 592.0 | 602.8 | 613.5 | 624.3 | 635.1 |
| 60 | 645.8 | 656.6 | 667.4 | 678.1 | 688.9 | 699.7 | 710.4 | 721.2 | 731.9 | 742.7 |
| 70 | 753.5 | 764.2 | 775.0 | 785.8 | 796.5 | 807.3 | 818.1 | 828.8 | 839.6 | 850.3 |
| 80 | 861.1 | 871.9 | 882.6 | 893.4 | 904.2 | 914.9 | 925.7 | 936.5 | 947.2 | 958.0 |
| 90 | 968.8 | 979.5 | 990.3 | 1001.0 | 1011.8 | 1022.6 | 1033.3 | 1044.1 | 1054.9 | 1065.6 |
| | 0 | 10 | 20 | 30 | 40 | 50 | 60 | 70 | 80 | 90 |
| | | | | | KILOLUX (1000 lux) | | | | | |
| 100 | 1.076 | 1.184 | 1.292 | 1.399 | 1.507 | 1.615 | 1.722 | 1.830 | 1.938 | 2.045 |
| 200 | 2.153 | 2.260 | 2.368 | 2.476 | 2.583 | 2.691 | 2.799 | 2.906 | 3.014 | 3.122 |
| 300 | 3.229 | 3.337 | 3.444 | 3.552 | 3.660 | 3.767 | 3.875 | 3.983 | 4.090 | 4.198 |
| 400 | 4.306 | 4.413 | 4.521 | 4.628 | 4.736 | 4.844 | 4.951 | 5.059 | 5.167 | 5.274 |
| 500 | 5.382 | 5.490 | 5.597 | 5.705 | 5.813 | 5.920 | 6.028 | 6.135 | 6.243 | 6.351 |
| 600 | 6.458 | 6.566 | 6.674 | 6.781 | 6.889 | 6.997 | 7.104 | 7.212 | 7.319 | 7.427 |
| 700 | 7.535 | 7.642 | 7.750 | 7.858 | 7.965 | 8.073 | 8.181 | 8.288 | 8.396 | 8.503 |
| 800 | 8.611 | 8.719 | 8.826 | 8.934 | 9.042 | 9.149 | 9.257 | 9.365 | 9.472 | 9.580 |
| 900 | 9.688 | 9.795 | 9.903 | 10.010 | 10.118 | 10.226 | 10.333 | 10.441 | 10.549 | 10.656 |
| 1000 | 10.764 | | | | | | | | | |

METRIC

## POUND-FORCE TO NEWTONS (1 lbf = 4.448 22 N)

| POUND-FORCE | 0 | 1 | 2 | 3 | 4 | 5 | 6 | 7 | 8 | 9 |
|---|---|---|---|---|---|---|---|---|---|---|
| | | | | | NEWTONS (N) | | | | | |
| 0 | . . . | 4.45 | 8.90 | 13.34 | 17.79 | 22.24 | 26.69 | 31.14 | 35.59 | 40.03 |
| 10 | 44.48 | 48.93 | 53.38 | 57.83 | 62.28 | 66.72 | 71.17 | 75.62 | 80.07 | 84.52 |
| 20 | 88.96 | 93.41 | 97.86 | 102.31 | 106.76 | 111.21 | 115.65 | 120.10 | 124.55 | 129.00 |
| 30 | 133.45 | 137.89 | 142.34 | 146.79 | 151.24 | 155.69 | 160.14 | 164.58 | 169.03 | 173.48 |
| 40 | 177.93 | 182.38 | 186.83 | 191.27 | 195.72 | 200.17 | 204.62 | 209.07 | 213.51 | 217.96 |
| 50 | 222.41 | 226.86 | 231.31 | 235.76 | 240.20 | 244.65 | 249.10 | 253.55 | 258.00 | 262.45 |
| 60 | 266.89 | 271.34 | 275.79 | 280.24 | 284.69 | 289.13 | 293.58 | 298.03 | 302.48 | 306.93 |
| 70 | 311.38 | 315.82 | 320.27 | 324.72 | 329.17 | 333.62 | 338.06 | 342.51 | 346.96 | 351.41 |
| 80 | 355.86 | 360.31 | 364.75 | 369.20 | 373.65 | 378.10 | 382.55 | 387.00 | 391.44 | 395.89 |
| 90 | 400.34 | 404.79 | 409.24 | 413.68 | 418.13 | 422.58 | 427.03 | 431.48 | 435.93 | 440.37 |

| POUND-FORCE | 0 | 10 | 20 | 30 | 40 | 50 | 60 | 70 | 80 | 90 |
|---|---|---|---|---|---|---|---|---|---|---|
| 100 | 444.8 | 489.3 | 533.8 | 578.3 | 622.8 | 667.2 | 711.7 | 756.2 | 800.7 | 845.2 |
| 200 | 889.6 | 934.1 | 978.6 | 1023.1 | 1067.6 | 1112.1 | 1156.5 | 1201.0 | 1245.5 | 1290.0 |
| 300 | 1334.5 | 1378.9 | 1423.4 | 1467.9 | 1512.4 | 1556.9 | 1601.4 | 1645.8 | 1690.3 | 1734.8 |
| 400 | 1779.3 | 1823.8 | 1868.3 | 1912.7 | 1957.2 | 2001.7 | 2046.2 | 2090.7 | 2135.1 | 2179.6 |
| 500 | 2224.1 | 2268.6 | 2313.1 | 2357.6 | 2402.0 | 2446.5 | 2491.0 | 2535.5 | 2580.0 | 2624.5 |
| 600 | 2668.9 | 2713.4 | 2757.9 | 2802.4 | 2846.9 | 2891.3 | 2935.8 | 2980.3 | 3024.8 | 3069.3 |
| 700 | 3113.8 | 3158.2 | 3202.7 | 3247.2 | 3291.7 | 3336.2 | 3380.6 | 3425.1 | 3469.6 | 3514.1 |
| 800 | 3558.6 | 3603.1 | 3647.5 | 3692.0 | 3736.5 | 3781.0 | 3835.5 | 3870.0 | 3914.4 | 3958.9 |
| 900 | 4003.4 | 4047.9 | 4092.4 | 4136.8 | 4181.3 | 4225.8 | 4270.3 | 4314.8 | 4359.3 | 4403.7 |
| 1000 | 4448.2 | 4492.7 | 4537.2 | 4581.7 | 4626.1 | 4670.6 | 4715.1 | 4759.6 | 4804.1 | 4848.6 |
| 1100 | 4893.0 | 4937.5 | 4982.0 | 5026.5 | 5071.0 | 5115.5 | 5159.9 | 5204.4 | 5248.9 | 5293.4 |
| 1200 | 5337.9 | 5382.3 | 5426.8 | 5471.3 | 5515.8 | 5560.3 | 5604.8 | 5649.2 | 5693.7 | 5738.2 |
| 1300 | 5782.7 | 5827.2 | 5871.7 | 5916.1 | 5960.6 | 6005.1 | 6049.6 | 6094.1 | 6138.5 | 6183.0 |
| 1400 | 6227.5 | 6272.0 | 6316.5 | 6361.0 | 6405.4 | 6449.9 | 6494.4 | 6538.9 | 6583.4 | 6627.8 |
| 1500 | 6672.3 | 6716.8 | 6761.3 | 6805.8 | 6850.3 | 6894.7 | 6939.2 | 6983.7 | 7028.2 | 7072.7 |
| 1600 | 7117.2 | 7161.6 | 7206.1 | 7250.6 | 7295.1 | 7339.6 | 7384.0 | 7428.5 | 7473.0 | 7517.5 |
| 1700 | 7562.0 | 7606.5 | 7650.9 | 7695.4 | 7739.9 | 7784.4 | 7828.9 | 7873.3 | 7917.8 | 7962.3 |
| 1800 | 8006.0 | 8051.3 | 8095.8 | 8140.2 | 8184.7 | 8229.2 | 8273.7 | 8318.2 | 8362.7 | 8407.1 |
| 1900 | 8451.6 | 8496.1 | 8540.6 | 8585.1 | 8629.5 | 8674.0 | 8718.5 | 8763.0 | 8807.5 | 8852.0 |
| 2000 | 8896.4 | | | | | | | | | |

NOTE: 1000 newtons (N) equal 1 kilonewton (1kN). The lower portion of the table could also have been shown in kilonewtons; for example, 4893.0 N = 4.8930 kN. The table can also be used for the conversion of kips (1000 lbf) to kilonewtons (kN), since a multiplier of 1000 applies to both measurements units.

METRIC

# Data Sources

# Index